Places, Towns and Townships

Sixth Edition, 2016

Places, Towns and Townships
Sixth Edition, 2016

Edited by Deirdre A. Gaquin
Mary Meghan Ryan

Lanham, MD

Published in the United States of America
by Bernan Press, a wholly owned subsidiary of
The Rowman & Littlefield Publishing Group, Inc.
4501 Forbes Boulevard, Suite 200
Lanham, Maryland 20706

Bernan Press
800-462-6420
www.rowman.com

ISBN-13: 978-1-59888-856-0
eISBN-13: 978-1-59888-857-7

∞™ The paper used in this publication meets the minimum requirements of American National
Standard for Information Sciences—Permanence of Paper for Printed Library Materials,
ANSI/NISO Z39.48-1992.
Manufactured in the United States of America.

Contents

ABOUT THE EDITORS

Deirdre A. Gaquin has been a data use consultant to private organizations, government agencies, and universities for over 30 years. Prior to that, she was Director of Data Access Services at Data Use & Access Laboratories, a pioneer in private sector distribution of federal statistical data. A former President of the Association of Public Data Users, Ms. Gaquin has served on numerous boards, panels, and task forces concerned with federal statistical data and has worked on five decennial censuses. She holds a Master of Urban Planning (MUP) degree from Hunter College. Ms. Gaquin is also an editor of Bernan Press's *County and City Extra; The Who, What, and Where of America: Understanding the American Community Survey; The Congressional District Atlas; The Almanac of American Education; Race and Employment in America; Families in America;* and the *State and Metropolitan Area Data Book.*

Mary Meghan Ryan is a senior research editor with Bernan Press. She is the editor for *Handbook of U.S. Labor Statistics, Patterns of Economic Change,* and associate editor for *Business Statistics of the United States.*

INTRODUCTION

Places, Towns and Townships contains statistical information about places in the United States and the people who live in them. Data are presented for all incorporated places, census designated places (CDPs), and consolidated cities—from the largest city to the smallest village. CDPs are unincorporated areas of relatively dense population for which boundaries were established by the Census Bureau in cooperation with state agencies and local census statistical area committees. Data are also provided in this volume for Minor Civil Divisions (MCDs) in the 12 states where MCDs serve as general-purpose local governments. MCDs are primary subdivisions of counties and are often called towns or townships.[1]

This book is divided into three tables. Table A presents data for more than 38,000 places (MCDs, CDPs, and incorporated places) in the United States. Included are the 2014 population estimates, 2010 census population, and education and home ownership data from the 2010–2014 5-year American Community Survey.

Tables B and C are limited to places with populations of 10,000 or more and Table B includes data on migration, income, employment, and household type from the 2010–2014 5-year estimates from the American Community Survey; the most recent available information on crime, residential construction, and local government finances. Table C contains establishment and employee data from the 2012 Economic Census.

Within each table, data are presented alphabetically by state, with place names listed alphabetically within each state.

What are cities and towns?

More than 62 percent of Americans live in incorporated cities, and many others live in unincorporated areas with concentrations of people and businesses. While nearly 58 million people (about 18 percent of the population) lived in the nation's 75 largest cities, 119 million (37 percent) lived in areas that were not incorporated as places in 2014. Incorporation laws and practices vary from state to state, and many of the unincorporated Census Designated Places (CDPs) are large urban centers. Nevada has four unincorporated CDPs with populations over 100,000 in 2010 (there are no 2014 population estimates for CDPs). About 75 percent of Maryland's residents live outside of incorporated cities,

but several of Maryland's CDPs are the principal cities of metropolitan areas. In states where MCDs serve as local governments, many large towns are also incorporated cities, but many towns contain no incorporated cities or several small incorporated villages. On New York's Long Island, four towns have populations over 250,000, ranking them among the 75 most populous cities in the United States.

Figure 1 shows the populations of the 10 largest cities—those with one million or more residents. These 10 cities house fully 8 percent of the U.S. population. Fifteen percent of people live in the 295 cities with more than 100,000 residents.

At the other extreme, a mere 2.9 percent of people live in cities with populations below 2,500, while almost two-thirds of all incorporated places fell into this smallest size category. Eighty-four percent of incorporated places had populations of less than 10,000, but these places include only 8.9 percent of the population. As place size increased, the number of places within the size class dropped markedly. Only 295 incorporated places had populations of 100,000 or more, an increase from 273 places in 2010. Thirty-four cities had populations of 500,000 or more.

The distribution of the population living in incorporated places was quite different from the distribution of the number of places. The largest population grouping consists of persons living in medium-sized places. One out of four persons lived in places of 10,000 to 100,000 in 2014. More than one-third of the population lived outside of incorporated places, ranging from the 350,000 in Urban Honolulu CDP to those who lived outside of any defined urban cluster.

Tables 1 provides 2014 population estimates, by state, of the population living in incorporated places of varied sizes and those living outside of places. Table 2 shows the percentage of people in each state by size of place.

Figure 2 represents the population density of the states, with the more densely populated states located on the East, West, Gulf, and Great Lakes Coasts. The lower-density Rocky Mountain and Plains states contain many of the places with fewer than 2,500 people. Densely populated states tend to have larger cities. California and Texas each have four cities among the 15 most populous, resulting in high densities despite their large land areas.

City size and growth patterns vary from state to state. Most of the older large cities in the East and the Midwest consolidated or annexed territory and grew to their current

---

1 See Appendix A for more complete definitions of CDPs and MCDs and a list of the 12 states for which MCD data are provided.

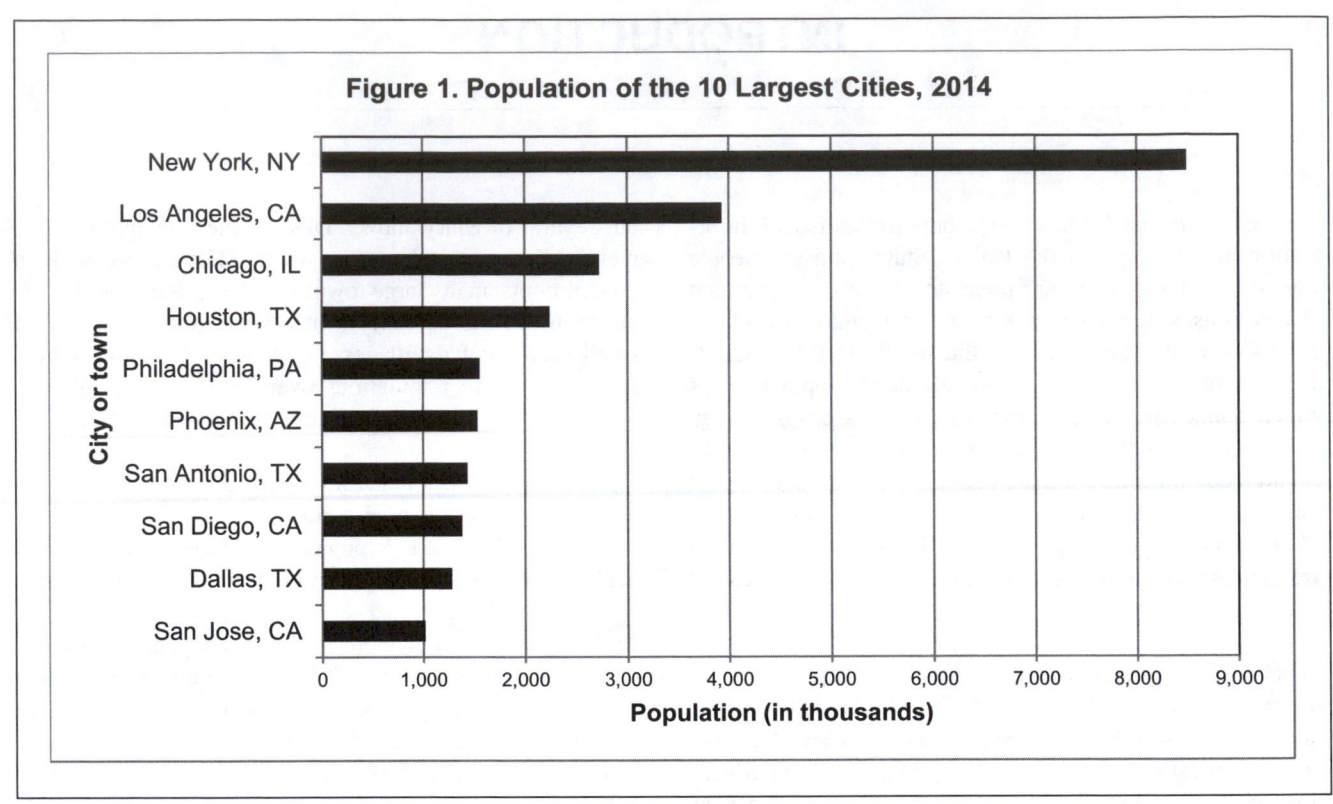

Figure 1. Population of the 10 Largest Cities, 2014

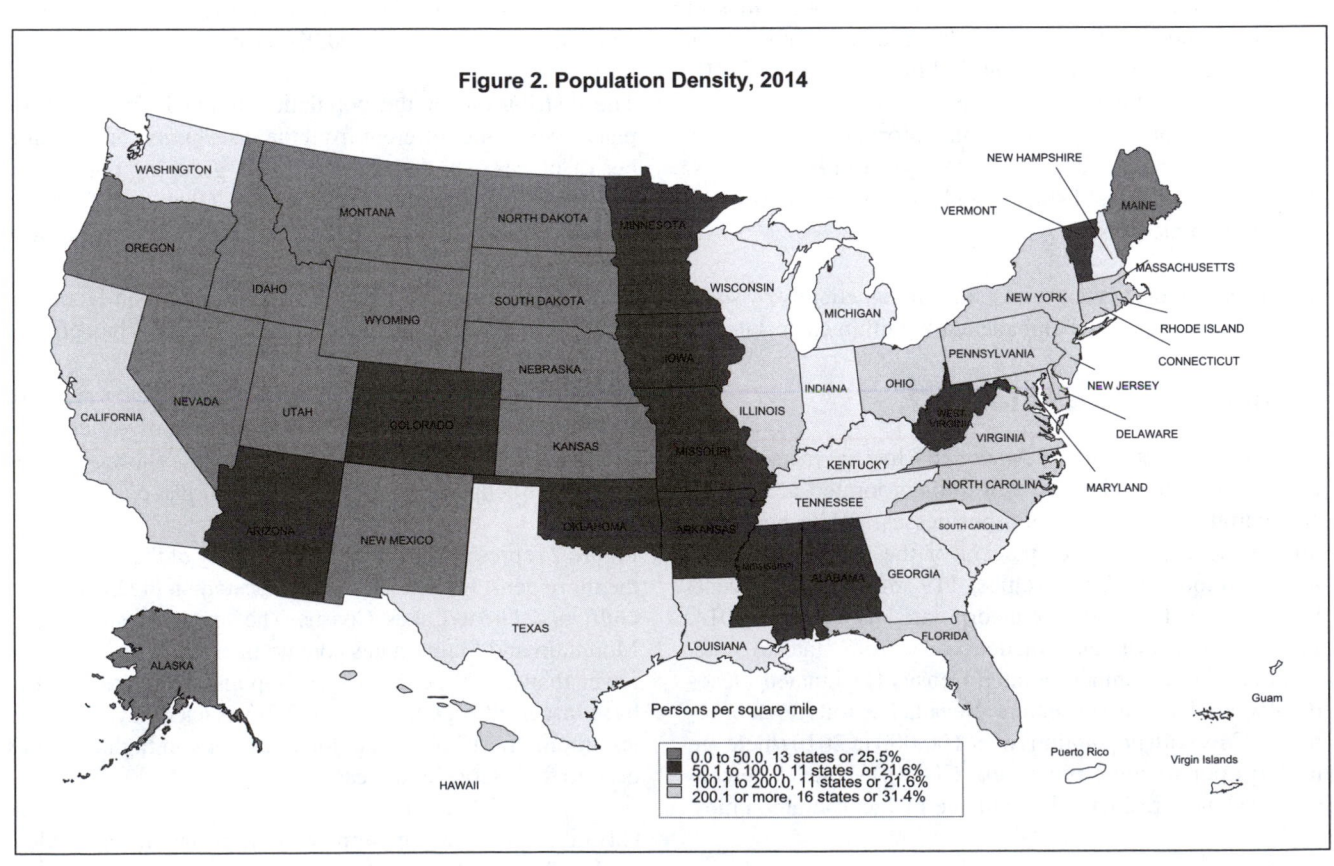

Figure 2. Population Density, 2014

geographic boundaries more than 100 years ago. In the early years of the 21st century, many of these older cities lost population, while some of their suburban counties experienced high levels of growth. While Chicago's population dropped by almost 7 percent between 2000 and 2010, nearby Kendall county more than doubled its population. At the same time, many large Western cities have continued to annex territory, with development at the edges of these cities helping to accommodate their growing populations. For example, the land area of Phoenix, AZ increased by 8.8 percent between 2000 and 2010 while its population grew by 9.4 percent. Meanwhile, nearby Maricopa city grew by 4,081 percent from 2000 to 2010, reflecting annexations of land that increased its area by 1,070 percent. Some cities have altered their boundaries through consolidation with surrounding areas. In 2003, Louisville, KY, consolidated its governmental functions with the surrounding county, forming the consolidated city Louisville-Jefferson County. Because of this, the Louisville-Jefferson County consolidated city ranked as the 18th most populous city in 2010, jumping from 65th at the time of the 2000 census. The five boroughs of New York were consolidated into a single incorporated city in 1898. Each borough remains an individual MCD, and four of the five would be among the top ten cities by 2014 population.

Between 2010 and 2014, Austin, TX was the fastest growing of the largest cities, increasing by 12.5 percent and moving ahead of Indianapolis, Jacksonville, and San Francisco to become the 11th largest city. New Orleans had the second highest growth, at 11.8 percent, continuing its increase as it recovers from a huge population loss after Hurricane Katrina in 2005. Despite steady growth, the New Orleans population is still only 84 percent of its pre-Katrina total. Other large cities with growth rates over 9 percent were Denver, Charlotte, Seattle, Fort Worth, and Washington.

New York, Los Angeles, Chicago, Houston, and Philadelphia were the five largest cities in 2014—as they have been since the 1990 census—and the top 10 cities retained the same order as in 2010. Among the 75 largest cities, 36 experienced growth rates of 5 percent or higher over the 2010–2014 time period, while 5 large cities lost population during the 4-year period: Pittsburgh, St. Louis, Cleveland, Toledo, and Detroit.

There were 34 incorporated cities and one town with more than 500,000 people in 2014. These 34 cities and towns represented only 23 states, with 6 cities in Texas, 5 in California, 2 each in New York, Arizona and Tennessee, and 1 each in 17 other states and the District of Columbia. Thirteen percent of the people in the United States lived in these 34 cities and towns. Forty-three percent of New York state's population resided in New York City, and almost one-third of Arizona's population lived in either Phoenix or Tucson. Between 20 and 30 percent of the populations of Texas, New Mexico, Illinois and Nevada lived in cities of 500,000 or more. California, despite its 4 cities in this size category, counted less than 20 percent of its population as living in those four cities.

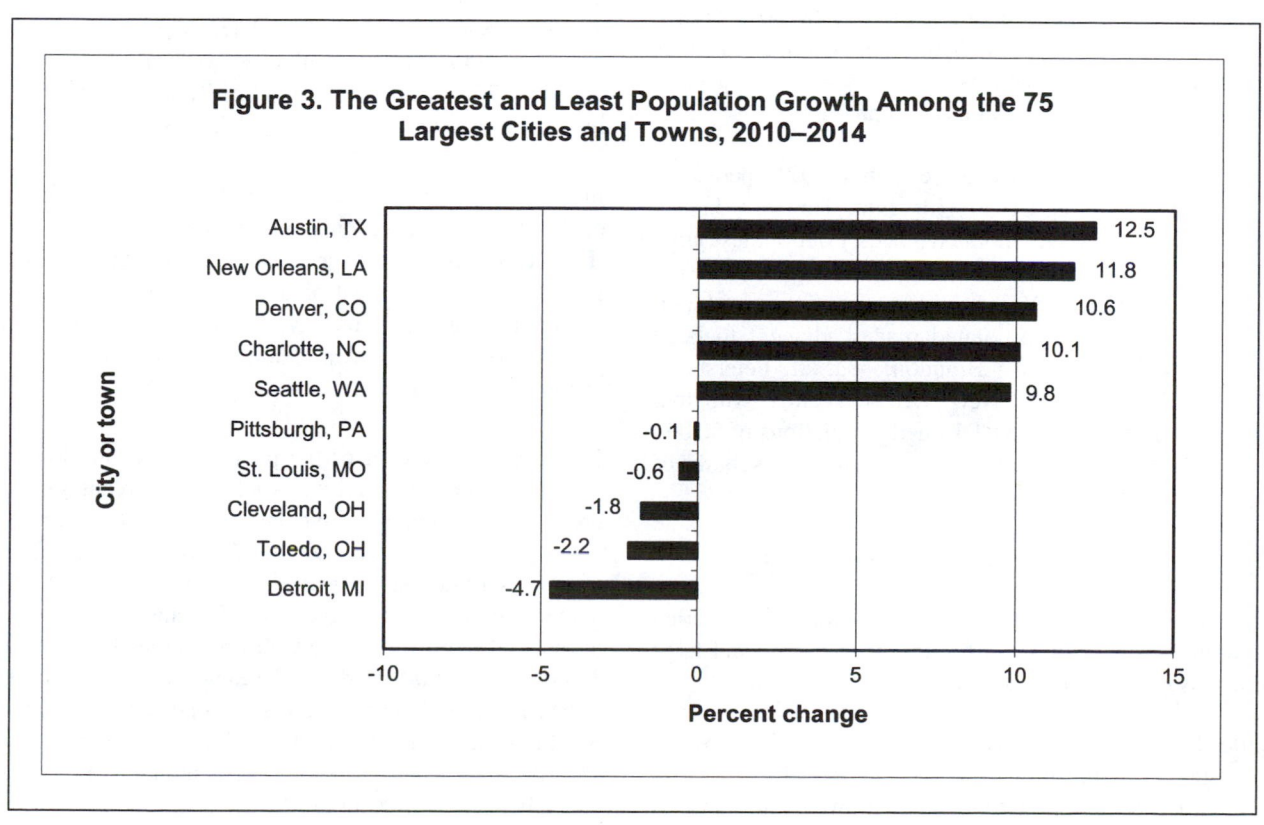

Figure 3. The Greatest and Least Population Growth Among the 75 Largest Cities and Towns, 2010–2014

At the other end of the spectrum are places with very small populations. There were 78 cities, CDPs, or MCDs where no people were counted in the 2010 census. Only four of these were incorporated cities. Some are remote unpopulated MCDs; some are CDPs that had populations in 2000. Two incorporated places had zero population in the 2014 estimates: Goss, a Missouri town where the last residents have moved away, and Carlton Landing, a newly incorporated town being developed in Oklahoma. There were 40 incorporated places with 10 or fewer people in 2014. Although these were located in 18 states, there were 9 in South Dakota, 5 each in North Dakota and Missouri, 4 in Nebraska, 3 in Oklahoma, and 2 in Idaho.

Thirty-seven percent of the population of the United States lived outside of incorporated places, but this group included very rural locations as well as major metropolitan areas. In the decennial censuses, census designated places (CDPs) are defined to represent concentrations of population that are identifiable by name but not located in any incorporated place. There has been increasing awareness that some of these CDPs are major residential and commercial centers. In 2000, the Office of Management and Budget issued new guidelines for defining metropolitan areas, and some unincorporated places are now identified as principal cities of metropolitan areas. For example, Bethesda, MD, together with the incorporated cities of Gaithersburg and Frederick, is now defined as a central city of the Bethesda-Gaithersburg-Frederick, MD Metropolitan Division, in the Washington-Arlington-Alexandria, DC-VA-MD-WV Metropolitan Statistical Area. In the 2010 census, the Bethesda CDP had a population of over 60,000. With a population of over 200,000, Arlington, Virginia—another principal city in this metropolitan area—is also a CDP because it is a county, not an incorporated city.

There are 9 CDPs that had more than 100,000 people in 2010. The largest is Urban Honolulu, Hawaii's largest city—Hawaii has no incorporated places. Four of these large CDPs are in Nevada, in the Las Vegas metropolitan area—Enterprise, Paradise, Spring Valley, and Sunrise Manor. Others are large unincorporated places adjacent to large cities—East Los Angeles; Brandon, near St. Petersburg, Florida; Metairie, near New Orleans; and Arlington, Virginia. An additional 56 CDPs had populations of 50,000 or more in the 2010 census. Most of these were suburbs of major metropolitan areas.

Who lives in the cities and towns?

America's cities are home to diverse populations of varied ethnic and racial groups, differing age patterns, and large variations in education, income, and employment.

While 62.8 percent of Americans identified as White alone, not Hispanic or Latino, the 2010–2014 American Community Survey (ACS) estimated over 3,400 places where all of the residents were non-Hispanic White. These were very small towns and villages. Most had fewer than 100 residents and barely a handful of towns had populations of 3,000 to 4,000. More than 10,000 additional places had non-Hispanic white populations of 95 percent or more. Most of these places were very small but there were 8 with populations over 25,000, including The Villages in Florida with 61,000 residents. Among the 75 largest cities, there are four with non-Hispanic White populations of 70 percent or more: Oyster Bay and Brookhaven, two suburban towns near New York City, Lexington-Fayette, Kentucky, and Portland, Oregon. Fewer than 10 percent of the residents of Detroit, Michigan and Santa Ana, California are non-Hispanic White.

The predominant ethnic and racial groups estimated by the ACS and included in this book are Hispanic or Latino (16.9 percent of the United States population); Black alone (12.2 percent); and Asian alone (4.9 percent). Because of small numbers, all other races are combined into a single group in this book: American Indian and Alaska native alone; Native Hawaiian and Other Pacific Islander alone; some other race alone; and two or more races, all not Hispanic or Latino. These combined groups make up 3.1 percent of the U.S. population.

There are 341 places where more than 95 percent of the residents are Latino. Though most are small cities or CDPs, thirteen of them have more than 25,000 residents, including Laredo, Texas and Hialeah, Florida, both with more than 200,000 residents. Among the 75 largest cities, El Paso, Texas and Santa Ana, California have the largest concentrations of Latino residents, both close to 80 percent. The proportion is 70 percent in Miami, Florida, and over 60 percent in San Antonio and Corpus Christi, Texas.

In 86 places, more than 95 percent of the residents are Black or African-American. Only one of these—East St. Louis, IL—has a population over 25,000. Among the largest cities, 80.7 percent of Detroit's residents are Black, while Baltimore and Memphis have African-American populations of 62 percent. Black residents number just under 60 percent in New Orleans.

In Hawaii, 37 percent of the people are Asian alone, not of Hispanic or Latino origin. Another 29 percent are in the group that combines native Hawaiians with other racial groups. Five Hawaiian CDPs, 6 California cities, and one CDP in Virginia have Asian populations of more than 60 percent. While most of the Hawaiian and Virginia CDPs have small populations, the California cities have between 30,000 and 70,000 residents. Among the 75 largest cities, Urban Honolulu's population is 53.6 percent Asian, while San Francisco and San Jose are both about one-third Asian. The Asian population is below 2 percent in ten of the largest cities, below one percent in Miami.

There are 343 cities where 90 percent or more of the residents are in the racial category that combines all other races and two or more races. These small places are mostly located on reservations and only a few have more than 5,000 residents. Among the 75 largest cities, Urban Honolulu has the largest proportion at 22.1 percent. There, the group consists primarily of Native Hawaiians. Anchorage, Alaska and Tulsa, Oklahoma also have large proportions (16.8 and 10.7 percent respectively) and in those cities the group mainly represents American Indian and Alaskan Native populations.

During the years 2010 through 2014, 13.1 percent of the residents of the United States were born in foreign countries. Some cities have larger immigrant populations than others. In 43 cities—mostly medium-sized cities and CDPs—more than half of the people are foreign-born. About half of these cities are in Florida, and Miami has the highest proportion of the 75 largest cities (57.6 percent). California has 13 cities where more than half of the residents are foreign-born. Among the 75 largest cities, three California cities follow Miami: Santa Ana (47.3 percent), San Jose (38.7 percent), and Los Angeles (38.6 percent). Los Angeles and New York have similar proportions of foreign-born residents—Los Angeles at 38.6 percent and New York at 37.1 percent—but New York has 3.1 million foreign-born residents, more than double the 1.5 million foreign-born residents in Los Angeles.

At the other extreme are several hundred small places with no foreign-born residents. There were a few thousand cities where about one percent or fewer of the residents were born in foreign countries, including nearly 80 cities with more than 10,000 residents. Four Midwestern cities have the lowest proportions among the 75 largest cities—Toledo, Cleveland, Cincinnati, and Detroit all have levels below six percent. The foreign-born populations of New Orleans and Memphis are also low, at 6 percent or just above.

The working-age population can be defined to include persons aged 18 to 64, though certainly younger and older persons are often employed. This 18-to-64 age group comprises 62.8 percent of the United States population, while many cities have larger or smaller proportions of working-age adults. While there are about 100 small towns with more than 90 percent of their populations in this age group, the larger of these towns tend to have predominantly student or military populations. At the other extreme are some small towns with fewer than 25 percent of their residents in the working-age group. Many of these are age-restricted retirement communities like Sun City, Arizona. Among the 75 largest cities, Seattle and Boston both have more than 73 percent of their residents in the 18-to-64 age group, and six other cities have levels above 70 percent. In Mesa, Arizona and Stockton, California, the proportion is barely 60 percent. Mesa has a high proportion of persons age 65 and older, while Stockton has a high proportion of persons under 18 years old.

Nationally, children under 18 comprise 23.5 percent of the population, but there are communities where more than 70 percent are children, while others have fewer than 10 percent. Most of these are very small cities and towns. Among places with more than 20,000 residents, there are a few where children make up about half of the population, mostly Orthodox Jewish communities in New York and New Jersey, and suburban cities in Utah. Places with low proportions of children tend to have disproportionately large working-age populations or age-restricted retirement communities. Among the largest cities, four California cities have under-18 populations of 28 percent or more. Five have levels of 17 percent or less—generally the same cities with large working-age populations. People age 65 and older make up 13.7 percent of the population, with levels above 70 percent in some places, mainly in Florida and Arizona. Among the 75 largest cities, Urban Honolulu has the highest proportion of retirement-age people at 18.3 percent. Oyster Bay, NY and Henderson, NV also have high levels, at 17.2 and 16 percent.

Education levels vary greatly from city to city; 31.5 percent of householders have earned bachelor's degrees or higher, while 37.4 percent have never attended college. In 108 cities and towns, more than 90 percent of householders are college graduates, while hundreds of small towns and villages have college-graduate proportions below 5 percent. Of the 75 largest cities, Seattle has the highest proportion of college graduates at 59.8 percent. Plano, San Francisco, Washington, Raleigh, and Atlanta all have levels over 50 percent. Newark, Detroit, and Santa Ana, have college-graduate proportions of 15 percent or below. In Santa Ana and Newark, 60 percent or more of their householders have no education beyond high school.

In the five-year period from 2010 through 2014, 63.9 percent of Americans age 16 and older were in the civilian labor force, and 9.2 percent of the labor force participants were unemployed. The 9.2 percent unemployment rate illustrates one of the issues inherent in using 5-year ACS data. The 2014 national unemployment rate measured by the 1-year ACS data was 7.2 percent, after steadily declining from a 2010 rate of 10.8 percent. While the 5-year data masks these changes, there is no 1-year data for most of the cities in this book. The official unemployment rate for 2014 was 6.2 percent, as measured by the Current Population Survey.

Labor force participation was over 80 percent in 26 of the cities with populations of 10,000 or more, and 12 of the largest cities had civilian labor force participation over 70 percent, led by Anchorage at 74.1 percent, with Minneapolis and Austin both at 73 percent. These three cities all had unemployment rates below the national rate of 9.2 percent, with Austin and Anchorage well below at 6.8 and 6.9 percent. Three of the largest cities had labor force participation rates below 60 percent: Detroit, Cleveland, and Philadelphia. Detroit's unemployment rate in the 2010–2014 period was

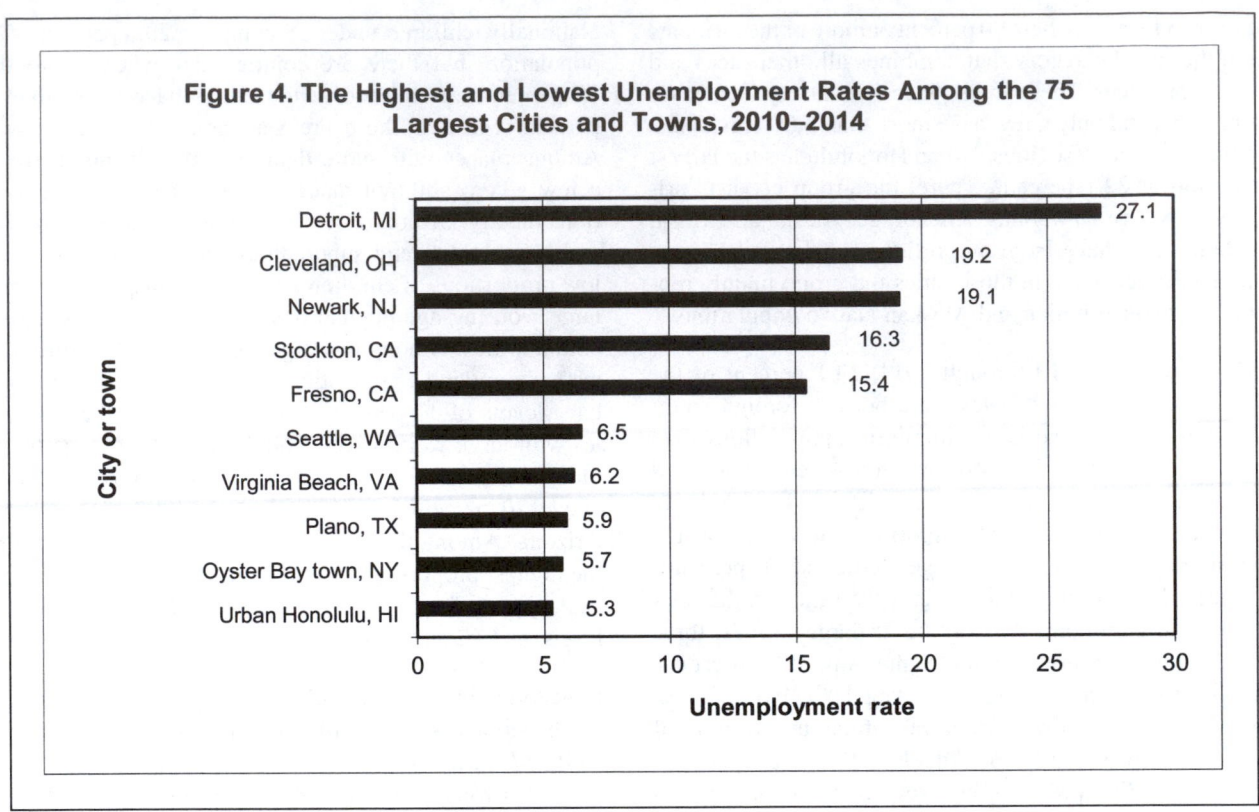

Figure 4. The Highest and Lowest Unemployment Rates Among the 75 Largest Cities and Towns, 2010–2014

27.1, the highest among the 75 largest cities, followed by Cleveland and Newark, both at 19 percent. Urban Honolulu, Oyster Bay Town, and Plano had the lowest unemployment rates among the 75 largest cities, all under 6 percent.

In the years 2010 through 2014, the median household income in the United States was $53,482. Half of all households had incomes above this level, and half had lower incomes. The median income is calculated from income groupings of $2,500, but the top group is simply "$250,000 or more" so no recorded median is ever over $250,000. This "top code" is necessary to protect the confidentiality of the respondents and to minimize sampling error because so few households are in this category. Among all households in the United States, 23.1 percent had incomes above $100,000. Nearly 500 cities or towns with populations of 10,000 or more had median incomes over $100,000, 11 with medians over $200,000. These 11 high-income cities and towns were in nine different states, led by Hillsborough, California with a median income of at least $250,000. The other ten are Scarsdale village and town, New York; Short Hills CDP, New Jersey; Great Falls CDP, Virginia; Piedmont, California; Travilah CDP, Maryland; Weston town, Connecticut; Winnetka village, Illinois; West University Place, Texas; Wolf Trap CDP, Virginia; and Weston town, Massachusetts. Among the 75 largest cities, Oyster Bay town, New York topped the list with a median income of $111,341. The three other large towns on New York's Long Island; San Jose, California; and Plano, Texas followed with median Incomes over $80,000. Among cities with populations of 10,000 or

more, there are ten with median incomes below $20,000. Among the 75 largest cities, Detroit and Cleveland had median incomes below $30,000.

In 2014, the average poverty threshold for a family of four was $24,230. It can be higher or lower depending on the number of persons in the household. Households with incomes below this level are considered to be in poverty. This poverty-level threshold has no regional variations, though the cost of living can vary dramatically from city to city throughout the nation. Nationally, 14.4 percent of households had incomes below the poverty level. In four cities of 10,000 or more population, more than half of the households had incomes below the poverty level: Kiryas Joel, New York, an Orthodox Jewish community with very large families; Boone, North Carolina, an Appalachian mountain town that's a recreational destination as well as home to a university; and two cities with large student populations: Isla Vista, California and Athens, Ohio. In another 32 of these cities, more than 40 percent of the households had poverty-level incomes. Among the 75 largest cities, Detroit had the highest proportion, at 36.2 percent, followed by Cleveland at 32.8 percent, while Miami, Newark, and Cincinnati all had levels above 28 percent.

Most Americans live in households, and nearly two-thirds of those households are occupied by their owners. There are hundreds of small towns where all households are owner-occupied, and a few small towns where none of the households are owner-occupied. Oyster Bay, Hempstead,

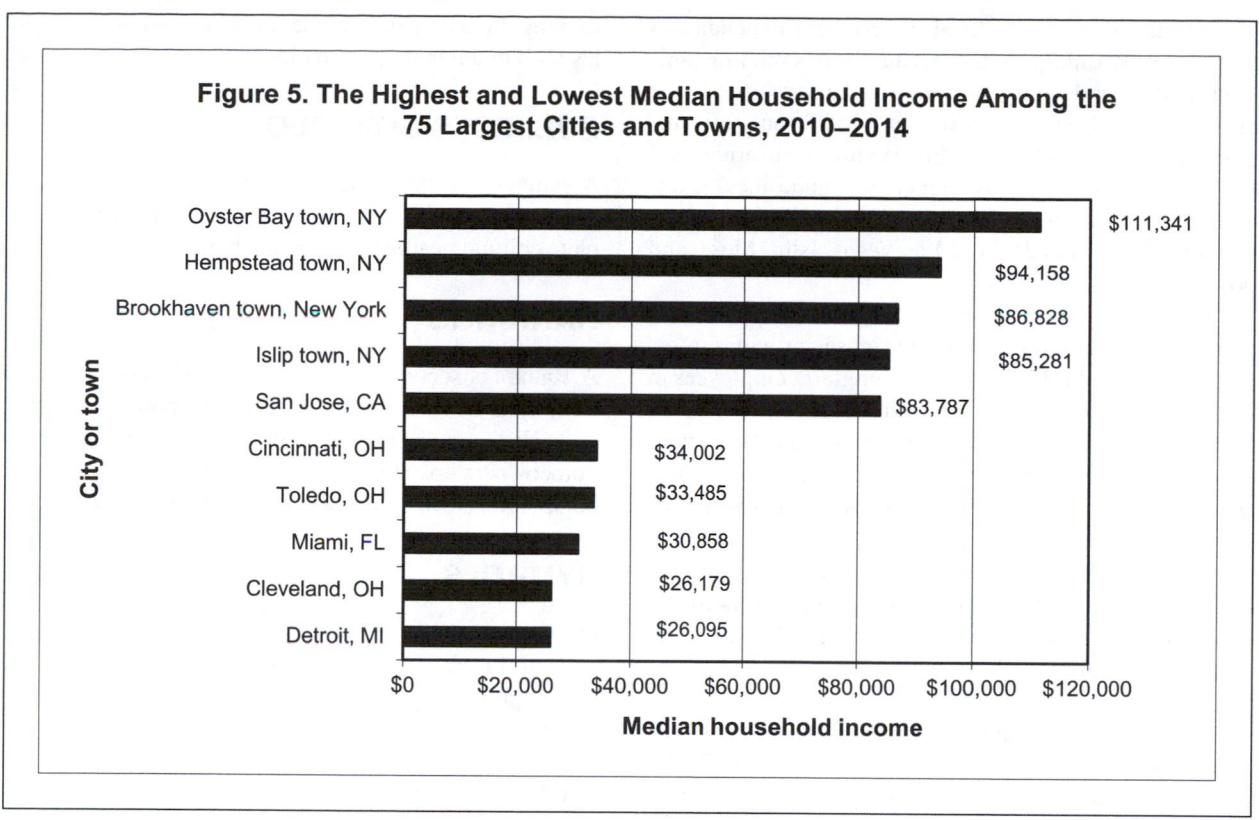

Figure 5. The Highest and Lowest Median Household Income Among the 75 Largest Cities and Towns, 2010–2014

Oyster Bay town, NY — $111,341
Hempstead town, NY — $94,158
Brookhaven town, New York — $86,828
Islip town, NY — $85,281
San Jose, CA — $83,787
Cincinnati, OH — $34,002
Toledo, OH — $33,485
Miami, FL — $30,858
Cleveland, OH — $26,179
Detroit, MI — $26,095

City or town (vertical axis)
Median household income (horizontal axis)

Brookhaven, and Islip—towns in the New York suburbs—have the highest homeownership rates of the 75 largest cities, all above 75 percent. At 22 percent, Newark has the lowest homeownership rate of the largest cities, while Miami and New York are both around 32 percent, and 5 other large cities have rates below 40 percent.

About two-thirds of all households are family households—people living in the same household who are related by birth, marriage, or adoption. Among cities with populations over 10,000, there are 31 where more than 90 percent of households are family households. These are varied cities, including suburban towns, CDPs with military bases, Orthodox Jewish communities, and cities near the Mexican border. Of the 75 largest cities, Santa Ana, California has the highest proportion of family households at 81.6 percent, and the New York suburbs of Oyster Bay, Hempstead, and Islip all had rates over 76 percent. In a few cities—mostly college towns—family households make up less than 30 percent of all households. Among the largest cities, there are 11 where fewer than half of all households are family households, with Washington DC the lowest at 42.5 percent.

Persons living alone comprise 27.6 percent of households. Of the cities with 10,000 or more residents, there are 8 where more than half of the households consist of a single person, topped by Laguna Woods and West Hollywood, California, both above 60 percent. One-person households make up more than 40 percent of households in 10 of the 75 largest cities. Atlanta and Washington have the highest levels, both above 45 percent.

What happens in cities and towns?

The FBI's Uniform Crime Reporting (UCR) Program compiles information on crime in the nation. Since the 1930s, they have published data received from over 18,000 city, university/college, county, state, tribal, and federal law enforcement agencies voluntarily participating in the program. Data are not available for many of the cities in this book—they may not have a separate law enforcement agency, they may not participate, or the data may represent only a portion of the entity used here. Nationally in 2014, there were 366 violent crimes and 2596 property crimes per 100,000 persons. In the largest cities, violent crime ranged from a high of 1990 per 100,000 people in Detroit to a low of 148 per 100,000 in Virginia Beach. Property crime ranged from highs of over 6000 in St. Louis and Seattle to lows of 1602 and 1030 in New York and Raleigh.

Data on construction authorized by building permits is compiled by the Census Bureau for about 19,000 permit-issuing places in the United States. Houston and Los Angeles had the highest construction values at 2.4 and 2.3 billion dollars in 2014, followed by Seattle and Austin at 1.1 billion each. Cleveland had the lowest value of the largest cities, at 7.4 million.

Per capita local taxes and local government expenditures are highest in Washington, DC because it has the functions of both a state and a city. Among the largest cities, New York has the highest local taxes, at $5,077, but residents of Nantucket, Massachusetts, Emeryville, California, and seven Connecticut cities pay higher per capita local taxes. Among the largest cities, the lowest per capita local taxes are under $400 for residents of Las Vegas, Islip, Mesa, and Brookhaven.

As shown in Table 4, the Economic Census provides information for about 111,251,646 private nonfarm employees in 18 sectors. Table B includes the number of establishments and employees in each of the cities with 10,000 or more residents. Nationally, Health Care and Social Assistance is the sector with the most employees—16.6 percent of the total—followed by Retail Trade with 13.2 percent. Accommodation and Food Services (10.8 percent) and Manufacturing (10.1 percent) also have large proportions. Each of the other sectors represents less than 10 percent of the national workforce.

Because of its large population, New York City has the most employees in most sectors, but its number of health care workers (688,569) is somewhat higher than might be expected on the basis of population alone. New York is one of four states where more than 20 percent of the workforce are in health care occupations. Los Angeles has the second highest number, but California is one of 10 states where fewer than 15 percent of employees work in the health care field.

Los Angeles and Houston have more manufacturing employees than New York. Everett, Washington, home of Boeing's assembly plant, has 43,136 manufacturing employees, ranking it after the four largest cities though it has a population of barely over 100,000. At the state level, Wisconsin and Indiana have nearly double the national proportion of manufacturing employees at about 19 percent each. Indianapolis and Milwaukee rank 7th and 15th for manufacturing employees in large cities, higher than their population ranks.

For employees in the information sector, San Francisco, Atlanta, Seattle, Boston, and Washington rank considerably higher than their population ranks. Burbank, California, with its large concentration of media companies, has 37,338 employees in the information sector and Mountain View, California, in the heart of Silicon Valley, has 27,874,

ranking them both among the top 7, outnumbering most cities with much larger populations.

SUBJECTS COVERED

A summary of the subjects covered in Tables A, B, and C appears on page xxxvi. Pages xxxvii–xxxviii show the complete column headings for each table.

RANKINGS

A Rankings section ranks the 75 largest cities by population, land area, population density, population change, race, Hispanic origin, age, education, income, poverty rate, homeownership rate, unemployment rate, employee numbers, violent crime rate, and per capita local taxes.

SYMBOLS

D Indicates that the number has been withheld to avoid disclosure of information pertaining to a specific organization or individual, or because the number does not meet statistical standards for publication.

NA Indicates that data are not available.

X Indicates that data are not applicable or are not meaningful for this geographic unit.

In this volume, where a figure is less than half the unit of measure shown, it will appear as zero.

SOURCES

The data in this volume have been obtained from federal government sources. For a complete list of sources, see Appendix B.

Data included in this volume meet the publication standards established by the U.S. Census Bureau and the other federal statistical agencies from which they were obtained. Every effort has been made to select data that are accurate, meaningful, and useful. All data from censuses, surveys, and administrative records are subject to errors arising from factors such as sampling variability, reporting errors, incomplete coverage, nonresponse, imputations, and processing error. Responsibility of the editors and publishers of this volume is limited to reasonable care in the reproduction and presentation of data obtained from sources believed to be reliable.

Table 1. Population by Residence in Incorporated Places and Size of Place, 2014

State	Total population	500,000 or more	100,000 to 499,999	50,000 to 99,999	25,000 to 49,999	10,000 to 24,999	2,500 to 9,999	Less than 2,500	Total in incorporated places	Not in incorporated places
United States	318,857,056	42,116,471	47,822,486	31,604,623	24,980,238	24,630,971	19,272,953	9,380,351	199,808,093	119,048,963
Alabama	4,849,377		795,629	364,674	371,180	678,464	475,662	266,034	2,951,643	1,897,734
Alaska	736,732		301,010		64,875		85,086	57,706	508,677	228,055
Arizona	6,731,484	2,065,030	1,892,311	481,546	512,549	188,324	158,913	22,104	5,320,777	1,410,707
Arkansas	2,966,369		197,706	509,511	380,668	273,761	337,026	241,784	1,940,456	1,025,913
California	38,802,500	7,694,173	11,538,902	7,522,927	3,261,279	1,755,256	461,935	41,088	32,275,560	6,526,940
Colorado	5,355,866	663,862	1,781,768	491,341	288,113	307,109	300,362	124,022	3,956,577	1,399,289
Connecticut	3,596,677		640,184	472,432	222,739	31,727	16,766	6,913	1,390,761	2,205,916
Delaware	935,614			71,817	70,363	41,259	49,938	32,378	265,755	669,859
District of Columbia	658,893	658,893							658,893	0
Florida	19,893,297	853,382	3,594,105	2,377,100	1,358,280	1,156,085	538,023	145,897	10,022,872	9,870,425
Georgia	10,097,343		1,373,229	611,915	639,623	793,483	603,214	248,505	4,269,969	5,827,374
Hawaii	1,419,561								0	1,419,561
Idaho	1,634,464		216,282	339,161	183,912	165,735	131,078	97,837	1,134,005	500,459
Illinois	12,880,580	2,722,389	987,389	1,401,943	2,110,767	2,141,919	1,234,119	599,896	11,198,422	1,682,158
Indiana	6,596,855	848,788	480,058	890,479	697,400	630,355	478,617	340,330	4,366,027	2,230,828
Iowa	3,107,126		440,863	525,369	262,875	308,756	468,316	464,119	2,470,298	636,828
Kansas	2,904,021		982,851	264,482	215,025	342,916	320,307	278,411	2,403,992	500,029
Kentucky	4,413,457	612,780	310,797	120,853	339,530	362,848	442,491	240,122	2,429,421	1,984,036
Louisiana	4,649,676		937,523	209,425	218,386	346,381	324,679	167,486	2,203,880	2,445,796
Maine	1,330,089			66,666	94,291	136,942	72,940	3,601	374,440	955,649
Maryland	5,976,407	622,793		258,799	170,199	196,188	226,089	75,727	1,549,795	4,426,612
Massachusetts	6,745,408	655,884	556,646	1,227,568	838,260	149,210			3,427,568	3,317,840
Michigan	9,909,877	680,250	693,022	1,291,161	698,554	735,336	660,087	309,350	5,067,760	4,842,117
Minnesota	5,457,173		816,249	1,002,561	676,555	986,675	628,766	379,170	4,489,976	967,197
Mississippi	2,994,079		171,155	123,574	340,065	477,335	240,636	171,044	1,523,809	1,470,270
Missouri	6,063,589		1,187,997	536,198	458,106	739,777	662,432	419,896	4,004,406	2,059,183
Montana	1,023,579		108,869	128,973	105,583	21,518	117,213	74,002	556,158	467,421
Nebraska	1,881,503		719,595	105,172	58,969	187,658	172,121	217,074	1,460,589	420,914
Nevada	2,839,099	613,599	745,223	149,230		71,860	28,044	6,707	1,614,663	1,224,436
New Hampshire	1,326,813		110,448	87,259	103,100	99,139	17,929		417,875	908,938
New Jersey	8,938,175		818,183	845,966	621,544	1,061,697	822,671	94,011	4,264,072	4,674,103
New Mexico	2,085,572	557,169	101,408	164,117	229,194	137,415	133,966	44,677	1,367,946	717,626
New York	19,746,227	8,491,079	813,616	487,491	752,419	818,545	912,235	366,039	12,641,424	7,104,803
North Carolina	9,943,964	809,958	1,795,105	625,119	669,584	716,749	686,886	277,902	5,581,303	4,362,661
North Dakota	739,482		115,863	124,953	79,768	83,150	45,030	118,141	566,905	172,577
Ohio	11,594,163	835,957	1,307,579	564,195	1,639,262	1,804,861	919,636	456,103	7,527,593	4,066,570
Oklahoma	3,878,051	620,602	622,448	353,243	239,122	456,021	409,640	274,450	2,975,526	902,525
Oregon	3,970,239	619,360	432,090	575,122	260,370	453,263	323,158	126,140	2,789,503	1,180,736
Pennsylvania	12,787,209	1,560,297	424,516	396,982	459,932	690,388	1,515,862	568,496	5,616,473	7,170,736
Rhode Island	1,055,173		179,154	234,499	88,559	43,417			545,629	509,544
South Carolina	4,832,482		368,929	210,015	358,905	353,913	309,920	136,672	1,738,354	3,094,128
South Dakota	853,175		168,586	72,638	27,800	124,534	77,122	127,776	598,456	254,719
Tennessee	6,549,352	1,300,875	625,819	370,189	559,135	391,393	466,247	208,179	3,921,837	2,627,515
Texas	26,956,058	7,361,367	4,994,419	1,966,542	1,673,702	1,796,442	1,459,405	635,696	19,887,573	7,069,385
Utah	2,942,902		551,100	597,470	696,789	366,774	280,904	112,522	2,605,559	337,343
Vermont	626,562				42,211	34,685	50,608	26,115	153,619	472,943
Virginia	8,326,289		1,618,051	413,763	337,676	309,636	257,949	119,708	3,056,783	5,269,506
Washington	7,061,530	668,342	955,227	1,162,051	633,843	617,344	414,698	121,034	4,572,539	2,488,991
West Virginia	1,850,326			50,404	138,651	134,384	168,463	147,518	639,420	1,210,906
Wisconsin	5,757,564	599,642	350,582	634,797	666,474	822,161	684,845	341,427	4,099,928	1,657,636
Wyoming	584,153			122,931	64,052	88,183	80,919	46,542	402,627	181,526

Table 2. Percent of Population in Incorporated Places, by Size of Place, 2014

State	Total population	500,000 or more	100,000 to 499,999	50,000 to 99,999	25,000 to 49,999	10,000 to 24,999	2,500 to 9,999	Less than 2,500	Total in incorporated places	Not in incorporated places
United States............	318,857,056	13.2	15.0	9.9	7.8	7.7	6.0	2.9	62.7	37.3
Alabama	4,849,377	0.0	16.4	7.5	7.7	14.0	9.8	5.5	60.9	39.1
Alaska............................	736,732	0.0	40.9	0.0	8.8	0.0	11.5	7.8	69.0	31.0
Arizona	6,731,484	30.7	28.1	7.2	7.6	2.8	2.4	0.3	79.0	21.0
Arkansas........................	2,966,369	0.0	6.7	17.2	12.8	9.2	11.4	8.2	65.4	34.6
California	38,802,500	19.8	29.7	19.4	8.4	4.5	1.2	0.1	83.2	16.8
Colorado	5,355,866	12.4	33.3	9.2	5.4	5.7	5.6	2.3	73.9	26.1
Connecticut....................	3,596,677	0.0	17.8	13.1	6.2	0.9	0.5	0.2	38.7	61.3
Delaware	935,614	0.0	0.0	7.7	7.5	4.4	5.3	3.5	28.4	71.6
District of Columbia	658,893	100.0	0.0	0.0	0.0	0.0	0.0	0.0	100.0	0.0
Florida............................	19,893,297	4.3	18.1	11.9	6.8	5.8	2.7	0.7	50.4	49.6
Georgia..........................	10,097,343	0.0	13.6	6.1	6.3	7.9	6.0	2.5	42.3	57.7
Hawaii............................	1,419,561	0.0	0.0	0.0	0.0	0.0	0.0	0.0	0.0	100.0
Idaho..............................	1,634,464	0.0	13.2	20.8	11.3	10.1	8.0	6.0	69.4	30.6
Illinois............................	12,880,580	21.1	7.7	10.9	16.4	16.6	9.6	4.7	86.9	13.1
Indiana...........................	6,596,855	12.9	7.3	13.5	10.6	9.6	7.3	5.2	66.2	33.8
Iowa...............................	3,107,126	0.0	14.2	16.9	8.5	9.9	15.1	14.9	79.5	20.5
Kansas...........................	2,904,021	0.0	33.8	9.1	7.4	11.8	11.0	9.6	82.8	17.2
Kentucky	4,413,457	13.9	7.0	2.7	7.7	8.2	10.0	5.4	55.0	45.0
Louisiana	4,649,676	0.0	20.2	4.5	4.7	7.4	7.0	3.6	47.4	52.6
Maine.............................	1,330,089	0.0	0.0	5.0	7.1	10.3	5.5	0.3	28.2	71.8
Maryland.........................	5,976,407	10.4	0.0	4.3	2.8	3.3	3.8	1.3	25.9	74.1
Massachusetts................	6,745,408	9.7	8.3	18.2	12.4	2.2	0.0	0.0	50.8	49.2
Michigan	9,909,877	6.9	7.0	13.0	7.0	7.4	6.7	3.1	51.1	48.9
Minnesota	5,457,173	0.0	15.0	18.4	12.4	18.1	11.5	6.9	82.3	17.7
Mississippi	2,994,079	0.0	5.7	4.1	11.4	15.9	8.0	5.7	50.9	49.1
Missouri	6,063,589	0.0	19.6	8.8	7.6	12.2	10.9	6.9	66.0	34.0
Montana.........................	1,023,579	0.0	10.6	12.6	10.3	2.1	11.5	7.2	54.3	45.7
Nebraska	1,881,503	0.0	38.2	5.6	3.1	10.0	9.1	11.5	77.6	22.4
Nevada	2,839,099	21.6	26.2	5.3	0.0	2.5	1.0	0.2	56.9	43.1
New Hampshire	1,326,813	0.0	8.3	6.6	7.8	7.5	1.4	0.0	31.5	68.5
New Jersey.....................	8,938,175	0.0	9.2	9.5	7.0	11.9	9.2	1.1	47.7	52.3
New Mexico	2,085,572	26.7	4.9	7.9	11.0	6.6	6.4	2.1	65.6	34.4
New York........................	19,746,227	43.0	4.1	2.5	3.8	4.1	4.6	1.9	64.0	36.0
North Carolina	9,943,964	8.1	18.1	6.3	6.7	7.2	6.9	2.8	56.1	43.9
North Dakota	739,482	0.0	15.7	16.9	10.8	11.2	6.1	16.0	76.7	23.3
Ohio................................	11,594,163	7.2	11.3	4.9	14.1	15.6	7.9	3.9	64.9	35.1
Oklahoma	3,878,051	16.0	16.1	9.1	6.2	11.8	10.6	7.1	76.7	23.3
Oregon...........................	3,970,239	15.6	10.9	14.5	6.6	11.4	8.1	3.2	70.3	29.7
Pennsylvania	12,787,209	12.2	3.3	3.1	3.6	5.4	11.9	4.4	43.9	56.1
Rhode Island	1,055,173	0.0	17.0	22.2	8.4	4.1	0.0	0.0	51.7	48.3
South Carolina...............	4,832,482	0.0	7.6	4.3	7.4	7.3	6.4	2.8	36.0	64.0
South Dakota.................	853,175	0.0	19.8	8.5	3.3	14.6	9.0	15.0	70.1	29.9
Tennessee	6,549,352	19.9	9.6	5.7	8.5	6.0	7.1	3.2	59.9	40.1
Texas	26,956,958	27.3	18.5	7.3	6.2	6.7	5.4	2.4	73.8	26.2
Utah...............................	2,942,902	0.0	18.7	20.3	23.7	12.5	9.5	3.8	88.5	11.5
Vermont	626,562	0.0	0.0	0.0	6.7	5.5	8.1	4.2	24.5	75.5
Virginia...........................	8,326,289	0.0	19.4	5.0	4.1	3.7	3.1	1.4	36.7	63.3
Washington.....................	7,061,530	9.5	13.5	16.5	9.0	8.7	5.9	1.7	64.8	35.2
West Virginia..................	1,850,326	0.0	0.0	2.7	7.5	7.3	9.1	8.0	34.6	65.4
Wisconsin	5,757,564	10.4	6.1	11.0	11.6	14.3	11.9	5.9	71.2	28.8
Wyoming.........................	584,153	0.0	0.0	21.0	11.0	15.1	13.9	8.0	68.9	31.1

Table 3. Population Change in the 75 Largest Cities and Towns, 2010–2014

Population rank 2014	City	Population 2014	Population 2010	Population rank 2010	Percent change 2010–2014
1	New York, NY	8,491,079	8,174,959	1	3.9
2	Los Angeles, CA	3,928,864	3,792,657	2	3.6
3	Chicago, IL	2,722,389	2,695,598	3	1.0
4	Houston, TX	2,239,558	2,096,661	4	6.8
5	Philadelphia, PA	1,560,297	1,526,006	5	2.2
6	Phoenix, AZ	1,537,058	1,447,617	6	6.2
7	San Antonio, TX	1,436,697	1,327,556	7	8.2
8	San Diego, CA	1,381,069	1,301,621	8	6.1
9	Dallas, TX	1,281,047	1,197,792	9	7.0
10	San Jose, CA	1,015,785	952,560	10	6.6
11	Austin, TX	912,791	811,458	13	12.5
12	Indianapolis, IN	858,325	829,668	11	3.5
13	Jacksonville, FL	853,382	821,784	12	3.8
14	San Francisco, CA	852,469	805,195	14	5.9
15	Columbus, OH	835,957	788,654	15	6.0
16	Fort Worth, FL	812,238	742,060	17	9.5
17	Charlotte, NC	809,958	735,758	19	10.1
18	Hempstead town, NY	770,116	759,933	16	1.3
19	Louisville/Jefferson County metro government, KY	760,026	741,096	18	2.6
20	Detroit, MI	680,250	713,862	20	-4.7
21	El Paso, TX	679,036	649,133	22	4.6
22	Nashville-Davidson metropolitan government, TN	668,347	626,663	23	6.7
23	Seattle, WA	668,342	608,658	26	9.8
24	Denver, CO	663,862	600,025	28	10.6
25	Washington, DC	658,893	601,767	27	9.5
26	Memphis, TN	656,861	651,858	21	0.8
27	Boston city, MA	655,884	617,680	25	6.2
28	Baltimore, MD	622,793	621,121	24	0.3
29	Oklahoma City, OK	620,602	580,008	32	7.0
30	Portland, OR	619,360	583,789	31	6.1
31	Las Vegas, NV	613,599	584,240	30	5.0
32	Milwaukee, WI	599,642	594,738	29	0.8
33	Albuquerque, NM	557,169	546,360	33	2.0
34	Tucson, AZ	527,972	520,561	34	1.4
35	Fresno, CA	515,986	496,080	35	4.0
36	Brookhaven, NY	489,403	486,040	36	0.7
37	Sacramento, CA	485,199	466,488	37	4.0
38	Long Beach, CA	473,577	462,257	38	2.4
39	Kansas City , MO	470,800	459,787	39	2.4
40	Mesa, AZ	464,704	439,865	40	5.6
41	Atlanta, GA	456,002	420,256	43	8.5
42	Virginia Beach, VA	450,980	437,966	41	3.0
43	Omaha, NE	446,599	423,327	42	5.5
44	Colorado Springs, CO	445,830	417,341	44	6.8
45	Raleigh, NC	439,896	403,971	45	8.9
46	Miami, FL	430,332	399,508	46	7.7
47	Oakland, CA	413,775	390,905	49	5.9
48	Minneapolis, MN	407,207	382,599	50	6.4
49	Tulsa, OK	399,682	391,922	48	2.0
50	Cleveland, OH	389,521	396,697	47	-1.8
51	Wichita city, KS	388,413	382,386	51	1.6
52	New Orleans, LA	384,320	343,829	54	11.8
53	Arlington, TX	383,204	365,361	52	4.9
54	Bakersfield, CA	368,759	347,587	53	6.1
55	Tampa, FL	358,699	335,715	57	6.8
56	Aurora city	353,108	324,688	60	8.8
57	Urban Honolulu, HI	350,399	337,256	55	3.9
58	Anaheim, CA	346,997	336,440	56	3.1
59	Islip town, NY	336,793	335,543	58	0.4
60	Santa Ana, CA	334,909	324,782	59	3.1
61	Corpus Christi, CA	320,434	305,215	63	5.0
62	Riverside, CA	319,504	303,987	64	5.1
63	St. Louis, MO	317,419	319,365	61	-0.6
64	Lexington-Fayette urban county, KY	310,797	295,803	66	5.1
65	Pittsburgh, PA	305,412	305,702	62	-0.1
66	Stockton, CA	302,389	291,731	69	3.7
67	Anchorage, AK	301,010	291,826	68	3.1
68	Cincinnati, OH	298,165	296,950	65	0.4
69	Oyster Bay town, NY	297,896	293,219	67	1.6
70	St. Paul, MN	297,640	285,068	71	4.4
71	Greensboro, NC	282,586	268,877	73	5.1
72	Toledo, OH	281,031	287,206	70	-2.2
73	Newark city, NJ	280,579	277,149	72	1.2
74	Plano, TX	278,480	259,841	74	7.2
75	Henderson, NV	277,440	257,354	75	7.8

Table 4.   Percent of Private Nonfarm Employment by Industry by State, 2012

State	Private nonfarm employment measured in Economic Census	Percentage of employment by sector							
		Mining, quarrying, and oil and gas extraction	Utilities	Construction	Manufacturing	Wholesale trade	Retail trade	Transportation and ware-housing	Information
United States.................	111,251,646	0.8	0.6	5.1	10.1	4.4	13.2	3.9	3.0
Alabama	1,503,351	0.6	1.0	5.2	15.5	4.0	14.5	3.8	2.3
Alaska.............................	265,000	5.7	0.8	9.1	4.7	2.9	12.7	7.2	2.5
Arizona*	1,998,086	0.6	0.6	6.2	6.6	3.7	14.3	4.0	2.5
Arkansas.........................	926,909	1.1	0.8	4.6	16.6	3.7	14.6	5.5	2.6
California	12,663,341	0.2	0.5	4.7	9.2	5.7	12.2	3.5	4.4
Colorado	1,957,343	1.7	0.4	6.3	5.9	3.9	12.6	3.2	4.2
Connecticut*	1,407,288	0.1	0.7	4.0	11.6	4.2	13.0	3.1	2.7
Delaware*	362,162	0.1	0.7	4.9	7.3	2.1	14.3	3.3	1.9
District of Columbia*........	430,035	0.0	0.4	2.1	0.3	0.8	4.6	2.0	5.1
Florida.............................	6,609,491	0.1	0.4	4.5	4.2	3.8	14.3	3.2	2.3
Georgia*	3,129,476	0.2	0.7	4.6	10.7	4.8	13.9	4.9	3.9
Hawaii*	466,888	0.0	0.7	5.9	2.5	3.6	14.6	5.7	1.8
Idaho*	476,837	0.7	0.8	6.7	10.9	4.5	15.3	3.6	2.6
Illinois.............................	4,898,221	0.2	0.6	4.2	11.1	5.2	12.1	4.7	2.5
Indiana............................	2,391,256	0.3	0.7	5.2	18.9	3.8	12.9	4.9	1.8
Iowa	1,219,153	0.2	0.6	5.4	16.7	4.8	14.3	4.6	2.5
Kansas............................	1,082,390	1.0	0.7	5.4	14.1	4.8	13.4	4.6	3.1
Kentucky.........................	1,427,082	1.4	0.6	4.5	15.0	4.0	14.2	5.9	2.3
Louisiana	1,583,727	3.5	0.7	8.6	8.6	4.1	13.9	4.4	1.6
Maine*	466,244	0.0	0.5	5.4	10.6	3.2	17.2	3.2	2.6
Maryland*	2,074,008	0.1	0.5	7.0	4.8	3.5	13.6	3.1	2.7
Massachusetts.................	2,851,670	0.0	0.5	4.2	8.2	4.0	12.3	2.7	4.1
Michigan*	3,279,920	0.2	0.7	4.0	15.7	4.0	13.5	3.2	2.0
Minnesota	2,372,457	0.3	0.5	4.8	12.6	4.6	12.2	3.5	2.7
Mississippi	837,890	0.8	1.1	5.0	15.8	3.6	16.2	4.0	1.7
Missouri	2,187,586	0.2	0.7	5.0	11.1	4.4	13.8	3.8	2.7
Montana..........................	337,840	2.6	0.9	7.1	4.7	3.9	16.4	3.5	2.7
Nebraska	777,291	0.1	0.1	5.2	11.9	4.4	13.6	3.5	2.7
Nevada*	1,010,655	1.5	0.5	5.4	3.8	2.7	12.9	4.3	1.7
New Hampshire	527,406	0.1	0.6	4.6	12.6	4.0	18.1	2.6	2.6
New Jersey	3,329,598	0.0	0.6	4.4	6.9	6.3	13.1	4.8	3.6
New Mexico	576,673	3.4	0.8	6.6	4.6	3.0	15.7	3.0	2.2
New York.........................	7,242,664	0.1	0.6	4.6	5.9	4.5	12.5	3.3	4.0
North Carolina	3,175,363	0.1	0.6	5.7	12.7	4.3	14.1	3.4	2.5
North Dakota*.................	330,971	7.5	1.1	7.8	7.1	5.7	14.3	5.7	2.1
Ohio................................	4,334,996	0.2	0.6	4.2	14.5	4.2	12.7	3.7	2.1
Oklahoma	1,257,305	4.7	0.7	5.5	10.6	4.0	13.4	3.5	2.3
Oregon............................	1,303,295	0.1	0.6	5.4	11.7	4.6	14.4	4.0	3.0
Pennsylvania	4,820,990	0.8	0.6	4.9	11.3	4.0	13.4	4.4	2.7
Rhode Island*.................	383,006	0.0	0.3	4.6	10.3	4.1	12.5	2.9	1.9
South Carolina................	1,465,106	0.1	0.8	4.7	14.2	3.8	15.0	3.3	2.3
South Dakota..................	321,302	0.4	0.7	6.2	13.1	4.9	15.5	3.0	2.1
Tennessee	2,243,591	0.1	0.1	4.5	13.1	4.1	13.6	5.9	2.1
Texas	9,101,233	3.1	0.6	6.3	8.4	4.5	12.6	4.2	2.5
Utah*..............................	998,624	1.3	0.4	6.5	10.8	4.4	13.4	4.6	3.8
Vermont*.........................	239,267	0.2	0.7	6.6	13.2	4.0	16.3	2.4	2.8
Virginia...........................	2,988,984	0.3	0.5	5.9	7.6	3.0	13.7	3.0	3.4
Washington.....................	2,299,935	0.1	0.4	6.0	10.8	4.5	13.4	3.8	5.6
West Virginia...................	556,970	7.2	1.1	4.8	8.7	3.0	15.3	2.8	2.0
Wisconsin	2,294,128	0.2	0.6	4.5	19.0	4.2	12.9	4.3	2.3
Wyoming*	215,602	14.9	1.1	9.9	4.7	3.2	14.0	4.7	1.9

* Includes one or more sectors where the number of employees was withheld to avoid disclosure. For those sectors, a range of employees was used. In this table, the midpoint of the range was used to derive an estimate.

Table 4. Percent of Private Nonfarm Employment by Industry by State, 2012—Continued

Percentage of employment by sector

State	Finance and insurance	Real estate and rental and leasing	Professional, scientific, and technical services	Management of companies and enterprises	Administrative and support and waste management and remediation services	Educational services	Health care and social assistance	Arts, entertainment, and recreation	Accommo- dation and food services	Other services (except public administration)
United States................	5.4	1.7	7.4	2.8	8.8	0.6	16.6	1.9	10.8	3.1
Alabama	4.8	1.5	6.0	1.2	8.9	0.3	16.2	1.1	10.5	2.5
Alaska.............................	2.7	1.6	6.7	2.4	7.5	0.5	18.4	1.9	10.1	2.7
Arizona*..........................	6.4	2.0	6.1	1.9	10.9	0.6	15.8	2.1	12.6	3.1
Arkansas.........................	3.8	1.4	3.5	4.3	5.7	0.2	18.0	1.0	10.3	2.4
California	4.8	2.2	10.3	2.2	8.8	0.8	14.0	2.4	11.0	3.1
Colorado.........................	5.0	2.0	9.2	2.8	10.7	0.7	13.2	2.6	12.3	3.3
Connecticut*...................	8.5	1.4	6.9	2.7	6.6	0.7	19.3	1.9	9.6	3.1
Delaware*.......................	10.1	1.5	10.4	4.8	6.3	0.5	17.1	2.2	9.8	2.7
District of Columbia*........	4.2	2.3	22.7	2.2	6.7	1.2	15.8	1.7	14.0	13.7
Florida.............................	5.1	2.1	6.7	2.0	18.3	0.6	15.0	2.6	11.9	3.0
Georgia*..........................	5.3	1.8	4.8	3.7	10.5	0.4	14.3	1.4	11.3	2.9
Hawaii*...........................	4.0	2.4	4.6	1.6	10.1	0.5	14.3	2.3	21.1	4.1
Idaho*.............................	4.6	1.3	6.7	1.6	7.1	0.4	17.5	1.9	11.4	2.6
Illinois............................	6.0	1.6	7.4	4.1	9.4	0.6	15.7	1.6	9.6	3.4
Indiana............................	4.1	1.3	4.2	2.3	7.5	0.4	16.6	1.4	10.7	3.1
Iowa................................	7.5	1.0	4.0	1.2	6.0	0.4	17.0	1.7	9.4	2.5
Kansas............................	5.5	1.3	5.6	1.9	6.5	0.4	17.8	1.3	9.9	2.7
Kentucky.........................	4.8	1.3	4.4	2.2	6.6	0.3	17.6	1.2	11.0	2.7
Louisiana	4.1	2.0	5.6	1.6	6.5	0.4	18.0	1.5	12.2	2.7
Maine*............................	5.5	1.3	4.9	1.6	4.8	0.6	23.4	1.6	10.7	3.0
Maryland*.......................	4.8	2.1	11.8	3.6	8.8	0.8	17.3	1.7	9.8	3.8
Massachusetts.................	7.1	1.5	8.9	3.4	6.7	0.8	20.6	1.9	9.6	3.3
Michigan*........................	4.6	1.5	4.6	3.0	9.6	0.5	17.9	1.4	10.6	2.9
Minnesota........................	6.6	1.5	5.9	4.8	6.9	0.5	18.6	1.8	9.4	3.1
Mississippi	4.1	1.2	3.6	0.9	5.7	0.2	18.8	1.1	13.9	2.3
Missouri..........................	6.1	1.5	6.3	3.3	6.8	0.4	18.3	1.7	10.9	2.9
Montana..........................	4.8	1.5	4.9	0.9	6.1	0.5	19.4	3.2	13.7	3.2
Nebraska	8.0	1.3	9.6	2.3	7.3	0.3	16.1	1.7	9.0	2.8
Nevada*..........................	3.4	2.2	4.7	1.7	9.3	0.5	10.7	2.6	29.4	2.5
New Hampshire...............	4.6	1.3	5.7	1.3	8.6	0.8	16.5	2.5	10.2	3.1
New Jersey......................	6.0	1.6	9.2	4.0	8.5	1.0	16.2	1.7	8.8	3.3
New Mexico	3.9	1.7	7.7	1.1	6.0	0.5	20.2	2.1	14.3	3.0
New York.........................	7.5	2.3	8.1	2.6	7.5	0.9	20.3	2.2	9.4	3.8
North Carolina	5.3	1.5	6.2	2.7	8.0	0.5	16.7	1.8	11.3	2.5
North Dakota*..................	5.2	1.6	4.1	1.5	3.8	0.2	17.1	1.5	10.8	2.8
Ohio................................	5.6	1.4	5.4	3.9	8.4	0.4	18.4	1.4	10.1	2.9
Oklahoma	4.6	1.7	5.7	2.4	7.4	0.4	17.0	2.1	11.4	2.6
Oregon............................	4.4	2.0	6.5	3.4	6.4	0.6	16.7	1.8	11.5	2.9
Pennsylvania	5.5	1.2	6.6	3.4	6.4	0.5	19.8	2.1	9.1	3.2
Rhode Island*..................	6.6	1.5	5.5	4.6	5.5	0.5	21.9	2.3	11.5	3.4
South Carolina.................	4.5	1.6	5.4	1.4	10.7	0.3	14.5	1.7	12.6	3.0
South Dakota...................	8.2	1.1	3.5	1.5	3.6	0.2	19.8	1.9	11.8	2.6
Tennessee	5.0	1.4	4.7	3.7	9.5	0.4	17.0	1.4	10.8	2.5
Texas	5.3	1.9	7.0	3.2	10.2	0.4	14.8	1.3	10.7	2.8
Utah*..............................	5.3	1.6	7.6	1.8	10.9	0.7	12.6	2.1	9.6	2.6
Vermont*.........................	3.8	1.3	6.7	0.7	3.1	0.7	18.5	3.0	13.1	3.0
Virginia...........................	5.1	1.8	14.4	2.1	8.4	0.6	13.8	1.8	10.7	3.8
Washington......................	4.2	2.0	7.3	3.1	6.1	0.7	16.3	2.6	10.2	3.0
West Virginia....................	3.2	1.1	4.5	0.9	5.7	0.2	23.2	1.5	11.9	3.0
Wisconsin	6.1	1.0	4.3	2.9	6.1	0.4	16.8	1.9	9.7	2.7
Wyoming*........................	3.1	2.1	4.2	0.3	3.0	0.6	14.5	1.8	12.8	3.1

* Includes one or more sectors where the number of employees was withheld to avoid disclosure. For those sectors, a range of employees was used. In this table, the midpoint of the range was used to derive an estimate.

75 Largest Cities and Towns by 2014 Population
Selected Rankings

	Population, 2014			Land area, 2010		
Population rank	City	Population [Table A col 2]	Population rank	Land area rank	City	Land area (square miles) [Table B col 1]
1	New York, NY	8,491,079	67	1	Anchorage, AK	1,704.9
2	Los Angeles, CA	3,928,864	13	2	Jacksonville, FL	747.4
3	Chicago, IL	2,722,389	29	3	Oklahoma City, OK	606.7
4	Houston, TX	2,239,558	4	4	Houston, TX	599.7
5	Philadelphia, PA	1,560,297	6	5	Phoenix, AZ	517.5
6	Phoenix, AZ	1,537,058	22	6	Nashville-Davidson metropolitan government, TN	504.0
7	San Antonio, TX	1,436,697	2	7	Los Angeles, CA	468.7
8	San Diego, CA	1,381,069	7	8	San Antonio, TX	461.0
9	Dallas, TX	1,281,047	19	9	Louisville/Jefferson County metro government, KY	380.4
10	San Jose, CA	1,015,785	12	10	Indianapolis, IN	366.5
11	Austin, TX	912,791	9	11	Dallas, TX	341.4
12	Indianapolis, IN	858,325	16	12	Fort Worth, TX	340.7
13	Jacksonville, FL	853,382	8	13	San Diego, CA	325.2
14	San Francisco, CA	852,469	26	14	Memphis, TN	317.4
15	Columbus, OH	835,957	39	15	Kansas City, MO	315.0
16	Fort Worth, FL	812,238	11	16	Austin, TX	312.4
17	Charlotte, NC	809,958	17	17	Charlotte, NC	303.4
18	Hempstead town, NY	770,116	1	18	New York, NY	301.5
19	Louisville/Jefferson County metro government, KY	760,026	64	19	Lexington-Fayette, KY	283.6
20	Detroit, MI	680,250	36	20	Brookhaven town, New York	259.5
21	El Paso, TX	679,036	21	21	El Paso, TX	256.7
22	Nashville-Davidson metropolitan government, TN	668,347	42	22	Virginia Beach, VA	249.7
23	Seattle, WA	668,342	34	23	Tucson, AZ	230.8
24	Denver, CO	663,862	3	24	Chicago, IL	227.8
25	Washington, DC	658,893	15	25	Columbus, OH	218.0
26	Memphis, TN	656,861	49	26	Tulsa, OK	196.9
27	Boston city, MA	655,884	44	27	Colorado Springs, CO	194.9
28	Baltimore, MD	622,793	33	28	Albuquerque, NM	188.1
29	Oklahoma, OK	620,602	10	29	San Jose, CA	176.6
30	Portland, OR	619,360	52	30	New Orleans, LA	169.4
31	Las Vegas, NV	613,599	61	31	Corpus Christi, TX	160.5
32	Milwaukee, WI	599,642	51	32	Wichita , KS	160.4
33	Albuquerque, NM	557,169	56	33	Aurora city	153.8
34	Tucson, AZ	527,972	24	34	Denver, CO	153.0
35	Fresno, CA	515,986	54	35	Bakersfield city, CA	148.5
36	Brookhaven, NY	489,403	45	36	Raleigh, NC	144.1
37	Sacramento, CA	485,199	20	37	Detroit city, MI	138.7
38	Long Beach, CA	473,577	40	38	Mesa, AZ	137.6
39	Kansas City , MO	470,800	5	39	Philadelphia, PA	134.1
40	Mesa, AZ	464,704	30	40	Portland, OR	133.5
41	Atlanta, GA	456,002	31	41	Las Vegas, NV	133.1
42	Virginia Beach, VA	450,980	41	41	Atlanta, GA	133.1
43	Omaha, NE	446,599	43	43	Omaha, NE	129.9
44	Colorado Springs, CO	445,830	71	44	Greensboro, NC	126.7
45	Raleigh, NC	439,896	18	45	Hempstead town, NY	118.7
46	Miami, FL	430,332	55	46	Tampa, FL	113.4
47	Oakland, CA	413,775	35	47	Fresno, CA	113.2
48	Minneapolis, MN	407,207	75	48	Henderson, NV	104.7
49	Tulsa, OK	399,682	59	49	Islip town, NY	103.9
50	Cleveland, OH	389,521	69	50	Oyster Bay town, NY	103.8
51	Wichita city, KS	388,413	37	51	Sacramento, CA	97.9
52	New Orleans, LA	384,320	32	52	Milwaukee, WI	96.1
53	Arlington, TX	383,204	53	53	Arlington, TX	95.9
54	Bakersfield, CA	368,759	23	54	Seattle, WA	83.8
55	Tampa, FL	358,699	62	55	Riverside, CA	81.2
56	Aurora city	353,108	28	56	Baltimore , MD	80.9
57	Urban Honolulu, HI	350,399	72	57	Toledo city, OH	80.7
58	Anaheim, CA	346,997	68	58	Cincinnati, OH	77.9
59	Islip town, NY	336,793	50	59	Cleveland, OH	77.7
60	Santa Ana, CA	334,909	74	60	Plano city, TX	71.7
61	Corpus Christi, CA	320,434	63	61	St. Louis, MO	62.0
62	Riverside, CA	319,504	66	62	Stockton, CA	61.7
63	St. Louis, MO	317,419	25	63	Washington, D.C.	61.0
64	Lexington-Fayette urban county, KY	310,797	57	64	Urban Honolulu, HI	60.5
65	Pittsburgh, PA	305,412	47	65	Oakland, CA	55.9
66	Stockton, CA	302,389	65	66	Pittsburgh , PA	55.4
67	Anchorage, AK	301,010	48	67	Minneapolis, MN	54.0
68	Cincinnati, OH	298,165	70	68	St. Paul, MN	52.0
69	Oyster Bay town, NY	297,896	38	69	Long Beach, CA	50.3
70	St. Paul, MN	297,640	58	70	Anaheim, CA	50.0
71	Greensboro, NC	282,586	27	71	Boston, MA	48.4
72	Toledo, OH	281,031	14	72	San Francisco, CA	46.9
73	Newark city, NJ	280,579	46	73	Miami, FL	35.9
74	Plano, TX	278,480	60	74	Santa Ana, CA	27.1
75	Henderson, NV	277,440	73	75	Newark city, NJ	24.2

75 Largest Cities and Towns by 2014 Population
Selected Rankings

		Population density, 2014				Percent population change, 2010–2014		
Population rank	Density rank	City	Density (persons per square mile) [Table B col 5]	Population rank	Percent change rank	City		Percent change [Table A col 3]
1	1	New York, NY..................................	28,163.4	11	1	Austin, TX..............................		12.5
14	2	San Francisco, CA...........................	18,179.1	52	2	New Orleans, LA.....................		11.8
27	3	Boston, MA....................................	13,560.9	24	3	Denver, CO............................		10.6
60	4	Santa Ana, CA...............................	12,337.5	17	4	Charlotte, NC........................		10.1
46	5	Miami, FL.....................................	11,989.7	23	5	Seattle, WA...........................		9.8
3	6	Chicago, IL...................................	11,952.6	16	6	Fort Worth, FL.......................		9.5
5	7	Philadelphia, PA............................	11,634.6	25	6	Washington city......................		9.5
73	8	Newark city, NJ.............................	11,597.3	45	8	Raleigh, NC..........................		8.9
25	9	Washington, D.C............................	10,793.0	56	9	Aurora city...........................		8.8
38	10	Long Beach, CA.............................	9,414.8	41	10	Atlanta, GA...........................		8.5
2	11	Los Angeles, CA............................	8,383.0	7	11	San Antonio, TX......................		8.2
23	12	Seattle, WA..................................	7,971.9	75	12	Henderson, NV.......................		7.8
28	13	Baltimore , MD..............................	7,694.1	46	13	Miami, FL..............................		7.7
48	14	Minneapolis, MN............................	7,539.3	74	14	Plano, TX..............................		7.2
47	15	Oakland, CA..................................	7,403.0	9	15	Dallas, TX............................		7.0
58	16	Anaheim, CA.................................	6,943.1	29	15	Oklahoma, OK........................		7.0
18	17	Hempstead town, NY.......................	6,489.2	4	17	Houston, TX..........................		6.8
32	18	Milwaukee, WI...............................	6,239.4	44	17	Colorado Springs, CO...............		6.8
57	19	Urban Honolulu, HI.........................	5,789.8	55	17	Tampa, FL.............................		6.8
10	20	San Jose, CA................................	5,752.9	22	20	Nashville-Davidson metropolitan government, TN		6.7
70	21	St. Paul, MN..................................	5,726.2	10	21	San Jose, CA.........................		6.6
65	22	Pittsburgh , PA..............................	5,515.2	48	22	Minneapolis, MN......................		6.4
63	23	St. Louis, MO................................	5,123.5	6	23	Phoenix, AZ...........................		6.2
50	24	Cleveland, OH...............................	5,012.8	27	23	Boston city, MA......................		6.2
37	25	Sacramento, CA.............................	4,954.9	8	25	San Diego, CA........................		6.1
66	26	Stockton, CA.................................	4,903.6	30	25	Portland, OR..........................		6.1
20	27	Detroit city, MI..............................	4,902.7	54	25	Bakersfield, CA.......................		6.1
30	28	Portland, OR.................................	4,641.1	15	28	Columbus, OH........................		6.0
31	29	Las Vegas, NV...............................	4,609.1	14	29	San Francisco, CA...................		5.9
35	30	Fresno, CA...................................	4,557.2	47	29	Oakland, CA..........................		5.9
24	31	Denver, CO...................................	4,337.9	40	31	Mesa, AZ..............................		5.6
8	32	San Diego, CA...............................	4,247.0	43	32	Omaha, NE............................		5.5
53	33	Arlington, TX.................................	3,996.0	62	33	Riverside, CA.........................		5.1
62	34	Riverside, CA................................	3,935.8	64	33	Lexington-Fayette urban county, KY...............		5.1
74	35	Plano city, TX................................	3,885.6	71	33	Greensboro, NC......................		5.1
15	36	Columbus, OH...............................	3,835.2	31	36	Las Vegas, NV........................		5.0
68	37	Cincinnati, OH...............................	3,825.5	61	36	Corpus Christi, CA...................		5.0
9	38	Dallas, TX....................................	3,752.7	53	38	Arlington, TX..........................		4.9
4	39	Houston, TX..................................	3,734.2	21	39	El Paso, TX...........................		4.6
72	40	Toledo city, OH.............................	3,481.5	70	40	St. Paul, MN..........................		4.4
43	41	Omaha, NE...................................	3,438.8	35	41	Fresno, CA............................		4.0
41	42	Atlanta, GA...................................	3,426.1	37	41	Sacramento, CA......................		4.0
40	43	Mesa, AZ.....................................	3,377.2	1	43	New York, NY.........................		3.9
59	44	Islip town, NY...............................	3,241.4	57	43	Urban Honolulu, HI...................		3.9
55	45	Tampa, FL....................................	3,163.0	13	45	Jacksonville, FL......................		3.8
7	46	San Antonio, TX............................	3,116.6	66	46	Stockton, CA.........................		3.7
45	47	Raleigh, NC..................................	3,052.3	2	47	Los Angeles, CA.....................		3.6
6	48	Phoenix, AZ..................................	2,970.1	12	48	Indianapolis, IN......................		3.5
33	49	Albuquerque, NM...........................	2,961.3	58	49	Anaheim, CA..........................		3.1
11	50	Austin, TX....................................	2,921.6	60	49	Santa Ana, CA.......................		3.1
69	51	Oyster Bay town, NY.......................	2,871.2	67	49	Anchorage, AK.......................		3.1
17	52	Charlotte, NC................................	2,669.2	42	52	Virginia Beach, VA...................		3.0
75	53	Henderson, NV..............................	2,650.9	19	53	Louisville/Jefferson County metro government, KY...........		2.6
21	54	El Paso, TX..................................	2,645.1	38	54	Long Beach, CA......................		2.4
54	55	Bakersfield city, CA........................	2,482.4	39	54	Kansas City , MO....................		2.4
51	56	Wichita , KS.................................	2,421.0	5	56	Philadelphia, PA.....................		2.2
16	57	Fort Worth, TX..............................	2,384.0	33	57	Albuquerque, NM.....................		2.0
12	58	Indianapolis, IN.............................	2,342.2	49	57	Tulsa, OK.............................		2.0
56	59	Aurora city....................................	2,295.5	51	59	Wichita city, KS......................		1.6
44	60	Colorado Springs, CO......................	2,287.8	69	59	Oyster Bay town, NY.................		1.6
34	61	Tucson, AZ...................................	2,287.5	34	61	Tucson, AZ...........................		1.4
52	62	New Orleans, LA............................	2,268.5	18	62	Hempstead town, NY................		1.3
71	63	Greensboro, NC.............................	2,230.8	73	63	Newark city, NJ......................		1.2
26	64	Memphis, TN.................................	2,069.7	3	64	Chicago, IL...........................		1.0
49	65	Tulsa, OK.....................................	2,030.3	26	65	Memphis, TN..........................		0.8
19	66	Louisville/Jefferson County metro government, KY...............	1,997.9	32	65	Milwaukee, WI........................		0.8
61	67	Corpus Christi, TX..........................	1,996.0	36	67	Brookhaven, NY......................		0.7
36	68	Brookhaven town, New York...............	1,886.2	59	68	Islip town, NY.........................		0.4
42	69	Virginia Beach, VA.........................	1,806.0	68	68	Cincinnati, OH........................		0.4
39	70	Kansas City, MO............................	1,494.8	28	70	Baltimore, MD........................		0.3
22	71	Nashville-Davidson metropolitan government, TN	1,326.0	65	71	Pittsburgh , PA......................		-0.1
13	72	Jacksonville, FL.............................	1,141.7	63	72	St. Louis, MO.........................		-0.6
64	73	Lexington-Fayette, KY......................	1,095.7	50	73	Cleveland, OH........................		-1.8
29	74	Oklahoma City, OK..........................	1,022.9	72	74	Toledo, OH............................		-2.2
67	75	Anchorage, AK..............................	176.6	20	75	Detroit, MI............................		-4.7

75 Largest Cities and Towns by 2014 Population
Selected Rankings

Percent White alone, not Hispanic or Latino 2010–2014				Percent Black alone, not Hispanic or Latino 2010–2014			
Population rank	Non-Hispanic White rank	City	Percent White alone, not Hispanic or Latino [Table A col 5]	Population rank	Non-Hispanic Black rank	City	Percent Black alone, not Hispanic or Latino [Table A col 6]
69	1	Oyster Bay town, NY	79.1	20	1	Detroit, MI	80.7
36	2	Brookhaven, NY	75.1	26	2	Memphis, TN	62.6
64	3	Lexington-Fayette urban county, KY	72.6	28	3	Baltimore, MD	62.5
30	4	Portland, OR	71.8	52	4	New Orleans, LA	59.2
19	5	Louisville/Jefferson County metro government, KY	69.9	41	5	Atlanta, GA	52.4
44	5	Colorado Springs, CO	69.9	50	6	Cleveland, OH	51.3
43	7	Omaha, NE	68.2	73	7	Newark city, NJ	49.0
75	8	Henderson, NV	67.8	25	8	Washington city	48.7
23	9	Seattle, WA	66.2	63	9	St. Louis, MO	47.9
65	10	Pittsburgh, PA	65.1	68	10	Cincinnati, OH	43.3
40	11	Mesa, AZ	64.1	5	11	Philadelphia, PA	41.8
51	12	Wichita city, KS	63.9	71	12	Greensboro, NC	40.2
42	13	Virginia Beach, VA	63.6	32	13	Milwaukee, WI	38.8
72	14	Toledo, OH	61.3	17	14	Charlotte, NC	34.4
67	15	Anchorage, AK	61.1	3	15	Chicago, IL	31.5
48	16	Minneapolis, MN	61.0	13	16	Jacksonville, FL	30.2
15	17	Columbus, OH	58.4	39	17	Kansas City , MO	28.9
12	18	Indianapolis, IN	57.8	45	18	Raleigh, NC	28.5
18	19	Hempstead town, NY	57.7	22	19	Nashville-Davidson metropolitan government, TN	27.5
22	20	Nashville-Davidson metropolitan government, TN	57.1	12	20	Indianapolis, IN	27.4
49	21	Tulsa, OK	57.0	15	20	Columbus, OH	27.4
74	22	Plano, TX	56.9	72	22	Toledo, OH	26.2
59	23	Islip town, NY	56.3	47	23	Oakland, CA	25.6
29	24	Oklahoma, OK	55.7	55	24	Tampa, FL	24.5
39	25	Kansas City , MO	55.1	9	25	Dallas, TX	24.3
70	26	St. Paul, MN	54.8	65	25	Pittsburgh, PA	24.3
13	27	Jacksonville, FL	54.2	4	27	Houston, TX	22.8
45	28	Raleigh, NC	54.0	27	28	Boston city, MA	22.7
24	29	Denver, CO	52.9	1	29	New York, NY	22.6
68	30	Cincinnati, OH	48.8	19	30	Louisville/Jefferson County metro government, KY	20.4
11	31	Austin, TX	48.7	53	31	Arlington, TX	19.3
31	32	Las Vegas, NV	46.3	16	32	Fort Worth, FL	18.7
34	32	Tucson, AZ	46.3	42	33	Virginia Beach, VA	18.6
56	32	Aurora city	46.3	48	34	Minneapolis, MN	17.6
6	35	Phoenix, AZ	46.0	46	35	Miami, FL	16.7
27	35	Boston city, MA	46.0	18	36	Hempstead town, NY	16.2
55	37	Tampa, FL	45.9	56	37	Aurora city	15.5
71	38	Greensboro, NC	45.4	70	38	St. Paul, MN	15.1
17	39	Charlotte, NC	43.9	49	39	Tulsa, OK	15.0
8	40	San Diego, CA	43.6	29	40	Oklahoma, OK	14.4
53	41	Arlington, TX	42.9	64	41	Lexington-Fayette urban county, KY	14.2
63	42	St. Louis, MO	42.8	37	42	Sacramento, CA	13.0
14	43	San Francisco, CA	41.4	43	43	Omaha, NE	12.7
33	44	Albuquerque, NM	41.3	38	44	Long Beach, CA	12.6
16	45	Fort Worth, FL	40.9	51	45	Wichita city, KS	11.2
32	46	Milwaukee, WI	36.6	31	46	Las Vegas, NV	11.0
41	47	Atlanta, GA	36.4	66	47	Stockton, CA	10.8
5	48	Philadelphia, PA	36.2	24	48	Denver, CO	9.5
54	49	Bakersfield, CA	35.8	2	49	Los Angeles, CA	8.9
25	50	Washington city	35.4	59	49	Islip town, NY	8.9
50	51	Cleveland, OH	34.3	54	51	Bakersfield, CA	7.8
37	52	Sacramento, CA	34.0	11	52	Austin, TX	7.5
1	53	New York, NY	32.7	35	52	Fresno, CA	7.5
3	54	Chicago, IL	32.2	74	54	Plano, TX	7.3
61	55	Corpus Christi, CA	32.0	23	55	Seattle, WA	7.2
62	55	Riverside, CA	32.0	6	56	Phoenix, AZ	6.5
52	57	New Orleans, LA	30.7	7	57	San Antonio, TX	6.4
9	58	Dallas, TX	29.3	8	57	San Diego, CA	6.4
35	59	Fresno, CA	28.6	30	59	Portland, OR	5.9
2	60	Los Angeles, CA	28.5	62	59	Riverside, CA	5.9
28	61	Baltimore, MD	28.1	44	61	Colorado Springs, CO	5.8
38	61	Long Beach, CA	28.1	67	62	Anchorage, AK	5.6
10	63	San Jose, CA	27.5	75	62	Henderson, NV	5.6
26	64	Memphis, TN	27.4	14	64	San Francisco, CA	5.5
58	65	Anaheim, CA	27.0	36	65	Brookhaven, NY	5.1
47	66	Oakland, CA	26.5	34	66	Tucson, AZ	4.6
7	67	San Antonio, TX	26.3	61	67	Corpus Christi, CA	4.0
4	68	Houston, TX	25.5	40	68	Mesa, AZ	3.3
66	69	Stockton, CA	22.3	21	69	El Paso, TX	3.1
57	70	Urban Honolulu, HI	16.6	10	70	San Jose, CA	2.9
21	71	El Paso, TX	14.8	33	70	Albuquerque, NM	2.9
46	72	Miami, FL	11.1	58	72	Anaheim, CA	2.3
73	72	Newark city, NJ	11.1	69	73	Oyster Bay town, NY	2.2
60	74	Santa Ana, CA	9.2	57	74	Urban Honolulu, HI	1.8
20	75	Detroit, MI	8.7	60	75	Santa Ana, CA	1.0

75 Largest Cities and Towns by 2014 Population
Selected Rankings

Asian alone, not Hispanic or Latino, 2010–2014				Percent all other races or 2 or more races, not Hispanic or Latino, 2010–2014			
Population rank	Asian alone not Hispanic or Latino rank	City	Percent Asian alone, not Hispanic or Latino [Table A col 7]	Population rank	All other races or 2 or more races rank	City	Percent All other races or 2 or more races, not Hispanic or Latino [Table A col 8]
57	1	Urban Honolulu, HI	53.6	57	1	Urban Honolulu, HI	22.1
14	2	San Francisco, CA	33.3	67	2	Anchorage, AK	16.8
10	3	San Jose, CA	32.9	49	3	Tulsa, OK	10.7
66	4	Stockton, CA	21.2	29	4	Oklahoma, OK	7.8
37	5	Sacramento, CA	18.4	37	5	Sacramento, CA	6.9
74	6	Plano, TX	18.1	23	6	Seattle, WA	6.1
8	7	San Diego, CA	16.4	33	7	Albuquerque, NM	5.9
47	7	Oakland, CA	16.4	48	8	Minneapolis, MN	5.8
70	9	St. Paul, MN	15.9	47	9	Oakland, CA	5.6
58	10	Anaheim, CA	15.5	30	10	Portland, OR	5.2
23	11	Seattle, WA	14.2	38	11	Long Beach, CA	4.8
1	12	New York, NY	13.2	70	12	St. Paul, MN	4.7
38	13	Long Beach, CA	12.8	14	13	San Francisco, CA	4.5
35	14	Fresno, CA	12.7	44	14	Colorado Springs, CO	4.4
2	15	Los Angeles, CA	11.4	51	14	Wichita city, KS	4.4
60	16	Santa Ana, CA	10.3	56	14	Aurora city	4.4
69	17	Oyster Bay town, NY	9.4	66	14	Stockton, CA	4.4
27	18	Boston city, MA	9.1	31	18	Las Vegas, NV	4.3
67	19	Anchorage, AK	8.3	34	18	Tucson, AZ	4.3
75	20	Henderson, NV	7.8	42	20	Virginia Beach, VA	4.2
30	21	Portland, OR	7.4	8	21	San Diego, CA	4.0
53	22	Arlington, TX	7.0	15	21	Columbus, OH	4.0
62	22	Riverside, CA	7.0	40	23	Mesa, AZ	3.9
5	24	Philadelphia, PA	6.6	6	24	Phoenix, AZ	3.8
11	25	Austin, TX	6.5	27	24	Boston city, MA	3.8
42	26	Virginia Beach, VA	6.4	72	24	Toledo, OH	3.8
54	26	Bakersfield, CA	6.4	75	24	Henderson, NV	3.8
4	28	Houston, TX	6.3	10	28	San Jose, CA	3.6
31	29	Las Vegas, NV	6.2	62	28	Riverside, CA	3.6
18	30	Hempstead town, NY	6.0	39	30	Kansas City , MO	3.4
48	31	Minneapolis, MN	5.8	73	31	Newark city, NJ	3.3
3	32	Chicago, IL	5.7	32	32	Milwaukee, WI	3.2
17	33	Charlotte, NC	5.5	35	32	Fresno, CA	3.2
56	34	Aurora city	5.0	43	32	Omaha, NE	3.2
65	35	Pittsburgh, PA	4.8	13	35	Jacksonville, FL	3.1
51	36	Wichita city, KS	4.7	54	35	Bakersfield, CA	3.1
15	37	Columbus, OH	4.4	65	35	Pittsburgh, PA	3.1
13	38	Jacksonville, FL	4.3	68	35	Cincinnati, OH	3.1
36	38	Brookhaven, NY	4.3	24	39	Denver, CO	3.0
45	38	Raleigh, NC	4.3	71	39	Greensboro, NC	3.0
29	41	Oklahoma, OK	4.2	74	39	Plano, TX	3.0
71	42	Greensboro, NC	3.9	12	42	Indianapolis, IN	2.8
41	43	Atlanta, GA	3.8	19	42	Louisville/Jefferson County metro government, KY	2.8
16	44	Fort Worth, FL	3.7	63	42	St. Louis, MO	2.8
32	44	Milwaukee, WI	3.7	64	42	Lexington-Fayette urban county, KY	2.8
55	44	Tampa, FL	3.7	1	46	New York, NY	2.7
25	47	Washington city	3.6	2	46	Los Angeles, CA	2.7
64	48	Lexington-Fayette urban county, KY	3.5	17	46	Charlotte, NC	2.7
24	49	Denver, CO	3.4	50	46	Cleveland, OH	2.7
6	50	Phoenix, AZ	3.3	55	50	Tampa, FL	2.6
22	51	Nashville-Davidson metropolitan government, TN .	3.1	11	51	Austin, TX	2.5
9	52	Dallas, TX	3.0	16	51	Fort Worth, FL	2.5
44	53	Colorado Springs, CO	2.9	25	51	Washington city	2.5
52	53	New Orleans, LA	2.9	28	51	Baltimore, MD	2.5
59	55	Islip town, NY	2.8	5	55	Philadelphia, PA	2.4
63	55	St. Louis, MO	2.8	22	55	Nashville-Davidson metropolitan government, TN .	2.4
43	57	Omaha, NE	2.7	58	55	Anaheim, CA	2.4
34	58	Tucson, AZ	2.6	45	58	Raleigh, NC	2.3
49	58	Tulsa, OK	2.6	53	59	Arlington, TX	2.2
28	60	Baltimore, MD	2.5	20	60	Detroit, MI	2.1
33	60	Albuquerque, NM	2.5	18	61	Hempstead town, NY	1.9
19	62	Louisville/Jefferson County metro government, KY	2.4	41	61	Atlanta, GA	1.9
39	62	Kansas City , MO	2.4	36	63	Brookhaven, NY	1.8
7	64	San Antonio, TX	2.3	52	63	New Orleans, LA	1.8
12	64	Indianapolis, IN	2.3	3	65	Chicago, IL	1.7
40	66	Mesa, AZ	1.9	9	65	Dallas, TX	1.7
68	66	Cincinnati, OH	1.9	26	65	Memphis, TN	1.7
61	68	Corpus Christi, CA	1.8	7	68	San Antonio, TX	1.6
73	68	Newark city, NJ	1.8	59	68	Islip town, NY	1.6
26	70	Memphis, TN	1.7	4	70	Houston, TX	1.5
50	70	Cleveland, OH	1.7	69	71	Oyster Bay town, NY	1.4
20	72	Detroit, MI	1.2	61	72	Corpus Christi, CA	1.3
72	72	Toledo, OH	1.2	21	73	El Paso, TX	1.2
21	74	El Paso, TX	1.1	60	74	Santa Ana, CA	0.9
46	75	Miami, FL	0.8	46	75	Miami, FL	0.7

75 Largest Cities and Towns by 2014 Population
Selected Rankings

Percent Hispanic or Latino,[1] 2010–2014				Percent Foreign-Born, 2010–2014			
Population rank	Hispanic or Latino rank	City	Percent Hispanic or Latino [Table A col 9]	Population rank	Foreign-born rank	City	Percent Foreign-born [Table B col 6]
21	1	El Paso, TX	79.7	46	1	Miami, FL	57.6
60	2	Santa Ana, CA	78.6	60	2	Santa Ana, CA	47.3
46	3	Miami, FL	70.7	10	3	San Jose, CA	38.7
7	4	San Antonio, TX	63.3	2	4	Los Angeles, CA	38.6
61	5	Corpus Christi, CA	60.8	1	5	New York, NY	37.1
58	6	Anaheim, CA	52.8	58	6	Anaheim, CA	37.0
62	7	Riverside, CA	51.5	14	7	San Francisco, CA	35.5
2	8	Los Angeles, CA	48.6	4	8	Houston, TX	28.4
35	9	Fresno, CA	48.0	73	9	Newark city, NJ	27.9
33	10	Albuquerque, NM	47.3	57	10	Urban Honolulu, HI	27.5
54	11	Bakersfield, CA	46.9	47	11	Oakland, CA	27.1
4	12	Houston, TX	43.9	27	12	Boston, MA	27.0
34	13	Tucson, AZ	42.2	8	13	San Diego, CA	26.3
9	14	Dallas, TX	41.7	66	14	Stockton, CA	26.2
38	14	Long Beach, CA	41.7	38	15	Long Beach, CA	26.1
66	16	Stockton, CA	41.3	21	16	El Paso, TX	24.9
6	17	Phoenix, AZ	40.5	9	17	Dallas, TX	24.2
11	18	Austin, TX	34.8	74	18	Plano city, TX	24.1
73	18	Newark city, NJ	34.8	62	19	Riverside, CA	22.9
16	20	Fort Worth, FL	34.2	37	20	Sacramento, CA	22.1
10	21	San Jose, CA	33.1	18	21	Hempstead town, NY	21.7
31	22	Las Vegas, NV	32.2	31	22	Las Vegas, NV	21.3
24	23	Denver, CO	31.2	35	23	Fresno, CA	21.1
59	24	Islip town, NY	30.4	3	24	Chicago, IL	20.9
8	25	San Diego, CA	29.5	6	25	Phoenix, AZ	20.2
3	26	Chicago, IL	28.9	56	25	Aurora city	20.2
56	26	Aurora city	28.9	53	27	Arlington, TX	19.7
1	28	New York, NY	28.8	59	27	Islip town, NY	19.7
53	29	Arlington, TX	28.7	54	29	Bakersfield city, CA	18.5
37	30	Sacramento, CA	27.6	11	30	Austin, TX	18.4
40	31	Mesa, AZ	26.8	70	31	St. Paul, MN	18.2
47	32	Oakland, CA	25.9	23	32	Seattle, WA	18.0
55	33	Tampa, FL	23.3	16	33	Fort Worth, TX	17.5
27	34	Boston city, MA	18.4	24	34	Denver, CO	16.0
18	35	Hempstead town, NY	18.2	55	35	Tampa, FL	15.4
29	36	Oklahoma, OK	18.0	17	36	Charlotte, NC	15.3
32	37	Milwaukee, WI	17.7	48	37	Minneapolis, MN	15.1
44	38	Colorado Springs, CO	17.0	69	38	Oyster Bay town, NY	15.0
51	39	Wichita city, KS	15.7	34	39	Tucson, AZ	14.9
14	40	San Francisco, CA	15.3	7	40	San Antonio, TX	14.2
75	41	Henderson, NV	14.9	25	41	Washington, D.C.	14.0
49	42	Tulsa, OK	14.8	30	41	Portland, OR	14.0
74	43	Plano, TX	14.7	45	43	Raleigh, NC	13.3
36	44	Brookhaven, NY	13.7	5	44	Philadelphia, PA	12.5
17	45	Charlotte, NC	13.4	29	45	Oklahoma City, OK	12.4
43	46	Omaha, NE	13.3	40	45	Mesa, AZ	12.4
5	47	Philadelphia, PA	13.0	75	47	Henderson, NV	12.1
45	48	Raleigh, NC	10.9	22	48	Nashville-Davidson metropolitan government, TN	11.8
39	49	Kansas City , MO	10.1	36	49	Brookhaven town, New York	11.5
50	50	Cleveland, OH	10.0	15	50	Columbus, OH	11.3
25	51	Washington city	9.9	71	51	Greensboro, NC	10.8
22	52	Nashville-Davidson metropolitan government, TN	9.8	33	52	Albuquerque, NM	10.7
48	52	Minneapolis, MN	9.8	51	53	Wichita , KS	10.2
12	54	Indianapolis, IN	9.6	49	54	Tulsa, OK	10.1
30	54	Portland, OR	9.6	32	55	Milwaukee, WI	9.8
70	56	St. Paul, MN	9.5	43	55	Omaha, NE	9.8
67	57	Anchorage, AK	8.3	13	57	Jacksonville, FL	9.7
13	58	Jacksonville, FL	8.2	67	57	Anchorage, AK	9.7
69	59	Oyster Bay town, NY	7.9	64	59	Lexington-Fayette, KY	9.1
72	60	Toledo, OH	7.6	42	60	Virginia Beach, VA	8.9
71	61	Greensboro, NC	7.4	12	61	Indianapolis, IN	8.6
20	62	Detroit, MI	7.3	44	62	Colorado Springs, CO	8.2
42	63	Virginia Beach, VA	7.2	61	63	Corpus Christi, TX	8.1
64	64	Lexington-Fayette urban county, KY	6.8	39	64	Kansas City, MO	7.6
26	65	Memphis, TN	6.5	41	64	Atlanta, GA	7.6
23	66	Seattle, WA	6.4	28	66	Baltimore , MD	7.5
57	67	Urban Honolulu, HI	5.9	65	66	Pittsburgh , PA	7.5
15	68	Columbus, OH	5.7	63	68	St. Louis, MO	6.8
41	69	Atlanta, GA	5.6	19	69	Louisville/Jefferson County metro government, KY	6.7
52	70	New Orleans, LA	5.4	26	70	Memphis, TN	6.2
19	71	Louisville/Jefferson County metro government, KY	4.6	52	71	New Orleans, LA	6.0
28	72	Baltimore, MD	4.5	20	72	Detroit city, MI	5.2
63	73	St. Louis, MO	3.7	68	73	Cincinnati, OH	5.1
68	74	Cincinnati, OH	3.0	50	74	Cleveland, OH	4.7
65	75	Pittsburgh, PA	2.7	72	75	Toledo city, OH	3.4

75 Largest Cities and Towns by 2014 Population
Selected Rankings

Percent under 18 years old, 2010–2014				Percent 65 years old and over, 2010–2014			
Population rank	Under 18 years old rank	City	Percent under 18 years old [Table A col 10]	Population rank	65 years and over rank	City	Percent 65 years old and over [Table A col 12]
54	1	Bakersfield, CA	30.5	57	1	Urban Honolulu, HI	18.3
35	2	Fresno, CA	29.7	69	2	Oyster Bay town, NY	17.2
60	3	Santa Ana, CA	29.4	75	3	Henderson, NV	16.0
66	4	Stockton, CA	29.2	46	4	Miami, FL	15.8
16	5	Fort Worth, FL	28.8	40	5	Mesa, AZ	15.3
21	6	El Paso, TX	28.0	18	6	Hempstead town, NY	14.6
6	7	Phoenix, AZ	27.2	14	7	San Francisco, CA	14.0
53	8	Arlington, TX	27.1	65	7	Pittsburgh, PA	14.0
56	9	Aurora city	27.0	19	9	Louisville/Jefferson County metro government, KY	13.8
32	10	Milwaukee, WI	26.8	31	10	Las Vegas, NV	13.3
51	11	Wichita city, KS	26.4	36	11	Brookhaven, NY	13.0
58	12	Anaheim, CA	26.3	33	12	Albuquerque, NM	12.8
7	13	San Antonio, TX	26.1	49	12	Tulsa, OK	12.8
9	14	Dallas, TX	25.9	72	14	Toledo, OH	12.7
62	14	Riverside, CA	25.9	34	15	Tucson, AZ	12.6
73	16	Newark city, NJ	25.7	1	16	New York, NY	12.5
29	17	Oklahoma, OK	25.6	50	17	Cleveland, OH	12.4
20	18	Detroit, MI	25.5	5	18	Philadelphia, PA	12.3
61	18	Corpus Christi, CA	25.5	59	19	Islip town, NY	12.2
4	20	Houston, TX	25.3	61	19	Corpus Christi, CA	12.2
26	20	Memphis, TN	25.3	71	19	Greensboro, NC	12.2
67	20	Anchorage, AK	25.3	20	22	Detroit, MI	12.1
43	23	Omaha, NE	25.2	51	23	Wichita city, KS	12.0
70	23	St. Paul, MN	25.2	28	24	Baltimore, MD	11.9
74	25	Plano, TX	25.0	13	25	Jacksonville, FL	11.7
12	26	Indianapolis, IN	24.8	47	25	Oakland, CA	11.7
17	26	Charlotte, NC	24.8	21	27	El Paso, TX	11.6
40	28	Mesa, AZ	24.7	39	28	Kansas City, MO	11.5
31	29	Las Vegas, NV	24.6	43	28	Omaha, NE	11.5
49	29	Tulsa, OK	24.6	44	28	Colorado Springs, CO	11.5
38	31	Long Beach, CA	24.4	52	28	New Orleans, LA	11.5
44	32	Colorado Springs, CO	24.3	29	32	Oklahoma, OK	11.4
59	32	Islip town, NY	24.3	37	32	Sacramento, CA	11.4
37	34	Sacramento, CA	24.2	42	32	Virginia Beach, VA	11.4
10	35	San Jose, CA	24.0	55	32	Tampa, FL	11.4
39	36	Kansas City, MO	23.8	23	36	Seattle, WA	11.3
33	37	Albuquerque, NM	23.6	25	36	Washington city	11.3
50	38	Cleveland, OH	23.5	8	38	San Diego, CA	11.2
72	39	Toledo, OH	23.4	68	38	Cincinnati, OH	11.2
13	40	Jacksonville, FL	23.3	63	40	St. Louis, MO	11.1
36	40	Brookhaven, NY	23.3	7	41	San Antonio, TX	11.0
42	40	Virginia Beach, VA	23.3	30	41	Portland, OR	11.0
15	43	Columbus, OH	23.1	64	41	Lexington-Fayette urban county, KY	11.0
18	44	Hempstead town, NY	22.9	2	44	Los Angeles, CA	10.9
19	44	Louisville/Jefferson County metro government, KY	22.9	10	44	San Jose, CA	10.9
45	46	Raleigh, NC	22.8	12	46	Indianapolis, IN	10.8
3	47	Chicago, IL	22.4	3	47	Chicago, IL	10.7
5	48	Philadelphia, PA	22.3	22	47	Nashville-Davidson metropolitan government, TN	10.7
55	48	Tampa, FL	22.3	26	47	Memphis, TN	10.7
2	50	Los Angeles, CA	22.2	24	50	Denver, CO	10.6
75	50	Henderson, NV	22.2	66	50	Stockton, CA	10.6
71	52	Greensboro, NC	22.1	27	52	Boston city, MA	10.4
34	53	Tucson, AZ	22.0	74	52	Plano, TX	10.4
68	53	Cincinnati, OH	22.0	41	54	Atlanta, GA	10.1
11	55	Austin, TX	21.9	58	55	Anaheim, CA	10.0
69	55	Oyster Bay town, NY	21.9	38	56	Long Beach, CA	9.8
22	57	Nashville-Davidson metropolitan government, TN	21.7	56	57	Aurora city	9.7
1	58	New York, NY	21.3	62	57	Riverside, CA	9.7
28	58	Baltimore, MD	21.3	35	59	Fresno, CA	9.6
8	60	San Diego, CA	21.2	4	60	Houston, TX	9.5
64	60	Lexington-Fayette urban county, KY	21.2	9	61	Dallas, TX	9.2
24	62	Denver, CO	21.0	32	61	Milwaukee, WI	9.2
47	63	Oakland, CA	20.9	6	63	Phoenix, AZ	9.1
52	64	New Orleans, LA	20.8	15	64	Columbus, OH	9.0
63	65	St. Louis, MO	20.6	17	64	Charlotte, NC	9.0
48	66	Minneapolis, MN	20.1	70	64	St. Paul, MN	9.0
30	67	Portland, OR	18.8	45	67	Raleigh, NC	8.9
41	67	Atlanta, GA	18.8	53	68	Arlington, TX	8.8
46	69	Miami, FL	18.6	54	68	Bakersfield, CA	8.8
57	70	Urban Honolulu, HI	17.5	16	70	Fort Worth, FL	8.6
25	71	Washington city	17.0	48	71	Minneapolis, MN	8.5
27	72	Boston city, MA	16.7	73	71	Newark city, NJ	8.5
65	73	Pittsburgh, PA	16.2	67	73	Anchorage, AK	8.1
23	74	Seattle, WA	15.5	11	74	Austin, TX	7.3
14	75	San Francisco, CA	13.4	60	75	Santa Ana, CA	7.2

75 Largest Cities and Towns by 2014 Population
Selected Rankings

Percent age 18 to 64 years old, 2010–2014				Percent owner-occupied households, 2010–2014			
Population rank	18 to 64 years old rank	City	Percent 18 to 64 years old [Table A col 11]	Population rank	Owner-occupied households rank	City	Percent owner-occupied households [Table A col 14]
23	1	Seattle, WA	73.2	69	1	Oyster Bay town, NY	87.5
27	2	Boston city, MA	73.0	18	2	Hempstead town, NY	80.4
14	3	San Francisco, CA	72.5	36	3	Brookhaven, NY	79.4
25	4	Washington city	71.7	59	4	Islip town, NY	76.1
48	5	Minneapolis, MN	71.5	42	5	Virginia Beach, VA	64.1
41	6	Atlanta, GA	71.0	74	6	Plano, TX	63.1
11	7	Austin, TX	70.7	19	7	Louisville/Jefferson County metro government, KY	62.2
30	8	Portland, OR	70.3	75	8	Henderson, NV	62.0
65	9	Pittsburgh, PA	69.7	51	9	Wichita city, KS	60.6
45	10	Raleigh, NC	68.5	40	10	Mesa, AZ	60.5
24	11	Denver, CO	68.4	13	11	Jacksonville, FL	60.3
63	12	St. Louis, MO	68.3	67	12	Anchorage, AK	59.8
15	13	Columbus, OH	68.0	21	13	El Paso, TX	59.3
64	13	Lexington-Fayette urban county, KY	68.0	33	13	Albuquerque, NM	59.3
52	15	New Orleans, LA	67.7	29	15	Oklahoma, OK	58.8
8	16	San Diego, CA	67.6	44	15	Colorado Springs, CO	58.8
47	16	Oakland, CA	67.6	43	17	Omaha, NE	58.1
22	18	Nashville-Davidson metropolitan government, TN	67.5	16	18	Fort Worth, FL	57.7
68	19	Cincinnati, OH	67.0	10	19	San Jose, CA	57.4
2	20	Los Angeles, CA	66.9	56	20	Aurora city	57.3
3	20	Chicago, IL	66.9	54	21	Bakersfield, CA	56.9
28	22	Baltimore, MD	66.8	53	22	Arlington, TX	56.7
67	23	Anchorage, AK	66.6	61	22	Corpus Christi, CA	56.7
55	24	Tampa, FL	66.4	17	24	Charlotte, NC	55.4
17	25	Charlotte, NC	66.2	39	24	Kansas City, MO	55.4
1	26	New York, NY	66.1	62	24	Riverside, CA	55.4
38	27	Long Beach, CA	65.9	7	27	San Antonio, TX	55.0
73	27	Newark city, NJ	65.9	64	28	Lexington-Fayette urban county, KY	54.9
46	29	Miami, FL	65.7	12	29	Indianapolis, IN	54.7
70	29	St. Paul, MN	65.7	72	30	Toledo, OH	54.6
71	31	Greensboro, NC	65.5	6	31	Phoenix, AZ	54.0
5	32	Philadelphia, PA	65.4	22	31	Nashville-Davidson metropolitan government, TN	54.0
4	33	Houston, TX	65.3	45	33	Raleigh, NC	53.2
34	33	Tucson, AZ	65.3	5	34	Philadelphia, PA	52.9
42	33	Virginia Beach, VA	65.3	49	34	Tulsa, OK	52.9
10	36	San Jose, CA	65.1	30	36	Portland, OR	52.8
9	37	Dallas, TX	64.9	31	37	Las Vegas, NV	52.5
13	37	Jacksonville, FL	64.9	71	38	Greensboro, NC	51.8
39	39	Kansas City, MO	64.7	20	39	Detroit, MI	50.7
74	40	Plano, TX	64.6	26	40	Memphis, TN	49.9
12	41	Indianapolis, IN	64.5	24	41	Denver, CO	49.7
62	41	Riverside, CA	64.5	34	42	Tucson, AZ	49.6
37	43	Sacramento, CA	64.4	55	42	Tampa, FL	49.6
57	44	Urban Honolulu, HI	64.3	66	42	Stockton, CA	49.6
32	45	Milwaukee, WI	64.1	70	45	St. Paul, MN	49.4
50	45	Cleveland, OH	64.1	65	46	Pittsburgh, PA	48.8
53	45	Arlington, TX	64.1	48	47	Minneapolis, MN	48.6
26	48	Memphis, TN	64.0	37	48	Sacramento, CA	47.6
44	48	Colorado Springs, CO	64.0	8	49	San Diego, CA	47.5
58	50	Anaheim, CA	63.8	35	50	Fresno, CA	47.4
72	50	Toledo, OH	63.8	58	50	Anaheim, CA	47.4
6	52	Phoenix, AZ	63.6	28	52	Baltimore, MD	47.2
36	52	Brookhaven, NY	63.6	52	53	New Orleans, LA	46.9
33	54	Albuquerque, NM	63.5	23	54	Seattle, WA	46.2
59	54	Islip town, NY	63.5	15	55	Columbus, OH	45.9
60	54	Santa Ana, CA	63.5	60	56	Santa Ana, CA	45.4
43	57	Omaha, NE	63.4	11	57	Austin, TX	44.8
19	58	Louisville/Jefferson County metro government, KY	63.2	3	58	Chicago, IL	44.7
56	59	Aurora city	63.1	4	59	Houston, TX	44.5
29	60	Oklahoma, OK	63.0	63	60	St. Louis, MO	44.2
7	61	San Antonio, TX	62.7	41	61	Atlanta, GA	44.1
49	62	Tulsa, OK	62.6	50	62	Cleveland, OH	43.5
18	63	Hempstead town, NY	62.5	57	63	Urban Honolulu, HI	43.1
16	64	Fort Worth, FL	62.4	9	64	Dallas, TX	43.0
20	64	Detroit, MI	62.4	32	64	Milwaukee, WI	43.0
61	66	Corpus Christi, CA	62.3	25	66	Washington city	41.6
31	67	Las Vegas, NV	62.2	38	67	Long Beach, CA	40.2
75	68	Henderson, NV	61.9	47	68	Oakland, CA	39.8
51	69	Wichita city, KS	61.5	68	69	Cincinnati, OH	39.4
69	70	Oyster Bay town, NY	60.9	2	70	Los Angeles, CA	37.2
35	71	Fresno, CA	60.7	14	71	San Francisco, CA	36.6
54	72	Bakersfield, CA	60.6	27	72	Boston city, MA	34.2
21	73	El Paso, TX	60.5	1	73	New York, NY	31.9
66	74	Stockton, CA	60.2	46	74	Miami, FL	31.6
40	75	Mesa, AZ	60.1	73	75	Newark city, NJ	22.3

75 Largest Cities and Towns by 2014 Population
Selected Rankings

Median household income, 2010–2014				Percent of households with income below the poverty level, 2010–2014			
Population rank	Median income rank	City	Median income (dollars) [Table B col 8]	Population rank	Poverty rate rank	City	Poverty rate [Table B col 10]
69	1	Oyster Bay town, NY	111,341	20	1	Detroit city, MI	36.2
18	2	Hempstead town, NY	94,158	50	2	Cleveland, OH	32.8
36	3	Brookhaven town, New York	86,828	46	3	Miami, FL	29.9
59	4	Islip town, NY	85,281	73	4	Newark city, NJ	29.3
10	5	San Jose, CA	83,787	68	5	Cincinnati, OH	28.1
74	6	Plano city, TX	82,944	52	6	New Orleans, LA	26.1
14	7	San Francisco, CA	78,378	72	7	Toledo city, OH	25.9
67	8	Anchorage, AK	78,121	32	8	Milwaukee, WI	25.6
25	9	Washington, D.C.	69,235	35	8	Fresno, CA	25.6
23	10	Seattle, WA	67,365	63	10	St. Louis, MO	25.1
42	11	Virginia Beach, VA	67,001	5	11	Philadelphia, PA	24.5
8	12	San Diego, CA	65,753	26	12	Memphis, TN	23.4
75	13	Henderson, NV	63,830	66	13	Stockton, CA	23.0
57	14	Urban Honolulu, HI	60,548	34	14	Tucson, AZ	22.7
58	15	Anaheim, CA	59,707	28	15	Baltimore , MD	22.2
54	16	Bakersfield city, CA	56,842	27	16	Boston, MA	21.7
62	17	Riverside, CA	56,089	65	17	Pittsburgh , PA	21.4
11	18	Austin, TX	55,216	41	18	Atlanta, GA	21.1
45	19	Raleigh, NC	54,581	21	19	El Paso, TX	20.9
27	20	Boston, MA	54,485	2	20	Los Angeles, CA	20.4
44	21	Colorado Springs, CO	54,228	3	21	Chicago, IL	20.3
17	22	Charlotte, NC	53,274	9	22	Dallas, TX	20.1
30	23	Portland, OR	53,230	48	22	Minneapolis, MN	20.1
53	24	Arlington, TX	53,055	60	24	Santa Ana, CA	19.9
47	25	Oakland, CA	52,962	70	24	St. Paul, MN	19.9
38	26	Long Beach, CA	52,944	37	26	Sacramento, CA	19.5
1	27	New York, NY	52,737	55	26	Tampa, FL	19.5
60	28	Santa Ana, CA	52,519	4	28	Houston, TX	19.4
16	29	Fort Worth, TX	52,492	1	29	New York, NY	19.3
56	30	Aurora city	52,275	6	30	Phoenix, AZ	19.2
24	31	Denver, CO	51,800	15	31	Columbus, OH	19.0
31	32	Las Vegas, NV	50,903	12	32	Indianapolis, IN	18.8
48	33	Minneapolis, MN	50,767	47	33	Oakland, CA	18.7
37	34	Sacramento, CA	50,013	7	34	San Antonio, TX	18.5
2	35	Los Angeles, CA	49,682	38	35	Long Beach, CA	18.1
61	36	Corpus Christi, TX	49,675	49	36	Tulsa, OK	17.9
43	37	Omaha, NE	48,751	64	36	Lexington-Fayette, KY	17.9
64	38	Lexington-Fayette, KY	48,667	39	38	Kansas City, MO	17.7
40	39	Mesa, AZ	48,259	71	38	Greensboro, NC	17.7
70	40	St. Paul, MN	48,258	54	40	Bakersfield city, CA	17.5
3	41	Chicago, IL	47,831	33	41	Albuquerque, NM	17.0
19	42	Louisville/Jefferson County metro government, KY	47,692	16	42	Fort Worth, TX	16.9
22	43	Nashville-Davidson metropolitan government, TN .	47,434	62	43	Riverside, CA	16.8
33	44	Albuquerque, NM	47,413	61	44	Corpus Christi, TX	16.7
29	45	Oklahoma City, OK	47,004	29	45	Oklahoma City, OK	16.5
6	46	Phoenix, AZ	46,881	30	45	Portland, OR	16.5
13	47	Jacksonville, FL	46,768	13	47	Jacksonville, FL	16.2
41	48	Atlanta, GA	46,439	51	47	Wichita , KS	16.2
7	49	San Antonio, TX	46,317	24	49	Denver, CO	16.1
51	50	Wichita , KS	45,907	22	50	Nashville-Davidson metropolitan government, TN	16.0
4	51	Houston, TX	45,728	19	51	Louisville/Jefferson County metro government, KY...	15.9
39	52	Kansas City, MO	45,376	11	52	Austin, TX	15.7
66	53	Stockton, CA	45,347	25	52	Washington, D.C.	15.7
15	54	Columbus, OH	44,774	43	54	Omaha, NE	15.5
55	55	Tampa, FL	43,740	31	55	Las Vegas, NV	15.4
9	56	Dallas, TX	43,359	53	56	Arlington, TX	14.9
12	57	Indianapolis, IN	42,169	58	56	Anaheim, CA	14.9
21	58	El Paso, TX	42,037	17	58	Charlotte, NC	14.8
49	59	Tulsa, OK	41,957	40	59	Mesa, AZ	14.0
28	60	Baltimore , MD	41,819	8	60	San Diego, CA	13.8
71	61	Greensboro, NC	41,518	14	61	San Francisco, CA	13.4
35	62	Fresno, CA	41,455	56	61	Aurora city	13.4
65	63	Pittsburgh , PA	40,009	45	63	Raleigh, NC	13.0
5	64	Philadelphia, PA	37,460	23	64	Seattle, WA	12.7
34	65	Tucson, AZ	37,149	44	64	Colorado Springs, CO	12.7
26	66	Memphis, TN	37,099	57	66	Urban Honolulu, HI	11.9
52	67	New Orleans, LA	36,964	10	67	San Jose, CA	10.6
32	68	Milwaukee, WI	35,489	75	68	Henderson, NV	9.4
63	69	St. Louis, MO	34,800	42	69	Virginia Beach, VA	7.8
73	70	Newark city, NJ	34,012	36	70	Brookhaven town, New York	7.4
68	71	Cincinnati, OH	34,002	18	71	Hempstead town, NY	7.1
72	72	Toledo city, OH	33,485	74	71	Plano city, TX	7.1
46	73	Miami, FL	30,858	59	73	Islip town, NY	7.0
50	74	Cleveland, OH	26,179	67	74	Anchorage, AK	6.5
20	75	Detroit city, MI	26,095	69	75	Oyster Bay town, NY	3.8

75 Largest Cities and Towns by 2014 Population
Selected Rankings

	Percent high school graduates or less, 2010–2014				Percent college graduates (bachelor's degree or more), 2010–2014		
Population rank	High school graduate or less rank	City	Percent high school graduate or less [Table A col 15]	Population rank	College graduate rank	City	Percent college graduates [Table A col 16]
60	1	Santa Ana, CA	62.3	23	1	Seattle, WA	59.8
73	2	Newark city, NJ	60.0	74	2	Plano, TX	58.8
50	3	Cleveland, OH	52.1	14	3	San Francisco, CA	57.4
46	4	Miami, FL	51.5	25	4	Washington city	56.8
20	5	Detroit, MI	50.0	45	5	Raleigh, NC	51.3
5	6	Philadelphia, PA	48.3	41	6	Atlanta, GA	50.9
72	7	Toledo, OH	45.4	11	7	Austin, TX	49.3
66	8	Stockton, CA	43.3	69	8	Oyster Bay town, NY	48.8
28	9	Baltimore, MD	43.1	48	9	Minneapolis, MN	48.4
32	10	Milwaukee, WI	42.9	30	10	Portland, OR	47.0
61	11	Corpus Christi, CA	42.5	27	11	Boston city, MA	46.9
21	12	El Paso, TX	42.4	8	12	San Diego, CA	46.8
35	13	Fresno, CA	42.2	24	12	Denver, CO	46.8
58	14	Anaheim, CA	41.4	10	14	San Jose, CA	43.9
26	15	Memphis, TN	41.3	17	15	Charlotte, NC	43.4
59	16	Islip town, NY	41.0	47	16	Oakland, CA	42.2
9	17	Dallas, TX	40.8	64	17	Lexington-Fayette urban county, KY	41.7
4	18	Houston, TX	40.5	18	18	Hempstead town, NY	40.7
12	19	Indianapolis, IN	39.7	70	18	St. Paul, MN	40.7
1	20	New York, NY	39.6	3	20	Chicago, IL	39.6
31	20	Las Vegas, NV	39.6	22	21	Nashville-Davidson metropolitan government, TN	39.5
7	22	San Antonio, TX	39.3	65	21	Pittsburgh, PA	39.5
54	23	Bakersfield, CA	39.2	71	23	Greensboro, NC	38.9
62	24	Riverside, CA	38.5	1	24	New York, NY	38.6
16	25	Fort Worth, FL	38.3	57	25	Urban Honolulu, HI	38.4
68	26	Cincinnati, OH	37.6	44	26	Colorado Springs, CO	37.6
2	27	Los Angeles, CA	37.3	55	27	Tampa, FL	36.6
6	28	Phoenix, AZ	36.7	2	28	Los Angeles, CA	36.2
13	29	Jacksonville, FL	36.6	52	29	New Orleans, LA	36.1
51	30	Wichita city, KS	36.4	15	30	Columbus, OH	35.8
36	31	Brookhaven, NY	36.3	42	31	Virginia Beach, VA	35.6
63	31	St. Louis, MO	36.3	43	32	Omaha, NE	35.5
29	33	Oklahoma, OK	35.9	33	33	Albuquerque, NM	35.2
19	34	Louisville/Jefferson County metro government, KY	35.8	67	34	Anchorage, AK	34.3
52	35	New Orleans, LA	35.7	75	35	Henderson, NV	33.9
55	36	Tampa, FL	35.6	9	36	Dallas, TX	33.8
3	37	Chicago, IL	35.4	4	37	Houston, TX	33.7
40	38	Mesa, AZ	35.0	36	38	Brookhaven, NY	33.5
49	38	Tulsa, OK	35.0	39	38	Kansas City, MO	33.5
39	40	Kansas City, MO	34.4	68	40	Cincinnati, OH	32.8
56	41	Aurora city	33.9	19	41	Louisville/Jefferson County metro government, KY	32.6
53	42	Arlington, TX	33.7	38	41	Long Beach, CA	32.6
65	43	Pittsburgh, PA	33.3	63	43	St. Louis, MO	32.5
34	44	Tucson, AZ	33.2	37	44	Sacramento, CA	32.2
38	45	Long Beach, CA	33.0	49	45	Tulsa, OK	31.5
15	46	Columbus, OH	32.9	28	46	Baltimore, MD	30.9
18	46	Hempstead town, NY	32.9	29	47	Oklahoma, OK	30.8
22	48	Nashville-Davidson metropolitan government, TN	32.6	53	48	Arlington, TX	30.7
27	49	Boston city, MA	32.5	56	49	Aurora city	30.2
70	50	St. Paul, MN	31.5	12	50	Indianapolis, IN	29.8
37	51	Sacramento, CA	31.3	16	50	Fort Worth, FL	29.8
43	52	Omaha, NE	31.0	6	52	Phoenix, AZ	29.6
57	53	Urban Honolulu, HI	30.6	59	53	Islip town, NY	29.5
33	54	Albuquerque, NM	30.2	51	54	Wichita city, KS	29.3
47	54	Oakland, CA	30.2	46	55	Miami, FL	28.1
71	56	Greensboro, NC	29.3	7	56	San Antonio, TX	27.8
75	57	Henderson, NV	28.3	13	57	Jacksonville, FL	27.6
10	58	San Jose, CA	28.1	58	57	Anaheim, CA	27.6
24	59	Denver, CO	27.2	34	59	Tucson, AZ	27.5
64	59	Lexington-Fayette urban county, KY	27.2	5	60	Philadelphia, PA	26.9
69	61	Oyster Bay town, NY	27.1	26	61	Memphis, TN	26.8
17	62	Charlotte, NC	26.4	40	62	Mesa, AZ	26.2
67	62	Anchorage, AK	26.4	62	63	Riverside, CA	25.9
41	64	Atlanta, GA	26.2	31	64	Las Vegas, NV	24.7
25	65	Washington city	25.7	21	65	El Paso, TX	24.5
42	66	Virginia Beach, VA	25.1	32	66	Milwaukee, WI	24.4
48	67	Minneapolis, MN	24.3	61	67	Corpus Christi, CA	23.2
44	68	Colorado Springs, CO	24.2	54	68	Bakersfield, CA	22.7
11	69	Austin, TX	23.5	35	69	Fresno, CA	22.5
8	70	San Diego, CA	22.8	66	70	Stockton, CA	19.5
30	71	Portland, OR	22.1	72	71	Toledo, OH	18.4
14	72	San Francisco, CA	21.2	50	72	Cleveland, OH	16.3
45	73	Raleigh, NC	20.2	60	73	Santa Ana, CA	15.0
74	74	Plano, TX	15.3	20	74	Detroit, MI	14.7
23	75	Seattle, WA	15.0	73	75	Newark city, NJ	13.9

75 Largest Cities and Towns by 2014 Population
Selected Rankings

	Unemployment rate, 2010–2014					Per capita local taxes, 2012		
Population rank	Unemployment rate rank	City	Unemployment rate [Table B col 12]		Population rank	Per capita local taxes rank	City	Per capita local taxes [Table B col 25]
20	1	Detroit city, MI	27.1		25	1	Washington, D.C.	9,344
50	2	Cleveland, OH	19.2		1	2	New York, NY	5,077
73	3	Newark city, NJ	19.1		14	3	San Francisco, CA	3,430
66	4	Stockton, CA	16.3		27	4	Boston, MA	2,844
35	5	Fresno, CA	15.4		5	5	Philadelphia, PA	2,089
72	6	Toledo city, OH	15.3		28	6	Baltimore, MD	1,989
5	7	Philadelphia, PA	14.9		22	7	Nashville-Davidson metropolitan government, TN	1,952
63	8	St. Louis, MO	14.1		67	8	Anchorage, AK	1,830
28	9	Baltimore, MD	13.9		42	9	Virginia Beach, VA	1,817
62	9	Riverside, CA	13.9		24	10	Denver, CO	1,748
37	11	Sacramento, CA	13.7		63	11	St. Louis, MO	1,706
26	12	Memphis, TN	13.4		39	12	Kansas City, MO	1,599
3	13	Chicago, IL	13.2		23	13	Seattle, WA	1,438
31	14	Las Vegas, NV	13.1		47	14	Oakland, CA	1,420
32	14	Milwaukee, WI	13.1		68	15	Cincinnati, OH	1,400
68	14	Cincinnati, OH	13.1		52	16	New Orleans, LA	1,349
41	17	Atlanta, GA	12.9		41	17	Atlanta, GA	1,173
46	18	Miami, FL	12.5		48	18	Minneapolis, MN	1,170
34	19	Tucson, AZ	12.1		65	19	Pittsburgh, PA	1,166
38	19	Long Beach, CA	12.1		13	20	Jacksonville, FL	1,104
47	21	Oakland, CA	11.8		73	21	Newark city, NJ	1,099
52	22	New Orleans, LA	11.6		20	22	Detroit city, MI	1,078
54	22	Bakersfield city, CA	11.6		50	23	Cleveland, OH	1,071
2	24	Los Angeles, CA	11.5		12	24	Indianapolis, IN	1,064
55	24	Tampa, FL	11.5		64	25	Lexington-Fayette, KY	1,045
13	26	Jacksonville, FL	11.4		30	26	Portland, OR	1,016
12	27	Indianapolis, IN	11.2		29	27	Oklahoma City, OK	1,003
58	28	Anaheim, CA	10.9		2	28	Los Angeles, CA	997
17	29	Charlotte, NC	10.8		46	29	Miami, FL	976
25	30	Washington, D.C.	10.6		15	30	Columbus, OH	958
1	31	New York, NY	10.3		3	31	Chicago, IL	930
75	31	Henderson, NV	10.3		74	32	Plano city, TX	907
56	33	Aurora city	10.1		43	33	Omaha, NE	903
27	34	Boston, MA	10.0		4	34	Houston, TX	888
71	34	Greensboro, NC	10.0		38	35	Long Beach, CA	877
6	36	Phoenix, AZ	9.9		10	36	San Jose, CA	876
60	36	Santa Ana, CA	9.9		9	37	Dallas, TX	872
10	38	San Jose, CA	9.8		49	38	Tulsa, OK	862
44	39	Colorado Springs, CO	9.7		8	39	San Diego, CA	838
70	40	St. Paul, MN	9.5		17	40	Charlotte, NC	803
30	41	Portland, OR	9.4		26	41	Memphis, TN	789
65	41	Pittsburgh, PA	9.4		16	42	Fort Worth, TX	783
19	43	Louisville/Jefferson County metro government, KY	9.3		58	43	Anaheim, CA	779
8	44	San Diego, CA	9.2		55	44	Tampa, FL	774
39	45	Kansas City, MO	9.1		37	45	Sacramento, CA	771
40	45	Mesa, AZ	9.1		69	46	Oyster Bay town, NY	729
48	47	Minneapolis, MN	9.0		71	47	Greensboro, NC	711
4	48	Houston, TX	8.9		11	48	Austin, TX	709
9	48	Dallas, TX	8.9		45	49	Raleigh, NC	679
15	48	Columbus, OH	8.9		6	50	Phoenix, AZ	663
53	51	Arlington, TX	8.8		33	50	Albuquerque, NM	663
51	52	Wichita, KS	8.7		53	52	Arlington, TX	644
16	53	Fort Worth, TX	8.6		56	53	Aurora city	638
21	53	El Paso, TX	8.6		62	54	Riverside, CA	631
33	55	Albuquerque, NM	8.5		60	55	Santa Ana, CA	621
7	56	San Antonio, TX	8.4		72	56	Toledo city, OH	618
45	57	Raleigh, NC	8.3		61	57	Corpus Christi, TX	614
22	58	Nashville-Davidson metropolitan government, TN	8.2		19	58	Louisville/Jefferson County metro government, KY	607
64	59	Lexington-Fayette, KY	8.0		70	59	St. Paul, MN	602
18	60	Hempstead town, NY	7.9		21	60	El Paso, TX	572
24	61	Denver, CO	7.8		66	61	Stockton, CA	544
49	62	Tulsa, OK	7.7		7	62	San Antonio, TX	534
59	62	Islip town, NY	7.7		34	62	Tucson, AZ	534
14	64	San Francisco, CA	7.6		35	64	Fresno, CA	529
43	65	Omaha, NE	7.3		32	65	Milwaukee, WI	505
61	66	Corpus Christi, TX	7.2		44	66	Colorado Springs, CO	494
67	67	Anchorage, AK	6.9		75	67	Henderson, NV	487
11	68	Austin, TX	6.8		18	68	Hempstead town, NY	449
29	69	Oklahoma City, OK	6.6		51	69	Wichita, KS	435
36	69	Brookhaven town, New York	6.6		54	70	Bakersfield city, CA	417
23	71	Seattle, WA	6.5		36	71	Brookhaven town, New York	361
42	72	Virginia Beach, VA	6.2		40	72	Mesa, AZ	346
74	73	Plano city, TX	5.9		59	73	Islip town, NY	340
69	74	Oyster Bay town, NY	5.7		31	74	Las Vegas, NV	336
57	75	Urban Honolulu, HI	5.3		57	NA	Urban Honolulu, HI	NA

75 Largest Cities and Towns by 2014 Population
Selected Rankings

Violent crime rate (violent crime known to police), 2014				Property crime rate (property crime known to police), 2014			
Population rank	Violent crime rank	City	Violent crime rate (per 100,000 population) [Table B col 17]	Population rank	Property crime rank	City	Property crime rate (per 100,000 population) [Table B col 18]
20	1	Detroit city, MI	1,990	63	1	St. Louis, MO	6,253
26	2	Memphis, TN	1,744	23	2	Seattle, WA	6,146
47	3	Oakland, CA	1,685	26	3	Memphis, TN	5,995
63	4	St. Louis, MO	1,679	34	4	Tucson, AZ	5,993
32	5	Milwaukee, WI	1,485	47	5	Oakland, CA	5,943
28	6	Baltimore , MD	1,339	41	6	Atlanta, GA	5,747
50	6	Cleveland, OH	1,339	68	7	Cincinnati, OH	5,604
66	8	Stockton, CA	1,331	50	8	Cleveland, OH	5,459
39	9	Kansas City, MO	1,258	33	9	Albuquerque, NM	5,446
12	10	Indianapolis, IN	1,255	7	10	San Antonio, TX	5,418
41	11	Atlanta, GA	1,227	14	11	San Francisco, CA	5,303
25	12	Washington, D.C.	1,185	30	12	Portland, OR	5,235
22	13	Nashville-Davidson metropolitan government, TN	1,125	49	13	Tulsa, OK	5,082
72	14	Toledo city, OH	1,091	25	14	Washington, D.C.	5,012
73	15	Newark city, NJ	1,078	39	15	Kansas City, MO	4,862
46	16	Miami, FL	1,060	46	16	Miami, FL	4,833
5	17	Philadelphia, PA	1,021	12	17	Indianapolis, IN	4,823
48	18	Minneapolis, MN	1,012	20	18	Detroit city, MI	4,819
4	19	Houston, TX	991	48	19	Minneapolis, MN	4,728
52	20	New Orleans, LA	974	51	20	Wichita , KS	4,723
68	21	Cincinnati, OH	913	28	21	Baltimore , MD	4,718
3	22	Chicago, IL	886	4	22	Houston, TX	4,694
33	23	Albuquerque, NM	883	32	23	Milwaukee, WI	4,588
67	24	Anchorage, AK	865	61	24	Corpus Christi, TX	4,420
31	25	Las Vegas, NV	841	29	25	Oklahoma City, OK	4,411
49	26	Tulsa, OK	805	66	26	Stockton, CA	4,390
65	27	Pittsburgh , PA	798	43	27	Omaha, NE	4,345
14	28	San Francisco, CA	795	15	28	Columbus, OH	4,278
29	29	Oklahoma City, OK	774	52	29	New Orleans, LA	4,232
51	30	Wichita , KS	758	19	30	Louisville/Jefferson County metro government, KY	4,196
27	31	Boston, MA	726	11	31	Austin, TX	4,142
13	32	Jacksonville, FL	684	35	32	Fresno, CA	4,112
9	33	Dallas, TX	665	16	33	Fort Worth, TX	4,001
70	34	St. Paul, MN	662	54	34	Bakersfield city, CA	3,972
61	35	Corpus Christi, TX	656	13	35	Jacksonville, FL	3,941
34	36	Tucson, AZ	653	64	36	Lexington-Fayette, KY	3,912
37	37	Sacramento, CA	615	67	37	Anchorage, AK	3,827
23	38	Seattle, WA	604	22	38	Nashville-Davidson metropolitan government, TN	3,767
24	39	Denver, CO	601	6	39	Phoenix, AZ	3,724
1	40	New York, NY	597	44	40	Colorado Springs, CO	3,668
19	41	Louisville/Jefferson County metro government, KY	592	71	41	Greensboro, NC	3,600
17	42	Charlotte, NC	590	9	42	Dallas, TX	3,589
55	43	Tampa, FL	582	17	43	Charlotte, NC	3,567
6	44	Phoenix, AZ	572	53	44	Arlington, TX	3,515
43	45	Omaha, NE	561	70	45	St. Paul, MN	3,484
15	46	Columbus, OH	558	5	46	Philadelphia, PA	3,388
16	46	Fort Worth, TX	558	24	47	Denver, CO	3,367
7	48	San Antonio, TX	539	65	48	Pittsburgh , PA	3,213
2	49	Los Angeles, CA	491	3	49	Chicago, IL	3,133
38	50	Long Beach, CA	489	37	50	Sacramento, CA	3,123
53	51	Arlington, TX	484	62	51	Riverside, CA	3,088
71	52	Greensboro, NC	477	31	52	Las Vegas, NV	2,923
30	53	Portland, OR	473	73	53	Newark city, NJ	2,851
35	54	Fresno, CA	464	56	54	Aurora city	2,839
40	55	Mesa, AZ	459	40	55	Mesa, AZ	2,800
54	56	Bakersfield city, CA	457	38	56	Long Beach, CA	2,640
44	57	Colorado Springs, CO	456	27	57	Boston, MA	2,639
62	58	Riverside, CA	433	10	58	San Jose, CA	2,434
56	59	Aurora city	407	55	59	Tampa, FL	2,428
11	60	Austin, TX	396	58	60	Anaheim, CA	2,362
21	61	El Paso, TX	393	42	61	Virginia Beach, VA	2,187
8	62	San Diego, CA	381	21	62	El Paso, TX	2,142
60	63	Santa Ana, CA	374	3	63	Los Angeles, CA	2,128
64	64	Lexington-Fayette, KY	337	72	64	Toledo city, OH	2,006
10	65	San Jose, CA	321	74	65	Plano city, TX	1,983
58	66	Anaheim, CA	317	75	66	Henderson, NV	1,978
74	67	Plano city, TX	165	8	67	San Diego, CA	1,959
75	67	Henderson, NV	165	60	68	Santa Ana, CA	1,719
45	69	Raleigh, NC	152	1	69	New York, NY	1,602
42	70	Virginia Beach, VA	148	45	70	Raleigh, NC	1,030
36	NA	Brookhaven town, New York	NA	36	NA	Brookhaven town, New York	NA
18	NA	Hempstead town, NY	NA	18	NA	Hempstead town, NY	NA
59	NA	Islip town, NY	NA	59	NA	Islip town, NY	NA
69	NA	Oyster Bay town, NY	NA	69	NA	Oyster Bay town, NY	NA
57	NA	Urban Honolulu, HI	NA	57	NA	Urban Honolulu, HI	NA

75 Largest Cities and Towns by 2014 Population
Selected Rankings

Value of new residential construction authorized by building permits, 2014

Population rank	Value of new residential construction rank	City	Value of new residential construction authorized by building permits, 2014 [Table B col 19]
4	1	Houston, TX	2,399,526
2	2	Los Angeles, CA	2,325,891
23	3	Seattle, WA	1,109,041
11	4	Austin, TX	1,105,477
3	5	Chicago, IL	959,625
22	6	Nashville-Davidson metropolitan government, TN	953,546
46	7	Miami, FL	950,530
6	8	Phoenix, AZ	935,003
5	9	Philadelphia, PA	879,066
24	10	Denver, CO	811,547
9	11	Dallas, TX	801,685
30	12	Portland, OR	773,329
29	13	Oklahoma City, OK	770,619
14	14	San Francisco, CA	768,892
16	15	Fort Worth, TX	749,094
7	16	San Antonio, TX	745,110
27	17	Boston, MA	687,770
45	18	Raleigh, NC	626,797
41	19	Atlanta, GA	618,660
10	20	San Jose, CA	595,056
13	21	Jacksonville, FL	543,925
8	22	San Diego, CA	524,088
15	23	Columbus, OH	449,879
21	24	El Paso, TX	416,264
55	25	Tampa, FL	406,253
25	26	Washington, D.C.	374,397
48	27	Minneapolis, MN	365,662
40	28	Mesa, AZ	333,102
54	29	Bakersfield city, CA	316,961
19	30	Louisville/Jefferson County metro government, KY	289,055
74	31	Plano city, TX	287,925
61	32	Corpus Christi, TX	285,268
39	33	Kansas City, MO	281,796
43	34	Omaha, NE	280,516
75	35	Henderson, NV	251,384
56	36	Aurora city	220,809
67	37	Anchorage, AK	211,518
33	38	Albuquerque, NM	209,154
34	39	Tucson, AZ	208,900
58	40	Anaheim, CA	206,092
31	41	Las Vegas, NV	202,296
52	42	New Orleans, LA	201,755
35	43	Fresno, CA	195,072
71	44	Greensboro, NC	188,669
1	45	New York, NY	185,203
49	46	Tulsa, OK	183,107
12	47	Indianapolis, IN	167,626
42	48	Virginia Beach, VA	158,800
64	49	Lexington-Fayette, KY	134,483
53	50	Arlington, TX	127,751
63	51	St. Louis, MO	123,458
51	52	Wichita, KS	105,584
28	53	Baltimore, MD	94,235
70	54	St. Paul, MN	92,655
62	55	Riverside, CA	70,655
73	56	Newark city, NJ	69,735
37	57	Sacramento, CA	60,400
38	58	Long Beach, CA	59,121
36	59	Brookhaven town, New York	55,645
18	60	Hempstead town, NY	52,372
68	61	Cincinnati, OH	50,826
69	62	Oyster Bay town, NY	49,652
47	63	Oakland, CA	49,131
65	64	Pittsburgh, PA	46,476
20	65	Detroit city, MI	33,443
72	66	Toledo city, OH	26,614
66	67	Stockton, CA	21,907
60	68	Santa Ana, CA	19,782
32	69	Milwaukee, WI	17,811
59	70	Islip town, NY	10,261
50	71	Cleveland, OH	7,350
17	NA	Charlotte, NC	NA
26	NA	Memphis, TN	NA
44	NA	Colorado Springs, CO	NA
57	NA	Urban Honolulu, HI	NA

Per capita general expenditures, 2012

Population rank	Per capita general expenditures rank	City	Per capita general expenditures [Table B col 27]
25	1	Washington, D.C.	17,636
1	2	New York, NY	9,701
14	3	San Francisco, CA	6,875
28	4	Baltimore, MD	5,874
27	5	Boston, MA	4,932
52	6	New Orleans, LA	4,334
67	7	Anchorage, AK	4,190
24	8	Denver, CO	4,139
42	9	Virginia Beach, VA	4,036
22	10	Nashville-Davidson metropolitan government, TN	3,888
12	11	Indianapolis, IN	3,777
38	12	Long Beach, CA	3,753
48	13	Minneapolis, MN	3,663
5	14	Philadelphia, PA	3,537
41	15	Atlanta, GA	3,530
26	16	Memphis, TN	3,451
63	17	St. Louis, MO	3,391
47	18	Oakland, CA	3,266
20	19	Detroit city, MI	3,227
73	20	Newark city, NJ	3,093
3	21	Chicago, IL	2,740
68	22	Cincinnati, OH	2,641
23	23	Seattle, WA	2,611
39	24	Kansas City, MO	2,489
50	25	Cleveland, OH	2,294
13	26	Jacksonville, FL	2,255
2	27	Los Angeles, CA	2,247
44	28	Colorado Springs, CO	2,233
30	29	Portland, OR	2,124
9	30	Dallas, TX	2,045
58	31	Anaheim, CA	1,917
55	32	Tampa, FL	1,817
49	33	Tulsa, OK	1,806
65	34	Pittsburgh, PA	1,791
6	35	Phoenix, AZ	1,780
46	36	Miami, FL	1,777
8	37	San Diego, CA	1,763
11	38	Austin, TX	1,746
70	39	St. Paul, MN	1,733
4	40	Houston, TX	1,708
37	41	Sacramento, CA	1,695
17	42	Charlotte, NC	1,671
32	42	Milwaukee, WI	1,671
15	44	Columbus, OH	1,670
75	45	Henderson, NV	1,594
62	46	Riverside, CA	1,551
71	47	Greensboro, NC	1,492
33	48	Albuquerque, NM	1,491
31	49	Las Vegas, NV	1,470
10	50	San Jose, CA	1,449
64	51	Lexington-Fayette, KY	1,443
16	52	Fort Worth, TX	1,434
51	53	Wichita, KS	1,410
72	54	Toledo city, OH	1,408
29	55	Oklahoma City, OK	1,392
43	56	Omaha, NE	1,333
40	57	Mesa, AZ	1,330
19	58	Louisville/Jefferson County metro government, KY	1,322
66	59	Stockton, CA	1,293
53	60	Arlington, TX	1,275
7	61	San Antonio, TX	1,258
69	62	Oyster Bay town, NY	1,257
61	63	Corpus Christi, TX	1,246
45	64	Raleigh, NC	1,245
74	65	Plano city, TX	1,240
60	66	Santa Ana, CA	1,181
56	67	Aurora city	1,180
34	68	Tucson, AZ	1,159
54	69	Bakersfield city, CA	1,069
35	70	Fresno, CA	1,045
21	71	El Paso, TX	920
36	72	Brookhaven town, New York	740
18	73	Hempstead town, NY	723
59	74	Islip town, NY	690
57	NA	Urban Honolulu, HI	NA

75 Largest Cities and Towns by 2014 Population
Selected Rankings

Number of healthcare and social assistance employees, 2012				Number of manufacturing employees, 2012			
Population rank	Healthcare and social assistance employees rank	City	Number of healthcare and social assistance employees [Table C col 24]	Population rank	Manufacturing employees rank	City	Number of manufacturing employees [Table C col 4]
1	1	New York, NY	688,569	2	1	Los Angeles, CA	101,103
2	2	Los Angeles, CA	205,046	4	2	Houston, TX	86,899
3	3	Chicago, IL	179,570	1	3	New York, NY	68,953
4	4	Houston, TX	175,483	3	4	Chicago, IL	58,435
5	5	Philadelphia, PA	152,972	9	5	Dallas, TX	42,824
27	6	Boston, MA	112,776	8	6	San Diego, CA	41,655
9	7	Dallas, TX	105,321	12	7	Indianapolis, IN	41,099
7	8	San Antonio, TX	102,675	19	8	Louisville/Jefferson County metro government, KY	40,666
6	9	Phoenix, AZ	88,736	16	9	Fort Worth, TX	39,747
8	10	San Diego, CA	85,519	6	10	Phoenix, AZ	38,642
12	11	Indianapolis, IN	80,905	10	11	San Jose, CA	32,421
28	12	Baltimore , MD	79,915	7	12	San Antonio, TX	27,947
15	13	Columbus, OH	75,569	30	13	Portland, OR	26,432
23	14	Seattle, WA	72,737	51	14	Wichita , KS	25,801
50	15	Cleveland, OH	69,208	32	15	Milwaukee, WI	22,779
25	16	Washington, D.C.	67,742	5	16	Philadelphia, PA	22,558
19	17	Louisville/Jefferson County metro government, KY	65,785	50	17	Cleveland, OH	22,075
22	18	Nashville-Davidson metropolitan government, TN	62,989	49	18	Tulsa, OK	22,012
14	19	San Francisco, CA	62,075	29	19	Oklahoma City, OK	21,675
65	20	Pittsburgh , PA	59,171	13	20	Jacksonville city	21,616
30	21	Portland, OR	56,678	17	21	Charlotte, NC	21,152
26	22	Memphis, TN	55,137	11	22	Austin, TX	20,866
48	23	Minneapolis, MN	54,418	23	23	Seattle, WA	20,323
24	24	Denver, CO	54,161	58	24	Anaheim, CA	19,991
11	25	Austin, TX	53,771	15	25	Columbus, OH	19,881
13	26	Jacksonville city	53,374	60	26	Santa Ana, CA	19,771
17	27	Charlotte, NC	52,599	26	27	Memphis, TN	18,847
32	28	Milwaukee, WI	50,163	22	28	Nashville-Davidson metropolitan government, TN	18,154
68	29	Cincinnati, OH	48,741	20	29	Detroit city, MI	17,613
29	30	Oklahoma City, OK	48,353	63	30	St. Louis, MO	17,422
33	31	Albuquerque, NM	46,890	39	31	Kansas City, MO	17,035
20	32	Detroit city, MI	46,219	24	32	Denver, CO	17,032
16	33	Fort Worth, TX	45,055	43	33	Omaha, NE	16,879
43	34	Omaha, NE	44,466	71	34	Greensboro, NC	16,855
39	35	Kansas City, MO	42,718	59	35	Islip town, NY	15,901
34	36	Tucson, AZ	41,707	68	36	Cincinnati, OH	12,881
49	37	Tulsa, OK	41,344	48	37	Minneapolis, MN	12,837
37	38	Sacramento, CA	40,520	35	38	Fresno, CA	12,295
70	39	St. Paul, MN	40,511	72	39	Toledo city, OH	11,821
21	40	El Paso, TX	39,853	28	40	Baltimore , MD	11,748
46	41	Miami, FL	39,678	21	41	El Paso, TX	11,607
41	42	Atlanta, GA	37,406	33	42	Albuquerque, NM	10,810
63	43	St. Louis, MO	35,572	53	43	Arlington, TX	9,679
10	44	San Jose, CA	34,064	62	44	Riverside, CA	9,041
55	45	Tampa, FL	34,012	44	45	Colorado Springs, CO	8,351
57	46	Urban Honolulu, HI	32,660	38	46	Long Beach, CA	8,027
35	47	Fresno, CA	32,532	64	47	Lexington-Fayette, KY	8,005
45	48	Raleigh, NC	31,918	37	48	Sacramento, CA	7,890
51	49	Wichita , KS	31,393	14	49	San Francisco, CA	7,506
31	50	Las Vegas, NV	30,509	41	50	Atlanta, GA	7,404
64	51	Lexington-Fayette, KY	29,625	40	51	Mesa, AZ	7,319
44	52	Colorado Springs, CO	26,896	65	52	Pittsburgh , PA	7,303
61	53	Corpus Christi, TX	26,176	27	53	Boston, MA	6,965
47	54	Oakland, CA	25,852	70	54	St. Paul, MN	6,867
18	55	Hempstead town, NY	25,765	73	55	Newark city, NJ	6,686
38	56	Long Beach, CA	25,677	34	56	Tucson, AZ	6,648
67	57	Anchorage, AK	25,616	47	57	Oakland, CA	6,555
72	58	Toledo city, OH	23,389	52	58	New Orleans, LA	6,049
71	59	Greensboro, NC	23,135	66	59	Stockton, CA	5,937
36	60	Brookhaven town, New York	22,909	55	60	Tampa, FL	5,894
59	61	Islip town, NY	22,253	42	61	Virginia Beach, VA	5,616
40	62	Mesa, AZ	21,915	57	62	Urban Honolulu, HI	5,599
52	63	New Orleans, LA	21,761	61	63	Corpus Christi, TX	5,412
69	64	Oyster Bay town, NY	21,570	45	64	Raleigh, NC	5,229
54	65	Bakersfield city, CA	21,024	36	65	Brookhaven town, New York	4,906
74	66	Plano city, TX	19,401	69	66	Oyster Bay town, NY	4,877
53	67	Arlington, TX	19,213	74	67	Plano city, TX	4,601
42	68	Virginia Beach, VA	18,362	46	68	Miami, FL	3,948
73	69	Newark city, NJ	17,437	75	69	Henderson, NV	3,591
62	70	Riverside, CA	17,360	18	70	Hempstead town, NY	3,256
66	71	Stockton, CA	16,417	31	71	Las Vegas, NV	2,631
58	72	Anaheim, CA	15,700	54	72	Bakersfield city, CA	2,541
56	73	Aurora city	13,962	56	73	Aurora city	2,400
60	74	Santa Ana, CA	13,396	67	74	Anchorage, AK	2,049
75	75	Henderson, NV	9,527	25	75	Washington, D.C.	1,361

75 Largest Cities and Towns by 2014 Population
Selected Rankings

Number of information employees, 2012				Number of retail trade employees, 2012			
Population rank	Information employees rank	City	Information employees [Table C col 12]	Population rank	Retail trade employees rank	City	Retail trade employees [Table C col 8]
1	1	New York, NY	182,826	1	1	New York, NY	318,004
2	2	Los Angeles, CA	78,511	2	2	Los Angeles, CA	133,706
3	3	Chicago, IL	52,959	4	3	Houston, TX	130,540
14	4	San Francisco, CA	49,681	3	4	Chicago, IL	85,388
4	5	Houston, TX	33,977	7	5	San Antonio, TX	72,437
41	6	Atlanta, GA	27,297	8	6	San Diego, CA	61,044
8	7	San Diego, CA	26,707	6	7	Phoenix, AZ	60,797
23	8	Seattle, WA	26,680	9	8	Dallas, TX	57,240
11	9	Austin, TX	25,007	5	9	Philadelphia, PA	50,185
27	10	Boston, MA	24,881	11	10	Austin, TX	49,905
9	11	Dallas, TX	22,962	15	11	Columbus, OH	46,211
5	12	Philadelphia, PA	22,421	13	12	Jacksonville city	43,471
25	13	Washington, D.C.	22,144	14	13	San Francisco, CA	43,378
6	14	Phoenix, AZ	20,074	12	14	Indianapolis, IN	42,887
17	15	Charlotte, NC	18,683	19	15	Louisville/Jefferson County metro government, KY	41,294
7	16	San Antonio, TX	16,436	10	16	San Jose, CA	40,525
24	17	Denver, CO	16,362	17	17	Charlotte, NC	39,240
10	18	San Jose, CA	14,483	22	18	Nashville-Davidson metropolitan government, TN	37,506
22	19	Nashville-Davidson metropolitan government, TN	14,161	26	19	Memphis, TN	35,878
15	20	Columbus, OH	13,835	23	20	Seattle, WA	34,652
39	21	Kansas City, MO	13,553	43	21	Omaha, NE	33,150
12	22	Indianapolis, IN	12,920	30	22	Portland, OR	32,426
65	23	Pittsburgh , PA	11,013	21	23	El Paso, TX	32,405
55	24	Tampa, FL	10,878	33	24	Albuquerque, NM	31,702
30	25	Portland, OR	10,512	16	25	Fort Worth, TX	31,491
43	26	Omaha, NE	10,349	29	26	Oklahoma City, OK	31,326
48	27	Minneapolis, MN	9,632	34	27	Tucson, AZ	30,599
19	28	Louisville/Jefferson County metro government, KY	9,381	31	28	Las Vegas, NV	29,614
44	29	Colorado Springs, CO	9,109	27	29	Boston, MA	28,148
21	30	El Paso, TX	9,075	18	30	Hempstead town, NY	27,859
29	31	Oklahoma City, OK	9,043	45	31	Raleigh, NC	27,148
45	32	Raleigh, NC	8,744	57	32	Urban Honolulu, HI	26,485
13	33	Jacksonville city	8,692	24	33	Denver, CO	26,469
49	34	Tulsa, OK	8,528	49	34	Tulsa, OK	26,411
32	35	Milwaukee, WI	7,866	41	35	Atlanta, GA	24,977
16	36	Fort Worth, TX	7,621	55	36	Tampa, FL	24,934
64	37	Lexington-Fayette, KY	7,262	44	37	Colorado Springs, CO	24,923
74	38	Plano city, TX	7,134	39	38	Kansas City, MO	24,531
20	39	Detroit city, MI	7,123	51	39	Wichita , KS	24,136
63	40	St. Louis, MO	7,096	42	40	Virginia Beach, VA	22,723
33	41	Albuquerque, NM	7,054	40	41	Mesa, AZ	22,342
69	42	Oyster Bay town, NY	6,785	35	42	Fresno, CA	22,005
70	43	St. Paul, MN	5,775	46	43	Miami, FL	21,175
26	44	Memphis, TN	5,694	74	44	Plano city, TX	20,770
37	45	Sacramento, CA	5,681	64	45	Lexington-Fayette, KY	19,820
59	46	Islip town, NY	5,507	25	46	Washington, D.C.	19,780
34	47	Tucson, AZ	5,465	71	47	Greensboro, NC	19,426
28	48	Baltimore , MD	5,324	54	48	Bakersfield city, CA	18,130
71	49	Greensboro, NC	5,087	37	49	Sacramento, CA	18,042
31	50	Las Vegas, NV	4,950	53	50	Arlington, TX	17,817
46	51	Miami, FL	4,917	65	51	Pittsburgh , PA	17,411
57	52	Urban Honolulu, HI	4,877	36	52	Brookhaven town, New York	16,945
68	53	Cincinnati, OH	4,774	69	53	Oyster Bay town, NY	16,468
73	54	Newark city, NJ	4,692	61	54	Corpus Christi, TX	16,278
50	55	Cleveland, OH	4,615	28	55	Baltimore , MD	15,747
51	56	Wichita , KS	4,591	32	56	Milwaukee, WI	15,652
47	57	Oakland, CA	4,534	56	57	Aurora city	15,374
42	58	Virginia Beach, VA	4,493	67	58	Anchorage, AK	15,253
67	59	Anchorage, AK	4,355	48	59	Minneapolis, MN	14,533
54	60	Bakersfield city, CA	4,165	62	60	Riverside, CA	13,943
35	61	Fresno, CA	3,673	75	61	Henderson, NV	13,600
18	62	Hempstead town, NY	3,433	68	62	Cincinnati, OH	13,549
38	63	Long Beach, CA	3,046	58	63	Anaheim, CA	13,333
60	64	Santa Ana, CA	2,862	38	64	Long Beach, CA	13,033
52	65	New Orleans, LA	2,737	72	65	Toledo city, OH	13,004
53	66	Arlington, TX	2,654	59	66	Islip town, NY	12,465
58	67	Anaheim, CA	2,477	52	67	New Orleans, LA	12,371
72	68	Toledo city, OH	2,231	20	68	Detroit city, MI	11,850
62	69	Riverside, CA	2,214	60	69	Santa Ana, CA	11,680
61	70	Corpus Christi, TX	2,007	66	70	Stockton, CA	10,893
40	71	Mesa, AZ	1,570	50	71	Cleveland, OH	10,637
36	72	Brookhaven town, New York	1,542	47	72	Oakland, CA	10,458
56	73	Aurora city	1,321	63	73	St. Louis, MO	9,422
75	74	Henderson, NV	1,228	70	74	St. Paul, MN	9,230
66	75	Stockton, CA	1,158	73	75	Newark city, NJ	5,918

SUBJECTS COVERED BY TYPE AND SIZE OF PLACE

	Incorporated places			Minor civil divisions (MCDs)			Census designated places (CDPs)		
	All places	10,000 or more population		All MCDs	10,000 or more population		All CDPs	10,000 or more population	
Subject	Table A	Table B	Table C	Table A	Table B	Table C	Table A	Table B	Table C
Land area		1			1			1	
Population									
Total persons, 2010	1	2		1	2		1	2	
Total persons, 2014	2	3		2	3		2	3	
Percent change, 2010–2014	3	4		3	4		3	4	
Total population estimate, 2010–2014	4			4			4		
Persons per square mile, 2014		5			5			5	
Race and Hispanic origin, 2010–2014	5–9			5–9			5–9		
Age distribution, 2010–2014	10–12			10–12			10–12		
Foreign–born, 2010–2014		6			6			6	
Households									
Total households, 2010–2014	13			13			13		
Owner–occupied, 2010–2014	14			14			14		
Family households, 2010–2014		13			13			13	
One–person households, 2010–2014		14			14			14	
Same residence as previous year, 2010–2014		7			7			7	
Income									
Median household income, 2010–2014		8			8			8	
Income of $100,000 or more, 2010–2014		9			9			9	
Income below poverty level, 2010–2014		10			10			10	
Education									
High school diploma or less, 2010–2014	15			15			15		
Bachelor's degree or more, 2010–2014	16			16			16		
Employment									
Percent in labor force, 2010–2014		11			11			11	
Unemployment rate, 2010–2014		12			12			12	
Crime									
Total number, 2014		15			15			15	
Total rate, 2014		16			16			16	
Violent crime rate, 2014		17			17			17	
Property crime rate, 2014		18			18			18	
New residential construction									
Value, 2014		19			19			19	
Number of units, 2014		20			20			20	
Percent singe family, 2014		21			21			21	
Local government finance									
General revenue, 2012		22–25			22–25			22–25	
Per capita taxes, 2012		25			25			25	
General expenditure, 2012		26–28			26–28			26–28	
Debt outstanding, 2012		29			29			29	
Utilities									
Number of establishments, 2012			1			1			1
Number of employees, 2012			2			2			2
Manufacturing									
Number of establishments, 2012			3			3			3
Number of employees, 2012			4			4			4
Wholesale Trade									
Number of establishments, 2012			5			5			5
Number of establishments, 2012			6			6			6
Retail Trade									
Number of establishments, 2012			7			7			7
Number of employees, 2012			8			8			8
Transportation and Warehousing									
Number of establishments, 2012			9			9			9
Number of employees, 2012			10			10			10
Information									
Number of establishments, 2012			11			11			11
Number of employees, 2012			12			12			12
Finance and insurance									
Number of establishments, 2012			13			13			13
Number of employees, 2012			14			14			14
Real Estate and Rental and Leasing									
Number of establishments, 2012			15			15			15
Number of employees, 2012			16			16			16
Professional, scientific, and technical services									
Number of establishments, 2012			17			17			17
Number of employees, 2012			18			18			18
Administration and support and waste management and mediation services									
Number of establishments, 2012			19			19			19
Number of employees, 2012			20			20			20
Educational services									
Number of establishments, 2012			21			21			21
Number of employees, 2012			22			22			22
Health care and social assistance									
Number of establishments, 2012			23			23			23
Number of employees, 2012			24			24			24
Arts, entertainment, and recreation									
Number of establishments, 2012			25			25			25
Number of employees, 2012			26			26			26
Accommodation and food services									
Number of establishments, 2012			27			27			27
Number of employees, 2012			28			28			28
Other services (except public administration)									
Number of establishments, 2012			29			29			29
Number of employees, 2012			30			30			30

COLUMN HEADINGS FOR TABLE A

Table A. All Places — **Population and Housing**

STATE City, town, township, borough, or CDP (county if applicable)	Population				Race and Hispanic or Latino origin (percent), 2010–2014					Age (percent), 2010–2014			Households, 2010–2014			
															Householders by level of education (percent)	
	2010 census total population	2014 estimated population	Percent change 2010–2014	ACS total population estimate 2010–2014	White alone, not Hispanic or Latino	Black alone, not Hispanic or Latino	Asian alone, not Hispanic or Latino	All other races or 2 or more races, not Hispanic or Latino	Hispanic or Latino[1]	Under 18 years old	Age 18 to 64 years old	Age 65 years and older	Total occupied housing units	Percent owner occupied	High school diploma or less	Bachelor's degree or more
	1	2	3	4	5	6	7	8	9	10	11	12	13	14	15	16

1 May be of any race.

COLUMN HEADINGS FOR TABLE B

Table B. Incorporated Places, Census Designated Places (CDPs), and Minor Civil Divisions (MCDs) of 10,000 or More Population — **Land Area, Population, and Households, and Employment**

STATE City, town, township, borough, or CDP (county if applicable)	Land area,[1] 2010 (sq mi)	Population				Population characteristics 2010–2014		Household income and poverty, 2010–2014			Employment, 2010–2014,[2]		Households, 2010–2014 (percent of households)	
									Percent of households					
		Total persons 2010	Total persons 2014	Percent change 2010–2014	Persons per square mile, 2014	Foreign born	Lives in same house as previous year	Median household income (dollars)	Income of $100,000 or more	Income below poverty level	Percent in labor force	Unemploy-ment rate	Family households	One person households
	1	2	3	4	5	6	7	8	9	10	11	12	13	14

1 Dry land or land partially or temporarily covered by water.   2 16 years old and over.

Table B. Incorporated Places, Census Designated Places (CDPs), and Minor Civil Divisions (MCDs) of 10,000 or More Population — **Crime, Construction, and Local Government Finance**

STATE City, town, township, borough, or CDP (county if applicable)	Serious crimes known to police, 2014[1]				New residential construction authorized by building permits, 2014			Local government finance, 2012							
		Rate[2]						General revenue				General expenditure			
									Intergovernmental				Per capita[3]		
	Total number	Total	Violent	Property	Value ($1,000)	Number of housing units	Percent single family	Total (mil dol)	Total (mil dol)	Percent from state gov.	Taxes per capita[3]	Total (mil dol)	Total	Capital outlays	Debt outstanding (mil dol)
	15	16	17	18	19	20	21	22	23	24	25	26	27	28	29

1 Data for serious crimes have not been adjusted for underreporting. This may affect comparability between geographic areas over time.   2 Per 100,000 population estimated by the FBI.   3 Based on population estimated as of July 1 of the year shown.

COLUMN HEADINGS FOR TABLE C

Table C. Incorporated Places, Census Designated Places (CDPs), and Minor Civil Divisions (MCDs) of 10,000 or More Population — **Economic Census**

STATE City, town, township, borough, or CDP (county if applicable)	Economic activity by sector, 2012														
	Utilities		Manufacturing		Wholesale trade[1]		Retail trade		Transportation and warehousing		Information		Finance and insurance		Real estate and rental and leasing
	Number of establish-ments	Number of employees	Number of establish-ments	Number of employees	Number of establish-ments	Number of employees	Number of establish-ments	Number of employees	Number of establish-ments	Number of employees	Number of establish-ments	Number of employees	Number of establish-ments	Number of employees	Number of establish-ments
	1	2	3	4	5	6	7	8	9	10	11	12	13	14	15

1 Merchant wholesalers, except manufacturers' sales branches and offices.

Table C. Incorporated Places, Census Designated Places (CDPs), and Minor Civil Divisions (MCDs) of 10,000 or More Population — **Economic Census**

STATE City, town, township, borough, or CDP (county if applicable)	Economic activity by sector, 2012														
	Real estate and rental and leasing	Professional, scientific, and technical services		Administration and support and waste management and mediation services		Educational services		Health care and social assistance		Arts, entertainment, and recreation		Accommodation and food services		Other services (except public administration)	
	Number of employees	Number of establish-ments	Number of employees	Number of establish-ments	Number of employees	Number of establish-ments	Number of employees	Number of establish-ments	Number of employees	Number of establish-ments	Number of employees	Number of establish-ments	Number of employees	Number of establish-ments	Number of employees
	16	17	18	19	20	21	22	23	24	25	26	27	28	29	30

TABLE A.

All Places

(For explanation of symbols see page xvi)

Table A — All Places

1

Table A. All Places — **Population and Housing**

STATE City, town, township, borough, or CDP (county if applicable)	Population: 2010 census total population	Population: 2014 estimated population	Population: Percent change 2010–2014	Population: ACS total population estimate 2010–2014	Race and Hispanic or Latino origin (percent), 2010–2014: White alone, not Hispanic or Latino	Black alone, not Hispanic or Latino	Asian alone, not Hispanic or Latino	All other races or 2 or more races, not Hispanic or Latino	Hispanic or Latino[1]	Age (percent), 2010–2014: Under 18 years old	Age 18 to 64 years old	Age 65 years and older	Households, 2010–2014: Total occupied housing units	Percent owner occupied	Householders by level of education (percent): High school diploma or less	Bachelor's degree or more
	1	2	3	4	5	6	7	8	9	10	11	12	13	14	15	16
UNITED STATES	308,758,105	318,857,056	3.3	314,107,084	62.8	12.2	4.9	3.1	16.9	23.5	62.8	13.7	116,211,092	64.4	37.4	31.5
ALABAMA	4,780,127	4,849,377	1.4	4,817,678	66.6	26.2	1.2	2.0	4.0	23.2	62.3	14.5	1,842,174	69.2	43.7	24.7
Abanda CDP	192	NA	NA	43	100.0	0.0	0.0	0.0	0.0	0.0	72.1	27.9	43	100.0	72.1	0.0
Abbeville city	2,688	2,624	-2.4	2,654	47.8	41.5	8.2	0.9	1.5	17.8	55.1	27.1	1,061	72.6	62.8	15.8
Adamsville city	4,522	4,435	-1.9	4,472	48.7	40.6	1.5	0.1	9.1	19.5	65.1	15.3	1,721	76.4	49.7	19.2
Addison town	756	749	-0.9	913	95.6	0.0	0.0	4.4	0.0	23.1	54.1	22.9	385	70.9	59.5	18.7
Akron town	356	338	-5.1	302	20.5	79.5	0.0	0.0	0.0	20.5	67.8	11.6	121	70.2	66.1	7.4
Alabaster city	30,360	31,545	3.9	30,978	73.2	13.2	0.4	1.7	11.5	28.1	61.9	10.1	10,416	83.3	30.7	38.9
Albertville city	21,127	21,458	1.6	21,363	67.2	1.3	0.0	1.5	29.9	29.4	57.8	12.7	7,215	61.3	58.8	13.5
Alexander City city	14,875	14,849	-0.2	14,815	57.0	36.3	0.0	0.6	6.0	25.9	57.6	16.7	5,808	55.8	50.8	15.2
Alexandria CDP	3,917	NA	NA	3,947	91.6	6.3	0.0	0.0	2.1	24.7	61.6	13.7	1,434	84.8	47.9	16.1
Aliceville city	2,481	2,388	-3.7	3,892	16.2	82.3	0.0	1.3	0.2	26.8	59.0	14.1	1,378	49.7	55.9	12.6
Allgood town	622	628	1.0	607	48.1	0.0	0.0	0.8	51.1	28.0	61.2	10.7	206	45.1	70.4	9.2
Altoona town	937	928	-1.0	764	91.6	3.3	0.0	2.1	3.0	22.3	56.9	20.8	317	55.2	64.7	10.7
Andalusia city	9,015	9,081	0.7	9,048	66.9	28.4	1.0	1.2	2.4	23.7	56.7	19.6	3,522	64.8	46.5	21.4
Anderson town	282	279	-1.1	322	89.8	0.0	0.0	0.9	9.3	22.9	60.3	16.8	117	65.0	44.4	21.4
Anniston city	23,120	22,457	-2.9	22,749	42.3	51.8	1.9	2.0	2.0	20.4	61.3	18.3	9,415	55.7	47.6	22.8
Arab city	8,087	8,284	2.4	8,241	95.9	0.4	0.8	1.1	1.8	24.1	57.7	18.3	3,335	68.6	40.1	24.5
Ardmore town	1,194	1,341	12.3	1,511	97.7	1.2	0.0	1.1	0.0	25.0	60.1	15.0	610	61.5	52.8	18.5
Argo town	4,071	4,187	2.8	4,127	94.5	3.5	0.1	1.8	0.0	17.1	73.2	9.7	1,624	89.7	53.9	19.3
Ariton town	762	745	-2.2	720	66.5	25.4	0.0	6.5	1.5	24.0	60.1	16.0	268	64.6	67.2	13.8
Arley town	359	356	-0.8	453	98.2	0.0	0.0	0.4	1.3	11.5	67.5	21.0	199	82.4	50.3	19.1
Ashford town	2,139	2,164	1.2	2,273	73.6	20.1	0.0	5.9	0.4	23.7	60.7	15.6	872	67.9	56.3	17.2
Ashland town	2,037	1,984	-2.6	2,494	66.9	21.9	0.0	1.6	9.6	21.7	60.8	17.5	1,046	48.7	47.9	6.9
Ashville city	2,212	2,255	1.9	2,225	63.3	29.2	0.7	3.4	3.5	26.0	56.3	17.6	736	80.2	60.7	6.3
Athens city	21,891	24,522	12.0	23,335	72.2	16.5	0.5	2.8	8.0	23.9	59.9	16.3	9,203	64.4	41.9	26.9
Atmore city	10,194	10,006	-1.8	10,096	49.0	46.6	0.4	3.0	1.0	17.8	68.9	13.2	3,263	60.0	63.7	13.1
Attalla city	6,048	5,940	-1.8	5,995	76.7	14.1	0.0	3.0	6.2	18.2	66.0	15.8	2,287	63.4	53.0	9.8
Auburn city	53,393	60,258	12.9	56,986	71.2	16.7	6.6	1.6	4.0	17.4	76.1	6.5	21,644	43.8	13.3	48.7
Autaugaville town	880	865	-1.7	1,101	24.6	72.1	0.0	2.3	1.0	23.6	66.2	10.3	385	71.7	72.5	8.6
Avon town	543	535	-1.5	579	79.6	12.3	3.1	5.0	0.0	29.2	52.8	18.1	203	74.4	60.1	14.3
Axis CDP	757	NA	NA	1,020	72.0	21.4	6.7	0.0	0.0	26.5	57.6	15.9	313	82.7	34.5	17.3
Babbie town	603	607	0.7	649	97.1	1.2	0.0	1.4	0.3	20.9	65.0	14.0	254	78.7	60.2	8.7
Baileyton town	614	620	1.0	742	96.4	1.1	0.4	2.2	0.0	27.6	56.7	15.8	274	71.2	55.5	9.1
Bakerhill town	279	269	-3.6	276	65.6	34.4	0.0	0.0	0.0	20.0	59.2	21.0	103	82.5	62.1	4.9
Ballplay CDP	1,580	NA	NA	1,444	96.7	0.0	0.0	3.3	0.0	25.1	59.1	15.7	526	78.3	61.8	6.8
Banks town	179	174	-2.8	184	75.5	22.3	0.0	0.0	2.2	32.1	54.4	13.6	82	51.2	64.6	24.4
Bay Minette city	8,318	9,049	8.8	8,682	60.8	36.0	0.3	1.5	1.5	26.7	58.1	15.1	2,835	58.0	50.3	17.8
Bayou La Batre city	2,557	2,636	3.1	2,661	40.2	17.3	30.4	4.9	7.2	27.5	60.6	11.8	884	57.0	76.6	2.3
Bear Creek town	1,070	1,052	-1.7	1,510	97.9	0.0	0.0	1.0	1.1	21.7	65.4	12.8	591	71.7	70.7	4.6
Beatrice town	302	289	-4.3	268	22.8	77.2	0.0	0.0	0.0	18.9	60.7	20.1	105	75.2	47.6	5.7
Beaverton town	195	189	-3.1	235	88.9	6.8	0.0	0.0	4.3	20.4	54.1	25.5	100	86.0	81.0	5.0
Belgreen CDP	129	NA	NA	94	100.0	0.0	0.0	0.0	0.0	6.4	77.7	16.0	54	100.0	31.5	11.1
Belk town	215	211	-1.9	282	100.0	0.0	0.0	0.0	0.0	29.1	53.5	17.4	106	84.0	68.9	9.4
Bellamy CDP	543	NA	NA	689	8.9	91.1	0.0	0.0	0.0	18.3	65.1	16.7	302	98.0	78.1	3.3
Belle Fontaine CDP	608	NA	NA	557	92.6	7.4	0.0	0.0	0.0	42.2	57.8	0.0	193	63.7	50.8	21.2
Benton town	49	46	-6.1	42	100.0	0.0	0.0	0.0	0.0	21.4	38.2	40.5	15	100.0	33.3	13.3
Berry town	1,148	1,120	-2.4	1,239	94.1	3.9	0.0	2.0	0.0	21.1	65.7	13.2	519	73.4	64.0	4.4
Bessemer city	27,463	26,949	-1.9	27,202	23.9	71.6	0.1	1.1	3.4	24.6	59.8	15.5	10,457	57.4	51.9	13.7
Billingsley town	144	142	-1.4	162	82.7	17.3	0.0	0.0	0.0	24.1	56.2	19.8	65	81.5	58.5	12.3
Birmingham city	212,193	212,247	0.0	211,705	21.3	73.1	1.0	1.1	3.5	21.0	66.0	12.9	88,817	48.5	39.8	25.4
Black town	207	207	0.0	146	97.9	0.0	0.0	2.1	0.0	16.5	74.7	8.9	77	72.7	59.7	6.5
Blountsville town	1,684	1,698	0.8	1,848	80.1	5.5	0.1	3.1	11.1	27.9	61.4	10.8	636	48.1	64.3	6.6
Blue Ridge CDP	1,341	NA	NA	1,531	98.5	0.0	0.0	0.0	1.5	19.6	61.9	18.4	525	97.9	18.9	49.9
Blue Springs town	96	93	-3.1	93	90.3	9.7	0.0	0.0	0.0	4.4	75.4	20.4	41	97.6	56.1	24.4
Boaz city	9,468	9,689	2.3	9,781	80.7	2.0	2.3	2.1	12.8	27.8	57.4	14.7	3,490	63.0	44.3	18.7
Boligee town	328	311	-5.2	609	6.4	93.6	0.0	0.0	0.0	38.3	56.0	5.7	244	36.1	57.8	14.8
Bon Air town	116	114	-1.7	117	99.1	0.9	0.0	0.0	0.0	34.2	54.7	11.1	35	74.3	80.0	0.0
Boykin CDP	275	NA	NA	104	0.0	100.0	0.0	0.0	0.0	23.0	51.9	25.0	32	100.0	75.0	0.0
Brantley town	808	808	0.0	1,016	58.1	36.6	1.1	1.8	2.5	30.4	54.7	14.7	410	55.4	58.5	22.2
Brantleyville CDP	884	NA	NA	941	72.2	9.7	0.0	11.4	6.8	38.3	58.5	3.0	332	81.6	50.9	10.2
Brent city	4,947	4,881	-1.3	4,911	48.8	48.3	0.1	2.1	0.7	18.7	69.5	11.8	1,320	58.1	68.9	8.1
Brewton city	5,401	5,391	-0.2	5,426	49.9	47.4	0.2	2.4	0.2	21.4	57.8	20.9	2,209	69.2	45.8	27.1
Bridgeport city	2,417	2,372	-1.9	2,416	76.0	13.2	0.0	8.2	2.6	23.9	59.9	16.2	998	63.5	72.6	8.2
Brighton city	2,945	2,885	-2.0	2,918	5.5	82.7	0.0	0.2	11.6	24.2	59.2	16.6	1,095	56.2	62.9	9.8
Brilliant town	900	887	-1.4	1,053	95.1	0.0	0.0	0.7	4.3	23.5	55.8	20.7	478	66.7	61.9	9.2
Bristow Cove CDP	683	NA	NA	336	100.0	0.0	0.0	0.0	0.0	21.1	63.1	15.8	147	80.3	50.3	10.9
Brook Highland CDP	6,746	NA	NA	7,281	64.7	19.1	5.4	1.2	9.6	20.1	74.4	5.6	3,243	43.2	12.9	58.2
Brookside town	1,363	1,340	-1.7	1,112	78.2	21.2	0.0	0.5	0.0	24.0	61.2	14.7	428	67.5	53.5	7.0
Brookwood town	1,828	1,834	0.3	1,918	87.1	10.6	0.5	0.2	1.7	26.5	68.0	5.6	640	72.0	54.1	17.3
Broomtown CDP	182	NA	NA	104	98.1	0.0	0.0	1.9	0.0	6.7	38.4	54.8	70	100.0	71.4	0.0
Brundidge city	2,076	2,001	-3.6	2,007	20.8	76.3	0.0	1.9	1.0	21.0	61.3	17.8	900	61.9	63.9	14.2
Bucks CDP	32	NA	NA	45	100.0	0.0	0.0	0.0	0.0	0.0	0.0	100.0	23	100.0	0.0	0.0
Butler town	1,890	1,819	-3.8	2,280	67.5	30.8	0.0	0.0	1.7	23.1	55.6	21.1	941	56.6	48.5	15.8
Calera city	11,606	12,972	11.8	12,376	67.1	24.9	0.3	2.7	4.9	27.2	63.2	9.5	4,724	80.3	29.8	41.8
Calvert CDP	277	NA	NA	154	46.8	53.2	0.0	0.0	0.0	33.7	48.1	18.2	42	66.7	100.0	0.0
Camden city	2,020	1,933	-4.3	2,770	44.3	54.6	0.0	0.6	0.5	31.6	53.0	15.3	873	67.5	52.8	15.1
Camp Hill town	1,014	992	-2.2	895	16.3	80.3	0.0	1.7	1.7	24.4	64.3	11.2	361	50.7	63.7	15.8
Carbon Hill city	2,025	1,980	-2.2	2,030	89.6	7.2	0.0	3.3	0.0	22.7	58.0	19.3	854	56.8	69.2	5.7
Cardiff town	55	54	-1.8	21	76.2	23.8	0.0	0.0	0.0	19.0	38.1	42.9	13	100.0	53.8	7.7
Carlisle-Rockledge CDP	2,137	NA	NA	2,745	83.2	3.8	0.0	1.0	12.0	25.7	64.6	9.6	773	85.6	66.4	5.2
Carlton CDP	65	NA	NA	173	22.0	78.0	0.0	0.0	0.0	39.3	55.5	5.2	77	76.6	42.9	0.0
Carolina town	297	299	0.7	299	92.3	0.0	0.0	7.0	0.7	20.7	63.6	15.7	132	80.3	43.9	21.2
Carrollton town	1,019	989	-2.9	1,138	49.7	41.5	0.0	5.8	3.0	18.5	68.5	13.1	383	58.0	60.8	9.7
Castleberry town	592	566	-4.4	565	55.4	42.7	0.0	1.6	0.4	13.8	62.9	23.4	283	67.1	66.4	5.7
Catherine CDP	22	NA	NA	23	0.0	100.0	0.0	0.0	0.0	0.0	100.0	0.0	10	100.0	100.0	0.0
Cedar Bluff town	1,825	1,816	-0.5	1,872	87.1	8.1	0.6	2.8	1.3	26.6	53.9	19.5	833	64.2	45.6	17.3
Center Point city	16,924	16,777	-0.9	16,876	28.7	67.4	0.0	1.5	2.4	26.7	61.4	11.8	6,303	59.0	43.1	17.9
Centre city	3,489	3,595	3.0	3,555	83.2	14.4	0.0	1.2	1.2	17.2	55.8	27.1	1,639	64.4	53.5	16.4
Centreville city	2,778	2,705	-2.6	2,727	70.8	28.3	0.0	0.8	0.0	22.5	57.5	20.1	851	60.0	56.5	14.3

1 May be of any race.

Table A. All Places — **Population and Housing**

STATE City, town, township, borough, or CDP (county if applicable)	Population				Race and Hispanic or Latino origin (percent), 2010–2014					Age (percent), 2010–2014			Households, 2010–2014		Householders by level of education (percent)	
	2010 census total population	2014 estimated population	Percent change 2010–2014	ACS total population estimate 2010–2014	White alone, not Hispanic or Latino	Black alone, not Hispanic or Latino	Asian alone, not Hispanic or Latino	All other races or 2 or more races, not Hispanic or Latino	Hispanic or Latino[1]	Under 18 years old	Age 18 to 64 years old	Age 65 years and older	Total occupied housing units	Percent owner occupied	High school diploma or less	Bachelor's degree or more
	1	2	3	4	5	6	7	8	9	10	11	12	13	14	15	16
ALABAMA—Con.																
Chatom town	1,288	1,237	-4.0	1,063	69.2	28.9	0.0	1.2	0.7	17.8	57.3	24.9	427	69.3	46.1	20.6
Chelsea city	10,488	11,758	12.1	11,051	87.2	6.0	1.8	0.9	4.1	28.7	63.3	8.1	3,696	89.0	20.3	51.3
Cherokee town	1,048	1,024	-2.3	1,000	87.6	11.2	0.0	0.9	0.3	28.3	50.4	21.3	430	65.6	61.2	11.2
Chickasaw city	6,106	5,981	-2.0	6,026	58.8	37.6	0.0	1.2	2.4	29.3	59.0	11.8	2,300	58.8	53.1	10.1
Childersburg city	5,182	5,068	-2.2	5,117	57.8	40.2	0.4	1.3	0.3	27.5	55.7	16.8	2,130	59.4	49.8	9.1
Choccolocco CDP	2,804	NA	NA	2,443	86.9	5.3	0.0	0.0	7.9	29.6	58.6	11.7	954	77.1	28.4	25.7
Chunchula CDP	210	NA	NA	153	74.5	25.5	0.0	0.0	0.0	0.0	75.9	24.2	75	100.0	72.0	0.0
Citronelle city	3,908	3,885	-0.6	3,892	69.0	22.0	0.0	8.9	0.0	20.2	64.9	15.0	1,562	71.3	58.9	11.8
Clanton city	8,619	8,727	1.3	8,672	72.0	19.0	0.8	1.8	6.3	20.5	63.9	15.7	3,358	63.6	55.5	15.2
Clay city	9,689	9,700	0.1	9,699	78.8	18.6	0.2	1.2	1.2	19.9	67.2	13.1	3,724	88.1	41.5	25.0
Clayhatchee town	589	576	-2.2	539	91.3	3.3	0.2	4.6	0.6	23.0	56.9	20.0	213	60.1	39.4	19.2
Clayton town	3,005	2,947	-1.9	2,971	30.5	65.4	0.1	2.5	1.6	10.4	77.8	11.8	649	64.7	68.0	10.8
Cleveland town	1,303	1,316	1.0	1,340	76.1	0.4	0.0	0.0	23.5	24.9	58.0	16.9	471	78.8	68.4	9.1
Clio city	1,399	1,547	10.6	1,575	32.2	42.9	0.0	1.7	23.3	14.8	71.8	13.4	379	74.1	75.5	7.4
Coaling town	1,660	1,663	0.2	1,778	88.1	8.0	0.0	3.7	0.1	25.2	68.4	6.4	567	82.9	54.3	11.1
Coats Bend CDP	1,394	NA	NA	1,908	89.3	7.4	0.0	1.4	1.9	26.9	64.2	8.9	555	87.0	48.1	4.9
Coffee Springs town	228	228	0.0	207	91.8	7.2	0.0	1.0	0.0	20.3	48.1	31.4	92	91.3	46.7	8.7
Coffeeville town	352	341	-3.1	374	57.8	42.2	0.0	0.0	0.0	32.3	46.0	21.7	130	73.1	67.7	3.8
Coker town	976	985	0.9	1,094	98.9	0.0	0.0	1.1	0.0	26.7	63.4	9.9	341	77.4	62.8	14.1
Collinsville town	1,983	1,976	-0.4	1,991	49.9	11.3	0.0	0.3	38.5	28.7	57.0	14.4	570	49.6	65.4	8.4
Colony town	268	271	1.1	265	8.7	85.3	0.0	4.9	1.1	22.3	65.4	12.5	93	74.2	53.8	5.4
Columbia town	740	741	0.1	780	81.4	16.4	0.3	1.9	0.0	22.2	57.8	20.0	345	67.8	55.7	9.6
Columbiana city	4,165	4,213	1.2	4,198	64.4	33.6	0.1	1.2	0.7	22.0	62.8	15.1	1,217	61.3	55.2	15.3
Concord CDP	1,837	NA	NA	1,724	100.0	0.0	0.0	0.0	0.0	16.2	58.1	25.9	762	81.4	42.5	15.5
Coosada town	1,224	1,230	0.5	1,193	50.0	49.3	0.0	0.7	0.0	29.0	54.7	16.2	418	79.9	48.8	27.0
Cordova city	2,095	2,035	-2.9	1,944	88.8	7.8	0.0	1.2	2.2	18.2	56.3	25.7	811	56.7	60.4	6.8
Cottondale CDP	0	NA	NA	3,480	61.1	26.8	0.0	4.8	7.4	18.9	70.2	10.8	1,208	69.1	46.7	20.4
Cottonwood town	1,289	1,275	-1.1	1,296	69.9	28.8	0.0	0.8	0.5	20.7	64.4	15.0	515	66.4	63.5	4.5
County Line town	258	261	1.2	276	97.8	0.0	0.7	1.4	0.0	9.0	79.7	11.2	120	96.7	75.8	4.2
Courtland town	617	604	-2.1	540	50.2	48.0	0.0	1.9	0.0	32.6	52.2	15.4	203	71.4	66.5	5.4
Cowarts town	1,894	1,953	3.1	1,897	82.0	9.4	0.1	5.2	3.3	24.4	60.5	15.1	739	75.5	56.2	14.5
Creola city	1,926	1,942	0.8	1,898	89.8	6.3	0.4	3.1	0.5	26.0	59.3	14.7	698	80.8	54.7	13.5
Crossville town	1,862	1,846	-0.9	2,201	82.9	0.2	0.9	2.0	14.1	26.7	59.2	14.0	729	67.4	62.3	9.2
Cuba town	346	323	-6.6	344	67.7	30.5	1.2	0.6	0.0	14.8	71.0	14.2	139	77.7	51.1	29.5
Cullman city	14,802	15,145	2.3	14,933	88.8	1.1	0.4	2.5	7.3	22.5	59.0	18.5	6,109	57.3	41.2	22.1
Cullomburg CDP	171	NA	NA	93	67.7	32.3	0.0	0.0	0.0	24.7	45.2	30.1	52	100.0	78.8	0.0
Cusseta town	123	123	0.0	133	99.2	0.0	0.8	0.0	0.0	12.8	71.5	15.8	53	84.9	52.8	7.5
Dadeville city	3,229	3,184	-1.4	3,203	56.9	41.9	0.0	1.1	0.1	21.0	62.5	16.5	1,247	51.1	56.5	24.0
Daleville city	5,295	5,142	-2.9	5,233	56.0	27.1	3.2	5.2	8.5	26.3	62.8	10.8	2,197	44.4	37.9	15.4
Daphne city	21,581	24,395	13.0	22,983	82.9	11.5	1.2	1.5	2.9	23.1	62.6	14.3	8,731	64.1	21.5	44.3
Dauphin Island town	1,238	1,242	0.3	1,291	92.6	0.7	1.9	3.6	1.2	20.4	57.1	22.5	520	84.6	34.0	28.1
Daviston town	214	212	-0.9	287	85.7	6.6	0.0	0.0	7.7	15.0	74.5	10.5	109	78.0	40.4	12.8
Dayton town	52	50	-3.8	41	80.5	19.5	0.0	0.0	0.0	39.0	31.7	29.3	20	100.0	0.0	20.0
Deatsville town	1,154	1,158	0.3	1,098	75.1	16.2	1.8	3.2	3.6	33.1	56.1	10.7	351	92.9	30.2	27.1
Decatur city	55,704	55,532	-0.3	55,641	61.7	21.4	1.0	2.9	13.0	23.0	61.5	15.6	22,006	61.6	43.3	24.5
Deer Park CDP	188	NA	NA	214	75.7	24.3	0.0	0.0	0.0	18.6	53.8	27.6	59	91.5	59.3	23.7
Delta CDP	197	NA	NA	149	92.6	7.4	0.0	0.0	0.0	7.4	45.7	47.0	112	90.2	33.9	13.4
Demopolis city	7,483	7,182	-4.0	7,323	45.2	50.9	0.8	0.0	3.1	28.3	55.8	16.0	2,985	59.0	45.6	24.3
Detroit town	237	230	-3.0	226	79.2	18.6	0.0	2.2	0.0	24.8	58.9	16.4	110	56.4	64.5	10.0
Dodge City town	593	599	1.0	805	80.6	0.0	0.0	5.8	13.5	24.6	63.9	11.4	276	73.6	54.7	11.2
Dora city	2,025	1,969	-2.8	2,253	82.0	14.6	0.0	3.1	0.4	23.4	61.6	15.0	803	74.8	51.4	15.7
Dothan city	65,916	68,409	3.8	67,574	61.1	32.7	1.2	2.2	2.8	24.3	60.6	15.0	25,935	59.3	40.2	25.6
Double Springs town	1,084	1,068	-1.5	1,388	90.0	5.1	0.2	4.5	0.2	18.0	62.9	19.1	450	68.2	62.9	10.9
Douglas town	744	757	1.7	990	93.4	0.0	0.1	0.3	6.2	34.6	58.1	7.3	309	58.3	58.6	9.7
Dozier town	329	332	0.9	322	67.1	28.0	0.0	4.7	0.3	22.9	57.1	19.9	135	57.8	60.0	14.1
Dunnavant CDP	981	NA	NA	831	96.3	0.0	0.0	0.0	3.7	26.9	58.4	14.8	308	81.2	40.6	17.9
Dutton town	315	312	-1.0	251	98.8	0.0	0.0	1.2	0.0	20.4	59.9	19.9	89	92.1	52.8	10.1
East Brewton city	2,478	2,426	-2.1	2,552	65.3	27.0	0.0	2.2	5.6	24.6	59.3	15.9	1,024	49.9	64.9	5.1
East Point CDP	201	NA	NA	166	100.0	0.0	0.0	0.0	0.0	0.0	64.5	35.5	69	100.0	0.0	56.5
Eclectic town	1,001	1,015	1.4	830	85.1	8.9	0.0	4.9	1.1	25.2	53.5	21.4	352	71.9	50.3	10.5
Edgewater CDP	883	NA	NA	804	37.2	62.8	0.0	0.0	0.0	24.4	66.7	8.7	329	53.5	37.1	4.3
Edwardsville town	202	204	1.0	202	99.5	0.0	0.0	0.5	0.0	14.8	70.8	14.4	83	78.3	33.7	8.4
Egypt CDP	932	NA	NA	1,153	95.5	4.5	0.0	0.0	0.0	20.4	67.6	12.0	408	79.4	46.8	0.0
Elba city	3,939	3,893	-1.2	3,935	57.5	37.8	0.7	1.2	2.7	24.1	58.3	17.6	1,334	59.4	56.9	16.0
Elberta town	1,515	1,634	7.9	1,470	92.4	0.8	0.0	0.7	6.1	17.2	63.7	19.2	659	52.8	43.4	28.1
Eldridge town	130	128	-1.5	166	95.2	4.8	0.0	0.0	0.0	27.7	63.8	8.4	42	83.3	47.6	16.7
Elkmont town	426	462	8.5	459	79.3	17.4	0.0	2.2	1.1	19.4	59.1	21.6	192	73.4	67.7	14.6
Elmore town	1,276	1,274	-0.2	1,738	46.7	32.3	0.0	0.2	20.8	33.0	59.6	7.4	545	70.1	59.6	16.7
Emelle town	53	50	-5.7	31	25.8	74.2	0.0	0.0	0.0	0.0	38.8	61.3	14	85.7	71.4	28.6
Emerald Mountain CDP	2,561	NA	NA	2,316	82.4	13.0	0.8	2.8	1.0	24.2	65.0	10.8	856	96.5	23.8	36.7
Enterprise city	26,615	27,772	4.3	27,375	67.1	19.9	1.8	2.7	8.4	25.6	60.1	14.4	10,182	63.1	33.8	31.2
Epes town	193	183	-5.2	108	13.0	87.0	0.0	0.0	0.0	18.5	64.0	17.6	53	60.4	54.7	22.6
Ethelsville town	76	74	-2.6	81	82.7	8.6	0.0	8.6	0.0	19.8	57.9	22.2	27	66.7	55.6	25.9
Eufaula city	13,134	12,781	-2.7	12,897	47.8	44.4	0.6	2.0	5.2	26.1	56.9	17.1	4,811	61.4	48.6	20.5
Eunola CDP	243	NA	NA	289	76.5	0.0	0.0	6.2	17.3	16.6	51.2	32.2	134	95.5	59.7	10.4
Eutaw town	2,934	2,788	-5.0	2,856	18.9	78.6	0.4	0.9	1.2	22.2	57.1	20.8	1,032	54.7	47.0	15.9
Eva town	515	512	-0.6	544	93.4	0.0	0.7	5.9	0.0	25.9	53.8	20.4	201	87.6	49.3	12.9
Evergreen city	3,947	3,773	-4.4	3,864	30.4	64.2	0.0	2.9	2.5	27.0	60.1	12.9	1,456	47.6	65.1	5.4
Excel town	723	682	-5.7	1,037	97.2	1.8	0.2	0.8	0.0	25.2	54.2	20.5	357	82.9	48.2	22.7
Fairfield city	11,117	10,988	-1.2	11,039	5.3	91.1	0.1	1.6	1.9	25.5	62.7	11.8	3,954	58.7	41.5	19.8
Fairford CDP	186	NA	NA	82	100.0	0.0	0.0	0.0	0.0	0.0	48.7	51.2	49	83.7	100.0	0.0
Fairhope city	15,338	18,089	17.9	16,661	89.5	5.3	1.8	0.9	2.5	24.3	52.5	23.2	6,631	72.3	21.5	50.1
Fairview town	448	452	0.9	483	84.5	0.0	0.2	0.0	15.3	24.3	57.2	18.4	182	74.7	63.7	11.5
Falkville town	1,279	1,270	-0.7	1,262	94.8	2.6	0.2	2.4	0.0	17.1	51.1	31.9	362	59.9	56.1	10.8
Faunsdale town	98	94	-4.1	83	73.5	18.1	0.0	8.4	0.0	22.8	59.0	18.1	34	100.0	52.9	41.2
Fayette city	4,619	4,524	-2.1	4,562	70.0	25.5	0.5	2.1	2.0	25.6	58.7	15.7	1,835	46.4	57.5	14.0
Fayetteville CDP	1,284	NA	NA	1,232	97.7	0.0	0.0	2.3	0.0	28.9	50.6	20.5	446	92.8	51.6	4.0
Fitzpatrick CDP	83	NA	NA	81	87.7	12.3	0.0	0.0	0.0	0.0	30.9	69.1	42	100.0	23.8	59.5
Five Points town	141	141	0.0	146	37.0	63.0	0.0	0.0	0.0	15.0	66.4	18.5	60	73.3	68.3	23.3
Flomaton town	1,440	1,417	-1.6	1,683	55.4	43.6	0.1	0.9	0.0	22.5	63.1	14.3	631	57.4	59.3	19.8

1 May be of any race.

Table A. All Places — **Population and Housing**

STATE City, town, township, borough, or CDP (county if applicable)	Population				Race and Hispanic or Latino origin (percent), 2010–2014					Age (percent), 2010–2014			Households, 2010–2014		Householders by level of education (percent)	
	2010 census total population	2014 estimated population	Percent change 2010–2014	ACS total population estimate 2010–2014	White alone, not Hispanic or Latino	Black alone, not Hispanic or Latino	Asian alone, not Hispanic or Latino	All other races or 2 or more races, not Hispanic or Latino	Hispanic or Latino[1]	Under 18 years old	Age 18 to 64 years old	Age 65 years and older	Total occupied housing units	Percent owner occupied	High school diploma or less	Bachelor's degree or more
	1	2	3	4	5	6	7	8	9	10	11	12	13	14	15	16
ALABAMA—Con.																
Florala town	1,980	1,981	0.1	2,210	76.5	17.7	0.0	3.3	2.5	24.5	54.7	20.8	870	63.2	60.8	6.8
Florence city	39,339	40,215	2.2	39,738	74.2	19.5	1.3	2.4	2.6	19.6	62.8	17.8	17,617	57.5	39.0	26.4
Foley city	14,658	16,243	10.8	15,428	75.1	18.0	0.2	2.6	4.1	19.3	55.2	25.5	6,644	63.2	36.3	28.6
Forestdale CDP	10,162	NA	NA	10,168	22.5	74.2	0.0	0.9	2.5	24.7	61.8	13.7	3,776	80.9	34.7	23.3
Forkland town	645	606	-6.0	757	15.2	84.8	0.0	0.0	0.0	34.5	53.1	12.5	223	83.0	61.4	8.1
Fort Deposit town	1,347	1,256	-6.8	1,366	28.0	72.0	0.0	0.0	0.0	33.5	52.5	14.1	469	55.4	61.6	16.2
Fort Payne city	14,113	14,125	0.1	14,115	65.9	4.2	0.5	1.7	27.7	25.5	59.6	14.9	5,122	65.3	55.6	15.4
Fort Rucker CDP	4,636	NA	NA	4,860	64.5	7.6	2.4	2.7	22.7	38.1	61.8	0.0	1,259	0.0	11.3	43.4
Franklin town	149	134	-10.1	184	65.8	33.7	0.0	0.0	0.5	23.3	69.0	7.6	81	88.9	32.1	40.7
Fredonia CDP	199	NA	NA	312	93.3	6.7	0.0	0.0	0.0	17.0	60.6	22.4	124	78.2	32.3	38.7
Frisco City town	1,309	1,239	-5.3	1,440	38.1	60.6	0.3	0.8	0.1	26.5	56.4	17.1	591	59.6	71.4	6.8
Fruitdale CDP	185	NA	NA	223	100.0	0.0	0.0	0.0	0.0	50.7	47.1	2.2	53	83.0	81.1	0.0
Fruithurst town	280	283	1.1	262	100.0	0.0	0.0	0.0	0.0	18.0	69.1	13.0	94	75.5	64.9	5.3
Fulton town	272	264	-2.9	269	89.2	10.8	0.0	0.0	0.0	21.5	59.0	19.3	101	72.3	73.3	5.0
Fultondale city	8,380	8,908	6.3	8,593	64.8	19.6	0.6	2.4	12.6	19.3	62.6	17.9	3,862	71.3	38.6	27.7
Fyffe town	1,018	1,024	0.6	1,376	93.0	1.5	0.0	5.1	0.4	25.3	64.6	10.0	464	73.1	42.0	13.6
Gadsden city	36,879	36,295	-1.6	36,621	55.5	36.3	0.9	2.5	4.8	23.0	60.1	17.1	14,689	59.6	48.1	15.4
Gainesville town	208	198	-4.8	151	21.9	57.6	20.5	0.0	0.0	30.5	63.0	6.6	51	70.6	66.7	13.7
Gallant CDP	855	NA	NA	1,005	100.0	0.0	0.0	0.0	0.0	20.5	60.3	19.5	398	91.5	30.9	13.1
Gantt town	222	223	0.5	210	57.6	42.4	0.0	0.0	0.0	19.9	68.1	11.9	77	90.9	55.8	14.3
Garden City town	492	491	-0.2	447	96.0	0.0	0.0	4.0	0.0	19.3	49.4	31.3	183	72.7	67.2	10.9
Gardendale city	13,881	13,729	-1.1	13,809	83.5	14.4	0.9	0.2	1.0	20.9	58.5	20.6	5,696	82.9	38.8	27.1
Gaylesville town	144	144	0.0	153	98.0	0.0	0.0	2.0	0.0	11.8	67.3	20.9	71	84.5	52.1	16.9
Geiger town	170	162	-4.7	198	50.5	47.0	0.0	0.0	2.5	36.8	49.0	14.1	72	66.7	80.6	16.7
Geneva city	4,457	4,454	-0.1	4,465	81.4	11.5	2.4	3.8	0.9	24.8	56.7	18.4	1,699	60.8	57.8	12.4
Georgiana town	1,738	1,680	-3.3	1,619	28.4	70.6	0.0	1.0	0.0	24.4	53.6	22.1	651	56.8	66.1	10.9
Geraldine town	899	901	0.2	795	89.4	0.0	0.0	6.0	4.5	28.4	53.9	17.6	316	66.8	54.1	18.0
Gilbertown town	215	208	-3.3	169	65.7	31.4	0.0	1.8	1.2	20.2	58.1	21.9	71	67.6	57.7	15.5
Glen Allen town	510	501	-1.8	472	80.3	19.1	0.0	0.6	0.0	20.6	57.8	21.6	190	80.5	51.1	4.2
Glencoe city	5,160	5,174	0.3	5,137	93.4	4.0	0.3	2.3	0.0	14.3	64.3	21.5	2,113	70.6	43.6	13.8
Glenwood town	187	189	1.1	215	66.0	32.6	0.0	1.4	0.0	15.9	61.3	22.8	92	85.9	54.3	18.5
Goldville town	55	55	0.0	54	100.0	0.0	0.0	0.0	0.0	31.5	46.4	22.2	19	94.7	47.4	31.6
Good Hope town	2,264	2,268	0.2	2,295	82.2	0.0	0.4	3.1	14.2	32.1	56.2	11.8	796	78.8	51.0	20.1
Goodwater town	1,475	1,357	-8.0	1,678	18.8	80.9	0.0	0.4	0.0	22.4	60.1	17.6	610	73.0	67.2	3.3
Gordo town	1,750	1,689	-3.5	1,504	58.6	39.8	0.0	0.0	1.7	24.1	53.3	22.5	603	54.1	61.4	13.6
Gordon town	330	329	-0.3	275	22.2	77.1	0.0	0.7	0.0	18.9	57.3	23.6	119	72.3	83.2	2.5
Gordonville town	326	308	-5.5	313	0.6	99.4	0.0	0.0	0.0	23.7	51.8	24.6	146	74.7	65.1	8.9
Goshen town	266	258	-3.0	299	82.3	13.7	0.0	0.7	3.3	27.8	50.5	21.7	117	65.0	59.0	19.7
Graham CDP	211	NA	NA	383	95.8	4.2	0.0	0.0	0.0	30.8	60.3	8.9	144	43.1	47.2	11.8
Grand Bay CDP	3,672	NA	NA	3,632	85.8	11.0	0.0	2.6	0.6	22.0	66.1	12.1	1,180	83.0	63.0	12.4
Grant town	896	903	0.8	823	99.0	0.0	0.0	1.0	0.0	25.9	56.6	17.6	310	69.0	44.8	23.5
Grayson Valley CDP	5,736	NA	NA	5,090	67.4	26.7	0.6	1.2	4.1	20.3	70.7	9.1	2,296	79.1	27.9	27.0
Graysville city	2,158	2,114	-2.0	2,091	82.4	17.1	0.4	0.0	0.0	23.0	57.5	19.6	807	81.0	63.3	11.6
Greensboro city	2,494	2,402	-3.7	2,448	37.2	61.8	0.2	0.8	0.0	23.5	60.0	16.7	984	57.6	67.0	7.5
Greenville city	8,135	7,902	-2.9	7,974	38.9	57.6	1.5	0.7	1.3	25.1	59.4	15.7	3,295	55.4	49.0	22.4
Grimes town	558	545	-2.3	521	54.7	42.4	1.2	1.7	0.0	23.2	63.2	13.6	202	65.3	58.9	11.9
Grove Hill town	1,569	1,509	-3.8	1,494	46.9	52.4	0.0	0.3	0.4	25.1	61.2	13.7	631	49.9	59.6	20.1
Guin city	2,376	2,333	-1.8	2,104	91.8	6.2	0.0	1.6	0.3	17.3	55.5	27.2	976	61.8	61.3	8.8
Gulfcrest CDP	161	NA	NA	123	100.0	0.0	0.0	0.0	0.0	40.6	39.0	20.3	37	100.0	0.0	35.1
Gulf Shores city	10,113	10,963	8.4	10,523	89.1	0.3	1.9	6.0	2.7	17.8	58.5	23.6	4,728	55.6	32.8	33.8
Guntersville city	8,197	8,358	2.0	8,316	81.3	11.1	2.6	1.7	3.4	21.1	58.1	20.8	3,201	63.4	40.5	27.1
Gurley town	801	792	-1.1	860	73.8	19.2	0.0	4.2	2.8	20.4	66.5	13.3	326	61.7	62.6	14.1
Gu-Win town	176	174	-1.1	111	100.0	0.0	0.0	0.0	0.0	18.9	63.9	17.1	48	87.5	66.7	0.0
Hackleburg town	1,516	1,490	-1.7	1,609	98.1	0.0	0.2	1.7	0.0	20.5	62.8	16.8	658	80.7	70.2	4.4
Hackneyville CDP	347	NA	NA	410	100.0	0.0	0.0	0.0	0.0	7.8	71.6	20.5	212	75.0	38.7	27.4
Haleburg town	103	101	-1.9	128	96.1	3.9	0.0	0.0	0.0	21.1	63.3	15.6	51	92.2	37.3	39.2
Haleyville city	4,178	4,122	-1.3	4,102	91.3	0.5	0.2	1.5	6.5	24.2	54.1	21.7	1,709	47.9	52.4	10.5
Hamilton city	6,885	6,790	-1.4	6,842	84.6	9.1	1.8	0.7	3.7	23.4	61.3	15.2	2,556	68.6	51.7	10.4
Hammondville town	488	487	-0.2	599	95.3	0.8	0.0	3.5	0.3	26.0	56.2	17.7	191	86.9	55.5	14.7
Hanceville city	3,109	3,238	4.1	3,163	91.6	4.2	0.6	2.7	1.0	19.3	57.3	23.4	1,210	49.3	54.8	7.8
Harpersville town	1,651	1,682	1.9	1,836	68.2	21.4	0.0	6.6	3.8	30.8	54.8	14.3	661	79.7	48.0	13.0
Hartford city	2,624	2,635	0.4	2,642	65.3	22.4	0.0	1.2	11.0	22.7	56.5	20.9	1,082	64.7	63.1	12.8
Hartselle city	14,247	14,459	1.5	14,393	88.8	8.0	0.0	1.9	1.3	26.0	59.9	14.2	5,299	73.4	35.4	28.7
Harvest CDP	5,281	NA	NA	5,213	69.7	23.9	0.3	1.9	4.2	30.5	59.2	10.2	1,697	81.9	26.3	37.4
Hatton CDP	261	NA	NA	173	91.9	0.0	0.0	8.1	0.0	23.1	72.8	4.0	74	81.1	40.5	12.2
Hayden town	1,333	1,341	0.6	1,255	92.7	0.8	0.1	5.2	1.3	28.9	61.3	9.8	422	82.0	45.7	18.2
Hayneville town	933	874	-6.3	1,113	13.5	83.3	0.0	0.0	3.2	26.2	59.1	14.6	394	45.4	62.4	14.0
Hazel Green CDP	3,630	NA	NA	3,272	89.0	6.6	0.5	3.9	0.0	20.9	64.0	15.0	1,262	75.6	46.5	15.8
Headland city	4,516	4,700	4.1	4,637	70.3	29.1	0.0	0.2	0.4	29.6	56.9	13.5	1,794	70.0	40.1	23.1
Heath town	256	258	0.8	292	75.3	12.0	0.0	12.0	0.7	18.1	67.9	13.7	107	70.1	41.1	15.0
Heflin city	3,485	3,517	0.9	3,497	81.1	9.3	0.3	2.5	6.8	27.6	55.5	16.9	1,237	60.6	59.7	12.2
Helena city	16,951	17,883	5.5	16,752	82.1	11.6	1.6	3.1	1.6	33.2	60.4	6.4	5,825	90.4	14.6	47.8
Henagar city	2,344	2,344	0.0	2,308	93.2	0.0	0.7	3.6	2.6	24.0	58.7	17.3	882	77.3	66.2	6.5
Highland Lake town	412	423	2.7	468	97.2	0.0	0.4	0.0	2.4	15.8	62.5	21.8	204	93.1	27.9	41.2
Highland Lakes CDP	3,926	NA	NA	4,679	78.5	10.5	7.7	2.1	1.2	26.8	61.6	11.4	1,606	94.8	6.0	74.6
Hillsboro town	547	527	-3.7	553	23.9	66.4	0.0	2.0	7.8	18.2	58.8	23.1	234	70.9	56.0	16.7
Hissop CDP	658	NA	NA	854	23.1	73.9	0.0	3.0	0.0	14.4	68.9	16.7	372	89.2	54.0	26.9
Hobson CDP	126	NA	NA	55	100.0	0.0	0.0	0.0	0.0	0.0	0.0	100.0	50	100.0	50.0	50.0
Hobson City town	771	764	-0.9	812	10.5	86.5	0.0	3.1	0.0	27.7	61.6	10.5	316	57.9	55.1	4.1
Hodges town	286	285	-0.3	307	100.0	0.0	0.0	0.0	0.0	20.8	63.2	16.0	130	70.0	64.6	6.9
Hokes Bluff city	4,284	4,325	1.0	4,313	97.3	0.0	0.0	0.6	2.1	19.9	63.3	16.8	1,898	81.6	40.8	21.8
Hollins CDP	545	NA	NA	811	96.4	3.6	0.0	0.0	0.0	42.2	51.1	6.7	253	55.3	70.0	5.9
Hollis Crossroads CDP	608	NA	NA	483	83.4	0.0	0.0	0.0	16.6	24.2	58.4	17.4	191	85.9	58.1	13.6
Holly Pond town	798	806	1.0	951	89.8	0.7	0.0	2.0	7.5	22.1	62.0	16.2	365	60.3	46.3	14.8
Hollywood town	1,000	982	-1.8	980	75.5	20.3	1.1	1.4	1.6	16.9	59.4	23.8	438	79.5	71.0	8.2
Holt CDP	3,638	NA	NA	3,812	32.7	52.3	0.7	0.5	13.8	28.4	64.4	7.2	1,134	62.5	62.7	7.3
Holtville CDP	4,096	NA	NA	4,466	92.6	5.3	0.0	0.8	1.4	25.2	64.5	10.4	1,686	82.3	40.3	22.8
Homewood city	25,165	25,802	2.5	25,420	76.2	15.2	1.7	1.0	5.8	23.1	68.2	8.7	9,306	54.1	17.6	60.3
Hoover city	81,024	84,353	4.1	82,849	70.9	14.8	5.6	1.7	7.0	25.4	61.0	13.6	32,375	67.4	13.0	59.2
Horn Hill town	228	230	0.9	268	85.8	0.0	0.0	14.2	0.0	22.4	57.9	19.8	117	68.4	61.5	2.6
Hueytown city	16,104	15,815	-1.8	15,956	69.9	26.1	0.4	1.3	2.2	23.3	59.1	17.6	6,008	77.9	42.9	17.7

1 May be of any race.

Table A. All Places — **Population and Housing**

STATE City, town, township, borough, or CDP (county if applicable)	Population: 2010 census total population	Population: 2014 estimated population	Population: Percent change 2010–2014	Population: ACS total population estimate 2010–2014	Race and Hispanic or Latino origin (percent), 2010–2014: White alone, not Hispanic or Latino	Race: Black alone, not Hispanic or Latino	Race: Asian alone, not Hispanic or Latino	Race: All other races or 2 or more races, not Hispanic or Latino	Race: Hispanic or Latino[1]	Age (percent), 2010–2014: Under 18 years old	Age: Age 18 to 64 years old	Age: Age 65 years and older	Households, 2010–2014: Total occupied housing units	Households: Percent owner occupied	Householders by level of education (percent): High school diploma or less	Householders by level of education (percent): Bachelor's degree or more
	1	2	3	4	5	6	7	8	9	10	11	12	13	14	15	16
ALABAMA—Con.																
Huguley CDP	2,540	NA	NA	2,449	74.5	25.1	0.0	0.0	0.4	21.2	64.7	14.1	1,056	64.7	56.6	10.5
Huntsville city	180,241	188,226	4.4	184,132	59.0	30.1	2.3	2.9	5.7	21.2	64.5	14.3	76,959	59.8	26.1	41.5
Hurtsboro town	553	601	8.7	494	32.8	64.6	0.0	1.8	0.8	30.6	45.5	23.9	206	62.1	63.1	13.1
Hytop town	354	351	-0.8	540	96.1	0.0	1.5	1.1	1.3	32.4	52.7	14.8	162	90.1	72.2	6.2
Ider town	723	716	-1.0	1,033	91.8	0.0	0.0	7.6	0.6	25.5	53.5	20.8	346	75.1	60.7	6.9
Indian Springs Village city	2,424	2,511	3.6	2,490	95.5	1.7	1.6	0.6	0.5	20.6	60.6	19.0	861	92.3	9.8	65.3
Irondale city	12,354	12,444	0.7	12,399	54.7	33.8	1.7	1.0	8.8	19.7	63.6	16.8	5,454	68.4	33.7	31.4
Ivalee CDP	879	NA	NA	709	100.0	0.0	0.0	0.0	0.0	14.8	60.0	25.2	317	96.2	71.6	8.8
Jackson city	5,224	5,025	-3.8	5,116	53.1	45.4	0.0	0.7	0.7	25.7	58.1	16.1	1,895	63.0	52.4	19.2
Jacksons' Gap town	823	808	-1.8	1,115	65.0	33.8	0.4	0.8	0.0	21.9	65.0	12.9	354	60.5	59.9	8.5
Jacksonville city	12,556	12,250	-2.4	12,416	72.0	23.2	0.9	1.2	2.7	17.7	70.7	11.5	4,364	49.1	30.1	30.3
Jasper city	14,386	14,109	-1.9	14,247	78.7	14.5	0.4	1.9	4.5	23.3	59.7	17.1	5,397	63.6	41.7	23.3
Jemison city	2,615	2,631	0.6	2,628	73.7	15.3	0.0	0.6	10.4	29.9	58.8	11.5	887	75.5	61.1	14.9
Joppa CDP	0	NA	NA	103	100.0	0.0	0.0	0.0	0.0	0.0	19.4	80.6	97	68.0	44.3	32.0
Kansas town	226	222	-1.8	204	100.0	0.0	0.0	0.0	0.0	12.8	67.2	20.1	88	75.0	55.7	5.7
Kellyton town	217	201	-7.4	381	94.2	4.5	0.0	0.0	1.3	29.1	52.8	18.1	136	77.2	92.6	0.0
Kennedy town	447	434	-2.9	431	76.3	19.3	0.5	2.6	1.4	15.3	60.9	23.7	210	70.5	71.0	8.1
Killen town	993	988	-0.5	1,169	83.1	3.8	1.9	0.3	10.8	21.4	61.8	16.8	437	79.9	45.1	18.5
Kimberly city	2,693	2,835	5.3	2,767	96.2	1.3	1.5	0.3	0.7	25.4	66.6	7.8	898	95.8	37.6	19.3
Kinsey town	2,198	2,206	0.4	2,246	44.4	49.3	0.0	2.5	3.8	28.1	59.8	12.1	840	61.8	57.0	8.1
Kinston town	540	538	-0.4	563	90.6	2.0	0.7	6.2	0.5	28.6	58.3	13.1	181	72.9	76.8	13.3
Ladonia CDP	3,142	NA	NA	2,947	83.8	12.8	0.0	1.0	2.4	23.8	60.2	16.0	1,174	68.1	49.4	10.0
La Fayette city	3,003	2,984	-0.6	2,993	29.1	70.8	0.0	0.1	0.0	24.1	56.3	19.6	1,100	49.0	64.1	17.0
Lakeview town	143	143	0.0	143	90.9	0.0	9.1	0.0	0.0	32.2	51.1	16.8	41	95.1	41.5	29.3
Lake View town	1,943	2,067	6.4	2,143	96.8	1.6	0.2	0.5	1.0	21.8	68.2	10.1	683	98.8	40.1	30.3
Lanett city	6,468	6,447	-0.3	6,455	32.8	64.3	0.1	1.1	1.6	23.7	57.4	18.8	2,617	53.6	61.1	12.6
Langston town	270	267	-1.1	270	93.7	5.6	0.0	0.7	0.0	15.5	58.5	25.9	105	85.7	50.5	18.1
Leeds city	11,772	11,939	1.4	12,063	75.9	14.3	0.4	1.2	8.2	25.2	58.9	15.9	4,590	74.1	45.1	23.6
Leesburg town	1,024	1,021	-0.3	1,056	95.0	0.6	0.4	4.1	0.0	20.9	58.7	20.5	471	73.9	60.1	6.8
Leighton town	729	718	-1.5	804	51.5	44.4	1.2	1.2	1.6	17.5	61.5	21.0	370	66.5	64.3	11.9
Leroy CDP	911	NA	NA	937	85.7	14.3	0.0	0.0	0.0	17.3	65.2	17.4	376	93.6	35.1	20.5
Lester town	111	121	9.0	115	100.0	0.0	0.0	0.0	0.0	18.3	63.4	18.3	51	96.1	80.4	5.9
Level Plains town	2,076	2,024	-2.5	2,020	76.3	6.9	4.4	3.2	9.3	21.8	63.5	14.7	750	85.2	38.8	11.7
Lexington town	735	728	-1.0	663	98.8	0.0	0.0	0.0	1.2	22.7	50.9	26.4	287	64.8	68.6	6.6
Libertyville town	115	116	0.9	120	88.3	0.0	0.0	0.0	11.7	14.2	63.3	22.5	51	92.2	66.7	9.8
Lincoln city	6,258	6,438	2.9	6,321	76.8	21.5	0.0	1.8	0.0	22.9	67.0	9.9	2,581	80.9	44.1	20.5
Linden city	2,123	2,034	-4.2	2,133	46.1	52.7	0.0	1.2	0.0	23.7	53.2	23.0	920	61.4	54.9	24.2
Lineville city	2,395	2,321	-3.1	2,597	56.8	32.1	0.0	4.0	7.1	30.0	51.0	19.2	1,062	62.3	55.9	11.7
Lipscomb city	2,210	2,175	-1.6	2,331	24.0	52.9	0.0	4.1	19.0	23.3	68.5	8.2	825	66.7	54.4	8.1
Lisman town	539	513	-4.8	694	3.2	95.7	1.2	0.0	0.0	29.9	53.8	16.1	244	77.5	51.6	9.0
Littleville town	1,011	996	-1.5	999	97.5	0.0	0.0	1.6	0.9	17.8	58.8	23.3	416	82.0	62.3	3.6
Livingston city	3,458	3,439	-0.5	3,465	36.8	57.9	4.8	0.0	0.5	15.1	73.3	11.6	1,140	45.2	40.8	23.6
Loachapoka town	180	189	5.0	170	52.4	43.5	0.0	2.4	1.8	23.6	70.5	5.9	82	63.4	29.3	37.8
Lockhart town	516	519	0.6	456	76.8	22.6	0.0	0.7	0.0	26.9	57.0	16.0	187	72.2	57.8	11.8
Locust Fork town	1,186	1,192	0.5	1,208	96.4	0.6	0.0	2.4	0.6	19.4	64.9	15.7	425	88.5	45.9	12.0
Lookout Mountain CDP	1,621	NA	NA	1,096	91.7	2.5	0.0	2.9	2.9	17.0	66.5	16.5	429	92.5	40.3	17.0
Louisville town	519	496	-4.4	487	53.6	36.8	0.0	1.0	8.6	24.8	60.1	15.0	175	67.4	57.7	18.9
Lowndesboro town	115	109	-5.2	167	92.8	7.2	0.0	0.0	0.0	30.5	52.8	16.8	71	91.5	8.5	71.8
Loxley town	1,628	1,725	6.0	2,170	75.0	10.5	0.7	3.9	9.9	28.3	59.3	12.4	779	55.8	42.7	21.6
Luverne city	2,798	2,835	1.3	2,818	57.6	33.0	6.6	1.2	1.6	20.0	56.4	23.5	1,120	51.2	54.5	13.9
Lynn town	658	648	-1.5	595	98.7	0.0	0.0	1.3	0.0	17.3	58.6	24.2	257	71.2	66.5	12.1
McDonald Chapel CDP	717	NA	NA	514	75.1	19.8	0.0	5.1	0.0	21.4	59.6	19.1	248	86.7	61.7	3.2
Macedonia CDP	292	NA	NA	146	13.7	86.3	0.0	0.0	0.0	17.1	36.9	45.9	74	94.6	81.1	0.0
McIntosh town	236	227	-3.8	415	35.4	60.2	0.0	3.9	0.5	34.5	59.2	6.3	105	81.0	43.8	12.4
McKenzie town	530	516	-2.6	645	71.0	29.0	0.0	0.0	0.0	21.5	63.5	15.0	238	71.8	75.2	2.9
McMullen town	10	10	0.0	20	0.0	100.0	0.0	0.0	0.0	0.0	70.0	30.0	8	100.0	100.0	0.0
Madison city	42,939	46,450	8.2	44,866	71.9	14.5	5.6	3.5	4.5	26.8	64.1	9.2	16,583	71.4	12.9	60.0
Madrid town	350	342	-2.3	385	76.9	16.4	1.8	4.7	0.3	17.1	70.4	12.5	159	89.9	76.7	5.7
Magnolia Springs town	723	782	8.2	766	90.7	0.0	1.8	0.4	7.0	15.9	53.5	30.4	342	89.5	32.5	40.1
Malcolm CDP	187	NA	NA	47	100.0	0.0	0.0	0.0	0.0	0.0	0.0	100.0	26	100.0	100.0	0.0
Malvern town	1,448	1,442	-0.4	1,771	86.3	3.1	0.0	0.7	9.9	23.0	62.1	15.0	664	77.7	67.9	8.0
Maplesville town	708	705	-0.4	732	82.4	17.2	0.0	0.4	0.0	26.8	63.2	10.0	274	63.5	52.2	10.6
Marbury CDP	1,418	NA	NA	1,836	98.5	0.2	0.0	0.0	1.3	28.4	65.6	6.0	594	69.0	69.2	14.3
Margaret town	4,420	4,506	1.9	4,475	78.6	14.9	0.6	4.4	1.3	37.2	58.8	3.9	1,286	94.2	41.5	16.7
Marion city	3,685	3,482	-5.5	3,587	33.0	62.5	0.5	1.8	2.3	21.7	63.5	14.6	804	60.6	52.4	14.9
Maytown town	385	376	-2.3	319	87.8	10.7	0.0	0.3	1.3	18.8	56.7	24.5	137	83.9	52.6	19.0
Meadowbrook CDP	8,769	NA	NA	8,550	89.0	6.2	2.0	1.0	1.7	24.2	67.0	8.8	3,235	77.7	12.2	63.4
Megargel CDP	62	NA	NA	77	100.0	0.0	0.0	0.0	0.0	0.0	26.0	74.0	42	100.0	47.6	52.4
Memphis town	29	28	-3.4	24	25.0	75.0	0.0	0.0	0.0	12.5	54.1	33.3	15	73.3	60.0	40.0
Mentone town	361	365	1.1	417	86.8	0.0	0.0	12.7	0.5	18.8	51.5	29.7	165	90.3	37.0	31.5
Meridianville CDP	6,021	NA	NA	6,073	67.8	19.9	1.3	5.6	5.5	22.5	65.0	12.6	2,247	83.7	29.3	32.2
Midfield city	5,363	5,263	-1.9	5,319	13.4	85.7	0.3	0.5	0.0	28.3	61.0	10.5	1,932	67.1	42.5	19.4
Midland City town	2,161	2,366	9.5	2,311	68.0	22.5	3.2	2.3	3.9	25.8	63.4	10.8	904	45.9	45.7	15.4
Midway town	499	493	-1.2	436	8.9	91.1	0.0	0.0	0.0	19.3	69.5	11.2	192	58.3	93.8	3.1
Mignon CDP	1,284	NA	NA	1,290	67.9	20.0	0.0	0.5	11.6	26.3	64.2	9.5	484	55.4	65.5	2.7
Millbrook city	14,637	15,169	3.6	14,858	75.7	19.2	1.1	2.3	1.7	25.0	64.6	10.5	5,778	68.3	36.0	28.3
Millerville CDP	278	NA	NA	321	96.6	3.4	0.0	0.0	0.0	19.3	54.1	26.5	157	75.2	66.9	15.9
Millport town	1,049	1,014	-3.3	942	68.0	29.5	0.0	2.4	0.0	19.4	55.2	25.3	436	60.8	60.8	12.8
Millry town	546	524	-4.0	535	61.9	35.3	0.0	2.2	0.6	21.9	56.3	21.9	212	75.9	60.4	2.8
Minor CDP	1,094	NA	NA	1,275	85.0	14.3	0.0	0.7	0.0	19.5	64.1	16.4	523	75.3	49.9	13.4
Mobile city	195,243	194,675	-0.3	194,942	43.8	50.8	1.2	1.4	2.7	23.5	62.2	14.3	75,653	57.1	36.6	29.4
Monroeville city	6,501	6,189	-4.8	6,343	39.4	58.2	0.5	0.1	1.8	27.9	53.8	18.3	2,148	67.7	56.7	19.1
Montevallo city	6,293	6,601	4.9	6,470	63.3	25.8	0.3	1.1	9.5	14.1	73.9	12.0	2,450	55.8	39.1	28.9
Montgomery city	205,595	200,481	-2.5	204,095	34.7	57.7	2.3	1.6	3.6	24.8	63.0	12.2	79,760	57.2	36.9	33.5
Moody city	11,727	12,457	6.2	12,124	86.5	10.8	1.2	0.8	0.7	20.8	66.6	12.5	4,785	77.8	37.2	21.4
Moores Mill CDP	5,682	NA	NA	5,819	65.9	21.1	0.3	3.5	9.2	23.4	67.1	9.4	2,105	90.1	28.3	28.2
Mooresville town	53	58	9.4	62	71.0	22.6	4.8	0.0	1.6	17.7	43.7	38.7	23	100.0	17.4	73.9
Morris town	1,859	1,912	2.9	1,806	98.1	0.3	0.0	0.4	1.1	25.6	61.4	13.0	707	78.5	43.7	18.5
Morrison Crossroads CDP	0	NA	NA	214	93.5	0.0	0.0	6.5	0.0	22.0	65.4	12.6	121	75.2	66.9	7.4
Mosses town	1,029	965	-6.2	1,069	0.6	99.4	0.0	0.0	0.0	19.8	69.3	10.9	457	48.6	84.2	6.1
Moulton city	3,469	3,375	-2.7	3,413	80.4	15.7	0.2	2.6	1.1	18.3	59.2	22.3	1,483	61.0	65.6	12.5

1 May be of any race.

Table A. All Places — **Population and Housing**

STATE City, town, township, borough, or CDP (county if applicable)	Population: 2010 census total population	Population: 2014 estimated population	Population: Percent change 2010–2014	Population: ACS total population estimate 2010–2014	Race and Hispanic or Latino origin (percent), 2010–2014: White alone, not Hispanic or Latino	Race: Black alone, not Hispanic or Latino	Race: Asian alone, not Hispanic or Latino	Race: All other races or 2 or more races, not Hispanic or Latino	Race: Hispanic or Latino[1]	Age (percent), 2010–2014: Under 18 years old	Age: Age 18 to 64 years old	Age: Age 65 years and older	Households, 2010–2014: Total occupied housing units	Households: Percent owner occupied	Householders by level of education (percent): High school diploma or less	Householders by level of education (percent): Bachelor's degree or more
	1	2	3	4	5	6	7	8	9	10	11	12	13	14	15	16
ALABAMA—Con.																
Moundville town	2,427	2,460	1.4	2,417	58.0	38.0	0.0	1.3	2.6	27.2	58.3	14.4	818	79.5	40.8	18.0
Mountain Brook city	20,484	20,734	1.2	20,484	95.9	1.0	1.2	0.5	1.3	29.7	55.8	14.6	7,481	85.8	2.5	86.3
Mount Olive CDP (Coosa)	371	NA	NA	358	58.9	41.1	0.0	0.0	0.0	29.1	60.0	10.9	141	90.1	80.9	0.0
Mount Olive CDP (Jefferson)	4,079	NA	NA	4,286	98.3	0.0	1.2	0.3	0.2	23.1	60.9	16.1	1,548	90.4	48.3	18.2
Mount Vernon town	1,572	1,559	-0.8	1,435	29.4	66.6	0.0	3.3	0.8	19.6	63.4	17.0	496	76.2	63.1	7.7
Movico CDP	305	NA	NA	149	0.0	100.0	0.0	0.0	0.0	16.1	73.1	10.7	63	34.9	63.5	23.8
Mulga town	836	822	-1.7	952	85.2	13.3	0.0	0.6	0.8	27.8	55.4	16.8	323	62.8	71.5	3.1
Munford town	1,292	1,262	-2.3	1,401	70.9	20.9	1.1	1.2	5.8	26.9	62.8	10.2	482	73.2	43.4	15.4
Muscle Shoals city	13,156	13,614	3.5	13,380	79.5	17.8	0.2	1.4	1.1	22.5	61.5	16.1	5,539	75.7	36.9	25.5
Myrtlewood town	130	124	-4.6	148	95.3	4.7	0.0	0.0	0.0	14.2	50.1	35.8	70	90.0	74.3	5.7
Nanafalia CDP	94	NA	NA	77	55.8	44.2	0.0	0.0	0.0	18.2	62.4	19.5	42	71.4	47.6	28.6
Nances Creek CDP	407	NA	NA	567	100.0	0.0	0.0	0.0	0.0	40.0	52.1	7.9	174	86.2	77.6	0.0
Napier Field town	354	346	-2.3	395	73.7	12.7	0.5	4.1	9.1	21.0	67.1	11.9	190	32.1	47.9	6.8
Natural Bridge town	37	37	0.0	43	100.0	0.0	0.0	0.0	0.0	9.3	58.2	32.6	17	88.2	88.2	0.0
Nauvoo town	217	213	-1.8	142	90.8	0.0	0.0	5.6	3.5	23.2	60.4	16.2	59	67.8	52.5	0.0
Nectar town	342	345	0.9	318	96.2	0.0	0.0	0.0	3.8	24.2	66.0	9.7	117	84.6	53.8	1.7
Needham town	95	92	-3.2	97	94.8	3.1	0.0	2.1	0.0	11.3	54.6	34.0	48	93.8	66.7	25.0
Newbern town	186	180	-3.2	164	32.3	66.5	0.0	0.0	1.2	17.0	62.8	20.1	77	85.7	54.5	0.0
New Brockton town	1,144	1,151	0.6	1,396	66.8	23.3	0.2	8.2	1.6	29.7	58.2	12.2	470	55.1	54.0	11.1
New Hope city	2,810	2,814	0.1	2,813	91.8	0.3	0.0	6.9	1.0	21.7	65.4	12.8	1,118	70.3	42.3	11.2
New Market CDP	1,597	NA	NA	1,596	69.7	16.2	0.0	2.8	11.3	28.3	62.5	9.3	666	71.8	50.3	18.3
New Site town	773	760	-1.7	807	81.9	17.5	0.0	0.0	0.6	19.9	61.6	18.5	314	88.9	66.2	11.5
Newton town	1,511	1,473	-2.5	1,581	83.2	8.0	0.0	5.7	3.1	16.8	65.9	17.1	626	71.6	51.8	7.5
New Union CDP	955	NA	NA	1,139	94.6	0.0	0.0	0.0	5.4	41.1	49.4	9.6	396	80.1	51.8	9.1
Newville town	539	522	-3.2	429	40.8	38.5	0.0	0.5	20.3	18.2	59.3	22.6	186	65.6	74.7	8.6
North Courtland town	632	618	-2.2	606	3.3	95.0	0.0	0.3	1.3	27.5	55.9	16.7	295	75.3	69.8	2.7
North Johns town	145	143	-1.4	212	50.5	47.6	0.0	1.9	0.0	33.0	59.3	7.5	62	58.1	85.5	1.6
Northport city	23,360	24,709	5.8	24,092	71.6	24.0	1.0	1.0	2.4	23.4	63.0	13.7	8,924	67.0	34.3	36.1
Notasulga town	965	868	-10.1	988	60.2	38.6	0.0	0.9	0.3	22.5	63.5	14.0	455	74.7	56.3	18.5
Oak Grove town	529	521	-1.5	629	90.5	2.4	0.0	0.0	7.2	23.4	59.7	16.9	263	70.0	69.6	8.4
Oak Hill town	26	25	-3.8	11	0.0	100.0	0.0	0.0	0.0	0.0	36.4	63.6	11	54.5	81.8	0.0
Oakman town	786	763	-2.9	771	83.7	13.6	0.0	2.7	0.0	18.8	62.1	19.1	316	68.4	64.2	10.1
Odenville town	3,592	3,687	2.6	3,641	89.8	7.4	0.2	0.6	2.0	20.9	65.3	13.7	1,422	87.6	57.3	9.4
Ohatchee town	1,156	1,144	-1.0	1,091	96.7	1.6	0.0	1.0	0.6	19.4	64.5	16.2	446	87.7	55.8	10.5
Oneonta city	6,563	6,627	1.0	6,623	62.7	9.7	0.1	3.0	24.4	25.0	56.5	18.4	2,441	53.3	54.0	15.0
Onycha town	184	185	0.5	207	98.1	0.0	1.0	0.0	1.0	33.3	54.5	12.1	68	76.5	72.1	16.2
Opelika city	26,425	29,171	10.4	27,956	50.3	40.7	1.3	1.8	5.9	22.8	62.4	14.7	11,183	60.4	41.3	27.8
Opp city	6,658	6,677	0.3	6,675	82.1	15.3	0.2	2.1	0.3	22.9	56.5	20.6	2,478	65.9	56.5	11.4
Orange Beach city	5,441	5,788	6.4	5,629	85.2	0.3	2.6	2.5	9.4	19.2	57.6	23.1	2,285	63.3	25.3	35.6
Orrville town	203	192	-5.4	114	28.9	71.1	0.0	0.0	0.0	12.3	52.6	35.1	67	58.2	73.1	7.5
Our Town CDP	641	NA	NA	717	99.4	0.0	0.0	0.6	0.0	9.8	57.4	32.8	327	91.4	59.0	21.7
Owens Cross Roads town	1,522	1,767	16.1	1,954	87.2	6.4	0.8	4.5	1.1	23.7	62.3	14.1	717	82.3	36.0	25.0
Oxford city	21,329	21,155	-0.8	21,250	76.9	13.5	0.8	2.4	6.5	25.9	61.4	12.8	7,543	71.3	45.8	20.4
Ozark city	14,899	14,700	-1.3	14,835	63.7	29.6	0.2	3.9	2.5	21.2	59.8	18.9	6,214	62.9	43.6	19.7
Paint Rock town	210	208	-1.0	212	95.3	0.9	0.0	3.8	0.0	16.0	67.0	17.0	95	64.2	63.2	8.4
Panola CDP	144	NA	NA	28	0.0	100.0	0.0	0.0	0.0	28.6	71.5	0.0	16	100.0	100.0	0.0
Parrish town	990	965	-2.5	954	72.3	21.8	0.0	4.9	0.9	25.6	58.6	15.8	377	68.2	54.9	8.8
Pelham city	21,448	22,699	5.8	22,106	79.0	8.6	1.8	0.9	9.6	22.4	66.1	11.4	8,619	82.8	26.4	37.5
Pell City city	12,684	13,573	7.0	13,128	82.0	14.6	2.0	0.5	0.9	25.1	58.5	16.4	5,111	59.4	49.0	21.4
Pennington town	220	212	-3.6	218	32.1	67.9	0.0	0.0	0.0	17.9	62.4	19.7	83	85.5	68.7	8.4
Penton CDP	201	NA	NA	316	83.9	16.1	0.0	0.0	0.0	28.5	55.1	16.5	145	83.4	60.7	26.2
Perdido Beach town	581	624	7.4	550	92.5	0.0	0.0	1.1	6.4	11.4	60.7	27.8	264	81.1	37.1	32.6
Peterman CDP	89	NA	NA	114	94.7	5.3	0.0	0.0	0.0	21.9	64.9	13.2	58	81.0	100.0	0.0
Petrey town	58	58	0.0	41	56.1	43.9	0.0	0.0	0.0	14.6	60.9	24.4	22	50.0	81.8	0.0
Phenix City city	32,871	37,540	14.2	35,753	45.4	45.5	1.2	2.3	5.5	27.7	61.3	10.8	13,787	49.3	41.5	19.4
Phil Campbell town	1,148	1,233	7.4	1,016	94.9	0.0	0.0	0.6	4.5	24.7	60.8	14.6	412	68.7	55.8	11.9
Pickensville town	604	581	-3.8	578	39.6	60.4	0.0	0.0	0.0	16.0	68.1	15.7	272	77.6	78.3	5.5
Piedmont city	4,878	4,736	-2.9	4,811	87.8	7.6	1.4	2.1	1.1	23.1	58.1	18.7	2,024	68.2	53.9	13.1
Pike Road town	5,424	7,933	46.3	6,605	73.3	22.8	2.5	0.7	0.7	26.7	62.4	10.9	2,440	91.9	18.2	54.8
Pinckard town	647	635	-1.9	532	89.5	5.6	0.0	1.1	3.8	19.5	63.0	17.5	235	63.8	52.8	11.9
Pine Apple town	132	126	-4.5	123	74.0	26.0	0.0	0.0	0.0	17.1	39.7	43.1	39	82.1	38.5	43.6
Pine Hill town	973	922	-5.2	1,045	42.4	57.6	0.0	0.0	0.0	38.4	49.3	12.2	315	61.9	61.6	14.6
Pine Level CDP	4,183	NA	NA	4,002	96.6	0.0	0.0	3.4	0.0	27.1	63.7	9.0	1,443	89.4	57.7	17.6
Pine Ridge town	282	283	0.4	189	70.9	3.7	0.0	4.2	21.2	30.7	54.4	14.8	69	68.1	66.7	2.9
Pinson city	7,144	7,143	0.0	7,141	75.1	21.5	0.6	0.8	1.9	19.7	68.6	11.6	2,798	86.1	34.8	26.4
Pisgah town	722	715	-1.0	802	96.9	0.9	0.0	1.5	0.7	23.5	54.5	21.9	326	77.6	38.7	21.5
Pleasant Grove city	10,110	10,325	2.1	10,230	50.8	48.2	0.3	0.2	0.5	22.6	63.0	14.3	3,605	91.3	36.6	21.3
Pleasant Groves town	420	416	-1.0	549	96.2	0.0	0.4	3.5	0.0	26.1	60.6	13.3	189	81.0	60.3	12.2
Point Clear CDP	2,125	NA	NA	2,388	62.5	36.9	0.0	0.6	0.0	25.9	53.3	20.6	858	78.9	30.1	54.1
Pollard town	137	135	-1.5	200	36.5	38.5	0.0	0.5	24.5	41.5	54.0	4.5	56	83.9	42.9	23.2
Powell town	955	957	0.2	981	92.9	2.2	0.0	2.5	2.3	17.6	68.3	14.2	293	71.3	61.8	10.9
Prattville city	33,974	35,317	4.0	34,349	75.7	17.1	1.5	2.0	3.6	26.8	59.9	13.2	12,480	68.4	32.5	34.6
Priceville town	2,657	3,061	15.2	2,848	92.6	1.6	0.0	3.2	2.6	27.4	56.6	15.9	1,013	90.5	37.9	33.7
Prichard city	22,671	22,312	-1.6	22,475	15.4	82.4	0.5	1.0	0.8	25.2	61.0	13.8	8,271	55.9	60.2	9.4
Providence town	224	215	-4.0	238	83.6	15.5	0.8	0.0	0.0	17.2	51.3	31.5	120	94.2	55.0	10.0
Putnam CDP	193	NA	NA	122	10.7	84.4	0.0	4.9	0.0	18.0	62.3	19.7	68	50.0	48.5	19.1
Ragland town	1,636	1,677	2.5	1,702	79.0	19.1	0.3	1.6	0.0	23.6	55.2	21.2	685	78.1	67.4	8.9
Rainbow City city	9,602	9,606	0.0	9,623	87.8	8.6	0.4	1.6	1.6	23.2	58.7	18.2	4,014	63.6	34.4	25.6
Rainsville city	4,948	5,011	1.3	4,984	95.8	0.0	0.0	3.5	0.7	19.7	64.3	16.0	2,001	67.5	51.7	11.8
Ranburne town	406	411	1.2	449	98.4	1.6	0.0	0.0	0.0	20.3	51.0	28.7	188	80.9	52.1	13.3
Ray CDP	443	NA	NA	555	71.5	5.0	0.0	0.0	23.4	10.2	70.7	18.9	225	89.3	44.9	0.0
Red Bay city	3,158	3,126	-1.0	3,143	97.3	1.5	0.3	0.0	1.0	20.0	56.8	23.2	1,345	64.4	67.5	11.0
Redland CDP	3,736	NA	NA	4,571	81.8	14.0	0.0	3.9	0.3	28.3	59.1	12.5	1,693	87.2	27.8	36.3
Red Level town	487	490	0.6	367	90.2	8.7	0.0	0.0	1.1	15.3	64.8	19.9	169	72.2	51.5	13.6
Redstone Arsenal CDP	1,946	NA	NA	1,565	67.3	14.6	0.9	7.0	10.2	22.4	75.1	2.5	278	0.0	10.4	33.5
Reece City town	653	637	-2.5	766	97.4	1.2	0.9	0.5	0.0	22.2	55.1	22.7	277	87.0	54.5	10.1
Reeltown CDP	766	NA	NA	456	96.5	0.0	0.0	3.5	0.0	2.9	75.0	22.1	185	100.0	34.1	7.6
Reform town	1,700	1,638	-3.6	2,044	46.5	51.5	0.0	0.5	1.5	24.6	58.9	16.5	808	57.7	60.0	8.7
Rehobeth town	1,292	1,440	11.5	1,609	96.7	1.4	0.0	0.0	1.9	25.0	64.8	10.2	567	85.7	54.0	19.8

1 May be of any race.

Table A. All Places — **Population and Housing**

STATE City, town, township, borough, or CDP (county if applicable)	Population				Race and Hispanic or Latino origin (percent), 2010–2014					Age (percent), 2010–2014			Households, 2010–2014			
															Householders by level of education (percent)	
	2010 census total population	2014 estimated population	Percent change 2010–2014	ACS total population estimate 2010–2014	White alone, not Hispanic or Latino	Black alone, not Hispanic or Latino	Asian alone, not Hispanic or Latino	All other races or 2 or more races, not Hispanic or Latino	Hispanic or Latino[1]	Under 18 years old	Age 18 to 64 years old	Age 65 years and older	Total occupied housing units	Percent owner occupied	High school diploma or less	Bachelor's degree or more
	1	2	3	4	5	6	7	8	9	10	11	12	13	14	15	16
ALABAMA—Con.																
Repton town	282	272	-3.5	160	73.8	26.3	0.0	0.0	0.0	20.6	63.9	15.6	63	82.5	76.2	4.8
Ridgeville town	107	106	-0.9	145	24.1	73.8	0.0	2.1	0.0	20.0	61.3	18.6	59	64.4	71.2	6.8
River Falls town	526	527	0.2	671	51.6	43.1	0.9	4.0	0.4	17.8	61.6	20.4	298	77.9	61.4	13.4
Riverside town	2,208	2,298	4.1	1,967	96.3	1.6	0.4	0.0	1.6	18.2	67.5	14.3	852	82.7	47.8	24.6
Riverview town	184	182	-1.1	160	85.6	0.0	0.0	0.0	14.4	25.6	52.0	22.5	52	82.7	59.6	9.6
Roanoke city	6,074	5,970	-1.7	6,013	49.2	47.2	0.0	1.7	1.9	25.6	57.5	17.0	2,440	55.2	50.4	10.0
Robertsdale city	5,276	5,773	9.4	5,556	82.0	5.5	0.1	0.9	11.5	21.3	65.9	12.7	1,900	62.8	52.3	21.0
Rock Creek CDP	1,456	NA	NA	1,377	97.5	2.5	0.0	0.0	0.0	20.6	62.8	16.6	561	89.1	58.6	21.2
Rockford town	477	449	-5.9	537	57.9	42.1	0.0	0.0	0.0	12.6	72.8	14.3	223	54.7	64.6	5.8
Rock Mills CDP	600	NA	NA	633	87.0	0.0	0.0	13.0	0.0	27.0	54.1	18.8	253	87.4	64.8	4.0
Rockville CDP	43	NA	NA	23	100.0	0.0	0.0	0.0	0.0	17.4	60.9	21.7	9	0.0	55.6	44.4
Rogersville town	1,257	1,241	-1.3	1,106	93.4	3.3	0.8	2.4	0.0	23.7	46.8	29.5	509	66.4	56.0	17.5
Rosa town	316	319	0.9	358	100.0	0.0	0.0	0.0	0.0	13.8	69.5	16.8	128	75.8	43.8	17.2
Russellville city	9,835	9,806	-0.3	9,836	51.4	11.6	0.0	1.5	35.6	28.8	55.3	15.9	3,553	50.8	65.2	11.4
Rutledge town	465	461	-0.9	442	80.5	11.1	0.0	7.7	0.7	26.9	54.2	18.8	183	62.3	55.2	21.3
St. Florian town	413	449	8.7	423	94.1	2.1	0.0	2.8	0.9	12.5	61.8	25.5	193	91.7	46.6	23.3
St. Stephens CDP	495	NA	NA	503	89.3	10.7	0.0	0.0	0.0	10.2	71.7	18.3	171	100.0	81.9	0.0
Saks CDP	10,744	NA	NA	10,445	64.3	25.8	0.3	4.7	4.9	26.0	60.1	13.8	4,056	73.2	50.7	15.4
Samson city	1,940	1,923	-0.9	2,134	70.9	21.6	0.0	2.1	5.3	29.6	55.8	14.7	897	44.5	70.7	5.2
Sand Rock town	560	562	0.4	539	96.1	0.0	0.0	2.6	1.3	17.1	60.2	22.8	225	85.3	51.6	19.1
Sanford town	246	248	0.8	269	95.5	1.9	0.0	1.5	1.1	29.4	59.9	10.8	90	68.9	47.8	13.3
Saraland city	13,631	13,744	0.8	13,657	77.5	11.7	3.7	3.1	4.1	22.7	59.2	18.0	5,058	72.5	52.7	19.1
Sardis City town	1,704	1,742	2.2	1,695	94.9	0.5	0.0	0.4	4.2	19.7	63.7	16.6	629	86.0	44.8	21.1
Satsuma city	6,168	6,167	0.0	6,145	88.7	8.4	0.8	1.3	0.8	22.6	64.5	13.1	2,322	88.6	45.2	16.1
Scottsboro city	14,778	14,748	-0.2	14,779	86.9	4.9	0.7	2.8	4.7	20.2	58.8	21.0	6,071	72.4	52.3	19.8
Section town	770	763	-0.9	880	94.1	0.6	0.0	3.0	2.4	28.1	58.6	13.4	319	65.5	51.4	10.3
Selma city	20,756	19,814	-4.5	20,276	17.2	80.4	0.2	1.6	0.6	26.6	59.0	14.4	7,765	47.4	57.7	17.4
Selmont-West Selmont CDP	2,671	NA	NA	2,887	1.4	98.1	0.0	0.0	0.5	31.6	60.0	8.4	867	50.4	67.9	5.2
Semmes city	2,997	3,257	8.7	3,059	81.5	3.5	0.2	3.1	11.6	30.3	55.8	13.8	1,029	54.9	52.5	10.6
Sheffield city	9,039	9,144	1.2	9,067	69.9	25.5	0.4	3.0	1.2	20.7	61.8	17.6	3,918	56.8	51.8	17.1
Shelby CDP	1,044	NA	NA	1,417	80.0	16.7	0.4	0.0	2.9	25.8	54.0	20.3	473	82.7	73.2	7.2
Shiloh town	274	274	0.0	336	86.9	1.8	1.2	5.7	4.5	24.1	63.0	13.1	112	70.5	59.8	17.0
Shoal Creek CDP	1,400	NA	NA	1,385	94.9	3.1	1.2	0.0	0.9	30.4	55.4	14.0	536	92.5	3.7	78.4
Shorter town	472	435	-7.8	497	15.1	84.9	0.0	0.0	0.0	21.3	59.6	18.9	191	75.9	65.4	14.7
Silas town	452	437	-3.3	605	75.7	23.1	0.0	0.0	1.2	24.1	64.8	11.1	194	76.3	54.1	5.2
Silverhill town	706	754	6.8	684	89.5	7.5	1.2	0.9	1.0	21.1	54.5	24.3	284	74.6	43.3	14.1
Sims Chapel CDP	153	NA	NA	259	53.3	0.0	39.4	7.3	0.0	39.0	60.9	0.0	67	100.0	40.3	0.0
Sipsey town	435	427	-1.8	381	51.4	37.3	0.0	1.8	9.4	12.9	71.0	16.0	175	76.6	59.4	1.1
Skyline town	851	843	-0.9	873	84.1	0.0	0.0	6.4	9.5	19.9	64.1	16.0	327	77.7	60.2	6.7
Slocomb city	1,980	1,970	-0.5	1,936	76.1	16.8	0.0	1.3	5.8	20.9	64.4	14.7	786	72.5	56.6	13.4
Smiths Station city	4,912	5,251	6.9	5,095	75.5	18.5	0.0	5.1	0.9	27.0	61.4	11.4	1,927	73.0	45.2	22.3
Smoke Rise CDP	1,825	NA	NA	2,277	97.3	0.0	0.0	1.1	1.6	24.6	67.5	7.9	706	99.4	42.8	40.8
Snead town	835	843	1.0	1,038	92.3	1.0	0.0	0.8	6.0	25.9	57.0	17.1	412	68.9	59.2	11.2
Somerville town	724	718	-0.8	657	94.5	3.2	0.0	2.3	0.0	21.0	67.1	12.0	259	68.7	61.8	16.6
Southside city	8,412	8,552	1.7	8,432	90.2	1.6	1.4	0.3	6.5	25.3	63.2	11.6	2,820	91.4	34.6	21.0
South Vinemont town	749	753	0.5	553	76.1	5.2	1.1	2.7	14.8	22.7	61.6	15.9	240	32.1	62.9	10.8
Spanish Fort city	6,900	7,806	13.1	7,357	88.4	4.0	0.4	3.6	3.6	23.4	63.4	13.2	2,955	53.5	27.9	50.3
Spring Garden CDP	238	NA	NA	183	100.0	0.0	0.0	0.0	0.0	35.5	64.5	0.0	73	39.7	38.4	61.6
Springville city	4,072	4,194	3.0	4,140	95.6	4.4	0.0	0.0	0.0	28.8	56.4	14.8	1,478	90.7	41.9	29.7
Spruce Pine CDP	222	NA	NA	0	0.0	0.0	0.0	0.0	0.0	0.0	0.0	0.0	0	0.0	0.0	0.0
Standing Rock CDP	168	NA	NA	52	100.0	0.0	0.0	0.0	0.0	0.0	100.1	0.0	28	71.4	100.0	0.0
Steele town	1,043	1,075	3.1	1,021	96.3	0.0	0.0	1.3	2.4	18.2	60.9	20.9	441	78.5	58.5	7.7
Sterrett CDP	712	NA	NA	622	96.1	0.0	0.0	3.9	0.0	15.1	49.6	35.2	266	92.5	49.6	4.1
Stevenson city	2,046	2,002	-2.2	2,739	78.7	13.3	1.5	3.5	3.0	26.5	64.9	8.5	988	63.9	60.8	7.8
Stewartville CDP	1,767	NA	NA	1,855	93.1	6.1	0.0	0.8	0.0	21.2	58.0	20.8	711	78.9	59.5	10.4
Sulligent city	1,927	1,870	-3.0	1,884	68.7	22.9	0.0	2.7	5.7	22.1	60.3	17.5	883	58.4	67.7	9.5
Sumiton city	2,515	2,423	-3.7	2,544	90.3	4.0	0.2	2.7	2.8	25.5	51.6	23.0	1,036	75.5	47.4	14.4
Summerdale town	896	1,005	12.2	1,076	77.6	14.2	0.0	2.6	5.6	24.2	57.7	18.2	373	74.8	49.3	21.7
Susan Moore town	763	771	1.0	850	90.7	0.0	0.0	0.0	9.3	19.8	69.7	10.4	309	81.2	57.9	14.6
Sweet Water town	258	247	-4.3	221	89.6	7.2	0.0	0.0	3.2	25.4	54.7	19.9	90	96.7	33.3	28.9
Sylacauga city	12,864	12,703	-1.3	12,786	63.9	29.6	0.0	3.2	3.2	25.9	57.4	16.7	5,078	59.8	52.7	15.9
Sylvania town	1,859	1,853	-0.3	1,979	89.7	0.3	0.3	2.8	6.9	28.1	60.7	11.2	613	78.6	60.7	10.0
Sylvan Springs town	1,542	1,533	-0.6	1,671	98.3	1.0	0.0	0.2	0.5	22.5	55.2	22.3	635	89.8	57.2	10.6
Talladega city	16,082	16,012	-0.4	16,034	46.6	46.8	1.4	0.8	4.5	20.9	64.9	14.2	5,508	55.9	60.6	10.8
Talladega Springs town	166	163	-1.8	228	85.5	13.2	0.0	0.0	1.3	31.6	53.9	14.5	62	85.5	51.6	4.8
Tallassee city	4,818	4,805	-0.3	5,011	70.5	19.0	6.2	3.5	0.9	24.6	57.5	17.8	2,032	51.7	55.5	20.5
Tarrant city	6,394	6,257	-2.1	6,331	36.3	51.4	0.6	5.7	6.0	19.2	63.8	17.0	2,573	56.4	58.7	10.7
Taylor town	2,372	2,415	1.8	2,995	91.3	3.3	0.0	0.4	5.0	35.2	57.0	7.7	967	68.1	43.4	15.2
Theodore CDP	6,130	NA	NA	6,051	73.0	12.8	4.5	3.6	6.2	26.8	59.2	13.9	2,299	78.3	49.9	11.9
Thomaston town	417	400	-4.1	391	45.0	49.1	0.0	5.9	0.0	24.0	54.3	21.7	163	74.2	34.4	25.2
Thomasville city	4,208	4,089	-2.8	4,136	47.4	49.9	0.5	2.2	0.0	22.3	59.7	18.0	1,747	59.9	41.0	16.9
Thorsby town	1,980	2,023	2.2	2,039	79.0	8.7	0.6	1.5	10.2	23.9	61.5	14.6	769	79.5	50.8	20.3
Tibbie CDP	41	NA	NA	7	100.0	0.0	0.0	0.0	0.0	0.0	0.0	100.0	7	100.0	0.0	100.0
Tidmore Bend CDP	1,245	NA	NA	1,031	98.1	0.0	0.0	1.9	0.0	10.1	60.5	29.5	433	93.5	61.0	8.5
Tillmans Corner CDP	17,398	NA	NA	19,105	78.7	12.5	3.0	3.8	2.0	26.9	60.0	13.4	6,907	66.2	52.9	14.0
Town Creek town	1,100	1,076	-2.2	940	63.0	22.2	0.0	11.8	3.0	32.4	59.4	8.2	379	71.5	68.1	6.3
Toxey town	137	132	-3.6	181	67.4	24.3	0.0	8.3	0.0	23.7	57.0	19.3	69	84.1	58.0	27.5
Trafford town	646	640	-0.9	652	94.5	3.5	0.0	2.0	0.0	27.5	57.4	15.0	239	62.3	67.4	4.2
Triana town	512	522	2.0	499	20.2	62.1	4.0	5.2	8.4	20.0	66.6	13.2	217	73.3	44.2	32.3
Trinity town	2,091	2,144	2.5	2,257	88.3	7.1	0.0	2.3	2.3	21.5	68.7	9.7	845	83.9	34.7	19.1
Troy city	18,180	19,138	5.3	18,636	54.5	38.7	3.5	1.3	2.0	17.2	73.0	10.0	6,762	49.2	36.9	31.8
Trussville city	19,997	20,702	3.5	20,229	91.0	5.4	1.3	2.1	0.2	26.7	59.4	13.9	7,124	88.7	24.3	45.3
Tuscaloosa city	90,524	96,122	6.2	93,325	49.6	43.6	2.4	1.2	3.2	19.0	70.2	10.8	31,794	50.0	33.9	36.2
Tuscumbia city	8,576	8,529	-0.5	8,565	77.9	14.9	0.1	5.8	1.3	23.1	56.9	19.9	3,776	58.8	42.6	21.5
Tuskegee city	9,816	8,993	-8.4	9,435	3.6	93.7	0.4	0.7	1.6	17.2	70.0	12.9	3,413	46.5	35.9	23.1
Twin town	396	390	-1.5	376	98.4	0.0	0.0	0.8	0.8	16.7	51.7	31.6	179	84.9	63.1	10.1
Underwood-Petersville CDP	3,247	NA	NA	3,139	90.3	5.6	1.7	1.8	0.5	17.1	66.8	16.0	1,391	63.9	56.7	13.3
Union town	237	225	-5.1	292	7.9	92.1	0.0	0.0	0.0	7.9	58.1	33.9	120	90.0	57.5	13.3
Union Grove town	77	79	2.6	77	100.0	0.0	0.0	0.0	0.0	10.4	55.9	33.8	34	82.4	55.9	5.9

1 May be of any race.

Table A. All Places — Population and Housing

STATE City, town, township, borough, or CDP (county if applicable)	Population 2010 census total population	2014 estimated population	Percent change 2010– 2014	ACS total population estimate 2010–2014	Race and Hispanic or Latino origin (percent), 2010–2014 White alone, not Hispanic or Latino	Black alone, not Hispanic or Latino	Asian alone, not Hispanic or Latino	All other races or 2 or more races, not Hispanic or Latino	Hispanic or Latino[1]	Age (percent), 2010–2014 Under 18 years old	Age 18 to 64 years old	Age 65 years and older	Households, 2010–2014 Total occupied housing units	Percent owner occupied	Householders by level of education (percent) High school diploma or less	Bachelor's degree or more
	1	2	3	4	5	6	7	8	9	10	11	12	13	14	15	16
ALABAMA—Con.																
Union Springs city	3,978	3,931	-1.2	3,903	17.1	70.3	0.0	1.6	11.0	26.8	61.0	12.2	1,240	60.1	49.9	23.0
Uniontown town	2,696	2,471	-8.3	2,982	8.8	90.7	0.5	0.0	0.0	31.7	58.2	10.1	990	47.0	60.1	10.8
Uriah CDP	294	NA	NA	278	90.6	0.0	0.0	9.4	0.0	6.8	54.3	38.8	152	88.8	46.7	33.6
Valley city	9,479	9,453	-0.3	9,456	59.5	37.0	2.1	1.3	0.0	20.8	61.9	17.3	3,698	64.6	49.4	15.5
Valley Grande city	4,025	3,878	-3.7	3,951	72.9	26.8	0.3	0.0	0.0	24.2	58.7	17.0	1,549	82.8	43.1	11.7
Valley Head town	557	552	-0.9	642	92.8	0.0	0.0	3.4	3.7	18.2	66.8	15.0	245	80.8	56.7	13.5
Vance town	1,516	1,523	0.5	1,274	89.8	2.5	0.0	1.5	6.2	21.4	71.3	7.2	442	83.3	45.2	18.8
Vandiver CDP	1,135	NA	NA	1,090	94.5	3.9	0.0	0.3	1.4	13.9	69.3	16.9	487	95.1	70.6	10.9
Vernon city	2,000	1,926	-3.7	2,185	82.8	14.1	0.0	0.0	3.1	24.3	62.0	13.6	977	57.3	62.1	13.1
Vestavia Hills city	34,055	34,124	0.2	34,061	89.3	3.3	5.2	0.8	1.4	25.5	58.6	15.9	13,637	73.3	12.5	68.9
Vina town	358	356	-0.6	358	95.0	0.0	0.0	3.1	2.0	22.6	55.9	21.5	155	64.5	76.1	0.0
Vincent town	2,078	2,119	2.0	1,850	75.4	24.0	0.0	0.6	0.0	18.5	65.0	16.4	738	88.9	65.4	10.2
Vinegar Bend CDP	192	NA	NA	249	0.0	53.8	0.0	26.1	20.1	49.3	32.5	18.1	60	100.0	35.0	45.0
Vredenburgh town	312	298	-4.5	142	10.6	89.4	0.0	0.0	0.0	8.4	82.4	9.2	50	52.0	100.0	0.0
Wadley town	751	736	-2.0	813	64.6	31.7	0.0	2.0	1.7	21.7	68.7	9.6	226	53.1	48.7	27.0
Waldo town	283	278	-1.8	279	64.9	34.8	0.0	0.0	0.4	26.1	56.5	17.6	108	65.7	77.8	5.6
Walnut Grove town	696	689	-1.0	930	94.9	0.0	0.0	1.6	3.4	28.4	58.5	13.2	288	82.3	58.0	10.1
Warrior city	3,176	3,190	0.4	3,191	72.9	21.9	0.0	1.2	4.0	22.2	64.1	13.7	1,287	80.3	53.7	4.7
Waterloo town	203	201	-1.0	147	94.6	0.0	0.0	0.0	5.4	28.6	50.4	21.1	59	64.4	44.1	20.3
Waverly town	145	148	2.1	260	73.1	23.8	1.2	1.9	0.0	12.2	70.4	17.3	98	63.3	45.9	24.5
Weaver city	3,035	3,081	1.5	3,072	81.2	14.3	1.5	0.8	2.2	20.6	59.3	20.0	1,307	80.0	41.9	12.0
Webb town	1,428	1,421	-0.5	1,342	70.9	21.7	0.0	2.2	5.2	22.5	64.3	13.3	507	73.0	62.3	10.8
Wedowee town	821	804	-2.1	896	66.2	31.8	0.0	0.0	2.0	18.2	57.5	24.3	402	58.5	65.7	12.4
Weogufka CDP	282	NA	NA	284	100.0	0.0	0.0	0.0	0.0	37.4	36.7	26.1	100	100.0	91.0	0.0
West Blocton town	1,291	1,259	-2.5	1,566	76.8	17.6	0.0	3.1	2.6	23.4	59.4	17.3	461	77.0	51.2	3.5
West End-Cobb Town CDP	3,465	NA	NA	3,821	71.7	23.9	0.0	2.3	2.1	23.2	60.6	16.2	1,445	76.5	64.3	5.9
West Jefferson town	340	338	-0.6	494	98.0	0.0	0.0	1.6	0.4	30.1	59.7	10.1	184	76.6	44.6	9.2
Westover town	1,240	1,446	16.6	1,104	93.8	2.0	1.2	1.0	2.0	24.3	62.5	13.0	418	84.0	37.3	32.8
West Point town	583	589	1.0	649	94.3	0.0	0.6	3.1	2.0	17.4	64.1	18.5	267	81.6	41.6	19.9
Wetumpka city	6,662	7,661	15.0	7,136	71.3	24.3	0.3	1.7	2.4	21.3	63.3	15.4	2,437	60.0	43.1	19.2
Whatley CDP	150	NA	NA	0	0.0	0.0	0.0	0.0	0.0	0.0	0.0	0.0	0	0.0	0.0	0.0
White Hall town	874	820	-6.2	801	6.6	93.4	0.0	0.0	0.0	27.4	55.8	16.6	301	77.1	71.8	4.7
White Plains CDP	811	NA	NA	544	100.0	0.0	0.0	0.0	0.0	19.8	73.8	6.3	204	86.8	35.8	29.9
Whitesboro CDP	2,138	NA	NA	1,979	97.1	0.0	0.0	0.8	2.2	31.1	51.5	17.4	696	71.8	47.8	11.9
Wilsonville town	1,900	1,970	3.7	2,112	88.1	7.7	0.0	2.9	1.2	28.4	55.5	15.9	792	76.1	46.7	18.9
Wilton town	679	690	1.6	767	70.7	27.2	0.0	0.9	1.2	22.4	65.6	12.0	287	78.4	55.7	16.4
Winfield city	4,654	4,593	-1.3	4,300	91.0	4.6	0.2	0.0	4.1	17.5	58.4	24.0	1,943	67.5	42.3	25.0
Woodland town	184	182	-1.1	269	99.6	0.4	0.0	0.0	0.0	22.6	54.4	23.0	103	76.7	46.6	15.5
Woodstock town	1,418	1,502	5.9	1,785	91.2	0.0	0.0	0.3	8.5	25.3	63.4	11.3	489	83.4	58.5	19.8
Woodville town	746	739	-0.9	705	89.2	1.7	0.4	5.4	3.3	28.2	55.2	16.5	260	74.2	56.9	9.6
Yellow Bluff town	186	178	-4.3	182	0.0	98.9	0.0	1.1	0.0	35.6	58.0	6.0	44	97.7	81.8	2.3
York city	2,538	2,408	-5.1	2,803	13.1	85.9	0.0	0.8	0.2	24.1	62.3	13.7	1,126	67.5	62.6	20.3
ALASKA	710,249	736,732	3.7	728,300	62.9	3.3	5.5	22.1	6.2	25.9	65.7	8.5	251,678	63.3	31.0	29.0
Adak city	326	333	2.1	114	38.6	0.0	1.8	39.5	20.2	28.1	68.4	3.5	36	66.7	44.4	30.6
Akhiok city	71	73	2.8	103	12.6	8.7	2.9	72.8	2.9	27.2	67.0	5.8	28	78.6	64.3	7.1
Akiachak CDP	627	NA	NA	590	6.9	0.5	0.0	91.4	1.2	36.8	57.4	5.8	135	77.8	50.4	8.1
Akiak city	346	363	4.9	407	1.7	0.0	0.5	92.6	5.2	37.7	59.0	3.4	91	74.7	53.8	9.9
Akutan city	1,027	1,041	1.4	879	9.3	19.5	39.4	11.5	20.4	1.9	94.5	3.8	40	42.5	85.0	0.0
Alakanuk city	677	726	7.2	733	4.8	0.1	0.4	94.7	0.0	43.8	48.3	7.9	159	74.8	76.1	1.3
Alatna CDP	37	NA	NA	2	0.0	0.0	0.0	100.0	0.0	0.0	100.0	0.0	2	100.0	100.0	0.0
Alcan Border CDP	33	NA	NA	0	0.0	0.0	0.0	0.0	0.0	0.0	0.0	0.0	0	0.0	0.0	0.0
Aleknagik city	219	226	3.2	231	16.9	0.0	0.0	83.1	0.0	28.5	63.6	7.8	59	67.8	39.0	27.1
Aleneva CDP	37	NA	NA	63	100.0	0.0	0.0	0.0	0.0	76.2	23.8	0.0	8	0.0	100.0	0.0
Allakaket city	105	104	-1.0	72	13.9	0.0	0.0	86.1	0.0	18.1	72.2	9.7	36	63.9	61.1	16.7
Ambler city	258	265	2.7	329	11.6	0.0	0.0	88.4	0.0	37.1	54.3	8.8	84	64.3	66.7	3.6
Anaktuvuk Pass city	324	337	4.0	233	3.0	0.0	0.0	95.7	1.3	39.5	57.6	3.0	61	63.9	70.5	3.3
Anchorage municipality	291,826	301,010	3.1	298,178	61.1	5.6	8.3	16.8	8.3	25.3	66.6	8.1	105,164	59.8	26.4	34.3
Anchor Point CDP	1,930	NA	NA	2,189	90.1	0.0	0.4	7.0	2.5	22.2	63.8	14.1	950	86.8	40.9	17.1
Anderson city	246	271	10.2	257	79.8	11.3	0.0	7.8	1.2	23.7	67.9	8.2	82	80.5	28.0	20.7
Angoon city	459	446	-2.8	416	14.4	0.0	4.6	77.9	3.1	20.2	68.2	11.8	140	55.0	55.0	17.9
Aniak city	501	526	5.0	519	21.6	0.0	3.5	75.0	0.0	32.0	62.4	5.6	172	59.3	54.1	20.9
Anvik city	85	85	0.0	86	0.0	0.0	0.0	100.0	0.0	45.4	44.2	10.5	34	64.7	50.0	5.9
Arctic Village CDP	152	NA	NA	118	5.1	0.0	0.0	94.9	0.0	32.2	56.7	11.0	51	66.7	51.0	9.8
Atka city	61	65	6.6	66	19.7	0.0	12.1	68.2	0.0	16.7	74.3	9.1	24	66.7	41.7	25.0
Atmautluak CDP	277	NA	NA	288	0.0	0.0	0.0	100.0	0.0	35.4	56.9	7.6	60	75.0	76.7	6.7
Atqasuk city	233	241	3.4	219	2.7	0.0	0.0	97.3	0.0	34.7	54.8	10.5	68	63.2	57.4	4.4
Attu Station CDP	21	NA	NA	11	63.6	0.0	0.0	0.0	36.4	0.0	100.0	0.0	0	0.0	0.0	0.0
Badger CDP	19,482	NA	NA	21,175	79.3	2.0	1.2	13.2	4.4	28.9	65.6	5.5	7,152	76.9	34.0	23.9
Barrow city	4,212	4,393	4.3	4,296	11.3	0.7	9.2	74.0	4.8	36.5	59.2	4.3	1,312	40.8	52.0	16.0
Bear Creek CDP	1,956	NA	NA	2,399	76.6	0.8	5.0	17.5	0.0	23.5	71.0	5.4	788	78.0	37.4	24.5
Beaver CDP	84	NA	NA	86	0.0	0.0	0.0	100.0	0.0	21.0	72.3	7.0	38	71.1	47.4	7.9
Beluga CDP	20	NA	NA	5	80.0	0.0	0.0	20.0	0.0	0.0	80.0	20.0	5	60.0	60.0	0.0
Bethel city	6,080	6,415	5.5	6,295	25.4	1.8	2.1	67.4	3.3	32.4	63.2	4.4	1,918	47.3	37.9	23.8
Bettles city	12	12	0.0	11	100.0	0.0	0.0	0.0	0.0	0.0	63.7	36.4	9	44.4	22.2	22.2
Big Delta CDP	591	NA	NA	590	72.0	0.8	0.5	8.6	18.0	21.0	67.7	11.2	174	74.1	43.7	40.8
Big Lake CDP	3,350	NA	NA	3,959	76.4	0.0	1.3	16.6	5.7	26.4	60.7	12.8	1,351	80.2	32.5	18.8
Birch Creek CDP	33	NA	NA	11	0.0	0.0	0.0	100.0	0.0	0.0	100.1	0.0	9	55.6	100.0	0.0
Brevig Mission city	388	399	2.8	439	0.5	0.0	0.0	99.5	0.0	42.2	56.5	1.4	96	41.7	77.1	3.1
Buckland city	416	428	2.9	582	2.2	0.0	0.0	97.1	0.7	41.4	54.7	3.8	122	50.8	64.8	12.3
Buffalo Soapstone CDP	855	NA	NA	878	84.2	0.0	1.3	10.9	3.6	30.8	59.4	9.9	296	88.2	37.8	33.4
Butte CDP	3,246	NA	NA	3,544	84.2	1.5	0.9	8.7	4.7	24.4	63.5	11.9	1,144	84.5	29.5	31.3
Cantwell CDP	219	NA	NA	197	81.7	0.0	1.0	17.3	0.0	22.8	58.3	18.8	89	78.7	40.4	30.3
Central CDP	96	NA	NA	91	96.7	0.0	0.0	3.3	0.0	23.1	59.4	17.6	45	77.8	31.1	15.6
Chalkyitsik CDP	69	NA	NA	85	3.5	0.0	0.0	96.5	0.0	44.7	44.9	10.6	30	60.0	63.3	10.0
Chase CDP	34	NA	NA	22	100.0	0.0	0.0	0.0	0.0	0.0	100.0	0.0	22	100.0	100.0	0.0
Chefornak city	418	439	5.0	474	3.8	0.0	0.0	96.2	0.0	39.5	54.1	6.3	80	83.8	70.0	5.0
Chena Ridge CDP	5,791	NA	NA	5,671	78.8	0.7	0.6	12.3	7.6	23.7	71.0	5.3	2,127	71.9	20.7	51.6
Chenega CDP	76	NA	NA	72	30.6	0.0	0.0	69.4	0.0	26.3	61.3	12.5	25	52.0	56.0	12.0

1 May be of any race.

Table A.   All Places — **Population and Housing**

STATE City, town, township, borough, or CDP (county if applicable)	Population 2010 census total population	Population 2014 estimated population	Population Percent change 2010–2014	Population ACS total population estimate 2010–2014	Race and Hispanic or Latino origin (percent), 2010–2014 White alone, not Hispanic or Latino	Black alone, not Hispanic or Latino	Asian alone, not Hispanic or Latino	All other races or 2 or more races, not Hispanic or Latino	Hispanic or Latino[1]	Age (percent), 2010–2014 Under 18 years old	Age 18 to 64 years old	Age 65 years and older	Households, 2010–2014 Total occupied housing units	Percent owner occupied	Householders by level of education (percent) High school diploma or less	Bachelor's degree or more
	1	2	3	4	5	6	7	8	9	10	11	12	13	14	15	16
ALASKA—Con.																
Chevak city	938	1,006	7.2	986	2.1	1.3	3.0	92.7	0.8	38.5	58.0	3.5	199	72.4	62.3	5.0
Chickaloon CDP	272	NA	NA	234	85.0	0.0	0.0	11.1	3.8	6.0	71.9	22.2	100	82.0	23.0	22.0
Chicken CDP	7	NA	NA	0	0.0	0.0	0.0	0.0	0.0	0.0	0.0	0.0	0	0.0	0.0	0.0
Chignik city	91	91	0.0	86	39.5	0.0	4.7	54.7	1.2	45.4	54.7	0.0	26	46.2	46.2	15.4
Chignik Lagoon CDP	78	NA	NA	60	25.0	0.0	0.0	75.0	0.0	21.7	73.2	5.0	26	69.2	50.0	38.5
Chignik Lake CDP	73	NA	NA	58	8.6	0.0	0.0	91.4	0.0	29.3	63.7	6.9	25	72.0	52.0	16.0
Chiniak CDP	47	NA	NA	14	100.0	0.0	0.0	0.0	0.0	0.0	57.1	42.9	8	100.0	0.0	0.0
Chisana CDP	0	NA	NA	0	0.0	0.0	0.0	0.0	0.0	0.0	0.0	0.0	0	0.0	0.0	0.0
Chistochina CDP	93	NA	NA	105	43.8	0.0	0.0	56.2	0.0	6.7	89.4	3.8	43	72.1	44.2	14.0
Chitina CDP	126	NA	NA	78	25.6	32.1	0.0	42.3	0.0	38.5	50.0	11.5	32	53.1	46.9	6.3
Chuathbaluk city	118	124	5.1	104	3.8	1.9	0.0	94.2	0.0	44.2	52.7	2.9	31	29.0	64.5	19.4
Circle CDP	104	NA	NA	103	10.7	0.0	0.0	70.9	18.4	46.6	41.6	11.7	36	55.6	83.3	0.0
Clam Gulch CDP	176	NA	NA	163	78.5	0.0	0.0	11.7	9.8	31.9	57.1	11.0	63	93.7	44.4	30.2
Clark's Point city	62	64	3.2	75	0.0	0.0	0.0	100.0	0.0	34.7	62.6	2.7	19	57.9	42.1	0.0
Coffman Cove city	178	182	2.2	131	96.2	0.0	0.0	3.8	0.0	8.4	76.2	15.3	78	75.6	70.5	0.0
Cohoe CDP	1,364	NA	NA	1,485	85.4	0.4	0.1	12.3	1.8	19.9	70.0	10.2	597	85.1	32.5	25.3
Cold Bay city	108	125	15.7	44	72.7	0.0	0.0	18.2	9.1	4.5	95.4	0.0	25	24.0	24.0	40.0
Coldfoot CDP	10	NA	NA	11	100.0	0.0	0.0	0.0	0.0	0.0	100.1	0.0	0	0.0	0.0	0.0
College CDP	12,964	NA	NA	14,568	68.3	4.4	4.5	15.9	6.8	20.0	72.0	7.9	4,961	58.3	20.7	39.3
Cooper Landing CDP	289	NA	NA	323	100.0	0.0	0.0	0.0	0.0	4.3	55.0	40.6	161	85.7	37.3	26.1
Copper Center CDP	328	NA	NA	378	47.4	0.0	0.0	51.1	1.6	29.4	64.9	5.8	120	73.3	39.2	15.8
Cordova city	2,239	2,226	-0.6	2,637	76.3	0.0	8.4	14.5	0.8	21.6	62.3	16.1	840	74.5	26.8	36.5
Covenant Life CDP	86	NA	NA	151	58.3	0.0	0.0	41.7	0.0	30.5	65.6	4.0	43	53.5	32.6	67.4
Craig city	1,201	1,254	4.4	1,295	67.5	0.3	0.9	27.5	3.8	25.7	67.2	7.0	486	66.5	41.2	23.0
Crooked Creek CDP	105	NA	NA	104	5.8	0.0	0.0	94.2	0.0	45.2	50.0	4.8	23	73.9	47.8	0.0
Crown Point CDP	74	NA	NA	84	100.0	0.0	0.0	0.0	0.0	28.6	71.4	0.0	33	100.0	30.3	69.7
Deering city	122	125	2.5	128	7.8	0.0	0.0	92.2	0.0	32.8	58.6	8.6	36	61.1	58.3	13.9
Delta Junction city	958	943	-1.6	1,070	87.7	0.1	0.3	4.9	7.1	24.4	66.8	8.9	352	64.5	24.4	31.0
Deltana CDP	2,251	NA	NA	2,122	91.3	0.0	0.2	4.7	3.8	32.9	54.5	12.7	670	76.7	33.1	12.8
Diamond Ridge CDP	1,156	NA	NA	1,144	91.0	0.0	2.6	6.4	0.0	28.7	62.6	8.7	444	85.1	21.2	43.0
Dillingham city	2,329	2,396	2.9	2,255	32.9	0.4	0.9	60.4	5.5	31.4	59.6	8.9	770	51.9	31.2	29.0
Diomede city	115	118	2.6	65	0.0	0.0	0.0	100.0	0.0	47.7	47.6	4.6	23	52.2	65.2	0.0
Dot Lake CDP	13	NA	NA	0	0.0	0.0	0.0	0.0	0.0	0.0	0.0	0.0	0	0.0	0.0	0.0
Dot Lake Village CDP	62	NA	NA	38	13.2	0.0	0.0	86.8	0.0	39.5	47.4	13.2	14	57.1	50.0	0.0
Dry Creek CDP	94	NA	NA	88	100.0	0.0	0.0	0.0	0.0	18.2	76.1	5.7	25	20.0	0.0	20.0
Eagle city	86	85	-1.2	74	97.3	0.0	0.0	2.7	0.0	14.9	74.4	10.8	28	64.3	46.4	17.9
Eagle Village CDP	67	NA	NA	11	18.2	0.0	0.0	81.8	0.0	0.0	63.7	36.4	11	45.5	54.5	0.0
Edna Bay CDP	42	NA	NA	21	100.0	0.0	0.0	0.0	0.0	0.0	0.0	100.0	10	0.0	100.0	0.0
Eek city	296	311	5.1	425	0.0	0.0	0.0	97.9	2.1	40.7	49.5	9.9	94	84.0	70.2	4.3
Egegik city	109	109	0.0	74	23.0	0.0	18.9	47.3	10.8	17.7	71.7	10.8	22	72.7	81.8	9.1
Eielson AFB CDP	2,647	NA	NA	2,647	61.5	11.3	1.2	10.7	15.4	36.1	63.8	0.0	695	1.6	10.4	25.8
Ekwok city	115	119	3.5	100	1.0	0.0	0.0	99.0	0.0	29.0	61.0	10.0	35	71.4	71.4	0.0
Elfin Cove CDP	20	NA	NA	42	78.6	0.0	0.0	21.4	0.0	23.8	61.8	14.3	19	68.4	57.9	15.8
Elim city	330	339	2.7	319	0.9	0.0	0.6	97.2	1.3	34.1	60.9	5.0	91	61.5	65.9	1.1
Emmonak city	762	826	8.4	819	4.6	0.0	0.1	95.2	0.0	37.1	58.6	4.3	195	76.4	57.4	16.4
Ester CDP	2,422	NA	NA	2,653	84.7	0.5	0.8	11.5	2.6	14.1	77.5	8.3	1,173	50.2	11.6	31.0
Eureka Roadhouse CDP	29	NA	NA	0	0.0	0.0	0.0	0.0	0.0	0.0	0.0	0.0	0	0.0	0.0	0.0
Evansville CDP	15	NA	NA	21	14.3	0.0	0.0	85.7	0.0	4.8	76.1	19.0	14	64.3	14.3	35.7
Excursion Inlet CDP	12	NA	NA	36	72.2	0.0	0.0	27.8	0.0	0.0	100.1	0.0	0	0.0	0.0	0.0
Fairbanks city	31,535	32,469	3.0	32,100	60.1	8.5	4.5	16.4	10.5	26.3	66.0	7.7	11,512	37.0	33.3	21.1
False Pass city	35	40	14.3	31	48.4	0.0	0.0	48.4	3.2	19.3	80.7	0.0	19	36.8	42.1	26.3
Farmers Loop CDP	4,853	NA	NA	4,062	85.4	0.0	0.0	10.2	4.4	24.4	66.6	9.1	1,475	71.4	28.3	34.9
Farm Loop CDP	1,028	NA	NA	1,018	92.6	0.0	0.3	5.3	1.8	18.7	70.6	10.6	346	85.5	23.7	39.0
Ferry CDP	33	NA	NA	7	100.0	0.0	0.0	0.0	0.0	0.0	100.0	0.0	7	100.0	0.0	0.0
Fishhook CDP	4,679	NA	NA	5,015	84.6	0.5	1.0	7.3	6.6	31.9	59.9	8.3	1,549	90.6	30.5	30.2
Flat CDP	0	NA	NA	0	0.0	0.0	0.0	0.0	0.0	0.0	0.0	0.0	0	0.0	0.0	0.0
Fort Greely CDP	539	NA	NA	560	80.2	12.3	1.1	1.4	5.0	41.5	57.3	1.3	162	0.0	18.5	53.1
Fort Yukon city	583	573	-1.7	514	7.4	0.0	0.0	92.6	0.0	27.1	58.6	14.4	229	68.1	61.6	10.9
Four Mile Road CDP	43	NA	NA	29	75.9	0.0	0.0	24.1	0.0	27.6	55.1	17.2	12	100.0	83.3	0.0
Fox CDP	417	NA	NA	510	49.4	0.0	11.4	26.5	12.7	2.7	90.0	7.3	277	53.1	42.2	40.1
Fox River CDP	685	NA	NA	685	100.0	0.0	0.0	0.0	0.0	45.7	53.3	1.0	141	81.6	78.7	9.9
Fritz Creek CDP	1,932	NA	NA	1,774	87.3	0.8	1.0	4.3	6.6	18.8	69.2	12.0	778	78.1	30.1	29.4
Funny River CDP	877	NA	NA	935	93.2	0.0	3.9	3.0	0.0	16.6	55.4	28.2	402	83.1	46.8	21.9
Gakona CDP	218	NA	NA	163	73.0	0.0	0.0	18.4	8.6	43.5	44.7	11.7	51	76.5	19.6	45.1
Galena city	470	468	-0.4	539	26.3	0.0	3.3	68.8	1.5	26.9	58.3	15.0	202	75.2	37.6	24.3
Gambell city	681	700	2.8	702	5.6	0.0	1.0	91.7	1.7	32.4	61.2	6.6	160	76.9	64.4	6.9
Game Creek CDP	18	NA	NA	38	100.0	0.0	0.0	0.0	0.0	63.2	36.8	0.0	7	0.0	0.0	100.0
Gateway CDP	5,552	NA	NA	5,367	84.0	2.1	0.8	9.0	4.1	27.2	65.5	7.5	1,790	83.0	21.1	31.5
Glacier View CDP	234	NA	NA	278	92.1	0.0	0.0	2.5	5.4	24.8	60.2	15.1	91	86.8	24.2	37.4
Glennallen CDP	483	NA	NA	389	96.9	0.0	0.0	2.1	1.0	20.5	74.3	5.1	116	66.4	23.3	35.3
Goldstream CDP	3,557	NA	NA	3,910	92.7	0.1	0.3	6.1	0.8	23.3	66.7	9.9	1,638	88.3	9.9	56.3
Golovin city	156	160	2.6	122	1.6	0.0	0.0	98.4	0.0	33.6	59.8	6.6	47	59.6	61.7	0.0
Goodnews Bay city	243	255	4.9	237	3.4	0.0	0.0	96.6	0.0	36.7	55.7	7.6	63	82.5	93.7	0.0
Grayling city	194	193	-0.5	151	0.0	0.0	0.0	100.0	0.0	31.8	57.6	10.6	44	47.7	59.1	2.3
Gulkana CDP	119	NA	NA	104	27.9	0.0	0.0	72.1	0.0	13.5	62.5	24.0	37	75.7	37.8	10.8
Gustavus city	442	426	-3.6	529	89.4	0.0	3.8	4.3	2.5	10.2	78.0	11.7	262	65.6	15.6	45.4
Haines CDP	1,713	NA	NA	1,951	81.0	0.1	2.5	14.8	1.6	20.8	64.6	14.5	883	67.2	33.1	31.4
Halibut Cove CDP	76	NA	NA	21	52.4	0.0	0.0	47.6	0.0	0.0	28.6	71.4	10	100.0	0.0	40.0
Happy Valley CDP	593	NA	NA	585	90.3	0.3	0.3	7.4	1.7	9.4	69.6	21.0	274	92.0	39.8	17.5
Harding-Birch Lakes CDP	299	NA	NA	155	92.3	0.0	0.0	7.7	0.0	20.7	74.3	5.2	84	73.8	35.7	36.9
Healy CDP	1,021	NA	NA	1,146	86.8	0.0	7.3	3.4	2.4	28.1	68.3	3.6	447	73.8	34.0	24.2
Healy Lake CDP	13	NA	NA	0	0.0	0.0	0.0	0.0	0.0	0.0	0.0	0.0	0	0.0	0.0	0.0
Hobart Bay CDP	1	NA	NA	0	0.0	0.0	0.0	0.0	0.0	0.0	0.0	0.0	0	0.0	0.0	0.0
Hollis CDP	112	NA	NA	129	82.2	0.0	0.0	17.8	0.0	11.6	88.4	0.0	39	64.1	20.5	56.4
Holy Cross city	178	177	-0.6	209	2.9	0.0	0.0	97.1	0.0	25.8	62.8	11.5	64	70.3	64.1	3.1
Homer city	5,020	5,415	7.9	5,229	83.1	0.7	1.6	10.7	3.9	24.1	62.8	13.1	2,122	62.8	23.8	33.0
Hoonah city	759	734	-3.3	772	34.6	1.6	0.4	63.0	0.5	20.8	63.0	16.1	323	55.1	45.5	13.6
Hooper Bay city	1,093	1,173	7.3	1,259	5.0	0.5	0.3	94.2	0.0	47.4	48.9	3.7	227	78.0	70.5	1.8
Hope CDP	192	NA	NA	57	59.6	0.0	0.0	0.0	40.4	7.0	59.7	33.3	20	45.0	20.0	55.0
Houston city	1,910	2,133	11.7	2,058	75.9	1.1	0.2	20.4	2.3	28.9	61.6	9.4	716	78.2	46.5	13.1
Hughes city	77	77	0.0	63	0.0	0.0	0.0	100.0	0.0	34.9	57.0	7.9	20	40.0	50.0	0.0

1 May be of any race.

Table A. All Places — **Population and Housing**

STATE City, town, township, borough, or CDP (county if applicable)	2010 census total population	2014 estimated population	Percent change 2010–2014	ACS total population estimate 2010–2014	White alone, not Hispanic or Latino	Black alone, not Hispanic or Latino	Asian alone, not Hispanic or Latino	All other races or 2 or more races, not Hispanic or Latino	Hispanic or Latino[1]	Under 18 years old	Age 18 to 64 years old	Age 65 years and older	Total occupied housing units	Percent owner occupied	High school diploma or less	Bachelor's degree or more
	1	2	3	4	5	6	7	8	9	10	11	12	13	14	15	16
ALASKA—Con.																
Huslia city	275	274	-0.4	379	5.3	0.0	0.0	94.7	0.0	40.6	51.0	8.4	92	68.5	52.2	7.6
Hydaburg city	375	393	4.8	356	7.6	0.0	0.3	91.9	0.3	23.8	63.1	12.9	121	74.4	61.2	8.3
Hyder CDP	87	NA	NA	12	100.0	0.0	0.0	0.0	0.0	0.0	41.7	58.3	12	58.3	41.7	0.0
Igiugig CDP	50	NA	NA	37	10.8	0.0	0.0	86.5	2.7	32.4	64.8	2.7	15	66.7	20.0	13.3
Iliamna CDP	109	NA	NA	71	39.4	0.0	0.0	57.7	2.8	12.6	67.6	19.7	31	58.1	38.7	16.1
Ivanof Bay CDP	7	NA	NA	0	0.0	0.0	0.0	0.0	0.0	0.0	0.0	0.0	0	0.0	0.0	0.0
Juneau city and borough	31,275	32,406	3.6	32,200	66.5	1.2	6.0	20.5	5.9	22.8	68.0	9.3	12,081	63.7	23.9	38.3
Kachemak city	476	486	2.1	594	88.2	0.0	1.0	10.3	0.5	13.8	69.1	17.2	268	78.7	21.3	44.0
Kake city	557	576	3.4	592	26.0	0.5	1.7	69.4	2.4	25.1	64.2	10.5	218	61.0	41.7	16.5
Kaktovik city	239	246	2.9	176	5.1	0.0	0.0	94.9	0.0	26.7	63.6	9.7	57	87.7	66.7	1.8
Kalifornsky CDP	7,850	NA	NA	7,806	82.9	0.7	0.3	11.1	5.1	30.4	61.1	8.6	2,931	78.5	30.5	23.4
Kaltag city	190	189	-0.5	200	6.0	0.0	0.0	94.0	0.0	20.0	70.0	10.0	60	85.0	70.0	5.0
Karluk CDP	37	NA	NA	30	0.0	0.0	0.0	100.0	0.0	30.0	66.6	3.3	9	66.7	66.7	0.0
Kasaan city	49	51	4.1	67	32.8	0.0	0.0	67.2	0.0	26.9	58.3	14.9	25	68.0	52.0	0.0
Kasigluk CDP	569	NA	NA	537	0.0	0.0	0.0	100.0	0.0	37.8	53.7	8.6	98	71.4	79.6	1.0
Kasilof CDP	549	NA	NA	396	60.9	0.0	2.8	8.1	28.3	36.6	57.6	5.8	134	73.1	32.8	38.8
Kenai city	7,112	7,568	6.4	7,348	76.7	0.2	0.7	20.1	2.2	25.2	64.1	10.6	2,896	57.9	39.4	23.3
Kenny Lake CDP	355	NA	NA	131	58.8	0.0	0.0	41.2	0.0	24.4	75.6	0.0	40	100.0	55.0	45.0
Ketchikan city	8,050	8,245	2.4	8,173	57.4	0.7	9.7	26.3	5.9	22.9	66.5	10.6	3,373	46.8	39.6	23.4
Kiana city	361	371	2.8	371	5.9	0.0	0.0	94.1	0.0	37.7	52.9	9.4	106	65.1	57.5	12.3
King Cove city	938	1,015	8.2	900	12.7	3.2	35.6	36.8	11.8	14.5	79.9	5.6	180	61.7	62.8	20.0
King Salmon CDP	374	NA	NA	335	61.2	0.3	0.0	28.1	10.4	25.1	71.9	3.3	137	44.5	36.5	23.4
Kipnuk CDP	639	NA	NA	700	0.3	0.0	0.0	99.7	0.0	36.5	57.2	6.3	157	84.1	79.6	2.5
Kivalina city	374	384	2.7	532	2.4	0.0	0.0	96.8	0.8	42.7	53.4	3.9	110	64.5	70.9	10.0
Klawock city	755	774	2.5	697	38.9	0.7	0.0	57.2	3.2	22.1	62.1	15.6	285	60.7	64.9	7.0
Klukwan CDP	95	NA	NA	66	18.2	0.0	0.0	81.8	0.0	10.6	59.1	30.3	32	68.8	34.4	37.5
Knik-Fairview CDP	14,923	NA	NA	15,797	83.4	0.2	2.2	11.6	2.7	29.4	64.5	6.1	5,032	80.8	38.7	19.3
Knik River CDP	744	NA	NA	690	91.7	0.4	0.0	4.1	3.8	19.4	70.8	9.7	265	79.2	33.2	25.3
Kobuk city	151	155	2.6	159	2.5	0.0	0.0	89.3	8.2	47.8	47.8	4.4	35	68.6	74.3	5.7
Kodiak city	6,130	6,304	2.8	6,280	35.2	0.0	41.7	12.7	10.4	25.2	65.3	9.5	1,969	52.8	38.4	19.6
Kodiak Station CDP	1,301	NA	NA	1,397	75.7	2.4	3.2	4.7	14.0	34.9	65.1	0.0	392	3.1	12.2	19.9
Kokhanok CDP	170	NA	NA	123	13.8	0.0	0.0	83.7	2.4	32.5	61.0	6.5	48	68.8	45.8	18.8
Koliganek CDP	209	NA	NA	164	3.0	0.0	0.0	97.0	0.0	43.9	50.6	5.5	45	62.2	62.2	8.9
Kongiganak CDP	439	NA	NA	368	1.6	0.0	0.0	94.6	3.8	35.1	58.8	6.3	70	85.7	64.3	2.9
Kotlik city	577	619	7.3	636	0.6	0.2	0.0	99.2	0.0	38.5	54.4	7.1	137	75.9	76.6	4.4
Kotzebue city	3,201	3,284	2.6	3,273	20.8	0.7	1.5	74.2	2.8	31.6	61.8	6.6	919	46.0	40.6	22.7
Koyuk city	332	341	2.7	265	1.5	0.0	0.0	98.5	0.0	45.0	47.1	7.9	65	70.8	69.2	4.6
Koyukuk city	96	95	-1.0	89	2.2	0.0	0.0	97.8	0.0	30.3	65.0	4.5	38	57.9	73.7	7.9
Kupreanof city	27	27	0.0	48	79.2	0.0	0.0	20.8	0.0	20.9	58.5	20.8	19	73.7	31.6	36.8
Kwethluk city	721	757	5.0	763	0.4	0.0	0.5	99.1	0.0	41.7	53.6	4.7	157	73.9	59.2	3.2
Kwigillingok CDP	321	NA	NA	325	0.0	0.0	0.0	99.1	0.9	36.6	59.4	4.0	62	75.8	54.8	0.0
Lake Louise CDP	46	NA	NA	42	81.0	0.0	0.0	19.0	0.0	0.0	57.1	42.9	14	100.0	57.1	0.0
Lake Minchumina CDP	13	NA	NA	19	73.7	0.0	0.0	26.3	0.0	21.1	36.8	42.1	9	66.7	0.0	55.6
Lakes CDP	8,364	NA	NA	9,345	81.6	0.7	0.9	13.0	3.8	28.4	62.3	9.3	2,996	78.4	31.6	25.7
Larsen Bay city	87	89	2.3	52	34.6	5.8	0.0	59.6	0.0	19.2	57.6	23.1	26	80.8	26.9	11.5
Lazy Mountain CDP	1,479	NA	NA	1,629	82.8	2.9	1.0	10.3	3.0	35.5	55.4	9.1	474	81.6	24.7	33.8
Levelock CDP	69	NA	NA	131	6.1	0.0	0.0	93.9	0.0	44.3	51.9	3.8	35	51.4	45.7	2.9
Lime Village CDP	29	NA	NA	22	0.0	0.0	0.0	100.0	0.0	0.0	86.4	13.6	8	50.0	75.0	25.0
Livengood CDP	13	NA	NA	10	100.0	0.0	0.0	0.0	0.0	0.0	40.0	60.0	6	100.0	0.0	0.0
Loring CDP	4	NA	NA	0	0.0	0.0	0.0	0.0	0.0	0.0	0.0	0.0	0	0.0	0.0	0.0
Lowell Creek CDP	80	NA	NA	66	100.0	0.0	0.0	0.0	0.0	0.0	0.0	100.0	31	100.0	100.0	0.0
Lower Kalskag city	282	296	5.0	340	1.5	0.0	10.3	88.2	0.0	33.3	59.8	7.1	87	83.9	81.6	3.4
Lutak CDP	49	NA	NA	12	0.0	0.0	0.0	100.0	0.0	0.0	100.0	0.0	12	100.0	100.0	0.0
McCarthy CDP	28	NA	NA	133	100.0	0.0	0.0	0.0	0.0	21.8	63.2	15.0	40	52.5	47.5	30.0
McGrath city	346	344	-0.6	344	34.6	2.9	3.5	57.3	1.7	24.1	62.8	13.1	130	60.8	44.6	16.9
McKinley Park CDP	185	NA	NA	429	83.2	2.3	2.3	7.9	4.2	0.0	97.2	3.0	85	42.4	12.9	42.4
Manley Hot Springs CDP	89	NA	NA	80	63.8	0.0	0.0	25.0	11.3	21.3	52.6	26.3	33	75.8	42.4	21.2
Manokotak city	442	455	2.9	673	5.5	0.0	5.2	89.0	0.3	30.0	62.5	7.4	125	77.6	58.4	4.8
Marshall city	414	444	7.2	320	0.0	0.0	0.0	100.0	0.0	40.6	53.5	5.9	84	77.4	56.0	0.0
Meadow Lakes CDP	7,570	NA	NA	7,139	84.8	0.1	1.5	10.0	3.6	27.2	63.9	8.8	2,574	80.6	44.9	11.9
Mekoryuk city	191	201	5.2	177	1.7	0.0	0.0	98.3	0.0	25.4	63.2	11.3	64	81.3	70.3	0.0
Mendeltna CDP	39	NA	NA	25	100.0	0.0	0.0	0.0	0.0	0.0	100.0	0.0	12	100.0	100.0	0.0
Mentasta Lake CDP	112	NA	NA	231	5.2	0.0	0.0	94.8	0.0	21.6	73.6	4.8	68	41.2	54.4	0.0
Mertarvik CDP	0	NA	NA	0	0.0	0.0	0.0	0.0	0.0	0.0	0.0	0.0	0	0.0	0.0	0.0
Metlakatla CDP	1,405	NA	NA	1,568	7.5	0.3	0.1	87.6	4.5	30.3	59.6	10.1	495	66.9	53.1	11.1
Minto CDP	210	NA	NA	252	3.2	0.0	0.0	96.8	0.0	32.9	58.9	8.3	72	81.9	59.7	4.2
Moose Creek CDP	747	NA	NA	728	99.7	0.0	0.0	0.3	0.0	27.9	68.1	4.1	317	32.2	18.6	10.7
Moose Pass CDP	219	NA	NA	464	89.9	0.0	0.0	7.8	2.4	24.8	61.2	14.0	163	97.5	45.4	22.7
Mosquito Lake CDP	309	NA	NA	119	89.1	0.0	0.0	10.9	0.0	9.2	74.8	16.0	75	100.0	48.0	8.0
Mountain Village city	813	872	7.3	781	3.6	0.0	0.0	96.4	0.0	42.3	52.3	5.5	163	72.4	72.4	3.1
Mud Bay CDP	212	NA	NA	131	95.4	0.0	0.0	4.6	0.0	0.0	79.3	20.6	66	62.1	0.0	80.3
Nabesna CDP	5	NA	NA	0	0.0	0.0	0.0	0.0	0.0	0.0	0.0	0.0	0	0.0	0.0	0.0
Naknek CDP	544	NA	NA	600	53.2	0.3	1.2	41.8	3.5	28.9	64.0	7.0	230	57.0	30.4	19.1
Nanwalek CDP	254	NA	NA	212	5.2	0.0	0.0	94.8	0.0	47.7	50.9	1.4	51	21.6	29.4	11.8
Napakiak city	354	372	5.1	365	0.3	0.0	0.3	99.5	0.0	43.5	48.5	7.9	98	74.5	78.6	0.0
Napaskiak city	405	425	4.9	430	7.7	0.0	0.0	92.3	0.0	37.3	52.0	10.7	93	79.6	69.9	2.2
Naukati Bay CDP	113	NA	NA	35	100.0	0.0	0.0	0.0	0.0	0.0	40.0	60.0	35	85.7	85.7	0.0
Nelchina CDP	59	NA	NA	124	100.0	0.0	0.0	0.0	0.0	49.2	40.3	10.5	28	100.0	67.9	0.0
Nelson Lagoon CDP	52	NA	NA	39	10.3	0.0	0.0	82.1	7.7	0.0	84.7	15.4	16	93.8	81.3	6.3
Nenana city	378	376	-0.5	438	54.1	0.5	0.0	44.5	0.9	21.9	63.4	14.6	175	62.9	40.6	12.6
New Allakaket CDP	66	NA	NA	71	0.0	0.0	0.0	100.0	0.0	23.9	59.1	16.9	18	72.2	61.1	0.0
Newhalen city	190	190	0.0	175	5.1	0.0	0.0	90.9	4.0	42.9	55.5	1.7	44	72.7	38.6	20.5
New Stuyahok city	510	525	2.9	574	1.0	0.0	0.0	99.0	0.0	35.1	54.8	10.3	107	64.5	74.8	0.0
Newtok CDP	354	NA	NA	384	0.0	0.0	0.0	100.0	0.0	44.1	48.4	7.6	60	78.3	65.0	5.0
Nightmute city	280	294	5.0	281	6.4	0.0	0.0	93.6	0.0	35.6	55.2	9.3	49	79.6	79.6	2.0
Nikiski CDP	4,493	NA	NA	4,536	85.0	0.0	0.8	6.1	8.0	20.6	65.2	14.1	1,705	78.6	40.9	19.0
Nikolaevsk CDP	318	NA	NA	196	100.0	0.0	0.0	0.0	0.0	23.0	68.4	8.7	92	77.2	57.6	12.0
Nikolai city	94	94	0.0	75	18.7	0.0	0.0	81.3	0.0	15.9	69.4	14.7	33	48.5	60.6	0.0
Nikolski CDP	18	NA	NA	34	32.4	0.0	5.9	61.8	0.0	20.6	55.8	23.5	19	31.6	78.9	5.3
Ninilchik CDP	883	NA	NA	730	84.2	0.0	1.1	14.7	0.0	14.4	62.9	22.7	349	72.8	34.1	28.1
Noatak CDP	514	NA	NA	452	0.2	0.2	0.0	99.6	0.0	35.6	54.5	10.0	92	83.7	82.6	1.1

1 May be of any race.

Table A. All Places — **Population and Housing**

STATE City, town, township, borough, or CDP (county if applicable)	2010 census total population	2014 estimated population	Percent change 2010–2014	ACS total population estimate 2010–2014	White alone, not Hispanic or Latino	Black alone, not Hispanic or Latino	Asian alone, not Hispanic or Latino	All other races or 2 or more races, not Hispanic or Latino	Hispanic or Latino[1]	Under 18 years old	Age 18 to 64 years old	Age 65 years and older	Total occupied housing units	Percent owner occupied	High school diploma or less	Bachelor's degree or more
	1	2	3	4	5	6	7	8	9	10	11	12	13	14	15	16
ALASKA—Con.																
Nome city	3,598	3,788	5.3	3,745	34.6	1.7	1.9	58.6	3.2	29.8	62.8	7.3	1,306	45.5	35.5	28.7
Nondalton city	164	164	0.0	214	5.6	0.0	0.0	94.4	0.0	35.0	60.2	4.7	64	78.1	78.1	1.6
Noorvik city	668	686	2.7	598	1.0	0.0	0.0	99.0	0.0	36.5	55.9	7.5	140	60.0	68.6	3.6
North Pole city	2,117	2,178	2.9	2,153	78.0	3.9	2.0	12.5	3.6	27.9	61.3	10.7	828	55.3	29.6	25.6
Northway CDP	71	NA	NA	139	27.3	0.0	0.0	72.7	0.0	22.2	75.4	2.2	33	81.8	15.2	12.1
Northway Junction CDP	54	NA	NA	62	16.1	0.0	0.0	83.9	0.0	43.6	53.2	3.2	18	83.3	55.6	16.7
Northway Village CDP	98	NA	NA	97	0.0	0.0	0.0	100.0	0.0	18.6	55.6	25.8	26	96.2	96.2	0.0
Nuiqsut city	402	416	3.5	371	6.2	0.0	0.0	93.8	0.0	32.6	61.3	5.9	100	69.0	74.0	6.0
Nulato city	264	263	-0.4	272	5.5	0.0	0.0	94.5	0.0	24.3	64.2	11.4	86	68.6	46.5	16.3
Nunam Iqua city	187	201	7.5	132	14.4	0.0	0.0	85.6	0.0	27.3	63.5	9.1	31	67.7	71.0	19.4
Nunapitchuk city	496	521	5.0	459	2.6	0.0	0.0	97.4	0.0	43.1	52.2	4.6	89	74.2	53.9	11.2
Old Harbor city	218	223	2.3	268	5.6	0.0	0.0	93.3	1.1	31.0	62.4	6.7	86	75.6	74.4	5.8
Oscarville CDP	70	NA	NA	29	0.0	0.0	0.0	100.0	0.0	31.0	37.8	31.0	9	100.0	66.7	0.0
Ouzinkie city	161	165	2.5	275	13.8	0.0	2.2	78.9	5.1	17.8	72.0	10.2	100	75.0	68.0	12.0
Palmer city	5,937	6,515	9.7	6,250	73.1	1.3	1.6	17.0	7.0	28.5	63.1	8.4	2,120	59.1	35.4	22.8
Paxson CDP	40	NA	NA	34	100.0	0.0	0.0	0.0	0.0	14.7	50.0	35.3	21	42.9	57.1	42.9
Pedro Bay CDP	42	NA	NA	22	31.8	0.0	0.0	68.2	0.0	36.3	45.4	18.2	11	63.6	36.4	27.3
Pelican city	88	86	-2.3	57	29.8	0.0	0.0	70.2	0.0	15.8	56.2	28.1	23	78.3	65.2	21.7
Perryville CDP	113	NA	NA	116	1.7	0.0	0.0	98.3	0.0	43.1	47.3	9.5	36	83.3	80.6	5.6
Petersburg CDP	2,948	NA	NA	2,926	70.2	2.5	1.9	17.1	8.3	19.2	70.2	10.6	1,267	65.9	34.6	21.9
Petersville CDP	4	NA	NA	0	0.0	0.0	0.0	0.0	0.0	0.0	0.0	0.0	0	0.0	0.0	0.0
Pilot Point city	68	68	0.0	47	0.0	0.0	0.0	100.0	0.0	23.4	63.8	12.8	25	80.0	56.0	20.0
Pilot Station city	568	609	7.2	567	0.0	0.0	0.0	100.0	0.0	37.0	57.9	4.9	121	81.8	63.6	2.5
Pitkas Point CDP	109	NA	NA	136	0.0	0.0	0.0	100.0	0.0	41.9	54.3	3.7	31	93.5	58.1	0.0
Platinum city	61	64	4.9	42	0.0	0.0	0.0	92.9	7.1	45.3	42.8	11.9	11	45.5	81.8	0.0
Pleasant Valley CDP	725	NA	NA	280	73.6	0.0	0.0	26.4	0.0	17.2	82.8	0.0	94	100.0	52.1	0.0
Point Baker CDP	15	NA	NA	48	56.3	0.0	0.0	43.8	0.0	0.0	75.1	25.0	35	100.0	34.3	0.0
Point Hope city	674	702	4.2	628	2.5	0.3	0.0	96.0	1.1	38.1	55.8	5.9	176	61.4	59.7	5.7
Point Lay CDP	189	NA	NA	246	13.0	0.0	0.0	85.8	1.2	39.5	59.3	1.2	68	44.1	60.3	10.3
Point MacKenzie CDP	529	NA	NA	473	65.5	4.4	0.2	27.9	1.9	5.8	79.5	14.8	86	89.5	59.3	18.6
Point Possession CDP	3	NA	NA	0	0.0	0.0	0.0	0.0	0.0	0.0	0.0	0.0	0	0.0	0.0	0.0
Pope-Vannoy Landing CDP	6	NA	NA	0	0.0	0.0	0.0	0.0	0.0	0.0	0.0	0.0	0	0.0	0.0	0.0
Portage Creek CDP	2	NA	NA	0	0.0	0.0	0.0	0.0	0.0	0.0	0.0	0.0	0	0.0	0.0	0.0
Port Alexander city	52	55	5.8	30	90.0	0.0	0.0	10.0	0.0	30.0	56.7	13.3	9	66.7	0.0	22.2
Port Alsworth CDP	159	NA	NA	147	62.6	5.4	0.0	25.9	6.1	40.2	57.1	2.7	47	36.2	21.3	27.7
Port Clarence CDP	24	NA	NA	43	46.5	0.0	0.0	0.0	53.5	0.0	100.0	0.0	0	0.0	0.0	0.0
Port Graham CDP	177	NA	NA	166	7.8	0.0	0.0	91.6	0.6	24.0	68.0	7.8	65	43.1	67.7	3.1
Port Heiden city	102	102	0.0	84	47.6	0.0	0.0	52.4	0.0	22.6	70.3	7.1	32	56.3	65.6	18.8
Port Lions city	194	198	2.1	230	42.2	0.9	0.0	51.3	5.7	22.6	60.1	17.4	93	78.5	62.4	8.6
Port Protection CDP	48	NA	NA	83	100.0	0.0	0.0	0.0	0.0	0.0	86.7	13.3	56	100.0	19.6	35.7
Primrose CDP	78	NA	NA	51	90.2	0.0	0.0	9.8	0.0	0.0	88.4	11.8	25	100.0	24.0	24.0
Prudhoe Bay CDP	2,174	NA	NA	2,570	84.2	0.4	2.3	10.4	2.8	0.0	96.1	3.9	0	0.0	0.0	0.0
Quinhagak city	669	702	4.9	616	2.8	0.0	0.0	97.2	0.0	36.2	57.1	6.7	150	84.0	79.3	2.7
Rampart CDP	24	NA	NA	15	53.3	0.0	0.0	46.7	0.0	0.0	86.6	13.3	7	100.0	100.0	0.0
Red Devil CDP	23	NA	NA	32	34.4	0.0	0.0	65.6	0.0	15.7	59.4	25.0	13	100.0	92.3	0.0
Red Dog Mine CDP	309	NA	NA	139	61.2	0.0	0.7	38.1	0.0	0.0	100.1	0.0	0	0.0	0.0	0.0
Ridgeway CDP	2,022	NA	NA	2,128	69.5	0.0	0.2	19.6	10.8	25.7	59.1	15.1	740	80.5	20.4	21.4
Ruby city	166	165	-0.6	208	5.3	0.0	0.0	94.7	0.0	31.3	60.1	8.7	69	78.3	71.0	7.2
Russian Mission city	312	335	7.4	404	10.9	0.0	0.0	89.1	0.0	41.0	57.4	1.5	75	78.7	61.3	6.7
St. George city	102	108	5.9	33	0.0	0.0	0.0	100.0	0.0	15.1	60.6	24.2	12	66.7	75.0	8.3
St. Mary's city	507	544	7.3	551	9.6	0.0	0.0	88.9	1.5	34.8	57.2	7.8	168	67.9	50.6	23.8
St. Michael city	401	412	2.7	406	4.9	0.0	0.0	94.8	0.2	44.6	52.4	3.0	94	52.1	70.2	7.4
St. Paul city	479	511	6.7	612	8.0	1.3	3.1	87.3	0.3	24.6	66.4	9.0	161	64.6	54.0	7.5
Salamatof CDP	980	NA	NA	1,049	68.1	2.4	1.7	24.1	3.7	17.3	74.7	8.0	249	70.7	39.8	18.5
Salcha CDP	1,095	NA	NA	957	97.2	0.0	0.4	0.0	2.4	32.2	59.4	8.5	377	81.7	24.7	31.8
Sand Point city	976	1,073	9.9	1,371	14.2	9.6	28.1	37.3	10.8	16.0	78.3	5.7	289	55.4	51.9	13.8
Savoonga city	671	690	2.8	872	1.1	0.0	0.0	98.9	0.0	38.7	52.9	8.6	173	79.2	71.7	4.6
Saxman city	411	418	1.7	470	17.7	0.2	0.4	75.5	6.2	20.9	64.3	14.9	145	62.1	55.2	9.7
Scammon Bay city	474	508	7.2	447	0.0	0.0	0.0	100.0	0.0	49.2	43.6	7.2	100	74.0	77.0	4.0
Selawik city	829	852	2.8	754	0.9	0.0	0.0	99.1	0.0	40.4	54.3	5.2	161	61.5	85.7	5.0
Seldovia city	254	272	7.1	264	71.2	2.7	1.5	24.6	0.0	14.0	61.4	24.6	146	66.4	37.0	32.2
Seldovia Village CDP	165	NA	NA	180	58.3	0.0	8.3	33.3	0.0	13.9	63.9	22.2	83	95.2	21.7	25.3
Seward city	2,693	2,528	-6.1	2,646	67.3	2.1	1.9	26.9	1.8	12.5	70.2	17.3	939	49.3	40.0	16.6
Shageluk city	83	83	0.0	58	3.4	0.0	0.0	96.6	0.0	29.2	60.3	10.3	27	81.5	81.5	7.4
Shaktoolik city	251	258	2.8	212	2.4	0.0	0.0	95.8	1.9	29.7	62.2	8.0	65	52.3	72.3	4.6
Shishmaref city	563	579	2.8	629	2.2	0.0	0.2	97.3	0.3	42.9	53.3	3.7	138	62.3	68.8	2.9
Shungnak city	262	269	2.7	308	1.9	0.0	1.6	96.4	0.0	40.9	53.2	5.8	64	68.8	84.4	0.0
Silver Springs CDP	114	NA	NA	170	82.4	0.0	0.0	14.1	3.5	24.1	68.2	7.6	62	83.9	19.4	56.5
Sitka city and borough	8,881	8,900	0.2	8,957	63.5	1.0	5.9	24.0	5.6	23.0	64.9	12.0	3,513	57.6	23.4	34.3
Skagway CDP	920	NA	NA	932	75.8	0.0	12.4	8.9	2.9	18.4	73.6	7.9	361	57.1	29.1	38.0
Skwentna CDP	37	NA	NA	47	100.0	0.0	0.0	0.0	0.0	19.1	55.2	25.5	21	100.0	38.1	0.0
Slana CDP	147	NA	NA	139	86.3	0.0	0.0	13.7	0.0	17.3	42.5	40.3	72	100.0	43.1	0.0
Sleetmute CDP	86	NA	NA	100	18.0	0.0	0.0	79.0	3.0	28.0	56.0	16.0	36	66.7	77.8	8.3
Soldotna city	4,163	4,445	6.8	4,345	86.8	0.2	2.0	9.5	1.6	25.1	60.5	14.2	1,651	63.1	31.5	21.3
South Naknek CDP	79	NA	NA	60	13.3	0.0	0.0	86.7	0.0	10.0	66.8	23.3	31	77.4	45.2	6.5
South Van Horn CDP	558	NA	NA	547	70.0	0.0	0.7	29.3	0.0	23.2	55.3	21.6	213	54.9	46.5	20.2
Stebbins city	556	572	2.9	538	0.4	0.0	0.0	99.6	0.0	44.1	51.8	4.1	123	65.9	62.6	1.6
Steele Creek CDP	6,662	NA	NA	6,180	85.3	0.0	1.6	9.5	3.6	19.7	71.0	9.3	2,395	83.6	15.5	37.9
Sterling CDP	5,617	NA	NA	5,748	92.0	1.0	0.6	4.9	1.4	22.0	64.2	13.6	2,098	84.8	39.2	18.2
Stevens Village CDP	78	NA	NA	69	0.0	7.2	0.0	34.8	58.0	55.0	33.2	11.6	12	83.3	66.7	0.0
Stony River CDP	54	NA	NA	61	0.0	0.0	0.0	100.0	0.0	52.5	44.3	3.3	19	47.4	78.9	0.0
Sunrise CDP	18	NA	NA	15	100.0	0.0	0.0	0.0	0.0	0.0	100.0	0.0	15	60.0	0.0	60.0
Susitna CDP	18	NA	NA	0	0.0	0.0	0.0	0.0	0.0	0.0	0.0	0.0	0	0.0	0.0	0.0
Susitna North CDP	1,260	NA	NA	1,420	93.5	0.0	0.0	6.5	0.0	15.2	64.9	19.8	602	92.7	45.8	16.1
Sutton-Alpine CDP	1,447	NA	NA	1,390	69.5	1.7	2.2	24.0	2.7	10.4	82.2	7.4	296	73.3	43.2	15.2
Takotna CDP	52	NA	NA	56	28.6	0.0	0.0	71.4	0.0	35.7	57.2	7.1	20	55.0	45.0	0.0
Talkeetna CDP	876	NA	NA	508	91.7	0.0	1.2	6.9	0.2	20.5	64.2	15.2	245	56.3	28.6	38.8
Tanacross CDP	136	NA	NA	176	9.1	0.0	0.0	90.3	0.6	24.4	60.3	15.3	53	77.4	50.9	0.0
Tanaina CDP	8,197	NA	NA	9,391	80.0	0.5	0.5	12.3	6.7	32.9	60.2	6.9	2,761	76.3	34.5	22.7
Tanana city	246	245	-0.4	248	16.1	0.0	0.0	83.9	0.0	27.7	63.7	8.5	94	69.1	46.8	13.8

1 May be of any race.

Table A. All Places — Population and Housing

STATE City, town, township, borough, or CDP (county if applicable)	Population — 2010 census total population	2014 estimated population	Percent change 2010–2014	ACS total population estimate 2010–2014	Race and Hispanic or Latino origin (percent), 2010–2014 — White alone, not Hispanic or Latino	Black alone, not Hispanic or Latino	Asian alone, not Hispanic or Latino	All other races or 2 or more races, not Hispanic or Latino	Hispanic or Latino[1]	Age (percent), 2010–2014 — Under 18 years old	Age 18 to 64 years old	Age 65 years and older	Households, 2010–2014 — Total occupied housing units	Percent owner occupied	Householders by level of education (percent) — High school diploma or less	Bachelor's degree or more
	1	2	3	4	5	6	7	8	9	10	11	12	13	14	15	16
ALASKA—Con.																
Tatitlek CDP	88	NA	NA	69	4.3	0.0	0.0	95.7	0.0	10.1	69.3	20.3	28	78.6	71.4	7.1
Tazlina CDP	297	NA	NA	323	53.9	0.0	0.0	45.5	0.6	9.6	73.1	17.3	118	75.4	33.1	26.3
Teller city	229	235	2.6	184	0.0	0.5	0.0	99.5	0.0	32.6	60.2	7.1	62	46.8	83.9	0.0
Tenakee Springs city	131	130	-0.8	117	93.2	0.0	0.0	0.0	6.8	9.4	71.9	18.8	65	89.2	36.9	20.0
Tetlin CDP	127	NA	NA	123	14.6	0.0	0.0	82.9	2.4	36.6	60.3	3.3	33	72.7	66.7	6.1
Thorne Bay city	471	488	3.6	536	91.4	0.0	0.0	8.6	0.0	22.9	65.4	11.6	252	76.6	36.1	40.1
Togiak city	817	842	3.1	765	3.9	0.4	0.0	95.7	0.0	36.7	59.6	3.8	159	65.4	61.0	8.2
Tok CDP	1,258	NA	NA	1,304	75.5	0.0	1.4	22.7	0.5	24.8	62.3	12.8	512	81.6	41.2	21.3
Toksook Bay city	590	619	4.9	650	2.0	0.0	0.0	98.0	0.0	37.1	55.8	7.1	123	75.6	69.9	8.1
Tolsona CDP	30	NA	NA	0	0.0	0.0	0.0	0.0	0.0	0.0	0.0	0.0	0	0.0	0.0	0.0
Tonsina CDP	78	NA	NA	16	100.0	0.0	0.0	0.0	0.0	0.0	100.0	0.0	7	100.0	0.0	0.0
Trapper Creek CDP	481	NA	NA	448	93.3	0.0	0.0	4.7	2.0	27.9	56.0	16.1	176	85.8	40.3	19.9
Tuluksak CDP	373	NA	NA	421	3.3	0.0	0.0	95.2	1.4	44.9	53.3	1.9	86	64.0	73.3	8.1
Tuntutuliak CDP	408	NA	NA	437	0.0	0.0	0.0	100.0	0.0	40.5	47.9	11.7	95	73.7	71.6	5.3
Tununak CDP	327	NA	NA	297	3.4	0.0	0.0	96.6	0.0	31.7	57.3	11.1	70	70.0	54.3	8.6
Twin Hills CDP	74	NA	NA	93	1.1	0.0	0.0	98.9	0.0	41.9	51.7	6.5	25	48.0	56.0	0.0
Two Rivers CDP	719	NA	NA	441	100.0	0.0	0.0	0.0	0.0	10.4	89.6	0.0	179	68.2	6.7	46.4
Tyonek CDP	171	NA	NA	226	5.3	0.0	0.0	94.7	0.0	29.2	67.3	3.5	73	65.8	64.4	6.8
Ugashik CDP	12	NA	NA	19	63.2	0.0	0.0	36.8	0.0	0.0	52.7	47.4	10	100.0	50.0	20.0
Unalakleet city	688	707	2.8	708	14.7	0.0	1.7	83.6	0.0	27.2	61.5	11.3	215	69.8	49.8	21.4
Unalaska city	4,376	4,516	3.2	4,536	29.9	5.3	42.1	10.8	11.9	15.7	78.9	5.2	853	27.0	42.1	21.6
Upper Kalskag city	210	221	5.2	257	1.2	0.0	0.0	96.5	2.3	40.5	52.2	7.4	64	87.5	65.6	0.0
Valdez city	3,977	3,921	-1.4	4,002	72.5	0.1	1.1	17.7	8.5	28.4	68.3	3.0	1,296	73.8	20.7	14.0
Venetie CDP	166	NA	NA	171	3.5	0.0	0.0	96.5	0.0	34.0	58.5	7.6	62	80.6	83.9	0.0
Wainwright city	556	580	4.3	482	1.2	0.0	0.0	98.1	0.6	31.8	58.9	9.3	135	71.1	64.4	0.0
Wales city	145	149	2.8	165	4.8	0.0	0.0	95.2	0.0	29.7	63.0	7.3	56	50.0	57.1	7.1
Wasilla city	7,831	8,849	13.0	8,406	77.4	2.1	2.1	14.9	3.5	28.7	61.8	9.3	3,094	53.4	35.3	20.2
Whale Pass CDP	31	NA	NA	39	100.0	0.0	0.0	0.0	0.0	0.0	100.0	0.0	27	100.0	55.6	0.0
White Mountain city	190	195	2.6	148	10.1	0.0	0.0	89.9	0.0	33.1	62.8	4.1	58	41.4	58.6	6.9
Whitestone CDP	97	NA	NA	244	90.6	0.0	7.0	0.0	2.5	4.9	84.5	10.7	17	0.0	0.0	0.0
Whitestone Logging Camp CDP	17	NA	NA	46	0.0	0.0	0.0	100.0	0.0	52.1	47.7	0.0	12	0.0	0.0	0.0
Whittier city	220	217	-1.4	246	68.3	0.0	10.6	14.2	6.9	17.9	73.2	8.9	106	34.9	38.7	23.6
Willow CDP	2,102	NA	NA	1,944	89.6	0.0	0.7	6.4	3.3	20.8	67.7	11.5	732	87.2	39.5	17.8
Willow Creek CDP	191	NA	NA	46	100.0	0.0	0.0	0.0	0.0	43.5	56.5	0.0	26	100.0	65.4	0.0
Wiseman CDP	14	NA	NA	13	100.0	0.0	0.0	0.0	0.0	30.8	69.3	0.0	5	100.0	100.0	0.0
Womens Bay CDP	719	NA	NA	854	63.0	7.4	1.4	18.0	10.2	20.5	71.0	8.5	288	85.4	28.1	23.6
Wrangell city and borough	2,365	2,364	0.0	2,383	71.2	0.2	3.1	24.5	1.0	16.5	58.4	25.1	1,163	72.0	43.3	19.4
Yakutat CDP	662	NA	NA	587	38.5	1.9	1.9	53.2	4.6	24.3	65.6	10.1	265	47.2	43.0	21.9
ARIZONA	6,392,310	6,731,484	5.3	6,561,516	56.9	3.9	2.8	6.2	30.1	24.7	60.3	14.9	2,387,246	63.4	32.9	30.1
Aguila CDP	798	NA	NA	901	1.9	2.2	0.0	0.6	95.3	20.9	71.2	8.1	179	72.1	92.2	0.0
Ajo CDP	3,304	NA	NA	3,787	41.0	1.3	3.6	15.2	38.9	20.7	51.6	27.7	1,585	60.7	53.6	19.2
Ak Chin CDP	30	NA	NA	25	0.0	0.0	0.0	100.0	0.0	24.0	76.0	0.0	7	100.0	42.9	0.0
Ak-Chin Village CDP	862	NA	NA	1,195	4.5	0.4	0.0	82.8	12.2	35.4	60.3	4.4	361	9.1	68.7	3.3
Alamo Lake CDP	25	NA	NA	22	100.0	0.0	0.0	0.0	0.0	0.0	100.0	0.0	11	100.0	81.8	0.0
Ali Chuk CDP	161	NA	NA	119	0.0	0.0	0.0	77.3	22.7	13.4	81.5	5.0	36	100.0	83.3	0.0
Ali Chukson CDP	132	NA	NA	107	0.0	0.0	0.0	100.0	0.0	22.4	60.7	16.8	36	80.6	100.0	0.0
Ali Molina CDP	71	NA	NA	142	0.0	0.0	0.0	100.0	0.0	40.8	51.3	7.7	39	100.0	74.4	0.0
Alpine CDP	145	NA	NA	127	100.0	0.0	0.0	0.0	0.0	0.0	47.2	52.8	62	35.5	56.5	0.0
Amado CDP	295	NA	NA	166	48.8	0.0	0.0	0.0	51.2	0.0	72.1	27.7	100	76.0	50.0	31.0
Anegam CDP	151	NA	NA	77	3.9	0.0	0.0	96.1	0.0	19.5	75.4	5.2	21	100.0	76.2	0.0
Antares CDP	126	NA	NA	127	100.0	0.0	0.0	0.0	0.0	0.0	62.9	37.0	73	67.1	58.9	0.0
Anthem CDP	21,700	NA	NA	23,995	78.4	2.1	3.6	0.9	15.1	35.5	53.4	10.9	7,879	73.6	12.8	48.5
Apache Junction city	35,838	38,131	6.4	36,965	77.9	1.3	0.8	3.2	16.8	20.0	52.7	27.4	15,519	72.7	44.4	14.3
Arivaca CDP	695	NA	NA	635	94.5	0.0	0.0	3.5	2.0	5.8	53.9	40.3	346	72.3	26.0	27.5
Arivaca Junction CDP	1,090	NA	NA	848	48.0	2.2	0.0	0.0	49.8	33.2	56.3	10.6	283	78.8	47.7	15.2
Arizona City CDP	10,475	NA	NA	9,573	52.4	7.1	0.0	3.1	37.4	23.9	64.1	12.0	3,692	65.6	45.2	13.9
Arizona Village CDP	946	NA	NA	737	42.5	0.0	0.0	39.3	18.2	30.3	42.9	26.7	239	43.9	62.3	6.3
Arlington CDP	194	NA	NA	38	100.0	0.0	0.0	0.0	0.0	0.0	57.8	42.1	19	100.0	42.1	15.8
Ash Fork CDP	396	NA	NA	767	37.8	0.0	0.0	0.0	62.2	43.2	41.6	15.3	212	73.1	64.6	10.8
Avenue B and C CDP	4,176	NA	NA	4,059	22.1	3.0	1.0	1.7	72.1	26.5	59.3	14.3	1,606	57.5	58.1	6.1
Avondale city	76,130	79,646	4.6	77,912	31.9	8.9	3.3	2.6	53.3	31.0	62.5	6.4	23,030	57.3	38.3	22.9
Avra Valley CDP	6,050	NA	NA	4,919	73.6	2.7	0.3	5.7	17.7	17.1	61.7	21.0	1,991	83.6	39.8	14.8
Aztec CDP	47	NA	NA	3	100.0	0.0	0.0	0.0	0.0	0.0	100.0	0.0	3	100.0	0.0	0.0
Bagdad CDP	1,876	NA	NA	1,932	77.3	1.4	0.0	1.7	19.7	35.8	63.3	0.9	621	1.4	53.5	7.1
Bear Flat CDP	18	NA	NA	9	100.0	0.0	0.0	0.0	0.0	0.0	44.4	55.6	4	100.0	0.0	0.0
Beaver Dam CDP	1,962	NA	NA	1,643	93.1	0.0	2.9	0.0	4.0	22.2	54.3	23.5	538	92.6	53.3	13.6
Beaver Valley CDP	231	NA	NA	173	100.0	0.0	0.0	0.0	0.0	0.0	56.7	43.4	82	64.6	12.2	0.0
Benson city	5,105	4,927	-3.5	5,075	73.4	0.3	0.4	2.8	23.1	16.8	46.6	36.6	2,374	68.5	39.3	23.0
Beyerville CDP	177	NA	NA	301	3.0	0.0	0.0	0.0	97.0	37.6	60.4	2.0	55	7.3	45.5	5.5
Bisbee city	5,571	5,308	-4.7	5,475	56.3	1.3	0.9	2.5	39.1	17.3	61.2	21.5	2,685	63.9	32.1	30.8
Bitter Springs CDP	452	NA	NA	362	1.9	0.0	0.0	98.1	0.0	21.5	66.8	11.6	93	87.1	81.7	0.0
Black Canyon City CDP	2,837	NA	NA	2,542	85.3	0.0	0.9	3.0	10.8	6.8	57.7	35.6	1,145	85.9	45.2	8.0
Blackwater CDP	1,062	NA	NA	1,246	3.0	1.5	1.6	82.8	11.0	33.5	56.6	9.9	335	35.5	77.3	0.0
Bluewater CDP	725	NA	NA	723	72.1	0.0	1.4	14.4	12.2	9.0	53.8	37.2	421	72.9	46.8	20.4
Bouse CDP	996	NA	NA	662	98.0	0.0	1.5	0.0	0.5	7.6	37.5	55.1	404	93.1	59.7	9.2
Bowie CDP	449	NA	NA	417	40.5	0.0	0.0	1.0	58.5	19.7	47.7	32.6	158	74.1	63.3	3.2
Brenda CDP	676	NA	NA	416	96.6	0.0	0.0	0.0	3.4	0.0	23.1	76.9	229	90.8	59.4	11.8
Bryce CDP	175	NA	NA	100	72.0	0.0	0.0	0.0	28.0	32.0	61.0	7.0	42	54.8	0.0	14.3
Buckeye town	50,891	59,470	16.9	54,927	50.5	7.1	1.6	3.2	37.6	30.4	61.3	8.3	15,396	66.4	36.7	19.8
Buckshot CDP	153	NA	NA	0	0.0	0.0	0.0	0.0	0.0	0.0	0.0	0.0	0	0.0	0.0	0.0
Bullhead City city	39,540	39,364	-0.4	39,480	73.9	1.2	1.5	2.1	21.4	19.2	53.6	27.3	16,796	60.4	48.0	14.8
Burnside CDP	537	NA	NA	648	13.6	0.0	0.0	86.4	0.0	32.7	61.2	6.0	145	35.2	46.2	20.0
Bylas CDP	1,962	NA	NA	1,595	1.4	0.6	0.0	94.5	3.4	29.7	63.2	7.3	393	76.1	68.7	3.1
Cactus Flats CDP	1,518	NA	NA	1,393	69.3	0.0	0.0	0.0	30.7	30.9	55.1	14.0	469	84.6	47.3	6.2
Cactus Forest CDP	594	NA	NA	491	85.1	0.0	0.0	0.0	14.9	33.2	47.4	19.3	210	56.2	60.0	14.3
Cameron CDP	885	NA	NA	1,241	4.1	0.2	0.0	93.4	2.3	31.5	58.3	10.2	314	79.0	64.6	7.0
Campo Bonito CDP	74	NA	NA	0	0.0	0.0	0.0	0.0	0.0	0.0	0.0	0.0	0	0.0	0.0	0.0
Camp Verde town	10,873	11,097	2.1	10,965	76.2	0.2	0.0	10.3	13.3	18.8	60.2	20.9	4,251	68.4	46.8	17.4

1 May be of any race.

Table A. All Places — **Population and Housing**

STATE City, town, township, borough, or CDP (county if applicable)	Population				Race and Hispanic or Latino origin (percent), 2010–2014					Age (percent), 2010–2014			Households, 2010–2014			
	2010 census total population	2014 estimated population	Percent change 2010–2014	ACS total population estimate 2010–2014	White alone, not Hispanic or Latino	Black alone, not Hispanic or Latino	Asian alone, not Hispanic or Latino	All other races or 2 or more races, not Hispanic or Latino	Hispanic or Latino[1]	Under 18 years old	Age 18 to 64 years old	Age 65 years and older	Total occupied housing units	Percent owner occupied	Householders by level of education (percent): High school diploma or less	Householders by level of education (percent): Bachelor's degree or more
	1	2	3	4	5	6	7	8	9	10	11	12	13	14	15	16
ARIZONA—Con.																
Cane Beds CDP	448	NA	NA	551	75.5	0.0	0.0	24.5	0.0	51.9	41.5	6.7	140	65.0	62.1	0.0
Canyon Day CDP	1,209	NA	NA	1,243	0.6	0.0	0.0	99.4	0.0	30.7	64.0	5.6	300	71.7	37.3	8.3
Carefree town	3,363	3,526	4.8	3,445	96.8	0.0	0.0	0.0	3.2	3.4	49.7	46.8	1,850	82.3	18.4	66.1
Carrizo CDP	127	NA	NA	182	0.0	0.0	0.0	100.0	0.0	36.8	50.4	12.6	40	100.0	75.0	0.0
Casa Blanca CDP	1,388	NA	NA	1,848	3.3	0.0	2.3	89.0	5.4	30.8	63.6	5.7	388	49.7	70.9	4.6
Casa Grande city	48,583	51,478	6.0	50,316	50.6	4.9	2.6	3.5	38.4	27.3	54.6	18.0	17,672	67.4	39.2	20.1
Casas Adobes CDP	66,795	NA	NA	68,525	70.3	1.3	3.1	2.8	22.5	21.8	60.0	18.4	27,593	64.8	24.0	37.1
Catalina CDP	7,569	NA	NA	7,527	73.4	0.6	0.2	1.9	23.9	21.7	58.0	20.2	2,866	84.3	35.4	25.8
Catalina Foothills CDP	50,796	NA	NA	50,643	79.9	1.9	5.4	2.7	10.2	15.6	57.1	27.2	23,549	72.1	10.0	67.2
Cave Creek town	4,819	5,253	9.0	5,014	92.5	0.8	0.5	2.3	3.8	15.7	61.0	23.3	2,137	83.3	15.6	52.2
Cedar Creek CDP	318	NA	NA	511	2.3	0.0	0.0	97.7	0.0	43.9	48.6	7.4	114	65.8	63.2	9.6
Centennial Park CDP	1,264	NA	NA	1,315	100.0	0.0	0.0	0.0	0.0	66.4	30.6	2.9	230	57.4	23.9	20.4
Central CDP	645	NA	NA	422	98.3	0.0	0.0	0.0	1.7	28.7	60.1	11.4	150	82.0	51.3	15.3
Central Heights-Midland City CDP	2,534	NA	NA	2,857	74.5	0.0	0.0	2.3	23.2	15.9	67.3	16.8	1,086	73.2	43.2	15.7
Chandler city	236,167	254,276	7.7	245,231	58.3	4.9	8.8	4.4	23.6	27.3	64.1	8.8	86,853	62.4	21.8	43.0
Charco CDP	52	NA	NA	23	0.0	0.0	0.0	100.0	0.0	0.0	82.6	17.4	23	17.4	100.0	0.0
Chiawuli Tak CDP	78	NA	NA	43	0.0	0.0	0.0	100.0	0.0	0.0	100.1	0.0	10	100.0	100.0	0.0
Chilchinbito CDP	506	NA	NA	738	0.0	1.1	0.0	98.9	0.0	34.1	56.2	9.6	185	54.6	73.5	7.0
Chinle CDP	4,518	NA	NA	4,743	7.9	0.6	0.8	85.0	5.8	41.6	50.8	7.6	1,133	31.3	36.7	25.4
Chino Valley town	10,817	11,019	1.9	10,879	88.1	0.2	0.3	2.7	8.8	19.5	57.2	23.3	4,422	74.9	36.9	17.2
Chloride CDP	271	NA	NA	197	85.8	0.0	0.0	14.2	0.0	6.6	34.9	58.4	137	83.2	50.4	11.7
Christopher Creek CDP	156	NA	NA	73	100.0	0.0	0.0	0.0	0.0	0.0	31.5	68.5	51	100.0	13.7	0.0
Chuichu CDP	269	NA	NA	260	0.0	0.0	0.0	100.0	0.0	23.8	76.2	0.0	48	10.4	56.3	0.0
Cibecue CDP	1,713	NA	NA	1,797	0.6	1.2	0.0	89.4	8.8	35.2	61.6	3.3	439	44.2	70.8	4.6
Cibola CDP	250	NA	NA	285	80.4	0.0	3.5	0.0	16.1	23.1	56.1	20.7	121	91.7	71.9	8.3
Cienega Springs CDP	1,798	NA	NA	1,897	94.3	0.0	0.0	0.0	5.7	13.7	56.0	30.2	1,037	67.3	37.3	13.3
Citrus Park CDP	4,028	NA	NA	4,379	77.5	0.0	6.3	3.6	12.6	21.0	68.5	10.3	1,434	84.3	17.2	28.5
Clacks Canyon CDP	173	NA	NA	166	100.0	0.0	0.0	0.0	0.0	22.9	55.4	21.7	50	100.0	18.0	26.0
Clarkdale town	4,092	4,165	1.8	4,101	74.8	0.6	0.0	11.5	13.1	12.7	54.8	32.6	1,786	73.6	32.6	17.4
Claypool CDP	1,538	NA	NA	1,958	62.8	0.0	0.0	0.0	37.2	28.5	50.3	21.2	690	72.8	52.2	4.1
Clay Springs CDP	401	NA	NA	679	81.3	0.0	0.0	18.7	0.0	57.0	38.3	4.7	128	82.0	65.6	0.0
Clifton town	3,311	3,626	9.5	3,430	31.7	2.2	0.3	4.2	61.6	33.9	60.1	6.0	1,233	23.7	55.0	11.4
Colorado City town	4,820	4,792	-0.6	4,816	99.9	0.0	0.0	0.1	0.0	54.8	43.7	1.6	534	9.6	58.8	7.1
Comobabi CDP	8	NA	NA	54	0.0	0.0	0.0	100.0	0.0	68.5	31.5	0.0	9	0.0	0.0	0.0
Concho CDP	38	NA	NA	285	6.0	0.0	0.0	27.7	66.3	45.6	28.8	25.6	56	100.0	69.6	0.0
Congress CDP	1,975	NA	NA	1,138	84.5	0.0	0.0	0.0	15.5	8.1	34.9	56.9	585	86.8	30.4	12.6
Coolidge city	11,825	12,209	3.2	12,058	50.4	4.7	0.4	6.7	37.8	29.5	57.9	12.6	3,839	62.9	52.5	8.9
Copper Hill CDP	108	NA	NA	19	100.0	0.0	0.0	0.0	0.0	0.0	100.0	0.0	9	100.0	0.0	0.0
Cordes Lakes CDP	2,633	NA	NA	2,758	89.1	0.0	0.0	1.0	9.9	9.5	57.6	32.9	1,365	76.1	64.0	7.6
Cornfields CDP	255	NA	NA	258	0.0	0.0	0.0	99.2	0.8	27.9	58.4	13.6	45	77.8	60.0	8.9
Cornville CDP	3,280	NA	NA	2,780	86.0	0.0	0.0	6.2	7.8	13.4	54.4	32.2	1,424	87.9	30.0	36.8
Corona de Tucson CDP	5,675	NA	NA	7,172	66.1	11.4	1.7	3.9	16.9	33.0	58.1	8.8	2,255	83.6	11.7	39.6
Cottonwood CDP	226	NA	NA	185	0.0	0.0	0.0	97.3	2.7	31.4	54.1	14.6	60	38.3	41.7	20.0
Cottonwood city	11,271	11,595	2.9	11,358	65.1	1.2	0.1	3.5	30.2	21.0	55.2	23.8	4,784	57.5	43.1	18.3
Cowlic CDP	135	NA	NA	95	0.0	0.0	0.0	100.0	0.0	25.2	65.2	9.5	17	100.0	100.0	0.0
Crozier CDP	14	NA	NA	24	62.5	4.2	0.0	4.2	29.2	0.0	79.3	20.8	11	18.2	36.4	0.0
Crystal Beach CDP	279	NA	NA	177	98.3	0.0	0.0	1.7	0.0	0.0	78.6	21.5	91	80.2	41.8	0.0
Cutter CDP	74	NA	NA	67	20.9	14.9	0.0	64.2	0.0	17.9	61.1	20.9	21	100.0	0.0	0.0
Dateland CDP	416	NA	NA	317	38.5	0.0	0.0	0.0	61.5	24.6	61.3	14.2	114	85.1	83.3	4.4
Deer Creek CDP	216	NA	NA	245	94.7	0.0	0.0	0.0	5.3	20.0	49.9	30.2	100	80.0	42.0	19.0
Del Muerto CDP	329	NA	NA	385	0.0	0.0	2.3	88.1	9.6	24.7	72.8	2.3	92	100.0	87.0	0.0
Dennehotso CDP	746	NA	NA	708	0.0	0.0	0.0	100.0	0.0	30.5	61.1	8.5	169	92.3	75.7	6.5
Desert Hills CDP	2,245	NA	NA	2,508	76.8	0.0	0.7	1.7	20.8	15.7	48.5	35.9	1,163	83.1	45.7	11.8
Dewey-Humboldt town	3,894	3,971	2.0	3,913	85.7	0.5	0.0	2.0	11.8	16.7	60.7	22.6	1,660	85.5	27.8	21.4
Dilkon CDP	1,184	NA	NA	1,380	0.0	0.0	0.0	97.3	2.7	35.1	54.8	9.9	329	36.5	51.4	6.1
Dolan Springs CDP	2,033	NA	NA	2,254	89.4	0.0	0.0	0.6	9.9	9.8	56.4	33.7	970	87.5	47.9	11.1
Doney Park CDP	5,395	NA	NA	5,860	75.8	1.0	0.7	9.2	13.4	26.9	66.9	6.3	1,919	78.2	28.5	33.9
Donovan Estates CDP	1,508	NA	NA	1,351	8.4	0.0	0.0	0.0	91.6	29.4	62.5	8.1	392	74.7	78.8	1.5
Douglas city	17,504	16,744	-4.3	17,137	16.4	5.3	1.7	1.4	75.3	22.5	66.7	10.7	4,216	59.9	55.0	15.6
Dragoon CDP	209	NA	NA	255	87.5	0.0	0.0	4.7	7.8	0.0	63.9	36.1	108	100.0	71.3	28.7
Drexel Heights CDP	27,749	NA	NA	28,291	22.4	0.8	0.4	4.7	71.7	29.5	60.1	10.3	8,781	75.3	49.4	13.6
Dripping Springs CDP	235	NA	NA	116	65.5	0.0	0.0	3.4	31.0	8.6	36.2	55.2	62	87.1	32.3	22.6
Drysdale CDP	272	NA	NA	175	5.7	0.0	0.0	0.0	94.3	40.0	57.1	2.9	60	73.3	100.0	0.0
Dudleyville CDP	959	NA	NA	454	26.4	0.0	0.0	0.0	73.6	20.3	53.1	26.7	176	80.1	48.9	0.0
Duncan town	696	783	12.5	655	65.0	0.0	0.0	2.7	32.2	22.3	62.1	15.4	290	73.8	53.8	12.8
Eagar town	4,893	4,913	0.4	4,935	73.1	0.4	0.0	8.7	17.8	37.1	49.0	13.9	1,466	81.5	41.0	15.0
East Fork CDP	699	NA	NA	507	0.0	0.0	0.0	100.0	0.0	21.3	64.9	13.8	161	75.2	96.3	0.0
East Globe CDP	226	NA	NA	137	0.0	0.0	38.7	61.3	0.0	35.8	64.2	0.0	45	100.0	57.8	42.2
East Verde Estates CDP	170	NA	NA	199	100.0	0.0	0.0	0.0	0.0	27.6	45.2	27.1	69	100.0	58.0	23.2
Ehrenberg CDP	1,470	NA	NA	1,017	81.0	0.0	1.3	0.0	17.7	23.2	65.8	11.0	432	53.5	49.8	5.1
El Capitan CDP	37	NA	NA	133	100.0	0.0	0.0	0.0	0.0	30.1	69.9	0.0	32	100.0	25.0	46.9
Elephant Head CDP	612	NA	NA	694	52.3	0.7	0.9	0.7	45.4	22.5	56.8	20.6	256	82.8	28.9	35.2
Elfrida CDP	459	NA	NA	285	48.8	0.0	0.0	4.6	46.7	29.2	57.9	13.0	118	75.4	49.2	10.2
Elgin CDP	161	NA	NA	198	82.3	0.0	0.0	9.1	8.6	25.7	49.6	24.7	74	89.2	32.4	35.1
El Mirage city	31,797	33,532	5.5	32,600	43.7	4.5	0.8	3.9	47.0	32.9	58.9	8.3	9,888	63.1	40.3	17.1
Eloy city	16,676	16,738	0.4	17,062	19.6	7.0	2.3	4.7	66.3	20.1	71.6	8.3	3,280	61.8	64.7	8.2
El Prado Estates CDP	504	NA	NA	337	3.9	0.0	0.0	0.0	96.1	37.1	61.7	1.2	103	40.8	85.4	3.9
First Mesa CDP	1,555	NA	NA	1,929	1.4	0.0	0.7	97.9	0.0	33.4	55.2	11.3	434	86.2	50.2	15.9
Flagstaff city	66,067	68,785	4.1	67,419	63.1	2.0	2.5	13.5	18.8	19.5	72.9	7.6	23,239	44.9	19.3	41.0
Florence town	25,526	26,912	5.4	26,513	47.4	5.8	0.6	4.4	41.9	9.4	73.4	17.2	5,232	72.8	42.2	15.6
Flowing Springs CDP	42	NA	NA	6	100.0	0.0	0.0	0.0	0.0	0.0	50.0	50.0	3	100.0	0.0	0.0
Flowing Wells CDP	16,419	NA	NA	16,062	54.8	0.9	2.2	3.3	38.8	21.2	60.1	18.8	6,728	70.0	45.2	11.5
Fort Apache CDP	143	NA	NA	123	4.9	0.0	0.0	66.7	28.5	27.6	63.5	8.9	26	57.7	19.2	42.3
Fort Defiance CDP	3,624	NA	NA	4,044	3.3	0.0	0.0	95.8	0.8	30.9	61.4	7.8	929	61.2	44.6	14.3
Fort Mohave CDP	14,364	NA	NA	13,862	80.0	0.0	2.2	2.4	15.3	15.1	59.2	25.7	5,956	71.1	47.4	13.1
Fort Thomas CDP	374	NA	NA	517	90.3	0.0	0.0	1.5	8.1	42.5	45.3	12.2	135	94.1	36.3	38.5
Fortuna Foothills CDP	26,265	NA	NA	27,181	77.8	0.3	1.1	2.7	18.1	14.4	43.4	42.2	12,475	85.1	39.8	21.4
Fort Valley CDP	779	NA	NA	962	66.9	0.0	0.0	12.3	20.8	24.6	66.8	8.6	336	94.3	4.5	59.2
Fountain Hills town	22,489	23,573	4.8	23,051	91.5	1.7	1.8	1.6	3.4	14.3	55.5	30.1	10,669	82.3	17.3	49.8
Franklin CDP	92	NA	NA	45	75.6	0.0	0.0	0.0	24.4	40.0	40.0	20.0	23	78.3	0.0	39.1

1 May be of any race.

Table A. All Places — **Population and Housing**

STATE City, town, township, borough, or CDP (county if applicable)	2010 census total population	2014 estimated population	Percent change 2010–2014	ACS total population estimate 2010–2014	White alone, not Hispanic or Latino	Black alone, not Hispanic or Latino	Asian alone, not Hispanic or Latino	All other races or 2 or more races, not Hispanic or Latino	Hispanic or Latino[1]	Under 18 years old	Age 18 to 64 years old	Age 65 years and older	Total occupied housing units	Percent owner occupied	High school diploma or less	Bachelor's degree or more
	1	2	3	4	5	6	7	8	9	10	11	12	13	14	15	16
ARIZONA—Con.																
Fredonia town	1,328	1,317	-0.8	1,670	78.8	0.0	2.5	16.2	2.5	29.4	53.6	16.9	554	78.9	38.8	19.5
Freedom Acres CDP	84	NA	NA	60	100.0	0.0	0.0	0.0	0.0	8.3	30.0	61.7	32	100.0	15.6	21.9
Gadsden CDP	678	NA	NA	714	1.1	0.0	0.0	0.0	98.9	33.6	60.4	6.0	216	63.4	60.2	11.6
Ganado CDP	1,210	NA	NA	1,149	3.2	0.0	1.2	94.2	1.4	34.8	51.3	13.8	294	59.9	36.7	18.4
Geronimo Estates CDP	60	NA	NA	202	84.2	0.0	0.0	0.0	15.8	44.6	31.7	23.8	52	34.6	19.2	15.4
Gila Bend town	1,921	2,001	4.2	1,965	22.3	0.9	0.5	4.3	72.0	34.3	54.6	11.0	647	58.7	66.2	13.4
Gila Crossing CDP	621	NA	NA	544	5.7	0.0	2.4	69.9	22.1	33.7	62.5	3.9	111	69.4	67.6	16.2
Gilbert town	208,399	239,277	14.8	223,131	71.5	3.2	6.2	3.6	15.6	32.1	60.7	7.2	71,614	71.3	17.4	43.9
Gisela CDP	570	NA	NA	620	78.4	0.0	0.0	1.3	20.3	24.0	55.2	20.6	266	66.2	34.2	32.7
Glendale city	226,437	237,517	4.9	231,978	50.1	5.7	3.6	3.6	36.9	27.3	63.0	9.7	78,496	55.8	37.5	24.3
Globe city	7,534	7,375	-2.1	7,463	47.0	1.2	1.6	6.1	44.1	23.6	55.2	21.0	2,722	60.8	41.0	21.5
Gold Canyon CDP	0	NA	NA	9,392	91.6	0.5	1.3	1.5	5.0	5.9	49.7	44.2	4,483	90.0	21.5	41.3
Golden Shores CDP	2,047	NA	NA	1,817	80.2	0.0	0.0	7.5	12.3	11.2	52.4	36.4	791	83.9	57.6	13.0
Golden Valley CDP	8,370	NA	NA	8,162	86.1	0.6	1.9	4.2	7.2	12.7	57.6	29.7	3,750	81.1	47.7	7.2
Goodyear city	65,225	75,664	16.0	70,148	56.2	7.8	3.9	3.7	28.4	26.4	61.0	12.7	22,873	69.4	28.3	32.2
Goodyear Village CDP	457	NA	NA	496	0.0	0.0	0.0	78.2	21.8	26.0	65.9	8.1	90	76.7	52.2	0.0
Grand Canyon Village CDP	2,004	NA	NA	1,345	66.1	3.2	1.3	16.1	13.4	6.9	86.4	6.6	416	31.0	14.7	29.3
Grand Canyon West CDP	2	NA	NA	0	0.0	0.0	0.0	0.0	0.0	0.0	0.0	0.0	0	0.0	0.0	0.0
Greasewood CDP	547	NA	NA	451	0.4	0.0	0.0	92.2	7.3	37.7	50.8	11.5	128	47.7	33.6	10.2
Green Valley CDP	21,391	NA	NA	22,519	92.7	0.2	0.5	0.4	6.3	2.6	25.1	72.4	13,226	82.9	23.8	43.7
Greer CDP	41	NA	NA	0	0.0	0.0	0.0	0.0	0.0	0.0	0.0	0.0	0	0.0	0.0	0.0
Guadalupe town	5,520	6,106	10.6	5,892	2.9	2.2	0.0	32.3	62.7	31.7	60.0	8.4	1,555	54.7	61.3	5.8
Gu Oidak CDP	188	NA	NA	96	0.0	0.0	0.0	100.0	0.0	24.0	76.0	0.0	24	70.8	29.2	0.0
Hackberry CDP	68	NA	NA	86	100.0	0.0	0.0	0.0	0.0	0.0	60.4	39.5	49	89.8	61.2	8.2
Haigler Creek CDP	19	NA	NA	8	100.0	0.0	0.0	0.0	0.0	0.0	50.0	50.0	4	100.0	100.0	0.0
Haivana Nakya CDP	96	NA	NA	251	0.0	0.0	0.0	100.0	0.0	33.9	60.2	6.0	55	76.4	81.8	0.0
Hard Rock CDP	94	NA	NA	65	0.0	0.0	0.0	100.0	0.0	40.0	37.1	23.1	13	100.0	76.9	0.0
Hayden town	662	648	-2.1	612	5.6	0.0	0.0	0.0	94.4	23.0	60.8	16.2	192	73.4	62.0	0.0
Heber-Overgaard CDP	2,822	NA	NA	3,006	64.3	0.0	0.3	17.6	17.7	28.2	56.6	15.2	960	61.5	59.2	16.1
Holbrook city	5,053	5,016	-0.7	5,003	52.8	0.4	1.2	23.5	22.2	28.2	58.6	13.2	1,625	69.2	39.4	18.3
Hondah CDP	812	NA	NA	1,020	7.4	1.9	0.0	79.2	11.6	37.0	58.8	4.3	301	54.2	46.5	13.0
Hotevilla-Bacavi CDP	957	NA	NA	1,300	2.7	0.0	0.0	95.7	1.6	35.8	53.7	10.5	311	71.7	47.3	13.2
Houck CDP	1,024	NA	NA	1,170	0.1	0.0	0.0	99.6	0.3	21.9	66.9	11.2	274	89.4	70.4	4.4
Huachuca City town	1,853	1,775	-4.2	2,246	56.0	11.4	1.2	2.4	29.0	30.5	58.1	11.6	925	55.9	38.4	10.2
Hunter Creek CDP	48	NA	NA	49	100.0	0.0	0.0	0.0	0.0	0.0	0.0	100.0	25	100.0	0.0	100.0
Icehouse Canyon CDP	677	NA	NA	832	48.2	4.0	0.0	13.6	34.3	25.5	56.4	18.1	330	52.1	44.2	14.5
Indian Wells CDP	255	NA	NA	146	0.0	0.0	0.0	95.2	4.8	21.9	62.9	15.1	40	75.0	52.5	0.0
Jakes Corner CDP	76	NA	NA	52	100.0	0.0	0.0	0.0	0.0	0.0	76.9	23.1	46	87.0	26.1	0.0
Jeddito CDP	293	NA	NA	282	0.4	0.0	0.7	98.9	0.0	40.1	50.7	9.2	73	31.5	63.0	12.3
Jerome town	444	451	1.6	392	87.2	0.8	2.3	3.3	6.4	8.9	74.5	16.6	206	58.3	17.0	48.1
Joseph City CDP	1,386	NA	NA	1,143	59.8	0.0	0.0	38.3	1.9	38.8	51.6	9.4	344	70.1	30.8	11.0
Kachina Village CDP	2,622	NA	NA	2,940	75.6	0.0	0.0	13.8	10.6	22.1	65.9	12.0	1,353	83.1	22.4	36.6
Kaibab CDP	124	NA	NA	202	17.8	0.0	0.0	79.7	2.5	37.2	45.7	17.3	71	32.4	31.0	0.0
Kaibito CDP	1,522	NA	NA	1,777	0.2	0.0	0.0	97.1	2.7	38.1	57.3	4.7	379	55.1	57.5	6.9
Kaka CDP	141	NA	NA	99	0.0	0.0	0.0	100.0	0.0	29.3	55.7	15.2	32	90.6	81.3	0.0
Katherine CDP	103	NA	NA	79	93.7	3.8	0.0	2.5	0.0	0.0	56.9	43.0	49	87.8	18.4	0.0
Kayenta CDP	5,189	NA	NA	5,094	3.1	0.0	1.1	91.2	4.7	36.9	58.1	5.1	1,325	48.8	53.1	18.1
Keams Canyon CDP	304	NA	NA	245	0.0	0.0	0.0	87.3	12.7	8.2	57.5	34.3	67	59.7	14.9	23.9
Kearny town	1,950	2,017	3.4	2,394	43.9	0.0	2.2	1.0	52.8	25.2	57.4	17.3	714	82.6	45.7	10.2
Kingman city	28,068	28,549	1.7	28,381	79.7	0.7	0.5	5.7	13.3	21.9	56.8	21.4	10,715	62.9	39.8	15.8
Kino Springs CDP	136	NA	NA	227	31.7	0.0	0.0	0.0	68.3	27.3	64.3	8.4	76	55.3	26.3	39.5
Klagetoh CDP	242	NA	NA	296	0.0	0.0	0.0	100.0	0.0	27.7	51.3	20.9	72	58.3	59.7	9.7
Kohatk CDP	27	NA	NA	21	0.0	0.0	0.0	100.0	0.0	0.0	100.0	0.0	21	100.0	100.0	0.0
Kohls Ranch CDP	46	NA	NA	32	100.0	0.0	0.0	0.0	0.0	0.0	34.4	65.6	19	100.0	0.0	36.8
Komatke CDP	821	NA	NA	1,418	2.8	0.4	1.1	82.0	13.8	47.2	49.4	3.2	282	42.9	68.8	6.0
Ko Vaya CDP	0	NA	NA	15	0.0	0.0	0.0	100.0	0.0	53.4	46.7	0.0	3	100.0	0.0	100.0
Kykotsmovi Village CDP	746	NA	NA	827	0.5	0.0	0.0	99.5	0.0	23.8	60.7	15.6	283	82.3	33.9	7.1
Lake Havasu City city	52,532	53,103	1.1	52,827	83.3	0.6	1.3	1.9	12.9	17.8	52.8	29.3	22,633	68.5	39.5	17.1
Lake Montezuma CDP	4,706	NA	NA	5,594	85.1	0.0	0.0	3.6	11.2	12.6	67.3	20.1	2,318	69.9	38.6	25.5
Lake of the Woods CDP	4,094	NA	NA	3,970	68.1	0.8	1.3	1.8	28.0	26.9	51.6	21.4	1,512	70.7	40.9	15.8
La Paz Valley CDP	699	NA	NA	644	93.3	0.0	0.0	2.5	4.2	0.0	0.0	100.0	419	88.8	63.0	0.0
Lazy Y U CDP	428	NA	NA	670	93.9	0.0	6.1	0.0	0.0	48.9	44.3	6.7	170	100.0	12.9	32.9
LeChee CDP	1,443	NA	NA	1,639	0.6	0.1	0.0	98.4	0.9	29.9	63.9	6.3	370	90.8	55.7	5.1
Leupp CDP	951	NA	NA	1,059	0.0	0.0	0.0	97.8	2.2	35.7	53.9	10.3	271	66.8	46.1	9.6
Linden CDP	2,597	NA	NA	2,605	91.3	0.0	1.4	2.0	5.3	26.8	58.8	14.3	999	84.4	28.6	16.4
Litchfield Park city	4,887	5,392	10.3	5,122	76.7	1.6	2.1	2.0	17.6	20.0	56.4	23.6	2,096	81.1	21.1	49.3
Littlefield CDP	308	NA	NA	303	77.9	0.0	0.0	1.7	20.5	37.3	29.4	33.3	90	73.3	33.3	0.0
Littletown CDP	873	NA	NA	503	27.0	0.0	0.0	3.0	70.0	39.4	55.5	5.2	177	77.4	55.4	22.0
Lower Santan Village CDP	374	NA	NA	525	3.0	0.0	0.0	92.4	4.6	33.1	64.7	2.3	124	83.1	83.1	0.0
Low Mountain CDP	757	NA	NA	751	0.0	0.0	0.0	100.0	0.0	34.1	53.5	12.5	198	82.3	65.7	8.1
Lukachukai CDP	1,701	NA	NA	1,790	0.5	0.0	1.2	97.4	0.9	36.3	58.1	5.6	349	84.5	55.9	14.6
Lupton CDP	25	NA	NA	20	0.0	0.0	0.0	100.0	0.0	0.0	100.0	0.0	7	57.1	57.1	0.0
McConnico CDP	70	NA	NA	0	0.0	0.0	0.0	0.0	0.0	0.0	0.0	0.0	0	0.0	0.0	0.0
McNary CDP	528	NA	NA	560	8.2	0.0	0.0	77.1	14.6	38.9	55.4	5.7	115	57.4	58.3	12.2
McNeal CDP	238	NA	NA	302	93.4	0.0	0.0	1.7	5.0	32.8	47.3	19.9	118	61.0	37.3	28.8
Maish Vaya CDP	158	NA	NA	117	0.0	0.0	0.0	100.0	0.0	36.8	54.6	8.5	36	58.3	75.0	8.3
Mammoth town	1,426	1,472	3.2	1,634	31.3	0.0	0.0	3.7	64.9	30.4	55.4	14.3	471	75.4	56.5	7.2
Many Farms CDP	1,348	NA	NA	1,556	0.6	0.0	0.3	96.9	2.2	40.1	54.2	5.7	329	51.7	38.9	31.0
Marana town	34,575	39,888	15.4	37,028	69.1	3.2	3.8	3.0	20.8	26.0	57.6	16.3	13,470	75.9	17.9	43.4
Maricopa city	43,482	47,442	9.1	45,388	60.4	10.5	3.7	4.3	21.2	29.6	62.4	7.9	14,481	78.0	27.6	29.0
Maricopa Colony CDP	709	NA	NA	547	8.6	0.0	0.0	77.7	13.7	37.6	61.6	0.9	110	59.1	54.5	22.7
Martinez Lake CDP	798	NA	NA	43	100.0	0.0	0.0	0.0	0.0	23.3	51.2	25.6	21	57.1	28.6	42.9
Mayer CDP	1,497	NA	NA	911	96.2	0.0	0.0	0.0	3.8	24.2	58.9	17.0	446	68.2	39.7	8.5
Mead Ranch CDP	38	NA	NA	30	36.7	0.0	0.0	0.0	63.3	46.7	53.4	0.0	14	100.0	0.0	78.6
Meadview CDP	1,224	NA	NA	687	83.0	3.9	0.0	10.6	2.5	0.0	47.5	52.4	406	79.3	34.7	7.1
Mesa city	439,865	464,704	5.6	452,091	64.1	3.3	1.9	3.9	26.8	24.7	60.1	15.3	167,609	60.5	35.0	26.2
Mesa del Caballo CDP	765	NA	NA	707	95.9	0.0	0.0	0.0	4.1	26.0	51.7	22.5	285	83.9	44.6	5.3
Mescal CDP	1,812	NA	NA	1,644	90.8	0.0	0.0	0.0	9.2	15.5	55.7	28.6	716	80.9	35.2	14.1
Mesquite Creek CDP	416	NA	NA	504	79.6	0.0	1.4	10.1	8.9	14.0	41.0	45.2	237	78.9	44.7	13.5
Miami town	1,829	1,781	-2.6	1,979	38.2	0.0	1.4	0.7	59.7	24.1	61.2	14.6	737	71.9	47.9	14.1

1 May be of any race.

STATE City, town, township, borough, or CDP (county if applicable)	2010 census total population	2014 estimated population	Percent change 2010–2014	ACS total population estimate 2010–2014	White alone, not Hispanic or Latino	Black alone, not Hispanic or Latino	Asian alone, not Hispanic or Latino	All other races or 2 or more races, not Hispanic or Latino	Hispanic or Latino[1]	Under 18 years old	Age 18 to 64 years old	Age 65 years and older	Total occupied housing units	Percent owner occupied	High school diploma or less	Bachelor's degree or more
	1	2	3	4	5	6	7	8	9	10	11	12	13	14	15	16
ARIZONA—Con.																
Miracle Valley CDP	644	NA	NA	357	88.2	0.0	0.0	0.0	11.8	16.0	60.6	23.5	135	100.0	8.1	10.4
Moccasin CDP	89	NA	NA	160	100.0	0.0	0.0	0.0	0.0	0.0	52.5	47.5	81	100.0	6.2	93.8
Moenkopi CDP	964	NA	NA	1,091	0.0	0.0	0.6	98.9	0.5	26.0	57.5	16.4	256	94.5	58.2	10.5
Mohave Valley CDP	2,616	NA	NA	2,868	70.3	0.0	0.0	2.9	26.8	21.8	60.9	17.4	1,089	65.2	53.0	6.3
Mojave Ranch Estates CDP	52	NA	NA	32	18.8	0.0	0.0	53.1	28.1	15.6	84.6	0.0	8	87.5	37.5	12.5
Morenci CDP	1,489	NA	NA	1,550	49.2	2.3	0.8	3.9	43.9	32.7	65.6	1.7	594	0.0	44.1	20.5
Morristown CDP	0	NA	NA	161	100.0	0.0	0.0	0.0	0.0	5.0	63.5	31.7	73	71.2	78.1	5.5
Mountainaire CDP	1,119	NA	NA	1,114	92.5	0.0	0.0	7.0	0.5	23.5	73.2	3.3	487	75.4	24.2	65.1
Munds Park CDP	631	NA	NA	721	92.5	0.0	0.0	0.0	7.5	8.2	36.7	55.2	312	91.7	9.3	52.2
Naco CDP	1,046	NA	NA	1,080	10.7	0.0	0.0	0.2	89.1	43.5	46.1	10.3	323	70.0	68.4	16.4
Nazlini CDP	489	NA	NA	377	0.0	0.0	0.0	100.0	0.0	36.1	51.2	12.7	95	77.9	53.7	3.2
Nelson CDP	259	NA	NA	954	48.5	7.8	0.0	3.9	39.8	18.2	79.9	1.8	102	88.2	44.1	15.7
New Kingman-Butler CDP	12,134	NA	NA	11,892	77.1	0.2	0.6	4.1	17.9	24.8	55.7	19.6	4,740	65.5	52.9	7.9
New River CDP	14,952	NA	NA	15,432	91.0	0.1	0.2	1.4	7.3	21.3	66.2	12.5	5,685	87.1	27.6	27.3
Nogales city	20,837	20,407	-2.1	20,699	6.0	0.2	0.6	0.4	92.8	30.2	54.8	15.1	6,529	51.2	60.6	15.9
Nolic CDP	37	NA	NA	0	0.0	0.0	0.0	0.0	0.0	0.0	0.0	0.0	0	0.0	0.0	0.0
North Fork CDP	1,417	NA	NA	1,763	5.0	0.4	1.9	84.7	7.9	30.4	66.0	3.6	422	63.5	44.1	19.0
Nutrioso CDP	26	NA	NA	93	100.0	0.0	0.0	0.0	0.0	0.0	39.8	60.2	64	57.8	42.2	0.0
Oak Springs CDP	63	NA	NA	84	0.0	0.0	0.0	100.0	0.0	32.2	56.1	11.9	13	100.0	61.5	0.0
Oatman CDP	135	NA	NA	126	100.0	0.0	0.0	0.0	0.0	0.0	73.8	26.2	89	18.0	82.0	0.0
Oljato-Monument Valley CDP	154	NA	NA	187	0.0	0.0	0.0	100.0	0.0	19.3	67.9	12.8	50	88.0	70.0	0.0
Oracle CDP	3,686	NA	NA	3,887	58.6	0.0	0.0	0.9	40.5	18.4	61.5	20.2	1,704	74.6	30.4	27.9
Orange Grove Mobile Manor CDP	594	NA	NA	600	0.0	0.0	0.0	0.0	100.0	22.8	45.1	32.2	191	100.0	100.0	0.0
Oro Valley town	41,007	42,018	2.5	41,493	82.6	1.2	3.1	2.2	10.8	19.2	52.9	27.8	17,364	74.8	13.3	55.2
Oxbow Estates CDP	217	NA	NA	145	96.6	0.0	0.0	3.4	0.0	11.0	68.9	20.0	61	78.7	54.1	45.9
Padre Ranchitos CDP	171	NA	NA	345	1.4	0.0	0.0	0.0	98.6	36.0	63.8	0.3	87	74.7	82.8	0.0
Page city	7,291	7,440	2.0	7,374	57.4	0.0	0.0	32.3	10.3	33.4	58.7	7.9	2,273	71.8	31.6	22.7
Palominas CDP	212	NA	NA	469	32.2	0.0	0.0	40.7	27.1	66.9	23.3	9.8	109	100.0	23.9	10.1
Paradise Valley town	12,780	13,663	6.9	13,243	87.3	0.4	3.2	1.4	7.7	21.0	55.2	23.8	5,217	93.1	6.3	76.0
Parker town	3,083	3,057	-0.8	3,057	32.5	0.9	0.8	25.4	40.5	26.4	62.8	10.8	1,085	71.2	47.0	12.5
Parker Strip CDP	662	NA	NA	548	97.4	0.0	0.0	0.9	1.6	3.8	45.0	51.1	343	74.1	46.1	29.7
Parks CDP	1,188	NA	NA	1,456	83.5	0.0	0.0	9.0	7.5	20.2	67.2	12.7	613	85.5	23.2	27.2
Patagonia town	913	898	-1.6	697	60.1	0.0	0.0	0.4	39.5	12.0	53.1	34.9	362	56.9	28.7	35.6
Paulden CDP	5,231	NA	NA	4,909	68.2	0.7	0.0	1.7	29.4	23.9	65.5	10.8	1,912	74.5	29.2	2.1
Payson town	15,299	15,245	-0.4	15,234	87.7	0.2	0.2	2.8	9.0	14.7	51.3	34.0	6,621	70.5	34.5	22.3
Peach Springs CDP	1,090	NA	NA	977	6.8	0.1	0.0	86.7	6.4	35.0	61.4	3.6	209	37.3	53.6	4.3
Peeples Valley CDP	428	NA	NA	586	96.8	0.3	0.0	1.5	1.4	27.5	47.0	25.6	251	74.1	53.4	17.9
Peoria city	154,083	166,934	8.3	160,231	70.3	3.0	3.8	3.1	19.7	25.1	59.8	15.1	58,203	70.0	28.1	31.3
Peridot CDP	1,350	NA	NA	1,638	0.0	0.0	0.0	96.0	4.0	39.1	53.6	7.3	353	79.6	59.2	13.3
Phoenix city	1,447,617	1,537,058	6.2	1,490,758	46.0	6.5	3.3	3.8	40.5	27.2	63.6	9.1	520,856	54.0	36.7	29.6
Picacho CDP	471	NA	NA	330	32.4	1.2	0.0	0.0	66.4	14.3	64.3	21.5	104	77.9	63.5	7.7
Picture Rocks CDP	9,563	NA	NA	8,775	81.5	0.6	0.2	3.3	14.3	23.4	60.4	16.1	3,462	79.7	41.2	16.8
Pima town	2,387	2,477	3.8	2,270	70.9	0.1	0.2	2.6	26.2	33.6	52.9	13.5	762	72.0	38.3	24.3
Pimaco Two CDP	682	NA	NA	382	84.8	0.0	0.0	4.5	10.7	0.0	52.4	47.6	222	82.4	42.8	7.2
Pinal CDP	439	NA	NA	280	74.3	0.0	1.8	0.0	23.9	0.0	58.6	41.4	167	67.1	63.5	31.1
Pine CDP	1,963	NA	NA	1,068	96.3	0.0	1.1	2.5	0.0	1.8	51.0	47.1	546	91.8	16.1	53.7
Pinedale CDP	487	NA	NA	560	100.0	0.0	0.0	0.0	0.0	37.7	52.1	10.4	172	92.4	22.7	18.6
Pine Lake CDP	138	NA	NA	88	54.5	0.0	0.0	0.0	45.5	21.6	52.3	26.1	48	100.0	20.8	0.0
Pinetop Country Club CDP	1,794	NA	NA	2,160	81.4	0.0	0.0	7.2	11.4	14.4	46.1	39.5	978	91.1	9.5	50.4
Pinetop-Lakeside town	4,294	4,318	0.6	4,297	90.3	0.0	1.4	4.7	3.5	23.3	55.1	21.7	1,709	74.0	29.0	35.3
Pinion Pines CDP	186	NA	NA	186	100.0	0.0	0.0	0.0	0.0	0.0	41.4	58.6	103	100.0	35.9	0.0
Pinon CDP	904	NA	NA	889	6.0	0.0	9.1	79.5	5.4	37.4	52.4	10.0	266	39.8	47.0	29.3
Pirtleville CDP	1,744	NA	NA	1,451	3.4	0.0	0.0	0.6	96.0	29.3	57.6	13.1	490	79.4	76.5	4.3
Pisinemo CDP	321	NA	NA	428	1.2	11.4	0.0	87.4	0.0	42.4	50.9	6.8	75	54.7	90.7	0.0
Poston CDP	285	NA	NA	346	1.2	0.0	0.0	28.0	70.8	22.8	74.3	2.9	143	43.4	77.6	0.0
Prescott city	39,827	40,958	2.8	40,240	87.1	0.7	1.6	3.1	7.5	13.1	53.8	33.1	18,691	65.7	19.5	41.0
Prescott Valley town	38,822	41,075	5.8	39,575	79.0	0.6	0.9	2.9	16.6	23.4	56.5	20.1	15,611	60.4	36.5	18.9
Quartzsite town	3,677	3,613	-1.7	3,646	95.9	0.0	0.0	0.1	4.0	0.1	31.4	68.5	2,281	90.7	46.5	16.8
Queen Creek town	26,348	32,236	22.3	28,529	76.4	2.5	1.2	2.2	17.7	39.4	54.2	6.5	8,307	79.4	18.1	39.7
Queen Valley CDP	788	NA	NA	813	78.8	0.0	0.0	0.0	21.2	10.2	14.3	75.4	431	91.2	46.6	9.5
Rainbow City CDP	968	NA	NA	1,188	0.0	0.0	0.0	100.0	0.0	31.8	63.5	4.6	217	71.0	80.6	0.0
Rancho Mesa Verde CDP	625	NA	NA	696	0.0	0.0	0.0	0.0	100.0	39.0	48.5	12.6	193	79.3	100.0	0.0
Red Mesa CDP	480	NA	NA	211	23.7	0.0	0.0	76.3	0.0	23.2	55.5	21.3	79	10.1	38.0	32.9
Red Rock CDP (Apache)	0	NA	NA	240	1.7	0.0	0.0	98.3	0.0	20.4	70.0	9.6	58	93.1	77.6	6.9
Red Rock CDP (Pinal)	169	NA	NA	1,980	63.8	5.3	2.1	4.0	24.8	36.3	59.9	3.6	632	85.1	27.4	26.7
Rillito CDP	97	NA	NA	366	7.1	4.4	0.0	0.0	88.5	33.9	43.8	22.4	84	34.5	84.5	0.0
Rincon Valley CDP	5,139	NA	NA	4,784	75.8	0.5	1.0	1.9	20.7	24.1	62.1	13.8	1,720	86.1	20.8	52.8
Rio Rico CDP	18,962	NA	NA	18,837	10.5	0.4	1.3	0.0	87.8	33.2	58.6	8.3	5,596	78.2	40.3	22.9
Rio Verde CDP	1,811	NA	NA	2,102	100.0	0.0	0.0	0.0	0.0	0.8	27.4	71.8	1,081	91.8	17.9	58.8
Rock House CDP	50	NA	NA	14	100.0	0.0	0.0	0.0	0.0	0.0	0.0	100.0	14	100.0	50.0	0.0
Rock Point CDP	642	NA	NA	449	0.0	0.0	0.9	99.1	0.0	44.6	47.0	8.5	110	67.3	55.5	15.5
Roosevelt CDP	28	NA	NA	54	72.2	0.0	0.0	0.0	27.8	0.0	61.2	38.9	21	100.0	76.2	0.0
Rough Rock CDP	414	NA	NA	499	3.2	0.0	0.0	96.8	0.0	44.0	47.6	8.2	98	46.9	32.7	25.5
Round Rock CDP	789	NA	NA	896	1.3	0.0	1.6	95.2	1.9	43.0	47.7	9.3	187	89.3	63.1	7.5
Round Valley CDP	487	NA	NA	613	92.5	0.0	0.0	7.5	0.0	21.1	58.8	20.2	186	85.5	12.4	39.2
Rye CDP	77	NA	NA	63	71.4	0.0	0.0	28.6	0.0	0.0	30.2	69.8	42	0.0	100.0	0.0
Sacate Village CDP	169	NA	NA	211	0.0	0.0	0.0	100.0	0.0	59.3	37.4	3.3	34	5.9	94.1	0.0
Sacaton CDP	2,672	NA	NA	3,131	3.3	0.5	0.7	85.5	10.0	22.1	69.7	8.2	655	51.0	58.3	9.2
Sacaton Flats Village CDP	541	NA	NA	436	0.0	0.0	0.0	82.8	17.2	35.1	60.8	4.1	170	78.8	41.8	6.5
Saddlebrooke CDP	9,614	NA	NA	9,392	94.9	0.2	0.2	0.2	4.4	5.2	32.8	61.9	4,700	96.0	11.3	60.0
Safford city	9,549	9,744	2.0	9,574	51.5	0.8	0.9	2.0	44.8	27.8	55.5	16.9	3,476	66.7	38.3	13.6
Sahuarita town	25,259	27,547	9.1	26,441	59.5	3.6	4.1	2.5	30.2	31.2	52.2	16.9	9,135	80.9	18.2	39.4
St. David CDP	1,699	NA	NA	1,837	89.8	0.0	0.1	0.0	10.1	43.1	42.4	14.3	659	77.8	18.7	37.2
St. Johns city	3,480	3,497	0.5	3,504	61.1	0.2	0.0	8.9	29.8	19.6	63.2	17.2	1,354	74.6	24.2	15.4
St. Johns CDP	476	NA	NA	316	1.3	4.1	0.0	83.2	11.4	34.2	58.5	7.3	73	72.6	63.0	0.0
St. Michaels CDP	1,443	NA	NA	1,434	8.6	0.2	0.8	89.3	1.0	25.7	65.2	9.2	286	87.1	46.2	23.1
Salome CDP	1,530	NA	NA	1,467	63.6	0.0	0.0	0.9	35.5	24.1	36.9	39.1	583	90.4	46.3	25.4

1 May be of any race.

Table A. All Places — **Population and Housing**

STATE City, town, township, borough, or CDP (county if applicable)	2010 census total population	2014 estimated population	Percent change 2010–2014	ACS total population estimate 2010–2014	White alone, not Hispanic or Latino	Black alone, not Hispanic or Latino	Asian alone, not Hispanic or Latino	All other races or 2 or more races, not Hispanic or Latino	Hispanic or Latino[1]	Under 18 years old	Age 18 to 64 years old	Age 65 years and older	Total occupied housing units	Percent owner occupied	High school diploma or less	Bachelor's degree or more
	1	2	3	4	5	6	7	8	9	10	11	12	13	14	15	16
ARIZONA—Con.																
San Carlos CDP	4,038	NA	NA	4,365	1.0	0.8	1.6	94.3	2.3	35.8	56.3	7.9	988	44.1	64.3	4.6
Sanders CDP	630	NA	NA	483	0.0	0.0	7.7	90.1	2.3	56.9	41.1	1.9	95	30.5	78.9	3.2
San Jose CDP	506	NA	NA	569	24.4	0.0	0.0	0.0	75.6	33.6	53.8	12.8	169	70.4	63.9	11.8
San Luis city	27,909	31,091	11.4	30,139	2.9	1.0	0.1	0.6	95.4	33.1	60.3	6.6	7,944	73.9	67.6	8.5
San Manuel CDP	3,551	NA	NA	3,961	46.8	0.1	0.0	0.6	52.6	31.7	53.4	15.0	1,372	64.4	40.5	14.9
San Miguel CDP	197	NA	NA	279	0.0	0.0	0.0	100.0	0.0	44.2	43.0	12.9	77	88.3	51.9	0.0
San Simon CDP	165	NA	NA	180	48.3	0.0	0.0	6.1	45.6	16.6	52.2	31.1	90	77.8	47.8	0.0
Santa Cruz CDP	37	NA	NA	0	0.0	0.0	0.0	0.0	0.0	0.0	0.0	0.0	0	0.0	0.0	0.0
San Tan Valley CDP	81,321	NA	NA	86,743	65.2	4.8	1.7	6.2	22.0	35.8	56.5	7.7	24,661	70.8	30.5	24.7
Santa Rosa CDP	628	NA	NA	654	3.4	0.0	0.6	96.0	0.0	24.3	56.0	19.7	203	67.0	64.0	0.0
Sawmill CDP	748	NA	NA	701	0.0	0.0	1.3	98.7	0.0	35.6	53.8	10.4	130	87.7	71.5	5.4
Scenic CDP	1,643	NA	NA	1,679	63.1	0.0	0.0	0.0	36.9	31.5	51.6	17.0	589	84.7	71.8	8.8
Scottsdale city	217,434	230,512	6.0	223,519	81.7	1.7	4.0	2.9	9.7	17.2	61.6	21.1	100,891	66.8	14.2	56.0
Seba Dalkai CDP	136	NA	NA	123	6.5	0.0	0.0	76.4	17.1	23.6	64.9	11.4	40	85.0	45.0	15.0
Second Mesa CDP	962	NA	NA	1,016	0.0	0.0	0.0	100.0	0.0	35.5	60.7	3.7	233	76.0	57.1	15.5
Sedona city	10,036	10,281	2.4	10,092	80.2	0.0	2.6	3.3	13.9	10.7	57.8	31.7	5,136	67.8	18.7	48.2
Sehili CDP	135	NA	NA	87	0.0	0.0	0.0	100.0	0.0	29.8	65.3	4.6	19	100.0	52.6	0.0
Seligman CDP	445	NA	NA	391	56.8	3.1	0.0	7.4	32.7	12.8	66.7	20.5	176	61.9	33.5	21.0
Sells CDP	2,495	NA	NA	1,893	4.1	0.2	1.5	91.4	2.8	30.2	60.3	9.5	488	59.8	58.6	13.5
Seven Mile CDP	707	NA	NA	888	0.0	0.0	0.0	100.0	0.0	28.4	65.9	5.7	223	67.3	55.2	0.0
Shongopovi CDP	831	NA	NA	996	0.0	0.0	0.0	96.6	3.4	34.6	55.5	9.8	173	86.1	69.4	3.5
Shonto CDP	591	NA	NA	455	1.3	0.0	0.0	98.0	0.7	35.8	53.6	10.8	121	50.4	53.7	22.3
Show Low city	10,667	10,841	1.6	10,754	82.1	0.3	0.6	6.0	10.9	22.6	52.4	25.0	4,244	62.3	37.3	16.8
Sierra Vista city	45,140	43,806	-3.0	45,365	61.3	7.0	3.7	6.0	22.0	25.3	59.5	15.2	16,911	53.7	23.5	35.1
Sierra Vista Southeast CDP	14,797	NA	NA	14,501	74.6	0.6	0.4	3.4	21.0	21.8	54.6	23.6	5,803	87.8	18.6	31.6
Six Shooter Canyon CDP	1,019	NA	NA	958	67.5	6.6	0.0	10.3	15.6	26.5	56.1	17.4	399	83.0	52.6	14.3
Snowflake town	5,590	5,644	1.0	5,595	92.1	0.5	0.3	1.0	6.1	35.6	53.1	11.3	1,644	81.5	26.6	20.7
So-Hi CDP	477	NA	NA	300	91.0	0.0	0.0	0.0	9.0	0.0	33.7	66.3	189	100.0	60.8	24.3
Solomon CDP	426	NA	NA	445	21.6	0.7	0.0	0.0	77.8	37.3	51.1	11.5	131	73.3	67.2	2.3
Somerton city	14,297	14,912	4.3	14,679	3.1	0.1	0.2	0.9	95.7	36.3	56.5	7.1	4,468	67.1	67.3	5.4
Sonoita CDP	818	NA	NA	837	93.0	0.0	0.5	0.2	6.3	13.7	51.6	34.8	417	86.8	15.6	49.4
South Komelik CDP	111	NA	NA	69	0.0	0.0	0.0	100.0	0.0	15.9	72.4	11.6	39	76.9	35.9	0.0
South Tucson city	5,652	5,730	1.4	5,675	7.6	3.3	0.2	6.7	82.1	31.7	57.3	11.0	1,829	28.8	65.2	4.8
Springerville town	1,958	1,964	0.3	1,738	71.7	0.0	0.0	6.0	22.3	29.3	55.6	15.1	655	67.3	41.7	17.1
Spring Valley CDP	1,148	NA	NA	1,226	93.4	0.0	1.1	1.7	3.8	14.3	51.2	34.4	550	83.8	48.0	9.5
Stanfield CDP	740	NA	NA	151	83.4	0.0	0.0	0.0	16.6	0.0	49.7	50.3	127	20.5	80.3	0.0
Star Valley town	2,312	2,276	-1.6	2,333	94.5	0.0	0.0	1.2	4.3	24.8	51.8	23.3	1,027	84.0	48.0	9.0
Steamboat CDP	284	NA	NA	439	0.0	0.0	0.0	97.9	2.1	32.8	54.7	12.5	83	89.2	65.1	4.8
Stotonic Village CDP	659	NA	NA	306	0.0	0.0	0.0	93.8	6.2	34.3	48.7	17.0	126	37.3	76.2	15.1
Strawberry CDP	961	NA	NA	507	92.1	0.0	0.0	3.9	3.9	1.6	39.6	58.8	288	80.2	58.7	15.6
Summerhaven CDP	40	NA	NA	141	100.0	0.0	0.0	0.0	0.0	56.7	43.3	0.0	30	50.0	0.0	50.0
Summit CDP	5,372	NA	NA	4,628	12.9	0.0	0.0	1.9	85.1	34.6	57.2	8.2	1,284	67.6	73.5	3.8
Sun City CDP	37,499	NA	NA	38,622	92.9	1.6	0.4	1.2	3.9	0.4	25.9	73.7	23,300	81.2	39.8	22.7
Sun City West CDP	24,535	NA	NA	24,066	97.2	0.3	1.6	0.4	0.6	0.0	15.3	84.6	14,490	88.2	27.2	39.1
Sunizona CDP	281	NA	NA	205	82.4	0.0	0.0	3.9	13.7	15.6	54.8	29.8	125	83.2	38.4	19.2
Sun Lakes CDP	13,975	NA	NA	13,885	95.6	0.4	0.7	1.0	2.2	1.3	22.6	76.0	7,956	92.6	24.6	40.5
Sun Valley CDP	316	NA	NA	256	76.2	0.0	0.0	0.0	23.8	0.0	82.7	17.2	135	100.0	49.6	43.0
Sunwest CDP	15	NA	NA	2	100.0	0.0	0.0	0.0	0.0	0.0	0.0	100.0	2	100.0	100.0	0.0
Supai CDP	208	NA	NA	54	0.0	0.0	0.0	100.0	0.0	24.1	70.5	5.6	12	75.0	66.7	0.0
Superior town	2,837	2,916	2.8	2,886	23.8	0.7	0.7	1.9	73.0	23.4	59.1	17.5	969	65.5	55.7	7.8
Surprise city	117,517	126,275	7.5	121,648	72.4	5.2	1.6	2.5	18.2	26.9	52.2	20.9	44,472	74.1	27.2	32.4
Sweet Water Village CDP	83	NA	NA	353	5.9	0.0	0.0	92.9	1.1	15.9	73.7	10.5	71	93.0	100.0	0.0
Swift Trail Junction CDP	2,935	NA	NA	2,913	59.8	4.6	1.0	3.7	30.8	27.3	68.0	4.7	652	81.6	46.2	6.3
Tacna CDP	602	NA	NA	605	49.9	0.0	9.8	0.0	40.3	28.1	48.2	23.6	233	76.0	47.6	12.4
Tanque Verde CDP	16,901	NA	NA	16,411	83.1	0.7	2.6	3.4	10.3	16.8	59.1	24.0	6,461	91.3	13.1	57.0
Tat Momoli CDP	10	NA	NA	0	0.0	0.0	0.0	0.0	0.0	0.0	0.0	0.0	0	0.0	0.0	0.0
Taylor town	4,119	4,144	0.6	4,112	75.6	0.0	0.9	6.6	17.0	33.5	52.4	14.0	1,374	71.0	32.3	29.0
Teec Nos Pos CDP	730	NA	NA	611	0.0	0.0	0.0	98.7	1.3	31.8	54.9	13.3	161	66.5	47.8	8.7
Tees Toh CDP	448	NA	NA	395	0.0	0.0	0.0	90.1	9.9	25.1	59.8	14.9	128	79.7	64.8	5.5
Tempe city	161,781	172,816	6.8	166,975	60.0	5.0	6.5	6.2	22.2	16.9	74.2	8.7	63,523	42.6	20.3	41.6
Thatcher town	4,861	5,023	3.3	4,894	65.0	2.7	0.7	3.2	28.3	28.3	57.8	13.9	1,606	70.7	32.8	25.5
Theba CDP	0	NA	NA	152	0.0	0.0	0.0	0.0	100.0	40.8	59.1	0.0	45	0.0	91.1	0.0
Three Points CDP	5,581	NA	NA	5,313	64.1	0.3	0.0	1.6	34.0	20.4	65.3	14.3	1,963	78.0	49.0	18.7
Tolani Lake CDP	280	NA	NA	316	0.0	0.0	0.0	98.1	1.9	33.8	60.1	6.0	75	60.0	65.3	0.0
Tolleson city	6,545	6,929	5.9	6,707	13.8	4.2	0.0	1.2	80.9	26.9	62.7	10.4	2,070	43.6	60.7	9.1
Tombstone city	1,380	1,322	-4.2	1,674	64.5	0.0	0.2	3.9	31.5	22.0	53.0	24.9	679	72.0	40.2	14.1
Tonalea CDP	549	NA	NA	403	2.7	0.0	0.0	95.8	1.5	35.8	54.4	9.9	121	57.9	48.8	13.2
Tonopah CDP	60	NA	NA	20	100.0	0.0	0.0	0.0	0.0	0.0	100.0	0.0	10	100.0	0.0	0.0
Tonto Basin CDP	1,424	NA	NA	1,453	100.0	0.0	0.0	0.0	0.0	13.7	44.1	42.3	721	96.8	28.6	8.7
Tonto Village CDP	256	NA	NA	150	100.0	0.0	0.0	0.0	0.0	24.7	48.0	27.3	53	100.0	9.4	66.0
Topawa CDP	299	NA	NA	250	0.0	0.0	0.0	100.0	0.0	34.8	61.2	4.0	64	75.0	64.1	0.0
Topock CDP	10	NA	NA	12	100.0	0.0	0.0	0.0	0.0	0.0	100.0	0.0	12	0.0	0.0	0.0
Top-of-the-World CDP	231	NA	NA	164	61.0	0.0	0.0	0.0	39.0	10.9	70.1	18.9	47	100.0	29.8	34.0
Toyei CDP	13	NA	NA	35	14.3	85.7	0.0	0.0	0.0	2.9	85.7	11.4	0	0.0	0.0	0.0
Truxton CDP	134	NA	NA	196	62.2	0.0	0.0	27.6	10.2	31.6	56.7	11.7	84	79.8	50.0	1.2
Tsaile CDP	1,205	NA	NA	1,234	15.7	2.0	1.8	72.8	7.7	32.5	65.0	2.7	217	42.4	41.9	19.8
Tubac CDP	1,191	NA	NA	1,256	78.5	0.0	0.0	2.5	18.9	3.9	51.2	44.8	698	63.3	12.9	55.0
Tuba City CDP	8,611	NA	NA	9,860	3.0	0.0	1.9	93.2	1.8	31.2	61.0	7.7	2,391	59.7	38.8	29.1
Tucson city	520,561	527,972	1.4	525,031	46.3	4.6	2.6	4.3	42.2	22.0	65.3	12.6	204,341	49.6	33.2	27.5
Tucson Estates CDP	12,192	NA	NA	12,829	62.7	2.0	1.0	5.2	29.1	16.6	55.1	28.4	5,118	82.7	34.5	21.1
Tumacacori-Carmen CDP	393	NA	NA	646	35.4	0.0	3.1	2.6	58.8	32.6	43.9	23.7	279	60.9	74.9	19.0
Turkey Creek CDP	294	NA	NA	351	0.0	0.0	0.0	100.0	0.0	51.6	46.9	1.4	72	52.8	65.3	8.3
Tusayan town	570	576	1.1	327	45.6	0.6	1.5	34.6	17.7	13.1	86.7	0.0	118	3.4	28.0	30.5
Upper Santan Village CDP	495	NA	NA	460	0.0	0.0	0.0	98.0	2.0	15.6	73.7	10.7	107	60.7	100.0	0.0
Utting CDP	126	NA	NA	99	35.4	0.0	0.0	0.0	64.6	23.2	41.4	35.4	39	59.0	41.0	23.1
Vail CDP	10,208	NA	NA	10,764	75.1	2.0	2.2	1.5	19.3	30.2	60.2	9.7	3,720	83.5	21.6	34.6
Vaiva Vo CDP	128	NA	NA	35	0.0	0.0	0.0	100.0	0.0	37.1	62.8	0.0	6	100.0	100.0	0.0
Valencia West CDP	9,355	NA	NA	10,051	21.5	2.6	1.2	3.5	71.2	32.7	59.8	7.5	3,122	86.8	38.7	15.5
Valentine CDP	38	NA	NA	38	7.9	0.0	0.0	92.1	0.0	15.8	84.2	0.0	12	41.7	25.0	0.0
Valle CDP	832	NA	NA	481	12.7	0.0	0.0	22.9	64.4	59.7	40.4	0.0	98	18.4	77.6	0.0

1 May be of any race.

Items 1–16

Table A. All Places — **Population and Housing**

STATE City, town, township, borough, or CDP (county if applicable)	2010 census total population	2014 estimated population	Percent change 2010–2014	ACS total population estimate 2010–2014	White alone, not Hispanic or Latino	Black alone, not Hispanic or Latino	Asian alone, not Hispanic or Latino	All other races or 2 or more races, not Hispanic or Latino	Hispanic or Latino[1]	Under 18 years old	Age 18 to 64 years old	Age 65 years and older	Total occupied housing units	Percent owner occupied	High school diploma or less	Bachelor's degree or more
	1	2	3	4	5	6	7	8	9	10	11	12	13	14	15	16
ARIZONA—Con.																
Valle Vista CDP	1,659	NA	NA	2,024	92.7	0.0	0.0	4.7	2.6	18.9	46.2	35.0	884	86.1	42.4	23.8
Ventana CDP	49	NA	NA	53	0.0	0.0	0.0	100.0	0.0	41.5	58.5	0.0	24	70.8	100.0	0.0
Verde Village CDP	11,605	NA	NA	12,739	73.9	0.7	0.4	2.1	22.9	27.4	54.0	18.7	4,779	71.8	41.3	20.7
Vernon CDP	122	NA	NA	35	100.0	0.0	0.0	0.0	0.0	0.0	100.1	0.0	16	100.0	50.0	50.0
Vicksburg CDP	597	NA	NA	1,025	62.8	0.0	0.0	1.5	35.7	24.6	34.6	40.8	436	72.0	69.5	8.0
Village of Oak Creek (Big Park) CDP	6,147	NA	NA	6,341	84.8	0.7	0.9	4.1	9.5	7.7	49.2	43.1	3,164	70.9	18.6	46.2
Wagon Wheel CDP	1,652	NA	NA	1,170	89.9	0.0	0.0	0.0	10.1	13.3	44.5	42.2	514	88.5	25.5	22.6
Wahak Hotrontk CDP	114	NA	NA	38	0.0	0.0	0.0	100.0	0.0	15.8	60.5	23.7	24	79.2	62.5	20.8
Wall Lane CDP	415	NA	NA	754	11.1	0.0	2.8	0.0	86.1	46.3	44.8	8.9	195	67.2	78.5	7.7
Walnut Creek CDP	562	NA	NA	446	100.0	0.0	0.0	0.0	0.0	13.2	44.1	42.6	204	82.4	34.3	7.4
Washington Park CDP	70	NA	NA	73	100.0	0.0	0.0	0.0	0.0	0.0	52.1	47.9	45	82.2	40.0	0.0
Wellton town	2,882	2,956	2.6	2,934	57.6	6.8	0.0	1.9	33.6	16.2	39.2	44.6	1,222	86.7	48.6	14.8
Wellton Hills CDP	258	NA	NA	243	68.3	0.0	14.8	11.5	5.3	18.5	74.8	6.6	125	77.6	49.6	0.0
Wenden CDP	728	NA	NA	674	33.8	0.0	0.0	2.7	63.5	19.9	66.7	13.5	259	66.4	71.0	10.8
Wet Camp Village CDP	229	NA	NA	277	1.4	0.0	0.0	97.8	0.7	35.4	58.5	6.1	40	62.5	100.0	0.0
Wheatfields CDP	785	NA	NA	914	60.2	0.0	0.0	7.7	32.2	33.8	44.7	21.6	352	76.1	62.8	1.1
Whetstone CDP	0	NA	NA	2,871	75.4	0.4	0.0	8.4	15.8	21.6	62.1	16.4	1,209	84.3	29.1	16.3
Whispering Pines CDP	148	NA	NA	197	100.0	0.0	0.0	0.0	0.0	29.9	46.7	23.4	56	100.0	41.1	12.5
Whitecone CDP	817	NA	NA	924	1.1	0.0	0.0	95.8	3.1	35.1	52.5	12.6	219	73.1	63.0	2.3
White Hills CDP	323	NA	NA	379	71.8	6.9	0.0	0.0	21.4	7.4	48.0	44.6	178	94.4	50.0	6.2
White Mountain Lake CDP	2,205	NA	NA	1,916	67.4	0.0	0.0	3.7	28.9	24.6	56.4	18.8	743	73.2	55.0	5.9
Whiteriver CDP	4,104	NA	NA	4,315	2.8	0.2	0.0	96.0	1.0	33.2	61.9	5.0	976	48.6	58.1	4.7
Why CDP	0	NA	NA	202	36.6	0.0	0.0	0.0	63.4	31.6	43.6	24.8	84	51.2	42.9	22.6
Wickenburg town	6,395	6,685	4.5	6,629	86.7	0.2	0.0	1.5	11.6	15.7	46.2	38.2	3,224	68.7	38.4	24.4
Wide Ruins CDP	176	NA	NA	119	38.7	23.5	0.0	0.0	37.8	0.0	90.9	9.2	7	0.0	100.0	0.0
Wikieup CDP	133	NA	NA	108	67.6	0.0	0.0	3.7	28.7	22.3	38.0	39.8	49	65.3	61.2	4.1
Wilhoit CDP	868	NA	NA	1,075	84.1	0.6	0.0	1.7	13.7	13.6	54.3	32.0	426	89.2	40.6	6.6
Willcox city	3,753	3,607	-3.9	3,698	37.3	0.0	0.0	2.1	60.6	22.8	62.2	14.9	1,396	70.2	60.2	11.7
Williams city	3,027	3,094	2.2	3,037	68.1	1.0	1.0	5.3	24.7	24.2	62.9	12.9	1,241	61.2	43.2	21.3
Williamson CDP	5,438	NA	NA	5,398	92.0	0.0	4.2	1.0	2.9	12.6	46.2	41.3	2,452	90.0	16.1	41.1
Willow Canyon CDP	1	NA	NA	0	0.0	0.0	0.0	0.0	0.0	0.0	0.0	0.0	0	0.0	0.0	0.0
Willow Valley CDP	1,062	NA	NA	1,042	89.3	0.0	0.0	10.6	0.2	14.7	57.3	27.9	531	70.8	62.7	2.4
Window Rock CDP	2,712	NA	NA	3,171	2.2	0.0	1.0	96.3	0.5	26.0	60.8	13.4	880	36.8	45.9	30.3
Winkelman town	353	346	-2.0	311	16.4	0.0	0.0	0.0	83.6	14.4	61.4	24.1	105	89.5	26.7	14.3
Winslow city	9,655	9,604	-0.5	9,570	32.0	2.4	0.3	27.9	37.3	27.4	63.2	9.3	2,654	54.9	37.5	15.3
Winslow West CDP	438	NA	NA	767	17.1	2.0	0.0	46.9	34.0	48.2	49.5	2.2	199	34.2	63.8	16.1
Wintersburg CDP	136	NA	NA	110	100.0	0.0	0.0	0.0	0.0	0.0	89.0	10.9	50	50.0	74.0	0.0
Wittmann CDP	763	NA	NA	376	47.3	0.0	0.0	4.0	48.7	43.4	56.6	0.0	119	65.5	66.4	0.0
Woodruff CDP	191	NA	NA	69	100.0	0.0	0.0	0.0	0.0	0.0	100.0	0.0	37	100.0	100.0	0.0
Yarnell CDP	649	NA	NA	552	92.9	1.3	0.0	0.0	5.8	0.0	50.4	49.6	335	87.5	44.8	12.5
York CDP	557	NA	NA	771	75.5	0.0	0.0	5.3	19.2	32.0	51.0	17.0	308	62.7	63.0	2.6
Young CDP	666	NA	NA	418	99.3	0.0	0.0	0.7	0.0	6.2	55.7	38.0	217	89.4	47.9	20.7
Youngtown town	6,147	6,542	6.4	6,299	59.6	1.8	1.0	0.8	36.8	27.5	56.4	16.1	2,292	50.9	48.7	14.6
Yucca CDP	126	NA	NA	89	74.2	0.0	0.0	7.9	18.0	19.1	50.5	30.3	40	82.5	67.5	0.0
Yuma city	90,702	93,400	3.0	93,078	36.2	2.7	1.8	2.4	56.8	27.9	58.6	13.4	32,523	60.0	43.9	16.2
ARKANSAS	2,915,958	2,966,369	1.7	2,947,036	73.9	15.5	1.3	2.6	6.7	24.1	61.0	15.0	1,132,488	66.5	47.1	21.9
Adona city	209	205	-1.9	114	100.0	0.0	0.0	0.0	0.0	16.7	68.4	14.9	49	93.9	85.7	2.0
Alexander city	2,902	2,864	-1.3	2,880	49.9	21.1	0.0	1.5	27.5	35.4	53.7	10.9	914	72.1	60.7	14.8
Alicia town	124	120	-3.2	153	98.7	0.0	0.0	0.0	1.3	19.7	53.6	26.8	63	61.9	71.4	3.2
Allport town	115	114	-0.9	228	1.8	96.5	0.0	1.8	0.0	34.2	54.5	11.4	64	89.1	62.5	3.1
Alma city	5,467	5,560	1.7	5,514	87.0	3.0	1.0	2.9	6.2	34.8	55.1	10.1	1,873	61.2	47.5	12.4
Almyra town	283	276	-2.5	336	98.2	0.0	0.0	1.8	0.0	24.1	66.3	9.5	134	85.1	64.2	5.2
Alpena town	392	394	0.5	436	93.6	0.0	1.4	0.9	4.1	34.1	57.8	8.0	147	57.1	65.3	1.4
Altheimer city	984	909	-7.6	1,012	9.2	87.9	1.0	0.4	1.5	28.7	56.9	14.3	375	66.1	69.3	7.2
Altus city	758	736	-2.9	843	95.4	0.0	0.0	1.7	3.0	27.8	56.8	15.3	308	66.6	57.1	6.5
Amagon town	98	94	-4.1	91	94.5	0.0	0.0	0.0	5.5	16.5	58.3	25.3	50	96.0	70.0	0.0
Amity city	723	704	-2.6	774	95.2	0.0	0.5	3.0	1.3	25.3	65.0	9.6	286	55.6	57.0	15.4
Anthonyville town	159	154	-3.1	216	5.1	94.9	0.0	0.0	0.0	9.3	46.2	44.4	108	88.9	87.0	3.7
Antoine town	117	114	-2.6	144	86.8	9.0	0.0	0.0	4.2	11.8	45.1	43.1	73	65.8	60.3	12.3
Arkadelphia city	10,714	10,649	-0.6	10,703	65.2	28.1	0.6	1.2	4.9	17.2	69.7	13.0	3,602	46.8	30.3	34.5
Arkansas City city	366	336	-8.2	543	61.1	36.6	0.0	2.2	0.0	22.3	62.1	15.5	229	81.2	84.3	3.5
Ashdown city	4,723	4,503	-4.7	4,611	63.5	34.7	0.0	1.0	0.8	26.0	56.8	17.3	1,933	71.0	52.6	7.3
Ash Flat city	1,082	1,064	-1.7	1,230	98.3	1.3	0.0	0.4	0.0	17.1	55.4	27.5	442	48.9	55.2	7.0
Atkins city	3,016	3,049	1.1	3,044	96.5	0.9	0.0	1.0	1.7	24.7	58.8	16.6	1,018	65.0	46.6	16.1
Aubrey town	170	159	-6.5	168	55.4	23.2	0.0	1.8	19.6	19.7	48.9	31.5	74	56.8	82.4	8.1
Augusta city	2,199	2,105	-4.3	2,385	48.1	46.5	0.0	4.7	0.6	24.1	58.9	17.1	1,053	53.9	71.4	11.0
Austin city	2,035	3,091	51.9	2,584	89.6	1.9	0.0	1.8	6.7	36.6	58.8	4.4	841	88.3	18.7	22.6
Avilla CDP	896	NA	NA	935	82.4	6.4	3.9	1.2	6.2	15.5	69.2	15.2	371	94.3	42.3	32.1
Avoca town	488	509	4.3	727	80.6	1.4	1.0	6.9	10.2	34.5	59.9	5.6	239	81.6	65.3	8.8
Bald Knob city	2,891	2,892	0.0	2,918	91.6	2.3	0.0	2.0	4.0	29.7	55.6	14.7	1,161	56.2	64.1	16.3
Banks town	124	121	-2.4	161	94.4	5.6	0.0	0.0	0.0	22.9	66.4	10.6	81	71.6	45.7	4.9
Barling city	4,702	4,720	0.4	4,722	82.7	1.0	5.4	1.4	9.5	21.7	59.9	18.4	1,936	66.9	60.7	6.2
Bassett town	173	164	-5.2	138	95.7	0.0	0.0	0.0	4.3	17.4	52.9	29.7	74	62.2	64.9	16.2
Batesville city	10,243	10,497	2.5	10,386	78.5	5.5	1.1	1.4	13.5	24.4	58.7	17.0	3,944	63.5	44.1	20.6
Bauxite town	487	506	3.9	511	89.4	7.8	0.0	1.0	1.8	29.4	59.1	11.5	174	66.1	56.3	8.0
Bay city	1,801	1,796	-0.3	2,020	93.5	3.1	0.0	0.7	2.6	24.5	61.4	14.2	799	58.1	57.2	11.8
Bearden city	966	916	-5.2	1,053	51.1	40.5	0.0	6.5	2.0	27.0	62.3	10.8	423	65.2	69.5	14.9
Beaver town	100	101	1.0	88	100.0	0.0	0.0	0.0	0.0	13.7	77.3	9.1	28	89.3	35.7	14.3
Beebe city	7,315	7,971	9.0	7,688	86.8	6.5	0.0	1.9	4.7	25.6	62.6	11.7	2,887	51.1	47.5	15.7
Beedeville town	107	103	-3.7	114	97.4	0.0	0.0	1.8	0.9	24.6	59.6	15.8	48	70.8	83.3	0.0
Bella Vista town	26,461	27,688	4.6	27,223	92.3	0.5	1.1	2.2	3.9	18.6	48.6	32.9	11,430	87.2	28.4	38.8
Bellefonte town	454	476	4.8	464	91.8	0.6	0.0	2.2	5.4	21.3	63.6	15.1	201	57.7	48.8	15.9
Belleville city	441	437	-0.9	348	58.6	0.0	10.6	0.6	30.2	23.6	63.3	13.2	126	77.0	69.8	6.3
Ben Lomond town	145	148	2.1	139	95.0	0.0	0.0	3.6	1.4	2.8	63.3	33.8	77	80.5	62.3	15.6
Benton city	30,683	33,625	9.6	32,208	83.3	7.5	0.8	3.3	5.2	26.1	60.9	13.1	11,851	68.9	35.4	28.3
Bentonville city	35,300	41,613	17.9	38,572	75.3	2.4	9.7	3.5	9.0	28.0	65.3	6.7	14,209	56.5	28.7	45.4
Bergman town	439	445	1.4	430	94.2	0.0	1.9	0.5	3.5	17.0	67.1	16.0	173	86.1	46.2	8.1
Berryville city	5,277	5,375	1.9	5,329	66.7	0.5	0.0	3.5	29.3	30.4	58.5	11.1	1,705	68.8	68.9	11.1

1 May be of any race.

Table A. All Places — **Population and Housing**

STATE City, town, township, borough, or CDP (county if applicable)	Population: 2010 census total population	Population: 2014 estimated population	Population: Percent change 2010–2014	Population: ACS total population estimate 2010–2014	Race and Hispanic or Latino origin (percent), 2010–2014: White alone, not Hispanic or Latino	Black alone, not Hispanic or Latino	Asian alone, not Hispanic or Latino	All other races or 2 or more races, not Hispanic or Latino	Hispanic or Latino[1]	Age (percent), 2010–2014: Under 18 years old	Age 18 to 64 years old	Age 65 years and older	Households, 2010–2014: Total occupied housing units	Percent owner occupied	Householders by level of education (percent): High school diploma or less	Bachelor's degree or more
	1	2	3	4	5	6	7	8	9	10	11	12	13	14	15	16
ARKANSAS—Con.																
Bethel Heights city	2,367	2,473	4.5	2,507	53.0	3.9	4.7	11.3	27.1	37.4	56.0	6.5	752	71.4	52.3	20.3
Bigelow town	315	309	-1.9	327	96.0	1.8	0.0	0.0	2.1	20.5	56.3	23.2	122	87.7	68.9	4.9
Big Flat town	105	103	-1.9	83	100.0	0.0	0.0	0.0	0.0	31.3	42.1	26.5	33	72.7	66.7	12.1
Biggers town	347	339	-2.3	342	95.0	0.3	0.0	2.3	2.3	23.4	56.1	20.5	143	86.0	57.3	7.0
Birdsong town	41	39	-4.9	23	0.0	100.0	0.0	0.0	0.0	0.0	47.7	52.2	18	88.9	83.3	16.7
Black Oak town	262	261	-0.4	321	97.5	0.0	0.0	0.0	2.5	25.2	61.1	13.7	123	61.0	61.8	5.7
Black Rock city	662	635	-4.1	680	95.7	0.0	0.0	4.0	0.3	20.9	55.8	23.4	249	68.3	55.8	10.0
Black Springs town	101	97	-4.0	39	100.0	0.0	0.0	0.0	0.0	20.5	59.0	20.5	16	100.0	87.5	12.5
Blevins city	315	311	-1.3	318	56.6	37.1	0.0	0.0	6.3	34.2	50.4	15.4	120	73.3	59.2	24.2
Blue Eye town	30	30	0.0	37	100.0	0.0	0.0	0.0	0.0	10.8	67.5	21.6	14	85.7	100.0	0.0
Blue Mountain town	124	122	-1.6	120	92.5	0.0	0.0	0.0	7.5	29.1	62.3	8.3	36	83.3	33.3	2.8
Bluff City town	124	121	-2.4	74	36.5	63.5	0.0	0.0	0.0	10.8	66.4	23.0	35	88.6	80.0	2.9
Blytheville city	15,620	14,884	-4.7	15,251	39.5	55.4	0.0	1.1	3.9	29.1	57.3	13.7	6,288	54.0	50.3	19.1
Bodcaw town	138	134	-2.9	215	87.4	7.9	0.0	0.0	4.7	11.2	72.5	16.3	77	85.7	45.5	19.5
Bonanza city	567	550	-3.0	608	91.4	0.0	0.0	7.7	0.8	24.2	65.4	10.5	222	73.0	46.8	11.3
Bono city	2,131	2,159	1.3	2,488	92.6	1.7	0.1	1.1	4.5	33.9	59.2	7.0	935	52.2	59.4	13.7
Booneville city	3,974	3,933	-1.0	3,955	90.7	3.0	0.4	0.3	5.7	19.0	57.9	23.0	1,670	50.7	54.0	13.3
Bradford city	759	756	-0.4	811	93.7	0.0	0.0	6.3	0.0	27.9	50.8	21.3	328	69.5	75.3	9.5
Bradley city	628	577	-8.1	532	42.9	55.6	0.0	0.0	1.5	26.6	59.5	14.1	218	56.9	69.7	6.4
Branch city	367	360	-1.9	398	96.2	0.0	0.0	0.0	3.8	24.6	59.2	16.1	136	80.9	71.3	11.8
Briarcliff city	236	233	-1.3	212	96.7	0.0	0.0	3.3	0.0	15.6	56.1	28.3	101	97.0	39.6	6.9
Brinkley city	3,184	2,960	-7.0	3,074	43.4	54.1	0.5	1.3	0.8	23.2	56.6	20.2	1,265	52.6	67.0	10.0
Brookland city	1,969	3,111	58.0	2,402	98.8	0.0	0.0	0.5	0.7	26.4	61.1	12.7	828	52.7	50.1	17.6
Bryant city	16,691	19,625	17.6	18,497	88.3	6.4	1.3	1.8	2.2	25.7	60.8	13.4	7,170	70.1	37.2	30.2
Buckner city	275	256	-6.9	375	40.3	56.5	2.7	0.0	0.5	21.6	64.9	13.3	139	82.0	74.1	6.5
Bull Shoals city	1,950	1,951	0.1	2,057	96.1	0.0	0.4	1.2	2.2	17.4	48.4	34.3	949	73.7	44.3	12.5
Burdette town	191	181	-5.2	169	65.1	18.3	0.0	0.0	16.6	27.3	53.4	19.5	61	73.8	59.0	13.1
Cabot city	23,792	25,627	7.7	24,768	90.5	1.2	1.2	2.6	4.5	29.0	60.2	10.9	9,106	69.1	33.0	24.7
Caddo Valley town	635	611	-3.8	641	81.4	9.0	0.2	2.0	7.3	26.1	57.0	16.8	266	72.2	33.5	24.1
Caldwell town	543	507	-6.6	745	79.5	12.8	0.7	0.0	7.1	18.2	70.6	11.0	324	60.2	57.1	8.6
Cale town	79	77	-2.5	87	97.7	0.0	0.0	0.0	2.3	21.8	58.5	19.5	37	100.0	48.6	5.4
Calico Rock city	1,543	1,692	9.7	1,422	88.1	8.7	1.0	1.3	0.9	15.2	69.4	15.5	365	52.9	58.1	11.2
Calion city	494	470	-4.9	424	56.8	43.2	0.0	0.0	0.0	15.8	67.2	17.0	199	78.4	62.3	9.5
Camden city	12,183	11,569	-5.0	11,861	39.4	54.7	0.3	2.7	2.8	25.0	56.7	18.3	5,013	57.3	52.8	16.5
Cammack Village city	768	754	-1.8	918	95.0	0.0	0.0	2.5	2.5	34.2	55.2	10.6	364	66.2	6.9	65.9
Campbell Station city	255	246	-3.5	273	95.6	2.6	0.0	1.8	0.0	25.0	58.3	16.8	112	72.3	62.5	5.4
Caraway city	1,279	1,263	-1.3	1,182	92.3	0.8	0.0	0.0	6.9	26.9	58.4	14.8	481	64.7	64.0	4.2
Carlisle city	2,214	2,202	-0.5	2,122	81.4	16.5	0.0	0.0	2.1	17.9	55.3	26.8	884	68.2	49.7	29.0
Carthage city	343	328	-4.4	511	8.8	82.4	0.0	0.0	8.8	25.8	58.8	15.5	189	82.5	74.6	4.2
Casa town	171	168	-1.8	132	98.5	0.0	0.0	1.5	0.0	25.7	67.4	6.8	42	64.3	38.1	7.1
Cash town	342	360	5.3	318	95.6	0.0	1.9	0.0	2.5	25.8	58.2	16.0	122	68.0	82.0	3.3
Caulksville town	213	209	-1.9	184	94.6	0.0	0.0	4.3	1.1	10.9	56.0	33.2	89	91.0	41.6	14.6
Cave City city	1,904	1,869	-1.8	2,238	94.9	1.1	0.1	2.9	0.9	30.7	53.7	15.5	855	53.6	53.9	7.4
Cave Springs city	1,729	2,455	42.0	2,230	89.6	2.2	0.9	1.1	6.2	29.4	61.7	8.9	727	82.1	31.2	38.2
Cedarville city	1,394	1,370	-1.7	1,695	92.9	0.0	0.2	4.1	2.8	22.8	67.4	9.9	595	83.7	60.5	6.7
Center Ridge CDP	388	NA	NA	567	98.9	1.1	0.0	0.0	0.0	31.2	48.6	20.1	197	82.7	65.5	31.0
Centerton city	9,526	11,193	17.5	10,278	74.9	1.8	7.1	6.1	10.1	35.9	60.5	3.5	3,485	65.3	32.3	39.1
Central City town	502	493	-1.8	459	91.5	0.0	0.4	2.6	5.4	17.9	60.5	21.6	210	78.1	64.8	9.0
Charleston city	2,522	2,500	-0.9	2,517	93.0	1.6	0.0	4.3	1.2	25.5	56.1	18.4	944	72.9	37.4	19.0
Cherokee City CDP	72	NA	NA	72	100.0	0.0	0.0	0.0	0.0	45.8	54.2	0.0	14	100.0	57.1	0.0
Cherokee Village city	4,707	4,596	-2.4	4,554	92.2	0.0	2.4	0.8	4.6	21.1	44.1	34.8	2,024	77.1	51.6	11.7
Cherry Valley city	651	616	-5.4	824	93.3	3.8	0.2	2.3	0.4	30.2	58.7	11.0	295	64.1	67.5	11.2
Chester town	163	160	-1.8	105	99.0	0.0	0.0	1.0	0.0	40.0	42.1	18.1	47	68.1	61.7	0.0
Chidester city	289	276	-4.5	218	45.0	55.0	0.0	0.0	0.0	9.1	61.1	29.8	114	81.6	71.9	7.0
Clarendon city	1,664	1,542	-7.3	1,504	61.8	30.2	0.2	1.7	6.2	19.5	59.7	20.5	689	58.8	65.6	5.4
Clarkedale city	371	359	-3.2	423	87.2	11.6	0.0	1.2	0.0	34.7	56.9	8.3	136	83.8	38.2	28.7
Clarksville city	9,180	9,391	2.3	9,286	69.8	4.0	1.9	3.0	21.3	23.6	62.2	14.1	3,633	54.3	61.7	19.5
Clinton city	2,596	2,549	-1.8	2,585	94.7	0.6	0.3	1.6	2.7	23.6	56.0	20.3	927	57.8	59.4	14.7
Coal Hill city	1,012	1,021	0.9	1,044	93.3	0.0	0.1	3.8	2.8	23.3	64.3	12.3	434	67.5	71.0	6.0
College City city	455	485	6.6	351	81.8	10.8	0.0	2.0	5.4	6.9	91.8	1.4	57	22.8	22.8	42.1
College Station CDP	600	NA	NA	807	8.9	91.1	0.0	0.0	0.0	21.7	59.0	19.3	260	72.3	65.4	10.8
Colt city	378	356	-5.8	396	93.7	3.0	0.0	0.0	3.3	14.2	58.1	27.8	203	49.8	80.8	3.0
Concord town	244	240	-1.6	218	95.9	0.0	0.0	0.0	4.1	16.9	61.1	22.0	81	100.0	74.1	3.7
Conway city	58,906	64,490	9.5	62,455	74.5	16.2	2.0	2.1	5.2	23.1	68.0	8.8	23,205	49.8	28.6	36.8
Corinth town	70	69	-1.4	74	100.0	0.0	0.0	0.0	0.0	2.8	96.0	1.4	22	100.0	95.5	0.0
Corning city	3,377	3,163	-6.3	3,267	98.3	0.0	0.0	0.4	1.3	21.1	55.1	23.7	1,570	59.9	69.7	10.8
Cotter city	970	947	-2.4	1,097	96.4	0.0	0.0	1.4	2.2	19.4	63.1	17.5	484	59.5	47.3	14.7
Cotton Plant city	649	619	-4.6	582	27.5	71.3	0.0	1.2	0.0	13.9	58.4	27.7	298	67.1	74.5	3.7
Cove town	382	373	-2.4	494	96.2	0.0	0.0	3.6	0.2	33.6	52.7	13.6	170	64.1	45.9	8.2
Coy town	96	96	0.0	129	51.9	46.5	0.0	0.8	0.8	38.8	53.6	7.8	32	90.6	75.0	6.3
Crawfordsville town	479	463	-3.3	503	53.7	38.4	0.4	2.8	4.8	25.0	57.0	18.1	196	72.4	60.7	8.7
Crossett city	5,507	5,252	-4.6	5,389	56.0	39.9	0.0	0.0	4.1	25.5	56.9	17.6	2,070	62.6	46.9	11.3
Cushman city	452	454	0.4	595	89.4	0.0	1.0	8.7	0.8	30.4	53.1	16.5	237	77.2	73.4	8.4
Daisy town	115	112	-2.6	111	98.2	0.0	0.0	1.8	0.0	19.8	71.1	9.0	45	93.3	53.3	2.2
Damascus town	382	383	0.3	477	96.0	0.4	0.0	2.1	1.5	28.3	62.3	9.4	175	65.7	46.9	20.6
Danville city	2,415	2,377	-1.6	2,686	32.0	2.0	1.1	1.1	63.8	39.6	51.9	8.6	635	51.8	80.9	11.5
Dardanelle city	4,745	4,710	-0.7	4,699	63.8	2.5	0.0	1.7	31.9	15.9	65.4	18.6	1,905	44.4	63.9	9.9
Datto town	100	94	-6.0	45	100.0	0.0	0.0	0.0	0.0	11.1	75.5	13.3	22	77.3	63.6	9.1
Decatur city	1,699	1,766	3.9	2,275	50.3	0.0	0.5	4.2	45.0	35.7	58.4	5.7	628	48.4	71.3	7.5
Delaplaine town	116	117	0.9	56	96.4	3.6	0.0	0.0	0.0	7.2	50.0	42.9	29	100.0	44.8	3.4
Delight city	279	273	-2.2	310	95.8	0.6	0.6	0.0	2.9	21.6	56.6	21.9	156	71.8	48.1	13.5
Dell town	223	211	-5.4	248	95.2	0.0	0.0	4.0	0.8	16.1	54.8	29.0	118	75.4	60.2	21.2
Dennard CDP	530	NA	NA	458	96.5	0.0	0.0	3.5	0.0	9.6	62.8	27.7	226	52.2	79.6	0.0
Denning town	314	308	-1.9	165	98.8	0.0	0.0	0.0	1.2	12.1	64.9	23.0	63	73.0	71.4	1.6
De Queen city	6,594	6,749	2.4	6,671	33.2	5.2	1.3	1.6	58.7	33.3	57.1	9.6	1,972	62.4	73.1	6.4
Dermott city	2,889	2,754	-4.7	2,814	28.9	69.5	0.0	0.0	1.6	20.5	63.4	16.0	961	60.6	69.2	9.4
Des Arc city	1,717	1,638	-4.6	1,997	84.6	9.5	0.0	2.3	3.6	20.6	60.6	19.0	854	60.0	63.7	7.7
De Valls Bluff city	619	587	-5.2	610	72.6	26.9	0.0	0.5	0.0	23.5	55.1	21.5	288	59.7	64.6	16.7
DeWitt city	3,292	3,215	-2.3	3,261	66.9	28.6	0.0	1.5	3.0	25.3	60.4	14.2	1,245	52.0	54.5	16.1
Diamond City city	782	782	0.0	929	87.6	0.0	0.0	3.0	9.4	13.7	47.3	39.0	443	79.7	60.7	15.8
Diaz city	1,318	1,274	-3.3	1,517	60.8	29.3	0.0	7.1	2.8	30.0	57.2	12.9	590	60.7	65.1	11.7

1 May be of any race.

Table A. All Places — **Population and Housing**

STATE City, town, township, borough, or CDP (county if applicable)	Population				Race and Hispanic or Latino origin (percent), 2010–2014					Age (percent), 2010–2014			Households, 2010–2014		Householders by level of education (percent)	
	2010 census total population	2014 estimated population	Percent change 2010–2014	ACS total population estimate 2010–2014	White alone, not Hispanic or Latino	Black alone, not Hispanic or Latino	Asian alone, not Hispanic or Latino	All other races or 2 or more races, not Hispanic or Latino	Hispanic or Latino[1]	Under 18 years old	Age 18 to 64 years old	Age 65 years and older	Total occupied housing units	Percent owner occupied	High school diploma or less	Bachelor's degree or more
	1	2	3	4	5	6	7	8	9	10	11	12	13	14	15	16
ARKANSAS—Con.																
Dierks city	1,133	1,108	-2.2	1,220	90.0	0.8	0.3	7.0	1.8	28.5	53.8	17.7	465	64.9	63.7	15.3
Donaldson town	301	301	0.0	300	97.0	0.0	0.0	3.0	0.0	20.7	63.1	16.3	119	89.1	68.1	6.7
Dover city	1,378	1,397	1.4	1,499	92.4	0.2	0.0	5.7	1.7	24.2	62.3	13.3	580	56.4	50.0	9.8
Dumas city	4,706	4,432	-5.8	4,551	34.5	62.0	0.0	0.7	2.8	25.6	59.9	14.4	1,848	49.8	64.5	10.0
Dyer city	876	861	-1.7	757	98.3	0.0	0.0	1.7	0.0	15.7	63.7	20.7	339	76.4	47.8	22.7
Dyess town	410	389	-5.1	436	87.8	0.0	0.0	2.1	10.1	33.7	57.5	8.7	127	68.5	65.4	10.2
Earle city	2,414	2,321	-3.9	2,505	16.4	82.7	0.0	0.9	0.0	25.6	63.2	11.1	830	52.0	63.6	8.7
East Camden town	931	880	-5.5	1,143	70.4	24.7	0.0	2.5	2.4	33.2	60.4	6.4	453	46.4	50.8	19.9
East End CDP	6,998	NA	NA	6,917	88.8	4.8	2.2	3.4	0.8	24.0	60.6	15.3	2,652	78.5	54.1	16.3
Edmondson town	427	410	-4.0	307	19.2	75.9	0.7	0.0	4.2	23.4	64.9	11.7	118	65.3	76.3	8.5
Egypt town	112	111	-0.9	108	98.1	0.0	0.0	1.9	0.0	29.6	47.2	23.1	45	51.1	77.8	2.2
Elaine city	636	572	-10.1	809	30.7	50.8	0.0	3.1	15.5	37.0	47.6	15.3	323	52.6	62.8	10.8
El Dorado city	18,884	18,352	-2.8	18,590	43.9	51.4	0.6	1.4	2.8	24.8	60.0	15.1	7,548	56.2	48.3	20.2
Elkins city	2,648	2,890	9.1	2,759	92.2	0.1	0.1	3.5	4.0	26.3	61.5	12.3	1,065	72.1	38.0	21.7
Elm Springs city	1,541	1,720	11.6	1,455	89.4	0.2	0.0	2.6	7.8	27.2	57.2	15.7	494	85.6	38.9	34.8
Emerson town	368	354	-3.8	322	72.0	25.2	0.6	2.2	0.0	30.7	58.0	11.2	123	65.0	64.2	4.1
Emmet city	518	497	-4.1	474	59.1	38.8	0.0	1.7	0.4	16.9	72.4	10.8	167	76.6	64.1	6.0
England city	2,825	2,786	-1.4	2,808	62.8	33.7	1.1	0.6	1.8	29.7	53.9	16.4	1,189	44.7	51.3	15.5
Enola town	338	344	1.8	399	91.2	0.0	0.0	6.5	2.3	25.8	57.3	16.8	152	73.7	59.9	13.2
Etowah town	351	333	-5.1	276	93.8	0.7	0.0	5.1	0.4	27.2	58.0	14.9	103	65.0	77.7	11.7
Eudora city	2,269	2,137	-5.8	2,169	9.4	88.8	0.0	0.9	0.9	23.6	59.3	17.2	887	60.8	68.7	9.9
Eureka Springs city	2,069	2,086	0.8	2,335	94.1	0.5	0.0	3.7	1.8	16.3	61.8	21.9	1,129	57.0	33.0	28.7
Evening Shade city	434	421	-3.0	606	99.2	0.3	0.0	0.3	0.2	24.5	53.9	21.6	236	76.3	48.7	14.0
Everton town	133	133	0.0	185	98.4	0.0	0.0	1.6	0.0	30.3	54.1	15.7	64	67.2	57.8	12.5
Fairfield Bay city	2,338	2,280	-2.5	2,213	93.5	0.0	0.0	0.5	6.0	13.0	33.8	53.3	1,121	83.1	37.5	27.5
Fargo town	98	92	-6.1	101	25.7	74.3	0.0	0.0	0.0	24.8	66.3	8.9	37	48.6	35.1	18.9
Farmington city	5,974	6,477	8.4	6,208	89.9	0.0	1.0	2.3	6.8	27.2	63.7	9.1	2,331	63.6	32.3	26.3
Fayetteville city	73,581	80,621	9.6	77,264	80.1	6.1	3.2	3.7	6.9	17.8	73.4	8.7	32,601	41.4	22.2	43.3
Felsenthal town	150	144	-4.0	84	86.9	6.0	0.0	4.8	2.4	3.6	47.7	48.8	48	87.5	68.8	20.8
Fifty-Six city	173	173	0.0	260	98.8	0.0	0.0	0.8	0.4	24.2	49.2	26.5	84	76.2	53.6	7.1
Fisher city	223	220	-1.3	299	95.0	0.0	0.0	0.7	4.3	18.4	67.5	14.0	112	73.2	67.0	2.7
Flippin city	1,355	1,350	-0.4	1,254	89.2	0.6	4.0	1.8	4.4	23.2	55.3	21.6	536	56.3	63.1	5.4
Fordyce city	4,300	4,107	-4.5	4,205	46.5	50.1	3.0	0.0	0.4	24.7	59.1	16.3	1,769	54.9	68.5	14.5
Foreman city	1,011	957	-5.3	1,303	69.2	28.9	0.0	1.8	0.0	19.5	62.1	18.5	561	75.8	60.6	19.3
Forrest City city	15,371	14,823	-3.6	15,122	25.1	65.0	0.3	4.0	5.5	23.6	67.3	9.1	4,115	44.8	49.6	15.1
Fort Smith city	86,261	87,351	1.3	87,193	63.2	8.5	5.7	5.6	17.0	25.1	62.3	12.7	34,542	54.3	44.4	22.4
Fouke city	870	864	-0.7	841	97.5	0.0	0.0	2.5	0.0	28.1	63.2	8.8	294	55.1	67.0	6.5
Fountain Hill town	175	168	-4.0	163	56.4	42.9	0.0	0.0	0.6	8.5	87.1	4.3	68	75.0	45.6	25.0
Fountain Lake town	503	510	1.4	559	92.3	3.9	0.0	3.2	0.5	30.9	51.6	17.4	198	70.7	49.5	15.7
Fourche town	62	61	-1.6	100	96.0	0.0	0.0	4.0	0.0	23.0	64.0	13.0	33	97.0	51.5	3.0
Franklin town	198	193	-2.5	216	85.6	0.0	0.0	6.5	7.9	14.8	59.8	25.5	103	66.0	38.8	10.7
Fredonia (Biscoe) town	359	343	-4.5	365	47.4	52.1	0.0	0.5	0.0	22.4	68.4	9.0	160	74.4	81.3	6.3
Friendship town	176	176	0.0	236	99.6	0.0	0.0	0.4	0.0	18.2	62.9	19.1	69	71.0	53.6	20.3
Fulton town	201	198	-1.5	209	51.2	43.5	0.0	0.0	5.3	28.2	48.2	23.4	96	72.9	58.3	7.3
Garfield town	502	524	4.4	508	87.4	2.2	0.0	4.5	5.9	25.4	59.9	14.8	197	82.7	53.3	21.3
Garland town	242	240	-0.8	396	27.8	72.0	0.0	0.3	0.0	30.6	53.4	16.2	149	62.4	77.9	2.7
Garner town	284	283	-0.4	174	100.0	0.0	0.0	0.0	0.0	16.1	68.9	14.9	65	73.8	84.6	0.0
Gassville city	2,078	2,121	2.1	2,206	94.7	0.4	0.5	0.6	3.8	21.0	63.3	15.6	811	64.5	64.9	10.2
Gateway town	405	423	4.4	438	97.7	0.0	0.0	1.4	0.9	31.1	59.9	9.1	147	79.6	69.4	6.8
Gentry city	3,158	3,367	6.6	3,291	79.1	0.2	1.0	5.0	14.8	34.1	55.3	10.7	1,149	62.6	57.4	15.4
Georgetown town	124	123	-0.8	79	100.0	0.0	0.0	0.0	0.0	8.8	69.6	21.5	33	93.9	87.9	0.0
Gibson CDP	3,543	NA	NA	3,433	90.6	2.0	0.6	0.9	5.9	22.7	65.6	11.8	1,386	70.9	37.2	12.9
Gilbert town	28	27	-3.6	104	99.0	0.0	0.0	1.0	0.0	8.7	84.6	6.7	26	100.0	61.5	11.5
Gillett city	691	687	-0.6	620	79.5	10.5	0.0	1.8	8.2	24.0	64.8	11.1	261	64.0	56.3	18.8
Gillham town	160	163	1.9	252	59.1	0.0	0.0	3.2	37.7	35.3	59.6	5.2	90	56.7	83.3	12.2
Gilmore city	265	256	-3.4	195	20.0	71.3	0.0	0.5	8.2	11.2	66.8	22.1	87	67.8	71.3	9.2
Glenwood city	2,228	2,179	-2.2	2,731	77.1	1.6	0.0	1.4	19.9	25.6	56.0	18.3	991	53.6	53.8	20.9
Goshen town	1,067	1,433	34.3	1,253	90.6	2.5	2.0	2.8	2.2	32.5	59.3	8.3	439	82.2	16.6	48.5
Gosnell city	3,548	3,352	-5.5	3,455	62.2	32.4	1.2	0.5	3.7	35.0	59.2	5.7	1,159	62.1	54.8	8.5
Gould city	837	794	-5.1	797	8.3	89.8	0.0	1.9	0.0	31.3	54.4	14.3	344	55.2	65.4	6.4
Grady city	449	422	-6.0	1,071	39.8	48.8	0.0	7.3	4.1	5.9	85.0	9.2	178	57.3	57.3	8.4
Grannis city	554	564	1.8	540	61.5	0.0	0.0	7.8	30.7	27.2	57.8	15.0	176	62.5	61.4	9.7
Gravette city	3,113	3,221	3.5	3,190	78.1	2.2	0.3	10.8	8.6	28.3	62.0	9.6	1,150	64.0	57.8	15.7
Greenbrier city	4,712	5,212	10.6	4,970	89.0	0.7	0.8	4.0	5.5	28.6	60.1	11.2	1,828	73.0	46.1	17.3
Green Forest city	2,761	2,776	0.5	2,762	46.9	0.8	2.2	3.6	46.4	29.6	57.6	12.7	1,025	57.2	72.3	9.9
Greenland city	1,294	1,377	6.4	1,475	87.0	2.0	0.2	9.0	1.8	30.2	56.1	13.8	559	70.7	47.6	23.1
Greenway city	209	196	-6.2	182	93.4	0.0	0.0	2.7	3.8	21.9	67.4	10.4	72	87.5	79.2	0.0
Greenwood city	9,067	9,263	2.2	9,222	93.9	0.0	2.5	3.0	0.6	30.0	60.5	9.5	3,336	72.4	38.7	27.6
Greers Ferry city	891	878	-1.5	807	98.0	0.0	0.0	0.7	1.2	12.0	61.9	26.1	345	80.0	59.1	10.7
Griffithville town	225	224	-0.4	143	99.3	0.7	0.0	0.0	0.0	10.5	65.8	23.8	72	86.1	77.8	4.2
Grubbs city	386	372	-3.6	549	99.5	0.0	0.0	0.5	0.0	23.7	51.1	25.1	226	74.8	82.3	1.3
Guion town	86	84	-2.3	78	100.0	0.0	0.0	0.0	0.0	16.6	50.1	33.3	35	77.1	54.3	0.0
Gum Springs town	120	117	-2.5	123	38.2	57.7	0.0	1.6	2.4	21.2	57.7	21.1	67	58.2	31.3	38.8
Gurdon city	2,212	2,150	-2.8	2,332	47.8	38.3	0.0	0.4	13.4	25.9	63.0	11.0	901	52.2	68.6	7.5
Guy city	705	718	1.8	739	95.3	2.7	0.0	2.0	0.0	33.0	55.7	11.2	213	80.8	45.1	16.0
Hackett city	775	816	5.3	804	82.2	0.0	0.0	17.8	0.0	23.1	62.7	14.3	297	73.4	63.3	12.5
Hagarville CDP	129	NA	NA	262	100.0	0.0	0.0	0.0	0.0	24.8	33.7	41.6	95	85.3	37.9	48.4
Hamburg city	2,894	2,810	-2.9	2,846	65.5	26.8	0.0	1.9	5.8	26.9	53.0	20.2	1,167	64.6	58.8	17.2
Hampton city	1,324	1,276	-3.6	1,735	60.5	37.3	0.0	1.3	0.8	19.8	54.4	25.9	712	68.0	67.6	6.6
Hardy city	776	760	-2.1	724	98.9	0.0	0.0	0.6	0.6	12.8	62.6	24.6	401	55.1	64.3	6.7
Harrell town	254	247	-2.8	278	38.1	58.6	0.0	2.2	1.1	18.7	66.3	15.1	123	87.8	70.7	5.7
Harrisburg city	2,296	2,317	0.9	2,440	92.0	4.5	0.0	1.9	1.6	27.3	57.5	15.1	792	50.3	62.8	10.1
Harrison city	12,941	13,130	1.5	13,103	92.2	0.3	1.0	3.3	3.2	26.4	53.7	19.9	5,507	58.8	43.7	18.6
Hartford city	653	641	-1.8	657	92.7	0.0	0.0	6.2	1.1	23.7	55.2	21.2	263	76.0	65.0	8.0
Hartman city	519	527	1.5	657	96.2	0.0	0.0	0.6	3.2	31.6	59.0	9.3	244	62.3	68.9	9.8
Haskell city	3,991	4,396	10.1	4,259	89.7	3.6	0.0	0.5	6.2	27.0	64.8	8.1	1,442	75.4	36.1	16.4
Hatfield town	413	403	-2.4	479	93.1	0.0	0.0	5.4	1.5	29.5	55.7	14.6	195	71.3	59.5	5.1
Havana city	375	372	-0.8	184	92.9	0.0	0.0	0.0	7.1	17.9	66.8	15.2	82	63.4	74.4	12.2
Haynes town	150	140	-6.7	165	16.4	83.6	0.0	0.0	0.0	28.5	60.0	11.5	50	78.0	56.0	18.0
Hazen city	1,468	1,403	-4.4	1,506	73.6	26.3	0.1	0.0	0.0	26.6	50.1	23.2	679	65.7	63.3	11.5
Heber Springs city	7,206	7,174	-0.4	7,177	97.1	0.3	0.6	0.6	1.4	22.5	57.8	19.9	2,715	61.6	39.7	26.5

1 May be of any race.

Table A. All Places — **Population and Housing**

STATE City, town, township, borough, or CDP (county if applicable)	Population: 2010 census total population	Population: 2014 estimated population	Population: Percent change 2010–2014	Population: ACS total population estimate 2010–2014	Race and Hispanic or Latino origin (percent), 2010–2014: White alone, not Hispanic or Latino	Race: Black alone, not Hispanic or Latino	Race: Asian alone, not Hispanic or Latino	Race: All other races or 2 or more races, not Hispanic or Latino	Race: Hispanic or Latino[1]	Age (percent), 2010–2014: Under 18 years old	Age: Age 18 to 64 years old	Age: Age 65 years and older	Households, 2010–2014: Total occupied housing units	Households: Percent owner occupied	Householders by level of education (percent): High school diploma or less	Householders by level of education (percent): Bachelor's degree or more
	1	2	3	4	5	6	7	8	9	10	11	12	13	14	15	16
ARKANSAS—Con.																
Hector town	450	452	0.4	380	86.8	0.0	0.0	6.8	6.3	16.4	66.4	17.4	153	81.7	69.9	5.2
Helena-West Helena city	12,282	11,320	-7.8	11,795	22.9	75.8	0.2	0.5	0.6	30.7	56.1	12.9	4,561	42.4	50.3	16.2
Hensley CDP	139	NA	NA	134	3.7	96.3	0.0	0.0	0.0	0.0	91.8	8.2	37	86.5	43.2	0.0
Hermitage city	830	808	-2.7	875	38.7	31.0	0.0	1.1	29.1	42.5	48.6	9.0	300	31.7	77.3	9.7
Hickory Ridge city	272	261	-4.0	307	98.0	0.0	0.0	1.3	0.7	23.4	65.9	10.7	137	63.5	75.2	5.1
Higden town	120	118	-1.7	138	100.0	0.0	0.0	0.0	0.0	23.9	47.9	28.3	61	91.8	31.1	27.9
Higginson town	621	643	3.5	758	89.7	1.2	0.0	1.8	7.3	23.4	62.1	14.4	298	71.8	72.5	6.7
Highfill town	585	628	7.4	596	84.4	0.5	9.1	5.0	1.0	24.1	65.3	10.6	226	73.9	59.3	19.0
Highland city	1,045	1,050	0.5	1,018	96.8	0.4	0.3	2.5	0.1	14.8	61.5	23.7	405	83.0	54.6	23.5
Hindsville town	61	61	0.0	48	95.8	0.0	0.0	4.2	0.0	4.2	69.0	27.1	16	75.0	87.5	6.3
Holiday Island CDP	2,373	NA	NA	2,800	92.5	3.8	0.0	1.0	2.7	15.7	41.6	42.8	1,393	78.5	35.7	22.9
Holland city	539	549	1.9	491	96.3	0.0	0.0	1.8	1.8	22.4	59.4	18.1	196	88.3	50.0	14.8
Holly Grove city	602	561	-6.8	680	17.4	81.9	0.0	0.7	0.0	34.0	52.2	13.8	246	51.6	61.4	13.4
Hope city	10,095	10,004	-0.9	10,033	34.0	42.4	0.0	1.3	22.3	33.3	52.6	14.2	3,435	57.8	62.2	10.7
Horatio city	1,044	1,070	2.5	1,201	55.3	4.6	0.0	3.9	36.2	32.6	62.1	5.2	369	64.0	58.3	6.2
Horseshoe Bend city	2,184	2,108	-3.5	2,250	93.5	1.1	0.0	2.7	2.7	9.9	49.1	41.0	1,219	82.7	49.1	13.3
Horseshoe Lake town	292	282	-3.4	265	94.3	1.9	0.0	3.0	0.8	9.1	65.2	25.7	134	71.6	52.2	12.7
Hot Springs city	35,193	35,673	1.4	35,486	68.4	18.5	1.8	2.4	8.9	21.1	57.6	21.4	15,115	53.6	43.1	21.2
Hot Springs Village CDP	12,807	NA	NA	13,510	96.5	1.3	0.4	1.0	0.8	3.7	33.4	62.9	7,088	91.4	22.3	39.2
Houston town	173	170	-1.7	365	100.0	0.0	0.0	0.0	0.0	24.9	61.6	13.4	113	75.2	70.8	7.1
Hoxie city	2,780	2,710	-2.5	2,746	93.0	0.9	0.0	4.8	1.2	20.9	61.5	17.6	1,124	59.0	58.3	6.4
Hughes city	1,440	1,341	-6.9	1,589	19.4	77.7	0.0	0.4	2.5	33.7	55.7	10.6	585	53.0	61.4	5.8
Humnoke city	284	283	-0.4	186	79.6	15.6	0.0	4.8	0.0	30.1	56.0	14.0	69	68.1	68.1	10.1
Humphrey city	557	530	-4.8	501	51.1	46.7	0.0	2.2	0.0	12.4	70.8	17.0	233	74.7	64.4	8.2
Hunter town	105	100	-4.8	84	98.8	0.0	0.0	1.2	0.0	13.1	52.5	34.5	46	84.8	93.5	2.2
Huntington city	636	625	-1.7	620	96.1	1.5	0.0	0.2	2.3	22.6	57.0	20.5	216	66.7	65.3	2.3
Huntsville city	2,349	2,378	1.2	2,168	80.9	0.0	3.0	2.5	13.6	29.5	56.7	13.9	813	49.8	68.0	8.7
Huttig city	597	568	-4.9	502	55.8	43.2	1.0	0.0	0.0	22.3	62.6	15.3	201	73.1	67.2	3.5
Imboden town	677	650	-4.0	555	97.3	0.0	0.0	0.0	2.7	19.6	52.1	28.1	268	61.2	61.2	14.2
Jacksonport town	212	207	-2.4	126	95.2	0.0	0.0	4.8	0.0	9.5	56.5	34.1	61	70.5	82.0	3.3
Jacksonville city	28,388	28,808	1.5	28,728	53.6	33.5	2.0	3.4	7.5	25.9	62.8	11.3	10,523	52.9	44.6	19.0
Jasper city	464	447	-3.7	606	90.4	0.0	1.0	7.9	0.7	20.3	47.4	32.3	274	46.0	60.2	12.4
Jennette town	115	111	-3.5	105	4.8	93.3	0.0	1.9	0.0	19.0	71.4	9.5	44	77.3	79.5	9.1
Jericho town	119	115	-3.4	60	0.0	100.0	0.0	0.0	0.0	23.3	68.4	8.3	27	88.9	59.3	11.1
Jerome town	39	39	0.0	69	72.5	4.3	0.0	0.0	23.2	18.8	78.1	2.9	27	55.6	88.9	11.1
Johnson city	3,383	3,601	6.4	3,509	70.4	5.9	2.2	5.4	16.2	31.0	61.7	7.6	1,298	55.7	34.3	36.1
Joiner city	576	546	-5.2	547	46.3	43.7	0.0	3.1	6.9	27.6	63.1	9.1	208	53.8	83.2	7.2
Jonesboro city	67,388	72,210	7.2	70,217	71.9	19.0	1.5	2.2	5.3	25.0	63.4	11.6	26,771	53.8	36.6	30.2
Judsonia city	2,019	2,019	0.0	2,362	80.2	9.3	0.0	2.1	8.4	26.3	51.7	21.9	842	65.8	73.9	4.2
Junction City city	581	552	-5.0	588	56.6	42.5	0.0	0.0	0.9	26.2	53.2	20.6	201	78.6	68.7	10.0
Keiser city	759	715	-5.8	595	91.4	2.7	0.0	3.0	2.9	28.7	53.9	17.3	207	61.8	67.1	4.8
Kensett city	1,648	1,647	-0.1	1,655	60.4	11.8	0.0	2.7	25.2	24.0	58.6	17.5	717	58.4	79.2	0.3
Keo town	256	261	2.0	217	69.6	20.3	0.0	0.0	10.1	11.9	70.2	18.0	93	71.0	55.9	14.0
Kibler city	961	944	-1.8	1,026	90.7	0.0	4.3	2.5	2.4	17.7	63.8	18.4	423	84.6	65.0	13.2
Kingsland city	447	428	-4.3	402	65.7	32.8	0.0	0.7	0.7	20.9	64.2	14.9	189	69.3	70.9	6.3
Kirby CDP	786	NA	NA	785	97.5	0.0	0.0	2.5	0.0	18.7	64.5	16.8	290	78.3	51.0	10.3
Knobel city	287	269	-6.3	255	99.2	0.0	0.0	0.8	0.0	20.8	67.1	12.2	102	90.2	68.6	4.9
Knoxville town	731	742	1.5	687	96.8	0.0	0.0	1.0	2.2	19.9	66.0	14.1	295	80.3	58.0	11.5
Lafe town	456	460	0.9	366	96.7	0.0	0.0	0.0	3.3	24.0	56.4	19.7	157	79.6	58.0	12.1
LaGrange town	89	83	-6.7	97	61.9	38.1	0.0	0.0	0.0	18.6	57.8	23.7	39	69.2	92.3	7.7
Lake City city	2,082	2,253	8.2	2,100	92.6	0.0	0.0	0.8	6.6	25.4	58.0	16.6	769	66.6	60.2	11.4
Lake Hamilton CDP	2,135	NA	NA	1,804	90.5	2.2	2.5	3.6	1.2	17.2	60.0	22.8	826	64.5	29.5	32.6
Lakeview city	741	722	-2.6	760	96.8	0.0	0.0	1.6	1.6	14.2	40.3	45.5	352	81.3	40.1	16.2
Lake View city	443	404	-8.8	411	0.5	99.5	0.0	0.0	0.0	23.0	62.2	14.6	197	49.2	52.3	13.2
Lake Village city	2,575	2,447	-5.0	2,724	35.0	55.7	0.6	1.2	7.5	28.5	55.0	16.5	1,041	58.9	59.2	16.1
Lamar city	1,607	1,658	3.2	1,524	82.9	1.2	0.0	0.0	15.9	22.9	60.2	17.0	592	72.8	67.9	10.5
Landmark CDP	3,555	NA	NA	2,782	75.1	17.5	0.0	3.5	3.8	16.0	65.9	18.1	1,136	75.4	55.6	10.8
Lavaca city	2,293	2,380	3.8	2,358	86.4	0.5	0.0	5.4	7.7	29.2	63.1	7.8	854	74.1	43.9	17.3
Leachville city	1,993	1,890	-5.2	1,693	84.6	0.2	0.0	0.0	15.1	27.9	54.6	17.6	665	64.8	61.5	8.1
Lead Hill town	271	274	1.1	291	90.4	0.0	0.7	0.3	8.6	23.4	59.4	17.2	131	58.0	51.1	13.0
Leola town	501	504	0.6	723	46.7	1.9	0.0	0.8	50.5	30.8	63.5	5.7	218	70.2	80.3	1.8
Lepanto city	1,893	1,853	-2.1	1,954	75.3	20.5	0.0	2.3	1.8	21.7	64.3	13.9	710	47.2	73.7	5.8
Leslie city	432	418	-3.2	499	92.8	0.0	0.0	6.8	0.4	26.8	57.2	15.8	196	57.7	62.2	8.2
Letona town	255	254	-0.4	270	95.6	0.0	0.0	2.2	2.2	32.9	57.0	10.0	102	65.7	80.4	2.0
Lewisville city	1,287	1,201	-6.7	1,215	37.2	57.8	0.0	1.2	3.9	21.2	60.3	18.4	462	64.5	80.3	5.6
Lexa town	286	261	-8.7	322	81.4	9.9	0.0	1.9	6.8	35.7	49.2	14.9	109	73.4	66.1	7.3
Lincoln city	2,249	2,413	7.3	2,132	89.0	2.3	0.0	5.3	3.4	30.5	52.5	16.9	860	56.5	69.2	7.2
Little Flock city	2,577	2,717	5.4	2,666	75.4	8.7	5.8	1.3	8.9	22.1	69.1	8.9	1,132	34.4	38.9	39.4
Little Rock city	193,524	197,706	2.2	196,188	47.2	42.0	3.1	1.9	5.8	24.1	63.8	12.2	78,658	57.1	28.4	40.3
Lockesburg city	739	749	1.4	780	83.5	13.8	0.0	0.6	2.1	23.2	62.3	14.5	302	59.9	54.6	8.9
London city	1,039	1,048	0.9	937	96.8	0.2	0.9	1.1	1.1	22.0	64.3	13.7	361	75.1	54.0	12.2
Lonoke city	4,245	4,260	0.4	4,255	69.1	25.6	1.2	0.3	3.8	24.8	55.5	19.8	1,532	70.3	51.8	14.7
Lonsdale town	94	95	1.1	148	99.3	0.0	0.0	0.7	0.0	28.4	59.6	12.2	52	63.5	57.7	3.8
Lost Bridge Village CDP	434	NA	NA	424	100.0	0.0	0.0	0.0	0.0	10.3	59.4	30.2	177	96.0	21.5	55.4
Louann town	164	156	-4.9	143	83.2	16.8	0.0	0.0	0.0	28.0	54.6	17.5	53	71.7	62.3	1.9
Lowell city	7,301	8,334	14.1	7,756	69.2	0.3	1.9	3.3	25.4	30.7	63.7	5.4	2,871	56.4	43.3	31.3
Luxora city	1,178	1,117	-5.2	1,036	25.3	72.7	0.0	2.0	0.0	35.3	54.3	10.4	359	35.1	70.5	7.2
Lynn town	288	280	-2.8	217	93.1	0.0	0.0	5.5	1.4	21.2	66.5	12.4	93	77.4	57.0	15.1
McAlmont CDP	1,873	NA	NA	1,721	19.9	80.1	0.0	0.0	0.0	22.2	64.6	13.1	602	52.8	63.6	9.0
McCaskill town	96	95	-1.0	89	93.3	0.0	0.0	0.0	6.7	3.4	91.0	5.6	27	40.7	85.2	0.0
McCrory city	1,733	1,642	-5.3	2,019	81.0	16.2	0.0	1.9	0.9	26.6	54.1	19.2	773	51.1	65.1	11.3
McDougal town	186	175	-5.9	165	100.0	0.0	0.0	0.0	0.0	24.2	55.8	20.0	67	77.6	91.0	0.0
McGehee city	4,219	4,024	-4.6	4,094	41.3	50.9	0.0	1.1	6.8	32.7	53.2	14.0	1,649	50.6	58.5	15.0
McNab town	68	67	-1.5	58	32.8	67.2	0.0	0.0	0.0	17.2	75.8	6.9	21	100.0	90.5	0.0
McNeil city	516	496	-3.9	493	30.4	68.8	0.0	0.8	0.0	29.1	66.2	4.7	219	37.4	36.5	3.7
McRae city	682	679	-0.4	806	92.3	2.7	0.0	5.0	0.0	26.8	58.2	15.0	314	64.0	67.8	7.0
Madison city	769	717	-6.8	850	11.4	88.6	0.0	0.0	0.0	29.9	58.2	12.0	364	51.6	68.1	11.0
Magazine city	847	835	-1.4	921	95.1	0.0	0.0	1.2	3.7	25.0	54.4	20.6	330	73.0	57.0	6.1
Magness town	202	203	0.5	209	71.3	0.0	0.0	0.0	28.7	42.1	50.7	7.2	54	90.7	74.1	7.4
Magnet Cove town	5	5	0.0	0	0.0	0.0	0.0	0.0	0.0	0.0	0.0	0.0	0	0.0	0.0	0.0
Magnolia city	11,577	11,489	-0.8	11,681	53.0	41.9	1.3	2.6	1.2	20.7	64.0	15.3	4,333	54.0	41.1	27.1

1 May be of any race.

Table A. All Places — **Population and Housing**

STATE City, town, township, borough, or CDP (county if applicable)	Population: 2010 census total population	Population: 2014 estimated population	Population: Percent change 2010–2014	Population: ACS total population estimate 2010–2014	Race (percent), 2010–2014: White alone, not Hispanic or Latino	Race: Black alone, not Hispanic or Latino	Race: Asian alone, not Hispanic or Latino	Race: All other races or 2 or more races, not Hispanic or Latino	Race: Hispanic or Latino[1]	Age (percent), 2010–2014: Under 18 years old	Age: Age 18 to 64 years old	Age: Age 65 years and older	Households, 2010–2014: Total occupied housing units	Households: Percent owner occupied	Householders by level of education (percent): High school diploma or less	Householders by level of education (percent): Bachelor's degree or more
	1	2	3	4	5	6	7	8	9	10	11	12	13	14	15	16
ARKANSAS—Con.																
Malvern city	10,320	10,826	4.9	10,695	60.5	34.7	0.0	1.2	3.5	19.4	65.4	15.3	3,782	52.4	54.1	17.0
Mammoth Spring city	977	963	-1.4	1,034	96.8	0.0	0.0	3.2	0.0	21.5	57.3	21.2	504	64.1	55.6	9.1
Manila city	3,346	3,261	-2.5	3,283	94.2	0.1	0.0	5.2	0.5	26.5	59.4	14.0	1,299	60.0	61.4	7.0
Mansfield city	1,139	1,105	-3.0	1,339	96.1	0.0	0.2	3.3	0.4	29.2	61.6	9.2	504	64.7	59.5	12.1
Marianna city	4,115	3,872	-5.9	4,024	21.7	78.1	0.0	0.2	0.0	25.2	57.4	17.4	1,603	41.5	65.7	9.2
Marie town	84	80	-4.8	45	95.6	0.0	0.0	0.0	4.4	13.3	73.3	13.3	27	63.0	55.6	18.5
Marion city	12,369	12,321	-0.4	12,354	67.5	27.0	0.1	1.9	3.5	29.7	63.3	6.9	4,409	70.2	40.0	24.4
Marked Tree city	2,566	2,525	-1.6	2,540	66.9	28.3	0.0	1.2	3.5	18.9	63.1	18.0	1,097	52.8	62.2	9.1
Marmaduke city	1,111	1,206	8.6	1,177	99.2	0.0	0.0	0.0	0.8	32.0	55.6	12.5	424	48.6	68.6	8.5
Marshall city	1,355	1,313	-3.1	1,601	82.8	1.6	4.1	3.1	8.4	27.3	46.7	25.9	578	61.8	55.0	11.6
Marvell city	1,186	1,074	-9.4	1,119	29.4	68.2	0.0	0.9	1.5	28.1	49.9	22.0	500	45.2	50.8	16.8
Maumelle city	17,168	17,804	3.7	17,565	73.6	20.7	2.1	1.8	1.8	27.7	60.5	11.8	6,758	74.1	16.9	51.6
Mayflower city	2,225	2,345	5.4	2,043	88.4	8.1	0.0	2.3	1.2	20.1	64.0	15.7	873	68.6	45.7	12.3
Maynard town	426	422	-0.9	396	95.5	0.0	0.0	2.8	1.8	17.2	55.1	27.5	199	62.8	57.8	2.5
Maysville CDP	130	NA	NA	19	100.0	0.0	0.0	0.0	0.0	26.3	73.7	0.0	5	100.0	100.0	0.0
Melbourne city	1,843	1,791	-2.8	1,637	96.6	0.1	0.0	3.0	0.3	17.5	51.5	31.0	774	61.5	45.5	16.3
Mena city	5,737	5,660	-1.3	5,701	93.0	0.1	0.8	3.9	2.2	18.3	56.2	25.4	2,505	65.9	48.6	12.7
Menifee town	302	299	-1.0	369	19.2	79.7	0.0	1.1	0.0	17.0	70.7	12.5	148	83.1	53.4	11.5
Midland town	326	320	-1.8	389	85.3	0.0	0.3	2.3	12.1	35.5	47.3	17.2	127	97.6	79.5	5.5
Midway CDP	1,084	NA	NA	1,025	100.0	0.0	0.0	0.0	0.0	12.5	70.4	17.2	547	48.1	46.8	11.9
Midway town	389	389	0.0	446	93.9	0.0	0.0	5.4	0.7	29.1	62.9	8.1	151	84.8	60.3	21.2
Mineral Springs city	1,208	1,178	-2.5	983	49.6	44.5	0.0	0.3	5.6	25.9	61.0	13.0	435	60.5	54.9	7.8
Minturn town	107	104	-2.8	85	100.0	0.0	0.0	0.0	0.0	20.0	54.1	25.9	41	63.4	87.8	2.4
Mitchellville city	360	339	-5.8	345	2.6	97.4	0.0	0.0	0.0	24.4	56.4	19.1	152	75.7	69.7	3.3
Monette city	1,496	1,523	1.8	1,437	95.2	0.0	0.3	2.6	1.9	20.9	57.6	21.5	589	77.4	54.5	16.6
Monticello city	9,467	9,696	2.4	9,718	57.5	37.1	0.0	1.9	3.5	19.7	67.6	12.7	3,706	44.9	42.2	25.4
Montrose city	354	337	-4.8	341	38.7	56.0	0.0	0.0	5.3	34.0	56.7	9.4	124	58.1	65.3	7.3
Moorefield town	137	137	0.0	154	98.7	0.0	0.0	0.0	1.3	22.0	56.3	21.4	68	82.4	30.9	36.8
Moro town	216	202	-6.5	309	91.9	8.1	0.0	0.0	0.0	21.0	62.1	16.8	147	70.1	57.8	8.2
Morrilton city	6,769	6,748	-0.3	6,764	71.8	17.6	0.0	1.5	9.2	25.1	58.3	16.6	2,616	58.3	49.6	19.3
Morrison Bluff town	64	63	-1.6	72	100.0	0.0	0.0	0.0	0.0	36.1	50.0	13.9	27	44.4	44.4	7.4
Mountainburg city	631	620	-1.7	542	96.5	0.0	0.0	3.5	0.0	27.3	56.6	16.1	246	54.1	49.2	9.8
Mountain Home city	12,448	12,278	-1.4	12,338	94.3	0.5	1.1	1.6	2.4	18.1	48.7	33.2	5,872	61.4	44.6	20.1
Mountain Pine city	770	781	1.4	761	61.2	31.7	1.6	3.2	2.4	26.8	57.3	16.0	269	71.7	72.5	3.3
Mountain View city	2,745	2,839	3.4	2,810	97.1	0.7	0.0	0.5	1.7	18.8	60.2	21.0	1,217	48.6	59.7	13.8
Mount Ida city	1,076	1,037	-3.6	1,160	89.0	0.9	0.0	3.4	6.6	16.8	51.4	31.8	470	68.9	44.5	17.9
Mount Pleasant town	417	405	-2.9	371	100.0	0.0	0.0	0.0	0.0	13.8	51.2	35.0	197	75.1	54.3	11.7
Mount Vernon town	145	148	2.1	195	99.0	0.0	0.0	0.0	1.0	25.2	62.0	12.8	67	73.1	74.6	1.5
Mulberry city	1,655	1,625	-1.8	1,725	92.4	0.6	0.0	4.3	2.7	26.1	57.3	16.6	690	68.8	59.9	10.0
Murfreesboro city	1,641	1,607	-2.1	1,802	85.4	5.9	0.4	2.2	6.1	27.2	53.1	19.8	710	64.4	55.9	13.9
Nashville city	4,624	4,548	-1.6	4,604	43.3	35.7	0.0	0.7	20.3	28.2	56.0	15.8	1,766	52.6	54.4	12.9
Natural Steps CDP	426	NA	NA	302	89.7	10.3	0.0	0.0	0.0	11.6	72.5	15.9	115	100.0	56.5	15.7
Newark city	1,176	1,180	0.3	1,536	96.0	2.3	0.0	0.6	1.1	27.9	58.7	13.5	595	61.2	62.5	6.4
New Blaine CDP	174	NA	NA	164	100.0	0.0	0.0	0.0	0.0	22.6	73.2	4.3	61	54.1	50.8	0.0
New Edinburg CDP	127	NA	NA	356	89.3	0.0	0.0	0.0	10.7	31.2	64.9	3.9	116	100.0	51.7	34.5
Newport city	7,879	7,783	-1.2	7,817	65.9	27.5	0.9	2.3	3.4	17.2	69.5	13.4	2,143	50.1	60.3	15.4
Nimmons town	69	65	-5.8	55	92.7	0.0	0.0	7.3	0.0	12.8	69.0	18.2	26	80.8	80.8	0.0
Norfork city	511	498	-2.5	519	99.2	0.0	0.0	0.8	0.0	14.4	60.7	24.9	223	76.2	39.9	26.0
Norman town	379	364	-4.0	271	92.6	0.0	0.0	0.7	6.6	25.8	50.0	24.4	127	66.9	69.3	7.9
Norphlet city	844	826	-2.1	843	86.4	4.4	0.0	4.0	5.2	28.0	58.5	13.5	325	74.8	41.8	20.9
North Crossett CDP	3,119	NA	NA	3,250	83.6	13.0	0.0	1.7	1.6	24.0	59.6	16.5	1,317	72.6	58.8	10.2
North Little Rock city	62,368	66,810	7.1	64,731	49.6	40.1	0.9	1.9	7.5	25.6	61.5	13.0	25,879	53.9	36.7	27.7
Oak Grove town	369	373	1.1	434	97.0	0.0	1.6	1.4	0.0	15.5	55.5	29.0	184	65.2	66.8	2.7
Oak Grove Heights town	889	963	8.3	834	96.0	0.0	0.0	0.0	4.0	24.3	67.7	8.0	301	78.1	61.5	15.6
Oakhaven town	63	62	-1.6	104	100.0	0.0	0.0	0.0	0.0	31.7	62.4	5.8	28	100.0	28.6	25.0
Oden town	232	222	-4.3	304	96.7	0.0	2.0	0.7	0.7	36.9	53.6	9.5	84	96.4	61.9	11.9
Ogden city	180	172	-4.4	173	75.1	19.1	0.0	5.8	0.0	18.6	70.0	11.6	73	56.2	47.9	15.1
Oil Trough town	260	261	0.4	258	92.2	2.3	0.0	5.0	0.4	29.5	51.1	19.4	105	68.6	55.2	9.5
O'Kean town	194	189	-2.6	205	97.1	0.0	0.0	0.0	2.9	20.1	65.4	14.6	91	90.1	72.5	4.4
Okolona town	147	143	-2.7	189	85.2	14.8	0.0	0.0	0.0	27.0	58.8	14.3	73	82.2	57.5	2.7
Ola city	1,273	1,262	-0.9	1,181	82.3	0.0	0.4	3.0	14.3	15.0	67.7	17.4	440	41.4	57.5	8.2
Omaha town	170	171	0.6	354	89.3	0.0	0.0	10.7	0.0	30.2	62.7	7.1	124	53.2	33.9	10.5
Oppelo city	781	772	-1.2	782	96.5	0.0	0.6	2.8	0.0	24.5	61.5	14.1	295	78.0	56.3	4.1
Osceola city	7,757	7,320	-5.6	7,535	45.0	51.0	0.7	2.9	0.4	26.8	60.7	12.6	2,763	45.6	55.4	9.7
Oxford city	670	652	-2.7	660	96.4	0.0	0.0	3.6	0.0	17.5	59.3	23.0	277	70.8	73.3	4.7
Ozan town	85	84	-1.2	62	54.8	45.2	0.0	0.0	0.0	16.1	51.7	32.3	33	84.8	63.6	0.0
Ozark city	3,684	3,614	-1.9	3,645	90.4	0.2	0.9	1.8	6.7	27.1	53.4	19.3	1,266	54.6	57.4	7.7
Palestine city	681	633	-7.0	759	80.2	15.5	0.0	3.0	1.2	28.3	56.3	15.3	256	59.0	65.2	7.4
Pangburn city	601	598	-0.5	650	92.0	0.0	0.0	1.2	6.8	25.2	55.2	19.5	288	55.2	60.1	4.5
Paragould city	26,111	27,465	5.2	26,859	93.7	1.3	0.1	1.9	3.0	24.6	60.5	14.9	10,831	57.1	56.0	15.2
Paris city	3,532	3,473	-1.7	3,503	92.0	4.3	2.5	1.2	0.0	21.8	59.4	19.0	1,399	68.7	59.0	13.2
Parkdale city	277	266	-4.0	296	11.5	75.7	0.0	0.0	12.8	29.7	61.5	8.8	95	68.4	75.8	1.1
Parkin city	1,104	1,055	-4.4	1,034	28.8	71.2	0.0	0.0	0.0	20.2	54.3	25.4	457	56.7	81.4	3.9
Patmos town	64	63	-1.6	83	100.0	0.0	0.0	0.0	0.0	26.6	63.8	9.6	29	86.2	48.3	31.0
Patterson city	452	423	-6.4	428	89.0	9.6	0.0	1.4	0.0	22.8	68.6	8.4	169	66.3	84.0	2.4
Peach Orchard city	135	127	-5.9	92	100.0	0.0	0.0	0.0	0.0	10.9	66.3	22.8	49	71.4	85.7	2.0
Pea Ridge city	4,792	5,117	6.8	4,956	92.6	0.5	0.6	1.9	4.4	30.7	57.6	11.7	1,622	75.0	51.7	9.4
Perla town	241	241	0.0	172	41.3	51.2	0.0	7.6	0.0	17.5	69.3	13.4	65	70.8	58.5	7.7
Perry town	270	268	-0.7	238	94.5	0.0	0.0	0.0	5.5	16.8	65.1	18.1	96	78.1	61.5	7.3
Perrytown town	272	268	-1.5	390	74.1	12.1	0.0	0.3	13.6	22.9	52.9	24.1	179	52.0	67.6	13.4
Perryville city	1,460	1,439	-1.4	1,542	92.6	0.3	0.0	1.5	5.6	28.0	56.6	15.4	548	61.3	50.7	9.9
Piggott city	3,849	3,659	-4.9	3,739	94.5	0.3	0.0	2.3	2.9	22.2	52.8	25.1	1,675	74.6	64.8	7.8
Pindall town	110	106	-3.6	231	100.0	0.0	0.0	0.0	0.0	18.6	58.3	23.4	63	84.1	68.3	6.3
Pine Bluff city	49,080	45,332	-7.6	47,058	20.1	76.3	1.0	1.2	1.4	24.7	62.1	13.2	17,998	55.2	48.6	19.2
Pineville town	238	231	-2.9	224	87.1	0.0	3.1	9.8	0.0	29.5	52.2	18.3	90	74.4	55.6	7.8
Piney CDP	4,699	NA	NA	3,921	91.4	1.1	0.0	4.3	3.2	17.9	62.2	20.1	1,803	62.5	38.2	16.7
Plainview city	610	605	-0.8	623	95.8	2.2	0.0	1.9	0.0	36.2	51.2	12.5	185	63.8	74.6	2.7
Pleasant Plains town	348	349	0.3	306	97.7	0.0	0.0	2.3	0.0	10.1	62.1	27.8	145	55.2	77.9	3.4
Plumerville city	826	810	-1.9	867	68.9	24.9	0.0	0.5	5.8	22.9	61.6	15.6	373	54.7	50.1	12.1
Pocahontas city	6,608	6,474	-2.0	6,543	96.1	1.2	0.0	1.1	1.6	22.2	56.9	21.0	2,694	59.8	43.1	15.0
Pollard city	222	208	-6.3	214	96.7	0.0	0.0	0.0	3.3	29.0	52.3	18.7	78	84.6	64.1	3.8

1 May be of any race.

Table A. All Places — **Population and Housing**

STATE City, town, township, borough, or CDP (county if applicable)	Population				Race and Hispanic or Latino origin (percent), 2010–2014					Age (percent), 2010–2014			Households, 2010–2014			
	2010 census total population	2014 estimated population	Percent change 2010–2014	ACS total population estimate 2010–2014	White alone, not Hispanic or Latino	Black alone, not Hispanic or Latino	Asian alone, not Hispanic or Latino	All other races or 2 or more races, not Hispanic or Latino	Hispanic or Latino[1]	Under 18 years old	Age 18 to 64 years old	Age 65 years and older	Total occupied housing units	Percent owner occupied	Householders by level of education (percent) High school diploma or less	Householders by level of education (percent) Bachelor's degree or more
	1	2	3	4	5	6	7	8	9	10	11	12	13	14	15	16
ARKANSAS—Con.																
Portia town	437	425	-2.7	544	96.1	0.7	0.0	3.1	0.0	19.3	59.6	21.1	228	63.2	71.1	7.9
Portland city	430	413	-4.0	430	56.3	43.7	0.0	0.0	0.0	19.7	55.6	24.4	192	80.7	53.6	17.2
Pottsville city	2,838	3,066	8.0	2,984	89.5	0.2	1.3	2.4	6.5	28.0	60.7	11.1	1,013	76.5	42.4	17.9
Powhatan town	72	70	-2.8	102	100.0	0.0	0.0	0.0	0.0	38.2	46.1	15.7	41	90.2	73.2	0.0
Poyen town	290	292	0.7	299	100.0	0.0	0.0	0.0	0.0	26.8	64.2	9.0	112	71.4	68.8	4.5
Prairie Creek CDP	2,066	NA	NA	2,163	96.4	0.0	0.0	0.6	2.9	19.4	52.7	28.0	944	78.7	33.8	28.4
Prairie Grove city	4,380	4,937	12.7	4,670	90.0	0.0	0.5	3.8	5.7	26.5	60.7	12.8	1,779	74.5	33.8	22.4
Prattsville town	305	307	0.7	480	97.7	2.3	0.0	0.0	0.0	33.2	56.4	10.4	136	86.0	54.4	8.8
Prescott city	3,296	3,194	-3.1	3,248	38.7	50.0	3.4	0.4	7.5	28.1	52.9	19.0	1,316	52.8	47.7	21.5
Pyatt town	221	218	-1.4	144	95.1	0.0	0.0	3.5	1.4	25.7	57.7	16.7	54	51.9	63.0	13.0
Quitman city	762	749	-1.7	976	93.6	0.0	0.6	3.3	2.5	31.8	51.6	16.7	320	67.2	62.8	13.8
Ratcliff city	202	198	-2.0	192	99.0	0.0	0.0	0.0	1.0	20.8	60.9	18.2	79	77.2	67.1	5.1
Ravenden town	470	457	-2.8	437	96.1	0.0	0.0	3.2	0.7	16.0	68.0	16.0	199	56.8	64.3	4.0
Ravenden Springs town	118	115	-2.5	122	99.2	0.0	0.0	0.8	0.0	13.9	70.4	15.6	66	77.3	60.6	0.0
Reader CDP	66	NA	NA	21	100.0	0.0	0.0	0.0	0.0	0.0	0.0	100.0	10	100.0	0.0	0.0
Rector city	1,977	1,843	-6.8	2,222	95.4	0.0	0.2	1.6	2.8	24.9	59.5	15.6	865	75.0	62.9	10.8
Redfield city	1,297	1,527	17.7	1,436	85.5	9.5	0.9	2.7	1.4	23.9	63.2	12.8	531	68.5	40.7	24.3
Reed town	172	161	-6.4	147	0.0	100.0	0.0	0.0	0.0	8.8	74.3	17.0	93	69.9	82.8	5.4
Reyno city	456	445	-2.4	478	96.4	0.0	0.0	1.0	2.5	23.4	60.1	16.3	219	52.5	54.3	11.0
Rison city	1,346	1,305	-3.0	1,432	50.2	45.1	0.0	4.4	0.3	26.2	54.8	18.9	509	63.5	61.1	8.8
Rockport city	755	754	-0.1	924	97.0	1.3	0.0	0.6	1.1	21.2	62.9	16.0	357	71.7	60.8	12.3
Rockwell CDP	3,780	NA	NA	3,613	94.9	1.7	0.0	0.8	2.7	25.6	53.1	21.3	1,480	81.3	26.0	31.4
Roe town	114	107	-6.1	104	95.2	0.0	0.0	3.8	1.0	35.6	54.0	10.6	38	50.0	68.4	5.3
Rogers city	55,983	61,464	9.8	58,944	61.6	1.2	2.4	2.8	31.9	29.4	60.6	9.9	20,289	60.3	45.6	29.0
Roland CDP	746	NA	NA	728	75.8	5.9	0.0	18.3	0.0	20.2	59.5	20.3	304	90.1	46.4	17.1
Rondo town	198	185	-6.6	289	39.1	60.9	0.0	0.0	0.0	19.8	54.0	26.3	128	70.3	66.4	7.0
Rose Bud town	482	480	-0.4	532	84.0	0.9	0.0	6.6	8.5	25.5	62.1	12.4	199	58.8	55.8	17.1
Rosston town	261	254	-2.7	348	46.0	51.1	0.0	0.0	2.9	36.5	54.6	8.9	119	74.8	55.5	16.0
Rudy town	61	60	-1.6	76	100.0	0.0	0.0	0.0	0.0	29.0	65.9	5.3	22	54.5	68.2	0.0
Russell town	216	215	-0.5	241	99.6	0.0	0.0	0.0	0.4	23.6	61.8	14.5	109	48.6	70.6	6.4
Russellville city	27,917	28,993	3.9	28,581	75.8	6.0	0.6	3.8	13.9	23.3	64.5	12.4	9,922	52.3	42.5	27.1
Rye CDP	146	NA	NA	112	100.0	0.0	0.0	0.0	0.0	36.6	51.9	11.6	38	65.8	65.8	0.0
St. Charles town	230	225	-2.2	271	100.0	0.0	0.0	0.0	0.0	13.6	71.2	15.1	123	83.7	61.8	18.7
St. Francis city	250	235	-6.0	189	91.5	0.0	0.0	5.3	3.2	25.8	64.4	9.5	79	62.0	64.6	3.8
St. Joe town	130	126	-3.1	71	94.4	1.4	0.0	4.2	0.0	9.8	56.2	33.8	35	94.3	48.6	25.7
St. Paul town	113	115	1.8	120	99.2	0.0	0.0	0.8	0.0	17.5	55.0	27.5	52	80.8	61.5	25.0
Salem city	1,635	1,623	-0.7	1,506	93.4	1.3	0.0	1.2	4.1	19.6	60.4	19.9	685	49.6	64.2	10.9
Salem CDP	2,607	NA	NA	2,678	97.1	0.0	0.4	1.3	1.2	25.2	60.0	14.9	1,044	89.1	46.9	18.6
Salesville city	450	446	-0.9	412	90.8	0.0	0.0	0.7	8.5	20.6	50.6	28.9	175	89.7	45.7	8.0
Scott CDP	72	NA	NA	21	100.0	0.0	0.0	0.0	0.0	0.0	100.0	0.0	10	100.0	0.0	100.0
Scranton city	224	223	-0.4	233	94.4	0.0	0.9	3.9	0.9	21.4	68.4	10.3	93	69.9	43.0	17.2
Searcy city	22,858	23,983	4.9	23,524	85.1	8.6	0.9	1.7	3.8	19.7	65.1	15.2	8,540	52.8	38.3	29.4
Sedgwick town	152	148	-2.6	162	100.0	0.0	0.0	0.0	0.0	26.0	59.8	14.2	61	75.4	52.5	11.5
Shannon Hills city	3,130	3,671	17.3	3,356	67.8	23.4	0.2	0.8	7.8	24.2	68.3	7.6	1,137	80.7	40.1	29.7
Sheridan city	4,603	4,845	5.3	4,749	97.1	0.7	1.2	1.0	0.1	28.0	57.6	14.5	1,750	59.1	39.3	25.7
Sherrill town	84	78	-7.1	53	34.0	66.0	0.0	0.0	0.0	20.8	56.5	22.6	27	66.7	55.6	7.4
Sherwood city	29,680	30,407	2.4	30,061	73.3	16.9	1.0	2.1	6.7	23.2	64.2	12.7	11,828	67.6	35.4	32.7
Shirley town	291	283	-2.7	397	95.2	0.0	0.0	0.0	4.8	24.7	55.8	19.4	175	58.3	60.0	9.1
Sidney town	189	185	-2.1	255	94.1	0.0	2.4	1.2	2.4	13.3	61.5	25.1	85	77.6	55.3	5.9
Siloam Springs city	15,038	15,944	6.0	15,614	67.2	2.5	3.5	8.0	18.8	29.1	60.9	9.9	5,103	55.3	49.2	22.4
Smackover city	1,865	1,790	-4.0	1,862	76.4	17.2	0.0	5.2	1.2	23.7	57.9	18.5	789	69.8	48.7	20.8
Smithville town	75	73	-2.7	63	100.0	0.0	0.0	0.0	0.0	33.3	49.4	17.5	29	89.7	51.7	13.8
South Lead Hill town	102	102	0.0	105	100.0	0.0	0.0	0.0	0.0	29.6	68.6	1.9	35	62.9	62.9	5.7
Sparkman city	427	409	-4.2	478	62.1	22.6	0.0	0.4	14.9	30.0	51.7	18.2	201	69.2	74.6	7.0
Springdale city	70,747	76,565	8.2	73,789	50.6	2.1	2.0	9.8	35.4	33.7	58.1	8.2	24,340	50.6	52.9	20.4
Springtown town	87	91	4.6	68	76.5	0.0	8.8	14.7	0.0	16.1	63.3	20.6	29	93.1	72.4	0.0
Stamps city	1,693	1,580	-6.7	1,863	32.9	61.9	0.2	0.6	4.3	24.2	53.4	22.4	721	67.5	58.3	12.2
Star City city	2,272	2,220	-2.3	2,470	77.4	19.8	0.0	0.6	2.1	28.5	52.5	18.9	891	59.3	59.9	15.4
Staves CDP	116	NA	NA	172	100.0	0.0	0.0	0.0	0.0	25.5	44.8	29.7	53	66.0	47.2	0.0
Stephens city	891	843	-5.4	945	38.3	61.2	0.0	0.5	0.0	20.6	61.9	17.4	341	66.9	71.6	4.7
Strawberry town	302	293	-3.0	308	94.5	0.0	0.0	2.3	3.2	12.6	51.5	35.7	154	70.8	72.7	7.8
Strong city	555	535	-3.6	416	21.6	78.4	0.0	0.0	0.0	18.9	53.8	27.2	235	71.9	70.2	14.5
Stuttgart city	9,326	9,132	-2.1	9,269	59.1	35.2	0.9	0.8	4.1	25.3	57.7	17.2	3,834	66.7	60.0	14.8
Subiaco town	572	566	-1.0	551	84.2	8.5	4.0	1.6	1.6	21.7	63.2	14.9	175	86.3	52.6	21.7
Success town	149	140	-6.0	112	93.8	0.0	0.0	2.7	3.6	12.6	72.3	15.2	61	68.9	80.3	6.6
Sulphur Rock town	456	458	0.4	515	79.6	1.9	0.0	17.9	0.6	28.3	63.8	8.0	232	60.8	59.9	19.0
Sulphur Springs city	511	525	2.7	396	84.8	1.8	0.8	8.3	4.3	27.8	52.1	20.2	160	76.9	48.8	11.3
Sulphur Springs CDP	1,101	NA	NA	1,260	91.2	3.6	0.0	5.2	0.0	15.1	64.1	20.8	559	74.8	61.4	5.2
Summit city	604	587	-2.8	581	96.9	0.0	0.0	2.4	0.7	20.8	58.3	21.0	271	64.6	73.8	3.7
Sunset town	198	191	-3.5	221	1.4	92.8	0.0	5.9	0.0	37.1	57.9	5.0	76	65.8	73.7	13.2
Sweet Home CDP	849	NA	NA	627	17.2	64.4	3.8	0.0	14.5	24.1	58.5	17.5	259	56.0	93.8	2.7
Swifton city	798	770	-3.5	734	98.2	1.1	0.0	0.4	0.3	16.9	63.7	19.3	327	74.6	70.0	9.5
Taylor city	566	544	-3.9	574	90.6	3.1	0.0	0.0	6.3	33.7	53.3	13.2	208	73.6	48.1	24.0
Texarkana city	29,911	30,014	0.3	30,015	61.0	33.1	0.1	2.6	3.1	24.4	61.9	13.7	11,825	58.5	49.2	15.5
Thornton city	407	396	-2.7	583	65.2	31.4	0.0	3.4	0.0	21.8	61.5	16.6	206	84.5	56.3	9.7
Tillar city	225	222	-1.3	301	81.4	14.3	0.0	4.3	0.0	32.9	58.2	9.0	101	76.2	76.2	6.9
Tinsman town	54	52	-3.7	24	100.0	0.0	0.0	0.0	0.0	12.5	41.7	45.8	9	100.0	55.6	22.2
Tollette town	240	235	-2.1	317	1.6	96.5	0.0	1.3	0.6	15.5	67.9	16.7	149	49.7	53.0	16.1
Tontitown city	2,460	2,719	10.5	2,577	95.7	0.0	1.3	2.2	0.8	21.6	63.2	15.2	957	81.4	40.6	27.5
Traskwood city	518	538	3.9	442	100.0	0.0	0.0	0.0	0.0	19.0	70.1	10.9	161	87.0	55.9	3.7
Trumann city	7,296	7,201	-1.3	7,222	87.2	7.7	0.2	1.2	3.8	29.2	54.8	15.9	2,772	52.2	66.1	10.3
Tuckerman city	1,862	1,790	-3.9	2,060	88.2	6.8	0.0	4.0	1.1	20.9	58.6	20.4	938	69.8	62.8	9.8
Tull town	448	451	0.7	654	91.7	0.2	0.2	2.6	5.4	28.3	61.2	10.6	223	69.5	54.3	12.6
Tumbling Shoals CDP	978	NA	NA	1,013	96.9	0.0	0.0	0.0	3.1	22.2	55.1	22.6	390	79.0	47.4	9.7
Tupelo town	180	174	-3.3	179	98.9	0.0	0.0	0.0	1.1	17.4	44.8	38.0	84	72.6	61.9	23.8
Turrell city	615	586	-4.7	484	30.0	69.2	0.0	0.0	0.8	14.7	63.0	22.3	217	46.1	67.7	9.2
Twin Groves town	335	341	1.8	413	34.9	63.4	0.0	1.0	0.7	16.7	61.8	21.5	137	72.3	69.3	1.5
Tyronza city	762	753	-1.2	917	99.7	0.0	0.0	0.3	0.0	23.5	59.5	17.0	371	58.8	69.3	7.0
Ulm town	170	164	-3.5	187	82.9	16.0	0.0	1.1	0.0	21.4	55.7	23.0	82	90.2	68.3	11.0
Valley Springs town	183	184	0.5	218	95.0	0.5	0.0	4.6	0.0	27.1	54.7	18.3	84	78.6	44.0	25.0
Van Buren city	22,791	23,070	1.2	22,955	76.3	2.4	2.9	6.0	12.4	27.7	59.9	12.4	8,769	67.5	45.4	19.8

1 May be of any race.

Table A. All Places — **Population and Housing**

STATE City, town, township, borough, or CDP (county if applicable)	Population				Race and Hispanic or Latino origin (percent), 2010–2014					Age (percent), 2010–2014			Households, 2010–2014		Householders by level of education (percent)	
	2010 census total population	2014 estimated population	Percent change 2010–2014	ACS total population estimate 2010–2014	White alone, not Hispanic or Latino	Black alone, not Hispanic or Latino	Asian alone, not Hispanic or Latino	All other races or 2 or more races, not Hispanic or Latino	Hispanic or Latino[1]	Under 18 years old	Age 18 to 64 years old	Age 65 years and older	Total occupied housing units	Percent owner occupied	High school diploma or less	Bachelor's degree or more
	1	2	3	4	5	6	7	8	9	10	11	12	13	14	15	16
ARKANSAS—Con.																
Vandervoort town	87	85	-2.3	113	95.6	0.0	0.0	4.4	0.0	36.3	61.2	2.7	36	61.1	52.8	11.1
Victoria town	37	35	-5.4	52	100.0	0.0	0.0	0.0	0.0	40.4	59.6	0.0	16	0.0	100.0	0.0
Vilonia city	3,818	4,337	13.6	4,091	99.3	0.0	0.0	0.6	0.1	29.3	59.6	11.0	1,446	73.4	32.6	31.7
Viola town	337	334	-0.9	573	88.1	0.0	0.0	1.4	10.5	25.7	55.9	18.5	237	70.9	48.5	8.9
Wabbaseka town	255	238	-6.7	228	18.4	81.6	0.0	0.0	0.0	22.8	52.2	25.0	105	65.7	69.5	4.8
Waldenburg town	61	60	-1.6	104	100.0	0.0	0.0	0.0	0.0	9.6	67.3	23.1	37	70.3	43.2	10.8
Waldo city	1,372	1,305	-4.9	1,303	34.9	60.1	0.0	1.9	3.1	25.6	60.0	14.6	541	63.6	73.6	5.0
Waldron city	3,618	3,447	-4.7	3,564	76.5	0.8	2.2	5.1	15.5	31.2	48.8	20.1	1,230	52.9	57.3	15.3
Walnut Ridge city	4,890	4,734	-3.2	4,800	95.6	1.4	0.0	0.9	2.0	22.3	55.7	21.9	1,882	62.6	59.5	20.7
Ward city	4,065	4,610	13.4	4,354	98.3	0.4	0.0	1.3	0.0	29.4	64.6	6.0	1,593	67.2	49.8	12.7
Warren city	6,003	5,829	-2.9	5,918	42.3	40.6	0.0	0.6	16.4	22.5	58.9	18.7	2,498	63.9	65.6	10.6
Washington city	180	178	-1.1	149	27.5	70.5	0.0	2.0	0.0	8.7	73.3	18.1	66	77.3	30.3	10.6
Watson city	211	197	-6.6	115	68.7	31.3	0.0	0.0	0.0	8.7	59.1	32.2	56	92.9	83.9	7.1
Weiner city	716	696	-2.8	792	87.4	2.3	0.0	3.5	6.8	30.4	53.4	16.3	308	70.8	53.9	13.6
Weldon town	75	72	-4.0	93	100.0	0.0	0.0	0.0	0.0	20.4	62.4	17.2	43	79.1	83.7	0.0
West Crossett CDP	1,256	NA	NA	1,253	49.6	50.4	0.0	0.0	0.0	23.8	61.3	14.9	549	82.3	63.8	10.7
Western Grove town	384	364	-5.2	340	95.6	0.0	0.9	3.5	0.0	16.8	61.5	21.8	150	76.0	60.0	12.0
West Fork city	2,324	2,506	7.8	2,424	92.9	0.4	0.2	4.9	1.6	28.8	58.0	13.2	858	71.3	44.4	20.9
West Memphis city	26,247	25,423	-3.1	25,767	32.4	65.4	0.3	1.3	0.6	27.8	59.0	13.1	9,675	47.1	54.0	12.1
West Point town	185	184	-0.5	194	96.9	3.1	0.0	0.0	0.0	18.1	70.5	11.3	65	69.2	86.2	3.1
Wheatley city	355	332	-6.5	241	82.2	17.8	0.0	0.0	0.0	14.1	55.2	30.7	126	77.0	65.9	11.1
Whelen Springs town	92	90	-2.2	52	100.0	0.0	0.0	0.0	0.0	15.4	71.1	13.5	18	83.3	66.7	0.0
White Hall city	5,526	5,242	-5.1	5,392	85.5	7.4	1.1	2.0	3.9	27.5	57.8	14.7	2,038	73.5	37.6	28.1
Wickes town	754	735	-2.5	626	58.9	0.0	0.0	0.5	40.6	29.4	61.7	8.9	226	58.4	66.8	3.1
Widener town	271	255	-5.9	263	30.0	65.8	0.0	0.0	4.2	22.4	64.7	12.9	112	48.2	68.8	9.8
Wiederkehr Village city	38	37	-2.6	40	100.0	0.0	0.0	0.0	0.0	0.0	87.5	12.5	23	91.3	13.0	47.8
Williford town	75	73	-2.7	38	89.5	0.0	0.0	10.5	0.0	21.1	42.1	36.8	24	100.0	75.0	0.0
Willisville town	152	148	-2.6	201	92.5	7.5	0.0	0.0	0.0	25.8	56.9	17.4	74	83.8	54.1	27.0
Wilmar city	511	506	-1.0	425	34.1	65.9	0.0	0.0	0.0	28.0	57.0	15.1	169	63.9	63.3	11.8
Wilmot city	550	522	-5.1	493	29.2	68.4	0.0	0.0	2.4	14.4	61.4	24.1	212	63.2	60.8	16.0
Wilson city	903	876	-3.0	927	57.4	32.9	0.4	0.0	9.3	29.8	59.9	10.5	326	58.9	58.3	18.4
Wilton city	374	356	-4.8	498	65.3	32.5	0.0	1.2	1.0	14.0	70.7	15.1	190	78.9	66.8	6.8
Winchester town	167	166	-0.6	206	11.7	88.3	0.0	0.0	0.0	31.6	51.9	16.5	67	55.2	73.1	6.0
Winslow city	391	417	6.6	362	91.4	0.0	0.0	2.8	5.8	21.3	64.8	13.8	154	70.1	45.5	16.2
Winthrop city	192	183	-4.7	139	100.0	0.0	0.0	0.0	0.0	14.4	50.4	35.3	63	63.5	63.5	4.8
Woodlawn CDP	209	NA	NA	198	97.0	0.0	3.0	0.0	0.0	32.8	61.1	6.1	58	75.9	56.9	0.0
Woodson CDP	403	NA	NA	384	11.5	88.5	0.0	0.0	0.0	14.4	65.0	20.8	134	60.4	64.9	23.1
Wooster town	857	971	13.3	1,119	95.4	1.3	0.6	1.8	1.0	36.6	51.8	11.6	349	83.4	32.1	29.8
Wrightsville city	2,114	2,105	-0.4	1,451	20.8	71.7	0.0	4.9	2.5	12.3	78.0	9.6	306	67.6	67.3	6.5
Wynne city	8,367	8,150	-2.6	8,296	60.9	32.1	1.3	2.4	3.3	27.3	59.5	13.2	3,156	51.3	57.4	16.1
Yarborough Landing CDP	487	NA	NA	511	100.0	0.0	0.0	0.0	0.0	15.1	67.3	17.6	200	88.5	64.0	5.5
Yellville city	1,204	1,181	-1.9	1,290	93.1	2.7	0.0	1.9	2.2	23.0	53.3	23.6	530	61.9	53.6	10.9
Zinc town	103	103	0.0	56	91.1	0.0	0.0	8.9	0.0	5.4	62.6	32.1	22	86.4	59.1	0.0
CALIFORNIA	37,254,503	38,802,500	4.2	38,066,920	39.2	5.7	13.3	3.7	38.2	24.2	63.7	12.1	12,617,280	54.8	32.7	34.9
Acalanes Ridge CDP	1,137	NA	NA	1,226	65.3	0.0	23.6	10.0	1.1	22.6	66.1	11.3	434	86.4	8.1	76.3
Acampo CDP	341	NA	NA	776	45.1	0.0	0.0	0.0	54.9	8.9	91.1	0.0	190	62.6	40.5	31.6
Acton CDP	7,596	NA	NA	6,956	78.7	1.6	1.7	3.2	14.9	19.1	68.2	12.9	2,533	87.9	32.5	31.4
Adelanto city	31,765	32,728	3.0	31,773	17.4	20.0	1.5	6.0	55.1	37.9	57.0	5.1	7,392	53.6	55.0	7.6
Adin CDP	272	NA	NA	215	98.6	0.0	0.0	1.4	0.0	42.3	45.6	12.1	64	76.6	29.7	0.0
Agoura Hills city	20,330	20,843	2.5	20,630	75.4	1.8	6.9	2.6	13.3	24.2	63.3	12.6	7,311	74.1	13.7	56.5
Agua Dulce CDP	3,342	NA	NA	2,898	66.6	0.2	2.0	9.6	21.6	18.6	62.5	18.8	1,064	92.9	28.3	30.5
Aguanga CDP	1,128	NA	NA	897	78.5	3.3	0.0	1.7	16.5	20.1	52.8	27.1	418	84.9	45.5	14.8
Ahwahnee CDP	2,246	NA	NA	2,165	96.4	0.0	0.0	2.1	1.4	22.1	48.1	29.8	905	71.2	39.9	9.0
Airport CDP	1,964	NA	NA	1,547	28.6	2.3	0.0	0.0	69.0	30.0	60.8	9.2	472	33.1	74.6	4.9
Alameda city	73,812	77,660	5.2	75,763	43.7	7.0	30.8	6.6	11.9	20.6	65.8	13.6	30,346	47.6	19.2	51.3
Alamo CDP	14,570	NA	NA	15,639	83.3	0.9	5.9	3.3	6.6	26.5	55.7	17.9	5,322	90.6	5.0	77.6
Albany city	18,543	19,488	5.1	19,020	48.0	5.3	27.7	7.5	11.6	26.8	63.5	9.7	7,292	46.1	8.0	72.8
Albion CDP	168	NA	NA	295	66.4	1.0	9.5	11.9	11.2	0.0	89.9	10.2	100	87.0	23.0	9.0
Alderpoint CDP	186	NA	NA	255	100.0	0.0	0.0	0.0	0.0	8.6	91.4	0.0	126	82.5	68.3	0.0
Alhambra city	83,089	85,569	3.0	84,400	10.1	1.3	51.5	1.8	35.3	18.3	66.6	15.0	29,061	39.9	34.3	38.4
Alhambra Valley CDP	924	NA	NA	499	91.6	0.0	5.4	1.8	1.2	5.6	68.0	26.3	214	87.9	20.1	52.3
Aliso Viejo city	48,053	50,231	4.5	49,437	60.4	2.7	15.2	5.2	16.5	25.7	67.2	7.1	18,351	62.1	11.7	61.6
Alleghany CDP	58	NA	NA	115	100.0	0.0	0.0	0.0	0.0	0.0	80.0	20.0	43	100.0	53.5	0.0
Allendale CDP	1,506	NA	NA	1,613	67.0	6.6	2.8	4.4	19.3	16.9	72.0	11.2	568	96.5	25.7	23.2
Allensworth CDP	471	NA	NA	480	1.3	4.2	1.0	0.4	93.1	43.5	54.3	2.1	118	37.3	86.4	0.0
Almanor CDP	0	NA	NA	0	0.0	0.0	0.0	0.0	0.0	0.0	0.0	0.0	0	0.0	0.0	0.0
Alondra Park CDP	8,592	NA	NA	8,833	20.3	9.7	19.2	3.6	47.2	25.2	62.3	12.6	2,616	51.9	41.5	23.5
Alpaugh CDP	1,026	NA	NA	969	18.9	0.0	0.0	2.6	78.5	42.1	54.6	3.3	243	56.4	79.4	3.7
Alpine CDP	14,236	NA	NA	14,580	75.6	1.3	1.4	3.1	18.6	19.9	61.3	19.0	5,329	67.1	29.1	28.0
Alpine Village CDP	114	NA	NA	105	60.0	0.0	0.0	40.0	0.0	6.7	65.8	27.6	25	88.0	24.0	32.0
Alta CDP	610	NA	NA	369	96.7	0.0	0.0	0.0	3.3	14.3	61.5	24.1	154	80.5	32.5	19.5
Altadena CDP	42,777	NA	NA	44,622	40.5	20.6	6.1	3.7	29.2	21.3	63.5	15.3	15,518	70.9	20.5	52.1
Alta Sierra CDP	6,911	NA	NA	6,902	90.8	0.0	2.0	2.9	4.3	18.1	55.0	27.0	2,851	84.8	21.1	31.1
Alto CDP	711	NA	NA	678	74.6	0.0	0.0	3.2	22.1	19.3	67.7	13.0	287	57.8	7.7	53.3
Alturas city	2,827	2,618	-7.4	2,714	81.0	0.5	0.1	4.8	13.7	24.1	58.5	17.4	1,240	59.7	41.8	20.2
Alum Rock CDP	15,536	NA	NA	10,992	11.2	2.3	12.6	1.9	72.1	25.9	63.5	10.4	2,628	58.9	56.3	14.1
Amador City city	185	186	0.5	164	87.2	0.0	0.0	6.1	6.7	18.2	66.5	15.2	86	61.6	44.2	32.6
American Canyon city	19,540	20,470	4.8	20,089	26.3	7.8	34.9	4.2	26.8	26.8	63.0	10.2	5,744	73.6	32.3	33.1
Amesti CDP	3,478	NA	NA	3,213	27.3	0.0	1.6	2.4	68.7	30.7	56.9	12.4	961	66.2	51.6	13.1
Anaheim city	336,440	346,997	3.1	342,973	27.0	2.3	15.5	2.4	52.8	26.3	63.8	10.0	99,208	47.4	41.4	27.6
Anchor Bay CDP	340	NA	NA	254	95.7	0.0	0.0	4.3	0.0	0.0	59.8	40.2	137	58.4	38.0	34.3
Anderson city	9,932	10,209	2.8	10,066	80.0	0.5	0.3	6.8	12.5	26.6	60.8	12.6	3,884	51.4	40.7	7.3
Angels city	3,836	3,756	-2.1	3,782	83.2	0.0	0.4	2.8	13.6	15.9	57.6	26.5	1,798	67.7	26.9	32.5
Angwin CDP	3,051	NA	NA	3,583	51.0	4.7	12.3	5.6	26.4	13.8	77.5	8.8	844	48.0	18.5	53.3
Antelope CDP	45,770	NA	NA	47,798	58.4	8.2	10.9	7.8	14.7	29.3	63.3	7.3	14,385	65.2	30.4	25.2
Antioch city	102,365	108,930	6.4	105,630	32.0	17.4	10.3	6.2	34.0	26.6	63.8	9.8	32,900	61.0	36.6	23.1
Anza CDP	3,014	NA	NA	2,356	62.9	0.4	0.0	8.1	28.5	22.7	58.1	19.3	897	57.3	30.9	10.7
Apple Valley town	69,139	71,595	3.6	70,561	57.8	8.0	3.0	2.5	28.7	25.1	58.7	16.3	23,987	67.1	38.5	18.3
Aptos CDP	6,220	NA	NA	5,872	77.3	1.9	4.1	4.1	12.6	19.7	64.6	15.8	2,416	66.7	17.3	48.6

1 May be of any race.

Table A. All Places — **Population and Housing**

	Population				Race and Hispanic or Latino origin (percent), 2010–2014					Age (percent), 2010–2014			Households, 2010–2014			
STATE City, town, township, borough, or CDP (county if applicable)	2010 census total population	2014 estimated population	Percent change 2010–2014	ACS total population estimate 2010–2014	White alone, not Hispanic or Latino	Black alone, not Hispanic or Latino	Asian alone, not Hispanic or Latino	All other races or 2 or more races, not Hispanic or Latino	Hispanic or Latino[1]	Under 18 years old	Age 18 to 64 years old	Age 65 years and older	Total occupied housing units	Percent owner occupied	Householders by level of education (percent) High school diploma or less	Householders by level of education (percent) Bachelor's degree or more
	1	2	3	4	5	6	7	8	9	10	11	12	13	14	15	16
CALIFORNIA—Con.																
Aptos Hills-Larkin Valley CDP	2,381	NA	NA	1,808	80.0	0.0	1.1	0.8	18.1	19.1	60.0	20.9	681	83.6	6.2	56.7
Arbuckle CDP	3,028	NA	NA	3,009	18.3	0.0	0.3	3.1	78.3	35.0	58.7	6.2	798	68.2	64.7	14.0
Arcadia city	56,364	58,232	3.3	57,251	25.0	1.0	58.4	2.9	12.7	21.5	62.2	16.2	19,463	60.0	17.7	57.9
Arcata city	17,231	17,730	2.9	17,679	74.9	2.2	1.8	7.2	14.0	13.6	78.0	8.5	6,891	32.0	16.0	42.0
Arden-Arcade CDP	92,186	NA	NA	92,844	61.4	8.3	6.3	5.2	18.8	21.7	62.6	15.6	40,152	45.9	24.1	36.2
Armona CDP	4,156	NA	NA	3,531	17.6	4.8	4.2	3.4	70.0	35.9	55.8	8.4	970	51.2	55.8	0.8
Arnold CDP	3,843	NA	NA	2,728	88.2	0.0	0.8	2.9	8.1	12.4	57.7	29.9	1,335	79.2	23.0	34.5
Aromas CDP	2,650	NA	NA	2,677	57.3	0.0	5.7	4.3	32.7	18.2	68.0	13.7	887	77.2	32.9	29.3
Arroyo Grande city	17,249	17,908	3.8	17,536	75.8	0.2	5.3	3.4	15.3	20.6	57.4	21.9	6,848	69.6	21.7	38.5
Artesia city	16,522	16,895	2.3	16,698	19.5	3.8	36.0	2.7	38.1	21.0	66.9	12.2	4,517	51.5	41.6	27.8
Artois CDP	295	NA	NA	194	100.0	0.0	0.0	0.0	0.0	57.3	37.6	5.2	37	100.0	89.2	10.8
Arvin city	19,304	20,583	6.6	20,028	6.9	0.8	0.4	0.6	91.3	35.4	60.3	4.2	4,595	47.2	76.3	2.8
Ashland CDP	21,925	NA	NA	23,360	13.7	19.3	17.4	4.4	45.1	30.3	62.4	7.2	7,610	31.7	50.3	19.2
Aspen Springs CDP	65	NA	NA	54	100.0	0.0	0.0	0.0	0.0	27.8	72.3	0.0	16	100.0	0.0	43.8
Atascadero city	28,306	29,134	2.9	28,792	78.3	1.8	1.9	2.3	15.8	21.2	63.4	15.4	11,065	63.5	25.4	30.2
Atherton town	6,920	7,147	3.3	7,034	78.5	0.2	12.2	4.0	5.0	22.7	55.7	21.5	2,373	90.8	4.5	87.5
Atwater city	28,172	29,022	3.0	28,686	34.5	3.4	6.4	4.2	51.5	32.6	56.9	10.5	8,672	49.6	47.6	16.1
Auberry CDP	2,369	NA	NA	2,347	65.1	0.3	0.6	1.6	32.4	19.5	63.1	17.6	915	81.5	33.2	13.2
Auburn city	13,305	13,960	4.9	13,690	84.8	1.7	2.4	5.0	6.2	17.3	61.9	20.6	5,992	54.0	22.6	37.1
Auburn Lake Trails CDP	3,426	NA	NA	3,839	96.4	0.3	0.0	2.6	0.7	26.3	57.7	15.9	1,366	87.0	12.2	41.7
August CDP	8,390	NA	NA	8,479	17.7	1.3	13.6	2.1	65.3	33.3	60.5	6.2	2,259	43.2	72.1	2.8
Avalon city	3,728	3,802	2.0	3,768	25.7	0.3	0.1	1.7	72.2	29.5	60.2	10.2	1,262	22.1	46.8	25.3
Avenal city	15,505	13,308	-14.2	14,553	12.7	4.9	0.6	2.6	79.2	26.9	68.3	4.9	2,482	42.2	81.7	6.5
Avery CDP	646	NA	NA	674	100.0	0.0	0.0	0.0	0.0	8.6	52.5	38.9	299	92.6	38.1	22.1
Avila Beach CDP	1,627	NA	NA	1,166	89.2	0.0	7.7	2.5	0.6	4.3	65.3	30.4	665	70.5	5.4	54.6
Avocado Heights CDP	15,411	NA	NA	15,432	7.4	0.0	9.5	0.6	82.5	23.1	62.7	14.1	3,856	78.1	47.0	20.8
Azusa city	46,361	48,799	5.3	47,420	19.8	2.8	9.8	2.3	65.2	24.2	67.8	7.9	11,816	51.2	48.3	22.0
Baker CDP	735	NA	NA	916	21.6	1.4	3.5	1.3	72.2	35.5	62.0	2.6	259	31.3	73.0	5.8
Bakersfield city	347,587	368,759	6.1	358,700	35.8	7.8	6.4	3.1	46.9	30.5	60.6	8.8	111,988	56.9	39.2	22.7
Baldwin Park city	75,390	77,119	2.3	76,411	3.5	1.2	16.3	1.1	77.9	26.7	64.3	9.1	17,434	58.7	67.3	11.4
Ballard CDP	467	NA	NA	323	78.6	0.0	0.0	0.0	21.4	9.9	65.6	24.5	144	77.1	20.8	62.5
Ballico CDP	406	NA	NA	333	52.3	2.4	1.2	0.9	43.2	27.0	60.6	12.3	110	64.5	60.0	6.4
Bangor CDP	646	NA	NA	575	92.5	0.0	0.0	7.1	0.3	22.6	55.9	21.4	234	72.6	25.6	23.5
Banning city	29,603	30,769	3.9	30,281	45.9	7.3	5.0	2.2	39.5	19.9	52.1	28.0	11,739	66.8	46.1	17.5
Barstow city	22,639	23,498	3.8	23,110	32.1	13.2	3.2	8.3	43.2	30.6	58.8	10.7	7,937	47.8	47.1	12.1
Bass Lake CDP	527	NA	NA	570	100.0	0.0	0.0	0.0	0.0	9.9	48.5	41.8	249	74.3	12.0	39.8
Bay Point CDP	21,349	NA	NA	21,586	19.6	12.0	8.4	3.7	56.2	30.8	62.1	7.2	6,431	50.1	54.3	12.7
Bayview CDP (Contra Costa)	1,754	NA	NA	2,025	34.1	14.9	16.3	2.0	32.6	30.6	55.9	13.7	647	82.8	43.0	29.5
Bayview CDP (Humboldt)	2,510	NA	NA	2,408	64.7	0.0	0.9	6.2	28.2	22.5	65.8	11.7	1,020	54.5	42.5	22.9
Beale AFB CDP	1,319	NA	NA	1,342	60.5	9.3	10.7	7.0	12.4	38.5	61.2	0.3	363	0.8	19.3	23.4
Bear Creek CDP	290	NA	NA	197	13.7	0.0	0.0	0.0	86.3	8.1	56.0	36.0	80	50.0	68.8	0.0
Bear Valley CDP (Alpine)	121	NA	NA	43	86.0	0.0	0.0	0.0	14.0	25.6	74.4	0.0	19	63.2	52.6	21.1
Bear Valley CDP (Mariposa)	125	NA	NA	201	100.0	0.0	0.0	0.0	0.0	33.3	29.5	37.3	92	80.4	26.1	29.3
Bear Valley Springs CDP	5,172	NA	NA	5,058	82.1	1.2	2.2	4.8	9.7	20.9	56.1	23.1	2,098	89.6	16.2	40.7
Beaumont city	36,878	42,277	14.6	39,620	44.1	5.0	10.2	2.8	37.9	29.8	58.9	11.3	12,721	76.5	30.8	27.6
Beckwourth CDP	432	NA	NA	290	92.1	0.0	0.0	0.0	7.9	5.2	63.2	31.7	170	94.1	27.6	47.1
Belden CDP	22	NA	NA	46	69.6	0.0	30.4	0.0	0.0	34.8	65.2	0.0	30	0.0	46.7	0.0
Bell city	35,477	36,217	2.1	35,896	5.0	1.3	0.6	0.4	92.7	30.2	62.5	7.4	8,998	28.8	71.7	5.6
Bella Vista CDP	2,781	NA	NA	2,717	84.5	0.3	0.0	7.0	8.2	20.3	62.2	17.5	944	79.3	40.5	13.1
Bell Canyon CDP	2,049	NA	NA	2,289	71.2	0.0	12.8	8.4	7.6	22.4	66.0	11.5	737	99.3	11.3	71.5
Bellflower city	76,610	78,236	2.1	77,521	19.1	13.7	11.0	2.1	54.2	28.2	62.4	9.3	23,473	39.5	49.4	14.9
Bell Gardens city	42,072	43,146	2.6	42,712	2.3	0.4	0.6	0.2	96.5	33.6	61.0	5.5	9,693	22.8	80.7	4.5
Belmont city	25,844	27,073	4.8	26,503	55.9	2.3	22.8	6.2	12.8	21.6	63.2	15.2	10,493	60.7	13.8	59.0
Belvedere city	2,068	2,129	2.9	2,036	83.1	0.2	3.5	6.5	6.6	21.5	44.2	34.3	906	78.1	4.7	79.6
Benbow CDP	321	NA	NA	314	86.3	0.0	0.0	0.0	13.7	6.7	57.8	35.7	124	91.1	7.3	47.6
Bend CDP	619	NA	NA	641	92.2	0.0	2.0	2.2	3.6	15.6	64.2	20.3	250	85.6	32.8	22.8
Benicia city	26,997	27,930	3.5	27,450	61.7	5.4	10.4	7.3	15.2	23.8	62.5	13.8	10,788	68.2	17.7	44.1
Ben Lomond CDP	6,234	NA	NA	6,485	85.6	0.0	1.8	3.1	9.5	19.9	68.6	11.5	2,595	72.6	18.0	42.2
Benton CDP	280	NA	NA	178	77.0	0.0	0.0	16.9	6.2	10.7	69.1	20.2	112	75.0	29.5	0.0
Berkeley city	112,489	118,853	5.7	115,688	55.8	8.3	19.5	5.5	10.9	12.7	74.1	13.0	45,569	41.9	11.6	66.5
Bermuda Dunes CDP	7,282	NA	NA	7,719	52.0	6.1	0.4	3.2	38.3	22.9	66.4	10.7	2,811	52.7	34.3	37.2
Berry Creek CDP	1,424	NA	NA	1,292	85.6	1.9	0.9	6.3	5.3	14.8	62.8	22.4	555	74.8	41.6	11.5
Bertsch-Oceanview CDP	2,436	NA	NA	2,568	76.8	0.0	0.0	12.7	10.4	27.0	57.4	15.5	806	76.3	45.9	17.4
Bethel Island CDP	2,137	NA	NA	2,158	81.1	0.0	0.0	3.8	15.0	6.4	58.5	35.3	1,066	81.0	39.1	9.7
Beverly Hills city	34,109	34,871	2.2	34,536	78.7	1.7	9.1	4.1	6.4	19.4	60.5	20.1	14,606	40.7	15.2	62.1
Bieber CDP	312	NA	NA	127	72.4	0.0	0.0	4.7	22.8	29.9	40.1	29.9	49	100.0	71.4	0.0
Big Bear City CDP	12,304	NA	NA	12,563	79.9	0.0	1.2	1.6	17.2	19.3	65.4	15.3	5,054	62.2	38.2	17.1
Big Bear Lake city	5,018	5,173	3.1	5,104	73.8	1.4	0.0	4.1	20.7	21.7	57.5	21.0	2,174	55.9	33.3	22.2
Big Bend CDP	102	NA	NA	87	86.2	3.4	0.0	10.3	0.0	10.3	44.7	44.8	49	59.2	51.0	16.3
Big Creek CDP	175	NA	NA	201	66.2	0.0	0.0	19.4	14.4	22.4	57.3	20.4	85	36.5	11.8	48.2
Biggs city	1,707	1,711	0.2	2,010	49.1	0.0	4.1	7.1	39.8	28.4	61.8	9.6	593	56.2	51.3	6.7
Big Lagoon CDP	93	NA	NA	142	47.9	0.0	0.0	47.2	4.9	16.2	71.2	12.7	65	95.4	4.6	38.5
Big Pine CDP	1,756	NA	NA	1,612	62.2	0.0	3.9	24.4	9.5	22.1	59.6	18.3	663	72.4	35.3	12.1
Big River CDP	1,327	NA	NA	1,061	78.8	0.0	0.0	7.9	13.3	10.5	49.2	40.2	581	84.5	42.7	14.5
Biola CDP	1,623	NA	NA	1,017	1.0	0.0	23.8	4.3	70.9	45.4	46.0	8.6	227	75.3	78.0	2.2
Bishop city	3,879	3,841	-1.0	3,851	66.5	0.3	1.8	2.4	29.1	24.6	57.5	17.8	1,710	41.6	42.1	23.1
Blackhawk CDP	9,354	NA	NA	9,297	73.3	1.9	18.9	1.5	4.3	20.5	63.5	15.9	3,667	88.7	5.6	74.3
Blacklake CDP	930	NA	NA	942	96.6	0.0	0.0	0.6	2.8	9.0	25.7	65.3	470	88.7	7.2	51.9
Black Point-Green Point CDP	1,306	NA	NA	1,111	91.8	0.0	6.8	0.7	0.7	24.4	55.4	20.3	441	83.2	14.3	66.0
Blairsden CDP	39	NA	NA	35	100.0	0.0	0.0	0.0	0.0	0.0	100.0	0.0	26	26.9	26.9	26.9
Bloomfield CDP	345	NA	NA	373	90.9	6.2	2.9	0.0	0.0	0.0	63.7	36.2	166	74.1	34.9	44.0
Bloomington CDP	23,851	NA	NA	25,228	10.0	2.6	0.6	1.1	85.7	31.2	61.9	7.0	5,530	72.2	63.7	7.1
Blue Lake city	1,253	1,243	-0.8	1,258	80.0	1.8	1.7	11.6	4.8	18.8	67.2	14.0	514	58.8	36.4	36.4
Bluewater CDP	172	NA	NA	174	96.6	0.0	0.0	0.0	3.4	0.0	11.5	88.5	105	92.4	47.6	9.5
Blythe city	20,817	19,258	-7.5	20,101	28.1	13.6	2.1	2.2	53.9	17.4	74.7	7.9	5,019	53.3	48.6	13.3
Bodega CDP	220	NA	NA	156	100.0	0.0	0.0	0.0	0.0	0.0	87.7	12.2	109	11.0	25.7	11.0
Bodega Bay CDP	1,077	NA	NA	603	98.0	0.0	0.0	0.0	2.0	0.0	69.6	30.3	308	89.9	21.1	65.9

1 May be of any race.

Table A. All Places — **Population and Housing**

STATE City, town, township, borough, or CDP (county if applicable)	Population 2010 census total population	2014 estimated population	Percent change 2010–2014	ACS total population estimate 2010–2014	Race and Hispanic or Latino origin (percent), 2010–2014 White alone, not Hispanic or Latino	Black alone, not Hispanic or Latino	Asian alone, not Hispanic or Latino	All other races or 2 or more races, not Hispanic or Latino	Hispanic or Latino[1]	Age (percent), 2010–2014 Under 18 years old	Age 18 to 64 years old	Age 65 years and older	Households, 2010–2014 Total occupied housing units	Percent owner occupied	Householders by level of education (percent) High school diploma or less	Bachelor's degree or more
	1	2	3	4	5	6	7	8	9	10	11	12	13	14	15	16
CALIFORNIA—Con.																
Bodfish CDP	1,956	NA	NA	1,961	68.1	0.7	0.0	8.4	22.8	13.0	57.8	29.2	1,043	73.9	40.8	20.9
Bolinas CDP	1,620	NA	NA	1,403	85.0	5.1	2.1	0.8	7.1	14.2	61.7	24.0	500	66.4	4.2	74.4
Bombay Beach CDP	295	NA	NA	171	75.4	10.5	4.1	0.0	9.9	18.8	37.5	43.9	119	68.1	80.7	13.4
Bonadelle Ranchos-Madera Ranchos CDP	8,569	NA	NA	8,503	64.8	2.3	1.3	3.5	28.2	22.3	65.5	12.4	2,727	85.3	31.0	24.2
Bonita CDP	12,538	NA	NA	13,864	38.2	4.0	8.0	4.2	45.6	18.1	62.0	19.8	4,445	75.5	24.8	43.5
Bonny Doon CDP	2,678	NA	NA	2,752	87.6	0.0	1.2	5.9	5.3	14.2	70.2	15.5	1,049	82.4	7.4	57.6
Bonsall CDP	3,982	NA	NA	4,138	63.8	1.0	4.2	4.3	26.7	18.4	61.6	19.9	1,539	74.2	23.3	42.2
Boonville CDP	1,035	NA	NA	1,090	35.0	0.0	0.0	3.3	61.7	23.8	57.8	18.3	367	56.1	50.1	14.7
Bootjack CDP	960	NA	NA	959	87.1	0.0	4.3	1.3	7.4	25.7	49.2	25.1	365	73.4	39.2	16.2
Boron CDP	2,253	NA	NA	2,241	63.5	16.6	1.5	2.1	16.2	31.8	50.8	17.4	830	58.3	60.8	9.9
Boronda CDP	1,710	NA	NA	1,278	23.4	0.0	3.0	1.8	71.8	24.5	57.2	18.2	384	29.7	68.8	2.1
Borrego Springs CDP	3,429	NA	NA	2,359	60.3	0.0	5.9	2.8	31.0	18.8	51.8	29.3	1,143	62.5	42.4	27.3
Bostonia CDP	15,379	NA	NA	16,460	51.9	5.5	2.0	4.5	36.1	26.4	62.3	11.5	5,602	41.1	46.4	11.8
Boulder Creek CDP	4,923	NA	NA	4,741	88.3	0.3	2.4	4.4	4.5	15.3	70.0	14.5	2,034	77.0	15.9	43.5
Boulevard CDP	315	NA	NA	434	41.2	0.0	0.0	48.2	10.6	37.1	40.6	22.4	178	58.4	86.5	0.0
Bowles CDP	166	NA	NA	182	57.1	0.0	0.0	0.0	42.9	23.6	43.4	33.0	39	53.8	38.5	0.0
Boyes Hot Springs CDP	6,656	NA	NA	7,664	38.0	0.4	3.4	1.6	56.7	29.1	59.4	11.5	2,452	52.4	42.1	29.4
Bradbury city	1,048	1,087	3.7	845	47.5	2.8	31.7	2.7	15.3	11.6	61.4	27.1	316	84.8	12.7	62.7
Bradley CDP	93	NA	NA	127	74.8	5.5	0.0	19.7	0.0	22.8	60.5	16.5	44	47.7	34.1	6.8
Brawley city	24,953	25,820	3.5	25,478	16.4	1.6	0.8	0.2	80.9	31.3	57.8	10.9	7,455	55.0	50.1	12.1
Brea city	39,189	41,508	5.9	40,443	49.4	1.1	18.4	3.2	27.9	22.4	64.2	13.3	14,153	61.6	20.4	43.7
Brentwood city	51,624	57,019	10.5	54,062	56.2	4.7	8.1	5.3	25.8	29.5	57.8	12.8	17,138	73.5	24.2	32.2
Bret Harte CDP	5,152	NA	NA	4,998	12.3	0.0	1.5	0.9	85.3	37.8	56.3	5.9	1,224	39.2	87.9	0.7
Bridgeport CDP	575	NA	NA	761	39.9	2.2	5.3	28.6	23.9	0.8	67.1	32.2	292	64.7	37.0	7.2
Brisbane city	4,282	4,612	7.7	4,421	41.8	2.0	32.3	2.6	21.2	17.7	67.5	14.9	1,743	63.8	18.8	56.9
Broadmoor CDP	4,176	NA	NA	4,734	25.1	0.3	55.4	3.5	15.7	17.1	70.2	12.6	1,496	74.9	22.6	42.6
Brookdale CDP	1,991	NA	NA	2,204	89.2	0.0	2.5	0.0	8.3	14.4	75.5	10.0	992	82.7	21.2	31.7
Brooktrails CDP	3,235	NA	NA	3,589	89.5	0.0	0.0	3.5	7.0	31.9	57.7	10.6	1,380	66.7	23.8	24.1
Buckhorn CDP	2,429	NA	NA	2,503	88.1	0.4	0.1	5.3	6.0	12.5	47.5	40.2	1,110	76.6	42.6	16.7
Buck Meadows CDP	31	NA	NA	50	0.0	0.0	16.0	0.0	84.0	0.0	100.0	0.0	23	0.0	82.6	17.4
Bucks Lake CDP	10	NA	NA	14	100.0	0.0	0.0	0.0	0.0	0.0	100.0	0.0	9	100.0	100.0	0.0
Buellton city	4,828	5,044	4.5	4,924	56.7	2.5	3.1	7.7	30.0	22.3	65.2	12.6	1,830	69.6	28.4	32.6
Buena Park city	80,613	83,105	3.1	82,191	26.2	4.0	29.2	2.6	38.1	23.9	64.8	11.3	23,223	55.7	35.5	29.7
Buena Vista CDP	429	NA	NA	284	85.9	0.0	0.0	0.0	14.1	21.1	58.1	20.8	109	90.8	31.2	0.0
Burbank city	103,340	105,368	2.0	104,484	56.7	1.7	11.4	4.4	25.8	19.6	66.0	14.3	41,414	41.6	26.1	40.9
Burbank CDP	4,926	NA	NA	5,869	32.5	1.6	8.6	4.0	53.4	22.0	72.4	5.7	2,097	45.3	28.9	30.5
Burlingame city	28,806	30,298	5.2	29,618	59.5	1.1	20.6	5.5	13.3	22.9	64.0	13.1	12,186	48.2	14.0	60.1
Burney CDP	3,154	NA	NA	3,172	91.0	1.0	0.4	4.3	3.2	21.0	56.8	22.2	1,336	53.6	55.1	9.1
Burnt Ranch CDP	281	NA	NA	308	97.1	0.0	0.0	2.3	0.6	12.7	64.6	22.7	116	73.3	42.2	25.9
Butte Creek Canyon CDP	1,086	NA	NA	805	92.5	0.0	0.0	2.1	5.3	10.6	68.6	20.9	401	93.5	10.7	52.1
Butte Meadows CDP	40	NA	NA	34	100.0	0.0	0.0	0.0	0.0	0.0	47.1	52.9	18	100.0	0.0	0.0
Butte Valley CDP	899	NA	NA	603	83.7	3.5	0.0	1.0	11.8	24.6	61.2	14.3	247	98.4	28.3	55.1
Buttonwillow CDP	1,508	NA	NA	1,371	16.8	5.5	0.1	1.4	76.2	34.9	56.7	8.2	378	44.4	71.4	3.2
Byron CDP	1,277	NA	NA	1,305	56.7	0.7	0.7	0.0	41.9	29.7	53.0	17.5	443	47.6	63.4	9.9
Bystrom CDP	4,008	NA	NA	3,805	19.2	0.0	3.8	0.6	76.4	30.7	61.5	7.8	1,160	38.1	80.2	2.9
Cabazon CDP	2,535	NA	NA	3,266	35.7	1.8	0.0	6.6	55.9	36.2	59.6	4.2	880	56.1	58.0	6.9
Calabasas city	23,462	24,296	3.6	23,956	76.6	2.2	8.9	5.7	6.6	25.3	61.1	13.7	8,792	70.8	11.1	67.8
Calexico city	38,573	39,799	3.2	39,281	1.8	0.2	1.2	0.0	96.9	30.0	57.8	12.3	9,213	51.6	60.1	12.1
California City city	14,120	13,263	-6.1	13,243	50.5	14.7	2.8	2.3	29.6	22.2	66.5	11.3	4,689	62.7	43.3	9.7
California Hot Springs CDP	37	NA	NA	74	81.1	0.0	0.0	1.4	17.6	17.6	51.4	31.1	32	75.0	50.0	15.6
California Pines CDP	520	NA	NA	367	71.9	0.0	0.0	6.5	21.5	34.7	59.7	5.7	159	66.7	46.5	33.3
Calimesa city	7,883	8,423	6.9	8,143	71.2	0.0	1.6	2.7	24.5	17.3	53.9	28.7	3,351	86.8	43.6	16.1
Calipatria city	7,705	7,519	-2.4	7,599	5.2	7.5	0.6	2.0	84.8	31.2	60.9	7.9	1,571	52.5	54.5	3.8
Calistoga city	5,155	5,303	2.9	5,244	59.0	0.9	3.5	3.8	32.8	19.6	58.9	21.4	2,187	62.9	27.2	32.7
Callender CDP	1,262	NA	NA	1,537	71.2	1.2	16.2	2.6	8.8	25.5	59.1	15.4	522	61.9	22.0	9.2
Calpella CDP	679	NA	NA	424	64.6	8.7	4.5	2.6	19.6	21.9	68.0	10.1	164	48.2	28.0	11.6
Calpine CDP	205	NA	NA	189	100.0	0.0	0.0	0.0	0.0	0.0	49.8	50.3	99	66.7	71.7	18.2
Calwa CDP	0	NA	NA	1,330	7.9	0.0	1.8	2.6	87.7	39.9	56.6	3.6	330	20.6	70.9	0.0
Camanche North Shore CDP	979	NA	NA	947	82.3	0.0	1.0	3.1	13.7	11.5	76.8	11.6	393	70.2	33.1	13.2
Camanche Village CDP	847	NA	NA	840	91.1	0.0	0.0	6.1	2.9	28.3	49.0	22.7	292	90.4	15.4	19.2
Camarillo city	65,221	66,923	2.6	65,985	59.2	2.0	10.2	3.2	25.5	22.6	59.3	18.2	24,270	70.1	20.4	44.5
Cambria CDP	6,032	NA	NA	6,246	75.6	0.1	0.5	2.3	21.4	13.1	49.7	37.3	2,827	71.7	18.7	51.9
Cambrian Park CDP	3,282	NA	NA	3,318	65.7	0.2	3.4	8.8	21.9	21.6	64.0	14.5	1,170	75.4	22.1	40.3
Cameron Park CDP	18,228	NA	NA	18,831	81.4	0.2	2.0	2.9	13.4	24.4	59.6	15.9	7,071	67.1	22.3	36.7
Camino CDP	1,750	NA	NA	1,833	94.8	0.2	0.7	0.8	3.5	20.7	58.2	21.1	737	71.1	15.3	26.3
Camino Tassajara CDP	2,197	NA	NA	1,789	32.5	1.0	59.5	5.3	1.7	33.0	59.1	7.7	579	90.3	8.5	77.4
Campbell city	39,348	41,119	4.5	40,327	57.5	1.9	15.7	4.9	20.0	20.8	68.2	11.0	15,763	50.9	18.1	51.9
Camp Nelson CDP	97	NA	NA	100	100.0	0.0	0.0	0.0	0.0	0.0	80.0	20.0	50	68.0	0.0	0.0
Campo CDP	2,684	NA	NA	3,031	62.1	1.4	1.5	2.5	32.6	26.3	63.6	10.1	960	75.7	38.2	18.1
Camp Pendleton North CDP	5,200	NA	NA	6,436	58.1	10.6	2.3	4.4	24.6	29.0	70.6	0.3	1,244	0.0	35.0	28.0
Camp Pendleton South CDP	10,616	NA	NA	12,691	51.9	15.7	3.7	6.4	22.4	40.8	59.1	0.0	2,943	0.0	43.6	15.7
Camptonville CDP	158	NA	NA	150	82.0	0.0	10.0	6.0	2.0	8.7	71.9	19.3	84	39.3	41.7	15.5
Canby CDP	315	NA	NA	693	46.3	8.9	2.9	10.5	31.3	25.3	61.1	13.6	106	30.2	50.0	0.0
Cantua Creek CDP	466	NA	NA	440	0.0	0.0	0.0	0.0	100.0	33.6	60.3	6.1	129	61.2	100.0	0.0
Canyondam CDP	31	NA	NA	78	37.2	0.0	0.0	0.0	62.8	0.0	100.0	0.0	49	100.0	100.0	0.0
Canyon Lake city	10,561	11,010	4.3	10,810	84.5	1.0	1.0	0.6	12.9	20.7	61.3	18.0	3,952	85.0	25.5	30.2
Capitola city	9,918	10,146	2.3	10,043	66.3	1.9	4.3	5.2	22.3	18.7	65.6	15.8	4,424	46.2	21.7	42.3
Caribou CDP	0	NA	NA	0	0.0	0.0	0.0	0.0	0.0	0.0	0.0	0.0	0	0.0	0.0	0.0
Carlsbad city	105,459	112,299	6.5	109,296	74.6	1.2	7.1	2.9	14.2	23.1	61.9	14.9	42,516	62.6	11.7	58.0
Carmel-by-the-Sea city	3,722	3,876	4.1	3,807	80.7	0.0	8.2	1.6	9.5	17.7	48.3	34.1	1,750	65.1	16.5	58.2
Carmel Valley Village CDP	4,407	NA	NA	4,321	86.7	0.9	2.2	4.9	5.3	18.9	60.8	20.2	1,758	68.8	15.8	46.9
Carmet CDP	47	NA	NA	14	100.0	0.0	0.0	0.0	0.0	0.0	42.9	57.1	6	100.0	0.0	100.0
Carmichael CDP	61,762	NA	NA	63,314	74.1	5.2	4.0	5.7	10.9	20.5	61.7	17.9	25,956	55.3	23.1	34.4
Carnelian Bay CDP	524	NA	NA	463	100.0	0.0	0.0	0.0	0.0	10.4	59.8	30.0	207	78.7	19.3	50.2
Carpinteria city	13,044	13,671	4.8	13,323	49.2	0.2	3.0	2.6	45.0	18.1	65.0	16.9	5,082	55.2	35.8	32.3
Carrick CDP	131	NA	NA	66	100.0	0.0	0.0	0.0	0.0	0.0	60.6	39.4	26	100.0	0.0	0.0

1 May be of any race.

Table A. All Places — **Population and Housing**

STATE City, town, township, borough, or CDP (county if applicable)	Population: 2010 census total population	Population: 2014 estimated population	Population: Percent change 2010–2014	Population: ACS total population estimate 2010–2014	Race and Hispanic or Latino origin (percent), 2010–2014: White alone, not Hispanic or Latino	Black alone, not Hispanic or Latino	Asian alone, not Hispanic or Latino	All other races or 2 or more races, not Hispanic or Latino	Hispanic or Latino[1]	Age (percent), 2010–2014: Under 18 years old	Age 18 to 64 years old	Age 65 years and older	Households, 2010–2014: Total occupied housing units	Percent owner occupied	Householders by level of education (percent): High school diploma or less	Bachelor's degree or more
	1	2	3	4	5	6	7	8	9	10	11	12	13	14	15	16
CALIFORNIA—Con.																
Carson city	91,714	93,271	1.7	92,475	7.2	20.4	25.5	7.2	39.6	22.4	63.5	14.2	24,729	74.7	36.9	26.8
Cartago CDP	92	NA	NA	38	100.0	0.0	0.0	0.0	0.0	0.0	60.5	39.5	33	100.0	78.8	21.2
Caruthers CDP	2,497	NA	NA	3,338	11.1	1.9	2.3	3.7	80.9	32.5	63.2	4.3	754	50.9	68.8	4.4
Casa Conejo CDP	3,249	NA	NA	3,699	58.4	0.0	6.2	2.7	32.7	24.8	63.8	11.4	1,031	83.1	28.6	25.9
Casa de Oro-Mount Helix CDP	18,762	NA	NA	21,076	66.8	4.9	2.0	4.0	22.3	22.5	58.7	18.9	7,455	69.9	22.7	45.2
Casmalia CDP	138	NA	NA	114	43.0	0.0	0.0	0.0	57.0	14.0	70.2	15.8	33	100.0	51.5	0.0
Caspar CDP	509	NA	NA	599	86.6	0.0	0.0	10.9	2.5	11.1	54.7	34.2	250	54.0	10.4	65.2
Cassel CDP	207	NA	NA	349	96.3	0.0	0.0	0.0	3.7	10.6	55.0	34.4	146	71.2	17.1	0.0
Castaic CDP	19,015	NA	NA	18,619	55.7	1.7	9.0	5.6	28.1	29.4	64.5	6.1	5,747	80.8	21.9	36.8
Castle Hill CDP	1,299	NA	NA	1,223	81.7	1.0	5.8	5.0	6.5	16.0	55.5	28.5	470	100.0	0.0	60.6
Castro Valley CDP	61,388	NA	NA	62,363	46.9	5.6	24.0	4.8	18.6	22.9	63.3	13.5	22,365	67.1	27.0	37.4
Castroville CDP	6,481	NA	NA	6,226	3.9	0.3	3.8	1.4	90.5	33.8	59.8	6.4	1,438	43.3	80.7	4.2
Cathedral City city	51,200	53,437	4.4	52,550	29.6	2.2	4.5	1.4	62.4	28.0	58.4	13.6	16,840	61.7	48.0	19.3
Catheys Valley CDP	825	NA	NA	878	79.5	0.0	0.0	11.2	9.3	9.6	59.8	30.6	396	72.2	42.9	31.8
Cayucos CDP	2,592	NA	NA	2,553	81.0	0.0	6.3	0.5	12.1	8.7	57.7	33.8	1,230	66.5	21.5	40.9
Cazadero CDP	354	NA	NA	312	86.2	1.6	0.0	6.7	5.4	18.6	66.4	15.1	143	67.1	52.4	18.9
Cedar Ridge CDP	1,132	NA	NA	1,132	90.9	0.4	0.6	3.4	4.8	12.9	64.6	22.5	491	87.6	33.6	22.6
Cedar Slope CDP	0	NA	NA	0	0.0	0.0	0.0	0.0	0.0	0.0	0.0	0.0	0	0.0	0.0	0.0
Cedarville CDP	514	NA	NA	297	86.5	0.0	0.7	2.4	10.4	13.2	54.3	32.7	153	69.9	30.1	17.6
Centerville CDP	392	NA	NA	348	75.0	3.4	0.0	1.4	20.1	18.4	74.1	7.5	138	64.5	32.6	31.2
Ceres city	45,897	47,343	3.2	46,570	30.3	1.7	5.8	3.5	58.7	29.2	61.7	9.2	13,110	58.4	56.1	11.7
Cerritos city	49,047	50,004	2.0	49,599	16.1	7.1	61.5	3.3	12.0	19.8	60.9	19.2	15,140	80.8	18.2	54.5
Chalfant CDP	651	NA	NA	714	100.0	0.0	0.0	0.0	0.0	20.1	64.0	15.8	311	88.1	44.4	14.8
Challenge-Brownsville CDP	1,148	NA	NA	952	81.2	0.0	0.0	2.6	16.2	26.7	52.0	21.1	408	64.0	29.4	16.2
Channel Islands Beach CDP	3,103	NA	NA	2,778	84.1	1.5	3.5	3.2	7.7	14.8	68.8	16.6	1,209	56.1	14.4	54.0
Charter Oak CDP	9,310	NA	NA	9,200	37.1	3.9	8.0	2.5	48.5	26.9	61.1	12.2	2,905	65.6	31.7	22.3
Cherokee CDP	69	NA	NA	80	78.8	0.0	21.3	0.0	0.0	22.6	41.3	36.3	32	100.0	59.4	15.6
Cherokee Strip CDP	227	NA	NA	295	25.1	0.0	0.0	0.0	74.9	36.3	48.9	14.9	68	67.6	66.2	0.0
Cherryland CDP	14,728	NA	NA	15,244	21.6	7.1	9.9	8.0	53.3	28.1	63.7	8.2	4,514	40.0	53.3	17.7
Cherry Valley CDP	6,362	NA	NA	6,823	68.4	1.4	2.8	1.7	25.7	12.7	56.7	30.7	2,705	78.8	36.0	25.8
Chester CDP	2,144	NA	NA	1,978	89.7	0.1	0.0	6.3	3.9	21.8	54.0	24.2	829	66.3	22.8	22.8
Chico city	86,198	89,180	3.5	87,517	72.4	1.8	4.1	4.7	17.0	19.5	69.4	11.1	34,314	43.8	19.4	34.3
Chilcoot-Vinton CDP	454	NA	NA	130	100.0	0.0	0.0	0.0	0.0	42.3	57.7	0.0	37	100.0	100.0	0.0
China Lake Acres CDP	1,876	NA	NA	1,376	82.5	0.0	0.0	11.6	5.9	15.4	55.5	29.3	607	72.5	37.4	6.3
Chinese Camp CDP	126	NA	NA	99	68.7	0.0	0.0	12.1	19.2	26.3	49.5	24.2	50	66.0	84.0	0.0
Chino city	77,972	84,723	8.7	80,810	24.1	5.2	11.5	4.5	54.7	23.7	67.7	8.6	20,468	69.6	37.3	28.4
Chino Hills city	74,799	77,005	2.9	76,187	32.1	4.1	31.6	3.3	28.9	25.5	66.5	8.0	23,039	79.2	19.0	50.0
Chowchilla city	18,782	18,909	0.7	18,411	42.4	11.8	2.0	4.7	39.0	19.2	71.2	9.6	3,873	48.5	50.3	14.2
Chualar CDP	1,190	NA	NA	1,255	3.3	0.6	0.0	0.2	95.9	29.5	63.9	6.8	271	50.6	81.9	5.2
Chula Vista city	243,916	260,988	7.0	253,031	19.8	4.2	14.0	3.6	58.4	26.8	62.5	10.8	77,062	58.2	33.8	29.3
Citrus CDP	10,866	NA	NA	11,446	18.0	0.9	8.5	1.2	71.5	26.0	65.9	8.2	2,634	68.4	58.7	14.2
Citrus Heights city	83,255	86,145	3.5	84,678	71.6	2.8	2.9	4.8	17.9	21.0	64.5	14.5	32,889	55.2	31.7	21.1
Claremont city	34,926	36,054	3.2	35,569	56.2	4.4	15.3	2.9	21.2	19.2	63.2	17.7	11,836	66.2	12.5	60.8
Clarksburg CDP	418	NA	NA	406	82.0	0.0	0.0	0.0	18.0	22.4	56.3	21.4	192	75.0	18.2	46.9
Clay CDP	1,195	NA	NA	1,153	70.3	0.0	3.5	2.2	24.0	17.9	67.4	14.6	418	87.6	47.4	21.3
Clayton city	10,918	11,690	7.1	11,328	77.8	2.0	6.9	5.4	7.9	23.4	60.1	16.6	4,134	91.4	11.9	58.0
Clear Creek CDP	169	NA	NA	182	90.7	0.0	0.0	2.2	7.1	15.3	63.5	20.9	87	41.4	11.5	18.4
Clearlake city	15,250	15,089	-1.1	15,121	64.6	6.7	0.6	6.0	22.1	21.7	62.7	15.6	6,861	56.6	44.4	8.9
Clearlake Oaks CDP	2,359	NA	NA	1,547	86.3	6.4	0.0	4.3	3.0	11.7	54.0	34.4	814	53.9	48.6	18.1
Clearlake Riviera CDP	3,090	NA	NA	2,912	79.8	1.1	0.0	3.1	16.0	18.2	67.0	14.6	1,226	68.4	36.1	19.5
Cleone CDP	618	NA	NA	679	72.2	0.0	0.0	0.0	27.8	17.9	62.5	19.7	238	84.9	38.7	30.3
Clio CDP	66	NA	NA	49	75.5	0.0	0.0	0.0	24.5	0.0	91.9	8.2	25	100.0	48.0	16.0
Clipper Mills CDP	142	NA	NA	0	0.0	0.0	0.0	0.0	0.0	0.0	0.0	0.0	0	0.0	0.0	0.0
Cloverdale city	8,618	8,796	2.1	8,692	58.6	0.9	4.2	4.3	32.1	22.5	61.9	15.6	3,345	63.9	35.2	20.7
Clovis city	95,633	102,189	6.9	98,815	55.8	2.7	10.5	3.4	27.6	28.2	60.4	11.4	33,555	60.2	26.3	31.8
Clyde CDP	678	NA	NA	680	57.2	2.4	15.9	13.5	11.0	19.0	75.1	5.7	279	66.3	12.2	21.5
Coachella city	40,704	44,132	8.4	42,576	1.8	1.0	0.1	0.4	96.8	37.4	58.1	4.6	9,694	63.9	78.0	4.8
Coalinga city	18,089	16,452	-9.0	17,235	34.9	5.9	2.1	3.6	53.5	25.4	67.3	7.4	4,807	51.4	39.1	15.9
Coarsegold CDP	1,840	NA	NA	1,172	96.7	0.0	0.0	0.0	3.3	7.0	60.4	32.6	625	78.1	27.8	29.1
Cobb CDP	1,778	NA	NA	1,147	84.5	0.0	5.7	2.0	7.8	25.5	56.0	18.5	446	72.9	22.4	36.1
Coffee Creek CDP	217	NA	NA	132	81.8	0.0	0.0	2.3	15.9	12.1	72.0	15.9	48	95.8	29.2	37.5
Cohasset CDP	847	NA	NA	808	92.8	0.0	0.0	2.4	4.8	16.2	65.5	18.4	328	76.2	27.4	36.6
Cold Springs CDP (El Dorado)	446	NA	NA	623	96.5	0.0	0.0	1.1	2.4	21.2	49.8	28.9	207	80.7	5.3	15.0
Cold Springs CDP (Tuolumne)	181	NA	NA	193	66.8	0.0	0.0	15.5	17.6	10.9	71.5	17.6	115	92.2	0.0	21.7
Coleville CDP	495	NA	NA	395	77.7	0.0	0.0	0.0	22.3	18.2	81.9	0.0	116	12.9	30.2	0.0
Colfax city	1,950	2,013	3.2	2,424	88.6	0.0	1.0	5.7	4.7	22.9	69.0	8.1	969	44.3	31.9	13.6
College City CDP	290	NA	NA	196	40.8	0.0	0.0	5.6	53.6	12.2	64.8	23.0	52	100.0	55.8	0.0
Collierville CDP	1,934	NA	NA	1,942	76.4	0.0	0.0	0.8	22.8	34.2	46.2	19.5	599	71.8	43.1	12.2
Colma town	1,447	1,514	4.6	1,837	9.4	2.3	32.4	3.5	52.4	21.4	69.9	8.9	479	53.2	34.0	34.7
Coloma CDP	529	NA	NA	761	91.1	0.0	1.7	0.0	7.2	7.8	66.6	25.8	345	75.4	21.7	8.1
Colton city	52,155	54,053	3.6	53,129	13.8	8.2	3.8	1.8	72.4	32.2	61.0	6.8	14,885	50.2	53.3	12.4
Columbia CDP	2,297	NA	NA	2,456	77.4	0.0	1.5	7.9	13.3	17.7	59.0	23.3	1,011	65.7	34.6	22.8
Colusa city	5,971	5,946	-0.4	5,962	35.0	0.7	2.1	2.8	59.4	27.8	60.0	12.3	2,097	63.7	42.9	16.7
Commerce city	12,827	13,076	1.9	12,975	1.7	0.9	0.9	0.4	96.0	26.3	61.3	12.4	3,528	43.4	72.7	5.6
Comptche CDP	159	NA	NA	77	100.0	0.0	0.0	0.0	0.0	0.0	78.0	22.1	42	100.0	0.0	0.0
Compton city	96,412	98,597	2.3	97,663	1.1	30.9	0.4	1.3	66.3	31.6	60.8	7.7	23,395	54.9	61.3	7.9
Concord city	122,282	127,522	4.3	125,017	49.4	4.0	10.9	5.7	30.1	22.5	64.9	12.6	44,987	59.0	30.0	34.9
Concow CDP	710	NA	NA	539	83.3	2.6	0.0	8.0	6.1	9.3	64.8	26.0	262	79.0	30.5	26.0
Contra Costa Centre CDP	0	NA	NA	6,031	58.3	3.3	22.2	7.4	8.9	10.2	78.4	11.3	3,369	22.9	9.2	71.6
Copperopolis CDP	3,671	NA	NA	4,365	84.3	0.4	2.3	2.8	10.2	22.3	58.8	18.8	1,699	82.6	27.5	21.1
Corcoran city	24,813	22,815	-8.1	23,634	18.8	13.1	1.3	3.6	63.2	18.6	75.9	5.6	3,615	43.5	62.8	4.5
Corning city	7,663	7,558	-1.4	7,617	48.0	1.7	0.9	3.5	46.0	34.8	53.5	11.9	2,345	43.2	59.0	8.3
Corona city	152,374	161,486	6.0	157,395	38.4	4.8	10.8	3.8	42.2	28.1	63.9	8.2	45,790	66.6	33.4	30.4
Coronado city	24,697	24,910	0.9	24,333	75.1	3.2	2.9	3.3	15.4	18.0	64.9	17.0	8,846	46.4	9.0	64.6
Coronita CDP	2,608	NA	NA	3,397	43.4	0.8	9.1	0.9	45.8	23.2	61.9	15.0	935	80.0	38.5	18.2
Corralitos CDP	2,326	NA	NA	2,812	59.5	0.0	1.7	1.4	37.4	24.1	65.3	10.6	896	80.7	9.5	52.1

1 May be of any race.

Table A. All Places — **Population and Housing**

STATE City, town, township, borough, or CDP (county if applicable)	Population				Race and Hispanic or Latino origin (percent), 2010–2014					Age (percent), 2010–2014			Households, 2010–2014			
	2010 census total population	2014 estimated population	Percent change 2010–2014	ACS total population estimate 2010–2014	White alone, not Hispanic or Latino	Black alone, not Hispanic or Latino	Asian alone, not Hispanic or Latino	All other races or 2 or more races, not Hispanic or Latino	Hispanic or Latino[1]	Under 18 years old	Age 18 to 64 years old	Age 65 years and older	Total occupied housing units	Percent owner occupied	Householders by level of education (percent): High school diploma or less	Householders by level of education (percent): Bachelor's degree or more
	1	2	3	4	5	6	7	8	9	10	11	12	13	14	15	16
CALIFORNIA—Con.																
Corte Madera town	9,253	9,916	7.2	9,478	78.6	1.0	9.4	3.3	7.7	24.6	58.0	17.4	3,797	71.9	12.2	70.2
Costa Mesa city	109,929	112,784	2.6	111,635	51.1	1.4	9.1	3.1	35.4	21.3	69.7	9.0	40,506	39.8	24.1	40.2
Cotati city	7,265	7,429	2.3	7,347	71.9	3.6	4.9	5.9	13.6	21.6	67.4	11.0	2,912	57.2	25.5	37.1
Coto de Caza CDP	14,866	NA	NA	14,647	80.3	0.6	8.0	2.3	8.8	28.4	61.2	10.5	4,848	88.7	7.4	68.6
Cottonwood CDP	3,316	NA	NA	4,178	70.4	0.5	0.0	6.4	22.8	28.6	60.1	11.2	1,328	68.2	42.5	11.1
Coulterville CDP	201	NA	NA	227	93.0	0.0	0.0	0.0	7.0	18.0	61.2	20.7	130	80.0	47.7	25.4
Country Club CDP	9,379	NA	NA	10,018	40.3	3.6	3.1	5.7	47.2	21.8	64.0	14.3	3,747	59.6	41.1	13.7
Courtland CDP	355	NA	NA	515	49.9	9.1	1.9	0.0	39.0	9.7	72.1	18.1	115	86.1	33.9	27.0
Covelo CDP	1,255	NA	NA	1,444	48.8	1.0	0.2	27.6	22.4	28.3	53.3	18.5	524	67.0	43.1	5.7
Covina city	47,796	49,002	2.5	48,429	25.5	3.6	11.6	2.3	57.0	26.1	62.4	11.5	15,340	57.8	30.7	28.2
Cowan CDP	318	NA	NA	510	31.8	0.0	0.0	21.4	46.9	32.7	59.4	8.0	137	62.8	62.0	11.7
Crescent City city	7,640	6,786	-11.2	7,295	54.2	7.7	1.8	5.6	30.7	12.8	79.3	7.9	1,726	29.5	40.8	23.9
Crescent Mills CDP	196	NA	NA	426	52.8	0.0	0.0	23.7	23.5	45.8	54.2	0.0	137	40.9	63.5	0.0
Cressey CDP	394	NA	NA	322	52.8	0.0	2.8	0.0	44.4	11.5	69.6	18.9	102	91.2	42.2	12.7
Crest CDP	2,593	NA	NA	2,393	83.6	0.0	2.4	5.3	8.7	15.2	65.2	19.4	969	84.0	30.9	28.3
Crestline CDP	10,770	NA	NA	9,437	75.6	1.8	0.8	3.6	18.1	23.0	58.5	18.5	3,920	70.7	30.1	22.4
Creston CDP	94	NA	NA	61	100.0	0.0	0.0	0.0	0.0	32.8	34.4	32.8	31	64.5	0.0	64.5
C-Road CDP	150	NA	NA	213	78.9	0.0	10.3	6.1	4.7	7.0	79.9	13.1	82	100.0	17.1	62.2
Crockett CDP	3,094	NA	NA	3,151	70.0	0.7	1.4	5.4	22.5	17.7	67.6	14.6	1,400	53.4	28.9	32.1
Cromberg CDP	261	NA	NA	172	97.1	0.0	0.0	0.0	2.9	0.0	84.9	15.1	128	64.1	29.7	38.3
Crowley Lake CDP	875	NA	NA	707	76.1	0.0	0.0	0.0	23.9	25.0	64.5	10.5	340	70.0	23.2	58.2
Crows Landing CDP	355	NA	NA	194	38.7	0.0	0.0	0.0	61.3	14.4	54.0	31.4	83	77.1	66.3	0.0
Cudahy city	23,805	24,291	2.0	24,073	1.4	0.2	0.7	0.3	97.4	34.0	61.2	4.7	5,615	17.3	79.4	4.1
Culver City city	38,885	39,691	2.1	39,353	48.8	7.8	15.5	5.0	22.9	19.4	65.7	15.0	16,515	55.0	16.3	56.9
Cupertino city	58,572	60,668	3.6	59,787	27.1	0.5	64.9	2.8	4.7	27.4	59.6	13.0	20,643	63.0	7.9	78.2
Cutler CDP	5,000	NA	NA	4,224	1.4	0.0	1.9	0.0	96.7	43.4	50.7	5.8	996	37.2	75.1	3.9
Cutten CDP	3,108	NA	NA	3,117	82.5	2.0	2.5	4.1	9.0	15.3	67.1	17.6	1,371	50.6	28.6	34.7
Cuyama CDP	57	NA	NA	72	29.2	0.0	5.6	0.0	65.3	40.2	38.9	20.8	22	63.6	81.8	0.0
Cypress city	47,863	49,240	2.9	48,748	42.8	2.8	31.9	3.9	18.5	21.9	64.3	13.8	15,905	68.0	21.8	43.0
Daly City city	101,146	106,094	4.9	103,897	12.8	3.0	57.3	3.7	23.2	19.2	66.4	14.5	31,008	55.2	29.1	35.8
Dana Point city	33,278	34,116	2.5	33,861	77.4	0.7	3.9	2.3	15.7	17.5	64.2	18.3	14,523	57.7	14.2	51.9
Danville town	41,859	43,909	4.9	42,891	78.7	1.1	11.4	3.0	5.8	27.3	56.9	15.8	15,685	84.3	8.6	67.3
Daphnedale Park CDP	184	NA	NA	20	100.0	0.0	0.0	0.0	0.0	0.0	0.0	100.0	9	100.0	0.0	0.0
Darwin CDP	43	NA	NA	18	100.0	0.0	0.0	0.0	0.0	0.0	55.6	44.4	13	38.5	0.0	61.5
Davenport CDP	408	NA	NA	303	55.8	0.0	2.3	0.0	41.9	14.2	73.7	12.2	127	63.0	11.8	29.9
Davis city	65,611	66,742	1.7	66,093	56.2	2.1	21.8	6.5	13.5	17.2	73.8	8.9	24,306	44.1	10.7	63.6
Day Valley CDP	3,409	NA	NA	3,869	78.7	0.0	0.0	6.5	14.8	20.2	57.0	22.6	1,336	81.0	19.0	46.5
Deer Park CDP	1,267	NA	NA	1,072	83.9	0.0	2.8	3.6	9.7	13.9	45.8	40.3	427	68.4	15.0	38.6
Del Aire CDP	10,001	NA	NA	10,406	33.7	4.6	11.1	4.3	46.4	24.3	66.4	9.5	3,277	66.4	32.3	40.1
Delano city	53,041	52,651	-0.7	52,883	7.1	4.8	13.1	1.7	73.4	29.4	64.1	6.4	10,549	55.3	68.6	8.7
Delft Colony CDP	454	NA	NA	164	0.0	0.0	0.0	0.0	100.0	61.6	38.4	0.0	63	0.0	68.3	0.0
Delhi CDP	10,755	NA	NA	9,918	15.2	2.8	2.2	4.1	75.7	34.1	58.7	7.2	2,838	71.9	59.3	9.9
Delleker CDP	705	NA	NA	798	57.3	0.0	0.0	4.8	38.0	31.3	44.4	24.2	296	81.1	35.5	30.4
Del Mar city	4,161	4,311	3.6	4,242	86.0	0.0	1.0	0.0	13.0	14.8	61.2	23.8	2,127	53.7	6.4	70.5
Del Monte Forest CDP	4,514	NA	NA	6,439	76.1	2.6	7.1	3.8	10.4	9.9	64.7	25.3	1,834	85.8	6.9	69.2
Del Rey CDP	1,639	NA	NA	1,489	1.0	0.0	3.4	0.0	95.6	37.3	57.3	5.4	374	61.0	71.7	0.0
Del Rey Oaks city	1,624	1,682	3.6	1,727	72.3	0.2	8.3	4.6	14.6	17.5	63.0	19.6	641	77.2	14.2	49.9
Del Rio CDP	1,270	NA	NA	1,769	76.2	0.0	4.2	0.0	19.6	24.2	56.0	19.8	583	93.1	8.9	55.9
Denair CDP	4,404	NA	NA	4,892	57.6	1.4	0.0	2.6	38.4	31.2	59.1	9.7	1,490	71.8	47.4	24.2
Derby Acres CDP	322	NA	NA	324	90.7	0.0	0.0	5.9	3.4	19.2	55.5	25.3	145	71.0	51.7	15.2
Descanso CDP	1,423	NA	NA	1,305	83.1	1.1	4.6	1.2	10.0	22.8	50.2	27.0	497	85.5	28.6	28.0
Desert Center CDP	204	NA	NA	208	57.2	0.5	0.0	2.9	39.4	19.2	62.5	18.3	69	73.9	40.6	18.8
Desert Edge CDP	3,822	NA	NA	4,244	69.8	0.0	1.2	0.5	28.5	11.4	40.7	47.9	2,184	84.3	51.0	17.6
Desert Hot Springs city	27,049	28,164	4.1	27,678	31.6	5.4	2.7	3.9	56.4	31.0	59.0	10.0	9,164	44.3	48.9	14.9
Desert Palms CDP	6,957	NA	NA	6,776	95.5	0.5	0.8	0.7	2.4	0.0	11.3	88.7	4,099	90.4	17.5	49.5
Desert Shores CDP	1,104	NA	NA	1,039	13.2	0.0	0.0	0.0	86.8	33.3	49.8	16.8	284	71.5	74.3	3.5
Desert View Highlands CDP	2,360	NA	NA	2,291	36.3	4.7	0.7	1.3	57.0	32.8	54.8	12.3	665	54.7	31.1	16.8
Diablo CDP	1,158	NA	NA	969	86.0	0.0	2.0	12.1	0.0	26.8	45.0	28.2	372	96.2	10.8	73.1
Diablo Grande CDP	826	NA	NA	1,083	53.6	6.0	3.0	5.2	32.2	26.6	70.0	3.4	385	74.3	24.4	30.9
Diamond Bar city	55,544	56,784	2.2	56,259	21.6	3.3	51.4	3.3	20.5	20.5	66.6	12.8	17,266	79.2	18.5	55.5
Diamond Springs CDP	11,037	NA	NA	12,105	79.2	0.6	1.0	5.7	13.4	20.0	60.6	19.3	4,406	71.2	35.1	20.3
Dillon Beach CDP	283	NA	NA	82	90.2	0.0	9.8	0.0	0.0	0.0	42.7	57.3	55	69.1	45.5	43.6
Dinuba city	21,453	23,667	10.3	22,828	11.5	0.0	1.3	0.5	86.7	33.9	58.4	7.6	5,964	52.6	61.8	8.7
Discovery Bay CDP	13,352	NA	NA	14,315	77.4	3.4	2.9	5.1	11.1	26.9	61.3	11.9	4,976	79.6	19.2	31.5
Dixon city	18,392	19,164	4.2	18,718	50.6	2.8	2.0	5.1	39.6	30.6	60.4	8.9	6,050	64.5	39.8	22.9
Dixon Lane-Meadow Creek CDP	2,645	NA	NA	2,447	76.3	0.0	0.0	1.5	22.2	18.2	53.1	28.7	1,140	86.4	49.2	18.1
Dobbins CDP	624	NA	NA	658	76.7	0.0	0.0	3.0	20.2	23.6	54.8	21.6	262	57.6	27.9	31.3
Dogtown CDP	2,506	NA	NA	2,475	71.4	0.0	1.4	2.9	24.3	24.8	60.4	14.7	815	80.6	35.5	33.1
Dollar Point CDP	1,215	NA	NA	1,076	84.1	2.7	0.0	0.0	13.2	13.8	71.9	14.1	481	71.1	9.4	45.9
Dorrington CDP	609	NA	NA	349	85.1	0.0	0.0	4.3	10.6	0.3	52.2	47.6	181	95.6	6.1	42.5
Dorris city	939	903	-3.8	1,115	62.8	0.4	0.0	4.4	32.5	34.1	56.4	9.5	381	65.1	52.8	5.5
Dos Palos city	4,950	5,082	2.7	5,023	27.9	0.9	0.0	0.5	70.7	32.2	56.1	11.7	1,487	67.7	60.8	6.6
Dos Palos Y CDP	323	NA	NA	171	28.7	0.0	0.0	1.8	69.6	22.8	54.4	22.8	75	26.7	80.0	0.0
Douglas City CDP	713	NA	NA	670	75.4	0.0	0.0	6.0	18.7	25.0	49.9	25.2	323	73.7	28.5	15.8
Downey city	111,791	114,172	2.1	113,082	16.5	3.5	6.7	1.5	71.8	25.2	64.4	10.5	33,169	50.6	44.1	23.4
Downieville CDP	282	NA	NA	233	98.3	0.0	0.0	0.0	1.7	26.2	55.8	18.0	107	49.5	30.8	30.8
Doyle CDP	678	NA	NA	382	95.3	0.0	0.0	2.4	2.4	9.9	62.1	28.0	219	79.0	21.0	0.0
Drytown CDP	167	NA	NA	148	37.2	0.0	62.8	0.0	0.0	17.5	56.8	25.7	51	100.0	49.0	0.0
Duarte city	21,321	22,006	3.2	21,676	29.3	6.9	16.6	3.3	43.9	21.3	62.1	16.7	7,030	64.0	34.7	37.3
Dublin city	46,036	54,695	18.8	49,694	42.8	6.6	31.8	6.0	12.8	23.1	68.7	8.2	16,476	62.9	13.5	60.9
Ducor CDP	612	NA	NA	646	12.8	0.0	0.0	0.0	87.2	36.9	57.3	6.0	176	56.3	67.6	11.4
Dunnigan CDP	1,416	NA	NA	1,017	38.4	6.1	9.9	3.7	41.8	15.3	69.7	15.0	372	75.0	51.1	11.3
Dunsmuir city	1,640	1,574	-4.0	1,482	83.3	1.9	1.3	3.6	10.0	13.8	63.8	22.4	751	56.7	30.5	24.4
Durham CDP	5,518	NA	NA	5,743	86.7	0.5	0.0	1.8	11.0	23.6	61.4	14.9	2,136	72.9	19.5	36.9
Dustin Acres CDP	652	NA	NA	295	96.6	0.0	0.0	3.4	0.0	17.2	62.8	20.0	128	96.9	35.2	9.4
Dutch Flat CDP	160	NA	NA	132	100.0	0.0	0.0	0.0	0.0	9.1	58.3	32.6	72	70.8	29.2	44.4
Eagleville CDP	59	NA	NA	70	68.6	0.0	2.9	0.0	28.6	17.1	71.3	11.4	32	53.1	37.5	15.6
Earlimart CDP	8,537	NA	NA	8,310	2.3	0.8	5.8	1.0	90.0	40.5	56.7	2.9	1,903	40.4	85.9	2.9
East Foothills CDP	8,269	NA	NA	6,479	39.9	1.6	22.7	2.1	33.6	19.2	63.6	17.2	2,259	82.6	23.4	45.1

1 May be of any race.

Table A. All Places — **Population and Housing**

STATE City, town, township, borough, or CDP (county if applicable)	2010 census total population	2014 estimated population	Percent change 2010–2014	ACS total population estimate 2010–2014	White alone, not Hispanic or Latino	Black alone, not Hispanic or Latino	Asian alone, not Hispanic or Latino	All other races or 2 or more races, not Hispanic or Latino	Hispanic or Latino[1]	Under 18 years old	Age 18 to 64 years old	Age 65 years and older	Total occupied housing units	Percent owner occupied	High school diploma or less	Bachelor's degree or more
	1	2	3	4	5	6	7	8	9	10	11	12	13	14	15	16
CALIFORNIA—Con.																
East Hemet CDP	17,418	NA	NA	18,188	52.5	3.2	0.8	3.4	40.1	29.7	58.8	11.5	5,410	63.6	47.4	13.4
East Los Angeles CDP	126,496	NA	NA	127,610	1.2	0.3	0.9	0.3	97.3	28.5	61.9	9.4	31,499	34.5	74.8	5.8
East Nicolaus CDP	225	NA	NA	251	54.2	0.0	2.0	0.0	43.8	32.2	54.4	13.5	97	70.1	54.6	7.2
East Oakdale CDP	2,762	NA	NA	2,901	76.7	0.0	2.3	2.2	18.7	21.8	60.2	17.8	1,045	88.4	25.7	33.7
Easton CDP	2,083	NA	NA	1,991	31.0	0.9	1.3	1.6	65.2	22.4	62.6	15.0	631	74.3	56.4	14.3
East Orosi CDP	495	NA	NA	321	1.2	0.0	0.0	21.8	76.9	27.1	67.0	5.9	70	50.0	65.7	0.0
East Palo Alto city	28,155	29,530	4.9	28,920	6.6	14.1	3.0	14.2	62.0	29.9	64.5	5.6	6,940	36.9	52.4	20.7
East Pasadena CDP	6,144	NA	NA	6,123	34.2	1.2	26.7	2.8	35.0	22.9	61.6	15.3	2,042	64.7	19.0	47.4
East Porterville CDP	6,767	NA	NA	6,585	21.3	0.0	0.8	0.5	77.4	35.3	57.7	6.9	1,660	51.4	77.5	2.2
East Quincy CDP	2,489	NA	NA	2,633	86.5	0.8	0.0	11.6	1.1	20.0	62.5	17.4	1,127	74.3	23.5	14.6
East Rancho Dominguez CDP	15,135	NA	NA	15,343	0.3	17.3	1.0	1.0	80.4	30.2	63.4	6.5	3,214	54.4	69.0	4.0
East Richmond Heights CDP	3,280	NA	NA	3,501	53.8	11.9	9.7	4.1	20.5	18.6	64.6	16.7	1,431	80.5	9.0	53.5
East San Gabriel CDP	14,874	NA	NA	15,573	20.6	0.8	53.1	3.2	22.3	20.4	64.6	14.9	5,140	58.2	26.2	47.4
East Shore CDP	156	NA	NA	203	74.9	0.0	20.7	0.0	4.4	18.7	49.3	32.0	70	80.0	27.1	34.3
East Sonora CDP	2,266	NA	NA	2,168	83.4	0.0	0.0	8.4	8.2	7.7	46.6	45.6	1,156	65.3	39.0	28.8
East Tulare Villa CDP	778	NA	NA	951	38.3	0.0	3.0	0.2	58.5	36.2	55.9	8.0	263	48.3	56.3	1.1
Eastvale city	53,683	57,016	6.2	55,298	21.8	9.3	26.9	3.0	39.0	32.3	60.8	6.9	13,050	78.5	22.0	43.0
East Whittier CDP	0	NA	NA	10,440	37.3	0.2	6.1	2.2	54.2	24.4	62.1	13.6	3,337	64.0	32.1	20.7
Edgewood CDP	43	NA	NA	30	86.7	0.0	0.0	13.3	0.0	23.3	76.7	0.0	11	45.5	0.0	9.1
Edmundson Acres CDP	279	NA	NA	274	37.2	17.2	0.0	1.5	44.2	42.0	44.1	13.9	54	50.0	85.2	7.4
Edna CDP	193	NA	NA	174	93.7	0.0	0.0	0.0	6.3	19.0	48.8	32.2	82	29.3	56.1	32.9
Edwards AFB CDP	2,063	NA	NA	2,503	68.2	10.4	2.2	5.7	13.5	37.3	62.5	0.0	619	1.6	5.8	40.5
El Cajon city	99,476	103,091	3.6	101,582	54.5	5.3	3.8	7.1	29.2	25.9	62.6	11.6	32,088	38.6	44.0	18.8
El Centro city	42,596	43,763	2.7	43,268	12.4	2.2	2.2	0.9	82.4	28.8	59.9	11.4	12,752	49.7	47.2	17.4
El Cerrito city	23,586	24,599	4.3	24,136	50.6	6.5	25.0	6.4	11.5	16.5	64.8	18.7	10,027	60.2	13.6	63.9
El Cerrito CDP	5,100	NA	NA	5,551	47.2	1.7	2.8	1.4	46.9	23.1	62.3	14.8	1,467	79.2	45.1	17.5
El Dorado Hills CDP	42,108	NA	NA	43,862	74.9	2.0	10.3	4.6	8.1	28.1	58.8	13.3	14,241	85.7	12.8	56.8
Eldridge CDP	1,233	NA	NA	1,333	75.3	3.4	3.7	1.7	15.9	23.9	60.1	16.2	455	65.1	39.8	17.6
El Granada CDP	5,467	NA	NA	5,377	76.9	0.0	3.0	3.7	16.4	20.1	68.1	11.8	2,026	76.3	8.8	69.3
Elizabeth Lake CDP	1,756	NA	NA	1,603	82.7	0.0	2.1	1.8	13.4	17.5	73.8	8.6	629	81.4	40.1	27.0
Elk Creek CDP	163	NA	NA	136	75.7	0.0	0.0	11.8	12.5	2.9	54.4	42.6	60	81.7	40.0	26.7
Elk Grove city	153,015	163,553	6.9	158,455	36.4	11.0	27.0	7.8	17.8	29.1	61.1	9.8	48,737	71.2	21.0	38.9
Elkhorn CDP	1,565	NA	NA	1,342	68.4	0.0	1.3	1.8	28.5	18.7	65.9	15.6	472	80.3	38.1	26.7
Elmira CDP	188	NA	NA	242	97.5	0.0	0.0	0.0	2.5	27.3	54.6	18.2	91	17.6	20.9	33.0
El Monte city	113,475	116,631	2.8	115,243	4.5	0.5	28.0	1.0	66.0	25.3	63.4	11.4	29,793	40.3	67.9	11.7
El Nido CDP	330	NA	NA	412	22.3	0.0	0.0	0.0	77.7	40.8	49.0	10.2	115	53.9	71.3	13.0
El Paso de Robles (Paso Robles) city	29,793	31,287	5.0	30,522	55.1	3.2	2.3	1.2	38.3	25.9	61.1	12.9	11,356	54.8	34.4	24.5
El Portal CDP	474	NA	NA	601	86.7	5.7	0.0	0.0	7.7	24.5	70.4	5.2	230	51.7	12.2	70.4
El Rancho CDP	124	NA	NA	16	0.0	0.0	0.0	0.0	100.0	0.0	100.1	0.0	7	0.0	100.0	0.0
El Rio CDP	7,198	NA	NA	6,785	12.4	0.4	1.6	0.2	85.4	27.6	62.6	9.7	1,673	68.7	70.9	4.5
El Segundo city	16,654	17,063	2.5	16,839	68.0	1.3	6.2	6.7	17.8	23.4	66.0	10.6	6,629	42.4	16.4	49.9
El Sobrante CDP (Contra Costa)	12,669	NA	NA	13,122	39.1	12.4	21.0	5.3	22.2	21.2	67.7	11.2	4,873	58.3	29.2	32.5
El Sobrante CDP (Riverside)	12,723	NA	NA	14,855	45.5	5.9	16.2	8.3	24.0	29.5	65.1	5.3	3,905	89.8	14.8	43.2
El Verano CDP	4,123	NA	NA	4,338	53.2	0.3	1.2	2.2	43.0	26.2	64.1	9.6	1,571	46.8	30.4	36.2
Elverta CDP	5,492	NA	NA	5,547	73.3	1.0	3.8	5.7	16.2	27.3	60.9	11.8	1,749	80.0	51.4	10.4
Emerald Lake Hills CDP	4,278	NA	NA	4,519	79.7	0.4	9.2	2.8	7.9	21.1	63.0	15.8	1,585	91.7	5.4	71.9
Emeryville city	10,015	11,227	12.1	10,497	43.6	15.5	25.7	5.3	9.9	10.3	76.1	13.5	5,997	36.1	8.7	71.5
Empire CDP	4,189	NA	NA	4,296	39.0	1.4	1.6	2.0	56.0	29.7	57.1	13.1	1,295	53.0	61.6	6.4
Encinitas city	59,518	62,254	4.6	61,008	78.1	0.4	5.1	2.5	13.9	20.9	65.0	14.1	23,208	65.4	13.2	60.6
Escalon city	7,132	7,388	3.6	7,252	76.3	0.0	1.1	1.8	20.8	26.2	59.0	14.8	2,587	73.6	34.1	23.0
Escondido city	143,913	150,243	4.4	147,603	41.6	2.0	5.4	2.2	48.8	26.4	63.4	10.3	44,798	49.0	42.2	24.8
Esparto CDP	3,108	NA	NA	3,229	40.1	0.0	5.5	0.3	54.0	30.5	57.4	12.1	919	72.0	51.1	9.1
Etna city	737	711	-3.5	750	85.5	0.0	0.8	5.7	8.0	28.5	47.6	23.9	310	68.7	30.0	13.2
Eucalyptus Hills CDP	5,313	NA	NA	5,352	66.2	7.8	5.5	5.9	14.6	30.2	55.8	14.0	1,769	69.9	26.5	29.5
Eureka city	27,191	26,925	-1.0	27,039	73.2	2.2	4.9	10.1	9.6	18.5	68.0	13.5	10,758	45.5	31.7	25.4
Exeter city	10,332	10,558	2.2	10,468	53.9	1.0	0.4	2.5	42.3	33.7	54.9	11.5	3,308	59.8	50.2	13.7
Fairbanks Ranch CDP	3,148	NA	NA	3,245	88.9	0.0	0.0	0.0	11.1	29.9	47.4	22.8	1,063	92.1	6.2	70.4
Fairfax town	7,441	7,638	2.6	7,546	85.4	1.5	2.2	3.1	7.8	20.5	67.0	12.4	3,330	63.6	10.2	61.4
Fairfield city	105,318	111,125	5.5	107,983	35.0	14.8	15.3	7.6	27.3	25.3	63.7	11.1	34,674	56.9	33.8	24.7
Fairmead CDP	1,447	NA	NA	1,983	20.1	3.7	1.3	15.4	59.6	27.6	69.1	3.3	401	45.4	60.6	6.7
Fair Oaks CDP	30,912	NA	NA	31,256	79.7	1.8	4.8	3.3	10.4	19.5	60.8	19.7	12,755	66.1	18.1	45.4
Fairview CDP	10,003	NA	NA	9,852	36.9	20.0	11.0	5.6	26.5	18.9	65.9	15.4	3,304	78.0	19.7	37.4
Fallbrook CDP	30,534	NA	NA	31,435	51.0	1.5	3.2	2.0	42.3	23.6	61.4	15.0	10,386	56.6	42.3	22.5
Fall River Mills CDP	573	NA	NA	712	76.4	0.0	0.6	2.2	20.8	21.3	60.4	18.4	229	49.8	63.3	20.5
Farmersville city	10,588	10,786	1.9	10,675	10.1	2.3	0.0	0.7	87.0	34.5	58.9	6.6	2,551	60.8	61.2	5.1
Farmington CDP	207	NA	NA	124	92.7	0.0	0.0	0.0	7.3	0.0	50.0	50.0	84	100.0	10.7	0.0
Fellows CDP	106	NA	NA	98	98.0	0.0	0.0	0.0	2.0	26.6	72.5	1.0	35	85.7	65.7	2.9
Felton CDP	4,057	NA	NA	3,957	84.1	0.0	3.8	6.0	6.1	21.9	63.0	15.0	1,593	73.2	10.3	45.8
Ferndale city	1,371	1,364	-0.5	1,456	90.9	0.0	0.7	4.2	4.3	14.5	59.5	26.0	696	62.2	26.6	32.5
Fetters Hot Springs-Agua Caliente CDP	4,144	NA	NA	4,866	46.9	0.0	3.4	2.0	47.7	23.8	65.8	10.5	1,619	58.7	43.7	34.5
Fiddletown CDP	235	NA	NA	86	90.7	0.0	0.0	0.0	9.3	0.0	58.1	41.9	52	46.2	34.6	34.6
Fieldbrook CDP	859	NA	NA	812	88.5	1.6	2.1	6.4	1.4	22.2	60.9	17.1	328	84.5	20.1	39.3
Fields Landing CDP	276	NA	NA	130	46.9	0.0	0.0	53.1	0.0	6.2	93.8	0.0	93	24.7	9.7	65.6
Fillmore city	15,002	15,420	2.8	15,203	19.1	0.0	0.8	0.9	79.1	32.5	57.6	10.0	4,131	67.3	53.5	12.0
Firebaugh city	7,558	8,300	9.8	7,935	5.8	0.7	0.0	2.1	91.4	33.0	60.5	6.4	2,171	51.1	75.4	6.6
Fish Camp CDP	59	NA	NA	44	36.4	0.0	0.0	63.6	0.0	0.0	70.5	29.5	29	44.8	100.0	0.0
Florence-Graham CDP	63,387	NA	NA	62,815	0.7	8.4	0.3	0.4	90.1	32.9	60.9	6.1	14,316	35.1	79.6	4.0
Florin CDP	47,513	NA	NA	50,791	19.6	14.3	28.1	8.8	29.3	28.5	60.2	11.4	15,279	52.2	51.5	12.5
Floriston CDP	73	NA	NA	58	100.0	0.0	0.0	0.0	0.0	0.0	89.6	10.3	37	100.0	0.0	16.2
Flournoy CDP	101	NA	NA	143	81.8	0.0	0.0	2.1	16.1	30.1	58.8	11.2	48	83.3	31.3	20.8
Folsom city	72,199	75,361	4.4	73,334	63.3	5.8	13.8	5.3	11.8	23.9	65.4	10.6	25,111	68.0	13.7	54.7
Fontana city	196,074	204,950	4.5	201,355	15.5	9.2	5.8	2.8	66.7	30.6	63.3	6.1	49,438	65.6	46.9	17.5
Foothill Farms CDP	33,121	NA	NA	33,024	54.9	8.3	5.4	8.0	23.5	27.0	63.8	9.1	11,829	55.5	38.6	15.0
Forbestown CDP	320	NA	NA	450	44.9	0.0	0.0	17.8	37.3	32.8	49.3	17.8	132	74.2	52.3	0.0
Ford City CDP	4,278	NA	NA	4,154	51.3	0.0	1.3	0.8	46.6	27.4	61.9	10.6	1,323	47.8	57.1	3.7

1 May be of any race.

Table A. All Places — **Population and Housing**

STATE City, town, township, borough, or CDP (county if applicable)	2010 census total population	2014 estimated population	Percent change 2010–2014	ACS total population estimate 2010–2014	White alone, not Hispanic or Latino	Black alone, not Hispanic or Latino	Asian alone, not Hispanic or Latino	All other races or 2 or more races, not Hispanic or Latino	Hispanic or Latino[1]	Under 18 years old	Age 18 to 64 years old	Age 65 years and older	Total occupied housing units	Percent owner occupied	High school diploma or less	Bachelor's degree or more
	1	2	3	4	5	6	7	8	9	10	11	12	13	14	15	16
CALIFORNIA—Con.																
Foresthill CDP	1,483	NA	NA	1,345	81.5	0.0	0.0	11.2	7.3	16.1	72.1	11.8	578	44.5	43.8	8.0
Forest Meadows CDP	1,249	NA	NA	1,674	92.7	0.0	0.0	0.0	7.3	15.5	57.2	27.3	644	80.9	9.0	42.5
Forest Ranch CDP	1,184	NA	NA	1,064	93.9	0.0	0.0	6.1	0.0	21.8	51.8	26.4	490	96.3	22.7	25.3
Forestville CDP	3,293	NA	NA	3,461	82.2	4.4	2.4	1.2	9.8	12.1	70.5	17.3	1,513	64.4	23.2	40.0
Fort Bidwell CDP	173	NA	NA	161	41.6	0.0	0.0	52.2	6.2	23.7	49.7	26.7	78	83.3	52.6	19.2
Fort Bragg city	7,273	7,302	0.4	7,274	55.6	0.6	1.7	4.6	37.5	25.8	56.6	17.4	2,887	41.0	41.9	22.1
Fort Irwin CDP	8,845	NA	NA	9,191	46.4	15.1	7.5	6.2	24.9	38.8	61.2	0.0	2,323	1.2	25.6	26.3
Fort Jones city	710	686	-3.4	848	84.9	0.0	0.4	7.2	7.5	34.0	56.9	9.2	324	64.2	35.8	17.3
Fortuna city	11,926	11,888	-0.3	11,863	74.5	0.6	2.2	5.0	17.7	26.7	56.7	16.5	4,178	59.5	40.4	15.7
Fort Washington CDP	233	NA	NA	430	100.0	0.0	0.0	0.0	0.0	23.7	43.3	33.0	135	90.4	8.9	79.3
Foster City city	30,567	32,754	7.2	31,809	41.9	1.9	45.8	4.9	5.5	21.2	62.7	16.2	12,188	58.6	8.9	69.1
Fountain Valley city	55,371	57,010	3.0	56,440	46.0	1.0	35.0	2.8	15.1	19.8	62.3	17.9	18,777	70.7	20.2	43.1
Fowler city	5,640	6,042	7.1	5,908	19.9	0.5	10.7	1.1	67.8	32.3	58.4	9.4	1,696	53.2	47.2	16.4
Franklin CDP (Merced)	6,149	NA	NA	6,840	29.0	5.1	8.6	4.0	53.4	34.2	57.9	8.1	1,964	70.1	57.7	10.0
Franklin CDP (Sacramento)	155	NA	NA	33	45.5	0.0	0.0	0.0	54.5	0.0	54.5	45.5	33	100.0	30.3	0.0
Frazier Park CDP	2,691	NA	NA	2,730	81.0	0.0	2.2	2.4	14.4	27.0	59.7	13.4	958	43.5	42.6	25.8
Freedom CDP	3,070	NA	NA	3,205	20.7	0.7	4.3	3.0	71.3	26.3	64.4	9.2	847	52.8	52.9	10.5
Freeport CDP	38	NA	NA	68	60.3	0.0	0.0	0.0	39.7	17.6	11.8	70.6	30	86.7	53.3	33.3
Fremont city	214,079	228,758	6.9	221,654	24.8	3.6	52.0	5.4	14.1	24.3	64.8	11.0	71,575	63.2	21.3	57.0
French Camp CDP	3,376	NA	NA	4,155	26.5	8.0	4.0	1.9	59.6	15.6	78.7	5.8	540	49.1	67.2	3.9
French Gulch CDP	346	NA	NA	441	94.6	0.0	0.0	5.2	0.2	12.0	72.1	15.9	185	74.6	50.3	9.7
French Valley CDP	23,067	NA	NA	26,753	51.6	4.8	10.9	5.6	27.1	32.0	61.4	6.6	7,115	77.2	24.4	27.2
Fresno city	496,093	515,986	4.0	506,132	28.6	7.5	12.7	3.2	48.0	29.7	60.7	9.6	160,172	47.4	42.2	22.5
Friant CDP	509	NA	NA	263	82.1	0.0	3.8	0.0	14.1	0.0	54.8	45.2	181	76.8	48.6	19.3
Fruitdale CDP	935	NA	NA	1,089	59.8	3.0	24.2	0.0	13.0	14.5	78.8	6.5	382	59.4	27.5	42.1
Fruitridge Pocket CDP	5,800	NA	NA	5,802	13.8	14.9	19.4	5.3	46.6	32.3	58.4	9.2	1,557	35.1	63.7	6.3
Fuller Acres CDP	991	NA	NA	924	9.1	0.0	1.5	0.0	89.4	34.5	57.2	8.2	262	46.2	80.2	1.9
Fullerton city	135,235	139,677	3.3	137,945	35.7	2.3	24.2	2.9	34.8	22.9	64.6	12.4	44,406	53.1	26.7	41.4
Fulton CDP	541	NA	NA	441	78.0	0.0	1.1	1.8	19.0	10.7	65.9	23.4	186	58.1	56.5	11.3
Furnace Creek CDP	24	NA	NA	187	77.0	0.0	0.0	11.2	11.8	0.5	85.6	13.9	158	60.1	67.7	7.6
Galt city	23,647	24,817	4.9	24,280	47.9	2.6	3.1	2.0	44.3	29.7	59.9	10.6	7,481	70.6	43.1	16.8
Garberville CDP	913	NA	NA	1,061	81.5	3.4	0.0	7.3	7.8	24.4	56.6	19.0	506	29.4	43.9	9.1
Gardena city	58,829	60,395	2.7	59,682	9.5	24.3	25.7	4.4	36.0	22.5	61.9	15.6	20,658	50.2	40.4	25.7
Garden Acres CDP	10,648	NA	NA	11,172	19.0	0.7	2.0	2.9	75.4	28.8	63.8	7.4	2,870	52.7	72.0	3.6
Garden Farms CDP	386	NA	NA	341	100.0	0.0	0.0	0.0	0.0	16.7	78.6	4.7	118	100.0	12.7	48.3
Garden Grove city	170,964	175,078	2.4	173,853	21.3	1.1	38.5	2.8	36.4	24.4	64.1	11.6	46,453	56.0	42.8	22.4
Garey CDP	68	NA	NA	74	25.7	0.0	0.0	0.0	74.3	46.0	51.4	2.7	18	44.4	33.3	11.1
Garnet CDP	7,543	NA	NA	6,380	18.1	4.5	0.6	3.7	73.1	33.4	58.1	8.6	1,928	73.1	62.9	11.9
Gasquet CDP	661	NA	NA	500	73.6	0.0	0.0	2.2	24.2	23.0	54.4	22.6	243	84.4	36.6	15.2
Gazelle CDP	70	NA	NA	76	75.0	0.0	0.0	6.6	18.4	3.9	36.9	59.2	46	65.2	80.4	0.0
Georgetown CDP	2,367	NA	NA	2,458	77.6	0.6	0.5	2.7	18.6	24.4	57.2	18.5	892	82.5	34.3	14.6
Gerber CDP	1,060	NA	NA	1,201	47.5	0.0	0.0	11.2	41.3	27.7	59.5	12.7	363	63.6	38.0	11.8
Geyserville CDP	862	NA	NA	879	54.0	1.8	2.6	5.0	36.5	20.3	66.1	13.7	303	48.8	40.9	22.8
Gilroy city	48,810	52,533	7.6	50,776	31.5	1.8	5.7	2.1	59.0	29.7	61.8	8.6	14,922	58.4	38.4	29.1
Glendale city	191,713	200,167	4.4	195,380	62.7	1.1	16.0	2.8	17.4	18.7	65.5	15.9	71,132	36.2	29.3	42.6
Glendora city	50,073	51,442	2.7	50,855	57.7	2.3	7.0	3.0	29.9	23.2	62.4	14.4	16,608	68.7	25.6	33.5
Glen Ellen CDP	784	NA	NA	614	96.1	0.0	0.0	0.0	3.9	7.6	60.3	32.1	354	45.5	25.4	31.9
Golden Hills CDP	8,656	NA	NA	8,398	63.9	1.5	1.0	2.2	31.5	27.1	61.0	11.8	2,937	67.7	30.9	17.4
Gold Mountain CDP	80	NA	NA	22	100.0	0.0	0.0	0.0	0.0	0.0	0.0	100.0	12	100.0	0.0	100.0
Gold River CDP	7,912	NA	NA	7,658	67.1	2.5	20.5	3.9	6.0	21.4	57.5	21.1	3,244	85.0	12.8	60.7
Goleta city	29,902	30,797	3.0	30,333	49.4	0.8	9.2	2.4	38.3	19.9	66.0	14.2	10,375	54.6	23.4	45.8
Gonzales city	8,154	8,440	3.5	8,336	4.8	0.2	1.0	0.3	93.8	36.9	58.5	4.7	1,961	51.9	66.2	6.3
Good Hope CDP	9,192	NA	NA	8,911	11.6	10.6	0.9	1.3	75.6	28.4	63.2	8.3	2,166	59.2	68.3	5.7
Goodyears Bar CDP	68	NA	NA	23	100.0	0.0	0.0	0.0	0.0	0.0	52.2	47.8	23	47.8	52.2	0.0
Goshen CDP	3,006	NA	NA	3,832	15.2	0.0	0.0	3.0	78.8	43.0	53.4	3.7	856	51.5	59.7	8.3
Graeagle CDP	737	NA	NA	546	83.2	0.0	0.0	5.3	11.5	4.4	49.0	46.5	317	84.2	9.8	34.1
Grand Terrace city	12,040	12,414	3.1	12,252	41.1	7.3	5.0	1.9	44.7	21.7	64.0	14.3	4,415	62.6	35.0	27.2
Grangeville CDP	469	NA	NA	607	59.3	7.1	5.9	4.4	23.2	25.3	68.3	6.3	239	66.9	36.8	21.8
Granite Bay CDP	20,402	NA	NA	22,646	80.4	1.0	6.2	6.8	5.6	25.8	59.6	14.6	7,723	89.5	13.2	59.4
Granite Hills CDP	3,035	NA	NA	3,438	80.9	0.0	3.1	3.0	12.9	17.1	62.1	20.7	1,096	83.2	13.1	42.7
Graniteville CDP	11	NA	NA	0	0.0	0.0	0.0	0.0	0.0	0.0	0.0	0.0	0	0.0	0.0	0.0
Grass Valley city	12,861	12,878	0.1	12,861	82.1	0.2	1.1	2.4	14.2	18.5	56.5	25.0	5,980	44.0	34.1	26.0
Graton CDP	1,707	NA	NA	1,626	66.1	0.4	1.7	3.9	28.0	17.3	66.5	16.1	706	60.3	28.5	52.1
Grayson CDP	952	NA	NA	888	14.9	8.3	0.0	0.0	76.8	32.2	60.7	7.2	272	57.0	77.2	0.0
Greeley Hill CDP	915	NA	NA	566	98.8	0.0	0.0	0.0	1.2	11.3	43.4	45.4	247	76.9	45.3	24.3
Greenacres CDP	5,566	NA	NA	4,949	75.1	1.1	2.5	5.8	15.4	24.3	58.4	17.4	1,905	81.3	36.4	16.3
Green Acres CDP	1,805	NA	NA	2,330	44.3	3.8	0.1	6.7	45.1	30.7	57.5	11.8	563	60.0	63.4	17.1
Greenfield CDP	3,991	NA	NA	3,974	33.1	2.0	0.2	1.6	63.1	27.4	62.2	10.4	1,174	58.4	67.5	3.8
Greenfield city	16,330	16,929	3.7	16,715	6.5	0.8	4.0	0.5	88.3	35.3	60.3	4.4	3,545	46.5	70.7	9.3
Greenhorn CDP	236	NA	NA	182	79.1	0.0	0.0	0.0	20.9	6.6	75.7	17.6	138	89.1	11.6	5.8
Green Valley CDP (Los Angeles)	1,027	NA	NA	1,022	81.3	0.0	5.4	6.8	6.5	15.6	70.5	13.9	445	75.3	36.0	30.8
Green Valley CDP (Solano)	1,625	NA	NA	1,217	79.0	0.0	1.1	6.1	13.9	4.2	55.4	40.4	603	98.0	10.8	60.0
Greenview CDP	201	NA	NA	183	96.7	0.0	0.0	3.3	0.0	0.0	69.4	30.6	85	100.0	30.6	43.5
Greenville CDP	1,129	NA	NA	950	88.7	0.0	0.0	2.6	8.6	17.5	53.3	29.2	455	63.3	49.9	5.3
Grenada CDP	367	NA	NA	421	81.7	0.0	0.0	13.5	4.8	17.3	57.3	25.2	216	32.9	51.9	5.1
Gridley city	6,579	6,578	0.0	6,566	44.0	0.1	2.5	2.8	50.5	27.3	60.3	12.2	2,065	59.3	49.0	14.6
Grimes CDP	391	NA	NA	419	31.3	0.0	0.0	0.0	68.7	46.3	35.5	18.1	123	29.3	56.1	19.5
Grizzly Flats CDP	1,066	NA	NA	771	89.9	0.0	1.4	1.4	7.3	36.3	54.4	9.2	246	100.0	32.9	21.5
Groveland CDP	601	NA	NA	725	91.0	0.0	0.0	5.2	3.7	15.5	57.8	26.8	337	39.2	83.1	0.0
Grover Beach city	13,156	13,505	2.7	13,337	60.9	2.5	4.0	4.9	27.6	22.1	65.7	12.4	5,205	41.2	38.7	21.5
Guadalupe city	7,080	7,271	2.7	7,160	6.7	0.9	2.4	4.8	85.1	33.8	58.1	8.2	1,887	49.5	64.3	5.5
Guerneville CDP	4,534	NA	NA	3,775	80.8	2.2	0.5	4.4	12.3	11.1	73.3	15.6	2,046	57.4	17.4	34.7
Guinda CDP	254	NA	NA	599	17.7	76.1	1.5	4.7	0.0	42.6	43.2	14.2	118	78.0	31.4	18.6
Gustine city	5,520	5,687	3.0	5,610	37.0	0.6	0.6	1.2	60.6	23.7	63.7	12.7	1,903	59.1	64.2	10.7
Hacienda Heights CDP	54,038	NA	NA	55,179	13.3	0.9	38.8	1.6	45.5	21.3	62.3	16.4	15,800	79.5	30.5	39.9
Half Moon Bay city	11,324	12,371	9.2	11,803	60.8	1.8	4.5	2.2	30.6	19.5	62.8	17.7	4,464	73.6	23.0	49.9
Hamilton Branch CDP	537	NA	NA	634	94.0	0.0	1.6	2.1	2.4	9.3	63.7	27.1	271	80.1	25.5	28.8
Hamilton City CDP	1,759	NA	NA	1,718	12.8	0.0	0.0	1.3	85.9	31.1	59.8	9.2	503	68.4	66.6	5.2

1 May be of any race.

Table A. All Places — **Population and Housing**

STATE City, town, township, borough, or CDP (county if applicable)	Population: 2010 census total population	Population: 2014 estimated population	Population: Percent change 2010–2014	Population: ACS total population estimate 2010–2014	Race and Hispanic or Latino origin (percent), 2010–2014: White alone, not Hispanic or Latino	Black alone, not Hispanic or Latino	Asian alone, not Hispanic or Latino	All other races or 2 or more races, not Hispanic or Latino	Hispanic or Latino[1]	Age (percent), 2010–2014: Under 18 years old	Age 18 to 64 years old	Age 65 years and older	Households, 2010–2014: Total occupied housing units	Percent owner occupied	Householders by level of education (percent): High school diploma or less	Bachelor's degree or more
	1	2	3	4	5	6	7	8	9	10	11	12	13	14	15	16
CALIFORNIA—Con.																
Hanford city	54,076	55,065	1.8	54,523	42.5	3.9	4.1	2.6	47.0	30.0	59.4	10.7	17,200	57.2	40.3	18.9
Happy Camp CDP	1,190	NA	NA	1,153	62.4	0.5	5.4	27.2	4.5	17.9	63.9	18.3	526	55.5	49.6	20.5
Harbison Canyon CDP	3,841	NA	NA	4,577	68.9	0.0	2.2	6.2	22.7	19.2	69.6	11.2	1,459	87.9	33.5	30.3
Hardwick CDP	138	NA	NA	184	40.2	0.0	3.3	0.5	56.0	37.5	60.3	2.2	47	48.9	85.1	14.9
Hartland CDP	30	NA	NA	0	0.0	0.0	0.0	0.0	0.0	0.0	0.0	0.0	0	0.0	0.0	0.0
Hartley CDP	2,510	NA	NA	2,458	71.6	2.8	2.1	6.0	17.5	19.3	63.0	17.8	840	77.4	25.2	25.8
Hasley Canyon CDP	1,137	NA	NA	1,296	72.6	0.0	1.4	4.0	22.0	23.4	64.7	11.8	427	82.4	31.1	27.9
Hat Creek CDP	309	NA	NA	215	64.7	0.0	0.0	7.4	27.9	4.2	47.4	48.4	117	58.1	51.3	6.0
Hawaiian Gardens city	14,259	14,557	2.1	14,432	9.6	3.4	11.7	1.1	74.2	29.6	60.4	9.9	3,799	39.4	59.1	12.7
Hawthorne city	84,293	87,583	3.9	85,889	9.7	25.3	6.1	5.3	53.6	27.3	64.8	7.9	29,145	25.5	42.5	20.7
Hayfork CDP	2,368	NA	NA	2,372	86.5	0.7	0.3	6.4	6.2	13.8	64.8	21.5	1,001	66.8	38.7	26.0
Hayward city	144,369	154,612	7.1	149,596	18.0	11.2	23.6	6.6	40.6	23.3	66.3	10.4	45,972	52.5	40.0	27.6
Healdsburg city	11,254	11,656	3.6	11,466	62.5	0.3	0.8	2.1	34.3	22.9	59.9	17.3	4,456	55.2	31.3	37.5
Heber CDP	4,275	NA	NA	4,256	0.4	0.0	0.0	0.0	99.6	31.7	55.8	12.3	1,030	64.6	65.9	6.7
Hemet city	78,658	83,032	5.6	81,203	48.8	6.8	3.0	3.9	37.6	24.9	52.5	22.5	30,585	58.2	47.4	13.5
Herald CDP	1,184	NA	NA	1,221	66.8	4.5	0.0	0.6	28.1	17.0	65.2	17.8	362	92.0	35.6	28.7
Hercules city	24,084	25,086	4.2	24,596	16.8	17.6	42.7	8.1	14.8	22.8	66.2	10.9	8,184	78.0	16.9	46.9
Herlong CDP	298	NA	NA	1,702	25.7	21.7	2.4	5.9	44.4	4.2	95.2	0.5	141	0.0	34.8	14.2
Hermosa Beach city	19,506	19,891	2.0	19,725	80.4	1.3	5.7	4.1	8.6	17.6	71.7	10.6	9,294	45.0	7.1	72.6
Hesperia city	90,173	92,749	2.9	91,757	39.8	6.8	1.6	2.5	49.3	30.8	59.4	9.7	26,203	63.3	49.3	11.2
Hickman CDP	641	NA	NA	479	73.9	0.0	0.4	1.9	23.8	25.1	59.7	15.2	170	67.1	50.6	5.3
Hidden Hills city	1,856	1,919	3.4	1,749	92.5	0.0	2.9	1.7	3.0	27.1	59.3	13.7	583	96.2	5.5	66.7
Hidden Meadows CDP	3,485	NA	NA	3,283	81.2	0.9	14.3	1.2	2.3	11.9	53.0	35.2	1,392	93.0	13.1	43.9
Hidden Valley Lake CDP	5,579	NA	NA	6,168	75.5	0.0	0.8	1.3	22.3	29.9	55.6	14.5	2,134	67.6	27.4	34.2
Highgrove CDP	3,988	NA	NA	4,067	22.4	1.3	3.6	0.6	72.1	27.9	63.6	8.3	1,130	44.4	59.4	7.9
Highland city	53,104	54,651	2.9	54,032	30.5	10.4	7.4	2.8	48.9	30.7	61.3	8.2	15,111	63.3	42.8	22.1
Highlands-Baywood Park CDP	4,027	NA	NA	4,298	58.7	0.5	29.7	5.2	5.9	22.4	56.2	21.4	1,498	84.8	3.5	72.8
Hillsborough town	10,825	11,413	5.4	11,148	63.5	0.6	27.2	3.8	4.9	27.2	53.6	19.1	3,598	93.9	6.2	81.0
Hilmar-Irwin CDP	5,197	NA	NA	5,266	74.5	0.3	1.0	2.6	21.6	24.5	57.5	18.0	1,837	71.0	59.0	8.7
Hiouchi CDP	301	NA	NA	413	88.1	0.0	1.5	5.1	5.3	21.6	56.7	21.8	137	73.0	42.3	20.4
Hollister city	34,898	37,086	6.3	36,067	25.6	1.1	2.5	2.6	68.2	30.7	61.8	7.6	10,188	56.8	46.5	18.2
Holtville city	5,939	6,290	5.9	6,067	20.4	0.2	0.0	0.4	79.0	33.3	53.8	12.8	1,666	52.5	62.2	11.0
Home Garden CDP	1,761	NA	NA	1,787	10.4	18.0	0.3	2.4	68.9	31.8	60.2	8.1	464	49.8	72.6	3.7
Home Gardens CDP	11,570	NA	NA	11,701	15.5	2.5	6.1	1.4	74.6	30.6	63.7	5.7	2,848	73.8	61.2	10.0
Homeland CDP	5,969	NA	NA	5,921	39.0	0.6	0.9	1.8	57.7	21.1	63.2	15.8	1,967	65.8	61.8	9.5
Homestead Valley CDP	3,032	NA	NA	3,366	85.4	0.0	4.1	2.2	8.3	17.3	59.0	23.7	1,363	77.0	52.5	11.2
Homewood Canyon CDP	44	NA	NA	20	100.0	0.0	0.0	0.0	0.0	0.0	100.0	0.0	20	100.0	100.0	0.0
Honcut CDP	370	NA	NA	145	20.7	0.0	0.0	16.6	62.8	13.1	73.0	13.8	76	75.0	23.7	63.2
Hood CDP	271	NA	NA	311	11.3	0.0	2.6	20.9	65.3	14.2	70.2	15.8	88	84.1	80.7	9.1
Hopland CDP	756	NA	NA	587	80.9	0.0	0.0	7.7	11.4	10.1	76.3	13.5	273	38.1	30.8	4.8
Hornbrook CDP	248	NA	NA	275	85.5	0.0	0.0	8.0	6.5	29.8	59.0	11.3	99	71.7	46.5	6.1
Hornitos CDP	75	NA	NA	56	100.0	0.0	0.0	0.0	0.0	44.6	55.4	0.0	16	100.0	0.0	100.0
Hughson city	6,640	7,227	8.8	6,895	50.1	1.3	1.0	5.6	42.0	29.9	57.8	12.2	2,324	64.6	46.4	13.9
Humboldt Hill CDP	3,414	NA	NA	3,704	70.0	1.6	3.8	16.7	7.9	15.6	67.6	16.7	1,370	64.7	32.3	20.7
Huntington Beach city	191,037	200,809	5.1	195,686	65.1	0.7	11.2	3.8	19.2	19.7	65.2	15.3	74,235	59.1	18.8	45.1
Huntington Park city	58,114	59,362	2.1	58,787	0.9	0.3	0.9	0.4	97.5	30.0	62.8	7.1	14,637	25.6	77.7	5.6
Huron city	6,745	6,806	0.9	6,777	1.0	1.1	0.0	0.0	97.9	38.0	55.8	6.2	1,629	30.6	90.5	0.0
Hyampom CDP	241	NA	NA	255	100.0	0.0	0.0	0.0	0.0	0.0	73.7	26.3	115	58.3	78.3	0.0
Hydesville CDP	1,237	NA	NA	1,354	85.4	3.0	1.5	4.4	5.8	26.3	58.8	14.8	510	67.5	24.9	31.2
Idlewild CDP	43	NA	NA	32	100.0	0.0	0.0	0.0	0.0	12.5	59.4	28.1	12	100.0	0.0	0.0
Idyllwild-Pine Cove CDP	3,874	NA	NA	2,562	87.1	0.0	2.2	0.8	10.0	7.9	65.6	26.4	1,150	72.8	22.3	44.7
Imperial city	14,752	16,811	14.0	15,782	18.5	2.5	1.6	2.3	75.1	33.4	58.2	8.4	4,607	69.8	29.3	23.4
Imperial Beach city	26,324	27,149	3.1	26,857	33.7	3.4	7.5	5.4	50.0	27.8	63.5	8.8	8,649	33.4	37.5	18.7
Independence CDP	669	NA	NA	681	70.0	0.1	0.3	18.4	11.2	8.6	71.2	20.1	323	68.1	31.3	20.1
Indian Falls CDP	54	NA	NA	23	100.0	0.0	0.0	0.0	0.0	0.0	100.0	0.0	15	40.0	0.0	40.0
Indianola CDP	823	NA	NA	889	77.1	0.0	0.0	4.7	18.2	20.8	65.1	14.1	384	81.8	23.4	23.7
Indian Wells city	4,958	5,219	5.3	5,089	87.9	1.2	7.4	0.8	2.7	3.4	35.6	60.9	2,744	81.0	14.5	57.1
Indio city	79,116	85,633	8.2	82,539	25.1	2.0	2.0	1.9	69.0	29.7	56.6	13.7	25,281	65.1	49.9	18.5
Indio Hills CDP	972	NA	NA	910	16.9	1.1	0.1	1.3	80.5	32.8	62.2	4.9	291	96.9	63.6	6.5
Industry city	219	208	-5.0	384	29.2	5.2	7.6	0.5	57.6	34.1	55.7	10.2	88	8.0	11.4	56.8
Inglewood city	109,673	111,905	2.0	111,133	3.3	42.1	1.2	2.7	50.7	26.0	64.1	9.9	36,309	35.7	41.2	20.3
Interlaken CDP	7,321	NA	NA	6,954	18.4	1.1	5.1	1.3	74.1	25.6	64.0	10.4	1,722	69.0	55.2	15.9
Inverness CDP	1,304	NA	NA	1,368	87.6	2.3	0.8	0.6	8.7	6.0	66.5	27.3	755	49.8	14.0	58.0
Inyokern CDP	1,099	NA	NA	665	86.5	2.4	0.0	11.1	0.0	6.6	47.9	45.6	347	82.1	42.9	30.3
Ione city	7,920	6,983	-11.8	7,318	59.5	8.5	2.2	5.0	24.8	14.1	73.9	11.8	1,397	77.7	26.9	21.5
Iron Horse CDP	297	NA	NA	343	100.0	0.0	0.0	0.0	0.0	40.8	59.3	0.0	98	68.4	16.3	38.8
Irvine city	211,906	248,531	17.3	229,850	44.4	1.9	38.7	5.1	9.9	22.1	68.3	9.5	83,321	49.2	8.1	68.1
Irwindale city	1,422	1,431	0.6	1,530	3.6	1.5	0.5	0.0	94.4	28.8	61.8	9.2	365	74.0	47.4	7.7
Isla Vista CDP	23,096	NA	NA	24,792	54.9	2.1	15.8	4.2	23.0	3.6	94.8	1.6	5,167	2.6	15.7	19.7
Isleton city	804	828	3.0	792	41.3	1.0	7.3	1.0	49.4	16.8	64.5	18.4	306	56.2	55.6	8.2
Ivanhoe CDP	4,495	NA	NA	4,044	16.8	0.0	1.4	0.4	81.3	31.9	63.3	4.8	1,064	69.1	76.6	4.8
Jackson city	4,666	4,604	-1.3	4,616	80.0	0.4	0.7	4.5	14.3	23.0	55.1	21.9	1,818	54.0	35.5	22.8
Jacumba CDP	561	NA	NA	77	100.0	0.0	0.0	0.0	0.0	0.0	58.4	41.6	61	100.0	0.0	0.0
Jamestown CDP	3,433	NA	NA	3,394	82.4	0.0	0.0	2.7	14.8	24.0	56.6	19.5	1,537	54.7	37.5	10.9
Jamul CDP	6,163	NA	NA	5,445	70.2	2.9	2.2	2.7	22.1	20.9	62.4	16.6	1,704	88.5	18.0	34.6
Janesville CDP	1,408	NA	NA	1,474	95.0	0.0	1.3	0.9	2.8	22.7	62.0	15.3	498	94.0	18.7	21.3
Jenner CDP	136	NA	NA	109	100.0	0.0	0.0	0.0	0.0	0.0	56.0	44.0	58	41.4	12.1	8.6
Johannesburg CDP	172	NA	NA	79	59.5	0.0	40.5	0.0	0.0	0.0	40.5	59.5	62	100.0	21.0	0.0
Johnstonville CDP	1,024	NA	NA	1,072	91.0	0.3	0.4	5.4	3.0	29.2	60.0	10.6	387	80.6	30.7	14.0
Johnsville CDP	20	NA	NA	35	40.0	0.0	0.0	60.0	0.0	0.0	100.0	0.0	21	100.0	0.0	0.0
Joshua Tree CDP	7,414	NA	NA	7,564	71.7	2.4	2.2	4.7	19.0	24.1	59.4	16.7	3,085	46.9	38.4	27.5
Julian CDP	1,502	NA	NA	1,345	86.7	0.0	0.7	1.8	10.9	23.7	52.5	23.9	563	80.3	31.6	38.0
Junction City CDP	680	NA	NA	920	90.0	0.0	0.7	2.0	7.4	22.1	60.4	17.4	271	78.2	41.3	16.2
June Lake CDP	629	NA	NA	589	90.0	0.0	0.0	0.0	10.0	18.5	81.6	0.0	156	23.7	33.3	5.8
Jurupa Valley city	95,004	98,842	4.0	97,247	23.8	2.9	2.8	1.7	68.7	28.6	62.8	8.5	24,684	64.9	54.7	11.3
Keddie CDP	66	NA	NA	89	100.0	0.0	0.0	0.0	0.0	21.3	69.7	9.0	37	59.5	0.0	37.8
Keeler CDP	66	NA	NA	80	93.8	0.0	0.0	0.0	6.3	15.0	25.1	60.0	40	100.0	0.0	40.0
Keene CDP	431	NA	NA	325	89.8	0.0	0.0	10.2	0.0	20.0	69.5	10.5	163	84.0	12.9	10.4
Kelly Ridge CDP	2,544	NA	NA	2,594	90.8	1.2	2.0	1.8	4.2	10.7	50.3	39.1	1,242	77.7	29.0	17.1
Kelseyville CDP	3,353	NA	NA	3,516	62.3	0.3	0.5	1.7	35.2	22.3	66.1	11.5	1,220	66.2	49.6	9.8

1 May be of any race.

Table A. All Places — **Population and Housing**

STATE City, town, township, borough, or CDP (county if applicable)	Population: 2010 census total population	Population: 2014 estimated population	Population: Percent change 2010–2014	Population: ACS total population estimate 2010–2014	Race and Hispanic or Latino origin (percent), 2010–2014: White alone, not Hispanic or Latino	Black alone, not Hispanic or Latino	Asian alone, not Hispanic or Latino	All other races or 2 or more races, not Hispanic or Latino	Hispanic or Latino[1]	Age (percent), 2010–2014: Under 18 years old	Age 18 to 64 years old	Age 65 years and older	Households, 2010–2014: Total occupied housing units	Percent owner occupied	Householders by level of education (percent): High school diploma or less	Bachelor's degree or more
	1	2	3	4	5	6	7	8	9	10	11	12	13	14	15	16
CALIFORNIA—Con.																
Kennedy CDP	3,254	NA	NA	3,487	8.2	4.9	4.6	2.7	79.6	33.6	55.6	10.8	847	55.6	70.0	3.5
Kennedy Meadows CDP	28	NA	NA	37	100.0	0.0	0.0	0.0	0.0	0.0	51.4	48.6	29	100.0	0.0	0.0
Kensington CDP	5,077	NA	NA	5,351	76.3	1.2	12.5	6.5	3.4	18.7	59.1	22.2	2,235	86.5	4.8	84.5
Kentfield CDP	6,485	NA	NA	6,667	89.8	2.1	2.3	2.4	3.4	24.6	52.8	22.6	2,631	73.5	5.4	73.6
Kenwood CDP	1,028	NA	NA	1,075	90.9	0.0	0.0	1.9	7.3	18.3	66.5	15.2	450	76.2	13.1	58.0
Kerman city	13,544	14,394	6.3	14,110	17.2	0.0	5.7	0.9	76.1	36.0	56.9	7.1	3,713	53.2	62.9	10.2
Kernville CDP	1,395	NA	NA	1,354	96.3	0.2	0.0	2.8	0.7	11.3	51.3	37.3	662	66.6	37.5	21.3
Keswick CDP	451	NA	NA	410	78.5	0.0	0.0	13.9	7.6	15.1	60.0	24.9	186	87.6	36.0	8.1
Kettleman City CDP	1,439	NA	NA	1,648	0.5	0.0	0.0	0.0	99.5	30.9	68.4	0.6	347	62.0	74.1	0.0
Keyes CDP	5,601	NA	NA	6,364	36.7	0.0	1.7	3.7	57.9	36.0	55.6	8.6	1,795	66.4	72.5	7.6
King City city	12,872	13,580	5.5	13,171	8.6	0.0	0.5	1.0	89.9	35.4	57.4	7.2	2,944	43.3	77.7	6.7
Kings Beach CDP	3,796	NA	NA	3,384	40.6	0.2	0.4	1.5	57.3	22.5	75.9	1.7	1,164	36.2	41.0	25.1
Kingsburg city	11,397	11,732	2.9	11,582	50.2	0.1	5.7	2.8	41.2	26.5	60.1	13.5	3,815	66.7	35.4	31.2
Kingvale CDP	143	NA	NA	177	100.0	0.0	0.0	0.0	0.0	0.0	100.0	0.0	73	54.8	45.2	54.8
Kirkwood CDP	158	NA	NA	98	54.1	0.0	3.1	2.0	40.8	0.0	88.8	11.2	23	0.0	52.2	21.7
Klamath CDP	779	NA	NA	955	53.8	0.5	0.0	41.2	4.5	23.6	58.7	17.7	342	56.4	43.0	12.6
Knightsen CDP	1,568	NA	NA	1,644	77.7	0.7	0.3	3.4	17.8	22.0	55.7	22.2	521	77.0	29.8	25.9
Knights Landing CDP	995	NA	NA	1,161	35.0	0.0	7.3	4.3	53.4	28.5	63.2	8.1	426	63.4	70.2	4.9
La Cañada Flintridge city	20,246	20,662	2.1	20,477	62.1	0.2	27.9	2.9	6.9	25.9	57.5	16.4	6,664	88.1	5.9	77.7
La Crescenta-Montrose CDP	19,653	NA	NA	20,241	55.2	0.7	28.0	2.9	13.1	22.6	63.9	13.4	7,004	63.8	14.0	53.9
Ladera CDP	1,426	NA	NA	1,497	86.2	0.0	3.9	8.2	1.6	28.6	50.6	20.8	513	100.0	0.0	87.7
Ladera Heights CDP	6,498	NA	NA	7,362	15.0	70.8	2.8	6.1	5.3	18.6	60.6	20.7	2,947	74.2	9.9	57.1
Ladera Ranch CDP	22,980	NA	NA	26,010	67.4	1.2	11.2	4.9	15.3	38.4	57.2	4.5	7,943	72.2	9.6	64.5
Lafayette city	23,794	25,473	7.1	24,685	76.0	1.1	9.0	4.7	9.1	25.4	56.7	17.6	9,150	74.8	5.4	76.3
Laguna Beach city	22,730	23,341	2.7	23,114	85.3	0.7	4.0	3.2	6.9	16.2	61.6	22.5	11,355	61.5	9.3	64.6
Laguna Hills city	30,257	30,972	2.4	30,768	61.4	1.9	13.3	4.9	18.6	20.5	64.6	14.9	10,261	70.2	18.2	50.3
Laguna Niguel city	62,985	65,448	3.9	64,299	68.3	2.4	8.8	4.6	15.8	21.2	64.8	13.9	24,538	71.8	11.5	57.2
Laguna Woods city	16,046	16,415	2.3	16,302	80.4	0.8	13.4	0.9	4.5	0.2	23.9	75.8	11,377	73.8	23.9	43.9
Lagunitas-Forest Knolls CDP	1,819	NA	NA	2,007	72.6	5.0	2.0	4.6	15.8	18.2	70.5	11.2	773	69.7	15.4	68.8
La Habra city	60,281	62,066	3.0	61,341	28.2	1.0	8.4	2.0	60.4	25.7	63.4	10.8	18,832	56.3	38.9	24.4
La Habra Heights city	5,325	5,466	2.6	5,398	65.2	0.6	18.3	2.6	13.2	22.5	49.7	27.7	1,863	93.2	23.7	55.4
La Honda CDP	928	NA	NA	741	96.1	0.3	0.0	1.6	2.0	21.7	55.5	22.7	295	66.8	22.4	61.0
Lake Almanor Country Club CDP	419	NA	NA	530	98.1	0.0	0.0	1.9	0.0	0.0	45.9	54.2	334	93.1	8.7	71.9
Lake Almanor Peninsula CDP	356	NA	NA	470	92.6	0.0	0.0	5.7	1.7	10.7	60.3	29.1	186	89.2	23.1	22.6
Lake Almanor West CDP	270	NA	NA	263	100.0	0.0	0.0	0.0	0.0	2.3	17.5	80.2	141	100.0	0.0	29.8
Lake Arrowhead CDP	12,424	NA	NA	11,255	71.1	0.1	1.0	1.8	26.0	26.6	56.8	16.6	4,089	77.2	24.3	31.8
Lake California CDP	3,054	NA	NA	2,851	81.7	0.0	2.2	5.1	11.0	20.4	58.8	20.8	1,115	71.0	35.2	16.0
Lake City CDP	61	NA	NA	35	94.3	5.7	0.0	0.0	0.0	0.0	28.6	71.4	27	100.0	85.2	7.4
Lake Davis CDP	45	NA	NA	45	100.0	0.0	0.0	0.0	0.0	0.0	100.0	0.0	30	100.0	56.7	0.0
Lake Don Pedro CDP	1,077	NA	NA	995	68.1	0.0	0.5	8.6	22.7	21.6	62.7	15.7	414	84.5	51.0	24.4
Lake Elsinore city	52,861	60,029	13.6	56,243	35.3	4.7	4.8	4.7	50.5	32.6	61.2	6.4	14,846	65.2	39.6	20.0
Lake Forest city	77,448	80,148	3.5	78,940	55.5	1.8	14.9	3.7	24.0	23.7	66.2	10.1	26,772	70.3	18.1	49.1
Lakehead CDP	461	NA	NA	493	79.3	0.0	10.1	8.1	2.4	14.6	62.8	22.5	204	78.9	19.1	22.5
Lake Hughes CDP	649	NA	NA	469	85.7	5.3	0.0	0.0	9.0	19.1	57.5	23.5	237	61.6	57.4	21.1
Lake Isabella CDP	3,466	NA	NA	3,093	84.9	0.0	0.0	2.7	12.5	13.9	54.1	32.0	1,417	56.0	54.3	2.5
Lakeland Village CDP	11,541	NA	NA	11,343	46.2	2.6	1.7	2.5	46.9	27.5	63.8	8.7	3,551	54.4	57.5	8.2
Lake Los Angeles CDP	12,328	NA	NA	11,948	30.2	10.5	2.3	3.0	54.0	28.3	59.8	12.0	3,388	66.1	56.0	6.4
Lake Mathews CDP	5,890	NA	NA	5,518	50.8	7.0	1.9	1.0	39.4	25.0	61.7	13.3	1,611	80.9	38.6	25.0
Lake Nacimiento CDP	2,411	NA	NA	2,497	81.9	1.2	0.0	0.9	15.9	20.2	62.2	17.7	1,027	78.3	33.8	21.9
Lake of the Pines CDP	3,917	NA	NA	3,563	88.3	0.0	0.3	1.2	10.2	14.5	58.3	27.3	1,516	80.5	16.1	34.2
Lake of the Woods CDP	917	NA	NA	539	94.1	0.0	2.4	0.0	3.5	9.5	70.7	19.9	292	58.6	48.3	9.9
Lakeport city	4,753	4,776	0.5	4,746	77.8	1.7	0.3	5.0	15.3	18.8	59.5	21.7	2,001	53.1	38.9	23.0
Lake Riverside CDP	1,173	NA	NA	858	60.7	0.0	0.0	2.8	36.5	23.9	57.1	18.9	277	88.1	31.4	6.1
Lake San Marcos CDP	4,437	NA	NA	4,679	79.0	0.0	0.6	9.1	11.2	13.2	46.4	40.5	2,413	68.3	12.1	45.5
Lake Sherwood CDP	1,527	NA	NA	1,526	81.9	3.7	3.9	2.5	7.9	17.7	64.6	17.8	540	92.0	12.6	71.1
Lakeside CDP	20,648	NA	NA	21,079	70.8	1.9	2.1	3.2	22.1	25.5	61.0	13.5	7,177	69.2	38.2	18.8
Lakeview CDP	2,104	NA	NA	1,723	35.9	0.0	0.0	1.2	62.9	25.1	63.6	11.3	443	65.7	50.6	7.2
Lake Wildwood CDP	4,991	NA	NA	5,293	80.1	0.8	1.3	5.3	12.6	16.0	45.4	38.9	2,280	77.6	17.3	42.3
Lakewood city	80,048	81,653	2.0	80,926	38.1	6.9	16.2	5.6	33.2	23.5	65.1	11.6	26,339	71.2	28.9	29.8
La Mesa city	57,065	59,177	3.7	58,239	55.8	7.0	4.9	6.6	25.7	19.9	65.8	14.4	23,566	43.9	23.4	36.9
La Mirada city	48,527	49,459	1.9	49,038	35.3	2.2	19.2	3.0	40.4	20.5	63.4	16.2	14,346	78.3	29.0	33.1
Lamont CDP	15,120	NA	NA	16,359	3.5	0.0	0.8	0.3	95.3	35.6	59.3	5.0	3,606	40.8	81.1	2.4
Lanare CDP	589	NA	NA	398	0.0	5.5	0.0	0.0	94.5	40.4	50.9	8.5	88	65.9	75.0	0.0
Lancaster city	156,633	161,043	2.8	159,092	34.2	20.4	4.1	3.6	37.7	29.4	61.7	9.1	47,872	58.3	41.4	18.5
La Palma city	15,526	15,911	2.5	15,791	28.8	5.2	45.4	4.1	16.5	21.1	61.7	17.0	4,989	71.8	20.3	45.1
La Porte CDP	26	NA	NA	12	100.0	0.0	0.0	0.0	0.0	0.0	0.0	100.0	12	100.0	0.0	0.0
La Presa CDP	34,169	NA	NA	34,739	28.1	10.5	9.0	3.4	48.9	26.3	63.0	10.6	10,311	62.5	36.0	19.1
La Puente city	39,816	40,735	2.3	40,342	3.6	1.4	8.9	0.5	85.6	28.2	62.4	9.4	9,002	56.2	65.3	9.9
La Quinta city	37,467	39,964	6.7	38,774	60.4	2.2	2.7	1.6	33.1	22.1	54.3	23.7	14,977	70.6	22.9	39.6
La Riviera CDP	10,802	NA	NA	11,529	59.1	10.0	5.0	6.0	19.8	23.4	62.5	14.0	4,477	54.9	19.5	40.0
Larkfield-Wikiup CDP	8,884	NA	NA	8,831	74.6	1.6	2.4	7.8	13.6	21.2	64.7	14.0	3,464	65.7	22.0	36.4
Larkspur city	11,926	12,325	3.3	12,131	80.9	1.7	5.3	4.4	7.6	19.9	56.3	23.7	5,881	44.6	11.9	66.0
La Selva Beach CDP	2,843	NA	NA	2,932	89.1	0.5	3.2	4.9	2.3	22.8	56.8	20.5	1,150	74.9	5.9	55.2
Las Flores CDP (Orange)	5,971	NA	NA	6,311	65.9	0.9	12.7	5.8	14.7	33.9	61.3	4.9	2,009	71.3	5.1	65.7
Las Flores CDP (Tehama)	187	NA	NA	154	57.8	0.0	0.0	14.3	27.9	7.1	75.9	16.9	66	84.8	53.0	15.2
Las Lomas CDP	3,024	NA	NA	3,409	6.9	0.0	0.0	0.2	92.9	31.2	66.4	2.3	599	55.9	79.5	0.0
Lathrop city	18,023	20,075	11.4	19,163	22.9	8.5	20.0	5.5	43.1	29.3	63.4	7.4	4,646	71.1	42.9	15.3
Laton CDP	1,824	NA	NA	1,144	23.2	0.0	0.0	0.0	76.8	26.2	58.4	15.4	416	56.7	67.1	7.5
La Verne city	31,063	32,288	3.9	31,592	51.4	3.7	8.8	3.6	32.5	21.1	61.3	17.6	10,993	73.3	22.3	40.3
La Vina CDP	279	NA	NA	436	0.0	0.0	0.0	0.0	100.0	37.2	62.9	0.0	78	42.3	100.0	0.0
Lawndale city	32,769	33,442	2.1	33,155	14.0	7.4	9.0	3.9	65.6	27.6	65.0	7.2	9,597	33.4	49.1	19.2
Laytonville CDP	1,227	NA	NA	1,227	56.6	0.0	2.6	28.3	12.6	24.4	63.1	12.4	474	35.9	58.6	7.8
Lebec CDP	1,468	NA	NA	1,333	56.6	0.0	9.2	2.6	31.7	37.1	58.2	4.9	404	53.0	67.6	10.6
Lee Vining CDP	222	NA	NA	234	9.0	0.0	0.0	80.8	10.3	71.8	28.3	0.0	32	100.0	65.6	34.4
Leggett CDP	122	NA	NA	54	53.7	0.0	0.0	5.6	40.7	38.9	61.2	0.0	26	46.2	42.3	26.9
Le Grand CDP	1,659	NA	NA	1,823	11.4	0.8	0.0	0.2	87.7	29.8	59.0	11.2	509	67.6	71.7	7.1
Lemon Cove CDP	308	NA	NA	214	79.9	0.0	3.3	2.3	14.5	22.4	42.8	34.6	99	68.7	21.2	20.2

1 May be of any race.

Table A. All Places — **Population and Housing**

STATE City, town, township, borough, or CDP (county if applicable)	Population: 2010 census total population	Population: 2014 estimated population	Population: Percent change 2010–2014	Population: ACS total population estimate 2010–2014	Race and Hispanic or Latino origin (percent), 2010–2014: White alone, not Hispanic or Latino	Black alone, not Hispanic or Latino	Asian alone, not Hispanic or Latino	All other races or 2 or more races, not Hispanic or Latino	Hispanic or Latino[1]	Age (percent), 2010–2014: Under 18 years old	Age 18 to 64 years old	Age 65 years and older	Households, 2010–2014: Total occupied housing units	Percent owner occupied	Householders by level of education (percent): High school diploma or less	Bachelor's degree or more
	1	2	3	4	5	6	7	8	9	10	11	12	13	14	15	16
CALIFORNIA—Con.																
Lemon Grove city	25,320	26,511	4.7	25,963	35.9	9.1	5.5	4.9	44.6	25.3	63.4	11.3	8,396	54.1	41.7	15.9
Lemon Hill CDP	13,729	NA	NA	12,767	20.3	9.6	17.6	5.3	47.2	30.7	60.8	8.5	3,991	39.8	65.3	6.8
Lemoore city	24,531	25,186	2.7	24,788	39.5	5.5	7.1	5.7	42.2	29.6	62.8	7.5	8,311	53.4	37.6	18.8
Lemoore Station CDP	7,438	NA	NA	6,913	48.8	13.9	7.4	8.8	21.2	33.0	67.1	0.0	1,584	0.7	23.0	20.6
Lennox CDP	22,753	NA	NA	22,039	2.1	3.7	0.9	0.6	92.7	30.6	63.8	5.6	5,362	29.8	74.8	6.7
Lenwood CDP	3,543	NA	NA	3,153	36.2	8.9	0.0	7.0	47.9	31.8	61.7	6.5	1,042	41.8	52.1	8.1
Leona Valley CDP	1,607	NA	NA	1,697	83.7	0.0	0.6	5.5	10.2	18.9	59.9	21.2	657	93.3	32.4	21.6
Lewiston CDP	1,193	NA	NA	1,480	89.4	0.0	0.0	4.5	6.1	15.2	66.2	18.7	590	73.9	25.9	17.6
Lexington Hills CDP	2,421	NA	NA	2,367	81.7	0.0	5.5	9.5	3.2	24.4	65.5	10.1	865	87.6	1.3	66.1
Likely CDP	63	NA	NA	31	100.0	0.0	0.0	0.0	0.0	0.0	100.0	0.0	15	100.0	0.0	0.0
Lincoln city	42,781	45,902	7.3	44,397	70.8	1.2	5.8	3.6	18.6	22.6	51.6	25.8	16,938	78.0	20.4	36.5
Lincoln Village CDP	4,381	NA	NA	3,996	55.7	7.5	3.5	4.4	29.0	22.8	61.6	15.6	1,475	66.4	22.1	24.7
Linda CDP	17,773	NA	NA	18,634	43.1	1.9	11.0	8.7	35.3	32.9	59.7	7.6	5,869	44.4	50.4	8.9
Lindcove CDP	406	NA	NA	520	27.7	0.0	0.0	6.5	65.8	22.2	70.3	7.7	148	59.5	64.2	8.8
Linden CDP	1,784	NA	NA	1,948	72.7	0.4	0.0	3.9	23.0	29.8	56.0	14.3	687	73.5	26.8	42.2
Lindsay city	11,744	13,192	12.3	12,688	8.7	0.3	1.7	1.3	87.9	37.7	56.1	6.1	3,245	48.2	68.5	5.4
Linnell Camp CDP	849	NA	NA	561	0.0	0.0	0.0	1.8	98.2	19.8	69.0	11.1	164	0.0	100.0	0.0
Litchfield CDP	195	NA	NA	129	91.5	0.0	0.0	0.0	8.5	17.8	43.4	38.8	60	56.7	45.0	0.0
Little Grass Valley CDP	2	NA	NA	0	0.0	0.0	0.0	0.0	0.0	0.0	0.0	0.0	0	0.0	0.0	0.0
Little River CDP	117	NA	NA	38	65.8	0.0	34.2	0.0	0.0	0.0	65.8	34.2	18	33.3	100.0	0.0
Littlerock CDP	1,377	NA	NA	2,040	15.0	1.4	0.0	1.2	82.4	37.1	57.0	5.9	465	79.8	74.6	13.5
Live Oak CDP	17,158	NA	NA	17,494	64.0	1.0	3.7	3.6	27.8	21.7	65.4	13.0	6,387	61.3	24.8	40.8
Live Oak city	8,473	8,488	0.2	8,500	29.0	0.3	10.3	4.8	55.5	29.2	59.6	11.3	2,405	67.4	61.1	9.5
Livermore city	81,108	86,870	7.1	83,901	65.1	1.6	9.8	3.4	20.0	24.1	64.5	11.4	29,956	69.9	22.4	43.1
Livingston city	13,027	13,815	6.0	13,461	3.7	0.5	21.2	2.0	72.6	32.7	58.4	8.9	3,104	61.8	70.9	7.2
Lockeford CDP	3,233	NA	NA	3,172	67.5	0.0	3.3	2.8	26.4	22.7	62.5	14.8	1,254	67.7	47.2	15.8
Lockwood CDP	379	NA	NA	389	59.6	0.0	0.0	0.0	40.4	33.4	49.6	17.0	146	54.1	11.0	24.7
Lodi city	62,134	63,950	2.9	63,158	51.9	1.2	7.9	2.7	36.3	28.2	57.8	13.9	21,988	53.0	42.4	19.7
Lodoga CDP	197	NA	NA	147	80.3	9.5	0.0	0.0	10.2	4.1	49.8	46.3	94	84.0	58.5	6.4
Loleta CDP	783	NA	NA	661	83.5	0.0	1.7	2.7	12.1	14.3	70.8	14.8	279	47.3	39.4	22.9
Loma Linda city	23,261	23,853	2.5	23,648	32.0	12.1	29.0	3.6	23.3	20.2	65.7	14.0	8,637	36.4	20.5	54.5
Loma Mar CDP	113	NA	NA	211	33.2	0.0	0.0	10.0	56.9	30.8	69.2	0.0	86	67.4	26.7	48.8
Loma Rica CDP	2,368	NA	NA	2,537	88.5	0.0	0.0	4.4	7.1	19.0	54.3	26.6	944	94.1	23.0	26.3
Lomita city	20,256	20,768	2.5	20,539	38.6	2.5	15.4	6.8	36.6	20.7	68.2	11.0	7,980	41.4	36.0	29.6
Lompico CDP	1,137	NA	NA	900	78.7	0.0	1.3	5.3	14.7	15.8	80.8	3.4	409	87.3	23.7	43.5
Lompoc city	42,438	44,013	3.7	43,045	34.9	4.5	2.9	4.5	53.2	27.9	62.5	9.5	13,359	44.7	46.0	18.3
London CDP	1,869	NA	NA	2,080	6.2	0.0	0.0	0.1	93.8	35.6	58.4	6.0	467	36.6	91.4	1.1
Lone Pine CDP	2,035	NA	NA	2,017	53.8	1.1	1.1	9.2	34.8	29.8	53.1	16.9	831	49.7	56.3	5.7
Long Barn CDP	155	NA	NA	291	100.0	0.0	0.0	0.0	0.0	16.2	83.8	0.0	129	36.4	100.0	0.0
Long Beach city	462,257	473,577	2.4	468,594	28.1	12.6	12.8	4.8	41.7	24.4	65.9	9.8	163,232	40.2	33.0	32.6
Lookout CDP	84	NA	NA	67	100.0	0.0	0.0	0.0	0.0	38.8	52.2	9.0	19	31.6	5.3	26.3
Loomis town	6,419	6,728	4.8	6,589	92.4	0.9	1.8	2.0	2.9	25.0	60.9	14.2	2,251	76.9	32.8	32.4
Los Alamitos city	11,409	11,716	2.7	11,598	55.2	3.1	12.8	8.8	20.2	24.1	62.5	13.4	4,072	47.8	23.3	42.4
Los Alamos CDP	1,890	NA	NA	1,166	48.6	0.0	3.1	3.8	44.5	20.0	65.3	14.4	447	63.1	22.8	26.4
Los Altos city	28,999	30,288	4.4	29,762	66.4	0.6	24.0	5.2	3.6	26.1	53.3	20.6	10,982	84.8	4.8	82.2
Los Altos Hills town	8,028	8,396	4.6	8,244	65.5	0.0	29.7	2.9	1.9	22.9	53.1	23.8	2,976	89.1	3.8	86.7
Los Angeles city	3,792,657	3,928,864	3.6	3,862,210	28.5	8.9	11.4	2.7	48.6	22.2	66.9	10.9	1,329,372	37.2	37.3	36.2
Los Banos city	35,967	37,126	3.2	36,626	23.5	2.4	2.9	1.7	69.6	32.7	58.1	9.4	10,303	52.9	55.5	13.3
Los Berros CDP	641	NA	NA	908	82.7	0.0	0.0	6.2	11.1	32.3	50.9	16.7	314	53.8	37.9	9.9
Los Gatos town	29,436	30,735	4.4	30,163	77.0	1.4	12.7	3.7	5.2	22.1	58.2	19.5	12,425	63.9	6.5	71.6
Los Molinos CDP	2,037	NA	NA	2,184	65.2	0.0	0.0	2.2	32.7	20.1	59.3	20.6	845	56.8	54.1	9.1
Los Olivos CDP	1,132	NA	NA	913	88.8	0.0	0.3	2.4	8.4	15.7	61.6	22.9	376	83.8	17.0	52.7
Los Osos CDP	14,276	NA	NA	14,778	79.2	0.3	5.1	4.4	10.9	15.5	63.4	21.1	6,462	64.8	16.9	43.2
Los Ranchos CDP	1,477	NA	NA	1,676	91.9	0.5	0.4	5.3	2.0	21.6	47.6	30.9	719	80.3	18.6	68.7
Lost Hills CDP	2,412	NA	NA	2,194	0.9	0.0	0.0	0.0	99.1	41.1	57.3	1.6	452	41.4	93.1	0.0
Lower Lake CDP	1,294	NA	NA	1,620	66.0	0.0	0.6	12.5	20.9	14.5	69.8	15.7	685	71.1	54.6	16.4
Loyalton city	766	710	-7.3	874	83.3	0.2	0.2	0.0	16.2	17.1	57.1	25.7	336	80.1	33.3	8.9
Loyola CDP	3,261	NA	NA	3,463	68.6	0.1	22.4	5.7	3.1	25.6	54.6	19.7	1,150	90.3	2.2	85.6
Lucas Valley-Marinwood CDP	6,094	NA	NA	6,168	81.9	0.6	7.9	3.0	6.6	21.0	57.9	21.1	2,368	82.8	12.4	66.6
Lucerne CDP	3,067	NA	NA	3,318	65.1	0.0	3.2	16.2	15.6	32.0	51.0	16.9	1,258	51.0	52.1	8.1
Lucerne Valley CDP	5,811	NA	NA	5,767	64.8	1.1	0.9	8.0	25.2	17.6	71.2	11.0	1,986	76.3	32.4	10.9
Lynwood city	69,772	71,839	3.0	70,789	2.0	8.1	0.6	0.4	88.8	31.5	62.1	6.4	15,206	44.1	73.0	5.9
Lytle Creek CDP	701	NA	NA	1,127	59.4	0.0	2.5	3.2	35.0	17.2	65.7	17.1	418	69.1	40.2	14.6
Mabie CDP	161	NA	NA	52	100.0	0.0	0.0	0.0	0.0	0.0	40.4	59.6	38	100.0	0.0	44.7
McArthur CDP	338	NA	NA	308	84.7	0.0	0.0	0.0	15.3	7.5	67.6	25.0	166	70.5	0.0	0.0
McClellan Park CDP	743	NA	NA	1,103	52.4	9.2	25.1	2.4	10.9	35.7	57.7	6.5	275	0.0	45.8	11.3
McClenney Tract CDP	10	NA	NA	6	100.0	0.0	0.0	0.0	0.0	0.0	100.0	0.0	4	50.0	50.0	0.0
McCloud CDP	1,101	NA	NA	1,111	83.6	0.0	2.5	5.9	7.9	15.8	55.6	28.4	516	61.8	27.1	23.8
Macdoel CDP	133	NA	NA	111	0.0	0.0	0.0	9.0	91.0	22.5	77.4	0.0	18	27.8	72.2	0.0
McFarland city	12,707	13,605	7.1	12,784	4.0	1.8	0.6	1.7	91.9	35.9	59.2	4.9	2,817	53.5	76.7	4.9
McGee Creek CDP	41	NA	NA	125	100.0	0.0	0.0	0.0	0.0	0.0	15.2	84.8	80	100.0	46.3	0.0
McKinleyville CDP	15,177	NA	NA	16,448	81.4	0.9	1.1	8.2	8.4	23.4	63.3	13.3	6,297	62.1	30.0	31.8
McKittrick CDP	115	NA	NA	112	69.6	0.0	0.0	3.6	26.8	11.6	82.3	6.3	38	78.9	55.3	0.0
McSwain CDP	4,171	NA	NA	4,531	56.5	0.6	6.9	2.5	33.6	24.2	60.4	15.4	1,418	88.4	28.2	22.1
Madera city	61,416	63,605	3.6	62,559	15.2	2.7	2.7	1.7	77.7	34.0	58.1	8.0	16,446	47.8	57.0	10.0
Madera Acres CDP	9,163	NA	NA	9,653	29.6	2.3	1.7	0.0	66.4	33.5	58.3	8.4	2,416	81.2	44.9	20.4
Madison CDP	503	NA	NA	526	19.2	0.0	1.7	0.0	79.1	32.3	59.4	8.2	143	72.0	49.7	5.6
Mad River CDP	420	NA	NA	398	75.1	0.0	0.0	19.6	5.3	9.8	65.7	24.6	200	59.5	61.0	24.0
Magalia CDP	11,310	NA	NA	11,467	87.0	0.0	0.0	4.5	8.5	17.1	57.9	25.0	4,855	77.5	37.7	17.9
Malaga CDP	947	NA	NA	935	5.1	0.0	0.0	0.0	94.9	27.4	63.4	9.2	241	51.0	88.8	4.1
Malibu city	12,645	12,958	2.5	12,830	83.6	1.4	4.6	3.0	7.4	17.8	60.5	21.7	5,245	71.5	10.6	64.1
Mammoth Lakes town	8,234	8,009	-2.7	8,154	58.3	0.3	0.6	2.1	38.8	22.0	70.7	7.2	2,691	43.1	30.0	37.3
Manchester CDP	195	NA	NA	193	38.9	0.0	0.0	0.0	61.1	25.9	58.9	15.0	84	56.0	56.0	20.2
Manhattan Beach city	35,135	35,881	2.1	35,534	77.6	0.6	9.0	4.5	8.3	24.3	61.1	14.7	13,951	68.5	7.5	78.4
Manila CDP	784	NA	NA	673	85.4	0.0	0.0	11.4	3.1	8.3	81.4	10.3	337	40.1	31.8	46.0
Manteca city	67,276	73,494	9.2	70,693	45.0	3.6	7.4	4.1	39.9	28.8	60.5	10.6	22,396	60.0	44.3	15.8
Manton CDP	347	NA	NA	341	82.7	2.1	3.8	3.5	7.9	11.8	56.7	31.7	157	85.4	36.3	18.5
March ARB CDP	1,159	NA	NA	1,129	58.3	14.2	3.4	1.8	22.4	9.0	42.6	48.3	508	9.3	16.1	51.8
Maricopa city	1,154	1,181	2.3	1,158	68.4	0.0	6.3	5.0	20.3	27.8	61.6	10.4	395	58.7	70.1	4.6
Marina city	19,718	20,817	5.6	20,198	37.6	6.3	15.5	11.6	29.0	21.6	65.8	12.8	6,897	42.6	32.6	28.4

1 May be of any race.

Table A. All Places — **Population and Housing**

STATE City, town, township, borough, or CDP (county if applicable)	Population				Race and Hispanic or Latino origin (percent), 2010–2014					Age (percent), 2010–2014			Households, 2010–2014			
	2010 census total population	2014 estimated population	Percent change 2010–2014	ACS total population estimate 2010–2014	White alone, not Hispanic or Latino	Black alone, not Hispanic or Latino	Asian alone, not Hispanic or Latino	All other races or 2 or more races, not Hispanic or Latino	Hispanic or Latino[1]	Under 18 years old	Age 18 to 64 years old	Age 65 years and older	Total occupied housing units	Percent owner occupied	Householders by level of education (percent): High school diploma or less	Householders by level of education (percent): Bachelor's degree or more
	1	2	3	4	5	6	7	8	9	10	11	12	13	14	15	16
CALIFORNIA—Con.																
Marina del Rey CDP	8,866	NA	NA	9,157	71.3	3.9	9.3	5.6	9.9	8.7	78.0	13.2	5,428	6.4	6.5	67.0
Marin City CDP	2,666	NA	NA	2,958	33.8	26.9	6.6	5.3	27.3	28.2	59.3	12.4	1,241	30.4	22.9	34.7
Mariposa CDP	2,173	NA	NA	1,524	65.0	1.6	0.0	14.2	19.3	22.1	52.2	25.6	692	37.4	48.4	20.8
Markleeville CDP	210	NA	NA	268	93.7	0.0	0.0	3.4	3.0	16.8	60.8	22.4	95	92.6	44.2	13.7
Martell CDP	282	NA	NA	94	100.0	0.0	0.0	0.0	0.0	0.0	100.0	0.0	85	28.2	0.0	0.0
Martinez city	36,040	37,567	4.2	36,876	68.3	3.0	7.2	5.1	16.4	20.2	66.7	13.1	14,192	65.5	21.5	38.7
Marysville city	12,072	12,231	1.3	12,144	59.8	5.1	5.2	4.3	25.6	25.1	62.9	11.9	4,631	37.5	38.7	13.6
Matheny CDP	1,212	NA	NA	1,098	33.8	2.0	0.0	0.8	63.4	31.8	58.0	10.4	291	41.6	75.3	5.8
Mather CDP	4,451	NA	NA	4,806	45.9	9.4	22.1	8.2	14.4	29.1	64.4	6.5	1,512	69.9	16.4	39.4
Maxwell CDP	1,103	NA	NA	1,076	52.2	0.0	0.0	0.0	47.8	33.5	53.3	13.2	349	58.5	53.3	11.7
Mayfair CDP	4,589	NA	NA	4,512	26.6	2.0	6.2	3.0	62.3	29.1	62.6	8.2	1,306	48.2	55.2	5.7
Mayflower Village CDP	5,515	NA	NA	5,779	37.2	1.3	32.3	2.6	26.5	24.6	62.7	12.8	1,874	77.1	26.7	43.4
Maywood city	27,395	27,937	2.0	27,703	1.4	0.4	0.1	0.2	97.9	33.0	61.4	5.7	6,287	25.8	80.7	4.5
Meadowbrook CDP	3,185	NA	NA	3,447	27.0	2.3	2.2	1.5	67.0	25.9	62.3	11.7	1,032	71.8	64.9	7.8
Meadow Valley CDP	464	NA	NA	435	89.2	3.9	0.0	0.0	6.9	17.5	55.5	27.1	194	100.0	30.4	25.8
Meadow Vista CDP	3,217	NA	NA	3,072	87.0	0.0	0.0	8.5	4.6	18.4	58.1	23.5	1,305	83.2	21.8	31.2
Mead Valley CDP	18,510	NA	NA	19,851	19.4	4.1	1.1	1.2	74.2	30.5	62.7	6.8	4,486	62.3	66.2	6.0
Mecca CDP	8,577	NA	NA	8,912	1.4	0.0	0.0	0.0	98.6	37.1	58.8	4.1	1,986	51.7	91.5	0.7
Meiners Oaks CDP	3,571	NA	NA	3,634	51.7	0.0	0.9	1.7	45.8	19.9	63.2	16.8	1,233	60.9	36.2	27.2
Mendocino CDP	894	NA	NA	826	76.2	0.0	5.0	10.7	8.2	13.5	53.7	32.7	447	85.0	5.4	65.3
Mendota city	11,148	11,412	2.4	11,360	1.0	0.3	0.6	0.1	98.0	33.6	61.1	5.3	2,884	39.2	84.5	0.7
Menifee city	77,519	85,182	9.9	81,658	52.9	5.5	4.8	3.1	33.6	24.7	56.5	18.7	26,955	75.1	35.9	18.6
Menlo Park city	32,026	33,309	4.0	32,792	62.9	4.9	10.9	5.4	15.9	24.5	62.1	13.5	12,397	55.9	10.3	76.5
Mentone CDP	8,720	NA	NA	9,388	56.2	6.6	3.6	3.6	30.0	24.0	66.7	9.2	3,034	60.4	31.5	24.5
Merced city	78,957	81,743	3.5	80,490	30.8	5.3	12.4	2.7	48.8	31.1	59.6	9.2	24,950	42.2	42.5	18.3
Meridian CDP	358	NA	NA	438	67.8	0.0	0.0	7.3	24.9	24.9	55.5	19.6	178	66.3	58.4	11.8
Mesa CDP	251	NA	NA	442	85.1	0.0	0.7	4.8	9.5	19.9	64.6	15.4	177	75.1	35.0	23.7
Mesa Verde CDP	1,023	NA	NA	1,004	28.4	8.5	0.0	2.2	61.0	32.6	51.5	16.1	342	74.3	56.4	5.6
Mesa Vista CDP	200	NA	NA	212	88.2	0.0	0.9	10.8	0.0	19.8	52.3	27.8	84	89.3	9.5	54.8
Mettler CDP	136	NA	NA	88	20.5	0.0	0.0	0.0	79.5	23.8	76.2	0.0	31	35.5	90.3	9.7
Mexican Colony CDP	281	NA	NA	216	1.4	0.0	0.0	0.0	98.6	36.6	58.8	4.6	63	34.9	76.2	0.0
Middletown CDP	1,323	NA	NA	1,073	83.9	0.0	0.0	1.9	14.3	25.4	49.0	25.6	511	54.2	12.5	13.5
Midpines CDP	1,204	NA	NA	689	91.0	0.0	1.5	0.0	7.5	15.4	70.8	13.9	343	86.3	8.5	25.9
Midway City CDP	8,485	NA	NA	9,104	20.5	0.1	46.9	3.8	28.6	17.6	69.6	12.8	2,680	37.4	47.1	23.7
Milford CDP	167	NA	NA	116	100.0	0.0	0.0	0.0	0.0	0.0	93.1	6.9	63	100.0	12.7	0.0
Millbrae city	21,532	22,703	5.4	22,177	38.0	1.0	42.7	3.8	14.5	19.9	61.1	18.9	8,023	64.4	22.5	45.2
Mill Valley city	13,903	14,403	3.6	14,178	84.6	0.6	3.9	4.2	6.6	24.5	54.9	20.5	5,975	68.3	4.8	79.3
Millville CDP	727	NA	NA	861	92.8	0.6	0.6	3.4	2.7	27.3	55.2	17.5	301	79.7	18.9	36.5
Milpitas city	66,815	73,672	10.3	69,346	14.0	2.2	63.0	4.2	16.6	21.5	67.9	10.6	19,973	64.7	24.0	49.6
Mineral CDP	123	NA	NA	222	96.4	0.0	0.0	1.4	2.3	14.9	63.2	22.1	116	49.1	17.2	35.3
Minkler CDP	1,003	NA	NA	1,066	68.9	0.0	2.0	2.3	26.7	23.2	52.7	24.2	409	88.8	25.2	37.7
Mira Monte CDP	6,854	NA	NA	7,306	80.4	0.1	1.0	2.4	16.2	17.5	56.7	25.8	2,911	74.4	21.4	31.0
Miranda CDP	520	NA	NA	536	100.0	0.0	0.0	0.0	0.0	29.8	70.1	0.0	185	43.2	30.3	13.0
Mission Canyon CDP	2,381	NA	NA	2,531	86.1	1.2	1.5	1.1	10.1	15.5	66.8	17.9	956	85.7	8.6	65.4
Mission Hills CDP	3,576	NA	NA	3,415	54.6	8.6	1.0	6.4	29.5	23.4	60.4	16.0	1,098	79.1	30.8	31.4
Mission Viejo city	93,105	97,209	4.4	95,246	70.4	1.5	8.3	3.9	16.0	21.2	63.1	15.9	33,640	77.3	16.7	49.4
Mi-Wuk Village CDP	941	NA	NA	1,069	63.8	0.0	0.8	11.0	24.3	16.6	49.8	33.5	414	83.3	37.7	12.1
Modesto city	203,116	209,286	3.0	205,984	47.7	3.5	7.2	4.4	37.2	26.0	61.6	12.3	70,310	53.8	40.6	21.0
Mohawk Vista CDP	159	NA	NA	109	100.0	0.0	0.0	0.0	0.0	22.0	65.9	11.9	58	86.2	34.5	0.0
Mojave CDP	4,238	NA	NA	4,172	33.3	12.6	0.2	1.0	52.9	28.1	61.7	10.1	1,516	46.7	57.9	5.9
Mokelumne Hill CDP	646	NA	NA	635	72.6	0.0	0.0	5.4	22.0	13.5	67.0	19.5	280	75.0	33.6	37.9
Monmouth CDP	152	NA	NA	184	24.5	3.3	0.0	0.0	72.3	21.8	55.4	22.8	68	63.2	48.5	8.8
Mono City CDP	172	NA	NA	67	34.3	0.0	0.0	28.4	37.3	58.2	29.9	11.9	22	22.7	0.0	77.3
Mono Vista CDP	3,127	NA	NA	1,979	92.3	0.5	0.4	0.6	6.3	19.5	56.6	24.0	891	82.0	23.8	19.5
Monrovia city	36,590	37,415	2.3	37,035	39.3	6.2	12.7	3.0	38.8	23.5	65.7	10.8	13,032	49.2	26.3	39.3
Monson CDP	188	NA	NA	191	13.1	0.0	0.0	0.0	86.9	32.9	61.9	5.2	48	93.8	56.3	6.3
Montague city	1,443	1,397	-3.2	1,504	86.2	0.5	0.9	4.5	8.0	23.6	63.9	12.6	574	60.5	41.3	9.6
Montalvin Manor CDP	2,876	NA	NA	3,055	20.0	4.7	14.2	1.6	59.4	22.8	59.3	18.0	846	72.1	43.3	12.2
Montara CDP	2,909	NA	NA	2,880	88.5	0.0	0.6	0.0	10.9	22.3	69.6	8.3	967	88.6	5.9	56.9
Montclair city	36,664	38,465	4.9	37,685	15.5	4.1	9.7	2.3	68.5	26.2	63.4	10.4	10,336	60.1	59.1	13.3
Montebello city	62,500	63,929	2.3	63,353	9.3	1.0	12.6	1.0	76.1	22.6	62.5	14.9	19,674	46.1	56.3	18.5
Montecito CDP	8,965	NA	NA	9,444	87.1	0.9	2.0	3.6	6.3	18.6	57.1	24.3	3,187	73.2	6.6	73.7
Monterey city	27,241	28,276	3.8	28,053	68.1	2.6	8.1	4.1	17.0	16.6	65.0	18.3	12,527	34.0	17.9	49.7
Monterey Park city	60,269	61,458	2.0	60,966	3.9	0.4	62.4	2.5	30.7	17.8	63.2	19.1	18,875	52.0	42.2	31.8
Monterey Park Tract CDP	133	NA	NA	273	67.0	0.0	0.0	0.0	33.0	32.6	67.4	0.0	53	0.0	100.0	0.0
Monte Rio CDP	1,152	NA	NA	1,031	84.5	2.4	0.6	5.5	7.0	12.0	67.5	20.5	553	55.7	28.8	27.1
Monte Sereno city	3,373	3,542	5.0	3,462	81.2	0.6	11.6	3.2	3.4	25.1	53.6	21.4	1,270	89.2	4.7	77.2
Montgomery Creek CDP	163	NA	NA	123	82.1	1.6	0.0	13.0	3.3	30.1	59.4	10.6	58	77.6	0.0	48.3
Monument Hills CDP	1,542	NA	NA	1,469	65.3	0.4	0.0	1.4	32.9	15.2	74.8	9.9	462	100.0	31.0	18.2
Moorpark city	34,421	35,550	3.3	35,033	60.3	0.8	6.6	2.6	29.8	25.4	66.2	8.4	10,634	75.3	22.4	42.0
Morada CDP	3,828	NA	NA	4,573	58.8	1.0	22.9	8.5	8.8	22.9	51.0	26.1	1,658	92.6	26.9	49.1
Moraga town	16,006	17,032	6.4	16,549	70.0	4.1	14.9	4.1	6.8	20.5	59.8	19.6	5,719	81.7	4.5	77.6
Moreno Valley city	193,365	202,976	5.0	198,872	18.3	17.1	5.7	3.3	55.5	30.8	62.1	7.1	50,650	60.5	45.9	16.8
Morgan Hill city	37,879	42,068	11.1	39,875	49.3	2.6	10.3	4.8	33.0	26.9	62.7	10.5	12,879	71.4	25.5	41.4
Morongo Valley CDP	3,552	NA	NA	3,605	72.5	0.0	0.2	0.4	26.9	20.8	60.5	18.7	1,599	70.0	35.6	20.3
Morro Bay city	10,234	10,544	3.0	10,383	79.0	0.0	2.1	1.0	17.9	14.4	62.3	23.1	5,038	48.4	23.3	38.4
Moskowite Corner CDP	211	NA	NA	172	90.7	0.0	0.0	3.5	5.8	12.2	64.0	23.8	76	85.5	47.4	25.0
Moss Beach CDP	3,103	NA	NA	3,435	59.9	0.4	1.1	1.4	37.1	27.4	56.6	15.9	1,138	78.2	31.0	44.4
Moss Landing CDP	204	NA	NA	200	18.5	0.0	0.0	0.0	81.5	3.5	89.5	7.0	70	34.3	32.9	10.0
Mountain Center CDP	63	NA	NA	75	8.0	0.0	0.0	0.0	92.0	61.3	30.7	8.0	18	33.3	66.7	0.0
Mountain Gate CDP	943	NA	NA	1,153	89.9	0.0	0.0	0.0	10.1	15.6	67.0	17.5	470	58.7	47.4	21.1
Mountain House CDP	9,675	NA	NA	12,088	26.5	14.3	29.1	13.1	17.0	34.9	60.4	4.6	3,416	73.8	14.2	49.4
Mountain Mesa CDP	777	NA	NA	454	88.8	2.6	0.0	6.2	2.4	21.6	42.5	35.9	156	88.5	51.3	37.8
Mountain Ranch CDP	1,628	NA	NA	1,369	90.4	6.1	0.0	2.1	1.4	15.2	61.9	22.9	684	87.0	25.0	10.1
Mountain View CDP	2,372	NA	NA	2,299	61.4	4.3	7.6	3.5	23.3	17.8	69.4	12.8	998	49.2	39.6	18.2
Mountain View city	74,020	79,378	7.2	76,741	45.9	1.9	27.0	4.3	20.9	20.6	68.6	10.8	32,432	41.3	14.0	66.9
Mountain View Acres CDP	3,130	NA	NA	3,502	32.4	7.4	1.1	1.5	57.5	24.6	65.5	9.9	1,009	75.6	45.9	5.3
Mount Hebron CDP	95	NA	NA	88	23.9	0.0	0.0	4.5	71.6	35.2	56.8	8.0	33	69.7	48.5	30.3
Mount Hermon CDP	1,037	NA	NA	1,027	77.7	0.0	1.1	0.0	21.2	27.8	64.7	7.6	385	54.3	12.7	50.4
Mount Laguna CDP	57	NA	NA	12	100.0	0.0	0.0	0.0	0.0	0.0	0.0	100.0	12	100.0	100.0	0.0
Mount Shasta city	3,394	3,285	-3.2	3,331	86.4	0.0	0.5	5.3	7.8	16.9	68.6	14.5	1,666	47.1	18.7	36.9

1 May be of any race.

Table A. All Places — **Population and Housing**

STATE City, town, township, borough, or CDP (county if applicable)	Population				Race and Hispanic or Latino origin (percent), 2010–2014					Age (percent), 2010–2014			Households, 2010–2014			
	2010 census total population	2014 estimated population	Percent change 2010–2014	ACS total population estimate 2010–2014	White alone, not Hispanic or Latino	Black alone, not Hispanic or Latino	Asian alone, not Hispanic or Latino	All other races or 2 or more races, not Hispanic or Latino	Hispanic or Latino[1]	Under 18 years old	Age 18 to 64 years old	Age 65 years and older	Total occupied housing units	Percent owner occupied	Householders by level of education (percent): High school diploma or less	Householders by level of education (percent): Bachelor's degree or more
	1	2	3	4	5	6	7	8	9	10	11	12	13	14	15	16
CALIFORNIA—Con.																
Muir Beach CDP	310	NA	NA	292	92.5	3.4	4.1	0.0	0.0	14.4	58.5	27.1	141	85.8	12.1	63.8
Murphys CDP	2,213	NA	NA	1,884	94.8	0.0	0.0	0.3	4.9	19.2	47.4	33.3	952	75.2	23.3	27.8
Murrieta city	103,429	108,368	4.8	106,326	53.1	7.0	7.9	5.4	26.6	29.7	59.8	10.5	32,568	67.9	24.4	31.9
Muscoy CDP	10,644	NA	NA	11,674	10.3	2.8	1.0	0.5	85.3	36.6	58.1	5.4	2,260	51.5	84.0	3.8
Myers Flat CDP	146	NA	NA	57	100.0	0.0	0.0	0.0	0.0	0.0	100.0	0.0	26	0.0	0.0	0.0
Myrtletown CDP	4,675	NA	NA	5,225	78.2	0.4	3.7	8.4	9.2	19.8	61.8	18.3	1,984	55.8	18.3	34.7
Napa city	76,989	80,011	3.9	78,511	55.8	0.9	2.3	2.0	38.9	24.0	62.1	13.9	28,476	55.2	35.1	31.4
National City city	58,578	60,343	3.0	59,543	10.0	4.4	18.3	2.2	65.1	24.3	64.7	11.1	15,523	31.9	53.8	12.5
Needles city	4,844	4,969	2.6	4,923	57.3	3.2	2.5	14.8	22.1	27.2	53.8	19.0	1,981	53.4	50.8	10.4
Nevada City city	3,064	3,028	-1.2	3,051	77.4	0.8	8.2	2.9	10.6	15.7	66.4	18.0	1,358	61.0	8.3	57.7
Newark city	42,573	44,723	5.1	43,635	27.9	4.5	29.3	5.2	33.1	21.6	66.5	11.8	13,474	69.0	37.3	34.7
Newcastle CDP	1,224	NA	NA	1,409	80.7	0.0	1.5	6.6	11.2	10.6	64.0	25.5	677	81.8	31.9	21.6
New Cuyama CDP	517	NA	NA	591	34.3	0.0	0.0	2.4	63.3	34.9	54.7	10.5	212	58.5	51.9	20.3
Newell CDP	449	NA	NA	429	24.9	0.0	2.8	0.0	72.3	43.0	52.1	5.1	132	54.5	57.6	6.1
Newman city	10,219	10,748	5.2	10,553	27.0	1.5	1.7	2.0	67.8	31.9	59.2	8.8	3,157	55.0	51.1	9.8
New Pine Creek CDP	98	NA	NA	84	90.5	0.0	0.0	9.5	0.0	0.0	54.7	45.2	51	100.0	100.0	0.0
Newport Beach city	85,199	87,266	2.4	86,594	81.2	0.4	7.4	2.8	8.2	17.9	62.5	19.7	38,451	55.4	9.3	66.9
Nicasio CDP	96	NA	NA	95	73.7	0.0	0.0	0.0	26.3	33.7	40.1	26.3	28	78.6	42.9	57.1
Nice CDP	2,731	NA	NA	2,156	79.8	1.7	3.0	5.0	10.6	10.9	68.1	21.0	1,170	45.2	54.7	8.7
Nicolaus CDP	211	NA	NA	205	79.5	0.0	12.7	0.0	7.8	14.7	69.4	16.1	82	74.4	18.3	22.0
Niland CDP	1,006	NA	NA	1,063	22.6	0.4	0.0	4.9	72.2	27.1	49.6	23.3	409	45.2	90.7	4.9
Nipinnawasee CDP	475	NA	NA	729	91.4	0.0	0.0	0.0	8.6	20.6	64.6	14.8	213	93.0	34.3	42.7
Nipomo CDP	16,714	NA	NA	17,115	59.1	1.0	1.9	2.3	35.7	25.8	59.7	14.4	5,727	70.7	30.2	29.0
Norco city	27,063	26,959	-0.4	27,143	56.5	5.4	4.1	4.1	29.9	21.6	66.9	11.4	7,027	77.6	37.6	23.7
Nord CDP	320	NA	NA	239	61.5	4.6	0.0	14.2	19.7	13.8	69.0	17.2	88	61.4	54.5	33.0
Norris Canyon CDP	957	NA	NA	1,227	54.2	0.0	42.0	3.8	0.0	36.1	61.2	2.9	303	90.4	8.9	70.3
North Auburn CDP	13,022	NA	NA	14,011	69.5	0.8	2.8	3.1	23.8	21.7	56.5	21.7	5,123	61.1	43.2	20.1
North Edwards CDP	1,058	NA	NA	966	79.5	9.0	0.0	3.9	7.6	27.5	58.5	14.1	412	56.3	45.1	15.0
North El Monte CDP	3,723	NA	NA	3,924	28.9	0.6	36.6	2.6	31.3	19.7	65.8	14.3	1,263	69.6	20.8	32.4
North Fair Oaks CDP	14,687	NA	NA	15,181	20.2	0.9	4.4	3.0	71.5	25.7	66.8	7.4	4,113	49.7	49.9	28.5
North Gate CDP	679	NA	NA	417	93.8	0.0	0.0	4.3	1.9	16.1	51.9	32.1	174	94.8	11.5	59.2
North Highlands CDP	42,694	NA	NA	44,899	53.2	11.5	6.1	4.9	24.3	28.2	60.6	11.1	15,088	47.5	40.6	12.5
North Lakeport CDP	3,314	NA	NA	2,676	80.3	0.0	3.0	2.5	14.3	17.4	60.2	22.5	1,257	72.6	34.0	23.3
North Richmond CDP	3,717	NA	NA	3,926	3.0	19.9	10.8	2.9	63.5	33.5	60.0	6.5	1,078	40.6	55.0	13.5
North San Juan CDP	269	NA	NA	281	56.2	0.0	0.0	43.8	0.0	31.3	40.3	28.5	87	88.5	44.8	11.5
North Shore CDP	3,477	NA	NA	3,184	6.3	0.4	0.0	0.0	93.3	38.3	55.9	5.7	700	71.3	80.7	4.6
North Tustin CDP	24,917	NA	NA	25,724	73.9	0.8	10.7	3.9	10.8	21.3	58.2	20.5	9,007	92.2	11.9	60.8
Norwalk city	105,549	107,096	1.5	106,455	11.6	3.8	12.7	1.5	70.3	25.7	63.6	10.7	27,132	65.3	48.0	17.4
Novato city	51,904	55,005	6.0	53,451	68.8	2.1	5.5	4.0	19.6	22.0	61.2	16.8	20,890	65.4	19.2	47.1
Nubieber CDP	50	NA	NA	15	86.7	0.0	0.0	0.0	13.3	0.0	53.3	46.7	7	100.0	0.0	100.0
Nuevo CDP	6,447	NA	NA	7,345	37.9	1.0	4.8	2.1	54.3	30.9	61.1	8.0	1,974	76.8	51.5	19.1
Oakdale city	20,675	21,854	5.7	21,260	65.2	1.2	2.0	4.4	27.2	28.7	58.5	12.7	7,389	56.5	37.5	18.4
Oak Glen CDP	638	NA	NA	694	47.0	5.3	0.0	3.0	44.7	22.5	64.9	12.7	194	63.9	18.6	49.5
Oak Hills CDP	8,879	NA	NA	10,308	53.3	3.8	2.1	2.0	38.8	24.8	64.0	11.1	3,045	88.3	37.1	23.3
Oakhurst CDP	2,829	NA	NA	2,482	87.3	1.0	0.0	1.8	9.9	15.3	58.1	26.6	988	69.9	33.4	17.9
Oakland city	390,905	413,775	5.9	402,339	26.5	25.6	16.4	5.6	25.9	20.9	67.6	11.7	155,918	39.8	30.2	42.2
Oakley city	35,428	39,224	10.7	37,391	43.0	7.0	8.3	5.0	36.9	28.0	63.7	8.2	11,136	74.7	40.5	19.1
Oak Park CDP	13,811	NA	NA	14,512	76.4	0.3	13.4	2.9	7.0	28.0	62.8	9.2	5,178	72.2	9.1	66.2
Oak Shores CDP	337	NA	NA	147	87.8	0.0	0.0	0.0	12.2	0.0	52.3	47.6	81	100.0	23.5	58.0
Oak View CDP	4,066	NA	NA	4,347	69.5	0.0	0.7	1.8	28.0	19.7	69.8	10.5	1,493	76.2	32.6	31.5
Oakville CDP	71	NA	NA	59	0.0	0.0	0.0	0.0	100.0	57.6	42.4	0.0	13	0.0	100.0	0.0
Oasis CDP	6,890	NA	NA	5,807	0.3	0.8	1.1	0.8	97.1	40.2	56.9	2.9	1,297	81.0	93.3	1.2
Occidental CDP	1,115	NA	NA	1,155	93.3	0.0	3.3	2.3	1.0	12.5	74.2	13.2	522	82.4	15.3	57.3
Oceano CDP	7,286	NA	NA	7,355	42.9	0.0	0.7	4.2	52.3	20.8	61.1	18.1	2,595	52.0	46.6	17.6
Oceanside city	167,086	174,558	4.5	171,400	48.0	4.7	6.4	5.1	35.8	23.0	63.7	13.2	59,144	56.3	30.8	29.2
Ocotillo CDP	266	NA	NA	221	98.2	0.0	0.0	1.8	0.0	43.0	39.9	17.2	64	79.7	14.1	59.4
Oildale CDP	32,684	NA	NA	33,879	74.4	1.6	0.3	4.5	19.2	30.0	59.9	10.1	12,308	42.1	51.4	10.2
Ojai city	7,461	7,627	2.2	7,558	78.8	0.0	1.8	2.8	16.6	22.9	59.1	18.1	2,928	55.5	18.1	50.7
Olancha CDP	192	NA	NA	287	39.0	2.4	0.0	38.3	20.2	28.9	52.5	18.5	112	71.4	11.6	21.4
Old Fig Garden CDP	5,365	NA	NA	5,186	65.5	1.5	6.4	1.3	25.4	21.5	60.6	17.9	2,106	72.6	20.3	44.9
Old Station CDP	51	NA	NA	52	100.0	0.0	0.0	0.0	0.0	21.2	59.7	19.2	18	100.0	44.4	0.0
Olivehurst CDP	13,656	NA	NA	13,928	46.1	0.7	5.6	8.6	39.0	31.3	59.9	8.8	4,225	66.2	52.7	7.0
Ontario city	163,924	169,089	3.2	166,892	17.2	5.6	4.9	2.2	70.2	28.1	64.2	7.6	45,680	54.7	50.3	15.7
Onyx CDP	475	NA	NA	599	71.8	0.0	0.0	0.0	28.2	10.5	73.8	15.7	217	56.7	41.0	18.4
Orange city	136,419	139,812	2.5	138,980	45.1	1.1	12.2	2.3	39.4	22.5	66.5	11.1	42,754	57.8	29.2	38.3
Orange Cove city	9,072	9,584	5.6	9,473	5.0	0.2	0.1	1.1	93.6	38.2	55.3	6.5	2,337	46.7	73.5	5.0
Orangevale CDP	33,960	NA	NA	34,449	82.6	1.3	2.3	4.1	9.7	22.5	63.7	13.7	12,862	72.8	28.5	28.4
Orcutt CDP	28,905	NA	NA	30,266	69.5	1.6	3.1	3.8	22.0	23.7	57.9	18.5	11,058	76.5	25.6	31.7
Orick CDP	357	NA	NA	281	84.3	0.0	0.0	4.6	11.0	11.1	71.5	17.4	139	56.8	35.3	13.7
Orinda city	17,751	19,003	7.1	18,390	76.1	1.5	10.3	5.9	6.3	24.7	55.4	20.1	6,647	89.2	5.0	83.0
Orland city	7,332	7,512	2.5	7,451	43.5	0.2	3.4	1.1	51.9	34.8	54.5	10.5	2,382	59.6	52.3	15.4
Orosi CDP	8,770	NA	NA	8,620	4.0	0.0	9.2	1.6	85.3	33.3	56.5	10.1	2,031	55.3	83.4	2.7
Oroville city	15,971	16,220	1.6	16,015	65.4	3.8	9.1	9.9	11.7	25.6	61.1	13.3	5,666	46.6	38.9	11.0
Oroville East CDP	8,280	NA	NA	8,782	74.5	2.8	3.2	11.3	8.2	23.4	54.8	21.8	3,337	81.3	43.8	12.2
Oxnard city	197,899	205,437	3.8	201,744	14.1	2.5	7.4	1.6	74.4	28.8	62.6	8.7	50,291	55.0	48.3	19.7
Pacheco CDP	3,685	NA	NA	4,295	57.9	2.0	9.9	9.6	20.6	14.0	71.9	14.0	1,649	71.4	37.9	22.8
Pacifica city	37,295	39,088	4.8	38,283	53.7	2.6	19.1	6.9	17.7	21.1	66.6	12.5	14,168	67.2	19.6	44.6
Pacific Grove city	15,039	15,601	3.7	15,365	76.8	1.8	5.5	3.5	12.4	15.6	61.8	22.7	6,878	48.4	17.3	55.6
Pajaro CDP	3,070	NA	NA	2,957	3.3	0.3	0.5	0.3	95.6	39.7	58.4	1.9	537	12.8	89.6	0.0
Pajaro Dunes CDP	144	NA	NA	269	62.5	2.6	5.9	0.0	29.0	16.4	64.2	19.3	132	85.6	28.8	51.5
Palermo CDP	5,382	NA	NA	5,419	69.3	2.1	0.3	5.2	23.1	22.4	59.5	18.1	1,871	73.5	50.9	10.5
Palmdale city	152,750	158,279	3.6	155,810	22.9	13.2	4.3	2.9	56.6	32.1	60.4	7.5	42,012	64.3	45.2	17.9
Palm Desert city	48,443	51,202	5.7	49,953	66.3	1.2	5.1	2.5	24.9	17.2	51.1	31.7	23,636	62.8	26.6	35.7
Palm Springs city	44,531	46,854	5.2	45,827	61.0	4.8	4.7	3.4	26.2	12.1	60.8	27.2	22,906	57.8	26.7	37.5
Palo Alto city	64,409	66,955	4.0	65,998	56.6	1.5	29.5	4.5	7.8	23.0	59.8	17.2	26,420	54.7	6.5	83.1
Palo Cedro CDP	1,269	NA	NA	1,626	80.7	0.0	0.0	9.7	9.6	31.7	53.3	15.1	582	85.4	18.0	23.5
Palos Verdes Estates city	13,438	13,680	1.8	13,568	69.1	1.7	19.8	4.3	5.0	25.1	51.2	23.5	4,777	88.4	5.6	80.8
Palo Verde CDP	171	NA	NA	17	100.0	0.0	0.0	0.0	0.0	0.0	0.0	100.0	17	0.0	100.0	0.0
Panorama Heights CDP	41	NA	NA	38	89.5	0.0	0.0	10.5	0.0	0.0	52.6	47.4	24	91.7	66.7	0.0
Paradise town	26,217	26,449	0.9	26,246	87.9	0.4	1.3	3.8	6.7	16.7	58.9	24.3	10,917	71.2	26.7	26.2
Paradise CDP	153	NA	NA	235	85.1	0.0	7.2	0.0	7.7	10.3	70.2	19.6	110	90.0	19.1	40.9

1 May be of any race.

Table A. All Places — **Population and Housing**

STATE City, town, township, borough, or CDP (county if applicable)	Population: 2010 census total population	Population: 2014 estimated population	Population: Percent change 2010–2014	Population: ACS total population estimate 2010–2014	Race and Hispanic or Latino origin (percent), 2010–2014: White alone, not Hispanic or Latino	Black alone, not Hispanic or Latino	Asian alone, not Hispanic or Latino	All other races or 2 or more races, not Hispanic or Latino	Hispanic or Latino[1]	Age (percent), 2010–2014: Under 18 years old	Age 18 to 64 years old	Age 65 years and older	Households, 2010–2014: Total occupied housing units	Percent owner occupied	Householders by level of education (percent): High school diploma or less	Bachelor's degree or more
	1	2	3	4	5	6	7	8	9	10	11	12	13	14	15	16
CALIFORNIA—Con.																
Paradise Park CDP	389	NA	NA	542	97.0	0.0	0.0	3.0	0.0	3.0	69.0	28.0	289	94.1	2.8	34.3
Paramount city	54,098	55,406	2.4	54,813	5.5	10.1	2.8	1.7	79.9	31.6	62.1	6.3	13,732	38.3	65.4	9.0
Parklawn CDP	1,337	NA	NA	1,191	7.2	0.0	0.0	3.5	89.3	23.8	69.1	7.2	348	64.4	94.0	1.7
Parksdale CDP	2,621	NA	NA	3,114	10.4	0.8	0.0	1.5	87.2	35.7	58.3	6.0	689	64.9	73.0	0.0
Parkway CDP	14,670	NA	NA	14,756	17.3	19.9	12.5	9.1	41.2	31.7	58.4	9.9	4,591	42.9	53.7	11.5
Parkwood CDP	2,268	NA	NA	2,879	13.7	2.5	4.3	1.5	78.0	38.1	54.6	7.3	596	52.7	58.6	12.2
Parlier city	14,508	14,990	3.3	14,750	2.1	0.5	0.7	0.0	96.7	35.4	59.1	5.5	3,611	45.1	78.4	5.3
Pasadena city	137,122	140,881	2.7	139,065	37.9	10.5	14.7	3.3	33.6	19.0	66.6	14.4	54,092	43.9	20.0	56.5
Pasatiempo CDP	1,041	NA	NA	1,016	73.3	0.0	6.5	3.0	17.2	15.4	50.8	33.8	434	94.9	2.8	65.0
Paskenta CDP	112	NA	NA	52	100.0	0.0	0.0	0.0	0.0	23.0	53.9	23.1	26	100.0	53.8	0.0
Patterson city	20,413	21,212	3.9	20,736	25.6	6.3	3.6	6.0	58.5	35.2	57.8	6.9	5,613	65.9	54.1	13.5
Patterson Tract CDP	1,752	NA	NA	2,041	36.3	0.0	9.0	0.0	54.8	25.1	64.2	10.7	570	63.2	58.6	6.7
Patton Village CDP	702	NA	NA	592	51.4	28.0	1.7	12.2	6.8	16.8	63.7	19.6	301	72.8	54.5	10.0
Paxton CDP	14	NA	NA	0	0.0	0.0	0.0	0.0	0.0	0.0	0.0	0.0	0	0.0	0.0	0.0
Paynes Creek CDP	57	NA	NA	41	92.7	0.0	4.9	2.4	0.0	7.3	53.6	39.0	23	87.0	39.1	8.7
Pearsonville CDP	17	NA	NA	23	100.0	0.0	0.0	0.0	0.0	0.0	52.2	47.8	6	100.0	0.0	0.0
Penngrove CDP	2,522	NA	NA	2,928	70.6	3.3	1.2	7.3	17.6	23.2	64.1	12.7	1,214	51.7	31.0	43.8
Penn Valley CDP	1,621	NA	NA	1,599	83.9	0.0	0.8	9.3	5.9	18.6	65.4	16.1	616	77.1	24.2	15.6
Penryn CDP	831	NA	NA	946	93.4	0.0	0.0	1.4	5.2	18.4	64.6	17.1	367	89.9	36.2	32.4
Perris city	68,383	73,756	7.9	71,377	11.1	10.4	3.3	1.4	73.7	35.0	59.9	4.9	16,242	64.1	59.1	8.5
Pescadero CDP	643	NA	NA	1,046	36.4	0.0	0.0	0.0	63.6	37.4	43.9	18.7	266	51.1	54.9	11.7
Petaluma city	57,941	59,953	3.5	58,912	67.2	0.7	4.9	3.8	23.4	23.3	62.2	14.4	21,538	65.6	26.0	39.9
Peters CDP	672	NA	NA	523	55.8	0.0	0.0	10.3	33.8	15.3	65.3	19.5	227	89.0	20.3	21.1
Phelan CDP	14,304	NA	NA	12,947	66.5	3.8	3.5	1.2	25.0	21.0	64.1	14.9	4,463	69.8	47.1	10.0
Phillipsville CDP	140	NA	NA	77	100.0	0.0	0.0	0.0	0.0	0.0	44.2	55.8	77	29.9	70.1	0.0
Philo CDP	349	NA	NA	317	6.0	1.6	0.0	4.4	88.0	30.3	69.7	0.0	118	10.2	81.4	0.0
Phoenix Lake CDP	4,269	NA	NA	4,712	85.8	1.4	0.2	0.6	12.1	20.7	54.1	25.3	1,775	88.6	26.6	36.6
Pico Rivera city	62,942	64,235	2.1	63,698	4.8	0.8	2.6	0.9	90.9	25.4	61.2	13.3	16,464	67.7	58.6	13.2
Piedmont city	10,686	11,236	5.1	10,957	71.2	0.7	18.1	3.9	6.0	27.5	57.3	15.2	3,748	88.6	3.2	87.5
Pierpoint CDP	52	NA	NA	23	100.0	0.0	0.0	0.0	0.0	0.0	0.0	100.0	12	100.0	0.0	0.0
Pike CDP	134	NA	NA	126	94.4	0.0	0.0	5.6	0.0	14.3	59.6	26.2	48	75.0	35.4	0.0
Pine Canyon CDP	1,822	NA	NA	2,243	24.3	3.2	0.0	11.9	60.7	34.1	53.9	11.9	642	85.2	53.3	15.1
Pine Flat CDP	166	NA	NA	130	92.3	0.0	0.0	7.7	0.0	11.4	43.8	44.6	81	85.2	42.0	19.8
Pine Grove CDP	2,219	NA	NA	1,865	92.0	0.0	1.4	1.4	5.2	7.4	51.7	40.9	930	78.8	24.2	25.3
Pine Hills CDP	3,131	NA	NA	3,160	83.9	0.4	2.2	5.6	7.9	23.8	54.8	21.4	1,244	71.8	24.4	27.2
Pine Mountain Club CDP	2,315	NA	NA	1,890	82.8	0.8	2.3	4.9	9.2	21.4	58.4	20.3	825	73.5	25.1	36.7
Pine Mountain Lake CDP	2,796	NA	NA	2,422	89.3	0.0	0.8	1.9	8.1	11.6	50.3	37.9	1,216	82.2	23.8	30.4
Pine Valley CDP	1,510	NA	NA	1,554	91.4	0.0	0.0	6.0	2.6	22.0	64.1	13.8	590	89.7	22.2	22.9
Pinole city	18,330	19,100	4.2	18,754	34.9	10.4	22.8	8.4	23.6	19.7	63.5	16.7	6,679	73.5	27.7	35.8
Piñon Hills CDP	7,272	NA	NA	6,654	70.2	0.8	0.0	1.8	27.1	17.3	65.6	17.0	2,443	70.2	46.4	17.1
Pioneer CDP	1,094	NA	NA	1,237	80.8	2.9	0.0	8.8	7.5	12.9	55.6	31.4	577	96.9	49.0	18.5
Piru CDP	2,063	NA	NA	2,078	10.6	0.0	0.0	0.2	89.2	30.7	61.3	7.9	559	69.2	59.2	7.7
Pismo Beach city	7,655	7,931	3.6	7,789	88.9	0.9	2.1	3.6	4.4	17.8	57.9	24.2	3,652	52.2	13.7	38.4
Pittsburg city	63,260	68,140	7.7	65,761	19.0	17.8	16.0	6.9	40.2	25.4	65.2	9.6	19,629	57.5	39.6	19.4
Pixley CDP	3,310	NA	NA	3,769	11.6	4.1	1.8	0.0	82.5	40.4	54.1	5.5	831	40.6	87.0	4.6
Placentia city	50,893	52,397	3.0	51,860	42.5	1.4	15.8	2.7	37.7	24.5	62.0	13.6	15,778	66.1	24.6	43.2
Placerville city	10,389	10,556	1.6	10,415	76.3	0.3	1.5	4.3	17.5	21.9	60.8	17.4	3,998	54.1	36.2	26.7
Plainview CDP	945	NA	NA	858	7.9	0.0	0.0	0.0	92.1	42.6	50.8	6.6	203	47.8	94.6	0.0
Planada CDP	4,584	NA	NA	4,465	4.2	1.7	0.0	0.0	94.2	30.5	61.8	7.9	1,130	56.7	66.9	7.3
Pleasant Hill city	33,110	34,497	4.2	33,842	66.4	1.5	12.8	4.9	14.3	18.9	66.6	14.5	13,774	57.5	14.8	55.3
Pleasanton city	70,317	77,682	10.5	73,164	56.6	2.2	26.1	4.1	11.0	26.9	61.2	12.0	25,222	69.5	13.6	61.0
Pleasure Point CDP	0	NA	NA	6,004	68.3	0.8	2.7	3.3	25.0	17.1	72.5	10.5	2,683	52.2	16.6	45.8
Plumas Eureka CDP	339	NA	NA	265	100.0	0.0	0.0	0.0	0.0	0.0	61.2	38.9	130	91.5	19.2	53.8
Plumas Lake CDP	5,853	NA	NA	6,380	64.2	9.6	3.4	5.2	17.5	36.5	58.6	4.8	1,888	87.0	18.8	30.0
Plymouth city	979	961	-1.8	1,185	78.6	2.7	0.3	2.0	16.4	25.9	59.7	14.3	421	68.2	46.8	8.8
Point Arena city	449	453	0.9	405	46.4	0.0	0.0	1.2	52.3	21.2	61.1	17.5	182	41.8	40.1	16.5
Point Reyes Station CDP	848	NA	NA	848	69.7	0.0	2.4	0.0	27.9	14.2	54.2	31.7	409	44.5	21.8	41.3
Pollock Pines CDP	6,871	NA	NA	6,540	91.0	0.0	0.1	2.0	6.9	17.7	65.0	17.5	2,699	77.3	31.7	21.5
Pomona city	149,058	153,350	2.9	151,142	12.6	7.1	9.1	1.8	69.4	27.6	63.9	8.4	38,894	52.6	51.4	19.4
Ponderosa CDP	16	NA	NA	100	100.0	0.0	0.0	0.0	0.0	0.0	8.0	92.0	50	100.0	0.0	16.0
Poplar-Cotton Center CDP	2,470	NA	NA	2,764	11.1	0.0	13.9	4.2	70.8	31.0	60.1	8.9	704	40.6	82.0	1.0
Port Costa CDP	190	NA	NA	302	100.0	0.0	0.0	0.0	0.0	4.0	67.9	28.1	170	37.6	38.8	31.2
Porterville city	54,165	55,466	2.4	54,949	27.7	0.6	5.1	1.9	64.6	32.8	56.4	10.8	16,060	57.4	52.0	11.7
Port Hueneme city	21,723	22,139	1.9	21,949	28.5	4.7	4.8	5.6	56.3	25.6	62.8	11.6	6,924	43.0	37.1	21.9
Portola city	2,104	1,928	-8.4	2,710	70.0	0.6	1.5	6.9	20.9	18.9	64.3	16.6	1,045	54.0	41.1	15.4
Portola Valley town	4,353	4,570	5.0	4,478	86.1	0.2	8.1	2.5	3.0	18.0	50.2	31.7	1,844	85.0	10.1	80.0
Posey CDP	10	NA	NA	8	75.0	0.0	0.0	25.0	0.0	0.0	50.0	50.0	4	50.0	50.0	0.0
Poso Park CDP	9	NA	NA	4	100.0	0.0	0.0	0.0	0.0	0.0	0.0	100.0	2	100.0	0.0	100.0
Potrero CDP	656	NA	NA	693	24.0	0.0	0.0	1.9	74.2	43.7	45.5	10.8	207	64.7	63.3	7.2
Potter Valley CDP	646	NA	NA	509	70.5	0.0	0.0	22.4	7.1	36.3	45.0	18.7	180	51.1	53.9	8.9
Poway city	47,811	49,848	4.3	49,040	65.6	1.5	11.7	5.0	16.3	24.4	62.3	13.2	15,936	75.5	18.4	51.0
Prattville CDP	33	NA	NA	12	100.0	0.0	0.0	0.0	0.0	0.0	0.0	100.0	7	100.0	0.0	100.0
Princeton CDP	303	NA	NA	232	63.8	0.0	0.0	0.0	36.2	4.7	67.7	27.6	90	98.9	40.0	26.7
Proberta CDP	267	NA	NA	280	96.4	0.0	0.0	0.0	3.6	0.0	87.5	12.5	103	33.0	68.0	0.0
Prunedale CDP	17,560	NA	NA	18,574	41.3	0.9	4.3	4.5	48.9	22.2	65.1	12.6	5,636	74.7	40.3	22.3
Quartz Hill CDP	10,912	NA	NA	11,002	56.7	6.0	2.1	2.0	33.2	23.2	64.8	12.0	3,760	70.7	43.9	19.9
Quincy CDP	1,728	NA	NA	1,439	84.8	2.6	0.0	4.0	8.5	18.8	60.8	20.3	696	39.9	22.8	28.7
Rackerby CDP	204	NA	NA	139	96.4	0.0	0.0	0.0	3.6	20.9	55.5	23.7	43	79.1	37.2	18.6
Rail Road Flat CDP	475	NA	NA	369	84.0	0.5	0.0	3.5	11.9	18.5	39.5	42.0	161	81.4	37.9	8.1
Rainbow CDP	1,832	NA	NA	1,678	63.1	1.0	1.3	4.4	30.3	13.1	63.7	23.2	637	76.3	31.6	33.0
Raisin City CDP	380	NA	NA	232	5.6	0.0	0.0	0.0	94.4	31.5	53.8	14.7	59	52.5	61.0	10.2
Ramona CDP	20,292	NA	NA	21,578	66.1	0.6	1.2	2.5	29.5	25.6	63.7	10.8	6,551	62.4	39.8	19.5
Rancho Calaveras CDP	5,325	NA	NA	5,736	72.3	0.0	0.3	10.1	17.3	23.7	61.9	14.4	2,094	80.0	32.2	14.9
Rancho Cordova city	64,805	69,740	7.6	67,167	52.0	9.6	11.3	6.9	20.1	25.6	63.5	10.9	23,908	54.3	30.9	26.9
Rancho Cucamonga city	165,350	174,305	5.4	170,170	39.8	8.5	12.0	3.7	36.1	24.7	66.3	9.0	55,410	63.9	22.8	35.7
Rancho Mirage city	17,218	17,982	4.4	17,634	81.9	2.4	3.0	2.0	10.7	9.6	45.0	45.4	8,962	75.9	20.5	48.7
Rancho Murieta CDP	5,488	NA	NA	5,804	79.4	1.9	3.8	6.8	8.1	18.8	54.4	26.6	2,378	91.1	16.4	53.2
Rancho Palos Verdes city	41,643	42,726	2.6	42,282	56.3	2.6	27.9	5.4	7.8	22.2	52.5	25.5	15,852	79.7	7.7	69.4
Rancho San Diego CDP	21,208	NA	NA	21,514	66.7	3.7	4.1	4.6	20.9	20.9	62.9	16.2	7,999	69.2	19.0	44.1
Rancho Santa Fe CDP	3,117	NA	NA	2,838	82.1	0.0	4.8	6.8	6.4	22.0	56.0	22.1	1,037	76.6	5.6	82.1

1 May be of any race.

Table A. All Places — **Population and Housing**

STATE City, town, township, borough, or CDP (county if applicable)	Population: 2010 census total population	Population: 2014 estimated population	Population: Percent change 2010–2014	Population: ACS total population estimate 2010–2014	Race and Hispanic or Latino origin (percent), 2010–2014: White alone, not Hispanic or Latino	Black alone, not Hispanic or Latino	Asian alone, not Hispanic or Latino	All other races or 2 or more races, not Hispanic or Latino	Hispanic or Latino[1]	Age (percent), 2010–2014: Under 18 years old	Age 18 to 64 years old	Age 65 years and older	Households, 2010–2014: Total occupied housing units	Percent owner occupied	Householders by level of education (percent): High school diploma or less	Bachelor's degree or more
	1	2	3	4	5	6	7	8	9	10	11	12	13	14	15	16
CALIFORNIA—Con.																
Rancho Santa Margarita city	47,855	49,359	3.1	48,758	66.6	1.3	10.1	3.2	18.7	28.1	65.4	6.3	16,559	72.2	17.1	51.8
Rancho Tehama Reserve CDP	1,485	NA	NA	2,300	56.5	0.0	0.0	8.0	35.5	27.7	60.9	11.4	877	87.8	57.5	7.2
Randsburg CDP	69	NA	NA	128	68.8	0.0	0.0	0.0	31.3	0.0	21.9	78.1	78	100.0	0.0	0.0
Red Bluff city	14,076	14,057	-0.1	14,069	68.9	0.1	2.9	5.7	22.4	28.5	56.9	14.5	5,097	48.4	43.4	14.1
Red Corral CDP	1,413	NA	NA	1,601	85.5	1.3	1.3	1.6	10.3	21.3	62.0	16.7	610	77.7	48.7	18.7
Redcrest CDP	89	NA	NA	52	92.3	0.0	0.0	7.7	0.0	7.7	71.2	21.2	30	63.3	63.3	36.7
Redding city	89,861	91,593	1.9	90,725	80.3	1.4	3.5	6.2	8.6	22.4	60.0	17.4	34,818	53.3	29.6	24.1
Redlands city	68,667	70,622	2.8	69,787	53.5	5.3	7.2	4.0	30.0	24.7	62.3	13.1	23,923	59.1	25.2	41.7
Redondo Beach city	66,748	68,149	2.1	67,511	61.8	3.0	12.0	5.2	17.9	21.1	67.8	10.9	27,929	50.7	12.5	60.9
Redway CDP	1,225	NA	NA	1,132	92.2	0.0	0.0	5.8	1.9	19.5	71.2	9.5	487	52.8	38.2	25.5
Redwood City city	76,802	82,881	7.9	79,736	42.5	1.9	11.6	3.5	40.5	24.8	63.9	11.3	28,129	52.1	28.4	45.6
Redwood Valley CDP	1,729	NA	NA	1,814	62.4	0.0	0.0	13.5	24.1	15.4	79.7	4.9	474	68.1	21.9	15.2
Reedley city	24,194	25,426	5.1	24,858	19.1	0.4	2.2	1.1	77.1	30.0	59.2	10.7	6,792	59.6	51.4	15.8
Reliez Valley CDP	3,101	NA	NA	3,677	75.3	2.1	13.6	3.4	5.5	17.4	58.7	23.8	1,518	78.9	13.2	71.8
Rialto city	99,150	102,741	3.6	101,367	10.6	13.4	1.7	2.6	71.6	32.2	60.1	7.8	24,810	62.8	54.2	11.7
Richfield CDP	306	NA	NA	278	89.2	0.0	0.0	8.3	2.5	29.8	44.6	25.5	114	72.8	20.2	16.7
Richgrove CDP	2,882	NA	NA	3,006	0.7	0.0	4.8	1.2	93.3	35.9	60.4	3.7	628	40.9	86.1	3.5
Richmond city	103,671	108,565	4.7	106,469	17.5	22.7	14.0	5.2	40.6	24.3	65.0	10.8	36,413	49.4	36.4	28.8
Richvale CDP	244	NA	NA	86	100.0	0.0	0.0	0.0	0.0	0.0	67.5	32.6	59	72.9	27.1	49.2
Ridgecrest city	27,616	28,726	4.0	28,282	69.3	5.1	6.0	4.7	14.9	26.3	60.3	13.3	10,948	60.4	25.9	33.2
Ridgemark CDP	3,016	NA	NA	3,471	69.8	0.9	3.4	1.6	24.3	21.3	55.6	23.0	1,300	80.6	18.2	42.8
Rio Dell city	3,368	3,377	0.3	3,373	80.3	0.0	0.4	5.6	13.8	19.2	64.6	16.1	1,425	59.9	43.4	14.0
Rio del Mar CDP	9,216	NA	NA	9,240	84.2	1.2	3.3	3.2	8.1	17.5	60.4	21.9	3,978	71.8	10.4	52.5
Rio Linda CDP	15,106	NA	NA	14,581	67.1	3.2	7.5	3.1	19.1	25.6	62.4	11.9	4,791	74.8	48.5	13.3
Rio Oso CDP	356	NA	NA	428	62.6	0.0	7.7	3.5	26.2	25.3	64.9	9.8	134	56.7	35.1	27.6
Rio Vista city	7,367	8,070	9.5	7,646	70.8	6.0	7.0	4.4	11.8	14.2	49.5	36.4	3,461	73.6	34.3	24.0
Ripley CDP	692	NA	NA	659	5.0	0.9	0.0	0.0	94.1	30.1	51.5	18.5	256	22.3	92.2	0.0
Ripon city	14,297	14,966	4.7	14,645	69.9	0.7	2.5	3.3	23.6	29.0	58.0	12.9	4,944	66.9	30.3	29.2
Riverbank city	22,682	23,798	4.9	23,310	38.2	1.7	3.3	3.2	53.6	30.1	60.7	9.2	6,688	69.3	46.7	15.4
Riverdale CDP	3,153	NA	NA	3,881	23.6	1.4	0.0	0.2	74.9	36.0	56.3	7.6	888	52.3	74.9	8.7
Riverdale Park CDP	1,128	NA	NA	922	46.6	0.2	5.0	0.0	48.2	29.4	59.8	10.7	251	45.0	66.9	4.0
River Pines CDP	379	NA	NA	309	26.9	0.0	0.0	21.0	52.1	27.5	59.8	12.6	97	77.3	22.7	77.3
Riverside city	303,987	319,504	5.1	313,041	32.0	5.9	7.0	3.6	51.5	25.9	64.5	9.7	90,690	55.4	38.5	25.9
Robbins CDP	323	NA	NA	355	34.4	0.0	0.0	13.5	52.1	23.4	65.9	10.7	152	54.6	63.8	4.6
Robinson Mill CDP	80	NA	NA	0	0.0	0.0	0.0	0.0	0.0	0.0	0.0	0.0	0	0.0	0.0	0.0
Rocklin city	57,019	60,344	5.8	59,002	71.4	1.9	8.5	5.9	12.2	27.0	62.3	10.8	21,276	65.7	17.8	41.4
Rodeo CDP	8,679	NA	NA	9,648	32.9	11.7	26.2	7.5	21.6	21.8	63.4	14.9	3,043	63.2	42.5	22.5
Rodriguez Camp CDP	156	NA	NA	192	0.0	0.0	0.0	0.0	100.0	41.7	54.1	4.2	39	0.0	100.0	0.0
Rohnert Park city	40,818	42,262	3.5	41,352	63.6	1.4	5.1	5.2	24.7	19.1	71.0	9.9	15,832	51.1	28.5	26.1
Rolling Hills city	1,860	1,902	2.3	1,689	69.2	0.6	21.1	5.3	3.8	17.7	48.9	33.4	617	98.9	5.3	74.2
Rolling Hills CDP	742	NA	NA	921	77.6	0.0	8.7	0.0	13.7	17.6	54.1	28.3	307	96.7	31.9	33.2
Rolling Hills Estates city	8,067	8,251	2.3	8,184	60.5	3.9	26.3	4.1	5.2	23.8	51.7	24.7	3,027	91.4	7.2	75.0
Rollingwood CDP	2,969	NA	NA	2,832	15.3	1.0	17.9	2.0	63.8	29.6	59.4	10.9	644	52.0	60.6	15.2
Romoland CDP	1,684	NA	NA	1,682	43.9	4.8	0.0	1.6	49.7	28.4	69.5	2.3	373	49.1	56.0	2.7
Rosamond CDP	18,150	NA	NA	18,658	44.9	8.7	4.3	4.6	37.5	27.8	62.8	9.2	5,847	62.7	44.6	13.9
Rosedale CDP	14,058	NA	NA	14,826	70.9	1.3	3.5	2.7	21.6	25.2	64.2	10.6	4,861	92.1	25.6	32.7
Rose Hills CDP	2,803	NA	NA	3,260	20.6	0.6	17.4	2.9	58.5	20.8	65.2	14.0	1,068	83.3	12.6	43.1
Roseland CDP	6,325	NA	NA	5,556	35.4	1.5	2.6	7.8	52.7	25.5	67.3	7.3	1,665	52.5	52.4	16.3
Rosemead city	53,764	54,947	2.2	54,457	4.8	0.2	61.5	1.2	32.2	20.6	65.2	14.2	14,604	47.5	58.0	17.5
Rosemont CDP	22,681	NA	NA	22,824	49.2	12.1	12.1	6.1	20.5	22.2	66.9	10.8	8,487	58.0	27.0	27.6
Roseville city	118,660	128,615	8.4	124,250	71.1	1.3	9.0	4.3	14.2	25.8	60.0	14.3	45,657	64.6	21.3	38.9
Ross town	2,415	2,483	2.8	2,227	89.4	0.0	1.9	3.0	5.7	30.4	55.0	14.7	743	90.4	1.7	88.2
Rossmoor CDP	10,244	NA	NA	10,816	75.1	0.1	10.7	3.6	10.6	23.3	57.0	19.7	3,818	86.9	11.4	62.5
Rough and Ready CDP	963	NA	NA	1,195	62.2	0.3	0.0	20.0	17.6	18.7	65.8	15.5	437	69.3	56.1	21.1
Round Mountain CDP	155	NA	NA	126	69.8	2.4	0.0	27.8	0.0	0.0	67.5	32.5	86	53.5	19.8	19.8
Round Valley CDP	435	NA	NA	436	59.9	12.4	2.8	7.3	17.7	2.3	87.2	10.6	164	41.5	32.9	28.0
Rouse CDP	2,005	NA	NA	1,757	12.1	0.0	2.2	5.5	80.1	31.7	60.2	8.1	515	35.1	86.4	0.0
Rowland Heights CDP	48,993	NA	NA	51,597	10.5	0.8	56.6	2.2	30.0	18.9	65.8	15.3	14,640	67.3	30.6	40.3
Running Springs CDP	4,862	NA	NA	4,833	79.6	0.8	1.3	3.8	14.4	22.9	64.7	12.4	1,820	71.3	17.7	26.1
Ruth CDP	195	NA	NA	164	100.0	0.0	0.0	0.0	0.0	10.4	62.7	26.8	83	51.8	54.2	15.7
Rutherford CDP	164	NA	NA	219	57.1	0.0	0.0	0.0	42.9	16.4	61.7	21.9	84	46.4	64.3	4.8
Sacramento city	466,488	485,199	4.0	476,075	34.0	13.0	18.4	6.9	27.6	24.2	64.4	11.4	177,578	47.6	31.3	32.2
St. Helena city	5,816	5,987	2.9	5,895	65.2	0.3	4.2	4.9	25.4	18.7	56.0	25.2	2,568	55.3	27.3	47.8
Salida CDP	13,722	NA	NA	14,509	41.8	1.6	6.5	3.0	47.0	30.8	61.5	7.8	4,085	75.5	50.0	16.5
Salinas city	150,498	156,677	4.1	154,077	15.1	1.4	6.8	1.3	75.4	31.5	61.0	7.5	40,441	42.6	54.5	14.1
Salmon Creek CDP	86	NA	NA	59	88.1	0.0	0.0	11.9	0.0	0.0	84.7	15.3	42	45.2	21.4	23.8
Salton City CDP	3,763	NA	NA	3,867	36.7	1.4	0.0	4.8	57.0	29.4	61.2	9.2	1,277	59.4	43.9	13.8
Salton Sea Beach CDP	422	NA	NA	757	40.8	0.0	0.0	2.6	56.5	34.1	49.4	16.5	259	63.7	86.1	0.0
Samoa CDP	258	NA	NA	305	81.3	0.3	0.0	8.5	9.8	15.1	78.1	6.9	102	0.0	40.2	26.5
San Andreas CDP	2,783	NA	NA	2,829	73.2	4.0	3.9	8.0	10.9	19.1	59.2	21.7	1,204	55.1	30.2	29.2
San Anselmo town	12,336	12,676	2.8	12,527	85.4	0.6	4.5	4.0	5.4	23.2	60.6	16.2	5,243	72.0	8.5	69.0
San Antonio Heights CDP	3,371	NA	NA	3,097	68.0	0.0	9.1	3.1	19.7	19.1	61.9	19.2	1,127	81.9	16.5	45.8
San Ardo CDP	517	NA	NA	647	16.4	0.0	0.9	0.0	82.7	34.0	59.1	7.0	198	13.6	80.3	1.5
San Bernardino city	209,961	215,213	2.5	213,044	17.9	13.2	4.5	3.2	61.2	30.9	60.9	8.3	57,577	48.9	53.1	13.4
San Bruno city	41,053	43,009	4.8	42,090	34.2	2.2	26.0	7.7	30.0	19.5	67.2	13.3	14,669	55.6	27.4	37.5
San Buenaventura (Ventura) city	107,231	109,484	2.1	108,449	59.3	1.5	3.3	3.2	32.7	22.0	63.5	14.4	41,306	54.3	22.1	38.5
San Carlos city	28,406	29,803	4.9	29,166	71.6	0.9	11.6	5.2	10.7	23.4	62.0	14.7	11,570	70.3	12.2	62.9
San Clemente city	63,497	65,326	2.9	64,673	72.1	0.9	3.3	4.4	19.3	25.3	60.6	14.3	24,126	64.6	14.0	49.9
Sand City city	334	338	1.2	355	56.1	2.3	0.6	3.1	38.0	26.2	68.5	5.4	154	14.9	40.9	18.8
San Diego city	1,301,621	1,381,069	6.1	1,341,510	43.6	6.4	16.4	4.0	29.5	21.2	67.6	11.2	479,079	47.5	22.8	46.8
San Diego Country Estates CDP	10,109	NA	NA	10,191	81.0	1.5	0.4	2.9	14.2	24.0	63.8	12.4	3,462	84.1	20.9	33.9
San Dimas city	33,371	34,637	3.8	33,896	48.3	3.8	13.0	4.9	30.0	19.7	63.6	16.7	11,840	71.6	22.1	39.7
San Fernando city	23,646	24,587	4.0	24,050	6.5	1.0	1.1	1.4	90.0	28.5	62.8	8.7	6,111	57.5	64.6	10.2
San Francisco city	805,195	852,469	5.9	829,072	41.4	5.5	33.3	4.5	15.3	13.4	72.5	14.0	348,832	36.6	21.2	57.4
San Gabriel city	39,718	40,519	2.0	40,173	11.7	0.6	59.7	1.6	26.4	18.5	66.5	14.9	12,051	49.6	37.2	34.7
Sanger city	24,270	24,810	2.2	24,587	15.1	1.0	1.1	1.1	81.7	30.9	58.1	11.0	6,904	57.4	53.3	12.2
San Geronimo CDP	446	NA	NA	369	97.3	2.7	0.0	0.0	0.0	21.4	58.7	19.8	153	63.4	0.0	88.2

1 May be of any race.

Table A. All Places — **Population and Housing**

STATE City, town, township, borough, or CDP (county if applicable)	Population: 2010 census total population	Population: 2014 estimated population	Population: Percent change 2010–2014	Population: ACS total population estimate 2010–2014	Race and Hispanic or Latino origin (percent), 2010–2014: White alone, not Hispanic or Latino	Black alone, not Hispanic or Latino	Asian alone, not Hispanic or Latino	All other races or 2 or more races, not Hispanic or Latino	Hispanic or Latino[1]	Age (percent), 2010–2014: Under 18 years old	Age 18 to 64 years old	Age 65 years and older	Households, 2010–2014: Total occupied housing units	Percent owner occupied	Householders by level of education (percent): High school diploma or less	Bachelor's degree or more
	1	2	3	4	5	6	7	8	9	10	11	12	13	14	15	16
CALIFORNIA—Con.																
San Jacinto city	44,199	46,490	5.2	45,497	33.2	6.4	4.1	4.2	52.2	30.3	58.0	11.5	13,269	67.2	49.9	12.6
San Joaquin city	3,982	4,019	0.9	4,010	4.1	0.0	0.3	0.0	95.6	42.5	53.0	4.4	937	41.8	85.3	3.5
San Jose city	952,560	1,015,785	6.6	986,320	27.5	2.9	32.9	3.6	33.1	24.0	65.1	10.9	310,584	57.4	28.1	43.9
San Juan Bautista city	1,862	1,937	4.0	2,219	47.7	0.0	0.0	0.7	51.6	24.5	61.9	13.6	796	43.7	28.9	21.4
San Juan Capistrano city	34,709	36,282	4.5	35,562	56.3	0.0	3.3	3.2	37.2	24.6	59.1	16.5	11,671	73.4	25.0	42.2
San Leandro city	84,950	89,351	5.2	87,159	23.9	10.9	31.9	5.3	28.0	20.6	65.8	13.7	31,226	55.4	37.6	29.9
San Lorenzo CDP	23,452	NA	NA	24,563	29.5	5.2	23.3	5.4	36.6	21.8	63.3	14.8	7,496	73.1	41.3	24.1
San Lucas CDP	269	NA	NA	243	8.6	0.0	0.0	0.0	91.4	28.4	63.4	8.2	63	38.1	65.1	7.9
San Luis Obispo city	45,170	46,730	3.5	45,911	71.0	2.5	6.7	2.9	16.8	12.4	76.6	10.9	17,855	36.4	15.1	42.9
San Marcos city	83,650	92,929	11.1	87,808	50.2	2.2	8.9	3.7	35.0	25.6	63.4	11.0	28,428	59.5	30.1	34.5
San Marino city	13,147	13,423	2.1	13,294	37.3	0.1	50.1	2.7	9.8	24.1	57.2	18.6	4,518	88.5	9.7	74.2
San Martin CDP	7,027	NA	NA	7,081	42.7	0.2	9.8	6.9	40.4	20.6	63.9	15.6	2,033	76.6	24.5	28.6
San Mateo city	97,207	102,893	5.8	100,114	46.9	2.0	19.0	5.9	26.2	20.5	65.0	14.6	38,011	53.0	21.4	50.0
San Miguel CDP (Contra Costa)	3,392	NA	NA	3,355	87.3	0.1	5.8	2.2	4.6	24.9	64.2	10.9	1,138	90.0	5.0	76.4
San Miguel CDP (San Luis Obispo)	2,336	NA	NA	2,638	42.2	0.0	0.1	8.7	49.1	32.0	63.8	4.0	754	51.3	48.3	15.6
San Pablo city	29,134	30,050	3.1	29,516	11.3	15.9	14.7	3.0	55.0	26.2	64.3	9.6	8,967	42.4	56.7	14.7
San Pasqual CDP	2,041	NA	NA	2,143	59.0	6.4	17.3	2.1	15.2	18.6	67.4	13.9	898	56.7	10.8	70.7
San Rafael city	57,717	59,237	2.6	58,588	58.0	2.6	6.5	4.0	28.9	19.6	63.4	17.1	22,907	52.7	21.3	50.3
San Ramon city	72,211	75,332	4.3	73,826	43.5	2.2	40.2	5.4	8.6	30.0	61.5	8.5	25,215	68.5	8.5	69.2
San Simeon CDP	462	NA	NA	477	22.0	0.0	0.0	0.8	77.1	20.1	67.2	12.6	180	31.7	56.1	3.9
Santa Ana city	324,782	334,909	3.1	331,266	9.2	1.0	10.3	0.9	78.6	29.4	63.5	7.2	74,437	45.4	62.3	15.0
Santa Barbara city	88,411	91,196	3.2	89,669	52.8	1.1	3.2	2.4	40.4	19.0	65.7	15.3	34,522	40.0	24.0	47.9
Santa Clara city	116,497	122,192	4.9	119,525	34.5	3.4	38.9	4.1	19.1	22.2	67.9	10.0	42,751	44.9	18.2	58.1
Santa Clarita city	176,313	181,557	3.0	179,030	52.4	2.3	9.3	4.6	31.4	25.8	63.5	10.8	59,314	69.0	24.6	34.4
Santa Cruz city	59,948	63,364	5.7	62,045	64.6	1.7	7.6	5.1	20.9	14.0	77.1	8.9	21,015	43.3	16.1	50.2
Santa Fe Springs city	16,229	17,537	8.1	16,859	11.1	3.7	5.1	1.3	78.8	25.5	60.9	13.6	4,848	57.8	50.8	16.1
Santa Margarita CDP	1,259	NA	NA	1,231	79.9	0.0	0.0	0.0	20.1	24.1	68.3	7.6	461	61.4	33.2	43.2
Santa Maria city	99,597	103,410	3.8	101,468	21.1	1.0	4.8	1.6	71.5	30.8	59.9	9.3	27,541	50.2	53.4	15.4
Santa Monica city	89,736	92,987	3.6	91,619	68.0	3.9	9.6	4.0	14.5	14.0	70.5	15.6	46,536	27.1	12.5	66.9
Santa Nella CDP	1,380	NA	NA	1,164	51.6	1.2	1.4	10.3	35.5	27.9	64.9	7.2	478	61.7	52.3	5.9
Santa Paula city	29,321	30,441	3.8	29,990	18.9	0.1	1.2	0.9	78.8	30.0	58.8	11.1	8,630	57.4	50.7	16.5
Santa Rosa city	167,834	174,170	3.8	170,782	57.7	2.0	5.2	4.6	30.4	23.7	62.6	13.6	63,213	53.5	27.4	35.0
Santa Rosa Valley CDP	3,334	NA	NA	3,422	85.3	2.1	3.4	0.6	8.6	22.3	62.6	15.1	1,129	94.3	13.3	65.0
Santa Susana CDP	1,037	NA	NA	989	73.0	7.4	0.0	0.0	19.6	10.3	84.2	5.5	411	80.3	19.0	32.1
Santa Venetia CDP	4,292	NA	NA	5,017	62.1	1.6	9.0	2.2	25.1	17.7	65.8	16.4	1,734	69.3	26.3	44.3
Santa Ynez CDP	4,418	NA	NA	4,909	73.9	1.2	1.1	7.9	15.8	19.3	63.4	17.5	1,806	71.2	25.8	40.6
Santee city	53,415	57,052	6.8	55,435	70.4	1.4	3.6	6.9	17.8	24.9	63.8	11.3	19,173	69.9	27.0	27.6
Saranap CDP	5,202	NA	NA	5,591	77.6	2.1	7.7	7.2	5.3	26.2	61.8	12.0	2,105	68.5	15.4	65.2
Saratoga city	29,971	31,001	3.4	30,627	47.6	0.4	45.0	3.7	3.3	23.0	57.2	19.8	10,704	86.4	4.8	83.1
Saticoy CDP	1,029	NA	NA	1,212	9.1	0.0	0.8	8.3	81.8	37.7	52.2	10.1	278	56.1	68.0	17.6
Sattley CDP	49	NA	NA	74	78.4	0.0	0.0	21.6	0.0	0.0	100.0	0.0	48	52.1	0.0	0.0
Sausalito city	6,943	7,135	2.8	7,043	86.8	1.8	3.6	1.5	6.3	7.7	68.4	23.9	3,958	46.6	5.5	74.7
Scotia CDP	850	NA	NA	864	86.3	3.9	0.0	8.6	1.2	29.3	68.5	2.1	290	0.0	47.6	3.8
Scotts Valley city	11,581	11,858	2.4	11,711	78.2	0.9	5.6	4.9	10.5	24.5	61.4	14.2	4,317	76.5	13.9	52.4
Seacliff CDP	3,267	NA	NA	3,373	66.2	0.3	4.9	5.1	23.5	18.2	67.5	14.2	1,491	56.1	17.7	48.5
Seal Beach city	24,072	24,662	2.5	24,477	73.6	0.5	8.8	2.8	14.2	13.0	49.3	37.7	12,517	74.5	18.8	47.0
Sea Ranch CDP	1,305	NA	NA	983	96.4	0.0	0.5	0.8	2.2	2.1	31.6	66.2	552	86.1	6.0	63.0
Searles Valley CDP	1,739	NA	NA	1,597	74.9	5.8	0.3	3.9	15.1	24.8	59.4	15.8	683	60.2	52.6	8.9
Seaside city	33,025	34,182	3.5	33,729	31.2	8.1	10.0	7.6	43.0	26.8	64.3	8.8	10,185	38.1	40.7	27.5
Sebastopol city	7,392	7,659	3.6	7,535	81.7	1.4	1.2	3.6	12.1	14.9	62.5	22.5	3,676	50.3	17.8	46.5
Seeley CDP	1,739	NA	NA	1,214	10.5	1.2	0.0	0.9	87.4	28.1	56.0	16.1	393	40.7	55.5	0.0
Selma city	23,219	24,283	4.6	23,808	13.9	0.4	6.1	2.2	77.4	29.9	58.4	11.6	6,540	57.4	58.5	11.3
Sequoia Crest CDP	10	NA	NA	26	100.0	0.0	0.0	0.0	0.0	0.0	0.0	100.0	13	100.0	0.0	0.0
Sereno del Mar CDP	126	NA	NA	51	100.0	0.0	0.0	0.0	0.0	0.0	37.2	62.7	30	100.0	0.0	70.0
Seville CDP	480	NA	NA	437	1.6	0.0	0.0	0.0	98.4	32.0	63.7	4.3	91	28.6	83.5	2.2
Shafter city	16,988	17,559	3.4	17,261	16.8	0.7	0.2	1.6	80.7	34.2	59.0	6.6	4,434	53.2	68.4	7.3
Shandon CDP	1,295	NA	NA	1,323	56.6	6.1	0.5	4.2	32.6	28.1	65.3	6.5	402	53.7	50.0	10.4
Shasta CDP	1,771	NA	NA	1,814	84.3	0.0	2.3	9.5	3.9	18.4	58.5	23.3	750	89.1	30.5	31.3
Shasta Lake city	10,164	10,166	0.0	10,143	81.9	0.0	1.8	5.0	11.3	24.0	58.9	17.1	4,010	63.2	35.4	13.4
Shaver Lake CDP	634	NA	NA	735	92.0	0.0	2.2	0.5	5.3	20.5	61.0	18.4	299	75.6	22.1	34.1
Shell Ridge CDP	959	NA	NA	1,139	57.2	0.0	9.6	8.1	25.2	32.0	47.5	20.3	361	100.0	3.6	71.5
Shelter Cove CDP	693	NA	NA	516	83.3	0.0	0.0	0.0	16.7	22.9	67.0	10.1	219	82.2	27.4	11.0
Sheridan CDP	1,238	NA	NA	1,465	64.0	0.0	0.0	4.1	31.9	21.2	71.2	7.6	415	84.6	29.4	22.4
Shingle Springs CDP	4,432	NA	NA	4,562	81.5	0.4	0.4	1.1	16.6	18.7	64.6	16.5	1,598	79.5	23.1	28.4
Shingletown CDP	2,283	NA	NA	2,241	73.6	2.1	5.0	13.9	5.4	20.4	48.9	30.6	915	86.3	32.1	21.1
Shoshone CDP	31	NA	NA	22	86.4	0.0	0.0	0.0	13.6	0.0	100.0	0.0	12	0.0	66.7	0.0
Sierra Brooks CDP	478	NA	NA	418	90.2	0.0	0.0	9.8	0.0	31.6	50.8	17.5	164	76.8	11.6	26.8
Sierra City CDP	221	NA	NA	263	93.9	0.0	0.0	2.3	3.8	18.6	71.5	9.9	126	95.2	4.8	40.5
Sierra Madre city	10,917	11,165	2.3	11,060	69.9	1.5	10.5	3.7	14.3	20.1	62.1	17.7	4,457	57.5	8.5	64.3
Sierra Village CDP	456	NA	NA	612	80.7	0.0	12.1	2.6	4.6	12.1	49.0	39.1	273	68.5	24.9	27.8
Sierraville CDP	200	NA	NA	133	25.6	1.5	0.8	0.0	72.2	36.0	38.5	25.6	46	50.0	50.0	50.0
Signal Hill city	11,016	11,526	4.6	11,245	27.5	12.9	21.5	6.5	31.6	26.0	67.0	7.0	3,975	46.2	29.1	38.4
Silverado Resort CDP	1,095	NA	NA	1,074	98.2	0.0	0.0	0.0	1.8	5.9	48.8	45.3	560	72.3	13.2	62.9
Silver City CDP	0	NA	NA	0	0.0	0.0	0.0	0.0	0.0	0.0	0.0	0.0	0	0.0	0.0	0.0
Silver Lakes CDP	5,623	NA	NA	5,706	74.4	4.7	3.3	1.8	15.7	21.6	57.8	20.4	2,082	71.9	29.4	34.4
Simi Valley city	124,239	126,871	2.1	125,699	61.7	1.1	8.9	3.9	24.4	23.7	64.5	12.0	41,803	73.1	25.2	35.4
Sisquoc CDP	183	NA	NA	276	47.1	0.0	0.0	19.9	33.0	35.5	52.8	11.6	83	56.6	43.4	6.0
Sky Valley CDP	2,406	NA	NA	2,493	52.5	1.6	0.0	3.0	42.9	21.2	54.5	24.4	973	73.1	40.2	20.5
Sleepy Hollow CDP	2,384	NA	NA	2,584	82.7	0.4	9.2	5.8	1.9	21.8	60.0	18.3	927	92.0	6.8	74.3
Smartsville CDP	177	NA	NA	143	93.0	0.7	0.0	5.6	0.7	25.2	68.6	6.3	74	35.1	29.7	10.8
Smith Corner CDP	524	NA	NA	661	4.7	0.0	0.0	0.0	95.3	39.6	59.3	0.9	137	56.9	86.9	13.1
Smith River CDP	866	NA	NA	871	62.3	0.0	2.1	6.1	29.5	37.9	47.7	14.4	307	50.5	34.9	2.6
Snelling CDP	231	NA	NA	116	92.2	0.0	0.0	7.8	0.0	11.2	66.4	22.4	68	66.2	33.8	10.3
Soda Bay CDP	1,016	NA	NA	1,369	78.7	0.0	0.0	0.0	21.3	6.3	48.5	45.2	613	83.5	28.9	21.4
Soda Springs CDP	81	NA	NA	80	100.0	0.0	0.0	0.0	0.0	0.0	100.1	0.0	65	0.0	0.0	76.9
Solana Beach city	12,867	13,337	3.7	13,146	71.9	0.2	3.1	2.4	22.4	17.6	62.2	20.2	5,437	58.3	15.4	66.2
Soledad city	25,740	25,336	-1.6	26,008	12.3	10.1	2.2	2.6	72.8	21.9	72.6	5.6	3,735	56.1	72.3	5.9
Solvang city	5,245	5,506	5.0	5,345	69.2	0.0	1.8	2.4	26.6	16.9	56.4	26.9	2,447	52.6	22.2	45.8
Sonoma city	10,652	11,017	3.4	10,818	84.9	0.2	2.2	1.6	11.1	16.5	55.1	28.6	4,978	54.5	14.7	42.9

1 May be of any race.

Table A. All Places — **Population and Housing**

STATE City, town, township, borough, or CDP (county if applicable)	2010 census total population	2014 estimated population	Percent change 2010–2014	ACS total population estimate 2010–2014	White alone, not Hispanic or Latino	Black alone, not Hispanic or Latino	Asian alone, not Hispanic or Latino	All other races or 2 or more races, not Hispanic or Latino	Hispanic or Latino[1]	Under 18 years old	Age 18 to 64 years old	Age 65 years and older	Total occupied housing units	Percent owner occupied	High school diploma or less	Bachelor's degree or more
	1	2	3	4	5	6	7	8	9	10	11	12	13	14	15	16
CALIFORNIA—Con.																
Sonora city	4,904	4,802	-2.1	4,844	77.1	3.2	4.4	5.4	9.9	18.6	62.5	18.9	2,256	38.7	34.5	22.1
Soquel CDP	9,644	NA	NA	10,275	71.0	0.0	2.9	4.9	21.1	21.0	65.8	13.1	3,865	71.4	18.7	44.3
Soulsbyville CDP	2,215	NA	NA	2,020	90.4	0.0	0.0	3.7	5.8	30.0	59.0	10.8	743	82.4	28.3	20.2
South Dos Palos CDP	1,620	NA	NA	2,464	1.0	7.3	0.0	0.0	91.7	28.3	63.7	8.0	561	66.0	57.8	4.1
South El Monte city	20,116	20,569	2.3	20,375	2.4	0.0	9.9	0.8	86.9	27.6	62.2	10.1	4,821	48.0	78.4	6.8
South Gate city	94,396	96,312	2.0	95,515	2.8	0.6	0.8	0.2	95.6	28.2	63.8	8.1	23,386	47.1	70.7	7.6
South Lake Tahoe city	21,400	21,529	0.6	21,394	58.3	1.4	4.6	3.4	32.3	19.4	68.8	11.8	8,585	45.9	33.6	25.4
South Monrovia Island CDP	6,777	NA	NA	6,929	13.7	6.5	5.8	1.6	72.5	23.1	66.2	10.7	1,627	69.0	53.3	11.9
South Oroville CDP	5,742	NA	NA	6,058	49.0	0.2	21.0	6.7	23.1	29.0	61.6	9.4	1,665	55.9	58.0	6.6
South Pasadena city	25,619	26,156	2.1	25,914	40.8	2.1	30.8	4.9	21.4	23.6	64.3	12.2	10,394	43.5	11.8	63.1
South San Francisco city	63,664	67,009	5.3	65,537	20.1	1.9	37.9	6.1	34.0	20.6	65.0	14.4	21,470	59.7	34.4	33.8
South San Gabriel CDP	8,070	NA	NA	8,281	5.8	0.9	57.4	1.0	34.9	16.5	61.8	21.6	2,167	74.3	38.6	30.4
South San Jose Hills CDP	20,551	NA	NA	21,012	4.6	1.5	6.9	1.3	85.7	28.4	61.9	9.7	4,033	74.1	71.0	9.4
South Taft CDP	2,169	NA	NA	1,680	53.7	3.8	0.0	2.4	40.1	30.7	61.7	7.7	471	45.9	60.1	8.7
South Whittier CDP	57,156	NA	NA	58,328	16.3	0.7	3.8	2.4	76.7	26.7	63.4	9.9	15,283	64.9	47.2	17.5
Spaulding CDP	178	NA	NA	197	95.4	0.0	0.0	4.6	0.0	12.2	39.7	48.2	96	86.5	45.8	24.0
Spreckels CDP	673	NA	NA	939	92.1	0.0	2.2	0.0	5.6	32.4	60.3	7.3	305	62.0	5.2	38.7
Spring Garden CDP	16	NA	NA	0	0.0	0.0	0.0	0.0	0.0	0.0	0.0	0.0	0	0.0	0.0	0.0
Spring Valley CDP (Lake)	845	NA	NA	1,000	94.6	0.0	0.0	0.0	5.4	6.0	67.4	26.6	441	88.0	31.3	19.0
Spring Valley CDP (San Diego)	28,205	NA	NA	29,841	45.1	11.0	5.1	5.5	33.3	26.9	61.8	11.3	9,363	60.3	31.3	24.2
Spring Valley Lake CDP	8,220	NA	NA	7,816	70.8	6.8	3.4	1.5	17.5	27.7	58.6	13.7	2,672	65.9	26.7	21.3
Springville CDP	934	NA	NA	502	82.1	0.0	0.0	9.2	8.8	7.4	47.5	45.2	303	76.2	33.0	23.1
Squaw Valley CDP	3,162	NA	NA	2,450	82.9	0.0	2.8	9.2	5.1	23.2	56.4	20.4	922	86.1	22.0	19.2
Squirrel Mountain Valley CDP	547	NA	NA	372	94.1	0.0	0.0	0.0	5.9	0.0	41.6	58.3	180	100.0	43.3	29.4
Stallion Springs CDP	2,488	NA	NA	2,983	92.5	0.0	2.0	0.0	5.4	21.5	57.6	20.9	1,146	77.4	42.4	15.6
Stanford CDP	13,809	NA	NA	13,506	48.6	5.0	26.4	6.5	13.4	7.8	87.7	4.5	2,970	27.8	1.8	96.9
Stanton city	37,827	38,719	2.4	38,455	21.4	2.5	23.7	2.8	49.7	26.3	63.4	10.5	11,586	48.7	47.7	21.4
Stevenson Ranch CDP	17,557	NA	NA	18,832	55.5	3.3	20.5	3.8	16.8	32.2	60.2	7.5	5,996	68.3	17.6	52.3
Stevenson CDP	313	NA	NA	171	100.0	0.0	0.0	0.0	0.0	18.7	56.8	24.6	41	70.7	70.7	0.0
Stinson Beach CDP	632	NA	NA	425	97.4	1.2	0.0	0.0	1.4	6.6	58.7	34.6	240	71.3	2.5	60.8
Stirling City CDP	295	NA	NA	154	100.0	0.0	0.0	0.0	0.0	19.5	28.6	51.9	53	100.0	56.6	17.0
Stockton city	291,731	302,389	3.7	297,223	22.3	10.8	21.2	4.4	41.3	29.2	60.2	10.6	91,304	49.6	43.3	19.5
Stonyford CDP	149	NA	NA	283	81.6	0.7	0.0	10.2	7.4	21.5	57.7	20.8	104	73.1	74.0	12.5
Storrie CDP	4	NA	NA	0	0.0	0.0	0.0	0.0	0.0	0.0	0.0	0.0	0	0.0	0.0	0.0
Stratford CDP	1,277	NA	NA	1,301	16.0	0.0	0.0	1.5	82.6	32.3	63.5	4.2	377	66.3	75.1	0.0
Strathmore CDP	2,819	NA	NA	3,626	13.9	0.0	0.0	0.0	86.1	32.6	61.4	6.0	825	35.3	65.2	2.9
Strawberry CDP (Marin)	5,393	NA	NA	5,684	71.5	2.3	15.2	6.2	4.8	19.1	64.0	16.8	2,482	36.3	7.7	70.7
Strawberry CDP (Tuolumne)	86	NA	NA	228	99.6	0.0	0.0	0.0	0.4	28.1	41.7	30.3	76	100.0	40.8	0.0
Sugarloaf Mountain Park CDP	0	NA	NA	0	0.0	0.0	0.0	0.0	0.0	0.0	0.0	0.0	0	0.0	0.0	0.0
Sugarloaf Saw Mill CDP	18	NA	NA	0	0.0	0.0	0.0	0.0	0.0	0.0	0.0	0.0	0	0.0	0.0	0.0
Sugarloaf Village CDP	10	NA	NA	0	100.0	0.0	0.0	0.0	0.0	0.0	33.3	66.7	6	100.0	33.3	33.3
Suisun City city	28,104	29,256	4.1	28,627	25.6	20.5	20.2	8.6	25.1	27.8	63.8	8.3	8,684	62.0	27.9	20.9
Sultana CDP	775	NA	NA	813	4.9	0.0	0.5	0.0	94.6	44.1	49.6	6.3	207	27.1	83.1	1.4
Summerland CDP	1,448	NA	NA	1,575	73.5	1.7	14.3	4.4	6.2	11.1	75.7	13.1	775	57.0	1.9	47.6
Sunnyside CDP	4,235	NA	NA	4,159	45.6	0.4	18.2	1.6	34.3	23.4	53.3	23.4	1,424	82.0	21.4	38.3
Sunnyside-Tahoe City CDP	1,557	NA	NA	1,845	78.4	0.0	2.1	2.1	17.4	22.8	68.5	8.6	737	65.5	13.7	56.9
Sunny Slopes CDP	182	NA	NA	137	100.0	0.0	0.0	0.0	0.0	0.0	100.0	0.0	66	100.0	0.0	16.7
Sunnyvale city	140,058	149,980	7.1	145,921	34.7	1.8	41.3	4.2	18.0	23.0	65.9	11.2	54,267	47.0	16.0	63.7
Sunol CDP	913	NA	NA	956	72.5	0.0	5.8	7.8	13.9	11.5	67.1	21.4	365	77.0	14.8	49.9
Sun Village CDP	11,565	NA	NA	11,613	23.1	9.0	0.9	1.8	65.2	29.6	60.5	9.8	2,992	78.4	56.7	9.2
Susanville city	17,943	15,543	-13.4	16,537	56.2	11.1	1.9	6.2	24.6	12.8	79.9	7.4	3,932	49.9	31.6	20.5
Sutter CDP	2,904	NA	NA	2,959	83.1	0.0	0.7	3.1	13.0	28.9	62.0	9.2	1,053	71.5	30.6	15.3
Sutter Creek city	2,514	2,467	-1.9	2,271	87.4	0.0	1.0	3.2	8.5	17.7	53.2	29.2	1,180	48.3	36.2	18.0
Swall Meadows CDP	220	NA	NA	259	99.2	0.0	0.0	0.0	0.8	16.2	72.6	11.2	106	93.4	3.8	72.6
Taft city	9,288	8,909	-4.1	9,063	55.9	2.0	2.2	3.2	36.7	20.9	69.7	9.4	2,313	54.6	44.3	15.8
Taft Heights CDP	1,949	NA	NA	2,612	75.4	0.8	1.1	2.1	20.6	35.6	58.3	6.1	901	27.7	41.5	6.1
Taft Mosswood CDP	1,530	NA	NA	1,398	5.6	6.9	22.8	0.6	64.2	28.4	63.9	7.6	340	47.6	86.8	5.0
Tahoe Vista CDP	1,433	NA	NA	1,332	57.5	0.0	2.3	0.0	40.2	16.8	70.8	12.5	497	55.7	12.3	51.9
Tahoma CDP	1,191	NA	NA	959	93.7	0.0	1.0	5.2	0.0	21.4	70.3	8.3	423	57.9	17.3	28.8
Talmage CDP	1,130	NA	NA	1,335	37.8	1.3	4.1	6.1	50.8	19.5	65.8	14.7	340	58.2	40.3	27.9
Tamalpais-Homestead Valley CDP	10,735	NA	NA	10,331	82.5	0.9	9.0	2.5	5.0	23.3	61.5	15.3	4,077	77.8	3.0	78.0
Tara Hills CDP	5,126	NA	NA	4,767	29.9	13.2	13.9	7.2	35.8	21.9	64.5	13.6	1,677	64.5	40.3	15.8
Tarpey Village CDP	3,888	NA	NA	3,246	65.3	5.8	9.8	0.7	18.4	25.1	57.7	17.2	1,036	90.0	36.6	24.2
Taylorsville CDP	140	NA	NA	185	88.1	0.0	0.0	0.0	11.9	0.0	87.6	12.4	106	100.0	37.7	40.6
Tecopa CDP	150	NA	NA	115	100.0	0.0	0.0	0.0	0.0	17.4	48.7	33.9	60	61.7	41.7	11.7
Tehachapi city	14,414	13,236	-8.2	13,818	55.5	6.5	1.3	2.1	34.6	19.4	71.6	8.9	3,269	58.2	44.4	14.9
Tehama city	418	414	-1.0	397	91.7	0.0	0.0	0.8	7.6	24.9	56.1	18.9	163	63.8	34.4	22.1
Temecula city	100,156	109,428	9.3	104,955	56.9	3.0	9.9	6.1	24.1	29.9	61.6	8.4	32,233	65.7	24.6	34.1
Temelec CDP	1,441	NA	NA	1,505	86.4	0.9	1.8	0.7	10.2	0.0	28.8	71.2	948	88.3	32.1	33.8
Temescal Valley CDP	22,535	NA	NA	24,714	51.8	7.8	8.0	3.6	28.8	25.9	62.5	11.6	7,760	86.4	26.2	35.1
Temple City city	35,558	36,334	2.2	36,006	19.7	0.5	56.5	2.0	21.2	21.6	62.1	16.2	11,393	66.0	28.6	39.3
Templeton CDP	7,674	NA	NA	7,753	77.7	0.5	2.2	3.3	16.2	23.9	60.6	15.5	2,799	72.2	26.7	33.4
Tennant CDP	41	NA	NA	115	44.3	0.0	0.0	3.5	52.2	29.6	43.4	27.0	45	71.1	11.1	8.9
Terminous CDP	381	NA	NA	409	74.6	0.0	1.2	1.2	23.0	7.3	54.1	38.6	214	81.3	40.7	18.2
Terra Bella CDP	3,310	NA	NA	2,912	4.6	1.4	1.2	0.0	92.8	37.7	55.9	6.4	687	59.5	83.0	3.2
Teviston CDP	1,214	NA	NA	1,823	8.0	6.2	0.0	0.0	85.8	47.7	46.6	5.7	407	36.6	82.3	1.5
Thermal CDP	2,865	NA	NA	3,570	0.1	0.0	0.0	0.4	99.6	30.3	63.5	6.1	949	41.6	80.3	0.0
Thermalito CDP	6,646	NA	NA	6,911	64.9	0.0	18.3	7.8	9.0	21.9	61.7	16.4	2,265	68.7	55.7	6.3
Thornton CDP	1,131	NA	NA	748	26.2	0.9	6.4	1.5	65.0	33.0	51.0	15.9	264	42.8	68.2	11.4
Thousand Oaks city	126,555	129,342	2.2	128,126	69.1	1.2	9.5	3.2	17.0	23.2	60.9	15.8	45,849	71.4	16.9	52.5
Thousand Palms CDP	7,715	NA	NA	7,956	33.7	2.5	0.0	1.6	62.2	21.0	57.3	21.8	2,895	72.7	41.0	20.3
Three Rivers CDP	2,182	NA	NA	2,278	87.8	0.5	0.3	4.0	7.5	12.6	56.1	31.3	1,116	77.0	27.0	39.3
Three Rocks CDP	246	NA	NA	51	0.0	0.0	0.0	0.0	100.0	23.5	76.5	0.0	11	0.0	100.0	0.0
Tiburon town	8,962	9,224	2.9	9,100	86.3	0.2	3.7	2.4	7.4	21.6	52.4	26.1	3,897	70.1	5.8	72.7

1 May be of any race.

Table A. All Places — **Population and Housing**

STATE City, town, township, borough, or CDP (county if applicable)	Population: 2010 census total population	Population: 2014 estimated population	Population: Percent change 2010–2014	Population: ACS total population estimate 2010–2014	Race and Hispanic or Latino origin (percent), 2010–2014: White alone, not Hispanic or Latino	Black alone, not Hispanic or Latino	Asian alone, not Hispanic or Latino	All other races or 2 or more races, not Hispanic or Latino	Hispanic or Latino[1]	Age (percent), 2010–2014: Under 18 years old	Age 18 to 64 years old	Age 65 years and older	Households, 2010–2014: Total occupied housing units	Percent owner occupied	Householders by level of education (percent): High school diploma or less	Bachelor's degree or more
	1	2	3	4	5	6	7	8	9	10	11	12	13	14	15	16
CALIFORNIA—Con.																
Timber Cove CDP	164	NA	NA	132	77.3	2.3	0.0	2.3	18.2	1.5	68.2	30.3	83	49.4	47.0	41.0
Tipton CDP	2,543	NA	NA	2,327	14.4	0.0	0.0	2.4	83.2	38.5	57.6	3.8	584	35.3	74.7	0.9
Tobin CDP	12	NA	NA	12	100.0	0.0	0.0	0.0	0.0	0.0	0.0	100.0	12	100.0	0.0	0.0
Tomales CDP	204	NA	NA	155	76.1	0.0	0.0	23.9	0.0	0.0	83.3	16.8	99	48.5	33.3	30.3
Tonyville CDP	316	NA	NA	764	0.0	0.0	0.0	0.0	100.0	23.4	76.6	0.0	135	23.7	76.3	0.0
Tooleville CDP	339	NA	NA	387	10.9	0.0	0.0	0.0	89.1	7.0	82.5	10.6	124	65.3	100.0	0.0
Topanga CDP	8,289	NA	NA	8,923	82.1	0.8	4.3	4.3	8.5	25.2	60.3	14.3	3,353	83.1	11.4	60.2
Topaz CDP	50	NA	NA	123	68.3	0.0	0.0	0.0	31.7	50.4	49.6	0.0	56	0.0	17.9	0.0
Toro Canyon CDP	1,508	NA	NA	1,476	80.6	0.0	2.0	0.8	16.6	17.4	55.3	27.2	628	59.7	15.8	38.5
Torrance city	145,438	148,495	2.1	147,181	42.0	2.7	33.6	5.4	16.3	20.9	62.8	16.2	55,279	55.6	20.2	47.7
Tracy city	83,101	85,841	3.3	84,573	34.0	6.4	14.1	6.5	39.0	31.4	60.9	7.7	24,480	63.6	37.8	24.4
Tranquillity CDP	799	NA	NA	897	24.4	0.0	0.0	0.0	75.6	35.6	39.4	25.1	256	59.8	73.8	7.4
Traver CDP	713	NA	NA	910	13.6	0.0	0.0	8.9	77.5	27.0	63.0	10.0	195	47.7	82.6	3.1
Tres Pinos CDP	476	NA	NA	457	67.0	1.8	1.1	2.4	27.8	23.9	69.2	7.0	175	54.9	33.1	28.6
Trinidad city	367	357	-2.7	236	89.8	0.0	0.4	5.9	3.8	4.2	61.5	34.3	142	59.9	13.4	62.0
Trinity Center CDP	267	NA	NA	239	99.6	0.0	0.0	0.4	0.0	8.4	39.7	51.9	136	83.1	34.6	23.5
Trinity Village CDP	297	NA	NA	211	93.8	0.0	0.0	0.5	5.7	11.4	63.0	25.6	111	69.4	37.8	13.5
Trona CDP	18	NA	NA	0	0.0	0.0	0.0	0.0	0.0	0.0	0.0	0.0	0	0.0	0.0	0.0
Trowbridge CDP	226	NA	NA	184	90.8	0.0	7.1	0.0	2.2	32.6	50.7	16.8	63	92.1	54.0	6.3
Truckee town	16,164	16,297	0.8	16,191	80.3	0.1	2.1	0.8	16.9	23.8	69.1	7.1	6,213	67.3	20.8	40.7
Tulare city	59,312	61,867	4.3	60,663	34.5	2.8	2.1	2.9	57.7	32.2	59.2	8.8	18,064	58.0	55.9	11.4
Tulelake city	1,010	989	-2.1	1,029	40.0	0.0	0.0	2.4	57.5	28.5	60.3	11.2	383	41.5	57.2	19.3
Tuolumne City CDP	1,779	NA	NA	1,824	82.2	0.0	0.1	4.8	12.9	15.9	55.7	28.6	875	59.7	29.1	19.0
Tupman CDP	161	NA	NA	176	82.4	0.0	0.0	0.0	17.6	31.8	54.9	13.1	45	66.7	91.1	0.0
Turlock city	68,549	71,245	3.9	69,875	50.9	2.2	5.8	4.5	36.6	26.4	61.1	12.6	23,606	53.1	42.2	24.7
Tustin city	75,314	80,621	7.0	77,765	32.4	2.4	20.2	3.6	41.4	25.4	65.6	9.0	25,517	50.2	27.5	44.2
Tuttle CDP	103	NA	NA	17	100.0	0.0	0.0	0.0	0.0	0.0	0.0	100.0	8	100.0	0.0	0.0
Tuttletown CDP	668	NA	NA	949	93.7	0.0	0.0	0.0	6.3	14.1	56.9	28.9	406	74.6	15.5	25.4
Twain CDP	82	NA	NA	0	0.0	0.0	0.0	0.0	0.0	0.0	0.0	0.0	0	0.0	0.0	0.0
Twain Harte CDP	2,226	NA	NA	2,374	92.3	0.0	1.0	0.8	5.9	11.0	64.0	25.1	1,125	67.8	44.7	23.1
Twentynine Palms city	25,048	25,902	3.4	25,601	60.7	7.8	3.1	5.8	22.6	24.8	69.0	6.2	8,217	31.9	40.9	16.6
Twin Lakes CDP	4,917	NA	NA	5,212	75.7	1.4	1.0	1.9	20.0	12.0	73.8	14.1	2,354	36.4	13.5	39.1
Ukiah city	16,075	15,977	-0.6	15,956	62.8	0.9	2.3	7.6	26.5	25.4	58.7	15.9	6,039	40.1	39.0	25.1
Union City city	69,524	73,621	5.9	71,675	14.0	5.6	51.6	6.8	22.0	22.7	64.4	13.0	20,529	65.1	33.0	39.2
University of California-Davis CDP	5,786	NA	NA	6,735	38.0	3.7	38.7	5.1	14.6	5.4	94.5	0.1	912	0.0	10.1	52.1
University of California-Merced CDP	0	NA	NA	0	0.0	0.0	0.0	0.0	0.0	0.0	0.0	0.0	0	0.0	0.0	0.0
Upland city	73,732	76,043	3.1	75,089	43.9	5.3	8.8	3.6	38.4	23.3	62.9	13.7	27,017	56.9	30.2	31.4
Upper Lake CDP	1,052	NA	NA	755	58.9	0.0	0.9	7.9	32.2	33.6	45.9	20.7	283	70.3	36.4	3.2
Vacaville city	92,422	95,856	3.7	93,994	54.6	9.0	6.8	6.1	23.6	22.6	66.2	11.1	31,224	60.5	28.1	25.3
Valinda CDP	22,822	NA	NA	23,818	6.9	1.0	11.2	1.2	79.6	26.6	63.9	9.5	4,911	78.2	58.1	15.8
Vallecito CDP	442	NA	NA	573	98.4	0.0	0.0	0.0	1.6	40.6	39.5	19.9	182	54.4	22.5	38.5
Vallejo city	115,940	120,228	3.7	118,078	24.6	20.7	23.9	6.5	24.2	22.0	64.6	13.3	40,848	57.2	32.6	23.9
Valle Vista CDP	14,578	NA	NA	15,995	59.0	2.4	2.7	4.9	31.1	25.1	57.7	17.2	5,641	72.4	45.8	15.8
Valley Acres CDP	527	NA	NA	717	67.4	0.0	0.7	2.5	29.4	25.5	61.4	13.1	227	58.1	41.4	4.8
Valley Center CDP	9,277	NA	NA	9,872	71.6	0.4	1.6	6.8	19.7	23.8	64.8	11.3	3,034	84.1	31.1	29.7
Valley Ford CDP	147	NA	NA	167	18.6	0.0	0.0	0.0	81.4	19.2	81.0	0.0	100	0.0	69.0	0.0
Valley Home CDP	228	NA	NA	292	68.8	0.7	0.7	1.0	28.8	18.2	66.5	15.4	93	66.7	66.7	8.6
Valley Ranch CDP	109	NA	NA	68	100.0	0.0	0.0	0.0	0.0	0.0	82.4	17.6	32	100.0	18.8	50.0
Valley Springs CDP	3,553	NA	NA	3,631	82.9	0.8	2.8	1.1	12.4	17.6	63.8	18.4	1,327	76.8	18.5	19.3
Valley Wells CDP	0	NA	NA	0	0.0	0.0	0.0	0.0	0.0	0.0	0.0	0.0	0	0.0	0.0	0.0
Val Verde CDP	2,468	NA	NA	2,550	23.5	4.8	1.3	3.7	66.7	28.1	67.3	4.7	662	71.3	37.5	15.7
Vandenberg AFB CDP	3,338	NA	NA	3,464	50.9	9.5	5.1	11.7	22.8	36.6	63.0	0.2	889	0.0	9.9	22.3
Vandenberg Village CDP	6,497	NA	NA	7,133	68.0	2.5	2.2	5.3	21.9	23.6	56.2	20.3	2,754	71.2	22.8	32.1
Verdi CDP	162	NA	NA	92	100.0	0.0	0.0	0.0	0.0	0.0	90.3	9.8	64	100.0	0.0	70.3
Vernon city	112	114	1.8	59	15.3	0.0	3.4	0.0	81.4	20.4	73.1	6.8	20	5.0	60.0	15.0
Victor CDP	293	NA	NA	605	3.1	0.0	0.0	0.0	96.9	53.4	39.4	7.3	144	25.0	93.8	0.0
Victorville city	115,921	121,901	5.2	119,603	25.1	15.5	4.8	2.5	52.1	33.4	58.2	8.4	31,440	58.8	43.3	13.7
View Park-Windsor Hills CDP	11,075	NA	NA	11,374	7.2	75.5	1.6	6.6	9.2	19.8	63.1	17.3	4,697	70.3	11.3	50.5
Villa Park city	5,822	5,968	2.5	5,911	70.8	1.7	18.6	3.0	5.9	18.1	56.6	25.3	1,954	93.8	12.4	63.5
Vina CDP	237	NA	NA	161	69.6	0.0	5.0	5.6	19.9	16.2	51.6	32.3	79	100.0	29.1	0.0
Vincent CDP	15,922	NA	NA	17,687	13.9	0.9	5.2	1.6	78.3	26.2	63.6	10.2	4,050	82.1	53.9	15.0
Vine Hill CDP	3,761	NA	NA	4,296	43.4	4.3	6.6	8.7	37.0	21.5	67.7	10.9	1,280	60.9	38.4	21.3
Vineyard CDP	24,836	NA	NA	25,640	36.0	9.3	30.5	5.7	18.5	29.8	62.9	7.2	7,612	76.9	29.2	33.5
Visalia city	124,457	129,281	3.9	126,942	43.0	1.9	5.0	2.6	47.5	29.8	59.0	11.1	41,554	60.1	36.2	23.6
Vista city	93,854	98,079	4.5	96,181	42.3	2.4	5.2	2.5	47.7	22.9	67.1	9.9	30,662	49.2	39.0	22.2
Vista Santa Rosa CDP	2,926	NA	NA	2,815	7.0	0.0	0.1	3.2	89.8	31.3	62.8	5.8	676	46.9	70.7	4.1
Volcano CDP	115	NA	NA	0	0.0	0.0	0.0	0.0	0.0	0.0	0.0	0.0	0	0.0	0.0	0.0
Volta CDP	246	NA	NA	257	38.1	1.9	0.0	0.0	59.9	19.5	65.8	14.8	79	72.2	34.2	0.0
Walker CDP	721	NA	NA	540	97.2	0.0	0.0	2.8	0.0	4.8	46.2	49.1	326	85.6	26.1	6.1
Wallace CDP	403	NA	NA	682	94.6	0.0	5.4	0.0	0.0	0.0	82.3	17.7	320	100.0	27.2	39.7
Walnut city	29,172	30,214	3.6	29,822	11.8	2.6	63.2	2.9	19.5	20.0	66.2	13.6	8,421	85.7	16.1	55.6
Walnut Creek city	64,174	67,673	5.5	65,923	71.8	1.7	13.0	3.3	10.1	16.6	56.2	27.2	30,328	64.6	10.5	64.7
Walnut Grove CDP	1,542	NA	NA	1,137	61.8	0.0	8.1	0.3	29.8	21.3	56.7	22.0	428	77.8	24.8	29.0
Walnut Park CDP	15,966	NA	NA	16,039	1.4	0.0	0.5	0.7	97.3	27.3	62.2	10.4	3,655	48.5	79.3	6.2
Warm Springs CDP	2,676	NA	NA	3,163	28.7	0.0	1.6	10.2	59.4	34.4	58.7	7.1	805	30.2	39.0	10.7
Warner Valley CDP	2	NA	NA	5	100.0	0.0	0.0	0.0	0.0	0.0	0.0	100.0	5	100.0	0.0	100.0
Wasco city	25,552	26,303	2.9	25,865	13.6	7.2	1.0	0.9	77.3	27.2	67.0	5.9	5,264	51.3	73.5	6.1
Washington CDP	185	NA	NA	17	100.0	0.0	0.0	0.0	0.0	0.0	100.0	0.0	17	100.0	100.0	0.0
Waterford city	8,456	8,732	3.3	8,579	44.7	0.7	1.9	3.1	49.7	32.9	62.0	5.2	2,318	64.3	57.5	10.1
Waterloo CDP	572	NA	NA	384	98.2	0.0	0.0	1.8	0.0	21.4	59.9	18.8	109	100.0	16.5	42.2
Watsonville city	51,199	53,111	3.7	52,085	14.9	0.2	3.0	1.2	80.8	30.3	60.5	9.1	14,148	41.3	60.9	11.4
Waukena CDP	108	NA	NA	173	63.6	0.0	0.0	0.6	35.8	39.9	53.8	6.4	51	56.9	35.3	17.6
Wawona CDP	169	NA	NA	167	85.0	0.0	6.0	4.2	4.8	30.6	50.4	19.2	54	50.0	16.7	22.2
Weaverville CDP	3,600	NA	NA	3,294	76.7	0.6	3.1	11.9	7.7	19.5	59.9	20.6	1,387	61.0	35.1	24.7
Weed city	2,967	2,865	-3.4	2,937	65.4	5.2	1.8	6.3	21.2	22.6	63.5	13.8	1,090	41.1	36.3	17.7
Weedpatch CDP	2,658	NA	NA	2,170	5.9	0.3	0.8	0.6	92.3	34.6	57.4	7.9	583	35.7	93.3	0.0
Weldon CDP	2,642	NA	NA	2,604	83.4	0.0	0.0	14.0	2.6	17.0	50.0	32.9	1,236	82.5	44.9	10.0
Weott CDP	288	NA	NA	152	100.0	0.0	0.0	0.0	0.0	10.5	89.5	0.0	56	100.0	33.9	25.0

1 May be of any race.

Table A. All Places — **Population and Housing**

STATE City, town, township, borough, or CDP (county if applicable)	Population: 2010 census total population	Population: 2014 estimated population	Population: Percent change 2010–2014	Population: ACS total population estimate 2010–2014	Race and Hispanic or Latino origin (percent), 2010–2014: White alone, not Hispanic or Latino	Black alone, not Hispanic or Latino	Asian alone, not Hispanic or Latino	All other races or 2 or more races, not Hispanic or Latino	Hispanic or Latino[1]	Age (percent), 2010–2014: Under 18 years old	Age 18 to 64 years old	Age 65 years and older	Households, 2010–2014: Total occupied housing units	Percent owner occupied	Householders by level of education (percent): High school diploma or less	Bachelor's degree or more
	1	2	3	4	5	6	7	8	9	10	11	12	13	14	15	16
CALIFORNIA—Con.																
West Athens CDP	8,729	NA	NA	8,615	1.8	41.7	1.3	4.1	51.1	24.9	64.8	10.4	2,646	45.9	50.2	17.3
West Bishop CDP	2,607	NA	NA	2,865	77.4	2.9	0.9	3.6	15.2	16.9	60.0	23.0	1,091	88.4	17.2	46.7
West Carson CDP	21,699	NA	NA	20,766	20.5	11.6	29.3	7.3	31.3	18.4	60.6	21.0	7,224	72.0	31.6	38.6
West Covina city	106,098	108,455	2.2	107,441	13.5	4.8	25.6	1.4	54.7	23.7	63.3	12.9	31,042	64.6	33.0	30.2
West Goshen CDP	511	NA	NA	633	21.3	0.0	0.0	0.0	78.7	44.6	50.2	5.2	165	19.4	66.7	0.0
Westhaven-Moonstone CDP	1,205	NA	NA	962	85.9	0.7	2.2	9.7	1.6	10.1	69.6	20.4	458	76.6	16.2	43.9
West Hollywood city	34,399	35,883	4.3	35,053	75.0	3.1	4.9	4.3	12.7	4.2	80.4	15.2	21,808	22.1	13.0	62.4
Westlake Village city	8,270	8,473	2.5	8,393	80.2	0.5	5.0	4.6	9.8	21.3	55.0	23.8	3,269	85.5	11.3	66.3
Westley CDP	603	NA	NA	853	7.6	0.0	0.0	0.0	92.4	50.6	45.2	4.1	174	5.7	100.0	0.0
West Menlo Park CDP	3,659	NA	NA	3,743	76.6	0.6	14.0	4.0	4.9	29.2	57.6	13.4	1,251	84.8	4.2	81.2
Westminster city	89,614	92,068	2.7	91,255	25.6	0.7	47.7	3.2	22.8	21.7	62.7	15.6	27,195	52.7	40.1	24.4
West Modesto CDP	5,682	NA	NA	5,534	25.4	3.2	8.1	5.6	57.7	32.7	57.6	9.8	1,506	48.7	68.5	6.3
Westmont CDP	31,853	NA	NA	30,835	1.9	52.4	0.0	2.0	43.7	28.4	61.8	10.0	10,037	31.9	55.1	9.2
Westmorland city	2,223	2,268	2.0	1,747	6.2	2.2	0.0	0.0	91.6	36.7	48.3	15.0	526	46.0	66.2	8.4
West Park CDP	1,157	NA	NA	792	9.5	8.0	6.2	3.7	72.7	21.2	64.5	14.3	244	65.2	70.1	2.5
West Point CDP	674	NA	NA	743	88.3	0.0	0.0	0.8	10.9	12.2	49.1	38.8	337	79.8	28.2	23.4
West Puente Valley CDP	22,636	NA	NA	23,868	5.4	1.8	8.9	0.8	83.1	24.8	63.0	12.1	5,175	75.7	63.6	8.8
West Rancho Dominguez CDP	5,669	NA	NA	21,739	1.6	52.8	1.6	1.5	42.4	27.7	59.9	12.5	6,119	63.1	45.3	11.7
West Sacramento city	48,744	51,847	6.4	49,946	47.5	4.0	9.8	6.8	31.9	26.2	63.0	10.8	17,571	53.8	36.2	27.4
West Whittier-Los Nietos CDP	25,540	NA	NA	26,590	9.2	0.7	1.0	0.9	88.1	23.5	65.0	11.6	6,730	74.5	58.6	11.6
Westwood CDP	1,647	NA	NA	1,509	89.7	0.0	1.0	5.9	3.4	24.3	62.5	13.3	690	52.0	17.1	18.8
Wheatland city	3,480	3,484	0.1	3,494	59.8	2.2	11.4	5.8	20.9	25.5	66.0	8.6	1,189	58.8	36.3	17.7
Whitehawk CDP	113	NA	NA	41	100.0	0.0	0.0	0.0	0.0	0.0	22.0	78.0	22	100.0	0.0	40.9
Whitewater CDP	0	NA	NA	469	40.9	36.0	5.5	1.1	16.4	42.5	43.0	14.5	172	55.8	62.2	8.7
Whitley Gardens CDP	285	NA	NA	166	90.4	0.0	0.0	9.6	0.0	10.8	79.4	9.6	88	51.1	19.3	18.2
Whittier city	85,328	87,318	2.3	86,400	26.3	1.0	3.8	2.0	66.9	24.4	63.1	12.4	27,449	57.4	35.1	25.8
Wildomar city	32,220	35,377	9.8	33,601	48.1	5.3	3.7	2.9	40.0	27.6	62.5	10.0	9,814	71.3	36.7	17.6
Wilkerson CDP	563	NA	NA	550	76.0	0.0	3.5	2.7	17.8	27.6	53.4	18.9	217	78.3	20.3	43.8
Williams city	5,123	5,192	1.3	5,166	20.6	0.3	0.7	0.8	77.6	29.9	61.2	8.8	1,446	57.7	71.9	5.7
Willits city	4,888	4,861	-0.6	4,853	74.5	0.1	0.9	7.4	17.1	17.0	66.6	16.4	2,142	44.9	41.7	12.7
Willowbrook CDP	35,983	NA	NA	20,897	0.6	25.3	0.6	1.8	71.8	34.9	59.8	5.2	4,851	37.8	60.8	7.7
Willow Creek CDP	1,710	NA	NA	1,425	75.2	0.0	0.0	15.0	9.8	15.3	65.4	19.2	752	66.0	24.9	28.1
Willows city	6,166	6,088	-1.3	6,118	58.0	2.0	3.0	6.6	30.4	22.1	65.8	12.1	2,374	43.9	37.7	21.6
Wilsonia CDP	5	NA	NA	0	0.0	0.0	0.0	0.0	0.0	0.0	0.0	0.0	0	0.0	0.0	0.0
Wilton CDP	5,363	NA	NA	4,670	69.0	2.4	6.3	6.1	16.1	22.5	57.9	19.7	1,742	88.0	24.8	30.0
Winchester CDP	2,534	NA	NA	2,717	70.7	1.4	1.8	4.3	21.9	22.6	63.4	13.9	790	81.5	62.2	9.6
Windsor town	26,795	27,414	2.3	27,113	65.1	0.2	3.8	2.6	28.3	25.7	61.0	13.3	9,435	74.4	30.1	30.4
Winter Gardens CDP	20,631	NA	NA	20,346	74.7	0.7	1.6	2.8	20.2	22.8	64.6	12.5	7,093	57.7	31.9	19.9
Winterhaven CDP	394	NA	NA	151	35.1	0.0	0.0	55.0	9.9	23.2	47.7	29.1	105	30.5	77.1	8.6
Winters city	6,624	6,941	4.8	6,843	47.8	0.4	2.2	3.9	45.6	22.4	65.8	11.8	2,479	71.8	36.7	29.6
Winton CDP	10,613	NA	NA	11,774	16.1	2.4	4.3	0.5	76.6	35.6	59.2	5.2	2,905	49.0	71.1	4.3
Wofford Heights CDP	2,200	NA	NA	2,043	98.2	0.0	0.0	0.5	1.3	18.6	45.6	35.9	992	86.3	29.9	10.6
Woodacre CDP	1,348	NA	NA	1,778	92.3	0.0	2.1	0.3	5.2	19.4	63.3	17.3	713	74.2	2.2	71.8
Woodbridge CDP	3,984	NA	NA	3,973	61.1	0.0	5.2	0.5	33.3	24.3	59.5	16.2	1,461	69.8	31.0	33.9
Woodcrest CDP	14,347	NA	NA	15,951	54.8	2.7	5.8	1.4	35.4	21.8	66.1	12.2	4,440	89.4	29.5	28.9
Woodlake city	7,279	7,659	5.2	7,452	9.9	0.4	0.1	1.7	87.9	33.3	58.8	8.0	2,004	59.1	69.1	9.3
Woodland city	55,468	57,432	3.5	56,390	42.0	0.7	6.7	2.9	47.7	25.9	62.4	11.8	19,348	56.0	40.0	25.3
Woodlands CDP	576	NA	NA	448	73.2	0.0	10.9	0.0	15.8	4.2	60.7	35.0	247	79.4	0.0	78.1
Woodside town	5,287	5,531	4.6	5,427	87.6	0.4	5.4	2.2	4.4	24.0	53.6	22.5	1,918	90.4	15.3	70.5
Woodville CDP	1,740	NA	NA	1,961	9.6	0.0	0.0	0.3	90.1	34.9	59.9	5.3	446	42.8	87.7	3.4
Wrightwood CDP	4,525	NA	NA	4,452	83.4	0.0	0.0	1.1	15.5	29.6	57.6	12.8	1,787	66.5	18.0	42.0
Yankee Hill CDP	333	NA	NA	242	82.2	0.0	0.0	5.4	12.4	5.3	53.0	41.7	156	87.2	38.5	11.5
Yettem CDP	211	NA	NA	285	0.0	0.0	0.0	0.0	100.0	42.4	57.6	0.0	61	0.0	100.0	0.0
Yolo CDP	450	NA	NA	561	12.7	0.0	0.0	0.0	87.3	35.0	59.6	5.5	175	41.7	64.0	0.0
Yorba Linda city	64,193	67,826	5.7	66,335	61.5	1.0	16.8	3.7	17.0	24.4	62.1	13.6	21,583	84.1	14.0	52.6
Yosemite Lakes CDP	4,952	NA	NA	4,668	83.6	0.3	0.4	2.7	13.0	21.8	56.8	21.4	1,708	81.5	28.2	26.9
Yosemite Valley CDP	1,035	NA	NA	877	84.3	2.3	5.5	0.9	7.1	9.2	87.4	3.4	140	0.0	22.1	52.9
Yountville city	2,933	3,014	2.8	2,977	85.8	3.8	0.9	2.0	7.4	8.9	43.4	47.7	1,307	65.1	17.2	54.4
Yreka city	7,765	7,564	-2.6	7,675	73.7	1.7	2.5	11.4	10.8	26.7	52.9	20.3	3,246	48.7	39.2	17.6
Yuba City city	64,925	65,773	1.3	65,141	45.7	2.4	18.1	5.6	28.2	26.9	60.2	12.9	21,557	55.6	39.2	20.9
Yucaipa city	51,371	53,096	3.4	52,406	63.0	1.4	1.7	3.0	30.9	25.4	60.1	14.6	17,834	71.6	36.1	24.1
Yucca Valley town	20,700	21,485	3.8	21,083	72.1	4.7	2.0	4.2	17.1	25.7	56.0	18.3	7,941	57.9	37.4	15.3
Zayante CDP	705	NA	NA	853	84.8	0.0	1.5	6.6	7.2	27.4	62.0	10.6	307	81.8	12.7	41.0
COLORADO	5,029,324	5,355,866	6.5	5,197,580	69.4	3.8	2.8	3.1	20.9	23.7	64.4	11.8	1,998,314	64.8	27.3	39.7
Acres Green CDP	3,007	NA	NA	3,035	81.0	0.4	4.3	3.7	10.6	26.5	65.2	8.3	1,041	91.0	22.5	45.5
Aetna Estates CDP	834	NA	NA	1,031	43.5	0.0	0.0	2.2	54.2	23.2	67.2	9.4	347	67.1	51.3	8.4
Aguilar town	538	479	-11.0	563	46.4	0.0	0.0	1.6	52.0	17.2	56.6	26.1	233	57.5	69.5	6.9
Air Force Academy CDP	6,680	NA	NA	6,046	77.4	8.6	1.6	4.3	8.2	12.5	87.3	0.2	425	0.0	5.2	31.8
Akron town	1,702	1,694	-0.5	1,906	79.9	2.6	0.3	2.2	15.0	18.0	61.4	20.7	762	68.6	54.2	15.2
Alamosa city	8,828	9,531	8.0	9,427	44.2	2.3	1.2	1.9	50.3	23.3	65.8	10.8	3,580	46.7	33.8	25.4
Alamosa East CDP	1,458	NA	NA	1,671	53.3	1.4	0.0	0.8	44.5	29.7	61.1	9.3	630	56.8	40.3	11.9
Allenspark CDP	528	NA	NA	632	93.2	0.3	6.5	0.0	0.0	13.1	60.5	26.3	333	69.7	19.5	64.6
Alma town	270	275	1.9	348	96.6	0.0	3.4	0.0	0.0	22.4	73.5	4.0	159	61.0	22.0	50.9
Alpine CDP	174	NA	NA	137	89.1	0.0	0.0	10.9	0.0	10.9	64.2	24.8	74	100.0	17.6	45.9
Altona CDP	501	NA	NA	544	89.9	0.0	0.0	0.0	10.1	21.5	72.9	5.7	213	71.4	5.2	85.9
Amherst CDP	58	NA	NA	35	100.0	0.0	0.0	0.0	0.0	0.0	100.0	0.0	35	0.0	48.6	0.0
Antonito town	781	775	-0.8	774	11.9	0.1	0.0	0.4	87.6	21.2	60.1	18.7	339	61.9	55.5	20.6
Applewood CDP	7,160	NA	NA	7,467	91.8	0.4	2.4	0.9	4.6	16.5	61.9	21.5	3,377	70.2	18.7	53.1
Arboles CDP	280	NA	NA	263	75.3	3.8	0.0	0.0	20.9	12.1	64.3	23.6	123	75.6	39.0	18.7
Aristocrat Ranchettes CDP	1,344	NA	NA	1,492	43.3	0.7	0.0	0.5	55.5	31.9	59.2	8.9	456	74.1	54.2	2.2
Arriba town	193	194	0.5	186	89.2	2.2	0.5	3.2	4.8	23.7	53.2	23.1	94	73.4	55.3	16.0
Arvada city	106,474	113,574	6.7	109,800	81.6	0.7	2.0	1.9	13.9	22.2	63.1	14.6	43,779	73.5	26.5	39.0
Aspen city	6,663	6,805	2.1	6,700	85.1	3.3	2.4	0.8	8.3	12.7	69.4	18.1	3,149	62.9	9.7	61.8
Aspen Park CDP	882	NA	NA	780	97.9	0.0	0.0	0.0	2.1	23.1	61.5	15.4	310	88.7	14.5	41.3
Atwood CDP	133	NA	NA	206	100.0	0.0	0.0	0.0	0.0	30.6	54.9	14.6	48	89.6	39.6	14.6

1 May be of any race.

Table A. All Places — Population and Housing

STATE City, town, township, borough, or CDP (county if applicable)	2010 census total population	2014 estimated population	Percent change 2010–2014	ACS total population estimate 2010–2014	White alone, not Hispanic or Latino	Black alone, not Hispanic or Latino	Asian alone, not Hispanic or Latino	All other races or 2 or more races, not Hispanic or Latino	Hispanic or Latino[1]	Under 18 years old	Age 18 to 64 years old	Age 65 years and older	Total occupied housing units	Percent owner occupied	High school diploma or less	Bachelor's degree or more
	1	2	3	4	5	6	7	8	9	10	11	12	13	14	15	16
COLORADO—Con.																
Ault town	1,519	1,603	5.5	1,558	64.6	0.0	0.4	2.1	33.0	32.9	53.4	13.6	578	71.5	39.6	14.9
Aurora city	324,688	353,108	8.8	339,480	46.3	15.5	5.0	4.4	28.9	27.0	63.1	9.7	123,344	57.3	33.9	30.2
Avon town	6,391	6,447	0.9	6,384	50.3	2.7	0.0	0.9	46.1	27.2	69.7	3.0	2,153	42.4	31.2	49.0
Avondale CDP	674	NA	NA	739	24.4	0.0	0.0	3.7	72.0	15.6	51.5	32.9	248	96.8	42.7	8.9
Bark Ranch CDP	213	NA	NA	336	100.0	0.0	0.0	0.0	0.0	18.2	81.8	0.0	137	100.0	0.0	66.4
Basalt town	3,856	3,919	1.6	3,891	79.1	1.2	2.4	1.1	16.2	18.4	69.5	12.0	1,553	69.5	12.5	59.6
Battlement Mesa CDP	4,471	NA	NA	4,540	74.5	0.0	0.5	2.3	22.7	27.5	54.7	17.8	1,726	62.6	32.0	27.3
Bayfield town	2,333	2,533	8.6	2,435	82.7	0.4	0.9	2.5	13.6	28.3	63.1	8.5	916	72.6	26.6	34.9
Bennett town	2,305	2,443	6.0	1,898	84.1	0.3	0.2	2.9	12.5	24.6	69.2	6.1	755	78.3	45.8	18.0
Berkley town	11,207	NA	NA	11,706	36.5	0.2	3.5	2.1	57.7	23.4	65.3	11.2	3,994	59.2	53.6	15.1
Berthoud town	5,122	5,807	13.4	5,323	89.9	0.5	0.3	1.6	7.7	27.4	58.8	13.9	2,061	84.8	24.9	26.8
Bethune town	237	240	1.3	315	51.4	0.0	0.0	0.0	48.6	35.5	52.2	12.1	93	71.0	66.7	2.2
Beulah Valley CDP	556	NA	NA	800	92.4	0.0	7.6	0.0	0.0	34.9	54.7	10.6	270	69.3	20.7	30.4
Black Forest CDP	13,116	NA	NA	12,959	90.4	0.4	1.5	3.4	4.4	24.9	62.7	12.4	4,669	94.6	12.3	55.1
Black Hawk city	118	126	6.8	130	75.4	0.0	0.0	5.4	19.2	0.0	84.6	15.4	55	25.5	38.2	16.4
Blanca town	385	372	-3.4	464	34.7	0.0	1.1	2.2	62.1	25.0	59.2	15.7	129	82.2	51.9	17.8
Blende CDP	878	NA	NA	739	45.6	2.4	0.0	0.5	51.4	33.2	43.1	23.5	280	69.6	58.9	21.1
Blue River town	849	882	3.9	645	100.0	0.0	0.0	0.0	0.0	17.4	70.0	12.7	268	86.2	4.9	60.1
Blue Sky CDP	24	NA	NA	0	0.0	0.0	0.0	0.0	0.0	0.0	0.0	0.0	0	0.0	0.0	0.0
Bonanza town	16	16	0.0	9	100.0	0.0	0.0	0.0	0.0	0.0	22.2	77.8	9	100.0	0.0	100.0
Bonanza Mountain Estates CDP	128	NA	NA	123	100.0	0.0	0.0	0.0	0.0	0.0	69.2	30.9	65	100.0	56.9	43.1
Boone town	339	342	0.9	351	72.6	0.3	0.0	0.6	26.5	28.0	56.6	15.4	130	75.4	63.1	6.2
Boulder city	97,468	105,112	7.8	102,002	82.7	0.9	4.7	2.9	8.9	13.8	76.5	9.7	41,687	48.0	9.1	64.7
Bow Mar town	866	921	6.4	1,062	93.8	0.0	1.5	2.2	2.5	30.4	55.3	14.2	343	89.5	4.1	84.5
Brandon CDP	21	NA	NA	32	100.0	0.0	0.0	0.0	0.0	0.4	78.2	21.9	17	41.2	76.5	0.0
Branson town	74	67	-9.5	38	68.4	0.0	0.0	0.0	31.6	21.1	44.8	34.2	19	73.7	36.8	36.8
Breckenridge town	4,527	4,749	4.9	4,604	84.1	0.2	1.7	2.0	11.9	12.1	72.5	15.6	1,682	67.0	10.2	56.5
Brick Center CDP	107	NA	NA	37	73.0	27.0	0.0	0.0	0.0	0.0	99.9	0.0	18	100.0	0.0	0.0
Brighton city	33,780	36,765	8.8	35,004	54.8	1.3	1.1	2.4	40.3	29.9	61.4	8.8	10,895	68.0	43.1	22.0
Brookside town	233	243	4.3	268	92.2	0.0	0.0	1.9	6.0	28.8	57.8	13.4	92	80.4	32.6	20.7
Broomfield city	55,860	62,138	11.2	59,027	78.7	1.0	5.9	2.8	11.6	25.3	63.6	11.0	22,651	69.6	17.7	51.4
Brush city	5,473	5,466	-0.1	5,493	55.6	1.1	0.0	3.6	39.7	29.7	56.5	13.8	1,967	48.3	52.2	17.5
Buena Vista town	2,617	2,734	4.5	2,675	90.2	2.0	0.6	1.2	6.0	24.7	57.8	17.3	1,121	65.5	27.4	33.0
Burlington city	4,254	4,014	-5.6	4,084	69.4	6.8	0.2	3.6	20.0	19.6	62.7	17.6	1,418	61.0	42.2	13.1
Byers CDP	1,160	NA	NA	1,361	91.9	0.5	0.0	1.7	5.9	19.1	66.4	14.5	514	64.4	48.2	16.3
Calhan town	780	797	2.2	800	95.3	0.0	0.3	2.3	2.3	26.2	57.0	16.8	314	66.6	49.0	15.3
Campo town	109	105	-3.7	39	100.0	0.0	0.0	0.0	0.0	0.0	15.3	84.6	26	73.1	38.5	26.9
Cañon City city	16,415	16,337	-0.5	16,410	83.4	3.6	1.4	2.7	8.9	20.1	59.5	20.4	6,699	61.6	37.3	21.5
Capulin CDP	200	NA	NA	73	13.7	6.8	0.0	0.0	79.5	27.4	49.2	23.3	33	69.7	100.0	0.0
Carbondale town	6,427	6,574	2.3	6,464	59.7	0.4	0.4	2.3	37.2	27.2	64.2	8.6	2,208	61.2	26.1	48.1
Cascade-Chipita Park CDP	1,655	NA	NA	1,588	83.6	1.0	0.0	9.3	6.0	18.2	62.4	19.3	676	75.0	20.6	42.3
Castle Pines city	10,360	10,796	4.2	10,626	87.8	0.8	2.5	2.7	6.2	31.1	57.9	11.1	3,671	83.3	5.8	70.6
Castle Pines Village CDP	0	NA	NA	4,013	84.4	0.4	5.6	3.2	6.4	31.8	56.0	12.2	1,297	95.2	7.7	79.3
Castle Rock town	48,262	55,747	15.5	51,802	83.3	0.9	1.4	2.9	11.5	30.6	61.9	7.4	17,767	76.0	19.3	48.8
Cathedral CDP	14	NA	NA	16	100.0	0.0	0.0	0.0	0.0	18.8	62.6	18.8	7	100.0	0.0	0.0
Catherine CDP	228	NA	NA	237	93.2	0.0	6.8	0.0	0.0	28.7	63.2	8.0	106	60.4	0.0	34.9
Cattle Creek CDP	641	NA	NA	853	1.3	0.2	0.2	0.0	98.2	29.9	64.2	6.0	170	100.0	85.9	0.0
Cedaredge town	2,253	2,187	-2.9	2,429	84.4	0.3	0.6	0.9	13.8	26.5	48.4	25.0	1,052	68.2	46.8	23.8
Centennial city	100,547	107,201	6.6	104,213	82.8	2.2	4.7	2.8	7.5	24.5	62.2	13.3	38,423	83.1	12.3	59.3
Center town	2,239	2,199	-1.8	2,077	9.6	0.0	0.9	0.0	89.6	30.9	60.3	8.8	699	52.2	74.7	8.4
Central City city	663	724	9.2	681	75.6	1.3	1.3	3.8	17.9	20.1	74.3	5.6	380	26.8	28.7	23.4
Chacra CDP	329	NA	NA	476	100.0	0.0	0.0	0.0	0.0	36.4	54.7	9.0	117	66.7	12.8	57.3
Cheraw town	252	249	-1.2	202	72.3	0.0	0.0	1.5	26.2	25.8	64.9	9.4	72	77.8	59.7	9.7
Cherry Creek CDP	11,120	NA	NA	12,113	79.1	1.5	8.1	1.8	9.4	28.8	62.9	8.4	4,409	67.6	10.4	67.3
Cherry Hills Village city	5,987	6,423	7.3	6,234	86.8	3.3	3.0	4.6	2.3	30.5	52.7	16.7	2,085	96.1	6.1	82.5
Cheyenne Wells town	846	860	1.7	980	72.2	0.6	1.9	1.4	23.8	20.0	65.8	14.3	399	73.7	47.4	20.1
Cimarron Hills CDP	16,161	NA	NA	16,698	66.9	4.8	2.2	9.6	16.5	28.5	64.2	7.2	5,968	65.8	32.2	21.1
City of Creede town	290	282	-2.8	188	89.9	2.7	0.5	2.7	4.3	4.7	70.2	25.0	100	88.0	31.0	40.0
Clifton CDP	19,889	NA	NA	20,262	73.0	1.0	0.2	2.5	23.2	26.7	63.5	9.9	7,754	65.9	49.0	10.3
Coal Creek CDP	2,400	NA	NA	1,939	92.5	0.0	0.5	0.4	6.7	10.6	82.4	7.0	1,052	90.3	12.6	56.0
Coal Creek town	343	339	-1.2	311	97.4	0.0	0.0	1.6	1.0	24.7	47.2	28.0	126	88.1	48.4	7.1
Coaldale CDP	255	NA	NA	296	98.0	0.0	2.0	0.0	0.0	30.1	62.8	7.1	140	50.0	19.3	28.6
Cokedale town	129	119	-7.8	145	71.7	0.0	0.0	4.8	23.4	33.7	53.7	12.4	62	59.7	17.7	37.1
Collbran town	703	706	0.4	604	82.6	1.0	1.0	4.8	10.6	25.0	66.2	8.8	181	71.8	39.8	21.0
Colona CDP	30	NA	NA	14	0.0	0.0	0.0	0.0	100.0	0.0	100.0	0.0	14	0.0	0.0	0.0
Colorado City CDP	2,193	NA	NA	1,801	88.9	0.0	1.7	4.2	5.3	22.2	50.3	27.6	750	86.3	27.2	28.8
Colorado Springs city	417,341	445,830	6.8	433,547	69.9	5.8	2.9	4.4	17.0	24.3	64.0	11.5	170,273	58.8	24.2	37.6
Columbine CDP	24,280	NA	NA	24,724	85.4	1.6	1.9	2.3	8.8	22.5	60.8	16.7	9,590	88.9	20.6	47.3
Columbine Valley town	1,256	1,328	5.7	1,258	91.9	1.4	3.3	1.6	1.8	20.4	54.8	24.7	494	96.8	5.1	73.5
Comanche Creek CDP	369	NA	NA	366	74.3	0.0	0.0	17.8	7.9	17.0	62.1	21.0	145	100.0	45.5	6.2
Commerce City city	45,917	51,762	12.7	48,792	46.5	3.2	2.5	2.2	45.5	33.7	60.2	6.2	14,581	71.9	47.8	22.1
Conejos CDP	58	NA	NA	114	9.6	0.0	0.0	0.0	90.4	17.5	71.0	11.4	45	82.2	28.9	28.9
Copper Mountain CDP	385	NA	NA	268	100.0	0.0	0.0	0.0	0.0	26.5	68.1	5.6	101	44.6	37.6	14.9
Cortez city	8,482	8,602	1.4	8,515	67.5	0.0	0.1	16.6	15.8	26.8	56.9	16.3	3,500	55.2	41.8	25.0
Cotopaxi CDP	47	NA	NA	7	100.0	0.0	0.0	0.0	0.0	0.0	100.0	0.0	7	100.0	0.0	0.0
Craig city	9,464	8,846	-6.5	9,092	80.2	0.3	1.1	1.6	16.7	29.3	60.6	10.0	3,286	66.3	43.7	17.0
Crawford town	430	411	-4.4	310	91.9	0.0	0.0	5.2	2.9	26.2	56.0	17.7	131	69.5	49.6	8.4
Crested Butte town	1,487	1,541	3.6	1,451	97.1	0.0	1.0	0.6	1.3	21.4	70.1	8.4	712	49.0	12.2	68.8
Crestone town	127	137	7.9	148	100.0	0.0	0.0	0.0	0.0	38.5	53.5	8.1	69	65.2	4.3	24.6
Cripple Creek city	1,189	1,172	-1.4	1,427	77.2	1.3	0.3	3.9	17.4	29.7	62.2	8.2	565	43.9	49.4	12.0
Crisman CDP	186	NA	NA	278	100.0	0.0	0.0	0.0	0.0	36.3	57.1	6.5	79	78.5	0.0	58.2
Crook town	110	109	-0.9	108	85.2	0.0	0.0	0.0	14.8	13.9	66.8	19.4	35	85.7	51.4	8.6
Crowley town	176	175	-0.6	405	32.1	1.0	0.0	0.0	66.9	14.1	69.2	16.8	106	76.4	35.8	21.7
Dacono city	4,155	4,544	9.4	4,355	62.8	0.5	2.3	0.3	34.1	26.0	63.0	10.9	1,617	67.4	50.6	14.2
Dakota Ridge CDP	32,005	NA	NA	33,583	82.0	1.1	3.3	2.0	11.6	24.8	67.3	8.0	12,376	82.7	19.2	45.9
De Beque town	500	496	-0.8	377	89.4	0.0	0.0	1.6	9.0	25.7	58.9	15.4	159	67.3	62.9	13.2
Deer Trail town	546	576	5.5	386	84.2	1.8	1.3	3.4	9.3	24.9	52.8	22.3	178	69.1	43.3	12.4
Del Norte town	1,686	1,629	-3.4	1,987	40.0	0.2	0.0	1.3	58.6	25.5	61.7	12.6	742	57.3	53.6	9.6
Delta city	8,882	8,720	-1.8	8,801	73.2	1.1	0.7	1.2	23.8	23.8	55.2	21.0	3,520	57.6	42.4	20.9

1 May be of any race.

Table A. All Places — **Population and Housing**

STATE City, town, township, borough, or CDP (county if applicable)	Population				Race and Hispanic or Latino origin (percent), 2010–2014					Age (percent), 2010–2014			Households, 2010–2014		Householders by level of education (percent)	
	2010 census total population	2014 estimated population	Percent change 2010–2014	ACS total population estimate 2010–2014	White alone, not Hispanic or Latino	Black alone, not Hispanic or Latino	Asian alone, not Hispanic or Latino	All other races or 2 or more races, not Hispanic or Latino	Hispanic or Latino[1]	Under 18 years old	Age 18 to 64 years old	Age 65 years and older	Total occupied housing units	Percent owner occupied	High school diploma or less	Bachelor's degree or more
	1	2	3	4	5	6	7	8	9	10	11	12	13	14	15	16
COLORADO—Con.																
Denver city	600,025	663,862	10.6	633,777	52.9	9.5	3.4	3.0	31.2	21.0	68.4	10.6	271,054	49.7	27.2	46.8
Derby CDP	7,685	NA	NA	8,638	30.4	2.6	0.5	6.7	59.8	33.5	58.0	8.7	2,345	64.5	73.6	4.6
Dillon town	906	937	3.4	926	72.9	0.0	0.3	5.3	21.5	16.6	68.4	15.0	482	47.9	18.0	51.2
Dinosaur town	339	312	-8.0	396	75.3	0.0	0.0	6.6	18.2	31.9	51.4	16.7	142	85.9	64.1	9.9
Divide CDP	127	NA	NA	98	100.0	0.0	0.0	0.0	0.0	0.0	100.0	0.0	26	100.0	0.0	69.2
Dolores town	936	948	1.3	987	91.5	0.0	0.0	2.4	6.1	23.7	67.9	8.4	479	57.2	42.2	28.0
Dotsero CDP	705	NA	NA	967	7.0	0.0	0.0	0.0	93.0	45.9	53.3	0.7	176	73.3	73.9	0.0
Dove Creek town	735	703	-4.4	690	82.2	0.0	0.0	9.6	8.3	27.8	50.7	21.4	323	72.8	52.0	22.6
Dove Valley CDP	5,243	NA	NA	5,401	66.6	5.5	9.1	6.6	12.1	25.4	72.5	2.1	2,296	45.1	20.6	46.8
Downieville-Lawson-Dumont CDP	594	NA	NA	430	83.0	0.0	0.0	0.0	17.0	10.9	81.3	7.7	163	78.5	70.6	0.0
Durango city	16,891	17,834	5.6	17,268	78.8	0.7	0.7	6.4	13.4	16.4	74.2	9.6	6,723	48.7	16.5	54.5
Eads town	609	599	-1.6	545	80.2	1.1	0.0	10.3	8.4	28.4	51.3	20.2	222	67.6	35.6	12.2
Eagle town	6,508	6,572	1.0	6,511	82.4	0.2	0.0	0.9	16.5	31.5	63.0	5.6	2,053	82.0	18.6	56.8
East Pleasant View CDP	356	NA	NA	333	52.0	0.0	0.0	0.0	48.0	14.1	57.6	28.2	140	90.0	24.3	65.7
Eaton town	4,365	4,815	10.3	4,570	75.3	0.2	0.0	0.0	24.4	31.5	54.9	13.6	1,521	80.3	28.4	21.4
Eckley town	257	255	-0.8	314	88.9	0.0	0.0	0.3	10.8	33.4	59.3	7.3	102	56.9	54.9	4.9
Edgewater city	5,159	5,289	2.5	5,217	58.6	0.6	2.3	3.2	35.4	19.9	69.7	10.3	2,359	34.4	40.3	25.6
Edwards CDP	10,266	NA	NA	9,385	62.8	0.3	0.9	1.3	34.6	25.9	66.6	7.5	3,288	65.5	29.0	50.6
Elbert CDP	230	NA	NA	174	93.7	0.0	0.0	4.0	2.3	33.9	56.4	9.8	62	69.4	59.7	12.9
Eldora CDP	142	NA	NA	124	100.0	0.0	0.0	0.0	0.0	22.6	66.9	10.5	78	19.2	0.0	19.2
Eldorado Springs CDP	585	NA	NA	540	95.9	0.0	1.5	0.0	2.6	22.2	46.0	31.9	239	90.8	5.0	75.7
Elizabeth town	1,358	1,395	2.7	1,270	87.5	0.0	0.0	0.2	12.3	31.2	61.9	6.9	427	66.0	45.0	22.0
El Jebel CDP	3,801	NA	NA	3,450	50.8	0.0	0.0	0.0	49.2	31.7	64.0	4.4	1,127	90.8	37.4	37.5
Ellicott CDP	1,131	NA	NA	771	79.2	0.0	0.0	0.0	20.8	22.8	63.7	13.5	287	72.8	39.7	21.6
El Moro CDP	221	NA	NA	367	83.1	0.0	0.0	5.7	11.2	24.2	63.4	12.3	117	87.2	19.7	37.6
Empire town	282	283	0.4	306	93.1	1.0	0.0	1.3	4.6	19.0	70.2	10.8	152	64.5	41.4	21.7
Englewood city	30,255	32,480	7.4	31,298	76.1	1.6	1.5	3.6	17.3	18.7	69.7	11.7	14,231	48.9	31.4	36.1
Erie town	18,133	20,493	13.0	19,305	81.8	0.4	6.1	2.7	9.0	30.3	63.3	6.3	6,489	85.9	7.8	61.5
Estes Park town	5,858	6,165	5.2	6,022	92.0	0.0	0.0	1.0	7.0	15.4	53.7	30.8	3,044	70.5	17.5	46.3
Evans city	18,545	20,473	10.4	19,535	48.7	0.3	1.0	1.7	48.3	32.9	60.4	6.7	6,377	59.2	43.7	18.5
Evergreen CDP	9,038	NA	NA	8,690	95.7	0.0	1.1	1.1	2.1	21.5	61.6	16.9	3,831	82.9	8.8	66.7
Fairmount CDP	7,559	NA	NA	8,093	87.4	0.1	3.2	4.0	5.3	20.9	65.3	14.0	2,961	87.3	26.0	45.9
Fairplay town	679	679	0.0	929	99.2	0.0	0.0	0.0	0.8	24.1	70.3	5.5	396	56.8	21.2	35.1
Federal Heights city	11,472	12,178	6.2	11,835	39.0	1.1	4.1	2.8	53.0	27.6	62.5	9.9	4,329	49.2	58.6	10.4
Firestone town	10,161	11,537	13.5	10,908	79.6	0.8	1.3	2.6	15.8	34.2	60.3	5.3	3,389	86.2	23.5	37.2
Flagler town	561	561	0.0	539	89.6	0.4	0.0	0.0	10.0	28.2	50.0	21.9	236	66.1	53.8	15.3
Fleming town	408	399	-2.2	548	95.1	0.7	0.0	3.1	1.1	28.8	60.7	10.4	173	82.7	32.4	11.0
Florence city	3,885	3,852	-0.8	3,875	81.9	0.1	1.9	1.7	14.5	28.2	50.5	21.3	1,551	68.3	39.2	12.9
Florissant CDP	104	NA	NA	53	100.0	0.0	0.0	0.0	0.0	15.1	85.0	0.0	35	31.4	31.4	0.0
Floyd Hill CDP	998	NA	NA	1,209	90.6	4.4	1.0	2.9	1.2	11.3	72.9	15.7	558	100.0	10.4	64.0
Fort Carson CDP	13,813	NA	NA	14,766	64.6	10.2	1.1	8.5	15.6	29.7	70.3	0.0	2,733	0.4	35.1	13.8
Fort Collins city	144,073	156,480	8.6	149,627	81.2	1.4	2.8	3.3	11.4	19.6	71.5	9.0	57,146	54.6	13.8	49.7
Fort Garland CDP	433	NA	NA	495	9.3	0.0	0.0	0.4	90.3	24.1	69.3	6.7	200	64.0	49.5	14.5
Fort Lupton city	7,401	7,783	5.2	7,595	47.5	0.3	1.2	1.0	50.1	29.9	59.9	10.2	2,601	63.8	61.2	11.2
Fort Morgan city	11,348	11,329	-0.2	11,397	51.7	5.6	0.2	1.7	40.7	30.9	54.0	15.0	4,131	61.3	53.9	13.2
Fountain city	25,885	27,631	6.7	26,881	62.6	10.7	2.6	7.7	16.4	33.6	60.8	5.4	9,144	63.3	24.8	23.2
Fowler town	1,182	1,155	-2.3	1,184	84.8	0.0	0.7	0.9	13.6	26.2	50.1	23.6	469	66.5	43.9	11.7
Foxfield town	685	741	8.2	678	86.6	3.5	5.5	1.0	3.4	19.6	54.4	26.0	270	85.6	21.9	50.0
Franktown CDP	395	NA	NA	192	100.0	0.0	0.0	0.0	0.0	20.3	61.6	18.2	90	100.0	24.4	61.1
Fraser town	1,224	1,165	-4.8	1,042	89.8	0.0	1.0	0.0	9.2	18.8	73.5	7.9	394	56.3	27.2	48.0
Frederick town	8,668	10,927	26.1	9,636	82.8	0.1	1.3	1.4	14.4	29.6	63.5	7.2	3,228	91.8	24.2	39.9
Frisco town	2,686	2,914	8.5	2,782	92.8	0.0	1.8	1.5	3.8	14.7	72.9	12.4	1,112	58.5	13.9	62.4
Fruita city	12,685	12,761	0.6	12,702	83.6	0.3	0.1	2.7	13.3	27.9	59.5	12.4	4,697	74.0	27.8	27.5
Fruitvale CDP	7,675	NA	NA	8,422	84.9	0.5	0.1	1.5	13.0	24.2	58.2	17.7	3,402	84.4	33.3	22.0
Fulford CDP	2	NA	NA	0	0.0	0.0	0.0	0.0	0.0	0.0	0.0	0.0	0	0.0	0.0	0.0
Garden City town	250	264	5.6	223	33.2	0.0	0.4	0.9	65.5	19.7	64.9	15.2	126	13.5	60.3	8.7
Garfield CDP	15	NA	NA	12	100.0	0.0	0.0	0.0	0.0	0.0	100.0	0.0	12	100.0	0.0	0.0
Genesee CDP	3,609	NA	NA	3,745	93.0	0.0	2.0	3.8	1.2	20.0	59.5	20.6	1,585	93.4	5.2	74.5
Genoa town	139	140	0.7	87	100.0	0.0	0.0	0.0	0.0	11.5	65.3	23.0	49	98.0	42.9	16.3
Georgetown town	1,034	1,038	0.4	1,069	90.7	1.5	0.0	1.6	6.2	15.2	69.6	15.0	466	66.7	22.5	38.6
Gerrard CDP	278	NA	NA	138	74.6	0.0	0.0	0.0	25.4	0.0	72.5	27.5	73	69.9	63.0	20.5
Gilcrest town	1,034	1,080	4.4	982	46.5	0.0	1.8	1.4	50.2	28.3	59.7	12.0	317	80.1	54.6	8.2
Glendale city	4,318	5,115	18.5	4,564	57.0	8.0	5.7	3.2	26.1	11.4	86.0	2.5	2,501	5.4	20.2	50.8
Glendale CDP	69	NA	NA	111	82.0	0.0	18.0	0.0	0.0	13.5	73.8	12.6	31	100.0	0.0	100.0
Gleneagle CDP	6,611	NA	NA	6,870	89.0	1.8	2.4	3.1	3.7	27.1	55.4	17.5	2,423	83.4	5.1	60.2
Glenwood Springs city	9,608	9,840	2.4	9,668	70.1	0.2	0.8	2.1	26.9	19.1	71.7	9.2	3,887	54.5	29.4	35.5
Golden city	18,905	20,201	6.9	19,759	82.5	1.0	2.6	4.2	9.8	18.9	72.0	9.1	7,581	56.8	16.0	55.6
Goldfield CDP	49	NA	NA	23	100.0	0.0	0.0	0.0	0.0	34.8	65.1	0.0	10	50.0	0.0	0.0
Gold Hill CDP	230	NA	NA	237	79.7	0.0	6.8	1.7	11.8	7.2	50.2	42.6	132	78.8	36.4	40.2
Granada town	517	490	-5.2	543	24.3	0.0	0.0	0.0	75.7	32.8	57.6	9.8	176	69.3	52.8	10.8
Granby town	1,869	1,808	-3.3	2,009	86.2	0.1	0.5	2.9	10.3	22.6	72.0	5.2	738	72.0	49.5	23.6
Grand Junction city	59,005	60,210	2.0	59,731	80.0	0.8	1.0	3.2	15.1	22.3	61.8	15.8	24,343	59.6	32.0	29.9
Grand Lake town	471	466	-1.1	321	88.2	0.0	2.2	7.8	1.9	5.3	59.7	34.9	166	53.6	33.7	28.3
Grand View Estates CDP	528	NA	NA	553	77.0	4.5	2.7	13.4	2.4	36.7	47.3	15.9	224	85.3	31.7	42.9
Greeley city	92,881	98,596	6.2	95,677	58.6	2.1	1.2	2.5	35.6	25.2	63.7	11.3	33,533	56.2	37.2	26.3
Green Mountain Falls town	640	676	5.6	687	80.2	0.9	1.6	8.2	9.2	20.2	63.1	16.7	339	69.6	14.5	37.2
Greenwood Village city	13,925	15,385	10.5	14,546	82.6	0.2	8.2	3.3	5.7	22.3	63.3	14.5	6,000	67.8	6.0	77.1
Grover town	137	145	5.8	79	89.9	8.9	0.0	1.3	0.0	19.0	49.3	31.6	38	55.3	36.8	18.4
Guffey CDP	98	NA	NA	65	100.0	0.0	0.0	0.0	0.0	0.0	73.9	26.2	55	100.0	0.0	100.0
Gunbarrel CDP	9,263	NA	NA	8,933	86.6	0.7	1.8	4.0	6.9	14.9	67.8	17.3	4,327	67.6	5.1	71.6
Gunnison city	5,829	5,973	2.5	5,927	80.9	0.6	0.1	1.5	16.9	14.7	79.2	6.3	2,166	36.6	25.5	32.3
Gypsum town	6,494	6,797	4.7	6,587	53.5	0.0	0.0	2.0	44.5	29.1	67.3	3.7	1,902	79.5	34.2	38.0
Hartman town	76	73	-3.9	63	65.1	0.0	0.0	0.0	34.9	23.8	66.8	9.5	33	48.5	45.5	0.0
Hasty CDP	144	NA	NA	145	95.9	0.0	0.0	0.0	4.1	20.7	48.2	31.0	72	90.3	45.8	27.8
Haswell town	68	68	0.0	64	96.9	0.0	0.0	0.0	3.1	15.7	64.2	20.3	27	96.3	48.1	11.1
Haxtun town	946	933	-1.4	899	96.0	0.1	0.3	2.6	1.0	24.1	54.9	21.0	357	68.1	39.2	26.6
Hayden town	1,810	1,837	1.5	1,788	86.1	0.0	0.2	1.7	12.0	25.4	66.2	8.3	733	70.7	40.0	22.9
Heeney CDP	76	NA	NA	16	100.0	0.0	0.0	0.0	0.0	0.0	0.0	100.0	16	100.0	0.0	0.0
Hidden Lake CDP	31	NA	NA	0	0.0	0.0	0.0	0.0	0.0	0.0	0.0	0.0	0	0.0	0.0	0.0

1 May be of any race.

Table A. All Places — **Population and Housing**

STATE City, town, township, borough, or CDP (county if applicable)	Population				Race and Hispanic or Latino origin (percent), 2010–2014					Age (percent), 2010–2014			Households, 2010–2014		Householders by level of education (percent)	
	2010 census total population	2014 estimated population	Percent change 2010–2014	ACS total population estimate 2010–2014	White alone, not Hispanic or Latino	Black alone, not Hispanic or Latino	Asian alone, not Hispanic or Latino	All other races or 2 or more races, not Hispanic or Latino	Hispanic or Latino[1]	Under 18 years old	Age 18 to 64 years old	Age 65 years and older	Total occupied housing units	Percent owner occupied	High school diploma or less	Bachelor's degree or more
	1	2	3	4	5	6	7	8	9	10	11	12	13	14	15	16
COLORADO—Con.																
Highlands Ranch CDP	96,713	NA	NA	101,350	83.4	0.9	5.7	2.8	7.2	31.1	61.1	7.8	35,041	81.2	10.3	65.2
Hillrose town	252	250	-0.8	255	73.3	0.8	0.0	0.0	25.9	21.2	63.9	14.9	108	80.6	46.3	16.7
Hoehne CDP	111	NA	NA	119	14.3	0.0	0.0	0.0	85.7	19.4	72.3	8.4	33	72.7	60.6	18.2
Holly town	794	766	-3.5	845	55.7	0.0	0.2	4.7	39.3	25.4	54.9	19.6	309	75.7	46.0	12.0
Holly Hills CDP	2,521	NA	NA	2,584	85.1	2.4	1.8	2.4	8.3	20.5	61.8	17.7	1,015	90.0	5.9	73.7
Holyoke city	2,313	2,263	-2.2	2,339	50.6	0.0	0.8	2.1	46.5	28.1	54.6	17.4	851	63.6	55.9	12.7
Hooper town	103	103	0.0	79	60.8	0.0	0.0	0.0	39.2	29.1	50.6	20.3	47	63.8	42.6	14.9
Hotchkiss town	942	907	-3.7	1,011	90.1	0.0	0.0	0.9	9.0	23.6	60.0	16.2	463	54.2	48.8	14.7
Hot Sulphur Springs town	663	656	-1.1	718	92.8	0.7	0.0	4.3	2.2	29.8	63.7	6.5	211	78.2	42.7	30.8
Howard CDP	723	NA	NA	1,057	97.4	0.0	0.0	0.0	2.6	11.7	63.3	25.1	548	74.1	28.1	44.9
Hudson town	2,344	2,569	9.6	2,475	63.4	0.0	0.8	0.0	35.9	27.9	62.0	10.1	904	64.4	57.4	5.6
Hugo town	730	731	0.1	654	89.0	3.7	0.0	0.6	6.7	15.8	51.0	33.0	283	62.5	44.5	10.2
Idaho Springs city	1,717	1,710	-0.4	1,971	88.1	2.7	0.0	0.0	9.2	22.3	61.1	16.6	883	60.0	44.3	25.1
Idalia CDP	88	NA	NA	69	87.0	0.0	0.0	2.9	10.1	17.3	70.8	11.6	37	35.1	16.2	5.4
Idledale CDP	252	NA	NA	267	100.0	0.0	0.0	0.0	0.0	18.0	76.0	6.0	115	72.2	36.5	13.9
Ignacio town	704	721	2.4	832	28.2	0.7	0.4	24.0	46.6	23.4	57.5	19.1	353	59.8	48.7	10.5
Iliff town	266	258	-3.0	239	84.5	0.0	0.0	0.8	14.6	28.9	52.3	18.8	79	74.7	57.0	11.4
Indian Hills CDP	1,280	NA	NA	1,181	78.1	0.8	0.0	2.8	18.4	23.3	62.6	13.9	486	74.3	13.4	41.2
Inverness CDP	1,532	NA	NA	1,968	65.0	5.9	20.1	2.1	6.9	5.6	89.1	5.1	1,124	17.6	6.0	85.7
Jackson Lake CDP	154	NA	NA	168	76.2	0.0	0.0	0.0	23.8	17.2	40.5	42.3	80	76.3	75.0	2.5
Jamestown town	274	262	-4.4	266	95.5	0.0	0.0	0.0	4.5	20.7	68.8	10.5	107	64.5	6.5	73.8
Jansen CDP	112	NA	NA	158	84.2	0.0	0.0	0.0	15.8	0.0	39.9	60.1	80	100.0	86.3	13.8
Joes CDP	80	NA	NA	60	100.0	0.0	0.0	0.0	0.0	26.6	58.3	15.0	26	65.4	38.5	26.9
Johnson Village CDP	246	NA	NA	276	100.0	0.0	0.0	0.0	0.0	29.0	53.5	17.4	89	50.6	10.1	0.0
Johnstown town	9,879	13,306	34.7	11,639	83.1	0.0	0.1	2.5	14.4	30.3	59.7	9.9	3,842	92.2	24.0	34.1
Julesburg town	1,225	1,211	-1.1	1,176	71.5	0.4	0.9	6.6	20.5	22.2	50.8	27.0	473	60.9	41.4	16.5
Keenesburg town	1,127	1,191	5.7	1,401	82.9	0.0	0.4	1.2	15.5	32.8	54.7	12.4	483	61.7	43.5	11.6
Ken Caryl CDP	32,438	NA	NA	32,944	85.0	0.7	2.1	1.9	10.2	23.3	67.2	9.5	12,985	83.2	18.6	45.9
Kersey town	1,451	1,560	7.5	1,533	68.3	0.1	0.0	0.1	31.4	27.3	59.2	13.4	503	77.7	57.7	10.5
Keystone CDP	1,079	NA	NA	1,243	73.1	0.0	1.8	0.0	25.1	0.9	96.6	2.5	464	33.6	61.4	19.0
Kim town	74	67	-9.5	64	71.9	0.0	0.0	0.0	28.1	6.2	70.3	23.4	33	75.8	57.6	9.1
Kiowa town	723	742	2.6	915	89.1	0.1	2.1	2.4	6.3	28.6	53.6	17.7	318	83.6	46.2	21.7
Kirk CDP	59	NA	NA	77	81.8	0.0	0.0	1.3	16.9	3.9	65.0	31.2	36	63.9	44.4	27.8
Kit Carson town	233	235	0.9	317	80.8	0.3	0.0	0.0	18.9	40.3	49.6	10.1	101	78.2	30.7	32.7
Kittredge CDP	1,304	NA	NA	1,314	96.0	0.5	1.0	0.0	2.5	31.0	63.4	5.8	500	56.6	12.2	55.2
Kremmling town	1,444	1,404	-2.8	1,957	74.9	0.0	1.6	0.8	22.7	34.0	58.3	7.7	591	66.7	41.3	19.5
Lafayette city	24,452	27,081	10.8	25,812	76.2	0.5	5.4	3.3	14.7	23.4	67.2	9.5	10,482	72.2	20.3	55.0
Laird CDP	47	NA	NA	51	100.0	0.0	0.0	0.0	0.0	0.0	43.2	56.9	37	100.0	43.2	0.0
La Jara town	823	817	-0.7	835	40.5	0.0	0.0	0.5	59.0	22.9	58.5	18.7	318	67.0	45.9	21.4
La Junta city	7,077	6,964	-1.6	7,040	50.6	0.2	1.4	4.2	43.5	21.2	60.7	18.1	2,835	54.5	44.8	17.1
La Junta Gardens CDP	153	NA	NA	22	100.0	0.0	0.0	0.0	0.0	0.0	68.2	31.8	11	100.0	100.0	0.0
Lake City town	408	378	-7.4	366	95.9	0.0	0.0	3.6	0.5	13.7	55.6	30.9	184	74.5	23.4	45.1
Lakeside town	8	8	0.0	4	100.0	0.0	0.0	0.0	0.0	0.0	100.0	0.0	3	0.0	33.3	0.0
Lakewood city	142,995	149,643	4.6	145,880	70.2	1.6	2.7	3.2	22.4	20.2	64.8	15.0	62,283	57.9	28.0	38.0
Lamar city	7,932	7,608	-4.1	7,810	59.7	0.4	0.0	1.2	38.7	26.7	59.0	14.4	3,126	61.6	45.4	14.7
Laporte CDP	2,450	NA	NA	2,878	84.9	0.0	1.2	6.0	8.0	15.8	67.2	16.9	1,215	68.1	17.4	30.9
Larkspur town	185	198	7.0	204	88.7	0.0	0.0	0.0	11.3	10.8	79.5	9.8	100	79.0	41.0	11.0
La Salle town	1,955	2,047	4.7	2,559	58.7	0.0	0.1	2.4	38.8	30.3	56.5	13.2	812	75.2	53.0	12.4
Las Animas city	2,410	2,198	-8.8	1,943	54.3	0.2	0.2	1.2	44.1	23.4	52.0	24.7	949	58.0	52.2	12.0
La Veta town	800	758	-5.3	867	83.9	0.0	0.0	0.0	16.1	16.7	60.2	23.1	385	71.7	28.8	40.3
Lazy Acres CDP	920	NA	NA	996	91.8	2.2	4.0	0.4	1.6	24.0	63.0	12.8	407	90.9	0.0	86.2
Leadville city	2,602	2,595	-0.3	2,590	89.2	0.0	1.5	4.6	4.7	14.0	75.9	10.2	1,380	43.5	19.9	49.8
Leadville North CDP	1,794	NA	NA	1,600	62.1	0.0	2.3	0.4	35.1	25.9	59.5	14.5	652	83.4	41.0	23.2
Lewis CDP	302	NA	NA	451	80.9	0.0	0.0	13.1	6.0	43.5	35.9	20.6	152	93.4	48.7	20.4
Leyner CDP	29	NA	NA	31	100.0	0.0	0.0	0.0	0.0	0.0	51.6	48.4	15	100.0	0.0	0.0
Limon town	1,882	1,887	0.3	1,688	87.5	3.8	0.0	1.4	7.3	23.2	56.7	19.9	730	56.8	41.8	26.2
Lincoln Park CDP	3,546	NA	NA	3,294	87.7	0.5	0.7	5.1	6.0	20.5	48.2	31.4	1,524	73.6	45.4	17.3
Littleton city	41,733	44,669	7.0	43,710	82.6	1.1	1.8	2.6	11.9	20.4	62.7	16.8	19,031	61.1	22.3	44.7
Lochbuie town	4,726	5,302	12.2	5,127	47.6	0.0	0.6	2.8	48.9	34.2	56.5	9.1	1,666	85.6	56.7	12.5
Loghill Village CDP	521	NA	NA	373	98.4	0.0	0.0	0.0	1.6	5.4	61.2	33.5	184	81.5	3.3	67.9
Log Lane Village town	873	872	-0.1	894	38.6	0.0	0.0	0.7	60.7	26.2	60.6	13.1	310	63.5	63.2	5.2
Loma CDP	1,293	NA	NA	1,442	97.1	0.0	1.5	0.0	1.5	21.0	73.4	5.4	542	79.2	48.2	22.5
Lone Tree city	11,104	13,545	22.0	12,328	81.3	0.5	10.3	2.0	5.9	27.1	63.1	9.7	4,752	59.5	12.2	66.6
Longmont city	86,303	90,237	4.6	88,547	67.5	1.1	2.9	2.7	25.9	25.7	62.4	11.9	33,859	61.9	29.3	38.7
Louisville city	18,405	20,112	9.3	19,171	87.1	0.3	4.1	3.0	5.5	23.1	65.8	11.0	7,870	73.2	8.6	70.8
Louviers CDP	269	NA	NA	157	100.0	0.0	0.0	0.0	0.0	0.0	54.1	45.9	71	100.0	59.2	4.2
Loveland city	66,824	72,651	8.7	70,093	85.4	0.3	1.4	2.4	10.5	23.0	61.2	15.6	29,227	63.5	28.9	34.9
Lynn CDP	12	NA	NA	0	0.0	0.0	0.0	0.0	0.0	0.0	0.0	0.0	0	0.0	0.0	0.0
Lyons town	2,033	2,108	3.7	2,225	88.3	1.4	0.4	4.1	5.8	22.1	68.0	10.0	870	72.9	14.4	63.3
McCoy CDP	24	NA	NA	16	100.0	0.0	0.0	0.0	0.0	0.0	100.0	0.0	5	100.0	0.0	0.0
Manassa town	991	978	-1.3	1,031	47.1	0.0	0.0	1.6	51.3	26.5	56.6	17.0	373	82.8	51.7	11.5
Mancos town	1,338	1,377	2.9	1,461	77.7	0.0	0.0	7.3	15.1	20.0	65.6	14.4	590	60.0	21.4	34.4
Manitou Springs city	4,992	5,314	6.5	5,175	89.7	0.5	0.9	2.9	6.0	14.3	73.0	12.8	2,598	56.0	18.9	44.9
Manzanola town	434	425	-2.1	385	39.5	0.0	0.0	3.9	56.6	22.3	61.5	16.1	165	47.3	64.8	10.3
Marble town	130	131	0.8	104	88.5	0.0	1.9	0.0	9.6	14.4	73.1	12.5	41	73.2	31.7	41.5
Maybell CDP	72	NA	NA	65	100.0	0.0	0.0	0.0	0.0	0.0	26.2	73.8	61	90.2	41.0	0.0
Maysville CDP	135	NA	NA	55	100.0	0.0	0.0	0.0	0.0	0.0	69.1	30.9	26	100.0	0.0	42.3
Mead town	3,432	4,104	19.6	3,781	85.4	0.0	4.5	1.7	8.4	28.5	62.0	9.7	1,347	93.9	24.4	46.2
Meeker town	2,475	2,429	-1.9	2,562	81.5	0.0	0.0	3.6	14.9	25.3	57.9	16.7	1,150	58.4	45.0	15.9
Meridian CDP	2,970	NA	NA	2,713	77.9	0.9	13.9	1.9	5.4	13.2	73.6	13.2	1,439	25.5	8.8	55.0
Morino town	204	202	-0.7	243	91.8	0.0	0.0	3.3	4.9	21.8	67.9	10.3	93	66.7	60.2	7.5
Midland CDP	156	NA	NA	295	68.1	0.0	12.2	0.0	19.7	26.1	54.2	19.7	123	86.2	17.1	37.4
Milliken town	5,612	6,091	8.5	5,837	68.9	0.0	0.0	0.9	30.1	28.5	65.2	6.3	1,898	82.7	48.8	19.2
Minturn town	1,029	1,035	0.6	1,041	61.5	4.7	0.0	6.1	27.7	15.6	74.6	9.9	353	41.9	22.4	45.9
Moffat town	116	116	0.0	134	90.3	6.0	0.0	1.5	2.2	1.5	64.2	34.3	81	87.7	21.0	28.4
Monte Vista city	4,444	4,311	-3.0	4,394	36.0	0.6	0.0	1.6	61.8	25.4	58.4	16.2	1,816	57.5	46.1	16.0
Montezuma town	65	67	3.1	57	91.2	0.0	0.0	8.8	0.0	15.8	84.1	0.0	26	57.7	0.0	53.8
Montrose city	19,143	19,045	-0.5	19,018	72.9	0.6	0.4	1.8	24.4	20.6	57.5	21.9	8,267	62.0	41.4	28.7
Monument town	6,005	6,391	6.4	6,226	83.5	0.1	3.9	6.3	6.2	33.3	58.4	8.2	1,883	86.0	10.4	54.1
Morgan Heights CDP	266	NA	NA	430	97.4	0.0	0.0	0.0	2.6	14.6	56.6	28.8	180	85.0	13.9	54.4
Morrison town	425	431	1.4	400	86.3	0.0	2.3	0.0	11.5	6.3	41.6	52.3	130	74.6	21.5	46.9

1 May be of any race.

Table A. All Places — **Population and Housing**

STATE City, town, township, borough, or CDP (county if applicable)	Population: 2010 census total population	Population: 2014 estimated population	Population: Percent change 2010–2014	Population: ACS total population estimate 2010–2014	Race and Hispanic or Latino origin (percent), 2010–2014: White alone, not Hispanic or Latino	Black alone, not Hispanic or Latino	Asian alone, not Hispanic or Latino	All other races or 2 or more races, not Hispanic or Latino	Hispanic or Latino[1]	Age (percent), 2010–2014: Under 18 years old	Age 18 to 64 years old	Age 65 years and older	Households, 2010–2014: Total occupied housing units	Percent owner occupied	Householders by level of education (percent): High school diploma or less	Bachelor's degree or more
	1	2	3	4	5	6	7	8	9	10	11	12	13	14	15	16
COLORADO—Con.																
Mountain Meadows CDP	274	NA	NA	173	100.0	0.0	0.0	0.0	0.0	9.8	64.2	26.0	86	100.0	0.0	70.9
Mountain View town	507	522	3.0	564	61.5	0.0	1.4	4.3	32.8	22.0	65.8	12.1	277	56.0	32.5	33.2
Mountain Village town	1,316	1,387	5.4	1,291	63.7	1.2	1.5	3.9	29.7	15.6	78.0	6.3	604	28.3	17.4	53.6
Mount Crested Butte town	801	809	1.0	799	95.1	1.0	0.0	3.9	0.0	12.6	77.2	10.4	413	57.9	7.3	72.6
Mulford CDP	174	NA	NA	199	66.8	0.0	0.0	0.0	33.2	23.7	50.7	25.6	82	76.8	26.8	62.2
Naturita town	546	530	-2.9	399	86.0	0.0	0.0	7.5	6.5	15.1	58.7	26.3	177	71.8	58.8	12.4
Nederland town	1,449	1,504	3.8	1,417	94.1	0.2	0.2	4.3	1.2	28.3	66.1	5.7	593	57.0	13.2	53.6
New Castle town	4,518	4,608	2.0	4,538	67.2	0.5	0.3	0.2	31.9	32.7	61.0	6.2	1,507	71.9	28.0	36.5
Niwot CDP	4,006	NA	NA	4,732	92.1	0.5	3.4	0.5	3.3	30.6	59.3	10.0	1,676	85.8	7.9	75.2
No Name CDP	123	NA	NA	192	100.0	0.0	0.0	0.0	0.0	0.0	65.7	34.4	105	50.5	10.5	34.3
Norrie CDP	7	NA	NA	0	0.0	0.0	0.0	0.0	0.0	0.0	0.0	0.0	0	0.0	0.0	0.0
Northglenn city	35,769	38,596	7.9	37,075	62.4	1.5	3.3	1.9	30.9	23.1	64.4	12.6	13,945	59.1	41.5	20.6
North La Junta CDP	512	NA	NA	394	65.7	0.0	0.0	1.3	33.0	34.3	43.6	22.1	172	79.7	46.5	5.2
North Washington CDP	484	NA	NA	303	64.4	0.0	0.0	0.0	35.6	9.6	69.4	21.1	164	54.3	60.4	5.5
Norwood town	518	554	6.9	536	95.1	0.0	0.0	0.0	4.9	24.1	58.1	17.9	207	66.2	35.7	31.4
Nucla town	711	704	-1.0	630	86.8	0.0	0.0	7.8	5.4	22.1	59.9	18.1	272	72.1	55.5	15.8
Nunn town	420	440	4.8	491	78.0	0.4	0.0	5.1	16.5	20.7	70.0	9.2	192	82.3	41.7	22.9
Oak Creek town	884	892	0.9	856	86.4	0.7	0.0	3.9	9.0	17.6	75.5	6.9	384	75.3	39.3	29.7
Olathe town	1,849	1,804	-2.4	1,591	44.2	0.0	0.3	1.6	53.9	34.4	51.1	14.5	495	46.7	63.4	10.7
Olney Springs town	345	334	-3.2	527	46.9	0.0	0.4	6.3	46.5	23.6	68.7	7.8	105	51.4	40.0	11.4
Ophir town	159	167	5.0	173	96.5	0.0	0.0	1.2	2.3	35.8	61.2	2.9	58	84.5	3.4	77.6
Orchard CDP	90	NA	NA	88	80.7	0.0	0.0	0.0	19.3	12.5	71.6	15.9	52	42.3	50.0	9.6
Orchard City town	3,119	3,025	-3.0	3,072	88.1	0.1	1.0	0.4	10.4	19.0	48.9	32.0	1,403	79.1	40.6	13.8
Orchard Mesa CDP	6,836	NA	NA	6,272	87.9	0.1	0.9	1.3	9.8	18.2	61.6	20.3	2,665	85.5	42.0	19.9
Ordway town	1,080	1,059	-1.9	1,159	67.7	0.9	0.3	0.8	30.2	21.2	63.9	14.8	395	71.4	45.1	15.4
Otis town	475	468	-1.5	423	88.9	0.0	0.0	0.7	10.4	25.8	49.3	24.8	205	60.0	43.9	19.5
Ouray city	1,000	1,021	2.1	796	91.5	0.0	0.0	2.3	6.3	14.2	63.8	22.2	343	66.2	23.0	51.0
Ovid town	318	308	-3.1	330	73.0	1.5	0.6	2.7	22.1	14.5	64.9	20.6	132	74.2	56.8	6.1
Padroni CDP	76	NA	NA	133	91.0	0.0	6.0	3.0	0.0	36.1	60.2	3.8	33	69.7	87.9	12.1
Pagosa Springs town	1,725	1,743	1.0	1,835	65.0	0.6	0.6	0.1	33.7	21.5	63.7	14.8	782	54.9	39.9	27.0
Palisade town	2,642	2,645	0.1	2,635	79.1	1.3	0.0	4.6	15.1	23.4	63.1	13.4	1,164	58.3	37.5	19.5
Palmer Lake town	2,420	2,579	6.6	2,507	82.4	0.0	0.2	3.4	13.9	25.4	66.2	8.1	1,037	63.9	31.1	41.2
Paoli town	34	33	-2.9	50	100.0	0.0	0.0	0.0	0.0	0.0	18.0	82.0	27	100.0	66.7	3.7
Paonia town	1,458	1,413	-3.1	1,351	85.1	0.0	0.0	6.1	8.7	18.7	63.9	17.5	630	63.0	38.3	27.3
Parachute town	1,085	1,098	1.2	1,172	61.3	1.6	0.7	3.4	32.9	38.5	55.3	6.2	385	48.3	60.3	16.1
Paragon Estates CDP	928	NA	NA	768	93.6	0.0	0.0	0.0	6.4	14.3	60.6	25.1	316	96.8	7.9	84.5
Parker town	45,297	49,857	10.1	47,515	85.1	1.3	2.6	3.3	7.6	31.6	63.1	5.4	16,282	79.6	14.5	54.1
Parshall CDP	47	NA	NA	15	100.0	0.0	0.0	0.0	0.0	0.0	0.0	100.0	15	100.0	100.0	0.0
Peetz town	238	237	-0.4	236	98.7	0.8	0.0	0.0	0.4	18.2	67.4	14.4	85	77.6	43.5	12.9
Penrose CDP	3,582	NA	NA	3,293	89.9	0.0	0.0	3.5	6.6	23.6	57.9	18.5	1,434	81.2	34.7	17.6
Peoria CDP	163	NA	NA	70	100.0	0.0	0.0	0.0	0.0	10.0	72.9	17.1	25	100.0	36.0	16.0
Perry Park CDP	1,646	NA	NA	1,634	93.3	1.8	1.5	0.2	3.2	13.8	61.9	24.2	676	96.3	15.7	54.9
Peyton CDP	250	NA	NA	329	39.5	0.0	10.6	10.9	38.9	50.5	45.3	4.3	92	100.0	54.3	45.7
Phippsburg CDP	0	NA	NA	154	100.0	0.0	0.0	0.0	0.0	4.5	90.9	4.5	88	90.9	39.8	31.8
Piedra CDP	28	NA	NA	59	100.0	0.0	0.0	0.0	0.0	11.9	50.9	37.3	22	100.0	27.3	31.8
Pierce town	834	871	4.4	914	71.0	0.0	0.0	4.8	24.2	17.6	66.4	16.1	396	80.1	56.1	17.4
Pine Brook Hill CDP	983	NA	NA	1,214	88.1	0.0	4.0	4.9	3.0	24.9	54.7	20.3	440	77.0	2.5	76.8
Pitkin town	66	67	1.5	65	100.0	0.0	0.0	0.0	0.0	6.2	60.0	33.8	34	100.0	52.9	38.2
Platteville town	2,480	2,608	5.2	2,548	58.2	0.1	0.0	0.6	41.0	25.5	63.9	10.6	879	69.7	56.3	7.5
Poncha Springs town	737	764	3.7	1,190	80.8	0.7	0.0	2.0	16.5	19.8	63.8	16.2	451	60.5	33.5	38.4
Ponderosa Park CDP	3,232	NA	NA	3,018	88.7	1.1	1.0	3.7	5.5	21.7	68.1	10.2	1,163	96.0	25.5	34.1
Portland CDP	135	NA	NA	192	96.9	0.0	0.0	0.0	3.1	17.7	78.7	3.6	66	90.9	33.3	50.0
Pritchett town	140	136	-2.9	156	100.0	0.0	0.0	0.0	0.0	7.7	67.9	24.4	79	87.3	54.4	2.5
Pueblo city	106,544	108,423	1.8	107,706	44.0	2.1	0.8	2.4	50.7	23.4	60.4	16.3	43,371	57.3	39.5	21.6
Pueblo West CDP	29,637	NA	NA	30,655	71.6	1.2	0.6	1.9	24.8	27.1	59.5	13.4	10,848	79.8	26.4	28.9
Ramah town	123	127	3.3	91	87.9	0.0	0.0	1.1	11.0	12.1	79.2	8.8	40	90.0	37.5	20.0
Rangely town	2,365	2,430	2.7	2,205	89.7	0.0	0.3	2.0	8.0	28.0	60.6	11.4	854	71.2	43.1	17.0
Raymer (New Raymer) town	96	102	6.3	91	91.2	4.4	0.0	0.0	4.4	28.6	52.8	18.7	35	88.6	65.7	20.0
Red Cliff town	267	270	1.1	268	46.6	0.0	0.0	5.6	47.8	18.3	74.3	7.5	92	71.7	34.8	29.3
Red Feather Lakes CDP	343	NA	NA	203	93.1	0.0	0.0	0.0	6.9	11.9	63.5	24.6	100	71.0	46.0	26.0
Redlands CDP	8,685	NA	NA	9,546	89.8	0.5	1.3	2.0	6.4	20.6	56.3	23.0	3,895	89.3	28.2	36.9
Redstone CDP	130	NA	NA	10	100.0	0.0	0.0	0.0	0.0	0.0	100.0	0.0	10	0.0	0.0	100.0
Redvale CDP	236	NA	NA	268	100.0	0.0	0.0	0.0	0.0	23.8	67.5	8.6	95	83.2	27.4	46.3
Rico town	265	256	-3.4	187	100.0	0.0	0.0	0.0	0.0	18.7	61.4	19.8	87	67.8	26.4	25.3
Ridgway town	924	953	3.1	990	91.8	0.0	0.0	1.6	6.6	24.7	59.7	15.5	412	62.4	18.4	55.8
Rifle city	9,365	9,488	1.3	9,397	74.3	0.4	0.4	1.8	23.1	30.8	61.0	8.3	3,146	59.7	49.0	18.2
Rock Creek Park CDP	58	NA	NA	0	0.0	0.0	0.0	0.0	0.0	0.0	0.0	0.0	0	0.0	0.0	0.0
Rockvale town	487	498	2.3	454	93.8	0.0	0.0	0.0	6.2	22.4	56.8	20.7	193	74.1	50.8	12.4
Rocky Ford city	3,957	3,873	-2.1	3,925	39.3	0.6	1.4	0.0	58.6	22.4	56.0	21.7	1,588	65.7	47.8	14.7
Rollinsville CDP	181	NA	NA	64	100.0	0.0	0.0	0.0	0.0	0.0	73.4	26.6	64	100.0	0.0	46.9
Romeo town	404	394	-2.5	335	16.4	0.0	0.0	0.6	83.0	30.1	58.6	11.3	126	81.7	73.0	7.9
Roxborough Park CDP	9,099	NA	NA	9,273	82.8	2.2	3.6	0.9	10.5	30.4	61.7	8.0	3,080	96.3	13.2	59.2
Rye town	153	154	0.7	221	75.6	0.9	0.0	7.7	15.8	20.4	61.1	18.6	96	53.1	25.0	20.8
Saddle Ridge CDP	56	NA	NA	40	72.5	0.0	0.0	0.0	27.5	12.5	42.5	45.0	12	100.0	0.0	41.7
Saguache town	485	480	-1.0	583	67.8	2.7	0.0	5.3	24.2	15.4	59.0	25.6	287	63.8	41.1	23.0
St. Ann Highlands CDP	288	NA	NA	363	95.3	0.0	0.0	0.0	4.7	19.0	45.0	36.1	144	87.5	0.0	90.3
St. Mary's CDP	283	NA	NA	113	100.0	0.0	0.0	0.0	0.0	10.6	70.8	18.6	66	100.0	16.7	31.8
Salida city	5,236	5,406	3.2	5,329	84.1	0.5	0.0	2.4	13.0	17.9	59.6	22.5	2,443	71.9	30.1	33.7
Salt Creek CDP	587	NA	NA	800	11.6	0.9	0.0	0.0	87.5	13.1	66.4	20.5	280	61.4	41.4	25.4
San Acacio CDP	40	NA	NA	11	36.4	0.0	0.0	0.0	63.6	0.0	0.0	100.0	11	100.0	63.6	36.4
Sanford town	879	870	-1.0	865	67.7	0.0	0.0	0.2	32.0	27.7	61.8	10.4	328	83.8	43.9	11.9
San Luis town	629	622	-1.1	709	8.7	0.0	0.0	0.4	90.8	25.3	55.2	19.5	223	56.5	61.4	7.6
Sawpit town	40	42	5.0	36	83.3	0.0	0.0	0.0	16.7	16.7	75.0	8.3	16	93.8	0.0	62.5
Security-Widefield CDP	32,882	NA	NA	33,566	61.8	7.8	3.0	7.7	19.7	27.7	60.3	11.9	11,393	80.5	28.4	22.2
Sedalia CDP	206	NA	NA	101	95.0	0.0	0.0	5.0	0.0	10.9	69.3	19.8	63	88.9	46.0	11.1
Sedgwick town	146	145	-0.7	184	60.3	0.0	1.1	0.0	38.6	10.8	74.3	14.7	75	73.3	42.7	8.0
Segundo CDP	98	NA	NA	125	60.8	0.0	0.0	0.0	39.2	35.2	49.6	15.2	50	38.0	56.0	0.0
Seibert town	181	218	20.4	178	95.5	0.0	0.0	0.0	4.5	15.7	52.8	31.5	80	86.3	52.5	7.5
Seven Hills CDP	121	NA	NA	129	86.0	14.0	0.0	0.0	0.0	12.4	68.3	19.4	65	58.5	0.0	76.9
Severance town	3,163	3,525	11.4	3,352	87.7	0.9	0.2	1.5	9.7	27.8	63.5	8.7	1,150	92.5	20.4	38.8

1 May be of any race.

Table A. All Places — Population and Housing

STATE City, town, township, borough, or CDP (county if applicable)	2010 census total population	2014 estimated population	Percent change 2010–2014	ACS total population estimate 2010–2014	White alone, not Hispanic or Latino	Black alone, not Hispanic or Latino	Asian alone, not Hispanic or Latino	All other races or 2 or more races, not Hispanic or Latino	Hispanic or Latino[1]	Under 18 years old	Age 18 to 64 years old	Age 65 years and older	Total occupied housing units	Percent owner occupied	High school diploma or less	Bachelor's degree or more
	1	2	3	4	5	6	7	8	9	10	11	12	13	14	15	16
COLORADO—Con.																
Shaw Heights CDP	5,116	NA	NA	4,749	55.1	1.1	7.1	1.4	35.3	20.4	66.2	13.3	1,594	77.3	46.1	17.6
Sheridan city	5,664	5,949	5.0	5,819	45.5	7.3	1.4	4.0	41.9	25.3	60.3	14.3	2,261	52.8	58.6	10.4
Sheridan Lake town	88	88	0.0	81	97.5	0.0	1.2	1.2	0.0	50.6	41.9	7.4	23	52.2	56.5	21.7
Sherrelwood CDP	18,287	NA	NA	19,275	33.6	0.5	0.9	1.4	63.5	26.9	63.4	9.7	6,002	59.2	59.8	10.6
Silt town	2,934	3,007	2.5	2,946	61.0	0.0	0.0	0.3	38.7	32.0	61.6	6.5	950	69.6	47.4	20.3
Silver Cliff town	587	584	-0.5	841	85.6	7.6	0.0	0.0	6.8	22.9	53.9	23.3	373	53.1	47.5	15.8
Silver Plume town	170	172	1.2	233	97.0	0.0	0.0	1.3	1.7	15.0	67.5	17.6	110	64.5	20.9	38.2
Silverthorne town	3,885	4,271	9.9	4,009	78.7	0.0	0.6	3.0	17.6	24.8	67.4	7.7	1,420	76.8	22.3	51.8
Silverton town	637	655	2.8	609	71.9	0.0	1.6	3.1	23.3	9.9	75.6	14.6	318	60.7	28.9	29.9
Simla town	618	627	1.5	568	91.5	0.0	0.0	3.2	5.3	28.9	58.0	13.2	193	80.3	57.5	20.7
Smeltertown CDP	120	NA	NA	122	100.0	0.0	0.0	0.0	0.0	0.0	99.9	0.0	37	56.8	32.4	24.3
Snowmass Village town	2,822	2,898	2.7	2,852	95.3	0.0	0.0	2.5	2.2	17.3	72.9	9.9	1,253	56.5	6.8	65.8
Snyder CDP	132	NA	NA	129	96.9	0.0	0.0	0.0	3.1	17.9	63.6	18.6	55	89.1	36.4	0.0
Southern Ute CDP	177	NA	NA	156	42.3	0.0	0.0	29.5	28.2	23.8	67.4	9.0	59	86.4	28.8	10.2
South Fork town	378	364	-3.7	675	90.8	2.1	3.3	1.8	2.1	23.1	48.6	28.1	279	80.3	39.8	22.2
Springfield town	1,451	1,405	-3.2	1,354	85.5	4.0	0.0	3.5	7.0	20.3	53.2	26.4	625	71.2	44.3	21.1
Starkville town	59	53	-10.2	39	30.8	0.0	0.0	0.0	69.2	5.1	66.7	28.2	23	91.3	56.5	34.8
Steamboat Springs city	12,088	12,260	1.4	12,044	88.6	0.7	1.5	1.0	8.2	18.3	72.7	9.0	5,027	65.9	12.0	55.6
Sterling city	14,777	14,629	-1.0	14,709	72.7	1.5	2.3	1.9	21.5	18.7	65.6	15.7	5,081	59.7	44.0	14.6
Stonegate CDP	8,962	NA	NA	8,755	85.2	0.2	4.7	2.0	7.8	31.5	64.0	4.4	2,999	92.5	6.9	69.1
Stonewall Gap CDP	67	NA	NA	81	97.5	0.0	0.0	0.0	2.5	19.8	60.5	19.8	33	100.0	0.0	48.5
Strasburg CDP	2,447	NA	NA	2,999	89.3	0.3	1.1	3.5	5.8	32.4	58.8	8.8	989	82.5	50.6	23.1
Stratmoor CDP	6,900	NA	NA	7,209	56.4	3.1	1.5	15.8	23.2	30.6	59.6	9.8	2,393	55.7	36.2	12.1
Stratton town	662	663	0.2	630	81.0	0.0	0.0	0.0	19.0	28.0	56.3	15.6	273	64.8	46.5	15.8
Sugar City town	258	253	-1.9	485	76.7	0.0	0.0	4.1	18.8	14.5	77.4	8.0	124	77.4	47.6	6.5
Sugarloaf CDP	261	NA	NA	235	74.9	0.0	0.0	0.0	25.1	23.8	65.5	10.6	112	100.0	10.7	51.8
Sunshine CDP	230	NA	NA	182	100.0	0.0	0.0	0.0	0.0	24.7	62.5	12.6	69	92.8	0.0	65.2
Superior town	12,483	12,855	3.0	12,716	74.5	0.9	15.4	1.9	7.2	29.5	67.2	3.4	4,410	68.2	3.0	81.7
Swink town	617	602	-2.4	775	74.8	0.4	1.0	0.4	23.4	34.1	52.8	13.2	277	62.1	26.4	17.7
Tabernash CDP	417	NA	NA	290	64.5	0.0	35.5	0.0	0.0	25.5	39.0	35.5	127	71.7	0.0	71.7
Tall Timber CDP	208	NA	NA	193	100.0	0.0	0.0	0.0	0.0	12.9	51.2	35.8	84	100.0	0.0	85.7
Telluride town	2,229	2,369	6.3	1,856	90.5	0.0	0.0	0.6	8.8	14.2	79.8	6.1	843	42.6	21.4	57.9
The Pinery CDP	10,517	NA	NA	11,087	88.4	1.0	2.0	4.2	4.4	28.5	63.7	7.8	3,728	93.4	12.8	64.1
Thornton city	118,792	130,307	9.7	124,707	59.7	1.5	4.5	2.6	31.7	29.2	63.2	7.6	41,632	69.0	35.6	28.7
Timnath town	627	1,983	216.3	1,210	91.2	0.0	0.6	0.3	7.9	36.6	52.2	11.2	390	91.3	16.9	53.1
Todd Creek CDP	3,768	NA	NA	3,673	81.8	4.8	4.1	4.2	5.2	23.1	64.2	12.6	1,233	97.4	11.8	42.8
Towaoc CDP	1,087	NA	NA	985	5.9	0.5	0.0	88.0	5.6	34.0	58.8	7.3	298	47.0	67.1	8.7
Towner CDP	22	NA	NA	60	71.7	0.0	0.0	0.0	28.3	55.0	38.4	6.7	19	47.4	15.8	36.8
Trail Side CDP	59	NA	NA	0	0.0	0.0	0.0	0.0	0.0	0.0	0.0	0.0	0	0.0	0.0	0.0
Trinidad city	9,096	8,193	-9.9	8,657	44.2	1.5	0.8	2.2	51.2	22.2	60.1	17.6	3,448	65.1	33.8	21.4
Twin Lakes CDP (Adams)	6,101	NA	NA	6,332	35.6	0.2	2.5	1.8	59.9	22.0	65.9	12.0	2,158	63.1	65.8	11.5
Twin Lakes CDP (Lake)	171	NA	NA	153	95.4	0.0	0.0	0.0	4.6	6.5	50.9	42.5	88	100.0	21.6	56.8
Two Buttes town	43	42	-2.3	72	97.2	0.0	0.0	0.0	2.8	15.3	72.4	12.5	38	73.7	47.4	5.3
Upper Bear Creek CDP	1,059	NA	NA	1,040	97.1	0.0	1.7	1.2	0.0	16.2	63.0	20.7	466	93.6	6.4	53.9
Vail town	5,305	5,328	0.4	5,280	90.5	1.8	0.8	2.2	4.8	8.6	79.2	12.1	2,451	54.3	14.9	57.2
Valdez CDP	47	NA	NA	22	13.6	0.0	0.0	0.0	86.4	9.1	0.0	90.9	10	70.0	60.0	40.0
Valmont CDP	59	NA	NA	124	100.0	0.0	0.0	0.0	0.0	8.8	67.7	23.4	72	100.0	6.9	37.5
Vernon CDP	29	NA	NA	13	61.5	0.0	0.0	0.0	38.5	0.0	100.0	0.0	8	0.0	0.0	0.0
Victor city	400	400	0.0	382	97.6	0.0	0.3	1.0	1.0	11.8	73.5	14.7	183	70.5	43.2	27.3
Vilas town	114	110	-3.5	212	86.3	0.0	0.0	0.0	13.7	53.3	39.1	7.5	61	50.8	27.9	14.8
Vineland CDP	251	NA	NA	121	70.2	0.0	0.0	10.7	19.0	32.2	43.0	24.8	53	84.9	39.6	0.0
Vona town	106	107	0.9	58	94.8	0.0	0.0	0.0	5.2	13.8	48.1	37.9	30	76.7	76.7	3.3
Walden town	608	601	-1.2	527	90.1	0.2	0.0	0.0	9.7	22.6	55.4	22.0	254	70.9	49.6	13.8
Walsenburg city	3,063	2,896	-5.5	2,959	33.2	1.4	0.3	5.4	59.7	20.5	59.5	19.9	1,160	52.9	49.7	17.8
Walsh town	546	524	-4.0	703	71.8	0.0	0.0	0.7	27.5	21.3	55.6	23.2	301	66.4	44.2	12.6
Ward town	150	154	2.7	107	90.7	0.0	0.0	9.3	0.0	16.8	77.6	5.6	50	92.0	16.0	18.0
Watkins CDP	0	NA	NA	510	93.7	1.4	3.3	0.0	1.6	10.2	81.7	8.0	190	84.7	34.7	44.7
Welby CDP	14,846	NA	NA	16,273	35.8	1.5	0.5	1.6	60.5	31.0	61.3	7.8	5,215	63.3	54.6	12.7
Weldona CDP	139	NA	NA	97	64.9	3.1	0.0	2.1	29.9	16.5	49.5	34.0	47	80.9	29.8	8.5
Wellington town	6,289	7,185	14.2	6,634	82.5	0.3	0.6	1.5	15.1	32.6	60.5	6.9	2,370	83.5	18.2	29.9
Westcliffe town	568	572	0.7	552	80.6	1.3	0.0	8.7	9.4	27.8	54.9	17.4	230	63.0	48.3	18.3
Westcreek CDP	129	NA	NA	150	92.7	0.0	0.0	0.0	7.3	22.0	72.0	6.0	60	80.0	13.3	50.0
Westminster city	106,129	112,090	5.6	109,296	68.1	1.5	5.4	3.2	21.7	23.9	65.9	10.0	41,821	63.5	27.9	37.5
Weston CDP	55	NA	NA	73	54.8	0.0	0.0	0.0	45.2	16.4	75.3	8.2	16	37.5	12.5	0.0
West Pleasant View CDP	3,840	NA	NA	3,598	82.0	2.9	0.7	3.8	10.6	16.3	72.5	11.3	1,564	63.4	34.8	26.2
Wheat Ridge city	30,192	31,034	2.8	30,655	73.9	0.2	1.4	2.1	22.4	18.4	62.8	18.6	13,895	53.9	34.6	34.6
Wiggins town	893	895	0.2	962	70.3	0.0	0.0	1.7	28.1	25.7	58.1	16.1	355	73.2	36.1	11.8
Wiley town	405	387	-4.4	359	73.3	0.0	0.0	8.9	17.8	22.0	64.8	13.1	174	72.4	47.1	26.4
Williamsburg town	662	653	-1.4	647	84.1	0.0	0.0	8.7	7.3	20.9	49.4	29.7	270	88.1	39.3	13.7
Windsor town	18,637	21,106	13.2	19,865	87.4	0.3	2.0	2.2	8.1	28.5	61.3	10.4	7,210	80.4	18.6	46.3
Winter Park town	999	955	-4.4	554	83.8	0.0	3.8	5.2	7.2	14.7	68.8	16.8	248	69.4	15.3	66.9
Wolcott CDP	15	NA	NA	0	0.0	0.0	0.0	0.0	0.0	0.0	0.0	0.0	0	0.0	0.0	0.0
Woodland Park city	7,172	7,194	0.3	7,187	91.3	0.0	0.3	2.2	6.2	23.4	64.6	12.1	2,854	79.8	19.2	39.6
Woodmoor CDP	8,741	NA	NA	8,155	88.2	1.3	1.2	2.3	7.1	26.4	60.6	12.9	2,756	94.2	4.1	71.7
Woody Creek CDP	263	NA	NA	390	82.3	0.0	0.0	0.0	17.7	21.0	70.4	8.5	134	67.9	17.2	44.0
Wray city	2,361	2,400	1.7	2,554	81.4	0.2	0.5	2.1	15.7	31.3	54.2	14.4	861	55.2	42.0	18.8
Yampa town	429	436	1.6	370	97.6	0.0	1.1	0.8	0.5	21.6	61.9	16.5	132	81.8	39.4	26.5
Yuma city	3,524	3,606	2.3	3,563	60.7	1.5	0.0	0.4	37.5	20.4	60.7	18.9	1,643	60.9	42.4	27.1
CONNECTICUT	3,574,096	3,596,677	0.6	3,592,053	69.6	9.5	4.0	2.3	14.3	22.1	63.1	14.8	1,356,206	67.3	34.7	39.0
Andover town (Tolland)	3,303	3,272	-0.9	3,181	91.4	2.1	1.2	3.8	1.5	23.3	63.4	13.3	1,145	88.1	28.4	39.6
Ansonia city & town (New Haven)	19,251	18,959	-1.5	19,128	66.6	7.5	2.2	1.1	22.6	22.8	63.3	14.0	7,240	54.6	57.9	15.7
Ashford town (Windham)	4,321	4,259	-1.4	4,297	94.3	1.8	0.0	2.1	1.8	20.7	67.1	12.2	1,707	84.1	32.0	42.3
Avon town (Hartford)	18,098	18,421	1.8	18,298	87.5	0.4	8.3	1.2	2.6	25.1	57.8	17.2	7,207	85.9	12.1	70.7
Baltic CDP	1,250	NA	NA	1,142	81.9	3.2	2.6	10.1	2.2	20.5	64.5	15.1	525	56.2	58.9	13.9
Bantam borough	759	740	-2.5	751	93.6	2.1	1.3	1.7	1.2	12.8	67.2	20.2	369	62.3	52.8	21.1
Barkhamsted town (Litchfield)	3,799	3,705	-2.5	3,749	98.4	0.0	0.6	0.2	0.7	22.0	64.5	13.6	1,475	89.6	26.5	44.1

1 May be of any race.

Table A. All Places — **Population and Housing**

STATE City, town, township, borough, or CDP (county if applicable)	Population				Race and Hispanic or Latino origin (percent), 2010–2014					Age (percent), 2010–2014			Households, 2010–2014			
	2010 census total population	2014 estimated population	Percent change 2010–2014	ACS total population estimate 2010–2014	White alone, not Hispanic or Latino	Black alone, not Hispanic or Latino	Asian alone, not Hispanic or Latino	All other races or 2 or more races, not Hispanic or Latino	Hispanic or Latino[1]	Under 18 years old	Age 18 to 64 years old	Age 65 years and older	Total occupied housing units	Percent owner occupied	High school diploma or less	Bachelor's degree or more
	1	2	3	4	5	6	7	8	9	10	11	12	13	14	15	16

CONNECTICUT—Con.

	1	2	3	4	5	6	7	8	9	10	11	12	13	14	15	16
Beacon Falls town (New Haven)...............	6,044	6,055	0.2	6,065	90.6	0.6	1.8	0.6	6.3	22.1	64.7	13.2	2,334	82.3	41.3	29.0
Berlin town (Hartford)	19,870	20,610	3.7	20,352	92.4	1.0	3.1	0.7	2.8	21.2	60.3	18.5	7,822	85.3	30.7	39.6
Bethany town (New Haven)...............	5,563	5,531	-0.6	5,546	95.8	0.0	1.7	1.2	1.3	24.0	63.1	12.9	2,034	90.6	22.2	58.8
Bethel town (Fairfield).......	18,584	19,372	4.2	19,078	85.1	1.2	4.5	2.4	6.8	22.8	64.3	13.0	7,071	77.5	29.8	43.2
Bethel CDP..................	9,549	NA	NA	9,471	82.0	1.8	7.3	2.7	6.3	21.9	66.7	11.4	3,986	67.4	35.1	35.9
Bethlehem town (Litchfield)	3,593	3,501	-2.6	3,551	98.1	0.5	0.2	0.3	0.9	20.8	63.5	15.9	1,353	85.9	29.9	36.2
Bethlehem Village CDP	2,021	NA	NA	1,783	98.9	0.7	0.0	0.0	0.4	12.9	70.9	16.3	742	83.0	30.3	33.0
Bloomfield town (Hartford)	20,486	20,819	1.6	20,626	34.1	54.6	1.9	4.2	5.2	14.6	60.8	24.6	8,417	73.0	29.9	40.4
Blue Hills CDP..............	2,901	NA	NA	2,735	7.7	88.5	0.0	0.3	3.5	14.5	68.6	16.9	935	84.0	62.2	10.6
Bolton town (Tolland)	4,977	4,952	-0.5	4,963	90.2	1.2	2.0	2.0	4.5	20.5	64.4	15.1	1,985	87.9	22.1	50.5
Bozrah town (New London)...............	2,627	2,622	-0.2	2,631	90.0	1.2	1.3	3.3	4.1	20.0	63.6	16.4	1,049	81.7	33.9	26.8
Branford town (New Haven)...............	28,026	28,225	0.7	28,066	88.1	1.2	4.2	1.3	5.2	17.5	61.4	21.2	12,410	68.3	28.1	43.4
Branford Center CDP........	5,819	NA	NA	6,255	91.3	2.0	0.9	0.7	5.1	16.8	61.7	21.4	3,046	44.6	31.4	42.0
Bridgeport city & town (Fairfield)...............	144,236	147,612	2.3	146,680	21.2	34.1	3.6	2.3	38.9	25.2	64.9	9.8	50,034	41.1	52.9	18.6
Bridgewater town (Litchfield)	1,727	1,675	-3.0	1,747	91.4	0.9	1.4	1.6	4.8	19.5	57.0	23.6	765	88.8	22.5	55.9
Bristol city & town (Hartford)...............	60,477	60,570	0.2	60,556	82.2	2.6	1.9	2.5	10.7	20.7	63.4	15.8	25,194	66.9	45.3	24.9
Broad Brook CDP............	4,069	NA	NA	4,526	80.8	5.4	0.3	2.0	11.5	27.4	64.4	8.0	1,726	65.2	44.0	23.9
Brookfield town (Fairfield).	16,452	17,055	3.7	16,774	87.5	0.7	5.6	1.7	4.4	23.0	61.1	15.9	6,010	85.4	21.1	54.8
Brooklyn CDP...............	981	NA	NA	889	68.3	10.2	1.6	5.2	14.7	0.0	75.6	24.4	144	81.3	15.3	61.8
Brooklyn town (Windham) ..	8,210	8,254	0.5	8,240	87.1	1.4	0.6	2.3	8.5	22.7	61.9	15.5	2,918	79.2	38.9	31.5
Burlington town (Hartford)	9,301	9,576	3.0	9,443	94.3	1.0	1.9	0.8	2.0	26.6	62.3	11.3	3,381	93.8	18.6	48.3
Byram CDP.................	4,146	NA	NA	4,885	54.1	3.1	5.4	0.9	36.5	23.4	66.1	10.3	1,659	41.4	29.5	48.6
Canaan CDP................	1,212	NA	NA	1,178	82.2	1.4	11.6	0.0	4.8	21.5	56.9	21.6	481	69.0	62.0	13.1
Canaan town (Litchfield)...	1,235	1,195	-3.2	1,240	96.8	0.0	0.2	1.0	2.1	16.2	63.3	20.6	575	70.1	29.9	36.0
Cannondale CDP............	141	NA	NA	173	94.2	0.0	0.0	5.8	0.0	31.8	47.3	20.8	58	58.6	0.0	69.0
Canterbury town (Windham)	5,132	5,088	-0.9	5,110	96.8	0.7	0.5	2.0	0.0	23.1	63.4	13.5	1,931	87.5	38.1	26.2
Canton town (Hartford).....	10,292	10,345	0.5	10,334	91.6	0.5	0.9	1.0	6.0	22.7	61.2	16.2	4,023	82.0	19.5	50.6
Canton Valley CDP..........	1,580	NA	NA	1,484	95.1	1.6	0.0	2.3	0.9	17.9	63.6	18.5	593	80.6	42.8	37.4
Chaplin town (Windham) ..	2,305	2,262	-1.9	2,256	91.6	1.1	0.0	2.1	5.2	20.1	66.1	13.7	865	80.9	37.9	30.8
Cheshire town (New Haven)...............	29,258	29,250	0.0	29,272	79.3	4.5	7.7	1.7	6.8	21.6	63.7	14.7	9,799	88.0	19.5	59.2
Cheshire Village CDP.......	5,786	NA	NA	5,264	85.3	1.4	6.7	2.1	4.6	19.8	56.9	23.2	2,141	80.3	18.1	58.9
Chester town (Middlesex)...	3,994	4,316	8.1	4,223	95.0	0.7	0.6	1.0	2.7	19.2	56.2	24.6	1,853	70.2	31.4	41.1
Chester Center CDP........	1,558	NA	NA	1,761	94.4	0.7	0.0	1.2	3.7	22.1	56.5	21.4	807	67.7	28.1	42.4
Clinton town (Middlesex) ..	13,260	13,129		13,188	90.3	0.3	1.6	1.3	6.5	21.1	63.1	15.8	5,313	80.9	31.8	40.0
Clinton CDP................	3,368	NA	NA	3,372	91.1	0.1	0.9	4.3	3.5	19.4	59.4	21.0	1,447	66.9	36.0	39.9
Colchester CDP.............	4,781	NA	NA	4,414	91.8	1.0	0.8	3.2	3.2	23.3	58.2	18.3	1,845	58.3	39.7	31.6
Colchester town (New London)...............	16,059	16,192	0.8	16,143	94.3	1.0	1.1	1.6	2.0	25.3	62.7	11.9	5,785	80.6	32.0	38.1
Colebrook town (Litchfield)	1,485	1,445	-2.7	1,594	96.8	0.3	0.6	0.7	1.6	18.1	66.4	15.5	615	92.5	35.1	28.8
Collinsville CDP.............	3,746	NA	NA	3,851	87.6	0.2	0.0	0.0	12.2	22.5	60.1	17.5	1,569	69.1	18.3	52.9
Columbia town (Tolland) ..	5,485	5,454	-0.6	5,472	88.7	2.3	1.0	8.0	0.0	20.7	63.5	15.9	2,079	86.6	26.8	40.9
Conning Towers Nautilus Park CDP.................	8,834	NA	NA	10,130	69.2	8.4	4.0	6.9	11.5	23.7	73.2	3.2	2,552	16.3	34.6	26.1
Cornwall town (Litchfield) .	1,420	1,398	-1.5	1,505	96.5	0.0	1.1	2.1	0.3	20.9	56.7	22.4	621	81.6	17.1	63.3
Cos Cob CDP...............	6,770	NA	NA	6,265	77.1	1.6	7.9	3.8	9.7	26.3	60.9	13.0	2,276	76.0	18.0	67.9
Coventry town (Tolland)....	12,435	12,419	-0.1	12,434	93.2	0.4	1.6	1.6	3.9	20.2	66.1	13.6	4,781	90.5	31.3	37.3
Coventry Lake CDP.........	2,990	NA	NA	3,417	94.3	0.0	1.9	0.4	3.5	19.3	68.1	12.8	1,404	92.2	40.2	19.5
Cromwell town (Middlesex)	14,005	14,113	0.8	14,077	82.2	7.3	3.6	1.3	5.6	18.4	64.4	17.3	5,501	82.6	31.4	42.6
Crystal Lake CDP............	1,945	NA	NA	2,378	94.6	0.0	3.0	0.0	2.4	30.0	64.1	6.0	779	81.6	27.2	44.4
Danbury city & town (Fairfield)...............	80,897	83,784	3.6	82,781	56.8	5.9	5.7	4.4	27.1	21.2	66.2	12.6	29,046	60.3	42.4	34.0
Danielson borough	4,051	3,999	-1.3	4,023	76.7	5.9	6.7	1.6	9.0	17.5	70.6	12.1	1,824	43.5	46.8	22.6
Darien CDP & town (Fairfield)...............	20,732	21,689	4.6	21,190	91.0	0.3	4.0	2.2	2.4	33.7	54.5	11.7	6,556	85.8	9.1	80.7
Deep River town (Middlesex)	4,629	4,571	-1.3	4,611	90.5	3.1	2.2	1.1	3.1	21.3	61.6	17.1	1,882	82.6	36.4	37.2
Deep River Center CDP ...	2,484	NA	NA	2,408	84.1	5.3	3.4	2.1	5.1	26.8	59.8	13.5	954	73.3	38.5	36.6
Derby city & town (New Haven)...............	12,900	12,768	-1.0	12,837	66.0	4.1	2.9	1.5	25.5	21.5	63.8	14.7	4,972	58.3	46.5	26.8
Durham CDP................	2,933	NA	NA	2,924	97.7	0.0	1.4	0.0	0.9	25.2	56.8	17.9	1,089	86.9	25.7	50.2
Durham town (Middlesex).	7,388	7,348	-0.5	7,371	92.1	0.2	2.0	2.5	3.2	24.3	61.0	14.7	2,582	91.2	21.6	53.5
East Brooklyn CDP..........	1,638	NA	NA	1,784	76.6	0.8	1.2	5.0	16.4	26.4	61.2	12.3	746	60.5	55.4	14.3
Eastford town (Windham) .	1,751	1,734	-1.0	1,726	94.1	0.3	1.6	2.0	1.9	19.1	65.5	15.4	689	84.6	34.5	28.7
East Granby town (Hartford)...............	5,148	5,212	1.2	5,098	85.0	6.2	3.4	1.9	3.6	24.3	59.3	16.4	2,131	73.9	26.9	47.1
East Haddam town (Middlesex)	9,126	9,127	0.0	9,142	93.8	0.9	1.0	2.0	2.2	23.4	63.2	13.2	3,500	84.4	25.3	39.5
East Hampton CDP..........	2,691	NA	NA	2,402	87.9	0.9	0.5	2.6	8.2	24.4	62.9	12.7	924	85.0	29.8	40.3
East Hampton town (Middlesex)	12,959	12,874	-0.7	12,936	88.6	0.5	3.6	1.7	5.6	22.3	63.9	13.8	4,990	87.9	27.8	44.3
East Hartford CDP & town (Hartford)...............	51,249	51,033	-0.4	51,211	38.3	24.2	5.7	2.7	29.1	22.0	64.6	13.3	20,157	57.5	46.0	20.5
East Haven CDP & town (New Haven)	29,209	29,044	-0.6	29,139	79.0	3.5	4.8	2.0	10.7	19.5	63.2	17.3	11,215	71.2	50.4	22.9
East Lyme town (New London)...............	19,159	19,140	-0.1	19,118	80.7	4.0	5.6	2.9	6.8	18.7	61.5	19.8	7,263	80.0	22.5	50.8
Easton town (Fairfield)......	7,490	7,631	1.9	7,593	89.6	0.5	2.9	1.5	5.5	26.7	56.8	16.6	2,598	94.6	17.7	62.6
East Windsor town (Hartford)...............	11,162	11,423	2.3	11,353	75.1	7.9	6.8	3.9	6.3	20.8	65.1	14.2	4,556	69.8	40.6	27.4
Ellington town (Tolland)	15,602	15,795	1.2	15,725	94.4	0.7	2.2	1.1	1.6	25.2	63.1	11.7	6,318	68.5	27.3	39.6

1 May be of any race.

Table A. All Places — **Population and Housing**

STATE City, town, township, borough, or CDP (county if applicable)	2010 census total population	2014 estimated population	Percent change 2010–2014	ACS total population estimate 2010–2014	White alone, not Hispanic or Latino	Black alone, not Hispanic or Latino	Asian alone, not Hispanic or Latino	All other races or 2 or more races, not Hispanic or Latino	Hispanic or Latino[1]	Under 18 years old	Age 18 to 64 years old	Age 65 years and older	Total occupied housing units	Percent owner occupied	High school diploma or less	Bachelor's degree or more
	1	2	3	4	5	6	7	8	9	10	11	12	13	14	15	16
CONNECTICUT—Con.																
Enfield town (Hartford)......	44,654	44,626	-0.1	44,713	81.7	5.5	2.4	2.1	8.3	18.8	65.6	15.6	16,192	75.1	41.5	26.9
Essex town (Middlesex)....	6,683	6,612	-1.1	6,643	97.3	0.4	0.2	0.5	1.6	20.6	52.7	26.7	2,916	82.4	18.5	58.1
Essex Village CDP..........	2,495	NA	NA	2,174	97.2	1.2	0.0	0.6	0.9	12.2	51.6	36.3	1,078	85.3	9.6	05.2
Fairfield town (Fairfield)....	59,404	61,347	3.3	60,678	86.4	1.3	4.7	2.5	5.2	25.4	59.6	15.0	20,194	82.6	17.2	64.3
Falls Village CDP..............	538	NA	NA	481	96.0	0.0	0.0	1.5	2.5	9.5	61.1	29.3	253	53.4	28.5	31.2
Farmington town (Hartford)......	25,340	25,627	1.1	25,515	83.0	2.2	9.5	2.4	3.0	21.7	60.8	17.5	10,400	74.5	20.1	59.2
Fenwick borough.......	43	44	2.3	65	100.0	0.0	0.0	0.0	0.0	0.0	13.8	86.2	36	97.2	5.6	47.2
Franklin town (New London)......	1,922	1,984	3.2	1,993	96.1	0.0	0.1	2.7	1.2	20.1	63.2	16.7	740	87.4	36.1	33.5
Gales Ferry CDP..............	1,162	NA	NA	885	94.2	5.2	0.0	0.6	0.0	32.4	56.7	10.8	345	100.0	33.9	33.9
Georgetown CDP............	1,805	NA	NA	1,819	86.7	0.0	6.5	1.5	5.3	24.2	63.0	12.6	739	78.2	9.5	58.1
Glastonbury town (Hartford)......	34,427	34,754	0.9	34,661	83.2	2.3	9.4	1.2	3.9	24.9	59.6	15.4	13,152	81.2	16.0	63.1
Glastonbury Center CDP..	7,387	NA	NA	7,418	85.8	3.2	8.6	0.3	2.2	22.4	56.8	20.7	3,320	67.4	23.1	55.0
Glenville CDP.................	2,327	NA	NA	2,383	87.3	0.1	6.2	4.8	1.6	18.4	64.4	17.2	911	73.1	22.5	54.8
Goshen town (Litchfield)...	2,976	2,914	-2.1	2,956	94.8	0.5	0.3	0.9	3.5	19.8	62.3	17.9	1,225	88.6	21.6	44.5
Granby town (Hartford).....	11,282	11,310	0.2	11,310	92.2	1.1	1.0	2.5	3.2	23.0	61.3	15.7	4,409	92.0	18.5	59.9
Greenwich town (Fairfield)	61,172	62,610	2.4	62,141	77.7	1.8	6.6	2.5	11.4	26.6	58.1	15.3	21,994	69.1	17.4	68.9
Greenwich CDP...............	12,942	NA	NA	13,221	72.4	2.5	9.0	2.1	14.0	22.0	62.0	16.1	5,473	48.6	24.9	63.3
Griswold town (New London)......	11,951	11,916	-0.3	11,952	89.1	0.8	2.8	3.1	4.2	25.0	63.8	11.3	4,404	73.0	54.3	20.4
Groton city..................	9,389	9,299	-1.0	9,348	64.5	10.3	6.0	4.5	14.7	22.0	67.7	10.2	4,307	36.6	42.5	30.3
Groton town (New London)......	40,115	40,167	0.1	40,136	73.5	6.1	5.0	5.5	9.9	20.4	65.9	13.5	16,283	47.4	34.2	35.6
Groton Long Point borough..............	518	517	-0.2	445	97.5	0.0	0.0	0.0	2.5	7.0	46.9	46.1	232	89.2	3.9	74.1
Guilford town (New Haven)......	22,375	22,413	0.2	22,405	91.9	0.6	2.1	1.5	4.0	21.9	58.5	19.5	8,814	85.6	15.3	61.6
Guilford Center CDP.......	2,597	NA	NA	2,394	96.5	0.3	0.4	0.0	2.8	15.4	57.4	27.2	1,250	61.1	15.0	56.7
Haddam town (Middlesex)	8,346	8,333	-0.2	8,356	94.6	0.3	2.2	0.4	2.5	22.6	62.8	14.6	3,192	90.6	24.7	45.8
Hamden town (New Haven)......	60,887	61,422	0.9	61,605	63.7	18.7	5.0	2.6	10.0	19.0	66.2	14.9	23,374	65.5	27.6	47.7
Hampton town (Windham)	1,863	1,859	-0.2	1,912	92.1	0.7	0.3	2.6	4.3	19.8	64.5	15.7	746	82.0	37.3	32.7
Hartford city & town (Hartford)......	124,775	124,705	-0.1	125,211	15.9	35.1	2.5	2.9	43.6	25.4	65.1	9.5	45,801	23.5	56.7	16.7
Hartland town (Hartford)...	2,114	2,129	0.7	2,211	95.0	0.6	1.7	0.5	2.2	22.2	62.6	15.2	761	92.9	31.9	36.5
Harwinton town (Litchfield)	5,642	5,531	-2.0	5,592	98.5	0.1	1.0	0.0	0.4	20.4	61.1	18.6	2,072	94.9	31.9	41.5
Hazardville CDP..............	4,599	NA	NA	4,863	86.3	0.4	3.0	4.4	5.8	22.5	61.0	16.6	1,848	86.3	47.5	25.2
Hebron town (Tolland)	9,686	9,564	-1.3	9,627	94.2	0.6	0.6	2.5	2.0	25.9	62.7	11.5	3,356	91.0	21.6	51.7
Heritage Village CDP........	3,736	NA	NA	4,126	93.5	0.0	0.2	0.0	6.3	6.5	25.1	68.3	2,758	80.5	27.0	36.8
Higganum CDP...............	1,698	NA	NA	1,673	96.7	0.0	0.8	1.2	1.4	22.7	63.2	14.0	655	80.2	22.0	54.5
Jewett City borough..........	3,487	3,468	-0.5	3,488	80.4	1.3	3.0	3.8	11.6	31.7	62.0	6.3	1,321	42.8	58.8	12.7
Kensington CDP..............	8,459	NA	NA	9,492	95.6	0.0	2.9	0.2	1.3	20.6	61.8	17.5	3,730	85.5	32.3	32.3
Kent town (Litchfield)	2,979	2,910	-2.3	2,951	90.8	6.6	0.3	2.0	0.2	20.7	58.5	20.8	1,125	64.4	22.2	51.5
Killingly town (Windham) ..	17,370	17,172	-1.1	17,281	89.9	1.8	2.7	1.1	4.5	20.6	65.7	13.7	6,959	70.0	42.8	20.5
Killingworth town (Middlesex)......	6,525	6,490	-0.5	6,516	92.1	0.0	1.2	3.7	3.0	20.5	59.1	20.4	2,590	94.9	22.5	47.2
Lake Pocotopaug CDP	3,436	NA	NA	2,994	90.3	0.0	4.5	1.8	3.4	21.6	58.9	19.4	1,318	84.0	26.1	51.1
Lakeville CDP	928	NA	NA	761	84.4	15.0	0.0	0.5	0.1	7.8	63.3	29.0	365	67.4	14.5	41.1
Lebanon town (New London)......	7,308	7,309	0.0	7,314	93.4	0.5	1.0	1.7	3.5	20.1	63.6	16.3	2,733	91.0	27.3	46.0
Ledyard town (New London)......	15,051	15,121	0.5	15,090	81.4	1.8	4.1	6.4	6.3	23.6	63.5	12.7	5,669	82.3	29.0	38.3
Lisbon town (New London)......	4,338	4,342	0.1	4,340	96.5	0.0	0.2	2.4	0.9	20.6	62.5	16.8	1,635	90.8	38.1	22.2
Litchfield borough.............	1,258	1,225	-2.6	1,430	94.9	0.0	1.0	0.8	3.3	18.8	60.3	20.8	586	63.0	25.4	49.7
Litchfield town (Litchfield) .	8,466	8,264	-2.4	8,365	96.7	0.4	0.9	0.8	1.2	21.3	60.3	18.4	3,454	78.4	31.1	45.2
Long Hill CDP.................	4,205	NA	NA	4,148	73.2	0.5	8.3	9.1	8.9	18.0	63.3	18.6	2,138	26.5	40.9	25.4
Lyme town (New London).	2,406	2,389	-0.7	2,367	95.1	0.0	1.9	0.7	2.3	16.3	55.3	28.3	1,060	84.1	19.3	58.5
Madison town (New Haven)......	18,269	18,259	-0.1	18,284	94.7	0.4	2.4	1.4	1.2	27.5	52.5	20.0	6,727	87.5	13.1	69.5
Madison Center CDP.......	2,290	NA	NA	2,415	99.4	0.2	0.0	0.2	0.1	22.6	41.9	35.5	1,075	62.2	14.6	58.3
Manchester CDP	30,577	NA	NA	30,621	63.0	13.5	3.1	2.6	17.8	22.9	64.9	12.2	12,589	54.2	37.6	27.9
Manchester town (Hartford)......	58,253	58,106	-0.3	58,270	62.5	11.6	8.4	2.5	15.1	21.6	65.0	13.5	24,005	56.1	31.2	37.8
Mansfield town (Tolland)..	26,543	25,977	-2.1	26,328	74.6	5.0	10.3	3.5	6.6	10.4	81.2	8.3	5,489	64.0	16.4	47.2
Mansfield Center CDP......	947	NA	NA	1,055	79.9	0.0	13.4	0.0	6.7	21.3	60.2	18.5	377	76.9	18.6	54.6
Marlborough town (Hartford)......	6,413	6,430	0.3	6,428	93.8	0.6	0.5	1.1	4.1	25.3	59.8	14.9	2,259	94.2	19.6	60.0
Mashantucket CDP..........	0	NA	NA	236	13.6	9.7	3.0	54.7	19.1	36.4	55.4	8.1	61	55.7	23.0	11.5
Meriden city & town (New Haven)......	60,868	60,293	-0.9	60,616	58.6	9.6	1.1	2.6	28.2	20.7	64.8	14.6	24,018	60.9	49.5	20.4
Middlebury town (New Haven)......	7,575	7,591	0.2	7,575	87.0	1.6	7.4	1.8	2.2	22.4	59.7	17.9	2,761	89.5	20.6	51.5
Middlefield town (Middlesex)......	4,425	4,424	0.0	4,426	94.7	0.5	3.3	0.0	1.5	22.0	62.5	15.4	1,729	91.2	32.8	40.5
Middletown city & town (Middlesex)......	47,648	47,043	-1.3	47,424	70.3	12.4	4.4	3.8	9.1	18.4	68.4	13.1	19,419	53.1	33.1	38.6
Milford city	52,759	53,358	1.1	53,039	85.9	1.9	5.0	1.9	5.3	19.7	63.5	16.7	21,199	77.3	31.5	43.3
Milford (balance).............	51,271	51,857	1.1	51,506	85.9	1.9	5.1	1.9	5.3	19.9	63.3	16.7	20,536	77.5	31.8	43.0
Milford town (New Haven).	52,759	53,358	1.1	53,039	85.9	1.9	5.0	1.9	5.3	19.7	63.5	16.7	21,199	77.3	31.5	43.3
Monroe town (Fairfield).....	19,480	19,867	2.0	19,744	89.8	0.7	3.2	1.5	4.8	25.9	59.7	14.3	6,602	93.5	25.2	55.8
Montville town (New London)......	19,571	19,635	0.3	19,649	73.8	5.5	6.0	7.1	7.7	20.3	64.2	15.5	6,846	80.7	43.6	25.9
Moodus CDP.................	1,413	NA	NA	1,403	99.1	0.0	0.0	0.9	0.0	24.8	66.9	8.1	565	86.2	23.2	37.5
Moosup CDP	3,231	NA	NA	3,032	81.4	3.1	0.0	1.0	14.4	18.2	67.2	14.4	1,234	63.7	47.9	14.7
Morris town (Litchfield)	2,388	2,314	-3.1	2,289	96.9	0.3	0.3	0.2	2.2	20.2	64.0	15.8	925	84.8	26.3	38.6
Mystic CDP...................	4,205	NA	NA	3,905	94.1	0.7	0.7	2.6	1.9	11.9	58.3	29.8	1,953	62.5	15.1	64.8
Naugatuck borough & town (New Haven)........	31,884	31,659	-0.7	31,790	80.3	4.9	2.8	2.1	9.9	22.8	63.5	13.6	12,157	66.5	40.8	26.9

1 May be of any race.

Items 1–16

CT(Enfield town (Hartford))—CT(Naugatuck borough & town (New Haven)) 47

Table A. All Places — **Population and Housing**

STATE City, town, township, borough, or CDP (county if applicable)	2010 census total population	2014 estimated population	Percent change 2010–2014	ACS total population estimate 2010–2014	White alone, not Hispanic or Latino	Black alone, not Hispanic or Latino	Asian alone, not Hispanic or Latino	All other races or 2 or more races, not Hispanic or Latino	Hispanic or Latino[1]	Under 18 years old	Age 18 to 64 years old	Age 65 years and older	Total occupied housing units	Percent owner occupied	High school diploma or less	Bachelor's degree or more
	1	2	3	4	5	6	7	8	9	10	11	12	13	14	15	16
CONNECTICUT—Con.																
New Britain city & town (Hartford)...........	73,202	72,878	-0.4	73,095	46.5	9.8	3.0	2.5	38.1	23.1	65.0	12.0	27,820	40.3	52.7	18.9
New Canaan town (Fairfield)............	19,749	20,314	2.9	20,073	89.9	1.1	3.0	1.7	4.3	31.9	52.8	15.2	6,833	79.7	8.6	77.2
New Fairfield town (Fairfield)............	13,881	14,149	1.9	14,079	89.3	0.4	1.3	1.4	7.6	25.3	60.7	14.0	4,815	96.1	23.1	46.7
New Hartford town (Litchfield).........	6,970	6,812	-2.3	6,910	95.9	0.8	1.0	0.0	2.3	23.5	61.1	15.4	2,702	90.7	27.2	45.5
New Hartford Center CDP	1,385	NA	NA	1,509	90.5	0.3	0.0	0.0	9.1	19.0	72.1	8.9	721	85.3	32.6	23.0
New Haven city & town (New Haven)...........	129,890	130,282	0.3	130,553	32.2	33.6	5.0	3.1	26.0	22.0	67.8	10.2	49,945	29.5	43.4	35.6
Newington CDP & town (Hartford)...........	30,562	30,685	0.4	30,652	78.5	5.1	6.0	2.0	8.4	18.9	61.6	19.4	12,634	82.2	32.1	41.0
New London city & town (New London)............	27,620	27,374	-0.9	27,536	48.5	15.8	3.3	3.1	29.3	18.7	71.8	9.5	10,224	36.3	47.6	21.9
New Milford CDP............	6,523	NA	NA	6,568	76.7	6.0	1.2	2.8	13.2	21.2	66.2	12.6	2,767	56.8	46.4	24.5
New Milford town (Litchfield).........	28,142	27,474	-2.4	27,821	87.3	2.3	2.3	1.7	6.3	22.9	63.8	13.4	10,642	79.2	31.2	40.9
New Preston CDP	1,182	NA	NA	932	93.5	0.0	0.0	0.6	5.9	18.2	59.3	22.6	439	80.0	19.6	57.4
Newtown borough..........	1,934	1,969	1.8	2,027	89.9	0.2	1.4	1.1	7.4	29.2	59.2	11.6	707	87.0	11.0	66.8
Newtown town (Fairfield) ..	27,559	28,152	2.2	27,960	87.8	1.1	2.1	1.0	8.1	25.8	59.7	14.5	9,624	88.8	21.8	57.7
Niantic CDP....................	3,114	NA	NA	3,032	90.0	3.6	1.6	1.6	3.1	14.8	56.5	28.7	1,416	74.5	28.0	42.2
Noank CDP....................	1,796	NA	NA	2,100	88.1	1.4	0.0	6.7	3.8	19.5	56.6	23.9	907	73.2	19.7	56.3
Norfolk CDP....................	553	NA	NA	666	86.9	0.0	0.0	12.3	0.8	26.5	50.9	22.8	287	59.9	26.5	43.2
Norfolk town (Litchfield)	1,709	1,655	-3.2	1,486	91.7	0.9	1.4	5.7	0.3	21.7	54.8	23.6	635	72.6	29.9	41.1
North Branford town (New Haven)...........	14,407	14,322	-0.6	14,387	94.0	1.1	1.5	0.9	2.5	19.7	61.1	19.1	5,549	87.8	31.6	41.6
North Canaan town (Litchfield)	3,314	3,214	-3.0	3,262	90.8	1.2	4.4	0.4	3.1	16.5	60.3	23.1	1,298	76.8	58.0	22.4
North Granby CDP.............	1,944	NA	NA	1,786	77.0	1.3	0.0	7.5	14.2	27.9	63.1	9.0	603	96.7	29.5	59.4
North Grosvenor Dale CDP	1,530	NA	NA	1,614	94.8	0.0	0.0	2.4	2.8	22.1	67.5	10.4	613	44.2	51.5	13.2
North Haven CDP & town (New Haven)...........	24,088	23,909	-0.7	23,997	86.2	2.8	6.1	1.1	3.7	19.9	60.3	19.7	8,590	86.0	34.3	42.2
North Stonington town (New London)	5,297	5,288	-0.2	5,293	89.7	2.1	1.7	3.3	3.1	19.6	64.4	16.0	2,036	86.9	37.0	36.9
Northwest Harwinton CDP	3,252	NA	NA	3,186	99.3	0.1	0.0	0.0	0.6	20.7	59.9	19.4	1,199	92.8	38.1	38.1
Norwalk city & town (Fairfield)............	85,621	88,145	2.9	87,214	56.2	14.4	5.3	2.2	21.9	19.2	66.5	14.3	35,450	62.1	33.5	43.6
Norwich city & town (New London)............	40,493	40,178	-0.8	40,378	61.4	10.6	8.1	5.9	14.1	22.8	64.2	13.1	16,331	52.2	44.7	22.4
Oakville CDP..................	9,047	NA	NA	9,118	89.9	3.1	0.8	1.3	4.9	20.5	60.8	18.7	3,524	75.0	43.1	20.7
Old Greenwich CDP.........	6,611	NA	NA	6,520	82.2	0.5	8.9	2.3	6.1	35.8	52.9	11.4	2,135	87.2	5.3	87.0
Old Lyme town (New London)...................	7,603	7,575	-0.4	7,587	95.0	0.2	2.4	1.1	1.3	20.4	55.7	24.0	3,216	81.5	17.5	54.8
Old Mystic CDP..............	3,554	NA	NA	3,559	89.2	1.5	4.4	1.6	3.3	19.8	64.8	15.3	1,491	79.3	24.6	44.3
Old Saybrook town (Middlesex)	10,242	10,217	-0.2	10,222	92.6	1.0	3.8	1.3	1.3	21.1	52.0	26.9	4,217	84.1	21.6	48.4
Old Saybrook Center CDP	2,039	NA	NA	2,182	93.6	0.0	5.8	0.0	0.6	25.2	44.4	30.4	901	73.5	18.3	56.5
Orange CDP & town (New Haven)...........	13,956	13,955	NA	13,947	85.4	1.4	7.6	0.9	4.7	22.3	59.5	18.2	4,841	88.2	21.2	59.2
Oxford town (New Haven).	12,690	12,914	1.8	12,831	93.2	0.3	1.0	1.0	4.6	25.2	61.2	13.8	4,411	88.2	25.7	47.5
Oxoboxo River CDP	3,165	NA	NA	3,230	89.4	0.9	1.8	5.4	2.5	20.9	56.8	22.4	1,411	76.2	46.8	19.2
Pawcatuck CDP..............	5,624	NA	NA	5,428	86.7	2.3	3.0	2.6	5.4	24.4	57.4	18.1	2,266	59.8	43.2	33.6
Pemberwick CDP............	3,680	NA	NA	4,058	81.0	0.5	3.3	4.3	11.0	22.8	61.8	15.4	1,413	67.7	30.3	54.3
Plainfield town (Windham)	15,399	15,135	-1.7	15,270	90.5	1.9	1.0	3.0	3.6	22.0	63.5	14.4	5,730	74.6	53.4	16.0
Plainfield Village CDP.......	2,557	NA	NA	2,117	87.6	4.6	1.8	1.3	4.7	19.2	60.7	20.2	837	69.2	50.5	8.5
Plainville town (Hartford) ..	17,716	17,801	0.5	17,791	87.2	2.3	1.9	1.4	7.3	19.8	63.6	16.7	7,699	68.0	42.8	25.5
Plymouth town (Litchfield)	12,243	11,914	-2.7	12,085	93.1	1.1	0.1	1.3	4.4	21.3	66.1	12.7	4,711	81.3	43.3	21.2
Pomfret town (Windham) ..	4,247	4,179	-1.6	4,216	95.6	1.0	1.9	0.2	1.3	25.6	62.5	11.9	1,513	79.2	35.8	41.9
Poquonock Bridge CDP....	1,727	NA	NA	1,649	46.7	15.3	13.0	8.0	17.0	18.8	75.3	5.9	599	42.6	49.4	17.4
Portland town (Middlesex)	9,508	9,444	-0.7	9,483	94.4	0.2	0.6	1.7	3.1	19.8	62.6	17.5	3,955	82.1	35.0	37.1
Portland CDP..................	5,862	NA	NA	5,634	93.9	0.1	0.6	1.6	3.8	16.7	61.3	22.2	2,546	74.0	37.4	29.9
Preston town (New London)...................	4,726	4,748	0.5	4,735	80.7	2.2	7.7	6.3	3.1	17.4	64.5	18.1	1,978	80.2	40.5	30.2
Prospect town (New Haven)...................	9,423	9,723	3.2	9,615	92.7	3.1	0.7	0.4	3.1	19.6	63.2	17.2	3,256	91.1	32.5	37.6
Putnam CDP..................	7,214	NA	NA	7,249	91.7	0.6	0.4	3.2	4.2	24.6	61.2	14.2	3,030	50.6	46.2	14.9
Putnam town (Windham) ..	9,582	9,416	-1.7	9,515	93.2	0.5	0.4	2.5	3.3	22.9	61.0	16.1	3,870	59.8	45.6	18.5
Quinebaug CDP..............	1,133	NA	NA	974	93.9	0.0	0.0	0.0	6.1	15.7	64.5	19.9	454	85.7	50.9	22.9
Redding town (Fairfield)....	9,158	9,309	1.6	9,267	91.9	1.3	1.3	2.3	3.2	24.1	55.7	20.3	3,548	80.3	8.4	74.4
Ridgefield CDP................	7,645	NA	NA	7,599	91.0	0.6	0.9	2.1	5.9	29.2	54.9	15.9	3,034	71.4	10.8	69.7
Ridgefield town (Fairfield) .	24,634	25,205	2.3	25,025	90.7	0.6	2.0	1.5	5.2	30.2	56.3	13.5	8,801	83.2	9.6	74.1
Riverside CDP................	8,416	NA	NA	8,682	78.1	1.6	7.2	2.5	10.6	31.5	54.7	13.8	2,821	83.2	12.7	70.7
Rockville CDP................	7,474	NA	NA	7,348	74.0	10.1	2.2	5.2	8.5	20.8	68.2	11.0	3,381	28.0	44.3	18.9
Rocky Hill town (Hartford).	19,709	20,094	2.0	19,838	77.1	2.7	10.7	2.8	6.8	19.8	64.2	15.9	8,127	67.7	26.1	48.0
Roxbury town (Windham) ..	2,260	2,201	-2.6	2,273	96.3	0.0	0.4	0.4	2.9	18.7	58.6	22.6	945	83.0	16.7	55.7
Salem town (New London)	4,151	4,184	0.8	4,176	89.4	1.7	2.8	3.9	2.2	26.0	62.1	11.7	1,493	94.3	23.5	47.3
Salisbury town (Litchfield).	3,741	3,665	-2.0	3,708	90.1	3.1	1.1	2.0	3.7	17.9	57.3	24.8	1,499	73.2	17.5	59.4
Salmon Brook CDP	2,324	NA	NA	2,766	93.6	0.8	0.8	2.7	2.1	19.3	62.4	18.2	1,122	84.1	23.3	52.3
Saybrook Manor CDP.......	1,052	NA	NA	1,045	92.1	0.0	1.5	1.8	4.6	19.4	50.8	29.8	459	83.4	19.8	52.7
Scotland town (Windham)	1,726	1,694	-1.9	1,709	94.3	0.2	0.0	0.9	4.6	23.3	63.1	13.6	589	89.6	33.1	34.3
Seymour town (New Haven)...................	16,533	16,537	0.0	16,551	81.4	4.1	3.0	2.6	8.9	22.2	65.2	12.4	6,090	75.6	39.4	32.6
Sharon CDP	729	NA	NA	662	80.8	1.1	0.0	16.0	2.1	17.7	50.8	31.4	263	77.2	26.6	41.8
Sharon town (Litchfield)....	2,782	2,725	-2.0	2,746	90.9	0.3	2.2	6.2	0.5	12.8	55.9	31.2	1,261	84.0	30.0	42.8
Shelton city & town (Fairfield)............	39,559	41,295	4.4	40,472	89.6	1.0	3.3	0.5	5.5	19.8	61.9	18.4	15,186	79.9	31.0	41.2
Sherman town (Fairfield) ..	3,581	3,671	2.5	3,636	94.8	0.0	1.9	1.3	2.0	23.6	56.5	19.9	1,381	93.0	12.2	59.6
Sherwood Manor CDP.....	5,410	NA	NA	5,449	92.0	4.3	1.3	0.6	1.8	20.4	59.2	20.4	2,126	93.8	38.6	30.0
Simsbury town (Hartford)..	23,511	23,975	2.0	23,681	87.9	1.9	3.5	1.6	5.0	25.5	59.6	15.0	8,731	85.8	11.2	68.8

1 May be of any race.

Table A. All Places — **Population and Housing**

STATE City, town, township, borough, or CDP (county if applicable)	Population 2010 census total population	2014 estimated population	Percent change 2010–2014	ACS total population estimate 2010–2014	Race and Hispanic or Latino origin (percent), 2010–2014 White alone, not Hispanic or Latino	Black alone, not Hispanic or Latino	Asian alone, not Hispanic or Latino	All other races or 2 or more races, not Hispanic or Latino	Hispanic or Latino[1]	Age (percent), 2010–2014 Under 18 years old	Age 18 to 64 years old	Age 65 years and older	Households, 2010–2014 Total occupied housing units	Percent owner occupied	Householders by level of education (percent) High school diploma or less	Bachelor's degree or more
	1	2	3	4	5	6	7	8	9	10	11	12	13	14	15	16
CONNECTICUT—Con.																
Simsbury Center CDP	5,836	NA	NA	5,843	88.4	0.9	2.5	0.7	7.6	24.4	59.9	15.7	2,171	88.2	8.5	65.2
Somers CDP	1,789	NA	NA	1,733	97.7	2.0	0.0	0.0	0.3	23.2	57.5	19.2	648	86.0	30.6	24.5
Somers town (Tolland)	11,444	11,303	-1.2	11,431	82.2	7.6	2.5	1.4	6.3	18.2	68.1	13.6	3,326	85.9	31.7	35.2
Southbury town (New Haven)	19,904	19,881	-0.1	19,876	89.4	1.7	3.4	1.2	4.3	21.6	51.9	26.6	7,841	86.0	23.1	46.8
South Coventry CDP	1,483	NA	NA	1,036	98.0	0.0	0.9	1.2	0.0	18.6	63.6	17.7	482	60.6	26.8	41.1
Southington town (Hartford)	43,072	43,815	1.7	43,509	92.5	1.1	2.1	0.9	3.4	21.8	59.4	18.5	17,115	83.1	33.3	37.0
Southport CDP	1,585	NA	NA	1,711	91.1	1.2	2.7	4.4	0.5	18.9	57.5	23.8	728	76.1	8.5	73.1
South Windham CDP	1,421	NA	NA	1,603	76.5	1.1	0.0	8.5	13.8	18.0	65.5	16.5	556	94.2	49.8	11.3
South Windsor town (Hartford)	25,703	25,823	0.5	25,795	77.9	5.1	10.3	1.1	5.6	23.5	60.8	15.5	9,606	88.3	24.3	53.5
Southwood Acres CDP	7,657	NA	NA	8,060	93.9	3.2	0.2	0.7	2.1	19.4	62.7	17.8	3,013	89.4	45.2	25.7
South Woodstock CDP	1,291	NA	NA	1,150	95.8	2.9	0.0	0.0	1.3	22.7	59.9	17.5	541	63.8	44.2	21.1
Sprague town (New London)	2,984	2,980	-0.1	2,993	89.6	1.6	1.2	5.1	2.5	18.2	67.2	14.7	1,287	68.8	46.9	20.5
Stafford town (Tolland)	12,087	11,881	-1.7	12,013	94.3	0.4	1.7	1.3	2.3	21.2	66.5	12.2	4,721	73.5	44.4	22.3
Stafford Springs CDP	4,988	NA	NA	4,734	89.5	0.2	3.7	1.5	5.1	22.2	65.3	12.5	2,020	53.2	42.7	20.8
Stamford city & town (Fairfield)	122,630	128,278	4.6	125,401	49.9	13.1	8.4	1.6	27.0	21.8	65.7	12.6	46,418	54.8	29.3	49.4
Sterling town (Windham)	3,836	3,773	-1.6	3,809	94.6	1.1	0.4	2.9	1.0	27.7	64.9	7.5	1,208	85.0	47.8	11.8
Stonington borough	929	917	-1.3	1,066	96.8	0.7	0.4	1.2	0.9	11.4	64.5	24.1	547	57.2	14.3	69.8
Stonington town (New London)	18,545	18,512	-0.2	18,539	91.5	0.9	2.1	1.7	3.7	19.0	59.7	21.2	7,881	72.4	27.8	50.0
Storrs CDP	15,344	NA	NA	15,374	74.7	4.5	11.0	4.1	5.7	3.0	92.4	4.5	1,427	38.7	19.6	39.9
Stratford CDP & town (Fairfield)	51,384	52,734	2.6	52,092	66.1	14.4	2.9	2.4	14.1	19.8	62.0	18.1	20,330	80.6	39.7	32.1
Suffield town (Hartford)	15,735	15,814	0.5	15,764	79.6	10.0	1.7	2.5	6.2	19.8	66.0	14.2	4,822	86.1	25.5	48.1
Suffield Depot CDP	1,325	NA	NA	1,372	94.7	0.0	0.7	1.2	3.4	28.6	55.6	15.6	571	65.3	15.2	65.5
Tariffville CDP	1,324	NA	NA	1,371	85.6	5.0	1.6	3.4	4.4	23.2	65.6	11.2	627	72.6	33.0	50.9
Terramuggus CDP	1,025	NA	NA	837	87.5	0.0	0.0	6.6	6.0	16.6	65.5	18.0	351	92.6	16.8	61.5
Terryville CDP	5,387	NA	NA	5,121	95.2	0.0	0.0	2.0	2.8	19.4	69.8	10.8	2,158	72.2	43.7	18.0
Thomaston CDP	1,910	NA	NA	1,727	95.8	0.6	0.5	0.0	3.1	14.6	62.2	23.1	855	56.4	53.8	20.7
Thomaston town (Litchfield)	7,887	7,683	-2.6	7,793	93.7	0.6	0.6	2.9	2.3	20.3	65.6	14.1	3,000	80.5	41.8	26.7
Thompson town (Windham)	9,460	9,308	-1.6	9,390	95.8	0.4	0.4	1.8	1.6	19.7	65.5	14.9	3,673	80.5	43.5	23.7
Thompsonville CDP	8,577	NA	NA	9,021	64.3	5.7	6.1	2.8	21.0	22.5	65.7	11.7	3,491	36.2	49.0	21.7
Tolland town (Tolland)	15,052	14,872	-1.2	14,971	91.7	0.3	1.7	1.7	4.6	25.6	60.4	14.0	5,427	93.8	21.9	48.5
Torrington city & town (Litchfield)	36,383	35,190	-3.3	35,774	84.7	1.7	3.3	1.7	8.6	19.3	63.4	17.3	14,820	67.2	48.9	21.7
Trumbull CDP & town (Fairfield)	36,011	36,578	1.6	36,444	83.5	2.1	4.4	1.9	8.1	25.1	56.2	18.7	12,205	89.3	23.0	56.8
Union town (Tolland)	854	846	-0.9	950	94.2	0.4	0.0	1.4	4.0	22.8	59.5	17.6	338	93.8	42.0	33.4
Vernon town (Tolland)	29,179	29,098	-0.3	29,162	81.9	4.5	3.5	2.7	7.4	17.5	65.8	16.7	13,167	54.7	32.2	36.0
Voluntown town (New London)	2,603	2,593	-0.4	2,602	93.2	0.0	0.5	4.6	1.7	20.6	64.4	15.0	1,038	85.9	45.6	21.1
Wallingford town (New Haven)	45,135	45,074	-0.1	45,154	84.3	1.7	3.3	1.6	9.1	20.0	62.7	17.3	17,169	75.0	34.7	37.9
Wallingford Center CDP	18,209	NA	NA	17,824	79.2	1.4	2.6	1.5	15.3	18.5	65.6	15.7	7,258	60.3	39.5	34.1
Warren town (Litchfield)	1,461	1,427	-2.3	1,390	94.9	0.0	0.7	1.3	3.1	19.1	61.4	19.5	575	86.1	28.2	47.5
Washington town (Litchfield)	3,578	3,487	-2.5	3,529	90.4	0.0	1.1	0.6	7.9	14.5	60.1	25.2	1,545	78.4	23.2	54.0
Waterbury city & town (New Haven)	110,331	109,307	-0.9	109,887	42.1	17.9	1.7	4.0	34.2	25.0	63.0	12.1	40,960	46.7	53.5	16.7
Waterford CDP	2,887	NA	NA	2,994	87.0	1.9	3.5	3.8	3.9	20.5	55.6	23.9	1,286	79.3	43.0	24.9
Waterford town (New London)	19,517	19,427	-0.5	19,499	85.1	2.2	3.8	2.4	6.5	19.8	60.0	20.0	7,931	84.9	35.2	35.3
Watertown CDP	3,574	NA	NA	3,549	95.4	0.5	0.0	0.5	3.7	22.2	64.4	13.4	1,386	78.9	21.4	40.5
Watertown town (Litchfield)	22,528	22,046	-2.1	22,286	91.5	1.5	1.1	1.2	4.8	21.4	61.7	17.0	8,476	82.3	33.3	32.2
Wauregan CDP	1,205	NA	NA	1,210	84.6	3.8	0.0	11.6	0.0	30.6	65.2	4.2	427	43.6	59.7	11.0
Weatogue CDP	2,776	NA	NA	3,012	87.2	1.1	8.4	1.3	2.0	24.5	61.9	13.5	1,071	85.0	10.4	71.4
Westbrook town (Middlesex)	6,938	6,902	-0.5	6,916	92.1	0.4	0.2	2.2	5.1	15.7	65.0	19.2	2,733	79.6	39.7	33.4
Westbrook Center CDP	2,413	NA	NA	2,182	97.1	1.1	0.3	1.4	0.0	8.2	72.7	19.2	986	62.2	53.5	23.4
West Hartford CDP & town (Hartford)	63,268	63,324	0.1	63,396	74.4	6.8	6.6	2.4	9.9	22.6	60.1	17.2	24,910	72.2	20.4	62.1
West Haven city & town (New Haven)	55,564	54,905	-1.2	55,290	53.3	20.8	3.5	3.2	19.3	21.5	65.5	12.9	20,463	54.5	45.4	22.7
Weston town (Fairfield)	10,179	10,388	2.1	10,319	89.1	1.3	3.4	2.6	3.7	33.4	55.3	11.4	3,285	95.6	4.7	87.0
Westport CDP & town (Fairfield)	26,391	27,561	4.4	27,055	86.8	0.8	5.9	2.0	4.6	28.6	55.0	16.4	9,558	85.9	11.7	77.2
West Simsbury CDP	2,447	NA	NA	2,446	92.7	0.3	4.2	2.7	0.1	21.9	56.4	21.7	843	88.3	10.1	75.8
Wethersfield CDP & town (Hartford)	26,668	26,446	-0.8	26,579	80.4	3.3	3.9	1.9	10.6	19.9	59.2	21.0	10,853	79.0	28.6	43.7
Willimantic CDP	17,737	NA	NA	17,845	49.8	5.7	2.2	2.0	40.3	19.0	72.0	8.8	5,826	34.6	56.1	18.2
Willington town (Tolland)	6,035	5,934	-1.7	5,994	89.9	0.0	1.5	2.7	5.9	18.9	69.8	11.2	2,312	67.5	35.5	34.6
Wilton town (Fairfield)	18,044	18,692	3.6	18,519	88.5	0.8	6.4	1.9	2.4	31.4	55.2	13.5	5,963	87.4	6.5	79.4
Wilton Center CDP	732	NA	NA	676	89.1	0.0	3.7	2.7	4.6	17.7	56.3	26.2	377	43.0	14.9	60.5
Winchester town (Litchfield)	11,242	10,929	-2.8	11,089	85.2	1.3	2.6	2.1	8.8	18.6	62.2	19.0	4,819	60.5	42.1	21.6
Windham town (Windham)	25,268	25,005		25,271	55.8	4.7	1.9	2.7	34.9	19.1	69.5	11.6	8,920	47.3	54.2	18.5
Windsor town (Hartford)	29,044	29,069	0.1	29,130	48.0	36.9	3.8	3.2	8.1	21.7	62.6	15.7	10,796	81.8	27.1	41.5
Windsor Locks CDP & town (Hartford)	12,498	12,565	0.5	12,554	81.5	4.4	7.3	2.5	4.4	17.9	65.4	16.7	5,224	78.6	41.0	27.5
Winsted CDP	7,712	NA	NA	7,876	82.3	1.5	1.8	2.5	12.0	19.9	60.4	19.6	3,384	50.9	46.0	19.4
Wolcott town (New Haven)	16,695	16,716	0.1	16,724	89.9	1.7	1.6	0.6	6.2	21.4	62.5	16.2	5,827	88.4	40.5	30.9
Woodbridge town (New Haven)	8,990	8,925	-0.7	8,969	83.1	1.0	12.1	0.9	3.0	23.8	56.1	20.0	3,090	90.6	15.3	67.0
Woodbury town (Litchfield)	9,977	9,719	-2.6	9,851	91.6	0.2	3.0	0.7	4.4	21.3	61.5	17.1	4,096	76.7	26.6	49.8

1 May be of any race.

Table A. All Places — **Population and Housing**

STATE City, town, township, borough, or CDP (county if applicable)	Population: 2010 census total population	Population: 2014 estimated population	Population: Percent change 2010–2014	Population: ACS total population estimate 2010–2014	Race and Hispanic or Latino origin (percent), 2010–2014: White alone, not Hispanic or Latino	Black alone, not Hispanic or Latino	Asian alone, not Hispanic or Latino	All other races or 2 or more races, not Hispanic or Latino	Hispanic or Latino[1]	Age (percent), 2010–2014: Under 18 years old	Age 18 to 64 years old	Age 65 years and older	Households, 2010–2014: Total occupied housing units	Percent owner occupied	Householders by level of education (percent): High school diploma or less	Bachelor's degree or more
	1	2	3	4	5	6	7	8	9	10	11	12	13	14	15	16
CONNECTICUT—Con.																
Woodbury Center CDP	1,294	NA	NA	1,421	77.7	0.0	17.9	0.0	4.4	22.6	62.6	14.7	662	41.2	25.1	49.4
Woodmont borough	1,488	1,501	0.9	1,530	87.8	2.2	1.3	2.1	6.7	15.6	66.2	18.1	663	70.4	22.6	50.8
Woodstock town (Windham)	7,964	7,860	-1.3	7,916	94.1	0.4	0.2	1.8	3.5	23.7	59.5	16.8	3,169	84.0	30.8	43.0
DELAWARE	897,936	935,614	4.2	917,060	64.4	21.1	3.4	2.6	8.6	22.3	62.3	15.4	339,046	71.6	38.5	32.2
Arden village	439	448	2.1	516	90.5	1.6	1.2	6.2	0.6	14.3	64.5	21.1	251	62.5	31.5	47.0
Ardencroft village	231	234	1.3	221	84.6	7.2	5.9	0.0	2.3	9.6	72.8	17.6	91	72.5	24.2	41.8
Ardentown village	264	271	2.7	289	87.5	2.1	0.0	8.3	2.1	15.2	64.5	20.4	150	66.0	12.0	58.0
Bear CDP	19,371	NA	NA	19,732	39.1	36.5	5.8	3.2	15.5	25.7	66.9	7.3	6,806	68.5	42.8	26.3
Bellefonte town	1,193	1,191	-0.2	1,400	92.1	2.4	2.0	1.1	2.4	18.0	72.5	9.4	569	83.7	32.9	41.8
Bethany Beach town	1,057	1,142	8.0	890	94.5	0.0	1.9	2.5	1.1	6.0	40.9	53.1	447	83.0	22.6	59.5
Bethel town	171	183	7.0	179	96.1	0.0	0.0	1.7	2.2	17.4	44.1	38.5	74	95.9	32.4	35.1
Blades town	1,240	1,323	6.7	1,335	47.3	28.5	0.7	6.5	17.0	26.4	61.1	12.6	452	55.1	65.0	8.2
Bowers town	333	354	6.3	272	88.6	4.8	0.0	2.2	4.4	12.5	70.8	16.5	120	68.3	37.5	31.7
Bridgeville town	2,050	2,205	7.6	2,359	57.6	20.9	0.5	1.0	20.0	20.9	51.0	28.2	965	70.3	45.4	24.4
Brookside CDP	14,353	NA	NA	13,585	61.6	21.5	4.1	3.6	9.1	21.2	65.9	12.9	5,095	64.9	42.0	25.4
Camden town	3,458	3,517	1.7	3,504	65.5	20.8	4.3	6.5	2.8	27.6	55.3	17.2	1,208	80.7	28.9	33.7
Cheswold town	1,364	1,420	4.1	1,307	45.1	38.2	3.5	9.0	4.1	23.6	61.0	15.5	424	91.3	53.8	16.3
Claymont CDP	8,253	NA	NA	9,242	63.3	25.9	3.4	2.8	4.6	24.9	62.2	13.1	3,579	63.4	41.1	24.4
Clayton town	2,912	3,073	5.5	2,989	65.1	27.9	0.0	2.1	4.9	30.3	61.0	8.8	893	81.0	48.6	21.5
Dagsboro town	780	839	7.6	939	69.0	5.9	0.0	10.9	14.3	28.1	58.3	13.5	355	58.3	32.4	23.4
Delaware City city	1,695	1,731	2.1	1,858	81.0	10.8	0.0	3.0	5.2	23.6	68.0	8.5	662	74.6	50.8	14.5
Delmar town	1,594	1,693	6.2	1,606	72.2	15.3	1.1	5.5	6.0	22.2	57.8	20.0	568	59.2	54.0	17.1
Dewey Beach town	336	363	8.0	254	96.9	0.0	0.4	0.0	2.8	3.5	56.7	39.8	142	82.4	16.9	54.9
Dover city	35,934	37,355	4.0	36,826	43.9	41.6	2.2	4.0	8.3	21.8	63.7	14.4	12,680	51.4	33.5	29.9
Dover Base Housing CDP	3,450	NA	NA	3,390	68.1	10.5	1.9	6.3	13.2	39.7	59.8	0.7	1,065	0.0	15.1	19.7
Edgemoor CDP	5,677	NA	NA	6,089	58.4	25.0	1.1	8.5	7.1	22.4	64.6	13.0	2,539	63.1	27.6	34.1
Ellendale town	381	404	6.0	335	58.8	29.3	0.0	1.8	10.1	28.1	58.5	13.7	105	67.6	66.7	7.6
Elsmere town	6,131	6,152	0.3	6,149	59.0	8.6	0.2	2.1	30.1	22.5	66.6	10.9	2,143	62.6	61.9	17.4
Farmington town	110	115	4.5	88	100.0	0.0	0.0	0.0	0.0	34.0	60.3	5.7	28	53.6	85.7	0.0
Felton town	1,298	1,386	6.8	1,519	75.6	18.1	0.0	1.3	5.0	27.9	63.4	8.8	534	65.4	47.2	21.7
Fenwick Island town	377	406	7.7	370	98.1	0.0	1.9	0.0	0.0	3.0	43.2	53.8	207	96.6	26.1	51.2
Frankford town	846	911	7.7	912	25.5	34.5	0.3	4.1	35.5	32.8	53.9	13.5	227	68.3	64.3	10.6
Frederica town	769	816	6.1	1,085	48.9	39.4	0.0	4.2	7.4	23.2	62.6	14.3	345	79.7	55.1	11.0
Georgetown town	6,422	6,891	7.3	6,650	38.2	12.3	0.1	2.8	46.6	28.3	60.3	11.3	1,623	48.4	55.7	18.1
Glasgow CDP	14,303	NA	NA	14,962	63.2	23.2	5.6	1.9	6.2	23.9	67.5	8.6	5,030	84.2	31.3	34.7
Greenville CDP	2,326	NA	NA	2,286	85.0	2.0	11.1	0.7	1.3	21.1	55.1	23.9	1,090	54.2	17.5	64.6
Greenwood town	973	1,045	7.4	1,182	61.1	18.2	0.0	4.8	15.9	23.2	64.1	12.8	416	49.5	56.0	13.2
Harrington city	3,550	3,704	4.3	3,643	63.9	22.4	3.0	5.9	4.8	27.6	60.0	12.5	1,355	45.8	40.4	20.1
Hartly town	70	71	1.4	48	100.0	0.0	0.0	0.0	0.0	23.0	68.8	8.3	20	90.0	45.0	45.0
Henlopen Acres town	122	132	8.2	133	100.0	0.0	0.0	0.0	0.0	3.8	32.4	63.9	70	94.3	8.6	71.4
Highland Acres CDP	3,459	NA	NA	3,962	75.3	13.0	4.0	6.4	1.3	26.2	57.7	16.1	1,338	78.6	31.3	43.6
Hockessin CDP	13,527	NA	NA	13,620	81.6	3.3	11.7	1.7	1.7	24.3	56.4	19.2	4,749	91.9	11.3	70.0
Houston town	366	388	6.0	391	77.5	4.9	9.2	2.3	6.1	17.4	70.3	12.3	130	84.6	56.2	10.8
Kent Acres CDP	1,890	NA	NA	1,828	58.6	16.5	10.2	9.7	5.0	28.1	60.4	11.7	645	86.5	35.0	32.1
Kenton town	248	263	6.0	242	68.6	2.9	0.0	3.3	25.2	42.1	54.7	3.3	72	58.3	75.0	0.0
Laurel town	3,705	3,983	7.5	3,842	42.5	41.1	0.0	5.5	10.9	33.7	57.7	8.5	1,222	56.1	58.0	11.3
Leipsic town	183	195	6.6	108	96.3	0.0	0.9	2.8	0.0	19.5	53.0	27.8	57	70.2	61.4	8.8
Lewes city	2,739	2,943	7.4	2,840	86.1	8.5	2.2	1.4	1.9	10.3	48.5	41.3	1,347	79.2	27.1	56.5
Little Creek town	218	232	6.4	211	90.5	0.0	0.0	0.0	9.5	22.3	65.0	12.8	74	78.4	47.3	5.4
Long Neck CDP	1,980	NA	NA	2,119	86.5	9.0	0.2	2.1	2.3	12.6	45.9	41.4	1,096	84.4	48.3	17.6
Magnolia town	219	233	6.4	198	78.3	19.2	0.0	0.5	2.0	17.7	67.7	14.6	78	71.8	51.3	14.1
Middletown town	18,871	19,910	5.5	19,469	61.7	26.5	3.4	3.2	5.2	32.7	56.5	10.8	6,263	79.5	28.9	40.1
Milford city	9,573	10,179	6.3	9,882	60.2	21.9	1.5	1.9	14.5	24.2	57.1	18.6	3,720	62.6	49.9	22.1
Millsboro town	3,864	4,120	6.6	3,987	73.0	19.6	0.6	5.7	1.1	21.6	58.8	19.6	1,687	51.0	45.7	19.8
Millville town	538	576	7.1	974	84.3	1.8	0.7	11.7	1.4	23.2	57.4	19.4	347	81.8	31.7	39.8
Milton town	2,571	2,759	7.3	2,656	73.0	16.9	0.4	1.1	8.7	18.8	61.1	20.1	1,096	60.9	44.6	35.9
Newark city	31,513	33,008	4.7	32,278	76.0	9.1	7.5	2.0	5.4	10.9	78.1	10.9	9,691	55.0	18.3	49.9
New Castle city	5,285	5,379	1.8	5,346	58.7	23.4	1.0	2.3	14.6	18.6	64.7	16.7	2,271	66.6	40.1	30.1
Newport town	1,055	1,060	0.5	1,064	53.3	13.6	1.9	5.5	25.7	23.4	65.7	10.7	425	40.5	50.1	17.2
North Star CDP	7,980	NA	NA	7,655	85.8	2.0	7.7	1.1	3.5	23.3	62.3	14.4	2,688	98.6	10.3	74.7
Ocean View town	1,839	1,986	8.0	1,776	90.5	0.1	3.4	1.9	4.2	7.6	46.2	46.3	829	92.5	27.7	44.8
Odessa town	364	374	2.7	643	82.6	5.9	0.0	4.5	7.0	16.9	61.4	21.9	235	77.0	25.5	34.9
Pike Creek CDP	7,898	NA	NA	8,142	73.2	6.3	13.8	0.8	5.9	22.5	64.4	13.0	3,145	89.8	11.0	66.7
Pike Creek Valley CDP	11,217	NA	NA	10,509	75.1	10.7	4.3	1.5	8.4	15.8	69.5	14.6	4,860	65.1	20.7	50.0
Rehoboth Beach city	1,323	1,424	7.6	1,082	98.5	0.0	0.5	1.0	0.0	1.9	55.6	42.4	579	85.8	10.0	71.3
Rising Sun-Lebanon CDP	3,391	NA	NA	3,597	62.7	19.8	0.5	10.4	6.6	24.0	66.2	9.8	1,286	57.7	30.6	33.8
Riverview CDP	2,456	NA	NA	2,761	81.5	11.3	0.6	5.8	0.8	27.2	60.3	12.6	887	94.9	34.9	27.2
Rodney Village CDP	1,487	NA	NA	1,320	45.8	39.3	7.5	5.8	1.6	12.5	71.4	15.9	523	62.9	30.0	36.1
St. Georges CDP	0	NA	NA	1,312	81.5	11.7	0.0	0.0	6.9	27.3	60.5	12.3	442	90.7	55.4	22.9
Seaford city	6,896	7,417	7.6	7,163	48.8	43.8	0.5	1.4	5.5	27.7	52.9	19.3	2,689	43.7	53.8	16.0
Selbyville town	2,182	2,342	7.3	2,535	55.6	5.4	0.3	3.2	35.5	31.6	55.7	12.7	827	63.8	50.8	16.6
Slaughter Beach town	207	225	8.7	177	96.6	0.0	0.6	2.8	0.0	6.2	67.8	26.0	98	75.5	25.5	48.0
Smyrna town	10,001	11,170	11.7	10,681	65.2	26.1	1.3	3.2	4.1	29.1	57.5	13.3	4,001	65.3	40.3	23.5
South Bethany town	449	485	8.0	393	93.9	0.0	0.0	2.5	3.6	3.0	36.1	60.8	223	95.5	21.5	63.2
Townsend town	2,049	2,109	2.9	2,556	60.1	31.0	0.5	4.9	3.5	39.4	56.0	4.5	645	89.3	23.6	45.7
Viola town	157	167	6.4	178	92.1	0.0	1.1	2.8	3.9	14.0	74.3	11.8	58	91.4	32.8	32.8
Wilmington city	70,852	71,817	1.4	71,263	28.9	54.6	1.1	1.8	13.6	23.5	64.1	12.4	29,085	46.4	46.5	28.7
Wilmington Manor CDP	7,889	NA	NA	8,049	59.1	14.4	0.3	2.8	23.4	24.8	62.3	13.0	2,856	81.5	57.4	14.0
Woodside town	181	194	7.2	124	90.3	2.4	0.0	4.8	2.4	17.0	68.6	14.5	47	66.0	63.8	6.4
Woodside East CDP	2,316	NA	NA	2,140	52.1	39.1	0.0	4.1	4.8	23.6	68.9	7.5	733	65.2	63.2	7.1
Wyoming town	1,312	1,442	9.9	1,628	70.2	23.9	0.2	2.1	3.6	24.0	66.1	9.9	583	70.0	29.5	30.4
DISTRICT OF COLUMBIA	601,767	658,893	9.5	633,736	35.4	48.7	3.6	2.5	9.9	17.0	71.7	11.3	267,415	41.6	25.7	56.8
Washington city	601,767	658,893	9.5	633,736	35.4	48.7	3.6	2.5	9.9	17.0	71.7	11.3	267,415	41.6	25.7	56.8
FLORIDA	18,804,623	19,893,297	5.8	19,361,792	56.6	15.4	2.5	2.2	23.3	20.8	61.1	18.2	7,217,508	66.1	37.6	30.0
Acacia Villas CDP	427	NA	NA	614	8.0	19.5	0.0	0.0	72.5	44.2	53.5	2.3	179	24.6	43.0	0.0

1 May be of any race.

Table A. All Places — **Population and Housing**

STATE City, town, township, borough, or CDP (county if applicable)	Population				Race and Hispanic or Latino origin (percent), 2010–2014					Age (percent), 2010–2014			Households, 2010–2014			
	2010 census total population	2014 estimated population	Percent change 2010–2014	ACS total population estimate 2010–2014	White alone, not Hispanic or Latino	Black alone, not Hispanic or Latino	Asian alone, not Hispanic or Latino	All other races or 2 or more races, not Hispanic or Latino	Hispanic or Latino[1]	Under 18 years old	Age 18 to 64 years old	Age 65 years and older	Total occupied housing units	Percent owner occupied	Householders by level of education (percent): High school diploma or less	Householders by level of education (percent): Bachelor's degree or more
	1	2	3	4	5	6	7	8	9	10	11	12	13	14	15	16
FLORIDA—Con.																
Alachua city	9,058	9,561	5.6	9,291	67.7	14.8	1.4	5.2	10.8	23.5	60.3	16.3	4,142	68.9	25.0	37.8
Alafaya CDP	78,113	NA	NA	85,561	44.4	7.7	7.9	3.0	36.9	26.8	66.4	6.8	27,930	62.8	19.3	42.4
Alford town	489	469	-4.1	487	96.1	0.0	0.0	0.8	3.1	23.9	60.9	15.2	188	77.1	60.6	9.6
Allentown CDP	894	NA	NA	990	82.8	0.0	0.6	10.6	6.0	19.2	62.7	18.3	382	90.8	34.3	10.7
Altamonte Springs city	41,499	42,225	1.7	41,889	57.9	14.0	2.7	2.0	23.4	17.0	68.2	14.8	16,481	49.0	26.4	39.4
Altha town	536	529	-1.3	619	92.7	1.8	0.0	2.6	2.9	26.8	62.7	10.5	216	67.1	50.5	11.6
Altoona CDP	89	NA	NA	103	100.0	0.0	0.0	0.0	0.0	39.8	50.5	9.7	37	48.6	67.6	0.0
Alturas CDP	4,185	NA	NA	3,948	80.9	0.5	0.0	0.1	18.5	20.4	64.8	14.9	1,284	83.3	59.7	11.1
Alva CDP	2,596	NA	NA	2,040	92.0	0.0	2.6	0.0	5.4	11.2	55.4	33.5	826	82.3	43.2	19.7
Andrews CDP	798	NA	NA	1,198	97.8	0.7	0.0	1.5	0.0	21.0	67.3	11.5	396	80.3	64.9	7.3
Anna Maria city	1,503	1,626	8.2	1,219	99.8	0.0	0.0	0.0	0.2	5.4	50.3	44.3	601	84.7	31.4	35.8
Apalachicola city	2,231	2,276	2.0	2,129	64.0	33.2	0.0	0.0	2.8	23.9	54.1	22.2	939	66.3	46.6	24.4
Apollo Beach CDP	14,055	NA	NA	15,648	78.1	6.1	3.5	2.0	10.4	21.6	63.7	14.8	6,019	79.6	24.7	35.4
Apopka city	41,671	47,084	13.0	44,462	45.7	19.9	3.6	3.7	27.1	25.9	62.3	11.8	14,819	76.3	33.0	28.6
Arcadia city	7,626	7,722	1.3	7,647	42.4	28.4	1.3	0.8	27.1	26.4	60.8	12.7	2,374	62.0	67.0	10.4
Archer city	1,118	1,158	3.6	1,105	62.8	32.2	0.4	2.3	2.4	34.0	53.0	13.0	401	62.8	45.1	9.2
Aripeka CDP	308	NA	NA	152	100.0	0.0	0.0	0.0	0.0	21.8	62.4	15.8	73	82.2	74.0	26.0
Asbury Lake CDP	8,700	NA	NA	8,165	78.8	4.1	1.7	2.3	13.2	26.9	61.1	11.8	2,908	92.8	35.7	28.0
Astatula town	1,809	1,867	3.2	1,736	75.3	0.7	1.6	2.2	20.2	25.4	57.2	17.4	590	85.9	57.8	9.8
Astor CDP	1,556	NA	NA	1,444	76.9	0.0	1.6	2.3	19.2	11.2	53.9	34.8	569	82.1	62.0	10.4
Atlantic Beach city	12,655	13,031	3.0	12,840	80.0	8.2	2.2	1.2	8.4	18.0	65.6	16.3	5,421	62.6	25.0	49.4
Atlantis city	2,005	2,083	3.9	2,063	89.9	3.0	0.8	0.0	6.3	13.5	36.3	50.2	919	93.1	18.8	55.6
Auburndale city	13,502	14,518	7.5	13,979	70.1	12.1	0.6	0.9	16.3	27.3	60.2	12.4	4,633	65.8	55.0	14.5
Aucilla CDP	100	NA	NA	106	67.0	33.0	0.0	0.0	0.0	26.5	41.5	32.1	37	59.5	83.8	0.0
Avalon CDP	679	NA	NA	620	82.1	0.0	14.8	3.1	0.0	20.3	65.6	14.2	255	83.1	27.1	16.1
Aventura city	35,762	37,451	4.7	36,979	59.6	2.9	0.9	0.9	35.6	18.1	52.6	29.4	18,102	67.8	21.4	51.8
Avon Park city	8,879	8,879	0.0	8,874	34.7	34.0	0.6	0.4	30.3	27.8	56.5	15.8	2,827	60.5	55.3	12.5
Azalea Park CDP	12,556	NA	NA	13,203	23.9	4.7	5.0	1.6	64.8	22.5	66.7	10.9	4,537	50.0	51.6	15.6
Babson Park CDP	1,356	NA	NA	1,240	60.7	18.7	3.5	6.3	10.8	19.0	67.0	14.2	317	76.7	42.6	14.8
Bagdad CDP	3,761	NA	NA	3,827	75.2	6.6	3.3	8.5	6.4	24.3	56.4	19.4	1,455	75.2	35.5	22.3
Baldwin town	1,425	1,440	1.1	1,822	69.4	20.7	0.0	3.6	6.3	28.3	58.8	12.7	613	58.2	61.0	3.4
Bal Harbour village	2,514	2,633	4.7	2,605	50.2	0.0	0.3	1.2	48.2	18.2	46.7	35.0	1,412	64.9	19.5	47.2
Balm CDP	1,457	NA	NA	1,688	47.0	23.2	9.1	4.5	16.2	29.8	60.6	9.6	505	90.7	43.6	18.4
Bardmoor CDP	9,732	NA	NA	9,635	84.1	6.4	2.6	2.4	4.3	19.6	61.7	18.6	3,858	81.0	37.1	29.8
Bartow city	17,298	18,420	6.5	17,766	63.0	24.4	0.5	1.3	10.9	27.5	57.7	14.7	5,847	63.7	52.0	16.8
Bascom town	121	118	-2.5	118	98.3	1.7	0.0	0.0	0.0	23.7	50.8	25.4	40	85.0	52.5	20.0
Bay Harbor Islands town	5,628	6,007	6.7	5,847	48.0	5.3	0.9	2.8	43.1	23.3	59.6	17.1	2,590	45.5	29.0	47.1
Bay Hill CDP	4,884	NA	NA	5,704	75.6	4.1	10.5	3.2	6.6	21.1	64.1	14.9	1,993	85.0	11.0	63.6
Bay Lake city	47	49	4.3	14	100.0	0.0	0.0	0.0	0.0	7.1	49.9	42.9	6	100.0	33.3	33.3
Bayonet Point CDP	23,467	NA	NA	24,412	85.1	1.9	0.5	1.7	10.8	16.9	51.7	31.3	10,982	71.7	53.6	12.3
Bay Pines CDP	2,931	NA	NA	3,061	91.7	0.5	3.9	0.9	3.0	13.6	60.6	25.8	1,322	87.9	37.0	23.1
Bayport CDP	43	NA	NA	352	100.0	0.0	0.0	0.0	0.0	22.4	69.7	8.0	104	14.4	73.1	26.9
Bayshore Gardens CDP	16,323	NA	NA	17,899	65.1	8.1	3.1	3.7	20.0	17.7	56.1	26.2	7,363	61.1	55.3	12.9
Beacon Square CDP	7,224	NA	NA	6,645	86.2	1.7	1.4	1.2	9.6	20.7	56.3	23.1	2,661	71.1	55.2	11.8
Bear Creek CDP	1,948	NA	NA	1,757	86.2	6.3	4.6	0.0	3.0	7.9	61.0	31.1	912	75.0	29.1	37.2
Bee Ridge CDP	9,598	NA	NA	9,796	91.4	1.3	0.3	0.3	6.8	15.9	49.7	34.2	4,462	74.7	32.3	35.2
Bell town	456	454	-0.4	557	94.6	1.3	0.0	1.6	2.5	30.3	60.8	9.0	190	52.6	67.9	8.9
Bellair-Meadowbrook Terrace CDP	13,343	NA	NA	13,578	60.2	15.7	3.0	4.4	16.7	21.1	64.3	14.8	5,336	46.9	36.8	15.1
Belleair town	3,869	3,949	2.1	3,903	91.0	1.2	2.4	0.0	5.4	21.2	50.3	28.6	1,735	83.1	15.0	54.2
Belleair Beach city	1,560	1,591	2.0	1,705	95.0	0.0	1.9	0.0	3.0	14.8	49.8	35.4	741	86.1	25.1	48.2
Belleair Bluffs city	2,031	2,071	2.0	2,098	93.5	2.3	1.0	0.9	2.3	9.6	58.2	32.4	1,136	69.0	26.0	37.7
Belleair Shore town	109	111	1.8	61	88.5	0.0	6.6	0.0	4.9	8.2	44.3	47.5	31	100.0	12.9	64.5
Belle Glade city	17,461	18,061	3.4	17,785	11.3	56.1	0.4	0.4	31.7	27.4	60.7	12.0	5,590	42.6	70.4	10.6
Belle Isle city	5,988	6,528	9.0	6,265	78.3	2.5	7.7	1.7	9.8	16.8	67.6	15.6	2,252	83.3	20.2	47.1
Belleview city	4,533	4,681	3.3	4,585	79.4	5.1	0.0	4.5	10.9	25.6	54.2	20.3	1,866	52.1	61.9	22.1
Bellview CDP	23,355	NA	NA	22,759	68.3	18.3	4.8	4.5	4.1	23.2	61.7	15.0	8,780	71.9	35.6	18.7
Berrydale CDP	441	NA	NA	326	69.9	21.5	0.0	5.2	3.4	8.7	80.7	10.7	81	81.5	58.0	42.0
Beverly Beach town	338	347	2.7	377	100.0	0.0	0.0	0.0	0.0	2.4	35.8	61.8	207	75.8	43.0	30.9
Beverly Hills CDP	8,445	NA	NA	8,518	82.7	2.9	0.9	1.0	12.5	17.2	51.0	31.9	4,046	66.5	54.3	11.4
Big Coppitt Key CDP	2,458	NA	NA	2,397	65.8	4.4	0.7	0.7	28.3	19.0	66.8	14.1	913	72.7	29.7	22.8
Big Pine Key CDP	4,252	NA	NA	4,511	79.4	1.3	0.5	3.4	15.5	10.2	65.7	24.1	1,798	74.9	36.2	24.6
Biscayne Park village	3,074	3,204	4.2	3,172	41.9	9.5	0.9	0.0	47.8	22.4	61.4	16.1	1,204	64.9	21.1	44.0
Bithlo CDP	8,268	NA	NA	8,486	63.4	7.7	3.2	3.7	22.1	28.1	64.2	7.7	2,659	77.4	45.4	32.9
Black Diamond CDP	1,101	NA	NA	924	98.9	0.0	0.0	0.0	1.1	14.6	50.1	35.3	318	66.7	11.3	81.4
Black Hammock CDP	1,144	NA	NA	922	89.0	1.0	0.0	2.0	8.0	10.5	66.6	22.9	382	92.1	28.8	33.5
Bloomingdale CDP	22,711	NA	NA	22,879	69.2	7.8	2.9	5.3	14.9	25.0	63.4	11.7	7,727	77.3	20.1	47.4
Blountstown city	2,505	2,497	-0.3	2,557	60.3	29.1	1.4	2.1	7.2	19.7	55.6	24.6	900	70.0	57.0	11.9
Boca Raton city	84,401	91,332	8.2	88,187	78.5	4.6	2.4	2.3	12.2	16.9	60.9	22.1	36,507	68.9	17.7	54.5
Bokeelia CDP	1,780	NA	NA	1,242	100.0	0.0	0.0	0.0	0.0	6.4	45.4	48.3	529	87.5	27.2	42.5
Bonifay city	2,805	2,761	-1.6	2,774	80.1	12.8	0.0	3.1	4.0	24.4	56.9	18.8	963	50.9	57.1	17.3
Bonita Springs city	43,832	49,299	12.5	46,384	69.4	0.8	1.5	0.8	27.5	14.8	51.6	33.6	18,761	74.2	35.6	36.8
Boulevard Gardens CDP	1,274	NA	NA	1,800	1.3	98.7	0.0	0.0	0.0	12.1	58.3	29.6	505	44.2	56.6	11.5
Bowling Green city	2,930	2,909	-0.7	2,925	25.4	7.5	0.3	0.5	66.3	32.3	54.4	13.2	740	69.1	77.3	7.2
Boynton Beach city	68,215	73,124	7.2	70,355	52.2	31.8	2.2	1.6	12.2	18.5	60.2	21.2	28,493	64.3	36.0	27.4
Bradenton city	49,283	52,769	7.1	50,777	62.3	16.6	0.9	1.3	18.8	20.8	56.8	22.4	20,483	53.2	46.6	24.1
Bradenton Beach city	1,171	1,219	4.1	1,142	94.2	0.4	0.3	1.7	3.4	12.2	51.4	36.3	636	62.9	40.7	32.9
Bradley Junction CDP	686	NA	NA	494	52.6	26.3	0.0	1.2	19.8	14.0	59.1	27.1	175	66.9	74.3	0.0
Brandon CDP	103,483	NA	NA	106,604	53.1	15.1	3.5	4.0	24.3	22.3	67.6	10.2	39,748	56.6	31.2	31.2
Branford town	712	723	1.5	1,184	54.6	23.6	0.0	7.4	14.3	25.5	65.1	9.3	339	46.0	59.3	8.0
Brent CDP	21,804	NA	NA	22,175	49.7	36.4	3.9	4.1	5.9	18.6	70.2	11.4	6,779	51.9	49.0	15.6
Briny Breezes town	601	601	0.0	753	98.7	0.0	0.0	0.3	1.1	0.3	23.6	76.1	458	91.5	31.0	45.6
Bristol city	998	972	-2.6	965	76.6	3.4	3.8	2.0	14.2	21.4	56.2	22.2	285	72.6	58.6	13.7
Broadview Park CDP	7,125	NA	NA	7,175	20.8	13.1	1.8	2.2	62.1	22.2	71.4	6.2	2,072	59.0	62.2	12.5
Bronson town	1,113	1,105	-0.7	1,125	57.2	25.4	3.1	5.0	9.2	22.5	62.5	15.2	418	77.3	46.7	16.3
Brooker town	338	332	-1.8	344	78.8	6.1	0.6	7.6	7.0	18.9	66.7	14.5	108	80.6	57.4	6.5
Brookridge CDP	4,420	NA	NA	4,750	89.8	1.6	0.0	0.0	8.7	11.0	37.2	51.9	2,390	89.1	51.5	9.9
Brooksville city	7,719	7,778	0.8	7,725	72.1	19.5	0.1	2.8	5.6	19.1	56.4	24.5	3,020	57.3	49.8	13.6
Brownsdale CDP	471	NA	NA	557	100.0	0.0	0.0	0.0	0.0	19.7	70.3	9.9	215	100.0	60.5	23.7
Brownsville CDP	15,313	NA	NA	14,835	2.0	71.6	0.0	0.1	26.3	27.4	60.0	12.5	4,664	37.0	71.7	7.1
Buckhead Ridge CDP	1,450	NA	NA	1,747	92.9	0.0	0.8	0.7	5.6	10.3	42.5	47.3	684	80.3	64.6	10.2

1 May be of any race.

Table A. All Places — **Population and Housing**

STATE City, town, township, borough, or CDP (county if applicable)	Population: 2010 census total population	Population: 2014 estimated population	Population: Percent change 2010–2014	Population: ACS total population estimate 2010–2014	Race and Hispanic or Latino origin (percent), 2010–2014: White alone, not Hispanic or Latino	Black alone, not Hispanic or Latino	Asian alone, not Hispanic or Latino	All other races or 2 or more races, not Hispanic or Latino	Hispanic or Latino[1]	Age (percent), 2010–2014: Under 18 years old	Age 18 to 64 years old	Age 65 years and older	Households, 2010–2014: Total occupied housing units	Percent owner occupied	Householders by level of education (percent): High school diploma or less	Bachelor's degree or more
	1	2	3	4	5	6	7	8	9	10	11	12	13	14	15	16
FLORIDA—Con.																
Buckingham CDP	4,036	NA	NA	4,142	95.4	0.2	0.0	0.0	4.4	19.6	65.6	14.8	1,480	73.1	44.4	26.4
Buenaventura Lakes CDP	26,079	NA	NA	30,324	14.8	9.7	2.3	2.5	70.6	25.1	63.0	11.7	8,415	69.0	49.4	13.9
Bunnell city	2,678	2,778	3.7	2,715	70.3	23.5	0.0	3.5	2.7	20.0	60.5	19.4	985	59.3	59.8	13.0
Burnt Store Marina CDP	1,793	NA	NA	1,799	99.4	0.0	0.0	0.0	0.6	0.4	27.8	71.8	942	97.7	17.3	54.9
Bushnell city	3,003	3,047	1.5	3,026	70.0	10.9	0.4	4.0	14.7	22.6	46.8	30.5	1,134	73.8	55.7	10.6
Butler Beach CDP	4,951	NA	NA	5,709	96.0	0.1	0.4	0.3	3.3	8.6	55.1	36.3	2,717	75.6	27.2	48.1
Cabana Colony CDP	2,391	NA	NA	2,103	75.8	0.0	14.6	1.4	8.2	26.4	60.0	13.7	834	69.7	53.7	14.1
Callahan town	1,123	1,177	4.8	1,187	93.0	5.3	0.0	0.5	1.2	27.7	60.5	11.8	513	47.2	52.4	16.6
Callaway city	14,336	15,006	4.7	14,617	66.2	15.6	4.9	7.1	6.2	25.3	60.0	14.9	5,159	62.2	38.4	13.1
Campbell CDP	2,479	NA	NA	2,705	81.3	1.6	1.6	0.0	15.6	10.0	36.0	54.2	1,307	56.9	44.0	22.3
Campbellton town	230	221	-3.9	187	52.9	47.1	0.0	0.0	0.0	10.1	71.0	18.7	85	81.2	36.5	15.3
Canal Point CDP	367	NA	NA	324	46.0	21.0	0.0	0.0	33.0	28.3	49.9	21.6	113	88.5	66.4	0.0
Cape Canaveral city	9,945	10,049	1.0	9,960	88.5	2.6	0.2	2.0	6.7	8.8	60.7	30.6	5,865	53.8	31.4	27.9
Cape Coral city	154,301	169,854	10.1	161,804	74.2	4.0	1.6	1.6	18.6	22.4	58.5	19.0	57,643	69.4	40.8	23.5
Captiva CDP	583	NA	NA	154	91.6	8.4	0.0	0.0	0.0	7.8	74.5	17.5	23	78.3	0.0	78.3
Carrabelle city	2,772	2,814	1.5	2,790	67.9	23.9	0.3	0.7	7.2	8.5	77.5	13.8	748	63.2	56.4	12.7
Carrollwood CDP	33,365	NA	NA	34,254	56.4	9.5	4.6	2.9	26.6	19.7	65.0	15.4	13,860	69.1	22.0	46.0
Caryville town	411	277	-32.6	382	76.2	21.5	0.0	2.4	0.0	25.1	65.0	9.9	83	61.4	68.7	9.6
Casselberry city	26,264	26,707	1.7	26,520	64.3	8.4	2.6	2.3	22.4	19.9	65.4	14.6	10,496	61.8	35.9	23.6
Cedar Grove CDP	3,397	NA	NA	3,257	52.4	35.5	0.5	4.2	7.4	23.9	63.8	12.2	1,219	55.2	55.2	12.6
Cedar Key city	705	698	-1.0	691	96.7	0.0	0.0	3.3	0.0	7.8	48.0	44.3	367	73.0	36.8	40.9
Celebration CDP	7,427	NA	NA	7,111	87.5	1.4	2.5	1.4	7.1	25.1	61.3	13.6	2,534	67.6	15.9	64.8
Center Hill city	988	1,143	15.7	1,385	33.5	8.4	0.0	1.2	56.8	36.3	51.3	12.4	378	66.9	67.5	8.7
Century town	1,698	1,752	3.2	1,488	38.6	56.5	0.2	4.7	0.1	16.6	63.7	19.6	654	57.2	67.7	8.9
Charleston Park CDP	218	NA	NA	274	14.2	82.8	0.0	0.0	2.9	13.1	17.1	69.7	54	85.2	85.2	0.0
Charlotte Harbor CDP	3,714	NA	NA	3,969	76.3	12.4	1.1	1.8	8.4	14.3	47.6	38.1	1,804	46.2	35.0	25.6
Charlotte Park CDP	2,325	NA	NA	2,243	91.6	0.0	3.2	5.2	0.0	8.2	39.5	52.3	1,129	90.8	44.4	13.3
Chattahoochee city	3,648	3,157	-13.5	3,342	47.7	47.0	0.0	0.9	4.5	15.0	72.8	12.3	917	54.5	46.8	24.8
Cheval CDP	10,702	NA	NA	10,992	68.5	2.6	8.5	1.5	18.9	27.8	61.4	10.7	4,292	51.1	21.2	42.7
Chiefland city	2,245	2,206	-1.7	2,301	61.7	33.3	0.0	2.0	3.0	27.2	58.8	14.1	906	36.3	68.3	6.8
Chipley city	3,605	3,520	-2.4	3,581	62.7	33.5	0.0	2.4	1.4	22.1	55.4	22.4	1,344	56.0	49.1	16.1
Chokoloskee CDP	359	NA	NA	421	100.0	0.0	0.0	0.0	0.0	45.6	43.5	10.9	147	60.5	3.4	46.3
Christmas CDP	1,146	NA	NA	2,188	91.0	0.0	0.0	0.0	9.0	11.7	76.0	12.2	792	90.5	52.5	23.1
Chuluota CDP	2,483	NA	NA	2,302	87.7	1.5	0.0	0.6	10.3	23.7	66.9	9.4	750	84.4	39.5	34.7
Chumuckla CDP	850	NA	NA	786	96.6	0.0	0.0	3.4	0.0	15.6	64.1	20.2	330	94.8	50.0	20.9
Cinco Bayou town	383	414	8.1	362	71.3	15.2	3.0	0.0	10.5	18.8	58.8	22.4	193	42.5	24.9	52.8
Citrus Hills CDP	7,470	NA	NA	8,191	81.8	5.5	6.3	1.6	4.9	7.4	41.0	51.5	3,741	90.7	27.2	38.2
Citrus Park CDP	24,252	NA	NA	25,329	51.7	5.7	3.4	5.5	33.6	24.2	65.1	10.6	8,989	68.3	33.4	34.3
Citrus Springs CDP	8,622	NA	NA	8,545	82.5	5.7	1.0	1.1	9.7	20.5	57.8	21.6	3,375	82.0	40.2	17.6
Clarcona CDP	2,990	NA	NA	2,926	78.3	6.3	1.1	6.6	7.7	16.1	64.8	19.1	1,276	73.1	56.1	13.4
Clearwater city	108,334	110,703	2.2	109,210	71.6	10.4	2.6	2.2	13.2	18.4	60.4	21.3	47,015	59.1	37.1	29.9
Clermont city	28,740	30,600	6.5	29,582	55.5	13.2	3.9	4.8	22.6	25.6	54.5	19.8	10,678	70.9	27.8	33.3
Cleveland CDP	2,990	NA	NA	2,933	85.2	0.0	0.0	3.4	11.4	13.0	47.5	39.4	1,253	77.1	52.9	7.4
Clewiston city	7,155	7,376	3.1	7,184	32.3	8.6	1.5	1.5	56.1	32.5	57.4	10.1	2,326	70.2	52.8	22.3
Cloud Lake town	135	143	5.9	93	59.1	2.2	0.0	0.0	38.7	11.9	62.4	25.8	45	51.1	40.0	20.0
Cobbtown CDP	67	NA	NA	44	100.0	0.0	0.0	0.0	0.0	22.7	77.3	0.0	17	41.2	41.2	0.0
Cocoa city	17,134	17,419	1.7	17,261	52.4	30.6	0.4	4.1	12.6	23.5	60.0	16.5	7,130	53.8	45.6	16.7
Cocoa Beach city	11,231	11,400	1.5	11,287	95.2	0.5	0.6	1.9	1.7	10.7	54.3	34.9	5,735	66.8	21.9	42.1
Cocoa West CDP	5,925	NA	NA	4,802	41.0	49.6	0.3	0.0	9.1	22.7	60.8	16.6	1,945	51.8	56.2	8.6
Coconut Creek city	52,934	58,536	10.6	55,590	56.8	12.9	4.4	2.5	23.4	22.4	59.7	18.0	22,067	65.4	32.1	35.7
Coleman city	694	838	20.7	648	61.4	33.5	0.0	0.3	4.8	11.6	69.6	18.8	284	76.8	74.6	3.5
Combee Settlement CDP	5,577	NA	NA	5,899	73.1	14.1	0.9	3.2	8.7	23.8	63.6	12.6	2,014	58.0	66.8	9.6
Connerton CDP	2,116	NA	NA	3,001	84.0	6.8	1.5	0.4	7.3	8.9	89.0	2.1	277	80.5	26.7	43.7
Conway CDP	13,467	NA	NA	15,382	72.9	2.2	1.1	2.4	21.4	21.8	64.7	13.6	5,552	76.1	29.6	30.0
Cooper City city	28,548	34,923	22.3	32,058	58.7	5.5	6.4	2.3	27.2	24.8	65.3	9.7	10,508	85.9	18.0	46.9
Coral Gables city	46,776	51,227	9.5	49,319	39.2	3.4	2.5	1.1	53.8	17.7	66.1	16.1	17,599	64.2	12.0	66.5
Coral Springs city	121,098	127,952	5.7	125,150	48.1	20.3	4.0	3.1	24.5	26.0	65.0	9.0	40,554	62.9	27.2	37.9
Coral Terrace CDP	24,376	NA	NA	25,318	10.1	0.9	0.7	0.3	88.1	18.2	60.6	21.3	7,469	67.7	51.1	24.3
Cortez CDP	4,241	NA	NA	4,114	93.0	0.4	1.4	0.0	5.1	8.5	45.6	45.8	2,128	79.5	34.3	37.9
Cottondale town	933	902	-3.3	739	67.4	21.5	0.0	2.0	9.1	29.6	57.3	13.1	276	48.6	62.7	6.5
Country Club CDP	47,105	NA	NA	48,349	9.3	10.1	1.7	0.3	78.5	24.9	65.2	9.7	15,435	53.0	37.0	28.7
Country Walk CDP	15,997	NA	NA	17,156	20.6	8.9	5.2	2.3	63.1	26.7	63.1	10.3	4,715	88.7	24.8	38.3
Crawfordville CDP	3,702	NA	NA	3,790	80.7	7.2	3.3	4.9	4.0	27.1	59.5	13.4	1,370	79.9	33.6	22.0
Crescent Beach CDP	931	NA	NA	884	91.4	0.0	0.0	0.5	8.1	4.2	52.0	43.7	496	64.9	25.6	36.9
Crescent City city	1,577	1,543	-2.2	1,935	49.6	26.0	1.7	6.5	16.2	16.9	58.9	24.1	759	64.8	52.6	12.5
Crestview city	20,980	22,955	9.4	22,099	64.0	20.2	2.3	6.1	7.3	26.5	65.3	8.2	7,862	60.8	32.0	19.5
Crooked Lake Park CDP	1,722	NA	NA	1,526	80.5	5.0	0.0	3.5	11.0	20.1	56.8	23.1	616	83.3	53.1	20.5
Cross City town	1,737	1,692	-2.6	2,159	64.0	33.5	0.0	2.5	0.0	27.0	55.7	17.3	794	61.6	71.4	3.8
Crystal Lake CDP	5,514	NA	NA	6,049	47.0	21.0	2.0	3.0	27.1	26.5	62.4	11.1	2,051	52.0	58.7	9.8
Crystal River city	3,098	3,054	-1.4	3,072	71.0	8.8	12.2	3.2	4.9	21.9	46.6	31.5	1,199	64.5	46.4	23.2
Crystal Springs CDP	1,327	NA	NA	923	87.5	0.0	0.0	0.8	11.7	19.6	57.5	22.9	367	73.3	57.8	19.1
Cudjoe Key CDP	1,763	NA	NA	1,703	90.1	0.7	0.3	0.7	8.2	8.8	56.3	34.8	858	78.9	22.5	50.1
Cutler Bay town	40,286	44,321	10.0	42,573	32.8	12.1	1.7	2.1	51.4	25.2	63.6	11.2	12,873	74.9	30.9	36.9
Cypress Gardens CDP	8,917	NA	NA	8,918	84.3	2.6	2.1	1.4	9.6	18.4	56.8	24.8	3,560	83.3	33.7	32.8
Cypress Lake CDP	11,846	NA	NA	12,177	88.9	1.3	0.2	1.1	8.5	10.4	47.9	41.8	5,937	69.3	35.9	30.6
Cypress Quarters CDP	1,215	NA	NA	869	29.5	66.9	0.0	1.7	2.0	27.3	58.6	14.3	294	62.2	59.5	14.6
Dade City city	6,444	6,750	4.7	6,548	56.0	21.9	0.3	0.9	20.9	20.5	57.9	21.5	2,522	53.2	52.3	17.4
Dade City North CDP	3,113	NA	NA	2,491	18.9	11.8	1.0	1.3	66.9	26.2	62.8	11.1	795	47.5	47.3	16.0
Dania Beach city	29,639	31,117	5.0	30,531	50.9	23.3	1.9	2.0	21.8	20.7	64.4	14.9	11,986	54.1	43.2	24.0
Davenport city	2,899	3,228	11.3	3,022	43.7	18.2	0.9	0.6	36.7	22.6	57.5	20.0	944	83.1	60.4	11.9
Davie town	91,992	98,895	7.5	95,721	51.8	8.8	5.1	2.1	32.1	23.0	65.5	11.5	33,170	72.0	31.0	35.7
Day CDP	116	NA	NA	178	100.0	0.0	0.0	0.0	0.0	6.8	93.2	0.0	55	70.9	41.8	5.5
Daytona Beach city	61,005	63,011	3.3	61,913	52.9	33.7	2.9	2.8	7.7	15.6	65.2	19.1	25,775	46.8	40.4	20.2
Daytona Beach Shores city	4,253	4,319	1.6	4,278	94.2	0.5	2.9	0.0	2.4	4.0	44.7	51.1	2,408	66.3	28.2	45.5
DeBary city	19,315	19,648	1.7	19,404	81.7	3.7	1.9	1.3	11.5	18.0	59.2	22.7	7,852	85.5	37.3	29.6
Deerfield Beach city	75,018	78,881	5.1	77,341	54.7	24.2	1.6	2.5	17.0	18.9	58.6	22.3	31,667	62.8	45.8	26.1
DeFuniak Springs city	5,162	5,601	8.5	5,410	63.3	20.0	0.0	2.3	14.5	22.2	53.7	24.1	2,113	66.4	52.4	20.5
DeLand city	26,957	29,194	8.3	27,872	64.1	15.6	3.0	2.6	14.8	22.6	56.8	20.5	10,079	55.4	39.4	25.4
DeLand Southwest CDP	1,052	NA	NA	988	19.4	66.2	0.7	7.0	6.7	26.2	59.8	14.0	375	32.0	58.4	0.0
De Leon Springs CDP	2,614	NA	NA	3,639	44.7	1.0	0.0	27.9	26.3	23.4	59.7	17.0	867	83.6	49.5	17.5

1 May be of any race.

Table A. All Places — **Population and Housing**

STATE City, town, township, borough, or CDP (county if applicable)	Population: 2010 census total population	Population: 2014 estimated population	Population: Percent change 2010–2014	Population: ACS total population estimate 2010–2014	Race and Hispanic or Latino origin (percent), 2010–2014: White alone, not Hispanic or Latino	Black alone, not Hispanic or Latino	Asian alone, not Hispanic or Latino	All other races or 2 or more races, not Hispanic or Latino	Hispanic or Latino[1]	Age (percent), 2010–2014: Under 18 years old	Age 18 to 64 years old	Age 65 years and older	Households, 2010–2014: Total occupied housing units	Percent owner occupied	Householders by level of education (percent): High school diploma or less	Bachelor's degree or more
	1	2	3	4	5	6	7	8	9	10	11	12	13	14	15	16
FLORIDA—Con.																
Delray Beach city	60,601	65,055	7.3	62,828	57.7	27.2	2.0	1.7	11.4	15.7	61.2	23.0	26,554	63.9	32.1	38.8
Deltona city	85,182	86,890	2.0	85,765	56.8	9.6	0.9	2.0	30.7	24.2	60.8	15.1	28,949	78.0	47.1	16.1
Desoto Lakes CDP	3,646	NA	NA	3,624	71.4	2.8	6.8	1.1	17.9	23.0	55.2	21.9	1,369	74.5	33.0	33.5
Destin city	12,305	13,355	8.5	12,840	87.9	0.8	1.0	3.8	6.6	16.8	65.9	17.3	5,544	68.6	29.5	39.7
Dickerson City CDP	146	NA	NA	79	100.0	0.0	0.0	0.0	0.0	0.0	0.0	100.0	79	36.7	0.0	19.0
Dixonville CDP	181	NA	NA	171	93.6	0.0	0.0	6.4	0.0	0.0	60.9	39.2	96	89.6	76.0	10.4
Doctor Phillips CDP	10,981	NA	NA	12,028	55.7	6.7	17.7	3.4	16.6	20.7	64.2	15.1	4,094	79.3	19.2	54.7
Doral city	45,709	54,116	18.4	49,363	14.2	1.3	3.8	1.0	79.7	30.2	63.3	6.2	14,507	54.6	18.8	59.6
Dover CDP	3,702	NA	NA	4,284	23.9	3.0	0.0	0.9	72.2	32.4	59.6	7.9	1,077	46.3	79.3	3.4
Duck Key CDP	621	NA	NA	621	87.8	5.2	0.0	0.0	7.1	8.8	59.8	31.4	271	80.8	27.7	30.6
Dundee town	3,717	3,976	7.0	3,833	69.0	12.5	0.7	5.8	12.1	23.1	59.3	17.5	1,499	67.6	45.9	9.8
Dunedin city	35,356	35,819	1.3	35,538	86.3	3.3	1.8	1.5	7.1	15.6	55.6	28.9	16,548	62.5	33.4	31.4
Dunnellon city	1,733	1,762	1.7	1,686	84.0	9.3	1.6	2.8	2.3	12.2	48.2	39.6	946	67.0	57.9	19.0
Eagle Lake city	2,255	2,417	7.2	2,590	68.6	6.6	1.2	2.8	20.8	29.5	56.4	14.1	911	67.7	53.8	9.7
East Bronson CDP	1,945	NA	NA	2,109	71.1	5.6	0.0	1.8	21.4	19.1	62.1	18.9	722	92.1	48.8	7.3
East Lake CDP	30,962	NA	NA	32,335	87.5	1.0	2.9	2.1	6.5	19.4	58.0	22.4	13,189	78.9	23.4	46.7
East Lake-Orient Park CDP	22,753	NA	NA	23,995	34.3	36.3	5.2	4.4	19.8	26.1	65.8	8.1	9,109	48.9	49.3	18.3
East Milton CDP	11,074	NA	NA	11,337	68.2	17.6	0.2	6.3	7.8	17.9	71.7	10.3	2,774	76.0	42.9	16.4
East Palatka CDP	1,654	NA	NA	1,883	78.7	19.5	0.0	0.0	1.9	22.4	62.9	14.7	524	84.4	48.7	21.9
Eastpoint CDP	2,337	NA	NA	1,953	93.5	2.0	0.0	0.0	4.5	22.9	59.3	18.0	756	77.2	68.8	7.4
East Williston CDP	694	NA	NA	529	16.4	81.9	0.0	1.7	0.0	11.7	72.8	15.5	176	77.8	66.5	0.0
Eatonville town	2,159	2,251	4.3	2,258	16.9	72.2	0.0	3.0	7.9	23.4	63.6	12.8	591	51.8	53.8	10.7
Ebro town	270	267	-1.1	266	92.9	0.8	0.0	4.1	2.3	30.9	55.3	13.9	92	63.0	65.2	10.9
Edgewater city	20,759	21,121	1.7	20,879	90.0	3.6	1.1	1.8	3.5	16.2	59.7	24.0	8,476	81.5	41.0	18.1
Edgewood city	2,503	2,728	9.0	2,624	64.1	14.3	7.0	2.4	12.2	21.2	64.5	14.3	1,028	85.4	21.2	46.5
Eglin AFB CDP	2,274	NA	NA	2,417	73.8	5.2	3.1	3.6	14.2	30.7	52.3	17.0	929	0.3	30.4	11.4
Egypt Lake-Leto CDP	35,282	NA	NA	36,735	26.6	7.9	5.0	1.0	59.4	21.0	66.3	12.7	13,266	42.8	48.9	18.5
Elfers CDP	13,986	NA	NA	14,301	79.0	3.7	3.9	1.3	12.2	20.7	59.9	19.5	5,584	69.6	56.5	10.8
Ellenton CDP	4,275	NA	NA	3,314	86.4	4.4	0.0	0.0	9.2	9.5	60.0	30.6	1,439	67.0	38.3	32.0
El Portal village	2,325	2,409	3.6	2,404	21.6	53.7	2.7	2.2	19.8	18.2	65.6	16.3	819	66.4	39.7	32.2
Englewood CDP	14,863	NA	NA	14,366	94.4	0.3	1.2	0.4	3.6	7.4	42.3	50.3	7,440	79.2	42.8	26.9
Ensley CDP	20,602	NA	NA	20,784	59.2	30.5	3.4	3.4	3.5	22.8	61.1	16.2	8,271	64.4	38.4	18.1
Estero CDP	22,612	NA	NA	22,649	87.4	3.1	2.2	0.6	6.7	11.3	46.5	42.2	10,562	84.9	25.0	47.0
Esto town	364	359	-1.4	326	88.0	4.9	0.0	1.8	5.2	24.3	60.4	15.3	104	77.9	56.7	5.8
Eustis city	18,490	19,455	5.2	18,920	68.6	16.9	2.6	2.3	9.6	21.6	55.7	22.6	7,394	63.4	47.6	18.1
Everglades city	400	410	2.5	327	98.8	0.0	0.3	0.0	0.9	21.2	52.4	26.6	121	90.1	47.9	33.9
Fairview Shores CDP	10,239	NA	NA	10,457	61.6	15.4	1.9	3.3	17.9	20.6	66.3	13.1	4,196	53.8	36.2	27.0
Fanning Springs city	988	974	-1.4	1,109	86.3	5.2	1.3	3.7	3.5	21.7	51.7	26.4	404	61.4	51.5	16.1
Feather Sound CDP	3,420	NA	NA	3,235	78.0	0.9	13.2	1.6	6.2	15.6	69.7	14.6	1,698	57.1	13.2	61.8
Fellsmere city	5,209	5,439	4.4	5,312	10.8	0.8	0.0	0.2	88.2	27.4	67.9	4.8	1,279	50.0	81.6	3.6
Fernandina Beach city	11,583	12,103	4.5	11,851	73.3	14.3	2.5	1.7	8.1	16.5	57.6	25.9	5,156	67.5	26.6	41.5
Ferndale CDP	472	NA	NA	277	57.8	0.0	0.0	0.0	42.2	11.6	65.7	22.7	137	71.5	38.7	0.0
Fern Park CDP	7,704	NA	NA	8,123	77.6	6.0	1.4	0.8	14.2	18.8	65.1	16.3	3,234	73.8	28.7	35.8
Ferry Pass CDP	28,921	NA	NA	31,204	71.9	16.2	1.8	4.2	5.9	19.2	64.8	16.1	12,726	45.5	25.2	30.0
Fidelis CDP	156	NA	NA	51	100.0	0.0	0.0	0.0	0.0	0.0	80.4	19.6	19	100.0	100.0	0.0
Fisher Island CDP	132	NA	NA	240	0.0	0.0	0.0	0.0	100.0	63.4	36.6	0.0	44	100.0	100.0	0.0
Fish Hawk CDP	14,087	NA	NA	15,823	79.1	3.4	2.5	2.4	12.6	36.5	57.3	6.2	4,836	84.3	12.0	61.8
Five Points CDP	1,265	NA	NA	673	86.8	6.4	0.0	0.0	6.8	5.9	81.9	12.0	305	64.9	63.9	8.9
Flagler Beach city	4,484	4,747	5.9	4,595	96.0	1.0	0.0	0.0	3.0	12.8	56.8	30.4	1,932	74.2	36.9	37.8
Flagler Estates CDP	3,215	NA	NA	2,739	91.0	0.8	0.0	0.8	7.4	25.2	65.8	8.8	910	93.2	55.2	16.4
Fleming Island CDP	27,126	NA	NA	29,656	84.3	3.1	2.8	2.9	6.9	26.5	60.2	13.3	10,033	80.2	18.3	49.8
Floral City CDP	5,217	NA	NA	4,883	92.1	0.9	0.0	1.7	5.3	12.6	52.5	34.8	2,271	84.6	49.7	16.5
Florida City city	11,245	12,062	7.3	11,853	7.0	47.9	0.0	2.5	42.6	33.6	59.3	7.2	2,745	29.2	69.1	5.6
Florida Ridge CDP	18,164	NA	NA	18,056	62.8	20.5	2.7	2.3	11.6	20.0	56.5	23.6	6,995	74.8	44.1	21.0
Floridatown CDP	244	NA	NA	267	90.3	6.7	3.0	0.0	0.0	7.1	84.2	8.6	105	66.7	43.8	39.0
Forest City CDP	13,854	NA	NA	14,724	60.5	7.3	4.2	2.6	25.3	26.4	62.1	11.3	4,728	61.0	32.4	29.1
Fort Denaud CDP	1,694	NA	NA	1,499	81.6	0.0	0.0	0.0	18.4	10.1	61.2	28.4	551	96.6	62.1	10.5
Fort Green CDP	101	NA	NA	118	100.0	0.0	0.0	0.0	0.0	2.5	97.5	0.0	37	89.2	56.8	10.8
Fort Green Springs CDP	231	NA	NA	292	100.0	0.0	0.0	0.0	0.0	27.1	71.3	1.7	92	62.0	27.2	19.6
Fort Lauderdale city	165,578	176,013	6.3	171,137	50.0	31.1	1.2	2.0	15.6	17.7	65.9	16.4	73,279	52.9	33.2	38.2
Fort Meade city	5,653	5,869	3.8	5,745	54.6	14.8	0.6	0.6	29.4	25.4	56.7	17.9	1,840	69.0	63.0	9.7
Fort Myers city	62,202	70,918	14.0	66,167	47.6	28.8	1.7	1.4	20.5	21.6	61.2	17.3	23,847	47.1	41.3	28.6
Fort Myers Beach town	6,277	6,811	8.5	6,539	94.8	0.9	0.4	1.3	2.6	4.0	47.4	48.7	3,556	77.2	26.9	41.0
Fort Myers Shores CDP	5,487	NA	NA	5,420	70.7	2.8	0.2	1.9	24.4	20.1	62.4	17.5	2,012	63.1	59.7	11.5
Fort Pierce city	41,853	43,601	4.2	42,744	40.6	37.2	0.4	0.5	21.3	25.1	58.8	16.1	16,283	45.3	55.9	14.5
Fort Pierce North CDP	6,474	NA	NA	6,901	18.3	67.1	0.0	2.8	11.8	24.3	60.4	15.3	2,346	65.7	68.4	8.0
Fort Pierce South CDP	5,062	NA	NA	4,887	56.0	19.8	0.0	1.2	22.9	18.0	66.8	15.2	1,851	69.9	59.3	20.4
Fort Walton Beach city	19,516	21,558	10.5	20,320	71.6	13.6	2.9	3.3	8.6	21.4	62.3	16.4	8,103	58.2	33.4	25.9
Fort White town	565	563	-0.4	682	73.8	22.0	0.0	1.2	3.1	33.3	53.0	13.6	222	70.3	49.1	11.7
Fountainebleau CDP	59,764	NA	NA	53,413	4.7	0.9	1.4	0.5	92.5	17.4	65.7	16.8	17,926	53.7	41.6	30.0
Four Corners CDP	26,116	NA	NA	32,154	52.1	9.5	3.1	3.7	31.6	23.9	63.3	12.7	11,129	53.8	33.5	28.7
Franklin Park CDP	860	NA	NA	1,000	0.0	98.0	0.0	0.0	2.0	33.7	64.0	2.3	371	14.3	50.1	1.9
Freeport city	1,775	1,985	11.8	2,119	85.7	1.3	0.6	5.8	6.6	27.5	61.0	11.6	750	64.3	41.9	17.5
Frostproof city	2,991	3,083	3.1	3,030	69.4	2.8	0.0	3.4	24.4	20.9	59.7	19.4	1,041	88.7	59.7	9.8
Fruit Cove CDP	29,362	NA	NA	30,770	85.2	3.3	2.8	2.3	6.4	27.0	61.6	11.4	9,928	86.3	14.3	54.6
Fruitland Park city	4,146	4,386	5.8	4,275	70.2	19.9	0.0	3.8	6.1	30.8	56.3	12.9	1,459	60.9	51.6	9.1
Fruitville CDP	13,224	NA	NA	13,462	86.1	1.7	2.3	1.3	8.5	18.7	60.2	21.0	5,610	65.1	32.7	31.7
Fuller Heights CDP	8,758	NA	NA	9,198	68.3	7.6	0.9	1.3	22.0	22.7	64.9	12.2	3,184	78.8	40.9	34.7
Fussels Corner CDP	5,561	NA	NA	5,152	88.2	2.3	0.0	1.5	8.0	14.2	45.7	40.1	2,222	80.7	52.9	17.2
Gainesville city	124,486	128,460	3.2	126,465	57.3	22.7	6.7	3.2	10.1	12.7	78.9	8.5	47,420	38.0	20.5	42.2
Garcon Point CDP	347	NA	NA	522	100.0	0.0	0.0	0.0	0.0	29.1	66.1	4.8	197	100.0	7.6	65.0
Garden Grove CDP	674	NA	NA	617	92.7	7.3	0.0	0.0	0.0	8.6	56.0	35.3	362	68.8	35.1	24.6
Gardner CDP	463	NA	NA	321	98.1	0.0	0.0	1.9	0.0	4.7	19.9	75.4	186	96.2	51.1	24.2
Gateway CDP	8,401	NA	NA	8,226	83.6	2.5	3.1	0.5	10.3	25.3	57.5	17.1	2,971	79.5	20.2	42.8
Geneva CDP	2,940	NA	NA	2,380	83.6	0.0	5.5	4.0	6.9	20.4	58.8	21.0	758	92.3	32.8	43.3
Gibsonton CDP	14,234	NA	NA	15,893	48.4	16.8	3.4	2.0	29.4	31.3	61.7	7.0	4,930	65.5	47.1	13.8
Gifford CDP	9,590	NA	NA	9,169	42.7	41.9	1.7	1.1	12.7	22.4	49.3	28.3	3,877	53.4	43.3	27.8
Gladeview CDP	11,535	NA	NA	11,825	0.7	76.1	0.1	0.8	22.3	31.5	59.2	9.3	3,498	36.6	70.6	6.6
Glencoe CDP	2,582	NA	NA	2,896	96.8	1.1	0.0	0.0	2.0	21.0	68.3	10.7	1,124	81.9	54.1	18.2
Glen Ridge town	219	231	5.5	199	71.4	0.0	1.5	0.0	27.1	18.6	69.7	11.6	71	84.5	35.2	16.9

1 May be of any race.

Table A. All Places — **Population and Housing**

STATE City, town, township, borough, or CDP (county if applicable)	Population				Race and Hispanic or Latino origin (percent), 2010–2014					Age (percent), 2010–2014			Households, 2010–2014			
	2010 census total population	2014 estimated population	Percent change 2010–2014	ACS total population estimate 2010–2014	White alone, not Hispanic or Latino	Black alone, not Hispanic or Latino	Asian alone, not Hispanic or Latino	All other races or 2 or more races, not Hispanic or Latino	Hispanic or Latino[1]	Under 18 years old	Age 18 to 64 years old	Age 65 years and older	Total occupied housing units	Percent owner occupied	Householders by level of education (percent): High school diploma or less	Householders by level of education (percent): Bachelor's degree or more
	1	2	3	4	5	6	7	8	9	10	11	12	13	14	15	16
FLORIDA—Con.																
Glen St. Mary town	439	435	-0.9	531	78.0	4.7	0.2	0.6	16.6	39.8	54.5	5.6	162	46.9	61.1	8.6
Glenvar Heights CDP	16,898	NA	NA	18,899	24.7	1.7	3.3	2.4	67.8	17.1	67.4	15.4	7,298	53.5	21.8	53.5
Golden Beach town	919	966	5.1	653	66.2	0.0	0.9	0.2	32.8	32.0	57.6	10.3	176	95.5	11.9	72.7
Golden Gate CDP	23,961	NA	NA	28,917	20.1	14.7	0.4	1.5	63.2	29.6	63.2	7.1	6,855	50.1	67.2	12.8
Golden Glades CDP	33,145	NA	NA	33,620	7.6	68.8	2.4	1.3	19.9	23.9	64.7	11.5	9,124	54.8	53.1	16.9
Goldenrod CDP	12,039	NA	NA	12,500	61.3	5.7	2.2	3.2	27.7	19.9	68.5	11.6	4,721	44.5	27.2	29.7
Golf village	252	266	5.6	218	100.0	0.0	0.0	0.0	0.0	7.8	28.5	63.8	106	97.2	3.8	78.3
Gonzalez CDP	13,273	NA	NA	13,936	82.8	8.0	1.0	4.4	3.8	24.5	60.9	14.7	4,778	82.6	24.0	32.8
Goodland CDP	267	NA	NA	285	100.0	0.0	0.0	0.0	0.0	0.0	53.0	47.0	159	66.7	38.4	28.3
Gotha CDP	1,915	NA	NA	2,007	64.9	3.6	12.8	4.3	14.3	31.3	62.6	6.1	584	89.7	14.7	65.4
Goulding CDP	4,102	NA	NA	4,539	18.3	73.8	0.0	5.0	2.9	15.7	69.9	14.4	1,012	51.0	76.9	4.2
Goulds CDP	10,103	NA	NA	11,210	4.9	52.8	0.2	2.1	40.0	32.0	55.9	12.1	2,745	50.8	56.5	15.6
Graceville city	2,278	2,223	-2.4	2,266	59.0	30.1	0.0	2.0	8.9	21.8	59.4	18.8	761	58.5	56.1	11.6
Grand Ridge town	904	873	-3.4	973	86.8	9.5	0.0	2.1	1.6	17.2	66.8	15.8	377	80.4	56.5	9.5
Grant-Valkaria town	3,850	3,968	3.1	3,908	89.2	3.6	0.7	4.5	2.1	14.0	60.6	25.4	1,558	92.6	29.1	34.5
Greenacres city	37,580	39,157	4.2	38,444	36.5	16.6	3.2	2.8	40.9	23.8	61.7	14.5	13,296	65.1	44.3	22.8
Greenbriar CDP	2,502	NA	NA	2,482	75.1	1.8	11.1	1.7	10.2	19.0	63.2	17.8	1,091	79.7	34.7	26.6
Green Cove Springs city	6,895	7,109	3.1	6,984	64.6	22.2	1.0	2.7	9.4	22.1	63.2	14.7	2,534	67.0	47.1	19.4
Greensboro town	639	611	-4.4	793	11.6	13.4	0.0	0.0	75.0	27.9	55.6	16.5	292	57.2	71.2	16.1
Greenville town	840	805	-4.2	681	17.9	75.8	0.4	1.9	4.0	25.3	55.6	19.2	258	67.4	55.8	6.2
Greenwood town	684	659	-3.7	823	53.5	36.2	0.0	3.4	6.9	27.3	51.9	20.8	242	81.4	48.8	16.9
Grenelefe CDP	1,752	NA	NA	1,813	62.8	14.9	0.0	0.6	21.7	24.4	60.1	15.3	717	48.0	34.3	32.4
Gretna city	1,463	1,398	-4.4	1,339	1.9	77.3	0.0	0.2	20.5	21.4	66.2	12.4	505	67.1	60.8	14.7
Grove City CDP	1,804	NA	NA	1,975	86.9	2.4	0.0	0.8	9.9	8.3	58.9	32.7	1,007	73.2	39.2	19.7
Groveland city	8,705	10,460	20.2	9,381	52.6	20.1	0.5	3.9	22.9	27.9	59.8	12.3	2,951	70.6	51.0	18.7
Gulf Breeze city	5,763	6,195	7.5	5,984	96.3	0.9	0.0	1.1	1.8	23.6	60.7	15.7	2,246	72.8	21.1	49.0
Gulf Gate Estates CDP	10,911	NA	NA	10,946	82.1	1.2	1.7	0.2	14.8	15.3	54.0	30.7	5,297	54.1	34.5	28.7
Gulfport city	12,029	12,198	1.4	12,102	77.9	10.7	3.1	2.3	6.0	12.9	59.5	27.5	5,846	64.7	30.6	34.4
Gulf Stream town	786	827	5.2	747	96.1	0.3	0.7	0.0	2.9	17.5	47.6	34.9	327	90.8	6.1	69.4
Gun Club Estates CDP	776	NA	NA	936	15.4	4.4	0.0	0.0	80.2	29.2	61.2	9.7	302	72.5	66.6	0.0
Haines City city	20,577	22,072	7.3	21,207	33.5	21.3	1.0	1.6	42.6	31.9	53.2	14.9	6,769	60.1	57.3	13.9
Hallandale Beach city	37,113	39,051	5.2	38,270	46.6	18.1	1.6	1.4	32.3	15.3	59.6	25.1	18,042	56.3	40.1	30.3
Hampton city	500	485	-3.0	469	72.5	19.2	0.0	1.5	6.8	17.5	63.5	19.0	162	69.8	76.5	4.9
Harbor Bluffs CDP	2,860	NA	NA	2,821	99.5	0.0	0.0	0.0	0.5	19.5	50.1	30.3	1,277	92.8	24.4	45.5
Harbour Heights CDP	2,987	NA	NA	3,392	92.2	5.0	0.7	0.1	2.0	11.2	48.7	40.1	1,401	76.4	39.3	27.5
Harlem CDP	2,658	NA	NA	2,580	3.8	92.4	0.0	1.4	2.4	38.4	50.4	11.2	775	59.7	75.9	10.3
Harlem Heights CDP	1,975	NA	NA	1,136	10.2	8.0	0.0	0.0	81.8	12.9	70.8	16.3	333	46.2	64.9	12.3
Harold CDP	823	NA	NA	850	99.2	0.0	0.0	0.8	0.0	18.8	64.4	16.6	345	89.0	33.6	19.7
Hastings town	580	620	6.9	611	56.6	39.4	0.0	3.3	0.7	14.0	56.2	29.6	251	81.3	50.2	19.1
Havana town	1,757	1,698	-3.4	2,244	40.9	58.2	0.0	0.4	0.5	27.3	55.3	17.5	865	74.5	46.4	24.3
Haverhill town	1,873	1,993	6.4	1,966	35.2	33.2	1.0	0.7	29.9	28.6	64.5	6.9	661	79.3	34.6	27.4
Hawthorne city	1,417	1,471	3.8	1,780	50.4	45.6	0.1	1.3	2.6	32.0	57.4	10.6	498	67.3	52.4	14.5
Heathrow CDP	5,896	NA	NA	5,943	74.3	6.3	13.1	0.7	5.7	17.6	61.5	20.9	2,265	75.9	10.3	63.1
Heritage Pines CDP	2,136	NA	NA	1,942	97.7	0.0	0.0	1.1	1.2	0.0	16.4	83.6	1,074	91.3	27.7	31.1
Hernando CDP	9,054	NA	NA	9,109	88.6	3.1	0.4	1.0	7.0	16.5	58.5	25.1	3,837	81.4	55.1	11.9
Hernando Beach CDP	2,299	NA	NA	2,098	97.4	0.0	1.4	0.0	1.2	8.0	60.2	31.8	1,027	77.2	36.8	26.0
Hialeah city	224,667	235,563	4.8	232,311	3.5	0.5	0.2	0.1	95.6	18.1	62.7	19.3	68,878	48.5	64.2	14.3
Hialeah Gardens city	21,744	23,555	8.3	22,660	3.0	0.7	0.0	0.1	96.2	20.1	66.5	13.4	6,348	66.4	56.7	16.4
Highland Beach town	3,539	3,687	4.2	3,614	93.6	2.4	1.0	0.2	2.9	4.4	44.0	51.3	1,964	84.5	16.9	58.9
Highland City CDP	10,834	NA	NA	10,040	75.7	10.5	3.4	0.5	9.8	23.5	64.7	11.9	3,507	85.5	34.2	31.0
Highland Park village	230	243	5.7	289	94.1	0.0	1.4	0.3	4.2	24.2	56.0	19.7	129	65.9	16.3	44.2
High Point CDP	3,686	NA	NA	3,467	89.4	1.0	3.0	2.0	4.7	8.8	45.6	45.4	1,674	91.2	58.8	11.6
High Springs city	5,350	5,672	6.0	5,499	79.7	15.4	0.0	1.0	4.0	30.7	57.8	11.5	1,801	78.8	36.8	26.9
Hillcrest Heights town	254	269	5.9	258	94.6	0.8	0.0	1.2	3.5	16.6	62.8	20.5	103	85.4	33.0	38.8
Hilliard town	3,086	3,123	1.2	3,112	82.6	13.6	0.2	1.1	2.6	29.7	57.5	12.8	1,015	50.6	50.2	7.7
Hill 'n Dale CDP	1,934	NA	NA	1,760	59.3	34.4	0.0	0.0	6.3	37.3	55.4	7.1	598	59.5	54.0	17.4
Hillsboro Beach town	1,875	1,981	5.7	1,635	87.3	0.6	0.9	1.2	10.1	5.2	41.7	53.2	969	75.4	21.7	56.7
Hillsboro Pines CDP	446	NA	NA	511	81.2	6.1	1.6	5.5	5.7	22.4	65.8	11.7	176	80.7	27.8	54.5
Hobe Sound CDP	11,521	NA	NA	13,205	81.2	8.1	0.0	0.8	9.9	15.7	52.6	31.8	5,735	73.5	37.9	29.0
Holden Heights CDP	3,679	NA	NA	4,107	49.6	21.0	8.5	1.7	19.2	16.3	67.3	16.4	1,357	59.5	35.3	29.4
Holiday CDP	22,403	NA	NA	21,049	79.2	4.5	1.6	2.0	12.8	20.2	59.0	20.9	8,761	66.0	54.2	14.1
Holley CDP	1,630	NA	NA	1,576	77.3	1.4	0.7	6.0	14.6	22.7	56.2	20.9	614	77.7	41.4	23.1
Holly Hill city	11,657	11,765	0.9	11,680	75.8	17.6	0.2	3.8	2.5	17.3	64.4	18.4	4,831	51.8	51.3	13.9
Hollywood city	140,769	148,047	5.2	145,128	47.0	16.2	2.5	2.8	31.5	20.3	64.3	15.4	55,823	59.9	39.2	30.2
Holmes Beach city	3,836	4,098	6.8	3,973	92.1	2.7	0.0	1.0	4.1	6.7	50.5	42.9	2,075	70.6	24.3	44.4
Homeland CDP	366	NA	NA	301	65.8	0.0	0.0	0.0	34.2	49.2	39.1	11.6	86	100.0	50.0	10.5
Homestead city	60,509	65,524	8.3	63,459	19.7	17.2	1.9	1.4	59.8	31.4	60.8	7.8	19,269	41.2	52.3	17.1
Homestead Base CDP	964	NA	NA	1,070	27.7	38.5	0.2	0.4	33.3	20.7	76.2	3.0	94	0.0	92.6	0.0
Homosassa CDP	2,578	NA	NA	2,143	96.9	0.1	0.0	2.4	0.6	10.0	43.1	46.9	972	92.0	50.0	29.9
Homosassa Springs CDP	13,791	NA	NA	13,403	92.8	0.2	1.8	2.6	2.7	16.0	55.9	28.1	5,356	79.5	54.0	8.7
Horizon West CDP	14,000	NA	NA	17,222	62.1	4.4	10.1	2.3	21.1	31.0	64.5	4.5	5,817	67.2	9.8	59.9
Horseshoe Beach town	169	167	-1.2	136	92.6	0.0	0.0	7.4	0.0	0.0	46.3	53.7	81	96.3	42.0	11.1
Hosford CDP	650	NA	NA	624	98.9	0.0	0.0	1.1	0.0	25.6	62.4	12.0	251	72.5	44.2	18.7
Howey-in-the-Hills town	1,098	1,145	4.3	1,089	89.1	0.6	0.0	2.5	7.8	12.8	59.0	28.2	519	80.7	27.2	31.4
Hudson CDP	12,158	NA	NA	11,730	91.1	1.6	0.9	1.1	5.3	12.6	52.4	35.0	5,410	73.4	45.5	18.1
Hunters Creek CDP	14,321	NA	NA	21,064	46.5	4.1	6.8	5.3	37.2	23.2	69.9	7.0	7,413	50.4	19.9	46.7
Hutchinson Island South CDP	5,201	NA	NA	4,877	97.1	0.0	0.1	0.8	1.9	1.5	31.9	66.7	2,978	75.3	31.0	41.0
Hypoluxo town	2,588	2,689	3.9	2,641	80.4	10.8	1.6	0.4	6.8	10.4	62.6	27.0	1,301	73.5	22.1	47.7
Immokalee CDP	24,154	NA	NA	24,021	3.9	18.5	0.1	0.8	76.7	33.1	61.6	5.4	4,495	43.5	83.5	5.5
Indialantic town	2,720	2,785	2.4	2,744	88.7	0.0	3.8	0.8	6.7	17.6	60.9	21.5	1,225	76.1	13.8	59.3
Indian Creek village	86	90	4.7	61	70.5	0.0	0.0	0.0	29.5	44.3	39.3	16.4	17	76.5	41.2	58.8
Indian Harbour Beach city	8,215	8,334	1.4	8,254	90.4	0.6	2.3	2.7	4.0	17.3	57.3	25.3	3,750	66.9	25.1	44.7
Indian River Estates CDP	6,220	NA	NA	5,953	92.1	3.4	2.1	0.9	1.5	14.3	55.2	30.4	2,548	87.4	46.9	20.1
Indian River Shores town	3,899	4,075	4.5	3,980	93.0	0.8	0.0	0.0	6.2	2.3	26.7	71.0	2,065	97.6	7.0	70.1
Indian Rocks Beach city	4,113	4,196	2.0	4,153	91.4	0.0	2.5	2.4	3.7	9.7	68.7	21.4	2,171	59.2	20.6	51.5
Indian Shores town	1,420	1,444	1.7	1,392	93.3	0.0	1.9	1.4	3.4	4.5	54.6	40.9	834	74.6	30.2	41.8
Indiantown CDP	6,083	NA	NA	5,981	20.7	16.1	0.6	1.8	60.8	28.6	58.4	13.0	1,383	71.8	67.9	17.3
Inglis town	1,325	1,303	-1.7	1,306	93.2	1.8	1.1	0.9	3.0	14.2	56.2	29.6	633	71.1	60.2	15.2
Interlachen town	1,403	1,358	-3.2	1,370	73.8	6.0	0.0	1.2	19.1	25.0	58.8	16.2	557	73.4	64.5	5.6
Inverness city	7,273	7,162	-1.5	7,205	84.9	8.2	0.5	2.7	3.7	19.9	45.3	34.8	3,242	69.2	45.2	20.9

1 May be of any race.

Table A. All Places — **Population and Housing**

STATE City, town, township, borough, or CDP (county if applicable)	Population: 2010 census total population	Population: 2014 estimated population	Population: Percent change 2010–2014	Population: ACS total population estimate 2010–2014	Race and Hispanic or Latino origin (percent), 2010–2014: White alone, not Hispanic or Latino	Black alone, not Hispanic or Latino	Asian alone, not Hispanic or Latino	All other races or 2 or more races, not Hispanic or Latino	Hispanic or Latino[1]	Age (percent), 2010–2014: Under 18 years old	Age 18 to 64 years old	Age 65 years and older	Households, 2010–2014: Total occupied housing units	Percent owner occupied	Householders by level of education (percent): High school diploma or less	Bachelor's degree or more
	1	2	3	4	5	6	7	8	9	10	11	12	13	14	15	16
FLORIDA—Con.																
Inverness Highlands North CDP	2,401	NA	NA	3,290	90.1	4.9	0.0	0.0	5.0	29.8	56.9	13.1	1,005	84.7	43.3	9.3
Inverness Highlands South CDP	6,542	NA	NA	6,566	86.8	3.8	2.2	1.2	5.9	20.7	50.3	29.2	2,652	87.1	47.7	16.1
Inwood CDP	6,403	NA	NA	6,468	55.2	26.8	0.4	5.9	11.7	29.4	55.8	14.7	2,309	59.1	69.6	7.1
Iona CDP	15,369	NA	NA	13,549	93.6	0.0	0.1	0.1	6.1	7.3	40.3	52.4	7,143	71.7	29.0	41.3
Islamorada	6,109	6,523	6.8	6,318	89.4	0.9	0.0	0.8	9.0	15.5	53.8	30.6	2,623	73.3	27.6	38.8
Islandia	0	0	0.0	0	0.0	0.0	0.0	0.0	0.0	0.0	0.0	0.0	0	0.0	0.0	0.0
Island Walk CDP	3,035	NA	NA	3,044	98.2	0.0	0.3	0.5	1.0	7.7	34.0	58.4	1,578	86.6	19.5	51.5
Istachatta CDP	116	NA	NA	116	100.0	0.0	0.0	0.0	0.0	39.6	34.5	25.9	26	38.5	100.0	0.0
Ives Estates CDP	19,525	NA	NA	19,980	20.8	45.3	2.3	1.8	29.8	21.1	66.6	12.2	6,781	67.5	33.6	31.1
Jacksonville city	821,784	853,382	3.8	837,533	54.2	30.2	4.3	3.1	8.2	23.3	64.9	11.7	315,619	60.3	36.6	27.6
Jacksonville Beach city	21,362	22,665	6.1	21,822	85.8	5.8	2.1	1.6	4.7	17.7	67.2	15.1	10,143	59.9	22.3	44.8
Jacob City city	250	244	-2.4	520	5.6	93.5	0.0	1.0	0.0	20.2	66.0	13.8	188	72.3	74.5	2.1
Jan Phyl Village CDP	5,573	NA	NA	5,161	60.1	22.8	2.2	3.5	11.4	32.1	53.9	14.0	1,619	73.4	57.1	9.2
Jasmine Estates CDP	18,989	NA	NA	18,470	76.5	5.0	1.9	2.1	14.5	21.1	60.0	19.0	7,210	65.1	49.8	10.8
Jasper city	4,546	3,954	-13.0	4,301	42.8	43.2	1.0	2.0	10.9	10.3	81.4	8.3	575	56.5	65.4	16.2
Jay town	533	566	6.2	433	93.3	0.0	0.5	2.3	3.9	16.2	61.4	22.4	186	75.8	55.9	14.5
Jennings town	878	866	-1.4	802	24.2	34.0	0.0	3.1	38.7	25.5	61.1	13.2	280	64.3	72.1	3.6
Jensen Beach CDP	11,707	NA	NA	12,000	94.7	2.1	0.1	0.9	2.2	13.9	58.3	27.8	5,259	73.9	34.0	24.5
June Park CDP	4,094	NA	NA	4,059	89.1	0.0	0.9	2.9	7.2	17.2	66.2	16.5	1,568	93.2	44.1	29.2
Juno Beach town	3,192	3,363	5.4	3,267	94.0	0.7	1.8	0.4	3.2	4.8	43.8	51.5	1,945	67.2	22.7	54.3
Juno Ridge CDP	718	NA	NA	537	84.2	4.8	0.6	1.5	8.9	11.1	87.5	1.3	319	14.7	43.3	22.6
Jupiter town	55,266	60,681	9.8	57,625	82.3	1.0	2.9	1.4	12.4	19.1	58.9	22.0	24,257	72.5	24.4	48.1
Jupiter Farms CDP	11,994	NA	NA	11,803	85.2	2.8	0.4	0.7	10.8	22.2	65.4	12.5	3,956	90.5	23.9	37.0
Jupiter Inlet Colony town	400	433	8.3	411	96.8	0.0	0.2	1.0	1.9	24.1	47.4	28.5	174	80.5	14.4	63.8
Jupiter Island town	817	864	5.8	630	81.7	7.5	2.5	1.7	6.5	4.6	39.9	55.6	282	90.1	11.0	74.1
Kathleen CDP	6,332	NA	NA	6,385	82.3	0.5	3.7	3.8	9.7	23.3	64.3	12.4	2,063	82.3	58.1	8.7
Kendale Lakes CDP	56,148	NA	NA	58,767	8.9	1.0	1.8	0.4	87.9	17.7	66.2	16.2	17,866	74.2	40.2	29.4
Kendall CDP	75,371	NA	NA	78,580	27.9	3.8	4.0	1.3	63.0	20.0	64.1	15.8	28,448	63.5	22.9	49.9
Kendall West CDP	36,154	NA	NA	38,673	7.8	1.6	1.2	0.6	88.7	19.7	66.8	13.5	11,215	62.9	38.1	30.0
Kenneth City town	4,964	5,026	1.2	4,986	69.8	7.9	10.7	1.4	10.2	15.2	60.0	24.8	1,819	74.4	50.0	21.6
Kensington Park CDP	3,901	NA	NA	4,228	56.3	8.3	2.2	2.0	31.2	20.3	59.4	20.4	1,529	75.4	48.6	16.9
Kenwood Estates CDP	1,283	NA	NA	1,140	27.3	8.8	0.0	0.0	63.9	26.7	64.2	9.1	278	53.6	74.5	13.3
Key Biscayne village	12,344	12,924	4.7	12,774	37.5	0.4	3.2	0.8	58.1	31.2	50.6	18.1	4,287	74.9	6.4	75.7
Key Colony Beach city	797	845	6.0	615	96.3	0.0	0.5	0.0	3.3	0.0	43.9	56.1	335	75.8	13.7	49.6
Key Largo CDP	10,433	NA	NA	10,781	66.5	2.9	2.1	1.9	26.6	13.4	65.3	21.3	4,395	68.4	34.4	32.8
Keystone CDP	24,039	NA	NA	22,678	80.0	3.5	4.6	1.2	10.7	25.6	61.9	12.6	7,735	91.9	17.1	53.2
Keystone Heights city	1,333	1,403	5.3	1,540	89.9	1.5	0.1	0.5	8.0	28.8	54.9	16.4	589	75.9	23.4	26.5
Key Vista CDP	1,757	NA	NA	1,640	91.5	0.6	2.4	2.4	3.1	27.7	46.3	26.0	540	98.1	13.9	42.4
Key West city	24,649	25,704	4.3	25,187	66.8	10.3	0.9	2.2	19.9	16.0	70.4	13.3	9,226	43.9	30.7	35.0
Kissimmee city	59,620	66,722	11.9	63,392	24.5	9.0	2.8	1.5	62.1	25.4	64.1	10.5	20,616	44.0	50.3	16.1
LaBelle city	4,648	4,693	1.0	4,633	44.2	6.3	0.1	1.0	48.5	28.9	54.3	16.7	1,400	65.1	59.0	9.6
Lacoochee CDP	1,714	NA	NA	1,446	64.7	6.8	2.1	0.2	26.2	31.0	54.5	14.5	476	62.6	64.3	3.8
La Crosse town	364	375	3.0	248	64.9	19.4	0.0	0.8	14.9	18.1	64.4	17.3	105	78.1	41.9	16.2
Lady Lake town	13,927	14,455	3.8	14,138	87.5	4.8	0.8	0.8	6.0	14.4	38.5	47.1	6,845	68.3	41.8	24.9
Laguna Beach CDP	3,932	NA	NA	3,700	85.3	2.5	1.2	3.8	7.2	11.0	68.9	20.3	1,840	57.9	41.0	32.4
Lake Alfred city	5,015	5,253	4.7	5,136	52.1	28.1	1.2	1.9	16.7	31.6	50.8	17.8	1,671	59.4	44.3	16.2
Lake Belvedere Estates CDP	3,334	NA	NA	3,568	25.3	27.5	5.4	3.2	38.6	32.7	59.5	7.8	962	81.7	24.4	43.0
Lake Buena Vista city	10	10	0.0	9	100.0	0.0	0.0	0.0	0.0	0.0	33.3	66.7	6	100.0	66.7	33.3
Lake Butler CDP	15,400	NA	NA	16,053	69.0	9.6	9.6	2.7	9.1	27.9	62.6	9.6	5,285	83.0	12.8	64.5
Lake Butler city	1,896	1,846	-2.6	2,227	58.8	29.4	0.5	5.7	5.6	31.9	61.2	7.0	729	43.1	58.8	7.7
Lake City city	12,031	12,100	0.6	12,059	52.5	38.8	0.6	2.4	5.8	23.7	59.1	17.2	4,552	47.1	41.5	17.7
Lake Clarke Shores town	3,376	3,508	3.9	3,445	63.6	2.1	2.2	0.9	31.1	15.2	66.9	17.7	1,423	79.6	28.0	47.4
Lake Hamilton town	1,231	1,313	6.7	1,258	61.8	19.6	0.0	0.0	18.5	24.8	61.2	13.9	430	69.8	64.2	7.7
Lake Harbor CDP	45	NA	NA	0	0.0	0.0	0.0	0.0	0.0	0.0	0.0	0.0	0	0.0	0.0	0.0
Lake Hart CDP	542	NA	NA	366	68.6	1.6	0.0	0.0	29.8	3.3	53.8	42.9	230	100.0	5.2	61.3
Lake Helen city	2,624	2,648	0.9	2,632	88.3	4.5	1.0	1.1	5.1	15.9	65.4	18.5	1,048	77.7	42.7	19.0
Lake Kathryn CDP	920	NA	NA	985	74.8	0.0	0.0	0.0	25.2	27.1	55.9	17.0	328	69.2	72.9	0.0
Lakeland city	97,433	102,346	5.0	99,942	62.5	19.5	1.6	2.2	14.1	21.1	58.2	20.8	39,497	55.3	42.2	27.2
Lakeland Highlands CDP	11,056	NA	NA	11,649	83.6	2.5	2.3	1.6	10.0	23.8	57.8	18.5	3,967	88.3	23.3	52.6
Lake Lindsey CDP	71	NA	NA	23	100.0	0.0	0.0	0.0	0.0	30.4	30.4	39.1	16	56.3	100.0	0.0
Lake Lorraine CDP	7,010	NA	NA	7,011	76.9	6.6	4.6	2.7	9.1	18.4	64.2	17.3	3,119	66.0	29.6	40.0
Lake Mack-Forest Hills CDP	1,010	NA	NA	727	100.0	0.0	0.0	0.0	0.0	15.7	63.8	20.5	365	77.0	53.4	0.0
Lake Magdalene CDP	28,509	NA	NA	28,966	62.7	8.4	2.0	1.9	25.0	18.7	64.4	17.1	11,773	69.1	30.3	38.6
Lake Mary city	13,818	15,801	14.4	14,605	74.4	5.6	6.8	3.4	9.8	21.1	64.4	14.7	5,083	78.9	19.7	47.0
Lake Mary Jane CDP	1,575	NA	NA	1,310	78.9	0.0	6.6	0.0	14.5	23.6	66.5	10.0	449	86.6	12.5	50.6
Lake Mystic CDP	500	NA	NA	394	100.0	0.0	0.0	0.0	0.0	21.6	72.2	6.3	150	88.7	46.0	10.7
Lake Panasoffkee CDP	3,551	NA	NA	3,409	96.2	0.0	0.0	1.7	2.1	13.2	51.9	35.0	1,643	77.5	56.9	9.9
Lake Park town	8,155	8,448	3.6	8,317	35.2	54.8	2.1	3.7	4.1	17.1	67.8	15.0	3,093	41.5	44.3	20.5
Lake Placid town	2,125	2,134	0.4	2,518	43.0	8.6	0.0	3.4	45.0	26.1	57.0	16.9	752	45.9	60.9	21.7
Lake Sarasota CDP	4,679	NA	NA	4,795	85.2	3.1	0.0	0.8	10.9	24.1	63.3	12.7	1,623	73.8	31.4	20.8
Lakeside CDP	30,943	NA	NA	31,522	75.3	8.8	2.8	3.0	10.0	23.1	62.7	14.3	11,291	73.6	36.8	25.2
Lake Wales city	14,205	15,140	6.6	14,665	54.0	22.9	0.6	2.8	19.7	29.8	48.1	22.1	5,497	57.6	47.1	23.4
Lakewood Park CDP	11,323	NA	NA	11,304	75.9	12.2	1.7	4.4	5.8	15.6	57.5	26.9	4,812	85.3	45.4	15.4
Lake Worth city	34,910	37,097	6.3	35,903	37.5	19.2	0.9	1.3	41.1	22.7	65.6	11.5	11,824	49.0	50.5	22.6
Lamont CDP	178	NA	NA	101	17.8	82.2	0.0	0.0	0.0	0.0	100.0	0.0	36	19.4	0.0	19.4
Land O' Lakes CDP	31,996	NA	NA	33,112	71.4	5.8	1.8	2.1	19.0	21.5	64.9	13.7	11,663	80.9	25.7	37.5
Lantana town	10,616	10,996	3.6	10,822	53.5	23.9	1.4	2.8	18.4	22.2	61.3	16.5	3,936	53.3	42.2	25.0
Largo city	78,135	79,019	1.1	78,391	76.6	5.7	2.3	2.8	12.6	16.1	59.1	24.8	35,683	56.2	44.1	22.0
Lauderdale-by-the-Sea town	6,056	6,388	5.5	6,241	90.9	0.5	0.3	1.2	7.1	6.0	53.8	40.3	3,773	71.1	27.9	44.3
Lauderdale Lakes city	32,653	34,410	5.4	33,710	8.8	81.1	1.9	1.6	6.6	24.4	60.7	15.1	11,328	58.8	53.5	14.3
Lauderhill city	66,954	70,626	5.5	69,082	11.2	76.0	2.0	2.2	8.7	24.3	62.7	13.0	23,265	57.5	46.0	20.8
Laurel CDP	8,171	NA	NA	8,888	95.1	0.5	0.2	2.3	1.9	12.9	51.9	35.2	4,244	79.2	34.7	28.8
Laurel Hill city	537	575	7.1	579	60.4	32.3	0.0	2.4	4.8	23.6	60.9	15.7	224	80.4	53.6	8.9
Lawtey city	730	714	-2.2	1,084	46.4	45.5	0.0	0.7	7.4	24.9	60.3	14.9	422	67.8	60.9	9.7
Layton city	184	190	3.3	113	87.6	0.0	0.0	0.0	12.4	0.0	57.5	42.5	63	68.3	15.9	23.8
Lazy Lake village	24	25	4.2	35	88.6	5.7	0.0	0.0	5.7	0.0	71.5	28.6	12	83.3	0.0	66.7

1 May be of any race.

Table A. All Places — **Population and Housing**

STATE City, town, township, borough, or CDP (county if applicable)	Population: 2010 census total population	Population: 2014 estimated population	Population: Percent change 2010–2014	Population: ACS total population estimate 2010–2014	Race and Hispanic or Latino origin (percent), 2010–2014: White alone, not Hispanic or Latino	Black alone, not Hispanic or Latino	Asian alone, not Hispanic or Latino	All other races or 2 or more races, not Hispanic or Latino	Hispanic or Latino[1]	Age (percent), 2010–2014: Under 18 years old	Age 18 to 64 years old	Age 65 years and older	Households, 2010–2014: Total occupied housing units	Percent owner occupied	Householders by level of education (percent): High school diploma or less	Bachelor's degree or more
	1	2	3	4	5	6	7	8	9	10	11	12	13	14	15	16
FLORIDA—Con.																
Lealman CDP	19,879	NA	NA	20,740	73.4	9.2	6.1	3.4	7.9	18.8	63.4	17.9	8,849	58.3	64.2	8.9
Lecanto CDP	5,882	NA	NA	5,394	92.0	3.7	0.4	0.4	3.5	15.2	59.2	25.7	1,992	83.7	53.2	14.5
Lee town	352	330	-6.3	618	53.1	18.1	0.0	13.4	15.4	25.5	67.9	6.5	181	68.0	50.3	8.3
Leesburg city	20,364	21,524	5.7	20,915	59.6	26.1	1.5	3.9	8.9	22.5	54.1	23.3	8,488	53.0	45.1	19.5
Lehigh Acres CDP	86,784	NA	NA	106,747	40.7	19.8	1.2	2.2	36.0	29.0	60.0	11.0	30,887	57.7	53.9	15.3
Leisure City CDP	22,655	NA	NA	24,125	8.1	18.6	1.4	0.4	71.6	27.3	64.6	8.3	6,196	56.0	67.3	11.2
Lely CDP	3,451	NA	NA	3,481	90.7	0.5	0.0	0.2	8.6	8.7	45.0	46.4	1,712	78.3	37.7	27.7
Lely Resort CDP	4,646	NA	NA	4,687	58.7	26.9	0.7	0.4	13.2	14.2	55.1	30.7	1,908	62.2	24.8	44.9
Lemon Grove CDP	657	NA	NA	702	63.4	0.0	0.0	0.9	35.8	26.2	64.6	9.3	221	64.7	54.3	10.9
Lighthouse Point city	10,344	10,953	5.9	10,693	87.5	2.1	1.6	0.2	8.6	15.5	62.6	21.8	4,890	79.6	22.6	47.2
Limestone CDP	132	NA	NA	324	82.7	17.3	0.0	0.0	0.0	31.8	62.6	5.6	97	100.0	100.0	0.0
Limestone Creek CDP	1,014	NA	NA	1,152	25.0	61.7	0.9	0.9	11.5	35.8	61.5	2.7	307	75.6	44.0	6.2
Lisbon CDP	260	NA	NA	108	63.9	0.0	0.0	0.0	36.1	13.0	50.1	37.0	51	70.6	84.3	0.0
Live Oak city	6,850	6,969	1.7	6,927	44.3	39.0	0.1	0.5	16.0	25.1	58.7	16.1	2,661	37.5	70.4	8.1
Lloyd CDP	215	NA	NA	362	27.6	72.4	0.0	0.0	0.0	43.4	52.3	4.4	113	94.7	31.9	33.6
Lochmoor Waterway Estates CDP	4,204	NA	NA	4,188	89.3	0.4	0.2	1.2	8.9	15.6	59.8	24.8	1,702	78.0	28.5	30.0
Lockhart CDP	13,060	NA	NA	14,489	48.3	22.5	3.7	5.8	19.8	25.9	65.5	8.4	5,015	64.2	43.0	24.7
Longboat Key town	6,888	7,143	3.7	7,003	92.3	0.0	2.5	1.9	3.3	3.3	31.6	65.2	3,851	90.7	12.7	64.6
Longwood city	13,659	13,877	1.6	13,776	69.8	8.5	3.5	1.7	16.6	18.6	63.0	18.3	4,591	73.6	37.2	25.9
Loughman CDP	2,680	NA	NA	2,578	57.0	12.1	0.3	1.2	29.3	23.3	68.8	7.9	965	46.2	48.7	15.3
Lower Grand Lagoon CDP	3,881	NA	NA	4,181	91.3	0.1	1.7	1.6	5.3	9.2	69.3	21.3	2,077	48.4	26.5	25.9
Loxahatchee Groves town	3,180	3,343	5.1	3,263	87.9	2.6	0.4	1.9	7.2	15.7	67.5	16.9	1,042	90.1	40.3	25.0
Lutz CDP	19,344	NA	NA	20,184	74.0	6.3	4.1	1.5	14.2	22.5	63.4	14.2	7,377	84.0	24.8	42.7
Lynn Haven city	18,474	19,792	7.1	19,049	77.4	11.9	2.2	4.1	4.4	26.6	60.1	13.3	7,316	63.5	34.4	31.6
Macclenny city	6,372	6,417	0.7	6,387	72.6	20.9	1.0	2.1	3.4	30.9	58.3	10.8	1,975	62.4	48.9	11.8
McGregor CDP	7,406	NA	NA	7,690	90.3	1.7	1.4	1.2	5.4	18.1	56.5	25.5	3,394	70.9	19.5	55.7
McIntosh town	450	456	1.3	269	93.3	0.0	0.0	0.0	6.7	11.6	55.8	32.7	153	85.0	24.2	38.6
Madeira Beach city	4,263	4,332	1.6	4,297	88.6	0.4	0.8	2.1	8.1	6.7	65.9	27.3	2,420	57.6	28.3	37.9
Madison city	3,049	2,901	-4.9	2,976	29.7	68.6	0.4	0.4	0.8	28.7	57.1	14.4	1,210	54.9	52.9	13.5
Maitland city	15,739	16,823	6.9	16,273	74.0	9.9	4.9	1.4	9.8	20.5	64.2	15.5	6,986	57.2	15.3	61.2
Malabar town	2,757	2,864	3.9	2,793	87.9	5.8	0.5	1.6	4.2	20.1	58.7	21.2	1,037	82.8	33.9	27.1
Malone town	2,088	2,189	4.8	2,187	43.6	35.6	0.9	7.2	12.8	10.9	83.8	5.3	285	74.4	40.7	20.0
Manalapan town	406	440	8.4	231	90.0	0.0	3.0	0.0	6.9	11.2	48.0	40.7	120	95.0	20.8	70.0
Manasota Key CDP	1,229	NA	NA	1,312	92.0	0.0	0.0	1.0	7.0	3.8	43.0	53.0	749	73.2	29.9	41.5
Manatee Road CDP	2,244	NA	NA	2,722	98.3	0.0	0.0	0.7	1.0	22.3	49.2	28.5	1,120	72.9	66.6	6.5
Mango CDP	11,313	NA	NA	12,062	53.1	15.3	0.8	2.5	28.3	29.9	61.8	8.3	4,314	50.5	57.5	13.1
Mangonia Park town	1,888	1,958	3.7	1,758	12.1	80.9	0.0	0.1	6.9	31.0	59.0	10.1	588	31.6	64.3	5.6
Marathon city	8,297	8,708	5.0	8,529	58.2	7.0	1.5	1.5	31.8	19.5	64.4	16.0	3,042	60.4	32.6	29.2
Marco Island city	16,413	17,460	6.4	16,921	91.7	0.6	1.0	0.4	6.2	9.6	41.5	49.0	8,100	85.5	21.0	51.2
Margate city	53,284	56,061	5.2	54,929	44.8	25.3	4.3	3.4	22.3	18.9	62.2	18.8	20,891	76.3	45.4	21.1
Marianna city	7,594	9,249	21.8	8,548	54.4	39.7	0.8	3.9	1.2	24.5	58.6	16.9	2,964	56.0	43.8	17.4
Marineland town	16	16	0.0	11	45.5	0.0	45.5	0.0	9.1	0.0	100.0	0.0	0	0.0	0.0	0.0
Mary Esther city	3,851	4,180	8.5	4,035	83.4	3.1	6.1	2.5	4.9	11.3	66.9	21.9	1,797	75.0	26.4	32.1
Masaryktown CDP	1,040	NA	NA	1,125	92.3	0.0	0.9	0.0	6.8	9.0	70.6	20.4	485	63.7	70.5	1.9
Mascotte city	5,091	5,344	5.0	5,197	43.5	2.3	0.0	3.2	51.0	30.4	59.5	10.2	1,413	82.7	57.8	3.8
Matlacha CDP	677	NA	NA	914	97.8	0.0	0.0	0.0	2.2	0.0	51.1	48.9	474	60.3	60.5	20.5
Matlacha Isles-Matlacha Shores CDP	229	NA	NA	411	100.0	0.0	0.0	0.0	0.0	5.1	64.9	30.2	186	94.1	58.1	37.6
Mayo town	1,214	1,251	3.0	1,412	46.3	31.8	0.4	1.3	20.2	17.4	64.9	17.6	465	61.1	64.3	4.3
Meadow Oaks CDP	2,442	NA	NA	2,490	93.9	0.0	1.4	0.0	4.7	15.4	61.8	22.7	993	83.2	42.4	20.8
Meadow Woods CDP	25,558	NA	NA	27,301	16.9	8.3	7.0	1.3	66.6	25.6	67.1	7.4	7,991	67.8	42.7	26.7
Medley town	838	851	1.6	940	4.5	0.0	0.0	2.7	92.9	19.4	58.8	21.8	341	54.8	61.0	15.0
Medulla CDP	8,892	NA	NA	8,114	74.1	10.0	0.6	2.0	13.3	23.6	66.5	9.8	3,098	59.8	38.2	26.9
Melbourne city	76,196	78,490	3.0	77,216	75.7	9.9	2.6	3.5	8.3	17.4	61.4	21.3	33,083	60.2	35.7	27.0
Melbourne Beach town	3,101	3,163	2.0	3,126	90.2	0.0	0.6	0.0	9.1	15.2	63.8	21.0	1,308	83.3	15.3	58.0
Melbourne Village town	662	678	2.4	722	96.3	0.0	1.0	0.0	2.8	13.5	64.5	21.7	307	93.5	11.7	53.7
Memphis CDP	7,848	NA	NA	8,722	41.7	33.1	0.0	2.1	23.1	25.0	57.6	17.3	2,756	72.4	50.5	18.2
Merritt Island CDP	34,743	NA	NA	35,063	82.6	5.2	2.2	2.8	7.2	18.0	59.8	22.3	14,410	75.6	28.8	34.7
Mexico Beach city	1,072	1,145	6.8	1,413	91.9	1.1	0.9	2.1	4.0	11.2	62.1	26.5	637	60.1	35.0	33.0
Miami city	399,508	430,332	7.7	416,432	11.1	16.7	0.8	0.7	70.7	18.6	65.7	15.8	152,525	31.6	51.5	28.1
Miami Beach city	87,784	91,732	4.5	90,669	39.2	3.5	1.7	2.0	53.5	15.3	68.7	16.0	43,650	35.9	28.0	47.4
Miami Gardens city	107,163	112,265	4.8	110,867	2.4	71.9	0.7	0.8	24.2	23.8	64.8	11.3	31,365	66.7	55.7	15.5
Miami Lakes town	29,364	30,791	4.9	30,396	13.3	2.7	1.5	0.5	82.0	22.8	63.1	13.9	9,741	65.3	27.2	37.2
Miami Shores village	10,329	10,861	5.2	10,736	44.9	20.5	2.0	3.0	29.6	21.9	65.6	12.6	3,398	85.3	22.4	52.7
Miami Springs city	13,809	14,415	4.4	14,255	25.6	0.5	2.4	0.7	70.9	20.0	61.8	18.3	5,015	59.4	38.4	27.9
Micanopy town	600	622	3.7	637	72.4	20.9	0.5	1.3	5.0	20.3	57.6	22.3	283	79.5	43.8	22.3
Micco CDP	9,052	NA	NA	8,555	95.6	0.8	0.0	0.7	2.9	6.1	43.2	50.8	4,394	86.3	53.7	12.2
Middleburg CDP	13,008	NA	NA	13,042	91.4	1.9	1.5	2.0	3.2	22.5	62.7	14.7	4,355	77.1	49.9	10.4
Midway city	3,007	3,299	9.7	3,200	9.5	85.3	0.0	1.3	3.8	28.8	65.6	5.6	1,239	75.6	46.7	26.3
Midway CDP (Santa Rosa)	16,115	NA	NA	17,640	89.8	1.2	1.1	4.6	3.2	23.4	62.4	14.1	6,687	75.9	24.3	39.2
Midway CDP (Seminole)	1,705	NA	NA	1,596	5.3	89.6	0.0	1.8	3.3	21.8	64.7	13.3	573	67.7	59.0	22.5
Milton city	8,826	9,445	7.0	9,149	75.3	13.8	3.0	5.4	2.5	18.2	64.5	17.3	3,930	51.8	38.6	23.8
Mims CDP	7,058	NA	NA	6,735	83.3	10.9	1.0	2.4	2.4	17.7	58.6	23.5	2,752	81.5	54.8	14.4
Minneola city	9,413	10,351	10.0	9,849	66.2	5.7	0.7	6.7	20.7	28.7	62.7	8.7	3,236	74.7	38.9	25.7
Miramar city	122,041	134,989	10.6	128,414	10.4	43.6	5.8	3.2	36.9	26.4	65.7	8.0	37,439	74.2	26.4	37.1
Miramar Beach CDP	6,146	NA	NA	6,835	91.6	0.1	2.8	4.0	1.5	9.3	59.2	31.5	3,444	71.1	15.5	46.1
Molino CDP	1,277	NA	NA	1,351	68.0	15.4	0.0	5.3	11.3	26.8	58.3	15.1	434	82.0	34.3	25.1
Monticello city	2,506	2,399	-4.3	2,711	45.7	49.4	0.0	0.1	4.8	17.0	65.1	17.8	992	70.5	49.1	28.9
Montura CDP	3,283	NA	NA	3,147	27.8	1.8	0.0	4.2	66.2	25.1	64.2	10.7	1,015	80.4	78.4	5.1
Montverde town	1,463	1,562	6.8	1,787	70.7	5.9	2.0	0.7	20.8	31.9	58.1	10.2	524	72.5	32.8	36.8
Moon Lake CDP	4,919	NA	NA	4,802	94.8	1.7	0.3	1.4	1.8	22.7	65.9	11.4	1,690	68.6	53.1	14.4
Moore Haven city	1,680	1,789	6.5	2,978	35.6	25.8	0.0	0.0	38.6	22.6	64.2	13.4	643	58.3	72.2	6.2
Morriston CDP	164	NA	NA	75	100.0	0.0	0.0	0.0	0.0	0.0	16.0	84.0	44	100.0	100.0	0.0
Mount Carmel CDP	227	NA	NA	219	96.8	0.0	0.0	3.2	0.0	29.7	57.5	12.8	100	85.0	37.0	21.0
Mount Dora city	12,151	13,182	8.5	12,663	68.5	16.1	1.7	2.3	11.5	18.0	56.7	25.3	5,343	51.3	34.1	33.8
Mount Plymouth CDP	4,011	NA	NA	4,991	85.3	5.4	0.8	2.3	6.1	24.2	64.5	11.1	1,574	89.7	51.3	13.8
Mulat CDP	259	NA	NA	263	95.8	0.4	3.8	0.0	0.0	30.3	59.3	10.3	73	53.4	32.9	67.1
Mulberry city	3,822	3,921	2.6	3,864	70.3	15.6	6.0	2.1	6.0	19.9	47.0	33.1	1,638	77.6	68.0	10.0
Munson CDP	372	NA	NA	462	99.1	0.9	0.0	0.0	0.0	28.4	59.7	11.9	178	90.4	36.5	5.1

1 May be of any race.

Table A. All Places — **Population and Housing**

STATE City, town, township, borough, or CDP (county if applicable)	Population: 2010 census total population	Population: 2014 estimated population	Population: Percent change 2010–2014	Population: ACS total population estimate 2010–2014	Race and Hispanic or Latino origin (percent), 2010–2014: White alone, not Hispanic or Latino	Black alone, not Hispanic or Latino	Asian alone, not Hispanic or Latino	All other races or 2 or more races, not Hispanic or Latino	Hispanic or Latino[1]	Age (percent), 2010–2014: Under 18 years old	Age 18 to 64 years old	Age 65 years and older	Households, 2010–2014: Total occupied housing units	Percent owner occupied	Householders by level of education (percent): High school diploma or less	Bachelor's degree or more
	1	2	3	4	5	6	7	8	9	10	11	12	13	14	15	16
FLORIDA—Con.																
Myrtle Grove CDP	15,870	NA	NA	17,475	60.1	22.1	2.7	6.8	8.3	23.3	64.7	12.1	6,155	49.4	42.0	13.6
Naples city	19,537	20,968	7.3	20,214	89.3	4.3	0.4	0.8	5.1	9.6	41.1	49.3	10,068	80.4	17.3	56.8
Naples Manor CDP	5,562	NA	NA	6,096	6.8	19.1	0.0	1.3	72.9	32.4	57.0	10.5	1,106	63.5	82.5	6.9
Naples Park CDP	5,967	NA	NA	7,178	70.8	1.1	0.0	1.1	27.0	18.9	65.3	15.9	2,520	54.4	32.4	30.2
Naranja CDP	8,303	NA	NA	8,379	7.5	36.4	1.6	3.6	50.9	34.1	58.0	7.9	2,402	31.4	60.9	18.9
Nassau Village-Ratliff CDP	5,337	NA	NA	5,506	97.0	0.1	0.0	1.9	1.0	21.2	64.6	14.1	1,832	83.1	54.0	8.6
Navarre CDP	31,378	NA	NA	32,586	79.6	6.2	2.2	6.0	6.0	26.3	65.1	8.6	11,962	67.2	24.4	35.1
Navarre Beach CDP	638	NA	NA	1,103	96.2	0.0	0.0	0.0	3.8	14.7	67.0	18.3	512	77.9	7.6	73.0
Neptune Beach city	7,037	7,180	2.0	6,733	91.8	0.4	0.9	1.2	5.7	18.3	63.1	18.6	2,925	64.9	16.6	55.0
Newberry city	4,954	5,412	9.2	5,185	69.3	20.6	1.3	2.0	6.8	30.6	60.1	9.3	1,875	81.2	29.7	29.8
New Port Richey city	14,903	15,527	4.2	15,063	82.0	1.9	0.9	2.6	12.6	18.6	56.3	25.2	6,298	56.0	57.4	13.2
New Port Richey East CDP	10,036	NA	NA	8,376	86.9	1.1	1.3	1.8	9.0	16.0	58.4	25.6	3,868	57.1	44.4	15.5
New Smyrna Beach city	22,556	23,658	4.9	22,993	90.0	5.4	0.8	0.7	3.1	14.1	54.5	31.4	10,780	69.0	30.2	35.0
Niceville city	12,752	14,387	12.8	13,562	81.3	4.7	4.3	6.3	3.4	24.2	61.3	14.3	5,243	69.3	26.0	36.6
Nobleton CDP	282	NA	NA	341	100.0	0.0	0.0	0.0	0.0	24.3	56.6	19.1	116	71.6	83.6	0.0
Nocatee CDP	4,524	NA	NA	5,923	89.6	4.2	4.1	0.4	1.8	34.2	56.0	9.7	1,962	82.9	14.2	67.3
Nokomis CDP	3,167	NA	NA	3,218	88.4	1.3	6.3	2.6	1.4	14.3	62.1	23.6	1,353	72.5	44.1	24.0
Noma town	211	208	-1.4	281	65.1	33.1	0.0	1.8	0.0	34.2	55.8	10.0	89	74.2	69.7	3.4
North Bay Village city	7,137	7,871	10.3	7,453	27.3	1.8	2.8	4.9	63.3	13.1	78.5	8.4	3,197	35.9	22.2	48.7
North Brooksville CDP	3,544	NA	NA	3,964	82.1	9.2	0.0	0.8	7.9	25.2	55.2	19.6	1,431	75.1	47.2	19.2
Northdale CDP	22,079	NA	NA	22,587	63.4	5.6	4.0	2.7	24.4	22.3	66.1	11.7	8,374	69.0	25.4	44.0
North DeLand CDP	1,450	NA	NA	1,540	78.4	1.5	0.3	0.0	19.8	29.3	50.4	20.4	493	69.4	60.6	9.3
North Fort Myers CDP	39,407	NA	NA	39,143	90.0	2.2	0.6	1.2	6.0	8.5	44.5	46.9	18,629	84.0	46.8	22.1
North Key Largo CDP	1,244	NA	NA	1,242	85.3	4.1	1.2	0.0	9.4	7.4	45.3	47.3	476	85.5	13.2	60.1
North Lauderdale city	41,055	43,214	5.3	42,354	16.0	53.5	3.8	2.1	24.6	27.4	65.4	7.2	12,047	55.0	54.7	16.1
North Miami city	58,896	61,420	4.3	60,756	12.7	57.0	2.2	1.3	26.8	22.2	67.1	10.6	18,038	49.0	45.9	22.1
North Miami Beach city	41,523	43,664	5.2	43,028	20.7	42.1	3.4	0.6	33.1	22.1	65.4	12.5	14,065	54.3	41.0	23.2
North Palm Beach village	12,013	12,483	3.9	12,272	91.1	0.7	0.5	1.5	6.2	14.8	54.3	30.9	6,215	75.9	25.1	46.0
North Port city	57,333	60,380	5.3	58,584	79.8	7.8	1.3	3.5	7.7	21.5	57.1	21.4	22,622	73.5	41.8	18.0
North Redington Beach town	1,417	1,446	2.0	1,472	95.2	0.2	1.0	0.7	2.9	8.0	48.0	44.0	743	59.1	24.8	48.6
North River Shores CDP	3,079	NA	NA	3,824	85.5	9.9	0.6	0.0	4.0	20.0	51.0	29.1	1,509	80.5	21.7	48.1
North Sarasota CDP	6,982	NA	NA	7,548	47.2	28.7	1.6	2.1	20.4	23.1	58.8	18.2	3,047	72.3	52.7	16.0
North Weeki Wachee CDP	8,524	NA	NA	8,463	88.8	0.8	0.9	0.2	9.3	18.0	50.2	31.9	3,622	89.0	38.8	28.9
Oak Hill city	1,799	1,816	0.9	1,899	85.7	10.7	0.1	3.2	0.3	20.6	57.0	22.4	745	80.9	51.1	12.2
Oakland town	2,538	2,762	8.8	2,652	65.8	20.8	4.4	4.4	4.5	27.4	65.2	7.3	835	79.3	27.7	33.8
Oakland Park city	41,394	43,800	5.8	42,795	42.5	24.8	2.6	2.0	28.0	21.0	69.2	9.7	17,031	55.3	37.9	26.3
Oakleaf Plantation CDP	20,315	NA	NA	22,318	53.3	24.6	8.3	4.8	9.1	36.9	58.4	4.7	6,536	77.8	19.2	39.0
Oak Ridge CDP	22,685	NA	NA	22,313	15.4	35.9	4.2	4.0	40.5	24.8	68.0	7.4	7,353	36.0	57.9	8.9
Ocala city	56,324	57,586	2.2	56,918	60.4	21.3	3.1	2.7	12.5	24.4	58.0	17.7	21,922	52.8	39.8	24.7
Ocean Breeze Park town	355	353	-0.6	258	99.2	0.0	0.8	0.0	0.0	1.6	38.0	60.5	172	68.0	31.4	19.8
Ocean City CDP	5,550	NA	NA	5,901	70.6	5.8	2.2	6.0	15.4	18.0	65.4	16.5	2,447	57.5	33.4	20.6
Ocean Ridge town	1,786	1,878	5.2	1,754	90.7	0.0	0.5	1.1	7.6	13.1	51.4	35.4	921	77.1	18.7	55.7
Ocoee city	35,736	41,073	14.9	38,340	52.7	19.4	4.5	3.9	19.5	27.2	62.8	9.9	12,049	74.4	34.0	34.2
Odessa CDP	7,267	NA	NA	7,348	83.0	5.4	1.6	0.9	9.2	29.8	59.3	10.9	2,573	80.2	34.7	38.2
Ojus CDP	18,036	NA	NA	18,761	43.8	6.2	3.2	1.6	45.2	22.9	62.4	14.7	6,676	73.8	25.0	40.4
Okahumpka CDP	267	NA	NA	40	100.0	0.0	0.0	0.0	0.0	0.0	100.0	0.0	16	100.0	0.0	0.0
Okeechobee city	5,621	5,553	-1.2	5,581	56.1	5.6	0.9	1.4	36.0	25.3	61.1	13.6	1,720	60.5	53.5	15.3
Oldsmar city	13,617	13,913	2.2	13,730	74.7	6.9	5.1	4.4	8.9	23.6	65.1	11.3	4,916	66.1	38.8	27.3
Olga CDP	1,952	NA	NA	2,216	84.9	11.6	0.0	0.3	3.2	18.3	66.2	15.3	801	72.3	54.2	13.0
Olympia Heights CDP	13,488	NA	NA	13,991	10.5	0.6	1.5	0.1	87.4	17.6	62.3	20.0	3,896	81.7	49.2	24.7
Ona CDP	0	NA	NA	108	100.0	0.0	0.0	0.0	0.0	42.6	29.6	27.8	28	0.0	100.0	0.0
Opa-locka city	15,219	16,460	8.2	15,867	2.4	59.7	0.1	0.1	37.6	33.4	57.4	9.2	4,901	36.8	63.8	9.4
Orange City city	10,962	11,056	0.9	10,968	74.3	3.0	1.8	0.7	20.2	18.0	53.4	28.6	4,875	49.0	43.8	16.9
Orange Park town	8,388	8,606	2.6	8,472	74.4	10.8	5.0	4.3	5.4	18.7	61.2	20.2	3,298	61.2	31.7	26.7
Orangetree CDP	4,406	NA	NA	5,351	48.8	3.8	4.0	2.4	41.1	30.5	53.7	15.7	1,471	83.2	33.7	39.7
Orchid town	415	431	3.9	389	99.5	0.0	0.0	0.0	0.5	1.8	26.6	71.7	201	97.0	2.5	90.5
Oriole Beach CDP	1,420	NA	NA	1,594	94.2	0.0	0.0	5.8	0.0	25.3	58.2	16.4	581	59.2	17.4	40.1
Orlando city	238,834	262,372	9.9	250,224	39.8	27.3	3.6	2.5	26.8	21.8	68.4	9.8	102,570	37.4	31.0	36.7
Orlovista CDP	6,123	NA	NA	5,917	24.9	33.8	7.0	11.7	22.6	26.4	63.5	10.0	2,014	63.6	52.0	10.5
Ormond Beach city	38,171	39,075	2.4	38,502	85.7	3.8	3.9	2.6	3.9	16.5	55.1	28.4	15,550	77.8	31.7	35.6
Ormond-by-the-Sea CDP	7,406	NA	NA	7,764	93.4	1.0	1.2	0.8	3.6	10.8	57.5	31.4	3,768	75.1	33.3	32.8
Osprey CDP	6,100	NA	NA	6,223	91.3	0.0	2.6	1.6	4.5	12.5	49.9	37.6	2,767	92.6	18.3	54.5
Otter Creek town	134	133	-0.7	209	91.9	5.7	0.0	0.0	2.4	20.6	66.5	12.9	71	100.0	69.0	0.0
Oviedo city	33,467	38,020	13.6	35,602	65.8	7.9	5.3	1.6	19.5	28.2	64.5	7.2	10,012	80.3	17.2	51.6
Pace CDP	20,039	NA	NA	21,272	82.9	2.3	2.8	5.2	6.8	27.7	61.0	11.4	7,362	80.3	31.8	29.0
Page Park CDP	514	NA	NA	750	70.4	9.5	0.0	0.0	20.1	40.0	51.2	8.8	308	3.9	69.5	7.1
Pahokee city	5,649	6,029	6.7	5,941	7.5	56.4	0.0	0.6	35.5	26.1	63.6	10.1	1,817	66.0	60.3	14.0
Paisley CDP	818	NA	NA	775	96.6	0.1	0.0	0.0	3.2	16.1	72.6	11.4	272	79.8	57.7	13.6
Palatka city	10,546	10,387	-1.5	10,464	42.2	50.3	0.2	1.3	6.0	28.2	57.0	14.6	3,835	42.2	54.1	13.5
Palm Bay city	103,203	105,838	2.6	104,342	63.2	16.6	1.6	3.0	15.7	22.7	60.7	16.6	37,249	73.5	43.2	20.0
Palm Beach town	8,161	8,503	4.2	8,344	94.6	0.7	1.4	0.4	2.9	6.8	36.6	56.7	4,694	87.6	12.8	62.2
Palm Beach Gardens city	48,567	51,919	6.9	50,147	77.9	5.9	3.5	2.5	10.2	15.8	57.0	27.4	22,675	71.2	19.4	51.1
Palm Beach Shores town	1,142	1,194	4.6	1,097	92.7	1.4	1.5	0.2	4.3	5.8	55.0	39.2	645	60.3	18.3	42.6
Palm City CDP	23,120	NA	NA	23,380	91.0	0.5	2.0	1.2	5.3	18.9	53.1	27.9	9,371	83.6	21.3	48.1
Palm Coast city	75,197	80,600	7.2	77,779	71.9	12.0	2.6	2.4	11.0	20.3	54.0	25.5	27,466	79.4	37.1	23.8
Palmetto city	12,629	13,082	3.6	12,856	63.0	9.9	0.2	1.5	25.3	20.8	52.0	27.2	5,092	67.4	50.2	22.6
Palmetto Bay village	23,408	24,513	4.7	24,214	49.1	6.1	3.9	2.1	38.8	27.9	59.1	13.0	7,251	84.4	13.0	61.1
Palmetto Estates CDP	13,535	NA	NA	15,969	12.4	36.4	2.6	1.5	47.2	22.4	65.9	11.7	3,972	81.7	38.5	33.2
Palm Harbor CDP	57,439	NA	NA	59,007	89.5	1.6	1.6	1.0	6.3	16.2	58.2	25.6	26,198	72.3	28.4	37.1
Palmona Park CDP	1,146	NA	NA	1,267	90.0	0.9	0.0	2.4	6.8	20.9	73.0	6.1	447	34.0	49.4	22.4
Palm River-Clair Mel CDP	21,024	NA	NA	22,667	28.3	25.4	2.5	1.8	42.1	25.7	64.0	10.4	7,551	59.1	57.1	16.8
Palm Shores town	900	992	10.2	1,125	88.4	1.1	0.8	1.5	8.2	20.3	69.3	10.5	431	80.0	26.0	27.1
Palm Springs village	20,825	21,728	4.3	21,302	30.7	15.3	1.8	1.8	50.4	23.2	65.4	11.5	7,900	51.5	53.1	12.9
Palm Springs North CDP	5,253	NA	NA	5,657	16.3	0.1	0.0	0.3	83.3	24.1	61.9	13.8	1,595	94.6	33.7	19.2
Palm Valley CDP	20,019	NA	NA	20,888	87.0	3.5	3.4	1.4	4.7	19.6	61.7	18.8	8,590	76.3	15.5	55.3
Panacea CDP	816	NA	NA	1,052	97.1	0.0	0.0	2.9	0.0	18.1	77.7	4.2	359	24.8	76.0	0.0
Panama City city	35,520	37,681	6.1	36,405	67.4	18.1	2.5	4.6	7.4	21.6	61.4	16.8	14,781	49.1	41.3	22.7
Panama City Beach city	11,554	12,408	7.4	11,884	84.4	3.3	1.7	3.4	7.1	18.0	67.4	14.6	5,146	53.3	29.8	24.5

1 May be of any race.

Table A. All Places — **Population and Housing**

STATE City, town, township, borough, or CDP (county if applicable)	Population: 2010 census total population	Population: 2014 estimated population	Population: Percent change 2010–2014	Population: ACS total population estimate 2010–2014	Race and Hispanic or Latino origin (percent), 2010–2014: White alone, not Hispanic or Latino	Black alone, not Hispanic or Latino	Asian alone, not Hispanic or Latino	All other races or 2 or more races, not Hispanic or Latino	Hispanic or Latino[1]	Age (percent), 2010–2014: Under 18 years old	Age 18 to 64 years old	Age 65 years and older	Households, 2010–2014: Total occupied housing units	Percent owner occupied	Householders by level of education (percent): High school diploma or less	Bachelor's degree or more
	1	2	3	4	5	6	7	8	9	10	11	12	13	14	15	16
FLORIDA—Con.																
Paradise Heights CDP	1,215	NA	NA	550	65.3	0.0	0.0	0.0	34.7	28.4	53.7	18.0	199	91.5	74.9	15.1
Parker city	4,317	4,554	5.5	4,419	72.7	17.4	4.6	1.0	4.3	13.4	63.9	22.7	2,077	64.0	41.8	17.1
Parkland city	23,960	28,131	17.4	25,895	66.7	6.5	6.3	1.3	19.3	31.4	60.7	7.8	7,827	85.9	11.6	66.1
Pasadena Hills CDP	7,570	NA	NA	8,190	73.2	6.2	4.0	7.2	9.4	20.0	54.5	25.3	3,305	79.4	42.0	23.9
Patrick AFB CDP	1,222	NA	NA	1,233	61.9	12.2	4.4	4.9	16.5	28.5	67.4	3.9	321	0.0	10.6	41.1
Paxton town	644	725	12.6	477	99.0	0.4	0.0	0.6	0.0	20.1	54.4	25.4	194	85.6	52.6	9.8
Pea Ridge CDP	3,587	NA	NA	3,758	82.4	6.8	0.9	5.3	4.6	29.8	62.0	8.2	1,320	63.0	31.6	14.0
Pebble Creek CDP	7,622	NA	NA	8,388	46.5	12.6	13.3	6.9	20.7	26.5	62.0	11.6	2,731	76.5	12.4	56.6
Pelican Bay CDP	6,346	NA	NA	5,426	99.3	0.0	0.3	0.1	0.3	1.4	21.2	77.4	3,100	95.0	13.2	66.1
Pembroke Park town	6,102	6,287	3.0	6,220	27.6	58.4	0.6	2.0	11.4	27.6	58.8	13.7	2,480	44.7	48.5	24.0
Pembroke Pines city	154,019	164,626	6.9	159,920	30.1	18.8	5.4	2.0	43.7	22.0	62.7	15.4	56,308	73.1	28.9	36.1
Penney Farms town	746	806	8.0	647	90.4	6.2	0.0	2.5	0.9	1.1	19.1	79.9	367	16.1	21.5	62.4
Pensacola city	51,956	53,068	2.1	52,505	62.9	25.4	2.9	4.2	4.5	20.0	62.3	17.7	22,062	59.5	28.1	37.0
Perry city	7,004	7,031	0.4	7,040	51.3	44.2	0.0	2.5	2.0	25.8	58.8	15.3	2,388	71.9	49.8	19.8
Pierson town	1,736	1,746	0.6	1,466	57.2	7.5	0.0	0.7	34.6	27.1	55.3	17.6	419	82.3	56.1	12.9
Pine Air CDP	2,024	NA	NA	2,433	16.0	7.9	2.1	2.4	71.6	22.3	68.6	9.2	678	45.6	63.7	17.8
Pine Castle CDP	10,805	NA	NA	10,668	27.7	16.3	7.3	0.8	48.0	25.5	67.0	7.2	3,587	41.0	60.1	14.5
Pinecrest village	18,223	19,251	5.6	18,914	48.3	1.2	6.2	2.7	41.6	28.0	59.6	12.4	5,991	79.1	14.0	65.6
Pine Hills CDP	60,076	NA	NA	64,516	11.4	71.9	3.1	2.2	11.3	29.1	61.6	9.3	19,709	55.6	53.8	12.7
Pine Island CDP	64	NA	NA	36	100.0	0.0	0.0	0.0	0.0	0.0	0.0	100.0	18	100.0	0.0	100.0
Pine Island Center CDP	1,854	NA	NA	2,002	89.5	0.4	0.0	5.0	5.1	8.7	59.0	32.2	845	64.7	49.6	24.0
Pine Lakes CDP	862	NA	NA	552	77.5	0.0	0.0	7.1	15.4	21.2	60.6	18.1	198	53.0	48.0	10.6
Pineland CDP	407	NA	NA	352	96.6	0.0	0.0	0.0	3.4	9.4	60.8	29.8	133	84.2	21.8	45.9
Pine Level CDP	227	NA	NA	215	100.0	0.0	0.0	0.0	0.0	15.3	61.3	23.3	87	64.4	57.5	35.6
Pinellas Park city	49,175	50,946	3.6	49,874	74.4	4.1	7.2	2.3	12.0	18.3	61.9	19.8	20,911	65.9	46.2	19.3
Pine Manor CDP	3,428	NA	NA	4,363	24.4	11.0	1.8	1.7	61.1	34.5	61.2	4.4	1,151	13.6	86.5	1.5
Pine Ridge CDP (Citrus)	9,598	NA	NA	9,569	88.0	5.9	2.0	0.4	3.7	13.0	42.6	44.4	4,343	84.5	36.8	26.2
Pine Ridge CDP (Collier)	1,918	NA	NA	1,993	87.3	1.8	5.6	0.5	4.9	19.4	51.2	29.5	817	91.1	22.3	55.8
Pinewood CDP	16,520	NA	NA	16,531	3.1	76.6	0.2	1.0	19.2	23.8	64.6	11.5	4,597	43.6	63.1	8.0
Pioneer CDP	697	NA	NA	828	62.0	1.7	0.0	0.0	36.4	22.3	56.2	21.5	322	73.0	47.2	13.4
Pittman CDP	180	NA	NA	309	98.1	1.9	0.0	0.0	0.0	9.7	78.3	12.0	108	96.3	34.3	27.8
Plantation city	84,877	91,457	7.8	88,486	52.1	20.0	4.1	1.8	22.0	21.4	64.7	13.8	33,521	66.4	21.4	44.7
Plantation CDP	4,919	NA	NA	4,873	97.5	0.2	0.5	0.8	1.0	3.0	29.0	68.1	2,665	88.3	28.8	45.9
Plantation Island CDP	163	NA	NA	616	100.0	0.0	0.0	0.0	0.0	63.2	31.3	5.5	161	100.0	60.9	12.4
Plantation Mobile Home Park CDP	1,260	NA	NA	1,031	33.0	0.0	0.0	13.2	53.8	17.6	69.7	12.7	315	47.9	65.7	10.8
Plant City city	34,688	36,627	5.6	35,866	53.3	15.2	1.1	1.3	29.2	28.7	60.5	10.8	12,329	56.9	50.0	19.1
Poinciana CDP	53,193	NA	NA	56,678	20.7	24.8	1.7	2.1	50.7	29.2	55.9	15.0	16,938	72.7	41.1	19.2
Point Baker CDP	2,991	NA	NA	3,391	76.0	8.4	1.4	8.0	6.2	29.3	63.8	7.0	1,097	66.9	37.1	21.9
Polk City town	1,725	1,838	6.6	2,016	86.1	3.7	0.5	0.9	8.8	24.6	59.8	15.6	681	69.3	57.6	12.3
Pomona Park town	912	880	-3.5	700	79.3	10.4	0.4	2.3	7.6	17.0	56.8	26.1	288	75.7	59.0	10.4
Pompano Beach city	99,844	106,105	6.3	103,234	49.0	30.1	1.4	1.6	17.9	19.0	61.9	19.1	41,138	55.5	44.5	26.7
Ponce de Leon town	573	557	-2.8	577	91.5	1.2	0.0	2.6	4.7	23.2	56.8	19.9	244	70.1	55.7	9.8
Ponce Inlet town	3,032	3,100	2.2	3,053	90.8	0.0	1.6	1.0	6.6	11.2	44.7	44.2	1,386	85.6	24.3	37.4
Port Charlotte CDP	54,392	NA	NA	55,206	78.5	9.0	2.3	1.9	8.2	16.3	55.1	28.7	23,118	76.7	42.0	20.7
Port LaBelle CDP	3,530	NA	NA	4,182	34.9	6.3	1.0	2.1	55.7	26.0	57.6	16.4	1,303	62.5	58.8	14.3
Port Orange city	56,595	58,742	3.8	57,218	88.1	3.8	1.8	2.1	4.2	17.6	58.1	24.2	23,941	75.1	37.2	27.2
Port Richey city	2,671	2,723	1.9	2,685	92.6	0.0	0.3	2.5	4.7	14.2	55.8	30.1	1,312	68.6	37.2	23.2
Port St. Joe city	3,445	3,415	-0.9	3,416	58.1	36.3	0.7	3.6	1.3	16.7	65.9	17.3	1,232	67.0	40.3	16.2
Port St. John CDP	12,267	NA	NA	11,444	82.5	7.2	1.6	1.2	7.5	21.8	66.4	11.9	4,301	77.9	32.7	22.5
Port St. Lucie city	164,716	174,110	5.7	169,260	58.9	16.6	2.1	3.1	19.4	24.2	58.9	17.0	59,101	77.8	40.2	21.0
Port Salerno CDP	10,091	NA	NA	10,070	77.9	8.0	0.9	2.2	11.0	18.8	57.0	24.1	4,093	72.7	40.7	21.7
Pretty Bayou CDP	3,206	NA	NA	3,189	89.5	1.9	0.0	2.0	6.6	19.2	56.1	24.8	1,328	73.1	31.1	28.5
Princeton CDP	22,038	NA	NA	26,164	13.6	25.1	1.3	0.9	59.1	32.6	61.4	6.1	6,398	63.3	48.3	21.9
Progress Village CDP	5,392	NA	NA	6,960	27.3	43.8	4.2	1.0	23.7	28.4	64.4	7.1	2,298	72.1	30.6	32.2
Punta Gorda city	16,641	17,596	5.7	16,984	89.6	2.4	0.5	2.5	4.9	6.3	42.1	51.5	8,495	79.0	27.5	39.0
Punta Rassa CDP	1,750	NA	NA	1,800	98.1	0.0	1.3	0.6	0.0	2.6	7.1	90.2	1,053	37.2	15.4	58.2
Quail Ridge CDP	1,040	NA	NA	1,171	83.7	2.9	0.3	2.0	11.0	27.0	64.5	8.6	462	76.0	17.1	50.0
Quincy city	8,174	7,914	-3.2	8,022	19.0	61.7	0.9	3.0	15.4	23.1	63.1	13.7	2,825	62.7	58.6	16.7
Raiford town	254	248	-2.4	142	92.3	7.0	0.0	0.7	0.0	35.9	54.3	9.9	53	41.5	62.3	1.9
Raleigh CDP	373	NA	NA	139	40.3	42.4	0.0	0.0	17.3	0.0	69.9	30.2	94	23.4	63.8	19.1
Reddick town	506	512	1.2	517	36.2	48.4	0.0	2.1	13.3	30.0	62.9	7.2	187	67.9	58.3	12.3
Redington Beach town	1,427	1,455	2.0	1,475	91.0	0.2	1.1	1.5	6.2	12.6	64.9	22.4	653	82.4	20.7	49.8
Redington Shores town	2,121	2,168	2.2	2,093	91.5	0.0	1.2	1.3	6.0	9.1	63.2	27.8	1,237	66.4	20.5	49.6
Richmond Heights CDP	8,541	NA	NA	8,895	3.2	70.6	0.0	1.0	25.2	16.0	66.6	17.3	2,450	81.1	48.5	25.4
Richmond West CDP	31,973	NA	NA	34,825	13.2	5.8	1.8	1.1	78.2	23.5	65.3	11.3	8,967	90.8	34.5	30.5
Ridgecrest CDP	2,558	NA	NA	3,526	30.7	60.6	0.0	4.0	4.7	35.9	52.1	12.2	1,030	63.4	42.1	10.7
Ridge Manor CDP	4,513	NA	NA	4,649	88.9	1.8	0.0	1.1	8.2	18.5	58.7	22.7	1,859	82.8	49.9	13.8
Ridge Wood Heights CDP	4,795	NA	NA	4,953	81.3	3.8	0.8	0.9	13.1	18.8	66.5	14.6	2,074	64.3	31.0	28.0
Rio CDP	965	NA	NA	1,059	88.8	3.7	2.2	2.7	2.6	5.8	78.9	15.2	484	68.2	23.6	32.4
Rio Pinar CDP	5,211	NA	NA	5,562	58.4	6.1	3.0	1.8	30.6	20.6	60.8	18.5	1,785	88.6	22.4	45.4
River Park CDP	5,222	NA	NA	5,352	82.6	4.8	0.3	2.3	9.9	11.6	58.1	30.3	2,512	79.6	51.8	13.3
River Ridge CDP	4,702	NA	NA	4,635	89.0	0.7	0.5	1.3	8.5	19.6	60.7	19.7	1,881	91.5	34.9	31.2
Riverview CDP	71,050	NA	NA	76,590	56.1	15.4	3.7	4.0	20.9	27.3	63.9	8.6	25,871	74.1	30.6	31.8
Riviera Beach city	32,488	33,649	3.6	33,123	22.1	64.1	2.3	2.5	9.0	24.1	61.4	14.4	11,950	55.2	46.5	24.0
Rockledge city	24,930	26,071	4.6	25,477	73.3	13.9	2.5	3.1	7.1	19.7	61.3	18.8	9,941	77.2	27.3	32.9
Roeville CDP	608	NA	NA	470	94.9	0.0	1.3	0.0	3.8	25.5	54.7	19.8	202	74.3	59.9	5.0
Roosevelt Gardens CDP	2,456	NA	NA	2,630	0.4	96.0	0.5	0.6	2.5	28.5	62.6	8.9	736	45.5	59.5	12.1
Roseland CDP	1,472	NA	NA	1,694	84.8	0.0	4.7	3.0	7.6	3.8	66.3	29.9	692	91.5	40.0	23.8
Rotonda CDP	8,759	NA	NA	8,616	96.4	2.0	0.0	0.3	1.3	10.5	39.5	49.9	4,195	81.0	40.2	29.0
Royal Palm Beach village	34,140	37,015	8.4	35,482	51.3	22.6	3.1	1.5	21.6	26.6	61.7	11.7	11,188	79.7	31.5	30.1
Royal Palm Estates CDP	3,025	NA	NA	2,780	28.5	20.8	0.3	0.6	49.8	28.6	65.7	5.7	751	31.7	69.6	9.7
Ruskin CDP	17,208	NA	NA	18,846	46.6	12.6	0.9	2.6	37.4	31.5	59.5	8.9	5,967	68.2	50.0	21.5
Safety Harbor city	16,885	17,234	2.1	17,017	83.9	3.8	2.5	3.1	6.7	17.8	60.4	21.9	7,301	81.8	26.9	40.9
St. Augustine city	12,975	13,841	6.7	13,440	79.5	11.7	0.9	1.3	6.6	12.7	66.8	20.5	5,383	54.1	27.9	39.0
St. Augustine Beach city	6,176	6,706	8.6	6,422	91.6	0.2	0.5	0.7	7.0	17.9	61.2	21.1	2,834	63.5	12.4	51.8
St. Augustine Shores CDP	7,359	NA	NA	7,824	90.1	2.5	0.6	3.0	3.8	16.7	51.7	31.6	3,699	68.6	27.2	31.8
St. Augustine South CDP	4,998	NA	NA	5,140	83.9	0.6	3.9	1.6	10.0	20.2	61.2	18.6	2,093	86.4	25.1	36.3
St. Cloud city	36,332	43,005	18.4	39,685	57.1	7.3	2.2	3.1	30.5	25.2	60.7	14.1	13,102	69.6	42.9	17.4
St. George Island CDP	0	NA	NA	645	94.9	0.0	0.0	0.0	5.1	9.8	57.9	32.4	309	90.0	4.2	57.0
St. James City CDP	3,784	NA	NA	3,741	95.1	0.0	0.4	0.0	4.5	8.3	39.0	53.0	1,844	88.8	38.4	24.8

1 May be of any race.

Table A. All Places — **Population and Housing**

STATE City, town, township, borough, or CDP (county if applicable)	Population: 2010 census total population	Population: 2014 estimated population	Population: Percent change 2010–2014	Population: ACS total population estimate 2010–2014	Race and Hispanic or Latino origin (percent), 2010–2014: White alone, not Hispanic or Latino	Black alone, not Hispanic or Latino	Asian alone, not Hispanic or Latino	All other races or 2 or more races, not Hispanic or Latino	Hispanic or Latino[1]	Age (percent), 2010–2014: Under 18 years old	Age 18 to 64 years old	Age 65 years and older	Households, 2010–2014: Total occupied housing units	Percent owner occupied	Householders by level of education (percent): High school diploma or less	Bachelor's degree or more
	1	2	3	4	5	6	7	8	9	10	11	12	13	14	15	16
FLORIDA—Con.																
St. Leo town	1,338	1,506	12.6	1,272	73.4	9.8	1.9	0.9	13.9	4.6	89.1	6.1	98	93.9	17.3	57.1
St. Lucie Village town	590	609	3.2	546	97.4	0.0	0.0	2.0	0.5	18.3	64.8	16.8	212	77.8	30.2	29.2
St. Marks city	293	297	1.4	245	96.7	0.8	0.0	0.0	2.4	17.6	61.2	21.2	115	55.7	50.4	16.5
St. Pete Beach city	9,346	9,496	1.6	9,408	95.2	0.6	1.6	0.5	2.2	10.4	57.0	32.6	4,936	68.2	15.6	53.5
St. Petersburg city	245,193	253,693	3.5	248,429	63.1	23.7	3.3	3.0	6.9	18.8	65.1	16.2	105,071	58.7	35.1	32.5
Samoset CDP	3,854	NA	NA	3,590	26.4	30.0	1.5	2.2	39.9	24.6	62.5	12.9	1,088	59.7	67.6	4.7
Samsula-Spruce Creek CDP	5,047	NA	NA	5,694	95.1	0.3	1.4	0.0	3.1	17.9	60.4	21.6	2,224	91.8	31.0	32.8
San Antonio city	1,147	1,250	9.0	1,062	88.0	4.5	0.0	0.3	7.2	25.6	61.0	13.5	416	76.2	24.3	34.9
San Carlos Park CDP	16,824	NA	NA	17,646	71.0	0.7	3.0	3.6	21.7	20.2	69.4	10.3	5,752	66.9	50.5	18.3
San Castle CDP	3,428	NA	NA	4,513	16.2	47.2	0.9	1.0	34.7	27.8	64.5	7.7	1,074	58.0	66.9	10.4
Sanford city	53,711	57,525	7.1	55,296	46.7	27.2	2.5	3.0	20.6	26.4	62.4	11.2	18,267	56.6	37.2	26.5
Sanibel city	6,469	7,056	9.1	6,761	97.3	0.7	0.2	0.6	1.2	7.9	40.7	51.3	3,459	87.4	11.9	66.1
Sarasota city	52,056	54,214	4.1	52,986	64.8	13.7	1.3	1.7	18.4	16.7	60.4	22.8	22,773	53.2	36.8	34.6
Sarasota Springs CDP	14,395	NA	NA	15,659	85.0	1.1	0.7	1.7	11.6	17.7	63.1	19.2	6,248	80.7	38.8	27.2
Satellite Beach city	10,109	10,418	3.1	10,262	89.3	2.0	1.2	2.1	5.5	22.4	57.8	19.8	4,009	75.7	21.3	42.3
Sawgrass CDP	4,880	NA	NA	5,089	93.1	0.5	1.6	3.0	1.8	14.0	54.2	31.7	2,465	78.7	3.7	68.4
Schall Circle CDP	1,117	NA	NA	1,129	30.9	30.3	1.3	0.7	36.8	37.2	55.9	6.9	398	41.0	60.3	7.0
Sea Ranch Lakes village	670	712	6.3	737	88.7	0.0	1.4	0.0	9.9	26.4	50.3	23.5	280	90.4	7.5	74.3
Sebastian city	21,929	23,344	6.5	22,485	85.0	6.8	0.5	1.8	5.9	19.3	52.5	28.2	9,128	80.3	41.5	19.8
Sebring city	10,413	10,372	-0.4	10,356	61.7	12.6	1.2	1.9	22.6	19.0	56.1	25.0	4,047	49.2	55.7	14.1
Seffner CDP	7,579	NA	NA	7,532	66.1	7.5	6.6	4.6	15.2	25.2	63.5	11.4	2,547	79.1	34.1	23.9
Seminole city	17,159	17,923	4.5	17,477	88.9	1.1	3.7	2.6	3.7	14.5	52.9	32.6	8,249	76.7	34.9	35.4
Seminole Manor CDP	2,621	NA	NA	2,464	41.0	27.2	0.0	0.0	31.8	28.7	54.4	16.9	804	70.9	50.2	10.1
Seville CDP	614	NA	NA	192	79.2	10.9	0.0	0.0	9.9	19.8	62.4	17.7	95	84.2	54.7	16.8
Sewall's Point town	1,996	2,100	5.2	1,994	91.6	1.3	0.1	0.4	6.7	20.8	52.9	26.5	787	88.8	13.5	62.9
Shady Hills CDP	11,523	NA	NA	10,687	92.4	0.3	0.0	1.3	6.0	18.8	61.2	20.0	3,979	89.4	51.4	12.5
Shalimar town	721	784	8.7	723	84.9	3.7	1.9	2.9	6.5	17.3	64.3	18.4	315	69.8	14.3	40.6
Sharpes CDP	3,411	NA	NA	3,059	90.2	3.7	0.0	3.3	2.8	17.0	64.1	18.9	1,268	70.7	53.5	23.3
Siesta Key CDP	6,565	NA	NA	6,158	95.0	0.4	0.6	1.2	2.8	9.3	46.9	43.7	3,056	81.5	14.5	61.5
Silver Lake CDP	1,879	NA	NA	1,641	79.5	9.2	2.6	0.0	8.7	18.2	63.0	18.8	713	75.9	26.9	46.6
Silver Springs Shores CDP	6,539	NA	NA	6,551	35.8	39.5	0.8	3.0	20.8	29.5	45.6	24.7	2,580	71.0	54.1	12.3
Sky Lake CDP	6,153	NA	NA	5,699	36.5	11.9	3.9	1.5	46.1	19.2	66.5	14.1	1,818	71.9	57.7	8.4
Sneads town	1,849	1,781	-3.7	2,061	71.7	14.3	0.0	2.6	11.5	21.0	57.4	21.7	804	74.3	62.3	15.8
Solana CDP	742	NA	NA	437	87.4	12.6	0.0	0.0	0.0	0.0	70.6	29.3	221	66.1	42.5	15.8
Sopchoppy city	449	456	1.6	308	57.5	36.7	0.0	5.8	0.0	19.5	63.7	16.9	134	74.6	50.0	15.7
Sorrento CDP	861	NA	NA	792	51.3	0.0	0.0	0.0	48.7	7.1	68.8	24.1	331	54.7	70.1	13.9
South Apopka CDP	5,728	NA	NA	5,565	15.7	56.0	0.2	0.8	27.3	26.2	69.8	4.0	1,655	46.8	59.6	10.6
South Bay city	4,876	5,015	2.9	4,941	14.9	55.9	0.3	1.5	27.3	19.3	75.8	4.7	625	58.7	64.0	10.2
South Beach CDP	3,501	NA	NA	3,432	98.0	0.0	0.0	1.7	0.3	7.0	40.2	52.7	1,734	92.2	2.8	68.6
South Bradenton CDP	22,178	NA	NA	22,814	66.4	10.5	1.9	2.8	18.5	18.7	57.5	23.9	10,174	50.8	54.9	13.6
South Brooksville CDP	4,007	NA	NA	3,923	79.8	10.4	0.4	3.8	5.6	16.1	53.3	30.5	1,698	77.3	47.1	22.9
Southchase CDP	15,921	NA	NA	16,131	27.2	15.6	8.2	2.0	47.0	25.7	67.3	7.1	4,788	70.4	37.6	30.6
South Daytona city	12,252	12,397	1.2	12,265	73.9	14.2	0.2	4.4	7.2	20.7	59.8	19.5	5,020	60.9	43.5	17.3
Southeast Arcadia CDP	6,554	NA	NA	7,855	30.8	6.1	0.6	0.3	62.2	30.1	63.7	6.4	2,123	55.7	78.1	6.3
Southgate CDP	7,173	NA	NA	7,220	85.9	0.9	2.5	2.1	8.5	16.0	58.3	25.8	3,332	73.2	29.5	38.0
South Gate Ridge CDP	5,688	NA	NA	5,906	87.8	1.0	0.5	2.0	8.6	19.8	62.8	17.4	2,413	71.8	45.7	22.5
South Highpoint CDP	5,195	NA	NA	4,942	49.8	12.1	4.1	3.8	30.2	26.2	64.7	9.3	1,697	50.0	58.9	9.1
South Miami city	11,655	12,183	4.5	12,036	31.9	17.3	2.6	1.9	46.3	22.3	66.6	11.1	4,121	61.8	22.8	46.8
South Miami Heights CDP	35,696	NA	NA	37,564	9.0	19.6	1.8	1.4	68.3	23.0	63.6	13.4	10,411	57.0	55.0	17.7
South Palm Beach town	1,358	1,409	3.8	1,277	93.3	0.9	0.8	0.6	4.4	3.7	35.2	61.1	775	76.6	17.0	49.3
South Pasadena city	4,964	5,033	1.4	4,993	91.8	1.0	2.2	0.0	5.0	6.4	36.9	56.6	3,080	53.8	30.4	38.2
South Patrick Shores CDP	5,875	NA	NA	6,173	87.2	2.2	3.2	1.7	5.7	15.8	62.1	22.3	2,536	79.2	22.5	45.4
South Sarasota CDP	4,950	NA	NA	4,531	86.3	1.2	2.8	2.1	7.5	13.8	54.9	31.2	2,260	70.9	21.1	46.3
South Venice CDP	13,949	NA	NA	14,637	90.8	0.2	0.8	2.3	5.9	15.2	57.9	26.8	6,231	78.4	44.4	21.2
Southwest Ranches town	7,344	7,761	5.7	7,583	51.4	7.5	1.9	2.8	36.3	19.2	66.3	14.5	2,154	91.3	28.7	40.9
Springfield city	8,902	9,355	5.1	9,095	65.8	18.2	3.0	8.3	4.7	21.1	64.3	14.7	3,496	51.7	55.3	12.3
Spring Hill CDP	98,621	NA	NA	100,270	76.6	4.6	1.3	2.6	14.8	21.4	55.6	23.1	38,703	76.9	47.1	15.2
Springhill CDP	160	NA	NA	102	100.0	0.0	0.0	0.0	0.0	17.6	62.8	19.6	40	75.0	57.5	25.0
Spring Lake CDP	458	NA	NA	354	93.2	0.0	0.0	0.0	6.8	1.4	62.4	36.2	164	100.0	29.9	14.0
Spring Ridge CDP	398	NA	NA	304	81.9	0.0	0.0	4.6	13.5	15.5	50.7	33.9	172	100.0	62.2	2.9
Stacey Street CDP	858	NA	NA	484	10.3	80.4	0.0	0.0	9.3	33.9	60.8	5.4	145	16.6	51.7	0.0
Starke city	5,446	5,360	-1.6	5,404	68.4	25.4	0.3	4.2	1.7	20.8	55.2	24.1	2,122	62.1	60.8	13.1
Steinhatchee CDP	1,047	NA	NA	934	95.3	0.0	0.0	0.0	4.7	10.4	25.7	63.9	581	82.4	29.3	5.7
Stock Island CDP	3,919	NA	NA	4,153	30.6	15.0	1.6	0.7	52.1	18.6	74.2	7.2	1,195	43.4	60.3	13.0
Stuart city	15,589	16,197	3.9	15,850	72.8	13.1	1.2	1.5	11.5	14.4	59.5	26.1	7,291	54.0	34.6	28.8
Sugarmill Woods CDP	8,287	NA	NA	9,495	93.7	0.6	1.7	1.1	2.9	9.0	40.5	50.6	4,418	89.0	39.6	24.0
Sumatra CDP	148	NA	NA	152	96.1	0.0	0.0	0.0	3.9	32.9	67.0	0.0	44	79.5	61.4	0.0
Sun City Center CDP	19,258	NA	NA	20,042	90.1	4.0	0.3	0.6	5.0	3.1	22.6	74.4	11,790	81.5	30.7	35.9
Suncoast Estates CDP	4,384	NA	NA	4,629	96.0	0.0	0.0	0.1	3.8	20.5	67.9	11.5	1,659	60.2	65.6	2.8
Sunny Isles Beach city	20,832	21,946	5.3	21,583	53.1	4.1	1.0	1.4	40.4	12.9	57.5	29.5	11,216	53.6	23.3	47.7
Sunrise city	84,381	91,256	8.1	88,391	35.6	30.6	3.8	2.3	27.7	21.4	63.4	15.5	31,343	69.6	36.9	28.8
Sunset CDP	16,389	NA	NA	17,097	13.8	0.3	2.3	0.9	82.7	19.9	61.9	18.1	5,312	83.0	30.2	39.6
Surfside town	5,743	5,996	4.4	5,927	61.6	0.2	1.3	6.8	30.0	27.2	51.4	21.6	2,215	63.3	20.1	61.7
Sweetwater city	19,958	20,751	4.0	20,562	2.3	0.7	1.5	0.1	95.4	19.9	65.7	14.4	5,489	40.4	61.5	20.5
Taft CDP	2,205	NA	NA	2,146	56.2	13.3	2.0	2.3	26.2	14.0	76.0	10.3	733	68.3	64.4	19.2
Tallahassee city	181,383	188,107	3.7	185,395	52.3	34.9	3.8	2.3	6.6	17.1	74.4	8.5	74,108	40.6	17.8	44.4
Tamarac city	60,503	63,793	5.4	62,478	45.7	23.6	1.7	2.0	27.1	17.0	56.5	26.5	27,011	72.6	40.1	27.4
Tamiami CDP	55,271	NA	NA	57,123	4.9	0.6	0.5	0.3	93.7	17.4	65.2	17.4	16,078	77.6	42.8	31.2
Tampa city	335,715	358,699	6.8	348,934	45.9	24.5	3.7	2.6	23.3	22.3	66.4	11.4	139,337	49.6	35.6	36.6
Tangelo Park CDP	2,231	NA	NA	2,260	2.4	84.2	0.0	1.9	11.4	25.1	59.3	15.7	749	64.2	57.3	7.2
Tangerine CDP	2,865	NA	NA	2,275	61.8	8.7	0.0	6.2	23.2	23.8	56.6	19.4	827	82.5	36.2	34.9
Tarpon Springs city	23,515	24,239	3.1	23,789	85.9	5.2	1.1	1.8	6.0	15.1	55.9	28.9	10,017	71.8	40.0	26.6
Tavares city	13,956	14,930	7.0	14,343	72.3	15.0	2.8	2.0	8.0	18.5	46.2	35.3	6,127	74.5	47.5	19.7
Tavernier CDP	2,136	NA	NA	2,252	84.2	0.5	0.4	1.9	13.0	16.2	69.3	14.6	821	63.6	34.2	31.5
Taylor Creek CDP	4,348	NA	NA	4,067	82.6	0.2	3.4	1.2	12.6	19.1	50.4	30.3	1,745	74.3	58.4	8.2
Temple Terrace city	24,501	25,419	3.7	25,098	59.0	17.7	4.8	3.4	15.0	21.4	65.9	12.6	9,939	54.0	24.6	44.9
Tequesta village	5,634	5,875	4.3	5,756	82.8	1.6	4.4	1.0	10.2	19.2	58.5	22.3	2,519	79.6	28.4	41.6
The Acreage CDP	38,704	NA	NA	37,773	64.9	14.1	2.3	1.7	17.0	24.0	65.3	10.6	11,120	90.4	41.1	20.3
The Crossings CDP	22,758	NA	NA	24,313	25.7	4.9	2.3	1.6	65.5	22.9	63.0	14.1	7,752	78.5	24.0	37.9

1 May be of any race.

Table A. All Places — **Population and Housing**

STATE City, town, township, borough, or CDP (county if applicable)	Population: 2010 census total population	Population: 2014 estimated population	Population: Percent change 2010–2014	Population: ACS total population estimate 2010–2014	Race and Hispanic or Latino origin (percent), 2010–2014: White alone, not Hispanic or Latino	Black alone, not Hispanic or Latino	Asian alone, not Hispanic or Latino	All other races or 2 or more races, not Hispanic or Latino	Hispanic or Latino[1]	Age (percent), 2010–2014: Under 18 years old	Age 18 to 64 years old	Age 65 years and older	Households, 2010–2014: Total occupied housing units	Percent owner occupied	Householders by level of education (percent): High school diploma or less	Bachelor's degree or more
	1	2	3	4	5	6	7	8	9	10	11	12	13	14	15	16
FLORIDA—Con.																
The Hammocks CDP	51,003	NA	NA	54,833	14.1	5.2	2.7	1.3	76.7	21.1	66.8	12.0	15,888	64.0	29.1	36.2
The Meadows CDP	3,994	NA	NA	3,851	94.2	3.6	0.0	0.0	2.1	8.2	37.2	54.7	2,061	80.2	21.1	52.0
The Villages CDP	51,442	NA	NA	61,046	96.7	0.4	0.8	0.3	1.8	0.0	25.6	74.4	33,361	96.5	25.3	42.2
Thonotosassa CDP	13,014	NA	NA	13,461	67.4	16.6	1.9	3.2	10.9	23.6	60.1	16.2	4,770	70.5	47.9	20.6
Three Lakes CDP	15,047	NA	NA	16,263	25.9	7.3	4.4	0.9	61.5	26.4	65.7	7.8	4,983	71.9	19.9	50.3
Three Oaks CDP	3,592	NA	NA	3,479	86.2	0.6	2.5	3.1	7.6	26.8	62.8	10.4	1,113	90.0	25.9	33.3
Tice CDP	4,470	NA	NA	4,245	23.3	7.1	2.1	0.0	67.6	25.2	68.4	6.5	1,105	45.4	68.1	6.7
Tierra Verde CDP	3,721	NA	NA	3,227	94.6	0.3	1.4	0.8	2.9	9.9	56.9	33.3	1,608	88.7	8.8	66.5
Tiger Point CDP	3,090	NA	NA	2,932	91.3	0.8	3.6	0.4	3.8	19.4	58.7	21.9	1,192	74.2	15.3	43.6
Tildenville CDP	511	NA	NA	1,710	16.0	72.6	0.0	5.2	6.3	35.0	60.1	5.0	525	8.6	73.7	0.0
Timber Pines CDP	5,386	NA	NA	5,300	98.3	0.2	0.2	0.4	0.9	0.4	16.7	83.0	3,165	89.0	32.8	35.5
Titusville city	43,749	44,557	1.8	44,032	73.1	16.0	2.2	2.3	6.3	18.8	57.7	23.4	18,438	65.9	37.7	23.5
Town 'n' Country CDP	78,442	NA	NA	82,506	41.4	6.7	3.6	1.8	46.5	20.8	66.6	12.5	30,444	58.6	37.7	28.5
Treasure Island city	6,705	6,810	1.6	6,749	93.9	0.0	1.3	0.8	4.0	11.4	60.6	27.9	3,578	67.4	27.5	44.7
Trenton city	1,999	2,023	1.2	2,298	72.4	17.7	1.3	0.8	7.7	26.6	58.7	14.7	819	55.1	48.6	10.0
Trilby CDP	419	NA	NA	449	74.2	11.4	0.0	0.0	14.5	24.1	65.2	10.9	269	40.9	53.2	6.7
Trinity CDP	10,907	NA	NA	10,550	88.9	2.4	2.5	1.5	4.7	23.8	52.8	23.3	3,979	94.2	19.1	46.1
Tyndall AFB CDP	2,994	NA	NA	3,330	58.2	12.8	2.2	12.4	14.5	38.2	60.5	1.2	786	0.0	7.5	32.2
Umatilla city	3,453	3,634	5.2	3,545	90.5	0.8	0.0	0.8	7.9	20.3	43.6	35.9	1,566	64.7	52.3	20.8
Union Park CDP	9,765	NA	NA	10,501	50.3	5.1	3.5	2.2	39.0	20.1	68.7	11.3	3,611	60.9	35.3	22.6
University CDP (Hillsborough)	41,163	NA	NA	41,732	32.7	28.9	4.4	2.8	31.3	20.8	70.8	8.3	16,922	13.9	42.6	19.3
University CDP (Orange)	31,084	NA	NA	30,926	55.9	10.1	6.4	2.2	25.5	13.2	83.2	3.6	6,102	45.4	27.1	34.8
University Park CDP	26,995	NA	NA	26,304	9.5	2.7	0.5	0.5	86.7	15.2	63.7	20.9	7,677	63.6	47.2	32.6
Upper Grand Lagoon CDP	13,963	NA	NA	14,917	89.0	2.6	1.0	3.5	3.9	20.9	65.8	13.2	6,070	64.0	28.3	30.6
Valparaiso city	5,033	5,188	3.1	5,109	78.3	5.2	1.6	8.8	6.1	13.3	74.1	12.4	1,601	65.1	26.0	35.4
Valrico CDP	35,545	NA	NA	36,603	68.0	9.3	2.7	3.1	16.9	24.7	61.4	13.6	12,664	84.1	29.0	36.1
Vamo CDP	4,727	NA	NA	4,752	95.1	0.0	0.1	0.0	4.8	9.4	44.2	46.5	2,463	54.0	36.8	39.2
Venice city	20,746	21,730	4.7	21,121	94.9	0.6	1.1	0.8	2.7	7.0	37.5	55.7	11,312	73.7	30.3	39.0
Venice Gardens CDP	7,104	NA	NA	7,381	91.6	0.1	1.7	0.4	6.2	12.9	52.4	34.7	3,414	78.8	37.1	32.6
Vernon city	687	671	-2.3	1,402	55.3	20.7	1.9	19.3	2.9	40.7	52.6	6.5	355	60.0	63.1	5.4
Vero Beach city	15,225	16,017	5.2	15,577	86.2	3.3	0.4	3.0	7.0	13.4	59.0	27.6	7,012	62.0	34.9	34.7
Vero Beach South CDP	23,092	NA	NA	23,343	83.6	4.8	0.5	2.2	9.0	20.3	56.0	23.9	9,248	72.5	40.1	26.8
Verona Walk CDP	1,782	NA	NA	2,375	88.6	0.0	5.2	1.5	4.7	10.1	51.6	38.4	1,128	80.9	24.6	44.9
Viera East CDP	10,757	NA	NA	10,998	76.9	5.3	6.2	2.2	9.4	20.2	50.4	29.2	4,417	82.7	17.7	48.5
Viera West CDP	6,641	NA	NA	8,163	67.7	3.9	7.7	2.5	18.3	24.6	55.0	20.5	3,114	74.0	15.3	61.7
Villano Beach CDP	2,678	NA	NA	2,808	93.2	0.0	0.0	2.1	4.8	18.7	59.2	21.9	1,078	75.7	28.8	48.7
Villas CDP	11,569	NA	NA	10,464	79.6	2.2	3.0	1.7	13.5	11.7	59.2	29.0	4,928	61.3	33.4	29.4
Vineyards CDP	3,375	NA	NA	3,643	91.6	0.1	0.5	0.4	7.5	11.3	42.9	45.7	1,583	91.5	10.2	64.6
Virginia Gardens village	2,375	2,475	4.2	2,632	20.6	0.0	0.8	0.0	78.6	22.4	61.2	16.5	922	50.9	51.1	23.3
Wabasso CDP	609	NA	NA	824	51.9	0.1	0.0	0.0	47.9	35.8	33.8	30.5	221	67.0	32.6	19.0
Wabasso Beach CDP	1,853	NA	NA	1,630	95.5	0.0	2.6	0.0	1.8	4.7	32.9	62.3	915	94.3	8.1	73.8
Wacissa CDP	386	NA	NA	150	53.3	46.7	0.0	0.0	0.0	16.0	67.3	16.7	62	88.7	46.8	0.0
Wahneta CDP	5,091	NA	NA	5,000	40.2	0.0	0.0	0.0	59.8	31.3	64.5	4.3	1,228	61.9	88.7	2.1
Waldo city	1,016	1,024	0.8	1,160	68.7	20.2	1.7	0.0	9.4	22.9	65.7	11.4	425	63.8	65.4	14.1
Wallace CDP	1,785	NA	NA	1,488	93.3	0.8	0.5	1.6	3.8	13.5	71.0	15.6	631	91.8	27.9	41.8
Warm Mineral Springs CDP	5,061	NA	NA	5,454	91.1	1.2	2.1	3.7	1.8	5.8	34.6	59.6	2,610	88.2	52.0	15.4
Warrington CDP	14,531	NA	NA	13,428	70.0	20.2	1.0	3.5	5.3	24.6	58.6	16.8	5,826	55.3	41.8	21.9
Washington Park CDP	1,672	NA	NA	1,514	2.7	87.1	0.0	0.0	10.2	32.8	56.2	10.9	450	68.9	58.9	6.7
Watergate CDP	2,942	NA	NA	3,142	68.1	5.6	5.3	6.5	14.6	24.0	66.2	9.7	968	65.3	44.8	13.5
Watertown CDP	2,829	NA	NA	2,871	59.1	25.0	0.0	8.6	7.3	18.7	60.6	20.8	1,031	55.7	37.1	14.1
Wauchula city	4,938	4,925	-0.3	4,930	47.3	9.3	0.4	4.0	39.0	29.6	55.1	15.4	1,435	64.9	64.0	18.3
Waukeenah CDP	272	NA	NA	208	63.0	26.4	0.0	0.0	10.6	24.1	64.9	11.1	71	71.8	56.3	0.0
Wausau town	381	370	-2.9	519	99.8	0.0	0.0	0.0	0.2	35.4	49.0	15.4	166	70.5	70.5	5.4
Waverly CDP	767	NA	NA	740	53.6	41.8	0.0	0.0	4.6	25.4	58.1	16.5	373	12.9	66.8	0.0
Webster city	785	955	21.7	845	44.7	27.3	0.0	1.5	26.4	25.9	62.1	12.1	286	73.1	64.0	11.9
Wedgefield CDP	6,705	NA	NA	7,337	45.6	17.9	2.9	6.5	27.0	29.3	63.0	7.8	2,330	86.4	34.1	31.8
Weeki Wachee city	12	12	0.0	1	100.0	0.0	0.0	0.0	0.0	0.0	0.0	100.0	1	100.0	0.0	0.0
Weeki Wachee Gardens CDP	1,146	NA	NA	1,237	96.0	3.2	0.0	0.0	0.8	2.5	56.1	41.5	727	74.7	52.0	4.8
Wekiwa Springs CDP	21,998	NA	NA	23,813	80.7	1.8	4.1	1.3	12.0	21.9	61.4	16.9	8,281	79.9	16.3	53.5
Welaka town	702	682	-2.8	752	64.4	25.7	0.0	1.6	8.4	27.8	46.7	25.4	303	69.6	54.5	15.8
Wellington village	56,712	61,485	8.4	59,022	62.5	12.5	4.0	2.0	19.0	26.1	60.7	13.3	19,770	79.4	19.9	47.2
Wesley Chapel CDP	44,092	NA	NA	46,935	59.2	10.8	6.0	4.3	19.7	29.5	60.6	9.9	16,148	73.7	24.1	44.1
West Bradenton CDP	4,192	NA	NA	4,511	85.1	0.5	1.0	2.3	11.2	20.6	54.7	24.8	1,640	81.6	41.6	29.5
Westchase CDP	21,747	NA	NA	22,897	69.4	8.8	6.7	2.6	12.5	28.2	62.4	9.4	8,353	63.2	10.5	62.3
Westchester CDP	29,862	NA	NA	29,921	7.0	0.3	0.2	0.3	92.2	17.3	60.0	22.5	9,202	66.1	47.9	26.6
West DeLand CDP	3,535	NA	NA	3,820	75.8	11.4	0.3	1.5	11.0	23.9	61.6	14.3	1,264	83.9	39.4	17.1
Westgate CDP	7,975	NA	NA	8,486	18.4	35.3	1.9	1.1	43.3	30.0	60.9	9.0	2,120	47.5	66.0	6.2
West Lealman CDP	15,651	NA	NA	15,257	76.4	3.4	7.0	2.3	10.9	15.5	57.0	27.3	7,440	72.9	48.5	18.5
West Little River CDP	34,699	NA	NA	31,226	1.8	49.1	0.3	0.9	48.0	21.4	63.4	15.1	9,029	60.8	63.7	10.1
West Melbourne city	18,370	20,078	9.3	19,208	81.5	3.4	4.8	3.8	6.5	22.1	56.8	21.3	7,318	69.9	27.5	35.8
West Miami city	5,965	6,326	6.1	6,197	8.6	0.2	0.9	0.3	90.0	17.9	60.8	21.3	2,039	59.2	47.2	21.9
Weston city	65,333	69,100	5.8	67,567	42.8	4.0	4.1	1.4	47.8	30.6	60.7	8.7	21,317	72.3	11.7	63.5
West Palm Beach city	100,347	104,031	3.7	102,283	41.5	30.5	2.5	1.6	23.8	19.4	63.4	17.3	41,411	50.5	35.2	35.0
West Park city	14,156	14,914	5.4	14,604	16.7	54.3	0.2	4.7	24.1	23.1	65.2	11.8	3,922	64.7	56.2	14.0
West Pensacola CDP	21,339	NA	NA	19,571	48.9	37.8	3.9	5.2	4.2	22.8	64.0	13.2	7,762	50.1	52.4	11.5
West Perrine CDP	9,460	NA	NA	10,317	7.4	57.7	1.3	1.9	31.7	23.8	65.4	10.9	2,928	55.3	50.5	25.2
West Samoset CDP	5,583	NA	NA	6,597	21.9	21.4	0.0	0.8	55.9	34.8	55.9	9.1	1,911	40.7	63.1	6.9
West Vero Corridor CDP	7,138	NA	NA	7,176	91.6	0.6	0.0	1.0	6.8	8.2	36.0	55.6	3,972	61.5	38.6	20.2
Westview CDP	9,650	NA	NA	10,365	3.3	66.6	0.8	0.6	28.8	22.7	64.9	12.4	2,906	63.6	60.7	13.4
Westville town	289	279	-3.5	389	99.5	0.0	0.0	0.5	0.0	27.2	60.0	12.9	121	86.8	62.8	6.6
Westwood Lakes CDP	11,838	NA	NA	11,860	12.1	0.4	0.5	0.0	86.9	14.8	65.1	20.0	3,237	79.4	57.7	24.6
Wewahitchka city	1,981	1,971	-0.5	2,285	75.7	16.3	3.0	1.0	4.0	16.0	67.7	16.2	877	69.1	53.4	10.0
Whiskey Creek CDP	4,655	NA	NA	4,964	90.5	0.0	0.6	3.3	5.6	13.8	54.4	31.8	2,132	90.3	13.8	50.8
White City CDP	3,719	NA	NA	3,716	90.4	0.8	2.3	0.4	6.1	20.0	63.1	16.9	1,330	73.2	39.2	23.2
White Springs town	777	769	-1.0	960	30.2	55.5	0.0	12.9	1.4	30.0	54.7	15.3	365	53.7	47.7	17.0
Whitfield CDP (Manatee)	2,882	NA	NA	2,762	87.9	0.8	2.5	1.7	7.1	13.6	57.3	29.1	1,208	77.9	17.5	26.2
Whitfield CDP (Santa Rosa)	295	NA	NA	170	60.6	0.0	30.6	8.8	0.0	11.8	55.3	32.9	75	76.0	48.0	13.3

1 May be of any race.

Table A. All Places — **Population and Housing**

STATE City, town, township, borough, or CDP (county if applicable)	Population — 2010 census total population	2014 estimated population	Percent change 2010–2014	ACS total population estimate 2010–2014	White alone, not Hispanic or Latino	Black alone, not Hispanic or Latino	Asian alone, not Hispanic or Latino	All other races or 2 or more races, not Hispanic or Latino	Hispanic or Latino[1]	Under 18 years old	Age 18 to 64 years old	Age 65 years and older	Total occupied housing units	Percent owner occupied	High school diploma or less	Bachelor's degree or more
	1	2	3	4	5	6	7	8	9	10	11	12	13	14	15	16
FLORIDA—Con.																
Wildwood city	6,540	7,181	9.8	6,782	77.3	17.7	0.3	2.4	2.3	14.6	47.3	38.1	3,014	82.5	38.4	29.4
Williamsburg CDP	7,646	NA	NA	7,973	68.6	2.7	5.9	2.8	20.0	12.4	66.3	21.3	3,522	78.4	34.6	33.0
Williston city	2,776	2,723	-1.9	2,748	58.1	31.3	2.9	0.7	7.0	22.8	56.2	20.8	1,032	60.5	54.5	10.1
Williston Highlands CDP	2,275	NA	NA	2,238	91.2	1.9	0.0	3.2	3.7	25.6	60.9	13.4	862	82.9	69.4	7.9
Willow Oak CDP	6,732	NA	NA	5,127	57.2	8.2	0.0	1.3	33.3	30.3	63.3	6.4	1,689	57.4	59.4	15.7
Wilton Manors city	11,632	12,243	5.3	11,994	67.1	13.9	1.5	1.1	16.4	10.6	71.5	18.1	6,245	52.1	29.2	40.8
Wimauma CDP	6,373	NA	NA	6,327	19.3	6.4	1.7	0.6	72.1	33.9	58.7	7.6	1,738	56.3	73.1	6.2
Windermere town	2,911	3,173	9.0	3,038	91.2	0.1	3.5	1.5	3.7	26.9	57.0	16.1	1,098	91.4	5.7	72.2
Windsor CDP	256	NA	NA	126	100.0	0.0	0.0	0.0	0.0	15.9	46.8	37.3	61	100.0	0.0	49.2
Winter Beach CDP	2,067	NA	NA	2,582	89.6	0.0	0.0	0.3	10.1	25.4	54.0	20.5	795	78.6	26.0	41.8
Winter Garden city	34,648	38,746	11.8	36,826	52.8	16.7	3.9	2.7	23.9	27.3	62.9	9.8	12,213	71.0	27.3	41.4
Winter Haven city	33,874	36,371	7.4	35,070	55.4	27.3	1.9	1.9	13.5	21.6	54.8	23.7	13,907	58.5	46.3	19.4
Winter Park city	27,856	29,442	5.7	28,771	77.3	8.1	2.8	2.3	9.5	19.3	61.2	19.4	11,747	63.1	17.1	55.1
Winter Springs city	33,282	34,169	2.7	33,673	70.3	4.7	2.1	2.4	20.5	21.7	64.2	14.2	11,214	77.9	22.7	42.4
Wiscon CDP	706	NA	NA	574	93.4	0.0	0.0	6.6	0.0	16.7	50.4	32.9	244	73.0	67.6	7.4
Woodlawn Beach CDP	1,785	NA	NA	1,746	94.3	0.0	0.0	0.0	5.7	16.5	55.8	27.7	675	92.6	39.3	22.8
Woodville CDP	2,978	NA	NA	2,786	73.3	22.0	0.0	1.6	3.1	20.8	68.3	10.9	1,064	83.6	65.1	11.2
World Golf Village CDP	12,310	NA	NA	13,326	81.0	5.7	1.1	2.2	10.0	31.0	55.6	13.4	4,747	78.4	23.0	47.8
Worthington Springs town	406	390	-3.9	537	57.2	30.9	0.0	4.5	7.4	34.1	61.1	4.8	149	21.5	61.7	6.0
Wright CDP	23,127	NA	NA	25,384	60.0	14.3	5.1	6.6	13.9	24.5	64.4	10.9	10,250	45.0	38.5	20.4
Yalaha CDP	1,364	NA	NA	1,244	86.0	1.2	4.7	0.0	8.1	7.3	55.5	37.3	593	87.7	23.3	42.3
Yankeetown town	502	498	-0.8	481	94.6	1.5	0.0	2.1	1.9	11.6	41.2	47.2	253	79.8	45.1	18.2
Yeehaw Junction CDP	240	NA	NA	168	100.0	0.0	0.0	0.0	0.0	7.1	66.6	26.2	77	100.0	81.8	0.0
Yulee CDP	11,491	NA	NA	11,609	87.7	7.0	1.6	1.8	1.9	22.1	63.0	14.8	4,287	78.0	45.5	15.5
Zellwood CDP	2,817	NA	NA	2,969	78.9	7.0	0.0	0.0	14.0	9.4	45.5	45.0	1,382	88.0	51.4	12.7
Zephyrhills city	13,538	14,381	6.2	14,041	83.2	5.2	1.7	1.9	8.0	14.6	55.9	29.4	6,562	67.6	50.5	16.4
Zephyrhills North CDP	2,600	NA	NA	2,173	87.6	4.9	4.0	2.1	1.4	8.4	48.8	42.8	1,140	86.3	60.7	6.9
Zephyrhills South CDP	5,276	NA	NA	6,059	88.1	1.0	3.2	0.5	7.1	12.7	47.0	40.3	2,720	80.3	63.6	4.4
Zephyrhills West CDP	5,865	NA	NA	5,378	93.0	0.5	1.7	0.1	4.6	9.9	30.4	59.6	2,681	85.8	57.0	10.4
Zolfo Springs town	1,817	1,797	-1.1	1,933	29.4	0.1	0.0	1.0	69.5	40.5	49.9	9.6	490	68.0	86.5	5.1
GEORGIA	9,688,681	10,097,343	4.2	9,907,756	55.0	30.4	3.5	2.1	9.1	25.2	63.3	11.5	3,540,690	64.2	38.9	30.9
Abbeville city	2,910	2,809	-3.5	2,874	33.5	58.7	1.2	1.6	4.9	8.8	81.3	9.9	372	54.3	70.7	7.5
Acworth city	20,439	21,867	7.0	21,169	52.6	29.6	4.6	3.1	10.1	26.9	64.3	9.0	8,000	63.9	28.2	34.0
Adairsville city	4,648	4,738	1.9	4,692	73.6	12.0	1.0	1.7	11.7	31.8	64.0	4.4	1,501	61.0	52.7	16.9
Adel city	5,332	5,339	0.1	5,294	40.0	49.5	0.0	0.4	10.1	29.4	55.8	14.6	1,872	60.1	59.9	17.7
Adrian city	664	651	-2.0	532	74.2	25.8	0.0	0.0	0.0	27.8	58.2	13.9	221	58.8	61.1	6.3
Ailey city	546	551	0.9	595	63.7	32.4	1.0	2.0	0.8	17.2	66.3	16.6	171	75.4	35.1	38.6
Alamo town	2,797	3,399	21.5	4,701	34.0	63.3	0.0	0.0	2.7	3.3	91.7	5.0	301	47.5	64.8	11.6
Alapaha town	668	647	-3.1	684	45.9	54.1	0.0	0.0	0.0	23.1	62.9	13.9	231	64.9	50.2	10.8
Albany city	77,434	75,769	-2.2	76,946	23.9	71.0	0.9	1.8	2.5	26.1	62.1	11.9	28,979	38.9	44.6	18.8
Aldora town	103	103	0.0	93	81.7	10.8	0.0	4.3	3.2	24.8	63.5	11.8	43	0.0	60.5	7.0
Allenhurst city	691	700	1.3	555	59.5	26.3	0.4	5.6	8.3	26.3	56.0	17.7	226	47.8	57.5	16.8
Allentown city	169	163	-3.6	242	57.9	42.1	0.0	0.0	0.0	27.6	52.6	19.8	86	82.6	68.6	10.5
Alma city	3,472	3,518	1.3	3,514	46.6	39.5	3.2	0.4	10.3	25.3	61.9	12.9	1,153	47.7	55.9	13.5
Alpharetta city	57,500	63,038	9.6	60,903	63.0	10.2	15.1	3.6	8.2	29.5	62.3	8.2	22,200	63.5	10.5	66.1
Alston town	159	159	0.0	157	94.3	2.5	3.2	0.0	0.0	19.8	60.4	19.7	65	66.2	67.7	10.8
Alto town	1,172	1,164	-0.7	1,103	51.9	0.0	1.5	0.0	46.5	28.5	64.6	6.9	337	64.4	78.6	7.4
Ambrose city	380	376	-1.1	502	58.2	13.1	0.0	1.6	27.1	35.4	52.8	12.0	157	63.7	79.0	4.5
Americus city	17,085	16,283	-4.7	16,557	34.6	59.2	0.4	2.3	3.6	26.4	60.0	13.7	6,287	45.9	48.2	22.4
Andersonville city	255	241	-5.5	232	62.1	26.7	0.0	0.0	11.2	29.8	47.0	23.3	73	60.3	58.9	2.7
Appling CDP	0	NA	NA	594	90.9	9.1	0.0	0.0	0.0	31.0	59.9	9.1	225	75.6	53.3	32.4
Arabi town	586	568	-3.1	517	71.6	27.1	1.4	0.0	0.0	22.5	63.7	13.9	208	60.6	55.3	13.9
Aragon city	1,249	1,232	-1.4	1,164	80.2	17.8	0.0	0.1	1.9	23.1	68.6	8.5	485	57.1	57.9	9.9
Arcade city	1,786	1,782	-0.2	1,506	86.5	2.4	0.3	4.6	6.2	20.8	69.9	9.4	553	75.4	71.2	9.4
Argyle town	212	213	0.5	240	71.7	28.3	0.0	0.0	0.0	13.8	77.6	8.8	54	66.7	61.1	11.1
Arlington city	1,476	1,409	-4.5	1,200	25.3	74.8	0.0	0.0	0.0	38.4	52.4	9.2	482	74.3	62.7	2.9
Arnoldsville city	357	349	-2.2	554	88.6	8.3	0.0	3.1	0.0	24.8	63.9	11.2	226	77.4	38.1	27.0
Ashburn city	4,152	3,791	-8.7	3,935	29.5	60.6	2.0	0.2	7.7	26.3	56.6	17.0	1,602	54.7	73.3	7.6
Athens-Clarke County unified government	116,707	120,938	3.6	119,681	56.6	26.3	4.2	2.3	10.6	17.5	73.5	9.1	42,107	42.6	27.9	41.4
Athens-Clarke County unified government (balance)	115,453	119,648	3.6	118,514	56.4	26.4	4.2	2.3	10.6	17.4	73.6	9.0	41,606	42.1	27.8	41.4
Atlanta city	420,256	456,002	8.5	440,641	36.4	52.4	3.8	1.9	5.6	18.8	71.0	10.1	181,681	44.1	26.2	50.9
Attapulgus city	449	438	-2.4	545	25.3	45.5	0.0	1.8	27.3	26.9	55.1	18.0	179	62.6	68.2	16.8
Auburn city	7,030	7,254	3.2	7,388	73.5	6.8	7.5	1.5	10.7	24.5	67.8	7.7	2,474	77.5	50.8	13.7
Augusta-Richmond County consolidated government	200,549	201,368	0.4	201,244	37.1	53.6	1.7	3.1	4.4	24.2	63.9	12.0	71,776	53.3	43.1	22.4
Augusta-Richmond County consolidated government (balance)	195,844	196,741	0.5	196,551	36.6	54.1	1.7	3.1	4.4	24.2	63.9	11.9	70,256	52.8	43.0	22.6
Austell city	6,658	6,985	4.9	6,944	20.7	65.4	0.4	0.5	12.9	31.3	61.5	7.0	2,267	64.3	44.6	26.1
Avalon town	213	204	-4.2	190	87.9	7.4	0.0	0.0	4.7	12.6	66.9	20.5	81	76.5	63.0	16.0
Avera city	246	237	-3.7	306	96.4	1.6	0.3	1.6	0.0	26.8	65.2	8.2	109	70.6	48.6	6.4
Avondale Estates city	2,714	2,832	4.3	2,777	84.4	7.7	3.2	2.3	2.3	24.1	60.9	15.0	1,181	88.7	5.5	80.6
Baconton city	914	879	-3.8	831	40.3	59.7	0.0	0.0	0.0	40.4	52.6	7.1	290	47.4	65.6	4.4
Bainbridge city	12,697	12,496	-1.6	12,600	37.6	59.0	0.0	1.2	2.3	24.3	58.7	16.9	5,113	51.1	50.9	20.2
Baldwin city	3,281	3,309	0.9	3,373	59.1	5.8	1.8	3.8	29.4	31.3	60.3	8.4	1,056	51.4	54.5	18.7
Ball Ground city	1,434	1,658	15.6	1,657	96.8	0.3	0.0	0.0	2.9	20.7	62.5	16.7	614	76.2	36.3	24.8
Barnesville city	6,753	6,670	-1.2	6,617	36.5	56.7	0.0	4.5	2.4	19.5	66.2	14.2	2,138	47.8	44.2	16.8
Bartow town	286	268	-6.3	301	46.8	53.2	0.0	0.0	0.0	14.2	63.4	22.3	117	67.5	67.5	4.3
Barwick city	386	378	-2.1	440	39.8	35.9	0.0	0.0	24.3	29.5	61.1	9.3	170	39.4	68.8	14.7
Baxley city	4,368	4,463	2.2	4,419	47.2	39.6	3.2	1.7	8.2	21.8	58.7	19.5	1,923	47.0	64.2	19.0
Bellville city	123	123	0.0	247	100.0	0.0	0.0	0.0	0.0	24.7	58.7	16.6	83	77.1	50.6	16.9
Belvedere Park CDP	15,152	NA	NA	16,446	18.7	74.5	0.5	2.4	3.9	25.0	66.5	8.6	5,877	54.2	41.2	28.4
Berkeley Lake city	1,841	1,983	7.7	1,739	72.5	5.4	13.9	1.7	6.6	19.4	63.9	16.7	616	94.3	9.1	76.1
Berlin city	558	562	0.7	565	55.6	28.8	0.0	0.0	15.6	20.5	60.1	19.5	216	68.5	63.9	9.7
Bethlehem town	613	652	6.4	747	82.5	1.7	1.2	2.5	12.0	27.3	60.4	12.4	255	71.8	63.5	12.9

1 May be of any race.

Table A. All Places — **Population and Housing**

STATE City, town, township, borough, or CDP (county if applicable)	Population				Race and Hispanic or Latino origin (percent), 2010–2014					Age (percent), 2010–2014			Households, 2010–2014		Householders by level of education (percent)	
	2010 census total population	2014 estimated population	Percent change 2010–2014	ACS total population estimate 2010–2014	White alone, not Hispanic or Latino	Black alone, not Hispanic or Latino	Asian alone, not Hispanic or Latino	All other races or 2 or more races, not Hispanic or Latino	Hispanic or Latino[1]	Under 18 years old	Age 18 to 64 years old	Age 65 years and older	Total occupied housing units	Percent owner occupied	High school diploma or less	Bachelor's degree or more
	1	2	3	4	5	6	7	8	9	10	11	12	13	14	15	16
GEORGIA—Con.																
Between town	296	314	6.1	371	85.7	4.0	0.0	0.0	10.2	29.9	55.9	14.3	123	78.9	35.0	34.1
Bishop town	224	238	6.3	278	78.8	0.0	0.0	0.0	21.2	41.4	52.4	6.1	82	65.9	18.3	40.2
Blackshear city	3,439	3,549	3.2	3,485	73.3	15.6	1.6	3.6	5.9	29.3	47.3	23.3	1,338	62.3	51.2	14.3
Blairsville city	652	553	-15.2	776	78.0	12.9	2.7	0.0	6.4	16.8	67.0	16.2	261	30.3	48.3	13.4
Blakely city	5,068	4,795	-5.4	4,882	32.7	63.1	0.5	0.6	3.1	29.2	53.8	17.2	1,904	54.2	52.2	15.0
Bloomingdale city	2,695	2,760	2.4	2,724	87.3	6.6	0.2	1.1	4.9	23.9	62.8	13.4	1,045	63.1	50.0	21.1
Blue Ridge city	1,288	1,263	-1.9	1,387	87.7	2.8	0.0	2.3	7.1	14.4	64.9	20.8	567	51.3	58.0	13.4
Bluffton town	103	101	-1.9	104	71.2	28.8	0.0	0.0	0.0	19.2	64.4	16.3	50	70.0	50.0	12.0
Blythe city	721	704	-2.4	691	79.0	16.5	0.0	1.6	2.9	18.4	60.2	21.4	257	87.5	54.1	16.7
Bogart town	1,034	1,036	0.2	1,254	73.4	3.9	1.8	1.8	19.1	24.6	63.2	12.1	442	64.9	45.5	19.7
Bonanza CDP	3,135	NA	NA	3,483	22.8	67.0	0.3	1.1	8.7	26.9	64.9	8.4	1,004	70.8	29.9	37.7
Boston city	1,315	1,322	0.5	1,484	21.8	74.8	0.0	0.5	3.0	27.4	51.3	21.1	557	56.2	68.0	10.1
Bostwick city	365	366	0.3	589	92.5	6.5	0.0	0.2	0.8	31.4	58.5	10.0	179	87.7	47.5	40.8
Bowdon city	2,040	2,053	0.6	1,856	68.0	24.6	0.0	6.3	1.1	24.4	55.5	20.2	769	43.2	68.3	8.2
Bowersville town	465	463	-0.4	408	76.2	19.6	0.0	2.7	1.5	20.8	64.9	14.5	153	86.9	65.4	8.5
Bowman city	862	825	-4.3	826	73.1	25.4	0.0	1.0	0.5	19.4	59.4	21.3	354	61.0	62.4	15.5
Boykin CDP	143	NA	NA	192	87.0	13.0	0.0	0.0	0.0	0.0	93.7	6.3	130	90.8	74.6	0.8
Braselton town	7,521	8,727	16.0	8,212	77.9	6.8	3.3	3.9	8.0	29.1	60.7	10.3	2,660	86.5	22.1	50.6
Braswell town	379	384	1.3	333	90.4	4.8	0.0	1.8	3.0	35.7	61.8	2.4	105	66.7	62.9	12.4
Bremen city	6,231	6,290	0.9	6,204	85.1	11.7	0.7	1.0	1.5	30.3	56.8	12.7	2,376	55.6	48.1	29.7
Brinson town	215	211	-1.9	322	37.9	62.1	0.0	0.0	0.0	20.5	67.8	11.8	109	87.2	54.1	15.6
Bronwood town	417	392	-6.0	302	24.2	75.8	0.0	0.0	0.0	28.2	44.1	27.8	114	57.9	79.8	3.5
Brookhaven city	49,219	51,079	3.8	50,181	56.3	9.3	5.1	2.6	26.6	21.2	69.7	9.0	21,153	49.1	22.4	62.1
Brooklet city	1,395	1,419	1.7	1,588	83.4	8.0	0.9	3.8	3.9	26.3	61.1	12.6	581	65.4	31.8	38.0
Brooks town	524	540	3.1	600	88.5	0.0	0.5	3.2	7.8	27.9	60.6	11.5	209	81.3	34.4	23.9
Broxton city	1,189	1,182	-0.6	1,075	59.4	28.7	0.3	0.6	11.0	22.9	58.9	18.1	440	70.5	71.6	12.0
Brunswick city	15,383	15,903	3.4	15,648	22.8	63.5	0.2	2.7	10.8	24.5	62.3	13.2	5,869	36.2	55.1	12.0
Buchanan city	1,104	1,145	3.7	1,209	76.8	16.5	0.0	2.6	4.1	19.0	63.7	17.4	356	43.8	75.3	3.1
Buckhead town	171	171	0.0	209	66.5	31.1	0.0	0.0	2.4	17.7	67.8	14.4	97	68.0	43.3	14.4
Buena Vista city	2,203	2,216	0.6	2,347	28.0	57.1	0.0	2.6	12.2	21.2	66.2	12.8	784	36.7	69.4	9.9
Buford city	12,235	13,392	9.5	12,864	48.1	11.4	2.5	0.9	37.0	29.8	59.9	10.4	4,065	57.9	56.4	18.5
Butler city	1,980	1,928	-2.6	1,711	43.8	50.4	0.0	0.0	5.8	17.9	65.4	16.6	783	57.3	67.3	8.4
Byromville town	546	526	-3.7	694	24.2	41.4	0.3	0.0	34.1	16.7	66.5	16.7	219	78.5	84.0	3.7
Byron city	4,513	4,947	9.6	4,725	57.0	34.5	2.6	0.9	5.1	25.4	58.2	16.4	1,823	65.7	32.8	23.8
Cadwell town	528	534	1.1	596	67.1	28.2	0.0	0.2	4.5	16.2	72.2	11.6	143	54.5	65.0	8.4
Cairo city	9,627	9,806	1.9	9,750	34.8	48.5	0.5	1.6	14.6	25.3	59.4	15.3	3,605	48.5	61.8	13.0
Calhoun city	15,667	16,052	2.5	15,837	56.2	9.0	1.8	0.9	32.1	27.7	59.6	12.9	5,477	47.4	58.1	20.9
Calvary CDP	161	NA	NA	71	63.4	8.5	0.0	0.0	28.2	0.0	84.6	15.5	32	28.1	46.9	0.0
Camak town	138	132	-4.3	156	23.7	66.0	0.0	8.3	1.9	26.9	63.6	9.6	46	65.2	45.7	13.0
Camilla city	5,140	5,010	-2.5	5,078	22.5	74.7	0.9	0.6	1.4	27.6	57.1	15.5	1,971	53.1	60.0	20.2
Candler-McAfee CDP	23,025	NA	NA	22,345	8.2	88.8	0.2	1.8	1.0	19.3	64.0	16.7	8,152	58.3	49.0	18.7
Canon city	804	802	-0.2	746	95.2	1.5	0.0	1.7	1.6	23.0	60.3	16.8	277	69.7	80.1	2.5
Canoochee CDP	71	NA	NA	93	69.9	30.1	0.0	0.0	0.0	18.3	63.4	18.3	47	91.5	89.4	0.0
Canton city	22,959	24,801	8.0	23,841	60.6	12.0	1.4	2.2	23.8	29.8	59.8	10.4	8,442	54.6	41.6	26.7
Carl town	198	208	5.1	252	73.0	1.2	18.7	0.0	7.1	27.5	60.8	11.9	72	55.6	56.9	19.4
Carlton city	260	261	0.4	292	69.5	22.3	0.0	4.8	3.4	13.0	67.0	19.9	126	87.3	60.3	21.4
Carnesville city	577	578	0.2	652	67.3	18.9	5.2	7.2	1.4	25.1	66.2	8.6	207	51.7	54.6	13.5
Carrollton city	24,392	26,690	9.4	25,138	53.0	29.5	2.3	1.7	13.6	22.7	67.7	9.6	8,496	40.3	42.0	28.9
Cartersville city	19,786	20,015	1.2	19,858	67.0	20.7	0.4	1.8	10.2	28.1	57.0	15.0	7,137	49.8	48.1	23.6
Cave Spring city	1,205	1,167	-3.2	1,353	90.5	7.8	0.2	1.5	0.0	26.2	58.0	15.8	476	62.0	44.5	22.1
Cecil city	284	280	-1.4	325	43.1	56.9	0.0	0.0	0.0	23.4	66.6	9.8	116	56.0	57.8	3.4
Cedar Springs CDP	74	NA	NA	22	100.0	0.0	0.0	0.0	0.0	0.0	100.0	0.0	11	100.0	0.0	0.0
Cedartown city	9,748	9,723	-0.3	9,760	39.8	23.0	0.7	2.0	34.4	29.5	56.2	14.3	3,270	40.5	70.2	11.9
Centerville city	7,148	7,584	6.1	7,468	59.4	22.8	6.6	1.9	9.4	25.0	62.7	12.4	2,646	58.6	28.3	30.4
Centralhatchee town	410	397	-3.2	456	90.8	7.5	0.9	0.9	0.0	31.3	56.1	12.5	152	67.8	61.8	17.8
Chamblee city	15,514	16,112	3.9	15,835	40.2	10.6	9.1	4.5	35.6	19.4	73.5	7.1	5,890	40.2	34.7	45.3
Chatsworth city	4,301	4,290	-0.3	4,285	72.1	1.7	0.5	0.6	25.1	22.2	63.8	13.9	1,668	46.6	52.7	13.5
Chattahoochee Hills city	2,378	2,610	9.8	2,511	77.7	14.9	0.0	1.0	6.4	17.6	63.9	18.5	1,005	92.8	33.4	24.6
Chattanooga Valley CDP	3,846	NA	NA	3,848	96.5	0.4	0.0	1.6	1.4	20.0	61.9	18.0	1,561	74.7	42.2	24.0
Chauncey city	342	328	-4.1	368	63.9	30.2	0.0	1.9	4.1	26.4	63.4	10.3	151	63.6	82.8	9.3
Cherry Log CDP	119	NA	NA	118	100.0	0.0	0.0	0.0	0.0	0.0	0.0	100.0	80	100.0	47.5	18.8
Chester town	1,596	1,564	-2.0	1,719	37.9	57.3	0.2	0.8	3.8	5.3	90.7	4.0	139	33.1	65.5	2.9
Chickamauga city	3,101	3,127	0.8	3,125	91.5	2.0	0.0	5.5	1.0	23.8	65.5	10.8	1,234	61.7	45.1	12.5
Clarkesville city	1,733	1,751	1.0	1,911	81.9	7.0	1.7	0.8	8.6	24.1	59.7	16.1	747	54.9	42.3	27.6
Clarkston city	7,553	7,846	3.9	7,717	15.0	52.1	31.1	0.3	1.4	31.3	63.3	5.6	2,264	22.4	47.9	22.2
Claxton city	2,390	2,364	-1.1	2,096	41.3	43.3	0.7	1.3	13.5	26.7	54.7	18.5	823	42.5	54.7	16.4
Clayton city	2,151	2,232	3.8	1,945	74.9	5.1	0.0	2.8	17.2	22.6	53.9	23.4	831	55.6	55.0	18.5
Clermont town	877	915	4.3	1,055	99.4	0.0	0.0	0.6	0.0	27.9	64.0	8.1	335	75.2	42.4	17.9
Cleveland city	3,457	3,727	7.8	3,624	80.7	12.9	0.7	0.7	5.0	27.2	62.5	10.3	1,410	48.4	43.8	18.2
Climax city	280	274	-2.1	198	64.6	26.3	0.0	1.0	8.1	12.6	57.6	29.8	91	79.1	60.4	9.9
Cobbtown city	351	350	-0.3	335	82.1	6.6	0.0	0.6	10.7	21.8	59.6	18.8	158	71.5	62.7	10.8
Cochran city	5,159	4,830	-6.4	4,917	42.1	54.5	0.2	1.1	2.1	15.9	67.9	16.2	1,334	61.5	60.2	15.9
Cohutta city	626	634	1.3	671	95.5	0.7	0.1	2.1	1.5	20.0	69.0	11.0	251	72.5	43.8	18.3
Colbert city	590	596	1.0	882	81.5	16.6	0.0	0.5	1.5	26.1	59.0	15.0	300	62.7	32.3	29.0
Coleman CDP	127	NA	NA	111	68.5	31.5	0.0	0.0	0.0	37.8	30.6	31.5	38	100.0	100.0	0.0
College Park city	13,942	14,598	4.7	14,019	9.7	80.4	0.3	2.8	6.7	29.4	64.6	6.0	5,235	25.4	49.0	17.9
Collins city	584	584	0.0	643	55.5	40.1	0.0	0.0	4.4	37.3	53.8	9.0	258	64.0	74.4	7.4
Colquitt city	1,992	1,929	-3.2	2,509	49.0	50.7	0.0	0.1	0.2	29.3	56.2	14.3	796	51.3	52.9	8.2
Columbus city	190,545	200,887	5.4	198,247	42.9	44.2	2.3	3.6	7.1	24.8	63.6	11.6	72,556	50.8	37.4	26.5
Comer city	1,126	1,132	0.5	1,320	64.2	18.5	12.1	4.4	0.8	23.6	61.2	15.2	436	70.0	45.0	22.0
Commerce city	6,540	6,580	0.6	6,535	75.8	11.2	0.6	2.3	10.1	26.5	58.8	14.7	2,255	53.2	60.8	13.4
Concord city	375	374	-0.3	349	76.5	19.5	0.0	0.0	4.0	30.2	52.6	17.2	118	74.6	40.7	22.0
Conley CDP	6,228	NA	NA	5,679	14.5	69.5	4.1	0.8	11.0	30.8	61.0	8.2	1,881	64.6	51.6	8.5
Conyers city	15,195	15,718	3.4	15,456	22.2	61.8	0.7	1.8	13.5	30.3	59.7	10.1	5,072	34.5	48.0	22.0
Coolidge city	525	526	0.2	571	49.9	39.1	0.0	5.3	5.8	21.2	62.0	16.8	227	54.6	71.8	2.6
Cordele city	11,147	10,939	-1.9	11,177	24.3	68.7	1.9	1.4	3.6	31.2	56.3	12.5	3,844	41.5	60.3	11.1
Cornelia city	4,173	4,210	0.9	4,187	54.4	8.2	1.2	2.5	33.6	30.4	51.7	18.0	1,502	59.5	65.4	18.5
Country Club Estates CDP	8,545	NA	NA	9,091	43.7	42.6	4.8	2.0	7.0	25.2	62.1	12.8	3,543	46.1	44.3	13.5
Covington city	13,116	13,667	4.2	13,342	45.4	45.6	1.3	1.4	6.3	21.5	64.0	14.5	5,042	41.7	52.2	15.2
Crawford city	826	816	-1.2	840	57.3	34.4	1.9	3.7	2.7	17.0	52.1	31.0	344	50.0	57.3	14.2

1 May be of any race.

Table A. All Places — **Population and Housing**

STATE City, town, township, borough, or CDP (county if applicable)	Population				Race and Hispanic or Latino origin (percent), 2010–2014					Age (percent), 2010–2014			Households, 2010–2014			
	2010 census total population	2014 estimated population	Percent change 2010–2014	ACS total population estimate 2010–2014	White alone, not Hispanic or Latino	Black alone, not Hispanic or Latino	Asian alone, not Hispanic or Latino	All other races or 2 or more races, not Hispanic or Latino	Hispanic or Latino[1]	Under 18 years old	Age 18 to 64 years old	Age 65 years and older	Total occupied housing units	Percent owner occupied	Householders by level of education (percent): High school diploma or less	Householders by level of education (percent): Bachelor's degree or more
	1	2	3	4	5	6	7	8	9	10	11	12	13	14	15	16
GEORGIA—Con.																
Crawfordville city	534	525	-1.7	594	35.7	56.4	0.0	1.9	6.1	20.5	61.9	17.5	251	53.0	77.7	5.2
Crooked Creek CDP	639	NA	NA	811	93.1	5.8	0.0	1.1	0.0	20.3	48.9	30.7	240	70.4	24.2	10.8
Culloden city	175	177	1.1	280	57.1	42.9	0.0	0.0	0.0	27.1	59.6	13.2	85	70.6	57.6	16.5
Cumming city	5,438	5,615	3.3	5,538	58.7	4.5	2.4	2.0	32.4	21.2	61.7	17.3	1,892	44.5	49.9	24.7
Cusseta-Chattahoochee County unified government	11,267	11,837	5.1	11,846	60.9	17.5	2.9	4.3	14.3	25.6	71.1	3.3	2,602	28.1	36.4	28.8
Cuthbert city	3,873	3,736	-3.5	3,731	13.2	83.2	1.1	2.1	0.4	26.3	58.6	15.0	1,390	52.2	65.3	9.0
Dacula city	4,442	4,971	11.9	4,664	52.7	12.7	0.0	0.8	33.9	32.4	56.4	11.1	1,579	86.2	52.6	27.9
Dahlonega city	5,242	6,337	20.9	5,884	81.2	3.7	0.9	2.6	11.5	9.8	72.1	18.1	2,119	35.2	26.7	44.9
Daisy city	145	144	-0.7	119	98.3	1.7	0.0	0.0	0.0	17.7	64.7	17.6	56	67.9	44.6	41.1
Dallas city	11,564	12,629	9.2	12,129	42.9	38.6	2.8	1.2	14.5	30.8	60.1	9.0	4,349	48.1	46.1	22.8
Dalton city	33,103	33,529	1.3	33,336	41.7	8.2	2.7	1.1	46.3	29.4	59.2	11.5	11,446	44.6	55.0	20.0
Damascus city	254	237	-6.7	302	36.4	62.6	0.0	0.0	1.0	22.5	57.6	19.9	104	49.0	78.8	3.8
Danielsville city	565	573	1.4	894	85.8	2.7	4.3	1.1	6.2	35.2	54.3	10.4	294	50.0	49.3	18.4
Danville town	238	219	-8.0	235	57.4	41.3	0.0	1.3	0.0	15.3	65.5	19.1	92	48.9	71.7	6.5
Darien city	1,958	1,903	-2.8	3,465	38.6	52.2	0.0	5.0	4.2	27.0	56.0	17.0	1,166	59.8	50.7	8.7
Dasher town	912	959	5.2	982	89.1	4.4	1.3	2.1	3.1	24.3	61.3	14.4	329	84.2	40.1	15.5
Davisboro city	2,010	1,763	-12.3	2,022	29.7	67.3	0.3	0.2	2.5	7.4	88.6	3.9	194	68.0	67.5	5.2
Dawson city	4,541	4,358	-4.0	4,447	12.9	82.8	0.4	1.0	2.8	29.7	58.5	11.8	1,379	39.2	76.1	5.7
Dawsonville city	2,442	2,497	2.3	2,671	89.0	1.9	0.2	5.1	3.8	28.6	58.8	12.6	911	61.4	42.0	16.9
Dearing town	549	542	-1.3	597	78.2	21.3	0.0	0.0	0.5	25.8	63.3	11.1	224	57.6	46.0	12.9
Decatur city	19,334	20,380	5.4	19,888	68.1	21.6	4.4	2.7	3.2	26.1	63.6	10.5	7,987	62.0	14.2	69.5
Deenwood CDP	2,146	NA	NA	1,514	87.0	13.0	0.0	0.0	0.0	24.2	61.6	14.1	690	66.2	44.6	15.9
Deepstep town	131	129	-1.5	153	100.0	0.0	0.0	0.0	0.0	13.1	57.0	30.1	57	98.2	26.3	43.9
Demorest city	1,823	2,047	12.3	1,857	75.1	6.7	3.8	3.2	11.3	14.0	74.3	11.8	516	64.5	30.0	30.4
Denton city	250	250	0.0	284	65.8	34.2	0.0	0.0	0.0	23.6	65.4	11.3	95	81.1	86.3	0.0
De Soto city	192	184	-4.2	264	23.5	60.6	0.0	0.0	15.9	29.9	57.5	12.5	91	61.5	72.5	7.7
Dewy Rose CDP	154	NA	NA	244	29.5	0.0	0.0	0.0	70.5	49.2	50.8	0.0	54	44.4	100.0	0.0
Dexter town	575	571	-0.7	605	63.3	35.7	1.0	0.0	0.0	28.8	53.9	17.2	193	73.6	61.1	14.5
Dillard city	344	335	-2.6	329	71.1	0.0	0.0	0.0	28.9	19.4	60.5	20.1	148	55.4	51.4	39.9
Dock Junction CDP	7,721	NA	NA	7,261	62.5	30.9	0.4	0.6	5.7	20.5	62.4	17.1	3,066	56.5	52.5	16.1
Doerun city	774	779	0.6	794	59.7	38.3	0.3	1.8	0.0	31.4	53.8	14.9	298	54.0	58.1	17.1
Donalsonville city	2,650	2,702	2.0	2,720	35.3	59.6	0.9	0.5	3.8	24.3	59.4	16.4	973	71.6	51.5	13.6
Dooling town	154	149	-3.2	349	8.3	80.2	0.0	0.0	11.5	35.6	56.3	8.0	117	79.5	88.0	6.8
Doraville city	10,326	10,714	3.8	10,513	22.2	12.4	12.0	2.7	50.6	26.6	66.7	6.7	3,200	46.6	49.5	28.4
Douglas city	11,590	11,665	0.6	11,738	32.1	57.1	0.2	3.1	7.5	27.3	59.3	13.4	4,221	47.0	57.2	14.8
Douglasville city	30,956	32,523	5.1	31,573	31.0	58.5	2.5	1.3	6.6	29.1	62.0	8.9	11,597	47.3	27.0	33.4
Druid Hills CDP	14,568	NA	NA	14,439	72.5	7.4	14.9	2.5	2.7	14.2	76.1	9.7	4,454	57.0	4.7	83.5
Dublin city	16,206	16,182	-0.1	16,200	36.4	59.4	2.0	0.9	1.2	25.6	56.3	18.1	6,190	48.9	55.0	19.8
Dudley city	575	571	-0.7	707	73.8	15.1	0.0	0.0	11.0	19.1	67.7	13.2	234	76.5	56.4	19.7
Duluth city	26,602	28,838	8.4	27,821	41.8	21.8	23.9	2.4	10.2	25.2	66.4	8.6	10,558	53.4	29.0	44.7
Dunwoody city	46,268	48,000	3.7	47,182	64.3	10.1	13.4	2.5	9.8	24.5	63.0	12.6	19,344	54.1	12.4	69.5
Du Pont town	120	123	2.5	215	36.3	63.7	0.0	0.0	0.0	23.8	63.8	12.6	86	75.6	88.4	4.7
Dutch Island CDP	1,257	NA	NA	1,040	89.0	4.4	1.7	1.7	3.1	29.0	45.2	25.8	387	100.0	14.0	59.9
Eagle Grove CDP	164	NA	NA	14	100.0	0.0	0.0	0.0	0.0	0.0	0.0	100.0	14	100.0	100.0	0.0
East Dublin city	2,441	2,400	-1.7	2,549	38.6	60.1	0.2	0.4	0.7	28.1	59.5	12.3	931	46.6	76.8	4.2
East Ellijay city	547	549	0.4	997	62.0	3.1	0.0	0.9	34.0	39.9	48.8	11.1	283	41.0	64.7	12.0
East Griffin CDP	1,451	NA	NA	1,248	56.3	37.1	1.1	1.3	4.2	33.5	54.1	12.4	453	48.3	67.8	3.8
Eastman city	5,590	5,331	-4.6	5,442	49.8	40.1	1.8	3.4	4.9	24.4	61.1	14.6	2,167	42.6	60.0	11.7
East Newnan CDP	1,321	NA	NA	1,771	54.9	24.8	0.0	0.0	20.3	20.3	58.3	21.5	694	34.3	84.7	0.0
East Point city	33,712	35,488	5.3	35,070	11.3	74.0	1.2	0.9	12.6	23.5	66.9	9.5	12,745	43.9	40.0	30.3
Eatonton city	6,486	6,466	-0.3	6,489	26.6	58.6	0.0	0.8	14.0	25.8	62.6	11.7	2,452	59.7	63.1	11.6
Edge Hill city	24	24	0.0	18	100.0	0.0	0.0	0.0	0.0	0.0	55.6	44.4	8	62.5	37.5	0.0
Edison city	1,531	1,477	-3.5	1,040	19.1	73.0	1.4	1.0	5.5	33.1	53.9	13.1	466	45.9	60.5	7.7
Elberton city	4,578	4,484	-2.1	4,494	45.3	45.3	0.0	1.0	8.3	25.0	55.3	19.7	1,863	56.8	65.4	12.6
Ellaville city	1,812	1,880	3.8	2,099	53.7	41.0	0.5	2.0	2.9	25.5	57.8	16.6	849	53.8	66.1	9.3
Ellenton town	281	280	-0.4	129	64.3	5.4	0.0	0.0	30.2	15.6	48.9	35.7	69	65.2	75.4	2.9
Ellijay city	1,619	1,647	1.7	1,579	71.9	0.8	0.0	1.4	26.0	19.1	62.9	17.9	611	41.6	60.4	15.1
Emerson city	1,482	1,506	1.6	1,397	66.4	8.2	6.2	0.3	19.0	19.7	64.4	15.9	512	72.3	54.1	25.0
Empire CDP	393	NA	NA	398	76.1	9.5	0.0	0.0	14.3	17.1	70.4	12.6	195	65.1	62.1	0.0
Enigma town	1,332	1,277	-4.1	1,052	70.1	6.1	0.0	2.8	21.1	28.1	66.4	5.6	376	52.9	70.5	2.1
Ephesus city	427	422	-1.2	529	90.9	0.2	0.0	1.1	7.8	30.3	56.0	13.6	172	80.2	53.5	12.8
Epworth CDP	480	NA	NA	252	100.0	0.0	0.0	0.0	0.0	7.5	54.7	37.7	132	70.5	67.4	0.0
Eton city	910	905	-0.5	879	58.4	0.0	1.6	0.0	40.0	29.1	62.1	9.0	284	76.4	55.3	10.6
Euharlee city	4,141	4,211	1.7	4,172	89.8	3.3	0.0	2.5	4.4	28.2	62.6	9.1	1,338	77.8	46.3	22.5
Evans CDP	29,011	NA	NA	32,591	74.9	14.0	6.6	1.2	3.3	27.7	60.5	11.8	10,420	84.3	17.3	51.5
Experiment CDP	2,894	NA	NA	2,241	49.4	42.6	1.1	6.8	0.0	16.2	63.1	20.8	836	47.0	68.9	5.1
Fairburn city	13,028	13,696	5.1	13,520	14.1	69.9	2.6	1.9	11.5	32.1	61.3	6.7	4,706	59.5	34.5	23.7
Fairmount city	720	733	1.8	773	95.9	3.2	0.3	0.3	0.4	17.5	63.4	19.3	309	55.7	73.8	8.7
Fair Oaks CDP	8,225	NA	NA	8,533	24.3	24.5	1.4	2.7	47.1	27.7	68.1	4.1	2,974	30.1	62.6	15.1
Fairview CDP	6,769	NA	NA	7,381	95.6	2.6	0.2	0.9	0.7	27.4	59.8	12.9	2,713	71.3	61.7	9.0
Fargo city	321	324	0.9	314	77.1	16.2	0.0	0.6	6.1	24.5	57.2	18.2	136	76.5	75.0	13.2
Fayetteville city	16,097	16,725	3.9	16,323	51.3	33.1	6.7	3.5	5.4	27.0	57.3	15.6	6,058	72.7	25.4	44.6
Fitzgerald city	9,072	9,039	-0.4	9,054	43.7	49.2	0.0	2.9	4.1	28.8	56.7	14.5	3,130	50.7	57.2	10.6
Flemington city	743	752	1.2	874	42.9	30.9	3.9	14.2	8.1	24.2	70.6	5.0	293	74.1	23.2	24.9
Flovilla city	653	639	-2.1	647	36.8	57.8	0.0	3.6	1.9	29.1	57.7	13.1	224	76.3	60.3	1.3
Flowery Branch city	5,686	6,385	12.3	6,012	75.7	10.0	1.1	3.2	10.0	27.8	63.2	9.0	2,315	53.6	24.7	43.7
Folkston city	4,153	5,206	25.4	5,233	48.9	40.2	0.1	1.2	9.6	13.8	69.7	16.3	1,329	71.5	56.5	19.6
Forest Park city	18,468	18,949	2.6	18,783	17.9	37.8	9.1	1.3	33.9	31.1	60.9	8.1	5,672	44.9	65.3	10.5
Forsyth city	3,844	3,993	3.9	3,964	28.0	66.3	1.7	1.2	2.7	28.1	59.0	12.7	1,424	46.9	66.2	11.1
Fort Gaines city	1,112	1,079	-3.0	1,126	17.9	78.3	0.0	3.8	0.0	37.8	48.0	14.1	396	38.6	65.4	8.3
Fort Oglethorpe city	9,262	9,590	3.5	9,368	89.1	6.1	1.8	2.8	0.2	21.8	57.9	20.3	3,926	55.9	43.8	16.8
Fort Stewart CDP	4,924	NA	NA	5,325	56.6	21.1	1.5	6.3	14.4	33.9	66.3	0.0	1,047	0.0	38.0	15.1
Fort Valley city	9,815	8,952	-8.8	9,448	17.4	74.6	0.8	0.9	6.3	23.2	66.9	10.0	3,116	39.2	49.5	15.6
Franklin city	992	974	-1.8	899	64.0	30.1	0.0	3.6	2.3	15.8	64.8	19.6	356	32.6	64.6	9.0
Franklin Springs city	952	1,143	20.1	981	77.6	12.4	1.8	1.1	7.0	8.6	81.9	9.6	238	53.4	34.0	32.8
Funston city	449	445	-0.9	743	43.5	38.5	0.0	2.6	15.5	39.1	52.9	8.2	222	61.3	78.4	5.9
Gainesville city	33,809	36,306	7.4	34,938	38.8	15.7	3.9	1.1	40.5	30.3	59.3	10.4	11,339	36.0	48.7	26.7
Garden City city	8,798	8,994	2.2	8,924	39.3	39.4	1.2	1.3	18.7	28.0	60.0	12.1	3,428	38.2	66.9	12.7
Garfield city	201	204	1.5	219	66.7	26.9	0.0	6.4	0.0	37.0	55.7	7.3	84	65.5	47.6	14.3

1 May be of any race.

Table A. All Places — **Population and Housing**

STATE City, town, township, borough, or CDP (county if applicable)	Population				Race and Hispanic or Latino origin (percent), 2010–2014					Age (percent), 2010–2014			Households, 2010–2014			
	2010 census total population	2014 estimated population	Percent change 2010–2014	ACS total population estimate 2010–2014	White alone, not Hispanic or Latino	Black alone, not Hispanic or Latino	Asian alone, not Hispanic or Latino	All other races or 2 or more races, not Hispanic or Latino	Hispanic or Latino[1]	Under 18 years old	Age 18 to 64 years old	Age 65 years and older	Total occupied housing units	Percent owner occupied	Householders by level of education (percent): High school diploma or less	Householders by level of education (percent): Bachelor's degree or more
	1	2	3	4	5	6	7	8	9	10	11	12	13	14	15	16
GEORGIA—Con.																
Gay town	89	86	-3.4	107	67.3	0.0	0.0	0.0	32.7	34.6	54.2	11.2	42	59.5	57.1	26.2
Geneva town	105	100	-4.8	89	44.9	50.6	0.0	4.5	0.0	7.8	71.8	20.2	36	94.4	44.4	11.1
Georgetown CDP	11,823	NA	NA	12,235	56.0	25.2	3.6	4.4	10.8	24.0	67.1	8.9	4,603	49.6	34.3	27.6
Georgetown-Quitman County unified government	2,513	2,315	-7.9	2,407	45.5	52.9	0.6	1.0	0.0	21.4	56.0	22.6	1,001	77.7	62.6	8.0
Gibson city	663	654	-1.4	623	79.5	18.8	0.0	1.8	0.0	22.0	41.2	36.9	243	58.8	61.3	19.3
Gillsville city	235	246	4.7	267	93.6	1.9	0.0	0.0	4.5	32.9	48.5	18.4	78	78.2	56.4	20.5
Girard town	156	153	-1.9	134	60.4	39.6	0.0	0.0	0.0	17.9	57.5	24.6	64	64.1	76.6	4.7
Glennville city	5,171	5,117	-1.0	5,166	60.1	32.4	0.3	2.8	4.4	17.1	73.1	9.8	1,490	62.1	39.1	24.4
Glenwood city	747	742	-0.7	610	79.5	19.8	0.0	0.7	0.0	20.0	56.1	23.9	322	44.4	82.9	2.8
Good Hope city	274	286	4.4	405	97.5	2.5	0.0	0.0	0.0	33.6	50.4	16.0	153	92.8	66.7	9.2
Gordon city	2,017	1,991	-1.3	2,133	39.6	59.6	0.0	0.4	0.4	22.5	63.3	14.2	764	67.9	74.3	4.8
Graham city	291	300	3.1	394	61.7	36.0	0.0	2.3	0.0	37.8	55.0	7.1	121	79.3	83.5	3.3
Grantville city	3,046	3,145	3.3	3,105	60.9	27.6	0.8	2.8	7.9	32.0	60.4	7.6	1,082	66.8	53.6	11.2
Gray city	3,263	3,294	1.0	3,276	62.4	33.7	0.0	0.1	3.8	28.5	56.9	14.7	1,071	57.9	41.7	27.1
Grayson city	2,552	2,780	8.9	2,665	51.9	35.5	7.4	1.3	4.0	24.2	60.9	14.7	800	87.1	25.9	35.4
Greensboro city	3,359	3,426	2.0	3,389	15.3	62.6	2.0	0.0	20.1	28.3	63.9	7.8	1,230	38.7	74.6	11.2
Greenville city	879	863	-1.8	844	22.4	77.6	0.0	0.0	0.0	20.6	65.5	14.0	334	46.1	63.5	6.0
Gresham Park CDP	7,432	NA	NA	7,947	11.5	78.8	1.2	2.1	6.4	23.5	65.7	10.9	2,800	60.2	53.3	22.4
Griffin city	23,637	23,329	-1.3	23,425	40.7	51.2	1.5	1.4	5.2	26.8	59.6	13.5	8,691	40.8	55.2	19.6
Grovetown city	11,272	12,746	13.1	12,179	51.3	23.2	1.3	4.2	20.0	31.8	62.7	5.6	3,914	64.2	31.7	26.9
Gumbranch city	264	267	1.1	208	98.1	0.0	0.0	0.0	1.9	24.0	63.5	12.5	86	55.8	69.8	0.0
Gumlog CDP	2,146	NA	NA	2,297	91.0	3.1	0.0	0.5	5.4	28.1	57.3	14.7	817	72.1	55.2	15.7
Guyton city	1,686	1,760	4.4	2,308	69.5	29.2	0.0	0.5	0.8	33.1	58.5	8.4	660	69.2	50.5	17.3
Hagan city	991	982	-0.9	884	75.7	19.7	0.0	0.3	4.3	26.5	63.4	10.0	347	62.2	51.6	22.2
Hahira city	2,737	2,861	4.5	2,804	78.1	13.9	1.1	1.1	5.8	30.6	57.1	12.3	984	71.2	39.1	20.6
Hamilton city	1,016	1,056	3.9	982	47.6	41.8	0.0	8.8	1.9	26.0	69.0	5.1	261	55.6	41.0	30.7
Hampton city	6,950	7,305	5.1	7,092	43.6	42.1	1.6	4.5	8.2	38.1	56.3	5.6	1,821	65.8	51.0	22.1
Hannahs Mill CDP	3,298	NA	NA	3,975	81.0	8.1	0.0	0.5	10.5	26.4	62.6	11.0	1,282	70.8	66.0	6.7
Hapeville city	6,373	6,669	4.6	6,611	29.6	37.2	1.6	2.3	29.2	27.2	64.5	8.3	2,447	35.5	43.8	22.0
Haralson town	163	173	6.1	197	92.4	5.6	0.0	1.0	1.0	25.3	64.5	10.2	64	68.8	65.6	10.9
Hardwick CDP	3,930	NA	NA	3,828	28.3	68.6	0.0	3.1	0.0	20.2	67.4	12.5	1,392	43.7	73.3	6.2
Harlem city	2,666	2,903	8.9	2,795	65.9	24.0	1.1	4.3	4.7	28.1	62.8	9.3	1,118	66.3	51.6	17.7
Harrison town	489	472	-3.5	404	19.8	77.2	0.2	2.0	0.7	24.6	56.6	18.8	129	80.6	82.9	2.3
Hartwell city	4,469	4,487	0.4	4,499	56.9	35.7	0.1	1.0	6.3	21.1	54.6	24.4	1,823	65.6	46.5	17.4
Hawkinsville city	5,721	5,507	-3.7	5,588	46.0	53.3	0.0	0.4	0.3	12.0	72.0	16.2	1,731	50.9	61.2	17.2
Hazlehurst city	4,226	4,181	-1.1	4,225	63.9	26.6	1.3	0.5	7.7	26.0	57.1	16.9	1,566	58.9	67.8	7.2
Helen city	510	526	3.1	269	88.1	1.1	1.9	5.6	3.3	7.0	68.3	24.5	147	44.2	27.9	30.6
Helena city	2,881	2,893	0.4	2,940	38.8	50.9	0.5	0.4	9.4	13.5	70.4	15.9	831	53.7	85.9	5.5
Henderson CDP	1,647	NA	NA	1,704	50.6	46.7	0.7	0.0	2.1	8.1	80.1	11.9	659	63.6	14.7	34.6
Hephzibah city	4,011	3,949	-1.5	4,026	55.4	36.7	0.0	4.5	3.5	25.9	62.2	11.8	1,273	74.6	49.6	11.8
Heron Bay CDP	3,384	NA	NA	3,435	49.2	39.2	0.5	8.5	2.6	31.4	61.5	7.1	1,188	92.5	31.1	29.9
Hiawassee city	880	907	3.1	930	91.7	1.9	0.6	0.2	5.5	6.7	49.2	44.1	438	52.5	32.4	35.6
Higgston town	323	317	-1.9	397	65.7	28.0	0.0	0.8	5.5	25.7	62.2	12.1	173	47.4	46.8	15.6
Hilltop CDP	262	NA	NA	439	3.9	84.5	0.0	11.6	0.0	38.7	49.4	11.8	111	77.5	92.8	7.2
Hiltonia town	342	327	-4.4	497	22.3	77.3	0.0	0.0	0.4	24.8	64.2	10.9	157	73.9	63.7	3.2
Hinesville city	33,439	34,815	4.1	34,253	35.2	43.9	2.5	5.2	13.1	28.3	66.2	5.6	12,747	46.3	34.8	19.9
Hiram city	3,550	3,705	4.4	3,628	68.6	27.9	0.0	1.4	2.2	20.6	68.8	10.8	1,581	72.6	35.9	32.6
Hoboken city	528	530	0.4	663	95.2	4.1	0.0	0.0	0.8	24.3	58.1	17.6	263	89.4	70.7	9.5
Hogansville city	3,038	3,090	1.7	3,063	42.1	51.1	3.2	2.8	0.8	29.2	53.9	16.8	1,111	63.3	64.4	9.3
Holly Springs city	9,188	10,237	11.4	9,678	79.5	7.1	1.5	3.6	8.2	32.9	62.7	4.5	3,446	79.1	24.0	38.3
Homeland city	913	860	-5.8	1,141	77.3	19.2	1.1	2.0	0.4	24.4	62.1	13.5	310	74.2	67.4	15.2
Homer town	1,145	1,131	-1.2	1,452	78.2	20.5	0.0	0.0	1.3	33.2	58.8	7.9	483	60.0	45.3	19.5
Homerville city	2,454	2,452	-0.1	2,573	49.8	47.0	0.4	1.9	0.9	29.7	54.0	16.3	994	48.7	62.4	10.4
Hoschton city	1,377	1,415	2.8	1,642	82.2	4.4	4.1	2.9	6.3	29.0	57.1	13.8	534	75.8	38.2	21.9
Howard CDP	110	NA	NA	0	0.0	0.0	0.0	0.0	0.0	0.0	0.0	0.0	0	0.0	0.0	0.0
Hull city	198	200	1.0	178	84.3	6.7	0.6	0.0	8.4	20.8	71.6	7.9	73	46.6	50.7	20.5
Ideal city	499	469	-6.0	542	18.1	81.2	0.0	0.4	0.4	30.8	47.4	21.8	170	53.5	63.5	6.5
Ila city	337	340	0.9	418	100.0	0.0	0.0	0.0	0.0	37.1	56.9	6.2	147	43.5	61.2	20.4
Indian Springs CDP	2,241	NA	NA	2,529	90.7	3.6	0.0	3.5	2.1	19.1	67.9	13.0	866	71.1	37.4	17.4
Iron City town	310	309	-0.3	287	87.5	10.8	0.0	0.0	1.7	18.0	52.9	28.9	137	87.6	59.9	13.1
Irondale CDP	7,446	NA	NA	7,927	11.6	64.1	4.4	2.3	17.6	33.3	61.7	5.0	2,269	67.1	41.0	27.6
Irwinton city	589	577	-2.0	708	47.3	43.5	0.0	0.0	9.2	18.2	67.6	14.1	220	65.9	63.2	21.4
Isle of Hope CDP	2,402	NA	NA	2,355	93.8	1.2	1.1	3.1	0.8	17.3	63.0	19.6	992	89.7	18.5	51.8
Ivey city	981	947	-3.5	947	98.6	0.0	0.0	0.2	1.2	28.3	54.7	17.1	369	77.0	63.1	6.8
Jackson city	5,047	4,891	-3.1	4,959	52.0	37.9	2.3	1.1	6.7	28.6	59.3	12.0	1,649	47.2	67.3	12.2
Jacksonville city	140	134	-4.3	198	24.7	19.2	0.0	0.0	56.1	20.7	69.7	9.6	59	76.3	86.4	3.4
Jakin city	155	150	-3.2	167	57.5	38.3	2.4	1.8	0.0	34.2	53.4	12.6	63	36.5	46.0	4.8
Jasper city	3,684	3,744	1.6	3,691	92.4	4.6	2.2	0.5	0.4	25.4	57.1	17.4	1,341	40.3	41.9	18.9
Jefferson city	9,459	9,867	4.3	9,630	78.8	12.6	2.3	1.3	5.1	31.0	57.0	12.1	3,473	72.1	36.3	26.4
Jeffersonville city	1,035	961	-7.1	1,160	36.6	62.3	0.0	0.8	0.3	22.5	57.1	20.4	350	66.3	75.7	4.0
Jenkinsburg city	370	368	-0.5	380	70.8	17.4	0.3	10.8	0.8	31.3	59.1	9.7	121	57.9	57.9	14.9
Jersey city	137	143	4.4	146	100.0	0.0	0.0	0.0	0.0	10.3	70.5	19.2	66	69.7	72.7	7.6
Jesup city	10,214	10,285	0.7	10,275	49.2	39.7	0.1	2.6	8.4	23.0	62.1	14.7	3,253	55.2	55.2	17.2
Johns Creek city	76,727	83,102	8.3	80,979	58.3	10.8	22.5	3.0	5.5	30.4	61.4	8.0	26,501	79.1	10.5	71.3
Jonesboro city	4,719	4,624	-2.0	4,661	34.8	56.3	1.8	0.8	6.3	20.7	71.8	7.4	1,136	46.9	58.5	15.6
Junction City town	177	167	-5.6	170	28.2	71.8	0.0	0.0	0.0	24.7	67.6	7.6	61	78.7	72.1	6.6
Kennesaw city	30,294	32,400	7.0	31,358	55.4	23.8	4.6	3.0	13.2	25.3	66.2	8.5	12,126	62.4	24.0	44.0
Keysville city	332	317	-4.5	292	17.1	71.9	0.0	0.0	11.0	23.0	65.3	11.6	84	84.5	79.8	1.2
Kings Bay Base CDP	1,777	NA	NA	1,905	66.0	14.0	0.9	3.1	16.0	26.8	73.2	0.0	345	0.0	31.6	11.0
Kingsland city	15,944	16,416	3.0	16,147	67.3	18.0	1.4	4.8	8.5	30.1	62.3	7.6	5,803	64.0	31.9	20.2
Kingston city	639	651	1.9	785	57.5	38.6	0.0	3.3	0.6	19.9	70.5	9.6	270	57.8	68.1	5.2
Kite city	241	229	-5.0	306	89.9	0.0	0.7	0.0	9.5	30.4	55.5	14.1	92	57.6	54.3	7.6
Knoxville CDP	69	NA	NA	68	57.4	42.6	0.0	0.0	0.0	0.0	82.3	17.6	6	100.0	0.0	0.0
LaFayette city	7,117	7,169	0.7	7,105	88.8	7.2	0.2	2.7	1.2	22.1	58.0	20.0	2,993	50.9	43.1	15.2
LaGrange city	29,430	30,557	3.8	30,138	40.3	49.0	2.7	2.2	5.8	27.4	60.7	12.0	10,713	39.6	48.1	21.4
Lake City city	2,612	2,671	2.3	2,631	24.7	48.8	9.9	1.8	14.7	20.6	61.1	18.2	819	51.0	49.6	9.2
Lakeland city	3,364	3,341	-0.7	3,385	47.9	48.9	0.7	0.9	1.6	24.5	59.5	15.9	1,174	35.0	51.8	12.5
Lake Park city	733	734	0.1	885	70.4	15.7	0.5	1.6	11.9	32.4	55.8	11.6	313	56.5	39.9	20.1
Lakeview CDP	4,839	NA	NA	5,603	87.6	4.9	0.3	2.6	4.7	20.0	63.4	16.4	2,119	72.1	55.5	14.8

1 May be of any race.

Table A. All Places — **Population and Housing**

STATE City, town, township, borough, or CDP (county if applicable)	Population: 2010 census total population	Population: 2014 estimated population	Population: Percent change 2010–2014	Population: ACS total population estimate 2010–2014	Race and Hispanic or Latino origin (percent), 2010–2014: White alone, not Hispanic or Latino	Black alone, not Hispanic or Latino	Asian alone, not Hispanic or Latino	All other races or 2 or more races, not Hispanic or Latino	Hispanic or Latino[1]	Age (percent), 2010–2014: Under 18 years old	Age 18 to 64 years old	Age 65 years and older	Households, 2010–2014: Total occupied housing units	Percent owner occupied	Householders by level of education (percent): High school diploma or less	Bachelor's degree or more
	1	2	3	4	5	6	7	8	9	10	11	12	13	14	15	16
GEORGIA—Con.																
Lakeview Estates CDP	2,695	NA	NA	2,427	7.7	0.0	0.0	0.0	92.3	42.0	56.8	1.2	512	47.5	93.8	0.0
Lavonia city	2,156	2,160	0.2	1,726	64.5	20.9	0.4	1.4	12.7	17.9	58.5	23.6	827	40.1	61.7	13.8
Lawrenceville city	28,391	30,212	6.4	29,364	35.4	33.9	6.1	3.3	21.3	28.3	59.8	11.6	9,679	52.6	42.9	21.1
Leary city	618	590	-4.5	536	19.6	80.4	0.0	0.0	0.0	23.5	48.5	28.0	256	84.4	57.8	16.0
Leesburg city	2,896	2,982	3.0	2,936	70.7	21.2	1.9	3.2	3.0	34.7	57.8	7.6	942	59.6	42.6	20.5
Lenox town	873	861	-1.4	807	56.5	35.8	0.0	1.0	6.7	26.0	63.7	10.4	290	71.7	64.1	3.1
Leslie city	409	392	-4.2	435	52.4	37.9	0.0	0.0	9.7	23.0	59.7	17.2	161	65.8	47.8	11.8
Lexington city	228	224	-1.8	367	77.1	22.6	0.0	0.3	0.0	34.6	47.3	18.0	129	71.3	45.7	25.6
Lilburn city	11,660	12,543	7.6	12,162	38.1	15.1	22.4	3.2	21.2	26.9	61.0	12.0	3,909	65.7	39.8	35.5
Lilly city	213	206	-3.3	237	44.3	50.6	0.0	0.0	5.1	35.0	60.7	4.2	101	53.5	77.2	0.0
Lincoln Park CDP	833	NA	NA	653	0.0	100.0	0.0	0.0	0.0	9.8	70.4	19.8	336	53.0	71.4	0.0
Lincolnton city	1,566	1,485	-5.2	1,559	58.1	39.6	0.6	1.5	0.3	19.4	65.7	14.9	665	62.1	57.7	16.5
Lindale CDP	4,191	NA	NA	4,266	85.7	2.9	1.3	2.2	7.8	30.1	53.2	16.6	1,586	66.6	59.4	11.7
Lithia Springs CDP	15,491	NA	NA	16,384	37.6	42.4	0.1	1.3	18.5	28.3	62.6	9.2	6,021	50.8	47.4	20.5
Lithonia city	1,924	1,998	3.8	1,975	7.5	80.5	0.0	5.8	6.2	29.5	58.8	11.7	759	33.6	48.4	10.5
Locust Grove city	5,403	5,702	5.5	5,573	50.7	40.5	0.0	2.0	6.7	29.9	62.2	7.8	1,766	72.5	45.5	21.6
Loganville city	10,458	11,022	5.4	10,711	64.6	20.2	2.8	5.4	7.0	26.8	58.5	14.8	3,581	75.0	39.1	21.7
Lone Oak town	92	89	-3.3	117	64.1	7.7	0.0	3.4	24.8	53.8	39.4	6.8	41	34.1	78.0	14.6
Lookout Mountain city	1,602	1,591	-0.7	1,756	93.7	0.6	0.2	2.7	2.8	30.7	55.0	14.4	607	83.9	8.1	80.7
Louisville city	2,490	2,370	-4.8	2,705	26.8	72.1	0.0	0.3	0.8	29.3	56.9	13.8	965	60.2	63.3	13.6
Lovejoy city	6,447	6,406	-0.6	6,433	8.0	75.7	0.1	1.5	14.7	28.6	66.3	5.2	2,009	51.5	31.2	18.8
Ludowici city	1,701	2,012	18.3	2,563	59.0	26.6	0.0	9.8	4.6	24.2	64.6	11.0	765	43.3	50.3	15.6
Lula city	2,762	2,867	3.8	2,771	81.4	8.5	0.1	2.2	7.8	32.6	57.0	10.4	927	74.4	60.9	8.7
Lumber City city	1,328	1,250	-5.9	894	40.3	58.2	0.0	0.4	1.1	19.0	59.8	21.1	388	57.0	88.9	2.8
Lumpkin city	1,145	1,104	-3.6	1,216	26.9	65.1	6.1	1.0	0.9	17.3	66.9	15.8	447	60.9	60.0	22.4
Luthersville city	874	828	-5.3	1,163	35.1	50.7	0.0	3.7	10.5	26.4	62.2	11.3	371	50.4	60.4	7.3
Lyerly town	535	526	-1.7	483	91.9	1.0	5.6	1.4	0.0	24.2	63.8	12.0	185	71.4	55.1	8.1
Lyons city	4,367	4,389	0.5	4,395	41.6	39.7	0.0	1.4	17.3	31.9	56.5	11.5	1,587	43.8	68.6	7.7
Mableton CDP	37,115	NA	NA	40,521	36.1	42.5	2.1	2.4	16.8	28.9	63.4	7.7	14,277	70.5	36.8	36.5
McCaysville city	1,056	1,059	0.3	1,327	97.1	0.0	0.7	1.7	0.5	27.6	50.6	21.7	559	45.8	60.3	7.7
McDonough city	22,019	23,004	4.5	22,560	30.5	58.0	3.5	2.8	5.2	27.7	62.6	9.7	8,374	47.6	33.5	23.3
McIntyre town	650	631	-2.9	893	19.3	65.8	0.0	0.0	14.9	23.5	54.1	22.4	261	65.9	81.2	3.4
Macon-Bibb County	155,292	153,691	-1.0	155,023	41.1	52.3	1.7	1.8	3.1	25.4	61.3	13.2	56,567	53.8	46.0	25.4
McRae city	5,656	5,972	5.6	5,762	55.8	42.3	0.0	0.0	1.8	26.9	55.1	18.1	2,297	53.6	57.6	24.4
Madison city	3,979	4,005	0.7	3,983	52.2	43.5	0.0	0.9	3.4	24.2	59.1	16.6	1,407	72.1	48.0	35.5
Manassas city	94	95	1.1	102	59.8	40.2	0.0	0.0	0.0	30.4	59.8	9.8	43	62.8	46.5	4.7
Manchester city	4,262	4,099	-3.8	4,190	45.2	54.7	0.0	0.1	0.0	32.1	49.9	17.9	1,483	50.6	71.4	8.1
Mansfield city	410	426	3.9	367	93.2	6.5	0.0	0.3	0.0	21.8	55.0	23.2	130	63.1	68.5	10.0
Marietta city	56,605	60,014	6.0	58,436	44.5	32.0	3.2	1.9	18.4	21.6	67.9	10.4	22,261	42.9	28.6	38.2
Marshallville city	1,448	1,353	-6.6	1,400	27.5	70.5	0.5	1.5	0.0	21.0	62.8	16.1	536	76.1	61.9	17.0
Martin town	381	367	-3.7	348	90.2	6.6	0.0	0.0	3.2	21.8	51.7	26.4	133	69.2	68.4	9.8
Martinez CDP	35,795	NA	NA	36,190	74.5	14.6	5.5	2.4	2.9	25.2	62.5	12.2	12,662	72.8	27.6	37.1
Matthews CDP	150	NA	NA	277	88.8	11.2	0.0	0.0	0.0	44.0	42.0	14.1	106	92.5	100.0	0.0
Maxeys town	224	221	-1.3	252	92.5	6.3	0.0	1.2	0.0	21.5	64.1	14.7	79	87.3	24.1	24.1
Maysville town	1,815	1,834	1.0	2,079	97.8	0.8	0.5	0.7	0.2	30.7	55.3	14.0	745	64.4	58.0	7.0
Meansville city	182	182	0.0	166	82.5	17.5	0.0	0.0	0.0	18.6	63.2	18.1	70	67.1	48.6	28.6
Meigs city	1,035	1,029	-0.6	921	19.7	68.2	0.0	0.0	12.2	27.4	62.2	10.3	374	44.4	86.4	1.6
Mendes CDP	122	NA	NA	63	100.0	0.0	0.0	0.0	0.0	14.3	42.8	42.9	31	100.0	48.4	22.6
Menlo city	474	466	-1.7	452	94.0	2.9	3.1	0.0	0.0	21.0	59.4	19.5	216	56.0	62.5	13.4
Metter city	4,120	4,079	-1.0	4,137	51.5	41.8	2.0	0.8	3.9	26.6	52.9	20.4	1,516	52.4	64.1	13.6
Midville city	269	263	-2.2	223	43.5	41.3	0.0	3.1	12.1	18.8	51.3	29.6	102	72.5	76.5	3.9
Midway city	2,121	2,103	-0.8	2,141	54.5	36.4	1.8	2.3	5.0	29.1	61.8	9.0	701	67.5	32.0	21.8
Milan city	700	771	10.1	632	81.2	18.0	0.0	0.8	0.0	19.6	52.1	28.2	285	68.4	61.8	20.0
Milledgeville city	18,380	19,211	4.5	18,840	50.3	42.8	2.6	1.4	2.9	16.4	71.9	11.7	6,126	36.4	41.2	21.5
Millen city	3,120	2,991	-4.1	3,042	32.8	61.1	0.0	4.9	1.1	34.0	47.3	18.7	1,093	62.9	57.7	12.3
Milner city	610	601	-1.5	1,144	85.0	14.2	0.0	0.3	0.5	32.7	59.2	8.2	359	51.5	55.4	13.4
Milton city	32,712	36,662	12.1	34,874	71.6	8.7	9.8	2.3	7.6	29.8	62.5	7.7	12,119	68.6	8.7	68.6
Mineral Bluff CDP	150	NA	NA	81	88.9	0.0	0.0	0.0	11.1	11.1	88.9	0.0	53	84.9	60.4	39.6
Mitchell town	199	200	0.5	189	79.4	3.2	0.0	4.2	13.2	24.9	66.5	8.5	66	80.3	36.4	24.2
Molena city	368	371	0.8	481	61.5	36.6	0.0	0.0	1.9	26.1	53.1	20.8	148	62.8	54.7	9.5
Monroe city	13,219	13,664	3.4	13,427	47.7	46.2	1.3	1.3	3.5	24.1	61.6	14.3	5,034	39.7	61.5	12.5
Montezuma city	3,460	3,232	-6.6	3,338	31.9	64.1	2.7	0.0	1.3	21.8	65.4	12.7	1,310	49.8	53.8	9.8
Montgomery CDP	4,523	NA	NA	4,560	87.0	5.1	1.0	1.0	5.9	16.8	71.8	11.5	1,838	69.3	43.4	30.8
Monticello city	2,662	2,579	-3.1	2,619	36.7	56.0	0.7	3.7	2.9	30.4	58.0	11.6	984	52.3	55.0	14.8
Montrose town	215	213	-0.9	231	49.4	48.1	0.4	0.4	1.7	27.7	61.5	10.8	64	84.4	29.7	9.4
Moody AFB CDP	886	NA	NA	726	76.9	14.3	0.0	2.6	6.2	45.6	53.4	0.8	220	0.0	31.4	21.8
Moreland town	399	418	4.8	428	69.4	28.7	0.0	0.5	1.4	29.9	58.8	11.2	140	84.3	56.4	20.0
Morgan city	1,861	1,830	-1.7	2,401	28.2	60.6	1.1	2.2	7.9	2.6	94.8	2.6	86	65.1	70.9	3.5
Morganton city	303	303	0.0	345	95.7	0.0	0.3	1.2	2.9	22.7	52.3	24.9	136	74.3	47.1	11.8
Morrow city	6,408	7,167	11.8	6,837	22.3	34.2	25.7	8.8	8.9	19.2	68.8	11.7	2,273	60.4	39.9	17.4
Morven city	565	528	-6.5	557	33.9	46.7	0.0	2.0	17.4	17.0	71.4	11.5	226	62.4	46.9	8.8
Moultrie city	14,268	14,507	1.7	14,467	38.9	47.9	0.0	0.6	12.6	29.7	56.5	13.8	5,342	41.4	65.1	12.2
Mountain City town	1,088	1,064	-2.2	767	94.5	0.0	0.0	0.0	5.5	17.8	51.9	30.4	337	70.3	65.0	14.2
Mountain Park city	547	579	5.9	529	92.2	0.0	0.9	0.0	6.8	16.0	73.1	11.2	261	83.5	15.7	59.0
Mountain Park CDP	11,554	NA	NA	12,510	64.9	17.6	12.9	1.9	2.8	22.9	61.8	15.3	4,370	82.7	24.0	47.0
Mount Airy town	1,284	1,290	0.5	1,224	68.4	2.9	2.6	1.1	25.1	25.5	62.0	12.4	443	76.1	51.5	13.5
Mount Vernon city	2,347	2,293	-2.3	2,207	49.8	38.9	0.0	1.9	9.3	20.6	65.0	14.3	834	60.7	66.4	14.9
Mount Zion city	1,705	1,721	0.9	1,817	91.5	5.7	0.7	1.3	0.8	29.5	62.5	7.8	577	69.0	63.4	11.1
Nahunta city	1,055	1,056	0.1	1,183	82.9	15.3	0.0	1.5	0.3	23.3	56.6	20.0	426	53.8	54.9	12.4
Nashville city	4,939	4,790	-3.0	4,918	77.9	20.9	0.2	0.6	0.4	25.5	54.6	19.8	1,854	59.4	56.4	13.2
Nelson city	1,314	1,342	2.1	1,306	88.6	2.8	2.0	5.4	1.2	25.3	58.2	16.6	477	78.6	41.9	15.3
Newborn town	696	720	3.4	736	78.7	21.2	0.0	0.1	0.0	25.9	60.4	13.6	237	70.0	52.3	16.0
Newington town	272	267	-1.8	342	75.1	24.9	0.0	0.0	0.0	31.8	52.0	16.1	125	60.0	56.8	20.0
Newnan city	33,191	36,203	9.1	34,457	56.0	27.9	2.5	2.3	11.4	29.6	60.8	9.8	12,697	54.0	39.7	29.5
Newton city	654	610	-6.7	707	53.5	44.8	0.0	0.0	1.7	16.8	63.4	19.8	308	56.5	79.2	3.2
Nicholls city	2,798	3,311	18.3	3,303	43.1	52.7	0.0	0.2	4.0	9.3	86.4	4.3	345	55.4	79.7	4.3
Nicholson city	1,708	1,704	-0.2	1,425	84.6	8.8	0.0	0.7	5.9	21.5	66.0	12.6	508	76.4	58.1	12.0
Norcross city	15,174	16,349	7.7	15,799	20.0	18.1	13.4	1.6	47.0	32.5	62.7	4.8	4,876	48.7	45.5	30.0
Norman Park city	972	966	-0.6	1,363	77.0	11.8	0.0	1.0	10.3	28.2	60.8	11.1	481	53.2	60.5	11.6
Norristown CDP	59	NA	NA	77	59.7	40.3	0.0	0.0	0.0	18.2	57.2	24.7	35	54.3	60.0	40.0
North Decatur CDP	16,698	NA	NA	17,023	70.9	9.4	10.9	2.2	6.6	17.5	67.6	14.9	8,020	49.3	12.1	62.7

1 May be of any race.

Table A. All Places — **Population and Housing**

STATE City, town, township, borough, or CDP (county if applicable)	Population				Race and Hispanic or Latino origin (percent), 2010–2014					Age (percent), 2010–2014			Households, 2010–2014		Householders by level of education (percent)	
	2010 census total population	2014 estimated population	Percent change 2010–2014	ACS total population estimate 2010–2014	White alone, not Hispanic or Latino	Black alone, not Hispanic or Latino	Asian alone, not Hispanic or Latino	All other races or 2 or more races, not Hispanic or Latino	Hispanic or Latino[1]	Under 18 years old	Age 18 to 64 years old	Age 65 years and older	Total occupied housing units	Percent owner occupied	High school diploma or less	Bachelor's degree or more
	1	2	3	4	5	6	7	8	9	10	11	12	13	14	15	16
GEORGIA—Con.																
North Druid Hills CDP	18,947	NA	NA	17,996	62.6	12.6	9.8	4.3	10.7	12.9	73.9	13.1	9,149	40.9	10.7	70.6
North High Shoals town	652	682	4.6	794	75.4	6.7	0.9	0.4	16.6	29.1	53.8	17.3	202	92.6	31.7	43.6
Norwood city	239	229	-4.2	403	21.3	78.4	0.0	0.2	0.0	12.1	70.6	17.4	126	81.0	84.9	11.9
Nunez city	147	149	1.4	110	42.7	28.2	0.0	4.5	24.5	20.9	64.5	14.5	33	72.7	48.5	30.3
Oak Park town	484	483	-0.2	718	79.8	0.3	0.0	1.8	18.1	31.4	59.6	8.8	225	81.8	66.7	2.7
Oakwood city	3,979	4,163	4.6	4,089	52.3	11.4	9.0	3.1	24.2	22.6	66.2	11.1	1,611	32.1	52.8	13.3
Ochlocknee town	676	680	0.6	730	68.6	28.1	0.3	1.6	1.4	23.9	63.0	13.0	281	53.0	60.5	6.0
Ocilla city	3,402	3,286	-3.4	3,462	30.6	67.6	0.2	0.2	1.4	22.2	65.1	12.7	1,106	64.1	49.8	9.6
Oconee city	259	251	-3.1	315	63.2	32.7	2.5	1.6	0.0	22.2	55.4	22.2	94	80.9	63.8	14.9
Odum city	504	498	-1.2	551	76.8	9.6	0.4	4.9	8.3	31.8	53.1	15.2	166	75.3	50.0	15.7
Offerman city	441	440	-0.2	432	72.0	10.2	0.0	0.7	17.1	17.7	70.6	11.8	166	81.9	71.1	3.6
Oglethorpe city	1,328	1,223	-7.9	1,468	24.7	71.3	1.8	1.7	0.4	18.9	66.5	14.6	617	53.5	66.8	12.8
Oliver city	239	227	-5.0	320	42.2	56.6	0.0	1.3	0.0	24.1	66.1	10.0	110	73.6	69.1	4.5
Omega city	1,221	1,229	0.7	1,346	45.8	10.7	0.0	0.0	43.5	32.2	55.6	12.0	399	67.2	78.4	0.3
Orchard Hill town	209	207	-1.0	193	63.7	19.7	0.0	4.1	12.4	25.4	60.2	14.5	80	60.0	88.8	1.3
Oxford city	2,134	2,262	6.0	2,273	50.4	37.8	9.4	1.3	1.1	17.7	71.2	11.1	656	61.3	54.0	18.9
Palmetto city	4,489	4,747	5.7	4,893	24.9	44.0	0.0	3.3	27.8	33.2	55.5	11.2	1,570	62.7	50.5	13.1
Panthersville CDP	9,749	NA	NA	9,474	5.3	90.4	0.0	2.8	1.4	25.8	62.3	12.0	3,380	50.5	45.1	18.1
Parrott town	158	152	-3.8	186	64.5	35.5	0.0	0.0	0.0	18.9	46.8	34.4	52	92.3	51.9	15.4
Patterson city	730	744	1.9	870	82.1	16.0	0.0	0.7	1.3	23.3	63.0	13.7	299	60.5	46.5	31.4
Pavo city	627	613	-2.2	749	63.7	36.0	0.0	0.0	0.3	15.2	59.7	25.0	291	78.7	66.7	5.8
Payne city	218	214	-1.8	214	23.8	67.3	0.0	5.6	3.3	36.4	61.5	1.9	93	9.7	67.7	4.3
Peachtree City city	34,364	35,063	2.0	34,701	76.8	8.3	4.7	2.3	7.9	26.3	60.6	13.1	12,633	72.7	16.0	58.8
Peachtree Corners city	38,011	40,531	6.6	39,381	49.7	24.2	8.4	2.2	15.5	25.6	66.4	7.8	14,699	55.9	21.4	53.0
Pearson city	2,113	2,072	-1.9	1,898	25.7	33.6	0.0	3.2	37.5	23.5	66.4	10.2	594	48.3	82.8	4.0
Pelham city	3,898	3,841	-1.5	3,887	46.4	45.5	0.0	5.2	2.9	27.1	53.1	19.8	1,639	46.1	68.0	3.8
Pembroke city	2,201	2,387	8.5	2,895	58.8	35.4	0.0	2.7	3.1	35.5	52.1	12.4	1,033	57.3	56.8	12.5
Pendergrass town	428	429	0.2	471	96.6	3.0	0.0	0.0	0.4	25.1	54.9	20.2	184	39.1	69.6	11.4
Perkins CDP	91	NA	NA	142	100.0	0.0	0.0	0.0	0.0	24.6	75.4	0.0	23	100.0	0.0	0.0
Perry city	13,829	15,144	9.5	14,714	52.8	40.1	1.9	1.9	3.3	24.5	63.1	12.7	4,818	56.2	38.2	26.2
Phillipsburg CDP	707	NA	NA	673	0.0	100.0	0.0	0.0	0.0	42.3	44.9	12.6	217	52.1	45.2	12.0
Pinehurst city	455	346	-24.0	493	53.5	43.6	0.0	0.0	2.8	23.7	55.6	20.7	201	70.1	59.2	14.9
Pine Lake city	730	754	3.3	674	77.3	9.1	0.4	3.1	10.1	14.3	69.3	16.2	355	72.1	14.1	58.6
Pine Mountain town	1,304	1,344	3.1	1,426	46.1	41.6	1.1	5.9	5.3	22.9	58.2	18.9	583	57.5	47.2	29.3
Pineview town	523	490	-6.3	592	13.9	78.7	3.4	1.0	3.0	32.3	47.7	20.3	176	67.6	47.2	5.7
Pitts city	320	308	-3.8	477	58.7	40.9	0.0	0.4	0.0	29.9	57.9	12.2	167	61.7	69.5	12.0
Plains city	774	758	-2.1	574	43.9	45.6	0.0	0.3	10.1	9.4	57.2	33.3	208	54.3	39.9	18.3
Plainville city	313	318	1.6	347	94.5	1.4	0.0	0.6	3.5	34.6	57.9	7.5	118	70.3	64.4	5.9
Pooler city	19,104	22,251	16.5	20,646	60.4	26.1	4.2	3.6	5.6	27.3	63.4	9.3	7,668	67.5	25.9	43.3
Portal town	638	620	-2.8	778	73.4	22.5	0.3	2.7	1.2	30.8	54.8	14.4	294	57.5	57.5	14.6
Porterdale city	1,429	1,465	2.5	1,701	57.6	32.6	0.0	6.5	3.4	21.9	65.4	12.7	601	40.8	57.1	22.6
Port Wentworth city	5,360	7,080	32.1	6,189	39.3	46.1	0.0	1.3	13.2	27.6	63.3	9.1	2,400	60.5	38.5	31.5
Poulan city	851	815	-4.2	1,175	65.1	30.9	0.0	4.0	0.0	21.7	62.6	15.7	446	69.1	76.0	9.9
Powder Springs city	13,939	14,590	4.7	14,271	34.4	51.0	0.5	4.0	10.0	29.9	59.2	11.1	4,901	76.9	29.1	34.5
Pulaski town	266	271	1.9	251	82.5	15.5	0.0	1.2	0.8	26.3	34.4	39.4	62	82.3	59.7	21.0
Putney CDP	2,898	NA	NA	2,716	56.5	41.0	0.0	0.7	1.8	16.4	65.0	18.6	1,092	84.7	51.2	16.1
Quitman city	3,927	3,746	-4.6	3,808	22.0	75.6	0.0	0.2	2.3	27.6	52.5	19.8	1,552	59.0	65.0	8.7
Ranger town	131	133	1.5	156	99.4	0.6	0.0	0.0	0.0	24.9	57.9	17.3	45	66.7	84.4	2.2
Raoul CDP	2,558	NA	NA	2,733	56.8	24.6	2.0	0.0	16.6	7.9	87.6	4.5	279	83.2	78.5	4.7
Ray City city	1,090	1,040	-4.6	1,343	82.4	9.5	1.3	4.0	2.8	25.0	64.1	10.9	492	59.8	38.8	19.7
Rayle town	199	191	-4.0	226	57.1	32.3	10.6	0.0	0.0	34.1	54.4	11.5	52	38.5	67.3	17.3
Rebecca town	187	171	-8.6	218	97.7	1.4	0.0	0.9	0.0	27.2	47.6	25.2	81	95.1	72.8	8.6
Redan CDP	33,015	NA	NA	33,603	3.0	91.8	1.2	2.4	1.6	26.3	67.2	6.7	11,549	65.1	28.2	29.7
Reed Creek CDP	2,604	NA	NA	3,297	97.8	1.5	0.0	0.0	0.7	18.4	53.8	27.8	1,413	87.9	46.1	29.0
Register town	175	173	-1.1	102	77.5	15.7	4.9	2.0	0.0	13.6	55.8	30.4	53	84.9	47.2	30.2
Reidsville city	2,601	2,617	0.6	2,618	41.6	51.0	0.0	2.9	4.6	27.3	58.5	14.3	1,086	51.1	52.9	16.6
Remerton city	1,123	1,130	0.6	1,386	55.2	32.0	2.5	1.9	8.4	10.0	89.0	1.0	596	3.4	9.9	19.1
Rentz city	295	293	-0.7	324	91.7	5.9	0.0	2.5	0.0	28.3	52.7	18.8	144	68.8	47.2	11.1
Resaca town	768	770	0.3	975	56.4	8.4	0.3	2.3	32.6	26.9	63.0	10.3	334	49.7	49.7	24.0
Rest Haven town	62	66	6.5	54	81.5	0.0	0.0	14.8	3.7	13.0	59.4	27.8	22	72.7	86.4	0.0
Reynolds city	1,085	1,041	-4.1	1,120	48.5	45.4	0.0	0.2	5.9	24.4	49.6	26.0	519	63.8	58.4	17.5
Rhine town	394	379	-3.8	552	62.5	26.8	0.9	0.9	8.9	23.5	53.4	23.2	241	68.0	68.5	7.5
Riceboro city	801	811	1.2	848	5.4	94.0	0.0	0.0	0.6	16.7	60.3	23.1	335	83.3	67.2	21.5
Richland city	1,473	1,427	-3.1	2,089	31.7	67.8	0.0	0.1	0.3	19.7	64.3	15.9	641	53.5	69.3	10.8
Richmond Hill city	9,281	11,229	21.0	10,334	69.6	17.7	1.7	3.0	7.9	30.5	63.0	6.6	3,712	51.3	26.9	37.4
Riddleville town	96	95	1.0	70	90.0	10.0	0.0	0.0	0.0	14.3	84.3	1.4	22	81.8	45.5	18.2
Rincon town	8,843	9,638	9.0	9,273	66.0	20.0	2.7	2.9	8.4	40.5	54.0	5.4	3,025	53.9	32.8	27.8
Ringgold city	3,580	3,679	2.8	3,647	79.1	3.2	5.8	1.3	10.7	26.3	59.7	14.1	1,502	57.7	39.3	14.8
Riverdale city	15,235	15,669	2.8	15,496	7.4	70.8	8.1	5.2	8.5	29.7	62.3	8.1	5,255	49.5	45.6	21.3
Riverside town	35	36	2.9	17	100.0	0.0	0.0	0.0	0.0	0.0	70.6	29.4	7	57.1	42.9	28.6
Roberta city	1,007	998	-0.9	866	60.9	32.9	2.4	3.8	0.0	20.2	55.6	24.4	346	45.1	57.2	15.0
Robins AFB CDP	1,170	NA	NA	1,413	69.1	13.1	1.7	4.7	11.5	32.2	67.4	0.6	281	0.0	14.2	37.4
Rochelle city	1,175	1,122	-4.5	1,012	50.5	48.4	0.0	1.1	0.0	17.6	60.3	22.0	461	71.8	73.1	6.7
Rockingham CDP	248	NA	NA	394	55.3	12.2	0.0	0.0	32.5	58.4	41.5	0.0	114	57.0	74.6	9.6
Rockmart city	4,187	4,264	1.8	4,174	75.9	21.3	2.9	0.0	0.0	22.3	64.8	12.9	1,670	59.4	49.9	14.0
Rocky Ford town	144	141	-2.1	166	77.1	22.9	0.0	0.0	0.0	15.7	66.7	17.5	71	83.1	69.0	7.0
Rome city	36,306	35,997	-0.9	36,099	51.6	28.5	2.0	1.9	16.0	25.0	60.0	14.9	13,577	46.4	47.1	22.9
Roopville town	218	223	2.3	283	86.2	11.3	0.0	2.5	0.0	21.9	56.5	21.6	103	76.7	53.4	19.4
Rossville city	4,105	4,027	-1.9	4,066	83.8	7.9	0.5	5.8	2.0	23.6	60.9	15.5	1,626	43.1	56.0	12.7
Roswell city	88,347	94,089	6.5	92,364	66.7	11.7	5.3	2.5	13.8	24.0	64.5	11.8	34,408	67.1	18.6	58.1
Royston city	2,573	2,574	0.0	2,578	71.1	24.7	0.0	0.8	3.5	23.4	55.3	21.4	1,071	37.8	55.2	9.9
Russell CDP	1,203	NA	NA	1,318	52.0	15.8	17.5	0.0	14.7	18.3	76.0	5.8	411	36.7	65.0	11.2
Rutledge city	781	790	1.2	708	63.1	35.3	1.6	0.0	0.0	14.5	66.0	19.4	317	79.5	60.6	19.2
St. Marys city	17,126	17,949	4.8	17,555	71.4	19.2	1.1	3.3	4.9	26.7	62.2	11.3	6,488	50.6	35.1	22.5
St. Simons CDP	12,743	NA	NA	12,807	90.6	2.4	2.0	1.8	3.1	16.2	55.0	28.8	6,158	71.3	12.3	58.8
Sale City city	380	360	-5.3	485	70.3	25.6	0.0	0.4	3.7	29.8	57.8	12.4	157	56.1	61.1	8.3
Salem CDP	310	NA	NA	295	0.0	100.0	0.0	0.0	0.0	11.2	69.8	19.0	154	79.2	81.2	1.3
Sandersville city	5,912	5,779	-2.2	5,839	35.3	62.0	0.0	0.9	1.8	27.7	59.9	12.5	2,144	59.6	60.5	14.7
Sandy Springs city	93,852	101,908	8.6	98,480	57.4	21.3	6.1	2.3	12.9	21.8	66.9	11.3	42,196	46.2	16.2	59.4
Santa Claus city	165	166	0.6	237	90.7	6.8	0.0	0.0	2.5	29.1	43.9	27.0	95	71.6	61.1	13.7
Sardis city	999	965	-3.4	1,058	37.8	62.0	0.0	0.2	0.0	32.8	57.7	9.5	376	64.9	67.3	11.4

1 May be of any race.

Table A. All Places — **Population and Housing**

STATE City, town, township, borough, or CDP (county if applicable)	Population: 2010 census total population	Population: 2014 estimated population	Population: Percent change 2010–2014	Population: ACS total population estimate 2010–2014	Race and Hispanic or Latino origin (percent), 2010–2014: White alone, not Hispanic or Latino	Black alone, not Hispanic or Latino	Asian alone, not Hispanic or Latino	All other races or 2 or more races, not Hispanic or Latino	Hispanic or Latino[1]	Age (percent), 2010–2014: Under 18 years old	Age 18 to 64 years old	Age 65 years and older	Households, 2010–2014: Total occupied housing units	Percent owner occupied	Householders by level of education (percent): High school diploma or less	Bachelor's degree or more
	1	2	3	4	5	6	7	8	9	10	11	12	13	14	15	16
GEORGIA—Con.																
Sasser town	279	264	-5.4	373	53.1	41.8	0.0	0.0	5.1	32.7	51.6	15.5	128	60.9	54.7	5.5
Satilla CDP	421	NA	NA	348	100.0	0.0	0.0	0.0	0.0	18.4	52.5	29.0	119	86.6	75.6	0.0
Sautee-Nacoochee CDP	363	NA	NA	198	79.3	20.7	0.0	0.0	0.0	10.1	55.1	34.8	112	71.4	15.2	46.4
Savannah city	136,340	144,352	5.9	141,298	37.1	54.1	2.2	1.8	4.9	21.8	66.1	12.1	52,264	45.0	37.6	28.3
Scotland city	366	345	-5.7	248	77.4	22.6	0.0	0.0	0.0	20.5	74.2	5.2	91	71.4	91.2	0.0
Scottdale CDP	10,631	NA	NA	9,847	30.7	38.9	18.0	7.4	5.2	24.5	69.5	6.1	3,879	35.4	32.6	41.3
Screven city	766	758	-1.0	861	55.4	36.1	0.0	1.7	6.7	33.4	53.4	13.2	322	67.1	59.3	5.6
Senoia city	3,328	3,959	19.0	3,627	70.0	20.1	3.1	0.3	6.5	28.1	64.4	7.3	1,308	69.7	34.9	27.7
Seville CDP	202	NA	NA	167	100.0	0.0	0.0	0.0	0.0	25.2	63.6	11.4	68	39.7	19.1	27.9
Shady Dale town	249	238	-4.4	217	55.3	16.1	0.0	0.0	28.6	20.7	69.1	10.1	86	70.9	57.0	20.9
Shannon CDP	1,862	NA	NA	1,862	95.9	2.6	0.0	1.5	0.0	32.8	53.4	13.9	714	63.9	39.8	18.6
Sharon city	140	139	-0.7	77	33.8	66.2	0.0	0.0	0.0	2.6	70.2	27.3	45	86.7	84.4	6.7
Sharpsburg town	341	351	2.9	459	73.2	18.5	0.0	3.9	4.4	18.1	76.6	5.2	162	48.1	47.5	25.9
Shellman city	1,083	1,004	-7.3	1,077	42.3	57.7	0.0	0.0	0.0	25.8	54.4	19.8	415	77.1	59.3	8.4
Shiloh city	447	440	-1.6	658	44.4	55.0	0.0	0.6	0.0	30.5	59.4	10.2	195	77.4	57.4	12.8
Siloam town	282	283	0.4	399	30.1	69.9	0.0	0.0	0.0	25.6	60.4	14.3	122	65.6	82.8	6.6
Skidaway Island CDP	8,341	NA	NA	7,798	93.4	0.9	2.7	0.7	2.3	13.5	38.9	47.6	3,625	94.0	4.0	78.2
Sky Valley city	272	267	-1.8	359	97.2	2.8	0.0	0.0	0.0	5.0	33.5	61.6	193	96.4	17.6	46.6
Smithville city	575	585	1.7	603	15.4	84.2	0.0	0.3	0.0	24.1	67.1	9.0	212	72.6	50.9	15.1
Smyrna city	51,265	54,958	7.2	52,922	45.8	31.5	6.9	1.4	14.4	22.2	69.9	7.8	23,305	50.2	20.9	53.6
Snellville city	18,265	19,439	6.4	18,939	47.7	32.2	5.3	2.1	12.7	24.2	61.3	14.5	6,176	78.9	25.4	35.7
Social Circle city	4,228	4,358	3.1	4,270	70.1	27.9	0.0	1.2	0.8	22.6	61.7	15.6	1,509	65.2	48.3	9.1
Soperton city	3,112	3,060	-1.7	3,082	34.6	62.6	0.0	2.4	0.5	25.4	56.3	18.4	1,077	55.3	66.9	15.3
Sparks town	2,049	2,025	-1.2	2,128	33.2	53.2	2.1	8.1	3.4	31.5	57.4	11.0	782	59.1	58.7	14.1
Sparta city	1,401	1,282	-8.5	2,103	14.2	80.4	0.0	2.4	3.0	13.9	71.8	14.5	578	58.3	53.3	13.8
Springfield city	2,809	2,781	-1.0	2,818	68.6	28.2	0.0	2.7	0.5	27.0	58.1	14.9	826	66.0	58.1	15.5
Stapleton city	438	413	-5.7	420	67.6	28.6	0.0	2.9	1.0	27.2	55.7	17.1	164	82.3	64.6	9.8
Statenville CDP	1,040	NA	NA	1,281	55.5	3.0	0.0	0.9	40.6	34.7	57.4	7.8	428	57.2	77.3	2.6
Statesboro city	28,404	30,367	6.9	29,630	51.4	40.6	2.5	2.7	2.8	14.1	78.7	7.0	10,127	22.8	25.5	23.1
Statham city	2,499	2,590	3.6	2,544	58.7	17.1	0.9	0.6	22.7	30.0	66.8	3.2	820	69.1	62.0	12.8
Stillmore city	532	530	-0.4	596	44.0	52.9	0.0	3.2	0.0	28.7	58.0	13.3	213	77.9	66.2	3.3
Stockbridge city	26,319	27,619	4.9	26,992	23.0	55.3	9.3	4.2	8.1	28.5	62.9	8.7	9,473	58.5	29.5	32.9
Stone Mountain city	5,802	6,025	3.8	5,924	18.2	74.2	1.8	2.0	3.8	22.2	65.7	11.9	2,419	56.9	39.4	30.9
Sugar Hill city	18,524	20,821	12.4	19,688	61.1	10.5	5.9	1.7	20.8	28.3	64.7	6.7	6,491	82.8	27.9	32.7
Summertown city	160	163	1.9	237	84.4	15.6	0.0	0.0	0.0	32.1	60.3	7.6	68	79.4	63.2	2.9
Summerville city	4,532	4,410	-2.7	4,442	74.5	24.6	0.2	0.6	0.0	20.6	57.5	21.9	1,894	51.3	72.7	5.2
Sumner town	427	407	-4.7	458	66.2	31.4	0.0	2.4	0.0	26.2	53.9	19.9	171	70.8	79.5	6.4
Sunny Side city	134	133	-0.7	87	96.6	0.0	0.0	0.0	3.4	13.7	77.9	8.0	44	56.8	34.1	31.8
Sunnyside CDP	1,303	NA	NA	1,453	91.1	2.9	1.4	4.1	0.6	23.0	59.4	17.7	555	86.8	33.3	34.1
Sunset Village CDP	846	NA	NA	993	98.3	0.0	0.0	0.0	1.7	32.9	52.4	14.6	306	87.6	60.8	12.1
Surrency town	201	207	3.0	158	62.7	36.1	0.0	0.0	1.3	13.9	67.1	19.0	70	80.0	75.7	12.9
Suwanee city	15,355	18,164	18.3	16,648	63.3	8.6	15.3	1.3	11.5	29.7	62.4	7.9	5,466	73.4	16.3	59.4
Swainsboro city	7,273	7,472	2.7	7,431	34.7	54.8	0.0	2.0	8.5	30.9	58.2	10.7	2,376	50.7	61.0	7.4
Sycamore city	712	668	-6.2	703	67.1	27.6	1.1	1.1	3.0	14.8	70.6	14.7	203	70.4	54.2	7.9
Sylvania city	2,613	2,539	-2.8	2,565	58.4	39.1	0.0	1.9	0.5	23.1	50.8	26.2	1,102	50.5	63.4	13.8
Sylvester city	6,188	6,097	-1.5	6,180	37.4	60.8	0.0	0.5	1.4	28.7	57.5	13.7	2,224	62.1	66.8	11.0
Talahi Island CDP	1,248	NA	NA	1,229	94.6	0.0	0.8	2.8	1.8	17.2	60.0	22.7	538	100.0	32.5	24.2
Talbotton city	957	893	-6.7	1,152	11.2	87.8	0.4	0.0	0.6	17.4	69.5	13.1	484	53.9	81.0	3.9
Talking Rock town	64	65	1.6	77	100.0	0.0	0.0	0.0	0.0	35.1	58.5	6.5	23	95.7	78.3	8.7
Tallapoosa city	3,173	3,150	-0.7	3,140	90.5	4.2	1.1	1.5	2.7	27.2	59.3	13.5	1,203	64.6	61.3	13.6
Tallulah Falls town	167	168	0.6	129	82.2	0.0	0.0	0.0	17.8	13.2	81.5	5.4	32	21.9	46.9	3.1
Talmo town	181	187	3.3	235	99.6	0.0	0.0	0.0	0.4	14.0	77.4	8.5	81	69.1	65.4	30.9
Tarrytown town	87	87	0.0	90	100.0	0.0	0.0	0.0	0.0	2.2	56.6	41.1	47	95.7	40.4	38.3
Tate City CDP	16	NA	NA	0	0.0	0.0	0.0	0.0	0.0	0.0	0.0	0.0	0	0.0	0.0	0.0
Taylorsville town	210	213	1.4	221	99.1	0.9	0.0	0.0	0.0	13.6	70.5	15.8	95	83.2	51.6	24.2
Temple city	4,228	4,262	0.8	4,244	68.7	26.8	0.0	0.0	4.5	27.6	61.0	11.5	1,525	76.9	66.1	17.9
Tennille city	1,539	1,689	9.7	1,395	31.3	68.7	0.0	0.0	0.0	29.8	56.4	13.8	558	51.8	64.5	10.8
The Rock CDP	160	NA	NA	123	94.3	0.0	0.0	5.7	0.0	10.6	44.0	45.5	54	100.0	55.6	0.0
Thomaston city	9,170	8,952	-2.4	9,068	54.5	43.1	0.0	1.0	1.4	25.2	56.1	18.8	3,471	40.7	53.8	13.6
Thomasville city	18,554	18,700	0.8	18,558	40.2	56.4	0.4	0.9	2.1	25.0	58.8	16.4	7,535	48.5	43.8	22.0
Thomson city	6,773	6,618	-2.3	6,682	28.3	68.6	0.0	0.5	2.6	34.0	51.7	14.4	2,516	38.2	65.3	13.4
Thunderbolt town	2,524	2,613	3.5	2,576	57.2	22.6	3.0	0.1	17.1	16.3	65.0	18.6	1,013	53.4	37.4	32.4
Tifton city	16,346	16,701	2.2	16,589	48.6	35.4	1.5	3.8	10.7	23.8	63.8	12.3	5,626	39.3	50.8	17.3
Tiger town	408	400	-2.0	374	88.8	0.0	0.0	9.4	1.9	25.4	55.4	19.3	155	63.9	38.7	17.4
Tignall town	546	516	-5.5	604	41.6	54.3	0.0	4.1	0.0	27.5	56.2	16.6	203	62.1	77.8	5.9
Toccoa city	8,448	8,257	-2.3	8,327	73.5	22.8	0.4	1.4	1.8	24.8	59.4	15.9	2,966	62.4	51.0	23.2
Toomsboro city	472	455	-3.6	314	37.3	60.8	0.3	0.0	1.6	5.7	57.3	36.9	131	64.9	74.0	8.4
Trenton city	2,301	2,275	-1.1	1,988	91.6	2.3	0.0	2.8	3.3	23.5	60.9	15.6	775	56.4	58.8	9.7
Trion town	1,827	1,779	-2.6	2,124	65.8	3.4	1.6	1.5	27.8	32.5	58.3	9.2	736	53.7	63.5	14.5
Tucker CDP	27,581	NA	NA	28,343	55.0	21.4	8.7	3.3	11.7	24.6	60.2	15.3	10,822	68.9	23.2	51.5
Tunnel Hill city	861	872	1.3	986	86.8	7.5	2.6	1.0	2.0	26.1	59.5	14.5	348	72.4	62.1	12.4
Turin town	246	336	36.6	427	90.4	8.0	0.0	0.0	1.6	34.5	55.0	10.5	148	77.7	33.8	46.6
Twin City city	1,742	1,676	-3.8	2,051	41.4	57.3	0.2	0.7	0.3	20.9	64.3	15.0	575	61.9	73.4	4.5
Tybee Island city	2,990	3,082	3.1	3,049	89.3	1.9	0.0	3.0	5.8	9.1	59.7	31.2	1,307	71.6	20.1	42.2
Tyrone town	6,923	7,135	3.1	7,028	64.7	19.4	2.6	2.1	11.3	23.4	65.7	10.8	2,381	81.2	28.0	41.6
Ty Ty city	725	727	0.3	986	52.1	29.6	0.0	0.3	18.0	28.9	61.5	9.7	295	65.1	55.6	10.2
Unadilla city	3,796	3,684	-3.0	3,716	31.2	63.2	0.0	0.2	5.5	11.4	76.2	12.4	716	62.4	74.4	10.3
Union City city	19,463	20,427	5.0	20,200	9.8	84.2	0.1	1.2	4.7	31.2	58.6	10.1	7,869	40.8	43.5	19.9
Union Point city	1,618	1,676	3.6	1,501	38.3	56.0	0.0	1.3	4.3	26.0	55.9	18.3	593	63.4	64.1	10.8
Unionville CDP	1,845	NA	NA	1,226	0.0	100.0	0.0	0.0	0.0	14.7	68.3	17.0	555	56.8	76.2	3.4
Uvalda city	595	589	-1.0	590	60.0	36.6	0.0	0.8	2.5	30.2	50.0	19.7	210	68.1	62.9	16.2
Valdosta city	54,764	56,595	3.3	56,324	40.1	50.3	1.7	2.9	5.0	22.6	67.0	10.3	21,199	38.8	37.8	23.0
Varnell city	1,756	1,781	1.4	1,766	85.1	2.8	0.0	0.7	11.5	22.7	68.0	9.1	555	77.5	47.9	22.0
Vernonburg town	122	129	5.7	116	100.0	0.0	0.0	0.0	0.0	15.5	58.5	25.9	41	82.9	9.8	61.0
Vidalia city	10,442	10,670	2.2	10,596	51.3	40.7	2.1	0.4	5.6	30.1	56.0	13.8	4,178	51.3	54.2	20.1
Vidette city	112	110	-1.8	117	93.2	6.8	0.0	0.0	0.0	25.6	58.1	16.2	35	100.0	45.7	17.1
Vienna city	4,011	3,823	-4.7	3,880	26.4	64.1	0.0	0.4	9.1	26.9	59.1	14.0	1,374	54.3	63.0	8.9
Villa Rica city	13,956	14,700	5.3	14,266	54.2	34.6	2.0	4.5	4.7	28.6	59.7	11.6	5,333	63.7	35.4	26.1
Vinings CDP	9,734	NA	NA	10,221	56.9	26.4	5.4	3.0	8.4	11.6	77.7	10.6	5,688	31.2	9.1	69.0
Waco city	516	514	-0.4	574	97.4	1.7	0.0	0.9	0.0	18.5	61.2	20.4	226	66.4	77.0	2.7
Wadley city	2,061	1,988	-3.5	2,013	13.6	83.4	0.0	0.1	2.9	28.0	60.2	11.9	715	58.2	73.6	4.6

1 May be of any race.

Table A. All Places — Population and Housing

STATE City, town, township, borough, or CDP (county if applicable)	2010 census total population	2014 estimated population	Percent change 2010– 2014	ACS total population estimate 2010–2014	White alone, not Hispanic or Latino	Black alone, not Hispanic or Latino	Asian alone, not Hispanic or Latino	All other races or 2 or more races, not Hispanic or Latino	Hispanic or Latino[1]	Under 18 years old	Age 18 to 64 years old	Age 65 years and older	Total occupied housing units	Percent owner occupied	High school diploma or less	Bachelor's degree or more
	1	2	3	4	5	6	7	8	9	10	11	12	13	14	15	16
GEORGIA—Con.																
Waleska city	644	871	35.2	615	71.4	19.3	1.6	5.9	1.8	6.2	86.3	7.6	83	59.0	51.8	21.7
Walnut Grove city	1,330	1,375	3.4	1,383	79.7	6.1	0.0	3.6	10.6	29.1	61.3	9.6	459	76.3	48.4	12.2
Walthourville city	4,130	4,170	1.0	4,142	26.1	57.3	0.0	6.6	9.9	33.0	62.5	4.6	1,609	53.1	43.1	13.5
Warm Springs city	425	410	-3.5	586	37.7	41.0	3.9	4.4	13.0	23.4	51.8	24.7	241	41.5	42.7	14.1
Warner Robins city	68,618	73,271	6.8	71,359	49.7	37.2	2.7	3.2	7.2	28.7	61.7	9.7	26,574	56.0	37.6	22.9
Warrenton city	1,937	1,833	-5.4	1,994	23.4	73.1	3.4	0.1	0.0	23.4	56.2	20.5	703	53.1	72.3	12.2
Warwick city	423	411	-2.8	430	34.7	64.7	0.0	0.7	0.0	19.6	68.1	12.3	202	67.3	65.8	6.4
Washington city	4,134	4,013	-2.9	4,031	40.1	57.7	1.2	0.8	0.2	17.0	58.8	24.4	1,845	62.2	63.7	16.7
Watkinsville city	2,832	2,855	0.8	2,881	80.9	9.4	5.3	1.4	2.9	25.5	61.9	12.4	1,016	73.7	22.5	48.3
Waverly Hall town	735	728	-1.0	1,032	42.0	54.3	0.6	3.0	0.2	12.4	67.1	20.4	306	79.1	56.2	21.6
Waycross city	14,651	14,166	-3.3	14,363	36.6	56.6	0.8	0.6	5.4	25.2	55.5	19.3	6,033	47.8	59.2	12.2
Waynesboro city	5,881	5,699	-3.1	5,820	27.3	71.2	0.2	1.1	0.2	32.4	55.5	12.1	2,055	45.8	57.5	13.3
Webster County unified government	2,801	2,649	-5.4	2,744	48.4	51.6	0.0	0.0	0.0	19.6	63.2	17.3	1,175	77.6	74.8	3.7
West Point city	3,460	3,770	9.0	3,402	39.4	58.8	0.8	0.0	1.0	23.1	55.8	21.1	1,564	42.3	65.9	18.7
Whigham city	471	466	-1.1	604	69.4	26.0	0.0	4.1	0.5	19.2	52.0	28.6	199	67.3	61.8	7.0
White city	670	674	0.6	740	95.8	0.4	0.0	3.4	0.4	29.1	59.7	11.2	245	49.0	68.6	5.7
Whitemarsh Island CDP	6,792	NA	NA	7,139	81.2	4.7	7.8	3.0	3.3	21.4	65.6	12.8	3,002	63.6	16.9	54.5
White Plains city	289	292	1.0	219	55.7	43.8	0.5	0.0	0.0	15.5	71.2	13.2	81	79.0	66.7	12.3
Whitesburg city	588	591	0.5	592	89.2	6.3	0.0	1.0	3.5	28.3	55.2	16.4	227	62.6	72.2	12.8
Willacoochee city	1,391	1,361	-2.2	1,632	36.7	32.9	0.0	5.3	25.1	30.4	56.9	12.7	497	65.6	64.8	4.6
Williamson city	352	354	0.6	436	80.5	14.0	0.5	0.0	5.0	25.7	59.1	15.1	143	51.7	47.6	8.4
Wilmington Island CDP	15,138	NA	NA	15,338	86.5	3.0	5.2	2.7	2.6	19.2	65.7	15.1	6,446	78.3	20.7	46.7
Winder city	14,139	14,930	5.6	14,495	69.5	18.2	1.7	3.5	7.1	30.4	56.5	13.0	4,693	57.8	54.3	16.1
Winterville city	1,121	1,155	3.0	1,019	73.6	17.6	1.6	1.0	6.3	23.0	56.9	19.9	434	83.9	27.2	46.8
Woodbine city	1,412	1,318	-6.7	1,503	47.9	44.6	2.2	0.0	5.3	25.7	59.9	14.2	522	62.5	55.6	10.9
Woodbury city	959	912	-4.9	753	42.6	55.9	0.0	1.5	0.0	24.6	56.8	18.6	349	51.9	73.9	4.0
Woodland city	403	372	-7.7	398	14.1	85.9	0.0	0.0	0.0	15.6	71.8	12.6	167	71.3	79.6	7.8
Woodstock city	23,904	27,823	16.4	25,672	76.3	8.4	8.4	6.0	3.3	29.6	61.0	9.4	9,617	69.4	21.3	42.5
Woodville city	321	329	2.5	385	35.6	63.1	0.0	0.0	1.3	16.3	69.3	14.3	142	85.9	64.8	12.0
Woolsey town	158	163	3.2	158	93.0	0.0	0.0	3.2	3.2	19.1	51.9	29.1	63	100.0	38.1	28.6
Wrens city	2,190	2,086	-4.7	2,587	34.4	62.7	0.2	0.4	2.3	29.7	56.9	13.3	1,038	43.5	60.0	8.0
Wrightsville city	3,754	3,672	-2.2	3,717	46.8	50.3	0.0	1.8	1.0	19.4	68.5	12.2	1,055	57.1	65.7	10.5
Yatesville town	359	342	-4.7	440	83.9	11.4	0.0	1.8	3.0	19.1	57.7	23.2	198	70.2	62.1	7.1
Yonah CDP	507	NA	NA	387	100.0	0.0	0.0	0.0	0.0	30.0	56.3	13.7	170	88.8	28.2	47.1
Young Harris city	899	1,237	37.6	1,040	92.2	3.4	0.0	1.4	3.0	12.8	83.4	3.8	145	33.8	26.2	27.6
Zebulon city	1,174	1,141	-2.8	1,522	62.5	34.8	0.0	2.6	0.0	26.9	58.1	15.0	631	46.1	53.6	9.8
HAWAII	1,360,301	1,419,561	4.4	1,392,704	22.9	1.8	37.2	28.6	9.6	22.0	62.7	15.2	450,299	57.1	31.1	34.3
Ahuimanu CDP	8,810	NA	NA	8,728	20.2	0.3	33.0	32.5	13.9	19.8	67.6	12.6	2,857	73.3	19.5	43.9
Aiea CDP	9,338	NA	NA	9,181	17.8	0.0	54.4	21.1	6.7	22.2	57.0	20.8	2,685	69.9	30.7	38.5
Ainaloa CDP	2,965	NA	NA	3,645	34.2	0.3	19.2	31.9	14.3	28.5	62.1	9.5	1,143	71.5	42.4	20.9
Anahola CDP	2,223	NA	NA	2,122	16.7	0.1	10.3	67.4	5.5	22.8	63.8	13.3	645	78.4	48.2	16.3
Captain Cook CDP	3,429	NA	NA	4,265	30.6	0.0	23.4	39.3	6.7	24.8	58.0	17.2	1,332	70.3	30.8	27.4
Discovery Harbour CDP	949	NA	NA	1,073	54.8	0.0	17.4	26.6	1.2	13.7	54.1	32.2	514	63.8	40.3	12.8
East Honolulu CDP	49,914	NA	NA	48,926	23.9	0.6	50.2	21.2	4.1	19.0	58.6	22.6	17,048	82.8	16.6	61.9
Eden Roc CDP	942	NA	NA	690	36.7	1.4	2.6	49.6	9.7	26.6	66.7	6.7	257	67.7	46.7	17.9
Eleele CDP	2,390	NA	NA	2,723	9.1	0.2	50.6	26.4	13.7	24.5	57.3	18.2	791	69.8	39.1	21.0
Ewa Beach CDP	14,955	NA	NA	14,291	8.0	0.5	50.9	29.7	11.0	23.6	59.4	17.1	3,053	68.9	46.9	18.1
Ewa Gentry CDP	22,690	NA	NA	22,663	17.0	4.1	39.7	28.6	10.5	25.8	66.5	7.7	6,816	70.6	23.3	35.2
Ewa Villages CDP	6,108	NA	NA	7,141	1.1	0.4	52.5	27.7	18.2	26.3	59.5	14.2	1,368	84.8	49.6	6.8
Fern Acres CDP	1,504	NA	NA	1,338	36.3	0.0	12.4	28.0	23.3	18.7	73.6	7.7	518	75.7	43.2	23.2
Fern Forest CDP	931	NA	NA	720	41.3	0.0	10.8	38.3	9.6	20.5	66.0	13.6	305	78.4	34.4	16.4
Haena CDP	431	NA	NA	277	80.1	0.0	2.2	13.0	4.7	17.3	80.1	2.5	124	83.1	12.1	24.2
Haiku-Pauwela CDP	8,118	NA	NA	7,689	56.1	0.0	7.0	30.7	6.3	22.7	66.6	10.7	2,857	60.3	26.1	39.3
Halaula CDP	469	NA	NA	562	26.3	0.0	23.0	33.5	17.3	22.1	60.1	17.8	139	48.9	49.6	29.5
Halawa CDP	14,014	NA	NA	14,363	9.9	0.4	51.4	27.5	10.8	20.8	60.2	18.9	4,168	64.2	31.3	33.7
Haleiwa CDP	3,970	NA	NA	3,883	29.1	2.1	27.4	29.3	12.1	25.4	63.0	11.7	1,190	50.8	32.1	20.5
Haliimaile CDP	964	NA	NA	928	12.3	0.0	39.4	35.9	12.4	24.2	60.0	15.8	265	69.4	52.8	11.3
Hana CDP	1,235	NA	NA	1,158	32.6	0.0	1.7	60.8	4.8	29.2	57.5	13.3	335	53.4	58.5	17.6
Hanalei CDP	450	NA	NA	320	55.9	0.0	14.4	19.1	10.6	23.5	54.9	21.6	133	69.9	39.1	30.8
Hanamaulu CDP	3,835	NA	NA	4,398	7.8	1.3	61.6	19.4	9.8	21.7	61.2	17.1	1,089	58.9	55.6	9.6
Hanapepe CDP	2,638	NA	NA	2,488	19.8	0.4	36.8	22.3	20.7	19.5	68.5	12.1	818	69.9	35.1	22.2
Hauula CDP	4,148	NA	NA	3,767	20.7	0.7	6.8	58.1	13.7	36.6	55.7	7.9	945	52.8	40.2	34.4
Hawaiian Acres CDP	2,700	NA	NA	2,155	48.3	3.8	4.8	30.8	12.3	18.5	63.8	17.6	835	85.1	31.6	19.8
Hawaiian Beaches CDP	4,280	NA	NA	4,467	18.3	1.1	16.6	45.6	18.4	29.2	54.6	16.2	1,378	66.7	35.8	19.1
Hawaiian Ocean View CDP	4,437	NA	NA	3,927	46.4	0.0	2.4	37.0	14.1	20.4	61.2	18.4	1,552	81.8	42.0	10.9
Hawaiian Paradise Park CDP	11,404	NA	NA	11,623	24.4	1.9	25.3	25.5	22.8	21.5	63.8	14.7	4,221	68.3	38.0	32.3
Hawi CDP	1,081	NA	NA	1,356	12.7	0.4	17.0	53.6	16.3	27.7	58.8	13.6	381	79.0	50.1	18.9
Heeia CDP	4,963	NA	NA	4,713	25.1	0.3	40.9	27.9	5.8	18.7	57.8	23.4	1,472	89.7	20.0	58.4
Hickam Housing CDP	6,920	NA	NA	8,573	64.2	7.6	4.6	8.1	15.6	40.7	59.1	0.3	2,381	0.0	7.1	35.4
Hilo CDP	43,263	NA	NA	44,549	15.0	0.6	32.5	41.3	10.6	21.6	59.9	18.3	15,091	64.1	34.9	31.5
Holualoa CDP	8,538	NA	NA	9,098	45.2	0.1	17.3	20.5	16.9	19.4	66.6	13.9	3,364	62.5	25.3	40.8
Honalo CDP	2,423	NA	NA	2,822	22.3	0.1	14.7	41.2	21.6	27.7	58.3	14.1	816	46.9	45.3	23.5
Honaunau-Napoopoo CDP	2,567	NA	NA	2,792	28.5	0.2	17.3	46.5	7.4	16.5	69.4	14.0	803	61.5	38.9	34.7
Honokaa CDP	2,258	NA	NA	2,522	26.2	0.0	42.8	27.5	3.5	22.7	61.4	15.9	716	58.1	43.7	12.0
Honomu CDP	509	NA	NA	409	36.7	0.0	30.6	24.2	8.6	8.4	69.8	21.8	189	70.4	26.5	35.4
Iroquois Point CDP	3,374	NA	NA	3,639	36.1	4.3	5.9	32.2	21.5	29.3	68.1	2.6	1,186	0.0	27.1	24.9
Kaaawa CDP	1,379	NA	NA	1,110	40.9	0.0	5.2	43.3	10.5	21.1	64.8	14.2	380	69.5	28.4	37.4
Kaanapali CDP	1,045	NA	NA	1,354	83.1	0.0	3.5	6.9	6.4	18.9	54.4	26.9	566	84.3	11.0	53.5
Kahaluu CDP	4,738	NA	NA	4,514	17.4	0.8	27.8	43.6	10.3	31.8	52.6	15.6	1,227	68.6	31.7	34.3
Kahaluu-Keauhou CDP	3,549	NA	NA	3,807	63.6	0.0	5.3	22.7	8.3	22.8	53.3	24.0	1,399	62.0	20.2	47.5
Kahuku CDP	2,614	NA	NA	2,391	7.0	0.9	27.7	52.0	12.4	32.3	55.4	12.2	543	60.4	52.3	19.7
Kahului CDP	26,337	NA	NA	27,339	8.7	0.8	48.9	31.6	10.0	23.1	60.9	16.0	7,016	55.1	46.8	21.3
Kailua CDP (Hawaii)	11,975	NA	NA	12,727	33.9	0.7	15.8	40.3	9.2	22.5	62.8	14.7	4,143	49.5	40.0	27.7
Kailua CDP (Honolulu)	38,635	NA	NA	39,353	43.1	0.6	20.4	28.4	7.5	20.2	63.1	16.7	12,962	72.4	18.7	53.0
Kalaeloa CDP	48	NA	NA	149	6.0	0.0	0.0	36.9	57.0	51.7	47.0	1.3	18	0.0	50.0	50.0

1 May be of any race.

Table A. All Places — **Population and Housing**

STATE City, town, township, borough, or CDP (county if applicable)	Population: 2010 census total population	Population: 2014 estimated population	Population: Percent change 2010–2014	Population: ACS total population estimate 2010–2014	Race and Hispanic or Latino origin (percent), 2010–2014: White alone, not Hispanic or Latino	Black alone, not Hispanic or Latino	Asian alone, not Hispanic or Latino	All other races or 2 or more races, not Hispanic or Latino	Hispanic or Latino[1]	Age (percent), 2010–2014: Under 18 years old	Age 18 to 64 years old	Age 65 years and older	Households, 2010–2014: Total occupied housing units	Percent owner occupied	Householders by level of education (percent): High school diploma or less	Bachelor's degree or more
	1	2	3	4	5	6	7	8	9	10	11	12	13	14	15	16
HAWAII—Con.																
Kalaheo CDP	4,595	NA	NA	4,127	32.6	0.0	29.3	21.3	16.8	23.7	57.9	18.4	1,465	63.5	26.7	38.8
Kalaoa CDP	9,644	NA	NA	10,257	51.4	0.3	8.5	24.8	15.1	18.2	70.4	11.5	3,599	68.7	28.7	30.3
Kalihiwai CDP	428	NA	NA	306	56.2	1.0	3.6	33.7	5.6	20.9	55.9	23.2	108	69.4	13.0	61.8
Kaneohe CDP	34,597	NA	NA	33,443	19.7	0.7	37.4	34.7	7.4	18.4	62.3	19.3	10,763	69.4	33.2	35.4
Kaneohe Station CDP	9,517	NA	NA	11,342	63.0	7.3	3.4	6.4	19.9	28.8	71.3	0.0	2,658	0.0	20.5	18.0
Kapaa CDP	10,699	NA	NA	10,582	30.9	2.2	25.3	31.3	10.3	21.5	61.4	17.0	3,415	63.3	27.6	24.6
Kapaau CDP	1,734	NA	NA	1,667	14.6	1.1	22.2	41.1	21.0	22.9	56.9	20.1	501	68.1	50.1	15.4
Kapalua CDP	353	NA	NA	363	77.1	0.0	3.0	10.7	9.1	11.9	60.6	27.5	160	74.4	8.8	46.3
Kapolei CDP	15,186	NA	NA	16,890	9.0	4.0	33.7	40.9	12.4	29.6	63.9	6.6	4,565	76.6	23.8	33.8
Kaumakani CDP	749	NA	NA	1,007	2.6	0.0	84.9	6.2	6.4	25.4	59.0	15.7	220	0.0	58.2	7.3
Kaunakakai CDP	3,425	NA	NA	3,239	21.8	0.0	18.4	53.3	6.5	23.0	53.8	23.2	1,240	55.6	39.4	24.7
Kawela Bay CDP	330	NA	NA	288	73.6	1.0	2.4	16.0	6.9	11.1	67.7	21.2	139	56.8	9.4	45.3
Keaau CDP	2,253	NA	NA	2,541	7.4	0.2	47.2	34.9	10.4	22.3	62.4	15.2	667	64.5	37.9	24.7
Kealakekua CDP	2,019	NA	NA	1,953	25.2	0.7	18.5	41.4	14.1	24.4	58.2	17.5	693	44.3	38.0	20.5
Kekaha CDP	3,537	NA	NA	2,616	15.1	0.1	42.2	33.0	9.6	18.8	62.2	19.1	864	68.3	53.8	15.2
Keokea CDP	1,612	NA	NA	1,855	22.0	0.8	6.1	59.1	12.0	28.9	59.0	12.0	617	75.5	45.2	20.6
Kihei CDP	20,881	NA	NA	22,314	46.3	0.9	15.8	23.1	14.0	22.9	65.8	11.1	8,196	46.7	33.5	27.3
Kilauea CDP	2,803	NA	NA	3,441	48.8	0.5	21.1	23.4	6.2	25.2	67.8	7.1	957	56.5	33.6	34.4
Koloa CDP	2,144	NA	NA	2,806	24.1	0.4	35.4	25.3	14.8	27.2	59.3	13.4	823	37.5	47.0	18.8
Ko Olina CDP	1,799	NA	NA	1,976	67.1	2.7	12.3	11.0	6.8	20.5	72.4	7.1	877	36.1	10.9	48.7
Kualapuu CDP	2,027	NA	NA	2,061	6.0	1.1	12.7	73.7	6.6	26.4	59.1	14.6	595	74.3	41.3	18.8
Kukuihaele CDP	336	NA	NA	396	24.5	0.0	9.1	64.6	1.8	30.5	55.9	13.4	103	80.6	35.9	27.2
Kula CDP	6,452	NA	NA	6,687	55.3	0.0	10.3	24.8	9.6	22.5	60.2	17.3	2,580	62.4	19.0	47.5
Kurtistown CDP	1,298	NA	NA	973	27.4	0.0	34.3	29.6	8.6	14.3	68.2	17.6	360	70.8	46.1	31.1
Lahaina CDP	11,704	NA	NA	11,941	25.7	0.3	35.4	31.7	7.0	21.3	66.0	12.5	3,472	49.4	39.8	21.7
Laie CDP	6,138	NA	NA	5,447	27.1	2.1	12.4	52.7	5.8	20.7	72.1	7.2	915	44.3	8.3	60.0
Lanai City CDP	3,102	NA	NA	3,514	11.4	1.0	48.3	22.4	16.8	27.0	57.8	15.2	1,134	49.6	37.0	27.2
Launiupoko CDP	588	NA	NA	575	74.1	1.0	2.1	10.1	12.7	19.9	70.8	9.4	212	67.9	4.2	41.0
Laupahoehoe CDP	581	NA	NA	575	26.4	0.0	17.9	45.6	10.1	28.4	50.4	21.0	223	57.4	24.7	13.0
Lawai CDP	2,363	NA	NA	2,209	46.1	0.0	26.2	15.3	12.4	20.3	61.6	18.2	893	72.7	26.8	38.0
Leilani Estates CDP	1,560	NA	NA	1,729	66.2	0.0	5.8	18.0	10.1	17.5	63.0	19.4	745	76.0	25.2	33.7
Lihue CDP	6,455	NA	NA	6,955	22.2	0.7	45.5	24.1	7.5	29.4	54.4	16.1	2,212	62.8	37.8	30.3
Maalaea CDP	352	NA	NA	326	83.1	0.0	7.7	4.9	4.3	5.8	50.3	43.9	205	68.8	12.2	47.8
Mahinahina CDP	880	NA	NA	1,049	60.1	0.4	17.7	14.7	7.1	17.2	72.3	10.6	425	70.8	22.1	34.4
Maili CDP	9,488	NA	NA	9,399	12.1	1.8	12.1	59.2	14.7	34.7	58.3	6.9	2,242	54.4	50.8	13.7
Makaha CDP	8,278	NA	NA	8,663	12.8	1.7	12.6	51.1	21.7	27.1	60.4	12.6	2,411	39.5	54.7	14.3
Makaha Valley CDP	1,341	NA	NA	1,307	24.3	8.4	10.6	33.4	23.3	28.8	60.7	10.6	500	45.0	34.0	33.2
Makakilo CDP	18,248	NA	NA	19,819	20.5	4.2	29.0	33.0	13.3	28.9	62.6	8.5	5,655	70.4	18.7	35.6
Makawao CDP	7,184	NA	NA	6,674	29.2	0.2	22.2	37.2	11.3	24.8	63.6	11.6	2,317	50.9	30.9	17.8
Makena CDP	99	NA	NA	99	70.7	0.0	5.1	24.2	0.0	27.3	67.7	5.1	45	51.1	33.3	60.0
Manele CDP	29	NA	NA	12	100.0	0.0	0.0	0.0	0.0	0.0	0.0	100.0	8	100.0	0.0	50.0
Maunaloa CDP	376	NA	NA	394	12.4	0.0	5.6	71.3	10.7	43.9	53.3	2.8	119	35.3	44.5	12.6
Maunawili CDP	2,040	NA	NA	2,114	34.7	0.6	40.9	22.8	1.0	17.9	56.4	25.7	679	88.5	16.3	63.2
Mililani Mauka CDP	21,039	NA	NA	21,051	18.3	1.9	45.9	26.5	7.4	30.1	62.1	7.7	7,105	77.7	17.6	50.1
Mililani Town CDP	27,629	NA	NA	28,217	16.3	1.7	40.4	31.2	10.3	22.0	63.2	15.0	9,014	76.5	24.2	36.6
Mokuleia CDP	1,811	NA	NA	1,670	58.2	1.5	11.0	18.6	10.7	15.7	68.5	15.8	725	52.3	17.5	45.0
Mountain View CDP	3,924	NA	NA	3,078	23.1	0.0	21.0	29.7	26.3	27.9	60.5	11.7	1,148	65.0	23.1	36.8
Naalehu CDP	866	NA	NA	923	7.0	0.0	69.1	19.9	3.9	22.2	59.1	18.7	217	77.4	70.0	8.8
Nanakuli CDP	12,666	NA	NA	12,181	5.2	1.6	6.8	72.8	13.6	31.2	59.3	9.5	2,582	72.9	55.3	9.1
Nanawale Estates CDP	1,426	NA	NA	1,661	36.7	1.1	14.6	37.1	10.5	28.2	63.2	8.5	602	67.1	47.3	19.3
Napili-Honokowai CDP	7,261	NA	NA	6,491	51.3	1.3	19.3	17.2	10.9	19.1	71.6	9.2	2,729	39.5	28.2	34.9
Ocean Pointe CDP	8,361	NA	NA	10,502	33.7	10.1	23.3	22.1	10.8	30.8	64.5	4.9	3,152	73.4	14.1	43.7
Olinda CDP	1,084	NA	NA	1,302	68.1	0.2	4.2	26.3	1.2	16.5	68.9	14.5	477	57.2	26.0	36.3
Olowalu CDP	80	NA	NA	69	75.4	0.0	1.4	23.2	0.0	18.8	66.6	14.5	28	78.6	46.4	25.0
Omao CDP	1,301	NA	NA	1,184	37.0	0.2	24.1	25.2	13.6	14.0	62.8	23.2	394	62.7	35.5	22.8
Orchidlands Estates CDP	2,815	NA	NA	3,315	23.4	1.3	28.3	37.5	9.6	22.2	67.9	9.9	1,025	71.8	34.9	30.8
Paauilo CDP	595	NA	NA	651	15.2	0.0	41.3	33.5	10.0	27.6	54.7	17.8	210	79.5	69.0	7.6
Pahala CDP	1,356	NA	NA	1,291	8.6	0.0	35.6	41.4	14.3	24.5	53.4	22.3	387	62.8	54.5	15.8
Pahoa CDP	945	NA	NA	862	21.7	0.0	35.5	38.9	3.9	21.1	67.9	11.0	295	55.9	33.9	27.5
Paia CDP	2,668	NA	NA	2,542	45.5	0.0	25.8	22.2	6.5	19.8	67.8	12.4	770	61.9	39.7	39.0
Pakala Village CDP	294	NA	NA	361	16.9	1.1	32.7	45.2	4.2	12.8	48.8	38.5	114	0.0	73.7	13.2
Papaikou CDP	1,314	NA	NA	1,194	19.5	0.0	28.1	41.3	11.1	18.7	58.4	22.9	392	71.7	53.1	17.9
Paukaa CDP	425	NA	NA	480	43.3	0.4	29.4	21.7	5.2	8.8	53.9	37.3	191	83.2	27.2	41.4
Pearl City CDP	47,698	NA	NA	47,277	12.7	1.7	52.3	23.7	9.6	21.0	57.9	21.0	14,004	72.3	34.4	31.7
Pepeekeo CDP	1,789	NA	NA	1,817	16.0	0.3	30.7	40.9	12.1	18.4	59.5	22.2	574	60.5	43.4	19.5
Poipu CDP	979	NA	NA	1,028	65.6	0.0	15.8	14.9	3.8	13.3	54.2	32.5	497	73.4	16.3	54.1
Princeville CDP	2,158	NA	NA	2,511	76.0	0.0	4.4	11.0	8.6	22.8	59.2	18.0	927	54.8	19.1	46.1
Puako CDP	772	NA	NA	724	74.0	0.3	11.3	14.4	0.0	8.0	67.1	24.9	328	63.7	10.1	59.1
Puhi CDP	2,906	NA	NA	3,572	18.2	0.0	54.8	18.6	8.4	25.7	60.7	13.5	984	64.4	38.2	19.6
Pukalani CDP	7,574	NA	NA	8,067	33.9	0.0	25.8	29.5	10.8	22.9	63.4	13.7	2,873	64.4	33.6	26.4
Punaluu CDP	1,164	NA	NA	1,102	31.3	3.0	13.2	42.7	9.7	17.5	61.7	20.9	410	40.2	27.6	35.1
Pupukea CDP	4,551	NA	NA	5,498	50.4	0.0	7.0	36.8	5.8	23.4	65.7	10.7	1,571	64.0	24.4	47.7
Royal Kunia CDP	14,525	NA	NA	14,779	13.2	2.4	54.5	22.6	7.3	24.0	64.0	12.2	4,055	69.1	30.7	29.0
Schofield Barracks CDP	16,370	NA	NA	19,525	48.9	17.0	3.5	9.6	21.0	34.8	65.1	0.1	4,366	0.0	27.6	15.5
Ualapue CDP	425	NA	NA	445	25.6	0.0	1.3	56.6	16.4	37.3	42.8	19.8	157	56.7	42.0	24.2
Urban Honolulu CDP	337,256	350,399	3.9	345,130	16.6	1.8	53.6	22.1	5.9	17.5	64.3	18.3	127,929	43.1	30.6	38.4
Volcano CDP	2,575	NA	NA	2,603	68.0	0.0	10.6	8.5	13.0	21.5	68.3	10.3	1,091	65.2	32.4	33.8
Wahiawa CDP	17,821	NA	NA	17,473	11.4	1.7	43.2	33.4	10.3	21.6	61.4	17.0	5,676	46.9	44.3	17.8
Waialua CDP	3,860	NA	NA	3,929	22.4	0.2	41.4	24.6	11.4	19.8	62.7	17.5	1,177	59.0	36.4	26.1
Waianae CDP	13,177	NA	NA	12,694	4.4	1.1	13.7	65.3	15.5	30.8	60.5	8.5	2,941	67.8	54.2	8.5
Waihee-Waiehu CDP	8,841	NA	NA	9,663	10.6	0.7	34.1	43.2	11.4	23.8	67.7	8.5	2,399	78.5	41.1	29.1
Waikane CDP	778	NA	NA	871	20.3	0.0	18.3	46.2	15.3	19.8	65.9	14.4	230	54.8	44.8	21.7
Waikapu CDP	2,965	NA	NA	3,689	21.8	0.0	33.3	33.4	11.5	28.1	62.7	9.4	1,028	78.1	38.4	25.4
Waikele CDP	7,479	NA	NA	7,868	10.0	4.6	56.5	23.0	6.0	20.8	70.4	8.6	2,881	67.7	18.4	48.7
Waikoloa Village CDP	6,362	NA	NA	6,841	47.8	0.7	15.2	31.0	5.3	25.7	58.3	15.8	2,321	74.3	20.1	29.7
Wailea CDP	5,938	NA	NA	6,107	70.9	0.0	7.0	15.6	6.4	15.8	61.6	22.5	2,743	66.2	20.8	46.1
Wailua CDP	2,254	NA	NA	2,361	25.9	0.3	33.9	28.7	11.2	19.7	59.7	20.5	886	65.5	25.7	28.2
Wailua Homesteads CDP	5,188	NA	NA	5,521	41.6	0.3	28.4	25.6	4.1	16.1	68.5	15.4	2,067	68.3	23.4	41.1
Wailuku CDP	15,313	NA	NA	16,196	17.1	0.8	31.5	36.3	14.3	22.7	61.0	16.3	5,731	57.9	36.9	27.9
Waimalu CDP	13,730	NA	NA	12,680	15.3	2.4	50.5	23.1	8.7	17.6	66.4	16.0	5,378	56.4	25.7	36.9
Waimanalo CDP	5,451	NA	NA	5,807	13.2	0.9	18.2	60.0	7.6	31.3	57.6	11.1	1,323	59.2	51.3	12.5

1 May be of any race.

Table A. All Places — **Population and Housing**

STATE City, town, township, borough, or CDP (county if applicable)	Population				Race and Hispanic or Latino origin (percent), 2010–2014					Age (percent), 2010–2014			Households, 2010–2014		Householders by level of education (percent)	
	2010 census total population	2014 estimated population	Percent change 2010–2014	ACS total population estimate 2010–2014	White alone, not Hispanic or Latino	Black alone, not Hispanic or Latino	Asian alone, not Hispanic or Latino	All other races or 2 or more races, not Hispanic or Latino	Hispanic or Latino[1]	Under 18 years old	Age 18 to 64 years old	Age 65 years and older	Total occupied housing units	Percent owner occupied	High school diploma or less	Bachelor's degree or more
	1	2	3	4	5	6	7	8	9	10	11	12	13	14	15	16
HAWAII—Con.																
Waimanalo Beach CDP	4,481	NA	NA	4,439	10.3	0.0	5.0	72.9	11.8	24.6	59.3	16.2	1,022	74.8	48.1	19.5
Waimea CDP (Hawaii)	9,212	NA	NA	9,642	33.2	1.8	12.9	44.1	8.0	31.2	57.9	10.8	3,051	66.6	34.1	35.3
Waimea CDP (Kauai)	1,855	NA	NA	1,859	19.6	0.0	53.3	25.7	1.4	22.2	63.6	14.2	640	47.7	45.5	25.2
Wainaku CDP	1,224	NA	NA	1,445	32.1	0.0	34.3	23.1	10.4	14.8	58.8	26.5	450	76.2	36.7	24.4
Wainiha CDP	318	NA	NA	145	59.3	0.0	8.3	20.7	11.7	19.3	73.0	7.6	63	60.3	30.2	54.0
Waiohinu CDP	213	NA	NA	67	9.0	0.0	9.0	77.6	4.5	23.9	58.3	17.9	24	79.2	45.8	25.0
Waipahu CDP	38,216	NA	NA	40,532	3.6	0.6	63.6	24.3	7.9	22.6	61.6	15.7	8,310	57.0	50.1	15.6
Waipio CDP	11,674	NA	NA	11,424	11.7	1.7	52.9	17.4	16.2	21.1	65.4	13.3	3,948	63.4	27.3	33.0
Waipio Acres CDP	5,236	NA	NA	4,807	18.3	3.0	32.1	37.4	9.2	20.7	67.9	11.3	1,814	51.1	30.3	26.6
West Loch Estate CDP	5,485	NA	NA	5,971	11.9	2.0	49.9	21.2	15.1	17.9	68.5	13.6	1,639	75.3	26.8	31.5
Wheeler AFB CDP	1,634	NA	NA	2,541	58.4	8.1	4.4	10.1	19.0	35.9	63.9	0.2	825	0.0	28.7	21.1
Whitmore Village CDP	4,499	NA	NA	5,254	3.3	2.2	57.7	29.4	7.5	27.3	62.6	10.1	1,097	56.1	46.9	14.9
IDAHO	1,567,652	1,634,464	4.3	1,599,464	83.3	0.5	1.3	3.2	11.7	26.9	59.8	13.3	585,259	69.2	35.0	27.1
Aberdeen city	1,994	1,951	-2.2	2,047	43.3	0.0	0.0	1.3	55.3	36.1	53.0	10.9	669	57.5	67.1	7.9
Acequia city	124	124	0.0	123	55.3	3.3	0.0	0.0	41.5	23.6	65.0	11.4	44	84.1	68.2	4.5
Albion city	265	272	2.6	210	89.0	0.0	0.0	0.0	11.0	17.6	54.4	28.1	86	72.1	41.9	25.6
American Falls city	4,457	4,314	-3.2	4,398	63.5	0.2	0.0	2.4	34.0	32.1	54.1	13.7	1,414	64.7	58.3	5.6
Ammon city	13,814	14,685	6.3	14,257	87.1	0.4	0.7	2.5	9.3	38.7	52.0	9.2	4,475	76.7	22.1	37.0
Arbon Valley CDP	599	NA	NA	730	69.3	0.0	0.3	10.8	19.6	31.9	53.8	14.4	276	79.3	44.9	16.3
Arco city	995	896	-9.9	1,018	91.2	0.1	0.9	6.9	1.0	23.2	58.0	18.8	366	63.4	48.9	19.7
Arimo city	354	356	0.6	319	90.0	0.0	0.3	5.0	4.7	29.7	54.0	16.3	110	92.7	33.6	26.4
Ashton city	1,127	1,064	-5.6	1,100	77.5	0.0	0.0	0.0	22.5	27.3	57.6	15.1	429	60.8	47.6	20.3
Athol city	692	694	0.3	751	98.0	0.0	0.0	2.0	0.0	28.4	54.4	17.3	277	83.8	47.3	12.6
Atomic City city	29	29	0.0	22	100.0	0.0	0.0	0.0	0.0	27.3	50.0	22.7	10	80.0	80.0	0.0
Bancroft city	377	371	-1.6	338	90.5	0.0	0.0	5.0	4.4	21.9	57.7	20.4	157	70.1	38.9	3.2
Banks CDP	17	NA	NA	11	100.0	0.0	0.0	0.0	0.0	0.0	0.0	100.0	11	100.0	100.0	0.0
Basalt city	394	389	-1.3	360	87.2	0.0	0.0	0.3	12.5	33.3	49.1	17.5	116	88.8	59.5	6.0
Bellevue city	2,329	2,300	-1.2	2,457	59.3	0.1	0.7	0.9	39.1	31.5	63.7	4.8	960	58.6	45.4	23.0
Bennington CDP	190	NA	NA	280	97.5	0.0	0.0	0.0	2.5	42.1	47.5	10.4	84	67.9	11.9	13.1
Blackfoot city	11,899	11,814	-0.7	11,891	77.0	0.5	2.0	3.1	17.3	31.6	56.8	11.7	4,280	58.9	41.8	22.2
Blanchard CDP	261	NA	NA	150	100.0	0.0	0.0	0.0	0.0	0.0	44.7	55.3	82	100.0	25.6	29.3
Bliss city	318	302	-5.0	403	60.0	0.0	2.0	2.2	35.7	24.0	66.2	9.7	169	58.6	65.7	14.2
Bloomington city	206	209	1.5	196	95.4	0.0	0.0	4.6	0.0	27.0	58.7	14.3	70	95.7	41.4	8.6
Boise City city	206,105	216,282	4.9	211,655	83.6	1.5	3.6	3.6	7.7	22.2	65.9	12.0	86,642	59.6	22.7	40.9
Bonners Ferry city	2,546	2,490	-2.2	2,812	86.8	0.2	0.1	9.1	3.8	22.0	57.0	21.0	1,151	63.0	54.0	13.3
Bovill city	260	255	-1.9	185	92.4	0.0	0.0	5.4	2.2	13.0	74.1	13.0	92	67.4	59.8	6.5
Buhl city	4,122	4,231	2.6	4,166	71.7	0.1	0.0	1.9	26.2	26.6	55.9	17.5	1,491	63.0	64.4	8.3
Burley city	10,345	10,480	1.3	10,352	66.1	0.4	1.0	1.4	31.1	30.9	53.9	15.4	3,564	65.1	45.3	13.9
Butte City city	74	67	-9.5	78	62.8	12.8	0.0	0.0	24.4	10.2	60.2	29.5	48	87.5	58.3	8.3
Caldwell city	46,301	50,224	8.5	48,114	61.2	0.3	1.0	2.5	34.9	30.8	58.8	10.3	15,641	65.5	48.7	16.6
Cambridge city	326	314	-3.7	208	96.2	0.0	0.0	3.8	0.0	14.8	61.5	23.6	106	75.5	53.8	8.5
Carey city	604	603	-0.2	539	87.4	0.0	0.0	0.0	12.6	28.9	58.2	12.8	200	72.5	27.0	19.5
Cascade city	935	919	-1.7	1,040	94.1	0.0	0.3	5.2	0.4	13.9	63.9	22.1	339	70.2	54.6	15.6
Castleford city	226	234	3.5	139	44.6	0.0	0.0	2.9	52.5	35.3	46.6	18.0	64	62.5	42.2	10.9
Challis city	1,102	1,056	-4.2	1,011	93.7	0.0	0.0	4.3	2.1	20.7	64.8	14.4	445	79.6	51.0	10.1
Chubbuck city	13,954	14,229	2.0	14,117	86.3	0.1	0.7	4.3	8.7	35.2	54.3	10.5	4,917	71.2	29.9	23.4
Clark Fork city	536	540	0.7	485	90.9	0.0	1.9	7.2	0.0	15.8	67.1	17.1	247	72.1	40.5	5.3
Clayton city	7	7	0.0	7	100.0	0.0	0.0	0.0	0.0	28.6	71.5	0.0	2	100.0	100.0	0.0
Clifton city	259	283	9.3	310	85.8	0.0	0.0	8.1	6.1	39.3	47.1	13.5	92	87.0	35.9	32.6
Coeur d'Alene city	44,137	47,912	8.6	45,848	90.1	0.3	1.8	2.6	5.2	23.3	61.8	15.1	18,860	57.2	31.6	24.4
Conkling Park CDP	43	NA	NA	51	100.0	0.0	0.0	0.0	0.0	0.0	35.2	64.7	26	69.2	50.0	26.9
Cottonwood city	900	918	2.0	928	92.6	0.9	0.6	1.5	4.4	24.9	61.1	14.0	338	68.9	47.6	23.4
Council city	839	812	-3.2	883	93.3	0.0	0.0	1.2	5.4	26.8	50.4	22.8	338	64.2	48.2	16.0
Craigmont city	501	503	0.4	479	92.5	0.0	0.6	2.3	4.6	16.1	65.0	18.8	228	89.5	41.2	19.7
Crouch city	162	156	-3.7	167	100.0	0.0	0.0	0.0	0.0	17.4	54.6	28.1	68	60.3	48.5	16.2
Culdesac city	380	379	-0.3	345	77.7	1.2	0.0	18.8	2.3	18.3	65.0	16.5	145	67.6	51.7	6.9
Dalton Gardens city	2,335	2,370	1.5	2,056	95.4	0.0	0.0	1.6	3.1	20.1	57.4	22.4	813	94.6	34.9	23.6
Dayton city	463	462	-0.2	456	84.6	0.0	0.0	0.0	15.4	39.7	48.8	11.4	126	85.7	23.0	27.0
Deary city	506	507	0.2	485	90.9	0.0	0.0	0.0	9.1	25.9	56.4	17.5	208	80.8	50.0	20.2
Declo city	343	352	2.6	545	47.7	0.0	0.0	3.7	48.6	34.1	60.3	5.5	147	61.2	53.7	12.9
De Smet CDP	175	NA	NA	184	5.4	0.0	0.0	94.6	0.0	27.1	62.1	10.9	73	49.3	41.1	0.0
Dietrich city	332	339	2.1	305	80.0	0.3	0.0	1.6	18.0	45.0	46.3	8.9	84	73.8	39.3	9.5
Donnelly city	146	144	-1.4	110	100.0	0.0	0.0	0.0	0.0	59.0	41.0	0.0	20	70.0	70.0	25.0
Dover city	556	607	9.2	817	96.9	0.0	0.4	1.1	1.6	31.5	52.8	15.8	293	76.5	17.7	45.4
Downey city	625	617	-1.3	593	97.3	1.7	0.0	0.5	0.5	25.6	48.0	26.3	238	81.9	37.8	14.7
Driggs city	1,660	1,662	0.1	2,141	78.0	0.0	0.0	0.0	22.0	33.0	62.4	4.7	730	47.4	38.2	34.4
Drummond city	16	15	-6.3	2	100.0	0.0	0.0	0.0	0.0	0.0	0.0	100.0	2	100.0	100.0	0.0
Dubois city	677	597	-11.8	575	44.0	0.0	0.0	0.0	56.0	32.3	55.4	12.3	191	69.6	57.1	16.8
Eagle city	19,921	22,502	13.0	21,102	90.5	0.1	0.9	3.4	5.1	29.5	57.1	13.4	7,595	81.4	16.8	48.5
East Hope city	210	214	1.9	209	90.4	0.0	0.0	3.8	5.7	17.2	57.9	24.9	103	68.0	20.4	30.1
Eden city	405	404	-0.2	379	89.7	0.0	0.0	0.0	10.3	22.2	55.3	22.7	164	67.1	56.1	9.8
Elk City CDP	0	NA	NA	203	100.0	0.0	0.0	0.0	0.0	24.1	42.9	33.0	75	81.3	42.7	37.3
Elk River city	125	120	-4.0	125	98.4	0.0	0.0	0.0	1.6	17.6	53.6	28.8	68	85.3	36.8	26.5
Emmett city	6,559	6,599	0.6	6,546	81.5	0.1	4.4	1.3	12.6	28.4	51.8	19.7	2,545	57.2	46.5	16.7
Fairfield city	416	381	-8.4	452	90.0	0.0	0.0	0.7	9.3	23.6	60.3	15.9	177	56.5	55.4	24.9
Ferdinand city	159	160	0.6	181	97.8	0.0	1.7	0.6	0.0	19.8	64.7	15.5	84	86.9	52.4	28.6
Fernan Lake Village city	169	172	1.8	141	94.3	0.0	0.7	1.4	3.5	17.0	49.7	33.3	62	96.8	12.9	54.8
Filer city	2,520	2,655	5.4	2,576	84.6	0.2	0.7	4.3	10.2	30.9	57.2	11.8	930	65.8	49.2	8.4
Firth city	477	471	-1.3	540	77.6	0.0	0.0	2.2	20.2	32.4	57.4	10.4	161	66.5	52.7	15.4
Fort Hall CDP	3,201	NA	NA	3,315	28.4	0.0	0.2	59.5	11.8	26.3	61.4	12.4	1,062	78.3	54.0	11.5
Franklin city	641	741	15.6	760	82.6	2.2	0.0	0.0	15.1	40.0	52.9	7.1	251	77.7	52.2	8.4
Fruitland city	4,690	4,949	5.5	4,761	77.2	0.7	0.9	4.3	16.9	34.0	55.0	11.0	1,770	85.4	44.4	12.8
Garden City city	10,977	11,420	4.0	11,223	83.4	0.4	1.0	2.2	13.0	20.9	59.6	19.4	4,904	60.0	35.7	34.6
Garden Valley CDP	394	NA	NA	150	76.7	1.3	0.0	20.0	2.0	27.3	69.4	3.3	50	72.0	48.0	18.0
Genesee city	955	956	0.1	965	94.8	0.2	0.0	3.5	1.5	29.1	60.9	9.9	370	83.5	22.4	37.8
Georgetown city	480	470	-2.1	455	94.7	2.0	0.0	1.5	1.8	26.2	54.4	19.3	186	90.3	62.9	6.5
Glenns Ferry city	1,319	1,241	-5.9	1,360	73.5	0.0	0.0	3.5	22.9	29.6	46.8	23.8	576	64.6	50.5	9.0
Gooding city	3,567	3,461	-3.0	3,508	63.7	0.0	1.0	1.3	34.0	27.8	52.4	19.7	1,391	68.3	55.2	9.3
Grace city	915	905	-1.1	914	88.5	0.0	0.0	0.5	10.9	25.5	53.8	20.7	352	85.5	49.7	10.8

1 May be of any race.

Table A. All Places — **Population and Housing**

STATE City, town, township, borough, or CDP (county if applicable)	Population: 2010 census total population	Population: 2014 estimated population	Population: Percent change 2010–2014	Population: ACS total population estimate 2010–2014	Race and Hispanic or Latino origin (percent), 2010–2014: White alone, not Hispanic or Latino	Black alone, not Hispanic or Latino	Asian alone, not Hispanic or Latino	All other races or 2 or more races, not Hispanic or Latino	Hispanic or Latino[1]	Age (percent), 2010–2014: Under 18 years old	Age 18 to 64 years old	Age 65 years and older	Households, 2010–2014: Total occupied housing units	Percent owner occupied	Householders by level of education (percent): High school diploma or less	Bachelor's degree or more
	1	2	3	4	5	6	7	8	9	10	11	12	13	14	15	16
IDAHO—Con.																
Grand View city	452	444	-1.8	442	84.4	0.0	0.5	1.6	13.6	30.5	50.6	19.0	169	58.0	57.4	5.3
Grangeville city	3,141	3,141	0.0	3,158	94.3	0.0	0.0	1.1	4.6	20.8	54.1	25.0	1,421	73.6	47.9	12.8
Greenleaf city	846	878	3.8	1,076	62.2	0.0	0.6	3.7	33.6	34.0	48.0	16.2	330	64.0	44.2	16.8
Groveland CDP	877	NA	NA	810	85.6	0.0	0.0	0.0	14.4	19.0	66.0	15.1	281	71.2	32.0	26.3
Hagerman city	872	856	-1.8	1,034	87.5	0.2	0.0	0.0	12.3	30.5	48.8	20.9	429	62.9	48.3	12.1
Hailey city	7,964	8,076	1.4	7,961	65.9	0.1	0.8	2.5	30.7	26.0	66.0	7.9	3,246	62.5	28.6	33.3
Hamer city	50	51	2.0	27	88.9	0.0	0.0	0.0	11.1	29.6	48.1	22.2	10	80.0	30.0	10.0
Hansen city	1,144	1,226	7.2	1,433	77.5	0.0	0.0	1.1	21.4	32.3	56.3	11.4	472	87.1	52.5	9.1
Harrison city	208	215	3.4	211	98.6	0.0	0.0	1.4	0.0	7.5	57.4	35.1	113	66.4	51.3	21.2
Hauser city	676	680	0.6	679	92.3	0.0	0.6	2.9	4.1	18.0	67.2	14.6	309	65.7	35.9	12.3
Hayden city	13,304	13,870	4.3	13,588	94.5	0.0	0.4	1.4	3.7	22.8	58.4	18.9	5,222	74.6	28.7	23.4
Hayden Lake city	576	590	2.4	605	94.7	0.0	0.0	0.7	4.6	15.6	55.5	29.1	278	74.8	11.5	56.5
Hazelton city	753	747	-0.8	771	50.7	0.0	0.0	1.8	47.5	25.6	61.4	13.1	301	56.8	65.1	6.0
Heyburn city	3,089	3,183	3.0	3,136	47.5	0.1	0.1	2.8	49.5	33.9	57.3	8.6	1,039	60.4	55.6	11.5
Hidden Spring CDP	2,280	NA	NA	2,238	95.8	0.0	0.2	3.2	0.8	36.2	57.8	6.1	770	86.2	4.4	63.8
Hollister city	272	274	0.7	244	75.4	0.0	0.0	1.2	23.4	19.7	67.7	12.7	93	66.7	37.6	2.2
Homedale city	2,633	2,582	-1.9	2,595	51.6	0.0	0.5	2.9	44.9	31.3	54.9	13.8	883	58.8	69.8	1.8
Hope city	86	88	2.3	67	97.0	0.0	0.0	3.0	0.0	22.4	65.6	11.9	34	50.0	50.0	23.5
Horseshoe Bend city	707	669	-5.4	858	93.6	0.0	0.0	4.2	2.2	23.6	60.5	15.9	333	73.0	57.4	10.5
Huetter city	100	101	1.0	82	90.2	4.9	0.0	1.2	3.7	25.7	66.0	8.5	27	25.9	70.4	0.0
Idaho City city	485	461	-4.9	506	81.0	2.0	0.0	7.1	9.9	29.9	53.2	17.0	203	65.5	59.6	13.8
Idaho Falls city	56,891	58,691	3.2	57,935	83.5	0.4	0.6	2.9	12.5	28.8	59.0	12.2	20,846	67.6	33.2	28.2
Inkom city	854	863	1.1	930	95.5	0.0	0.6	1.6	2.3	35.7	49.6	14.6	299	85.3	31.8	20.7
Iona city	1,803	1,953	8.3	1,986	95.1	0.0	0.0	0.0	4.9	39.7	48.7	11.7	571	88.3	37.7	22.1
Irwin city	219	221	0.9	214	99.5	0.0	0.0	0.5	0.0	8.9	72.4	18.7	100	79.0	47.0	14.0
Island Park city	284	273	-3.9	175	96.0	0.0	0.0	4.0	0.0	17.8	67.5	14.9	74	100.0	36.5	24.3
Jerome city	10,890	11,189	2.7	11,046	58.2	0.2	0.4	2.3	38.9	34.5	55.3	10.3	3,771	59.7	66.8	8.7
Juliaetta city	579	578	-0.2	667	94.0	0.0	0.3	1.3	4.3	16.8	63.3	19.6	303	81.8	36.6	17.2
Kamiah city	1,295	1,297	0.2	1,310	80.5	0.2	1.1	10.4	7.9	20.9	55.0	24.2	582	60.5	45.5	13.6
Kellogg city	2,120	2,063	-2.7	2,275	90.7	0.8	0.0	4.2	4.2	24.0	58.0	18.0	967	47.7	49.9	14.3
Kendrick city	303	299	-1.3	394	92.9	0.0	0.0	4.8	2.3	18.3	48.8	33.0	182	73.1	57.1	15.9
Ketchum city	2,719	2,720	0.0	2,703	95.5	0.0	0.0	0.0	4.5	9.3	66.0	24.8	1,618	61.8	10.2	61.0
Kimberly city	3,264	3,510	7.5	3,363	86.1	0.0	0.0	2.2	11.8	32.7	54.0	13.1	1,094	81.0	34.5	17.2
Kooskia city	607	604	-0.5	572	90.7	0.0	0.0	6.1	3.1	20.6	51.9	27.4	246	76.4	70.3	5.7
Kootenai city	748	770	2.9	832	93.3	0.0	3.1	2.8	0.8	32.1	57.2	10.7	340	50.6	55.0	9.1
Kuna city	15,234	16,999	11.6	16,188	91.3	0.0	0.6	1.7	6.4	33.2	58.9	7.9	5,279	83.2	30.7	22.9
Lapwai city	1,137	1,149	1.1	1,251	20.9	1.0	1.5	68.1	8.4	35.4	56.9	7.7	383	52.7	35.2	18.0
Lava Hot Springs city	407	406	-0.2	425	99.1	0.0	0.5	0.0	0.5	22.1	63.3	14.6	171	63.7	48.5	35.7
Leadore city	105	102	-2.9	199	98.5	0.0	0.0	1.5	0.0	30.7	55.1	14.1	78	33.3	46.2	10.3
Lewiston city	31,894	32,482	1.8	32,178	92.1	0.3	1.2	3.3	3.2	20.7	60.2	18.9	13,361	68.0	37.6	25.0
Lewisville city	458	476	3.9	488	91.8	0.0	0.0	1.2	7.0	24.0	59.3	16.8	153	85.6	38.6	22.2
Lincoln CDP	3,647	NA	NA	2,771	73.6	0.0	3.0	0.0	23.3	40.8	54.4	4.7	898	65.9	41.8	32.2
Lost River city	68	NA	NA	25	100.0	0.0	0.0	0.0	0.0	0.0	32.0	68.0	8	100.0	0.0	100.0
Lowman CDP	42	NA	NA	19	100.0	0.0	0.0	0.0	0.0	0.0	0.0	100.0	11	100.0	54.5	45.5
McCall city	2,975	3,006	1.0	2,925	89.6	0.0	0.4	0.8	9.2	23.5	60.5	16.0	848	60.7	18.2	53.5
McCammon city	809	797	-1.5	577	86.5	0.5	0.0	5.9	7.1	28.6	56.0	15.4	204	83.8	45.6	23.0
Mackay city	512	483	-5.7	495	90.1	0.0	0.0	4.4	5.5	12.1	53.7	34.1	239	60.3	51.9	33.1
Malad City city	2,095	2,017	-3.7	2,189	97.8	0.0	0.0	1.1	1.2	28.3	50.5	21.1	860	80.1	47.8	13.7
Malta city	193	199	3.1	225	80.9	0.0	0.0	0.0	19.1	28.9	47.6	23.6	82	59.8	39.0	32.9
Marsing city	1,319	1,295	-1.8	1,269	50.8	0.0	0.0	6.4	42.8	30.4	56.7	13.0	436	45.6	70.9	2.5
Melba city	513	529	3.1	568	79.6	0.0	0.0	1.9	18.5	34.2	53.6	12.3	180	65.0	47.2	16.7
Menan city	741	747	0.8	848	83.1	0.0	0.0	1.9	15.0	31.1	61.7	7.2	244	88.1	41.4	12.7
Meridian city	75,130	87,743	16.8	81,025	88.2	0.7	1.8	2.1	7.1	31.1	59.0	9.9	28,431	75.2	25.4	36.6
Middleton city	5,524	6,420	16.2	5,898	81.7	0.0	1.1	5.1	12.1	34.8	56.6	8.6	1,972	71.2	49.4	15.6
Midvale city	169	165	-2.4	150	96.7	0.0	0.0	3.3	0.0	8.0	53.3	38.7	76	60.5	59.2	5.3
Minidoka city	112	112	0.0	66	28.8	0.0	0.0	16.7	54.5	40.9	40.8	18.2	24	79.2	100.0	0.0
Montpelier city	2,597	2,536	-2.3	2,540	92.4	0.0	1.8	0.4	5.5	27.4	56.3	16.4	1,052	73.2	55.3	11.2
Moore city	189	172	-9.0	174	100.0	0.0	0.0	0.0	0.0	31.0	49.2	19.5	73	84.9	57.5	2.7
Moreland CDP	1,278	NA	NA	1,490	65.8	0.4	0.0	2.8	31.1	38.1	55.7	6.2	371	87.9	56.1	10.5
Moscow city	23,809	24,767	4.0	24,406	88.7	0.8	3.2	3.1	4.3	15.9	76.5	7.6	9,643	39.8	12.1	49.3
Mountain Home city	14,209	13,780	-3.0	13,871	78.3	2.8	2.8	5.3	10.8	26.3	63.0	10.5	5,392	62.5	39.1	14.8
Mountain Home AFB CDP	3,238	NA	NA	3,133	72.6	5.6	9.3	5.0	7.5	32.9	67.0	0.0	782	0.0	19.3	23.3
Moyie Springs city	721	702	-2.6	870	92.0	0.2	0.0	1.4	6.4	26.8	58.2	14.9	307	74.3	51.5	11.1
Mud Lake city	357	369	3.4	384	48.4	0.5	2.6	0.5	47.9	47.6	45.9	6.5	100	75.0	61.0	15.0
Mullan city	692	673	-2.7	647	87.5	0.0	0.8	2.2	9.6	19.6	59.8	20.6	328	79.9	62.2	12.5
Murphy CDP	97	NA	NA	82	96.3	0.0	0.0	2.4	1.2	0.0	75.5	24.4	27	40.7	40.7	59.3
Murtaugh city	115	120	4.3	97	88.7	0.0	0.0	4.1	7.2	33.0	52.6	14.4	38	89.5	52.6	13.2
Nampa city	81,748	88,211	7.9	84,660	72.1	0.7	0.8	3.0	23.4	32.3	56.6	11.1	28,098	63.2	44.7	17.0
Newdale city	323	309	-4.3	379	75.2	1.6	0.0	0.0	23.2	31.9	57.3	10.8	134	70.9	39.6	14.9
New Meadows city	496	475	-4.2	458	95.4	0.0	0.0	2.2	2.4	21.4	65.1	13.5	198	75.8	58.6	9.1
New Plymouth city	1,538	1,510	-1.8	1,943	82.6	0.0	0.3	3.1	14.1	25.7	58.1	16.2	728	69.6	58.9	16.6
Nezperce city	466	467	0.2	478	90.8	0.0	0.0	6.3	2.9	18.2	60.4	21.3	190	72.6	38.4	20.5
Notus city	531	545	2.6	497	63.6	0.0	0.0	1.6	34.8	28.3	56.3	15.3	172	85.5	64.5	5.8
Oakley city	763	790	3.5	937	77.1	0.0	0.0	7.3	15.7	40.2	46.8	12.9	289	71.6	45.3	15.2
Oldtown city	184	181	-1.6	227	97.8	0.0	0.0	0.0	2.2	17.6	66.8	15.4	94	42.6	59.6	5.3
Onaway city	187	189	1.1	189	95.2	0.0	0.0	1.6	3.2	14.2	70.8	14.8	75	88.0	46.7	12.0
Orofino city	3,163	3,096	-2.1	3,089	86.8	0.6	0.7	5.9	6.0	14.0	71.3	14.8	1,040	61.0	46.8	14.7
Osburn city	1,555	1,504	-3.3	1,366	95.8	0.0	0.0	3.1	1.1	18.8	56.0	25.0	673	75.2	48.7	14.4
Oxford city	48	48	0.0	71	90.1	0.0	0.0	9.9	0.0	33.8	54.8	11.3	23	100.0	65.2	4.3
Paris city	513	508	-1.0	476	95.0	0.0	0.0	1.1	4.0	21.0	52.1	26.9	223	88.3	40.4	23.3
Parker city	305	298	-2.3	352	94.0	0.0	0.0	0.0	6.0	36.3	51.8	11.9	127	63.8	47.2	9.4
Parkline CDP	0	NA	NA	53	73.6	0.0	0.0	26.4	0.0	17.0	43.4	39.6	27	74.1	66.7	7.4
Parma city	1,983	2,066	4.2	1,931	68.7	0.0	0.5	5.3	25.5	30.6	55.5	13.8	692	65.5	58.4	16.9
Paul city	1,169	1,188	1.6	1,165	59.3	0.0	0.1	5.2	35.5	28.9	52.5	18.8	424	81.8	56.8	14.4
Payette city	7,476	7,422	-0.7	7,447	70.8	0.2	0.1	5.4	23.6	26.7	59.5	13.8	2,669	60.5	51.6	8.1
Peck city	197	201	2.0	192	95.8	0.0	0.0	4.2	0.0	18.7	55.7	25.5	83	95.2	42.2	28.9
Pierce city	508	490	-3.5	668	94.2	0.0	0.6	1.6	3.6	19.8	59.4	20.7	282	87.9	47.5	17.7
Pinehurst city	1,622	1,575	-2.9	1,743	91.6	0.0	0.0	2.1	6.3	22.8	54.9	22.2	819	70.9	54.5	15.6
Placerville city	53	52	-1.9	26	100.0	0.0	0.0	0.0	0.0	0.0	69.2	30.8	13	100.0	15.4	46.2
Plummer city	1,044	1,026	-1.7	1,041	40.8	3.1	0.4	40.6	15.1	34.4	56.1	9.3	366	56.8	50.5	14.5
Pocatello city	54,230	54,292	0.1	54,466	86.3	0.9	1.5	3.4	7.9	26.0	63.1	10.8	20,379	63.6	30.4	30.6

1 May be of any race.

Table A. All Places — **Population and Housing**

STATE City, town, township, borough, or CDP (county if applicable)	Population				Race and Hispanic or Latino origin (percent), 2010–2014					Age (percent), 2010–2014			Households, 2010–2014			
															Householders by level of education (percent)	
	2010 census total population	2014 estimated population	Percent change 2010–2014	ACS total population estimate 2010–2014	White alone, not Hispanic or Latino	Black alone, not Hispanic or Latino	Asian alone, not Hispanic or Latino	All other races or 2 or more races, not Hispanic or Latino	Hispanic or Latino[1]	Under 18 years old	Age 18 to 64 years old	Age 65 years and older	Total occupied housing units	Percent owner occupied	High school diploma or less	Bachelor's degree or more
	1	2	3	4	5	6	7	8	9	10	11	12	13	14	15	16
IDAHO—Con.																
Ponderay city	1,136	1,136	0.0	1,143	96.1	0.0	0.0	0.6	3.3	23.7	58.7	17.8	504	31.7	48.8	17.1
Post Falls city	27,572	29,896	8.4	28,786	91.0	0.7	0.6	3.9	3.9	28.4	60.4	11.2	11,202	67.7	34.2	22.5
Potlatch city	804	806	0.2	773	87.6	0.4	0.1	6.0	6.0	28.6	57.1	14.2	325	70.2	54.8	17.2
Preston city	5,204	5,217	0.2	5,172	91.6	0.0	0.0	2.9	5.5	30.9	56.0	13.0	1,798	76.0	48.3	20.5
Priest River city	1,743	1,751	0.5	1,770	95.2	0.0	1.4	1.6	1.8	22.4	61.0	16.6	734	67.2	54.0	10.1
Princeton CDP	148	NA	NA	59	100.0	0.0	0.0	0.0	0.0	56.0	25.4	18.6	13	38.5	100.0	0.0
Rathdrum city	6,841	7,283	6.5	7,046	88.5	0.0	0.0	3.0	8.5	31.8	57.9	10.4	2,505	73.2	43.0	22.0
Reubens city	71	72	1.4	73	100.0	0.0	0.0	0.0	0.0	27.4	56.1	16.4	30	76.7	46.7	26.7
Rexburg city	25,468	27,094	6.4	26,301	91.0	0.8	1.3	2.3	4.6	22.4	73.5	4.2	7,238	33.1	8.7	30.0
Richfield city	482	489	1.5	457	77.2	0.0	0.7	1.1	21.0	28.9	58.7	12.5	141	78.0	63.8	6.4
Rigby city	3,967	4,037	1.8	4,007	83.2	0.5	0.0	2.9	13.4	32.3	54.1	13.6	1,377	70.6	46.0	21.3
Riggins city	419	416	-0.7	353	89.2	0.0	0.0	0.0	10.8	7.0	61.4	31.4	173	54.9	39.9	24.3
Ririe city	636	636	0.0	770	72.5	0.0	0.0	4.4	23.1	34.6	56.1	9.4	236	76.3	62.7	6.8
Riverside CDP	838	NA	NA	1,120	51.1	0.0	0.0	25.4	23.5	39.9	48.6	11.4	297	90.6	44.8	11.1
Roberts city	580	576	-0.7	579	34.7	0.5	0.7	1.2	62.9	32.5	60.8	6.9	171	63.7	67.8	13.5
Robie Creek CDP	1,162	NA	NA	1,509	95.1	1.0	0.0	1.1	2.8	20.3	68.4	11.3	625	90.1	10.6	30.6
Rockford CDP	276	NA	NA	450	61.8	0.0	0.0	0.0	38.2	21.3	70.4	8.2	117	100.0	51.3	31.6
Rockford Bay CDP	184	NA	NA	245	94.3	1.2	1.6	0.8	2.0	6.1	44.1	49.8	126	96.8	15.9	38.9
Rockland city	295	288	-2.4	297	99.0	0.0	0.0	0.0	1.0	29.7	50.1	20.2	128	88.3	52.3	7.8
Rupert city	5,548	5,673	2.3	5,583	52.5	0.1	0.1	3.1	44.3	31.0	55.7	13.4	1,895	63.1	59.0	8.1
St. Anthony city	3,542	3,454	-2.5	3,490	79.1	0.1	0.3	4.0	16.5	27.2	63.8	9.0	1,202	69.3	45.7	13.1
St. Charles city	131	135	3.1	94	100.0	0.0	0.0	0.0	0.0	24.4	36.3	39.4	42	100.0	38.1	21.4
St. Maries city	2,402	2,347	-2.3	2,350	94.6	0.1	0.2	2.6	2.5	20.8	55.6	23.4	990	61.6	56.2	12.9
Salmon city	3,112	3,033	-2.5	3,070	91.5	0.2	0.3	4.0	4.0	20.6	58.9	20.4	1,518	56.9	42.7	22.4
Sandpoint city	7,366	7,760	5.3	7,497	92.0	0.2	0.3	2.9	4.7	24.5	58.2	17.4	3,447	47.2	40.7	21.2
Shelley city	4,409	4,382	-0.6	4,428	81.1	0.0	0.8	0.0	18.1	40.4	52.0	7.7	1,313	67.5	44.2	12.9
Shoshone city	1,459	1,493	2.3	1,614	68.1	0.0	0.0	5.8	26.1	26.2	57.5	16.1	570	65.6	60.5	8.9
Smelterville city	626	603	-3.7	636	91.5	0.0	0.0	1.1	7.4	23.8	58.4	17.6	307	47.2	47.9	9.1
Smiths Ferry CDP	75	NA	NA	166	100.0	0.0	0.0	0.0	0.0	9.0	67.5	23.5	37	100.0	70.3	0.0
Soda Springs city	3,058	2,980	-2.6	3,004	96.4	0.0	0.2	0.6	2.8	27.6	54.8	17.7	1,244	84.4	45.4	16.8
Spencer city	37	33	-10.8	17	100.0	0.0	0.0	0.0	0.0	5.9	58.8	35.3	14	100.0	42.9	21.4
Spirit Lake city	1,932	2,040	5.6	2,003	95.0	0.4	0.4	1.8	2.3	26.6	60.3	12.9	750	73.1	47.5	8.9
Stanley city	63	68	7.9	96	81.3	0.0	0.0	7.3	11.5	5.2	82.3	12.5	45	33.3	11.1	48.9
Star city	5,810	7,295	25.6	6,379	87.6	0.3	2.1	3.9	6.2	38.4	54.2	7.4	2,016	77.1	24.2	25.2
State Line city	43	44	2.3	22	100.0	0.0	0.0	0.0	0.0	18.2	81.9	0.0	13	30.8	69.2	0.0
Stites city	221	221	0.0	213	92.0	0.0	0.0	7.5	0.5	22.5	60.1	17.4	101	64.4	64.4	5.9
Sugar City city	1,511	1,367	-9.5	1,399	75.7	0.0	0.1	0.8	23.4	35.4	55.2	9.4	414	81.2	35.5	34.5
Sun Valley city	1,408	1,412	0.3	1,392	88.0	0.6	3.6	2.2	5.6	10.6	57.3	32.0	613	74.7	10.8	76.0
Swan Valley city	204	215	5.4	120	98.3	0.0	0.0	0.0	1.7	21.7	53.4	25.0	52	88.5	53.8	19.2
Sweetwater CDP	143	NA	NA	142	45.8	0.0	0.0	54.2	0.0	11.9	47.0	40.8	51	80.4	41.2	5.9
Tensed city	123	121	-1.6	114	57.9	0.0	0.0	30.7	11.4	9.7	57.9	32.5	51	43.1	68.6	3.9
Teton city	735	712	-3.1	993	64.7	3.2	0.0	3.5	28.6	32.8	58.9	8.4	305	73.4	56.7	5.6
Tetonia city	269	272	1.1	286	52.1	0.0	0.0	1.4	46.5	23.0	69.8	7.0	91	83.5	36.3	30.8
Troy city	862	881	2.2	906	92.7	1.1	0.8	5.1	0.3	30.0	59.0	11.0	313	81.5	23.6	32.9
Twin Falls city	44,308	46,528	5.0	45,362	78.6	0.8	2.0	2.5	16.1	27.7	58.9	13.4	16,412	59.3	38.9	17.7
Tyhee CDP	0	NA	NA	1,134	93.7	0.0	0.0	0.0	6.3	24.5	59.8	15.8	366	91.5	34.4	21.0
Ucon city	1,108	1,128	1.8	1,546	95.4	0.0	0.0	0.8	3.8	32.4	58.5	9.1	393	86.0	32.1	17.6
Victor city	1,927	1,945	0.9	2,247	72.1	0.4	0.0	1.1	26.5	30.2	59.3	10.4	756	52.8	31.2	32.3
Wallace city	784	760	-3.1	822	86.5	0.0	0.9	4.7	7.9	11.7	66.6	21.8	370	54.9	43.2	21.4
Wardner city	188	185	-1.6	213	93.9	0.0	0.0	1.9	4.2	29.1	61.6	9.4	82	53.7	37.8	9.8
Warm River city	3	3	0.0	0	0.0	0.0	0.0	0.0	0.0	0.0	0.0	0.0	0	0.0	0.0	0.0
Weippe city	433	411	-5.1	437	94.7	0.0	0.0	1.8	3.4	22.6	54.3	23.1	201	78.1	59.7	10.0
Weiser city	5,507	5,356	-2.7	5,407	67.7	0.0	0.9	2.2	29.2	26.7	55.9	17.4	1,951	64.7	55.4	15.2
Wendell city	2,782	2,707	-2.7	2,736	55.3	0.0	0.0	0.4	44.3	34.0	53.9	12.1	909	69.5	62.9	14.9
Weston city	437	448	2.5	485	99.2	0.0	0.0	0.0	0.8	37.1	52.3	10.5	152	88.2	42.8	22.4
White Bird city	92	93	1.1	75	98.7	0.0	0.0	0.0	1.3	8.0	60.0	32.0	43	86.0	67.4	0.0
Wilder city	1,533	1,597	4.2	1,417	16.7	0.0	0.0	6.1	77.3	40.8	52.5	6.8	416	38.5	80.5	7.0
Winchester city	340	343	0.9	307	91.9	0.0	0.0	6.2	2.0	15.7	51.3	32.9	155	74.2	48.4	9.0
Worley city	257	254	-1.2	213	54.5	0.0	0.0	40.4	5.2	17.4	60.0	22.5	95	67.4	29.5	12.6
Yellow Pine CDP	32	NA	NA	94	100.0	0.0	0.0	0.0	0.0	0.0	73.4	26.6	67	100.0	74.6	0.0
ILLINOIS	12,831,587	12,880,580	0.4	12,868,747	62.9	14.2	4.8	1.9	16.3	23.7	63.1	13.2	4,778,633	66.9	35.4	34.0
Abingdon city	3,286	3,226	-1.8	2,777	93.0	2.6	0.0	2.7	1.8	23.7	57.3	18.8	1,187	67.4	55.2	12.6
Adair CDP	210	NA	NA	214	100.0	0.0	0.0	0.0	0.0	21.5	56.5	22.0	87	77.0	81.6	11.5
Addieville village	252	243	-3.6	280	100.0	0.0	0.0	0.0	0.0	27.2	67.8	5.0	94	84.0	43.6	16.0
Addison village	36,964	37,297	0.9	37,215	49.7	4.0	5.3	0.9	40.2	26.6	61.9	11.5	12,302	67.7	51.2	21.2
Adeline village	85	83	-2.4	72	100.0	0.0	0.0	0.0	0.0	12.6	63.9	23.6	32	87.5	56.3	9.4
Albany village	903	883	-2.2	1,047	96.5	0.0	0.9	1.1	1.6	21.9	59.4	18.6	430	82.3	57.7	15.6
Albers village	1,190	1,180	-0.8	1,163	92.0	0.9	1.0	1.2	4.8	26.8	63.0	10.2	386	84.2	32.9	28.0
Albion city	1,988	1,957	-1.6	2,139	93.1	0.9	0.7	1.9	3.4	24.7	57.2	18.1	899	73.5	40.4	10.5
Aledo city	3,646	3,588	-1.6	3,724	95.0	0.6	0.6	0.5	3.4	21.1	54.2	24.9	1,578	66.7	41.3	14.6
Alexis village	831	818	-1.6	862	99.2	0.3	0.0	0.0	0.5	21.9	56.1	21.8	377	82.8	41.9	16.4
Algonquin village	30,049	30,410	1.2	30,189	82.9	1.7	7.5	1.3	6.7	26.4	64.1	9.5	10,393	88.5	21.7	44.9
Alhambra village	681	665	-2.3	675	99.3	0.7	0.0	0.0	0.0	14.2	58.1	27.7	248	65.3	36.7	18.5
Allendale village	475	461	-2.9	633	94.9	0.0	0.0	0.8	4.3	31.4	59.4	9.2	206	81.6	26.2	17.0
Allenville village	148	146	-1.4	130	100.0	0.0	0.0	0.0	0.0	7.7	50.0	42.3	59	100.0	67.8	5.1
Allerton village	291	289	-0.7	244	97.1	1.2	0.0	1.6	0.0	15.9	68.9	15.2	104	76.0	51.0	6.7
Alma village	320	316	-1.3	382	96.1	0.0	0.8	3.1	0.0	23.6	60.2	16.2	165	64.2	52.7	12.1
Alorton village	2,034	1,954	-3.9	1,729	0.4	98.5	0.0	0.3	0.8	32.3	59.4	8.3	649	44.1	62.4	7.9
Alpha village	671	652	-2.8	595	94.6	0.0	0.0	1.0	4.4	14.6	65.9	19.5	296	83.8	50.7	15.5
Alsey village	227	222	-2.2	264	92.0	0.0	0.0	8.0	0.0	31.0	53.4	15.5	103	70.9	81.6	6.8
Alsip village	19,277	19,427	0.8	19,385	59.7	15.2	1.4	1.4	22.3	23.6	63.5	13.0	7,003	62.8	43.3	17.6
Altamont city	2,319	2,304	-0.6	2,257	97.5	0.0	0.3	1.4	0.8	23.1	54.4	22.6	836	74.6	47.5	14.0
Alton city	27,918	27,177	-2.7	27,517	69.0	24.0	0.6	3.9	2.5	24.1	61.3	14.7	11,737	59.1	39.1	18.1
Altona village	529	517	-2.3	482	95.6	0.0	1.0	0.6	2.7	26.1	62.5	11.2	195	75.4	54.4	16.9
Alto Pass village	391	383	-2.0	486	85.8	0.8	0.4	0.4	12.6	29.3	59.1	11.7	171	84.2	36.3	14.0
Alvan village	270	266	-1.5	255	91.0	0.0	2.7	0.8	5.5	20.5	65.9	13.7	99	78.8	58.6	7.1
Amboy city	2,500	2,383	-4.7	2,319	92.1	0.1	0.0	0.2	7.6	21.4	59.1	19.5	987	69.0	61.5	10.4
Anchor village	146	146	0.0	130	96.9	1.5	0.0	1.5	0.0	23.8	56.1	20.0	54	90.7	64.8	1.9
Andalusia village	1,178	1,183	0.4	1,471	98.1	0.7	0.1	0.4	0.7	22.5	66.7	10.9	505	94.9	44.2	18.2

1 May be of any race.

Table A. All Places — **Population and Housing**

STATE City, town, township, borough, or CDP (county if applicable)	Population: 2010 census total population	Population: 2014 estimated population	Population: Percent change 2010–2014	Population: ACS total population estimate 2010–2014	Race and Hispanic or Latino origin (percent), 2010–2014: White alone, not Hispanic or Latino	Black alone, not Hispanic or Latino	Asian alone, not Hispanic or Latino	All other races or 2 or more races, not Hispanic or Latino	Hispanic or Latino[1]	Age (percent), 2010–2014: Under 18 years old	Age 18 to 64 years old	Age 65 years and older	Households, 2010–2014: Total occupied housing units	Percent owner occupied	Householders by level of education (percent): High school diploma or less	Bachelor's degree or more
	1	2	3	4	5	6	7	8	9	10	11	12	13	14	15	16
ILLINOIS—Con.																
Andover village	578	574	-0.7	582	98.5	0.0	0.0	0.0	1.5	20.1	55.7	24.2	234	98.3	53.0	11.5
Anna city	4,444	4,331	-2.5	4,385	93.4	1.7	0.4	1.0	3.5	20.1	58.0	21.9	1,840	63.8	48.0	18.6
Annapolis CDP	55	NA	NA	55	100.0	0.0	0.0	0.0	0.0	45.5	54.7	0.0	16	81.3	0.0	43.8
Annawan town	878	861	-1.9	930	92.9	1.0	0.3	2.6	3.2	25.2	56.4	18.5	401	67.3	46.4	20.0
Antioch village	14,456	14,411	-0.3	14,395	84.6	1.6	4.0	2.4	7.3	29.6	62.0	8.4	5,077	74.8	33.6	33.7
Apple Canyon Lake CDP	558	NA	NA	382	100.0	0.0	0.0	0.0	0.0	0.0	53.9	46.1	208	100.0	35.1	44.2
Apple River village	365	358	-1.9	485	97.5	0.2	0.0	1.6	0.6	28.5	60.6	10.9	195	66.7	59.5	4.1
Arcola city	2,914	2,893	-0.7	3,017	71.3	0.7	0.2	0.0	27.8	25.1	58.5	16.2	1,131	72.6	48.5	15.7
Arenzville village	409	398	-2.7	317	94.3	0.0	0.0	1.9	3.8	23.8	54.2	22.1	134	85.1	47.0	25.4
Argenta village	946	924	-2.3	972	93.6	0.4	0.0	5.3	0.6	27.3	56.9	15.7	391	77.7	46.3	15.9
Arlington village	193	187	-3.1	180	92.8	0.0	0.0	1.7	5.6	17.8	66.2	16.1	82	75.6	63.4	7.3
Arlington Heights village	75,101	76,024	1.2	75,577	83.2	1.6	7.8	1.3	6.1	21.6	60.6	17.9	30,283	75.9	21.2	55.4
Armington village	343	340	-0.9	359	96.4	0.0	0.0	0.8	2.8	32.2	60.3	7.2	146	78.1	53.4	7.5
Aroma Park village	741	719	-3.0	624	81.4	1.3	0.6	1.3	15.4	23.8	61.1	15.1	241	89.6	42.7	20.7
Arrowsmith village	294	295	0.3	344	90.7	0.3	1.7	5.8	1.5	36.6	52.4	11.0	115	86.1	31.3	28.7
Arthur village	2,288	2,281	-0.3	2,448	91.9	0.3	0.0	2.4	5.4	27.3	54.4	18.4	979	72.3	49.4	17.2
Ashkum village	761	744	-2.2	807	97.9	0.7	0.0	1.0	0.4	25.6	64.1	10.3	323	72.4	42.4	16.1
Ashland village	1,335	1,289	-3.4	1,200	97.3	0.0	0.0	1.4	1.3	23.7	62.4	14.1	459	80.6	56.2	12.9
Ashley city	536	511	-4.7	505	88.9	0.0	0.0	4.4	6.7	23.5	62.3	14.1	232	70.3	51.7	9.1
Ashmore village	785	771	-1.8	870	98.5	0.3	0.0	0.9	0.2	22.2	66.9	10.9	349	75.4	41.5	14.0
Ashton village	972	927	-4.6	947	96.3	0.3	0.0	0.0	3.4	20.9	58.3	20.9	426	67.6	54.9	10.3
Assumption city	1,168	1,128	-3.4	1,266	96.4	0.6	0.0	1.6	1.3	29.0	51.8	19.2	554	73.3	65.9	10.6
Astoria town	1,141	1,100	-3.6	1,141	94.0	0.6	2.0	1.3	2.0	25.5	54.0	20.6	453	77.7	54.3	8.8
Athens city	1,988	1,960	-1.4	1,996	95.5	1.6	0.0	2.5	0.5	25.4	60.9	14.0	745	80.7	44.7	26.8
Atkinson town	972	953	-2.0	1,034	96.9	0.0	0.0	1.4	1.7	22.8	61.7	15.6	450	87.8	50.2	14.4
Atlanta city	1,692	1,663	-1.7	1,243	94.9	0.6	0.2	3.8	0.6	25.9	53.6	20.6	559	78.4	52.8	17.0
Atwood village	1,222	1,199	-1.9	1,164	97.9	0.3	0.0	1.1	0.8	19.8	61.1	19.1	520	74.6	57.7	15.4
Auburn city	4,812	4,815	0.1	5,004	99.3	0.0	0.0	0.3	0.3	29.3	59.4	11.6	1,806	81.8	48.6	19.5
Augusta village	587	566	-3.6	609	99.3	0.0	0.0	0.0	0.7	13.0	62.5	24.6	292	84.2	45.5	9.9
Aurora city	197,952	200,456	1.3	199,878	38.2	9.8	7.2	2.2	42.7	30.7	62.2	7.1	61,506	67.5	40.2	33.6
Ava city	654	639	-2.3	703	96.2	0.0	0.0	2.0	1.8	28.9	59.5	11.7	279	76.3	43.7	12.9
Aviston village	1,945	2,073	6.6	2,092	95.7	0.0	0.3	1.1	2.9	27.4	59.5	13.1	744	84.7	29.4	29.0
Avon village	799	767	-4.0	711	96.1	0.4	0.0	3.0	0.6	24.5	59.4	16.2	299	74.2	52.8	11.7
Baldwin village	373	353	-5.4	396	91.9	0.0	0.0	2.3	5.8	21.2	67.9	10.9	122	85.2	58.2	11.5
Banner village	189	183	-3.2	188	93.6	0.0	0.0	6.4	0.0	21.8	58.1	20.2	79	87.3	48.1	16.5
Bannockburn village	1,583	1,575	-0.5	1,460	79.0	4.4	7.5	3.8	5.2	11.4	79.9	8.6	283	68.2	8.5	80.6
Bardolph village	251	245	-2.4	243	96.7	0.0	0.0	0.8	2.5	25.9	57.6	16.5	101	72.3	50.5	19.8
Barrington village	10,321	10,373	0.5	10,830	86.3	0.2	6.7	0.7	6.1	29.6	52.8	17.5	3,809	75.4	10.7	68.6
Barrington Hills village	4,221	4,259	0.9	3,653	90.1	1.4	8.4	0.0	0.1	17.9	57.0	24.9	1,418	98.3	13.4	64.7
Barry city	1,318	1,280	-2.9	1,287	96.7	0.0	0.5	1.5	1.3	24.0	55.6	20.4	564	77.0	56.0	10.1
Bartelso village	595	598	0.5	653	99.1	0.0	0.0	0.6	0.3	26.8	64.3	8.9	207	90.8	46.9	20.8
Bartlett village	41,227	41,632	1.0	41,529	70.4	2.0	15.0	1.1	11.5	26.9	63.7	9.3	13,797	88.9	22.4	44.8
Bartonville village	6,471	6,423	-0.7	6,440	96.6	0.5	0.0	0.8	2.1	23.2	60.3	16.6	2,639	77.0	54.3	12.0
Basco village	98	96	-2.0	85	98.8	0.0	0.0	1.2	0.0	12.9	58.8	28.2	47	87.2	61.7	2.1
Batavia city	26,158	26,424	1.0	25,905	88.5	1.6	1.3	1.5	7.0	26.6	61.4	12.1	9,471	78.5	17.3	52.5
Batchtown village	214	208	-2.8	193	96.4	0.0	0.0	2.1	1.6	11.4	78.2	10.4	79	83.5	29.1	22.8
Bath village	333	310	-6.9	268	96.6	0.0	3.4	0.0	0.0	23.8	55.6	20.5	122	75.4	59.8	6.6
Baylis village	205	200	-2.4	182	97.3	0.0	0.0	0.0	2.7	11.0	67.0	22.0	84	66.7	57.1	1.2
Bay View Gardens village	380	392	3.2	354	96.9	0.0	0.0	2.0	1.1	19.5	67.7	12.7	168	75.6	57.7	6.5
Beach Park village	13,795	13,988	1.4	13,851	54.3	10.4	3.9	2.9	28.4	23.0	63.8	13.1	4,663	85.4	37.9	25.1
Beardstown city	6,127	5,882	-4.0	6,336	58.8	6.0	0.0	1.1	34.1	28.4	59.9	11.6	2,273	63.5	64.1	11.7
Beason CDP	189	NA	NA	185	95.7	1.1	0.0	3.2	0.0	10.3	81.1	8.6	79	45.6	86.1	3.8
Beaverville village	362	347	-4.1	314	93.3	0.3	0.6	1.6	4.1	30.3	50.0	19.7	132	81.8	59.1	9.8
Beckemeyer village	1,040	1,019	-2.0	988	94.7	0.0	2.4	1.0	1.8	17.1	61.8	21.2	404	93.1	61.6	6.2
Bedford Park village	580	576	-0.7	604	65.2	0.0	0.5	0.0	34.3	25.7	61.5	12.7	219	87.2	52.1	17.8
Beecher village	4,359	4,461	2.3	4,568	88.3	3.1	1.4	0.7	6.4	25.7	58.6	15.8	1,675	73.9	38.1	20.2
Beecher City village	463	456	-1.5	415	98.6	1.2	0.0	0.0	0.2	28.7	56.0	15.2	170	71.2	56.5	4.7
Belgium village	409	402	-1.7	379	97.6	1.6	0.0	0.3	0.5	21.9	64.0	14.2	166	72.3	57.2	9.6
Belknap village	104	105	1.0	75	100.0	0.0	0.0	0.0	0.0	36.0	48.0	16.0	29	93.1	62.1	0.0
Belle Prairie City town	54	53	-1.9	63	100.0	0.0	0.0	0.0	0.0	14.3	65.1	20.6	23	100.0	56.5	17.4
Belle Rive village	361	361	0.0	373	96.5	0.0	0.0	0.0	3.5	23.6	55.2	21.2	149	82.6	50.3	14.8
Belleville city	44,074	42,529	-3.5	43,296	68.5	23.0	1.5	3.8	3.2	22.2	64.4	13.5	17,652	62.0	31.4	24.9
Bellevue village	1,984	1,963	-1.1	1,576	89.2	3.2	4.1	1.8	1.6	21.0	63.8	15.2	711	92.1	56.4	15.6
Bellflower village	360	353	-1.9	353	99.2	0.0	0.0	0.0	0.8	19.5	69.7	10.8	133	94.7	46.6	12.8
Bellmont village	276	269	-2.5	193	100.0	0.0	0.0	0.0	0.0	22.3	52.4	25.4	89	88.8	61.8	3.4
Bellwood village	19,071	19,152	0.4	19,149	5.4	75.0	0.3	2.0	17.4	25.2	62.4	12.3	6,116	73.7	45.3	14.8
Belvidere city	25,585	25,282	-1.2	25,713	64.7	2.3	1.1	1.5	30.4	28.8	60.0	11.2	8,810	74.0	54.8	13.7
Bement village	1,730	1,692	-2.2	1,765	93.3	0.0	0.2	5.3	1.2	23.7	60.1	16.2	696	81.5	49.4	13.9
Benld city	1,556	1,503	-3.4	1,773	94.9	0.0	0.2	1.6	3.2	26.9	57.1	16.0	726	68.0	46.6	14.5
Bensenville village	18,352	18,487	0.7	18,457	42.6	3.7	3.9	0.6	49.1	24.1	65.7	10.2	6,214	53.3	50.9	21.4
Benson village	429	428	-0.2	403	97.0	0.0	0.0	2.5	0.5	22.5	61.8	15.6	184	80.4	52.7	14.1
Bentley town	35	34	-2.9	47	83.0	0.0	0.0	17.0	0.0	12.8	78.7	8.5	24	62.5	45.8	20.8
Benton city	7,087	7,016	-1.0	7,185	92.4	0.4	0.4	2.4	4.4	22.8	59.2	18.0	2,884	64.1	39.7	19.3
Berkeley village	5,209	5,230	0.4	5,219	31.3	31.0	6.0	2.6	29.1	26.2	62.3	11.6	1,808	86.1	36.2	23.1
Berlin village	180	180	0.0	133	100.0	0.0	0.0	0.0	0.0	6.1	73.6	20.3	64	73.4	76.6	3.1
Berwyn city	56,657	56,693	0.1	56,762	29.9	7.2	2.4	1.3	59.1	27.1	63.1	10.0	18,401	60.3	45.7	23.5
Bethalto village	9,521	9,382	-1.5	9,443	96.3	0.6	0.1	1.4	1.5	25.9	60.7	13.5	3,715	68.0	39.8	24.0
Bethany village	1,352	1,322	-2.2	1,269	99.7	0.0	0.0	0.0	0.3	29.7	56.1	14.0	520	69.4	55.0	11.7
Biggsville village	304	287	-5.6	273	100.0	0.0	0.0	0.0	0.0	19.5	49.9	30.8	126	88.9	66.7	10.3
Big Rock village	1,134	1,160	2.3	1,053	96.3	1.4	0.0	0.9	1.3	19.5	61.0	19.5	410	93.2	38.3	21.7
Bingham village	83	83	0.0	77	97.4	0.0	0.0	2.6	0.0	26.0	62.4	11.7	28	71.4	64.3	7.1
Bishop Hill village	128	126	-1.6	137	97.8	0.7	0.0	1.5	0.0	2.2	77.9	19.7	69	91.3	27.5	47.8
Bismarck village	579	560	-3.3	544	100.0	0.0	0.0	0.0	0.0	16.1	61.2	22.6	222	78.8	47.3	20.3
Blandinsville village	651	628	-3.5	695	95.7	0.0	0.0	4.3	0.0	14.6	61.1	24.3	342	76.0	44.4	17.8
Bloomingdale village	22,063	22,299	1.1	22,208	74.7	2.9	12.4	1.0	9.0	17.5	64.4	18.1	9,013	72.0	27.8	41.9
Bloomington city	76,616	78,730	2.8	77,883	73.2	11.1	7.4	2.7	5.6	24.2	65.4	10.4	30,558	62.2	26.2	46.1
Blue Island city	23,706	23,785	0.3	23,453	21.0	27.6	0.6	1.4	49.4	27.7	61.2	11.2	8,208	57.8	48.6	17.5
Blue Mound village	1,158	1,124	-2.9	1,169	99.5	0.0	0.0	0.0	0.5	27.8	57.7	14.5	474	80.2	54.2	11.8
Bluffs village	715	691	-3.4	742	99.1	0.0	0.0	0.0	0.9	24.9	63.4	11.6	275	72.4	50.5	12.4
Bluford village	688	678	-1.5	611	97.4	0.0	0.0	1.8	0.8	22.3	60.2	17.5	249	89.2	43.4	9.6
Bolingbrook village	73,366	74,180	1.1	74,112	42.0	21.5	9.9	2.9	23.7	29.0	63.7	7.3	22,124	82.0	29.1	38.5

1 May be of any race.

Table A. All Places — **Population and Housing**

STATE City, town, township, borough, or CDP (county if applicable)	Population: 2010 census total population	Population: 2014 estimated population	Population: Percent change 2010–2014	Population: ACS total population estimate 2010–2014	Race and Hispanic or Latino origin (percent), 2010–2014: White alone, not Hispanic or Latino	Black alone, not Hispanic or Latino	Asian alone, not Hispanic or Latino	All other races or 2 or more races, not Hispanic or Latino	Hispanic or Latino[1]	Age (percent), 2010–2014: Under 18 years old	Age 18 to 64 years old	Age 65 years and older	Households, 2010–2014: Total occupied housing units	Percent owner occupied	Householders by level of education (percent): High school diploma or less	Bachelor's degree or more
	1	2	3	4	5	6	7	8	9	10	11	12	13	14	15	16
ILLINOIS—Con.																
Bondville village	443	447	0.9	516	95.5	1.7	0.0	2.3	0.4	23.6	66.0	10.3	224	51.8	42.9	12.1
Bone Gap village	246	244	-0.8	211	99.5	0.0	0.0	0.0	0.5	22.3	63.5	14.2	91	85.7	52.7	4.4
Bonfield village	382	375	-1.8	299	95.7	0.0	1.0	0.7	2.7	18.1	67.4	14.7	114	90.4	44.7	14.9
Bonnie village	397	389	-2.0	456	96.9	0.0	0.0	0.0	3.1	13.8	69.8	16.4	209	79.9	57.9	17.2
Boody CDP	276	NA	NA	249	100.0	0.0	0.0	0.0	0.0	25.7	69.0	5.2	92	94.6	52.2	4.3
Boulder Hill CDP	8,108	NA	NA	8,349	71.2	4.0	2.0	1.4	21.5	26.5	61.0	12.6	2,958	80.0	45.5	18.7
Bourbonnais village	18,645	18,534	-0.6	18,641	76.8	12.9	1.7	2.6	6.1	23.4	65.9	10.8	6,120	67.4	27.3	30.3
Bowen village	494	478	-3.2	489	99.6	0.0	0.0	0.4	0.0	27.2	61.2	11.5	201	90.5	52.7	16.4
Braceville village	792	775	-2.1	831	91.5	0.0	0.0	3.4	5.2	25.7	63.9	10.5	299	76.6	56.5	5.7
Bradford village	768	741	-3.5	798	95.4	0.8	0.0	1.5	2.4	29.4	49.8	20.8	315	86.0	46.7	15.2
Bradley village	15,895	15,677	-1.4	15,822	82.9	6.5	1.5	0.8	8.3	24.3	64.1	11.6	6,129	62.8	37.5	20.7
Braidwood city	6,219	6,185	-0.5	6,191	96.8	0.3	0.4	0.4	2.1	20.9	65.5	13.7	2,501	78.8	49.8	10.5
Breese city	4,442	4,502	1.4	4,577	93.9	0.1	0.4	1.1	4.4	24.7	60.1	15.2	1,768	84.4	39.0	24.2
Bridgeport city	1,886	1,813	-3.9	1,267	98.0	0.0	0.1	0.0	1.9	30.2	48.2	21.8	564	76.6	53.4	9.0
Bridgeview village	16,446	16,491	0.3	16,550	73.2	2.0	4.5	3.2	17.1	27.1	59.4	13.4	5,530	71.9	57.3	14.1
Brighton village	2,254	2,217	-1.6	2,122	96.5	0.1	0.0	2.5	0.8	27.1	56.9	16.0	794	79.8	44.3	9.2
Brimfield village	868	862	-0.7	963	96.0	0.0	0.0	2.8	1.2	33.9	54.6	11.3	353	75.1	35.7	26.1
Broadlands village	349	356	2.0	350	95.7	0.6	1.1	0.6	2.0	24.6	58.2	17.1	139	83.5	48.2	18.7
Broadview village	7,932	7,959	0.3	7,956	21.6	67.5	2.3	1.5	7.2	19.6	65.6	15.1	3,181	62.0	40.8	19.3
Broadwell village	145	143	-1.4	101	94.1	0.0	0.0	5.0	1.0	17.9	60.5	21.8	47	70.2	59.6	10.6
Brocton village	322	305	-5.3	390	93.6	0.0	0.0	4.9	1.5	34.1	54.5	11.5	143	73.4	59.4	7.0
Brookfield village	18,978	19,023	0.2	19,022	78.2	2.4	1.6	1.4	16.5	22.8	66.5	10.4	7,006	74.1	25.2	37.6
Brooklyn village	749	723	-3.5	807	0.7	98.5	0.0	0.7	0.0	32.3	58.3	9.4	343	35.9	55.4	10.5
Brookport city	984	941	-4.4	924	80.5	13.7	0.0	1.3	4.4	16.6	62.4	20.9	433	74.6	54.0	8.8
Broughton village	194	192	-1.0	286	97.6	0.0	0.0	2.4	0.0	46.1	39.9	13.6	84	83.3	86.9	7.1
Browning village	137	134	-2.2	80	96.3	0.0	0.0	0.0	3.8	8.8	61.5	30.0	43	93.0	53.5	4.7
Browns village	134	133	-0.7	145	96.6	0.0	0.0	3.4	0.0	9.6	78.6	11.7	66	90.9	69.7	0.0
Brownstown village	759	747	-1.6	700	98.7	0.0	0.0	1.3	0.0	20.0	60.7	19.3	285	74.4	58.2	8.8
Brussels village	141	138	-2.1	128	93.8	0.8	0.0	3.1	2.3	18.8	61.9	19.5	47	70.2	44.7	8.5
Bryant village	222	215	-3.2	174	97.1	0.0	0.0	1.7	1.1	20.0	65.4	14.4	81	85.2	46.9	14.8
Buckingham village	300	295	-1.7	337	94.7	0.0	0.3	3.6	1.5	30.3	63.7	5.9	100	78.0	64.0	5.0
Buckley village	600	575	-4.2	621	94.4	0.0	0.0	0.0	5.6	16.4	62.9	20.5	250	82.0	50.8	8.4
Buckner village	462	451	-2.4	522	98.7	0.0	0.0	0.0	1.3	24.3	59.4	16.3	204	79.4	50.0	17.2
Buda village	538	523	-2.8	671	92.5	0.0	4.0	2.1	1.3	25.6	58.9	15.5	251	83.7	64.9	6.0
Buffalo village	503	494	-1.8	483	96.7	0.0	0.0	1.4	1.9	24.2	62.9	12.8	202	62.4	54.5	22.3
Buffalo Grove village	41,431	41,701	0.7	41,613	74.7	1.9	17.8	1.7	3.9	22.9	63.8	13.2	16,276	80.2	13.0	66.5
Bull Valley village	1,122	1,107	-1.3	1,202	86.9	0.5	0.6	2.1	10.0	16.8	65.2	18.0	473	93.0	21.8	53.9
Bulpitt village	222	216	-2.7	291	100.0	0.0	0.0	0.0	0.0	28.8	55.8	15.5	118	74.6	66.1	4.2
Buncombe village	203	205	1.0	216	96.8	0.0	0.0	0.0	3.2	31.5	58.7	9.7	77	74.0	49.4	10.4
Bunker Hill city	1,772	1,727	-2.5	1,644	95.9	0.0	0.0	0.9	3.2	16.8	62.0	21.1	730	68.5	44.1	14.7
Burbank city	28,925	29,218	1.0	29,097	66.0	1.7	3.0	1.4	27.8	24.5	62.5	13.0	8,795	80.1	57.1	13.7
Bureau Junction village	321	312	-2.8	237	85.2	0.0	0.0	6.8	8.0	17.0	74.6	8.4	101	78.2	68.3	7.9
Burlington village	623	636	2.1	623	99.4	0.0	0.0	0.0	0.6	24.2	68.7	7.1	238	71.0	31.5	12.6
Burnham village	4,206	4,229	0.5	4,225	13.8	62.3	2.1	0.3	21.6	26.2	63.7	10.2	1,396	60.3	44.6	12.9
Burnt Prairie village	52	51	-1.9	67	100.0	0.0	0.0	0.0	0.0	9.0	58.3	32.8	35	100.0	45.7	5.7
Burr Ridge village	10,559	10,761	1.9	10,678	76.1	3.8	15.6	0.3	4.2	22.5	57.8	19.8	4,019	90.7	11.5	73.1
Bush village	275	274	-0.4	293	96.2	0.0	0.7	3.1	0.0	17.4	58.0	24.6	125	79.2	69.6	3.2
Bushnell city	3,117	3,014	-3.3	3,049	93.3	1.8	0.5	3.0	1.4	22.7	60.8	16.5	1,295	76.8	51.5	11.0
Butler village	180	176	-2.2	138	98.6	0.0	0.0	1.4	0.0	27.5	64.3	8.0	60	81.7	46.7	16.7
Byron city	3,753	3,665	-2.3	3,694	94.0	0.3	0.0	1.6	4.1	30.9	56.1	13.0	1,312	71.4	34.1	23.2
Cabery village	266	258	-3.0	390	90.8	0.0	0.0	2.3	6.9	20.3	70.6	9.0	146	72.6	47.3	4.1
Cahokia village	15,238	14,588	-4.3	14,905	34.5	60.5	0.0	3.0	2.0	29.5	61.0	9.5	4,977	51.4	54.3	8.1
Cairo city	2,831	2,576	-9.0	2,688	28.4	68.8	0.3	2.1	0.4	30.1	53.4	16.5	1,078	45.5	50.2	6.1
Caledonia village	197	196	-0.5	215	84.2	0.0	4.7	0.5	10.7	25.1	69.2	5.6	76	90.8	50.0	21.1
Calhoun village	172	171	-0.6	190	100.0	0.0	0.0	0.0	0.0	12.6	57.9	29.5	81	96.3	54.3	8.6
Calumet City city	37,042	37,213	0.5	37,197	13.2	70.0	0.3	1.6	14.9	28.2	59.5	12.4	14,127	58.2	38.2	16.6
Calumet Park village	7,830	7,903	0.9	8,189	5.6	85.7	0.0	0.3	8.3	21.0	65.1	13.8	3,025	66.7	34.6	16.4
Camargo village	445	446	0.2	531	95.5	0.0	3.6	0.0	0.9	30.0	59.4	10.5	190	87.9	38.9	15.3
Cambria village	1,228	1,260	2.6	1,500	97.5	0.7	0.0	0.0	1.8	19.0	72.9	8.1	585	69.2	43.4	9.7
Cambridge village	2,162	2,121	-1.9	2,189	93.8	3.0	1.6	0.0	1.6	21.8	63.6	14.7	885	75.7	49.2	18.0
Camden village	86	84	-2.3	123	100.0	0.0	0.0	0.0	0.0	17.1	48.7	34.1	59	98.3	81.4	10.2
Campbell Hill village	333	325	-2.4	247	100.0	0.0	0.0	0.0	0.0	10.5	69.7	19.8	116	81.9	56.0	14.7
Camp Point village	1,132	1,126	-0.5	1,343	95.6	0.7	0.0	3.6	0.0	21.5	59.7	19.0	484	77.3	53.3	7.9
Campton Hills village	11,106	11,317	1.9	10,908	92.6	0.6	1.1	1.4	4.3	28.1	64.0	8.0	3,410	94.5	20.7	56.1
Campus village	166	162	-2.4	172	97.7	0.0	0.0	2.3	0.0	27.3	65.6	7.0	65	70.8	35.4	3.1
Candlewick Lake CDP	0	NA	NA	4,453	81.1	2.4	1.8	0.2	14.6	23.3	67.2	9.6	1,372	94.8	37.8	30.3
Canton city	14,704	14,307	-2.7	14,650	88.8	5.3	0.3	2.4	3.3	19.5	63.7	16.9	5,589	63.2	37.4	19.7
Cantrall village	139	139	0.0	121	98.3	0.0	0.0	1.7	0.0	18.1	63.6	18.2	63	82.5	39.7	19.0
Capron village	1,376	1,356	-1.5	1,793	66.7	0.2	0.9	0.8	31.3	35.7	57.7	6.6	530	75.1	65.5	10.4
Carbon Cliff village	2,087	2,046	-2.0	2,013	70.9	13.8	1.0	5.3	9.0	31.4	51.8	17.0	813	62.1	45.3	15.6
Carbondale city	26,229	26,324	0.4	26,374	57.7	24.8	5.6	5.2	6.7	14.4	78.9	6.8	9,416	25.9	17.8	39.3
Carbon Hill village	345	349	1.2	404	85.4	0.0	2.7	0.0	11.9	28.5	59.9	11.6	148	81.8	60.1	4.7
Carlinville city	5,918	5,756	-2.7	5,615	95.7	0.5	0.0	3.1	0.7	20.4	57.8	21.6	2,264	62.8	45.0	21.3
Carlock village	552	559	1.3	777	91.4	8.1	0.0	0.0	0.5	26.7	64.1	9.1	267	84.3	35.6	37.8
Carlyle city	3,287	3,238	-1.5	3,317	88.6	2.2	2.5	3.3	3.3	24.5	62.5	12.9	1,253	77.2	33.3	26.6
Carmi city	5,240	5,136	-2.0	5,307	96.6	0.7	0.8	0.9	0.9	22.0	54.5	23.4	2,314	64.4	48.0	14.6
Carol Stream village	39,718	40,349	1.6	40,136	63.3	5.2	16.4	1.1	13.9	22.6	67.9	9.4	14,735	67.0	28.2	39.8
Carpentersville village	37,691	38,407	1.9	38,128	36.7	6.5	4.2	1.6	50.9	33.3	61.3	5.5	10,987	72.5	49.9	22.1
Carrier Mills village	1,653	1,629	-1.5	1,813	81.0	14.5	0.3	4.2	0.0	17.4	63.2	19.5	823	69.5	49.5	13.2
Carrollton city	2,488	2,405	-3.3	2,631	99.1	0.3	0.1	0.4	0.1	20.5	55.5	24.0	1,237	74.8	42.0	18.1
Carterville city	5,502	5,770	4.9	5,635	89.2	2.0	1.7	2.5	4.7	30.5	58.1	11.5	2,117	73.5	25.3	33.1
Carthage city	2,605	2,542	-2.4	2,600	95.8	0.6	0.7	0.9	2.0	21.0	56.2	22.8	1,129	66.3	39.9	31.0
Cary village	18,269	17,991	-1.5	18,115	85.5	1.3	2.6	1.4	9.2	28.9	64.3	6.9	5,844	87.6	17.9	51.5
Casey city	2,777	2,744	-1.2	2,477	95.9	0.2	0.2	0.5	3.1	22.1	54.9	22.9	1,053	63.2	49.3	17.7
Caseyville village	4,212	4,092	-2.8	4,080	72.0	12.7	0.0	3.9	11.4	22.4	61.3	16.1	1,613	78.8	54.1	7.7
Catlin village	2,040	2,022	-0.9	2,157	94.6	2.7	0.0	0.6	2.0	31.4	53.8	14.7	777	83.1	25.6	26.5
Cave-In-Rock village	318	302	-5.0	304	96.4	2.6	0.0	0.0	1.0	20.7	58.0	21.7	114	69.3	57.9	10.5
Cedar Point village	277	271	-2.2	307	78.5	1.0	4.6	0.7	15.3	28.0	62.0	10.1	108	83.3	48.1	13.0
Cedarville village	741	726	-2.0	603	99.2	0.3	0.5	0.0	0.0	17.8	60.5	21.7	260	86.9	27.7	32.3
Central City village	1,172	1,138	-2.9	1,076	92.6	1.0	0.6	2.6	3.3	29.2	55.0	15.8	435	72.0	52.0	6.0
Centralia city	13,034	12,742	-2.2	12,880	82.4	10.0	1.0	4.1	2.4	20.9	58.1	21.0	5,639	66.5	40.9	16.0

1 May be of any race.

Table A. All Places — **Population and Housing**

STATE City, town, township, borough, or CDP (county if applicable)	Population: 2010 census total population	Population: 2014 estimated population	Population: Percent change 2010–2014	Population: ACS total population estimate 2010–2014	Race and Hispanic or Latino origin (percent), 2010–2014: White alone, not Hispanic or Latino	Black alone, not Hispanic or Latino	Asian alone, not Hispanic or Latino	All other races or 2 or more races, not Hispanic or Latino	Hispanic or Latino[1]	Age (percent), 2010–2014: Under 18 years old	Age 18 to 64 years old	Age 65 years and older	Households, 2010–2014: Total occupied housing units	Percent owner occupied	Householders by level of education (percent): High school diploma or less	Bachelor's degree or more
	1	2	3	4	5	6	7	8	9	10	11	12	13	14	15	16
ILLINOIS—Con.																
Centreville city	5,327	5,090	-4.4	5,208	0.8	98.4	0.0	0.2	0.6	29.3	55.5	15.3	2,109	44.0	58.1	8.5
Cerro Gordo village	1,403	1,359	-3.1	1,298	95.5	0.5	0.0	3.8	0.3	23.9	58.1	18.1	498	77.3	45.4	15.7
Chadwick village	551	529	-4.0	454	91.4	0.0	0.0	3.7	4.8	17.4	54.9	27.8	190	85.8	43.2	14.7
Champaign city	81,072	84,513	4.2	82,848	64.2	15.5	12.2	2.4	5.8	17.1	74.7	8.2	32,734	47.6	19.5	46.8
Chandlerville village	553	535	-3.3	671	99.6	0.0	0.0	0.0	0.4	29.3	51.7	19.1	266	78.2	64.3	10.9
Channahon village	12,560	12,616	0.4	12,422	93.3	0.0	0.4	1.2	5.2	31.8	60.4	7.9	3,803	88.5	32.5	25.6
Channel Lake CDP	1,664	NA	NA	1,337	94.8	0.0	0.0	3.4	1.8	12.9	71.3	15.8	643	91.1	44.3	18.8
Chapin village	512	499	-2.5	461	99.1	0.0	0.0	0.9	0.0	20.4	56.3	23.4	200	87.0	62.0	12.0
Charleston city	21,836	21,838	0.0	22,065	85.7	7.4	2.0	2.0	3.0	12.8	77.3	9.7	7,876	45.5	24.7	32.7
Chatham village	11,599	12,212	5.3	12,131	90.4	1.4	0.7	3.7	3.7	29.2	60.1	10.5	4,474	82.9	20.3	45.8
Chatsworth town	1,206	1,167	-3.2	1,136	86.2	0.0	6.9	0.7	6.3	27.3	55.3	17.3	494	61.7	69.6	5.7
Chebanse village	1,062	1,030	-3.0	1,140	96.9	0.3	1.1	1.2	0.5	31.0	58.9	10.2	394	76.4	44.7	12.4
Chemung CDP	308	NA	NA	211	41.7	0.0	0.0	0.0	58.3	42.6	57.3	0.0	74	67.6	90.5	0.0
Chenoa city	1,783	1,777	-0.3	1,806	94.0	2.0	0.7	0.8	2.5	22.2	62.5	15.2	728	74.6	54.0	20.6
Cherry village	482	468	-2.9	429	97.0	0.0	1.6	1.4	0.0	20.3	62.0	17.9	189	79.9	54.0	14.8
Cherry Valley village	3,162	3,110	-1.6	2,884	88.4	2.0	2.8	3.2	3.6	13.3	64.8	21.9	1,361	71.7	37.0	31.2
Chester city	8,586	8,421	-1.9	8,495	69.5	25.2	0.4	0.8	4.1	18.3	68.9	12.8	2,168	66.9	56.8	12.2
Chesterfield village	188	183	-2.7	224	100.0	0.0	0.0	0.0	0.0	23.2	66.5	10.3	86	93.0	76.7	2.3
Chestnut CDP	246	NA	NA	163	70.6	0.0	29.4	0.0	0.0	36.2	54.7	9.2	64	62.5	64.1	28.1
Chicago city	2,695,598	2,722,389	1.0	2,712,608	32.2	31.5	5.7	1.7	28.9	22.4	66.9	10.7	1,028,829	44.7	35.4	39.6
Chicago Heights city	30,321	30,436	0.4	30,410	23.4	40.9	0.1	2.2	33.4	27.6	61.5	10.9	10,341	58.9	49.2	15.3
Chicago Ridge village	14,308	14,434	0.9	14,410	72.4	7.8	3.3	2.4	14.2	25.2	64.2	10.7	5,504	50.3	44.4	15.8
Chillicothe city	6,097	6,135	0.6	6,181	94.0	0.2	0.2	0.5	5.1	22.9	61.4	15.6	2,526	70.7	44.6	15.5
Chrisman city	1,343	1,290	-3.9	1,389	96.3	1.6	0.0	1.1	1.0	18.3	51.9	29.8	558	78.9	43.9	11.6
Christopher city	2,817	2,773	-1.6	2,828	99.4	0.0	0.0	0.0	0.6	24.1	54.9	21.0	1,237	68.9	43.3	8.6
Cicero town	84,241	84,354	0.1	84,423	8.3	3.5	0.3	0.2	87.7	32.9	61.2	5.9	21,792	50.9	70.0	8.0
Cisco village	261	256	-1.9	243	89.7	0.8	0.0	8.2	1.2	22.6	54.7	22.6	99	76.8	49.5	18.2
Cisne village	672	663	-1.3	696	95.3	0.0	3.2	0.0	1.6	26.4	47.4	26.1	289	90.0	45.0	7.6
Cissna Park village	846	816	-3.5	806	99.5	0.5	0.0	0.0	0.0	17.9	48.5	33.7	400	68.8	51.0	12.5
Claremont village	176	175	-0.6	227	88.5	0.0	0.0	1.3	10.1	23.4	56.7	19.8	93	80.6	44.1	16.1
Clarendon Hills village	8,427	8,658	2.7	8,548	82.0	2.1	6.9	1.1	7.9	32.3	55.3	12.4	3,163	75.0	8.3	71.3
Clay City village	962	937	-2.6	959	99.9	0.0	0.0	0.1	0.0	18.8	54.6	26.5	380	82.1	67.9	8.2
Clayton village	709	697	-1.7	651	95.1	2.8	0.0	1.2	0.9	21.0	61.7	17.1	275	77.5	69.8	4.0
Clear Lake village	229	229	0.0	262	94.3	0.0	0.0	1.9	3.8	18.3	59.5	22.1	112	88.4	71.4	7.1
Cleveland village	188	186	-1.1	137	90.5	2.9	0.0	1.5	5.1	21.2	66.4	12.4	59	96.6	49.2	5.1
Clifton village	1,468	1,420	-3.3	1,432	96.2	0.0	0.5	1.9	1.4	27.2	60.7	12.1	520	68.3	53.1	15.0
Clinton city	7,228	7,078	-2.1	6,931	93.2	1.1	0.2	1.6	3.9	22.8	59.4	17.8	3,014	68.7	53.5	12.6
Coal City village	5,587	5,521	-1.2	5,460	93.6	1.0	0.7	3.1	1.7	28.4	61.3	10.3	2,017	78.0	47.7	16.6
Coalton village	304	296	-2.6	265	100.0	0.0	0.0	0.0	0.0	18.8	61.3	19.6	117	96.6	65.0	10.3
Coal Valley village	3,719	3,743	0.6	3,692	94.8	1.6	0.2	0.9	2.5	20.7	63.3	16.1	1,499	91.7	31.6	31.4
Coatsburg village	147	146	-0.7	137	99.3	0.0	0.0	0.7	0.0	19.7	67.8	12.4	54	74.1	50.0	5.6
Cobden village	1,157	1,144	-1.1	1,359	61.7	7.5	0.0	2.9	27.8	24.6	64.3	11.1	452	70.1	44.0	26.8
Coffeen city	685	668	-2.5	446	96.6	0.0	0.4	2.7	0.2	26.1	51.8	22.2	201	83.6	60.2	6.0
Colchester city	1,399	1,354	-3.2	1,391	98.5	0.4	0.0	1.1	0.0	19.6	62.7	17.8	614	72.1	57.7	14.0
Coleta village	164	159	-3.0	244	95.9	0.0	2.0	0.0	2.0	43.4	41.8	14.8	81	90.1	59.3	18.5
Colfax village	1,061	1,055	-0.6	1,096	94.3	0.0	0.0	4.9	0.8	25.0	59.7	15.2	403	78.9	39.7	18.4
Collinsville city	25,558	24,883	-2.6	25,282	82.9	10.3	0.5	2.3	4.0	23.4	64.4	12.3	10,723	61.5	35.3	27.9
Colona city	5,121	5,099	-0.4	5,057	92.5	0.0	0.0	3.4	4.1	25.7	65.2	9.2	1,932	84.7	48.5	10.7
Colp village	225	224	-0.4	269	61.7	34.2	0.0	3.3	0.7	38.2	53.9	7.8	80	70.0	47.5	7.5
Columbia city	9,691	10,121	4.4	9,889	94.3	0.9	0.9	0.5	3.5	22.2	61.8	16.0	3,933	78.5	34.9	35.8
Columbus village	99	99	0.0	119	83.2	16.8	0.0	0.0	0.0	34.4	50.4	15.1	37	94.6	56.8	2.7
Como CDP	567	NA	NA	321	97.5	2.5	0.0	0.0	0.0	11.8	53.8	34.3	154	94.2	61.7	15.6
Compton village	303	289	-4.6	298	91.9	0.0	0.0	0.7	7.4	24.5	62.1	13.4	128	79.7	40.6	8.6
Concord village	167	165	-1.2	137	100.0	0.0	0.0	0.0	0.0	15.3	72.9	11.7	57	89.5	40.4	24.6
Congerville village	477	492	3.1	500	97.8	0.0	0.8	0.8	0.6	30.0	56.6	13.4	162	80.9	38.9	21.6
Cooksville village	185	185	0.0	197	99.0	0.0	0.0	0.0	1.0	19.3	60.0	20.8	92	75.0	47.8	16.3
Cordova village	672	665	-1.0	648	98.3	0.0	0.0	0.0	1.7	16.4	70.8	12.7	282	79.8	35.8	20.9
Cornell village	467	455	-2.6	366	98.4	0.0	0.5	0.3	0.8	22.7	61.7	15.6	163	76.7	44.2	22.7
Cornland CDP	93	NA	NA	51	100.0	0.0	0.0	0.0	0.0	0.0	62.8	37.3	29	100.0	79.3	20.7
Cortland town	4,270	4,341	1.7	4,375	74.9	2.2	2.0	4.9	16.0	33.8	63.5	2.8	1,285	82.8	22.1	28.8
Coulterville village	945	918	-2.9	993	93.7	2.6	0.6	2.4	0.7	28.5	51.7	19.5	331	85.5	61.0	10.3
Country Club Hills city	16,543	16,865	1.9	16,752	9.3	82.4	0.9	2.2	5.3	25.0	62.1	12.8	5,802	80.0	24.0	34.1
Countryside city	5,895	6,023	2.2	5,974	79.2	5.4	1.8	1.8	11.8	19.9	63.0	17.1	2,486	73.8	40.5	26.4
Cowden village	615	593	-3.6	579	97.8	0.0	0.0	0.5	1.7	18.2	65.3	16.6	234	74.4	81.6	1.7
Coyne Center CDP	827	NA	NA	900	98.6	0.0	0.0	0.4	1.0	18.8	51.1	30.2	334	74.3	61.7	13.2
Crab Orchard CDP	333	NA	NA	354	96.9	0.0	0.0	3.1	0.0	25.1	61.6	13.3	150	79.3	36.0	11.3
Crainville village	1,273	1,364	7.1	1,278	96.9	0.0	1.6	0.4	1.2	20.1	61.3	18.7	566	73.7	28.3	37.8
Creal Springs city	543	533	-1.8	574	93.2	0.0	2.1	0.0	4.7	21.6	68.8	9.6	243	84.8	57.2	5.3
Crescent City village	615	602	-2.1	703	97.7	0.0	0.3	0.7	1.3	23.2	58.9	17.8	274	83.9	43.8	22.6
Crest Hill city	20,840	20,771	-0.3	20,444	52.6	20.9	2.8	3.9	19.8	20.1	65.4	14.5	7,336	65.9	38.5	20.7
Creston village	662	657	-0.8	792	83.5	0.4	0.0	0.4	15.8	21.1	70.1	8.6	283	61.8	45.9	15.2
Crestwood village	10,950	11,029	0.7	11,006	84.4	7.1	0.6	0.6	7.3	19.0	60.0	21.0	4,772	79.4	38.0	23.1
Crete village	8,252	8,227	-0.3	8,284	67.8	26.4	1.7	2.3	1.9	24.8	60.3	14.9	3,120	80.8	22.3	38.8
Creve Coeur village	5,464	5,367	-1.8	5,717	98.1	0.6	0.0	1.2	0.0	18.8	69.1	12.2	2,384	64.2	58.0	5.6
Crossville village	745	727	-2.4	656	94.5	0.0	0.9	1.7	2.9	21.3	61.3	17.4	302	68.2	46.0	10.6
Crystal Lake city	40,739	40,493	-0.6	40,598	83.5	1.3	2.9	1.3	11.0	26.0	62.2	11.8	14,491	76.6	25.6	41.7
Crystal Lawns CDP	1,872	NA	NA	2,306	77.0	0.0	0.7	0.0	22.4	26.7	64.1	9.1	793	85.5	38.5	10.6
Cuba city	1,294	1,239	-4.3	1,431	94.8	0.3	0.0	2.9	2.1	26.3	58.1	15.7	533	71.5	44.5	12.0
Cullom village	560	538	-3.9	633	88.8	0.3	0.0	6.3	4.6	30.3	51.5	18.2	246	74.8	56.1	16.7
Curran village	212	212	0.0	180	94.4	0.0	0.0	0.0	5.6	31.1	59.6	9.4	78	76.9	61.5	3.8
Cutler village	441	424	-3.9	443	99.8	0.0	0.0	0.2	0.0	17.3	71.7	11.1	150	86.0	74.0	6.7
Cypress village	234	236	0.9	295	98.3	0.0	0.0	0.0	1.7	21.3	61.7	16.9	117	82.9	63.2	0.0
Dahlgren village	525	512	-2.5	389	98.5	0.0	0.0	0.3	1.3	11.6	60.3	28.3	223	74.4	35.0	16.6
Dakota village	506	486	-4.0	538	95.2	1.1	0.0	2.8	0.9	29.8	62.5	7.8	200	67.0	51.5	9.0
Dallas City city	945	910	-3.7	1,153	97.1	0.3	0.7	0.7	1.2	29.2	49.7	21.0	466	74.0	51.5	15.0
Dalton City village	544	528	-2.9	504	96.0	0.0	0.0	0.0	4.0	20.3	69.6	10.1	194	90.2	59.3	14.4
Dalzell village	717	688	-4.0	732	97.8	0.0	0.4	0.3	1.5	20.9	57.8	21.2	316	91.1	41.5	18.0
Damiansville village	491	493	0.4	504	86.1	0.0	1.2	1.4	11.3	21.5	69.5	9.1	156	80.8	36.5	19.9
Dana village	159	155	-2.5	97	82.5	0.0	0.0	7.2	10.3	12.4	68.0	19.6	46	76.1	71.7	4.3
Danforth village	604	581	-3.8	543	91.9	0.0	1.7	0.4	6.1	18.6	47.7	33.7	211	63.0	40.8	19.4
Danvers village	1,154	1,147	-0.6	1,117	92.6	0.6	0.4	3.8	2.7	23.1	65.7	11.4	429	81.4	32.9	34.5

1 May be of any race.

Table A. All Places — **Population and Housing**

STATE City, town, township, borough, or CDP (county if applicable)	Population				Race and Hispanic or Latino origin (percent), 2010–2014					Age (percent), 2010–2014			Households, 2010–2014			
	2010 census total population	2014 estimated population	Percent change 2010–2014	ACS total population estimate 2010–2014	White alone, not Hispanic or Latino	Black alone, not Hispanic or Latino	Asian alone, not Hispanic or Latino	All other races or 2 or more races, not Hispanic or Latino	Hispanic or Latino[1]	Under 18 years old	Age 18 to 64 years old	Age 65 years and older	Total occupied housing units	Percent owner occupied	Householders by level of education (percent): High school diploma or less	Householders by level of education (percent): Bachelor's degree or more
	1	2	3	4	5	6	7	8	9	10	11	12	13	14	15	16
ILLINOIS—Con.																
Danville city	33,019	32,243	-2.4	32,483	58.3	31.5	1.8	2.1	6.2	26.0	58.5	15.3	12,446	58.0	50.3	16.9
Darien city	22,087	22,315	1.0	22,251	77.4	4.1	11.2	3.2	4.1	20.6	60.2	19.2	9,058	82.2	23.1	47.9
Darmstadt CDP	68	NA	NA	0	0.0	0.0	0.0	0.0	0.0	0.0	0.0	0.0	0	0.0	0.0	0.0
Davis village	677	653	-3.5	838	96.4	0.0	1.3	1.6	0.7	35.6	53.2	11.2	268	76.1	45.5	11.6
Davis Junction village	2,373	2,293	-3.4	2,566	76.3	1.9	0.7	2.1	18.9	34.4	59.9	5.7	759	92.0	32.4	18.1
Dawson village	509	500	-1.8	520	100.0	0.0	0.0	0.0	0.0	19.9	66.6	13.5	223	84.3	59.6	10.3
Dayton CDP	537	NA	NA	521	95.2	0.4	0.0	2.5	1.9	12.2	78.6	9.4	204	81.4	44.1	16.7
Decatur city	76,126	74,010	-2.8	75,088	70.2	21.6	1.3	4.6	2.3	22.2	60.8	17.1	31,481	61.7	43.9	21.1
Deer Creek village	704	694	-1.4	781	86.8	0.0	0.5	2.6	10.1	24.5	65.8	9.9	295	71.9	40.0	22.7
Deerfield village	18,233	18,385	0.8	18,476	90.5	0.5	3.6	0.9	4.5	28.4	56.2	15.4	6,601	88.6	9.2	77.3
Deer Grove village	48	47	-2.1	67	98.5	0.0	0.0	0.0	1.5	32.9	61.2	6.0	27	63.0	33.3	3.7
Deer Park village	3,209	3,245	1.1	3,247	89.7	0.5	5.6	0.8	3.4	25.2	62.9	11.7	1,106	97.4	6.0	73.1
DeKalb city	44,117	44,054	-0.1	44,092	67.7	13.0	3.9	2.2	13.2	19.6	71.7	8.6	14,937	43.0	23.8	32.3
De Land village	446	427	-4.3	487	95.7	0.0	0.0	2.7	1.6	20.4	64.6	15.0	211	79.1	63.5	4.7
Delavan city	1,689	1,663	-1.5	1,543	93.5	2.5	0.0	1.2	2.8	24.9	54.2	20.9	630	73.3	45.1	17.3
De Pue village	1,833	1,760	-4.0	1,787	29.5	1.5	0.1	0.6	68.4	27.4	60.8	11.6	599	65.6	71.6	9.5
De Soto village	1,590	1,585	-0.3	1,475	87.1	1.6	4.7	2.5	4.2	23.6	61.5	14.8	600	64.5	32.7	31.8
Des Plaines city	58,364	58,947	1.0	58,802	66.1	1.6	13.1	1.5	17.7	19.9	62.5	17.7	22,418	79.9	33.7	37.8
Detroit village	83	81	-2.4	147	100.0	0.0	0.0	0.0	0.0	27.9	67.9	4.1	35	88.6	65.7	0.0
De Witt village	184	181	-1.6	203	95.6	0.0	0.0	4.4	0.0	20.7	59.4	19.7	89	75.3	62.9	11.2
Diamond village	2,527	2,501	-1.0	2,764	84.5	3.1	0.9	2.9	8.6	32.2	59.5	8.3	994	66.9	42.8	15.5
Dieterich village	617	608	-1.5	646	99.1	0.2	0.0	0.8	0.0	29.1	51.0	20.0	236	83.1	48.3	20.3
Divernon village	1,172	1,163	-0.8	1,363	96.0	0.0	1.5	2.5	0.0	27.9	57.7	14.4	540	77.6	43.5	10.4
Dix village	459	459	0.0	456	99.6	0.0	0.0	0.0	0.4	18.0	63.9	18.2	249	36.1	42.2	7.6
Dixmoor village	3,644	3,622	-0.6	3,635	5.9	44.5	0.0	3.0	46.6	36.9	55.1	7.9	1,086	52.9	64.5	10.1
Dixon city	15,735	15,285	-2.9	14,963	79.9	9.1	1.0	3.0	7.0	19.3	66.0	14.7	5,564	67.0	40.5	18.9
Dolton village	23,153	23,307	0.7	23,262	4.6	89.3	0.2	1.3	4.6	24.4	64.3	11.5	7,728	67.6	35.7	21.6
Dongola village	726	714	-1.7	780	99.0	0.0	0.0	0.0	1.0	27.8	57.5	14.7	280	71.4	47.5	8.2
Donnellson village	210	205	-2.4	185	100.0	0.0	0.0	0.0	0.0	28.6	58.3	13.0	84	86.9	70.2	6.0
Donovan village	304	300	-1.3	350	95.7	0.0	0.0	0.3	4.0	28.3	58.3	13.4	133	72.2	60.2	12.0
Dorchester village	151	147	-2.6	147	89.8	0.0	5.4	4.8	0.0	22.4	60.5	17.0	57	91.2	57.9	15.8
Dover village	168	163	-3.0	151	100.0	0.0	0.0	0.0	0.0	23.2	57.5	19.2	57	87.7	35.1	19.3
Dowell village	408	396	-2.9	303	99.7	0.0	0.0	0.3	0.0	15.5	63.5	21.1	149	77.2	65.8	6.7
Downers Grove village	48,867	49,715	1.7	49,372	85.1	2.7	6.3	1.3	4.6	23.5	61.1	15.4	19,018	76.9	18.6	54.7
Downs village	1,005	997	-0.8	1,017	97.1	0.3	0.3	2.1	0.3	27.9	61.8	10.3	386	80.1	44.6	28.8
Du Bois village	205	200	-2.4	184	98.4	1.6	0.0	0.0	0.0	13.6	68.5	17.9	76	85.5	56.6	2.6
Dunfermline village	300	291	-3.0	296	93.9	0.0	0.0	0.7	5.4	27.4	60.5	12.2	118	79.7	50.0	16.9
Dunlap village	1,383	1,389	0.4	1,592	93.2	1.2	4.0	0.8	0.8	34.0	59.8	6.2	513	81.5	20.1	52.2
Dupo village	4,130	3,969	-3.9	4,045	95.6	1.6	0.0	1.8	0.9	23.6	66.2	10.3	1,682	79.9	46.1	14.4
Du Quoin city	6,109	5,908	-3.3	6,012	83.9	10.6	0.3	3.5	1.6	20.2	61.1	18.7	2,540	62.4	45.5	13.3
Durand village	1,450	1,418	-2.2	1,203	94.8	0.7	0.4	3.7	0.4	17.8	63.5	18.5	497	76.1	52.7	23.3
Dwight village	4,260	4,119	-3.3	4,104	95.0	0.8	0.0	0.8	3.4	23.7	57.8	18.4	1,661	64.1	38.5	21.3
Eagarville village	127	124	-2.4	161	93.8	1.2	1.9	3.1	0.0	23.0	69.0	8.1	64	90.6	53.1	14.1
Earlville city	1,701	1,646	-3.2	1,729	92.9	0.0	0.6	0.9	5.6	20.6	62.6	16.8	709	67.8	59.0	11.8
East Alton village	6,301	6,215	-1.4	6,231	95.3	0.0	1.2	2.9	0.5	15.8	66.7	17.3	2,820	63.3	48.8	13.5
East Brooklyn village	106	105	-0.9	147	95.2	0.0	0.0	0.0	4.8	16.4	60.5	23.1	60	76.7	61.7	10.0
East Cape Girardeau village	387	347	-10.3	672	87.9	8.5	0.3	2.7	0.6	25.1	60.3	14.7	244	65.6	54.5	9.0
East Carondelet village	503	481	-4.4	546	85.0	13.2	0.0	1.8	0.0	20.2	72.4	7.5	177	66.1	68.4	0.0
East Dubuque city	1,711	1,671	-2.3	1,751	94.8	0.6	0.8	1.8	2.0	28.0	49.1	22.9	758	70.3	51.7	11.6
East Dundee village	2,868	3,198	11.5	3,003	82.7	0.7	0.2	0.0	16.5	18.3	62.1	19.8	1,326	71.9	38.4	28.9
East Galesburg village	816	806	-1.2	814	96.8	2.0	0.0	0.0	1.2	20.8	62.4	17.0	328	71.0	55.2	16.8
East Gillespie village	270	271	0.4	219	97.3	0.0	1.4	1.4	0.0	19.2	52.5	28.3	95	88.4	56.8	18.9
East Hazel Crest village	1,543	1,552	0.6	1,652	30.1	51.2	2.5	3.4	12.8	19.9	65.6	14.5	656	54.9	42.4	12.2
East Moline city	21,302	21,175	-0.6	21,294	60.4	14.0	4.0	2.5	19.2	23.6	57.2	19.2	8,546	61.7	47.9	17.7
Easton village	321	306	-4.7	345	100.0	0.0	0.0	0.0	0.0	19.1	57.5	23.5	135	84.4	48.1	13.3
East Peoria city	23,437	23,375	-0.3	23,225	93.3	1.8	0.6	2.2	2.1	20.5	61.5	17.9	9,733	74.2	40.6	19.0
East St. Louis city	26,917	26,672	-0.9	26,697	1.3	96.1	0.4	1.7	0.5	28.2	58.0	13.7	10,368	45.1	52.5	8.5
Eddyville village	101	97	-4.0	85	100.0	0.0	0.0	0.0	0.0	24.6	53.0	22.4	30	60.0	60.0	0.0
Edgewood village	440	429	-2.5	492	93.1	0.0	6.7	0.0	0.2	25.8	58.1	16.1	200	77.0	63.0	13.0
Edinburg village	1,078	1,056	-2.0	1,065	95.6	0.6	0.0	0.5	3.4	20.3	65.4	14.4	438	74.2	51.8	18.0
Edwardsville city	24,293	24,758	1.9	24,464	84.3	9.4	2.8	2.2	1.3	20.8	67.6	11.6	8,685	68.4	17.4	52.5
Effingham city	12,329	12,577	2.0	12,428	95.6	0.7	0.2	1.0	2.5	23.9	57.2	18.9	5,491	64.6	39.3	21.7
Elburn village	5,602	5,682	1.4	5,733	92.4	0.0	1.5	0.9	5.1	31.3	60.3	8.3	1,884	86.0	33.7	37.3
El Dara village	78	76	-2.6	116	98.3	0.0	0.0	1.7	0.0	6.9	88.8	4.3	57	96.5	5.3	10.5
Eldorado city	4,133	4,076	-1.4	4,139	95.1	1.1	0.0	3.0	0.8	25.3	58.3	16.3	1,563	69.4	45.2	11.3
Eldred village	201	196	-2.5	191	97.4	0.0	0.0	1.0	1.6	17.2	60.6	22.0	104	53.8	48.1	0.0
Elgin city	108,146	111,117	2.7	110,906	41.3	6.5	6.2	1.5	44.4	28.7	61.8	9.5	34,755	67.9	43.2	25.9
Elizabeth village	764	752	-1.6	819	98.4	0.0	0.0	0.9	0.7	22.5	55.0	22.5	376	61.4	44.1	20.2
Elizabethtown village	311	295	-5.1	255	96.9	0.0	0.0	0.0	3.1	24.4	59.3	16.5	115	71.3	47.0	4.3
Elk Grove Village village	33,127	33,379	0.8	33,288	76.8	0.6	10.7	1.8	10.0	20.5	64.4	15.0	13,393	74.4	29.3	36.0
Elkhart village	405	398	-1.7	377	79.8	0.3	0.8	18.6	0.5	26.7	50.3	22.8	166	81.9	45.2	19.3
Elkville village	928	910	-1.9	1,048	88.6	3.3	0.0	1.2	6.8	25.7	62.7	11.8	375	64.5	51.5	8.5
Elliott village	295	284	-3.7	264	95.8	0.0	0.0	0.8	3.4	14.4	66.6	18.9	106	95.3	63.2	10.4
Ellis Grove village	366	356	-2.7	500	86.8	0.2	0.0	0.0	13.0	24.6	58.2	17.2	204	76.5	50.5	7.8
Ellisville village	96	93	-3.1	122	100.0	0.0	0.0	0.0	0.0	32.8	52.5	14.8	36	83.3	47.2	0.0
Ellsworth village	195	195	0.0	249	98.0	0.0	0.0	2.0	0.0	16.4	77.3	6.0	87	81.6	63.2	10.3
Elmhurst city	44,136	45,751	3.7	45,105	84.3	1.8	5.8	1.4	6.7	26.8	58.4	14.8	15,655	81.0	16.4	59.6
Elmwood city	2,097	2,100	0.1	2,235	97.3	0.6	0.0	0.8	1.3	28.3	54.5	17.2	850	82.5	32.0	35.1
Elmwood Park village	24,883	24,954	0.3	24,960	69.4	2.1	3.6	1.2	23.7	19.0	65.1	15.8	9,372	67.5	41.6	26.9
El Paso city	2,810	2,804	-0.2	2,582	95.7	0.0	0.5	1.0	2.7	28.9	55.9	15.1	982	73.4	47.0	24.6
Elsah village	673	667	-0.9	698	94.6	3.2	0.0	1.7	0.6	2.3	91.8	5.7	81	39.5	13.6	72.8
Elvaston village	165	161	-2.4	104	96.2	0.0	0.0	0.0	3.8	18.2	53.8	27.9	49	91.8	51.0	4.1
Elwood village	2,279	2,267	-0.5	2,165	91.8	2.7	0.0	2.7	2.8	25.8	59.0	15.1	823	84.6	45.3	19.4
Emden village	485	477	-1.6	347	93.7	0.0	0.0	5.2	1.2	20.8	53.1	26.2	163	78.5	64.4	15.3
Emington village	117	114	-2.6	122	100.0	0.0	0.0	0.0	0.0	33.7	60.8	5.7	49	81.6	67.3	2.0
Energy village	1,146	1,145	-0.1	1,039	94.7	2.0	1.3	1.4	0.6	15.6	59.7	24.5	452	54.2	31.4	14.8
Enfield village	596	581	-2.5	655	100.0	0.0	0.0	0.0	0.0	22.2	59.9	18.0	261	80.8	48.3	15.7
Equality village	595	560	-5.9	643	98.1	0.3	0.0	1.6	0.0	22.0	58.3	19.8	274	82.1	45.6	16.1
Erie village	1,602	1,547	-3.4	1,594	94.4	0.4	0.0	1.1	4.1	24.1	59.2	16.9	670	80.0	41.8	22.5
Essex village	802	778	-3.0	905	93.3	0.0	0.0	1.0	5.7	30.3	61.3	8.4	297	92.9	42.4	15.2

1 May be of any race.

Table A. All Places — **Population and Housing**

STATE City, town, township, borough, or CDP (county if applicable)	Population				Race and Hispanic or Latino origin (percent), 2010–2014					Age (percent), 2010–2014			Households, 2010–2014		Householders by level of education (percent)	
	2010 census total population	2014 estimated population	Percent change 2010–2014	ACS total population estimate 2010–2014	White alone, not Hispanic or Latino	Black alone, not Hispanic or Latino	Asian alone, not Hispanic or Latino	All other races or 2 or more races, not Hispanic or Latino	Hispanic or Latino[1]	Under 18 years old	Age 18 to 64 years old	Age 65 years and older	Total occupied housing units	Percent owner occupied	High school diploma or less	Bachelor's degree or more
	1	2	3	4	5	6	7	8	9	10	11	12	13	14	15	16
ILLINOIS—Con.																
Eureka city	5,323	5,373	0.9	5,638	94.4	2.1	0.3	1.5	1.7	22.9	56.9	20.2	2,010	65.4	38.3	34.7
Evanston city	74,486	75,658	1.6	75,282	60.4	17.2	9.1	3.2	10.1	20.1	67.6	12.4	28,939	55.4	12.5	68.8
Evansville village	701	682	-2.7	702	94.7	0.0	0.1	0.4	4.7	23.4	63.5	13.1	255	82.7	64.3	7.5
Evergreen Park village	19,852	19,935	0.4	19,924	67.2	19.4	0.7	1.2	11.4	24.8	61.3	13.8	7,260	82.2	33.7	37.1
Ewing village	307	303	-1.3	305	96.4	0.0	0.0	3.6	0.0	24.2	60.7	15.1	112	81.3	46.4	5.4
Exeter village	65	64	-1.5	119	100.0	0.0	0.0	0.0	0.0	16.8	74.8	8.4	48	93.8	75.0	4.2
Fairbury city	3,773	3,678	-2.5	3,842	93.1	0.2	1.3	0.0	5.4	21.7	58.1	20.1	1,658	67.4	52.1	22.8
Fairfield city	5,154	5,080	-1.4	5,080	94.1	1.4	0.7	2.1	1.6	21.9	57.1	20.8	2,435	64.6	42.4	11.7
Fairmont CDP	2,459	NA	NA	2,384	23.4	45.5	1.0	2.1	28.1	24.4	62.6	13.1	804	66.5	51.2	8.6
Fairmont City village	2,629	2,529	-3.8	2,650	25.4	1.8	0.0	0.3	72.6	29.2	59.8	11.0	848	61.4	75.1	3.4
Fairmount village	642	623	-3.0	534	99.6	0.0	0.0	0.4	0.0	19.7	55.0	25.3	231	78.8	51.1	6.9
Fairview village	522	497	-4.8	515	98.8	0.4	0.0	0.2	0.6	26.2	53.6	20.2	204	87.3	46.1	18.6
Fairview Heights city	17,078	16,901	-1.0	17,250	64.7	26.4	3.1	2.1	3.6	18.0	65.5	16.4	7,394	75.0	27.6	35.4
Farina village	518	510	-1.5	663	98.3	0.0	0.0	0.3	1.4	29.6	54.2	16.1	235	72.8	59.1	13.2
Farmer City city	2,028	2,005	-1.1	2,054	98.5	0.0	0.0	1.5	0.0	19.6	62.9	17.7	854	77.5	44.0	15.2
Farmersville village	724	706	-2.5	568	98.9	0.0	0.4	0.4	0.4	27.3	62.3	10.4	234	82.5	53.0	14.5
Farmington city	2,445	2,356	-3.6	2,283	91.7	0.0	0.0	1.8	6.5	24.6	60.4	14.9	872	84.1	46.7	19.7
Fayetteville village	366	346	-5.5	441	93.0	0.0	0.2	1.4	5.4	24.7	61.5	13.8	154	77.9	51.3	6.5
Ferris village	156	152	-2.6	166	93.4	0.0	0.0	0.0	6.6	18.0	67.3	14.5	70	84.3	41.4	12.9
Fidelity village	114	110	-3.5	140	100.0	0.0	0.0	0.0	0.0	32.8	58.7	8.6	50	54.0	68.0	4.0
Fieldon village	239	230	-3.8	224	98.7	0.0	0.0	1.3	0.0	19.2	61.1	19.6	97	89.7	55.7	2.1
Fillmore village	330	322	-2.4	289	98.6	0.0	1.4	0.0	0.0	31.1	49.6	19.4	116	87.1	62.9	3.4
Findlay village	683	664	-2.8	777	97.8	0.8	0.0	0.8	0.6	24.9	56.9	18.1	331	72.2	55.0	10.6
Fisher village	1,879	1,960	4.3	1,792	98.5	0.0	0.6	0.8	0.1	23.2	60.5	16.4	724	84.0	42.1	17.5
Fithian village	485	473	-2.5	481	94.2	0.0	0.0	3.5	2.3	20.0	72.1	7.9	188	89.4	48.4	12.8
Flanagan village	1,110	1,086	-2.2	1,111	94.9	0.0	0.6	0.1	4.4	24.0	52.3	23.9	460	74.3	48.7	18.5
Flat Rock village	331	325	-1.8	338	94.4	0.0	0.6	5.0	0.0	20.0	50.1	29.9	139	95.7	44.6	12.9
Flora city	5,074	4,977	-1.9	5,045	96.3	0.6	0.2	2.6	0.3	27.7	53.7	18.6	1,973	65.6	47.9	15.2
Floraville CDP	53	NA	NA	0	0.0	0.0	0.0	0.0	0.0	0.0	0.0	0.0	0	0.0	0.0	0.0
Florence village	38	37	-2.6	28	100.0	0.0	0.0	0.0	0.0	0.0	57.1	42.9	22	63.6	81.8	0.0
Flossmoor village	9,464	9,522	0.6	9,339	45.0	46.9	2.0	2.7	3.4	25.0	57.9	17.0	3,249	91.9	10.5	67.7
Foosland village	101	102	1.0	123	91.9	8.1	0.0	0.0	0.0	28.5	57.8	13.8	38	78.9	44.7	0.0
Ford Heights village	2,763	2,785	0.8	2,777	0.6	96.3	0.0	2.5	0.6	28.2	59.7	12.1	931	37.5	71.1	8.1
Forest City village	246	235	-4.5	232	100.0	0.0	0.0	0.0	0.0	19.0	61.5	19.4	92	81.5	69.6	0.0
Forest Lake CDP	1,659	NA	NA	1,750	90.3	0.0	3.4	0.0	6.3	24.7	70.3	4.9	613	81.6	20.7	59.7
Forest Park village	14,167	14,196	0.2	14,202	45.0	32.7	8.5	2.1	11.7	16.9	70.4	12.8	7,178	50.0	26.4	44.3
Forest View village	698	697	-0.1	774	61.5	0.0	0.4	0.4	37.7	17.9	57.8	24.3	304	88.2	47.7	19.7
Forrest village	1,220	1,193	-2.2	1,202	95.2	0.0	0.0	1.0	3.8	26.2	61.8	12.0	462	72.1	56.9	15.4
Forreston village	1,446	1,393	-3.7	1,657	97.2	0.0	0.0	1.4	1.3	27.6	60.3	12.2	650	72.2	50.3	16.6
Forsyth village	3,490	3,592	2.9	3,690	88.6	2.5	6.0	1.9	1.0	24.9	56.0	19.2	1,477	91.7	25.7	59.4
Fox Lake village	10,623	10,578	-0.4	10,757	80.6	0.2	4.3	1.9	12.9	20.5	64.0	15.5	4,511	68.8	38.0	19.9
Fox Lake Hills CDP	2,591	NA	NA	2,274	93.6	1.4	0.0	0.0	5.1	19.1	67.6	13.3	886	83.5	35.7	16.1
Fox River Grove village	4,791	4,704	-1.8	4,749	86.6	0.0	1.6	2.1	9.7	28.4	64.5	7.2	1,566	84.7	27.4	45.7
Frankfort village	17,808	18,446	3.6	18,100	86.8	7.0	2.5	1.5	2.2	29.1	58.3	12.6	5,689	93.8	18.0	57.7
Frankfort Square CDP	9,276	NA	NA	9,143	86.9	2.5	0.8	2.0	7.7	28.2	65.5	6.4	2,892	92.5	30.7	29.1
Franklin village	610	598	-2.0	564	97.2	0.9	0.0	1.6	0.4	27.4	59.7	12.9	225	77.3	41.3	20.4
Franklin Grove village	1,021	977	-4.3	1,232	93.0	0.8	3.1	0.6	2.5	31.0	49.3	19.7	376	78.7	48.7	14.9
Franklin Park village	18,330	18,404	0.4	18,389	50.0	0.3	3.0	0.9	45.9	22.2	66.0	11.6	6,219	73.6	54.1	17.7
Freeburg village	4,356	4,280	-1.7	4,252	96.7	1.4	0.0	1.2	0.8	21.9	64.0	14.2	1,641	79.6	29.3	31.0
Freeman Spur village	292	290	-0.7	262	93.5	6.5	0.0	0.0	0.0	17.2	69.5	13.4	103	77.7	53.4	11.7
Freeport city	25,637	24,851	-3.1	25,225	74.4	16.1	0.9	3.4	5.2	22.7	57.0	20.4	10,541	62.5	43.1	18.0
Fulton city	3,483	3,360	-3.5	3,538	94.8	1.2	1.1	1.8	1.1	19.3	61.0	19.6	1,587	71.5	43.9	20.6
Fults village	26	26	0.0	22	100.0	0.0	0.0	0.0	0.0	9.0	90.9	0.0	7	100.0	85.7	0.0
Gages Lake CDP	10,198	NA	NA	10,330	75.3	4.5	2.7	2.3	15.2	24.1	67.2	8.6	3,781	80.3	26.4	39.8
Galatia village	933	921	-1.3	808	98.4	0.0	0.0	1.0	0.6	22.7	51.5	25.9	337	78.0	34.1	11.6
Galena city	3,419	3,327	-2.7	3,358	88.0	0.4	0.0	0.1	11.5	14.5	58.4	27.1	1,611	69.3	43.2	25.9
Galesburg city	32,189	31,659	-1.6	31,898	76.6	13.3	1.3	1.3	7.6	19.0	61.8	19.3	13,082	58.5	48.8	18.2
Galva city	2,589	2,528	-2.4	2,560	97.5	0.2	1.1	0.5	0.6	20.8	60.2	18.9	1,170	71.9	44.4	18.3
Garden Prairie CDP	352	NA	NA	230	94.3	0.0	0.0	0.0	5.7	17.0	67.1	16.1	91	69.2	65.9	5.5
Gardner village	1,463	1,443	-1.4	1,325	92.6	0.0	0.5	2.6	4.3	27.9	61.6	10.5	481	79.6	43.9	14.1
Garrett village	162	162	0.0	123	95.1	0.0	0.0	0.8	4.1	21.1	63.4	15.4	51	88.2	76.5	0.0
Gays village	281	277	-1.4	310	97.4	0.0	0.0	1.3	1.3	24.9	64.7	10.6	114	84.2	49.1	13.2
Geneseo city	6,623	6,537	-1.3	6,500	92.7	0.3	0.1	3.7	3.3	26.0	53.0	21.0	2,508	75.1	40.3	28.7
Geneva city	21,495	21,742	1.1	21,662	90.9	1.0	2.3	0.4	5.3	25.4	62.1	12.6	7,906	81.2	15.3	60.0
Genoa city	5,193	5,223	0.6	5,716	88.2	0.0	2.2	1.6	7.9	24.1	66.3	9.5	2,181	61.8	49.7	15.1
Georgetown CDP	404	NA	NA	531	84.4	1.9	11.9	0.4	1.5	23.1	58.9	17.9	242	93.0	19.4	56.6
Georgetown city	3,474	3,386	-2.5	3,437	97.1	2.4	0.0	0.4	0.0	25.0	58.3	16.7	1,352	67.2	58.9	10.8
Germantown village	1,281	1,288	0.5	1,142	96.9	0.1	0.0	0.3	2.7	22.2	59.2	18.7	454	91.2	47.8	19.2
Germantown Hills village	3,391	3,510	3.5	3,439	94.2	0.1	3.4	0.9	1.4	31.7	61.7	6.8	1,179	94.7	14.5	50.2
German Valley village	463	456	-1.5	481	97.9	0.0	1.2	0.0	0.8	23.1	62.9	13.9	184	83.7	44.6	19.0
Gibson City city	3,415	3,395	-0.6	3,542	95.7	0.2	0.2	4.0	0.0	23.2	56.0	20.7	1,513	63.3	48.2	17.3
Gifford village	975	999	2.5	923	95.4	0.4	0.0	0.0	4.1	23.9	58.4	17.8	338	87.3	46.4	23.4
Gilberts village	6,879	7,556	9.8	7,256	66.2	3.9	10.5	2.6	16.8	31.7	62.5	5.8	2,217	92.4	20.5	52.7
Gillespie city	3,319	3,209	-3.3	3,346	97.7	0.0	0.6	0.7	1.1	24.4	62.0	13.7	1,420	70.7	47.3	16.5
Gilman city	1,814	1,765	-2.7	1,703	76.0	0.3	0.5	2.7	20.4	24.2	53.6	22.2	657	65.6	60.1	12.5
Gilson CDP	190	NA	NA	179	100.0	0.0	0.0	0.0	0.0	4.5	77.6	17.9	76	50.0	82.9	0.0
Girard city	2,103	2,042	-2.9	1,804	94.3	0.3	0.9	3.3	1.2	23.2	59.4	17.4	706	65.9	56.8	8.5
Gladstone village	281	273	-2.8	257	100.0	0.0	0.0	0.0	0.0	19.9	53.3	26.8	128	87.5	69.5	2.3
Glasford village	1,022	1,011	-1.1	1,018	97.5	0.0	0.6	1.2	0.7	26.6	61.0	12.5	407	75.7	59.7	13.5
Glasgow village	141	138	-2.1	130	96.9	0.0	0.0	3.1	0.0	14.6	65.5	20.0	52	86.5	84.6	0.0
Glen Carbon village	12,936	12,947	0.1	13,095	80.6	11.7	2.1	2.3	3.3	26.1	59.5	14.5	4,992	67.1	18.4	51.4
Glencoe village	8,723	8,923	2.3	8,824	93.4	0.7	1.7	1.3	2.8	30.9	54.2	15.0	3,052	93.7	4.6	85.6
Glendale Heights village	34,212	34,530	0.9	34,436	36.9	5.9	23.2	2.8	31.2	25.0	66.7	8.2	11,351	68.7	38.4	31.9
Glen Ellyn village	27,369	27,763	1.4	27,394	82.0	3.7	7.9	1.8	4.5	26.0	59.6	14.5	10,443	75.0	17.0	62.3
Glenview village	44,695	46,767	4.6	45,400	76.6	1.3	12.0	1.7	8.3	24.0	55.4	20.7	16,801	81.6	16.4	64.9
Glenwood village	8,990	9,036	0.5	9,040	22.0	65.9	0.0	2.9	9.2	22.3	61.0	16.6	3,258	82.6	32.4	30.5
Godfrey village	18,007	17,782	-1.2	17,911	90.8	5.7	0.4	1.7	1.4	21.9	57.8	20.1	7,319	82.5	30.5	29.1
Godley village	602	670	11.3	622	86.2	0.0	0.5	1.4	11.9	29.5	63.9	6.6	203	74.4	38.4	6.9
Golconda city	670	640	-4.5	822	89.9	3.3	1.8	1.2	3.8	19.8	57.0	23.2	299	46.5	53.5	9.0
Golden village	644	637	-1.1	706	95.3	0.0	0.0	0.0	4.7	25.5	55.5	19.0	267	74.9	52.8	14.6
Golden Gate village	68	68	0.0	48	100.0	0.0	0.0	0.0	0.0	10.4	45.9	43.8	27	100.0	74.1	14.8

1 May be of any race.

Table A. All Places — **Population and Housing**

STATE City, town, township, borough, or CDP (county if applicable)	Population: 2010 census total population	Population: 2014 estimated population	Population: Percent change 2010–2014	Population: ACS total population estimate 2010–2014	Race and Hispanic or Latino origin (percent), 2010–2014: White alone, not Hispanic or Latino	Black alone, not Hispanic or Latino	Asian alone, not Hispanic or Latino	All other races or 2 or more races, not Hispanic or Latino	Hispanic or Latino[1]	Age (percent), 2010–2014: Under 18 years old	Age 18 to 64 years old	Age 65 years and older	Households, 2010–2014: Total occupied housing units	Percent owner occupied	Householders by level of education (percent): High school diploma or less	Bachelor's degree or more
	1	2	3	4	5	6	7	8	9	10	11	12	13	14	15	16
ILLINOIS—Con.																
Golf village	500	506	1.2	490	86.1	0.0	3.7	0.2	10.0	32.8	53.9	13.3	146	99.3	2.7	84.9
Goodfield village	864	913	5.7	1,044	87.0	0.0	1.0	11.8	0.3	31.3	59.4	9.6	321	96.6	36.8	29.9
Good Hope village	396	387	-2.3	389	93.6	0.0	0.0	0.8	5.7	16.7	61.8	21.6	188	83.0	43.1	31.4
Goofy Ridge CDP	350	NA	NA	242	100.0	0.0	0.0	0.0	0.0	27.7	67.5	5.0	128	80.5	90.6	0.0
Goreville village	1,050	1,067	1.6	1,189	98.2	0.0	0.0	0.4	1.3	30.2	53.1	16.7	462	62.8	37.2	18.6
Gorham village	236	234	-0.8	168	97.6	0.0	0.0	0.0	2.4	21.3	55.9	22.6	81	80.2	81.5	2.5
Grafton city	674	660	-2.1	719	88.3	3.2	1.0	1.8	5.7	24.9	53.3	21.8	327	67.3	37.3	24.8
Grand Detour CDP	429	NA	NA	394	100.0	0.0	0.0	0.0	0.0	4.5	65.9	29.4	208	92.3	34.6	25.5
Grand Ridge village	560	538	-3.9	512	88.5	0.0	0.6	0.8	10.2	27.6	56.2	16.2	195	84.6	35.4	21.0
Grand Tower city	605	590	-2.5	407	97.3	1.0	0.5	1.2	0.0	15.7	59.0	25.3	180	75.0	58.9	8.3
Grandview village	1,441	1,433	-0.6	1,351	81.3	14.4	0.7	3.0	0.7	29.2	56.9	13.8	552	66.1	45.8	10.1
Grandwood Park CDP	5,202	NA	NA	5,606	66.8	5.1	11.3	4.0	12.7	31.8	60.0	8.2	1,730	83.4	23.4	53.5
Granite City city	29,849	29,183	-2.2	29,764	86.5	5.5	0.7	2.3	4.9	21.4	62.0	16.6	12,423	67.3	53.5	14.5
Grantfork village	337	330	-2.1	393	98.0	0.0	0.0	1.5	0.5	27.5	64.4	8.1	157	90.4	44.6	20.4
Grant Park village	1,331	1,299	-2.4	1,323	93.3	0.3	0.5	1.8	4.0	19.8	68.4	11.9	504	71.4	47.0	14.1
Granville village	1,427	1,363	-4.5	1,457	89.4	0.0	0.0	4.0	6.7	25.6	62.3	12.1	609	72.7	54.7	12.5
Grayslake village	20,883	21,018	0.6	20,863	76.1	3.1	8.1	2.7	10.0	27.1	65.0	8.0	7,579	71.8	18.9	52.7
Grayville city	1,668	1,639	-1.7	1,722	97.6	0.5	0.0	1.3	0.5	15.8	55.6	28.8	797	73.7	44.0	10.0
Greenfield city	1,071	1,029	-3.9	1,346	99.7	0.0	0.0	0.3	0.0	24.5	61.1	14.6	559	79.1	60.3	13.1
Green Oaks village	3,852	3,854	0.1	3,844	80.1	1.0	11.0	2.0	5.8	30.5	60.8	8.8	1,142	99.5	10.0	76.5
Greenup village	1,513	1,487	-1.7	1,794	98.7	0.4	0.7	0.3	0.0	21.2	56.8	22.0	760	74.3	54.9	14.5
Green Valley village	709	694	-2.1	786	96.7	0.0	0.0	2.5	0.8	24.7	63.6	11.7	321	77.3	47.4	12.5
Greenview village	778	761	-2.2	924	92.2	0.8	0.0	1.0	6.1	23.8	64.2	12.0	348	77.9	50.3	12.1
Greenville city	7,037	6,885	-2.2	6,860	79.0	8.9	3.1	4.0	5.0	20.5	64.7	14.9	2,197	58.6	36.5	26.6
Greenwood village	255	252	-1.2	400	94.3	0.0	0.3	0.0	5.5	26.1	65.9	8.5	122	70.5	35.2	18.9
Gridley village	1,432	1,448	1.1	1,377	96.2	0.2	0.6	1.6	1.4	25.3	58.4	16.2	520	84.0	41.7	23.5
Griggsville city	1,226	1,182	-3.6	955	94.5	0.8	0.0	0.0	4.7	26.4	49.3	24.4	418	81.6	57.7	12.7
Gulf Port village	54	51	-5.6	24	100.0	0.0	0.0	0.0	0.0	0.0	87.5	12.5	11	100.0	45.5	0.0
Gurnee village	31,232	31,207	-0.1	31,182	65.5	8.5	11.1	2.8	12.1	26.4	63.1	10.5	11,603	72.7	24.7	47.5
Hainesville village	3,688	3,682	-0.2	3,682	73.6	0.8	8.3	1.3	16.1	31.6	60.4	7.9	1,234	80.8	20.3	55.7
Hamburg village	128	125	-2.3	124	99.2	0.0	0.0	0.8	0.0	11.2	63.6	25.0	56	82.1	44.6	7.1
Hamel village	816	807	-1.1	878	95.3	1.4	0.5	2.8	0.0	31.1	54.0	14.9	317	81.1	24.3	43.8
Hamilton city	2,951	2,861	-3.0	3,059	97.6	1.0	0.3	0.2	1.0	21.1	59.1	19.8	1,257	73.0	50.8	16.5
Hammond village	509	487	-4.3	418	94.3	0.0	0.0	1.2	4.5	22.7	59.6	17.7	190	68.9	57.4	1.6
Hampshire village	5,568	5,976	7.3	6,053	78.8	0.8	0.0	0.0	20.4	31.9	59.1	9.0	1,972	83.1	24.2	30.1
Hampton village	1,863	1,848	-0.8	2,061	83.9	5.8	0.5	2.5	7.3	21.8	60.0	18.2	793	84.9	39.3	23.1
Hanaford village	327	317	-3.1	312	100.0	0.0	0.0	0.0	0.0	8.0	64.2	27.9	169	74.0	60.4	4.7
Hanna City village	1,225	1,229	0.3	1,308	94.9	0.7	0.8	0.7	3.0	22.5	63.6	13.8	537	78.8	42.8	13.6
Hanover village	841	818	-2.7	794	93.3	0.4	1.0	2.8	2.5	15.5	55.2	29.5	398	75.4	50.5	17.1
Hanover Park village	37,958	38,476	1.4	38,302	36.9	8.3	15.4	2.0	37.5	28.9	64.1	6.9	11,134	77.3	43.2	26.5
Hardin village	967	943	-2.5	1,046	99.3	0.3	0.0	0.4	0.0	20.8	52.0	27.2	402	76.1	57.7	10.2
Harmon village	120	115	-4.2	121	97.5	0.0	0.0	0.8	1.7	17.3	62.9	19.8	53	73.6	77.4	5.7
Harrisburg city	9,025	8,914	-1.2	8,989	87.4	6.1	1.1	2.1	3.4	22.8	59.0	18.2	3,771	62.6	46.2	14.3
Harrison CDP	970	NA	NA	982	98.7	0.0	0.0	1.3	0.0	33.2	46.8	20.0	358	86.6	38.5	20.1
Harristown village	1,367	1,341	-1.9	1,431	96.6	0.3	2.5	0.6	0.0	24.0	61.2	14.8	549	92.3	53.0	13.7
Hartford village	1,429	1,388	-2.9	1,529	99.4	0.0	0.0	0.5	0.1	21.7	63.6	14.9	647	75.3	57.3	4.5
Hartsburg village	314	311	-1.0	221	94.1	0.0	0.0	4.5	1.4	26.2	59.8	14.0	96	77.1	47.9	15.6
Harvard city	9,435	9,230	-2.2	9,829	47.7	0.1	0.0	0.2	52.0	36.7	56.2	6.9	2,780	61.9	62.8	10.7
Harvel village	223	217	-2.7	155	98.1	0.0	0.0	0.6	1.3	20.7	58.1	21.3	81	80.2	53.1	11.1
Harvey city	25,282	25,347	0.3	25,225	2.8	76.5	0.5	1.7	18.5	29.4	59.5	11.2	8,647	45.4	62.4	9.2
Harwood Heights village	8,612	8,675	0.7	8,656	85.1	0.5	3.5	0.5	10.3	15.5	66.0	18.5	3,628	59.7	48.0	26.5
Havana city	3,301	3,121	-5.5	3,243	96.5	2.0	0.9	0.2	0.4	19.4	57.4	23.3	1,447	62.0	54.1	15.7
Hawthorn Woods village	7,738	7,875	1.8	7,727	85.8	2.0	6.6	1.2	4.4	25.2	62.2	12.6	2,583	98.5	13.9	70.9
Hazel Crest village	14,100	14,182	0.6	14,102	7.6	85.1	0.3	1.3	5.8	27.8	58.6	13.7	4,907	68.5	29.1	25.2
Hebron village	1,216	1,205	-0.9	1,094	81.8	0.8	1.6	2.9	12.9	19.5	67.3	13.3	406	69.0	44.6	13.1
Hecker village	486	489	0.6	503	93.0	0.0	0.0	7.0	0.0	29.0	54.3	16.7	176	77.8	52.8	13.6
Henderson village	255	253	-0.8	228	94.7	0.0	0.9	1.3	3.1	15.4	67.1	17.5	113	78.8	48.7	2.7
Hennepin village	757	722	-4.6	979	87.5	0.3	0.0	0.0	12.2	28.5	59.0	12.6	407	75.4	47.9	8.8
Henning village	251	247	-1.6	364	100.0	0.0	0.0	0.0	0.0	29.9	59.7	10.2	117	85.5	43.6	0.0
Henry city	2,464	2,336	-5.2	2,367	96.6	0.1	1.4	1.2	0.6	20.7	56.7	22.7	987	75.9	49.5	15.6
Heritage Lake CDP	1,520	NA	NA	1,292	100.0	0.0	0.0	0.0	0.0	35.2	61.9	2.9	438	100.0	15.8	57.5
Herrick village	436	429	-1.6	446	98.0	0.0	0.0	0.0	2.0	27.2	57.2	15.7	170	92.4	73.5	3.5
Herrin city	12,523	12,852	2.6	12,721	95.3	2.2	0.1	0.4	1.9	22.9	59.3	17.7	5,341	69.3	35.2	24.2
Herscher village	1,591	1,566	-1.6	1,519	97.4	0.0	0.5	1.4	0.7	27.3	55.2	17.4	609	72.4	35.8	23.6
Hettick village	181	176	-2.8	254	99.2	0.0	0.0	0.8	0.0	20.5	71.3	8.3	99	85.9	61.6	11.1
Heyworth village	2,838	2,906	2.4	3,028	95.9	0.9	0.4	2.7	0.2	30.4	61.2	8.5	1,060	79.0	45.0	29.9
Hickory Hills city	14,049	14,177	0.9	14,117	82.3	2.4	1.3	1.7	12.3	22.8	62.4	14.8	4,965	72.7	43.5	26.1
Hidalgo village	106	105	-0.9	88	97.7	0.0	0.0	1.1	1.1	22.6	66.0	11.4	35	91.4	57.1	5.7
Highland city	9,913	9,894	-0.2	9,738	93.9	0.3	0.5	1.6	3.7	23.4	58.1	18.4	4,033	66.1	40.7	26.1
Highland Park city	29,728	29,871	0.5	29,819	86.7	2.3	2.5	1.3	7.2	25.2	54.1	20.7	11,549	81.7	12.3	71.4
Highwood city	5,423	5,387	-0.7	5,400	48.7	2.9	1.8	0.3	46.3	23.3	62.2	14.4	2,040	43.7	40.7	36.4
Hillcrest village	1,326	1,292	-2.6	1,203	71.7	0.3	0.0	3.5	24.5	26.4	64.0	9.6	397	87.2	53.7	19.4
Hillsboro city	6,207	6,089	-1.9	8,371	70.7	23.5	0.6	2.0	3.3	13.9	77.2	9.0	1,634	69.5	45.8	15.9
Hillsdale village	517	511	-1.2	507	92.7	0.0	0.0	1.4	5.9	22.6	64.9	12.4	220	79.5	53.2	11.4
Hillside village	8,157	8,195	0.5	8,192	24.2	40.2	1.0	1.9	32.6	21.6	63.3	15.1	2,991	67.8	44.0	25.7
Hillview village	193	188	-2.6	152	100.0	0.0	0.0	0.0	0.0	29.6	50.7	19.7	51	62.7	72.5	3.9
Hinckley village	2,070	2,070	0.0	2,052	91.2	0.9	0.6	1.3	6.0	23.1	64.5	12.3	814	74.7	41.2	22.0
Hindsboro village	313	308	-1.6	341	91.8	1.5	0.6	2.9	3.2	18.5	64.8	16.7	144	85.4	51.4	9.7
Hinsdale village	16,816	17,446	3.7	16,898	84.0	0.5	8.4	1.5	5.7	34.0	53.2	12.8	5,400	86.4	7.0	78.7
Hodgkins village	1,897	1,881	-0.8	2,185	51.8	0.9	0.0	1.2	46.1	24.8	60.0	15.1	678	64.7	63.6	8.4
Hoffman village	508	496	-2.4	555	96.4	2.9	0.0	0.7	0.0	28.6	60.8	10.5	191	86.9	28.8	14.1
Hoffman Estates village	51,890	52,347	0.9	52,271	53.1	4.5	24.7	2.1	15.6	25.0	65.3	9.9	17,731	75.2	23.4	47.7
Holiday Hills village	601	593	-1.3	654	94.0	0.0	0.5	0.5	5.0	19.0	69.3	11.8	248	89.5	48.0	14.9
Holiday Shores CDP	2,882	NA	NA	2,918	93.1	3.1	0.9	2.9	0.0	24.6	66.3	9.2	1,065	98.5	26.1	45.5
Hollowayville village	84	82	-2.4	51	98.0	2.0	0.0	0.0	0.0	9.8	60.9	29.4	16	93.8	62.5	6.3
Homer village	1,193	1,207	1.2	1,159	97.0	0.0	1.2	1.3	0.5	26.4	56.2	17.4	452	82.1	46.9	14.4
Homer Glen village	24,224	24,364	0.6	24,322	89.6	0.7	1.3	1.0	7.4	23.2	62.5	14.4	8,232	92.7	30.7	37.0
Hometown city	4,349	4,365	0.4	4,358	80.2	0.0	0.0	0.4	19.4	20.6	62.4	16.8	1,910	79.5	46.5	15.3
Homewood village	19,323	19,464	0.7	19,642	52.0	35.5	0.9	3.1	8.5	23.8	61.8	14.4	7,267	80.6	20.4	47.7
Hoopeston city	5,351	5,258	-1.7	5,474	85.1	1.1	0.0	0.3	13.5	23.4	56.1	20.4	2,271	67.2	68.1	12.5
Hooppole village	204	201	-1.5	293	99.7	0.0	0.0	0.3	0.0	29.7	45.4	24.9	97	90.7	54.6	7.2

1 May be of any race.

Table A. All Places — **Population and Housing**

STATE City, town, township, borough, or CDP (county if applicable)	Population: 2010 census total population	Population: 2014 estimated population	Population: Percent change 2010–2014	Population: ACS total population estimate 2010–2014	Race and Hispanic or Latino origin (percent), 2010–2014: White alone, not Hispanic or Latino	Black alone, not Hispanic or Latino	Asian alone, not Hispanic or Latino	All other races or 2 or more races, not Hispanic or Latino	Hispanic or Latino[1]	Age (percent), 2010–2014: Under 18 years old	Age 18 to 64 years old	Age 65 years and older	Households, 2010–2014: Total occupied housing units	Percent owner occupied	Householders by level of education (percent): High school diploma or less	Bachelor's degree or more
	1	2	3	4	5	6	7	8	9	10	11	12	13	14	15	16
ILLINOIS—Con.																
Hopedale village	865	857	-0.9	1,018	97.5	2.0	0.5	0.0	0.0	20.3	54.1	25.4	388	63.1	46.9	11.1
Hopewell village	410	405	-1.2	421	96.7	0.7	0.0	0.0	2.6	22.6	64.9	12.6	157	96.8	25.5	38.2
Hopkins Park village	603	584	-3.2	495	13.5	81.2	1.4	3.4	0.4	18.9	61.0	20.0	236	49.6	61.4	9.3
Hoyleton village	531	514	-3.2	586	81.4	8.9	0.2	4.4	5.1	33.8	52.6	13.7	189	79.4	39.7	18.5
Hudson village	1,838	1,858	1.1	1,918	97.5	0.6	0.2	0.9	0.8	27.4	60.7	11.7	642	92.7	24.8	40.5
Huey village	169	167	-1.2	209	100.0	0.0	0.0	0.0	0.0	18.7	66.9	14.4	74	91.9	45.9	20.3
Hull village	461	442	-4.1	450	90.7	0.2	0.9	0.7	7.6	25.0	64.5	10.4	177	76.8	65.0	9.0
Humboldt village	437	432	-1.1	430	86.3	0.0	0.0	0.0	13.7	23.0	61.1	15.8	176	73.9	64.2	8.5
Hume village	380	368	-3.2	399	98.0	0.0	0.0	2.0	0.0	22.3	56.9	20.8	173	79.8	64.7	6.4
Huntley village	24,292	25,603	5.4	25,200	81.9	0.3	6.5	2.4	8.9	23.7	46.5	29.9	10,211	94.4	26.5	36.0
Hurst city	795	792	-0.4	841	96.3	0.0	0.0	3.4	0.2	16.5	65.0	18.7	371	73.0	59.3	9.7
Hutsonville village	554	546	-1.4	468	90.4	0.9	0.0	6.6	2.1	20.6	62.2	17.3	183	77.0	37.7	17.5
Illiopolis village	891	886	-0.6	913	98.5	0.0	0.0	0.8	0.8	25.6	61.1	13.0	352	79.3	44.9	21.0
Ina village	2,338	2,329	-0.4	2,301	58.4	30.3	0.0	2.3	9.0	7.5	86.6	6.0	276	59.1	49.6	9.4
Indian Creek village	545	546	0.2	591	64.1	3.0	30.3	0.7	1.9	27.8	59.7	12.5	191	89.0	12.0	78.0
Indian Head Park village	3,809	3,839	0.8	3,837	88.5	3.6	2.6	0.6	4.7	15.7	55.4	28.9	1,861	90.5	19.5	56.5
Indianola village	276	272	-1.4	381	97.9	0.8	0.0	1.3	0.0	26.5	60.4	13.1	123	88.6	68.3	0.8
Industry village	478	462	-3.3	432	95.4	1.6	0.0	2.1	0.9	24.3	53.6	22.0	188	89.4	49.5	20.7
Ingalls Park CDP	3,314	NA	NA	3,368	56.7	8.0	3.3	0.8	31.2	27.4	65.6	7.1	1,206	72.2	60.3	15.4
Inverness village	7,399	7,592	2.6	7,516	86.8	0.2	10.8	1.3	0.8	22.5	55.7	21.8	2,726	95.9	12.2	69.9
Iola village	141	139	-1.4	131	100.0	0.0	0.0	0.0	0.0	33.6	52.8	13.7	40	70.0	77.5	0.0
Ipava village	470	450	-4.3	594	88.6	0.0	1.7	7.9	1.9	23.5	59.3	17.3	233	86.3	45.9	13.7
Iroquois village	154	150	-2.6	166	91.6	0.0	0.0	7.8	0.6	10.2	67.8	21.7	81	97.5	38.3	16.0
Irving village	495	483	-2.4	377	99.2	0.5	0.0	0.0	0.3	23.7	56.2	20.2	168	81.0	58.3	6.5
Irvington village	665	642	-3.5	735	97.4	0.7	0.0	1.0	1.0	20.2	67.2	12.7	307	65.5	45.3	13.7
Irwin village	74	73	-1.4	107	93.5	0.0	0.0	0.0	6.5	46.7	37.4	15.9	34	67.6	41.2	8.8
Island Lake village	8,077	8,031	-0.6	8,033	81.9	0.7	0.7	3.6	13.1	26.4	66.0	7.5	3,017	80.7	30.3	24.9
Itasca village	8,649	8,800	1.7	8,579	76.6	0.3	8.0	2.6	12.4	22.3	63.2	14.3	3,279	70.5	28.5	40.8
Iuka village	489	474	-3.1	480	96.0	0.0	2.7	0.6	0.6	26.4	59.0	14.6	186	83.3	57.0	2.2
Ivesdale village	267	271	1.5	288	99.0	0.0	0.0	1.0	0.0	22.2	66.3	11.5	116	85.3	47.4	19.0
Jacksonville city	19,446	19,159	-1.5	19,315	83.1	10.8	0.5	2.3	3.3	19.6	62.7	17.6	7,287	58.3	47.4	23.6
Jeffersonville village	367	358	-2.5	434	99.1	0.9	0.0	0.0	0.0	27.9	61.2	10.8	179	70.9	59.2	7.8
Jeisyville village	107	104	-2.8	131	100.0	0.0	0.0	0.0	0.0	22.9	53.4	23.7	55	81.8	87.3	1.8
Jerome village	1,677	1,662	-0.9	1,532	90.3	2.7	2.0	4.2	0.8	11.6	64.3	24.3	800	80.9	31.3	31.0
Jerseyville city	8,465	8,532	0.8	8,305	97.0	0.3	0.4	0.7	1.6	21.1	57.7	21.1	3,430	69.9	47.5	14.6
Jewett village	223	220	-1.3	310	96.8	0.0	0.0	2.3	1.0	31.3	64.6	4.2	103	68.0	65.0	1.9
Johnsburg village	6,337	6,297	-0.6	6,322	88.7	2.3	1.7	1.2	6.2	24.1	64.1	11.8	2,048	90.2	34.5	33.1
Johnsonville village	77	77	0.0	64	100.0	0.0	0.0	0.0	0.0	31.3	46.8	21.9	30	93.3	63.3	13.3
Johnston City city	3,557	3,506	-1.4	3,541	92.0	0.2	0.4	5.0	2.4	26.1	59.5	14.5	1,413	59.9	50.4	7.3
Joliet city	147,459	147,928	0.3	147,786	52.5	15.5	2.1	2.2	27.7	29.6	61.7	8.5	46,992	71.5	40.3	25.1
Jonesboro city	1,821	1,772	-2.7	2,052	96.1	0.5	0.0	0.8	2.6	25.6	57.1	17.4	762	71.9	45.3	19.2
Joppa village	360	349	-3.1	319	79.6	11.3	0.0	9.1	0.0	27.5	55.4	16.9	99	54.5	64.6	7.1
Joy village	417	396	-5.0	410	96.6	0.0	1.0	0.0	2.4	26.3	59.9	13.7	161	82.6	57.1	11.2
Junction village	129	123	-4.7	88	97.7	0.0	0.0	2.3	0.0	13.7	60.2	26.1	43	95.3	60.5	0.0
Junction City village	482	466	-3.3	506	97.4	1.8	0.4	0.0	0.4	23.7	63.9	12.3	203	90.6	70.4	3.9
Justice village	12,926	13,022	0.7	13,001	62.2	19.0	1.8	1.4	15.7	27.9	64.9	7.1	4,362	53.4	52.2	14.4
Kampsville village	328	319	-2.7	387	98.7	0.3	0.3	0.5	0.3	33.2	52.0	15.0	150	61.3	40.7	4.7
Kane village	438	422	-3.7	338	95.6	1.5	0.0	3.0	0.0	24.6	67.1	8.3	148	69.6	59.5	5.4
Kaneville village	482	491	1.9	523	90.6	0.0	4.6	1.0	3.8	26.2	60.2	13.8	201	84.1	35.3	28.9
Kangley village	251	245	-2.4	348	78.4	0.3	0.0	0.9	20.4	22.1	62.7	15.2	117	75.2	58.1	12.0
Kankakee city	27,537	26,860	-2.5	27,145	41.7	37.3	0.5	2.5	18.0	28.8	58.0	13.4	9,455	49.5	49.7	12.3
Kansas village	787	753	-4.3	834	98.7	0.0	0.0	0.8	0.5	26.3	55.4	18.3	355	69.0	58.6	9.6
Kappa village	230	239	3.9	325	98.5	0.0	0.0	0.0	1.5	26.7	68.4	4.9	110	85.5	25.5	37.3
Karnak village	499	468	-6.2	611	98.0	1.1	0.0	0.8	0.0	28.8	58.7	12.6	209	87.1	49.3	6.2
Kaskaskia village	14	14	0.0	9	100.0	0.0	0.0	0.0	0.0	0.0	0.0	100.0	5	100.0	100.0	0.0
Keenes village	83	83	0.0	76	94.7	0.0	1.3	3.9	0.0	14.5	48.6	36.8	35	100.0	65.7	0.0
Keensburg village	210	205	-2.4	197	93.9	0.0	0.5	5.6	0.0	28.9	61.4	9.6	76	93.4	46.1	0.0
Keithsburg city	609	586	-3.8	598	97.7	0.0	0.0	1.8	0.5	19.0	59.1	21.7	294	81.0	68.0	2.7
Kell village	219	216	-1.4	212	96.2	0.0	0.0	0.5	3.3	24.1	64.5	11.3	78	93.6	38.5	2.6
Kempton village	231	223	-3.5	141	95.7	0.0	1.4	2.8	0.0	26.2	63.1	10.6	63	82.5	36.5	7.9
Kenilworth village	2,513	2,562	1.9	2,648	94.0	1.0	1.9	1.1	1.9	35.8	49.3	14.8	819	91.0	0.9	91.5
Kenney village	326	321	-1.5	325	98.5	0.0	0.0	1.5	0.0	18.7	64.4	16.6	147	91.2	69.4	10.2
Kewanee city	12,916	12,596	-2.5	12,694	79.2	4.5	0.4	1.7	14.1	24.7	58.3	16.9	5,175	65.8	53.5	16.3
Keyesport village	421	405	-3.8	489	97.1	0.6	0.4	0.2	1.6	21.4	57.8	20.7	212	70.3	60.8	3.3
Kilbourne village	302	288	-4.6	278	100.0	0.0	0.0	0.0	0.0	18.0	64.4	17.6	124	78.2	64.5	2.4
Kildeer village	3,910	3,958	1.2	3,917	80.3	1.3	9.3	3.0	6.2	25.8	64.4	9.8	1,255	95.6	8.0	68.9
Kincaid village	1,505	1,451	-3.6	1,666	90.9	0.1	0.7	3.4	5.0	25.1	59.4	15.5	707	78.2	63.1	8.5
Kinderhook village	216	211	-2.3	284	99.3	0.0	0.0	0.7	0.0	28.8	57.4	13.7	106	97.2	62.3	8.5
Kingston village	1,160	1,163	0.3	1,029	90.5	0.7	0.0	3.3	5.5	30.6	62.3	7.0	338	77.2	42.9	17.2
Kingston Mines village	302	301	-0.3	253	96.4	0.8	0.0	1.6	1.2	21.7	65.9	12.3	107	85.0	63.6	1.9
Kinmundy city	796	778	-2.3	1,025	98.0	0.0	0.0	1.6	0.5	32.2	54.7	13.2	387	81.7	50.4	4.9
Kinsman village	99	98	-1.0	124	85.5	0.0	0.0	0.0	14.5	40.2	43.5	16.1	41	80.5	56.1	2.4
Kirkland village	1,744	1,744	0.0	1,791	92.5	0.0	0.0	1.6	5.9	27.6	63.4	8.9	629	80.0	50.2	13.5
Kirkwood village	714	715	0.1	782	99.9	0.0	0.0	0.0	0.1	28.6	56.0	15.2	289	83.7	62.3	12.5
Knollwood CDP	1,747	NA	NA	1,519	77.0	2.5	3.0	0.0	17.5	19.3	68.7	12.0	561	83.4	18.0	50.8
Knoxville city	2,913	2,872	-1.4	2,954	98.0	0.3	0.0	0.3	1.4	20.2	55.4	24.5	1,227	75.2	44.7	17.0
Lacon city	1,937	1,832	-5.4	1,759	98.8	0.4	0.1	0.0	0.7	19.5	52.4	27.9	726	85.0	53.2	14.2
Ladd village	1,295	1,251	-3.4	1,231	95.5	0.2	1.2	0.3	2.8	21.3	60.5	18.0	536	75.4	38.1	22.0
La Fayette village	223	217	-2.7	266	97.7	1.1	0.0	0.0	1.1	28.6	48.2	23.3	96	89.6	68.8	4.2
La Grange village	15,550	15,759	1.3	15,675	81.3	5.6	1.7	0.6	10.9	30.7	55.6	13.7	5,329	80.1	18.1	63.3
La Grange Park village	13,579	13,665	0.6	13,624	81.8	3.8	1.2	0.5	12.7	24.7	58.2	17.1	5,347	66.7	20.8	49.4
La Harpe city	1,235	1,200	-2.8	1,387	98.1	0.0	0.0	1.7	0.1	24.3	53.6	22.0	581	82.8	44.6	22.4
Lake Barrington village	4,982	4,985	0.1	4,903	91.7	1.8	2.2	1.5	2.8	14.5	50.7	34.8	2,319	83.1	17.3	63.4
Lake Bluff village	5,705	5,698	-0.1	5,867	88.5	0.9	6.1	2.9	1.6	26.7	55.7	17.5	2,079	84.8	6.0	82.7
Lake Camelot CDP	1,686	NA	NA	1,910	90.3	0.0	1.5	0.0	8.2	26.5	64.2	9.2	653	96.6	25.0	39.4
Lake Catherine CDP	1,379	NA	NA	1,718	91.5	2.3	0.0	3.8	2.4	20.8	66.9	12.3	646	73.8	44.6	19.8
Lake Forest city	19,377	19,379	0.0	18,914	90.6	1.2	4.2	1.4	2.6	24.5	56.5	19.0	6,606	87.8	9.5	77.3
Lake Holiday CDP	4,761	NA	NA	4,738	95.3	0.0	0.5	0.6	3.6	24.2	64.4	11.5	1,660	91.7	39.2	31.9
Lake in the Hills village	28,971	28,893	-0.3	28,926	80.1	1.5	4.1	2.3	11.9	29.3	64.2	6.5	9,925	89.9	30.0	34.5
Lake Ka-Ho village	237	225	-5.1	232	96.1	0.0	0.0	0.0	3.9	19.4	59.4	21.1	113	88.5	62.8	8.8
Lakemoor village	6,014	6,005	-0.1	6,576	78.2	0.5	0.9	0.9	19.6	27.1	66.9	6.0	2,360	65.5	37.3	26.1

1 May be of any race.

Table A. All Places — **Population and Housing**

STATE City, town, township, borough, or CDP (county if applicable)	Population				Race and Hispanic or Latino origin (percent), 2010–2014					Age (percent), 2010–2014			Households, 2010–2014		Householders by level of education (percent)	
	2010 census total population	2014 estimated population	Percent change 2010–2014	ACS total population estimate 2010–2014	White alone, not Hispanic or Latino	Black alone, not Hispanic or Latino	Asian alone, not Hispanic or Latino	All other races or 2 or more races, not Hispanic or Latino	Hispanic or Latino[1]	Under 18 years old	Age 18 to 64 years old	Age 65 years and older	Total occupied housing units	Percent owner occupied	High school diploma or less	Bachelor's degree or more
	1	2	3	4	5	6	7	8	9	10	11	12	13	14	15	16
ILLINOIS—Con.																
Lake of the Woods CDP	2,912	NA	NA	2,855	97.3	0.0	0.0	2.7	0.0	26.9	59.7	13.3	1,236	79.2	39.7	21.4
Lake Petersburg CDP	719	NA	NA	667	96.3	0.0	3.7	0.0	0.0	8.8	56.4	34.6	355	97.7	36.3	40.8
Lake Summerset CDP	2,048	NA	NA	1,755	97.2	0.0	0.0	1.4	1.4	18.3	45.2	36.5	786	93.1	23.2	41.1
Lake Villa village	8,677	8,825	1.7	8,860	75.6	4.4	4.5	2.8	12.6	31.1	59.6	9.3	2,998	76.7	22.9	46.8
Lakewood village	3,854	3,811	-1.1	4,411	89.3	3.6	3.7	2.0	1.4	27.5	61.2	11.3	1,425	95.4	9.7	72.4
Lakewood Shores CDP	1,347	NA	NA	1,250	96.2	0.0	0.0	1.4	2.3	22.4	65.3	12.2	477	91.8	50.3	8.0
Lake Zurich village	19,676	20,054	1.9	19,849	81.3	0.9	8.8	1.9	7.1	27.7	64.3	8.0	6,633	88.8	19.6	56.5
La Moille village	726	705	-2.9	825	95.9	0.2	0.6	1.6	1.7	24.0	57.7	18.3	297	80.1	53.2	10.1
Lanark city	1,457	1,383	-5.1	1,650	94.5	0.2	0.6	2.7	2.1	26.1	58.0	16.0	681	81.1	41.3	14.8
Langleyville CDP	432	NA	NA	356	100.0	0.0	0.0	0.0	0.0	18.7	70.4	10.7	157	89.2	51.6	11.5
Lansing village	28,374	28,522	0.5	28,486	49.7	34.1	1.2	0.9	14.1	22.8	62.1	15.2	11,221	71.3	38.4	20.7
LaPlace CDP	259	NA	NA	146	92.5	0.0	0.0	7.5	0.0	15.8	76.0	8.2	63	100.0	63.5	11.1
La Prairie village	47	47	0.0	74	97.3	0.0	0.0	2.7	0.0	16.3	58.3	25.7	27	81.5	48.1	14.8
La Rose village	144	137	-4.9	129	100.0	0.0	0.0	0.0	0.0	17.1	60.6	22.5	61	95.1	63.9	18.0
LaSalle city	9,630	9,328	-3.1	9,537	86.8	0.1	0.6	2.3	10.2	22.6	62.5	14.9	4,007	63.1	45.1	13.5
Latham village	380	366	-3.7	265	96.6	0.0	0.0	3.4	0.0	27.9	45.6	26.4	115	72.2	38.3	12.2
Lawrenceville city	4,418	4,397	-0.5	4,665	87.0	6.0	0.2	3.3	3.5	26.9	47.6	25.5	2,019	65.7	52.8	13.5
Leaf River village	443	424	-4.3	586	91.0	0.3	0.0	8.0	0.7	28.7	53.2	18.1	246	70.3	58.9	9.8
Lebanon city	4,457	4,466	0.2	3,998	71.6	19.9	1.9	2.9	3.7	18.0	61.9	20.1	1,450	63.7	37.9	30.6
Lee village	337	330	-2.1	335	91.3	3.9	0.0	3.6	1.2	26.9	56.6	16.7	134	70.9	43.3	12.7
Leland village	977	951	-2.7	888	93.8	0.1	0.0	0.0	6.1	25.1	64.2	10.8	330	80.9	40.3	17.6
Leland Grove city	1,489	1,533	3.0	1,521	94.7	0.8	0.3	1.1	3.2	15.8	58.0	26.3	713	93.1	10.1	71.8
Lemont village	16,091	16,661	3.5	16,376	89.8	0.7	0.9	1.6	7.0	25.0	59.2	15.8	5,674	85.9	27.6	43.5
Lena village	2,912	2,840	-2.5	2,888	97.5	0.0	0.2	1.7	0.6	23.1	57.6	19.2	1,182	75.1	50.6	18.3
Lenzburg village	518	498	-3.9	524	79.6	0.0	15.1	1.7	3.6	33.8	55.2	11.1	188	66.5	41.5	11.2
Leonore village	130	127	-2.3	77	93.5	0.0	0.0	0.0	6.5	15.6	62.4	22.1	45	100.0	55.6	17.8
Lerna village	286	283	-1.0	315	95.6	0.0	0.0	0.0	4.4	27.3	59.9	12.7	100	69.0	56.0	6.0
Le Roy city	3,564	3,602	1.1	3,565	97.6	0.4	0.2	0.2	1.6	26.2	56.9	16.9	1,313	81.0	38.5	35.3
Lewistown city	2,384	2,292	-3.9	2,433	92.9	1.2	0.0	1.6	4.3	17.8	60.6	21.7	1,037	74.9	46.4	14.5
Lexington city	2,064	2,068	0.2	2,213	96.6	0.0	0.8	1.0	1.6	24.3	58.7	17.0	892	84.4	35.7	30.6
Liberty village	516	513	-0.6	466	86.5	0.4	0.0	0.0	13.1	30.6	48.7	20.6	165	81.8	35.8	29.1
Libertyville village	20,327	20,512	0.9	20,398	89.1	1.0	4.9	1.1	4.0	23.7	59.9	16.2	7,633	78.7	11.7	67.5
Lily Lake village	993	1,024	3.1	1,082	93.2	0.9	0.0	0.9	5.0	29.0	63.0	7.9	326	91.4	20.9	34.4
Lima village	161	160	-0.6	179	94.4	0.0	0.0	0.0	5.6	21.3	68.1	10.6	68	94.1	76.5	8.8
Limestone village	1,603	1,573	-1.9	1,452	93.9	2.5	0.5	1.6	1.5	23.2	61.9	14.9	558	88.0	37.1	21.9
Lincoln city	14,502	14,162	-2.3	14,382	88.3	2.8	1.1	6.3	1.5	22.0	58.1	20.0	6,566	61.5	45.6	19.2
Lincolnshire village	7,274	7,292	0.2	7,270	86.5	0.7	8.1	2.1	2.7	20.5	47.7	31.6	2,929	81.6	9.6	74.7
Lincolnwood village	12,590	12,687	0.8	12,653	60.0	2.6	28.6	1.4	7.4	21.4	54.6	23.9	4,179	86.6	20.9	60.1
Lindenhurst village	14,384	14,468	0.6	14,412	82.1	1.2	5.4	3.2	8.0	29.5	61.3	9.4	5,018	86.9	18.9	47.6
Lisbon village	285	295	3.5	333	99.4	0.0	0.0	0.6	0.0	32.1	55.2	12.6	127	69.3	48.8	19.7
Lisle village	22,451	22,827	1.7	22,626	70.4	5.3	10.9	3.5	9.9	20.7	66.5	12.9	9,170	59.0	15.5	54.3
Litchfield city	7,128	6,930	-2.8	6,913	97.1	1.4	0.4	0.2	0.8	23.8	53.4	22.8	3,262	67.7	53.3	14.0
Littleton village	181	177	-2.2	205	95.1	0.0	0.0	0.0	4.9	19.5	65.3	15.1	91	79.1	60.4	20.9
Little York village	331	335	1.2	289	98.3	0.7	0.0	0.0	1.0	21.4	67.0	11.4	125	79.2	42.4	4.8
Liverpool village	129	125	-3.1	115	100.0	0.0	0.0	0.0	0.0	27.8	54.7	17.4	45	48.9	75.6	0.0
Livingston village	858	833	-2.9	855	95.3	0.9	0.1	2.7	0.9	18.7	63.7	17.5	388	76.0	51.0	9.5
Loami village	745	754	1.2	840	88.8	0.4	0.2	3.9	6.7	31.6	59.3	8.9	309	79.0	42.1	17.8
Lockport city	24,886	25,119	0.9	25,063	86.8	1.8	1.7	1.5	8.3	27.8	62.7	9.5	9,005	87.3	29.6	33.1
Loda village	407	400	-1.7	420	94.3	2.6	0.0	0.7	2.4	23.0	67.2	9.8	163	80.4	54.6	8.6
Lomax village	454	421	-7.3	328	93.0	0.0	0.0	2.4	4.6	14.1	54.6	31.4	165	73.3	69.1	7.3
Lombard village	43,395	43,893	1.1	43,853	76.4	5.0	8.8	1.9	7.9	19.4	65.2	15.4	17,781	73.8	24.6	42.6
London Mills village	392	383	-2.3	413	92.5	0.0	0.0	3.1	4.4	26.4	57.1	16.5	143	87.4	48.3	16.8
Long Creek village	1,324	1,318	-0.5	1,383	93.3	0.0	0.7	3.8	2.2	24.1	60.5	15.2	480	92.9	46.3	25.2
Long Grove village	8,048	8,181	1.7	8,017	76.5	3.0	12.1	3.4	5.1	26.0	62.3	11.7	2,371	97.8	8.3	70.8
Long Lake CDP	3,515	NA	NA	3,217	62.9	1.1	1.4	1.9	32.7	27.1	62.0	10.9	1,169	78.1	50.1	14.6
Long Point village	226	220	-2.7	203	93.6	0.0	0.0	2.5	3.9	19.7	60.6	19.7	94	94.7	50.0	12.8
Longview village	153	155	1.3	172	96.5	0.0	0.0	0.0	3.5	25.1	60.0	15.1	70	97.1	68.6	11.4
Loraine village	313	311	-0.6	279	95.0	0.0	0.0	1.1	3.9	19.0	59.9	21.1	120	81.7	63.3	8.3
Lostant village	506	485	-4.2	365	97.3	0.3	0.5	0.3	1.6	24.3	54.8	20.8	145	86.2	42.8	18.6
Lost Nation CDP	708	NA	NA	594	100.0	0.0	0.0	0.0	0.0	12.1	65.1	22.7	262	96.2	32.8	36.6
Louisville village	1,148	1,125	-2.0	1,022	97.8	1.4	0.2	0.6	0.0	21.5	57.4	21.0	416	75.0	46.2	14.4
Loves Park city	24,001	23,551	-1.9	24,435	83.7	3.7	2.6	1.9	8.1	24.2	61.9	13.9	9,670	71.1	39.6	23.9
Lovington village	1,130	1,109	-1.9	1,030	96.3	0.2	0.0	3.5	0.0	20.5	67.8	11.8	452	68.6	62.8	5.5
Ludlow village	371	367	-1.1	446	94.6	3.6	0.0	1.8	0.0	29.4	64.2	6.5	153	58.8	44.4	9.8
Lyndon village	648	625	-3.5	724	92.3	2.5	0.4	2.8	2.1	30.7	52.6	16.7	266	85.3	53.0	12.8
Lynnville village	117	116	-0.9	68	92.6	0.0	0.0	4.4	2.9	20.5	66.2	13.2	33	93.9	57.6	15.2
Lynwood village	9,053	9,313	2.9	9,260	20.9	67.7	0.9	1.1	9.5	25.6	62.2	12.1	3,137	80.1	25.5	33.9
Lyons village	10,729	10,773	0.4	10,667	46.5	3.9	1.8	1.8	45.9	21.6	64.5	13.9	3,811	63.1	50.4	19.4
McClure village	402	364	-9.5	348	99.7	0.0	0.0	0.3	0.0	18.4	63.9	17.8	130	76.2	64.6	5.4
McCook village	228	231	1.3	212	75.0	0.0	5.2	1.4	18.4	16.5	64.2	19.3	90	46.7	43.3	30.0
McCullom Lake village	1,049	1,026	-2.2	1,001	82.4	0.7	0.4	2.1	14.4	21.8	68.0	10.3	394	63.5	56.6	4.1
Macedonia village	63	63	0.0	52	100.0	0.0	0.0	0.0	0.0	0.0	57.7	42.3	23	95.7	43.5	0.0
McHenry city	26,994	26,630	-1.3	26,803	82.3	0.3	2.4	1.6	13.4	24.3	62.2	13.5	10,194	75.0	38.9	24.7
Machesney Park village	23,495	23,036	-2.0	23,180	88.9	2.0	1.8	1.7	5.6	24.3	62.8	12.9	8,610	78.8	46.5	15.0
Mackinaw village	1,950	1,950	0.0	2,407	93.0	0.0	0.7	0.5	5.8	27.6	58.3	14.1	892	71.5	38.6	22.8
McLean village	830	823	-0.8	841	99.0	0.0	0.4	0.2	0.4	19.4	60.4	20.3	354	88.4	48.0	13.8
McLeansboro city	2,883	2,826	-2.0	2,753	95.4	1.3	0.0	0.4	2.9	22.0	50.3	27.8	1,206	67.1	52.0	12.9
McNabb village	285	273	-4.2	376	96.8	0.0	1.6	0.0	1.6	30.8	60.9	8.2	131	84.0	42.0	13.7
Macomb city	19,294	18,943	-1.8	19,193	83.7	7.8	2.7	2.0	3.8	12.5	75.6	11.8	7,014	46.6	24.8	41.0
Macon city	1,138	1,142	0.4	1,168	96.2	0.0	0.0	3.3	0.5	22.2	56.2	21.5	493	79.3	45.0	15.4
Madison city	3,891	3,893	0.1	4,061	37.6	54.8	0.7	2.4	4.5	25.6	61.1	13.3	1,655	51.5	61.1	7.1
Maeystown village	159	158	-0.6	160	96.3	0.0	0.0	0.0	3.8	30.7	48.8	20.6	67	85.1	23.9	29.9
Magnolia village	260	260	0.0	345	94.8	0.0	0.0	1.7	3.5	30.7	60.8	8.4	117	66.7	70.1	15.4
Mahomet village	7,259	7,955	9.6	7,592	92.6	0.1	1.6	4.5	1.1	30.5	58.6	10.9	2,734	81.3	16.1	55.9
Makanda village	561	547	-2.5	530	75.1	2.6	20.4	1.1	0.8	13.8	76.0	10.4	239	86.6	20.9	55.2
Malden village	362	352	-2.8	427	97.4	0.0	0.0	2.6	0.0	30.0	57.5	12.4	152	77.6	51.3	7.9
Malta village	1,164	1,159	-0.4	1,115	89.1	3.3	1.1	3.0	3.5	35.1	52.4	12.3	366	80.1	41.0	15.6
Manchester village	292	286	-2.1	385	96.9	0.0	1.0	2.1	0.0	24.2	57.9	17.9	136	88.2	50.0	14.7
Manhattan village	7,051	7,302	3.6	7,017	90.5	0.1	0.7	1.0	7.7	31.5	60.8	7.6	2,422	85.3	27.2	34.2
Manito village	1,642	1,550	-5.6	1,752	98.0	0.0	0.0	0.5	1.5	24.5	59.4	16.0	696	78.7	45.7	12.9
Manlius village	359	349	-2.8	408	94.9	0.0	0.0	1.0	4.2	25.7	49.5	24.8	169	84.0	58.0	4.1

1 May be of any race.

Table A. All Places — **Population and Housing**

STATE City, town, township, borough, or CDP (county if applicable)	Population: 2010 census total population	Population: 2014 estimated population	Population: Percent change 2010–2014	Population: ACS total population estimate 2010–2014	Race and Hispanic or Latino origin (percent), 2010–2014: White alone, not Hispanic or Latino	Black alone, not Hispanic or Latino	Asian alone, not Hispanic or Latino	All other races or 2 or more races, not Hispanic or Latino	Hispanic or Latino[1]	Age (percent), 2010–2014: Under 18 years old	Age 18 to 64 years old	Age 65 years and older	Households, 2010–2014: Total occupied housing units	Percent owner occupied	Householders by level of education (percent): High school diploma or less	Bachelor's degree or more
	1	2	3	4	5	6	7	8	9	10	11	12	13	14	15	16
ILLINOIS—Con.																
Mansfield village	906	872	-3.8	941	95.9	0.0	0.4	2.6	1.2	18.9	60.9	20.3	407	79.6	57.2	9.1
Manteno village	9,204	9,026	-1.9	9,585	90.7	0.6	1.4	1.6	5.8	25.7	59.2	15.1	3,854	74.1	40.3	29.2
Maple Park village	1,310	1,313	0.2	1,366	89.8	0.4	1.6	2.9	5.4	32.6	56.7	10.7	505	76.8	29.1	24.2
Mapleton village	270	276	2.2	310	99.0	0.0	0.0	0.0	1.0	26.7	63.9	9.4	107	86.9	55.1	11.2
Maquon village	289	286	-1.0	370	97.3	0.0	0.0	0.0	2.7	23.3	67.0	9.7	137	79.6	51.1	5.8
Marengo city	7,648	7,508	-1.8	7,451	79.3	2.2	0.3	1.5	16.8	25.5	62.8	11.6	2,628	65.5	43.6	21.9
Marietta village	112	109	-2.7	198	96.5	0.0	0.0	0.0	3.5	5.1	83.9	11.1	76	92.1	84.2	1.3
Marine village	960	939	-2.2	1,199	98.9	0.0	0.0	0.9	0.2	16.6	67.6	15.8	499	72.9	40.5	25.5
Marion city	17,192	17,438	1.4	17,353	86.4	6.7	1.9	2.7	2.3	21.1	59.4	19.6	7,424	61.5	31.3	26.5
Marissa village	1,977	1,882	-4.8	2,253	99.4	0.0	0.0	0.6	0.0	25.1	58.4	16.5	840	71.8	53.5	10.0
Mark village	555	547	-1.4	615	90.6	0.0	1.3	2.9	5.2	26.2	62.2	11.5	244	75.4	38.1	15.2
Markham city	12,508	12,688	1.4	12,625	9.7	80.7	0.4	0.7	8.6	26.9	59.1	14.1	4,478	69.8	46.1	13.7
Maroa city	1,801	1,756	-2.5	1,853	88.3	0.3	0.1	7.9	3.3	23.4	58.3	18.2	715	79.9	49.1	16.4
Marquette Heights city	2,824	2,790	-1.2	2,789	93.3	0.6	0.3	3.0	2.8	27.6	61.7	10.6	968	87.1	47.2	12.3
Marseilles city	5,117	4,994	-2.4	4,832	92.5	0.0	0.6	1.7	5.2	26.3	58.0	15.7	1,832	72.4	56.1	6.4
Marshall city	3,933	3,921	-0.3	3,895	95.0	1.0	0.5	2.0	1.5	24.7	55.2	20.2	1,700	59.2	45.9	17.9
Martinsville city	1,167	1,151	-1.4	1,150	92.3	0.9	0.3	1.8	4.8	21.1	58.6	20.3	505	61.8	47.7	15.2
Martinton village	381	375	-1.6	316	96.8	0.9	0.6	0.0	1.6	26.9	65.7	7.3	113	75.2	41.6	9.7
Maryville village	7,487	7,826	4.5	7,727	92.6	1.9	1.5	1.7	2.2	20.7	62.4	17.0	3,004	82.4	28.3	46.0
Mascoutah city	7,509	7,869	4.8	7,675	89.3	5.2	0.5	4.2	0.9	28.5	59.8	11.8	2,753	68.5	29.7	27.2
Mason town	345	343	-0.6	404	98.3	0.0	1.5	0.2	0.0	30.0	57.0	13.1	138	84.1	79.7	3.6
Mason City city	2,343	2,212	-5.6	2,374	96.0	0.5	1.2	1.6	0.7	23.0	56.6	20.6	1,047	70.7	56.8	8.3
Matherville village	721	689	-4.4	941	95.0	0.0	0.5	2.0	2.4	24.1	66.2	9.7	405	76.8	61.0	5.2
Matteson village	19,009	19,156	0.8	19,097	14.6	81.0	0.4	1.0	3.0	25.1	61.9	13.2	6,778	79.7	26.6	36.1
Mattoon city	18,555	18,211	-1.9	17,906	94.0	1.4	0.3	2.2	2.2	22.3	59.6	18.1	7,632	60.6	47.4	16.4
Maunie village	139	137	-1.4	102	100.0	0.0	0.0	0.0	0.0	16.7	68.6	14.7	44	84.1	90.9	0.0
Maywood village	24,090	24,133	0.2	24,148	4.8	72.5	0.3	0.7	21.8	24.9	62.2	13.0	7,635	62.0	51.9	12.9
Mazon village	1,015	996	-1.9	1,093	91.1	0.0	1.0	5.0	2.8	30.7	55.4	13.9	401	68.3	48.6	15.0
Mechanicsburg village	590	605	2.5	570	94.2	3.2	0.4	0.7	1.6	27.4	60.8	11.8	218	86.2	44.5	12.4
Media village	107	101	-5.6	126	99.2	0.0	0.0	0.8	0.0	6.4	74.7	19.0	63	92.1	90.5	4.8
Medora village	419	408	-2.6	434	91.7	0.0	0.9	7.4	0.0	19.9	69.6	10.6	169	74.6	57.4	11.8
Melrose Park village	25,414	25,511	0.4	25,514	20.1	4.4	1.0	0.5	73.9	29.6	60.4	9.9	7,555	50.6	63.0	11.7
Melvin village	452	436	-3.5	478	90.0	2.7	0.0	0.2	7.1	26.9	54.7	18.4	192	83.3	67.2	14.6
Mendon village	953	944	-0.9	851	98.6	0.6	0.1	0.7	0.0	25.0	55.8	19.3	323	69.0	42.1	15.5
Mendota city	7,372	7,254	-1.6	7,161	70.8	1.8	0.9	2.0	24.5	25.6	57.5	17.0	2,624	70.2	59.0	12.7
Menominee village	252	247	-2.0	239	99.2	0.0	0.0	0.4	0.4	30.5	49.7	19.7	88	63.6	37.5	12.5
Meredosia village	1,044	1,022	-2.1	1,045	98.5	0.3	0.0	1.0	0.3	23.5	59.7	16.9	453	68.4	59.2	5.5
Merrionette Park village	1,900	1,897	-0.2	1,748	81.8	7.8	2.2	1.5	6.6	15.9	74.2	10.0	782	69.7	44.6	19.7
Metamora village	3,658	3,736	2.1	3,544	95.8	0.1	2.1	0.8	1.3	26.5	55.7	17.8	1,309	75.2	43.3	27.8
Metcalf village	189	183	-3.2	249	96.8	0.0	0.0	3.2	0.0	26.9	56.5	16.5	101	91.1	72.3	0.0
Metropolis city	6,570	6,390	-2.7	6,466	90.2	6.3	0.9	1.4	1.2	21.6	57.2	21.1	2,735	57.8	53.0	13.5
Mettawa village	563	571	1.4	455	79.8	0.0	4.8	8.8	6.6	22.3	60.0	17.6	186	90.9	11.8	71.0
Middletown village	324	317	-2.2	296	90.2	0.0	1.4	8.1	0.3	18.2	58.5	23.3	142	76.1	62.7	6.3
Midlothian village	14,819	14,911	0.6	14,901	66.5	7.4	2.1	2.8	21.1	23.9	65.4	10.6	5,472	75.0	44.9	16.8
Milan village	5,160	5,105	-1.1	5,122	89.2	2.6	0.5	4.5	3.2	16.9	62.8	20.1	2,448	66.3	52.0	12.4
Milford village	1,306	1,254	-4.0	1,281	92.1	0.0	0.0	1.2	6.6	21.8	56.5	21.9	556	71.9	64.7	10.6
Millbrook village	335	347	3.6	329	89.7	0.0	0.6	0.0	9.7	13.1	76.4	10.6	133	94.0	31.6	24.8
Mill Creek village	65	64	-1.5	48	100.0	0.0	0.0	0.0	0.0	8.4	87.7	4.2	21	100.0	61.9	9.5
Milledgeville village	1,032	989	-4.2	1,034	99.3	0.1	0.0	0.5	0.1	21.8	58.1	20.0	428	82.5	59.3	10.0
Millington village	665	665	0.0	665	98.8	0.0	0.0	0.0	1.2	29.1	61.5	9.3	223	91.5	48.4	14.3
Mill Shoals village	215	212	-1.4	168	95.2	0.0	0.0	0.0	4.8	13.2	65.0	22.0	76	81.6	59.2	3.9
Millstadt village	3,986	3,924	-1.6	3,955	99.6	0.0	0.0	0.0	0.4	21.5	62.1	16.5	1,561	86.8	36.3	30.9
Milton village	271	265	-2.2	296	99.3	0.0	0.0	0.0	0.7	29.8	56.1	14.2	90	91.1	72.2	5.6
Mineral village	237	230	-3.0	246	95.5	1.2	0.0	2.0	1.2	28.9	56.6	14.6	100	75.0	57.0	3.0
Minier village	1,252	1,245	-0.6	1,206	98.3	0.0	0.0	0.8	0.8	24.0	59.3	16.6	491	78.4	46.2	20.6
Minonk city	2,078	2,061	-0.8	2,160	98.3	0.0	0.0	0.0	1.7	25.7	56.8	17.5	855	84.6	49.8	14.4
Minooka village	10,924	11,194	2.5	11,225	85.0	2.4	0.0	1.4	11.2	31.7	62.6	5.8	3,551	83.6	29.4	30.2
Mitchell CDP	1,356	NA	NA	1,301	94.2	0.0	5.8	0.0	0.0	14.9	69.1	15.9	561	83.6	46.0	14.8
Modesto village	189	184	-2.6	167	97.6	0.0	0.0	0.0	2.4	27.0	56.4	16.8	60	85.0	46.7	8.3
Mokena village	18,738	19,447	3.8	18,804	92.3	0.7	1.3	1.1	4.6	23.6	65.9	10.5	6,276	91.7	23.5	40.9
Moline city	43,471	42,685	-1.8	43,087	75.6	4.8	2.3	1.6	15.8	22.5	62.0	15.7	18,114	66.7	38.2	25.7
Momence city	3,310	3,240	-2.1	3,155	68.5	6.9	0.0	1.2	23.4	22.9	65.5	11.8	1,096	70.5	59.2	7.8
Monee village	5,146	5,105	-0.8	5,133	74.7	8.9	4.1	1.9	10.5	27.4	56.9	15.7	1,866	90.8	38.2	26.6
Monmouth city	9,444	9,527	0.9	9,565	77.5	4.6	2.3	1.2	14.6	23.2	62.1	14.7	3,458	63.5	49.4	18.7
Monroe Center village	471	459	-2.5	473	94.7	0.0	1.1	1.5	2.7	27.3	60.9	11.6	175	83.4	46.3	22.3
Montgomery village	18,377	19,301	5.0	18,780	55.4	5.3	3.6	1.2	34.5	32.9	60.8	6.2	5,826	86.0	30.2	31.0
Monticello city	5,548	5,516	-0.6	5,400	97.5	0.6	0.0	0.4	1.5	23.9	56.4	19.5	2,233	80.9	34.3	36.9
Montrose village	201	200	-0.5	248	79.4	0.0	0.0	6.5	14.1	27.8	54.4	17.7	97	76.3	62.9	12.4
Morris city	13,636	14,135	3.7	13,929	84.2	1.6	0.5	0.1	13.6	23.2	62.2	14.5	5,455	60.3	41.9	26.8
Morrison city	4,188	4,136	-1.2	4,118	89.8	1.7	0.2	3.2	5.1	21.7	58.3	20.0	1,621	73.9	43.6	18.7
Morrisonville village	1,056	1,033	-2.2	885	99.2	0.0	0.0	0.8	0.0	25.4	55.3	19.2	353	88.1	57.5	9.3
Morton village	16,273	16,499	1.4	16,493	93.5	1.4	1.2	1.1	2.7	24.3	56.8	18.9	6,498	77.1	24.0	42.6
Morton Grove village	23,270	23,497	1.0	23,424	59.3	1.7	29.1	3.7	6.3	19.0	58.6	22.4	8,343	91.7	28.9	45.2
Mound City city	595	558	-6.2	603	42.8	47.9	0.3	0.0	9.0	29.1	56.7	14.3	217	61.3	67.3	9.2
Mounds city	810	763	-5.8	1,225	29.3	68.3	0.7	0.6	1.1	32.8	55.1	12.2	402	62.9	47.0	11.2
Mound Station village	122	120	-1.6	134	94.0	0.0	0.0	6.0	0.0	24.7	61.9	13.4	44	86.4	56.8	6.8
Mount Auburn village	480	468	-2.5	535	96.4	0.0	0.7	2.8	0.0	25.0	61.4	13.6	217	86.6	64.1	2.3
Mount Carmel city	7,284	7,034	-3.4	7,155	95.1	0.4	1.1	1.5	1.8	19.8	60.4	19.8	3,060	70.7	39.5	21.2
Mount Carroll city	1,717	1,634	-4.8	1,670	95.1	0.4	0.6	3.0	0.9	20.8	53.8	25.3	754	79.7	53.3	15.8
Mount Clare village	278	271	-2.5	222	98.6	0.0	0.0	1.4	0.0	11.3	62.8	26.1	100	88.0	67.0	10.0
Mount Erie village	88	88	0.0	112	97.3	0.0	2.7	0.0	0.0	26.0	63.5	10.7	45	75.6	40.0	4.4
Mount Morris village	2,998	2,905	-3.1	3,155	92.2	0.1	0.0	0.0	7.7	26.5	55.8	17.7	1,237	62.3	46.7	13.7
Mount Olive city	2,106	2,032	-3.5	2,085	99.8	0.0	0.0	0.2	0.0	22.9	60.2	16.9	870	84.0	52.1	11.3
Mount Prospect village	54,243	54,951	1.3	54,589	67.2	2.2	11.9	1.8	17.0	23.4	61.8	14.9	20,288	71.4	30.3	40.2
Mount Pulaski city	1,566	1,528	-2.4	1,257	94.8	0.0	0.0	4.9	0.2	27.6	47.2	25.2	528	82.4	47.9	21.6
Mount Sterling city	2,025	1,973	-2.6	2,165	91.0	3.2	2.6	3.1	0.0	20.2	64.8	15.1	882	69.0	49.8	12.2
Mount Vernon city	15,283	15,177	-0.7	15,069	77.7	13.5	2.1	4.0	2.7	22.6	58.5	18.9	6,603	55.5	42.0	16.4
Mount Zion village	5,833	5,888	0.9	5,830	92.9	3.0	0.0	1.3	2.8	27.7	58.1	14.1	2,153	82.8	26.1	39.8
Moweaqua village	1,831	1,777	-2.9	1,793	97.7	0.8	0.4	0.6	0.5	23.1	58.9	17.9	755	69.7	57.6	16.6
Muddy village	69	69	0.0	37	78.4	0.0	0.0	10.8	10.8	10.8	67.5	21.6	17	23.5	29.4	0.0
Mulberry Grove village	634	605	-4.6	744	96.8	1.6	0.0	1.6	0.0	33.4	54.8	11.7	243	78.6	63.0	6.2

1 May be of any race.

Table A. All Places — **Population and Housing**

STATE City, town, township, borough, or CDP (county if applicable)	Population: 2010 census total population	Population: 2014 estimated population	Population: Percent change 2010–2014	Population: ACS total population estimate 2010–2014	Race and Hispanic or Latino origin (percent), 2010–2014: White alone, not Hispanic or Latino	Black alone, not Hispanic or Latino	Asian alone, not Hispanic or Latino	All other races or 2 or more races, not Hispanic or Latino	Hispanic or Latino[1]	Age (percent), 2010–2014: Under 18 years old	Age 18 to 64 years old	Age 65 years and older	Households, 2010–2014: Total occupied housing units	Percent owner occupied	Householders by level of education (percent): High school diploma or less	Bachelor's degree or more
	1	2	3	4	5	6	7	8	9	10	11	12	13	14	15	16
ILLINOIS—Con.																
Mulkeytown CDP	175	NA	NA	130	100.0	0.0	0.0	0.0	0.0	15.4	58.4	26.2	64	100.0	40.6	59.4
Muncie village	146	144	-1.4	151	100.0	0.0	0.0	0.0	0.0	17.9	68.2	13.9	74	75.7	35.1	16.2
Mundelein village	31,012	31,562	1.8	31,498	57.8	1.6	8.1	1.7	30.8	25.0	65.3	9.6	10,808	75.8	28.6	45.6
Murphysboro city	7,967	7,811	-2.0	8,189	82.9	12.1	0.5	3.5	1.0	18.5	61.5	19.9	3,617	60.1	41.0	23.4
Murrayville village	587	573	-2.4	573	99.8	0.0	0.0	0.0	0.2	21.7	61.9	16.6	248	65.3	61.3	10.9
Naperville city	142,087	146,128	2.8	144,108	69.6	4.5	16.8	2.8	6.3	27.4	62.6	10.0	49,741	75.7	11.5	68.8
Naplate village	496	485	-2.2	497	91.5	3.2	0.0	0.8	4.4	18.7	62.1	19.1	226	66.8	50.0	6.6
Naples town	130	127	-2.3	61	100.0	0.0	0.0	0.0	0.0	6.6	70.5	23.0	26	100.0	88.5	0.0
Nashville city	3,258	3,148	-3.4	3,352	96.7	1.2	1.2	0.0	1.0	23.5	52.1	24.4	1,334	68.6	32.3	31.4
Nason city	236	236	0.0	218	99.1	0.0	0.9	0.0	0.0	5.5	69.8	24.8	114	87.7	56.1	0.0
Nauvoo city	1,149	1,110	-3.4	1,195	93.0	2.3	1.0	2.3	1.4	19.9	50.2	29.9	488	66.6	41.8	29.3
Nebo village	340	332	-2.4	381	95.8	0.0	0.0	2.6	1.6	22.5	64.8	12.6	161	93.2	78.9	0.0
Nelson village	170	164	-3.5	219	93.2	0.0	0.0	0.5	6.4	30.6	65.8	3.7	58	86.2	62.1	15.5
Neoga city	1,636	1,607	-1.8	1,598	95.5	0.3	0.6	1.4	2.3	22.0	58.5	19.5	625	75.5	45.4	16.8
Neponset village	473	451	-4.7	523	90.4	0.2	1.5	2.1	5.7	24.1	66.3	9.6	194	91.2	43.3	11.9
Newark village	987	1,017	3.0	1,108	93.8	0.0	0.2	0.0	6.0	29.3	59.0	11.8	382	79.3	42.7	18.6
New Athens village	2,058	1,977	-3.9	2,108	97.4	1.0	0.0	0.3	1.2	26.2	57.8	15.9	777	80.6	39.8	20.1
New Baden village	3,349	3,330	-0.6	3,413	90.8	4.5	2.0	1.4	1.3	23.9	63.1	13.0	1,242	78.0	25.2	25.8
New Bedford village	75	73	-2.7	73	98.6	0.0	1.4	0.0	0.0	21.8	45.1	32.9	34	100.0	67.6	2.9
New Berlin village	1,346	1,356	0.7	1,444	99.0	0.7	0.0	0.0	0.3	28.1	58.7	13.2	553	68.9	32.9	33.3
New Boston city	683	658	-3.7	707	96.0	0.0	1.6	0.3	2.1	20.6	65.6	13.7	306	83.7	58.8	3.3
New Burnside village	211	213	0.9	188	97.9	0.0	0.0	2.1	0.0	22.8	50.1	27.1	74	87.8	59.5	8.1
New Canton town	359	350	-2.5	391	98.0	0.0	0.0	2.0	0.0	24.5	60.8	14.6	176	61.9	66.5	0.0
New Douglas village	319	319	0.0	372	94.4	1.9	0.0	3.8	0.0	25.0	63.8	11.3	134	73.9	45.5	25.4
New Grand Chain village	210	200	-4.8	194	90.2	0.0	0.0	3.1	6.7	25.8	64.0	10.3	84	72.6	38.1	14.3
New Haven village	433	406	-6.2	406	94.8	0.0	0.0	5.2	0.0	17.0	61.6	21.4	180	81.1	52.2	2.2
New Holland village	269	265	-1.5	173	97.7	0.0	0.0	1.7	0.6	16.1	56.6	27.2	84	85.7	45.2	19.0
New Lenox village	24,381	25,426	4.3	24,747	90.8	0.8	1.6	0.9	5.9	29.2	61.4	9.3	8,137	86.5	28.4	37.4
Newman city	865	855	-1.2	895	97.4	1.3	0.0	0.3	0.9	22.3	56.5	21.1	372	75.0	45.7	12.6
New Milford village	697	676	-3.0	756	84.3	4.0	6.9	0.4	4.5	27.3	60.1	12.4	294	73.5	49.3	11.2
New Minden village	215	208	-3.3	222	100.0	0.0	0.0	0.0	0.0	22.1	64.1	14.0	86	90.7	53.5	7.0
New Salem village	137	134	-2.2	135	94.1	5.9	0.0	0.0	0.0	34.1	55.5	10.4	51	76.5	33.3	11.8
Newton city	2,849	2,821	-1.0	2,872	99.0	0.4	0.0	0.2	0.3	20.5	58.6	20.8	1,258	73.1	43.6	19.6
Niantic village	707	682	-3.5	621	93.6	0.0	0.0	6.4	0.0	19.9	65.8	14.5	303	86.5	51.8	14.2
Niles village	29,803	30,000	0.7	29,939	67.7	1.6	17.7	1.7	11.3	17.1	57.4	25.5	11,398	75.4	41.7	29.3
Nilwood town	239	233	-2.5	226	92.9	0.4	3.1	3.5	0.0	19.0	66.0	15.0	91	83.5	65.9	14.3
Noble village	677	671	-0.9	553	98.9	0.2	0.4	0.5	0.0	20.1	61.2	18.8	245	81.6	51.4	10.6
Nokomis city	2,256	2,195	-2.7	2,358	97.9	0.3	0.6	0.3	0.9	29.0	46.3	24.8	1,002	76.7	51.4	19.4
Nora village	117	115	-1.7	104	100.0	0.0	0.0	0.0	0.0	8.7	69.1	22.1	49	69.4	93.9	2.0
Normal town	52,535	54,594	3.9	54,082	81.1	7.4	3.7	2.6	5.2	17.9	73.4	8.7	18,877	57.8	20.3	46.6
Norridge village	14,572	14,674	0.7	14,713	86.3	0.4	4.9	0.3	8.1	16.3	59.5	24.0	5,506	85.1	49.0	21.3
Norris village	213	206	-3.3	194	100.0	0.0	0.0	0.0	0.0	30.4	56.7	12.9	76	86.8	47.4	14.5
Norris City village	1,275	1,251	-1.9	1,576	99.7	0.0	0.0	0.3	0.0	28.8	54.0	17.2	669	76.8	41.6	9.4
North Aurora village	16,732	17,342	3.6	16,927	72.1	7.1	6.8	2.6	11.4	26.4	64.7	8.8	5,776	78.2	25.5	42.6
North Barrington village	3,022	3,029	0.2	3,105	92.1	0.0	2.5	3.2	2.3	21.7	63.2	14.9	1,090	95.5	8.1	70.4
Northbrook village	33,173	33,655	1.5	33,396	82.7	0.7	11.7	2.3	2.7	24.1	52.3	23.5	12,287	87.6	10.9	72.7
North Chicago city	32,575	30,395	-6.7	30,760	34.2	28.5	4.1	4.6	28.5	21.9	73.5	4.6	6,765	37.4	49.1	20.9
North City village	608	596	-2.0	891	98.8	0.0	0.0	1.2	0.0	29.5	57.4	13.1	301	89.4	43.2	18.6
Northfield village	5,420	5,483	1.2	5,332	89.6	0.0	7.5	1.2	1.7	24.5	52.3	23.2	2,072	87.6	7.3	75.3
North Henderson village	187	181	-3.2	201	100.0	0.0	0.0	0.0	0.0	21.4	63.8	14.9	77	76.6	45.5	26.0
Northlake city	12,326	12,372	0.4	12,368	35.1	2.5	3.1	1.4	57.9	26.6	60.8	12.7	3,650	71.3	57.5	13.9
North Pekin village	1,569	1,596	1.7	1,464	97.7	0.0	1.4	1.0	0.0	24.9	60.8	14.2	581	84.9	57.5	6.5
North Riverside village	6,672	6,698	0.4	6,940	60.7	6.2	1.3	3.3	28.6	21.0	60.3	18.6	2,765	66.7	41.7	23.9
North Utica village	1,350	1,356	0.4	1,381	94.7	0.0	1.6	0.0	3.7	23.6	59.7	16.7	547	88.7	41.0	15.4
Norwood village	478	477	-0.2	453	93.4	1.5	0.0	3.8	1.3	15.8	61.2	23.2	191	91.1	57.6	8.9
Oak Brook village	7,883	8,065	2.3	7,967	65.9	2.2	22.0	6.0	3.9	16.5	53.6	29.9	3,048	93.8	13.7	72.6
Oakbrook Terrace city	2,134	2,171	1.7	2,061	70.2	7.5	12.4	3.1	6.8	13.9	67.6	18.5	968	50.6	15.9	50.7
Oakdale village	221	214	-3.2	195	97.4	0.0	0.0	0.0	2.6	27.7	55.0	17.4	81	91.4	30.9	19.8
Oakford village	286	283	-1.0	280	93.2	0.0	0.0	1.4	5.4	23.5	62.5	13.9	124	79.0	50.8	6.5
Oak Forest city	27,962	28,174	0.8	28,104	77.7	5.0	1.7	2.8	12.8	21.2	66.3	12.4	10,145	79.8	37.0	26.8
Oak Grove village	595	574	-3.5	756	88.5	5.6	0.4	2.0	3.6	32.2	59.0	8.7	305	67.5	58.4	5.9
Oakland city	880	886	0.7	751	98.4	0.0	0.8	0.0	0.8	15.7	56.2	28.4	363	84.3	50.4	18.2
Oak Lawn village	56,687	57,034	0.6	56,969	74.9	4.8	1.6	2.1	16.6	21.2	60.9	17.8	21,701	81.3	39.2	28.8
Oak Park village	51,878	52,008	0.3	51,988	63.2	20.8	5.2	3.6	7.2	24.4	63.9	11.5	21,658	59.7	10.9	68.7
Oak Run CDP	547	NA	NA	434	96.3	0.9	2.8	0.0	0.0	6.2	56.2	37.6	230	100.0	16.5	47.4
Oakwood village	1,595	1,542	-3.3	1,750	91.8	0.0	0.6	1.6	6.1	25.3	59.5	15.1	694	77.5	45.0	16.9
Oakwood Hills village	2,083	2,070	-0.6	2,079	93.1	0.0	1.1	1.5	4.3	16.8	72.3	10.9	798	91.9	25.6	37.2
Oblong village	1,466	1,426	-2.7	1,569	95.1	0.7	0.0	4.1	0.1	24.4	54.6	20.8	626	81.6	47.9	16.0
Oconee village	180	178	-1.1	159	98.7	0.0	0.0	1.3	0.0	31.4	53.9	14.5	64	75.0	45.3	4.7
Odell village	1,046	1,015	-3.0	1,014	96.8	0.0	0.0	0.0	3.2	25.9	57.0	17.1	416	72.1	48.8	14.9
Odin village	1,076	1,046	-2.8	1,033	99.3	0.0	0.0	0.3	0.4	17.6	53.0	29.3	398	79.4	43.7	7.0
O'Fallon city	28,674	29,069	1.4	29,100	75.9	14.7	2.5	3.8	3.1	28.4	62.0	9.7	10,525	70.4	19.4	49.1
Ogden village	810	811	0.1	777	98.2	0.0	0.0	1.2	0.6	25.2	63.5	11.5	292	90.4	36.6	21.6
Oglesby city	3,791	3,676	-3.0	3,667	93.2	0.7	0.0	0.0	6.2	25.1	59.5	15.5	1,513	78.6	42.6	18.2
Ohio village	513	498	-2.9	446	97.8	0.0	0.0	0.4	1.8	24.2	54.0	21.7	182	68.7	59.9	18.1
Ohlman village	135	132	-2.2	88	95.5	1.1	0.0	3.4	0.0	17.0	63.6	19.3	41	87.8	85.4	4.9
Okawville village	1,434	1,403	-2.2	1,410	97.0	1.8	0.0	0.3	0.9	22.7	59.8	17.4	591	77.5	29.1	27.9
Old Mill Creek village	222	224	0.9	151	72.2	0.0	15.2	2.6	9.9	17.2	64.9	17.9	79	63.3	22.8	48.1
Old Ripley village	108	104	-3.7	87	97.7	0.0	0.0	2.3	0.0	18.4	65.4	16.1	31	100.0	67.7	3.2
Old Shawneetown village	193	179	-7.3	199	100.0	0.0	0.0	0.0	0.0	29.1	59.1	11.6	76	77.6	68.4	5.3
Olive Branch CDP	864	NA	NA	719	94.4	0.0	0.0	0.0	5.6	16.4	55.9	27.8	251	87.3	57.4	9.2
Olivet CDP	428	NA	NA	384	92.7	0.5	2.1	0.0	4.7	17.7	58.2	24.2	138	87.0	47.8	11.6
Olmsted village	333	317	-4.8	475	80.0	15.4	0.0	0.0	4.6	28.5	48.9	22.5	170	80.0	58.8	6.5
Olney city	9,121	9,026	-1.0	8,997	95.5	0.8	0.8	1.8	1.2	21.5	56.4	22.2	3,901	64.9	42.8	20.1
Olympia Fields village	4,988	5,045	1.1	5,022	24.2	71.5	2.1	1.4	0.8	14.1	54.4	31.6	2,098	88.9	16.7	57.7
Omaha village	266	254	-4.5	249	98.0	0.0	0.0	2.0	0.0	16.1	61.7	22.1	117	79.5	47.0	10.3
Onarga village	1,365	1,329	-2.6	1,404	57.8	0.4	0.0	0.6	41.3	26.2	61.3	12.5	484	68.4	57.0	9.3
Oneida city	702	688	-2.0	813	96.9	0.0	0.0	0.5	2.6	31.7	54.1	14.1	297	77.1	45.8	20.9
Opdyke CDP	254	NA	NA	389	97.4	0.0	0.5	0.0	2.1	30.8	60.3	9.0	120	90.8	46.7	12.5
Oquawka village	1,371	1,301	-5.1	1,380	94.6	1.0	0.2	2.3	1.8	22.4	54.5	23.0	610	75.6	73.8	10.8
Orangeville village	793	768	-3.2	1,014	98.3	0.0	0.0	0.2	1.5	27.9	62.2	9.8	397	72.0	52.9	10.1

1 May be of any race.

Table A. All Places — **Population and Housing**

STATE City, town, township, borough, or CDP (county if applicable)	Population: 2010 census total population	Population: 2014 estimated population	Population: Percent change 2010–2014	Population: ACS total population estimate 2010–2014	Race and Hispanic or Latino origin (percent), 2010–2014: White alone, not Hispanic or Latino	Black alone, not Hispanic or Latino	Asian alone, not Hispanic or Latino	All other races or 2 or more races, not Hispanic or Latino	Hispanic or Latino[1]	Age (percent), 2010–2014: Under 18 years old	Age 18 to 64 years old	Age 65 years and older	Households, 2010–2014: Total occupied housing units	Percent owner occupied	Householders by level of education (percent): High school diploma or less	Bachelor's degree or more
	1	2	3	4	5	6	7	8	9	10	11	12	13	14	15	16
ILLINOIS—Con.																
Oreana village	875	847	-3.2	958	92.7	1.0	1.1	3.7	1.5	28.4	52.4	19.1	370	85.9	43.0	20.8
Oregon city	3,721	3,605	-3.1	3,592	94.9	1.5	0.0	2.3	1.3	17.4	61.0	21.6	1,589	60.8	43.2	16.9
Orient city	358	354	-1.1	377	96.8	0.0	0.0	2.7	0.5	17.3	65.9	17.0	166	73.5	56.6	4.8
Orion village	1,861	1,833	-1.5	1,957	95.2	0.0	0.6	3.5	0.7	26.7	54.5	18.8	778	84.8	37.7	24.3
Orland Hills village	7,210	7,277	0.9	7,252	77.8	5.9	4.7	2.9	8.8	26.9	66.3	6.8	2,324	74.4	34.6	29.9
Orland Park village	56,680	58,666	3.5	57,802	83.2	2.3	6.6	1.5	6.4	20.9	59.8	19.4	21,678	89.1	27.5	43.4
Oswego village	30,345	33,099	9.1	31,723	75.2	7.6	4.4	2.5	10.3	32.2	60.6	7.2	9,999	84.3	19.0	47.3
Ottawa city	18,758	18,428	-1.8	18,992	87.2	3.0	0.8	1.6	7.3	23.4	59.1	17.6	7,668	64.3	45.1	20.4
Otterville town	126	121	-4.0	118	100.0	0.0	0.0	0.0	0.0	13.5	60.0	26.3	54	75.9	70.4	5.6
Owaneco village	239	233	-2.5	165	98.2	0.0	0.0	0.0	1.8	25.5	54.0	20.6	67	89.6	58.2	14.9
Paderborn CDP	43	NA	NA	53	100.0	0.0	0.0	0.0	0.0	0.0	100.0	0.0	21	100.0	38.1	61.9
Palatine village	68,555	69,387	1.2	69,015	63.8	2.9	14.6	1.6	17.1	24.8	63.8	11.3	26,163	68.5	24.0	52.0
Palestine village	1,369	1,330	-2.8	1,466	97.4	0.0	1.1	1.5	0.0	23.8	53.1	23.1	624	75.8	52.7	10.4
Palmer village	229	223	-2.6	161	100.0	0.0	0.0	0.0	0.0	16.2	55.3	28.6	72	97.2	80.6	5.6
Palmyra village	698	680	-2.6	558	96.2	0.0	0.0	2.9	0.9	19.9	57.0	23.1	276	57.6	62.3	9.4
Palos Heights city	12,515	12,597	0.7	12,572	90.2	2.7	2.7	0.8	3.7	16.2	54.7	29.1	4,779	94.4	22.5	47.1
Palos Hills city	17,484	17,627	0.8	17,584	81.3	5.0	3.2	2.0	8.5	18.0	63.9	18.2	7,093	79.4	37.1	20.2
Palos Park village	4,847	4,906	1.2	4,919	87.2	1.0	2.5	1.1	8.3	17.5	54.7	27.9	2,057	86.9	19.9	42.9
Pana city	5,844	5,656	-3.2	5,601	95.8	1.2	0.0	2.6	0.4	24.2	54.0	21.7	2,505	68.5	59.4	8.9
Panama village	343	333	-2.9	235	94.0	0.0	0.0	0.0	6.0	23.3	56.4	20.4	107	84.1	53.3	0.0
Panola village	51	51	0.0	39	100.0	0.0	0.0	0.0	0.0	17.9	64.1	17.9	15	93.3	46.7	26.7
Papineau village	171	166	-2.9	291	90.0	0.0	0.3	7.2	2.4	25.1	71.8	3.1	77	77.9	68.8	3.9
Paris city	8,857	8,498	-4.1	8,702	97.4	0.8	0.6	0.1	1.0	21.3	59.4	19.4	3,922	67.3	55.7	14.3
Park City city	7,559	7,440	-1.6	7,551	20.0	11.4	8.4	2.2	57.9	34.3	59.1	6.6	2,558	56.8	60.8	10.6
Parkersburg village	199	198	-0.5	171	100.0	0.0	0.0	0.0	0.0	24.0	66.1	9.9	76	96.1	57.9	0.0
Park Forest village	21,971	22,034	0.3	22,490	27.1	63.3	0.6	2.6	6.4	26.9	60.2	12.8	8,511	63.2	29.7	28.8
Park Ridge city	37,480	37,856	1.0	37,511	87.8	0.9	3.9	0.9	6.5	23.3	58.1	18.5	14,138	82.6	18.5	58.1
Patoka village	584	568	-2.7	597	97.7	1.0	0.0	0.3	1.0	20.9	64.6	14.6	222	83.8	55.9	8.1
Pawnee village	2,739	2,725	-0.5	2,786	95.2	0.5	0.9	1.1	2.3	29.1	59.2	11.7	1,037	76.7	39.9	22.0
Paw Paw village	870	830	-4.6	825	95.0	1.5	0.0	0.2	3.3	17.4	67.0	15.4	355	69.9	47.3	14.9
Paxton city	4,489	4,345	-3.2	4,361	95.6	1.0	0.5	0.2	2.7	23.7	56.5	19.9	1,763	77.4	43.8	15.5
Payson village	1,026	1,011	-1.5	1,322	97.6	2.4	0.0	0.0	0.0	22.1	63.3	14.7	473	85.6	46.7	11.0
Pearl village	138	135	-2.2	266	85.7	0.0	0.0	14.3	0.0	38.7	47.1	14.3	94	81.9	79.8	8.5
Pearl City village	838	818	-2.4	940	95.6	0.0	0.0	0.1	4.3	29.9	58.6	11.6	376	72.9	53.5	18.1
Pecatonica village	2,203	2,138	-3.0	2,265	92.2	0.0	0.0	2.6	5.1	25.5	59.9	14.6	905	77.0	47.6	14.4
Pekin city	34,096	33,824	-0.8	33,928	94.0	1.8	0.5	1.7	2.1	22.3	61.8	15.9	13,912	68.6	43.2	19.3
Penfield CDP	193	NA	NA	189	80.4	0.0	3.7	9.5	6.3	15.4	64.5	20.1	86	62.8	53.5	0.0
Peoria city	115,021	115,828	0.7	115,718	59.3	26.1	5.1	3.9	5.5	25.1	61.5	13.3	47,286	55.6	34.4	35.0
Peoria Heights village	6,087	6,020	-1.1	6,056	84.7	7.8	0.5	6.2	0.8	18.5	66.8	14.6	2,737	62.1	32.2	23.3
Peotone village	4,142	4,136	-0.1	4,122	96.5	0.0	0.0	0.0	3.5	25.1	64.6	10.3	1,523	81.5	31.9	27.6
Percy village	970	938	-3.3	800	82.5	0.0	0.0	0.4	17.1	20.2	61.7	18.3	356	67.4	68.5	0.8
Perry village	397	382	-3.8	355	95.2	0.0	0.0	4.8	0.0	10.2	57.9	31.8	188	83.5	54.8	14.4
Peru city	10,297	10,016	-2.7	10,172	91.8	0.8	0.5	0.4	6.4	20.1	58.6	21.3	4,291	73.5	40.5	21.7
Pesotum village	551	549	-0.4	474	96.6	0.4	0.0	0.0	3.0	18.0	64.5	17.5	206	92.7	38.8	31.1
Petersburg city	2,260	2,216	-1.9	2,173	93.5	1.0	0.4	3.7	1.3	24.9	54.6	20.5	949	60.6	42.7	14.5
Phillipstown village	44	44	0.0	24	100.0	0.0	0.0	0.0	0.0	8.4	20.9	70.8	15	40.0	86.7	0.0
Philo village	1,466	1,475	0.6	1,652	98.8	0.0	0.2	0.7	0.3	31.9	59.9	8.3	596	81.9	27.0	28.7
Phoenix village	1,964	1,969	0.3	2,143	2.7	89.5	0.2	1.1	6.5	25.4	60.0	14.7	824	52.9	43.3	10.7
Pierron village	600	573	-4.5	459	94.3	0.0	0.0	3.3	2.4	22.1	60.2	17.4	202	71.8	48.5	15.8
Pinckneyville city	5,648	5,536	-2.0	5,600	70.1	20.4	1.2	1.5	6.8	17.9	68.8	13.3	1,522	70.2	46.1	16.8
Pingree Grove village	4,532	5,878	29.7	5,062	57.3	0.0	2.1	3.9	36.7	32.4	58.3	9.3	1,475	82.2	27.7	39.1
Piper City village	826	789	-4.5	807	93.9	0.0	0.1	0.5	5.5	19.9	58.5	21.7	280	74.6	49.6	6.8
Pistakee Highlands CDP	3,454	NA	NA	3,364	94.3	0.0	0.2	0.7	4.9	23.1	64.9	12.0	1,267	89.7	45.5	18.4
Pittsburg village	572	561	-1.9	599	98.7	0.0	0.3	0.7	0.3	16.2	64.2	19.4	249	80.3	60.2	8.4
Pittsfield city	4,583	4,493	-2.0	4,730	93.6	3.3	1.0	0.7	1.4	20.5	57.7	21.8	1,913	68.0	53.9	20.3
Plainfield village	39,840	42,138	5.8	40,641	73.1	6.0	8.4	2.0	10.5	33.6	60.6	6.0	11,973	85.7	16.0	55.4
Plainville village	264	263	-0.4	317	98.1	0.0	0.0	0.0	1.9	31.5	52.9	15.5	106	86.8	59.4	4.7
Plano city	10,859	11,175	2.9	11,371	61.4	4.5	0.1	2.8	31.2	31.1	63.6	5.3	3,720	69.4	50.6	17.7
Plattville village	242	251	3.7	262	94.3	0.0	0.0	0.8	5.0	26.7	64.9	8.4	93	83.9	24.7	25.8
Pleasant Hill village	966	943	-2.4	1,191	91.3	0.0	0.0	7.3	1.4	28.1	59.2	12.8	442	80.8	61.8	4.8
Pleasant Plains village	802	804	0.2	892	96.4	0.2	0.0	1.2	2.1	28.9	59.5	11.5	319	79.9	33.9	29.2
Plymouth village	505	486	-3.8	495	97.8	0.0	0.0	2.2	0.0	14.1	70.7	15.2	240	74.6	56.7	8.8
Pocahontas village	784	756	-3.6	633	98.1	0.0	0.0	1.3	0.6	18.6	60.7	20.7	259	75.3	66.0	4.6
Polo city	2,355	2,274	-3.4	2,122	93.2	0.0	0.0	0.5	6.3	24.9	55.1	20.0	869	78.9	48.3	14.3
Pontiac city	11,931	11,599	-2.8	12,012	82.1	10.8	0.3	1.4	5.5	19.9	65.5	14.6	4,311	67.3	50.9	21.1
Pontoon Beach village	5,836	5,671	-2.8	5,804	83.5	8.3	1.0	2.6	4.7	17.2	72.7	10.3	2,210	68.7	48.2	12.4
Pontoosuc village	146	143	-2.1	88	96.6	0.0	0.0	3.4	0.0	19.3	62.4	18.2	43	88.4	51.2	11.6
Poplar Grove village	5,008	5,169	3.2	5,498	83.7	7.1	1.8	2.1	5.2	31.7	52.6	15.6	1,835	88.3	48.1	20.6
Port Barrington village	1,517	1,508	-0.6	1,503	83.6	0.9	8.0	1.1	6.5	28.9	61.2	10.0	540	98.3	30.4	45.9
Port Byron village	1,647	1,650	0.2	1,707	93.6	0.0	0.0	1.1	5.3	21.9	63.6	14.4	684	82.9	24.6	30.1
Posen village	5,987	6,021	0.6	5,934	33.0	12.3	0.0	0.2	54.6	27.6	66.1	6.2	1,965	73.3	56.6	12.5
Potomac village	750	729	-2.8	728	94.6	0.0	0.0	2.5	2.9	28.7	56.8	14.6	277	71.5	60.3	8.3
Prairie City village	379	371	-2.1	526	92.8	4.2	1.7	1.0	0.4	27.0	55.5	17.5	165	87.3	51.5	11.5
Prairie du Rocher village	604	580	-4.0	690	95.9	0.0	1.9	1.7	0.4	28.1	64.4	7.5	246	80.9	69.5	8.9
Prairie Grove village	1,907	1,876	-1.6	1,812	89.8	0.9	3.6	0.6	5.1	27.0	62.3	10.8	642	83.0	18.8	55.5
Prestbury CDP	1,722	NA	NA	1,597	81.7	0.0	5.3	0.0	13.0	12.6	54.5	33.0	687	92.4	16.2	54.3
Preston Heights CDP	2,575	NA	NA	2,720	21.1	57.5	0.0	2.8	18.6	24.1	62.5	13.4	923	66.2	53.7	9.3
Princeton city	7,662	7,415	-3.2	7,698	93.9	0.8	0.8	1.1	3.5	21.0	57.3	21.6	3,545	66.3	42.4	20.4
Princeville village	1,738	1,733	-0.3	2,077	93.7	1.8	0.0	0.0	4.5	31.0	53.6	15.5	770	79.9	42.2	17.9
Prophetstown city	2,080	2,007	-3.5	2,146	89.7	0.8	0.3	2.0	7.2	26.3	53.7	19.9	818	73.8	41.4	21.0
Prospect Heights city	16,256	16,418	1.0	16,344	60.2	0.1	7.4	0.7	31.6	23.1	62.0	15.0	6,175	72.3	39.1	38.0
Pulaski village	206	193	-6.3	172	45.9	52.3	0.0	1.7	0.0	15.7	65.1	19.2	74	70.3	62.2	5.4
Quincy city	40,636	40,805	0.4	40,782	89.4	5.7	1.2	2.1	1.6	22.9	59.0	18.2	16,810	63.5	41.7	21.7
Radom village	220	213	-3.2	139	97.8	0.0	0.0	0.0	2.2	13.7	59.8	26.6	69	95.7	58.0	8.7
Raleigh village	350	348	-0.6	272	97.8	0.0	0.0	0.0	2.2	23.2	52.1	24.6	122	82.0	39.3	4.9
Ramsey village	1,037	1,024	-1.3	1,168	99.7	0.0	0.0	0.3	0.0	28.0	61.5	10.5	431	80.5	56.1	4.9
Rankin village	561	544	-3.0	418	100.0	0.0	0.0	0.0	0.0	19.6	64.9	15.6	179	71.5	68.7	8.9
Ransom village	384	376	-2.1	325	97.5	0.0	0.0	0.3	2.2	16.0	72.4	11.7	136	79.4	48.5	6.6
Rantoul village	12,941	13,100	1.2	13,214	57.2	20.9	1.1	6.6	14.2	29.4	59.3	11.3	4,974	49.2	47.4	17.3
Rapids City village	959	956	-0.3	959	93.6	0.6	1.0	3.1	1.6	19.9	66.2	13.8	382	91.1	31.2	22.8
Raritan village	138	130	-5.8	97	95.9	0.0	0.0	4.1	0.0	12.4	48.5	39.2	44	81.8	54.5	20.5

1 May be of any race.

Table A. All Places — **Population and Housing**

STATE City, town, township, borough, or CDP (county if applicable)	Population				Race and Hispanic or Latino origin (percent), 2010–2014					Age (percent), 2010–2014			Households, 2010–2014			
	2010 census total population	2014 estimated population	Percent change 2010–2014	ACS total population estimate 2010–2014	White alone, not Hispanic or Latino	Black alone, not Hispanic or Latino	Asian alone, not Hispanic or Latino	All other races or 2 or more races, not Hispanic or Latino	Hispanic or Latino[1]	Under 18 years old	Age 18 to 64 years old	Age 65 years and older	Total occupied housing units	Percent owner occupied	Householders by level of education (percent): High school diploma or less	Householders by level of education (percent): Bachelor's degree or more
	1	2	3	4	5	6	7	8	9	10	11	12	13	14	15	16
ILLINOIS—Con.																
Raymond village	1,006	981	-2.5	732	98.2	0.0	1.4	0.1	0.3	26.9	51.5	21.6	308	82.1	53.2	16.2
Red Bud city	3,698	3,609	-2.4	3,648	97.1	0.4	0.0	0.0	2.5	23.7	54.1	22.3	1,455	79.1	46.8	17.6
Reddick village	163	159	-2.5	389	100.0	0.0	0.0	0.0	0.0	29.3	61.0	9.8	126	77.0	44.4	8.7
Redmon village	173	167	-3.5	177	100.0	0.0	0.0	0.0	0.0	18.0	55.4	26.6	76	81.6	39.5	5.3
Rentchler CDP	34	NA	NA	0	0.0	0.0	0.0	0.0	0.0	0.0	0.0	0.0	0	0.0	0.0	0.0
Reynolds village	539	523	-3.0	514	97.5	0.4	0.6	1.6	0.0	31.1	53.9	14.8	195	92.3	42.1	14.4
Richmond village	1,874	1,895	1.1	2,120	89.6	1.1	2.4	2.9	4.0	19.1	66.5	14.1	972	53.0	39.6	23.4
Richton Park village	13,646	13,751	0.8	13,718	13.1	79.6	3.0	1.4	2.9	21.9	68.1	10.2	5,304	60.8	24.2	35.0
Richview village	253	241	-4.7	188	94.1	5.3	0.0	0.5	0.0	21.3	65.5	13.3	84	76.2	59.5	7.1
Ridge Farm village	882	860	-2.5	836	99.2	0.0	0.0	0.2	0.6	14.9	61.2	23.9	376	77.9	57.7	5.3
Ridgway village	869	821	-5.5	741	98.2	0.0	0.0	1.8	0.0	15.5	60.7	23.9	373	78.0	46.6	8.6
Ridott village	164	161	-1.8	122	100.0	0.0	0.0	0.0	0.0	19.7	64.0	16.4	47	80.9	44.7	10.6
Ringwood village	836	825	-1.3	752	93.5	0.8	0.7	1.6	3.5	25.4	67.8	6.8	262	86.3	40.8	22.1
Rio village	220	218	-0.9	214	91.1	0.0	0.0	0.9	7.9	20.1	59.7	20.1	85	78.8	70.6	8.2
Ripley village	86	85	-1.2	96	100.0	0.0	0.0	0.0	0.0	21.8	64.7	13.5	34	82.4	67.6	0.0
Riverdale village	13,549	13,604	0.4	13,278	3.3	92.7	0.0	2.4	1.6	27.8	66.4	5.8	4,873	48.9	42.8	15.9
River Forest village	11,172	11,208	0.3	11,211	80.9	5.0	7.2	2.3	4.6	24.9	60.1	15.0	3,895	90.0	7.5	76.9
River Grove village	10,227	10,271	0.4	10,268	74.7	0.4	2.7	1.1	21.1	20.0	65.4	14.5	4,159	62.1	45.2	19.9
Riverside village	8,875	8,881	0.1	8,915	82.2	0.7	1.2	0.6	15.2	25.9	59.5	14.8	3,290	79.6	18.7	64.7
Riverton village	3,455	3,472	0.5	3,468	95.2	0.0	0.8	1.4	2.5	30.8	59.5	9.8	1,329	64.6	45.4	16.2
Riverwoods village	3,660	3,659	0.0	3,792	91.4	0.3	4.2	2.4	1.7	25.9	55.6	18.4	1,282	98.6	4.5	77.1
Roanoke village	2,078	2,080	0.1	2,169	96.2	0.0	0.0	0.2	3.6	18.9	61.9	19.1	920	78.5	38.8	22.1
Robbins village	5,337	5,480	2.7	5,221	3.2	95.9	0.2	0.2	0.4	22.8	59.3	18.0	1,823	50.1	48.5	5.8
Roberts village	362	349	-3.6	352	79.0	0.0	0.0	0.3	20.7	25.5	57.6	16.8	152	93.4	65.8	7.9
Robinson city	7,713	7,622	-1.2	7,264	85.1	6.3	1.1	2.9	4.6	18.3	64.3	17.6	2,770	68.9	40.7	20.1
Rochelle city	9,574	9,390	-1.9	9,492	71.8	2.7	1.1	1.3	23.1	25.9	57.3	16.9	3,789	59.4	49.2	19.9
Rochester village	3,689	3,771	2.2	3,725	95.2	0.2	1.9	1.5	1.2	27.6	59.4	13.3	1,367	89.0	18.5	55.0
Rockbridge village	169	165	-2.4	195	94.9	0.0	0.0	1.0	4.1	12.3	62.6	25.1	89	85.4	80.9	7.9
Rock City village	315	311	-1.3	333	98.8	0.0	0.0	0.6	0.6	30.6	54.6	14.7	124	79.8	51.6	12.1
Rockdale village	1,976	1,957	-1.0	1,974	56.5	1.6	0.0	1.4	40.5	24.5	64.6	11.0	787	49.2	50.4	13.3
Rock Falls city	9,398	9,062	-3.6	9,111	81.5	1.6	0.5	1.6	14.7	22.7	60.2	17.1	4,021	66.2	55.0	9.6
Rockford city	153,054	149,123	-2.6	151,290	56.1	21.1	2.9	2.8	17.1	26.1	59.8	14.2	58,746	55.8	45.1	22.0
Rock Island city	39,005	38,642	-0.9	38,888	66.1	17.7	1.6	3.7	10.9	23.0	60.9	16.1	15,422	67.2	42.6	22.8
Rock Island Arsenal CDP	149	NA	NA	117	37.6	21.4	0.0	41.0	0.0	32.4	67.6	0.0	36	5.6	25.0	58.3
Rockton village	7,685	7,554	-1.7	7,461	94.2	1.0	1.9	1.2	1.7	23.6	63.8	12.5	2,729	76.9	33.7	30.4
Rockwood village	42	41	-2.4	61	100.0	0.0	0.0	0.0	0.0	29.6	50.8	19.7	25	100.0	24.0	40.0
Rolling Meadows city	24,094	24,279	0.8	23,646	63.0	3.5	7.9	1.0	24.6	21.8	65.9	12.3	8,959	71.6	31.0	33.2
Rome CDP	1,738	NA	NA	1,746	98.1	0.2	0.0	0.8	0.9	17.9	63.2	18.8	700	74.1	58.3	18.0
Romeoville village	39,611	39,679	0.2	39,675	49.3	8.6	7.6	2.7	31.8	30.6	60.9	8.5	11,747	85.2	35.5	27.7
Roodhouse city	1,814	1,750	-3.5	1,810	96.6	0.0	0.0	1.6	1.8	24.5	56.8	18.6	812	70.2	61.2	10.1
Roscoe village	10,782	10,603	-1.7	10,724	90.7	2.7	2.5	1.8	2.4	29.6	59.6	10.7	3,894	67.8	31.4	30.3
Rose Hill village	80	80	0.0	69	100.0	0.0	0.0	0.0	0.0	7.2	72.2	20.3	39	76.9	89.7	2.6
Roselle village	22,746	23,030	1.2	22,951	73.0	6.8	8.4	1.8	10.0	24.9	64.2	11.1	8,450	78.7	24.3	39.0
Rosemont village	4,202	4,226	0.6	4,043	57.1	2.9	4.3	0.3	35.4	22.5	63.7	13.6	1,664	28.3	50.4	13.6
Roseville village	989	993	0.4	1,125	95.3	1.1	0.7	0.5	2.4	20.3	59.9	19.7	453	75.3	44.6	27.2
Rosewood Heights CDP	4,038	NA	NA	4,011	96.9	1.3	0.0	0.0	1.8	17.5	64.7	18.0	1,704	75.7	54.8	9.8
Rosiclare city	1,160	1,107	-4.6	1,011	93.9	0.8	1.9	0.5	3.0	26.3	57.3	16.2	406	70.4	51.7	6.4
Rossville village	1,331	1,293	-2.9	1,495	98.6	0.0	0.0	0.8	0.6	27.0	57.0	16.1	543	71.3	54.1	11.2
Round Lake village	18,310	18,536	1.2	18,399	56.9	7.1	8.3	2.8	25.0	32.6	60.7	6.5	5,761	79.8	28.4	39.4
Round Lake Beach village	28,108	28,012	-0.3	28,048	43.7	3.3	3.4	1.1	48.5	30.8	62.8	6.3	8,087	80.3	54.2	17.0
Round Lake Heights village	2,742	2,734	-0.3	2,757	46.2	5.4	3.8	2.4	42.2	36.2	58.4	5.4	811	76.0	50.2	25.0
Round Lake Park village	7,455	7,371	-1.1	7,758	44.9	3.3	3.2	2.0	46.6	26.4	49.2	24.4	2,721	82.1	53.7	14.8
Roxana village	1,542	1,495	-3.0	1,569	92.0	0.4	0.0	1.1	6.4	25.7	58.4	15.9	656	61.6	49.5	18.3
Royal village	293	299	2.0	257	95.7	0.0	0.0	1.2	3.1	22.5	53.6	23.7	117	99.1	46.2	16.2
Royal Lakes village	197	192	-2.5	132	44.7	50.0	0.8	3.0	1.5	27.3	46.9	25.8	52	73.1	57.7	9.6
Royalton village	1,151	1,138	-1.1	1,032	95.4	2.5	0.3	1.0	0.8	18.2	60.6	21.1	460	72.6	56.3	7.4
Ruma village	317	318	0.3	382	99.0	0.0	0.0	1.0	0.0	34.6	56.8	8.6	120	88.3	50.8	4.2
Rushville city	3,209	3,108	-3.1	3,218	96.2	0.3	0.0	3.2	0.3	24.1	52.8	22.9	1,389	74.9	44.2	17.6
Russellville village	94	92	-2.1	66	100.0	0.0	0.0	0.0	0.0	24.2	45.4	30.3	33	81.8	81.8	9.1
Rutland village	318	311	-2.2	265	98.1	1.1	0.0	0.8	0.0	10.1	70.4	19.6	117	86.3	76.1	0.9
Sadorus village	416	422	1.4	434	97.0	0.5	0.0	1.6	0.9	17.9	70.1	12.0	158	84.2	59.5	13.3
Sailor Springs village	95	94	-1.1	103	100.0	0.0	0.0	0.0	0.0	25.2	64.3	10.7	38	84.2	73.7	0.0
St. Anne village	1,259	1,230	-2.3	1,606	79.5	0.2	0.0	1.3	19.1	25.7	61.9	12.5	620	67.6	51.0	10.2
St. Augustine village	122	121	-0.8	117	100.0	0.0	0.0	0.0	0.0	13.7	53.9	32.5	62	90.3	51.6	4.8
St. Charles city	32,949	33,387	1.3	33,422	85.1	1.6	3.3	1.1	8.9	23.2	62.3	14.4	12,880	71.7	25.2	50.8
St. David village	589	563	-4.4	550	97.3	0.0	0.0	2.7	0.0	17.1	62.0	20.9	238	76.1	51.3	4.6
St. Elmo city	1,426	1,405	-1.5	1,470	98.8	0.0	0.0	0.6	0.6	26.6	53.2	20.3	560	73.8	52.1	9.1
Ste. Marie village	244	243	-0.4	257	100.0	0.0	0.0	0.0	0.0	24.5	55.2	20.2	118	85.6	44.1	14.4
St. Francisville city	697	670	-3.9	519	100.0	0.0	0.0	0.0	0.0	28.7	47.9	23.3	220	79.5	68.2	4.5
St. Jacob village	1,098	1,147	4.5	1,287	93.4	0.0	1.7	2.4	2.5	25.9	57.2	16.8	476	89.1	24.6	33.2
St. Johns village	219	211	-3.7	156	94.9	0.0	0.0	5.1	0.0	25.7	52.6	21.8	67	77.6	61.2	11.9
St. Joseph village	4,002	4,082	2.0	4,076	97.1	0.0	0.6	1.3	0.9	33.5	57.2	9.4	1,546	77.9	21.7	31.3
St. Libory village	609	597	-2.0	550	98.7	0.0	0.0	1.3	0.0	20.7	61.0	18.4	244	83.2	36.1	11.5
St. Peter village	359	357	-0.6	349	99.7	0.0	0.0	0.3	0.0	11.5	77.0	11.5	147	94.6	53.7	10.9
Salem city	7,480	7,334	-2.0	7,135	94.7	1.2	0.8	2.1	1.2	23.8	56.7	19.6	3,021	66.7	45.8	15.9
Sammons Point village	279	277	-0.7	350	91.4	0.0	0.0	3.7	4.9	19.8	60.5	19.7	125	81.6	59.2	7.2
Sandoval village	1,274	1,240	-2.7	1,150	94.1	0.8	1.0	1.7	2.5	32.5	57.0	10.4	441	68.9	53.3	10.4
Sandwich city	7,421	7,410	-0.1	7,513	82.5	0.2	0.5	1.2	15.7	22.4	63.1	14.5	2,641	67.1	44.5	16.0
San Jose village	642	619	-3.6	582	97.3	1.4	0.0	0.7	0.7	22.0	64.7	13.2	218	83.0	54.6	9.2
Sauget village	159	153	-3.8	318	99.1	0.0	0.0	0.9	0.0	10.0	76.1	13.8	122	54.9	50.0	4.1
Sauk Village village	10,506	10,545	0.4	10,545	26.2	62.8	0.1	1.8	9.1	32.8	59.5	7.7	3,242	67.0	46.7	13.8
Saunemin village	420	409	-2.6	361	95.3	0.0	0.0	1.7	3.0	31.0	58.5	10.5	130	90.0	64.6	3.1
Savanna city	3,063	2,906	-5.1	2,993	86.9	3.9	0.2	1.5	7.5	23.3	59.2	17.4	1,291	59.8	62.0	18.0
Savoy village	7,322	7,879	7.6	7,835	63.9	9.8	13.9	3.7	8.8	21.3	64.1	14.7	3,129	51.2	11.8	64.1
Sawyerville village	279	272	-2.5	253	94.9	0.0	0.0	4.0	1.2	19.0	62.0	19.0	113	77.9	62.8	13.3
Saybrook village	693	689	-0.6	789	95.8	0.6	0.0	0.8	2.8	29.2	57.5	13.3	288	74.7	51.4	12.2
Scales Mound village	385	380	-1.3	451	93.1	0.0	0.0	0.7	6.2	25.4	62.7	11.8	172	73.8	44.2	10.5
Schaumburg village	74,227	74,896	0.9	74,560	64.7	3.5	20.1	2.2	9.6	20.3	67.4	12.5	30,389	63.1	23.7	48.2
Schiller Park village	11,793	11,857	0.5	11,842	61.7	1.2	8.6	3.5	25.1	20.2	68.1	11.7	4,422	64.5	47.1	20.0
Schram City village	586	572	-2.4	462	95.9	1.7	0.0	0.0	2.4	20.1	48.3	31.6	226	77.4	71.2	6.2

1 May be of any race.

Table A. All Places — **Population and Housing**

STATE City, town, township, borough, or CDP (county if applicable)	Population: 2010 census total population	Population: 2014 estimated population	Population: Percent change 2010–2014	Population: ACS total population estimate 2010–2014	Race and Hispanic or Latino origin (percent), 2010–2014: White alone, not Hispanic or Latino	Black alone, not Hispanic or Latino	Asian alone, not Hispanic or Latino	All other races or 2 or more races, not Hispanic or Latino	Hispanic or Latino[1]	Age (percent), 2010–2014: Under 18 years old	Age 18 to 64 years old	Age 65 years and older	Households, 2010–2014: Total occupied housing units	Percent owner occupied	Householders by level of education (percent): High school diploma or less	Bachelor's degree or more
	1	2	3	4	5	6	7	8	9	10	11	12	13	14	15	16
ILLINOIS—Con.																
Sciota village	61	60	-1.6	86	97.7	0.0	0.0	0.0	2.3	36.0	46.4	17.4	37	59.5	45.9	10.8
Scott AFB CDP	3,612	NA	NA	3,314	68.5	21.9	1.1	3.9	4.6	39.9	60.1	0.0	1,006	1.1	5.1	33.1
Scottville village	116	113	-2.6	81	100.0	0.0	0.0	0.0	0.0	24.7	51.9	23.5	31	100.0	61.3	32.3
Seaton village	222	215	-3.2	246	99.2	0.0	0.0	0.0	0.8	24.0	56.5	19.5	101	95.0	56.4	13.9
Seatonville village	314	311	-1.0	329	90.9	0.0	1.2	0.0	7.9	18.9	64.0	17.0	136	83.8	47.8	15.4
Secor village	374	371	-0.8	403	94.5	0.0	0.0	0.0	5.5	29.5	56.6	13.9	151	87.4	57.6	11.3
Seneca village	2,365	2,306	-2.5	2,629	93.6	0.0	0.3	0.8	5.3	28.9	59.6	11.6	883	75.3	48.4	13.8
Sesser city	1,931	1,903	-1.5	1,962	92.5	0.3	0.5	4.8	1.9	23.8	57.4	18.9	791	75.3	44.4	14.3
Seymour CDP	303	NA	NA	269	74.7	13.4	2.6	9.3	0.0	33.1	52.9	14.1	135	68.9	40.7	5.9
Shabbona village	939	939	0.0	877	89.4	1.0	0.3	1.4	7.9	18.8	55.9	25.3	346	59.5	44.2	14.2
Shannon village	757	718	-5.2	701	91.9	0.0	0.3	0.3	7.6	20.1	56.0	23.8	327	81.0	56.9	11.9
Shawneetown city	1,239	1,171	-5.5	1,224	93.8	1.6	1.0	2.6	1.1	28.2	50.7	20.9	513	67.3	53.6	4.9
Sheffield village	926	897	-3.1	900	98.2	0.0	0.0	0.4	1.3	20.7	55.7	23.7	361	80.1	54.6	15.0
Shelbyville city	4,697	4,662	-0.7	5,211	96.4	0.2	0.0	1.6	1.8	20.5	56.3	23.2	2,248	71.3	40.8	15.9
Sheldon village	1,070	1,033	-3.5	1,264	93.6	1.3	0.1	0.5	4.6	30.6	57.0	12.3	442	65.6	63.6	5.4
Sheridan village	2,137	2,111	-1.2	2,026	51.0	34.7	1.5	1.2	11.5	11.4	85.1	3.3	298	66.4	57.0	4.4
Sherman village	4,148	4,511	8.8	4,016	97.4	0.0	1.4	1.2	0.0	24.3	56.3	19.5	1,564	85.6	21.2	54.1
Sherrard village	640	614	-4.1	819	93.5	1.7	0.6	0.5	3.7	24.2	59.1	16.7	324	79.9	54.3	11.4
Shiloh village	12,411	12,907	4.0	12,706	70.8	20.3	2.0	3.3	3.6	24.1	65.5	10.4	4,394	76.7	19.9	46.5
Shipman town	624	608	-2.6	665	95.0	0.3	0.0	2.6	2.1	28.9	64.0	7.2	214	76.2	39.7	16.4
Shorewood village	15,615	16,569	6.1	16,186	75.9	7.4	3.2	2.4	11.1	26.1	61.1	12.7	5,289	88.7	27.2	39.9
Shumway village	202	201	-0.5	171	95.3	0.0	4.7	0.0	0.0	19.9	67.4	12.9	70	95.7	65.7	4.3
Sibley village	272	262	-3.7	324	95.1	1.5	1.9	0.0	1.5	24.0	61.5	14.5	138	85.5	56.5	10.1
Sidell village	617	597	-3.2	688	100.0	0.0	0.0	0.0	0.0	26.6	60.5	12.8	245	90.6	69.8	7.3
Sidney village	1,233	1,240	0.6	1,377	96.9	1.1	0.6	0.2	1.2	23.6	60.9	15.5	552	77.2	42.6	16.3
Sigel town	373	365	-2.1	353	97.7	0.0	0.0	0.0	2.3	26.0	54.2	19.5	128	80.5	45.3	7.8
Silvis city	7,506	7,526	0.3	7,525	73.7	8.4	1.8	2.0	14.2	27.3	55.6	17.3	3,142	65.6	39.4	19.4
Simpson village	60	61	1.7	107	100.0	0.0	0.0	0.0	0.0	49.5	43.9	6.5	26	96.2	57.7	19.2
Sims village	252	251	-0.4	335	100.0	0.0	0.0	0.0	0.0	25.4	64.9	9.9	121	94.2	64.5	1.7
Skokie village	64,784	65,112	0.5	65,056	54.0	6.3	26.5	2.7	10.5	20.9	61.4	17.7	22,532	72.9	24.0	50.4
Sleepy Hollow village	3,304	3,340	1.1	3,336	85.2	0.8	3.7	1.6	8.7	27.4	60.6	11.9	1,103	89.8	26.7	43.0
Smithboro village	177	171	-3.4	150	97.3	0.0	2.7	0.0	0.0	17.3	69.9	12.7	59	93.2	69.5	3.4
Smithfield village	230	223	-3.0	202	95.5	0.0	0.0	4.5	0.0	21.3	52.1	26.7	85	85.9	52.9	11.8
Smithton village	3,688	3,729	1.1	3,706	91.7	2.3	1.1	0.4	4.4	25.3	57.4	17.2	1,316	91.3	34.7	24.5
Somonauk village	1,893	1,884	-0.5	2,191	90.5	2.4	0.2	3.0	4.0	31.2	55.4	13.4	763	79.9	44.2	15.7
Sorento village	498	476	-4.4	734	86.4	0.0	2.5	2.2	9.0	34.5	54.2	11.4	225	77.3	73.3	3.6
South Barrington village	4,576	4,822	5.4	4,811	57.6	1.0	33.2	5.2	3.1	21.8	60.2	17.8	1,521	99.3	6.9	77.2
South Beloit city	7,892	7,719	-2.2	8,129	86.6	2.3	0.6	1.2	9.3	30.3	60.4	9.2	2,865	71.4	45.1	17.8
South Chicago Heights village	4,139	4,157	0.4	4,164	41.9	18.9	0.0	3.8	35.4	30.7	57.4	11.9	1,454	68.6	52.1	12.2
South Elgin village	21,985	22,226	1.1	22,126	77.2	2.5	7.1	1.1	12.2	30.6	62.7	6.8	7,293	86.7	23.7	37.9
Southern View village	1,661	1,646	-0.9	1,936	92.9	2.9	1.0	1.2	2.0	21.7	61.9	16.5	817	71.6	35.6	20.3
South Holland village	22,030	22,144	0.5	22,123	16.6	77.8	0.8	0.9	3.9	22.5	59.9	17.6	7,448	88.0	27.3	33.0
South Jacksonville village	3,331	3,271	-1.8	3,309	93.7	2.2	0.0	1.8	2.2	18.5	57.8	23.7	1,557	75.7	43.4	28.1
South Pekin village	1,146	1,138	-0.7	1,160	98.4	0.0	0.8	0.0	0.9	28.8	63.8	7.4	427	78.5	59.0	4.9
South Roxana village	2,053	2,010	-2.1	2,294	99.2	0.2	0.0	0.4	0.2	27.0	62.5	10.5	857	61.4	55.5	8.4
South Wilmington village	681	666	-2.2	688	92.9	0.0	0.0	0.4	6.7	21.8	65.9	12.4	280	81.1	50.4	18.2
Sparland village	406	387	-4.7	483	95.4	0.0	0.0	1.9	2.7	15.5	67.9	16.6	166	82.5	60.2	4.8
Sparta city	4,302	4,456	3.6	4,338	73.9	25.4	0.0	0.6	0.1	14.2	67.5	18.4	1,822	70.0	55.0	19.5
Spaulding village	873	870	-0.3	791	95.3	1.3	0.8	2.4	0.3	28.6	57.1	14.5	259	87.6	34.4	24.7
Spillertown village	203	202	-0.5	242	92.1	0.0	5.4	0.0	2.5	26.9	61.1	12.0	94	86.2	42.6	13.8
Spring Bay village	472	465	-1.5	556	95.1	0.4	0.9	1.8	1.8	26.9	62.1	11.0	214	70.6	53.3	8.4
Springerton village	110	109	-0.9	88	100.0	0.0	0.0	0.0	0.0	23.8	59.0	17.0	44	97.7	72.7	6.8
Springfield city	116,365	116,809	0.4	116,815	73.1	19.6	2.3	2.6	2.4	22.4	62.6	14.8	50,732	63.1	31.4	37.4
Spring Grove village	5,772	5,725	-0.8	5,390	94.0	0.0	0.6	0.9	4.5	28.1	62.0	9.9	1,806	94.8	27.9	31.3
Spring Valley city	5,558	5,359	-3.6	5,441	80.9	1.8	1.8	1.6	13.9	20.3	62.6	17.1	2,308	73.1	44.4	17.5
Standard village	220	211	-4.1	228	89.9	0.0	1.8	5.3	3.1	26.7	54.4	18.9	101	71.3	42.6	6.9
Standard City village	152	148	-2.6	225	98.7	0.0	0.0	1.3	0.0	31.9	59.4	8.4	78	82.1	41.0	7.7
Stanford village	596	588	-1.3	603	85.9	0.0	1.3	11.3	1.5	26.4	64.0	9.6	212	86.8	54.2	11.8
Staunton city	5,205	5,056	-2.9	4,780	96.0	0.0	0.0	2.3	1.8	20.2	58.0	21.8	2,273	65.9	41.2	17.3
Steeleville village	2,083	2,006	-3.7	1,930	99.1	0.0	0.0	0.4	0.5	23.3	54.8	21.9	818	76.7	47.3	14.4
Steger village	9,570	9,557	-0.1	9,569	57.8	19.1	1.2	4.1	17.8	24.5	60.4	15.1	3,885	55.7	49.4	14.8
Sterling city	15,438	15,011	-2.8	15,208	72.1	1.3	0.5	1.0	25.1	25.2	57.9	16.9	5,902	65.1	44.8	16.2
Steward village	256	246	-3.9	322	90.1	2.5	0.0	0.0	7.5	30.4	54.5	14.9	115	75.7	43.5	15.7
Stewardson village	734	716	-2.5	738	94.9	0.0	4.9	0.0	0.3	21.7	54.3	24.0	305	76.1	48.2	16.4
Stickney village	6,786	6,818	0.5	6,810	48.5	0.3	2.5	0.9	47.8	24.5	61.6	14.0	2,440	76.5	47.3	8.4
Stillman Valley village	1,120	1,083	-3.3	978	97.5	0.5	1.0	0.9	0.0	23.2	66.6	10.0	383	72.6	41.5	24.5
Stockton village	1,869	1,809	-3.2	1,948	99.1	0.3	0.4	0.2	0.0	25.1	51.4	23.3	828	72.0	55.6	17.8
Stonefort village	297	295	-0.7	348	100.0	0.0	0.0	0.0	0.0	24.4	62.3	13.2	127	85.0	54.3	0.0
Stone Park village	4,946	4,957	0.2	4,959	6.4	0.5	0.6	0.4	92.1	32.4	61.5	6.4	1,302	59.0	65.1	6.9
Stonington village	932	899	-3.5	889	94.0	0.0	0.0	0.0	6.0	25.7	55.8	18.3	350	80.0	51.7	17.1
Stoy village	115	113	-1.7	160	100.0	0.0	0.0	0.0	0.0	21.9	50.7	27.5	78	93.6	3.8	48.7
Strasburg village	467	453	-3.0	601	98.2	0.0	0.5	1.3	0.0	20.0	63.9	16.3	238	86.1	34.9	16.0
Strawn village	100	97	-3.0	136	97.1	0.0	0.0	2.9	0.0	25.7	63.3	11.0	59	74.6	71.2	1.7
Streamwood village	39,858	40,345	1.2	40,746	50.8	2.5	15.4	1.4	29.8	24.7	66.5	8.8	13,041	86.2	36.8	32.3
Streator city	13,705	13,289	-3.0	13,152	81.8	2.0	1.2	1.1	13.9	22.6	57.9	19.7	5,297	69.1	58.3	11.7
Stronghurst village	883	829	-6.1	995	95.1	0.7	0.0	2.6	1.6	24.0	52.9	22.8	392	59.4	40.8	14.8
Sublette village	449	432	-3.8	431	94.0	0.0	0.0	1.2	4.9	15.5	54.6	29.9	210	74.8	51.9	15.2
Sugar Grove village	8,997	9,192	2.2	9,096	83.9	1.2	0.5	1.7	12.7	25.7	66.1	8.2	3,260	87.7	20.0	42.0
Sullivan city	4,450	4,458	0.2	4,637	97.5	0.4	0.2	0.7	1.2	20.0	58.2	21.8	1,956	67.9	51.4	19.1
Summerfield village	432	408	-5.6	576	92.5	2.4	0.7	3.8	0.5	18.9	72.3	8.9	201	78.6	50.2	7.5
Summit village	11,054	11,447	3.6	11,367	21.7	8.9	2.1	0.5	66.9	28.4	63.2	8.4	3,136	53.1	62.3	11.3
Sumner city	3,174	3,145	-0.9	5,556	29.1	56.5	0.1	2.6	11.8	3.2	94.2	2.6	230	76.5	42.2	10.0
Sun River Terrace village	528	522	-1.1	459	1.5	93.9	0.0	1.1	3.5	26.2	52.4	21.4	197	48.2	42.6	9.1
Swansea village	13,455	13,651	1.5	13,870	71.5	16.3	1.4	6.1	4.7	24.2	60.4	15.6	5,367	73.8	29.1	36.1
Sycamore city	17,519	17,753	1.3	17,473	85.9	2.5	2.4	1.7	7.5	22.3	66.1	11.8	6,796	63.8	24.0	40.2
Symerton village	87	89	2.3	88	84.1	0.0	0.0	0.0	15.9	34.2	55.9	10.2	31	100.0	48.4	6.5
Table Grove village	416	405	-2.6	375	98.7	0.0	0.0	1.3	0.0	27.5	55.7	16.8	154	89.0	35.7	22.1
Tallula village	488	484	-0.8	477	98.3	0.0	0.0	1.7	0.0	20.9	62.9	16.4	200	79.0	61.0	6.5
Tamaroa village	638	614	-3.8	528	98.5	0.0	0.0	1.5	0.0	25.9	53.7	20.3	204	86.8	63.2	2.0
Tamms village	1,043	984	-5.7	739	54.5	41.7	0.0	3.2	0.5	18.9	63.4	17.5	245	68.2	69.0	1.2

1 May be of any race.

Table A. All Places — **Population and Housing**

STATE City, town, township, borough, or CDP (county if applicable)	Population				Race and Hispanic or Latino origin (percent), 2010–2014					Age (percent), 2010–2014			Households, 2010–2014			
															Householders by level of education (percent)	
	2010 census total population	2014 estimated population	Percent change 2010–2014	ACS total population estimate 2010–2014	White alone, not Hispanic or Latino	Black alone, not Hispanic or Latino	Asian alone, not Hispanic or Latino	All other races or 2 or more races, not Hispanic or Latino	Hispanic or Latino[1]	Under 18 years old	Age 18 to 64 years old	Age 65 years and older	Total occupied housing units	Percent owner occupied	High school diploma or less	Bachelor's degree or more
	1	2	3	4	5	6	7	8	9	10	11	12	13	14	15	16
ILLINOIS—Con.																
Tampico village	790	758	-4.1	674	95.7	0.0	1.0	0.0	3.3	24.6	57.1	18.2	289	69.9	65.7	6.6
Taylor Springs village	690	675	-2.2	578	99.0	0.0	0.5	0.0	0.5	16.2	50.5	33.6	225	77.8	63.1	10.2
Taylorville city	11,278	10,971	-2.7	11,761	95.6	2.7	0.3	0.0	1.4	19.9	61.4	18.7	4,956	64.0	51.2	17.6
Tennessee village	115	112	-2.6	202	100.0	0.0	0.0	0.0	0.0	21.3	73.3	5.4	77	84.4	46.8	20.8
Teutopolis village	1,533	1,577	2.9	1,863	98.8	0.1	0.0	0.9	0.2	27.1	61.4	11.4	646	82.4	35.4	30.3
Thawville village	241	268	11.2	189	89.4	0.0	0.0	2.6	7.9	29.6	48.1	22.2	71	85.9	71.8	8.5
Thayer village	693	686	-1.0	614	97.7	0.0	1.3	1.0	0.0	16.6	73.0	10.4	274	79.2	43.1	12.8
Thebes village	437	391	-10.5	593	59.0	36.9	1.0	0.7	2.4	36.4	55.1	8.4	174	62.1	74.7	9.8
The Galena Territory CDP	1,058	NA	NA	1,116	93.8	1.8	0.0	0.4	3.9	4.8	45.0	50.2	519	98.5	16.0	48.9
Third Lake village	1,184	1,194	0.8	1,370	91.5	0.1	0.4	1.5	6.5	26.3	64.7	9.1	451	93.6	12.4	65.2
Thomasboro village	1,126	1,141	1.3	1,147	95.5	2.4	0.6	1.2	0.3	21.6	62.7	15.7	509	72.1	47.2	12.4
Thompsonville village	543	535	-1.5	782	95.7	0.0	0.0	1.2	3.2	30.8	60.5	8.7	253	70.8	55.7	6.7
Thomson village	590	565	-4.2	818	90.7	2.2	0.0	0.0	7.1	26.3	56.2	17.4	313	65.5	55.6	11.8
Thornton village	2,392	2,401	0.4	2,826	77.7	9.6	0.2	1.1	11.4	23.5	61.5	15.0	1,132	79.2	55.1	9.9
Tilden village	934	901	-3.5	695	98.8	0.1	0.0	1.0	0.0	23.1	61.3	15.8	301	72.8	65.8	6.0
Tilton village	2,724	2,647	-2.8	2,686	86.2	0.0	0.0	2.3	11.5	24.1	56.2	19.8	1,177	75.9	64.0	6.9
Timberlane village	934	954	2.1	1,052	95.8	0.0	0.2	0.7	3.3	28.6	66.9	4.6	325	100.0	19.1	39.4
Time village	23	22	-4.3	17	100.0	0.0	0.0	0.0	0.0	0.0	47.1	52.9	7	100.0	100.0	0.0
Tinley Park village	56,736	57,280	1.0	57,099	81.2	3.6	4.1	1.2	9.9	23.0	63.4	13.4	21,058	84.4	29.7	36.3
Tiskilwa village	829	796	-4.0	950	98.0	0.0	0.0	0.1	1.9	30.7	53.9	15.4	342	82.2	52.9	11.7
Toledo village	1,238	1,214	-1.9	1,221	96.6	2.5	0.0	0.4	0.6	28.1	57.4	14.5	470	68.1	58.5	10.0
Tolono village	3,447	3,501	1.6	3,141	94.3	0.1	0.5	0.5	4.7	28.0	61.0	11.0	1,165	83.7	25.5	31.8
Toluca city	1,414	1,335	-5.6	1,310	79.2	2.7	0.2	1.0	16.9	18.0	59.0	22.9	542	80.3	43.9	17.5
Tonica village	768	744	-3.1	753	94.4	0.0	0.3	1.1	4.2	21.7	59.0	19.4	315	80.0	43.2	17.8
Topeka village	76	73	-3.9	37	100.0	0.0	0.0	0.0	0.0	2.7	40.5	56.8	21	85.7	47.6	23.8
Toulon city	1,292	1,254	-2.9	1,275	94.9	1.2	0.2	2.4	1.3	20.0	54.5	25.5	486	75.5	40.5	22.6
Tovey village	512	494	-3.5	483	90.1	0.0	0.0	1.9	8.1	19.7	57.8	22.6	219	79.9	74.0	6.4
Towanda village	480	481	0.2	531	94.0	0.0	0.2	1.9	4.0	21.9	53.6	24.7	208	80.8	53.4	19.7
Tower Hill village	611	600	-1.8	528	98.1	0.0	0.8	0.4	0.8	21.5	64.4	13.8	181	82.9	67.4	11.6
Tower Lakes village	1,274	1,264	-0.8	1,297	93.2	0.0	1.3	1.5	4.0	27.4	59.6	12.9	421	95.2	5.5	75.5
Tremont village	2,236	2,210	-1.2	2,120	96.0	0.0	0.7	1.5	1.8	22.9	55.8	21.0	937	78.5	38.4	27.7
Trenton city	2,715	2,682	-1.2	2,716	95.7	0.3	1.3	0.4	2.4	21.3	59.8	18.8	1,114	70.5	37.4	24.8
Trout Valley village	537	530	-1.3	528	94.1	0.4	1.3	1.1	3.0	19.7	62.3	18.0	191	95.8	8.4	69.1
Troy city	9,888	9,996	1.1	9,931	88.6	3.3	0.7	2.3	5.0	26.1	64.7	9.1	3,562	68.1	35.5	23.8
Troy Grove village	250	244	-2.4	236	89.8	0.0	0.0	0.0	10.2	24.5	66.6	8.9	97	75.3	52.6	5.2
Tuscola city	4,480	4,461	-0.4	4,307	90.0	1.1	2.7	0.1	6.0	21.5	62.1	16.4	1,814	76.1	54.7	18.7
Twin Grove CDP	1,564	NA	NA	1,803	91.1	7.3	0.8	0.8	0.0	17.9	69.2	12.8	693	88.0	19.8	49.4
Ullin village	463	436	-5.8	473	68.3	23.9	0.0	7.4	0.4	9.7	63.2	27.1	192	66.1	40.1	14.1
Union village	580	562	-3.1	516	96.7	0.0	0.0	0.0	3.3	28.8	60.3	10.9	161	89.4	46.6	18.6
Union Hill village	58	57	-1.7	61	100.0	0.0	0.0	0.0	0.0	54.0	37.8	8.2	15	93.3	33.3	6.7
University Park village	7,119	7,095	-0.3	6,852	6.2	87.1	0.7	3.3	2.7	30.1	62.1	7.8	2,557	53.7	23.5	27.6
Urbana city	41,452	42,044	1.4	41,760	57.9	16.2	18.0	3.0	4.9	11.2	80.8	8.0	15,803	36.4	18.7	51.2
Ursa village	626	623	-0.5	596	98.2	0.0	0.3	0.0	1.5	17.1	65.1	17.8	266	74.1	51.9	13.9
Valier village	669	658	-1.6	633	99.1	0.0	0.0	0.0	0.9	14.6	59.6	25.8	293	91.8	47.8	8.2
Valley City village	13	13	0.0	4	100.0	0.0	0.0	0.0	0.0	0.0	50.0	50.0	2	100.0	100.0	0.0
Valmeyer village	1,251	1,259	0.6	1,407	97.9	0.0	0.0	0.4	1.7	33.9	59.4	7.0	471	76.9	51.6	20.8
Vandalia city	7,043	6,984	-0.8	6,247	84.9	10.4	0.1	0.7	3.9	16.9	68.9	14.2	2,043	66.8	52.6	20.4
Varna village	384	366	-4.7	418	96.7	0.0	0.0	3.1	0.2	27.1	47.7	25.4	160	96.3	59.4	12.5
Venedy village	138	134	-2.9	108	98.1	1.9	0.0	0.0	0.0	16.7	64.0	19.4	50	82.0	68.0	4.0
Venetian Village CDP	2,826	NA	NA	2,852	87.3	4.4	0.2	1.2	6.9	18.8	67.7	13.5	1,092	92.7	38.6	18.2
Venice city	1,890	1,927	2.0	1,751	1.3	96.7	0.3	1.1	0.6	24.5	63.9	11.6	728	50.5	58.2	7.1
Vergennes village	298	295	-1.0	322	92.9	0.0	0.0	0.0	7.1	30.1	55.6	14.3	121	85.1	43.0	8.3
Vermilion village	225	217	-3.6	239	100.0	0.0	0.0	0.0	0.0	26.7	50.5	22.6	90	81.1	76.7	3.3
Vermont village	667	651	-2.4	754	91.6	5.0	0.0	3.3	0.0	21.4	63.7	14.9	318	90.6	57.5	12.3
Vernon village	129	127	-1.6	99	82.8	0.0	0.0	1.0	16.2	29.3	48.6	22.2	42	92.9	52.4	0.0
Vernon Hills village	25,024	25,911	3.5	25,535	64.5	0.7	20.0	3.2	11.6	26.4	63.3	10.4	9,430	71.5	18.4	61.2
Verona village	215	213	-0.9	235	71.5	0.0	0.0	0.0	28.5	38.3	49.4	12.3	69	98.6	52.2	8.7
Versailles village	478	464	-2.9	449	89.3	0.0	6.9	3.8	0.0	21.0	64.2	14.9	191	72.8	55.0	0.0
Victoria village	316	313	-0.9	348	100.0	0.0	0.0	0.0	0.0	23.9	63.7	12.6	126	89.7	57.1	14.3
Vienna city	1,434	1,436	0.1	1,383	95.8	1.2	0.0	2.2	0.9	17.5	56.4	26.2	609	48.1	55.8	11.0
Villa Grove city	2,537	2,511	-1.0	2,270	95.0	0.0	0.6	0.4	4.1	22.3	59.2	18.5	995	74.3	46.0	18.4
Villa Park village	21,907	22,038	0.6	22,073	68.0	3.6	5.6	0.7	22.0	23.9	65.5	10.6	7,713	70.1	30.9	36.5
Viola village	955	927	-2.9	1,013	94.0	0.0	0.0	1.3	4.7	23.4	53.2	23.3	440	87.3	44.5	10.9
Virden city	3,525	3,430	-2.7	3,600	98.3	0.2	0.0	1.5	0.0	25.4	60.4	14.1	1,417	67.0	49.4	10.8
Virgil village	329	336	2.1	347	99.7	0.3	0.0	0.0	0.0	26.8	67.5	5.8	116	88.8	37.9	23.3
Virginia city	1,611	1,551	-3.7	1,369	93.6	0.6	0.0	1.0	4.8	17.3	63.9	18.8	592	66.9	64.0	9.5
Volo village	2,949	3,870	31.2	3,658	70.1	8.7	5.9	1.3	14.0	26.8	67.8	5.4	1,296	88.7	15.0	46.9
Wadsworth village	3,756	3,759	0.1	3,714	73.8	9.2	6.4	0.0	10.6	21.4	61.4	17.1	1,155	86.0	22.9	42.2
Waggoner village	266	259	-2.6	164	100.0	0.0	0.0	0.0	0.0	28.1	64.0	7.9	65	69.2	67.7	4.6
Walnut village	1,416	1,361	-3.9	1,520	93.6	0.6	0.1	0.7	5.0	29.1	53.5	17.4	568	71.0	48.2	25.4
Walnut Hill village	108	107	-0.9	66	100.0	0.0	0.0	0.0	0.0	22.7	65.2	12.1	29	79.3	62.1	13.8
Walshville village	64	62	-3.1	32	100.0	0.0	0.0	0.0	0.0	12.5	78.2	9.4	11	100.0	90.9	0.0
Waltonville village	434	434	0.0	429	99.8	0.0	0.0	0.0	0.2	30.0	56.3	13.5	166	67.5	43.4	7.2
Wamac city	1,185	1,152	-2.8	1,440	89.2	3.1	0.0	1.3	6.4	26.6	60.0	13.4	553	64.7	64.6	3.1
Wapella village	558	543	-2.7	600	96.3	0.0	0.0	3.3	0.3	21.7	65.9	12.5	245	93.9	49.0	15.1
Warren village	1,428	1,390	-2.7	1,541	98.0	0.0	0.0	1.0	1.0	19.4	61.2	19.5	632	81.6	52.4	18.8
Warrensburg village	1,210	1,176	-2.8	1,143	86.0	2.4	0.0	4.3	7.3	28.4	59.6	11.6	439	72.7	37.1	29.2
Warrenville city	13,176	13,336	1.2	13,361	71.5	3.6	3.8	3.8	17.3	22.7	68.0	9.3	4,882	79.5	21.6	44.8
Warsaw city	1,607	1,556	-3.2	1,441	95.6	0.0	0.8	1.9	1.7	17.5	64.7	17.8	640	81.1	46.4	16.9
Washburn village	1,148	1,132	-1.4	1,022	94.3	0.8	0.0	1.7	3.2	29.5	59.0	11.5	366	75.4	61.7	12.3
Washington city	15,201	15,816	4.0	15,525	93.5	0.2	2.5	1.2	2.6	28.8	57.2	13.9	5,813	80.8	25.9	39.9
Washington Park village	4,196	4,040	-3.7	4,120	5.6	92.9	0.0	0.7	0.7	26.6	65.1	8.3	1,379	51.3	53.9	6.7
Wataga village	843	828	-1.8	883	94.3	0.0	0.0	3.1	2.6	24.4	64.6	11.1	367	70.3	44.1	9.0
Waterloo city	9,982	10,178	2.0	10,102	98.7	0.0	0.2	0.1	1.0	23.0	63.0	13.9	3,999	77.2	36.7	26.9
Waterman village	1,506	1,503	-0.2	1,481	91.8	0.0	0.8	3.3	4.1	27.8	63.7	8.6	482	73.0	36.5	23.7
Watseka city	5,297	5,113	-3.5	5,463	90.4	2.9	1.2	0.0	5.5	19.8	55.2	25.1	2,480	68.8	56.0	12.7
Watson village	754	744	-1.3	619	98.2	0.0	0.0	1.6	0.2	26.5	65.7	7.8	239	90.4	58.6	12.1
Wauconda village	13,635	13,896	1.9	13,189	73.1	0.6	6.0	2.1	18.2	26.5	63.1	10.4	4,818	75.3	29.8	41.0
Waukegan city	89,099	88,915	-0.2	88,671	22.4	17.2	4.7	2.4	53.4	28.9	62.9	8.1	28,725	51.0	51.5	20.6
Waverly city	1,307	1,274	-2.5	1,237	100.0	0.0	0.0	0.0	0.0	25.7	56.3	18.0	520	83.3	52.7	19.0
Wayne village	2,409	2,442	1.4	2,445	96.2	0.7	2.6	0.0	0.5	18.0	69.7	12.2	881	97.0	15.9	59.6

1 May be of any race.

Table A. All Places — **Population and Housing**

STATE City, town, township, borough, or CDP (county if applicable)	Population: 2010 census total population	Population: 2014 estimated population	Population: Percent change 2010–2014	Population: ACS total population estimate 2010–2014	Race and Hispanic or Latino origin (percent), 2010–2014: White alone, not Hispanic or Latino	Black alone, not Hispanic or Latino	Asian alone, not Hispanic or Latino	All other races or 2 or more races, not Hispanic or Latino	Hispanic or Latino[1]	Age (percent), 2010–2014: Under 18 years old	Age 18 to 64 years old	Age 65 years and older	Households, 2010–2014: Total occupied housing units	Percent owner occupied	Householders by level of education (percent): High school diploma or less	Bachelor's degree or more
	1	2	3	4	5	6	7	8	9	10	11	12	13	14	15	16
ILLINOIS—Con.																
Wayne City village	1,032	1,020	-1.2	1,138	98.3	0.4	0.0	0.2	1.1	30.2	46.4	23.4	451	76.5	51.9	15.1
Waynesville village	428	422	-1.4	511	97.8	0.0	0.0	2.2	0.0	16.5	66.9	16.6	209	91.4	55.5	15.8
Weldon village	429	423	-1.4	438	92.9	0.0	0.0	5.7	1.4	26.8	58.8	14.4	171	91.8	46.2	11.7
Wellington village	242	235	-2.9	239	90.8	0.0	4.2	1.7	3.3	15.8	56.9	27.2	118	81.4	44.1	11.0
Wenona city	1,056	998	-5.5	1,119	94.8	0.0	0.0	0.4	4.7	24.0	61.5	14.6	458	74.2	46.9	15.3
Wenonah village	37	36	-2.7	34	94.1	0.0	0.0	5.9	0.0	47.1	29.4	23.5	12	100.0	83.3	16.7
West Brooklyn village	142	137	-3.5	124	91.1	0.0	0.0	0.0	8.9	25.8	57.2	16.9	50	90.0	64.0	0.0
Westchester village	16,718	16,807	0.5	16,786	63.2	15.6	4.0	1.3	15.9	20.1	57.3	22.6	6,693	90.3	33.6	34.8
West Chicago city	27,200	27,507	1.1	27,416	39.6	2.4	6.2	0.7	51.2	30.4	61.4	8.2	7,743	66.9	44.7	28.5
West City village	661	653	-1.2	702	97.4	0.0	0.0	1.4	1.1	17.7	57.2	25.1	362	57.7	52.8	6.1
West Dundee village	7,331	7,391	0.8	7,367	80.5	3.5	9.9	1.0	5.1	21.1	69.5	9.4	2,940	67.5	19.8	50.2
Western Springs village	12,975	13,284	2.4	13,066	94.8	0.1	0.9	0.5	3.6	31.0	54.0	14.8	4,317	94.9	5.1	78.5
Westervelt CDP	128	NA	NA	93	100.0	0.0	0.0	0.0	0.0	34.5	18.3	47.3	54	100.0	42.6	0.0
Westfield village	601	589	-2.0	719	99.3	0.0	0.0	0.7	0.0	22.1	57.0	20.9	295	84.7	58.3	11.9
West Frankfort city	8,177	8,056	-1.5	8,247	95.7	0.1	0.8	2.6	0.7	23.9	59.2	17.0	3,407	62.4	50.1	8.2
Westmont village	24,663	24,963	1.2	25,236	66.8	8.1	12.9	3.4	8.7	19.5	64.4	16.0	10,595	50.3	27.3	43.6
West Peoria city	4,466	4,452	-0.3	4,453	84.0	12.0	1.3	2.1	0.6	16.6	64.1	19.3	2,014	79.9	29.8	22.7
West Point village	178	174	-2.2	222	97.3	0.0	0.0	2.7	0.0	29.3	61.0	9.9	72	93.1	56.9	12.5
West Salem village	897	884	-1.4	962	97.5	2.0	0.0	0.5	0.0	27.8	54.0	18.4	391	84.4	52.7	12.3
West Union CDP	288	NA	NA	339	95.9	1.5	0.0	0.9	1.8	27.4	66.2	6.5	126	71.4	23.8	16.7
Westville village	3,197	3,126	-2.2	3,264	96.3	0.0	0.0	2.6	1.1	21.9	60.9	17.0	1,359	77.6	48.4	13.1
West York CDP	129	NA	NA	124	100.0	0.0	0.0	0.0	0.0	22.5	72.6	4.8	57	100.0	66.7	10.5
Wheaton city	52,978	53,644	1.3	53,406	83.2	3.5	6.2	2.2	4.9	23.1	63.3	13.6	19,194	72.1	13.7	63.7
Wheeler village	147	146	-0.7	97	100.0	0.0	0.0	0.0	0.0	19.5	65.9	14.4	47	80.9	53.2	4.3
Wheeling village	37,636	38,010	1.0	37,886	49.3	1.7	15.5	0.8	32.6	21.9	65.9	12.2	14,334	63.6	34.3	40.0
Whiteash village	241	240	-0.4	354	98.9	0.0	0.0	0.0	1.1	27.3	64.9	7.6	131	78.6	46.6	9.9
White City village	232	230	-0.9	189	94.7	0.0	0.5	1.1	3.7	18.6	60.7	20.6	84	85.7	54.8	11.9
White Hall city	2,520	2,436	-3.3	2,704	98.0	0.3	0.0	1.4	0.2	25.1	56.6	18.3	1,035	74.0	58.9	9.3
White Heath CDP	290	NA	NA	247	96.8	0.0	0.0	0.0	3.2	8.5	87.9	3.6	114	56.1	40.4	6.1
Williamsfield village	578	566	-2.1	574	96.2	1.0	0.0	1.6	1.2	21.9	58.3	19.7	237	78.1	50.6	13.5
Williamson village	230	225	-2.2	208	96.2	2.9	0.0	1.0	0.0	19.3	64.4	16.3	78	85.9	67.9	2.6
Williamsville village	1,476	1,494	1.2	1,668	93.0	0.0	2.5	1.6	3.0	27.7	62.7	9.8	581	92.1	22.2	30.1
Willisville village	633	609	-3.8	425	99.8	0.0	0.2	0.0	0.0	22.2	60.7	17.2	183	79.8	74.9	2.2
Willowbrook village	8,542	8,631	1.0	8,607	71.3	5.2	17.7	2.0	3.8	17.5	60.8	21.7	3,999	68.9	23.8	47.5
Willowbrook CDP	2,076	NA	NA	2,048	63.5	31.5	1.0	0.8	3.1	12.3	71.4	16.4	781	90.9	14.7	48.3
Willow Hill village	230	229	-0.4	201	97.0	0.0	0.0	3.0	0.0	20.4	67.8	11.9	78	74.4	67.9	9.0
Willow Springs village	5,662	5,709	0.8	5,692	85.8	1.8	4.3	1.2	6.9	18.2	65.0	16.8	2,375	86.2	34.1	39.9
Wilmette village	27,087	27,446	1.3	27,345	80.4	0.9	12.7	1.4	4.6	28.9	53.3	17.8	9,604	85.6	5.4	81.5
Wilmington village	142	138	-2.8	148	97.3	0.0	0.0	1.4	1.4	29.7	61.6	8.8	57	84.2	75.4	5.3
Wilmington city	5,720	5,712	-0.1	5,934	84.8	2.0	1.0	2.4	9.8	25.2	60.6	14.2	2,278	65.3	53.9	18.2
Wilsonville village	586	571	-2.6	592	93.6	0.0	0.0	6.1	0.3	17.4	72.1	10.5	227	78.0	60.4	4.0
Winchester city	1,593	1,547	-2.9	1,644	99.5	0.0	0.0	0.5	0.0	25.8	54.3	19.8	676	69.1	56.4	15.4
Windsor village	748	716	-4.3	935	97.4	0.3	0.0	1.5	0.7	26.2	58.6	15.3	375	70.4	53.9	18.4
Windsor city	1,187	1,175	-1.0	1,366	97.4	0.0	0.2	0.8	1.6	29.1	55.5	15.4	525	72.6	45.1	11.2
Winfield village	9,077	9,569	5.4	9,368	89.0	1.3	1.3	2.2	6.3	21.6	63.5	14.9	3,563	93.1	18.1	52.9
Winnebago village	3,101	3,026	-2.4	3,203	89.4	3.9	0.0	2.7	4.0	25.3	62.0	12.7	1,169	83.6	33.9	24.0
Winnetka village	12,187	12,490	2.5	12,366	88.9	0.2	4.6	3.7	2.6	33.4	52.0	14.7	4,043	90.8	3.1	90.1
Winslow village	338	333	-1.5	235	96.6	0.0	1.3	0.9	1.3	20.4	61.4	18.3	106	63.2	48.1	7.5
Winthrop Harbor village	6,760	6,730	-0.4	6,744	87.6	1.1	2.3	2.6	6.3	20.4	66.3	13.3	2,525	78.5	33.7	23.7
Witt city	903	875	-3.1	775	95.4	4.5	0.0	0.0	0.1	28.8	54.0	17.0	333	86.5	57.1	6.9
Wonder Lake village	4,014	3,944	-1.7	3,769	89.4	0.0	0.0	0.5	10.1	23.5	67.0	9.6	1,354	92.3	26.5	28.4
Wood Dale city	13,770	13,945	1.3	13,882	71.0	1.1	4.4	0.9	22.7	22.4	60.2	17.3	5,116	82.1	40.7	23.4
Woodhull village	811	792	-2.3	1,076	95.2	0.3	0.0	1.1	3.4	27.7	57.8	14.4	413	77.7	47.5	14.5
Woodland village	324	327	0.9	370	94.9	0.5	0.0	1.9	2.7	30.8	59.8	9.5	144	71.5	61.1	0.0
Woodlawn village	698	698	0.0	616	94.3	0.6	0.3	2.6	2.1	23.2	58.5	18.3	242	84.7	43.4	19.8
Woodridge village	32,967	33,378	1.2	33,227	64.5	8.1	11.4	3.1	13.0	22.3	68.4	9.3	12,935	65.5	20.0	48.7
Wood River city	10,657	10,355	-2.8	10,477	93.9	0.5	0.8	0.4	4.4	21.2	62.1	16.7	4,573	72.8	38.2	16.0
Woodson village	512	499	-2.5	438	94.7	0.0	0.0	2.3	3.0	21.4	64.1	14.4	191	91.6	55.5	17.8
Woodstock city	24,771	25,178	1.6	25,121	73.2	3.4	1.8	1.0	20.5	26.2	64.1	9.7	9,397	64.2	32.1	31.9
Worden village	1,044	1,030	-1.3	1,136	95.5	0.4	1.6	2.5	0.0	23.1	63.1	13.7	447	80.3	50.8	13.6
Worth village	10,789	10,838	0.5	10,827	86.7	2.4	1.3	1.0	8.6	22.2	66.2	11.4	4,171	71.6	48.7	16.5
Wyanet village	991	963	-2.8	1,172	94.1	0.0	0.0	2.5	3.4	27.8	60.2	11.9	421	83.6	50.1	5.7
Wyoming city	1,429	1,383	-3.2	1,553	96.3	0.0	0.9	1.2	1.5	27.8	51.1	21.2	609	76.5	54.5	12.8
Xenia village	392	385	-1.8	508	92.9	0.0	0.0	0.2	6.9	25.4	56.5	17.9	171	82.5	53.8	4.7
Yale village	86	86	0.0	74	85.1	0.0	5.4	0.0	9.5	31.1	54.1	14.9	23	100.0	39.1	8.7
Yates City village	691	678	-1.9	804	94.2	0.0	0.0	5.6	0.2	29.2	53.1	17.9	281	84.7	49.8	7.1
Yorkville city	16,919	18,096	7.0	17,980	82.2	5.1	2.3	1.2	9.2	32.3	59.9	7.7	6,000	77.2	23.2	35.8
Zeigler city	1,801	1,762	-2.2	1,850	97.4	0.2	0.0	0.9	1.5	26.0	57.7	16.3	640	74.5	51.7	10.5
Zion city	24,346	24,264	-0.3	24,292	33.8	32.0	3.0	4.3	26.9	29.4	61.0	9.7	8,115	55.7	47.6	16.1
INDIANA	6,484,192	6,596,855	1.7	6,542,411	80.8	9.0	1.7	2.1	6.3	24.4	62.0	13.6	2,492,183	69.5	44.1	24.8
Aberdeen CDP	1,875	NA	NA	1,831	87.8	0.0	4.2	1.5	6.6	27.8	59.1	13.2	744	71.1	6.2	68.3
Advance town	477	509	6.7	488	100.0	0.0	0.0	0.0	0.0	29.1	60.5	10.5	168	78.0	56.5	13.1
Akron town	1,167	1,145	-1.9	1,337	70.9	0.0	0.0	0.6	28.5	35.2	52.9	11.9	440	70.5	65.2	3.4
Alamo town	65	65	0.0	59	98.3	0.0	0.0	1.7	0.0	13.6	83.0	3.4	24	95.8	79.2	4.2
Albany town	2,165	2,127	-1.8	1,849	97.1	0.0	0.0	2.4	0.5	17.7	62.9	19.3	860	74.4	54.1	17.9
Albion town	2,349	2,319	-1.3	2,347	96.8	0.8	0.0	0.7	1.7	23.9	61.4	14.5	878	63.6	58.2	11.2
Alexandria city	5,145	5,067	-1.5	5,100	91.1	1.4	0.0	0.1	7.4	23.4	58.8	17.8	2,202	60.1	51.3	9.6
Alfordsville town	101	105	4.0	84	98.8	0.0	0.0	0.0	1.2	20.2	47.7	32.1	41	87.8	51.2	0.0
Alton town	55	55	0.0	40	97.5	2.5	0.0	0.0	0.0	0.0	75.0	25.0	17	100.0	76.5	5.9
Altona town	197	197	0.0	255	94.1	0.0	0.0	4.3	1.6	17.6	66.2	16.1	105	73.3	84.8	1.0
Ambia town	239	236	-1.3	256	75.0	0.0	0.0	2.0	23.0	35.6	56.8	7.8	88	75.0	60.2	4.5
Amboy town	384	378	-1.6	348	96.6	0.0	0.0	0.9	2.6	22.1	55.4	22.4	146	85.6	63.0	12.3
Americus CDP	423	NA	NA	535	100.0	0.0	0.0	0.0	0.0	29.7	53.9	16.4	199	67.8	77.4	10.1
Amo town	401	413	3.0	495	99.8	0.0	0.0	0.2	0.0	25.1	61.4	13.5	169	64.5	50.9	15.4
Anderson city	56,176	55,455	-1.3	55,789	77.6	13.5	0.6	3.3	5.0	22.5	61.6	16.0	23,132	57.0	53.6	14.6
Andrews town	1,151	1,134	-1.5	1,099	96.3	0.0	0.4	2.6	0.7	23.2	64.9	11.8	470	67.7	70.4	4.3
Angola city	8,606	8,624	0.2	8,610	87.7	1.6	0.9	5.8	3.9	22.3	63.4	14.2	3,039	55.9	40.7	23.9
Arcadia town	1,666	1,680	0.8	1,276	94.8	0.1	1.0	0.5	3.6	26.7	55.3	18.0	500	67.0	64.4	8.8
Argos town	1,691	1,666	-1.5	1,783	96.7	0.0	0.1	0.9	2.2	30.7	58.2	11.2	648	66.2	64.4	8.0

1 May be of any race.

Table A. All Places — **Population and Housing**

STATE City, town, township, borough, or CDP (county if applicable)	Population: 2010 census total population	Population: 2014 estimated population	Population: Percent change 2010–2014	Population: ACS total population estimate 2010–2014	Race and Hispanic or Latino origin (percent), 2010–2014: White alone, not Hispanic or Latino	Black alone, not Hispanic or Latino	Asian alone, not Hispanic or Latino	All other races or 2 or more races, not Hispanic or Latino	Hispanic or Latino[1]	Age (percent), 2010–2014: Under 18 years old	Age 18 to 64 years old	Age 65 years and older	Households, 2010–2014: Total occupied housing units	Percent owner occupied	Householders by level of education (percent): High school diploma or less	Bachelor's degree or more
	1	2	3	4	5	6	7	8	9	10	11	12	13	14	15	16
INDIANA—Con.																
Arlington CDP	433	NA	NA	471	97.0	0.0	0.0	3.0	0.0	31.6	53.8	14.6	145	94.5	73.8	7.6
Ashley town	983	982	-0.1	1,255	96.5	0.1	0.0	0.6	2.8	29.1	61.5	9.6	492	65.4	50.4	7.5
Atlanta town	725	740	2.1	690	93.9	0.0	0.0	2.8	3.3	25.4	61.0	13.6	249	80.7	61.4	4.0
Attica city	3,245	3,132	-3.5	3,365	93.5	0.9	0.4	0.6	4.6	20.0	60.8	19.1	1,475	60.2	56.8	16.0
Auburn city	12,742	12,834	0.7	12,972	94.5	0.2	0.6	1.0	3.7	24.0	60.1	15.8	5,421	74.5	42.5	22.6
Aurora city	3,750	3,705	-1.2	3,762	97.6	0.0	1.1	0.6	0.7	23.6	61.5	14.8	1,563	53.2	54.6	9.2
Austin city	4,295	4,163	-3.1	4,294	95.3	2.2	0.0	0.3	2.3	26.8	61.0	12.1	1,636	64.0	66.0	6.6
Avilla town	2,401	2,411	0.4	2,332	92.9	0.2	2.9	1.8	2.1	25.0	59.9	15.2	966	77.4	51.0	14.1
Avoca CDP	583	NA	NA	821	100.0	0.0	0.0	0.0	0.0	37.3	59.6	3.2	248	95.2	13.7	18.5
Avon town	13,566	15,971	17.7	14,570	77.2	6.8	1.8	4.6	9.5	31.4	60.2	8.3	4,916	83.6	20.9	41.9
Bainbridge town	750	742	-1.1	885	98.8	0.0	0.0	0.5	0.8	28.1	62.3	9.6	292	51.7	59.6	8.2
Bargersville town	5,885	6,627	12.6	6,324	97.2	0.0	0.9	1.9	0.0	28.6	58.9	12.5	2,349	71.9	44.3	27.1
Bass Lake CDP	1,195	NA	NA	1,298	92.4	0.0	0.0	4.9	2.8	19.6	64.5	15.9	552	73.6	53.1	13.0
Batesville city	6,524	6,541	0.3	6,397	96.4	0.3	2.2	0.2	0.9	26.1	56.1	17.7	2,422	70.2	37.0	34.4
Battle Ground town	1,334	1,459	9.4	1,053	97.0	0.0	0.5	1.3	1.2	20.2	67.9	11.9	427	92.0	19.4	50.1
Bedford city	13,407	13,355	-0.4	13,384	94.3	0.6	1.6	0.8	2.8	22.7	58.1	19.5	5,648	60.5	52.3	13.2
Beech Grove city	14,194	14,514	2.3	14,301	90.8	2.8	0.4	2.6	3.4	26.3	57.6	16.2	5,534	55.7	51.7	15.7
Berne city	3,999	4,038	1.0	3,810	94.0	0.2	1.0	0.7	4.0	24.0	50.6	25.5	1,539	63.7	50.1	22.2
Bethany town	81	81	0.0	109	98.2	0.0	0.0	0.0	1.8	23.8	65.2	11.0	42	81.0	54.8	0.0
Beverly Shores town	599	610	1.8	539	98.9	0.0	0.0	0.0	1.1	12.1	50.6	37.3	264	87.1	12.1	69.7
Bicknell city	2,913	2,892	-0.7	2,961	99.3	0.1	0.0	0.0	0.6	22.2	61.0	17.0	1,230	58.0	63.3	6.8
Birdseye town	416	407	-2.2	380	100.0	0.0	0.0	0.0	0.0	20.8	60.5	18.7	175	63.4	72.6	5.7
Blanford CDP	342	NA	NA	284	100.0	0.0	0.0	0.0	0.0	13.4	74.6	12.0	101	100.0	85.1	0.0
Bloomfield town	2,386	2,356	-1.3	2,724	94.2	0.4	0.0	3.0	2.3	26.5	57.2	16.2	1,092	66.1	53.8	16.4
Bloomingdale town	335	333	-0.6	305	98.7	0.0	0.0	1.3	0.0	28.8	60.3	10.8	110	94.5	46.4	8.2
Bloomington city	80,307	83,322	3.8	81,963	79.3	3.9	9.2	3.5	4.1	11.6	80.4	8.0	30,085	34.3	16.5	49.3
Blountsville town	134	132	-1.5	108	98.1	1.9	0.0	0.0	0.0	22.3	62.1	15.7	41	82.9	63.4	19.5
Bluffton city	9,896	9,969	0.7	9,621	94.7	0.6	0.1	2.2	2.4	23.5	57.6	19.0	4,101	67.3	51.4	16.1
Boonville city	6,246	6,164	-1.3	6,220	93.6	0.2	0.0	2.3	3.9	22.4	57.2	20.5	2,423	71.8	49.5	14.7
Borden town	821	876	6.7	681	95.9	0.0	0.0	0.9	3.2	26.3	56.5	17.2	273	76.6	57.5	10.3
Boston town	138	136	-1.4	175	100.0	0.0	0.0	0.0	0.0	23.9	53.6	22.3	74	81.1	74.3	4.1
Boswell town	778	763	-1.9	728	78.8	0.0	0.8	1.4	19.0	25.1	59.8	14.8	302	68.2	60.6	18.2
Bourbon town	1,810	1,791	-1.0	1,687	92.3	0.0	2.0	1.3	4.4	26.0	59.5	14.4	725	72.4	57.2	13.0
Brazil city	8,071	8,114	0.5	8,022	93.4	0.7	0.0	4.1	1.8	27.4	56.9	15.8	3,059	60.1	65.1	11.6
Bremen town	4,588	4,589	0.0	4,581	89.9	0.3	0.3	0.0	9.5	25.0	57.4	17.5	1,829	58.3	48.2	17.8
Bright CDP	5,693	NA	NA	5,079	94.2	0.7	0.4	1.1	3.6	23.2	62.6	14.2	1,959	84.8	47.2	24.7
Bristol town	1,602	1,650	3.0	1,889	79.5	3.9	1.6	3.9	11.1	21.2	61.5	17.2	728	68.3	57.0	16.8
Brook town	1,001	986	-1.5	1,164	86.9	0.0	0.0	4.8	8.2	26.9	55.8	17.2	434	68.4	63.4	7.6
Brooklyn town	1,595	1,604	0.6	1,634	92.1	0.3	0.4	1.3	5.9	26.9	61.8	11.4	566	74.9	49.1	10.1
Brooksburg town	81	81	0.0	66	100.0	0.0	0.0	0.0	0.0	21.2	71.2	7.6	32	65.6	62.5	0.0
Brookston town	1,554	1,544	-0.6	1,582	93.9	1.3	1.4	2.7	0.7	29.3	58.6	12.1	607	72.0	53.7	13.8
Brookville town	2,596	2,575	-0.8	2,598	98.0	0.0	0.3	0.0	1.7	24.4	53.0	22.5	1,185	57.5	54.1	16.3
Brownsburg town	21,542	23,322	8.3	22,618	90.6	3.4	1.7	1.3	3.1	25.6	61.9	12.4	8,918	75.1	31.3	39.8
Brownstown town	2,936	2,956	0.7	2,960	97.5	0.1	0.0	0.0	2.4	25.0	56.4	18.6	1,211	58.1	50.3	13.8
Bruceville town	481	477	-0.8	710	95.4	3.1	0.0	1.5	0.0	28.8	62.7	8.5	275	73.8	54.2	8.0
Bryant town	252	256	1.6	285	96.5	0.0	2.8	0.7	0.0	30.9	54.5	14.7	87	82.8	79.3	1.1
Buck Creek CDP	207	NA	NA	202	100.0	0.0	0.0	0.0	0.0	10.4	82.7	6.9	66	100.0	18.2	12.1
Buffalo CDP	692	NA	NA	1,016	87.5	0.0	0.0	0.8	11.7	20.1	65.0	14.9	359	81.1	68.0	3.6
Bunker Hill town	888	860	-3.2	560	89.8	8.4	0.9	0.4	0.5	21.4	62.7	16.1	241	69.7	53.1	11.6
Burket town	195	195	0.0	159	93.1	0.0	0.0	6.9	0.0	30.1	57.7	11.9	58	79.3	62.1	3.4
Burlington town	603	598	-0.8	698	93.3	2.7	0.0	0.6	3.4	25.3	51.0	23.9	315	68.9	46.0	17.1
Burnettsville town	346	343	-0.9	383	90.1	0.5	1.8	5.2	2.3	25.3	58.4	16.2	166	78.9	63.9	9.6
Burns City CDP	117	NA	NA	93	100.0	0.0	0.0	0.0	0.0	3.2	69.9	26.9	39	71.8	69.2	0.0
Burns Harbor town	1,156	1,571	35.9	1,476	93.8	0.7	0.7	1.5	3.3	29.4	62.4	8.2	499	80.6	47.5	30.5
Butler city	2,685	2,690	0.2	2,908	97.2	0.0	0.0	1.3	1.4	28.0	60.6	11.5	1,001	66.8	66.2	9.2
Butlerville CDP	282	NA	NA	248	100.0	0.0	0.0	0.0	0.0	0.0	92.3	7.7	149	36.2	89.9	10.1
Cadiz town	147	145	-1.4	162	93.8	0.6	0.0	5.6	0.0	35.2	56.7	8.0	45	60.0	66.7	11.1
Cambridge City town	1,860	1,806	-2.9	1,871	98.6	0.1	0.3	1.0	0.0	19.8	59.4	20.7	822	71.8	56.2	11.6
Camden town	611	602	-1.5	749	98.1	0.0	0.0	0.8	1.1	26.9	58.5	14.4	273	85.0	64.1	12.8
Campbellsburg town	585	578	-1.2	628	92.2	7.8	0.0	0.0	0.0	38.5	47.9	13.7	234	72.2	65.8	3.8
Canaan CDP	90	NA	NA	96	100.0	0.0	0.0	0.0	0.0	25.0	75.0	0.0	36	44.4	44.4	0.0
Cannelburg town	149	154	3.4	174	100.0	0.0	0.0	0.0	0.0	28.1	64.2	7.5	62	74.2	74.2	8.1
Cannelton city	1,563	1,532	-2.0	1,562	92.7	0.2	0.5	3.2	3.4	27.7	59.4	13.0	639	44.1	64.5	6.7
Carbon town	397	390	-1.8	577	100.0	0.0	0.0	0.0	0.0	32.9	58.3	8.7	178	79.2	84.8	6.2
Carlisle town	692	676	-2.3	704	98.6	0.0	0.0	1.4	0.0	26.9	60.6	12.6	243	74.5	44.0	25.5
Carmel city	79,191	86,682	9.5	83,474	81.6	2.7	9.7	2.5	3.5	28.5	60.1	11.5	30,594	78.5	9.6	71.9
Carthage town	927	901	-2.8	767	98.8	0.0	0.0	0.9	0.3	27.3	56.1	16.4	313	58.1	62.6	7.0
Cayuga town	1,162	1,117	-3.9	1,016	97.3	0.0	0.0	2.2	0.5	18.0	63.6	18.4	424	83.7	70.0	12.0
Cedar Grove town	156	155	-0.6	211	98.6	0.0	0.0	1.4	0.0	21.3	68.1	10.4	100	58.0	44.0	10.0
Cedar Lake town	11,560	11,854	2.5	11,653	90.8	0.3	0.3	1.9	6.6	27.9	61.7	10.5	4,013	80.6	53.4	15.5
Center Point town	242	239	-1.2	223	99.6	0.0	0.4	0.0	0.0	25.1	58.3	16.6	90	75.6	40.0	12.2
Centerville town	2,643	2,603	-1.5	2,637	90.1	2.2	1.9	4.2	1.6	27.9	58.1	14.0	1,033	73.1	46.1	16.7
Chalmers town	508	506	-0.4	439	92.0	0.0	0.0	2.7	5.2	30.2	56.2	13.4	172	82.0	55.8	12.8
Chandler town	3,423	3,377	-1.3	3,236	95.2	0.0	0.0	3.8	1.0	32.8	57.8	9.4	1,161	70.6	54.3	10.1
Charlestown city	7,585	8,054	6.2	7,802	82.3	4.0	0.0	2.1	11.6	25.7	62.6	11.9	2,903	63.0	48.3	15.9
Chesterfield town	2,550	2,504	-1.8	2,528	92.7	0.7	0.0	6.2	0.4	21.3	62.8	16.0	1,094	72.4	53.8	8.7
Chesterton town	13,092	13,403	2.4	13,894	84.7	3.3	3.8	1.4	6.8	26.1	61.5	12.5	4,985	71.6	31.3	37.8
Chrisney town	485	484	-0.2	469	98.5	0.0	0.9	0.6	0.0	23.9	63.8	12.4	180	83.3	55.0	14.4
Churubusco town	1,796	1,790	-0.3	1,806	95.6	0.0	0.3	1.9	2.1	25.0	60.3	14.7	757	81.2	52.7	11.0
Cicero town	4,812	4,891	1.6	4,870	92.1	0.0	0.3	1.8	5.8	21.6	64.6	13.8	1,943	78.8	40.8	25.7
Clarksburg CDP	149	NA	NA	326	100.0	0.0	0.0	0.0	0.0	16.2	83.7	0.0	169	63.3	63.3	0.0
Clarks Hill town	614	665	8.3	592	97.1	0.0	0.0	1.7	1.2	27.2	63.2	9.6	231	70.6	68.8	3.9
Clarksville town	21,724	21,879	0.7	21,579	81.0	5.1	0.5	2.8	10.6	23.6	60.6	15.9	8,794	60.3	45.8	20.0
Clay City town	861	843	-2.1	764	100.0	0.0	0.0	0.0	0.0	22.5	57.8	19.8	333	72.7	51.4	14.4
Claypool town	431	432	0.2	313	93.0	0.0	0.0	2.9	4.2	23.1	65.6	11.5	124	70.2	69.4	2.4
Clayton town	972	1,001	3.0	1,029	94.7	0.3	1.0	2.8	1.3	27.4	62.4	10.1	384	69.3	52.1	14.1
Clear Lake town	339	341	0.6	503	98.0	0.0	0.0	2.0	0.0	8.0	52.4	39.8	242	92.6	32.6	38.0
Clermont town	1,356	1,402	3.4	1,388	87.5	8.1	0.0	2.3	2.0	19.1	66.5	14.4	570	83.7	37.0	32.5
Clifford town	225	232	3.1	276	100.0	0.0	0.0	0.0	0.0	31.1	58.1	10.5	99	50.5	63.6	0.0
Clinton city	4,893	4,812	-1.7	4,821	95.7	0.5	0.4	1.3	2.0	25.4	58.8	15.8	1,954	63.3	60.8	15.8
Cloverdale town	2,158	2,098	-2.8	2,051	97.3	0.1	0.0	2.1	0.5	25.4	51.5	23.1	839	71.9	56.7	13.5

1 May be of any race.

Table A. All Places — **Population and Housing**

STATE City, town, township, borough, or CDP (county if applicable)	Population: 2010 census total population	Population: 2014 estimated population	Population: Percent change 2010–2014	Population: ACS total population estimate 2010–2014	Race and Hispanic or Latino origin (percent), 2010–2014: White alone, not Hispanic or Latino	Black alone, not Hispanic or Latino	Asian alone, not Hispanic or Latino	All other races or 2 or more races, not Hispanic or Latino	Hispanic or Latino[1]	Age (percent), 2010–2014: Under 18 years old	Age 18 to 64 years old	Age 65 years and older	Households, 2010–2014: Total occupied housing units	Percent owner occupied	Householders by level of education (percent): High school diploma or less	Bachelor's degree or more
	1	2	3	4	5	6	7	8	9	10	11	12	13	14	15	16
INDIANA—Con.																
Coalmont CDP	402	NA	NA	331	99.1	0.0	0.0	0.9	0.0	30.5	65.3	4.2	122	49.2	93.4	6.6
Coatesville town	523	542	3.6	580	97.1	0.9	0.0	2.1	0.0	28.1	62.0	9.8	209	83.7	66.5	10.5
Colburn CDP	193	NA	NA	240	100.0	0.0	0.0	0.0	0.0	25.5	64.1	10.4	67	43.3	19.4	0.0
Colfax town	691	683	-1.2	754	98.4	0.0	0.0	1.1	0.5	28.4	52.7	19.0	256	71.1	64.1	7.0
Collegeville CDP	330	NA	NA	337	81.6	11.3	0.0	5.6	1.5	0.0	96.8	3.3	23	100.0	0.0	0.0
Columbia City city	8,750	8,829	0.9	9,057	92.3	1.0	0.4	2.0	4.3	23.2	61.3	15.5	3,708	64.4	44.1	22.0
Columbus city	44,077	46,124	4.6	45,522	83.1	2.9	7.3	2.2	4.5	24.8	60.3	14.9	18,420	62.1	38.1	35.0
Connersville city	13,506	13,032	-3.5	13,267	94.5	2.4	0.6	1.1	1.4	21.8	58.8	19.3	5,464	58.7	65.3	8.8
Converse town	1,265	1,234	-2.5	1,491	96.6	0.0	0.0	0.9	2.5	30.3	59.3	10.3	549	64.1	61.2	13.8
Cordry Sweetwater Lakes CDP	1,128	NA	NA	1,034	97.7	0.0	0.0	2.3	0.0	6.3	69.8	24.1	510	91.8	48.0	26.5
Corunna town	254	254	0.0	243	88.9	0.0	4.1	6.6	0.4	35.7	57.2	7.0	84	85.7	66.7	2.4
Corydon town	3,122	3,123	0.0	3,114	94.7	0.0	0.0	4.0	1.3	28.4	56.5	15.4	1,377	59.9	59.7	16.0
Country Club Heights town	79	78	-1.3	114	92.1	7.9	0.0	0.0	0.0	16.6	62.3	21.1	43	100.0	27.9	46.5
Country Squire Lakes CDP	3,571	NA	NA	3,096	91.5	1.4	0.3	0.0	6.8	24.6	66.4	9.0	1,149	71.6	70.1	4.3
Covington city	2,645	2,579	-2.5	2,641	97.3	0.8	0.3	1.1	0.5	22.2	55.4	22.4	1,076	72.5	46.4	12.0
Crandall town	152	151	-0.7	137	100.0	0.0	0.0	0.0	0.0	24.8	50.2	24.8	58	81.0	43.1	20.7
Crane town	184	183	-0.5	177	97.2	0.0	0.0	1.7	1.1	18.6	53.2	28.2	77	71.4	64.9	13.0
Crawfordsville city	15,924	15,988	0.4	15,988	88.6	2.2	0.2	1.7	7.2	23.9	60.0	16.1	5,993	56.5	54.9	15.2
Cromwell town	512	504	-1.6	496	79.6	0.0	0.0	0.8	19.6	26.2	63.5	10.3	207	56.5	73.4	7.2
Crothersville town	1,585	1,599	0.9	1,573	95.7	0.0	0.4	2.6	1.3	20.1	62.9	16.8	671	75.6	56.8	5.8
Crown Point city	27,837	28,623	2.8	28,259	82.3	7.3	2.0	1.6	6.7	20.8	62.5	16.8	10,773	77.1	37.1	34.7
Crows Nest town	73	75	2.7	113	98.2	1.8	0.0	0.0	0.0	9.7	66.5	23.9	43	100.0	4.7	90.7
Culver town	1,353	1,392	2.9	1,513	86.3	1.1	0.2	3.5	8.9	22.9	55.0	22.1	611	64.8	32.7	35.7
Cumberland town	5,279	5,389	2.1	5,243	83.1	7.9	0.8	2.1	6.2	24.2	61.2	14.6	1,985	60.2	50.3	19.8
Cynthiana town	545	539	-1.1	592	90.4	0.0	0.5	5.7	3.4	18.8	68.0	13.2	248	85.1	54.0	7.7
Dale town	1,593	1,556	-2.3	1,834	75.5	1.3	0.1	1.4	21.6	23.9	54.7	21.4	707	73.1	59.8	8.1
Daleville town	1,647	1,615	-1.9	1,650	95.9	0.1	0.7	3.3	0.0	23.0	62.7	14.4	687	68.0	38.1	18.3
Dana town	608	581	-4.4	538	95.2	0.0	0.0	1.9	3.0	15.8	62.9	21.2	221	72.9	52.9	10.0
Danville town	9,006	9,593	6.5	9,258	97.0	0.6	0.1	1.6	0.7	27.9	57.8	14.5	3,420	69.4	31.1	29.9
Darlington town	843	839	-0.5	757	99.5	0.3	0.0	0.3	0.0	26.0	61.1	12.9	299	70.2	53.2	14.4
Darmstadt town	1,407	1,456	3.5	1,468	95.7	0.5	1.2	2.6	0.0	17.5	64.5	17.8	586	91.3	29.7	37.2
Dayton town	1,420	1,550	9.2	1,462	85.0	3.1	0.5	1.1	10.3	30.2	60.8	8.9	546	74.5	43.2	21.1
Decatur city	9,405	9,432	0.3	9,511	86.3	2.1	0.5	0.7	10.4	23.5	61.6	15.1	4,020	68.4	60.1	13.4
Decker town	248	246	-0.8	229	99.1	0.0	0.0	0.0	0.9	20.6	59.4	20.1	79	88.6	82.3	2.5
Delphi city	2,893	2,868	-0.9	2,787	84.4	1.3	0.0	1.5	12.8	25.9	53.4	20.7	1,076	66.8	56.8	10.6
De Motte town	3,814	3,978	4.3	3,899	89.7	3.8	0.5	1.6	4.4	25.6	55.7	18.6	1,530	77.6	53.3	5.9
Denver town	482	469	-2.7	544	91.7	0.0	0.0	7.4	0.9	20.2	65.6	14.3	185	89.2	67.6	7.0
Deputy CDP	86	NA	NA	13	100.0	0.0	0.0	0.0	0.0	0.0	46.2	53.8	13	53.8	100.0	0.0
Dillsboro town	1,334	1,321	-1.0	1,473	91.9	0.4	2.2	4.8	0.8	28.8	50.4	20.7	515	50.7	60.4	13.4
Dover Hill CDP	114	NA	NA	130	100.0	0.0	0.0	0.0	0.0	22.3	59.2	18.5	62	100.0	48.4	0.0
Dresser CDP	104	NA	NA	131	82.4	14.5	0.0	3.1	0.0	3.1	68.0	29.0	53	100.0	88.7	0.0
Dublin town	801	779	-2.7	684	95.5	0.0	0.0	0.4	4.1	18.0	60.7	21.2	302	77.8	69.2	7.0
Dubois CDP	488	NA	NA	483	85.5	14.5	0.0	0.0	0.0	25.3	55.6	19.3	222	64.4	57.2	16.7
Dugger town	920	902	-2.0	832	99.5	0.0	0.0	0.1	0.4	19.7	61.6	18.8	363	81.3	68.9	8.8
Dune Acres town	182	186	2.2	235	96.2	0.0	3.0	0.0	0.9	7.2	37.1	55.7	119	95.8	9.2	77.3
Dunkirk city	2,362	2,348	-0.6	2,365	98.4	0.4	0.0	0.3	0.9	29.4	57.3	13.5	948	66.1	74.3	6.2
Dunlap CDP	6,235	NA	NA	6,557	85.2	2.2	0.2	2.0	10.5	30.6	57.4	12.1	2,157	86.8	45.6	23.7
Dunreith town	177	174	-1.7	203	97.5	0.0	0.0	2.0	0.5	27.7	55.6	16.7	75	82.7	62.7	6.7
Dupont town	339	339	0.0	316	99.4	0.0	0.0	0.3	0.3	22.2	71.8	6.0	113	72.6	56.6	7.1
Dyer town	16,390	16,169	-1.3	16,322	81.4	4.0	1.8	2.6	10.2	20.7	62.7	16.6	5,772	91.6	38.7	30.8
Earl Park town	348	336	-3.4	386	95.3	0.3	0.0	1.8	2.6	16.8	72.0	11.1	172	80.2	65.7	2.9
East Chicago city	29,698	28,990	-2.4	29,387	10.3	39.1	0.2	0.4	50.0	31.0	58.2	10.6	9,890	43.4	62.2	6.5
East Enterprise CDP	148	NA	NA	500	100.0	0.0	0.0	0.0	0.0	42.6	47.8	9.6	161	63.4	95.0	0.0
East Germantown town	395	379	-4.1	244	100.0	0.0	0.0	0.0	0.0	12.2	60.6	27.0	114	70.2	64.0	12.3
Eaton town	1,805	1,758	-2.6	1,736	97.2	0.0	0.2	2.5	0.0	27.5	56.7	15.6	683	72.8	54.2	13.2
Economy town	185	182	-1.6	188	93.6	0.0	0.0	6.4	0.0	30.9	46.3	22.9	79	78.5	77.2	10.1
Edgewood town	1,913	1,885	-1.5	1,879	96.9	3.1	0.0	0.0	0.0	23.1	50.4	26.4	822	91.5	27.7	38.1
Edinburgh town	4,479	4,533	1.2	4,023	91.1	0.8	0.1	0.2	7.8	26.5	60.1	13.5	1,540	52.5	68.1	8.4
Edwardsport town	302	300	-0.7	313	99.7	0.0	0.0	0.0	0.3	24.0	64.9	11.2	124	90.3	71.0	4.0
Elberfeld town	625	643	2.9	691	100.0	0.0	0.0	0.0	0.0	23.2	59.6	17.2	263	88.6	44.5	12.5
Elizabeth town	162	160	-1.2	192	97.9	0.0	0.0	2.1	0.0	23.4	56.8	19.8	69	88.4	59.4	15.9
Elizabethtown town	512	518	1.2	561	88.1	2.1	0.0	4.3	5.5	33.6	63.2	3.2	166	59.6	78.9	4.2
Elkhart city	50,904	51,421	1.0	51,539	58.1	13.5	1.8	2.8	23.8	29.0	60.1	11.0	19,064	51.0	57.2	14.1
Ellettsville town	6,207	6,475	4.3	6,352	92.3	2.1	0.0	2.7	2.8	24.7	61.2	14.2	2,573	70.7	41.6	29.7
Elnora town	640	654	2.2	497	94.8	0.0	0.0	2.2	3.0	16.7	64.1	19.1	226	73.5	52.7	7.5
Elwood city	8,600	8,480	-1.4	8,569	92.3	0.0	0.3	3.6	3.8	27.3	60.2	12.5	3,320	58.7	56.7	8.9
Emison CDP	154	NA	NA	128	100.0	0.0	0.0	0.0	0.0	26.5	56.1	17.2	46	65.2	47.8	19.6
English town	645	641	-0.6	802	93.9	1.9	0.0	2.0	2.2	23.0	59.7	17.3	349	59.9	72.5	5.7
Etna Green town	586	587	0.2	679	99.0	0.4	0.0	0.6	0.0	26.1	59.2	14.6	249	79.1	57.8	15.7
Evansville city	120,081	120,346	0.2	120,220	80.7	12.4	0.6	3.2	3.1	22.5	62.9	14.6	51,335	53.3	44.1	20.4
Fairland town	315	316	0.3	334	97.0	0.0	0.0	0.9	2.1	25.5	60.3	14.4	136	67.6	62.5	11.8
Fairmount town	2,954	2,880	-2.5	2,998	93.2	0.3	0.8	4.7	1.1	25.9	58.7	15.4	1,109	74.6	54.5	16.0
Fairview Park town	1,386	1,333	-3.8	1,200	96.8	0.2	1.3	0.9	0.8	18.8	56.9	24.4	566	75.6	50.7	15.9
Farmersburg town	1,118	1,098	-1.8	1,163	97.2	0.3	0.0	0.4	2.1	23.5	60.9	15.6	499	70.7	50.3	14.4
Farmland town	1,333	1,294	-2.9	1,413	94.6	0.3	0.0	3.3	1.9	22.2	58.5	19.3	593	77.2	55.6	14.7
Ferdinand town	2,157	2,180	1.1	1,984	98.6	0.0	0.0	0.0	1.4	20.2	56.5	23.4	739	77.1	49.7	19.6
Fillmore town	533	526	-1.3	565	99.6	0.0	0.2	0.0	0.2	25.7	64.1	10.1	219	73.1	56.6	7.8
Fishers town	76,880	86,325	12.3	81,060	84.3	4.6	5.4	2.5	3.3	32.4	61.1	6.4	28,216	83.1	11.4	63.2
Fish Lake CDP	1,016	NA	NA	751	94.8	5.2	0.0	0.0	0.0	21.4	64.5	14.1	344	87.5	60.8	28.2
Flora town	2,036	1,994	-2.1	2,184	98.1	0.3	0.0	0.0	1.6	25.0	56.6	18.4	903	67.7	55.0	15.0
Florence CDP	80	NA	NA	129	100.0	0.0	0.0	0.0	0.0	7.8	48.1	44.2	63	77.8	100.0	0.0
Fontanet CDP	423	NA	NA	260	93.5	3.8	0.0	2.7	0.0	16.2	80.7	3.1	103	66.0	36.9	9.7
Fort Branch town	2,779	2,810	1.1	3,194	95.5	0.8	0.6	3.0	0.0	22.7	60.4	17.0	1,314	74.4	45.7	20.8
Fortville town	3,905	3,953	1.2	4,055	98.4	0.0	0.0	1.6	0.0	27.2	61.1	11.9	1,472	59.8	56.7	29.6
Fort Wayne city	253,700	258,522	1.9	255,784	69.4	15.4	3.6	3.6	8.1	26.3	61.4	12.5	101,549	63.2	38.2	25.8
Fountain City town	811	791	-2.5	815	94.6	0.0	1.5	3.9	0.0	30.1	55.7	14.1	289	72.3	42.6	16.3
Fowler town	2,317	2,274	-1.9	2,340	93.2	2.6	0.0	1.0	3.2	21.7	55.8	22.7	959	70.3	63.4	14.1
Fowlerton town	261	256	-1.9	318	100.0	0.0	0.0	0.0	0.0	32.4	61.0	6.6	101	73.3	76.2	5.0

1 May be of any race.

Table A. All Places — **Population and Housing**

STATE City, town, township, borough, or CDP (county if applicable)	Population: 2010 census total population	Population: 2014 estimated population	Population: Percent change 2010–2014	Population: ACS total population estimate 2010–2014	Race and Hispanic or Latino origin (percent), 2010–2014: White alone, not Hispanic or Latino	Black alone, not Hispanic or Latino	Asian alone, not Hispanic or Latino	All other races or 2 or more races, not Hispanic or Latino	Hispanic or Latino[1]	Age (percent), 2010–2014: Under 18 years old	Age 18 to 64 years old	Age 65 years and older	Households, 2010–2014: Total occupied housing units	Percent owner occupied	Householders by level of education (percent): High school diploma or less	Bachelor's degree or more
	1	2	3	4	5	6	7	8	9	10	11	12	13	14	15	16
INDIANA—Con.																
Francesville town	879	844	-4.0	1,023	96.5	0.0	0.1	0.9	2.5	15.4	68.8	15.8	381	81.1	64.0	7.6
Francisco town	470	473	0.6	771	98.3	0.0	0.0	1.7	0.0	36.5	56.0	7.5	254	84.3	62.6	7.1
Frankfort city	16,442	16,153	-1.8	16,488	71.8	1.4	0.1	0.5	26.2	28.0	58.3	13.7	5,777	60.1	64.5	9.9
Franklin city	23,731	24,356	2.6	24,193	92.2	2.1	0.8	2.1	2.9	26.1	58.9	14.9	8,725	60.8	43.1	23.2
Frankton town	1,862	1,831	-1.7	1,775	90.4	0.0	0.8	1.8	7.0	25.1	60.7	14.1	703	79.1	64.6	10.8
Fredericksburg CDP	85	NA	NA	70	100.0	0.0	0.0	0.0	0.0	12.9	38.6	48.6	32	93.8	56.3	37.5
Freelandville CDP	643	NA	NA	495	100.0	0.0	0.0	0.0	0.0	12.3	65.9	21.6	182	72.5	45.1	5.5
Freetown CDP	385	NA	NA	159	100.0	0.0	0.0	0.0	0.0	0.0	79.2	20.8	71	100.0	100.0	0.0
Fremont town	2,138	2,149	0.5	2,340	85.4	0.0	2.4	10.1	2.1	28.1	61.8	9.9	900	77.4	52.1	9.6
French Lick town	1,801	1,798	-0.2	1,969	85.1	6.0	0.8	3.0	5.0	23.5	54.2	22.2	801	51.1	68.8	5.7
Fulton town	333	327	-1.8	464	97.8	0.2	0.0	1.7	0.2	34.6	58.1	7.1	134	81.3	73.1	6.7
Galena CDP	1,818	NA	NA	1,818	99.1	0.0	0.9	0.0	0.0	33.1	57.3	9.4	565	85.3	34.3	31.0
Galveston town	1,311	1,288	-1.8	1,149	96.7	0.0	0.0	1.8	1.5	24.8	57.7	17.4	504	73.6	50.2	16.1
Garrett city	6,310	6,319	0.1	6,213	97.1	0.1	0.1	2.0	0.7	30.7	57.7	11.6	2,256	66.0	51.5	17.7
Gary city	80,314	77,909	-3.0	79,165	10.6	82.1	0.4	1.4	5.5	27.3	57.5	15.3	30,746	51.7	49.7	13.3
Gas City city	6,167	6,032	-2.2	6,093	92.0	0.9	1.0	2.7	3.4	21.4	59.4	19.1	2,403	69.3	56.7	13.5
Gaston town	871	864	-0.8	896	97.5	0.3	0.3	1.2	0.6	29.4	58.2	12.3	321	81.6	53.3	12.1
Geneva town	1,293	1,313	1.5	1,384	92.8	1.1	0.0	3.0	3.0	17.8	66.9	15.2	597	69.7	63.5	8.7
Gentryville town	268	271	1.1	294	99.3	0.0	0.0	0.3	0.3	27.8	62.2	9.9	109	78.0	61.5	4.6
Georgetown town	2,875	3,162	10.0	3,036	96.5	0.5	0.1	1.9	1.0	30.4	61.9	7.6	1,018	88.5	36.9	29.8
Glenwood town	250	244	-2.4	277	99.6	0.0	0.4	0.0	0.0	31.4	55.2	13.4	100	64.0	71.0	0.0
Goodland town	1,043	1,028	-1.4	1,101	99.3	0.0	0.0	0.2	0.5	19.3	65.3	15.3	463	73.4	68.7	14.7
Goshen city	31,613	32,267	2.1	32,297	63.4	4.0	1.0	3.6	28.0	27.1	58.2	14.5	11,946	57.0	53.5	21.7
Gosport town	826	806	-2.4	848	94.6	0.0	0.0	0.4	5.1	25.7	51.2	23.1	327	53.8	54.4	15.0
Grabill town	1,063	1,121	5.5	1,440	93.1	2.6	0.0	3.1	1.1	29.5	57.6	12.9	540	72.8	45.9	17.0
Grandview town	749	734	-2.0	794	96.7	2.0	0.1	0.4	0.8	34.8	55.3	9.9	251	65.7	68.5	12.4
Granger CDP	30,465	NA	NA	29,400	88.1	2.6	5.2	1.8	2.3	27.4	59.2	13.5	10,040	96.1	20.5	55.1
Greencastle city	10,315	10,362	0.5	10,307	90.8	2.4	3.3	1.4	2.0	18.3	68.3	13.3	3,049	56.1	51.3	20.3
Greendale city	4,520	4,450	-1.5	4,545	92.4	5.0	0.3	0.2	2.2	25.9	60.0	14.0	1,795	79.0	38.2	32.0
Greenfield city	20,624	21,398	3.8	21,012	94.1	0.9	0.9	2.1	2.0	25.1	59.8	15.0	8,027	63.8	42.5	21.5
Greensboro town	143	141	-1.4	168	100.0	0.0	0.0	0.0	0.0	30.3	52.6	17.3	74	79.7	77.0	6.8
Greensburg city	11,492	11,817	2.8	12,160	93.7	2.0	1.1	0.5	2.8	26.0	59.5	14.5	4,724	59.8	54.6	16.2
Greens Fork town	423	416	-1.7	416	94.2	0.0	0.5	0.7	4.6	13.8	70.1	16.1	167	79.6	45.5	23.4
Greentown town	2,415	2,397	-0.7	2,570	98.4	0.3	0.2	0.5	0.6	27.3	57.6	15.1	965	65.4	49.5	11.3
Greenville town	600	669	11.5	593	92.9	0.0	4.0	3.0	0.0	19.6	69.0	11.5	203	88.2	27.1	28.6
Greenwood city	50,979	54,491	6.9	52,799	85.5	3.0	4.1	2.5	4.9	24.7	62.8	12.6	20,807	61.5	38.6	27.6
Griffin town	172	168	-2.3	144	100.0	0.0	0.0	0.0	0.0	20.1	66.6	13.2	62	87.1	56.5	1.6
Griffith town	16,893	16,516	-2.2	16,765	69.8	13.1	2.4	1.5	13.2	25.1	62.7	12.1	6,345	65.9	45.2	18.1
Grissom AFB CDP	5,537	NA	NA	2,258	85.3	10.5	0.0	1.7	2.6	22.9	70.2	6.9	642	23.4	49.4	7.5
Hagerstown town	1,787	1,751	-2.0	1,537	97.6	0.2	0.0	1.2	1.0	23.4	59.1	17.4	665	75.5	44.8	20.9
Hamilton town	1,530	1,540	0.7	1,744	90.5	0.0	2.6	4.7	2.2	21.9	56.1	21.9	779	74.2	52.1	15.5
Hamlet town	800	778	-2.8	936	93.4	0.0	0.0	4.4	2.2	29.8	58.2	12.1	340	72.1	58.2	14.4
Hammond city	80,823	78,384	-3.0	79,585	40.0	20.9	0.9	2.2	36.0	26.3	63.0	10.6	28,678	61.8	53.8	13.4
Hanna CDP	463	NA	NA	245	100.0	0.0	0.0	0.0	0.0	12.3	77.2	10.6	116	73.3	47.4	6.9
Hanover town	3,546	3,555	0.3	3,682	91.6	4.2	1.0	1.0	2.3	18.5	70.4	11.1	1,067	56.5	59.8	15.8
Hardinsburg town	248	245	-1.2	234	94.9	0.0	0.0	0.0	5.1	16.2	75.6	8.1	112	83.0	58.9	3.6
Harlan CDP	1,634	NA	NA	1,718	97.4	0.5	0.0	0.0	2.0	21.2	66.0	12.9	652	81.6	58.3	17.8
Harmony town	656	640	-2.4	659	95.9	0.0	0.0	3.2	0.9	18.5	70.6	10.9	308	76.6	64.6	10.7
Harrodsburg CDP	691	NA	NA	761	100.0	0.0	0.0	0.0	0.0	34.9	49.4	15.8	219	96.3	38.8	13.2
Hartford City city	6,220	6,042	-2.9	6,166	96.6	0.0	0.1	2.2	1.0	22.0	59.4	18.4	2,602	71.9	61.6	8.2
Hartsville town	369	383	3.8	358	97.8	0.0	0.0	2.2	0.0	24.1	65.3	10.6	141	79.4	69.5	9.2
Hatfield CDP	813	NA	NA	756	98.8	0.0	1.2	0.0	0.0	15.8	68.7	15.5	328	90.2	80.8	3.0
Haubstadt town	1,574	1,637	4.0	1,712	97.8	1.9	0.0	0.0	0.3	25.9	59.3	14.9	632	81.5	48.9	23.1
Hayden CDP	521	NA	NA	1,123	87.9	12.1	0.0	0.0	0.0	35.7	58.2	6.1	309	69.9	66.3	9.1
Hazleton town	257	257	0.0	307	89.9	0.0	0.0	8.5	1.6	25.0	61.0	14.0	129	93.0	52.7	5.4
Hebron town	3,716	3,713	-0.1	3,714	91.8	7.5	0.0	0.0	0.7	26.9	62.7	10.3	1,394	65.6	52.5	13.2
Henryville CDP	1,905	NA	NA	1,916	100.0	0.0	0.0	0.0	0.0	23.3	64.7	12.2	776	75.1	48.6	15.2
Herbst CDP	112	NA	NA	83	100.0	0.0	0.0	0.0	0.0	25.3	74.7	0.0	31	67.7	41.9	25.8
Heritage Lake CDP	2,880	NA	NA	2,958	97.3	1.5	0.0	0.3	0.9	20.5	65.5	13.9	1,124	94.3	50.7	16.4
Hidden Valley CDP	5,387	NA	NA	5,174	97.3	0.0	0.0	1.3	1.4	25.6	57.9	16.4	1,832	92.5	34.0	28.3
Highland town	23,727	23,127	-2.5	23,429	77.3	3.3	1.9	2.2	15.2	21.2	60.9	17.9	9,571	78.1	38.8	29.9
Highland CDP	4,489	NA	NA	4,379	94.1	1.2	3.3	1.4	0.0	20.1	63.9	16.0	1,730	93.9	22.8	35.6
Hillsboro town	538	522	-3.0	568	95.2	0.0	0.0	0.9	3.9	29.4	51.2	19.4	225	73.3	50.2	8.0
Hoagland CDP	821	NA	NA	855	99.2	0.0	0.0	0.8	0.0	18.0	64.3	17.8	348	87.6	51.4	23.3
Hobart city	29,349	28,635	-2.4	29,136	78.0	6.1	0.7	1.9	13.3	22.1	63.4	14.4	11,542	71.9	45.6	16.9
Holland town	626	619	-1.1	712	97.9	0.0	0.0	0.0	2.1	31.5	54.5	13.9	266	71.8	58.3	9.0
Holton town	480	468	-2.5	573	95.5	0.7	0.0	2.3	1.6	32.3	57.0	10.6	214	74.8	72.0	7.5
Homecroft town	718	740	3.1	694	95.8	0.3	0.0	2.0	1.9	17.7	69.7	12.5	294	90.5	25.2	45.9
Hope town	2,112	2,157	2.1	2,292	97.6	0.3	1.3	0.8	0.0	26.4	59.9	13.7	871	77.0	50.2	13.0
Howe CDP	807	NA	NA	691	76.3	1.4	0.6	0.0	21.7	16.0	58.5	25.5	275	82.9	66.9	10.5
Hudson town	518	516	-0.4	604	92.2	0.0	0.7	2.5	4.6	35.4	54.5	10.1	224	80.4	56.7	13.4
Hudson Lake CDP	1,297	NA	NA	1,409	98.8	0.0	0.0	1.2	0.0	26.3	62.4	11.4	565	85.7	55.4	5.0
Huntertown town	5,065	5,349	5.6	5,326	89.7	2.5	1.0	2.3	4.5	30.0	61.3	8.6	1,815	90.6	26.1	31.0
Huntingburg city	6,057	6,042	-0.2	6,489	75.5	0.3	0.0	2.5	21.8	27.5	57.6	15.0	2,333	67.9	61.6	12.6
Huntington city	17,367	17,166	-1.2	17,284	94.0	1.1	1.3	0.9	2.7	22.5	63.5	14.2	6,749	66.1	57.0	14.8
Hymera town	795	778	-2.1	723	99.0	0.0	0.0	0.7	0.3	22.9	58.4	18.7	267	76.4	57.3	15.0
Idaville CDP	461	NA	NA	762	99.3	0.7	0.0	0.0	0.0	28.2	59.6	12.3	191	46.1	71.2	13.6
Indianapolis city	829,668	858,325	3.5	844,449	57.8	27.4	2.3	2.8	9.6	24.8	64.5	10.8	332,300	54.7	39.7	29.8
Indianapolis city (balance)	820,441	848,788	3.5	835,097	57.6	27.6	2.4	2.8	9.6	24.9	64.4	10.7	328,423	54.6	39.7	29.7
Indian Village town	133	132	-0.8	91	89.0	6.6	4.4	0.0	0.0	13.2	60.5	26.4	44	90.9	36.4	38.6
Ingalls town	2,394	2,390	-0.2	2,152	88.7	2.5	0.4	5.2	3.3	33.0	58.8	8.3	761	80.4	53.1	11.2
Jalapa CDP	171	NA	NA	152	80.9	9.9	0.0	9.2	0.0	9.2	82.4	8.6	62	100.0	17.7	16.1
Jamestown town	958	939	-2.0	1,057	98.6	0.0	0.0	0.0	1.4	20.3	66.0	13.7	451	72.3	50.8	21.7
Jasonville city	2,222	2,188	-1.5	2,406	98.4	0.0	0.0	0.3	1.3	25.9	56.0	17.8	996	67.2	62.8	12.0
Jasper city	15,048	15,325	1.8	15,177	91.4	0.4	0.9	0.6	6.7	24.2	59.0	16.7	5,935	71.5	44.7	23.3
Jeffersonville city	45,031	46,440	3.1	45,869	78.0	12.9	1.5	3.7	3.9	22.9	64.1	13.0	17,650	69.5	42.1	23.1
Jonesboro city	1,756	1,711	-2.6	1,702	96.5	0.0	0.3	1.5	1.7	25.4	62.1	12.5	654	72.3	72.2	7.5
Jonesville town	178	183	2.8	111	97.3	0.0	0.0	0.0	2.7	15.3	57.6	27.0	56	87.5	60.7	7.1
Kempton town	335	317	-5.4	377	98.9	0.0	0.0	1.1	0.0	26.2	57.7	16.2	132	85.6	52.3	4.5
Kendallville city	9,862	9,905	0.4	9,847	90.3	0.0	1.3	2.0	6.4	26.6	60.6	12.8	3,970	61.2	48.0	18.0
Kennard town	471	464	-1.5	516	99.6	0.0	0.0	0.4	0.0	32.3	55.5	12.2	155	80.6	61.3	11.6

1 May be of any race.

Table A. All Places — **Population and Housing**

STATE City, town, township, borough, or CDP (county if applicable)	Population				Race and Hispanic or Latino origin (percent), 2010–2014					Age (percent), 2010–2014			Households, 2010–2014			
	2010 census total population	2014 estimated population	Percent change 2010–2014	ACS total population estimate 2010–2014	White alone, not Hispanic or Latino	Black alone, not Hispanic or Latino	Asian alone, not Hispanic or Latino	All other races or 2 or more races, not Hispanic or Latino	Hispanic or Latino[1]	Under 18 years old	Age 18 to 64 years old	Age 65 years and older	Total occupied housing units	Percent owner occupied	Householders by level of education (percent): High school diploma or less	Householders by level of education (percent): Bachelor's degree or more
	1	2	3	4	5	6	7	8	9	10	11	12	13	14	15	16
INDIANA—Con.																
Kent CDP	70	NA	NA	99	100.0	0.0	0.0	0.0	0.0	0.0	100.0	0.0	36	100.0	55.6	0.0
Kentland town	1,748	1,722	-1.5	1,918	91.8	0.3	0.3	1.5	6.1	26.9	57.4	15.7	734	64.6	62.1	12.1
Kewanna town	615	606	-1.5	774	97.9	0.0	0.0	1.0	1.0	28.5	61.3	10.2	267	70.8	64.0	16.1
Kimmell CDP	422	NA	NA	473	92.4	0.0	0.0	1.9	5.7	25.6	70.0	4.4	171	73.1	88.3	0.0
Kingman town	511	490	-4.1	457	94.7	2.2	0.0	0.0	3.1	34.8	52.1	13.1	176	65.3	59.7	8.0
Kingsbury town	248	246	-0.8	381	91.6	0.0	0.0	2.1	6.3	32.0	56.2	11.8	131	77.1	58.8	6.9
Kingsford Heights town	1,435	1,428	-0.5	1,558	84.0	6.6	0.0	5.4	4.0	25.9	66.3	7.8	586	70.1	61.1	5.8
Kirklin town	788	779	-1.1	925	92.2	0.0	3.4	0.2	4.2	27.7	57.8	14.5	320	71.3	56.6	12.2
Knightstown town	2,182	2,124	-2.7	2,055	99.4	0.0	0.0	0.5	0.1	21.6	61.0	17.4	882	64.1	61.6	13.3
Knightsville town	872	855	-1.9	877	97.7	1.4	0.0	0.3	0.6	21.2	63.7	15.1	339	83.5	51.3	14.2
Knox city	3,704	3,622	-2.2	3,658	92.6	0.4	0.0	0.2	6.8	24.1	60.0	15.8	1,441	61.5	72.0	7.5
Kokomo city	56,842	57,085	0.4	56,958	82.6	9.8	1.4	2.6	3.5	22.9	59.8	17.3	24,823	61.7	47.3	18.1
Koontz Lake CDP	1,557	NA	NA	1,465	98.4	1.6	0.0	0.0	0.0	19.9	66.4	13.9	560	86.8	48.0	22.7
Kouts town	1,879	1,949	3.7	1,992	95.2	0.0	1.7	0.0	3.2	32.0	56.3	11.7	702	78.2	47.6	20.1
Laconia town	50	49	-2.0	74	98.6	0.0	1.4	0.0	0.0	9.5	82.6	8.1	52	23.1	17.3	0.0
La Crosse town	555	541	-2.5	671	97.3	0.0	0.0	2.1	0.6	24.8	63.4	11.8	277	74.7	56.7	13.7
Ladoga town	986	982	-0.4	1,055	96.4	1.5	0.0	1.8	0.3	31.0	55.3	13.7	360	71.1	49.2	14.2
Lafayette city	68,867	70,654	2.6	69,982	75.8	7.7	2.2	1.8	12.6	23.7	65.1	11.3	29,448	48.4	38.8	26.9
La Fontaine town	875	863	-1.4	776	94.5	0.0	0.0	3.7	1.8	19.4	55.3	25.1	298	74.5	58.1	11.4
Lagrange town	2,609	2,691	3.1	2,652	84.8	0.3	0.0	5.4	9.6	24.9	54.2	21.0	1,028	59.7	62.7	6.6
Lagro town	415	408	-1.7	594	93.8	0.0	1.3	3.9	1.0	33.2	59.6	7.2	205	79.5	67.8	9.3
Lake Dalecarlia CDP	1,355	NA	NA	1,334	93.9	0.0	0.0	2.0	4.0	21.1	66.7	12.1	504	84.3	33.5	9.3
Lake Holiday CDP	910	NA	NA	931	97.7	2.3	0.0	0.0	0.0	18.4	72.7	8.9	374	90.9	47.1	20.9
Lake Santee CDP	820	NA	NA	809	94.4	0.0	0.0	5.6	0.0	21.1	55.5	23.5	319	97.8	33.5	15.7
Lakes of the Four Seasons CDP	7,033	NA	NA	6,854	87.4	1.6	1.5	0.3	9.2	19.3	65.5	15.2	2,585	97.0	32.5	32.3
Lake Station city	12,572	12,175	-3.2	12,369	66.6	2.4	0.5	1.2	29.4	25.6	61.2	13.3	4,566	68.1	64.1	5.5
Laketon CDP	623	NA	NA	473	81.4	0.0	0.0	1.3	17.3	29.6	51.1	19.5	185	65.9	70.3	13.0
Lake Village CDP	765	NA	NA	585	96.6	0.0	0.0	0.0	3.4	6.0	72.4	21.5	251	68.5	72.9	0.0
Lakeville town	786	785	-0.1	856	92.8	1.6	0.0	4.7	0.9	23.8	63.9	12.0	351	52.4	56.1	8.8
Landess CDP	188	NA	NA	330	100.0	0.0	0.0	0.0	0.0	40.9	57.0	2.1	86	75.6	17.4	0.0
Lanesville town	564	565	0.2	579	94.5	0.0	1.6	4.0	0.0	23.0	52.0	25.0	268	75.0	37.3	20.9
La Paz town	561	559	-0.4	571	96.7	0.0	0.0	0.5	2.8	32.8	51.1	16.1	195	71.3	56.9	5.1
Lapel town	2,068	2,051	-0.8	1,760	98.9	0.0	0.0	1.1	0.0	16.7	64.1	19.1	840	76.9	55.8	22.4
La Porte city	22,043	22,007	-0.2	22,153	85.0	1.9	0.2	1.7	11.2	24.8	59.8	15.5	9,156	58.7	55.7	15.0
Larwill town	283	283	0.0	347	99.4	0.0	0.3	0.3	0.0	36.3	54.8	8.9	117	76.1	70.1	5.1
Laurel town	512	507	-1.0	478	94.8	0.0	0.0	0.0	5.2	34.2	51.3	14.4	167	68.3	77.2	0.6
Lawrence city	46,003	47,550	3.4	46,796	58.2	23.4	1.3	4.8	12.3	29.0	61.2	9.9	17,316	68.3	32.4	33.8
Lawrenceburg city	5,042	4,977	-1.3	5,022	96.4	1.7	0.5	1.1	0.4	22.2	62.5	15.3	1,957	52.7	54.9	11.4
Leavenworth town	238	234	-1.7	243	97.5	1.2	0.0	1.2	0.0	12.4	53.1	34.6	89	71.9	48.3	20.2
Lebanon city	15,794	15,836	0.3	15,688	93.1	1.0	0.3	0.8	4.8	24.1	61.6	14.3	6,481	62.0	51.8	18.8
Leesburg town	555	560	0.9	649	86.6	2.3	0.8	0.6	9.7	29.1	56.8	14.0	228	92.1	42.5	21.1
Leo-Cedarville town	3,603	3,818	6.0	3,742	94.9	0.4	0.5	2.0	2.2	34.0	53.7	12.3	1,140	94.0	30.4	39.2
Lewisville town	366	360	-1.6	357	97.5	0.8	0.0	0.6	1.1	19.1	63.3	17.6	133	73.7	51.9	9.0
Liberty town	2,133	2,056	-3.6	2,139	94.2	0.8	2.4	2.4	0.1	27.4	56.1	16.6	797	67.1	50.2	13.7
Ligonier city	4,405	4,393	-0.3	4,344	48.2	0.6	0.0	1.6	49.6	30.9	57.8	11.4	1,412	53.5	73.9	4.0
Linden town	759	755	-0.5	864	96.9	0.0	0.0	1.7	1.4	30.2	59.9	10.0	309	69.9	55.0	16.2
Linton city	5,409	5,331	-1.4	5,368	96.6	0.8	0.4	1.8	0.4	22.1	56.6	21.3	2,261	65.4	50.7	11.9
Little York town	192	190	-1.0	199	86.9	0.0	0.0	0.0	13.1	24.6	64.2	11.1	66	90.9	77.3	0.0
Livonia town	128	127	-0.8	113	94.7	0.0	0.0	0.0	5.3	23.9	58.3	17.7	47	89.4	61.7	8.5
Lizton town	489	497	1.6	543	96.1	0.0	0.7	0.0	3.1	23.9	68.6	7.6	226	58.0	47.3	23.5
Logansport city	18,266	18,019	-1.4	17,933	70.2	2.8	2.0	1.4	23.7	26.2	60.3	13.7	6,626	62.6	61.4	11.9
Long Beach town	1,164	1,160	-0.3	1,206	95.9	1.7	1.7	0.2	0.3	13.2	49.8	37.1	577	92.9	13.5	62.6
Loogootee city	2,749	2,706	-1.6	2,721	94.6	0.7	2.3	1.9	0.5	26.4	57.1	16.5	1,162	67.6	54.3	10.0
Losantville town	237	232	-2.1	244	97.1	0.0	0.0	2.9	0.0	21.4	58.2	20.5	98	69.4	75.5	4.1
Lowell town	9,276	9,402	1.4	9,347	96.7	0.3	0.0	0.4	2.5	25.8	62.1	12.0	3,075	78.3	40.6	20.5
Lynn town	1,097	1,063	-3.1	1,083	96.0	0.1	0.0	0.6	3.3	23.1	58.8	18.1	414	70.8	59.9	9.2
Lynnville town	888	911	2.6	1,011	96.9	0.0	0.5	1.5	1.1	28.8	56.6	14.5	366	82.5	57.4	10.9
Lyons town	742	731	-1.5	787	92.5	1.1	1.9	0.3	4.2	23.7	55.5	20.8	285	67.0	64.2	8.4
McCordsville town	4,800	5,445	13.4	5,037	73.9	10.7	0.0	4.5	10.9	25.9	70.6	3.6	1,844	86.1	15.3	52.0
Mackey town	106	106	0.0	116	100.0	0.0	0.0	0.0	0.0	12.9	73.3	13.8	47	57.4	72.3	4.3
Macy town	209	206	-1.4	225	97.8	0.0	0.4	1.8	0.0	31.6	56.5	12.0	66	90.9	57.6	7.6
Madison city	11,967	12,035	0.6	12,033	90.6	3.7	1.9	1.1	2.8	19.3	62.2	18.4	5,073	58.8	44.0	25.3
Manilla CDP	267	NA	NA	220	100.0	0.0	0.0	0.0	0.0	0.0	88.7	11.4	108	87.0	53.7	13.9
Marengo town	828	825	-0.4	789	95.4	0.0	0.0	0.0	4.6	24.2	55.7	20.0	335	57.6	79.4	0.0
Marion city	29,920	29,308	-2.0	29,403	75.5	14.3	0.8	3.6	5.8	19.3	64.2	16.7	11,952	58.5	54.2	17.3
Markle town	1,095	1,092	-0.3	1,083	92.1	0.3	0.2	4.3	3.1	19.4	56.3	24.1	434	81.1	54.6	9.0
Markleville town	528	522	-1.1	486	99.8	0.0	0.0	0.2	0.0	27.9	62.7	9.3	164	78.0	51.8	15.2
Marshall town	324	324	0.0	271	99.6	0.0	0.0	0.4	0.0	19.9	66.2	14.0	100	85.0	64.0	3.0
Martinsville city	11,771	11,744	-0.2	11,756	97.0	0.6	0.4	0.9	1.1	23.4	61.6	15.0	4,499	58.2	58.3	12.4
Matthews town	591	573	-3.0	597	100.0	0.0	0.0	0.0	0.0	17.0	61.2	21.8	237	79.3	66.7	5.1
Mauckport town	81	80	-1.2	54	98.1	0.0	0.0	1.9	0.0	22.3	68.6	9.3	22	72.7	68.2	4.5
Mecca town	328	326	-0.6	396	98.7	0.0	0.3	1.0	0.0	39.9	43.6	16.7	135	80.7	76.3	0.7
Medaryville town	614	595	-3.1	600	85.0	0.0	1.0	0.0	14.0	25.3	59.0	15.7	203	61.6	77.8	1.5
Medora town	700	699	-0.1	582	96.0	0.0	0.0	2.6	1.4	24.6	57.5	18.0	225	78.7	86.2	3.1
Mellott town	197	190	-3.6	181	93.4	0.0	0.0	1.7	5.0	21.5	47.6	30.9	82	84.1	87.8	2.4
Melody Hill CDP	3,628	NA	NA	3,824	90.7	5.6	0.5	1.6	1.6	23.0	59.8	17.1	1,440	95.6	33.4	26.9
Memphis CDP	695	NA	NA	624	98.4	0.0	0.0	0.0	1.6	26.8	63.3	9.9	254	80.3	40.9	30.7
Mentone town	997	989	-0.8	922	95.2	0.2	0.3	1.7	2.5	29.9	57.7	12.4	332	75.9	63.9	10.2
Meridian Hills town	1,616	1,673	3.5	1,682	86.8	1.7	1.5	7.2	2.9	25.7	55.1	19.1	631	91.6	4.0	84.2
Merom town	228	226	-0.9	177	98.3	0.0	0.0	1.7	0.0	28.2	60.4	11.3	76	73.7	50.0	10.5
Merrillville town	34,969	35,450	1.4	35,262	36.5	46.8	1.0	2.1	13.6	26.2	60.6	13.2	13,225	63.3	42.3	21.4
Metamora CDP	188	NA	NA	135	100.0	0.0	0.0	0.0	0.0	0.0	65.9	34.1	72	50.0	88.9	0.0
Mexico CDP	836	NA	NA	706	98.6	0.0	0.0	1.4	0.0	16.4	56.8	26.8	312	96.8	54.8	9.9
Michiana Shores town	307	305	-0.7	329	97.0	0.0	0.0	0.0	3.0	10.7	55.0	34.3	161	92.5	18.6	59.6
Michigan City city	31,484	31,487	0.0	31,369	61.8	26.6	1.0	4.3	6.2	21.6	63.9	14.4	12,718	54.4	49.2	15.9
Michigantown town	467	459	-1.7	426	94.1	0.0	0.0	3.8	2.1	28.7	60.3	11.0	160	55.6	42.5	19.4
Middlebury town	3,420	3,527	3.1	3,456	85.4	0.0	0.0	2.9	11.7	28.8	55.3	15.9	1,215	78.3	43.7	19.3
Middletown town	2,317	2,264	-2.3	2,347	98.3	0.5	0.4	0.8	0.0	23.5	61.7	15.0	970	63.5	61.4	8.8
Mier CDP	78	NA	NA	162	100.0	0.0	0.0	0.0	0.0	24.7	47.5	27.8	60	71.7	0.0	21.7
Milan town	1,899	1,877	-1.2	1,897	98.4	0.0	0.0	0.6	1.0	23.2	56.6	20.3	738	67.9	60.0	9.2

1 May be of any race.

Table A. All Places — **Population and Housing**

STATE City, town, township, borough, or CDP (county if applicable)	Population: 2010 census total population	Population: 2014 estimated population	Population: Percent change 2010–2014	Population: ACS total population estimate 2010–2014	Race and Hispanic or Latino origin (percent), 2010–2014: White alone, not Hispanic or Latino	Black alone, not Hispanic or Latino	Asian alone, not Hispanic or Latino	All other races or 2 or more races, not Hispanic or Latino	Hispanic or Latino[1]	Age (percent), 2010–2014: Under 18 years old	Age 18 to 64 years old	Age 65 years and older	Households, 2010–2014: Total occupied housing units	Percent owner occupied	Householders by level of education (percent): High school diploma or less	Bachelor's degree or more
	1	2	3	4	5	6	7	8	9	10	11	12	13	14	15	16
INDIANA—Con.																
Milford town	1,557	1,566	0.6	1,615	84.8	1.1	0.7	0.0	13.3	26.2	59.6	14.2	618	67.6	65.7	8.6
Millersburg town	903	926	2.5	1,022	87.9	0.0	0.0	5.1	7.0	29.4	61.3	9.3	393	57.0	66.7	6.6
Millhousen town	127	131	3.1	197	100.0	0.0	0.0	0.0	0.0	29.4	60.0	10.7	75	100.0	42.7	21.3
Milltown town	818	807	-1.3	918	97.7	0.0	0.0	2.3	0.0	25.3	54.7	20.0	399	61.9	69.4	9.0
Milroy CDP	604	NA	NA	742	99.7	0.0	0.0	0.3	0.0	31.3	55.8	12.8	240	55.8	89.2	3.8
Milton town	486	471	-3.1	521	94.8	0.0	0.0	3.8	1.3	29.8	59.7	10.6	186	72.6	57.5	12.4
Mishawaka city	48,260	48,174	-0.2	48,120	82.4	6.6	2.4	2.8	5.8	22.6	63.8	13.6	20,544	49.7	43.1	25.3
Mitchell city	4,345	4,284	-1.4	4,320	93.6	0.0	0.8	1.8	3.7	20.2	59.9	19.8	1,903	69.9	69.3	10.5
Modoc town	196	192	-2.0	261	97.3	0.0	0.0	0.4	2.3	29.9	51.7	18.4	104	65.4	81.7	3.8
Monon town	1,777	1,758	-1.1	1,872	64.3	0.0	0.0	3.3	32.4	35.6	53.0	11.3	607	59.6	63.3	5.4
Monroe town	842	857	1.8	717	97.1	0.0	0.0	0.3	2.6	29.1	49.6	21.3	290	80.3	53.1	20.0
Monroe City town	538	536	-0.4	579	98.4	0.0	0.0	1.2	0.3	32.6	52.0	15.4	212	84.0	39.2	10.8
Monroeville town	1,235	1,292	4.6	1,294	94.5	0.0	0.0	1.9	3.6	22.9	63.3	13.9	513	78.4	56.5	10.9
Monrovia town	1,063	1,354	27.4	1,631	94.6	1.5	2.5	0.2	1.2	36.5	58.5	5.0	513	81.5	47.2	12.7
Monterey town	218	211	-3.2	249	76.3	0.0	0.0	0.0	23.7	35.3	44.4	20.1	91	71.4	64.8	9.9
Montezuma town	1,022	1,005	-1.7	1,105	96.2	0.0	0.0	0.9	2.9	30.4	56.9	12.8	394	71.3	62.7	3.6
Montgomery town	335	347	3.6	370	100.0	0.0	0.0	0.0	0.0	22.7	59.5	17.8	156	76.3	66.0	10.9
Monticello city	5,378	5,352	-0.5	5,355	88.6	0.3	0.0	1.1	10.0	21.2	56.3	22.7	2,109	66.9	51.9	15.5
Montmorenci CDP	243	NA	NA	128	100.0	0.0	0.0	0.0	0.0	4.7	39.0	56.3	64	100.0	62.5	23.4
Montpelier city	1,805	1,750	-3.0	1,864	97.3	0.0	0.4	0.5	1.8	27.7	55.1	17.2	770	56.9	66.1	7.7
Mooreland town	371	365	-1.6	316	100.0	0.0	0.0	0.0	0.0	26.0	59.2	14.9	117	88.9	59.8	7.7
Moores Hill town	597	588	-1.5	654	99.1	0.0	0.0	0.0	0.9	34.2	53.4	12.5	232	72.8	66.8	6.0
Mooresville town	9,335	9,576	2.6	9,459	97.1	0.3	0.5	0.0	2.1	22.2	61.4	16.4	3,794	67.9	43.9	14.3
Morgantown town	986	988	0.2	1,033	94.1	0.8	0.0	4.7	0.4	36.8	51.7	11.5	337	61.4	60.2	3.0
Morocco town	1,139	1,130	-0.8	1,248	95.2	0.0	0.0	3.3	1.5	22.7	57.1	20.2	516	69.6	58.1	14.5
Morristown town	1,218	1,326	8.9	1,329	98.4	0.0	0.0	0.8	0.8	21.4	60.7	18.1	521	65.6	67.6	6.3
Mount Auburn town	110	108	-1.8	116	100.0	0.0	0.0	0.0	0.0	23.3	56.0	20.7	47	70.2	53.2	14.9
Mount Ayr town	122	121	-0.8	128	95.3	0.0	0.0	0.0	4.7	18.0	68.8	13.3	57	80.7	82.5	5.3
Mount Carmel town	86	85	-1.2	113	97.3	0.0	0.0	2.7	0.0	29.1	68.9	1.8	35	60.0	82.9	5.7
Mount Etna town	105	103	-1.9	84	100.0	0.0	0.0	0.0	0.0	17.9	75.1	7.1	38	71.1	57.9	21.1
Mount Summit town	352	346	-1.7	442	96.8	0.0	0.0	0.0	3.2	19.7	63.9	16.3	165	75.2	49.7	19.4
Mount Vernon city	6,687	6,573	-1.7	6,607	92.0	2.7	0.4	2.2	2.6	25.9	57.5	16.6	2,728	71.8	50.2	20.2
Mulberry town	1,254	1,247	-0.6	1,289	96.9	0.0	0.0	1.2	1.9	22.1	53.0	24.8	457	72.4	56.9	17.1
Muncie city	70,201	70,211	0.0	70,035	82.4	8.4	1.5	5.1	2.4	16.9	69.4	13.8	27,662	50.4	40.2	22.8
Munster town	23,560	23,103	-1.9	23,325	77.6	3.9	5.2	1.5	11.7	22.6	57.5	19.8	8,644	84.2	27.7	43.3
Napoleon town	234	228	-2.6	172	83.1	0.0	0.0	2.9	14.0	27.8	51.7	20.3	77	55.8	58.4	0.0
Nappanee city	6,648	6,715	1.0	6,639	92.4	1.0	0.0	0.1	6.5	30.6	57.0	12.5	2,423	68.8	53.2	17.2
Nashville town	1,100	1,076	-2.2	1,051	97.0	1.4	0.0	1.0	0.6	14.1	51.5	34.3	470	48.7	36.8	27.2
New Albany city	36,345	36,589	0.7	36,496	84.5	7.4	0.5	3.4	4.1	22.0	64.0	14.1	15,312	55.5	51.0	17.4
New Amsterdam town	27	27	0.0	16	93.8	0.0	0.0	6.3	0.0	12.6	25.1	62.5	7	100.0	57.1	14.3
Newberry town	193	192	-0.5	183	98.4	0.0	0.0	1.1	0.5	13.7	63.4	23.0	78	87.2	61.5	2.6
Newburgh town	3,325	3,278	-1.4	3,312	92.9	0.0	2.1	0.0	5.0	22.2	61.4	16.5	1,379	77.5	29.9	30.8
New Carlisle town	1,829	1,848	1.0	2,056	92.5	0.7	0.3	3.1	3.5	28.2	59.1	12.7	783	78.0	43.4	24.4
New Castle city	18,106	17,653	-2.5	17,859	94.0	1.8	0.7	1.7	1.8	21.9	61.4	16.7	7,301	57.9	55.5	13.3
New Chicago town	2,035	1,993	-2.1	1,954	58.9	2.8	0.3	1.9	36.2	21.9	66.6	11.5	776	68.6	62.9	9.1
New Goshen CDP	390	NA	NA	419	95.7	0.0	0.0	4.3	0.0	19.1	58.0	22.9	164	100.0	32.3	20.7
New Harmony town	791	770	-2.7	711	93.1	2.7	3.7	0.6	0.0	9.3	54.4	36.3	336	69.3	45.8	24.4
New Haven city	14,794	15,608	5.5	15,612	90.4	1.4	0.3	1.1	6.8	25.1	60.4	14.3	6,193	75.0	47.8	20.3
New Market town	629	629	0.0	640	95.6	0.0	0.0	0.8	3.6	29.4	56.9	13.8	237	80.6	64.6	7.2
New Middletown town	93	92	-1.1	33	100.0	0.0	0.0	0.0	0.0	21.2	69.8	9.1	17	94.1	52.9	5.9
New Palestine town	2,073	2,105	1.5	2,385	94.3	0.0	0.9	4.5	0.3	30.6	54.9	14.3	872	78.3	43.5	28.6
New Paris CDP	1,494	NA	NA	1,088	98.5	0.0	0.1	0.7	0.6	29.2	61.5	9.4	452	81.0	39.4	14.4
New Pekin town	1,401	1,383	-1.3	1,382	95.7	1.7	0.0	0.7	2.0	25.0	60.1	14.9	565	62.1	66.7	11.3
New Point town	333	343	3.0	406	92.9	2.5	0.0	3.0	1.7	22.3	60.3	17.2	118	84.7	67.8	3.4
Newport town	515	490	-4.9	433	98.8	0.2	0.9	0.0	0.0	13.4	59.9	26.6	175	88.0	65.7	6.9
New Richmond town	333	333	0.0	432	97.0	0.0	3.0	0.0	0.0	29.0	61.3	9.7	144	81.3	54.2	11.8
New Ross town	345	345	0.0	328	98.8	0.0	0.0	0.6	0.6	37.5	46.8	15.9	114	84.2	49.1	9.6
New Salisbury CDP	613	NA	NA	509	100.0	0.0	0.0	0.0	0.0	36.7	43.4	19.8	174	85.1	65.5	0.0
Newtown town	256	249	-2.7	282	96.1	0.0	0.0	2.5	1.4	18.4	79.3	2.1	112	72.3	62.5	6.3
New Trenton CDP	252	NA	NA	419	100.0	0.0	0.0	0.0	0.0	4.5	89.8	5.7	205	82.0	56.6	25.4
New Washington CDP	566	NA	NA	481	92.9	0.0	0.0	7.1	0.0	28.7	62.5	8.9	188	54.8	32.4	14.9
New Whiteland town	5,486	5,810	5.9	5,646	97.9	0.0	0.9	0.0	1.2	28.2	60.7	11.0	2,061	83.4	42.7	10.9
Noblesville city	52,135	57,584	10.5	56,576	87.1	4.0	1.9	2.4	4.6	28.4	61.5	10.0	20,952	70.8	21.6	49.1
North Crows Nest town	45	46	2.2	54	74.1	0.0	5.6	20.4	0.0	35.2	39.0	25.9	17	100.0	0.0	94.1
North Judson town	1,772	1,753	-1.1	1,930	86.6	0.8	0.5	0.4	11.8	25.6	56.2	18.2	772	62.3	55.4	15.5
North Liberty town	1,913	1,913	0.0	1,847	94.9	0.6	0.2	0.9	3.5	38.2	49.5	12.4	637	64.5	51.8	17.9
North Manchester town	6,112	5,989	-2.0	6,080	93.2	2.2	0.0	2.0	2.5	19.3	59.3	21.4	2,204	61.7	46.0	25.9
North Salem town	507	525	3.6	493	97.0	0.0	0.0	3.0	0.0	17.5	68.9	13.6	188	71.8	55.9	11.7
North Terre Haute CDP	4,305	NA	NA	4,595	97.6	1.1	0.0	1.3	0.0	22.5	59.7	17.9	1,680	64.3	52.7	11.7
North Vernon city	6,728	6,636	-1.4	6,736	93.6	1.2	0.2	3.3	1.8	25.9	59.5	14.6	2,586	55.7	67.7	8.9
North Webster town	1,151	1,160	0.8	1,235	93.3	0.0	0.0	2.6	4.1	25.6	60.5	13.8	552	54.9	50.2	22.3
Norway CDP	386	NA	NA	440	76.6	0.0	0.0	0.0	23.4	23.0	59.9	17.0	204	76.5	47.5	0.0
Notre Dame CDP	5,973	NA	NA	7,123	79.3	2.0	7.4	4.3	7.0	0.1	98.5	1.5	96	0.0	0.0	93.8
Oakland City city	2,415	2,433	0.7	2,542	95.6	1.3	0.0	1.4	1.7	18.7	61.7	19.4	1,017	59.2	51.3	15.9
Oaktown town	605	601	-0.7	637	94.8	0.3	0.0	0.5	4.4	21.2	54.2	24.6	231	63.2	57.1	6.9
Odon town	1,356	1,394	2.8	1,565	98.6	0.0	0.0	0.4	1.0	27.3	50.0	22.6	698	63.0	56.3	11.9
Ogden Dunes town	1,110	1,114	0.4	1,236	94.5	0.3	1.5	1.8	1.9	15.7	57.8	26.5	564	95.0	11.9	62.6
Oldenburg town	674	669	-0.7	715	98.2	1.0	0.0	0.0	0.8	20.3	48.4	31.6	233	69.5	56.2	14.6
Onward town	100	99	-1.0	167	98.2	1.2	0.0	0.6	0.0	32.4	63.0	4.8	54	51.9	46.3	3.7
Oolitic town	1,178	1,164	-1.2	1,203	98.4	0.0	0.0	0.5	1.1	23.1	58.2	18.6	530	76.2	61.7	6.2
Orestes town	414	411	-0.7	439	88.2	5.5	0.2	4.8	1.4	28.0	60.1	11.8	126	77.0	73.8	3.2
Orland town	434	437	0.7	455	91.4	0.0	0.9	5.9	1.8	20.0	64.1	15.8	186	74.7	72.0	4.8
Orleans town	2,142	2,132	-0.5	2,197	96.7	2.5	0.3	0.5	0.0	24.6	57.1	18.4	880	65.7	65.5	8.2
Osceola town	2,463	2,469	0.2	2,789	91.7	0.2	0.4	2.5	5.2	27.8	56.8	15.5	965	86.2	51.0	15.6
Osgood town	1,624	1,601	-1.4	1,785	95.8	0.3	3.1	0.3	0.6	30.2	56.0	13.8	657	61.3	61.8	11.1
Ossian town	3,289	3,326	1.1	3,512	93.2	0.2	1.0	0.7	4.9	25.5	59.8	14.8	1,339	74.9	39.4	14.3
Otterbein town	1,262	1,253	-0.7	1,402	95.9	0.0	0.3	1.4	2.4	30.7	60.2	9.1	549	60.1	48.6	14.9
Otwell CDP	434	NA	NA	345	100.0	0.0	0.0	0.0	0.0	17.1	67.3	15.7	151	71.5	89.4	0.0
Owensburg CDP	406	NA	NA	792	100.0	0.0	0.0	0.0	0.0	21.8	68.2	10.0	230	94.3	58.7	23.9
Owensville town	1,278	1,287	0.7	1,296	94.8	1.3	0.2	2.5	1.1	25.5	52.8	21.8	439	82.2	52.8	18.9
Oxford town	1,162	1,142	-1.7	1,282	99.3	0.0	0.0	0.0	0.7	24.1	63.5	12.4	517	67.7	58.8	17.0

1 May be of any race.

Table A. All Places — **Population and Housing**

STATE City, town, township, borough, or CDP (county if applicable)	Population: 2010 census total population	Population: 2014 estimated population	Population: Percent change 2010–2014	Population: ACS total population estimate 2010–2014	Race and Hispanic or Latino origin (percent), 2010–2014: White alone, not Hispanic or Latino	Black alone, not Hispanic or Latino	Asian alone, not Hispanic or Latino	All other races or 2 or more races, not Hispanic or Latino	Hispanic or Latino[1]	Age (percent), 2010–2014: Under 18 years old	Age 18 to 64 years old	Age 65 years and older	Households, 2010–2014: Total occupied housing units	Percent owner occupied	Householders by level of education (percent): High school diploma or less	Bachelor's degree or more
	1	2	3	4	5	6	7	8	9	10	11	12	13	14	15	16
INDIANA—Con.																
Painted Hills CDP	677	NA	NA	626	97.8	0.0	0.0	0.0	2.2	18.4	61.1	20.4	254	100.0	33.1	44.1
Palmyra town	930	928	-0.2	1,198	94.3	0.0	3.8	1.9	0.0	27.0	60.9	12.0	459	59.9	51.0	8.9
Paoli town	3,677	3,632	-1.2	3,883	95.9	0.9	0.0	1.3	2.0	23.9	61.1	14.9	1,452	69.1	68.4	12.0
Paragon town	659	662	0.5	683	99.7	0.0	0.0	0.0	0.3	24.5	68.0	7.6	279	51.6	58.1	0.7
Parker City town	1,419	1,380	-2.7	1,320	95.8	1.4	0.0	1.7	1.1	21.2	55.7	22.9	547	71.8	59.6	13.2
Parkers Settlement CDP	711	NA	NA	702	98.6	0.0	0.0	0.0	1.4	17.1	69.5	13.4	290	82.4	39.7	14.8
Patoka town	729	730	0.1	886	93.7	1.6	0.8	2.9	1.0	31.5	52.3	16.1	301	89.0	55.8	9.3
Patriot town	209	205	-1.9	303	100.0	0.0	0.0	0.0	0.0	34.4	57.5	8.3	100	54.0	58.0	7.0
Pendleton town	4,221	4,212	-0.2	4,279	88.9	2.5	0.7	7.5	0.4	19.3	61.7	18.9	1,701	64.7	45.8	28.2
Pennville town	701	694	-1.0	806	100.0	0.0	0.0	0.0	0.0	28.6	58.5	12.7	304	64.8	72.4	3.9
Perrysville town	456	438	-3.9	547	98.9	0.9	0.2	0.0	0.0	26.6	56.1	17.2	218	72.9	50.5	8.7
Peru city	11,417	11,079	-3.0	11,199	86.1	9.5	0.1	2.6	1.7	24.7	59.8	15.5	4,364	64.8	55.6	9.4
Petersburg city	2,383	2,351	-1.3	2,513	98.4	0.8	0.0	0.4	0.4	24.9	56.0	19.1	941	63.2	59.4	13.6
Pierceton town	1,018	1,029	1.1	1,154	87.8	0.0	0.0	5.6	6.6	35.6	52.0	12.5	421	64.6	54.6	14.0
Pine Village town	217	213	-1.8	207	85.5	0.0	1.0	9.7	3.9	21.2	60.3	18.4	92	63.0	57.6	6.5
Pittsboro town	2,926	3,188	9.0	3,069	93.5	0.0	3.2	0.7	2.6	29.6	59.9	10.5	1,048	90.1	36.9	25.7
Plainfield town	27,634	30,409	10.0	29,220	82.3	7.5	4.6	1.5	4.1	23.8	64.0	12.2	10,494	73.7	38.9	28.9
Plainville town	476	490	2.9	588	99.3	0.0	0.0	0.0	0.7	32.1	48.9	19.0	220	80.0	58.6	10.0
Plymouth city	10,033	10,095	0.6	10,048	71.8	0.3	0.4	0.6	26.8	30.0	56.0	14.1	3,751	60.5	61.7	16.3
Point Isabel CDP	91	NA	NA	90	100.0	0.0	0.0	0.0	0.0	13.3	68.9	17.8	34	100.0	73.5	0.0
Poneto town	166	166	0.0	148	96.6	0.0	2.7	0.0	0.7	19.0	66.1	14.9	62	96.8	58.1	6.5
Portage city	36,828	36,760	-0.2	37,008	73.3	7.5	0.9	1.1	17.2	23.4	63.3	13.4	13,992	73.4	49.9	16.8
Porter town	4,858	4,881	0.5	4,883	95.1	0.0	0.3	0.2	4.4	27.6	64.0	8.4	1,872	83.8	38.8	27.0
Portland city	6,223	6,204	-0.3	6,408	90.5	0.6	0.0	1.3	7.6	25.1	58.6	16.3	2,701	62.1	61.4	8.8
Poseyville town	1,045	1,029	-1.5	1,278	100.0	0.0	0.0	0.0	0.0	27.1	52.7	20.0	510	78.4	54.1	18.6
Pottawattamie Park town	235	233	-0.9	272	84.9	7.4	0.0	0.0	7.7	22.4	55.1	22.4	111	95.5	11.7	47.7
Princes Lakes town	1,307	1,326	1.5	1,417	95.1	0.7	0.0	3.2	1.0	20.8	66.6	12.5	544	90.1	47.6	18.8
Princeton city	8,642	8,608	-0.4	8,600	88.3	4.2	0.1	3.8	3.5	24.6	58.7	16.8	3,331	65.6	46.8	15.3
Purdue University CDP	12,183	NA	NA	10,954	66.7	3.3	23.7	1.9	4.3	3.2	96.4	0.2	1,059	1.1	14.0	60.1
Raglesville CDP	141	NA	NA	70	100.0	0.0	0.0	0.0	0.0	0.0	100.0	0.0	56	75.0	75.0	25.0
Ragsdale CDP	129	NA	NA	122	78.7	0.0	0.0	21.3	0.0	30.4	49.2	20.5	36	100.0	75.0	0.0
Redkey town	1,353	1,348	-0.4	1,337	97.8	0.0	0.4	1.0	0.7	30.6	55.7	13.7	495	70.9	61.0	6.9
Remington town	1,185	1,167	-1.5	1,274	96.9	0.2	0.0	0.5	2.4	23.5	60.8	15.6	526	62.5	51.1	12.2
Rensselaer city	5,983	5,937	-0.8	5,787	91.5	1.7	0.7	2.3	3.8	19.3	63.0	17.7	2,378	60.5	48.1	19.8
Reynolds town	533	527	-1.1	575	84.5	0.0	1.7	2.6	11.1	27.5	58.9	13.6	226	76.1	58.8	14.2
Richland town	426	411	-3.5	471	96.6	0.8	0.0	0.6	1.9	32.9	54.5	12.5	170	90.6	54.1	9.4
Richmond city	36,797	36,159	-1.7	36,527	82.6	7.2	1.5	4.5	4.2	22.4	61.0	16.6	15,288	55.9	52.9	18.6
Ridgeville town	803	776	-3.4	676	92.0	0.0	0.0	2.1	5.9	22.3	61.2	16.6	287	75.6	68.3	6.3
Riley town	221	220	-0.5	165	100.0	0.0	0.0	0.0	0.0	18.7	53.9	27.3	78	84.6	50.0	10.3
Rising Sun city	2,301	2,242	-2.6	2,291	93.6	4.9	0.0	1.2	0.3	17.4	60.0	22.6	972	58.1	64.8	7.7
River Forest town	22	22	0.0	33	81.8	0.0	0.0	18.2	0.0	9.1	78.7	12.1	13	100.0	7.7	46.2
Roachdale town	919	898	-2.3	867	99.2	0.0	0.0	0.7	0.1	31.2	55.4	13.3	298	55.7	59.7	8.1
Roann town	479	472	-1.5	496	98.0	0.0	0.0	0.4	1.6	31.6	56.1	12.1	191	69.6	52.9	14.1
Roanoke town	1,721	1,702	-1.1	1,605	97.4	0.3	0.0	1.7	0.5	25.3	62.5	12.1	633	80.7	37.0	31.3
Rochester city	6,218	6,119	-1.6	6,151	93.5	0.4	0.0	1.6	4.4	20.0	58.6	21.2	2,922	60.7	54.0	13.8
Rockport city	2,270	2,240	-1.3	2,279	94.9	2.9	0.1	1.9	0.2	23.5	56.6	20.0	926	54.4	60.8	6.7
Rockville town	2,611	2,596	-0.6	2,587	88.2	8.6	0.0	1.8	1.4	16.6	70.0	13.5	834	66.9	57.4	12.8
Rocky Ripple town	606	625	3.1	648	83.5	8.0	0.0	4.8	3.7	23.3	65.2	11.4	290	68.3	22.8	37.6
Rolling Prairie CDP	582	NA	NA	560	97.3	2.7	0.0	0.0	0.0	40.1	52.1	7.7	151	76.8	26.5	45.7
Rome City town	1,361	1,377	1.2	1,263	96.0	0.0	1.4	2.1	0.5	15.2	65.7	19.2	559	72.8	58.5	14.8
Rosedale town	717	715	-0.3	788	97.7	0.0	0.8	1.0	0.5	31.7	56.6	11.7	325	78.8	48.3	9.8
Roseland town	626	625	-0.2	560	71.4	9.1	5.2	5.0	9.3	14.9	68.7	16.4	236	64.4	42.8	31.8
Roselawn CDP	4,131	NA	NA	3,863	83.3	0.3	0.3	0.2	16.0	27.2	62.3	10.4	1,239	88.2	59.6	10.7
Rossville town	1,653	1,637	-1.0	1,612	93.1	1.1	0.7	1.6	3.5	30.3	47.9	21.8	550	74.4	46.4	18.9
Royal Center town	861	847	-1.6	1,006	89.1	0.7	0.3	4.3	5.7	29.5	57.3	13.3	395	75.2	56.7	11.9
Rushville city	6,341	6,158	-2.9	6,314	92.9	2.5	0.0	1.8	2.8	22.7	60.0	17.4	2,723	55.9	64.5	10.0
Russellville town	354	349	-1.4	380	99.7	0.0	0.0	0.0	0.3	21.4	71.9	6.6	143	72.7	75.5	6.3
Russiaville town	1,094	1,088	-0.5	1,160	95.6	0.0	0.7	2.0	1.7	25.2	62.0	12.7	473	75.5	39.5	20.5
St. Bernice CDP	646	NA	NA	454	97.6	0.0	0.0	1.8	0.7	26.8	57.0	16.1	156	83.3	62.8	4.5
St. Joe town	462	462	0.0	438	96.8	0.0	0.0	3.0	0.2	29.2	61.4	9.4	158	81.0	61.4	9.5
St. John town	14,853	16,117	8.5	15,456	85.8	0.3	1.1	2.6	10.2	26.8	61.0	12.3	5,409	96.1	24.7	41.9
St. Leon town	678	671	-1.0	629	98.9	0.0	0.0	0.0	1.1	21.0	61.9	17.2	222	73.0	56.3	18.0
St. Mary of the Woods CDP	797	NA	NA	722	92.8	2.6	0.7	0.0	3.9	2.8	68.6	28.7	181	33.7	68.5	0.0
St. Meinrad CDP	706	NA	NA	517	99.4	0.0	0.6	0.0	0.0	16.6	52.1	31.3	206	83.5	63.1	11.7
St. Paul town	1,031	1,052	2.0	1,181	95.9	0.3	0.0	0.8	3.0	22.9	63.9	13.3	462	69.7	66.7	5.4
Salamonia town	157	157	0.0	156	71.2	12.8	0.0	2.6	13.5	37.8	50.7	11.5	53	66.0	50.9	0.0
Salem city	6,320	6,236	-1.3	6,264	96.1	0.3	0.0	1.1	2.5	26.2	56.0	17.9	2,507	65.1	60.4	15.2
Salt Creek Commons CDP	2,117	NA	NA	2,604	84.0	0.3	2.0	3.0	10.7	36.0	58.6	5.4	786	76.6	44.0	17.8
Saltillo town	92	91	-1.1	102	92.2	0.0	0.0	7.8	0.0	13.7	56.9	29.4	52	78.8	75.0	3.8
Sandborn town	414	411	-0.7	381	100.0	0.0	0.0	0.0	0.0	19.7	55.6	24.7	175	90.9	49.7	16.0
San Pierre CDP	144	NA	NA	90	100.0	0.0	0.0	0.0	0.0	0.0	70.0	30.0	53	100.0	54.7	0.0
Santa Claus town	2,483	2,479	-0.2	2,821	97.2	0.4	0.2	0.6	1.6	29.6	54.7	15.5	1,014	86.4	35.2	36.2
Saratoga town	254	248	-2.4	192	93.2	0.0	0.5	0.0	6.3	29.2	55.1	15.6	89	69.7	73.0	3.4
Schererville town	29,243	28,926	-1.1	29,082	78.7	5.0	3.1	1.3	11.8	21.8	63.1	15.1	11,528	75.2	37.4	32.5
Schneider town	277	271	-2.2	287	98.6	0.0	0.0	1.4	0.0	22.3	68.0	9.8	114	65.8	72.8	6.1
Scipio CDP	153	NA	NA	123	100.0	0.0	0.0	0.0	0.0	0.0	70.0	30.1	78	100.0	92.3	7.7
Scotland CDP	134	NA	NA	51	100.0	0.0	0.0	0.0	0.0	37.2	47.0	15.7	32	100.0	28.1	25.0
Scottsburg city	6,771	6,662	-1.6	6,700	96.3	0.5	0.0	0.5	2.7	22.9	59.6	17.5	2,655	55.7	52.4	20.8
Seelyville town	1,029	1,027	-0.2	930	97.0	0.3	0.3	2.0	0.3	17.1	69.5	13.4	406	67.0	51.0	12.6
Sellersburg town	7,833	8,066	3.0	8,004	98.0	1.3	0.2	0.5	0.0	26.6	61.2	12.2	2,873	73.8	42.9	24.9
Selma town	866	848	-2.1	849	93.5	0.2	4.5	1.8	0.0	20.7	66.0	13.3	370	64.9	47.6	8.1
Seymour city	18,021	19,094	6.0	18,686	83.1	1.1	1.9	2.4	11.5	25.7	60.8	13.5	7,274	62.9	58.3	18.8
Shadeland town	1,610	1,751	8.8	1,778	94.8	0.6	1.3	1.3	2.1	16.1	62.0	21.8	749	85.8	51.9	21.2
Shamrock Lakes town	231	226	-2.2	397	87.2	0.0	12.3	0.5	0.0	24.8	63.3	12.1	135	98.5	35.6	35.6
Sharpsville town	607	585	-3.6	638	95.9	0.0	0.0	0.8	3.3	25.1	59.2	15.8	252	78.2	61.5	16.7
Shelburn town	1,254	1,228	-2.1	1,254	99.4	0.0	0.0	0.3	0.3	22.8	65.6	11.6	483	65.8	70.4	8.3
Shelby CDP	539	NA	NA	526	100.0	0.0	0.0	0.0	0.0	31.9	63.3	4.8	205	92.2	66.8	5.4
Shelbyville city	19,152	19,163	0.1	19,216	85.8	2.6	1.2	2.5	7.9	25.3	61.0	13.5	7,737	55.1	55.7	14.1
Shepardsville CDP	237	NA	NA	420	88.1	6.7	0.0	5.2	0.0	39.1	58.6	2.4	112	93.8	61.6	31.3

1 May be of any race.

Table A. All Places — **Population and Housing**

STATE City, town, township, borough, or CDP (county if applicable)	Population: 2010 census total population	Population: 2014 estimated population	Population: Percent change 2010–2014	Population: ACS total population estimate 2010–2014	Race and Hispanic or Latino origin (percent), 2010–2014: White alone, not Hispanic or Latino	Black alone, not Hispanic or Latino	Asian alone, not Hispanic or Latino	All other races or 2 or more races, not Hispanic or Latino	Hispanic or Latino[1]	Age (percent), 2010–2014: Under 18 years old	Age 18 to 64 years old	Age 65 years and older	Households, 2010–2014: Total occupied housing units	Percent owner occupied	Householders by level of education (percent): High school diploma or less	Bachelor's degree or more
	1	2	3	4	5	6	7	8	9	10	11	12	13	14	15	16
INDIANA—Con.																
Sheridan town	2,665	2,893	8.6	3,084	93.4	0.5	0.0	0.3	5.7	27.1	58.7	14.1	1,277	64.8	53.6	9.6
Shipshewana town	654	677	3.5	660	94.7	0.0	0.0	1.4	3.9	21.9	59.9	18.0	299	59.2	59.5	19.7
Shirley town	830	828	-0.2	859	96.9	0.0	0.3	0.9	1.9	27.4	63.2	9.4	306	64.1	64.7	7.8
Shoals town	797	781	-2.0	798	98.9	0.0	0.0	1.1	0.0	16.3	57.2	26.6	387	69.3	75.5	7.8
Shorewood Forest CDP	2,708	NA	NA	2,495	92.4	2.2	2.0	1.5	1.8	18.3	66.4	15.5	914	96.6	21.8	57.1
Sidney town	83	83	0.0	95	96.8	0.0	0.0	0.0	3.2	21.0	53.7	25.3	36	88.9	75.0	0.0
Silver Lake town	918	925	0.8	962	96.2	0.3	0.3	0.8	2.4	27.6	58.4	13.9	375	83.2	67.2	5.3
Simonton Lake CDP	4,678	NA	NA	4,354	87.8	6.3	2.0	0.8	3.1	21.3	61.1	17.8	1,907	80.3	40.8	23.9
Sims CDP	156	NA	NA	342	98.0	0.0	0.0	0.0	2.0	39.8	50.0	10.2	132	72.7	56.1	0.0
Smithville-Sanders CDP	3,184	NA	NA	3,234	96.0	0.0	1.9	1.4	0.6	22.5	59.9	17.7	1,319	81.1	23.9	44.4
Somerset CDP	401	NA	NA	437	96.8	0.0	0.0	3.2	0.0	29.9	49.2	20.8	178	74.7	64.6	7.9
Somerville town	289	290	0.3	211	96.2	2.8	0.0	0.9	0.0	25.1	49.2	25.6	85	89.4	75.3	10.6
South Bend city	101,046	101,190	0.1	100,422	55.5	26.7	1.3	3.9	12.6	27.0	60.2	12.8	39,866	58.7	44.1	24.5
South Haven CDP	5,282	NA	NA	5,304	86.4	2.4	0.0	1.6	9.6	23.3	67.2	9.5	1,927	77.5	46.1	13.9
Southport city	1,712	1,753	2.4	1,778	94.3	0.4	0.2	0.7	4.4	23.9	63.2	12.7	715	72.6	46.7	25.6
South Whitley town	1,784	1,752	-1.8	1,956	98.2	0.1	0.0	0.9	0.9	30.9	57.1	12.2	748	77.7	60.6	8.0
Speedway town	11,812	12,101	2.4	12,012	68.3	19.3	1.0	3.7	7.6	18.0	64.1	17.8	5,783	44.4	39.4	24.9
Spencer town	2,345	2,280	-2.8	2,453	94.7	0.7	0.8	1.2	2.6	19.1	61.3	19.7	1,098	54.8	64.3	7.7
Spiceland town	888	867	-2.4	900	97.9	0.0	0.8	1.2	0.1	30.6	57.0	12.3	333	78.4	58.0	12.9
Spring Grove town	339	335	-1.2	281	81.1	12.1	5.3	1.1	0.4	11.7	48.7	39.5	106	76.4	35.8	37.7
Spring Hill town	98	101	3.1	93	74.2	21.5	2.2	2.2	0.0	4.3	51.6	44.1	53	96.2	5.7	88.7
Spring Lake town	218	218	0.0	292	99.3	0.7	0.0	0.0	0.0	17.1	65.4	17.5	117	96.6	41.0	21.4
Springport town	146	144	-1.4	174	94.8	0.0	2.3	2.3	0.6	20.1	63.2	16.7	67	89.6	53.7	14.9
Spurgeon town	207	203	-1.9	163	100.0	0.0	0.0	0.0	0.0	11.7	65.1	23.3	84	85.7	64.3	7.1
Star City CDP	344	NA	NA	278	100.0	0.0	0.0	0.0	0.0	30.6	58.3	11.2	121	94.2	60.3	20.7
State Line City town	143	140	-2.1	133	100.0	0.0	0.0	0.0	0.0	18.8	70.1	11.3	63	87.3	66.7	1.6
Staunton town	535	519	-3.0	452	98.2	0.0	0.0	0.0	1.8	22.8	66.6	10.6	162	67.9	58.0	14.2
Stilesville town	316	326	3.2	276	92.4	4.0	0.0	3.6	0.0	23.5	47.5	29.0	119	77.3	51.3	9.2
Stinesville town	203	210	3.4	149	96.6	0.0	0.0	3.4	0.0	8.8	69.1	22.1	68	72.1	48.5	20.6
Stockwell CDP	545	NA	NA	513	93.2	0.0	0.0	0.0	6.8	16.0	59.2	24.8	220	100.0	59.1	15.9
Straughn town	222	219	-1.4	257	99.6	0.0	0.0	0.4	0.0	27.6	61.4	10.9	80	71.3	67.5	16.3
Sullivan city	4,247	4,171	-1.8	4,203	98.3	0.0	0.0	0.2	1.5	20.6	61.6	17.9	1,842	50.8	53.5	12.9
Sulphur Springs town	392	386	-1.5	433	99.3	0.0	0.5	0.2	0.0	27.5	57.0	15.7	147	80.3	69.4	4.8
Summitville town	1,004	991	-1.3	1,078	96.2	0.0	0.0	1.4	2.4	22.0	65.3	12.5	389	74.3	60.9	10.0
Sunman town	1,049	1,034	-1.4	903	85.8	0.0	0.9	0.0	13.3	29.2	59.0	11.8	352	61.6	60.2	13.1
Swayzee town	981	963	-1.8	993	99.4	0.1	0.0	0.4	0.1	26.5	54.0	19.2	391	87.2	58.3	13.0
Sweetser town	1,229	1,207	-1.8	1,210	93.6	0.0	0.0	0.3	6.1	29.2	51.6	19.3	498	74.3	53.0	20.5
Switz City town	293	293	0.0	328	95.4	0.0	1.5	0.9	2.1	27.4	55.8	16.8	135	74.1	53.3	6.7
Syracuse town	2,857	2,882	0.9	2,878	86.3	2.9	0.4	1.8	8.6	31.9	57.2	10.9	1,142	66.8	51.6	12.3
Taylorsville CDP	919	NA	NA	926	96.0	1.3	0.0	0.0	2.7	26.1	62.7	11.2	365	79.5	43.6	24.4
Tecumseh CDP	658	NA	NA	843	97.4	0.0	1.7	0.9	0.0	25.8	61.7	12.5	295	97.3	41.4	26.8
Tell City city	7,272	7,257	-0.2	7,251	97.0	0.5	0.1	1.1	1.3	23.4	57.4	19.3	3,109	72.6	59.8	12.1
Tennyson town	279	287	2.9	323	94.1	0.0	0.0	0.0	5.9	26.3	58.2	15.5	114	77.2	75.4	4.4
Terre Haute city	60,785	60,956	0.3	61,040	81.5	9.8	1.6	3.7	3.3	19.8	67.6	12.6	21,812	53.7	42.7	22.3
Thorntown town	1,522	1,484	-2.5	1,563	93.3	0.0	0.4	3.7	2.6	26.6	60.2	13.4	596	63.9	58.4	5.0
Tipton city	5,383	5,192	-3.5	5,288	95.4	0.4	0.3	2.3	1.7	24.7	56.0	19.4	2,163	64.0	50.3	11.5
Toad Hop CDP	108	NA	NA	69	100.0	0.0	0.0	0.0	0.0	0.0	100.0	0.0	54	100.0	100.0	0.0
Topeka town	1,155	1,190	3.0	1,010	82.3	0.0	0.3	15.9	1.5	39.5	53.2	7.1	358	57.8	78.8	9.8
Town of Pines town	708	705	-0.4	732	90.6	2.7	2.0	1.2	3.4	20.0	66.0	13.8	285	70.9	63.2	10.5
Trafalgar town	1,101	1,145	4.0	1,123	97.4	0.9	0.1	0.0	1.6	29.8	61.7	8.5	383	77.5	53.0	15.4
Trail Creek town	2,067	2,036	-1.5	1,872	91.7	4.9	0.4	2.5	0.6	21.4	57.9	20.6	826	95.2	42.7	16.9
Tri-Lakes CDP	1,421	NA	NA	1,340	100.0	0.0	0.0	0.0	0.0	14.7	69.1	16.1	641	94.5	33.7	35.9
Troy town	385	375	-2.6	299	96.0	0.0	0.0	0.0	4.0	14.4	60.3	25.4	158	78.5	77.8	5.1
Ulen town	117	124	6.0	119	98.3	0.0	0.0	0.0	1.7	15.2	41.2	43.7	54	96.3	13.0	70.4
Union City city	3,584	3,478	-3.0	3,606	87.6	0.2	0.0	1.3	10.9	28.9	54.0	17.1	1,511	59.8	62.7	7.9
Uniondale town	309	310	0.3	308	92.9	0.0	0.6	1.6	4.9	27.0	59.5	13.6	120	83.3	48.3	11.7
Universal town	362	345	-4.7	329	98.8	0.0	0.0	0.0	1.2	30.7	49.7	19.8	130	88.5	70.0	10.8
Upland town	3,845	3,802	-1.1	4,068	95.7	2.2	1.0	0.2	0.9	17.3	74.2	8.7	987	68.7	32.5	44.4
Utica town	776	795	2.4	828	77.3	5.7	0.0	12.0	5.1	28.2	60.8	11.0	307	77.5	44.6	21.8
Vallonia CDP	336	NA	NA	252	100.0	0.0	0.0	0.0	0.0	11.5	74.6	13.9	134	83.6	85.8	7.5
Valparaiso city	31,734	32,369	2.0	31,745	84.2	4.0	2.2	1.6	8.0	22.2	64.0	13.9	12,092	57.7	29.6	38.7
Van Bibber Lake CDP	485	NA	NA	307	100.0	0.0	0.0	0.0	0.0	14.6	65.8	19.5	150	97.3	66.7	0.0
Van Buren town	864	842	-2.5	764	99.7	0.0	0.0	0.3	0.0	19.1	59.7	21.3	317	70.0	56.8	9.1
Veedersburg town	2,180	2,107	-3.3	2,126	97.0	0.0	0.0	0.4	2.6	23.0	58.9	18.0	911	79.6	69.0	7.5
Vera Cruz town	80	80	0.0	106	94.3	0.0	0.0	2.8	2.8	29.3	58.5	12.3	41	56.1	36.6	17.1
Vernon town	318	312	-1.9	334	89.5	0.0	0.0	0.0	10.5	29.4	58.5	12.3	132	74.2	40.2	11.4
Versailles town	2,113	2,088	-1.2	2,007	91.0	4.9	0.0	0.6	3.4	22.7	59.4	17.9	864	61.0	53.6	20.6
Vevay town	1,683	1,666	-1.0	1,379	94.3	0.7	0.6	3.5	0.9	12.3	66.8	21.2	603	56.7	67.7	8.8
Vincennes city	18,422	18,032	-2.1	18,233	89.9	6.1	0.3	1.3	2.5	21.0	63.4	15.7	7,101	54.4	49.2	14.4
Wabash city	10,670	10,433	-2.2	10,534	95.8	0.0	0.6	1.7	1.9	22.8	59.4	17.8	4,417	68.3	51.5	12.0
Wakarusa town	1,758	1,798	2.3	1,960	92.7	1.6	0.0	1.3	4.4	28.9	50.4	20.6	645	74.9	44.0	25.9
Waldron CDP	804	NA	NA	747	100.0	0.0	0.0	0.0	0.0	19.8	67.4	12.7	250	79.6	68.8	2.8
Walkerton town	2,145	2,256	5.2	1,982	92.7	0.4	0.0	1.4	5.5	24.7	57.6	17.7	776	71.0	52.4	12.4
Wallace town	102	99	-2.9	127	100.0	0.0	0.0	0.0	0.0	30.8	48.0	21.3	56	89.3	58.9	8.9
Walton town	1,049	1,034	-1.4	950	86.2	0.0	0.0	1.4	12.4	19.5	59.3	21.3	413	72.4	59.3	11.9
Wanatah town	1,047	1,029	-1.7	1,076	90.0	0.2	0.5	3.3	6.1	26.1	58.2	15.8	433	82.2	57.5	12.2
Warren town	1,243	1,225	-1.4	1,476	94.4	0.0	0.0	1.0	4.6	24.8	57.5	17.7	635	52.3	61.6	12.3
Warren Park town	1,480	1,531	3.4	1,596	69.5	13.0	0.3	1.2	16.0	20.7	51.5	27.8	748	34.1	52.0	19.1
Warsaw city	13,562	14,280	5.3	14,179	80.4	1.2	4.6	0.7	13.1	22.3	63.2	14.4	5,798	63.0	47.4	26.0
Washington city	11,497	12,020	4.5	11,758	84.9	2.9	0.4	0.8	11.1	26.8	57.3	15.9	4,614	64.0	62.5	13.4
Waterloo town	2,242	2,243	0.0	2,437	92.3	0.2	2.4	0.3	4.8	38.4	57.1	4.6	790	73.3	62.0	9.7
Waveland town	420	420	0.0	358	94.4	0.3	0.0	0.8	4.5	24.0	56.7	19.3	141	77.3	60.3	14.9
Waynetown town	958	954	-0.4	1,042	89.2	0.0	0.9	3.1	6.9	27.3	57.5	15.2	396	75.8	55.8	16.9
West Baden Springs town	574	565	-1.6	564	92.7	7.3	0.0	0.0	0.0	20.7	60.1	19.3	256	63.7	60.9	7.0
West College Corner town	676	650	-3.8	771	93.5	0.0	0.0	6.5	0.0	33.0	53.0	13.9	330	48.8	59.7	11.8
Westfield city	30,090	35,297	17.3	32,426	86.2	3.7	2.9	3.3	3.8	32.4	61.4	6.2	11,491	79.5	15.4	59.4
West Harrison town	289	285	-1.4	387	98.7	0.0	0.0	0.0	1.3	20.2	68.3	11.6	171	49.1	73.7	3.5
West Lafayette city	29,596	32,109	8.5	30,843	71.1	3.1	19.7	2.8	3.3	11.7	79.8	8.6	11,924	31.2	13.8	52.3
West Lebanon town	723	710	-1.8	767	96.5	0.0	0.0	2.1	1.4	26.4	60.0	13.7	310	52.6	67.1	6.5
Westphalia CDP	202	NA	NA	84	76.2	0.0	0.0	23.8	0.0	13.1	53.5	33.3	46	78.3	82.6	17.4
West Point CDP	594	NA	NA	655	100.0	0.0	0.0	0.0	0.0	36.4	49.3	14.2	215	100.0	60.9	19.5

1 May be of any race.

Table A. All Places — **Population and Housing**

STATE City, town, township, borough, or CDP (county if applicable)	Population: 2010 census total population	Population: 2014 estimated population	Population: Percent change 2010–2014	Population: ACS total population estimate 2010–2014	Race and Hispanic or Latino origin (percent), 2010–2014: White alone, not Hispanic or Latino	Black alone, not Hispanic or Latino	Asian alone, not Hispanic or Latino	All other races or 2 or more races, not Hispanic or Latino	Hispanic or Latino[1]	Age (percent), 2010–2014: Under 18 years old	Age 18 to 64 years old	Age 65 years and older	Households, 2010–2014: Total occupied housing units	Percent owner occupied	Householders by level of education (percent): High school diploma or less	Bachelor's degree or more
	1	2	3	4	5	6	7	8	9	10	11	12	13	14	15	16
INDIANA—Con.																
Westport town	1,379	1,423	3.2	1,400	96.7	0.0	0.6	0.9	1.8	24.5	62.2	13.1	567	65.6	67.2	7.6
West Terre Haute town	2,236	2,226	-0.4	2,480	96.9	0.2	0.0	0.2	2.8	30.1	58.4	11.3	885	64.6	65.8	5.4
Westville town	5,801	5,959	2.7	6,895	61.4	28.3	0.8	2.4	7.2	8.7	88.3	3.0	776	72.3	49.9	11.2
Wheatfield town	853	844	-1.1	885	87.9	1.0	0.0	0.1	11.0	27.1	61.8	11.1	330	66.4	52.1	13.6
Wheatland town	478	474	-0.8	513	94.2	0.2	0.0	1.0	4.7	27.5	60.3	12.3	199	66.3	50.3	9.0
Wheeler CDP	443	NA	NA	246	81.7	0.0	0.0	0.0	18.3	13.4	72.8	13.8	108	80.6	57.4	10.2
Whiteland town	4,167	4,303	3.3	4,226	96.4	0.0	0.3	2.7	0.6	25.7	66.2	8.1	1,460	87.7	41.5	27.9
Whitestown town	3,132	5,258	67.9	4,125	85.3	6.2	2.0	3.5	3.0	33.3	62.5	4.2	1,483	81.9	21.1	50.9
Whitewater town	72	71	-1.4	71	95.8	0.0	0.0	4.2	0.0	25.3	59.1	15.5	28	50.0	71.4	0.0
Whiting city	4,997	4,856	-2.8	4,930	52.5	4.2	0.3	1.5	41.4	24.3	65.3	10.3	1,816	65.0	47.5	20.3
Wilkinson town	460	451	-2.0	535	99.1	0.0	0.0	0.0	0.9	29.2	58.8	12.1	179	73.7	54.7	8.9
Williams CDP	286	NA	NA	298	100.0	0.0	0.0	0.0	0.0	20.4	68.1	11.4	117	100.0	41.9	16.2
Williams Creek town	407	419	2.9	355	96.3	1.4	1.1	0.8	0.3	28.5	50.3	21.4	130	97.7	2.3	86.9
Williamsport town	1,898	1,867	-1.6	2,020	94.2	0.4	0.5	1.0	3.8	22.7	55.5	21.9	755	70.9	60.5	12.3
Winamac town	2,490	2,417	-2.9	2,627	93.2	0.0	1.0	1.9	3.8	20.8	62.0	17.2	1,110	61.3	52.9	20.5
Winchester city	4,957	4,809	-3.0	4,760	97.4	0.1	0.1	2.1	0.3	24.7	55.4	19.7	2,036	65.3	64.2	11.0
Windfall City town	708	679	-4.1	892	96.0	0.1	0.0	0.0	3.9	28.7	57.7	13.6	329	73.6	54.4	12.8
Winfield town	4,529	5,260	16.1	4,888	72.7	8.9	2.7	1.1	14.5	28.7	56.8	14.5	1,620	85.9	35.9	27.0
Wingate town	262	262	0.0	236	97.0	0.0	1.3	0.0	1.7	12.7	70.1	17.4	123	64.2	68.3	8.1
Winona Lake town	4,908	4,969	1.2	4,934	85.7	0.6	0.8	4.5	8.4	18.4	67.7	13.9	1,698	60.7	26.6	50.8
Winslow town	864	849	-1.7	1,099	99.5	0.3	0.0	0.3	0.0	27.8	59.9	12.3	394	70.8	67.8	6.9
Wolcott town	1,001	995	-0.6	1,129	84.8	0.4	1.2	5.2	8.5	29.0	53.8	17.4	433	69.7	56.4	6.9
Wolcottville town	989	1,009	2.0	864	91.6	0.0	0.0	5.3	3.1	26.9	62.9	10.2	342	61.7	76.0	3.5
Woodburn city	1,520	1,601	5.3	1,609	98.9	0.0	0.0	0.4	0.6	28.3	61.4	10.4	607	81.9	47.0	20.4
Woodlawn Heights town	79	78	-1.3	50	94.0	0.0	0.0	2.0	4.0	10.0	58.0	32.0	25	100.0	12.0	44.0
Worthington town	1,463	1,442	-1.4	1,383	98.2	0.0	0.0	0.5	1.3	25.6	58.3	16.0	564	75.0	61.3	7.8
Wynnedale town	231	238	3.0	181	71.8	28.2	0.0	0.0	0.0	12.2	57.4	30.4	80	97.5	5.0	77.5
Yeoman town	139	138	-0.7	119	100.0	0.0	0.0	0.0	0.0	33.7	54.7	11.8	50	82.0	76.0	10.0
Yorktown town	11,303	11,220	-0.7	11,265	93.3	1.2	1.1	3.2	1.3	26.2	57.4	16.3	4,410	79.3	36.0	35.5
Zanesville town	600	609	1.5	646	97.4	0.5	0.0	0.6	1.5	27.4	60.2	12.4	233	90.6	57.9	14.6
Zionsville town	23,520	25,734	9.4	24,559	91.8	1.4	4.6	1.0	1.2	31.3	58.8	9.7	8,621	80.8	11.1	70.6
IOWA	3,046,869	3,107,126	2.0	3,078,116	87.8	3.0	1.9	1.9	5.3	23.6	61.1	15.3	1,232,228	71.8	38.5	27.3
Ackley city	1,589	1,550	-2.5	1,546	93.7	0.0	0.0	0.0	6.3	17.4	47.6	34.9	697	78.2	48.1	19.5
Ackworth city	83	83	0.0	39	100.0	0.0	0.0	0.0	0.0	12.8	72.0	15.4	18	72.2	50.0	16.7
Adair city	781	752	-3.7	890	95.4	0.7	0.6	0.1	3.3	22.4	61.7	16.0	406	76.8	44.8	20.7
Adel city	3,707	4,171	12.5	3,940	94.0	0.6	0.0	1.8	3.7	26.4	59.7	13.8	1,593	67.3	46.3	26.7
Afton city	845	842	-0.4	917	92.5	0.9	0.0	2.5	4.1	21.8	62.9	15.5	390	68.7	51.5	11.5
Agency city	638	636	-0.3	694	88.8	0.0	6.6	2.7	1.9	25.6	56.2	18.3	307	71.0	47.6	13.0
Ainsworth city	567	568	0.2	589	58.1	0.8	0.0	0.7	40.4	28.7	59.7	11.5	205	85.4	68.3	20.5
Akron city	1,486	1,456	-2.0	1,364	96.8	0.4	0.0	0.0	2.8	25.2	49.9	24.9	585	74.2	53.5	13.7
Albert City city	699	700	0.1	672	91.8	4.8	0.3	2.4	0.7	24.0	54.9	21.3	285	77.2	34.0	22.1
Albia city	3,766	3,782	0.4	3,788	98.5	0.4	0.2	0.9	0.0	23.2	54.6	22.3	1,629	63.9	51.0	22.4
Albion city	505	469	-7.1	430	94.7	0.0	0.0	3.7	1.6	18.2	61.4	20.5	191	92.7	47.6	10.5
Alburnett city	673	690	2.5	612	99.7	0.0	0.0	0.3	0.0	22.3	64.5	13.4	229	90.4	44.1	18.3
Alden city	787	763	-3.0	756	94.3	0.0	0.0	0.0	5.7	20.4	61.1	18.5	307	76.2	49.5	11.7
Alexander city	175	172	-1.7	190	98.9	1.1	0.0	0.0	0.0	25.8	63.7	10.5	86	62.8	64.0	10.5
Algona city	5,560	5,479	-1.5	5,513	96.2	0.0	0.5	1.1	2.2	21.1	52.7	26.2	2,524	77.6	35.7	26.3
Alleman city	432	438	1.4	592	98.8	0.0	0.3	0.0	0.8	28.7	61.2	10.0	206	99.0	24.8	38.3
Allerton city	501	497	-0.8	474	91.6	1.3	0.0	7.2	0.0	29.5	47.2	23.2	180	82.2	53.3	7.8
Allison city	1,029	1,034	0.5	1,184	94.3	0.3	2.1	1.1	2.2	20.5	55.3	24.2	481	82.1	42.2	13.5
Alta city	1,905	1,952	2.5	1,919	87.0	0.4	0.3	0.6	11.7	26.8	55.9	17.1	766	72.3	43.5	21.1
Alta Vista city	266	263	-1.1	293	100.0	0.0	0.0	0.0	0.0	26.6	53.9	19.5	132	75.0	59.1	10.6
Alton city	1,216	1,256	3.3	1,190	83.6	0.4	0.5	1.3	14.2	23.9	63.6	12.5	473	79.9	48.6	24.1
Altoona city	14,541	16,105	10.8	15,317	93.4	0.6	0.7	2.1	3.3	27.5	61.7	10.9	5,843	72.5	32.7	34.1
Alvord city	196	193	-1.5	236	88.1	0.0	1.3	1.3	9.3	27.1	60.5	12.3	79	84.8	60.8	3.8
Amana CDP	442	NA	NA	334	89.5	6.9	0.0	0.0	3.6	18.3	49.2	32.6	172	100.0	34.3	34.9
Ames city	58,967	63,266	7.3	61,276	82.0	3.3	8.9	2.6	3.2	12.9	78.7	8.3	23,566	41.5	12.6	51.9
Anamosa city	5,537	5,425	-2.0	5,526	88.1	6.9	0.6	0.9	3.5	19.9	63.4	16.8	1,966	63.8	48.7	14.5
Anderson CDP	65	NA	NA	12	100.0	0.0	0.0	0.0	0.0	0.0	100.0	0.0	7	100.0	0.0	0.0
Andover city	103	100	-2.9	101	97.0	0.0	0.0	0.0	3.0	24.8	63.5	11.9	35	85.7	62.9	22.9
Andrew city	434	424	-2.3	399	95.0	0.5	0.0	4.5	0.0	25.6	62.6	11.8	155	72.9	65.2	8.4
Anita city	980	957	-2.3	927	96.5	0.0	0.0	0.0	3.5	23.8	52.9	23.2	402	71.1	40.0	18.7
Ankeny city	45,582	53,801	18.0	49,488	92.5	0.9	2.3	2.3	2.0	26.8	64.0	9.3	19,324	74.9	17.9	44.1
Anthon city	565	565	0.0	713	95.8	0.0	2.8	0.3	1.1	25.3	58.1	16.4	291	78.4	54.6	15.1
Aplington city	1,128	1,120	-0.7	1,104	100.0	0.0	0.0	0.0	0.0	26.5	50.7	22.8	433	77.6	46.0	15.7
Arcadia city	484	471	-2.7	563	91.1	0.0	0.0	3.6	5.3	31.0	53.3	16.0	207	91.8	57.0	17.9
Archer city	131	128	-2.3	121	76.9	0.8	0.0	1.7	20.7	27.2	44.6	28.1	50	88.0	40.0	24.0
Aredale city	74	74	0.0	70	94.3	0.0	0.0	0.0	5.7	17.2	55.8	27.1	37	100.0	81.1	0.0
Arion city	108	108	0.0	139	82.0	0.0	0.0	0.0	18.0	29.4	60.3	10.1	51	84.3	80.4	0.0
Arispe city	100	100	0.0	46	100.0	0.0	0.0	0.0	0.0	15.2	65.2	19.6	29	79.3	37.9	17.2
Arlington city	429	414	-3.5	557	96.1	0.0	0.9	3.1	0.0	25.1	59.0	16.0	223	80.7	51.1	13.9
Armstrong city	926	912	-1.5	924	99.5	0.0	0.0	0.5	0.0	22.2	56.4	21.5	403	80.9	43.9	9.9
Arnolds Park city	1,126	1,207	7.2	1,109	92.5	1.1	0.2	1.4	4.8	13.2	59.0	27.8	598	65.1	41.0	22.7
Arthur city	206	205	-0.5	161	98.1	0.0	0.6	1.2	0.0	14.9	54.6	30.4	87	87.4	60.9	12.6
Asbury city	4,395	5,171	17.7	4,848	85.9	3.6	6.9	0.7	2.9	34.6	55.8	9.5	1,559	92.9	26.6	51.3
Ashton city	458	436	-4.8	417	96.9	0.5	0.0	1.4	1.2	20.1	62.4	17.5	199	80.9	58.3	12.1
Aspinwall city	40	40	0.0	25	100.0	0.0	0.0	0.0	0.0	12.0	68.0	20.0	15	80.0	53.3	6.7
Atalissa city	311	303	-2.6	401	92.0	0.7	0.0	0.0	7.2	27.2	61.2	11.5	144	83.3	62.5	3.5
Athelstan CDP	19	NA	NA	45	100.0	0.0	0.0	0.0	0.0	40.0	60.0	0.0	12	58.3	41.7	0.0
Atkins city	1,670	1,753	5.0	1,812	97.6	0.6	0.8	0.7	0.3	28.9	60.2	11.0	636	88.5	31.1	33.2
Atlantic city	7,112	6,842	-3.8	6,983	94.5	0.4	0.4	0.9	3.7	21.4	56.7	22.0	3,298	66.2	51.3	21.5
Auburn city	322	314	-2.5	260	99.6	0.4	0.0	0.0	0.0	23.9	53.9	22.3	115	73.0	68.7	8.7
Audubon city	2,176	2,035	-6.5	2,089	96.9	0.0	0.1	1.5	1.4	20.9	50.5	28.8	976	84.7	47.8	20.5
Aurelia city	1,036	1,016	-1.9	1,084	91.1	0.0	0.7	0.7	7.4	21.4	57.1	21.4	460	80.7	48.7	21.3
Aurora city	185	171	-7.6	222	89.6	1.4	1.8	6.8	0.5	24.9	68.1	7.2	86	82.6	58.1	18.6
Avoca city	1,508	1,506	-0.1	1,328	97.7	0.0	0.0	1.8	0.5	24.5	56.0	19.6	597	73.5	48.9	13.9
Ayrshire city	143	139	-2.8	158	100.0	0.0	0.0	0.0	0.0	30.4	51.9	17.7	74	81.1	66.2	6.8
Badger city	561	547	-2.5	495	97.8	0.0	1.2	0.0	1.0	23.5	59.0	17.8	193	84.5	38.9	9.8
Bagley city	303	297	-2.0	419	90.9	0.0	0.0	0.5	8.6	28.9	58.2	12.9	158	82.9	58.2	10.8

1 May be of any race.

Table A. All Places — **Population and Housing**

STATE City, town, township, borough, or CDP (county if applicable)	Population				Race and Hispanic or Latino origin (percent), 2010–2014					Age (percent), 2010–2014			Households, 2010–2014		Householders by level of education (percent)	
	2010 census total population	2014 estimated population	Percent change 2010–2014	ACS total population estimate 2010–2014	White alone, not Hispanic or Latino	Black alone, not Hispanic or Latino	Asian alone, not Hispanic or Latino	All other races or 2 or more races, not Hispanic or Latino	Hispanic or Latino[1]	Under 18 years old	Age 18 to 64 years old	Age 65 years and older	Total occupied housing units	Percent owner occupied	High school diploma or less	Bachelor's degree or more
	1	2	3	4	5	6	7	8	9	10	11	12	13	14	15	16
IOWA—Con.																
Baldwin city	109	106	-2.8	101	99.0	0.0	0.0	1.0	0.0	18.8	62.6	18.8	53	75.5	64.2	11.3
Balltown city	65	65	0.0	59	100.0	0.0	0.0	0.0	0.0	17.0	51.0	32.2	31	96.8	58.1	6.5
Bancroft city	734	716	-2.5	698	96.3	0.0	0.0	1.0	2.7	23.1	50.9	25.9	305	74.4	48.9	9.2
Bankston city	25	25	0.0	78	100.0	0.0	0.0	0.0	0.0	5.2	93.6	1.3	22	100.0	22.7	4.5
Barnes City city	176	176	0.0	219	99.1	0.0	0.0	0.0	0.9	23.8	50.2	26.0	96	78.1	54.2	9.4
Barnum city	191	189	-1.0	248	88.7	0.0	0.0	0.0	11.3	45.6	49.8	4.4	75	72.0	46.7	17.3
Bartlett CDP	50	NA	NA	11	100.0	0.0	0.0	0.0	0.0	0.0	0.0	100.0	5	100.0	100.0	0.0
Bassett city	66	65	-1.5	82	100.0	0.0	0.0	0.0	0.0	3.7	87.8	8.5	38	92.1	84.2	0.0
Batavia city	499	510	2.2	549	96.9	0.0	0.0	0.0	3.1	21.1	64.6	14.2	249	82.3	65.5	2.8
Battle Creek city	713	700	-1.8	676	96.6	0.0	1.9	1.5	0.0	21.7	47.4	31.1	319	74.3	49.5	12.5
Baxter city	1,101	1,101	0.0	971	97.7	0.0	0.0	2.3	0.0	26.8	54.6	18.8	370	71.1	32.7	24.3
Bayard city	471	460	-2.3	488	99.0	0.4	0.0	0.6	0.0	23.3	60.5	16.2	189	84.7	54.0	6.9
Beacon city	494	487	-1.4	502	99.0	0.0	0.8	0.2	0.0	26.7	56.8	16.7	195	86.2	63.6	7.2
Beaconsfield city	15	15	0.0	25	100.0	0.0	0.0	0.0	0.0	0.0	60.0	40.0	15	60.0	80.0	0.0
Beaman city	191	191	0.0	199	98.5	0.0	0.0	0.0	1.5	30.6	56.6	12.6	77	81.8	55.8	20.8
Beaver city	48	48	0.0	73	82.2	0.0	0.0	17.8	0.0	30.2	51.9	17.8	26	73.1	46.2	11.5
Beaverdale CDP	952	NA	NA	1,231	83.4	10.0	2.4	2.7	1.5	36.9	51.8	11.4	369	87.0	45.0	16.8
Bedford city	1,440	1,404	-2.5	1,495	92.2	1.3	1.2	1.6	3.7	24.8	54.8	20.5	646	79.6	55.6	10.7
Belle Plaine city	2,534	2,489	-1.8	2,605	89.4	0.7	0.1	4.4	5.4	28.3	52.7	19.1	1,059	68.9	52.5	15.6
Bellevue city	2,193	2,167	-1.2	2,158	98.7	0.0	0.0	0.6	0.7	20.6	51.4	28.2	995	71.7	50.8	14.1
Belmond city	2,376	2,322	-2.3	2,391	90.4	0.0	0.4	0.2	9.0	21.7	57.2	21.1	1,104	75.1	42.7	16.9
Bennett city	405	401	-1.0	369	96.2	0.0	0.0	2.7	1.1	24.1	53.8	22.0	159	83.0	63.5	9.4
Bentley CDP	118	NA	NA	111	100.0	0.0	0.0	0.0	0.0	0.0	83.7	16.2	49	100.0	36.7	20.4
Benton city	43	42	-2.3	52	100.0	0.0	0.0	0.0	0.0	17.3	69.2	13.5	20	100.0	55.0	5.0
Berkley city	32	32	0.0	16	100.0	0.0	0.0	0.0	0.0	0.0	56.4	43.8	10	100.0	70.0	0.0
Bernard city	110	109	-0.9	112	95.5	0.0	0.0	3.6	0.9	15.2	64.2	20.5	56	80.4	69.6	8.9
Bertram city	294	300	2.0	334	93.7	2.1	0.0	0.0	4.2	24.9	56.4	18.9	116	97.4	38.8	29.3
Bettendorf city	33,213	35,122	5.7	34,247	87.8	3.4	4.3	1.3	3.2	25.1	59.9	15.1	13,623	76.5	22.1	50.3
Bevington city	63	62	-1.6	23	82.6	0.0	0.0	17.4	0.0	17.4	52.2	30.4	11	100.0	45.5	0.0
Birmingham city	448	439	-2.0	471	96.0	0.0	0.0	0.0	4.0	18.2	65.9	15.9	218	84.9	49.1	12.4
Blairsburg city	215	210	-2.3	116	100.0	0.0	0.0	0.0	0.0	10.4	50.9	38.8	56	85.7	46.4	8.9
Blairstown city	692	673	-2.7	724	89.2	0.0	0.0	3.6	7.2	24.3	57.9	17.7	298	70.5	60.7	8.7
Blakesburg city	296	287	-3.0	273	98.5	0.0	0.0	1.5	0.0	19.8	53.9	26.4	130	73.8	55.4	10.0
Blanchard city	38	37	-2.6	41	100.0	0.0	0.0	0.0	0.0	17.1	82.9	0.0	16	93.8	50.0	0.0
Blencoe city	224	217	-3.1	244	96.3	0.0	0.0	3.7	0.0	19.7	55.2	25.0	107	74.8	65.4	11.2
Blockton city	192	189	-1.6	175	98.9	0.0	0.0	0.0	1.1	22.2	55.4	22.3	89	62.9	41.6	22.5
Bloomfield city	2,639	2,632	-0.3	2,636	95.1	0.2	0.8	0.4	3.6	24.3	53.8	21.8	1,073	69.2	47.4	15.6
Blue Grass city	1,452	1,623	11.8	1,612	96.0	0.6	0.0	0.6	2.7	23.7	54.3	21.8	610	90.5	44.3	18.7
Bode city	302	297	-1.7	370	82.2	0.0	0.0	0.0	17.8	24.3	62.6	13.0	143	74.8	46.2	5.6
Bolan CDP	33	NA	NA	35	82.9	0.0	0.0	0.0	17.1	60.0	22.9	17.1	14	57.1	0.0	0.0
Bonaparte city	433	425	-1.8	400	99.3	0.0	0.0	0.8	0.0	29.9	58.1	12.5	168	78.6	41.7	8.3
Bondurant city	3,860	4,806	24.5	4,332	93.2	0.0	1.8	0.7	4.2	39.1	57.2	3.8	1,347	77.7	26.2	28.8
Boone city	12,661	12,633	-0.2	12,619	93.4	1.8	0.9	1.3	2.5	22.2	61.9	15.8	5,245	69.4	40.9	20.9
Bouton city	127	135	6.3	213	93.9	0.0	0.0	3.3	2.8	32.8	60.5	6.6	65	75.4	50.8	9.2
Boxholm city	195	195	0.0	238	99.2	0.0	0.8	0.0	0.0	24.4	51.4	24.4	107	75.7	61.7	5.6
Boyden city	707	709	0.3	697	87.4	0.0	0.4	1.3	10.9	24.1	59.0	16.9	269	82.9	46.5	11.5
Braddyville city	159	155	-2.5	147	91.2	0.0	0.0	8.8	0.0	14.9	68.0	17.0	70	87.1	47.1	10.0
Bradford CDP	99	NA	NA	65	100.0	0.0	0.0	0.0	0.0	0.0	40.0	60.0	37	100.0	78.4	0.0
Bradgate city	86	84	-2.3	114	82.5	0.0	1.8	0.0	15.8	7.9	82.5	9.6	53	90.6	77.4	1.9
Brandon city	309	308	-0.3	325	96.6	0.0	0.0	0.6	2.8	21.9	65.9	12.3	152	75.0	63.8	11.8
Brayton city	128	120	-6.3	132	100.0	0.0	0.0	0.0	0.0	22.7	56.0	21.2	66	60.6	60.6	10.6
Breda city	483	477	-1.2	456	98.9	0.0	0.0	0.0	1.1	23.7	61.9	14.5	197	87.3	44.7	11.7
Bridgewater city	182	178	-2.2	162	100.0	0.0	0.0	0.0	0.0	22.9	56.2	21.0	75	85.3	58.7	9.3
Brighton city	655	658	0.5	550	96.5	0.0	0.0	1.5	2.0	21.1	58.0	20.9	243	74.5	64.2	8.6
Bristow city	160	161	0.6	149	100.0	0.0	0.0	0.0	0.0	21.5	66.4	12.1	64	78.1	68.8	4.7
Britt city	2,069	2,026	-2.1	1,985	90.3	0.9	0.5	1.6	6.8	23.4	52.3	24.2	875	82.4	47.1	17.5
Bronson city	322	322	0.0	396	97.0	0.5	0.0	2.0	0.5	32.3	50.5	17.2	133	82.7	51.9	18.0
Brooklyn city	1,478	1,453	-1.7	1,279	95.3	0.1	1.3	0.9	2.4	24.8	57.4	17.6	541	66.0	48.2	17.2
Brunsville city	151	149	-1.3	98	100.0	0.0	0.0	0.0	0.0	12.2	79.6	8.2	49	91.8	38.8	26.5
Buckeye city	108	107	-0.9	90	100.0	0.0	0.0	0.0	0.0	32.3	49.8	17.8	30	90.0	76.7	13.3
Buck Grove city	43	43	0.0	31	100.0	0.0	0.0	0.0	0.0	16.2	58.3	25.8	14	85.7	64.3	0.0
Buffalo city	1,273	1,298	2.0	1,120	95.4	1.1	0.0	0.4	3.2	19.5	62.8	17.6	479	77.7	52.4	9.4
Buffalo Center city	905	891	-1.5	877	96.4	0.9	0.0	2.7	0.0	25.6	49.0	25.3	397	79.3	40.1	21.7
Burchinal CDP	40	NA	NA	62	100.0	0.0	0.0	0.0	0.0	35.5	45.2	19.4	19	100.0	31.6	0.0
Burlington city	25,625	25,539	-0.3	25,559	85.3	8.2	0.3	2.7	3.4	23.5	58.2	18.1	10,882	67.9	38.8	20.6
Burr Oak CDP	166	NA	NA	204	89.7	0.0	0.0	4.4	5.9	16.6	66.1	17.2	102	72.5	72.5	2.9
Burt city	533	515	-3.4	544	83.3	1.1	0.6	14.5	0.6	29.4	52.9	17.6	194	84.5	55.7	9.3
Bussey city	422	416	-1.4	441	97.7	0.0	0.0	1.6	0.7	26.1	53.9	20.0	180	73.9	58.9	10.0
Calamus city	439	418	-4.8	380	97.6	0.8	0.5	0.5	0.5	22.4	56.5	21.1	165	80.0	37.6	14.5
California Junction CDP	85	NA	NA	94	100.0	0.0	0.0	0.0	0.0	14.8	69.1	16.0	56	100.0	37.5	0.0
Callender city	376	363	-3.5	436	99.3	0.7	0.0	0.0	0.0	28.2	56.5	15.1	173	75.1	59.0	9.8
Calmar city	978	961	-1.7	1,032	95.0	2.5	0.0	0.0	2.5	22.0	64.7	13.2	460	69.6	41.1	13.9
Calumet city	170	170	0.0	309	76.4	0.0	2.3	2.9	18.4	33.1	58.9	8.1	116	81.0	49.1	7.8
Camanche city	4,448	4,358	-2.0	4,401	92.8	0.7	0.0	1.0	5.6	24.9	57.9	17.3	1,939	85.0	39.1	20.5
Cambridge city	827	822	-0.6	842	92.9	0.7	0.5	0.7	5.2	31.5	57.1	11.5	329	84.8	36.5	20.1
Cantril city	222	222	0.0	168	99.4	0.0	0.6	0.0	0.0	14.9	55.4	29.8	84	86.9	63.1	7.1
Carbon city	34	33	-2.9	21	90.5	0.0	0.0	4.8	4.8	0.0	66.7	33.3	12	100.0	83.3	0.0
Carlisle city	3,876	4,098	5.7	4,062	92.0	3.7	1.6	2.0	0.6	30.2	53.6	16.1	1,498	76.9	39.0	24.8
Carpenter city	109	108	-0.9	110	82.7	0.0	17.3	0.0	0.0	11.8	71.7	16.4	51	90.2	51.0	2.0
Carroll city	10,103	10,007	-1.0	10,051	94.6	2.5	0.0	0.4	2.5	23.1	58.0	19.1	4,319	71.4	46.2	19.5
Carson city	812	812	0.0	860	93.6	0.0	0.0	5.8	0.6	28.2	55.0	16.7	317	78.9	48.9	18.3
Carter Lake city	3,785	3,766	-0.5	3,771	84.1	2.4	0.0	3.5	10.0	24.7	62.6	12.8	1,446	74.1	47.9	14.9
Cascade city	2,166	2,252	4.0	2,000	92.7	0.0	0.0	0.0	7.4	25.4	55.8	19.3	862	76.0	46.1	26.1
Casey city	426	407	-4.5	447	94.0	0.0	0.0	1.1	4.9	23.7	63.2	13.2	181	70.2	53.0	14.9
Castalia city	173	169	-2.3	175	100.0	0.0	0.0	0.0	0.0	14.8	56.1	29.1	88	80.7	61.4	9.1
Castana city	142	137	-3.5	94	100.0	0.0	0.0	0.0	0.0	7.5	61.7	30.9	55	92.7	61.8	1.8
Cedar Falls city	39,260	40,859	4.1	40,009	91.9	2.4	3.1	0.9	1.8	16.8	71.0	12.2	14,290	64.3	21.4	44.1
Cedar Rapids city	126,326	129,195	2.3	128,009	85.3	6.1	2.0	3.1	3.5	22.9	63.7	13.3	53,125	69.3	30.6	31.4
Center Junction city	111	111	0.0	111	100.0	0.0	0.0	0.0	0.0	23.4	61.2	15.3	49	93.9	53.1	6.1
Center Point city	2,421	2,494	3.0	2,632	97.0	1.3	0.0	0.8	0.8	31.0	62.4	6.6	944	79.9	36.2	23.1
Centerville city	5,534	5,433	-1.8	5,480	94.7	0.7	0.4	1.6	2.6	19.6	58.5	21.8	2,420	59.5	43.7	19.0

1 May be of any race.

Table A. All Places — **Population and Housing**

STATE City, town, township, borough, or CDP (county if applicable)	Population: 2010 census total population	Population: 2014 estimated population	Population: Percent change 2010–2014	Population: ACS total population estimate 2010–2014	Race and Hispanic or Latino origin (percent), 2010–2014: White alone, not Hispanic or Latino	Black alone, not Hispanic or Latino	Asian alone, not Hispanic or Latino	All other races or 2 or more races, not Hispanic or Latino	Hispanic or Latino[1]	Age (percent), 2010–2014: Under 18 years old	Age 18 to 64 years old	Age 65 years and older	Households, 2010–2014: Total occupied housing units	Percent owner occupied	Householders by level of education (percent): High school diploma or less	Bachelor's degree or more
	1	2	3	4	5	6	7	8	9	10	11	12	13	14	15	16
IOWA—Con.																
Central City city	1,257	1,272	1.2	1,284	97.3	0.0	0.0	2.2	0.5	28.1	61.0	10.9	530	76.4	41.9	14.0
Centralia city	131	130	-0.8	119	100.0	0.0	0.0	0.0	0.0	19.3	70.4	10.1	47	85.1	61.7	12.8
Chapin CDP	87	NA	NA	161	100.0	0.0	0.0	0.0	0.0	9.3	72.7	18.0	49	57.1	28.6	0.0
Chariton city	4,321	4,227	-2.2	4,263	97.4	0.2	0.3	1.7	0.4	24.1	52.8	23.0	1,881	68.3	51.8	13.7
Charles City city	7,652	7,513	-1.8	7,562	91.5	4.5	0.8	1.1	2.0	22.4	54.8	22.9	3,512	62.2	45.0	15.7
Charlotte city	394	375	-4.8	383	89.6	0.0	0.0	3.4	7.0	31.0	59.3	9.7	141	68.8	48.9	13.5
Charter Oak city	502	498	-0.8	503	87.7	0.0	0.0	0.0	12.3	21.5	56.1	22.7	233	85.4	48.9	17.6
Chatsworth city	79	80	1.3	68	98.5	0.0	0.0	1.5	0.0	8.8	69.1	22.1	26	84.6	61.5	3.8
Chelsea city	265	261	-1.5	188	62.2	0.0	0.0	1.1	36.7	27.6	48.5	23.9	85	100.0	61.2	11.8
Cherokee city	5,256	5,139	-2.2	5,203	92.8	0.5	0.4	2.5	3.8	18.9	56.3	24.9	2,442	67.0	45.6	17.6
Chester city	127	126	-0.8	263	98.1	0.0	1.9	0.0	0.0	30.8	48.7	20.5	103	83.5	69.9	0.0
Chillicothe city	97	97	0.0	102	97.1	2.9	0.0	0.0	0.0	12.8	63.7	23.5	47	93.6	66.0	17.0
Churdan city	386	376	-2.6	340	95.0	0.0	0.6	3.2	1.2	27.1	52.0	20.9	149	70.5	47.7	14.1
Cincinnati city	357	348	-2.5	299	94.6	0.0	0.0	4.3	1.0	17.5	58.8	23.7	136	86.8	64.0	9.6
Clare city	146	141	-3.4	190	100.0	0.0	0.0	0.0	0.0	18.4	70.0	11.6	85	87.1	40.0	10.6
Clarence city	974	965	-0.9	907	98.1	0.0	0.0	0.0	1.9	17.0	55.0	28.0	427	74.2	51.3	10.1
Clarinda city	5,583	5,362	-4.0	5,490	90.0	4.6	1.1	2.1	2.2	20.9	59.8	19.3	2,007	66.6	38.8	21.8
Clarion city	2,850	2,773	-2.7	2,795	86.4	0.6	1.5	1.6	9.8	27.0	51.1	21.9	1,107	69.5	47.4	16.7
Clarksville city	1,439	1,419	-1.4	1,388	96.6	2.2	0.0	1.2	0.0	28.7	53.5	17.8	556	77.3	57.6	12.1
Clayton city	43	42	-2.3	37	100.0	0.0	0.0	0.0	0.0	0.0	45.9	54.1	23	82.6	43.5	26.1
Clearfield city	363	342	-5.8	378	92.3	0.0	0.0	1.1	6.6	19.8	53.3	26.7	167	79.6	59.9	7.8
Clear Lake city	7,777	7,682	-1.2	7,718	92.4	0.9	1.5	1.1	4.2	22.1	57.9	20.0	3,400	76.7	31.4	29.9
Cleghorn city	237	232	-2.1	194	96.4	0.0	0.0	1.5	2.1	22.7	52.1	25.3	91	93.4	42.9	24.2
Clemons city	148	150	1.4	125	97.6	0.0	0.0	0.0	2.4	29.6	51.2	19.2	50	86.0	66.0	2.0
Clermont city	632	615	-2.7	672	100.0	0.0	0.0	0.0	0.0	27.5	51.9	20.5	265	87.9	56.6	15.1
Climbing Hill CDP	97	NA	NA	172	100.0	0.0	0.0	0.0	0.0	38.4	55.7	5.8	51	100.0	47.1	0.0
Clinton city	26,885	26,246	-2.4	26,611	88.5	5.0	1.1	2.5	3.0	21.9	60.1	18.1	11,239	68.0	47.6	18.1
Clio city	80	81	1.3	125	93.6	0.0	0.0	0.0	6.4	30.4	44.8	24.8	44	86.4	61.4	9.1
Clive city	15,407	17,052	10.7	16,246	83.5	1.8	3.1	2.5	9.1	26.4	62.1	11.5	6,132	76.2	18.3	59.4
Clutier city	213	210	-1.4	256	86.7	0.0	0.0	12.5	0.8	17.6	64.9	17.6	115	83.5	48.7	7.0
Coalville CDP	610	NA	NA	646	87.0	0.0	0.0	4.0	9.0	29.7	55.8	14.4	288	78.1	66.3	7.3
Coburg city	42	41	-2.4	47	100.0	0.0	0.0	0.0	0.0	27.6	68.0	4.3	14	92.9	64.3	7.1
Coggon city	658	656	-0.3	705	99.6	0.0	0.0	0.0	0.4	29.2	51.1	19.7	287	75.3	52.6	11.5
Coin city	193	188	-2.6	205	100.0	0.0	0.0	0.0	0.0	22.9	48.3	28.8	89	80.9	51.7	15.7
Colesburg city	404	395	-2.2	366	98.4	0.0	0.5	1.1	0.0	17.5	59.4	23.0	150	87.3	68.0	6.7
Colfax city	2,093	2,061	-1.5	1,835	97.4	0.3	0.1	1.9	0.3	28.8	56.3	15.1	736	80.6	51.6	15.5
College Springs city	214	209	-2.3	216	98.1	0.0	0.0	1.9	0.0	25.4	54.6	19.9	85	82.4	45.9	23.5
Collins city	495	485	-2.0	428	98.8	0.0	0.0	1.2	0.0	36.0	52.0	11.9	155	73.5	52.3	18.7
Colo city	876	863	-1.5	805	96.5	0.0	0.0	1.4	2.1	27.1	53.0	20.0	332	73.5	48.2	15.7
Columbus City city	391	373	-4.6	417	40.8	0.0	2.6	0.0	56.6	21.4	65.1	13.4	160	85.6	70.6	6.9
Columbus Junction city	1,896	1,857	-2.1	2,021	37.3	2.0	7.0	0.2	53.5	30.2	58.1	11.7	711	59.4	67.9	9.3
Colwell city	73	72	-1.4	51	100.0	0.0	0.0	0.0	0.0	15.6	62.7	21.6	28	50.0	39.3	21.4
Conesville city	432	421	-2.5	462	21.2	0.9	3.0	2.2	72.7	33.9	60.3	5.6	128	71.1	80.5	3.9
Conrad city	1,108	1,100	-0.7	1,088	95.1	0.0	0.2	0.0	4.7	22.3	53.1	24.6	451	78.5	44.3	14.6
Conroy CDP	259	NA	NA	335	100.0	0.0	0.0	0.0	0.0	18.5	65.2	16.4	156	94.9	64.7	16.7
Conway city	41	40	-2.4	22	100.0	0.0	0.0	0.0	0.0	40.9	36.2	22.7	8	100.0	62.5	0.0
Coon Rapids city	1,305	1,269	-2.8	1,408	97.2	1.6	0.0	0.6	0.6	28.1	47.8	23.9	587	70.2	43.8	19.4
Coppock city	47	47	0.0	62	100.0	0.0	0.0	0.0	0.0	30.6	53.2	16.1	28	85.7	42.9	10.7
Coralville city	18,908	20,349	7.6	19,677	76.4	9.1	7.7	1.2	5.6	24.0	68.1	7.7	7,710	56.5	16.4	60.4
Corley CDP	26	NA	NA	28	100.0	0.0	0.0	0.0	0.0	0.0	64.3	35.7	28	100.0	100.0	0.0
Corning city	1,638	1,564	-4.5	1,625	95.6	1.6	0.2	1.4	1.3	16.8	58.8	24.5	753	72.0	48.5	14.9
Correctionville city	821	805	-1.9	848	90.9	0.0	1.1	2.1	5.9	22.8	48.7	28.7	343	84.8	53.6	17.2
Corwith city	309	269	-12.9	262	96.2	0.0	0.0	1.5	2.3	15.6	61.2	23.3	121	85.1	47.1	13.2
Corydon city	1,585	1,587	0.1	1,430	98.0	0.3	0.0	1.7	0.0	16.4	53.3	30.1	644	77.2	52.8	16.5
Cotter city	48	47	-2.1	67	77.6	0.0	0.0	0.0	22.4	19.4	59.8	20.9	30	80.0	86.7	6.7
Coulter city	281	277	-1.4	349	81.1	0.0	2.0	0.0	16.9	20.4	69.1	10.3	152	79.6	44.1	8.6
Council Bluffs city	62,228	62,245	0.0	62,261	86.1	1.5	0.6	2.7	9.1	23.9	62.3	13.8	24,769	63.6	43.0	18.5
Craig city	89	88	-1.1	52	100.0	0.0	0.0	0.0	0.0	15.3	78.6	5.8	17	64.7	52.9	41.2
Crawfordsville city	264	268	1.5	287	84.7	0.0	0.0	1.4	13.9	23.6	61.6	14.6	118	76.3	44.1	10.2
Crescent city	617	622	0.8	515	98.1	0.0	0.0	1.6	0.4	19.6	66.5	13.8	203	94.1	46.8	17.7
Cresco city	3,868	3,849	-0.5	3,871	94.2	0.2	0.3	1.9	3.5	27.0	54.7	18.4	1,610	69.4	47.3	16.5
Creston city	7,834	7,839	0.1	7,846	94.1	2.0	0.1	1.0	2.7	22.5	59.0	18.7	3,322	70.0	39.1	19.8
Cromwell city	107	107	0.0	87	100.0	0.0	0.0	0.0	0.0	13.8	69.9	16.1	38	86.8	36.8	10.5
Crystal Lake city	250	246	-1.6	164	98.8	0.0	0.0	0.0	1.2	11.6	50.6	37.8	102	75.5	55.9	9.8
Cumberland city	262	253	-3.4	371	98.9	0.0	0.0	0.5	0.5	39.9	47.5	12.7	131	66.4	49.6	19.1
Cumming city	351	397	13.1	383	90.9	0.0	0.3	1.8	7.0	29.5	61.0	9.4	138	94.2	15.9	39.9
Curlew city	58	56	-3.4	70	100.0	0.0	0.0	0.0	0.0	22.8	65.7	11.4	39	97.4	82.1	0.0
Cushing city	220	222	0.9	200	99.5	0.0	0.5	0.0	0.0	23.5	51.5	25.0	91	71.4	61.5	5.5
Cylinder city	88	85	-3.4	68	100.0	0.0	0.0	0.0	0.0	23.5	66.1	10.3	27	96.3	33.3	11.1
Dakota City city	843	822	-2.5	769	97.9	0.0	0.0	1.3	0.8	23.9	60.6	15.5	326	88.7	48.2	9.8
Dallas Center city	1,631	1,788	9.6	1,757	97.4	0.0	0.0	0.1	2.5	27.3	58.2	14.5	621	77.8	29.8	36.1
Dana city	71	70	-1.4	72	86.1	0.0	0.0	0.0	13.9	25.1	72.2	2.8	28	57.1	60.7	7.1
Danbury city	348	342	-1.7	372	97.6	0.0	0.0	2.4	0.0	24.2	54.7	21.2	166	78.3	57.8	10.8
Danville city	934	934	0.0	989	94.0	0.0	0.5	3.8	1.6	29.6	55.3	15.2	369	79.4	34.7	23.6
Davenport city	99,687	102,448	2.8	101,316	75.4	11.5	2.1	2.8	8.2	23.9	63.4	12.8	40,912	61.5	36.0	29.3
Davis City city	204	195	-4.4	276	96.4	1.8	0.0	1.8	0.0	25.7	50.7	23.6	109	73.4	69.7	8.3
Dawson city	131	139	6.1	217	53.9	0.0	4.6	0.0	41.5	42.5	50.6	6.9	65	66.2	40.0	0.0
Dayton city	837	803	-4.1	860	98.6	0.0	0.0	1.0	0.3	25.1	48.8	26.2	348	67.5	46.0	15.2
Decatur City city	197	188	-4.6	218	95.0	3.7	0.0	0.0	1.4	26.1	60.1	13.8	81	84.0	60.5	4.9
Decorah city	8,131	7,957	-2.1	8,058	95.3	1.8	0.6	0.2	2.1	12.6	66.8	20.7	2,841	64.7	32.7	43.2
Dedham city	266	264	-0.8	220	99.5	0.0	0.0	0.0	0.5	30.5	52.4	17.3	85	92.9	41.2	12.9
Deep River city	279	275	-1.4	330	92.7	0.0	0.0	3.9	3.3	27.5	51.8	20.6	131	81.7	61.1	12.2
Defiance city	284	280	-1.4	254	90.9	0.0	0.0	0.4	8.7	19.7	55.9	24.4	111	85.6	73.0	5.4
Delaware city	159	156	-1.9	176	97.2	0.0	0.0	2.8	0.0	21.6	66.4	11.9	78	84.6	69.2	7.7
Delhi city	460	470	2.2	393	99.7	0.0	0.0	0.0	0.3	13.1	59.4	27.5	216	75.0	61.1	17.1
Delmar city	525	505	-3.8	499	95.0	0.0	0.0	2.6	2.4	23.4	56.8	19.6	205	86.3	58.5	12.7
Deloit city	264	265	0.4	369	59.1	19.2	0.0	0.0	21.7	31.4	48.5	20.1	145	66.2	60.0	1.4
Delphos city	25	25	0.0	20	100.0	0.0	0.0	0.0	0.0	25.0	45.0	30.0	8	62.5	100.0	0.0
Delta city	328	318	-3.0	285	93.0	0.0	0.0	1.4	5.6	30.2	54.5	15.4	119	79.0	61.3	10.9
Denison city	8,301	8,390	1.1	8,370	49.7	1.5	0.6	1.3	46.9	31.0	53.5	15.5	2,700	69.5	62.7	12.2
Denmark CDP	423	NA	NA	309	100.0	0.0	0.0	0.0	0.0	15.5	65.8	18.8	162	88.9	39.5	14.8

1 May be of any race.

Table A. All Places — **Population and Housing**

STATE City, town, township, borough, or CDP (county if applicable)	Population: 2010 census total population	Population: 2014 estimated population	Population: Percent change 2010–2014	Population: ACS total population estimate 2010–2014	Race and Hispanic or Latino origin (percent), 2010–2014: White alone, not Hispanic or Latino	Black alone, not Hispanic or Latino	Asian alone, not Hispanic or Latino	All other races or 2 or more races, not Hispanic or Latino	Hispanic or Latino[1]	Age (percent), 2010–2014: Under 18 years old	Age 18 to 64 years old	Age 65 years and older	Households, 2010–2014: Total occupied housing units	Percent owner occupied	Householders by level of education (percent): High school diploma or less	Bachelor's degree or more
	1	2	3	4	5	6	7	8	9	10	11	12	13	14	15	16
IOWA—Con.																
Denver city	1,780	1,820	2.2	1,844	98.9	0.1	0.0	0.7	0.3	28.3	55.0	16.7	703	77.7	33.9	29.4
Derby city	115	113	-1.7	103	80.6	0.0	0.0	19.4	0.0	25.3	46.7	28.2	42	85.7	47.6	2.4
Des Moines city	204,186	209,220	2.5	206,702	68.9	10.7	5.0	3.1	12.3	25.2	64.0	10.9	81,239	61.7	39.8	26.8
De Soto city	1,044	1,098	5.2	1,142	98.3	0.0	0.0	0.4	1.3	32.8	56.6	10.5	391	78.0	38.6	24.6
De Witt city	5,322	5,253	-1.3	5,297	98.3	0.0	0.0	0.6	1.1	24.8	60.5	14.7	2,153	72.8	33.0	27.9
Dexter city	603	638	5.8	751	99.2	0.0	0.0	0.8	0.0	27.0	64.4	8.7	295	74.9	32.5	29.2
Diagonal city	330	328	-0.6	310	90.3	0.0	0.0	6.1	3.5	16.1	47.3	36.5	119	69.7	43.7	22.7
Diamondhead Lake CDP	366	NA	NA	343	99.1	0.0	0.0	0.9	0.0	20.7	51.9	27.4	146	100.0	48.6	21.9
Dickens city	185	182	-1.6	176	99.4	0.0	0.0	0.0	0.6	20.5	60.2	19.3	73	87.7	64.4	1.4
Dike city	1,209	1,257	4.0	1,300	96.8	0.0	0.2	1.8	1.2	28.8	55.4	15.8	536	86.4	34.7	33.4
Dixon city	243	248	2.1	208	99.0	0.0	0.0	1.0	0.0	21.1	60.1	18.8	92	83.7	43.5	15.2
Dolliver city	66	66	0.0	78	94.9	0.0	0.0	0.0	5.1	21.8	52.4	25.6	33	97.0	69.7	6.1
Donahue city	356	369	3.7	461	98.7	0.0	0.0	0.7	0.7	29.6	61.5	8.7	151	93.4	58.3	6.0
Donnellson city	912	899	-1.4	815	98.7	0.0	0.0	1.3	0.0	22.8	53.5	23.7	357	67.2	54.3	13.2
Doon city	577	588	1.9	533	98.7	0.0	0.0	0.0	1.3	24.4	57.7	17.8	238	81.9	53.8	11.3
Douds CDP	152	NA	NA	47	100.0	0.0	0.0	0.0	0.0	14.9	68.1	17.0	34	76.5	23.5	0.0
Dougherty city	58	57	-1.7	70	100.0	0.0	0.0	0.0	0.0	17.1	64.3	18.6	31	80.6	45.2	22.6
Dow City city	510	505	-1.0	561	87.9	0.0	0.0	2.5	9.6	22.1	58.4	19.4	256	68.4	58.2	10.9
Dows city	538	519	-3.5	442	92.5	0.7	0.2	1.1	5.4	12.3	53.8	33.9	234	75.6	62.0	13.7
Drakesville city	184	186	1.1	210	100.0	0.0	0.0	0.0	0.0	11.9	65.4	22.9	93	84.9	53.8	5.4
Dubuque city	57,532	58,436	1.6	58,068	90.5	2.1	1.4	3.8	2.2	20.6	62.5	16.8	24,025	64.2	38.9	30.2
Dumont city	637	633	-0.6	682	97.5	0.0	0.0	0.0	2.5	22.8	46.2	30.9	280	81.4	58.2	9.3
Duncan CDP	131	NA	NA	113	67.3	9.7	0.0	23.0	0.0	13.3	77.8	8.8	24	70.8	20.8	50.0
Duncombe city	410	392	-4.4	397	98.5	0.0	0.0	1.0	0.5	30.0	51.1	18.9	176	71.6	52.3	4.5
Dundee city	174	170	-2.3	155	99.4	0.0	0.0	0.6	0.0	23.2	53.5	23.2	63	90.5	60.3	7.9
Dunkerton city	852	844	-0.9	897	96.5	2.2	0.0	0.8	0.4	30.4	56.8	12.8	333	77.2	60.7	12.0
Dunlap city	1,042	994	-4.6	1,172	94.3	0.0	0.4	4.3	1.0	26.2	52.3	21.6	449	76.2	51.7	16.3
Durango city	24	24	0.0	17	94.1	5.9	0.0	0.0	0.0	0.0	53.0	47.1	9	66.7	100.0	0.0
Durant city	1,832	1,825	-0.4	2,041	96.1	0.0	0.1	1.6	2.2	24.3	56.2	19.5	843	75.6	46.6	19.7
Dyersville city	4,058	4,149	2.2	4,178	98.2	0.0	0.2	0.0	1.6	25.6	55.9	18.4	1,756	80.9	50.6	20.0
Dysart city	1,379	1,367	-0.9	1,532	99.3	0.0	0.0	0.1	0.7	23.1	54.0	23.0	596	86.7	41.9	21.6
Eagle Grove city	3,583	3,452	-3.7	3,506	79.9	0.3	0.0	1.6	18.2	23.1	58.0	18.8	1,339	71.8	45.6	20.2
Earlham city	1,445	1,403	-2.9	1,778	96.0	2.0	0.0	0.6	1.3	31.0	59.0	10.0	630	75.4	33.8	27.5
Earling city	437	427	-2.3	588	94.0	0.0	0.0	5.4	0.5	32.8	43.7	23.6	201	83.6	47.8	14.9
Earlville city	812	793	-2.3	780	97.7	0.3	0.0	0.8	1.3	22.7	63.8	13.5	320	88.8	59.1	11.6
Early city	557	532	-4.5	647	93.2	2.3	0.0	3.4	1.1	23.1	62.8	14.1	290	66.6	44.1	16.6
East Amana CDP	56	NA	NA	46	100.0	0.0	0.0	0.0	0.0	0.0	47.8	52.2	25	100.0	72.0	28.0
East Peru city	125	122	-2.4	72	100.0	0.0	0.0	0.0	0.0	12.6	55.8	31.9	31	93.5	83.9	6.5
Eddyville city	1,024	1,016	-0.8	1,227	87.4	1.5	0.0	9.6	1.5	30.3	55.8	13.8	457	80.5	55.4	16.4
Edgewood city	866	861	-0.6	836	99.4	0.0	0.0	0.6	0.0	18.5	57.0	24.4	377	72.7	58.9	11.9
Elberon city	196	193	-1.5	170	100.0	0.0	0.0	0.0	0.0	20.6	61.7	17.6	78	87.2	74.4	3.8
Eldon city	927	915	-1.3	988	94.5	0.5	0.0	1.4	3.5	21.5	60.3	18.1	444	71.4	65.3	7.2
Eldora city	2,732	2,698	-1.2	2,707	87.8	2.4	4.1	4.2	1.5	27.9	51.9	20.2	959	71.4	40.6	26.9
Eldridge city	5,652	6,162	9.0	5,908	96.4	1.8	0.0	0.7	1.2	30.4	54.9	14.7	2,242	72.7	31.0	34.1
Elgin city	683	655	-4.1	793	98.0	0.0	0.4	1.6	0.0	26.0	54.3	19.5	347	72.3	44.4	17.6
Elkader city	1,273	1,220	-4.2	1,208	98.7	0.3	0.0	1.0	0.0	14.2	57.9	27.6	608	76.5	50.0	26.3
Elkhart city	683	716	4.8	597	98.0	0.0	0.0	0.8	1.2	22.3	72.7	5.2	278	72.7	33.5	34.5
Elk Horn city	662	647	-2.3	638	98.6	0.0	0.0	1.4	0.0	15.6	47.5	36.8	263	75.7	44.5	18.3
Elkport city	37	36	-2.7	33	100.0	0.0	0.0	0.0	0.0	24.2	69.6	6.1	17	52.9	52.9	0.0
Elk Run Heights city	1,117	1,131	1.3	1,020	94.6	0.4	0.0	3.4	1.6	16.0	64.9	19.1	460	88.7	66.3	7.8
Elliott city	350	336	-4.0	379	98.9	0.0	0.0	1.1	0.0	29.2	54.9	15.8	141	80.9	59.6	6.4
Ellston city	43	42	-2.3	42	100.0	0.0	0.0	0.0	0.0	31.0	40.5	28.6	17	100.0	70.6	5.9
Ellsworth city	531	506	-4.7	632	90.7	0.0	0.3	0.8	8.2	36.7	51.3	12.0	208	85.1	38.0	29.3
Elma city	546	534	-2.2	629	98.6	0.0	0.0	0.6	0.8	18.7	51.4	29.9	285	71.6	55.8	14.7
Ely city	1,776	2,001	12.7	1,966	96.4	0.2	1.1	0.3	2.0	30.5	63.5	6.0	712	84.1	19.0	37.4
Emerson city	438	426	-2.7	471	97.5	1.1	0.0	1.5	0.0	23.8	60.8	15.5	182	89.6	56.6	13.7
Emmetsburg city	3,904	3,790	-2.9	3,844	93.6	1.5	1.0	0.9	3.0	19.1	57.7	23.2	1,642	71.9	32.3	22.2
Epworth city	1,860	1,943	4.5	1,963	96.9	0.0	0.0	3.1	0.0	26.7	64.1	9.4	686	84.1	40.2	26.5
Essex city	798	774	-3.0	912	96.3	0.0	0.0	3.2	0.5	19.6	61.7	18.6	416	76.4	46.6	19.5
Estherville city	6,360	6,121	-3.8	6,177	83.5	1.1	0.2	1.1	14.1	22.0	61.1	16.8	2,479	74.6	44.7	15.7
Evansdale city	4,751	4,793	0.9	4,768	89.0	5.3	0.2	2.6	3.0	23.3	64.0	12.7	1,921	71.2	60.6	10.8
Everly city	596	584	-2.0	530	98.7	0.0	0.0	0.0	1.3	29.4	52.2	18.3	219	87.2	43.8	17.8
Exira city	840	778	-7.4	828	97.8	1.4	0.0	0.7	0.0	20.5	53.0	26.4	383	80.7	63.2	6.5
Exline city	160	158	-1.3	124	99.2	0.0	0.0	0.0	0.8	8.9	42.6	48.4	66	87.9	75.8	1.5
Fairbank city	1,113	1,107	-0.5	1,129	98.9	0.0	0.0	1.1	0.0	28.9	58.7	12.4	444	80.0	52.5	17.6
Fairfax city	2,123	2,409	13.5	2,332	95.1	0.8	0.6	2.1	1.5	30.5	58.7	10.7	846	93.7	23.4	35.6
Fairfield city	9,464	9,750	3.0	9,615	79.0	2.7	11.1	3.0	4.3	16.9	66.4	16.8	3,990	60.8	31.3	42.8
Farley city	1,537	1,639	6.6	1,527	96.3	0.4	0.0	2.6	0.7	27.3	61.7	10.9	568	91.0	55.5	12.5
Farmersburg city	302	278	-7.9	264	97.3	0.4	0.0	0.8	1.5	28.0	55.7	16.3	112	81.3	49.1	8.0
Farmington city	664	658	-0.9	822	93.7	0.0	0.0	5.8	0.5	19.0	63.0	18.0	344	69.5	59.9	12.8
Farnhamville city	371	360	-3.0	339	97.6	0.0	0.0	0.9	1.5	15.4	61.3	23.3	177	70.6	41.2	15.8
Farragut city	485	449	-7.4	561	99.6	0.0	0.0	0.4	0.0	18.3	60.8	20.9	259	78.4	46.7	15.1
Fayette city	1,338	1,469	9.8	1,206	73.6	9.2	6.0	2.2	9.0	11.4	73.3	15.4	344	59.3	35.8	31.1
Fenton city	279	264	-5.4	290	100.0	0.0	0.0	0.0	0.0	16.9	60.7	22.4	137	92.0	53.3	15.3
Ferguson city	126	127	0.8	108	95.4	0.0	0.0	4.6	0.0	12.0	61.1	26.9	53	88.7	45.3	0.0
Fertile city	370	374	1.1	333	93.4	0.0	0.9	0.0	5.7	15.0	58.2	26.7	153	80.4	58.8	15.0
Floris city	138	140	1.4	170	100.0	0.0	0.0	0.0	0.0	27.6	57.7	14.7	59	93.2	62.7	6.8
Floyd city	335	330	-1.5	390	99.7	0.0	0.0	0.3	0.0	20.3	61.0	18.7	155	85.2	65.2	8.4
Fonda city	631	613	-2.9	541	92.8	0.0	0.0	1.1	6.1	22.6	51.6	25.9	229	68.6	48.0	14.8
Fontanelle city	672	653	-2.8	700	96.6	0.0	0.4	0.6	2.4	18.5	54.9	26.6	308	80.5	58.1	11.0
Forest City city	4,151	3,982	-4.1	4,142	91.9	1.4	1.2	0.1	5.3	21.4	63.0	15.7	1,734	67.2	41.0	18.2
Fort Atkinson city	349	337	-3.4	326	95.4	0.0	0.0	2.8	1.8	25.8	49.5	24.8	151	82.1	58.9	10.6
Fort Dodge city	25,206	24,594	-2.4	24,846	86.0	5.2	1.2	2.6	5.0	21.1	62.3	16.6	10,169	60.9	40.4	20.8
Fort Madison city	11,051	10,764	-2.6	10,929	85.0	5.8	1.1	2.6	5.5	22.8	60.8	16.3	4,500	70.7	51.6	15.4
Fostoria city	244	240	-1.6	124	93.5	0.0	0.0	0.0	6.5	21.8	59.6	18.5	58	94.8	60.3	19.0
Franklin city	143	142	-0.7	103	99.0	0.0	0.0	0.0	1.0	13.6	65.1	21.4	46	89.1	56.5	21.7
Fraser city	102	102	0.0	129	100.0	0.0	0.0	0.0	0.0	25.6	66.0	8.5	47	78.7	55.3	4.3
Fredericksburg city	931	926	-0.5	1,034	89.9	0.0	0.0	2.3	7.7	28.3	49.4	22.4	480	76.3	58.5	12.7
Frederika city	183	182	-0.5	176	95.5	2.8	0.0	0.0	1.7	17.1	55.1	27.8	85	83.5	47.1	12.9
Fredonia city	244	239	-2.0	254	46.9	5.1	0.0	0.0	48.0	28.4	67.4	4.3	87	85.1	73.6	0.0
Fremont city	743	736	-0.9	644	95.7	0.0	0.0	2.0	2.3	27.9	60.5	11.6	254	66.1	56.3	13.4

1 May be of any race.

Table A. All Places — **Population and Housing**

STATE City, town, township, borough, or CDP (county if applicable)	Population: 2010 census total population	Population: 2014 estimated population	Population: Percent change 2010–2014	Population: ACS total population estimate 2010–2014	Race and Hispanic or Latino origin (percent), 2010–2014: White alone, not Hispanic or Latino	Black alone, not Hispanic or Latino	Asian alone, not Hispanic or Latino	All other races or 2 or more races, not Hispanic or Latino	Hispanic or Latino[1]	Age (percent), 2010–2014: Under 18 years old	Age 18 to 64 years old	Age 65 years and older	Households, 2010–2014: Total occupied housing units	Percent owner occupied	Householders by level of education (percent): High school diploma or less	Bachelor's degree or more
	1	2	3	4	5	6	7	8	9	10	11	12	13	14	15	16
IOWA—Con.																
Fruitland city	977	977	0.0	1,296	96.6	0.0	0.0	0.3	3.1	29.9	64.8	5.3	380	97.4	37.1	16.3
Frytown CDP	165	NA	NA	85	100.0	0.0	0.0	0.0	0.0	20.0	44.7	35.3	35	100.0	42.9	57.1
Galt city	32	31	-3.1	78	78.2	0.0	0.0	0.0	21.8	25.7	67.9	6.4	22	100.0	40.9	22.7
Galva city	434	435	0.2	484	97.9	0.0	0.0	0.2	1.9	30.1	57.3	12.6	186	81.7	60.2	11.3
Garber city	88	86	-2.3	121	94.2	0.0	5.0	0.8	0.0	29.7	63.7	6.6	46	100.0	41.3	6.5
Garden City CDP	89	NA	NA	36	100.0	0.0	0.0	0.0	0.0	13.9	75.0	11.1	20	100.0	20.0	80.0
Garden Grove city	211	202	-4.3	228	97.8	0.0	2.2	0.0	0.0	29.8	60.9	9.2	80	86.3	26.3	16.3
Garnavillo city	745	729	-2.1	854	91.8	2.1	0.0	0.1	6.0	21.7	50.3	28.2	362	83.4	52.8	14.1
Garner city	3,129	3,095	-1.1	3,107	94.2	0.1	0.0	2.1	3.6	27.6	58.2	14.2	1,138	86.1	39.5	27.8
Garrison city	371	365	-1.6	349	90.5	0.0	0.0	3.2	6.3	20.7	68.5	10.9	143	73.4	56.6	4.9
Garwin city	527	512	-2.8	516	92.6	5.6	0.0	1.6	0.2	28.8	56.0	15.3	204	85.8	50.5	11.8
Geneva city	165	162	-1.8	166	94.0	2.4	0.0	0.0	3.6	26.4	58.8	14.5	66	84.8	54.5	9.1
George city	1,080	1,059	-1.9	1,115	94.7	0.0	0.6	2.1	2.6	21.5	48.2	30.2	477	78.2	54.9	16.6
Gibson city	61	60	-1.6	48	100.0	0.0	0.0	0.0	0.0	10.5	75.3	14.6	29	55.2	31.0	13.8
Gilbert city	1,076	1,099	2.1	1,398	95.6	0.6	0.7	2.2	0.9	35.3	60.1	4.4	437	78.5	18.5	43.5
Gilbertville city	717	749	4.5	633	95.7	0.0	0.0	4.3	0.0	12.6	65.6	22.0	306	81.7	57.2	10.5
Gillett Grove city	49	48	-2.0	68	94.1	0.0	0.0	5.9	0.0	23.5	58.7	17.6	30	60.0	26.7	6.7
Gilman city	509	507	-0.4	692	99.1	0.0	0.0	0.0	0.9	26.0	60.2	13.7	285	77.9	47.7	7.0
Gilmore City city	504	501	-0.6	465	99.8	0.0	0.2	0.0	0.0	19.3	63.5	17.2	227	74.4	64.3	11.0
Gladbrook city	945	897	-5.1	819	98.3	1.0	0.0	0.6	0.1	18.6	50.4	31.1	357	74.8	49.6	19.3
Glenwood city	5,269	5,242	-0.5	5,253	95.4	0.9	0.0	2.4	1.4	22.9	62.1	14.8	1,789	72.4	37.9	25.3
Glidden city	1,146	1,131	-1.3	1,403	95.7	1.1	0.0	0.7	2.6	28.1	59.5	12.4	515	77.9	36.7	19.6
Goldfield city	635	612	-3.6	666	92.9	0.0	0.3	0.0	6.8	21.7	56.6	21.9	289	76.1	50.2	9.3
Goodell city	139	135	-2.9	181	86.7	0.0	0.0	0.0	13.3	34.9	50.3	14.9	71	77.5	74.6	0.0
Goose Lake city	240	236	-1.7	275	100.0	0.0	0.0	0.0	0.0	35.7	54.2	10.2	87	92.0	46.0	18.4
Gowrie city	1,037	990	-4.5	1,090	92.0	0.0	0.6	4.3	3.1	24.2	55.4	20.5	438	71.2	40.9	19.4
Graettinger city	844	813	-3.7	698	97.0	3.0	0.0	0.0	0.0	21.0	60.9	18.1	341	68.9	48.7	19.4
Graf city	79	78	-1.3	75	100.0	0.0	0.0	0.0	0.0	30.7	56.1	13.3	29	93.1	31.0	51.7
Grafton city	252	255	1.2	290	93.1	2.4	0.0	4.1	0.3	25.5	56.9	17.6	134	78.4	55.2	9.0
Grand Junction city	824	807	-2.1	854	98.7	0.0	0.0	0.2	1.1	26.9	58.8	14.3	309	73.5	51.5	10.4
Grand Mound city	642	623	-3.0	554	95.3	0.4	0.0	2.0	2.3	23.3	61.7	15.0	208	87.0	51.4	7.7
Grand River city	236	226	-4.2	259	100.0	0.0	0.0	0.0	0.0	26.6	46.3	27.0	111	65.8	64.9	6.3
Grandview city	556	535	-3.8	478	84.1	0.0	4.0	0.4	11.5	24.1	54.8	21.1	197	79.7	54.8	15.2
Granger city	1,244	1,416	13.8	1,408	97.9	0.0	0.0	1.1	1.0	32.5	56.2	11.3	481	79.4	30.4	37.8
Grant city	92	90	-2.2	51	100.0	0.0	0.0	0.0	0.0	11.8	39.3	49.0	31	96.8	54.8	0.0
Granville city	312	316	1.3	348	89.4	0.6	0.0	0.0	10.1	28.4	55.9	15.5	148	78.4	45.3	14.9
Gravity city	188	185	-1.6	146	92.5	0.0	0.0	7.5	0.0	8.3	65.6	26.0	87	86.2	63.2	2.3
Gray city	63	59	-6.3	94	100.0	0.0	0.0	0.0	0.0	17.0	67.0	16.0	49	71.4	34.7	0.0
Greeley city	256	251	-2.0	320	99.4	0.0	0.0	0.6	0.0	26.0	62.8	11.3	114	79.8	74.6	2.6
Greene city	1,130	1,127	-0.3	1,128	98.6	0.1	0.4	1.0	0.0	22.2	49.6	28.2	507	84.0	39.6	18.1
Greenfield city	1,982	1,939	-2.2	2,045	96.6	0.6	0.8	0.7	1.3	21.6	54.8	23.6	921	70.0	48.2	14.7
Green Mountain CDP	126	NA	NA	122	100.0	0.0	0.0	0.0	0.0	23.8	58.2	18.0	59	100.0	33.9	25.4
Greenville city	75	74	-1.3	61	88.5	0.0	0.0	11.5	0.0	19.7	67.2	13.1	30	46.7	46.7	0.0
Grimes city	8,256	9,786	18.5	9,037	96.6	0.0	1.8	0.9	0.6	31.7	61.9	6.3	3,380	83.0	19.4	50.9
Grinnell city	9,221	9,069	-1.6	9,136	88.3	1.9	3.9	2.2	3.8	19.4	62.8	17.8	3,541	63.2	34.1	33.2
Griswold city	1,036	994	-4.1	1,182	95.3	0.0	0.0	3.7	1.0	26.2	53.5	20.2	470	75.1	56.2	11.5
Grundy Center city	2,706	2,705	0.0	2,704	100.0	0.0	0.0	0.0	0.0	23.2	54.9	21.8	1,109	75.4	41.8	21.8
Gruver city	94	94	0.0	76	96.1	0.0	0.0	0.0	3.9	18.4	40.7	40.8	37	91.9	51.4	5.4
Guernsey city	63	62	-1.6	73	100.0	0.0	0.0	0.0	0.0	20.5	51.8	27.4	37	70.3	62.2	13.5
Guthrie Center city	1,565	1,523	-2.7	1,621	93.3	2.1	0.1	1.2	3.4	25.5	53.5	21.0	663	68.9	48.6	16.6
Guttenberg city	1,919	1,861	-3.0	1,884	97.3	0.0	0.0	1.9	0.7	18.2	53.5	28.1	862	79.4	42.5	14.5
Halbur city	246	242	-1.6	231	100.0	0.0	0.0	0.0	0.0	35.1	46.3	18.6	86	84.9	43.0	26.7
Hamburg city	1,187	1,105	-6.9	1,076	87.6	0.0	0.0	4.1	8.3	26.8	56.7	16.5	462	63.9	51.9	17.3
Hamilton city	130	130	0.0	181	100.0	0.0	0.0	0.0	0.0	39.7	58.7	1.7	55	89.1	45.5	41.8
Hampton city	4,461	4,343	-2.6	4,402	75.6	1.5	0.0	0.9	22.0	26.7	54.1	19.3	1,751	70.8	53.7	16.8
Hancock city	196	194	-1.0	219	97.3	0.0	0.0	2.7	0.0	18.2	59.9	21.9	90	83.3	56.7	5.6
Hanlontown city	226	228	0.9	177	87.0	0.0	1.1	1.1	10.7	14.1	72.9	13.0	90	74.4	31.1	23.3
Hansell city	98	96	-2.0	120	99.2	0.0	0.0	0.8	0.0	18.3	64.9	16.7	52	94.2	50.0	0.0
Harcourt city	303	293	-3.3	246	89.8	5.3	0.0	4.9	0.0	22.3	59.1	18.7	113	76.1	48.7	11.5
Hardy city	47	46	-2.1	92	95.7	4.3	0.0	0.0	0.0	40.2	53.2	6.5	23	95.7	73.9	8.7
Harlan city	5,106	5,013	-1.8	5,047	93.6	0.2	0.7	1.4	4.2	22.3	54.5	23.2	2,258	71.8	39.8	24.1
Harper city	114	112	-1.8	115	100.0	0.0	0.0	0.0	0.0	16.5	63.5	20.0	54	87.0	51.9	5.6
Harpers Ferry city	328	323	-1.5	291	99.3	0.0	0.0	0.7	0.0	5.9	52.2	41.9	170	85.9	56.5	18.8
Harris city	170	165	-2.9	150	93.3	0.7	0.0	6.0	0.0	10.7	72.0	17.3	72	62.5	65.3	5.6
Hartford city	771	760	-1.4	705	98.3	0.0	0.0	1.1	0.6	34.2	53.8	11.9	253	93.7	58.1	7.9
Hartley city	1,672	1,628	-2.6	1,599	88.4	0.4	1.0	1.5	8.7	23.9	50.5	25.6	726	78.5	51.4	13.2
Hartwick city	86	85	-1.2	75	86.7	0.0	0.0	13.3	0.0	20.0	54.7	25.3	32	96.9	65.6	6.3
Harvey city	235	236	0.4	308	96.4	0.0	0.0	3.2	0.3	21.0	62.6	16.2	131	78.6	61.8	5.3
Hastings city	152	150	-1.3	185	100.0	0.0	0.0	0.0	0.0	24.9	57.4	17.8	70	72.9	68.6	8.6
Havelock city	138	136	-1.4	185	100.0	0.0	0.0	0.0	0.0	31.9	58.3	9.7	83	74.7	45.8	4.8
Haverhill city	173	175	1.2	175	99.4	0.0	0.6	0.0	0.0	17.2	66.8	16.0	63	98.4	33.3	23.8
Hawarden city	2,546	2,543	-0.1	2,556	78.6	0.2	0.0	0.3	21.0	24.5	55.8	19.6	1,050	76.5	53.0	19.0
Hawkeye city	449	428	-4.7	602	91.0	0.0	1.7	6.0	1.3	34.3	47.5	18.3	233	76.8	44.6	12.4
Hayesville city	50	49	-2.0	45	100.0	0.0	0.0	0.0	0.0	22.3	57.7	20.0	22	86.4	50.0	4.5
Hayfield CDP	43	NA	NA	0	0.0	0.0	0.0	0.0	0.0	0.0	0.0	0.0	0	0.0	0.0	0.0
Hazleton city	823	820	-0.4	811	96.4	1.2	0.0	1.0	1.4	27.9	62.5	9.5	347	76.7	50.7	4.9
Hedrick city	765	749	-2.1	964	98.0	0.0	0.0	1.7	0.3	29.4	53.9	16.6	379	69.4	54.6	12.4
Henderson city	185	183	-1.1	171	100.0	0.0	0.0	0.0	0.0	28.0	62.5	9.4	72	86.1	65.3	4.2
Hepburn city	23	23	0.0	61	100.0	0.0	0.0	0.0	0.0	31.1	60.8	8.2	18	50.0	44.4	0.0
Hiawatha city	7,024	7,157	1.9	7,109	85.5	5.0	6.1	1.8	1.6	24.6	62.2	13.2	3,034	61.4	28.0	36.9
High Amana CDP	115	NA	NA	124	100.0	0.0	0.0	0.0	0.0	29.1	59.8	11.3	76	85.5	11.8	26.3
Hills city	703	806	14.7	812	85.5	5.7	0.0	8.9	0.0	25.4	57.3	17.4	317	59.0	47.0	20.8
Hillsboro city	180	182	1.1	222	94.1	0.0	0.0	4.5	1.4	32.5	51.1	16.7	86	77.9	48.8	9.3
Hinton city	952	943	-0.9	892	99.1	0.0	0.2	0.4	0.2	30.8	53.2	16.0	333	85.9	35.4	23.4
Holiday Lake CDP	433	NA	NA	559	98.7	0.0	0.0	0.0	1.3	19.0	58.1	22.9	285	92.6	38.6	31.6
Holland city	282	279	-1.1	240	99.2	0.0	0.0	0.8	0.0	27.5	55.9	16.7	99	90.9	54.5	9.1
Holstein city	1,396	1,393	-0.2	1,408	94.8	0.0	0.2	1.3	3.6	19.0	56.7	24.4	646	74.1	38.5	21.5
Holy Cross city	374	378	1.1	369	98.4	0.0	0.0	1.6	0.0	26.9	53.9	19.2	166	77.7	52.4	9.6
Homestead CDP	148	NA	NA	129	100.0	0.0	0.0	0.0	0.0	34.1	46.5	19.4	50	82.0	56.0	26.0
Hopkinton city	628	611	-2.7	578	99.1	0.0	0.0	0.9	0.0	18.3	57.6	24.0	276	82.6	63.0	7.6
Hornick city	225	225	0.0	264	89.0	0.0	0.0	8.7	2.3	22.3	54.6	23.1	107	90.7	52.3	2.8

1 May be of any race.

Table A. All Places — **Population and Housing**

STATE City, town, township, borough, or CDP (county if applicable)	Population: 2010 census total population	Population: 2014 estimated population	Population: Percent change 2010–2014	Population: ACS total population estimate 2010–2014	Race and Hispanic or Latino origin (percent), 2010–2014: White alone, not Hispanic or Latino	Black alone, not Hispanic or Latino	Asian alone, not Hispanic or Latino	All other races or 2 or more races, not Hispanic or Latino	Hispanic or Latino[1]	Age (percent), 2010–2014: Under 18 years old	Age 18 to 64 years old	Age 65 years and older	Households, 2010–2014: Total occupied housing units	Percent owner occupied	Householders by level of education (percent): High school diploma or less	Bachelor's degree or more
	1	2	3	4	5	6	7	8	9	10	11	12	13	14	15	16
IOWA—Con.																
Hospers city	698	712	2.0	769	93.8	0.0	1.4	0.5	4.3	27.4	51.6	21.1	296	82.1	37.8	17.9
Houghton city	146	145	-0.7	143	99.3	0.7	0.0	0.0	0.0	28.7	51.8	19.6	53	86.8	58.5	30.2
Hubbard city	845	829	-1.9	862	93.0	0.0	0.0	0.0	7.0	21.5	48.9	29.7	360	81.9	47.8	13.9
Hudson city	2,282	2,369	3.8	2,393	97.7	0.0	0.1	0.9	1.2	24.5	62.3	13.1	933	83.1	31.3	34.8
Hull city	2,175	2,227	2.4	2,263	83.7	0.1	1.8	2.5	11.8	30.0	54.7	15.4	808	81.2	50.6	18.8
Humboldt city	4,689	4,625	-1.4	4,663	92.1	0.2	0.5	2.4	4.9	23.4	53.0	23.7	2,069	65.9	44.9	21.0
Humeston city	494	491	-0.6	513	98.8	0.0	0.0	0.0	1.2	23.8	52.3	24.0	225	75.6	52.0	9.8
Hutchins CDP	28	NA	NA	10	100.0	0.0	0.0	0.0	0.0	0.0	100.0	0.0	6	100.0	100.0	0.0
Huxley city	3,304	3,484	5.4	3,370	96.8	0.5	1.4	0.0	1.3	30.0	58.0	12.0	1,297	76.3	34.7	28.6
Ida Grove city	2,142	2,121	-1.0	2,093	95.7	0.1	0.2	1.1	2.9	20.7	53.2	26.2	1,008	67.9	53.1	18.4
Imogene city	72	68	-5.6	56	96.4	0.0	0.0	0.0	3.6	37.6	51.8	10.7	22	100.0	31.8	31.8
Independence city	5,966	5,986	0.3	5,955	94.9	0.9	1.1	0.5	2.7	22.5	57.6	19.7	2,601	71.6	43.7	19.8
Indianola city	14,777	15,305	3.6	15,014	94.9	0.7	0.5	1.9	2.0	23.9	61.0	15.2	5,614	69.0	33.8	30.3
Inwood city	814	817	0.4	772	95.7	0.0	0.6	0.0	3.6	20.3	48.9	30.7	342	78.1	54.1	15.5
Ionia city	291	288	-1.0	387	98.7	0.0	0.0	0.0	1.3	37.7	48.3	14.0	139	87.1	69.8	5.8
Iowa City city	67,894	73,415	8.1	70,597	78.1	5.7	7.9	3.0	5.2	15.5	75.9	8.6	28,843	48.1	14.2	52.8
Iowa Falls city	5,238	5,173	-1.2	5,193	91.0	1.0	0.4	0.8	6.7	20.5	58.8	20.8	2,128	69.3	41.1	21.0
Ireton city	609	604	-0.8	652	95.9	0.6	0.0	1.8	1.7	25.2	59.8	15.0	262	81.7	51.9	13.4
Irvington CDP	38	NA	NA	25	100.0	0.0	0.0	0.0	0.0	44.0	56.0	0.0	6	100.0	0.0	0.0
Irwin city	341	334	-2.1	435	97.5	0.0	0.0	2.1	0.5	20.9	51.0	28.0	193	77.2	49.2	21.2
Jackson Junction city	58	57	-1.7	55	92.7	0.0	0.0	7.3	0.0	27.3	65.6	7.3	21	66.7	38.1	14.3
Jacksonville CDP	30	NA	NA	36	100.0	0.0	0.0	0.0	0.0	0.0	66.7	33.3	29	69.0	100.0	0.0
Jamaica city	224	220	-1.8	224	78.1	0.4	0.0	0.0	21.4	24.1	61.2	14.7	93	72.0	46.2	6.5
Janesville city	930	947	1.8	888	99.7	0.0	0.0	0.3	0.0	23.1	57.9	18.9	384	77.1	46.4	19.0
Jefferson city	4,345	4,276	-1.6	4,296	94.4	0.1	0.7	1.9	3.0	19.9	56.0	24.0	1,883	74.7	40.3	21.2
Jesup city	2,520	2,649	5.1	2,642	96.8	0.0	0.0	1.3	1.9	25.5	60.0	14.3	1,066	79.6	43.1	18.1
Jewell Junction city	1,215	1,177	-3.1	1,198	91.5	0.4	0.8	2.4	4.9	28.0	58.5	13.6	468	72.0	35.3	22.6
Johnston city	17,266	20,359	17.9	18,874	91.5	1.1	3.8	1.2	2.3	28.0	61.4	10.6	7,211	77.7	10.7	63.9
Joice city	222	224	0.9	207	100.0	0.0	0.0	0.0	0.0	19.3	68.5	12.1	94	73.4	29.8	7.4
Jolley city	39	27	-30.8	38	100.0	0.0	0.0	0.0	0.0	15.8	39.6	44.7	18	77.8	61.1	27.8
Kalona city	2,371	2,479	4.6	2,501	97.6	0.2	0.2	0.5	1.4	23.5	51.1	25.3	1,185	67.6	48.0	22.2
Kamrar city	199	193	-3.0	190	87.4	0.0	2.6	0.0	10.0	21.6	57.8	20.5	88	85.2	61.4	4.5
Kanawha city	652	626	-4.0	603	93.2	0.0	1.3	0.5	5.0	16.1	48.8	35.0	294	72.8	66.3	9.5
Kellerton city	315	311	-1.3	394	96.4	0.8	0.0	2.0	0.8	34.7	52.3	12.9	154	66.9	45.5	5.2
Kelley city	309	307	-0.6	338	95.9	0.0	0.9	0.0	3.3	20.5	72.0	7.7	141	68.1	44.0	20.6
Kellogg city	599	595	-0.7	759	97.8	0.0	1.1	0.0	1.2	24.0	63.6	12.5	303	65.7	47.2	8.6
Kensett city	266	269	1.1	251	96.0	0.0	0.0	0.0	4.0	18.0	61.1	21.1	125	80.8	56.0	12.0
Kent CDP	61	NA	NA	18	100.0	0.0	0.0	0.0	0.0	0.0	33.3	66.7	6	100.0	0.0	0.0
Keokuk city	10,780	10,692	-0.8	10,742	88.9	3.6	0.6	3.5	3.4	22.7	59.5	17.8	4,356	62.6	51.8	16.3
Keomah Village city	84	84	0.0	74	100.0	0.0	0.0	0.0	0.0	5.5	67.6	27.0	39	92.3	30.8	25.6
Keosauqua city	1,006	995	-1.1	1,078	96.7	0.7	0.0	0.2	2.4	21.1	48.8	30.1	431	81.4	44.5	29.9
Keota city	1,009	980	-2.9	907	94.7	0.0	0.0	4.5	0.8	23.9	55.4	20.7	386	77.5	53.9	17.4
Keswick city	246	241	-2.0	226	90.7	0.0	0.0	9.3	0.0	27.5	43.8	28.8	94	90.4	44.7	6.4
Keystone city	622	607	-2.4	657	99.5	0.0	0.0	0.5	0.0	20.6	51.1	28.5	277	89.9	45.8	10.1
Kimballton city	322	301	-6.5	300	94.7	0.0	1.3	2.7	1.3	20.6	51.1	28.3	138	72.5	68.8	5.8
Kingsley city	1,411	1,407	-0.3	1,430	96.1	0.0	0.0	1.3	2.6	29.5	53.1	17.3	523	74.0	32.9	16.6
Kinross city	73	72	-1.4	60	100.0	0.0	0.0	0.0	0.0	10.0	75.0	15.0	33	93.9	75.8	3.0
Kirkman city	64	63	-1.6	61	100.0	0.0	0.0	0.0	0.0	3.3	72.2	24.6	43	67.4	58.1	4.7
Kirkville city	167	171	2.4	173	100.0	0.0	0.0	0.0	0.0	17.3	69.3	13.3	77	93.5	51.9	5.2
Kiron city	279	280	0.4	277	80.5	0.0	0.0	0.0	19.5	24.9	50.6	24.5	111	81.1	61.3	10.8
Klemme city	507	487	-3.9	523	95.2	2.3	0.0	1.3	1.1	32.7	51.0	16.3	203	74.4	68.0	7.9
Knierim city	60	60	0.0	93	100.0	0.0	0.0	0.0	0.0	37.7	50.7	11.8	33	100.0	27.3	24.2
Knoxville city	7,313	7,244	-0.9	7,257	93.0	0.4	0.2	1.4	5.1	26.0	54.4	19.6	3,041	68.3	43.4	17.9
Lacona city	361	361	0.0	427	89.7	0.0	0.0	1.9	8.4	30.0	57.8	12.4	171	73.1	64.3	11.1
Ladora city	283	283	0.0	286	100.0	0.0	0.0	0.0	0.0	22.3	68.7	8.7	130	74.6	56.9	7.7
Lake City city	1,727	1,677	-2.9	1,754	96.1	1.2	0.4	1.4	0.9	18.5	54.4	27.3	777	77.5	45.0	20.1
Lake Mills city	2,100	2,056	-2.1	1,878	93.8	0.3	0.1	4.0	1.8	20.3	53.7	26.0	879	71.3	44.6	19.5
Lake Panorama CDP	1,309	NA	NA	1,196	98.3	0.0	0.0	0.3	1.3	11.2	51.8	36.9	564	100.0	28.0	43.3
Lake Park city	1,105	1,128	2.1	1,065	96.7	0.4	0.0	0.7	2.3	24.2	55.7	20.3	440	78.0	38.2	13.9
Lakeside city	700	709	1.3	650	62.6	1.7	2.8	2.2	30.8	18.1	62.8	19.1	246	82.5	42.7	33.3
Lake View city	1,142	1,124	-1.6	1,172	99.3	0.0	0.0	0.3	0.4	15.4	52.5	32.3	587	80.7	46.3	17.0
Lakota city	294	288	-2.0	226	99.1	0.0	0.0	0.9	0.0	16.4	50.1	33.6	111	85.6	58.6	5.4
Lambs Grove city	172	172	0.0	175	94.9	0.0	0.0	0.0	5.1	28.0	52.6	19.4	66	97.0	18.2	37.9
Lamoni city	2,324	2,404	3.4	2,547	84.9	4.6	0.0	3.8	6.8	17.4	68.0	14.4	788	49.5	29.6	30.8
Lamont city	461	458	-0.7	354	98.9	0.0	0.0	0.0	1.1	20.6	61.9	17.5	163	87.1	66.9	5.5
La Motte city	260	254	-2.3	228	95.6	0.0	0.0	4.4	0.0	20.2	62.2	17.5	101	93.1	56.4	8.9
Lanesboro city	118	116	-1.7	111	100.0	0.0	0.0	0.0	0.0	29.7	53.1	17.1	43	79.1	62.8	4.7
Lansing city	999	962	-3.7	881	95.6	0.0	1.1	1.4	1.9	19.1	51.1	29.9	392	73.7	46.4	16.8
La Porte City city	2,285	2,290	0.2	2,403	93.4	0.0	1.0	1.6	4.1	30.9	54.5	14.5	917	74.0	44.6	17.1
Larchwood city	866	873	0.8	1,004	91.9	0.2	0.2	0.3	7.4	32.4	50.5	17.3	377	88.1	55.4	20.2
Larrabee city	139	136	-2.2	155	91.6	0.0	0.0	8.4	0.0	27.8	56.8	15.5	72	83.3	50.0	4.2
Latimer city	507	490	-3.4	456	84.6	0.0	2.4	1.1	11.8	17.8	57.0	25.2	210	79.5	48.6	16.2
Laurel city	239	242	1.3	361	93.6	0.0	0.0	4.4	1.9	29.1	51.4	19.4	124	71.0	62.1	12.1
Laurens city	1,258	1,227	-2.5	1,268	90.2	4.9	0.3	1.3	3.2	21.5	57.7	20.9	605	69.3	42.8	15.9
Lawler city	439	426	-3.0	313	97.4	0.0	0.0	0.3	2.2	10.2	60.4	29.4	175	81.1	56.0	10.3
Lawton city	908	947	4.3	904	98.3	0.7	0.0	0.0	1.0	31.0	52.8	16.5	321	80.7	40.8	28.7
Leando CDP	115	NA	NA	28	67.9	0.0	32.1	0.0	0.0	0.0	32.1	67.9	18	50.0	0.0	0.0
Le Claire city	3,744	3,929	4.9	3,846	93.4	1.7	0.0	1.8	3.1	24.6	62.6	12.7	1,538	85.2	28.5	42.0
Ledyard city	130	127	-2.3	110	97.3	0.0	0.0	1.8	0.9	19.1	52.5	28.2	55	92.7	69.1	7.3
Le Grand city	938	944	0.6	954	93.0	0.9	0.7	2.3	3.0	27.3	57.9	14.8	386	78.2	39.6	17.1
Lehigh city	416	397	-4.6	419	96.9	0.0	0.0	1.0	2.1	10.1	67.6	22.4	224	65.6	53.1	13.4
Leighton city	162	162	0.0	192	100.0	0.0	0.0	0.0	0.0	27.6	52.1	20.3	66	83.3	59.1	21.2
Leland city	289	284	-1.7	290	77.9	0.0	2.1	0.7	19.3	25.8	64.4	9.7	121	71.9	63.6	13.2
Le Mars city	9,826	9,764	-0.6	9,783	91.1	0.6	0.4	3.0	5.0	23.2	58.7	18.2	4,177	75.5	43.4	17.5
Lenox city	1,407	1,370	-2.6	1,430	75.9	0.0	0.0	0.0	24.1	20.5	53.7	25.8	690	51.6	53.2	13.5
Leon city	1,977	1,909	-3.4	1,996	97.2	0.7	1.0	0.1	1.1	23.8	55.9	20.3	780	55.5	59.4	13.7
Le Roy city	15	14	-6.7	2	100.0	0.0	0.0	0.0	0.0	0.0	0.0	100.0	2	100.0	0.0	0.0
Lester city	294	290	-1.4	299	96.3	0.3	0.0	1.0	2.3	28.7	48.5	22.7	120	83.3	52.5	11.7
Letts city	384	376	-2.1	378	93.7	0.0	0.0	0.0	6.3	24.3	58.5	17.2	140	90.0	50.0	8.6
Lewis city	433	415	-4.2	467	94.4	0.0	0.0	4.5	1.1	22.5	62.3	15.2	201	76.6	62.7	4.0
Libertyville city	315	327	3.8	346	93.4	0.0	0.0	0.0	6.6	22.0	62.9	15.0	154	74.7	57.8	16.2

1 May be of any race.

Table A. All Places — **Population and Housing**

STATE City, town, township, borough, or CDP (county if applicable)	Population: 2010 census total population	Population: 2014 estimated population	Population: Percent change 2010–2014	Population: ACS total population estimate 2010–2014	Race and Hispanic or Latino origin (percent), 2010–2014: White alone, not Hispanic or Latino	Black alone, not Hispanic or Latino	Asian alone, not Hispanic or Latino	All other races or 2 or more races, not Hispanic or Latino	Hispanic or Latino[1]	Age (percent), 2010–2014: Under 18 years old	Age 18 to 64 years old	Age 65 years and older	Households, 2010–2014: Total occupied housing units	Percent owner occupied	Householders by level of education (percent): High school diploma or less	Bachelor's degree or more
	1	2	3	4	5	6	7	8	9	10	11	12	13	14	15	16
IOWA—Con.																
Lidderdale city	180	177	-1.7	213	97.2	0.0	0.0	2.8	0.0	33.4	45.0	21.6	79	92.4	63.3	11.4
Lime Springs city	505	492	-2.6	475	97.1	0.0	1.5	1.5	0.0	22.3	51.0	26.7	206	89.8	67.5	3.9
Lincoln city	162	158	-2.5	134	98.5	0.0	0.0	0.0	1.5	26.1	48.4	25.4	65	76.9	63.1	6.2
Linden city	199	212	6.5	175	94.9	0.0	0.0	5.1	0.0	13.2	64.5	22.3	78	89.7	43.6	16.7
Lineville city	217	219	0.9	244	93.4	0.0	2.9	3.7	0.0	20.9	55.3	23.8	113	88.5	69.9	6.2
Linn Grove city	154	155	0.6	129	86.8	0.0	0.0	0.0	13.2	20.2	65.3	14.7	69	94.2	43.5	21.7
Lisbon city	2,152	2,184	1.5	1,812	97.5	0.6	0.0	1.0	1.0	28.0	55.5	16.6	762	81.1	42.4	22.0
Liscomb city	301	305	1.3	265	98.9	0.0	0.0	1.1	0.0	24.5	65.3	10.2	104	82.7	62.5	3.8
Little Cedar CDP	60	NA	NA	49	100.0	0.0	0.0	0.0	0.0	0.0	26.5	73.5	30	100.0	53.3	0.0
Little Rock city	459	444	-3.3	466	97.4	0.0	0.4	0.0	2.1	20.2	57.9	21.9	193	88.6	52.8	10.9
Little Sioux city	170	163	-4.1	156	96.2	0.0	0.0	2.6	1.3	18.5	59.0	22.4	69	79.7	69.6	0.0
Livermore city	384	370	-3.6	407	95.8	0.0	0.0	0.5	3.7	25.8	55.8	18.4	175	80.6	46.3	12.6
Lockridge city	268	279	4.1	252	94.8	0.0	0.0	2.4	2.8	23.0	68.3	8.7	108	78.7	56.5	11.1
Logan city	1,534	1,474	-3.9	1,618	97.0	0.2	0.3	2.0	0.5	27.6	57.8	14.5	607	75.6	40.2	22.7
Lohrville city	368	354	-3.8	413	98.5	0.0	0.2	0.2	1.0	33.2	54.1	12.8	156	82.7	48.1	18.6
Lone Rock city	146	143	-2.1	125	96.8	0.0	0.0	0.0	3.2	12.0	51.2	36.8	65	89.2	53.8	20.0
Lone Tree city	1,300	1,408	8.3	1,394	92.8	0.0	0.2	2.4	4.6	26.9	57.1	15.9	586	66.4	41.1	15.5
Long Grove city	810	840	3.7	940	96.1	0.6	0.4	0.2	2.7	33.8	57.1	9.1	302	93.7	25.8	47.0
Lorimor city	360	355	-1.4	419	98.3	0.0	0.0	0.5	1.2	28.3	58.7	12.9	181	67.4	74.0	4.4
Lost Nation city	446	429	-3.8	502	97.8	0.0	0.0	1.8	0.4	35.3	49.0	15.9	176	64.2	50.0	15.9
Loveland CDP	35	NA	NA	37	100.0	0.0	0.0	0.0	0.0	0.0	99.9	0.0	18	100.0	100.0	0.0
Lovilia city	538	532	-1.1	580	99.5	0.0	0.0	0.5	0.0	27.6	54.4	18.1	225	76.4	68.4	4.4
Lowden city	789	774	-1.9	769	93.2	0.8	0.0	3.4	2.6	23.4	52.1	24.4	365	74.8	53.2	15.1
Low Moor city	288	281	-2.4	186	99.5	0.0	0.0	0.5	0.0	35.4	47.9	16.7	73	84.9	58.9	8.2
Luana city	269	275	2.2	293	92.5	0.0	0.0	0.7	6.8	17.0	68.2	14.7	129	77.5	50.4	14.0
Lucas city	216	213	-1.4	188	97.9	2.1	0.0	0.0	0.0	12.2	70.2	17.6	82	86.6	50.0	11.0
Luther city	122	122	0.0	157	91.7	0.0	0.0	0.0	8.3	13.9	73.3	12.7	76	89.5	23.7	22.4
Lu Verne city	261	256	-1.9	266	95.1	0.8	0.0	0.4	3.8	29.7	53.1	17.3	106	74.5	59.4	4.7
Luxemburg city	240	252	5.0	192	100.0	0.0	0.0	0.0	0.0	9.4	66.5	24.0	88	87.5	45.5	5.7
Luzerne city	96	95	-1.0	83	100.0	0.0	0.0	0.0	0.0	24.1	64.9	10.8	31	90.3	51.6	0.0
Lynnville city	379	391	3.2	483	99.0	0.0	0.0	0.0	1.0	17.1	68.6	14.1	198	86.4	64.6	7.6
Lytton city	316	304	-3.8	319	97.2	0.0	0.0	0.3	2.5	19.1	63.1	17.9	131	87.0	51.9	9.2
McCallsburg city	333	335	0.6	365	97.0	0.0	0.0	3.0	0.0	32.0	55.2	12.6	154	72.7	36.4	13.6
McCausland city	303	314	3.6	319	98.1	0.0	0.0	1.6	0.3	19.1	66.7	14.1	130	84.6	36.9	11.5
McClelland city	151	150	-0.7	129	93.8	0.0	0.0	0.0	6.2	28.8	58.1	13.2	48	83.3	39.6	22.9
Macedonia city	246	244	-0.8	270	100.0	0.0	0.0	0.0	0.0	15.6	69.5	14.8	127	77.2	36.2	6.3
McGregor city	871	838	-3.8	884	96.6	0.1	0.6	1.4	1.4	23.5	50.3	26.1	398	75.9	43.2	21.1
McIntire city	122	121	-0.8	79	100.0	0.0	0.0	0.0	0.0	16.4	32.9	50.6	46	80.4	80.4	4.3
Macksburg city	113	110	-2.7	175	91.4	0.0	5.7	2.3	0.6	29.6	55.4	14.9	66	80.3	54.5	9.1
Madrid city	2,543	2,553	0.4	2,548	97.3	0.0	0.0	0.6	2.1	27.8	55.7	16.4	1,001	72.3	52.7	13.2
Magnolia city	183	175	-4.4	148	100.0	0.0	0.0	0.0	0.0	3.4	77.8	18.9	65	92.3	78.5	10.8
Maharishi Vedic City city	1,294	1,300	0.5	682	28.3	0.1	54.5	17.0	0.0	1.1	95.1	3.8	121	43.8	4.1	83.5
Malcom city	287	283	-1.4	306	95.1	1.3	2.0	1.0	0.7	15.1	57.9	27.1	155	80.0	58.1	17.4
Mallard city	274	266	-2.9	334	98.5	1.2	0.0	0.0	0.3	18.0	60.0	22.2	173	78.0	56.1	7.5
Maloy city	29	29	0.0	22	100.0	0.0	0.0	0.0	0.0	27.3	63.5	9.1	8	100.0	37.5	50.0
Malvern city	1,142	1,118	-2.1	1,042	97.8	0.2	0.0	0.8	1.2	21.1	64.5	14.4	391	81.8	37.9	24.3
Manchester city	5,180	5,087	-1.8	5,126	96.9	0.5	0.0	1.2	1.4	24.5	52.9	22.6	2,201	65.6	51.8	13.9
Manilla city	776	777	0.1	997	88.1	0.0	0.0	1.1	10.8	26.3	50.6	22.9	404	70.3	43.6	17.6
Manly city	1,323	1,325	0.2	1,444	93.4	0.0	0.2	1.5	4.9	30.1	52.1	17.9	545	72.3	38.9	13.4
Manning city	1,516	1,485	-2.0	1,554	94.3	0.4	1.1	0.8	3.4	22.1	53.5	24.5	679	73.3	51.7	18.0
Manson city	1,690	1,627	-3.7	1,724	95.6	0.3	0.0	2.3	1.8	22.5	54.5	22.9	806	71.3	41.6	17.7
Mapleton city	1,224	1,217	-0.6	1,454	98.4	0.0	0.0	0.0	1.6	25.0	50.8	24.2	647	74.2	53.5	21.0
Maquoketa city	6,141	6,012	-2.1	6,064	93.2	0.3	0.4	4.5	1.6	24.2	56.2	19.6	2,627	65.7	54.1	14.5
Marathon city	239	241	0.8	286	85.7	0.0	0.0	9.1	5.2	30.7	56.8	12.2	109	78.9	53.2	7.3
Marble Rock city	307	303	-1.3	292	95.2	0.3	0.0	4.5	0.0	19.8	59.6	20.5	141	76.6	48.2	9.2
Marcus city	1,117	1,096	-1.9	1,230	96.1	0.0	0.0	2.4	1.5	22.2	55.2	22.7	551	80.9	41.6	24.9
Marengo city	2,528	2,513	-0.6	2,502	88.9	2.2	0.0	1.4	7.5	26.4	59.4	14.3	974	63.7	45.9	10.8
Marion city	34,768	36,774	5.8	35,809	92.9	1.8	2.0	1.7	1.5	26.1	60.4	13.5	14,590	75.3	26.0	36.6
Marne city	120	116	-3.3	76	100.0	0.0	0.0	0.0	0.0	15.8	72.4	11.8	32	90.6	46.9	12.5
Marquette city	462	453	-1.9	426	95.1	0.0	1.9	2.8	0.2	20.6	59.8	19.5	222	54.1	45.9	11.3
Marshalltown city	27,552	27,727	0.6	27,749	66.5	2.2	3.5	1.9	25.9	26.5	56.9	16.6	10,054	66.7	43.1	22.4
Martelle city	255	254	-0.4	242	100.0	0.0	0.0	0.0	0.0	14.0	58.0	28.1	122	74.6	44.3	6.6
Martensdale city	465	464	-0.2	482	95.6	0.0	0.0	0.0	4.4	26.9	62.3	10.6	190	65.8	38.4	10.0
Martinsburg city	112	110	-1.8	151	93.4	0.0	0.0	4.0	2.6	35.8	54.9	9.3	52	92.3	76.9	3.8
Marysville city	66	66	0.0	22	100.0	0.0	0.0	0.0	0.0	45.4	36.3	18.2	6	100.0	33.3	0.0
Mason City city	28,079	27,458	-2.2	27,775	90.8	1.2	1.4	1.9	4.7	21.5	60.7	17.9	12,873	66.6	40.5	21.0
Masonville city	127	124	-2.4	115	100.0	0.0	0.0	0.0	0.0	23.5	67.9	8.7	60	61.7	70.0	0.0
Massena city	355	345	-2.8	367	99.5	0.0	0.5	0.0	0.0	24.5	56.6	18.8	172	74.4	47.7	10.5
Matlock city	87	88	1.1	94	100.0	0.0	0.0	0.0	0.0	13.8	74.5	11.7	39	76.9	56.4	2.6
Maurice city	275	277	0.7	297	77.4	0.3	0.0	3.7	18.5	26.7	61.6	11.8	113	84.1	54.9	12.4
Maxwell city	922	914	-0.9	997	95.8	0.0	1.6	2.1	0.5	24.5	64.4	10.8	403	74.7	31.8	18.6
Maynard city	518	501	-3.3	541	97.4	0.0	0.0	1.5	1.1	23.8	62.7	13.5	235	82.6	44.7	22.6
Maysville city	176	179	1.7	161	100.0	0.0	0.0	0.0	0.0	11.2	68.8	19.9	74	77.0	39.2	12.2
Mechanicsville city	1,144	1,117	-2.4	1,063	96.3	0.0	0.0	2.9	0.8	22.2	56.8	21.1	457	81.4	55.8	15.5
Mediapolis city	1,560	1,589	1.9	1,398	95.0	2.4	0.0	0.4	2.2	20.8	53.9	25.3	606	75.6	42.4	24.4
Melbourne city	830	826	-0.5	868	96.7	0.3	0.2	2.5	0.2	27.7	53.7	18.5	345	79.7	44.6	19.4
Melcher-Dallas city	1,288	1,276	-0.9	1,170	99.1	0.0	0.0	0.9	0.0	18.6	62.3	19.0	531	77.6	55.2	11.5
Melrose city	112	112	0.0	121	96.7	1.7	1.7	0.0	0.0	14.9	56.2	28.9	58	79.3	67.2	0.0
Melvin city	214	208	-2.8	255	87.8	0.0	0.0	0.0	12.2	22.0	61.9	16.1	118	89.8	50.8	12.7
Menlo city	353	346	-2.0	363	99.7	0.0	0.0	0.0	0.3	29.5	55.5	14.9	149	89.3	57.7	12.1
Meriden city	157	153	-2.5	181	100.0	0.0	0.0	0.0	0.0	24.3	58.4	17.1	87	54.0	49.4	19.5
Merrill city	755	737	-2.4	862	97.3	0.0	0.0	2.7	0.0	26.5	60.1	13.5	335	83.3	48.4	14.6
Meservey city	256	250	-2.3	232	96.1	0.0	0.9	0.0	3.0	17.6	62.6	19.8	109	83.5	56.9	11.9
Meyer CDP	31	NA	NA	0	0.0	0.0	0.0	0.0	0.0	0.0	0.0	0.0	0	0.0	0.0	0.0
Middle Amana CDP	581	NA	NA	595	100.0	0.0	0.0	0.0	0.0	24.2	43.0	32.8	220	95.0	28.6	43.2
Middletown city	318	336	5.7	302	90.7	0.0	1.7	5.6	2.0	26.7	57.0	16.2	115	90.4	35.7	8.7
Miles city	456	443	-2.9	437	97.5	0.0	0.0	1.6	0.9	23.8	55.7	20.4	204	74.5	58.8	14.7
Milford city	2,898	2,985	3.0	2,955	97.5	0.0	0.4	1.0	1.0	24.6	58.6	16.7	1,303	69.4	46.3	15.9
Miller CDP	60	NA	NA	0	0.0	0.0	0.0	0.0	0.0	0.0	0.0	0.0	0	0.0	0.0	0.0
Millersburg city	159	159	0.0	186	100.0	0.0	0.0	0.0	0.0	9.8	74.7	15.6	93	65.6	62.4	9.7
Millerton city	45	45	0.0	44	100.0	0.0	0.0	0.0	0.0	38.6	59.1	2.3	16	100.0	37.5	50.0

1 May be of any race.

Table A. All Places — **Population and Housing**

STATE City, town, township, borough, or CDP (county if applicable)	Population: 2010 census total population	Population: 2014 estimated population	Population: Percent change 2010–2014	Population: ACS total population estimate 2010–2014	Race and Hispanic or Latino origin (percent), 2010–2014: White alone, not Hispanic or Latino	Black alone, not Hispanic or Latino	Asian alone, not Hispanic or Latino	All other races or 2 or more races, not Hispanic or Latino	Hispanic or Latino[1]	Age (percent), 2010–2014: Under 18 years old	Age 18 to 64 years old	Age 65 years and older	Households, 2010–2014: Total occupied housing units	Percent owner occupied	Householders by level of education (percent): High school diploma or less	Bachelor's degree or more
	1	2	3	4	5	6	7	8	9	10	11	12	13	14	15	16
IOWA—Con.																
Millville city	30	29	-3.3	21	100.0	0.0	0.0	0.0	0.0	4.8	42.8	52.4	11	100.0	100.0	0.0
Milo city	775	769	-0.8	758	94.3	0.0	0.1	0.0	5.5	28.4	57.5	14.2	291	83.8	48.5	11.3
Milton city	443	417	-5.9	428	97.7	0.2	0.0	1.9	0.2	25.1	64.2	10.5	155	83.9	54.8	14.2
Minburn city	364	388	6.6	359	97.8	0.0	0.0	0.0	2.2	26.8	57.2	15.9	143	76.9	48.3	17.5
Minden city	599	592	-1.2	578	100.0	0.0	0.0	0.0	0.0	29.3	48.7	22.1	225	83.1	44.4	20.0
Mineola CDP	166	NA	NA	152	100.0	0.0	0.0	0.0	0.0	26.3	54.0	19.7	75	82.7	18.7	42.7
Mingo city	302	301	-0.3	248	96.0	0.0	0.0	1.2	2.8	20.5	56.2	23.0	108	90.7	38.0	21.3
Missouri Valley city	2,837	2,692	-5.1	2,752	98.2	0.0	0.4	0.0	1.4	22.1	58.9	19.1	1,162	64.8	50.5	13.0
Mitchell city	138	136	-1.4	120	100.0	0.0	0.0	0.0	0.0	21.7	55.0	23.3	56	100.0	50.0	8.9
Mitchellville city	2,254	2,217	-1.6	2,396	87.7	5.7	0.2	4.0	2.4	16.9	73.3	9.7	681	75.8	46.8	21.9
Modale city	283	269	-4.9	241	99.2	0.0	0.0	0.8	0.0	28.7	56.8	14.5	99	71.7	57.6	8.1
Mona CDP	34	NA	NA	34	100.0	0.0	0.0	0.0	0.0	41.2	58.8	0.0	20	35.0	65.0	0.0
Mondamin city	402	378	-6.0	336	97.6	0.0	0.0	0.6	1.8	16.7	62.9	20.5	158	65.8	52.5	13.3
Monmouth city	153	149	-2.6	99	97.0	0.0	2.0	1.0	0.0	7.0	72.6	20.2	50	74.0	64.0	2.0
Monona city	1,549	1,510	-2.5	1,625	98.3	0.0	0.0	1.6	0.1	18.0	59.5	22.4	760	76.1	59.7	13.3
Monroe city	1,830	1,831	0.1	1,800	97.8	0.0	0.2	0.9	1.1	27.0	60.2	12.7	740	66.4	40.0	16.9
Montezuma city	1,462	1,444	-1.2	1,698	99.8	0.0	0.0	0.0	0.2	26.7	52.5	20.8	664	66.3	47.3	22.1
Monticello city	3,784	3,809	0.7	3,801	98.5	0.1	0.4	0.8	0.3	22.5	55.5	22.0	1,666	75.8	52.5	12.2
Montour city	249	248	-0.4	268	96.6	0.0	0.0	0.0	3.4	17.1	65.0	17.9	112	89.3	66.1	7.1
Montrose city	898	880	-2.0	916	97.2	0.0	0.0	2.5	0.3	24.2	55.6	20.3	377	72.9	51.2	14.3
Moorhead city	226	219	-3.1	243	99.2	0.0	0.8	0.0	0.0	17.3	56.3	26.3	122	84.4	52.5	16.4
Moorland city	169	163	-3.6	199	91.5	0.0	0.0	0.0	8.5	21.1	60.1	18.6	86	82.6	40.7	8.1
Moravia city	665	651	-2.1	843	96.2	0.0	0.0	2.3	1.5	28.4	50.9	20.8	331	79.8	52.0	15.7
Morley city	115	115	0.0	155	91.6	0.0	3.9	4.5	0.0	25.2	58.6	16.1	66	77.3	45.5	12.1
Morning Sun city	836	821	-1.8	1,033	97.3	0.0	0.0	1.0	1.7	29.9	54.3	15.8	356	82.3	43.5	11.5
Morrison city	94	93	-1.1	68	100.0	0.0	0.0	0.0	0.0	19.1	63.2	17.6	31	93.5	41.9	9.7
Moulton city	605	592	-2.1	592	96.1	0.0	0.0	2.4	1.5	28.4	49.3	22.5	244	79.5	46.7	14.3
Mount Auburn city	150	148	-1.3	106	100.0	0.0	0.0	0.0	0.0	17.9	64.2	17.9	46	87.0	50.0	4.3
Mount Ayr city	1,691	1,680	-0.7	1,609	93.4	0.4	1.9	2.2	2.0	17.6	50.2	32.1	716	70.8	44.0	23.6
Mount Pleasant city	8,668	8,647	-0.2	8,682	82.0	4.4	4.4	3.1	6.2	22.4	63.4	14.3	3,047	64.8	40.4	25.0
Mount Sterling CDP	36	NA	NA	36	97.2	0.0	0.0	2.8	0.0	11.1	33.4	55.6	17	100.0	17.6	64.7
Mount Union city	107	108	0.9	105	92.4	0.0	0.0	0.0	7.6	38.1	50.6	11.4	43	97.7	37.2	23.3
Mount Vernon city	4,506	4,522	0.4	4,532	85.3	0.9	0.7	4.4	8.7	26.0	62.8	11.3	1,273	85.3	18.6	58.3
Moville city	1,618	1,626	0.5	1,436	97.2	0.0	0.0	1.0	1.7	27.7	56.9	15.3	561	82.7	36.0	26.2
Murray city	756	734	-2.9	555	99.6	0.0	0.0	0.4	0.0	20.5	60.2	19.3	270	80.4	64.1	8.1
Muscatine city	23,772	23,888	0.5	23,857	77.1	2.2	1.3	1.3	18.0	26.9	58.4	14.7	9,413	68.8	45.5	18.8
Mystic city	425	415	-2.4	444	98.9	0.0	0.0	0.9	0.2	27.0	58.0	14.9	173	80.3	67.6	7.5
Nashua city	1,663	1,636	-1.6	1,632	98.2	0.0	0.2	1.5	0.0	24.1	55.8	20.0	731	77.2	44.7	16.0
Nemaha city	85	83	-2.4	85	68.2	0.0	0.0	0.0	31.8	23.6	61.1	15.3	36	94.4	58.3	25.0
Neola city	845	856	1.3	874	96.2	0.0	0.0	1.8	1.9	30.2	54.7	15.0	345	74.2	39.1	20.3
Nevada city	6,792	6,779	-0.2	6,794	93.6	1.0	0.5	0.5	4.4	25.3	60.4	14.2	2,809	72.2	36.7	20.8
New Albin city	522	504	-3.4	504	98.4	0.0	0.0	1.6	0.0	26.2	49.9	24.0	241	77.2	51.5	16.2
Newell city	876	877	0.1	1,239	91.0	0.0	0.1	0.6	8.3	34.6	49.4	16.1	446	78.0	55.2	18.4
Newhall city	875	853	-2.5	956	97.5	0.0	0.0	2.0	0.5	26.3	54.5	19.1	376	88.3	35.4	25.5
New Hampton city	3,571	3,546	-0.7	3,555	94.6	1.0	1.1	0.2	3.1	25.0	55.4	19.7	1,546	61.2	55.3	18.2
New Hartford city	516	511	-1.0	598	92.8	0.0	0.0	0.0	7.2	25.3	62.9	11.9	265	66.8	50.2	12.8
New Haven CDP	91	NA	NA	37	100.0	0.0	0.0	0.0	0.0	0.0	54.1	45.9	29	100.0	31.0	0.0
New Liberty city	139	142	2.2	159	96.9	0.0	1.3	1.9	0.0	34.6	52.7	12.6	54	94.4	48.1	11.1
New London city	1,897	1,893	-0.2	1,844	96.4	0.0	1.6	1.6	0.5	18.6	55.5	25.9	770	86.0	40.8	19.4
New Market city	415	405	-2.4	426	99.5	0.0	0.0	0.5	0.0	24.0	53.2	22.8	200	76.5	56.0	11.5
New Providence city	228	227	-0.4	217	98.2	0.0	0.0	1.8	0.0	20.7	60.3	18.9	90	78.9	55.6	23.3
New Sharon city	1,293	1,301	0.6	1,315	93.5	0.0	0.2	2.7	3.6	24.6	58.7	16.7	523	78.8	52.2	13.4
Newton city	15,254	15,150	-0.7	15,139	96.0	1.1	0.9	1.4	0.6	22.9	58.1	19.0	6,399	63.0	47.4	22.1
New Vienna city	407	426	4.7	420	92.6	0.0	0.0	7.4	0.0	18.8	62.6	18.8	214	88.8	55.1	11.7
New Virginia city	489	484	-1.0	491	100.0	0.0	0.0	0.0	0.0	31.4	52.3	16.3	187	76.5	43.3	17.1
Nichols city	372	372	0.0	383	84.3	1.3	1.3	0.0	13.1	20.4	63.8	15.9	156	81.4	56.4	7.1
Nodaway city	114	110	-3.5	142	98.6	0.0	0.0	1.4	0.0	34.5	55.0	10.6	61	68.9	36.1	21.3
Nora Springs city	1,431	1,402	-2.0	1,517	96.1	0.5	0.0	1.6	1.8	21.8	63.9	14.2	653	78.7	31.7	13.6
Northboro city	58	57	-1.7	39	100.0	0.0	0.0	0.0	0.0	7.8	69.2	23.1	19	100.0	57.9	0.0
North Buena Vista city	121	115	-5.0	109	100.0	0.0	0.0	0.0	0.0	3.6	79.7	16.5	73	84.9	86.3	4.1
North English city	1,041	1,026	-1.4	1,054	96.6	0.0	0.0	2.6	0.9	29.1	48.7	22.3	422	75.1	44.3	16.4
North Liberty city	13,374	15,386	15.0	14,503	84.2	5.3	2.7	1.7	6.2	26.5	69.6	3.9	5,942	68.4	16.2	47.9
North Washington city	117	116	-0.9	144	95.1	0.7	0.0	0.0	4.2	26.5	66.6	6.9	57	87.7	64.9	10.5
Northwood city	1,989	2,003	0.7	2,083	94.0	1.8	0.0	1.5	2.6	20.3	58.6	21.0	958	76.6	45.5	21.2
Norwalk city	8,978	9,859	9.8	9,444	94.7	0.0	0.5	1.9	2.9	27.6	63.2	9.1	3,459	72.8	19.7	39.0
Norway city	545	529	-2.9	581	99.3	0.0	0.0	0.7	0.0	23.4	55.0	21.5	258	89.9	39.5	13.2
Numa city	92	91	-1.1	65	100.0	0.0	0.0	0.0	0.0	12.3	56.8	30.8	32	87.5	71.9	9.4
Oakland city	1,527	1,506	-1.4	1,621	90.7	0.0	0.3	0.9	8.1	28.8	52.9	18.3	599	71.5	46.4	20.0
Oakland Acres city	156	156	0.0	135	97.8	0.7	1.5	0.0	0.0	25.9	60.7	13.3	57	96.5	31.6	35.1
Oakville city	173	169	-2.3	123	98.4	0.0	0.0	0.0	1.6	26.8	60.9	12.2	54	81.5	55.6	7.4
Ocheyedan city	490	472	-3.7	446	97.8	1.8	0.0	0.4	0.0	16.4	60.7	22.9	223	88.8	64.6	13.5
Odebolt city	1,014	977	-3.6	1,217	98.3	0.6	0.0	0.0	1.2	24.5	53.2	22.3	508	82.3	50.6	21.7
Oelwein city	6,415	6,181	-3.6	6,321	94.2	0.3	0.2	1.4	4.0	20.3	57.3	22.5	2,764	68.7	51.9	16.6
Ogden city	2,044	2,034	-0.5	2,199	98.4	0.0	0.0	0.7	0.9	24.8	58.0	17.4	848	78.2	45.5	24.2
Okoboji city	810	809	-0.1	923	94.4	0.0	0.9	0.5	4.2	15.9	58.8	25.2	434	80.0	18.4	40.6
Olds city	229	235	2.6	247	93.1	0.0	0.0	1.2	5.7	30.0	56.0	14.2	83	79.5	45.8	12.0
Olin city	698	692	-0.9	668	98.2	0.0	0.7	0.6	0.4	21.3	58.4	20.1	299	72.9	64.9	3.3
Ollie city	215	211	-1.9	207	99.5	0.0	0.0	0.5	0.0	16.4	63.4	20.3	104	87.5	64.4	6.7
Onawa city	2,998	2,891	-3.6	2,954	91.0	0.9	0.0	6.1	2.0	23.8	53.9	22.4	1,233	63.4	51.4	15.2
Onslow city	197	196	-0.5	218	91.7	0.9	0.9	0.5	6.0	20.2	66.6	13.3	103	77.7	60.2	3.9
Orange City city	6,064	6,151	1.4	6,130	89.9	0.4	1.4	0.7	7.7	22.8	61.2	15.9	1,972	81.7	37.3	35.3
Orchard city	71	70	-1.4	59	100.0	0.0	0.0	0.0	0.0	32.2	44.1	23.7	22	86.4	45.5	13.6
Orient city	408	393	-3.7	385	96.9	0.0	0.0	0.0	3.1	20.2	62.3	17.4	182	70.3	52.7	9.3
Orleans city	610	610	0.0	486	100.0	0.0	0.0	0.0	0.0	13.4	50.6	36.0	224	92.9	27.2	50.0
Osage city	3,619	3,653	0.9	3,628	96.3	0.8	0.0	1.2	1.7	20.5	54.3	25.2	1,615	76.8	45.2	19.3
Osceola city	4,927	4,949	0.4	4,981	80.1	0.1	0.3	0.0	19.6	26.3	55.7	18.1	2,038	57.9	62.5	14.7
Oskaloosa city	11,502	11,541	0.3	11,555	91.9	2.4	1.3	2.2	2.2	22.5	60.4	17.1	4,932	61.8	42.5	25.0
Ossian city	845	824	-2.5	934	96.3	0.0	0.0	1.4	2.4	25.6	57.3	17.1	379	81.8	48.0	14.5
Osterdock city	59	57	-3.4	67	100.0	0.0	0.0	0.0	0.0	18.0	61.3	20.9	33	93.9	60.6	6.1
Otho city	542	520	-4.1	526	97.5	0.0	0.0	0.0	2.5	19.0	67.1	14.1	234	70.9	50.9	2.1
Oto city	108	108	0.0	76	98.7	0.0	1.3	0.0	0.0	13.1	59.1	27.6	35	74.3	57.1	0.0

1 May be of any race.

Table A. All Places — **Population and Housing**

STATE City, town, township, borough, or CDP (county if applicable)	Population: 2010 census total population	Population: 2014 estimated population	Population: Percent change 2010–2014	Population: ACS total population estimate 2010–2014	Race and Hispanic or Latino origin (percent), 2010–2014: White alone, not Hispanic or Latino	Black alone, not Hispanic or Latino	Asian alone, not Hispanic or Latino	All other races or 2 or more races, not Hispanic or Latino	Hispanic or Latino[1]	Age (percent), 2010–2014: Under 18 years old	Age 18 to 64 years old	Age 65 years and older	Households, 2010–2014: Total occupied housing units	Percent owner occupied	Householders by level of education (percent): High school diploma or less	Bachelor's degree or more
	1	2	3	4	5	6	7	8	9	10	11	12	13	14	15	16
IOWA—Con.																
Otranto CDP	27	NA	NA	7	100.0	0.0	0.0	0.0	0.0	0.0	0.0	100.0	7	100.0	100.0	0.0
Ottosen city	55	42	-23.6	56	91.1	0.0	0.0	0.0	8.9	25.0	57.1	17.9	27	74.1	66.7	11.1
Ottumwa city	25,023	24,682	-1.4	24,847	83.6	1.9	1.1	1.8	11.7	22.8	61.5	15.8	10,253	68.0	50.0	15.9
Owasa city	43	43	0.0	44	100.0	0.0	0.0	0.0	0.0	22.7	65.8	11.4	14	92.9	85.7	7.1
Oxford city	807	829	2.7	877	94.9	0.1	2.2	0.1	2.7	26.2	63.4	10.4	352	81.0	37.8	21.0
Oxford Junction city	496	487	-1.8	493	97.4	0.0	0.0	0.4	2.2	23.5	56.3	20.1	226	65.5	60.2	2.7
Oyens city	103	101	-1.9	83	100.0	0.0	0.0	0.0	0.0	47.0	52.9	0.0	27	81.5	25.9	0.0
Pacific Junction city	471	459	-2.5	384	94.0	3.6	0.0	0.0	2.3	19.5	63.3	17.2	148	81.8	61.5	10.8
Packwood city	204	212	3.9	306	100.0	0.0	0.0	0.0	0.0	33.0	53.9	13.1	104	76.0	43.3	12.5
Palmer city	165	162	-1.8	153	92.2	0.0	0.0	0.0	7.8	13.1	64.7	22.2	85	85.9	76.5	4.7
Palo city	953	1,044	9.5	902	98.0	1.3	0.0	0.0	0.7	31.8	59.5	8.6	331	88.8	38.7	21.5
Panama city	221	216	-2.3	196	96.4	0.0	0.0	2.0	1.5	19.9	60.2	19.9	88	88.6	40.9	8.0
Panora city	1,121	1,093	-2.5	1,241	97.2	0.0	0.5	2.3	0.0	28.7	52.8	18.5	482	71.2	42.7	21.2
Panorama Park city	129	139	7.8	110	98.2	0.0	1.8	0.0	0.0	10.9	62.1	27.3	50	100.0	62.0	8.0
Parkersburg city	1,870	1,957	4.7	1,859	95.6	0.0	0.0	1.6	2.9	24.7	56.5	18.7	821	76.7	48.1	22.0
Park View CDP	2,389	NA	NA	2,476	92.5	1.1	0.0	1.1	5.3	26.2	68.0	5.8	923	62.8	24.2	41.4
Parnell city	193	207	7.3	227	98.7	0.0	0.0	1.3	0.0	26.4	62.6	11.0	91	87.9	47.3	11.0
Paton city	236	233	-1.3	294	96.6	0.0	0.0	0.3	3.1	31.3	59.8	8.8	120	74.2	49.2	6.7
Patterson city	147	161	9.5	131	100.0	0.0	0.0	0.0	0.0	24.4	60.3	15.3	50	94.0	64.0	2.0
Paullina city	1,056	1,026	-2.8	944	96.0	1.9	0.0	1.1	1.1	24.6	49.0	26.5	451	85.8	53.7	16.0
Pella city	10,357	10,337	-0.2	10,343	94.0	1.4	2.5	1.0	1.1	23.7	59.9	16.4	3,748	64.3	33.1	33.5
Peosta city	1,388	1,560	12.4	1,587	90.7	1.4	0.0	5.0	2.8	40.7	54.1	5.4	477	79.5	28.3	23.7
Percival CDP	87	NA	NA	21	100.0	0.0	0.0	0.0	0.0	0.0	0.0	100.0	16	62.5	31.3	0.0
Perry city	7,703	8,151	5.8	7,986	61.9	1.5	1.5	1.3	33.7	28.8	57.8	13.5	2,818	66.6	55.9	14.7
Persia city	319	301	-5.6	302	98.7	0.0	0.0	1.3	0.0	26.1	56.6	17.2	120	73.3	47.5	7.5
Peterson city	332	320	-3.6	320	92.5	3.8	1.6	1.6	0.6	16.9	59.3	23.8	174	83.9	44.8	21.3
Pierson city	366	357	-2.5	423	91.5	0.0	1.4	3.8	3.3	27.5	56.9	15.6	180	76.7	42.2	11.7
Pilot Mound city	173	173	0.0	162	100.0	0.0	0.0	0.0	0.0	8.6	56.2	35.2	95	68.4	60.0	5.3
Pioneer city	23	23	0.0	7	100.0	0.0	0.0	0.0	0.0	28.6	57.2	14.3	2	100.0	50.0	50.0
Pisgah city	251	240	-4.4	237	97.9	0.0	0.0	1.7	0.4	19.9	57.1	23.2	112	71.4	57.1	6.3
Plainfield city	436	428	-1.8	443	98.2	0.0	0.0	1.8	0.0	24.3	57.2	18.3	193	79.3	63.2	10.9
Plano city	70	69	-1.4	73	100.0	0.0	0.0	0.0	0.0	17.8	56.2	26.0	31	74.2	64.5	12.9
Pleasant Hill city	8,785	9,159	4.3	9,011	85.0	4.1	1.6	0.8	8.5	24.7	63.9	11.2	3,482	76.3	32.5	36.2
Pleasanton city	48	46	-4.2	15	100.0	0.0	0.0	0.0	0.0	26.6	66.6	6.7	6	100.0	83.3	0.0
Pleasant Plain city	93	97	4.3	55	100.0	0.0	0.0	0.0	0.0	14.6	61.8	23.6	28	96.4	50.0	7.1
Pleasantville city	1,694	1,687	-0.4	1,953	96.1	0.0	1.5	2.0	0.4	27.1	58.3	14.6	805	71.2	42.1	18.9
Plover city	77	76	-1.3	39	100.0	0.0	0.0	0.0	0.0	15.3	58.9	25.6	24	79.2	37.5	0.0
Plymouth city	382	375	-1.8	398	98.0	0.0	0.0	0.3	1.8	20.3	67.4	12.3	174	86.2	29.9	12.6
Pocahontas city	1,789	1,754	-2.0	1,732	97.8	1.3	0.0	0.6	0.3	17.5	52.0	30.5	846	80.6	40.2	25.8
Polk City city	3,418	4,177	22.2	3,770	94.8	0.0	1.6	1.3	2.3	29.8	59.7	10.4	1,303	86.4	20.8	47.0
Pomeroy city	662	633	-4.4	887	90.6	2.8	0.0	2.4	4.2	27.3	45.8	26.8	339	82.9	50.4	13.3
Popejoy city	79	78	-1.3	63	100.0	0.0	0.0	0.0	0.0	36.5	58.7	4.8	18	77.8	50.0	0.0
Portland CDP	35	NA	NA	17	100.0	0.0	0.0	0.0	0.0	0.0	70.6	29.4	11	100.0	100.0	0.0
Portsmouth city	195	191	-2.1	183	96.2	0.5	1.1	1.1	1.1	8.7	50.3	41.0	99	69.7	63.6	6.1
Postville city	2,227	2,155	-3.2	2,329	62.2	5.8	0.4	0.5	31.1	32.8	52.9	14.2	849	61.2	56.9	10.4
Prairieburg city	178	179	0.6	199	100.0	0.0	0.0	0.0	0.0	25.5	62.6	11.6	81	77.8	59.3	0.0
Prairie City city	1,680	1,695	0.9	1,656	96.5	0.0	0.0	1.4	2.1	27.1	57.5	15.3	650	78.8	46.3	21.7
Prescott city	257	252	-1.9	294	95.6	0.0	1.7	2.4	0.3	24.2	59.7	16.0	118	78.8	46.6	9.3
Preston city	1,012	984	-2.8	981	96.6	0.0	0.0	1.3	2.0	25.5	56.0	18.5	436	69.7	50.2	7.8
Primghar city	909	888	-2.3	949	93.3	0.3	2.0	0.2	4.2	30.1	51.9	18.1	344	77.9	44.5	20.3
Princeton city	886	928	4.7	1,038	96.0	0.0	0.0	1.4	2.6	27.1	58.2	14.8	405	94.3	37.0	21.7
Promise City city	111	112	0.9	230	100.0	0.0	0.0	0.0	0.0	3.4	80.3	16.1	69	95.7	44.9	1.4
Protivin city	283	280	-1.1	248	99.2	0.0	0.8	0.0	0.0	12.0	53.7	34.3	129	77.5	52.7	7.8
Pulaski city	260	272	4.6	295	98.0	0.0	0.0	0.7	1.4	23.7	58.7	17.6	120	83.3	62.5	13.3
Quasqueton city	554	550	-0.7	457	98.9	0.0	0.0	0.4	0.7	13.8	64.4	21.9	232	77.2	65.9	5.6
Quimby city	317	310	-2.2	280	96.4	0.0	0.7	0.0	2.9	24.3	53.2	22.5	116	87.1	68.1	12.1
Radcliffe city	545	538	-1.3	556	96.2	0.0	0.0	0.0	3.8	23.1	57.1	20.0	241	78.4	53.9	14.1
Rake city	225	221	-1.8	175	89.7	0.0	0.0	0.0	10.3	19.5	50.4	30.3	95	72.6	41.1	15.8
Ralston city	77	76	-1.3	84	100.0	0.0	0.0	0.0	0.0	31.0	50.1	19.0	36	88.9	69.4	2.8
Randalia city	68	66	-2.9	56	100.0	0.0	0.0	0.0	0.0	16.1	71.5	12.5	25	88.0	44.0	4.0
Randall city	173	168	-2.9	146	96.6	0.0	1.4	0.0	2.1	11.6	71.9	16.4	75	72.0	36.0	26.7
Randolph city	168	158	-6.0	185	98.4	0.0	0.0	1.6	0.0	23.8	55.7	20.5	79	78.5	50.6	11.4
Rathbun city	89	88	-1.1	64	100.0	0.0	0.0	0.0	0.0	9.4	65.7	25.0	37	94.6	62.2	8.1
Raymond city	788	807	2.4	872	94.8	0.0	0.0	4.1	1.0	26.1	64.1	10.0	300	93.0	43.0	24.7
Readlyn city	808	824	2.0	851	97.4	0.0	0.0	0.7	1.9	26.1	59.2	14.9	335	91.0	45.1	18.5
Reasnor city	152	153	0.7	138	97.8	0.0	0.0	2.2	0.0	13.1	60.7	26.1	61	88.5	41.0	9.8
Redding city	82	81	-1.2	90	100.0	0.0	0.0	0.0	0.0	27.7	47.7	24.4	36	80.6	63.9	0.0
Redfield city	835	885	6.0	844	89.5	1.2	0.0	8.6	0.7	19.2	61.2	19.7	359	73.8	59.1	8.1
Red Oak city	5,742	5,573	-2.9	5,644	92.0	0.0	0.0	3.1	4.9	23.8	55.7	20.5	2,480	64.1	50.7	14.5
Reinbeck city	1,671	1,639	-1.9	1,824	95.0	0.4	0.4	1.3	2.9	22.3	57.3	20.5	806	74.2	45.7	20.6
Rembrandt city	204	206	1.0	163	85.3	3.7	0.0	0.0	11.0	24.0	59.5	16.6	80	68.8	57.5	8.8
Remsen city	1,663	1,643	-1.2	1,869	97.7	0.0	0.0	1.7	0.6	32.0	46.6	21.6	694	79.7	51.7	14.0
Renwick city	242	238	-1.7	317	92.7	0.0	0.3	1.9	5.0	30.3	51.8	18.0	131	75.6	55.0	8.4
Rhodes city	305	309	1.3	310	95.2	0.6	0.0	1.9	2.3	22.0	60.4	17.7	134	76.1	53.0	11.9
Riceville city	785	802	2.2	805	97.6	0.0	0.0	1.5	0.9	18.9	50.6	30.3	377	84.1	57.0	14.1
Richland city	584	567	-2.9	665	100.0	0.0	0.0	0.0	0.0	26.4	55.5	18.2	255	80.4	42.4	18.8
Rickardsville city	180	179	-0.6	171	100.0	0.0	0.0	0.0	0.0	20.4	54.3	25.1	71	100.0	50.7	16.9
Ricketts city	145	145	0.0	146	84.9	0.0	0.0	7.5	7.5	29.4	54.8	15.8	59	89.8	50.8	1.7
Ridgeway city	315	310	-1.6	322	100.0	0.0	0.0	0.0	0.0	23.0	63.1	14.0	162	64.2	55.6	14.8
Rinard city	52	52	0.0	60	96.7	0.0	0.0	3.3	0.0	15.0	66.7	18.3	30	93.3	63.3	13.3
Ringsted city	422	406	-3.8	413	98.1	0.0	0.0	1.9	0.0	24.9	54.0	21.1	188	84.6	41.0	11.2
Rippey city	292	289	-1.0	206	95.1	0.5	0.0	0.0	4.4	21.8	62.7	15.5	88	80.7	67.0	5.7
Riverdale city	405	415	2.5	531	91.5	0.4	0.0	3.6	4.5	19.2	61.1	19.6	207	89.9	25.6	36.7
Riverside city	993	1,042	4.9	1,034	97.5	0.3	0.0	1.2	1.1	25.7	62.0	12.3	468	65.2	40.6	20.5
River Sioux CDP	59	NA	NA	138	100.0	0.0	0.0	0.0	0.0	33.3	26.8	39.9	50	90.0	64.0	0.0
Riverton city	304	288	-5.3	348	96.6	0.0	0.0	0.9	2.6	27.0	59.8	13.2	139	89.9	66.9	0.7
Robins city	3,142	3,389	7.9	3,282	90.2	0.4	5.5	1.6	2.2	27.2	61.6	11.2	1,130	96.7	15.6	59.7
Rochester CDP	133	NA	NA	40	100.0	0.0	0.0	0.0	0.0	0.0	100.0	0.0	20	100.0	0.0	0.0
Rock Falls city	155	153	-1.3	159	100.0	0.0	0.0	0.0	0.0	20.0	57.7	22.0	70	92.9	45.7	12.9
Rockford city	860	851	-1.0	734	98.5	0.7	0.0	0.4	0.4	22.7	57.6	19.8	321	77.3	46.4	15.6
Rock Rapids city	2,549	2,580	1.2	2,579	98.3	0.0	0.2	0.3	1.2	24.2	55.5	20.1	1,081	74.7	47.5	23.7

1 May be of any race.

Table A. All Places — **Population and Housing**

STATE City, town, township, borough, or CDP (county if applicable)	Population: 2010 census total population	Population: 2014 estimated population	Population: Percent change 2010–2014	Population: ACS total population estimate 2010–2014	Race and Hispanic or Latino origin (percent), 2010–2014: White alone, not Hispanic or Latino	Black alone, not Hispanic or Latino	Asian alone, not Hispanic or Latino	All other races or 2 or more races, not Hispanic or Latino	Hispanic or Latino[1]	Age (percent), 2010–2014: Under 18 years old	Age 18 to 64 years old	Age 65 years and older	Households, 2010–2014: Total occupied housing units	Percent owner occupied	Householders by level of education (percent): High school diploma or less	Bachelor's degree or more
	1	2	3	4	5	6	7	8	9	10	11	12	13	14	15	16
IOWA—Con.																
Rock Valley city	3,357	3,626	8.0	3,495	94.5	1.2	0.0	0.2	4.1	29.1	55.6	15.2	1,286	79.8	50.0	17.3
Rockwell city	1,039	1,023	-1.5	1,028	92.8	1.0	0.0	0.2	6.0	20.0	53.3	26.8	471	84.1	46.3	12.1
Rockwell City city	2,220	2,149	-3.2	2,074	89.9	4.1	0.6	3.0	2.5	19.3	60.3	20.2	796	72.7	44.0	15.8
Rodman city	45	43	-4.4	49	100.0	0.0	0.0	0.0	0.0	12.3	59.2	28.6	30	86.7	36.7	0.0
Rodney city	60	58	-3.3	73	93.2	0.0	0.0	6.8	0.0	38.3	42.5	19.2	34	85.3	85.3	0.0
Roland city	1,284	1,295	0.9	1,463	96.7	0.3	0.1	1.4	1.4	36.0	55.6	8.4	523	84.3	22.2	41.9
Rolfe city	584	568	-2.7	560	88.9	0.0	0.0	0.4	10.7	19.5	58.7	22.0	239	71.5	52.3	18.4
Rome city	117	118	0.9	153	90.2	9.8	0.0	0.0	0.0	28.1	68.7	3.3	58	41.4	63.8	13.8
Rose Hill city	168	168	0.0	132	99.2	0.0	0.0	0.8	0.0	19.8	69.8	10.6	62	90.3	54.8	4.8
Roseville CDP	49	NA	NA	0	0.0	0.0	0.0	0.0	0.0	0.0	0.0	0.0	0	0.0	0.0	0.0
Rossie city	70	71	1.4	85	100.0	0.0	0.0	0.0	0.0	24.7	71.9	3.5	37	64.9	54.1	10.8
Rowan city	158	154	-2.5	186	98.9	0.0	0.0	0.0	1.1	23.6	48.8	27.4	74	63.5	63.5	9.5
Rowley city	264	267	1.1	246	92.3	7.7	0.0	0.0	0.0	24.8	61.8	13.4	98	86.7	55.1	15.3
Royal city	446	430	-3.6	540	96.3	1.1	0.0	2.6	0.0	28.0	64.1	8.0	218	62.8	38.1	12.8
Rudd city	369	364	-1.4	368	93.8	1.6	0.0	1.4	3.3	14.7	61.1	24.2	182	78.0	47.3	12.6
Runnells city	507	513	1.2	585	96.6	0.7	0.2	0.9	1.7	30.1	60.9	9.1	208	74.0	54.8	5.8
Russell city	554	538	-2.9	522	97.7	0.0	0.0	2.3	0.0	28.8	47.2	23.9	221	80.5	57.0	8.6
Ruthven city	737	701	-4.9	651	96.3	0.0	1.2	2.2	0.3	23.3	55.2	21.4	285	64.9	33.7	18.9
Rutland city	126	127	0.8	109	100.0	0.0	0.0	0.0	0.0	30.3	52.4	17.4	51	74.5	76.5	5.9
Ryan city	361	358	-0.8	354	98.9	0.0	0.0	0.8	0.3	17.2	67.4	15.3	162	77.8	51.9	9.9
Sabula city	576	556	-3.5	516	96.7	0.0	0.0	3.3	0.0	15.8	57.7	26.6	271	69.0	66.4	8.1
Sac City city	2,222	2,143	-3.6	2,175	94.7	1.7	0.9	1.4	1.3	17.4	57.2	25.5	1,031	75.8	44.4	24.3
Sageville city	104	103	-1.0	75	98.7	0.0	0.0	1.3	0.0	9.3	74.8	16.0	39	84.6	61.5	12.8
St. Ansgar city	1,107	1,146	3.5	1,062	97.2	0.0	0.9	0.0	1.9	21.5	50.5	28.1	483	79.7	42.2	24.4
St. Anthony city	102	103	1.0	125	92.0	2.4	0.0	5.6	0.0	39.2	54.4	6.4	36	86.1	66.7	2.8
St. Benedict CDP	39	NA	NA	29	100.0	0.0	0.0	0.0	0.0	24.1	75.7	0.0	13	100.0	23.1	23.1
St. Charles city	649	629	-3.1	662	96.8	0.3	1.1	0.0	1.8	21.9	63.0	15.1	261	73.9	43.3	21.1
St. Donatus city	135	132	-2.2	105	95.2	0.0	0.0	4.8	0.0	22.9	61.0	16.2	49	79.6	40.8	4.1
St. Joseph CDP	61	NA	NA	43	100.0	0.0	0.0	0.0	0.0	72.1	27.9	0.0	6	50.0	50.0	0.0
St. Lucas city	143	139	-2.8	143	100.0	0.0	0.0	0.0	0.0	11.9	52.5	35.7	78	89.7	38.5	12.8
St. Marys city	127	127	0.0	187	91.4	0.0	0.0	0.0	8.6	17.7	44.0	38.5	79	82.3	44.3	31.6
St. Olaf city	108	107	-0.9	122	98.4	0.0	1.6	0.0	0.0	22.9	64.0	13.1	54	85.2	64.8	11.1
St. Paul city	129	130	0.8	83	100.0	0.0	0.0	0.0	0.0	18.0	66.2	15.7	41	78.0	34.1	17.1
Salem city	383	378	-1.3	413	94.7	0.0	2.4	2.9	0.0	22.3	61.1	16.7	171	73.7	55.6	8.2
Salix city	363	372	2.5	356	97.2	0.0	0.3	1.1	1.4	26.4	61.3	12.4	146	78.1	38.4	11.6
Sanborn city	1,404	1,372	-2.3	1,216	98.1	0.0	0.0	0.4	1.5	22.1	46.9	31.0	544	78.3	50.0	17.8
Sandyville city	51	51	0.0	71	78.9	0.0	0.0	4.2	16.9	28.1	67.7	4.2	24	79.2	58.3	33.3
Saylorville CDP	3,301	NA	NA	2,944	100.0	0.0	0.0	0.0	0.0	21.0	60.7	18.1	1,211	87.3	37.7	36.4
Scarville city	72	71	-1.4	99	84.8	5.1	0.0	3.0	7.1	35.4	51.6	13.1	44	86.4	38.6	20.5
Schaller city	772	746	-3.4	803	88.2	0.0	0.0	0.2	11.6	27.8	54.5	17.7	314	88.2	52.2	16.6
Schleswig city	882	888	0.7	859	83.7	0.0	0.0	7.2	9.1	19.7	56.6	23.9	395	79.0	53.4	11.6
Scranton city	557	543	-2.5	567	90.7	0.0	0.0	0.2	9.2	26.0	55.6	18.5	241	77.2	52.7	11.2
Searsboro city	148	146	-1.4	165	93.9	0.0	0.0	6.1	0.0	23.0	70.9	6.1	68	61.8	52.9	5.9
Sergeant Bluff city	4,227	4,417	4.5	4,300	93.0	0.0	3.0	1.8	2.1	36.2	55.4	8.4	1,429	79.6	26.7	39.0
Sexton CDP	37	NA	NA	46	100.0	0.0	0.0	0.0	0.0	47.9	34.8	17.4	15	100.0	53.3	46.7
Seymour city	701	700	-0.1	871	98.6	0.5	0.0	0.9	0.0	27.0	50.5	22.5	322	76.1	57.5	12.7
Shambaugh city	191	186	-2.6	200	91.5	0.0	0.0	0.5	8.0	15.5	70.0	14.5	85	90.6	41.2	8.2
Shannon City city	71	71	0.0	62	100.0	0.0	0.0	0.0	0.0	32.3	54.9	12.9	25	76.0	80.0	4.0
Sharpsburg city	89	87	-2.2	113	95.6	0.0	0.0	4.4	0.0	13.3	70.8	15.9	57	45.6	66.7	3.5
Sheffield city	1,172	1,162	-0.9	1,057	98.6	0.0	0.4	1.0	0.0	24.4	50.9	24.5	427	85.0	41.0	15.9
Shelby city	641	620	-3.3	617	96.6	0.0	0.8	2.3	0.3	17.4	62.8	19.9	270	68.1	39.3	17.0
Sheldahl city	319	319	0.0	232	97.8	1.3	0.0	0.9	0.0	22.8	61.3	15.9	97	92.8	52.6	16.5
Sheldon city	5,191	5,106	-1.6	5,047	91.8	0.6	0.9	1.5	5.1	17.3	60.5	22.3	2,348	60.7	45.7	23.8
Shell Rock city	1,296	1,328	2.5	1,242	98.6	0.0	0.0	1.0	0.3	23.4	54.8	21.8	531	74.2	45.2	16.8
Shellsburg city	983	964	-1.9	1,013	100.0	0.0	0.0	0.0	0.0	26.3	57.5	16.1	396	79.5	52.0	7.6
Shenandoah city	5,150	5,032	-2.3	5,079	89.2	0.0	2.3	2.6	6.0	22.4	55.6	22.1	2,180	68.9	43.7	18.5
Sherrill city	175	176	0.6	191	100.0	0.0	0.0	0.0	0.0	21.0	62.9	16.2	79	82.3	69.6	6.3
Shueyville city	577	674	16.8	506	89.3	0.0	8.9	1.8	0.0	29.7	61.5	8.9	181	92.8	34.8	39.8
Sibley city	2,798	2,692	-3.8	2,712	88.5	0.1	0.8	1.3	9.3	22.8	57.5	19.8	1,109	68.3	52.2	15.0
Sidney city	1,138	1,062	-6.7	1,010	98.6	0.3	0.0	0.5	0.6	21.8	55.2	22.8	404	71.5	35.9	23.8
Sigourney city	2,059	2,017	-2.0	2,273	96.2	0.4	0.9	0.2	2.3	21.9	54.3	23.7	978	77.2	45.4	20.3
Silver City city	245	242	-1.2	154	97.4	0.0	0.0	0.0	2.6	14.8	58.2	26.6	66	90.9	43.9	21.2
Sioux Center city	7,049	7,389	4.8	7,218	84.0	0.4	1.1	0.8	13.7	24.5	61.0	14.6	2,227	74.1	37.4	37.9
Sioux City city	82,684	82,517	-0.2	82,719	72.1	3.2	2.8	4.2	17.6	25.9	61.0	13.0	31,419	64.2	46.6	21.1
Sioux Rapids city	775	784	1.2	678	96.3	1.2	0.0	0.0	2.5	28.2	51.9	19.9	297	71.7	40.4	14.8
Slater city	1,489	1,506	1.1	1,587	95.8	0.0	0.0	0.9	3.3	32.7	57.1	10.1	564	81.9	22.5	39.2
Sloan city	973	975	0.2	1,031	92.0	0.0	0.0	6.6	1.4	22.2	61.4	16.5	403	72.2	39.0	21.8
Smithland city	224	224	0.0	164	100.0	0.0	0.0	0.0	0.0	11.0	61.0	28.0	78	71.8	59.0	3.8
Soldier city	174	169	-2.9	165	96.4	0.0	0.0	1.8	1.8	24.3	47.2	28.5	75	80.0	53.3	20.0
Solon city	2,040	2,396	17.5	2,460	95.0	0.3	0.2	2.2	2.3	33.1	55.7	11.1	852	75.4	22.1	33.7
Somers city	113	110	-2.7	111	91.0	0.0	0.9	0.0	8.1	13.5	59.4	27.0	58	86.2	34.5	6.9
South Amana CDP	159	NA	NA	160	100.0	0.0	0.0	0.0	0.0	22.5	59.6	18.1	67	91.0	29.9	0.0
South English city	212	208	-1.9	237	90.7	0.0	0.0	5.9	3.4	30.8	60.3	8.9	90	95.6	47.8	8.9
Spencer city	11,241	11,206	-0.3	11,177	94.1	0.0	0.0	1.6	4.2	21.7	57.8	20.5	5,015	70.1	44.1	19.3
Spillville city	367	353	-3.8	356	99.7	0.0	0.0	0.0	0.3	24.4	55.0	20.5	165	70.3	52.7	17.6
Spirit Lake city	4,871	4,945	1.5	4,916	96.3	0.0	0.3	1.8	1.5	20.0	60.1	19.9	2,354	64.4	32.0	26.6
Spragueville city	81	81	0.0	102	100.0	0.0	0.0	0.0	0.0	25.5	60.9	13.7	48	85.4	50.0	6.3
Springbrook city	144	141	-2.1	166	98.2	0.6	0.0	1.2	0.0	14.4	71.0	14.5	71	100.0	66.2	4.2
Spring Hill city	63	63	0.0	21	100.0	0.0	0.0	0.0	0.0	0.0	61.9	38.1	14	92.9	71.4	14.3
Springville city	1,074	1,123	4.6	1,021	98.7	0.0	0.0	1.3	0.0	20.2	61.3	18.6	439	75.2	38.0	19.4
Stacyville city	490	477	-2.7	553	98.6	0.0	0.0	0.7	0.7	19.4	54.2	26.4	258	86.8	70.9	5.4
Stanhope city	422	409	-3.1	421	94.8	0.0	0.5	3.3	1.4	15.2	67.5	17.3	176	76.7	48.3	15.9
Stanley city	125	125	0.0	97	94.8	0.0	0.0	3.1	2.1	22.7	60.9	16.5	42	97.6	69.0	7.1
Stanton city	689	656	-4.8	708	99.2	0.0	0.4	0.0	0.4	20.5	57.3	22.2	291	77.3	39.5	15.8
Stanwood city	684	667	-2.5	634	97.0	0.0	0.5	0.3	2.2	24.0	58.6	17.5	272	66.2	45.2	10.7
State Center city	1,468	1,471	0.2	1,475	92.9	0.0	0.4	0.9	5.8	28.6	56.9	14.7	540	74.1	33.9	24.3
Steamboat Rock city	310	308	-0.6	254	99.6	0.0	0.0	0.0	0.4	17.3	61.5	21.3	117	73.5	53.0	12.0
Stockport city	296	296	0.0	287	97.2	0.0	0.0	2.1	0.7	25.0	55.0	19.9	112	80.4	35.7	12.5
Stockton city	197	197	0.0	217	91.7	0.0	0.0	8.3	0.0	36.4	53.9	9.7	71	66.2	47.9	11.3
Stone City CDP	192	NA	NA	231	100.0	0.0	0.0	0.0	0.0	21.6	56.4	22.1	79	88.6	36.7	16.5
Storm Lake city	10,641	10,895	2.4	10,743	42.5	3.8	11.1	3.5	39.0	25.9	61.1	12.9	3,665	60.5	54.4	17.4

1 May be of any race.

Table A. All Places — **Population and Housing**

STATE City, town, township, borough, or CDP (county if applicable)	2010 census total population	2014 estimated population	Percent change 2010–2014	ACS total population estimate 2010–2014	White alone, not Hispanic or Latino	Black alone, not Hispanic or Latino	Asian alone, not Hispanic or Latino	All other races or 2 or more races, not Hispanic or Latino	Hispanic or Latino[1]	Under 18 years old	Age 18 to 64 years old	Age 65 years and older	Total occupied housing units	Percent owner occupied	High school diploma or less	Bachelor's degree or more
	1	2	3	4	5	6	7	8	9	10	11	12	13	14	15	16
IOWA—Con.																
Story City city	3,431	3,431	0.0	3,430	93.3	0.6	2.2	1.9	1.9	21.7	53.6	24.5	1,495	64.3	36.1	29.0
Stout city	224	222	-0.9	237	100.0	0.0	0.0	0.0	0.0	24.5	66.0	9.7	90	91.1	46.7	3.3
Stratford city	743	720	-3.1	671	99.0	0.0	0.3	0.7	0.0	20.0	58.4	21.8	272	76.8	61.0	8.5
Strawberry Point city	1,279	1,243	-2.8	1,371	97.8	0.1	0.0	1.1	0.9	23.8	50.6	25.6	578	72.0	52.4	15.9
Struble city	78	77	-1.3	62	100.0	0.0	0.0	0.0	0.0	19.3	66.2	14.5	29	72.4	51.7	13.8
Stuart city	1,648	1,615	-2.0	1,699	97.9	0.8	0.0	0.4	0.9	26.5	54.9	18.7	687	74.4	47.2	15.0
Sully city	821	823	0.2	796	98.7	0.5	0.0	0.6	0.1	26.8	54.1	19.2	322	80.4	61.5	18.0
Sumner city	2,028	2,021	-0.3	2,081	97.0	0.2	1.3	1.2	0.2	24.5	52.5	23.1	901	80.2	47.2	16.5
Sun Valley Lake CDP	161	NA	NA	181	100.0	0.0	0.0	0.0	0.0	0.0	50.8	49.2	97	100.0	29.9	46.4
Superior city	130	129	-0.8	155	98.1	0.0	0.0	1.9	0.0	32.9	54.8	12.3	55	87.3	67.3	0.0
Sutherland city	649	625	-3.7	591	99.3	0.0	0.5	0.2	0.0	17.4	54.7	27.9	286	78.0	51.0	9.8
Swaledale city	165	161	-2.4	174	90.8	0.0	0.0	2.3	6.9	27.5	50.9	21.3	74	67.6	79.7	0.0
Swan city	72	72	0.0	61	91.8	0.0	0.0	6.6	1.6	27.9	42.7	29.5	24	66.7	54.2	4.2
Swea City city	536	526	-1.9	592	93.1	0.0	0.5	1.0	5.4	22.5	58.6	18.9	260	79.6	42.7	16.2
Swisher city	879	932	6.0	805	98.5	0.0	0.2	1.2	0.0	26.8	60.3	13.0	312	90.7	26.3	38.1
Tabor city	1,040	985	-5.3	1,212	95.1	0.0	0.0	1.6	3.3	29.9	54.5	15.7	435	66.7	37.7	16.8
Tama city	2,877	2,830	-1.6	2,835	69.4	0.5	0.8	7.4	21.9	31.1	56.1	12.6	1,032	71.0	57.6	19.1
Templeton city	351	345	-1.7	370	99.5	0.5	0.0	0.0	0.0	24.1	53.2	22.7	154	87.0	49.4	15.6
Tennant city	68	66	-2.9	40	100.0	0.0	0.0	0.0	0.0	10.0	60.0	30.0	21	85.7	57.1	4.8
Terril city	367	363	-1.1	379	98.4	0.5	0.0	0.8	0.3	22.4	58.1	19.5	183	66.7	42.1	11.5
Thayer city	59	59	0.0	70	100.0	0.0	0.0	0.0	0.0	24.3	67.2	8.6	29	100.0	44.8	6.9
Thompson city	502	488	-2.8	568	92.8	0.0	1.6	0.5	5.1	23.8	56.1	20.1	263	79.1	63.9	12.2
Thor city	186	183	-1.6	189	97.9	0.0	0.0	2.1	0.0	26.5	61.9	11.6	81	82.7	63.0	8.6
Thornburg city	67	61	-9.0	83	100.0	0.0	0.0	0.0	0.0	22.8	73.3	3.6	33	100.0	63.6	18.2
Thornton city	422	410	-2.8	422	98.3	0.2	0.2	0.2	0.9	16.8	65.0	18.2	189	70.9	39.7	15.9
Thurman city	229	217	-5.2	197	97.5	0.0	0.0	0.0	2.5	27.5	58.3	14.2	83	79.5	71.1	12.0
Tiffin city	1,947	2,444	25.5	1,921	84.1	1.1	0.8	1.1	12.9	26.1	66.0	7.9	832	72.5	20.9	38.8
Tingley city	184	181	-1.6	198	100.0	0.0	0.0	0.0	0.0	23.2	49.1	27.8	85	81.2	49.4	10.6
Tipton city	3,221	3,202	-0.6	3,207	97.5	0.1	1.9	0.1	0.4	21.9	56.8	21.3	1,394	75.5	48.8	18.9
Titonka city	479	459	-4.2	394	93.1	0.0	0.0	1.0	5.8	14.2	52.0	33.8	201	85.1	40.8	19.9
Toeterville CDP	48	NA	NA	36	100.0	0.0	0.0	0.0	0.0	13.9	38.9	47.2	27	100.0	29.6	37.0
Toledo city	2,341	2,250	-3.9	2,208	75.5	1.7	0.4	1.9	20.6	23.8	52.3	23.9	847	69.2	51.6	11.9
Toronto city	124	121	-2.4	164	95.7	0.0	0.0	1.2	3.0	21.9	68.8	9.1	54	88.9	61.1	0.0
Traer city	1,703	1,665	-2.2	1,814	96.6	0.0	0.7	1.7	1.0	24.9	50.9	24.1	724	66.6	47.7	15.6
Treynor city	919	940	2.3	993	99.0	0.0	0.0	0.7	0.3	27.1	54.5	18.0	387	79.3	29.5	35.4
Tripoli city	1,313	1,332	1.4	1,557	93.7	0.0	0.0	5.0	1.3	29.0	53.7	17.3	516	76.9	53.3	12.8
Truesdale city	81	82	1.2	148	85.8	0.0	0.0	0.0	14.2	14.9	75.7	9.5	61	78.7	59.0	4.9
Truro city	486	477	-1.9	544	88.6	2.2	0.6	7.0	1.7	33.7	55.9	10.5	178	61.2	53.4	9.0
Turin city	68	66	-2.9	100	96.0	0.0	0.0	4.0	0.0	30.0	46.0	24.0	41	78.0	70.7	0.0
Twin Lakes CDP	334	NA	NA	288	100.0	0.0	0.0	0.0	0.0	0.0	73.9	26.0	164	100.0	12.8	50.0
Udell city	47	47	0.0	34	100.0	0.0	0.0	0.0	0.0	11.7	23.5	64.7	17	82.4	47.1	11.8
Underwood city	941	938	-0.3	925	98.7	0.0	0.0	0.0	1.3	37.3	53.5	9.2	314	77.4	37.9	28.3
Union city	397	387	-2.5	522	87.2	0.0	0.8	8.2	3.8	28.7	46.6	24.7	192	79.2	59.9	15.6
Unionville city	102	101	-1.0	73	100.0	0.0	0.0	0.0	0.0	10.9	69.8	19.2	39	74.4	64.1	5.1
University Heights city	1,051	1,125	7.0	1,214	95.4	0.7	1.2	0.6	2.2	16.0	73.4	10.5	534	59.6	5.4	75.8
University Park city	487	484	-0.6	555	84.5	5.4	0.0	6.5	3.6	29.3	62.6	7.9	198	54.5	36.4	19.7
Urbana city	1,458	1,452	-0.4	1,431	97.6	1.6	0.1	0.6	0.0	25.3	66.5	8.2	544	83.5	37.9	28.7
Urbandale city	39,457	43,150	9.4	41,157	89.1	3.0	2.8	2.3	2.8	25.8	61.3	12.9	16,289	81.6	20.3	50.8
Ute city	374	355	-5.1	433	99.8	0.0	0.2	0.0	0.0	27.2	50.4	22.4	185	76.8	73.0	2.2
Vail city	438	430	-1.8	385	79.5	0.0	1.0	0.5	19.0	23.9	60.8	15.3	161	82.0	71.4	13.0
Valeria city	57	57	0.0	65	100.0	0.0	0.0	0.0	0.0	35.4	54.0	10.8	22	100.0	31.8	45.5
Van Horne city	685	667	-2.6	742	89.5	0.0	0.1	4.4	5.9	25.4	62.6	12.0	300	82.3	42.7	13.7
Van Meter city	1,020	1,133	11.1	1,463	97.3	0.0	0.3	1.4	1.0	32.9	58.0	9.1	478	90.2	27.6	39.1
Van Wert city	225	215	-4.4	197	76.6	0.0	13.2	5.6	4.6	24.8	61.5	13.7	81	84.0	59.3	7.4
Varina city	71	70	-1.4	108	61.1	0.0	0.0	0.0	38.9	48.2	49.1	2.8	31	93.5	77.4	12.9
Ventura city	717	721	0.6	667	99.0	0.0	0.4	0.0	0.6	11.6	60.3	27.7	348	78.7	29.0	32.8
Victor city	893	889	-0.4	996	98.5	0.1	0.0	0.2	1.2	25.3	57.4	17.1	449	71.5	47.2	13.6
Villisca city	1,252	1,211	-3.3	1,282	96.8	0.0	0.0	0.6	2.6	24.5	56.1	19.2	565	68.5	49.2	11.2
Vincent city	174	168	-3.4	219	72.1	0.0	0.0	0.0	27.9	32.5	55.8	11.9	71	78.9	52.1	16.9
Vining city	50	49	-2.0	78	97.4	0.0	0.0	2.6	0.0	20.6	62.7	16.7	33	93.9	69.7	12.1
Vinton city	5,257	5,159	-1.9	5,211	97.6	1.0	0.2	1.2	0.0	24.5	55.9	19.6	2,113	74.6	35.6	26.0
Volga city	208	206	-1.0	216	100.0	0.0	0.0	0.0	0.0	20.4	61.1	18.5	102	67.6	55.9	15.7
Wadena city	262	254	-3.1	354	89.8	0.0	0.3	0.0	7.9	36.6	51.5	11.9	118	73.7	44.9	14.4
Wahpeton city	341	343	0.6	345	96.2	0.6	1.2	0.6	1.4	7.0	47.6	45.5	184	85.3	27.7	41.3
Walcott city	1,619	1,630	0.7	1,702	95.5	0.6	0.0	0.5	3.4	24.9	61.0	14.1	694	80.8	48.1	19.3
Walford city	1,458	1,459	0.1	1,607	97.6	0.3	0.2	0.2	1.6	35.4	60.7	3.9	495	92.5	24.0	44.6
Walker city	791	792	0.1	712	99.2	0.8	0.0	0.0	0.0	26.3	61.6	12.2	276	93.5	46.4	11.2
Wallingford city	197	193	-2.0	165	92.1	1.2	0.0	1.2	5.5	24.9	64.3	10.9	67	85.1	55.2	6.0
Wall Lake city	819	803	-2.0	698	98.4	1.6	0.0	0.0	0.0	21.3	50.2	28.4	293	76.8	45.1	18.1
Walnut city	785	773	-1.5	694	95.8	0.0	0.4	2.0	1.7	16.9	55.8	27.4	334	69.8	65.0	11.7
Wapello city	2,067	2,037	-1.5	1,903	84.8	0.3	0.3	2.6	12.1	24.9	52.0	23.1	748	71.8	53.3	15.2
Washburn CDP	876	NA	NA	957	91.3	0.0	0.0	0.0	8.7	21.4	61.3	17.3	406	95.8	43.3	21.7
Washington city	7,270	7,349	1.1	7,315	86.2	1.9	0.5	1.7	9.7	23.8	54.1	21.9	3,161	66.2	42.5	21.9
Washta city	248	242	-2.4	271	97.0	0.0	0.7	0.0	2.2	32.8	48.0	19.2	112	79.5	51.8	9.8
Waterloo city	68,406	68,364	-0.1	68,392	74.4	15.6	1.3	2.8	5.9	23.8	61.5	14.8	28,834	64.2	46.1	21.5
Waterville city	144	141	-2.1	138	97.8	0.0	0.0	0.0	2.2	18.8	68.8	12.3	65	81.5	55.4	4.6
Watkins CDP	118	NA	NA	123	100.0	0.0	0.0	0.0	0.0	10.6	59.3	30.1	39	100.0	100.0	0.0
Waucoma city	259	259	0.0	286	89.2	1.4	0.3	7.0	2.1	24.1	56.8	18.9	124	61.3	52.4	7.3
Waukee city	13,800	17,705	28.3	15,944	90.8	0.0	2.1	2.5	4.6	31.1	60.8	8.2	5,748	82.5	18.7	53.5
Waukon city	3,910	3,795	-2.9	3,846	95.9	0.0	0.0	3.1	1.0	20.8	56.2	23.1	1,714	70.1	51.8	15.1
Waverly city	9,876	10,106	2.3	9,998	96.6	2.5	0.4	0.8	1.8	19.2	63.6	17.3	3,533	74.9	30.3	35.4
Wayland city	966	977	1.1	1,062	88.5	7.3	0.0	2.3	1.9	23.5	51.4	25.0	417	68.1	49.6	19.2
Webb city	141	139	-1.4	145	100.0	0.0	0.0	0.0	0.0	24.9	48.1	26.9	65	90.8	58.5	12.3
Webster city	88	73	-17.0	115	91.3	0.0	0.0	1.7	7.0	26.1	62.7	11.3	44	84.1	45.5	6.8
Webster City city	8,070	7,788	-3.5	7,905	90.2	0.4	3.4	0.6	5.4	22.3	55.8	21.9	3,411	64.8	40.4	15.3
Weldon city	125	120	-4.0	144	96.5	0.0	2.1	1.4	0.0	20.9	57.7	21.5	60	90.0	71.7	5.0
Wellman city	1,411	1,426	1.1	1,537	91.4	0.8	0.5	2.4	4.9	25.9	55.2	18.9	600	81.3	43.3	19.5
Wellsburg city	707	696	-1.6	971	98.6	0.0	0.5	0.9	0.0	25.9	54.6	19.5	408	87.0	43.6	13.5
Welton city	165	161	-2.4	157	98.7	0.0	0.0	1.3	0.0	28.7	54.9	16.6	58	79.3	60.3	6.9
Wesley city	390	382	-2.1	326	97.5	0.0	0.0	0.0	2.5	19.3	62.6	18.1	147	80.3	59.2	6.1
West Amana CDP	135	NA	NA	222	100.0	0.0	0.0	0.0	0.0	8.6	91.5	0.0	96	25.0	0.0	53.1

1 May be of any race.

Table A. All Places — **Population and Housing**

STATE City, town, township, borough, or CDP (county if applicable)	Population: 2010 census total population	Population: 2014 estimated population	Population: Percent change 2010–2014	Population: ACS total population estimate 2010–2014	Race and Hispanic or Latino origin (percent), 2010–2014: White alone, not Hispanic or Latino	Black alone, not Hispanic or Latino	Asian alone, not Hispanic or Latino	All other races or 2 or more races, not Hispanic or Latino	Hispanic or Latino[1]	Age (percent), 2010–2014: Under 18 years old	Age 18 to 64 years old	Age 65 years and older	Households, 2010–2014: Total occupied housing units	Percent owner occupied	Householders by level of education (percent): High school diploma or less	Bachelor's degree or more
	1	2	3	4	5	6	7	8	9	10	11	12	13	14	15	16
IOWA—Con.																
West Bend city	785	762	-2.9	922	94.7	0.1	0.1	0.5	4.6	22.6	51.6	25.9	417	71.7	39.8	11.8
West Branch city	2,322	2,349	1.2	2,684	94.4	0.0	0.4	1.4	3.8	28.8	60.2	11.0	1,047	78.0	28.7	32.2
West Burlington city	3,012	3,051	1.3	3,026	91.6	3.3	0.5	2.0	2.6	19.2	60.3	20.4	1,368	70.5	47.3	10.5
West Chester city	146	148	1.4	115	96.5	2.6	0.0	0.0	0.9	11.3	56.7	32.2	56	96.4	67.9	3.6
West Des Moines city	56,700	63,325	11.7	59,815	82.3	3.7	6.5	1.6	5.9	23.2	65.7	11.0	25,261	60.3	17.7	54.7
Westfield city	132	130	-1.5	175	74.9	0.0	0.0	4.0	21.1	34.9	51.9	13.1	68	67.6	60.3	17.6
Westgate city	211	205	-2.8	273	100.0	0.0	0.0	0.0	0.0	27.8	63.1	9.2	103	77.7	58.3	5.8
West Liberty city	3,753	3,733	-0.5	3,750	43.2	0.3	2.7	2.2	51.6	29.1	62.0	8.9	1,119	63.8	55.0	13.2
West Okoboji city	289	293	1.4	332	99.1	0.3	0.0	0.0	0.6	10.2	53.5	36.1	171	74.9	24.0	36.8
Weston CDP	92	NA	NA	237	100.0	0.0	0.0	0.0	0.0	50.2	38.4	11.4	58	100.0	48.3	51.7
Westphalia city	127	126	-0.8	122	100.0	0.0	0.0	0.0	0.0	22.2	60.6	17.2	54	70.4	35.2	9.3
West Point city	966	960	-0.6	1,100	95.9	0.0	0.0	0.0	4.1	21.0	60.4	18.6	491	81.5	50.1	17.7
Westside city	299	302	1.0	358	99.2	0.0	0.0	0.8	0.0	22.1	57.8	20.1	155	94.8	41.9	14.8
West Union city	2,486	2,433	-2.1	2,642	96.9	0.9	0.5	1.6	0.2	23.0	56.9	20.2	1,140	70.4	42.7	25.4
Westwood city	112	113	0.9	121	98.3	0.0	0.0	1.7	0.0	28.0	44.5	27.3	42	97.6	11.9	57.1
What Cheer city	646	627	-2.9	703	98.7	0.0	0.0	0.4	0.9	29.7	54.1	16.2	281	72.2	66.2	7.8
Wheatland city	764	740	-3.1	670	98.5	0.0	0.0	1.2	0.3	24.8	50.2	25.1	246	78.5	39.8	13.4
Whiting city	762	746	-2.1	878	96.8	0.5	0.0	0.5	2.3	24.4	55.6	20.2	340	71.2	47.6	22.4
Whittemore city	504	492	-2.4	459	98.9	0.0	0.0	0.9	0.2	19.8	60.1	20.3	219	82.2	43.4	13.7
Whitten city	149	148	-0.7	128	97.7	0.0	0.0	2.3	0.0	30.4	40.7	28.9	52	92.3	65.4	0.0
Willey city	88	101	14.8	71	100.0	0.0	0.0	0.0	0.0	22.6	66.1	11.3	28	100.0	64.3	7.1
Williams city	344	333	-3.2	517	86.3	2.3	0.4	10.6	0.4	34.2	53.7	12.0	197	66.5	51.8	14.2
Williamsburg city	3,068	3,175	3.5	3,105	97.9	0.0	0.0	0.5	1.6	26.5	56.0	17.5	1,271	67.2	33.8	26.8
Williamson city	152	150	-1.3	123	96.7	0.0	0.0	3.3	0.0	23.6	61.9	14.6	58	77.6	62.1	3.4
Wilton city	2,788	2,795	0.3	2,783	97.7	0.1	0.3	0.5	1.3	22.3	64.5	13.2	1,213	69.9	41.9	22.8
Windsor Heights city	4,860	4,875	0.3	4,877	87.7	1.5	3.3	3.5	3.8	23.2	57.9	18.9	2,062	71.5	19.7	44.3
Winfield city	1,134	1,149	1.3	951	93.8	0.0	0.0	1.5	4.7	25.9	54.8	19.6	353	71.4	34.8	24.9
Winterset city	5,190	5,141	-0.9	5,165	95.8	0.0	1.4	0.4	2.4	26.7	53.1	20.2	2,125	59.2	55.7	18.2
Winthrop city	850	851	0.1	956	94.9	0.0	0.0	4.2	0.9	29.1	58.6	12.1	388	82.2	51.3	16.5
Wiota city	116	112	-3.4	88	97.7	0.0	0.0	2.3	0.0	10.2	65.9	23.9	48	87.5	54.2	2.1
Woden city	229	223	-2.6	228	82.0	3.9	0.0	5.3	8.8	21.0	55.7	23.2	115	89.6	51.3	7.8
Woodbine city	1,485	1,424	-4.1	1,668	97.1	0.0	0.2	1.1	1.6	22.4	55.1	22.7	746	61.7	52.8	18.1
Woodburn city	202	199	-1.5	239	97.5	0.0	0.4	2.1	0.0	11.7	73.6	14.6	96	67.7	49.0	11.5
Woodward city	1,466	1,512	3.1	1,485	87.8	4.4	0.0	5.5	2.3	27.8	60.9	11.2	463	62.4	39.7	15.8
Woolstock city	168	164	-2.4	193	96.9	0.5	0.0	2.6	0.0	16.0	58.5	25.4	91	91.2	45.1	4.4
Worthington city	409	411	0.5	355	98.9	0.0	0.0	0.8	0.3	19.4	61.4	19.2	160	86.3	56.3	15.6
Wyoming city	515	514	-0.2	432	99.3	0.0	0.0	0.7	0.0	21.8	60.6	17.6	205	79.5	45.4	17.1
Yale city	246	245	-0.4	244	97.5	0.0	0.0	0.8	1.6	20.9	54.2	25.0	120	73.3	52.5	11.7
Yetter city	34	33	-2.9	21	100.0	0.0	0.0	0.0	0.0	14.3	61.9	23.8	11	90.9	72.7	0.0
Yorktown city	85	83	-2.4	100	75.0	0.0	0.0	25.0	0.0	41.0	45.0	14.0	32	75.0	59.4	15.6
Zearing city	554	536	-3.2	639	95.9	0.5	0.0	3.6	0.0	22.9	62.9	14.2	252	81.0	44.8	16.7
Zwingle city	91	89	-2.2	123	90.2	1.6	1.6	6.5	0.0	24.4	68.3	7.3	57	78.9	54.4	5.3
KANSAS	2,853,132	2,904,021	1.8	2,882,946	77.4	5.7	2.5	3.5	11.0	25.1	61.3	13.7	1,112,335	67.1	34.1	31.6
Abbyville city	87	88	1.1	106	97.2	0.0	0.0	2.8	0.0	21.7	49.1	29.2	46	80.4	43.5	2.2
Abilene city	6,844	6,590	-3.7	6,729	91.9	0.4	0.2	4.0	3.4	24.5	55.7	19.8	2,797	68.6	50.7	21.0
Ada CDP	100	NA	NA	53	100.0	0.0	0.0	0.0	0.0	0.0	54.7	45.3	39	100.0	38.5	0.0
Admire city	156	154	-1.3	120	83.3	0.0	0.0	0.0	16.7	25.8	51.5	22.5	46	91.3	56.5	19.6
Agenda city	68	66	-2.9	87	100.0	0.0	0.0	0.0	0.0	18.3	64.3	17.2	37	100.0	27.0	13.5
Agra city	267	255	-4.5	268	96.6	0.0	0.4	3.0	0.0	25.4	54.1	20.5	124	79.8	49.2	18.5
Albert city	175	174	-0.6	158	95.6	0.0	0.0	3.8	0.6	14.6	62.1	23.4	86	82.6	43.0	20.9
Alden city	148	147	-0.7	108	97.2	0.0	0.9	1.9	0.0	11.1	70.4	18.5	42	76.2	59.5	19.0
Alexander city	65	63	-3.1	34	94.1	0.0	0.0	5.9	0.0	0.0	82.5	17.6	18	100.0	38.9	22.2
Allen city	177	175	-1.1	333	77.2	0.0	0.0	21.3	1.5	33.3	60.0	6.6	115	81.7	33.9	15.7
Alma city	832	813	-2.3	826	96.6	0.0	0.2	1.2	1.9	21.7	59.2	19.0	325	79.1	49.2	24.0
Almena city	408	397	-2.7	524	94.8	0.0	0.0	4.8	0.4	20.7	61.8	17.6	273	67.8	37.7	10.3
Altamont city	1,080	1,049	-2.9	1,099	92.8	0.2	0.0	6.7	0.3	29.0	57.2	13.8	399	73.4	34.6	24.3
Alta Vista city	444	436	-1.8	474	90.5	0.0	0.0	5.7	3.8	21.5	64.2	14.3	204	73.5	53.4	18.6
Alton city	103	101	-1.9	133	94.0	0.0	6.0	0.0	0.0	21.0	54.3	24.8	62	79.0	35.5	25.8
Altoona city	413	390	-5.6	390	92.8	0.0	0.0	4.6	2.6	31.0	52.1	16.9	160	76.9	65.0	7.5
Americus city	894	879	-1.7	822	97.8	0.0	0.0	1.5	0.7	21.6	67.9	10.3	337	81.3	51.3	17.5
Andale city	928	981	5.7	879	96.8	0.0	0.0	0.2	3.0	35.9	55.1	9.2	278	80.9	31.3	38.5
Andover city	11,791	12,509	6.1	12,113	86.2	2.8	2.2	2.2	6.7	32.4	59.8	7.8	4,262	81.5	17.6	48.2
Anthony city	2,269	2,234	-1.5	2,340	94.2	0.3	0.0	2.3	3.2	23.7	52.3	24.0	1,088	76.1	48.0	17.8
Arcadia city	310	310	0.0	410	96.8	0.0	0.0	2.4	0.7	31.5	55.5	12.9	157	79.0	68.2	6.4
Argonia city	508	492	-3.1	585	85.0	0.3	0.0	12.5	2.2	36.9	48.6	14.5	202	71.3	44.1	17.8
Arkansas City city	12,405	12,205	-1.6	12,316	73.1	3.3	0.8	5.1	17.7	26.2	58.1	15.6	4,751	58.5	38.0	14.8
Arlington city	473	459	-3.0	503	91.1	0.8	0.4	6.4	1.4	16.9	60.1	23.1	249	72.7	48.6	10.4
Arma city	1,481	1,464	-1.1	1,484	95.9	0.0	0.0	1.6	2.5	26.9	52.9	20.2	612	65.8	50.3	23.7
Asherville CDP	28	NA	NA	0	0.0	0.0	0.0	0.0	0.0	0.0	0.0	0.0	0	0.0	0.0	0.0
Ashland city	867	835	-3.7	798	82.5	0.9	0.0	4.1	12.5	22.5	51.4	26.3	379	76.8	39.3	31.4
Assaria city	413	412	-0.2	560	97.9	0.0	0.0	0.9	1.3	29.5	60.2	10.4	210	88.1	35.2	23.3
Atchison city	11,027	10,771	-2.3	10,920	85.2	6.6	0.2	5.0	2.9	25.0	61.6	13.6	3,825	67.4	44.3	19.5
Athol city	44	43	-2.3	55	100.0	0.0	0.0	0.0	0.0	1.8	65.6	32.7	25	100.0	56.0	8.0
Atlanta city	195	194	-0.5	278	83.5	0.0	0.0	4.0	12.6	34.5	45.1	20.5	101	76.2	31.7	19.8
Attica city	626	592	-5.4	754	84.2	0.0	0.4	6.2	9.2	30.1	52.7	17.1	290	70.0	42.4	19.3
Atwood city	1,194	1,222	2.3	1,019	93.3	1.2	0.0	2.9	2.6	20.9	49.7	29.3	507	71.2	33.3	29.2
Auburn city	1,227	1,217	-0.8	1,322	91.9	0.4	0.5	1.1	6.1	28.1	60.9	11.0	539	72.0	37.5	17.1
Augusta city	9,274	9,242	-0.3	9,239	90.2	0.8	0.1	3.7	5.2	25.8	56.9	17.4	3,745	65.5	41.3	25.3
Aurora city	60	60	0.0	48	100.0	0.0	0.0	0.0	0.0	25.1	64.6	10.4	21	100.0	28.6	4.8
Axtell city	406	409	0.7	411	99.5	0.0	0.0	0.5	0.0	20.5	57.1	22.4	184	85.9	56.5	15.8
Baileyville CDP	181	NA	NA	172	100.0	0.0	0.0	0.0	0.0	11.0	64.4	24.4	82	75.6	76.8	17.1
Baldwin City city	4,515	4,585	1.6	4,552	88.8	0.9	0.5	6.0	3.9	24.7	62.5	12.8	1,596	66.4	29.1	35.3
Barnard city	70	69	-1.4	56	100.0	0.0	0.0	0.0	0.0	8.9	64.3	26.8	33	87.9	39.4	15.2
Barnes city	159	154	-3.1	113	100.0	0.0	0.0	0.0	0.0	14.2	49.6	36.3	59	100.0	50.8	3.4
Bartlett city	80	78	-2.5	68	64.7	0.0	0.0	23.5	11.8	19.2	80.9	0.0	33	57.6	42.4	24.2
Basehor city	4,638	5,119	10.4	4,831	90.5	0.2	1.6	2.4	5.3	26.7	63.0	10.2	1,680	82.4	26.7	39.8
Bassett city	15	14	-6.7	15	100.0	0.0	0.0	0.0	0.0	13.4	80.0	6.7	11	100.0	0.0	18.2
Baxter Springs city	4,238	4,073	-3.9	4,161	86.2	0.0	0.1	12.9	0.8	21.9	63.3	15.0	1,558	72.0	40.4	15.4
Bazine city	334	335	0.3	440	63.4	0.0	0.0	0.0	36.6	28.9	43.9	27.3	180	90.0	73.3	10.0

1 May be of any race.

Table A. All Places — **Population and Housing**

STATE City, town, township, borough, or CDP (county if applicable)	Population: 2010 census total population	Population: 2014 estimated population	Population: Percent change 2010–2014	Population: ACS total population estimate 2010–2014	Race and Hispanic or Latino origin (percent), 2010–2014: White alone, not Hispanic or Latino	Black alone, not Hispanic or Latino	Asian alone, not Hispanic or Latino	All other races or 2 or more races, not Hispanic or Latino	Hispanic or Latino[1]	Age (percent), 2010–2014: Under 18 years old	Age 18 to 64 years old	Age 65 years and older	Households, 2010–2014: Total occupied housing units	Percent owner occupied	Householders by level of education (percent): High school diploma or less	Bachelor's degree or more
	1	2	3	4	5	6	7	8	9	10	11	12	13	14	15	16
KANSAS—Con.																
Beattie city	200	197	-1.5	239	97.1	0.4	0.0	0.0	2.5	13.0	67.8	19.2	94	76.6	68.1	12.8
Bel Aire city	6,769	7,284	7.6	6,923	77.4	11.8	5.2	1.2	4.4	27.8	60.6	11.6	2,414	85.8	15.1	55.5
Belle Plaine city	1,681	1,627	-3.2	1,680	93.2	0.5	0.7	2.9	2.8	30.5	58.1	11.3	593	67.8	36.3	18.4
Belleville city	1,991	1,917	-3.7	1,869	93.6	0.0	1.1	2.5	2.8	18.5	49.3	32.3	903	67.9	50.4	21.6
Beloit city	3,835	3,792	-1.1	3,927	95.0	0.2	1.1	1.2	2.5	22.7	57.2	20.1	1,672	64.9	41.4	23.0
Belpre city	84	84	0.0	148	34.5	0.0	0.0	0.7	64.9	37.2	56.2	6.8	55	54.5	61.8	9.1
Belvue city	205	207	1.0	205	87.8	0.0	0.0	0.0	12.2	25.4	64.4	10.2	85	77.6	50.6	4.7
Bendena CDP	117	NA	NA	65	100.0	0.0	0.0	0.0	0.0	18.5	43.0	38.5	36	100.0	19.4	55.6
Benedict city	73	71	-2.7	70	88.6	0.0	5.7	5.7	0.0	12.8	45.7	41.4	39	89.7	64.1	0.0
Bennington city	672	665	-1.0	764	97.1	0.0	0.0	0.7	2.2	33.5	58.4	8.0	281	86.5	29.5	22.1
Bentley city	530	524	-1.1	515	88.7	1.4	0.4	3.9	5.6	22.6	61.8	15.7	187	90.4	48.7	13.9
Benton city	880	872	-0.9	1,013	89.0	5.7	0.3	2.2	2.8	25.9	63.0	11.1	405	74.1	28.9	30.6
Bern city	166	165	-0.6	186	76.9	11.8	0.0	1.6	9.7	29.0	54.0	17.2	83	86.7	51.8	27.7
Beverly city	162	159	-1.9	232	91.8	2.2	0.0	0.0	6.0	28.4	57.3	14.2	100	74.0	52.0	16.0
Bird City city	447	439	-1.8	470	75.5	0.0	0.6	6.2	17.7	24.9	56.3	18.9	212	70.3	42.9	10.8
Bison city	255	247	-3.1	171	94.7	0.0	0.0	5.3	0.0	15.8	63.8	20.5	84	81.0	36.9	22.6
Blue Mound city	275	275	0.0	303	99.0	0.0	0.0	0.0	1.0	30.3	53.4	16.2	126	78.6	57.9	1.6
Blue Rapids city	1,019	997	-2.2	1,025	98.6	0.1	0.0	0.6	0.7	32.5	44.9	22.5	386	80.6	61.9	11.7
Bluff City city	65	62	-4.6	57	100.0	0.0	0.0	0.0	0.0	24.5	54.4	21.1	22	86.4	63.6	4.5
Bogue city	143	142	-0.7	219	97.7	2.3	0.0	0.0	0.0	19.1	56.1	24.7	92	81.5	41.3	21.7
Bonner Springs city	7,314	7,553	3.3	7,420	75.7	7.2	1.1	2.7	13.3	26.5	60.5	13.0	2,758	69.1	40.7	21.8
Brewster city	305	304	-0.3	293	95.9	0.0	0.3	0.7	3.1	24.6	45.7	29.7	121	76.9	31.4	15.7
Bronson city	323	311	-3.7	406	93.6	3.7	0.0	0.0	2.7	33.0	51.4	15.8	141	78.0	51.1	7.8
Brookville city	262	266	1.5	360	93.9	4.4	0.0	0.0	1.7	35.0	59.0	6.1	131	78.6	32.8	15.3
Brownell city	29	29	0.0	63	100.0	0.0	0.0	0.0	0.0	20.7	41.3	38.1	30	100.0	36.7	20.0
Bucklin city	794	803	1.1	1,120	79.7	0.4	0.7	9.6	9.6	33.8	50.7	15.4	350	78.9	36.6	16.9
Bucyrus CDP	193	NA	NA	221	96.8	0.0	0.0	3.2	0.0	11.8	67.4	20.8	80	100.0	91.3	0.0
Buffalo city	232	224	-3.4	294	90.8	0.0	0.7	1.4	7.1	31.0	59.6	9.5	120	90.0	50.0	5.0
Buhler city	1,340	1,335	-0.4	1,485	97.8	0.1	0.0	0.2	1.8	29.3	52.1	18.5	495	71.5	27.7	35.4
Bunker Hill city	95	95	0.0	104	97.1	0.0	0.0	2.9	0.0	27.8	44.2	27.9	52	90.4	51.9	11.5
Burden city	535	536	0.2	531	88.7	0.0	0.8	4.3	6.2	28.3	57.8	13.7	201	77.6	36.3	18.4
Burdett city	247	244	-1.2	275	95.3	0.0	0.0	2.5	2.2	28.0	51.4	20.7	101	70.3	25.7	24.8
Burlingame city	932	900	-3.4	861	95.9	0.0	0.0	1.2	2.9	22.4	61.0	16.5	404	61.6	49.5	13.1
Burlington city	2,674	2,635	-1.5	2,648	91.4	0.5	1.2	2.5	4.4	21.2	58.5	20.4	1,152	65.5	45.7	21.7
Burns city	228	222	-2.6	258	99.2	0.0	0.0	0.8	0.0	16.6	64.7	18.6	100	88.0	62.0	20.0
Burr Oak city	174	168	-3.4	154	95.5	0.0	0.0	1.9	2.6	5.8	68.5	25.3	86	93.0	61.6	18.6
Burrton city	901	893	-0.9	904	93.3	0.0	0.0	1.5	5.2	32.4	51.9	15.7	333	56.8	57.1	15.3
Bushong city	34	34	0.0	47	70.2	2.1	0.0	27.7	0.0	34.1	63.8	2.1	11	100.0	63.6	36.4
Bushton city	279	277	-0.7	265	84.2	4.2	0.0	7.9	3.8	20.4	49.8	29.8	117	71.8	41.0	13.7
Byers city	35	36	2.9	94	97.9	0.0	0.0	2.1	0.0	36.2	62.9	1.1	33	81.8	18.2	0.0
Caldwell city	1,068	1,034	-3.2	1,178	88.5	0.4	0.0	9.4	1.6	20.8	53.7	25.3	509	77.6	42.8	16.9
Cambridge city	84	83	-1.2	60	100.0	0.0	0.0	0.0	0.0	13.3	50.0	36.7	26	96.2	46.2	3.8
Caney city	2,220	2,125	-4.3	2,117	90.4	0.0	0.0	7.8	1.8	24.8	52.1	23.1	834	67.5	45.7	15.0
Canton city	748	749	0.1	1,006	96.7	0.2	0.0	0.7	2.4	25.7	64.6	9.9	352	84.9	51.7	11.1
Carbondale city	1,437	1,405	-2.2	1,367	92.5	0.0	0.0	5.3	2.1	27.1	61.9	10.9	561	61.1	45.5	14.1
Carlton city	42	42	0.0	15	100.0	0.0	0.0	0.0	0.0	0.0	59.9	40.0	9	100.0	55.6	22.2
Cassoday city	129	128	-0.8	83	98.8	0.0	0.0	1.2	0.0	25.3	48.1	26.5	42	88.1	35.7	14.3
Catharine CDP	104	NA	NA	64	89.1	0.0	0.0	10.9	0.0	42.2	57.8	0.0	22	63.6	0.0	0.0
Cawker City city	469	456	-2.8	527	97.9	0.2	0.4	0.0	1.5	18.4	52.5	29.2	267	81.6	46.8	16.9
Cedar city	14	14	0.0	0	0.0	0.0	0.0	0.0	0.0	0.0	0.0	0.0	0	0.0	0.0	0.0
Cedar Point city	28	27	-3.6	23	73.9	0.0	0.0	26.1	0.0	21.7	34.7	43.5	14	35.7	42.9	0.0
Cedar Vale city	579	546	-5.7	477	96.0	0.0	0.0	4.0	0.0	25.2	48.8	26.0	206	85.4	42.7	23.3
Centralia city	512	508	-0.8	524	94.1	0.8	0.6	4.2	0.4	31.9	47.7	20.4	209	82.3	52.2	17.2
Chanute city	9,119	9,295	1.9	9,194	87.8	1.5	0.1	3.7	6.9	24.5	57.0	18.5	3,710	63.6	39.6	20.5
Chapman city	1,393	1,379	-1.0	1,441	89.7	0.1	0.3	1.2	8.6	24.3	58.9	16.9	569	62.2	36.9	25.1
Chase city	477	465	-2.5	576	72.0	0.7	0.0	13.7	13.5	30.0	59.2	10.8	203	84.2	68.5	10.8
Chautauqua city	111	106	-4.5	59	94.9	0.0	0.0	5.1	0.0	8.5	57.8	33.9	33	90.9	84.8	12.1
Cheney city	2,099	2,153	2.6	1,916	98.0	0.0	0.0	0.9	1.1	27.6	59.1	13.6	745	83.1	38.7	32.5
Cherokee city	714	716	0.3	663	94.7	1.1	0.0	0.8	3.5	32.5	51.0	16.4	263	77.9	54.0	7.2
Cherryvale city	2,378	2,283	-4.0	2,116	92.0	0.0	0.0	6.7	1.4	22.8	61.0	16.2	824	67.7	45.9	14.4
Chetopa city	1,125	1,091	-3.0	1,146	87.5	1.7	0.0	10.2	0.6	22.6	50.6	26.7	459	68.2	56.0	9.6
Chicopee CDP	408	NA	NA	431	94.2	0.0	0.0	5.8	0.0	28.5	61.2	10.0	172	94.8	19.8	41.3
Cimarron city	2,184	2,240	2.6	2,057	74.6	0.0	0.0	0.5	24.9	35.4	52.5	12.2	703	62.6	37.7	23.5
Circleville city	170	171	0.6	154	88.3	0.0	1.9	2.6	7.1	26.6	51.0	22.1	68	86.8	52.9	19.1
Claflin city	645	638	-1.1	665	90.7	0.0	0.0	3.6	5.7	22.9	62.6	14.6	279	74.9	41.6	19.0
Clay Center city	4,339	4,177	-3.7	4,280	94.4	0.8	1.0	1.8	2.0	25.7	51.8	22.5	1,730	76.6	35.3	26.7
Clayton city	59	58	-1.7	92	98.9	0.0	0.0	0.0	1.1	19.5	69.5	10.9	52	63.5	34.6	9.6
Clearwater city	2,488	2,531	1.7	2,525	97.7	0.1	0.0	0.9	1.2	26.9	57.6	15.4	910	74.0	38.4	29.2
Clifton city	554	537	-3.1	577	98.6	0.7	0.0	0.0	0.7	22.3	49.7	27.7	204	82.4	46.1	15.2
Climax city	72	69	-4.2	167	100.0	0.0	0.0	0.0	0.0	44.3	44.9	10.8	49	98.0	40.8	57.1
Clyde city	716	703	-1.8	796	99.1	0.0	0.0	0.0	0.9	20.4	54.5	25.1	335	78.2	41.8	14.9
Coats city	83	85	2.4	159	85.5	0.0	0.0	0.0	14.5	30.8	53.4	15.7	53	92.5	79.2	1.9
Coffeyville city	10,295	9,876	-4.1	10,034	71.6	11.5	0.9	10.0	6.0	21.3	59.5	19.0	4,060	61.8	46.7	13.8
Colby city	5,387	5,388	0.0	5,411	90.9	2.3	0.1	1.6	5.2	20.3	63.4	16.2	2,206	70.2	32.9	27.8
Coldwater city	828	855	3.3	704	94.9	0.0	0.9	1.4	2.8	19.4	55.3	25.1	346	73.7	41.9	17.3
Collyer city	109	106	-2.8	97	94.8	3.1	0.0	0.0	2.1	16.5	56.6	26.8	43	90.7	37.2	20.9
Colony city	408	402	-1.5	404	97.8	0.5	0.0	1.2	0.5	17.8	53.8	28.5	185	84.3	61.6	10.8
Columbus city	3,311	3,186	-3.8	3,244	87.2	0.0	0.0	9.1	3.7	21.4	55.2	23.3	1,441	59.4	54.2	16.8
Colwich city	1,327	1,362	2.6	1,368	97.2	0.0	0.0	1.0	1.8	31.3	58.5	10.3	446	78.9	37.4	30.3
Concordia city	5,400	5,311	-1.6	5,327	91.1	0.4	1.4	2.4	4.6	20.1	60.9	19.1	2,177	64.1	36.7	19.4
Conway Springs city	1,272	1,239	-2.6	1,539	97.2	0.0	0.0	2.5	0.3	34.9	49.3	15.7	502	69.5	50.6	16.7
Coolidge city	95	93	-2.1	107	67.3	0.0	0.0	0.0	32.7	31.7	51.3	16.8	44	63.6	40.9	27.3
Copeland city	310	303	-2.3	292	88.7	0.0	0.0	0.7	10.6	27.0	56.3	16.8	117	82.1	45.3	23.1
Corning city	157	156	-0.6	143	80.4	0.0	0.0	19.6	0.0	32.9	56.0	11.2	52	82.7	50.0	19.2
Cottonwood Falls city	904	877	-3.0	1,012	92.0	3.0	0.0	1.4	3.7	21.8	57.8	20.2	405	76.5	41.2	20.0
Council Grove city	2,182	2,105	-3.5	2,200	92.0	0.5	0.5	1.9	5.0	18.2	55.3	26.5	982	67.8	49.2	17.8
Courtland city	285	277	-2.8	383	100.0	0.0	0.0	0.0	0.0	31.3	52.5	16.2	152	77.6	37.5	21.1
Coyville city	46	44	-4.3	38	94.7	0.0	0.0	5.3	0.0	26.3	65.9	7.9	19	100.0	47.4	5.3
Cuba city	156	150	-3.8	171	98.8	0.0	0.0	1.2	0.0	12.9	49.1	38.0	83	85.5	41.0	15.7
Cullison city	101	104	3.0	48	100.0	0.0	0.0	0.0	0.0	16.7	64.5	18.8	22	77.3	18.2	4.5
Culver city	121	121	0.0	107	91.6	0.0	0.0	6.5	1.9	12.1	64.3	23.4	42	90.5	54.8	14.3

1 May be of any race.

Table A. All Places — **Population and Housing**

STATE City, town, township, borough, or CDP (county if applicable)	2010 census total population	2014 estimated population	Percent change 2010–2014	ACS total population estimate 2010–2014	White alone, not Hispanic or Latino	Black alone, not Hispanic or Latino	Asian alone, not Hispanic or Latino	All other races or 2 or more races, not Hispanic or Latino	Hispanic or Latino[1]	Under 18 years old	Age 18 to 64 years old	Age 65 years and older	Total occupied housing units	Percent owner occupied	High school diploma or less	Bachelor's degree or more
	1	2	3	4	5	6	7	8	9	10	11	12	13	14	15	16
KANSAS—Con.																
Cunningham city	473	470	-0.6	374	92.5	0.8	0.0	1.6	5.1	23.3	47.2	29.4	162	83.3	29.0	27.2
Damar city	132	132	0.0	223	98.2	0.0	1.8	0.0	0.0	29.2	52.4	18.4	89	71.9	24.7	20.2
Danville city	38	36	-5.3	35	97.1	0.0	0.0	2.9	0.0	11.4	74.4	14.3	19	84.2	31.6	26.3
Dearing city	431	408	-5.3	478	84.7	0.6	7.9	4.8	1.9	19.7	66.7	13.6	215	81.4	37.2	20.0
Deerfield city	700	687	-1.9	791	36.4	0.6	0.0	0.3	62.7	32.3	50.3	17.3	226	86.3	57.5	7.1
Delia city	169	170	0.6	177	87.0	0.0	0.0	4.5	8.5	31.6	58.6	9.6	62	74.2	48.4	8.1
Delphos city	359	351	-2.2	407	98.8	0.0	0.0	0.2	1.0	19.9	53.1	27.0	174	81.0	44.3	14.9
Denison city	187	188	0.5	191	80.6	0.0	0.0	7.9	11.5	28.2	57.6	14.1	73	79.5	57.5	6.8
Denton city	148	148	0.0	179	98.3	0.0	0.0	1.7	0.0	7.8	78.1	14.0	82	92.7	35.4	30.5
Derby city	22,227	23,234	4.5	23,419	87.7	2.4	1.3	3.3	5.3	26.2	61.3	12.4	8,914	70.7	20.5	39.0
De Soto city	5,720	6,038	5.6	5,888	75.3	4.9	0.0	4.5	15.3	30.3	60.7	9.1	2,071	57.1	35.5	27.1
Detroit CDP	114	NA	NA	448	100.0	0.0	0.0	0.0	0.0	46.4	49.8	3.8	106	100.0	52.8	22.6
Dexter city	278	276	-0.7	347	93.4	0.0	0.0	6.6	0.0	17.3	42.0	40.9	135	83.0	33.3	14.1
Dighton city	1,038	1,000	-3.7	930	89.8	0.1	0.0	0.6	9.5	23.1	54.0	22.9	480	76.7	44.4	16.7
Dodge City city	27,340	28,117	2.8	27,950	34.3	2.7	1.5	1.6	60.0	31.6	60.0	8.5	8,695	61.0	55.4	16.3
Dorrance city	185	186	0.5	175	100.0	0.0	0.0	0.0	0.0	20.0	62.9	17.1	84	90.5	54.8	3.6
Douglass city	1,700	1,692	-0.5	2,089	94.9	0.4	1.4	1.8	1.4	32.6	57.9	9.4	718	72.8	45.3	14.2
Downs city	900	873	-3.0	1,033	98.3	0.6	0.0	1.1	0.1	15.5	56.3	28.3	487	74.7	39.6	22.6
Dresden city	41	40	-2.4	83	100.0	0.0	0.0	0.0	0.0	36.1	42.1	21.7	35	74.3	62.9	20.0
Dunlap city	30	29	-3.3	14	100.0	0.0	0.0	0.0	0.0	0.0	71.3	28.6	6	33.3	33.3	33.3
Durham city	112	108	-3.6	144	80.6	2.1	0.0	15.3	2.1	30.6	46.0	23.6	55	70.9	63.6	16.4
Dwight city	272	263	-3.3	231	88.7	0.0	3.5	2.2	5.6	29.4	48.6	22.1	96	82.3	45.8	19.8
Earlton city	55	53	-3.6	59	98.3	0.0	0.0	1.7	0.0	28.9	51.0	20.3	24	91.7	58.3	0.0
Eastborough city	773	769	-0.5	728	97.0	1.1	1.6	0.3	0.0	25.0	59.1	16.1	285	90.2	9.5	73.7
Easton city	253	257	1.6	337	96.7	0.0	0.0	0.0	3.3	19.9	59.1	21.1	89	75.3	53.9	22.5
Edgerton city	1,671	1,703	1.9	1,573	92.7	0.8	0.0	2.2	4.3	24.6	65.1	10.4	563	82.6	35.9	21.1
Edna city	49	48	-2.0	45	100.0	0.0	0.0	0.0	0.0	24.5	75.7	0.0	14	100.0	64.3	0.0
Edmond city	442	430	-2.7	415	93.7	0.0	0.5	5.8	0.0	27.4	50.3	22.2	177	78.5	38.4	22.6
Edwardsville city	4,340	4,380	0.9	4,367	86.3	5.3	0.6	2.2	5.6	28.1	61.2	10.6	1,458	72.4	51.0	16.8
Effingham city	546	526	-3.7	566	92.2	0.0	1.2	3.2	3.4	31.6	50.0	18.6	226	68.1	55.8	14.6
Elbing city	229	227	-0.9	273	99.6	0.0	0.0	0.0	0.4	31.2	51.2	17.6	87	85.1	28.7	36.8
El Dorado city	13,026	12,879	-1.1	12,931	90.5	1.3	0.4	3.4	4.3	26.3	58.8	15.0	5,005	58.9	38.1	19.1
Elgin city	89	85	-4.5	97	82.5	0.0	0.0	15.5	2.1	12.3	59.8	27.8	51	88.2	68.6	3.9
Elk City city	325	314	-3.4	373	86.6	0.0	0.0	9.1	4.3	25.8	53.1	21.2	141	85.8	53.9	5.7
Elk Falls city	107	101	-5.6	50	88.0	0.0	0.0	12.0	0.0	8.0	58.0	34.0	33	93.9	54.5	9.1
Elkhart city	2,205	2,113	-4.2	2,298	71.8	0.6	1.2	2.3	24.2	25.6	57.7	16.7	845	68.0	50.3	15.1
Ellinwood city	2,131	2,098	-1.5	2,494	90.9	1.0	0.0	2.8	5.3	25.7	55.9	18.4	1,008	78.4	46.2	13.3
Ellis city	2,062	2,074	0.6	2,028	91.2	0.4	1.6	0.9	5.9	25.4	58.4	16.3	904	78.8	44.9	30.0
Ellsworth city	3,120	3,076	-1.4	3,097	79.6	7.8	0.0	3.9	8.8	15.3	66.4	18.1	1,055	71.6	34.9	32.4
Elmdale city	55	53	-3.6	45	100.0	0.0	0.0	0.0	0.0	0.0	75.4	24.4	17	88.2	23.5	0.0
Elsmore city	77	74	-3.9	93	100.0	0.0	0.0	0.0	0.0	10.8	54.9	34.4	48	81.3	60.4	4.2
Elwood city	1,224	1,204	-1.6	1,116	77.5	11.9	0.0	2.9	7.7	25.3	61.2	13.5	483	65.8	63.1	3.1
Emmett city	191	191	0.0	158	89.2	0.0	0.0	0.0	10.8	43.1	38.4	18.4	51	80.4	52.9	3.9
Emporia city	24,923	24,560	-1.5	24,787	65.3	2.5	2.8	3.1	26.3	22.4	65.4	12.1	9,723	51.7	39.7	25.3
Englewood city	77	75	-2.6	112	63.4	0.0	0.0	36.6	0.0	18.8	56.3	25.0	50	86.0	46.0	0.0
Ensign city	187	184	-1.6	252	60.7	0.0	0.0	0.4	38.9	21.5	59.5	19.0	105	96.2	66.7	13.3
Enterprise city	855	825	-3.5	958	92.0	0.0	0.5	1.3	6.3	25.0	59.4	15.7	325	67.4	50.2	14.5
Erie city	1,150	1,108	-3.7	1,024	92.6	0.1	0.4	2.3	4.6	23.2	55.7	21.1	395	72.2	33.4	22.3
Esbon city	99	98	-1.0	135	94.1	0.0	0.0	0.7	5.2	30.3	39.2	30.4	55	89.1	40.0	14.5
Eskridge city	534	520	-2.6	494	97.6	0.0	0.0	1.2	1.2	22.7	57.0	20.4	180	77.2	46.1	24.4
Eudora city	6,137	6,303	2.7	6,152	91.2	2.4	1.7	3.2	1.5	31.4	60.2	8.3	2,259	62.2	28.2	34.5
Eureka city	2,633	2,485	-5.6	2,449	93.5	0.5	0.0	2.4	3.6	22.1	53.3	24.6	1,131	70.7	45.1	14.7
Everest city	284	281	-1.1	258	94.6	1.6	0.0	2.7	1.2	21.7	63.1	15.1	118	65.3	50.0	17.8
Fairview city	260	255	-1.9	254	90.9	3.5	0.0	5.5	0.0	20.8	49.4	29.9	127	89.8	43.3	13.4
Fairway city	3,882	3,969	2.2	3,946	96.3	0.3	1.0	2.1	0.4	20.3	66.9	12.7	1,860	84.7	4.0	79.2
Fall River city	162	154	-4.9	163	96.3	0.0	0.0	3.7	0.0	16.0	62.4	21.5	79	87.3	62.0	6.3
Falun CDP	87	NA	NA	118	85.6	0.0	0.0	14.4	0.0	0.0	75.6	24.6	45	82.2	62.2	0.0
Florence city	467	444	-4.9	511	88.6	3.5	0.0	1.8	6.1	23.3	52.1	24.7	223	70.4	58.3	9.0
Fontana city	224	222	-0.9	151	95.4	0.0	0.0	2.0	2.6	23.2	60.8	15.9	67	89.6	61.2	7.5
Ford city	216	220	1.9	216	85.2	3.7	0.0	0.0	11.1	17.6	62.1	20.4	89	76.4	59.6	10.1
Formoso city	93	92	-1.1	108	98.1	0.0	0.9	0.9	0.0	34.3	38.0	27.8	45	77.8	71.1	2.2
Fort Dodge CDP	165	NA	NA	162	95.7	0.0	3.7	0.6	0.0	3.7	50.6	45.7	90	0.0	40.0	25.6
Fort Riley CDP	7,761	NA	NA	7,444	65.7	12.0	2.9	3.9	15.5	32.6	67.4	0.0	1,244	0.8	35.0	6.8
Fort Scott city	8,087	7,874	-2.6	7,957	89.2	6.3	1.0	0.9	2.5	23.5	58.2	18.1	3,161	58.4	41.0	19.4
Fowler city	590	560	-5.1	463	90.9	0.0	0.0	0.0	9.1	26.0	50.9	23.3	208	78.8	32.7	24.0
Frankfort city	726	711	-2.1	649	100.0	0.0	0.0	0.0	0.0	15.4	48.8	35.9	286	86.4	45.5	16.4
Franklin CDP	375	NA	NA	488	99.2	0.0	0.0	0.8	0.0	13.7	59.6	26.6	206	82.5	46.6	0.0
Frederick city	18	18	0.0	7	100.0	0.0	0.0	0.0	0.0	0.0	57.2	42.9	5	60.0	100.0	0.0
Fredonia city	2,482	2,372	-4.4	2,400	89.7	0.3	0.0	7.3	2.8	24.8	53.8	21.3	1,023	66.4	48.6	11.6
Freeport city	5	5	0.0	0	0.0	0.0	0.0	0.0	0.0	0.0	0.0	0.0	0	0.0	0.0	0.0
Frontenac city	3,437	3,444	0.2	3,456	88.5	0.1	0.0	4.7	6.7	24.6	59.0	16.3	1,304	64.0	36.2	26.8
Fulton city	163	160	-1.8	152	89.5	0.0	1.3	1.3	7.9	19.0	61.3	19.7	59	72.9	69.5	13.6
Galatia city	39	39	0.0	43	100.0	0.0	0.0	0.0	0.0	0.0	55.8	44.2	26	100.0	0.0	15.4
Galena city	3,085	2,966	-3.9	3,022	92.4	0.0	0.0	0.4	7.1	26.9	59.9	13.1	1,081	74.4	45.2	17.8
Galesburg city	126	122	-3.2	108	85.2	0.0	0.0	0.9	13.9	31.5	54.6	13.9	42	90.5	33.3	16.7
Galva city	870	898	3.2	908	99.1	0.2	0.2	0.4	0.0	24.5	51.4	23.9	388	78.1	45.1	17.0
Garden City city	26,666	27,004	1.3	26,924	41.0	2.7	4.7	1.7	50.0	30.7	59.6	9.7	9,361	61.0	48.8	18.7
Garden Plain city	849	879	3.5	812	97.7	0.0	0.0	1.4	1.0	28.7	56.5	14.8	322	73.9	46.3	27.6
Gardner city	19,115	20,667	8.1	20,128	84.3	3.4	2.3	2.7	7.3	33.3	60.6	6.2	7,014	70.4	29.8	31.4
Garfield city	190	188	-1.1	207	91.8	0.5	0.0	2.9	4.8	14.5	70.9	14.5	85	84.7	49.4	14.1
Garnett city	3,415	3,295	-3.5	3,345	96.4	0.4	0.0	2.7	0.6	26.9	49.2	23.8	1,457	57.0	46.6	16.3
Gas city	564	532	-5.7	509	91.4	0.0	0.0	6.1	2.6	24.8	59.4	15.9	197	77.7	49.7	9.6
Gaylord city	114	111	-2.6	172	78.5	0.0	0.0	19.2	2.3	36.6	44.7	18.6	71	70.4	56.3	12.7
Gem city	88	88	0.0	74	98.6	0.0	0.0	0.0	1.4	25.7	69.1	5.4	29	93.1	31.0	13.8
Geneseo city	267	267	0.0	316	87.7	1.3	0.0	6.6	4.4	24.0	57.0	19.0	143	79.7	54.5	4.9
Geuda Springs city	187	183	-2.1	191	69.6	0.0	0.0	29.8	0.5	32.4	57.5	9.9	75	90.7	45.3	4.0
Girard city	2,789	2,773	-0.6	2,779	84.9	2.4	2.3	3.0	7.4	22.2	60.8	17.0	994	64.9	38.6	24.2
Glade city	96	94	-2.1	81	98.8	0.0	0.0	1.2	0.0	13.6	69.3	17.3	46	97.8	47.8	4.3
Glasco city	498	487	-2.2	437	97.9	1.1	0.0	0.0	0.9	14.2	51.2	34.8	202	84.7	41.6	21.3
Glen Elder city	445	435	-2.2	478	99.2	0.0	0.0	0.0	0.8	27.8	54.5	17.8	226	75.2	35.0	15.9
Goddard city	4,381	4,692	7.1	4,583	89.9	0.2	1.3	1.3	7.3	36.0	56.1	7.8	1,478	79.2	31.7	33.2

1 May be of any race.

Table A. All Places — **Population and Housing**

	Population				Race and Hispanic or Latino origin (percent), 2010–2014					Age (percent), 2010–2014			Households, 2010–2014			
STATE City, town, township, borough, or CDP (county if applicable)	2010 census total population	2014 estimated population	Percent change 2010–2014	ACS total population estimate 2010–2014	White alone, not Hispanic or Latino	Black alone, not Hispanic or Latino	Asian alone, not Hispanic or Latino	All other races or 2 or more races, not Hispanic or Latino	Hispanic or Latino[1]	Under 18 years old	Age 18 to 64 years old	Age 65 years and older	Total occupied housing units	Percent owner occupied	High school diploma or less	Bachelor's degree or more
	1	2	3	4	5	6	7	8	9	10	11	12	13	14	15	16
KANSAS—Con.																
Goessel city	539	514	-4.6	545	82.2	4.6	0.0	3.7	9.5	21.9	52.2	26.1	211	75.4	34.6	15.6
Goff city	126	125	-0.8	120	100.0	0.0	0.0	0.0	0.0	38.3	45.1	16.7	43	79.1	53.5	23.3
Goodland city	4,492	4,554	1.4	4,879	82.3	2.7	0.4	0.7	13.9	23.6	59.0	17.5	2,185	49.6	39.7	13.4
Gorham city	334	335	0.3	322	94.4	0.3	0.0	5.3	0.0	20.5	63.7	15.8	174	62.1	43.7	22.4
Gove City city	80	80	0.0	118	95.8	0.0	0.0	4.2	0.0	23.7	54.2	22.0	56	66.1	39.3	14.3
Grainfield city	277	275	-0.7	343	95.6	0.0	0.0	2.6	1.7	26.2	52.7	21.0	161	82.0	47.8	12.4
Grandview Plaza city	1,558	1,670	7.2	1,989	58.8	18.1	1.2	12.4	9.5	21.4	70.6	7.9	844	33.5	38.5	4.5
Grantville CDP	180	NA	NA	66	83.3	0.0	0.0	16.7	0.0	0.0	57.6	42.4	42	100.0	100.0	0.0
Great Bend city	15,995	15,840	-1.0	15,942	74.8	2.0	0.2	1.9	21.2	26.4	57.4	16.2	6,590	61.1	49.4	16.7
Greeley city	302	296	-2.0	237	97.9	0.4	0.0	1.7	0.0	24.5	52.8	22.8	119	82.4	46.2	5.0
Greeley County unified government	1,177	1,228	4.3	1,107	75.6	0.5	0.1	2.1	21.7	21.3	55.8	22.9	429	76.2	34.0	22.8
Greeley County unified government (balance)	436	454	4.1	419	80.2	0.0	0.0	0.2	19.6	19.4	64.7	16.0	164	75.0	29.9	26.2
Green city	128	128	0.0	144	100.0	0.0	0.0	0.0	0.0	32.7	56.8	10.4	58	65.5	43.1	20.7
Greenleaf city	331	314	-5.1	378	85.7	1.9	0.3	5.8	6.3	19.8	54.5	25.7	168	69.0	61.3	7.7
Greensburg city	772	779	0.9	933	92.3	0.1	1.5	0.5	5.6	21.3	62.5	16.3	452	51.3	33.6	23.0
Grenola city	216	203	-6.0	196	98.0	0.0	0.5	1.5	0.0	22.0	38.8	39.3	83	88.0	43.4	18.1
Gridley city	341	337	-1.2	310	94.2	0.0	1.9	2.9	1.0	23.2	53.9	22.9	153	69.3	48.4	15.0
Grinnell city	259	258	-0.4	277	99.6	0.0	0.0	0.4	0.0	16.2	49.4	34.3	149	84.6	45.0	19.5
Gypsum city	405	395	-2.5	380	96.8	0.0	0.0	1.3	1.8	20.8	61.0	18.2	167	74.3	52.7	12.0
Haddam city	104	100	-3.8	96	96.9	0.0	0.0	1.0	2.1	3.1	62.6	34.4	57	94.7	45.6	8.8
Halstead city	2,085	2,084	0.0	2,339	95.6	2.6	0.0	1.0	0.8	30.5	54.7	14.7	774	76.2	39.1	23.8
Hamilton city	268	255	-4.9	246	98.0	0.0	0.0	2.0	0.0	33.0	57.9	8.9	103	75.7	50.5	10.7
Hamlin city	46	45	-2.2	56	91.1	0.0	8.9	0.0	0.0	32.2	51.8	16.1	18	94.4	66.7	11.1
Hanover city	682	665	-2.5	549	97.8	0.5	0.0	0.4	1.3	24.0	48.3	27.7	239	89.5	50.2	14.2
Hanston city	206	207	0.5	288	79.2	0.0	0.0	2.4	18.4	24.7	57.1	18.4	118	78.0	45.8	22.9
Hardtner city	172	175	1.7	154	96.8	0.0	0.0	2.6	0.6	23.3	49.9	26.6	73	91.8	31.5	31.5
Harper city	1,473	1,398	-5.1	1,304	85.9	0.2	0.0	2.1	11.8	19.2	61.4	19.6	590	67.3	50.0	11.0
Harris CDP	51	NA	NA	9	100.0	0.0	0.0	0.0	0.0	0.0	0.0	100.0	9	100.0	100.0	0.0
Hartford city	371	367	-1.1	398	96.2	0.5	1.3	2.0	0.0	23.1	61.3	15.6	164	70.1	54.9	22.0
Harveyville city	236	246	4.2	243	88.9	0.0	3.7	5.3	2.1	29.2	57.6	13.2	91	83.5	44.0	14.3
Havana city	104	100	-3.8	162	92.0	0.0	0.0	8.0	0.0	27.8	53.7	18.5	67	82.1	53.7	22.4
Haven city	1,237	1,225	-1.0	1,135	86.2	1.4	0.4	9.5	2.6	19.6	69.2	11.1	463	84.4	37.8	19.9
Havensville city	133	144	8.3	118	82.2	0.0	10.2	5.1	2.5	6.7	76.9	16.1	57	82.5	66.7	14.0
Haviland city	701	684	-2.4	769	88.6	2.1	0.0	5.6	3.8	24.0	56.8	19.2	252	68.3	19.4	25.4
Hays city	20,533	21,044	2.5	20,886	90.4	1.4	1.6	1.8	4.9	20.6	67.0	12.5	8,573	54.6	25.4	34.1
Haysville city	10,826	11,112	2.6	11,235	88.0	0.4	0.9	4.9	5.7	30.6	56.2	13.1	3,895	73.3	40.9	14.6
Hazelton city	93	95	2.2	129	84.5	1.6	0.0	4.7	9.3	24.8	61.4	14.0	54	87.0	63.0	13.0
Healy CDP	234	NA	NA	238	87.8	0.0	0.0	0.4	11.8	23.6	60.5	16.0	104	68.3	52.9	22.1
Hepler city	132	132	0.0	137	92.0	0.0	0.0	0.0	8.0	16.0	63.5	20.4	58	93.1	67.2	12.1
Herington city	2,526	2,413	-4.5	2,353	89.3	1.2	1.2	1.5	6.7	22.0	57.2	20.9	1,026	69.6	48.5	9.9
Herndon city	129	133	3.1	136	100.0	0.0	0.0	0.0	0.0	16.2	57.2	26.5	69	75.4	44.9	18.8
Hesston city	3,691	3,734	1.2	3,621	87.8	1.2	2.1	3.1	5.7	25.2	60.0	14.9	1,294	69.4	23.8	36.9
Hiawatha city	3,172	3,108	-2.0	3,144	90.7	1.1	0.2	4.5	3.5	22.1	57.9	20.0	1,410	58.2	51.0	22.1
Highland city	1,012	1,015	0.3	1,078	78.8	12.9	2.1	2.2	4.0	6.6	80.7	12.7	282	62.8	29.8	26.2
Hill City city	1,474	1,454	-1.4	1,533	86.3	4.7	1.0	3.3	4.7	19.8	52.9	27.2	699	76.1	38.2	25.0
Hillsboro city	2,993	2,893	-3.3	2,940	93.0	2.6	0.7	1.2	2.6	20.2	58.1	21.7	966	73.3	33.7	34.5
Hillsdale CDP	229	NA	NA	223	97.3	0.0	0.0	2.7	0.0	17.0	47.9	35.0	76	80.3	38.2	26.3
Hoisington city	2,706	2,664	-1.6	2,687	94.0	0.8	0.6	2.4	2.3	30.1	51.9	17.8	1,088	62.5	48.3	19.9
Holcomb city	2,089	2,120	1.5	2,181	68.1	0.9	0.0	2.8	28.2	42.4	55.3	2.4	618	77.3	49.2	17.8
Hollenberg city	21	20	-4.8	21	85.7	0.0	0.0	0.0	14.3	0.0	66.7	33.3	14	92.9	28.6	21.4
Holton city	3,329	3,316	-0.4	3,298	83.7	1.3	0.6	7.5	6.9	21.3	58.9	19.9	1,444	55.4	47.1	21.2
Holyrood city	447	437	-2.2	332	97.0	0.0	0.0	0.0	3.0	14.1	51.9	33.7	173	74.6	41.6	14.5
Home CDP	160	NA	NA	210	100.0	0.0	0.0	0.0	0.0	12.4	59.5	28.1	92	100.0	88.0	5.4
Hope city	368	348	-5.4	353	92.6	0.0	0.0	2.5	4.8	24.9	55.7	19.3	161	75.2	43.5	17.4
Horace city	70	73	4.3	116	86.2	3.4	0.9	4.3	5.2	25.0	68.8	6.0	42	90.5	61.9	11.9
Horton city	1,776	1,732	-2.5	1,751	81.2	0.7	0.9	10.9	6.3	24.8	52.2	23.0	767	57.0	60.4	10.2
Howard city	687	642	-6.6	667	87.7	2.4	0.7	2.2	6.9	19.1	47.0	33.7	312	66.7	50.0	22.1
Hoxie city	1,201	1,189	-1.0	1,330	90.8	0.0	0.0	3.3	5.9	19.0	54.7	26.2	603	69.0	42.0	17.2
Hoyt city	669	662	-1.0	746	84.2	0.0	1.2	6.3	8.3	30.0	58.8	11.3	272	67.3	43.8	16.2
Hudson city	129	125	-3.1	161	88.8	0.0	0.0	11.2	0.0	27.9	58.9	13.0	63	84.1	47.6	17.5
Hugoton city	3,904	3,966	1.6	3,903	56.8	0.0	0.7	2.4	40.0	30.8	56.7	12.6	1,339	82.7	55.3	16.1
Humboldt city	1,953	1,886	-3.4	1,977	82.4	1.2	0.0	5.5	10.9	27.1	53.4	19.5	842	65.2	43.2	20.1
Hunnewell city	67	66	-1.5	66	100.0	0.0	0.0	0.0	0.0	19.6	68.1	12.1	24	83.3	58.3	4.2
Hunter city	57	56	-1.8	67	100.0	0.0	0.0	0.0	0.0	12.0	64.2	23.9	38	76.3	50.0	2.6
Huron city	54	53	-1.9	50	100.0	0.0	0.0	0.0	0.0	24.0	66.0	10.0	17	58.8	52.9	5.9
Hutchinson city	42,192	41,642	-1.3	41,946	81.0	4.0	0.7	3.0	11.4	22.8	60.2	16.9	16,868	61.4	34.7	20.6
Independence city	9,483	9,162	-3.4	9,282	74.8	6.7	1.3	5.1	12.1	28.9	56.2	14.9	3,682	61.3	38.0	19.0
Ingalls city	306	304	-0.7	296	81.1	0.0	0.0	0.0	18.9	27.1	67.3	5.7	104	67.3	32.7	26.9
Inman city	1,377	1,374	-0.2	1,240	98.0	0.0	0.0	1.7	0.3	20.5	49.1	30.6	514	79.2	49.0	21.0
Iola city	5,703	5,553	-2.6	5,650	90.7	3.9	0.7	3.3	1.5	23.9	57.1	18.9	2,292	59.5	42.6	15.8
Isabel city	90	91	1.1	99	85.9	0.0	0.0	0.0	14.1	15.2	61.7	23.2	39	100.0	53.8	0.0
Iuka city	163	168	3.1	211	77.3	1.4	0.0	0.5	20.9	31.7	50.1	18.0	81	88.9	38.3	19.8
Jamestown city	286	283	-1.0	321	96.3	0.0	0.0	0.0	3.7	24.6	62.2	13.1	119	82.4	47.9	7.6
Jennings city	96	95	-1.0	137	90.5	1.5	0.0	8.0	0.0	10.2	48.9	40.9	77	67.5	51.9	28.6
Jetmore city	867	864	-0.3	857	87.0	0.0	0.0	1.4	11.6	24.8	51.7	23.6	364	74.5	34.9	18.1
Jewell city	432	424	-1.9	436	97.9	0.0	0.0	0.5	1.6	25.6	49.8	24.8	202	75.7	45.5	13.4
Johnson City city	1,495	1,413	-5.5	1,473	54.6	1.4	0.0	3.5	40.5	28.5	55.8	15.8	581	76.8	43.2	17.7
Junction City city	23,349	24,665	5.6	24,691	55.7	18.9	3.3	8.1	14.0	28.4	63.8	7.7	9,161	47.8	38.9	19.5
Kanopolis city	492	479	-2.6	444	93.0	0.0	0.0	2.3	4.7	19.4	56.1	24.5	218	86.2	55.0	11.0
Kanorado city	153	157	2.6	148	78.4	0.0	0.0	0.0	21.6	11.5	59.6	29.1	85	91.8	60.0	7.1
Kansas City city	145,786	149,636	2.6	147,598	39.9	25.9	3.3	2.7	28.2	28.4	60.9	10.9	53,802	58.5	49.7	16.6
Kechi city	1,909	1,982	3.8	2,291	92.5	2.4	0.7	2.6	1.8	28.6	60.6	10.8	780	96.3	21.9	47.3
Kensington city	473	461	-2.5	393	95.4	0.8	0.0	2.8	1.0	17.6	44.6	37.9	184	83.2	50.5	16.3
Kickapoo Site 1 CDP	101	NA	NA	143	5.6	0.0	0.0	85.3	9.1	47.6	52.5	0.0	37	45.9	54.1	0.0
Kickapoo Site 2 CDP	34	NA	NA	35	0.0	0.0	0.0	100.0	0.0	34.3	60.1	5.7	9	88.9	11.1	0.0
Kickapoo Site 5 CDP	66	NA	NA	35	5.7	0.0	0.0	85.7	8.6	25.7	65.8	8.6	17	64.7	76.5	5.9
Kickapoo Site 6 CDP	15	NA	NA	21	0.0	0.0	0.0	100.0	0.0	23.8	76.2	0.0	5	100.0	0.0	0.0
Kickapoo Site 7 CDP	66	NA	NA	67	0.0	0.0	0.0	73.1	26.9	29.9	55.4	14.9	36	33.3	52.8	25.0

1 May be of any race.

Table A. All Places — **Population and Housing**

STATE City, town, township, borough, or CDP (county if applicable)	2010 census total population	2014 estimated population	Percent change 2010–2014	ACS total population estimate 2010–2014	White alone, not Hispanic or Latino	Black alone, not Hispanic or Latino	Asian alone, not Hispanic or Latino	All other races or 2 or more races, not Hispanic or Latino	Hispanic or Latino[1]	Under 18 years old	Age 18 to 64 years old	Age 65 years and older	Total occupied housing units	Percent owner occupied	High school diploma or less	Bachelor's degree or more
	1	2	3	4	5	6	7	8	9	10	11	12	13	14	15	16
KANSAS—Con.																
Kickapoo Tribal Center CDP	194	NA	NA	195	9.7	7.2	0.0	79.5	3.6	26.7	52.8	20.5	78	60.3	34.6	17.9
Kincaid city	122	119	-2.5	138	96.4	0.7	0.0	2.9	0.0	39.8	44.1	15.9	53	81.1	52.8	3.8
Kingman city	3,177	3,094	-2.6	3,151	92.4	0.3	0.0	3.9	3.3	23.5	52.6	23.9	1,318	65.3	39.7	19.1
Kinsley city	1,457	1,451	-0.4	1,488	76.7	2.1	0.7	2.2	18.3	23.9	53.1	22.8	624	77.2	54.2	14.9
Kiowa city	1,026	1,028	0.2	1,117	91.8	0.7	0.0	4.7	2.9	26.0	54.1	19.9	468	70.9	46.6	21.4
Kipp CDP	59	NA	NA	159	100.0	0.0	0.0	0.0	0.0	69.2	30.8	0.0	39	25.6	74.4	0.0
Kirwin city	171	164	-4.1	174	93.7	0.0	0.0	4.6	1.7	22.4	60.3	17.2	79	72.2	68.4	12.7
Kismet city	459	467	1.7	404	59.9	0.5	0.0	4.7	34.9	30.5	57.4	12.1	127	73.2	36.2	9.4
Labette city	78	76	-2.6	40	90.0	0.0	0.0	10.0	0.0	7.5	70.0	22.5	26	100.0	50.0	7.7
La Crosse city	1,342	1,290	-3.9	1,377	94.5	2.1	0.0	2.0	1.4	16.6	55.7	27.6	680	67.1	40.6	18.5
La Cygne city	1,149	1,116	-2.9	1,347	97.8	0.3	0.0	0.7	1.2	30.2	54.1	15.7	530	55.5	54.0	10.2
La Harpe city	578	552	-4.5	606	87.5	0.0	4.6	4.6	3.3	22.2	65.1	12.7	251	75.3	50.6	8.8
Lake Quivira city	906	934	3.1	957	96.3	0.3	1.4	0.9	1.0	22.6	53.9	23.5	351	97.7	7.1	79.2
Lakin city	2,216	2,180	-1.6	1,913	71.8	1.5	0.0	1.4	25.3	28.7	55.6	15.7	679	66.3	45.2	21.5
Lancaster city	298	292	-2.0	322	91.0	0.0	0.0	9.0	0.0	22.6	62.0	15.2	128	95.3	58.6	14.8
Lane city	225	222	-1.3	237	93.7	0.0	3.4	0.8	2.1	8.8	72.3	19.0	126	72.2	65.1	1.6
Langdon city	42	41	-2.4	31	100.0	0.0	0.0	0.0	0.0	3.2	48.5	48.4	21	81.0	52.4	9.5
Lansing city	11,265	11,713	4.0	11,535	76.2	9.4	2.4	5.9	6.1	22.9	69.1	8.0	3,135	77.0	25.6	41.0
Larned city	4,054	4,023	-0.8	4,044	85.8	3.1	0.0	3.0	8.2	22.5	56.9	20.5	1,709	67.3	30.8	28.7
Latham city	139	138	-0.7	127	86.6	0.0	0.0	13.4	0.0	13.4	65.2	21.3	53	56.6	60.4	3.8
Latimer city	20	19	-5.0	41	87.8	0.0	0.0	12.2	0.0	34.2	58.5	7.3	14	78.6	78.6	14.3
Lawrence city	87,643	92,763	5.8	90,194	77.6	4.3	5.0	6.6	6.5	17.4	74.2	8.3	34,926	45.6	17.6	50.8
Leavenworth city	35,251	36,000	2.1	35,738	70.7	13.6	2.2	5.2	8.3	25.9	63.0	11.0	12,347	49.9	34.8	32.8
Leawood city	31,867	34,395	7.9	32,842	90.8	1.4	3.6	2.3	1.9	27.0	56.7	16.4	12,306	93.0	5.9	78.3
Lebanon city	218	212	-2.8	274	91.2	0.0	0.0	8.8	0.0	24.4	55.0	20.4	123	79.7	55.3	8.1
Lebo city	940	915	-2.7	887	98.9	0.0	0.5	0.7	0.0	26.9	53.2	19.8	349	74.5	51.3	18.1
Lecompton city	625	637	1.9	642	84.3	0.0	0.0	12.9	2.8	25.7	59.1	15.3	245	77.1	33.5	22.9
Lehigh city	175	169	-3.4	164	98.8	0.0	0.0	0.0	1.2	30.5	58.0	11.6	67	88.1	35.8	22.4
Lenexa city	48,190	51,042	5.9	49,573	79.7	5.5	3.9	2.9	8.0	24.3	64.1	11.4	19,694	62.6	15.2	56.0
Lenora city	250	240	-4.0	265	94.7	0.4	0.0	1.5	3.4	17.0	45.6	37.4	137	73.7	26.3	26.3
Leon city	704	697	-1.0	572	95.8	0.0	0.0	3.7	0.5	23.8	59.1	17.0	243	77.4	40.7	5.8
Leona city	53	53	0.0	71	88.7	0.0	0.0	11.3	0.0	12.7	80.3	7.0	27	77.8	66.7	0.0
Leonardville city	450	455	1.1	361	98.6	0.8	0.6	0.0	0.0	11.3	59.5	29.1	159	68.6	56.6	13.8
Leoti city	1,534	1,496	-2.5	1,478	62.4	0.0	0.3	1.2	36.1	29.4	52.7	17.8	576	72.0	50.7	20.1
LeRoy city	561	550	-2.0	566	93.6	0.9	0.0	1.6	3.9	25.6	56.6	17.8	235	67.7	51.1	9.8
Levant CDP	61	NA	NA	59	100.0	0.0	0.0	0.0	0.0	0.0	81.3	18.6	40	47.5	27.5	10.0
Lewis city	451	445	-1.3	393	67.9	0.0	0.0	0.0	32.1	18.8	59.0	22.1	171	76.6	53.8	11.7
Liberal city	20,525	21,012	2.4	20,846	32.5	4.0	3.1	1.4	59.0	31.7	58.9	9.2	6,681	63.5	61.0	13.2
Liberty city	123	119	-3.3	228	92.5	0.0	0.0	7.5	0.0	26.8	64.4	8.8	97	92.8	33.0	3.1
Liebenthal city	103	100	-2.9	103	98.1	0.0	0.0	0.0	1.9	2.9	72.0	25.2	64	98.4	50.0	9.4
Lincoln Center city	1,297	1,266	-2.4	1,343	96.8	0.1	0.2	0.2	2.7	22.8	50.1	27.0	603	74.5	44.6	15.3
Lincolnville city	201	194	-3.5	244	95.9	1.2	1.6	0.8	0.4	27.1	49.6	23.4	109	76.1	58.7	18.3
Lindsborg city	3,458	3,438	-0.6	3,473	83.8	1.8	1.0	2.8	10.6	23.0	59.6	17.3	1,253	65.5	25.3	40.5
Linn city	410	398	-2.9	419	82.1	1.2	0.0	1.2	15.5	18.4	43.2	38.4	171	70.8	57.9	14.6
Linn Valley city	804	799	-0.6	958	92.2	1.5	0.4	3.7	2.3	18.8	54.2	26.8	453	96.5	32.7	28.0
Linwood city	375	384	2.4	381	95.5	0.0	0.0	1.6	2.9	27.3	59.8	12.9	144	81.9	60.4	10.4
Little River city	557	549	-1.4	564	96.1	0.0	0.0	3.9	0.0	26.9	50.6	22.3	209	64.1	43.5	15.8
Logan city	589	569	-3.4	492	95.7	0.0	0.0	3.0	1.2	20.4	49.6	30.1	236	80.5	47.9	20.3
Lone Elm city	25	24	-4.0	22	90.9	0.0	0.0	0.0	9.1	9.1	45.4	45.5	9	66.7	66.7	22.2
Longford city	79	77	-2.5	206	100.0	0.0	0.0	0.0	0.0	3.4	85.4	11.2	77	84.4	26.0	5.2
Long Island city	134	131	-2.2	157	84.7	0.6	0.0	0.0	14.6	19.7	65.6	14.6	67	71.6	44.8	23.9
Longton city	348	322	-7.5	373	89.8	0.0	0.5	5.4	4.3	28.7	55.1	16.1	168	78.6	33.3	20.8
Lorraine city	138	137	-0.7	129	93.8	0.0	0.0	1.6	4.7	19.4	63.7	17.1	57	73.7	35.1	17.5
Lost Springs city	70	68	-2.9	57	87.7	0.0	12.3	0.0	0.0	19.3	38.7	42.1	30	100.0	70.0	3.3
Louisburg city	4,315	4,322	0.2	4,313	96.6	0.0	0.0	1.2	2.2	30.7	57.7	11.6	1,652	66.0	32.3	26.2
Louisville city	188	202	7.4	304	85.2	0.0	0.0	0.7	14.1	35.6	57.2	7.2	124	56.5	62.9	10.5
Lowell CDP	283	NA	NA	216	100.0	0.0	0.0	0.0	0.0	0.0	43.6	56.5	94	74.5	37.2	0.0
Lucas city	393	393	0.0	518	93.1	2.3	0.0	3.5	1.2	21.3	53.8	25.1	233	76.0	42.9	17.2
Luray city	194	195	0.5	224	97.8	0.0	0.0	0.0	2.2	12.1	63.0	25.0	112	75.9	34.8	31.3
Lyndon city	1,058	1,030	-2.6	1,080	95.1	1.5	0.0	0.8	2.6	24.5	64.5	11.0	409	74.3	39.6	28.6
Lyons city	3,740	3,737	-0.1	3,746	73.7	0.7	0.4	2.0	23.1	24.5	56.9	18.5	1,442	69.3	43.8	15.2
McConnell AFB CDP	1,777	NA	NA	1,428	64.4	6.4	2.2	5.3	21.7	33.5	66.5	0.0	346	0.9	6.4	14.2
McCracken city	190	184	-3.2	239	93.7	0.0	0.0	6.3	0.0	24.7	55.7	19.7	106	76.4	37.7	17.0
McCune city	405	405	0.0	504	94.8	0.0	0.0	4.4	0.8	19.3	71.1	9.5	223	67.7	57.0	8.5
McDonald city	160	165	3.1	139	62.6	0.0	0.0	1.4	36.0	12.2	61.3	26.6	72	68.1	61.1	15.3
McFarland city	260	257	-1.2	326	85.6	0.0	0.0	7.1	7.4	26.0	59.9	14.1	117	76.1	53.0	7.7
Macksville city	549	543	-1.1	529	75.8	0.0	0.4	0.2	23.6	31.0	51.9	17.0	196	81.6	43.9	19.9
McLouth city	880	854	-3.0	1,204	92.9	0.7	0.0	4.3	2.1	32.0	61.0	7.1	422	73.9	39.8	15.9
McPherson city	13,157	13,189	0.2	13,205	91.5	1.5	0.8	2.3	4.0	24.3	59.2	16.6	5,543	74.0	32.2	31.6
Madison city	701	661	-5.7	859	82.4	0.0	0.2	1.4	15.9	36.9	47.1	16.1	322	78.9	41.6	13.0
Mahaska city	83	80	-3.6	45	97.8	0.0	0.0	2.2	0.0	15.5	64.5	20.0	21	95.2	66.7	0.0
Maize city	3,442	4,073	18.3	3,984	86.6	0.0	1.4	0.2	11.7	34.1	55.5	10.4	1,230	74.6	26.2	31.2
Manchester city	97	98	1.0	122	89.3	0.0	0.0	10.7	0.0	27.9	63.2	9.0	56	55.4	78.6	3.6
Manhattan city	52,297	56,078	7.2	55,112	78.7	5.7	5.7	3.6	6.3	14.8	78.0	7.4	20,476	38.9	14.7	45.9
Mankato city	869	858	-1.3	830	90.4	0.4	1.1	4.7	3.5	19.5	54.1	26.4	388	69.3	45.4	9.8
Manter city	171	163	-4.7	192	75.5	0.0	3.1	4.7	16.7	14.6	70.3	15.1	98	58.2	33.7	19.4
Maple Hill city	620	626	1.0	684	96.3	0.4	0.0	1.6	1.6	41.7	48.5	9.8	222	95.9	32.9	34.2
Mapleton city	84	83	-1.2	115	100.0	0.0	0.0	0.0	0.0	39.2	50.5	10.4	41	92.7	48.8	12.2
Marienthal CDP	71	NA	NA	33	72.7	0.0	0.0	27.3	0.0	0.0	78.8	21.2	27	48.1	18.5	0.0
Marion city	1,927	1,861	-3.4	1,943	93.5	0.1	0.0	2.3	4.1	26.1	53.0	20.8	873	74.1	49.4	16.0
Marquette city	641	632	-1.4	613	94.1	0.0	0.3	1.0	4.6	22.9	56.5	20.6	254	80.3	48.8	15.4
Marysville city	3,298	3,295	-0.1	3,301	94.1	1.0	1.0	1.2	2.7	22.4	57.8	19.8	1,529	61.9	46.9	19.8
Matfield Green city	47	45	-4.3	44	100.0	0.0	0.0	0.0	0.0	15.9	45.4	38.6	23	95.7	34.8	8.7
Mayetta city	341	342	0.3	471	69.2	0.0	1.1	24.2	5.5	33.1	61.9	5.1	157	95.5	45.2	21.7
Mayfield city	113	110	-2.7	82	100.0	0.0	0.0	0.0	0.0	31.7	42.7	25.6	36	83.3	38.9	25.0
Meade city	1,721	1,637	-4.9	1,604	91.6	3.2	1.5	0.0	3.6	28.9	49.7	21.4	622	75.6	41.3	25.1
Medicine Lodge city	2,009	2,021	0.6	2,132	95.5	0.0	0.5	0.7	3.4	25.8	57.4	16.8	928	68.3	41.3	19.2
Melvern city	385	369	-4.2	456	97.6	0.0	0.2	2.2	0.0	30.3	59.6	10.1	164	67.7	47.0	15.9
Menlo city	61	61	0.0	40	100.0	0.0	0.0	0.0	0.0	57.5	42.5	0.0	11	90.9	54.5	27.3
Meriden city	813	791	-2.7	940	92.4	0.0	0.0	4.0	3.5	27.1	61.3	11.6	356	64.3	56.7	15.2

1 May be of any race.

Table A. All Places — **Population and Housing**

STATE City, town, township, borough, or CDP (county if applicable)	Population: 2010 census total population	Population: 2014 estimated population	Population: Percent change 2010–2014	Population: ACS total population estimate 2010–2014	Race and Hispanic or Latino origin (percent), 2010–2014: White alone, not Hispanic or Latino	Race: Black alone, not Hispanic or Latino	Race: Asian alone, not Hispanic or Latino	Race: All other races or 2 or more races, not Hispanic or Latino	Race: Hispanic or Latino[1]	Age (percent), 2010–2014: Under 18 years old	Age: Age 18 to 64 years old	Age: Age 65 years and older	Households, 2010–2014: Total occupied housing units	Households: Percent owner occupied	Households: Householders by level of education (percent): High school diploma or less	Households: Householders by level of education (percent): Bachelor's degree or more
	1	2	3	4	5	6	7	8	9	10	11	12	13	14	15	16
KANSAS—Con.																
Merriam city	11,032	11,290	2.3	11,191	79.1	7.3	2.3	2.1	9.2	18.0	68.4	13.7	4,950	55.2	26.2	37.8
Milan city	82	80	-2.4	69	76.8	0.0	0.0	2.9	20.3	24.6	59.2	15.9	37	78.4	40.5	16.2
Mildred city	28	27	-3.6	35	100.0	0.0	0.0	0.0	0.0	57.2	42.9	0.0	8	12.5	100.0	0.0
Milford city	530	594	12.1	519	83.2	1.0	1.2	1.7	12.9	33.9	52.3	13.9	206	54.4	34.5	10.7
Milton CDP	155	NA	NA	43	100.0	0.0	0.0	0.0	0.0	23.3	60.5	16.3	20	100.0	35.0	0.0
Miltonvale city	539	526	-2.4	490	98.0	0.2	0.0	1.2	0.6	16.3	59.8	23.9	221	77.4	39.4	13.6
Minneapolis city	2,032	2,029	-0.1	2,160	94.3	0.2	0.0	3.4	2.1	28.1	54.1	17.7	836	67.7	41.7	18.1
Minneola city	745	724	-2.8	706	86.1	0.0	1.8	1.1	10.9	26.2	51.6	22.2	296	60.5	35.5	29.7
Mission city	9,323	9,501	1.9	9,451	79.3	7.7	2.9	2.5	7.6	19.5	68.9	11.6	4,904	49.3	19.1	51.3
Mission Hills city	3,498	3,597	2.8	3,555	95.8	0.0	1.1	0.5	2.6	26.7	53.5	19.8	1,281	100.0	0.9	89.0
Mission Woods city	178	182	2.2	166	96.4	0.0	3.0	0.6	0.0	16.8	56.5	26.5	72	95.8	5.6	87.5
Moline city	371	344	-7.3	283	94.3	0.0	0.0	2.1	3.5	7.5	54.8	37.8	161	76.4	52.2	10.6
Montezuma city	966	979	1.3	969	90.2	0.0	0.7	1.7	7.4	21.7	51.7	26.5	357	69.7	44.5	16.2
Moran city	558	529	-5.2	503	94.6	0.4	0.0	0.4	4.6	21.9	54.4	23.9	203	73.9	48.8	10.8
Morganville city	192	187	-2.6	213	95.8	0.0	0.0	2.3	1.9	34.7	50.3	15.0	75	88.0	40.0	16.0
Morland city	154	153	-0.6	110	100.0	0.0	0.0	0.0	0.0	22.7	55.5	21.8	55	87.3	32.7	43.6
Morrill city	230	227	-1.3	321	86.3	0.0	0.0	0.0	13.7	34.5	60.6	5.0	115	73.9	59.1	20.9
Morrowville city	155	150	-3.2	155	100.0	0.0	0.0	0.0	0.0	34.9	49.0	16.1	54	94.4	55.6	11.1
Moscow city	318	322	1.3	359	61.3	0.6	0.0	0.3	37.9	37.9	49.5	12.8	114	64.9	43.9	13.2
Mound City city	694	682	-1.7	870	96.8	1.8	0.0	0.6	0.8	25.1	57.5	17.5	336	74.7	38.4	22.6
Moundridge city	1,737	1,726	-0.6	1,782	95.8	0.2	0.6	2.0	1.4	20.2	52.2	27.7	754	71.4	50.4	15.6
Mound Valley city	407	390	-4.2	452	78.3	0.0	0.0	14.2	7.5	28.9	56.9	14.2	165	72.7	44.8	9.7
Mount Hope city	813	814	0.1	790	95.7	1.1	0.4	1.5	1.3	20.7	59.0	20.4	314	66.9	29.0	34.4
Mulberry city	520	512	-1.5	547	85.4	0.4	0.0	11.5	2.7	21.7	60.1	18.5	241	71.0	63.1	4.1
Mullinville city	255	250	-2.0	247	79.8	0.0	0.0	3.2	17.0	28.3	52.2	19.4	98	68.4	32.7	12.2
Mulvane city	6,143	6,289	2.4	6,000	92.4	0.0	1.2	3.2	3.2	24.6	60.2	15.3	2,297	87.2	26.2	35.9
Munden city	100	96	-4.0	148	96.6	0.0	0.0	0.0	3.4	35.1	54.9	10.1	58	86.2	39.7	13.8
Munjor CDP	213	NA	NA	176	100.0	0.0	0.0	0.0	0.0	0.0	36.5	63.6	98	100.0	83.7	10.2
Muscotah city	176	172	-2.3	147	93.9	2.7	0.0	2.7	0.7	32.0	56.3	11.6	56	82.1	53.6	12.5
Narka city	94	91	-3.2	94	100.0	0.0	0.0	0.0	0.0	21.3	59.7	19.1	51	70.6	51.0	2.0
Nashville city	64	63	-1.6	77	98.7	0.0	0.0	1.3	0.0	14.3	55.9	29.9	44	54.5	27.3	15.9
Natoma city	335	323	-3.6	304	88.2	1.0	0.0	3.6	7.2	17.4	56.9	25.7	151	81.5	55.0	17.9
Neodesha city	2,486	2,400	-3.5	2,229	91.2	0.3	1.7	2.8	4.0	24.1	57.8	18.2	954	59.6	53.0	17.2
Neosho Falls city	141	135	-4.3	153	81.0	0.0	0.0	11.8	7.2	24.1	56.1	19.6	59	72.9	64.4	0.0
Neosho Rapids city	265	262	-1.1	229	92.1	0.0	1.3	3.5	3.1	21.4	56.5	22.3	95	89.5	57.9	11.6
Ness City city	1,456	1,454	-0.1	1,509	89.6	0.7	0.0	1.5	8.2	20.8	54.7	24.4	665	77.1	49.8	18.9
Netawaka city	143	146	2.1	163	85.3	0.0	0.0	14.7	0.0	28.8	64.8	6.1	65	90.8	52.3	7.7
New Albany city	56	54	-3.6	31	71.0	0.0	0.0	29.0	0.0	6.5	74.3	19.4	16	100.0	81.3	12.5
New Cambria city	126	126	0.0	140	80.7	1.4	0.0	0.0	17.9	22.1	60.8	17.1	51	80.4	43.1	3.9
New Strawn city	394	404	2.5	427	89.5	1.2	0.0	3.3	6.1	20.7	71.2	8.2	190	78.9	24.7	41.1
Newton city	19,139	19,120	-0.1	19,144	77.8	1.8	0.6	2.9	17.0	25.4	57.1	17.6	7,691	65.7	42.6	23.7
Nickerson city	1,070	1,041	-2.7	1,174	99.7	0.0	0.0	0.1	0.3	28.3	60.6	11.2	438	77.2	40.0	10.3
Niotaze city	82	78	-4.9	113	74.3	0.0	0.0	25.7	0.0	17.7	71.8	10.6	47	78.7	55.3	4.3
Norcatur city	151	149	-1.3	172	93.0	0.0	0.0	7.0	0.0	18.5	47.0	34.3	90	93.3	47.8	12.2
North Newton city	1,759	1,788	1.6	1,926	88.1	0.9	1.7	2.2	7.1	14.8	56.9	28.3	702	61.8	23.4	51.1
Norton city	2,904	2,846	-2.0	2,878	94.2	0.8	0.0	1.4	3.6	25.0	53.3	21.7	1,267	73.8	38.4	14.3
Nortonville city	637	615	-3.5	566	97.7	0.0	0.0	1.9	0.4	25.4	50.0	24.6	202	84.2	59.9	11.9
Norwich city	491	475	-3.3	421	95.7	0.0	0.0	4.3	0.0	35.9	48.4	15.9	134	81.3	35.8	19.4
Oak Hill city	24	23	-4.2	15	100.0	0.0	0.0	0.0	0.0	13.3	53.4	33.3	9	88.9	55.6	0.0
Oaklawn-Sunview CDP	3,276	NA	NA	2,838	63.2	2.3	19.4	2.4	12.8	28.7	64.7	6.7	1,000	54.1	69.1	1.8
Oakley city	2,045	2,075	1.5	1,939	90.4	0.0	3.6	1.0	5.0	21.3	56.5	22.1	881	68.2	41.4	19.9
Oberlin city	1,788	1,749	-2.2	1,877	95.6	0.4	0.0	0.9	3.0	18.4	51.7	29.9	950	74.7	50.9	21.6
Odin CDP	101	NA	NA	77	100.0	0.0	0.0	0.0	0.0	19.5	50.7	29.9	38	100.0	63.2	0.0
Offerle city	199	200	0.5	250	85.2	0.0	0.0	2.8	12.0	32.0	52.8	15.2	87	87.4	20.7	34.5
Ogden city	2,087	2,138	2.4	1,987	71.6	8.0	0.0	3.3	17.1	35.6	58.2	6.1	750	49.9	37.9	15.5
Oketo city	66	65	-1.5	56	96.4	0.0	0.0	0.0	3.6	17.8	53.6	28.6	28	89.3	71.4	3.6
Olathe city	125,875	133,062	5.7	129,913	76.5	4.8	4.6	3.3	10.8	29.6	62.5	7.9	45,166	71.8	20.9	47.2
Olivet city	67	66	-1.5	85	100.0	0.0	0.0	0.0	0.0	20.0	64.7	15.3	44	93.2	65.9	4.5
Olmitz city	114	113	-0.9	140	100.0	0.0	0.0	0.0	0.0	18.5	62.7	18.6	65	81.5	73.8	7.7
Olpe city	546	537	-1.6	576	95.7	0.5	0.0	3.8	0.0	28.3	59.0	12.8	248	73.8	44.8	25.4
Olsburg city	219	226	3.2	205	92.2	0.0	0.0	0.0	7.8	28.3	60.0	11.7	86	91.9	45.3	10.5
Onaga city	702	702	0.0	764	91.4	0.5	0.7	3.3	4.2	26.2	53.1	20.7	304	67.4	46.1	21.1
Oneida city	75	75	0.0	55	90.9	5.5	3.6	0.0	0.0	11.0	43.5	45.5	26	96.2	69.2	11.5
Osage City city	2,943	2,862	-2.8	2,910	94.6	0.4	1.5	2.4	1.1	25.5	49.5	24.9	1,222	65.1	48.9	22.3
Osawatomie city	4,443	4,357	-1.9	4,403	94.3	2.4	0.1	1.6	1.7	27.5	60.1	12.4	1,737	68.5	49.9	1.5
Osborne city	1,436	1,396	-2.8	1,403	94.9	0.1	2.0	0.7	2.2	22.1	52.0	25.9	640	75.0	46.1	19.8
Oskaloosa city	1,113	1,086	-2.4	1,292	89.6	2.3	0.0	3.9	4.2	25.5	58.6	15.9	500	72.0	54.0	15.8
Oswego city	1,829	1,781	-2.6	2,018	82.5	3.2	0.3	12.5	1.5	24.7	56.7	18.7	770	74.9	43.8	14.0
Otis city	282	274	-2.8	333	95.5	0.0	0.0	4.2	0.3	23.4	60.6	15.9	140	81.4	46.4	17.1
Ottawa city	12,651	12,403	-2.0	12,548	89.0	2.0	0.7	3.2	5.1	23.8	63.4	12.8	5,042	60.4	43.7	19.3
Overbrook city	1,058	1,029	-2.7	1,056	95.6	0.0	0.0	0.9	3.5	27.4	52.3	20.4	400	71.3	40.0	24.8
Overland Park city	173,333	184,525	6.5	178,945	79.5	4.8	6.7	2.5	6.5	24.1	62.4	13.5	74,058	64.2	13.7	59.7
Oxford city	1,049	1,022	-2.6	1,178	94.6	0.0	0.0	2.9	2.5	23.8	55.2	20.8	458	77.1	33.2	23.1
Ozawkie city	645	631	-2.2	743	88.0	1.5	0.5	0.9	9.0	29.6	54.2	16.2	241	90.0	33.6	35.7
Palco city	277	282	1.8	159	97.5	0.0	0.0	1.9	0.6	25.8	40.3	34.0	78	96.2	50.0	23.1
Palmer city	111	107	-3.6	158	77.8	0.0	0.0	0.0	22.2	34.2	56.9	8.9	63	79.4	31.7	14.3
Paola city	5,602	5,593	-0.2	5,589	88.8	1.9	0.0	4.0	5.3	32.5	50.4	17.0	2,009	64.4	41.0	23.3
Paradise city	49	49	0.0	30	96.7	0.0	0.0	3.3	0.0	6.7	39.9	53.3	20	100.0	15.0	30.0
Park city	126	125	-0.8	98	99.0	0.0	0.0	1.0	0.0	35.8	52.0	12.2	46	60.9	60.9	8.7
Park City city	7,297	7,556	3.5	7,194	83.1	2.1	3.3	1.8	9.8	28.0	62.7	9.3	2,560	78.3	34.4	21.3
Parker city	277	273	-1.4	307	96.4	0.0	0.0	2.0	1.6	17.6	67.0	15.3	153	81.0	59.5	5.2
Parkerfield city	420	417	-0.7	352	94.3	0.0	0.0	2.0	3.7	17.1	65.6	17.3	148	94.6	39.2	31.8
Parkerville city	59	57	-3.4	70	95.7	0.0	0.0	4.3	0.0	10.0	68.6	21.4	28	92.9	67.9	10.7
Parsons city	10,500	10,174	-3.1	10,307	83.1	6.0	0.0	4.7	6.2	23.9	61.3	14.9	4,161	61.0	38.5	20.9
Partridge city	248	245	-1.2	300	82.3	0.0	0.0	4.3	13.3	22.0	63.0	15.0	92	81.5	60.9	17.4
Pawnee Rock city	252	244	-3.2	213	91.5	0.0	0.0	5.2	3.3	25.8	57.3	16.9	96	71.9	50.0	11.5
Paxico city	221	218	-1.4	239	69.9	6.3	0.0	20.1	3.8	33.1	55.2	11.7	88	63.6	33.0	8.0
Peabody city	1,210	1,156	-4.5	1,185	94.0	0.4	0.0	5.0	0.6	23.9	51.0	25.1	456	61.0	48.2	13.6
Penalosa city	17	17	0.0	11	90.9	0.0	0.0	0.0	9.1	0.0	54.6	45.5	6	83.3	66.7	0.0
Perry city	929	904	-2.7	961	94.5	0.8	0.0	3.0	1.7	27.1	48.7	24.0	416	81.0	52.2	26.2
Peru city	139	133	-4.3	144	75.7	2.8	0.0	21.5	0.0	18.0	62.7	19.4	70	72.9	64.3	4.3

1 May be of any race.

Table A. All Places — **Population and Housing**

STATE City, town, township, borough, or CDP (county if applicable)	Population				Race and Hispanic or Latino origin (percent), 2010–2014					Age (percent), 2010–2014			Households, 2010–2014			
	2010 census total population	2014 estimated population	Percent change 2010–2014	ACS total population estimate 2010–2014	White alone, not Hispanic or Latino	Black alone, not Hispanic or Latino	Asian alone, not Hispanic or Latino	All other races or 2 or more races, not Hispanic or Latino	Hispanic or Latino[1]	Under 18 years old	Age 18 to 64 years old	Age 65 years and older	Total occupied housing units	Percent owner occupied	Householders by level of education (percent): High school diploma or less	Householders by level of education (percent): Bachelor's degree or more
	1	2	3	4	5	6	7	8	9	10	11	12	13	14	15	16
KANSAS—Con.																
Phillipsburg city	2,584	2,556	-1.1	2,556	95.1	0.2	0.7	1.6	2.4	26.1	53.2	20.7	1,108	73.6	40.1	20.4
Piqua CDP	107	NA	NA	152	74.3	0.0	0.0	0.0	25.7	29.5	67.1	3.3	67	92.5	88.1	6.0
Pittsburg city	20,233	20,394	0.8	20,336	84.7	3.4	2.5	3.8	5.7	20.5	67.4	12.3	7,981	46.1	25.3	29.6
Plains city	1,146	1,093	-4.6	1,184	56.9	0.0	1.5	0.4	41.1	29.1	58.2	12.8	452	64.4	58.2	17.9
Plainville city	1,903	1,889	-0.7	1,776	95.0	0.0	2.3	1.5	1.2	20.9	53.8	25.2	843	65.8	41.2	16.4
Pleasanton city	1,216	1,180	-3.0	1,213	94.2	0.2	1.2	1.6	2.9	30.5	50.2	19.2	572	63.6	46.3	7.3
Plevna city	98	97	-1.0	88	100.0	0.0	0.0	0.0	0.0	22.7	51.2	26.1	45	80.0	24.4	22.2
Pomona city	832	807	-3.0	761	88.7	0.8	0.0	8.4	2.1	24.0	58.1	17.9	340	71.5	62.9	10.0
Portis city	103	101	-1.9	94	100.0	0.0	0.0	0.0	0.0	31.9	53.3	14.9	39	82.1	43.6	12.8
Potwin city	449	436	-2.9	534	93.4	0.0	0.0	0.6	6.0	27.2	60.6	12.4	210	86.7	43.3	16.2
Powhattan city	77	76	-1.3	105	89.5	0.0	0.0	8.6	1.9	34.3	52.4	13.3	36	72.2	47.2	11.1
Prairie View city	134	131	-2.2	167	90.4	0.0	0.0	7.2	2.4	29.4	58.8	12.0	61	75.4	45.9	41.0
Prairie Village city	21,447	21,877	2.0	21,730	93.6	1.6	1.1	1.2	2.4	21.8	59.1	19.1	9,754	79.2	8.6	70.1
Pratt city	6,835	6,963	1.9	6,889	88.2	0.7	0.1	3.5	7.5	22.2	58.7	19.2	2,973	61.6	36.7	22.4
Prescott city	264	260	-1.5	217	93.5	0.0	0.0	6.5	0.0	20.8	53.0	26.3	91	68.1	42.9	7.7
Preston city	158	162	2.5	159	95.6	0.0	0.0	2.5	1.9	20.1	59.6	20.1	72	75.0	51.4	8.3
Pretty Prairie city	683	681	-0.3	821	91.7	0.0	1.3	5.0	1.9	28.6	51.9	19.4	306	70.6	36.3	7.8
Princeton city	277	267	-3.6	289	95.8	0.0	0.3	0.3	3.5	29.4	58.4	12.1	105	73.3	48.6	14.3
Protection city	514	527	2.5	521	87.7	0.0	0.0	0.0	12.3	21.3	42.4	36.3	194	81.4	28.9	18.6
Quenemo city	388	373	-3.9	488	85.2	0.2	0.0	13.9	0.6	27.0	62.8	10.0	188	61.2	78.2	2.7
Quinter city	918	960	4.6	1,026	96.5	0.8	0.0	1.8	1.0	26.2	47.5	26.3	405	76.8	39.3	25.9
Radium city	25	25	0.0	46	100.0	0.0	0.0	0.0	0.0	6.5	89.2	4.3	30	96.7	66.7	0.0
Ramona city	187	181	-3.2	113	89.4	0.0	0.0	3.5	7.1	39.8	52.2	8.0	37	91.9	51.4	21.6
Randall city	65	64	-1.5	80	96.3	0.0	0.0	1.3	2.5	21.4	60.2	18.8	37	91.9	70.3	8.1
Randolph city	163	169	3.7	170	94.7	0.0	1.2	4.1	0.0	23.5	68.3	8.2	74	78.4	40.5	23.0
Ransom city	294	289	-1.7	278	97.1	1.8	0.0	1.1	0.0	18.0	49.0	33.1	135	85.9	38.5	17.8
Rantoul city	184	182	-1.1	125	88.8	0.0	3.2	5.6	2.4	10.4	72.8	16.8	65	78.5	67.7	12.3
Raymond city	79	78	-1.3	59	96.6	0.0	0.0	3.4	0.0	0.0	79.6	20.3	31	80.6	38.7	6.5
Reading city	231	228	-1.3	279	86.4	0.0	0.0	12.2	1.4	39.8	56.5	3.6	87	82.8	50.6	11.5
Redfield city	146	143	-2.1	96	56.3	3.1	0.0	40.6	0.0	36.4	50.1	13.5	33	84.8	39.4	21.2
Republic city	116	112	-3.4	111	96.4	0.0	0.0	1.8	1.8	14.4	63.9	21.6	62	85.5	40.3	1.6
Reserve city	84	83	-1.2	58	82.8	0.0	0.0	17.2	0.0	17.3	55.1	27.6	26	57.7	61.5	0.0
Rexford city	232	231	-0.4	313	66.1	0.0	0.0	0.0	33.9	45.1	44.2	10.9	85	71.8	49.4	24.7
Richfield city	43	42	-2.3	44	100.0	0.0	0.0	0.0	0.0	20.4	54.5	25.0	17	88.2	47.1	35.3
Richmond city	464	457	-1.5	535	91.6	0.0	0.2	5.2	3.0	32.3	50.4	17.2	175	76.0	46.3	14.9
Riley city	958	994	3.8	1,002	91.4	2.2	0.0	2.9	3.5	27.7	61.7	10.8	384	70.1	34.4	19.8
Riverton CDP	929	NA	NA	1,124	97.9	0.0	0.0	1.2	1.0	27.9	57.4	14.9	435	79.8	43.7	20.2
Robinson city	234	231	-1.3	257	95.7	0.0	2.3	0.8	1.2	33.4	53.7	12.8	97	75.3	42.3	17.5
Roeland Park city	6,731	6,840	1.6	6,799	79.6	2.6	2.0	2.9	12.9	20.5	69.3	10.4	2,979	74.8	15.6	54.3
Rolla city	442	429	-2.9	357	67.5	10.6	1.1	2.5	18.2	30.2	57.3	12.3	141	58.9	46.1	21.3
Rosalia CDP	171	NA	NA	93	97.8	0.0	0.0	2.2	0.0	27.9	56.9	15.1	30	76.7	46.7	10.0
Rose Hill city	3,931	3,960	0.7	4,009	90.3	0.7	2.5	2.0	4.4	28.4	58.7	12.9	1,415	79.8	30.2	27.5
Roseland city	77	75	-2.6	89	89.9	0.0	0.0	10.1	0.0	29.1	65.3	5.6	35	71.4	42.9	5.7
Rossville city	1,151	1,139	-1.0	1,015	85.6	1.1	0.0	10.5	2.8	21.3	59.4	19.3	378	73.3	46.3	30.7
Roxbury CDP	104	NA	NA	55	100.0	0.0	0.0	0.0	0.0	0.0	52.7	47.3	26	100.0	50.0	0.0
Rozel city	156	154	-1.3	226	100.0	0.0	0.0	0.0	0.0	31.5	56.4	12.4	82	74.4	42.7	14.6
Rush Center city	170	165	-2.9	148	89.2	0.0	0.0	2.7	8.1	15.6	57.6	27.0	78	78.2	43.6	6.4
Russell city	4,506	4,484	-0.5	4,513	93.2	2.9	0.0	1.2	2.8	22.5	55.7	21.8	2,052	71.4	46.4	25.3
Russell Springs city	24	24	0.0	22	68.2	0.0	0.0	31.8	0.0	22.7	59.0	18.2	11	63.6	54.5	0.0
Sabetha city	2,571	2,564	-0.3	2,562	96.0	1.4	0.0	1.0	1.6	19.7	50.7	29.5	1,120	65.1	40.7	27.9
St. Francis city	1,329	1,312	-1.3	1,257	91.6	0.0	1.5	0.2	6.7	16.1	53.6	30.3	667	76.5	38.1	26.1
St. George city	639	773	21.0	845	75.7	17.4	0.8	2.8	3.2	42.5	51.4	6.2	269	68.8	14.5	32.0
St. John city	1,295	1,244	-3.9	1,325	78.0	1.4	0.0	1.5	19.1	27.8	53.4	18.9	531	72.3	38.0	22.4
St. Marys city	2,627	2,664	1.4	2,808	85.0	1.5	0.0	4.9	8.5	34.9	48.4	16.7	911	66.8	39.2	18.3
St. Paul city	629	610	-3.0	758	89.7	1.2	0.0	7.8	1.3	40.1	41.6	18.3	244	77.9	31.6	15.6
Salina city	47,707	47,867	0.3	47,894	79.3	3.2	2.8	3.5	11.3	24.8	60.2	15.2	19,393	63.8	41.4	24.2
Satanta city	1,133	1,117	-1.4	1,103	54.8	0.0	3.8	0.5	41.0	27.2	59.1	13.8	372	67.7	55.1	14.8
Savonburg city	109	104	-4.6	120	87.5	0.0	0.0	0.8	11.7	25.0	59.2	15.8	41	85.4	61.0	12.2
Sawyer city	124	127	2.4	84	98.8	0.0	0.0	1.2	0.0	19.0	63.1	17.9	45	86.7	57.8	15.6
Scammon city	482	461	-4.4	390	94.9	0.0	0.0	5.1	0.0	24.1	53.1	22.8	163	77.3	52.8	14.7
Scandia city	372	359	-3.5	437	97.5	0.0	0.0	1.4	1.1	26.4	55.0	18.8	187	82.4	40.1	24.1
Schoenchen city	207	208	0.5	190	92.6	0.0	0.0	3.2	4.2	22.6	66.8	10.5	79	93.7	46.8	29.1
Scott City city	3,816	3,927	2.9	3,631	74.4	0.0	0.6	1.6	23.5	24.4	56.7	18.8	1,574	74.5	42.3	27.8
Scottsville city	25	25	0.0	14	100.0	0.0	0.0	0.0	0.0	0.0	100.0	0.0	7	100.0	100.0	0.0
Scranton city	710	693	-2.4	752	91.8	0.0	0.0	6.9	1.3	33.0	55.6	11.4	275	57.1	55.3	9.5
Sedan city	1,124	1,065	-5.2	1,247	85.7	1.2	0.0	6.3	6.8	19.8	57.4	22.9	555	74.2	43.6	18.9
Sedgwick city	1,695	1,701	0.4	1,925	96.1	0.0	0.0	2.9	1.0	31.0	56.8	12.1	642	73.8	32.9	19.8
Selden city	219	218	-0.5	327	94.5	0.0	0.0	2.4	3.1	29.6	62.4	8.0	138	73.9	32.6	12.3
Seneca city	2,001	2,006	0.2	1,819	96.3	0.2	0.0	1.3	2.2	18.2	54.3	27.5	904	76.5	53.2	18.3
Severance city	94	94	0.0	75	100.0	0.0	0.0	0.0	0.0	22.6	46.8	30.7	31	93.5	58.1	12.9
Severy city	259	241	-6.9	293	90.4	0.0	0.0	9.6	0.0	19.8	59.9	20.5	127	89.8	53.5	3.9
Seward city	64	62	-3.1	55	89.1	0.0	1.8	0.0	9.1	38.2	36.5	25.5	22	86.4	72.7	0.0
Sharon city	158	161	1.9	161	93.8	0.0	1.2	4.3	0.6	11.1	70.2	18.6	77	89.6	66.2	5.2
Sharon Springs city	748	756	1.1	697	93.4	0.3	0.4	0.1	5.7	22.3	47.4	30.4	321	72.3	48.6	21.8
Shawnee city	62,209	64,599	3.8	63,597	82.6	4.4	2.3	4.0	6.7	27.4	61.9	10.7	23,688	72.1	22.0	45.4
Silver Lake city	1,439	1,426	-0.9	1,692	92.7	0.5	0.2	1.3	5.3	31.6	56.5	12.0	603	73.0	35.0	24.9
Simpson city	86	85	-1.2	50	100.0	0.0	0.0	0.0	0.0	2.0	76.0	22.0	31	100.0	35.5	0.0
Smith Center city	1,665	1,641	-1.4	1,634	96.8	1.0	0.4	0.1	1.7	21.2	51.2	27.5	761	78.6	40.5	20.0
Smolan city	215	215	0.0	238	98.3	0.0	1.7	0.0	0.0	31.5	56.1	12.2	97	87.6	37.1	25.8
Soldier city	136	141	3.7	105	85.7	3.8	0.0	6.7	3.8	26.7	41.2	32.4	43	79.1	69.8	0.0
Solomon city	1,095	1,061	-3.1	1,177	94.3	0.0	0.0	1.6	4.1	31.0	59.3	9.8	454	80.2	45.6	9.9
South Haven city	363	353	-2.8	288	87.2	0.0	0.0	11.1	1.7	25.1	59.7	15.3	123	74.0	42.3	13.8
South Hutchinson city	2,457	2,544	3.5	2,267	88.3	0.8	0.3	1.9	8.7	14.0	59.7	26.3	1,043	57.7	52.6	12.6
Spearville city	773	806	4.3	829	96.0	0.0	0.0	0.5	3.5	20.7	57.1	22.3	353	82.2	43.6	18.7
Speed city	37	36	-2.7	75	76.0	0.0	0.0	24.0	0.0	36.0	64.1	0.0	19	100.0	52.6	26.3
Spivey city	78	76	-2.6	59	81.4	0.0	0.0	0.0	18.6	17.0	54.4	28.8	28	67.9	53.6	3.6
Spring Hill city	5,449	5,896	8.2	5,618	93.3	2.0	1.0	1.4	2.3	29.2	60.9	9.9	1,948	74.4	30.6	27.9
Stafford city	1,042	1,002	-3.8	1,092	83.7	1.8	0.6	2.8	11.0	22.8	51.1	26.1	482	84.9	37.8	22.4
Stark city	72	70	-2.8	70	95.7	0.0	0.0	4.3	0.0	25.7	60.1	14.3	28	82.1	53.6	0.0
Sterling city	2,328	2,303	-1.1	2,333	90.5	2.6	1.0	2.1	3.8	16.8	66.4	16.8	832	64.4	32.5	35.5
Stockton city	1,329	1,315	-1.1	1,311	95.1	1.8	0.0	1.6	1.5	21.6	60.7	17.6	584	76.4	34.8	28.3

1 May be of any race.

Table A. All Places — Population and Housing

STATE City, town, township, borough, or CDP (county if applicable)	2010 census total population	2014 estimated population	Percent change 2010–2014	ACS total population estimate 2010–2014	White alone, not Hispanic or Latino	Black alone, not Hispanic or Latino	Asian alone, not Hispanic or Latino	All other races or 2 or more races, not Hispanic or Latino	Hispanic or Latino[1]	Under 18 years old	Age 18 to 64 years old	Age 65 years and older	Total occupied housing units	Percent owner occupied	High school diploma or less	Bachelor's degree or more
	1	2	3	4	5	6	7	8	9	10	11	12	13	14	15	16
KANSAS—Con.																
Strong City city	485	461	-4.9	485	98.4	0.8	0.0	0.8	0.0	20.4	63.7	15.9	201	67.2	61.7	10.9
Sublette city	1,453	1,399	-3.7	1,603	73.6	0.0	0.2	0.7	25.5	26.5	60.5	13.1	574	82.4	39.4	24.2
Summerfield city	156	154	-1.3	146	95.2	0.7	0.0	4.1	0.0	16.4	51.4	32.2	77	81.8	79.2	3.9
Sun City city	53	54	1.9	64	100.0	0.0	0.0	0.0	0.0	3.1	51.6	45.3	32	93.8	62.5	6.3
Susank city	34	34	0.0	39	100.0	0.0	0.0	0.0	0.0	12.8	66.8	20.5	20	95.0	65.0	5.0
Sylvan Grove city	279	268	-3.9	295	92.5	0.0	2.0	2.7	2.7	17.3	53.3	29.5	151	88.7	45.0	27.8
Sylvia city	218	215	-1.4	288	78.1	0.0	0.7	2.8	18.4	36.5	48.4	15.3	97	70.1	43.3	13.4
Syracuse city	1,812	1,750	-3.4	1,712	63.2	0.1	0.0	2.0	34.7	29.3	57.0	13.6	678	77.3	48.5	13.4
Talmage CDP	99	NA	NA	119	100.0	0.0	0.0	0.0	0.0	38.7	61.4	0.0	41	70.7	0.0	0.0
Tampa city	112	108	-3.6	105	99.0	0.0	0.0	0.0	1.0	27.6	41.9	30.5	40	92.5	55.0	17.5
Tescott city	319	318	-0.3	285	96.5	0.0	0.0	1.4	2.1	28.1	57.0	15.1	113	79.6	40.7	17.7
Thayer city	497	474	-4.6	549	92.2	0.0	0.0	5.1	2.7	33.7	55.2	11.1	194	73.2	33.0	9.8
Timken city	76	74	-2.6	60	100.0	0.0	0.0	0.0	0.0	58.3	23.3	18.3	16	87.5	56.3	6.3
Tipton city	210	207	-1.4	214	100.0	0.0	0.0	0.0	0.0	21.0	43.3	35.5	108	82.4	37.0	35.2
Tonganoxie city	4,996	5,192	3.9	4,802	90.7	1.0	1.7	0.9	5.7	29.4	57.5	13.0	1,857	56.9	48.4	28.9
Topeka city	127,474	127,215	-0.2	127,660	69.1	10.1	1.3	5.9	13.6	24.2	61.1	14.7	53,411	56.8	38.9	28.8
Toronto city	281	265	-5.7	315	96.2	0.0	0.0	2.9	1.0	21.0	47.9	31.1	167	86.2	47.3	13.8
Towanda city	1,450	1,427	-1.6	1,666	92.4	0.9	0.0	5.6	1.1	35.4	54.7	9.8	555	69.9	37.5	15.1
Tribune city	741	774	4.5	688	72.8	0.9	0.1	3.2	23.0	22.4	50.5	27.2	265	77.0	36.6	20.8
Troy city	1,010	998	-1.2	1,037	96.6	0.0	0.2	1.8	1.4	21.8	61.1	17.4	451	70.5	44.1	11.1
Turon city	387	378	-2.3	301	83.1	3.3	0.7	2.7	10.3	21.3	55.5	23.3	137	79.6	58.4	8.0
Tyro city	220	213	-3.2	254	67.7	0.0	0.0	31.1	1.2	26.5	64.6	9.1	115	80.9	33.0	15.7
Udall city	753	738	-2.0	803	93.4	0.0	0.0	0.9	5.7	25.9	58.7	15.6	362	63.3	48.9	13.5
Ulysses city	6,161	6,160	0.0	6,010	43.5	0.0	0.0	2.8	53.7	32.7	57.7	9.6	2,114	71.0	60.2	20.9
Uniontown city	272	267	-1.8	439	87.7	0.0	0.9	11.2	0.2	42.9	47.7	9.6	146	71.9	31.5	26.0
Utica city	158	159	0.6	132	100.0	0.0	0.0	0.0	0.0	14.4	43.9	41.7	76	89.5	61.8	10.5
Valley Center city	6,822	7,057	3.4	6,449	91.2	0.2	1.1	2.2	5.3	28.3	59.5	12.2	2,385	78.6	34.3	29.2
Valley Falls city	1,192	1,158	-2.9	1,149	96.3	1.0	0.0	1.7	1.0	17.2	57.2	25.8	518	68.7	51.2	16.0
Vassar CDP	530	NA	NA	723	88.9	0.0	0.0	0.0	11.1	24.2	55.4	20.3	296	92.9	54.1	15.2
Vermillion city	112	110	-1.8	95	84.2	0.0	2.1	5.3	8.4	16.9	45.3	37.9	50	82.0	52.0	14.0
Victoria city	1,214	1,225	0.9	1,129	99.1	0.0	0.0	0.5	0.4	19.1	55.7	25.3	522	80.3	38.1	24.5
Vining city	45	43	-4.4	41	90.2	0.0	9.8	0.0	0.0	34.2	41.5	24.4	20	75.0	55.0	0.0
Viola city	130	131	0.8	166	71.7	1.2	0.0	20.5	6.6	24.6	67.4	7.8	65	81.5	63.1	9.2
Virgil city	71	68	-4.2	30	100.0	0.0	0.0	0.0	0.0	13.4	40.0	46.7	21	95.2	71.4	0.0
Wakarusa CDP	260	NA	NA	398	69.6	0.0	0.0	7.3	23.1	16.1	66.8	17.1	182	85.7	28.6	24.7
WaKeeney city	1,862	1,797	-3.5	1,896	95.1	0.0	0.4	2.4	2.1	21.8	55.6	22.6	864	72.5	36.6	22.6
Wakefield city	980	967	-1.3	1,034	96.2	0.9	0.3	1.3	1.4	28.7	56.9	14.6	388	67.8	27.6	25.8
Waldo city	30	30	0.0	53	98.1	0.0	0.0	1.9	0.0	15.1	47.3	37.7	26	84.6	30.8	30.8
Waldron city	11	11	0.0	9	100.0	0.0	0.0	0.0	0.0	0.0	0.0	100.0	9	77.8	44.4	0.0
Wallace city	57	58	1.8	50	100.0	0.0	0.0	0.0	0.0	24.0	56.0	20.0	25	68.0	24.0	16.0
Walnut city	220	220	0.0	307	86.6	0.3	1.6	6.8	4.6	34.5	59.9	5.5	95	91.6	44.2	7.4
Walton city	235	239	1.7	210	85.7	3.3	0.0	3.8	7.1	13.8	69.7	16.7	91	81.3	45.1	13.2
Wamego city	4,372	4,578	4.7	4,401	92.3	0.0	0.6	1.7	5.4	28.5	57.7	13.8	1,631	68.2	18.2	41.6
Washington city	1,131	1,087	-3.9	1,258	94.3	1.0	0.6	1.8	2.3	24.6	54.9	20.5	538	70.3	53.9	11.3
Waterville city	680	662	-2.6	682	92.8	0.0	1.6	1.5	4.1	25.2	56.5	18.3	285	84.2	48.4	8.4
Wathena city	1,368	1,352	-1.2	1,281	94.8	0.0	0.3	2.3	2.5	20.4	54.9	24.6	558	73.3	39.6	19.5
Waverly city	592	568	-4.1	587	96.3	0.0	0.0	3.7	0.0	26.1	50.3	23.7	260	70.0	38.5	18.8
Webber city	25	25	0.0	27	100.0	0.0	0.0	0.0	0.0	0.0	74.1	25.9	15	100.0	20.0	13.3
Weir city	686	657	-4.2	585	86.0	0.0	0.0	13.2	0.9	19.6	67.0	13.5	267	77.9	33.0	33.0
Welda CDP	129	NA	NA	76	100.0	0.0	0.0	0.0	0.0	0.0	68.4	31.6	38	100.0	65.8	0.0
Wellington city	8,168	7,942	-2.8	8,028	84.1	0.4	0.2	3.6	11.7	23.8	59.2	16.9	3,158	69.9	44.3	20.5
Wellsville city	1,857	1,822	-1.9	1,786	93.2	1.1	0.0	2.8	2.9	35.2	52.2	12.7	669	65.8	30.2	23.3
Weskan CDP	161	NA	NA	171	90.1	0.0	0.0	9.9	0.0	21.6	64.3	14.0	65	70.8	44.6	13.8
West Mineral city	185	179	-3.2	215	95.3	0.0	0.0	3.7	0.9	22.8	66.8	10.2	82	75.6	47.6	7.3
Westmoreland city	778	777	-0.1	818	96.3	0.0	0.0	2.0	1.7	24.4	52.9	22.7	316	77.5	39.9	21.5
Westphalia city	163	159	-2.5	230	97.0	0.0	0.0	2.2	0.9	34.8	46.9	18.3	97	68.0	69.1	11.3
Westwood city	1,506	1,534	1.9	1,699	87.4	0.9	2.0	2.3	7.4	22.1	62.9	14.9	728	85.4	8.9	70.9
Westwood Hills city	359	364	1.4	401	90.0	1.0	2.7	1.2	5.0	19.1	62.5	18.2	178	92.1	6.2	82.6
Wetmore city	368	366	-0.5	355	82.8	0.6	3.4	9.0	4.2	30.1	61.9	7.9	147	59.9	48.3	15.0
Wheaton city	95	100	5.3	196	63.3	13.3	1.5	0.0	21.9	49.4	44.9	5.6	50	68.0	42.0	26.0
White City city	618	588	-4.9	590	93.1	0.0	1.0	5.6	0.3	27.0	56.4	16.6	217	75.1	46.5	6.5
White Cloud city	176	175	-0.6	235	52.3	3.0	0.0	43.8	0.9	32.8	46.4	20.9	101	55.4	62.4	3.0
Whitewater city	718	707	-1.5	728	88.9	0.0	0.4	8.5	2.2	27.7	53.8	18.5	252	81.0	37.7	33.7
Whiting city	187	188	0.5	192	81.3	0.0	0.0	9.4	9.4	25.5	54.2	20.3	92	75.0	55.4	15.2
Wichita city	382,386	388,413	1.6	385,518	63.9	11.2	4.7	4.4	15.7	26.4	61.5	12.0	150,282	60.6	36.4	29.3
Willard city	92	92	0.0	96	96.9	0.0	0.0	0.0	3.1	34.3	59.5	6.3	35	71.4	37.1	17.1
Williamsburg city	401	387	-3.5	314	89.8	0.0	0.0	2.5	7.6	24.2	56.4	19.4	131	75.6	51.9	12.2
Willis city	38	38	0.0	24	100.0	0.0	0.0	0.0	0.0	8.4	62.5	29.2	13	92.3	15.4	23.1
Willowbrook city	87	86	-1.1	105	100.0	0.0	0.0	0.0	0.0	16.2	39.1	44.8	43	93.0	16.3	69.8
Wilmore city	53	55	3.8	19	100.0	0.0	0.0	0.0	0.0	10.5	84.3	5.3	11	100.0	54.5	9.1
Wilroads Gardens CDP	609	NA	NA	309	47.9	0.0	0.0	0.0	52.1	15.5	59.2	25.2	112	100.0	47.3	13.4
Wilsey city	153	148	-3.3	177	97.2	0.0	0.0	1.1	1.7	19.8	55.3	24.9	67	95.5	65.7	6.0
Wilson city	781	766	-1.9	758	94.9	0.7	0.8	2.6	1.1	16.5	56.0	27.4	340	75.3	43.2	22.4
Winchester city	551	536	-2.7	527	96.6	0.4	0.0	0.8	2.3	18.2	51.3	30.6	240	63.3	59.6	12.5
Windom city	130	129	-0.8	147	68.0	0.0	0.0	5.4	26.5	38.1	38.1	23.8	55	83.6	52.7	7.3
Winfield city	12,347	12,258	-0.7	12,324	80.0	3.8	4.1	4.7	7.4	22.8	62.5	14.7	4,489	64.1	32.1	27.9
Winona city	162	164	1.2	178	97.8	0.0	0.0	0.0	2.2	18.0	61.3	20.8	82	76.8	53.7	12.2
Woodbine city	170	172	1.2	208	75.0	0.0	0.0	3.8	21.2	32.3	62.5	5.3	67	97.0	43.3	16.4
Woodston city	136	136	0.0	158	86.1	0.0	0.0	13.9	0.0	22.8	64.0	13.3	57	87.7	54.4	7.0
Wright CDP	163	NA	NA	117	100.0	0.0	0.0	0.0	0.0	14.5	58.9	26.5	57	93.0	22.8	19.3
Yates Center city	1,417	1,350	-4.7	1,285	98.1	0.1	0.0	1.6	0.2	21.7	55.6	22.7	640	76.4	43.6	24.1
Yoder CDP	194	NA	NA	269	100.0	0.0	0.0	0.0	0.0	28.3	48.7	23.0	91	100.0	37.4	29.7
Zenda city	90	88	-2.2	103	100.0	0.0	0.0	0.0	0.0	16.4	62.2	21.4	43	69.8	41.9	9.3
Zurich city	99	99	0.0	102	100.0	0.0	0.0	0.0	0.0	13.7	73.3	12.7	52	90.4	53.8	1.9
KENTUCKY	4,339,349	4,413,457	1.7	4,383,272	85.8	7.8	1.2	2.0	3.2	23.2	62.8	14.0	1,702,235	67.7	47.1	23.0
Adairville city	892	889	-0.3	1,150	75.8	12.2	0.0	1.8	10.2	27.7	50.6	21.7	474	56.8	75.7	9.1
Ages CDP	0	NA	NA	324	100.0	0.0	0.0	0.0	0.0	27.5	52.0	20.7	111	91.0	71.2	0.0
Albany city	2,031	2,010	-1.0	1,743	90.0	2.2	0.0	0.5	7.2	21.9	53.9	24.2	790	57.8	69.5	10.1
Alexandria city	8,489	8,790	3.5	8,654	95.6	0.6	0.5	2.7	0.6	28.2	60.3	11.5	3,151	83.6	35.6	32.5

1 May be of any race.

Table A. All Places — **Population and Housing**

STATE City, town, township, borough, or CDP (county if applicable)	Population: 2010 census total population	Population: 2014 estimated population	Population: Percent change 2010–2014	Population: ACS total population estimate 2010–2014	Race and Hispanic or Latino origin (percent), 2010–2014: White alone, not Hispanic or Latino	Black alone, not Hispanic or Latino	Asian alone, not Hispanic or Latino	All other races or 2 or more races, not Hispanic or Latino	Hispanic or Latino[1]	Age (percent), 2010–2014: Under 18 years old	Age 18 to 64 years old	Age 65 years and older	Households, 2010–2014: Total occupied housing units	Percent owner occupied	Householders by level of education (percent): High school diploma or less	Bachelor's degree or more
	1	2	3	4	5	6	7	8	9	10	11	12	13	14	15	16
KENTUCKY—Con.																
Allen city	193	187	-3.1	180	96.1	0.0	0.0	3.9	0.0	14.5	70.7	15.0	64	40.6	54.7	12.5
Allensville city	157	NA	NA	143	88.8	11.2	0.0	0.0	0.0	42.7	51.8	5.6	47	83.0	68.1	27.7
Anchorage city	2,348	2,408	2.6	2,154	93.9	0.6	3.4	0.9	1.2	33.6	53.0	13.4	678	92.6	6.9	82.7
Annville CDP	1,095	NA	NA	766	94.1	0.4	0.0	5.5	0.0	21.7	51.7	26.5	344	57.8	62.2	0.0
Anthoston CDP	0	NA	NA	74	100.0	0.0	0.0	0.0	0.0	0.0	74.3	25.7	24	100.0	100.0	0.0
Arjay CDP	0	NA	NA	508	100.0	0.0	0.0	0.0	0.0	36.8	52.4	10.8	190	49.5	71.6	0.0
Arlington city	324	316	-2.5	383	84.9	4.2	0.0	8.4	2.6	23.2	53.0	23.8	186	73.7	62.9	2.7
Artemus CDP	590	NA	NA	610	97.9	2.1	0.0	0.0	0.0	8.7	67.5	23.8	279	79.2	79.2	0.0
Ashland city	21,684	21,335	-1.6	21,551	93.1	2.5	0.9	2.1	1.4	21.0	61.3	18.0	9,372	61.4	42.3	19.8
Auburn city	1,340	1,346	0.4	1,556	87.9	4.6	0.0	1.7	5.8	29.0	56.4	14.5	623	58.7	47.7	9.0
Audubon Park city	1,473	1,502	2.0	1,348	97.3	0.5	0.0	0.8	1.4	12.5	70.3	17.1	573	84.8	20.4	46.4
Augusta city	1,190	1,174	-1.3	1,183	100.0	0.0	0.0	0.0	0.0	20.2	60.3	19.5	536	58.0	56.0	15.7
Auxier CDP	669	NA	NA	366	100.0	0.0	0.0	0.0	0.0	27.5	64.5	7.9	155	63.9	19.4	11.0
Bancroft city	494	506	2.4	470	83.4	0.6	8.7	0.6	6.6	21.2	56.1	22.8	177	96.0	15.3	60.5
Bandana CDP	203	NA	NA	106	77.4	0.0	0.0	0.0	22.6	0.0	83.9	16.0	58	100.0	39.7	0.0
Barbourmeade city	1,218	1,251	2.7	1,375	95.3	2.0	0.1	0.5	2.1	22.9	54.1	23.0	555	93.5	7.0	66.7
Barbourville city	3,166	3,154	-0.4	3,176	90.0	6.2	0.0	3.6	0.3	20.7	61.2	18.2	1,111	43.7	52.9	28.7
Bardstown city	12,604	12,998	3.1	12,833	78.8	13.5	0.4	2.8	4.4	28.2	59.9	11.9	5,030	56.1	56.0	17.5
Bardwell city	723	708	-2.1	783	94.5	2.4	0.5	0.0	2.6	20.0	53.4	26.7	330	51.2	52.4	14.8
Barlow city	675	675	0.0	805	91.6	4.7	0.4	0.7	2.6	24.1	59.7	16.0	324	64.8	67.9	7.4
Beattyville city	1,307	1,257	-3.8	1,806	96.4	0.8	1.1	0.2	1.6	27.9	61.9	10.2	619	41.0	56.2	4.2
Beaver Dam city	3,505	3,541	1.0	3,532	87.6	4.4	0.0	0.0	8.0	23.4	62.7	14.0	1,241	56.6	61.8	4.7
Bedford city	610	609	-0.2	687	99.3	0.0	0.0	0.0	0.7	20.5	69.4	10.2	263	47.9	61.6	6.8
Beech Grove CDP	243	NA	NA	448	100.0	0.0	0.0	0.0	0.0	35.3	54.4	10.5	127	100.0	43.3	18.1
Beechmont CDP	689	NA	NA	911	100.0	0.0	0.0	0.0	0.0	29.8	51.5	18.8	344	76.5	71.8	2.3
Beechwood Village city	1,324	1,359	2.6	1,321	94.9	2.0	1.2	0.8	1.1	19.8	66.5	13.6	634	70.3	19.7	53.8
Belfry CDP	0	NA	NA	148	100.0	0.0	0.0	0.0	0.0	16.2	46.6	37.2	79	92.4	49.4	20.3
Bellefonte city	888	871	-1.9	747	96.8	0.8	0.3	0.7	1.5	16.5	59.2	24.2	302	89.7	15.2	51.0
Bellemeade city	865	889	2.8	818	96.8	0.5	0.6	1.7	0.4	23.5	49.8	26.7	374	93.3	13.6	58.8
Belleview CDP	343	NA	NA	617	100.0	0.0	0.0	0.0	0.0	26.3	70.3	3.4	166	64.5	47.6	7.2
Bellevue city	5,955	5,919	-0.6	5,933	93.9	0.0	2.0	1.6	2.5	20.6	65.7	13.7	2,563	72.1	41.7	30.2
Bellewood city	321	330	2.8	362	97.0	0.0	0.6	0.8	1.7	25.4	60.4	14.1	132	90.2	11.4	71.2
Benham city	505	480	-5.0	533	95.9	3.4	0.0	0.8	0.0	18.7	54.4	26.8	246	82.5	49.6	22.4
Benton city	4,408	4,329	-1.8	4,380	98.7	0.6	0.3	0.4	0.1	21.7	55.4	23.0	1,748	76.5	45.0	20.2
Berea city	13,561	14,658	8.1	14,209	88.8	3.9	1.5	2.6	3.3	20.6	65.5	13.8	5,228	55.0	43.5	28.7
Berry city	264	260	-1.5	243	97.5	0.0	0.0	0.0	2.5	21.8	66.7	11.5	95	80.0	69.5	8.4
Betsy Layne CDP	688	NA	NA	764	96.6	0.0	0.0	1.0	2.4	36.4	56.4	7.2	273	96.0	49.8	15.0
Big Clifty CDP	0	NA	NA	283	100.0	0.0	0.0	0.0	0.0	16.2	72.0	11.7	107	84.1	65.4	7.5
Blackey city	120	160	33.3	207	100.0	0.0	0.0	0.0	0.0	41.1	49.6	9.2	66	60.6	54.5	12.1
Blaine city	47	47	0.0	71	93.0	0.0	0.0	0.0	7.0	25.4	63.4	11.3	21	76.2	76.2	14.3
Blandville city	90	NA	NA	48	100.0	0.0	0.0	0.0	0.0	31.3	52.2	16.7	16	100.0	50.0	50.0
Bloomfield city	1,017	1,044	2.7	1,038	86.9	9.8	0.1	2.6	0.6	25.9	64.8	9.4	370	67.3	64.3	15.7
Blue Ridge Manor city	767	789	2.9	761	85.5	9.7	2.8	0.8	1.2	15.9	60.8	23.3	420	83.6	13.3	50.7
Bonnieville city	255	262	2.7	321	96.6	1.2	0.6	0.0	1.6	29.6	56.4	14.0	119	63.9	72.3	5.9
Booneville city	81	77	-4.9	62	100.0	0.0	0.0	0.0	0.0	16.1	69.4	14.5	36	69.4	75.0	2.8
Boston CDP	266	NA	NA	499	100.0	0.0	0.0	0.0	0.0	28.6	46.4	24.8	168	77.4	72.0	0.0
Bowling Green city	58,888	62,479	6.1	60,660	72.6	14.3	4.1	2.4	6.6	20.3	68.8	10.9	23,153	38.8	39.5	25.6
Bradfordsville city	294	296	0.7	388	99.7	0.0	0.0	0.3	0.0	31.6	56.2	12.1	155	58.1	71.0	3.2
Brandenburg city	2,673	2,919	9.2	2,812	85.6	5.9	0.5	3.7	4.3	26.0	58.9	15.1	1,055	51.6	54.7	17.5
Breckinridge Center CDP	2,080	NA	NA	2,216	49.4	36.4	2.5	2.0	9.7	13.4	85.3	1.4	287	40.1	83.3	0.0
Bremen city	197	195	-1.0	167	97.6	0.0	1.2	1.2	0.0	10.8	69.0	20.4	73	75.3	69.9	4.1
Briarwood city	435	445	2.3	537	82.5	4.1	4.8	0.0	8.6	20.3	59.7	19.9	267	79.4	15.0	45.7
Brodhead city	1,211	1,197	-1.2	1,341	94.6	0.5	0.2	4.5	0.2	17.8	57.1	25.2	486	53.3	69.5	9.7
Broeck Pointe city	272	279	2.6	253	88.9	4.3	0.0	0.0	6.7	27.2	50.4	22.1	88	92.0	8.0	62.5
Bromley city	802	808	0.7	735	93.7	4.2	0.0	1.9	0.1	22.3	64.1	13.7	297	60.9	53.2	6.7
Brooks CDP	2,401	NA	NA	2,964	96.6	0.8	0.0	2.6	0.0	25.4	62.7	11.8	1,112	86.7	62.9	10.1
Brooksville city	648	644	-0.6	474	100.0	0.0	0.0	0.0	0.0	24.5	51.5	24.1	232	54.7	57.8	16.8
Brownsboro Farm city	648	662	2.2	786	97.8	0.4	1.1	0.4	0.3	33.6	49.0	17.6	263	91.3	12.5	62.7
Brownsboro Village city	319	327	2.5	303	95.4	0.7	0.0	2.3	1.7	11.2	65.1	23.8	168	82.7	7.7	70.2
Brownsville city	836	826	-1.2	772	96.4	1.7	0.4	0.8	0.8	13.8	49.4	36.8	378	50.3	70.6	6.9
Buckhorn city	164	159	-3.0	122	86.1	9.8	0.0	2.5	1.6	27.9	60.6	11.5	40	77.5	20.0	32.5
Buckner CDP	5,837	NA	NA	5,539	83.6	13.5	0.0	1.2	1.7	16.8	77.1	6.1	835	87.9	14.5	59.8
Buffalo CDP	498	NA	NA	535	100.0	0.0	0.0	0.0	0.0	19.3	63.4	17.4	207	86.0	40.6	28.5
Burgin city	965	964	-0.1	1,153	88.8	3.0	0.2	8.0	0.0	21.7	59.1	19.1	479	70.8	60.5	8.6
Burkesville city	1,535	1,513	-1.4	1,459	83.6	15.1	0.0	1.0	0.3	20.2	58.5	21.4	646	45.7	64.1	8.8
Burlington CDP	15,926	NA	NA	16,479	90.5	2.3	1.1	1.9	4.1	29.3	62.5	8.5	5,590	74.9	27.4	31.8
Burna CDP	257	NA	NA	251	100.0	0.0	0.0	0.0	0.0	4.8	92.6	2.8	116	80.2	87.1	0.0
Burnside city	819	829	1.2	873	97.7	0.0	0.0	1.4	0.9	24.3	52.2	23.4	360	79.2	45.8	18.9
Butler city	612	593	-3.1	513	98.1	1.9	0.0	0.0	0.0	23.6	45.6	30.8	216	45.8	72.2	6.5
Cadiz city	2,625	2,631	0.2	2,633	75.4	18.5	0.0	4.3	1.8	24.8	53.9	21.2	1,129	53.7	53.8	17.8
Calhoun city	763	761	-0.3	934	96.5	0.2	0.0	2.7	0.6	21.0	51.2	27.9	375	64.5	65.3	7.5
California city	86	87	1.2	142	100.0	0.0	0.0	0.0	0.0	40.2	53.3	6.3	36	83.3	72.2	13.9
Calvert City city	2,566	2,498	-2.7	2,586	92.6	0.4	0.2	3.8	3.1	29.9	49.6	20.4	925	67.4	45.4	15.1
Camargo city	1,081	1,119	3.5	1,327	91.0	1.8	0.0	4.6	2.6	28.8	55.1	16.0	472	72.2	62.9	9.3
Cambridge city	175	177	1.1	171	95.3	0.0	0.0	2.3	2.3	26.4	60.2	13.5	85	78.8	25.9	43.5
Campbellsburg city	813	825	1.5	766	94.3	3.0	0.0	1.6	1.2	28.1	52.4	19.6	292	69.2	59.6	8.9
Campbellsville city	10,638	11,282	6.1	11,126	82.1	8.8	1.7	3.5	3.9	21.9	59.6	18.6	4,272	56.0	57.8	16.9
Campton city	436	428	-1.8	522	100.0	0.0	0.0	0.0	0.0	24.3	58.5	17.0	210	49.0	64.3	8.1
Caneyville city	609	621	2.0	628	99.4	0.6	0.0	0.0	0.0	19.3	63.9	16.7	261	57.1	60.9	13.4
Cannonsburg CDP	856	NA	NA	721	97.9	0.0	0.0	2.1	0.0	28.3	52.9	18.9	313	71.9	69.3	3.8
Carlisle city	2,010	1,981	-1.4	2,135	98.1	1.2	0.0	0.0	0.7	19.1	56.1	24.9	983	57.7	59.4	10.9
Carrollton city	3,938	3,931	-0.2	3,954	86.9	2.4	0.0	2.1	8.6	26.6	57.2	16.4	1,547	44.6	58.7	11.7
Carrsville city	50	49	-2.0	46	100.0	0.0	0.0	0.0	0.0	2.2	56.5	41.3	27	88.9	70.4	0.0
Catlettsburg city	1,856	1,827	-1.6	1,875	93.5	4.9	0.0	0.8	0.9	17.4	63.4	19.3	756	49.9	58.7	2.4
Cave City city	2,240	2,294	2.4	2,214	80.4	15.3	0.4	2.8	1.2	22.4	59.6	18.0	965	42.3	72.1	12.2
Cawood CDP	731	NA	NA	658	100.0	0.0	0.0	0.0	0.0	10.6	57.1	32.2	282	82.6	83.7	0.0
Cayce CDP	123	NA	NA	68	100.0	0.0	0.0	0.0	0.0	8.8	35.3	55.9	39	66.7	87.2	0.0
Cecilia CDP	572	NA	NA	320	100.0	0.0	0.0	0.0	0.0	5.6	86.0	8.4	159	100.0	15.1	64.8
Centertown city	437	440	0.7	320	100.0	0.0	0.0	0.0	0.0	15.7	68.4	15.9	122	83.6	77.9	3.3
Central City city	5,978	5,899	-1.3	5,932	85.5	13.2	0.0	0.7	0.6	19.1	65.7	15.2	1,938	70.3	56.8	8.3
Cerulean CDP	314	NA	NA	270	38.5	61.5	0.0	0.0	0.0	15.6	62.2	22.2	130	90.8	76.2	0.0

1 May be of any race.

Table A. All Places — **Population and Housing**

STATE City, town, township, borough, or CDP (county if applicable)	Population				Race and Hispanic or Latino origin (percent), 2010–2014					Age (percent), 2010–2014			Households, 2010–2014			
	2010 census total population	2014 estimated population	Percent change 2010–2014	ACS total population estimate 2010–2014	White alone, not Hispanic or Latino	Black alone, not Hispanic or Latino	Asian alone, not Hispanic or Latino	All other races or 2 or more races, not Hispanic or Latino	Hispanic or Latino[1]	Under 18 years old	Age 18 to 64 years old	Age 65 years and older	Total occupied housing units	Percent owner occupied	Householders by level of education (percent): High school diploma or less	Householders by level of education (percent): Bachelor's degree or more
	1	2	3	4	5	6	7	8	9	10	11	12	13	14	15	16
KENTUCKY—Con.																
Chaplin CDP	418	NA	NA	382	96.3	0.0	0.0	3.7	0.0	17.8	60.0	22.3	172	95.9	80.8	9.9
Clarkson city	874	894	2.3	1,007	94.5	2.0	0.0	3.2	0.3	25.3	62.0	12.9	431	43.4	69.8	8.4
Claryville CDP	2,355	NA	NA	2,601	94.0	2.0	0.7	0.0	3.3	30.9	55.0	14.1	813	86.6	37.6	31.0
Clay city	1,181	1,148	-2.8	1,274	97.8	0.0	0.0	0.0	2.2	25.8	63.1	11.1	499	71.5	56.7	11.4
Clay City city	1,077	1,063	-1.3	1,354	97.5	0.0	0.0	1.8	0.7	26.5	57.0	16.5	503	53.3	72.2	2.8
Cleaton CDP	0	NA	NA	186	95.2	4.8	0.0	0.0	0.0	16.6	80.2	3.2	70	90.0	88.6	0.0
Clinton city	1,388	1,348	-2.9	1,406	70.3	26.6	0.0	0.5	2.6	17.8	57.8	24.3	548	69.9	61.3	11.7
Cloverport city	1,152	1,147	-0.4	1,276	95.1	3.3	0.5	0.0	1.1	22.0	63.3	14.5	505	66.7	60.0	5.1
Coal Run Village city	1,708	1,633	-4.4	1,804	89.9	2.4	1.2	2.4	4.1	24.4	67.2	8.4	705	67.8	45.4	23.0
Coldiron CDP	223	NA	NA	144	100.0	0.0	0.0	0.0	0.0	6.3	75.1	18.8	81	90.1	55.6	0.0
Cold Spring city	5,898	6,161	4.5	6,093	96.8	0.7	0.1	1.4	1.1	20.3	57.3	22.3	2,719	87.0	25.1	38.6
Coldstream city	1,100	1,130	2.7	1,135	56.6	37.5	2.0	2.0	1.9	25.6	70.6	3.7	447	92.4	21.0	42.5
Columbia city	4,452	4,880	9.6	4,792	87.1	7.7	0.5	2.4	2.3	10.9	69.2	19.8	1,872	52.7	53.8	18.5
Columbus city	170	164	-3.5	182	61.0	36.8	0.0	2.2	0.0	6.5	70.7	22.5	83	90.4	86.7	1.2
Combs CDP	0	NA	NA	542	77.7	0.0	0.0	22.3	0.0	41.9	58.2	0.0	151	41.7	75.5	0.0
Concord city	35	35	0.0	18	100.0	0.0	0.0	0.0	0.0	27.8	66.7	5.6	6	50.0	100.0	0.0
Corbin city	7,314	7,308	-0.1	7,051	94.8	0.1	1.4	1.6	2.1	25.1	54.0	20.9	2,686	54.7	51.9	16.8
Corinth city	232	234	0.9	310	99.7	0.0	0.0	0.0	0.3	19.0	67.1	13.9	111	55.9	48.6	2.7
Corydon city	720	713	-1.0	748	83.0	13.4	0.3	2.0	1.3	26.7	62.9	10.6	278	76.6	70.9	10.8
Covington city	40,516	40,944	1.1	40,712	81.0	11.1	0.2	3.8	3.8	22.9	65.9	11.1	16,863	50.3	46.7	20.8
Coxton CDP	0	NA	NA	241	84.6	7.5	0.0	7.9	0.0	11.7	81.3	7.1	115	73.0	73.0	7.0
Crab Orchard city	841	832	-1.1	973	92.8	0.0	0.0	3.4	3.8	23.3	55.1	21.5	444	58.3	83.1	2.3
Crayne CDP	173	NA	NA	143	100.0	0.0	0.0	0.0	0.0	7.7	79.1	13.3	90	96.7	31.1	7.8
Creekside city	305	314	3.0	325	81.2	15.1	0.3	3.4	0.0	10.5	63.2	26.5	148	95.3	16.9	60.1
Crescent Springs city	3,936	3,987	1.3	3,958	76.6	2.2	15.4	3.9	1.9	30.8	58.4	10.6	1,548	49.1	35.7	43.9
Crestview city	475	484	1.9	392	96.9	0.0	0.0	0.5	2.6	24.1	66.5	9.4	148	88.5	41.9	30.4
Crestview Hills city	3,111	3,328	7.0	3,310	95.0	3.7	0.2	0.2	1.1	18.5	59.9	21.5	1,413	71.7	27.5	47.5
Crestwood city	4,531	4,788	5.7	4,640	93.2	0.2	2.2	0.7	3.7	34.2	60.2	5.6	1,650	70.6	29.9	49.6
Crittenden city	3,815	3,863	1.3	3,819	91.3	0.0	0.0	6.7	1.9	33.9	60.7	5.4	1,317	48.4	36.4	15.7
Crofton city	768	765	-0.4	903	75.5	15.2	0.3	4.7	4.3	34.3	51.4	14.4	345	58.6	64.9	7.0
Crossgate city	225	228	1.3	258	91.1	0.4	5.8	2.7	0.0	20.6	58.6	20.9	87	90.8	3.4	79.3
Cumberland city	2,237	2,140	-4.3	2,282	96.8	1.9	0.0	1.1	0.2	23.7	55.9	20.3	967	58.6	59.5	13.3
Cunningham CDP	0	NA	NA	304	100.0	0.0	0.0	0.0	0.0	17.7	70.2	12.2	125	91.2	37.6	31.2
Cynthiana city	6,443	6,365	-1.2	6,388	90.9	5.2	0.1	2.5	1.3	24.1	56.9	18.9	2,617	45.0	56.9	15.1
Danville city	16,218	16,620	2.5	16,471	81.4	10.3	0.8	3.7	3.8	19.5	63.2	17.3	6,243	55.6	40.0	29.8
Dawson Springs city	2,764	2,744	-0.7	2,753	96.1	0.5	0.5	2.9	0.0	21.7	55.8	22.4	1,172	61.0	68.6	5.5
Dayton city	5,340	5,427	1.6	5,382	95.8	0.0	0.7	2.4	1.2	26.2	63.6	10.2	2,045	60.7	54.4	12.3
Dexter CDP	277	NA	NA	374	97.1	2.9	0.0	0.0	0.0	10.7	82.2	7.0	128	93.0	57.0	7.0
Diablock CDP	453	NA	NA	325	100.0	0.0	0.0	0.0	0.0	14.2	63.4	22.5	155	55.5	77.4	9.0
Dixon city	920	901	-2.1	976	95.2	4.8	0.0	0.0	0.0	16.5	74.0	9.6	358	64.8	64.0	12.3
Doe Valley CDP	1,931	NA	NA	1,739	94.9	0.0	0.0	1.3	3.9	15.5	67.5	17.0	669	94.6	34.2	44.1
Douglass Hills city	5,484	5,640	2.8	5,566	85.3	2.4	5.7	1.1	5.5	19.0	63.4	17.8	2,284	66.8	17.5	47.7
Dover city	252	246	-2.4	288	96.5	0.0	0.0	3.5	0.0	23.6	62.7	13.5	108	80.6	63.9	2.8
Drakesboro city	515	509	-1.2	483	92.8	0.6	0.0	3.9	2.7	28.8	60.5	10.8	198	84.8	70.2	8.1
Druid Hills city	308	317	2.9	386	99.7	0.0	0.0	0.0	0.3	26.5	61.5	11.9	163	96.3	6.1	73.6
Dry Ridge city	2,191	2,215	1.1	2,315	93.1	0.1	0.1	0.6	6.0	26.8	60.1	13.0	868	39.4	60.6	13.7
Dunmor CDP	0	NA	NA	290	100.0	0.0	0.0	0.0	0.0	28.7	66.7	4.8	121	81.8	74.4	9.1
Dwale CDP	329	NA	NA	230	100.0	0.0	0.0	0.0	0.0	14.3	63.0	22.6	129	46.5	30.2	16.3
Dycusburg city	26	NA	NA	18	100.0	0.0	0.0	0.0	0.0	0.0	100.0	0.0	10	0.0	100.0	0.0
Earlington city	1,413	1,400	-0.9	1,596	71.4	22.2	0.0	5.8	0.6	27.2	61.5	11.4	552	59.4	54.7	11.6
East Bernstadt CDP	716	NA	NA	891	98.1	0.0	0.0	1.9	0.0	27.2	56.8	16.2	357	68.3	59.1	7.6
Eddyville city	2,554	2,609	2.2	2,600	86.4	10.5	1.2	1.2	0.8	13.5	71.5	14.9	918	60.3	56.8	11.4
Edgewood city	8,605	8,741	1.6	8,665	98.8	0.1	0.7	0.3	0.1	23.8	59.4	16.6	3,196	89.9	16.9	54.2
Edmonton city	1,593	1,580	-0.8	1,665	94.1	2.2	0.0	3.2	0.5	20.7	54.3	25.1	732	53.8	72.4	10.4
Ekron city	154	152	-1.3	128	96.1	3.9	0.0	0.0	0.0	24.2	61.0	14.8	47	74.5	57.4	2.1
Elizabethtown city	28,541	29,974	5.0	29,464	78.1	11.4	3.4	3.3	3.7	23.6	63.0	13.4	11,765	51.4	38.4	30.5
Elizaville CDP	181	NA	NA	175	100.0	0.0	0.0	0.0	0.0	29.7	46.9	23.4	62	93.5	59.7	0.0
Elk Creek CDP	0	NA	NA	1,512	90.5	5.2	1.6	0.0	2.7	20.9	67.2	11.8	540	98.7	25.4	45.0
Elkhorn City city	985	951	-3.5	855	97.9	0.6	0.0	1.5	0.0	11.8	57.6	30.5	364	70.3	57.4	12.4
Elkton city	2,146	2,170	1.1	2,392	77.1	18.3	0.0	2.3	2.3	29.9	54.5	15.7	880	59.2	49.9	8.3
Elsmere city	8,391	8,507	1.4	8,451	77.8	9.1	0.4	3.4	9.2	28.5	60.8	10.6	2,889	72.3	45.6	17.0
Eminence city	2,498	2,526	1.1	2,505	75.8	10.8	0.0	2.7	10.7	27.7	58.4	13.9	1,007	52.6	70.0	9.0
Emlyn CDP	427	NA	NA	248	84.3	15.7	0.0	0.0	0.0	9.3	74.6	16.1	128	59.4	40.6	25.8
Erlanger city	18,127	18,647	2.9	18,370	90.6	3.2	0.9	2.3	3.0	23.5	63.8	12.7	6,997	70.8	40.6	25.6
Eubank city	319	324	1.6	327	88.1	0.9	0.0	1.8	9.2	31.8	54.8	13.5	131	70.2	52.7	11.5
Evarts city	960	935	-2.6	1,001	89.3	5.3	0.0	3.4	2.0	24.4	64.7	11.0	294	72.8	62.6	14.3
Ewing city	260	264	1.5	253	100.0	0.0	0.0	0.0	0.0	33.6	57.3	9.1	82	78.0	47.6	14.6
Ezel CDP	235	NA	NA	241	100.0	0.0	0.0	0.0	0.0	24.4	56.0	19.5	119	63.9	73.1	6.7
Fairfield city	113	114	0.9	117	98.3	0.0	0.0	1.7	0.0	14.5	59.9	25.6	45	86.7	73.3	4.4
Fairview CDP	286	NA	NA	320	100.0	0.0	0.0	0.0	0.0	54.7	38.1	7.2	72	86.1	86.1	13.9
Fairview city	143	145	1.4	166	97.0	0.0	0.0	3.0	0.0	18.6	68.5	12.7	68	91.2	58.8	2.9
Falmouth city	2,205	2,132	-3.3	2,278	97.3	2.2	0.0	0.3	0.2	24.5	61.9	13.5	882	56.3	64.1	13.2
Fancy Farm CDP	458	NA	NA	634	98.4	0.0	0.0	0.0	1.6	22.2	51.4	26.3	221	81.4	54.8	8.1
Farley CDP	4,701	NA	NA	4,443	93.3	3.3	0.2	0.7	2.5	20.8	65.2	14.1	1,797	74.9	62.3	8.5
Farmers CDP	284	NA	NA	123	100.0	0.0	0.0	0.0	0.0	0.0	78.9	21.1	94	40.4	87.2	12.8
Farmington CDP	245	NA	NA	150	100.0	0.0	0.0	0.0	0.0	41.3	53.3	5.3	76	78.9	17.1	22.4
Ferguson city	926	935	1.0	1,036	95.8	0.2	0.1	1.9	2.0	23.7	60.8	15.5	406	57.9	63.1	8.6
Fincastle city	817	844	3.3	865	60.3	20.9	6.8	4.3	7.6	24.6	63.5	11.8	310	91.0	23.9	37.1
Flat Lick CDP	960	NA	NA	1,036	98.7	0.0	0.0	1.3	0.0	23.8	52.5	23.6	416	63.0	85.6	6.0
Flatwoods city	7,508	7,405	-1.4	7,483	97.3	0.5	0.0	1.0	1.2	21.2	55.6	23.2	3,121	68.5	45.2	15.3
Fleming-Neon city	771	735	-4.7	1,002	94.7	4.1	0.0	0.0	1.2	25.0	62.6	12.6	347	60.2	71.5	3.5
Flemingsburg city	2,667	2,702	1.3	2,696	88.6	7.6	0.0	2.0	1.7	19.9	57.1	23.1	1,168	51.6	57.4	8.0
Florence city	29,953	31,888	6.5	31,038	86.1	5.6	3.8	2.5	2.0	24.6	60.2	15.1	12,684	50.9	38.0	28.6
Fordsville city	524	527	0.6	463	97.2	1.7	0.0	1.1	0.0	20.7	57.7	21.6	186	66.7	60.8	0.5
Forest Hills city	444	455	2.5	468	97.0	0.0	0.0	0.4	2.6	17.9	63.9	17.9	194	88.7	26.8	35.6
Fort Campbell North CDP	13,685	NA	NA	14,015	59.2	16.6	3.0	5.4	15.8	35.9	64.1	0.0	2,767	0.4	33.5	14.3
Fort Knox CDP	10,124	NA	NA	10,240	58.4	19.4	2.4	5.4	14.4	35.4	64.3	0.2	2,405	0.7	25.4	21.8
Fort Mitchell city	8,164	8,266	1.2	8,209	88.2	2.8	4.5	1.9	2.6	25.4	63.0	11.5	3,219	54.5	27.6	42.1
Fort Thomas city	16,194	16,329	0.8	16,250	94.1	2.0	0.7	1.9	1.3	24.1	61.4	14.5	6,536	71.0	22.8	50.1
Fort Wright city	5,678	5,760	1.4	5,726	92.8	2.1	1.3	1.6	2.1	20.6	65.0	14.5	2,315	65.6	21.4	47.9
Fountain Run city	217	212	-2.3	267	87.6	3.4	0.0	3.7	5.2	31.1	48.3	20.6	119	68.9	67.2	4.2
Fox Chase city	447	472	5.6	439	95.0	0.0	0.0	5.0	0.0	11.3	63.3	25.5	173	99.4	39.9	31.2

1 May be of any race.

Table A. All Places — **Population and Housing**

STATE City, town, township, borough, or CDP (county if applicable)	Population				Race and Hispanic or Latino origin (percent), 2010–2014					Age (percent), 2010–2014			Households, 2010–2014			
	2010 census total population	2014 estimated population	Percent change 2010–2014	ACS total population estimate 2010–2014	White alone, not Hispanic or Latino	Black alone, not Hispanic or Latino	Asian alone, not Hispanic or Latino	All other races or 2 or more races, not Hispanic or Latino	Hispanic or Latino[1]	Under 18 years old	Age 18 to 64 years old	Age 65 years and older	Total occupied housing units	Percent owner occupied	Householders by level of education (percent): High school diploma or less	Householders by level of education (percent): Bachelor's degree or more
	1	2	3	4	5	6	7	8	9	10	11	12	13	14	15	16
KENTUCKY—Con.																
Francisville CDP	7,944	NA	NA	9,217	89.3	1.3	5.8	1.3	2.3	35.4	57.8	6.7	2,782	86.5	17.5	60.8
Frankfort city	27,269	27,557	1.1	27,389	74.3	16.1	1.6	3.2	4.7	18.9	66.6	14.4	12,099	49.4	42.8	28.0
Franklin city	8,453	8,695	2.9	8,563	76.6	16.7	1.4	2.9	2.5	27.3	57.9	15.0	3,290	53.5	62.0	15.3
Fredonia city	401	394	-1.7	379	97.1	1.3	0.0	1.6	0.0	21.6	58.6	19.8	162	78.4	67.3	8.0
Freeburn CDP	399	NA	NA	176	100.0	0.0	0.0	0.0	0.0	11.4	71.7	17.0	91	54.9	54.9	0.0
Frenchburg city	531	525	-1.1	545	100.0	0.0	0.0	0.0	0.0	26.0	57.2	16.7	249	38.6	69.9	7.6
Fulton city	2,446	2,246	-8.2	2,497	65.4	29.9	0.3	4.4	0.0	27.0	54.0	18.9	1,059	42.1	59.2	13.6
Gamaliel city	376	367	-2.4	440	92.0	0.0	0.0	0.0	8.0	28.0	59.0	13.2	175	63.4	76.0	9.1
Garrison CDP	866	NA	NA	570	100.0	0.0	0.0	0.0	0.0	19.3	60.2	20.5	227	96.9	85.5	0.0
Georgetown city	29,119	31,653	8.7	30,349	84.8	7.3	1.0	2.7	4.2	26.5	64.3	9.1	11,270	64.3	39.2	29.0
Germantown city	154	153	-0.6	162	100.0	0.0	0.0	0.0	0.0	12.4	70.5	17.3	61	80.3	77.0	0.0
Ghent city	323	324	0.3	376	87.8	3.5	0.0	7.2	1.6	24.0	66.2	9.8	150	56.0	64.0	16.7
Gilbertsville CDP	458	NA	NA	212	100.0	0.0	0.0	0.0	0.0	17.9	70.7	11.3	120	52.5	87.5	12.5
Glasgow city	14,049	14,339	2.1	14,152	85.9	7.9	0.4	1.7	4.1	23.0	57.2	19.9	5,948	49.9	57.2	17.0
Glencoe city	359	357	-0.6	456	95.4	0.0	0.0	3.5	1.1	34.9	56.0	9.2	144	64.6	70.8	2.1
Glenview city	531	543	2.3	461	92.6	0.0	5.0	0.7	1.7	10.7	56.2	33.2	204	89.7	3.9	77.5
Glenview Hills city	319	328	2.8	369	97.3	0.0	0.5	1.4	0.8	27.9	47.9	24.1	137	100.0	3.6	75.9
Glenview Manor city	191	194	1.6	167	100.0	0.0	0.0	0.0	0.0	17.4	52.2	30.5	80	92.5	17.5	57.5
Goose Creek city	294	303	3.1	306	87.6	8.2	0.0	4.2	0.0	27.8	50.2	22.2	114	95.6	10.5	64.0
Goshen city	909	962	5.8	1,072	89.2	5.7	0.6	2.1	2.4	29.1	61.9	9.1	377	81.4	16.2	49.3
Gracey CDP	138	NA	NA	46	32.6	28.3	39.1	0.0	0.0	0.0	71.7	28.3	28	100.0	46.4	0.0
Grand Rivers city	382	376	-1.6	429	91.8	0.0	8.2	0.0	0.0	20.3	52.9	26.8	186	64.0	37.6	23.7
Gratz city	78	77	-1.3	50	100.0	0.0	0.0	0.0	0.0	26.0	56.0	18.0	24	91.7	70.8	8.3
Graymoor-Devondale city	2,870	2,937	2.3	2,902	83.0	11.5	1.0	2.5	1.9	15.8	56.9	27.4	1,120	71.8	12.8	59.1
Grayson city	4,148	4,105	-1.0	4,148	93.7	3.6	0.2	1.8	0.8	14.9	70.5	14.7	1,548	43.4	59.4	11.8
Greensburg city	2,163	2,130	-1.5	2,442	93.1	5.6	0.0	1.2	0.0	23.4	52.4	24.2	1,012	53.3	62.4	8.5
Green Spring city	715	736	2.9	615	93.0	2.8	2.9	1.3	0.0	20.0	53.8	26.2	266	96.2	10.9	68.8
Greenup city	1,188	1,165	-1.9	1,191	88.8	9.0	0.0	1.6	0.6	16.1	66.4	17.5	469	66.1	52.0	17.9
Greenville city	4,485	4,402	-1.9	4,442	94.0	3.7	0.0	1.2	1.0	19.0	58.8	22.2	1,801	64.4	45.9	22.0
Guthrie city	1,419	1,438	1.3	1,552	65.1	24.3	0.3	1.7	8.7	25.8	61.1	13.0	608	40.0	58.4	6.7
Hanson city	742	736	-0.8	779	96.9	1.8	0.0	0.5	0.8	19.8	47.7	32.6	308	86.7	43.2	17.9
Hardin city	615	597	-2.9	581	95.0	0.0	0.0	0.0	5.0	25.8	57.0	17.0	222	64.4	75.2	4.5
Hardinsburg city	2,339	2,319	-0.9	2,371	88.4	9.7	0.0	0.6	1.3	20.2	57.0	22.8	924	60.9	64.6	17.1
Hardyville CDP	156	NA	NA	283	98.9	0.0	0.0	1.1	0.0	25.4	61.2	13.4	102	72.5	45.1	23.5
Harlan city	1,745	1,667	-4.5	1,683	88.1	5.6	4.2	1.5	0.5	21.4	55.6	23.0	777	55.2	51.4	17.9
Harrodsburg city	8,363	8,361	0.0	8,359	86.4	9.1	0.8	1.8	1.9	27.1	55.3	17.5	3,534	55.3	60.0	15.9
Hartford city	2,672	2,696	0.9	2,692	93.0	2.6	0.0	1.8	2.6	23.2	55.1	21.8	987	70.3	62.0	13.8
Hawesville city	984	1,010	2.6	1,111	97.1	1.5	0.0	1.4	0.0	27.3	61.3	11.5	463	64.4	53.8	7.8
Hazard city	5,499	5,346	-2.8	5,453	93.7	2.1	3.0	1.0	0.2	19.2	67.5	13.3	2,314	52.3	43.7	25.0
Hazel city	407	411	1.0	499	89.0	4.6	0.6	3.0	2.8	27.2	61.6	11.0	204	64.7	35.8	18.6
Hazel Green CDP	228	NA	NA	280	100.0	0.0	0.0	0.0	0.0	5.4	68.9	25.7	132	94.7	81.8	14.4
Hebron CDP	5,929	NA	NA	5,976	84.3	3.6	0.0	2.6	9.6	30.0	65.3	4.6	2,015	79.2	35.6	25.2
Hebron Estates city	1,078	1,134	5.2	1,103	93.2	0.0	6.8	0.0	0.0	17.6	64.1	18.1	439	77.0	51.0	13.9
Henderson city	28,757	28,900	0.5	28,840	81.8	10.9	0.4	4.5	2.4	22.1	62.2	15.6	12,405	54.9	47.7	17.8
Hendron CDP	4,687	NA	NA	4,365	86.3	7.2	1.7	1.1	3.6	19.7	59.4	20.9	1,856	73.9	39.3	33.0
Heritage Creek city	1,076	1,111	3.3	1,114	93.7	5.8	0.0	0.2	0.3	22.1	65.8	11.9	383	93.2	57.7	13.8
Hickman city	2,395	2,212	-7.6	2,455	61.1	34.0	0.1	1.4	3.4	18.6	67.5	13.7	944	59.4	69.4	6.3
Hickory CDP	0	NA	NA	185	89.7	3.8	0.0	0.5	5.9	2.7	61.1	36.2	74	100.0	82.4	17.6
Hickory Hill city	114	116	1.8	164	69.5	29.3	0.0	1.2	0.0	37.8	44.4	17.7	58	86.2	41.4	31.0
High Bridge CDP	242	NA	NA	146	100.0	0.0	0.0	0.0	0.0	0.0	100.0	0.0	73	83.6	63.0	0.0
Highland Heights city	6,921	7,194	3.9	7,152	87.8	6.4	1.3	3.7	0.8	14.0	74.1	11.7	2,477	61.0	36.2	33.6
Hills and Dales city	142	144	1.4	166	98.8	0.0	1.2	0.0	0.0	15.0	57.7	27.1	65	98.5	9.2	70.8
Hillview city	7,591	8,002	5.4	7,785	95.0	0.0	0.3	2.5	2.1	26.3	60.0	13.6	2,823	76.1	48.5	10.8
Hindman city	777	751	-3.3	1,016	97.3	0.2	0.0	0.1	2.4	33.6	55.5	10.9	291	55.3	58.4	21.3
Hiseville CDP	240	NA	NA	197	100.0	0.0	0.0	0.0	0.0	9.2	72.1	18.8	108	63.9	83.3	7.4
Hodgenville city	3,240	3,242	0.1	3,236	87.1	9.8	0.0	1.4	1.8	18.0	62.8	19.2	1,344	46.7	69.7	10.6
Hollow Creek city	783	806	2.9	889	87.4	10.3	0.3	0.4	1.5	18.1	52.4	29.4	323	95.0	27.6	31.0
Hollyvilla city	537	549	2.2	433	94.9	3.0	0.0	2.1	0.0	20.1	59.6	20.3	193	90.2	73.1	1.6
Hopkinsville city	32,035	32,634	1.9	32,507	61.9	28.0	1.0	3.4	5.6	23.5	61.8	14.7	13,064	49.6	44.6	17.1
Horse Cave city	2,311	2,360	2.1	2,138	84.2	12.8	0.0	2.4	0.5	22.4	57.9	19.6	891	51.9	61.5	14.0
Houston Acres city	490	501	2.2	470	85.3	11.1	0.4	1.1	2.1	23.3	61.7	14.9	190	89.5	19.5	50.5
Hunters Hollow city	359	377	5.0	366	90.2	0.8	0.0	0.8	8.2	23.5	66.9	9.6	130	75.4	50.0	9.2
Hurstbourne city	4,216	4,336	2.8	4,280	79.6	3.3	12.3	2.6	2.2	18.7	50.9	30.6	1,846	74.3	18.1	60.7
Hurstbourne Acres city	1,811	1,863	2.9	1,611	52.5	8.9	30.1	3.4	5.2	14.3	75.2	10.6	846	17.7	22.1	48.8
Hustonville city	405	399	-1.5	476	97.7	0.6	0.0	1.7	0.0	16.3	60.0	23.7	242	66.9	57.9	14.0
Hyden city	365	356	-2.5	461	99.6	0.0	0.4	0.0	0.0	9.7	52.6	37.7	191	50.3	52.4	22.5
Independence city	24,753	26,378	6.6	25,638	93.4	1.6	0.9	1.9	2.1	32.2	60.6	7.2	8,497	78.6	33.7	30.6
Indian Hills city	2,868	2,946	2.7	2,904	97.2	0.7	0.7	1.0	0.5	23.8	51.2	24.9	1,082	98.0	3.2	84.9
Inez city	716	695	-2.9	1,021	98.4	0.0	0.0	0.2	1.4	20.9	63.0	16.1	415	62.4	61.0	7.0
Ironville CDP	0	NA	NA	516	100.0	0.0	0.0	0.0	0.0	29.5	45.6	25.0	212	85.4	39.6	14.2
Irvine city	2,475	2,432	-1.7	2,206	96.4	0.0	0.0	3.4	0.2	22.3	56.0	21.8	878	53.9	62.4	7.9
Irvington city	1,174	1,178	0.3	1,098	75.7	15.3	0.0	1.8	7.2	26.7	55.6	17.9	502	69.5	62.4	7.2
Island city	458	457	-0.2	450	98.7	0.0	0.0	0.2	1.1	16.4	66.3	17.3	189	84.1	72.5	2.1
Jackson city	2,228	2,143	-3.8	2,022	97.2	0.8	1.4	0.2	0.3	17.8	66.6	15.5	880	58.2	57.0	17.8
Jamestown city	1,800	1,816	0.9	2,027	88.9	2.3	0.0	2.1	6.8	25.4	58.0	16.7	750	47.9	66.3	10.7
Jeff CDP	323	NA	NA	335	100.0	0.0	0.0	0.0	0.0	32.0	59.2	9.0	126	79.4	67.5	0.0
Jeffersontown city	26,595	26,949	1.3	26,862	77.5	12.9	2.0	2.7	5.0	22.7	64.0	13.4	10,721	64.6	26.3	39.6
Jeffersonville city	1,641	1,697	3.4	1,637	99.1	0.0	0.0	0.0	0.9	22.7	59.7	17.5	667	77.8	72.9	4.8
Jenkins city	2,203	2,095	-4.9	2,314	97.0	0.6	0.0	1.0	1.4	21.0	66.0	13.1	886	62.4	60.6	7.7
Junction City city	2,193	2,224	1.4	2,575	94.6	2.1	0.2	2.1	0.9	26.1	64.6	9.4	1,027	54.2	62.9	6.6
Kenton Vale city	110	112	1.8	106	74.5	0.0	0.0	0.0	25.5	19.8	60.3	19.8	45	68.9	68.9	8.9
Kenvir CDP	297	NA	NA	316	100.0	0.0	0.0	0.0	0.0	27.5	72.4	0.0	111	79.3	83.8	0.0
Kevil city	376	376	0.0	343	100.0	0.0	0.0	0.0	0.0	18.4	60.6	21.0	161	75.2	50.9	10.6
Kingsley city	381	391	2.6	359	97.8	0.3	1.1	0.3	0.6	21.4	60.8	17.8	169	93.5	14.8	68.0
Kuttawa city	660	670	1.5	677	86.0	11.4	0.0	1.6	1.0	12.0	46.7	41.4	294	92.9	51.7	24.1
La Center city	1,009	1,008	-0.1	1,030	81.1	17.2	0.0	1.0	0.8	25.0	55.9	19.1	384	60.4	60.9	12.5
LaFayette city	174	173	-0.6	150	89.3	6.7	0.0	1.3	2.7	24.0	55.4	20.7	66	62.1	57.6	6.1
La Grange city	8,082	8,516	5.4	8,283	83.2	3.3	1.3	2.5	9.8	27.1	59.6	13.4	3,164	65.3	36.0	22.4
Lakeside Park city	2,722	2,768	1.7	2,745	89.1	4.1	1.3	1.0	4.5	21.2	61.4	17.5	1,178	66.6	22.2	39.0
Lakeview Heights city	229	232	1.3	256	98.4	1.6	0.0	0.0	0.0	30.5	50.8	18.8	96	95.8	10.4	62.5
Lancaster city	3,792	3,765	-0.7	3,779	88.0	6.7	0.1	2.9	2.3	24.0	54.5	21.4	1,494	54.0	67.4	13.0
Langdon Place city	936	964	3.0	993	68.4	11.8	11.5	6.8	1.5	22.4	64.1	13.4	360	87.2	13.1	62.8

1 May be of any race.

Table A. All Places — **Population and Housing**

STATE City, town, township, borough, or CDP (county if applicable)	Population: 2010 census total population	Population: 2014 estimated population	Population: Percent change 2010–2014	Population: ACS total population estimate 2010–2014	Race and Hispanic or Latino origin (percent), 2010–2014: White alone, not Hispanic or Latino	Black alone, not Hispanic or Latino	Asian alone, not Hispanic or Latino	All other races or 2 or more races, not Hispanic or Latino	Hispanic or Latino[1]	Age (percent), 2010–2014: Under 18 years old	Age 18 to 64 years old	Age 65 years and older	Households, 2010–2014: Total occupied housing units	Percent owner occupied	Householders by level of education (percent): High school diploma or less	Bachelor's degree or more
	1	2	3	4	5	6	7	8	9	10	11	12	13	14	15	16
KENTUCKY—Con.																
Lawrenceburg city	10,908	11,093	1.7	11,014	94.9	2.5	0.4	0.9	1.3	24.9	62.8	12.2	4,511	67.3	54.7	18.9
Lebanon city	5,539	5,617	1.4	5,594	73.1	22.5	0.0	1.4	3.0	27.5	56.0	16.5	2,314	55.8	56.8	13.3
Lebanon Junction city	1,813	1,898	4.7	1,814	98.4	0.0	0.0	0.2	1.4	21.7	64.9	13.5	727	71.1	67.7	11.8
Ledbetter CDP	1,683	NA	NA	1,757	100.0	0.0	0.0	0.0	0.0	28.0	56.9	15.1	610	77.7	51.1	17.9
Leitchfield city	6,700	6,872	2.6	6,781	93.4	3.0	0.0	3.2	0.4	22.6	60.3	17.0	2,658	50.4	58.3	5.6
Lewisburg city	810	807	-0.4	800	94.9	3.8	0.5	0.9	0.0	25.2	61.7	13.5	331	62.5	68.0	8.8
Lewisport city	1,672	1,709	2.2	1,656	88.1	3.4	0.0	2.7	5.8	24.2	57.0	18.8	710	58.9	51.0	14.8
Lexington-Fayette urban county	295,803	310,797	5.1	304,473	72.6	14.2	3.5	2.8	6.8	21.2	68.0	11.0	124,101	54.9	27.2	41.7
Liberty city	2,168	2,173	0.2	1,987	98.4	1.1	0.0	0.4	0.2	22.1	56.6	21.2	803	52.6	58.0	17.6
Lincolnshire city	148	150	1.4	126	92.1	0.8	0.8	1.6	4.8	14.4	57.9	27.8	56	96.4	39.3	37.5
Livermore city	1,365	1,352		1,330	98.3	0.7	0.0	0.7	0.3	27.4	55.8	16.9	499	71.9	61.1	7.4
Livingston city	226	223	-1.3	138	100.0	0.0	0.0	0.0	0.0	14.4	68.0	17.4	68	52.9	72.1	2.9
London city	7,978	8,126	1.9	8,062	89.3	3.7	0.5	1.7	4.8	20.8	63.5	15.8	3,375	38.3	57.7	17.0
Loretto city	713	717	0.6	626	97.6	0.6	0.6	0.6	0.5	25.3	57.3	17.6	250	80.4	74.4	4.8
Louisa city	2,466	2,463	-0.1	2,912	98.6	0.6	0.0	0.7	0.2	23.2	59.1	17.8	1,117	43.9	61.8	12.2
Louisville/Jefferson County metro government	741,096	760,026	2.6	751,485	69.9	20.4	2.4	2.8	4.6	22.9	63.2	13.8	306,511	62.2	35.8	32.6
Louisville/Jefferson County metro government (balance)	597,265	612,780	2.6	605,762	67.9	22.4	2.2	2.9	4.6	23.3	63.6	13.1	244,662	60.8	39.0	29.2
Lovelaceville CDP	148	NA	NA	234	100.0	0.0	0.0	0.0	0.0	52.2	41.9	6.0	68	76.5	75.0	0.0
Lowes CDP	98	NA	NA	104	100.0	0.0	0.0	0.0	0.0	0.0	100.1	0.0	46	60.9	39.1	60.9
Loyall city	688	665	-3.3	519	96.0	0.0	0.0	0.0	4.0	17.5	65.2	17.1	245	50.6	59.2	9.8
Ludlow city	4,537	4,543	0.1	4,533	98.7	0.5	0.4	0.2	0.3	22.0	68.3	9.7	1,878	65.2	43.9	25.6
Lynch city	747	720	-3.6	696	79.6	20.4	0.0	0.0	0.0	16.8	60.9	22.4	291	73.5	40.9	12.7
Lyndon city	11,002	11,311	2.8	11,167	73.1	11.1	4.3	2.9	8.7	20.4	66.5	13.1	5,121	43.3	21.8	44.3
Lynnview city	914	937	2.5	881	90.8	1.5	0.0	2.0	5.7	17.1	64.0	18.8	381	78.7	51.2	12.9
McCarr CDP	164	NA	NA	165	97.0	0.0	0.0	0.0	3.0	26.0	58.9	15.2	67	91.0	29.9	26.9
McDowell CDP	0	NA	NA	952	99.4	0.0	0.0	0.6	0.0	28.1	63.1	8.9	332	62.0	69.0	8.7
Maceo CDP	413	NA	NA	354	100.0	0.0	0.0	0.0	0.0	24.6	68.7	6.8	134	71.6	67.2	0.0
McHenry city	388	390	0.5	447	90.2	0.0	0.0	0.9	8.9	22.3	67.1	10.5	155	77.4	63.9	5.2
McKee city	805	787	-2.2	972	94.8	0.0	0.0	4.2	1.0	21.9	63.3	14.8	492	18.5	75.2	4.3
McKinney CDP	0	NA	NA	452	100.0	0.0	0.0	0.0	0.0	46.1	41.3	12.6	146	86.3	64.4	0.0
Mackville city	222	224	0.9	199	99.5	0.0	0.0	0.0	0.5	24.2	51.6	24.1	78	75.6	30.8	42.3
McRoberts CDP	784	NA	NA	802	96.0	2.7	0.0	0.0	1.2	5.1	68.6	26.3	342	73.7	65.5	16.1
Madisonville city	19,929	19,622	-1.5	19,807	80.5	11.3	1.0	4.0	3.2	24.1	59.2	16.6	8,121	60.8	48.3	16.8
Magnolia CDP	524	NA	NA	416	100.0	0.0	0.0	0.0	0.0	24.3	68.9	6.7	161	87.0	57.1	21.1
Manchester city	1,447	1,407	-2.8	1,661	85.6	14.1	0.0	0.1	0.2	16.2	68.8	15.0	756	51.5	67.5	11.4
Manitou CDP	181	NA	NA	107	100.0	0.0	0.0	0.0	0.0	0.0	75.7	24.3	62	77.4	61.3	12.9
Manor Creek city	226	229	1.3	253	77.5	11.1	4.7	4.3	2.4	24.0	56.5	19.4	81	100.0	8.6	65.4
Marion city	3,039	3,002	-1.2	3,020	96.3	2.7	0.0	0.6	0.5	20.0	56.2	23.7	1,335	68.6	54.1	8.1
Marrowbone CDP	217	NA	NA	209	100.0	0.0	0.0	0.0	0.0	26.8	46.9	26.3	71	100.0	100.0	0.0
Martin city	627	608	-3.0	687	98.7	1.0	0.0	0.3	0.0	25.5	58.6	15.9	301	45.8	75.4	10.3
Maryhill Estates city	179	181	1.1	159	100.0	0.0	0.0	0.0	0.0	30.8	57.7	11.3	50	96.0	10.0	74.0
Masonville CDP	1,014	NA	NA	1,060	91.4	0.0	0.0	3.5	5.1	35.3	54.8	10.0	430	76.3	34.7	29.3
Massac CDP	4,505	NA	NA	4,223	88.0	5.2	0.3	3.6	3.0	24.0	60.9	15.1	1,844	67.7	26.2	33.0
Mayfield city	10,024	10,122	1.0	10,091	70.6	14.9	0.0	3.0	11.4	27.1	56.4	16.5	3,862	49.0	59.1	14.9
Mayking CDP	487	NA	NA	158	95.6	0.0	0.0	0.0	4.4	21.6	67.2	11.4	79	70.9	13.9	32.9
Mays Lick CDP	242	NA	NA	177	89.3	9.6	0.0	1.1	0.0	7.4	67.3	25.4	81	93.8	64.2	1.2
Maysville city	9,011	8,851	-1.8	8,951	83.0	11.4	0.5	4.4	0.7	23.0	59.1	18.0	3,575	58.7	55.2	15.6
Maytown CDP	0	NA	NA	315	100.0	0.0	0.0	0.0	0.0	37.5	62.5	0.0	82	100.0	48.8	28.0
Meadowbrook Farm city	136	138	1.5	166	65.1	27.7	0.0	1.2	6.0	39.7	52.3	7.8	45	91.1	26.7	48.9
Meadow Vale city	736	754	2.4	673	89.0	2.5	1.0	0.0	7.4	20.5	55.4	24.1	278	89.2	27.7	38.8
Meadowview Estates city	363	371	2.2	376	79.5	15.2	0.5	0.8	4.0	12.5	62.8	24.7	187	42.8	25.1	50.8
Melbourne city	401	405	1.0	371	99.5	0.0	0.0	0.0	0.5	15.9	62.6	21.6	130	89.2	73.8	8.5
Mentor city	210	211	0.5	207	100.0	0.0	0.0	0.0	0.0	33.3	54.1	12.6	79	81.0	54.4	20.3
Middlesborough city	10,191	9,872	-3.1	10,035	90.1	5.5	1.6	2.3	0.5	22.2	58.8	18.9	4,215	54.9	68.8	9.8
Middletown city	7,220	7,422	2.8	7,333	85.5	6.7	3.6	3.5	0.7	21.7	59.5	18.9	3,301	76.2	21.0	43.9
Midway city	1,641	1,656	0.9	1,688	84.2	4.4	0.5	2.9	8.0	19.0	69.5	11.4	640	71.4	24.4	48.0
Millersburg city	792	790	-0.3	843	95.6	3.0	0.0	1.3	0.1	17.0	70.2	12.9	348	64.1	58.6	18.7
Millstone CDP	117	NA	NA	44	100.0	0.0	0.0	0.0	0.0	0.0	100.0	0.0	20	55.0	55.0	0.0
Milton city	574	574	0.0	660	97.3	0.0	0.3	2.0	0.5	21.5	57.6	20.9	303	63.4	60.1	9.6
Mockingbird Valley city	167	169	1.2	154	96.8	0.0	1.9	0.6	0.6	17.5	42.7	39.6	67	97.0	1.5	89.6
Monterey city	138	135	-2.2	160	100.0	0.0	0.0	0.0	0.0	30.7	58.9	10.6	69	82.6	52.2	2.9
Monticello city	6,182	6,095	-1.4	6,163	90.8	0.8	0.0	0.7	7.6	20.7	63.9	15.4	2,462	49.4	62.8	9.2
Moorland city	431	441	2.3	366	95.4	0.5	1.1	1.9	1.1	17.2	71.1	11.7	182	70.3	34.1	22.5
Morehead city	6,845	6,978	1.9	6,896	93.7	2.4	0.5	1.8	1.5	9.5	78.8	11.7	2,063	44.1	32.4	36.1
Morganfield city	3,255	3,598	10.5	3,554	76.6	19.9	0.0	3.0	0.5	22.8	56.7	20.7	1,518	62.5	51.0	10.7
Morgantown city	2,445	2,466	0.9	2,407	90.3	2.7	0.0	0.8	6.1	25.2	48.3	26.5	1,006	39.8	78.8	4.5
Mortons Gap city	863	854	-1.0	958	99.6	0.4	0.0	0.0	0.0	21.9	62.6	15.2	368	76.4	67.1	7.9
Mount Olivet city	296	286	-3.4	350	96.6	0.0	0.0	3.4	0.0	21.2	51.1	27.7	161	47.8	63.4	11.8
Mount Sterling city	6,902	7,178	4.0	7,030	86.7	7.0	0.2	2.6	3.6	20.3	64.5	15.3	3,045	49.6	48.3	26.4
Mount Vernon city	2,510	2,482	-1.1	2,545	98.2	0.7	0.3	0.9	0.0	26.1	55.5	18.3	1,007	55.2	54.2	12.2
Mount Washington city	11,718	12,246	4.5	11,956	97.6	0.2	0.0	1.3	1.0	27.5	60.2	12.1	4,598	84.7	49.2	20.8
Muldraugh city	947	1,036	9.4	1,173	81.2	8.3	2.1	3.1	5.3	23.0	70.0	7.0	479	34.9	59.1	3.1
Munfordville city	1,615	1,651	2.2	1,765	77.1	13.9	0.0	2.0	7.0	21.4	60.6	18.0	776	44.2	71.8	6.6
Murray city	17,736	18,630	5.0	18,375	85.2	6.1	3.2	2.4	3.0	15.2	70.2	14.5	7,051	42.2	32.7	32.0
Murray Hill city	582	601	3.3	505	96.2	0.8	1.2	0.8	1.0	13.9	42.4	43.8	273	49.5	28.6	45.8
Nebo city	236	232	-1.7	210	79.0	5.7	0.0	15.2	0.0	31.9	52.0	16.2	70	77.1	40.0	21.4
New Castle city	912	923	1.2	1,117	95.5	1.5	0.0	3.0	0.0	28.0	46.6	25.4	438	45.0	61.2	11.0
New Haven city	855	882	3.2	788	97.1	0.0	0.0	2.0	0.9	22.8	62.2	15.0	354	65.8	52.5	9.6
New Hope CDP	129	NA	NA	213	87.3	0.0	0.0	12.7	0.0	14.1	77.9	8.0	87	88.5	88.5	0.0
Newport city	15,449	15,426	-0.1	15,467	84.8	8.3	0.0	2.5	4.4	18.5	70.1	11.5	6,174	46.0	49.9	20.5
Nicholasville city	28,038	29,097	3.8	28,483	89.9	4.4	0.2	2.0	3.5	27.0	62.0	11.1	10,767	55.0	47.4	22.1
Norbourne Estates city	441	452	2.5	448	98.2	0.0	0.7	0.0	1.1	26.8	60.8	12.5	176	97.2	4.0	82.4
North Corbin CDP	1,773	NA	NA	1,819	100.0	0.0	0.0	0.0	0.0	23.0	61.5	15.4	718	61.8	76.9	6.1
Northfield city	1,020	1,045	2.5	934	88.0	4.7	5.5	1.5	0.3	21.4	52.7	25.9	372	66.1	11.3	58.3
North Middletown city	643	643	0.0	928	89.4	4.4	0.0	0.0	6.1	29.4	62.0	8.5	290	61.4	72.4	9.3
Nortonville city	1,204	1,193	-0.9	1,162	97.1	1.2	0.0	0.6	1.1	20.0	57.4	22.5	492	61.2	59.1	9.1
Norwood city	370	379	2.4	300	85.7	0.3	1.7	1.3	11.0	20.0	60.7	19.3	132	81.8	14.4	59.1

1 May be of any race.

Table A. All Places — **Population and Housing**

STATE City, town, township, borough, or CDP (county if applicable)	Population				Race and Hispanic or Latino origin (percent), 2010–2014					Age (percent), 2010–2014			Households, 2010–2014			
	2010 census total population	2014 estimated population	Percent change 2010–2014	ACS total population estimate 2010–2014	White alone, not Hispanic or Latino	Black alone, not Hispanic or Latino	Asian alone, not Hispanic or Latino	All other races or 2 or more races, not Hispanic or Latino	Hispanic or Latino[1]	Under 18 years old	Age 18 to 64 years old	Age 65 years and older	Total occupied housing units	Percent owner occupied	Householders by level of education (percent): High school diploma or less	Householders by level of education (percent): Bachelor's degree or more
	1	2	3	4	5	6	7	8	9	10	11	12	13	14	15	16
KENTUCKY—Con.																
Oakbrook CDP	9,036	NA	NA	9,091	89.5	3.1	0.4	0.8	6.2	24.3	64.1	11.6	3,478	87.5	24.0	35.7
Oak Grove city	7,489	7,515	0.3	7,522	66.2	15.7	1.2	10.8	6.0	37.7	61.7	0.6	2,688	34.9	37.7	10.9
Oakland city	225	231	2.7	145	92.4	7.6	0.0	0.0	0.0	22.8	54.5	22.8	57	86.0	43.9	33.3
Old Brownsboro Place city	353	363	2.8	395	94.2	0.3	1.5	0.0	4.1	27.9	49.2	22.8	143	100.0	9.1	80.4
Olive Hill city	1,634	1,609	-1.5	1,728	99.6	0.0	0.4	0.0	0.0	22.9	58.0	19.0	726	61.4	57.7	18.2
Oneida CDP	410	NA	NA	256	96.9	3.1	0.0	0.0	0.0	23.5	76.7	0.0	53	43.4	43.4	30.2
Onton CDP	141	NA	NA	32	100.0	0.0	0.0	0.0	0.0	46.9	53.2	0.0	15	100.0	0.0	0.0
Orchard Grass Hills city	1,595	1,689	5.9	1,692	74.7	18.1	1.6	4.6	1.0	31.8	59.1	9.1	588	94.4	25.0	37.1
Owensboro city	57,412	58,374	1.7	58,000	85.8	7.1	1.0	3.1	3.1	24.0	59.3	16.7	23,761	57.7	47.0	19.5
Owenton city	1,510	1,511	0.1	1,721	96.2	1.4	0.8	0.6	1.0	24.0	56.2	19.6	819	37.7	66.8	6.8
Owingsville city	1,511	1,581	4.6	1,643	93.9	4.1	0.0	1.6	0.4	29.9	46.4	23.7	615	56.4	55.3	20.8
Paducah city	25,027	24,978	-0.2	25,046	72.4	21.4	0.4	3.3	2.4	20.8	59.0	20.2	11,317	49.8	40.3	23.6
Paintsville city	4,232	4,258	0.6	4,254	93.6	0.7	1.8	2.9	1.0	22.2	60.0	17.7	1,787	56.0	51.2	20.1
Paris city	9,759	9,747	-0.1	9,746	77.8	13.1	0.1	0.8	8.1	26.2	58.6	15.1	3,827	48.5	52.7	14.8
Park City city	537	549	2.2	532	90.4	8.5	0.0	1.1	0.0	18.1	66.0	16.0	212	72.6	49.5	13.7
Park Hills city	2,985	2,997	0.4	2,987	83.5	5.5	0.9	2.4	7.7	21.4	63.6	15.0	1,245	56.5	25.5	49.9
Parkway Village city	650	663	2.0	694	95.5	0.9	1.0	1.6	1.0	18.8	68.5	12.7	317	79.5	27.4	36.9
Pathfork CDP	379	NA	NA	483	100.0	0.0	0.0	0.0	0.0	17.9	67.7	14.5	195	86.7	77.4	3.1
Payne Gap CDP	329	NA	NA	372	98.9	0.0	0.5	0.5	0.0	19.9	60.5	19.6	147	95.9	49.7	15.0
Pembroke city	869	890	2.4	766	64.1	28.5	0.0	5.1	2.3	22.9	57.7	19.5	304	54.3	47.0	15.1
Perryville city	751	759	1.1	969	93.1	3.3	0.1	1.5	2.0	17.5	61.3	21.3	383	63.7	58.0	13.1
Petersburg CDP	620	NA	NA	364	100.0	0.0	0.0	0.0	0.0	9.0	63.8	27.2	165	100.0	65.5	5.5
Pewee Valley city	1,451	1,522	4.9	1,431	90.1	0.8	1.5	3.2	4.5	22.2	52.2	25.6	484	91.5	18.8	61.0
Phelps CDP	893	NA	NA	1,179	100.0	0.0	0.0	0.0	0.0	20.1	72.5	7.5	442	52.9	82.8	5.9
Pikeville city	6,895	7,327	6.3	7,313	92.5	4.2	1.3	0.9	1.1	21.0	64.3	14.8	3,022	46.2	38.4	39.5
Pine Knot CDP	1,621	NA	NA	1,772	86.1	9.9	0.0	0.6	3.4	22.4	56.3	21.4	662	63.7	75.4	3.0
Pineville city	1,850	1,791	-3.2	1,971	91.6	2.3	0.0	5.9	0.1	16.9	68.2	14.9	772	42.9	51.7	19.2
Pioneer Village city	2,706	2,810	3.8	2,740	93.6	0.2	3.3	2.1	0.7	16.5	62.6	21.0	1,177	93.0	46.6	16.0
Pippa Passes city	533	644	20.8	508	97.0	1.2	1.2	0.6	0.0	6.7	90.8	2.6	43	7.0	2.3	86.0
Plano CDP	1,117	NA	NA	1,240	97.9	2.1	0.0	0.0	0.0	16.6	76.6	6.7	497	90.7	30.0	32.0
Plantation city	832	855	2.8	833	67.9	19.9	1.7	6.4	4.1	26.6	63.5	10.0	323	69.7	25.4	41.5
Pleasant View CDP	350	NA	NA	299	100.0	0.0	0.0	0.0	0.0	15.4	73.9	10.7	181	85.6	71.8	0.0
Pleasureville city	834	841	0.8	918	93.7	1.7	0.0	1.2	3.4	29.3	56.6	13.9	371	57.7	67.7	7.3
Plum Springs city	453	480	6.0	529	85.4	7.9	0.2	2.5	4.0	22.8	65.2	11.9	201	80.6	48.3	10.4
Poole CDP	0	NA	NA	302	100.0	0.0	0.0	0.0	0.0	45.7	45.1	9.3	112	50.0	66.1	0.0
Poplar Hills city	362	370	2.2	366	17.5	29.0	0.0	10.7	42.9	24.1	74.6	1.4	201	0.0	62.7	1.5
Powderly city	745	734	-1.5	735	92.7	0.0	0.0	0.0	7.3	14.0	65.5	20.4	320	79.4	71.9	4.7
Prestonsburg city	3,252	3,277	0.8	3,323	90.9	3.3	2.2	1.2	2.5	18.3	57.8	23.9	1,496	42.1	50.1	17.5
Prestonville city	161	161	0.0	101	100.0	0.0	0.0	0.0	0.0	12.9	62.4	24.8	47	57.4	80.9	0.0
Princeton city	6,334	6,199	-2.1	6,274	87.2	9.8	0.0	1.8	1.1	22.8	60.1	17.1	2,758	61.3	59.4	15.8
Prospect city	4,698	4,860	3.4	4,774	89.9	3.5	4.1	0.8	1.6	20.9	57.0	22.1	1,934	92.4	6.0	71.5
Providence city	3,193	3,085	-3.4	3,140	79.3	16.8	0.0	1.9	2.0	19.0	59.1	21.9	1,256	68.3	54.1	6.9
Pryorsburg CDP	311	NA	NA	236	86.9	13.1	0.0	0.0	0.0	23.7	55.9	20.3	138	79.7	93.5	0.0
Rabbit Hash CDP	315	NA	NA	396	100.0	0.0	0.0	0.0	0.0	34.1	52.0	13.9	115	100.0	14.8	57.4
Raceland city	2,407	2,385	-0.9	2,607	93.8	0.0	2.0	3.1	1.2	20.2	65.0	14.9	1,064	69.0	45.9	14.8
Radcliff city	22,305	22,952	2.9	22,939	54.4	24.8	3.0	8.0	9.8	27.8	61.4	10.7	8,773	47.6	35.3	18.5
Ravenna city	605	595	-1.7	614	98.0	0.0	0.0	2.0	0.0	20.2	56.0	23.9	269	59.5	59.5	13.8
Raywick city	134	135	0.7	281	100.0	0.0	0.0	0.0	0.0	8.9	76.6	14.6	121	90.9	89.3	0.0
Reidland CDP	4,491	NA	NA	4,601	90.4	7.0	0.0	1.2	1.4	26.9	60.7	12.5	1,609	92.0	44.4	27.5
Richlawn city	405	415	2.5	425	96.5	2.6	0.9	0.0	0.0	23.8	63.2	12.9	177	89.3	9.0	68.4
Richmond city	31,369	33,556	7.0	32,706	84.3	8.6	1.6	3.4	2.0	17.9	71.7	10.4	12,760	38.8	35.1	29.6
Rineyville CDP	0	NA	NA	3,436	93.8	4.2	0.0	1.4	0.6	31.1	64.4	4.5	1,045	70.3	40.3	20.7
River Bluff city	403	427	6.0	449	90.4	1.6	2.0	0.9	5.1	26.9	53.5	19.6	162	96.9	11.7	58.0
Riverwood city	446	457	2.5	480	98.5	0.0	0.4	0.4	0.6	25.3	57.3	17.3	177	96.0	1.1	79.7
Robards city	515	514	-0.2	555	96.8	0.0	0.0	2.3	0.9	24.8	61.4	13.9	179	89.4	44.7	12.3
Rochester city	152	155	2.0	202	99.0	0.0	0.0	1.0	0.0	25.2	55.0	19.8	86	93.0	66.3	12.8
Rockholds CDP	390	NA	NA	848	100.0	0.0	0.0	0.0	0.0	49.0	44.1	7.0	256	87.5	87.5	5.1
Rockport city	266	268	0.8	310	95.8	0.0	0.0	0.0	4.2	24.8	54.1	21.0	119	76.5	68.1	1.7
Rolling Fields city	646	660	2.2	694	98.3	0.0	1.3	0.3	0.1	32.7	47.2	20.2	248	94.4	4.4	83.5
Rolling Hills city	959	985	2.7	963	79.0	11.8	0.0	1.5	7.7	22.0	61.9	16.1	402	67.9	38.6	35.3
Rosine CDP	113	NA	NA	0	0.0	0.0	0.0	0.0	0.0	0.0	0.0	0.0	0	0.0	0.0	0.0
Russell city	3,312	3,258	-1.6	3,278	96.8	0.3	1.8	0.3	0.7	20.3	62.5	17.3	1,196	74.1	34.9	35.4
Russell Springs city	2,443	2,512	2.8	2,469	97.4	0.0	0.1	1.3	1.2	16.2	59.4	24.2	1,197	58.1	59.4	8.9
Russellville city	6,960	7,038	1.1	6,998	76.3	18.5	0.1	2.6	2.6	20.8	59.3	19.9	3,013	55.2	59.5	15.5
Ryland Heights city	1,022	1,037	1.5	1,083	98.6	0.0	0.2	0.8	0.4	23.8	64.8	11.3	352	79.8	66.2	11.9
Sacramento city	460	458	-0.4	488	97.3	1.8	0.0	0.0	0.8	25.2	60.5	14.3	200	65.5	62.5	12.5
Sadieville city	301	325	8.0	286	95.1	0.0	0.0	1.0	3.8	35.7	55.0	9.1	101	73.3	53.5	13.9
St. Charles city	277	273	-1.4	272	97.8	0.0	0.0	0.0	2.2	21.7	62.6	15.8	110	92.7	86.4	1.8
St. Matthews city	17,468	17,911	2.5	17,686	86.9	4.3	1.9	1.7	5.2	15.8	68.5	15.6	8,672	52.2	19.6	52.8
St. Regis Park city	1,456	1,495	2.7	1,551	95.9	0.5	0.3	0.3	3.0	18.6	59.8	21.3	625	95.5	19.8	48.8
Salem city	752	742	-1.3	881	91.5	1.9	0.0	3.0	3.6	18.8	51.2	30.1	350	81.7	57.1	9.7
Salt Lick city	303	320	5.6	342	100.0	0.0	0.0	0.0	0.0	30.4	63.8	5.8	109	56.0	61.5	11.9
Salvisa CDP	420	NA	NA	669	94.3	3.6	0.0	2.1	0.0	21.4	69.5	9.0	279	60.9	51.6	7.9
Salyersville city	1,881	1,829	-2.8	1,791	93.5	0.1	0.0	2.6	3.8	27.2	53.1	19.6	695	53.7	60.3	12.1
Sanders city	238	239	0.4	235	91.9	7.7	0.0	0.4	0.0	14.4	66.0	19.6	73	80.8	72.6	1.4
Sandy Hook city	643	629	-2.2	540	98.3	1.7	0.0	0.0	0.0	26.4	48.1	25.6	233	50.6	73.0	9.9
Sardis city	103	101	-1.9	116	100.0	0.0	0.0	0.0	0.0	14.6	60.4	25.0	46	87.0	87.0	0.0
Science Hill city	693	698	0.7	715	93.8	0.4	0.0	0.0	5.7	26.8	56.6	16.6	267	56.2	70.8	12.7
Scottsville city	4,226	4,346	2.8	4,295	94.1	5.1	0.0	0.7	0.1	25.4	59.5	15.0	1,782	49.0	56.4	13.0
Sebree city	1,603	1,561	-2.6	1,556	71.0	0.4	0.3	0.8	27.6	27.0	60.0	13.1	477	56.6	59.1	8.8
Sedalia CDP	295	NA	NA	367	91.6	0.0	0.0	8.4	0.0	23.4	31.8	44.7	129	90.7	59.7	40.3
Seneca Gardens city	696	710	2.0	622	97.6	0.0	0.0	1.9	0.5	18.1	58.0	24.0	261	85.4	5.4	77.4
Sharpsburg city	323	342	5.9	471	75.6	17.0	0.0	0.0	7.4	20.2	56.9	22.9	212	68.4	69.3	9.0
Shelbyville city	14,049	14,985	6.7	14,558	66.3	11.0	2.3	3.2	17.3	29.4	59.1	11.3	5,247	50.9	51.2	17.7
Shepherdsville city	11,309	11,856	4.8	11,573	92.3	2.8	0.2	3.1	1.6	27.7	64.5	7.9	4,208	60.9	50.7	12.7
Shively city	15,264	15,643	2.5	15,450	41.2	49.0	1.0	4.5	4.2	23.6	60.5	15.9	6,493	59.3	46.9	13.3
Silver Grove city	1,102	1,118	1.5	1,272	95.0	0.0	0.0	4.0	1.0	31.3	57.4	11.3	424	48.6	59.7	7.5
Simpsonville city	2,487	2,655	6.8	2,581	81.5	4.8	0.4	2.6	10.8	29.0	63.6	7.4	903	69.7	30.9	34.6
Slaughters city	216	210	-2.8	273	95.2	0.0	0.0	1.5	3.3	23.9	62.0	14.3	94	78.7	66.0	9.6
Smithfield city	106	107	0.9	66	100.0	0.0	0.0	0.0	0.0	7.6	62.1	30.3	34	52.9	76.5	0.0
Smithland city	301	296	-1.7	452	91.2	1.5	0.0	2.9	4.4	23.0	58.4	18.6	178	65.2	60.1	10.1
Smiths Grove city	714	719	0.7	706	79.2	17.8	1.0	2.0	0.0	26.1	61.2	12.5	276	80.4	50.7	22.8

1 May be of any race.

Table A. All Places — **Population and Housing**

STATE City, town, township, borough, or CDP (county if applicable)	Population: 2010 census total population	Population: 2014 estimated population	Population: Percent change 2010–2014	Population: ACS total population estimate 2010–2014	Race and Hispanic or Latino origin (percent), 2010–2014: White alone, not Hispanic or Latino	Black alone, not Hispanic or Latino	Asian alone, not Hispanic or Latino	All other races or 2 or more races, not Hispanic or Latino	Hispanic or Latino[1]	Age (percent), 2010–2014: Under 18 years old	Age 18 to 64 years old	Age 65 years and older	Households, 2010–2014: Total occupied housing units	Percent owner occupied	Householders by level of education (percent): High school diploma or less	Bachelor's degree or more
	1	2	3	4	5	6	7	8	9	10	11	12	13	14	15	16
KENTUCKY—Con.																
Somerset city	11,194	11,422	2.0	11,311	92.7	2.8	0.1	1.2	3.1	20.5	60.1	19.5	5,171	46.9	56.2	14.9
Sonora city	513	499	-2.7	702	93.7	0.3	0.4	1.9	3.7	29.5	61.1	9.4	243	87.7	43.6	16.5
South Carrollton city	184	182	-1.1	136	100.0	0.0	0.0	0.0	0.0	15.5	61.7	22.8	73	84.9	54.8	5.5
Southgate city	3,772	3,849	2.0	3,809	84.3	11.4	2.1	1.9	0.3	23.4	66.1	10.5	1,609	60.5	35.7	25.3
South Park View city	7	7	0.0	8	100.0	0.0	0.0	0.0	0.0	0.0	50.0	50.0	4	100.0	75.0	0.0
South Shore city	1,122	1,107	-1.3	1,337	98.1	0.0	1.3	0.6	0.0	22.3	55.9	21.8	542	61.1	55.2	8.9
South Wallins CDP	859	NA	NA	776	90.7	0.0	0.0	4.0	5.3	28.0	59.9	12.1	293	82.9	68.3	20.5
South Williamson CDP	602	NA	NA	646	80.2	1.5	18.3	0.0	0.0	25.0	58.9	16.1	266	66.9	53.0	16.5
Sparta city	268	264	-1.5	234	84.6	3.0	0.0	3.8	8.5	30.8	61.1	8.1	81	71.6	74.1	3.7
Spottsville CDP	325	NA	NA	190	100.0	0.0	0.0	0.0	0.0	23.1	55.7	21.1	85	84.7	69.4	0.0
Springfield city	2,519	2,651	5.2	2,578	75.1	17.0	0.7	1.0	6.1	23.8	58.7	17.6	1,097	63.9	52.4	14.4
Spring Mill city	287	296	3.1	315	97.5	1.9	0.0	0.0	0.6	21.5	59.7	18.7	114	99.1	29.8	43.0
Spring Valley city	654	668	2.1	808	91.3	1.1	1.5	2.2	3.8	34.2	54.5	11.4	268	97.4	2.2	76.1
Stamping Ground city	636	691	8.6	691	96.2	1.6	0.0	1.0	1.2	21.2	65.7	13.2	321	49.2	67.0	14.0
Stanford city	3,704	3,667	-1.0	3,686	83.9	10.3	2.0	0.9	2.9	29.6	56.6	13.8	1,461	48.5	52.8	15.3
Stanton city	2,735	2,698	-1.4	2,724	94.2	0.4	0.0	2.2	3.2	22.1	57.4	20.4	982	58.7	63.4	19.9
Stearns CDP	1,416	NA	NA	1,395	100.0	0.0	0.0	0.0	0.0	20.5	55.3	24.2	649	72.9	63.0	19.4
Strathmoor Manor city	337	344	2.1	349	93.1	0.0	2.6	1.1	3.2	24.1	66.3	9.7	138	96.4	0.7	79.0
Strathmoor Village city	648	661	2.0	687	92.9	1.3	2.9	2.9	0.0	23.8	65.8	10.5	275	88.4	7.3	62.9
Sturgis city	1,898	1,922	1.3	2,308	85.3	12.0	0.6	1.9	0.1	24.5	59.0	16.8	985	55.5	59.1	5.6
Summer Shade CDP	307	NA	NA	339	92.6	0.0	0.0	0.0	7.4	16.5	75.0	8.6	121	100.0	76.9	9.1
Summersville CDP	568	NA	NA	493	86.8	8.1	5.1	0.0	0.0	30.0	48.6	21.3	234	62.4	78.2	16.2
Sycamore city	160	162	1.3	165	66.7	30.9	0.0	1.8	0.6	7.8	56.4	35.8	81	96.3	13.6	40.7
Symsonia CDP	615	NA	NA	539	94.1	0.0	0.0	0.0	5.9	17.2	23.9	58.8	299	78.3	54.5	4.3
Taylor Mill city	6,648	6,728	1.2	6,682	99.3	0.1	0.0	0.6	0.0	22.2	66.7	11.3	2,627	75.0	33.0	29.6
Taylorsville city	763	790	3.5	816	87.6	3.3	0.0	3.4	5.6	26.4	63.8	9.9	396	22.0	49.0	8.1
Ten Broeck city	103	104	1.0	95	93.7	0.0	2.1	4.2	0.0	5.3	72.7	22.1	46	100.0	17.4	54.3
Thornhill city	180	182	1.1	182	100.0	0.0	0.0	0.0	0.0	25.8	50.9	23.1	73	100.0	6.8	79.5
Tolu CDP	88	NA	NA	160	93.8	0.0	0.0	0.0	6.3	6.9	76.4	16.9	90	37.8	54.4	20.0
Tompkinsville city	2,348	2,297	-2.2	2,177	84.4	6.1	0.0	1.1	8.4	17.2	59.9	22.8	954	54.6	66.9	9.2
Trenton city	384	385	0.3	393	76.1	20.6	0.0	1.5	1.8	14.5	60.4	25.2	188	82.4	41.0	32.4
Union city	5,375	5,733	6.7	5,569	82.9	0.0	7.5	2.2	7.4	34.6	60.9	4.4	1,632	94.2	15.9	57.0
Uniontown city	1,002	976	-2.6	851	86.1	8.6	0.0	4.6	0.7	28.0	60.9	11.0	398	69.8	60.8	4.0
Upton city	690	674	-2.3	767	94.0	1.4	0.0	4.2	0.4	26.9	62.0	11.2	289	67.5	71.3	5.5
Utica CDP	0	NA	NA	114	100.0	0.0	0.0	0.0	0.0	10.5	78.9	10.5	52	78.8	34.6	0.0
Vanceburg city	1,466	1,466	0.0	1,554	98.5	1.2	0.2	0.2	0.0	19.5	64.7	15.6	623	40.0	63.4	8.7
Verona CDP	1,455	NA	NA	1,232	96.8	2.7	0.0	0.0	0.5	22.1	59.7	18.0	498	90.6	47.0	26.1
Versailles city	8,833	9,054	2.5	8,908	78.5	8.0	0.0	3.0	10.5	23.5	62.0	14.5	3,513	54.3	49.1	25.4
Vicco city	334	320	-4.2	304	94.4	0.0	0.0	5.6	0.0	36.9	54.4	8.9	107	68.2	66.4	1.9
Villa Hills city	7,311	7,426	1.6	7,359	98.2	0.0	0.1	0.0	1.6	19.6	65.6	14.9	2,688	88.4	22.5	49.5
Vine Grove city	4,928	5,621	14.1	5,296	69.7	20.2	3.2	3.0	3.9	24.2	62.8	13.0	2,106	77.4	33.3	30.6
Virgie CDP	279	NA	NA	264	100.0	0.0	0.0	0.0	0.0	19.3	64.3	16.3	111	91.0	64.9	0.0
Wallins Creek city	157	152	-3.2	120	99.2	0.0	0.0	0.8	0.0	15.8	64.2	20.0	59	74.6	72.9	1.7
Walton city	3,644	3,870	6.2	3,977	93.1	1.7	0.0	0.3	4.9	33.7	59.8	6.6	1,259	68.1	42.7	28.9
Warfield city	268	259	-3.4	296	95.6	0.0	0.7	3.7	0.0	22.3	61.8	15.9	131	78.6	61.1	3.1
Warsaw city	1,681	1,686	0.3	1,860	75.1	6.1	4.1	8.5	6.2	22.2	59.5	18.3	762	40.6	62.5	11.0
Water Valley city	279	283	1.4	332	97.0	1.2	0.0	0.0	1.8	16.5	64.6	18.7	136	75.7	61.8	2.2
Watterson Park city	976	997	2.2	1,500	53.5	15.4	0.0	2.9	28.2	31.5	59.0	9.5	552	31.9	53.6	16.7
Waverly city	308	313	1.6	326	90.2	7.4	0.0	1.8	0.6	22.4	65.9	11.7	120	74.2	56.7	11.7
Wayland city	426	413	-3.1	377	100.0	0.0	0.0	0.0	0.0	28.4	55.2	16.4	143	60.8	62.9	6.3
Wellington city	565	577	2.1	569	93.3	0.5	0.0	5.8	0.4	17.0	67.2	15.8	261	92.7	9.2	67.4
West Buechel city	1,230	1,264	2.8	1,245	42.4	36.5	2.7	6.7	11.7	22.4	70.8	7.0	517	14.1	41.4	21.5
West Liberty city	3,433	3,271	-4.7	3,248	86.4	7.0	2.2	2.5	2.0	16.8	68.2	15.1	950	56.5	52.7	24.2
West Point city	797	772	-3.1	901	87.6	0.0	1.0	5.1	6.3	29.6	60.5	10.0	344	61.0	58.1	6.4
Westport CDP	268	NA	NA	201	100.0	0.0	0.0	0.0	0.0	10.0	69.2	20.9	96	95.8	33.3	41.7
Westwood CDP	4,746	NA	NA	4,655	96.3	0.7	0.0	3.0	0.0	22.6	57.5	19.8	1,905	73.5	65.1	7.7
Westwood city	634	648	2.2	591	87.5	9.3	0.8	1.2	1.2	23.2	57.5	19.5	200	99.0	16.0	66.0
Wheatcroft city	160	156	-2.5	169	95.9	0.0	0.0	4.1	0.0	17.8	60.5	21.9	72	93.1	84.7	0.0
Wheelwright city	783	556	-29.0	1,036	86.6	6.9	0.0	6.3	0.3	15.9	75.1	8.9	230	70.4	71.7	10.9
White Plains city	884	874	-1.1	909	95.4	0.6	0.7	3.4	0.0	22.0	64.7	13.6	369	81.8	56.6	7.9
Whitesburg city	2,132	2,027	-4.9	1,832	95.6	1.7	0.8	0.4	1.4	17.5	61.6	20.8	732	52.2	50.0	23.8
Whitesville city	552	539	-2.4	443	98.6	0.7	0.0	0.7	0.0	21.6	57.5	20.8	187	77.5	71.1	8.6
Whitley City CDP	1,170	NA	NA	1,172	94.2	5.2	0.0	0.0	0.6	11.5	78.6	9.8	393	80.2	65.1	5.3
Wickliffe city	688	688	0.0	625	93.3	4.3	0.0	2.4	0.0	19.1	64.5	16.3	277	71.1	60.3	10.5
Wilder city	3,030	3,097	2.2	3,060	97.3	1.1	0.5	0.0	1.1	15.8	71.3	12.9	1,394	66.7	19.1	42.0
Wildwood city	261	269	3.1	246	94.7	1.6	2.4	1.2	0.0	20.7	51.7	27.6	118	87.3	17.8	56.8
Williamsburg city	5,247	5,274	0.5	5,260	94.7	2.3	0.7	1.1	1.2	13.2	71.1	15.7	1,870	46.6	49.2	30.7
Williamstown city	3,925	3,960	0.9	3,932	93.6	0.6	0.0	2.1	3.7	32.1	57.2	10.6	1,079	67.8	57.1	16.7
Willisburg city	283	285	0.7	324	97.5	2.5	0.0	0.0	0.0	21.3	58.4	20.4	103	82.5	79.6	1.9
Wilmore city	5,920	6,123	3.4	5,995	90.5	1.7	4.2	1.5	2.1	19.7	66.0	14.2	1,785	57.1	14.5	58.4
Winchester city	18,370	18,443	0.4	18,363	86.2	8.4	0.6	1.2	3.6	23.9	61.8	14.2	7,794	49.2	52.8	18.2
Windy Hills city	2,385	2,427	1.8	2,331	91.0	4.3	1.7	1.6	1.4	17.3	54.9	27.7	1,074	96.3	7.6	66.0
Wingo city	632	642	1.6	847	93.6	4.8	0.0	1.2	0.4	18.7	61.1	20.1	302	77.8	56.6	10.9
Woodburn city	355	371	4.5	362	97.8	1.1	0.0	1.1	0.0	9.1	61.9	29.0	138	79.0	65.9	11.6
Woodbury city	90	92	2.2	84	100.0	0.0	0.0	0.0	0.0	38.1	48.8	13.1	35	77.1	54.3	34.3
Woodland Hills city	696	713	2.4	695	91.2	4.2	1.3	1.4	1.9	26.4	59.2	14.4	267	85.8	21.7	49.8
Woodlawn city	231	232	0.4	295	96.6	0.3	0.0	3.1	0.0	23.4	66.8	9.8	105	81.9	32.4	28.6
Woodlawn Park city	942	968	2.8	938	95.1	3.5	0.3	0.3	0.7	23.9	56.9	19.3	390	87.7	16.4	63.1
Worthington city	1,609	1,586	-1.4	1,391	98.3	0.4	0.0	0.4	0.9	24.3	56.0	19.6	555	92.4	44.9	18.0
Worthington Hills city	1,447	1,487	2.8	1,562	56.3	28.9	3.1	5.4	6.1	24.8	69.4	5.7	628	82.2	22.3	35.7
Worthville city	185	185	0.0	216	89.4	8.8	0.0	1.9	0.0	26.4	68.1	5.6	82	57.3	62.2	4.9
Wurtland city	995	1,050	5.5	894	95.1	0.0	0.0	4.6	0.3	23.3	53.9	22.8	410	78.0	58.3	6.1
LOUISIANA	4,533,479	4,649,676	2.6	4,601,049	59.7	31.9	1.6	2.1	4.6	24.3	62.9	12.9	1,718,876	66.3	47.5	23.6
Abbeville city	12,255	12,446	1.6	12,341	48.6	41.6	4.1	4.3	1.4	30.3	56.4	13.2	4,461	54.2	67.3	10.3
Abita Springs town	2,367	2,479	4.7	2,512	91.1	2.7	0.5	2.5	3.1	21.2	66.4	12.5	976	85.8	24.1	43.0
Addis town	3,593	4,431	23.3	4,004	57.1	37.4	2.5	0.2	2.8	29.4	61.7	8.8	1,540	72.9	48.4	26.6
Albany village	1,088	1,098	0.9	1,545	93.7	2.7	0.0	0.0	3.6	31.1	58.4	10.5	531	59.3	53.3	15.1
Alexandria city	47,587	48,175	1.2	47,983	35.3	59.3	2.6	1.6	1.2	27.7	57.9	14.6	17,237	54.2	47.0	21.2
Ama CDP	1,316	NA	NA	1,362	67.0	31.4	0.0	0.0	1.7	14.9	66.8	18.3	529	85.4	61.4	21.0
Amelia CDP	2,459	NA	NA	2,290	44.0	18.7	10.6	2.4	24.3	20.0	71.6	8.4	866	69.6	84.2	3.9

1 May be of any race.

Table A. All Places — **Population and Housing**

STATE City, town, township, borough, or CDP (county if applicable)	Population				Race and Hispanic or Latino origin (percent), 2010–2014					Age (percent), 2010–2014			Households, 2010–2014			
															Householders by level of education (percent)	
	2010 census total population	2014 estimated population	Percent change 2010–2014	ACS total population estimate 2010–2014	White alone, not Hispanic or Latino	Black alone, not Hispanic or Latino	Asian alone, not Hispanic or Latino	All other races or 2 or more races, not Hispanic or Latino	Hispanic or Latino[1]	Under 18 years old	Age 18 to 64 years old	Age 65 years and older	Total occupied housing units	Percent owner occupied	High school diploma or less	Bachelor's degree or more
	1	2	3	4	5	6	7	8	9	10	11	12	13	14	15	16
LOUISIANA—Con.																
Amite City town	4,141	4,327	4.5	4,234	37.6	58.3	0.0	3.9	0.2	19.0	66.2	14.7	1,323	74.0	48.5	30.8
Anacoco village	869	867	-0.2	1,077	92.7	2.0	0.6	2.1	2.5	25.8	57.9	16.2	410	77.3	45.6	22.2
Angie village	251	243	-3.2	251	67.7	25.5	0.0	2.0	4.8	19.6	61.5	19.1	92	81.5	52.2	23.9
Arabi CDP	3,635	NA	NA	4,521	71.2	13.1	2.7	1.5	11.5	27.5	62.2	10.2	1,584	65.5	49.7	16.0
Arcadia town	2,993	2,883	-3.7	2,939	33.9	60.8	0.0	3.4	1.8	23.6	59.3	17.1	1,147	53.9	52.4	18.0
Arnaudville town	1,057	1,067	0.9	1,238	89.1	10.5	0.0	0.4	0.0	27.7	54.9	17.4	422	72.7	69.9	7.8
Ashland village	269	264	-1.9	279	89.6	8.2	0.7	1.4	0.0	27.9	53.5	18.6	108	82.4	63.9	20.4
Athens village	249	235	-5.6	280	53.6	43.6	0.0	2.1	0.7	18.1	69.0	12.9	125	84.8	51.2	12.8
Atlanta village	163	156	-4.3	118	73.7	24.6	0.0	1.7	0.0	16.9	70.3	12.7	47	80.9	53.2	21.3
Avondale CDP	4,954	NA	NA	5,262	47.5	37.3	8.2	2.0	5.0	29.2	54.8	16.0	1,765	72.4	70.7	1.9
Baker city	13,888	13,776	-0.8	13,838	18.4	75.5	1.5	1.3	3.2	26.6	61.7	11.8	4,828	64.3	50.4	18.4
Baldwin town	2,436	2,361	-3.1	2,087	36.5	55.6	0.0	5.5	2.4	22.2	60.8	17.0	846	83.3	62.5	13.4
Ball town	3,993	4,010	0.4	4,005	89.1	4.6	3.5	0.3	2.4	22.1	64.6	13.3	1,413	74.9	39.6	19.6
Banks Springs CDP	1,192	NA	NA	1,292	57.6	39.1	0.0	3.3	0.0	28.6	54.9	16.5	522	41.4	82.2	8.6
Barataria CDP	1,109	NA	NA	908	100.0	0.0	0.0	0.0	0.0	13.6	57.7	28.7	452	80.1	63.9	13.1
Basile town	1,821	1,811	-0.5	1,965	58.5	23.5	0.8	8.9	8.3	26.5	61.9	11.7	581	63.2	72.3	9.0
Baskin village	254	248	-2.4	291	91.8	8.2	0.0	0.0	0.0	30.6	51.9	17.5	122	82.8	60.7	4.9
Bastrop city	11,365	10,881	-4.3	11,075	20.8	77.3	0.3	1.3	0.4	27.4	59.4	13.2	4,141	51.4	63.6	11.6
Baton Rouge city	229,447	228,895	-0.2	229,353	36.6	54.7	3.5	2.0	3.3	21.4	66.7	11.9	88,576	50.1	34.3	33.5
Bawcomville CDP	3,588	NA	NA	3,682	88.8	2.0	0.0	1.4	7.8	27.4	60.7	11.8	1,359	53.1	68.4	4.9
Bayou Blue CDP	12,352	NA	NA	12,659	79.1	13.6	0.5	4.0	2.8	29.8	61.6	8.6	4,305	78.7	64.2	11.0
Bayou Cane CDP	19,355	NA	NA	20,627	72.7	12.1	1.4	5.3	8.5	25.1	61.7	13.4	7,788	59.7	53.4	16.8
Bayou Corne CDP	0	NA	NA	177	100.0	0.0	0.0	0.0	0.0	12.4	80.8	6.8	103	82.5	61.2	21.4
Bayou Country Club CDP	1,396	NA	NA	1,397	81.0	15.0	0.9	2.7	0.4	21.5	60.7	17.9	523	94.5	17.4	59.5
Bayou Gauche CDP	2,071	NA	NA	2,594	99.1	0.0	0.0	0.9	0.0	26.0	63.8	10.1	942	94.4	62.4	8.1
Bayou Goula CDP	612	NA	NA	459	24.8	75.2	0.0	0.0	0.0	21.8	62.1	16.1	185	75.7	65.9	29.2
Bayou L'Ourse CDP	1,978	NA	NA	1,375	82.7	0.7	4.5	3.1	9.0	28.6	61.4	10.0	558	72.0	66.5	14.0
Bayou Vista CDP	4,652	NA	NA	5,092	78.9	8.2	1.7	1.9	9.3	27.1	60.3	12.7	1,969	64.6	69.4	8.4
Belcher village	263	259	-1.5	253	49.8	18.6	6.7	4.3	20.6	24.5	59.2	16.2	93	76.3	40.9	31.2
Belle Chasse CDP	12,679	NA	NA	13,171	81.4	4.8	2.3	2.8	8.7	28.4	60.7	10.7	4,895	53.8	45.2	20.5
Belle Rose CDP	1,902	NA	NA	1,579	44.4	55.2	0.0	0.4	0.0	22.0	56.9	21.2	655	77.4	75.7	4.3
Belmont CDP	361	NA	NA	753	79.4	2.9	5.8	8.4	3.5	34.9	50.8	14.5	261	81.6	43.3	24.1
Benton town	1,948	2,043	4.9	1,878	46.1	48.5	0.0	2.1	3.3	27.5	61.8	10.9	660	57.6	50.8	14.5
Bernice town	1,689	1,654	-2.1	1,373	20.1	61.3	0.0	0.8	17.8	28.8	51.2	20.2	519	67.6	65.1	1.3
Berwick town	4,946	4,810	-2.7	4,857	76.2	13.5	1.8	3.0	5.6	26.7	62.4	10.9	1,789	73.4	67.8	12.7
Bienville village	218	211	-3.2	213	77.0	21.6	0.0	0.0	1.4	22.1	66.2	11.7	97	73.2	54.6	6.2
Blanchard town	2,900	2,910	0.3	2,911	82.7	10.0	2.8	1.6	2.9	24.0	61.4	14.6	1,231	75.2	54.0	16.8
Bogalusa city	12,232	11,926	-2.5	12,071	43.0	48.1	0.2	2.6	6.2	26.9	57.9	15.4	4,497	60.5	64.3	13.4
Bonita village	284	269	-5.3	197	21.3	67.5	0.0	0.0	11.2	14.2	61.1	24.9	81	66.7	92.6	2.5
Boothville CDP	854	NA	NA	901	46.9	22.9	14.8	14.2	1.2	22.5	68.4	9.1	358	87.2	88.8	4.7
Bordelonville CDP	525	NA	NA	865	95.8	3.1	0.0	0.0	1.0	31.4	54.5	14.2	344	59.9	73.0	9.9
Bossier City city	61,631	67,472	9.5	64,895	61.5	26.3	1.8	3.1	7.4	25.3	62.0	12.7	24,933	55.4	38.6	26.7
Bourg CDP	2,579	NA	NA	2,358	75.7	13.9	0.6	9.0	0.8	29.8	62.0	8.2	888	79.7	66.2	9.6
Boutte CDP	3,075	NA	NA	2,436	40.1	51.5	0.0	4.5	3.9	24.0	68.1	7.9	947	77.8	52.4	31.9
Boyce town	1,004	986	-1.8	1,456	28.1	71.2	0.0	0.7	0.0	22.0	66.7	11.3	528	58.7	61.0	12.7
Branch CDP	388	NA	NA	123	79.7	20.3	0.0	0.0	0.0	0.0	100.0	0.0	56	100.0	100.0	0.0
Breaux Bridge city	8,139	8,327	2.3	8,232	50.4	46.6	1.4	1.2	0.3	31.3	56.7	11.9	2,832	65.5	63.3	16.0
Bridge City CDP	7,706	NA	NA	7,163	31.8	50.3	2.6	1.6	13.6	28.4	60.4	11.2	2,426	60.1	69.0	7.0
Broussard city	8,357	10,356	23.9	9,041	74.0	17.8	0.5	3.3	4.4	27.9	62.6	9.5	3,468	72.1	42.0	26.9
Brownfields CDP	5,401	NA	NA	5,562	25.2	72.8	0.0	1.2	0.9	30.3	55.3	14.4	2,027	78.1	46.5	25.2
Brownsville CDP	4,317	NA	NA	4,356	67.4	24.7	0.0	0.7	7.2	24.4	63.4	12.2	1,695	55.4	69.0	6.9
Brusly town	2,589	2,706	4.5	2,603	79.8	16.1	0.0	2.3	1.8	27.3	60.1	12.5	897	84.2	37.3	25.4
Bryceland village	108	104	-3.7	128	74.2	1.6	0.0	24.2	0.0	38.3	42.2	19.5	45	88.9	40.0	31.1
Bunkie city	4,178	4,071	-2.6	4,127	35.3	62.2	0.0	0.6	1.9	28.2	52.8	19.1	1,614	59.7	68.3	14.3
Buras CDP	945	NA	NA	860	83.3	0.0	9.9	6.9	0.0	28.1	64.5	7.4	386	84.7	68.9	14.0
Cade CDP	1,723	NA	NA	1,213	64.4	33.8	0.0	0.0	1.8	9.1	72.7	18.1	574	85.2	33.1	30.3
Calhoun CDP	679	NA	NA	729	100.0	0.0	0.0	0.0	0.0	35.6	59.1	5.3	331	64.4	73.4	16.3
Calvin village	238	228	-4.2	207	81.6	8.7	0.0	9.7	0.0	32.3	55.0	12.6	75	74.7	70.7	5.3
Cameron CDP	406	NA	NA	346	99.1	0.3	0.0	0.6	0.0	25.4	62.5	12.1	137	100.0	77.4	16.8
Campti town	1,056	1,042	-1.3	853	20.8	76.7	0.0	2.6	0.0	33.5	53.8	12.7	309	50.8	59.2	13.6
Cankton village	484	490	1.2	713	72.9	17.3	0.0	2.2	7.6	30.7	64.5	4.6	257	82.5	78.2	3.1
Carencro city	7,646	8,453	10.6	8,084	56.3	37.8	0.4	1.3	4.1	26.3	60.6	13.2	3,217	61.4	56.0	16.8
Carlyss CDP	4,670	NA	NA	5,089	91.0	6.4	0.4	1.3	0.9	32.5	57.4	10.1	1,766	68.2	60.8	12.6
Castor village	258	249	-3.5	193	73.6	21.8	0.5	3.1	1.0	31.1	56.0	13.0	69	59.4	60.9	11.6
Catahoula CDP	1,094	NA	NA	1,114	98.0	0.0	0.0	0.0	2.0	34.6	52.0	13.4	312	100.0	63.1	2.2
Cecilia CDP	1,980	NA	NA	1,020	74.1	25.9	0.0	0.0	0.0	25.7	66.9	7.3	408	74.8	39.2	25.7
Center Point CDP	492	NA	NA	293	95.2	4.8	0.0	0.0	0.0	14.3	42.6	43.0	116	100.0	45.7	13.8
Central city	26,867	28,119	4.7	27,505	86.8	9.8	0.3	1.7	1.5	22.9	61.0	16.1	10,097	85.3	44.6	21.7
Chackbay CDP	5,177	NA	NA	5,299	89.6	5.2	0.0	2.8	2.4	27.7	60.8	11.6	1,815	91.7	66.2	15.4
Chalmette CDP	16,751	NA	NA	19,375	67.8	15.8	3.3	2.6	10.5	27.0	64.3	8.7	6,813	58.5	51.8	14.4
Charenton CDP	1,903	NA	NA	1,934	50.6	17.2	1.7	24.5	6.0	21.6	60.3	17.9	759	88.4	72.9	7.9
Chataignier village	364	360	-1.1	435	46.9	51.3	0.0	0.7	1.1	19.1	69.1	11.7	169	63.3	72.8	7.7
Chatham town	557	549	-1.4	595	44.7	54.3	0.3	0.0	0.7	20.5	61.6	17.8	280	59.6	71.1	16.1
Chauvin CDP	2,912	NA	NA	3,220	90.5	0.6	0.2	7.0	1.8	28.9	57.8	13.1	1,052	83.7	75.6	5.8
Cheneyville town	625	612	-2.1	490	25.5	73.5	0.0	1.0	0.0	14.0	62.2	23.7	196	63.8	58.7	11.2
Choctaw CDP	879	NA	NA	796	89.8	0.0	0.0	10.2	0.0	19.0	57.2	23.9	344	97.4	81.4	0.0
Choudrant village	845	933	10.4	1,097	85.8	9.4	0.5	0.8	3.5	20.6	67.8	11.7	443	61.6	31.6	44.5
Church Point town	4,554	4,536	-0.4	4,529	62.7	34.0	0.0	2.2	1.1	27.2	57.3	15.6	1,722	53.5	70.2	1.3
Claiborne CDP	11,507	NA	NA	11,575	93.0	2.7	1.1	1.2	2.0	26.3	61.2	12.5	4,528	66.3	37.5	29.3
Clarence village	499	489	-2.0	381	15.7	83.2	1.0	0.0	0.0	23.8	63.2	12.9	139	61.2	74.1	10.8
Clarks village	1,017	1,000	-1.7	866	63.9	30.9	0.0	0.8	4.4	19.4	69.3	11.3	203	84.2	76.8	1.5
Clayton town	711	697	-2.0	718	20.3	79.7	0.0	0.0	0.0	23.0	64.4	12.5	272	54.4	77.2	5.1
Clinton town	1,652	1,589	-3.8	1,657	40.1	59.8	0.1	0.0	0.0	23.7	63.2	13.1	714	65.8	48.9	15.7
Colfax town	1,558	1,532	-1.7	1,684	24.9	70.0	0.3	3.8	1.0	25.9	58.6	15.4	569	53.8	65.7	6.0
Collinston village	287	272	-5.2	199	50.3	42.2	4.0	0.0	3.5	12.5	61.6	25.6	96	64.6	77.1	6.3
Columbia town	390	379	-2.8	438	55.3	32.0	2.1	6.4	4.3	18.0	66.2	16.0	181	77.3	56.4	11.6
Convent CDP	711	NA	NA	623	36.4	61.0	0.0	0.3	2.2	21.7	60.1	18.3	214	78.5	74.8	11.7
Converse village	440	440	0.0	428	86.7	3.7	0.0	7.9	1.6	22.8	56.4	20.6	155	71.6	67.7	11.6
Cottonport town	2,006	1,956	-2.5	2,850	41.1	51.3	0.0	4.6	3.1	22.5	67.8	9.9	674	57.4	69.4	9.3
Cotton Valley town	1,009	980	-2.9	961	54.0	43.0	0.0	1.4	1.7	22.9	56.9	20.2	429	69.7	66.0	19.1
Coushatta town	1,964	1,869	-4.8	2,361	18.4	79.3	0.0	0.6	1.7	33.8	53.9	12.5	732	39.8	77.0	8.6
Covington city	8,774	9,686	10.4	9,151	66.8	25.3	1.5	1.0	5.5	20.8	66.0	13.2	3,294	61.4	32.0	37.5

1 May be of any race.

Table A. All Places — **Population and Housing**

STATE City, town, township, borough, or CDP (county if applicable)	Population				Race and Hispanic or Latino origin (percent), 2010–2014					Age (percent), 2010–2014			Households, 2010–2014			
	2010 census total population	2014 estimated population	Percent change 2010–2014	ACS total population estimate 2010–2014	White alone, not Hispanic or Latino	Black alone, not Hispanic or Latino	Asian alone, not Hispanic or Latino	All other races or 2 or more races, not Hispanic or Latino	Hispanic or Latino[1]	Under 18 years old	Age 18 to 64 years old	Age 65 years and older	Total occupied housing units	Percent owner occupied	Householders by level of education (percent): High school diploma or less	Householders by level of education (percent): Bachelor's degree or more
	1	2	3	4	5	6	7	8	9	10	11	12	13	14	15	16
LOUISIANA—Con.																
Creola village	213	210	-1.4	311	95.8	3.2	0.0	0.6	0.3	38.6	60.6	0.6	86	2.3	54.7	7.0
Crescent CDP	959	NA	NA	794	25.9	72.5	0.0	0.0	1.5	17.9	53.7	28.5	269	100.0	27.5	32.7
Crowley city	13,263	13,189	-0.6	13,219	61.0	31.5	0.2	3.4	4.0	27.6	58.6	13.7	4,832	51.0	67.6	13.4
Cullen town	1,163	1,134	-2.5	937	18.4	80.5	0.0	0.2	1.0	29.7	48.4	21.8	415	48.7	71.6	5.5
Cut Off CDP	5,976	NA	NA	5,498	88.8	0.3	1.3	7.1	2.5	25.1	58.9	15.9	2,040	85.1	72.4	9.5
Delcambre town	1,866	1,859	-0.4	1,973	78.6	14.7	0.4	0.3	6.1	26.5	55.7	17.7	725	66.8	64.8	9.4
Delhi town	2,939	2,941	0.1	2,972	31.6	63.9	0.0	1.7	2.8	24.3	61.2	14.8	1,090	51.1	65.0	15.5
Delta village	284	270	-4.9	247	95.5	4.5	0.0	0.0	0.0	21.0	64.3	14.6	110	63.6	70.0	4.5
Denham Springs city	10,215	10,097	-1.2	10,148	78.0	17.2	0.7	1.5	2.6	22.7	60.3	16.9	3,876	61.4	57.4	14.1
DeQuincy city	3,235	3,174	-1.9	3,201	82.7	13.9	0.0	3.2	0.1	23.0	56.5	20.5	1,228	68.1	54.6	12.7
DeRidder city	10,578	10,799	2.1	10,846	53.1	34.3	1.6	4.7	6.3	27.3	60.5	12.3	3,875	58.3	47.2	23.9
Des Allemands CDP	2,505	NA	NA	1,773	87.6	4.8	1.9	5.1	0.6	12.3	61.7	26.1	724	83.1	82.6	5.5
Destrehan CDP	11,535	NA	NA	11,250	68.2	19.7	2.7	1.4	8.1	25.4	66.1	8.5	3,933	79.8	34.8	36.0
Deville CDP	1,764	NA	NA	1,968	100.0	0.0	0.0	0.0	0.0	30.8	58.0	11.3	749	69.3	67.8	7.2
Dixie Inn village	273	266	-2.6	283	31.8	56.9	0.0	9.5	1.8	29.3	61.4	9.2	115	41.7	52.2	8.7
Dodson village	337	323	-4.2	340	86.8	11.8	0.0	0.0	1.5	39.9	42.1	17.9	115	53.9	62.6	8.7
Donaldsonville city	7,436	7,635	2.7	7,507	24.4	74.6	0.0	0.4	0.6	29.0	59.9	11.1	2,515	63.1	65.5	10.9
Downsville village	141	139	-1.4	210	98.6	0.0	0.0	0.0	1.4	17.7	72.4	10.0	75	82.7	37.3	41.3
Doyline village	818	800	-2.2	999	73.5	23.9	0.1	1.0	1.5	26.0	59.5	14.4	366	65.0	55.5	7.1
Dry Prong village	440	439	-0.2	527	89.6	0.4	0.8	8.3	0.9	33.2	49.8	16.9	167	87.4	43.7	16.8
Dubach town	961	977	1.7	857	57.1	39.2	2.7	1.1	0.0	25.1	65.8	9.0	331	50.5	56.8	16.9
Dubberly village	273	266	-2.6	221	91.4	6.8	0.0	0.0	1.8	19.0	58.7	22.2	91	79.1	59.3	15.4
Dulac CDP	1,463	NA	NA	1,116	56.0	3.0	0.0	41.0	0.0	19.9	68.6	11.6	443	75.6	79.7	4.7
Duson town	1,744	1,774	1.7	1,801	58.1	34.2	0.6	1.8	5.4	28.8	60.7	10.3	640	63.9	72.3	8.9
East Hodge village	289	281	-2.8	331	0.0	100.0	0.0	0.0	0.0	35.6	51.5	12.7	139	34.5	49.6	6.5
Eastwood CDP	4,093	NA	NA	4,387	86.0	5.7	0.5	0.6	7.3	31.8	59.9	8.3	1,531	81.5	33.8	23.1
Eden Isle CDP	7,041	NA	NA	7,302	88.1	4.8	2.6	0.9	3.7	20.1	62.8	17.1	2,929	83.9	32.3	33.0
Edgard CDP	2,441	NA	NA	2,170	2.7	97.3	0.0	0.0	0.0	21.6	58.5	19.9	860	77.4	49.2	11.6
Edgefield village	218	207	-5.0	182	76.4	0.0	0.0	5.5	18.1	34.1	43.7	22.0	66	100.0	62.1	19.7
Egan CDP	631	NA	NA	352	100.0	0.0	0.0	0.0	0.0	13.1	75.4	11.6	174	67.2	78.2	20.7
Elizabeth town	532	555	4.3	570	95.1	0.7	0.0	4.2	0.0	33.2	54.8	11.9	190	61.1	63.2	9.5
Elmwood CDP	4,635	NA	NA	4,758	56.7	23.2	8.0	3.6	8.4	15.9	76.6	7.4	2,681	17.6	17.1	53.8
Elton town	1,128	1,129	0.1	1,141	42.1	43.2	0.2	10.3	4.2	23.2	58.7	18.1	479	63.9	69.5	10.4
Empire CDP	993	NA	NA	1,098	57.6	33.9	7.2	0.0	1.4	25.0	58.1	16.7	449	94.0	62.8	9.4
Epps village	854	848	-0.7	1,165	43.8	51.2	0.0	1.5	3.6	8.6	81.0	10.2	180	66.7	71.7	5.0
Erath town	2,114	2,110	-0.2	2,167	82.6	5.5	6.5	3.7	1.8	21.2	60.3	18.4	899	64.8	67.5	11.3
Eros town	155	151	-2.6	151	94.7	0.0	0.0	0.0	5.3	28.5	59.6	11.9	57	66.7	64.9	8.8
Erwinville CDP	2,192	NA	NA	2,284	96.7	3.3	0.0	0.0	0.0	21.7	60.5	17.7	867	91.6	71.5	15.7
Estelle CDP	16,377	NA	NA	15,236	54.4	28.4	6.2	1.2	9.8	24.9	65.7	9.5	5,130	82.9	55.4	14.2
Estherwood village	889	939	5.6	846	90.1	7.3	0.0	2.6	0.0	29.8	55.0	15.2	285	78.6	71.2	12.6
Eunice city	10,398	10,330	-0.7	10,325	58.8	34.2	1.0	2.2	3.7	24.8	59.4	15.9	3,965	52.7	66.9	8.9
Evergreen town	310	302	-2.6	303	67.0	30.0	1.3	0.7	1.0	16.9	65.1	18.2	149	34.2	76.5	2.7
Farmerville town	3,921	3,881	-1.0	3,892	32.1	60.4	0.0	5.5	2.0	27.8	58.2	14.1	1,479	67.1	49.9	10.5
Fenton village	383	374	-2.3	359	22.3	64.3	2.8	10.0	0.6	25.3	48.9	25.6	164	77.4	67.1	26.2
Ferriday town	3,509	3,440	-2.0	3,479	19.8	79.4	0.0	0.3	0.4	37.7	49.6	12.9	1,270	39.1	63.4	10.2
Fifth Ward CDP	800	NA	NA	873	100.0	0.0	0.0	0.0	0.0	19.6	61.2	19.2	371	81.9	62.3	22.6
Fisher village	230	228	-0.9	186	71.0	19.4	0.0	8.6	1.1	15.6	60.3	24.2	69	84.1	76.8	0.0
Florien village	633	630	-0.5	500	53.2	32.6	0.0	11.8	2.4	25.6	61.0	13.4	182	63.7	58.8	18.1
Folsom village	716	755	5.4	666	70.4	25.7	0.0	0.3	3.6	19.6	65.5	15.0	267	72.3	44.2	18.0
Fordoche town	928	910	-1.9	883	83.4	10.5	3.3	0.8	2.0	13.9	62.0	24.0	379	97.1	74.1	8.4
Forest village	355	350	-1.4	307	77.5	0.0	1.3	0.0	21.2	31.2	49.2	19.5	119	75.6	67.2	16.8
Forest Hill village	816	801	-1.8	679	53.5	0.0	0.6	1.8	44.2	42.1	50.9	7.1	194	68.0	64.4	9.8
Fort Jesup CDP	509	NA	NA	407	85.5	0.0	0.0	0.0	14.5	25.6	65.1	9.3	155	80.6	61.3	33.5
Fort Polk North CDP	2,864	NA	NA	2,625	56.0	20.9	0.9	5.3	16.9	28.9	71.2	0.0	962	0.7	29.7	15.5
Fort Polk South CDP	9,038	NA	NA	9,635	61.0	13.5	1.1	4.6	19.9	36.5	63.0	0.6	2,139	0.7	29.5	19.2
Franklin city	7,660	7,368	-3.8	7,483	34.7	58.1	1.8	1.3	4.1	26.3	58.8	14.9	2,626	58.2	62.8	11.8
Franklinton town	3,856	3,776	-2.1	3,809	48.0	50.9	0.0	0.6	0.5	24.6	54.0	21.2	1,353	57.0	51.6	18.7
French Settlement village	1,116	1,112	-0.4	1,283	98.5	0.5	0.0	0.7	0.2	19.6	67.5	12.9	484	84.7	57.4	6.8
Frierson CDP	143	NA	NA	557	61.8	23.5	0.0	2.2	12.6	26.5	46.6	26.9	119	58.0	29.4	0.0
Galliano CDP	7,676	NA	NA	7,830	80.8	1.3	0.8	7.9	9.3	27.3	59.3	13.3	2,816	73.4	70.6	4.0
Gardere CDP	10,580	NA	NA	10,594	20.6	59.5	0.3	0.7	18.9	28.9	68.9	2.3	3,506	34.8	40.1	26.6
Garyville CDP	2,811	NA	NA	2,517	45.6	54.4	0.0	0.0	0.0	32.7	52.3	15.0	932	75.4	70.6	5.7
Georgetown village	327	327	0.0	421	97.6	0.0	0.0	1.7	0.7	40.7	54.7	4.8	121	66.1	59.5	7.4
Gibsland town	979	953	-2.7	1,037	12.4	84.7	0.0	2.9	0.0	21.4	64.6	13.9	436	49.1	55.7	13.3
Gilbert village	575	568	-1.2	347	73.5	26.5	0.0	0.0	0.0	28.5	52.0	19.6	141	71.6	70.9	4.3
Gilliam village	164	161	-1.8	142	53.5	46.5	0.0	0.0	0.0	11.9	59.7	28.2	61	63.9	59.0	16.4
Gillis CDP	657	NA	NA	465	98.9	0.0	0.0	0.0	1.1	13.5	58.2	28.2	233	73.0	74.2	0.0
Glencoe CDP	211	NA	NA	393	31.3	58.3	0.0	0.0	10.4	27.4	70.3	2.3	140	50.0	84.3	0.0
Glenmora town	1,344	1,328	-1.2	1,291	49.7	42.5	0.3	0.9	6.6	29.7	56.1	14.2	496	55.8	68.1	7.9
Gloster CDP	94	NA	NA	0	0.0	0.0	0.0	0.0	0.0	0.0	0.0	0.0	0	0.0	0.0	0.0
Golden Meadow town	2,101	2,076	-1.2	1,786	84.5	0.0	0.9	1.3	13.3	19.1	61.6	19.3	749	78.9	79.4	6.3
Goldonna village	432	425	-1.6	406	86.9	0.0	0.0	11.3	1.7	20.5	56.7	22.9	155	91.0	63.9	12.9
Gonzales city	9,782	10,457	6.9	10,137	46.5	46.0	0.5	1.5	5.5	23.6	61.6	14.8	3,986	67.1	50.5	18.3
Grambling city	4,949	5,124	3.5	5,015	7.5	90.1	0.4	0.2	1.8	20.7	71.5	7.7	1,478	35.3	30.8	28.1
Gramercy town	3,613	3,466	-4.1	3,523	49.6	48.3	0.0	0.8	1.2	26.4	59.2	14.3	1,293	83.4	47.1	19.4
Grand Cane village	242	244	0.8	309	90.0	10.0	0.0	0.0	0.0	14.6	71.8	13.6	117	75.2	54.7	20.5
Grand Coteau town	928	935	0.8	914	19.7	80.1	0.0	0.0	0.2	21.4	54.9	23.6	364	70.6	66.5	16.5
Grand Isle town	1,296	1,382	6.6	1,002	98.6	0.1	0.1	1.2	0.0	20.9	59.1	20.2	387	71.8	71.6	4.4
Grand Point CDP	2,473	NA	NA	2,164	72.0	24.2	3.3	0.0	0.6	22.2	67.3	10.5	821	85.5	57.7	9.6
Gray CDP	5,584	NA	NA	5,202	53.7	38.5	0.5	4.4	2.9	31.7	60.5	7.6	1,804	72.6	71.3	9.3
Grayson village	532	518	-2.6	437	89.0	11.0	0.0	0.0	0.0	22.7	54.9	22.4	206	63.6	52.9	10.7
Greensburg town	721	688	-4.6	650	46.6	50.2	0.0	3.2	0.0	18.5	62.6	18.9	241	60.6	59.3	10.0
Greenwood town	3,219	3,201	-0.6	3,239	63.9	30.5	0.0	1.5	4.1	18.7	63.9	17.4	1,530	79.2	40.2	30.9
Gretna city	17,734	17,845	0.6	17,801	44.1	33.4	3.3	3.2	15.9	22.6	63.3	14.1	6,844	49.9	57.4	16.8
Grosse Tete village	647	641	-0.9	700	46.4	43.7	0.3	4.3	5.3	18.2	66.1	15.7	280	75.7	66.1	7.5
Gueydan town	1,398	1,400	0.1	1,580	88.9	10.4	0.0	0.5	0.3	20.0	59.4	20.6	668	78.6	70.1	10.0
Hackberry CDP	1,261	NA	NA	1,284	95.6	0.0	0.0	1.2	3.2	21.2	60.9	17.9	494	87.7	61.5	6.9
Hahnville CDP	3,344	NA	NA	3,338	44.7	45.0	0.0	4.6	5.8	19.2	69.9	10.9	1,198	78.3	61.5	13.1
Hall Summit village	300	286	-4.7	367	76.0	18.8	0.0	0.0	5.2	35.7	54.5	9.8	135	74.8	58.5	8.9
Hammond city	20,015	20,363	1.7	20,207	47.1	46.1	1.3	1.3	4.2	19.2	69.3	11.5	6,854	44.4	42.6	26.6
Harahan city	9,277	9,334	0.6	9,324	94.5	0.9	0.1	2.3	2.2	18.6	63.7	17.7	3,927	74.7	36.0	29.1
Harrisonburg village	348	338	-2.9	433	63.0	37.0	0.0	0.0	0.0	31.4	60.2	8.3	161	57.8	71.4	14.9

1 May be of any race.

STATE City, town, township, borough, or CDP (county if applicable)	Population				Race and Hispanic or Latino origin (percent), 2010–2014					Age (percent), 2010–2014			Households, 2010–2014			
	2010 census total population	2014 estimated population	Percent change 2010–2014	ACS total population estimate 2010–2014	White alone, not Hispanic or Latino	Black alone, not Hispanic or Latino	Asian alone, not Hispanic or Latino	All other races or 2 or more races, not Hispanic or Latino	Hispanic or Latino[1]	Under 18 years old	Age 18 to 64 years old	Age 65 years and older	Total occupied housing units	Percent owner occupied	Householders by level of education (percent): High school diploma or less	Householders by level of education (percent): Bachelor's degree or more
	1	2	3	4	5	6	7	8	9	10	11	12	13	14	15	16
LOUISIANA—Con.																
Harvey CDP	20,348	NA	NA	21,247	34.8	40.9	6.8	1.7	15.8	23.6	64.5	11.9	7,788	59.7	52.6	18.3
Haughton town	3,473	3,400	-2.1	3,458	77.7	18.0	0.0	3.6	0.6	26.7	61.8	11.7	1,312	77.8	48.9	14.5
Hayes CDP	780	NA	NA	509	100.0	0.0	0.0	0.0	0.0	33.4	60.5	6.1	127	100.0	88.2	0.0
Haynesville town	2,327	2,194	-5.7	2,548	44.0	52.2	0.0	2.9	0.9	24.2	56.5	19.2	1,021	49.4	60.8	13.4
Heflin village	240	234	-2.5	210	86.2	4.8	0.0	7.6	1.4	28.6	60.6	11.0	72	90.3	52.8	23.6
Henderson town	1,674	1,722	2.9	1,696	64.0	12.3	5.8	5.5	12.5	19.6	71.4	8.9	563	78.0	79.0	2.3
Hessmer village	802	781	-2.6	837	74.6	23.1	1.0	1.4	0.0	17.7	60.1	22.2	391	76.2	62.4	6.9
Hester CDP	498	NA	NA	442	86.7	11.5	0.0	0.0	1.8	21.5	70.5	8.1	161	95.0	47.2	29.2
Hodge village	470	457	-2.8	376	41.2	58.0	0.0	0.8	0.0	21.9	54.2	23.9	165	49.7	42.4	17.6
Homer town	3,237	3,036	-6.2	3,129	25.1	71.8	0.0	3.2	0.0	25.7	59.2	15.2	1,145	59.1	58.7	14.0
Hornbeck town	480	477	-0.6	468	97.9	0.0	0.0	0.4	1.7	24.8	60.1	15.2	168	76.2	41.7	14.3
Hosston village	316	311	-1.6	298	74.8	17.4	0.7	7.0	0.0	20.1	56.3	23.5	127	82.7	65.4	15.0
Houma city	33,703	34,124	1.2	33,807	62.9	25.0	1.0	6.1	5.0	25.9	61.1	12.9	12,297	64.3	58.3	16.3
Ida village	220	217	-1.4	204	95.6	4.4	0.0	0.0	0.0	8.4	63.2	28.4	109	91.7	70.6	3.7
Independence town	1,665	1,687	1.3	1,913	47.2	45.4	0.0	1.5	5.9	33.3	55.7	10.9	636	52.0	57.7	14.5
Inniswold CDP	6,180	NA	NA	6,633	79.7	14.3	3.8	2.1	0.0	26.9	59.8	13.5	2,781	56.0	26.6	43.4
Iota town	1,500	1,485	-1.0	1,790	93.4	3.7	0.0	2.9	0.0	27.5	63.2	9.2	736	59.2	62.9	9.5
Iowa town	2,996	3,174	5.9	3,083	65.4	30.5	0.0	2.9	1.3	23.3	67.8	8.9	1,154	70.8	55.2	13.0
Jackson town	3,842	3,800	-1.1	3,819	41.4	55.5	0.0	2.1	0.9	12.8	77.9	9.1	724	61.0	67.7	16.3
Jamestown village	139	134	-3.6	196	98.0	0.0	0.0	2.0	0.0	27.6	61.9	10.7	66	63.6	72.7	9.1
Jeanerette city	5,530	5,530	0.0	5,547	34.0	64.6	0.0	1.4	0.0	32.6	54.3	13.2	1,889	71.3	72.3	9.5
Jean Lafitte town	1,903	1,956	2.8	2,110	84.8	0.9	0.0	10.8	3.5	25.5	64.0	10.3	683	91.9	63.3	5.6
Jefferson CDP	11,193	NA	NA	11,068	64.5	21.5	0.4	2.1	11.4	14.4	70.0	15.6	5,137	54.4	43.8	27.2
Jena town	3,398	3,387	-0.3	3,396	86.2	11.5	0.0	0.3	2.0	16.5	63.1	20.3	1,452	74.0	61.0	16.8
Jennings city	10,383	10,183	-1.9	10,265	68.8	28.3	0.1	1.5	1.4	26.2	58.2	15.7	3,790	62.6	61.0	13.5
Jonesboro town	4,704	4,623	-1.7	4,680	49.6	49.9	0.0	0.1	0.4	22.5	62.2	15.4	1,638	52.9	61.4	13.5
Jonesville town	2,265	2,187	-3.4	2,212	28.2	66.9	0.0	4.1	0.8	27.7	58.0	14.4	792	58.8	64.4	11.1
Jordan Hill CDP	211	NA	NA	91	100.0	0.0	0.0	0.0	0.0	26.4	73.7	0.0	35	20.0	22.9	57.1
Joyce CDP	384	NA	NA	215	94.4	0.0	0.0	0.0	5.6	4.7	81.4	14.0	120	39.2	73.3	0.0
Junction City village	584	570	-2.4	524	39.7	48.7	0.0	8.0	3.6	31.3	48.0	20.8	210	51.0	81.9	1.9
Kaplan city	4,607	4,609	0.0	4,604	76.9	14.8	3.3	3.4	1.6	21.8	63.0	15.2	1,933	66.8	70.5	9.6
Keachi town	291	294	1.0	357	81.0	10.1	0.0	3.4	5.6	27.1	62.1	10.6	118	79.7	54.2	15.3
Kenner city	66,705	67,064	0.5	66,926	50.5	21.4	3.8	1.9	22.3	21.2	65.0	13.8	24,704	59.6	45.6	23.9
Kentwood town	2,198	2,310	5.1	2,181	28.9	69.6	0.0	0.2	1.2	22.9	58.6	18.6	863	63.7	70.5	6.7
Kilbourne village	416	410	-1.4	481	84.2	13.5	0.0	2.3	0.0	30.7	51.6	17.7	177	72.3	76.3	5.6
Killian town	1,206	1,290	7.0	969	85.8	10.1	0.0	2.2	2.0	25.8	61.5	12.7	423	85.1	47.8	14.9
Killona CDP	793	NA	NA	585	2.2	97.8	0.0	0.0	0.0	34.9	62.3	2.7	238	82.4	72.3	0.0
Kinder town	2,477	2,451	-1.0	2,746	60.2	28.9	1.6	8.5	0.9	29.3	55.5	15.1	1,113	59.4	65.0	6.9
Kraemer CDP	934	NA	NA	997	92.3	0.0	0.0	5.8	1.9	22.9	59.3	17.6	409	91.4	81.2	10.3
Krotz Springs town	1,198	1,205	0.6	1,063	99.6	0.0	0.0	0.0	0.4	20.6	55.3	24.1	445	71.0	74.2	7.6
Labadieville CDP	1,854	NA	NA	2,009	77.2	18.8	0.0	0.0	4.1	25.6	62.0	12.4	722	78.3	63.2	13.9
Lacassine CDP	480	NA	NA	432	100.0	0.0	0.0	0.0	0.0	29.2	61.8	9.0	135	94.8	34.1	37.0
Lacombe CDP	8,679	NA	NA	7,726	68.0	24.4	0.0	2.8	4.8	18.5	60.7	20.6	3,182	82.7	48.4	16.7
Lafayette city	121,131	126,066	4.1	123,528	60.6	31.0	2.0	1.7	4.6	21.6	66.3	12.1	49,556	55.5	33.7	35.4
Lafitte CDP	972	NA	NA	1,276	98.0	0.0	0.0	2.0	0.0	22.9	48.8	28.3	448	89.5	83.5	8.7
Lafourche Crossing CDP	2,002	NA	NA	2,301	85.5	10.9	1.7	0.0	1.8	20.9	65.7	13.5	815	85.4	51.8	25.0
Lake Arthur town	2,738	2,746	0.3	2,739	79.2	16.2	0.0	2.8	1.7	24.0	57.4	18.7	993	76.0	71.1	14.2
Lake Charles city	72,033	74,889	4.0	73,503	43.7	48.5	2.1	2.5	3.2	23.8	62.7	13.6	29,705	53.7	42.0	24.4
Lake Providence town	3,995	3,821	-4.4	3,899	14.6	84.4	0.0	0.7	0.2	31.6	55.6	12.8	1,506	47.7	66.3	12.9
Lakeshore CDP	1,930	NA	NA	1,591	74.8	10.9	9.3	0.0	5.0	20.7	58.4	20.7	718	75.9	45.8	23.3
Lakeview CDP	948	NA	NA	1,056	82.4	10.9	1.7	3.4	1.6	17.4	70.5	12.2	485	80.4	44.7	4.7
Laplace CDP	29,872	NA	NA	28,736	41.8	48.0	0.9	2.7	6.5	25.5	64.3	10.2	9,907	76.4	48.4	20.1
Larose CDP	7,400	NA	NA	7,030	76.6	3.5	2.3	6.4	11.2	23.1	59.6	17.3	2,565	81.2	66.2	14.2
Lawtell CDP	1,198	NA	NA	1,306	65.5	28.9	0.0	5.7	0.0	20.6	69.5	9.9	498	91.4	56.0	26.7
Lecompte town	1,227	1,199	-2.3	891	27.5	72.1	0.1	0.0	0.3	27.8	54.6	17.5	404	51.0	64.9	6.2
Leesville city	6,613	6,528	-1.3	6,656	49.7	36.5	2.9	5.1	5.9	24.8	63.0	12.3	2,460	44.8	44.7	19.4
Lemannville CDP	860	NA	NA	887	29.8	68.7	0.0	0.2	1.4	19.1	67.5	13.4	122	95.9	59.0	4.9
Leonville town	1,086	1,098	1.1	991	44.9	52.3	0.0	0.0	2.8	18.1	66.8	15.0	352	83.0	75.3	7.1
Lillie village	118	116	-1.7	104	75.0	7.7	0.0	1.0	16.3	1.0	73.9	25.0	43	86.0	60.5	16.3
Lisbon village	185	175	-5.4	262	82.8	17.2	0.0	0.0	0.0	34.7	48.9	16.4	85	92.9	50.6	18.8
Livingston town	1,769	1,905	7.7	1,922	88.3	8.2	0.7	0.5	2.3	23.8	58.5	17.6	650	76.3	61.1	19.2
Livonia town	1,442	1,419	-1.6	1,561	89.9	3.7	0.0	6.3	0.2	27.0	60.5	12.6	587	84.5	58.4	12.4
Lockport town	2,578	2,550	-1.1	2,561	89.0	1.4	0.0	2.8	6.8	25.2	59.6	15.4	990	65.2	69.7	11.1
Lockport Heights CDP	1,286	NA	NA	1,074	96.4	0.0	0.0	3.6	0.0	16.6	68.6	14.8	439	82.2	72.9	14.1
Logansport town	1,555	1,573	1.2	1,880	59.5	37.8	0.0	1.5	1.2	34.8	51.7	13.7	718	54.0	50.8	8.1
Longstreet village	157	158	0.6	361	91.7	7.2	0.0	1.1	0.0	39.6	53.4	6.9	83	53.0	68.7	3.6
Longville CDP	635	NA	NA	891	100.0	0.0	0.0	0.0	0.0	40.5	54.5	4.9	286	72.4	34.3	37.8
Loreauville village	887	895	0.9	680	84.1	14.3	0.0	0.9	0.7	26.7	53.9	19.6	290	71.0	74.8	12.1
Lucky village	272	263	-3.3	265	49.8	49.8	0.0	0.4	0.0	20.7	58.1	21.1	106	75.5	79.2	9.4
Luling CDP	12,119	NA	NA	12,375	77.1	15.9	1.3	1.9	3.8	26.3	62.8	11.0	4,298	84.3	44.9	21.5
Lutcher town	3,559	3,401	-4.4	3,471	55.1	41.6	0.0	0.0	3.3	23.5	58.8	17.7	1,353	73.3	49.6	14.4
Lydia CDP	952	NA	NA	715	100.0	0.0	0.0	0.0	0.0	21.1	49.2	29.7	317	95.6	72.2	14.8
McNary village	209	205	-1.9	144	63.9	9.7	25.7	0.7	0.0	20.9	57.0	22.2	64	48.4	60.9	25.0
Madisonville town	748	803	7.4	841	93.7	2.3	1.9	1.0	1.2	23.8	62.8	13.2	347	65.4	19.9	47.0
Mamou town	3,242	3,186	-1.7	3,211	65.1	31.9	0.0	2.8	0.2	30.1	46.8	23.0	1,355	41.3	69.4	11.4
Mandeville city	11,931	12,236	2.6	12,102	81.7	6.4	3.8	1.7	6.4	21.9	62.4	15.8	4,670	60.3	24.4	49.5
Mangham town	672	656	-2.4	819	52.1	46.2	0.2	1.5	0.0	35.6	50.1	14.3	309	68.6	70.2	10.4
Mansfield city	4,992	5,006	0.3	5,012	22.1	72.5	0.4	0.6	4.3	27.1	59.4	13.5	1,771	60.0	64.8	8.5
Mansura town	1,419	1,386	-2.3	1,622	25.2	61.7	0.0	6.1	7.0	31.0	56.1	12.9	605	55.4	64.5	7.9
Many town	2,853	2,797	-2.0	2,818	40.2	53.9	0.0	4.9	1.0	26.9	55.8	17.4	1,014	40.0	58.3	13.0
Maringouin town	1,098	1,077	-1.9	1,007	12.5	87.5	0.0	0.0	0.0	20.3	61.6	18.1	402	70.4	67.9	13.9
Marion town	765	757	-1.0	647	41.3	56.7	1.2	0.8	0.0	21.4	52.0	26.7	297	62.3	62.6	12.5
Marksville city	5,703	5,553	-2.6	5,635	48.6	41.8	3.2	6.0	0.5	24.8	60.4	14.7	2,019	43.9	65.8	12.2
Marrero CDP	33,141	NA	NA	33,263	37.7	50.5	3.8	1.7	6.3	26.6	59.0	14.4	12,191	63.7	62.4	10.3
Martin village	594	568	-4.4	661	93.0	6.4	0.0	0.2	0.5	23.2	62.1	14.4	223	87.0	63.7	10.8
Mathews CDP	2,209	NA	NA	2,280	98.4	0.0	0.0	0.7	0.9	29.9	62.5	7.3	779	83.2	59.9	20.5
Maurice village	1,059	1,170	10.5	1,490	71.1	11.4	0.6	1.3	15.6	20.2	64.1	15.8	518	63.1	48.1	19.7
Melville town	1,039	1,047	0.8	1,099	31.4	64.6	0.0	0.9	3.1	32.5	55.4	12.1	431	62.4	75.4	4.4
Meraux CDP	5,816	NA	NA	6,627	73.7	12.9	0.6	4.0	8.7	23.3	68.7	8.0	2,144	84.3	58.3	11.9
Mermentau village	661	656	-0.8	725	89.5	8.4	0.0	1.4	0.7	33.7	52.0	14.3	283	62.5	77.7	9.5
Mer Rouge village	622	597	-4.0	624	74.5	25.0	0.0	0.5	0.0	27.6	53.1	19.2	190	55.8	65.8	24.2
Merrydale CDP	9,772	NA	NA	9,601	6.0	90.3	0.5	1.7	1.6	27.0	66.6	6.4	3,234	71.2	35.9	23.2

1 May be of any race.

Table A. All Places — **Population and Housing**

STATE City, town, township, borough, or CDP (county if applicable)	Population: 2010 census total population	Population: 2014 estimated population	Population: Percent change 2010–2014	Population: ACS total population estimate 2010–2014	Race (percent), 2010–2014: White alone, not Hispanic or Latino	Race: Black alone, not Hispanic or Latino	Race: Asian alone, not Hispanic or Latino	Race: All other races or 2 or more races, not Hispanic or Latino	Race: Hispanic or Latino[1]	Age (percent), 2010–2014: Under 18 years old	Age: Age 18 to 64 years old	Age: Age 65 years and older	Households, 2010–2014: Total occupied housing units	Households: Percent owner occupied	Householders by level of education (percent): High school diploma or less	Householders by level of education (percent): Bachelor's degree or more
	1	2	3	4	5	6	7	8	9	10	11	12	13	14	15	16
LOUISIANA—Con.																
Merryville town	1,103	1,109	0.5	988	73.7	17.6	1.4	5.8	1.5	22.6	54.0	23.6	443	58.0	67.0	1.6
Metairie CDP	138,481	NA	NA	140,074	70.2	9.6	4.0	1.7	14.5	19.5	63.0	17.4	58,759	61.8	34.5	34.7
Midway CDP	1,291	NA	NA	1,624	51.9	43.4	0.0	2.7	2.0	33.8	58.8	7.6	620	72.1	70.3	4.7
Milton CDP	3,030	NA	NA	3,030	93.7	2.2	4.1	0.0	0.0	28.6	59.7	11.6	1,019	87.2	33.8	34.9
Minden city	13,082	12,808	-2.1	12,988	40.2	57.0	1.2	0.7	0.9	27.0	56.9	16.1	4,786	59.2	57.4	14.4
Minorca CDP	2,317	NA	NA	1,866	74.1	25.0	0.0	0.9	0.0	26.3	62.5	11.0	670	85.5	68.5	4.3
Monroe city	49,154	49,601	0.9	49,455	32.0	64.2	1.0	1.2	1.6	27.7	59.2	13.1	18,390	45.5	46.0	27.5
Montegut CDP	1,540	NA	NA	1,446	96.3	0.1	0.0	3.3	0.3	23.9	66.3	9.8	474	97.9	75.9	7.4
Monterey CDP	439	NA	NA	538	99.8	0.0	0.0	0.0	0.2	40.1	54.1	5.8	188	89.4	35.1	31.4
Montgomery town	721	723	0.3	641	73.6	22.2	1.4	2.8	0.0	17.8	63.0	19.3	283	73.1	75.6	5.7
Monticello CDP	5,172	NA	NA	5,431	15.2	77.9	2.6	4.3	0.0	24.4	65.9	9.6	1,957	94.8	32.5	33.4
Montpelier village	266	252	-5.3	249	42.2	50.6	0.0	1.6	5.6	35.4	50.4	14.1	82	75.6	63.4	7.3
Montz CDP	1,918	NA	NA	2,007	71.5	22.8	0.3	1.4	3.9	26.5	65.4	8.1	643	84.9	56.3	17.3
Moonshine CDP	194	NA	NA	114	18.4	81.6	0.0	0.0	0.0	39.5	45.6	14.9	40	100.0	75.0	0.0
Mooringsport town	793	789	-0.5	821	77.2	18.9	1.2	0.6	2.1	26.9	54.7	18.5	349	64.8	58.2	10.9
Moreauville village	929	906	-2.5	968	68.6	26.4	0.0	5.0	0.0	28.7	52.7	18.5	408	75.2	71.1	12.3
Morgan City city	12,404	11,943	-3.7	12,153	65.0	21.9	0.2	5.1	7.8	23.8	61.4	14.8	4,819	59.2	60.1	15.4
Morganza village	610	598	-2.0	808	67.6	31.1	0.4	1.0	0.0	25.1	56.7	18.2	303	71.3	67.3	13.9
Morse village	812	806	-0.7	924	98.5	0.0	0.0	1.1	0.4	27.5	64.6	7.9	312	75.3	77.2	2.6
Moss Bluff CDP	11,557	NA	NA	12,443	85.4	5.6	1.8	3.0	4.2	27.5	61.5	11.1	4,187	84.2	40.2	23.5
Mound village	19	18	-5.3	6	100.0	0.0	0.0	0.0	0.0	33.4	33.3	33.3	3	66.7	66.7	33.3
Mount Lebanon town	83	80	-3.6	49	79.6	20.4	0.0	0.0	0.0	8.2	65.4	26.5	31	100.0	41.9	38.7
Napoleonville village	660	647	-2.0	615	11.5	84.4	0.0	4.1	0.0	22.6	63.2	14.1	212	53.8	69.3	11.8
Natalbany CDP	2,984	NA	NA	2,900	38.7	39.6	7.8	0.0	13.9	23.1	70.8	6.2	1,013	34.6	45.4	17.6
Natchez village	597	587	-1.7	358	8.4	91.1	0.0	0.6	0.0	26.0	62.9	11.2	140	61.4	79.3	6.4
Natchitoches city	18,545	18,384	-0.9	18,460	37.6	58.7	0.4	1.4	1.8	23.2	63.3	13.5	7,014	45.6	42.3	24.0
Newellton town	1,187	1,095	-7.8	1,267	28.7	69.8	0.0	0.8	0.7	33.5	49.2	17.3	455	58.2	61.3	11.0
New Iberia city	30,617	30,745	0.4	30,750	50.5	39.8	2.7	2.0	5.1	28.5	57.5	14.1	11,409	59.3	59.2	15.7
New Llano town	2,597	2,547	-1.9	2,606	40.1	35.6	5.8	6.4	12.1	28.7	62.0	9.1	1,019	47.7	45.2	16.5
New Orleans city	343,829	384,320	11.8	368,471	30.7	59.2	2.9	1.8	5.4	20.8	67.7	11.5	150,409	46.9	35.7	36.1
New Roads city	4,831	4,734	-2.0	4,791	31.4	65.6	0.7	0.8	1.5	23.1	59.3	17.5	1,810	56.9	58.4	23.9
New Sarpy CDP	1,464	NA	NA	1,472	64.9	32.7	0.0	1.0	1.4	24.5	60.7	14.9	571	82.0	65.5	5.8
Noble village	252	251	-0.4	300	68.0	0.7	2.7	21.0	7.7	19.9	68.3	11.7	96	91.7	65.6	12.5
Norco CDP	3,074	NA	NA	3,044	91.3	5.9	0.0	1.2	1.5	26.4	56.1	17.3	1,149	82.8	55.1	9.6
North Hodge village	388	381	-1.8	442	70.4	19.2	0.5	5.2	4.8	29.5	59.4	11.1	183	53.6	57.4	12.0
North Vacherie CDP	2,346	NA	NA	2,261	28.0	70.3	0.0	0.0	1.6	21.9	64.0	14.1	804	78.6	48.1	25.5
Norwood village	322	315	-2.2	286	82.2	17.8	0.0	0.0	0.0	17.1	58.3	24.5	139	71.9	65.5	10.1
Oakdale city	7,784	7,723	-0.8	7,741	54.8	25.1	1.7	5.0	13.4	19.0	67.3	13.8	2,126	60.6	54.4	12.5
Oak Grove town	1,727	1,700	-1.6	1,718	67.6	24.4	1.0	3.9	3.0	30.4	47.5	21.9	663	61.7	62.1	15.4
Oak Hills Place CDP	8,195	NA	NA	8,568	70.0	16.3	4.2	0.9	8.6	18.7	67.5	13.9	3,680	68.9	13.0	67.9
Oak Ridge village	144	136	-5.6	120	95.8	2.5	0.0	1.7	0.0	26.6	51.6	21.7	47	89.4	19.1	55.3
Oberlin town	1,770	1,754	-0.9	2,069	59.2	30.6	1.2	7.3	1.7	33.3	52.7	14.2	686	57.9	59.9	9.6
Oil City town	1,008	1,001	-0.7	735	49.4	46.3	0.5	0.0	3.8	28.4	61.2	10.2	341	45.5	59.8	12.3
Old Jefferson CDP	6,980	NA	NA	7,182	69.2	19.2	6.8	1.8	3.0	25.4	64.2	10.3	2,833	80.3	27.6	36.8
Olla town	1,391	1,375	-1.2	1,306	96.1	0.0	0.0	3.5	0.4	27.9	55.0	17.1	533	75.8	57.2	12.2
Opelousas city	16,758	16,617	-0.8	16,668	20.6	76.0	0.6	1.8	1.0	31.5	53.9	14.6	5,820	48.6	68.1	12.2
Oretta CDP	418	NA	NA	469	100.0	0.0	0.0	0.0	0.0	39.5	49.8	10.9	133	94.0	93.2	0.0
Ossun CDP	2,144	NA	NA	2,181	41.3	49.4	0.0	5.6	3.7	39.2	54.4	6.3	691	71.6	58.5	14.2
Paincourtville CDP	911	NA	NA	1,155	64.3	32.1	2.5	0.2	0.9	32.2	50.2	17.6	398	85.4	48.5	26.1
Palmetto village	164	163	-0.6	130	56.2	43.8	0.0	0.0	0.0	16.1	50.8	33.1	60	60.0	85.0	10.0
Paradis CDP	1,298	NA	NA	1,396	82.2	3.6	1.8	0.4	12.0	31.8	62.9	5.2	441	77.6	49.4	11.8
Parks village	667	671	0.6	587	45.5	51.1	0.0	0.7	2.7	14.1	67.9	17.7	260	81.9	53.1	24.6
Patterson city	6,112	6,107	-0.1	6,100	49.4	42.4	0.0	4.9	3.3	29.4	57.3	13.4	2,238	65.6	59.3	11.0
Paulina CDP	1,178	NA	NA	1,251	93.0	7.0	0.0	0.0	0.0	29.3	54.8	15.9	439	83.8	59.2	12.3
Pearl River town	2,409	2,472	2.6	2,912	92.9	0.9	0.0	0.9	5.4	27.1	58.9	13.8	1,003	74.5	56.5	14.2
Pierre Part CDP	3,169	NA	NA	2,840	96.3	0.0	0.0	3.7	0.0	18.6	67.4	13.9	1,214	86.2	72.8	4.9
Pine Prairie village	1,607	1,593	-0.9	1,502	66.1	22.4	0.0	0.8	10.7	16.0	75.6	8.4	333	62.5	62.5	9.6
Pineville city	14,508	14,425	-0.6	14,486	60.7	32.1	0.4	3.5	3.3	24.2	63.0	12.7	5,111	52.3	42.2	25.7
Pioneer village	156	154	-1.3	148	55.4	44.6	0.0	0.0	0.0	16.3	67.7	16.2	58	65.5	65.5	13.8
Pitkin CDP	576	NA	NA	568	94.9	0.0	0.0	5.1	0.0	31.2	52.1	16.7	222	77.0	71.2	0.0
Plain Dealing town	1,015	988	-2.7	907	50.8	46.3	0.0	1.9	1.0	23.2	47.7	29.3	353	65.2	65.7	14.2
Plaquemine city	7,119	6,963	-2.2	7,055	46.2	50.4	0.0	0.5	2.9	26.4	61.0	12.5	2,811	67.0	57.2	14.2
Plaucheville village	248	240	-3.2	174	97.7	1.7	0.0	0.0	0.6	24.7	52.3	23.0	83	60.2	57.8	10.8
Pleasant Hill village	723	718	-0.7	866	49.3	44.7	0.2	2.7	3.1	25.5	59.9	14.4	275	60.4	65.1	5.8
Pleasure Bend CDP	250	NA	NA	332	100.0	0.0	0.0	0.0	0.0	34.3	52.9	12.7	123	78.0	72.4	0.0
Pointe a la Hache CDP	187	NA	NA	119	0.0	100.0	0.0	0.0	0.0	0.0	100.0	0.0	33	100.0	84.8	0.0
Point Place CDP	400	NA	NA	308	49.7	23.4	0.0	24.7	2.3	9.1	51.2	39.6	146	89.0	69.2	17.8
Pollock town	485	479	-1.2	454	96.7	1.5	0.0	1.8	0.0	32.2	58.2	9.5	168	55.4	45.8	7.7
Ponchatoula city	6,562	6,907	5.3	6,751	49.6	39.5	3.0	4.9	3.0	31.0	56.4	12.6	2,646	58.1	47.6	16.0
Port Allen city	5,180	5,144	-0.7	5,150	37.7	60.3	0.3	0.7	1.1	18.5	66.1	15.2	2,237	62.3	50.3	21.1
Port Barre town	2,091	2,111	1.0	1,813	78.1	20.5	0.0	0.0	1.4	31.1	59.4	9.3	696	55.2	71.3	3.3
Port Sulphur CDP	1,760	NA	NA	2,093	20.6	74.6	0.4	4.0	0.4	31.8	56.5	11.7	710	94.1	73.5	2.1
Port Vincent village	742	737	-0.7	907	98.0	0.7	0.0	0.3	1.0	22.7	63.7	13.6	345	86.7	52.2	23.8
Powhatan village	135	132	-2.2	104	0.0	100.0	0.0	0.0	0.0	13.4	42.4	44.2	45	35.6	86.7	6.7
Poydras CDP	2,351	NA	NA	2,309	75.0	15.2	0.0	1.9	7.9	24.6	64.6	10.7	819	91.5	75.8	8.8
Prairieville CDP	26,895	NA	NA	28,465	79.0	13.8	1.2	2.4	3.6	30.3	62.1	7.6	9,576	88.9	31.7	41.1
Presquille CDP	1,807	NA	NA	1,611	87.5	0.7	4.0	3.8	3.9	26.0	63.8	10.0	500	100.0	70.8	12.4
Prien CDP	7,810	NA	NA	8,142	83.6	8.0	3.5	3.7	1.2	28.8	57.6	13.7	2,953	90.6	33.9	32.5
Prospect CDP	476	NA	NA	667	100.0	0.0	0.0	0.0	0.0	46.1	50.3	3.3	161	71.4	43.5	23.0
Provencal village	611	607	-0.7	602	96.5	0.0	2.8	0.7	0.0	27.4	59.8	12.8	227	56.4	65.6	11.9
Quitman village	181	176	-2.8	156	96.2	1.9	0.0	1.9	0.0	20.5	50.6	28.8	68	82.4	44.1	14.7
Raceland CDP	10,193	NA	NA	9,976	65.4	30.0	0.1	2.5	2.0	23.7	62.3	14.1	3,756	81.5	67.7	13.5
Rayne city	7,939	8,039	1.3	7,984	63.8	32.8	0.7	1.7	0.9	23.9	60.4	15.7	3,173	58.0	65.1	7.7
Rayville town	3,695	3,720	0.7	3,745	27.6	71.2	0.0	0.9	0.3	29.6	57.0	13.4	1,368	42.5	59.7	15.2
Red Chute CDP	6,261	NA	NA	6,643	82.3	8.8	0.7	1.6	6.7	25.7	61.7	12.8	2,480	88.5	36.9	27.1
Reddell CDP	733	NA	NA	686	60.8	39.2	0.0	0.0	0.0	37.6	49.0	13.4	285	63.5	40.7	14.7
Reeves village	232	230	-0.9	293	94.5	0.7	0.0	2.7	2.0	34.5	51.1	14.3	87	92.0	59.8	12.6
Reserve CDP	9,766	NA	NA	9,976	36.9	58.5	0.0	0.6	4.0	26.6	61.4	12.0	3,342	77.7	61.6	12.6
Richmond village	577	555	-3.8	542	73.4	23.2	0.0	0.2	3.1	17.1	50.1	32.8	172	70.9	56.4	13.4
Richwood town	3,392	3,375	-0.5	5,846	18.7	78.6	0.0	0.4	2.3	10.1	86.2	3.7	660	35.3	58.6	8.0
Ridgecrest town	694	678	-2.3	630	64.4	27.0	0.0	0.5	8.1	19.8	60.0	20.0	296	70.3	60.5	5.7
Ringgold town	1,495	1,443	-3.5	1,642	26.4	72.7	0.0	0.5	0.4	30.3	50.8	18.9	639	54.9	66.7	7.4

1 May be of any race.

Table A. All Places — **Population and Housing**

STATE City, town, township, borough, or CDP (county if applicable)	Population: 2010 census total population	Population: 2014 estimated population	Population: Percent change 2010–2014	Population: ACS total population estimate 2010–2014	Race and Hispanic or Latino origin (percent), 2010–2014: White alone, not Hispanic or Latino	Race: Black alone, not Hispanic or Latino	Race: Asian alone, not Hispanic or Latino	Race: All other races or 2 or more races, not Hispanic or Latino	Race: Hispanic or Latino[1]	Age (percent), 2010–2014: Under 18 years old	Age: Age 18 to 64 years old	Age: Age 65 years and older	Households, 2010–2014: Total occupied housing units	Households: Percent owner occupied	Householders by level of education (percent): High school diploma or less	Householders by level of education (percent): Bachelor's degree or more
	1	2	3	4	5	6	7	8	9	10	11	12	13	14	15	16
LOUISIANA—Con.																
River Ridge CDP	13,494	NA	NA	13,835	78.1	11.8	0.4	1.4	8.3	20.4	60.9	18.7	5,774	72.8	31.3	36.9
Roanoke CDP	546	NA	NA	318	93.7	6.3	0.0	0.0	0.0	11.0	69.8	19.2	164	89.6	60.4	23.2
Robeline village	174	170	-2.3	106	67.9	13.2	0.0	14.2	4.7	8.4	57.6	34.0	58	44.8	55.2	8.6
Rock Hill CDP	274	NA	NA	191	100.0	0.0	0.0	0.0	0.0	11.0	69.1	19.9	108	100.0	70.4	24.1
Rodessa village	269	265	-1.5	272	61.0	23.9	0.0	15.1	0.0	18.7	68.8	12.5	106	67.0	80.2	5.7
Romeville CDP	130	NA	NA	262	33.6	66.4	0.0	0.0	0.0	26.7	62.7	10.7	82	68.3	54.9	0.0
Rosedale village	793	781	-1.5	1,021	59.6	36.4	0.8	0.0	3.1	22.7	65.4	11.8	422	84.6	61.8	6.9
Roseland town	1,123	1,186	5.6	1,059	29.2	68.6	0.5	0.0	1.7	22.6	62.1	15.3	408	73.0	72.1	14.0
Rosepine town	1,692	1,673	-1.1	1,855	76.9	8.2	0.2	3.1	11.6	22.4	67.0	10.5	650	44.5	63.2	14.0
Ruston city	21,907	22,301	1.8	22,149	48.9	44.5	3.1	1.9	1.6	19.0	70.0	10.9	7,973	37.3	24.9	40.5
St. Francisville town	1,763	1,716	-2.7	1,917	76.2	17.7	0.0	1.6	4.5	28.5	60.0	11.5	616	64.0	29.1	36.5
St. Gabriel city	6,677	6,993	4.7	6,796	38.0	56.0	0.0	4.4	1.6	12.7	82.0	5.4	1,230	68.5	51.6	22.4
St. James CDP	828	NA	NA	934	8.4	91.6	0.0	0.0	0.0	20.3	62.0	17.9	344	76.2	55.5	12.2
St. Joseph town	1,176	1,076	-8.5	913	21.5	74.5	0.0	0.0	4.1	24.3	60.1	15.6	379	56.2	62.0	9.5
St. Martinville city	6,114	6,092	-0.4	6,109	25.7	68.3	0.0	2.2	3.7	28.2	57.2	14.6	2,315	70.8	63.6	14.8
St. Maurice CDP	323	NA	NA	496	23.4	76.6	0.0	0.0	0.0	18.1	68.5	13.3	266	57.5	71.8	0.0
St. Rose CDP	8,122	NA	NA	9,125	43.1	47.0	0.2	0.5	9.2	32.4	57.8	9.8	2,970	70.8	45.3	18.1
Saline village	277	268	-3.2	376	70.5	24.5	0.0	2.4	2.7	34.3	58.0	7.7	124	80.6	61.3	15.3
Sarepta town	891	872	-2.1	919	97.6	0.5	0.0	1.8	0.0	30.7	53.6	15.7	318	78.9	59.1	14.2
Schriever CDP	6,853	NA	NA	7,564	65.5	26.7	0.0	4.8	3.0	25.9	65.7	8.4	2,516	76.3	58.4	15.5
Scott city	8,638	8,910	3.1	8,775	73.2	22.2	0.0	1.1	3.5	20.5	66.1	13.7	3,641	76.1	46.6	22.2
Shenandoah CDP	18,399	NA	NA	19,266	80.5	14.6	1.9	0.7	2.3	22.9	65.1	12.0	7,339	77.6	18.5	52.4
Shongaloo village	182	177	-2.7	181	99.4	0.0	0.6	0.0	0.0	28.2	60.2	11.6	62	91.9	38.7	25.8
Shreveport city	200,410	198,242	-1.1	200,692	39.2	55.2	1.3	1.6	2.7	24.9	61.6	13.5	77,726	56.0	41.6	27.9
Sibley town	1,218	1,193	-2.1	1,381	66.8	27.8	0.2	2.6	2.5	23.7	59.0	17.3	509	79.8	61.1	9.6
Sicily Island village	526	509	-3.2	527	20.7	78.6	0.0	0.8	0.0	36.7	49.7	13.5	159	62.9	69.2	11.9
Sikes village	119	114	-4.2	115	94.8	0.0	0.0	5.2	0.0	24.4	56.4	19.1	47	70.2	74.5	2.1
Simmesport town	2,161	2,118	-2.0	1,844	41.0	58.0	0.0	0.9	0.1	29.3	56.5	14.3	598	43.1	75.3	6.4
Simpson village	638	635	-0.5	816	94.7	1.1	0.0	0.0	4.2	33.6	57.2	9.3	258	81.4	31.8	17.4
Simsboro village	841	857	1.9	1,217	66.6	28.0	0.0	0.3	5.1	20.5	68.2	11.1	407	68.1	60.9	10.8
Singer CDP	287	NA	NA	545	96.9	0.0	0.0	3.1	0.0	10.6	59.3	30.1	190	88.9	62.6	16.3
Siracusaville CDP	422	NA	NA	602	4.2	95.8	0.0	0.0	0.0	27.0	68.6	4.5	167	61.1	76.6	0.0
Slaughter town	997	970	-2.7	1,159	87.4	10.4	0.0	1.6	0.5	23.4	63.1	13.5	414	85.7	54.1	14.7
Slidell city	27,071	27,622	2.0	27,372	73.2	17.5	0.7	2.4	6.2	23.5	60.1	16.5	10,091	69.9	39.4	24.7
Sorrel CDP	766	NA	NA	845	33.7	47.2	0.0	17.3	1.8	25.1	61.0	13.7	278	100.0	88.1	2.9
Sorrento town	1,418	1,551	9.4	1,598	85.2	11.4	0.1	0.8	2.4	26.3	59.7	14.0	652	81.4	68.9	5.5
South Mansfield village	346	349	0.9	503	6.2	91.1	0.0	0.0	2.8	24.0	64.6	11.5	205	31.2	70.2	5.4
South Vacherie CDP	3,642	NA	NA	3,606	61.6	38.4	0.0	0.0	0.0	18.4	66.3	15.3	1,421	81.5	63.1	11.2
Spearsville village	137	134	-2.2	178	100.0	0.0	0.0	0.0	0.0	17.4	45.4	37.1	84	57.1	51.2	20.2
Spokane CDP	442	NA	NA	347	86.7	7.5	2.0	3.7	0.0	13.8	58.4	28.0	175	87.4	50.3	24.0
Springfield town	478	491	2.7	426	90.6	8.0	0.0	0.0	1.4	13.9	65.7	20.4	162	76.5	67.9	18.5
Springhill city	5,269	5,148	-2.3	5,239	68.2	29.1	0.0	0.2	2.5	18.1	61.2	20.8	2,175	59.6	50.9	19.7
Stanley village	107	108	0.9	137	91.2	6.6	0.0	2.2	0.0	9.5	68.5	21.9	59	76.3	50.8	6.8
Starks CDP	664	NA	NA	650	94.5	4.9	0.0	0.6	0.0	27.3	56.7	16.0	264	78.4	77.3	3.4
Start CDP	905	NA	NA	940	92.7	7.3	0.0	0.0	0.0	29.4	60.0	10.5	414	63.5	46.9	23.7
Sterlington town	1,594	2,187	37.2	1,821	73.0	19.4	0.0	1.0	6.5	32.3	58.8	9.0	649	55.3	37.9	24.8
Stonewall town	1,846	2,019	9.4	1,954	84.8	9.1	0.6	3.6	1.9	22.4	62.9	14.6	743	83.3	43.3	22.3
Sugartown CDP	54	NA	NA	10	100.0	0.0	0.0	0.0	0.0	0.0	60.0	40.0	4	100.0	0.0	100.0
Sulphur city	20,408	20,206	-1.0	20,275	89.4	4.5	0.7	0.7	4.7	27.4	59.2	13.4	7,748	70.4	47.4	21.7
Sun village	469	479	2.1	306	85.6	11.4	0.0	2.9	0.0	23.8	62.8	13.4	131	87.8	64.1	6.9
Sunset town	2,897	2,928	1.1	2,904	48.7	44.1	0.0	7.2	0.0	28.3	58.1	13.7	1,186	64.0	62.6	18.3
Supreme CDP	1,052	NA	NA	903	14.6	83.9	0.0	1.4	0.0	33.9	59.1	7.1	325	81.2	79.1	0.0
Swartz CDP	4,536	NA	NA	4,977	73.5	22.1	2.4	0.5	1.5	22.4	60.0	17.6	1,823	79.5	38.0	22.3
Taft CDP	63	NA	NA	48	100.0	0.0	0.0	0.0	0.0	0.0	100.0	0.0	48	60.4	39.6	60.4
Tallulah city	7,335	7,181	-2.1	7,267	20.3	75.5	0.2	2.4	1.7	23.6	64.8	11.5	2,551	50.4	60.3	12.3
Tangipahoa village	755	796	5.4	517	7.4	92.6	0.0	0.0	0.0	18.5	72.3	9.1	191	54.5	59.2	6.8
Terrytown CDP	23,319	NA	NA	23,900	33.7	40.1	5.2	2.4	18.6	27.4	63.0	9.5	8,475	50.5	49.0	15.0
Thibodaux city	14,571	14,603	0.2	14,570	59.5	36.1	1.3	1.9	1.2	17.6	66.9	15.6	5,518	56.5	49.5	25.3
Tickfaw village	694	732	5.5	790	80.1	9.0	0.9	2.0	8.0	24.5	67.6	7.8	267	68.5	58.1	7.9
Timberlane CDP	10,243	NA	NA	10,891	43.6	36.8	5.6	1.9	12.1	25.9	63.4	10.7	3,492	67.6	43.0	25.8
Triumph CDP	216	NA	NA	93	100.0	0.0	0.0	0.0	0.0	6.5	93.6	0.0	55	81.8	40.0	25.5
Tullos town	385	384	-0.3	398	96.5	0.8	0.0	2.3	0.5	31.9	51.5	16.6	151	80.1	80.1	8.6
Turkey Creek village	441	443	0.5	330	98.8	0.0	0.0	0.9	0.3	29.3	58.1	12.7	125	76.0	57.6	11.2
Union CDP	892	NA	NA	1,060	14.9	83.8	0.0	1.3	0.0	32.3	55.8	12.0	349	89.7	67.0	6.6
Urania town	1,313	1,309	-0.3	1,124	57.6	38.3	0.0	1.8	2.4	7.7	78.9	13.3	215	80.9	54.0	17.2
Varnado village	336	328	-2.4	367	80.1	16.3	1.9	1.1	0.5	27.0	61.8	11.2	144	42.4	80.6	2.1
Venice CDP	202	NA	NA	217	82.9	0.0	0.0	10.1	6.9	28.2	51.7	20.3	82	80.5	61.0	0.0
Ventress CDP	890	NA	NA	1,060	79.7	18.9	0.0	1.4	0.0	18.8	53.9	27.3	480	68.8	42.1	3.3
Vidalia town	4,299	4,193	-2.5	4,238	67.8	27.6	1.4	0.6	2.7	23.0	60.3	16.7	1,687	61.8	57.9	17.0
Vienna town	386	389	0.8	447	93.7	3.6	0.0	0.7	2.0	24.0	62.8	13.2	170	78.2	28.8	44.1
Vienna Bend CDP	1,251	NA	NA	1,477	43.5	42.7	0.0	5.3	8.5	31.7	64.1	4.3	498	66.1	41.8	17.9
Village St. George CDP	7,104	NA	NA	7,190	63.9	28.3	3.5	2.2	2.2	24.4	65.8	9.7	2,717	79.9	25.4	51.6
Ville Platte city	7,431	7,287	-1.9	7,336	38.7	60.0	0.0	0.9	0.4	30.2	53.7	16.1	2,796	39.9	64.8	8.5
Vinton town	3,395	3,365	-0.9	3,391	66.9	24.1	0.0	0.0	9.0	20.5	60.0	19.5	1,474	54.4	68.7	8.4
Violet CDP	4,973	NA	NA	6,102	38.7	55.3	0.0	1.3	4.8	28.2	63.0	8.9	1,912	79.3	61.1	7.1
Vivian town	3,673	3,641	-0.9	3,682	59.7	32.4	0.0	4.6	3.3	19.8	61.7	18.5	1,675	53.0	61.9	9.1
Waggaman CDP	10,015	NA	NA	9,857	27.8	70.1	0.0	1.5	0.6	26.2	61.4	12.2	3,431	68.9	50.0	17.5
Walker town	6,138	6,238	1.6	6,176	87.3	11.3	0.0	1.4	0.0	26.3	62.6	11.2	2,303	75.5	37.4	22.7
Wallace CDP	671	NA	NA	803	4.6	95.4	0.0	0.0	0.0	26.4	62.9	10.6	253	78.3	72.7	1.2
Wallace Ridge CDP	710	NA	NA	228	92.5	7.5	0.0	0.0	0.0	21.5	43.4	35.1	109	92.7	65.1	21.1
Washington town	962	957	-0.5	656	47.0	52.6	0.2	0.3	0.0	25.6	55.7	18.6	288	60.4	54.9	27.4
Waterproof town	684	622	-9.1	768	2.9	94.8	0.0	1.3	1.0	34.0	48.6	17.2	262	56.1	71.8	3.8
Watson CDP	1,047	NA	NA	748	100.0	0.0	0.0	0.0	0.0	19.7	48.3	32.0	354	85.6	81.4	10.7
Welcome CDP	800	NA	NA	1,014	0.0	100.0	0.0	0.0	0.0	41.7	53.0	5.2	243	73.3	63.4	6.2
Welsh town	3,226	3,236	0.3	3,229	66.7	26.5	0.0	4.9	1.9	28.2	56.6	15.2	1,148	61.1	55.7	10.4
Westlake city	4,564	4,612	1.1	4,585	73.3	21.8	0.0	2.2	2.6	24.7	60.7	14.6	1,821	75.9	53.5	9.2
Westminster CDP	3,008	NA	NA	3,187	78.4	5.1	7.9	0.0	8.5	21.3	65.0	13.7	1,356	69.5	6.6	63.6
West Monroe city	13,064	12,985	-0.6	13,073	63.9	31.9	1.0	2.0	1.3	25.3	58.5	16.1	5,447	43.6	51.7	19.8
Westwego city	8,534	8,545	0.1	8,531	74.1	20.1	0.2	2.5	3.1	20.7	62.2	17.1	3,770	56.9	62.2	9.4
White Castle town	1,883	1,856	-1.4	2,317	10.6	86.1	0.0	0.0	3.3	30.8	56.5	12.8	870	52.2	69.4	6.8
Wilson village	595	577	-3.0	593	20.6	79.4	0.0	0.0	0.0	25.0	57.7	17.2	198	66.7	79.8	6.1
Winnfield city	4,842	4,629	-4.4	4,725	54.1	41.4	0.0	2.6	1.9	25.2	59.0	15.7	1,861	50.7	59.8	14.8

1 May be of any race.

Table A. All Places — Population and Housing

STATE City, town, township, borough, or CDP (county if applicable)	Population				Race and Hispanic or Latino origin (percent), 2010–2014					Age (percent), 2010–2014			Households, 2010–2014			
	2010 census total population	2014 estimated population	Percent change 2010–2014	ACS total population estimate 2010–2014	White alone, not Hispanic or Latino	Black alone, not Hispanic or Latino	Asian alone, not Hispanic or Latino	All other races or 2 or more races, not Hispanic or Latino	Hispanic or Latino[1]	Under 18 years old	Age 18 to 64 years old	Age 65 years and older	Total occupied housing units	Percent owner occupied	High school diploma or less	Bachelor's degree or more
	1	2	3	4	5	6	7	8	9	10	11	12	13	14	15	16
LOUISIANA—Con.																
Winnsboro city	4,910	4,785	-2.5	4,856	32.1	65.4	0.0	2.5	0.0	36.7	48.1	15.1	1,865	46.4	70.7	10.3
Wisner town	964	936	-2.9	966	68.2	31.8	0.0	0.0	0.0	25.6	52.4	22.2	332	63.0	62.3	9.6
Woodmere CDP	12,080	NA	NA	12,124	11.5	79.3	3.0	1.5	4.6	26.5	67.0	6.4	3,071	81.4	43.3	21.9
Woodworth town	1,094	1,089	-0.5	1,264	91.4	3.3	0.0	3.9	1.4	20.5	62.1	17.5	526	70.3	39.9	27.6
Youngsville city	8,157	11,006	34.9	9,358	87.4	6.4	1.7	2.9	1.5	32.6	60.5	6.7	3,237	85.4	28.9	37.1
Zachary city	14,942	16,219	8.5	15,579	55.4	40.9	0.8	1.7	1.1	31.4	57.2	11.3	5,119	75.7	26.4	36.6
Zwolle town	1,982	1,975	-0.4	2,218	35.0	42.0	0.8	15.8	6.4	30.2	59.0	10.7	724	58.0	70.4	5.8
MAINE	1,328,361	1,330,089	0.1	1,328,535	94.0	1.1	1.1	2.4	1.4	20.0	63.0	17.0	553,086	71.4	39.3	29.7
Abbot town (Piscataquis)..	714	701	-1.8	656	99.7	0.0	0.0	0.0	0.3	19.0	65.4	15.5	297	86.5	58.6	14.1
Acton town (York)	2,447	2,545	4.0	2,497	94.5	0.4	0.0	3.2	1.9	20.1	62.5	17.3	938	86.5	35.3	26.9
Addison town (Washington)	1,266	1,236	-2.4	1,170	95.9	0.0	0.3	2.0	1.8	17.0	62.2	20.9	545	82.9	47.5	19.1
Albion town (Kennebec)....	2,041	2,049	0.4	1,825	98.2	0.0	0.3	0.0	1.5	19.7	63.5	16.7	760	82.0	55.4	22.0
Alexander town (Washington)	503	490	-2.6	437	97.9	0.0	0.0	2.1	0.0	13.3	66.2	20.6	194	90.2	46.9	17.0
Alfred CDP	0	NA	NA	666	97.6	0.0	0.0	1.2	1.2	8.3	60.7	31.2	338	72.5	47.0	29.9
Alfred town (York)	3,019	3,076	1.9	3,051	96.9	0.6	0.0	1.8	0.8	15.0	61.2	23.9	1,231	84.6	42.2	24.6
Allagash town (Aroostook)	239	228	-4.6	215	95.8	0.0	0.0	2.3	1.9	6.6	53.6	40.0	118	82.2	44.9	26.3
Alna town (Lincoln)	709	714	0.7	650	100.0	0.0	0.0	0.0	0.0	18.0	65.5	16.5	265	97.0	28.7	38.9
Alton town (Penobscot).....	890	872	-2.0	893	97.6	0.0	0.6	1.8	0.0	21.5	64.7	13.9	370	78.6	43.8	17.0
Amherst town (Hancock) ..	265	264	-0.4	190	97.9	0.0	0.0	1.6	0.5	8.5	74.3	17.4	91	95.6	50.5	27.5
Amity town (Aroostook)	238	230	-3.4	188	81.9	4.3	0.0	13.8	0.0	24.0	63.4	12.8	73	95.9	27.4	15.1
Andover town (Oxford)......	821	807	-1.7	519	100.0	0.0	0.0	0.0	0.0	10.1	56.5	33.5	242	92.6	51.7	14.9
Anson CDP	752	NA	NA	734	96.5	0.0	0.0	3.5	0.0	21.7	62.4	15.5	284	77.5	72.5	9.5
Anson town (Somerset)	2,511	2,463	-1.9	2,593	95.7	0.0	0.0	3.3	1.0	21.2	64.6	14.3	1,085	78.1	61.9	11.0
Appleton town (Knox)	1,316	1,330	1.1	1,474	94.3	0.5	0.5	4.6	0.0	25.2	63.0	11.7	557	89.4	48.7	26.9
Argyle UT (Penobscot)	277	274	-1.1	235	99.1	0.0	0.0	0.9	0.0	13.6	68.1	18.3	109	97.2	40.4	22.0
Arrowsic town (Sagadahoc)	427	436	2.1	450	98.0	0.0	0.0	2.0	0.0	12.2	59.4	28.4	224	98.7	24.6	48.7
Arundel town (York)	4,022	4,176	3.8	4,100	90.5	3.7	1.5	2.9	1.4	20.0	69.9	10.0	1,591	78.0	42.5	28.2
Ashland CDP	709	NA	NA	737	95.8	0.0	0.0	3.5	0.7	22.7	57.4	19.9	310	62.6	51.0	13.5
Ashland town (Aroostook)	1,302	1,252	-3.8	1,300	96.8	0.0	0.6	2.2	0.4	21.4	57.7	20.8	554	73.1	58.8	8.7
Athens town (Somerset) ...	1,019	1,005	-1.4	1,072	98.7	0.0	0.0	1.3	0.0	25.2	58.5	16.3	406	82.0	48.5	12.3
Atkinson town (Piscataquis)	326	318	-2.5	249	98.0	0.0	1.6	0.4	0.0	12.0	64.1	23.7	120	86.7	55.8	10.0
Auburn city & MCD (Androscoggin)	23,052	22,912	-0.6	22,960	90.8	1.5	1.2	4.9	1.7	22.8	60.6	16.7	9,800	56.7	42.4	25.0
Augusta city & MCD (Kennebec)	19,132	18,705	-2.2	18,898	93.4	0.8	0.9	2.7	2.2	18.9	62.5	18.7	8,537	53.2	44.0	26.1
Aurora town (Hancock)	114	114	0.0	144	97.2	0.0	0.0	0.0	2.8	48.6	45.2	6.3	38	84.2	31.6	21.1
Avon town (Franklin)	461	455	-1.3	616	92.5	0.5	0.0	5.0	1.9	20.6	67.7	11.7	263	65.8	57.0	17.9
Baileyville town (Washington)	1,521	1,467	-3.6	1,409	98.6	0.2	0.3	0.4	0.6	14.6	66.9	18.5	640	82.0	50.3	16.6
Baldwin town (Cumberland)	1,525	1,579	3.5	1,511	99.1	0.0	0.2	0.7	0.0	20.3	65.0	14.6	561	93.8	49.0	22.5
Bancroft town (Aroostook)	68	66	-2.9	70	87.1	0.0	0.0	12.9	0.0	8.5	54.3	37.1	46	97.8	52.2	15.2
Bangor city & MCD (Penobscot)	33,037	32,568	-1.4	32,800	92.0	1.6	2.1	2.2	2.1	18.1	67.0	15.0	14,287	44.2	35.7	29.5
Bar Harbor CDP	2,552	NA	NA	2,524	92.0	0.9	5.0	1.7	0.4	15.2	70.8	14.1	1,130	45.8	22.7	48.8
Bar Harbor town (Hancock)..	5,235	5,308	1.4	5,269	90.9	0.4	4.7	1.7	2.3	16.2	68.4	15.5	2,359	62.4	23.3	51.1
Baring plantation (Washington)	251	242	-3.6	265	89.4	0.0	0.0	10.6	0.0	20.7	69.8	9.4	123	66.7	43.9	22.8
Bath city & MCD (Sagadahoc)	8,514	8,324	-2.2	8,396	93.2	1.4	0.8	2.3	2.3	22.3	61.3	16.3	3,875	55.7	33.1	29.1
Beals town (Washington)..	508	498	-2.0	485	97.1	0.0	0.2	0.4	2.3	18.8	51.2	30.1	227	88.1	65.6	15.4
Beaver Cove town (Piscataquis)	122	118	-3.3	169	100.0	0.0	0.0	0.0	0.0	15.4	56.9	27.8	78	73.1	19.2	41.0
Beddington town (Washington)	50	48	-4.0	40	90.0	0.0	2.5	2.5	5.0	5.0	60.0	35.0	24	100.0	45.8	25.0
Belfast city & MCD (Waldo)	6,668	6,677	0.1	6,664	95.9	0.4	2.0	0.8	0.9	23.5	53.1	23.4	2,771	61.5	37.7	40.1
Belgrade town (Kennebec)	3,189	3,154	-1.1	3,171	97.6	0.0	0.0	1.1	1.2	20.5	63.4	16.2	1,343	91.4	27.3	34.7
Belmont town (Waldo)	942	923	-2.0	1,084	96.3	0.4	0.0	3.0	0.4	20.6	61.3	18.2	454	79.5	49.3	15.2
Benton town (Kennebec)..	2,732	2,683	-1.8	2,696	98.2	0.0	0.0	1.4	0.4	19.7	62.4	17.9	1,137	91.3	53.6	10.7
Berwick CDP	2,187	NA	NA	2,048	88.5	1.8	0.0	8.5	1.2	25.0	69.5	5.4	755	71.5	35.5	24.1
Berwick town (York)	7,246	7,492	3.4	7,408	92.8	0.6	0.5	3.8	2.4	23.2	65.0	11.7	2,704	84.0	33.9	28.4
Bethel town (Oxford)	2,603	2,632	1.1	2,615	99.0	0.0	0.3	0.0	0.7	23.1	60.2	16.7	1,052	82.4	40.7	36.3
Biddeford city & MCD (York)	21,277	21,337	0.3	21,303	93.3	0.2	2.6	1.8	2.1	19.1	65.9	14.8	8,716	47.7	44.4	23.1
Bingham CDP	758	NA	NA	747	100.0	0.0	0.0	0.0	0.0	21.8	61.0	17.3	355	64.2	55.5	11.5
Bingham town (Somerset)	922	887	-3.8	1,015	96.0	0.0	0.0	4.0	0.0	21.2	60.2	18.5	455	72.1	47.7	21.3
Blaine CDP	301	NA	NA	395	98.5	0.0	0.0	1.0	0.5	29.6	60.5	9.9	149	71.1	35.6	18.8
Blaine town (Aroostook) ...	726	700	-3.6	772	97.3	0.0	0.0	2.3	0.4	26.1	60.1	13.6	298	78.2	45.3	21.1
Blanchard UT (Piscataquis)	98	97	-1.0	57	100.0	0.0	0.0	0.0	0.0	0.0	75.4	24.6	32	100.0	37.5	12.5
Blue Hill CDP	943	NA	NA	1,102	95.0	0.9	2.5	1.6	0.0	17.3	63.8	18.9	589	53.1	34.0	30.4
Blue Hill town (Hancock)...	2,686	2,676	-0.4	2,680	97.4	0.4	1.6	0.7	0.0	16.4	65.7	18.0	1,351	71.7	36.8	39.6
Boothbay town (Lincoln) ...	3,120	3,099	-0.7	3,102	98.0	0.0	0.2	0.4	1.4	10.5	54.1	27.3	1,418	92.7	27.9	34.2
Boothbay Harbor CDP......	1,086	NA	NA	881	98.0	0.0	0.3	1.1	0.6	9.2	61.6	29.3	468	69.7	34.0	30.6
Boothbay Harbor town (Lincoln)	2,165	2,170	0.2	2,011	97.5	0.4	0.1	1.7	0.2	10.2	51.7	38.1	998	71.7	31.4	36.2
Bowdoin town (Sagadahoc)	3,061	3,089	0.9	3,076	94.8	0.8	0.6	3.1	0.6	20.5	68.6	11.0	1,233	86.3	39.7	18.7
Bowdoinham CDP	722	NA	NA	508	90.7	6.9	0.0	1.2	1.2	27.8	63.0	9.3	179	92.2	36.3	30.2
Bowdoinham town (Sagadahoc)	2,889	2,891	0.1	2,883	95.2	1.2	0.3	0.4	2.9	22.6	64.3	13.0	1,195	90.1	35.4	36.2
Bowerbank town (Piscataquis)	116	114	-1.7	122	100.0	0.0	0.0	0.0	0.0	8.2	58.1	33.6	61	93.4	34.4	42.6
Bradford town (Penobscot)	1,290	1,268	-1.7	1,114	93.8	1.5	0.3	0.8	3.6	23.7	61.5	14.8	421	83.4	44.2	20.7

1 May be of any race.

Table A. All Places — Population and Housing

STATE City, town, township, borough, or CDP (county if applicable)	Population				Race and Hispanic or Latino origin (percent), 2010–2014					Age (percent), 2010–2014			Households, 2010–2014			
	2010 census total population	2014 estimated population	Percent change 2010– 2014	ACS total population estimate 2010–2014	White alone, not Hispanic or Latino	Black alone, not Hispanic or Latino	Asian alone, not Hispanic or Latino	All other races or 2 or more races, not Hispanic or Latino	Hispanic or Latino[1]	Under 18 years old	Age 18 to 64 years old	Age 65 years and older	Total occupied housing units	Percent owner occupied	Householders by level of education (percent) High school diploma or less	Bachelor's degree or more
	1	2	3	4	5	6	7	8	9	10	11	12	13	14	15	16
MAINE—Con.																
Bradley town (Penobscot).	1,492	1,485	-0.5	1,420	96.6	0.0	0.0	3.2	0.2	16.1	61.6	22.5	652	80.1	49.4	26.4
Bremen town (Lincoln)......	806	798	-1.0	894	97.4	0.6	0.0	2.0	0.0	23.6	51.5	24.9	369	95.4	28.7	46.6
Brewer city & MCD (Penobscot)..................	9,482	9,317	-1.7	9,391	97.0	0.7	0.3	1.9	0.1	19.6	65.0	15.3	3,982	63.3	34.3	32.9
Bridgewater town (Aroostook)	610	590	-3.3	618	89.6	2.8	2.3	2.1	3.2	22.5	56.2	21.4	264	83.7	51.1	12.1
Bridgton CDP................	2,071	NA	NA	2,182	97.4	0.6	1.3	0.1	0.5	16.6	61.9	21.5	971	60.9	29.8	29.2
Bridgton town (Cumberland)	5,210	5,344	2.6	5,291	94.4	0.7	1.3	3.0	0.5	23.2	58.6	18.3	2,118	67.7	37.2	30.2
Brighton plantation (Somerset)	70	68	-2.9	60	100.0	0.0	0.0	0.0	0.0	6.7	81.6	11.7	25	100.0	52.0	8.0
Bristol town (Lincoln)	2,755	2,728		2,738	96.6	0.8	0.0	0.3	2.4	9.3	57.8	33.0	1,441	94.7	37.0	33.7
Brooklin town (Hancock)...	824	819	-0.6	858	93.9	1.3	0.6	2.4	1.7	7.4	60.2	32.2	389	88.4	28.0	40.4
Brooks town (Waldo)	1,075	1,086	1.0	889	89.7	2.5	0.0	7.8	0.1	21.1	57.2	21.5	429	60.4	56.9	18.6
Brooksville town (Hancock)..................	934	928	-0.6	885	98.2	0.0	0.9	0.9	0.0	15.1	50.7	34.1	396	90.9	34.8	47.2
Brownfield town (Oxford) ..	1,597	1,607	0.6	1,261	99.0	0.3	0.2	0.6	0.0	20.1	63.2	16.7	491	91.9	46.6	25.1
Brownville town (Piscataquis).............	1,246	1,207	-3.1	1,104	94.2	0.0	0.5	5.0	0.3	20.0	55.1	24.8	517	81.8	57.6	9.9
Brunswick CDP................	15,175	NA	NA	15,275	92.1	0.7	2.2	3.1	2.0	15.4	63.3	21.1	6,198	66.5	31.5	39.7
Brunswick town (Cumberland)	20,278	20,441	0.8	20,329	93.2	0.7	1.7	2.6	1.8	16.8	62.8	20.5	8,316	68.2	31.8	41.8
Brunswick Station CDP.....	578	NA	NA	478	84.3	5.9	0.0	2.3	7.5	15.3	80.5	4.2	222	0.0	24.3	33.3
Buckfield town (Oxford)	2,010	2,000	-0.5	2,015	92.6	0.0	0.0	5.2	2.3	24.0	61.7	14.3	778	82.9	55.1	22.0
Bucksport CDP................	2,885	NA	NA	2,453	98.3	0.5	0.3	0.3	0.6	20.1	66.9	13.1	1,200	53.8	42.2	24.5
Bucksport town (Hancock)	4,926	4,939	0.3	4,936	98.8	0.2	0.1	0.5	0.3	20.3	65.6	14.0	2,153	72.3	43.2	22.9
Burlington town (Penobscot)................	363	407	12.1	268	97.8	0.0	1.1	0.0	1.1	16.1	61.2	22.8	116	87.9	64.7	5.2
Burnham town (Waldo).....	1,164	1,173	0.8	1,166	94.4	0.4	0.0	4.2	0.9	20.2	64.9	14.9	500	82.2	73.4	10.0
Buxton town (York)	8,037	8,143	1.3	8,079	94.2	2.4	0.6	0.2	2.6	20.7	66.8	12.6	3,293	83.7	39.9	24.0
Byron town (Oxford).........	145	144	-0.7	109	95.4	0.0	0.0	4.6	0.0	17.4	66.1	16.5	42	78.6	42.9	14.3
Calais city & MCD (Washington)..............	3,123	3,004	-3.8	3,063	97.7	0.1	0.1	0.9	1.2	18.8	56.9	24.3	1,500	55.4	47.9	19.2
Cambridge town (Somerset)	462	447	-3.2	493	99.4	0.0	0.0	0.6	0.0	14.5	65.2	20.3	206	84.0	73.3	6.8
Camden CDP	3,570	NA	NA	3,351	99.8	0.0	0.0	0.0	0.2	13.0	57.3	29.8	1,744	65.0	25.2	46.2
Camden town (Knox)........	4,850	4,838	-0.2	4,839	99.9	0.0	0.0	0.0	0.1	13.8	57.3	28.9	2,430	73.2	21.9	46.0
Canaan town (Somerset)..	2,275	2,237	-1.7	2,199	97.5	0.0	0.0	1.3	1.2	20.9	63.1	15.9	836	87.8	43.9	17.7
Canton town (Oxford)	990	977	-1.3	1,023	96.3	0.0	1.3	2.4	0.0	22.7	60.6	16.6	353	81.3	53.5	19.3
Cape Elizabeth town (Cumberland)................	9,015	9,185	1.9	9,093	94.8	2.0	0.8	1.0	1.3	23.2	58.1	18.8	3,678	88.3	11.4	66.9
Cape Neddick CDP	2,568	NA	NA	2,984	98.0	0.0	0.0	0.5	1.4	12.7	62.8	24.4	1,432	84.8	22.6	36.4
Caratunk town (Somerset)	69	67	-2.9	107	90.7	0.0	9.3	0.0	0.0	7.5	84.0	8.4	56	89.3	26.8	35.7
Caribou city & MCD (Aroostook)	8,189	7,871	-3.9	8,025	92.7	1.2	0.5	3.8	1.7	20.0	60.7	19.4	3,566	63.5	45.7	20.4
Carmel town (Penobscot).	2,794	2,796	0.1	2,794	97.8	0.0	0.8	1.4	0.0	19.3	69.6	10.8	1,072	85.7	45.1	19.3
Carrabassett Valley town (Franklin)	778	776	-0.3	561	97.1	0.0	0.0	1.2	1.6	11.8	63.5	24.6	255	92.5	10.2	63.9
Carroll plantation (Penobscot)................	153	151	-1.3	115	90.4	0.0	0.0	9.6	0.0	13.0	66.9	20.0	51	100.0	60.8	29.4
Carthage town (Franklin) ..	560	553	-1.3	738	95.0	0.0	0.0	0.1	4.9	23.2	63.8	13.0	256	85.9	57.0	14.5
Cary plantation (Aroostook)	218	211	-3.2	249	91.6	0.0	7.2	0.4	0.8	7.6	64.5	27.7	137	84.7	59.1	16.1
Casco CDP.....................	587	NA	NA	668	99.4	0.4	0.0	0.0	0.1	23.6	64.6	11.7	260	90.0	33.5	28.1
Casco town (Cumberland)	3,742	3,845	2.8	3,796	94.4	0.1	0.0	3.2	2.2	22.0	64.2	13.9	1,565	84.2	37.4	26.7
Castine CDP....................	1,029	NA	NA	984	97.6	0.0	1.0	0.9	0.5	3.6	80.4	15.9	198	61.1	17.7	58.6
Castine town (Hancock)....	1,366	1,358	-0.6	1,425	98.2	0.0	0.7	0.8	0.4	9.0	73.5	17.3	381	68.2	14.2	55.6
Castle Hill town (Aroostook)	425	403	-5.2	432	86.3	0.0	0.0	11.8	1.9	27.3	49.5	23.1	164	79.9	59.1	12.2
Caswell town (Aroostook) .	306	289	-5.6	246	92.3	0.0	0.0	3.3	4.5	16.3	47.5	36.2	121	85.1	68.6	5.8
Central Aroostook UT (Aroostook)	119	115	-3.4	123	100.0	0.0	0.0	0.0	0.0	7.3	85.4	7.3	73	100.0	47.9	0.0
Central Hancock UT (Hancock)..................	117	117	0.0	94	100.0	0.0	0.0	0.0	0.0	12.7	70.3	17.0	50	80.0	42.0	16.0
Central Somerset UT (Somerset)	338	334	-1.2	259	91.9	8.1	0.0	0.0	0.0	18.5	64.8	16.6	122	93.4	55.7	17.2
Chapman town (Aroostook)	468	452	-3.4	427	100.0	0.0	0.0	0.0	0.0	16.9	70.3	12.9	172	92.4	44.8	18.0
Charleston town (Penobscot)................	1,409	1,390	-1.3	1,275	93.1	1.9	0.0	2.5	2.5	22.8	68.4	8.7	404	77.7	52.2	15.1
Charlotte town (Washington).............	332	320	-3.6	279	91.0	0.0	0.7	8.2	0.0	18.0	57.7	24.4	122	93.4	34.4	26.2
Chebeague Island town (Cumberland)	341	346	1.5	431	99.5	0.0	0.0	0.0	0.5	11.7	47.3	41.1	237	82.7	24.9	54.4
Chelsea town (Kennebec)	2,721	2,706	-0.6	2,709	98.7	0.4	0.4	0.5	0.0	24.7	62.4	13.0	991	84.0	48.9	20.0
Cherryfield town (Washington)..............	1,232	1,182	-4.1	1,271	98.8	0.0	0.2	0.7	0.3	22.2	60.4	17.5	535	73.6	52.9	17.8
Chester town (Penobscot)	546	541	-0.9	522	95.8	0.4	0.6	2.9	0.4	18.6	59.3	22.0	226	86.3	56.6	13.3
Chesterville town (Franklin)	1,355	1,340	-1.1	1,464	99.6	0.0	0.0	0.4	0.0	19.6	64.9	15.6	608	87.2	54.4	22.0
China town (Kennebec)	4,330	4,280	-1.2	4,296	94.3	1.4	0.9	2.1	1.3	23.7	64.3	12.0	1,735	80.1	53.9	15.5
Chisholm CDP.................	1,380	NA	NA	1,019	98.5	0.0	0.0	1.5	0.0	17.9	55.1	27.1	420	80.7	48.6	20.7
Clifton town (Penobscot)...	921	916	-0.5	926	98.2	0.0	0.0	0.8	1.1	20.5	64.1	15.4	351	78.9	45.9	18.2
Clinton CDP....................	1,419	NA	NA	1,254	100.0	0.0	0.0	0.0	0.0	21.4	62.7	15.9	493	69.4	64.7	12.6
Clinton town (Kennebec) ..	3,486	3,375	-3.2	3,426	99.0	0.0	0.0	0.0	1.0	24.4	62.7	12.9	1,368	81.8	58.0	12.1
Codyville plantation (Washington)................	24	23	-4.2	14	100.0	0.0	0.0	0.0	0.0	14.3	64.3	21.4	5	60.0	100.0	0.0
Columbia town (Washington)................	486	469	-3.5	530	96.6	0.0	0.0	0.8	2.6	32.1	55.0	13.0	192	75.5	49.5	21.4
Columbia Falls town (Washington)..............	560	540	-3.6	539	99.1	0.0	0.4	0.0	0.6	14.7	60.0	25.4	269	80.7	53.5	25.3
Connor UT (Aroostook)	457	442	-3.3	432	89.6	2.5	0.0	6.0	1.9	17.8	56.3	25.9	190	79.5	55.8	7.9

1 May be of any race.

STATE City, town, township, borough, or CDP (county if applicable)	2010 census total population	2014 estimated population	Percent change 2010–2014	ACS total population estimate 2010–2014	White alone, not Hispanic or Latino	Black alone, not Hispanic or Latino	Asian alone, not Hispanic or Latino	All other races or 2 or more races, not Hispanic or Latino	Hispanic or Latino[1]	Under 18 years old	Age 18 to 64 years old	Age 65 years and older	Total occupied housing units	Percent owner occupied	High school diploma or less	Bachelor's degree or more
	1	2	3	4	5	6	7	8	9	10	11	12	13	14	15	16

MAINE—Con.

STATE City, town, township, borough, or CDP (county if applicable)	1	2	3	4	5	6	7	8	9	10	11	12	13	14	15	16
Cooper town (Washington)	154	149	-3.2	133	100.0	0.0	0.0	0.0	0.0	11.3	63.9	24.8	63	82.5	38.1	22.2
Coplin plantation (Franklin)	166	162	-2.4	102	88.2	0.0	2.0	2.0	7.8	12.7	53.1	34.3	54	100.0	72.2	14.8
Corinna town (Penobscot)	2,199	2,189	-0.5	1,954	98.2	0.0	0.0	0.0	1.8	20.3	59.0	20.8	834	76.7	61.0	15.9
Corinth town (Penobscot)	2,874	2,850	-0.8	2,868	95.1	0.5	0.0	3.3	1.1	25.3	63.0	11.6	1,131	87.2	50.3	13.7
Cornish town (York)	1,403	1,418	1.1	1,383	99.1	0.0	0.0	0.9	0.0	25.7	57.5	16.8	563	70.9	41.0	24.9
Cornville town (Somerset)	1,315	1,317	0.2	1,229	99.8	0.1	0.0	0.2	0.0	20.7	67.8	11.3	494	87.0	44.1	14.2
Cousins Island CDP	490	NA	NA	513	100.0	0.0	0.0	0.0	0.0	26.9	60.0	13.3	205	100.0	10.2	76.6
Cranberry Isles town (Hancock)	141	140	-0.7	123	74.0	0.0	0.8	25.2	0.0	14.6	64.3	21.1	57	84.2	38.6	50.9
Crawford town (Washington)	101	97	-4.0	94	96.8	0.0	0.0	0.0	3.2	19.2	66.1	14.9	37	83.8	32.4	16.2
Criehaven UT (Knox)	1	1	0.0	0	0.0	0.0	0.0	0.0	0.0	0.0	0.0	0.0	0	0.0	0.0	0.0
Crystal town (Aroostook)	269	260	-3.3	259	99.2	0.0	0.0	0.8	0.0	19.7	52.1	28.2	117	98.3	57.3	10.3
Cumberland town (Cumberland)	7,202	7,550	4.8	7,338	94.7	0.0	2.7	1.6	1.0	26.5	59.3	14.1	2,728	89.2	13.8	63.6
Cumberland Center CDP	2,499	NA	NA	2,636	94.8	0.0	2.9	1.4	0.9	31.4	56.7	11.9	925	87.8	11.6	72.9
Cushing town (Knox)	1,534	1,511	-1.5	1,415	98.9	0.0	0.1	0.8	0.3	24.7	60.7	14.5	544	74.3	53.7	22.8
Cutler town (Washington)	507	495	-2.4	468	93.6	1.1	1.3	2.6	1.5	31.2	54.1	14.7	182	79.7	48.9	24.2
Cyr plantation (Aroostook)	103	100	-2.9	101	100.0	0.0	0.0	0.0	0.0	18.9	68.4	12.9	45	95.6	44.4	31.1
Dallas plantation (Franklin)	305	297	-2.6	340	93.8	0.9	1.5	0.3	3.5	23.3	58.0	18.8	146	69.9	18.5	35.6
Damariscotta CDP	1,142	NA	NA	982	97.9	0.0	0.0	0.6	1.5	11.4	45.2	43.4	495	58.4	15.8	64.0
Damariscotta town (Lincoln)	2,218	2,214	-0.2	2,001	97.9	0.0	0.0	1.4	0.7	18.1	52.7	28.8	911	65.1	25.7	46.2
Danforth town (Washington)	589	578	-1.9	566	97.3	0.0	0.0	2.7	0.0	17.1	56.4	26.5	233	81.1	72.5	11.2
Dayton town (York)	1,961	2,018	2.9	1,989	96.6	0.0	0.6	2.6	0.2	23.8	63.9	12.3	725	93.5	39.4	28.8
Deblois town (Washington)	57	55	-3.5	44	100.0	0.0	0.0	0.0	0.0	18.2	52.2	29.5	19	89.5	89.5	10.5
Dedham town (Hancock)	1,681	1,688	0.4	1,584	96.6	0.0	0.3	0.6	2.5	24.3	65.5	10.3	636	81.6	36.9	28.0
Deer Isle town (Hancock)	1,975	1,965	-0.5	1,853	97.7	0.3	0.6	1.3	0.0	15.8	53.7	30.4	846	73.0	46.5	32.4
Denmark town (Oxford)	1,148	1,144	-0.3	1,210	90.9	5.2	0.7	2.6	0.5	21.4	59.3	19.3	471	89.2	38.9	28.7
Dennistown plantation (Somerset)	33	32	-3.0	20	100.0	0.0	0.0	0.0	0.0	20.0	60.0	20.0	8	100.0	100.0	0.0
Dennysville town (Washington)	342	330	-3.5	324	97.8	0.0	0.3	1.9	0.0	16.7	64.0	19.4	151	81.5	58.9	27.2
Detroit town (Somerset)	852	824	-3.3	967	94.7	0.0	0.8	1.2	3.2	18.6	67.4	14.1	396	76.0	55.6	16.9
Dexter CDP	2,158	NA	NA	1,904	98.1	0.0	1.4	0.0	0.6	25.0	50.8	24.3	875	61.6	48.1	17.7
Dexter town (Penobscot)	3,895	3,827	-1.7	3,857	96.1	0.4	1.1	1.5	0.9	18.1	60.9	21.1	1,686	71.8	57.9	13.4
Dixfield CDP	1,076	NA	NA	948	95.5	0.0	0.0	2.1	2.4	26.3	54.8	19.1	381	70.9	54.6	16.0
Dixfield town (Oxford)	2,550	2,487	-2.5	2,273	97.0	0.0	0.0	1.3	1.7	25.7	57.6	16.7	873	76.7	57.5	15.7
Dixmont town (Penobscot)	1,181	1,159	-1.9	1,203	94.5	0.0	0.4	4.2	0.8	17.9	65.8	16.4	503	86.9	47.1	22.5
Dover-Foxcroft town (Piscataquis)	4,213	4,056	-3.7	4,128	97.5	0.0	0.0	2.0	0.5	16.1	61.0	22.9	1,758	76.2	42.9	28.3
Dover-Foxcroft CDP	2,528	NA	NA	2,542	99.8	0.0	0.0	0.2	0.0	17.4	58.9	23.6	1,124	69.6	37.1	32.2
Dresden town (Lincoln)	1,672	1,650	-1.3	1,740	97.7	0.0	0.2	1.4	0.7	22.6	60.5	16.8	754	85.1	46.2	29.3
Drew plantation (Penobscot)	46	46	0.0	46	100.0	0.0	0.0	0.0	0.0	30.4	58.8	10.9	17	94.1	58.8	0.0
Durham town (Androscoggin)	3,848	3,908	1.6	3,879	96.0	0.0	0.7	3.3	0.0	21.8	67.4	10.8	1,526	93.3	34.3	42.4
Dyer Brook town (Aroostook)	206	202	-1.9	237	100.0	0.0	0.0	0.0	0.0	22.8	66.3	11.0	96	88.5	56.3	18.8
Eagle Lake CDP	625	NA	NA	519	97.9	1.3	0.2	0.6	0.0	13.1	63.8	23.1	197	66.5	62.9	12.7
Eagle Lake town (Aroostook)	864	834	-3.5	755	98.5	0.9	0.1	0.4	0.0	12.9	54.6	32.5	305	76.4	57.7	12.8
Eastbrook town (Hancock)	423	423	0.0	415	99.3	0.0	0.0	0.7	0.0	16.1	63.3	20.5	222	81.5	58.6	16.7
East Central Franklin UT (Franklin)	808	800	-1.0	522	95.0	0.0	1.0	4.0	0.0	16.4	66.0	17.4	234	78.2	53.0	27.8
East Central Penobscot UT (Penobscot)	343	340	-0.9	244	93.0	0.0	0.0	7.0	0.0	22.6	56.9	20.5	120	70.0	60.8	6.7
East Central Washington UT (Washington)	728	701	-3.7	809	94.3	0.5	0.1	4.0	1.1	21.7	60.7	17.6	343	87.8	43.4	24.2
East Hancock UT (Hancock)	92	92	0.0	77	93.5	0.0	0.0	6.5	0.0	26.0	65.0	9.1	31	74.2	41.9	3.2
East Machias town (Washington)	1,365	1,316	-3.6	1,381	97.5	0.1	0.1	1.2	1.0	21.9	62.9	15.2	553	80.5	44.5	25.3
East Millinocket town (Penobscot)	1,723	1,688	-2.0	1,812	97.2	0.0	0.0	1.7	1.1	22.9	56.8	20.3	789	77.6	53.0	12.8
East Millinocket CDP	1,567	NA	NA	1,521	97.3	0.0	0.0	1.4	1.3	19.5	56.9	23.7	698	74.6	52.7	13.8
Easton town (Aroostook)	1,287	1,236	-4.0	1,198	95.5	0.0	0.0	3.6	0.9	22.3	55.9	21.7	506	72.1	42.5	20.4
Eastport city & MCD (Washington)	1,331	1,272	-4.4	1,414	88.8	0.6	0.6	8.8	1.2	11.6	58.9	29.5	746	72.1	43.2	27.1
Eddington town (Penobscot)	2,225	2,230	0.2	2,374	99.9	0.0	0.0	0.0	0.1	19.5	68.5	12.1	960	82.9	42.1	23.8
Edgecomb town (Lincoln)	1,249	1,238	-0.9	1,154	95.3	1.8	0.0	2.9	0.0	20.6	57.2	22.2	483	77.6	28.4	38.1
Edinburg town (Penobscot)	131	130	-0.8	117	100.0	0.0	0.0	0.0	0.0	7.7	65.7	26.5	51	88.2	41.2	13.7
Eliot town (York)	6,204	6,298	1.5	6,234	95.7	0.5	0.2	1.7	1.8	21.2	64.0	14.8	2,392	79.4	28.8	40.2
Ellsworth city & MCD (Hancock)	7,741	7,843	1.3	7,804	95.8	1.6	0.8	0.6	1.3	20.1	59.2	20.6	3,441	63.9	31.2	33.5
Embden town (Somerset)	939	937	-0.2	984	99.2	0.0	0.0	0.8	0.0	13.5	62.5	24.0	417	97.8	55.6	21.1
Enfield town (Penobscot)	1,607	1,582	-1.6	1,714	93.5	0.0	0.0	5.2	1.3	21.6	56.5	21.8	675	84.9	55.7	12.0
Etna town (Penobscot)	1,252	1,231	-1.7	1,299	97.5	0.3	0.2	0.5	1.5	20.6	66.2	13.3	505	79.0	46.1	17.4
Eustis town (Franklin)	618	614	-0.6	527	99.4	0.0	0.0	0.6	0.0	13.9	67.2	18.8	202	73.3	72.3	5.9
Exeter town (Penobscot)	1,092	1,085	-0.6	1,012	93.8	0.0	0.0	0.0	6.2	22.2	61.0	16.8	396	90.9	56.8	14.6
Fairfield CDP	2,638	NA	NA	2,773	90.2	0.0	0.0	7.0	2.8	28.4	56.5	15.1	1,148	64.8	47.7	23.6
Fairfield town (Somerset)	6,735	6,567	-2.5	6,655	94.3	0.0	0.9	3.6	1.2	24.2	61.5	14.5	2,803	77.2	46.2	21.7
Falmouth CDP	1,855	NA	NA	2,179	91.7	1.6	5.9	0.0	0.8	17.0	62.0	21.0	976	61.2	13.0	68.3
Falmouth town (Cumberland)	11,185	11,734	4.9	11,424	93.5	1.0	1.8	2.2	1.6	21.0	60.0	19.0	4,648	80.4	10.1	68.5
Falmouth Foreside CDP	1,511	NA	NA	1,593	88.8	4.3	0.0	1.3	5.6	19.0	50.7	30.4	614	83.7	8.5	68.2

1 May be of any race.

Table A. All Places — Population and Housing

STATE City, town, township, borough, or CDP (county if applicable)	2010 census total population	2014 estimated population	Percent change 2010–2014	ACS total population estimate 2010–2014	White alone, not Hispanic or Latino	Black alone, not Hispanic or Latino	Asian alone, not Hispanic or Latino	All other races or 2 or more races, not Hispanic or Latino	Hispanic or Latino[1]	Under 18 years old	Age 18 to 64 years old	Age 65 years and older	Total occupied housing units	Percent owner occupied	High school diploma or less	Bachelor's degree or more
	1	2	3	4	5	6	7	8	9	10	11	12	13	14	15	16
MAINE—Con.																
Farmingdale CDP	1,970	NA	NA	2,056	93.3	0.0	0.0	3.5	3.2	20.4	48.6	31.1	1,032	63.3	46.4	29.1
Farmingdale town (Kennebec)	2,959	2,915	-1.5	2,938	95.0	0.0	0.0	2.8	2.2	23.0	49.3	27.7	1,433	67.3	44.7	30.0
Farmington CDP	4,288	NA	NA	4,142	95.2	1.3	0.2	1.7	1.6	9.8	67.7	22.5	1,482	34.8	26.9	37.6
Farmington town (Franklin)	7,758	7,610	-1.9	7,667	97.1	0.7	0.1	1.3	0.9	14.1	65.5	20.4	2,968	63.2	28.1	34.3
Fayette town (Kennebec)	1,140	1,133	-0.6	1,143	94.5	0.0	0.0	5.5	0.0	19.2	64.6	16.1	448	92.6	44.2	28.8
Fort Fairfield CDP	1,825	NA	NA	1,692	98.5	0.0	0.0	1.5	0.0	25.3	54.9	19.9	806	56.0	60.2	14.5
Fort Fairfield town (Aroostook)	3,496	3,402	-2.7	3,447	97.9	0.0	0.0	0.8	1.3	24.2	59.7	15.9	1,487	65.1	52.7	14.9
Fort Kent CDP	2,488	NA	NA	2,468	96.0	0.4	0.1	2.6	0.9	17.7	64.9	17.4	1,115	54.6	47.3	25.3
Fort Kent town (Aroostook)	4,097	4,012	-2.1	4,068	94.7	0.2	2.0	2.4	0.7	18.0	67.5	14.7	1,760	69.0	44.7	26.5
Frankfort town (Waldo)	1,124	1,136	1.1	1,202	97.9	0.5	0.2	1.3	0.0	20.8	64.7	14.6	513	83.6	50.5	20.5
Franklin town (Hancock)	1,478	1,496	1.2	1,433	93.9	0.0	0.3	5.4	0.3	20.6	62.6	17.0	618	74.4	53.4	18.0
Freedom town (Waldo)	719	721	0.3	639	90.0	1.1	0.0	5.6	3.3	22.1	58.4	19.4	264	84.5	37.1	31.1
Freeport CDP	1,485	NA	NA	1,414	93.9	0.2	3.7	2.1	0.0	21.8	52.7	25.5	599	51.6	25.9	43.4
Freeport town (Cumberland)	7,879	8,224	4.4	8,049	95.2	1.0	2.3	1.1	0.5	23.4	59.9	16.7	3,133	78.6	21.9	49.2
Frenchboro town (Hancock)	61	61	0.0	79	100.0	0.0	0.0	0.0	0.0	51.9	48.2	0.0	22	86.4	77.3	0.0
Frenchville town (Aroostook)	1,087	1,051	-3.3	1,030	96.9	0.0	0.3	2.4	0.4	17.4	56.6	26.0	428	87.4	55.1	18.5
Friendship town (Knox)	1,152	1,141	-0.9	1,057	97.4	0.0	0.0	2.1	0.5	16.8	53.5	30.0	470	92.8	43.8	25.1
Fryeburg CDP	1,631	NA	NA	1,614	97.0	0.7	2.2	0.0	0.0	14.8	63.9	21.2	651	67.9	40.2	29.6
Fryeburg town (Oxford)	3,447	3,398	-1.4	3,410	98.3	0.4	1.1	0.3	0.0	18.4	61.3	20.5	1,308	74.3	44.0	29.1
Frye Island town (Cumberland)	5	5	0.0	60	96.7	0.0	0.0	0.0	3.3	0.0	23.3	76.7	35	100.0	8.6	85.7
Gardiner city & MCD (Kennebec)	5,800	5,675	-2.2	5,737	94.3	0.4	1.1	1.3	2.9	20.1	64.5	15.4	2,498	63.6	41.8	20.3
Garfield plantation (Aroostook)	81	78	-3.7	106	97.2	0.0	0.0	2.8	0.0	28.3	52.7	18.9	41	87.8	58.5	12.2
Garland town (Penobscot)	1,105	1,086	-1.7	1,227	97.3	0.3	0.0	1.6	0.7	25.8	60.2	14.0	499	90.0	56.3	14.8
Georgetown town (Sagadahoc)	1,042	1,036	-0.6	1,050	98.0	1.2	0.3	0.2	0.3	21.0	49.2	29.9	442	82.8	27.1	48.6
Gilead town (Oxford)	209	206	-1.4	89	95.5	0.0	0.0	4.5	0.0	3.4	74.0	22.5	43	74.4	41.9	20.9
Glenburn town (Penobscot)	4,598	4,626	0.6	4,615	94.0	0.0	0.5	3.6	1.9	23.0	66.9	10.1	1,682	78.2	46.0	19.3
Glenwood plantation (Aroostook)	3	3	0.0	0	0.0	0.0	0.0	0.0	0.0	0.0	0.0	0.0	0	0.0	0.0	0.0
Gorham CDP	6,882	NA	NA	6,596	93.3	2.2	0.7	2.1	1.7	16.8	68.1	15.1	2,213	71.1	18.5	50.9
Gorham town (Cumberland)	16,380	17,024	3.9	16,677	93.6	1.1	1.1	3.2	0.9	20.8	66.9	12.2	5,928	82.7	22.9	45.4
Gouldsboro town (Hancock)	1,739	1,740	0.1	1,675	99.6	0.0	0.0	0.4	0.0	21.9	55.1	23.0	694	82.1	45.8	26.4
Grand Isle town (Aroostook)	467	452	-3.2	488	98.8	0.0	0.0	1.2	0.0	14.2	53.7	32.2	229	85.6	66.4	8.3
Grand Lake Stream plantation (Washington)	109	105	-3.7	118	96.6	0.0	0.0	3.4	0.0	11.0	42.3	46.6	62	88.7	29.0	33.9
Gray CDP	884	NA	NA	1,139	96.2	0.0	0.0	2.5	1.3	42.3	45.3	12.6	366	56.6	54.6	24.6
Gray town (Cumberland)	7,761	7,962	2.6	7,860	95.0	0.5	0.1	3.0	1.5	24.8	65.1	10.0	2,916	78.1	40.3	29.5
Great Pond town (Hancock)	58	58	0.0	37	100.0	0.0	0.0	0.0	0.0	5.4	72.9	21.6	20	65.0	45.0	0.0
Greenbush town (Penobscot)	1,491	1,503	0.8	1,441	96.7	0.8	0.0	2.4	0.0	17.8	72.5	9.6	571	82.8	52.4	13.7
Greene town (Androscoggin)	4,351	4,358	0.2	4,349	96.3	0.0	0.2	3.0	0.4	22.3	65.1	12.6	1,710	82.0	34.0	25.9
Greenville CDP	1,257	NA	NA	1,487	91.9	0.1	1.3	5.9	0.9	32.2	49.0	18.8	571	67.4	44.7	20.3
Greenville town (Piscataquis)	1,646	1,606	-2.4	1,841	92.9	0.1	1.0	5.3	0.7	26.3	53.7	20.0	755	72.6	39.1	27.3
Greenwood town (Oxford)	830	830	0.0	967	92.3	3.1	0.0	4.1	0.4	21.5	66.6	11.9	324	83.0	53.1	21.0
Guilford CDP	903	NA	NA	915	97.0	0.0	1.3	0.4	1.2	16.3	60.7	23.0	402	48.5	54.2	5.2
Guilford town (Piscataquis)	1,521	1,494	-1.8	1,542	96.9	1.4	0.8	0.3	0.7	18.3	62.5	19.1	677	58.9	51.3	8.9
Hallowell city & MCD (Kennebec)	2,378	2,329	-2.1	2,471	92.7	0.0	5.6	1.3	0.4	16.4	61.9	21.7	1,192	52.3	24.5	46.0
Hamlin town (Aroostook)	219	212	-3.2	359	99.4	0.0	0.0	0.6	0.0	29.8	44.6	25.6	122	98.4	54.9	6.6
Hammond town (Aroostook)	118	114	-3.4	83	96.4	0.0	3.6	0.0	0.0	18.0	62.5	19.3	38	92.1	71.1	0.0
Hampden CDP	4,343	NA	NA	3,944	95.2	0.0	2.9	1.9	0.0	17.4	62.4	20.2	1,600	78.8	22.2	43.6
Hampden town (Penobscot)	7,257	7,392	1.9	7,297	95.5	0.0	1.8	1.0	1.7	22.5	62.9	14.5	2,694	84.6	23.6	46.4
Hancock town (Hancock)	2,394	2,395	0.0	2,183	96.5	0.2	0.8	1.3	1.2	16.6	59.6	23.7	1,055	71.0	46.5	23.5
Hanover town (Oxford)	238	249	4.6	155	100.0	0.0	0.0	0.0	0.0	12.9	56.1	31.0	73	89.0	27.4	46.6
Harmony town (Somerset)	939	926	-1.4	816	97.4	0.0	0.0	2.6	0.0	21.1	51.6	27.3	369	88.3	62.3	11.4
Harpswell town (Cumberland)	4,740	4,836	2.0	4,780	98.7	0.0	0.6	0.5	0.2	17.4	50.2	32.4	2,069	84.4	22.2	50.9
Harrington town (Washington)	1,004	970	-3.4	985	95.2	0.1	0.1	0.0	4.6	18.2	56.3	25.4	421	84.1	58.7	19.7
Harrison town (Cumberland)	2,734	2,793	2.2	2,757	96.7	0.7	0.4	2.3	0.0	15.1	61.6	23.4	1,196	87.5	31.9	32.6
Hartford town (Oxford)	1,184	1,190	0.5	1,405	96.3	0.0	0.4	2.8	0.6	18.9	61.7	19.3	521	89.1	56.8	19.6
Hartland town (Oxford)	813	NA	NA	829	89.5	0.0	2.7	0.0	7.8	22.0	58.5	19.5	298	73.8	58.4	0.0
Hartland town (Somerset)	1,782	1,726	-3.1	1,831	94.5	0.0	1.7	0.2	3.5	18.6	63.7	17.8	725	80.3	57.5	9.9
Haynesville town (Aroostook)	121	117	-3.3	118	92.4	0.0	0.0	7.6	0.0	24.5	61.1	14.4	49	100.0	77.6	12.2
Hebron town (Oxford)	1,416	1,400	-1.1	1,643	86.1	1.6	0.0	11.0	1.3	22.0	69.6	8.6	466	87.3	39.1	24.0
Hermon town (Penobscot)	5,412	5,762	6.5	5,598	97.1	0.1	0.0	2.4	0.4	22.4	65.6	12.1	2,119	76.4	37.6	31.2
Hersey town (Aroostook)	83	80	-3.6	41	100.0	0.0	0.0	0.0	0.0	14.6	43.9	41.5	18	100.0	72.2	0.0
Hibberts gore (Lincoln)	1	1	0.0	0	0.0	0.0	0.0	0.0	0.0	0.0	0.0	0.0	0	0.0	0.0	0.0
Highland plantation (Somerset)	73	71	-2.7	45	97.8	0.0	0.0	2.2	0.0	2.2	46.6	51.1	25	100.0	72.0	16.0

1 May be of any race.

Table A. All Places — **Population and Housing**

STATE City, town, township, borough, or CDP (county if applicable)	Population 2010 census total population	2014 estimated population	Percent change 2010–2014	ACS total population estimate 2010–2014	White alone, not Hispanic or Latino	Black alone, not Hispanic or Latino	Asian alone, not Hispanic or Latino	All other races or 2 or more races, not Hispanic or Latino	Hispanic or Latino[1]	Under 18 years old	Age 18 to 64 years old	Age 65 years and older	Total occupied housing units	Percent owner occupied	High school diploma or less	Bachelor's degree or more
	1	2	3	4	5	6	7	8	9	10	11	12	13	14	15	16
MAINE—Con.																
Hiram town (Oxford)	1,620	1,610	-0.6	1,711	96.9	0.9	0.5	1.7	0.0	25.7	58.8	15.7	581	88.3	49.9	14.6
Hodgdon town (Aroostook)	1,309	1,292	-1.3	1,426	98.5	0.8	0.0	0.5	0.2	22.8	63.9	13.4	559	78.9	48.3	11.8
Holden town (Penobscot)	3,076	3,090	0.5	3,085	90.0	3.8	0.0	4.4	1.8	21.7	65.5	12.9	1,201	80.8	25.3	41.4
Hollis town (York)	4,285	4,407	2.8	4,343	98.6	0.0	0.0	0.6	0.7	20.6	66.9	12.5	1,726	85.5	45.5	21.6
Hope town (Knox)	1,536	1,659	8.0	1,651	97.9	0.0	0.0	0.7	1.4	24.3	62.7	13.0	634	86.0	34.2	34.4
Houlton CDP	4,856	NA	NA	4,840	94.3	0.3	0.4	3.6	1.4	16.3	58.5	25.3	2,169	52.3	47.3	21.5
Houlton town (Aroostook)	6,123	5,946	-2.9	6,041	91.7	0.3	0.5	6.1	1.5	17.1	59.6	23.2	2,677	56.0	47.3	20.3
Howland town (Penobscot)	1,241	1,216	-2.0	1,346	94.3	0.0	0.0	5.7	0.0	21.0	61.3	17.7	493	74.8	57.2	10.8
Howland CDP	1,096	NA	NA	1,144	94.7	0.0	0.0	5.3	0.0	21.4	59.5	19.1	432	74.3	56.7	11.3
Hudson town (Penobscot)	1,536	1,526	-0.7	1,484	92.3	0.0	0.0	7.3	0.4	20.0	63.1	16.8	603	84.6	50.2	16.7
Industry town (Franklin)	927	919	-0.9	950	92.9	0.0	0.5	6.0	0.5	16.4	67.9	15.6	374	84.5	41.7	32.4
Island Falls town (Aroostook)	844	814	-3.6	940	97.1	0.2	0.0	1.8	0.9	19.7	57.2	23.1	393	82.4	38.9	21.1
Isle au Haut town (Knox)	73	72	-1.4	61	72.1	0.0	0.0	27.9	0.0	26.2	60.7	13.1	27	70.4	55.6	44.4
Islesboro town (Waldo)	566	568	0.4	643	96.6	0.0	0.5	1.6	1.4	8.7	58.6	32.7	335	80.3	26.9	45.4
Jackman town (Somerset)	862	851	-1.3	804	96.5	0.0	0.0	1.9	1.6	17.5	64.6	17.9	321	63.6	53.9	25.2
Jackson town (Waldo)	548	555	1.3	682	87.2	0.0	0.0	12.8	0.0	34.7	53.2	12.0	235	82.1	44.7	14.0
Jay town (Franklin)	4,848	4,785	-1.3	4,827	95.9	0.0	0.0	3.1	1.0	20.2	63.5	16.3	1,722	86.6	43.8	19.8
Jefferson town (Lincoln)	2,427	2,397	-1.2	2,535	99.9	0.0	0.0	0.1	0.0	18.4	63.7	17.9	1,013	79.6	41.8	28.8
Jonesboro town (Washington)	583	576	-1.2	495	98.0	0.4	0.0	0.6	1.0	24.8	54.9	20.2	224	80.4	42.9	23.2
Jonesport town (Washington)	1,370	1,329	-3.0	1,239	97.2	0.9	0.6	1.2	0.2	17.1	57.8	25.3	550	80.5	49.1	23.8
Kenduskeag town (Penobscot)	1,348	1,337	-0.8	1,271	92.8	0.0	1.4	2.9	2.9	18.9	69.2	12.0	589	79.5	46.0	16.3
Kennebunk CDP	5,214	NA	NA	5,575	98.2	0.0	0.0	1.5	0.3	20.2	49.6	30.1	2,467	70.8	22.8	52.2
Kennebunk town (York)	10,798	11,111	2.9	10,972	98.7	0.2	0.0	0.9	0.2	20.9	53.7	25.4	4,577	78.0	24.3	53.2
Kennebunkport CDP	1,238	NA	NA	1,182	100.0	0.0	0.0	0.0	0.0	22.1	63.5	14.2	504	83.3	14.3	65.5
Kennebunkport town (York)	3,474	3,551	2.2	3,510	96.7	0.0	0.3	1.7	1.4	18.6	56.4	25.1	1,490	83.8	20.3	59.1
Kingfield town (Franklin)	997	970	-2.7	1,012	95.7	0.0	1.6	2.8	0.0	21.0	61.2	17.9	406	87.4	32.3	31.5
Kingman UT (Penobscot)	174	172	-1.1	102	100.0	0.0	0.0	0.0	0.0	7.8	49.0	43.1	63	90.5	71.4	0.0
Kingsbury plantation (Piscataquis)	28	27	-3.6	14	100.0	0.0	0.0	0.0	0.0	0.0	64.3	35.7	8	100.0	25.0	0.0
Kittery CDP	4,562	NA	NA	4,766	92.3	1.2	1.7	0.5	4.4	13.8	67.4	18.9	2,253	49.4	31.1	36.0
Kittery town (York)	9,490	9,649	1.7	9,573	94.5	0.9	2.1	0.3	2.2	14.7	65.2	20.1	4,364	65.2	30.4	39.2
Kittery Point CDP	1,012	NA	NA	977	100.0	0.0	0.0	0.0	0.0	17.2	56.7	26.1	467	82.7	31.9	50.7
Knox town (Waldo)	806	800	-0.7	793	99.6	0.0	0.0	0.4	0.0	20.3	63.5	16.1	305	88.2	59.0	10.5
Lagrange town (Penobscot)	708	694	-2.0	605	98.3	0.0	0.0	1.7	0.0	16.3	74.0	9.8	266	81.2	50.8	17.7
Lake Arrowhead CDP	3,071	NA	NA	2,890	96.3	0.0	0.7	2.1	0.9	35.4	58.4	6.2	932	90.7	20.9	34.8
Lake View plantation (Piscataquis)	89	87	-2.2	66	75.8	0.0	0.0	24.2	0.0	3.0	53.0	43.9	37	83.8	29.7	13.5
Lakeville town (Penobscot)	105	104	-1.0	113	100.0	0.0	0.0	0.0	0.0	17.7	41.7	40.7	51	90.2	58.8	11.8
Lamoine town (Hancock)	1,600	1,639	2.4	1,689	95.9	0.0	0.1	2.1	1.9	16.6	63.4	20.1	762	77.4	30.1	34.6
Lebanon town (York)	6,031	6,119	1.5	6,077	99.9	0.1	0.0	0.0	0.0	27.0	61.8	11.0	2,218	86.4	49.7	14.5
Lee town (Penobscot)	922	904	-2.0	1,268	93.9	2.1	0.7	2.2	1.1	26.9	57.1	16.0	398	91.2	53.0	12.6
Leeds town (Androscoggin)	2,325	2,309	-0.7	2,010	94.4	0.0	0.4	4.5	0.7	22.1	65.4	12.6	821	84.8	45.6	16.7
Levant town (Penobscot)	2,857	2,971	4.0	2,902	98.1	0.0	0.2	1.7	0.0	21.5	62.0	16.5	1,179	79.2	47.4	20.6
Lewiston city & MCD (Androscoggin)	36,592	36,299	-0.8	36,410	87.1	3.5	1.3	5.3	2.9	20.4	63.9	15.8	15,497	47.4	50.2	15.6
Liberty town (Waldo)	913	925	1.3	721	98.1	0.0	0.0	1.4	0.6	16.9	60.9	22.2	337	81.9	39.2	28.2
Limerick town (York)	2,892	2,919	0.9	2,905	95.8	2.5	0.9	0.8	0.0	28.3	62.0	9.6	994	84.7	43.8	22.4
Limestone CDP	1,075	NA	NA	1,233	91.1	3.7	0.0	2.2	3.0	29.9	51.9	18.2	413	48.9	61.0	18.9
Limestone town (Aroostook)	2,314	2,240	-3.2	2,091	88.4	5.2	1.3	1.4	3.7	26.2	53.6	20.2	752	60.5	52.3	22.2
Limington town (York)	3,713	3,759	1.2	3,734	97.5	0.0	0.0	0.4	2.1	21.4	67.8	10.6	1,392	87.6	47.4	23.6
Lincoln plantation (Oxford)	45	44	-2.2	31	100.0	0.0	0.0	0.0	0.0	0.0	67.8	32.3	17	70.6	64.7	11.8
Lincoln CDP	2,884	NA	NA	2,947	100.0	0.0	0.0	0.0	0.0	26.2	52.3	21.6	1,236	52.7	50.6	12.8
Lincoln town (Penobscot)	5,085	5,064	-0.4	5,088	98.7	0.0	0.0	1.3	0.0	24.3	54.7	20.9	2,043	65.0	50.4	12.5
Lincolnville town (Waldo)	2,164	2,203	1.8	2,269	95.5	0.0	0.4	2.7	1.4	17.9	59.9	21.9	1,008	82.4	36.8	35.0
Linneus town (Aroostook)	985	946	-4.0	935	98.2	0.2	0.0	1.6	0.0	20.3	63.5	16.1	373	73.5	48.5	15.8
Lisbon town (Androscoggin)	9,009	8,883	-1.4	8,936	94.7	0.3	0.1	4.5	0.4	23.4	64.1	12.5	3,602	71.0	42.8	19.9
Lisbon Falls CDP	4,100	NA	NA	4,135	95.2	0.4	0.2	3.6	0.5	24.3	65.5	10.2	1,655	65.8	32.4	27.3
Litchfield town (Kennebec)	3,624	3,604	-0.6	3,613	95.5	0.0	0.7	3.8	0.0	19.1	65.0	16.0	1,449	89.6	48.9	20.0
Little Falls CDP	708	NA	NA	408	86.3	3.4	0.0	10.3	0.0	14.2	83.1	2.7	175	74.3	33.7	29.7
Littlejohn Island CDP	118	NA	NA	123	100.0	0.0	0.0	0.0	0.0	26.0	59.3	14.6	51	76.5	17.6	41.2
Littleton town (Aroostook)	1,068	1,026	-3.9	1,122	88.8	0.0	0.0	10.3	0.9	24.8	58.9	16.3	428	80.8	49.1	9.8
Livermore town (Androscoggin)	2,095	2,102	0.3	2,055	98.1	0.0	0.0	1.0	0.9	21.1	60.2	18.6	864	86.1	48.4	12.3
Livermore Falls CDP	1,594	NA	NA	1,623	96.9	0.0	0.0	3.1	0.0	24.9	55.3	20.0	703	64.9	71.7	9.0
Livermore Falls town (Androscoggin)	3,187	3,144	-1.3	3,162	95.7	0.0	0.0	3.4	0.9	24.4	55.8	19.7	1,295	69.5	71.0	9.2
Long Island town (Cumberland)	230	237	3.0	239	97.5	0.0	1.3	1.3	0.0	10.0	55.7	34.3	122	86.9	24.6	46.7
Louds Island UT (Lincoln)	0	0	0.0	0	0.0	0.0	0.0	0.0	0.0	0.0	0.0	0.0	0	0.0	0.0	0.0
Lovell town (Oxford)	1,140	1,134	-0.5	1,131	91.8	0.4	0.8	1.9	5.1	22.6	60.9	16.4	454	90.7	38.5	33.9
Lowell town (Penobscot)	358	362	1.1	329	97.0	0.0	1.2	1.5	0.3	13.9	66.0	20.1	144	81.9	66.0	13.9
Lubec CDP	349	NA	NA	415	96.4	0.0	0.0	1.2	2.4	13.3	56.1	30.6	184	76.1	40.2	22.8
Lubec town (Washington)	1,359	1,304	-4.0	1,485	96.2	0.0	0.2	2.6	0.9	16.1	56.9	27.0	693	79.1	47.8	20.1
Ludlow town (Aroostook)	403	386	-4.2	397	96.2	0.3	0.3	2.5	0.8	21.1	62.0	16.9	168	89.9	56.5	17.9
Lyman town (York)	4,344	4,387	1.0	4,356	94.3	0.0	0.3	2.3	3.2	23.6	62.0	14.5	1,679	92.0	46.0	17.9
Machias CDP	1,274	NA	NA	1,186	96.5	0.3	0.0	2.4	0.9	22.6	53.4	23.9	552	47.1	43.7	26.4
Machias town (Washington)	2,221	2,132	-4.0	2,209	93.8	1.2	0.1	3.3	1.4	23.3	59.4	17.3	873	53.5	42.3	24.4
Machiasport town (Washington)	1,119	1,088	-2.8	1,185	98.1	1.1	0.0	0.5	0.3	15.7	66.3	17.9	432	83.8	43.8	28.5

1 May be of any race.

Table A. All Places — **Population and Housing**

STATE City, town, township, borough, or CDP (county if applicable)	2010 census total population	2014 estimated population	Percent change 2010–2014	ACS total population estimate 2010–2014	White alone, not Hispanic or Latino	Black alone, not Hispanic or Latino	Asian alone, not Hispanic or Latino	All other races or 2 or more races, not Hispanic or Latino	Hispanic or Latino[1]	Under 18 years old	Age 18 to 64 years old	Age 65 years and older	Total occupied housing units	Percent owner occupied	High school diploma or less	Bachelor's degree or more
	1	2	3	4	5	6	7	8	9	10	11	12	13	14	15	16
MAINE—Con.																
Macwahoc plantation (Aroostook)	79	76	-3.8	63	84.1	0.0	9.5	6.3	0.0	1.6	74.7	23.8	33	75.8	60.6	21.2
Madawaska CDP	2,967	NA	NA	2,825	95.2	2.7	0.2	1.6	0.3	14.9	53.6	31.5	1,410	68.9	54.0	16.7
Madawaska town (Aroostook)	4,035	3,892	-3.5	3,965	96.5	1.9	0.1	1.2	0.2	15.7	57.5	26.9	1,878	75.4	52.8	16.4
Madison CDP	2,630	NA	NA	2,648	95.1	1.6	0.0	1.0	2.3	22.0	57.4	20.6	1,112	66.8	56.3	11.1
Madison town (Somerset).	4,854	4,705	-3.1	4,791	96.9	1.2	0.0	0.6	1.3	20.9	59.2	19.8	1,915	76.4	52.5	13.4
Magalloway plantation (Oxford)	46	45	-2.2	30	90.0	0.0	0.0	10.0	0.0	6.7	50.0	43.3	12	100.0	75.0	25.0
Manchester town (Kennebec)	2,580	2,556	-0.9	2,575	99.1	0.2	0.0	0.7	0.0	20.1	61.3	18.6	1,052	82.2	33.6	41.9
Mapleton CDP	683	NA	NA	738	99.1	0.0	0.0	0.9	0.0	20.3	68.8	11.0	321	71.7	35.5	17.8
Mapleton town (Aroostook)	1,948	1,888	-3.1	1,952	97.8	0.0	0.0	2.0	0.2	21.3	66.0	12.8	795	86.3	40.0	21.8
Mariaville town (Hancock)	513	522	1.8	588	95.9	0.3	0.0	2.6	1.2	17.4	67.8	14.8	223	93.7	50.2	22.0
Marshall Island UT (Hancock)	0	0	0.0	0	0.0	0.0	0.0	0.0	0.0	0.0	0.0	0.0	0	0.0	0.0	0.0
Marshfield town (Washington)	521	509	-2.3	462	96.1	0.4	0.0	0.0	3.5	25.3	59.1	15.6	182	95.6	30.8	31.3
Mars Hill CDP	980	NA	NA	955	96.0	0.6	0.0	2.9	0.4	19.6	51.5	28.7	420	61.7	43.6	16.2
Mars Hill town (Aroostook)	1,493	1,447	-3.1	1,480	96.6	0.9	0.0	1.9	0.7	19.9	57.9	22.4	621	69.1	43.0	19.2
Masardis town (Aroostook)	249	241	-3.2	296	98.6	0.0	0.0	1.4	0.0	19.9	60.1	19.9	132	96.2	56.8	12.1
Matinicus Isle plantation (Knox)	74	73	-1.4	58	100.0	0.0	0.0	0.0	0.0	31.0	50.0	19.0	23	100.0	34.8	43.5
Mattawamkeag town (Penobscot)	683	671	-1.8	779	95.3	0.0	0.0	2.1	2.7	16.3	65.3	18.4	355	76.1	62.8	9.0
Maxfield town (Penobscot)	97	102	5.2	171	87.1	0.0	0.0	4.1	8.8	19.9	71.4	8.8	58	100.0	67.2	20.7
Mechanic Falls town (Androscoggin)	3,031	3,008	-0.8	3,011	95.8	0.1	0.5	2.5	1.1	25.6	62.5	12.0	1,136	69.7	60.2	13.6
Mechanic Falls CDP	2,237	NA	NA	1,698	92.9	0.2	0.8	4.2	1.9	25.9	58.3	15.8	694	67.9	60.1	20.5
Meddybemps town (Washington)	157	151	-3.8	121	98.3	0.0	0.0	1.7	0.0	10.8	71.0	18.2	57	94.7	36.8	17.5
Medford town (Piscataquis)	259	256	-1.2	204	95.1	0.0	0.0	4.9	0.0	14.7	73.0	12.3	83	91.6	49.4	16.9
Medway town (Penobscot)	1,349	1,327	-1.6	1,157	97.1	0.0	0.0	2.9	0.0	21.2	59.5	19.2	508	86.8	57.1	5.5
Mercer town (Somerset)	665	658	-1.1	628	95.9	0.6	0.0	1.1	2.4	16.2	66.8	17.0	261	87.7	43.7	24.5
Merrill town (Aroostook)	273	266	-2.6	226	88.1	0.0	0.0	9.3	2.7	15.1	69.2	15.9	106	79.2	47.2	14.2
Mexico CDP	1,743	NA	NA	1,650	96.1	0.4	2.4	1.2	0.0	21.7	54.9	23.5	723	59.9	69.8	6.9
Mexico town (Oxford)	2,681	2,610	-2.6	2,648	93.7	0.2	5.0	1.1	0.0	21.2	58.4	20.4	1,120	70.2	63.4	5.1
Milbridge town (Washington)	1,353	1,305	-3.5	1,409	91.4	0.0	0.0	0.6	7.9	17.6	52.4	30.0	639	81.2	51.5	25.5
Milford CDP	2,233	NA	NA	2,256	96.8	1.1	0.8	1.3	0.0	17.6	68.0	14.5	969	69.8	35.8	22.4
Milford town (Penobscot)	3,070	3,037	-1.1	3,054	96.1	0.8	0.6	1.4	1.0	16.4	69.5	14.0	1,270	70.5	36.7	21.4
Millinocket town (Penobscot)	4,504	4,401	-2.3	4,451	94.5	0.0	0.0	3.9	1.6	17.0	56.0	27.1	1,941	74.3	57.7	10.3
Millinocket CDP	4,466	NA	NA	4,451	94.5	0.0	0.0	3.9	1.6	17.0	56.0	27.1	1,941	74.3	57.7	10.3
Milo CDP	1,847	NA	NA	1,932	94.7	0.0	0.8	2.8	1.7	23.0	58.5	18.7	922	62.4	57.6	13.0
Milo town (Piscataquis)	2,335	2,273	-2.7	2,365	95.7	0.0	0.6	2.3	1.4	21.4	59.0	19.5	1,115	65.0	57.2	12.6
Milton UT (Oxford)	143	141	-1.4	118	100.0	0.0	0.0	0.0	0.0	40.6	50.7	8.5	40	82.5	60.0	15.0
Minot town (Androscoggin)	2,610	2,590	-0.8	2,610	94.4	0.1	1.3	1.6	2.6	24.1	63.9	12.0	937	92.3	46.7	23.3
Monhegan plantation (Lincoln)	69	68	-1.4	39	100.0	0.0	0.0	0.0	0.0	12.8	69.2	17.9	23	100.0	0.0	39.1
Monmouth town (Kennebec)	4,099	4,071	-0.7	4,076	97.0	0.0	0.0	0.8	2.2	22.8	64.9	12.2	1,584	82.4	40.2	25.4
Monroe town (Waldo)	890	899	1.0	910	98.5	0.0	0.0	1.5	0.0	16.3	62.9	20.7	390	83.8	45.9	29.2
Monson town (Piscataquis)	686	666	-2.9	648	97.1	0.0	0.0	1.5	1.4	14.1	62.4	23.5	297	88.9	48.8	20.9
Monticello town (Aroostook)	790	764	-3.3	665	93.7	0.0	1.4	5.0	0.0	20.6	64.8	14.6	282	84.4	54.3	6.0
Montville town (Waldo)	1,032	1,042	1.0	829	93.4	0.0	0.0	1.4	5.2	16.7	65.8	17.4	369	90.5	37.1	36.6
Moose River town (Somerset)	218	215	-1.4	182	95.6	0.0	0.0	1.6	2.7	18.1	62.5	19.4	87	92.0	51.7	11.5
Moro plantation (Aroostook)	38	37	-2.6	11	100.0	0.0	0.0	0.0	0.0	0.0	54.6	45.5	8	100.0	62.5	0.0
Morrill town (Waldo)	884	889	0.6	831	95.9	0.0	0.0	3.6	0.5	19.6	65.7	14.7	321	89.4	43.0	23.1
Moscow town (Somerset).	512	509	-0.6	555	98.2	0.0	0.0	1.8	0.0	16.2	63.4	20.4	247	92.3	80.2	0.4
Mount Chase town (Penobscot)	201	199	-1.0	197	93.9	0.0	0.0	2.0	4.1	10.1	62.5	27.4	103	89.3	63.1	15.5
Mount Desert town (Hancock)	2,053	2,068	0.7	2,174	96.6	0.2	2.1	0.5	0.7	11.5	61.7	26.8	1,086	77.1	24.9	52.0
Mount Vernon town (Kennebec)	1,640	1,638	-0.1	1,668	98.3	0.3	0.0	1.2	0.2	24.8	58.6	16.6	712	85.1	33.0	28.5
Muscle Ridge Islands UT (Knox)	6	6	0.0	0	0.0	0.0	0.0	0.0	0.0	0.0	0.0	0.0	0	0.0	0.0	0.0
Naples CDP	428	NA	NA	433	99.3	0.7	0.0	0.0	0.0	4.1	64.1	31.6	266	85.0	50.0	24.4
Naples town (Cumberland)	3,872	3,952	2.1	3,908	97.0	0.8	0.0	1.2	0.9	24.5	60.1	15.6	1,684	88.8	45.2	21.3
Nashville plantation (Aroostook)	46	44	-4.3	64	81.3	0.0	0.0	18.8	0.0	18.7	61.1	20.3	24	100.0	50.0	25.0
Newburgh town (Penobscot)	1,551	1,531	-1.3	1,503	95.1	0.3	0.0	3.8	0.9	21.1	63.8	15.1	632	82.0	43.2	27.5
New Canada town (Aroostook)	321	314	-2.2	329	92.1	0.0	0.0	7.6	0.3	32.5	55.2	12.2	106	94.3	50.0	18.9
Newcastle CDP	667	NA	NA	684	95.6	1.2	2.6	0.0	0.6	17.7	55.2	27.2	370	52.4	26.2	47.6
Newcastle town (Lincoln)..	1,752	1,734	-1.0	1,775	97.5	0.5	1.2	0.5	0.3	21.4	52.6	26.0	802	70.7	29.1	45.4
Newfield town (York)	1,522	1,563	2.7	1,499	92.8	0.0	0.0	3.9	3.3	17.4	61.8	20.7	634	76.5	49.8	14.5
New Gloucester town (Cumberland)	5,542	5,644	1.8	5,590	97.2	0.1	0.0	0.7	2.0	21.6	69.6	9.0	2,092	84.1	33.9	29.9
New Limerick town (Aroostook)	510	491	-3.7	439	96.4	0.0	0.0	3.6	0.0	12.9	56.3	30.8	212	80.7	48.1	17.0

1 May be of any race.

Table A. All Places — **Population and Housing**

STATE City, town, township, borough, or CDP (county if applicable)	Population				Race and Hispanic or Latino origin (percent), 2010–2014					Age (percent), 2010–2014			Households, 2010–2014			
	2010 census total population	2014 estimated population	Percent change 2010–2014	ACS total population estimate 2010–2014	White alone, not Hispanic or Latino	Black alone, not Hispanic or Latino	Asian alone, not Hispanic or Latino	All other races or 2 or more races, not Hispanic or Latino	Hispanic or Latino[1]	Under 18 years old	Age 18 to 64 years old	Age 65 years and older	Total occupied housing units	Percent owner occupied	High school diploma or less	Bachelor's degree or more
	1	2	3	4	5	6	7	8	9	10	11	12	13	14	15	16
MAINE—Con.																
Newport town (Penobscot)	3,274	3,248	-0.8	3,254	97.4	0.9	0.6	1.1	0.0	22.0	60.9	17.1	1,419	66.9	51.9	16.3
Newport CDP	1,776	NA	NA	1,725	98.3	0.0	0.6	1.1	0.0	26.4	58.5	15.0	809	54.6	52.4	16.3
New Portland town (Somerset)	718	708	-1.4	781	96.5	0.6	0.0	2.8	0.0	16.1	58.0	26.0	392	89.0	55.9	15.8
Newry town (Oxford)	329	341	3.6	332	100.0	0.0	0.0	0.0	0.0	19.5	65.8	14.5	138	92.8	38.4	35.5
New Sharon town (Franklin)	1,407	1,402	-0.4	1,346	97.2	0.0	0.1	2.7	0.0	19.8	63.2	16.9	525	87.4	45.1	26.7
New Sweden town (Aroostook)	602	589	-2.2	611	94.9	0.0	0.0	2.6	2.5	16.8	67.0	16.0	268	85.8	44.4	31.3
New Vineyard town (Franklin)	761	775	1.8	654	96.5	0.5	0.2	2.9	0.0	20.4	64.7	15.0	273	88.3	54.9	21.2
Nobleboro town (Lincoln)	1,643	1,625	-1.1	1,702	96.6	0.0	0.2	2.1	1.2	19.3	60.2	20.5	771	84.3	31.3	36.6
Norridgewock CDP	1,438	NA	NA	1,254	98.4	1.6	0.0	0.0	0.0	11.1	66.6	22.3	592	83.6	51.4	16.4
Norridgewock town (Somerset)	3,367	3,316	-1.5	3,341	98.9	0.6	0.0	0.0	0.5	18.4	62.7	18.8	1,441	83.0	60.0	11.7
North Berwick CDP	1,615	NA	NA	1,588	94.9	1.6	0.2	1.8	1.4	23.3	58.0	18.6	602	63.0	33.2	23.4
North Berwick town (York)	4,578	4,650	1.6	4,602	96.0	0.6	0.3	1.3	1.8	22.0	62.5	15.6	1,796	79.5	42.9	24.0
Northeast Piscataquis UT (Piscataquis)	277	273	-1.4	321	98.8	0.0	0.0	1.2	0.0	7.5	62.5	29.9	163	89.0	42.3	11.7
Northeast Somerset UT (Somerset)	390	385	-1.3	333	94.3	0.0	0.0	5.7	0.0	9.6	61.2	29.1	163	88.3	14.7	28.8
Northfield town (Washington)	148	143	-3.4	174	98.3	0.0	0.0	1.7	0.0	20.1	71.3	8.6	72	90.3	19.4	15.3
North Franklin UT (Franklin)	61	60	-1.6	37	100.0	0.0	0.0	0.0	0.0	0.0	72.9	27.0	23	47.8	47.8	52.2
North Haven town (Knox)	355	350	-1.4	410	94.6	0.5	0.0	2.7	2.2	15.6	53.0	31.5	191	69.6	30.9	49.2
North Oxford UT (Oxford)	24	24	0.0	0	0.0	0.0	0.0	0.0	0.0	0.0	0.0	0.0	0	0.0	0.0	0.0
North Penobscot UT (Penobscot)	462	457	-1.1	370	96.5	0.0	3.5	0.0	0.0	9.0	70.4	20.5	178	89.9	55.1	24.7
Northport town (Waldo)	1,520	1,545	1.6	1,492	99.1	0.0	0.3	0.3	0.3	18.9	56.9	24.4	669	84.5	30.2	42.3
North Washington UT (Washington)	499	480	-3.8	686	64.3	7.9	12.1	2.2	13.6	11.6	71.7	16.8	180	80.0	50.0	16.7
Northwest Aroostook UT (Aroostook)	10	10	0.0	78	100.0	0.0	0.0	0.0	0.0	0.0	51.3	48.7	41	92.7	92.7	0.0
Northwest Hancock UT (Hancock)	2	2	0.0	6	100.0	0.0	0.0	0.0	0.0	0.0	100.0	0.0	3	100.0	0.0	0.0
Northwest Piscataquis UT (Piscataquis)	147	145	-1.4	145	92.4	0.0	0.0	7.6	0.0	0.0	45.5	54.5	89	87.6	16.9	73.0
Northwest Somerset UT (Somerset)	62	61	-1.6	16	100.0	0.0	0.0	0.0	0.0	0.0	0.0	100.0	13	100.0	100.0	0.0
North Windham CDP	4,904	NA	NA	4,573	96.9	2.6	0.0	0.0	0.5	28.8	60.0	11.3	1,742	78.1	25.9	36.8
North Yarmouth town (Cumberland)	3,574	3,704	3.6	3,625	94.3	0.0	1.4	4.0	0.3	23.5	64.7	11.7	1,339	88.4	17.9	60.4
Norway CDP	2,748	NA	NA	2,286	97.1	0.1	0.6	2.2	0.0	21.6	57.6	20.9	1,036	56.8	57.7	9.9
Norway town (Oxford)	5,014	4,942	-1.4	4,978	98.7	0.0	0.3	1.0	0.0	19.9	61.2	18.8	1,938	74.1	51.9	17.0
Oakfield town (Aroostook)	737	710	-3.7	682	95.5	0.4	1.6	1.3	1.2	21.4	62.2	16.3	268	79.1	54.1	11.2
Oakland CDP	2,602	NA	NA	2,516	95.4	0.8	2.0	1.3	0.5	16.6	60.0	23.5	1,186	58.2	44.4	23.8
Oakland town (Kennebec)	6,240	6,216	-0.4	6,215	96.3	0.3	0.8	2.1	0.4	19.3	62.7	18.1	2,557	70.9	42.1	23.1
Ogunquit town (York)	892	912	2.2	1,141	100.0	0.0	0.0	0.0	0.0	5.8	54.4	40.1	594	90.1	16.5	61.4
Old Orchard Beach CDP & town (York)	8,624	8,756	1.5	8,679	92.2	2.1	0.3	3.6	1.8	11.4	66.3	22.3	4,308	57.7	37.5	31.3
Old Town city & MCD (Penobscot)	7,846	7,693	-2.0	7,756	93.0	0.9	2.5	3.5	0.1	16.4	70.3	13.4	3,322	57.0	36.0	26.6
Orient town (Aroostook)	147	142	-3.4	171	98.8	1.2	0.0	0.0	0.0	15.1	56.6	28.1	77	85.7	51.9	22.1
Orland town (Hancock)	2,225	2,214	-0.5	2,126	97.4	0.1	0.3	0.6	1.6	15.9	65.0	19.0	915	78.6	32.9	35.8
Orono town (Penobscot)	10,356	10,670	3.0	10,515	91.9	1.9	2.0	3.0	1.2	8.7	80.0	11.4	2,955	45.5	17.6	52.6
Orono CDP	9,474	NA	NA	9,514	91.5	2.1	2.2	3.1	1.1	8.4	80.5	11.1	2,521	40.5	16.5	54.6
Orrington town (Penobscot)	3,733	3,707	-0.7	3,721	98.5	0.0	0.0	1.2	0.2	20.0	65.1	14.9	1,591	87.7	33.9	36.4
Osborn town (Hancock)	67	67	0.0	93	89.2	0.0	0.0	10.8	0.0	36.6	49.7	14.0	33	97.0	42.4	39.4
Otis town (Hancock)	672	671	-0.1	587	99.8	0.0	0.0	0.2	0.0	13.6	71.7	14.7	276	88.8	35.5	24.6
Otisfield town (Oxford)	1,770	1,759	-0.6	2,120	97.5	0.1	0.0	1.9	0.5	24.9	61.2	14.0	764	92.8	49.3	20.8
Owls Head town (Knox)	1,578	1,581	0.2	1,669	97.1	0.7	0.4	1.7	0.1	19.3	53.6	27.1	705	88.5	40.0	29.8
Oxbow plantation (Aroostook)	66	64	-3.0	48	100.0	0.0	0.0	0.0	0.0	0.0	39.7	60.4	28	92.9	46.4	28.6
Oxford CDP	1,263	NA	NA	1,401	100.0	0.0	0.0	0.0	0.0	20.5	68.9	10.6	603	81.4	52.4	14.4
Oxford town (Oxford)	4,110	4,053	-1.4	4,090	98.5	0.0	0.0	1.5	0.0	19.5	65.8	14.9	1,633	88.0	56.0	19.5
Palermo town (Waldo)	1,535	1,542	0.5	1,534	99.1	0.0	0.0	0.8	0.1	20.2	63.3	16.5	652	87.1	40.5	25.9
Palmyra town (Somerset)	1,986	1,936	-2.5	2,075	96.9	0.0	0.0	2.7	0.4	24.1	56.8	19.1	830	91.1	60.0	20.2
Paris town (Oxford)	5,183	5,113	-1.4	5,141	94.0	0.6	1.1	1.7	2.7	16.4	64.4	19.3	2,125	56.0	53.7	14.8
Parkman town (Piscataquis)	843	828	-1.8	742	90.4	0.0	0.0	2.4	7.1	17.9	64.7	17.4	318	91.8	52.8	15.1
Parsonsfield town (York)	1,898	1,917	1.0	1,746	92.5	0.0	0.0	5.4	2.1	19.3	67.4	13.5	746	74.5	55.6	17.6
Passadumkeag town (Penobscot)	374	363	-2.9	426	93.4	0.2	0.0	4.9	1.4	17.9	58.8	23.5	188	76.6	59.0	5.3
Passamaquoddy Indian Township Reservation (Washington)	718	692	-3.6	769	7.0	0.1	0.0	91.8	1.0	32.8	60.9	6.5	308	41.2	57.8	1.3
Passamaquoddy Pleasant Point Reservation (Washington)	749	722	-3.6	787	10.7	0.0	0.4	88.1	0.9	31.6	60.5	7.8	301	50.8	47.2	13.3
Patten town (Penobscot)	1,017	1,002	-1.5	1,042	98.2	0.0	0.3	0.5	1.1	12.6	61.4	25.9	460	72.0	68.7	11.1
Pembroke town (Washington)	840	799	-4.9	881	96.3	0.0	0.3	3.4	0.0	21.2	58.7	20.1	391	87.2	43.5	25.8
Penobscot town (Hancock)	1,263	1,258	-0.4	1,153	98.5	0.0	0.6	0.9	0.0	14.0	57.8	28.3	533	82.2	31.0	34.3
Penobscot Indian Island Reservation (Aroostook)	0	0	0.0	0	0.0	0.0	0.0	0.0	0.0	0.0	0.0	0.0	0	0.0	0.0	0.0
Penobscot Indian Island Reservation (Penobscot)	610	604	-1.0	827	8.6	0.2	1.9	80.3	8.9	29.5	62.4	8.1	319	56.7	29.8	19.7
Perham town (Aroostook)	386	369	-4.4	454	90.7	0.0	0.0	6.8	2.4	22.9	63.2	13.9	163	79.8	52.8	15.3

1 May be of any race.

Table A. All Places — **Population and Housing**

STATE City, town, township, borough, or CDP (county if applicable)	Population 2010 census total population	Population 2014 estimated population	Population Percent change 2010–2014	Population ACS total population estimate 2010–2014	White alone, not Hispanic or Latino	Black alone, not Hispanic or Latino	Asian alone, not Hispanic or Latino	All other races or 2 or more races, not Hispanic or Latino	Hispanic or Latino[1]	Under 18 years old	Age 18 to 64 years old	Age 65 years and older	Total occupied housing units	Percent owner occupied	High school diploma or less	Bachelor's degree or more
	1	2	3	4	5	6	7	8	9	10	11	12	13	14	15	16
Perkins UT (Sagadahoc) ..	0	0	0.0	0	0.0	0.0	0.0	0.0	0.0	0.0	0.0	0.0	0	0.0	0.0	0.0
Perry town (Washington) ..	889	941	5.8	825	92.4	0.0	0.0	7.6	0.0	19.8	64.7	15.6	357	86.6	37.0	27.7
Peru town (Oxford)	1,541	1,514	-1.8	1,339	97.8	0.0	0.4	1.1	0.7	17.8	61.9	20.2	555	92.4	54.2	13.7
Phillips town (Franklin)......	1,028	1,016	-1.2	1,005	99.8	0.2	0.0	0.0	0.0	19.5	61.6	19.2	407	83.3	47.7	20.4
Phippsburg town (Sagadahoc)	2,216	2,223	0.3	1,983	99.2	0.0	0.0	0.4	0.5	12.0	63.5	24.4	903	84.5	41.0	32.4
Pittsfield CDP	3,150	NA	NA	3,063	95.1	1.4	0.8	2.3	0.4	22.2	62.5	15.2	1,043	68.8	45.1	21.3
Pittsfield town (Somerset)..	4,215	4,092	-2.9	4,164	96.4	1.0	0.6	1.7	0.3	22.1	62.4	15.5	1,450	76.6	45.7	21.9
Pittston town (Kennebec)..	2,666	2,631	-1.3	2,644	96.7	0.0	1.1	1.1	1.2	15.5	68.4	16.3	1,167	83.8	43.8	21.2
Pleasant Ridge plantation (Somerset)	93	91	-2.2	88	100.0	0.0	0.0	0.0	0.0	14.8	45.5	39.8	47	80.9	76.6	4.3
Plymouth town (Penobscot)..................	1,376	1,365	-0.8	1,302	97.6	0.1	0.4	1.9	0.0	21.5	64.1	14.4	523	83.7	43.8	6.7
Poland town (Androscoggin).............	5,376	5,517	2.6	5,424	93.6	0.2	0.0	5.9	0.2	24.6	63.1	12.2	2,181	86.2	45.6	22.6
Portage Lake town (Aroostook)	391	381	-2.6	435	97.2	0.0	0.0	2.5	0.2	13.5	58.0	28.5	212	91.0	50.9	17.0
Porter town (Oxford)	1,498	1,484	-0.9	1,774	95.6	0.0	2.6	1.8	0.0	25.4	58.7	16.0	617	79.9	53.8	18.6
Portland city & MCD (Cumberland)	66,194	66,666	0.7	66,317	82.7	7.1	3.7	3.1	3.4	17.1	70.6	12.2	30,107	43.7	26.0	47.4
Pownal town (Cumberland)	1,474	1,510	2.4	1,513	97.8	0.0	0.1	2.0	0.0	26.2	56.4	17.3	570	87.2	34.9	43.3
Prentiss UT (Penobscot)...	214	212	-0.9	214	100.0	0.0	0.0	0.0	0.0	27.6	60.2	12.1	79	92.4	72.2	10.1
Presque Isle city & MCD (Aroostook)	9,692	9,317	-3.9	9,494	93.1	0.5	0.6	4.9	0.9	18.7	64.1	17.3	4,198	56.6	45.7	21.2
Princeton town (Washington)	832	796	-4.3	803	96.9	0.0	0.0	2.5	0.6	19.5	65.0	15.6	375	80.5	43.5	13.6
Prospect town (Waldo)	709	716	1.0	700	98.7	0.0	0.0	0.9	0.4	15.5	73.1	11.4	299	90.6	47.8	23.7
Randolph CDP & town (Kennebec)	1,772	1,724	-2.7	1,837	98.0	0.0	0.0	0.4	1.5	21.6	55.1	23.2	827	69.4	48.6	15.1
Rangeley town (Franklin)..	1,175	1,162	-1.1	1,140	93.5	0.0	0.0	0.5	6.0	16.1	60.6	23.3	505	85.5	31.7	28.7
Rangeley plantation (Franklin)	189	185	-2.1	175	98.3	0.0	0.0	0.6	1.1	2.8	54.8	42.3	101	82.2	35.6	37.6
Raymond town (Cumberland)	4,438	4,501	1.4	4,460	98.5	0.2	0.0	1.3	0.0	17.4	66.1	16.7	1,915	82.8	26.3	35.1
Readfield town (Kennebec)	2,598	2,548	-1.9	2,567	97.2	0.4	2.2	0.2	0.0	20.2	65.3	14.8	1,089	93.1	27.3	43.5
Reed plantation (Aroostook)	161	156	-3.1	179	97.2	1.1	0.0	1.7	0.0	20.1	61.9	17.9	70	71.4	54.3	8.6
Richmond CDP..................	1,760	NA	NA	2,034	97.8	0.0	0.0	1.8	0.4	23.0	64.8	12.1	860	70.8	36.9	26.0
Richmond town (Sagadahoc)	3,411	3,383	-0.8	3,391	97.8	0.0	0.0	1.4	0.8	19.4	65.7	14.9	1,486	73.1	41.3	22.6
Ripley town (Somerset)	488	479	-1.8	422	99.1	0.0	0.5	0.5	0.0	13.9	68.5	17.5	178	80.3	58.4	21.9
Robbinston town (Washington)................	574	554	-3.5	533	94.0	0.0	1.1	4.9	0.0	19.1	59.4	21.6	233	96.6	43.3	15.9
Rockland city & MCD (Knox)	7,297	7,219	-1.1	7,241	95.5	0.8	2.2	0.8	0.7	15.2	62.7	22.2	3,446	61.7	40.9	35.9
Rockport town (Knox)	3,330	3,360	0.9	3,338	92.6	0.7	0.7	1.7	4.3	25.1	51.8	22.9	1,358	85.9	32.3	43.4
Rome town (Kennebec)....	1,010	997	-1.3	1,157	99.0	0.1	0.0	0.5	0.4	15.7	62.9	21.3	525	85.5	32.8	33.3
Roque Bluffs town (Washington)................	303	292	-3.6	262	100.0	0.0	0.0	0.0	0.0	11.4	60.0	28.6	127	95.3	46.5	32.3
Roxbury town (Oxford)......	369	362	-1.9	317	99.4	0.0	0.6	0.0	0.0	11.7	68.4	19.9	139	91.4	57.6	9.4
Rumford CDP	4,218	NA	NA	4,395	94.3	0.1	0.0	3.1	2.4	19.6	62.3	18.0	1,753	54.8	54.9	12.7
Rumford town (Oxford)	5,841	5,697	-2.5	5,770	94.9	0.1	0.3	2.5	2.2	18.8	62.0	19.2	2,428	62.0	55.0	14.5
Sabattus town (Androscoggin).............	4,876	5,022	3.0	4,964	98.7	0.0	0.0	1.3	0.0	21.0	61.9	17.1	2,159	82.9	55.0	23.9
Saco city & MCD (York)	18,482	19,014	2.9	18,757	92.6	1.1	1.9	2.1	2.4	20.5	63.9	15.7	7,794	64.1	38.7	31.3
St. Agatha town (Aroostook)	747	726	-2.8	578	99.5	0.3	0.0	0.2	0.0	14.2	56.4	29.4	310	77.1	66.8	16.8
St. Albans town (Somerset)	2,009	1,972	-1.8	1,960	97.4	0.4	0.4	1.9	0.0	23.5	62.7	13.9	744	84.5	55.1	7.1
St. Francis town (Aroostook)	485	463	-4.5	403	99.5	0.0	0.0	0.0	0.5	15.6	65.5	18.9	205	78.0	76.1	6.3
St. George town (Knox)	2,591	2,584	-0.3	2,586	94.9	0.0	0.5	3.9	0.7	17.2	52.9	29.9	1,148	91.6	37.6	35.5
St. John plantation (Aroostook)	267	258	-3.4	253	93.7	0.8	0.0	5.5	0.0	14.7	68.8	16.6	116	91.4	62.1	11.2
Sandy River plantation (Franklin)	133	130	-2.3	158	100.0	0.0	0.0	0.0	0.0	7.6	68.4	24.1	79	91.1	26.6	54.4
Sanford city & MCD (York)	20,796	20,906	0.5	20,853	94.5	0.2	1.4	2.2	1.7	23.1	60.7	16.2	8,686	62.8	47.9	18.2
Sangerville town (Piscataquis)	1,343	1,289	-4.0	1,428	96.0	0.0	1.5	0.2	2.2	20.5	56.9	22.5	620	78.4	55.8	14.7
Scarborough CDP	4,403	NA	NA	4,931	89.2	3.4	5.9	0.2	1.3	25.0	53.8	21.2	1,841	66.1	25.2	48.0
Scarborough town (Cumberland)	18,919	19,524	3.2	19,209	91.4	1.3	4.3	1.1	2.0	23.1	57.8	19.1	7,395	76.5	20.9	50.6
Searsmont town (Waldo) ..	1,392	1,409	1.2	1,637	97.3	0.4	0.0	0.4	2.0	26.5	62.3	11.4	679	86.0	29.6	34.5
Searsport CDP	992	NA	NA	964	89.9	0.0	0.0	4.6	5.5	13.8	63.4	22.7	556	44.1	42.3	42.3
Searsport town (Waldo)....	2,615	2,627	0.5	2,629	94.8	0.0	1.0	1.7	2.5	18.9	60.5	20.8	1,299	66.7	47.1	29.3
Sebago town (Cumberland)	1,719	1,763	2.6	1,603	96.7	0.3	1.4	1.1	0.5	14.6	67.5	17.9	750	85.2	44.1	27.2
Sebec town (Piscataquis).	630	605	-4.0	630	94.8	0.0	1.1	2.1	2.1	17.0	60.5	22.5	268	93.7	51.5	16.4
Seboeis plantation (Penobscot)..................	35	35	0.0	51	100.0	0.0	0.0	0.0	0.0	11.7	62.8	25.5	21	90.5	52.4	9.5
Seboomook Lake UT (Somerset)	47	47	0.0	39	100.0	0.0	0.0	0.0	0.0	0.0	0.0	100.0	20	100.0	100.0	0.0
Sedgwick town (Hancock)	1,196	1,187	-0.8	1,137	90.8	0.3	0.0	2.7	6.2	20.8	56.7	22.5	491	80.7	35.2	40.9
Shapleigh town (York).......	2,668	2,688	0.7	2,676	96.0	0.0	1.1	2.6	0.2	20.2	65.2	14.6	1,083	91.8	44.6	16.5
Sherman town (Aroostook)	846	816	-3.5	817	96.1	0.2	0.0	3.7	0.0	15.2	63.5	21.4	361	81.2	52.1	11.1
Shirley town (Piscataquis)	233	225	-3.4	291	99.7	0.0	0.3	0.0	0.0	18.2	64.9	16.8	113	89.4	53.1	17.7
Sidney town (Kennebec)...	4,212	4,251	0.9	4,212	97.3	0.0	0.0	1.3	1.4	22.1	63.9	14.1	1,660	79.7	41.0	23.3
Skowhegan CDP	6,297	NA	NA	6,219	97.7	0.5	0.2	1.2	0.4	20.8	60.4	18.7	2,907	56.8	54.2	15.9

1 May be of any race.

Table A. All Places — **Population and Housing**

STATE City, town, township, borough, or CDP (county if applicable)	Population				Race and Hispanic or Latino origin (percent), 2010–2014					Age (percent), 2010–2014			Households, 2010–2014			
	2010 census total population	2014 estimated population	Percent change 2010–2014	ACS total population estimate 2010–2014	White alone, not Hispanic or Latino	Black alone, not Hispanic or Latino	Asian alone, not Hispanic or Latino	All other races or 2 or more races, not Hispanic or Latino	Hispanic or Latino[1]	Under 18 years old	Age 18 to 64 years old	Age 65 years and older	Total occupied housing units	Percent owner occupied	High school diploma or less	Bachelor's degree or more
	1	2	3	4	5	6	7	8	9	10	11	12	13	14	15	16
MAINE—Con.																
Skowhegan town (Somerset)	8,589	8,458	-1.5	8,540	96.5	0.4	0.2	2.3	0.7	20.3	61.5	18.3	3,873	62.6	53.6	15.5
Smithfield town (Somerset)	1,033	1,003	-2.9	1,071	98.4	0.6	0.0	1.0	0.0	20.8	60.7	18.5	452	91.6	48.9	23.7
Smyrna town (Aroostook) .	442	432	-2.3	465	99.4	0.0	0.0	0.6	0.0	28.3	60.7	10.8	156	87.2	59.6	16.0
Solon town (Somerset)	1,053	1,047	-0.6	1,037	85.4	0.0	4.1	9.5	1.0	19.9	62.5	17.6	431	81.7	39.9	12.1
Somerville town (Lincoln) .	548	557	1.6	433	94.5	0.0	4.4	0.0	1.2	20.3	60.8	18.7	188	82.4	42.6	21.3
Sorrento town (Hancock)..	274	273	-0.4	285	95.4	0.0	0.7	2.5	1.4	15.8	57.7	26.7	125	90.4	29.6	36.0
South Aroostook UT (Aroostook)	388	375	-3.4	464	99.1	0.0	0.0	0.9	0.0	9.9	56.7	33.4	207	98.6	28.5	12.1
South Berwick town (York)	7,220	7,316	1.3	7,276	95.4	0.2	0.9	3.2	0.4	26.7	62.4	10.9	2,688	75.4	26.6	42.6
South Bristol town (Lincoln)	892	890	-0.2	952	98.9	0.0	0.0	0.0	1.1	12.3	52.1	35.6	453	84.8	27.2	44.4
Southeast Piscataquis UT (Piscataquis)	253	248	-2.0	199	92.0	0.0	0.0	6.5	1.5	16.5	57.6	25.6	82	75.6	58.5	9.8
South Eliot CDP	3,550	NA	NA	3,708	97.0	0.4	0.0	0.6	2.1	22.1	60.3	17.5	1,409	78.4	28.8	36.3
South Franklin UT (Franklin)	69	67	-2.9	238	100.0	0.0	0.0	0.0	0.0	37.8	43.2	18.9	65	95.4	70.8	4.6
South Oxford UT (Oxford).	583	583	0.0	426	100.0	0.0	0.0	0.0	0.0	14.7	62.6	22.5	183	79.8	57.4	19.1
South Paris CDP	2,267	NA	NA	2,906	91.1	1.1	2.0	2.2	3.7	17.7	62.7	19.5	1,217	43.6	54.7	11.1
Southport town (Lincoln) ..	606	594	-2.0	622	98.6	0.0	1.4	0.0	0.0	7.6	45.9	46.6	346	78.3	24.0	45.1
South Portland city & MCD (Cumberland).......	25,002	25,424	1.7	25,154	90.8	1.8	3.6	2.0	1.8	20.0	64.4	15.5	10,852	59.8	26.3	40.6
South Thomaston town (Knox)	1,560	1,597	2.4	1,495	95.6	0.9	0.0	3.0	0.5	19.1	60.3	20.5	616	84.4	41.4	28.7
Southwest Harbor CDP	720	NA	NA	693	89.6	0.0	0.0	6.8	3.6	10.8	63.3	25.8	377	49.9	34.7	30.8
Southwest Harbor town (Hancock)	1,764	1,771	0.4	1,976	92.0	0.0	0.1	3.6	4.3	17.8	59.6	22.6	955	60.1	35.0	32.1
South Windham CDP.......	1,374	NA	NA	1,190	88.7	4.7	0.2	6.4	0.1	5.4	83.5	10.9	290	88.6	32.4	30.3
Springfield town (Penobscot)	409	419	2.4	413	99.3	0.0	0.0	0.7	0.0	20.4	59.4	20.1	159	94.3	57.2	10.7
Square Lake UT (Aroostook)	594	574	-3.4	475	100.0	0.0	0.0	0.0	0.0	10.5	37.7	51.8	238	90.3	50.0	29.0
Stacyville town (Penobscot)	396	387	-2.3	404	91.8	0.0	1.7	6.4	0.0	25.3	54.7	20.0	163	90.2	55.8	11.7
Standish CDP	469	NA	NA	340	100.0	0.0	0.0	0.0	0.0	20.0	46.8	33.2	200	54.5	54.5	19.0
Standish town (Cumberland)	9,872	10,020	1.5	9,942	97.4	0.9	1.0	0.2	0.5	19.6	67.9	12.5	3,674	90.7	35.2	27.3
Starks town (Somerset)	636	628	-1.3	535	86.9	0.0	0.0	3.7	9.3	13.5	72.3	14.2	242	84.7	56.6	21.5
Steep Falls CDP	1,139	NA	NA	1,245	94.2	0.1	5.7	0.0	0.0	24.0	65.2	10.9	444	94.6	55.2	26.8
Stetson town (Penobscot).	1,200	1,209	0.8	1,237	98.9	0.0	0.0	1.1	0.0	23.6	62.4	14.0	487	94.7	49.5	15.2
Steuben town (Washington)	1,131	1,098	-2.9	1,017	89.7	0.9	0.0	8.4	1.1	20.0	59.5	20.6	449	80.6	59.2	22.5
Stockholm town (Aroostook)	253	245	-3.2	223	92.4	0.0	2.7	4.9	0.0	13.4	66.4	20.2	104	81.7	33.7	29.8
Stockton Springs town (Waldo)	1,591	1,601	0.6	1,423	98.1	0.0	0.0	1.9	0.0	13.9	57.1	29.0	655	83.7	35.3	35.3
Stoneham town (Oxford)...	236	235	-0.4	291	99.0	0.0	0.0	1.0	0.0	21.2	57.8	21.0	118	89.8	47.5	22.9
Stonington town (Hancock)	1,043	1,038	-0.5	1,312	97.2	0.4	0.0	0.8	1.6	20.7	58.6	20.8	587	70.2	45.7	23.9
Stow town (Oxford)	385	411	6.8	416	97.6	1.4	0.0	0.0	1.0	20.2	63.6	16.3	153	96.7	53.6	17.0
Strong town (Franklin)	1,213	1,196	-1.4	1,341	95.8	1.0	0.0	0.1	3.1	27.5	58.8	13.7	487	80.7	50.3	16.6
Sullivan town (Hancock) ...	1,241	1,243	0.2	1,083	91.3	0.3	0.8	6.1	1.5	16.2	67.1	16.7	485	81.4	51.1	21.2
Sumner town (Oxford)	939	937	-0.2	1,061	91.5	0.0	0.0	2.2	6.3	22.7	61.8	15.6	387	87.3	54.8	26.4
Surry town (Hancock)	1,466	1,467	0.1	1,666	93.7	1.1	0.2	2.9	2.1	17.3	62.8	19.9	752	77.0	32.2	43.5
Swans Island town (Hancock)	332	331	-0.3	302	93.4	0.0	0.7	3.6	2.3	23.9	53.7	22.5	126	82.5	46.0	36.5
Swanville town (Waldo).....	1,388	1,376	-0.9	1,262	99.0	0.0	0.0	0.6	0.3	19.8	65.7	14.4	519	78.4	50.9	21.2
Sweden town (Oxford)	391	393	0.5	391	95.9	0.0	0.3	3.1	0.8	19.4	52.5	28.1	171	91.8	38.6	35.7
Talmadge town (Washington)	64	62	-3.1	83	100.0	0.0	0.0	0.0	0.0	22.9	43.4	33.7	43	83.7	48.8	9.3
Temple town (Franklin)	528	523	-0.9	608	99.0	0.0	0.0	1.0	0.0	22.1	61.2	16.8	257	84.0	43.6	32.7
The Forks plantation (Somerset)	37	36	-2.7	24	100.0	0.0	0.0	0.0	0.0	0.0	54.2	45.8	16	100.0	43.8	31.3
Thomaston CDP	1,875	NA	NA	2,052	89.2	4.1	1.0	1.7	4.0	21.4	60.8	17.8	911	61.7	39.1	31.5
Thomaston town (Knox)....	2,781	2,768	-0.5	2,768	90.8	3.0	0.7	1.8	3.6	19.2	62.7	18.3	1,217	67.1	43.7	28.9
Thorndike town (Waldo)....	890	890	0.0	836	99.4	0.2	0.0	0.0	0.4	23.1	61.9	15.1	347	77.5	44.4	22.8
Topsfield town (Washington)	237	229	-3.4	215	99.1	0.0	0.0	0.9	0.0	20.9	62.3	16.7	85	94.1	45.9	18.8
Topsham CDP	5,931	NA	NA	6,228	92.8	0.3	1.4	4.1	1.4	20.0	58.1	22.0	2,625	75.0	29.8	43.5
Topsham town (Sagadahoc)	8,784	8,715	-0.8	8,728	92.6	0.2	1.8	3.7	1.6	17.9	61.1	20.8	3,712	79.2	27.2	43.9
Tremont town (Hancock)...	1,563	1,593	1.9	1,764	94.6	0.3	0.0	4.6	0.4	22.8	59.8	17.2	789	71.2	45.0	26.1
Trenton town (Hancock)....	1,483	1,525	2.8	1,555	94.0	0.3	1.0	3.5	1.1	17.7	64.7	17.6	701	70.3	40.9	28.2
Troy town (Waldo)	1,030	1,040	1.0	924	97.3	0.3	0.3	1.1	1.0	15.7	67.3	17.0	399	80.2	47.1	19.5
Turner town (Androscoggin).............	5,734	5,756	0.4	5,737	95.7	0.5	0.0	2.4	1.4	24.0	62.6	13.3	2,235	86.7	38.7	23.9
Twombly Ridge UT (Penobscot)..............	0	0	0.0	0	0.0	0.0	0.0	0.0	0.0	0.0	0.0	0.0	0	0.0	0.0	0.0
Union town (Knox)	2,259	2,233	-1.2	2,090	99.1	0.0	0.3	0.5	0.0	15.7	65.5	18.9	911	87.6	40.6	29.5
Unity UT (Kennebec)	43	42	-2.3	41	100.0	0.0	0.0	0.0	0.0	14.6	53.7	31.7	15	100.0	60.0	26.7
Unity CDP	469	NA	NA	535	95.9	0.0	0.0	4.1	0.0	26.7	54.8	18.5	249	46.2	57.4	25.3
Unity town (Waldo)	2,099	2,087	-0.6	2,499	91.4	1.6	1.3	2.4	3.3	19.9	69.5	10.5	768	71.4	50.0	24.5
Upton town (Oxford)	113	111	-1.8	61	100.0	0.0	0.0	0.0	0.0	8.2	54.1	37.7	34	85.3	47.1	20.6
Van Buren CDP	1,937	NA	NA	1,999	98.3	0.5	0.0	0.7	0.5	16.9	56.6	26.9	941	57.7	65.7	11.2
Van Buren town (Aroostook)	2,171	2,085	-4.0	2,315	97.8	0.4	0.0	0.7	1.1	19.1	57.3	23.6	1,030	60.2	64.4	12.1
Vanceboro town (Washington)	140	135	-3.6	111	95.5	0.0	0.0	4.5	0.0	21.6	53.1	25.2	49	69.4	59.2	6.1
Vassalboro town (Kennebec)..............	4,343	4,306	-0.9	4,337	98.1	0.4	0.0	1.3	0.2	25.0	64.1	10.8	1,614	77.1	45.5	17.5
Veazie town (Penobscot) ..	1,919	1,883	-1.9	1,959	93.8	0.0	1.3	4.3	0.6	20.3	61.2	18.4	832	66.3	26.0	36.7

1 May be of any race.

Table A. All Places — Population and Housing

STATE City, town, township, borough, or CDP (county if applicable)	Population				Race and Hispanic or Latino origin (percent), 2010–2014					Age (percent), 2010–2014			Households, 2010–2014			
	2010 census total population	2014 estimated population	Percent change 2010–2014	ACS total population estimate 2010–2014	White alone, not Hispanic or Latino	Black alone, not Hispanic or Latino	Asian alone, not Hispanic or Latino	All other races or 2 or more races, not Hispanic or Latino	Hispanic or Latino[1]	Under 18 years old	Age 18 to 64 years old	Age 65 years and older	Total occupied housing units	Percent owner occupied	High school diploma or less	Bachelor's degree or more
	1	2	3	4	5	6	7	8	9	10	11	12	13	14	15	16
MAINE—Con.																
Verona Island town (Hancock)	544	542	-0.4	571	89.5	0.0	0.0	10.5	0.0	13.3	69.9	16.8	261	85.1	53.6	13.0
Vienna town (Kennebec)	570	578	1.4	552	98.0	0.0	0.0	0.9	1.1	7.1	65.8	27.2	274	89.8	45.3	23.0
Vinalhaven town (Knox)	1,165	1,144	-1.8	1,327	94.8	0.0	2.7	2.5	0.0	22.3	61.3	16.2	578	82.4	56.9	20.4
Wade town (Aroostook)	283	274	-3.2	207	97.6	1.0	0.0	1.4	0.0	18.3	65.2	16.4	87	93.1	36.8	27.6
Waite town (Washington)	101	97	-4.0	91	94.5	0.0	0.0	5.5	0.0	14.3	75.9	9.9	43	81.4	51.2	4.7
Waldo town (Waldo)	765	828	8.2	875	98.4	0.0	0.0	0.2	1.4	17.8	69.7	12.5	406	84.2	44.1	19.2
Waldoboro CDP	1,233	NA	NA	832	91.2	0.0	0.0	0.0	8.8	24.4	57.8	17.8	431	66.1	36.0	30.2
Waldoboro town (Lincoln)	5,075	5,015	-1.2	5,035	96.7	0.0	0.6	1.1	1.7	23.0	60.6	16.5	1,947	80.7	49.8	26.4
Wales town (Androscoggin)	1,616	1,632	1.0	1,963	90.7	0.0	1.9	6.4	1.0	27.5	62.7	9.8	628	90.1	56.2	14.2
Wallagrass town (Aroostook)	546	533	-2.4	481	95.6	0.0	0.6	3.7	0.0	10.7	68.6	20.6	229	85.6	59.0	22.3
Waltham town (Hancock)	353	345	-2.3	295	99.0	0.0	0.0	1.0	0.0	14.9	65.8	19.3	125	85.6	60.8	10.4
Warren town (Knox)	4,751	4,687	-1.3	4,715	97.7	0.7	0.0	1.1	0.4	19.3	70.9	9.9	1,598	86.9	45.4	19.5
Washburn CDP	997	NA	NA	1,015	98.7	0.0	0.0	0.7	0.6	22.7	60.2	16.9	437	65.9	54.0	14.0
Washburn town (Aroostook)	1,687	1,618	-4.1	1,662	95.8	0.0	0.0	1.6	2.6	23.2	60.2	16.5	703	72.0	53.1	12.1
Washington town (Knox)	1,527	1,522	-0.3	1,459	97.7	0.8	0.0	1.0	0.5	21.1	59.6	19.4	585	83.9	51.3	25.3
Waterboro town (York)	7,693	7,771	1.0	7,747	94.6	0.6	2.1	2.1	0.6	27.5	64.6	8.0	2,674	90.2	34.0	22.1
Waterford town (Oxford)	1,553	1,547	-0.4	1,596	99.1	0.2	0.0	0.3	0.5	15.2	60.3	24.6	634	86.0	56.5	17.4
Waterville city & MCD (Kennebec)	15,722	16,182	2.9	15,886	89.4	3.6	1.5	3.5	2.0	18.2	66.6	15.1	6,539	46.8	46.7	25.0
Wayne town (Kennebec)	1,189	1,166	-1.9	1,050	100.0	0.0	0.0	0.0	0.0	15.9	58.7	25.2	482	94.2	20.7	48.5
Webster plantation (Penobscot)	85	84	-1.2	80	97.5	0.0	0.0	2.5	0.0	15.1	67.7	17.5	29	96.6	72.4	6.9
Weld town (Franklin)	419	413	-1.4	461	94.8	0.0	0.0	5.2	0.0	10.9	55.1	34.1	184	91.8	33.2	41.8
Wellington town (Piscataquis)	260	249	-4.2	245	96.3	0.0	0.0	3.3	0.4	11.8	57.2	31.0	122	91.0	58.2	9.8
Wells town (York)	9,589	10,009	4.4	9,783	98.3	0.3	0.6	0.4	0.4	19.2	55.3	25.5	4,300	82.7	29.6	31.5
Wesley town (Washington)	98	94	-4.1	77	96.1	0.0	0.0	2.6	1.3	0.0	46.8	53.2	53	84.9	54.7	13.2
West Bath town (Sagadahoc)	1,877	1,886	0.5	2,091	97.2	0.3	0.2	1.7	0.6	22.2	58.5	19.4	814	85.5	35.7	36.5
Westbrook city & MCD (Cumberland)	17,494	17,886	2.2	17,662	89.8	3.2	1.2	2.8	3.0	20.4	63.1	16.5	7,900	62.0	41.9	26.4
West Central Franklin UT (Franklin)	0	0	0.0	0	0.0	0.0	0.0	0.0	0.0	0.0	0.0	0.0	0	0.0	0.0	0.0
Westfield town (Aroostook)	549	527	-4.0	687	97.1	0.7	0.0	1.6	0.6	15.4	70.0	14.6	233	90.1	52.4	10.7
West Forks plantation (Somerset)	60	58	-3.3	31	100.0	0.0	0.0	0.0	0.0	0.0	74.3	25.8	16	81.3	68.8	18.8
West Gardiner town (Kennebec)	3,474	3,408	-1.9	3,436	96.7	0.0	0.4	2.3	0.5	22.5	64.7	13.0	1,432	80.4	41.8	27.4
West Kennebunk CDP	1,176	NA	NA	1,131	98.1	1.9	0.0	0.0	0.0	33.6	57.4	8.9	406	76.6	38.4	42.1
Westmanland town (Aroostook)	62	60	-3.2	89	95.5	0.0	0.0	0.0	4.5	11.2	69.6	19.1	34	97.1	38.2	29.4
Weston town (Aroostook)	228	220	-3.5	171	99.4	0.0	0.0	0.0	0.6	9.9	53.8	36.3	77	97.4	55.8	18.2
West Paris town (Oxford)	1,812	1,811	-0.1	1,808	95.9	0.9	0.0	1.7	1.5	20.7	60.8	18.4	633	78.8	51.8	13.6
Westport Island town (Lincoln)	718	720	0.3	835	98.2	0.4	0.5	1.0	0.0	20.5	53.1	26.5	363	84.3	28.1	39.1
Whitefield town (Lincoln)	2,300	2,286	-0.6	2,336	96.8	0.4	0.0	1.3	1.5	20.4	60.0	19.5	924	93.3	44.6	23.5
Whiting town (Washington)	487	481	-1.2	467	90.6	0.0	0.0	7.5	1.9	18.3	63.5	18.2	182	85.2	33.0	45.1
Whitney UT (Penobscot)	5	5	0.0	0	0.0	0.0	0.0	0.0	0.0	0.0	0.0	0.0	0	0.0	0.0	0.0
Whitneyville town (Washington)	220	212	-3.6	173	99.4	0.0	0.0	0.6	0.0	12.8	66.3	20.8	89	82.0	58.4	9.0
Willimantic town (Piscataquis)	150	144	-4.0	105	100.0	0.0	0.0	0.0	0.0	13.4	54.2	32.4	56	87.5	53.6	16.1
Wilton CDP	2,198	NA	NA	2,097	91.2	0.0	5.0	2.1	1.7	23.5	62.8	13.6	855	65.0	64.0	23.3
Wilton town (Franklin)	4,116	3,999	-2.8	4,068	94.8	0.1	3.1	1.1	0.9	24.9	59.6	15.5	1,572	76.3	52.9	19.5
Windham town (Cumberland)	16,997	17,589	3.5	17,300	95.3	2.2	0.0	2.1	0.5	22.5	65.1	12.3	6,453	83.1	34.3	34.4
Windsor town (Kennebec)	2,575	2,566	-0.3	2,576	98.6	0.0	0.0	0.3	1.1	18.7	69.1	12.2	1,113	81.7	46.7	19.4
Winn town (Penobscot)	411	405	-1.5	508	97.8	0.4	0.0	1.8	0.0	16.1	62.9	21.1	225	92.4	56.4	10.7
Winslow CDP & town (Kennebec)	7,792	7,637	-2.0	7,709	96.4	0.5	1.5	1.3	0.3	20.9	60.2	18.8	3,278	76.3	41.4	25.6
Winter Harbor CDP	426	NA	NA	400	99.5	0.0	0.0	0.5	0.0	17.1	65.5	17.8	205	71.7	36.1	23.9
Winter Harbor town (Hancock)	516	516	0.0	475	98.1	0.8	0.6	0.4	0.0	14.3	68.5	17.3	239	72.0	37.7	25.1
Winterport CDP	1,340	NA	NA	1,168	98.2	0.5	0.1	1.2	0.0	15.3	75.5	9.2	530	73.0	22.1	46.4
Winterport town (Waldo)	3,757	3,793	1.0	3,771	98.9	0.4	0.0	0.6	0.0	20.6	71.7	7.8	1,604	85.7	26.3	37.3
Winterville plantation (Aroostook)	224	216	-3.6	189	94.7	0.0	0.0	0.0	5.3	19.0	55.0	25.9	90	93.3	48.9	25.6
Winthrop CDP	2,650	NA	NA	2,651	93.0	0.0	0.0	2.4	4.6	22.7	59.5	17.8	1,140	66.9	31.4	33.7
Winthrop town (Kennebec)	6,094	5,987	-1.8	6,046	95.7	0.0	0.5	1.1	2.8	20.6	62.8	16.6	2,431	75.1	31.7	32.9
Wiscasset CDP	1,097	NA	NA	1,302	82.9	0.0	14.3	2.8	0.0	13.6	62.8	23.7	572	50.7	45.8	24.7
Wiscasset town (Lincoln)	3,732	3,672	-1.6	3,683	89.1	0.4	5.4	5.1	0.1	14.4	71.1	14.6	1,436	63.1	41.4	22.0
Woodland town (Aroostook)	1,213	1,175	-3.1	1,193	97.2	0.0	0.0	1.4	1.4	21.7	59.6	18.7	502	88.4	53.6	16.7
Woodland CDP	952	NA	NA	896	98.9	0.1	0.0	0.2	0.8	16.0	67.2	17.0	407	77.1	49.9	19.2
Woodstock town (Oxford)	1,277	1,266	-0.9	1,243	93.4	0.0	0.0	3.2	3.4	18.2	60.1	21.6	481	87.1	43.5	22.7
Woodville town (Penobscot)	248	247	-0.4	212	100.0	0.0	0.0	0.0	0.0	12.8	81.6	5.7	95	89.5	53.7	5.3
Woolwich town (Sagadahoc)	3,072	3,062	-0.3	3,054	97.9	1.0	0.0	0.6	0.5	22.9	59.1	18.1	1,224	94.2	42.9	34.9
Wyman UT (Franklin)	88	87	-1.1	12	100.0	0.0	0.0	0.0	0.0	0.0	66.7	33.3	9	100.0	0.0	100.0
Yarmouth CDP	5,869	NA	NA	5,645	93.9	0.4	0.9	1.3	3.5	19.9	64.7	15.4	2,370	67.1	19.7	55.2
Yarmouth town (Cumberland)	8,349	8,509	1.9	8,433	94.4	0.2	1.6	1.2	2.5	20.8	62.5	16.6	3,425	75.7	15.8	58.1
York town (York)	12,529	12,803	2.2	12,661	97.6	0.0	1.1	0.8	0.5	16.7	62.3	21.1	5,697	78.1	22.3	47.7
York Harbor CDP	3,033	NA	NA	3,190	98.1	0.0	1.4	0.0	0.5	17.1	55.7	27.0	1,472	53.3	22.9	53.4

1 May be of any race.

Table A. All Places — **Population and Housing**

STATE City, town, township, borough, or CDP (county if applicable)	Population: 2010 census total population	Population: 2014 estimated population	Population: Percent change 2010–2014	Population: ACS total population estimate 2010–2014	Race and Hispanic or Latino origin (percent), 2010–2014: White alone, not Hispanic or Latino	Black alone, not Hispanic or Latino	Asian alone, not Hispanic or Latino	All other races or 2 or more races, not Hispanic or Latino	Hispanic or Latino[1]	Age (percent), 2010–2014: Under 18 years old	Age 18 to 64 years old	Age 65 years and older	Households, 2010–2014: Total occupied housing units	Percent owner occupied	Householders by level of education (percent): High school diploma or less	Bachelor's degree or more
	1	2	3	4	5	6	7	8	9	10	11	12	13	14	15	16
MARYLAND	5,773,785	5,976,407	3.5	5,887,776	53.6	29.0	5.8	2.8	8.8	22.9	64.1	13.0	2,155,983	67.1	31.8	40.7
Aberdeen city	14,981	15,434	3.0	15,137	54.6	31.2	3.1	4.3	6.8	22.1	64.9	13.1	6,022	62.3	43.2	19.3
Aberdeen Proving Ground CDP	2,093	NA	NA	2,411	49.8	27.1	5.4	12.4	5.4	31.4	67.5	1.1	635	0.0	8.8	49.9
Accident town	325	319	-1.8	309	99.4	0.0	0.0	0.3	0.3	25.3	52.0	22.7	134	70.9	47.8	18.7
Accokeek CDP	10,573	NA	NA	10,806	20.4	68.4	4.3	2.9	3.9	22.7	67.6	9.6	3,688	92.8	23.9	42.6
Adamstown CDP	2,372	NA	NA	2,628	84.7	3.2	1.6	4.4	6.1	34.6	57.0	8.3	737	95.4	17.2	62.3
Adelphi CDP	15,086	NA	NA	15,885	14.9	34.5	9.3	2.2	39.2	20.5	71.1	8.5	5,280	48.6	36.4	43.2
Algonquin CDP	1,241	NA	NA	1,561	95.8	0.0	0.6	0.0	3.6	16.9	62.3	20.9	640	90.3	50.9	32.0
Allen CDP	210	NA	NA	88	53.4	46.6	0.0	0.0	0.0	0.0	53.4	46.6	88	46.6	0.0	100.0
Andrews AFB CDP	2,973	NA	NA	3,356	55.5	17.1	3.1	11.4	13.0	41.1	58.5	0.4	943	1.6	18.2	28.3
Annapolis city	38,274	38,856	1.5	38,599	55.9	22.5	1.7	1.5	18.4	21.6	64.7	13.8	15,781	51.6	27.2	49.3
Annapolis Neck CDP	10,950	NA	NA	11,266	80.8	9.1	2.1	3.1	4.9	22.1	58.0	20.0	4,516	85.2	11.3	70.3
Antietam CDP	89	NA	NA	115	78.3	21.7	0.0	0.0	0.0	11.3	69.5	19.1	52	53.8	25.0	61.5
Aquasco CDP	981	NA	NA	758	52.6	43.5	0.0	2.4	1.5	14.4	61.7	24.0	285	81.1	55.4	11.6
Arbutus CDP	20,483	NA	NA	21,404	69.8	12.8	9.0	4.3	4.1	21.1	67.1	11.7	8,019	67.6	35.3	31.9
Arden on the Severn CDP	1,953	NA	NA	2,245	96.7	0.0	0.0	1.1	2.1	22.1	67.2	10.7	873	94.0	23.9	54.8
Arnold CDP	23,106	NA	NA	23,131	86.2	3.5	3.0	3.1	4.1	25.1	60.9	14.0	8,215	83.9	18.3	54.6
Ashton-Sandy Spring CDP	5,628	NA	NA	5,555	62.6	15.0	8.9	4.2	9.2	22.3	57.4	19.9	1,838	84.1	16.5	65.8
Aspen Hill CDP	48,759	NA	NA	51,603	34.4	21.9	10.3	3.0	30.3	23.9	63.2	12.9	17,003	64.1	28.0	47.5
Baden CDP	2,128	NA	NA	1,942	53.5	42.8	0.7	1.0	2.0	18.1	59.6	22.3	753	91.5	46.6	24.8
Bagtown CDP	333	NA	NA	249	78.7	0.0	0.0	10.0	11.2	15.6	67.3	16.9	118	100.0	61.9	9.3
Bakersville CDP	30	NA	NA	0	0.0	0.0	0.0	0.0	0.0	0.0	0.0	0.0	0	0.0	0.0	0.0
Ballenger Creek CDP	18,274	NA	NA	18,400	59.1	18.1	8.3	3.3	11.1	26.5	65.1	8.4	6,904	62.4	23.5	38.9
Baltimore city	621,121	622,793	0.3	622,271	28.1	62.5	2.5	2.5	4.5	21.3	66.8	11.9	242,212	47.2	43.1	30.9
Baltimore Highlands CDP	7,019	NA	NA	7,078	50.5	21.5	3.6	3.2	21.1	26.9	63.5	9.6	2,383	50.4	60.9	6.7
Barclay town	120	119	-0.8	54	94.4	0.0	0.0	0.0	5.6	3.7	77.9	18.5	36	83.3	61.1	22.2
Barnesville town	172	178	3.5	160	84.4	1.3	3.1	0.0	11.3	23.2	60.7	16.3	47	87.2	6.4	61.7
Barrelville CDP	73	NA	NA	83	100.0	0.0	0.0	0.0	0.0	32.6	60.2	7.2	29	100.0	75.9	24.1
Barton town	454	437	-3.7	537	97.0	0.0	0.9	0.9	1.1	28.4	55.8	16.0	203	71.4	52.7	7.9
Bartonsville CDP	1,451	NA	NA	1,387	68.8	15.6	0.0	4.8	10.7	26.4	63.0	10.5	488	93.2	27.9	47.1
Beaver Creek CDP	251	NA	NA	97	100.0	0.0	0.0	0.0	0.0	19.6	59.8	20.6	58	86.2	50.0	36.2
Bel Air CDP	1,258	NA	NA	1,119	89.1	0.1	1.3	1.2	8.3	22.6	53.4	24.0	523	80.7	29.1	38.4
Bel Air town	10,132	10,264	1.3	10,240	86.0	4.8	3.6	2.7	2.9	24.4	58.9	16.7	4,201	66.8	23.7	40.6
Bel Air North CDP	30,568	NA	NA	30,758	90.0	3.3	2.2	2.0	2.5	25.6	62.2	12.3	10,434	89.7	21.6	47.8
Bel Air South CDP	47,709	NA	NA	46,614	83.5	6.5	4.2	1.9	4.0	24.5	62.6	12.9	17,757	81.5	25.8	43.4
Beltsville CDP	16,772	NA	NA	17,580	24.1	34.4	12.2	3.5	25.8	25.1	62.4	12.5	5,693	64.1	37.6	32.5
Benedict CDP	261	NA	NA	372	90.9	0.0	0.0	9.1	0.0	0.0	51.4	48.7	160	90.0	46.9	37.5
Bensville CDP	0	NA	NA	12,024	40.3	46.5	3.2	3.3	6.7	29.3	61.4	9.2	4,030	92.1	25.1	48.0
Berlin town	4,486	4,552	1.5	4,520	68.9	21.1	1.5	2.1	6.4	22.8	60.4	16.8	1,635	66.2	38.5	30.9
Berwyn Heights town	3,123	3,262	4.5	3,201	47.8	12.2	7.2	3.0	29.8	22.5	66.0	11.4	1,002	86.7	28.3	45.6
Bethesda CDP	60,858	NA	NA	62,024	76.8	2.4	10.5	3.0	7.3	23.0	59.0	18.1	25,141	68.3	5.5	84.9
Betterton town	345	334	-3.2	337	90.8	1.8	0.0	7.4	0.0	9.5	79.1	11.6	136	79.4	25.7	33.1
Bier CDP	173	NA	NA	194	100.0	0.0	0.0	0.0	0.0	35.1	57.8	7.2	83	37.3	20.5	0.0
Big Pool CDP	82	NA	NA	53	100.0	0.0	0.0	0.0	0.0	0.0	30.2	69.8	23	100.0	100.0	0.0
Big Spring CDP	84	NA	NA	105	100.0	0.0	0.0	0.0	0.0	6.7	83.8	9.5	56	71.4	50.0	0.0
Bishopville CDP	531	NA	NA	254	81.5	9.8	0.0	8.7	0.0	2.4	62.6	35.0	160	91.3	45.0	20.6
Bivalve CDP	201	NA	NA	266	100.0	0.0	0.0	0.0	0.0	40.3	50.8	9.0	105	52.4	100.0	0.0
Bladensburg town	9,156	9,583	4.7	9,371	3.7	63.9	1.9	0.6	30.0	25.5	64.1	10.3	3,679	21.4	52.4	14.9
Bloomington CDP	305	NA	NA	236	97.0	0.0	0.0	0.0	3.0	7.2	58.9	33.9	100	93.0	84.0	8.0
Boonsboro town	3,444	3,449	0.1	3,452	91.1	3.1	1.9	0.6	3.3	24.0	59.1	16.8	1,280	82.5	33.8	28.0
Bowie city	54,930	57,646	4.9	56,335	38.1	47.0	4.0	4.3	6.7	24.1	64.2	11.7	19,402	85.0	16.4	53.9
Bowleys Quarters CDP	6,755	NA	NA	6,419	88.3	6.3	1.3	1.7	2.4	19.2	67.5	13.2	2,541	69.3	46.3	19.9
Bowling Green CDP	1,077	NA	NA	1,400	78.4	17.5	0.0	2.9	1.2	12.4	72.1	15.5	463	68.9	44.7	19.4
Bowmans Addition CDP	627	NA	NA	717	99.0	0.0	0.0	1.0	0.0	26.7	49.6	23.7	277	92.4	57.8	13.4
Braddock Heights CDP	2,608	NA	NA	2,451	95.5	0.7	0.0	2.6	1.3	19.9	58.8	21.3	1,007	91.1	29.8	46.7
Brandywine CDP	6,719	NA	NA	8,791	20.2	66.9	0.5	4.5	7.8	26.9	64.6	8.7	2,769	89.8	25.9	32.5
Breathedsville CDP	254	NA	NA	321	100.0	0.0	0.0	0.0	0.0	25.3	64.9	10.0	153	52.3	42.5	46.4
Brentwood town	3,046	3,174	4.2	3,107	10.4	36.5	1.2	1.5	50.4	21.2	69.5	9.3	927	50.9	56.6	22.8
Brock Hall CDP	9,552	NA	NA	10,427	4.5	85.3	1.1	3.6	5.6	28.4	63.9	7.6	3,377	86.7	10.2	62.5
Brookeville town	134	138	3.0	156	98.1	0.0	0.0	0.0	1.9	20.5	59.0	20.5	51	90.2	15.7	68.6
Brooklyn Park CDP	14,373	NA	NA	14,136	70.9	16.4	3.2	5.6	3.9	22.9	61.3	15.8	5,046	75.9	53.0	15.0
Brookmont CDP	3,468	NA	NA	3,758	85.1	3.3	6.5	2.6	2.4	26.8	56.4	16.8	1,377	77.3	4.9	93.0
Brookview town	60	59	-1.7	58	93.1	6.9	0.0	0.0	0.0	17.3	65.4	17.2	25	92.0	40.0	12.0
Broomes Island CDP	405	NA	NA	433	100.0	0.0	0.0	0.0	0.0	27.5	53.9	18.7	152	100.0	23.7	18.4
Brownsville CDP	89	NA	NA	309	100.0	0.0	0.0	0.0	0.0	33.0	67.0	0.0	98	100.0	0.0	51.0
Brunswick city	5,870	6,102	4.0	6,006	88.8	4.8	0.1	2.2	4.2	27.2	61.3	11.4	2,212	73.6	41.4	31.0
Bryans Road CDP	7,244	NA	NA	7,772	37.8	51.9	1.9	5.0	3.4	24.6	64.4	11.1	2,650	85.5	34.9	22.9
Bryantown CDP	655	NA	NA	825	69.2	15.5	0.0	15.3	0.0	25.0	54.3	20.6	260	92.7	26.2	37.3
Buckeystown CDP	1,019	NA	NA	1,017	97.9	0.0	0.0	1.0	1.1	16.2	44.1	39.7	538	51.7	28.6	60.2
Burkittsville town	151	156	3.3	153	98.7	0.0	0.0	1.3	0.0	17.6	67.4	15.0	69	60.9	40.6	36.2
Burtonsville CDP	8,323	NA	NA	8,541	29.4	35.9	17.1	7.5	10.1	26.0	65.0	9.1	2,905	79.4	14.6	62.9
Butlertown CDP	505	NA	NA	356	37.9	60.4	0.0	1.7	0.0	31.4	53.9	14.6	119	93.3	74.8	5.9
Cabin John CDP	2,280	NA	NA	2,135	85.4	0.7	4.5	6.2	3.1	23.2	65.0	11.9	791	97.7	14.7	73.6
California CDP	11,857	NA	NA	12,132	70.3	16.0	3.0	3.1	7.7	27.3	64.3	8.4	4,625	66.7	26.6	42.8
Calvert Beach CDP	808	NA	NA	717	84.0	7.4	3.9	2.9	1.8	22.9	64.1	13.0	253	80.6	34.8	26.1
Calverton CDP	17,724	NA	NA	18,488	29.6	36.6	14.7	2.9	16.2	20.7	57.3	21.9	6,925	64.9	18.3	58.8
Cambridge city	12,382	12,569	1.5	12,511	42.6	49.5	1.4	1.9	4.6	24.9	60.0	15.3	5,215	38.8	52.4	19.1
Camp Springs CDP	19,096	NA	NA	19,600	10.8	77.0	3.5	2.8	6.0	21.3	64.9	13.8	7,191	79.7	33.3	33.7
Cape St. Claire CDP	8,747	NA	NA	8,858	86.3	2.3	3.4	2.1	5.9	27.1	62.6	10.5	3,203	84.7	21.6	46.1
Capitol Heights town	4,337	4,546	4.8	4,452	2.1	91.4	0.0	1.9	4.6	23.1	65.0	11.7	1,463	73.4	49.1	14.5
Carlos CDP	153	NA	NA	123	100.0	0.0	0.0	0.0	0.0	21.1	62.5	16.3	45	100.0	66.7	0.0
Carney CDP	29,941	NA	NA	28,194	72.7	14.8	6.2	2.5	3.8	20.3	61.0	18.9	12,278	57.5	35.3	32.3
Catonsville CDP	41,567	NA	NA	42,437	73.8	14.0	4.7	2.2	5.3	20.2	62.8	16.9	15,145	68.1	25.1	49.8
Cavetown CDP	1,473	NA	NA	1,665	90.4	0.7	2.7	1.0	5.2	24.0	55.1	20.8	540	86.9	47.6	24.3
Cearfoss CDP	178	NA	NA	155	100.0	0.0	0.0	0.0	0.0	25.1	67.1	7.7	46	78.3	47.8	0.0
Cecilton town	663	672	1.4	675	71.6	23.0	0.0	0.0	5.5	30.4	62.1	7.4	245	49.0	60.8	10.6
Cedarville CDP	717	NA	NA	610	70.3	14.3	0.0	15.4	0.0	5.2	60.4	34.4	298	82.2	52.0	2.3
Centreville town	4,285	4,574	6.7	4,451	88.3	10.2	0.0	0.0	1.4	26.2	54.2	19.5	1,605	76.7	21.4	51.5
Chance CDP	353	NA	NA	300	81.0	16.3	0.0	0.0	2.7	6.0	32.9	61.0	154	98.1	55.2	22.1

1 May be of any race.

Table A. All Places — **Population and Housing**

STATE City, town, township, borough, or CDP (county if applicable)	Population: 2010 census total population	Population: 2014 estimated population	Population: Percent change 2010–2014	Population: ACS total population estimate 2010–2014	Race and Hispanic or Latino origin (percent), 2010–2014: White alone, not Hispanic or Latino	Black alone, not Hispanic or Latino	Asian alone, not Hispanic or Latino	All other races or 2 or more races, not Hispanic or Latino	Hispanic or Latino[1]	Age (percent), 2010–2014: Under 18 years old	Age 18 to 64 years old	Age 65 years and older	Households, 2010–2014: Total occupied housing units	Percent owner occupied	Householders by level of education (percent): High school diploma or less	Bachelor's degree or more
	1	2	3	4	5	6	7	8	9	10	11	12	13	14	15	16
MARYLAND—Con.																
Charlestown town	1,183	1,197	1.2	1,085	96.5	3.5	0.0	0.0	0.0	22.7	62.1	15.1	427	90.2	45.0	18.5
Charlotte Hall CDP	1,420	NA	NA	1,403	71.2	25.9	0.4	2.5	0.0	19.1	45.5	35.4	334	74.6	65.0	3.3
Charlton CDP	171	NA	NA	161	60.9	0.0	6.8	32.3	0.0	32.3	46.6	21.1	58	100.0	39.7	25.9
Chesapeake Beach town	5,753	5,874	2.1	5,816	84.9	7.5	0.2	5.3	2.1	29.9	65.2	5.0	2,060	69.6	29.1	32.8
Chesapeake City town	683	690	1.0	703	89.3	6.8	0.0	3.1	0.7	18.5	59.3	22.2	327	65.1	37.0	31.5
Chesapeake Ranch Estates CDP	10,519	NA	NA	10,385	79.5	10.8	1.7	4.3	3.7	31.7	63.5	4.8	3,368	81.6	29.0	26.5
Chester CDP	4,167	NA	NA	4,520	84.9	3.8	1.0	5.9	4.3	17.4	65.0	17.5	1,822	77.7	24.4	43.2
Chestertown town	5,252	5,125	-2.4	5,221	71.8	22.1	2.9	0.9	2.3	11.7	61.4	26.8	1,868	49.7	33.5	36.4
Cheverly town	6,173	6,449	4.5	6,307	26.8	61.6	0.6	1.7	9.3	23.1	66.0	10.8	2,379	71.3	26.8	52.0
Chevy Chase town	2,824	2,959	4.8	2,907	88.5	0.6	2.2	3.9	4.8	28.0	57.3	14.7	1,034	95.4	1.0	95.2
Chevy Chase CDP	9,545	NA	NA	9,435	78.4	4.2	5.8	3.1	8.5	24.2	54.6	21.2	3,675	73.9	4.7	86.4
Chevy Chase Section Five village	658	689	4.7	736	93.9	0.3	0.3	2.0	3.5	27.2	56.1	16.7	246	95.9	0.8	91.1
Chevy Chase Section Three village	760	794	4.5	708	87.3	2.5	3.0	4.5	2.7	28.4	57.4	14.3	240	97.9	2.1	94.2
Chevy Chase View town	920	969	5.3	939	91.1	1.2	2.3	1.2	4.3	27.1	56.5	16.3	322	96.3	1.9	91.6
Chevy Chase Village town	1,953	2,047	4.8	1,974	93.9	0.0	1.0	2.9	2.2	25.0	54.9	20.3	683	96.9	2.5	94.6
Chewsville CDP	238	NA	NA	137	89.1	0.0	0.0	10.9	0.0	21.9	70.8	7.3	71	87.3	52.1	11.3
Chillum CDP	33,513	NA	NA	36,684	3.4	47.3	1.8	0.9	46.7	23.8	67.4	8.9	11,051	38.7	51.8	23.0
Choptank CDP	129	NA	NA	136	84.6	0.0	15.4	0.0	0.0	3.7	70.7	25.7	62	80.6	62.9	37.1
Church Creek town	125	124	-0.8	149	83.9	0.0	0.7	10.1	5.4	16.2	66.4	17.4	71	74.6	46.5	28.2
Church Hill town	745	736	-1.2	952	76.8	8.9	0.1	2.8	11.3	31.1	56.3	12.6	318	68.2	53.1	22.3
Clarksburg CDP	13,766	NA	NA	15,941	39.9	12.7	32.8	4.0	10.6	32.7	61.6	5.6	4,808	89.2	8.6	67.6
Clarysville CDP	73	NA	NA	103	100.0	0.0	0.0	0.0	0.0	26.2	47.5	26.2	37	100.0	37.8	0.0
Clear Spring town	358	353	-1.4	423	96.5	0.0	0.0	0.0	3.5	17.9	68.1	13.9	161	46.6	60.2	7.5
Clinton CDP	35,970	NA	NA	38,873	7.9	81.6	2.6	1.9	6.0	22.3	64.9	12.6	12,721	88.1	31.7	31.9
Cloverly CDP	15,126	NA	NA	15,467	40.3	28.3	17.4	3.1	10.9	22.9	61.9	15.2	4,840	91.7	16.4	64.6
Cobb Island CDP	1,166	NA	NA	662	93.5	1.2	3.9	1.4	0.0	16.8	50.2	33.1	292	82.2	44.2	15.8
Cockeysville CDP	20,776	NA	NA	21,006	58.9	17.1	13.4	3.5	7.1	20.4	66.9	12.8	9,208	34.9	19.5	49.4
Colesville CDP	14,647	NA	NA	14,574	35.1	26.5	19.9	5.6	12.9	22.1	59.2	18.7	4,860	91.9	24.3	56.9
College Park city	30,413	32,256	6.1	31,387	55.8	17.3	13.5	2.7	10.7	9.4	85.2	5.4	6,580	46.8	23.0	45.6
Colmar Manor town	1,404	1,460	4.0	1,737	5.7	33.8	9.3	0.4	50.8	29.5	63.1	7.3	407	80.3	58.2	15.7
Columbia CDP	99,615	NA	NA	102,116	50.1	25.2	12.2	4.1	8.4	23.3	64.5	12.1	39,978	66.3	12.8	67.3
Coral Hills CDP	9,895	NA	NA	10,196	3.1	87.6	0.0	1.0	8.3	26.4	64.4	9.2	3,657	57.0	53.4	14.5
Cordova CDP	562	NA	NA	601	98.3	1.0	0.7	0.0	0.0	18.3	67.9	14.0	262	67.6	56.1	9.9
Corriganville CDP	455	NA	NA	391	100.0	0.0	0.0	0.0	0.0	23.7	54.0	22.3	163	71.8	62.0	6.1
Cottage City town	1,305	1,363	4.4	1,070	17.7	37.6	3.0	2.5	39.3	19.7	62.7	17.7	429	64.8	57.6	19.8
Crellin CDP	264	NA	NA	192	100.0	0.0	0.0	0.0	0.0	23.5	70.9	5.7	100	70.0	58.0	30.0
Cresaptown CDP	4,592	NA	NA	5,048	68.2	27.2	0.7	2.1	1.9	12.1	75.3	12.4	1,195	88.5	48.5	15.0
Crisfield city	2,727	2,671	-2.1	2,698	55.2	38.3	0.5	4.1	1.9	30.3	50.5	19.1	1,034	44.3	59.4	17.3
Crofton CDP	27,348	NA	NA	28,140	75.7	11.7	3.8	3.8	5.0	27.0	64.5	8.6	10,312	78.9	13.4	58.9
Croom CDP	2,631	NA	NA	3,028	51.1	33.7	1.5	2.2	11.5	17.4	68.8	13.8	933	90.4	42.4	30.2
Crownsville CDP	1,757	NA	NA	2,070	92.6	6.4	0.0	0.0	1.0	23.0	64.8	12.0	662	82.5	28.5	51.2
Cumberland city	20,830	20,235	-2.9	20,557	88.2	6.7	1.1	2.7	1.3	21.6	59.0	19.6	8,892	56.6	50.9	17.8
Damascus CDP	15,257	NA	NA	15,094	70.4	8.0	7.0	3.3	11.2	27.1	64.3	8.4	4,840	90.1	22.1	50.9
Dames Quarter CDP	167	NA	NA	177	94.9	5.1	0.0	0.0	0.0	24.3	65.1	10.7	86	86.0	37.2	9.3
Danville CDP	271	NA	NA	344	100.0	0.0	0.0	0.0	0.0	11.3	81.3	7.3	141	92.9	80.1	0.0
Dargan CDP	165	NA	NA	182	100.0	0.0	0.0	0.0	0.0	16.5	72.5	11.0	87	79.3	70.1	0.0
Darlington CDP	409	NA	NA	495	100.0	0.0	0.0	0.0	0.0	14.7	61.8	23.4	171	81.3	49.1	18.7
Darnestown CDP	6,802	NA	NA	6,841	69.5	3.6	12.6	8.1	6.3	25.3	61.2	13.5	2,221	96.4	15.6	73.8
Dawson CDP	103	NA	NA	108	100.0	0.0	0.0	0.0	0.0	18.6	69.5	12.0	37	78.4	62.2	24.3
Deale CDP	4,945	NA	NA	5,057	86.0	3.6	0.2	3.2	6.9	21.2	64.7	14.0	1,947	86.3	32.5	32.2
Deal Island CDP	471	NA	NA	419	94.7	1.0	0.0	4.3	0.0	8.6	59.0	32.5	233	83.3	48.1	15.9
Deer Park town	395	385	-2.5	427	95.3	0.0	0.2	4.4	0.0	27.6	59.5	12.9	165	72.7	63.0	7.9
Delmar town	2,998	3,021	0.8	3,007	61.4	24.7	3.8	1.3	8.7	27.9	61.4	10.7	1,116	48.7	37.2	22.5
Denton town	4,409	4,344	-1.5	4,361	63.9	23.1	0.7	1.2	11.1	28.7	57.6	13.7	1,460	57.8	47.9	11.6
Derwood CDP	2,381	NA	NA	2,178	40.8	13.2	26.6	10.1	9.2	33.5	57.4	9.1	699	69.1	20.9	66.7
Detmold CDP	71	NA	NA	192	100.0	0.0	0.0	0.0	0.0	32.3	67.8	0.0	47	38.3	0.0	61.7
District Heights city	5,837	6,109	4.7	5,977	3.1	94.0	0.2	1.3	1.4	24.6	63.7	11.7	2,112	70.5	45.9	20.1
Downsville CDP	355	NA	NA	269	100.0	0.0	0.0	0.0	0.0	21.5	62.8	15.6	110	100.0	39.1	23.6
Drum Point CDP	2,731	NA	NA	2,947	87.8	7.0	0.0	0.9	4.4	16.2	70.7	13.2	1,202	82.6	39.1	21.2
Dundalk CDP	63,597	NA	NA	62,186	78.3	10.0	3.0	4.0	4.7	21.8	61.8	16.3	23,786	67.3	59.1	10.1
Dunkirk CDP	0	NA	NA	2,334	81.3	9.0	2.7	4.4	2.7	22.9	64.8	12.4	869	90.8	32.5	33.8
Eagle Harbor town	63	66	4.8	42	35.7	50.0	0.0	14.3	0.0	35.7	50.1	14.3	14	64.3	64.3	0.0
Eakles Mill CDP	27	NA	NA	0	0.0	0.0	0.0	0.0	0.0	0.0	0.0	0.0	0	0.0	0.0	0.0
East New Market town	400	394	-1.5	468	70.9	21.8	0.0	0.9	6.4	26.9	55.7	17.3	161	82.0	44.7	26.7
Easton town	16,190	16,675	3.0	16,541	69.3	15.9	2.5	1.6	10.7	20.7	55.1	24.2	7,163	57.8	39.3	29.3
East Riverdale CDP	15,509	NA	NA	15,975	9.5	32.9	2.0	1.7	54.0	30.7	63.5	5.8	4,368	51.0	60.3	15.4
Eckhart Mines CDP	932	NA	NA	863	100.0	0.0	0.0	0.0	0.0	15.5	65.5	19.0	397	71.8	66.2	10.6
Eden CDP	823	NA	NA	761	58.9	37.1	4.1	0.0	0.0	7.0	71.3	21.8	436	81.9	66.3	6.4
Edesville CDP	169	NA	NA	145	91.0	9.0	0.0	0.0	0.0	9.0	68.8	22.1	71	81.7	71.8	0.0
Edgemere CDP	8,669	NA	NA	8,295	91.9	4.5	0.0	1.4	2.2	17.9	61.7	20.5	3,276	79.4	55.3	12.9
Edgemont CDP	231	NA	NA	210	100.0	0.0	0.0	0.0	0.0	12.8	41.5	45.7	121	100.0	36.4	33.1
Edgewater CDP	9,023	NA	NA	9,192	87.6	1.7	2.8	2.5	5.4	22.3	64.6	13.1	3,548	82.5	30.7	37.3
Edgewood CDP	25,562	NA	NA	26,479	46.8	39.3	1.9	5.0	6.9	28.6	62.5	8.8	9,422	67.9	42.2	19.3
Edmonston town	1,445	1,509	4.4	1,395	18.4	33.5	1.0	2.5	44.6	21.7	71.4	6.7	485	64.1	54.6	20.2
Eldersburg CDP	30,531	NA	NA	31,799	88.8	3.5	2.8	2.6	2.3	24.9	60.5	14.5	10,660	89.5	22.5	49.0
Eldorado town	59	58	-1.7	100	74.0	0.0	0.0	26.0	0.0	41.0	56.0	3.0	28	78.6	50.0	0.0
Elkridge CDP	15,593	NA	NA	16,750	54.6	23.6	9.7	3.1	9.0	25.8	68.1	6.1	6,097	69.7	24.4	53.7
Elkton town	15,515	15,852	2.2	15,673	76.3	13.4	3.2	0.6	6.5	26.3	63.3	10.5	5,454	53.0	45.4	28.2
Ellerslie CDP	572	NA	NA	482	85.9	0.0	0.0	3.5	10.6	21.4	54.0	24.7	191	87.4	57.1	15.7
Ellicott City CDP	65,834	NA	NA	68,507	59.9	9.4	23.6	2.9	4.1	26.2	60.6	13.2	24,261	75.1	14.1	68.4
Elliott CDP	52	NA	NA	20	100.0	0.0	0.0	0.0	0.0	0.0	70.0	30.0	16	100.0	75.0	0.0
Emmitsburg town	2,814	3,026	7.5	3,001	92.4	2.1	3.7	0.4	1.4	28.1	54.2	17.9	1,097	69.1	38.8	23.2
Ernstville CDP	56	NA	NA	0	0.0	0.0	0.0	0.0	0.0	0.0	0.0	0.0	0	0.0	0.0	0.0
Essex CDP	39,262	NA	NA	37,380	65.5	25.1	1.9	2.3	5.2	22.8	63.4	13.9	14,704	55.9	55.8	12.2
Fairland CDP	23,681	NA	NA	24,127	17.3	53.5	15.2	4.7	9.2	25.2	66.9	7.9	8,694	46.8	20.4	49.7
Fairlee CDP	490	NA	NA	276	82.6	5.4	0.0	12.0	0.0	32.7	54.7	12.7	97	59.8	33.0	26.8
Fairmount CDP	457	NA	NA	313	90.7	9.3	0.0	0.0	0.0	5.8	54.5	39.6	210	66.7	69.5	6.2
Fairmount Heights town	1,494	1,561	4.5	1,529	1.1	81.6	1.8	3.5	11.9	21.5	65.5	12.8	558	69.0	53.2	14.7
Fairplay CDP	580	NA	NA	417	100.0	0.0	0.0	0.0	0.0	16.8	74.7	8.6	160	76.3	18.8	7.5

1 May be of any race.

Table A. All Places — **Population and Housing**

STATE City, town, township, borough, or CDP (county if applicable)	Population				Race and Hispanic or Latino origin (percent), 2010–2014					Age (percent), 2010–2014			Households, 2010–2014			
	2010 census total population	2014 estimated population	Percent change 2010–2014	ACS total population estimate 2010–2014	White alone, not Hispanic or Latino	Black alone, not Hispanic or Latino	Asian alone, not Hispanic or Latino	All other races or 2 or more races, not Hispanic or Latino	Hispanic or Latino[1]	Under 18 years old	Age 18 to 64 years old	Age 65 years and older	Total occupied housing units	Percent owner occupied	Householders by level of education (percent): High school diploma or less	Householders by level of education (percent): Bachelor's degree or more
	1	2	3	4	5	6	7	8	9	10	11	12	13	14	15	16
MARYLAND—Con.																
Fairview CDP	76	NA	NA	0	0.0	0.0	0.0	0.0	0.0	0.0	0.0	0.0	0	0.0	0.0	0.0
Fairwood CDP	5,031	NA	NA	5,249	13.7	70.5	10.9	2.4	2.4	25.0	65.8	9.3	1,621	92.5	7.0	74.2
Fallston CDP	8,958	NA	NA	9,056	97.6	0.0	0.0	0.8	1.6	22.6	59.0	18.5	3,071	95.0	14.8	48.6
Federalsburg town	2,738	2,667	-2.6	2,695	53.4	41.9	0.0	3.7	0.9	31.0	55.2	13.7	936	46.5	59.9	12.5
Ferndale CDP	16,746	NA	NA	18,577	56.8	18.7	4.9	4.3	15.4	23.1	64.2	12.6	6,510	61.1	45.8	19.4
Finzel CDP	547	NA	NA	539	100.0	0.0	0.0	0.0	0.0	20.2	45.8	34.1	238	89.5	73.1	5.9
Fishing Creek CDP	163	NA	NA	121	94.2	0.0	5.8	0.0	0.0	0.0	65.2	34.7	55	100.0	50.9	14.5
Flintstone CDP	177	NA	NA	160	81.3	0.0	18.8	0.0	0.0	5.0	73.8	21.3	87	74.7	12.6	33.3
Forest Glen CDP	6,582	NA	NA	7,393	48.4	21.3	5.4	5.6	19.4	22.3	64.8	13.0	2,830	62.2	20.7	65.3
Forest Heights town	2,447	2,559	4.6	2,496	5.6	71.4	5.8	1.6	15.7	20.9	62.3	16.8	881	84.2	43.8	19.5
Forestville CDP	12,353	NA	NA	11,286	3.7	87.9	0.2	2.1	6.1	22.4	65.7	12.0	4,389	67.1	50.3	20.0
Fort Meade CDP	9,327	NA	NA	9,809	56.2	19.4	2.6	6.1	15.6	40.1	59.6	0.2	2,577	1.4	9.5	24.6
Fort Ritchie CDP	314	NA	NA	306	98.0	0.0	0.0	2.0	0.0	39.2	58.2	2.6	94	8.5	42.6	18.1
Fort Washington CDP	23,717	NA	NA	24,062	12.6	66.9	9.1	4.2	7.2	18.5	62.2	19.3	8,525	87.7	22.1	44.4
Fountainhead-Orchard Hills CDP	5,666	NA	NA	5,754	85.6	5.5	2.9	1.7	4.3	22.8	59.9	17.3	2,320	74.0	28.7	39.9
Four Corners CDP	7,945	NA	NA	8,486	57.2	8.9	8.2	3.5	22.2	26.2	60.9	12.9	2,773	82.1	19.6	63.6
Franklin CDP	290	NA	NA	282	98.9	1.1	0.0	0.0	0.0	11.0	25.9	63.1	93	35.5	80.6	0.0
Frederick city	65,287	68,400	4.8	66,646	55.1	18.2	6.2	4.2	16.3	23.3	65.5	11.1	26,157	53.6	28.0	40.3
Frenchtown-Rumbly CDP	100	NA	NA	29	100.0	0.0	0.0	0.0	0.0	0.0	48.3	51.7	15	100.0	46.7	53.3
Friendly CDP	9,250	NA	NA	9,881	8.0	74.2	2.9	1.3	13.6	21.9	65.8	12.3	3,155	93.0	36.4	31.2
Friendship CDP	447	NA	NA	287	100.0	0.0	0.0	0.0	0.0	13.6	43.9	42.5	138	88.4	32.6	35.5
Friendship Heights Village CDP	4,698	NA	NA	4,829	74.5	2.2	12.5	1.2	9.6	6.9	58.6	34.6	3,390	34.1	5.8	84.1
Friendsville town	491	480	-2.2	502	97.0	0.0	0.0	1.8	1.2	21.0	64.5	14.7	211	66.4	60.7	13.3
Frostburg city	8,978	8,684	-3.3	8,802	83.2	10.5	2.4	3.0	0.9	12.6	73.5	13.7	3,201	41.4	33.7	26.1
Fruitland city	4,842	5,121	5.8	5,028	65.6	21.0	7.2	3.0	3.2	24.8	62.3	12.8	1,928	64.5	43.7	34.8
Fulton CDP	2,049	NA	NA	2,114	75.0	8.0	12.7	3.7	0.6	24.2	56.0	20.0	675	97.3	19.0	66.4
Funkstown town	885	887	0.2	963	92.2	1.9	0.0	0.8	5.1	23.2	66.4	10.5	374	50.8	50.3	11.8
Gaithersburg city	59,897	66,816	11.6	63,491	37.7	16.0	18.6	3.5	24.1	25.3	64.3	10.4	22,818	55.3	21.8	56.3
Galena town	612	601	-1.8	822	81.0	1.6	0.1	2.2	15.1	25.8	56.7	17.6	306	73.5	51.0	22.9
Galestown town	138	137	-0.7	132	78.8	0.0	17.4	3.8	0.0	18.9	71.2	9.8	65	60.0	58.5	10.8
Galesville CDP	684	NA	NA	707	89.8	10.2	0.0	0.0	0.0	1.8	63.9	34.4	322	79.2	32.9	20.2
Gambrills CDP	2,800	NA	NA	2,619	77.5	7.8	9.0	1.6	4.1	21.0	62.6	16.5	924	95.3	25.9	48.2
Gapland CDP	109	NA	NA	78	100.0	0.0	0.0	0.0	0.0	17.9	82.2	0.0	45	57.8	28.9	0.0
Garrett Park town	987	1,036	5.0	1,090	82.2	3.5	2.8	1.6	10.0	27.3	55.0	17.5	375	89.1	2.4	86.4
Garretts Mill CDP	234	NA	NA	391	100.0	0.0	0.0	0.0	0.0	26.4	39.1	34.5	159	90.6	75.5	12.6
Garrison CDP	8,823	NA	NA	8,139	60.9	29.2	6.0	2.6	1.3	22.9	62.8	14.3	3,353	57.9	17.1	56.9
Georgetown CDP	143	NA	NA	139	71.2	28.8	0.0	0.0	0.0	12.9	49.7	37.4	64	100.0	84.4	0.0
Germantown CDP	86,395	NA	NA	88,717	33.8	21.7	20.1	4.0	20.5	27.0	67.0	5.9	31,324	67.5	19.8	51.8
Gilmore CDP	127	NA	NA	130	100.0	0.0	0.0	0.0	0.0	5.4	82.3	12.3	54	51.9	51.9	0.0
Girdletree CDP	149	NA	NA	179	73.2	17.3	0.0	0.0	9.5	28.0	63.1	8.9	98	36.7	24.5	18.4
Glassmanor CDP	17,295	NA	NA	18,389	1.3	84.0	1.0	2.0	11.7	24.1	68.5	7.4	6,452	32.0	51.5	15.9
Glenarden city	6,000	6,290	4.8	6,145	0.0	88.7	3.7	2.0	5.6	26.4	60.5	13.0	2,098	67.0	45.9	29.1
Glen Burnie CDP	67,639	NA	NA	67,559	59.3	23.4	4.7	4.8	7.7	20.7	67.1	12.3	26,611	59.4	41.3	20.8
Glen Echo town	255	269	5.5	255	90.2	0.4	4.7	2.7	2.0	28.6	55.4	16.1	99	93.9	1.0	93.9
Glenmont CDP	13,529	NA	NA	15,412	26.2	24.9	9.8	3.2	35.9	22.4	64.8	12.8	5,047	60.7	33.2	47.0
Glenn Dale CDP	13,466	NA	NA	13,584	18.6	59.3	6.2	3.7	12.2	21.7	66.6	11.6	4,506	81.8	22.8	46.0
Golden Beach CDP	3,796	NA	NA	3,820	85.7	6.1	1.0	4.7	2.5	22.0	63.7	14.3	1,256	85.1	51.8	8.0
Goldsboro town	246	241	-2.0	165	86.7	0.0	0.0	0.0	13.3	27.3	52.8	20.0	67	68.7	76.1	7.5
Gorman CDP	106	NA	NA	35	100.0	0.0	0.0	0.0	0.0	0.0	0.0	100.0	17	100.0	100.0	0.0
Grahamtown CDP	364	NA	NA	280	97.5	2.5	0.0	0.0	0.0	11.1	80.2	8.9	150	68.7	38.0	8.7
Grantsville town	767	769	0.3	802	98.6	0.0	0.0	0.5	0.9	17.9	61.0	20.9	386	45.9	43.0	19.2
Grasonville CDP	3,425	NA	NA	3,379	77.3	14.3	0.8	2.7	5.0	26.9	63.7	9.4	1,138	80.5	42.8	29.9
Greenbelt city	23,048	24,125	4.7	23,612	24.2	48.8	8.0	3.7	15.2	23.6	68.2	8.1	9,264	45.5	25.6	46.4
Greensboro town	1,906	1,859	-2.5	2,195	80.7	12.0	0.1	3.7	3.6	30.0	61.7	8.3	729	63.2	48.8	17.6
Greensburg CDP	229	NA	NA	216	100.0	0.0	0.0	0.0	0.0	12.5	78.4	9.3	91	76.9	54.9	33.0
Hagerstown city	39,729	40,364	1.6	40,295	70.1	17.0	2.0	4.9	5.9	26.1	62.1	11.8	16,295	38.9	46.8	18.6
Halfway CDP	10,701	NA	NA	10,609	86.8	4.7	2.6	2.9	3.0	25.1	58.9	16.1	4,204	70.6	49.0	21.6
Hampstead town	6,326	6,363	0.6	6,342	96.3	0.3	0.2	1.6	1.6	30.2	60.4	9.4	2,340	79.7	34.4	31.0
Hampton CDP	5,052	NA	NA	4,968	90.7	2.0	2.9	0.9	3.5	21.5	53.7	24.6	1,855	96.8	12.7	67.0
Hancock town	1,562	1,555	-0.4	1,776	96.6	0.1	0.7	2.4	0.3	25.0	59.7	15.5	746	53.6	66.0	6.4
Havre de Grace city	12,982	13,512	4.1	13,360	73.3	16.2	3.2	3.3	4.0	18.7	63.9	17.3	5,730	62.5	34.9	38.9
Hebron town	1,084	1,085	0.1	994	80.6	15.6	0.0	3.2	0.6	27.9	57.8	13.9	380	75.0	37.9	26.8
Henderson town	146	143	-2.1	198	84.3	1.0	0.0	0.5	14.1	21.8	68.3	10.1	69	69.6	94.2	2.9
Herald Harbor CDP	2,603	NA	NA	2,403	95.8	0.0	1.2	0.5	2.5	26.4	63.1	10.6	992	86.7	13.8	53.1
Highfield-Cascade CDP	1,112	NA	NA	972	95.7	0.1	0.0	4.2	0.0	25.1	58.1	17.0	391	92.6	57.8	12.8
Highland CDP	1,034	NA	NA	1,040	96.3	0.0	2.2	1.5	0.0	27.0	59.5	13.5	352	94.0	9.1	87.2
Highland Beach town	96	100	4.2	103	24.3	66.0	2.9	6.8	0.0	7.8	63.2	29.1	44	84.1	22.7	68.2
Hillandale CDP	6,043	NA	NA	5,819	42.7	20.1	11.1	4.8	21.3	21.4	60.0	18.7	1,851	85.7	23.9	57.1
Hillcrest Heights CDP	16,469	NA	NA	15,604	2.8	93.1	0.5	1.2	2.4	22.4	64.6	13.0	6,514	50.8	43.3	18.1
Hillsboro town	161	158	-1.9	107	73.8	3.7	0.0	20.6	1.9	35.5	43.0	21.5	39	84.6	33.3	46.2
Hughesville CDP	2,197	NA	NA	2,556	69.5	17.5	2.9	8.8	1.3	22.7	67.6	9.9	869	78.6	32.9	35.0
Huntingtown CDP	0	NA	NA	3,840	69.8	22.7	0.3	7.2	0.0	29.6	63.8	6.7	1,002	95.0	26.6	47.4
Hurlock town	2,092	2,057	-1.7	2,056	56.6	31.9	0.9	3.5	7.1	26.4	59.2	14.4	796	64.8	57.9	10.9
Hutton CDP	86	NA	NA	70	100.0	0.0	0.0	0.0	0.0	30.0	70.0	0.0	25	100.0	60.0	0.0
Hyattsville city	17,656	18,420	4.3	18,049	25.6	35.6	3.3	2.9	32.5	21.8	70.2	8.1	6,326	45.4	38.4	40.0
Ilchester CDP	23,476	NA	NA	24,959	55.7	13.7	20.2	4.4	6.1	27.3	66.2	6.4	8,627	79.9	13.5	67.9
Indian Head town	3,844	3,873	0.8	3,885	31.9	58.7	0.6	6.7	2.0	27.0	62.9	9.9	1,386	72.9	43.2	19.0
Indian Springs CDP	64	NA	NA	50	100.0	0.0	0.0	0.0	0.0	20.0	80.0	0.0	15	100.0	100.0	0.0
Jarrettsville CDP	2,916	NA	NA	3,408	95.7	0.7	1.3	0.5	1.8	24.0	62.0	14.1	1,070	95.0	34.5	36.6
Jefferson CDP	2,111	NA	NA	2,192	93.4	0.9	2.5	0.0	3.2	21.5	61.7	16.8	888	84.7	28.3	45.8
Jennings CDP	113	NA	NA	80	100.0	0.0	0.0	0.0	0.0	10.0	71.4	18.8	27	100.0	85.2	0.0
Jessup CDP	7,137	NA	NA	7,535	39.3	52.7	0.5	1.9	5.7	5.2	90.1	4.7	644	68.0	61.6	18.8
Jesterville CDP	188	NA	NA	284	44.7	55.3	0.0	0.0	0.0	0.0	84.9	15.1	135	53.3	46.7	9.6
Joppatowne CDP	12,616	NA	NA	12,948	72.2	14.7	2.5	2.1	8.6	23.3	62.0	14.7	4,982	81.0	37.2	31.7
Jugtown CDP	204	NA	NA	204	100.0	0.0	0.0	0.0	0.0	23.0	77.0	0.0	59	88.1	62.7	0.0
Keedysville town	1,155	1,162	0.6	1,274	86.5	4.0	0.2	5.7	3.6	32.1	62.8	5.0	406	84.2	32.0	35.0
Kemp Mill CDP	12,564	NA	NA	11,850	62.9	15.0	7.4	4.7	10.1	25.1	57.3	17.4	4,131	81.6	16.4	67.9
Kemps Mill CDP	126	NA	NA	86	100.0	0.0	0.0	0.0	0.0	0.0	100.1	0.0	50	0.0	100.0	0.0
Kennedyville CDP	199	NA	NA	208	100.0	0.0	0.0	0.0	0.0	32.2	64.6	3.4	112	28.6	17.9	82.1
Kensington town	2,198	2,313	5.2	1,909	77.1	7.9	6.7	2.9	5.6	27.9	54.7	17.3	725	60.8	6.6	80.6

1 May be of any race.

Table A. All Places — **Population and Housing**

STATE City, town, township, borough, or CDP (county if applicable)	Population: 2010 census total population	Population: 2014 estimated population	Population: Percent change 2010–2014	Population: ACS total population estimate 2010–2014	Race and Hispanic or Latino origin (percent), 2010–2014: White alone, not Hispanic or Latino	Black alone, not Hispanic or Latino	Asian alone, not Hispanic or Latino	All other races or 2 or more races, not Hispanic or Latino	Hispanic or Latino[1]	Age (percent), 2010–2014: Under 18 years old	Age 18 to 64 years old	Age 65 years and older	Households, 2010–2014: Total occupied housing units	Percent owner occupied	Householders by level of education (percent): High school diploma or less	Bachelor's degree or more
	1	2	3	4	5	6	7	8	9	10	11	12	13	14	15	16
MARYLAND—Con.																
Kent Narrows CDP	567	NA	NA	436	95.0	0.0	2.8	2.3	0.0	2.8	51.3	45.9	248	54.0	25.8	46.0
Kettering CDP	12,790	NA	NA	13,331	4.4	88.0	3.8	1.8	2.0	19.6	63.1	17.3	5,075	87.6	21.6	41.2
Kingstown CDP	1,733	NA	NA	1,880	82.7	17.3	0.0	0.0	0.0	20.6	57.1	22.1	705	80.1	51.1	32.2
Kingsville CDP	4,318	NA	NA	4,479	97.7	0.7	0.7	0.4	0.4	17.6	60.1	22.3	1,575	96.6	31.0	40.3
Kitzmiller town	321	313	-2.5	307	95.1	0.0	0.0	1.6	3.3	20.8	65.8	13.4	114	83.3	62.3	16.7
Klondike CDP	118	NA	NA	155	100.0	0.0	0.0	0.0	0.0	36.1	57.4	6.5	47	72.3	100.0	0.0
Konterra CDP	2,527	NA	NA	2,712	21.1	47.6	4.9	6.5	20.0	24.0	54.4	21.7	910	90.2	37.3	38.0
Lake Arbor CDP	9,776	NA	NA	11,052	3.2	89.1	3.6	2.0	2.1	24.2	67.9	7.8	4,236	68.5	13.3	51.4
Lake Shore CDP	19,477	NA	NA	19,045	92.1	3.8	0.8	1.7	1.6	22.7	64.1	13.3	7,134	92.8	30.4	35.7
Landover CDP	23,078	NA	NA	23,112	1.5	81.4	1.0	1.1	14.9	28.5	63.0	8.6	8,123	44.6	52.1	15.7
Landover Hills town	1,726	1,801	4.3	2,000	10.0	38.4	3.2	4.9	43.7	30.9	63.2	6.1	539	76.1	52.9	12.4
Langley Park CDP	18,755	NA	NA	21,318	3.9	13.1	1.4	1.2	80.5	20.6	75.8	3.6	5,380	25.3	71.9	14.4
Lanham CDP	10,157	NA	NA	10,102	6.4	60.2	3.6	1.8	28.0	27.2	61.1	11.7	3,062	79.8	41.6	34.4
Lansdowne CDP	8,409	NA	NA	8,714	51.5	33.3	3.1	3.4	8.8	29.1	60.8	10.0	2,975	48.6	61.7	7.7
La Plata town	8,743	8,988	2.8	8,903	60.1	29.6	2.8	2.8	4.8	25.9	60.2	13.6	3,030	69.4	25.0	39.5
Largo CDP	10,709	NA	NA	10,301	3.7	89.7	3.3	1.9	1.3	21.1	69.9	9.1	4,196	60.3	19.6	44.1
Laurel city	25,115	26,160	4.2	25,673	22.6	48.4	7.7	3.4	17.8	23.5	68.8	7.7	9,934	46.8	29.5	43.9
La Vale CDP	3,551	NA	NA	3,117	94.0	2.2	2.3	0.6	0.9	17.7	60.0	22.2	1,303	77.5	35.4	21.7
Layhill CDP	5,169	NA	NA	5,066	27.0	36.4	15.9	5.0	15.7	20.1	61.5	18.3	1,550	89.2	15.6	64.7
Laytonsville town	353	370	4.8	334	82.9	6.3	3.6	2.4	4.8	17.1	67.8	15.3	119	78.2	20.2	59.7
Leisure World CDP	8,749	NA	NA	9,089	68.9	17.4	6.3	2.0	5.5	4.1	25.7	70.4	5,729	81.2	29.3	50.4
Leitersburg CDP	573	NA	NA	633	97.2	2.8	0.0	0.0	0.0	10.5	68.3	21.2	284	96.5	47.2	14.8
Leonardtown town	2,942	3,511	19.3	3,262	71.6	20.4	3.6	2.6	1.8	23.4	56.0	20.7	1,170	54.4	39.1	28.2
Lexington Park CDP	11,626	NA	NA	12,516	50.2	30.2	4.5	5.9	9.1	31.2	63.2	5.5	4,701	45.3	34.1	34.7
Libertytown CDP	950	NA	NA	1,256	92.4	0.0	2.1	5.6	0.0	25.2	63.1	11.5	438	75.3	49.8	28.5
Linganore CDP	8,543	NA	NA	9,154	85.3	4.6	3.1	1.9	5.1	30.4	61.3	8.3	3,032	91.7	17.5	57.8
Linthicum CDP	10,324	NA	NA	10,466	92.6	1.3	3.8	1.5	0.8	20.2	61.7	18.0	3,871	86.4	39.3	27.7
Little Orleans CDP	42	NA	NA	19	100.0	0.0	0.0	0.0	0.0	0.0	0.0	100.0	10	100.0	100.0	0.0
Lochearn CDP	25,333	NA	NA	25,888	12.4	80.3	1.7	1.7	4.0	19.2	63.8	17.1	10,178	67.1	31.6	31.5
Loch Lynn Heights town	552	540	-2.2	729	96.2	0.0	0.0	3.7	0.1	40.3	46.9	12.6	257	52.5	62.6	9.7
Lonaconing town	1,188	1,151	-3.1	1,149	93.4	4.0	0.3	1.8	0.5	21.0	58.4	20.7	436	55.3	62.8	13.3
Long Beach CDP	1,821	NA	NA	2,055	79.1	12.3	0.8	1.7	6.2	21.9	67.1	10.9	667	91.2	22.9	39.3
Luke town	65	64	-1.5	91	94.5	0.0	0.0	0.0	5.5	22.0	57.2	20.9	41	63.4	58.5	7.3
Lusby CDP	1,835	NA	NA	1,504	80.9	6.8	0.0	0.7	11.6	27.2	57.8	15.0	613	70.1	40.3	28.7
Lutherville CDP	6,504	NA	NA	6,476	83.0	1.9	7.8	2.8	4.6	21.0	59.9	19.0	2,574	85.6	20.1	60.2
McCoole CDP	511	NA	NA	514	100.0	0.0	0.0	0.0	0.0	24.1	66.0	9.7	201	88.1	84.1	4.0
Madison CDP	204	NA	NA	197	83.2	6.6	5.1	0.0	5.1	18.3	45.3	36.5	75	100.0	25.3	44.0
Manchester town	4,808	4,821	0.3	4,810	90.6	1.8	0.4	1.5	5.8	27.2	64.2	8.6	1,634	84.4	34.1	31.8
Mapleville CDP	238	NA	NA	243	100.0	0.0	0.0	0.0	0.0	9.9	69.5	20.6	125	100.0	51.2	41.6
Mardela Springs town	347	348	0.3	322	96.3	3.4	0.0	0.3	0.0	20.2	62.7	17.1	133	75.9	52.6	10.5
Marlboro Meadows CDP	3,672	NA	NA	3,577	8.1	86.5	0.7	2.7	2.0	20.4	67.0	12.6	1,222	93.4	31.5	35.0
Marlboro Village CDP	9,438	NA	NA	10,046	4.9	89.0	0.8	1.7	3.5	21.9	73.2	4.9	3,763	80.2	16.9	45.2
Marlow Heights CDP	5,618	NA	NA	5,667	2.3	84.0	4.1	1.3	8.3	24.5	63.7	11.9	2,206	39.2	44.3	16.8
Marlton CDP	9,031	NA	NA	9,460	12.7	82.3	1.0	3.3	0.7	25.8	66.1	8.1	3,323	73.6	23.7	46.9
Martin's Additions village	933	982	5.3	977	89.5	0.6	2.8	2.0	5.1	31.4	54.4	14.0	315	92.7	1.0	93.7
Marydel town	136	134	-1.5	184	35.3	0.0	1.6	0.0	63.0	22.3	55.4	22.3	48	52.1	77.1	0.0
Maryland City CDP	16,093	NA	NA	17,000	33.6	47.2	4.7	2.5	12.0	23.6	70.4	6.2	6,611	59.1	22.4	47.7
Maugansville CDP	3,071	NA	NA	3,077	86.6	7.1	1.2	2.2	3.0	25.6	58.5	15.9	1,211	71.3	42.5	26.3
Mayo CDP	8,298	NA	NA	8,560	91.7	1.8	0.7	3.7	2.1	22.6	64.9	12.4	3,083	89.2	27.1	43.0
Mays Chapel CDP	11,420	NA	NA	11,957	80.7	1.9	13.4	1.6	2.4	22.8	60.3	17.0	4,803	84.3	14.1	67.0
Mechanicsville CDP	1,508	NA	NA	1,708	88.9	9.5	0.2	0.8	0.5	24.1	65.2	10.7	594	81.0	41.9	34.0
Melwood CDP	0	NA	NA	2,720	17.7	76.6	1.7	1.7	2.3	21.3	58.5	20.3	1,157	82.1	39.3	33.0
Mercersville CDP	130	NA	NA	83	100.0	0.0	0.0	0.0	0.0	0.0	65.0	34.9	51	64.7	82.4	0.0
Middleburg CDP	70	NA	NA	19	100.0	0.0	0.0	0.0	0.0	0.0	100.0	0.0	19	100.0	0.0	0.0
Middle River CDP	25,191	NA	NA	26,652	63.8	22.9	2.8	3.1	7.5	24.6	62.3	13.0	9,765	61.5	48.1	17.1
Middletown town	4,278	4,460	4.3	4,396	84.9	1.9	4.7	2.1	6.3	29.4	60.1	10.5	1,433	89.9	19.9	62.9
Midland town	450	432	-4.0	639	96.4	0.0	0.8	2.8	0.0	18.7	61.6	19.7	262	67.2	59.5	10.3
Midlothian CDP	320	NA	NA	299	100.0	0.0	0.0	0.0	0.0	23.7	52.9	23.4	127	100.0	47.2	7.9
Milford Mill CDP	29,042	NA	NA	29,758	7.6	82.6	1.6	2.2	5.9	24.9	64.5	10.6	11,735	47.9	32.4	33.3
Millington town	642	623	-3.0	658	74.6	10.3	1.1	1.8	12.2	22.2	68.0	9.9	210	85.2	61.4	17.1
Mitchellville CDP	10,967	NA	NA	10,819	8.8	80.3	3.1	3.3	4.5	20.0	65.7	14.3	3,670	91.3	16.5	49.9
Monrovia CDP	416	NA	NA	348	81.6	8.3	0.0	10.1	0.0	17.2	74.1	8.6	120	82.5	15.8	48.3
Montgomery Village CDP	32,032	NA	NA	33,027	34.6	22.4	11.6	4.0	27.4	23.9	67.2	9.0	11,731	72.8	22.9	49.3
Morningside town	1,998	2,082	4.2	1,367	21.9	52.9	4.8	4.4	16.0	12.0	77.9	10.2	599	63.6	42.9	35.1
Moscow CDP	240	NA	NA	234	97.9	0.0	0.0	2.1	0.0	6.4	69.7	23.9	107	95.3	62.6	8.4
Mount Aetna CDP	561	NA	NA	700	95.3	0.7	0.1	1.4	2.4	23.6	48.5	28.0	251	86.1	19.5	38.2
Mountain Lake Park town	2,149	2,123	-1.2	2,368	97.8	0.5	0.3	1.3	0.1	22.0	62.8	15.2	942	61.1	46.2	26.2
Mount Airy town	9,286	9,388	1.1	9,333	91.6	1.8	2.1	2.8	1.8	29.0	60.5	10.4	3,201	85.3	25.6	45.0
Mount Briar CDP	160	NA	NA	222	100.0	0.0	0.0	0.0	0.0	23.0	77.1	0.0	86	76.7	23.3	19.8
Mount Lena CDP	515	NA	NA	532	97.0	0.0	3.0	0.0	0.0	10.2	69.8	19.9	192	77.1	40.1	26.6
Mount Rainier city	8,080	8,430	4.3	8,277	12.7	45.9	0.6	3.8	37.0	24.3	69.4	6.4	3,345	27.4	44.1	30.9
Mount Savage CDP	873	NA	NA	791	96.2	3.5	0.0	0.3	0.0	12.8	69.8	17.4	340	85.0	52.6	11.2
Mount Vernon CDP	779	NA	NA	737	92.9	3.1	3.9	0.0	0.0	28.5	52.7	18.7	272	79.8	47.8	14.7
Myersville town	1,630	1,703	4.5	1,859	92.1	1.4	0.3	0.9	5.3	32.5	61.0	6.3	590	88.8	18.3	57.6
Nanticoke CDP	225	NA	NA	328	39.6	60.4	0.0	0.0	0.0	25.3	51.2	23.5	122	65.6	12.3	40.2
Nanticoke Acres CDP	103	NA	NA	167	100.0	0.0	0.0	0.0	0.0	18.0	82.1	0.0	42	61.9	66.7	0.0
National CDP	56	NA	NA	11	100.0	0.0	0.0	0.0	0.0	0.0	100.0	0.0	11	100.0	0.0	0.0
National Harbor CDP	3,788	NA	NA	3,776	9.2	65.1	10.1	3.6	11.9	16.6	75.7	7.6	1,495	51.0	41.3	28.4
Naval Academy CDP	4,802	NA	NA	5,517	70.8	6.1	3.5	7.6	12.0	5.1	94.9	0.1	131	0.0	34.4	62.6
Newark CDP	336	NA	NA	315	94.6	0.0	0.0	0.0	5.4	21.6	67.0	11.4	109	93.6	62.4	30.3
New Carrollton city	12,134	12,708	4.7	12,412	8.1	64.0	2.4	4.3	21.3	26.0	64.4	9.5	4,141	56.7	41.9	28.1
New Market town	664	693	4.4	699	85.6	1.6	4.7	3.3	4.9	29.8	61.6	8.6	253	83.8	27.7	45.1
New Windsor town	1,396	1,402	0.4	1,237	91.6	3.6	0.4	3.0	1.5	27.4	61.6	11.0	461	79.8	39.5	28.0
Nikep CDP	116	NA	NA	72	100.0	0.0	0.0	0.0	0.0	27.8	43.0	29.2	23	56.5	0.0	0.0
North Beach town	1,978	2,015	1.9	2,183	79.8	6.3	0.6	8.8	4.5	23.3	63.5	13.3	964	43.9	40.0	29.8
North Bethesda CDP	43,828	NA	NA	46,738	61.8	6.6	14.6	3.5	13.5	18.6	65.9	15.8	20,347	52.6	9.7	75.9
North Brentwood town	517	538	4.1	509	5.1	58.5	3.3	1.2	31.8	16.9	68.6	14.5	164	84.1	51.8	22.6
North Chevy Chase village	555	585	5.4	596	83.4	6.2	3.4	1.2	5.9	23.0	60.0	16.9	216	92.1	3.7	88.0
North East town	3,660	3,715	1.5	3,696	86.2	8.7	0.6	1.1	3.5	21.1	66.2	12.7	1,533	51.9	43.9	29.7
North Kensington CDP	9,514	NA	NA	9,850	50.2	9.3	8.9	5.9	25.8	22.1	62.9	15.0	3,576	73.0	23.0	56.4
North Laurel CDP	4,474	NA	NA	21,437	35.6	36.6	14.9	5.8	7.1	28.2	66.5	5.3	7,578	58.6	19.7	51.7

1 May be of any race.

Table A. All Places — **Population and Housing**

STATE City, town, township, borough, or CDP (county if applicable)	Population: 2010 census total population	Population: 2014 estimated population	Population: Percent change 2010–2014	Population: ACS total population estimate 2010–2014	Race and Hispanic or Latino origin (percent), 2010–2014: White alone, not Hispanic or Latino	Black alone, not Hispanic or Latino	Asian alone, not Hispanic or Latino	All other races or 2 or more races, not Hispanic or Latino	Hispanic or Latino[1]	Age (percent), 2010–2014: Under 18 years old	Age 18 to 64 years old	Age 65 years and older	Households, 2010–2014: Total occupied housing units	Percent owner occupied	Householders by level of education (percent): High school diploma or less	Bachelor's degree or more
	1	2	3	4	5	6	7	8	9	10	11	12	13	14	15	16
MARYLAND—Con.																
North Potomac CDP	24,410	NA	NA	24,003	52.4	5.1	34.6	3.3	4.7	26.7	63.5	9.8	7,889	81.8	9.7	79.8
Oakland town	1,913	1,905	-0.4	2,165	88.6	5.9	1.0	2.4	2.0	14.1	62.4	23.4	918	49.9	40.5	29.0
Ocean CDP	32	NA	NA	9	100.0	0.0	0.0	0.0	0.0	0.0	0.0	100.0	9	100.0	0.0	100.0
Ocean City town	7,102	7,089	-0.2	7,093	92.6	0.7	0.5	0.2	6.0	9.8	55.5	34.7	3,359	79.3	30.9	40.2
Ocean Pines CDP	11,710	NA	NA	10,727	91.6	3.2	0.1	1.4	3.7	12.4	51.1	36.5	4,693	89.6	24.5	42.7
Odenton CDP	37,132	NA	NA	38,787	61.0	22.0	5.2	5.8	6.1	24.9	64.9	10.3	14,945	69.8	20.4	48.8
Oldtown CDP	86	NA	NA	79	10.1	89.9	0.0	0.0	0.0	12.7	62.0	25.3	19	57.9	42.1	0.0
Olney CDP	33,844	NA	NA	35,017	63.8	12.8	11.7	3.0	8.7	24.6	63.6	11.7	11,635	89.1	11.5	66.0
Overlea CDP	12,275	NA	NA	12,197	69.9	16.8	4.7	5.1	3.6	21.3	61.7	16.8	4,941	73.5	36.7	32.1
Owings CDP	2,149	NA	NA	2,745	82.5	14.3	1.5	0.7	1.0	31.1	56.1	12.8	800	93.1	34.6	25.8
Owings Mills CDP	30,622	NA	NA	32,927	29.4	52.5	8.6	3.2	6.3	23.7	68.2	8.0	12,898	44.3	18.9	53.4
Oxford town	651	624	-4.1	524	96.6	2.7	0.0	0.2	0.6	15.7	43.2	41.4	266	86.1	6.4	72.9
Oxon Hill CDP	17,722	NA	NA	18,723	4.8	73.2	5.7	1.8	14.5	20.4	67.3	12.4	7,104	57.5	41.6	23.9
Paramount-Long Meadow CDP	2,571	NA	NA	2,407	84.9	4.5	3.1	1.7	5.9	19.0	57.3	23.7	881	75.5	26.2	40.2
Parkville CDP	30,734	NA	NA	31,606	58.0	32.3	3.2	1.8	4.7	22.7	63.8	13.6	12,625	63.2	40.2	26.6
Parole CDP	15,922	NA	NA	17,060	84.1	5.8	2.8	1.7	5.6	13.2	59.5	27.3	8,130	67.1	15.2	57.9
Parsonsburg CDP	339	NA	NA	272	53.7	29.8	0.0	16.5	0.0	22.4	53.3	24.3	137	68.6	62.8	27.0
Pasadena CDP	24,287	NA	NA	25,030	82.4	6.7	1.7	3.7	5.5	23.9	66.8	9.5	8,835	86.0	37.0	31.6
Pecktonville CDP	167	NA	NA	179	100.0	0.0	0.0	0.0	0.0	36.3	63.7	0.0	49	83.7	87.8	0.0
Peppermill Village CDP	4,895	NA	NA	4,795	0.6	93.2	0.0	0.4	5.8	25.7	57.8	16.5	1,699	73.1	40.0	18.6
Perry Hall CDP	28,474	NA	NA	28,924	75.9	10.3	8.1	2.1	3.6	21.7	64.8	13.6	11,320	77.0	29.3	42.0
Perryman CDP	2,342	NA	NA	2,581	77.8	19.8	0.0	2.4	0.0	25.0	57.4	17.6	1,042	61.6	42.9	16.9
Perryville town	4,363	4,429	1.5	4,391	68.4	9.3	3.0	4.4	14.9	20.8	68.3	10.9	1,680	53.5	55.8	20.4
Pikesville CDP	30,764	NA	NA	32,125	74.8	14.3	5.6	2.5	2.8	19.9	55.1	24.9	13,785	65.8	20.0	59.1
Pinesburg CDP	449	NA	NA	507	100.0	0.0	0.0	0.0	0.0	19.7	68.5	11.6	189	100.0	79.4	10.1
Piney Point CDP	864	NA	NA	780	88.8	0.0	4.9	6.3	0.0	28.0	51.0	20.9	330	87.0	46.7	24.2
Pittsville town	1,417	1,421	0.3	1,540	93.0	1.2	1.2	2.1	2.6	27.7	61.0	11.1	594	76.3	53.5	12.3
Pleasant Grove CDP	353	NA	NA	339	100.0	0.0	0.0	0.0	0.0	14.4	69.3	16.2	158	64.6	65.8	7.0
Pleasant Hills CDP	3,379	NA	NA	3,434	92.8	2.1	0.6	1.5	3.0	21.2	61.4	17.4	1,133	93.4	26.2	48.1
Pocomoke City city	4,178	4,160	-0.4	4,170	45.8	50.6	1.1	2.3	0.1	27.9	57.3	14.8	1,484	52.8	55.3	17.3
Point of Rocks CDP	1,466	NA	NA	1,700	73.4	19.7	0.4	2.9	3.6	27.7	66.4	5.7	575	93.0	25.9	51.7
Pomfret CDP	517	NA	NA	470	42.6	34.7	0.0	18.3	4.5	12.1	76.9	10.9	203	80.3	29.1	7.9
Pondsville CDP	158	NA	NA	71	100.0	0.0	0.0	0.0	0.0	0.0	87.4	12.7	20	100.0	45.0	55.0
Poolesville town	4,883	5,160	5.7	5,042	76.1	8.7	8.2	0.3	6.8	26.8	67.2	6.0	1,546	91.8	10.3	64.3
Port Deposit town	653	659	0.9	639	90.1	4.1	1.4	2.8	1.6	15.4	69.2	15.2	264	44.3	48.5	29.9
Port Tobacco Village town	13	13	0.0	5	100.0	0.0	0.0	0.0	0.0	0.0	0.0	100.0	4	100.0	0.0	50.0
Potomac CDP	44,965	NA	NA	46,475	67.3	5.0	17.1	2.5	8.3	25.0	55.7	19.3	16,093	87.1	5.8	84.7
Potomac Heights CDP	1,117	NA	NA	1,125	91.6	0.0	0.0	7.5	1.0	31.4	58.5	10.1	480	91.3	45.6	6.7
Potomac Park CDP	2,530	NA	NA	1,889	61.1	35.0	0.0	3.1	0.8	11.5	77.3	11.3	435	78.6	51.0	16.6
Powellville CDP	189	NA	NA	75	100.0	0.0	0.0	0.0	0.0	0.0	89.3	10.7	33	100.0	51.5	0.0
Preston town	710	690	-2.8	967	90.1	3.2	2.9	3.8	0.0	33.6	56.2	10.2	333	61.6	53.2	22.2
Prince Frederick CDP	2,538	NA	NA	3,213	59.8	30.7	1.7	2.4	5.5	27.4	55.5	17.3	1,157	39.0	57.6	26.0
Princess Anne town	3,288	3,330	1.3	3,337	34.2	55.0	1.0	5.2	4.7	15.5	71.6	13.0	1,553	38.7	39.5	13.9
Pylesville CDP	693	NA	NA	772	100.0	0.0	0.0	0.0	0.0	18.9	60.4	20.6	216	100.0	27.3	29.2
Quantico CDP	133	NA	NA	110	100.0	0.0	0.0	0.0	0.0	21.8	43.6	34.5	38	44.7	0.0	44.7
Queen Anne CDP	1,280	NA	NA	1,135	28.3	67.0	0.0	0.0	4.8	29.4	56.9	13.7	366	97.3	23.0	62.0
Queen Anne town	222	218	-1.8	282	87.6	10.3	2.1	0.0	0.0	24.5	64.2	11.3	101	86.1	45.5	9.9
Queensland CDP	0	NA	NA	1,713	18.5	76.4	2.2	1.2	1.8	20.9	71.4	7.6	578	86.7	8.7	63.8
Queenstown town	661	656	-0.8	689	75.5	6.7	5.1	5.4	7.4	24.7	54.7	20.6	274	79.9	36.5	33.2
Randallstown CDP	32,430	NA	NA	33,815	14.2	80.1	1.3	1.9	2.5	23.5	62.8	14.0	12,077	69.9	27.7	37.6
Rawlings CDP	693	NA	NA	714	100.0	0.0	0.0	0.0	0.0	20.7	56.2	23.0	269	92.2	28.3	9.7
Redland CDP	17,242	NA	NA	17,443	38.4	14.5	16.6	4.0	26.6	24.5	64.2	11.2	5,625	73.1	23.4	55.6
Reid CDP	54	NA	NA	29	100.0	0.0	0.0	0.0	0.0	0.0	0.0	100.0	13	100.0	100.0	0.0
Reisterstown CDP	25,968	NA	NA	27,493	48.8	30.3	8.9	1.8	10.3	24.4	64.6	11.1	10,094	55.9	29.1	37.9
Ridgely town	1,637	1,616	-1.3	1,370	78.8	12.3	0.0	2.3	6.6	25.1	63.4	11.5	497	74.0	41.0	23.5
Ringgold CDP	166	NA	NA	162	100.0	0.0	0.0	0.0	0.0	15.4	48.8	35.8	67	85.1	92.5	7.5
Rising Sun town	2,854	2,877	0.8	2,870	93.5	0.0	0.3	2.1	4.1	30.8	56.4	12.8	1,037	56.4	53.3	12.7
Riva CDP	4,076	NA	NA	3,955	92.8	0.5	1.1	0.3	5.3	22.7	59.5	17.7	1,478	92.2	17.3	56.2
Riverdale Park town	6,956	7,266	4.5	7,119	18.6	24.6	3.0	1.3	52.5	30.2	63.5	6.3	1,957	50.3	52.6	24.5
Riverside CDP	6,425	NA	NA	7,150	62.9	22.4	4.4	3.2	7.2	24.3	70.3	5.4	2,595	70.1	23.5	38.8
Riviera Beach CDP	12,677	NA	NA	12,811	89.7	6.4	1.8	1.3	0.9	23.9	64.6	11.8	4,423	88.0	40.6	22.0
Robinwood CDP	6,918	NA	NA	7,431	73.4	12.1	3.9	3.5	7.1	26.7	59.5	13.8	2,818	43.2	27.0	32.1
Rock Hall town	1,310	1,312	0.2	1,377	85.1	8.7	0.4	0.3	5.4	13.3	58.4	28.2	566	71.6	49.3	25.3
Rock Point CDP	107	NA	NA	99	75.8	0.0	24.2	0.0	0.0	0.0	77.8	22.2	49	63.3	69.4	0.0
Rockville city	61,285	65,937	7.6	63,402	52.5	8.8	19.6	3.2	16.0	20.7	64.0	15.3	24,567	59.5	16.3	67.0
Rohrersville CDP	175	NA	NA	93	100.0	0.0	0.0	0.0	0.0	15.1	85.0	0.0	49	100.0	61.2	0.0
Rosaryville CDP	10,697	NA	NA	11,268	13.3	78.9	2.5	4.2	1.2	24.0	65.2	10.6	3,624	91.3	23.5	40.9
Rosedale CDP	19,257	NA	NA	18,779	56.0	34.5	1.2	3.1	5.2	21.4	62.4	16.1	6,965	74.5	46.2	18.4
Rosemont village	294	306	4.1	341	97.7	0.6	0.0	1.2	0.6	16.5	65.6	17.9	126	86.5	42.1	38.1
Rossville CDP	15,147	NA	NA	15,298	46.4	31.8	10.3	3.6	7.9	20.3	66.5	13.1	6,012	54.3	31.7	31.0
Sabillasville CDP	354	NA	NA	298	80.2	19.8	0.0	0.0	0.0	30.5	64.5	5.0	104	80.8	48.1	28.8
St. George Island CDP	257	NA	NA	302	96.4	0.0	0.0	3.6	0.0	8.3	76.8	14.9	112	67.0	10.7	23.2
St. James CDP	2,953	NA	NA	3,338	68.2	13.8	2.4	0.0	15.6	23.0	62.9	14.1	1,165	84.3	41.8	27.2
St. Leonard CDP	742	NA	NA	574	86.8	5.7	0.0	0.0	7.5	34.5	52.1	13.4	196	77.6	34.7	17.9
St. Michaels town	1,029	1,046	1.7	1,061	69.3	25.0	0.8	0.8	4.2	21.3	52.1	26.7	465	47.7	41.5	30.8
Salisbury city	30,352	32,563	7.3	31,334	52.3	34.5	3.1	3.7	6.5	23.0	65.8	11.2	11,635	33.3	37.1	27.8
Sandy Hook CDP	188	NA	NA	154	100.0	0.0	0.0	0.0	0.0	35.7	44.1	20.1	56	100.0	100.0	0.0
San Mar CDP	384	NA	NA	185	89.2	9.2	0.0	1.6	0.0	4.9	29.2	65.9	60	80.0	16.7	46.7
Savage CDP	7,054	NA	NA	6,139	55.7	24.3	14.8	3.0	2.2	23.6	66.8	9.7	2,434	59.9	21.0	53.2
Scaggsville CDP	0	NA	NA	9,204	66.4	7.3	18.1	4.3	3.0	26.7	63.7	9.6	2,986	91.4	13.9	70.2
Seabrook CDP	17,287	NA	NA	17,115	11.5	67.8	5.5	2.3	12.8	25.1	65.7	9.2	5,691	58.5	33.4	33.3
Seat Pleasant city	4,542	4,752	4.6	4,656	1.0	89.7	0.0	0.8	8.5	26.8	60.9	12.4	1,739	56.2	52.5	17.1
Secretary town	535	532	-0.6	855	76.3	0.0	2.6	0.9	20.2	33.8	51.1	15.2	283	72.8	49.5	8.8
Severn CDP	44,231	NA	NA	45,396	46.2	32.9	8.9	5.1	6.9	24.4	66.1	9.6	16,525	73.2	28.1	41.9
Severna Park CDP	37,634	NA	NA	38,177	88.3	3.6	3.5	2.2	2.3	25.1	60.3	14.5	13,056	92.3	18.9	60.4
Shady Side CDP	5,803	NA	NA	6,550	81.2	14.9	0.0	0.6	3.4	27.9	62.3	9.7	2,378	85.4	30.9	27.8
Shaft CDP	235	NA	NA	311	100.0	0.0	0.0	0.0	0.0	36.7	44.4	19.0	86	100.0	40.7	12.8
Sharpsburg town	709	706	-0.4	829	96.9	0.0	0.0	2.2	1.0	25.1	64.8	10.1	315	69.8	45.4	20.3
Sharptown town	646	643	-0.5	927	90.1	1.1	4.0	4.2	0.6	26.9	60.8	12.2	322	80.1	40.4	14.0
Silver Hill CDP	5,950	NA	NA	5,335	4.0	93.9	0.1	1.0	1.0	26.6	64.7	8.9	2,265	34.8	48.1	19.9
Silver Spring CDP	71,452	NA	NA	75,748	35.6	25.5	8.1	3.0	27.7	21.8	69.7	8.5	30,290	38.0	21.9	59.5

1 May be of any race.

Table A. All Places — **Population and Housing**

STATE City, town, township, borough, or CDP (county if applicable)	Population				Race and Hispanic or Latino origin (percent), 2010–2014					Age (percent), 2010–2014			Households, 2010–2014		Householders by level of education (percent)	
	2010 census total population	2014 estimated population	Percent change 2010–2014	ACS total population estimate 2010–2014	White alone, not Hispanic or Latino	Black alone, not Hispanic or Latino	Asian alone, not Hispanic or Latino	All other races or 2 or more races, not Hispanic or Latino	Hispanic or Latino[1]	Under 18 years old	Age 18 to 64 years old	Age 65 years and older	Total occupied housing units	Percent owner occupied	High school diploma or less	Bachelor's degree or more
	1	2	3	4	5	6	7	8	9	10	11	12	13	14	15	16
MARYLAND—Con.																
Smith Island CDP	276	NA	NA	176	100.0	0.0	0.0	0.0	0.0	13.7	52.2	34.1	80	93.8	75.0	13.8
Smithsburg town	2,985	3,002	0.6	3,001	93.1	1.3	0.0	1.7	3.9	31.3	61.6	7.1	976	72.8	33.4	28.1
Snow Hill town	2,103	2,091	-0.6	2,720	60.1	35.1	0.6	2.8	1.4	22.0	63.3	14.7	912	59.0	49.9	25.7
Solomons CDP	2,368	NA	NA	1,822	88.5	4.1	0.7	2.6	4.1	6.3	42.7	50.9	1,052	49.4	18.7	58.4
Somerset town	1,216	1,278	5.1	1,148	88.1	1.1	2.3	4.2	4.4	27.4	50.1	22.5	405	95.8	0.7	92.1
South Kensington CDP	8,462	NA	NA	8,387	83.6	2.7	3.7	3.3	6.7	28.9	55.1	16.0	2,966	88.5	6.9	81.6
South Laurel CDP	26,112	NA	NA	25,633	17.8	59.8	8.8	2.4	11.2	27.0	63.7	9.3	9,451	42.3	26.7	40.2
Spencerville CDP	1,594	NA	NA	1,588	44.7	29.8	22.0	2.1	1.4	20.7	63.6	15.7	493	86.8	17.8	57.8
Springdale CDP	2,994	NA	NA	3,126	1.8	87.9	7.7	2.6	0.0	23.9	65.7	10.5	885	92.7	25.5	51.2
Spring Gap CDP	55	NA	NA	36	100.0	0.0	0.0	0.0	0.0	0.0	50.0	50.0	17	100.0	100.0	0.0
Spring Ridge CDP	5,795	NA	NA	5,895	83.6	0.9	8.4	0.6	6.5	30.9	57.1	12.1	2,097	75.3	22.6	49.5
Stevensville CDP	6,803	NA	NA	6,393	97.0	0.4	0.4	0.8	1.4	24.7	66.1	9.3	2,135	90.4	26.1	37.8
Stockton CDP	92	NA	NA	86	54.7	45.3	0.0	0.0	0.0	0.0	100.0	0.0	42	100.0	35.7	0.0
Sudlersville town	505	502	-0.6	411	76.9	6.6	0.0	5.8	10.7	24.8	57.5	17.8	176	45.5	38.1	22.7
Suitland CDP	25,825	NA	NA	24,180	1.8	91.5	0.5	1.1	5.1	25.1	66.4	8.4	9,651	39.9	45.6	16.4
Summerfield CDP	10,898	NA	NA	11,970	1.6	91.3	1.2	2.0	4.0	23.8	66.3	9.9	4,881	52.6	29.2	30.7
Swanton CDP	58	NA	NA	49	100.0	0.0	0.0	0.0	0.0	0.0	100.0	0.0	27	100.0	0.0	70.4
Sykesville town	4,436	4,432	-0.1	4,426	92.6	3.4	2.2	0.0	1.8	24.7	62.4	12.8	1,803	65.8	34.4	39.0
Takoma Park city	16,715	17,670	5.7	17,307	43.8	33.7	4.4	3.1	15.1	22.8	67.0	10.3	6,483	52.0	25.5	56.9
Tall Timbers CDP	462	NA	NA	298	96.3	0.0	3.7	0.0	0.0	9.4	61.1	29.5	151	100.0	0.0	76.2
Taneytown city	6,730	6,752	0.3	6,738	86.6	5.1	2.2	3.5	2.7	27.2	57.2	15.6	2,374	80.7	41.5	27.3
Taylors Island CDP	173	NA	NA	146	100.0	0.0	0.0	0.0	0.0	15.0	59.5	25.3	66	74.2	81.8	18.2
Temple Hills CDP	7,852	NA	NA	8,069	4.4	92.4	0.9	0.8	1.4	24.5	68.3	7.2	3,192	33.2	37.4	25.4
Templeville town	114	113	-0.9	175	15.4	0.0	0.0	0.0	84.6	4.6	93.8	1.7	47	21.3	51.1	0.0
Thurmont town	6,169	6,439	4.4	6,333	93.1	1.5	0.3	1.8	3.2	24.2	63.1	12.6	2,543	72.5	39.8	29.1
Tilghman Island CDP	784	NA	NA	971	98.2	0.0	0.0	1.8	0.0	9.1	69.4	21.5	395	86.8	51.4	32.4
Tilghmanton CDP	465	NA	NA	546	97.3	0.0	0.0	2.7	0.0	17.6	72.4	10.1	157	88.5	68.8	10.8
Timonium CDP	9,925	NA	NA	10,280	80.6	2.1	9.4	2.4	5.5	16.7	55.8	27.5	4,117	74.4	23.3	54.0
Tolchester CDP	329	NA	NA	259	96.1	3.9	0.0	0.0	0.0	5.4	59.8	34.7	125	100.0	55.2	23.2
Towson CDP	55,197	NA	NA	57,146	76.6	11.4	6.1	2.1	3.7	17.4	67.2	15.3	20,976	58.8	15.8	63.3
Trappe town	1,077	1,030	-4.4	1,196	62.0	29.0	0.4	2.5	6.1	22.4	64.3	13.5	508	65.4	39.4	25.8
Travilah CDP	12,159	NA	NA	11,989	54.1	4.6	30.5	2.7	8.2	28.3	57.3	14.5	3,636	94.1	7.2	85.0
Trego-Rohrersville Station CDP	172	NA	NA	86	100.0	0.0	0.0	0.0	0.0	0.0	0.0	100.0	44	100.0	20.5	0.0
Tyaskin CDP	236	NA	NA	192	35.9	64.1	0.0	0.0	0.0	0.0	66.7	33.3	67	100.0	38.8	61.2
Union Bridge town	975	974	-0.1	874	85.2	10.2	0.2	1.9	2.4	26.7	56.8	16.4	348	49.1	62.1	17.5
University Park town	2,548	2,653	4.1	2,596	75.6	6.1	3.5	3.7	11.0	22.3	60.0	17.7	969	87.9	3.3	89.5
Upper Marlboro town	629	833	32.4	646	38.4	50.9	1.4	1.7	7.6	19.0	69.1	11.8	301	82.7	22.6	36.2
Urbana CDP	9,175	NA	NA	9,990	60.0	7.6	19.0	6.3	7.1	35.9	60.2	4.0	3,101	91.5	8.4	66.1
Vale Summit CDP	139	NA	NA	47	100.0	0.0	0.0	0.0	0.0	34.0	31.9	34.0	15	100.0	60.0	40.0
Vienna town	278	277	-0.4	204	79.9	10.8	0.0	0.0	9.3	8.9	63.8	27.5	102	85.3	39.2	28.4
Waldorf CDP	67,752	NA	NA	71,358	30.7	54.2	4.2	4.9	6.0	28.0	64.7	7.4	24,884	69.6	32.3	29.8
Walker Mill CDP	11,302	NA	NA	11,001	1.1	94.0	0.3	2.6	2.0	22.5	63.9	13.6	4,380	51.7	39.6	22.9
Walkersville town	5,802	6,058	4.4	5,966	91.0	2.5	1.4	2.3	2.8	26.0	59.3	14.7	2,173	77.2	28.9	48.1
Washington Grove town	545	573	5.1	615	73.7	11.5	4.4	4.6	5.9	19.4	63.2	17.4	256	90.6	14.5	72.7
Waterview CDP	40	NA	NA	31	100.0	0.0	0.0	0.0	0.0	0.0	51.6	48.4	31	48.4	51.6	48.4
West Denton CDP	52	NA	NA	150	39.3	52.7	0.0	8.0	0.0	20.0	80.0	0.0	52	0.0	76.9	0.0
Westernport town	1,888	1,821	-3.5	1,807	99.7	0.0	0.0	0.3	0.0	21.9	57.5	20.5	746	74.0	58.7	13.7
West Laurel CDP	4,230	NA	NA	4,385	67.6	14.3	5.6	2.1	10.3	19.3	59.4	21.3	1,487	95.9	22.3	53.1
Westminster city	18,586	18,724	0.7	18,656	83.7	6.2	1.9	2.0	6.2	22.5	63.0	14.5	6,890	50.7	41.2	29.3
West Ocean City CDP	4,375	NA	NA	4,586	83.7	3.7	1.6	3.3	7.8	20.2	55.3	24.5	1,820	74.6	36.5	32.7
Westphalia CDP	7,266	NA	NA	7,217	11.4	78.6	2.1	5.5	2.4	22.7	66.9	10.3	2,739	93.0	30.6	37.0
West Pocomoke CDP	454	NA	NA	534	76.2	11.6	3.7	0.0	8.4	24.0	56.9	19.1	216	82.4	49.5	29.6
Whaleyville CDP	149	NA	NA	185	90.3	0.0	0.0	0.0	9.7	8.1	74.0	17.8	61	100.0	50.8	32.8
Wheaton CDP	48,284	NA	NA	49,831	23.9	18.8	13.4	3.0	40.9	23.8	67.0	9.2	14,906	65.6	38.8	40.0
Whitehaven CDP	43	NA	NA	63	100.0	0.0	0.0	0.0	0.0	0.0	54.0	46.0	29	100.0	44.8	55.2
White Marsh CDP	9,513	NA	NA	9,671	70.4	12.2	13.2	2.5	1.6	23.6	65.3	11.0	3,568	81.9	32.1	42.2
White Oak CDP	17,403	NA	NA	18,101	21.7	50.4	5.3	3.1	19.4	22.6	68.0	9.5	6,833	34.2	27.5	46.0
Willards town	958	970	1.3	1,058	81.3	9.1	1.3	7.2	1.1	28.2	62.3	9.5	380	71.6	51.6	12.4
Williamsport town	2,137	2,167	1.4	2,384	92.6	4.2	0.0	2.3	0.9	21.0	56.4	22.7	1,012	36.2	56.5	9.7
Williston CDP	155	NA	NA	103	100.0	0.0	0.0	0.0	0.0	9.7	53.3	36.9	64	70.3	0.0	71.9
Wilson-Conococheague CDP	2,282	NA	NA	2,117	99.0	1.0	0.0	0.0	0.0	16.5	63.8	19.7	842	88.4	69.0	21.3
Woodland CDP	113	NA	NA	88	100.0	0.0	0.0	0.0	0.0	11.4	71.7	17.0	22	100.0	100.0	0.0
Woodlawn CDP (Baltimore)	37,879	NA	NA	39,518	21.8	60.2	9.2	3.6	5.1	24.4	63.9	11.7	14,620	64.4	29.8	34.8
Woodlawn CDP (Prince George's)	6,334	NA	NA	7,439	4.5	53.2	3.6	4.8	34.0	26.8	65.1	8.0	2,209	70.4	52.6	17.9
Woodmore CDP	3,936	NA	NA	3,940	9.8	85.5	0.6	3.0	1.1	26.9	63.0	10.1	1,297	95.6	7.7	67.2
Woodsboro town	1,141	1,193	4.6	1,202	86.0	2.0	0.5	3.4	8.1	24.6	59.7	15.6	453	80.6	41.5	30.9
Worton CDP	249	NA	NA	52	100.0	0.0	0.0	0.0	0.0	0.0	55.7	44.2	38	100.0	60.5	39.5
Yarrowsburg CDP	133	NA	NA	14	100.0	0.0	0.0	0.0	0.0	0.0	0.0	100.0	14	100.0	100.0	0.0
Zihlman CDP	362	NA	NA	357	100.0	0.0	0.0	0.0	0.0	17.1	66.1	16.8	151	79.5	84.1	10.6
MASSACHUSETTS	6,547,817	6,745,408	3.0	6,657,291	75.0	6.4	5.7	2.6	10.2	21.1	64.6	14.4	2,538,485	62.3	32.8	41.9
Abington CDP & town (Plymouth)	15,988	16,197	1.3	16,081	93.3	1.4	2.1	1.5	1.7	21.4	66.7	11.9	6,032	70.8	30.6	33.9
Acton town (Middlesex)	21,924	23,237	6.0	22,614	74.6	0.7	20.6	2.2	2.0	27.1	61.5	11.3	8,489	74.9	8.0	77.5
Acushnet town (Bristol)	10,303	10,410	1.0	10,329	94.7	0.0	0.1	2.6	2.7	18.5	64.4	17.2	3,873	85.9	53.5	21.3
Acushnet Center CDP	3,073	NA	NA	2,786	95.8	0.1	0.3	2.5	1.3	16.3	61.7	22.0	1,184	73.3	64.4	11.2
Adams town (Berkshire)	8,485	8,271	-2.5	8,382	96.3	0.6	0.0	2.1	1.0	21.4	61.0	17.5	3,741	64.5	51.2	19.4
Adams CDP	5,515	NA	NA	5,460	96.0	0.8	0.0	2.4	0.9	22.4	60.0	17.6	2,493	61.4	50.5	19.3
Agawam Town city & MCD (Hampden)	28,438	28,772	1.2	28,626	89.2	1.1	2.3	1.8	5.6	20.0	62.7	17.5	11,495	74.9	36.2	31.7
Alford town (Berkshire)	494	490	-0.8	471	96.8	1.1	0.6	0.8	0.6	13.8	55.4	30.8	207	92.3	13.0	55.1
Amesbury Town city & MCD (Essex)	16,283	16,794	3.1	16,554	92.5	0.9	1.4	3.6	1.6	20.2	68.4	11.5	6,812	70.7	25.1	45.6
Amherst town (Hampshire)	37,819	39,774	5.2	39,260	73.1	5.2	12.2	2.7	6.7	9.1	84.3	6.7	8,844	43.8	11.4	59.9
Amherst Center CDP	19,065	NA	NA	19,543	75.8	5.5	10.3	2.6	5.7	4.7	90.1	5.2	2,787	38.8	9.8	62.3
Andover CDP	8,762	NA	NA	8,953	78.9	2.9	6.7	1.9	9.6	21.0	60.4	18.7	3,438	57.5	18.9	62.0

1 May be of any race.

Table A. All Places — **Population and Housing**

STATE City, town, township, borough, or CDP (county if applicable)	2010 census total population	2014 estimated population	Percent change 2010–2014	ACS total population estimate 2010–2014	White alone, not Hispanic or Latino	Black alone, not Hispanic or Latino	Asian alone, not Hispanic or Latino	All other races or 2 or more races, not Hispanic or Latino	Hispanic or Latino[1]	Under 18 years old	Age 18 to 64 years old	Age 65 years and older	Total occupied housing units	Percent owner occupied	High school diploma or less	Bachelor's degree or more
	1	2	3	4	5	6	7	8	9	10	11	12	13	14	15	16
MASSACHUSETTS—Con.																
Andover town (Essex).......	33,209	35,085	5.6	34,251	80.8	1.7	11.4	1.8	4.3	26.3	59.8	13.9	12,079	79.5	12.8	70.7
Aquinnah town (Dukes)	311	323	3.9	363	51.2	0.6	0.6	47.7	0.0	21.8	68.2	9.9	120	62.5	22.5	38.3
Arlington CDP & town (Middlesex)	42,844	44,461	3.8	43,728	82.6	1.8	9.0	2.8	3.8	21.5	63.4	15.2	18,726	61.2	15.6	69.5
Ashburnham town (Worcester)	6,081	6,181	1.6	6,133	95.5	1.2	0.0	2.3	1.0	22.4	66.7	10.9	2,235	92.6	31.2	40.0
Ashby town (Middlesex)....	3,074	3,208	4.4	3,147	96.7	0.5	1.2	0.0	1.6	19.8	66.8	13.3	1,073	88.9	35.0	28.9
Ashfield town (Franklin) ...	1,740	1,731	-0.5	1,749	96.7	0.2	0.2	2.6	0.3	20.3	65.5	14.2	744	81.7	20.3	49.1
Ashland town (Middlesex)	16,593	17,312	4.3	16,985	84.7	2.8	7.3	2.0	3.1	23.3	63.9	12.8	6,560	80.0	20.9	60.2
Athol town (Worcester)	11,577	11,621	0.4	11,617	90.0	0.3	0.9	1.6	7.2	20.7	64.1	15.2	4,750	70.7	52.6	16.3
Athol CDP.......................	8,265	NA	NA	8,340	88.8	0.2	1.1	1.3	8.5	23.4	63.2	13.3	3,427	65.2	53.5	15.1
Attleboro city & MCD (Bristol)..........................	43,593	43,970	0.9	43,774	82.8	3.7	4.5	2.3	6.6	22.7	63.8	13.2	16,619	63.6	39.6	32.3
Auburn town (Worcester)..	16,188	16,387	1.2	16,294	92.6	2.5	0.9	0.7	3.2	20.0	61.0	19.0	6,346	84.7	35.9	38.9
Avon town (Norfolk)	4,356	4,464	2.5	4,421	77.1	12.9	5.0	1.6	3.3	19.4	63.6	17.0	1,636	83.2	36.7	32.2
Ayer town (Middlesex)	7,427	7,952	7.1	7,716	84.4	2.8	3.0	4.4	5.5	20.8	66.8	12.3	3,229	59.4	33.9	31.8
Ayer CDP.......................	2,868	NA	NA	2,930	81.1	3.2	5.1	6.1	4.6	17.6	65.4	16.8	1,360	47.6	42.0	25.6
Baldwinville CDP	2,028	NA	NA	2,327	98.0	0.2	0.0	1.7	0.1	17.0	64.6	18.4	891	73.3	60.2	14.4
Barnstable Town city & MCD (Barnstable)	45,189	44,529	-1.5	44,750	89.0	3.3	0.8	3.3	3.6	17.5	60.9	21.6	19,262	74.9	28.4	40.1
Barre CDP	1,009	NA	NA	910	99.2	0.0	0.0	0.8	0.0	30.7	39.7	29.5	420	51.9	44.3	7.4
Barre town (Worcester)....	5,398	5,463	1.2	5,414	96.6	0.2	1.8	0.1	1.3	26.4	59.8	13.7	1,943	80.2	42.7	21.7
Becket town (Berkshire)....	1,779	1,777	-0.1	1,790	95.7	0.6	0.3	1.9	1.6	13.2	65.6	21.2	791	91.2	29.5	40.7
Bedford town (Middlesex) .	13,320	14,205	6.6	13,788	81.4	1.4	11.2	1.4	4.5	25.0	58.5	16.4	5,012	70.3	11.5	70.4
Belchertown CDP	2,899	NA	NA	3,010	86.7	1.3	1.4	1.3	9.3	24.0	60.8	15.1	1,307	49.5	51.3	29.4
Belchertown town (Hampshire)	14,649	14,846	1.3	14,774	92.5	0.9	1.8	2.2	2.6	24.7	63.4	12.0	5,730	78.8	31.1	40.0
Bellingham town (Norfolk)	16,336	16,770	2.7	16,564	93.2	0.6	3.1	1.5	1.5	21.4	66.6	12.0	6,162	80.6	39.2	31.5
Bellingham CDP	4,854	NA	NA	5,055	90.0	0.3	5.7	2.1	1.8	20.0	66.2	13.7	1,976	74.7	39.9	30.5
Belmont CDP & town (Middlesex)	24,729	25,496	3.1	25,173	78.3	2.3	12.0	2.2	5.2	24.5	60.1	15.6	9,292	61.9	10.9	75.0
Berkley town (Bristol).......	6,411	6,580	2.6	6,492	95.3	0.3	0.0	1.5	2.9	26.2	63.8	10.0	2,140	95.6	37.0	30.4
Berlin town (Worcester)....	2,866	2,978	3.9	2,917	94.8	0.4	1.8	0.2	2.8	20.0	62.0	17.9	1,052	85.2	26.1	49.3
Bernardston town (Franklin)	2,129	2,113	-0.8	2,173	92.2	0.6	2.0	1.3	3.9	18.4	58.3	23.3	976	84.3	39.4	29.4
Beverly city & MCD (Essex)........................	39,502	40,952	3.7	40,370	91.3	1.7	2.1	1.4	3.5	18.4	66.1	15.4	15,925	61.0	27.0	46.6
Billerica town (Middlesex).	40,243	42,264	5.0	41,446	89.3	1.6	4.8	1.5	2.8	21.2	65.8	13.0	14,435	82.7	34.0	36.2
Blackstone town (Worcester)	9,026	9,091	0.7	9,055	92.1	1.5	0.6	1.3	4.5	22.1	66.4	11.4	3,451	68.0	38.9	27.3
Blandford CDP	393	NA	NA	425	97.6	0.0	1.6	0.7	0.0	17.2	69.9	12.7	167	95.8	37.1	36.5
Blandford town (Hampden)...................	1,233	1,255	1.8	1,186	98.9	0.0	0.6	0.3	0.3	18.5	67.2	14.2	483	94.0	36.2	35.0
Bliss Corner CDP	5,280	NA	NA	5,908	91.0	0.6	1.5	6.2	0.8	16.6	54.4	28.9	2,389	65.9	57.9	24.0
Bolton town (Worcester) ...	4,897	5,132	4.8	5,019	93.0	0.3	2.2	0.9	3.6	28.1	61.6	10.1	1,622	89.8	15.3	70.0
Boston city & MCD (Suffolk)........................	617,680	655,884	6.2	639,594	46.0	22.7	9.1	3.8	18.4	16.7	73.0	10.4	251,212	34.2	32.5	46.9
Bourne CDP	1,418	NA	NA	1,148	97.2	0.0	0.0	0.0	2.8	14.0	55.7	30.4	487	91.0	21.4	52.4
Bourne town (Barnstable).	19,754	19,711	-0.2	19,749	91.4	2.8	0.7	2.2	2.9	18.0	59.6	22.4	8,152	77.4	28.7	36.9
Boxborough town (Middlesex)	4,996	5,171	3.5	5,102	78.0	0.4	19.5	1.6	0.5	24.4	65.2	10.4	2,101	77.3	6.7	78.4
Boxford CDP.....................	2,339	NA	NA	2,228	95.2	0.0	2.4	1.8	0.6	28.2	55.8	16.2	763	100.0	20.2	65.4
Boxford town (Essex)........	7,965	8,213	3.1	8,105	92.4	0.0	4.0	1.8	1.8	25.3	59.4	15.2	2,671	97.5	17.4	63.6
Boylston town (Worcester)	4,355	4,475	2.8	4,399	93.0	1.0	2.5	2.0	1.4	23.1	62.8	14.2	1,611	87.9	18.7	58.5
Braintree Town city & MCD (Norfolk)	35,739	37,362	4.5	36,543	82.5	4.7	7.8	2.3	2.7	22.3	61.7	16.1	13,226	71.2	32.5	39.7
Brewster CDP	2,000	NA	NA	2,306	97.7	0.1	0.2	0.6	1.4	10.1	52.7	37.2	1,082	79.3	16.5	51.1
Brewster town (Barnstable)	9,820	9,954	1.4	9,858	96.9	0.8	0.3	0.7	1.3	15.8	55.1	29.0	4,262	83.6	17.7	50.6
Bridgewater CDP	7,841	NA	NA	8,374	80.7	8.3	1.4	3.5	6.1	9.9	80.8	9.3	2,293	41.2	38.6	30.6
Bridgewater town (Plymouth)	26,567	27,472	3.4	26,931	85.2	6.9	1.2	2.6	4.0	18.4	70.0	11.6	7,772	77.5	30.0	43.1
Brimfield town (Hampden)	3,609	3,723	3.2	3,667	98.8	0.0	0.0	0.0	1.2	20.6	64.0	15.5	1,504	78.7	25.1	40.6
Brockton city & MCD (Plymouth)	93,810	94,779	1.0	94,267	43.4	37.3	1.7	7.6	10.0	26.3	61.1	12.7	32,966	55.9	49.1	19.1
Brookfield CDP	833	NA	NA	902	99.3	0.0	0.0	0.7	0.0	18.0	69.6	12.3	350	54.0	45.1	16.9
Brookfield town (Worcester)	3,390	3,399	0.3	3,396	96.4	0.3	0.4	2.9	0.0	20.9	62.1	16.9	1,368	78.7	42.5	27.0
Brookline CDP & town (Norfolk)	58,618	59,334	1.2	59,016	73.4	2.5	16.1	2.3	5.6	18.4	66.6	15.0	25,408	49.8	9.4	77.9
Buckland town (Franklin) ..	1,899	1,874	-1.3	1,961	98.6	0.0	0.0	1.0	0.4	15.3	64.6	19.9	791	75.6	39.1	36.0
Burlington CDP & town (Middlesex)	24,498	25,683	4.8	25,190	78.1	3.7	14.1	2.1	2.0	21.2	60.9	17.9	9,423	68.9	24.5	52.4
Buzzards Bay CDP	3,859	NA	NA	3,176	90.8	4.4	0.4	1.9	2.6	15.3	66.0	18.7	1,283	74.4	35.9	29.7
Cambridge city & MCD (Middlesex)	105,201	109,694	4.3	106,844	63.0	10.6	14.9	4.1	7.4	11.9	77.3	10.8	44,013	36.1	14.3	74.1
Canton town (Norfolk).......	21,572	22,510	4.3	22,036	81.4	6.3	6.7	1.7	4.0	22.7	59.2	18.2	8,873	76.3	19.9	54.0
Carlisle town (Middlesex) .	4,852	5,071	4.5	4,967	87.2	0.3	7.7	3.4	1.4	26.5	57.8	15.6	1,724	94.3	6.4	83.2
Carver town (Plymouth)....	11,509	11,583	0.6	11,541	95.0	0.2	0.7	1.8	0.3	21.2	60.9	17.8	4,437	92.4	47.0	23.0
Charlemont town (Franklin)	1,266	1,246	-1.6	1,218	95.6	0.7	0.5	2.3	1.0	17.3	60.8	22.0	566	73.7	36.9	27.4
Charlton town (Worcester)	12,981	13,312	2.5	13,126	97.0	0.6	0.4	1.1	0.9	23.3	65.1	11.6	4,617	80.7	33.5	37.1
Chatham CDP	1,421	NA	NA	1,470	74.5	15.9	1.4	0.0	8.2	19.1	50.8	30.1	657	67.6	22.5	43.7
Chatham town (Barnstable)	6,125	6,151	0.4	6,129	90.9	5.2	0.7	1.1	2.2	14.0	50.7	35.3	2,827	83.0	20.2	51.6
Chelmsford town (Middlesex)	33,802	34,960	3.4	34,495	87.4	0.4	8.1	1.3	2.7	21.0	61.5	17.5	13,838	82.5	23.1	51.8
Chelsea city & MCD (Suffolk)........................	35,177	38,861	10.5	37,084	24.9	5.3	3.3	3.8	62.8	26.5	64.9	8.6	11,862	28.0	60.2	18.5
Cheshire CDP	514	NA	NA	571	96.5	0.0	0.0	0.0	3.5	37.1	56.8	6.1	192	72.4	32.8	30.2
Cheshire town (Berkshire)	3,235	3,181	-1.7	3,211	98.4	0.7	0.0	0.2	0.6	21.4	58.8	19.7	1,372	86.1	45.8	21.6
Chester CDP	627	NA	NA	727	93.1	0.4	0.0	1.8	4.7	24.4	66.3	9.4	264	81.4	48.5	10.6

1 May be of any race.

STATE City, town, township, borough, or CDP (county if applicable)	2010 census total population	2014 estimated population	Percent change 2010–2014	ACS total population estimate 2010–2014	White alone, not Hispanic or Latino	Black alone, not Hispanic or Latino	Asian alone, not Hispanic or Latino	All other races or 2 or more races, not Hispanic or Latino	Hispanic or Latino[1]	Under 18 years old	Age 18 to 64 years old	Age 65 years and older	Total occupied housing units	Percent owner occupied	High school diploma or less	Bachelor's degree or more
	1	2	3	4	5	6	7	8	9	10	11	12	13	14	15	16
MASSACHUSETTS—Con.																
Chester town (Hampden) .	1,337	1,365	2.1	1,528	93.7	1.0	0.8	1.6	2.9	25.5	65.2	9.3	558	86.6	45.2	18.5
Chesterfield town (Hampshire)	1,222	1,248	2.1	1,221	98.0	0.0	0.0	1.2	0.8	18.4	68.7	12.9	487	91.2	27.3	45.6
Chicopee city & MCD (Hampden)	55,298	55,795	0.9	55,603	77.1	2.7	1.4	2.1	16.7	20.4	63.0	16.7	22,921	56.9	49.6	17.8
Chilmark town (Dukes)	866	921	6.4	905	96.7	0.7	0.0	2.7	0.0	15.8	62.3	22.0	307	87.6	16.3	59.9
Clarksburg town (Berkshire)	1,702	1,672	-1.8	1,580	98.9	0.3	0.3	0.6	0.0	19.5	59.8	20.6	680	89.4	49.4	22.2
Clinton town (Worcester)..	13,606	13,749	1.1	13,675	82.2	0.8	1.3	4.7	11.1	18.5	67.6	13.8	5,777	57.9	35.1	36.7
Clinton CDP	7,389	NA	NA	7,488	78.2	0.9	1.1	6.4	13.3	21.0	66.2	12.6	3,070	45.4	38.1	33.8
Cochituate CDP	6,569	NA	NA	6,637	81.8	2.0	13.7	0.6	1.9	23.3	57.4	19.3	2,584	85.0	12.5	75.7
Cohasset town (Norfolk) ...	7,540	8,334	10.5	8,100	98.7	0.0	0.0	0.8	0.5	27.9	57.0	15.1	2,900	80.8	12.5	67.2
Colrain town (Franklin)	1,671	1,656	-0.9	1,680	93.4	0.4	1.4	3.8	1.0	19.1	63.0	18.0	704	74.7	40.9	25.1
Concord town (Middlesex)	17,668	19,535	10.6	18,834	84.1	2.9	5.4	2.9	4.8	22.6	58.3	19.0	6,734	77.4	8.2	79.8
Conway town (Franklin)	1,897	1,887	-0.5	1,663	95.9	0.5	0.5	2.0	1.1	17.1	67.9	15.0	708	92.1	16.4	58.5
Cordaville CDP	2,650	NA	NA	2,550	68.3	0.1	29.2	2.0	0.5	34.3	59.3	6.4	796	100.0	11.7	75.6
Cummington town (Hampshire)	872	872	0.0	925	94.1	3.4	0.0	0.5	2.1	21.3	55.3	23.4	428	81.8	32.0	45.3
Dalton town (Berkshire)....	6,756	6,693	-0.9	6,735	95.2	0.8	0.1	0.7	3.2	19.9	59.1	21.0	2,740	78.9	34.7	34.3
Danvers CDP & town (Essex)	26,493	27,460	3.7	27,075	92.3	1.3	2.8	1.0	2.7	21.3	60.2	18.3	10,330	68.7	24.4	46.4
Dartmouth town (Bristol)...	34,032	34,415	1.1	34,384	88.7	2.3	2.4	3.9	2.7	16.0	66.5	17.4	11,287	78.5	40.1	33.7
Dedham CDP & town (Norfolk)	24,729	25,473	3.0	25,111	82.4	5.5	3.9	2.0	6.1	20.4	60.6	19.1	9,710	68.9	24.9	50.4
Deerfield CDP	643	NA	NA	818	72.4	0.4	5.5	18.2	3.5	26.2	69.1	4.6	230	3.5	3.5	48.7
Deerfield town (Franklin)...	5,122	5,054	-1.3	5,097	91.7	0.5	1.2	4.0	2.6	20.3	65.7	13.9	2,093	67.7	16.6	48.4
Dennis CDP	2,407	NA	NA	2,431	97.3	0.0	0.3	1.4	1.0	9.3	45.8	45.0	1,227	89.6	24.4	52.9
Dennis town (Barnstable) .	14,207	14,037	-1.2	14,113	92.1	3.2	0.7	1.9	2.1	13.8	51.9	34.4	6,781	77.7	28.0	39.3
Dennis Port CDP	3,162	NA	NA	2,936	98.2	0.6	0.0	1.2	0.0	13.2	65.1	21.7	1,487	60.3	30.6	33.0
Devens CDP	1,840	NA	NA	1,745	60.5	15.5	1.9	6.8	15.2	9.3	80.5	10.1	194	76.3	29.9	39.2
Dighton town (Bristol)	7,086	7,315	3.2	7,173	95.7	0.1	0.1	2.2	2.0	24.7	61.1	14.3	2,416	92.8	42.5	32.9
Douglas town (Worcester)	8,470	8,681	2.5	8,578	93.8	0.4	0.1	1.9	3.7	27.5	62.9	9.6	3,101	81.8	29.8	40.0
Dover CDP	2,265	NA	NA	2,249	81.3	6.1	7.3	3.4	1.9	31.0	53.6	15.4	748	91.8	1.1	85.2
Dover town (Norfolk)	5,592	5,879	5.1	5,727	84.2	3.6	7.9	1.5	2.8	30.5	53.7	15.8	1,909	92.5	4.6	85.6
Dracut town (Middlesex) ...	29,457	31,079	5.5	30,350	85.8	2.8	4.9	1.3	5.2	23.1	64.1	12.8	10,968	79.5	42.8	26.3
Dudley town (Worcester) ..	11,390	11,818	3.8	11,633	92.4	1.6	0.7	3.2	2.2	23.6	64.9	11.5	4,135	75.1	38.4	27.2
Dunstable town (Middlesex)	3,179	3,389	6.6	3,299	94.6	0.0	3.3	1.8	0.3	26.3	61.5	12.3	1,140	95.8	23.5	56.8
Duxbury CDP	1,802	NA	NA	1,197	95.1	0.0	0.7	2.2	2.1	27.6	52.7	19.6	483	81.8	5.8	84.7
Duxbury town (Plymouth) .	15,059	15,384	2.2	15,208	96.4	0.8	0.8	0.7	1.2	28.1	54.9	17.0	5,305	90.1	13.1	67.3
East Bridgewater town (Plymouth)	13,790	14,243	3.3	13,996	95.6	0.3	1.2	1.3	1.7	22.1	61.7	16.2	4,860	85.0	34.0	25.2
East Brookfield town (Worcester)	2,183	2,186	0.1	2,263	96.0	0.8	0.3	1.9	1.1	18.8	65.3	15.8	833	80.8	36.4	32.3
East Brookfield CDP........	1,323	NA	NA	1,312	93.6	1.3	0.0	3.3	1.8	20.5	67.4	12.2	517	75.2	37.3	25.3
East Dennis CDP.............	2,753	NA	NA	2,928	93.5	2.8	0.0	0.0	3.7	17.8	43.8	38.4	1,309	86.4	20.8	43.5
East Douglas CDP	2,557	NA	NA	2,912	91.3	0.0	0.0	4.4	4.3	29.7	64.5	5.8	1,096	57.0	37.0	32.8
East Falmouth CDP..........	6,038	NA	NA	5,818	82.5	5.9	2.6	6.4	2.6	19.2	50.1	30.7	2,526	77.7	25.5	41.1
Eastham town (Barnstable)	4,956	4,928	-0.6	4,932	96.5	0.0	1.1	0.3	2.1	9.7	58.6	32.0	2,222	84.4	25.7	51.6
Easthampton Town city & MCD (Hampshire)	16,053	16,036	-0.1	16,066	89.3	0.7	3.5	2.0	4.5	15.6	68.1	16.1	7,359	58.1	36.1	34.2
East Harwich CDP............	4,872	NA	NA	4,749	89.5	3.0	3.3	1.9	2.4	15.5	55.4	29.2	1,984	90.3	28.9	42.9
East Longmeadow town (Hampden)	15,720	16,123	2.6	15,917	91.0	3.5	1.6	0.9	3.0	22.0	58.1	20.0	6,033	86.6	26.2	44.3
Easton town (Bristol)	23,112	23,907	3.4	23,548	88.4	4.0	1.7	1.7	4.2	22.9	65.5	11.6	7,608	83.5	20.9	52.9
East Pepperell CDP..........	2,059	NA	NA	1,967	92.0	2.7	0.0	0.5	4.8	22.5	67.2	10.2	711	58.5	37.3	23.6
East Sandwich CDP	3,940	NA	NA	3,861	93.8	0.0	0.0	3.9	2.4	19.6	56.8	23.5	1,511	90.9	16.2	51.0
Edgartown CDP...............	0	NA	NA	999	98.9	0.1	0.0	0.7	0.3	4.4	58.4	37.1	369	75.1	35.8	38.5
Edgartown town (Dukes) ..	4,067	4,308	5.9	4,186	95.9	1.6	0.2	1.9	0.3	12.6	69.6	17.8	1,379	76.3	32.6	43.7
Egremont town (Berkshire)	1,225	1,217	-0.7	1,062	97.5	0.2	0.0	1.2	1.1	10.8	57.7	31.5	537	80.3	27.4	49.7
Erving town (Franklin).......	1,800	1,788	-0.7	1,832	91.9	2.3	1.0	1.6	3.1	23.5	63.3	13.3	741	77.1	40.1	26.5
Essex CDP	1,471	NA	NA	1,733	98.2	0.0	0.0	0.9	1.0	18.4	68.7	13.0	636	71.2	21.4	41.7
Essex town (Essex)	3,504	3,637	3.8	3,580	96.9	0.0	1.0	1.4	0.7	19.6	65.0	15.3	1,401	68.3	28.1	42.8
Everett city & MCD (Middlesex)	41,667	44,231	6.2	42,758	54.4	15.9	4.0	4.8	20.8	22.5	66.1	11.4	15,350	38.9	57.2	16.0
Fairhaven town (Bristol)	15,873	16,034	1.0	15,971	93.7	0.2	2.4	2.7	1.0	17.8	62.0	20.4	6,764	72.5	39.7	26.7
Fall River city & MCD (Bristol)	88,857	88,712	-0.2	88,756	81.9	3.4	2.1	4.1	8.6	20.8	63.1	16.0	38,655	35.8	59.2	14.6
Falmouth CDP	3,799	NA	NA	3,785	83.6	5.5	6.9	3.1	0.8	10.0	50.6	39.4	1,977	49.6	28.4	44.8
Falmouth town (Barnstable)	31,531	31,631	0.3	31,576	87.5	3.9	3.5	3.1	2.1	17.7	54.2	28.1	13,646	77.6	26.8	45.8
Fiskdale CDP	2,583	NA	NA	2,213	90.1	0.0	0.8	2.4	6.6	26.7	53.6	19.8	958	57.7	28.1	34.2
Fitchburg city & MCD (Worcester)	40,318	40,445	0.3	40,419	66.6	3.6	3.8	2.1	23.9	22.3	64.7	13.2	14,782	54.7	46.4	20.2
Florida town (Berkshire) ...	752	738	-1.9	788	91.9	1.8	0.4	3.9	2.0	20.6	60.9	18.7	361	83.7	57.3	20.5
Forestdale CDP	4,099	NA	NA	4,381	95.6	0.0	0.0	0.3	4.0	27.9	64.6	7.6	1,335	82.2	21.3	43.1
Foxborough town (Norfolk)	16,865	17,376	3.0	17,129	91.4	1.3	4.0	1.0	2.3	23.4	63.5	13.3	6,403	69.9	23.2	48.7
Foxborough CDP	5,625	NA	NA	5,013	87.1	2.1	5.4	0.0	5.4	20.6	62.3	17.1	2,127	47.1	27.4	36.2
Framingham CDP & town (Middlesex)	68,326	70,746	3.5	69,900	67.6	6.7	7.4	4.2	14.1	21.4	64.8	13.8	26,724	55.5	32.0	46.8
Franklin Town city & MCD (Norfolk)	31,635	32,836	3.8	32,393	90.8	0.8	3.9	1.4	3.1	27.0	61.7	11.4	10,992	79.3	22.3	53.2
Freetown town (Bristol).....	8,870	9,093	2.5	8,957	96.5	0.3	0.1	2.3	0.7	22.5	64.7	12.9	3,093	86.2	42.0	28.6
Gardner city & MCD (Worcester)	20,228	20,381	0.8	20,279	86.6	1.9	1.3	2.1	8.0	20.9	64.5	14.6	8,132	52.0	45.9	17.6
Georgetown town (Essex)	8,183	8,530	4.2	8,379	95.4	0.5	0.5	2.6	1.0	27.0	59.0	14.1	2,970	82.4	23.2	50.0
Gill town (Franklin)	1,500	1,496	-0.3	1,573	92.0	0.1	0.0	2.2	5.8	13.0	73.1	13.9	562	84.9	35.1	32.2
Gloucester city & MCD (Essex)	28,789	29,626	2.9	29,237	94.2	0.6	0.6	1.7	2.9	17.7	62.7	19.6	12,201	62.4	37.0	34.4
Goshen town (Hampshire)	1,054	1,069	1.4	1,151	96.3	0.0	1.5	0.5	1.7	22.5	62.5	14.8	455	92.1	35.4	43.5

1 May be of any race.

Table A. All Places — **Population and Housing**

STATE City, town, township, borough, or CDP (county if applicable)	2010 census total population	2014 estimated population	Percent change 2010–2014	ACS total population estimate 2010–2014	White alone, not Hispanic or Latino	Black alone, not Hispanic or Latino	Asian alone, not Hispanic or Latino	All other races or 2 or more races, not Hispanic or Latino	Hispanic or Latino[1]	Under 18 years old	Age 18 to 64 years old	Age 65 years and older	Total occupied housing units	Percent owner occupied	High school diploma or less	Bachelor's degree or more
	1	2	3	4	5	6	7	8	9	10	11	12	13	14	15	16
MASSACHUSETTS—Con.																
Gosnold town (Dukes)	75	77	2.7	99	100.0	0.0	0.0	0.0	0.0	0.0	83.0	17.2	51	66.7	27.5	29.4
Grafton town (Worcester) .	17,765	18,371	3.4	18,047	84.3	2.6	7.0	2.6	3.5	25.2	62.6	12.1	6,733	69.2	23.7	50.0
Granby CDP	1,368	NA	NA	1,514	91.8	0.0	0.0	0.0	8.2	18.5	64.3	17.2	627	62.0	49.8	31.3
Granby town (Hampshire) .	6,240	6,333	1.5	6,301	93.6	0.0	0.0	0.5	5.9	21.5	64.2	14.3	2,440	79.8	42.0	33.7
Granville town (Hampden) .	1,566	1,620	3.4	1,518	98.5	0.3	0.0	0.7	0.5	18.3	61.4	20.2	582	88.3	33.3	34.7
Great Barrington CDP	2,231	NA	NA	2,324	65.8	0.2	2.3	1.9	29.9	15.7	66.2	18.0	1,126	49.4	43.3	32.4
Great Barrington town (Berkshire)	7,104	6,945	-2.2	7,029	78.7	1.3	1.7	5.4	12.9	17.4	64.3	18.4	2,616	63.8	38.2	41.2
Greenfield Town city & MCD (Franklin)............	17,456	17,368	-0.5	17,484	88.9	1.4	1.7	1.9	6.1	18.6	64.2	17.1	7,710	55.5	36.6	28.7
Green Harbor-Cedar Crest CDP	2,609	NA	NA	2,782	96.2	0.0	0.0	1.4	2.4	22.6	64.6	12.8	1,045	94.4	26.3	46.5
Groton CDP	1,124	NA	NA	939	91.1	2.1	0.0	2.2	4.6	8.2	52.6	39.2	505	58.6	17.0	63.6
Groton town (Middlesex) ...	10,646	11,222	5.4	10,997	92.6	1.0	3.6	1.1	1.7	25.5	61.8	12.7	4,014	84.7	15.2	66.9
Groveland town (Essex) ...	6,459	7,059	9.3	6,805	95.3	0.7	1.5	0.0	2.6	23.0	60.3	16.7	2,406	85.0	29.6	39.2
Hadley town (Hampshire) .	5,250	5,301	1.0	5,285	91.3	2.7	1.1	0.3	4.7	15.9	62.2	21.9	2,162	68.5	28.6	47.9
Halifax town (Plymouth)....	7,518	7,767	3.3	7,629	94.2	0.0	0.0	2.1	3.7	22.0	63.2	14.7	2,903	90.5	42.5	22.5
Hamilton town (Essex)......	7,764	8,188	5.5	8,098	88.8	3.0	4.4	1.5	2.3	26.6	59.8	13.8	2,838	76.3	12.2	70.8
Hampden town (Hampden)	5,139	5,195	1.1	5,174	97.6	0.4	0.0	1.0	1.0	19.3	59.3	21.6	1,906	91.7	30.4	37.9
Hancock town (Berkshire) .	717	713	-0.6	726	96.4	0.7	0.7	2.2	0.0	25.2	61.1	13.5	266	77.4	39.1	28.6
Hanover town (Plymouth) .	13,879	14,360	3.5	14,120	95.5	0.3	1.6	1.7	0.9	26.7	60.3	12.9	4,718	81.9	24.6	52.6
Hanscom AFB CDP.........	0	NA	NA	1,893	74.6	2.6	1.1	5.4	16.3	47.9	52.1	0.0	499	0.0	5.2	54.3
Hanson CDP..................	2,118	NA	NA	1,718	99.0	0.0	0.0	1.0	0.0	23.4	61.0	15.7	597	94.3	31.0	33.0
Hanson town (Plymouth) ..	10,209	10,441	2.3	10,316	93.7	1.9	0.5	1.9	2.1	24.2	63.4	12.3	3,438	88.4	30.7	31.4
Hardwick town (Worcester)	2,990	3,010	0.7	3,006	92.9	0.0	0.6	2.0	4.6	18.4	63.4	18.4	1,221	71.1	49.1	21.9
Harvard town (Worcester) .	6,520	6,566	0.7	6,558	80.6	7.3	3.4	2.7	6.0	23.0	63.9	13.2	1,911	90.8	9.2	79.0
Harwich town (Barnstable)	12,243	12,188	-0.4	12,205	92.1	2.0	2.5	1.6	1.8	15.2	57.2	27.7	5,358	82.3	26.0	45.3
Harwich Center CDP	1,798	NA	NA	1,902	94.2	4.3	0.0	0.0	1.5	16.8	64.2	19.1	834	71.8	29.7	43.3
Harwich Port CDP	1,644	NA	NA	1,772	90.2	0.3	8.6	0.5	0.4	9.1	51.1	39.7	907	79.6	16.1	62.4
Hatfield CDP	1,318	NA	NA	1,420	95.1	0.1	4.2	0.5	0.0	18.0	59.7	22.2	666	79.4	30.2	43.8
Hatfield town (Hampshire)	3,279	3,290	0.3	3,293	95.3	0.9	1.8	0.8	1.2	16.9	59.7	23.5	1,573	75.3	37.8	39.6
Haverhill city & MCD (Essex)	60,879	62,488	2.6	61,769	76.8	2.0	1.3	2.5	17.4	22.9	64.1	13.0	23,529	61.8	38.3	29.8
Hawley town (Franklin)	337	331	-1.8	435	97.0	0.0	1.6	0.5	0.9	17.7	60.9	21.4	162	88.9	45.7	32.1
Heath town (Franklin)	706	700	-0.8	629	95.9	0.0	0.3	1.4	2.4	13.3	66.6	20.0	269	88.1	40.5	31.6
Hingham CDP.................	5,650	NA	NA	5,199	96.7	0.0	0.8	2.0	0.6	27.7	57.7	14.6	1,875	80.4	13.4	71.7
Hingham town (Plymouth) .	22,157	22,964	3.6	22,550	95.4	0.4	2.1	1.2	1.0	26.4	53.2	20.4	8,375	80.1	15.2	67.1
Hinsdale town (Berkshire)	2,032	1,980	-2.6	2,161	97.0	1.0	0.0	1.2	0.7	22.4	62.2	15.5	869	88.1	42.6	25.0
Holbrook CDP & town (Norfolk)	10,802	11,026	2.1	10,925	79.4	7.6	2.7	1.9	8.3	17.4	66.8	15.9	4,343	79.1	44.1	24.0
Holden town (Worcester)..	17,346	18,476	6.5	17,802	92.8	1.2	2.9	1.0	2.1	24.0	61.9	14.4	6,299	89.7	21.4	56.0
Holland CDP..................	1,464	NA	NA	1,405	92.2	3.8	0.4	0.8	2.8	15.7	71.1	13.2	607	84.8	32.3	37.2
Holland town (Hampden)..	2,481	2,502	0.8	2,491	92.7	2.2	0.2	0.8	4.2	16.8	71.1	12.1	1,052	85.1	38.6	33.9
Holliston town (Middlesex)	13,547	14,388	6.2	14,008	93.4	0.7	2.1	1.2	2.6	27.1	59.4	13.6	5,028	81.8	16.9	59.5
Holyoke city & MCD (Hampden)	39,880	40,124	0.6	40,079	46.1	4.0	1.7	1.3	47.0	24.6	61.4	14.1	15,599	40.2	50.1	22.2
Hopedale town (Worcester)	5,911	5,950	0.7	5,934	92.8	0.3	1.4	0.0	5.5	25.9	61.0	13.0	2,240	79.6	32.4	41.3
Hopedale CDP................	3,753	NA	NA	3,858	96.7	0.5	1.3	0.0	1.6	24.9	60.6	14.4	1,476	76.4	33.3	35.0
Hopkinton CDP...............	2,550	NA	NA	2,509	93.3	0.7	0.0	2.2	3.7	24.4	58.5	17.2	1,025	62.3	25.1	53.0
Hopkinton town (Middlesex)	14,925	16,311	9.3	15,604	91.0	0.7	5.1	1.6	1.6	30.9	60.2	8.9	5,219	86.0	14.0	67.2
Housatonic CDP	1,109	NA	NA	814	98.8	0.0	0.0	1.2	0.0	21.0	56.9	22.2	343	62.1	29.4	50.1
Hubbardston town (Worcester)	4,382	4,522	3.2	4,452	96.8	2.6	0.2	0.4	0.0	25.7	63.6	10.7	1,558	91.7	40.8	28.6
Hudson town (Middlesex) .	19,063	19,754	3.6	19,464	88.5	0.9	2.4	4.5	3.6	20.7	61.9	17.3	7,657	75.2	33.1	38.1
Hudson CDP..................	14,907	NA	NA	15,212	88.0	1.1	2.3	4.5	4.1	20.0	61.7	18.5	6,079	69.9	37.4	32.1
Hull CDP & town (Plymouth)...............	10,293	10,365	0.7	10,324	92.5	0.7	0.9	2.8	3.1	16.6	63.8	19.6	4,766	72.4	28.8	45.1
Huntington CDP..............	936	NA	NA	785	86.9	0.0	0.0	7.6	5.5	16.3	70.0	13.6	371	54.7	43.9	12.4
Huntington town (Hampshire)	2,180	2,179	0.0	2,034	90.0	3.4	0.0	4.3	2.3	23.3	62.5	14.2	801	75.2	43.3	14.5
Ipswich CDP	4,222	NA	NA	4,003	95.8	0.4	1.2	0.6	1.9	17.9	64.0	18.0	1,827	59.8	30.8	42.1
Ipswich town (Essex)........	13,175	13,661	3.7	13,480	96.8	0.2	0.5	1.0	1.4	19.9	60.8	19.4	5,679	76.4	22.7	48.9
Kingston CDP	5,591	NA	NA	6,103	91.0	4.1	1.3	1.6	2.0	19.9	67.8	12.2	2,334	74.1	31.6	36.8
Kingston town (Plymouth).	12,629	13,154	4.2	12,846	92.5	2.0	1.1	2.3	2.1	21.5	62.3	16.3	4,625	82.3	31.1	38.7
Lakeville town (Plymouth).	10,602	11,208	5.7	10,933	95.3	0.7	0.7	1.3	2.0	23.6	62.6	13.9	3,745	86.7	36.8	38.8
Lancaster town (Worcester)	8,055	8,111	0.7	8,026	84.4	5.9	1.3	2.3	6.1	20.1	67.0	12.9	2,330	82.8	18.9	39.7
Lanesborough town (Berkshire)	3,091	3,015	-2.5	3,064	95.7	0.0	3.6	0.7	0.0	23.7	64.1	12.4	1,161	92.9	33.5	37.0
Lawrence city & MCD (Essex)	76,377	78,197	2.4	77,364	17.7	2.3	3.3	1.0	75.7	27.9	63.1	8.9	26,328	28.0	61.3	13.0
Lee CDP......................	2,051	NA	NA	1,914	86.7	0.5	8.1	0.0	4.7	16.6	65.4	17.9	886	42.9	41.5	29.6
Lee town (Berkshire)	5,943	5,861	-1.4	5,922	94.2	0.2	2.6	0.0	3.0	17.7	62.2	20.1	2,472	74.1	33.7	40.6
Leicester town (Worcester)	10,970	11,270	2.7	11,147	91.6	1.0	1.3	0.7	5.4	17.6	67.1	15.3	4,200	73.0	33.9	26.7
Lenox CDP	1,675	NA	NA	1,655	92.3	0.1	2.7	0.7	4.2	20.1	46.7	33.2	905	36.8	28.4	46.4
Lenox town (Berkshire)	5,078	5,004	-1.5	5,043	92.0	1.0	3.1	1.2	2.6	19.1	48.9	32.1	2,368	65.1	23.8	47.3
Leominster city & MCD (Worcester)	40,759	41,150	1.0	40,954	75.1	4.9	2.5	2.5	15.1	20.2	65.1	14.7	16,751	54.6	41.2	28.6
Leverett town (Franklin)	1,854	1,856	0.1	1,836	92.4	1.1	1.7	2.3	2.5	17.8	59.0	23.1	786	85.2	12.6	68.3
Lexington CDP & town (Middlesex)	31,394	33,075	5.4	32,306	72.2	1.1	21.9	3.0	1.8	26.2	55.3	18.3	11,594	81.9	8.2	80.5
Leyden town (Franklin)	711	718	1.0	650	99.4	0.0	0.0	0.0	0.6	14.4	73.3	12.2	300	95.0	30.3	37.0
Lincoln town (Middlesex)..	6,362	7,289	14.6	7,181	79.7	3.3	6.9	3.1	7.1	31.6	54.3	14.2	2,502	68.0	6.0	76.9
Littleton town (Middlesex)	8,924	9,396	5.3	9,157	90.8	0.3	4.7	3.1	1.1	22.9	63.1	13.9	3,346	84.3	16.3	61.7
Littleton Common CDP	2,789	NA	NA	2,845	95.7	0.0	3.2	1.1	0.0	23.4	61.1	15.3	1,092	81.2	25.3	51.6
Longmeadow CDP & town (Hampden)	15,784	15,882	0.6	15,858	88.4	0.7	6.3	1.0	3.7	24.5	55.1	20.3	5,725	90.4	13.8	66.7

1 May be of any race.

Table A. All Places — Population and Housing

STATE City, town, township, borough, or CDP (county if applicable)	2010 census total population	2014 estimated population	Percent change 2010–2014	ACS total population estimate 2010–2014	White alone, not Hispanic or Latino	Black alone, not Hispanic or Latino	Asian alone, not Hispanic or Latino	All other races or 2 or more races, not Hispanic or Latino	Hispanic or Latino[1]	Under 18 years old	Age 18 to 64 years old	Age 65 years and older	Total occupied housing units	Percent owner occupied	High school diploma or less	Bachelor's degree or more
	1	2	3	4	5	6	7	8	9	10	11	12	13	14	15	16
MASSACHUSETTS—Con.																
Lowell city & MCD (Middlesex)	106,519	109,945	3.2	108,491	50.3	6.7	20.8	4.1	18.2	22.4	67.2	10.4	38,639	44.4	50.2	23.7
Ludlow town (Hampden)...	21,103	21,436	1.6	21,288	91.5	1.6	0.7	0.9	5.4	18.6	63.6	17.7	8,228	76.7	46.1	24.2
Lunenburg CDP................	1,760	NA	NA	1,831	88.6	0.1	6.1	5.2	0.0	22.1	54.6	23.3	767	82.3	33.8	38.6
Lunenburg town (Worcester)...............	10,086	11,107	10.1	10,797	91.0	1.6	1.5	1.5	4.4	21.9	62.4	15.7	4,247	80.5	36.6	35.2
Lynn city & MCD (Essex)..	90,329	92,137	2.0	91,289	43.6	11.2	7.6	3.3	34.2	25.2	63.3	11.4	32,764	45.6	49.8	20.4
Lynnfield CDP & town (Essex)......................	11,596	12,668	9.2	12,058	92.4	1.2	3.5	1.0	2.0	22.4	59.7	17.8	4,303	86.8	25.0	48.5
Madaket CDP	236	NA	NA	273	98.5	0.0	1.5	0.0	0.0	22.7	60.6	16.8	124	83.9	2.4	79.0
Malden city & MCD (Middlesex)	59,464	60,859	2.3	60,309	47.7	12.9	23.8	4.5	11.1	19.0	69.9	10.9	22,851	41.4	39.9	34.7
Manchester-by-the-Sea town (Essex)................	5,136	5,336	3.9	5,247	97.4	0.0	0.0	0.5	2.1	23.9	54.7	21.3	2,108	65.5	15.5	57.0
Mansfield town (Bristol)	23,184	23,595	1.8	23,389	86.7	2.9	5.2	2.7	2.5	28.5	63.0	8.5	8,223	72.4	22.3	52.5
Mansfield Center CDP........	7,360	NA	NA	7,861	90.2	1.7	2.3	3.8	2.0	24.3	65.3	10.4	3,089	55.6	26.4	46.5
Marblehead CDP & town (Essex)......................	19,808	20,454	3.3	20,163	95.2	0.6	0.8	0.8	2.6	25.1	55.5	19.4	8,127	79.8	11.2	71.1
Marion town (Plymouth).......	4,907	5,048	2.9	4,935	91.2	1.2	1.1	5.0	1.5	21.9	54.2	23.9	1,872	74.6	21.5	49.4
Marion Center CDP.........	1,111	NA	NA	1,176	93.5	4.5	0.0	0.0	2.0	21.8	49.6	28.7	457	58.6	18.2	50.5
Marlborough city & MCD (Middlesex)	38,499	39,612	2.9	39,141	74.3	1.9	4.5	6.6	12.8	20.5	66.7	12.9	15,740	55.9	35.7	41.5
Marshfield CDP	4,335	NA	NA	4,227	93.6	0.0	1.1	4.0	1.4	18.3	63.6	18.0	1,850	63.8	33.0	37.9
Marshfield town (Plymouth)................	25,132	25,635	2.0	25,430	94.4	0.1	0.9	3.6	1.0	24.2	61.3	14.5	9,577	80.2	22.1	49.8
Marshfield Hills CDP.........	2,356	NA	NA	2,423	92.5	0.0	1.4	5.4	0.7	20.9	60.6	18.4	865	85.5	9.8	59.1
Mashpee town (Barnstable)	14,006	14,049	0.3	13,988	89.5	1.6	1.0	5.1	2.8	18.4	54.8	26.7	6,083	85.3	30.2	37.4
Mashpee Neck CDP	1,000	NA	NA	666	94.6	0.0	0.0	0.0	5.4	17.8	49.0	33.5	290	89.3	11.4	43.8
Mattapoisett town (Plymouth)................	6,045	6,221	2.9	6,138	97.3	0.5	0.7	1.3	0.1	23.9	57.2	18.9	2,289	79.7	21.8	50.6
Mattapoisett Center CDP..	2,915	NA	NA	3,199	96.5	1.0	1.4	1.1	0.0	25.5	57.6	16.7	1,185	71.2	19.5	52.2
Maynard CDP & town (Middlesex)	10,110	10,474	3.6	10,314	86.8	2.7	4.5	2.3	3.7	21.6	65.2	13.4	4,257	67.4	30.4	48.7
Medfield CDP	6,483	NA	NA	5,964	94.9	0.1	3.5	0.5	1.0	27.0	57.7	15.5	2,229	85.5	20.4	63.6
Medfield town (Norfolk).....	12,024	12,394	3.1	12,236	91.1	0.1	3.4	1.0	4.4	29.6	58.9	11.5	4,106	90.7	13.4	71.8
Medford city & MCD (Middlesex)	56,253	57,437	2.1	56,981	75.9	8.7	7.4	3.3	4.6	15.2	70.4	14.3	22,126	57.5	28.3	48.9
Medway town (Norfolk)	12,758	13,184	3.3	12,965	90.3	0.4	3.9	1.6	3.8	25.9	62.5	11.6	4,530	84.0	21.2	54.8
Melrose city & MCD (Middlesex)	26,983	27,969	3.7	27,509	88.3	2.6	4.1	1.1	3.9	20.8	63.2	15.8	11,304	67.2	21.7	55.1
Mendon town (Worcester)	5,839	5,960	2.1	5,895	90.8	0.7	1.3	2.2	5.1	26.2	61.4	12.5	2,045	92.0	15.8	53.8
Merrimac town (Essex).....	6,338	6,724	6.1	6,536	97.7	0.1	0.0	0.1	2.1	23.3	61.3	15.5	2,516	85.2	25.9	45.9
Methuen Town city & MCD (Essex)......................	47,255	49,112	3.9	48,159	72.2	1.8	3.2	1.3	21.4	23.4	62.3	14.3	17,584	71.2	38.8	31.1
Middleborough town (Plymouth)................	23,116	24,103	4.3	23,541	94.0	2.1	1.0	1.3	1.6	22.2	62.3	15.4	8,347	77.5	36.1	29.5
Middleborough Center CDP......................	7,319	NA	NA	7,432	93.4	0.9	0.3	2.9	2.5	27.6	59.8	12.4	2,668	49.4	46.8	19.6
Middlefield town (Hampshire)	521	528	1.3	514	95.3	0.0	0.0	4.7	0.0	13.6	63.4	23.0	234	93.2	41.9	26.1
Middleton town (Essex)	8,987	9,578	6.6	9,273	81.9	3.0	4.8	1.2	9.0	19.9	65.7	14.4	2,643	84.9	29.0	49.2
Milford town (Worcester)...	27,993	28,439	1.6	28,203	81.5	2.8	2.7	4.5	8.5	23.4	63.7	12.9	10,706	67.0	34.8	37.0
Milford CDP	25,055	NA	NA	25,422	80.5	3.0	2.7	4.5	9.3	23.7	63.0	13.1	9,674	63.7	36.8	34.3
Millbury town (Worcester) .	13,261	13,460	1.5	13,350	92.8	0.7	2.5	0.8	3.2	20.5	64.1	15.6	5,141	73.2	41.8	31.3
Millers Falls CDP	1,139	NA	NA	855	93.5	0.0	0.0	4.8	1.8	15.2	63.5	21.4	399	83.7	35.8	37.3
Millis town (Norfolk)	7,891	8,099	2.6	8,007	93.1	0.0	2.8	0.4	3.6	23.6	64.7	11.5	2,961	77.5	21.3	50.1
Millis-Clicquot CDP	4,403	NA	NA	4,260	96.0	0.1	2.7	0.0	1.2	21.8	63.7	14.3	1,650	74.8	22.7	47.8
Millville town (Worcester)..	3,190	3,223	1.0	3,208	93.4	1.2	1.0	1.6	2.8	25.9	64.0	10.2	1,056	78.9	40.6	29.6
Milton CDP & town (Norfolk)...................	27,003	27,360	1.3	27,204	74.4	13.3	5.7	2.0	4.6	25.1	60.0	14.9	8,995	79.2	15.5	64.9
Monomoscoy Island CDP .	147	NA	NA	170	100.0	0.0	0.0	0.0	0.0	8.8	42.4	48.8	66	89.4	56.1	33.3
Monroe town (Franklin).....	121	120	-0.8	118	98.3	0.0	0.0	1.7	0.0	13.5	71.1	15.3	66	80.3	51.5	24.2
Monson town (Hampden) .	8,560	8,754	2.3	8,660	95.7	0.5	0.3	2.1	1.4	20.8	64.0	15.2	3,432	82.4	41.5	28.1
Monson Center CDP	2,107	NA	NA	1,935	92.4	0.4	1.2	5.4	0.5	21.0	64.3	14.7	868	56.2	34.8	30.8
Montague town (Franklin)...	8,437	8,325	-1.3	8,394	89.7	0.6	1.0	3.9	4.8	20.5	61.2	18.3	3,633	64.2	37.9	28.9
Monterey town (Berkshire) .	961	954	-0.7	777	95.5	1.4	0.0	1.4	1.7	15.6	55.0	29.3	340	82.9	25.0	51.2
Montgomery town (Hampden)	838	860	2.6	950	98.7	0.0	0.5	0.7	0.0	16.8	68.1	15.1	360	95.8	27.5	38.3
Monument Beach CDP	2,790	NA	NA	3,224	93.8	5.4	0.9	0.0	0.0	17.7	61.1	21.1	1,316	85.5	21.3	43.4
Mount Washington town (Berkshire)	167	164	-1.8	151	92.1	4.6	0.0	2.6	0.7	4.6	57.6	37.7	75	100.0	26.7	45.3
Nahant CDP & town (Essex)......................	3,410	3,479	2.0	3,451	93.4	2.7	0.2	0.0	3.7	15.4	62.2	22.5	1,593	65.9	20.2	49.5
Nantucket CDP................	7,446	NA	NA	7,787	71.7	10.9	1.4	6.9	9.1	22.2	66.7	11.1	2,822	60.2	30.3	45.4
Nantucket town (Nantucket)................	10,172	10,856	6.7	10,414	77.8	8.1	1.2	5.6	7.2	21.0	66.2	12.8	3,978	64.2	24.6	49.8
Natick town (Middlesex)....	33,002	35,523	7.6	34,230	84.4	1.5	9.3	1.6	3.2	23.9	61.6	14.6	14,044	73.4	16.6	67.6
Needham CDP & town (Norfolk)...................	28,890	30,205	4.6	29,540	86.5	2.0	6.7	2.3	2.5	27.1	55.4	17.3	10,536	82.5	9.1	78.0
New Ashford town (Berkshire)	228	224	-1.8	238	94.5	1.7	0.8	0.8	2.1	18.9	68.5	12.6	91	84.6	28.6	49.5
New Bedford city & MCD (Bristol)......................	95,072	94,845	-0.2	94,873	67.0	6.7	1.2	7.7	17.5	22.6	62.2	15.2	39,088	42.5	57.5	16.0
New Braintree town (Worcester)...............	999	1,022	2.3	1,109	97.8	0.6	0.4	0.0	1.2	24.4	62.6	13.0	376	89.1	33.0	37.0
Newbury town (Essex)......	6,666	6,926	3.9	6,794	97.9	0.3	0.5	0.6	0.7	20.1	63.3	16.6	2,677	82.2	13.9	61.3
Newburyport city & MCD (Essex)......................	17,416	17,926	2.9	17,662	94.3	0.7	1.1	1.3	2.6	20.5	62.0	17.6	7,395	71.6	15.9	60.9
New Marlborough town (Berkshire)	1,509	1,492	-1.1	1,497	95.1	0.7	1.2	1.3	1.7	16.9	59.3	23.8	634	85.3	35.5	41.2

1 May be of any race.

Table A. All Places — **Population and Housing**

	Population				Race and Hispanic or Latino origin (percent), 2010–2014					Age (percent), 2010–2014			Households, 2010–2014			
								All other races or 2 or more								Householders by level of education (percent)	
STATE City, town, township, borough, or CDP (county if applicable)	2010 census total population	2014 estimated population	Percent change 2010–2014	ACS total population estimate 2010–2014	White alone, not Hispanic or Latino	Black alone, not Hispanic or Latino	Asian alone, not Hispanic or Latino	races not Hispanic or Latino	Hispanic or Latino[1]	Under 18 years old	Age 18 to 64 years old	Age 65 years and older	Total occupied housing units	Percent owner occupied	High school diploma or less	Bachelor's degree or more
	1	2	3	4	5	6	7	8	9	10	11	12	13	14	15	16

MASSACHUSETTS—Con.

	1	2	3	4	5	6	7	8	9	10	11	12	13	14	15	16
New Salem town (Franklin)	990	1,000	1.0	1,089	97.0	1.4	0.5	0.8	0.4	19.5	64.4	16.2	454	89.6	23.3	40.1
New Seabury CDP	717	NA	NA	1,005	87.6	0.0	2.9	0.0	9.6	16.7	47.2	36.0	513	85.6	7.2	71.3
Newton city & MCD (Middlesex)	85,174	88,287	3.7	86,945	75.1	3.6	13.3	2.6	5.4	22.2	62.1	15.8	31,175	69.7	10.8	76.4
Norfolk town (Norfolk)	11,227	11,800	5.1	11,529	85.7	7.3	1.2	1.1	4.8	21.9	68.9	9.1	3,185	94.3	15.8	66.0
North Adams city & MCD (Berkshire)	13,708	13,354	-2.6	13,563	92.0	0.1	0.3	2.5	3.2	16.7	65.0	18.2	6,069	50.8	49.8	22.0
North Amherst CDP	6,819	NA	NA	7,517	71.7	6.2	15.1	1.6	5.4	7.1	89.1	3.8	1,911	27.7	9.0	53.1
Northampton city & MCD (Hampshire)	28,549	28,554	0.0	28,637	81.3	2.6	6.6	1.9	7.6	16.5	68.3	15.0	11,637	57.2	19.7	59.1
North Andover town (Essex)	28,352	29,478	4.0	28,963	85.4	1.6	6.4	1.5	5.1	23.5	62.1	14.4	10,609	73.5	18.9	59.3
North Attleborough town (Bristol)	28,712	28,908	0.7	28,779	92.0	1.7	3.3	1.0	2.0	26.9	62.2	10.8	10,302	75.7	26.3	43.8
Northborough CDP	6,167	NA	NA	6,613	86.4	2.5	5.1	1.1	4.9	24.4	62.0	13.7	2,427	76.8	20.3	57.6
Northborough town (Worcester)	14,155	14,834	4.8	14,644	84.3	1.5	8.8	1.7	3.7	24.4	61.7	14.1	5,156	82.7	18.8	59.6
Northbridge town (Worcester)	15,707	16,407	4.5	16,100	93.8	0.3	1.4	2.1	2.5	25.4	61.6	13.1	5,913	66.2	36.2	32.6
North Brookfield CDP	2,265	NA	NA	2,079	96.4	2.0	0.4	0.0	1.2	23.5	62.5	14.0	815	64.9	58.5	14.7
North Brookfield town (Worcester)	4,680	4,748	1.5	4,715	96.6	1.8	0.5	0.6	0.6	22.9	63.9	13.2	1,815	71.5	47.6	20.8
North Eastham CDP	1,806	NA	NA	1,917	97.8	0.0	2.2	0.0	0.0	10.2	51.9	37.9	838	85.3	25.8	51.0
North Falmouth CDP	3,084	NA	NA	2,957	91.5	0.8	0.6	2.6	4.4	16.2	54.2	29.6	1,336	85.6	17.0	49.5
Northfield CDP	1,089	NA	NA	1,060	89.7	0.0	6.0	0.0	4.2	23.1	59.8	17.1	495	63.4	25.9	45.7
Northfield town (Franklin)	3,032	3,012	-0.7	3,031	95.0	0.2	2.1	0.4	2.3	22.1	63.1	15.0	1,255	78.7	32.6	40.0
North Lakeville CDP	2,630	NA	NA	2,409	95.8	1.9	0.0	2.3	0.0	16.1	63.0	20.7	1,068	70.1	49.8	33.6
North Pembroke CDP	3,292	NA	NA	3,313	89.9	1.8	0.0	0.9	7.5	26.3	61.6	12.3	1,199	57.5	29.1	36.9
North Plymouth CDP	3,600	NA	NA	3,747	93.2	1.5	0.0	2.3	3.0	22.5	63.5	14.0	1,561	42.0	45.4	22.8
North Reading town (Middlesex)	14,892	15,509	4.1	15,249	89.4	0.8	6.3	1.8	1.7	23.2	63.2	13.6	5,424	85.6	22.7	56.2
North Scituate CDP	5,077	NA	NA	4,962	97.2	0.1	0.6	1.2	0.8	26.5	60.1	13.5	1,788	84.5	16.8	62.6
North Seekonk CDP	2,643	NA	NA	2,660	94.0	2.8	0.6	0.0	2.6	18.9	68.8	12.4	957	93.4	36.6	29.7
Northwest Harwich CDP	3,929	NA	NA	3,782	95.1	0.2	0.0	2.6	2.0	17.0	58.7	24.4	1,633	79.4	26.0	39.8
North Westport CDP	4,571	NA	NA	4,540	96.2	0.8	1.1	1.7	0.3	16.6	60.4	23.0	1,801	78.1	44.3	25.4
Norton town (Bristol)	19,031	19,396	1.9	19,280	93.4	1.4	2.7	1.5	1.0	20.3	68.1	11.6	6,290	82.5	28.1	39.0
Norton Center CDP	2,671	NA	NA	2,870	82.3	4.4	6.0	3.3	4.0	11.2	85.0	3.8	368	83.7	18.2	53.0
Norwell town (Plymouth)	10,506	10,817	3.0	10,651	95.6	0.2	1.3	1.8	1.1	28.0	55.2	16.8	3,541	91.7	19.3	60.0
Norwood CDP & town (Norfolk)	28,604	29,056	1.6	28,844	81.6	4.0	6.3	3.4	4.7	21.2	61.9	16.8	11,623	57.2	29.7	43.8
Oak Bluffs town (Dukes)	4,527	4,698	3.8	4,599	94.2	2.6	2.4	0.8	0.0	22.5	53.1	24.3	1,824	78.1	25.8	42.2
Oakham town (Worcester)	1,902	1,921	1.0	1,791	98.6	0.0	0.0	0.8	0.6	21.4	67.0	11.4	640	88.9	31.6	38.8
Ocean Bluff-Brant Rock CDP	4,970	NA	NA	5,198	98.5	0.2	0.0	1.1	0.3	20.8	64.0	15.2	2,085	80.6	21.0	43.5
Ocean Grove CDP	2,811	NA	NA	2,674	95.3	0.5	1.0	3.0	0.3	18.1	66.1	15.9	1,045	75.2	38.0	23.0
Onset CDP	1,573	NA	NA	1,068	66.2	2.2	0.0	31.6	0.0	22.6	59.6	18.0	587	64.6	65.8	2.9
Orange CDP	4,018	NA	NA	3,944	95.8	1.4	1.0	0.9	0.9	22.8	63.6	13.6	1,584	57.8	47.3	14.3
Orange town (Franklin)	7,839	7,713	-1.6	7,793	95.4	0.7	1.1	1.2	1.6	22.6	60.9	16.4	3,215	66.2	49.6	15.4
Orleans CDP	1,621	NA	NA	1,531	91.0	1.9	0.0	1.8	5.4	5.5	54.5	40.0	946	59.5	25.6	39.2
Orleans town (Barnstable)	5,890	5,863	-0.5	5,874	96.8	0.6	0.3	0.5	1.8	8.5	50.4	41.1	2,956	76.5	18.9	52.2
Otis town (Berkshire)	1,612	1,585	-1.7	1,470	94.4	0.6	2.1	0.6	2.2	17.6	58.8	23.6	632	92.2	34.2	27.5
Oxford CDP	6,103	NA	NA	6,525	97.2	0.4	0.0	0.6	1.8	25.2	62.1	12.9	2,280	75.8	40.8	26.1
Oxford town (Worcester)	13,709	13,853	1.1	13,772	92.4	0.4	0.4	2.1	4.7	23.5	64.3	11.9	5,170	75.3	40.7	26.4
Palmer Town city & MCD (Hampden)	12,140	12,174	0.3	12,155	95.9	0.4	0.1	1.0	2.6	21.0	65.0	14.0	4,872	68.6	47.1	17.2
Paxton town (Worcester)	4,806	4,854	1.0	4,839	84.1	3.2	0.5	1.5	10.7	20.2	65.9	14.1	1,513	89.4	14.1	52.9
Peabody city & MCD (Essex)	51,251	52,376	2.2	51,868	86.5	1.8	2.4	1.5	7.8	18.8	60.6	20.7	21,686	63.8	41.1	30.9
Pelham town (Hampshire)	1,321	1,327	0.5	1,350	86.1	2.7	1.0	0.7	9.6	18.9	61.5	19.6	554	82.7	17.3	68.2
Pembroke town (Plymouth)	17,837	18,197	2.0	18,006	94.6	0.3	0.5	2.1	2.5	24.9	63.3	11.9	6,248	86.2	32.3	35.8
Pepperell CDP	2,504	NA	NA	2,361	90.1	0.3	2.1	1.5	6.1	26.0	60.7	13.0	938	43.0	45.8	23.6
Pepperell town (Middlesex)	11,497	11,975	4.2	11,782	92.7	0.7	1.6	2.1	3.0	25.4	63.6	11.0	4,203	75.8	34.7	37.3
Peru town (Berkshire)	847	846	-0.1	871	94.7	1.3	0.3	3.0	0.7	17.7	72.8	9.5	356	94.9	39.3	27.8
Petersham CDP	243	NA	NA	269	87.0	0.0	8.6	4.5	0.0	13.7	56.9	29.4	125	77.6	11.2	64.0
Petersham town (Worcester)	1,234	1,247	1.1	1,277	95.6	0.5	2.0	1.3	0.6	17.2	63.2	19.7	491	88.4	25.7	45.4
Phillipston town (Worcester)	1,689	1,715	1.5	1,647	94.2	0.0	0.8	1.6	3.4	20.8	70.6	8.7	587	94.4	40.7	27.4
Pinehurst CDP	7,152	NA	NA	7,452	89.7	1.6	6.8	0.6	1.2	23.2	64.4	12.3	2,545	96.2	37.5	27.3
Pittsfield city & MCD (Berkshire)	44,737	43,697	-2.3	44,226	85.0	5.6	1.4	2.7	5.3	19.9	62.1	18.0	19,541	60.7	40.6	26.8
Plainfield town (Hampshire)	648	650	0.3	605	91.7	2.1	1.8	3.5	0.8	17.7	59.0	23.3	256	91.8	27.7	50.0
Plainville town (Norfolk)	8,264	8,910	7.8	8,581	93.8	0.3	3.0	2.6	0.3	21.2	66.7	12.1	3,391	74.6	30.2	42.7
Plymouth CDP	7,494	NA	NA	7,567	90.3	2.2	0.8	6.1	0.5	16.9	66.3	16.9	3,330	45.3	37.4	28.2
Plymouth town (Plymouth)	56,468	58,271	3.2	57,414	92.1	2.0	0.9	2.7	2.3	20.8	62.3	17.0	21,833	78.6	29.0	37.3
Plympton town (Plymouth)	2,820	2,873	1.9	2,840	97.1	0.0	0.6	0.5	1.8	18.8	65.7	15.5	987	93.9	26.4	36.2
Pocasset CDP	2,851	NA	NA	2,932	88.6	5.0	2.3	2.2	1.8	9.1	49.2	41.6	1,462	69.2	24.5	43.1
Popponesset CDP	220	NA	NA	227	100.0	0.0	0.0	0.0	0.0	0.0	46.3	53.7	171	100.0	5.8	83.6
Popponesset Island CDP	26	NA	NA	24	66.7	0.0	0.0	0.0	33.3	0.0	37.5	62.5	16	100.0	0.0	100.0
Princeton town (Worcester)	3,413	3,443	0.9	3,432	91.1	0.8	1.3	0.7	6.0	24.3	64.5	11.2	1,234	85.7	15.2	65.5
Provincetown town (Barnstable)	2,942	2,980	1.3	2,959	88.6	3.1	1.0	2.2	5.1	4.4	71.0	24.6	1,737	64.8	22.2	50.8
Provincetown CDP	2,642	NA	NA	2,777	88.0	3.3	0.9	2.3	5.4	4.1	71.2	24.6	1,591	64.9	23.0	50.3
Quincy city & MCD (Norfolk)	92,271	93,397	1.2	92,920	63.2	5.4	25.8	2.6	3.1	16.5	68.9	14.7	39,643	47.6	33.3	43.2
Randolph CDP & town (Norfolk)	32,108	33,629	4.7	33,135	37.7	41.3	11.0	3.2	6.8	20.7	64.2	15.1	11,903	69.2	37.8	29.6

1 May be of any race.

Table A. All Places — Population and Housing

	Population				Race and Hispanic or Latino origin (percent), 2010–2014					Age (percent), 2010–2014			Households, 2010–2014			
STATE City, town, township, borough, or CDP (county if applicable)	2010 census total population	2014 estimated population	Percent change 2010–2014	ACS total population estimate 2010–2014	White alone, not Hispanic or Latino	Black alone, not Hispanic or Latino	Asian alone, not Hispanic or Latino	All other races or 2 or more races, not Hispanic or Latino	Hispanic or Latino[1]	Under 18 years old	Age 18 to 64 years old	Age 65 years and older	Total occupied housing units	Percent owner occupied	High school diploma or less	Bachelor's degree or more
	1	2	3	4	5	6	7	8	9	10	11	12	13	14	15	16
MASSACHUSETTS—Con.																
Raynham town (Bristol)	13,383	13,691	2.3	13,517	85.0	4.3	4.3	3.9	2.6	24.1	60.9	15.0	4,773	75.2	30.4	36.3
Raynham Center CDP......	4,100	NA	NA	4,480	71.1	11.3	8.7	4.4	4.5	30.4	58.5	11.0	1,398	70.5	24.0	39.4
Reading CDP & town (Middlesex)	24,733	25,508	3.1	25,176	91.0	1.1	4.3	0.8	2.8	24.8	60.4	14.8	9,294	79.7	17.3	59.7
Rehoboth town (Bristol)	11,608	11,926	2.7	11,742	97.9	0.2	0.5	1.0	0.5	21.1	66.2	12.7	3,967	88.9	28.5	34.9
Revere city & MCD (Suffolk)	51,733	54,157	4.7	53,258	61.4	4.2	5.9	2.3	26.2	18.9	67.3	13.8	20,110	49.4	54.0	21.1
Richmond town (Berkshire)	1,475	1,440	-2.4	1,535	96.2	0.1	0.8	1.2	1.6	13.4	57.7	28.9	687	85.3	20.4	51.5
Rochester town (Plymouth)................	5,232	5,443	4.0	5,348	90.4	0.8	3.2	3.9	1.7	24.5	63.0	12.5	1,830	91.6	37.2	41.0
Rockland town (Plymouth)	17,480	17,761	1.6	17,616	91.3	3.9	0.9	2.7	1.1	21.3	63.2	15.5	6,626	74.0	41.1	27.3
Rockport CDP...............	4,966	NA	NA	4,832	96.6	0.2	0.0	0.7	2.5	15.5	56.2	28.2	2,235	63.4	20.9	49.8
Rockport town (Essex)	6,952	7,175	3.2	7,078	94.8	1.6	0.5	1.0	2.2	16.8	56.0	27.4	3,199	68.6	22.9	50.5
Rowe town (Franklin)........	393	387	-1.5	452	95.1	0.7	0.2	1.3	2.7	26.7	52.2	21.0	181	77.9	37.6	29.3
Rowley CDP...................	1,416	NA	NA	1,444	95.6	1.6	0.0	0.0	2.8	12.3	66.2	21.5	627	83.4	36.5	23.4
Rowley town (Essex)	5,856	6,202	5.9	5,995	97.9	0.4	0.4	0.0	1.3	24.6	62.3	13.0	2,203	83.7	32.3	37.0
Royalston town (Worcester)	1,258	1,269	0.9	1,230	95.9	0.2	1.0	1.3	1.5	19.6	65.8	14.7	475	86.3	49.1	16.6
Russell CDP	786	NA	NA	544	91.9	0.0	0.0	6.1	2.0	6.5	73.8	19.9	265	92.1	51.3	19.6
Russell town (Hampden) ..	1,775	1,787	0.7	1,532	88.4	0.3	0.3	3.8	7.3	23.3	63.5	13.4	601	91.2	47.9	20.6
Rutland CDP	2,111	NA	NA	2,478	94.9	1.5	0.0	1.5	2.1	27.2	58.3	14.5	863	77.5	28.7	31.4
Rutland town (Worcester) .	7,973	8,349	4.7	8,188	93.9	0.6	1.7	0.9	2.9	25.3	64.4	10.3	2,843	85.7	26.2	40.3
Sagamore CDP	3,623	NA	NA	3,589	97.3	0.0	0.7	0.0	2.0	19.5	59.1	21.3	1,462	87.8	33.8	37.5
Salem city & MCD (Essex)	41,340	42,824	3.6	42,321	74.4	4.9	2.2	2.5	16.0	18.0	69.1	13.1	18,148	49.2	31.8	39.1
Salisbury CDP	4,869	NA	NA	4,757	93.7	0.3	3.2	1.7	1.1	12.8	68.8	18.4	2,059	63.4	35.5	29.2
Salisbury town (Essex)	8,283	8,706	5.1	8,495	94.6	0.8	1.8	2.0	0.8	17.0	66.8	16.1	3,297	70.7	39.1	29.7
Sandisfield town (Berkshire)	915	919	0.4	896	90.8	0.0	4.0	3.8	1.3	16.6	63.1	20.3	358	86.3	43.3	34.6
Sandwich CDP	2,962	NA	NA	2,847	94.7	0.0	3.5	0.0	1.8	13.1	59.1	27.8	1,329	78.4	31.9	43.4
Sandwich town (Barnstable)	20,675	20,536	-0.7	20,605	96.2	0.3	0.6	1.0	2.0	23.0	61.2	15.9	7,594	84.6	22.1	44.7
Saugus CDP & town (Essex)........................	26,636	27,921	4.8	27,369	90.3	2.0	2.4	1.4	3.9	18.4	63.8	17.8	10,345	77.1	43.7	27.5
Savoy town (Berkshire).....	692	681	-1.6	703	93.0	2.7	0.0	3.0	1.3	20.7	66.7	12.5	300	91.0	56.3	22.3
Scituate CDP	5,245	NA	NA	5,623	91.8	1.3	0.6	4.7	1.6	24.0	58.5	17.4	2,293	74.3	19.6	55.3
Scituate town (Plymouth)..	18,135	18,413	1.5	18,240	93.9	0.5	0.6	3.6	1.3	25.9	57.5	16.6	6,705	82.8	18.6	58.4
Seabrook CDP.................	455	NA	NA	445	100.0	0.0	0.0	0.0	0.0	9.4	47.3	43.1	221	100.0	22.6	50.7
Seconsett Island CDP	100	NA	NA	23	100.0	0.0	0.0	0.0	0.0	0.0	65.2	34.8	16	50.0	0.0	100.0
Seekonk town (Bristol)	13,722	14,683	7.0	14,131	95.2	1.3	1.7	0.5	1.4	20.0	63.8	16.1	5,094	91.4	36.6	34.6
Sharon town (Norfolk).......	17,610	18,121	2.9	17,879	74.4	3.7	16.6	2.8	2.5	28.2	58.3	13.6	6,333	86.7	10.5	74.9
Sharon CDP	5,658	NA	NA	6,010	82.9	2.4	8.9	4.6	1.1	30.9	60.1	9.0	2,091	85.4	6.8	76.9
Sheffield town (Berkshire)	3,257	3,208	-1.5	3,230	96.3	0.4	1.5	1.1	0.7	18.2	61.0	20.9	1,426	82.7	34.6	37.8
Shelburne town (Franklin).	1,893	1,883	-0.5	1,979	98.2	0.3	0.4	1.1	0.0	15.4	63.7	20.9	890	65.3	21.9	48.3
Shelburne Falls CDP	1,731	NA	NA	1,699	98.5	0.4	0.0	1.2	0.0	13.7	63.0	23.2	823	52.1	30.3	37.2
Sherborn town (Middlesex)	4,119	4,279	3.9	4,200	93.1	0.0	4.9	1.0	1.0	29.0	55.6	15.5	1,441	88.4	6.4	87.6
Shirley CDP	1,441	NA	NA	1,321	88.1	0.0	0.0	3.1	8.8	17.4	64.9	17.7	635	55.7	34.5	27.1
Shirley town (Middlesex)...	7,211	7,372	2.2	7,404	71.6	8.4	0.9	4.2	14.9	19.0	70.7	10.2	2,283	66.2	35.0	32.4
Shrewsbury town (Worcester)	35,608	36,580	2.7	36,114	75.1	2.6	16.4	2.4	3.5	26.1	60.3	13.6	12,968	73.7	21.7	58.5
Shutesbury town (Franklin)	1,771	1,770	-0.1	1,804	89.0	0.7	0.7	4.2	5.4	22.1	67.4	10.6	753	89.2	15.7	66.4
Siasconset CDP	205	NA	NA	200	95.0	0.0	0.0	5.0	0.0	26.5	67.0	6.5	63	100.0	23.8	0.0
Smith Mills CDP..............	4,760	NA	NA	4,741	92.2	2.4	0.6	1.7	3.0	19.4	57.6	23.1	1,923	71.0	37.8	26.1
Somerset CDP & town (Bristol)......................	18,165	18,278	0.6	18,262	95.2	0.9	0.9	2.4	0.6	18.3	59.6	22.2	6,854	82.2	42.4	28.7
Somerville city & MCD (Middlesex)	75,635	78,901	4.3	77,560	70.8	6.6	9.5	3.7	9.5	13.6	77.2	9.2	31,784	34.3	29.3	56.4
South Amherst CDP	4,994	NA	NA	5,267	64.3	7.7	15.1	2.8	10.2	15.6	78.6	5.9	1,445	40.0	11.3	63.9
Southampton town (Hampshire)	5,792	6,078	4.9	5,958	97.1	0.6	0.0	1.9	0.3	21.5	62.2	16.4	2,350	82.9	36.2	24.9
South Ashburnham CDP ..	1,062	NA	NA	1,042	82.1	2.8	0.0	11.6	3.6	34.0	58.2	7.7	304	82.2	32.9	38.2
Southborough town (Worcester)	9,767	9,943	1.8	9,869	81.0	1.7	14.8	1.6	0.9	27.8	60.6	11.6	3,296	89.4	12.3	70.9
Southbridge Town city & MCD (Worcester)	16,719	16,825	0.6	16,775	61.2	2.3	2.9	1.3	32.4	23.3	62.7	14.0	6,642	44.7	52.3	19.5
South Deerfield CDP	1,880	NA	NA	1,733	93.3	0.0	0.9	3.2	2.6	16.3	65.2	18.5	831	59.7	21.5	43.6
South Dennis CDP	3,643	NA	NA	3,599	83.7	9.6	0.2	4.2	2.3	15.4	53.5	31.2	1,704	80.0	34.3	32.0
South Duxbury CDP	3,360	NA	NA	3,752	98.8	0.1	0.5	0.6	0.0	33.4	54.9	11.5	1,226	94.5	7.5	76.4
Southfield CDP	0	NA	NA	0	0.0	0.0	0.0	0.0	0.0	0.0	0.0	0.0	0	0.0	0.0	0.0
South Hadley town (Hampshire)	17,514	17,691	1.0	17,745	87.4	3.7	2.7	1.6	4.6	15.6	67.3	17.0	6,988	73.8	26.4	40.4
South Lancaster CDP.......	1,894	NA	NA	1,812	88.0	0.0	0.7	4.8	6.5	19.6	67.6	12.8	607	58.6	27.0	35.7
Southwick town (Hampden)	9,502	9,689	2.0	9,599	96.2	0.0	1.6	1.7	0.5	19.7	64.3	16.1	3,593	82.7	36.9	34.9
South Yarmouth CDP........	11,092	NA	NA	11,482	92.0	2.3	2.1	1.3	2.3	16.3	55.3	28.5	5,293	72.7	31.6	30.8
Spencer CDP...................	5,700	NA	NA	5,670	91.8	0.7	0.0	0.9	6.6	23.3	60.4	16.2	2,410	45.3	49.3	22.0
Spencer town (Worcester)	11,688	11,805	1.0	11,746	93.5	0.4	0.3	0.7	5.1	21.5	64.4	14.1	4,662	63.9	44.4	26.8
Springfield city & MCD (Hampden)	153,195	153,991	0.5	153,836	34.6	19.2	2.1	2.6	41.4	26.6	62.2	11.3	56,130	47.8	52.5	18.1
Sterling town (Worcester) .	7,808	7,938	1.7	7,870	94.8	0.9	1.2	0.7	2.5	24.8	61.7	13.6	2,800	85.9	21.4	53.2
Stockbridge town (Berkshire)	1,947	1,950	0.2	2,127	90.6	2.8	1.9	2.9	1.8	13.9	55.8	30.2	948	68.4	25.4	45.1
Stoneham CDP & town (Middlesex)	21,275	21,886	2.9	21,611	91.7	1.4	3.2	0.9	2.9	17.8	63.9	18.3	9,032	67.1	31.0	41.8
Stoughton town (Norfolk)..	26,955	28,396	5.3	27,833	80.9	10.7	2.6	2.9	2.9	20.2	61.9	18.0	10,628	74.7	37.1	36.7
Stow town (Middlesex)......	6,586	7,033	6.8	6,841	92.2	0.0	2.2	2.2	3.4	26.7	58.7	14.6	2,460	92.2	12.8	67.9
Sturbridge CDP	2,253	NA	NA	2,265	92.3	0.8	1.3	0.0	5.6	28.1	62.5	9.4	824	74.3	16.9	51.9
Sturbridge town (Worcester)	9,268	9,463	2.1	9,363	94.4	0.2	1.2	0.9	3.4	26.3	57.2	16.6	3,578	81.0	24.6	46.3
Sudbury town (Middlesex)	17,659	18,766	6.3	18,197	87.4	0.0	7.7	2.8	2.1	30.4	55.9	13.7	6,011	94.7	6.6	82.3

1 May be of any race.

Table A. All Places — **Population and Housing**

STATE City, town, township, borough, or CDP (county if applicable)	2010 census total population	2014 estimated population	Percent change 2010–2014	ACS total population estimate 2010–2014	White alone, not Hispanic or Latino	Black alone, not Hispanic or Latino	Asian alone, not Hispanic or Latino	All other races or 2 or more races, not Hispanic or Latino	Hispanic or Latino[1]	Under 18 years old	Age 18 to 64 years old	Age 65 years and older	Total occupied housing units	Percent owner occupied	High school diploma or less	Bachelor's degree or more
	1	2	3	4	5	6	7	8	9	10	11	12	13	14	15	16
MASSACHUSETTS—Con.																
Sunderland town (Franklin)	3,684	3,679	-0.1	3,683	82.0	1.3	9.0	3.0	4.7	11.8	80.0	8.1	1,471	46.4	15.3	51.4
Sutton town (Worcester)	8,964	9,202	2.7	9,078	98.1	0.6	0.4	0.8	0.0	24.9	62.6	12.4	3,104	89.1	24.3	47.0
Swampscott CDP & town (Essex)	13,787	14,014	1.6	13,912	91.6	0.7	1.4	1.7	4.6	22.2	61.0	16.7	5,490	76.2	22.2	54.7
Swansea town (Bristol)	15,865	16,150	1.8	16,005	96.9	0.4	0.5	1.1	1.1	18.7	63.1	18.2	6,050	85.6	40.9	28.7
Taunton city & MCD (Bristol)	55,874	56,544	1.2	56,056	84.5	5.3	1.1	2.6	6.6	21.4	64.3	14.3	21,859	63.4	49.8	19.6
Teaticket CDP	1,692	NA	NA	1,441	92.5	1.5	0.0	4.2	1.8	6.3	47.1	46.6	806	82.0	28.2	40.1
Templeton town (Worcester)	8,013	8,155	1.8	8,091	99.1	0.1	0.0	0.5	0.3	21.2	62.8	16.1	3,008	84.5	48.1	17.4
Tewksbury town (Middlesex)	28,953	30,260	4.5	29,718	92.1	1.8	2.5	1.9	1.8	20.6	63.5	15.9	11,153	85.0	34.8	36.7
The Pinehills CDP	955	NA	NA	1,020	98.6	0.0	0.0	0.0	1.4	2.8	44.3	52.9	556	84.7	9.4	71.2
Tisbury town (Dukes)	3,949	4,128	4.5	4,036	93.6	2.1	0.4	3.7	0.2	19.1	67.6	13.4	1,216	69.7	28.7	38.7
Tolland town (Hampden)	485	492	1.4	569	91.7	0.0	1.2	5.1	1.9	18.5	67.0	14.4	209	87.6	33.5	48.3
Topsfield CDP	2,717	NA	NA	2,983	92.2	0.0	5.4	2.3	0.0	24.1	55.7	20.2	1,037	90.6	14.9	63.7
Topsfield town (Essex)	6,085	6,505	6.9	6,286	94.5	0.0	4.0	1.4	0.0	24.3	57.1	18.5	2,175	93.1	13.0	65.1
Townsend CDP	1,128	NA	NA	1,227	91.0	0.0	0.1	6.3	2.6	29.9	55.9	14.3	496	62.3	39.9	18.5
Townsend town (Middlesex)	8,926	9,404	5.4	9,183	94.3	0.1	2.1	1.8	1.7	25.1	64.7	10.2	3,288	82.8	31.5	38.3
Truro town (Barnstable)	2,003	2,011	0.4	1,738	96.4	0.0	0.0	2.0	1.6	7.5	62.6	30.0	887	86.1	21.4	50.3
Turners Falls CDP	4,470	NA	NA	4,719	90.5	0.0	0.1	3.9	5.5	22.8	61.4	15.7	2,032	52.4	44.3	23.2
Tyngsborough town (Middlesex)	11,292	12,149	7.6	11,867	89.6	0.5	5.5	1.6	2.8	22.8	66.9	10.3	4,114	86.2	29.1	43.9
Tyringham town (Berkshire)	327	324	-0.9	418	98.8	0.0	0.7	0.5	0.0	11.2	50.2	38.5	174	87.4	28.7	51.7
Upton CDP	3,013	NA	NA	3,319	94.2	0.1	1.5	1.4	2.9	27.2	60.0	12.8	1,332	70.6	28.1	41.0
Upton town (Worcester)	7,542	7,699	2.1	7,641	92.1	0.2	2.6	3.7	1.3	28.1	60.7	11.2	2,680	84.7	21.2	50.4
Uxbridge town (Worcester)	13,457	13,783	2.4	13,609	95.3	0.6	2.0	0.9	1.2	22.8	64.7	12.5	4,752	82.2	33.4	39.5
Vineyard Haven CDP	2,114	NA	NA	2,384	93.2	3.0	0.4	3.1	0.4	20.2	67.9	12.1	588	70.9	31.8	45.2
Wakefield CDP & town (Middlesex)	25,094	26,774	6.7	25,835	93.0	0.5	3.1	0.7	2.6	20.7	64.5	14.9	9,951	73.9	27.3	47.9
Wales town (Hampden)	1,838	1,878	2.2	1,923	98.4	0.4	0.0	1.1	0.2	21.2	60.8	17.9	778	83.8	54.0	15.2
Walpole CDP	5,918	NA	NA	5,910	96.7	0.0	0.7	1.8	0.8	22.9	56.0	21.0	2,353	83.7	25.7	48.9
Walpole town (Norfolk)	24,069	24,933	3.6	24,571	90.1	2.7	3.6	1.7	1.9	23.2	60.8	16.0	8,822	82.5	23.8	50.7
Waltham city & MCD (Middlesex)	60,632	63,014	3.9	61,908	65.9	5.7	11.4	2.9	14.1	14.6	72.6	12.7	23,873	49.3	29.9	50.8
Ware CDP	6,170	NA	NA	5,816	93.7	0.0	0.3	2.9	3.2	23.0	60.7	16.5	2,550	56.2	47.9	22.4
Ware town (Hampshire)	9,872	9,878	0.1	9,886	95.1	0.2	0.3	2.2	2.1	21.6	62.6	15.7	4,173	69.9	46.9	23.7
Wareham town (Plymouth)	21,822	22,473	3.0	22,247	86.2	1.9	1.2	9.0	1.8	17.7	64.6	17.8	9,148	80.3	43.3	22.3
Wareham Center CDP	2,896	NA	NA	3,218	83.7	3.0	0.0	12.4	0.9	16.5	67.2	16.3	1,502	57.3	40.2	23.3
Warren CDP	1,405	NA	NA	1,456	97.1	0.0	0.0	0.0	2.9	20.3	66.9	13.3	636	44.3	44.2	4.6
Warren town (Worcester)	5,135	5,178	0.8	5,153	98.9	0.0	0.0	0.3	0.8	24.1	62.7	13.3	2,044	63.1	45.7	14.9
Warwick town (Franklin)	780	769	-1.4	695	95.4	0.0	1.4	0.6	2.6	12.4	62.5	25.0	355	87.6	33.2	38.3
Washington town (Berkshire)	538	536	-0.4	546	98.5	0.0	1.3	0.0	0.2	10.7	70.0	19.4	244	98.4	39.3	33.6
Watertown Town city & MCD (Middlesex)	31,915	34,127	6.9	32,880	78.0	3.3	7.2	3.1	8.4	15.9	69.3	14.9	14,449	52.5	21.7	61.0
Wayland town (Middlesex)	12,994	13,541	4.2	13,294	84.4	1.1	11.2	0.9	2.5	25.3	55.8	18.9	5,153	87.1	10.3	78.3
Webster town (Worcester)	16,767	16,844	0.5	16,806	82.8	3.5	2.8	2.0	8.8	19.7	62.8	17.6	6,734	53.7	49.0	23.7
Webster CDP	11,412	NA	NA	12,135	78.8	3.9	3.4	2.7	11.3	20.7	62.9	16.4	4,746	42.5	52.5	18.4
Wellesley CDP & town (Norfolk)	27,971	29,362	5.0	28,858	79.8	2.0	10.8	2.5	4.9	26.9	59.4	13.8	8,594	82.6	6.3	85.1
Wellfleet town (Barnstable)	2,750	2,754	0.1	3,011	96.5	1.3	0.0	2.1	0.1	10.0	46.7	43.4	1,605	78.6	13.8	56.4
Wendell town (Franklin)	848	871	2.7	898	87.9	6.2	1.8	3.2	0.9	14.4	68.0	17.4	420	77.1	29.8	50.7
Wenham town (Essex)	4,875	5,165	5.9	5,039	93.8	1.6	2.0	1.1	1.5	18.3	67.4	14.4	1,363	87.2	18.0	63.4
Westborough town (Worcester)	18,272	18,756	2.6	18,481	70.7	2.9	18.2	1.6	6.5	23.9	62.6	13.5	7,085	59.9	16.4	65.9
Westborough CDP	4,045	NA	NA	4,061	83.3	0.1	11.7	1.7	3.1	18.2	69.3	12.6	1,780	52.5	24.8	49.4
West Boylston town (Worcester)	7,669	7,871	2.6	7,792	86.3	5.8	0.6	2.4	4.9	14.9	69.3	15.8	2,213	83.2	22.1	45.5
West Bridgewater town (Plymouth)	6,916	7,060	2.1	6,981	86.5	5.6	0.2	3.4	4.3	23.2	60.4	16.4	2,315	86.4	36.1	34.0
West Brookfield CDP	1,413	NA	NA	1,352	91.8	7.8	0.0	0.4	0.0	16.6	61.5	21.8	592	57.9	56.4	19.6
West Brookfield town (Worcester)	3,701	3,763	1.7	3,738	93.0	3.4	0.8	1.8	0.9	17.6	65.0	17.5	1,522	67.0	43.7	32.4
West Chatham CDP	1,410	NA	NA	1,352	92.0	3.8	0.0	4.2	0.0	18.3	55.2	26.6	592	82.3	31.4	36.7
West Concord CDP	6,028	NA	NA	7,085	75.6	6.3	6.4	3.1	8.7	18.8	63.9	17.2	2,396	65.9	9.3	77.4
West Dennis CDP	2,242	NA	NA	2,219	90.3	0.3	3.9	2.0	3.6	11.4	49.2	39.2	1,054	73.6	27.0	39.3
West Falmouth CDP	1,738	NA	NA	1,967	93.5	0.0	2.8	2.7	0.9	19.4	48.6	32.2	795	93.2	19.0	62.9
Westfield city & MCD (Hampden)	41,094	41,608	1.3	41,371	84.7	2.0	2.9	2.0	8.5	20.9	65.0	14.0	14,909	67.3	37.6	30.3
Westford town (Middlesex)	21,951	23,678	7.9	22,854	80.0	0.6	14.8	2.1	2.6	29.6	59.3	11.1	7,738	91.8	10.5	73.2
Westhampton town (Hampshire)	1,607	1,634	1.7	1,586	93.1	0.0	1.1	1.0	4.8	18.9	65.8	15.3	609	90.0	35.6	38.8
Westminster town (Worcester)	7,277	7,463	2.6	7,361	96.6	0.9	0.0	0.9	1.6	20.7	67.5	11.8	2,836	88.0	26.3	38.2
West Newbury town (Essex)	4,235	4,495	6.1	4,370	95.1	0.0	0.3	1.1	3.4	28.5	59.8	11.9	1,502	90.2	16.2	59.4
Weston town (Middlesex)	11,264	11,992	6.5	11,704	79.4	2.4	11.5	2.5	4.3	28.6	53.5	17.9	3,768	86.5	7.9	83.9
Westport town (Bristol)	15,532	15,742	1.4	15,647	98.2	0.2	0.3	1.1	0.2	19.1	58.9	22.0	6,046	83.4	40.1	35.1
West Springfield Town city & MCD (Hampden)	28,391	28,627	0.8	28,554	79.8	2.9	4.1	3.5	9.7	21.4	63.3	15.3	11,400	60.3	39.1	28.3
West Stockbridge town (Berkshire)	1,306	1,282	-1.8	1,349	88.4	1.9	1.1	7.6	0.9	18.7	61.5	19.8	582	86.6	23.4	52.9
West Tisbury town (Dukes)	2,740	2,901	5.9	2,727	97.2	1.0	0.3	0.0	1.5	23.3	62.2	14.6	942	90.1	17.8	61.3
West Wareham CDP	2,064	NA	NA	3,070	86.1	2.8	1.9	7.6	1.6	15.8	62.0	22.1	1,167	88.4	47.4	15.7
Westwood town (Norfolk)	14,616	14,979	2.5	14,809	89.3	0.3	6.5	1.1	2.7	28.1	52.8	19.1	5,400	86.8	12.5	73.9

1 May be of any race.

Table A. All Places — **Population and Housing**

	Population				Race and Hispanic or Latino origin (percent), 2010–2014					Age (percent), 2010–2014			Households, 2010–2014			
								All other races or 2 or more races, not Hispanic or Latino							Householders by level of education (percent)	
STATE City, town, township, borough, or CDP (county if applicable)	2010 census total population	2014 estimated population	Percent change 2010–2014	ACS total population estimate 2010–2014	White alone, not Hispanic or Latino	Black alone, not Hispanic or Latino	Asian alone, not Hispanic or Latino		Hispanic or Latino[1]	Under 18 years old	Age 18 to 64 years old	Age 65 years and older	Total occupied housing units	Percent owner occupied	High school diploma or less	Bachelor's degree or more
	1	2	3	4	5	6	7	8	9	10	11	12	13	14	15	16
MASSACHUSETTS—Con.																
West Yarmouth CDP	6,012	NA	NA	5,882	91.7	2.7	1.5	2.4	1.7	14.7	61.1	24.3	2,715	67.9	32.3	30.7
Weweantic CDP..............	2,105	NA	NA	1,662	84.4	3.1	0.0	10.9	1.6	11.8	58.4	29.8	797	82.2	37.5	30.1
Weymouth Town city & MCD (Norfolk)	53,743	55,643	3.5	54,815	86.3	3.4	4.9	2.8	2.5	20.5	63.3	16.1	22,559	66.9	33.7	34.8
Whately town (Franklin)	1,496	1,515	1.3	1,384	95.1	0.2	0.8	1.7	2.2	19.5	65.4	15.2	585	88.9	26.5	42.2
White Island Shores CDP.	2,106	NA	NA	1,917	99.0	0.0	0.0	0.0	1.0	27.9	66.2	5.9	652	92.6	55.2	15.2
Whitinsville CDP..............	6,704	NA	NA	6,478	91.3	0.3	1.6	4.1	2.7	25.1	61.6	13.3	2,358	57.1	37.4	28.5
Whitman town (Plymouth)	14,489	14,790	2.1	14,643	94.3	0.7	1.3	1.8	1.9	22.8	65.4	11.7	5,399	73.0	36.6	29.8
Wilbraham CDP..............	3,915	NA	NA	3,765	95.4	2.8	0.0	1.1	0.8	15.6	59.5	24.9	1,335	93.3	15.7	50.4
Wilbraham town (Hampden)	14,219	14,509	2.0	14,363	92.9	2.1	1.1	1.3	2.5	21.5	58.2	20.5	5,366	88.9	26.1	47.3
Williamsburg town (Hampshire)	2,482	2,472	-0.4	2,583	94.0	0.5	0.3	1.2	4.0	16.1	67.6	16.3	1,156	77.9	22.8	50.6
Williamstown CDP	4,325	NA	NA	4,173	79.3	3.6	4.6	5.9	6.6	12.7	72.3	15.0	1,107	66.6	16.2	64.4
Williamstown town (Berkshire)	7,754	7,605	-1.9	7,624	84.5	2.2	4.4	4.6	4.3	14.9	64.1	21.0	2,377	74.6	19.1	62.8
Wilmington CDP & town (Middlesex)	22,325	23,370	4.7	22,907	91.3	0.8	4.6	1.6	1.7	24.5	61.9	13.5	7,585	86.1	31.9	40.7
Winchendon CDP	4,213	NA	NA	3,714	93.0	1.3	0.0	2.3	3.4	20.5	59.6	19.9	1,691	51.6	55.4	10.1
Winchendon town (Worcester)	10,300	10,615	3.1	10,466	90.5	0.6	3.2	2.5	3.2	23.0	62.1	14.8	4,025	72.8	44.6	21.2
Winchester CDP & town (Middlesex)	21,374	22,270	4.2	21,863	84.7	0.8	11.6	1.3	1.5	28.8	54.4	16.7	7,564	84.3	12.3	73.4
Windsor town (Berkshire) .	899	897	-0.2	879	96.8	0.2	0.0	2.0	0.9	20.4	62.4	17.2	354	97.2	25.1	35.9
Winthrop Town city & MCD (Suffolk)	17,497	18,352	4.9	17,992	87.5	0.8	0.6	2.4	8.7	19.2	64.3	16.5	7,447	55.9	31.4	37.7
Woburn city & MCD (Middlesex)	38,134	39,272	3.0	38,826	82.9	4.6	6.5	1.7	4.3	19.4	65.2	15.4	14,914	61.4	35.8	38.3
Woods Hole CDP	781	NA	NA	953	90.3	0.2	6.1	0.0	3.4	14.7	52.9	32.5	420	67.6	14.8	72.9
Worcester city & MCD (Worcester)	181,041	183,016	1.1	182,511	59.1	11.1	6.7	2.6	20.5	21.9	65.9	12.2	68,000	44.0	41.4	32.0
Worthington town (Hampshire)	1,156	1,179	2.0	1,154	95.6	0.3	1.0	2.3	0.9	13.3	69.1	17.8	540	88.5	35.2	41.9
Wrentham town (Norfolk)..	10,955	11,422	4.3	11,169	97.7	0.2	0.6	0.5	1.0	25.8	62.8	11.4	3,904	83.9	24.7	52.5
Yarmouth town (Barnstable)	23,797	23,592	-0.9	23,680	92.7	1.9	1.8	1.5	2.0	14.8	55.4	29.7	10,999	76.7	29.8	34.9
Yarmouth Port CDP	5,320	NA	NA	4,906	95.3	0.5	1.8	1.1	1.3	9.6	50.7	39.6	2,462	92.0	22.5	46.4
MICHIGAN......................	9,884,133	9,909,877	0.3	9,889,024	76.1	13.8	2.6	2.8	4.6	23.0	62.5	14.6	3,827,880	71.5	37.2	27.9
Acme township (Grand Traverse)	4,375	4,625	5.7	4,498	97.4	0.5	0.2	1.4	0.6	20.0	61.6	18.4	1,851	79.4	17.9	47.8
Ada township (Kent)	13,135	14,040	6.9	13,575	92.6	0.6	3.4	1.5	1.9	29.0	60.2	10.7	4,544	94.9	10.6	68.4
Adams township (Arenac)	563	540	-4.1	543	98.7	0.0	0.0	0.4	0.9	24.3	67.5	8.1	201	89.6	59.7	14.4
Adams township (Hillsdale)	2,493	2,447	-1.8	2,301	94.6	0.0	1.6	0.4	3.3	17.8	62.3	19.9	959	79.2	50.6	16.1
Adams township (Houghton)	2,573	2,538	-1.4	2,563	96.1	0.0	0.9	2.1	1.0	27.6	61.1	11.0	907	86.5	50.4	14.6
Addison village	605	597	-1.3	650	86.5	1.8	0.0	4.3	7.4	32.4	57.9	9.7	258	62.4	50.8	9.7
Addison township (Oakland)	6,351	6,503	2.4	6,432	91.0	3.5	2.0	0.8	2.8	24.7	63.2	12.0	2,296	91.6	33.1	33.8
Adrian city & MCD (Lenawee)	21,193	20,840	-1.7	21,008	74.6	3.9	0.4	3.3	17.8	22.7	63.1	14.3	7,840	53.5	52.1	20.4
Adrian township (Lenawee)	5,978	6,278	5.0	6,128	90.2	0.7	0.0	0.9	8.2	18.1	59.4	22.3	2,474	89.2	40.8	26.7
Advance CDP (Mecosta)	328	NA	NA	269	98.1	0.0	0.0	1.9	0.0	9.7	42.8	47.6	128	83.6	43.0	35.2
Aetna township (Mecosta)	2,299	2,304	0.2	2,297	95.6	0.0	0.2	0.9	3.2	25.0	62.3	12.8	834	80.7	53.1	8.3
Aetna township (Missaukee)	413	418	1.2	443	87.6	0.5	0.0	0.0	12.0	19.4	62.9	17.6	170	79.4	71.2	8.8
Ahmeek village	146	150	2.7	128	100.0	0.0	0.0	0.0	0.0	20.3	62.6	17.2	61	78.7	57.4	16.4
Akron village	402	394	-2.0	397	82.1	1.5	0.0	8.8	7.6	23.7	63.0	13.4	159	73.6	54.1	9.4
Akron township (Tuscola) .	1,503	1,465	-2.5	1,581	96.0	0.0	0.0	1.8	2.3	24.6	59.2	16.2	602	82.9	49.0	10.6
Alabaster township (Iosco)	487	479	-1.6	506	99.6	0.0	0.0	0.0	0.4	14.1	50.5	35.4	234	91.0	45.7	26.5
Alaiedon township (Ingham)	2,892	2,910	0.6	2,904	89.2	1.5	1.2	2.1	6.1	20.3	61.3	18.4	1,087	88.9	24.7	43.4
Alamo township (Kalamazoo)	3,762	3,858	2.6	3,814	91.7	1.1	0.4	2.5	4.2	24.4	58.3	17.3	1,439	91.7	35.2	29.3
Alanson village	738	747	1.2	585	87.7	0.0	0.0	11.6	0.7	20.9	66.4	12.6	260	76.9	46.2	14.6
Alba CDP	295	NA	NA	318	98.7	0.0	0.0	1.3	0.0	14.4	66.6	18.9	129	69.0	74.4	2.3
Albee township (Saginaw)	2,160	2,087	-3.4	1,991	93.2	0.5	0.0	2.7	3.7	17.6	65.8	16.5	781	93.5	58.8	8.5
Albert township (Montmorency)	2,526	2,405	-4.8	2,345	97.8	0.0	0.0	1.3	0.9	17.0	52.8	30.3	1,056	81.5	49.9	9.6
Albion city & MCD (Calhoun)	8,616	8,267	-4.1	8,416	62.4	29.5	0.5	3.5	4.2	20.5	64.2	15.3	3,114	57.8	48.5	17.8
Albion township (Calhoun)	1,123	1,110	-1.2	941	95.4	1.0	0.4	0.7	2.4	15.1	62.3	22.6	378	81.7	63.2	17.2
Alcona township (Alcona).	968	927	-4.2	946	98.2	0.0	0.6	0.3	0.8	9.8	44.3	45.9	474	96.0	37.6	27.0
Alden CDP	125	NA	NA	135	98.5	0.0	0.0	0.0	1.5	8.9	57.0	34.1	77	94.8	27.3	42.9
Algansee township (Branch)	1,974	1,947	-1.4	2,013	97.0	0.0	0.2	0.0	2.8	30.6	52.1	17.6	650	87.7	52.9	19.7
Algoma township (Kent)....	9,932	10,663	7.4	10,285	95.5	0.0	1.3	1.1	2.1	31.0	59.1	9.9	3,433	93.5	28.1	40.1
Algonac city & MCD (St. Clair)	4,110	4,056	-1.3	4,065	96.6	0.1	0.7	1.2	1.5	18.4	63.5	18.1	1,883	65.1	47.9	21.1
Allegan city & MCD (Allegan)	4,998	5,070	1.4	5,030	89.7	4.9	0.7	2.0	2.7	23.6	60.9	15.6	2,067	56.5	55.8	15.5
Allegan township (Allegan)	4,406	4,490	1.9	4,445	92.5	2.7	0.0	0.7	4.2	20.8	56.3	22.9	1,808	92.0	44.5	23.2
Allen village	191	188	-1.6	227	87.2	0.9	0.4	0.4	11.5	23.9	56.0	20.3	96	68.8	66.7	6.3
Allen township (Hillsdale) .	1,657	1,625	-1.9	1,528	92.5	1.6	0.7	0.4	4.8	20.5	61.8	17.7	597	84.3	52.6	10.6
Allendale CDP	17,579	NA	NA	18,393	88.3	2.4	2.0	1.9	5.4	18.7	76.8	4.5	4,882	60.3	27.2	25.0
Allendale charter township (Ottawa)	20,708	21,655	4.6	21,152	88.5	2.4	1.9	2.0	5.2	18.6	77.1	4.4	5,753	61.9	27.5	24.1
Allen Park city & MCD (Wayne)	28,210	27,566	-2.3	27,869	87.5	2.1	0.2	1.5	8.6	20.7	62.7	16.6	10,956	86.2	39.2	24.2

1 May be of any race.

Table A. All Places — **Population and Housing**

STATE City, town, township, borough, or CDP (county if applicable)	2010 census total population	2014 estimated population	Percent change 2010–2014	ACS total population estimate 2010–2014	White alone, not Hispanic or Latino	Black alone, not Hispanic or Latino	Asian alone, not Hispanic or Latino	All other races or 2 or more races, not Hispanic or Latino	Hispanic or Latino[1]	Under 18 years old	Age 18 to 64 years old	Age 65 years and older	Total occupied housing units	Percent owner occupied	High school diploma or less	Bachelor's degree or more
	1	2	3	4	5	6	7	8	9	10	11	12	13	14	15	16
MICHIGAN—Con.																
Allis township (Presque Isle)	948	919	-3.1	964	95.1	0.0	0.0	3.8	1.0	21.5	60.1	18.3	400	90.0	63.5	9.0
Allouez township (Keweenaw)	1,571	1,615	2.8	1,510	99.7	0.2	0.0	0.1	0.0	23.6	56.3	20.3	651	86.9	50.7	13.8
Alma city & MCD (Gratiot)	9,378	9,232	-1.6	9,289	87.5	2.5	0.0	2.1	7.9	20.3	65.0	14.8	3,394	54.4	37.5	22.5
Almena township (Van Buren)	4,992	4,943		4,960	94.6	1.6	0.0	1.2	2.6	25.4	60.6	14.0	1,742	96.6	23.0	38.3
Almer township (Tuscola)	2,115	2,056	-2.8	2,017	90.1	0.3	0.0	0.4	9.1	20.9	57.0	22.2	829	86.1	47.3	20.4
Almira township (Benzie)	3,645	3,660	0.4	3,645	98.1	0.2	0.0	0.2	1.6	25.7	58.9	15.3	1,538	93.0	25.3	33.3
Almont village	2,674	2,694	0.7	2,670	93.2	0.0	2.5	1.1	3.2	23.9	64.7	11.5	1,047	80.8	44.1	15.4
Almont township (Lapeer)	6,583	6,670	1.3	6,589	95.0	0.0	1.0	0.9	3.1	22.4	59.8	17.8	2,496	90.0	41.9	19.0
Aloha township (Cheboygan)	947	930	-1.8	861	98.0	0.0	0.0	0.9	1.0	19.5	55.5	25.0	406	93.1	36.9	23.9
Alpena city & MCD (Alpena)	10,483	10,247	-2.3	10,336	95.2	0.9	0.5	2.1	1.3	20.8	60.0	19.1	4,623	63.7	38.7	18.8
Alpena township (Alpena)	9,060	8,916	-1.6	8,997	96.5	0.4	0.2	1.8	1.1	18.6	57.0	24.4	4,025	83.8	38.1	18.3
Alpha village	145	138	-4.8	83	97.6	0.0	0.0	2.4	0.0	10.8	48.1	41.0	55	92.7	67.3	5.5
Alpine township (Kent)	13,321	13,787	3.5	13,531	73.2	7.3	0.5	3.0	16.0	23.4	66.1	10.6	5,210	55.3	42.5	21.9
Amasa CDP	283	NA	NA	351	98.6	0.0	0.0	1.4	0.0	25.0	57.4	17.7	165	82.4	63.0	6.7
Amber township (Mason)	2,535	2,546	0.4	2,535	93.6	0.8	0.0	2.6	2.9	17.1	62.2	20.7	1,107	58.1	40.5	23.1
Amboy township (Hillsdale)	1,173	1,155	-1.5	1,009	97.0	0.0	0.0	1.7	1.3	15.9	67.2	16.8	418	89.7	58.6	11.7
Ann Arbor city & MCD (Washtenaw)	113,947	117,770	3.4	115,985	69.1	7.5	14.8	4.0	4.6	14.3	75.5	10.2	46,497	45.7	9.9	68.2
Ann Arbor charter township (Washtenaw)	4,357	4,524	3.8	4,439	75.7	1.6	17.1	2.5	3.1	22.6	60.0	17.3	1,730	71.7	6.0	80.8
Antioch township (Wexford)	815	818	0.4	844	95.6	0.0	0.0	0.9	3.1	26.6	58.2	15.4	339	81.1	42.5	22.1
Antrim township (Shiawassee)	2,161	2,115	-2.1	2,547	96.7	0.0	0.2	0.5	2.6	25.0	60.0	14.9	876	92.7	53.8	8.2
Antwerp township (Van Buren)	12,182	12,086	-0.8	12,121	90.5	0.6	1.3	1.4	6.1	27.4	61.6	10.9	4,330	82.3	34.1	28.9
Applegate village	248	241	-2.8	314	91.1	4.5	0.0	0.0	4.5	31.8	58.3	9.9	102	80.4	41.2	6.9
Arbela township (Tuscola)	3,070	2,976	-3.1	3,037	97.1	1.0	0.0	0.6	1.3	21.8	63.1	15.1	1,113	87.2	59.6	10.5
Arcada township (Gratiot)	1,681	1,660	-1.2	1,712	89.3	0.0	0.2	2.5	8.0	23.5	59.5	17.1	669	82.5	41.3	23.9
Arcadia township (Lapeer)	3,113	3,107	-0.2	3,110	96.2	0.6	0.0	0.0	3.2	21.7	62.0	16.2	1,127	96.3	47.3	14.3
Arcadia CDP	291	NA	NA	244	97.5	0.0	0.0	2.5	0.0	7.4	43.5	49.2	132	87.9	18.9	41.7
Arcadia township (Manistee)	639	630	-1.4	528	96.2	1.7	0.0	1.7	0.4	11.0	52.3	36.9	263	90.1	28.9	36.5
Arenac township (Arenac)	903	864	-4.3	776	98.7	0.4	0.0	0.6	0.3	16.0	63.1	21.0	320	84.7	61.9	10.3
Argentine CDP	2,525	NA	NA	2,345	97.2	0.0	0.3	1.4	1.0	21.6	61.4	17.1	913	81.6	36.6	29.1
Argentine township (Genesee)	6,913	6,687	-3.3	6,792	96.8	0.0	0.1	1.3	1.8	26.1	61.7	12.3	2,438	86.2	39.1	21.8
Argyle township (Sanilac)	759	731	-3.7	874	97.7	0.7	0.0	1.5	0.1	27.0	59.9	13.0	288	88.9	68.8	6.9
Arlington township (Van Buren)	2,073	2,033	-1.9	2,129	78.2	0.5	0.0	3.6	17.7	25.0	56.4	18.9	742	87.6	51.5	17.1
Armada village	1,730	1,744	0.8	2,012	94.6	0.2	0.0	1.4	3.7	30.5	53.2	16.3	723	74.6	43.4	25.9
Armada township (Macomb)	5,379	5,442	1.2	5,407	97.5	0.2	0.0	0.6	1.6	21.8	62.1	16.1	1,962	88.8	38.2	26.7
Arthur township (Clare)	647	641	-0.9	876	96.5	0.6	0.0	0.7	2.3	32.3	51.6	16.1	313	87.2	37.7	19.5
Arvon township (Baraga)	450	443	-1.6	368	97.0	0.0	0.8	0.8	1.4	7.0	45.7	47.3	207	96.6	47.3	21.3
Ash township (Monroe)	7,783	7,729	-0.7	7,759	93.4	1.1	1.0	2.3	2.1	21.3	63.5	15.2	2,969	89.2	45.6	14.7
Ashland township (Newaygo)	2,773	2,736	-1.3	2,765	86.3	1.4	0.1	1.2	11.0	29.7	58.5	11.8	872	85.1	58.4	7.7
Ashley village	563	556	-1.2	501	96.8	0.0	0.0	0.6	2.6	18.6	53.2	28.3	188	71.8	63.8	5.9
Assyria township (Barry)	1,988	2,001	0.7	1,971	94.0	0.0	0.5	4.1	1.4	19.4	67.8	12.8	753	92.6	46.2	12.7
Athens village	1,024	1,012	-1.2	1,071	96.0	0.2	0.3	1.4	2.1	26.0	61.6	12.2	392	81.1	47.4	13.5
Athens township (Calhoun)	2,554	2,516	-1.5	2,535	91.2	0.3	0.8	5.8	1.9	23.5	57.5	19.1	933	83.7	48.8	8.7
Atlanta CDP	827	NA	NA	896	98.7	1.0	0.0	0.3	0.0	14.5	65.2	20.2	350	79.7	65.7	9.1
Atlas township (Genesee)	7,993	7,829	-2.1	7,892	98.4	0.1	0.0	0.7	0.9	25.8	61.0	13.2	2,763	89.7	25.4	37.9
Attica CDP	994	NA	NA	782	93.1	0.0	0.0	3.3	3.6	21.9	60.3	17.8	269	88.1	69.1	2.6
Attica township (Lapeer)	4,755	4,738	-0.4	4,737	93.0	2.2	0.0	1.9	3.0	22.5	62.2	15.2	1,686	86.3	44.5	10.5
Auburn city & MCD (Bay)	2,087	2,121	1.6	2,063	89.9	0.0	1.6	5.2	3.2	21.8	58.7	19.5	937	63.2	32.1	29.2
Auburn Hills city & MCD (Oakland)	21,412	21,845	2.0	21,639	62.3	15.3	9.2	4.2	9.1	18.8	70.4	10.7	8,803	48.9	23.8	42.9
Au Gres city & MCD (Arenac)	889	863	-2.9	782	96.9	0.3	0.0	1.7	1.2	21.7	53.5	24.9	403	64.0	52.4	11.9
Au Gres township (Arenac)	953	923	-3.1	982	99.3	0.0	0.1	0.4	0.2	16.4	59.1	24.5	428	86.9	49.8	11.0
Augusta village	885	903	2.0	870	91.7	0.9	0.0	5.1	2.3	25.5	60.5	13.9	355	72.4	51.3	11.0
Augusta charter township (Washtenaw)	6,745	7,006	3.9	6,879	85.2	5.2	0.0	9.0	0.6	27.2	61.1	11.6	2,134	90.0	40.0	20.2
Aurelius township (Ingham)	3,525	4,228	19.9	3,925	92.6	2.9	0.8	0.2	3.5	27.6	62.4	10.0	1,285	88.0	24.4	27.8
Au Sable CDP	1,404	NA	NA	1,327	94.9	0.0	0.5	2.7	2.0	13.0	60.3	26.5	621	85.5	44.8	15.0
Au Sable charter township (Iosco)	2,047	2,016	-1.5	1,804	96.2	0.0	0.3	2.0	1.4	12.9	57.8	29.4	847	80.6	44.2	16.8
Au Sable township (Roscommon)	255	300	17.6	325	99.1	0.0	0.0	0.0	0.9	27.4	56.5	16.0	135	78.5	46.7	11.1
Austin township (Mecosta)	1,561	1,569	0.5	1,644	95.9	2.9	0.0	0.4	0.9	29.5	57.0	13.4	588	82.8	45.8	16.7
Austin township (Sanilac)	665	640	-3.8	589	100.0	0.0	0.0	0.0	0.0	20.5	61.0	18.3	216	90.3	68.1	10.2
Au Train township (Alger)	1,138	1,117	-1.8	1,174	88.1	0.0	0.0	10.8	1.1	15.1	56.0	29.0	543	98.0	47.1	24.3
Avery township (Montmorency)	646	612	-5.3	608	98.8	0.0	0.0	0.0	1.2	13.4	55.3	31.4	284	97.9	50.4	10.6
Backus township (Roscommon)	330	322	-2.4	442	95.0	0.0	0.0	3.4	1.6	26.4	56.9	16.5	166	91.6	44.6	17.5
Bad Axe city & MCD (Huron)	3,129	3,029	-3.2	3,082	96.4	0.5	1.2	0.8	1.1	21.1	55.5	23.3	1,341	59.5	52.8	15.7
Bagley township (Otsego)	5,879	5,873	-0.1	5,863	94.4	0.2	2.0	2.7	0.7	25.1	60.3	14.7	2,249	77.5	27.9	22.7
Bainbridge township (Berrien)	2,850	2,822	-1.0	2,837	80.8	2.0	0.5	0.5	16.2	24.8	58.7	16.5	981	80.7	47.3	14.3

1 May be of any race.

Table A. All Places — Population and Housing

STATE City, town, township, borough, or CDP (county if applicable)	Population				Race and Hispanic or Latino origin (percent), 2010–2014					Age (percent), 2010–2014			Households, 2010–2014		Householders by level of education (percent)	
	2010 census total population	2014 estimated population	Percent change 2010–2014	ACS total population estimate 2010–2014	White alone, not Hispanic or Latino	Black alone, not Hispanic or Latino	Asian alone, not Hispanic or Latino	All other races or 2 or more races, not Hispanic or Latino	Hispanic or Latino[1]	Under 18 years old	Age 18 to 64 years old	Age 65 years and older	Total occupied housing units	Percent owner occupied	High school diploma or less	Bachelor's degree or more
	1	2	3	4	5	6	7	8	9	10	11	12	13	14	15	16
MICHIGAN—Con.																
Baldwin township (Delta)..	759	750	-1.2	710	93.9	0.3	0.0	2.8	3.0	17.7	67.3	14.9	315	90.2	54.9	17.8
Baldwin township (Iosco)..	1,694	1,665	-1.7	1,624	93.8	1.7	0.2	2.2	2.0	11.7	60.5	27.8	744	85.3	41.7	26.2
Baldwin village	1,206	1,187	-1.6	1,535	55.1	26.5	0.3	8.7	9.4	20.0	62.9	16.9	478	36.8	49.8	2.3
Baltimore township (Barry)	1,861	1,867	0.3	2,097	96.5	0.0	0.1	0.4	3.0	26.1	61.4	12.6	752	89.6	55.1	10.1
Bancroft village	545	526	-3.5	660	95.0	0.0	0.3	3.6	1.1	34.8	55.2	9.8	217	79.3	50.2	6.9
Bangor charter township (Bay)	14,641	14,369	-1.9	14,519	92.6	0.4	0.8	3.6	2.7	17.8	60.6	21.8	6,190	73.0	46.8	17.7
Bangor city & MCD (Van Buren)	1,885	1,858	-1.4	2,026	62.8	8.5	0.1	5.9	22.6	27.2	59.9	12.8	792	59.6	50.3	11.6
Bangor township (Van Buren)	2,147	2,103	-2.0	2,157	75.6	1.8	0.0	3.1	19.5	23.1	64.9	12.0	769	80.9	57.6	15.6
Banks township (Antrim)...	1,609	1,584	-1.6	1,766	94.1	0.0	0.3	0.6	5.0	22.6	60.4	16.8	675	84.9	45.3	23.1
Baraga village	2,053	2,014	-1.9	2,875	38.4	51.4	0.4	8.4	1.4	7.8	86.8	5.5	325	60.6	52.0	12.6
Baraga township (Baraga)	3,815	3,739	-2.0	3,802	49.7	39.0	0.4	9.5	1.3	12.3	80.2	7.4	776	79.4	46.0	17.5
Bark River township (Delta)	1,578	1,560	-1.1	1,608	92.4	0.1	0.2	5.1	2.2	26.2	61.9	12.1	595	87.4	41.8	17.3
Barnes Lake-Millers Lake CDP	1,093	NA	NA	932	100.0	0.0	0.0	0.0	0.0	37.4	37.9	24.8	349	79.4	38.7	14.9
Baroda village	873	856	-1.9	824	93.3	0.0	1.7	0.7	4.2	18.7	69.0	12.3	366	76.0	51.6	13.7
Baroda township (Berrien)	2,801	2,746	-2.0	2,782	93.3	0.9	0.5	1.5	3.7	20.8	63.0	16.2	1,129	87.8	44.8	15.7
Barry township (Barry)......	3,378	3,402	0.7	3,381	97.4	0.0	0.0	1.5	1.0	26.4	58.8	14.6	1,373	84.0	37.2	28.4
Barryton village	355	359	1.1	392	96.4	0.3	0.0	3.3	0.0	25.8	53.7	20.4	159	61.6	63.5	10.1
Barton township (Newaygo)	717	750	4.6	541	94.3	0.2	0.0	4.3	1.3	13.3	65.3	21.3	254	90.6	57.9	19.7
Barton Hills village	294	303	3.1	313	79.2	7.7	2.9	4.2	6.1	15.6	57.2	27.2	114	94.7	0.0	97.4
Batavia township (Branch)	1,339	1,317	-1.6	1,221	98.1	0.0	0.0	0.0	1.9	18.7	61.4	19.8	489	79.1	62.8	11.9
Bates township (Iron)........	921	887	-3.7	1,021	95.2	0.0	1.0	0.8	3.0	17.5	56.6	26.0	471	95.3	39.9	23.8
Bath CDP	2,083	NA	NA	2,008	90.1	1.3	0.5	1.2	6.8	30.0	51.0	18.9	743	91.0	36.7	27.3
Bath charter township (Clinton)	11,616	11,946	2.8	11,794	84.6	3.1	2.6	3.8	5.9	20.2	68.9	10.9	4,317	68.4	20.2	43.2
Battle Creek city & MCD (Calhoun)	52,347	51,833	-1.0	51,963	67.0	17.8	2.8	4.9	7.5	25.5	59.8	14.6	20,502	60.7	40.5	21.5
Bay township (Charlevoix)	1,122	1,133	1.0	1,195	95.2	0.0	0.0	3.0	1.8	17.6	58.7	23.7	463	96.5	26.6	41.0
Bay City city & MCD (Bay)	34,932	34,149	-2.2	34,578	84.5	2.7	0.5	3.5	8.7	24.7	63.2	12.1	14,134	69.1	48.0	16.5
Bay de Noc township (Delta)	305	301	-1.3	280	99.3	0.0	0.0	0.7	0.0	14.6	56.1	29.3	135	96.3	42.2	21.5
Bay Mills township (Chippewa)	1,477	1,477	0.0	1,576	40.1	1.5	0.1	57.2	1.1	26.1	56.9	17.1	605	71.6	36.5	20.8
Bay Port CDP	477	NA	NA	429	98.6	0.0	0.0	1.4	0.0	15.0	69.1	16.1	196	85.7	56.1	8.2
Bay Shore CDP	0	NA	NA	682	94.6	0.0	0.0	5.4	0.0	18.6	59.9	21.6	287	89.9	49.1	24.4
Bay View CDP	133	NA	NA	189	97.9	0.0	2.1	0.0	0.0	3.2	44.5	52.4	86	93.0	8.1	52.3
Beal City CDP	357	NA	NA	420	99.3	0.0	0.7	0.0	0.0	27.8	58.7	13.6	121	93.4	65.3	19.0
Bear Creek township (Emmet)	6,202	6,301	1.6	6,261	91.2	0.9	1.2	5.6	1.2	25.0	60.2	14.8	2,425	67.4	27.4	32.7
Bearinger township (Presque Isle)..............	369	359	-2.7	340	95.9	0.0	0.6	2.6	0.9	15.0	56.2	28.8	161	95.7	48.4	21.7
Bear Lake CDP	327	NA	NA	357	98.3	0.0	0.0	0.6	1.1	12.5	58.8	28.6	179	100.0	43.6	25.1
Bear Lake township (Kalkaska)	667	676	1.3	686	87.2	0.0	0.0	6.3	6.6	13.8	61.3	24.8	321	88.5	50.5	18.4
Bear Lake village	286	282	-1.4	267	98.5	0.0	0.0	1.1	0.4	25.9	55.0	19.1	123	75.6	37.4	24.4
Bear Lake township (Manistee)..............	1,751	1,724	-1.5	1,761	93.1	0.3	0.0	1.8	4.8	21.5	55.0	23.5	715	91.5	41.0	28.7
Beaugrand township (Cheboygan)	1,168	1,146	-1.9	1,291	91.0	0.0	0.0	5.3	3.7	22.1	46.0	31.9	549	84.2	57.0	17.5
Beaver township (Bay)......	2,885	2,856	-1.0	2,871	96.4	0.1	0.3	1.5	1.7	23.0	59.0	18.1	1,037	93.2	50.4	14.5
Beaver township (Newaygo)	509	501	-1.6	505	96.0	0.0	0.0	1.6	2.4	18.2	63.7	18.0	213	87.3	64.8	4.2
Beaver Creek township (Crawford)	1,736	1,685	-2.9	1,846	93.1	0.0	0.3	1.1	5.5	19.6	62.5	17.7	736	94.6	40.9	18.5
Beaverton city & MCD (Gladwin)	1,071	1,060	-1.0	1,042	93.1	0.1	0.0	2.6	4.2	18.3	60.2	21.3	512	52.5	48.4	13.9
Beaverton township (Gladwin)	1,964	1,941	-1.2	1,970	96.9	0.1	0.0	1.4	1.7	23.1	61.3	15.7	753	87.9	47.5	11.0
Bedford charter township (Calhoun)	9,354	9,484	1.4	9,378	81.9	13.6	0.3	2.5	1.8	21.6	61.0	17.2	3,796	83.3	46.0	15.1
Bedford township (Monroe)	31,085	30,944	-0.5	31,036	94.8	0.0	0.6	1.8	2.5	24.5	59.7	15.9	12,075	85.3	34.0	27.2
Beecher CDP	10,232	NA	NA	10,230	24.7	64.6	0.0	6.4	4.3	28.6	57.9	13.6	3,628	61.4	49.1	6.1
Beechwood CDP	3,015	NA	NA	3,090	55.6	4.8	8.2	9.0	22.4	23.5	66.1	10.4	1,202	77.7	41.6	16.6
Belding city & MCD (Ionia)	5,757	5,784	0.5	5,764	90.2	0.3	0.6	3.9	4.9	27.8	58.8	13.4	2,100	64.1	54.7	11.9
Belknap township (Presque Isle)	751	730	-2.8	773	96.6	0.0	0.0	1.6	1.8	17.6	61.9	20.4	331	93.4	62.8	9.7
Bellaire village	1,086	1,071	-1.4	943	84.0	1.6	0.6	7.8	5.9	20.5	62.0	17.5	392	63.3	37.8	18.4
Belleville city & MCD (Wayne)	3,991	3,872	-3.0	3,914	85.0	7.2	0.8	1.1	5.8	27.1	59.9	12.8	1,587	58.5	39.2	20.4
Bellevue village	1,282	1,276	-0.5	1,304	94.1	0.9	0.5	3.5	1.0	20.5	63.1	16.3	525	69.9	59.0	9.3
Bellevue township (Eaton)	3,150	3,141	-0.3	3,140	89.6	0.8	0.2	8.1	1.4	21.9	62.6	15.7	1,257	83.8	55.7	15.6
Belvidere township (Montcalm)	2,209	2,203	-0.3	2,032	93.5	0.9	0.0	3.1	2.6	17.3	64.1	18.6	932	86.4	44.2	9.7
Bendon CDP	208	NA	NA	197	97.5	0.0	0.0	2.5	0.0	16.8	60.4	22.8	101	75.2	66.3	14.9
Bengal township (Clinton).	1,188	1,209	1.8	1,346	90.9	0.0	0.0	2.8	6.2	27.5	62.5	10.0	406	91.9	35.5	16.5
Bennington township (Shiawassee)	3,168	3,105	-2.0	3,119	95.5	0.3	0.8	0.5	2.9	20.3	57.5	22.2	1,252	94.1	40.5	24.0
Benona township (Oceana)	1,437	1,434	-0.2	1,308	91.8	0.0	0.0	0.4	7.8	13.8	61.7	24.5	570	90.5	30.2	29.6
Bentley township (Gladwin)	844	833	-1.3	809	95.7	0.0	0.0	4.1	0.2	21.6	67.1	11.2	320	89.1	55.9	13.4
Benton charter township (Berrien)	14,749	14,527	-1.5	14,625	40.7	47.4	0.3	2.7	8.9	27.4	57.2	15.5	5,600	55.3	57.4	10.9
Benton township (Cheboygan)	3,206	3,150	-1.7	3,170	89.1	0.0	0.9	9.8	0.3	18.6	55.0	26.1	1,443	87.7	49.1	21.6
Benton township (Eaton) ..	2,796	2,814	0.6	2,792	90.9	1.6	0.2	2.5	4.8	20.6	60.7	18.6	1,084	91.4	37.3	19.7

1 May be of any race.

Table A. All Places — **Population and Housing**

STATE City, town, township, borough, or CDP (county if applicable)	2010 census total population	2014 estimated population	Percent change 2010–2014	ACS total population estimate 2010–2014	White alone, not Hispanic or Latino	Black alone, not Hispanic or Latino	Asian alone, not Hispanic or Latino	All other races or 2 or more races, not Hispanic or Latino	Hispanic or Latino[1]	Under 18 years old	Age 18 to 64 years old	Age 65 years and older	Total occupied housing units	Percent owner occupied	High school diploma or less	Bachelor's degree or more
	1	2	3	4	5	6	7	8	9	10	11	12	13	14	15	16
MICHIGAN—Con.																
Benton Harbor city & MCD (Berrien)	10,038	10,018	-0.2	10,056	6.9	86.6	0.7	4.3	1.5	33.0	59.1	8.0	3,741	34.6	61.8	4.9
Benton Heights CDP	4,084	NA	NA	4,467	21.5	64.9	0.8	1.5	11.4	36.7	53.4	10.0	1,415	51.4	70.1	4.4
Benzonia village	497	493	-0.8	443	86.9	0.0	0.0	1.8	11.3	27.5	57.7	14.7	183	64.5	45.4	22.4
Benzonia township (Benzie)	2,727	2,728	0.0	2,722	88.5	2.1	0.0	6.0	3.3	16.7	56.2	27.1	1,098	74.6	34.4	28.7
Bergland township (Ontonagon)	467	426	-8.8	543	96.1	0.0	0.0	2.8	1.1	11.1	58.6	30.4	267	88.4	43.4	20.2
Berkley city & MCD (Oakland)	14,970	15,273	2.0	15,136	91.8	2.8	1.3	2.3	1.8	21.3	67.4	11.1	6,618	79.7	17.5	50.8
Berlin township (Ionia)	2,116	2,150	1.6	2,251	93.2	0.5	0.7	4.3	1.3	28.0	55.4	16.7	842	81.9	42.3	18.3
Berlin charter township (Monroe)	9,299	9,160	-1.5	9,211	92.3	0.8	0.2	1.7	4.9	25.1	63.4	11.6	3,320	84.4	43.6	15.6
Berlin township (St. Clair)	3,285	3,239	-1.4	3,246	91.8	0.0	0.2	1.4	6.6	20.9	62.1	17.1	1,198	93.5	44.3	14.9
Berrien township (Berrien)	5,084	5,035		5,047	77.4	4.8	3.2	3.7	10.9	21.5	59.3	19.1	1,593	87.3	31.1	38.2
Berrien Springs village	1,800	1,776	-1.3	1,338	68.9	11.1	5.1	5.2	9.6	22.2	58.5	19.4	570	59.3	29.1	40.7
Bertrand township (Berrien)	2,657	2,632	-0.9	2,644	94.0	0.3	0.2	2.2	3.3	19.7	63.6	16.8	982	90.2	39.6	30.3
Bessemer city & MCD (Gogebic)	1,905	1,810	-5.0	1,974	95.2	1.0	0.0	3.4	0.4	19.4	63.2	17.5	860	69.3	38.4	18.6
Bessemer township (Gogebic)	1,176	1,126	-4.3	1,172	98.3	0.7	0.0	0.8	0.3	19.2	51.7	29.1	535	79.4	52.0	14.2
Bethany township (Gratiot)	1,407	1,384	-1.6	1,338	86.8	5.6	0.0	2.2	5.5	18.6	63.6	17.9	470	91.3	53.4	11.9
Bethel township (Branch)	1,434	1,411	-1.6	1,481	86.2	3.6	0.0	1.6	8.6	27.2	60.3	12.5	512	80.7	53.1	7.4
Beulah village	342	342	0.0	268	85.4	4.5	0.0	1.5	8.6	15.7	45.3	38.8	126	68.3	31.7	50.0
Beverly Hills village	10,267	10,448	1.8	10,368	86.1	7.3	1.5	3.0	2.1	25.1	57.9	17.0	4,032	88.1	7.3	74.5
Big Bay CDP	319	NA	NA	183	97.8	0.0	0.0	2.2	0.0	3.3	67.2	29.5	110	89.1	41.8	32.7
Big Creek township (Oscoda)	2,827	2,735	-3.3	2,783	95.3	0.9	0.0	1.9	1.9	16.2	58.3	25.7	1,259	85.6	56.9	11.8
Big Prairie township (Newaygo)	2,573	2,519	-2.1	2,532	96.1	0.9	0.9	0.9	1.1	21.8	58.3	19.9	1,020	86.2	59.1	5.5
Big Rapids city & MCD (Mecosta)	10,432	10,443	0.1	10,543	84.7	6.8	1.9	4.0	2.7	12.1	80.6	7.2	3,077	39.5	28.0	23.7
Big Rapids charter township (Mecosta)	4,377	4,559	4.2	4,448	95.7	0.1	2.0	0.0	2.2	15.1	69.5	15.3	1,740	72.1	29.2	37.5
Billings township (Gladwin)	2,416	2,387	-1.2	2,181	97.5	0.0	0.0	2.0	0.5	13.9	51.5	34.5	1,036	91.7	55.3	11.6
Bingham township (Clinton)	2,859	2,899	1.4	2,889	90.2	0.0	0.0	5.2	4.6	25.2	62.5	12.3	1,074	80.9	38.7	19.6
Bingham township (Huron)	1,709	1,657	-3.0	1,549	99.3	0.7	0.0	0.0	0.0	23.4	59.9	16.7	641	81.0	57.4	15.1
Bingham township (Leelanau)	2,497	2,523	1.0	2,511	90.1	0.6	0.3	3.1	5.9	20.9	62.3	16.7	1,034	89.9	24.8	37.7
Bingham Farms village	1,111	1,131	1.8	1,220	76.6	12.5	3.9	6.0	1.0	19.2	44.4	36.2	496	88.9	8.9	78.0
Birch Run village	1,555	1,495	-3.9	1,537	89.1	2.0	0.0	1.4	7.5	25.7	58.6	15.7	615	58.0	46.3	19.2
Birch Run township (Saginaw)	6,033	5,853	-3.0	5,942	89.9	0.8	0.0	2.8	6.5	25.1	59.7	15.3	2,298	86.3	43.7	21.6
Birmingham city & MCD (Oakland)	20,103	20,757	3.3	20,382	89.7	3.5	2.1	2.2	2.5	25.9	60.7	13.4	8,733	74.8	6.8	78.7
Bismarck township (Presque Isle)	386	375	-2.8	426	95.5	0.2	0.0	2.6	1.6	15.0	50.7	34.3	204	95.6	38.7	27.5
Blackman charter township (Jackson)	24,051	23,923	-0.5	24,024	77.3	14.5	1.3	3.3	3.6	16.1	69.3	14.3	8,011	54.2	45.9	18.9
Blaine township (Benzie)	551	551	0.0	555	95.7	0.0	0.0	3.6	0.7	22.3	51.2	26.5	234	83.8	35.9	30.3
Blair township (Grand Traverse)	8,209	8,580	4.5	8,404	88.4	0.4	0.0	6.7	4.5	28.2	64.7	7.1	2,842	84.8	47.5	15.0
Blendon township (Ottawa)	5,772	6,147	6.5	5,940	92.5	1.6	0.9	1.4	3.6	28.0	60.4	11.6	1,931	87.7	35.6	27.7
Bliss township (Emmet)	620	630	1.6	649	86.6	0.0	0.0	11.9	1.5	27.4	51.9	20.6	259	91.5	40.9	24.7
Blissfield village	3,344	3,267	-2.3	3,304	91.3	0.0	0.5	3.3	4.9	23.7	62.1	14.1	1,455	79.1	32.5	28.6
Blissfield township (Lenawee)	3,973	3,883	-2.3	3,925	91.7	0.0	0.4	2.8	5.1	22.8	63.0	14.3	1,659	80.2	34.1	28.9
Bloomer township (Montcalm)	3,904	3,681	-5.7	3,811	65.5	23.1	1.0	5.5	4.9	13.8	77.9	8.2	564	83.5	42.7	17.7
Bloomfield township (Huron)	455	441	-3.1	528	90.0	0.9	0.2	2.8	6.1	21.8	56.8	21.4	199	89.4	75.4	3.0
Bloomfield township (Missaukee)	531	536	0.9	352	99.4	0.0	0.0	0.6	0.0	15.6	64.2	20.2	157	91.1	46.5	22.3
Bloomfield charter township (Oakland)	41,070	41,967	2.2	41,571	79.8	7.5	8.5	3.0	1.2	22.2	55.6	22.3	16,446	86.2	9.3	72.4
Bloomfield Hills city & MCD (Oakland)	3,869	3,990	3.1	3,925	85.5	1.4	7.7	3.9	1.5	26.2	52.3	21.5	1,304	89.0	5.0	85.0
Bloomingdale village	454	445	-2.0	612	85.9	3.1	0.0	8.7	2.3	26.8	62.6	10.6	224	64.3	61.6	4.5
Bloomingdale township (Van Buren)	3,103	3,041	-2.0	3,070	92.7	2.6	0.0	2.3	2.4	15.7	62.9	21.4	1,364	80.1	61.7	5.1
Blue Lake township (Kalkaska)	387	394	1.8	363	99.4	0.0	0.0	0.6	0.0	3.3	49.0	47.7	204	96.1	42.2	31.4
Blue Lake township (Muskegon)	2,399	2,417	0.8	2,340	91.9	0.9	0.3	4.1	2.8	29.5	59.9	10.5	778	82.5	41.0	22.9
Blumfield township (Saginaw)	1,960	1,900	-3.1	1,863	96.7	0.5	0.0	0.4	2.4	20.7	60.5	18.8	746	93.7	43.0	22.0
Boardman township (Kalkaska)	1,530	1,549	1.2	1,500	95.5	0.3	0.0	1.4	2.8	28.9	58.3	12.8	566	79.7	53.0	11.0
Bohemia township (Ontonagon)	82	75	-8.5	73	100.0	0.0	0.0	0.0	0.0	0.0	48.0	52.1	49	91.8	59.2	22.4
Bois Blanc township (Mackinac)	95	94	-1.1	72	97.2	0.0	0.0	2.8	0.0	0.0	58.2	41.7	51	84.3	45.1	9.8
Boon CDP	167	NA	NA	203	95.6	0.0	0.0	4.4	0.0	8.9	68.4	22.7	82	90.2	69.5	6.1
Boon township (Wexford)	687	693	0.9	710	96.9	0.0	0.0	1.8	1.3	18.8	65.1	16.1	270	87.4	49.3	7.0
Boston township (Ionia)	5,706	5,749	0.8	5,722	90.9	0.4	0.4	6.3	1.9	27.0	60.5	12.6	2,092	79.5	40.7	20.6
Bourret township (Gladwin)	461	456	-1.1	440	99.1	0.0	0.0	0.5	0.5	10.5	61.9	27.5	198	90.9	63.1	6.6
Bowne township (Kent)	3,084	3,276	6.2	3,181	93.9	0.8	0.7	0.7	4.0	31.0	59.5	9.6	1,051	90.8	28.6	34.0

1 May be of any race.

Table A. All Places — **Population and Housing**

STATE City, town, township, borough, or CDP (county if applicable)	2010 census total population	2014 estimated population	Percent change 2010–2014	ACS total population estimate 2010–2014	White alone, not Hispanic or Latino	Black alone, not Hispanic or Latino	Asian alone, not Hispanic or Latino	All other races or 2 or more races, not Hispanic or Latino	Hispanic or Latino[1]	Under 18 years old	Age 18 to 64 years old	Age 65 years and older	Total occupied housing units	Percent owner occupied	High school diploma or less	Bachelor's degree or more
	1	2	3	4	5	6	7	8	9	10	11	12	13	14	15	16
MICHIGAN—Con.																
Boyne City city & MCD (Charlevoix)	3,739	3,760	0.6	3,753	94.5	0.2	0.6	3.9	0.9	24.3	60.8	14.9	1,577	65.8	31.8	24.4
Boyne Falls village	294	294	0.0	291	85.6	2.1	0.0	9.3	3.1	21.6	59.7	18.6	109	78.0	54.1	19.3
Boyne Valley township (Charlevoix)	1,195	1,199	0.3	1,366	94.2	0.4	0.0	4.4	1.0	21.2	62.4	16.5	512	90.4	53.1	19.3
Brady township (Kalamazoo)	4,252	4,443	4.5	4,340	93.4	1.3	0.0	1.5	3.8	24.5	60.4	15.3	1,584	86.5	37.1	21.5
Brady township (Saginaw)	2,218	2,138	-3.6	2,207	93.1	0.0	2.1	0.5	4.3	23.1	62.7	14.3	814	90.3	47.9	9.2
Brampton township (Delta)	1,050	1,039		894	97.9	0.0	0.0	1.7	0.4	16.1	55.2	28.5	389	98.7	41.6	17.0
Branch township (Mason)	1,328	1,334	0.5	1,353	91.4	1.8	0.8	2.4	3.6	25.0	55.5	19.6	602	84.1	54.2	9.1
Brandon charter township (Oakland)	15,175	15,572	2.6	15,359	92.9	0.3	0.4	1.9	4.4	26.8	63.6	9.8	5,391	90.5	32.7	25.9
Brant township (Saginaw)	2,012	1,957	-2.7	2,042	96.3	0.3	0.0	1.5	2.0	21.6	64.9	13.6	772	92.7	54.3	10.2
Breckenridge village	1,328	1,309	-1.4	1,282	91.5	1.6	0.0	1.5	5.5	23.7	60.7	15.6	538	69.3	61.0	7.4
Breedsville village	199	197	-1.0	153	56.2	0.0	0.0	20.3	23.5	26.8	60.8	12.4	59	83.1	69.5	3.4
Breen township (Dickinson)	499	495	-0.8	450	89.6	0.2	0.2	9.8	0.2	29.3	52.3	18.4	167	86.2	57.5	6.0
Breitung charter township (Dickinson)	5,853	5,807	-0.8	5,845	96.0	0.9	0.1	1.1	2.0	21.1	59.3	19.6	2,369	90.6	46.3	27.9
Brethren CDP	410	NA	NA	327	95.7	0.0	0.0	4.3	0.0	19.9	58.7	21.4	152	72.4	58.6	5.9
Brevort township (Mackinac)	594	589	-0.8	484	67.1	4.8	0.0	26.4	1.7	10.7	68.0	21.3	224	94.6	67.0	10.7
Bridgehampton township (Sanilac)	854	823	-3.6	942	91.7	1.6	0.0	0.8	5.8	29.0	56.8	14.2	325	71.7	56.0	10.5
Bridgeport CDP	6,950	NA	NA	6,615	55.3	31.0	0.0	4.5	9.2	22.7	60.1	17.1	2,795	76.6	58.9	12.2
Bridgeport charter township (Saginaw)	10,514	10,190	-3.1	10,350	65.0	21.4	0.0	5.4	8.2	21.7	59.6	18.7	4,249	81.6	57.2	11.0
Bridgeton township (Newaygo)	2,141	2,109	-1.5	2,091	90.5	0.1	0.0	1.1	8.3	20.8	67.0	12.2	788	84.1	50.3	15.0
Bridgewater township (Washtenaw)	1,674	1,723	2.9	1,667	96.4	0.2	0.8	1.7	0.8	23.2	61.3	15.4	632	93.4	30.5	32.9
Bridgman city & MCD (Berrien)	2,291	2,261	-1.3	1,963	96.7	1.0	0.9	0.0	1.4	23.4	55.5	21.0	805	72.4	31.6	27.7
Brighton city & MCD (Livingston)	7,444	7,636	2.6	7,562	96.6	0.5	1.0	0.1	1.8	17.4	61.5	21.1	3,745	61.7	26.6	39.8
Brighton township (Livingston)	17,790	18,132	1.9	17,933	95.4	0.5	1.2	1.5	1.4	23.6	63.5	13.0	6,283	94.5	22.1	47.6
Briley township (Montmorency)	1,860	1,786	-4.0	1,899	96.8	0.5	0.0	0.4	2.3	16.7	60.2	23.3	753	87.0	58.7	13.0
Britton village	586	574	-2.0	703	94.9	0.3	0.0	4.1	0.7	30.2	63.3	6.5	272	70.2	43.0	16.5
Brockway township (St. Clair)	2,023	2,005	-0.9	1,901	95.1	0.0	0.0	2.6	2.3	22.4	62.2	15.5	699	92.4	44.9	16.2
Bronson city & MCD (Branch)	2,349	2,325	-1.0	2,420	80.7	0.2	1.7	4.3	13.0	32.4	56.6	10.9	784	66.8	58.5	13.1
Bronson township (Branch)	1,349	1,337	-0.9	1,282	97.8	0.0	0.9	0.0	1.2	23.6	64.7	11.7	461	85.9	51.4	15.6
Brookfield township (Eaton)	1,537	1,546	0.6	1,671	96.9	0.0	0.2	1.5	1.4	25.3	62.3	12.4	576	85.9	43.1	16.7
Brookfield township (Huron)	760	738	-2.9	702	90.7	0.0	0.7	3.0	5.6	21.2	57.0	21.8	301	91.4	68.8	6.6
Brooklyn village	1,206	1,199	-0.6	1,240	96.0	0.1	0.5	2.3	1.1	23.6	51.1	25.2	536	57.8	43.7	14.4
Brooks township (Newaygo)	3,508	3,469	-1.1	3,475	94.7	0.2	0.5	0.2	4.4	17.2	60.5	22.1	1,586	91.0	52.6	9.4
Broomfield township (Isabella)	1,849	1,829	-1.1	1,620	95.7	0.4	0.0	1.5	2.3	16.9	64.0	19.0	678	87.6	43.4	22.0
Brown township (Manistee)	747	738	-1.2	628	98.4	0.0	0.0	1.6	0.0	16.0	61.1	22.8	294	86.4	46.6	16.7
Brown City city	1,325	1,279	-3.5	1,243	92.0	0.2	0.0	5.1	2.7	26.3	60.7	12.9	509	66.4	59.7	6.7
Brown City city (Lapeer)	9	9	0.0	0	0.0	0.0	0.0	0.0	0.0	0.0	0.0	0.0	0	0.0	0.0	0.0
Brown City city (Sanilac)	1,316	1,270	-3.5	1,243	92.0	0.2	0.0	5.1	2.7	26.3	60.7	12.9	509	66.4	59.7	6.7
Brownlee Park CDP	2,108	NA	NA	2,016	90.1	0.4	2.5	4.5	2.5	26.3	62.7	11.3	750	74.1	67.5	2.4
Brownstown charter township (Wayne)	30,627	30,770	0.5	30,615	77.8	7.9	6.4	1.6	6.2	25.7	63.5	10.7	11,013	77.0	38.9	26.3
Bruce township (Chippewa)	2,128	2,121	-0.3	2,304	87.4	1.1	0.2	11.2	0.1	17.3	59.9	22.7	919	89.2	46.8	20.2
Bruce township (Macomb)	8,700	8,968	3.1	8,797	91.0	3.1	0.1	2.6	3.2	19.9	65.1	15.0	3,050	94.3	33.0	29.4
Brutus CDP	218	NA	NA	172	76.7	0.6	0.0	6.4	16.3	22.1	61.0	16.9	77	83.1	50.6	18.2
Buchanan city & MCD (Berrien)	4,456	4,390	-1.5	4,426	83.9	9.1	0.3	2.9	3.8	20.7	61.7	17.6	2,005	61.9	56.4	12.9
Buchanan township (Berrien)	3,523	3,504	-0.5	3,516	93.8	3.8	0.1	2.2	0.0	25.0	58.7	16.1	1,252	90.3	40.2	24.8
Buckeye township (Gladwin)	1,308	1,284	-1.8	1,442	97.2	0.0	0.0	0.6	2.2	21.2	62.1	16.8	539	87.9	68.1	3.9
Buckley village	697	703	0.9	624	92.8	0.0	0.2	3.2	3.8	35.3	57.4	7.4	196	67.3	43.9	19.4
Buel township (Sanilac)	1,265	1,216	-3.9	1,138	90.6	0.0	0.0	1.5	7.9	23.8	56.8	19.5	450	84.2	56.9	10.7
Buena Vista CDP	6,816	NA	NA	6,302	10.8	71.9	0.0	9.9	7.4	27.8	53.6	18.6	2,608	57.2	54.7	5.8
Buena Vista charter township (Saginaw)	8,674	8,335	-3.9	8,501	28.1	57.2	0.0	7.5	7.3	27.3	54.9	17.9	3,402	64.8	51.2	7.9
Bunker Hill township (Ingham)	2,115	2,106	-0.4	2,125	96.7	0.0	0.4	1.2	1.7	30.7	59.5	9.7	724	87.0	44.3	17.3
Burdell township (Osceola)	1,331	1,307	-1.8	1,238	97.3	0.0	0.0	1.7	1.1	25.2	58.3	16.6	482	86.9	58.7	15.6
Burleigh township (Iosco)	787	769	-2.3	841	92.2	0.0	0.0	3.2	4.6	24.4	57.2	18.4	296	84.1	62.5	4.7
Burlington village	261	258	-1.1	273	97.8	0.0	0.7	1.5	0.0	24.9	65.3	9.9	102	88.2	47.1	11.8
Burlington township (Calhoun)	1,941	1,907	-1.8	1,989	98.7	0.2	0.1	1.0	0.0	21.8	62.9	15.3	710	87.6	52.3	12.8
Burlington township (Lapeer)	1,478	1,472	-0.4	1,556	90.9	0.9	0.6	2.8	4.8	25.1	62.9	12.2	564	85.3	64.0	6.9
Burns township (Shiawassee)	3,457	3,380	-2.2	3,416	94.3	0.0	0.1	2.5	3.0	23.6	62.6	13.6	1,251	79.5	54.4	14.2
Burnside township (Lapeer)	1,861	1,854	-0.4	1,915	94.8	1.4	0.0	2.2	1.6	27.2	62.7	10.2	686	88.9	55.7	7.6

1 May be of any race.

Table A. All Places — **Population and Housing**

STATE City, town, township, borough, or CDP (county if applicable)	2010 census total population	2014 estimated population	Percent change 2010– 2014	ACS total population estimate 2010–2014	White alone, not Hispanic or Latino	Black alone, not Hispanic or Latino	Asian alone, not Hispanic or Latino	All other races or 2 or more races, not Hispanic or Latino	Hispanic or Latino[1]	Under 18 years old	Age 18 to 64 years old	Age 65 years and older	Total occupied housing units	Percent owner occupied	High school diploma or less	Bachelor's degree or more
	1	2	3	4	5	6	7	8	9	10	11	12	13	14	15	16
MICHIGAN—Con.																
Burr Oak village	828	820	-1.0	817	93.8	0.0	0.4	1.0	4.9	29.7	60.0	10.0	277	71.1	72.9	4.7
Burr Oak township (St. Joseph)	2,611	2,606	-0.2	2,595	96.8	0.4	0.6	0.3	1.9	25.5	59.5	15.2	923	81.9	59.6	10.0
Burt township (Alger)........	522	513	-1.7	382	96.3	0.0	0.0	3.7	0.0	5.8	46.4	47.9	192	89.1	47.9	22.4
Burt township (Cheboygan)	680	670	-1.5	665	86.5	0.0	0.0	11.4	2.1	8.5	51.3	40.5	358	95.8	38.8	30.2
Burt CDP	1,228	NA	NA	1,095	92.1	4.4	0.0	1.0	2.6	26.9	59.4	13.7	330	88.2	58.5	8.5
Burtchville township (St. Clair)	4,008	3,954	-1.3	3,970	94.7	0.4	0.6	2.8	1.5	22.7	61.5	15.7	1,622	76.4	43.3	15.5
Burton city & MCD (Genesee)	29,999	28,974	-3.4	29,429	86.6	6.0	0.3	3.4	3.6	22.0	64.0	14.1	11,643	73.2	44.1	16.4
Bushnell township (Montcalm)	1,604	1,591	-0.8	1,793	93.2	1.8	0.0	2.3	2.7	21.4	64.9	13.7	607	87.5	53.9	4.3
Butler township (Branch) ..	1,467	1,446	-1.4	1,429	99.2	0.0	0.0	0.1	0.6	31.2	51.5	17.1	486	81.7	63.4	10.9
Butman township (Gladwin)	1,999	1,989	-0.5	1,852	98.7	0.1	0.0	0.9	0.4	10.1	48.3	41.5	890	91.8	38.1	28.2
Butterfield township (Missaukee)	489	495	1.2	472	94.1	0.0	0.0	4.2	1.7	15.7	65.3	19.1	199	82.4	52.8	7.5
Byron township (Kent)	20,317	22,097	8.8	21,125	89.0	2.5	2.6	2.2	3.7	26.4	58.8	14.8	7,722	86.0	36.5	31.7
Byron village	581	562	-3.3	545	96.1	0.0	0.9	0.6	2.4	29.0	58.2	12.8	206	76.7	57.3	8.3
Byron Center CDP	5,822	NA	NA	6,057	94.2	0.0	2.4	0.5	2.9	27.0	57.0	16.1	2,161	95.5	30.1	38.9
Caberfae CDP	64	NA	NA	21	100.0	0.0	0.0	0.0	0.0	0.0	19.1	81.0	17	82.4	41.2	58.8
Cadillac city & MCD (Wexford)	10,356	10,335	-0.2	10,306	93.7	0.3	1.4	3.3	1.3	23.6	58.6	17.9	4,266	59.6	46.6	15.4
Caldwell township (Missaukee)	1,319	1,333	1.1	1,561	93.9	0.0	2.2	2.8	1.1	25.8	60.8	13.5	573	79.2	52.0	11.7
Caledonia township (Alcona)	1,161	1,110	-4.4	1,071	99.3	0.0	0.0	0.4	0.3	12.1	48.1	39.9	507	95.1	46.2	14.0
Caledonia village	1,511	1,572	4.0	1,595	93.7	0.2	0.4	3.8	1.9	33.5	60.6	6.0	564	68.3	34.4	34.6
Caledonia township (Kent)	12,338	13,470	9.2	12,835	92.5	0.5	2.4	1.4	3.2	29.9	60.7	9.4	4,332	86.8	25.9	40.5
Caledonia charter township (Shiawassee) .	4,475	4,380	-2.1	4,407	97.7	0.0	0.0	0.5	1.7	20.0	62.1	17.8	1,793	82.0	42.7	16.7
California township (Branch)	1,040	1,026	-1.3	1,065	95.3	0.0	2.3	0.2	2.3	37.6	53.9	8.4	324	81.5	71.6	4.6
Calumet village	726	708	-2.5	765	91.6	0.9	0.0	3.5	3.9	22.8	64.1	12.9	366	31.7	59.3	12.3
Calumet charter township (Houghton)	6,487	6,400	-1.3	6,463	94.6	0.1	0.0	3.1	2.2	23.1	60.3	16.6	2,666	74.2	52.8	21.5
Calvin township (Cass)	2,037	2,028	-0.4	1,836	81.4	9.8	1.0	5.1	2.7	25.1	57.2	17.8	689	81.6	58.8	16.5
Cambria township (Hillsdale)	2,533	2,483	-2.0	2,299	98.3	0.0	0.5	0.2	1.0	17.2	64.7	17.9	981	80.7	46.0	16.9
Cambridge township (Lenawee)	5,740	5,683	-1.0	5,708	95.7	0.0	0.3	1.0	3.0	19.8	61.7	18.4	2,416	85.0	37.0	28.1
Camden village	512	503	-1.8	562	97.7	0.0	0.0	1.1	1.2	28.4	64.6	6.9	185	57.8	62.2	5.9
Camden township (Hillsdale)	2,047	2,008	-1.9	2,196	98.7	0.0	0.2	0.7	0.4	31.4	56.8	11.7	692	74.6	62.6	8.7
Campbell township (Ionia)	2,391	2,411	0.8	2,487	97.9	0.0	1.0	0.2	0.8	24.6	63.6	12.0	909	86.9	45.0	13.8
Canada Creek Ranch CDP	304	NA	NA	276	97.5	0.0	0.0	2.5	0.0	9.1	32.3	58.7	133	100.0	31.6	21.8
Canadian Lakes CDP	2,756	NA	NA	2,793	88.4	7.6	0.2	1.6	2.2	12.9	45.6	41.4	1,299	93.4	24.0	36.9
Cannon township (Kent) ...	13,336	14,154	6.1	13,725	93.0	1.2	1.0	1.5	3.3	28.0	61.3	10.7	4,652	93.6	19.3	49.5
Canton charter township (Wayne)...........................	90,173	89,701	-0.5	89,672	69.5	9.9	14.6	3.1	2.9	26.8	63.6	9.7	31,081	76.4	20.3	50.3
Capac village	1,890	1,856	-1.8	2,036	73.6	0.6	0.0	1.7	24.1	30.3	61.3	8.3	709	70.0	57.8	7.6
Carleton village	2,345	2,350	0.2	2,332	90.1	2.7	3.4	1.3	2.4	23.5	65.3	11.2	951	80.8	45.6	14.1
Carlton township (Barry)...	2,391	2,404	0.5	2,323	93.5	0.0	1.5	2.7	2.3	21.9	66.1	12.1	883	89.4	43.9	19.0
Carmel township (Eaton) ..	2,855	2,881	0.9	2,870	97.4	0.0	0.3	0.4	1.8	20.8	60.5	18.6	1,116	93.5	36.1	20.5
Carney village	192	190		274	96.4	0.0	0.0	2.2	1.5	17.5	63.4	19.0	108	80.6	38.9	26.9
Caro city & MCD (Tuscola)	4,229	4,116	-2.7	4,164	90.2	0.7	2.5	0.6	5.9	19.4	60.2	20.5	1,764	54.8	44.7	17.7
Carp Lake CDP	357	NA	NA	474	92.2	0.0	0.0	7.0	0.8	13.3	46.2	40.5	210	81.4	41.4	7.1
Carp Lake township (Emmet)	759	770	1.4	854	90.2	0.1	0.0	9.3	0.5	16.0	51.9	32.0	361	85.3	46.0	7.8
Carp Lake township (Ontonagon)	722	661	-8.4	623	94.2	0.0	1.0	3.0	1.8	9.1	47.5	43.3	316	93.7	42.4	16.5
Carrollton township (Saginaw)	6,103	5,899	-3.3	6,009	63.1	15.1	0.8	3.0	18.0	23.5	63.5	12.9	2,235	73.6	45.7	19.0
Carson City city & MCD (Montcalm)	1,091	1,090	-0.1	1,080	89.6	0.0	0.9	2.1	7.3	23.6	52.3	24.2	445	65.4	47.6	17.1
Carsonville village............	527	512	-2.8	494	89.5	3.0	0.0	1.6	5.9	36.5	49.8	13.8	177	68.9	59.9	7.3
Cascade charter township (Kent)	17,135	18,316	6.9	17,715	94.9	0.3	2.9	0.5	1.2	27.9	56.7	15.4	6,416	92.4	12.1	67.5
Casco township (Allegan).	2,823	2,945	4.3	2,866	84.2	1.6	1.2	2.5	10.5	27.1	58.0	15.1	972	84.3	51.1	29.4
Casco township (St. Clair).	4,105	4,051	-1.3	4,063	96.6	0.0	0.0	0.0	3.4	23.7	61.3	14.8	1,456	91.7	44.0	19.0
Case township (Presque Isle)	903	878	-2.8	825	95.0	0.0	0.1	1.7	3.2	16.2	54.1	29.7	400	91.3	65.0	14.5
Caseville city & MCD (Huron)	774	749	-3.2	843	93.7	0.0	0.0	2.0	4.3	17.4	53.6	28.9	432	67.1	51.2	17.4
Caseville township (Huron)	1,796	1,739	-3.2	1,867	97.6	0.0	0.2	1.0	1.2	15.2	50.3	34.4	885	91.2	33.8	18.9
Casnovia village	319	325	1.9	479	68.9	0.0	0.6	3.1	27.3	26.1	63.9	10.0	144	79.9	56.3	8.3
Casnovia township (Muskegon)	2,805	2,817	0.4	2,806	88.1	0.8	0.2	2.1	8.8	22.6	65.5	12.0	955	85.9	54.1	9.7
Caspian city & MCD (Iron)	906	871	-3.9	790	98.5	0.0	0.0	1.5	0.0	15.5	60.3	24.1	401	79.6	62.8	11.7
Cass City village	2,428	2,366	-2.6	2,592	94.4	0.3	0.3	0.3	4.8	22.5	57.7	20.0	1,026	78.4	38.1	19.1
Cassopolis village............	1,774	1,738	-2.0	1,770	48.6	24.7	1.2	15.6	9.8	30.0	55.7	14.4	617	52.7	51.4	9.4
Castleton township (Barry)	3,471	3,470	0.0	3,457	93.3	0.0	0.0	2.4	4.4	22.7	61.2	16.2	1,349	68.1	54.9	8.5
Cato township (Montcalm)	2,735	2,736	0.0	2,732	96.4	0.3	0.3	1.2	1.8	27.8	54.8	17.4	1,039	80.3	46.8	16.1
Cedar CDP	93	NA	NA	85	96.5	0.0	0.0	3.5	0.0	27.0	54.0	18.8	37	83.8	43.2	13.5
Cedar township (Osceola)	455	446	-2.0	465	97.0	0.0	0.0	3.0	0.0	21.7	55.8	22.4	188	88.8	47.3	18.1
Cedar Creek township (Muskegon)	3,186	3,167	-0.6	3,170	95.7	0.0	0.0	0.6	3.7	21.6	65.5	12.8	1,214	90.0	48.2	17.9
Cedar Creek township (Wexford)	1,757	1,767	0.6	1,798	90.4	0.5	0.0	3.6	5.6	26.6	61.8	11.6	604	87.6	55.3	11.9

1 May be of any race.

Table A. All Places — **Population and Housing**

	Population				Race and Hispanic or Latino origin (percent), 2010–2014					Age (percent), 2010–2014			Households, 2010–2014			
STATE City, town, township, borough, or CDP (county if applicable)	2010 census total population	2014 estimated population	Percent change 2010–2014	ACS total population estimate 2010–2014	White alone, not Hispanic or Latino	Black alone, not Hispanic or Latino	Asian alone, not Hispanic or Latino	All other races or 2 or more races, not Hispanic or Latino	Hispanic or Latino[1]	Under 18 years old	Age 18 to 64 years old	Age 65 years and older	Total occupied housing units	Percent owner occupied	Householders by level of education (percent) High school diploma or less	Householders by level of education (percent) Bachelor's degree or more
	1	2	3	4	5	6	7	8	9	10	11	12	13	14	15	16
MICHIGAN—Con.																
Cedar Springs city & MCD (Kent)	3,509	3,601	2.6	3,544	92.3	1.2	0.9	3.3	2.3	29.1	60.3	10.9	1,297	62.8	53.8	13.0
Cedarville township (Menominee)	253	251	-0.8	279	98.6	0.0	0.0	0.0	1.4	10.8	53.8	35.5	154	91.6	49.4	29.2
Cement City village	441	428	-2.9	481	93.8	0.0	0.4	0.4	5.4	21.6	67.4	11.0	184	75.5	62.5	2.2
Center township (Emmet)	568	578	1.8	576	87.8	0.0	0.0	10.8	1.4	20.6	63.9	15.5	229	89.5	48.5	20.5
Center Line city & MCD (Macomb)	8,257	8,316	0.7	8,279	75.0	14.9	5.6	2.6	2.0	22.7	59.6	17.6	3,600	51.4	48.9	9.1
Centerville township (Leelanau)	1,274	1,284	0.8	1,366	90.8	0.6	0.1	0.9	7.6	20.6	54.6	24.8	509	84.3	32.6	33.2
Central Lake village	952	940	-1.3	1,063	95.4	0.0	0.0	2.8	1.8	24.0	62.2	13.7	411	68.9	58.9	13.1
Central Lake township (Antrim)	2,198	2,170	-1.3	2,138	97.2	0.0	0.0	1.6	1.1	17.6	60.7	21.7	906	80.4	45.5	20.9
Centreville village	1,425	1,416	-0.6	1,700	91.4	2.2	0.0	4.5	1.9	20.8	64.8	14.3	541	74.1	46.6	18.9
Champion township (Marquette)	297	300	1.0	312	98.4	0.0	0.0	1.0	0.6	26.9	57.2	15.7	131	82.4	68.7	9.2
Chandler township (Charlevoix)	248	248	0.0	264	90.9	0.0	0.0	3.8	5.3	24.3	55.9	19.7	105	88.6	41.0	14.3
Chandler township (Huron)	472	458	-3.0	483	97.9	0.0	0.0	0.6	1.4	23.6	66.3	10.1	168	81.5	47.6	11.3
Chapin township (Saginaw)	1,060	1,020	-3.8	927	94.2	0.0	0.2	3.9	1.7	22.2	65.5	12.3	353	85.3	62.3	4.0
Charleston township (Kalamazoo)	1,975	2,031	2.8	1,954	92.3	0.5	1.3	4.2	1.7	24.3	62.0	13.7	722	90.6	36.8	29.2
Charlevoix city & MCD (Charlevoix)	2,513	2,529	0.6	2,527	94.3	0.9	1.6	2.4	0.8	17.9	54.0	28.1	1,270	53.5	33.5	36.1
Charlevoix township (Charlevoix)	1,645	1,651	0.4	1,539	94.2	0.0	0.0	3.3	2.5	22.9	54.3	22.7	590	91.9	21.9	39.3
Charlotte city & MCD (Eaton)	9,074	9,056	-0.2	9,053	90.2	1.0	1.0	3.6	4.1	22.3	59.1	18.5	3,729	62.0	37.2	17.3
Charlton township (Otsego)	1,354	1,352	-0.1	1,281	98.8	0.0	0.0	1.2	0.0	15.1	50.5	34.3	625	94.6	55.5	15.2
Chase township (Lake)	1,137	1,119	-1.6	1,042	96.7	0.4	0.0	1.4	1.4	18.7	61.2	20.2	365	85.8	59.2	7.9
Chassell township (Houghton)	1,812	1,793	-1.0	1,841	95.9	0.0	0.3	1.6	2.3	28.2	55.5	16.2	710	83.1	35.8	29.9
Chatham village	220	214	-2.7	227	97.4	0.0	0.0	2.6	0.0	22.4	45.9	31.7	76	80.3	71.1	7.9
Cheboygan city & MCD (Cheboygan)	4,867	4,779	-1.8	4,801	90.2	0.5	0.6	7.0	1.6	23.1	58.3	18.6	2,034	61.4	55.5	8.3
Chelsea city & MCD (Washtenaw)	4,944	5,211	5.4	5,085	95.5	0.6	0.6	0.7	2.5	22.2	52.1	25.6	2,292	61.3	26.2	40.7
Cherry Grove township (Wexford)	2,377	2,395	0.8	2,125	96.7	1.1	0.0	1.2	1.0	21.4	61.0	17.7	827	84.9	33.7	34.3
Cherry Valley township (Lake)	396	389	-1.8	462	88.3	9.3	0.0	1.9	0.4	12.2	61.9	26.0	158	89.2	73.4	7.6
Chesaning village	2,394	2,308	-3.6	2,412	90.6	0.8	0.7	0.9	7.0	25.7	57.2	17.1	1,020	63.4	47.2	13.9
Chesaning township (Saginaw)	4,659	4,509	-3.2	4,587	93.9	0.4	0.4	1.6	3.7	22.5	59.5	18.0	1,871	75.3	47.5	16.4
Cheshire township (Allegan)	2,199	2,224	1.1	1,878	92.0	1.9	0.0	3.4	2.7	22.1	63.9	14.0	780	83.1	50.9	16.5
Chester township (Eaton)	1,747	1,760	0.7	1,829	95.2	0.9	0.3	2.0	1.6	23.6	60.2	16.0	664	90.5	44.9	15.4
Chester township (Otsego)	1,292	1,291	-0.1	1,263	99.5	0.0	0.0	0.5	0.0	21.3	61.8	16.7	500	85.2	48.4	15.8
Chester township (Ottawa)	2,017	2,058	2.0	1,940	93.0	1.6	0.7	2.3	2.4	19.9	67.3	12.7	737	87.4	42.6	23.3
Chesterfield township (Macomb)	43,381	44,385	2.3	43,814	88.7	5.5	1.2	1.7	2.9	25.4	64.1	10.5	16,484	81.1	35.5	23.4
Chestonia township (Antrim)	511	501	-2.0	557	98.6	0.0	0.0	1.1	0.4	16.1	60.8	23.0	230	91.3	71.7	7.8
Chikaming township (Berrien)	3,100	3,092	-0.3	3,094	95.8	2.4	0.3	0.3	1.3	10.0	54.4	35.7	1,422	91.4	25.6	44.2
China township (St. Clair)	3,551	3,490	-1.7	3,502	96.1	0.0	1.1	1.6	1.2	25.5	59.6	15.0	1,231	96.2	43.4	20.2
Chippewa township (Chippewa)	213	212	-0.5	144	91.0	0.0	0.0	9.0	0.0	22.3	50.8	27.1	74	77.0	62.2	12.2
Chippewa township (Isabella)	4,654	4,601	-1.1	4,636	69.0	1.8	0.8	20.5	7.8	25.4	63.8	10.8	1,744	76.5	51.0	17.1
Chippewa township (Mecosta)	1,212	1,217	0.4	1,021	97.3	0.6	0.0	1.8	0.4	11.5	57.3	31.1	471	82.2	43.7	15.7
Chocolay charter township (Marquette)	5,903	5,984	1.4	5,958	92.8	0.5	0.1	5.0	1.6	20.5	62.2	17.5	2,385	83.4	31.3	38.1
Chums Corner CDP	946	NA	NA	862	97.8	0.0	0.0	2.2	0.0	28.9	65.3	5.8	279	71.3	37.6	17.9
Churchill township (Ogemaw)	1,713	1,660	-3.1	1,614	97.1	0.0	0.0	0.3	2.5	16.9	58.3	24.9	702	90.6	50.1	12.8
Clam Lake township (Wexford)	2,286	2,303	0.7	2,411	98.8	0.0	0.2	0.5	0.5	19.8	62.4	17.8	905	90.8	39.7	24.9
Clam Union township (Missaukee)	882	893	1.2	971	91.8	0.0	0.2	3.6	4.4	22.9	59.3	17.9	419	80.4	62.8	5.7
Clare city	3,118	3,089	-0.9	3,056	94.2	0.6	0.3	4.3	0.6	22.9	59.9	17.1	1,335	50.0	53.9	15.7
Clare city (Clare)	3,071	3,042	-0.9	3,056	94.2	0.6	0.3	4.3	0.6	22.9	59.9	17.1	1,335	50.0	53.9	15.7
Clare city (Isabella)	47	47	0.0	0	0.0	0.0	0.0	0.0	0.0	0.0	0.0	0.0	0	0.0	0.0	0.0
Clarence township (Calhoun)	1,985	1,959	-1.3	1,966	98.8	0.2	0.3	0.4	0.4	18.0	59.5	22.6	823	82.9	45.1	22.0
Clarendon township (Calhoun)	1,139	1,127	-1.1	1,172	97.0	0.0	0.0	1.4	1.6	24.7	64.3	10.9	374	83.4	50.0	7.8
Clark township (Mackinac)	2,056	2,043	-0.6	2,106	83.5	0.0	0.3	16.1	0.0	15.9	56.3	27.8	1,018	77.2	43.4	22.4
Clarksville village	394	399	1.3	397	95.2	0.0	2.5	0.3	2.0	23.7	55.3	20.9	164	70.7	43.9	10.4
Clawson city & MCD (Oakland)	11,825	12,049	1.9	11,943	90.7	1.0	1.4	3.2	3.7	17.4	67.4	15.2	5,417	69.8	29.8	34.8
Clay township (St. Clair)	9,066	8,897	-1.9	8,947	98.6	0.0	0.3	0.5	0.5	17.6	61.5	21.0	3,903	86.3	48.7	18.1
Claybanks township (Oceana)	777	772	-0.6	788	93.7	0.4	0.0	0.3	5.7	19.2	57.9	22.8	325	90.8	32.6	23.7
Clayton township (Arenac)	1,097	1,060	-3.4	1,073	97.4	0.6	0.8	0.9	0.3	19.5	63.1	17.2	389	84.3	60.2	9.8
Clayton charter township (Genesee)	7,581	7,339	-3.2	7,447	87.7	3.6	0.1	4.0	4.6	20.5	60.8	18.7	2,920	89.9	34.3	26.4

1 May be of any race.

Table A. All Places — Population and Housing

STATE City, town, township, borough, or CDP (county if applicable)	Population 2010 census total population	Population 2014 estimated population	Population Percent change 2010–2014	Population ACS total population estimate 2010–2014	White alone, not Hispanic or Latino	Black alone, not Hispanic or Latino	Asian alone, not Hispanic or Latino	All other races or 2 or more races, not Hispanic or Latino	Hispanic or Latino[1]	Under 18 years old	Age 18 to 64 years old	Age 65 years and older	Total occupied housing units	Percent owner occupied	High school diploma or less	Bachelor's degree or more
	1	2	3	4	5	6	7	8	9	10	11	12	13	14	15	16
MICHIGAN—Con.																
Clayton village	344	340	-1.2	356	80.1	1.1	0.0	8.4	10.4	34.5	54.6	11.0	118	68.6	55.9	10.2
Clearwater township (Kalkaska)	2,444	2,481	1.5	2,440	95.9	1.1	0.2	0.9	1.9	20.4	59.3	20.3	1,062	85.5	46.5	16.2
Clement township (Gladwin)......................	901	891	-1.1	793	95.7	0.3	0.0	3.8	0.3	10.8	54.3	34.8	382	93.5	53.7	14.1
Cleon township (Manistee)	957	939	-1.9	911	94.8	0.0	0.0	0.8	4.4	14.4	66.8	19.0	418	87.6	62.0	10.3
Cleveland township (Leelanau)....................	1,031	1,043	1.2	1,008	93.3	0.0	0.0	4.7	2.1	18.3	54.6	27.1	464	87.9	36.9	38.8
Clifford village	324	324	0.0	320	94.1	0.0	0.6	1.6	3.8	21.9	63.4	14.7	126	81.0	69.8	4.8
Climax village	767	780	1.7	785	96.1	0.9	0.0	2.5	0.5	26.4	60.6	13.1	281	82.9	35.2	19.6
Climax township (Kalamazoo)..................	2,463	2,510	1.9	2,499	96.2	1.0	0.0	2.0	0.7	26.5	58.6	14.9	909	90.9	42.1	17.2
Clinton village	2,334	2,290	-1.9	2,229	90.1	0.3	2.2	3.7	3.8	26.9	63.0	10.1	903	79.5	39.5	27.7
Clinton township (Lenawee).....................	3,604	3,550	-1.5	3,571	92.6	0.7	1.3	2.3	3.1	26.6	59.4	14.0	1,385	86.0	44.5	25.9
Clinton charter township (Macomb).....................	96,796	99,084	2.4	97,848	78.7	14.3	2.1	2.5	2.4	19.5	63.2	17.4	42,768	65.7	38.4	21.8
Clinton township (Oscoda)	441	427	-3.2	431	98.6	0.0	0.0	1.4	0.0	14.6	58.8	26.5	215	94.4	55.3	9.3
Clio city & MCD (Genesee)....................	2,646	2,554	-3.5	2,601	94.3	0.1	1.2	4.2	0.3	24.3	60.0	15.6	1,232	47.9	47.9	13.5
Clyde township (Allegan)..	2,084	2,118	1.6	1,998	61.7	0.9	0.0	0.7	36.7	29.4	56.6	14.3	733	91.7	60.7	10.0
Clyde township (St. Clair) .	5,579	5,494	-1.5	5,515	93.7	0.0	0.0	2.0	4.3	20.7	63.7	15.4	2,106	89.0	41.2	17.3
Coe township (Isabella)	3,079	3,058	-0.7	3,087	92.9	0.0	0.1	3.2	3.8	19.5	65.9	14.6	1,217	80.2	38.3	21.0
Cohoctah township (Livingston)....................	3,317	3,403	2.6	3,376	97.2	0.6	1.5	0.7	0.1	22.0	68.0	10.2	1,245	93.2	49.6	18.7
Coldsprings township (Kalkaska).....................	1,464	1,485	1.4	1,510	96.5	0.3	0.5	2.3	0.4	17.1	60.9	22.1	678	92.8	56.3	8.8
Coldwater city & MCD (Branch).....................	10,945	10,811	-1.2	10,863	88.7	1.1	0.3	2.0	7.8	28.0	58.0	14.0	3,953	61.0	50.9	14.3
Coldwater township (Branch).....................	6,102	4,888	-19.9	5,112	75.5	16.5	0.1	4.0	3.9	14.5	71.9	13.4	1,207	89.8	37.4	21.7
Coldwater township (Isabella)	777	765	-1.5	799	94.7	0.5	0.5	3.8	0.5	19.2	62.9	18.0	312	82.1	58.3	12.5
Coleman city & MCD (Midland).....................	1,243	1,211	-2.6	1,162	92.5	0.0	0.0	1.4	6.1	20.5	59.4	20.2	555	52.1	62.7	11.4
Colfax township (Benzie)..	657	652	-0.8	753	90.2	0.0	0.5	7.3	2.0	17.3	67.1	15.5	277	84.1	49.1	14.1
Colfax township (Huron) ...	1,884	1,822	-3.3	1,859	93.7	1.1	2.6	0.4	2.1	23.7	56.2	20.1	686	84.8	57.4	14.4
Colfax township (Mecosta)	1,933	1,949	0.8	2,148	93.6	0.5	0.1	4.0	1.8	25.2	60.4	14.2	800	88.1	37.1	32.4
Colfax township (Oceana)	462	452	-2.2	470	71.3	1.5	0.0	1.7	25.5	20.6	55.1	24.3	171	94.7	55.0	4.7
Colfax township (Wexford)	840	845	0.6	982	98.0	0.0	0.0	1.7	0.3	24.3	57.0	18.8	359	89.4	61.0	15.6
Coloma city & MCD (Berrien).....................	1,483	1,463	-1.3	1,705	92.1	0.5	0.1	6.2	1.1	29.6	58.6	12.0	647	75.9	44.5	14.8
Coloma charter township (Berrien).....................	5,020	4,972	-1.0	4,998	94.7	0.1	1.0	3.7	0.5	18.8	64.0	17.1	2,018	85.9	45.8	18.5
Colon village	1,173	1,159	-1.2	1,214	98.5	0.2	0.5	0.4	0.4	23.3	59.0	17.6	491	71.3	50.1	18.3
Colon township (St. Joseph).....................	3,329	3,299	-0.9	3,317	96.9	0.1	0.2	1.8	1.1	28.1	56.9	14.9	1,210	79.5	52.4	18.0
Columbia township (Jackson).....................	7,420	7,422	0.0	7,410	96.7	0.0	0.5	1.5	1.3	19.5	59.0	21.4	2,910	85.9	40.4	25.3
Columbia township (Tuscola)....................	1,284	1,249	-2.7	1,160	97.3	0.3	0.0	0.8	1.6	22.2	54.1	23.8	482	87.8	44.4	18.0
Columbia township (Van Buren)	2,588	2,547	-1.6	2,557	68.6	3.0	1.3	4.2	22.9	23.6	62.7	13.7	874	87.2	61.1	9.7
Columbiaville village	787	781	-0.8	856	92.6	0.0	0.0	4.4	2.9	24.9	60.8	14.4	299	74.2	56.2	6.7
Columbus township (Luce)	204	198	-2.9	192	91.1	0.0	0.0	7.8	1.0	9.9	68.9	21.4	78	92.3	60.3	5.1
Columbus township (St. Clair)	4,070	4,015	-1.4	4,020	96.6	0.0	0.3	2.6	0.4	22.0	65.2	12.8	1,476	87.8	43.0	15.5
Comins township (Oscoda)	1,970	1,906	-3.2	1,880	95.3	0.0	0.0	3.7	1.1	23.6	49.8	26.6	790	74.2	55.6	11.6
Commerce charter township (Oakland)	40,186	42,112	4.8	41,102	92.0	1.3	2.6	1.8	2.3	24.6	63.2	12.1	15,247	90.1	25.0	45.0
Comstock charter township (Kalamazoo) ..	14,854	15,336	3.2	15,124	85.5	7.7	2.7	1.4	2.7	22.4	63.7	14.1	6,316	70.9	36.5	28.4
Comstock Northwest CDP	5,455	NA	NA	5,769	69.8	17.6	8.3	1.9	2.5	23.9	64.6	11.5	2,653	49.1	28.7	35.3
Comstock Park CDP.........	10,088	NA	NA	10,407	68.0	8.4	0.5	3.3	19.8	24.3	66.6	9.1	4,165	45.6	40.4	21.7
Concord village...............	1,050	1,049	-0.1	1,124	99.8	0.0	0.0	0.2	0.0	28.6	54.8	16.6	435	80.7	37.0	21.6
Concord township (Jackson).....................	2,723	2,718	-0.2	2,716	97.0	0.0	0.0	0.1	2.9	28.6	57.2	14.2	969	86.3	40.0	18.6
Constantine village	2,076	2,061	-0.7	1,760	83.5	8.4	0.0	0.6	7.5	25.9	64.1	10.0	646	64.9	58.2	11.1
Constantine township (St. Joseph).....................	4,217	4,196	-0.5	4,188	88.6	3.5	0.0	2.7	5.1	24.2	62.6	13.0	1,607	79.2	57.4	11.4
Convis township (Calhoun)	1,636	1,624	-0.7	1,625	91.1	1.6	0.6	3.1	3.6	21.0	61.6	17.4	633	89.9	47.6	22.1
Conway CDP	204	NA	NA	302	82.5	0.0	0.0	16.2	1.3	28.5	64.5	7.0	125	62.4	24.0	8.8
Conway township (Livingston)....................	3,546	3,634	2.5	3,584	91.2	0.2	1.9	2.4	4.2	29.0	61.5	9.4	1,105	89.3	45.5	15.2
Cooper charter township (Kalamazoo)..................	10,111	10,510	3.9	10,293	90.6	2.6	3.2	1.7	1.9	21.3	63.2	15.4	4,004	80.3	34.9	30.1
Coopersville city & MCD (Ottawa)	4,275	4,344	1.6	4,309	92.2	0.1	0.0	3.7	4.1	27.7	61.5	11.0	1,642	72.2	39.4	17.2
Copemish village	194	192		165	97.6	0.0	0.0	0.0	2.4	6.0	81.2	12.7	83	61.4	66.3	13.3
Copper City village	190	188	-1.1	253	99.6	0.0	0.4	0.0	0.0	31.6	57.0	11.5	91	85.7	50.5	18.7
Copper Harbor CDP.........	108	NA	NA	102	100.0	0.0	0.0	0.0	0.0	1.0	63.8	35.3	73	80.8	16.4	34.2
Cornell township (Delta) ...	593	587	-1.0	567	94.0	0.2	0.0	5.3	0.5	20.0	55.8	24.2	234	95.3	59.0	13.2
Corunna city & MCD (Shiawassee)...............	3,497	3,418	-2.3	3,450	95.1	3.4	0.0	0.3	1.2	21.6	61.8	16.6	1,387	47.2	36.8	23.1
Corwith township (Otsego)	1,748	1,745	-0.2	1,752	95.2	0.7	0.0	2.3	1.8	21.2	62.0	17.0	731	80.7	58.1	11.9
Cottrellville township (St. Clair)	3,559	3,507	-1.5	3,525	96.4	0.0	0.0	1.6	2.0	20.4	65.4	14.2	1,330	89.0	43.9	10.0
Courtland township (Kent)	7,674	8,202	6.9	7,942	95.6	0.1	1.0	1.9	1.4	26.5	62.5	11.1	2,663	92.3	27.8	34.0
Covert township (Van Buren)	2,888	2,837	-1.8	2,848	42.3	23.9	0.0	4.4	29.4	28.3	59.3	12.3	873	77.2	58.1	10.1

1 May be of any race.

Table A. All Places — **Population and Housing**

STATE City, town, township, borough, or CDP (county if applicable)	Population 2010 census total population	2014 estimated population	Percent change 2010–2014	ACS total population estimate 2010–2014	Race and Hispanic or Latino origin (percent), 2010–2014 White alone, not Hispanic or Latino	Black alone, not Hispanic or Latino	Asian alone, not Hispanic or Latino	All other races or 2 or more races, not Hispanic or Latino	Hispanic or Latino[1]	Age (percent), 2010–2014 Under 18 years old	Age 18 to 64 years old	Age 65 years and older	Households, 2010–2014 Total occupied housing units	Percent owner occupied	Householders by level of education (percent) High school diploma or less	Bachelor's degree or more
	1	2	3	4	5	6	7	8	9	10	11	12	13	14	15	16
MICHIGAN—Con.																
Covington township (Baraga)	476	462	-2.9	662	94.3	0.8	0.2	0.0	4.8	17.2	57.6	25.2	284	93.0	48.6	14.4
Crockery township (Ottawa)	3,960	4,297	8.5	4,129	95.5	1.2	0.6	1.6	1.0	25.1	61.8	13.1	1,497	87.0	45.5	22.4
Cross Village CDP	93	NA	NA	88	86.4	0.0	0.0	13.6	0.0	26.1	53.4	20.5	39	82.1	38.5	20.5
Cross Village township (Emmet)	281	286	1.8	242	84.7	0.0	0.0	11.2	4.1	19.1	50.8	30.2	116	89.7	41.4	31.0
Croswell city & MCD (Sanilac)	2,447	2,350	-4.0	2,573	79.4	0.5	0.0	1.2	18.9	28.2	61.6	10.3	910	59.2	48.2	6.7
Croton township (Newaygo)	3,228	3,202	-0.8	3,226	98.3	0.0	0.0	0.0	1.7	23.9	62.6	13.5	1,270	88.7	62.9	15.2
Crystal township (Montcalm)	2,691	2,685	-0.2	2,683	93.4	1.3	0.0	0.0	5.3	25.2	57.2	17.5	1,065	77.6	50.1	11.1
Crystal township (Oceana)	838	833	-0.6	1,009	52.7	0.0	0.0	1.2	46.1	25.6	65.4	9.1	260	73.8	65.4	8.5
Crystal Downs Country Club CDP	47	NA	NA	59	100.0	0.0	0.0	0.0	0.0	8.5	30.6	61.0	37	91.9	8.1	73.0
Crystal Falls city & MCD (Iron)	1,469	1,420	-3.3	1,544	96.5	0.5	0.1	2.1	0.7	21.0	58.0	21.2	690	75.4	52.9	21.4
Crystal Falls township (Iron)	1,743	1,686	-3.3	1,839	95.8	0.8	0.8	0.8	1.8	15.8	52.8	31.3	748	90.9	44.4	24.3
Crystal Lake township (Benzie)	957	958	0.1	1,046	97.5	0.1	0.0	0.0	2.4	14.6	51.3	33.9	485	86.8	28.2	39.6
Crystal Mountain CDP	54	NA	NA	34	100.0	0.0	0.0	0.0	0.0	14.7	47.1	38.2	16	100.0	12.5	75.0
Cumming township (Ogemaw)	698	675	-3.3	692	94.5	0.0	0.0	4.3	1.2	25.2	51.7	23.1	294	81.0	44.6	16.7
Curtis township (Alcona)	1,236	1,177	-4.8	1,281	95.6	0.0	0.2	1.6	2.5	14.7	48.7	36.6	611	90.3	64.6	7.5
Custer township (Antrim)	1,136	1,122	-1.2	1,126	96.1	0.0	0.2	3.7	0.0	15.3	58.5	26.3	499	95.4	38.3	20.4
Custer village	284	285	0.4	247	94.3	1.6	2.0	1.6	0.4	23.1	59.2	17.8	98	82.7	53.1	14.3
Custer township (Mason)	1,254	1,260	0.5	1,244	88.7	3.1	0.4	3.9	3.8	15.9	65.8	18.2	492	89.2	48.8	16.5
Custer township (Sanilac)	1,006	967	-3.9	930	96.0	0.0	0.0	1.3	2.7	17.6	55.8	26.6	392	92.6	60.7	11.2
Cutlerville CDP	14,370	NA	NA	14,533	81.3	6.6	2.2	3.3	6.7	24.6	61.6	13.8	5,783	69.3	41.8	21.6
Dafter township (Chippewa)	1,263	1,259	-0.3	1,184	78.2	0.1	0.0	21.0	0.7	22.4	65.4	12.2	420	91.7	38.8	22.1
Daggett village	258	256	-0.8	268	78.4	0.0	0.0	0.7	20.9	29.9	50.9	19.4	103	84.5	60.2	20.4
Daggett township (Menominee)	714	708	-0.8	663	90.8	0.0	0.0	0.8	8.4	23.2	54.9	21.9	270	90.4	55.9	17.0
Dallas township (Clinton)	2,369	2,413	1.9	2,283	96.3	0.0	2.5	0.7	0.5	30.2	54.3	15.4	754	89.3	41.6	14.9
Dalton township (Muskegon)	9,300	9,297	0.0	9,266	89.7	4.5	0.0	1.9	3.9	28.4	61.5	10.2	3,310	89.9	39.0	12.8
Danby township (Ionia)	2,988	3,007	0.6	2,988	96.6	0.1	0.0	1.9	1.3	28.9	58.5	12.5	1,043	94.5	32.6	27.3
Dansville village	563	556	-1.2	470	95.5	0.0	0.0	4.5	0.0	29.9	64.0	6.0	162	87.7	38.9	13.6
Davison city & MCD (Genesee)	5,173	5,000	-3.3	5,085	96.9	0.5	0.0	1.0	1.6	23.7	60.7	15.6	2,370	53.3	39.2	21.9
Davison township (Genesee)	19,575	19,071	-2.6	19,307	85.9	6.5	1.3	2.7	3.7	21.3	63.4	15.3	8,127	64.8	32.8	22.3
Day township (Montcalm)	1,172	1,168	-0.3	934	93.7	0.0	0.0	3.9	2.5	21.7	57.4	20.9	387	85.5	46.8	5.7
Dayton township (Newaygo)	1,949	1,931	-0.9	2,061	90.8	0.8	0.1	1.0	7.3	25.1	58.7	16.2	679	90.1	44.2	18.3
Dayton township (Tuscola)	1,848	1,798	-2.7	1,557	91.8	4.4	0.4	2.2	1.2	18.5	61.5	19.9	629	88.2	61.7	11.3
Dearborn city & MCD (Wayne)	98,146	95,535	-2.7	96,739	87.3	3.5	2.1	3.6	3.5	29.7	58.2	12.0	31,647	68.3	36.8	32.6
Dearborn Heights city & MCD (Wayne)	57,774	56,415	-2.4	57,063	81.3	8.4	2.0	3.9	4.3	24.6	59.9	15.5	20,984	74.8	44.2	21.1
Decatur village	1,810	1,772	-2.1	2,095	75.3	6.0	0.0	5.2	13.5	26.4	62.0	11.7	719	65.8	58.3	12.4
Decatur township (Van Buren)	3,726	3,651	-2.0	3,671	79.8	4.2	0.0	7.3	8.7	24.4	62.0	13.6	1,318	70.4	58.0	9.8
Deckerville village	830	802	-3.4	903	91.5	0.8	0.0	2.5	5.2	25.8	56.4	17.8	313	60.1	60.7	12.8
Deep River township (Arenac)	2,149	2,075	-3.4	2,157	96.5	0.4	0.0	1.3	1.8	22.3	57.8	19.8	830	86.4	57.3	11.7
Deerfield township (Isabella)	3,188	3,198	0.3	3,219	95.1	0.1	0.5	3.2	1.1	23.4	61.4	15.1	1,192	94.5	31.0	35.7
Deerfield township (Lapeer)	5,695	5,720	0.4	5,703	97.7	0.0	0.0	1.1	1.2	25.2	62.5	12.1	1,905	88.0	57.3	11.7
Deerfield village	898	880	-2.0	839	95.4	0.0	0.0	3.8	0.8	27.8	56.5	15.6	311	83.3	45.0	16.1
Deerfield township (Lenawee)	1,568	1,544	-1.5	1,521	93.6	0.0	0.0	3.0	3.4	26.1	56.7	17.2	544	89.0	45.8	17.6
Deerfield township (Livingston)	4,170	4,280	2.6	4,227	93.2	0.4	1.3	4.4	0.7	23.8	62.9	13.2	1,522	94.7	36.9	25.2
Deerfield township (Mecosta)	1,816	1,821	0.3	2,161	95.9	0.9	0.1	1.5	1.5	33.4	56.8	9.7	609	83.6	55.0	9.7
Delaware township (Sanilac)	856	826	-3.5	770	98.4	0.0	0.0	0.0	1.6	16.3	60.8	22.9	340	86.2	57.4	16.8
Delhi charter township (Ingham)	25,877	26,247	1.4	26,028	81.9	6.0	4.4	3.2	4.4	25.4	62.7	12.1	10,338	74.2	24.4	34.5
Delta charter township (Eaton)	32,408	32,921	1.6	32,657	73.0	11.0	4.8	3.6	7.6	20.1	64.2	15.9	14,520	62.4	24.1	39.5
Delton CDP	872	NA	NA	855	98.9	0.0	0.0	1.1	0.0	20.0	64.6	15.6	374	76.2	37.4	25.7
Denmark township (Tuscola)	3,068	2,973	-3.1	3,015	94.2	0.1	0.6	0.9	4.2	20.3	57.6	22.2	1,344	81.1	41.8	19.5
Denton township (Roscommon)	5,557	5,410	-2.6	5,470	98.5	0.0	0.0	0.9	0.6	15.6	55.5	28.8	2,774	78.8	50.3	10.5
Denver township (Isabella)	1,148	1,134	-1.2	1,053	85.6	0.3	0.0	8.9	5.2	20.5	68.0	11.4	391	87.7	51.7	17.9
Denver township (Newaygo)	1,928	1,898	-1.6	1,943	90.7	0.0	0.3	3.1	5.9	26.5	57.9	15.5	753	80.5	62.2	5.3
Detour township (Chippewa)	807	806	-0.1	707	81.9	0.8	0.7	16.5	0.0	13.3	44.7	42.0	379	86.8	42.0	27.7
De Tour Village village	325	324	-0.3	214	84.1	0.0	0.0	15.9	0.0	9.4	36.9	53.7	128	94.5	43.0	26.6
Detroit city & MCD (Wayne)	713,862	680,250	-4.7	695,437	8.7	80.7	1.2	2.1	7.3	25.5	62.4	12.1	254,197	50.7	50.0	14.7
Detroit Beach CDP	2,087	NA	NA	2,209	95.8	0.2	0.0	0.8	3.2	25.9	63.6	10.6	927	74.0	37.4	9.3
DeWitt city & MCD (Clinton)	4,507	4,688	4.0	4,606	95.6	0.0	2.6	0.0	1.7	28.4	60.7	10.9	1,770	74.7	22.1	45.3

1 May be of any race.

Table A. All Places — Population and Housing

STATE City, town, township, borough, or CDP (county if applicable)	2010 census total population	2014 estimated population	Percent change 2010–2014	ACS total population estimate 2010–2014	White alone, not Hispanic or Latino	Black alone, not Hispanic or Latino	Asian alone, not Hispanic or Latino	All other races or 2 or more races, not Hispanic or Latino	Hispanic or Latino[1]	Under 18 years old	Age 18 to 64 years old	Age 65 years and older	Total occupied housing units	Percent owner occupied	High school diploma or less	Bachelor's degree or more
	1	2	3	4	5	6	7	8	9	10	11	12	13	14	15	16
MICHIGAN—Con.																
DeWitt charter township (Clinton)	14,325	14,691	2.6	14,542	91.3	0.7	1.2	2.2	4.6	24.0	60.9	15.2	5,710	80.2	27.2	30.9
Dexter village	4,070	4,484	10.2	4,482	91.4	0.0	1.2	1.4	6.0	31.4	57.3	11.3	1,716	66.1	17.3	60.3
Dexter township (Washtenaw)	6,042	6,413	6.1	6,235	96.0	0.2	0.0	2.7	1.2	24.9	61.0	14.0	2,213	90.6	14.1	53.4
Dickson township (Manistee)	993	975	-1.8	921	94.6	0.0	0.0	3.1	2.3	13.2	58.7	28.2	449	82.6	57.7	8.0
Dimondale village	1,234	1,243	0.7	1,209	94.3	1.7	0.2	3.1	0.7	26.3	57.2	16.5	440	80.7	32.3	32.3
Dollar Bay CDP	1,082	NA	NA	896	98.4	0.0	0.8	0.8	0.0	31.6	57.0	11.5	349	75.6	32.7	27.5
Dorr township (Allegan)	7,439	7,626	2.5	7,512	94.4	0.5	0.0	2.7	2.4	28.6	63.5	7.8	2,386	89.5	51.4	17.8
Douglas city & MCD (Allegan)	1,232	1,266	2.8	1,046	98.0	0.3	0.1	0.0	1.6	13.0	55.5	31.5	540	81.7	31.9	42.0
Douglass township (Montcalm)	2,180	2,173	-0.3	2,073	95.7	0.0	0.0	1.6	2.7	18.1	62.7	19.3	796	89.7	47.4	13.8
Dover township (Lake)	395	389	-1.5	345	95.7	0.0	0.0	2.3	2.0	12.2	62.3	25.5	129	81.4	51.9	12.4
Dover township (Lenawee)	1,834	1,804	-1.6	1,841	82.1	0.1	0.2	2.8	14.7	24.3	61.0	14.7	707	83.6	57.3	11.5
Dover township (Otsego)	561	562	0.2	617	97.4	0.0	0.0	1.8	0.8	26.0	63.1	11.0	212	89.2	47.2	24.5
Dowagiac city & MCD (Cass)	5,879	5,748	-2.2	5,822	65.4	17.2	0.0	10.4	6.9	28.3	57.6	14.2	2,277	59.3	45.2	10.0
Dowling CDP	374	NA	NA	375	98.4	0.0	0.0	0.0	1.6	23.2	60.7	16.0	144	81.9	43.8	18.1
Doyle township (Schoolcraft)	624	600	-3.8	612	87.1	1.1	1.3	9.2	1.3	12.6	67.0	20.4	254	98.0	51.2	24.4
Drummond township (Chippewa)	1,058	1,058	0.0	1,117	86.5	0.0	0.0	13.5	0.0	12.9	48.7	38.5	577	87.7	38.6	26.7
Dryden village	951	943	-0.8	1,239	97.7	0.0	0.0	1.5	0.9	22.9	66.8	10.1	446	64.8	50.0	10.3
Dryden township (Lapeer)	4,768	4,763	-0.1	4,772	99.0	0.0	0.0	0.7	0.3	24.1	63.5	12.6	1,749	86.1	37.1	20.8
Duncan township (Houghton)	236	234	-0.8	228	96.5	0.0	1.8	0.9	0.9	6.6	51.9	41.7	121	95.9	61.2	8.3
Dundee village	3,951	3,953	0.1	3,943	95.6	0.0	1.3	2.6	0.5	25.5	61.0	13.5	1,670	66.3	39.9	15.7
Dundee township (Monroe)	6,759	6,728	-0.5	6,732	96.0	0.0	0.8	2.2	1.1	22.7	62.6	14.7	2,854	71.6	42.0	19.3
Duplain township (Clinton)	2,363	2,400	1.6	2,271	94.2	0.5	0.0	2.0	3.3	19.8	63.2	17.0	826	79.9	52.4	9.2
Durand city & MCD (Shiawassee)	3,446	3,355	-2.6	3,396	96.3	0.5	0.3	2.2	0.6	22.4	56.3	21.2	1,440	58.9	55.3	9.8
Dwight township (Huron)	758	735	-3.0	837	97.4	0.0	0.0	0.6	2.0	19.7	60.1	20.2	357	83.2	63.3	9.2
Eagle village	123	125	1.6	147	99.3	0.0	0.0	0.0	0.7	27.3	61.8	10.9	58	93.1	36.2	10.3
Eagle township (Clinton)	2,671	2,726	2.1	2,709	93.9	0.3	0.0	1.1	4.7	21.9	62.3	15.8	991	92.1	23.3	34.1
Eagle Harbor CDP	76	NA	NA	122	99.2	0.0	0.8	0.0	0.0	2.5	31.2	66.4	69	95.7	20.3	52.2
Eagle Harbor township (Keweenaw)	217	224	3.2	330	93.3	2.1	0.3	3.9	0.3	7.5	36.6	55.8	163	95.7	13.5	49.7
Eagle River CDP	71	NA	NA	67	79.1	14.9	0.0	0.0	6.0	1.5	82.1	16.4	34	97.1	20.6	47.1
East Bay township (Grand Traverse)	10,663	11,253	5.5	10,957	94.8	0.8	1.7	1.0	1.6	21.2	64.9	14.0	4,283	84.6	29.7	34.5
East China township (St. Clair)	3,788	3,749	-1.0	3,762	95.5	3.5	0.0	1.0	0.1	15.4	58.4	26.3	1,592	72.2	47.4	21.2
East Grand Rapids city & MCD (Kent)	10,692	11,258	5.3	10,999	95.3	0.6	1.0	1.4	1.7	31.8	58.2	10.0	4,014	91.4	4.5	78.3
East Jordan city & MCD (Charlevoix)	2,351	2,361	0.4	2,335	95.8	0.1	0.0	1.1	3.0	24.8	59.7	15.4	899	72.7	58.7	15.8
Eastlake village	512	506	-1.2	496	89.5	2.6	0.0	6.5	1.4	14.5	55.8	29.6	228	89.0	58.8	3.9
East Lansing city	48,557	48,648	0.2	48,611	73.7	7.6	11.2	4.0	3.6	7.9	85.8	6.4	13,705	34.8	7.2	54.9
East Lansing city (Clinton)	1,947	1,976	1.5	1,962	59.8	15.2	13.9	4.6	6.5	11.4	85.4	3.2	716	53.9	8.0	54.2
East Lansing city (Ingham)	46,610	46,672	0.1	46,649	74.3	7.3	11.0	4.0	3.4	7.7	85.8	6.5	12,989	33.7	7.2	54.9
Easton township (Ionia)	3,082	3,090	0.3	3,082	93.3	0.0	0.4	1.0	5.3	24.5	62.1	13.4	1,180	92.1	50.8	12.1
Eastpointe city & MCD (Macomb)	32,442	32,654	0.7	32,526	53.2	39.2	1.6	2.8	3.3	26.3	62.1	11.6	12,399	70.8	45.9	15.6
Eastport CDP	218	NA	NA	137	100.0	0.0	0.0	0.0	0.0	0.0	36.5	63.5	85	100.0	52.9	28.2
East Tawas city & MCD (Iosco)	2,808	2,758	-1.8	2,773	96.1	0.4	0.0	0.0	3.5	18.7	54.8	26.5	1,293	71.1	44.8	23.0
Eastwood CDP	6,340	NA	NA	6,734	60.6	28.9	0.5	4.1	5.9	28.6	63.0	8.5	2,603	55.5	33.2	20.7
Eaton township (Eaton)	4,073	4,113	1.0	4,082	95.2	1.1	0.2	1.8	1.7	24.6	60.6	14.9	1,437	90.0	32.4	24.8
Eaton Rapids city & MCD (Eaton)	5,223	5,220	-0.1	5,221	95.4	0.8	0.7	0.0	3.1	28.3	59.9	12.0	1,971	59.5	40.1	18.4
Eaton Rapids township (Eaton)	4,104	4,142	0.9	4,125	94.6	1.6	0.0	1.3	2.4	23.2	63.7	13.2	1,473	90.1	25.8	24.2
Eau Claire village	625	621	-0.6	569	60.3	2.1	0.0	4.6	33.0	30.4	62.0	7.6	186	79.6	45.7	14.0
Echo township (Antrim)	877	864	-1.5	934	95.5	0.0	1.1	1.9	1.5	21.1	55.0	24.0	380	88.7	48.2	21.6
Eckford township (Calhoun)	1,303	1,289	-1.1	1,382	94.2	3.3	0.3	1.3	0.9	28.6	54.3	17.2	508	82.9	39.8	19.7
Ecorse city & MCD (Wayne)	9,508	9,311	-2.1	9,401	38.4	42.5	0.3	4.2	14.5	25.8	60.3	13.9	3,476	60.8	63.3	8.6
Eden township (Lake)	489	478	-2.2	561	95.4	0.7	0.0	3.9	0.0	33.4	53.6	13.2	179	74.3	75.4	1.1
Eden township (Mason)	582	585	0.5	668	96.6	0.0	0.0	2.7	0.7	23.0	56.3	20.5	243	90.5	53.5	11.9
Edenville township (Midland)	2,551	2,526	NA	2,541	98.7	0.0	1.1	0.2	0.0	17.9	68.1	14.0	1,018	87.0	35.5	24.1
Edgemont Park CDP	2,358	NA	NA	2,242	64.9	15.0	0.0	1.0	19.1	24.2	61.9	13.9	995	72.1	27.5	35.0
Edmore village	1,192	1,193	0.1	1,219	85.2	4.4	0.5	4.9	4.9	24.6	60.2	15.1	476	64.7	56.9	16.0
Edwards township (Ogemaw)	1,413	1,369	-3.1	1,437	96.9	0.0	0.0	0.0	3.1	21.7	57.4	20.8	607	87.6	53.4	13.0
Edwardsburg village	1,259	1,231	-2.2	1,232	89.3	1.7	4.3	2.5	2.2	28.2	61.3	10.5	471	61.0	54.4	9.8
Egelston township (Muskegon)	9,909	9,840	-0.7	9,852	87.8	2.4	0.3	3.7	5.8	28.3	59.6	12.2	3,448	92.1	49.9	7.1
Elba township (Gratiot)	1,396	1,372	-1.7	1,274	96.8	0.0	0.5	1.0	1.6	24.6	56.0	19.5	483	77.4	54.2	11.2
Elba township (Lapeer)	5,250	5,241	-0.2	5,236	95.2	3.1	0.0	0.4	1.3	17.4	65.9	16.4	2,071	88.7	37.4	26.8
Elberta village	374	371	-0.8	221	100.0	0.0	0.0	0.0	0.0	13.1	57.5	29.4	110	78.2	54.5	21.8
Elbridge township (Oceana)	971	962	-0.9	1,180	68.6	0.0	0.0	1.7	29.7	33.8	54.8	11.4	361	75.6	62.6	11.1
Elk township (Lake)	985	973	-1.2	859	99.2	0.0	0.0	0.5	0.3	13.8	51.8	34.5	382	94.0	44.8	18.3
Elk township (Sanilac)	1,526	1,477	-3.2	1,662	94.5	1.7	0.0	2.0	1.7	24.3	59.1	16.5	535	87.1	59.4	7.3
Elkland township (Tuscola)	3,528	3,433	-2.7	3,471	94.9	0.2	0.2	0.7	4.0	23.2	55.5	21.3	1,394	80.1	42.8	15.5
Elk Rapids village	1,642	1,622	-1.2	1,558	94.5	0.0	1.2	1.9	2.4	16.4	51.3	32.3	719	81.2	22.7	38.9

1 May be of any race.

Table A. All Places — **Population and Housing**

STATE City, town, township, borough, or CDP (county if applicable)	Population				Race and Hispanic or Latino origin (percent), 2010–2014					Age (percent), 2010–2014			Households, 2010–2014			
	2010 census total population	2014 estimated population	Percent change 2010–2014	ACS total population estimate 2010–2014	White alone, not Hispanic or Latino	Black alone, not Hispanic or Latino	Asian alone, not Hispanic or Latino	All other races or 2 or more races, not Hispanic or Latino	Hispanic or Latino[1]	Under 18 years old	Age 18 to 64 years old	Age 65 years and older	Total occupied housing units	Percent owner occupied	High school diploma or less	Bachelor's degree or more
	1	2	3	4	5	6	7	8	9	10	11	12	13	14	15	16
MICHIGAN—Con.																
Elk Rapids township (Antrim)	2,631	2,603	-1.1	2,606	96.2	0.0	0.7	1.4	1.7	17.1	51.1	31.8	1,189	80.7	22.0	41.2
Elkton village	808	784	-3.0	871	94.0	0.0	0.0	2.1	3.9	31.6	55.6	12.9	338	62.7	54.4	13.6
Ellington township (Tuscola)	1,332	1,295	-2.8	1,375	94.4	1.1	0.5	1.8	2.2	27.4	58.7	13.9	487	78.2	44.1	12.5
Ellis township (Cheboygan)	596	585	-1.8	579	94.5	0.0	0.7	4.8	0.0	20.0	64.2	15.7	230	89.6	49.6	11.3
Ellsworth village	349	344	-1.4	427	86.2	0.0	1.2	0.0	12.6	18.5	70.7	10.8	154	75.3	38.3	18.8
Ellsworth township (Lake)	817	802	-1.8	680	92.6	0.4	0.0	2.6	4.3	24.6	53.2	22.4	238	92.0	44.1	8.8
Elmer township (Oscoda)	1,138	1,098	-3.5	1,166	99.2	0.1	0.0	0.4	0.3	25.0	55.7	19.4	415	96.9	61.9	8.9
Elmer township (Sanilac)	806	776	-3.7	910	93.4	0.8	0.0	0.3	5.5	21.4	63.8	14.9	306	89.2	64.1	5.9
Elmira township (Otsego)	1,687	1,689	0.1	1,716	91.8	1.5	0.0	1.9	4.8	22.7	50.8	26.5	663	96.5	35.1	32.9
Elm River township (Houghton)	177	175	-1.1	162	100.0	0.0	0.0	0.0	0.0	10.6	64.4	25.3	75	97.3	32.0	38.7
Elmwood charter township (Leelanau)	4,503	4,552	1.1	4,509	96.9	0.3	0.4	1.2	1.2	12.5	57.1	30.6	1,943	83.7	20.1	42.3
Elmwood township (Tuscola)	1,207	1,173	-2.8	1,063	93.5	0.5	0.8	1.0	4.1	16.6	65.1	18.3	437	81.9	51.5	14.4
Elsie village	966	978	1.2	1,007	92.0	1.1	0.0	2.1	4.9	18.0	65.9	16.1	376	74.2	59.8	3.7
Ely township (Marquette)	1,952	1,974	1.1	2,106	97.0	0.0	0.1	1.9	0.9	24.2	62.2	13.7	801	92.1	58.1	17.2
Emerson township (Gratiot)	952	938	-1.5	887	92.0	0.0	0.7	2.0	5.3	28.2	58.4	13.3	336	78.0	47.3	19.9
Emmett charter township (Calhoun)	11,770	11,686	-0.7	11,695	93.1	2.0	0.8	2.4	1.7	21.4	63.5	15.3	4,549	76.6	37.6	21.2
Emmett village	269	264	-1.9	323	97.5	0.0	0.0	2.5	0.0	29.5	57.6	13.0	100	72.0	58.0	10.0
Emmett township (St. Clair)	2,654	2,614	-1.5	2,620	98.4	0.0	0.0	0.5	1.2	25.5	64.1	10.4	931	92.4	48.1	10.4
Empire village	375	378	0.8	396	97.7	0.0	0.0	0.0	2.3	9.6	57.4	33.1	213	73.2	24.4	45.5
Empire township (Leelanau)	1,182	1,191	0.8	1,254	95.7	0.0	0.2	0.0	4.1	11.2	56.1	32.5	614	87.9	23.6	48.5
Ensign township (Delta)	748	741	-0.9	751	91.9	0.0	0.0	8.0	0.1	11.7	60.5	27.8	335	90.4	44.5	20.0
Ensley township (Newaygo)	2,635	2,616	-0.7	2,629	91.9	0.4	0.4	3.8	3.4	26.8	61.9	11.2	936	93.6	55.0	11.1
Enterprise township (Missaukee)	194	198	2.1	156	94.9	0.0	0.0	2.6	2.6	30.7	59.1	10.3	57	73.7	42.1	10.5
Erie township (Monroe)	4,517	4,420	-2.1	4,460	91.7	0.1	1.0	0.4	6.7	19.9	63.7	16.3	1,713	85.1	48.9	11.7
Erwin township (Gogebic)	326	307	-5.8	306	94.1	0.0	0.0	4.9	1.0	19.2	64.0	16.7	136	92.6	39.7	19.9
Escanaba city & MCD (Delta)	12,616	12,413	-1.6	12,529	92.1	0.9	0.0	5.7	1.3	20.0	58.4	21.7	5,780	63.7	41.3	15.4
Escanaba township (Delta)	3,482	3,445	-1.1	3,460	97.1	0.0	0.1	2.4	0.3	15.1	71.8	13.3	1,517	91.2	40.5	20.2
Essex township (Clinton)	1,910	1,945	1.8	1,869	95.7	0.0	0.0	1.7	2.7	23.8	62.7	13.5	709	90.3	46.8	18.2
Essexville city & MCD (Bay)	3,478	3,415	-1.8	3,451	89.6	3.6	1.4	1.0	4.4	22.7	58.6	18.9	1,472	91.9	22.5	30.6
Estral Beach village	418	408	-2.4	462	98.7	0.2	0.0	0.0	1.1	17.9	68.5	13.6	189	86.8	49.2	9.5
Eureka township (Montcalm)	3,959	3,971	0.3	3,968	92.6	0.0	1.4	1.9	4.2	27.0	59.9	13.1	1,434	92.1	45.5	24.6
Evangeline township (Charlevoix)	712	719	1.0	778	96.8	0.5	0.0	1.8	0.9	18.1	56.8	25.3	309	83.8	33.3	34.3
Evart city & MCD (Osceola)	1,903	1,871	-1.7	1,469	92.9	0.5	0.0	2.6	4.0	25.2	55.0	19.9	655	48.1	62.9	8.2
Evart township (Osceola)	1,483	1,460	-1.6	1,487	97.3	0.9	0.0	0.7	1.1	20.8	58.3	20.8	575	85.6	56.9	9.6
Eveline township (Charlevoix)	1,484	1,498	0.9	1,580	88.0	0.2	0.0	3.2	8.6	17.5	56.7	25.8	639	90.0	29.6	37.6
Everett township (Newaygo)	1,862	1,821	-2.2	1,638	92.4	2.8	0.0	4.0	0.9	21.3	58.9	19.8	658	81.8	68.5	4.6
Evergreen township (Montcalm)	2,858	2,849	-0.3	2,854	99.5	0.0	0.0	0.5	0.0	15.1	66.4	18.5	1,285	81.2	48.8	11.4
Evergreen township (Sanilac)	924	889	-3.8	900	96.8	1.7	0.0	0.8	0.8	29.4	53.7	16.9	307	80.1	62.9	7.2
Ewing township (Marquette)	160	161	0.6	114	98.2	0.0	1.8	0.0	0.0	7.0	50.0	43.0	65	95.4	40.0	15.4
Excelsior township (Kalkaska)	953	964	1.2	934	96.7	0.0	0.0	1.8	1.5	25.0	56.9	18.1	376	84.6	52.1	10.4
Exeter township (Monroe)	3,977	3,908	-1.7	3,930	95.9	2.0	0.0	1.4	0.6	20.1	68.0	11.9	1,401	89.5	50.7	10.0
Fabius township (St. Joseph)	3,248	3,233	-0.5	3,233	98.0	0.4	0.0	0.4	1.2	12.5	65.1	22.5	1,407	94.7	38.9	25.9
Fairbanks township (Delta)	281	278	-1.1	313	72.5	0.0	1.6	24.9	1.0	25.6	44.8	29.7	142	94.4	56.3	9.9
Fairfield township (Lenawee)	1,764	1,735	-1.6	1,672	88.8	0.5	0.0	4.4	6.3	24.5	61.6	13.9	634	80.1	56.5	12.9
Fairfield township (Shiawassee)	755	737	-2.4	712	94.9	0.0	0.1	1.1	3.8	27.7	57.5	14.6	266	85.7	53.0	12.8
Fairgrove village	563	545	-3.2	488	95.1	0.0	0.8	3.1	1.0	22.1	58.9	19.1	216	82.4	46.3	15.3
Fairgrove township (Tuscola)	1,579	1,534	-2.8	1,489	89.1	0.4	0.3	2.8	7.5	22.5	62.2	15.4	610	85.1	43.8	16.6
Fairhaven township (Huron)	1,107	1,067	-3.6	955	98.8	0.0	0.0	0.9	0.2	18.0	62.8	19.4	438	83.1	57.1	9.4
Fair Plain CDP	7,631	NA	NA	8,043	51.7	43.3	0.1	3.0	1.9	25.7	59.3	15.1	3,221	65.3	41.6	19.1
Fairplain township (Montcalm)	1,836	1,828	-0.4	1,695	95.3	0.1	0.0	1.8	2.7	20.9	65.9	13.2	619	80.3	43.3	13.4
Faithorn township (Menominee)	243	241	-0.8	273	98.5	0.0	0.0	0.0	1.5	20.9	59.4	19.8	113	99.1	46.9	15.9
Farmington city & MCD (Oakland)	10,372	10,554	1.8	10,472	67.4	11.1	16.0	3.7	1.8	21.6	62.5	15.9	4,690	59.3	17.0	55.2
Farmington Hills city & MCD (Oakland)	79,740	81,435	2.1	80,682	64.7	18.3	10.9	3.0	3.1	20.6	62.1	17.2	34,219	62.1	19.0	55.1
Farwell village	873	859	-1.6	733	97.3	0.0	0.0	0.8	1.9	19.0	56.6	24.4	347	68.9	57.9	7.5
Fawn River township (St. Joseph)	1,477	1,456	-1.4	1,323	87.2	0.0	2.5	0.2	10.1	21.9	62.1	16.0	478	84.3	54.4	12.8
Fayette township (Hillsdale)	3,326	3,268	-1.7	3,309	93.2	1.8	0.0	2.2	2.9	25.4	52.6	22.1	1,322	83.1	45.7	23.1

1 May be of any race.

Table A. All Places — **Population and Housing**

STATE City, town, township, borough, or CDP (county if applicable)	Population				Race and Hispanic or Latino origin (percent), 2010–2014					Age (percent), 2010–2014			Households, 2010–2014			
	2010 census total population	2014 estimated population	Percent change 2010–2014	ACS total population estimate 2010–2014	White alone, not Hispanic or Latino	Black alone, not Hispanic or Latino	Asian alone, not Hispanic or Latino	All other races or 2 or more races, not Hispanic or Latino	Hispanic or Latino[1]	Under 18 years old	Age 18 to 64 years old	Age 65 years and older	Total occupied housing units	Percent owner occupied	High school diploma or less	Bachelor's degree or more
	1	2	3	4	5	6	7	8	9	10	11	12	13	14	15	16
MICHIGAN—Con.																
Felch township (Dickinson)	754	748	-0.8	726	98.9	0.3	0.0	0.8	0.0	20.7	60.8	18.6	293	91.1	53.9	16.4
Fennville city & MCD (Allegan)	1,398	1,398	0.0	1,757	44.6	3.4	0.4	1.5	50.1	37.5	55.4	7.1	584	55.0	70.5	9.8
Fenton city	11,756	11,463	-2.5	11,601	92.1	0.9	0.0	2.6	4.3	24.2	60.8	15.0	4,763	58.5	39.8	26.3
Fenton city (Genesee)	11,746	11,453	-2.5	11,601	92.1	0.9	0.0	2.6	4.3	24.2	60.8	15.0	4,763	58.5	39.8	26.3
Fenton city (Livingston)	10	10	0.0	0	0.0	0.0	0.0	0.0	0.0	0.0	0.0	0.0	0	0.0	0.0	0.0
Fenton city (Oakland)	0	0	0.0	0	0.0	0.0	0.0	0.0	0.0	0.0	0.0	0.0	0	0.0	0.0	0.0
Fenton charter township (Genesee)	15,552	15,261	-1.9	15,356	94.7	0.4	1.0	2.4	1.6	23.2	62.2	14.6	5,886	85.7	27.0	33.3
Ferndale city & MCD (Oakland)	19,900	20,256	1.8	20,102	82.6	8.0	1.3	4.2	3.9	17.5	74.0	8.3	9,381	60.3	24.9	44.3
Ferris township (Montcalm)	1,422	1,414	-0.6	1,447	95.3	0.0	0.3	2.6	1.7	23.8	59.3	16.9	528	90.0	67.2	7.0
Ferry township (Oceana) ..	1,292	1,266	-2.0	1,081	95.6	0.0	0.0	0.8	3.6	18.2	61.3	20.4	457	87.5	49.5	16.0
Ferrysburg city & MCD (Ottawa)	2,892	2,984	3.2	2,939	95.6	1.0	0.5	0.4	2.4	14.2	65.0	21.0	1,383	78.5	26.1	37.8
Fife Lake village	443	455	2.7	342	95.0	0.0	0.0	0.0	5.0	17.5	66.0	16.4	166	77.7	44.0	7.2
Fife Lake township (Grand Traverse)	2,791	2,829	1.4	2,830	67.5	22.9	0.0	7.0	2.7	8.3	81.4	10.4	584	86.0	40.9	20.5
Filer charter township (Manistee)	2,325	2,298	-1.2	2,480	94.7	0.0	1.3	3.3	0.6	22.1	55.1	23.0	1,018	89.7	43.3	24.0
Filer City CDP	116	NA	NA	128	93.0	0.0	0.0	5.5	1.6	20.3	63.3	16.4	42	100.0	64.3	0.0
Fillmore township (Allegan)	2,681	2,716	1.3	2,691	85.7	0.4	0.0	0.6	13.3	28.5	59.4	12.1	937	81.5	57.1	16.5
Flat Rock city	9,878	9,854	-0.2	9,859	85.1	8.1	0.6	0.6	5.6	26.6	63.3	10.0	3,608	75.1	40.3	21.1
Flat Rock city (Monroe)	0	0	0.0	0	0.0	0.0	0.0	0.0	0.0	0.0	0.0	0.0	0	0.0	0.0	0.0
Flat Rock city (Wayne)......	9,878	9,854	-0.2	9,859	85.1	8.1	0.6	0.6	5.6	26.6	63.3	10.0	3,608	75.1	40.3	21.1
Flint city & MCD (Genesee)	102,400	99,002	-3.3	100,569	36.9	54.7	0.4	4.3	3.8	26.4	61.9	11.7	40,509	55.5	49.6	11.8
Flint charter township (Genesee)	31,929	30,892	-3.2	31,351	65.1	26.2	2.1	3.5	3.0	23.1	59.3	17.7	12,944	63.3	40.7	19.0
Florence township (St. Joseph)	1,242	1,233	-0.7	1,240	96.4	0.4	0.0	2.1	1.1	21.8	61.6	16.5	486	88.5	50.2	10.5
Flowerfield township (St. Joseph)	1,562	1,557	-0.3	1,396	91.2	0.6	4.4	2.4	1.4	17.1	67.8	15.0	579	85.8	47.5	16.1
Flushing city & MCD (Genesee)	8,397	8,135	-3.1	8,252	90.8	2.3	0.9	1.9	4.1	21.4	58.4	20.2	3,426	68.4	34.6	28.1
Flushing charter township (Genesee)	10,632	10,337	-2.8	10,468	91.2	1.6	0.4	3.8	3.0	27.5	56.7	15.8	3,870	94.2	31.1	32.6
Flynn township (Sanilac) ..	1,050	1,013	-3.5	1,012	98.2	0.0	0.0	0.7	1.1	30.4	55.6	13.8	328	85.7	57.9	9.5
Ford River township (Delta)	2,054	2,035	-0.9	2,118	95.6	0.0	0.3	2.2	1.9	20.3	62.9	16.8	861	93.0	39.6	20.1
Forest township (Cheboygan)	1,045	1,022	-2.2	960	96.0	0.0	0.0	1.1	2.8	15.2	63.1	21.9	471	89.6	67.3	3.0
Forest township (Genesee)	4,702	4,566	-2.9	4,523	97.3	0.3	0.2	0.7	1.5	20.0	62.2	17.8	1,816	90.9	54.0	11.2
Forest township (Missaukee)	1,157	1,166	0.8	1,041	97.1	0.0	0.0	1.8	1.1	26.4	57.0	16.6	406	74.1	54.2	12.6
Forester township (Sanilac)	1,011	977	-3.4	981	96.4	0.4	0.3	1.1	1.7	16.5	57.7	25.8	418	84.0	54.5	20.1
Forest Hills CDP	25,867	NA	NA	27,072	94.6	0.4	2.8	0.8	1.4	29.1	58.6	12.3	9,281	94.4	10.4	70.3
Forest Home township (Antrim)	1,720	1,701	-1.1	1,732	94.0	0.1	0.3	2.1	3.5	15.1	53.8	31.2	793	92.3	30.5	30.1
Forestville village	136	132	-2.9	69	100.0	0.0	0.0	0.0	0.0	26.1	37.6	36.2	33	100.0	54.5	24.2
Fork township (Mecosta) ..	1,604	1,613	0.6	1,578	95.5	0.6	0.0	2.6	1.3	21.7	55.6	22.7	646	85.6	57.7	12.4
Forsyth township (Marquette)	6,162	6,233	1.2	6,223	91.5	0.4	1.4	4.7	1.9	21.2	60.2	18.7	2,489	71.1	45.5	23.4
Fort Gratiot charter township (St. Clair)........	11,115	11,095	-0.2	11,102	92.0	2.7	1.1	2.1	2.1	21.2	58.2	20.6	4,552	74.6	37.6	29.1
Foster township (Ogemaw)	843	818	-3.0	735	96.9	0.0	0.0	0.3	2.9	13.6	59.6	26.8	352	87.5	42.6	8.5
Fostoria CDP	694	NA	NA	539	100.0	0.0	0.0	0.0	0.0	16.6	70.3	13.4	198	81.8	52.0	13.6
Fountain village	193	194	0.5	161	89.4	0.0	0.0	8.7	1.9	31.0	54.6	14.3	63	81.0	41.3	6.3
Fowler village	1,208	1,232	2.0	1,252	95.8	0.0	2.0	1.0	1.0	31.5	52.6	15.9	437	86.3	42.6	16.2
Fowlerville village	2,886	2,960	2.6	2,929	94.3	0.0	0.0	0.6	5.2	27.4	59.8	12.7	1,186	60.7	40.3	13.7
Frankenlust township (Bay)	3,562	3,561	0.0	3,564	94.8	1.7	1.2	0.8	1.5	20.8	59.7	19.4	1,403	75.5	29.3	37.4
Frankenmuth city & MCD (Saginaw)	4,966	4,951	-0.3	4,934	98.6	0.2	0.9	0.0	0.4	18.4	52.4	29.2	2,307	68.7	24.6	39.1
Frankenmuth township (Saginaw)	1,937	1,894	-2.2	2,240	94.1	0.5	0.6	1.6	3.2	24.7	58.9	16.2	766	91.1	33.7	41.3
Frankfort city & MCD (Benzie)	1,286	1,287	0.1	1,417	92.8	0.2	0.7	1.6	4.7	19.5	49.9	30.8	591	63.1	40.9	34.2
Franklin township (Clare)..	825	813	-1.5	742	98.2	0.1	0.0	1.6	0.0	12.9	58.6	28.6	368	91.0	48.1	11.7
Franklin township (Houghton)	1,466	1,447	-1.3	1,400	97.2	0.0	0.0	1.4	1.4	29.5	58.4	12.0	528	79.0	37.7	24.1
Franklin township (Lenawee)	3,167	3,192	0.8	3,173	96.1	0.0	0.3	2.5	1.0	23.8	60.4	15.8	1,172	92.4	41.2	23.0
Franklin village	3,150	3,231	2.6	3,106	86.3	4.8	6.9	1.1	0.8	27.6	55.5	16.9	1,108	93.6	8.7	75.3
Fraser township (Bay)	3,192	3,155	-1.2	3,177	95.6	0.0	0.0	1.4	3.0	18.5	57.5	23.9	1,319	93.0	59.0	9.0
Fraser city & MCD (Macomb)	14,480	14,622	1.0	14,544	87.2	8.3	1.5	1.1	1.9	21.3	61.5	17.1	6,163	71.2	39.8	21.2
Frederic township (Crawford)	1,341	1,347	0.4	1,459	90.9	0.3	0.0	4.9	3.8	22.0	57.6	20.6	590	87.8	51.5	13.2
Fredonia township (Calhoun)	1,626	1,608	-1.1	1,415	96.6	0.3	0.6	1.7	0.8	20.2	63.6	16.0	596	86.2	45.6	21.5
Freedom township (Washtenaw)	1,428	1,471	3.0	1,446	89.6	0.0	0.5	0.8	9.1	12.2	67.9	20.0	601	82.0	29.0	36.8
Freeland CDP	6,969	NA	NA	7,608	82.7	10.6	1.3	1.2	4.2	27.2	62.9	9.7	2,232	81.6	28.6	44.8
Freeman township (Clare)	1,159	1,141	-1.6	993	94.4	0.0	0.0	4.1	1.5	12.0	49.9	37.9	448	92.4	62.5	2.2
Freeport village	483	483	0.0	493	93.7	0.0	0.0	5.1	1.2	30.4	59.3	10.3	171	83.6	61.4	10.5

1 May be of any race.

Table A. All Places — **Population and Housing**

STATE City, town, township, borough, or CDP (county if applicable)	Population				Race and Hispanic or Latino origin (percent), 2010–2014					Age (percent), 2010–2014			Households, 2010–2014			
	2010 census total population	2014 estimated population	Percent change 2010–2014	ACS total population estimate 2010–2014	White alone, not Hispanic or Latino	Black alone, not Hispanic or Latino	Asian alone, not Hispanic or Latino	All other races or 2 or more races, not Hispanic or Latino	Hispanic or Latino[1]	Under 18 years old	Age 18 to 64 years old	Age 65 years and older	Total occupied housing units	Percent owner occupied	High school diploma or less	Bachelor's degree or more
	1	2	3	4	5	6	7	8	9	10	11	12	13	14	15	16
MICHIGAN—Con.																
Free Soil village	144	145	0.7	138	91.3	1.4	0.0	5.8	1.4	18.7	59.9	21.0	68	79.4	55.9	5.9
Free Soil township (Mason)	822	826	0.5	857	91.1	0.9	2.0	3.9	2.1	21.0	60.6	18.4	362	86.2	45.9	15.7
Fremont township (Isabella)	1,455	1,434	-1.4	1,554	94.3	0.0	0.3	1.6	3.7	22.7	66.8	10.6	542	76.6	56.3	5.4
Fremont city & MCD (Newaygo)	4,087	4,034	-1.3	4,065	93.7	1.2	0.6	1.1	3.4	23.0	57.0	20.1	1,652	74.8	37.0	20.7
Fremont township (Saginaw)	2,096	2,048	-2.3	1,996	94.3	0.0	0.4	2.9	2.4	22.2	62.8	15.0	771	86.1	39.9	19.2
Fremont township (Sanilac)	1,051	1,013	-3.6	1,009	91.6	0.9	0.6	0.1	6.8	27.5	59.4	13.2	352	85.5	53.7	8.2
Fremont township (Tuscola)	3,312	3,214	-3.0	3,258	94.0	0.6	0.0	4.9	0.5	13.9	68.4	17.7	1,309	71.6	54.4	10.1
Frenchtown township (Monroe)	20,428	20,032	-1.9	20,215	91.2	2.8	0.3	1.1	4.6	23.8	62.0	14.3	7,923	73.5	51.0	14.5
Friendship township (Emmet)	889	907	2.0	825	95.6	0.8	0.7	2.3	0.5	20.1	60.0	19.9	354	87.0	33.6	39.8
Frost township (Clare)	1,045	1,030	-1.4	1,037	93.5	0.3	0.0	6.2	0.0	13.8	58.5	27.7	483	91.3	62.3	13.0
Fruitland township (Muskegon)	5,543	5,577	0.6	5,550	89.4	0.9	0.4	3.4	5.8	20.8	61.8	17.6	2,109	87.2	33.1	32.1
Fruitport village	1,093	1,104	1.0	1,270	96.2	0.0	0.0	2.1	1.7	24.3	58.8	16.8	509	83.1	38.7	22.4
Fruitport charter township (Muskegon)	13,598	13,752	1.1	13,632	92.6	1.0	1.1	3.0	2.3	25.7	60.0	14.2	5,082	89.4	38.9	21.3
Fulton township (Gratiot) ..	2,521	2,484	-1.5	2,622	94.7	0.0	0.0	0.1	5.2	23.5	58.4	18.0	948	89.2	43.1	12.8
Gaastra city & MCD (Iron)	347	333	-4.0	318	98.1	0.3	0.0	1.6	0.0	20.4	56.9	22.6	128	84.4	56.3	9.4
Gagetown village	388	380	-2.1	368	92.4	0.0	0.5	1.4	5.7	17.9	66.9	15.2	146	71.9	62.3	8.9
Gaines village	380	371	-2.4	377	94.7	0.0	0.0	0.5	4.8	19.9	61.6	18.6	176	66.5	55.1	11.9
Gaines township (Genesee)	6,820	6,623	-2.9	6,718	93.5	0.5	0.0	1.5	4.6	23.5	62.6	13.9	2,493	91.1	41.2	16.8
Gaines charter township (Kent)	25,145	26,151	4.0	25,633	81.1	8.2	2.7	3.7	4.3	25.7	63.2	11.1	9,838	70.1	36.3	26.4
Galesburg city & MCD (Kalamazoo).................	2,009	2,039	1.5	1,876	90.7	2.8	1.0	3.0	2.5	22.7	64.0	13.3	713	65.2	44.5	8.8
Galien village	549	536	-2.4	538	93.7	0.0	0.0	3.2	3.2	23.3	66.8	9.7	213	65.7	67.6	8.0
Galien township (Berrien).	1,452	1,426	-1.8	1,454	95.3	0.0	0.0	3.6	1.2	22.6	61.7	15.6	567	82.4	61.0	9.5
Ganges township (Allegan)......................	2,530	2,593	2.5	2,572	86.1	0.5	0.0	0.0	13.3	23.8	55.6	20.7	1,028	88.2	31.6	35.6
Garden village	221	218	-1.4	210	82.9	0.0	0.0	17.1	0.0	13.4	55.3	31.4	96	92.7	49.0	15.6
Garden township (Delta)..	750	742	-1.1	678	90.6	0.0	0.0	9.4	0.0	15.9	49.4	34.5	324	96.3	43.8	19.8
Garden City city & MCD (Wayne)......................	27,692	27,052	-2.3	27,356	92.0	2.2	0.5	2.5	2.7	21.5	64.3	14.2	10,279	81.5	50.7	13.6
Garfield township (Bay)	1,743	1,719	-1.4	1,845	97.8	0.2	0.0	0.7	1.4	23.8	63.5	12.8	724	89.4	54.7	10.4
Garfield township (Clare)..	1,882	1,855	-1.4	1,958	98.1	0.0	0.0	1.9	0.0	18.8	53.1	28.1	857	94.2	50.5	11.2
Garfield charter township (Grand Traverse)	16,256	16,803	3.4	16,565	92.4	0.4	0.7	3.5	3.1	21.6	57.0	21.2	7,086	56.9	31.3	29.3
Garfield township (Kalkaska)	804	817	1.6	852	97.3	0.0	0.4	0.8	1.5	17.7	61.3	21.1	385	87.5	61.3	13.0
Garfield township (Mackinac)	1,146	1,144	-0.2	1,160	84.0	0.8	0.0	14.6	0.7	22.3	45.4	32.2	521	85.2	43.6	17.3
Garfield township (Newaygo)....................	2,526	2,504	-0.9	2,494	86.9	0.2	0.0	1.9	10.9	29.9	52.0	18.2	829	83.1	51.6	21.6
Gaylord city & MCD (Otsego)....................	3,652	3,648	-0.1	3,651	91.7	0.3	0.0	7.3	0.7	20.7	59.5	19.7	1,702	49.4	58.5	20.9
Genesee charter township (Genesee)	21,577	20,732	-3.9	21,102	85.9	7.9	0.1	3.2	2.9	21.2	62.8	16.0	8,394	76.3	51.6	11.0
Geneva township (Midland)	1,056	1,033	-2.2	1,080	97.5	0.0	0.0	1.4	1.1	22.2	60.1	17.8	436	88.3	49.5	10.6
Geneva township (Van Buren)	3,573	3,491	-2.3	3,526	63.2	6.2	0.0	5.4	25.2	34.1	51.9	13.9	1,048	84.4	48.3	6.4
Genoa township (Livingston)	19,791	20,281	2.5	20,034	94.7	0.8	0.6	1.0	2.8	22.7	60.8	16.6	7,868	82.9	25.7	39.4
Georgetown charter township (Ottawa)	46,985	49,646	5.7	48,237	94.2	0.9	1.0	1.2	2.6	27.1	58.7	13.9	17,101	82.3	32.1	32.1
Germfask township (Schoolcraft)	486	467	-3.9	524	93.9	0.0	0.0	4.2	1.9	27.7	56.1	16.2	194	75.3	54.1	1.0
Gerrish township (Roscommon)	2,993	2,939	-1.8	2,963	92.8	0.0	2.5	3.8	0.8	19.0	51.6	29.6	1,328	89.2	27.7	30.9
Gibraltar city & MCD (Wayne)......................	4,656	4,547	-2.3	4,602	92.7	2.5	0.2	3.2	1.4	19.3	65.2	15.3	1,813	79.6	42.7	18.1
Gibson township (Bay)......	1,210	1,182	-2.3	1,242	93.0	0.6	0.0	4.8	1.7	29.4	58.2	12.6	418	87.1	55.0	11.2
Gilead township (Branch) .	661	653	-1.2	677	93.8	0.1	0.0	0.3	5.8	20.7	63.5	16.0	249	93.2	61.8	8.8
Gilford township (Tuscola)	741	719	-3.0	777	88.3	0.0	0.0	0.3	11.5	23.4	63.6	13.0	283	85.9	56.2	12.4
Gilmore township (Benzie)	821	815	-0.7	777	96.5	0.0	0.0	0.5	3.0	18.0	60.6	21.5	330	90.6	38.8	27.9
Gilmore township (Isabella)	1,459	1,447	-0.8	1,411	90.9	0.0	0.0	2.3	6.9	18.9	62.8	18.4	554	86.3	52.2	15.7
Girard township (Branch)..	1,780	1,756	-1.3	1,788	95.9	0.9	0.3	2.2	0.7	15.6	62.7	21.8	771	82.1	40.9	19.5
Gladstone city & MCD (Delta)......................	4,973	4,868	-2.1	4,920	94.2	0.0	1.0	4.1	0.8	24.9	54.0	20.9	1,943	75.3	42.9	25.3
Gladwin city & MCD (Gladwin)...................	2,933	2,908	-0.9	2,928	97.6	0.7	0.7	1.0	0.0	24.8	51.5	23.7	1,321	56.4	47.9	20.7
Gladwin township (Gladwin)...................	1,116	1,102	-1.3	1,239	97.5	0.0	2.1	0.4	0.0	28.3	58.7	12.9	421	90.3	61.8	11.4
Glen Arbor CDP..............	229	NA	NA	215	100.0	0.0	0.0	0.0	0.0	6.5	36.7	56.7	106	88.7	19.8	46.2
Glen Arbor township (Leelanau)	859	869	1.2	687	96.9	1.0	0.0	0.0	2.0	9.3	41.5	49.2	331	90.6	21.1	51.4
Gobles city & MCD (Van Buren)	829	811	-2.2	763	88.7	0.4	0.5	6.9	3.4	21.2	66.1	12.7	303	67.0	55.1	13.5
Golden township (Oceana)	1,735	1,723	-0.7	1,681	96.5	0.0	0.0	0.8	2.7	15.8	56.5	27.8	718	87.7	43.0	22.8
Goodar township (Ogemaw)	398	387	-2.8	419	95.2	0.2	0.0	3.8	0.7	12.3	57.4	30.1	204	96.1	58.3	12.7

1 May be of any race.

Table A. All Places — **Population and Housing**

	Population				Race and Hispanic or Latino origin (percent), 2010–2014					Age (percent), 2010–2014			Households, 2010–2014			
STATE City, town, township, borough, or CDP (county if applicable)	2010 census total population	2014 estimated population	Percent change 2010–2014	ACS total population estimate 2010–2014	White alone, not Hispanic or Latino	Black alone, not Hispanic or Latino	Asian alone, not Hispanic or Latino	All other races or 2 or more races, not Hispanic or Latino	Hispanic or Latino[1]	Under 18 years old	Age 18 to 64 years old	Age 65 years and older	Total occupied housing units	Percent owner occupied	High school diploma or less	Bachelor's degree or more
	1	2	3	4	5	6	7	8	9	10	11	12	13	14	15	16
MICHIGAN—Con.																
Goodland township (Lapeer)	1,828	1,823	-0.3	1,679	94.0	0.4	0.0	2.1	3.5	23.9	61.2	14.8	592	87.2	49.2	11.8
Goodrich village	1,860	1,831	-1.6	1,851	98.0	0.3	0.0	0.6	1.1	30.8	57.8	11.4	650	84.6	32.5	29.1
Goodwell township (Newaygo)	547	539	-1.5	564	94.1	0.4	0.0	2.3	3.2	20.0	61.5	18.6	201	94.0	57.2	10.0
Gore township (Huron)	144	140	-2.8	213	94.4	0.0	0.0	2.3	3.3	16.9	48.5	34.7	102	92.2	54.9	12.7
Gourley township (Menominee)	420	417	-0.7	425	88.2	0.0	1.4	3.3	7.1	25.4	55.0	19.5	163	89.0	61.3	11.7
Grand Beach village	272	272	0.0	249	98.4	1.2	0.4	0.0	0.0	16.0	45.3	38.6	113	92.9	10.6	69.0
Grand Blanc city & MCD (Genesee)	8,276	8,033	-2.9	8,147	82.2	11.6	2.7	2.0	1.5	24.5	58.5	17.1	3,500	57.5	24.5	38.6
Grand Blanc charter township (Genesee)	37,508	36,733	-2.1	37,019	79.6	11.5	4.2	2.4	2.2	26.1	60.5	13.5	14,354	67.8	24.9	37.3
Grand Haven city & MCD (Ottawa)	10,412	10,965	5.3	10,687	97.0	0.2	0.8	0.4	1.6	19.8	61.4	18.6	4,898	68.2	28.0	31.6
Grand Haven charter township (Ottawa)	15,178	15,990	5.3	15,553	90.5	0.2	2.1	2.1	5.2	26.0	61.6	12.4	5,655	83.5	28.5	43.4
Grand Island township (Alger)	47	46	-2.1	75	54.7	0.0	0.0	45.3	0.0	42.7	44.0	13.3	25	76.0	48.0	32.0
Grand Ledge city	7,800	7,792	-0.1	7,779	95.5	0.2	0.0	1.6	2.7	22.1	62.2	15.7	3,324	64.0	31.3	27.8
Grand Ledge city (Clinton)	2	2	0.0	0	0.0	0.0	0.0	0.0	0.0	0.0	0.0	0.0	0	0.0	0.0	0.0
Grand Ledge city (Eaton)	7,798	7,790	-0.1	7,779	95.5	0.2	0.0	1.6	2.7	22.1	62.2	15.7	3,324	64.0	31.3	27.8
Grand Rapids city & MCD (Kent)	188,051	193,792	3.1	190,739	58.3	20.3	1.9	3.8	15.7	24.9	63.9	11.3	72,536	55.1	34.7	31.9
Grand Rapids charter township (Kent)	16,656	17,773	6.7	17,211	88.0	1.5	5.6	2.0	3.0	26.1	56.5	17.3	6,084	87.7	17.5	60.7
Grandville city & MCD (Kent)	15,378	15,857	3.1	15,613	86.6	3.1	1.2	3.0	6.0	23.9	60.5	15.4	6,041	71.0	29.9	35.8
Grant township (Cheboygan)	846	838	-0.9	791	96.1	0.0	0.0	3.0	0.9	13.4	50.1	36.5	367	93.5	49.9	16.6
Grant township (Clare)	3,259	3,265	0.2	3,253	97.3	0.0	0.3	0.7	1.7	23.3	59.5	17.1	1,299	81.9	51.2	14.2
Grant township (Grand Traverse)	1,061	1,125	6.0	1,233	94.6	0.0	3.8	0.7	0.8	24.6	60.3	15.2	472	89.8	40.7	20.6
Grant township (Huron)	913	893	-2.2	833	92.4	0.6	0.0	2.5	4.4	24.3	60.2	15.5	302	91.4	64.9	9.6
Grant township (Iosco)	1,546	1,522	-1.6	1,681	99.1	0.0	0.0	0.9	0.0	15.1	57.8	27.1	766	87.1	61.7	7.3
Grant township (Keweenaw)	219	225	2.7	180	99.4	0.0	0.0	0.0	0.6	0.6	59.5	40.0	118	86.4	24.6	39.8
Grant township (Mason)	909	922	1.4	764	99.2	0.0	0.0	0.8	0.0	13.3	67.3	19.2	336	89.6	48.2	20.2
Grant township (Mecosta)	686	700	2.0	737	96.9	0.0	0.5	2.3	0.3	17.5	63.6	18.9	285	93.0	51.2	14.0
Grant city & MCD (Newaygo)	894	881	-1.5	809	92.0	0.0	0.0	0.6	7.4	25.8	58.2	16.2	356	54.2	53.1	10.7
Grant township (Newaygo)	3,294	3,284	-0.3	3,287	81.5	0.8	0.6	0.5	16.6	28.8	57.9	13.4	1,048	88.4	56.2	15.2
Grant township (Oceana)	2,976	2,896	-2.7	2,941	85.8	0.2	0.0	3.8	10.1	27.0	60.7	12.1	1,007	86.3	50.8	7.6
Grant township (St. Clair)	1,891	1,860	-1.6	1,986	96.3	0.0	0.6	0.9	2.3	23.7	63.2	13.1	717	91.2	46.3	17.0
Grass Lake village	1,173	1,168	-0.4	1,300	95.2	0.0	0.0	3.1	1.8	21.1	69.2	9.7	529	68.2	37.6	23.8
Grass Lake charter township (Jackson)	5,684	5,847	2.9	5,757	95.6	1.4	0.3	1.1	1.5	24.9	62.1	12.9	2,187	83.1	29.8	27.3
Grattan township (Kent)	3,621	3,795	4.8	3,709	96.5	1.1	0.0	1.0	1.4	18.5	64.9	16.6	1,437	96.3	33.8	28.7
Grawn CDP	772	NA	NA	947	93.8	0.0	0.0	0.0	6.2	40.2	56.7	3.3	311	87.1	62.4	7.4
Grayling city & MCD (Crawford)	1,884	1,838	-2.4	1,798	97.3	0.4	0.0	1.4	0.8	21.3	57.3	21.5	722	47.1	53.3	10.4
Grayling charter township (Crawford)	5,827	5,683	-2.5	5,766	96.8	1.0	0.6	0.8	0.8	20.2	57.4	22.4	2,355	82.4	44.2	18.9
Green township (Alpena)	1,228	1,200	-2.3	1,217	98.4	0.0	0.0	1.3	0.3	19.5	57.1	23.3	539	90.4	61.6	10.6
Green charter township (Mecosta)	3,292	3,311	0.6	3,307	95.3	0.0	0.1	3.6	1.0	29.4	55.9	14.7	1,098	73.3	43.4	21.0
Greenbush township (Alcona)	1,409	1,348	-4.3	1,478	96.8	0.6	0.0	1.8	0.8	11.7	52.8	35.5	707	91.4	42.6	21.1
Greenbush township (Clinton)	2,199	2,242	2.0	2,208	93.0	1.0	0.1	3.4	2.5	23.3	60.1	16.4	812	92.5	49.4	14.0
Greendale township (Midland)	1,751	1,731	-1.1	1,849	93.0	0.5	0.4	1.7	4.4	25.5	60.4	14.2	684	80.6	55.8	15.9
Green Lake township (Grand Traverse)	5,789	6,098	5.3	5,947	89.0	2.6	1.4	2.4	4.7	22.3	66.9	10.7	2,061	89.9	34.2	27.3
Greenland township (Ontonagon)	790	712	-9.9	717	99.7	0.0	0.0	0.3	0.0	16.8	59.2	24.3	331	96.4	55.3	10.3
Greenleaf township (Sanilac)	781	752	-3.7	903	97.0	0.0	0.0	1.3	1.7	30.0	52.3	17.7	273	92.3	60.4	9.9
Green Oak township (Livingston)	17,476	18,237	4.4	17,842	94.7	0.4	1.3	1.9	1.7	24.5	62.9	12.7	6,801	87.0	25.0	37.7
Greenville city & MCD (Montcalm)	8,481	8,431	-0.6	8,434	93.7	0.3	0.0	2.3	3.7	28.4	54.0	17.6	3,365	57.0	40.9	23.1
Greenwood township (Clare)	1,039	1,031	-0.8	1,196	96.5	0.0	1.3	1.0	1.3	16.8	57.3	25.8	553	90.4	53.9	8.1
Greenwood township (Oceana)	1,184	1,187	0.3	1,207	91.6	0.0	1.5	6.3	0.6	28.2	58.8	13.0	397	80.6	49.6	11.1
Greenwood township (Oscoda)	1,121	1,096	-2.2	1,151	95.5	0.1	0.0	3.6	0.9	16.4	55.3	28.2	559	90.9	56.0	6.3
Greenwood township (St. Clair)	1,538	1,526	-0.8	1,467	98.6	0.0	0.3	0.3	0.7	25.9	61.5	12.4	534	91.8	42.7	9.0
Greenwood township (Wexford)	587	597	1.7	613	97.4	0.0	0.0	1.1	1.5	26.4	59.4	14.2	212	93.4	49.1	8.0
Greilickville CDP	1,530	NA	NA	1,960	99.1	0.2	0.0	0.7	0.0	12.9	42.6	44.5	870	80.5	18.5	43.2
Grim township (Gladwin)	136	135	-0.7	140	99.3	0.0	0.0	0.7	0.0	25.7	60.1	14.3	61	73.8	72.1	3.3
Grosse Ile township (Wayne)	10,371	10,181	-1.8	10,264	93.1	0.6	2.4	0.7	3.3	20.0	59.6	20.2	4,073	87.6	18.3	47.0
Grosse Pointe city & MCD (Wayne)	5,421	5,262	-2.9	5,350	88.1	0.6	2.4	6.5	2.4	26.5	56.5	17.0	2,120	81.1	9.4	71.1
Grosse Pointe Farms city & MCD (Wayne)	9,479	9,285	-2.0	9,371	93.5	1.3	1.1	1.6	2.5	29.0	53.7	17.3	3,531	97.1	8.1	74.4
Grosse Pointe Park city & MCD (Wayne)	11,553	11,288	-2.3	11,412	83.4	9.6	1.2	2.6	3.3	25.4	60.3	14.4	4,329	74.3	10.1	69.3

1   May be of any race.

Table A. All Places — Population and Housing

STATE City, town, township, borough, or CDP (county if applicable)	Population				Race and Hispanic or Latino origin (percent), 2010–2014					Age (percent), 2010–2014			Households, 2010–2014			
	2010 census total population	2014 estimated population	Percent change 2010–2014	ACS total population estimate 2010–2014	White alone, not Hispanic or Latino	Black alone, not Hispanic or Latino	Asian alone, not Hispanic or Latino	All other races or 2 or more races, not Hispanic or Latino	Hispanic or Latino[1]	Under 18 years old	Age 18 to 64 years old	Age 65 years and older	Total occupied housing units	Percent owner occupied	High school diploma or less	Bachelor's degree or more
	1	2	3	4	5	6	7	8	9	10	11	12	13	14	15	16
MICHIGAN—Con.																
Grosse Pointe Woods city & MCD (Wayne)	16,120	15,835	-1.8	15,943	90.8	5.8	0.9	1.7	0.9	22.8	59.4	17.8	6,117	89.8	11.0	62.1
Grout township (Gladwin) .	1,964	1,943	-1.1	2,000	97.5	1.6	0.0	0.4	0.7	24.5	58.9	17.1	675	94.7	58.4	9.6
Groveland township (Oakland)	5,476	5,593	2.1	5,532	95.0	2.5	0.8	1.4	0.4	23.6	64.4	11.7	1,873	90.5	29.6	28.6
Gun Plain township (Allegan).....................	5,893	5,990	1.6	5,934	95.7	0.8	0.0	0.7	2.8	21.2	64.4	14.5	2,235	91.4	43.2	25.2
Gustin township (Alcona)..	795	756	-4.9	713	95.9	0.1	0.0	3.9	0.0	14.8	60.8	24.4	336	77.4	55.7	12.2
Gwinn CDP	1,917	NA	NA	2,063	95.4	0.0	1.6	3.0	0.0	17.0	64.1	19.0	893	78.3	50.6	17.5
Hadley township (Lapeer).	4,528	4,532	0.1	4,526	96.8	0.6	0.4	0.5	1.7	23.8	63.3	12.9	1,614	93.4	33.2	20.3
Hagar township (Berrien)..	3,671	3,631	-1.1	3,655	86.5	5.2	0.0	2.4	5.8	22.9	58.8	18.4	1,522	73.3	35.2	21.6
Haight township (Ontonagon).................	212	193	-9.0	212	96.7	0.0	0.0	0.9	2.4	8.0	62.7	29.2	113	90.3	53.1	11.5
Hamburg township (Livingston)	21,165	21,691	2.5	21,428	95.8	0.1	0.5	1.8	1.9	22.6	63.2	14.3	8,127	91.9	23.5	38.0
Hamilton township (Clare)	1,829	1,808	-1.1	1,745	96.6	0.0	0.0	1.0	2.4	13.1	60.0	27.0	836	89.7	59.9	6.3
Hamilton township (Gratiot)......................	465	458	-1.5	407	95.6	0.0	0.2	2.2	2.0	15.0	70.8	14.3	172	83.1	55.8	11.6
Hamilton township (Van Buren).........................	1,489	1,457	-2.1	1,430	87.3	2.2	0.0	1.5	9.0	24.0	60.1	15.9	498	90.0	47.0	18.7
Hamlin township (Eaton) ..	3,341	3,379	1.1	3,360	90.1	0.0	1.0	6.9	2.0	27.5	60.1	12.4	1,151	84.8	36.9	14.8
Hamlin township (Mason) .	3,408	3,425	0.5	3,417	98.2	0.0	0.0	0.7	1.1	18.3	61.2	20.5	1,473	89.7	36.8	25.7
Hampton charter township (Bay)	9,652	9,494	-1.6	9,587	91.8	1.0	0.4	1.6	5.3	19.7	59.8	20.6	4,032	66.5	41.1	20.6
Hamtramck city & MCD (Wayne)	22,417	22,099	-1.4	22,256	56.0	13.8	23.8	5.3	1.1	31.5	60.7	7.7	6,148	48.1	63.0	12.6
Hancock city & MCD (Houghton)	4,634	4,581	-1.1	4,622	96.0	0.4	1.3	1.7	0.6	14.1	65.5	20.4	2,033	54.0	31.3	33.2
Hancock township (Houghton)	461	456	-1.1	509	96.9	0.0	0.4	2.8	0.0	29.6	54.8	15.5	188	84.6	36.2	25.5
Handy township (Livingston)	8,006	8,213	2.6	8,116	95.9	0.2	0.2	0.5	3.1	26.0	63.3	10.8	2,989	78.8	38.0	15.8
Hanover village	441	433	-1.8	423	97.6	0.0	0.0	1.9	0.5	27.6	62.9	9.5	140	77.1	61.4	10.7
Hanover township (Jackson).....................	3,695	3,696	0.0	3,708	96.9	0.4	0.0	2.6	0.1	25.1	60.1	14.8	1,315	93.1	30.4	21.8
Hanover township (Wexford)...................	1,560	1,570	0.6	1,417	96.2	0.0	0.1	2.0	1.7	26.8	60.3	13.1	507	76.7	51.5	11.8
Harbor Beach city & MCD (Huron)	1,703	1,644	-3.5	1,780	91.7	0.3	2.2	3.0	2.8	23.6	56.6	19.8	797	64.6	53.6	15.9
Harbor Springs city & MCD (Emmet)	1,194	1,205	0.9	986	84.7	1.7	1.8	11.5	0.3	12.7	49.9	37.4	464	76.1	25.4	34.9
Hardwood Acres CDP	432	NA	NA	518	100.0	0.0	0.0	0.0	0.0	31.8	64.8	3.3	150	100.0	39.3	22.0
Haring CDP	328	NA	NA	571	100.0	0.0	0.0	0.0	0.0	29.4	70.7	0.0	167	77.2	35.9	32.9
Haring charter township (Wexford)...................	3,353	3,379	0.8	3,353	98.0	0.0	0.7	0.3	1.0	25.6	56.8	17.6	1,207	88.9	48.0	18.8
Harper Woods city & MCD (Wayne)	14,236	13,907	-2.3	14,058	43.7	49.3	1.7	2.5	2.9	24.6	64.2	11.3	5,455	65.1	35.3	26.9
Harrietta village...............	143	144	0.7	128	99.2	0.0	0.0	0.0	0.8	20.4	61.1	18.8	58	81.0	53.4	1.7
Harris township (Menominee)................	1,968	1,944	-1.2	1,793	71.7	1.3	0.5	25.0	1.5	25.2	61.0	13.9	702	74.9	52.3	11.7
Harrison city & MCD (Clare)	2,114	2,148	1.6	2,128	90.3	4.0	1.2	1.8	2.7	18.7	65.6	15.7	904	58.6	49.4	13.2
Harrison charter township (Macomb)...................	24,587	24,918	1.3	24,738	83.4	10.2	0.2	2.6	3.5	19.2	65.6	15.2	11,015	69.7	35.6	24.2
Harrisville city & MCD (Alcona).....................	493	474	-3.9	387	93.5	2.3	0.5	2.1	1.6	12.6	56.6	30.7	180	65.6	44.4	16.7
Harrisville township (Alcona).....................	1,348	1,291	-4.2	1,275	94.9	0.0	1.9	1.7	1.5	15.2	55.7	29.0	588	83.5	43.5	11.7
Hart city & MCD (Oceana)	2,126	2,107	-0.9	2,128	71.5	1.6	0.0	3.9	22.9	28.1	49.2	22.7	703	54.5	51.5	16.2
Hart township (Oceana) ...	1,860	1,837	-1.2	1,904	82.5	0.5	0.4	2.1	14.6	25.4	57.4	17.2	704	80.7	47.9	19.0
Hartford city & MCD (Van Buren)	2,688	2,630	-2.2	2,660	66.2	1.2	1.9	6.0	24.7	33.4	56.8	9.8	842	67.3	59.0	7.6
Hartford township (Van Buren)	3,274	3,199	-2.3	3,227	78.8	2.3	0.9	3.4	14.7	24.0	63.9	12.0	1,205	77.8	53.7	9.5
Hartland township (Livingston)	14,664	15,033	2.5	14,839	96.2	0.3	0.5	1.5	1.5	28.1	60.7	11.2	5,062	83.9	22.9	38.9
Hartwick township (Osceola)....................	567	556	-1.9	537	92.7	1.1	0.0	3.4	2.8	14.7	59.4	25.9	218	82.1	70.6	7.8
Harvey CDP....................	1,393	NA	NA	1,733	96.4	0.9	0.0	1.4	1.3	17.5	67.4	15.0	714	66.5	43.6	35.0
Haslett CDP....................	19,220	NA	NA	20,061	82.9	3.7	6.0	3.3	4.1	18.6	65.3	16.1	8,983	57.8	13.1	56.8
Hastings city & MCD (Barry)	7,350	7,302	-0.7	7,313	93.4	1.2	0.6	2.3	2.4	24.6	59.5	15.8	2,994	64.8	45.1	14.0
Hastings charter township (Barry)	2,948	2,963	0.5	2,940	95.4	0.5	0.4	0.6	3.1	21.3	58.1	20.6	1,079	84.9	49.3	16.3
Hatton township (Clare)....	933	921	-1.3	895	95.9	0.0	0.6	1.6	2.0	23.8	60.2	16.0	338	82.5	42.6	13.3
Hawes township (Alcona) .	1,107	1,059	-4.3	1,035	95.1	0.2	0.0	2.4	2.3	14.8	51.9	33.2	483	88.2	52.0	12.8
Hay township (Gladwin)....	1,362	1,343	-1.4	1,358	97.3	0.0	0.7	0.6	1.5	15.1	64.1	21.0	600	90.8	58.7	8.8
Hayes township (Charlevoix).................	1,919	1,931	0.6	1,953	92.2	0.0	0.0	7.0	0.8	22.2	59.6	18.1	775	94.7	31.7	35.4
Hayes township (Clare)	4,677	4,627	-1.1	4,657	96.0	0.2	0.0	1.8	2.0	19.9	62.8	17.2	2,102	81.7	52.4	4.6
Hayes township (Otsego) .	2,619	2,620	0.0	2,611	95.8	0.0	0.0	0.5	3.7	24.5	62.6	12.9	922	90.7	39.7	18.8
Haynes township (Alcona) .	722	691	-4.3	693	98.1	0.0	0.1	0.9	0.9	12.1	51.7	36.2	329	95.7	37.7	21.3
Hazel Park city & MCD (Oakland)	16,422	16,604	1.1	16,532	83.3	10.4	1.1	4.1	1.0	22.7	65.7	11.7	6,822	59.2	58.5	13.8
Hazelton township (Shiawassee)................	2,071	2,020	-2.5	1,847	94.0	1.9	0.0	2.5	1.5	22.4	59.1	18.5	726	87.5	43.1	15.0
Heath township (Allegan) .	3,317	3,403	2.6	3,336	95.3	0.2	0.3	1.4	2.8	26.5	65.5	8.1	1,162	91.5	50.0	24.6
Hebron township (Cheboygan)	269	264	-1.9	290	88.6	0.0	0.0	10.0	1.4	25.2	62.3	12.4	115	81.7	44.3	26.1
Helena township (Antrim) .	1,001	990	-1.1	960	98.5	0.0	0.0	0.9	0.5	13.5	51.2	35.3	449	89.5	27.2	42.1
Hematite township (Iron) ..	338	325	-3.8	368	98.6	0.0	0.0	1.4	0.0	23.9	57.2	19.0	177	83.6	61.6	9.0
Hemlock CDP..................	1,466	NA	NA	1,397	95.3	1.3	0.0	1.4	2.0	25.9	58.9	15.2	542	70.5	44.8	16.4

1 May be of any race.

Table A. All Places — Population and Housing

STATE City, town, township, borough, or CDP (county if applicable)	2010 census total population	2014 estimated population	Percent change 2010–2014	ACS total population estimate 2010–2014	White alone, not Hispanic or Latino	Black alone, not Hispanic or Latino	Asian alone, not Hispanic or Latino	All other races or 2 or more races, not Hispanic or Latino	Hispanic or Latino[1]	Under 18 years old	Age 18 to 64 years old	Age 65 years and older	Total occupied housing units	Percent owner occupied	High school diploma or less	Bachelor's degree or more
	1	2	3	4	5	6	7	8	9	10	11	12	13	14	15	16
MICHIGAN—Con.																
Henderson CDP	399	NA	NA	380	88.7	0.0	5.0	1.1	5.3	27.9	55.4	16.6	146	71.2	52.7	21.9
Henderson township (Wexford)	163	164	0.6	152	98.0	0.0	0.0	2.0	0.0	13.8	56.0	30.3	74	90.5	63.5	10.8
Hendricks township (Mackinac)	153	153	0.0	186	76.9	0.0	0.0	21.0	2.2	17.7	53.9	28.5	94	90.4	69.1	7.4
Henrietta township (Jackson)	4,705	4,691	-0.3	4,693	94.2	0.4	0.6	1.6	3.3	23.8	61.4	14.8	1,755	91.3	42.8	19.5
Hersey village	350	348	-0.6	363	97.5	0.3	0.0	0.0	2.2	19.6	67.6	12.9	149	71.1	46.3	6.0
Hersey township (Osceola)	1,950	1,919	-1.6	2,036	97.3	1.0	0.2	1.0	0.4	23.9	60.0	16.2	743	81.8	55.3	10.8
Hesperia village	954	938	-1.7	911	86.8	0.0	0.0	2.4	10.8	25.4	58.7	15.8	372	54.6	59.9	6.2
Hiawatha township (Schoolcraft)	1,302	1,258	-3.4	1,332	90.5	0.2	0.3	8.9	0.1	13.5	58.2	28.5	580	95.9	51.9	21.9
Hickory Corners CDP	322	NA	NA	286	88.1	0.0	0.0	11.9	0.0	38.8	54.1	7.0	119	75.6	0.0	31.1
Higgins township (Roscommon)	1,932	1,897	-1.8	1,716	91.8	2.2	0.0	2.9	3.1	13.4	61.4	25.3	794	64.6	42.9	16.0
Highland charter township (Oakland)	19,202	19,725	2.7	19,452	96.1	0.3	1.0	0.9	1.7	23.8	62.8	13.4	7,270	91.8	34.4	31.2
Highland township (Osceola)	1,250	1,229	-1.7	1,329	98.9	0.0	0.4	0.8	0.0	29.3	58.9	11.7	467	88.9	55.7	15.0
Highland Park city & MCD (Wayne)	11,776	10,375	-11.9	10,951	5.8	90.6	0.2	3.2	0.3	24.1	61.0	15.0	4,229	37.1	51.8	11.9
Hill township (Ogemaw)	1,361	1,320	-3.0	1,475	96.7	0.1	0.2	1.4	1.6	15.9	53.9	30.2	709	87.0	49.2	10.6
Hillman village	701	672	-4.1	723	94.7	0.4	0.0	3.7	1.1	14.5	49.5	36.0	290	73.8	56.9	7.6
Hillman township (Montmorency)	2,170	2,064	-4.9	2,352	95.9	0.1	0.0	3.7	0.3	14.6	58.6	26.7	895	83.8	45.9	9.8
Hillsdale city & MCD (Hillsdale)	8,297	8,149	-1.8	8,222	92.2	1.1	0.8	2.7	3.3	21.9	63.6	14.5	2,906	51.1	43.2	20.8
Hillsdale township (Hillsdale)	2,041	2,011	-1.5	1,951	93.3	0.9	1.1	3.1	1.6	20.1	61.0	19.1	775	87.5	32.8	35.1
Hinton township (Mecosta)	1,126	1,132	0.5	1,016	98.1	0.0	0.0	1.3	0.6	15.4	64.3	20.4	395	85.6	58.0	7.1
Holland township (Missaukee)	248	249	0.4	261	95.0	0.0	0.0	3.4	1.5	24.1	59.7	16.1	111	90.1	60.4	7.2
Holland city	33,051	33,644	1.8	33,342	65.3	3.8	4.2	2.2	24.5	24.2	63.0	12.7	11,452	63.9	38.3	31.7
Holland city (Allegan)	7,016	7,073	0.8	7,029	67.2	3.9	3.2	2.7	23.0	26.0	58.0	16.1	2,664	72.0	44.7	24.5
Holland city (Ottawa)	26,035	26,571	2.1	26,313	64.9	3.8	4.4	2.1	24.9	23.8	64.5	11.8	8,788	61.4	36.4	33.9
Holland charter township (Ottawa)	35,636	37,433	5.0	36,541	62.4	1.6	8.8	2.8	24.3	27.7	62.2	10.1	12,940	69.9	42.8	27.3
Holly village	6,086	6,195	1.8	6,142	89.2	2.1	0.2	2.8	5.8	27.6	60.9	11.4	2,233	71.5	43.4	15.2
Holly township (Oakland)	11,362	11,570	1.8	11,474	91.6	2.3	1.0	1.6	3.5	26.2	61.2	12.6	4,168	79.3	35.8	27.2
Holmes township (Menominee)	335	330	-1.5	403	99.0	0.5	0.0	0.0	0.5	13.8	50.3	35.7	190	93.7	58.4	14.7
Holt CDP	23,973	NA	NA	24,267	81.6	6.3	4.1	3.4	4.5	26.4	62.2	11.4	9,612	72.7	24.5	35.0
Holton township (Muskegon)	2,515	2,502	-0.5	2,502	92.5	0.2	0.0	3.0	4.4	30.6	61.7	7.8	813	82.9	51.0	7.5
Home township (Montcalm)	2,542	2,540	-0.1	2,537	84.2	4.7	0.2	4.8	6.0	24.2	59.6	16.1	956	70.8	49.4	19.4
Home township (Newaygo)	232	228	-1.7	219	88.1	0.9	1.4	7.3	2.3	21.0	57.1	21.9	93	87.1	52.7	15.1
Homer village	1,668	1,640	-1.7	1,793	96.0	0.2	0.0	0.3	3.5	34.9	55.0	10.2	634	63.9	62.0	10.7
Homer township (Calhoun)	3,015	2,971	-1.5	2,981	96.3	0.4	0.0	0.6	2.6	30.8	57.6	11.5	1,046	69.5	60.6	10.6
Homer township (Midland)	4,003	3,985	-0.4	4,002	94.4	0.0	0.4	2.9	2.3	22.1	63.4	14.5	1,487	94.5	41.1	21.5
Homestead township (Benzie)	2,357	2,352	-0.2	2,354	95.8	0.4	0.0	2.8	0.9	20.2	60.1	19.7	943	86.5	55.4	9.3
Honor village	328	326	-0.6	291	86.3	0.0	0.0	6.2	7.6	24.4	54.9	20.6	136	73.5	50.7	11.0
Hope township (Barry)	3,239	3,222	-0.5	3,221	100.0	0.0	0.0	0.0	0.0	19.2	58.4	22.4	1,428	86.8	55.3	14.0
Hope township (Midland)	1,361	1,375	1.0	1,439	93.1	1.7	0.0	4.3	1.0	21.5	53.0	25.5	594	91.4	50.3	17.0
Hopkins village	610	609	-0.2	654	94.6	0.2	0.0	3.1	2.1	32.0	57.5	10.6	235	86.8	52.8	8.1
Hopkins township (Allegan)	2,601	2,667	2.5	2,628	95.9	0.3	0.6	2.1	1.1	27.0	57.2	15.7	963	88.1	55.3	15.9
Horton township (Ogemaw)	927	894	-3.6	1,075	96.0	0.0	0.0	3.6	0.4	22.3	56.4	21.2	428	88.8	60.3	11.7
Horton Bay CDP	512	NA	NA	496	94.4	0.0	0.0	4.8	0.8	18.4	59.6	22.0	193	95.3	35.2	35.2
Houghton city & MCD (Houghton)	7,708	7,932	2.9	7,897	82.2	2.1	10.3	3.2	2.1	10.8	79.8	9.5	2,481	39.9	22.2	44.4
Houghton township (Keweenaw)	82	84	2.4	98	81.6	10.2	0.0	0.0	8.2	6.1	71.4	22.4	48	85.4	27.1	41.7
Houghton Lake CDP	3,427	NA	NA	2,926	96.8	0.1	0.0	2.7	0.5	12.1	60.3	27.7	1,538	70.6	51.2	9.9
Howard township (Cass)	6,207	6,150	-0.9	6,178	92.7	2.2	0.3	1.3	3.4	18.7	60.6	20.7	2,526	91.2	46.5	18.8
Howard City village	1,808	1,788	-1.1	1,849	93.6	0.0	0.5	1.7	4.2	32.5	58.6	8.9	669	65.0	64.6	4.9
Howell city & MCD (Livingston)	9,480	9,598	1.2	9,543	90.3	1.0	1.8	3.0	3.8	24.7	61.9	13.3	4,022	53.0	34.4	23.8
Howell township (Livingston)	6,702	6,866	2.4	6,781	95.4	0.1	0.5	2.7	1.4	21.1	64.1	14.6	2,608	87.8	31.9	25.4
Hubbard Lake CDP	1,002	NA	NA	863	99.9	0.0	0.0	0.1	0.0	4.4	34.2	61.3	479	94.6	38.6	23.2
Hubbardston village	395	400	1.3	321	94.7	1.2	0.0	1.2	2.8	25.4	53.9	20.6	110	84.5	70.9	4.5
Hubbell CDP	946	NA	NA	1,068	99.8	0.0	0.2	0.0	0.0	29.6	56.5	13.9	377	82.5	50.4	17.5
Hudson township (Charlevoix)	691	696	0.7	632	98.4	0.3	0.0	1.3	0.0	16.0	66.1	18.0	243	95.9	45.3	17.3
Hudson city & MCD (Lenawee)	2,307	2,259	-2.1	2,431	91.5	0.3	0.0	1.2	7.0	32.0	61.0	7.0	857	63.7	53.0	16.3
Hudson township (Lenawee)	1,497	1,496	-0.1	1,446	95.0	1.0	0.0	2.5	1.5	17.3	53.6	29.1	630	92.1	61.1	8.3
Hudson township (Mackinac)	181	186	2.8	156	72.4	0.0	1.3	26.3	0.0	7.1	60.9	32.1	86	93.0	69.8	5.8
Hudsonville city & MCD (Ottawa)	7,116	7,323	2.9	7,217	89.7	1.1	4.5	3.1	1.7	25.8	61.3	13.0	2,495	74.0	41.0	29.5
Hulbert township (Chippewa)	168	167	-0.6	121	99.2	0.0	0.0	0.8	0.0	11.5	53.7	34.7	56	96.4	55.4	7.1
Humboldt township (Marquette)	464	469	1.1	500	97.0	0.0	0.2	0.8	2.0	23.0	55.6	21.4	185	84.3	57.8	11.4

1 May be of any race.

Table A. All Places — **Population and Housing**

STATE City, town, township, borough, or CDP (county if applicable)	2010 census total population	2014 estimated population	Percent change 2010–2014	ACS total population estimate 2010–2014	White alone, not Hispanic or Latino	Black alone, not Hispanic or Latino	Asian alone, not Hispanic or Latino	All other races or 2 or more races, not Hispanic or Latino	Hispanic or Latino[1]	Under 18 years old	Age 18 to 64 years old	Age 65 years and older	Total occupied housing units	Percent owner occupied	High school diploma or less	Bachelor's degree or more
	1	2	3	4	5	6	7	8	9	10	11	12	13	14	15	16
MICHIGAN—Con.																
Hume township (Huron)....	749	724	-3.3	723	98.1	0.0	0.0	1.9	0.0	15.8	59.0	25.3	324	91.4	48.8	18.8
Huntington Woods city & MCD (Oakland)............	6,238	6,357	1.9	6,310	93.9	2.2	1.6	1.8	0.6	26.5	58.8	14.6	2,409	96.7	4.7	82.2
Huron township (Huron)...	437	420	-3.9	400	93.0	0.0	0.0	1.3	5.8	15.8	43.4	41.0	188	95.2	62.8	11.7
Huron charter township (Wayne)......................	15,879	15,678	-1.3	15,782	90.5	3.7	0.6	3.0	2.2	23.9	64.9	11.3	5,564	87.6	41.8	20.9
Ida township (Monroe)......	4,964	4,873	-1.8	4,920	94.9	0.5	0.0	1.2	3.4	19.2	67.1	13.6	1,881	93.5	37.2	21.1
Imlay township (Lapeer) ...	3,128	3,135	0.2	3,127	73.6	0.7	1.3	1.9	22.5	28.4	60.6	11.2	1,001	88.7	48.2	14.2
Imlay City city & MCD (Lapeer)	3,597	3,573	-0.7	3,588	70.8	0.0	2.3	2.3	24.6	28.3	58.7	13.0	1,371	55.4	53.5	19.3
Independence charter township (Oakland).......	34,683	36,145	4.2	35,332	89.8	2.6	1.9	2.4	3.3	24.9	62.6	12.5	13,210	81.8	24.4	41.4
Indianfields township (Tuscola)...................	2,805	2,575	-8.2	2,694	88.8	3.8	0.2	1.9	5.2	17.1	62.1	20.9	1,075	93.7	51.0	19.4
Indian River CDP.............	1,959	NA	NA	1,977	94.3	0.0	0.0	4.3	1.4	20.5	53.9	25.4	854	72.5	43.8	24.6
Ingallston township (Menominee)................	935	925	-1.1	981	98.6	0.0	0.3	1.1	0.0	14.3	55.9	30.0	477	92.5	37.7	22.6
Ingersoll township (Midland)......................	2,751	2,727	-0.9	2,748	96.9	0.1	0.3	0.8	1.9	19.7	63.4	16.7	1,033	91.0	36.2	26.5
Ingham township (Ingham)	2,452	2,459	0.3	2,441	97.4	0.0	0.0	2.0	0.6	26.6	59.9	13.6	807	93.6	37.4	28.7
Inkster city & MCD (Wayne)......................	25,366	24,786	-2.3	25,056	17.5	76.1	0.9	3.3	2.2	29.2	60.0	11.0	9,466	51.2	47.8	11.0
Inland township (Benzie) ..	2,070	2,061	-0.4	1,856	95.9	0.0	1.5	2.1	0.5	18.6	66.3	15.0	850	86.2	50.0	17.2
Interior township (Ontonagon)................	336	304	-9.5	324	96.9	0.0	0.0	0.3	2.8	15.8	50.8	33.3	164	91.5	51.8	13.4
Interlochen CDP..............	583	NA	NA	424	97.9	0.0	0.0	0.0	2.1	29.5	58.3	12.3	186	65.1	45.2	8.1
Inverness township (Cheboygan)................	2,261	2,216	-2.0	2,445	92.6	1.1	0.1	5.6	0.6	16.2	63.5	20.4	1,038	81.9	44.6	16.3
Inwood township (Schoolcraft)................	733	705	-3.8	694	82.4	0.0	1.4	13.7	2.4	15.3	51.9	32.9	281	94.7	53.4	13.5
Ionia city & MCD (Ionia)....	11,394	11,439	0.4	11,388	71.7	15.7	0.2	4.5	7.8	17.4	74.9	7.9	2,846	56.7	46.9	14.5
Ionia township (Ionia)	3,779	3,786	0.2	3,780	92.0	1.1	0.0	3.2	3.7	26.5	62.0	11.7	1,358	82.5	46.2	13.9
Iosco township (Livingston).................	3,801	3,896	2.5	3,842	96.6	0.4	0.0	0.5	2.5	27.3	62.9	9.7	1,268	95.0	26.7	32.1
Ira township (St. Clair)	5,178	5,013	-3.2	5,072	96.8	0.7	1.0	1.2	0.3	20.7	66.3	13.0	2,072	78.5	39.2	15.6
Iron Mountain city & MCD (Dickinson).................	7,624	7,554	-0.9	7,593	94.9	0.4	0.7	2.6	1.4	24.9	58.1	17.1	3,287	73.9	46.2	23.9
Iron River city & MCD (Iron)..........................	3,029	2,915	-3.8	2,979	95.1	0.3	0.0	2.2	2.3	19.8	50.6	29.7	1,483	77.4	50.1	19.5
Iron River township (Iron) .	1,027	988	-3.8	903	93.0	3.7	0.0	2.4	0.9	9.8	70.5	19.8	442	88.7	58.8	20.8
Ironton CDP....................	140	NA	NA	184	100.0	0.0	0.0	0.0	0.0	20.1	52.8	27.2	74	93.2	21.6	32.4
Ironwood city & MCD (Gogebic)	5,387	5,113	-5.1	5,237	96.0	1.1	0.2	1.6	1.2	18.4	60.3	21.2	2,529	70.0	42.6	14.8
Ironwood charter township (Gogebic)	2,331	2,243	-3.8	2,190	97.5	0.4	0.4	0.8	0.9	13.8	65.2	20.8	994	81.8	36.1	26.7
Irving township (Barry)	3,250	3,268	0.6	3,254	95.3	0.2	0.3	1.9	2.2	30.8	60.4	8.8	1,159	88.3	44.4	22.6
Isabella township (Isabella).....................	2,253	2,230	-1.0	2,093	91.1	1.1	0.0	6.5	1.0	20.6	61.1	18.3	855	84.8	55.8	13.0
Ishpeming city & MCD (Marquette)	6,470	6,532	1.0	6,514	97.7	0.0	0.2	1.2	0.8	23.0	62.7	14.3	2,742	71.0	40.6	20.4
Ishpeming township (Marquette)	3,515	3,553	1.1	3,538	97.5	0.0	0.1	1.4	0.9	18.1	61.0	20.9	1,457	94.8	33.6	31.2
Ithaca city & MCD (Gratiot).....................	2,910	2,849	-2.1	2,875	92.6	4.1	0.0	0.6	2.7	21.5	62.2	16.2	1,267	69.0	45.4	14.1
Jackson city & MCD (Jackson)...................	33,534	33,200	-1.0	33,317	67.3	22.6	0.5	4.0	5.6	29.1	60.4	10.6	12,851	51.2	43.5	15.4
James township (Saginaw)....................	2,023	1,958	-3.2	1,842	94.4	0.0	0.5	0.6	4.5	18.6	63.3	18.2	731	95.2	42.1	18.6
Jamestown charter township (Ottawa)	7,034	7,694	9.4	7,364	96.1	0.3	1.2	0.3	2.1	31.5	59.0	9.6	2,472	92.2	34.4	32.7
Jasper CDP....................	412	NA	NA	403	78.7	0.0	0.0	16.9	4.5	31.0	60.3	8.7	146	72.6	45.2	5.5
Jasper township (Midland)	1,180	1,147	-2.8	1,117	95.4	0.0	0.0	1.5	3.0	23.3	61.3	15.5	445	84.0	55.1	10.1
Jefferson township (Cass)	2,541	2,535	-0.2	2,541	90.9	5.4	0.0	2.1	1.7	19.9	60.0	20.1	961	91.5	44.2	17.1
Jefferson township (Hillsdale)....................	3,063	2,993	-2.3	3,020	96.4	1.5	0.0	0.4	1.7	19.2	65.1	15.9	1,259	82.4	57.1	14.8
Jenison CDP...................	16,538	NA	NA	17,271	96.4	0.6	0.2	1.3	1.5	25.5	56.2	18.2	6,403	84.6	37.6	25.1
Jennings CDP.................	264	NA	NA	202	100.0	0.0	0.0	0.0	0.0	15.9	61.9	22.3	85	68.2	49.4	0.0
Jerome township (Midland)......................	4,796	4,725	-1.5	4,768	94.9	0.0	0.4	2.5	2.2	22.1	61.4	16.6	2,023	82.1	42.5	24.5
Johnstown township (Barry).......................	3,008	3,031	0.8	3,010	95.9	1.1	0.3	2.7	0.0	17.2	64.1	18.9	1,262	84.2	39.0	14.2
Jonesfield township (Saginaw)....................	1,667	1,618	-2.9	1,617	92.2	0.4	0.0	0.6	6.7	24.1	60.3	15.4	617	87.5	46.8	16.9
Jonesville village..............	2,258	2,217	-1.8	2,226	94.3	2.6	0.0	2.1	0.9	25.8	52.5	21.9	911	77.3	47.1	22.1
Jordan township (Antrim)..	992	977	-1.5	999	93.8	0.3	0.1	2.3	3.5	23.4	63.5	13.0	365	86.3	52.9	14.8
Joyfield township (Benzie)	799	797	-0.3	783	95.7	0.0	0.0	4.0	0.4	25.0	56.2	18.8	306	93.5	55.9	15.7
Juniata township (Tuscola)	1,567	1,519	-3.1	1,832	96.3	0.9	0.0	0.2	2.6	22.9	63.1	14.1	683	88.9	51.4	12.7
Kalamazoo city & MCD (Kalamazoo)...............	74,262	75,922	2.2	75,190	65.9	20.4	2.7	4.2	6.8	19.9	70.4	9.5	28,064	45.5	25.5	32.4
Kalamazoo charter township (Kalamazoo) ..	21,918	22,482	2.6	22,216	70.3	18.4	1.1	4.0	6.2	22.6	64.1	13.2	9,530	61.1	29.5	35.1
Kalamo township (Eaton) .	1,842	1,851	0.5	1,884	95.3	0.0	0.0	0.7	4.0	21.2	63.5	15.3	707	95.0	50.4	9.6
Kaleva village..................	470	464	-1.3	469	95.5	0.0	0.0	2.8	1.7	17.7	69.6	12.8	207	76.8	52.9	11.1
Kalkaska village...............	2,020	2,053	1.6	2,176	91.8	2.3	2.0	3.2	0.6	26.1	59.5	14.3	902	47.1	65.7	7.3
Kalkaska township (Kalkaska)...................	4,722	4,795	1.5	4,735	95.1	1.1	0.9	1.7	1.2	24.3	60.6	14.9	1,883	65.8	56.2	14.6
Kasson township (Leelanau)...................	1,609	1,624	0.9	1,515	95.7	0.0	0.8	1.7	1.8	25.7	59.3	15.0	587	83.5	38.2	25.6
Kawkawlin township (Bay)	4,848	4,766	-1.7	4,811	95.7	0.0	0.4	2.0	1.9	18.4	64.0	17.8	1,955	88.0	40.6	18.0
Kearney township (Antrim)	1,765	1,745	-1.1	1,803	91.1	1.2	0.2	6.0	1.5	19.2	54.3	26.5	689	72.6	37.6	25.4
Keego Harbor city & MCD (Oakland)	2,970	3,027	1.9	3,003	74.8	5.9	7.6	1.0	10.8	24.2	67.2	8.9	1,369	59.3	40.0	29.8

1 May be of any race.

Table A. All Places — Population and Housing

STATE City, town, township, borough, or CDP (county if applicable)	2010 census total population	2014 estimated population	Percent change 2010–2014	ACS total population estimate 2010–2014	White alone, not Hispanic or Latino	Black alone, not Hispanic or Latino	Asian alone, not Hispanic or Latino	All other races or 2 or more races, not Hispanic or Latino	Hispanic or Latino[1]	Under 18 years old	Age 18 to 64 years old	Age 65 years and older	Total occupied housing units	Percent owner occupied	High school diploma or less	Bachelor's degree or more
	1	2	3	4	5	6	7	8	9	10	11	12	13	14	15	16
MICHIGAN—Con.																
Keeler township (Van Buren)	2,176	2,177	0.0	2,082	71.7	0.4	1.0	0.2	26.7	22.7	60.4	17.0	740	84.7	52.7	12.7
Keene township (Ionia)	1,831	1,848	0.9	1,893	90.7	1.4	0.2	1.6	6.1	29.7	60.5	9.8	654	87.3	43.7	16.5
Kenockee township (St. Clair)	2,470	2,431	-1.6	2,460	98.4	0.0	0.1	1.4	0.1	22.2	66.4	11.3	942	92.4	45.4	18.0
Kent City village	1,057	1,085	2.6	1,113	76.2	2.6	0.0	0.9	20.3	31.5	61.5	6.9	380	73.7	51.6	10.5
Kentwood city & MCD (Kent)	48,707	50,764	4.2	49,736	62.5	16.5	7.6	4.8	8.6	23.8	64.8	11.4	19,708	59.1	34.6	33.9
Kimball township (St. Clair)	9,358	9,200	-1.7	9,259	91.2	1.0	0.1	4.6	3.0	23.5	61.2	15.4	3,695	84.9	48.4	16.8
Kinde village	448	435	-2.9	488	96.3	0.0	0.4	2.5	0.8	25.5	53.1	21.5	204	85.3	68.1	4.4
Kinderhook township (Branch)	1,497	1,478	-1.3	1,451	97.7	0.0	0.8	1.1	0.5	14.0	60.5	25.5	629	91.4	32.9	22.4
Kingsford city & MCD (Dickinson)	5,133	5,101	-0.6	5,115	95.5	0.7	1.3	1.6	0.8	19.0	60.1	20.8	2,296	76.1	41.7	21.6
Kingsley village	1,480	1,545	4.4	1,568	94.6	0.0	0.0	3.1	2.4	29.4	59.5	11.0	567	74.3	42.2	12.9
Kingston village	440	431	-2.0	432	91.7	0.9	0.0	5.1	2.3	23.4	61.8	14.8	152	69.1	52.0	9.9
Kingston township (Tuscola)	1,574	1,532	-2.7	1,652	93.5	0.0	0.0	3.2	3.3	25.3	62.7	12.1	563	78.2	51.7	9.9
Kinross charter township (Chippewa)	7,714	7,576	-1.8	7,664	52.0	23.6	0.6	19.3	4.5	18.0	76.9	5.2	1,423	56.1	37.3	19.4
K. I. Sawyer CDP	2,624	NA	NA	2,933	82.7	0.9	0.8	10.4	5.1	32.7	61.2	6.3	1,048	21.9	40.9	15.4
Klacking township (Ogemaw)	614	592	-3.6	552	98.2	0.4	0.0	0.5	0.9	17.6	55.8	26.4	244	88.5	60.7	12.3
Kochville township (Saginaw)	5,078	5,007	-1.4	5,051	81.5	8.8	2.8	2.6	4.4	9.7	80.6	9.7	1,366	76.4	34.3	23.4
Koehler township (Cheboygan)	1,283	1,259	-1.9	1,134	92.9	1.0	0.0	5.8	0.4	26.2	55.3	18.4	458	85.8	47.4	13.3
Koylton township (Tuscola)	1,585	1,542	-2.7	1,598	96.5	0.3	0.0	2.1	1.1	27.7	59.5	12.8	582	87.8	51.5	13.4
Krakow township (Presque Isle)	705	684	-3.0	740	99.9	0.0	0.0	0.1	0.0	10.8	49.1	40.1	363	91.7	52.6	12.7
Lafayette township (Gratiot)	591	583	-1.4	547	98.0	0.0	0.0	0.0	2.0	21.3	58.7	19.9	221	90.5	55.2	16.3
LaGrange township (Cass)	3,500	3,429	-2.0	3,473	65.8	16.5	1.5	11.2	5.0	23.2	60.0	16.8	1,265	64.3	46.0	14.9
Laingsburg city & MCD (Shiawassee)	1,283	1,276	-0.5	1,283	96.8	0.0	0.3	1.8	1.1	29.1	61.2	9.7	443	73.4	41.8	12.6
Laird township (Houghton)	555	548	-1.3	487	98.4	0.0	0.6	1.0	0.0	22.7	61.9	15.6	211	87.7	51.2	12.8
Lake township (Benzie)	759	762	0.4	661	95.9	0.0	0.0	1.1	3.0	3.8	41.0	55.4	362	91.4	12.7	64.1
Lake charter township (Berrien)	2,972	2,941	-1.0	2,962	96.7	1.2	0.0	1.9	0.2	19.8	53.3	27.0	1,216	84.9	44.1	27.8
Lake township (Huron)	855	830	-2.9	661	98.8	0.0	0.0	0.0	1.2	11.3	52.3	36.5	336	97.0	49.4	9.8
Lake township (Lake)	862	848	-1.6	675	96.9	0.0	0.0	0.4	2.7	5.4	50.6	44.3	319	96.2	58.6	6.9
Lake township (Menominee)	556	550	-1.1	583	95.4	0.7	0.0	2.1	1.9	16.0	57.1	26.8	280	91.1	57.1	12.1
Lake township (Missaukee)	2,798	2,843	1.6	2,827	96.8	0.0	0.0	1.8	1.4	22.1	55.8	22.3	1,218	83.1	38.7	22.8
Lake township (Roscommon)	1,215	1,188	-2.2	1,048	97.7	0.0	0.6	1.2	0.5	10.8	50.9	38.2	526	90.1	56.1	10.8
Lake Angelus city & MCD (Oakland)	290	297	2.4	264	95.8	1.5	1.9	0.8	0.0	11.8	55.4	33.0	120	95.0	11.7	79.2
Lake Ann village	268	266	-0.7	267	84.3	2.6	0.0	2.6	10.5	18.3	59.4	22.1	119	67.2	37.0	35.3
Lake City city & MCD (Missaukee)	836	850	1.7	1,000	88.2	1.6	0.3	1.7	8.2	23.4	61.4	15.2	367	69.2	49.3	13.9
Lake Fenton CDP	5,559	NA	NA	5,456	95.8	0.0	0.8	1.6	1.8	19.7	64.4	15.9	2,255	81.7	25.0	32.6
Lakefield township (Luce)	1,061	1,023	-3.6	1,108	96.3	0.0	0.0	3.2	0.5	17.3	55.7	27.0	442	85.7	43.4	24.4
Lakefield township (Saginaw)	1,029	1,005	-2.3	1,086	98.5	0.0	0.0	0.0	1.5	20.8	62.7	16.6	410	87.3	51.2	13.4
Lake Isabella village	1,681	1,655	-1.5	1,811	97.8	0.2	0.0	0.5	1.5	21.5	56.5	22.1	750	94.8	40.4	27.2
Lake Leelanau CDP	253	NA	NA	183	56.8	0.0	14.2	20.2	8.7	20.8	51.2	27.9	102	77.5	30.4	21.6
Lake Linden village	1,007	994	-1.3	1,108	94.8	0.0	1.1	2.3	1.8	24.4	53.7	21.8	469	68.7	47.1	25.6
Lake Michigan Beach CDP	1,216	NA	NA	1,153	84.9	0.8	0.0	0.9	13.4	24.1	51.6	24.2	526	75.3	34.2	22.4
Lake Odessa village	2,018	2,029	0.5	1,949	84.2	0.0	0.9	2.6	12.3	20.0	66.5	13.4	800	75.1	54.9	11.5
Lake Orion village	2,973	3,053	2.7	3,036	96.5	0.1	1.4	0.1	2.0	21.2	61.7	17.1	1,343	65.0	25.2	32.8
Lakes of the North CDP	0	NA	NA	824	97.8	0.0	0.0	0.0	2.2	21.1	55.5	23.4	352	89.2	26.1	25.6
Laketon township (Muskegon)	7,563	7,586	0.3	7,557	92.0	1.7	0.2	2.6	3.6	21.3	62.5	16.2	2,886	89.9	25.4	33.3
Laketown township (Allegan)	5,505	5,665	2.9	5,567	93.8	0.2	0.9	0.1	4.9	19.8	59.2	21.1	2,295	85.3	24.8	47.5
Lake Victoria CDP	930	NA	NA	889	92.1	0.0	0.0	3.1	4.7	22.5	63.3	13.8	358	95.5	24.6	34.1
Lakeview village	1,007	1,008	0.1	1,127	96.5	0.0	0.6	1.2	1.7	32.0	50.1	17.9	421	64.6	50.8	16.9
Lakewood Club village	1,291	1,288	-0.2	1,200	92.2	2.5	0.0	2.3	3.0	22.0	68.1	9.8	438	90.9	51.4	7.5
Lambertville CDP	9,953	NA	NA	9,988	94.5	0.2	0.7	0.6	4.0	24.1	61.1	14.7	3,732	86.3	29.2	30.4
Lamotte township (Sanilac)	919	886	-3.6	884	99.1	0.0	0.0	0.7	0.2	23.6	59.5	16.9	332	83.7	63.0	5.7
L'Anse village	2,011	1,952	-2.9	2,077	94.4	1.4	0.4	3.0	0.7	21.6	54.4	24.0	995	73.2	45.4	17.9
L'Anse township (Baraga)	3,843	3,736	-2.8	3,661	90.6	0.9	0.8	7.2	0.5	23.8	53.7	22.5	1,660	80.5	45.5	18.4
Lansing city	114,299	114,620	0.3	114,382	55.3	21.1	4.1	7.0	12.6	23.7	66.2	10.2	48,288	51.6	32.5	26.9
Lansing city (Clinton)	0	0	0.0	6	100.0	0.0	0.0	0.0	0.0	0.0	100.0	0.0	0	0.0	0.0	0.0
Lansing city (Eaton)	4,734	4,750	0.3	4,743	33.9	45.0	0.9	5.6	14.5	26.0	65.4	8.6	2,002	39.9	30.6	16.9
Lansing city (Ingham)	109,565	109,870	0.3	109,633	56.2	20.0	4.2	7.0	12.5	23.5	66.2	10.2	46,286	52.1	32.5	27.4
Lansing charter township (Ingham)	8,126	8,113	-0.2	8,116	62.1	18.1	1.0	4.6	14.0	20.7	69.0	10.2	3,802	47.4	22.2	33.4
Lapeer city & MCD (Lapeer)	8,841	8,762	-0.9	8,801	85.7	7.2	0.8	1.6	4.6	21.5	63.3	15.3	3,504	50.8	44.9	18.4
Lapeer township (Lapeer)	5,056	5,053	-0.1	5,049	95.3	0.0	0.3	1.7	2.7	18.1	63.0	19.0	2,027	89.3	37.2	22.8
Larkin charter township (Midland)	5,136	5,307	3.3	5,225	97.1	1.9	0.5	0.0	0.6	26.5	62.9	10.5	1,836	94.1	23.0	54.4
La Salle township (Monroe)	4,894	4,808	-1.8	4,850	95.1	0.4	1.3	1.2	2.0	20.0	66.4	13.7	1,912	83.5	49.4	18.5

1 May be of any race.

Table A. All Places — **Population and Housing**

STATE City, town, township, borough, or CDP (county if applicable)	Population				Race and Hispanic or Latino origin (percent), 2010–2014					Age (percent), 2010–2014			Households, 2010–2014			
								All other races or 2 or more races, not Hispanic or Latino							Householders by level of education (percent)	
	2010 census total population	2014 estimated population	Percent change 2010–2014	ACS total population estimate 2010–2014	White alone, not Hispanic or Latino	Black alone, not Hispanic or Latino	Asian alone, not Hispanic or Latino	All other races or 2 or more races, not Hispanic or Latino	Hispanic or Latino[1]	Under 18 years old	Age 18 to 64 years old	Age 65 years and older	Total occupied housing units	Percent owner occupied	High school diploma or less	Bachelor's degree or more
	1	2	3	4	5	6	7	8	9	10	11	12	13	14	15	16

MICHIGAN—Con.

STATE City, town, township, borough, or CDP (county if applicable)	1	2	3	4	5	6	7	8	9	10	11	12	13	14	15	16
Lathrup Village city & MCD (Oakland)	4,075	4,147	1.8	4,109	27.4	68.5	0.9	2.9	0.3	20.1	65.4	14.5	1,535	89.3	14.5	57.1
Laurium village	1,977	1,952	-1.3	2,001	96.4	0.0	0.1	1.6	1.8	28.6	57.3	13.9	772	72.5	43.3	24.1
Lawrence village	996	986	-1.0	1,049	73.6	2.3	0.0	6.9	17.3	29.8	59.0	11.1	402	58.7	50.7	13.4
Lawrence township (Van Buren)	3,259	3,231	-0.9	3,240	86.1	1.8	0.0	2.2	9.8	23.6	61.5	14.9	1,273	73.3	39.8	17.8
Lawton village	1,900	1,871	-1.5	1,698	87.2	1.5	0.0	3.0	8.4	24.9	60.3	14.8	630	55.7	49.7	16.7
Leavitt township (Oceana)	891	875	-1.8	778	80.2	1.0	0.0	3.7	15.0	28.1	55.4	16.6	292	82.5	58.9	4.5
Lebanon township (Clinton)	605	614	1.5	637	91.1	0.0	0.0	1.7	7.2	23.7	63.4	13.0	220	82.7	53.6	13.6
Lee township (Allegan)	4,015	4,015	0.0	4,003	66.6	11.7	0.8	0.0	20.9	27.2	63.5	9.2	1,264	70.3	51.8	12.9
Lee township (Calhoun)	1,215	1,203	-1.0	1,088	90.7	0.0	0.5	1.4	7.4	24.7	60.9	14.2	360	85.6	50.8	15.0
Lee township (Midland)	4,315	4,233	-1.9	4,278	94.8	0.4	0.0	1.6	3.2	24.1	62.6	13.3	1,555	88.3	41.7	15.8
Leelanau township (Leelanau)	2,027	2,046	0.9	2,200	92.8	0.0	0.3	2.1	4.8	14.2	47.3	38.5	990	91.4	20.6	54.0
Leighton township (Allegan)	4,934	5,304	7.5	5,078	96.0	0.0	0.8	3.2	0.0	28.5	59.7	11.7	1,787	85.8	40.0	27.1
Leland CDP	377	NA	NA	495	100.0	0.0	0.0	0.0	0.0	14.5	53.2	32.3	238	79.8	16.8	61.3
Leland township (Leelanau)	2,043	2,062	0.9	1,957	88.6	2.5	1.8	2.9	4.2	21.1	52.7	26.3	831	86.5	24.2	45.2
Lennon village	511	502	-1.8	408	90.9	0.5	3.2	3.4	2.0	20.2	63.9	15.9	169	89.9	50.3	10.7
Lenox township (Macomb)	10,470	10,680	2.0	10,568	78.9	13.6	2.3	4.3	0.9	23.8	66.2	9.9	3,272	79.6	47.3	15.6
Leonard village	403	410	1.7	407	94.1	0.0	0.0	0.0	5.9	28.0	61.0	11.1	159	85.5	44.7	21.4
Leoni township (Jackson)	13,807	13,753	-0.4	13,786	93.9	0.1	0.3	2.0	3.7	22.1	62.1	15.8	5,734	75.3	47.9	17.0
Leonidas township (St. Joseph)	1,185	1,178	-0.6	971	96.4	1.2	0.4	1.2	0.7	25.0	56.1	18.9	374	81.8	64.2	10.7
Leroy township (Calhoun)	3,712	3,701	-0.3	3,696	92.9	0.2	4.1	0.4	2.4	21.5	64.8	13.8	1,492	95.6	35.3	18.5
Leroy township (Ingham)	3,530	3,516	-0.4	3,512	92.9	1.3	0.0	5.0	0.8	24.6	65.7	9.9	1,320	77.4	38.3	19.5
Le Roy village	256	253	-1.2	305	93.8	0.0	0.0	4.9	1.3	22.5	65.0	12.5	119	87.4	50.4	13.4
Le Roy township (Osceola)	1,212	1,194	-1.5	1,371	94.3	0.0	0.5	3.5	1.7	29.8	57.8	12.3	453	86.3	51.0	13.2
Leslie city & MCD (Ingham)	1,851	1,857	0.3	1,798	93.9	0.6	0.8	1.8	2.9	28.4	57.3	14.2	618	76.4	45.6	12.5
Leslie township (Ingham)	2,389	2,391	0.1	2,417	93.5	0.7	0.0	0.9	4.9	25.8	60.7	13.6	885	87.0	44.4	17.2
Level Park-Oak Park CDP	3,409	NA	NA	3,438	91.1	3.7	0.6	3.8	0.8	18.9	64.9	16.2	1,457	88.6	50.8	16.0
Levering CDP	215	NA	NA	255	71.8	0.0	3.1	25.1	0.0	18.9	75.3	5.9	98	79.6	74.5	11.2
Lewiston CDP	1,392	NA	NA	1,329	97.0	0.0	0.0	1.4	1.6	23.9	48.8	27.2	591	72.4	43.1	9.3
Lexington village	1,178	1,131	-4.0	1,067	97.2	0.0	0.0	2.1	0.7	15.2	47.2	37.7	578	67.8	41.7	20.9
Lexington township (Sanilac)	3,658	3,529	-3.5	3,596	98.1	0.0	0.0	1.4	0.5	15.0	56.6	28.3	1,658	84.0	57.6	17.6
Liberty township (Jackson)	2,961	2,960	0.0	2,958	98.8	0.4	0.3	0.1	0.4	19.9	61.6	18.6	1,159	88.9	35.8	26.3
Liberty township (Wexford)	861	864	0.3	940	91.7	0.7	0.0	2.1	5.4	24.1	58.0	17.9	340	88.5	55.0	11.8
Lilley township (Newaygo)	797	787	-1.3	757	86.5	4.0	0.0	4.9	4.6	17.3	55.1	27.5	351	86.3	55.3	9.4
Lima township (Washtenaw)	3,307	3,670	11.0	3,540	91.1	0.0	2.5	2.4	4.0	25.4	64.0	10.7	1,314	96.7	22.2	37.1
Limestone township (Alger)	438	429	-2.1	406	94.8	0.0	0.0	5.2	0.0	19.0	60.4	20.7	164	94.5	40.9	17.7
Lincoln village	337	323	-4.2	297	92.9	0.3	0.0	4.0	2.7	24.2	49.6	26.3	160	53.1	53.8	13.8
Lincoln township (Arenac)	942	909	-3.5	1,032	95.6	0.3	0.6	1.6	1.9	24.1	58.8	17.4	414	81.9	62.8	9.9
Lincoln charter township (Berrien)	14,691	14,559	-0.9	14,620	90.7	1.5	3.4	2.1	2.4	22.8	59.7	17.6	5,948	79.2	27.8	41.6
Lincoln township (Clare)	1,824	1,797	-1.5	1,845	91.3	1.2	0.3	4.8	2.3	17.9	61.4	20.8	756	83.2	59.4	12.2
Lincoln township (Huron)	807	783	-3.0	797	98.4	0.0	0.3	1.0	0.4	23.2	58.2	18.7	345	89.0	54.2	9.3
Lincoln township (Isabella)	2,115	2,097	-0.9	1,967	90.6	0.1	0.6	5.4	3.4	23.1	63.2	13.6	742	90.3	35.7	29.4
Lincoln township (Midland)	2,474	2,457	-0.7	2,401	97.3	0.0	0.2	1.0	1.5	18.0	58.5	23.4	1,050	89.6	39.6	22.8
Lincoln township (Newaygo)	1,275	1,252	-1.8	1,379	89.3	3.2	0.0	5.8	1.7	17.4	66.2	16.5	547	87.6	45.2	9.5
Lincoln township (Osceola)	1,500	1,474	-1.7	1,445	97.4	0.6	0.1	1.5	0.4	23.8	59.3	16.9	591	82.2	58.2	12.0
Lincoln Park city & MCD (Wayne)	38,144	37,231	-2.4	37,648	75.3	5.4	0.1	2.5	16.6	24.3	64.3	11.5	14,659	71.1	56.7	8.8
Linden city & MCD (Genesee)	3,991	3,860	-3.3	3,919	99.0	0.4	0.0	0.3	0.4	26.2	53.7	20.1	1,482	82.7	33.6	31.2
Litchfield city & MCD (Hillsdale)	1,369	1,345	-1.8	1,257	94.9	0.3	0.0	0.5	4.3	22.3	63.6	14.0	511	65.2	51.9	11.0
Litchfield township (Hillsdale)	1,003	980	-2.3	1,021	98.0	0.4	0.0	0.7	0.9	24.9	58.6	16.5	375	86.4	56.8	11.7
Littlefield township (Emmet)	2,978	3,018	1.3	2,996	94.3	0.0	0.0	5.5	0.2	25.6	60.1	14.3	1,144	89.8	42.4	23.3
Little Traverse township (Emmet)	2,380	2,423	1.8	2,323	94.2	0.6	0.3	4.0	1.0	20.6	62.2	17.0	1,013	81.8	25.4	34.6
Livingston township (Otsego)	2,525	2,532	0.3	2,525	96.9	0.4	0.0	1.2	1.1	17.9	66.5	15.4	1,019	83.5	36.9	28.8
Livonia city & MCD (Wayne)	96,942	94,958	-2.0	95,888	90.0	3.1	2.9	1.6	2.4	20.0	61.9	17.9	37,262	84.8	26.7	38.6
Locke township (Ingham)	1,791	1,807	0.9	1,707	90.0	0.3	0.1	0.6	9.0	21.3	64.5	14.4	569	89.5	41.7	23.4
Lockport township (St. Joseph)	3,787	3,773	-0.4	3,786	83.3	7.7	1.7	3.0	4.3	25.8	55.3	18.7	1,425	88.4	47.8	26.5
Lodi township (Washtenaw)	6,058	6,377	5.3	6,241	89.3	0.9	4.3	3.7	1.8	24.6	59.7	15.5	2,247	96.0	12.1	66.0
Logan township (Mason)	312	313	0.3	324	92.6	0.0	0.0	1.9	5.6	8.1	56.8	35.2	178	81.5	49.4	15.2
Logan township (Ogemaw)	551	533	-3.3	570	99.8	0.2	0.0	0.0	0.0	17.1	59.1	23.9	236	91.1	58.5	5.1
London township (Monroe)	3,039	2,974	-2.1	3,008	89.1	6.8	0.5	2.4	1.3	23.5	65.4	11.0	1,078	89.9	53.7	13.0
Long Lake township (Grand Traverse)	8,662	9,145	5.6	8,909	96.9	0.1	0.0	1.4	1.7	23.3	62.5	14.2	3,442	88.2	31.6	30.5
Long Rapids township (Alpena)	1,010	990	-2.0	1,017	97.8	0.0	0.6	0.9	0.7	19.1	61.6	19.1	436	90.4	50.2	10.6
Loomis CDP	213	NA	NA	182	100.0	0.0	0.0	0.0	0.0	20.8	64.7	14.3	72	91.7	51.4	5.6
Lost Lake Woods CDP	312	NA	NA	352	100.0	0.0	0.0	0.0	0.0	9.9	38.1	52.0	176	97.7	33.5	29.0

1   May be of any race.

Table A. All Places — **Population and Housing**

STATE City, town, township, borough, or CDP (county if applicable)	Population				Race and Hispanic or Latino origin (percent), 2010–2014					Age (percent), 2010–2014			Households, 2010–2014		Householders by level of education (percent)	
	2010 census total population	2014 estimated population	Percent change 2010–2014	ACS total population estimate 2010–2014	White alone, not Hispanic or Latino	Black alone, not Hispanic or Latino	Asian alone, not Hispanic or Latino	All other races or 2 or more races, not Hispanic or Latino	Hispanic or Latino[1]	Under 18 years old	Age 18 to 64 years old	Age 65 years and older	Total occupied housing units	Percent owner occupied	High school diploma or less	Bachelor's degree or more
	1	2	3	4	5	6	7	8	9	10	11	12	13	14	15	16
MICHIGAN—Con.																
Loud township (Montmorency)	293	277	-5.5	236	94.5	0.0	0.0	4.2	1.3	13.1	53.5	33.5	113	97.3	54.0	9.7
Lovells township (Crawford)	626	610	-2.6	530	98.5	0.0	0.0	0.8	0.8	3.3	54.2	42.6	299	93.0	48.5	22.4
Lowell city & MCD (Kent)	3,783	3,890	2.8	3,838	96.0	0.4	0.0	1.8	1.8	26.1	56.3	17.6	1,468	63.9	39.2	20.0
Lowell charter township (Kent)	5,949	6,318	6.2	6,126	93.8	1.6	0.0	1.4	3.2	26.6	64.4	8.9	2,142	90.4	34.5	33.9
Ludington city & MCD (Mason)	8,076	8,078	0.0	8,061	89.2	1.0	0.8	2.7	6.3	20.9	58.5	20.5	3,598	57.5	41.2	21.3
Luna Pier city & MCD (Monroe)	1,436	1,395	-2.9	1,397	94.5	1.9	0.9	1.1	1.6	24.9	62.5	12.5	621	69.1	34.3	17.6
Lupton CDP	348	NA	NA	263	96.6	0.0	0.0	3.4	0.0	13.3	62.2	24.3	124	90.3	54.8	14.5
Luther village	318	313	-1.6	435	92.0	0.9	0.2	1.6	5.3	29.4	55.8	14.5	126	73.0	47.6	4.8
Lyndon township (Washtenaw)	2,720	2,767	1.7	2,747	84.9	4.2	1.4	4.8	4.7	18.6	66.2	15.1	1,008	94.2	22.4	45.5
Lynn township (St. Clair)	1,229	1,217	-1.0	1,289	93.3	0.0	0.0	1.1	5.6	27.1	60.5	12.4	450	88.9	47.3	17.1
Lyon charter township (Oakland)	14,545	17,215	18.4	15,736	92.2	1.2	1.1	2.5	3.1	28.3	61.6	10.1	5,578	86.4	31.3	39.9
Lyon township (Roscommon)	1,370	1,348	-1.6	1,185	97.9	0.3	0.0	1.7	0.2	13.0	56.0	31.1	605	88.9	33.7	20.2
Lyons village	789	793	0.5	943	91.9	2.5	1.0	0.1	4.5	22.1	65.6	12.3	321	86.6	50.2	6.5
Lyons township (Ionia)	3,465	3,487	0.6	3,476	97.3	0.5	0.3	0.0	2.0	25.1	61.3	13.5	1,307	84.4	49.8	11.9
McBain city & MCD (Missaukee)	656	666	1.5	694	94.2	0.3	0.0	0.6	4.9	23.6	50.9	25.5	275	58.5	49.8	16.0
McBride village	205	205	0.0	131	98.5	0.0	0.0	1.5	0.0	22.2	48.8	29.0	62	85.5	53.2	12.9
Mackinac Island city & MCD (Mackinac)	492	489	-0.6	600	53.5	14.5	0.8	21.2	10.0	15.7	69.1	15.3	245	42.9	32.7	36.3
Mackinaw township (Cheboygan)	539	530	-1.7	417	87.5	7.0	0.0	4.1	1.4	14.9	57.5	27.6	206	69.4	43.7	28.6
Mackinaw City village	806	808	0.2	719	87.8	4.7	0.0	5.1	2.4	14.0	67.4	18.5	338	65.7	30.8	27.5
McKinley township (Emmet)	1,297	1,311	1.1	1,251	80.7	0.0	0.6	15.8	2.9	22.5	68.3	9.1	518	69.5	56.8	8.9
McKinley township (Huron)	445	431	-3.1	479	99.4	0.0	0.0	0.0	0.6	15.6	54.5	29.9	213	79.8	58.7	6.1
McMillan township (Luce)	2,692	2,589	-3.8	2,581	82.3	0.3	0.5	16.0	0.9	20.1	58.4	21.4	1,177	66.9	59.3	11.0
McMillan township (Ontonagon)	478	437	-8.6	426	100.0	0.0	0.0	0.0	0.0	14.3	58.8	27.0	211	80.6	44.5	19.4
Macomb township (Macomb)	79,580	85,459	7.4	82,204	88.9	3.4	3.6	1.9	2.1	27.7	61.9	10.3	27,667	92.9	29.2	37.5
Macon township (Lenawee)	1,482	1,469	-0.9	1,387	91.1	3.8	0.0	3.5	1.7	24.8	62.3	13.0	518	88.2	45.4	27.2
Madison charter township (Lenawee)	8,621	8,499	-1.4	8,520	74.1	10.8	0.0	5.4	9.7	19.4	65.7	14.9	2,450	86.9	50.0	17.6
Madison Heights city & MCD (Oakland)	29,694	30,267	1.9	30,028	83.7	7.2	4.0	4.0	1.0	19.3	66.7	13.9	12,945	62.4	41.5	21.9
Mancelona village	1,390	1,372	-1.3	1,661	95.5	1.0	1.1	2.1	0.4	31.2	57.3	11.4	584	69.9	50.3	6.5
Mancelona township (Antrim)	4,400	4,322	-1.8	4,360	96.3	0.4	0.4	2.1	0.9	27.2	58.6	14.2	1,567	81.4	53.0	12.9
Manchester village	2,091	2,163	3.4	2,374	95.4	0.3	0.0	3.6	0.7	28.1	60.0	12.0	900	75.2	30.6	28.8
Manchester township (Washtenaw)	4,569	4,744	3.8	4,664	95.7	0.5	0.6	1.8	1.3	24.9	61.6	13.4	1,769	85.1	28.5	32.1
Manistee city & MCD (Manistee)	6,226	6,098	-2.1	6,160	89.9	0.6	0.3	5.3	3.9	22.3	57.8	20.0	2,861	59.0	41.2	28.3
Manistee township (Manistee)	4,084	4,108	0.6	4,072	73.4	13.7	0.4	9.6	2.9	11.0	67.4	21.6	1,309	88.2	43.5	21.2
Manistee Lake CDP	456	NA	NA	367	98.1	0.0	0.0	1.9	0.0	8.4	60.9	30.5	188	86.7	52.7	11.2
Manistique city & MCD (Schoolcraft)	3,097	2,983	-3.7	3,043	84.3	0.6	2.8	11.6	0.7	22.3	56.7	20.8	1,297	67.2	61.1	15.0
Manistique township (Schoolcraft)	1,095	1,054	-3.7	1,041	79.7	0.0	0.0	19.6	0.7	19.6	61.2	19.1	397	86.6	58.7	16.9
Manitou Beach-Devils Lake CDP	2,019	NA	NA	2,129	98.5	0.0	0.0	0.6	0.8	9.7	67.4	22.9	1,059	91.9	37.1	26.2
Manlius township (Allegan)	3,017	3,081	2.1	3,031	90.6	1.0	1.1	1.0	6.4	27.8	58.5	13.6	1,134	89.3	47.2	23.5
Mansfield township (Iron)	241	231	-4.1	224	98.2	0.0	0.0	0.0	1.8	8.0	54.8	37.1	99	97.0	50.5	17.2
Manton city & MCD (Wexford)	1,287	1,340	4.1	1,315	91.0	0.9	0.0	2.0	6.1	28.8	57.7	13.6	489	60.5	53.4	5.3
Maple City CDP	207	NA	NA	250	97.2	0.0	0.0	2.8	0.0	40.0	49.2	10.8	83	66.3	47.0	9.6
Maple Forest township (Crawford)	653	632	-3.2	655	92.4	0.0	0.0	7.6	0.0	21.1	64.0	14.8	255	91.0	37.3	12.9
Maple Grove township (Barry)	1,593	1,597	0.3	1,411	96.0	1.1	0.3	0.9	1.8	20.8	64.3	14.9	514	85.0	54.7	13.0
Maple Grove CDP	132	NA	NA	76	100.0	0.0	0.0	0.0	0.0	0.0	46.1	53.9	58	100.0	0.0	100.0
Maple Grove township (Manistee)	1,316	1,294	-1.7	1,223	92.6	3.4	0.0	2.5	1.6	15.7	67.1	17.3	544	84.2	57.7	11.6
Maple Grove township (Saginaw)	2,668	2,596	-2.7	2,625	99.0	0.0	0.0	0.0	1.0	27.6	58.6	13.9	931	92.4	58.8	13.2
Maple Rapids village	672	683	1.6	644	92.4	0.0	0.0	4.3	3.3	20.0	63.7	16.3	255	76.5	55.7	11.4
Maple Ridge township (Alpena)	1,690	1,650	-2.4	1,663	96.3	0.2	0.0	2.0	1.5	19.7	64.4	16.0	706	93.6	38.2	17.7
Maple Ridge township (Delta)	766	756	-1.3	794	92.8	0.0	0.0	5.5	1.6	22.2	61.9	16.0	335	92.5	57.3	13.1
Maple River township (Emmet)	1,348	1,365	1.3	1,405	93.2	0.3	0.3	3.5	2.8	26.8	63.0	10.3	502	81.5	37.6	20.9
Maple Valley township (Montcalm)	1,944	1,938	-0.3	2,028	94.7	0.8	0.0	2.2	2.3	22.8	59.7	17.5	752	79.7	54.3	8.5
Maple Valley township (Sanilac)	1,221	1,178	-3.5	1,354	97.3	0.0	0.0	1.2	1.5	35.6	52.7	11.7	393	87.5	59.5	9.7
Marathon township (Lapeer)	4,568	4,540	-0.6	4,553	92.8	0.1	0.0	3.4	3.8	22.6	65.0	12.6	1,648	86.8	53.9	14.3
Marcellus village	1,198	1,163	-2.9	1,024	94.9	3.8	0.0	0.6	0.7	28.3	59.1	12.7	387	79.3	53.5	15.5
Marcellus township (Cass)	2,539	2,489	-2.0	2,305	95.4	2.1	0.0	0.7	1.8	21.0	65.6	13.5	874	84.4	48.7	15.8

1 May be of any race.

Table A. All Places — **Population and Housing**

STATE City, town, township, borough, or CDP (county if applicable)	Population				Race and Hispanic or Latino origin (percent), 2010–2014					Age (percent), 2010–2014			Households, 2010–2014			
	2010 census total population	2014 estimated population	Percent change 2010–2014	ACS total population estimate 2010–2014	White alone, not Hispanic or Latino	Black alone, not Hispanic or Latino	Asian alone, not Hispanic or Latino	All other races or 2 or more races, not Hispanic or Latino	Hispanic or Latino[1]	Under 18 years old	Age 18 to 64 years old	Age 65 years and older	Total occupied housing units	Percent owner occupied	High school diploma or less	Bachelor's degree or more
	1	2	3	4	5	6	7	8	9	10	11	12	13	14	15	16
MICHIGAN—Con.																
Marengo township (Calhoun)	2,213	2,204	-0.4	2,293	95.5	0.6	0.0	1.3	2.7	23.7	56.7	19.5	840	83.7	42.4	22.0
Marenisco CDP	254	NA	NA	231	97.0	0.0	0.0	1.7	1.3	14.7	46.4	39.0	119	86.6	39.5	25.2
Marenisco township (Gogebic)	1,727	1,704	-1.3	1,731	59.8	33.7	0.0	3.5	2.9	2.2	86.8	11.0	288	94.1	41.7	25.0
Marilla township (Manistee)	393	387	-1.5	336	98.2	0.0	0.3	0.9	0.6	13.7	63.9	22.6	148	89.9	46.6	11.5
Marine City city & MCD (St. Clair)	4,248	4,165	-2.0	4,193	96.0	0.5	0.0	2.8	0.7	21.4	63.3	15.3	1,828	72.9	46.7	13.6
Marion township (Charlevoix)	1,714	1,738	1.4	1,551	97.2	0.1	1.5	0.6	0.6	21.6	65.2	13.3	626	89.9	31.6	32.1
Marion township (Livingston)	9,996	10,246	2.5	10,140	95.7	0.3	0.2	1.0	2.8	26.2	61.1	12.8	3,443	93.4	26.4	31.8
Marion village	872	855	-1.9	793	94.3	0.0	1.4	0.6	3.7	25.1	56.6	18.2	302	69.2	51.7	11.3
Marion township (Osceola)	1,692	1,659	-2.0	1,603	94.2	0.0	0.7	2.2	2.9	23.8	59.5	16.8	610	78.7	50.8	12.3
Marion township (Saginaw)	923	901	-2.4	906	95.3	0.1	0.0	0.2	4.4	28.5	60.5	11.0	338	76.0	63.6	7.4
Marion township (Sanilac)	1,659	1,601	-3.5	1,624	95.1	0.4	0.0	1.4	3.1	21.5	59.9	18.6	624	75.6	64.3	10.3
Markey township (Roscommon)	2,360	2,301	-2.5	2,648	95.8	0.5	0.0	0.8	2.9	15.3	54.3	30.4	1,357	79.0	48.4	9.9
Marlette city & MCD (Sanilac)	1,875	1,807	-3.6	1,646	94.6	0.1	0.0	0.8	4.5	25.2	59.1	15.7	698	59.2	50.4	11.5
Marlette township (Sanilac)	1,763	1,703	-3.4	1,583	95.6	2.1	0.0	0.2	2.1	21.2	56.7	21.9	567	86.8	63.1	9.7
Marquette township (Mackinac)	603	609	1.0	646	86.4	0.0	0.8	12.8	0.0	12.2	70.0	17.8	295	94.9	37.6	12.9
Marquette city & MCD (Marquette)	21,367	21,441	0.3	21,430	88.9	4.5	0.9	4.5	1.2	12.4	74.8	12.8	7,896	48.5	23.4	37.5
Marquette charter township (Marquette)	3,893	3,955	1.6	3,933	89.9	0.9	2.5	5.1	1.6	14.8	66.4	18.8	1,684	63.1	27.8	33.3
Marshall city & MCD (Calhoun)	7,086	7,035	-0.7	7,054	88.1	1.7	0.4	3.0	6.8	19.1	61.4	19.5	3,027	66.8	33.1	28.4
Marshall township (Calhoun)	3,117	3,124	0.2	3,115	91.4	0.1	0.0	0.4	8.2	22.2	62.5	15.3	1,175	86.8	27.8	39.2
Martin village	410	416	1.5	418	86.6	0.0	0.0	8.4	5.0	31.6	55.6	12.9	152	56.6	55.3	17.1
Martin township (Allegan)	2,629	2,666	1.4	2,649	80.0	0.7	0.3	3.0	16.0	25.9	61.3	12.8	911	80.5	56.9	13.4
Martiny township (Mecosta)	1,625	1,630	0.3	1,564	94.0	1.8	0.9	3.3	0.0	16.6	60.9	22.6	677	87.3	49.9	16.1
Marysville city & MCD (St. Clair)	9,959	9,793	-1.7	9,842	96.8	0.2	1.2	0.5	1.3	22.2	59.3	18.5	4,227	81.4	38.8	26.7
Mason township (Arenac)	851	821	-3.5	910	90.0	0.0	0.0	2.2	7.8	24.0	60.4	15.6	340	87.4	68.2	5.0
Mason township (Cass)	2,945	2,905	-1.4	2,931	97.1	0.2	1.3	1.1	0.3	28.4	60.6	10.8	1,013	81.2	48.2	13.3
Mason city & MCD (Ingham)	8,252	8,319	0.8	8,266	88.8	3.0	0.8	2.2	5.2	23.8	63.2	13.0	3,116	58.2	30.3	29.7
Masonville township (Delta)	1,734	1,715	-1.1	1,884	90.7	0.0	1.0	7.1	1.3	24.4	54.9	20.8	727	79.9	46.7	22.0
Mastodon township (Iron)	656	630	-4.0	491	98.2	0.0	0.0	0.4	1.4	8.2	55.8	36.0	257	95.7	46.7	24.1
Matchwood township (Ontonagon)	94	86	-8.5	67	94.0	1.5	0.0	0.0	4.5	1.5	59.8	38.8	39	87.2	66.7	12.8
Mathias township (Alger)	554	542	-2.2	461	96.7	0.0	0.0	3.0	0.2	15.4	56.0	28.6	217	92.6	57.6	13.4
Mattawan village	1,997	1,955	-2.1	2,075	91.1	1.1	1.3	3.0	3.5	27.8	62.2	10.0	822	79.6	41.6	17.4
Matteson township (Branch)	1,218	1,205	-1.1	1,119	99.0	0.0	0.0	0.3	0.7	24.0	58.0	17.9	460	81.7	52.0	15.0
Maybee village	563	550	-2.3	540	97.0	0.0	0.0	0.2	2.8	23.0	66.4	10.7	203	79.8	56.7	17.2
Mayfield township (Grand Traverse)	1,550	1,626	4.9	1,518	93.6	0.1	0.0	3.9	2.4	34.4	52.7	12.8	493	79.3	48.7	14.0
Mayfield township (Lapeer)	7,955	7,905	-0.6	7,921	96.5	0.3	0.4	1.2	1.6	23.0	60.0	17.1	3,020	87.3	40.4	15.2
Mayville village	950	925	-2.6	926	95.8	2.3	0.0	1.5	0.4	21.1	58.5	20.5	355	57.5	55.5	14.1
Meade township (Huron)	720	696	-3.3	791	98.4	0.0	0.0	1.6	0.0	17.6	65.3	17.2	322	87.6	60.6	12.7
Meade township (Mason)	181	182	0.6	176	89.2	0.0	0.0	8.0	2.8	12.5	65.4	22.2	90	96.7	48.9	20.0
Mecosta village	457	458	0.2	563	83.3	6.0	0.0	7.3	3.4	27.1	61.6	11.4	173	68.2	63.0	2.9
Mecosta township (Mecosta)	2,615	2,638	0.9	2,638	97.2	0.0	0.3	2.4	0.2	24.7	61.0	14.1	1,032	77.9	50.0	20.1
Medina township (Lenawee)	1,090	1,089	-0.1	1,002	97.9	0.6	0.0	0.0	1.5	26.2	55.6	18.4	386	87.3	62.7	9.3
Mellen township (Menominee)	1,150	1,136	-1.2	1,091	97.6	0.2	0.0	1.5	0.7	15.9	59.9	24.1	493	89.0	60.4	7.1
Melrose township (Charlevoix)	1,399	1,408	0.6	1,439	95.3	0.1	0.5	2.7	1.5	22.6	60.6	16.7	510	82.5	32.7	22.7
Melvin village	180	175	-2.8	196	90.8	0.0	0.0	6.6	2.6	25.5	63.9	10.7	70	75.7	64.3	12.9
Melvindale city & MCD (Wayne)	10,715	10,441	-2.6	10,584	67.7	13.0	1.7	5.0	12.6	27.0	61.1	12.1	4,204	59.6	53.2	12.6
Memphis city	1,183	1,184	0.1	1,200	93.1	0.3	0.0	4.5	2.1	28.2	60.7	11.2	438	71.0	42.9	15.1
Memphis city (Macomb)	823	830	0.9	792	93.7	0.0	0.0	3.9	2.4	25.3	63.6	11.1	292	70.2	46.6	16.1
Memphis city (St. Clair)	360	354	-1.7	408	91.9	1.0	0.0	5.6	1.5	33.8	55.0	11.3	146	72.6	35.6	13.0
Mendon village	870	860	-1.1	881	94.2	0.6	0.6	3.4	1.2	34.4	56.2	9.3	290	81.7	40.3	17.2
Mendon township (St. Joseph)	2,719	2,688	-1.1	2,705	93.3	0.8	0.4	2.1	3.4	25.2	53.4	21.3	1,023	85.8	53.7	14.8
Menominee city & MCD (Menominee)	8,599	8,458	-1.6	8,516	95.2	0.3	0.1	3.0	1.4	22.3	59.1	18.7	4,007	69.0	46.9	16.1
Menominee township (Menominee)	3,488	3,449	-1.1	3,459	96.1	0.0	0.7	2.4	0.9	16.1	64.3	19.8	1,603	96.2	47.7	22.6
Mentor township (Cheboygan)	818	804	-1.7	829	92.8	1.6	0.5	5.2	0.0	16.3	68.0	15.7	358	91.9	49.7	18.4
Mentor township (Oscoda)	1,143	1,109	-3.0	1,114	97.6	0.2	0.0	1.2	1.1	22.4	55.5	22.3	505	76.8	46.3	6.5
Meridian charter township (Ingham)	39,688	41,776	5.3	40,635	79.3	3.6	9.8	3.7	3.6	19.6	65.2	15.2	17,605	60.6	10.7	64.2
Merrill township (Newaygo)	667	657	-1.5	589	80.0	18.7	0.0	0.7	0.7	17.3	59.6	23.1	255	77.6	55.3	1.6
Merrill village	778	755	-3.0	723	90.9	0.6	0.0	0.3	8.3	27.9	57.4	14.7	259	76.1	45.2	18.5

1 May be of any race.

Table A. All Places — **Population and Housing**

STATE City, town, township, borough, or CDP (county if applicable)	Population				Race and Hispanic or Latino origin (percent), 2010–2014					Age (percent), 2010–2014			Households, 2010–2014			
	2010 census total population	2014 estimated population	Percent change 2010–2014	ACS total population estimate 2010–2014	White alone, not Hispanic or Latino	Black alone, not Hispanic or Latino	Asian alone, not Hispanic or Latino	All other races or 2 or more races, not Hispanic or Latino	Hispanic or Latino[1]	Under 18 years old	Age 18 to 64 years old	Age 65 years and older	Total occupied housing units	Percent owner occupied	High school diploma or less	Bachelor's degree or more
	1	2	3	4	5	6	7	8	9	10	11	12	13	14	15	16

MICHIGAN—Con.

STATE City, town, township, borough, or CDP (county if applicable)	1	2	3	4	5	6	7	8	9	10	11	12	13	14	15	16
Merritt township (Bay)	1,441	1,420	-1.5	1,269	97.2	0.2	0.2	0.7	1.8	21.6	58.4	20.1	527	91.3	44.6	17.1
Mesick village	394	397	0.8	379	97.9	0.0	0.0	0.5	1.6	25.8	59.6	14.5	141	73.8	60.3	12.1
Metamora village	565	566	0.2	603	94.7	0.0	0.0	3.0	2.3	37.5	54.4	8.0	200	78.5	32.0	32.5
Metamora township (Lapeer)	4,249	4,234	-0.4	4,233	96.2	0.0	0.0	2.3	1.4	24.2	59.9	15.9	1,558	83.7	28.0	31.1
Metz township (Presque Isle)	302	294	-2.6	227	93.4	0.0	0.4	1.3	4.8	14.6	57.3	28.2	118	88.1	69.5	8.5
Meyer township (Menominee)	1,001	990	-1.1	968	98.2	0.0	0.0	1.8	0.0	17.1	62.2	20.8	426	89.4	64.1	7.0
Michiana village	182	183	0.5	190	96.8	0.0	3.2	0.0	0.0	5.4	47.3	47.4	111	98.2	7.2	83.8
Michigamme CDP	271	NA	NA	262	97.3	0.0	0.0	0.0	2.7	12.5	53.5	34.0	121	95.9	34.7	32.2
Michigamme township (Marquette)	349	353	1.1	301	95.7	0.0	0.0	0.0	4.3	11.0	54.2	34.9	142	96.5	35.9	34.5
Michigan Center CDP	4,672	NA	NA	4,586	95.9	0.2	0.0	2.0	2.0	24.0	60.8	15.2	1,802	71.0	54.1	20.6
Middle Branch township (Osceola)	843	831	-1.4	834	98.9	0.0	0.0	1.1	0.0	22.1	56.9	21.1	315	87.9	61.6	6.3
Middlebury township (Shiawassee)	1,510	1,476	-2.3	1,617	93.9	0.0	0.0	1.2	4.9	20.3	66.5	13.2	606	88.0	43.9	9.4
Middletown CDP	897	NA	NA	742	98.0	0.0	0.0	0.0	2.0	10.9	68.8	20.2	358	63.4	48.6	10.3
Middleville village	3,319	3,313	-0.2	3,307	96.1	1.5	0.0	1.4	1.1	32.4	53.1	14.4	1,249	67.1	53.1	15.3
Midland city	41,869	41,957	0.2	42,067	89.1	2.0	4.3	2.2	2.4	22.9	61.4	15.6	17,603	63.4	24.9	42.9
Midland city (Bay)	157	153	-2.5	283	100.0	0.0	0.0	0.0	0.0	22.6	68.2	9.2	102	100.0	41.2	34.3
Midland city (Midland)	41,712	41,804	0.2	41,784	89.1	2.0	4.3	2.2	2.4	22.9	61.5	15.6	17,501	63.2	24.8	43.0
Midland charter township (Midland)	2,287	2,258	-1.3	2,208	94.4	0.8	0.0	2.9	1.9	24.8	61.9	13.2	792	89.9	36.2	24.1
Mikado township (Alcona)	947	902	-4.8	1,129	96.7	0.0	0.0	1.4	1.9	20.1	62.7	17.3	444	86.5	43.2	7.7
Milan township (Monroe)	1,601	1,564	-2.3	1,516	97.3	0.1	0.0	0.7	1.9	17.0	68.3	14.8	592	92.1	42.7	19.8
Milan city	5,836	5,950	2.0	5,724	91.1	0.5	1.9	2.6	3.9	25.6	61.8	12.8	2,270	70.0	30.7	29.3
Milan city (Monroe)	2,066	2,046	-1.0	1,891	90.3	1.5	1.9	1.3	5.0	24.0	60.5	15.4	785	58.0	45.6	22.5
Milan city (Washtenaw)	3,770	3,904	3.6	3,833	91.5	0.0	1.9	3.2	3.4	26.3	62.3	11.4	1,485	76.4	22.8	32.9
Milford village	6,175	6,461	4.6	6,325	95.5	0.5	0.0	1.8	2.2	21.8	64.0	14.2	2,602	70.0	26.5	40.9
Milford charter township (Oakland)	15,736	16,486	4.8	16,109	94.4	0.9	0.8	1.4	2.5	22.2	64.3	13.5	6,119	81.1	23.9	44.3
Millbrook township (Mecosta)	1,113	1,117	0.4	975	94.1	0.5	0.0	0.7	4.7	21.6	58.2	20.4	369	87.5	60.4	11.9
Millen township (Alcona)	404	384	-5.0	304	100.0	0.0	0.0	0.0	0.0	7.9	57.9	34.2	160	88.8	74.4	8.8
Millersburg village	206	201	-2.4	199	93.5	0.0	0.5	6.0	0.0	19.5	51.6	28.6	95	77.9	61.1	26.3
Millington village	1,072	1,043	-2.7	934	96.4	1.1	0.4	2.1	0.0	25.3	58.7	16.2	402	60.4	59.7	8.0
Millington township (Tuscola)	4,354	4,244	-2.5	4,286	96.9	0.3	0.1	1.7	1.0	27.7	54.8	17.5	1,647	86.2	50.7	13.2
Mills township (Midland)	1,939	1,912	-1.4	1,823	92.7	4.3	0.4	0.9	1.8	21.5	64.4	14.0	688	93.0	53.3	15.8
Mills township (Ogemaw)	4,291	4,155	-3.2	4,225	93.1	0.5	0.9	4.1	1.3	19.7	59.4	21.0	1,934	80.9	69.5	5.8
Milton township (Antrim)	2,204	2,180	-1.1	2,085	90.3	1.0	0.0	5.4	3.3	19.6	51.5	28.9	855	93.7	24.9	37.7
Milton township (Cass)	3,878	3,838	-1.0	3,859	90.5	2.1	1.8	1.6	4.1	19.0	57.3	23.6	1,330	95.7	44.2	27.1
Minden township (Sanilac)	545	529	-2.9	560	92.1	0.0	0.0	1.4	6.4	24.1	64.3	11.6	208	88.5	66.8	7.7
Minden City village	197	191	-3.0	209	100.0	0.0	0.0	0.0	0.0	29.2	60.7	10.0	68	77.9	57.4	7.4
Mio CDP	1,826	NA	NA	1,943	95.8	1.0	0.0	2.5	0.7	23.6	58.6	17.7	785	71.0	54.5	9.3
Mitchell township (Alcona)	352	335	-4.8	345	93.6	0.0	0.0	3.8	2.6	9.0	54.5	36.5	188	88.3	61.2	16.5
Moffatt township (Arenac)	1,184	1,144	-3.4	997	95.0	2.8	0.2	0.5	1.5	14.2	58.7	26.9	460	91.3	50.4	12.8
Moltke township (Presque Isle)	296	288	-2.7	266	96.2	0.0	1.5	0.8	1.5	11.2	63.2	25.6	122	96.7	58.2	16.4
Monitor charter township (Bay)	10,735	10,623	-1.0	10,695	95.5	0.0	0.4	1.8	2.3	19.2	58.2	22.5	4,291	92.8	37.3	22.4
Monroe city & MCD (Monroe)	20,733	20,198	-2.6	20,455	85.2	6.4	0.2	3.4	4.8	24.1	62.7	13.2	8,099	61.3	42.6	19.9
Monroe charter township (Monroe)	14,568	14,355	-1.5	14,448	89.3	4.1	1.0	2.7	2.9	22.6	60.9	16.7	5,731	77.3	47.0	17.6
Monroe township (Newaygo)	320	315	-1.6	320	96.3	0.0	0.0	0.6	3.1	14.1	62.7	23.1	150	89.3	44.7	11.3
Montague city & MCD (Muskegon)	2,361	2,357	-0.2	2,263	90.3	1.0	0.4	1.5	6.7	26.4	56.1	17.5	962	71.4	40.4	23.1
Montague township (Muskegon)	1,600	1,610	0.6	1,790	89.8	0.1	0.2	2.1	7.8	25.4	60.1	14.5	634	85.3	47.0	18.9
Montcalm township (Montcalm)	3,350	3,326	-0.7	3,327	95.1	0.0	0.0	2.0	2.9	23.8	61.9	14.3	1,247	91.7	49.4	10.0
Monterey township (Allegan)	2,356	2,384	1.2	2,412	94.7	0.0	1.1	3.9	0.4	26.2	66.2	7.5	850	84.4	49.1	11.4
Montgomery village	342	337	-1.5	329	99.1	0.0	0.0	0.9	0.0	28.0	58.1	14.0	118	57.6	67.8	2.5
Montmorency township (Montmorency)	1,122	1,068	-4.8	1,110	96.0	0.0	0.0	3.7	0.3	12.0	51.8	36.1	516	94.4	40.9	15.3
Montrose city & MCD (Genesee)	1,657	1,599	-3.5	1,735	95.1	2.0	0.5	0.9	1.4	27.6	58.8	13.5	660	61.7	49.8	9.7
Montrose charter township (Genesee)	6,224	6,030	-3.1	6,127	91.2	1.1	0.1	2.6	4.9	22.9	60.4	16.6	2,186	88.4	46.6	10.8
Moore township (Sanilac)	1,203	1,160	-3.6	1,088	97.4	0.7	0.0	0.0	1.8	26.8	57.5	15.6	376	87.8	55.3	12.0
Moorland township (Muskegon)	1,575	1,588	0.8	1,660	88.1	0.0	0.3	0.6	11.0	28.4	61.3	10.4	576	88.2	49.5	5.4
Moran township (Mackinac)	994	986	-0.8	933	69.7	0.2	1.0	27.8	1.4	20.1	65.4	14.5	393	88.3	45.0	27.2
Morenci city & MCD (Lenawee)	2,221	2,200	-0.9	2,412	89.8	1.2	0.0	2.9	6.1	24.5	63.3	12.3	919	68.9	49.3	6.4
Morley village	493	499	1.2	710	95.8	0.0	0.0	1.5	2.7	30.4	61.3	8.5	235	72.3	54.5	9.4
Morrice village	927	902	-2.7	1,065	93.8	1.0	0.9	2.7	1.5	25.2	65.2	9.5	373	79.6	48.5	15.0
Morton township (Mecosta)	4,311	4,379	1.6	4,374	90.3	5.4	0.1	2.6	1.5	15.4	51.1	33.4	1,853	89.2	27.7	29.7
Moscow township (Hillsdale)	1,470	1,440	-2.0	1,636	96.8	0.0	0.0	1.5	1.7	32.9	54.0	13.3	548	90.1	59.5	10.8
Mottville township (St. Joseph)	1,436	1,432	-0.3	1,663	95.7	0.8	0.2	1.6	1.7	21.9	64.7	13.5	611	84.1	62.5	7.2
Mount Clemens city & MCD (Macomb)	16,314	16,408	0.6	16,345	66.0	27.4	1.3	3.3	2.0	18.3	66.5	15.1	6,893	57.4	43.0	19.7

1 May be of any race.

Table A. All Places — **Population and Housing**

STATE City, town, township, borough, or CDP (county if applicable)	Population 2010 census total population	2014 estimated population	Percent change 2010–2014	ACS total population estimate 2010–2014	Race and Hispanic or Latino origin (percent), 2010–2014 White alone, not Hispanic or Latino	Black alone, not Hispanic or Latino	Asian alone, not Hispanic or Latino	All other races or 2 or more races, not Hispanic or Latino	Hispanic or Latino[1]	Age (percent), 2010–2014 Under 18 years old	Age 18 to 64 years old	Age 65 years and older	Households, 2010–2014 Total occupied housing units	Percent owner occupied	Householders by level of education (percent) High school diploma or less	Bachelor's degree or more
	1	2	3	4	5	6	7	8	9	10	11	12	13	14	15	16
MICHIGAN—Con.																
Mount Forest township (Bay)	1,392	1,383	-0.6	1,403	94.3	0.0	0.0	1.9	3.8	15.2	69.6	15.1	563	92.5	52.6	8.5
Mount Haley township (Midland)	1,678	1,666	-0.7	1,740	95.1	0.2	0.0	2.6	2.1	25.5	61.2	13.3	679	93.1	41.8	18.9
Mount Morris city & MCD (Genesee)	3,086	2,985	-3.3	3,032	76.9	15.4	0.8	5.7	1.2	27.0	64.2	8.7	1,140	44.8	54.2	4.2
Mount Morris township (Genesee)	21,501	20,797	-3.3	21,112	52.1	39.3	0.6	3.6	4.3	25.5	59.9	14.6	8,021	72.4	46.7	12.5
Mount Pleasant city & MCD (Isabella)	26,016	25,971	-0.2	26,095	83.8	3.5	3.5	6.1	3.2	12.4	80.3	7.4	8,116	35.1	21.1	35.3
Mueller township (Schoolcraft)	234	225	-3.8	255	92.2	0.0	0.0	5.9	2.0	19.7	48.2	32.2	123	85.4	69.1	8.9
Muir village	604	606	0.3	582	93.8	0.0	0.0	0.0	6.2	32.6	55.9	11.3	214	72.9	52.3	8.4
Mullett township (Cheboygan)	1,312	1,286	-2.0	1,211	95.9	0.5	0.0	2.6	1.1	15.5	52.2	32.3	522	93.3	37.4	28.9
Milliken village	553	557	0.7	588	92.7	0.3	0.0	3.4	3.6	30.8	59.8	9.4	216	77.3	53.7	9.3
Mundy township (Genesee)	15,120	14,722	-2.6	14,888	86.7	4.7	1.3	4.7	2.6	22.6	61.3	15.9	5,869	82.5	31.8	24.0
Munising city & MCD (Alger)	2,351	2,309	-1.8	2,116	94.1	1.6	0.0	3.4	0.9	16.5	59.6	24.0	866	70.7	46.8	25.5
Munising township (Alger)	2,987	2,973	-0.5	2,980	67.8	21.1	0.4	8.0	2.7	15.1	71.2	13.8	836	86.5	55.5	16.3
Munro township (Cheboygan)	571	561	-1.8	608	97.4	0.0	0.2	1.2	1.3	10.1	48.6	41.3	285	95.1	32.3	36.5
Muskegon city & MCD (Muskegon)	38,403	38,393	0.0	37,822	54.6	31.4	0.5	6.3	7.3	22.5	65.7	11.7	13,825	49.6	48.8	14.5
Muskegon charter township (Muskegon)	17,840	17,774	-0.4	17,777	86.1	4.7	0.2	3.6	5.4	24.2	61.2	14.5	6,484	76.9	46.5	12.0
Muskegon Heights city & MCD (Muskegon)	10,856	10,799	-0.5	10,807	16.4	77.4	0.1	4.9	1.2	32.5	57.3	10.3	4,155	50.7	56.0	5.4
Mussey township (St. Clair)	4,206	4,138	-1.6	4,162	79.0	0.3	0.9	2.6	17.1	30.1	62.7	7.2	1,416	79.3	47.3	10.1
Nadeau township (Menominee)	1,161	1,146	-1.3	1,129	97.1	0.0	0.0	2.2	0.7	22.7	59.3	17.9	473	84.1	54.1	17.1
Nahma township (Delta)	495	490	-1.0	470	97.0	0.0	0.0	3.0	0.0	15.7	49.9	34.3	210	86.7	39.0	22.9
Napoleon CDP	1,258	NA	NA	1,239	99.4	0.0	0.0	0.0	0.6	28.4	58.4	13.2	492	85.8	55.7	4.3
Napoleon township (Jackson)	6,776	6,764	-0.2	6,765	98.0	0.1	0.0	1.1	0.8	21.6	63.4	15.0	2,714	87.1	36.3	19.0
Nashville village	1,628	1,632	0.2	1,764	92.1	0.0	0.0	3.9	4.0	29.0	59.3	11.6	603	58.2	51.6	6.0
Negaunee city & MCD (Marquette)	4,568	4,616	1.1	4,608	94.1	0.4	0.2	3.7	1.7	21.9	59.6	18.5	1,909	70.7	35.0	29.8
Negaunee township (Marquette)	3,088	3,125	1.2	3,114	96.9	0.0	0.1	2.4	0.5	24.6	63.2	12.2	1,141	89.0	27.9	31.6
Nelson township (Kent)	4,764	4,945	3.8	4,869	96.0	0.1	0.0	0.1	3.9	27.8	61.9	10.2	1,681	86.7	47.9	19.0
Nessen City CDP	97	NA	NA	150	85.3	0.0	0.0	14.7	0.0	24.0	67.4	8.7	49	77.6	59.2	0.0
Nester township (Roscommon)	293	288	-1.7	314	96.8	0.0	1.6	1.6	0.0	16.0	52.5	31.5	145	92.4	50.3	13.1
Newark township (Gratiot)	1,093	1,073	-1.8	1,232	87.3	3.8	0.0	0.8	8.1	28.7	56.7	14.6	418	81.8	54.1	17.2
Newaygo city & MCD (Newaygo)	1,989	1,958	-1.6	1,986	89.8	0.7	1.2	4.6	3.7	30.4	54.0	15.8	763	50.2	43.4	13.6
New Baltimore city & MCD (Macomb)	12,084	12,269	1.5	12,144	94.7	1.0	0.7	1.5	2.0	27.0	60.1	13.0	4,483	82.9	30.2	26.2
Newberg township (Cass)	1,632	1,606	-1.6	1,534	92.9	1.0	0.1	3.2	2.8	21.0	61.7	17.4	583	90.4	50.6	16.5
Newberry village	1,519	1,459	-3.9	1,633	85.4	0.4	0.9	12.1	1.3	26.2	57.0	16.8	638	64.3	50.8	12.9
New Buffalo city & MCD (Berrien)	1,883	1,878	-0.3	1,890	88.4	5.0	0.3	0.8	5.6	19.8	59.4	20.7	815	72.3	41.6	33.9
New Buffalo township (Berrien)	2,386	2,404	0.8	2,261	97.1	1.4	0.3	0.0	1.2	19.6	53.3	27.1	975	79.0	27.3	47.2
New Era village	451	446	-1.1	562	92.9	0.0	0.0	0.9	6.2	29.2	57.7	13.2	198	86.9	33.3	36.4
Newfield township (Oceana)	2,401	2,337	-2.7	2,417	91.7	0.3	1.7	3.5	2.8	26.5	55.1	18.4	924	81.0	55.3	11.4
New Haven township (Gratiot)	1,004	985	-1.9	970	92.6	0.0	0.0	1.3	6.1	25.7	59.6	14.7	376	77.9	48.4	15.2
New Haven village	4,642	4,707	1.4	4,665	72.2	20.0	0.5	6.0	1.4	26.3	65.8	7.8	1,388	74.1	48.4	18.2
New Haven township (Shiawassee)	1,329	1,297	-2.4	1,397	97.7	0.4	0.0	0.9	1.0	21.1	60.9	18.1	507	91.7	42.8	18.5
Newkirk township (Lake)	630	618	-1.9	837	98.1	0.8	0.1	0.8	0.1	18.2	58.0	23.9	289	76.8	61.9	5.5
New Lothrop village	581	564	-2.9	476	92.6	2.9	0.0	3.2	1.3	18.7	59.6	21.6	210	67.1	36.2	21.4
Newton township (Calhoun)	2,551	2,540	-0.4	2,527	98.0	0.0	0.2	0.7	1.0	25.6	60.1	14.3	906	93.0	41.4	26.9
Newton township (Mackinac)	427	426	-0.2	405	86.9	0.0	0.0	11.4	1.7	15.3	59.4	25.2	183	84.2	55.7	13.7
New Troy CDP	497	NA	NA	558	93.0	0.0	0.0	4.8	2.2	26.7	57.6	15.8	206	74.8	71.4	3.9
Niles city	11,599	11,400	-1.7	11,479	78.8	11.2	0.1	3.7	6.2	28.0	57.2	14.7	4,552	57.7	50.1	14.5
Niles city (Berrien)	11,598	11,399	-1.7	11,479	78.8	11.2	0.1	3.7	6.2	28.0	57.2	14.7	4,552	57.7	50.1	14.5
Niles city (Cass)	1	1	0.0	0	0.0	0.0	0.0	0.0	0.0	0.0	0.0	0.0	0	0.0	0.0	0.0
Niles township (Berrien)	14,165	13,957	-1.5	14,057	87.1	3.8	0.8	3.9	4.4	21.8	61.2	17.3	5,322	78.1	50.8	16.0
Noble township (Branch)	520	512	-1.5	620	97.4	0.0	1.0	0.8	0.8	26.1	62.0	11.9	202	86.6	62.4	11.4
Norman township (Manistee)	1,553	1,523	-1.9	1,596	97.1	0.0	0.0	1.3	1.6	16.2	62.4	21.4	725	80.7	49.5	10.2
North Adams village	477	470	-1.5	634	97.6	0.0	0.0	0.2	2.2	31.4	54.5	14.2	222	74.3	53.2	7.2
North Allis township (Presque Isle)	521	505	-3.1	377	100.0	0.0	0.0	0.0	0.0	17.3	52.9	30.0	188	97.3	60.6	16.5
North Branch village	1,033	1,028	-0.5	979	91.8	0.0	0.0	0.8	7.4	27.8	59.4	12.9	416	59.4	48.8	12.5
North Branch township (Lapeer)	3,645	3,633	-0.3	3,647	94.3	0.0	0.0	0.2	5.5	25.3	61.7	13.0	1,322	84.8	47.4	18.2
Northfield township (Washtenaw)	8,245	8,589	4.2	8,409	93.3	0.2	0.5	2.8	3.3	24.1	63.9	12.0	3,313	82.9	27.0	33.8
North Muskegon city & MCD (Muskegon)	3,784	3,776	-0.2	3,769	93.4	0.9	0.0	4.3	1.4	18.9	56.3	25.0	1,713	79.0	32.5	39.2
North Plains township (Ionia)	1,279	1,287	0.6	1,259	93.4	1.0	0.0	2.8	2.8	26.1	59.9	14.0	445	81.1	55.1	3.4
Northport village	526	530	0.8	665	96.5	0.0	0.3	1.4	1.8	18.2	52.3	29.6	289	91.3	15.6	54.0

1 May be of any race.

Table A. All Places — Population and Housing

STATE City, town, township, borough, or CDP (county if applicable)	Population				Race and Hispanic or Latino origin (percent), 2010–2014					Age (percent), 2010–2014			Households, 2010–2014			
								All other races or 2 or more races not Hispanic or Latino							Householders by level of education (percent)	
	2010 census total population	2014 estimated population	Percent change 2010–2014	ACS total population estimate 2010–2014	White alone, not Hispanic or Latino	Black alone, not Hispanic or Latino	Asian alone, not Hispanic or Latino		Hispanic or Latino[1]	Under 18 years old	Age 18 to 64 years old	Age 65 years and older	Total occupied housing units	Percent owner occupied	High school diploma or less	Bachelor's degree or more
	1	2	3	4	5	6	7	8	9	10	11	12	13	14	15	16
MICHIGAN—Con.																
North Shade township (Gratiot)	665	656	-1.4	608	95.9	0.0	0.0	0.5	3.6	22.9	58.0	19.2	232	88.4	49.1	14.7
North Star township (Gratiot)	888	875	-1.5	919	92.9	0.0	0.8	0.4	5.9	20.6	59.2	20.2	356	87.9	52.2	13.5
Northview CDP	14,541	NA	NA	14,954	88.1	3.7	0.5	2.5	5.2	21.6	63.3	15.1	6,319	74.6	31.6	31.4
Northville city	5,970	6,014	0.7	6,001	90.4	1.3	3.2	2.4	2.7	20.6	61.2	18.0	2,547	71.6	13.9	65.0
Northville city (Oakland)	3,231	3,322	2.8	3,279	89.6	1.3	3.4	1.1	4.6	21.2	62.0	16.6	1,333	81.9	10.7	68.4
Northville city (Wayne)	2,739	2,692	-1.7	2,722	91.3	1.3	2.9	4.1	0.5	19.9	60.4	19.8	1,214	60.3	17.4	61.3
Northville township (Wayne)	28,497	28,809	1.1	28,682	76.0	3.0	14.7	2.0	4.2	23.9	59.0	17.1	11,086	75.6	13.5	64.1
Norton Shores city & MCD (Muskegon)	23,994	24,081	0.4	23,941	87.0	2.3	2.2	3.2	5.2	19.9	61.2	18.8	10,061	84.8	35.4	30.7
Norvell township (Jackson)	2,963	2,961	-0.1	2,962	95.7	1.5	0.5	0.3	1.9	16.1	64.9	19.0	1,245	85.1	48.0	14.5
Norway city & MCD (Dickinson)	2,845	2,817	-1.0	2,843	98.4	0.0	0.0	0.0	1.6	15.0	62.6	22.5	1,300	87.0	44.6	18.0
Norway township (Dickinson)	1,489	1,480	-0.6	1,665	97.8	0.0	1.0	1.2	0.0	20.7	61.2	18.1	680	85.0	41.8	31.0
Norwich township (Missaukee)	611	618	1.1	608	93.4	0.0	0.0	5.9	0.7	12.7	59.0	28.1	276	90.6	62.7	11.2
Norwich township (Newaygo)	607	601	-1.0	671	94.6	2.2	0.4	1.3	1.3	27.1	60.1	12.8	215	95.3	41.4	21.9
Norwood CDP	142	NA	NA	154	99.4	0.0	0.6	0.0	0.0	31.1	48.5	20.1	52	96.2	34.6	38.5
Norwood township (Charlevoix)	723	728	0.7	809	95.2	0.5	0.1	3.6	0.6	22.5	56.9	20.6	323	92.0	26.6	31.9
Nottawa township (Isabella)	2,282	2,255	-1.2	2,376	91.9	0.2	0.5	6.5	0.9	27.6	58.6	13.8	830	91.1	54.2	20.6
Nottawa township (St. Joseph)	3,858	3,865	0.2	3,839	94.7	1.2	0.2	2.3	1.7	22.5	58.9	18.5	1,337	82.0	43.7	17.4
Novesta township (Tuscola)	1,491	1,444	-3.2	1,472	96.3	0.0	0.0	0.6	3.1	22.7	61.0	16.1	580	89.0	56.9	11.4
Novi city & MCD (Oakland)	55,224	58,416	5.8	56,887	69.9	7.3	17.6	2.4	2.8	24.3	62.3	13.2	23,001	65.9	16.7	58.5
Novi township (Oakland)	150	153	2.0	157	87.3	1.9	4.5	3.8	2.5	16.5	71.4	12.1	60	96.7	10.0	83.3
Nunda township (Cheboygan)	1,042	1,020	-2.1	1,091	97.7	0.0	0.0	2.3	0.0	17.1	66.0	16.9	456	92.3	56.4	12.1
Oakfield township (Kent)	5,782	6,026	4.2	5,899	94.3	0.7	0.0	1.0	4.0	27.6	60.4	11.9	2,019	95.1	38.0	23.4
Oak Hill CDP	569	NA	NA	610	92.1	0.0	0.0	6.9	1.0	23.9	62.8	13.3	247	81.4	35.2	9.3
Oakland charter township (Oakland)	16,779	18,820	12.2	17,705	87.2	3.3	6.1	0.8	2.6	25.5	60.2	14.3	6,115	91.5	15.1	60.9
Oakley village	290	280	-3.4	168	91.7	0.0	1.2	1.8	5.4	10.1	71.5	18.5	79	96.2	62.0	5.1
Oak Park city & MCD (Oakland)	29,319	29,834	1.8	29,622	32.8	57.7	1.7	6.5	1.3	24.4	62.3	13.4	11,385	57.3	29.7	31.1
Oceola township (Livingston)	11,975	12,266	2.4	12,121	94.4	0.5	0.7	2.1	2.2	27.4	59.9	12.7	4,274	89.9	23.5	39.9
Ocqueoc township (Presque Isle)	655	638	-2.6	583	98.5	0.0	0.0	0.3	1.2	12.6	52.5	34.6	307	96.7	45.9	29.6
Oden CDP	363	NA	NA	600	92.3	0.0	0.0	7.7	0.0	27.0	50.3	22.8	219	89.0	51.1	23.3
Odessa township (Ionia)	3,778	3,806	0.7	3,787	87.7	0.9	0.8	2.4	8.1	25.1	60.2	14.6	1,413	78.6	48.4	14.5
Ogden township (Lenawee)	973	959	-1.4	1,049	93.5	0.0	0.0	3.4	3.1	24.5	62.3	13.1	361	88.1	42.7	18.6
Ogemaw township (Ogemaw)	1,223	1,188	-2.9	1,034	99.0	0.0	0.0	1.0	0.0	18.4	58.5	23.1	414	87.9	41.8	17.6
Okemos CDP	21,369	NA	NA	21,827	76.5	3.4	12.5	4.1	3.5	20.3	65.2	14.4	9,058	64.8	8.0	70.6
Olive township (Clinton)	2,476	2,528	2.1	2,510	94.5	1.4	0.0	2.6	1.5	24.2	59.3	16.4	946	88.9	34.0	22.6
Olive township (Ottawa)	4,735	4,957	4.7	4,834	74.2	4.4	1.6	3.2	16.6	30.7	62.9	6.5	1,403	93.6	49.3	13.1
Oliver township (Huron)	1,483	1,434	-3.3	1,521	96.2	0.0	0.0	1.3	2.5	29.4	55.9	14.6	583	74.1	52.7	11.1
Oliver township (Kalkaska)	281	284	1.1	271	94.8	0.0	0.0	5.2	0.0	17.4	61.7	21.0	124	87.9	54.0	7.3
Olivet city & MCD (Eaton)	1,605	1,611	0.4	1,631	86.6	7.5	2.0	2.8	1.1	15.7	75.6	8.7	394	55.3	39.8	26.4
Omena CDP	267	NA	NA	220	97.7	0.0	0.0	2.3	0.0	18.2	34.5	47.3	81	100.0	21.0	42.0
Omer city & MCD (Arenac)	313	300	-4.2	342	97.4	0.3	0.3	2.0	0.0	22.1	57.6	20.2	142	84.5	60.6	3.5
Onaway city & MCD (Presque Isle)	880	852	-3.2	829	95.3	1.9	0.0	1.8	1.0	25.3	60.0	14.7	339	85.5	51.0	6.5
Oneida charter township (Eaton)	3,855	3,902	1.2	3,883	92.6	1.1	0.3	0.7	5.3	23.5	61.4	15.2	1,462	92.8	30.6	25.4
Onekama village	411	406	-1.2	475	89.9	0.0	0.0	7.6	2.5	17.0	63.2	19.8	223	68.6	47.1	19.7
Onekama township (Manistee)	1,329	1,312	-1.3	1,489	91.7	1.0	0.0	3.0	4.3	17.9	55.4	26.8	663	82.2	34.7	32.7
Onondaga township (Ingham)	3,158	3,155	-0.1	3,160	95.7	0.9	0.0	1.4	1.9	25.3	64.3	10.5	1,096	92.2	40.0	19.6
Onota township (Alger)	352	345	-2.0	330	91.8	0.6	0.0	6.1	1.5	18.8	53.5	27.6	149	90.6	34.2	34.9
Onsted village	917	908	-1.0	820	94.9	0.0	0.0	0.7	4.4	26.0	53.8	20.2	352	72.4	42.9	14.2
Ontonagon village	1,494	1,361	-8.9	1,457	93.1	2.5	1.2	2.5	0.7	13.6	55.4	31.1	728	71.3	44.8	17.3
Ontonagon township (Ontonagon)	2,579	2,352	-8.8	2,586	94.7	1.4	0.7	2.4	0.9	15.9	58.0	26.0	1,267	82.9	43.7	19.7
Ontwa township (Cass)	6,549	6,493	-0.9	6,528	92.4	0.6	2.3	3.2	1.5	24.6	61.2	14.3	2,426	85.7	48.6	18.0
Orange township (Ionia)	987	994	0.7	1,030	94.7	0.0	0.2	2.1	3.0	25.4	61.4	13.1	378	82.3	48.7	15.9
Orange township (Kalkaska)	1,233	1,248	1.2	1,340	96.6	0.0	0.0	1.9	1.4	27.3	59.9	12.7	479	80.8	61.0	2.7
Orangeville township (Barry)	3,311	3,326	0.5	3,308	95.4	0.0	0.2	1.6	2.8	18.2	63.8	17.9	1,324	81.9	52.9	16.4
Orchard Lake Village city & MCD (Oakland)	2,375	2,412	1.6	2,343	81.7	7.9	5.4	3.1	1.9	20.3	61.5	18.1	779	97.7	10.7	66.4
Oregon township (Lapeer)	5,786	5,772	-0.2	5,773	93.1	0.0	1.0	1.6	4.3	20.5	65.8	13.7	2,026	92.2	38.0	21.1
Orient township (Osceola)	773	762	-1.4	831	97.6	0.4	0.0	1.4	0.6	25.2	54.7	20.0	302	88.7	47.7	12.6
Orion charter township (Oakland)	35,394	36,777	3.9	36,029	87.4	3.0	2.8	2.0	4.7	27.2	62.7	9.9	12,960	80.4	22.4	41.4
Orleans township (Ionia)	2,743	2,752	0.3	2,725	89.1	2.0	0.0	3.7	5.2	23.6	64.4	12.1	956	84.6	60.7	6.6
Oronoko charter township (Berrien)	9,193	9,138	-0.6	9,170	46.8	24.3	10.8	5.8	12.2	15.9	71.9	12.1	2,407	57.7	21.0	48.2
Ortonville village	1,442	1,467	1.7	1,488	86.2	2.0	0.0	5.2	6.6	31.2	59.9	8.9	546	63.9	28.2	24.2

1 May be of any race.

Table A. All Places — Population and Housing

STATE City, town, township, borough, or CDP (county if applicable)	Population				Race and Hispanic or Latino origin (percent), 2010–2014					Age (percent), 2010–2014			Households, 2010–2014			
	2010 census total population	2014 estimated population	Percent change 2010–2014	ACS total population estimate 2010–2014	White alone, not Hispanic or Latino	Black alone, not Hispanic or Latino	Asian alone, not Hispanic or Latino	All other races or 2 or more races, not Hispanic or Latino	Hispanic or Latino[1]	Under 18 years old	Age 18 to 64 years old	Age 65 years and older	Total occupied housing units	Percent owner occupied	High school diploma or less	Bachelor's degree or more
	1	2	3	4	5	6	7	8	9	10	11	12	13	14	15	16
MICHIGAN—Con.																
Osceola township (Houghton)	1,888	1,862	-1.4	1,930	98.4	0.3	0.5	0.2	0.6	29.5	59.4	11.0	725	80.3	43.7	21.8
Osceola township (Osceola)	1,076	1,057	-1.8	1,163	92.4	1.6	0.4	3.4	2.1	24.2	51.4	24.5	370	93.5	54.1	13.8
Oscoda CDP	903	NA	NA	807	83.4	0.0	7.3	0.0	9.3	22.4	54.3	23.3	323	76.8	25.7	28.5
Oscoda charter township (Iosco)	6,997	6,880	-1.7	6,886	92.8	0.9	1.1	2.7	2.5	17.1	56.0	26.9	3,173	74.9	45.8	16.5
Oshtemo charter township (Kalamazoo)	21,701	22,458	3.5	22,119	75.0	13.4	3.5	3.7	4.4	18.5	65.5	15.9	9,806	52.5	18.4	42.5
Ossineke CDP	938	NA	NA	996	98.4	0.0	0.0	1.4	0.2	25.1	59.5	15.2	385	74.3	51.4	16.9
Ossineke township (Alpena)	1,675	1,634	-2.4	1,664	95.4	0.0	1.1	2.2	1.3	19.2	57.8	22.9	710	85.5	46.8	9.4
Otisco township (Ionia)	2,282	2,304	1.0	2,328	91.8	0.0	0.0	0.1	8.2	27.7	60.2	12.0	835	88.6	43.1	15.9
Otisville village	864	832	-3.7	798	100.0	0.0	0.0	0.0	0.0	16.6	58.0	25.6	389	79.4	59.6	14.1
Otsego city & MCD (Allegan)	3,956	3,985	0.7	3,961	97.5	0.0	0.0	1.8	0.6	23.5	57.1	19.2	1,625	67.6	46.4	14.2
Otsego township (Allegan)	5,596	5,688	1.6	5,613	93.4	0.3	0.3	2.0	4.0	25.3	59.9	14.9	2,142	83.0	46.3	16.9
Otsego Lake township (Otsego)	2,847	2,846	0.0	2,847	98.3	0.1	0.3	0.4	0.9	23.1	56.3	20.8	1,188	86.1	38.9	29.3
Otter Lake village	389	387	-0.5	402	96.8	0.0	0.0	1.7	1.5	20.4	66.1	13.4	155	72.9	61.9	7.1
Otto township (Oceana)	826	803	-2.8	736	98.1	0.0	0.0	0.0	1.9	20.8	63.3	15.8	300	93.7	56.3	7.7
Overisel township (Allegan)	2,911	2,978	2.3	2,941	93.1	0.0	2.5	0.6	3.8	30.7	57.8	11.6	986	94.9	45.0	20.6
Ovid township (Branch)	2,326	2,299	-1.2	2,343	98.7	0.1	0.4	0.3	0.4	14.8	61.1	24.2	1,085	90.4	42.8	29.7
Ovid village	1,603	1,623	1.2	1,594	93.8	0.0	0.0	0.2	6.0	25.7	57.8	16.4	546	70.3	44.5	13.6
Ovid township (Clinton)	3,795	3,853	1.5	3,821	92.1	0.3	0.0	0.1	7.4	24.4	59.3	16.2	1,310	84.7	40.7	20.1
Owendale village	241	234	-2.9	265	85.7	0.0	0.4	2.3	11.7	26.0	60.0	14.0	98	86.7	73.5	0.0
Owosso city & MCD (Shiawassee)	15,194	14,779	-2.7	14,922	92.1	0.1	0.0	2.6	5.1	24.7	62.5	12.8	6,157	60.4	39.9	14.1
Owosso charter township (Shiawassee)	4,821	4,714	-2.2	4,772	92.3	1.6	2.5	0.9	2.7	23.8	57.2	19.0	1,770	81.2	50.7	15.4
Oxford village	3,436	3,537	2.9	3,488	98.1	0.9	0.0	0.0	0.9	20.4	64.8	14.8	1,531	66.4	27.6	29.5
Oxford charter township (Oakland)	20,526	21,343	4.0	20,882	92.9	0.9	0.8	1.8	3.6	26.2	60.8	13.1	7,783	82.9	29.9	40.3
Palmer CDP	418	NA	NA	525	97.1	0.0	0.0	0.0	2.9	28.2	61.2	10.5	185	95.7	53.5	16.8
Palmyra township (Lenawee)	2,084	2,041	-2.1	2,208	86.3	4.0	0.3	1.2	8.2	22.1	62.3	15.4	780	88.6	54.2	11.9
Paradise township (Grand Traverse)	4,713	4,942	4.9	4,808	97.4	0.0	0.0	1.0	1.6	27.0	66.1	7.1	1,580	85.9	46.8	14.6
Parchment city & MCD (Kalamazoo)	1,804	1,845	2.3	1,867	74.4	11.8	0.5	9.4	3.9	23.8	63.7	12.5	803	57.4	30.0	22.5
Paris township (Huron)	481	466	-3.1	470	100.0	0.0	0.0	0.0	0.0	20.9	64.1	15.1	194	85.6	72.2	12.4
Park township (Ottawa)	17,802	18,537	4.1	18,149	86.8	1.1	1.1	2.1	8.8	25.9	58.8	15.5	6,486	88.5	23.0	44.2
Park township (St. Joseph)	2,600	2,585	-0.6	2,592	92.8	0.3	0.7	4.6	1.5	22.9	60.3	16.7	892	85.3	41.3	25.2
Parkdale CDP	704	NA	NA	603	84.9	6.1	0.0	3.2	5.8	5.5	49.8	44.8	246	89.0	39.8	19.5
Parma village	769	762	-0.9	989	95.4	0.0	0.6	1.1	2.8	35.8	57.7	6.7	319	82.4	37.3	20.4
Parma township (Jackson)	2,726	2,718	-0.3	2,720	91.7	4.9	1.9	0.6	0.8	27.8	57.8	14.3	1,022	82.6	48.8	17.4
Pavilion township (Kalamazoo)	6,218	6,332	1.8	6,291	92.6	0.5	0.6	3.1	3.1	25.5	61.7	12.8	2,263	93.8	38.4	18.5
Paw Paw village	3,534	3,469	-1.8	3,494	87.2	0.4	1.8	7.1	3.5	21.3	69.9	8.8	1,281	40.0	49.6	21.9
Paw Paw township (Van Buren)	7,041	6,938	-1.5	6,979	90.0	0.9	1.2	3.6	4.4	19.1	64.5	16.6	2,721	67.8	41.9	24.5
Paw Paw Lake CDP	3,511	NA	NA	3,639	95.1	0.0	0.7	2.2	1.9	18.6	61.9	19.5	1,504	79.7	42.9	18.0
Peacock township (Lake)	492	483	-1.8	305	94.8	0.0	1.0	0.0	4.3	3.9	56.2	40.0	169	89.3	71.6	3.6
Peaine township (Charlevoix)	292	295	1.0	280	96.8	0.0	1.8	1.1	0.4	14.9	50.4	34.6	127	92.9	26.8	44.9
Pearl Beach CDP	2,829	NA	NA	3,114	99.5	0.0	0.2	0.4	0.0	13.5	59.0	27.5	1,430	88.3	45.9	20.1
Peck village	632	614	-2.8	750	95.2	1.2	0.0	1.6	2.0	25.4	58.4	16.0	218	85.8	59.6	7.3
Pellston village	822	832	1.2	881	82.7	0.0	0.0	13.2	4.1	29.3	64.6	6.2	353	64.0	43.6	8.2
Peninsula township (Grand Traverse)	5,433	5,736	5.6	5,586	99.1	0.0	0.6	0.3	0.0	13.9	53.6	32.6	2,577	89.2	9.6	66.4
Penn township (Cass)	1,774	1,743	-1.7	1,968	84.9	5.0	4.1	2.8	3.3	20.6	57.0	22.6	768	87.9	46.2	23.4
Pennfield charter township (Calhoun)	9,004	8,948	-0.6	8,965	87.9	4.3	0.5	4.0	3.3	23.9	60.1	15.9	3,607	71.8	38.9	18.5
Pentland township (Luce)	2,674	2,616	-2.2	2,631	68.4	22.7	0.2	6.7	2.1	14.7	72.3	12.9	648	77.0	49.1	21.3
Pentwater village	857	849	-0.9	977	90.3	0.0	0.0	0.7	9.0	16.8	48.7	34.5	445	76.9	18.4	40.0
Pentwater township (Oceana)	1,515	1,513	-0.1	1,464	92.1	0.0	0.0	1.0	7.0	13.0	48.0	39.1	691	83.8	16.8	43.7
Pere Marquette charter township (Mason)	2,366	2,397	1.3	2,470	92.0	0.0	0.7	2.6	4.7	24.8	52.5	22.8	974	82.1	32.3	25.6
Perrinton village	406	400	-1.5	496	86.5	0.0	0.0	0.0	13.5	30.6	56.7	12.5	188	63.3	60.1	4.3
Perry city & MCD (Shiawassee)	2,162	2,109	-2.5	1,923	88.7	1.5	0.0	3.8	6.0	26.5	63.4	10.1	814	57.7	39.4	15.6
Perry township (Shiawassee)	4,353	4,234	-2.7	4,274	97.4	0.4	0.2	1.5	0.4	26.0	63.8	10.1	1,624	90.6	51.3	18.3
Petersburg city & MCD (Monroe)	1,146	1,129	-1.5	1,395	94.7	3.6	0.0	1.4	0.4	23.4	65.5	11.1	565	70.1	57.2	13.1
Petoskey city & MCD (Emmet)	5,668	5,738	1.2	5,705	89.7	1.6	0.5	5.4	2.8	15.5	66.0	18.4	2,684	56.0	24.3	41.6
Pewamo village	469	476	1.5	439	98.6	0.0	0.0	0.0	1.4	21.9	58.4	19.8	186	80.1	62.4	9.1
Pickford township (Chippewa)	1,595	1,591	-0.3	1,832	92.0	0.0	0.1	7.5	0.4	20.6	64.2	15.1	824	84.3	40.9	19.9
Pierson village	172	172	0.0	207	97.1	0.0	0.0	2.9	0.0	34.8	58.8	6.3	71	83.1	81.7	2.8
Pierson township (Montcalm)	3,216	3,209	-0.2	3,202	98.1	0.6	0.2	0.7	0.5	24.7	67.6	7.6	1,181	89.7	57.2	14.1
Pigeon village	1,208	1,173	-2.9	1,221	96.8	0.3	0.7	0.0	2.2	20.0	53.4	26.5	550	70.4	49.1	25.6
Pilgrim CDP	11	NA	NA	41	100.0	0.0	0.0	0.0	0.0	0.0	46.3	53.7	20	100.0	0.0	100.0
Pinckney village	2,427	2,487	2.5	2,596	94.3	0.0	0.2	2.6	2.9	27.5	63.8	8.9	956	73.7	31.6	25.6
Pinconning city & MCD (Bay)	1,307	1,278	-2.2	1,380	89.2	2.4	0.0	5.7	2.8	24.5	58.0	17.4	590	67.8	54.9	14.1
Pinconning township (Bay)	2,431	2,398	-1.4	2,244	96.3	0.0	0.0	0.4	3.3	21.8	59.0	19.3	911	89.4	52.5	15.4

1 May be of any race.

Table A. All Places — Population and Housing

STATE City, town, township, borough, or CDP (county if applicable)	Population				Race and Hispanic or Latino origin (percent), 2010–2014					Age (percent), 2010–2014			Households, 2010–2014			
	2010 census total population	2014 estimated population	Percent change 2010–2014	ACS total population estimate 2010–2014	White alone, not Hispanic or Latino	Black alone, not Hispanic or Latino	Asian alone, not Hispanic or Latino	All other races or 2 or more races, not Hispanic or Latino	Hispanic or Latino[1]	Under 18 years old	Age 18 to 64 years old	Age 65 years and older	Total occupied housing units	Percent owner occupied	High school diploma or less	Bachelor's degree or more
	1	2	3	4	5	6	7	8	9	10	11	12	13	14	15	16
MICHIGAN—Con.																
Pine township (Montcalm)	1,834	1,832	-0.1	1,755	94.8	0.1	0.3	1.9	2.9	20.5	62.9	16.6	666	87.7	47.9	15.3
Pine Grove township (Van Buren)	2,949	2,934	-0.5	2,930	95.6	0.7	0.0	0.4	3.3	23.1	64.4	12.7	1,101	94.4	40.9	24.0
Pine River township (Gratiot)	2,284	2,244	-1.8	2,348	95.5	1.4	0.3	0.9	1.9	21.6	58.0	20.6	910	91.0	47.4	18.9
Pinora township (Lake)	717	702	-2.1	839	96.5	0.1	0.0	2.4	1.0	24.1	60.8	15.0	264	86.0	67.8	9.5
Pioneer township (Missaukee)	451	456	1.1	518	96.9	0.0	0.8	1.2	1.2	22.8	57.6	19.7	199	84.9	62.3	11.1
Pipestone township (Berrien)	2,312	2,277	-1.5	2,428	82.0	2.6	0.0	3.7	11.7	22.9	59.5	17.6	811	85.7	47.0	16.9
Pittsfield charter township (Washtenaw)	34,804	37,548	7.9	36,081	63.5	13.2	13.9	5.4	4.0	21.5	69.4	9.2	13,792	54.9	15.0	58.5
Pittsford township (Hillsdale)	1,603	1,571	-2.0	1,436	91.7	0.7	1.0	4.0	2.6	20.2	56.0	23.6	569	87.2	53.6	14.1
Plainfield township (Iosco)	3,799	3,713	-2.3	3,742	96.1	0.0	0.3	2.6	1.0	15.0	51.0	34.0	1,767	86.1	52.1	9.1
Plainfield charter township (Kent)	30,967	32,538	5.1	31,693	91.5	2.1	0.8	2.1	3.5	24.3	62.0	13.8	12,512	83.7	28.1	34.5
Plainwell city & MCD (Allegan)	3,804	3,824	0.5	3,798	94.5	0.5	0.0	2.4	2.6	22.4	61.7	15.8	1,574	57.2	45.1	21.3
Platte township (Benzie)	354	354	0.0	336	91.7	0.0	0.0	8.3	0.0	19.4	54.4	26.2	150	92.7	46.0	22.7
Pleasanton township (Manistee)	818	805	-1.6	807	96.5	0.0	0.0	0.0	3.5	19.9	51.5	28.6	358	87.4	48.6	20.1
Pleasant Plains township (Lake)	1,581	1,555	-1.6	1,996	68.3	19.9	0.3	5.2	6.3	20.4	61.9	17.8	733	69.6	49.0	11.3
Pleasant Ridge city & MCD (Oakland)	2,526	2,564	1.5	2,544	87.0	1.7	6.1	3.8	1.5	17.8	64.0	18.3	1,138	91.7	10.9	70.1
Pleasantview township (Emmet)	823	841	2.2	958	99.6	0.0	0.1	0.1	0.2	21.4	58.0	20.6	383	82.8	21.1	42.6
Plymouth city & MCD (Wayne)	9,132	8,933	-2.2	9,029	90.9	1.6	2.3	2.4	2.8	21.5	65.2	13.3	4,170	59.7	17.3	56.2
Plymouth charter township (Wayne)	27,524	27,039	-1.8	27,255	90.6	2.3	3.8	2.0	1.3	22.9	59.5	17.4	10,598	81.3	17.8	53.3
Pointe Aux Barques township (Huron)	10	10	0.0	17	82.4	0.0	0.0	0.0	17.6	0.0	29.4	70.6	11	100.0	18.2	63.6
Pokagon township (Cass)	2,029	1,993	-1.8	2,305	86.9	1.7	0.0	6.7	4.6	19.0	65.9	15.1	851	86.1	46.2	20.2
Polkton charter township (Ottawa)	2,423	2,529	4.4	2,558	94.5	0.3	0.5	1.2	3.6	27.0	59.1	14.0	878	87.7	39.0	28.0
Ponshewaing CDP	69	NA	NA	20	30.0	0.0	0.0	70.0	0.0	10.0	80.0	10.0	5	0.0	0.0	60.0
Pontiac city & MCD (Oakland)	59,515	59,808	0.5	59,658	25.5	50.7	2.3	4.9	16.6	27.2	62.9	10.0	23,238	44.4	53.6	11.2
Portage charter township (Houghton)	3,221	3,183	-1.2	3,216	91.6	2.5	3.9	2.0	0.0	18.4	64.7	17.0	1,200	73.8	32.5	40.2
Portage city & MCD (Kalamazoo)	46,287	47,837	3.3	47,137	85.6	5.6	2.9	2.9	3.0	24.8	61.5	13.6	19,293	67.8	22.1	41.2
Portage township (Mackinac)	981	972	-0.9	784	90.2	0.0	0.0	8.3	1.5	11.0	46.7	42.3	398	84.2	62.6	12.1
Port Austin village	664	644	-3.0	715	97.6	0.6	0.3	1.0	0.6	14.3	53.5	32.3	376	69.7	40.7	20.7
Port Austin township (Huron)	1,424	1,378	-3.2	1,515	97.9	0.3	0.6	0.5	0.7	12.6	51.7	35.8	764	82.6	44.0	19.9
Porter township (Cass)	3,798	3,791	-0.2	3,801	91.7	1.8	0.0	3.2	3.3	19.7	59.8	20.4	1,615	82.9	49.5	19.5
Porter township (Midland)	1,277	1,265	-0.9	1,241	94.4	0.0	0.0	1.2	4.4	19.7	67.1	13.1	475	89.9	46.3	12.4
Porter township (Van Buren)	2,466	2,440	-1.1	2,358	94.8	0.0	0.0	1.2	4.0	25.5	54.0	20.6	942	86.4	36.6	23.1
Port Hope village	267	259	-3.0	231	98.3	0.0	0.0	0.0	1.7	9.9	44.9	45.0	123	91.9	77.2	6.5
Port Huron city & MCD (St. Clair)	30,177	29,168	-3.3	29,534	81.4	8.2	0.8	4.9	4.7	24.9	60.5	14.6	12,106	55.3	44.5	16.9
Port Huron charter township (St. Clair)	10,654	10,448	-1.9	10,521	87.1	4.5	0.1	3.4	4.9	23.0	63.9	13.1	3,918	65.3	51.4	15.8
Portland city & MCD (Ionia)	3,895	3,921	0.7	3,899	92.6	0.8	0.3	2.1	4.2	26.0	63.2	10.6	1,521	69.9	30.6	23.7
Portland township (Ionia)	3,392	3,428	1.1	3,409	87.7	6.9	0.0	1.1	4.3	25.8	60.5	13.6	1,188	87.5	33.0	23.0
Port Sanilac village	623	606	-2.7	506	87.2	0.4	1.8	5.9	4.7	15.0	53.9	31.0	227	70.0	47.1	22.0
Port Sheldon township (Ottawa)	4,240	4,443	4.8	4,331	90.6	0.0	1.9	1.2	6.3	21.6	62.4	16.1	1,702	95.4	37.8	35.7
Portsmouth charter township (Bay)	3,306	3,249	-1.7	3,277	93.3	0.1	0.3	0.1	6.2	18.2	61.6	20.2	1,371	96.8	45.7	18.5
Posen village	234	228	-2.6	239	95.8	0.0	0.0	4.2	0.0	28.0	53.5	18.4	117	74.4	50.4	8.5
Posen township (Presque Isle)	850	828	-2.6	879	96.4	0.1	0.2	3.3	0.0	20.5	60.2	19.3	378	86.8	59.8	7.7
Potterville city & MCD (Eaton)	2,617	2,615	-0.1	2,621	90.1	2.4	2.2	1.5	3.9	25.9	67.1	7.0	1,051	63.7	32.1	20.1
Powell township (Marquette)	814	822	1.0	427	94.8	1.2	0.0	4.0	0.0	7.2	62.4	30.4	229	91.7	47.6	23.6
Powers village	422	420	-0.5	436	90.8	7.6	0.0	0.9	0.7	11.0	45.3	43.8	135	60.0	61.5	10.4
Prairie Ronde township (Kalamazoo)	2,250	2,353	4.6	2,375	96.1	1.0	0.2	0.8	1.9	25.0	63.0	12.0	813	96.7	32.0	31.0
Prairieville township (Barry)	3,404	3,410	0.2	3,398	92.2	0.7	0.0	0.1	7.0	16.6	71.3	12.2	1,259	84.2	34.6	33.0
Prescott village	266	258	-3.0	291	89.7	0.0	0.0	3.4	6.9	27.1	63.9	8.9	99	92.9	44.4	8.1
Presque Isle township (Presque Isle)	1,656	1,614	-2.5	1,683	97.0	0.1	0.2	2.3	0.4	13.7	55.9	30.4	792	94.8	21.7	30.6
Presque Isle Harbor CDP	600	NA	NA	561	97.5	0.4	0.0	1.1	1.1	5.5	50.7	43.9	310	97.1	16.1	40.6
Prudenville CDP	1,682	NA	NA	1,673	97.5	0.0	0.0	1.4	1.0	18.3	51.1	30.4	897	79.7	47.2	7.2
Pulaski township (Jackson)	2,075	2,067	-0.4	2,005	97.4	0.4	0.0	1.0	1.2	18.7	62.7	18.4	813	90.8	49.2	14.0
Pulawski township (Presque Isle)	343	334	-2.6	343	99.1	0.0	0.0	0.3	0.6	21.3	51.0	27.7	142	93.7	71.1	3.5
Putnam township (Livingston)	8,248	8,456	2.5	8,346	94.8	0.4	0.2	2.3	2.3	21.8	65.1	13.0	3,174	81.4	35.6	25.1
Quincy village	1,652	1,636		1,650	97.7	0.1	0.8	0.4	0.9	25.2	67.6	7.3	667	58.8	58.6	7.3
Quincy township (Branch)	4,285	4,238	-1.1	4,263	97.6	0.4	0.3	0.5	1.2	22.3	60.9	16.8	1,717	78.7	56.7	10.9

1 May be of any race.

Table A. All Places — Population and Housing

	Population				Race and Hispanic or Latino origin (percent), 2010–2014					Age (percent), 2010–2014			Households, 2010–2014			
STATE City, town, township, borough, or CDP (county if applicable)	2010 census total population	2014 estimated population	Percent change 2010–2014	ACS total population estimate 2010–2014	White alone, not Hispanic or Latino	Black alone, not Hispanic or Latino	Asian alone, not Hispanic or Latino	All other races or 2 or more races, not Hispanic or Latino	Hispanic or Latino[1]	Under 18 years old	Age 18 to 64 years old	Age 65 years and older	Total occupied housing units	Percent owner occupied	High school diploma or less	Bachelor's degree or more
	1	2	3	4	5	6	7	8	9	10	11	12	13	14	15	16
MICHIGAN—Con.																
Quincy township (Houghton)	270	267	-1.1	278	93.9	2.9	0.7	0.4	2.2	26.3	62.4	11.5	104	77.9	35.6	34.6
Quinnesec CDP	1,191	NA	NA	1,105	98.0	1.6	0.4	0.0	0.0	24.9	54.2	20.7	408	100.0	65.4	11.0
Raber township (Chippewa)	647	645	-0.3	585	95.0	0.0	1.2	3.2	0.5	17.0	44.7	38.1	267	86.1	56.6	13.5
Raisin township (Lenawee)	7,578	7,573	-0.1	7,539	90.6	0.6	0.3	3.9	4.7	25.4	61.9	12.8	2,634	94.0	28.2	23.3
Raisinville township (Monroe)	5,816	5,798	-0.3	5,803	95.3	0.7	0.7	0.6	2.8	26.2	59.7	14.0	1,941	94.6	41.6	16.6
Ransom township (Hillsdale)	932	912	-2.1	865	96.5	0.0	0.0	2.5	0.9	26.4	56.2	17.3	301	90.7	55.8	14.3
Rapid City CDP	1,352	NA	NA	1,490	94.0	1.7	0.0	1.1	3.1	19.2	63.7	17.2	652	80.5	56.4	9.4
Rapid River township (Kalkaska)	1,145	1,159	1.2	1,151	90.6	1.3	0.2	6.4	1.5	25.8	63.0	11.2	480	85.2	59.0	9.0
Ravenna village	1,219	1,213	-0.5	1,193	94.0	0.0	0.0	1.3	4.8	29.5	55.0	15.4	441	78.7	35.1	30.6
Ravenna township (Muskegon)	2,905	2,921	0.6	2,895	88.3	0.0	0.3	1.5	9.8	27.8	58.8	13.3	999	85.7	42.3	28.4
Ray township (Macomb)	3,735	3,928	5.2	3,870	96.8	0.5	0.0	1.0	1.7	17.9	65.6	16.4	1,521	91.8	39.0	25.2
Reading city & MCD (Hillsdale)	1,078	1,056	-2.0	1,244	96.2	0.4	0.4	3.0	0.0	31.6	59.9	8.4	417	65.2	55.6	4.1
Reading township (Hillsdale)	1,765	1,733	-1.8	1,784	98.0	0.2	0.2	1.7	0.0	24.3	54.1	21.6	679	92.6	49.8	18.6
Readmond township (Emmet)	581	593	2.1	672	89.0	0.0	0.6	8.0	2.4	16.9	60.7	22.5	292	95.5	36.0	32.5
Redding township (Clare)	526	520	-1.1	430	95.8	0.0	0.5	1.2	2.6	16.6	57.4	26.0	186	83.9	72.0	3.2
Redford charter township (Wayne)	48,362	47,446	-1.9	47,930	60.6	32.0	0.4	3.5	3.6	22.8	64.9	12.2	18,186	78.7	42.2	20.1
Reed City city & MCD (Osceola)	2,425	2,402	-0.9	2,816	91.8	0.7	0.2	3.7	3.5	28.7	55.6	15.7	1,061	50.9	55.8	11.6
Reeder township (Missaukee)	1,128	1,141	1.2	1,118	98.1	0.0	0.0	1.3	0.5	30.6	48.4	21.0	374	86.1	51.1	12.6
Reese village	1,459	1,414	-3.1	1,590	90.4	0.0	0.6	1.7	7.3	22.7	58.4	19.0	735	76.2	37.8	21.9
Reno township (Iosco)	590	578	-2.0	659	96.7	0.0	0.0	2.3	1.1	23.7	59.1	17.1	246	87.8	66.3	4.1
Republic CDP	570	NA	NA	494	99.6	0.0	0.0	0.0	0.4	17.1	55.9	26.7	260	71.5	50.0	10.8
Republic township (Marquette)	1,060	1,072	1.1	948	97.6	0.0	0.0	0.5	1.9	16.9	52.2	31.0	477	83.6	45.9	18.7
Resort township (Emmet)	2,699	2,750	1.9	2,705	92.3	0.5	0.7	5.1	1.3	24.9	56.1	19.1	1,020	91.1	32.4	37.4
Reynolds township (Montcalm)	5,310	5,253	-1.1	5,271	94.3	0.0	0.7	1.1	3.9	24.5	61.6	13.8	1,994	81.7	59.9	9.2
Rich township (Lapeer)	1,623	1,617	-0.4	1,640	94.8	0.7	1.3	1.5	1.7	29.1	57.9	13.0	543	93.6	39.4	13.8
Richfield township (Genesee)	8,730	8,433	-3.4	8,565	92.1	1.6	0.0	3.5	2.7	24.5	59.1	16.5	3,174	92.4	37.1	21.0
Richfield township (Roscommon)	3,733	3,656	-2.1	3,677	96.7	0.0	0.4	0.8	2.2	13.1	58.9	28.1	1,851	80.7	58.0	10.0
Richland village	751	774	3.1	858	93.4	0.3	0.8	2.1	3.4	23.7	54.4	22.0	334	80.8	19.5	46.7
Richland township (Kalamazoo)	7,580	7,930	4.6	7,744	90.6	3.8	0.5	1.5	3.7	25.1	60.9	14.0	2,934	75.0	24.3	45.9
Richland township (Missaukee)	1,491	1,511	1.3	1,416	96.7	0.4	0.2	1.1	1.6	21.3	65.2	13.7	582	86.6	52.4	18.4
Richland township (Montcalm)	2,778	2,766	-0.4	2,768	91.8	0.8	2.5	1.5	3.4	23.3	60.5	16.1	1,011	83.4	52.5	13.0
Richland township (Ogemaw)	914	885	-3.2	1,087	91.0	0.0	0.0	4.0	5.0	23.3	60.1	16.6	414	88.9	52.4	10.6
Richland township (Saginaw)	4,144	4,031	-2.7	4,078	93.7	1.0	0.2	0.7	4.4	23.9	58.5	17.5	1,567	82.5	45.4	18.7
Richmond city	5,773	5,833	1.0	5,806	85.2	4.3	0.0	2.6	7.9	27.0	60.8	12.4	2,373	70.7	42.1	15.7
Richmond city (Macomb)	5,771	5,831	1.0	5,800	85.2	4.3	0.0	2.6	7.9	27.0	60.7	12.4	2,370	70.7	42.0	15.7
Richmond city (St. Clair)	2	2	0.0	6	100.0	0.0	0.0	0.0	0.0	0.0	100.0	0.0	3	100.0	100.0	0.0
Richmond township (Macomb)	3,627	3,659	0.9	3,631	98.1	0.9	0.0	0.3	0.7	22.4	61.1	16.4	1,169	92.0	45.1	20.6
Richmond township (Marquette)	884	896	1.4	906	96.1	0.0	0.0	0.8	3.1	22.9	64.0	13.1	350	90.3	55.4	13.7
Richmond township (Osceola)	1,554	1,539	-1.0	1,621	97.5	1.1	0.0	0.8	0.6	19.4	64.3	16.5	623	86.8	46.9	24.4
Ridgeway township (Lenawee)	1,546	1,515	-2.0	1,662	94.2	0.1	0.8	2.3	2.5	24.2	64.0	11.7	640	78.1	40.3	18.8
Riga township (Lenawee)	1,406	1,373	-2.3	1,395	96.2	0.0	0.0	0.3	3.5	26.8	59.7	13.5	512	80.7	37.3	19.9
Riley township (Clinton)	2,024	2,072	2.4	2,218	94.5	0.0	0.5	2.0	3.1	27.5	57.8	14.8	712	94.9	39.2	25.1
Riley township (St. Clair)	3,353	3,301	-1.6	3,316	97.0	0.8	0.1	0.9	1.3	24.6	62.8	12.5	1,193	89.0	39.6	13.3
River Rouge city & MCD (Wayne)	7,903	7,618	-3.6	7,761	30.5	54.5	0.5	2.4	12.2	26.9	61.3	11.9	2,828	56.9	59.7	6.4
Riverside township (Missaukee)	1,179	1,193	1.2	1,052	97.9	0.4	0.0	0.4	1.3	31.4	57.3	11.5	347	90.5	60.5	19.0
Riverton township (Mason)	1,153	1,158	0.4	1,219	89.7	0.2	1.0	0.8	8.3	28.2	58.9	12.9	437	88.6	31.8	19.9
Riverview city & MCD (Wayne)	12,486	12,222	-2.1	12,347	85.3	4.8	0.5	2.4	7.0	21.5	55.8	22.6	4,895	66.2	37.2	24.8
Rives township (Jackson)	4,683	4,657	-0.6	4,664	93.0	2.2	0.0	2.3	2.6	24.8	62.9	12.5	1,653	87.9	35.6	14.6
Robin Glen-Indiantown CDP	722	NA	NA	894	80.8	3.1	0.0	1.7	14.4	30.0	63.4	6.7	329	76.9	30.7	14.0
Robinson township (Ottawa)	6,084	6,389	5.0	6,221	93.8	0.0	1.1	1.0	4.1	27.4	61.6	11.2	2,057	94.1	36.5	27.4
Rochester city & MCD (Oakland)	12,711	12,995	2.2	12,872	84.3	4.8	6.8	1.5	2.6	24.3	62.2	13.5	5,488	64.2	12.2	59.5
Rochester Hills city & MCD (Oakland)	70,995	73,125	3.0	72,195	78.9	5.5	9.9	2.4	3.3	23.1	62.6	14.2	27,790	75.5	17.2	54.4
Rockford city & MCD (Kent)	5,723	6,058	5.9	5,876	93.8	1.9	0.4	1.2	2.7	31.2	58.8	10.1	2,322	71.8	24.7	38.2
Rockland township (Ontonagon)	228	208	-8.8	181	95.0	0.0	0.0	1.7	3.3	16.6	49.3	34.3	92	89.1	50.0	10.9
Rock River township (Alger)	1,212	1,185	-2.2	1,592	94.9	0.0	0.0	5.0	0.1	16.8	60.7	22.6	617	87.2	51.7	19.6

1 May be of any race.

Table A. All Places — **Population and Housing**

	Population				Race and Hispanic or Latino origin (percent), 2010–2014					Age (percent), 2010–2014			Households, 2010–2014			
								All other races or 2 or more races, not Hispanic or Latino							Householders by level of education (percent)	
STATE City, town, township, borough, or CDP (county if applicable)	2010 census total population	2014 estimated population	Percent change 2010–2014	ACS total population estimate 2010–2014	White alone, not Hispanic or Latino	Black alone, not Hispanic or Latino	Asian alone, not Hispanic or Latino		Hispanic or Latino[1]	Under 18 years old	Age 18 to 64 years old	Age 65 years and older	Total occupied housing units	Percent owner occupied	High school diploma or less	Bachelor's degree or more
	1	2	3	4	5	6	7	8	9	10	11	12	13	14	15	16
MICHIGAN—Con.																
Rockwood city & MCD (Wayne)	3,289	3,216	-2.2	3,243	91.1	0.3	4.9	0.6	3.1	19.5	67.0	13.4	1,297	69.2	57.4	8.0
Rogers township (Presque Isle)	984	959	-2.5	1,099	95.5	0.0	0.7	1.4	2.4	19.3	53.3	27.4	467	94.4	43.5	18.8
Rogers City city & MCD (Presque Isle)	2,827	2,747	-2.8	2,774	96.3	1.3	0.7	1.5	0.2	15.1	53.7	31.3	1,379	69.0	50.4	21.2
Rolland township (Isabella)	1,305	1,292	-1.0	1,762	97.7	1.1	0.0	0.7	0.5	28.1	62.5	9.5	523	88.0	53.7	14.5
Rollin township (Lenawee)	3,270	3,257	-0.4	3,249	96.6	0.4	0.0	1.6	1.4	16.2	60.1	23.6	1,466	85.1	45.8	21.2
Rome township (Lenawee)	1,791	1,769	-1.2	1,632	93.3	1.5	0.9	2.4	2.0	21.3	61.9	16.7	634	89.0	43.8	12.9
Romeo village	3,596	3,628	0.9	3,608	84.9	5.3	0.0	5.8	3.9	18.4	65.8	15.8	1,534	69.8	35.8	27.9
Romulus city & MCD (Wayne)	23,989	23,496	-2.1	23,721	47.3	42.4	2.9	4.6	2.9	26.8	62.4	10.9	8,741	65.1	48.7	10.5
Ronald township (Ionia)	1,869	1,874	0.3	1,541	93.2	3.6	0.3	0.8	2.1	20.1	61.9	18.0	620	90.2	50.5	11.6
Roosevelt Park city & MCD (Muskegon)	3,831	3,818	-0.3	3,817	85.7	5.8	0.7	2.6	5.1	24.4	57.5	18.1	1,708	60.7	35.4	20.7
Roscommon village	1,075	1,065	-0.9	970	87.0	3.8	0.0	4.5	4.6	18.1	62.2	19.8	393	42.2	40.5	10.7
Roscommon township (Roscommon)	4,411	4,306	-2.4	4,353	95.0	0.3	0.4	3.5	0.8	14.1	57.2	28.6	2,115	77.4	50.9	11.4
Rose township (Oakland)	6,250	6,406	2.5	6,339	93.5	1.9	0.1	1.7	2.9	19.2	67.2	13.5	2,431	91.1	28.6	31.4
Rose township (Ogemaw)	1,368	1,337	-2.3	1,204	98.9	0.0	0.3	0.7	0.0	14.7	56.3	29.0	575	92.2	57.2	9.6
Rosebush village	368	366	-0.5	373	96.2	0.5	0.0	1.1	2.1	25.4	55.7	18.8	184	57.1	52.2	14.7
Rose City city & MCD (Ogemaw)	653	636	-2.6	641	97.2	0.8	0.0	0.3	1.7	27.0	49.0	24.0	226	60.6	54.0	10.2
Rose Lake township (Osceola)	1,373	1,350	-1.7	1,230	95.4	1.2	0.7	2.7	0.0	20.1	59.0	20.7	494	90.1	55.5	11.3
Roseville city & MCD (Macomb)	47,299	47,598	0.6	47,408	77.1	14.1	1.8	4.3	2.7	23.2	63.5	13.2	19,669	65.1	50.0	11.0
Ross township (Kalamazoo)	4,664	4,820	3.3	4,754	95.2	0.5	0.0	2.2	2.1	19.5	61.9	18.5	1,879	82.3	21.6	48.6
Rothbury village	432	425	-1.6	346	89.9	0.0	0.0	2.9	7.2	17.7	69.6	12.7	119	73.1	52.1	10.1
Roxand township (Eaton)	1,848	1,862	0.8	2,093	95.6	0.1	0.0	1.4	2.9	25.5	60.3	14.1	765	85.0	44.1	14.5
Royal Oak city & MCD (Oakland)	57,236	59,069	3.2	58,382	89.8	3.2	2.7	1.8	2.5	16.2	70.5	13.4	28,269	67.0	18.5	54.5
Royal Oak charter township (Oakland)	2,419	2,462	1.8	2,707	2.6	90.4	0.0	6.7	0.3	26.7	56.1	17.3	1,063	31.5	48.1	9.4
Royalton township (Berrien)	4,766	4,765	0.0	4,770	86.8	3.8	4.0	1.4	4.0	25.1	57.0	17.7	1,572	87.4	25.2	46.1
Rubicon township (Huron)	732	707	-3.4	715	98.7	0.0	0.0	0.7	0.6	13.8	51.4	35.0	348	89.7	58.3	8.3
Rudyard township (Chippewa)	1,370	1,365	-0.4	1,224	81.3	1.5	0.3	14.9	2.0	26.0	58.1	16.0	477	88.9	42.6	17.4
Rush township (Shiawassee)	1,291	1,260	-2.4	1,212	93.5	0.0	1.6	1.2	3.7	18.5	61.5	20.0	490	86.3	56.9	17.6
Rust township (Montmorency)	561	531	-5.3	490	94.9	0.0	0.0	0.0	5.1	20.4	58.7	21.0	196	92.3	60.2	12.8
Rutland charter township (Barry)	3,987	3,983	-0.1	3,970	93.0	0.4	0.4	1.5	4.7	28.3	53.3	18.4	1,369	81.7	50.6	24.1
Sage township (Gladwin)	2,457	2,428	-1.2	2,765	93.0	2.6	0.8	0.9	2.7	26.7	53.5	19.7	1,034	87.3	54.2	10.0
Saginaw city & MCD (Saginaw)	51,507	49,844	-3.2	50,700	37.5	44.1	0.5	3.4	14.5	26.1	62.4	11.4	19,376	60.9	52.5	12.7
Saginaw charter township (Saginaw)	40,840	39,982	-2.1	40,469	79.2	9.1	3.5	1.4	6.7	19.1	60.0	20.8	17,783	63.7	31.8	33.4
Sagola township (Dickinson)	1,106	1,098	-0.7	1,105	97.6	0.5	0.0	1.5	0.4	14.5	62.8	22.8	510	91.4	59.6	9.0
St. Charles village	2,054	1,981	-3.6	2,016	94.6	0.1	0.0	0.9	4.3	22.2	62.1	15.6	822	74.3	42.0	11.4
St. Charles township (Saginaw)	3,330	3,236	-2.8	3,281	95.3	0.0	0.0	1.3	3.3	23.6	61.4	15.1	1,272	82.0	46.1	12.6
St. Clair city & MCD (St. Clair)	5,485	5,400	-1.5	5,428	96.1	0.1	1.2	0.8	1.9	22.7	62.7	14.5	2,376	73.0	37.9	27.1
St. Clair township (St. Clair)	6,817	6,736	-1.2	6,757	97.0	0.0	0.4	0.5	2.1	23.6	61.3	15.2	2,537	92.2	33.7	24.4
St. Clair Shores city & MCD (Macomb)	59,730	60,036	0.5	59,865	90.2	4.6	1.1	2.0	2.1	19.4	62.1	18.5	26,663	78.4	36.0	25.2
St. Helen CDP	2,668	NA	NA	2,774	96.0	0.0	0.5	0.6	2.9	14.2	60.0	25.8	1,404	77.3	56.1	8.3
St. Ignace city & MCD (Mackinac)	2,452	2,424	-1.1	2,615	66.3	1.0	1.0	30.1	1.6	21.1	59.9	19.0	1,126	59.3	43.7	16.2
St. Ignace township (Mackinac)	939	927	-1.3	933	65.3	1.3	0.4	33.0	0.0	20.9	59.1	19.9	432	77.1	57.4	10.6
St. James CDP	205	NA	NA	218	97.7	0.0	0.0	2.3	0.0	19.2	48.7	32.1	98	85.7	51.0	20.4
St. James township (Charlevoix)	365	369	1.1	317	98.4	0.0	0.0	1.6	0.0	18.3	49.0	32.8	141	89.4	46.8	25.5
St. Johns city & MCD (Clinton)	7,865	7,971	1.3	7,933	89.5	2.0	0.0	2.8	5.0	25.3	56.8	17.8	3,222	69.0	40.8	21.7
St. Joseph city & MCD (Berrien)	8,365	8,325	-0.5	8,310	90.2	4.5	1.9	2.4	1.0	12.7	69.0	18.3	3,932	61.9	23.8	44.8
St. Joseph charter township (Berrien)	10,028	9,919	-1.1	9,974	81.5	12.9	3.2	1.5	0.9	23.0	57.5	19.5	4,090	89.0	27.7	40.8
St. Louis city & MCD (Gratiot)	7,482	7,249	-3.1	7,347	65.5	25.0	0.1	3.3	6.1	13.5	77.4	9.3	1,475	62.6	54.6	12.8
Salem township (Allegan)	4,446	4,664	4.9	4,537	94.4	0.0	2.6	0.3	2.6	27.3	64.2	8.3	1,534	97.3	54.4	10.4
Salem township (Washtenaw)	5,627	5,911	5.0	5,778	93.8	1.6	0.8	2.1	1.7	20.9	64.4	14.7	2,030	95.1	37.4	25.4
Saline city & MCD (Washtenaw)	8,810	9,158	4.0	9,000	92.3	0.6	2.4	1.3	3.4	24.1	59.4	16.6	3,891	74.6	17.2	57.5
Saline township (Washtenaw)	1,896	2,060	8.6	1,749	90.3	1.1	0.2	4.2	4.1	19.8	65.0	15.2	690	84.2	38.8	35.2
Sanborn township (Alpena)	2,116	2,065	-2.4	2,133	97.0	0.0	0.0	1.2	1.8	26.7	58.3	15.1	855	77.5	52.4	11.7
Sand Beach township (Huron)	1,221	1,182	-3.2	1,065	97.4	0.0	0.0	2.3	0.4	21.5	56.9	21.6	452	88.7	58.0	13.9
Sand Lake CDP	1,412	NA	NA	1,535	98.7	0.0	0.0	1.0	0.3	11.8	54.5	33.6	731	89.2	61.3	9.2

1 May be of any race.

Table A. All Places — **Population and Housing**

STATE City, town, township, borough, or CDP (county if applicable)	2010 census total population	2014 estimated population	Percent change 2010–2014	ACS total population estimate 2010–2014	White alone, not Hispanic or Latino	Black alone, not Hispanic or Latino	Asian alone, not Hispanic or Latino	All other races or 2 or more races, not Hispanic or Latino	Hispanic or Latino[1]	Under 18 years old	Age 18 to 64 years old	Age 65 years and older	Total occupied housing units	Percent owner occupied	High school diploma or less	Bachelor's degree or more
	1	2	3	4	5	6	7	8	9	10	11	12	13	14	15	16
MICHIGAN—Con.																
Sand Lake village	500	518	3.6	503	92.2	0.0	0.0	0.8	7.0	26.0	62.3	11.7	196	59.7	50.0	12.8
Sands township (Marquette)	2,285	2,303	0.8	2,694	97.0	0.1	0.4	1.3	1.2	25.3	66.1	8.7	975	90.3	28.9	38.4
Sandstone township (Jackson)	3,984	3,992	0.2	3,983	94.3	0.0	0.0	5.0	0.7	21.1	59.8	19.2	1,437	91.6	41.9	21.7
Sandusky city & MCD (Sanilac)	2,679	2,604	-2.8	2,638	89.0	0.9	0.5	3.3	6.2	18.3	62.8	18.7	1,060	53.8	54.2	12.3
Sanford village	859	847	-1.4	950	98.5	0.0	0.0	0.9	0.5	20.5	65.1	14.4	414	65.0	45.7	18.1
Sanilac township (Sanilac)	2,431	2,343	-3.6	2,242	93.4	0.1	0.8	2.0	3.7	13.0	58.6	28.3	1,025	88.1	51.9	21.9
Saranac village	1,321	1,333	0.9	1,469	82.8	1.5	0.0	10.9	4.8	33.0	55.7	11.4	590	53.7	56.1	11.2
Sauble township (Lake)	333	328	-1.5	291	98.6	0.0	0.0	1.4	0.0	5.2	46.0	48.8	148	91.9	43.2	13.5
Saugatuck city & MCD (Allegan)	951	963	1.3	883	92.5	1.0	0.2	0.5	5.8	17.6	55.3	27.1	455	67.3	26.2	48.4
Saugatuck township (Allegan)	2,918	3,062	4.9	2,977	95.8	0.2	0.0	1.8	2.3	25.4	57.0	17.5	1,144	93.1	32.8	39.3
Sault Ste. Marie city & MCD (Chippewa)..........	14,144	13,959	-1.3	14,121	74.4	4.0	1.1	19.5	1.0	22.6	64.8	12.7	5,785	56.2	42.6	20.2
Schoolcraft township (Houghton)	1,841	1,816	-1.4	1,785	94.6	0.0	1.1	1.8	2.6	26.9	55.9	17.4	720	77.9	45.1	22.6
Schoolcraft village	1,525	1,563	2.5	1,657	96.0	1.3	0.4	2.1	0.3	19.8	65.3	15.0	671	63.9	52.8	17.7
Schoolcraft township (Kalamazoo).................	8,219	8,621	4.9	8,421	95.9	0.6	0.1	2.7	0.7	24.7	59.6	15.8	3,308	77.8	40.0	24.3
Scio township (Washtenaw)	20,072	21,332	6.3	20,748	77.4	5.3	9.2	3.4	4.8	27.4	60.5	12.1	7,889	78.3	15.4	66.5
Sciota township (Shiawassee)	1,833	1,792	-2.2	1,633	96.8	0.1	0.2	1.6	1.2	22.3	66.7	11.1	648	89.2	30.2	23.8
Scipio township (Hillsdale)	1,884	1,839	-2.4	1,842	96.3	0.2	0.0	2.2	1.3	25.9	60.4	13.6	668	80.1	44.0	13.0
Scottville city & MCD (Mason)	1,214	1,218	0.3	1,209	88.9	0.0	1.4	2.5	7.2	31.2	55.9	12.8	428	65.4	46.0	16.1
Sebewa township (Ionia) ..	1,171	1,177	0.5	1,167	96.5	0.0	0.0	0.8	2.7	21.1	64.0	15.0	453	88.5	41.3	17.7
Sebewaing village	1,759	1,702	-3.2	1,654	91.7	0.0	1.1	1.2	5.9	14.2	62.7	23.1	747	77.2	57.0	13.9
Sebewaing township (Huron)	2,724	2,636	-3.2	2,668	94.0	0.0	0.7	1.0	4.2	19.1	62.1	18.9	1,123	80.9	54.9	13.4
Secord township (Gladwin)	1,151	1,139	-1.0	1,084	96.3	0.2	0.0	1.7	1.8	7.8	53.1	39.1	571	93.7	50.8	11.9
Selma township (Wexford)	2,093	2,099	0.3	2,053	96.5	0.0	0.7	0.9	1.9	17.2	65.0	17.7	866	81.6	49.9	22.2
Seneca township (Lenawee)	1,229	1,201	-2.3	1,112	97.3	0.4	0.4	0.0	1.9	24.1	59.0	16.9	429	92.8	52.7	15.4
Seney township (Schoolcraft)	119	115	-3.4	55	80.0	20.0	0.0	0.0	0.0	16.4	69.2	14.5	24	66.7	41.7	12.5
Seville township (Gratiot)..	2,173	2,132	-1.9	2,016	94.3	2.2	0.0	0.6	2.8	26.1	55.0	18.8	772	89.2	51.3	14.6
Sharon township (Washtenaw)	1,737	1,805	3.9	2,045	92.8	4.3	0.3	0.0	2.6	19.3	64.5	16.3	745	90.9	30.9	36.8
Shelby charter township (Macomb)	73,804	76,859	4.1	75,178	90.2	2.8	3.5	1.7	1.8	22.2	61.6	16.0	28,974	75.8	31.8	34.1
Shelby village	2,065	2,028	-1.8	1,793	49.7	0.0	0.0	2.5	47.8	32.4	54.3	13.3	613	57.3	59.1	14.0
Shelby township (Oceana)	4,069	4,023	-1.1	4,025	70.3	0.0	0.0	1.7	28.0	30.1	60.1	10.0	1,344	69.9	46.8	21.6
Shepherd village..............	1,515	1,508	-0.5	1,564	89.7	0.0	0.1	6.3	3.8	18.4	65.8	15.7	712	67.1	43.7	21.3
Sheridan township (Calhoun)	1,936	1,905	-1.6	2,123	89.9	4.0	0.3	3.8	2.0	28.2	55.1	16.8	740	82.2	51.6	13.2
Sheridan township (Clare)	1,575	1,554	-1.3	1,412	90.9	0.2	0.0	5.0	3.8	36.2	50.4	13.5	502	85.1	50.2	10.8
Sheridan township (Huron)	712	689	-3.2	735	97.7	0.0	0.5	0.0	1.8	27.5	54.5	17.8	254	89.8	53.5	9.4
Sheridan township (Mason).................	1,072	1,075	0.3	1,084	97.8	0.4	0.6	0.7	0.6	16.6	57.3	26.0	512	86.1	44.3	15.4
Sheridan township (Mecosta)	1,393	1,396	0.2	1,401	83.4	2.4	0.5	6.3	7.4	19.0	64.5	16.6	535	90.3	49.3	10.7
Sheridan village	649	650	0.2	624	98.2	0.5	0.0	1.0	0.3	19.6	61.3	19.1	271	81.2	46.5	14.0
Sheridan charter township (Newaygo).................	2,504	2,486	-0.7	2,679	87.9	0.0	0.4	2.0	9.7	25.7	58.9	15.4	942	84.3	44.9	18.7
Sherman township (Gladwin).................	1,043	1,033	-1.0	1,010	96.4	0.0	2.2	0.5	0.9	20.5	51.9	27.5	443	86.9	57.6	10.4
Sherman township (Huron)	1,083	1,047	-3.3	921	95.8	0.0	0.3	2.8	1.1	15.0	60.7	24.3	419	91.4	67.8	11.2
Sherman township (Iosco)	448	440	-1.8	411	91.2	0.0	0.0	0.7	8.0	14.6	63.2	22.1	178	84.3	69.1	15.7
Sherman township (Isabella)	2,991	2,935	-1.9	2,981	97.3	0.5	0.0	0.7	1.4	23.2	58.3	18.6	1,238	86.4	51.0	13.7
Sherman township (Keweenaw)	67	69	3.0	79	100.0	0.0	0.0	0.0	0.0	7.6	62.0	30.4	41	100.0	41.5	41.5
Sherman township (Mason).................	1,186	1,192	0.5	1,184	88.9	0.2	0.0	3.7	7.2	27.0	57.6	15.5	457	88.6	38.1	15.3
Sherman township (Newaygo).................	2,109	2,083	-1.2	2,049	91.1	0.3	1.0	3.6	4.0	22.3	56.4	21.2	731	89.9	48.3	17.5
Sherman township (Osceola)	1,042	1,028	-1.3	926	96.3	0.9	0.0	2.8	0.0	22.5	59.0	18.7	348	84.2	44.5	20.1
Sherman township (St. Joseph)	3,205	3,229	0.7	3,210	95.7	0.0	1.2	1.4	1.7	24.0	51.9	24.0	1,203	93.3	40.4	20.4
Sherwood village	309	308	-0.3	317	94.0	0.0	0.0	3.5	2.5	29.3	60.0	10.7	105	84.8	59.0	2.9
Sherwood township (Branch)	2,094	2,061	-1.6	1,969	97.1	0.0	0.0	2.3	0.6	19.9	62.6	17.4	753	89.5	56.3	8.5
Shiawassee township (Shiawassee)	2,840	2,773	-2.4	2,793	96.0	0.0	1.4	2.4	0.3	24.3	61.6	14.0	1,035	88.1	45.8	14.8
Shields CDP	6,587	NA	NA	6,430	92.1	1.2	1.1	1.8	3.8	21.8	55.3	22.8	2,606	80.5	40.4	26.3
Shoreham village	862	854	-0.9	832	79.2	8.4	6.3	0.8	5.3	21.1	57.1	21.8	357	79.6	17.1	61.1
Shorewood-Tower Hills-Harbert CDP	1,344	NA	NA	1,188	96.8	0.0	0.8	0.0	2.4	11.0	49.7	39.3	594	93.4	24.4	41.8
Sidney township (Montcalm)	2,574	2,562	-0.5	2,564	92.7	2.9	0.0	0.3	4.0	21.5	63.8	14.7	1,001	80.4	49.2	13.7
Sigel township (Huron)	465	451	-3.0	437	98.6	0.0	0.5	0.0	0.9	23.8	59.5	16.5	177	89.8	63.8	15.3
Silver Creek township (Cass)	3,211	3,166	-1.4	3,190	91.7	2.9	0.1	2.3	3.0	20.2	56.6	23.4	1,224	95.4	31.5	28.6
Sims township (Arenac)....	1,095	1,063	-2.9	955	96.1	0.0	0.1	1.5	2.3	15.8	49.3	34.8	454	93.4	48.2	20.0

1 May be of any race.

Table A. All Places — Population and Housing

STATE City, town, township, borough, or CDP (county if applicable)	2010 census total population	2014 estimated population	Percent change 2010–2014	ACS total population estimate 2010–2014	White alone, not Hispanic or Latino	Black alone, not Hispanic or Latino	Asian alone, not Hispanic or Latino	All other races or 2 or more races, not Hispanic or Latino	Hispanic or Latino[1]	Under 18 years old	Age 18 to 64 years old	Age 65 years and older	Total occupied housing units	Percent owner occupied	High school diploma or less	Bachelor's degree or more
	1	2	3	4	5	6	7	8	9	10	11	12	13	14	15	16
MICHIGAN—Con.																
Skandia township (Marquette)	826	833	0.8	804	90.9	0.9	0.2	7.8	0.1	17.3	69.1	13.7	361	85.3	49.3	24.1
Skidway Lake CDP	3,392	NA	NA	3,329	92.6	0.7	0.6	4.9	1.2	17.5	63.5	19.1	1,541	80.9	74.4	4.2
Slagle township (Wexford)	503	506	0.6	558	93.5	0.0	0.0	1.1	5.4	24.2	57.4	18.5	232	83.6	54.3	14.2
Snover CDP	448	NA	NA	457	98.0	0.0	0.0	0.0	2.0	27.8	57.4	14.9	153	81.0	47.1	7.8
Sodus township (Berrien)	1,932	1,937	0.3	1,929	76.7	5.9	2.5	1.8	13.1	17.6	60.4	21.9	840	81.5	46.0	15.2
Solon township (Kent)	5,974	6,349	6.3	6,153	86.8	1.5	0.1	7.2	4.4	29.1	58.1	12.7	2,233	88.9	49.7	13.7
Solon township (Leelanau)	1,509	1,522	0.9	1,440	94.7	0.1	1.8	3.1	0.3	19.0	63.5	17.5	577	91.3	30.5	33.1
Somerset township (Hillsdale)	4,623	4,568	-1.2	4,597	98.3	0.0	0.0	0.5	1.2	13.9	65.1	21.1	2,087	87.8	42.5	26.9
Soo township (Chippewa)	3,141	3,144	0.1	3,167	65.6	0.8	1.4	31.3	0.9	19.8	64.0	16.3	1,264	73.7	44.4	30.5
South Arm township (Charlevoix)	1,873	1,883	0.5	1,848	93.9	1.3	0.0	4.4	0.3	18.2	56.3	25.5	688	93.6	46.7	25.9
South Boardman CDP	536	NA	NA	571	91.8	0.0	0.0	0.9	7.4	27.5	63.9	8.8	211	64.5	59.2	8.5
South Branch township (Crawford)	2,007	1,950	-2.8	1,887	98.0	0.0	1.7	0.3	0.0	13.4	62.3	24.3	824	89.1	41.0	15.0
South Branch township (Wexford)	383	383	0.0	285	99.3	0.0	0.0	0.7	0.0	12.7	56.5	30.9	124	88.7	44.4	19.4
Southfield city & MCD (Oakland)	71,739	73,002	1.8	72,480	25.0	69.0	1.4	3.4	1.3	20.1	61.5	18.3	31,930	49.8	24.2	38.7
Southfield township (Oakland)	14,547	14,829	1.9	14,694	85.4	7.2	2.8	2.8	1.7	25.1	56.1	18.6	5,636	89.2	7.7	74.9
Southgate city & MCD (Wayne)	30,047	29,416	-2.1	29,710	84.1	5.5	1.8	2.2	6.5	18.0	64.7	17.3	12,749	63.9	43.3	18.1
South Gull Lake CDP	1,182	NA	NA	1,357	99.3	0.0	0.0	0.7	0.0	15.6	62.8	21.7	552	82.8	2.5	75.9
South Haven city	4,397	4,363	-0.8	4,367	79.6	14.8	1.2	3.1	1.3	20.2	55.9	23.9	2,024	57.4	32.7	22.8
South Haven city (Van Buren)	4,394	4,360	-0.8	4,367	79.6	14.8	1.2	3.1	1.3	20.2	55.9	23.9	2,024	57.4	32.7	22.8
South Haven charter township (Van Buren)	3,989	3,924	-1.6	3,946	81.0	7.3	0.0	2.3	9.4	24.8	54.9	20.3	1,718	72.5	48.4	16.2
South Lyon city & MCD (Oakland)	11,327	11,713	3.4	11,514	91.9	1.7	1.7	1.1	3.6	24.3	61.6	14.2	4,843	73.0	27.4	39.1
South Monroe CDP	6,433	NA	NA	6,622	87.4	5.2	1.8	2.8	2.9	20.8	58.7	20.8	2,810	70.5	46.8	15.6
South Range village	758	749	-1.2	761	95.4	0.0	2.4	0.5	1.7	24.1	60.6	15.4	314	76.1	47.1	26.1
South Rockwood village	1,681	1,642	-2.3	1,943	90.3	0.6	0.0	3.1	6.0	22.0	66.0	12.0	694	66.6	50.6	15.7
Spalding township (Menominee)	1,674	1,656	-1.1	1,793	91.9	2.3	0.0	4.0	1.8	19.5	59.5	21.2	699	79.3	56.1	10.6
Sparta village	4,140	4,264	3.0	4,199	90.3	1.3	1.0	2.8	4.7	26.9	60.6	12.6	1,734	62.5	45.9	19.8
Sparta township (Kent)	9,112	9,359	2.7	9,234	88.8	2.3	0.9	2.6	5.4	27.7	59.6	12.6	3,505	75.7	46.1	19.2
Spaulding township (Saginaw)	2,156	2,083	-3.4	2,140	69.8	13.2	0.0	3.8	13.2	23.1	58.9	18.2	788	84.3	49.6	8.6
Speaker township (Sanilac)	1,483	1,432	-3.4	1,419	98.5	0.0	0.0	0.9	0.6	22.2	62.4	15.4	503	85.9	54.1	8.3
Spencer township (Kent)	3,960	4,083	3.1	4,011	91.3	0.1	1.2	1.3	6.0	23.6	61.8	14.7	1,552	92.8	43.4	16.8
Spring Arbor CDP	2,881	NA	NA	2,795	90.5	4.0	0.9	0.5	4.0	8.2	73.6	18.1	745	67.1	40.5	38.9
Spring Arbor township (Jackson)	8,267	8,269	0.0	8,269	94.6	1.4	0.3	1.2	2.5	21.1	62.5	16.4	2,696	84.7	31.5	35.3
Springdale township (Manistee)	781	777	-0.5	812	98.8	0.0	0.0	0.2	1.0	28.2	55.4	16.4	319	85.0	51.1	15.7
Springfield city & MCD (Calhoun)	5,260	5,211	-0.9	5,231	74.7	8.2	11.4	4.7	1.1	23.8	64.8	11.4	2,131	50.7	55.6	13.7
Springfield township (Kalkaska)	1,523	1,542	1.2	1,422	95.9	0.9	0.0	2.3	0.7	17.5	61.4	21.0	565	86.4	54.2	13.8
Springfield charter township (Oakland)	13,940	14,344	2.9	14,155	95.1	0.7	0.3	0.7	3.2	25.4	62.0	12.5	5,091	90.8	25.8	40.6
Spring Lake village	2,323	2,449	5.4	2,413	95.2	0.5	0.3	2.2	1.8	18.7	58.1	23.2	1,094	82.7	26.3	36.6
Spring Lake township (Ottawa)	14,300	14,887	4.1	14,555	94.4	0.1	2.2	1.4	1.9	22.3	59.0	18.7	5,922	75.2	23.9	38.9
Springport village	800	792	-1.0	748	94.5	2.0	1.2	0.7	1.6	31.4	56.6	11.9	287	57.8	56.4	8.4
Springport township (Jackson)	2,159	2,151	-0.4	2,221	96.4	0.7	0.4	0.7	1.8	23.7	64.0	12.3	871	79.8	43.9	11.0
Springvale township (Emmet)	2,140	2,175	1.6	2,210	97.3	0.0	0.2	1.9	0.6	28.9	58.7	12.4	774	93.4	31.1	34.9
Springville township (Wexford)	1,755	1,756	0.1	1,863	94.3	2.4	0.0	3.0	0.4	28.0	59.6	12.5	665	76.7	57.3	11.4
Spurr township (Baraga)	276	274	-0.7	247	99.6	0.0	0.0	0.0	0.4	6.1	60.4	33.6	128	95.3	37.5	39.8
Stambaugh township (Iron)	1,140	1,101	-3.4	1,138	92.9	1.7	0.2	3.9	1.4	13.2	57.4	29.3	519	94.4	40.7	32.4
Standish city & MCD (Arenac)	1,509	1,461	-3.2	1,742	85.9	7.0	0.5	4.0	2.6	20.4	65.8	13.7	618	54.4	58.9	14.9
Standish township (Arenac)	1,900	1,833	-3.5	1,702	97.2	0.0	0.0	2.4	0.4	19.0	60.2	20.4	711	90.3	56.8	10.4
Stannard township (Ontonagon)	792	718	-9.3	696	95.8	0.0	0.0	3.7	0.4	16.2	56.2	27.3	352	86.6	58.0	5.4
Stanton township (Houghton)	1,419	1,401	-1.3	1,299	98.8	0.2	0.2	0.8	0.0	28.8	49.3	21.9	459	94.8	44.9	28.5
Stanton city & MCD (Montcalm)	1,417	1,412	-0.4	1,589	92.6	2.6	0.0	0.8	4.0	28.8	56.3	14.9	586	54.1	46.8	8.9
Stanwood village	211	214	1.4	165	97.6	0.0	0.0	0.0	2.4	24.9	61.6	13.3	72	68.1	68.1	11.1
Star township (Antrim)	926	915	-1.2	888	97.3	0.0	0.0	0.8	1.9	26.2	59.7	14.0	324	78.1	44.8	17.9
Stephenson city & MCD (Menominee)	862	848	-1.6	877	98.4	1.1	0.0	0.2	0.2	19.6	53.8	26.6	338	74.0	53.0	14.8
Stephenson township (Menominee)	670	665	-0.7	605	99.0	0.0	0.0	0.5	0.5	22.5	59.8	17.9	280	90.0	50.4	17.5
Sterling village	530	515	-2.8	543	97.1	1.7	0.0	0.0	1.3	21.2	55.0	23.8	194	75.8	50.5	10.3
Sterling Heights city & MCD (Macomb)	129,699	131,741	1.6	130,604	83.9	5.1	6.7	2.3	2.0	20.7	63.5	15.9	49,387	73.1	36.8	29.3
Stevensville village	1,142	1,122	-1.8	1,312	89.0	1.0	1.8	7.1	1.1	20.6	55.4	24.2	598	72.7	37.6	31.3
Stockbridge village	1,218	1,224	0.5	1,111	96.8	0.0	0.0	0.5	2.6	21.7	59.5	18.8	487	69.2	38.6	20.7
Stockbridge township (Ingham)	3,896	3,916	0.5	3,915	93.9	0.0	0.0	0.3	5.7	20.7	63.3	16.2	1,445	83.7	46.4	17.9
Stony Point CDP	1,724	NA	NA	1,410	98.7	0.0	0.0	1.3	0.0	24.0	61.3	14.6	519	81.9	42.0	10.8

1 May be of any race.

Table A. All Places — **Population and Housing**

STATE City, town, township, borough, or CDP (county if applicable)	2010 census total population	2014 estimated population	Percent change 2010–2014	ACS total population estimate 2010–2014	White alone, not Hispanic or Latino	Black alone, not Hispanic or Latino	Asian alone, not Hispanic or Latino	All other races or 2 or more races, not Hispanic or Latino	Hispanic or Latino[1]	Under 18 years old	Age 18 to 64 years old	Age 65 years and older	Total occupied housing units	Percent owner occupied	High school diploma or less	Bachelor's degree or more
	1	2	3	4	5	6	7	8	9	10	11	12	13	14	15	16
MICHIGAN—Con.																
Stronach CDP..................	162	NA	NA	222	87.8	0.0	0.0	9.0	3.2	43.8	49.4	7.2	71	93.0	45.1	2.8
Stronach township (Manistee).....................	821	812	-1.1	821	91.4	0.0	0.0	6.7	1.9	22.9	62.0	15.1	368	89.7	45.7	8.7
Sturgis city & MCD (St. Joseph).....................	10,994	10,901	-0.8	10,923	73.9	1.7	0.3	2.6	21.5	29.8	58.2	12.0	4,085	60.2	53.5	16.3
Sturgis township (St. Joseph).....................	2,261	2,230	-1.4	2,504	82.4	0.8	0.0	0.5	16.3	27.0	58.9	14.2	942	67.4	57.1	10.0
Sugar Island township (Chippewa).................	652	650	-0.3	703	76.5	0.0	1.8	19.9	1.7	15.2	51.5	33.3	327	95.1	39.8	23.9
Sullivan township (Muskegon).................	2,441	2,469	1.1	2,178	96.0	1.7	0.0	1.1	1.2	22.3	60.4	17.3	821	94.2	50.7	14.0
Summerfield township (Clare)........................	456	450	-1.3	524	98.7	0.0	0.0	0.4	1.0	12.9	58.5	28.6	236	88.6	58.1	3.8
Summerfield township (Monroe).....................	3,308	3,253	-1.7	3,281	95.8	0.6	0.3	0.9	2.4	23.6	60.2	16.2	1,176	89.5	47.9	23.1
Summit township (Jackson)......................	22,508	22,474	-0.2	22,475	84.8	7.6	1.5	2.5	3.6	21.2	60.0	18.7	8,989	77.5	29.9	31.0
Summit township (Mason)	924	928	0.4	795	92.5	2.6	1.3	0.5	3.1	17.9	54.0	28.1	369	93.8	37.1	29.8
Sumner township (Gratiot)	1,930	1,893	-1.9	1,997	95.3	0.3	0.0	1.0	3.5	22.7	61.3	16.2	761	83.6	62.9	4.6
Sumpter township (Wayne).....................	9,549	9,360	-2.0	9,435	82.3	9.0	0.3	2.6	5.9	23.8	65.3	11.2	3,569	89.2	46.4	14.9
Sunfield village	578	582	0.7	651	91.7	0.6	0.3	0.2	7.2	28.9	62.6	8.4	242	66.5	55.8	4.1
Sunfield township (Eaton).	1,997	2,012	0.8	1,946	93.2	0.2	0.1	0.3	6.2	19.5	67.3	13.1	815	85.3	49.3	9.0
Superior township (Chippewa).................	1,337	1,332	-0.4	1,280	68.9	1.5	0.5	29.1	0.0	24.9	60.2	14.9	519	92.3	34.9	34.1
Superior charter township (Washtenaw).................	13,058	13,572	3.9	13,317	55.0	25.9	6.4	7.4	5.3	25.6	63.1	11.3	4,831	78.7	27.3	41.8
Surrey township (Clare)....	3,606	3,555	-1.4	3,576	95.9	0.0	0.2	2.0	1.9	21.6	57.0	21.4	1,501	80.7	55.2	12.9
Suttons Bay village	618	624	1.0	569	89.6	0.4	0.5	6.9	2.6	13.6	43.8	42.5	266	68.4	14.7	62.0
Suttons Bay township (Leelanau).................	2,982	3,009	0.9	2,984	72.0	0.9	1.0	18.8	7.3	19.9	58.8	21.2	1,171	75.1	24.2	38.6
Swan Creek township (Saginaw).................	2,456	2,424	-1.3	2,380	94.7	0.4	0.2	1.2	3.5	17.7	67.5	14.7	912	95.1	48.4	15.2
Swartz Creek city & MCD (Genesee).....................	5,758	5,589	-2.9	5,664	91.2	4.5	1.1	0.2	3.0	22.4	55.3	22.4	2,377	75.7	41.6	18.3
Sweetwater township (Lake)........................	245	241	-1.6	271	89.3	3.0	0.0	2.6	5.2	13.6	58.7	27.7	86	90.7	51.2	17.4
Sylvan township (Osceola)	1,099	1,085	-1.3	926	90.7	1.1	1.3	2.9	4.0	20.9	57.6	21.4	352	90.6	54.5	6.8
Sylvan township (Washtenaw).................	2,833	2,929	3.4	2,879	96.3	0.8	0.4	1.7	0.7	19.4	65.0	15.5	1,159	90.5	24.4	45.0
Sylvan Lake city & MCD (Oakland).................	1,720	1,799	4.6	1,591	93.7	4.1	0.3	0.0	1.9	15.7	67.2	17.2	788	80.3	17.5	63.7
Tallmadge charter township (Ottawa)	7,575	7,881	4.0	7,716	97.1	0.2	0.0	1.2	1.5	26.1	62.8	11.2	2,773	85.0	39.1	24.6
Tawas township (Iosco)	1,744	1,715	-1.7	1,820	94.9	0.2	0.3	4.3	0.3	23.4	56.1	20.7	667	89.7	42.7	15.3
Tawas City city & MCD (Iosco).....................	1,827	1,793	-1.9	1,686	91.8	3.5	1.2	2.8	0.7	13.7	59.9	26.4	677	75.0	51.0	15.1
Taylor city & MCD (Wayne).....................	63,131	61,594	-2.4	62,331	73.3	15.9	1.4	3.3	6.1	23.9	61.6	14.3	23,553	66.5	51.9	9.5
Taymouth township (Saginaw).....................	4,520	4,390	-2.9	4,466	92.5	1.6	0.0	2.4	3.6	23.3	63.8	12.9	1,540	93.4	46.9	13.4
Tecumseh city & MCD (Lenawee).....................	8,482	8,400	-1.0	8,407	93.8	0.7	0.2	1.4	4.0	23.1	61.3	15.5	3,624	66.1	32.2	24.7
Tecumseh township (Lenawee).....................	1,989	1,973	-0.8	1,787	93.1	1.5	0.8	2.5	2.0	18.5	65.1	16.5	728	92.9	29.8	30.6
Tekonsha village	717	709	-1.1	672	96.7	0.0	0.0	3.3	0.0	23.1	57.5	19.5	257	77.0	59.5	8.6
Tekonsha township (Calhoun).................	1,645	1,626	-1.2	1,600	96.5	0.0	0.0	2.8	0.7	22.9	56.1	21.1	602	79.2	46.8	15.3
Temperance CDP	8,517	NA	NA	9,402	95.8	0.4	0.0	1.4	2.4	26.7	56.9	16.4	3,536	83.9	36.4	29.8
Texas charter township (Kalamazoo).................	14,701	16,162	9.9	15,461	85.9	3.5	4.5	3.4	2.6	27.5	60.6	12.0	5,140	93.8	16.6	52.9
Thetford township (Genesee).....................	7,049	6,797	-3.6	6,915	89.9	4.5	0.0	1.4	4.2	20.7	66.1	13.3	2,616	84.9	47.0	11.7
Thomas township (Saginaw).....................	11,985	11,685	-2.5	11,855	93.5	1.0	0.9	1.5	3.0	20.4	58.7	21.0	4,714	87.9	38.3	25.5
Thompson township (Schoolcraft).................	795	764	-3.9	789	94.4	0.0	0.0	5.1	0.5	18.2	62.0	19.8	345	92.5	46.4	22.6
Thompsonville village	441	438	-0.7	554	84.5	2.3	0.5	10.1	2.5	19.3	63.6	17.1	218	77.1	67.9	4.1
Thornapple township (Barry).....................	7,884	7,901	0.2	7,883	96.8	0.8	1.4	0.6	0.5	29.8	55.0	15.1	2,798	82.5	40.6	24.3
Three Oaks village...........	1,622	1,589	-2.0	1,685	87.4	0.2	0.5	7.7	4.2	28.3	58.5	13.2	663	71.5	45.2	14.8
Three Oaks township (Berrien).....................	2,574	2,528	-1.8	2,541	91.6	0.2	0.4	5.1	2.8	24.2	60.5	15.4	1,020	76.1	43.4	14.8
Three Rivers city & MCD (St. Joseph).................	7,811	7,745	-0.8	7,765	78.6	11.5	1.1	3.2	5.6	29.3	59.6	11.3	2,962	54.9	53.5	10.7
Tilden township (Marquette).................	1,013	1,022	0.9	1,158	99.1	0.0	0.0	0.2	0.8	23.5	61.1	15.4	448	93.5	55.4	18.8
Tittabawassee township (Saginaw).....................	9,726	9,809	0.9	9,786	84.7	9.1	1.1	1.5	3.6	25.5	62.0	12.7	3,174	86.0	30.3	41.5
Tobacco township (Gladwin).....................	2,566	2,539	-1.1	2,546	97.5	0.1	0.0	0.3	2.1	16.1	61.8	22.1	1,071	91.5	52.7	14.0
Tompkins township (Jackson).....................	2,671	2,646	-0.9	2,655	97.3	0.0	0.5	0.9	1.3	20.5	64.1	15.4	1,050	85.1	43.7	11.0
Torch Lake township (Antrim).....................	1,194	1,183	-0.9	1,045	98.0	0.0	0.0	0.8	1.2	7.7	45.5	46.8	541	100.0	28.1	45.5
Torch Lake township (Houghton).................	1,880	1,862	-1.0	2,059	98.6	0.0	0.0	0.3	0.2	25.8	52.4	21.8	813	86.0	38.6	29.0
Traverse City city	14,674	15,042	2.5	15,006	93.1	1.3	0.9	1.5	3.1	19.2	65.6	15.2	6,500	62.0	22.2	42.1
Traverse City city (Grand Traverse).....................	14,482	14,852	2.6	14,698	93.0	1.4	0.9	1.5	3.2	18.5	65.8	15.6	6,415	62.0	22.5	41.8
Traverse City city (Leelanau).....................	192	190	-1.0	308	100.0	0.0	0.0	0.0	0.0	51.0	49.0	0.0	85	58.8	0.0	62.4

1 May be of any race.

Table A. All Places — Population and Housing

STATE City, town, township, borough, or CDP (county if applicable)	2010 census total population	2014 estimated population	Percent change 2010–2014	ACS total population estimate 2010–2014	White alone, not Hispanic or Latino	Black alone, not Hispanic or Latino	Asian alone, not Hispanic or Latino	All other races or 2 or more races, not Hispanic or Latino	Hispanic or Latino[1]	Under 18 years old	Age 18 to 64 years old	Age 65 years and older	Total occupied housing units	Percent owner occupied	High school diploma or less	Bachelor's degree or more
	1	2	3	4	5	6	7	8	9	10	11	12	13	14	15	16
MICHIGAN—Con.																
Trenton city & MCD (Wayne)	18,853	18,427	-2.3	18,635	90.5	2.7	0.8	1.5	4.5	19.4	59.6	21.0	7,890	78.9	38.0	27.1
Trout Lake township (Chippewa)	384	384	0.0	439	98.9	0.0	0.0	1.1	0.0	11.2	57.1	31.9	212	82.5	46.2	23.6
Trowbridge township (Allegan)	2,502	2,520	0.7	2,497	96.6	0.4	0.5	2.1	0.3	20.4	64.2	15.3	995	85.1	57.4	15.2
Trowbridge Park CDP	2,176	NA	NA	2,227	87.7	1.3	4.1	5.2	1.8	14.4	70.2	15.6	936	69.6	32.3	27.1
Troy township (Newaygo)	283	279	-1.4	281	91.1	0.0	0.4	3.6	5.0	22.1	64.3	13.5	113	82.3	68.1	9.7
Troy city & MCD (Oakland)	80,980	83,107	2.6	82,106	69.9	3.9	21.6	2.4	2.2	23.2	62.1	14.7	30,635	73.5	17.3	61.0
Turin township (Marquette)	153	154	0.7	126	96.8	0.0	0.0	3.2	0.0	12.8	50.0	37.3	62	100.0	61.3	11.3
Turner village	114	111	-2.6	65	96.9	0.0	0.0	3.1	0.0	20.1	56.9	23.1	31	87.1	74.2	6.5
Turner township (Arenac)	550	530	-3.6	499	98.0	0.0	0.0	1.0	1.0	13.0	60.4	26.5	233	94.8	67.8	9.0
Tuscarora township (Cheboygan)	3,038	2,988	-1.6	3,015	94.4	0.0	0.0	4.7	0.9	20.0	59.7	20.5	1,300	73.7	45.4	27.0
Tuscola township (Tuscola)	2,082	2,031	-2.4	2,214	97.6	0.0	0.0	1.8	0.6	19.6	62.3	18.2	853	89.2	51.6	14.4
Tustin village	230	227	-1.3	189	97.9	0.0	0.0	2.1	0.0	24.9	64.1	11.1	64	81.3	48.4	17.2
Twining village	181	176	-2.8	169	86.4	0.0	0.0	2.4	11.2	34.3	58.6	7.1	61	88.5	86.9	0.0
Twin Lake CDP	1,720	NA	NA	1,858	97.2	0.0	0.0	0.3	2.5	24.1	66.8	9.0	740	87.0	24.2	14.2
Tyrone township (Kent)	4,729	4,887	3.3	4,806	84.2	3.0	0.2	1.7	10.9	25.9	62.9	11.3	1,640	87.4	52.9	13.0
Tyrone township (Livingston)	10,020	10,265	2.4	10,143	94.8	0.2	1.8	2.0	1.2	26.0	61.8	12.1	3,416	88.4	25.5	36.7
Ubly village	858	832	-3.0	750	98.5	1.5	0.0	0.0	0.0	22.6	56.4	20.9	347	72.0	54.8	17.6
Unadilla township (Livingston)	3,366	3,453	2.6	3,407	96.3	0.1	0.0	2.1	1.5	20.8	66.4	12.7	1,327	91.8	36.5	17.6
Union township (Branch)	2,868	2,835	-1.2	2,849	96.1	0.0	0.8	0.8	2.2	26.1	58.4	15.5	1,131	78.2	48.3	11.9
Union township (Grand Traverse)	405	426	5.2	350	97.1	0.3	0.0	2.3	0.3	21.4	65.9	12.6	153	85.6	28.1	34.0
Union charter township (Isabella)	12,927	13,588	5.1	13,054	84.6	4.7	1.3	4.2	5.1	15.5	78.9	5.3	4,826	36.4	24.4	23.5
Union City village	1,599	1,581	-1.1	1,622	96.1	0.0	1.5	1.5	0.9	31.5	58.0	10.7	615	68.6	48.6	13.5
Unionville village	508	497	-2.2	449	98.4	0.0	0.0	0.0	1.6	16.3	58.9	24.9	213	83.6	45.5	16.4
Utica city & MCD (Macomb)	4,757	4,783	0.5	4,747	87.9	5.0	1.3	1.0	4.7	17.3	65.5	17.3	2,163	56.2	40.2	19.5
Valley township (Allegan)	2,018	2,059	2.0	2,104	95.7	0.0	0.0	2.6	1.7	22.2	62.9	15.0	836	88.4	49.4	20.8
Van Buren charter township (Wayne)	28,821	28,315	-1.8	28,553	64.0	28.5	2.5	2.8	2.1	23.6	66.1	10.2	11,345	65.6	33.8	28.1
Vandalia village	301	295	-2.0	322	43.5	22.4	19.6	5.3	9.3	21.7	59.0	19.3	131	66.4	55.7	8.4
Vanderbilt village	562	562	0.0	609	89.2	2.0	0.0	3.8	5.1	19.9	64.3	15.8	268	70.9	67.2	2.6
Vandercook Lake CDP	4,721	NA	NA	4,690	95.4	1.9	0.0	0.6	2.1	27.2	59.4	13.3	1,760	82.3	45.0	12.4
Vassar city & MCD (Tuscola)	2,697	2,628	-2.6	2,662	85.0	9.0	0.0	3.1	2.9	34.3	55.5	10.1	930	67.5	49.0	17.1
Vassar township (Tuscola)	4,093	3,957	-3.3	4,012	96.4	0.0	0.4	1.1	2.0	24.1	64.3	11.8	1,427	91.0	57.8	10.9
Venice township (Shiawassee)	2,578	2,514	-2.5	2,548	97.1	0.1	0.5	0.5	1.8	21.4	65.4	13.4	1,002	87.3	50.6	9.5
Vergennes township (Kent)	4,189	4,494	7.3	4,329	97.5	0.0	0.4	0.4	1.6	28.5	61.3	10.3	1,441	93.5	24.9	42.4
Vermontville village	759	760	0.1	782	96.5	0.0	0.0	1.7	1.8	33.4	53.6	13.0	264	72.0	51.5	11.4
Vermontville township (Eaton)	2,053	2,064	0.5	1,899	96.1	0.0	0.0	1.5	2.4	25.0	57.4	17.6	674	81.3	47.8	13.6
Vernon township (Isabella)	1,369	1,356	-0.9	1,290	94.3	0.0	0.0	4.3	1.4	21.6	60.7	17.7	458	86.0	37.8	20.1
Vernon village	783	763	-2.6	1,020	97.2	0.0	0.0	0.6	2.3	23.9	57.7	18.2	391	73.1	46.3	20.5
Vernon township (Shiawassee)	4,614	4,470	-3.1	4,516	97.9	0.0	0.3	0.8	1.1	20.9	59.8	19.3	1,827	86.6	46.6	10.0
Verona township (Huron)	1,259	1,220	-3.1	1,125	87.6	3.6	0.8	1.4	6.7	23.0	63.4	13.6	417	96.2	48.9	18.7
Vevay township (Ingham)	3,537	3,540	0.1	3,535	92.3	0.6	0.0	0.2	6.9	22.5	61.3	16.2	1,287	89.4	27.4	29.1
Vicksburg village	2,906	3,181	9.5	2,894	91.8	0.6	0.0	4.4	3.1	29.7	58.8	11.7	1,111	75.1	36.8	18.8
Victor township (Clinton)	3,460	3,534	2.1	3,512	96.7	0.0	0.0	2.1	1.2	23.1	63.6	13.2	1,343	91.7	29.8	24.9
Victory township (Mason)	1,383	1,385	0.1	1,345	94.8	0.5	0.4	2.5	1.9	22.7	59.3	17.9	475	84.0	53.3	15.2
Vienna charter township (Genesee)	13,255	12,862	-3.0	13,038	92.5	2.9	0.5	1.7	2.4	20.9	61.2	17.7	4,989	81.9	47.4	17.0
Vienna township (Montmorency)	587	557	-5.1	466	92.3	1.5	0.0	6.2	0.0	23.4	54.8	21.9	172	93.0	60.5	9.3
Village of Clarkston city & MCD (Oakland)	882	898	1.8	852	98.6	0.0	0.5	0.4	0.6	22.2	51.4	26.5	378	65.3	25.4	52.6
Village of Grosse Pointe Shores city	3,008	2,946	-2.1	3,031	92.7	1.9	3.4	0.6	1.4	19.6	53.5	27.1	1,227	93.1	10.4	66.3
Village of Grosse Pointe Shores city (Macomb)	73	74	1.4	116	79.3	20.7	0.0	0.0	0.0	5.2	74.1	20.7	54	100.0	0.0	94.4
Village of Grosse Pointe Shores city (Wayne)	2,935	2,872	-2.1	2,915	93.2	1.2	3.6	0.6	1.4	20.3	52.5	27.3	1,173	92.8	10.9	65.0
Vineyard Lake CDP	980	NA	NA	900	98.8	0.1	0.1	1.0	0.0	9.9	70.6	19.4	416	85.8	67.1	4.8
Volinia township (Cass)	1,112	1,084	-2.5	1,100	90.2	2.5	0.5	3.7	3.1	23.7	55.4	20.8	409	87.0	44.3	19.3
Wacousta CDP	1,440	NA	NA	1,347	96.0	2.9	0.5	0.6	0.0	11.2	68.2	20.6	595	97.0	24.0	44.2
Wakefield city & MCD (Gogebic)	1,852	1,762	-4.9	1,837	94.7	1.1	0.8	2.8	0.6	18.0	52.0	29.9	845	74.1	38.5	18.7
Wakefield township (Gogebic)	304	289	-4.9	257	98.4	0.0	0.8	0.8	0.0	16.7	56.3	26.8	129	94.6	41.1	27.9
Wakeshma township (Kalamazoo)	1,301	1,329	2.2	1,395	96.3	0.0	0.0	2.9	0.9	23.2	60.7	16.3	522	92.0	52.3	9.0
Waldron village	538	530	-1.5	618	97.7	0.0	0.0	1.8	0.5	31.6	57.2	11.2	216	70.4	65.7	7.9
Wales township (St. Clair)	3,248	3,243	-0.2	3,227	93.5	0.8	0.0	2.4	3.3	23.8	61.9	14.4	1,277	88.0	42.2	15.5
Walker township (Cheboygan)	327	320	-2.1	414	88.9	0.2	0.5	10.4	0.0	29.2	54.7	16.2	120	90.8	62.5	6.7
Walker city & MCD (Kent)	23,537	24,468	4.0	24,015	87.6	3.1	2.2	2.3	4.9	22.7	65.4	12.1	10,149	60.9	32.4	31.4
Walkerville village	247	243	-1.6	158	89.2	0.0	0.0	2.5	8.2	17.7	59.5	22.8	71	73.2	60.6	2.8
Walled Lake city & MCD (Oakland)	6,999	7,129	1.9	7,065	82.9	2.9	2.8	3.8	7.6	19.7	66.0	14.3	3,324	58.8	36.3	27.7
Walloon Lake CDP	290	NA	NA	393	99.7	0.3	0.0	0.0	0.0	12.0	67.6	20.4	160	63.8	26.9	31.3
Walton township (Eaton)	2,264	2,281	0.8	1,966	91.4	0.7	0.1	0.6	7.3	26.9	59.5	13.5	719	85.5	48.1	19.2
Warner township (Antrim)	416	410	-1.4	369	98.1	0.0	0.0	1.9	0.0	22.7	69.1	8.1	131	90.8	51.1	13.0

1 May be of any race.

Table A. All Places — Population and Housing

STATE City, town, township, borough, or CDP (county if applicable)	Population				Race and Hispanic or Latino origin (percent), 2010–2014					Age (percent), 2010–2014			Households, 2010–2014			
	2010 census total population	2014 estimated population	Percent change 2010–2014	ACS total population estimate 2010–2014	White alone, not Hispanic or Latino	Black alone, not Hispanic or Latino	Asian alone, not Hispanic or Latino	All other races or 2 or more races, not Hispanic or Latino	Hispanic or Latino[1]	Under 18 years old	Age 18 to 64 years old	Age 65 years and older	Total occupied housing units	Percent owner occupied	High school diploma or less	Bachelor's degree or more
	1	2	3	4	5	6	7	8	9	10	11	12	13	14	15	16
MICHIGAN—Con.																
Warren city & MCD (Macomb)	134,056	135,099	0.8	134,398	74.4	15.1	5.8	2.9	1.9	23.0	61.2	15.8	52,936	72.4	47.1	18.4
Warren township (Midland)	2,119	2,065	-2.5	2,214	95.3	0.1	0.4	1.4	2.9	21.8	61.5	16.5	858	90.2	57.1	9.4
Washington township (Gratiot)	870	857	-1.5	909	95.9	0.0	0.3	0.6	3.2	23.1	61.3	15.6	326	88.3	47.5	8.3
Washington township (Macomb)	25,143	26,469	5.3	25,721	88.3	1.9	0.9	2.5	6.3	24.0	61.5	14.4	9,554	81.4	28.7	35.4
Washington township (Sanilac)	1,659	1,590	-4.2	1,538	93.2	2.8	0.7	1.1	2.2	24.5	56.8	18.6	588	86.6	55.6	9.7
Waterford charter township (Oakland)	71,705	73,139	2.0	72,503	83.4	5.4	1.5	2.9	6.9	21.1	65.7	13.4	30,166	70.7	33.5	27.3
Waterloo township (Jackson)	2,856	2,832	-0.8	2,839	96.0	0.4	0.0	2.0	1.5	19.5	66.7	13.7	1,104	95.2	41.3	28.7
Watersmeet CDP	428	NA	NA	407	65.1	0.0	2.0	32.9	0.0	24.8	52.8	22.4	177	83.1	44.6	14.7
Watersmeet township (Gogebic)	1,419	1,383	-2.5	1,338	74.1	0.1	1.1	23.7	0.9	16.2	45.8	38.0	600	86.0	43.0	20.8
Watertown charter township (Clinton)	4,836	5,173	7.0	5,008	89.6	3.2	0.8	3.8	2.5	24.1	61.7	14.3	1,894	93.2	26.5	40.1
Watertown township (Sanilac)	1,320	1,276	-3.3	1,397	95.3	0.0	0.8	0.7	3.2	25.1	58.2	16.8	491	85.9	53.2	17.7
Watertown township (Tuscola)	2,202	2,140	-2.8	2,108	97.8	0.9	0.0	1.3	0.0	19.7	63.1	17.2	801	88.1	56.6	10.9
Watervliet city & MCD (Berrien)	1,735	1,703	-1.8	1,949	90.3	0.9	1.9	4.0	3.0	30.9	56.7	12.6	662	71.0	51.4	10.1
Watervliet township (Berrien)	3,106	3,075	-1.0	3,084	86.3	0.0	0.2	2.1	11.3	27.0	57.1	16.0	1,167	77.7	49.8	14.8
Watson township (Allegan)	2,063	2,092	1.4	2,282	96.4	0.0	0.1	2.4	1.1	26.9	62.9	10.3	776	94.5	52.1	15.7
Waucedah township (Dickinson)	804	797	-0.9	718	97.2	0.0	0.0	2.8	0.0	12.5	62.0	25.5	346	94.5	33.8	23.4
Waverly township (Cheboygan)	457	449	-1.8	488	91.6	0.0	0.0	4.9	3.5	14.1	63.8	22.1	221	92.3	54.8	14.5
Waverly CDP	23,925	NA	NA	24,470	70.1	13.0	4.8	4.0	7.9	18.5	64.8	16.6	11,373	54.0	25.9	37.6
Waverly township (Van Buren)	2,554	2,508	-1.8	2,522	92.2	0.0	0.0	1.9	5.9	25.7	63.2	11.2	959	90.5	41.8	20.8
Wawatam township (Emmet)	661	671	1.5	612	91.7	1.0	0.0	5.1	2.3	13.5	66.1	20.4	282	74.1	26.6	33.0
Wayland city & MCD (Allegan)	4,079	4,139	1.5	4,082	93.3	0.0	1.3	2.5	2.9	31.9	59.3	8.8	1,353	65.2	46.5	28.1
Wayland township (Allegan)	3,088	3,176	2.8	3,129	94.3	0.1	0.5	3.6	1.5	22.5	63.2	14.1	1,247	88.2	42.7	16.8
Wayne township (Cass)	2,654	2,609	-1.7	2,630	98.9	0.1	0.0	1.0	0.1	19.1	64.3	16.7	993	84.7	45.5	11.6
Wayne city & MCD (Wayne)	17,593	17,091	-2.9	17,314	76.6	15.8	1.3	3.5	2.7	23.2	63.3	13.5	6,869	57.5	48.3	12.1
Weare township (Oceana)	1,210	1,201	-0.7	1,208	90.2	1.2	0.0	5.2	3.3	19.6	58.7	21.6	444	86.3	38.1	18.0
Webber township (Lake)	1,699	1,668	-1.8	1,416	68.9	19.2	0.0	9.6	2.3	14.6	58.3	27.1	545	61.8	50.1	11.9
Webberville village	1,275	1,268	-0.5	1,186	96.5	0.3	0.0	1.6	1.6	22.2	67.9	9.9	506	76.3	39.5	10.5
Webster township (Washtenaw)	6,784	7,121	5.0	6,974	97.1	0.0	1.2	1.0	0.7	26.3	61.3	12.2	2,476	95.3	16.2	58.2
Wedgewood CDP	237	NA	NA	201	97.0	0.0	0.0	0.0	3.0	17.9	53.7	28.4	79	100.0	20.3	67.1
Weesaw township (Berrien)	1,936	1,909	-1.4	1,766	90.9	0.1	0.5	2.8	5.6	19.0	63.6	17.4	727	86.8	55.7	17.7
Weidman CDP	959	NA	NA	1,015	92.9	1.1	0.0	3.9	2.1	28.7	60.2	11.2	400	78.3	46.0	5.0
Weldon township (Benzie)	542	542	0.0	545	88.3	2.4	0.6	6.2	2.6	22.5	59.7	18.0	224	77.7	57.6	9.4
Wellington township (Alpena)	307	300	-2.3	253	95.3	0.0	0.0	0.4	4.3	26.0	53.6	20.2	98	89.8	59.2	6.1
Wells township (Delta)	4,885	4,839	-0.9	4,865	97.7	0.0	0.0	2.3	0.0	21.3	60.2	18.5	1,853	88.9	42.3	14.1
Wells township (Marquette)	231	233	0.9	206	100.0	0.0	0.0	0.0	0.0	6.3	61.8	32.0	98	98.0	71.4	6.1
Wells township (Tuscola)	1,773	1,717	-3.2	1,673	96.0	0.6	0.0	1.8	1.6	22.4	64.2	13.3	599	85.3	46.4	9.2
Wellston CDP	311	NA	NA	284	99.3	0.0	0.0	0.0	0.7	7.8	64.0	28.2	155	62.6	44.5	13.5
West Bloomfield charter township (Oakland)	64,690	65,957	2.0	65,419	73.6	13.1	8.7	3.0	1.7	23.3	58.1	18.6	24,420	80.9	16.4	60.2
West Branch township (Dickinson)	61	60	-1.6	37	91.9	0.0	0.0	2.7	5.4	29.7	43.2	27.0	15	86.7	46.7	26.7
West Branch township (Marquette)	1,623	1,645	1.4	1,615	85.3	1.3	0.7	9.8	3.0	25.5	67.5	6.9	666	45.8	37.5	18.2
West Branch township (Missaukee)	466	471	1.1	496	95.0	0.0	0.6	2.6	1.8	23.8	58.3	17.9	195	86.7	64.6	8.7
West Branch city & MCD (Ogemaw)	2,139	2,077	-2.9	2,051	93.0	1.0	1.4	0.9	3.8	22.2	54.0	23.5	963	43.6	46.8	21.6
West Branch township (Ogemaw)	2,593	2,513	-3.1	2,562	97.5	0.0	0.0	1.7	0.4	20.4	57.9	21.7	1,096	92.0	40.7	17.9
West Ishpeming CDP	2,662	NA	NA	2,687	97.5	0.0	0.0	1.3	1.2	17.3	62.4	20.3	1,115	92.8	37.0	29.6
Westland city & MCD (Wayne)	84,097	82,314	-2.1	83,188	72.4	18.6	3.7	2.8	2.6	20.9	64.3	14.8	34,002	59.4	42.2	18.5
West Monroe CDP	3,503	NA	NA	3,248	88.8	3.8	0.0	2.4	5.0	23.4	65.1	11.6	1,293	76.3	62.5	9.4
Westphalia village	923	944	2.3	838	97.1	0.0	0.2	0.4	2.3	22.2	48.0	29.7	342	84.5	48.5	17.8
Westphalia township (Clinton)	2,365	2,415	2.1	2,355	93.2	0.2	0.1	2.7	3.9	28.0	52.2	19.8	836	85.9	45.2	17.8
West Traverse township (Emmet)	1,606	1,642	2.2	1,692	93.9	0.2	0.7	4.3	0.9	16.7	52.5	30.9	792	88.9	15.7	57.4
Westwood CDP	8,653	NA	NA	9,091	74.9	14.2	0.3	3.5	7.0	15.5	67.5	17.1	4,347	55.2	20.8	50.3
Wexford township (Wexford)	1,072	1,072	0.0	974	95.9	0.6	0.2	2.9	0.4	26.3	60.5	13.1	376	88.8	50.3	11.2
Wheatfield township (Ingham)	1,630	1,639	0.6	1,802	94.6	0.3	0.7	2.1	2.3	24.0	62.1	14.0	655	93.3	22.6	44.1
Wheatland township (Hillsdale)	1,351	1,322	-2.1	1,391	98.0	0.0	0.0	1.2	0.9	27.1	58.3	14.7	487	89.7	55.0	14.4
Wheatland township (Mecosta)	1,403	1,408	0.4	1,374	89.4	3.0	0.0	6.0	1.5	22.8	55.5	21.8	540	81.9	50.0	16.5

1 May be of any race.

Table A. All Places — **Population and Housing**

STATE City, town, township, borough, or CDP (county if applicable)	Population				Race and Hispanic or Latino origin (percent), 2010–2014					Age (percent), 2010–2014			Households, 2010–2014			
	2010 census total population	2014 estimated population	Percent change 2010–2014	ACS total population estimate 2010–2014	White alone, not Hispanic or Latino	Black alone, not Hispanic or Latino	Asian alone, not Hispanic or Latino	All other races or 2 or more races, not Hispanic or Latino	Hispanic or Latino[1]	Under 18 years old	Age 18 to 64 years old	Age 65 years and older	Total occupied housing units	Percent owner occupied	High school diploma or less	Bachelor's degree or more
	1	2	3	4	5	6	7	8	9	10	11	12	13	14	15	16
MICHIGAN—Con.																
Wheatland township (Sanilac)	488	468	-4.1	475	93.7	0.0	0.0	5.5	0.8	21.9	60.1	17.9	177	88.1	66.7	5.6
Wheeler township (Gratiot)	2,786	2,741	-1.6	2,760	91.4	0.7	0.0	0.7	7.2	22.3	59.6	18.0	1,119	80.3	62.0	7.7
White Cloud city & MCD (Newaygo)	1,408	1,384	-1.7	1,502	80.4	11.8	0.1	3.2	4.6	21.8	66.4	11.7	461	57.0	53.6	11.7
Whitefish township (Chippewa)	575	575	0.0	530	82.6	0.0	0.0	17.2	0.2	10.2	53.0	37.0	254	91.7	50.4	17.7
Whiteford township (Monroe)	4,602	4,510	-2.0	4,544	93.7	3.9	1.2	0.0	1.3	22.3	62.5	15.2	1,692	83.9	44.6	19.3
Whitehall city & MCD (Muskegon)	2,706	2,697	-0.3	2,694	92.8	2.5	0.0	1.9	2.8	24.6	54.8	20.8	1,145	65.9	33.6	21.0
Whitehall township (Muskegon)	1,739	1,740	0.1	1,929	91.6	0.2	0.3	3.1	4.9	26.1	60.0	13.9	696	91.4	31.8	21.0
White Lake charter township (Oakland)	30,019	30,955	3.1	30,552	93.2	2.1	1.0	1.6	2.3	21.7	65.0	13.3	11,612	89.2	32.2	34.0
White Oak township (Ingham)	1,173	1,181	0.7	1,130	97.3	0.0	0.3	1.0	1.4	20.1	64.9	15.1	443	92.1	41.8	20.8
White Pigeon village	1,522	1,512	-0.7	1,528	93.7	0.3	0.6	1.2	4.2	24.8	59.9	15.4	574	69.2	69.3	3.8
White Pigeon township (St. Joseph)	3,753	3,740	-0.3	3,748	96.7	0.1	1.0	0.5	1.7	25.3	58.9	15.8	1,312	71.8	59.3	10.9
White Pine CDP	474	NA	NA	402	96.0	0.0	1.5	1.7	0.7	9.2	49.2	41.5	202	90.1	42.1	13.4
White River township (Muskegon)	1,335	1,366	2.3	1,311	92.4	0.4	0.0	5.6	1.6	21.0	51.3	27.6	515	96.7	26.2	26.8
Whitewater township (Grand Traverse)	2,597	2,742	5.6	2,678	92.8	0.0	1.0	6.0	0.2	19.7	61.8	18.6	994	87.5	34.5	35.9
Whitmore Lake CDP	6,423	NA	NA	6,380	91.6	0.7	1.4	3.0	3.2	19.6	68.6	11.8	2,818	72.6	27.0	32.0
Whitney township (Arenac)	1,001	967	-3.4	1,072	95.6	0.6	0.7	0.9	2.1	12.1	53.7	34.2	466	92.5	49.1	16.3
Whittemore city & MCD (Iosco)	384	376	-2.1	442	97.3	0.0	0.7	1.4	0.7	19.0	61.1	19.9	193	68.9	68.9	5.7
Wilber township (Iosco)	729	716	-1.8	629	96.3	0.0	0.3	2.2	1.1	13.4	58.5	28.1	280	90.4	58.2	11.1
Wilcox township (Newaygo)	1,098	1,076	-2.0	1,069	94.9	0.7	0.0	1.6	2.7	23.4	63.4	13.2	421	84.6	58.0	7.8
Williams charter township (Bay)	4,772	4,888	2.4	4,815	95.2	0.0	1.0	1.3	2.5	23.3	62.7	13.9	1,736	93.8	41.2	26.3
Williamston city & MCD (Ingham)	3,856	3,853	-0.1	3,855	93.2	0.4	0.4	2.1	3.9	29.4	56.8	13.6	1,503	71.4	28.5	38.5
Williamstown township (Ingham)	4,978	5,027	1.0	5,009	93.7	0.8	0.3	2.2	3.0	16.9	64.3	18.7	1,946	92.9	16.5	56.7
Wilmot township (Cheboygan)	878	858	-2.3	761	95.5	0.0	0.0	4.5	0.0	25.4	56.0	18.5	313	85.6	60.1	8.0
Wilson township (Alpena)	2,029	1,986	-2.1	1,962	98.5	0.1	0.0	0.7	0.7	18.2	64.5	17.2	868	85.6	42.4	11.6
Wilson charter township (Charlevoix)	1,964	1,975	0.6	1,872	95.1	0.6	0.0	3.9	0.3	22.2	58.9	19.0	721	91.5	44.2	19.8
Windsor charter township (Eaton)	6,838	6,868	0.4	6,836	88.2	3.0	1.7	3.7	3.4	23.0	57.7	19.2	2,671	92.4	37.7	26.2
Winfield township (Montcalm)	2,235	2,235	0.0	2,469	94.2	0.0	0.0	5.8	0.0	27.0	63.3	9.9	759	91.8	48.1	15.7
Winsor township (Huron)	1,907	1,849	-3.0	1,954	97.3	0.2	0.6	0.0	1.9	17.9	58.0	24.2	846	74.9	55.3	20.4
Winterfield township (Clare)	459	454	-1.1	463	95.0	0.0	0.0	0.0	5.0	18.5	62.1	19.2	191	90.6	52.4	7.3
Wise township (Isabella)	1,397	1,379	-1.3	1,509	96.2	0.3	0.0	0.8	2.7	20.3	61.2	18.4	555	86.3	58.7	6.7
Wisner township (Tuscola)	690	670	-2.9	628	96.0	0.0	0.0	0.0	4.0	12.4	65.8	22.0	295	89.8	62.4	8.1
Wixom city & MCD (Oakland)	13,498	13,744	1.8	13,640	75.7	10.3	4.9	1.7	7.4	24.2	68.8	6.9	6,178	51.4	22.6	38.0
Wolf Lake CDP	4,104	NA	NA	4,360	87.5	0.0	0.0	6.3	6.2	28.4	58.7	12.9	1,573	92.5	52.1	7.2
Wolverine township	244	240	-1.6	223	98.2	0.0	0.0	1.8	0.0	20.6	60.5	18.8	90	87.8	68.9	14.4
Wolverine Lake village	4,312	4,396	1.9	4,357	93.9	0.0	0.7	1.0	4.4	20.4	67.3	12.1	1,764	82.1	35.1	29.3
Woodbridge township (Hillsdale)	1,325	1,296	-2.2	1,367	96.2	0.3	0.0	0.2	3.3	32.3	58.4	9.4	432	78.0	57.2	13.4
Woodhaven city & MCD (Wayne)	12,875	12,594	-2.2	12,747	86.9	4.8	2.5	2.3	3.5	23.4	63.6	13.0	4,979	72.0	26.8	27.0
Woodhull township (Shiawassee)	3,810	3,729	-2.1	3,769	92.4	1.7	0.6	3.7	1.6	20.8	63.4	15.7	1,521	93.2	29.9	28.1
Woodland village	425	425	0.0	421	94.1	0.0	0.0	1.2	4.8	21.2	61.3	17.3	171	80.1	59.1	7.0
Woodland township (Barry)	2,047	2,057	0.5	2,108	90.6	0.5	0.6	1.9	6.4	25.2	60.0	15.0	787	83.2	42.3	15.4
Woodland Beach CDP	2,049	NA	NA	1,728	94.8	0.0	0.0	4.5	0.7	19.8	68.4	11.7	726	73.8	50.3	14.3
Woodstock township (Lenawee)	3,505	3,465	-1.1	3,472	96.2	0.0	0.5	1.2	2.0	19.2	61.5	19.1	1,460	85.2	49.0	16.7
Worth township (Sanilac)	3,894	3,761	-3.4	3,821	98.1	0.0	0.0	1.6	0.3	23.5	56.5	20.0	1,528	90.0	41.5	17.9
Wright township (Hillsdale)	1,655	1,629	-1.6	2,007	98.1	0.2	0.2	1.3	0.1	34.3	54.3	11.3	649	78.3	62.7	10.3
Wright township (Ottawa)	3,147	3,246	3.1	3,202	94.9	0.3	0.2	2.1	2.4	23.4	63.2	13.2	1,094	92.5	51.7	13.2
Wyandotte city & MCD (Wayne)	25,883	25,151	-2.8	25,470	92.2	1.1	0.4	1.2	5.1	20.0	66.1	14.0	10,611	73.6	45.9	16.3
Wyoming city & MCD (Kent)	72,122	74,826	3.7	73,434	69.5	4.9	3.2	2.9	19.6	25.4	65.5	9.1	27,253	65.3	42.8	21.1
Yale city & MCD (St. Clair)	1,954	1,917	-1.9	1,843	93.2	0.0	0.0	1.6	5.2	22.9	58.6	18.5	766	66.4	50.9	12.1
Yankee Springs township (Barry)	4,065	4,077	0.3	4,062	96.6	0.0	0.0	2.0	1.4	19.8	61.3	18.8	1,617	94.3	27.0	29.1
Yates township (Lake)	761	748	-1.7	852	67.4	27.6	0.0	5.0	0.0	16.9	59.5	23.7	304	78.0	49.0	14.5
York charter township (Washtenaw)	8,708	9,049	3.9	8,856	79.4	7.2	1.5	4.1	7.8	22.7	69.5	7.8	2,306	91.3	14.4	52.0
Ypsilanti city & MCD (Washtenaw)	19,569	20,081	2.6	19,844	60.0	26.6	3.1	6.3	4.0	14.8	77.1	8.2	7,853	32.4	22.3	33.4
Ypsilanti charter township (Washtenaw)	53,362	52,139	-2.3	53,013	54.2	32.1	2.5	5.4	5.7	24.2	66.5	9.5	21,574	57.4	30.5	30.2
Zeba CDP	480	NA	NA	357	63.0	0.8	5.0	31.1	0.0	30.2	58.8	10.9	141	87.9	47.5	14.2
Zeeland city & MCD (Ottawa)	5,505	5,626	2.2	5,566	84.7	0.9	1.0	4.4	8.9	25.3	52.5	22.2	2,304	64.2	41.2	28.2

1 May be of any race.

Table A. All Places — **Population and Housing**

STATE City, town, township, borough, or CDP (county if applicable)	Population				Race and Hispanic or Latino origin (percent), 2010–2014					Age (percent), 2010–2014			Households, 2010–2014			
	2010 census total population	2014 estimated population	Percent change 2010–2014	ACS total population estimate 2010–2014	White alone, not Hispanic or Latino	Black alone, not Hispanic or Latino	Asian alone, not Hispanic or Latino	All other races or 2 or more races, not Hispanic or Latino	Hispanic or Latino[1]	Under 18 years old	Age 18 to 64 years old	Age 65 years and older	Total occupied housing units	Percent owner occupied	High school diploma or less	Bachelor's degree or more
	1	2	3	4	5	6	7	8	9	10	11	12	13	14	15	16
MICHIGAN—Con.																
Zeeland charter township (Ottawa)	9,970	10,690	7.2	10,342	85.0	0.6	4.3	1.5	8.7	30.6	60.4	9.1	3,393	94.5	38.3	25.5
Zilwaukee city & MCD (Saginaw)	1,658	1,597	-3.7	1,699	89.2	1.1	0.0	2.3	7.5	19.7	63.5	16.8	668	83.7	44.3	12.0
Zilwaukee township (Saginaw)	67	65	-3.0	157	57.3	1.9	1.3	2.5	36.9	46.5	46.3	7.0	37	62.2	43.2	10.8
MINNESOTA	5,303,925	5,457,173	2.9	5,383,661	82.1	5.3	4.3	3.4	4.9	23.8	62.7	13.6	2,115,337	72.1	31.6	34.4
Aastad township (Otter Tail)	213	213	0.0	191	99.5	0.0	0.5	0.0	0.0	23.0	65.5	11.5	75	97.3	36.0	20.0
Acoma township (McLeod)	1,149	1,131	-1.6	1,159	99.1	0.0	0.4	0.0	0.4	23.8	66.4	9.7	430	96.7	33.0	24.2
Acton township (Meeker)	375	375	0.0	400	89.8	0.0	1.3	1.0	8.0	28.1	56.0	16.3	147	85.0	46.3	15.6
Ada city & MCD (Norman)	1,707	1,650	-3.3	1,702	89.8	0.2	0.6	1.8	7.6	25.5	55.9	18.4	726	69.8	47.1	17.5
Adams city & MCD (Mower)	787	785	-0.3	717	98.6	1.0	0.0	0.4	0.0	20.8	51.1	28.2	295	76.3	38.6	20.7
Adams township (Mower)	452	457	1.1	519	100.0	0.0	0.0	0.0	0.0	34.7	49.7	15.6	168	89.9	34.5	27.4
Adrian city & MCD (Nobles)	1,209	1,217	0.7	1,239	96.0	0.7	1.5	1.3	0.5	24.7	54.8	20.7	502	84.9	51.4	13.1
Adrian township (Watonwan)	142	141	-0.7	159	99.4	0.0	0.0	0.0	0.6	14.4	56.5	28.9	74	89.2	41.9	20.3
Aetna township (Pipestone)	194	190	-2.1	168	100.0	0.0	0.0	0.0	0.0	26.8	48.7	24.4	64	92.2	59.4	15.6
Afton city & MCD (Washington)	2,879	2,953	2.6	2,912	86.6	0.0	4.2	0.5	8.7	20.3	63.7	16.0	1,133	93.0	18.3	56.0
Agassiz township (Lac qui Parle)	103	98	-4.9	85	100.0	0.0	0.0	0.0	0.0	27.1	56.5	16.5	36	100.0	63.9	5.6
Agder township (Marshall)	109	109	0.0	117	100.0	0.0	0.0	0.0	0.0	21.4	61.4	17.1	46	95.7	52.2	17.4
Agram township (Morrison)	572	570	-0.3	490	94.1	0.0	1.0	4.5	0.4	26.9	58.5	14.5	181	91.7	47.5	17.1
Aitkin city & MCD (Aitkin)	2,165	2,079	-4.0	2,351	96.7	0.5	0.2	2.0	0.6	21.3	51.8	26.8	1,105	54.0	61.0	12.4
Aitkin township (Aitkin)	856	838	-2.1	966	98.7	0.0	0.0	0.3	1.0	29.2	51.3	19.4	385	91.7	44.7	22.1
Akeley city & MCD (Hubbard)	432	431	-0.2	376	81.6	0.5	0.0	16.5	1.3	24.0	63.1	12.8	148	84.5	48.6	2.7
Akeley township (Hubbard)	551	559	1.5	443	96.4	0.0	0.0	2.5	1.1	12.6	52.7	34.5	211	88.6	36.0	19.0
Akron township (Big Stone)	168	168	0.0	148	100.0	0.0	0.0	0.0	0.0	14.9	63.5	21.6	60	95.0	38.3	28.3
Akron township (Wilkin)	133	132	-0.8	117	94.9	0.0	0.0	5.1	0.0	13.7	63.4	23.1	49	95.9	59.2	14.3
Alango township (St. Louis)	258	259	0.4	299	91.6	0.0	3.0	4.0	1.3	20.7	62.1	17.4	128	91.4	50.0	20.3
Alaska township (Beltrami)	217	221	1.8	212	91.5	0.0	0.0	7.5	0.9	25.4	59.8	14.6	86	90.7	34.9	34.9
Alba township (Jackson)	170	170	0.0	200	99.5	0.0	0.0	0.0	0.5	22.5	67.0	10.5	92	85.9	45.7	14.1
Albany city & MCD (Stearns)	2,573	2,618	1.7	2,599	98.0	0.0	0.2	0.5	1.2	24.4	55.0	20.5	1,135	71.6	46.5	14.7
Albany township (Stearns)	968	985	1.8	960	97.1	0.0	1.1	1.8	0.0	28.4	62.1	9.7	326	93.3	48.8	12.3
Alberta township (Benton)	826	840	1.7	887	99.2	0.0	0.0	0.8	0.0	24.4	62.7	13.1	319	97.2	59.2	7.8
Alberta city & MCD (Stevens)	103	102	-1.0	104	100.0	0.0	0.0	0.0	0.0	28.9	59.6	11.5	41	85.4	39.0	7.3
Albert Lea city & MCD (Freeborn)	18,053	17,815	-1.3	17,931	82.6	1.5	1.0	1.8	13.0	20.2	56.2	23.5	8,041	69.2	47.4	15.9
Albert Lea township (Freeborn)	646	638	-1.2	633	94.0	0.5	0.0	0.0	5.5	22.2	60.3	17.7	259	88.8	35.9	13.1
Albertville city & MCD (Wright)	7,044	7,281	3.4	7,159	79.5	3.2	7.2	5.3	4.7	38.8	56.2	5.1	2,161	86.4	20.0	38.5
Albin township (Brown)	348	341	-2.0	368	99.2	0.0	0.0	0.5	0.3	31.3	54.1	14.7	136	92.6	47.1	19.1
Albion township (Wright)	1,249	1,288	3.1	1,278	98.1	0.1	0.0	0.2	1.6	27.4	61.7	10.8	442	90.7	46.2	18.3
Alborn township (St. Louis)	462	463	0.2	487	82.3	0.4	0.0	14.6	2.7	21.6	67.8	10.7	183	94.0	42.6	12.0
Alden city & MCD (Freeborn)	661	650	-1.7	626	98.1	0.0	0.5	0.0	1.4	21.0	64.4	14.7	255	83.1	50.2	12.9
Alden township (Freeborn)	306	302	-1.3	357	100.0	0.0	0.0	0.0	0.0	30.3	53.2	16.5	123	91.1	49.6	11.4
Alden township (St. Louis)	213	214	0.5	177	94.9	0.0	0.0	4.5	0.6	23.2	67.8	9.0	75	89.3	37.3	34.7
Aldrich city & MCD (Wadena)	48	47	-2.1	73	100.0	0.0	0.0	0.0	0.0	31.5	50.5	17.8	30	70.0	20.0	10.0
Aldrich township (Wadena)	427	424	-0.7	524	92.2	1.9	0.0	3.4	2.5	23.3	59.6	17.2	209	86.6	38.3	7.7
Alexandria city & MCD (Douglas)	11,070	11,680	5.5	11,465	96.9	0.9	0.2	1.5	0.5	20.1	59.5	20.4	5,530	52.4	37.0	20.0
Alexandria township (Douglas)	4,098	4,120	0.5	4,087	97.0	0.3	0.0	2.2	0.4	24.6	56.9	18.4	1,492	92.4	29.2	31.9
Alfsborg township (Sibley)	319	314	-1.6	242	99.2	0.0	0.8	0.0	0.0	16.1	64.2	19.4	108	91.7	55.6	7.4
Alliance township (Clay)	235	241	2.6	200	99.5	0.0	0.0	0.0	0.5	19.5	59.0	21.5	84	94.0	33.3	33.3
Alma township (Marshall)	88	88	0.0	63	100.0	0.0	0.0	0.0	0.0	14.3	71.4	14.3	31	93.5	32.3	22.6
Almond township (Big Stone)	110	108	-1.8	122	100.0	0.0	0.0	0.0	0.0	9.0	75.5	15.6	53	100.0	24.5	17.0
Alpha city & MCD (Jackson)	128	128	0.0	252	84.1	0.0	12.7	2.0	1.2	37.8	58.1	4.4	78	100.0	32.1	3.8
Alta Vista township (Lincoln)	175	173	-1.1	159	97.5	0.6	1.9	0.0	0.0	17.0	61.6	21.4	69	87.0	56.5	17.4
Alton township (Waseca)	434	438	0.9	414	97.1	0.7	2.2	0.0	0.0	25.2	58.4	16.4	164	94.5	42.7	26.2
Altona township (Pipestone)	153	148	-3.3	85	100.0	0.0	0.0	0.0	0.0	35.3	57.8	7.1	35	94.3	54.3	11.4
Altura city & MCD (Winona)	493	491	-0.4	467	97.4	0.0	0.9	1.7	0.0	29.4	57.3	13.5	175	85.7	36.0	22.3
Alvarado city & MCD (Marshall)	363	357	-1.7	437	81.0	1.8	0.0	1.4	15.8	28.9	62.1	8.9	172	78.5	52.9	19.2
Alvwood township (Itasca)	42	42	0.0	48	100.0	0.0	0.0	0.0	0.0	0.0	77.1	22.9	22	95.5	63.6	0.0
Amador township (Chisago)	885	892	0.8	929	98.2	0.3	0.1	0.6	0.8	28.6	62.0	9.3	330	96.7	38.8	20.3
Amboy city & MCD (Blue Earth)	534	525	-1.7	499	95.4	0.0	0.0	0.4	4.2	16.4	59.4	24.0	241	82.2	53.9	13.3

1 May be of any race.

Table A. All Places — **Population and Housing**

STATE City, town, township, borough, or CDP (county if applicable)	Population				Race and Hispanic or Latino origin (percent), 2010–2014					Age (percent), 2010–2014			Households, 2010–2014			
	2010 census total population	2014 estimated population	Percent change 2010–2014	ACS total population estimate 2010–2014	White alone, not Hispanic or Latino	Black alone, not Hispanic or Latino	Asian alone, not Hispanic or Latino	All other races or 2 or more races, not Hispanic or Latino	Hispanic or Latino[1]	Under 18 years old	Age 18 to 64 years old	Age 65 years and older	Total occupied housing units	Percent owner occupied	High school diploma or less	Bachelor's degree or more
	1	2	3	4	5	6	7	8	9	10	11	12	13	14	15	16
MINNESOTA—Con.																
Amboy township (Cottonwood)	164	163	-0.6	144	97.2	0.0	0.0	2.8	0.0	20.1	52.8	27.1	63	95.2	47.6	17.5
Amherst township (Fillmore)	378	384	1.6	395	99.5	0.0	0.0	0.5	0.0	38.0	46.5	15.4	116	86.2	53.4	9.5
Amiret township (Lyon)	245	244	-0.4	235	96.2	3.4	0.0	0.4	0.0	21.3	59.6	19.1	85	87.1	51.8	22.4
Amo township (Cottonwood)	132	131	-0.8	157	100.0	0.0	0.0	0.0	0.0	35.8	51.6	12.7	49	85.7	14.3	42.9
Amor township (Otter Tail)	495	493	-0.4	596	95.6	0.0	1.2	2.9	0.3	19.6	40.8	39.6	232	97.8	22.4	37.5
Andover city & MCD (Anoka)	30,598	31,996	4.6	31,271	91.8	1.2	2.6	2.4	2.0	29.5	62.6	7.9	10,131	93.1	26.8	35.3
Andover township (Polk).	119	118	-0.8	187	92.0	0.0	0.0	0.0	8.0	30.0	58.8	11.2	66	87.9	22.7	50.0
Andrea township (Wilkin)..	65	64	-1.5	32	100.0	0.0	0.0	0.0	0.0	15.6	50.0	34.4	12	100.0	41.7	0.0
Angle township (Lake of the Woods)	119	NA	NA	38	100.0	0.0	0.0	0.0	0.0	0.0	86.9	13.2	30	56.7	83.3	0.0
Angle Inlet CDP	60	NA	NA	25	100.0	0.0	0.0	0.0	0.0	0.0	100.0	0.0	25	48.0	100.0	0.0
Angora township (St. Louis)	249	250	0.4	241	94.6	0.0	0.0	5.4	0.0	17.8	70.9	11.2	103	89.3	46.6	16.5
Angus township (Polk)	76	76	0.0	61	100.0	0.0	0.0	0.0	0.0	18.0	60.7	21.3	28	85.7	53.6	7.1
Ann township (Cottonwood)	179	178	-0.6	172	96.5	0.0	0.0	0.0	3.5	21.0	58.7	20.3	72	94.4	41.7	23.6
Annandale city & MCD (Wright)	3,228	3,295	2.1	3,281	95.3	3.0	0.0	0.8	0.8	25.2	55.7	19.1	1,290	77.6	47.3	21.0
Ann Lake township (Kanabec)	447	434	-2.9	444	93.9	0.0	1.6	2.5	2.0	19.0	63.7	17.3	189	91.0	53.4	8.5
Anoka city & MCD (Anoka)	17,142	17,276	0.8	17,202	85.3	6.4	1.1	3.2	4.0	21.3	63.3	15.4	7,247	54.5	35.7	21.4
Ansel township (Cass)	97	96	-1.0	53	100.0	0.0	0.0	0.0	0.0	17.0	49.1	34.0	26	84.6	84.6	0.0
Anthony township (Norman)	62	60	-3.2	47	100.0	0.0	0.0	0.0	0.0	10.7	66.0	23.4	21	100.0	47.6	4.8
Antrim township (Watonwan)	240	238	-0.8	220	98.2	0.9	0.9	0.0	0.0	13.7	64.5	21.8	108	78.7	61.1	16.7
Appleton city & MCD (Swift)	1,412	1,356	-4.0	1,510	91.9	3.5	0.1	2.9	1.7	22.7	52.9	24.3	692	61.7	49.6	12.3
Appleton township (Swift).	203	196	-3.4	181	99.4	0.0	0.0	0.0	0.6	14.4	64.1	21.5	90	85.6	38.9	36.7
Apple Valley city & MCD (Dakota)	49,084	50,487	2.9	49,911	80.6	5.8	5.0	4.3	4.2	24.9	64.1	11.1	19,284	79.5	18.7	46.7
Arago township (Hubbard)	607	607	0.0	672	98.2	0.7	0.0	1.0	0.0	22.4	58.9	18.8	271	95.9	35.1	27.7
Arbo township (Itasca)......	867	874	0.8	1,012	95.8	0.0	0.6	0.6	3.0	21.5	63.4	15.2	415	93.0	38.3	18.1
Arco city & MCD (Lincoln)	75	73	-2.7	91	96.7	0.0	0.0	3.3	0.0	27.5	52.8	19.8	45	77.8	64.4	8.9
Arctander township (Kandiyohi)	381	381	0.0	375	98.4	0.0	0.0	0.0	1.6	19.5	65.6	14.9	150	92.0	43.3	19.3
Arden Hills city & MCD (Ramsey)	9,552	9,876	3.4	9,700	89.4	0.8	5.3	1.7	2.7	15.5	68.1	16.5	3,023	85.0	16.0	61.8
Ardenhurst township (Itasca)	164	165	0.6	173	94.8	1.7	0.0	0.6	2.9	12.7	52.0	35.3	69	95.7	21.7	29.0
Arena township (Lac qui Parle)	122	116	-4.9	117	100.0	0.0	0.0	0.0	0.0	19.7	54.7	25.6	55	89.1	40.0	10.9
Arendahl township (Fillmore)	337	342	1.5	278	99.3	0.0	0.0	0.7	0.0	27.8	57.3	15.1	97	78.4	34.0	25.8
Argyle city & MCD (Marshall)	639	637	-0.3	536	99.6	0.0	0.0	0.4	0.0	17.5	44.5	38.1	274	67.2	60.9	14.2
Arlington city & MCD (Sibley)	2,233	2,179	-2.4	2,196	80.0	0.3	2.2	1.0	16.6	27.5	54.7	17.5	880	62.3	49.5	11.5
Arlington township (Sibley)	543	534	-1.7	611	96.9	0.0	0.2	0.3	2.6	23.0	62.3	14.6	225	91.6	50.7	17.8
Arlone township (Pine)	358	347	-3.1	466	87.1	0.0	4.3	3.2	5.4	21.5	65.5	13.1	188	89.4	55.9	5.9
Arna township (Pine)	112	111	-0.9	84	97.6	0.0	0.0	2.4	0.0	13.1	52.5	34.5	42	88.1	52.4	11.9
Arnold CDP	2,960	NA	NA	3,002	98.6	0.4	0.0	1.0	0.0	19.5	68.7	12.0	1,269	91.2	29.4	19.5
Arrowhead township (St. Louis)	223	224	0.4	205	84.4	4.4	0.0	11.2	0.0	22.5	58.1	19.5	65	92.3	52.3	12.3
Arthur township (Kanabec)	1,843	1,803	-2.2	1,819	97.1	0.3	0.0	0.5	2.1	21.8	63.8	14.2	643	89.9	44.6	19.3
Arthur township (Traverse)	81	77	-4.9	93	100.0	0.0	0.0	0.0	0.0	20.5	59.3	20.4	39	84.6	35.9	2.6
Artichoke township (Big Stone)	79	78	-1.3	66	100.0	0.0	0.0	0.0	0.0	9.0	66.6	24.2	35	88.6	48.6	17.1
Arveson township (Kittson)	96	94	-2.1	78	100.0	0.0	0.0	0.0	0.0	26.9	64.0	9.0	22	100.0	31.8	18.2
Ashby city & MCD (Grant)	446	436	-2.2	473	94.3	0.0	0.0	0.8	4.9	26.4	47.2	26.4	203	69.5	33.0	12.3
Ash Lake township (Lincoln)	151	150	-0.7	152	96.1	0.0	0.0	0.0	3.9	19.1	48.8	32.2	68	86.8	58.8	10.3
Ashland township (Dodge)	319	324	1.6	360	100.0	0.0	0.0	0.0	0.0	22.8	52.5	24.7	143	79.0	37.8	16.8
Ashley township (Stearns)	262	263	0.4	270	100.0	0.0	0.0	0.0	0.0	24.8	61.6	13.7	99	96.0	58.6	13.1
Askov city & MCD (Pine) ..	364	354	-2.7	371	97.0	0.0	0.0	3.0	0.0	18.1	60.0	21.8	196	57.7	61.2	15.3
Athens township (Isanti) ...	2,177	2,199	1.0	1,712	97.6	0.2	0.0	2.2	0.0	19.9	63.5	16.5	670	88.7	51.6	10.9
Atherton township (Wilkin)	145	143	-1.4	117	100.0	0.0	0.0	0.0	0.0	17.1	64.1	18.8	49	95.9	55.1	20.4
Atkinson township (Carlton)	406	411	1.2	368	95.7	1.1	0.5	2.7	0.0	28.3	63.3	8.4	140	92.9	36.4	25.7
Atlanta township (Becker).	119	120	0.8	119	95.0	0.0	0.0	5.0	0.0	26.0	63.7	10.1	49	83.7	51.0	6.1
Atwater city & MCD (Kandiyohi)	1,133	1,122	-1.0	1,012	93.2	0.7	2.0	0.0	4.2	25.2	60.5	14.1	433	76.9	49.7	12.7
Audubon city & MCD (Becker)	519	513	-1.2	546	81.3	0.4	0.0	17.2	1.1	28.7	64.2	7.0	202	56.4	43.6	7.4
Audubon township (Becker)	541	551	1.8	513	92.8	0.0	0.0	5.5	1.8	24.1	55.2	20.7	209	95.2	36.8	24.9
Augsburg township (Marshall)	74	74	0.0	54	92.6	0.0	0.0	7.4	0.0	20.5	48.2	31.5	22	81.8	59.1	22.7
Augusta township (Lac qui Parle)	110	105	-4.5	111	100.0	0.0	0.0	0.0	0.0	12.6	60.3	27.0	54	88.9	57.4	22.2
Ault township (St. Louis) ...	109	109	0.0	109	94.5	0.0	0.0	0.0	5.5	0.0	77.9	22.0	66	89.4	47.0	15.2
Aurdal township (Otter Tail)	1,450	1,461	0.8	1,688	96.5	1.5	0.0	1.3	0.7	27.0	62.4	10.6	587	97.8	27.1	37.5
Aurora city.........................	1,682	1,674	-0.5	1,587	99.0	0.1	0.0	0.9	0.1	17.0	59.0	24.1	767	72.5	54.4	12.8
Aurora township (Steele)..	574	574	0.0	535	98.1	0.0	0.0	1.9	0.0	25.8	54.9	19.3	192	94.8	56.3	10.9

1 May be of any race.

Table A.   All Places — **Population and Housing**

STATE City, town, township, borough, or CDP (county if applicable)	2010 census total population	2014 estimated population	Percent change 2010–2014	ACS total population estimate 2010–2014	White alone, not Hispanic or Latino	Black alone, not Hispanic or Latino	Asian alone, not Hispanic or Latino	All other races or 2 or more races, not Hispanic or Latino	Hispanic or Latino[1]	Under 18 years old	Age 18 to 64 years old	Age 65 years and older	Total occupied housing units	Percent owner occupied	High school diploma or less	Bachelor's degree or more
	1	2	3	4	5	6	7	8	9	10	11	12	13	14	15	16
MINNESOTA—Con.																
Austin city & MCD (Mower)	24,720	24,716	0.0	24,760	75.7	3.4	2.8	2.5	15.6	24.8	57.4	17.8	9,903	64.7	43.3	19.4
Austin township (Mower)	1,004	1,019	1.5	1,104	97.0	0.0	0.3	1.4	1.4	24.7	60.9	14.4	423	92.7	41.6	17.5
Automba township (Carlton)	140	141	0.7	125	93.6	0.0	0.0	6.4	0.0	24.8	57.6	17.6	51	80.4	64.7	7.8
Avoca city & MCD (Murray)	147	142	-3.4	95	88.4	0.0	0.0	0.0	11.6	12.7	63.1	24.2	50	90.0	48.0	12.0
Avon city & MCD (Stearns)	1,396	1,436	2.9	1,548	98.7	0.0	0.8	0.0	0.5	25.0	63.2	11.8	593	79.4	40.1	19.6
Avon township (Stearns)	2,294	2,365	3.1	2,355	96.9	0.0	0.5	1.1	1.6	23.7	63.8	12.5	822	92.9	45.3	20.4
Babbitt city & MCD (St. Louis)	1,475	1,530	3.7	1,456	97.3	0.1	0.0	2.5	0.1	16.3	53.7	30.0	722	80.2	49.3	13.2
Backus city & MCD (Cass)	250	245	-2.0	283	96.8	0.0	1.4	1.8	0.0	14.5	65.7	19.8	156	76.3	60.3	7.1
Badger township (Polk)	117	116	-0.9	138	89.1	10.9	0.0	0.0	0.0	17.4	69.3	13.0	53	88.7	58.5	11.3
Badger city & MCD (Roseau)	375	373	-0.5	479	91.2	0.2	0.0	6.7	1.9	25.1	62.3	12.7	238	70.2	47.5	6.7
Badoura township (Hubbard)	128	126	-1.6	139	88.5	0.0	0.0	8.6	2.9	30.9	44.0	25.2	47	87.2	40.4	23.4
Bagley city & MCD (Clearwater)	1,382	1,392	0.7	1,420	87.7	1.1	0.4	10.6	0.4	20.9	51.7	27.4	657	51.6	57.4	15.2
Baker CDP	55	NA	NA	50	100.0	0.0	0.0	0.0	0.0	22.0	50.0	28.0	22	100.0	22.7	36.4
Baker township (Stevens)	114	113	-0.9	123	100.0	0.0	0.0	0.0	0.0	22.7	63.4	13.8	42	85.7	16.7	23.8
Balaton city & MCD (Lyon)	643	626	-2.6	575	92.0	2.6	0.0	4.5	0.9	19.7	54.4	26.1	241	77.2	49.8	21.2
Baldwin township (Sherburne)	6,739	6,896	2.3	6,814	96.0	0.0	0.0	3.3	0.7	24.8	65.6	9.6	2,424	94.4	36.7	20.0
Balkan township (St. Louis)	832	839	0.8	844	100.0	0.0	0.0	0.0	0.0	16.7	67.1	16.0	367	94.6	45.2	11.4
Ball Bluff township (Aitkin)	278	271	-2.5	236	91.1	0.0	8.9	0.0	0.0	8.9	60.1	30.9	115	89.6	42.6	14.8
Ball Club CDP	342	NA	NA	371	48.5	0.0	0.0	41.0	10.5	26.9	64.8	8.1	117	60.7	62.4	5.1
Balsam township (Aitkin)	42	40	-4.8	30	100.0	0.0	0.0	0.0	0.0	6.7	19.9	73.3	17	88.2	41.2	5.9
Balsam township (Itasca)	553	559	1.1	648	86.7	0.0	3.5	2.0	7.7	17.9	60.2	21.8	270	97.0	43.3	25.6
Bancroft township (Freeborn)	946	936	-1.1	1,020	98.3	0.2	1.0	0.0	0.5	22.1	55.1	22.8	393	92.1	43.5	15.3
Bandon township (Renville)	175	168	-4.0	138	100.0	0.0	0.0	0.0	0.0	21.7	57.9	20.3	64	85.9	59.4	7.8
Bangor township (Pope)	185	187	1.1	184	100.0	0.0	0.0	0.0	0.0	24.0	66.2	9.8	74	94.6	58.1	6.8
Barber township (Faribault)	248	243	-2.0	221	99.5	0.0	0.0	0.0	0.5	24.0	52.1	24.0	87	85.1	47.1	25.3
Barclay township (Cass)	559	559	0.0	431	99.1	0.0	0.0	0.0	0.9	20.4	68.0	11.6	199	81.9	43.7	17.1
Barnesville city & MCD (Clay)	2,557	2,569	0.5	2,574	94.8	0.6	0.3	3.3	1.0	29.7	51.2	19.4	1,027	82.5	47.6	21.3
Barnesville township (Clay)	153	156	2.0	207	96.6	0.0	0.0	0.0	3.4	18.9	67.2	14.0	75	96.0	25.3	24.0
Barnett township (Roseau)	139	140	0.7	174	100.0	0.0	0.0	0.0	0.0	24.2	64.3	11.5	64	96.9	43.8	14.1
Barnum city & MCD (Carlton)	613	600	-2.1	724	97.8	0.0	0.0	2.2	0.0	27.1	58.0	14.8	294	56.8	34.0	26.9
Barnum township (Carlton)	1,061	1,073	1.1	1,063	98.4	0.0	0.3	1.0	0.3	26.7	58.9	14.5	384	98.2	40.1	20.3
Barrett city & MCD (Grant)	415	406	-2.2	340	98.2	0.0	0.0	1.8	0.0	21.8	41.4	36.8	128	83.6	44.5	11.7
Barry city & MCD (Big Stone)	16	15	-6.3	11	100.0	0.0	0.0	0.0	0.0	9.1	91.0	0.0	4	100.0	75.0	0.0
Barry township (Pine)	585	568	-2.9	543	93.9	0.0	0.0	5.2	0.9	18.8	65.2	16.0	247	76.5	61.1	15.4
Barsness township (Pope)	149	153	2.7	116	94.8	0.0	0.0	5.2	0.0	24.2	59.4	16.4	47	83.0	38.3	8.5
Bartlett township (Todd)	445	435	-2.2	533	96.2	0.0	0.0	3.2	0.6	39.0	48.2	12.9	157	93.0	56.7	7.0
Barto township (Roseau)	138	139	0.7	142	96.5	0.0	0.0	0.0	3.5	28.8	62.6	8.5	51	96.1	51.0	3.9
Bashaw township (Brown)	241	238	-1.2	307	99.3	0.0	0.0	0.0	0.7	35.8	49.1	15.0	104	88.5	53.8	25.0
Bassett township (St. Louis)	41	41	0.0	40	100.0	0.0	0.0	0.0	0.0	10.0	65.0	25.0	25	92.0	48.0	20.0
Bath township (Freeborn)	440	434	-1.4	399	98.2	0.0	0.5	0.0	1.3	16.1	70.0	14.0	161	95.0	41.6	22.4
Battle township (Beltrami)	50	51	2.0	38	76.3	0.0	7.9	15.8	0.0	31.7	47.4	21.1	15	80.0	66.7	20.0
Battle Lake city & MCD (Otter Tail)	875	879	0.5	865	94.5	0.2	2.0	2.5	0.8	20.6	44.6	34.7	398	73.4	30.2	24.9
Battle Plain township (Rock)	199	196	-1.5	208	99.0	0.0	0.0	1.0	0.0	29.3	48.6	22.1	70	94.3	61.4	22.9
Baudette city & MCD (Lake of the Woods)	1,106	1,059	-4.2	1,039	92.0	0.9	0.0	3.1	4.0	25.7	52.5	21.8	448	66.1	46.0	19.4
Baudette township (Lake of the Woods)	345	NA	NA	302	99.7	0.0	0.0	0.3	0.0	8.9	48.7	42.4	147	91.8	23.1	34.0
Baxter city & MCD (Crow Wing)	7,610	7,826	2.8	7,710	99.1	0.2	0.5	0.2	0.0	25.9	58.5	15.8	3,094	68.2	27.1	29.5
Baxter township (Lac qui Parle)	200	190	-5.0	160	100.0	0.0	0.0	0.0	0.0	20.6	52.6	26.9	69	92.8	39.1	31.9
Bay Lake township (Crow Wing)	929	949	2.2	851	93.9	0.0	0.0	3.3	2.8	8.7	47.8	43.5	425	95.3	35.5	36.0
Bayport city & MCD (Washington)	3,471	3,692	6.4	3,581	78.3	13.0	1.1	5.8	1.8	14.4	69.8	15.7	1,139	66.5	32.7	29.7
Baytown township (Washington)	1,619	1,806	11.6	1,574	98.2	0.0	1.0	0.4	0.4	21.1	66.7	12.1	562	95.2	17.1	53.7
Bear Creek township (Clearwater)	111	113	1.8	98	99.0	0.0	0.0	0.0	1.0	14.2	57.2	28.6	46	100.0	39.1	19.6
Beardsley city & MCD (Big Stone)	233	225	-3.4	191	96.3	0.0	0.0	0.0	3.7	19.9	61.9	18.3	98	83.7	69.4	3.1
Bear Park township (Norman)	192	186	-3.1	117	98.3	0.0	0.0	0.0	1.7	15.4	44.4	40.2	62	98.4	54.8	19.4
Bearville township (Itasca)	205	208	1.5	177	97.2	0.0	0.0	2.8	0.0	20.9	42.9	36.2	79	96.2	24.1	34.2
Beatty township (St. Louis)	374	378	1.1	427	98.1	0.0	0.0	0.7	1.2	5.8	46.0	48.0	217	96.8	28.6	44.7
Beauford township (Blue Earth)	406	406	0.0	461	100.0	0.0	0.0	0.0	0.0	26.9	61.6	11.5	178	92.7	47.2	22.5
Beaulieu CDP	48	NA	NA	69	59.4	0.0	0.0	40.6	0.0	10.1	44.8	44.9	33	87.9	63.6	18.2
Beaulieu township (Mahnomen)	108	111	2.8	124	54.0	0.0	0.0	46.0	0.0	20.2	37.8	41.9	56	82.1	35.7	21.4

1 May be of any race.

Table A. All Places — **Population and Housing**

STATE City, town, township, borough, or CDP (county if applicable)	2010 census total population	2014 estimated population	Percent change 2010–2014	ACS total population estimate 2010–2014	White alone, not Hispanic or Latino	Black alone, not Hispanic or Latino	Asian alone, not Hispanic or Latino	All other races or 2 or more races, not Hispanic or Latino	Hispanic or Latino[1]	Under 18 years old	Age 18 to 64 years old	Age 65 years and older	Total occupied housing units	Percent owner occupied	High school diploma or less	Bachelor's degree or more
	1	2	3	4	5	6	7	8	9	10	11	12	13	14	15	16
MINNESOTA—Con.																
Beaver township (Aitkin)...	53	51	-3.8	82	100.0	0.0	0.0	0.0	0.0	8.5	69.4	22.0	43	100.0	34.9	9.3
Beaver township (Fillmore)	242	245	1.2	274	99.6	0.0	0.0	0.0	0.4	28.8	58.3	12.8	94	87.2	53.2	13.8
Beaver township (Roseau)	107	108	0.9	138	100.0	0.0	0.0	0.0	0.0	28.2	55.0	16.7	50	98.0	82.0	6.0
Beaver Bay city & MCD (Lake)	181	176	-2.8	141	96.5	0.0	0.0	3.5	0.0	31.1	42.6	26.2	56	83.9	41.1	28.6
Beaver Bay township (Lake)	473	475	0.4	579	95.9	0.0	0.0	3.1	1.0	12.8	58.2	29.0	280	90.4	37.1	25.0
Beaver Creek city & MCD (Rock)	297	295	-0.7	310	98.1	1.9	0.0	0.0	0.0	29.9	58.3	11.6	125	80.0	47.2	24.8
Beaver Creek township (Rock)	386	385	-0.3	395	97.2	0.5	0.3	2.0	0.0	28.1	56.9	14.9	148	93.2	47.3	22.3
Beaver Falls township (Renville)	197	189	-4.1	173	100.0	0.0	0.0	0.0	0.0	17.3	62.3	20.2	78	82.1	56.4	15.4
Becker township (Cass)....	517	518	0.2	472	99.2	0.0	0.0	0.8	0.0	26.5	57.7	15.9	217	72.8	53.5	6.0
Becker city & MCD (Sherburne)	4,538	4,687	3.3	4,626	95.0	0.0	2.6	2.3	0.0	33.9	60.7	5.4	1,510	68.3	23.0	34.2
Becker township (Sherburne)	4,842	5,117	5.7	4,950	96.0	3.1	0.0	0.9	0.0	29.3	62.8	7.9	1,608	90.0	18.8	35.2
Bejou city & MCD (Mahnomen)	89	91	2.2	106	80.2	12.3	0.0	7.5	0.0	35.8	57.5	6.6	35	82.9	57.1	5.7
Bejou township (Mahnomen)	79	81	2.5	53	88.7	0.0	0.0	3.8	7.5	18.8	37.7	43.4	20	90.0	65.0	5.0
Belfast township (Murray) .	192	187	-2.6	196	96.9	3.1	0.0	0.0	0.0	28.1	52.0	19.9	75	92.0	40.0	13.3
Belgium township (Polk) ...	81	81	0.0	75	94.7	0.0	0.0	5.3	0.0	6.7	78.8	14.7	35	94.3	68.6	0.0
Belgrade township (Nicollet)	1,049	1,038	-1.0	1,009	98.1	0.2	0.2	0.5	1.0	20.8	64.9	14.3	385	95.3	38.4	27.3
Belgrade city & MCD (Stearns)	740	752	1.6	717	98.9	0.0	0.3	0.0	0.8	22.3	54.6	23.2	309	71.5	41.7	12.3
Bellechester city	175	175	0.0	232	84.9	0.0	0.0	0.9	14.2	30.2	58.0	11.6	81	86.4	54.3	14.8
Bellechester city (Goodhue)	133	134	0.8	183	91.3	0.0	0.0	1.1	7.7	30.6	59.7	9.8	65	89.2	49.2	15.4
Bellechester city (Wabasha)	42	41	-2.4	49	61.2	0.0	0.0	0.0	38.8	28.5	53.1	18.4	16	75.0	75.0	12.5
Belle Creek township (Goodhue)	501	504	0.6	448	99.3	0.0	0.4	0.2	0.0	26.1	63.1	10.9	173	85.5	50.9	20.8
Belle Plaine city & MCD (Scott)	6,659	6,902	3.6	6,794	96.8	0.1	1.2	1.7	0.1	30.2	60.3	9.5	2,413	85.5	35.5	27.2
Belle Plaine township (Scott)	880	921	4.7	854	98.4	0.0	1.1	0.1	0.5	23.5	63.7	12.8	280	95.0	44.3	20.4
Belle Prairie township (Morrison)	1,090	1,083	-0.6	1,238	98.1	0.4	0.5	0.6	0.3	20.7	65.9	13.3	497	92.0	38.4	27.8
Belle River township (Douglas)	345	347	0.6	352	99.4	0.6	0.0	0.0	0.0	23.5	53.7	22.7	144	86.8	48.6	8.3
Bellevue township (Morrison)	1,093	1,085	-0.7	1,040	96.7	1.6	0.0	0.0	1.6	29.3	59.4	11.3	361	95.0	41.0	15.0
Bellingham city & MCD (Lac qui Parle)	168	160	-4.8	164	100.0	0.0	0.0	0.0	0.0	18.9	48.7	32.3	70	88.6	58.6	7.1
Belmont township (Jackson)	218	218	0.0	176	98.3	0.0	0.0	1.7	0.0	23.8	52.5	23.9	79	87.3	46.8	19.0
Beltrami city & MCD (Polk)	107	106	-0.9	107	88.8	0.0	0.0	1.9	9.3	17.7	67.4	15.0	51	88.2	21.6	25.5
Belvidere township (Goodhue)	462	465	0.6	427	98.6	0.0	0.0	0.2	1.2	26.8	66.6	6.8	152	85.5	54.6	13.8
Belview city & MCD (Redwood)	384	364	-5.2	401	93.5	0.0	0.7	5.7	0.0	18.9	51.8	29.2	168	73.2	58.3	10.1
Bemidji city & MCD (Beltrami)	14,076	14,453	2.7	14,319	79.4	1.1	0.6	17.1	1.8	19.2	64.0	16.9	5,711	50.2	28.6	29.4
Bemidji township (Beltrami)	2,793	3,150	12.8	2,933	87.1	0.4	0.0	12.4	0.0	26.7	64.0	9.4	1,028	85.3	28.8	34.3
Bena city & MCD (Cass)...	119	117	-1.7	122	21.3	0.0	0.0	78.7	0.0	43.5	41.9	14.8	42	78.6	54.8	2.4
Bennington township (Mower)	169	170	0.6	130	99.2	0.0	0.0	0.8	0.0	15.3	62.3	22.3	60	91.7	51.7	13.3
Benson city & MCD (Swift)	3,240	3,107	-4.1	3,165	94.4	1.4	0.7	0.0	3.5	18.1	57.4	24.5	1,531	66.8	51.5	20.4
Benson township (Swift) ...	334	323	-3.3	332	93.1	4.5	0.0	2.4	0.0	24.1	61.6	14.2	111	85.6	36.0	32.4
Benton township (Carver).	786	800	1.8	800	99.6	0.0	0.0	0.0	0.4	18.5	63.5	18.1	295	93.6	62.7	15.6
Benville township (Beltrami)	86	87	1.2	75	100.0	0.0	0.0	0.0	0.0	34.7	58.7	6.7	26	100.0	80.8	3.8
Ben Wade township (Pope)	250	253	1.2	308	96.1	0.0	1.6	2.3	0.0	23.1	68.8	8.1	102	85.3	33.3	15.7
Bergen township (McLeod)	1,006	988	-1.8	1,005	95.7	0.0	0.0	0.0	4.3	26.9	60.2	13.1	356	93.5	41.0	18.5
Berlin township (Steele)....	519	520	0.2	432	100.0	0.0	0.0	0.0	0.0	17.8	68.4	13.9	168	89.9	42.9	19.0
Bernadotte township (Nicollet)	278	274	-1.4	238	96.2	0.0	0.0	0.0	3.8	22.7	64.0	13.4	101	92.1	44.6	12.9
Bertha city & MCD (Todd).	497	475	-4.4	541	97.8	0.0	0.0	1.8	0.4	26.8	55.2	18.1	242	69.8	36.4	15.7
Bertha township (Todd).....	408	396	-2.9	422	90.0	1.4	0.7	7.1	0.7	28.7	54.6	16.6	163	84.7	47.2	9.8
Beseman township (Carlton)	137	136	-0.7	171	91.2	0.0	0.0	0.6	8.2	24.0	61.4	14.6	65	98.5	44.6	15.4
Bethel city & MCD (Anoka)	466	470	0.9	401	95.0	1.7	0.2	0.5	2.5	25.2	65.9	9.0	156	85.3	53.2	10.9
Beulah township (Cass)....	64	63	-1.6	52	100.0	0.0	0.0	0.0	0.0	5.7	26.9	67.3	33	93.9	69.7	3.0
Big Bend township (Chippewa)	240	236	-1.7	269	95.2	0.0	0.0	0.7	4.1	23.4	67.7	8.9	109	87.2	46.8	21.1
Bigelow city & MCD (Nobles)	235	237	0.9	244	76.6	0.0	0.0	0.0	23.4	23.0	66.7	10.2	82	75.6	68.3	11.0
Bigelow township (Nobles)	373	376	0.8	371	99.7	0.0	0.0	0.0	0.3	26.8	58.6	14.6	125	95.2	24.8	30.4
Big Falls city & MCD (Koochiching)	236	225	-4.7	225	94.7	0.0	0.0	5.3	0.0	14.1	54.2	31.6	132	65.2	56.8	7.6
Bigfork city & MCD (Itasca)	446	447	0.2	404	93.3	0.0	0.0	5.9	0.7	12.1	43.5	44.3	194	66.0	45.9	7.2
Bigfork township (Itasca) ..	308	310	0.6	308	88.0	0.0	0.0	8.8	3.2	24.7	47.5	27.6	122	95.1	45.9	9.8
Big Lake CDP	443	NA	NA	298	72.8	0.0	0.0	27.2	0.0	10.8	62.9	26.5	142	75.4	40.8	26.1

1 May be of any race.

Table A. All Places — **Population and Housing**

STATE City, town, township, borough, or CDP (county if applicable)	2010 census total population	2014 estimated population	Percent change 2010–2014	ACS total population estimate 2010–2014	White alone, not Hispanic or Latino	Black alone, not Hispanic or Latino	Asian alone, not Hispanic or Latino	All other races or 2 or more races, not Hispanic or Latino	Hispanic or Latino[1]	Under 18 years old	Age 18 to 64 years old	Age 65 years and older	Total occupied housing units	Percent owner occupied	High school diploma or less	Bachelor's degree or more
	1	2	3	4	5	6	7	8	9	10	11	12	13	14	15	16
MINNESOTA—Con.																
Big Lake city & MCD (Sherburne)..............	10,060	10,360	3.0	10,230	88.8	2.4	0.2	0.6	8.0	32.5	62.6	5.1	3,373	84.5	35.3	19.5
Big Lake township (Sherburne)...............	7,386	7,571	2.5	7,471	96.3	0.3	1.6	0.9	0.8	24.1	66.8	9.2	2,383	95.3	28.9	36.0
Big Stone township (Big Stone)...................	273	270	-1.1	268	97.4	0.0	0.0	2.6	0.0	16.8	56.9	26.5	107	98.1	51.4	28.0
Big Woods township (Marshall)................	53	53	0.0	49	100.0	0.0	0.0	0.0	0.0	38.7	55.1	6.1	13	100.0	15.4	46.2
Bingham Lake city & MCD (Cottonwood)	126	128	1.6	141	87.9	0.0	4.3	1.4	6.4	27.0	55.3	17.7	59	94.9	49.2	6.8
Birch township (Beltrami)..	118	120	1.7	61	80.3	0.0	0.0	19.7	0.0	11.5	69.0	19.7	25	100.0	52.0	8.0
Birch Cooley township (Renville).................	245	235	-4.1	196	96.4	0.0	0.0	3.6	0.0	27.6	54.7	17.9	85	77.6	52.9	20.0
Birch Creek township (Pine)	233	227	-2.6	192	100.0	0.0	0.0	0.0	0.0	12.5	65.2	22.4	87	96.6	57.5	3.4
Birchdale township (Todd)	856	843	-1.5	744	98.8	0.0	0.0	1.1	0.1	15.2	64.5	20.4	340	92.4	46.5	15.6
Birch Lake township (Cass)...................	524	528	0.8	641	97.0	0.0	0.3	2.2	0.5	12.4	54.2	33.5	328	93.0	50.9	20.4
Birch Lake UT (St. Louis)..	505	508	0.6	341	100.0	0.0	0.0	0.0	0.0	7.9	50.8	41.3	172	93.0	20.9	58.7
Birchwood Village city & MCD (Washington)........	873	878	0.6	891	97.9	0.4	0.7	0.8	0.2	16.3	64.3	19.3	377	86.2	14.1	59.7
Bird Island city & MCD (Renville).................	1,042	1,004	-3.6	915	95.7	0.0	0.5	0.3	3.4	18.7	58.3	23.0	457	84.7	48.6	13.1
Bird Island township (Renville).................	205	197	-3.9	251	100.0	0.0	0.0	0.0	0.0	29.5	60.0	10.8	89	95.5	29.2	23.6
Biscay city & MCD (McLeod).................	113	111	-1.8	96	80.2	0.0	0.0	0.0	19.8	30.2	57.3	12.5	35	97.1	48.6	17.1
Bismarck township (Sibley)...................	314	310	-1.3	302	100.0	0.0	0.0	0.0	0.0	22.2	54.6	23.2	94	89.4	45.7	12.8
Biwabik city & MCD (St. Louis)	969	995	2.7	1,096	97.8	0.0	0.0	2.2	0.0	20.2	55.1	24.7	548	72.3	42.9	11.5
Biwabik township (St. Louis)...................	804	808	0.5	824	94.1	0.0	0.8	3.2	1.9	12.5	68.1	19.4	392	93.1	29.3	22.2
Blackberry township (Itasca)...................	880	885	0.6	778	97.4	0.0	0.3	0.5	1.8	20.2	62.9	16.8	314	98.1	35.4	13.7
Blackduck city & MCD (Beltrami).................	784	788	0.5	703	87.5	4.4	0.1	6.0	2.0	24.0	52.5	23.6	304	53.6	55.9	7.9
Black Hammer township (Houston).................	245	242	-1.2	264	99.2	0.0	0.0	0.4	0.4	12.1	73.1	14.8	112	78.6	44.6	25.0
Blackhoof township (Carlton).................	893	904	1.2	1,043	94.3	1.8	1.2	1.7	1.0	32.1	53.5	14.4	350	95.1	40.0	23.4
Black River township (Pennington)................	82	82	0.0	64	100.0	0.0	0.0	0.0	0.0	15.6	75.0	9.4	29	100.0	27.6	24.1
Blaine city..................	57,177	61,190	7.0	59,295	81.2	4.0	8.1	3.7	3.1	26.1	64.2	9.7	21,881	86.4	27.1	33.6
Blaine city (Anoka)...........	57,177	61,190	7.0	59,295	81.2	4.0	8.1	3.7	3.1	26.1	64.2	9.7	21,881	86.4	27.1	33.6
Blaine city (Ramsey).........	0	0	0.0	0	0.0	0.0	0.0	0.0	0.0	0.0	0.0	0.0	0	0.0	0.0	0.0
Blakeley township (Scott) .	418	436	4.3	417	85.9	0.2	3.6	10.3	0.0	24.0	58.3	17.7	153	84.3	47.7	24.8
Blind Lake township (Cass)...................	82	81	-1.2	81	92.6	0.0	0.0	7.4	0.0	17.3	70.2	12.3	37	94.6	45.9	16.2
Blomkest city & MCD (Kandiyohi).............	157	160	1.9	120	97.5	0.0	0.0	0.0	2.5	11.7	69.0	19.2	56	91.1	48.2	12.5
Bloom township (Nobles)..	158	159	0.6	145	95.2	0.0	0.0	0.0	4.8	9.0	80.1	11.0	67	80.6	65.7	10.4
Bloomer township (Marshall)................	89	89	0.0	86	100.0	0.0	0.0	0.0	0.0	23.2	65.2	11.6	31	100.0	41.9	9.7
Bloomfield township (Fillmore).................	353	358	1.4	311	99.4	0.6	0.0	0.0	0.0	22.8	57.8	19.3	128	92.2	49.2	8.6
Blooming Grove township (Waseca).................	525	531	1.1	433	94.2	0.7	2.1	2.8	0.2	16.0	61.9	22.2	188	88.8	32.4	20.7
Blooming Prairie city........	1,996	1,976	-1.0	1,836	93.3	0.0	0.0	0.0	6.7	23.4	52.1	24.6	781	78.9	49.8	21.3
Blooming Prairie city (Dodge)..................	0	0	0.0	0	0.0	0.0	0.0	0.0	0.0	0.0	0.0	0.0	0	0.0	0.0	0.0
Blooming Prairie city (Steele).................	1,996	1,976	-1.0	1,836	93.3	0.0	0.0	0.0	6.7	23.4	52.1	24.6	781	78.9	49.8	21.3
Blooming Prairie township (Steele).................	430	431	0.2	463	95.9	0.0	0.0	0.0	4.1	24.6	65.5	9.9	165	84.2	51.5	14.5
Bloomington city & MCD (Hennepin).................	82,893	86,314	4.1	85,136	75.8	7.3	6.3	3.4	7.2	19.2	62.0	18.7	36,608	68.9	24.9	42.4
Blowers township (Otter Tail)...................	321	321	0.0	363	95.6	3.0	0.0	0.8	0.6	35.5	54.8	9.6	137	85.4	44.5	8.8
Blueberry township (Wadena)...............	721	714	-1.0	717	95.4	1.8	0.8	2.0	0.0	31.2	49.9	19.0	270	84.4	39.6	24.4
Blue Earth city & MCD (Faribault)................	3,353	3,269	-2.5	3,309	89.1	1.3	0.5	1.9	7.3	22.7	52.1	25.3	1,447	68.4	44.9	20.6
Blue Earth City township (Faribault)................	387	384	-0.8	336	100.0	0.0	0.0	0.0	0.0	16.7	61.6	21.7	152	94.7	38.8	19.7
Blue Hill township (Sherburne)...............	2,176	2,226	2.3	2,280	96.8	0.1	1.2	1.9	0.0	36.2	60.2	3.6	695	98.1	32.7	16.5
Blue Mounds township (Pope)...................	186	189	1.6	189	97.9	0.0	0.0	2.1	0.0	20.6	59.2	20.1	78	94.9	42.3	23.1
Bluffton city & MCD (Otter Tail)...................	207	210	1.4	202	87.6	0.0	0.0	0.0	12.4	33.1	53.0	13.9	69	85.5	69.6	8.7
Bluffton township (Otter Tail)...................	479	480	0.2	403	98.5	0.0	0.0	0.0	1.5	29.3	57.6	13.2	140	87.9	33.6	11.4
Bock city & MCD (Mille Lacs)...................	106	106	0.0	94	100.0	0.0	0.0	0.0	0.0	13.8	68.0	18.1	46	65.2	67.4	10.9
Bogus Brook township (Mille Lacs)...............	1,421	1,411	-0.7	1,513	98.1	0.0	0.0	1.6	0.3	28.7	63.0	8.2	500	95.6	37.0	19.6
Bondin township (Murray).	268	265	-1.1	288	93.8	1.4	1.7	0.0	3.1	30.9	56.0	13.2	102	92.2	51.0	13.7
Boone township (Lake of the Woods)...............	36	NA	NA	20	100.0	0.0	0.0	0.0	0.0	35.0	65.0	0.0	7	100.0	0.0	0.0
Boon Lake township (Renville).................	378	363	-4.0	396	94.2	1.0	0.0	0.0	4.8	21.0	64.9	14.1	151	94.0	49.0	10.6

1 May be of any race.

Table A. All Places — Population and Housing

STATE City, town, township, borough, or CDP (county if applicable)	Population				Race and Hispanic or Latino origin (percent), 2010–2014					Age (percent), 2010–2014			Households, 2010–2014			
	2010 census total population	2014 estimated population	Percent change 2010–2014	ACS total population estimate 2010–2014	White alone, not Hispanic or Latino	Black alone, not Hispanic or Latino	Asian alone, not Hispanic or Latino	All other races or 2 or more races, not Hispanic or Latino	Hispanic or Latino[1]	Under 18 years old	Age 18 to 64 years old	Age 65 years and older	Total occupied housing units	Percent owner occupied	High school diploma or less	Bachelor's degree or more
	1	2	3	4	5	6	7	8	9	10	11	12	13	14	15	16
MINNESOTA—Con.																
Borgholm township (Mille Lacs)	1,718	1,707	-0.6	1,575	95.9	0.0	1.5	2.1	0.5	26.8	61.9	11.2	568	91.2	47.0	13.6
Borup city & MCD (Norman)	110	107	-2.7	104	89.4	0.0	2.9	0.0	7.7	17.3	71.1	11.5	49	85.7	44.9	30.6
Bovey city & MCD (Itasca)	804	817	1.6	867	84.3	0.8	0.9	11.6	2.3	24.4	60.3	15.2	369	66.4	36.0	13.6
Bowlus city & MCD (Morrison)	290	284	-2.1	320	99.7	0.0	0.0	0.3	0.0	31.5	58.5	10.0	131	77.1	60.3	5.3
Bowstring township (Itasca)	230	231	0.4	262	89.3	0.0	1.9	3.8	5.0	6.1	66.1	27.9	146	92.5	55.5	18.5
Bowstring Lake UT (Itasca)	1,166	1,173	0.6	1,150	50.3	0.4	0.0	44.0	5.2	26.1	60.4	13.5	389	72.0	52.7	14.4
Boxville township (Marshall)	39	39	0.0	40	100.0	0.0	0.0	0.0	0.0	17.5	62.5	20.0	18	88.9	72.2	5.6
Boyd city & MCD (Lac qui Parle)	175	166	-5.1	130	100.0	0.0	0.0	0.0	0.0	14.6	58.5	26.9	64	87.5	75.0	7.8
Boy Lake township (Cass)	256	257	0.4	245	54.7	0.0	0.0	45.3	0.0	20.3	49.9	29.8	114	68.4	56.1	12.3
Boy River city & MCD (Cass)	47	46	-2.1	36	97.2	0.0	0.0	2.8	0.0	13.9	66.6	19.4	23	95.7	82.6	0.0
Boy River township (Cass)	86	85	-1.2	66	87.9	0.0	0.0	12.1	0.0	18.2	66.7	15.2	31	90.3	58.1	0.0
Bradbury township (Mille Lacs)	268	267	-0.4	307	97.1	0.0	0.0	2.6	0.3	35.2	53.5	11.4	91	91.2	72.5	13.2
Bradford township (Isanti)	3,380	3,429	1.4	3,409	94.7	0.3	0.9	3.1	0.9	25.9	64.3	9.7	1,129	95.7	56.0	14.2
Bradford township (Wilkin)	91	90	-1.1	72	100.0	0.0	0.0	0.0	0.0	43.1	55.6	1.4	28	85.7	21.4	0.0
Braham city	1,793	1,790	-0.2	1,885	92.6	1.4	0.4	5.5	0.1	33.1	54.3	12.6	675	64.7	49.9	12.1
Braham city (Isanti)	1,793	1,790	-0.2	1,885	92.6	1.4	0.4	5.5	0.1	33.1	54.3	12.6	675	64.7	49.9	12.1
Braham city (Kanabec)	0	0	0.0	0	0.0	0.0	0.0	0.0	0.0	0.0	0.0	0.0	0	0.0	0.0	0.0
Brainerd city & MCD (Crow Wing)	13,586	13,425	-1.2	13,521	91.7	2.3	0.7	2.3	3.0	25.2	59.0	15.7	5,929	49.4	34.7	17.7
Brandon city & MCD (Douglas)	483	478	-1.0	497	100.0	0.0	0.0	0.0	0.0	22.5	56.6	20.7	199	87.4	40.2	7.5
Brandon township (Douglas)	719	729	1.4	819	96.0	0.0	1.0	1.7	1.3	18.4	59.0	22.7	313	96.8	46.3	17.6
Brandrup township (Wilkin)	158	156	-1.3	232	100.0	0.0	0.0	0.0	0.0	28.0	63.8	8.2	73	97.3	41.1	13.7
Brandsvold township (Polk)	245	248	1.2	216	92.6	1.9	0.0	5.6	0.0	21.8	55.5	22.7	92	88.0	44.6	25.0
Brandt township (Polk)	50	50	0.0	61	100.0	0.0	0.0	0.0	0.0	27.9	59.1	13.1	21	95.2	28.6	0.0
Bray township (Pennington)	64	64	0.0	58	100.0	0.0	0.0	0.0	0.0	20.7	58.6	20.7	20	100.0	30.0	30.0
Breckenridge city & MCD (Wilkin)	3,390	3,340	-1.5	3,378	94.6	0.4	0.3	2.9	1.9	23.5	56.3	20.4	1,483	65.1	37.0	13.1
Breckenridge township (Wilkin)	255	258	1.2	303	90.4	0.7	0.0	2.0	6.9	30.4	54.2	15.5	105	100.0	21.9	21.0
Breezy Point city & MCD (Crow Wing)	2,313	2,347	1.5	2,050	96.0	0.0	0.0	1.9	2.1	31.1	56.4	12.4	745	93.4	19.5	32.6
Breitung township (St. Louis)	605	609	0.7	630	99.0	0.0	0.0	1.0	0.0	18.9	59.8	21.3	280	92.5	22.9	26.8
Bremen township (Pine)	240	237	-1.3	211	97.6	0.9	0.0	1.4	0.0	9.5	70.6	19.9	96	93.8	55.2	16.7
Brevator township (St. Louis)	1,269	1,276	0.6	1,294	70.8	0.0	1.0	28.2	0.0	26.9	62.6	10.6	462	82.7	38.1	22.3
Brewster city & MCD (Nobles)	473	470	-0.6	468	90.0	0.0	0.0	0.0	10.0	31.9	54.3	13.9	198	80.3	47.0	11.6
Bricelyn city & MCD (Faribault)	365	350	-4.1	336	86.3	0.0	1.8	0.3	11.6	22.1	59.4	18.8	166	61.4	52.4	15.1
Bridgewater township (Rice)	1,786	1,816	1.7	1,856	96.2	0.1	1.2	0.0	2.5	19.4	66.9	13.7	710	92.5	29.9	41.1
Brighton township (Nicollet)	149	147	-1.3	163	98.8	0.0	0.0	0.0	1.2	24.6	54.7	20.9	61	78.7	62.3	11.5
Brislet township (Polk)	53	53	0.0	66	65.2	0.0	13.6	21.2	0.0	31.8	59.1	9.1	19	100.0	0.0	21.1
Bristol township (Fillmore)	396	401	1.3	414	99.0	0.0	1.0	0.0	0.0	30.8	57.3	11.8	135	90.4	45.9	15.6
Brockway township (Stearns)	2,702	2,792	3.3	2,752	95.7	0.0	1.6	2.4	0.3	25.7	63.8	10.5	1,041	93.7	28.7	27.6
Brookfield township (Renville)	156	150	-3.8	151	100.0	0.0	0.0	0.0	0.0	17.2	55.6	27.2	62	90.3	35.5	24.2
Brook Lake UT (Beltrami)	231	235	1.7	197	79.2	0.0	0.0	20.8	0.0	14.2	67.1	18.8	104	94.2	27.9	5.8
Brooklyn Center city & MCD (Hennepin)	30,130	30,729	2.0	30,549	42.5	29.5	15.2	3.9	8.9	27.3	61.4	11.3	11,135	61.6	41.5	21.3
Brooklyn Park city & MCD (Hennepin)	75,784	78,728	3.9	77,579	48.1	25.7	15.1	3.8	7.4	29.2	62.0	8.6	26,345	70.0	29.0	32.2
Brook Park city & MCD (Pine)	139	136	-2.2	141	100.0	0.0	0.0	0.0	0.0	11.3	79.4	9.2	60	78.3	81.7	8.3
Brook Park township (Pine)	522	507	-2.9	467	94.6	0.0	0.0	5.4	0.0	21.6	59.7	18.6	194	94.3	66.5	7.7
Brooks city & MCD (Red Lake)	141	140	-0.7	109	100.0	0.0	0.0	0.0	0.0	19.3	65.3	15.6	62	67.7	77.4	0.0
Brookston city & MCD (St. Louis)	139	139	0.0	115	78.3	7.0	0.0	14.8	0.0	9.5	66.8	23.5	31	90.3	58.1	16.1
Brookville township (Redwood)	224	217	-3.1	222	96.8	0.0	0.0	0.0	3.2	31.5	48.4	20.3	73	97.3	38.4	19.2
Brooten city	743	739	-0.5	624	97.4	0.0	0.0	0.8	1.8	26.6	45.0	28.4	247	72.5	54.3	20.6
Brooten city (Pope)	0	0	0.0	0	0.0	0.0	0.0	0.0	0.0	0.0	0.0	0.0	0	0.0	0.0	0.0
Brooten city (Stearns)	743	739	-0.5	624	97.4	0.0	0.0	0.8	1.8	26.6	45.0	28.4	247	72.5	54.3	20.6
Browerville city & MCD (Todd)	790	761	-3.7	677	94.1	4.0	0.0	1.3	0.6	26.4	52.2	21.4	262	76.7	55.3	18.3
Browns Creek township (Red Lake)	48	48	0.0	36	100.0	0.0	0.0	0.0	0.0	22.2	52.8	25.0	16	100.0	43.8	12.5
Brownsdale city & MCD (Mower)	690	690	0.0	746	96.1	0.0	0.0	0.0	3.9	20.3	62.6	17.0	323	74.9	48.0	10.8
Browns Valley township (Big Stone)	125	123	-1.6	98	100.0	0.0	0.0	0.0	0.0	13.3	61.3	25.5	48	97.9	45.8	2.1
Browns Valley city & MCD (Traverse)	589	556	-5.6	585	74.2	0.0	0.0	25.8	0.0	17.6	49.9	32.5	273	70.0	47.3	15.8

1 May be of any race.

STATE City, town, township, borough, or CDP (county if applicable)	2010 census total population	2014 estimated population	Percent change 2010–2014	ACS total population estimate 2010–2014	White alone, not Hispanic or Latino	Black alone, not Hispanic or Latino	Asian alone, not Hispanic or Latino	All other races or 2 or more races, not Hispanic or Latino	Hispanic or Latino[1]	Under 18 years old	Age 18 to 64 years old	Age 65 years and older	Total occupied housing units	Percent owner occupied	High school diploma or less	Bachelor's degree or more
	1	2	3	4	5	6	7	8	9	10	11	12	13	14	15	16
MINNESOTA—Con.																
Brownsville city & MCD (Houston)	466	459	-1.5	508	94.9	0.0	0.0	4.7	0.4	15.6	65.2	19.3	221	75.1	48.9	12.2
Brownsville township (Houston)	445	441	-0.9	384	100.0	0.0	0.0	0.0	0.0	15.9	64.0	20.1	171	93.0	44.4	18.7
Brownton city & MCD (McLeod)	762	739	-3.0	738	91.2	0.0	3.0	1.2	4.6	26.0	61.3	12.7	307	79.2	50.5	12.1
Bruce township (Todd)	585	568	-2.9	600	99.3	0.0	0.7	0.0	0.0	15.1	69.0	15.8	242	82.6	47.9	12.0
Bruno city & MCD (Pine)	102	100	-2.0	85	95.3	0.0	0.0	4.7	0.0	29.5	43.6	27.1	34	79.4	73.5	2.9
Bruno township (Pine)	184	178	-3.3	157	98.7	0.0	0.0	1.3	0.0	8.2	66.9	24.8	78	89.7	51.3	11.5
Brunswick township (Kanabec)	1,333	1,299	-2.6	1,290	98.5	0.2	0.3	0.0	1.0	21.3	64.9	13.8	495	86.9	44.0	7.9
Brush Creek township (Faribault)	225	220	-2.2	158	98.1	0.0	0.0	0.0	1.9	24.0	53.1	22.8	67	95.5	49.3	20.9
Buckman city & MCD (Morrison)	270	272	0.7	256	99.2	0.0	0.0	0.0	0.8	34.1	53.2	12.9	96	85.4	53.1	8.3
Buckman township (Morrison)	733	727	-0.8	650	96.0	0.0	0.0	2.0	2.0	25.1	66.5	8.3	238	89.5	41.6	7.1
Buffalo city & MCD (Wright)	15,459	15,912	2.9	15,710	94.4	0.6	1.0	1.6	2.4	29.2	56.5	14.2	5,766	67.7	34.0	23.0
Buffalo township (Wright)	1,802	1,862	3.3	1,938	98.7	0.0	0.2	0.4	0.7	27.2	58.6	14.0	608	93.6	35.2	26.6
Buffalo Lake city & MCD (Renville)	733	697	-4.9	810	77.4	0.0	0.0	6.9	15.7	32.7	44.9	22.5	270	76.3	54.4	14.1
Buh township (Morrison)	520	518	-0.4	407	100.0	0.0	0.0	0.0	0.0	24.9	61.2	14.0	161	87.6	56.5	7.5
Buhl city & MCD (St. Louis)	1,000	997	-0.3	1,106	86.9	1.4	1.4	7.5	2.8	24.0	56.7	19.4	464	78.9	49.4	14.0
Bullard township (Wadena)	219	215	-1.8	201	100.0	0.0	0.0	0.0	0.0	23.9	53.4	22.9	91	96.7	59.3	9.9
Bull Moose township (Cass)	133	131	-1.5	176	97.2	0.0	0.0	2.8	0.0	31.9	56.2	11.9	54	79.6	59.3	13.0
Bungo township (Cass)	188	188	0.0	176	98.3	1.7	0.0	0.0	0.0	31.8	52.3	15.9	67	92.5	67.2	14.9
Burbank township (Kandiyohi)	566	565	-0.2	480	99.6	0.0	0.0	0.0	0.4	21.8	68.5	9.6	194	95.4	39.2	17.0
Burke township (Pipestone)	209	204	-2.4	251	97.2	0.0	0.0	0.0	2.8	29.9	54.8	15.5	83	86.7	47.0	20.5
Burleene township (Todd)	345	337	-2.3	323	97.2	1.5	0.0	0.3	0.9	22.6	60.9	16.4	143	96.5	42.0	9.8
Burlington township (Becker)	1,545	1,579	2.2	1,465	93.0	0.0	0.3	5.1	1.6	30.1	60.1	9.8	539	91.5	34.3	25.2
Burnhamville township (Todd)	759	745	-1.8	712	99.6	0.0	0.0	0.4	0.0	18.9	60.2	20.9	319	90.6	59.2	14.1
Burnstown township (Brown)	268	264	-1.5	240	95.8	0.0	4.2	0.0	0.0	21.7	61.0	17.5	95	92.6	45.3	17.9
Burnsville city & MCD (Dakota)	60,307	61,630	2.2	61,059	71.2	11.3	4.9	3.6	8.9	23.2	64.4	12.4	24,445	65.4	26.9	37.5
Burton township (Yellow Medicine)	148	144	-2.7	131	100.0	0.0	0.0	0.0	0.0	18.4	62.5	19.1	61	85.2	49.2	21.3
Burtrum city & MCD (Todd)	144	140	-2.8	112	98.2	0.0	0.0	1.8	0.0	21.5	62.8	16.1	57	84.2	75.4	7.0
Buse township (Otter Tail)	495	498	0.6	493	94.9	0.8	0.0	1.4	2.8	21.0	65.5	13.8	204	87.7	32.8	26.0
Butler township (Otter Tail)	283	283	0.0	342	96.8	0.0	0.9	0.0	2.3	24.6	62.6	12.9	132	75.8	56.8	10.6
Butterfield city & MCD (Watonwan)	586	602	2.7	612	61.8	0.0	11.6	2.5	24.2	23.3	57.3	19.6	226	77.4	65.0	8.4
Butterfield township (Watonwan)	213	211	-0.9	210	98.6	0.0	1.4	0.0	0.0	27.6	52.4	20.0	87	89.7	54.0	24.1
Butternut Valley township (Blue Earth)	325	324	-0.3	322	99.4	0.0	0.0	0.0	0.6	22.1	62.4	15.5	126	96.0	39.7	19.8
Buzzle township (Beltrami)	310	311	0.3	259	99.2	0.0	0.0	0.0	0.8	17.0	62.9	20.1	107	89.7	51.4	24.3
Bygland township (Polk)	272	275	1.1	263	97.7	0.4	0.0	0.8	1.1	22.7	63.9	13.3	105	94.3	31.4	31.4
Byron township (Cass)	144	142	-1.4	142	100.0	0.0	0.0	0.0	0.0	15.4	64.8	19.7	57	87.7	52.6	5.3
Byron city & MCD (Olmsted)	4,914	5,191	5.6	5,023	97.9	0.2	0.0	1.9	0.0	32.1	60.8	7.1	1,690	82.4	18.7	38.6
Byron township (Waseca)	230	228	-0.9	183	96.2	0.0	0.0	2.2	1.6	25.7	56.4	18.0	70	97.1	50.0	27.1
Cairo township (Renville)	232	222	-4.3	244	90.2	0.0	1.6	0.4	7.8	21.7	56.9	21.3	111	63.1	62.2	7.2
Caledonia city & MCD (Houston)	2,868	2,793	-2.6	2,824	95.7	0.7	0.0	2.4	1.2	21.9	54.3	23.7	1,202	75.1	49.5	14.0
Caledonia township (Houston)	641	637	-0.6	588	99.1	0.0	0.0	0.2	0.7	23.4	66.1	10.5	213	88.7	46.0	23.5
Callaway city & MCD (Becker)	234	235	0.4	242	39.7	0.0	6.6	48.3	5.4	33.5	58.6	7.9	79	86.1	55.7	11.4
Callaway township (Becker)	287	289	0.7	261	61.3	0.0	0.0	37.2	1.5	35.3	49.3	15.3	95	96.8	50.5	12.6
Calumet city	367	363	-1.1	398	90.2	1.5	0.0	8.3	0.0	32.6	55.8	11.6	165	77.6	44.8	5.5
Cambria township (Blue Earth)	260	259	-0.4	267	99.3	0.0	0.0	0.7	0.0	11.6	75.0	13.5	119	86.6	40.3	28.6
Cambridge city & MCD (Isanti)	8,114	8,323	2.6	8,223	94.2	1.1	0.6	3.1	1.0	24.3	55.5	20.1	3,186	64.4	41.0	18.5
Cambridge township (Isanti)	2,376	2,405	1.2	2,623	97.6	0.8	0.6	0.9	0.0	29.2	59.0	11.7	903	88.7	43.0	21.9
Camden township (Carver)	921	947	2.8	929	97.4	0.0	0.0	1.8	0.0	22.6	66.2	11.3	330	92.4	51.8	19.4
Cameron township (Murray)	137	132	-3.6	117	98.3	0.0	0.0	0.0	1.7	29.1	61.6	9.4	46	97.8	69.6	6.5
Camp township (Renville)	186	178	-4.3	136	97.1	0.0	0.0	2.9	0.0	11.0	65.6	23.5	63	90.5	46.0	11.1
Camp 5 township (St. Louis)	35	35	0.0	11	100.0	0.0	0.0	0.0	0.0	0.0	91.0	9.1	6	100.0	83.3	0.0
Campbell city & MCD (Wilkin)	158	156	-1.3	197	98.5	1.5	0.0	0.0	0.0	25.5	60.9	13.7	80	86.3	32.5	2.5
Campbell township (Wilkin)	62	61	-1.6	52	94.2	0.0	0.0	5.8	0.0	13.5	67.3	19.2	23	95.7	73.9	0.0
Camp Lake township (Swift)	213	206	-3.3	172	100.0	0.0	0.0	0.0	0.0	18.6	57.6	23.8	76	90.8	47.4	13.2
Camp Release township (Lac qui Parle)	315	302	-4.1	296	97.3	0.7	0.0	0.7	1.4	21.3	61.5	17.2	122	88.5	46.7	12.3

1 May be of any race.

Table A. All Places — **Population and Housing**

STATE City, town, township, borough, or CDP (county if applicable)	Population 2010 census total population	2014 estimated population	Percent change 2010–2014	ACS total population estimate 2010–2014	Race and Hispanic or Latino origin (percent), 2010–2014 White alone, not Hispanic or Latino	Black alone, not Hispanic or Latino	Asian alone, not Hispanic or Latino	All other races or 2 or more races, not Hispanic or Latino	Hispanic or Latino[1]	Age (percent), 2010–2014 Under 18 years old	Age 18 to 64 years old	Age 65 years and older	Households, 2010–2014 Total occupied housing units	Percent owner occupied	Householders by level of education (percent) High school diploma or less	Bachelor's degree or more
	1	2	3	4	5	6	7	8	9	10	11	12	13	14	15	16
MINNESOTA—Con.																
Canby city & MCD (Yellow Medicine)	1,795	1,742	-3.0	1,837	91.4	0.0	0.8	0.9	6.9	18.5	53.8	27.9	794	68.5	47.4	14.1
Candor township (Otter Tail)	561	556	-0.9	613	94.5	0.0	0.0	5.2	0.3	19.9	64.3	15.8	260	94.2	39.6	16.2
Canisteo township (Dodge)	654	663	1.4	651	98.2	0.0	0.0	0.0	1.8	26.0	63.4	10.6	234	93.2	24.4	39.3
Cannon township (Kittson)	20	19	-5.0	32	100.0	0.0	0.0	0.0	0.0	21.9	59.5	18.8	11	100.0	63.6	36.4
Cannon City township (Rice)	1,215	1,233	1.5	1,214	98.1	0.0	0.3	0.0	1.6	20.3	60.4	19.0	455	91.6	53.6	20.7
Cannon Falls city & MCD (Goodhue)	4,083	4,068	-0.4	4,072	93.0	1.7	0.0	3.1	2.2	24.4	57.0	18.7	1,761	74.5	43.4	20.6
Cannon Falls township (Goodhue)	1,070	1,079	0.8	964	93.7	2.0	1.9	2.2	0.3	18.9	62.3	18.9	359	86.9	36.2	29.5
Canosia township (St. Louis)	2,158	2,188	1.4	2,342	92.7	0.0	0.0	5.3	2.0	26.2	60.7	13.0	860	91.2	26.2	35.5
Canton city & MCD (Fillmore)	346	346	0.0	302	99.3	0.0	0.0	0.0	0.7	21.1	58.0	20.9	144	90.3	67.4	3.5
Canton township (Fillmore)	724	733	1.2	559	98.2	0.0	0.0	1.3	0.5	34.7	55.5	10.0	173	84.4	49.7	20.8
Caribou township (Kittson)	48	47	-2.1	35	100.0	0.0	0.0	0.0	0.0	5.7	82.9	11.4	15	100.0	86.7	0.0
Carimona township (Fillmore)	296	301	1.7	320	100.0	0.0	0.0	0.0	0.0	21.2	60.6	18.1	138	91.3	40.6	23.2
Carlisle township (Otter Tail)	156	156	0.0	149	99.3	0.0	0.0	0.0	0.7	24.8	57.7	17.4	60	100.0	41.7	13.3
Carlos city & MCD (Douglas)	502	492	-2.0	552	94.7	0.5	0.0	0.7	4.0	29.1	63.4	7.4	226	70.8	48.7	22.1
Carlos township (Douglas)	2,048	2,078	1.5	1,971	98.6	0.3	0.8	0.0	0.4	22.8	58.7	18.7	787	93.6	21.9	37.6
Carlston township (Freeborn)	305	301	-1.3	235	98.7	0.0	0.9	0.4	0.0	21.7	59.2	19.1	104	90.4	36.5	21.2
Carlton city & MCD (Carlton)	862	891	3.4	938	94.6	0.9	0.0	2.3	2.2	14.4	60.2	25.4	342	55.6	47.4	14.9
Carpenter township (Itasca)	179	181	1.1	236	81.8	8.1	0.0	10.2	0.0	14.8	53.6	31.4	86	90.7	58.1	9.3
Carrolton township (Fillmore)	314	318	1.3	343	95.3	3.5	0.0	0.0	1.2	19.3	60.2	20.4	126	81.0	34.1	31.0
Carson township (Cottonwood)	280	279	-0.4	277	98.2	0.0	0.4	1.1	0.4	25.3	59.4	15.2	105	84.8	30.5	21.0
Carsonville township (Becker)	220	221	0.5	224	91.1	0.0	0.0	8.0	0.9	31.3	55.3	13.4	85	97.6	41.2	27.1
Carver city & MCD (Carver)	3,726	4,259	14.3	4,025	84.1	4.3	3.1	7.8	0.7	39.1	57.6	3.4	1,239	93.1	15.3	51.3
Cascade township (Olmsted)	2,823	2,861	1.3	2,847	92.9	0.3	5.0	0.3	1.5	23.6	62.1	14.3	1,047	96.6	22.6	54.3
Cashel township (Swift)	174	168	-3.4	115	97.4	0.0	1.7	0.0	0.9	33.9	44.3	21.7	44	90.9	59.1	20.5
Cass Lake city & MCD (Cass)	764	748	-2.1	645	26.8	0.0	0.3	65.4	7.4	27.2	57.7	15.2	302	47.4	46.7	11.3
Castle Rock township (Dakota)	1,342	1,368	1.9	1,372	97.9	0.0	0.1	1.7	0.2	24.3	63.4	12.3	508	88.4	35.8	26.6
Cedar township (Marshall)	86	86	0.0	61	100.0	0.0	0.0	0.0	0.0	6.6	60.8	32.8	31	100.0	74.2	3.2
Cedar township (Martin)	223	217	-2.7	175	98.3	0.0	1.1	0.0	0.6	21.2	58.4	20.6	67	91.0	35.8	26.9
Cedarbend township (Roseau)	221	221	0.0	225	76.9	7.1	0.4	13.8	1.8	27.1	62.6	10.2	100	74.0	55.0	12.0
Cedar Lake township (Scott)	2,779	2,931	5.5	2,858	96.2	0.0	0.8	1.5	1.6	29.4	62.4	8.2	883	97.1	26.2	40.8
Cedar Mills city & MCD (Meeker)	45	44	-2.2	45	100.0	0.0	0.0	0.0	0.0	20.0	64.4	15.6	22	100.0	40.9	18.2
Cedar Mills township (Meeker)	460	459	-0.2	457	99.6	0.0	0.0	0.2	0.2	24.5	61.8	13.6	180	90.6	40.6	13.9
Cedar Valley township (St. Louis)	195	196	0.5	240	97.5	0.8	0.0	0.0	1.7	24.6	52.4	22.9	100	96.0	30.0	28.0
Center township (Crow Wing)	910	930	2.2	993	98.9	0.0	0.0	1.1	0.0	20.6	61.5	18.0	412	92.7	39.8	25.5
Center City city & MCD (Chisago)	632	630	-0.3	666	89.5	0.3	1.1	4.2	5.0	20.3	68.1	11.9	251	79.3	27.9	30.7
Center Creek township (Martin)	217	212	-2.3	227	84.1	0.0	0.0	15.9	0.0	26.0	56.4	17.6	88	85.2	36.4	19.3
Centerville city & MCD (Anoka)	3,792	3,906	3.0	3,832	94.1	0.0	4.0	1.0	0.9	30.4	61.8	8.0	1,238	88.9	28.9	34.2
Ceresco township (Blue Earth)	239	238	-0.4	256	87.9	0.8	0.0	9.4	2.0	29.7	52.7	17.6	96	78.1	52.1	18.8
Cerro Gordo township (Lac qui Parle)	197	187	-5.1	236	90.3	0.0	1.3	3.4	5.1	20.8	68.7	10.6	83	97.6	43.4	20.5
Ceylon city & MCD (Martin)	369	360	-2.4	330	86.7	0.0	0.9	6.4	6.1	23.6	60.2	16.1	150	82.0	40.0	14.0
Champion township (Wilkin)	53	52	-1.9	80	82.5	0.0	0.0	0.0	17.5	0.0	61.4	38.8	44	75.0	18.2	43.2
Champlin city & MCD (Hennepin)	23,091	23,818	3.1	23,591	86.5	5.1	3.0	2.8	2.6	25.0	67.4	7.7	8,800	86.9	22.6	37.5
Chanarambie township (Murray)	206	203	-1.5	241	93.4	2.5	1.7	2.5	0.0	21.5	61.4	17.0	89	96.6	58.4	6.7
Chandler city & MCD (Murray)	270	260	-3.7	266	67.3	0.0	0.0	1.1	31.6	17.7	60.1	22.2	124	60.5	64.5	12.1
Chanhassen city	22,998	24,967	8.6	24,003	89.6	0.9	5.9	1.3	2.3	29.4	62.1	8.6	8,531	86.1	14.2	62.1
Chanhassen city (Carver)	22,950	24,918	8.6	23,952	89.6	0.9	5.9	1.3	2.2	29.4	62.0	8.6	8,514	86.0	14.2	62.1
Chanhassen city (Hennepin)	48	49	0.0	51	62.7	0.0	0.0	0.0	37.3	33.3	66.7	0.0	17	100.0	0.0	100.0
Charlestown township (Redwood)	208	201	-3.4	244	81.1	0.0	0.0	0.0	18.9	31.1	52.0	16.8	82	81.7	43.9	18.3
Chaska city & MCD (Carver)	23,770	24,838	4.5	24,238	85.5	1.8	2.4	2.1	8.2	27.9	64.6	7.4	9,084	69.7	24.5	43.9
Chatfield city	2,779	2,787	0.3	2,828	94.8	0.0	0.2	1.3	3.7	27.7	54.7	17.8	1,145	68.6	37.1	25.2
Chatfield city (Fillmore)	1,573	1,550	-1.5	1,527	93.1	0.0	0.0	2.5	4.5	25.0	54.2	20.8	640	57.7	43.0	23.3

1 May be of any race.

Table A. All Places — **Population and Housing**

STATE City, town, township, borough, or CDP (county if applicable)	2010 census total population	2014 estimated population	Percent change 2010–2014	ACS total population estimate 2010–2014	White alone, not Hispanic or Latino	Black alone, not Hispanic or Latino	Asian alone, not Hispanic or Latino	All other races or 2 or more races, not Hispanic or Latino	Hispanic or Latino[1]	Under 18 years old	Age 18 to 64 years old	Age 65 years and older	Total occupied housing units	Percent owner occupied	High school diploma or less	Bachelor's degree or more
	1	2	3	4	5	6	7	8	9	10	11	12	13	14	15	16
MINNESOTA—Con.																
Chatfield city (Olmsted)	1,206	1,237	2.6	1,301	96.8	0.0	0.4	0.0	2.8	30.8	55.1	14.3	505	82.4	29.7	27.7
Chatfield township (Fillmore)	531	535	0.8	587	98.8	0.0	1.0	0.0	0.2	30.6	51.9	17.4	213	91.5	27.2	41.3
Chatham township (Wright)	1,298	1,342	3.4	1,287	98.8	0.0	0.0	1.2	0.0	27.9	62.3	9.7	423	96.2	34.0	38.1
Chengwatana township (Pine)	988	971	-1.7	949	96.0	0.3	0.2	3.3	0.2	24.6	59.6	15.8	395	88.4	39.5	19.5
Cherry township (St. Louis)	860	863	0.3	830	97.0	0.5	0.0	1.4	1.1	15.6	70.1	14.5	365	98.1	29.6	18.6
Cherry Grove township (Goodhue)	397	399	0.5	393	99.5	0.0	0.5	0.0	0.0	24.0	62.9	13.2	142	89.4	48.6	19.7
Chester township (Polk)....	75	75	0.0	75	100.0	0.0	0.0	0.0	0.0	18.7	60.2	21.3	30	96.7	56.7	3.3
Chester township (Wabasha)	455	452	-0.7	428	100.0	0.0	0.0	0.0	0.0	25.7	61.7	12.6	158	84.8	60.1	19.0
Chickamaw Beach city & MCD (Cass)	114	112	-1.8	107	93.5	0.0	0.0	0.0	6.5	13.1	57.1	29.9	57	86.0	22.8	14.0
Chief township (Mahnomen)	96	98	2.1	80	82.5	0.0	0.0	17.5	0.0	8.8	72.8	18.8	34	88.2	64.7	11.8
Chilgren township (Lake of the Woods)	182	NA	NA	137	94.9	0.0	5.1	0.0	0.0	0.0	75.9	24.1	70	100.0	62.9	0.0
Chippewa Falls township (Pope)	228	231	1.3	244	98.4	0.0	0.0	1.6	0.0	17.7	55.7	26.6	108	80.6	40.7	22.2
Chisago City city & MCD (Chisago)	4,937	4,937	0.0	4,951	95.6	0.1	0.0	2.3	2.0	20.6	58.5	20.7	2,065	73.2	41.6	20.2
Chisago Lake township (Chisago)	4,679	4,742	1.3	4,697	97.3	0.8	0.2	0.7	0.9	25.1	65.7	9.2	1,659	96.9	29.8	30.2
Chisholm city & MCD (St. Louis)	4,976	5,017	0.8	5,001	92.7	0.6	0.0	4.0	2.6	22.6	62.0	15.5	2,109	71.2	44.8	14.0
Chokio city & MCD (Stevens)	400	391	-2.3	421	96.0	0.0	0.0	4.0	0.0	22.1	48.1	29.9	185	71.9	50.8	20.0
Christiania township (Jackson)	249	253	1.6	240	99.2	0.0	0.0	0.0	0.8	15.4	63.8	20.8	115	77.4	40.0	28.7
Circle Pines city & MCD (Anoka)	4,918	4,949	0.6	4,935	87.8	0.7	5.9	3.8	1.8	20.6	67.0	12.4	1,964	79.0	23.9	34.3
Clara City city & MCD (Chippewa)	1,360	1,320	-2.9	1,306	97.5	0.0	0.0	0.4	2.1	22.9	52.7	24.4	528	69.1	54.4	8.0
Claremont city & MCD (Dodge)	548	540	-1.5	485	84.3	0.0	0.0	0.6	15.1	21.4	67.5	11.1	197	83.8	61.9	8.1
Claremont township (Dodge)	461	469	1.7	480	92.7	0.0	0.0	0.0	7.3	25.3	59.8	15.2	182	86.8	42.3	19.2
Clarissa city & MCD (Todd)	681	658	-3.4	763	92.4	0.8	1.3	2.0	3.5	21.4	50.1	28.4	321	72.3	57.0	4.4
Clark township (Aitkin)......	170	167	-1.8	129	98.4	0.0	1.6	0.0	0.0	16.3	72.9	10.9	73	93.2	39.7	17.8
Clark township (Faribault).	254	249	-2.0	257	100.0	0.0	0.0	0.0	0.0	22.2	58.0	19.8	110	90.0	34.5	23.6
Clarkfield city & MCD (Yellow Medicine)	863	831	-3.7	750	96.4	0.0	0.4	2.5	0.7	19.1	53.9	27.1	339	71.4	51.3	14.7
Clarks Grove city & MCD (Freeborn)	706	688	-2.5	600	81.8	0.3	12.2	2.2	3.5	24.3	62.8	12.8	244	82.0	60.2	2.0
Clay township (Hubbard) ..	73	73	0.0	96	85.4	0.0	9.4	0.0	5.2	5.2	48.0	46.9	48	100.0	18.8	54.2
Clayton township (Mower)	158	159	0.6	125	100.0	0.0	0.0	0.0	0.0	17.6	58.4	24.0	50	92.0	42.0	16.0
Clearbrook city & MCD (Clearwater)	518	518	0.0	502	91.4	0.0	0.0	7.2	1.4	22.8	48.2	29.3	218	56.4	40.8	16.1
Clear Creek UT (Carlton)..	160	161	0.6	124	93.5	0.0	0.0	0.0	6.5	17.8	79.7	2.4	62	95.2	61.3	9.7
Clear Lake city & MCD (Sherburne)	545	625	14.7	554	98.2	0.0	0.0	1.8	0.0	37.4	57.8	4.9	188	86.7	22.9	34.6
Clear Lake township (Sherburne)	1,539	1,571	2.1	1,568	98.4	0.6	0.0	0.8	0.2	17.4	65.6	16.9	589	92.0	31.6	31.4
Clearwater city	1,735	1,780	2.6	1,719	93.7	2.0	0.3	0.6	3.4	32.1	55.5	12.4	634	75.1	32.5	19.1
Clearwater city (Stearns)..	0	0	0.0	0	0.0	0.0	0.0	0.0	0.0	0.0	0.0	0.0	0	0.0	0.0	0.0
Clearwater city (Wright)	1,735	1,780	2.6	1,719	93.7	2.0	0.3	0.6	3.4	32.1	55.5	12.4	634	75.1	32.5	19.1
Clearwater township (Wright)	1,306	1,346	3.1	1,444	98.3	0.6	0.0	0.8	0.4	30.1	59.8	10.2	493	87.4	42.0	20.7
Clements city & MCD (Redwood)	153	150	-2.0	190	73.2	0.0	10.5	0.0	16.3	23.2	60.6	16.3	76	90.8	75.0	5.3
Cleveland city & MCD (Le Sueur)	719	707	-1.7	611	96.2	0.0	2.1	0.7	1.0	21.1	65.2	13.7	248	89.5	47.2	11.3
Cleveland township (Le Sueur)	661	667	0.9	760	98.3	0.0	0.5	0.4	0.8	27.2	61.3	11.6	290	87.6	36.9	27.6
Clifton township (Lyon)	249	248	-0.4	286	87.4	0.0	3.1	0.7	8.7	26.6	61.3	11.9	105	75.2	43.8	19.0
Clifton township (Traverse)	75	71	-5.3	36	100.0	0.0	0.0	0.0	0.0	11.1	64.0	25.0	19	68.4	42.1	15.8
Climax city & MCD (Polk) .	267	266	-0.4	237	94.1	0.0	0.0	1.3	4.6	29.6	58.6	11.8	107	69.2	42.1	23.4
Clinton city & MCD (Big Stone)	449	428	-4.7	397	96.5	0.0	0.0	2.0	1.5	23.6	49.3	27.0	193	74.6	59.1	12.4
Clinton township (Rock)....	277	272	-1.8	251	100.0	0.0	0.0	0.0	0.0	23.9	67.5	8.8	96	82.3	51.0	15.6
Clinton township (St. Louis)	1,015	1,016	0.1	1,001	96.6	0.0	0.3	3.1	0.0	22.5	61.6	16.0	424	87.5	40.8	12.7
Clinton Falls township (Steele)	351	352	0.3	326	97.5	0.0	0.0	1.8	0.6	20.6	60.2	19.3	132	91.7	38.6	21.2
Clitherall city & MCD (Otter Tail)	112	114	1.8	67	97.0	0.0	0.0	3.0	0.0	6.0	35.9	58.2	31	87.1	77.4	3.2
Clitherall township (Otter Tail)	455	457	0.4	469	94.9	0.0	0.0	0.2	4.9	13.8	51.3	34.8	228	97.4	36.4	30.3
Clontarf city & MCD (Swift)	164	159	-3.0	130	100.0	0.0	0.0	0.0	0.0	19.2	67.0	13.8	63	90.5	71.4	6.3
Clontarf township (Swift)...	86	83	-3.5	91	100.0	0.0	0.0	0.0	0.0	5.5	61.6	33.0	38	81.6	47.4	2.6
Cloquet city & MCD (Carlton)	12,124	12,081	-0.4	12,064	83.1	0.1	1.2	14.4	1.2	25.7	59.2	15.1	4,847	69.0	44.8	23.8
Clover township (Clearwater)	113	115	1.8	60	100.0	0.0	0.0	0.0	0.0	0.0	78.4	21.7	34	100.0	67.6	20.6
Clover township (Hubbard)	154	158	2.6	146	94.5	0.0	0.0	0.0	5.5	17.8	49.9	32.2	59	100.0	33.9	27.1

1 May be of any race.

Table A. All Places — **Population and Housing**

STATE City, town, township, borough, or CDP (county if applicable)	Population				Race and Hispanic or Latino origin (percent), 2010–2014					Age (percent), 2010–2014			Households, 2010–2014		Householders by level of education (percent)	
	2010 census total population	2014 estimated population	Percent change 2010–2014	ACS total population estimate 2010–2014	White alone, not Hispanic or Latino	Black alone, not Hispanic or Latino	Asian alone, not Hispanic or Latino	All other races or 2 or more races, not Hispanic or Latino	Hispanic or Latino[1]	Under 18 years old	Age 18 to 64 years old	Age 65 years and older	Total occupied housing units	Percent owner occupied	High school diploma or less	Bachelor's degree or more
	1	2	3	4	5	6	7	8	9	10	11	12	13	14	15	16
MINNESOTA—Con.																
Clover township (Mahnomen)	121	124	2.5	81	29.6	0.0	0.0	70.4	0.0	25.8	62.9	11.1	35	65.7	54.3	11.4
Clover township (Pine)	410	397	-3.2	385	93.2	2.3	1.0	2.1	1.3	28.3	50.2	21.3	149	87.9	32.2	21.5
Cloverleaf township (Pennington)	84	84	0.0	91	98.9	0.0	0.0	1.1	0.0	18.7	71.5	9.9	36	86.1	38.9	2.8
Clow township (Kittson)	46	45	-2.2	58	100.0	0.0	0.0	0.0	0.0	27.6	58.6	13.8	21	85.7	0.0	57.1
Coates city & MCD (Dakota)	161	163	1.2	140	100.0	0.0	0.0	0.0	0.0	17.8	70.1	12.1	49	61.2	61.2	18.4
Cobden city & MCD (Brown)	36	35	-2.8	32	87.5	0.0	0.0	12.5	0.0	15.7	69.0	15.6	15	86.7	46.7	13.3
Cohasset city & MCD (Itasca)	2,698	2,754	2.1	2,733	96.5	0.2	0.2	3.0	0.0	19.8	60.9	19.3	1,131	87.1	30.1	31.5
Cokato city & MCD (Wright)	2,694	2,725	1.2	2,720	91.0	0.3	0.0	3.7	5.0	30.2	54.5	15.4	1,058	69.7	45.2	21.1
Cokato township (Wright)	1,311	1,349	2.9	1,456	94.8	2.1	0.3	0.6	2.3	43.5	48.2	8.4	374	92.8	43.3	24.3
Cold Spring city & MCD (Stearns)	4,025	4,044	0.5	4,033	93.1	0.1	0.5	0.1	6.2	30.1	53.6	16.3	1,567	76.9	51.2	21.4
Coleraine city & MCD (Itasca)	1,970	2,003	1.7	1,724	95.8	0.0	0.0	3.2	0.9	24.2	58.7	17.1	682	80.2	25.5	26.0
Colfax township (Kandiyohi)	547	549	0.4	600	97.3	0.2	0.0	0.0	2.5	17.0	64.8	18.2	246	95.5	40.2	20.3
Collegeville township (Stearns)	3,343	3,441	2.9	3,438	87.7	3.0	6.0	1.0	2.3	11.3	80.0	8.6	647	99.8	27.5	34.9
Collins township (McLeod)	473	464	-1.9	465	96.8	0.0	0.6	2.2	0.4	17.0	58.5	24.5	202	92.6	48.5	17.3
Collinwood township (Meeker)	1,113	1,109	-0.4	1,096	99.5	0.0	0.5	0.0	0.0	23.0	65.6	11.6	407	94.3	35.9	20.4
Cologne city & MCD (Carver)	1,519	1,546	1.8	1,564	91.7	0.3	1.7	4.1	2.2	34.5	58.8	6.6	551	82.4	36.1	32.1
Columbia township (Polk)	470	474	0.9	379	85.5	0.3	1.6	11.1	1.6	24.9	60.2	15.0	158	86.7	50.0	13.9
Columbia Heights city & MCD (Anoka)	19,496	19,675	0.9	19,605	61.7	18.0	5.0	3.8	11.5	21.8	63.7	14.5	7,999	65.3	40.8	23.2
Columbus city & MCD (Anoka)	3,914	3,980	1.7	3,940	99.2	0.0	0.5	0.0	0.3	19.2	66.7	14.1	1,510	95.2	34.3	30.3
Colvin township (St. Louis)	317	318	0.3	322	99.4	0.0	0.0	0.6	0.0	14.6	60.3	24.8	148	86.5	31.8	16.9
Comfort township (Kanabec)	1,078	1,067	-1.0	1,164	97.5	0.0	0.0	1.5	1.0	25.6	57.3	17.0	404	94.3	47.0	19.1
Comfrey city	384	374	-2.6	382	95.5	0.0	0.8	0.0	3.7	28.5	52.0	19.4	159	81.1	42.8	18.2
Comfrey city (Brown)	368	358	-2.7	361	95.3	0.0	0.8	0.0	3.9	28.5	52.3	19.1	150	80.7	44.7	17.3
Comfrey city (Cottonwood)	16	16	0.0	21	100.0	0.0	0.0	0.0	0.0	28.6	47.8	23.8	9	88.9	11.1	33.3
Como township (Marshall)	39	39	0.0	30	70.0	0.0	0.0	0.0	30.0	20.0	59.9	20.0	13	69.2	53.8	15.4
Compton township (Otter Tail)	801	810	1.1	780	98.2	0.3	0.9	0.6	0.0	32.8	54.9	12.2	271	91.9	41.0	18.1
Comstock city & MCD (Clay)	93	93	0.0	118	94.9	0.0	0.0	0.8	4.2	27.2	53.5	19.5	47	100.0	44.7	31.9
Comstock township (Marshall)	105	105	0.0	111	100.0	0.0	0.0	0.0	0.0	12.6	49.5	37.8	53	84.9	45.3	26.4
Concord township (Dodge)	574	582	1.4	642	96.4	0.0	0.0	0.5	3.1	19.2	66.1	14.8	239	86.6	39.3	22.6
Conger city & MCD (Freeborn)	146	144	-1.4	160	80.6	0.0	0.0	1.9	17.5	32.5	65.1	2.5	55	96.4	27.3	9.1
Connelly township (Wilkin)	118	117	-0.8	122	96.7	0.0	0.0	3.3	0.0	20.5	68.0	11.5	51	84.3	21.6	19.6
Cook city & MCD (St. Louis)	575	570	-0.9	635	84.7	0.0	0.0	15.3	0.0	19.0	58.7	22.4	293	70.0	43.7	13.3
Coon Creek township (Lyon)	244	243	-0.4	263	96.2	1.1	0.0	0.4	2.3	24.8	60.7	14.4	104	92.3	46.2	16.3
Coon Rapids city & MCD (Anoka)	61,476	62,112	1.0	61,809	84.3	5.1	3.1	3.8	3.7	23.2	64.4	12.3	23,730	77.4	32.4	27.0
Copley township (Clearwater)	877	900	2.6	711	94.2	0.3	1.4	4.1	0.0	22.3	64.7	13.1	272	91.2	41.5	18.4
Corcoran city & MCD (Hennepin)	5,381	5,526	2.7	5,482	91.5	0.2	2.8	1.4	4.1	22.5	67.6	9.9	1,855	95.1	28.6	30.7
Cordova township (Le Sueur)	472	477	1.1	484	98.3	0.0	0.2	0.2	1.2	22.5	60.6	16.9	189	88.4	50.3	16.9
Corinna township (Wright)	2,328	2,385	2.4	2,064	97.0	0.8	0.0	1.1	1.0	17.1	62.7	20.3	851	98.4	34.4	30.4
Corliss township (Otter Tail)	493	491	-0.4	591	99.5	0.0	0.5	0.0	0.0	28.0	59.6	12.4	212	97.2	39.2	14.6
Cormant township (Beltrami)	158	161	1.9	127	100.0	0.0	0.0	0.0	0.0	25.2	53.4	21.3	52	96.2	63.5	0.0
Cormorant township (Becker)	1,039	1,064	2.4	1,012	98.8	0.0	0.5	0.7	0.0	13.7	57.8	28.7	451	95.8	28.8	35.9
Cornish township (Aitkin)	28	27	-3.6	32	90.6	0.0	0.0	0.0	9.4	18.7	43.8	37.5	15	100.0	6.7	53.3
Cornish township (Sibley)	243	239	-1.6	221	94.6	0.0	0.0	0.0	5.4	30.3	60.7	9.0	85	88.2	37.6	15.3
Correll city & MCD (Big Stone)	34	33	-2.9	21	85.7	0.0	0.0	14.3	0.0	9.5	52.3	38.1	12	100.0	66.7	0.0
Cosmos city & MCD (Meeker)	473	460	-2.7	513	91.0	5.5	0.0	1.0	2.5	17.7	62.7	19.5	269	66.9	45.0	7.1
Cosmos township (Meeker)	228	225	-1.3	209	99.5	0.0	0.0	0.0	0.5	18.2	62.6	19.1	86	87.2	46.5	8.1
Cottage Grove city & MCD (Washington)	34,589	35,630	3.0	35,169	83.5	2.7	6.3	3.5	3.9	28.7	62.3	9.1	11,923	88.6	29.9	33.3
Cotton township (St. Louis)	445	447	0.4	535	97.6	0.0	0.0	2.4	0.0	19.1	65.6	15.3	215	93.5	36.7	20.0
Cottonwood township (Brown)	840	829	-1.3	781	100.0	0.0	0.0	0.0	0.0	19.3	65.5	15.4	332	94.3	53.9	16.9
Cottonwood city & MCD (Lyon)	1,221	1,211	-0.8	1,067	91.0	0.6	0.7	0.9	6.8	22.2	60.4	17.4	486	63.0	43.6	21.8
Courtland city & MCD (Nicollet)	611	633	3.6	706	99.2	0.0	0.0	0.4	0.4	24.9	65.0	10.2	269	89.2	39.4	31.6
Courtland township (Nicollet)	630	620	-1.6	511	98.4	0.2	0.0	0.0	1.4	20.6	61.2	18.2	203	95.1	50.7	25.1

1   May be of any race.

Table A. All Places — **Population and Housing**

STATE City, town, township, borough, or CDP (county if applicable)	2010 census total population	2014 estimated population	Percent change 2010–2014	ACS total population estimate 2010–2014	White alone, not Hispanic or Latino	Black alone, not Hispanic or Latino	Asian alone, not Hispanic or Latino	All other races or 2 or more races, not Hispanic or Latino	Hispanic or Latino[1]	Under 18 years old	Age 18 to 64 years old	Age 65 years and older	Total occupied housing units	Percent owner occupied	High school diploma or less	Bachelor's degree or more
	1	2	3	4	5	6	7	8	9	10	11	12	13	14	15	16
MINNESOTA—Con.																
Crane Lake township (St. Louis)	82	82	0.0	65	92.3	0.0	0.0	7.7	0.0	4.5	74.0	21.5	38	84.2	28.9	39.5
Crate township (Chippewa)	211	208	-1.4	219	100.0	0.0	0.0	0.0	0.0	26.5	57.9	15.5	85	98.8	35.3	11.8
Credit River township (Scott)	5,096	5,447	6.9	5,281	94.5	3.2	0.4	0.7	1.1	28.5	61.5	10.0	1,686	96.4	26.8	43.0
Croke township (Traverse)	75	71	-5.3	91	91.2	0.0	0.0	0.0	8.8	22.0	50.6	27.5	35	88.6	28.6	8.6
Cromwell city & MCD (Carlton)	234	230	-1.7	190	98.9	0.0	0.0	1.1	0.0	16.3	47.8	35.8	106	43.4	41.5	12.3
Cromwell township (Clay)	345	357	3.5	365	99.2	0.0	0.8	0.0	0.0	22.5	60.0	17.5	139	92.8	36.7	33.1
Crooked Creek township (Houston)	285	279	-2.1	247	98.0	0.0	2.0	0.0	0.0	23.5	56.3	20.2	104	88.5	56.7	11.5
Crooked Lake township (Cass)	560	565	0.9	570	89.6	0.0	3.0	4.4	3.0	11.4	46.6	42.1	295	91.2	40.7	28.5
Crooks township (Renville)	191	183	-4.2	180	97.8	2.2	0.0	0.0	0.0	21.6	59.5	18.9	67	91.0	40.3	20.9
Crookston city & MCD (Polk)	7,891	7,920	0.4	7,899	82.1	0.9	1.6	3.2	12.1	19.3	66.3	14.4	3,002	61.1	42.4	21.8
Crookston township (Polk)	413	419	1.5	434	95.9	1.2	0.0	1.4	1.6	28.3	56.6	15.0	147	97.3	32.0	24.5
Crosby city & MCD (Crow Wing)	2,386	2,359	-1.1	2,397	92.3	0.0	2.2	2.8	2.8	19.6	54.4	26.0	1,156	54.4	49.1	13.8
Crosby township (Pine)	93	91	-2.2	82	100.0	0.0	0.0	0.0	0.0	9.7	58.5	31.7	37	75.7	59.5	13.5
Crosslake city & MCD (Crow Wing)	2,146	2,196	2.3	2,022	99.0	0.0	0.5	0.4	0.0	13.4	51.7	35.0	992	86.0	27.7	34.4
Crow Lake township (Stearns)	318	326	2.5	312	100.0	0.0	0.0	0.0	0.0	24.3	60.2	15.4	133	90.2	51.9	14.3
Crow River township (Stearns)	327	335	2.4	306	100.0	0.0	0.0	0.0	0.0	23.5	64.8	11.8	112	94.6	50.9	12.5
Crow Wing township (Crow Wing)	1,966	1,990	1.2	1,880	97.8	0.0	0.0	2.0	0.3	23.3	64.6	12.0	735	89.4	40.5	18.2
Crow Wing Lake township (Hubbard)	332	332	0.0	276	100.0	0.0	0.0	0.0	0.0	8.3	54.8	37.0	131	98.5	29.8	36.6
Crystal city & MCD (Hennepin)	22,142	22,605	2.1	22,459	74.6	10.9	4.3	3.3	6.9	22.2	63.9	13.9	9,234	71.9	33.2	32.3
Crystal Bay township (Lake)	474	476	0.4	459	98.5	0.0	0.0	0.0	1.5	10.4	71.0	18.5	230	90.0	46.5	18.3
Cuba township (Becker)	277	278	0.4	272	97.4	0.0	0.0	0.0	2.6	35.8	56.3	8.1	87	92.0	26.4	26.4
Culdrum township (Morrison)	487	480	-1.4	477	99.6	0.0	0.0	0.4	0.0	26.2	62.5	11.3	189	81.5	43.9	11.6
Culver township (St. Louis)	292	293	0.3	360	87.5	5.3	0.0	5.6	1.7	25.0	58.7	16.4	125	92.0	38.4	15.2
Currie city & MCD (Murray)	233	228	-2.1	207	98.1	0.0	0.0	0.0	1.9	18.8	55.9	25.1	98	94.9	60.2	9.2
Cushing township (Morrison)	714	708	-0.8	759	97.6	0.0	0.3	0.8	1.3	22.5	66.5	10.8	306	95.1	41.2	17.0
Custer township (Lyon)	203	202	-0.5	161	99.4	0.0	0.0	0.6	0.0	18.0	60.2	21.7	71	93.0	47.9	32.4
Cuyuna city & MCD (Crow Wing)	332	341	2.7	266	91.7	3.4	1.1	0.4	3.4	26.3	62.0	11.7	113	84.1	45.1	8.8
Cyrus city & MCD (Pope)	288	283	-1.7	341	97.4	0.0	0.9	0.9	0.9	24.6	56.3	19.1	143	77.6	49.7	10.5
Daggett Brook township (Crow Wing)	554	564	1.8	529	98.1	0.0	0.6	0.6	0.8	20.5	65.4	14.2	208	89.4	51.9	16.3
Dahlgren township (Carver)	1,327	1,353	2.0	1,272	97.8	1.8	0.0	0.4	0.0	22.1	64.7	13.2	476	89.1	50.4	21.0
Dailey township (Mille Lacs)	234	233	-0.4	259	99.6	0.0	0.0	0.4	0.0	18.5	60.9	20.5	119	87.4	44.5	5.9
Dakota city & MCD (Winona)	323	318	-1.5	335	100.0	0.0	0.0	0.0	0.0	25.4	61.4	13.4	132	96.2	42.4	16.7
Dalbo township (Isanti)	743	750	0.9	750	99.7	0.0	0.0	0.0	0.3	22.9	69.5	7.6	286	87.1	55.9	10.8
Dale township (Cottonwood)	151	150	-0.7	147	100.0	0.0	0.0	0.0	0.0	25.9	54.5	19.7	58	89.7	44.8	10.3
Dalton city & MCD (Otter Tail)	253	253	0.0	328	97.9	1.8	0.0	0.3	0.0	35.7	56.8	7.6	119	65.5	49.6	13.4
Dane Prairie township (Otter Tail)	883	877	-0.7	878	93.4	0.3	0.0	0.8	4.9	21.6	55.1	23.2	352	91.5	28.7	27.6
Danforth township (Pine)	78	77	-1.3	65	100.0	0.0	0.0	0.0	0.0	23.1	55.4	21.5	27	92.6	37.0	22.2
Danielson township (Meeker)	295	292	-1.0	262	96.6	0.0	1.9	0.0	1.5	21.4	60.6	17.9	102	95.1	41.2	15.7
Danube city & MCD (Renville)	505	476	-5.7	515	87.4	0.0	0.0	0.8	11.8	30.4	56.6	12.8	198	83.8	49.0	18.2
Danvers city & MCD (Swift)	97	94	-3.1	108	100.0	0.0	0.0	0.0	0.0	34.3	54.8	11.1	41	78.0	51.2	14.6
Danville township (Blue Earth)	240	239	-0.4	216	97.2	0.0	0.9	0.9	0.9	21.3	62.5	16.2	90	94.4	38.9	24.4
Darfur city & MCD (Watonwan)	108	107	-0.9	122	100.0	0.0	0.0	0.0	0.0	25.4	62.3	12.3	57	94.7	80.7	0.0
Darling township (Morrison)	535	532	-0.6	569	97.0	0.0	1.1	1.9	0.0	21.0	58.3	20.7	224	90.2	42.4	8.0
Darnen township (Stevens)	292	293	0.3	347	83.9	0.0	0.0	0.6	15.6	23.9	65.7	10.4	116	82.8	37.1	10.3
Darwin city & MCD (Meeker)	350	350	0.0	407	99.5	0.0	0.0	0.0	0.5	19.9	63.6	16.5	176	75.6	42.0	6.8
Darwin township (Meeker)	681	677	-0.6	600	99.5	0.0	0.0	0.0	0.5	20.8	59.3	19.8	254	89.8	39.8	22.0
Dassel city & MCD (Meeker)	1,469	1,442	-1.8	1,493	92.4	0.0	0.6	1.5	5.6	27.4	50.9	21.6	611	68.4	35.7	24.5
Dassel township (Meeker)	1,526	1,524	-0.1	1,497	99.2	0.0	0.0	0.5	0.3	30.0	56.2	13.8	538	91.4	30.3	30.3
Davidson UT (Aitkin)	42	40	-4.8	41	100.0	0.0	0.0	0.0	0.0	0.0	61.0	39.0	25	100.0	64.0	0.0
Davis township (Kittson)	30	29	-3.3	40	100.0	0.0	0.0	0.0	0.0	2.5	62.5	35.0	22	100.0	9.1	13.6
Dawson city & MCD (Lac qui Parle)	1,540	1,454	-5.6	1,538	95.4	1.5	0.0	1.2	2.0	22.1	53.1	24.8	677	69.4	52.1	20.8
Dayton city	4,664	4,976	6.7	4,840	88.1	0.0	1.7	2.0	8.2	25.5	64.7	10.0	1,652	95.5	32.6	27.7
Dayton city (Hennepin)	4,610	4,921	6.7	4,778	88.0	0.0	1.7	2.0	8.3	25.7	64.1	10.1	1,619	95.4	31.2	28.2

1 May be of any race.

Table A. All Places — **Population and Housing**

STATE City, town, township, borough, or CDP (county if applicable)	2010 census total population	2014 estimated population	Percent change 2010–2014	ACS total population estimate 2010–2014	White alone, not Hispanic or Latino	Black alone, not Hispanic or Latino	Asian alone, not Hispanic or Latino	All other races or 2 or more races, not Hispanic or Latino	Hispanic or Latino[1]	Under 18 years old	Age 18 to 64 years old	Age 65 years and older	Total occupied housing units	Percent owner occupied	High school diploma or less	Bachelor's degree or more
	1	2	3	4	5	6	7	8	9	10	11	12	13	14	15	16
MINNESOTA—Con.																
Dayton city (Wright).........	54	55	1.9	62	100.0	0.0	0.0	0.0	0.0	0.0	100.0	0.0	33	100.0	100.0	0.0
Dead Lake township (Otter Tail).................	494	491	-0.6	410	93.9	4.4	0.0	0.0	1.7	23.4	51.2	25.4	163	93.3	55.2	11.7
Decoria township (Blue Earth)...........................	1,104	1,112	0.7	1,117	95.0	0.0	3.0	1.3	0.7	24.4	66.6	9.0	409	93.9	33.0	32.8
Deephaven city & MCD (Hennepin).................	3,658	3,807	4.1	3,741	96.5	0.2	0.2	1.5	1.6	29.3	58.4	12.3	1,302	94.9	8.6	71.7
Deer township (Roseau)...	105	106	1.0	109	100.0	0.0	0.0	0.0	0.0	22.9	61.4	15.6	45	95.6	46.7	11.1
Deer Creek city & MCD (Otter Tail).................	322	322	0.0	224	99.1	0.0	0.0	0.0	0.9	18.7	54.5	26.8	110	88.2	53.6	7.3
Deer Creek township (Otter Tail).................	344	344	0.0	382	100.0	0.0	0.0	0.0	0.0	32.7	54.0	13.4	127	94.5	46.5	12.6
Deerfield township (Cass)	118	117	-0.8	114	99.1	0.0	0.9	0.0	0.0	19.3	57.0	23.7	49	89.8	61.2	4.1
Deerfield township (Steele)...........................	517	517	0.0	502	98.2	0.0	0.0	0.0	1.8	24.3	60.8	15.1	193	89.6	37.3	21.8
Deerhorn township (Wilkin)...........................	97	96	-1.0	85	94.1	0.0	0.0	5.9	0.0	4.7	69.5	25.9	42	85.7	54.8	23.8
Deer Lake UT (Itasca)......	3,496	3,537	1.2	3,518	94.0	0.6	0.0	3.6	1.8	19.6	60.9	19.6	1,425	89.6	37.5	31.9
Deer Park township (Pennington)................	126	125	-0.8	191	89.5	0.0	0.0	0.0	10.5	36.6	53.3	9.9	49	91.8	16.3	16.3
Deer River city & MCD (Itasca).......................	930	940	1.1	914	77.5	0.0	0.2	19.5	2.8	24.0	50.6	25.3	387	58.1	39.0	13.4
Deer River township (Itasca).......................	703	707	0.6	815	83.3	0.0	0.0	15.6	1.1	27.0	58.7	14.5	285	92.3	41.4	16.5
Deerwood city & MCD (Crow Wing)................	525	522	-0.6	470	93.2	0.0	0.0	6.4	0.4	26.2	54.0	19.8	213	61.0	55.4	10.3
Deerwood township (Crow Wing).....................	1,313	1,340	2.1	1,316	96.8	1.4	0.9	0.8	0.0	17.6	53.8	28.6	566	95.4	33.9	31.4
Deerwood township (Kittson)........................	153	149	-2.6	122	98.4	0.8	0.0	0.8	0.0	8.2	62.4	29.5	58	96.6	43.1	29.3
De Graff city & MCD (Swift)............................	115	128	11.3	118	100.0	0.0	0.0	0.0	0.0	24.5	64.3	11.0	55	76.4	61.8	9.1
Delafield township (Jackson)........................	226	228	0.9	218	98.6	0.0	0.0	1.4	0.0	27.6	52.3	20.2	82	87.8	43.9	14.6
Delano city & MCD (Wright)...........................	5,465	5,767	5.5	5,598	97.0	0.0	0.9	1.5	0.5	33.7	57.2	9.1	1,931	81.8	34.9	39.4
Delavan city & MCD (Faribault).....................	179	175	-2.2	217	79.3	0.0	0.0	0.0	20.7	31.4	57.1	11.5	86	81.4	43.0	20.9
Delavan township (Faribault).....................	228	225	-1.3	215	100.0	0.0	0.0	0.0	0.0	24.2	60.6	15.3	91	81.3	34.1	20.9
Delaware township (Grant)............................	102	102	0.0	84	97.6	0.0	0.0	0.0	2.4	28.6	38.1	33.3	30	93.3	50.0	30.0
Delhi city & MCD (Redwood).....................	70	68	-2.9	46	100.0	0.0	0.0	0.0	0.0	8.7	67.3	23.9	26	92.3	73.1	7.7
Delhi township (Redwood)	293	286	-2.4	247	97.6	0.0	0.8	1.6	0.0	17.8	61.4	20.6	98	90.8	43.9	25.5
Dell Grove township (Pine).............................	697	681	-2.3	621	98.4	1.0	0.0	0.6	0.0	15.6	58.7	25.6	282	85.5	45.0	14.2
Dellwood city & MCD (Washington)................	1,071	1,083	1.1	1,145	96.4	0.3	1.3	0.3	1.7	27.3	58.3	14.4	409	95.4	7.1	74.3
Delton township (Cottonwood)..............	123	123	0.0	165	95.8	0.0	0.0	0.0	4.2	29.6	66.0	4.2	61	96.7	49.2	19.7
Denham city & MCD (Pine).............................	35	34	-2.9	38	100.0	0.0	0.0	0.0	0.0	5.3	60.5	34.2	23	95.7	87.0	0.0
Denmark township (Washington)................	1,739	1,796	3.3	1,724	96.4	0.0	0.5	2.1	0.9	21.6	63.9	14.4	638	92.5	23.4	43.3
Dennison city..................	212	213	0.5	150	100.0	0.0	0.0	0.0	0.0	26.6	62.6	10.7	64	82.8	46.9	17.2
Dennison city (Goodhue)..	199	200	0.5	147	100.0	0.0	0.0	0.0	0.0	27.1	61.7	10.9	62	85.5	48.4	17.7
Dennison city (Rice).........	13	13	0.0	3	100.0	0.0	0.0	0.0	0.0	0.0	100.0	0.0	2	0.0	0.0	0.0
Dent city & MCD (Otter Tail)..............................	192	192	0.0	132	98.5	0.0	0.0	1.5	0.0	12.9	57.5	29.5	72	72.2	55.6	6.9
Denver township (Rock) ...	173	170	-1.7	200	99.5	0.0	0.0	0.0	0.5	21.5	69.0	9.5	69	91.3	53.6	13.0
Derrynane township (Le Sueur).........................	508	516	1.6	497	98.4	0.0	0.6	1.0	0.0	23.3	59.5	17.1	201	91.5	49.3	14.9
Des Moines township (Jackson)........................	232	234	0.9	213	99.5	0.0	0.5	0.0	0.0	16.4	65.7	17.8	86	98.8	40.7	19.8
Des Moines River township (Murray)	133	128	-3.8	113	100.0	0.0	0.0	0.0	0.0	18.6	64.5	16.8	51	84.3	56.9	9.8
Detroit township (Becker) .	1,982	2,022	2.0	1,903	91.1	0.0	1.1	5.5	2.3	20.8	58.1	21.1	792	89.0	36.2	22.2
Detroit Lakes city & MCD (Becker).......................	8,627	8,961	3.9	8,834	91.0	0.7	0.4	5.5	2.3	21.5	55.7	22.8	3,980	61.4	38.5	25.5
Dewald township (Nobles)	254	256	0.8	243	100.0	0.0	0.0	0.0	0.0	18.4	56.4	25.1	98	88.8	53.1	11.2
Dewey township (Roseau)	122	123	0.8	105	81.9	0.0	0.0	0.0	18.1	29.5	60.0	10.5	37	78.4	13.5	40.5
Dexter city & MCD (Mower).......................	341	343	0.6	274	90.1	9.1	0.4	0.4	0.0	23.0	64.1	12.8	119	68.9	51.3	10.9
Dexter township (Mower)..	310	312	0.6	240	95.0	0.0	0.8	0.4	3.8	26.3	49.9	23.8	88	88.6	59.1	12.5
Diamond Lake township (Lincoln)........................	207	208	0.5	189	100.0	0.0	0.0	0.0	0.0	32.2	50.3	17.5	69	89.9	42.0	34.8
Dieter township (Roseau).	148	150	1.4	157	94.9	0.0	3.8	1.3	0.0	17.8	65.5	16.6	65	89.2	50.8	12.3
Dilworth city & MCD (Clay)............................	4,024	4,188	4.1	4,104	92.1	0.0	0.0	3.9	4.0	28.6	60.5	11.0	1,645	69.2	34.7	26.1
Dodge Center city & MCD (Dodge).......................	2,671	2,691	0.7	2,686	85.1	0.0	0.0	1.7	13.2	35.7	54.5	9.9	917	77.6	51.8	15.5
Dollymount township (Traverse)....................	77	73	-5.2	44	100.0	0.0	0.0	0.0	0.0	36.3	59.0	4.5	14	78.6	35.7	7.1
Donaldson city & MCD (Kittson).......................	42	41	-2.4	48	100.0	0.0	0.0	0.0	0.0	27.1	60.5	12.5	18	72.2	61.1	0.0
Donnelly township (Marshall).....................	19	19	0.0	22	100.0	0.0	0.0	0.0	0.0	0.0	95.4	4.5	10	100.0	30.0	10.0
Donnelly city & MCD (Stevens)......................	241	242	0.4	274	89.8	0.0	0.0	0.0	10.2	24.1	53.0	23.0	119	83.2	44.5	10.1

1 May be of any race.

Table A. All Places — **Population and Housing**

STATE City, town, township, borough, or CDP (county if applicable)	Population				Race and Hispanic or Latino origin (percent), 2010–2014					Age (percent), 2010–2014			Households, 2010–2014			
	2010 census total population	2014 estimated population	Percent change 2010– 2014	ACS total population estimate 2010–2014	White alone, not Hispanic or Latino	Black alone, not Hispanic or Latino	Asian alone, not Hispanic or Latino	All other races or 2 or more races, not Hispanic or Latino	Hispanic or Latino[1]	Under 18 years old	Age 18 to 64 years old	Age 65 years and older	Total occupied housing units	Percent owner occupied	High school diploma or less	Bachelor's degree or more
	1	2	3	4	5	6	7	8	9	10	11	12	13	14	15	16
MINNESOTA—Con.																
Donnelly township (Stevens)............	100	99	-1.0	74	100.0	0.0	0.0	0.0	0.0	21.6	66.3	12.2	31	100.0	32.3	41.9
Dora township (Otter Tail).	725	719	-0.8	729	98.2	0.0	0.7	0.8	0.3	10.4	55.4	34.2	343	91.8	39.1	26.8
Doran city & MCD (Wilkin)	55	54	-1.8	33	87.9	0.0	0.0	12.1	0.0	12.2	45.5	42.4	16	100.0	68.8	0.0
Douglas township (Dakota)	716	726	1.4	780	92.3	0.0	1.2	3.1	3.5	24.2	64.3	11.5	281	90.7	50.9	20.6
Dover city & MCD (Olmsted)...........	735	748	1.8	798	98.2	0.0	0.0	0.6	1.1	37.3	55.7	7.0	272	91.2	42.3	18.8
Dover township (Olmsted)	389	392	0.8	328	96.3	0.0	0.0	0.0	3.7	19.6	62.8	17.7	122	91.8	47.5	22.1
Dovray city & MCD (Murray)............	57	55	-3.5	72	100.0	0.0	0.0	0.0	0.0	6.9	27.8	65.3	46	89.1	56.5	0.0
Dovray township (Murray).	152	148	-2.6	142	98.6	1.4	0.0	0.0	0.0	12.6	70.4	16.9	65	83.1	41.5	6.2
Dovre township (Kandiyohi)	2,119	2,137	0.8	2,111	91.5	0.0	4.1	0.2	4.2	22.3	64.0	13.8	801	90.4	21.7	46.2
Drammen township (Lincoln)	118	115	-2.5	125	97.6	0.0	0.0	0.0	2.4	32.8	51.2	16.0	46	76.1	39.1	26.1
Dresbach township (Winona)	456	456	0.0	425	98.6	0.0	0.0	0.5	0.9	14.8	63.3	21.9	165	90.9	26.7	44.8
Dryden township (Sibley)..	287	282	-1.7	226	99.1	0.0	0.0	0.0	0.9	16.8	65.9	17.3	98	82.7	63.3	5.1
Dublin township (Swift)	152	147	-3.3	199	71.9	0.0	0.0	1.5	26.6	16.5	72.3	11.1	74	74.3	40.5	13.5
Dudley township (Clearwater)	400	406	1.5	476	97.5	0.0	0.0	2.5	0.0	27.3	62.5	10.3	169	88.2	50.3	11.2
Duluth city & MCD (St. Louis)...........	86,266	86,238	0.0	86,239	89.3	2.7	1.6	4.7	1.7	18.4	67.3	14.3	35,548	59.8	27.9	32.7
Duluth township (St. Louis)...........	1,941	2,017	3.9	1,871	97.3	0.3	0.0	1.1	1.3	22.9	60.2	16.9	745	93.6	29.4	39.9
Dumont city & MCD (Traverse)	100	95	-5.0	79	97.5	0.0	0.0	0.0	2.5	24.1	65.9	10.1	38	94.7	39.5	13.2
Dunbar township (Faribault)	283	277	-2.1	219	100.0	0.0	0.0	0.0	0.0	21.5	60.6	17.8	99	81.8	56.6	13.1
Dundas city & MCD (Rice)	1,345	1,446	7.5	1,623	87.6	0.2	2.2	0.8	9.1	32.5	61.2	6.4	591	88.2	30.6	30.5
Dundee city & MCD (Nobles).............	68	70	2.9	89	100.0	0.0	0.0	0.0	0.0	8.9	68.5	22.5	49	93.9	89.8	0.0
Dunn township (Otter Tail)	905	898	-0.8	759	97.1	0.4	0.4	1.7	0.4	9.3	57.0	33.6	386	94.3	25.1	39.4
Dunnell city & MCD (Martin)	167	163	-2.4	188	100.0	0.0	0.0	0.0	0.0	11.2	62.3	26.6	88	86.4	72.7	13.6
Durand township (Beltrami)	211	214	1.4	251	92.4	0.0	0.0	7.2	0.0	27.1	59.1	13.9	98	95.9	44.9	24.5
Eagan city & MCD (Dakota)	64,205	66,084	2.9	65,053	78.2	5.8	8.0	3.3	4.7	24.5	66.7	8.9	25,919	70.4	16.9	52.2
Eagle township (Carlton) ..	581	587	1.0	553	99.5	0.0	0.0	0.5	0.0	20.3	56.9	23.0	236	88.1	43.6	19.9
Eagle Bend city & MCD (Todd).............	535	513	-4.1	473	87.9	0.4	0.0	2.1	9.5	22.7	51.7	25.8	227	79.7	43.6	9.3
Eagle Lake city & MCD (Blue Earth)	2,422	2,688	11.0	2,532	86.2	10.5	0.0	0.5	2.8	29.2	64.0	7.0	903	80.2	29.0	36.2
Eagle Lake township (Otter Tail)	378	376	-0.5	360	93.1	0.0	0.0	4.2	2.8	16.7	59.3	23.9	161	89.4	34.2	23.6
Eagle Point township (Marshall)	17	17	0.0	2	100.0	0.0	0.0	0.0	0.0	0.0	0.0	100.0	2	100.0	0.0	0.0
Eagles Nest township (St. Louis)...........	242	244	0.8	259	96.1	1.2	0.0	2.3	0.4	5.8	55.2	39.0	133	100.0	17.3	53.4
Eagle Valley township (Todd).............	541	528	-2.4	388	94.6	0.0	0.0	1.8	3.6	20.8	61.9	17.3	165	89.7	52.1	9.7
Eagle View township (Becker)...........	131	134	2.3	232	49.6	0.0	0.9	48.3	1.3	29.3	51.0	19.8	101	69.3	39.6	18.8
East Bethel city & MCD (Anoka)	11,626	11,642	0.1	11,614	98.0	0.0	0.2	1.4	0.5	24.0	66.7	9.3	4,092	96.0	43.2	19.8
East Cass UT (Cass)........	62	61	-1.6	105	100.0	0.0	0.0	0.0	0.0	53.4	42.9	3.8	26	100.0	15.4	0.0
East Chain township (Martin)	296	288	-2.7	298	96.0	0.0	0.0	0.0	4.0	29.5	58.8	11.7	105	87.6	37.1	23.8
East Cook UT (Cook)	775	789	1.8	889	89.4	2.9	2.5	5.1	0.1	6.7	59.3	33.9	466	86.3	21.9	58.2
Eastern township (Otter Tail)	230	230	0.0	190	100.0	0.0	0.0	0.0	0.0	14.7	57.9	27.4	82	93.9	48.8	4.9
East Grand Forks city & MCD (Polk)........	8,601	8,651	0.6	8,621	89.2	2.5	0.0	4.0	4.0	27.4	59.2	13.7	3,460	62.8	33.1	22.0
East Gull Lake city & MCD (Cass)	1,004	1,003	-0.1	947	98.9	0.0	0.0	1.1	0.0	22.2	57.5	20.2	389	92.8	21.3	44.2
East Koochiching UT (Koochiching)..........	355	NA	NA	300	99.3	0.0	0.0	0.0	0.7	17.3	63.0	19.7	151	82.1	49.0	11.9
East Lake Lillian township (Kandiyohi)...........	199	198	-0.5	212	96.2	0.0	0.0	0.0	3.8	20.7	60.3	18.9	90	80.0	38.9	18.9
Easton city & MCD (Faribault)...........	199	195	-2.0	209	94.7	0.0	0.0	5.3	0.0	20.6	60.6	18.7	98	94.9	37.8	16.3
East Park township (Marshall)	23	23	0.0	22	100.0	0.0	0.0	0.0	0.0	18.2	54.4	27.3	8	100.0	87.5	0.0
East Side township (Mille Lacs)	620	616	-0.6	588	99.1	0.0	0.0	0.9	0.0	11.9	55.8	32.1	286	92.3	50.7	20.3
East Valley township (Marshall)	43	43	0.0	38	100.0	0.0	0.0	0.0	0.0	7.9	42.3	50.0	17	88.2	88.2	0.0
Ebro CDP	64	NA	NA	80	26.3	0.0	0.0	67.5	6.3	45.1	47.6	7.5	23	73.9	73.9	0.0
Echo city & MCD (Yellow Medicine)	278	270	-2.9	325	96.3	0.0	1.5	2.2	0.0	35.8	50.3	13.8	119	79.8	55.5	10.1
Echo township (Yellow Medicine)	145	141	-2.8	117	99.1	0.0	0.0	0.0	0.9	21.4	48.8	29.9	51	88.2	51.0	11.8
Eckles township (Beltrami)	1,510	1,504	-0.4	1,542	78.5	0.3	0.5	19.8	0.8	34.7	58.5	6.9	546	73.3	37.4	22.9
Eckvoll township (Marshall)	77	77	0.0	63	100.0	0.0	0.0	0.0	0.0	17.4	74.5	7.9	25	92.0	40.0	20.0
Eddy township (Clearwater)	339	344	1.5	288	96.9	0.0	3.1	0.0	0.0	25.7	57.9	16.3	120	89.2	40.8	22.5
Eden township (Brown)	254	250	-1.6	271	98.9	0.0	0.0	0.0	1.1	22.8	61.2	15.9	110	87.3	39.1	15.5

1 May be of any race.

Table A. All Places — **Population and Housing**

STATE City, town, township, borough, or CDP (county if applicable)	2010 census total population	2014 estimated population	Percent change 2010–2014	ACS total population estimate 2010–2014	White alone, not Hispanic or Latino	Black alone, not Hispanic or Latino	Asian alone, not Hispanic or Latino	All other races or 2 or more races, not Hispanic or Latino	Hispanic or Latino[1]	Under 18 years old	Age 18 to 64 years old	Age 65 years and older	Total occupied housing units	Percent owner occupied	High school diploma or less	Bachelor's degree or more
	1	2	3	4	5	6	7	8	9	10	11	12	13	14	15	16
MINNESOTA—Con.																
Eden township (Pipestone)...............	278	271	-2.5	256	99.2	0.0	0.0	0.4	0.4	25.4	53.2	21.5	95	89.5	54.7	13.7
Eden township (Polk)........	168	169	0.6	173	86.1	0.0	3.5	5.8	4.6	20.8	58.4	20.8	75	86.7	61.3	13.3
Eden Lake township (Stearns)...............	1,542	1,588	3.0	1,607	99.2	0.7	0.0	0.1	0.0	25.4	55.8	18.7	596	94.3	50.0	16.3
Eden Prairie city & MCD (Hennepin)	60,751	63,228	4.1	62,096	77.8	5.5	10.5	3.1	3.1	26.1	64.6	9.3	24,088	73.7	11.1	63.2
Eden Valley city	1,042	1,033	-0.9	964	92.5	0.0	1.0	4.6	1.9	27.7	56.4	15.9	447	62.6	57.0	13.6
Eden Valley city (Meeker) .	553	545	-1.4	498	86.5	0.0	2.0	7.8	3.6	29.5	51.6	18.7	249	64.7	56.2	15.3
Eden Valley city (Stearns).	489	488	-0.2	466	98.9	0.0	0.0	1.1	0.0	25.8	61.4	12.9	198	60.1	58.1	11.6
Edgerton city & MCD (Pipestone).................	1,189	1,143	-3.9	1,193	95.0	0.0	0.4	0.8	3.8	23.0	47.4	29.5	487	83.8	48.7	20.7
Edina city & MCD (Hennepin)	47,940	49,596	3.5	48,940	85.2	2.1	6.7	2.9	3.2	24.5	55.2	20.3	20,833	73.1	11.2	68.4
Edison township (Swift)	106	103	-2.8	109	100.0	0.0	0.0	0.0	0.0	16.5	53.2	30.3	49	91.8	32.7	24.5
Edna township (Otter Tail)	897	893	-0.4	885	97.6	0.8	0.2	0.9	0.5	21.1	57.0	21.8	339	95.9	33.6	33.3
Edwards township (Kandiyohi)	242	241	-0.4	261	97.3	2.3	0.0	0.0	0.4	18.8	70.1	11.1	86	93.0	26.7	14.0
Effie city & MCD (Itasca) ..	123	124	0.8	153	96.7	0.0	1.3	2.0	0.0	32.7	62.1	5.2	61	86.9	65.6	8.2
Effie UT (Itasca)............	216	217	0.5	201	94.0	0.0	0.0	6.0	0.0	27.9	50.4	21.9	67	89.6	56.7	7.5
Effington township (Otter Tail)......................	264	264	0.0	182	98.9	0.0	0.0	0.0	1.1	13.7	58.1	28.0	86	81.4	54.7	19.8
Eglon township (Clay).......	508	523	3.0	548	97.6	0.5	0.0	1.5	0.4	27.9	51.3	20.6	193	96.4	31.1	29.0
Eidsvold township (Lyon)..	236	235	-0.4	268	98.5	0.0	0.0	0.0	1.5	36.2	53.6	10.1	94	93.6	47.9	23.4
Eitzen city & MCD (Houston)	243	242	-0.4	226	100.0	0.0	0.0	0.0	0.0	19.9	54.4	25.7	110	92.7	58.2	8.2
Elba city & MCD (Winona)	152	156	2.6	138	94.9	0.0	0.0	0.0	5.1	22.4	55.0	22.5	53	83.0	66.0	5.7
Elba township (Winona)....	311	312	0.3	302	87.1	0.0	0.0	0.0	12.9	23.6	67.5	8.9	100	97.0	36.0	21.0
Elbow Lake CDP	95	NA	NA	100	27.0	0.0	2.0	71.0	0.0	28.0	62.0	10.0	47	44.7	57.4	12.8
Elbow Lake city & MCD (Grant)...................	1,176	1,156	-1.7	1,186	97.4	0.5	0.0	1.5	0.6	22.9	58.3	18.9	570	69.1	33.0	16.1
Elbow Lake township (Grant)......................	141	140	-0.7	139	100.0	0.0	0.0	0.0	0.0	20.1	61.9	18.0	64	95.3	25.0	15.6
Eldorado township (Stevens)......................	94	93	-1.1	52	100.0	0.0	0.0	0.0	0.0	11.5	76.9	11.5	19	100.0	47.4	15.8
Elgin city & MCD (Wabasha)................	1,089	1,064	-2.3	1,156	93.0	0.0	0.0	2.9	4.2	31.8	60.3	8.0	431	79.1	48.5	24.1
Elgin township (Wabasha)	733	730	-0.4	792	94.8	0.0	0.0	3.5	1.6	29.8	57.9	12.2	276	87.0	35.1	27.5
Elizabeth city & MCD (Otter Tail)	173	173	0.0	197	94.9	0.0	0.0	5.1	0.0	28.5	61.9	9.6	91	78.0	41.8	4.4
Elizabeth township (Otter Tail)	819	808	-1.3	792	92.7	0.5	0.0	6.8	0.0	23.2	55.2	21.6	328	92.7	26.8	29.6
Elk township (Nobles).......	253	255	0.8	252	97.6	0.0	0.0	0.0	2.4	23.5	58.8	17.9	97	85.6	45.4	13.4
Elk Lake township (Grant)	281	280	-0.4	296	94.3	0.0	3.0	0.3	2.4	19.6	64.5	15.9	94	96.8	36.2	12.8
Elko New Market city & MCD (Scott)	4,110	4,665	13.5	4,414	96.7	1.2	0.4	1.4	0.3	36.5	60.8	2.8	1,405	85.6	21.0	43.6
Elk River city & MCD (Sherburne)................	22,974	23,746	3.4	23,346	91.7	1.1	2.7	2.8	1.7	28.6	61.0	10.3	8,122	77.3	25.7	34.2
Elkton township (Clay)......	308	314	1.9	347	98.8	0.0	0.0	0.3	0.9	25.4	62.5	12.1	127	93.7	44.9	21.3
Elkton city & MCD (Mower)...................	141	142	0.7	130	96.2	0.0	0.0	0.0	3.8	38.5	51.5	10.0	50	74.0	42.0	2.0
Ellendale city & MCD (Steele)	691	688	-0.4	656	97.6	0.0	0.5	2.0	0.0	29.1	54.9	16.0	279	78.9	61.6	18.6
Ellington township (Dodge)...................	261	264	1.1	319	92.8	0.0	0.0	6.0	1.3	19.1	70.5	10.3	116	86.2	33.6	21.6
Ellsborough township (Murray)...................	145	140	-3.4	131	90.8	0.0	0.0	0.0	9.2	16.1	61.8	22.1	53	100.0	60.4	17.0
Ellsburg township (St. Louis)	219	220	0.5	200	100.0	0.0	0.0	0.0	0.0	9.5	61.5	29.0	109	91.7	63.3	14.7
Ellsworth township (Meeker)...................	848	845	-0.4	909	96.5	0.0	1.8	0.9	0.9	19.2	59.0	21.9	383	97.1	45.2	21.1
Ellsworth city & MCD (Nobles)..................	463	459	-0.9	453	92.9	1.3	0.0	4.9	0.9	19.2	46.8	34.0	188	82.4	49.5	13.8
Elm Creek township (Martin)...................	188	183	-2.7	176	94.3	0.0	0.0	5.7	0.0	15.9	62.5	21.6	70	87.1	47.1	24.3
Elmdale city & MCD (Morrison)................	116	114	-1.7	91	100.0	0.0	0.0	0.0	0.0	23.1	42.9	34.1	37	89.2	73.0	0.0
Elmdale township (Morrison)................	1,010	1,003	-0.7	955	97.9	0.3	1.3	0.0	0.5	24.1	64.0	11.9	362	91.7	56.1	12.7
Elmer township (Pipestone).................	231	226	-2.2	241	100.0	0.0	0.0	0.0	0.0	22.8	70.2	7.1	97	89.7	46.4	14.4
Elmer township (St. Louis)	151	152	0.7	143	100.0	0.0	0.0	0.0	0.0	11.9	67.9	20.3	63	93.7	76.2	3.2
Elmira township (Olmsted)	354	377	6.5	363	96.1	0.8	0.6	2.5	0.0	16.5	65.8	17.6	151	80.1	40.4	21.2
Elmo township (Otter Tail).	331	326	-1.5	309	97.4	1.3	0.0	0.6	0.6	17.4	62.0	20.4	137	89.1	63.5	10.9
Elmore city & MCD (Faribault).................	663	644	-2.9	634	92.1	1.6	0.0	1.3	5.0	29.2	49.6	21.3	265	79.2	61.5	14.0
Elmore township (Faribault).................	181	177	-2.2	193	96.9	0.0	0.0	0.0	3.1	16.6	54.4	29.0	88	96.6	43.2	21.6
Elmwood township (Clay) .	415	430	3.6	456	94.5	0.7	0.0	4.6	0.2	25.0	54.7	20.2	166	99.4	34.9	24.7
Elrosa city & MCD (Stearns)................	211	212	0.5	170	98.8	0.6	0.0	0.0	0.6	17.1	47.0	35.9	74	89.2	60.8	9.5
Ely city & MCD (St. Louis)	3,461	3,455	-0.2	3,459	98.1	0.1	1.4	0.4	0.0	15.7	63.0	21.3	1,661	68.0	33.1	32.3
Elysian city..................	652	669	2.6	523	99.8	0.0	0.2	0.0	0.0	19.0	59.8	21.2	227	87.7	47.1	28.2
Elysian city (Le Sueur)......	650	667	2.6	523	99.8	0.0	0.2	0.0	0.0	19.0	59.8	21.2	227	87.7	47.1	28.2
Elysian city (Waseca)......	2	2	0.0	0	0.0	0.0	0.0	0.0	0.0	0.0	0.0	0.0	0	0.0	0.0	0.0
Elysian township (Le Sueur)......................	1,042	1,050	0.8	1,107	94.0	0.0	0.0	0.6	5.3	22.6	56.1	21.4	421	86.7	39.9	22.8
Emardville township (Red Lake).......................	195	194	-0.5	248	95.6	0.0	0.0	0.0	4.4	19.7	66.2	14.1	97	83.5	62.9	8.2
Embarrass township (St. Louis)	607	609	0.3	491	96.5	0.0	1.6	1.8	0.0	15.9	55.2	29.1	242	96.3	58.7	12.0

1 May be of any race.

Table A. All Places — **Population and Housing**

STATE City, town, township, borough, or CDP (county if applicable)	Population 2010 census total population	2014 estimated population	Percent change 2010–2014	ACS total population estimate 2010–2014	Race and Hispanic or Latino origin (percent), 2010–2014 White alone, not Hispanic or Latino	Black alone, not Hispanic or Latino	Asian alone, not Hispanic or Latino	All other races or 2 or more races, not Hispanic or Latino	Hispanic or Latino[1]	Age (percent), 2010–2014 Under 18 years old	Age 18 to 64 years old	Age 65 years and older	Households, 2010–2014 Total occupied housing units	Percent owner occupied	Householders by level of education (percent) High school diploma or less	Bachelor's degree or more
	1	2	3	4	5	6	7	8	9	10	11	12	13	14	15	16
MINNESOTA—Con.																
Emerald township (Faribault)	222	218	-1.8	186	98.9	0.0	0.0	1.1	0.0	19.3	65.1	15.6	73	90.4	20.5	28.8
Emily city & MCD (Crow Wing)	813	825	1.5	837	95.2	0.0	1.0	1.7	2.2	14.2	51.2	34.6	417	88.5	46.8	20.6
Emmet township (Renville)	226	217	-4.0	251	96.8	0.0	2.0	0.0	1.2	23.1	66.8	10.4	93	93.5	32.3	15.1
Emmons city & MCD (Freeborn)	391	386	-1.3	440	90.0	0.0	0.0	1.8	8.2	30.2	52.7	17.0	182	85.2	40.1	17.0
Empire township (Dakota)	2,443	2,721	11.4	2,571	87.4	0.2	1.6	6.1	4.7	34.3	58.6	7.0	794	88.0	22.9	24.7
Enstrom township (Roseau)	455	451	-0.9	457	94.3	0.0	0.0	1.8	3.9	23.9	66.5	9.8	185	84.9	58.4	10.8
Enterprise township (Jackson)	187	187	0.0	184	98.9	0.0	1.1	0.0	0.0	23.9	58.1	17.9	84	77.4	38.1	25.0
Equality township (Red Lake)	131	130	-0.8	120	91.7	0.0	0.0	1.7	6.7	21.7	51.7	26.7	50	88.0	70.0	6.0
Erdahl township (Grant)	347	345	-0.6	399	96.2	0.0	0.0	1.0	2.8	21.8	55.3	23.1	161	90.7	26.7	28.0
Erhard city & MCD (Otter Tail)	148	148	0.0	111	94.6	0.0	0.0	4.5	0.9	16.2	48.6	35.1	46	89.1	67.4	13.0
Erhards Grove township (Otter Tail)	442	436	-1.4	473	95.1	0.0	0.0	0.0	4.9	20.7	63.2	16.1	195	92.3	49.2	16.9
Ericson township (Renville)	206	198	-3.9	244	94.7	0.0	0.0	2.0	3.3	24.6	65.5	9.8	91	86.8	47.3	9.9
Erie township (Becker)	1,642	1,673	1.9	1,863	89.6	0.2	0.0	7.7	2.5	27.3	55.8	16.9	675	93.8	44.4	18.5
Erin township (Rice)	859	867	0.9	789	99.2	0.0	0.3	0.5	0.0	25.8	57.8	16.2	293	90.8	52.9	15.0
Erskine city & MCD (Polk)	500	490	-2.0	538	84.6	0.0	0.0	3.3	12.1	29.3	53.5	17.3	236	63.1	55.1	8.5
Esko CDP	1,869	NA	NA	1,747	95.5	0.3	0.0	3.1	1.0	31.6	57.0	11.4	591	80.2	37.9	39.4
Espelie township (Marshall)	39	39	0.0	50	100.0	0.0	0.0	0.0	0.0	4.0	96.0	0.0	26	92.3	46.2	7.7
Esther township (Polk)	165	164	-0.6	177	98.3	0.0	1.7	0.0	0.0	17.5	69.0	13.6	60	100.0	31.7	20.0
Euclid township (Polk)	151	150	-0.7	190	96.8	0.0	0.0	3.2	0.0	27.4	56.4	16.3	82	74.4	35.4	14.6
Eureka township (Dakota)	1,426	1,448	1.5	1,500	99.1	0.0	0.3	0.1	0.5	21.1	66.6	12.5	545	94.5	32.7	28.8
Evan city & MCD (Brown)	86	83	-3.5	37	97.3	0.0	0.0	2.7	0.0	8.1	48.6	43.2	22	100.0	72.7	4.5
Evansville city & MCD (Douglas)	612	602	-1.6	597	97.3	0.0	0.0	1.7	1.0	17.2	55.3	27.3	278	75.5	56.8	7.6
Evansville township (Douglas)	242	243	0.4	257	99.6	0.0	0.0	0.4	0.0	24.9	59.0	16.0	90	95.6	38.9	10.0
Eveleth city & MCD (St. Louis)	3,718	3,698	-0.5	3,708	92.1	0.8	0.0	6.4	0.7	20.4	60.9	18.5	1,698	56.4	42.0	17.7
Everglade township (Stevens)	108	107	-0.9	111	100.0	0.0	0.0	0.0	0.0	28.8	52.2	18.9	30	100.0	26.7	26.7
Evergreen township (Becker)	340	344	1.2	508	96.9	0.0	0.0	0.0	3.1	46.0	47.3	6.7	142	86.6	62.0	8.5
Everts township (Otter Tail)	658	651	-1.1	784	95.9	1.3	1.5	0.6	0.6	16.0	48.3	35.6	358	94.4	24.3	42.2
Ewington township (Jackson)	244	244	0.0	271	90.8	0.0	0.4	0.4	8.5	26.2	57.3	16.6	101	87.1	42.6	9.9
Excel township (Marshall)	300	300	0.0	270	100.0	0.0	0.0	0.0	0.0	17.8	68.3	14.1	121	81.0	41.3	17.4
Excelsior city & MCD (Hennepin)	2,198	2,256	2.6	2,248	91.9	1.1	1.9	1.8	3.3	20.9	64.6	14.6	1,118	43.1	21.9	38.7
Eyota city & MCD (Olmsted)	1,977	2,037	3.0	2,120	94.2	0.0	1.5	2.4	2.0	32.2	57.1	10.6	768	83.3	33.6	27.9
Eyota township (Olmsted)	466	481	3.2	446	97.5	0.7	0.7	0.2	0.9	28.7	56.1	15.2	151	84.8	44.4	28.5
Fahlun township (Kandiyohi)	335	335	0.0	356	100.0	0.0	0.0	0.0	0.0	18.9	66.6	14.6	153	92.2	29.4	17.6
Fairbanks township (St. Louis)	63	63	0.0	58	100.0	0.0	0.0	0.0	0.0	18.9	55.1	25.9	28	96.4	28.6	32.1
Fairfax township (Polk)	198	199	0.5	193	96.9	0.0	0.0	3.1	0.0	11.9	66.9	21.2	85	87.1	27.1	20.0
Fairfax city & MCD (Renville)	1,235	1,183	-4.2	943	89.8	1.3	0.0	1.5	7.4	13.8	56.3	29.9	437	77.8	57.0	14.4
Fairfield township (Crow Wing)	347	354	2.0	289	99.3	0.0	0.0	0.7	0.0	10.4	45.4	44.3	149	94.0	35.6	14.8
Fairfield township (Swift)	128	124	-3.1	161	100.0	0.0	0.0	0.0	0.0	14.3	75.7	9.9	67	92.5	38.8	20.9
Fairhaven CDP	358	NA	NA	356	94.7	0.0	0.0	5.3	0.0	23.3	64.3	12.4	139	85.6	55.4	15.1
Fair Haven township (Stearns)	1,507	1,502	-0.3	1,407	97.9	0.3	0.0	1.4	0.4	18.7	66.1	15.4	582	91.4	45.4	16.3
Fairmont city & MCD (Martin)	10,666	10,328	-3.2	10,474	92.4	0.5	0.7	0.6	5.8	21.8	55.8	22.4	4,623	70.6	49.2	17.6
Fairmont township (Martin)	318	310	-2.5	304	98.4	0.0	1.0	0.0	0.7	16.8	59.1	24.0	119	91.6	43.7	35.3
Fairview township (Cass)	821	829	1.0	869	94.6	0.0	0.0	3.0	2.4	24.8	58.4	16.8	342	95.6	17.3	42.7
Fairview township (Lyon)	394	391	-0.8	514	95.1	1.8	0.0	0.8	2.3	18.4	73.2	8.6	145	96.6	46.2	26.2
Falcon Heights city & MCD (Ramsey)	5,321	5,513	3.6	5,439	76.0	4.4	12.8	2.8	4.1	17.8	68.2	14.1	2,152	55.0	14.0	68.2
Falk township (Clearwater)	284	288	1.4	305	63.6	0.0	0.0	33.1	3.3	27.8	59.6	12.5	108	88.9	54.6	6.5
Fall Lake township (Lake)	549	551	0.4	590	98.1	0.0	0.0	1.4	0.5	10.7	52.2	37.1	307	87.3	16.3	53.7
Falun township (Roseau)	251	256	2.0	246	98.4	0.0	0.0	0.0	1.6	22.4	57.5	20.3	104	92.3	47.1	22.1
Fanny township (Polk)	100	100	0.0	82	100.0	0.0	0.0	0.0	0.0	17.0	65.7	17.1	34	100.0	35.3	20.6
Farden township (Hubbard)	1,137	1,132	-0.4	930	88.3	0.0	0.4	10.1	1.2	22.9	56.9	20.2	405	85.2	31.9	38.8
Faribault city & MCD (Rice)	23,352	23,594	1.0	23,460	76.3	7.7	1.3	2.9	11.7	25.0	61.2	13.8	8,287	67.6	44.5	20.4
Farley township (Polk)	45	45	0.0	26	100.0	0.0	0.0	0.0	0.0	34.6	38.4	26.9	10	100.0	40.0	20.0
Farming township (Stearns)	987	1,007	2.0	961	99.5	0.0	0.5	0.0	0.0	27.8	62.2	9.8	335	85.1	51.0	11.9
Farmington city & MCD (Dakota)	21,087	22,571	7.0	21,861	90.2	2.1	2.8	2.2	2.7	31.1	62.4	6.5	7,546	87.7	23.4	37.9
Farmington township (Olmsted)	444	445	0.2	485	98.6	0.0	0.2	0.0	1.2	18.8	56.4	24.7	195	79.0	45.6	21.0
Farm Island township (Aitkin)	1,101	1,080	-1.9	1,101	98.5	1.4	0.0	0.0	0.2	17.7	53.1	29.2	491	93.1	40.7	16.1
Farwell city & MCD (Pope)	51	52	2.0	74	100.0	0.0	0.0	0.0	0.0	33.8	43.3	23.0	28	96.4	78.6	7.1

1 May be of any race.

Table A. All Places — **Population and Housing**

STATE City, town, township, borough, or CDP (county if applicable)	2010 census total population	2014 estimated population	Percent change 2010–2014	ACS total population estimate 2010–2014	White alone, not Hispanic or Latino	Black alone, not Hispanic or Latino	Asian alone, not Hispanic or Latino	All other races or 2 or more races, not Hispanic or Latino	Hispanic or Latino[1]	Under 18 years old	Age 18 to 64 years old	Age 65 years and older	Total occupied housing units	Percent owner occupied	High school diploma or less	Bachelor's degree or more
	1	2	3	4	5	6	7	8	9	10	11	12	13	14	15	16
MINNESOTA—Con.																
Fawn Lake township (Todd)	555	548	-1.3	628	90.3	0.0	0.0	9.4	0.3	29.2	58.4	12.3	238	83.6	29.0	18.5
Faxon township (Sibley)	701	693	-1.1	706	93.9	0.1	2.8	2.7	0.4	33.5	59.0	7.4	246	96.3	32.1	31.7
Fayal township (St. Louis)	1,809	1,824	0.8	1,883	94.5	0.0	1.0	3.0	1.4	17.2	62.2	20.4	811	99.3	25.4	33.7
Featherstone township (Goodhue)	782	789	0.9	748	98.3	0.0	0.0	1.2	0.5	19.6	65.4	15.1	292	93.5	46.6	21.6
Federal Dam city & MCD (Cass)	110	107	-2.7	134	74.6	0.0	1.5	23.9	0.0	30.7	56.0	13.4	51	72.5	52.9	7.8
Feeley township (Itasca)	306	308	0.7	292	99.3	0.0	0.0	0.7	0.0	15.1	50.4	34.6	141	88.7	36.9	29.8
Felton city & MCD (Clay)	177	180	1.7	123	100.0	0.0	0.0	0.0	0.0	11.4	75.6	13.0	64	87.5	53.1	10.9
Felton township (Clay)	86	86	0.0	61	100.0	0.0	0.0	0.0	0.0	27.9	47.6	24.6	26	96.2	46.2	19.2
Fenton township (Murray)	177	173	-2.3	156	98.1	0.0	0.0	0.0	1.9	26.9	59.6	13.5	52	90.4	42.3	9.6
Fergus Falls city & MCD (Otter Tail)	13,138	13,304	1.3	13,215	94.3	1.1	0.7	1.3	2.7	19.8	59.7	20.5	5,757	60.7	35.1	29.3
Fergus Falls township (Otter Tail)	1,006	1,010	0.4	959	98.4	0.5	0.0	0.0	1.0	22.2	57.6	20.2	390	90.0	31.5	30.5
Fern township (Hubbard)	270	270	0.0	346	92.5	0.0	0.0	5.8	1.7	23.9	66.9	9.0	143	95.1	53.8	16.1
Fertile city & MCD (Polk)	842	844	0.2	921	88.5	0.0	3.0	0.9	7.6	24.8	50.7	24.4	411	67.6	51.8	17.3
Field township (St. Louis)	390	391	0.3	383	97.1	0.0	0.0	2.9	0.0	15.7	63.9	20.4	174	93.1	54.6	18.4
Fieldon township (Watonwan)	209	207	-1.0	228	93.9	3.5	0.0	0.0	2.6	26.3	59.9	13.6	87	70.1	52.9	10.3
Fifty Lakes city & MCD (Crow Wing)	387	397	2.6	289	98.6	0.0	0.0	1.4	0.0	10.1	55.8	34.3	151	94.7	29.1	28.5
Fillmore township (Fillmore)	457	461	0.9	373	99.7	0.0	0.0	0.3	0.0	23.0	57.2	19.8	148	89.2	43.9	17.6
Fine Lakes township (St. Louis)	134	134	0.0	147	97.3	0.0	0.0	2.7	0.0	8.8	60.5	30.6	70	100.0	55.7	14.3
Finland CDP	195	NA	NA	215	99.5	0.0	0.0	0.0	0.5	5.6	74.8	19.5	116	86.2	61.2	12.1
Finlayson city & MCD (Pine)	315	312	-1.0	209	96.7	0.0	0.5	1.9	1.0	19.2	64.7	16.3	107	53.3	40.2	15.0
Finlayson township (Pine)	456	443	-2.9	478	96.4	1.7	0.4	1.5	0.0	26.3	60.1	13.4	178	94.4	61.2	5.1
First Assessment UT (Crow Wing)	5,428	5,555	2.3	5,488	96.4	0.0	0.0	3.6	0.0	26.0	59.4	14.4	2,110	88.4	29.8	39.6
Fisher city & MCD (Polk)	435	433	-0.5	407	91.9	3.2	1.2	0.7	2.9	30.5	52.7	16.7	168	63.1	30.4	25.0
Fisher township (Polk)	200	199	-0.5	160	98.1	0.0	0.0	1.9	0.0	24.4	65.2	10.6	56	91.1	19.6	33.9
Fish Lake CDP	51	NA	NA	53	100.0	0.0	0.0	0.0	0.0	0.0	60.3	39.6	31	100.0	16.1	38.7
Fish Lake township (Chisago)	2,019	2,043	1.2	1,765	95.5	0.3	0.1	4.1	0.0	21.9	61.9	16.1	702	93.2	40.2	17.0
Fleming township (Aitkin)	312	306	-1.9	406	95.3	0.0	0.2	3.0	1.5	17.5	54.8	27.6	185	92.4	53.0	11.4
Fleming township (Pine)	141	138	-2.1	137	98.5	0.0	0.0	0.0	1.5	32.9	45.9	21.2	56	92.9	44.6	32.1
Flensburg city & MCD (Morrison)	225	228	1.3	190	100.0	0.0	0.0	0.0	0.0	24.2	59.0	16.8	68	88.2	44.1	8.8
Flom township (Norman)	218	212	-2.8	261	90.8	0.0	0.0	9.2	0.0	25.6	50.1	24.1	104	82.7	54.8	16.3
Floodwood city & MCD (St. Louis)	528	526	-0.4	555	98.4	0.0	0.0	1.3	0.4	24.9	56.9	18.2	274	64.6	60.6	8.8
Floodwood township (St. Louis)	280	281	0.4	277	99.3	0.0	0.0	0.7	0.0	21.7	57.1	21.3	114	96.5	57.0	7.0
Flora township (Renville)	188	180	-4.3	181	100.0	0.0	0.0	0.0	0.0	20.4	44.8	34.8	67	89.6	40.3	19.4
Florence township (Goodhue)	1,581	1,592	0.7	1,447	97.0	0.0	0.0	2.7	0.3	19.9	58.2	21.9	597	87.9	42.4	24.5
Florence city & MCD (Lyon)	39	39	0.0	28	96.4	0.0	0.0	0.0	3.6	7.2	82.1	10.7	13	100.0	30.8	7.7
Florida township (Yellow Medicine)	129	125	-3.1	133	100.0	0.0	0.0	0.0	0.0	19.6	61.7	18.8	58	87.9	34.5	13.8
Flowing township (Clay)	77	77	0.0	61	100.0	0.0	0.0	0.0	0.0	18.0	68.9	13.1	25	92.0	40.0	12.0
Foldahl township (Marshall)	62	62	0.0	60	100.0	0.0	0.0	0.0	0.0	30.0	56.6	13.3	23	91.3	43.5	13.0
Folden township (Otter Tail)	299	299	0.0	300	99.3	0.0	0.7	0.0	0.0	17.7	53.6	28.7	126	96.8	50.0	11.9
Foley city & MCD (Benton)	2,629	2,658	1.1	2,632	94.6	2.2	0.0	2.1	1.2	29.1	58.2	12.6	961	70.4	39.8	14.8
Folsom township (Traverse)	128	123	-3.9	80	100.0	0.0	0.0	0.0	0.0	16.3	43.9	40.0	38	92.1	55.3	26.3
Forada city & MCD (Douglas)	185	190	2.7	214	98.1	0.0	0.0	0.0	1.9	14.0	59.9	26.2	101	90.1	50.5	8.9
Ford township (Kanabec)	195	192	-1.5	170	94.1	0.0	0.0	4.7	1.2	19.5	61.2	19.4	67	94.0	56.7	16.4
Forest township (Becker)	77	79	2.6	148	95.9	0.0	0.0	4.1	0.0	13.6	58.2	28.4	66	95.5	28.8	42.4
Forest township (Rice)	1,233	1,253	1.6	1,249	96.8	0.0	0.0	0.6	2.6	21.4	66.0	12.8	433	91.5	36.0	29.6
Forest Area township (Lake of the Woods)	5	NA	NA	0	0.0	0.0	0.0	0.0	0.0	0.0	0.0	0.0	0	0.0	0.0	0.0
Forest City township (Meeker)	653	650	-0.5	608	93.1	0.0	0.0	1.0	5.9	28.1	56.1	16.0	225	89.8	44.4	15.6
Forest Lake city & MCD (Washington)	18,377	19,399	5.6	18,933	91.4	0.5	2.5	1.9	3.6	27.6	60.2	12.3	6,999	74.8	31.8	29.8
Foreston city & MCD (Mille Lacs)	533	521	-2.3	628	95.1	1.0	1.3	2.2	0.5	32.9	61.8	5.4	193	72.0	49.2	11.9
Forest Prairie township (Meeker)	972	968	-0.4	1,008	97.7	0.0	0.0	1.7	0.6	27.4	56.4	16.4	365	89.0	59.2	10.7
Forestville township (Fillmore)	356	360	1.1	262	95.4	0.0	0.0	4.2	0.4	22.2	59.6	18.3	115	82.6	55.7	13.9
Fork township (Marshall)	10	10	0.0	6	100.0	0.0	0.0	0.0	0.0	0.0	0.0	100.0	4	100.0	100.0	0.0
Fortier township (Yellow Medicine)	99	96	-3.0	91	100.0	0.0	0.0	0.0	0.0	19.8	57.2	23.1	45	73.3	68.9	6.7
Fort Ripley city & MCD (Crow Wing)	69	69	0.0	109	96.3	0.0	1.8	1.8	0.0	33.0	53.2	13.8	45	95.6	48.9	11.1
Fort Ripley township (Crow Wing)	883	900	1.9	938	97.5	1.0	0.0	0.3	1.2	25.3	58.4	16.3	375	93.9	42.9	20.5
Fort Snelling UT (Hennepin)	149	NA	NA	147	55.8	24.5	0.0	12.9	6.8	0.0	85.0	15.0	133	0.0	56.4	23.3
Fosston city & MCD (Polk)	1,527	1,508	-1.2	1,723	94.0	0.2	1.2	1.7	2.8	25.3	50.8	24.0	748	60.7	48.7	21.1
Fossum township (Norman)	156	151	-3.2	175	90.9	0.0	3.4	5.7	0.0	23.5	62.8	13.7	70	97.1	32.9	18.6

1 May be of any race.

Table A. All Places — **Population and Housing**

STATE City, town, township, borough, or CDP (county if applicable)	Population				Race and Hispanic or Latino origin (percent), 2010–2014					Age (percent), 2010–2014			Households, 2010–2014			
	2010 census total population	2014 estimated population	Percent change 2010–2014	ACS total population estimate 2010–2014	White alone, not Hispanic or Latino	Black alone, not Hispanic or Latino	Asian alone, not Hispanic or Latino	All other races or 2 or more races, not Hispanic or Latino	Hispanic or Latino[1]	Under 18 years old	Age 18 to 64 years old	Age 65 years and older	Total occupied housing units	Percent owner occupied	High school diploma or less	Bachelor's degree or more
	1	2	3	4	5	6	7	8	9	10	11	12	13	14	15	16
MINNESOTA—Con.																
Foster township (Big Stone)	112	111	-0.9	124	100.0	0.0	0.0	0.0	0.0	15.3	45.8	38.7	58	100.0	46.6	12.1
Foster township (Faribault)	239	234	-2.1	212	100.0	0.0	0.0	0.0	0.0	18.0	60.4	21.7	100	99.0	61.0	12.0
Fountain city & MCD (Fillmore)	410	410	0.0	421	99.5	0.0	0.0	0.5	0.0	28.3	59.4	12.4	175	81.7	32.0	22.9
Fountain township (Fillmore)	315	318	1.0	274	74.8	3.6	0.0	0.0	21.5	16.4	64.6	19.0	111	86.5	55.0	18.9
Fountain Prairie township (Pipestone)	188	182	-3.2	184	100.0	0.0	0.0	0.0	0.0	32.0	51.1	16.8	61	86.9	63.9	11.5
Foxhome city & MCD (Wilkin)	116	115	-0.9	131	100.0	0.0	0.0	0.0	0.0	24.5	62.0	13.7	60	71.7	68.3	10.0
Foxhome township (Wilkin)	103	102	-1.0	119	94.1	0.0	0.0	0.0	5.9	36.9	56.3	6.7	35	94.3	22.9	17.1
Fox Lake township (Martin)	256	248	-3.1	241	94.6	0.0	2.1	3.3	0.0	14.2	63.5	22.4	105	86.7	43.8	12.4
Framnas township (Stevens)	305	308	1.0	286	100.0	0.0	0.0	0.0	0.0	21.3	58.1	20.3	108	97.2	37.0	29.6
Franconia township (Chisago)	1,805	1,827	1.2	1,808	96.3	2.2	0.0	0.4	1.1	18.9	66.7	14.3	584	94.5	34.4	27.7
Frankford township (Mower)	371	376	1.3	381	99.5	0.5	0.0	0.0	0.0	29.6	58.5	12.1	143	97.9	47.6	18.2
Franklin city & MCD (Renville)	510	483	-5.3	653	91.0	0.9	1.5	5.7	0.9	28.8	53.5	17.6	251	69.7	54.2	4.8
Franklin township (Wright)	2,759	2,848	3.2	2,807	97.8	0.0	0.7	0.4	1.1	23.3	57.4	19.3	1,075	98.7	39.3	25.5
Fraser township (Martin)...	304	296	-2.6	253	99.2	0.0	0.0	0.8	0.0	27.6	58.8	13.4	107	79.4	46.7	14.0
Frazee city & MCD (Becker)	1,350	1,374	1.8	1,250	84.6	2.8	2.3	9.6	0.6	19.8	59.6	20.6	560	67.3	56.6	13.8
Fredenberg township (St. Louis)	1,337	1,352	1.1	1,447	94.4	0.4	0.8	3.5	1.0	20.5	62.7	16.9	564	93.6	24.6	39.0
Freeborn city & MCD (Freeborn)	297	293	-1.3	299	95.0	0.0	0.0	0.7	4.3	28.7	53.4	17.7	113	84.1	39.8	17.7
Freeborn township (Freeborn)	267	264	-1.1	305	100.0	0.0	0.0	0.0	0.0	13.7	69.8	16.4	130	81.5	49.2	6.2
Freedom township (Waseca)	326	328	0.6	286	99.0	0.0	0.0	0.0	1.0	20.9	56.5	22.4	116	91.4	44.0	15.5
Freeland township (Lac qui Parle)	102	97	-4.9	106	100.0	0.0	0.0	0.0	0.0	16.9	62.3	20.8	43	100.0	55.8	27.9
Freeman township (Freeborn)	496	490	-1.2	525	95.2	0.0	1.0	1.7	2.1	22.5	57.9	19.6	188	92.6	59.6	14.9
Freeport city & MCD (Stearns)	632	656	3.8	582	99.7	0.0	0.0	0.0	0.3	19.4	60.5	20.1	258	90.7	54.7	10.9
Fremont township (Winona)	355	355	0.0	291	91.1	0.0	1.0	3.1	4.8	29.5	51.9	18.6	102	83.3	55.9	16.7
French township (St. Louis)	567	571	0.7	473	100.0	0.0	0.0	0.0	0.0	9.3	64.0	26.6	244	98.0	22.5	29.1
French Lake township (Wright)	1,172	1,209	3.2	1,079	98.4	0.0	0.0	0.4	1.2	19.8	64.9	15.5	401	90.0	51.6	23.4
Friberg township (Otter Tail)	809	802	-0.9	773	96.8	0.0	0.0	3.2	0.0	16.5	66.5	16.9	332	88.9	38.3	22.9
Fridley city & MCD (Anoka)	27,208	27,670	1.7	27,494	69.7	13.8	5.7	4.8	6.1	23.5	63.1	13.4	11,054	64.3	34.7	27.5
Friendship township (Yellow Medicine)	192	186	-3.1	179	99.4	0.0	0.0	0.0	0.6	12.9	66.0	21.2	78	84.6	57.7	7.7
Frohn township (Beltrami).	1,429	1,452	1.6	1,521	82.1	0.0	0.5	16.8	0.6	22.1	60.5	17.4	609	92.6	32.0	29.2
Frontenac CDP...............	282	NA	NA	194	100.0	0.0	0.0	0.0	0.0	13.9	59.3	26.8	108	94.4	60.2	15.7
Frost city & MCD (Faribault)	198	194	-2.0	220	85.5	0.0	7.7	0.0	6.8	20.9	64.5	14.5	99	84.8	46.5	7.1
Fulda city & MCD (Murray)	1,318	1,257	-4.6	1,301	93.7	0.3	1.3	3.0	1.7	18.9	56.2	25.0	588	69.7	45.9	12.1
Funkley city & MCD (Beltrami)	5	5	0.0	3	100.0	0.0	0.0	0.0	0.0	0.0	100.0	0.0	3	100.0	100.0	0.0
Gail Lake township (Crow Wing)	97	99	2.1	54	100.0	0.0	0.0	0.0	0.0	14.9	39.1	46.3	30	90.0	73.3	10.0
Galena township (Martin) .	246	240	-2.4	190	100.0	0.0	0.0	0.0	0.0	23.2	57.4	19.5	74	93.2	40.5	17.6
Gales township (Redwood)	137	132	-3.6	130	100.0	0.0	0.0	0.0	0.0	27.8	43.9	28.5	50	96.0	56.0	4.0
Garden township (Polk)	212	215	1.4	174	98.9	0.0	0.0	1.1	0.0	12.1	59.2	28.7	81	92.6	45.7	23.5
Garden City CDP.............	255	NA	NA	318	100.0	0.0	0.0	0.0	0.0	27.1	65.5	7.5	121	90.1	43.8	24.8
Garden City township (Blue Earth)	689	695	0.9	797	99.5	0.0	0.0	0.5	0.0	24.8	63.6	11.5	305	90.8	39.7	30.2
Garfield city & MCD (Douglas)	354	345	-2.5	233	94.8	3.0	1.3	0.4	0.4	20.5	63.6	15.9	109	84.4	43.1	15.6
Garfield township (Lac qui Parle)	145	138	-4.8	135	100.0	0.0	0.0	0.0	0.0	20.0	63.8	16.3	56	100.0	30.4	23.2
Garfield township (Polk)....	461	469	1.7	488	89.5	0.0	0.0	5.1	5.3	30.1	54.8	15.0	170	94.7	40.6	21.8
Garnes township (Red Lake)	190	189	-0.5	186	97.8	2.2	0.0	0.0	0.0	22.1	65.2	12.9	69	100.0	55.1	21.7
Garrison city & MCD (Crow Wing)	208	203	-2.4	197	94.9	0.0	0.0	0.5	4.6	15.2	56.3	28.4	97	74.2	59.8	15.5
Garrison township (Crow Wing)........................	756	772	2.1	769	93.6	0.0	0.1	4.9	1.3	17.6	53.8	28.6	339	92.3	40.1	23.6
Garvin city & MCD (Lyon).	135	135	0.0	120	99.2	0.0	0.0	0.8	0.0	25.8	66.6	7.5	50	88.0	66.0	20.0
Gary city & MCD (Norman)	214	208	-2.8	222	91.4	4.1	0.0	4.5	0.0	28.5	56.0	15.8	89	88.8	55.1	11.2
Gaylord city & MCD (Sibley)	2,305	2,253	-2.3	2,171	81.5	0.6	1.1	0.9	15.9	22.3	56.4	21.2	920	71.1	57.1	18.0
Gem Lake city & MCD (Ramsey)	393	447	13.7	350	91.1	0.0	7.4	0.0	1.4	23.5	60.2	16.3	131	86.3	26.7	36.6
Geneva city & MCD (Freeborn)	555	548	-1.3	453	98.5	0.0	0.0	0.0	1.5	27.5	48.3	24.1	162	90.1	48.8	9.3
Geneva township (Freeborn)	421	416	-1.2	522	99.4	0.0	0.0	0.0	0.6	28.0	61.6	10.3	169	87.6	49.1	15.4

1 May be of any race.

Table A.   All Places — **Population and Housing**

STATE City, town, township, borough, or CDP (county if applicable)	2010 census total population	2014 estimated population	Percent change 2010–2014	ACS total population estimate 2010–2014	White alone, not Hispanic or Latino	Black alone, not Hispanic or Latino	Asian alone, not Hispanic or Latino	All other races or 2 or more races, not Hispanic or Latino	Hispanic or Latino[1]	Under 18 years old	Age 18 to 64 years old	Age 65 years and older	Total occupied housing units	Percent owner occupied	High school diploma or less	Bachelor's degree or more
	1	2	3	4	5	6	7	8	9	10	11	12	13	14	15	16
MINNESOTA—Con.																
Gennessee township (Kandiyohi)	413	413	0.0	428	99.1	0.0	0.0	0.5	0.5	21.7	66.8	11.4	175	90.3	38.3	13.7
Genola city & MCD (Morrison)	75	74	-1.3	82	81.7	0.0	0.0	0.0	18.3	25.6	61.0	13.4	31	77.4	58.1	3.2
Gentilly township (Polk)	280	284	1.4	325	96.0	0.0	0.0	0.0	4.0	27.6	61.5	10.8	126	98.4	47.6	10.3
Georgetown city & MCD (Clay)	129	129	0.0	102	88.2	0.0	0.0	0.0	11.8	32.3	58.8	8.8	31	100.0	35.5	25.8
Georgetown township (Clay)	156	159	1.9	137	95.6	0.0	0.0	3.6	0.7	21.9	59.0	19.0	60	100.0	35.0	35.0
Germania township (Todd)	500	489	-2.2	472	98.5	0.0	0.2	0.0	1.3	35.4	51.3	13.3	152	87.5	63.2	9.9
Germantown township (Cottonwood)	207	206	-0.5	194	96.4	0.0	0.0	0.0	3.6	30.9	53.5	15.5	68	86.8	60.3	22.1
Gervais township (Red Lake)	226	224	-0.9	219	87.2	0.0	0.0	11.0	1.8	27.9	53.8	18.3	80	88.8	50.0	15.0
Getty township (Stearns) ..	376	386	2.7	400	90.5	0.0	0.0	4.3	5.3	37.1	55.7	7.5	111	83.8	51.4	3.6
Gheen UT (St. Louis)	18	18	0.0	20	100.0	0.0	0.0	0.0	0.0	0.0	50.0	50.0	10	100.0	0.0	0.0
Ghent city & MCD (Lyon)..	370	367	-0.8	317	89.0	0.9	0.0	1.3	8.8	31.5	58.7	9.8	122	90.2	28.7	23.8
Gibbon city & MCD (Sibley)	772	754	-2.3	879	88.3	1.6	0.1	4.8	5.2	30.9	54.6	14.6	331	78.9	47.7	16.0
Gilbert city & MCD (St. Louis)	1,799	1,799	0.0	1,823	97.9	1.6	0.0	0.1	0.3	19.2	66.5	14.3	859	76.3	38.9	17.8
Gilchrist township (Pope)..	194	197	1.5	190	94.2	0.0	1.6	4.2	0.0	18.4	55.8	25.8	96	91.7	35.4	29.2
Gillford township (Wabasha)	572	567	-0.9	541	98.0	0.0	0.4	0.0	1.7	26.2	60.6	13.3	190	84.7	52.1	26.3
Gilman city & MCD (Benton)	223	224	0.4	184	95.1	0.0	0.0	0.0	4.9	28.7	59.1	12.0	78	84.6	32.1	12.8
Gilmanton township (Benton)	808	822	1.7	732	97.7	0.0	1.9	0.0	0.4	23.9	61.5	14.8	297	94.3	48.5	20.5
Girard township (Otter Tail)	736	731	-0.7	790	98.2	0.8	0.0	0.6	0.4	23.0	46.6	30.4	314	95.2	31.5	45.9
Glasgow township (Wabasha)	247	245	-0.8	156	99.4	0.0	0.0	0.6	0.0	19.2	69.8	10.9	62	88.7	38.7	17.7
Glen township (Aitkin)	446	437	-2.0	479	99.2	0.8	0.0	0.0	0.0	14.6	49.3	36.1	240	90.8	53.3	20.4
Glencoe city & MCD (McLeod)	5,631	5,525	-1.9	5,575	83.3	0.6	0.0	0.1	16.0	26.3	54.8	18.7	2,193	70.5	43.0	18.9
Glencoe township (McLeod)	491	482	-1.8	404	97.0	0.0	0.0	1.0	2.0	14.4	67.2	18.6	189	91.0	58.2	10.6
Glendorado township (Benton)	762	780	2.4	724	97.7	0.0	0.0	1.5	0.8	22.6	63.2	14.1	272	86.0	46.7	15.1
Glenville city & MCD (Freeborn)	643	635	-1.2	606	94.9	0.0	1.3	0.5	3.3	22.6	60.7	16.7	265	83.8	50.2	13.6
Glenwood city & MCD (Pope)	2,564	2,528	-1.4	2,530	100.0	0.0	0.0	0.0	0.0	22.6	51.3	26.0	1,185	56.5	46.3	21.6
Glenwood township (Pope)	1,058	1,041	-1.6	906	99.1	0.0	0.0	0.0	0.9	16.1	61.0	22.7	411	93.7	30.7	29.4
Glyndon city & MCD (Clay)	1,392	1,386	-0.4	1,553	86.0	0.5	0.0	3.3	10.2	34.5	57.7	7.8	519	91.9	41.0	19.8
Glyndon township (Clay)...	280	286	2.1	315	98.4	0.0	0.0	0.0	1.6	23.8	68.3	7.9	108	90.7	30.6	41.7
Gnesen township (St. Louis)	1,683	1,718	2.1	1,626	94.9	0.7	2.7	1.4	0.3	19.6	65.1	15.3	704	93.0	31.3	40.6
Godfrey township (Polk) ...	313	317	1.3	369	97.3	0.0	0.0	1.9	0.8	19.8	57.5	22.8	154	95.5	38.3	22.1
Golden Valley city & MCD (Hennepin)	20,351	20,866	2.5	20,683	80.4	7.9	5.4	4.0	2.3	20.2	59.8	20.0	8,467	76.1	19.0	57.1
Golden Valley township (Roseau)	189	191	1.1	159	97.5	0.6	0.0	1.9	0.0	10.0	76.7	13.2	77	88.3	64.9	5.2
Gonvick city & MCD (Clearwater)	282	286	1.4	223	84.8	0.0	0.0	10.8	4.5	27.8	50.2	22.0	100	78.0	52.0	7.0
Good Hope township (Itasca)	99	100	1.0	198	98.5	0.5	0.0	1.0	0.0	25.7	57.6	16.7	74	97.3	66.2	10.8
Good Hope township (Norman)	43	42	-2.3	46	95.7	4.3	0.0	0.0	0.0	26.1	52.1	21.7	17	82.4	29.4	11.8
Goodhue city & MCD (Goodhue)	1,176	1,178	0.2	1,135	89.0	0.3	0.0	0.6	10.1	37.6	52.1	10.4	375	80.5	40.3	17.6
Goodhue township (Goodhue)	525	528	0.6	511	91.4	0.2	0.0	0.6	7.8	25.3	62.1	12.5	186	80.6	48.4	18.3
Goodland township (Itasca)	466	470	0.9	455	100.0	0.0	0.0	0.0	0.0	18.9	62.8	18.2	191	96.3	31.4	22.0
Goodridge city & MCD (Pennington)	132	131	-0.8	122	86.1	2.5	0.0	0.0	11.5	18.0	66.4	15.6	60	95.0	56.7	6.7
Goodridge township (Pennington)	79	79	0.0	50	90.0	0.0	0.0	0.0	10.0	40.0	50.0	10.0	20	90.0	35.0	0.0
Good Thunder city & MCD (Blue Earth)	583	580	-0.5	509	96.7	0.0	2.0	0.0	1.4	15.6	70.1	14.3	222	88.3	46.8	20.3
Goodview city & MCD (Winona)	4,025	4,020	-0.1	4,019	96.0	0.0	0.0	0.8	3.2	20.0	63.6	16.4	1,749	67.8	28.7	30.9
Goose Prairie township (Clay)	175	178	1.7	194	95.9	0.0	1.0	0.0	3.1	30.4	59.4	10.3	65	95.4	52.3	23.1
Gordon township (Todd) ...	659	646	-2.0	683	98.8	0.0	0.3	0.7	0.1	22.0	59.6	18.6	273	90.8	41.8	16.5
Gorman township (Otter Tail)	465	461	-0.9	445	98.9	0.0	0.0	1.1	0.0	22.1	57.4	20.4	181	95.6	53.6	16.6
Gorton township (Grant)...	49	49	0.0	29	100.0	0.0	0.0	0.0	0.0	17.2	72.4	10.3	15	86.7	46.7	13.3
Gould township (Cass)	224	225	0.4	201	40.8	0.0	5.5	50.2	3.5	19.0	62.3	18.9	91	74.7	54.9	9.9
Grace township (Chippewa)	95	93	-2.1	132	100.0	0.0	0.0	0.0	0.0	17.4	57.5	25.0	52	94.2	48.1	28.8
Graceville city & MCD (Big Stone)	577	565	-2.1	601	99.0	0.3	0.3	0.0	0.3	19.6	47.9	32.4	271	74.9	58.3	11.1
Graceville township (Big Stone)	197	193	-2.0	146	100.0	0.0	0.0	0.0	0.0	39.7	46.6	13.7	35	68.6	68.6	0.0
Grafton township (Sibley) .	238	234	-1.7	259	97.7	0.0	0.0	0.0	2.3	15.1	70.3	14.7	101	87.1	56.4	12.9
Graham township (Benton)	582	595	2.2	572	96.9	0.0	0.0	1.0	2.1	28.7	55.7	15.6	204	82.4	53.9	15.7

1 May be of any race.

Table A. All Places — **Population and Housing**

STATE City, town, township, borough, or CDP (county if applicable)	2010 census total population	2014 estimated population	Percent change 2010–2014	ACS total population estimate 2010–2014	White alone, not Hispanic or Latino	Black alone, not Hispanic or Latino	Asian alone, not Hispanic or Latino	All other races or 2 or more races, not Hispanic or Latino	Hispanic or Latino[1]	Under 18 years old	Age 18 to 64 years old	Age 65 years and older	Total occupied housing units	Percent owner occupied	High school diploma or less	Bachelor's degree or more
	1	2	3	4	5	6	7	8	9	10	11	12	13	14	15	16
MINNESOTA—Con.																
Graham Lakes township (Nobles)	218	220	0.9	201	100.0	0.0	0.0	0.0	0.0	21.9	65.8	12.4	78	94.9	51.3	23.1
Granada city & MCD (Martin)	303	295	-2.6	297	99.0	0.3	0.0	0.7	0.0	20.9	63.7	15.5	132	64.4	65.2	9.8
Granby township (Nicollet)	246	242	-1.6	203	100.0	0.0	0.0	0.0	0.0	19.3	61.5	19.2	84	90.5	50.0	19.0
Grand Forks township (Polk)	179	181	1.1	169	94.7	0.0	0.0	0.0	5.3	20.2	60.3	19.5	63	88.9	38.1	17.5
Grand Lake township (St. Louis)	2,780	2,800	0.7	2,788	95.2	0.9	0.4	2.3	1.2	22.0	63.7	14.3	1,039	92.3	34.8	31.0
Grand Marais city & MCD (Cook)	1,350	1,341	-0.7	1,037	91.9	0.3	0.3	5.3	2.2	18.9	54.8	26.2	540	60.6	38.3	35.4
Grand Meadow city & MCD (Mower)	1,139	1,146	0.6	1,159	93.3	5.0	0.9	0.3	0.5	29.8	52.3	18.0	435	75.4	51.0	9.0
Grand Meadow township (Mower)	306	308	0.7	219	100.0	0.0	0.0	0.0	0.0	17.8	68.5	13.7	87	78.2	54.0	20.7
Grand Plain township (Marshall)	55	55	0.0	47	100.0	0.0	0.0	0.0	0.0	38.3	42.5	19.1	16	93.8	43.8	50.0
Grand Portage UT (Cook)	565	570	0.9	549	30.8	0.0	1.8	67.2	0.2	30.7	57.4	11.7	254	39.8	61.0	5.5
Grand Prairie township (Nobles)	206	208	1.0	243	93.8	0.0	0.8	0.0	5.3	27.5	52.6	19.8	87	88.5	49.4	14.9
Grand Rapids city & MCD (Itasca)	10,869	11,097	2.1	10,950	95.3	0.6	0.4	3.5	0.3	22.1	56.8	21.0	4,616	61.2	36.5	25.0
Grandview township (Lyon)	288	287	-0.3	298	98.7	0.0	0.7	0.7	0.0	27.5	63.2	9.4	105	84.8	25.7	23.8
Grange township (Pipestone)	203	199	-2.0	192	97.9	0.0	0.0	1.6	0.5	20.4	61.3	18.2	80	95.0	52.5	15.0
Granite township (Morrison)	481	480	-0.2	501	97.6	0.4	0.0	1.4	0.6	38.2	52.2	9.8	145	96.6	65.5	6.9
Granite Falls township (Chippewa)	253	249	-1.6	245	98.0	0.0	0.0	0.4	1.6	21.2	62.4	16.3	94	86.2	46.8	14.9
Granite Falls city	2,897	2,796	-3.5	2,493	86.4	0.1	0.6	7.9	5.0	21.7	55.5	22.8	1,172	66.7	43.5	20.0
Granite Falls city (Chippewa)	853	825	-3.3	719	91.9	0.0	1.7	6.4	0.0	15.9	61.7	22.4	404	61.1	32.2	22.0
Granite Falls city (Yellow Medicine)	2,044	1,971	-3.6	1,774	84.2	0.1	0.2	8.5	7.0	23.9	52.9	22.9	768	69.7	49.5	18.9
Granite Ledge township (Benton)	743	756	1.7	728	93.7	0.0	2.1	2.3	1.9	18.0	61.0	21.0	289	95.2	61.2	11.8
Granite Rock township (Redwood)	225	218	-3.1	195	100.0	0.0	0.0	0.0	0.0	24.5	65.1	10.3	75	86.7	28.0	22.7
Grant city & MCD (Washington)	4,082	4,142	1.5	4,122	97.0	0.1	0.3	0.8	1.9	21.6	61.7	16.6	1,501	96.7	15.3	46.4
Grant Valley township (Beltrami)	2,029	2,042	0.6	2,427	89.7	0.5	0.5	7.8	1.5	28.5	61.4	10.3	885	78.9	34.6	23.1
Granville township (Kittson)	83	81	-2.4	94	95.7	0.0	0.0	0.0	4.3	26.6	64.9	8.5	33	97.0	33.3	24.2
Grass Lake township (Kanabec)	1,038	1,017	-2.0	1,031	94.1	0.0	2.1	3.4	0.4	23.5	61.5	14.9	389	87.7	58.6	11.6
Grasston city & MCD (Kanabec)	158	156	-1.3	241	95.9	0.8	0.0	3.3	0.0	30.7	56.0	13.3	72	90.3	69.4	2.8
Grattan township (Itasca)	44	44	0.0	60	78.3	3.3	0.0	0.0	18.3	56.6	36.7	6.7	12	58.3	8.3	8.3
Gray township (Pipestone)	220	215	-2.3	227	100.0	0.0	0.0	0.0	0.0	26.0	56.3	17.6	91	97.8	34.1	27.5
Great Bend township (Cottonwood)	298	297	-0.3	304	94.1	0.0	3.3	1.3	1.3	25.0	57.6	17.4	115	95.7	50.4	15.7
Great Scott township (St. Louis)	392	393	0.3	319	89.0	0.9	5.0	2.2	2.8	19.7	58.4	21.9	141	98.6	31.2	24.8
Greenbush township (Mille Lacs)	1,293	1,284	-0.7	1,249	91.7	0.8	0.4	3.0	4.1	24.4	59.5	16.1	459	86.3	43.8	18.7
Greenbush city & MCD (Roseau)	719	718	-0.1	825	97.1	1.2	0.6	1.1	0.0	26.2	53.5	20.1	324	68.5	41.7	14.8
Greenfield city & MCD (Hennepin)	2,771	2,885	4.1	2,830	98.0	0.0	0.3	1.3	0.4	26.7	63.3	10.0	988	91.4	32.7	39.3
Greenfield township (Wabasha)	1,349	1,340	-0.7	1,411	99.1	0.0	0.0	0.0	0.9	18.3	57.4	24.5	597	96.6	34.8	20.1
Green Isle city & MCD (Sibley)	559	541	-3.2	512	93.9	0.0	0.0	0.8	5.3	27.5	56.9	15.6	204	99.0	51.5	11.3
Green Isle township (Sibley)	524	516	-1.5	551	94.9	1.1	0.0	0.2	3.8	23.5	62.1	14.5	209	95.2	49.8	13.4
Green Lake township (Kandiyohi)	1,576	1,587	0.7	1,541	97.8	0.0	0.0	0.0	2.2	18.8	59.8	21.3	625	95.4	25.4	36.8
Greenleaf township (Meeker)	676	673	-0.4	814	92.9	0.0	1.5	0.0	5.7	19.2	64.5	16.3	328	86.9	46.6	23.8
Green Meadow township (Norman)	108	105	-2.8	70	100.0	0.0	0.0	0.0	0.0	25.7	48.6	25.7	23	95.7	52.2	13.0
Green Prairie township (Morrison)	748	746	-0.3	737	96.7	0.0	0.0	2.0	1.2	26.4	65.3	8.0	293	99.3	44.7	12.6
Greenvale township (Dakota)	803	822	2.4	847	98.0	0.4	0.0	1.4	0.2	24.5	57.4	18.2	283	94.0	33.2	38.2
Green Valley township (Becker)	376	380	1.1	296	99.0	0.0	0.0	0.3	0.7	22.9	57.7	19.3	125	93.6	47.2	10.4
Greenwald city & MCD (Stearns)	222	223	0.5	216	99.5	0.0	0.0	0.0	0.5	11.6	68.5	19.9	106	90.6	56.6	5.7
Greenway township (Itasca)	1,939	1,942	0.2	1,847	90.1	0.3	0.0	8.8	0.8	21.5	60.7	17.9	844	83.4	47.6	10.5
Greenwood township (Clearwater)	83	84	1.2	106	97.2	0.0	0.0	2.8	0.0	25.5	52.9	21.7	42	95.2	83.3	2.4
Greenwood city & MCD (Hennepin)	690	712	3.2	740	94.5	0.3	2.3	0.7	2.3	14.0	69.8	16.2	327	90.5	9.8	69.7
Greenwood township (St. Louis)	939	956	1.8	1,086	72.0	0.0	1.1	25.0	1.9	12.2	48.8	39.0	529	89.4	25.1	33.3
Gregory township (Mahnomen)	74	76	2.7	54	81.5	0.0	0.0	18.5	0.0	16.7	64.8	18.5	25	100.0	56.0	20.0

1 May be of any race.

Table A. All Places — **Population and Housing**

STATE City, town, township, borough, or CDP (county if applicable)	2010 census total population	2014 estimated population	Percent change 2010–2014	ACS total population estimate 2010–2014	White alone, not Hispanic or Latino	Black alone, not Hispanic or Latino	Asian alone, not Hispanic or Latino	All other races or 2 or more races, not Hispanic or Latino	Hispanic or Latino[1]	Under 18 years old	Age 18 to 64 years old	Age 65 years and older	Total occupied housing units	Percent owner occupied	High school diploma or less	Bachelor's degree or more
	1	2	3	4	5	6	7	8	9	10	11	12	13	14	15	16
MINNESOTA—Con.																
Grey Cloud Island township (Washington)..	295	298	1.0	235	88.9	0.4	0.9	9.4	0.4	8.6	64.0	27.7	114	87.7	44.7	29.8
Grey Eagle city & MCD (Todd)	348	333	-4.3	453	96.9	0.0	2.0	1.1	0.0	29.4	54.1	16.6	179	78.2	51.4	10.6
Grey Eagle township (Todd)	638	623	-2.4	579	94.8	0.0	0.3	3.3	1.6	15.9	58.3	25.9	265	94.7	51.7	17.7
Grimstad township (Roseau)	146	148	1.4	139	100.0	0.0	0.0	0.0	0.0	32.4	53.3	14.4	46	84.8	69.6	6.5
Grove township (Stearns).	493	508	3.0	475	98.3	0.0	0.0	0.4	1.3	30.4	58.8	10.9	166	93.4	57.2	11.4
Grove City city & MCD (Meeker)	635	619	-2.5	722	95.4	0.0	0.0	0.0	4.6	33.0	54.6	12.2	272	72.8	59.6	6.3
Grove Lake township (Pope)	255	257	0.8	215	89.8	3.3	0.9	1.4	4.7	21.4	56.5	22.3	92	80.4	62.0	8.7
Grove Park-Tilden township	282	285	1.1	333	94.9	0.0	0.0	4.5	0.6	21.3	60.0	18.6	123	95.9	56.1	17.1
Grygla city & MCD (Marshall)	221	218	-1.4	186	88.7	0.0	0.0	8.6	2.7	19.4	64.1	16.7	92	65.2	55.4	20.7
Gudrid township (Lake of the Woods)	219	NA	NA	246	100.0	0.0	0.0	0.0	0.0	11.0	81.4	7.7	99	100.0	43.4	50.5
Gully city & MCD (Polk)	66	66	0.0	85	100.0	0.0	0.0	0.0	0.0	22.3	60.1	17.6	45	64.4	57.8	8.9
Gully township (Polk)........	136	135	-0.7	118	90.7	3.4	0.0	5.9	0.0	33.0	54.1	12.7	47	91.5	34.0	44.7
Guthrie township (Hubbard)	555	550	-0.9	547	95.1	0.0	0.0	4.9	0.0	27.3	61.1	11.7	208	92.3	35.1	31.3
Hackensack city & MCD (Cass)	313	310	-1.0	329	79.6	0.0	3.6	14.3	2.4	21.9	60.4	17.9	164	36.6	60.4	12.2
Hadley city & MCD (Murray)	61	59	-3.3	51	100.0	0.0	0.0	0.0	0.0	13.7	54.9	31.4	25	96.0	48.0	0.0
Hagali township (Beltrami)	370	370	0.0	326	93.6	0.0	0.0	1.5	4.9	22.1	60.5	17.5	134	94.8	29.1	20.1
Hagen township (Clay)	154	157	1.9	213	95.8	0.0	0.0	2.3	1.9	33.3	55.8	10.8	74	77.0	48.6	13.5
Halden township (St. Louis)	129	129	0.0	129	100.0	0.0	0.0	0.0	0.0	21.0	56.8	22.5	57	87.7	64.9	8.8
Hale township (McLeod)...	942	925	-1.8	856	98.8	0.5	0.0	0.0	0.7	15.9	66.6	17.4	356	90.7	60.1	8.7
Hallock city & MCD (Kittson)	981	954	-2.8	883	95.1	0.3	1.6	0.1	2.8	15.9	53.4	30.8	404	78.2	35.1	27.5
Hallock township (Kittson)	104	101	-2.9	133	100.0	0.0	0.0	0.0	0.0	42.8	44.3	12.8	37	100.0	10.8	67.6
Halma city & MCD (Kittson)	61	60	-1.6	56	94.6	0.0	0.0	5.4	0.0	19.7	59.0	21.4	27	100.0	37.0	22.2
Halstad city & MCD (Norman)	597	574	-3.9	598	91.8	0.0	0.0	5.7	2.5	21.7	52.9	25.3	240	68.3	54.2	15.4
Halstad township (Norman)	108	105	-2.8	96	91.7	0.0	0.0	0.0	8.3	16.7	63.8	19.8	38	100.0	28.9	39.5
Hamburg city & MCD (Carver)	513	520	1.4	500	95.8	0.0	0.0	2.0	2.2	22.6	66.0	11.4	204	84.8	52.0	14.2
Hamden township (Becker)	206	207	0.5	219	95.4	0.0	0.0	4.6	0.0	26.0	67.2	6.8	88	97.7	33.0	13.6
Ham Lake city & MCD (Anoka)	15,296	15,888	3.9	15,565	92.2	0.4	2.0	2.1	3.3	26.2	62.5	11.3	5,277	92.8	30.6	35.1
Hamlin township (Lac qui Parle)	165	157	-4.8	170	99.4	0.0	0.0	0.6	0.0	22.4	58.3	19.4	73	78.1	46.6	21.9
Hammer township (Yellow Medicine)	196	190	-3.1	216	99.1	0.0	0.9	0.0	0.0	23.6	58.2	18.1	85	96.5	37.6	32.9
Hammond township (Polk)	44	44	0.0	53	66.0	0.0	0.0	34.0	0.0	33.9	47.2	18.9	15	60.0	33.3	0.0
Hammond city & MCD (Wabasha)	132	135	2.3	87	95.4	4.6	0.0	0.0	0.0	19.5	75.6	4.6	34	61.8	44.1	5.9
Hampden township (Kittson)	38	37	-2.6	40	100.0	0.0	0.0	0.0	0.0	32.5	47.5	20.0	14	78.6	21.4	57.1
Hampton city & MCD (Dakota)	687	691	0.6	791	91.5	0.0	0.6	4.6	3.3	34.7	63.2	2.0	278	72.3	43.5	14.4
Hampton township (Dakota)	905	923	2.0	932	94.0	0.0	4.7	1.1	0.2	19.2	67.2	13.6	335	87.8	40.3	22.1
Hamre township (Beltrami)	13	13	0.0	13	100.0	0.0	0.0	0.0	0.0	23.1	69.3	7.7	8	37.5	37.5	0.0
Hancock township (Carver)	345	350	1.4	328	92.1	0.0	0.6	0.0	7.3	18.2	65.3	16.5	136	85.3	51.5	14.0
Hancock city & MCD (Stevens)	765	758	-0.9	846	85.6	0.0	3.9	5.6	5.0	30.6	60.8	8.5	284	71.8	35.2	17.3
Hangaard township (Clearwater)	5	5	0.0	6	0.0	0.0	0.0	50.0	50.0	0.0	100.0	0.0	3	0.0	100.0	0.0
Hanley Falls city & MCD (Yellow Medicine)	304	295	-3.0	296	73.3	0.0	0.0	1.4	25.3	36.8	54.8	8.4	101	74.3	57.4	7.9
Hanover city	2,938	3,182	8.3	2,930	94.5	0.1	0.9	2.5	2.0	27.6	67.1	5.2	1,044	95.9	17.1	46.2
Hanover city (Hennepin)...	609	661	8.5	547	89.9	0.0	0.9	3.3	5.9	30.4	59.3	10.4	186	97.3	26.3	51.6
Hanover city (Wright)........	2,329	2,521	8.2	2,383	95.6	0.1	0.9	2.3	1.1	27.1	68.9	4.0	858	95.6	15.2	45.0
Hanska city & MCD (Brown)	402	381	-5.2	388	99.2	0.0	0.0	0.5	0.0	22.9	60.8	16.2	172	81.4	56.4	12.8
Hansonville township (Lincoln)	90	88	-2.2	84	100.0	0.0	0.0	0.0	0.0	21.5	72.6	6.0	34	73.5	70.6	5.9
Hantho township (Lac qui Parle)	105	100	-4.8	109	99.1	0.0	0.0	0.9	0.0	18.4	56.8	24.8	47	78.7	14.9	34.0
Harding city & MCD (Morrison)	125	126	0.8	137	100.0	0.0	0.0	0.0	0.0	27.0	60.4	12.4	38	81.6	68.4	5.3
Hardwick city & MCD (Rock)	198	195	-1.5	166	94.0	0.0	0.0	5.4	0.6	19.8	56.5	23.5	73	78.1	63.0	8.2
Harmony city & MCD (Fillmore)	1,020	997	-2.3	1,014	97.0	0.5	0.0	0.5	2.0	15.7	51.4	32.9	492	67.3	51.4	20.3
Harmony township (Fillmore)	387	393	1.6	388	100.0	0.0	0.0	0.0	0.0	24.2	61.7	14.2	152	89.5	48.0	19.1
Harris city & MCD (Chisago)	1,132	1,127	-0.4	999	94.9	0.7	0.0	2.6	1.8	27.1	57.7	15.1	389	88.2	45.0	14.1
Harris township (Itasca)....	3,253	3,289	1.1	3,266	97.4	0.2	0.3	0.8	1.3	20.1	65.9	14.0	1,269	92.4	27.7	33.3
Harrison township (Kandiyohi)	576	578	0.3	588	99.5	0.0	0.0	0.5	0.0	14.1	62.7	23.1	268	89.6	39.2	17.9

1 May be of any race.

Table A. All Places — **Population and Housing**

STATE City, town, township, borough, or CDP (county if applicable)	Population 2010 census total population	2014 estimated population	Percent change 2010–2014	ACS total population estimate 2010–2014	Race and Hispanic or Latino origin (percent), 2010–2014 White alone, not Hispanic or Latino	Black alone, not Hispanic or Latino	Asian alone, not Hispanic or Latino	All other races or 2 or more races, not Hispanic or Latino	Hispanic or Latino[1]	Age (percent), 2010–2014 Under 18 years old	Age 18 to 64	Age 65 years and older	Households, 2010–2014 Total occupied housing units	Percent owner occupied	Householders by level of education (percent) High school diploma or less	Bachelor's degree or more
	1	2	3	4	5	6	7	8	9	10	11	12	13	14	15	16
MINNESOTA—Con.																
Hart township (Winona)....	357	355	-0.6	264	100.0	0.0	0.0	0.0	0.0	20.1	66.1	13.6	100	83.0	46.0	12.0
Hartford township (Todd) ..	662	648	-2.1	760	99.6	0.0	0.0	0.0	0.4	32.7	55.3	11.8	259	90.3	52.1	12.0
Hart Lake township (Hubbard).....................	509	505	-0.8	521	86.0	0.0	0.2	10.4	3.5	27.3	54.2	18.6	205	78.5	40.0	22.4
Hartland city & MCD (Freeborn).....................	315	311	-1.3	316	98.1	0.6	0.6	0.0	0.6	25.9	56.1	18.0	123	78.9	39.8	22.8
Hartland township (Freeborn).....................	256	253	-1.2	214	100.0	0.0	0.0	0.0	0.0	25.7	56.6	17.8	72	93.1	43.1	20.8
Harvey township (Meeker)	374	372	-0.5	347	100.0	0.0	0.0	0.0	0.0	21.8	64.0	14.1	134	89.6	56.7	14.9
Hassan Valley township (McLeod).....................	691	678	-1.9	744	96.1	1.5	0.0	2.4	0.0	28.5	55.9	15.7	262	89.7	48.9	16.0
Hastings city..................	22,174	22,566	1.8	22,355	92.5	1.1	0.6	2.0	3.8	23.1	63.3	13.6	8,635	74.8	36.5	27.5
Hastings city (Dakota)	22,174	22,564	1.8	22,355	92.5	1.1	0.6	2.0	3.8	23.1	63.3	13.6	8,635	74.8	36.5	27.5
Hastings city (Washington)	0	2	0.0	0	0.0	0.0	0.0	0.0	0.0	0.0	0.0	0.0	0	0.0	0.0	0.0
Hatfield city & MCD (Pipestone).....................	59	57	-3.4	33	90.9	0.0	0.0	6.1	3.0	21.2	51.6	27.3	16	81.3	68.8	0.0
Haugen township (Aitkin)..	177	172	-2.8	138	100.0	0.0	0.0	0.0	0.0	1.4	55.0	43.5	79	94.9	41.8	13.9
Havana township (Steele).	570	570	0.0	628	87.9	0.0	2.5	0.8	8.8	24.8	55.8	19.4	235	86.8	61.3	13.6
Havelock township (Chippewa).....................	181	176	-2.8	143	90.2	0.0	0.0	0.0	9.8	13.3	65.1	21.7	62	85.5	62.9	17.7
Haven township (Sherburne).................	1,986	2,034	2.4	1,923	97.7	0.8	0.0	1.3	0.1	18.7	66.2	15.2	718	96.5	28.4	30.8
Haverhill township (Olmsted).....................	1,483	1,522	2.6	1,555	90.2	0.3	5.3	1.9	2.4	22.4	63.5	14.1	569	96.7	13.7	61.9
Hawk Creek township (Renville).....................	201	193	-4.0	190	94.7	1.1	0.0	2.6	1.6	18.4	63.2	18.4	83	89.2	34.9	22.9
Hawley city & MCD (Clay)	2,067	2,098	1.5	1,894	97.2	0.8	0.0	1.1	0.8	30.2	54.4	15.4	784	68.5	43.9	20.3
Hawley township (Clay)	474	490	3.4	457	98.5	0.0	0.0	1.5	0.0	24.7	60.0	15.3	155	98.7	28.4	36.8
Hay Brook township (Kanabec).....................	252	246	-2.4	265	100.0	0.0	0.0	0.0	0.0	21.2	60.3	18.5	107	95.3	57.0	6.5
Hay Creek township (Goodhue).....................	882	890	0.9	856	95.4	0.0	0.4	3.5	0.7	23.5	66.2	10.6	301	92.7	47.2	29.6
Hayes township (Swift)	199	193	-3.0	203	99.0	0.0	0.0	0.0	1.0	22.7	63.1	14.3	81	87.7	43.2	21.0
Hayfield city & MCD (Dodge).....................	1,340	1,328	-0.9	1,242	91.1	4.9	0.7	1.5	1.8	26.8	54.6	18.4	492	74.4	48.6	19.1
Hayfield township (Dodge)	465	474	1.9	451	96.5	0.0	0.7	0.0	2.9	25.3	62.0	12.6	153	98.7	31.4	22.2
Hay Lake UT (St. Louis)....	83	83	0.0	64	100.0	0.0	0.0	0.0	0.0	0.0	87.5	12.5	37	100.0	21.6	27.0
Hayland township (Mille Lacs).....................	501	496	-1.0	549	97.3	0.0	0.0	0.0	2.7	26.8	63.1	10.2	202	92.6	51.0	15.8
Hayward city & MCD (Freeborn).....................	250	247	-1.2	246	87.8	0.0	6.9	0.0	5.3	15.0	64.8	20.3	112	88.4	46.4	12.5
Hayward township (Freeborn).....................	381	376	-1.3	403	95.0	2.0	0.0	0.5	2.5	20.0	58.4	21.6	150	92.7	54.0	20.0
Hazel Run city & MCD (Yellow Medicine)	63	61	-3.2	18	100.0	0.0	0.0	0.0	0.0	0.0	38.9	61.1	8	100.0	37.5	12.5
Hazel Run township (Yellow Medicine)	193	187	-3.1	257	86.4	0.0	0.8	12.8	0.0	28.4	57.7	14.0	93	84.9	37.6	25.8
Hazelton township (Aitkin)	842	827	-1.8	755	94.0	0.9	0.1	4.9	0.0	15.1	48.6	36.3	376	87.8	37.0	27.9
Hazelton township (Kittson).....................	104	102	-1.9	77	97.4	0.0	0.0	2.6	0.0	27.3	59.8	13.0	31	93.5	35.5	3.2
Hector city & MCD (Renville).....................	1,151	1,089	-5.4	1,051	94.0	0.2	0.0	0.0	5.8	22.8	58.3	18.7	452	75.7	48.5	11.1
Hector township (Renville)	226	217	-4.0	244	100.0	0.0	0.0	0.0	0.0	21.0	61.6	17.6	94	84.0	44.7	10.6
Hegbert township (Swift) ..	93	90	-3.2	87	87.4	0.0	0.0	6.9	5.7	17.2	56.2	26.4	39	84.6	64.1	17.9
Hegne township (Norman)	40	39	-2.5	57	82.5	0.0	0.0	17.5	0.0	22.8	45.6	31.6	24	100.0	62.5	25.0
Heidelberg city & MCD (Le Sueur).....................	122	124	1.6	107	97.2	0.0	0.0	0.0	2.8	17.7	75.6	6.5	42	92.9	31.0	47.6
Heier township (Mahnomen).................	143	146	2.1	154	90.3	0.0	0.0	9.7	0.0	25.9	66.7	7.1	55	85.5	47.3	3.6
Height of Land township (Becker).....................	673	687	2.1	636	96.7	0.0	0.0	1.7	1.6	23.4	56.9	19.7	254	87.8	50.0	15.7
Helen township (McLeod).	863	847	-1.9	929	97.7	0.0	0.3	0.5	1.4	22.9	61.3	15.8	344	96.8	50.0	21.2
Helena township (Scott) ...	1,640	1,725	5.2	1,734	97.9	0.0	0.2	1.1	0.8	31.6	58.2	10.1	523	93.9	34.8	29.6
Helga township (Hubbard)	1,401	1,479	5.6	1,453	92.3	1.2	0.5	4.2	1.9	25.9	63.6	10.3	509	93.3	28.5	32.0
Helgeland township (Polk)	54	54	0.0	57	100.0	0.0	0.0	0.0	0.0	17.6	65.0	17.5	21	90.5	23.8	52.4
Henderson city & MCD (Sibley).....................	886	874	-1.4	873	97.8	0.3	0.0	1.5	0.3	25.2	59.2	15.6	386	72.8	56.5	15.3
Henderson township (Sibley).....................	728	716	-1.6	667	97.8	0.3	0.0	0.6	1.3	19.9	63.7	16.2	280	82.5	50.7	21.1
Hendricks city & MCD (Lincoln).....................	713	694	-2.7	643	98.3	0.0	0.0	1.2	0.5	16.8	47.3	35.9	298	70.8	51.3	25.2
Hendricks township (Lincoln).....................	201	201	0.0	202	100.0	0.0	0.0	0.0	0.0	20.8	56.9	22.3	79	97.5	58.2	19.0
Hendrickson township (Hubbard).....................	314	316	0.6	340	91.5	0.0	0.0	1.8	6.8	32.4	50.6	17.1	128	94.5	48.4	15.6
Hendrum city & MCD (Norman).....................	307	298	-2.9	281	90.4	0.0	2.1	3.9	3.6	26.4	63.7	10.0	109	92.7	54.1	11.9
Hendrum township (Norman).....................	95	92	-3.2	100	88.0	0.0	2.0	10.0	0.0	16.0	69.0	15.0	46	100.0	47.8	23.9
Henning city & MCD (Otter Tail).....................	802	798	-0.5	860	95.5	1.4	0.0	1.5	1.6	23.6	42.8	33.6	384	63.8	49.0	13.3
Henning township (Otter Tail)	378	370	-2.1	367	96.7	0.0	1.4	1.4	0.5	17.7	64.8	17.4	160	95.6	41.9	18.1
Henrietta township (Hubbard).....................	1,479	1,478	-0.1	1,552	97.3	0.1	0.0	0.7	1.9	21.2	58.3	20.5	643	89.0	31.7	28.8
Henriette city & MCD (Pine).....................	71	70	-1.4	50	96.0	0.0	4.0	0.0	0.0	18.0	40.0	42.0	22	68.2	63.6	9.1
Henryville township (Renville).....................	208	199	-4.3	187	100.0	0.0	0.0	0.0	0.0	20.3	70.5	9.1	79	87.3	60.8	11.4
Hereim township (Roseau)	228	230	0.9	226	96.5	3.5	0.0	0.0	0.0	19.1	64.6	16.4	102	84.3	47.1	9.8

1 May be of any race.

Table A. All Places — Population and Housing

STATE City, town, township, borough, or CDP (county if applicable)	Population				Race and Hispanic or Latino origin (percent), 2010–2014					Age (percent), 2010–2014			Households, 2010–2014		Householders by level of education (percent)	
	2010 census total population	2014 estimated population	Percent change 2010–2014	ACS total population estimate 2010–2014	White alone, not Hispanic or Latino	Black alone, not Hispanic or Latino	Asian alone, not Hispanic or Latino	All other races or 2 or more races, not Hispanic or Latino	Hispanic or Latino[1]	Under 18 years old	Age 18 to 64 years old	Age 65 years and older	Total occupied housing units	Percent owner occupied	High school diploma or less	Bachelor's degree or more
	1	2	3	4	5	6	7	8	9	10	11	12	13	14	15	16

MINNESOTA—Con.

STATE City, town, township, borough, or CDP (county if applicable)	1	2	3	4	5	6	7	8	9	10	11	12	13	14	15	16
Herman city & MCD (Grant)	437	433	-0.9	452	89.8	0.0	2.0	6.4	1.8	23.5	50.6	25.9	213	80.8	51.6	14.6
Hermantown city & MCD (St. Louis)	9,414	9,704	3.1	9,588	93.0	2.2	0.3	2.8	1.9	19.6	64.8	15.5	3,452	71.3	35.6	35.8
Heron Lake city & MCD (Jackson)	698	689	-1.3	626	81.8	0.5	0.0	0.0	17.7	25.9	55.0	19.2	267	79.8	44.2	14.2
Heron Lake township (Jackson)	327	333	1.8	291	99.3	0.0	0.0	0.7	0.0	15.5	61.0	23.7	115	85.2	58.3	12.2
Hersey township (Nobles)	219	221	0.9	226	83.6	0.0	11.9	4.4	0.0	30.0	56.7	13.3	78	84.6	47.4	19.2
Hewitt city & MCD (Todd)	266	250	-6.0	217	92.6	0.0	0.5	4.1	2.8	21.2	60.3	18.4	93	92.5	61.3	14.0
Hibbing city & MCD (St. Louis)	16,361	16,302	-0.4	16,330	93.8	0.9	0.5	2.6	2.1	23.6	59.0	17.5	7,382	69.5	40.0	16.8
Hickory township (Pennington)	80	80	0.0	85	98.8	0.0	0.0	1.2	0.0	35.3	49.5	15.3	26	92.3	53.8	15.4
Higdem township (Polk)	84	84	0.0	75	86.7	0.0	0.0	0.0	13.3	24.0	61.3	14.7	30	93.3	23.3	6.7
High Forest township (Olmsted)	980	1,011	3.2	988	99.1	0.6	0.2	0.1	0.0	18.5	64.4	17.1	378	91.8	29.6	27.5
Highland township (Wabasha)	462	458	-0.9	405	97.5	0.0	1.2	0.2	1.0	23.2	70.5	6.2	144	91.0	52.8	18.8
Highland Grove township (Clay)	288	294	2.1	242	98.3	0.0	0.0	0.8	0.8	18.2	57.4	24.4	96	95.8	40.6	17.7
Highlanding township (Pennington)	194	193	-0.5	196	95.9	1.5	0.0	2.6	0.0	29.1	53.6	17.3	66	90.9	63.6	10.6
Highwater township (Cottonwood)	166	165	-0.6	163	98.8	0.0	0.0	1.2	0.0	26.3	48.5	25.2	66	69.7	53.0	18.2
Hill township (Kittson)	15	15	0.0	2	100.0	0.0	0.0	0.0	0.0	0.0	0.0	100.0	1	100.0	100.0	0.0
Hill City city & MCD (Aitkin)	631	608	-3.6	530	93.4	0.6	0.2	3.2	2.6	22.5	62.6	14.9	276	47.8	44.2	7.6
Hill Lake township (Aitkin)	432	422	-2.3	395	93.4	0.0	0.0	6.1	0.5	26.1	58.3	15.7	164	96.3	47.6	20.1
Hillman township (Kanabec)	438	428	-2.3	421	84.8	0.0	0.0	14.5	0.7	24.0	59.7	16.4	168	88.1	47.6	17.3
Hillman city & MCD (Morrison)	38	37	-2.6	41	100.0	0.0	0.0	0.0	0.0	34.2	63.4	2.4	14	100.0	57.1	0.0
Hillman township (Morrison)	197	193	-2.0	223	96.0	0.0	0.4	0.0	3.6	34.9	54.8	10.3	71	88.7	57.7	4.2
Hill River township (Polk)	157	156	-0.6	122	100.0	0.0	0.0	0.0	0.0	25.5	50.0	24.6	55	87.3	60.0	21.8
Hills city & MCD (Rock)	684	674	-1.5	755	97.6	2.1	0.0	0.0	0.3	32.0	45.7	22.3	276	74.3	58.3	15.2
Hillsdale township (Winona)	923	889	-3.7	1,026	84.8	0.0	0.0	6.7	8.5	24.7	65.2	10.1	354	81.4	50.6	9.6
Hilltop city & MCD (Anoka)	744	738	-0.8	828	64.3	3.6	4.0	7.1	21.0	19.9	69.1	11.0	402	69.2	66.7	3.7
Hinckley city & MCD (Pine)	1,800	1,782	-1.0	1,727	71.7	0.5	0.2	25.0	2.6	25.0	61.5	13.6	797	46.7	58.0	11.8
Hinckley township (Pine)	806	790	-2.0	894	93.1	0.7	3.7	0.4	2.1	28.1	57.6	14.2	300	88.7	52.3	14.0
Hines township (Beltrami)	689	693	0.6	647	90.0	0.0	0.0	3.1	7.0	20.8	55.0	24.3	266	89.1	33.1	21.8
Hiram township (Cass)	316	318	0.6	296	99.7	0.0	0.0	0.0	0.3	16.9	40.2	42.9	143	93.7	39.2	40.6
Hitterdal city & MCD (Clay)	201	202	0.5	195	100.0	0.0	0.0	0.0	0.0	18.4	64.1	17.4	87	93.1	49.4	9.2
Hobart township (Otter Tail)	778	774	-0.5	804	97.8	0.5	0.0	0.0	1.7	19.5	59.2	21.4	330	93.3	38.5	29.7
Hodges township (Stevens)	277	297	7.2	170	80.0	0.0	0.0	0.0	20.0	26.0	59.3	14.7	65	80.0	36.9	20.0
Hoff township (Pope)	152	156	2.6	134	100.0	0.0	0.0	0.0	0.0	16.4	59.6	23.9	63	92.1	54.0	15.9
Hoffman city & MCD (Grant)	681	678	-0.4	686	95.0	0.0	0.7	0.6	3.6	29.3	50.6	20.0	284	72.2	55.6	10.9
Hokah city & MCD (Houston)	580	561	-3.3	559	83.2	0.0	0.0	15.0	1.8	22.2	67.8	10.0	264	68.9	50.4	15.9
Hokah township (Houston)	497	492	-1.0	491	95.5	0.0	0.0	3.9	0.6	20.0	65.5	14.7	204	89.7	43.6	27.0
Holden township (Goodhue)	454	457	0.7	555	95.9	0.0	0.5	0.0	3.6	30.1	57.4	12.4	186	91.9	29.6	34.9
Holding township (Stearns)	1,139	1,174	3.1	1,241	99.8	0.0	0.0	0.0	0.2	26.7	65.0	8.3	431	94.4	47.8	12.5
Holdingford city & MCD (Stearns)	708	704	-0.6	647	98.6	0.0	0.0	0.0	1.4	25.3	60.7	13.9	305	75.7	53.4	14.1
Holland township (Kandiyohi)	338	336	-0.6	347	97.1	0.0	0.0	2.9	0.0	33.2	58.8	8.1	116	94.0	31.9	16.4
Holland city & MCD (Pipestone)	187	181	-3.2	202	96.5	0.0	0.0	0.5	3.0	19.8	62.0	18.3	97	81.4	61.9	14.4
Hollandale city & MCD (Freeborn)	303	299	-1.3	281	91.1	0.0	0.0	0.0	8.9	32.0	55.8	12.1	109	69.7	35.8	13.8
Holloway city & MCD (Swift)	92	89	-3.3	105	100.0	0.0	0.0	0.0	0.0	10.5	71.5	18.1	54	79.6	59.3	7.4
Holly township (Murray)	127	122	-3.9	103	93.2	0.0	0.0	6.8	0.0	31.1	55.5	13.6	45	91.1	53.3	0.0
Hollywood township (Carver)	1,041	1,055	1.3	1,083	95.9	0.0	0.5	2.4	1.2	20.2	66.3	13.5	413	84.7	50.8	18.4
Holmes City township (Douglas)	804	813	1.1	676	96.7	0.0	0.0	0.3	3.0	17.3	62.4	20.4	302	93.7	40.4	18.9
Holmesville township (Becker)	505	513	1.6	458	86.9	0.2	0.0	10.0	2.8	15.3	71.4	13.3	202	87.6	29.2	22.8
Holst township (Clearwater)	369	374	1.4	463	96.8	0.0	0.0	0.4	2.8	30.5	54.5	15.1	161	99.4	49.7	19.3
Holt township (Fillmore)	271	276	1.8	251	98.4	0.0	0.0	0.4	1.2	22.3	55.1	22.7	109	90.8	50.5	18.3
Holt city & MCD (Marshall)	88	88	0.0	107	94.4	0.0	0.0	5.6	0.0	34.6	56.1	9.3	38	97.4	73.7	2.6
Holt township (Marshall)	132	132	0.0	149	98.7	0.0	0.0	0.0	1.3	13.4	59.7	26.8	68	88.2	57.4	2.9
Holy Cross township (Clay)	140	143	2.1	128	97.7	0.0	0.0	0.0	2.3	19.5	66.4	14.1	51	92.2	41.2	19.6
Holyoke township (Carlton)	182	183	0.5	261	97.3	0.0	0.0	1.9	0.8	21.1	69.7	9.2	103	83.5	35.0	17.5
Home township (Brown)	545	539	-1.1	524	99.8	0.0	0.0	0.0	0.2	20.4	62.4	17.2	225	92.4	55.6	15.1
Home Brook township (Cass)	255	254	-0.4	266	98.9	0.8	0.0	0.0	0.4	28.6	53.7	17.7	97	84.5	51.5	7.2

1 May be of any race.

Table A. All Places — **Population and Housing**

STATE City, town, township, borough, or CDP (county if applicable)	Population				Race and Hispanic or Latino origin (percent), 2010–2014					Age (percent), 2010–2014			Households, 2010–2014			
	2010 census total population	2014 estimated population	Percent change 2010–2014	ACS total population estimate 2010–2014	White alone, not Hispanic or Latino	Black alone, not Hispanic or Latino	Asian alone, not Hispanic or Latino	All other races or 2 or more races, not Hispanic or Latino	Hispanic or Latino[1]	Under 18 years old	Age 18 to 64 years old	Age 65 years and older	Total occupied housing units	Percent owner occupied	High school diploma or less	Bachelor's degree or more
	1	2	3	4	5	6	7	8	9	10	11	12	13	14	15	16
MINNESOTA—Con.																
Home Lake township (Norman)	148	144	-2.7	177	100.0	0.0	0.0	0.0	0.0	24.3	60.0	15.8	57	96.5	33.3	26.3
Homer CDP	181	NA	NA	139	100.0	0.0	0.0	0.0	0.0	19.4	52.5	28.1	54	96.3	38.9	31.5
Homer township (Winona)	1,356	1,361	0.4	1,271	99.4	0.0	0.0	0.0	0.6	17.9	67.3	14.8	519	92.1	35.5	30.8
Homestead township (Otter Tail)	362	362	0.0	385	99.7	0.0	0.0	0.3	0.0	31.7	56.7	11.7	146	91.8	46.6	14.4
Honner township (Redwood)	79	76	-3.8	81	95.1	0.0	0.0	4.9	0.0	22.2	58.0	19.8	32	96.3	31.3	31.3
Hope township (Lincoln)	272	269	-1.1	333	98.5	0.0	0.6	0.9	0.0	28.2	55.2	16.5	114	94.7	32.5	34.2
Hopkins city & MCD (Hennepin)	17,601	18,056	2.6	17,909	57.8	17.1	7.7	5.7	11.6	23.8	65.1	11.2	7,956	33.7	28.6	40.1
Hornet township (Beltrami)	234	238	1.7	196	91.3	0.0	0.0	8.7	0.0	24.9	57.6	17.3	82	92.7	64.6	11.0
Horton township (Stevens)	174	173	-0.6	189	100.0	0.0	0.0	0.0	0.0	37.6	56.2	6.3	59	74.6	27.1	13.6
Houston city & MCD (Houston)	979	969	-1.0	1,014	94.8	0.8	0.1	3.8	0.5	25.7	42.6	31.7	416	70.4	53.4	19.0
Houston township (Houston)	396	395	-0.3	401	95.5	1.7	0.0	2.5	0.2	23.1	58.9	18.0	156	82.1	42.3	32.7
Howard Lake city & MCD (Wright)	1,971	2,041	3.6	2,049	87.4	0.0	0.1	1.0	11.5	32.2	56.6	11.2	790	62.5	48.0	10.9
Hoyt Lakes city & MCD (St. Louis)	2,017	2,016	0.0	2,003	98.5	0.1	0.0	1.4	0.0	16.7	60.1	23.1	858	88.0	43.4	14.1
Hubbard township (Hubbard)	784	786	0.3	829	97.8	0.6	0.0	1.6	0.0	22.5	55.1	22.4	345	88.4	30.7	31.3
Hubbard township (Polk)	75	75	0.0	62	95.2	0.0	0.0	4.8	0.0	17.8	53.2	29.0	24	75.0	20.8	20.8
Hudson township (Douglas)	876	888	1.4	972	92.2	0.1	0.4	0.6	6.7	22.8	61.1	16.3	382	89.8	37.7	27.0
Hugo city & MCD (Washington)	13,336	14,239	6.8	13,850	90.8	1.8	1.4	2.3	3.8	27.1	65.2	7.8	5,051	89.2	23.0	42.2
Humboldt township (Clay)	275	281	2.2	288	97.6	0.0	0.0	0.0	2.4	35.8	53.7	10.4	99	89.9	38.4	29.3
Humboldt city & MCD (Kittson)	45	44	-2.2	21	85.7	0.0	0.0	14.3	0.0	9.5	76.2	14.3	11	90.9	36.4	0.0
Hunter township (Jackson)	224	226	0.9	279	100.0	0.0	0.0	0.0	0.0	23.6	59.3	17.2	108	89.8	40.7	26.9
Huntersville township (Wadena)	119	117	-1.7	78	100.0	0.0	0.0	0.0	0.0	26.9	59.1	14.1	34	76.5	52.9	5.9
Huntly township (Marshall)	77	77	0.0	64	95.3	0.0	0.0	0.0	4.7	14.1	62.5	23.4	32	71.9	65.6	25.0
Huntsville township (Polk)	464	473	1.9	459	91.3	0.0	1.1	0.2	7.4	14.9	66.4	18.7	185	92.4	38.9	16.8
Huss township (Roseau)	120	121	0.8	152	92.1	0.0	0.0	0.0	7.9	17.8	58.1	24.3	59	86.4	55.9	5.1
Hutchinson city & MCD (McLeod)	14,180	13,872	-2.2	13,983	93.0	0.3	1.0	2.2	3.4	24.1	58.7	17.2	5,979	67.7	36.8	21.7
Hutchinson township (McLeod)	1,220	1,200	-1.6	1,261	97.8	0.0	1.7	0.3	0.2	22.0	58.5	19.6	488	94.7	34.0	18.6
Hyde Park township (Wabasha)	286	283	-1.0	287	99.7	0.0	0.0	0.3	0.0	28.3	49.1	22.6	113	72.6	56.6	16.8
Ida township (Douglas)	1,228	1,245	1.4	1,248	97.3	0.0	0.2	0.1	2.4	13.8	55.5	30.4	542	97.2	39.7	26.2
Ideal township (Crow Wing)	1,088	1,114	2.4	1,189	99.4	0.0	0.0	0.3	0.3	18.4	49.1	32.5	540	89.1	22.0	44.6
Idun township (Aitkin)	259	253	-2.3	287	96.9	0.0	0.0	3.1	0.0	23.3	65.1	11.5	123	80.5	41.5	12.2
Ihlen city & MCD (Pipestone)	63	61	-3.2	43	93.0	0.0	0.0	0.0	7.0	4.7	48.9	46.5	26	96.2	65.4	15.4
Independence city & MCD (Hennepin)	3,536	3,707	4.8	3,634	97.9	0.1	0.0	1.0	0.9	22.4	62.8	14.8	1,342	93.2	20.2	51.7
Indian Lake township (Nobles)	232	234	0.9	226	100.0	0.0	0.0	0.0	0.0	20.8	62.6	16.8	89	91.0	30.3	24.7
Industrial township (St. Louis)	797	800	0.4	938	95.1	0.0	0.0	1.4	3.5	29.3	60.7	9.9	339	94.1	33.0	21.2
Inger CDP	212	NA	NA	316	20.6	0.0	0.0	79.4	0.0	24.1	74.7	1.3	89	60.7	58.4	23.6
Inguadona township (Cass)	190	192	1.1	221	93.2	0.0	0.0	2.3	4.5	10.5	52.1	37.6	117	83.8	60.7	14.5
Inman township (Otter Tail)	290	290	0.0	310	100.0	0.0	0.0	0.0	0.0	25.1	58.0	16.8	119	86.6	49.6	11.8
International Falls city & MCD (Koochiching)	6,423	6,171	-3.9	6,329	93.9	1.5	0.6	3.6	0.4	21.1	59.9	18.8	2,933	65.3	47.8	17.5
Inver Grove Heights city & MCD (Dakota)	33,882	34,709	2.4	34,258	79.6	3.9	4.2	2.5	9.9	23.4	62.9	13.9	13,640	70.9	31.2	35.0
Iona city & MCD (Murray)	137	132	-3.6	123	96.7	0.0	3.3	0.0	0.0	17.8	53.7	28.5	65	92.3	58.5	6.2
Iona township (Murray)	163	157	-3.7	134	100.0	0.0	0.0	0.0	0.0	22.4	63.4	14.2	57	93.0	33.3	17.5
Iona township (Todd)	490	479	-2.2	508	96.7	0.0	0.0	1.8	1.6	40.5	52.9	6.5	151	82.8	62.9	6.6
Iosco township (Waseca)	550	554	0.7	492	95.3	0.0	0.0	4.3	0.4	15.6	63.3	20.9	202	91.1	42.6	27.7
Irondale township (Crow Wing)	1,134	1,116	-1.6	1,193	96.8	0.7	0.0	2.5	0.0	18.3	58.9	22.9	476	90.5	43.9	23.5
Iron Junction city & MCD (St. Louis)	86	86	0.0	93	93.5	0.0	3.2	3.2	0.0	24.7	59.1	16.1	43	95.3	53.5	23.3
Iron Range township (Itasca)	649	654	0.8	688	89.7	0.3	0.7	4.8	4.5	27.2	59.0	13.8	278	80.6	36.7	11.2
Ironton city & MCD (Crow Wing)	572	564	-1.4	807	91.8	0.0	2.1	3.8	2.2	32.2	60.6	7.2	341	47.8	49.9	13.8
Irving township (Kandiyohi)	906	910	0.4	938	99.0	0.0	0.0	0.3	0.6	16.9	58.6	24.4	383	90.6	35.5	35.5
Isanti city & MCD (Isanti)	5,316	5,424	2.0	5,396	94.6	0.0	0.0	2.1	3.2	27.2	67.3	5.4	2,251	69.8	41.4	16.9
Isanti township (Isanti)	2,248	2,276	1.2	2,743	95.6	0.2	0.7	1.1	2.5	24.0	64.1	12.0	882	96.9	39.1	26.9
Island Lake township (Lyon)	175	173	-1.1	169	100.0	0.0	0.0	0.0	0.0	29.0	50.9	20.1	63	84.1	58.7	15.9
Island Lake township (Mahnomen)	233	236	1.3	274	79.6	0.0	0.4	17.2	2.9	25.8	48.5	25.5	120	90.0	60.0	17.5
Isle city & MCD (Mille Lacs)	776	786	1.3	743	80.9	0.5	0.0	16.8	1.7	14.7	55.7	29.6	352	64.5	42.9	15.3
Isle Harbor township (Mille Lacs)	570	564	-1.1	622	90.4	0.0	0.6	7.2	1.8	22.5	51.5	26.0	252	86.5	50.0	19.4
Itasca township (Clearwater)	132	134	1.5	111	99.1	0.0	0.0	0.0	0.9	19.8	60.3	19.8	55	96.4	27.3	29.1

1 May be of any race.

Table A. All Places — **Population and Housing**

	Population				Race and Hispanic or Latino origin (percent), 2010–2014					Age (percent), 2010–2014			Households, 2010–2014			
STATE City, town, township, borough, or CDP (county if applicable)	2010 census total population	2014 estimated population	Percent change 2010–2014	ACS total population estimate 2010–2014	White alone, not Hispanic or Latino	Black alone, not Hispanic or Latino	Asian alone, not Hispanic or Latino	All other races or 2 or more races, not Hispanic or Latino	Hispanic or Latino[1]	Under 18 years old	Age 18 to 64 years old	Age 65 years and older	Total occupied housing units	Percent owner occupied	High school diploma or less	Bachelor's degree or more
	1	2	3	4	5	6	7	8	9	10	11	12	13	14	15	16

MINNESOTA—Con.

STATE City, town, township, borough, or CDP (county if applicable)	1	2	3	4	5	6	7	8	9	10	11	12	13	14	15	16
Ivanhoe city & MCD (Lincoln)	570	554	-2.8	500	96.6	2.4	0.0	0.8	0.2	12.8	56.6	30.6	247	71.7	50.2	20.6
Jackson city & MCD (Jackson)	3,299	3,294	-0.2	3,300	90.4	0.3	5.3	1.2	2.8	20.0	56.5	23.6	1,549	65.3	44.0	22.1
Jackson township (Scott)	1,464	1,529	4.4	1,558	65.7	0.0	2.0	0.1	32.2	32.4	59.1	8.5	478	87.2	51.0	18.2
Jadis township (Roseau)	575	581	1.0	547	99.8	0.2	0.0	0.0	0.0	24.9	60.4	14.6	210	96.2	36.2	24.3
Jamestown township (Blue Earth)	693	700	1.0	767	97.8	0.0	0.4	0.7	1.2	26.9	59.8	13.6	285	93.3	35.1	31.6
Janesville city & MCD (Waseca)	2,256	2,249	-0.3	2,685	90.2	1.7	2.2	2.2	3.6	26.9	59.6	13.4	1,033	86.2	45.1	20.9
Janesville township (Waseca)	513	519	1.2	464	99.1	0.9	0.0	0.0	0.0	20.9	56.2	22.8	198	87.9	36.4	25.8
Janette Lake UT (St. Louis)	295	296	0.3	260	100.0	0.0	0.0	0.0	0.0	8.1	70.0	21.9	141	82.3	27.0	18.4
Jasper city	643	617	-4.0	570	97.7	0.0	0.0	0.9	1.4	20.5	46.5	33.0	290	73.4	63.4	11.0
Jasper city (Pipestone)	573	548	-4.4	523	97.7	0.0	0.0	1.0	1.3	21.4	45.1	33.7	262	73.3	64.9	8.8
Jasper city (Rock)	70	69	-1.4	47	97.9	0.0	0.0	0.0	2.1	10.6	63.9	25.5	28	75.0	50.0	32.1
Jay township (Martin)	237	231	-2.5	240	100.0	0.0	0.0	0.0	0.0	23.4	57.5	19.2	93	90.3	45.2	12.9
Jeffers city & MCD (Cottonwood)	369	360	-2.4	420	84.0	0.0	0.0	2.1	13.8	30.7	55.3	13.8	159	84.9	57.2	8.2
Jefferson township (Houston)	129	126	-2.3	133	100.0	0.0	0.0	0.0	0.0	18.8	61.7	19.5	51	96.1	58.8	13.7
Jenkins city & MCD (Crow Wing)	430	437	1.6	340	94.7	0.0	2.4	2.9	0.0	26.2	60.7	12.9	130	87.7	48.5	11.5
Jenkins township (Crow Wing)	359	368	2.5	338	99.4	0.0	0.6	0.0	0.0	9.5	45.6	45.0	157	91.7	29.9	31.8
Jessenland township (Sibley)	444	437	-1.6	406	96.6	0.0	0.0	1.0	2.5	24.6	59.7	15.5	153	89.5	55.6	13.7
Jevne township (Aitkin)	322	315	-2.2	252	94.4	0.0	0.0	5.6	0.0	19.9	56.0	24.2	109	80.7	45.0	22.0
Jewett UT (Aitkin)	47	45	-4.3	43	95.3	0.0	0.0	4.7	0.0	30.3	58.2	11.6	11	100.0	27.3	0.0
Jo Daviess township (Faribault)	245	240	-2.0	218	96.8	0.0	0.9	0.5	1.8	17.0	66.9	16.1	102	87.3	51.0	6.9
Johnson city & MCD (Big Stone)	29	28	-3.4	7	100.0	0.0	0.0	0.0	0.0	0.0	71.4	28.6	6	100.0	100.0	0.0
Johnson township (Polk)	51	51	0.0	59	100.0	0.0	0.0	0.0	0.0	30.5	42.5	27.1	31	83.9	61.3	16.1
Johnsonville township (Redwood)	152	147	-3.3	185	100.0	0.0	0.0	0.0	0.0	42.7	45.4	11.9	59	67.8	33.9	28.8
Jones township (Beltrami)	277	282	1.8	150	91.3	0.0	0.7	8.0	0.0	19.4	54.1	26.7	66	92.4	45.5	27.3
Jordan township (Fillmore)	352	357	1.4	361	98.3	0.0	0.0	1.7	0.0	25.8	59.8	14.4	139	91.4	46.0	23.0
Jordan city & MCD (Scott)	5,470	5,970	9.1	5,784	91.8	0.0	0.5	1.9	5.8	31.2	60.3	8.4	2,034	75.7	36.0	33.6
Judson township (Blue Earth)	554	561	1.3	551	99.5	0.4	0.2	0.0	0.0	14.2	55.2	30.5	231	91.8	35.9	27.3
Jupiter township (Kittson)	111	108	-2.7	96	100.0	0.0	0.0	0.0	0.0	12.5	57.4	30.2	45	91.1	37.8	20.0
Kabetogama township (St. Louis)	135	135	0.0	145	98.6	0.0	0.0	0.7	0.7	6.9	55.3	37.9	77	89.6	36.4	24.7
Kalevala township (Carlton)	327	331	1.2	325	99.4	0.0	0.0	0.6	0.0	16.3	67.3	16.3	137	93.4	42.3	12.4
Kalmar township (Olmsted)	1,046	1,083	3.5	1,150	96.7	0.0	1.5	0.3	1.6	19.5	61.1	19.4	446	92.2	38.8	33.0
Kanabec township (Kanabec)	943	921	-2.3	958	97.4	0.0	0.0	1.7	0.9	26.5	58.0	15.7	343	82.8	65.9	5.8
Kanaranzi township (Rock)	247	243	-1.6	252	100.0	0.0	0.0	0.0	0.0	25.9	57.1	17.1	90	95.6	65.6	6.7
Kandiyohi city & MCD (Kandiyohi)	491	488	-0.6	596	98.0	0.0	0.0	0.5	1.5	32.9	56.7	10.4	233	64.4	42.1	9.9
Kandiyohi township (Kandiyohi)	636	637	0.2	597	93.3	0.0	1.2	0.0	5.5	16.9	61.5	21.6	248	89.1	32.7	18.1
Kandota township (Todd)	729	716	-1.8	749	98.4	0.4	0.0	1.2	0.0	25.3	54.2	20.6	283	90.1	38.9	24.7
Karlstad city & MCD (Kittson)	760	736	-3.2	766	98.3	0.7	0.4	0.7	0.0	27.0	46.1	26.8	328	55.5	56.7	16.2
Kasota city & MCD (Le Sueur)	675	666	-1.3	833	94.4	2.3	1.6	1.8	0.0	23.7	68.3	8.0	325	78.8	51.4	5.2
Kasota township (Le Sueur)	1,581	1,604	1.5	1,617	95.5	2.7	0.0	0.4	1.4	21.6	61.7	16.8	647	89.0	37.6	26.4
Kasson city & MCD (Dodge)	5,931	6,074	2.4	6,017	96.5	0.1	0.6	0.7	2.0	30.2	57.7	12.0	2,291	82.8	31.6	30.4
Kathio township (Mille Lacs)	1,627	1,619	-0.5	1,528	31.3	1.8	0.7	64.9	1.3	30.4	54.8	14.8	540	64.1	51.7	6.7
Keene township (Clay)	155	156	0.6	121	100.0	0.0	0.0	0.0	0.0	25.7	64.4	9.9	45	97.8	46.7	22.2
Keewatin city & MCD (Itasca)	1,068	1,059	-0.8	1,052	98.0	1.0	0.0	1.0	0.0	25.9	58.6	15.6	454	77.8	48.5	6.2
Kego township (Cass)	505	509	0.8	673	71.8	0.0	0.0	27.9	0.3	26.9	49.1	24.1	278	76.3	57.6	16.5
Kelliher city & MCD (Beltrami)	262	262	0.0	292	98.3	0.0	0.0	1.7	0.0	27.4	55.1	17.5	121	71.9	44.6	14.9
Kelliher township (Beltrami)	130	132	1.5	129	90.7	0.0	0.0	9.3	0.0	17.0	66.9	16.3	56	92.9	46.4	19.6
Kellogg city & MCD (Wabasha)	456	439	-3.7	386	95.6	0.0	2.1	2.3	0.0	12.2	61.5	26.4	194	89.2	65.5	9.3
Kelsey township (St. Louis)	140	140	0.0	146	91.1	0.0	2.7	6.2	0.0	14.4	67.9	17.8	70	97.1	57.1	12.9
Kelso township (Sibley)	292	287	-1.7	311	98.1	0.0	0.6	1.3	0.0	22.3	55.3	22.5	128	91.4	49.2	21.9
Kennedy city & MCD (Kittson)	193	188	-2.6	245	99.6	0.0	0.0	0.0	0.4	20.4	61.5	18.0	103	88.3	37.9	20.4
Kenneth city & MCD (Rock)	68	67	-1.5	67	100.0	0.0	0.0	0.0	0.0	26.9	61.3	11.9	29	69.0	62.1	6.9
Kensington city & MCD (Douglas)	292	290	-0.7	303	93.1	0.0	0.0	4.0	3.0	23.0	62.8	14.2	141	87.2	55.3	1.4
Kent city & MCD (Wilkin)	81	80	-1.2	80	97.5	0.0	0.0	2.5	0.0	26.3	60.2	13.8	32	93.8	50.0	43.8
Kenyon city & MCD (Goodhue)	1,815	1,817	0.1	1,849	83.1	0.9	0.6	0.3	15.0	21.2	59.0	19.7	777	72.1	38.6	19.0

1 May be of any race.

Table A. All Places — **Population and Housing**

STATE City, town, township, borough, or CDP (county if applicable)	2010 census total population	2014 estimated population	Percent change 2010–2014	ACS total population estimate 2010–2014	White alone, not Hispanic or Latino	Black alone, not Hispanic or Latino	Asian alone, not Hispanic or Latino	All other races or 2 or more races, not Hispanic or Latino	Hispanic or Latino[1]	Under 18 years old	Age 18 to 64 years old	Age 65 years and older	Total occupied housing units	Percent owner occupied	High school diploma or less	Bachelor's degree or more
	1	2	3	4	5	6	7	8	9	10	11	12	13	14	15	16
MINNESOTA—Con.																
Kenyon township (Goodhue)	393	395	0.5	385	98.2	0.0	0.0	0.0	1.8	22.6	59.0	18.4	151	96.7	49.7	21.9
Kerkhoven city & MCD (Swift)	759	726	-4.3	784	84.6	0.0	0.0	0.5	14.9	28.7	55.7	15.6	308	70.5	48.7	14.3
Kerkhoven township (Swift)	236	228	-3.4	224	100.0	0.0	0.0	0.0	0.0	19.6	59.1	21.4	95	91.6	44.2	15.8
Kerrick city & MCD (Pine)	65	64	-1.5	48	85.4	0.0	0.0	14.6	0.0	14.6	64.6	20.8	28	85.7	75.0	0.0
Kerrick township (Pine)	325	322	-0.9	308	98.1	0.0	0.6	0.0	1.3	14.6	62.3	23.1	140	92.1	49.3	20.0
Kertsonville township (Polk)	94	94	0.0	77	98.7	0.0	0.0	0.0	1.3	19.5	53.3	27.3	34	94.1	52.9	11.8
Kettle River city & MCD (Carlton)	180	179	-0.6	122	91.0	0.0	5.7	3.3	0.0	22.2	56.6	21.3	65	63.1	35.4	12.3
Kettle River township (Pine)	504	505	0.2	550	96.9	0.0	0.0	2.2	0.9	28.0	53.6	18.5	213	81.2	50.2	24.4
Keystone township (Polk)	91	91	0.0	78	100.0	0.0	0.0	0.0	0.0	14.1	77.0	9.0	27	96.3	40.7	22.2
Kiel township (Lake of the Woods)	1	NA	NA	0	0.0	0.0	0.0	0.0	0.0	0.0	0.0	0.0	0	0.0	0.0	0.0
Kiester city & MCD (Faribault)	501	484	-3.4	541	97.8	0.0	0.0	0.0	2.2	17.2	59.7	22.9	260	71.9	53.1	12.3
Kiester township (Faribault)	260	255	-1.9	207	92.3	0.0	0.0	0.0	7.7	17.0	65.6	17.4	97	82.5	41.2	13.4
Kildare township (Swift)	151	146	-3.3	102	100.0	0.0	0.0	0.0	0.0	14.7	56.9	28.4	45	88.9	62.2	2.2
Kilkenny city & MCD (Le Sueur)	134	134	0.0	290	92.1	0.0	0.0	7.9	0.0	28.3	60.0	11.7	120	55.0	71.7	10.8
Kilkenny township (Le Sueur)	404	409	1.2	365	99.2	0.0	0.8	0.0	0.0	16.4	66.5	17.0	150	96.7	68.0	10.7
Kimball township (Jackson)	129	129	0.0	125	100.0	0.0	0.0	0.0	0.0	35.2	45.6	19.2	42	76.2	45.2	16.7
Kimball city & MCD (Stearns)	762	764	0.3	880	96.6	0.1	0.3	2.3	0.7	20.2	64.8	15.0	375	70.9	58.7	13.1
Kimberly township (Aitkin)	199	194	-2.5	157	98.1	0.0	0.6	0.0	1.3	13.4	61.1	25.5	77	94.8	45.5	9.1
Kinbrae city & MCD (Nobles)	12	12	0.0	4	100.0	0.0	0.0	0.0	0.0	0.0	100.0	0.0	2	100.0	100.0	0.0
King township (Polk)	219	220	0.5	173	98.8	0.0	0.0	1.2	0.0	20.2	57.7	22.0	74	89.2	51.4	16.2
Kinghurst township (Itasca)	106	107	0.9	110	100.0	0.0	0.0	0.0	0.0	8.1	49.1	42.7	53	88.7	41.5	13.2
Kingman township (Renville)	201	193	-4.0	175	100.0	0.0	0.0	0.0	0.0	16.7	64.1	19.4	77	100.0	48.1	11.7
Kingston city & MCD (Meeker)	161	159	-1.2	132	95.5	0.0	3.0	1.5	0.0	31.0	53.9	15.2	46	82.6	43.5	6.5
Kingston township (Meeker)	1,256	1,250	-0.5	1,246	97.2	0.0	0.0	2.1	0.7	27.1	56.2	16.9	445	89.9	49.0	19.3
Kinney city & MCD (St. Louis)	169	170	0.6	170	98.8	0.0	0.0	0.0	1.2	17.7	62.4	20.0	76	89.5	48.7	11.8
Kintire township (Redwood)	182	176	-3.3	145	84.8	0.0	0.0	2.1	13.1	20.1	64.3	15.9	62	85.5	48.4	21.0
Klondike UT (Kittson)	0	0	0.0	0	0.0	0.0	0.0	0.0	0.0	0.0	0.0	0.0	0	0.0	0.0	0.0
Knife Lake township (Kanabec)	1,156	1,144	-1.0	985	96.6	0.0	0.9	1.6	0.8	20.7	59.3	20.0	416	87.7	53.1	12.7
Knute township (Polk)	522	527	1.0	488	98.2	0.0	0.0	1.0	0.8	14.1	47.9	37.9	191	97.4	39.3	35.6
Kragero township (Chippewa)	125	122	-2.4	117	93.2	0.0	0.0	0.0	6.8	16.2	57.3	26.5	54	64.8	31.5	40.7
Kragnes township (Clay)	293	301	2.7	263	99.2	0.0	0.0	0.0	0.8	18.3	63.9	17.9	120	94.2	39.2	30.0
Krain township (Stearns)	981	1,010	3.0	914	99.8	0.0	0.0	0.0	0.2	26.3	58.2	15.5	329	93.0	55.6	9.7
Kratka township (Pennington)	131	130	-0.8	175	93.1	0.0	2.3	0.0	4.6	34.8	54.3	10.9	56	87.5	25.0	37.5
Kroschel township (Kanabec)	216	215	-0.5	228	90.8	0.0	0.0	9.2	0.0	19.7	63.3	17.1	93	67.7	45.2	10.8
Kugler township (St. Louis)	175	176	0.6	191	82.2	0.0	0.0	16.8	1.0	28.8	57.6	13.6	66	100.0	34.8	3.0
Kurtz township (Clay)	293	305	4.1	272	97.1	0.0	0.0	2.9	0.0	25.7	67.0	7.4	85	92.9	18.8	42.4
Lac qui Parle township (Lac qui Parle)	178	169	-5.1	172	100.0	0.0	0.0	0.0	0.0	16.9	67.4	15.7	77	81.8	36.4	29.9
La Crescent city	4,863	4,793	-1.4	4,871	98.4	0.0	0.5	0.7	0.4	24.3	60.1	15.5	2,072	75.4	28.4	29.3
La Crescent city (Houston)	4,863	4,793	-1.4	4,827	98.3	0.0	0.5	0.7	0.4	24.1	60.2	15.6	2,061	75.3	28.6	29.5
La Crescent city (Winona)	0	0	0.0	44	100.0	0.0	0.0	0.0	0.0	50.0	50.0	0.0	11	100.0	0.0	0.0
La Crescent township (Houston)	1,413	1,400	-0.9	1,390	98.3	0.0	0.0	1.7	0.0	16.5	66.9	16.5	542	96.9	26.4	38.6
La Crosse township (Jackson)	156	156	0.0	143	95.1	0.0	2.1	2.8	0.0	21.0	60.2	18.9	62	98.4	22.6	14.5
Lafayette city & MCD (Nicollet)	504	490	-2.8	492	98.0	0.0	0.0	1.4	0.6	23.6	61.1	15.4	231	80.5	55.4	15.2
Lafayette township (Nicollet)	694	683	-1.6	678	99.6	0.0	0.0	0.4	0.0	26.2	59.2	14.6	263	83.7	52.9	18.6
La Garde township (Mahnomen)	157	160	1.9	194	46.4	0.0	0.0	50.5	3.1	19.5	61.4	19.1	64	92.2	34.4	1.6
La Grand township (Douglas)	4,210	4,269	1.4	4,220	97.3	0.7	0.0	2.0	0.0	20.7	56.0	23.3	1,768	89.4	30.3	36.5
Lake township (Roseau)	2,090	2,082	-0.4	2,294	88.6	0.1	7.2	4.1	0.0	30.8	60.0	9.2	852	85.6	48.6	19.2
Lake township (Wabasha)	442	438	-0.9	546	95.4	0.0	1.3	2.4	0.9	24.4	58.7	16.8	212	96.2	32.5	37.7
Lake Alice township (Hubbard)	93	94	1.1	76	86.8	0.0	0.0	13.2	0.0	15.7	77.6	6.6	34	58.8	55.9	11.8
Lake Andrew township (Kandiyohi)	982	986	0.4	998	99.2	0.0	0.0	0.0	0.8	16.3	52.4	31.2	423	97.2	35.2	27.2
Lake Belt township (Martin)	189	184	-2.6	236	92.8	0.8	0.0	5.5	0.8	19.1	61.1	19.9	103	82.5	41.7	15.5
Lake Benton city & MCD (Lincoln)	683	662	-3.1	669	90.9	0.0	0.4	2.1	6.6	22.2	52.7	25.1	333	71.5	47.4	20.4
Lake Benton township (Lincoln)	241	242	0.4	195	100.0	0.0	0.0	0.0	0.0	23.6	49.8	26.7	80	86.3	40.0	23.8

1 May be of any race.

Table A. All Places — **Population and Housing**

STATE City, town, township, borough, or CDP (county if applicable)	Population				Race and Hispanic or Latino origin (percent), 2010–2014					Age (percent), 2010–2014			Households, 2010–2014			
	2010 census total population	2014 estimated population	Percent change 2010–2014	ACS total population estimate 2010–2014	White alone, not Hispanic or Latino	Black alone, not Hispanic or Latino	Asian alone, not Hispanic or Latino	All other races or 2 or more races, not Hispanic or Latino	Hispanic or Latino[1]	Under 18 years old	Age 18 to 64 years old	Age 65 years and older	Total occupied housing units	Percent owner occupied	Householders by level of education (percent) High school diploma or less	Bachelor's degree or more
	1	2	3	4	5	6	7	8	9	10	11	12	13	14	15	16
MINNESOTA—Con.																
Lake Bronson city & MCD (Kittson)	229	224	-2.2	263	100.0	0.0	0.0	0.0	0.0	26.6	53.5	19.8	115	75.7	65.2	5.2
Lake City city	5,063	4,957	-2.1	5,093	95.6	0.0	0.0	1.1	3.3	18.6	58.0	23.4	2,219	77.3	48.0	23.0
Lake City city (Goodhue)	747	747	0.0	839	96.9	0.1	0.1	2.9	0.0	21.1	47.8	31.0	339	68.1	41.6	23.0
Lake City city (Wabasha)	4,316	4,210	-2.5	4,254	95.3	0.0	0.0	0.8	3.9	18.2	60.0	21.9	1,880	78.9	49.1	23.0
Lake Crystal city & MCD (Blue Earth)	2,549	2,528	-0.8	2,539	97.1	0.0	1.2	0.5	1.2	30.7	53.4	15.9	950	79.5	35.6	22.7
Lake Edward township (Crow Wing)	2,085	2,129	2.1	1,830	97.1	0.0	0.4	0.8	1.6	13.1	61.1	25.7	877	92.1	27.1	28.5
Lake Elizabeth township (Kandiyohi)	233	232	-0.4	213	98.6	0.0	0.0	1.4	0.0	21.6	58.2	20.2	81	87.7	43.2	7.4
Lake Elmo city & MCD (Washington)	8,051	8,306	3.2	8,123	94.7	0.0	2.7	1.1	1.5	25.5	61.3	13.1	2,857	92.4	23.0	50.2
Lake Emma township (Hubbard)	985	986	0.1	1,063	97.8	0.0	0.0	0.4	1.8	11.8	55.0	33.2	518	91.7	26.4	41.5
Lake Eunice township (Becker)	1,545	1,577	2.1	1,497	95.9	0.0	0.0	4.1	0.0	20.2	59.2	20.6	671	93.6	36.2	25.3
Lakefield city & MCD (Jackson)	1,700	1,691	-0.5	1,528	94.8	0.1	1.2	0.5	3.4	20.8	61.9	17.3	713	76.2	44.9	16.8
Lake Fremont township (Martin)	162	158	-2.5	181	100.0	0.0	0.0	0.0	0.0	21.0	65.8	13.3	76	65.8	32.9	18.4
Lake George CDP	230	NA	NA	199	91.5	0.0	0.0	5.0	3.5	20.0	51.5	28.1	92	78.3	34.8	23.9
Lake George township (Hubbard)	378	377	-0.3	315	87.3	1.0	0.0	5.7	6.0	18.7	57.8	23.5	150	81.3	48.7	19.3
Lake George township (Stearns)	335	345	3.0	320	100.0	0.0	0.0	0.0	0.0	28.8	58.1	13.1	103	86.4	58.3	7.8
Lake Grove township (Mahnomen)	189	194	2.6	186	47.8	0.0	0.5	48.9	2.7	22.7	61.4	16.1	75	84.0	44.0	18.7
Lake Hanska township (Brown)	339	332	-2.1	296	99.0	0.0	0.3	0.7	0.0	20.2	61.7	17.9	125	88.0	49.6	24.0
Lake Hattie township (Hubbard)	202	201	-0.5	185	91.4	0.0	0.0	8.6	0.0	22.8	60.6	16.8	73	89.0	56.2	16.4
Lake Henry city & MCD (Stearns)	103	103	0.0	87	100.0	0.0	0.0	0.0	0.0	19.5	63.1	17.2	45	84.4	71.1	6.7
Lake Henry township (Stearns)	278	287	3.2	264	100.0	0.0	0.0	0.0	0.0	23.1	61.7	15.2	97	90.7	70.1	6.2
Lake Ida township (Norman)	160	155	-3.1	171	97.7	0.0	0.0	2.3	0.0	24.6	58.1	17.5	58	100.0	32.8	31.0
Lake Jessie township (Itasca)	303	305	0.7	304	99.7	0.0	0.0	0.3	0.0	22.3	57.0	20.7	132	91.7	53.0	7.6
Lake Johanna township (Pope)	139	142	2.2	158	91.8	0.0	0.0	1.3	7.0	23.4	62.0	14.6	65	83.1	44.6	35.4
Lakeland city & MCD (Washington)	1,796	1,832	2.0	1,761	96.3	0.6	0.7	1.0	1.4	24.0	63.1	12.9	665	96.1	29.3	40.9
Lakeland Shores city & MCD (Washington)	309	313	1.3	306	98.4	0.0	1.0	0.0	0.7	19.0	71.3	9.8	122	92.6	23.8	44.3
Lake Lillian city & MCD (Kandiyohi)	238	237	-0.4	235	96.6	0.4	1.3	0.4	1.3	22.2	50.7	27.2	109	89.0	67.0	12.8
Lake Lillian township (Kandiyohi)	190	189	-0.5	200	90.0	0.0	2.0	0.0	8.0	21.5	66.0	12.5	75	88.0	22.7	20.0
Lake Marshall township (Lyon)	561	563	0.4	476	95.4	3.6	0.2	0.0	0.8	20.5	68.1	11.6	198	89.4	40.9	30.3
Lake Mary township (Douglas)	1,098	1,110	1.1	1,101	98.2	0.0	0.0	0.2	1.6	24.2	53.8	22.0	412	98.1	35.4	21.1
Lake No. 1 UT (Lake)	152	152	0.0	105	100.0	0.0	0.0	0.0	0.0	0.0	100.0	0.0	29	100.0	0.0	0.0
Lake No. 2 UT (Lake)	2,094	2,095	0.0	2,210	100.0	0.0	0.0	0.0	0.0	22.2	59.5	18.4	956	99.0	36.9	31.5
Lake Park city & MCD (Becker)	783	783	0.0	738	94.0	0.0	0.4	4.9	0.7	27.2	61.0	11.8	312	72.4	58.3	16.3
Lake Park township (Becker)	481	491	2.1	487	99.8	0.0	0.0	0.2	0.0	24.2	56.0	19.9	169	96.4	46.7	20.1
Lake Pleasant township (Red Lake)	103	102	-1.0	111	92.8	0.0	2.7	0.0	4.5	23.4	58.5	18.0	35	91.4	42.9	11.4
Lakeport township (Hubbard)	845	846	0.1	873	88.2	1.0	0.0	8.8	1.9	21.3	53.5	25.1	360	87.8	34.7	29.2
Lake Prairie township (Nicollet)	672	662	-1.5	693	93.5	0.9	5.3	0.0	0.3	24.4	61.6	14.0	237	95.8	26.2	32.9
Lake St. Croix Beach city & MCD (Washington)	1,060	1,072	1.1	1,100	93.8	0.0	0.9	1.6	3.6	17.8	70.1	12.3	481	76.3	26.4	28.9
Lake Sarah township (Murray)	393	389	-1.0	425	98.8	0.0	0.0	0.7	0.5	25.2	50.3	24.5	188	86.7	46.3	25.0
Lake Shore city & MCD (Cass)	1,004	1,016	1.2	1,130	90.4	0.0	0.3	6.0	3.3	14.2	56.0	29.9	552	87.0	29.7	30.1
Lake Shore township (Lac qui Parle)	191	182	-4.7	194	84.0	0.0	0.0	0.0	16.0	20.7	64.5	14.9	82	85.4	52.4	9.8
Lakeside township (Aitkin)	463	451	-2.6	388	99.5	0.0	0.0	0.5	0.0	14.2	38.7	47.2	204	92.6	45.6	8.8
Lakeside township (Cottonwood)	237	236	-0.4	246	98.4	0.0	0.0	0.0	1.6	19.5	61.3	19.1	90	98.9	41.1	20.0
Lake Stay township (Lincoln)	156	153	-1.9	158	100.0	0.0	0.0	0.0	0.0	27.2	52.0	20.9	59	96.6	50.8	28.8
Laketown township (Carver)	2,211	2,368	7.1	2,241	96.3	0.1	1.7	0.6	1.3	24.2	67.6	7.9	661	90.5	19.5	54.6
Lake Valley township (Traverse)	237	229	-3.4	202	99.5	0.0	0.0	0.0	0.5	16.9	57.4	25.7	91	89.0	44.0	9.9
Lake View township (Becker)	1,678	1,713	2.1	1,875	94.3	0.1	0.0	5.4	0.2	19.0	62.9	18.2	802	88.9	29.8	31.3
Lakeview township (Carlton)	179	181	1.1	177	91.5	0.0	0.0	8.5	0.0	14.1	45.8	40.1	86	82.6	47.7	11.6
Lakeville city & MCD (Dakota)	55,954	59,866	7.0	57,715	88.0	1.7	4.5	2.2	3.6	30.7	62.7	6.4	19,314	88.1	20.0	48.8
Lake Wilson city & MCD (Murray)	251	242	-3.6	241	92.5	0.0	0.0	1.7	5.8	16.2	54.7	29.0	125	87.2	56.0	14.4

1 May be of any race.

Table A. All Places — **Population and Housing**

STATE City, town, township, borough, or CDP (county if applicable)	Population				Race and Hispanic or Latino origin (percent), 2010–2014					Age (percent), 2010–2014			Households, 2010–2014			
	2010 census total population	2014 estimated population	Percent change 2010–2014	ACS total population estimate 2010–2014	White alone, not Hispanic or Latino	Black alone, not Hispanic or Latino	Asian alone, not Hispanic or Latino	All other races or 2 or more races, not Hispanic or Latino	Hispanic or Latino[1]	Under 18 years old	Age 18 to 64 years old	Age 65 years and older	Total occupied housing units	Percent owner occupied	High school diploma or less	Bachelor's degree or more
	1	2	3	4	5	6	7	8	9	10	11	12	13	14	15	16
MINNESOTA—Con.																
Lakewood township (Lake of the Woods)..............	85	NA	NA	58	100.0	0.0	0.0	0.0	0.0	0.0	100.0	0.0	31	100.0	41.9	35.5
Lakewood township (St. Louis).......................	2,190	2,228	1.7	2,329	94.9	0.0	1.1	2.1	1.9	28.8	60.1	11.2	809	93.0	22.1	47.1
Lakin township (Morrison)	450	444	-1.3	429	94.2	0.0	0.7	1.9	3.3	28.0	63.0	9.1	141	94.3	60.3	3.5
Lambert township (Red Lake)........................	129	128	-0.8	140	100.0	0.0	0.0	0.0	0.0	27.1	53.6	19.3	58	93.1	37.9	10.3
Lamberton city & MCD (Redwood)....................	824	796	-3.4	875	91.2	0.2	0.0	0.0	8.6	24.3	52.1	23.4	354	80.8	50.3	9.0
Lamberton township (Redwood)....................	193	187	-3.1	159	100.0	0.0	0.0	0.0	0.0	14.5	63.7	22.0	70	94.3	54.3	20.0
Lammers township (Beltrami).....................	592	592	0.0	536	90.9	0.0	0.0	3.9	5.2	23.3	65.8	10.8	213	87.8	42.7	20.7
Lancaster city & MCD (Kittson)....................	340	332	-2.4	393	87.0	0.0	0.0	1.3	11.7	30.0	51.8	18.1	162	81.5	51.9	22.8
Land township (Grant)......	261	260	-0.4	239	92.5	0.0	0.0	0.0	7.5	18.8	67.3	13.8	90	66.7	48.9	16.7
Landfall city & MCD (Washington)................	706	738	4.5	796	54.1	1.9	3.0	2.4	38.6	27.2	68.1	4.9	294	95.6	70.4	2.4
Lanesboro city & MCD (Fillmore)....................	754	735	-2.5	762	95.4	0.0	0.0	3.5	1.0	20.7	57.1	22.2	352	72.4	35.2	29.5
Lanesburgh township (Le Sueur).....................	2,035	2,066	1.5	2,047	97.9	0.0	0.1	0.1	1.9	26.8	61.2	12.0	717	90.5	43.1	18.3
Langhei township (Pope)..	177	180	1.7	134	100.0	0.0	0.0	0.0	0.0	13.5	47.6	38.8	69	63.8	47.8	8.7
Langola township (Benton)....................	909	932	2.5	1,011	92.1	1.2	0.2	0.0	6.5	24.6	62.4	13.0	377	94.7	44.8	18.8
Langor township (Beltrami)....................	211	214	1.4	155	94.2	0.0	0.0	5.8	0.0	23.8	64.5	11.6	62	100.0	50.0	25.8
Lansing CDP...............	181	NA	NA	164	99.4	0.0	0.0	0.6	0.0	26.9	42.6	30.5	66	86.4	69.7	0.0
Lansing township (Mower)	939	949	1.1	897	91.2	0.3	0.0	4.0	4.5	23.7	59.6	16.6	357	86.8	31.4	15.7
Laona township (Roseau).	543	540	-0.6	474	98.7	0.0	0.0	1.3	0.0	20.7	60.0	19.2	211	85.3	60.2	17.1
Laporte city & MCD (Hubbard)....................	111	113	1.8	228	72.8	0.0	0.0	27.2	0.0	38.6	45.5	15.8	80	67.5	52.5	21.3
La Prairie township (Clearwater).................	356	361	1.4	398	20.9	0.0	0.0	77.4	1.8	36.4	53.4	10.1	150	68.7	61.3	3.3
La Prairie city & MCD (Itasca).....................	665	664	-0.2	807	95.9	0.1	0.0	4.0	0.0	32.9	52.1	15.1	296	79.4	47.0	20.9
Larkin township (Nobles)..	188	190	1.1	220	98.2	0.0	0.0	1.8	0.0	21.7	65.4	12.7	79	75.9	46.8	8.9
La Salle city & MCD (Watonwan).................	87	86	-1.1	71	100.0	0.0	0.0	0.0	0.0	28.1	70.2	1.4	30	96.7	36.7	33.3
Lastrup city & MCD (Morrison)...................	104	102	-1.9	146	100.0	0.0	0.0	0.0	0.0	16.4	69.2	14.4	74	71.6	50.0	17.6
Lauderdale city & MCD (Ramsey)...................	2,379	2,484	4.4	2,422	60.7	14.1	15.6	1.7	7.9	15.6	73.7	10.6	1,056	45.9	16.4	69.1
Lavell township (St. Louis)	303	304	0.3	331	98.2	0.0	0.0	1.8	0.0	19.9	67.8	12.1	141	96.5	49.6	4.3
Lawrence township (Grant).....................	84	84	0.0	104	100.0	0.0	0.0	0.0	0.0	21.1	42.3	36.5	43	83.7	53.5	23.3
Lawrence township (Itasca).....................	435	438	0.7	509	95.3	0.0	0.0	2.2	2.6	24.3	58.1	17.5	212	92.5	49.1	12.3
Leaf Lake township (Otter Tail).......................	560	556	-0.7	545	95.8	0.2	0.0	3.1	0.9	26.6	47.2	26.2	216	96.8	48.1	16.2
Leaf Mountain township (Otter Tail)...............	326	321	-1.5	344	100.0	0.0	0.0	0.0	0.0	30.6	55.0	14.5	132	81.8	53.0	13.6
Leaf River township (Wadena)...................	531	527	-0.8	687	92.7	3.6	0.0	2.9	0.7	24.5	56.2	19.1	227	94.7	53.7	16.3
Leaf Valley township (Douglas)..................	457	463	1.3	469	100.0	0.0	0.0	0.0	0.0	17.7	54.7	27.5	203	97.0	48.3	18.7
Leavenworth township (Brown).....................	287	282	-1.7	267	98.1	0.0	1.1	0.0	0.7	23.6	58.8	17.6	112	93.8	54.5	12.5
Le Center city & MCD (Le Sueur).....................	2,499	2,474	-1.0	2,292	77.7	0.4	0.0	0.2	21.6	27.3	59.4	13.4	958	70.5	50.8	17.3
Lee township (Aitkin)........	50	48	-4.0	26	100.0	0.0	0.0	0.0	0.0	0.0	57.7	42.3	17	100.0	70.6	17.6
Lee township (Beltrami)....	51	52	2.0	55	89.1	0.0	0.0	10.9	0.0	30.9	50.8	18.2	19	100.0	57.9	0.0
Lee township (Norman)	128	124	-3.1	114	97.4	0.0	2.6	0.0	0.0	25.5	57.1	17.5	43	95.3	27.9	25.6
Leech Lake township (Cass).....................	436	437	0.2	412	80.3	0.0	0.0	17.0	2.7	18.7	49.8	31.6	189	82.5	34.4	29.1
Leeds township (Murray) ..	210	207	-1.4	237	88.6	0.0	0.0	0.0	11.4	30.4	53.7	16.0	81	91.4	39.5	19.8
Leenthrop township (Chippewa)................	243	239	-1.6	279	84.6	0.0	3.2	9.0	3.2	27.6	53.9	18.6	101	83.2	44.6	16.8
Leiding township (St. Louis).....................	400	403	0.8	410	80.0	0.0	0.0	19.8	0.2	16.3	52.1	31.5	198	89.4	42.4	19.7
Leigh township (Morrison)	212	208	-1.9	250	87.2	5.6	0.0	7.2	0.0	28.8	62.0	9.2	94	97.9	66.0	3.2
Lemond township (Steele)	501	501	0.0	490	93.1	0.0	0.0	3.9	3.1	23.9	61.2	14.9	176	93.8	55.1	15.3
Lengby city & MCD (Polk).	86	86	0.0	92	75.0	0.0	0.0	25.0	0.0	14.1	46.7	39.1	46	87.0	65.2	8.7
Lent township (Chisago)...	3,092	3,071	-0.7	3,077	96.2	0.0	1.5	1.8	0.4	24.4	65.9	9.7	1,098	96.7	34.4	19.7
Leon township (Clearwater).................	345	350	1.4	359	99.2	0.0	0.0	0.8	0.0	23.4	59.1	17.5	140	98.6	36.4	18.6
Leon township (Goodhue)	885	893	0.9	910	97.1	0.0	0.0	1.9	1.0	18.6	64.9	16.5	350	92.9	40.0	20.9
Leonard city & MCD (Clearwater).................	41	42	2.4	32	100.0	0.0	0.0	0.0	0.0	21.9	71.9	6.3	12	100.0	91.7	0.0
Leonardsville township (Traverse).................	107	102	-4.7	118	100.0	0.0	0.0	0.0	0.0	22.1	65.2	12.7	52	90.4	21.2	13.5
Leonidas city & MCD (St. Louis).....................	52	52	0.0	59	81.4	0.0	0.0	10.2	8.5	25.4	56.0	18.6	34	88.2	52.9	5.9
Leota CDP.................	209	NA	NA	161	98.8	0.0	1.2	0.0	0.0	11.2	44.6	44.1	87	94.3	63.2	3.4
Leota township (Nobles)...	390	393	0.8	335	98.8	0.0	0.6	0.0	0.6	17.4	52.3	30.4	153	94.1	63.4	10.5
Le Ray township (Blue Earth)...................	746	751	0.7	740	97.6	0.7	0.0	0.3	1.5	20.2	62.6	17.3	305	94.4	38.4	41.6
Le Roy city & MCD (Mower)...................	929	927	-0.2	802	87.7	0.0	0.5	3.7	8.1	22.1	56.4	21.6	372	79.0	60.2	19.4
Le Roy township (Mower).	354	359	1.4	301	99.7	0.0	0.0	0.3	0.0	24.3	51.9	23.9	119	84.9	59.7	6.7

1 May be of any race.

Table A. All Places — **Population and Housing**

STATE City, town, township, borough, or CDP (county if applicable)	2010 census total population	2014 estimated population	Percent change 2010–2014	ACS total population estimate 2010–2014	White alone, not Hispanic or Latino	Black alone, not Hispanic or Latino	Asian alone, not Hispanic or Latino	All other races or 2 or more races, not Hispanic or Latino	Hispanic or Latino[1]	Under 18 years old	Age 18 to 64 years old	Age 65 years and older	Total occupied housing units	Percent owner occupied	High school diploma or less	Bachelor's degree or more
	1	2	3	4	5	6	7	8	9	10	11	12	13	14	15	16
MINNESOTA—Con.																
Le Sauk township (Stearns)	1,693	1,701	0.5	1,695	93.7	2.9	2.1	0.8	0.5	19.8	67.6	12.7	693	88.6	32.3	35.8
Leslie township (Todd)	642	628	-2.2	603	98.0	1.0	0.0	1.0	0.0	15.9	53.3	30.7	272	91.2	52.9	9.2
Lessor township (Polk)	175	176	0.6	142	100.0	0.0	0.0	0.0	0.0	21.1	62.6	16.2	63	82.5	55.6	9.5
Lester Prairie city & MCD (McLeod)	1,730	1,686	-2.5	1,666	82.9	0.4	0.0	1.9	14.8	31.2	57.7	10.9	651	77.4	54.8	12.0
Le Sueur city	4,058	4,023	-0.9	4,019	82.8	0.6	1.3	2.4	12.9	23.0	57.9	18.9	1,757	71.7	46.7	21.1
Le Sueur city (Le Sueur)	4,048	4,013	-0.9	4,019	82.8	0.6	1.3	2.4	12.9	23.0	57.9	18.9	1,757	71.7	46.7	21.1
Le Sueur city (Nicollet)	10	10	0.0	0	0.0	0.0	0.0	0.0	0.0	0.0	0.0	0.0	0	0.0	0.0	0.0
Le Sueur city (Sibley)	0	0	0.0	0	0.0	0.0	0.0	0.0	0.0	0.0	0.0	0.0	0	0.0	0.0	0.0
Leven township (Pope)	499	487	-2.4	574	100.0	0.0	0.0	0.0	0.0	17.8	60.4	22.0	262	90.8	34.0	31.7
Lewis township (Mille Lacs)	52	52	0.0	43	100.0	0.0	0.0	0.0	0.0	35.0	60.5	4.7	15	100.0	53.3	26.7
Lewiston city & MCD (Winona)	1,620	1,581	-2.4	1,526	88.1	5.1	0.0	1.5	5.2	28.6	59.7	11.9	557	70.0	46.9	19.4
Lewisville city & MCD (Watonwan)	250	248	-0.8	209	87.6	0.0	0.0	0.0	12.4	20.0	53.5	26.3	89	84.3	70.8	3.4
Lexington city & MCD (Anoka)	2,058	2,022	-1.7	2,019	88.3	2.8	3.1	5.0	0.8	29.9	63.1	7.1	769	63.6	45.3	16.6
Lexington township (Le Sueur)	709	716	1.0	791	96.1	0.0	0.1	0.0	3.8	20.3	66.9	12.8	309	89.6	53.4	10.4
Libby township (Aitkin)	45	43	-4.4	47	100.0	0.0	0.0	0.0	0.0	4.3	42.5	53.2	29	89.7	48.3	6.9
Liberty township (Beltrami)	730	733	0.4	775	87.2	0.1	2.2	8.8	1.7	27.0	63.3	9.5	292	87.0	41.8	23.3
Liberty township (Itasca)	62	62	0.0	50	100.0	0.0	0.0	0.0	0.0	12.0	48.0	40.0	23	91.3	65.2	8.7
Liberty township (Polk)	108	107	-0.9	69	100.0	0.0	0.0	0.0	0.0	11.5	68.0	20.3	29	96.6	24.1	13.8
Lida township (Otter Tail)	757	753	-0.5	720	96.3	0.0	0.0	2.4	1.4	13.0	56.7	30.6	326	97.5	27.3	37.7
Lien township (Grant)	111	111	0.0	114	100.0	0.0	0.0	0.0	0.0	24.6	55.2	20.2	43	90.7	25.6	20.9
Lilydale city & MCD (Dakota)	623	876	40.6	747	96.3	0.0	0.4	2.1	1.2	6.8	44.8	48.3	434	63.4	9.0	67.1
Lima township (Cass)	101	100	-1.0	90	85.6	3.3	0.0	8.9	2.2	4.4	60.0	35.6	43	81.4	46.5	16.3
Lime township (Blue Earth)	1,398	1,399	0.1	1,341	93.7	1.7	1.0	0.3	3.3	22.6	59.9	17.4	512	91.2	26.0	33.2
Lime Lake township (Murray)	181	178	-1.7	226	99.6	0.0	0.0	0.0	0.4	24.8	62.1	13.3	94	86.2	51.1	16.0
Limestone township (Lincoln)	136	133	-2.2	121	100.0	0.0	0.0	0.0	0.0	14.8	61.9	23.1	50	100.0	54.0	24.0
Lincoln township (Blue Earth)	200	199	-0.5	200	96.0	0.0	4.0	0.0	0.0	13.0	69.5	17.5	86	96.5	48.8	15.1
Lincoln township (Marshall)	117	117	0.0	116	92.2	0.0	1.7	4.3	1.7	10.3	64.6	25.0	59	78.0	50.8	23.7
Lind township (Roseau)	56	57	1.8	26	100.0	0.0	0.0	0.0	0.0	3.8	53.8	42.3	14	85.7	42.9	35.7
Linden township (Brown)	295	290	-1.7	323	99.1	0.0	0.0	0.0	0.9	25.0	56.9	18.0	121	95.9	46.3	19.8
Linden Grove township (St. Louis)	145	145	0.0	159	98.1	0.0	0.0	1.9	0.0	22.6	71.6	5.7	63	92.1	46.0	20.6
Lindstrom city & MCD (Chisago)	4,442	4,412	-0.7	4,405	97.2	0.0	0.9	0.0	2.0	23.0	55.4	21.7	1,826	80.8	40.0	30.1
Lino Lakes city & MCD (Anoka)	20,216	20,948	3.6	20,671	89.9	2.2	2.1	3.1	2.6	27.9	65.8	6.3	6,536	92.1	22.0	44.6
Linsell township (Marshall)	29	29	0.0	38	100.0	0.0	0.0	0.0	0.0	2.6	79.0	18.4	16	100.0	93.8	0.0
Linwood township (Anoka)	5,123	5,288	3.2	5,205	96.5	0.0	0.2	1.2	2.0	23.5	65.7	10.8	1,862	92.7	40.5	22.8
Lisbon township (Yellow Medicine)	201	195	-3.0	224	98.2	0.0	0.4	0.0	1.3	29.0	55.1	16.1	75	96.0	38.7	21.3
Lismore city & MCD (Nobles)	227	229	0.9	254	92.5	0.8	0.0	0.0	6.7	34.2	47.9	17.7	96	84.4	54.2	9.4
Lismore township (Nobles)	175	176	0.6	179	92.7	0.0	0.0	0.0	7.3	22.4	60.9	16.8	67	86.6	49.3	7.5
Litchfield city & MCD (Meeker)	6,726	6,668	-0.9	6,689	92.1	0.5	0.0	0.8	6.6	23.9	57.6	18.6	2,747	67.3	48.8	18.9
Litchfield township (Meeker)	832	829	-0.4	853	98.7	0.4	0.0	0.8	0.1	23.9	61.1	15.1	349	86.0	41.8	30.4
Little Canada city & MCD (Ramsey)	9,773	10,228	4.7	10,015	69.0	7.9	12.7	5.2	5.2	19.1	65.8	15.1	4,510	60.6	28.9	33.3
Little Elbow township (Mahnomen)	259	262	1.2	372	30.9	1.6	0.3	64.2	3.0	33.3	58.5	8.3	143	84.6	45.5	18.2
Little Elk township (Todd)	285	279	-2.1	372	94.4	0.0	3.5	1.1	1.1	28.5	54.0	17.5	132	93.2	45.5	6.8
Little Falls city & MCD (Morrison)	8,356	8,201	-1.9	8,291	95.1	0.9	0.0	2.9	1.1	19.3	57.4	23.3	3,840	62.2	49.9	19.9
Little Falls township (Morrison)	1,680	1,676	-0.2	1,753	95.0	0.0	0.0	3.9	0.4	27.5	60.2	12.3	620	95.0	35.0	31.3
Littlefork city & MCD (Koochiching)	647	623	-3.7	707	94.2	0.0	0.0	5.8	0.0	24.4	52.1	23.3	303	71.0	40.9	17.8
Little Pine township (Crow Wing)	86	87	1.2	87	100.0	0.0	0.0	0.0	0.0	11.5	66.6	21.8	42	85.7	42.9	28.6
Little Rock CDP	1,208	NA	NA	1,407	0.5	2.5	9.8	84.4	2.8	33.8	60.9	5.3	366	53.0	32.2	6.3
Little Rock township (Nobles)	211	213	0.9	212	90.6	0.0	3.3	4.7	1.4	24.0	60.3	15.6	81	92.6	35.8	16.0
Little Sand Lake UT (Itasca)	349	351	0.6	326	98.2	0.0	0.0	1.8	0.0	15.0	64.7	20.2	145	94.5	62.8	4.1
Little Sauk township (Todd)	829	815	-1.7	869	98.0	0.0	1.2	0.3	0.5	26.7	60.2	13.1	291	88.7	35.1	12.0
Livonia township (Sherburne)	5,951	6,103	2.6	6,017	95.1	0.0	0.0	2.6	2.3	34.0	60.2	5.6	1,855	89.1	29.2	23.8
Lockhart township (Norman)	50	49	-2.0	70	98.6	0.0	0.0	1.4	0.0	42.8	41.4	15.7	22	68.2	68.2	22.7
Lodi township (Mower)	270	272	0.7	222	100.0	0.0	0.0	0.0	0.0	28.5	59.1	12.6	75	92.0	50.7	6.7
Logan township (Aitkin)	184	178	-3.3	155	100.0	0.0	0.0	0.0	0.0	9.0	55.5	35.5	87	86.2	63.2	3.4
Logan township (Grant)	93	93	0.0	89	97.8	0.0	0.0	0.0	2.2	10.1	58.3	31.5	45	91.1	55.6	6.7
London township (Freeborn)	315	311	-1.3	276	98.2	0.0	0.0	0.0	1.8	19.2	65.9	14.9	111	93.7	48.6	1.8
Lone Pine township (Itasca)	410	415	1.2	350	97.7	0.0	0.3	1.1	0.9	11.4	63.4	25.1	188	94.1	25.5	29.8

1 May be of any race.

Table A. All Places — Population and Housing

STATE City, town, township, borough, or CDP (county if applicable)	Population: 2010 census total population	2014 estimated population	Percent change 2010–2014	ACS total population estimate 2010–2014	Race and Hispanic or Latino origin (percent), 2010–2014: White alone, not Hispanic or Latino	Black alone, not Hispanic or Latino	Asian alone, not Hispanic or Latino	All other races or 2 or more races, not Hispanic or Latino	Hispanic or Latino[1]	Age (percent), 2010–2014: Under 18 years old	Age 18 to 64 years old	Age 65 years and older	Households, 2010–2014: Total occupied housing units	Percent owner occupied	Householders by level of education (percent): High school diploma or less	Bachelor's degree or more
	1	2	3	4	5	6	7	8	9	10	11	12	13	14	15	16
MINNESOTA—Con.																
Lone Tree township (Chippewa)	199	194	-2.5	205	90.2	0.0	0.0	1.5	8.3	26.8	54.5	18.5	71	81.7	56.3	4.2
Long Beach city & MCD (Pope)	335	412	23.0	343	91.5	4.7	2.3	0.9	0.6	18.7	56.5	24.8	161	96.9	36.6	32.9
Long Lake township (Crow Wing)	1,036	1,058	2.1	1,220	92.1	0.0	1.0	6.0	0.9	23.3	62.0	14.7	469	91.9	40.3	13.4
Long Lake city & MCD (Hennepin)	1,756	1,798	2.4	1,889	95.5	1.2	0.4	1.2	1.8	25.3	61.5	13.2	767	65.4	25.4	40.5
Long Lake township (Watonwan)	338	336	-0.6	299	98.7	1.0	0.0	0.0	0.3	15.7	57.5	26.8	132	93.9	36.4	16.7
Long Lost Lake township (Clearwater)	43	44	2.3	92	69.6	0.0	0.0	30.4	0.0	15.2	63.1	21.7	43	76.7	27.9	41.9
Long Prairie city & MCD (Todd)	3,464	3,360	-3.0	3,422	67.9	0.6	0.0	0.2	31.2	27.9	53.2	18.8	1,367	63.1	50.5	21.4
Long Prairie township (Todd)	838	823	-1.8	749	93.5	0.0	1.1	1.2	4.3	25.8	56.4	17.5	283	92.2	39.2	21.6
Longville city & MCD (Cass)	156	156	0.0	103	100.0	0.0	0.0	0.0	0.0	9.7	33.0	57.3	68	66.2	55.9	11.8
Lonsdale city & MCD (Rice)	3,674	3,804	3.5	3,760	98.1	0.0	0.3	0.2	1.4	34.9	60.3	4.7	1,333	84.6	36.9	20.1
Loon Lake township (Cass)	540	541	0.2	491	99.8	0.0	0.2	0.0	0.0	25.5	52.8	22.0	201	96.5	43.8	21.9
Lorain township (Nobles)	297	299	0.7	340	95.6	0.0	1.5	0.3	2.6	22.7	54.7	22.6	133	88.0	47.4	13.5
Loretto city & MCD (Hennepin)	650	667	2.6	701	96.9	0.0	0.3	0.0	2.9	27.7	55.9	16.4	274	82.8	33.6	23.4
Louisburg city & MCD (Lac qui Parle)	47	45	-4.3	30	100.0	0.0	0.0	0.0	0.0	16.7	70.1	13.3	13	76.9	30.8	30.8
Louisville township (Red Lake)	187	186	-0.5	176	96.0	0.0	0.0	0.0	4.0	21.0	63.6	15.3	73	97.3	43.8	15.1
Louisville township (Scott)	1,266	1,325	4.7	1,202	96.1	0.0	2.0	1.2	0.7	24.0	67.3	8.7	379	93.9	26.4	34.0
Louriston township (Chippewa)	165	161	-2.4	151	100.0	0.0	0.0	0.0	0.0	24.4	66.9	8.6	56	92.9	39.3	17.9
Lowell township (Polk)	298	297	-0.3	331	84.0	2.1	0.0	3.9	10.0	19.9	70.6	9.4	96	91.7	62.5	12.5
Lower Red Lake UT (Beltrami)	5,786	5,860	1.3	5,857	2.5	1.1	2.6	88.9	4.9	39.4	55.1	5.3	1,600	48.9	53.3	6.9
Lowry city & MCD (Pope)	299	296	-1.0	285	97.9	0.0	0.0	0.0	2.1	30.8	55.2	14.0	120	78.3	41.7	17.5
Lowville township (Murray)	169	165	-2.4	215	98.6	0.0	0.0	1.4	0.0	40.9	50.8	8.4	69	92.8	34.8	13.0
Lucan city & MCD (Redwood)	191	185	-3.1	183	92.9	1.1	0.0	0.0	6.0	26.3	55.4	18.6	81	80.2	63.0	13.6
Lucas township (Lyon)	237	236	-0.4	277	97.5	0.0	0.7	0.0	1.8	32.9	58.6	8.7	102	78.4	51.0	14.7
Lund township (Douglas)	325	330	1.5	390	95.9	0.3	0.0	0.0	3.8	22.5	63.0	14.4	154	76.0	42.9	16.2
Lura township (Faribault)	163	160	-1.8	163	98.8	0.0	0.0	1.2	0.0	22.7	55.2	22.1	69	88.4	46.4	15.9
Lutsen CDP	190	NA	NA	495	93.9	4.0	0.0	1.8	0.2	22.3	72.2	5.5	273	44.7	26.4	23.8
Lutsen township (Cook)	415	423	1.9	675	95.3	3.0	0.0	1.6	0.1	17.7	69.1	13.2	377	58.9	23.6	33.4
Luverne city & MCD (Rock)	4,739	4,669	-1.5	4,688	92.9	0.0	1.5	1.8	3.8	23.9	51.8	24.4	2,102	66.3	52.9	18.5
Luverne township (Rock)	485	482	-0.6	459	100.0	0.0	0.0	0.0	0.0	25.2	52.3	22.4	163	94.5	36.2	25.8
Luxemburg township (Stearns)	637	659	3.5	666	98.0	0.0	0.0	0.0	2.0	28.6	57.9	13.8	208	94.2	56.7	7.7
Lyle city & MCD (Mower)	551	547	-0.7	477	99.2	0.0	0.0	0.8	0.0	20.6	55.6	24.1	198	76.8	43.9	16.7
Lyle township (Mower)	356	360	1.1	392	87.5	0.0	0.0	2.0	10.5	31.6	54.6	13.8	135	92.6	47.4	15.6
Lynd city & MCD (Lyon)	448	437	-2.5	547	77.7	1.6	0.5	0.2	19.9	24.0	70.0	6.0	179	92.7	39.7	15.1
Lynd township (Lyon)	423	420	-0.7	420	96.4	0.0	0.7	1.0	1.9	23.4	61.4	15.2	150	96.0	34.7	33.3
Lynden township (Stearns)	1,938	1,986	2.5	2,042	97.7	0.3	0.3	1.4	0.2	25.0	62.6	12.4	719	94.2	42.1	16.1
Lynn township (McLeod)	550	540	-1.8	584	99.7	0.0	0.0	0.0	0.3	22.1	64.4	13.5	223	83.9	35.9	12.6
Lyons township (Lyon)	199	199	0.0	169	100.0	0.0	0.0	0.0	0.0	19.5	68.7	11.8	77	77.9	36.4	37.7
Lyons township (Wadena)	192	189	-1.6	218	95.0	3.7	0.0	1.4	0.0	26.2	51.4	22.5	90	81.1	51.1	6.7
Lyra township (Blue Earth)	327	325	-0.6	284	97.5	0.0	0.4	1.4	0.7	18.0	59.2	22.9	121	94.2	39.7	19.8
Mabel city & MCD (Fillmore)	780	761	-2.4	783	98.0	0.0	0.0	0.8	1.3	20.6	51.3	28.2	333	79.0	49.2	17.4
McCauleyville township (Wilkin)	55	54	-1.8	32	100.0	0.0	0.0	0.0	0.0	31.2	43.8	25.0	13	100.0	76.9	7.7
McCormack UT (St. Louis)	209	210	0.5	170	100.0	0.0	0.0	0.0	0.0	28.8	56.4	14.7	75	100.0	46.7	24.0
McCrea township (Marshall)	241	241	0.0	290	98.6	1.0	0.0	0.3	0.0	33.8	47.3	19.0	110	83.6	32.7	22.7
McDavitt township (St. Louis)	459	460	0.2	400	98.0	0.0	0.0	2.0	0.0	14.8	65.2	20.3	173	96.5	44.5	16.8
McDonaldsville township (Norman)	175	170	-2.9	164	97.0	3.0	0.0	0.0	0.0	21.3	57.8	20.7	63	88.9	61.9	12.7
McDougald township (Lake of the Woods)	225	NA	NA	255	94.5	5.5	0.0	0.0	0.0	40.4	59.5	0.0	72	100.0	63.9	8.3
McGrath city & MCD (Aitkin)	80	77	-3.8	75	93.3	2.7	0.0	2.7	1.3	20.1	54.6	25.3	35	94.3	80.0	0.0
McGregor city & MCD (Aitkin)	391	373	-4.6	498	88.2	1.0	0.6	10.2	0.0	24.8	51.8	23.1	226	50.0	65.5	8.4
McGregor township (Aitkin)	105	101	-3.8	91	100.0	0.0	0.0	0.0	0.0	18.7	67.1	14.3	37	81.1	70.3	0.0
McIntosh city & MCD (Polk)	625	622	-0.5	509	95.3	0.0	0.0	2.8	2.0	19.7	43.6	36.7	238	58.4	52.5	9.7
McKinley township (Cass)	133	131	-1.5	140	93.6	0.0	0.0	5.7	0.7	16.4	67.0	16.4	72	69.4	33.3	11.1
McKinley UT (Kittson)	38	37	-2.6	53	100.0	0.0	0.0	0.0	0.0	18.9	50.9	30.2	23	82.6	56.5	0.0
McKinley city & MCD (St. Louis)	128	128	0.0	102	96.1	0.0	0.0	2.0	2.0	16.6	67.7	15.7	44	90.9	63.6	2.3
McPherson township (Blue Earth)	466	469	0.6	401	99.8	0.2	0.0	0.0	0.0	27.1	62.7	10.0	143	88.8	37.8	19.6
Macsville township (Grant)	114	114	0.0	136	100.0	0.0	0.0	0.0	0.0	19.9	62.5	17.6	60	90.0	38.3	13.3
Macville township (Aitkin)	206	202	-1.9	181	91.2	0.0	0.0	5.0	3.9	25.4	58.1	16.6	77	89.6	44.2	31.2
Madelia city & MCD (Watonwan)	2,308	2,279	-1.3	2,419	72.5	0.2	0.0	3.3	23.9	26.0	53.8	20.3	931	68.0	52.3	19.0

1 May be of any race.

Table A. All Places — Population and Housing

STATE City, town, township, borough, or CDP (county if applicable)	2010 census total population	2014 estimated population	Percent change 2010–2014	ACS total population estimate 2010–2014	White alone, not Hispanic or Latino	Black alone, not Hispanic or Latino	Asian alone, not Hispanic or Latino	All other races or 2 or more races, not Hispanic or Latino	Hispanic or Latino[1]	Under 18 years old	Age 18 to 64 years old	Age 65 years and older	Total occupied housing units	Percent owner occupied	High school diploma or less	Bachelor's degree or more
	1	2	3	4	5	6	7	8	9	10	11	12	13	14	15	16
MINNESOTA—Con.																
Madelia township (Watonwan)	351	348	-0.9	376	92.3	0.0	0.0	0.0	7.7	23.1	59.7	17.3	144	95.8	40.3	23.6
Madison city & MCD (Lac qui Parle)	1,551	1,470	-5.2	1,559	93.0	0.6	2.1	2.5	1.9	17.9	48.7	33.5	712	72.2	44.1	18.7
Madison township (Lac qui Parle)	216	205	-5.1	216	97.7	0.0	2.3	0.0	0.0	21.8	50.2	28.2	98	88.8	25.5	30.6
Madison Lake city & MCD (Blue Earth)	1,017	1,062	4.4	1,039	99.5	0.0	0.2	0.3	0.0	22.6	72.1	5.4	407	58.2	39.6	25.1
Magnolia city & MCD (Rock)	222	219	-1.4	203	77.8	2.5	8.4	3.9	7.4	19.3	68.1	12.8	86	84.9	66.3	2.3
Magnolia township (Rock)	212	208	-1.9	211	95.3	0.0	0.0	0.0	4.7	26.0	69.6	4.3	74	86.5	54.1	10.8
Mahnomen city & MCD (Mahnomen)	1,214	1,234	1.6	1,293	47.7	0.5	0.6	47.8	3.4	26.0	51.5	22.4	516	64.3	54.7	13.8
Mahnomen CDP	239	NA	NA	299	7.7	0.0	0.0	92.3	0.0	47.5	49.9	2.7	91	26.4	44.0	15.4
Mahtomedi city & MCD (Washington)	7,727	8,064	4.4	7,923	93.5	1.0	2.2	1.9	1.4	25.2	60.6	14.2	2,861	84.0	15.6	52.5
Mahtowa CDP	370	NA	NA	343	93.0	0.0	1.7	2.9	2.3	27.7	62.1	10.2	134	90.3	34.3	9.7
Mahtowa township (Carlton)	613	617	0.7	567	93.7	0.0	2.1	2.8	1.4	24.5	63.8	11.6	232	91.8	36.6	11.6
Maine township (Otter Tail)	653	649	-0.6	661	97.4	0.6	0.0	2.0	0.0	18.2	55.2	26.6	285	93.3	31.2	30.2
Maine Prairie township (Stearns)	1,887	1,888	0.1	1,778	97.1	0.0	0.6	0.9	1.4	24.8	62.7	12.4	681	94.6	47.1	17.0
Makinen UT (St. Louis)	1,310	1,317	0.5	1,260	96.3	0.0	0.0	1.7	2.0	10.6	67.3	22.1	619	95.3	37.2	28.8
Malmo township (Aitkin)	337	330	-2.1	342	94.2	0.3	0.0	4.4	1.2	18.4	51.1	30.4	167	88.0	53.3	13.8
Malta township (Big Stone)	98	95	-3.1	72	100.0	0.0	0.0	0.0	0.0	36.1	47.2	16.7	25	92.0	48.0	8.0
Malung township (Roseau)	438	433	-1.1	476	99.2	0.0	0.6	0.2	0.0	24.4	65.4	10.3	191	95.3	48.7	23.0
Mamre township (Kandiyohi)	385	383	-0.5	353	88.7	0.0	0.0	2.0	9.3	29.1	55.5	15.3	130	87.7	30.0	23.8
Manannah township (Meeker)	604	602	-0.3	538	97.6	0.6	1.3	0.6	0.0	25.5	58.1	16.5	211	91.9	57.3	9.5
Manchester city & MCD (Freeborn)	57	56	-1.8	33	100.0	0.0	0.0	0.0	0.0	0.0	63.8	36.4	20	85.0	85.0	0.0
Manchester township (Freeborn)	424	419	-1.2	407	92.6	0.0	0.0	6.9	0.5	24.3	56.7	18.9	143	88.1	43.4	11.2
Mandt township (Chippewa)	152	148	-2.6	151	100.0	0.0	0.0	0.0	0.0	23.1	61.4	15.2	58	84.5	43.1	15.5
Manfred township (Lac qui Parle)	99	94	-5.1	67	100.0	0.0	0.0	0.0	0.0	16.5	43.4	40.3	34	85.3	70.6	14.7
Manhattan Beach city & MCD (Crow Wing)	57	58	1.8	41	100.0	0.0	0.0	0.0	0.0	0.0	41.5	58.5	22	90.9	50.0	27.3
Mankato city	39,338	40,411	2.7	39,871	87.8	3.7	2.7	2.7	3.1	16.4	72.7	10.8	15,351	54.1	25.4	31.1
Mankato city (Blue Earth)	39,334	40,407	2.7	39,871	87.8	3.7	2.7	2.7	3.1	16.4	72.7	10.8	15,351	54.1	25.4	31.1
Mankato city (Le Sueur)	4	4	0.0	0	0.0	0.0	0.0	0.0	0.0	0.0	0.0	0.0	0	0.0	0.0	0.0
Mankato city (Nicollet)	0	0	0.0	0	0.0	0.0	0.0	0.0	0.0	0.0	0.0	0.0	0	0.0	0.0	0.0
Mankato township (Blue Earth)	1,931	1,943	0.6	1,915	94.6	1.7	2.3	0.8	0.6	18.7	66.0	15.3	688	96.8	26.9	45.5
Mansfield township (Freeborn)	237	234	-1.3	223	98.7	0.0	0.9	0.0	0.4	26.8	55.1	17.9	90	86.7	43.3	20.0
Manston township (Wilkin)	48	47	-2.1	37	100.0	0.0	0.0	0.0	0.0	16.2	59.4	24.3	21	95.2	76.2	19.0
Mantorville city & MCD (Dodge)	1,197	1,206	0.8	1,189	93.9	1.1	0.7	2.9	1.4	22.1	63.2	14.8	465	85.2	35.7	25.2
Mantorville township (Dodge)	1,926	1,960	1.8	1,894	98.9	0.0	0.5	0.3	0.3	27.1	64.5	8.4	634	94.0	23.7	39.7
Mantrap township (Hubbard)	519	530	2.1	523	96.0	0.0	0.0	0.4	3.6	16.4	61.6	22.0	218	95.9	28.0	38.5
Manyaska township (Martin)	306	298	-2.6	305	100.0	0.0	0.0	0.0	0.0	17.1	62.2	20.7	123	93.5	42.3	22.0
Maple township (Cass)	377	378	0.3	317	100.0	0.0	0.0	0.0	0.0	18.9	68.4	12.6	133	91.7	47.4	16.5
Maple Grove township (Becker)	455	466	2.4	465	39.1	0.0	1.7	57.0	2.2	25.9	52.5	21.5	196	88.8	47.4	14.3
Maple Grove township (Crow Wing)	774	791	2.2	777	99.2	0.0	0.0	0.6	0.1	19.4	61.5	19.2	312	96.2	43.9	13.8
Maple Grove city & MCD (Hennepin)	61,569	66,945	8.7	64,364	85.3	3.8	6.4	2.4	2.1	26.4	65.0	8.7	24,397	85.0	17.0	52.1
Maple Lake city & MCD (Wright)	2,059	2,092	1.6	2,061	98.4	0.1	0.0	1.0	0.5	31.0	56.4	12.6	799	67.1	43.7	20.0
Maple Lake township (Wright)	2,048	2,114	3.2	2,087	97.5	0.1	0.0	0.2	2.2	21.6	65.2	13.3	784	88.4	38.5	27.6
Maple Plain city & MCD (Hennepin)	1,742	1,780	2.2	1,765	86.2	0.9	1.6	2.3	9.0	25.6	58.7	15.7	690	66.8	36.8	30.3
Maple Ridge township (Beltrami)	104	106	1.9	134	76.1	0.0	0.0	21.6	2.2	17.9	66.5	15.7	48	100.0	43.8	27.1
Maple Ridge township (Isanti)	761	771	1.3	634	97.9	0.0	0.3	1.7	0.0	16.5	68.7	14.8	258	95.3	46.1	18.6
Mapleton city & MCD (Blue Earth)	1,756	1,741	-0.9	1,687	94.6	0.3	1.0	0.3	3.8	29.3	51.9	18.8	612	76.0	42.2	15.7
Mapleton township (Blue Earth)	310	309	-0.3	240	94.3	0.0	1.2	4.5	0.0	27.6	58.0	13.4	91	83.5	57.1	20.0
Mapleview city & MCD (Mower)	176	177	0.6	202	93.1	0.0	2.5	0.0	4.5	18.3	65.0	16.8	94	74.5	55.3	4.3
Maplewood township (Otter Tail)	318	318	0.0	399	96.5	0.3	0.0	1.0	2.3	22.6	60.3	17.3	159	81.1	45.3	15.7
Maplewood city & MCD (Ramsey)	38,018	40,199	5.7	39,261	68.7	7.6	14.5	3.5	5.8	23.8	60.5	15.7	15,168	72.0	33.3	32.0
Marble city	701	699	-0.3	602	89.9	0.0	0.0	7.8	2.3	19.1	55.1	25.9	265	78.1	56.2	6.0
Marble township (Lincoln)	161	160	-0.6	171	100.0	0.0	0.0	0.0	0.0	30.5	58.6	11.1	67	91.0	38.8	11.9
Marcell township (Itasca)	467	472	1.1	393	99.5	0.0	0.0	0.5	0.0	12.4	50.5	36.9	180	91.1	31.7	33.9

1 May be of any race.

Table A. All Places — **Population and Housing**

STATE City, town, township, borough, or CDP (county if applicable)	2010 census total population	2014 estimated population	Percent change 2010–2014	ACS total population estimate 2010–2014	White alone, not Hispanic or Latino	Black alone, not Hispanic or Latino	Asian alone, not Hispanic or Latino	All other races or 2 or more races, not Hispanic or Latino	Hispanic or Latino[1]	Under 18 years old	Age 18 to 64 years old	Age 65 years and older	Total occupied housing units	Percent owner occupied	High school diploma or less	Bachelor's degree or more
	1	2	3	4	5	6	7	8	9	10	11	12	13	14	15	16
MINNESOTA—Con.																
Marietta city & MCD (Lac qui Parle)	162	154	-4.9	215	99.1	0.0	0.0	0.9	0.0	34.4	45.2	20.5	96	94.8	42.7	1.0
Marine on St. Croix city & MCD (Washington)	687	695	1.2	686	93.4	0.6	0.4	5.5	0.0	20.5	58.1	21.3	299	87.6	7.7	61.9
Marion township (Olmsted)	3,672	3,826	4.2	3,750	95.6	1.7	0.3	1.6	0.7	19.3	66.8	13.8	1,390	92.2	24.6	34.9
Marshall city & MCD (Lyon)	13,687	13,641	-0.3	13,609	82.5	4.2	3.2	1.3	8.7	23.7	64.3	12.2	5,342	55.5	34.9	32.5
Marshall township (Mower)	361	363	0.6	430	93.5	0.0	0.5	0.0	6.0	39.3	50.6	10.0	135	89.6	34.8	15.6
Marshan township (Dakota)	1,106	1,132	2.4	1,075	93.7	0.1	0.7	4.7	0.8	20.0	65.3	14.8	409	89.0	40.8	24.2
Marsh Creek township (Mahnomen)	152	156	2.6	75	92.0	0.0	0.0	8.0	0.0	30.7	57.4	12.0	27	96.3	37.0	18.5
Marshfield township (Lincoln)	242	239	-1.2	222	98.6	0.0	0.0	0.0	1.4	26.7	55.5	18.0	88	100.0	33.0	15.9
Marsh Grove township (Marshall)	143	143	0.0	106	100.0	0.0	0.0	0.0	0.0	28.4	52.0	19.8	41	87.8	36.6	41.5
Martin township (Rock)	384	380		394	99.7	0.0	0.0	0.0	0.3	22.6	69.4	7.9	143	90.2	39.9	19.6
Martin Lake CDP	933	NA	NA	1,009	100.0	0.0	0.0	0.0	0.0	26.8	68.6	4.8	360	91.7	30.6	22.8
Martinsburg township (Renville)	197	189	-4.1	190	100.0	0.0	0.0	0.0	0.0	27.4	56.8	15.8	76	81.6	51.3	14.5
Mary township (Norman)	83	81	-2.4	83	94.0	0.0	0.0	6.0	0.0	28.9	56.4	14.5	29	82.8	44.8	0.0
Marysland township (Swift)	96	93	-3.1	112	100.0	0.0	0.0	0.0	0.0	29.4	55.5	15.2	52	84.6	57.7	3.8
Marysville township (Wright)	2,146	2,204	2.7	2,310	90.6	0.0	0.9	2.0	6.5	28.7	62.0	9.2	791	93.3	42.6	16.6
Mason township (Murray)	299	295	-1.3	283	100.0	0.0	0.0	0.0	0.0	17.7	52.2	30.0	129	90.7	45.0	21.7
Max township (Itasca)	142	143	0.7	141	73.0	0.0	14.9	9.2	2.8	32.6	39.7	27.7	60	88.3	46.7	21.7
Maxwell township (Lac qui Parle)	179	170	-5.0	155	100.0	0.0	0.0	0.0	0.0	19.4	73.7	7.1	71	83.1	52.1	12.7
May township (Cass)	852	851	-0.1	973	96.9	0.2	0.0	2.4	0.5	30.1	57.1	12.8	373	90.1	41.6	16.6
May township (Washington)	2,779	2,852	2.6	2,822	96.9	0.0	2.8	0.2	0.0	15.8	67.2	17.0	1,087	96.9	28.6	39.7
Mayer city & MCD (Carver)	1,749	1,856	6.1	1,792	92.5	0.0	2.9	2.5	2.1	32.9	60.6	6.5	577	92.7	26.7	37.3
Mayfield township (Pennington)	51	51	0.0	31	100.0	0.0	0.0	0.0	0.0	6.5	64.6	29.0	16	100.0	62.5	6.3
Mayhew Lake township (Benton)	827	847	2.4	944	97.2	0.0	0.4	1.5	0.8	30.4	60.9	8.8	312	91.3	48.4	12.8
Maynard city & MCD (Chippewa)	366	353	-3.6	379	76.0	0.0	6.6	0.5	16.9	21.9	64.5	13.5	150	74.7	64.7	10.0
Mayville township (Houston)	409	406	-0.7	422	92.9	0.0	0.0	0.7	6.4	24.6	53.0	22.3	165	92.1	51.5	8.5
Maywood township (Benton)	954	971	1.8	993	97.0	0.0	0.5	2.1	0.4	26.7	57.5	15.7	378	91.8	58.5	9.0
Mazeppa city & MCD (Wabasha)	840	829	-1.3	805	91.6	0.0	2.6	2.6	3.2	23.1	63.9	13.0	338	81.7	57.1	18.9
Mazeppa township (Wabasha)	705	699	-0.9	701	95.6	0.0	1.1	2.4	0.9	22.1	62.9	14.8	272	88.2	39.0	25.4
Meadow township (Wadena)	217	213	-1.8	226	100.0	0.0	0.0	0.0	0.0	13.7	58.8	27.4	102	99.0	69.6	4.9
Meadow Brook township (Cass)	226	226	0.0	220	96.4	0.0	2.3	1.4	0.0	10.9	66.9	22.3	97	93.8	35.1	3.1
Meadowlands city & MCD (St. Louis)	134	134	0.0	90	95.6	0.0	0.0	4.4	0.0	13.4	61.2	25.6	51	52.9	54.9	13.7
Meadowlands township (St. Louis)	304	305	0.3	247	100.0	0.0	0.0	0.0	0.0	20.3	58.2	21.5	110	91.8	44.5	15.5
Meadows township (Wilkin)	38	38	0.0	34	88.2	0.0	0.0	0.0	11.8	14.7	79.2	5.9	16	81.3	62.5	0.0
Medford city & MCD (Steele)	1,239	1,236	-0.2	1,382	92.3	0.3	0.4	0.7	6.3	31.3	57.6	11.2	468	92.5	43.6	24.1
Medford township (Steele)	813	804	-1.1	870	80.1	0.0	0.2	2.3	17.4	32.3	57.7	10.0	300	92.0	58.3	9.3
Medicine Lake city & MCD (Hennepin)	355	370	4.2	325	94.2	1.5	0.6	2.5	1.2	13.8	69.3	16.9	157	68.8	10.8	63.1
Medina city & MCD (Hennepin)	4,890	5668	15.9	5,163	94.2	0.5	0.9	1.6	2.7	29.8	57.0	13.3	1,744	93.8	13.8	59.1
Medo township (Blue Earth)	364	365	0.3	378	97.1	0.0	0.3	2.6	0.0	30.7	53.8	15.6	127	94.5	42.5	21.3
Mehurin township (Lac qui Parle)	77	73	-5.2	92	100.0	0.0	0.0	0.0	0.0	24.0	53.3	22.8	38	86.8	42.1	5.3
Meire Grove city & MCD (Stearns)	179	179	0.0	178	100.0	0.0	0.0	0.0	0.0	24.2	50.4	25.3	81	63.0	50.6	14.8
Melrose city & MCD (Stearns)	3,598	3,593	-0.1	3,599	71.5	0.3	2.4	0.5	25.2	31.5	48.5	20.2	1,265	79.0	52.6	16.2
Melrose township (Stearns)	759	768	1.2	753	92.7	0.0	0.0	0.0	7.3	23.6	59.1	17.3	262	93.5	41.2	17.6
Melville township (Renville)	225	216	-4.0	212	98.1	0.9	0.0	0.9	0.0	24.1	53.0	23.1	88	88.6	50.0	10.2
Menahga city & MCD (Wadena)	1,306	1,335	2.2	1,395	94.1	0.8	0.4	2.5	2.2	23.9	49.5	26.5	629	54.7	66.0	8.7
Mendota city & MCD (Dakota)	198	206	4.0	221	73.8	0.0	5.9	10.0	10.4	29.3	64.8	5.9	78	51.3	29.5	25.6
Mendota Heights city & MCD (Dakota)	11,071	11,222	1.4	11,131	87.9	1.4	2.8	2.3	5.7	20.8	59.9	19.2	4,528	88.9	13.0	65.4
Mentor city & MCD (Polk)	153	152	-0.7	182	94.5	0.0	0.0	3.3	2.2	23.6	59.6	16.5	83	73.5	66.3	6.0
Meriden township (Steele)	621	621	0.0	709	98.3	1.0	0.6	0.0	0.1	30.0	59.1	10.9	241	88.8	49.8	15.4
Merrifield CDP	140	NA	NA	99	100.0	0.0	0.0	0.0	0.0	4.0	47.5	48.5	51	82.4	29.4	29.4
Merton township (Steele)	348	349	0.3	354	98.6	0.0	0.3	0.3	0.8	24.3	60.3	15.5	127	87.4	44.9	18.9
Mickinock township (Roseau)	301	304	1.0	331	98.8	0.0	0.0	1.2	0.0	27.1	60.4	12.4	128	91.4	56.3	17.2

1 May be of any race.

Table A. All Places — **Population and Housing**

STATE City, town, township, borough, or CDP (county if applicable)	2010 census total population	2014 estimated population	Percent change 2010–2014	ACS total population estimate 2010–2014	White alone, not Hispanic or Latino	Black alone, not Hispanic or Latino	Asian alone, not Hispanic or Latino	All other races or 2 or more races, not Hispanic or Latino	Hispanic or Latino[1]	Under 18 years old	Age 18 to 64 years old	Age 65 years and older	Total occupied housing units	Percent owner occupied	High school diploma or less	Bachelor's degree or more
	1	2	3	4	5	6	7	8	9	10	11	12	13	14	15	16
MINNESOTA—Con.																
Middle River city & MCD (Marshall)	303	298	-1.7	335	95.8	0.0	0.0	2.7	1.5	31.7	48.3	20.3	143	72.7	52.4	11.9
Middle River township (Marshall)	78	78	0.0	84	100.0	0.0	0.0	0.0	0.0	11.9	72.8	15.5	38	89.5	36.8	23.7
Middletown township (Jackson)	227	229	0.9	252	95.6	0.0	1.2	0.0	3.2	19.8	57.4	22.6	115	87.0	33.9	26.1
Middleville township (Wright)	928	954	2.8	1,036	96.3	0.1	0.2	2.2	1.2	26.4	61.7	12.1	351	93.7	51.6	24.2
Midway township (Cottonwood)	219	218	-0.5	196	91.8	0.0	3.6	0.0	4.6	14.8	59.7	25.5	89	88.8	43.8	21.3
Midway CDP	26	NA	NA	12	8.3	0.0	0.0	91.7	0.0	58.3	41.7	0.0	4	25.0	0.0	0.0
Midway township (St. Louis)	1,398	1,410	0.9	1,438	97.4	0.0	0.0	2.6	0.0	23.6	59.8	16.3	555	88.1	32.4	24.7
Miesville city & MCD (Dakota)	125	131	4.8	163	88.3	0.0	0.0	0.0	11.7	21.5	63.8	14.7	74	71.6	48.6	4.1
Milaca city & MCD (Mille Lacs)	2,946	2,900	-1.6	2,907	92.9	0.6	0.1	2.1	4.3	24.5	53.2	22.5	1,288	56.0	41.8	18.7
Milaca township (Mille Lacs)	1,617	1,612	-0.3	1,566	98.5	0.2	0.1	0.6	0.6	25.2	64.9	9.8	579	93.6	40.4	17.1
Milan city & MCD (Chippewa)	369	360	-2.4	397	55.2	0.0	3.5	29.5	11.8	27.5	56.4	16.1	142	64.8	54.2	12.7
Milford township (Brown)	694	685	-1.3	747	98.8	0.4	0.0	0.7	0.1	21.7	62.0	16.3	283	95.8	50.9	16.6
Millerville city & MCD (Douglas)	106	105	-0.9	188	100.0	0.0	0.0	0.0	0.0	9.1	84.0	6.9	73	76.7	26.0	11.0
Millerville township (Douglas)	338	341	0.9	317	98.4	0.0	0.6	0.0	0.9	26.5	52.1	21.5	117	90.6	58.1	5.1
Millville city & MCD (Wabasha)	182	179	-1.6	152	91.4	8.6	0.0	0.0	0.0	23.7	55.4	21.1	63	82.5	65.1	3.2
Millward township (Aitkin)	72	69	-4.2	37	81.1	8.1	0.0	10.8	0.0	8.1	62.1	29.7	21	100.0	57.1	0.0
Millwood township (Stearns)	972	1,001	3.0	1,048	99.7	0.0	0.0	0.2	0.1	26.9	60.0	13.1	344	94.2	56.1	16.0
Milo township (Mille Lacs)	1,385	1,376	-0.6	1,467	98.3	0.0	0.0	1.4	0.3	28.0	59.0	13.0	528	95.1	44.1	11.0
Milroy city & MCD (Redwood)	252	244	-3.2	203	100.0	0.0	0.0	0.0	0.0	21.2	66.4	12.3	106	74.5	45.3	21.7
Milton township (Dodge)	734	743	1.2	705	91.5	0.0	0.4	0.9	7.2	28.5	52.2	19.1	250	89.2	37.6	22.0
Miltona city & MCD (Douglas)	424	430	1.4	335	93.1	0.3	0.0	1.2	5.4	27.2	56.8	16.1	146	71.2	44.5	8.2
Miltona township (Douglas)	806	815	1.1	728	99.2	0.0	0.0	0.0	0.8	9.3	58.5	32.1	348	94.5	37.6	20.4
Minden township (Benton)	1,549	1,583	2.2	1,552	98.8	0.0	0.0	1.0	0.3	20.8	62.8	16.3	629	91.3	37.4	24.3
Minerva township (Clearwater)	261	265	1.5	212	83.0	0.0	0.0	6.1	10.8	25.9	57.5	16.5	83	96.4	57.8	12.0
Minneapolis city & MCD (Hennepin)	382,599	407,207	6.4	394,424	61.0	17.6	5.8	5.8	9.8	20.1	71.5	8.5	166,824	48.6	24.3	48.4
Minneiska city	111	109	-1.8	105	95.2	0.0	2.9	1.9	0.0	8.6	61.1	30.5	52	92.3	23.1	36.5
Minneiska city (Wabasha)	61	60	-1.6	57	91.2	0.0	5.3	3.5	0.0	14.1	63.3	22.8	24	91.7	12.5	20.8
Minneiska city (Winona)	50	49	-2.0	48	100.0	0.0	0.0	0.0	0.0	2.1	58.4	39.6	28	92.9	32.1	50.0
Minneiska township (Wabasha)	185	182	-1.6	175	100.0	0.0	0.0	0.0	0.0	22.9	56.6	20.6	78	97.4	37.2	17.9
Minneola township (Goodhue)	629	635	1.0	743	94.6	0.0	2.3	0.5	2.6	25.1	58.3	16.6	278	91.7	42.1	25.9
Minneota township (Jackson)	259	263	1.5	407	98.8	0.0	0.0	0.7	0.5	31.0	46.0	22.9	149	73.2	60.4	13.4
Minneota city & MCD (Lyon)	1,392	1,365	-1.9	1,343	94.0	0.4	0.0	1.0	4.5	22.7	55.7	21.7	579	81.5	45.1	27.3
Minnesota City city & MCD (Winona)	204	201	-1.5	165	93.9	0.0	0.0	2.4	3.6	28.4	57.5	13.9	66	77.3	54.5	18.2
Minnesota Falls township (Yellow Medicine)	429	416	-3.0	469	57.4	1.3	1.1	38.6	1.7	21.4	66.0	12.8	184	91.3	42.4	20.1
Minnesota Lake city	687	669	-2.6	622	96.5	0.0	0.0	0.0	3.5	16.4	60.3	23.3	281	86.8	56.2	10.0
Minnesota Lake city (Blue Earth)	4	4	0.0	4	100.0	0.0	0.0	0.0	0.0	0.0	0.0	100.0	2	100.0	0.0	0.0
Minnesota Lake city (Faribault)	683	665	-2.6	618	96.4	0.0	0.0	0.0	3.6	16.5	60.8	22.8	279	86.7	56.6	10.0
Minnesota Lake township (Faribault)	190	186	-2.1	206	90.8	0.0	3.4	4.9	1.0	22.8	62.6	14.6	83	91.6	42.2	18.1
Minnetonka city & MCD (Hennepin)	49,723	51,486	3.5	50,897	86.7	4.3	3.6	3.0	2.4	20.1	62.4	17.5	22,306	72.2	14.2	57.3
Minnetonka Beach city & MCD (Hennepin)	540	558	3.3	587	93.0	0.0	1.2	4.1	1.7	33.4	57.9	8.9	205	91.2	8.3	76.6
Minnetrista city & MCD (Hennepin)	6,376	6885	8.0	6,661	91.5	1.3	1.6	3.4	2.2	30.6	58.4	11.0	2,243	94.7	22.0	56.8
Minnewaska township (Pope)	500	492	-1.6	557	92.6	4.5	0.0	2.9	0.0	24.7	52.0	23.3	216	95.4	21.8	29.2
Minnie township (Beltrami)	26	26	0.0	29	100.0	0.0	0.0	0.0	0.0	20.7	62.1	17.2	15	86.7	40.0	0.0
Mission township (Crow Wing)	815	832	2.1	684	99.6	0.4	0.0	0.0	0.0	16.3	53.4	30.3	343	90.1	34.1	26.8
Mission Creek township (Pine)	635	617	-2.8	692	97.1	0.0	1.9	0.6	0.4	24.2	63.3	12.7	268	82.8	53.0	6.3
Mitchell township (Wilkin)	85	84	-1.2	100	95.0	0.0	0.0	0.0	5.0	34.0	59.0	7.0	34	94.1	29.4	35.3
Mizpah city & MCD (Koochiching)	56	55	-1.8	90	100.0	0.0	0.0	0.0	0.0	21.1	48.8	30.0	43	100.0	81.4	4.7
Moe township (Douglas)	784	794	1.3	760	93.6	0.0	0.7	0.8	5.0	20.2	58.2	21.4	303	100.0	32.7	32.7
Moland township (Clay)	299	310	3.7	281	98.9	0.0	0.0	0.7	0.4	22.8	66.9	10.3	110	88.2	28.2	20.9
Moltke township (Sibley)	279	274	-1.8	283	99.6	0.0	0.0	0.0	0.4	25.2	54.8	20.1	117	86.3	51.3	13.7
Money Creek township (Houston)	597	592	-0.8	648	99.2	0.0	0.0	0.8	0.0	22.4	67.8	9.9	250	88.0	45.6	15.6
Monroe township (Lyon)	200	199	-0.5	269	98.9	0.0	0.0	0.0	1.1	30.9	58.7	10.4	95	89.5	45.3	15.8
Monson township (Traverse)	133	128	-3.8	146	82.2	0.0	0.0	6.2	11.6	27.4	43.1	29.5	57	94.7	49.1	7.0

1   May be of any race.

Table A. All Places — **Population and Housing**

STATE City, town, township, borough, or CDP (county if applicable)	2010 census total population	2014 estimated population	Percent change 2010–2014	ACS total population estimate 2010–2014	White alone, not Hispanic or Latino	Black alone, not Hispanic or Latino	Asian alone, not Hispanic or Latino	All other races or 2 or more races, not Hispanic or Latino	Hispanic or Latino[1]	Under 18 years old	Age 18 to 64 years old	Age 65 years and older	Total occupied housing units	Percent owner occupied	High school diploma or less	Bachelor's degree or more
	1	2	3	4	5	6	7	8	9	10	11	12	13	14	15	16

MINNESOTA—Con.

STATE City, town, township, borough, or CDP (county if applicable)	1	2	3	4	5	6	7	8	9	10	11	12	13	14	15	16
Montevideo city & MCD (Chippewa)	5,383	5,221	-3.0	5,283	88.9	1.2	0.0	2.1	7.8	23.9	54.6	21.4	2,243	66.1	41.4	19.7
Montgomery city & MCD (Le Sueur)	2,956	2,935	-0.7	2,935	88.6	1.3	0.9	4.6	4.7	26.7	58.8	14.4	1,129	77.0	55.3	11.9
Montgomery township (Le Sueur)	665	672	1.1	628	99.5	0.0	0.0	0.0	0.5	16.0	69.0	15.1	271	94.5	57.9	13.3
Monticello city & MCD (Wright)	12,759	13,136	3.0	12,974	89.1	0.8	0.6	2.1	7.4	31.1	60.2	8.7	4,693	75.0	31.8	31.4
Monticello township (Wright)	3,181	3,287	3.3	3,220	96.8	0.0	0.8	2.2	0.2	23.8	66.8	9.3	1,088	96.6	37.9	24.4
Montrose city & MCD (Wright)	2,847	3,046	7.0	2,952	96.6	0.0	0.0	0.5	2.9	36.9	59.5	3.6	1,016	80.2	29.0	19.7
Moonshine township (Big Stone)	102	101	-1.0	157	96.2	0.0	0.0	0.0	3.8	28.7	63.8	7.6	55	96.4	21.8	16.4
Moore township (Stevens)	243	242	-0.4	234	89.7	0.0	0.0	0.0	10.3	28.7	67.2	4.3	79	68.4	46.8	6.3
Moorhead city & MCD (Clay)	38,065	39,857	4.7	39,053	87.1	2.2	1.7	4.1	4.8	20.8	68.1	11.1	14,454	61.2	27.4	34.0
Moorhead township (Clay)	169	174	3.0	183	97.8	0.0	0.0	1.6	0.5	10.4	66.6	23.0	78	100.0	46.2	24.4
Moose township (Roseau)	114	115	0.9	81	100.0	0.0	0.0	0.0	0.0	25.9	55.5	18.5	32	87.5	31.3	21.9
Moose Creek township (Clearwater)	230	233	1.3	231	99.1	0.0	0.0	0.9	0.0	16.5	60.7	22.9	117	83.8	40.2	37.6
Moose Lake township (Beltrami)	228	232	1.8	219	98.6	0.0	0.0	0.0	1.4	20.5	58.4	21.0	91	98.9	56.0	19.8
Moose Lake city & MCD (Carlton)	2,751	2,804	1.9	2,773	78.4	8.6	0.4	9.1	3.5	11.5	69.4	19.0	858	57.5	42.9	21.7
Moose Lake township (Carlton)	1,061	1,075	1.3	1,008	99.2	0.0	0.0	0.0	0.0	13.6	60.0	26.4	399	83.0	29.1	30.1
Moose Lake township (Cass)	111	109	-1.8	154	96.1	0.0	0.0	3.9	0.0	15.5	70.7	13.6	67	95.5	62.7	4.5
Moose Park township (Itasca)	68	68	0.0	51	100.0	0.0	0.0	0.0	0.0	5.9	35.4	58.8	28	85.7	64.3	10.7
Moose River township (Marshall)	25	25	0.0	28	67.9	0.0	0.0	32.1	0.0	21.4	57.0	21.4	12	100.0	66.7	8.3
Mora city & MCD (Kanabec)	3,571	3,488	-2.3	3,534	94.2	0.0	0.4	2.4	3.0	22.2	54.4	23.4	1,500	48.9	51.3	14.6
Moran township (Todd)	508	495	-2.6	514	96.9	0.4	1.4	0.8	0.6	19.7	67.9	12.5	199	96.5	51.8	12.6
Moranville township (Roseau)	887	886	-0.1	902	96.1	0.0	0.9	0.8	2.2	26.8	58.0	15.0	312	90.4	51.6	18.6
Morcom township (St. Louis)	94	94	0.0	112	96.4	0.0	0.0	3.6	0.0	24.1	57.4	18.8	48	97.9	81.3	4.2
Morgan city & MCD (Redwood)	896	872	-2.7	904	94.1	0.0	0.0	3.3	2.5	27.9	50.2	21.8	388	76.8	48.5	18.3
Morgan township (Redwood)	257	251	-2.3	274	99.3	0.0	0.0	0.7	0.0	26.6	58.3	15.0	104	94.2	50.0	10.6
Morken township (Clay)	156	159	1.9	142	100.0	0.0	0.0	0.0	0.0	19.8	74.6	5.6	60	86.7	33.3	20.0
Morrill township (Morrison)	696	688	-1.1	694	98.0	0.0	0.0	0.6	1.4	27.5	62.7	9.7	270	94.1	61.1	7.8
Morris city & MCD (Stevens)	5,286	5,357	1.3	5,324	88.8	1.0	2.3	4.9	2.9	17.3	65.4	17.2	2,055	56.4	31.8	27.4
Morris township (Stevens)	396	399	0.8	439	97.7	0.0	0.0	0.0	2.3	28.2	57.2	14.6	155	92.3	32.3	32.9
Morrison township (Aitkin)	200	196	-2.0	253	97.6	2.0	0.0	0.4	0.0	16.2	59.8	24.1	120	80.8	45.0	10.0
Morristown city & MCD (Rice)	987	990	0.3	928	82.8	0.0	0.0	1.0	16.3	24.8	60.5	14.8	379	81.3	59.9	4.7
Morristown township (Rice)	697	704	1.0	509	97.2	0.6	1.2	1.0	0.0	21.0	65.4	13.6	212	81.1	52.4	19.3
Morse township (Itasca)	615	619	0.7	598	81.3	0.0	0.0	16.6	2.2	27.1	60.3	12.5	220	93.6	41.8	10.9
Morse township (St. Louis)	1,212	1,223	0.9	1,312	97.6	0.0	0.0	2.0	0.5	12.4	63.5	24.2	637	93.2	24.6	40.8
Morton city & MCD (Renville)	411	387	-5.8	403	79.9	0.0	3.0	13.4	3.7	24.8	62.0	13.2	181	72.4	44.2	8.3
Moscow township (Freeborn)	538	531	-1.3	489	88.1	0.6	0.0	0.0	11.2	19.8	60.2	20.0	196	88.3	51.5	11.7
Motley city (Cass)	671	651	-3.0	595	89.7	0.0	0.0	0.7	9.6	27.6	55.2	17.1	275	54.9	55.3	6.5
Motley city (Cass)	11	11	0.0	37	40.5	0.0	0.0	0.0	59.5	48.6	51.3	0.0	5	100.0	0.0	0.0
Motley city (Morrison)	660	640	-3.0	558	93.0	0.0	0.0	0.7	6.3	26.2	55.6	18.3	270	54.1	56.3	6.7
Motley township (Morrison)	202	200	-1.0	189	100.0	0.0	0.0	0.0	0.0	20.1	54.5	25.4	82	90.2	54.9	17.1
Moulton township (Murray)	206	203	-1.5	242	88.4	0.0	7.9	3.7	0.0	33.4	57.8	8.7	84	79.8	53.6	14.3
Mound city & MCD (Hennepin)	9,047	9,302	2.8	9,205	92.3	1.0	2.1	2.1	2.6	19.1	68.5	12.2	4,132	77.2	23.6	42.8
Mound township (Rock)	252	248	-1.6	208	96.2	0.0	0.0	0.0	3.8	23.1	68.3	8.7	75	89.3	40.0	28.0
Mound Prairie township (Houston)	606	601	-0.8	648	99.7	0.0	0.0	0.3	0.0	23.1	64.6	12.5	267	89.5	37.5	25.1
Mounds View city & MCD (Ramsey)	12,155	12,657	4.1	12,412	79.8	4.8	5.9	3.7	5.8	24.4	62.1	13.4	4,875	70.4	37.2	28.6
Mountain Iron city & MCD (St. Louis)	2,869	2,890	0.7	2,874	98.2	0.0	0.4	1.2	0.2	17.4	64.1	18.6	1,371	58.7	33.8	23.1
Mountain Lake city & MCD (Cottonwood)	2,104	2,134	1.4	2,175	76.6	0.0	9.3	4.6	9.4	26.1	53.8	20.1	879	79.1	45.7	14.6
Mountain Lake township (Cottonwood)	384	383	-0.3	277	94.2	0.0	0.0	0.0	5.8	26.0	60.1	13.7	85	85.9	45.9	23.5
Mount Morris township (Morrison)	93	91	-2.2	80	96.3	0.0	0.0	3.8	0.0	22.6	72.5	5.0	35	80.0	62.9	14.3
Mount Pleasant township (Wabasha)	447	441	-1.3	438	99.3	0.0	0.0	0.7	0.0	26.9	64.0	9.1	154	94.8	35.1	26.6
Mount Vernon township (Winona)	273	271	-0.7	241	88.8	0.0	0.0	0.0	11.2	23.3	61.0	15.8	89	83.1	46.1	20.2
Moyer township (Swift)	88	85	-3.4	65	100.0	0.0	0.0	0.0	0.0	16.9	58.4	24.6	31	77.4	67.7	12.9
Moylan township (Marshall)	98	98	0.0	122	96.7	0.0	0.0	0.0	3.3	20.5	58.1	21.3	50	92.0	56.0	14.0
Mudgett township (Mille Lacs)	84	84	0.0	63	98.4	0.0	0.0	1.6	0.0	11.1	66.5	22.2	25	96.0	64.0	8.0
Mud Lake UT (Marshall)	0	0	0.0	0	0.0	0.0	0.0	0.0	0.0	0.0	0.0	0.0	0	0.0	0.0	0.0

1 May be of any race.

Table A. All Places — **Population and Housing**

	Population				Race and Hispanic or Latino origin (percent), 2010–2014					Age (percent), 2010–2014			Households, 2010–2014			
STATE City, town, township, borough, or CDP (county if applicable)	2010 census total population	2014 estimated population	Percent change 2010–2014	ACS total population estimate 2010–2014	White alone, not Hispanic or Latino	Black alone, not Hispanic or Latino	Asian alone, not Hispanic or Latino	All other races or 2 or more races, not Hispanic or Latino	Hispanic or Latino[1]	Under 18 years old	Age 18 to 64 years old	Age 65 years and older	Total occupied housing units	Percent owner occupied	Householders by level of education (percent) — High school diploma or less	Householders by level of education (percent) — Bachelor's degree or more
	1	2	3	4	5	6	7	8	9	10	11	12	13	14	15	16
MINNESOTA—Con.																
Mulligan township (Brown)	218	215	-1.4	211	97.6	0.5	0.0	0.0	1.9	20.3	58.8	20.9	91	92.3	61.5	9.9
Munch township (Pine)	301	301	0.0	290	95.2	0.0	0.0	4.8	0.0	13.8	71.0	15.2	122	91.8	44.3	6.6
Munson township (Stearns)	1,466	1,489	1.6	1,505	99.7	0.0	0.0	0.3	0.1	28.6	57.7	13.6	534	97.2	45.1	20.0
Murdock city & MCD (Swift)	278	269	-3.2	284	82.4	0.0	0.0	0.0	17.6	26.1	62.4	11.6	115	79.1	51.3	11.3
Murray township (Murray)	177	175	-1.1	149	100.0	0.0	0.0	0.0	0.0	10.8	60.3	28.9	74	86.5	45.9	16.2
Myhre township (Lake of the Woods)	180	NA	NA	159	100.0	0.0	0.0	0.0	0.0	22.0	56.6	21.4	82	100.0	58.5	4.9
Myrtle city & MCD (Freeborn)	48	47	-2.1	57	56.1	0.0	0.0	0.0	43.9	50.8	33.3	15.8	20	45.0	70.0	0.0
Nashua city & MCD (Wilkin)	68	67	-1.5	73	50.7	0.0	0.0	0.0	49.3	41.1	53.4	5.5	20	100.0	80.0	0.0
Nashville township (Martin)	195	190	-2.6	227	85.5	0.0	0.0	0.0	14.5	24.6	62.2	13.2	90	86.7	44.4	8.9
Nashwauk city	983	977	-0.6	933	97.2	0.0	0.0	2.8	0.0	19.7	56.5	23.8	448	65.4	44.0	10.7
Nashwauk township (Itasca)	1,681	1,681	0.0	1,699	97.2	0.0	0.0	2.6	0.2	17.3	58.3	24.3	778	76.7	41.0	12.6
Nassau city & MCD (Lac qui Parle)	72	69	-4.2	51	90.2	0.0	0.0	0.0	9.8	27.4	62.7	9.8	22	95.5	54.5	18.2
Naytahwaush CDP	578	NA	NA	452	2.2	0.0	0.7	92.3	4.9	48.4	43.8	7.7	123	35.8	72.4	0.0
Nebish township (Beltrami)	288	287	-0.3	328	98.5	0.0	0.0	1.5	0.0	24.1	60.7	15.2	123	86.2	51.2	23.6
Nelson city & MCD (Douglas)	187	186	-0.5	179	93.9	0.0	0.0	0.6	5.6	20.1	63.1	16.8	81	70.4	51.9	7.4
Nelson township (Watonwan)	287	284	-1.0	264	98.9	0.0	0.0	0.4	0.8	21.2	60.4	18.2	111	89.2	47.7	9.9
Nelson Park township (Marshall)	125	125	0.0	151	96.0	0.0	0.0	2.6	1.3	15.9	68.1	15.9	63	90.5	44.4	14.3
Nereson township (Roseau)	58	59	1.7	45	100.0	0.0	0.0	0.0	0.0	17.8	60.1	22.2	25	84.0	40.0	8.0
Nerstrand city & MCD (Rice)	295	299	1.4	290	94.8	0.0	0.7	1.4	3.1	30.4	61.0	8.6	106	95.3	34.9	21.7
Nesbit township (Polk)	99	99	0.0	120	96.7	0.0	0.0	0.0	3.3	29.2	57.5	13.3	42	97.6	19.0	16.7
Ness township (St. Louis)	62	62	0.0	70	100.0	0.0	0.0	0.0	0.0	22.9	62.9	14.3	28	96.4	46.4	17.9
Nessel township (Chisago)	1,944	1,967	1.2	1,893	94.5	0.8	0.2	2.1	2.4	23.1	60.2	16.9	699	89.4	42.9	18.9
Nett Lake CDP	284	NA	NA	313	11.2	0.0	7.7	80.8	0.3	22.7	64.4	12.8	108	39.8	56.5	4.6
Nett Lake UT (Koochiching)	101	NA	NA	122	10.7	0.0	19.7	69.7	0.0	14.8	78.7	6.6	51	17.6	41.2	9.8
Nett Lake UT (St. Louis)	319	320	0.3	332	6.9	0.0	0.0	87.7	5.4	39.4	49.9	10.5	89	42.7	51.7	5.6
Nevada township (Mower)	338	342	1.2	421	92.2	0.0	0.7	0.0	7.1	21.5	58.0	20.7	157	82.2	43.3	15.3
Nevis city & MCD (Hubbard)	390	398	2.1	411	84.2	0.0	0.2	2.9	12.7	29.7	49.0	21.2	171	71.3	40.4	18.1
Nevis township (Hubbard)	1,009	1,009	0.0	953	97.4	0.0	0.6	0.7	1.3	17.0	53.4	29.7	414	91.1	37.0	30.7
New Auburn city & MCD (Sibley)	456	440	-3.5	527	96.6	0.0	0.0	0.2	3.2	31.2	62.0	6.8	202	85.6	60.9	8.4
New Auburn township (Sibley)	418	411	-1.7	476	99.8	0.0	0.2	0.0	0.0	25.4	57.6	17.0	178	89.9	64.6	10.1
New Avon township (Redwood)	191	185	-3.1	206	100.0	0.0	0.0	0.0	0.0	20.3	63.0	16.5	93	66.7	29.0	26.9
New Brighton city & MCD (Ramsey)	21,456	22,266	3.8	21,899	76.3	10.4	5.3	3.7	3.8	22.1	60.3	17.4	9,169	63.7	25.9	43.4
Newburg township (Fillmore)	379	382	0.8	364	100.0	0.0	0.0	0.0	0.0	15.1	67.8	17.0	166	86.7	44.6	7.8
New Dosey township (Pine)	74	75	1.4	64	98.4	0.0	0.0	1.6	0.0	14.1	36.1	50.0	31	90.3	83.9	0.0
Newfolden city & MCD (Marshall)	368	372	1.1	382	98.4	0.0	0.0	1.6	0.0	28.3	58.3	13.4	168	68.5	36.3	15.5
New Folden township (Marshall)	230	230	0.0	190	97.4	0.0	0.0	2.6	0.0	26.9	59.0	14.2	78	97.4	55.1	14.1
New Germany city & MCD (Carver)	373	383	2.7	425	89.9	1.6	0.0	1.4	7.1	31.2	60.4	8.2	168	79.2	46.4	12.5
New Hartford township (Winona)	890	888	-0.2	877	97.9	0.2	1.1	0.0	0.7	23.9	63.6	12.5	302	87.1	46.7	25.2
New Haven township (Olmsted)	1,176	1,227	4.3	1,179	98.5	0.0	0.0	1.2	0.3	18.0	63.3	18.6	482	88.6	37.6	24.7
New Hope city & MCD (Hennepin)	20,346	20,792	2.2	20,648	66.3	17.9	3.9	3.5	8.5	22.2	59.2	18.5	8,680	53.4	32.3	34.0
New Independence township (St. Louis)	301	302	0.3	279	91.0	0.0	0.0	9.0	0.0	20.4	71.4	8.2	111	91.0	43.2	16.2
New London city & MCD (Kandiyohi)	1,251	1,305	4.3	1,387	96.7	0.0	0.0	0.0	3.3	26.2	53.2	20.6	547	70.9	40.0	21.8
New London township (Kandiyohi)	2,943	2,954	0.4	2,942	98.2	0.0	0.6	1.2	0.0	20.1	59.9	20.0	1,232	97.1	31.9	30.0
New Maine township (Marshall)	199	199	0.0	230	100.0	0.0	0.0	0.0	0.0	25.7	61.3	13.0	93	97.8	59.1	5.4
New Market township (Scott)	3,440	3,618	5.2	3,535	95.8	0.0	1.0	2.7	0.4	20.8	65.9	13.4	1,274	95.6	24.6	34.1
New Munich city & MCD (Stearns)	320	323	0.9	332	100.0	0.0	0.0	0.0	0.0	25.5	47.4	26.8	141	83.7	64.5	13.5
Newport city & MCD (Washington)	3,435	3,469	1.0	3,455	77.3	6.5	6.7	5.6	3.9	22.4	65.9	11.5	1,374	66.4	43.0	21.4
New Prague city	7,329	7,546	3.0	7,434	96.3	0.0	0.1	0.9	2.7	32.0	56.4	11.6	2,710	76.8	31.3	29.2
New Prague city (Le Sueur)	3,041	3,065	0.8	3,048	96.5	0.1	0.0	1.2	2.2	36.9	55.9	7.2	1,010	83.2	27.1	39.5
New Prague city (Scott)	4,288	4,481	4.5	4,386	96.1	0.0	0.2	0.7	3.0	28.5	56.9	14.6	1,700	72.9	33.8	23.1
New Prairie township (Pope)	197	201	2.0	192	100.0	0.0	0.0	0.0	0.0	11.5	57.8	30.7	92	85.9	47.8	9.8
New Richland city & MCD (Waseca)	1,203	1,192	-0.9	1,200	92.5	0.0	0.9	0.0	6.6	22.0	56.3	21.8	498	73.9	53.6	13.1

1 May be of any race.

Table A. All Places — **Population and Housing**

STATE City, town, township, borough, or CDP (county if applicable)	Population				Race and Hispanic or Latino origin (percent), 2010–2014					Age (percent), 2010–2014			Households, 2010–2014			
	2010 census total population	2014 estimated population	Percent change 2010–2014	ACS total population estimate 2010–2014	White alone, not Hispanic or Latino	Black alone, not Hispanic or Latino	Asian alone, not Hispanic or Latino	All other races or 2 or more races, not Hispanic or Latino	Hispanic or Latino[1]	Under 18 years old	Age 18 to 64 years old	Age 65 years and older	Total occupied housing units	Percent owner occupied	Householders by level of education (percent)	
															High school diploma or less	Bachelor's degree or more
	1	2	3	4	5	6	7	8	9	10	11	12	13	14	15	16
MINNESOTA—Con.																
New Richland township (Waseca)	443	449	1.4	473	98.3	0.0	1.5	0.0	0.2	25.4	58.7	16.1	166	94.6	34.9	22.9
Newry township (Freeborn)	450	444	-1.3	567	92.6	0.0	0.0	1.8	5.6	35.2	53.8	10.9	183	89.1	35.5	18.0
New Solum township (Marshall)	325	325	0.0	333	97.9	0.0	0.0	1.2	0.9	29.4	65.1	5.4	123	95.1	44.7	13.8
New Sweden township (Nicollet)	297	292	-1.7	289	91.0	0.0	1.7	1.0	6.2	20.1	61.6	18.3	119	79.8	31.1	31.1
Newton township (Otter Tail)	746	738	-1.1	787	97.0	0.0	0.0	1.3	1.8	27.5	57.8	14.7	302	86.4	52.0	12.6
New Trier city & MCD (Dakota)	112	113	0.9	154	95.5	0.0	0.0	0.0	4.5	40.9	52.6	6.5	46	84.8	34.8	19.6
New Ulm city & MCD (Brown)	13,522	13,258	-2.0	13,328	96.7	0.2	0.4	1.1	1.6	19.1	60.9	19.9	5,824	73.6	44.0	24.6
New York Mills city & MCD (Otter Tail)	1,199	1,225	2.2	1,388	96.3	0.2	0.0	2.5	1.0	18.0	62.8	19.3	630	54.9	41.0	19.0
Nickerson township (Pine)	167	162	-3.0	163	97.5	0.0	0.0	2.5	0.0	24.6	53.9	21.5	64	93.8	51.6	12.5
Nicollet city & MCD (Nicollet)	1,093	1,129	3.3	1,157	94.9	0.0	0.0	0.2	4.9	23.7	64.7	11.6	462	78.4	45.0	15.6
Nicollet township (Nicollet)	527	519	-1.5	529	98.3	0.0	0.0	0.9	0.8	21.8	64.1	14.0	205	97.6	44.4	20.5
Nidaros township (Otter Tail)	316	313	-0.9	348	96.8	0.0	2.9	0.3	0.0	13.5	50.6	35.9	157	94.9	49.7	29.9
Nielsville city & MCD (Polk)	90	90	0.0	127	68.5	0.0	0.0	0.0	31.5	32.2	55.1	12.6	58	89.7	43.1	5.2
Nilsen township (Wilkin)	60	59	-1.7	84	91.7	0.0	0.0	8.3	0.0	32.1	60.7	7.1	29	100.0	24.1	13.8
Nimrod city & MCD (Wadena)	69	68	-1.4	81	100.0	0.0	0.0	0.0	0.0	14.9	70.3	14.8	41	78.0	56.1	0.0
Nininger township (Dakota)	948	961	1.4	860	99.2	0.0	0.0	0.6	0.2	14.1	55.4	30.6	423	72.3	40.2	25.5
Nisswa city & MCD (Crow Wing)	1,971	2,014	2.2	2,386	96.3	0.0	1.2	2.5	0.0	17.2	58.8	23.9	965	86.7	24.5	40.2
Nokay Lake township (Crow Wing)	830	846	1.9	926	97.4	0.2	0.0	1.3	1.1	23.2	62.3	14.4	360	86.9	43.6	19.4
Nora township (Clearwater)	442	448	1.4	490	85.3	0.0	0.0	12.9	1.8	25.9	55.6	18.6	185	87.0	50.3	17.3
Nora township (Pope)	205	209	2.0	211	93.4	1.4	3.8	1.4	0.0	22.2	60.2	17.5	90	84.4	33.3	33.3
Norcross city & MCD (Grant)	70	70	0.0	50	92.0	0.0	0.0	8.0	0.0	16.0	44.0	40.0	22	100.0	54.5	22.7
Norden township (Pennington)	379	368	-2.9	355	99.7	0.0	0.0	0.3	0.0	12.9	67.1	20.0	163	92.6	55.2	11.7
Nordick township (Wilkin)	87	86	-1.1	85	100.0	0.0	0.0	0.0	0.0	15.3	68.4	16.5	42	92.9	38.1	38.1
Nordland township (Aitkin)	972	951	-2.2	1,019	99.3	0.1	0.2	0.3	0.1	15.5	51.2	33.3	485	96.3	40.8	22.1
Nordland township (Lyon)	213	210	-1.4	197	82.7	0.0	0.0	2.5	14.7	24.9	64.4	10.7	69	85.5	46.4	18.8
Nore township (Itasca)	57	57	0.0	98	83.7	0.0	0.0	14.3	2.0	39.8	45.9	14.3	31	67.7	38.7	9.7
Norfolk township (Renville)	161	154	-4.3	159	95.6	0.0	0.0	0.0	4.4	16.3	70.9	12.6	75	69.3	48.0	17.3
Norman township (Pine)	251	254	1.2	223	92.4	3.1	0.0	1.3	3.1	24.7	55.2	20.2	100	92.0	51.0	21.0
Norman township (Yellow Medicine)	264	256	-3.0	212	100.0	0.0	0.0	0.0	0.0	22.6	64.5	12.7	87	100.0	28.7	23.0
Normania township (Yellow Medicine)	191	185	-3.1	170	95.9	0.0	3.5	0.0	0.6	24.7	54.1	21.2	66	93.9	36.4	16.7
Normanna township (St. Louis)	796	799	0.4	830	95.3	0.0	0.8	1.2	2.7	30.9	61.5	7.5	279	98.2	25.4	42.3
North township (Pennington)	678	691	1.9	797	89.2	1.1	3.8	1.4	4.5	26.5	60.8	12.7	267	85.8	33.7	33.0
North Beltrami UT (Beltrami)	34	35	2.9	22	59.1	0.0	0.0	18.2	22.7	22.7	31.8	45.5	9	100.0	22.2	77.8
North Branch city & MCD (Chisago)	10,125	10,160	0.3	10,099	93.4	1.0	0.9	1.9	2.7	28.1	61.4	10.5	3,700	80.6	44.7	20.0
North Branch township (Isanti)	1,779	1,802	1.3	1,655	90.8	1.2	4.4	2.0	1.6	25.3	60.6	14.0	589	94.7	45.7	17.3
North Carlton UT (Carlton)	982	995	1.3	738	70.3	1.2	2.8	19.8	5.8	22.0	63.9	14.1	274	80.7	62.4	12.0
North Cass UT (Cass)	261	259	-0.8	213	34.7	0.0	0.0	54.0	11.3	31.9	57.7	10.3	95	58.9	64.2	6.3
North Central Cass UT (Cass)	28	28	0.0	10	100.0	0.0	0.0	0.0	0.0	0.0	0.0	100.0	10	100.0	100.0	0.0
North Clearwater UT (Clearwater)	87	88	1.1	37	0.0	0.0	0.0	100.0	0.0	0.0	99.9	0.0	17	58.8	0.0	0.0
Northeast Aitkin UT (Aitkin)	11	11	0.0	8	100.0	0.0	0.0	0.0	0.0	0.0	50.0	50.0	4	100.0	100.0	0.0
Northeast Itasca UT (Itasca)	1,179	1,192	1.1	1,156	86.2	0.4	2.2	9.9	1.2	16.5	56.0	27.5	527	90.1	47.8	23.9
Northeast St. Louis UT (St. Louis)	246	249	1.2	184	100.0	0.0	0.0	0.0	0.0	12.0	44.1	44.0	78	100.0	26.9	48.7
Northern township (Beltrami)	4,351	4,522	3.9	4,482	91.6	1.7	1.7	4.4	0.6	26.0	60.8	13.2	1,634	87.1	22.7	41.0
Northfield city	20,017	20,356	1.7	20,303	83.3	2.1	4.4	2.2	8.0	17.9	69.3	12.8	6,227	68.6	23.6	47.8
Northfield city (Dakota)	1,147	1,190	3.7	1,123	99.3	0.0	0.0	0.7	0.0	30.5	54.5	15.0	420	86.4	6.2	61.4
Northfield city (Rice)	18,870	19,166	1.6	19,180	82.3	2.2	4.7	2.3	8.5	17.1	70.3	12.6	5,807	67.3	24.9	46.8
Northfield township (Rice)	842	855	1.5	776	95.2	0.0	0.5	0.0	4.3	23.4	63.9	12.6	289	90.3	31.5	40.8
North Fork township (Stearns)	247	255	3.2	226	99.1	0.0	0.0	0.0	0.9	30.1	55.2	14.6	79	69.6	45.6	13.9
North Germany township (Wadena)	313	307	-1.9	319	93.4	0.0	0.0	6.6	0.0	26.4	54.3	19.4	118	72.9	54.2	8.5
North Hero township (Redwood)	161	156	-3.1	163	88.3	0.0	11.7	0.0	0.0	11.1	67.5	21.5	71	78.9	64.8	15.5
Northland township (Polk)	160	159	-0.6	97	100.0	0.0	0.0	0.0	0.0	10.3	62.9	26.8	51	80.4	43.1	13.7
Northland township (St. Louis)	169	170	0.6	157	100.0	0.0	0.0	0.0	0.0	13.4	78.8	7.6	69	92.8	39.1	17.4
North Mankato city	13,397	13,432	0.3	13,403	91.1	4.2	0.3	1.1	3.3	23.3	63.2	13.5	5,691	71.5	27.2	35.6
North Mankato city (Blue Earth)	0	0	0.0	0	0.0	0.0	0.0	0.0	0.0	0.0	0.0	0.0	0	0.0	0.0	0.0

1 May be of any race.

Table A. All Places — Population and Housing

STATE City, town, township, borough, or CDP (county if applicable)	2010 census total population	2014 estimated population	Percent change 2010–2014	ACS total population estimate 2010–2014	White alone, not Hispanic or Latino	Black alone, not Hispanic or Latino	Asian alone, not Hispanic or Latino	All other races or 2 or more races, not Hispanic or Latino	Hispanic or Latino[1]	Under 18 years old	Age 18 to 64 years old	Age 65 years and older	Total occupied housing units	Percent owner occupied	High school diploma or less	Bachelor's degree or more
	1	2	3	4	5	6	7	8	9	10	11	12	13	14	15	16
MINNESOTA—Con.																
North Mankato city (Nicollet)	13,397	13,432	0.3	13,403	91.1	4.2	0.3	1.1	3.3	23.3	63.2	13.5	5,691	71.5	27.2	35.6
North Oaks city & MCD (Ramsey)	4,469	4,807	7.6	4,617	89.7	0.1	6.3	1.5	2.4	19.6	52.3	28.2	1,713	79.5	2.3	78.6
Northome city & MCD (Koochiching)	200	194	-3.0	226	77.9	0.0	0.4	21.7	0.0	16.8	64.6	18.6	95	85.3	51.6	13.7
Northome UT (Koochiching)	447	NA	NA	442	83.9	0.0	0.0	15.2	0.9	26.6	57.5	15.8	190	75.8	52.1	11.6
North Ottawa township (Grant)	50	50	0.0	47	100.0	0.0	0.0	0.0	0.0	23.4	55.4	21.3	18	100.0	22.2	33.3
North Red River UT (Kittson)	0	0	0.0	0	0.0	0.0	0.0	0.0	0.0	0.0	0.0	0.0	0	0.0	0.0	0.0
Northrop city & MCD (Martin)	227	221	-2.6	317	97.8	0.0	1.9	0.3	0.0	28.4	62.3	9.5	121	86.0	41.3	5.8
North Roseau UT (Roseau)	139	140	0.7	82	100.0	0.0	0.0	0.0	0.0	0.0	52.5	47.6	43	100.0	58.1	41.9
North St. Paul city & MCD (Ramsey)	11,460	12,224	6.7	11,775	75.4	6.4	9.4	2.8	6.1	20.0	67.3	12.5	4,694	66.5	43.4	25.2
North Star township (Brown)	287	283	-1.4	321	99.4	0.0	0.6	0.0	0.0	28.3	63.6	8.1	127	87.4	43.3	15.0
North Star township (St. Louis)	190	191	0.5	184	92.9	0.0	1.6	5.4	0.0	13.5	66.9	19.6	90	100.0	20.0	31.1
Northwest Aitkin UT (Aitkin)	342	335	-2.0	271	96.3	0.0	0.0	3.7	0.0	6.3	63.1	30.6	153	91.5	43.1	4.6
Northwest Koochiching UT (Koochiching)	463	NA	NA	444	98.9	0.0	0.7	0.5	0.0	16.9	58.7	24.3	209	87.1	54.5	15.8
Northwest Roseau UT (Roseau)	25	25	0.0	24	100.0	0.0	0.0	0.0	0.0	0.0	100.0	0.0	11	54.5	0.0	45.5
Northwest St. Louis UT (St. Louis)	301	303	0.7	406	91.1	0.0	0.0	8.9	0.0	19.8	64.4	16.0	164	87.8	56.7	11.0
Norton township (Winona)	490	490	0.0	688	89.8	0.4	1.6	2.3	5.8	25.7	62.3	11.9	260	65.8	49.6	26.5
Norway township (Fillmore)	343	348	1.5	331	98.2	0.0	1.2	0.6	0.0	23.2	61.1	15.4	137	90.5	48.9	25.5
Norway township (Kittson)	91	89	-2.2	82	96.3	1.2	0.0	2.4	0.0	8.6	70.9	20.7	40	97.5	52.5	7.5
Norway Lake township (Kandiyohi)	274	273	-0.4	233	99.1	0.0	0.0	0.9	0.0	9.8	65.3	24.9	118	94.1	46.6	12.7
Norwegian Grove township (Otter Tail)	300	300	0.0	232	99.1	0.4	0.0	0.0	0.4	18.5	54.2	27.2	99	93.9	38.4	18.2
Norwood Young America city & MCD (Carver)	3,569	3,665	2.7	3,617	84.5	0.9	0.2	2.8	11.6	28.8	59.8	11.6	1,328	65.3	42.5	20.9
Nowthen city & MCD (Anoka)	4,443	4,555	2.5	4,493	91.1	0.5	1.0	1.3	6.1	26.5	65.8	7.9	1,529	91.7	35.8	22.0
Numedal township (Pennington)	90	90	0.0	77	97.4	0.0	0.0	0.0	2.6	22.1	72.8	5.2	34	100.0	41.2	14.7
Nunda township (Freeborn)	321	317	-1.2	238	96.6	0.0	0.0	2.9	0.4	18.5	52.4	29.0	101	85.1	55.4	10.9
Oak township (Stearns)	595	585	-1.7	655	99.7	0.0	0.0	0.3	0.0	30.8	62.2	6.9	219	80.4	51.6	16.0
Oakdale city & MCD (Washington)	27,365	28,033	2.4	27,705	77.4	8.3	7.5	3.2	3.6	23.7	63.8	12.4	10,859	75.2	29.7	31.6
Oak Grove city & MCD (Anoka)	8,031	8,324	3.6	8,145	86.0	1.2	3.6	1.4	7.7	25.5	64.2	10.4	2,667	94.7	36.6	20.2
Oakland township (Freeborn)	396	391	-1.3	419	94.5	0.7	0.0	0.0	4.8	30.8	56.2	12.9	139	79.9	47.5	18.0
Oakland township (Mahnomen)	295	297	0.7	262	55.3	0.0	0.0	43.5	1.1	27.5	58.1	14.5	87	94.3	60.9	14.9
Oak Lawn township (Crow Wing)	1,792	1,829	2.1	1,645	97.1	1.3	0.3	1.0	0.3	21.5	63.4	15.3	672	85.4	38.8	13.4
Oak Park township (Marshall)	131	131	0.0	155	100.0	0.0	0.0	0.0	0.0	23.8	60.0	16.1	63	87.3	33.3	15.9
Oak Park Heights city & MCD (Washington)	4,444	4,795	7.9	4,671	87.2	5.7	1.2	3.6	2.3	12.6	59.4	28.0	1,992	53.5	23.6	39.0
Oakport CDP	1,387	NA	NA	1,333	97.9	0.5	0.0	1.1	0.5	24.9	63.8	11.4	495	95.4	24.4	41.2
Oakport township (Clay)	1,797	1,860	3.5	1,830	98.5	0.4	0.0	0.8	0.3	25.9	60.8	13.4	660	95.5	25.8	41.5
Oak Valley township (Otter Tail)	355	355	0.0	363	97.5	0.0	0.0	0.0	2.5	22.9	55.8	21.5	140	95.7	48.6	17.9
Oakwood township (Wabasha)	405	403	-0.5	369	97.3	0.0	0.0	0.5	2.2	20.9	69.0	10.0	138	82.6	41.3	18.1
O'Brien township (Beltrami)	58	59	1.7	47	100.0	0.0	0.0	0.0	0.0	12.8	53.2	34.0	21	85.7	61.9	23.8
Odessa city & MCD (Big Stone)	135	131	-3.0	132	100.0	0.0	0.0	0.0	0.0	18.2	61.9	19.7	62	90.3	62.9	9.7
Odessa township (Big Stone)	132	130	-1.5	253	97.2	0.0	0.0	0.0	2.8	38.7	45.9	15.4	74	97.3	66.2	9.5
Odin city & MCD (Watonwan)	106	105	-0.9	104	100.0	0.0	0.0	0.0	0.0	21.2	54.9	24.0	46	95.7	41.3	6.5
Odin township (Watonwan)	170	168	-1.2	155	94.2	0.0	1.9	3.9	0.0	14.2	67.8	18.1	70	90.0	37.1	12.9
Ogema city & MCD (Becker)	184	185	0.5	165	32.7	1.2	0.0	63.6	2.4	40.0	51.0	9.1	67	59.7	49.3	16.4
Ogema township (Pine)	352	346	-1.7	424	43.4	0.0	2.1	52.6	1.9	40.6	48.1	11.3	147	53.1	55.1	6.8
Ogilvie city & MCD (Kanabec)	369	356	-3.5	453	93.2	0.9	2.6	2.6	0.7	23.6	64.1	12.4	178	64.0	66.9	7.9
Okabena city & MCD (Jackson)	188	188	0.0	180	92.8	0.0	0.0	0.0	7.2	26.1	60.6	13.3	74	87.8	37.8	18.9
Oklee city & MCD (Red Lake)	435	424	-2.5	382	89.8	2.6	1.6	6.0	0.0	18.8	52.9	28.3	196	77.0	69.9	10.2
Olivia city & MCD (Renville)	2,484	2,374	-4.4	2,394	84.3	3.2	0.3	0.5	11.7	20.3	59.6	20.1	1,024	69.9	47.1	20.3
Olney township (Nobles)	205	207	1.0	229	98.3	0.4	0.0	0.0	1.3	18.3	68.6	13.1	93	91.4	69.9	6.5
Omro township (Yellow Medicine)	161	156	-3.1	209	96.7	0.0	0.0	0.0	3.3	37.8	56.4	5.7	74	67.6	54.1	12.2

1 May be of any race.

Table A. All Places — Population and Housing

STATE City, town, township, borough, or CDP (county if applicable)	Population				Race and Hispanic or Latino origin (percent), 2010–2014					Age (percent), 2010–2014			Households, 2010–2014			
	2010 census total population	2014 estimated population	Percent change 2010–2014	ACS total population estimate 2010–2014	White alone, not Hispanic or Latino	Black alone, not Hispanic or Latino	Asian alone, not Hispanic or Latino	All other races or 2 or more races, not Hispanic or Latino	Hispanic or Latino[1]	Under 18 years old	Age 18 to 64 years old	Age 65 years and older	Total occupied housing units	Percent owner occupied	Householders by level of education (percent) High school diploma or less	Householders by level of education (percent) Bachelor's degree or more
	1	2	3	4	5	6	7	8	9	10	11	12	13	14	15	16
MINNESOTA—Con.																
Onamia city & MCD (Mille Lacs)	878	869	-1.0	907	82.4	4.3	0.0	12.7	0.7	23.1	47.0	29.9	392	45.7	48.2	15.1
Onamia township (Mille Lacs)	575	570	-0.9	523	83.7	0.0	1.0	9.6	5.7	23.0	62.1	14.9	198	75.8	52.5	10.1
Onstad township (Polk)	71	71	0.0	108	89.8	0.0	0.0	0.0	10.2	34.2	35.2	30.6	40	80.0	62.5	12.5
Orange township (Douglas)	313	313	0.0	317	98.1	0.0	0.0	0.6	1.3	28.0	56.6	15.1	124	90.3	52.4	4.8
Orion township (Olmsted)	592	614	3.7	607	96.2	0.5	0.0	1.8	1.5	22.4	61.9	15.7	248	81.9	42.3	24.6
Ormsby city	131	129	-1.5	134	100.0	0.0	0.0	0.0	0.0	8.2	59.6	32.1	82	100.0	80.5	2.4
Ormsby city (Martin)	56	55	-1.8	74	100.0	0.0	0.0	0.0	0.0	9.5	69.1	21.6	49	100.0	89.8	4.1
Ormsby city (Watonwan)	75	74	-1.3	60	100.0	0.0	0.0	0.0	0.0	6.7	48.4	45.0	33	100.0	66.7	0.0
Orono city & MCD (Hennepin)	7,450	7,898	6.0	7,690	93.5	1.3	2.1	2.0	1.1	25.2	61.9	12.9	3,195	83.8	12.6	63.4
Oronoco city & MCD (Olmsted)	1,300	1,411	8.5	1,379	94.1	2.5	2.2	0.9	0.2	34.2	59.4	6.3	452	93.1	20.6	44.9
Oronoco township (Olmsted)	2,232	2,304	3.2	1,930	90.0	1.0	3.6	2.0	3.4	18.0	72.3	9.7	785	92.9	24.7	48.9
Orr city & MCD (St. Louis)	267	303	13.5	293	74.7	0.0	4.8	16.7	3.8	16.7	63.4	19.8	140	57.9	33.6	12.1
Orrock township (Sherburne)	3,451	3,536	2.5	3,480	96.2	0.0	0.6	0.7	2.4	23.5	65.5	10.9	1,244	93.7	36.2	26.3
Orton township (Wadena)	204	200	-2.0	165	98.8	0.0	0.0	0.0	1.2	12.7	55.7	31.5	81	84.0	51.9	8.6
Ortonville city & MCD (Big Stone)	1,916	1,848	-3.5	2,002	95.9	0.6	0.0	2.1	1.4	17.8	52.9	29.0	971	69.6	53.3	23.1
Ortonville township (Big Stone)	97	96	-1.0	85	100.0	0.0	0.0	0.0	0.0	27.0	30.7	42.4	33	100.0	60.6	12.1
Orwell township (Otter Tail)	170	170	0.0	140	91.4	2.9	0.0	5.0	0.7	23.5	69.9	6.4	55	90.9	32.7	25.5
Osage CDP	323	NA	NA	255	98.4	0.0	0.0	1.6	0.0	17.7	56.2	26.3	118	89.0	59.3	10.2
Osage township (Becker)	895	916	2.3	868	99.0	0.1	0.0	0.9	0.0	27.3	55.9	16.8	333	94.0	50.2	17.4
Osakis city	1,740	1,717	-1.3	1,687	89.4	1.5	0.6	3.5	5.0	27.2	49.6	23.2	698	70.6	47.9	14.8
Osakis city (Douglas)	1,591	1,573	-1.1	1,507	89.3	1.7	0.7	2.7	5.6	28.4	49.7	21.9	619	67.7	46.8	15.8
Osakis city (Todd)	149	144	-3.4	180	90.0	0.0	0.0	10.0	0.0	17.8	47.7	34.4	79	93.7	55.7	6.3
Osakis township (Douglas)	595	598	0.5	772	100.0	0.0	0.0	0.0	0.0	27.0	57.7	15.3	293	90.4	42.0	12.3
Osborne township (Pipestone)	286	284	-0.7	281	99.3	0.0	0.0	0.4	0.4	28.5	53.2	18.5	105	93.3	40.0	25.7
Oscar township (Otter Tail)	207	207	0.0	145	91.0	0.0	0.0	0.0	9.0	24.1	58.1	17.9	66	98.5	56.1	34.8
Osceola township (Renville)	158	152	-3.8	160	97.5	0.0	0.0	0.0	2.5	26.2	57.7	16.3	61	96.7	34.4	18.0
Oshawa township (Nicollet)	502	494	-1.6	661	96.4	0.0	0.6	2.1	0.9	31.4	59.6	9.2	207	97.6	27.1	45.4
Oshkosh township (Yellow Medicine)	210	204	-2.9	224	98.7	0.0	0.0	0.9	0.4	29.0	55.3	15.6	83	92.8	39.8	27.7
Oslo city & MCD (Marshall)	330	322	-2.4	247	70.0	0.0	0.0	1.6	28.3	25.5	56.6	17.8	104	86.5	65.4	9.6
Osseo city & MCD (Hennepin)	2,430	2,612	7.5	2,480	86.6	2.7	5.2	4.0	1.5	14.8	56.2	29.2	1,138	54.5	41.7	19.2
Ostrander city & MCD (Fillmore)	254	254	0.0	249	99.2	0.0	0.0	0.8	0.0	15.2	60.1	24.5	101	80.2	50.5	4.0
Oteneagen township (Itasca)	310	312	0.6	228	88.6	1.8	0.9	8.3	0.4	25.0	62.3	12.7	92	93.5	47.8	7.6
Otisco township (Waseca)	599	604	0.8	414	97.1	0.0	1.0	0.0	1.9	27.5	54.1	18.4	165	82.4	35.8	20.0
Otrey township (Big Stone)	87	86	-1.1	82	100.0	0.0	0.0	0.0	0.0	28.1	59.8	12.2	35	100.0	48.6	14.3
Otsego city & MCD (Wright)	13,571	15,047	10.9	14,257	93.4	1.7	1.0	3.2	0.7	29.7	64.4	6.0	5,056	94.2	30.9	32.0
Ottawa township (Le Sueur)	283	282	-0.4	233	95.3	0.0	0.0	0.9	3.9	13.3	61.5	25.3	100	86.0	46.0	23.0
Ottertail city & MCD (Otter Tail)	572	598	4.5	532	96.8	0.4	0.6	1.7	0.6	15.0	66.1	18.8	254	75.2	32.3	19.7
Otter Tail township (Otter Tail)	491	487	-0.8	481	95.4	0.0	0.4	3.7	0.4	11.2	46.6	42.2	246	83.7	37.8	27.6
Otter Tail Peninsula township (Cass)	54	54	0.0	44	95.5	0.0	0.0	4.5	0.0	0.0	45.6	54.5	25	80.0	60.0	24.0
Otto township (Otter Tail)	554	548	-1.1	498	96.6	0.0	0.0	0.6	2.8	24.1	59.4	16.3	216	87.5	46.8	19.9
Owatonna city & MCD (Steele)	25,601	25,625	0.1	25,550	85.6	3.3	1.0	2.2	7.9	25.9	59.2	14.9	10,214	72.4	40.5	28.3
Owatonna township (Steele)	607	609	0.3	601	95.5	0.0	0.0	1.0	3.5	21.2	58.1	21.0	252	86.5	48.4	22.2
Owens township (St. Louis)	263	264	0.4	225	94.2	0.9	0.0	1.8	3.1	16.5	50.2	33.3	115	86.1	61.7	13.9
Oxford township (Isanti)	888	900	1.4	938	91.5	0.0	0.0	3.0	5.5	28.5	60.4	11.1	312	83.7	52.6	18.3
Paddock township (Otter Tail)	346	346	0.0	207	100.0	0.0	0.0	0.0	0.0	24.1	56.0	19.8	83	89.2	42.2	13.3
Page township (Mille Lacs)	743	737	-0.8	675	97.8	0.0	0.0	1.3	0.9	23.9	60.4	15.6	258	93.0	47.7	15.9
Palisade city & MCD (Aitkin)	167	161	-3.6	152	88.8	0.0	2.0	6.6	2.6	11.1	47.4	41.4	77	92.2	51.9	5.2
Palmer township (Sherburne)	2,354	2,410	2.4	2,477	97.7	0.0	0.5	0.7	1.1	23.2	62.7	14.3	923	92.6	34.3	24.5
Palmville township (Roseau)	39	39	0.0	14	100.0	0.0	0.0	0.0	0.0	7.1	50.0	42.9	7	100.0	14.3	71.4
Palmyra township (Renville)	179	172	-3.9	212	99.1	0.0	0.5	0.5	0.0	25.0	63.7	11.3	79	87.3	31.6	21.5
Park township (Pine)	37	38	2.7	27	100.0	0.0	0.0	0.0	0.0	0.0	88.9	11.1	20	90.0	50.0	20.0
Parke township (Clay)	485	500	3.1	485	99.6	0.0	0.0	0.0	0.4	23.3	61.0	15.7	213	91.1	35.7	24.9
Parker township (Marshall)	35	35	0.0	31	93.5	6.5	0.0	0.0	0.0	22.6	64.7	12.9	13	100.0	30.8	23.1
Parker township (Morrison)	474	470	-0.8	491	98.0	0.0	0.0	0.4	1.6	30.7	57.4	11.8	165	95.8	47.3	15.8
Parkers Prairie city & MCD (Otter Tail)	1,011	1,006	-0.5	1,098	98.1	0.4	0.2	1.3	0.1	28.8	45.1	26.1	447	68.2	59.7	10.7

1 May be of any race.

Table A. All Places — Population and Housing

STATE City, town, township, borough, or CDP (county if applicable)	2010 census total population	2014 estimated population	Percent change 2010–2014	ACS total population estimate 2010–2014	White alone, not Hispanic or Latino	Black alone, not Hispanic or Latino	Asian alone, not Hispanic or Latino	All other races or 2 or more races, not Hispanic or Latino	Hispanic or Latino[1]	Under 18 years old	Age 18 to 64 years old	Age 65 years and older	Total occupied housing units	Percent owner occupied	High school diploma or less	Bachelor's degree or more
	1	2	3	4	5	6	7	8	9	10	11	12	13	14	15	16
MINNESOTA—Con.																
Parkers Prairie township (Otter Tail)	348	348	0.0	321	99.4	0.0	0.0	0.6	0.0	15.5	63.5	20.9	144	94.4	55.6	10.4
Park Rapids city & MCD (Hubbard)	3,872	3,927	1.4	3,894	95.2	1.2	1.3	2.0	0.2	20.5	52.9	26.6	1,856	50.2	47.4	14.5
Parnell township (Polk)	64	64	0.0	55	100.0	0.0	0.0	0.0	0.0	31.0	63.7	5.5	16	87.5	62.5	12.5
Parnell township (Traverse)	60	57	-5.0	26	100.0	0.0	0.0	0.0	0.0	0.0	65.3	34.6	15	86.7	46.7	26.7
Partridge township (Pine)	639	626	-2.0	671	96.1	0.0	0.0	3.6	0.3	27.3	56.9	15.8	257	91.8	52.9	16.0
Paxton township (Redwood)	555	546	-1.6	544	64.0	0.6	0.0	34.2	1.3	25.1	62.0	13.1	210	90.0	42.4	24.8
Paynesville city & MCD (Stearns)	2,432	2,418	-0.6	2,466	96.3	0.6	0.5	0.2	2.5	19.9	51.2	28.8	1,132	70.6	51.0	15.4
Paynesville township (Stearns)	1,421	1,457	2.5	1,270	99.2	0.0	0.0	0.2	0.6	16.9	61.0	22.0	563	97.2	34.8	32.5
Peace township (Kanabec)	937	933	-0.4	877	94.6	1.3	0.0	4.1	0.0	15.0	65.8	19.2	377	89.4	58.1	8.5
Pease city & MCD (Mille Lacs)	242	241	-0.4	213	89.2	0.0	2.3	0.0	8.5	27.3	61.9	10.8	79	72.2	67.1	1.3
Peatland UT (Kittson)	9	9	0.0	1	100.0	0.0	0.0	0.0	0.0	0.0	100.0	0.0	1	100.0	100.0	0.0
Pelan township (Kittson)	45	44	-2.2	56	100.0	0.0	0.0	0.0	0.0	9.0	84.1	7.1	20	95.0	40.0	15.0
Pelican township (Crow Wing)	455	466	2.4	565	98.8	1.2	0.0	0.0	0.0	19.5	48.9	31.5	228	95.2	26.3	27.2
Pelican township (Otter Tail)	627	622	-0.8	569	95.1	0.4	0.0	2.6	1.9	19.2	67.0	13.9	228	96.5	28.9	31.1
Pelican Lake township (Grant)	450	444	-1.3	440	97.3	0.0	0.0	2.7	0.0	10.7	64.7	24.5	198	89.4	41.4	28.3
Pelican Rapids city & MCD (Otter Tail)	2,462	2,457	-0.2	2,322	59.2	13.2	5.1	1.9	20.6	28.2	53.3	18.5	916	63.2	53.1	15.4
Pemberton city & MCD (Blue Earth)	247	248	0.4	357	93.3	0.0	0.0	0.0	6.7	26.5	66.4	7.0	117	84.6	48.7	7.7
Pembina township (Mahnomen)	707	715	1.1	642	59.5	1.1	1.1	34.9	3.4	36.1	53.0	10.9	207	68.1	52.2	11.6
Penn township (McLeod)	315	309	-1.9	296	98.3	0.0	0.0	1.7	0.0	25.7	50.2	24.3	123	87.8	64.2	14.6
Pennock city & MCD (Kandiyohi)	508	513	1.0	620	71.5	1.5	0.0	0.8	26.3	41.0	54.6	4.4	191	83.2	39.8	11.5
Pepin township (Wabasha)	378	374	-1.1	369	94.6	1.1	1.1	2.4	0.8	19.5	62.1	18.4	162	87.7	52.5	11.7
Pepperton township (Stevens)	134	133	-0.7	115	98.3	0.0	0.0	1.7	0.0	20.0	65.3	14.8	45	86.7	35.6	13.3
Pequaywan township (St. Louis)	130	131	0.8	155	88.4	0.0	9.7	1.9	0.0	5.7	69.1	25.2	71	100.0	15.5	49.3
Pequot Lakes city & MCD (Crow Wing)	2,162	2,240	3.6	2,410	95.7	2.9	0.4	0.2	0.7	26.2	55.1	18.7	961	58.5	41.3	20.8
Perch Lake township (Carlton)	1,046	1,060	1.3	875	76.9	0.0	0.8	21.7	0.6	19.3	64.1	16.7	345	84.3	50.4	21.4
Percy township (Kittson)	31	30	-3.2	20	100.0	0.0	0.0	0.0	0.0	0.0	85.0	15.0	12	91.7	58.3	0.0
Perham city & MCD (Otter Tail)	2,979	3,185	6.9	3,045	85.3	0.3	0.4	1.7	12.4	22.2	53.1	24.7	1,343	64.0	45.0	17.9
Perham township (Otter Tail)	833	876	5.2	800	91.5	0.0	0.0	2.1	6.4	25.2	59.3	15.5	306	88.6	39.5	22.5
Perley city & MCD (Norman)	92	89	-3.3	117	70.1	0.0	0.0	3.4	26.5	11.2	76.1	12.8	53	92.5	43.4	3.8
Perry township (Lac qui Parle)	101	96	-5.0	90	91.1	0.0	8.9	0.0	0.0	11.0	68.8	20.0	41	82.9	48.8	7.3
Perry Lake township (Crow Wing)	302	307	1.7	338	100.0	0.0	0.0	0.0	0.0	15.1	66.1	18.9	141	97.2	48.9	15.6
Petersburg township (Jackson)	232	234	0.9	188	100.0	0.0	0.0	0.0	0.0	20.8	59.0	20.2	75	90.7	34.7	17.3
Peterson city & MCD (Fillmore)	198	198	0.0	194	100.0	0.0	0.0	0.0	0.0	17.1	59.1	23.7	86	84.9	54.7	11.6
Pickerel Lake township (Freeborn)	673	664	-1.3	682	98.1	0.0	0.0	0.3	1.6	22.1	62.9	15.1	249	84.7	39.0	38.2
Pierz city & MCD (Morrison)	1,393	1,366	-1.9	1,295	98.5	0.0	0.8	0.3	0.5	21.8	50.6	27.5	536	67.2	56.0	8.8
Pierz township (Morrison)	535	533	-0.4	569	97.0	0.0	0.0	0.4	2.6	29.5	60.7	9.8	200	88.5	61.5	10.5
Pike township (St. Louis)	417	418	0.2	373	98.7	0.0	0.0	1.3	0.0	15.5	67.6	16.9	180	93.9	46.1	18.3
Pike Bay township (Cass)	1,616	1,623	0.4	1,613	27.2	1.0	0.9	67.6	3.3	32.5	55.9	11.6	639	67.6	45.2	12.4
Pike Creek township (Morrison)	957	951	-0.6	1,029	95.1	0.0	0.0	1.3	3.6	23.4	62.5	14.1	418	95.5	46.9	9.3
Pillager city & MCD (Cass)	469	454	-3.2	436	95.9	0.0	0.5	3.0	0.7	29.9	51.9	18.3	195	68.2	40.5	14.9
Pillsbury township (Swift)	254	246	-3.1	255	96.5	0.0	0.0	0.8	2.7	30.1	62.0	7.8	85	84.7	31.8	14.1
Pilot Grove township (Faribault)	156	153	-1.9	166	100.0	0.0	0.0	0.0	0.0	21.7	61.8	16.3	69	81.2	47.8	17.4
Pilot Mound township (Fillmore)	338	342	1.2	270	96.3	1.1	0.7	1.9	0.0	17.0	66.7	16.3	102	88.2	43.1	20.6
Pine Bend CDP	28	NA	NA	8	37.5	0.0	0.0	62.5	0.0	0.0	50.0	50.0	5	40.0	80.0	0.0
Pine City city & MCD (Pine)	3,133	3,076	-1.8	3,098	95.7	1.2	0.4	1.4	1.4	20.7	55.0	24.1	1,380	61.0	52.8	13.7
Pine City township (Pine)	1,394	1,357	-2.7	1,324	98.0	0.5	0.5	0.2	0.8	22.6	58.6	18.8	550	92.9	44.9	11.6
Pine Island city	3,271	3,324	1.6	3,434	95.5	1.0	1.3	0.3	2.0	27.7	58.5	13.9	1,441	70.5	31.4	29.3
Pine Island city (Goodhue)	2,560	2,590	1.2	2,579	95.2	1.4	1.7	0.3	1.4	23.9	59.3	16.8	1,154	67.9	33.3	26.9
Pine Island city (Olmsted)	711	734	3.2	855	96.4	0.0	0.0	0.0	3.6	39.0	55.8	5.3	287	80.8	23.7	39.0
Pine Island township (Goodhue)	540	546	1.1	684	96.8	0.0	1.3	1.2	0.7	21.6	66.6	11.7	243	88.9	32.5	17.3
Pine Lake township (Cass)	207	209	1.0	197	91.9	0.0	0.0	8.1	0.0	17.3	52.8	29.9	95	95.8	35.8	28.4
Pine Lake township (Clearwater)	414	414	0.0	551	97.6	0.0	0.7	1.6	0.0	22.9	53.3	23.8	210	86.7	52.9	18.1
Pine Lake township (Otter Tail)	639	634	-0.8	745	98.1	0.3	0.8	0.1	0.7	22.4	54.1	23.6	294	95.6	38.8	36.4

1 May be of any race.

Table A. All Places — **Population and Housing**

STATE City, town, township, borough, or CDP (county if applicable)	Population				Race and Hispanic or Latino origin (percent), 2010–2014					Age (percent), 2010–2014			Households, 2010–2014			
	2010 census total population	2014 estimated population	Percent change 2010–2014	ACS total population estimate 2010–2014	White alone, not Hispanic or Latino	Black alone, not Hispanic or Latino	Asian alone, not Hispanic or Latino	All other races or 2 or more races, not Hispanic or Latino	Hispanic or Latino[1]	Under 18 years old	Age 18 to 64 years old	Age 65 years and older	Total occupied housing units	Percent owner occupied	Householders by level of education (percent) High school diploma or less	Householders by level of education (percent) Bachelor's degree or more
	1	2	3	4	5	6	7	8	9	10	11	12	13	14	15	16
MINNESOTA—Con.																
Pine Lake township (Pine)	583	567	-2.7	624	95.2	2.2	0.0	1.3	1.3	16.5	63.5	20.0	246	89.0	50.0	20.7
Pine Point CDP	338	NA	NA	260	5.4	0.0	1.2	88.8	4.6	41.2	56.5	2.3	72	41.7	56.9	4.2
Pine Point township (Becker)	400	411	2.8	335	22.4	0.0	0.9	73.1	3.6	37.3	56.0	6.9	115	61.7	53.0	17.4
Pine River city & MCD (Cass)	944	927	-1.8	736	97.3	1.6	0.0	1.1	0.0	16.6	58.3	25.3	387	47.0	59.2	11.6
Pine River township (Cass)	1,156	1,163	0.6	1,210	93.2	1.5	1.0	4.0	0.2	23.9	61.2	14.8	550	80.2	48.4	11.5
Pine Springs city & MCD (Washington)	388	395	1.8	388	88.1	1.0	3.9	1.3	5.7	16.3	66.9	16.8	135	95.6	16.3	57.8
Pipestone city & MCD (Pipestone)	4,317	4,156	-3.7	4,221	85.6	2.3	2.1	3.6	6.4	23.6	56.8	19.4	1,858	61.6	46.2	17.6
Plainview city & MCD (Wabasha)	3,340	3,270	-2.1	3,297	95.7	0.1	0.0	0.3	3.9	29.2	55.3	15.6	1,331	86.5	51.7	19.2
Plainview township (Wabasha)	443	439	-0.9	462	93.9	0.0	0.0	1.9	4.1	27.7	60.7	11.5	171	74.3	33.9	24.6
Plato city & MCD (McLeod)	320	316	-1.3	329	97.0	0.0	0.0	0.0	3.0	20.1	66.2	13.7	151	91.4	44.4	18.5
Platte township (Morrison)	357	352	-1.4	365	96.7	0.0	1.6	1.6	0.0	28.5	58.0	13.4	148	90.5	49.3	8.1
Platte Lake township (Crow Wing)	414	420	1.4	378	97.1	0.8	0.0	0.3	1.9	25.7	60.2	14.0	154	94.2	51.9	3.2
Pleasant Grove township (Olmsted)	805	827	2.7	848	98.7	0.0	0.0	0.4	0.9	24.9	59.0	16.2	332	84.3	38.6	21.4
Pleasant Hill township (Winona)	531	531	0.0	507	99.0	0.0	0.0	0.0	1.0	20.9	61.7	17.4	195	92.8	59.0	14.4
Pleasant Mound township (Blue Earth)	214	213	-0.5	175	94.9	0.0	0.0	0.0	5.1	15.4	53.6	30.9	77	75.3	70.1	3.9
Pleasant Prairie township (Martin)	243	237	-2.5	242	98.8	0.0	0.0	1.2	0.0	23.6	59.5	16.9	104	93.3	40.4	14.4
Pleasant Valley township (Mower)	304	306	0.7	351	98.3	1.1	0.0	0.0	0.6	25.9	62.6	11.4	111	90.1	49.5	18.0
Pleasant View township (Norman)	108	105	-2.8	112	98.2	0.0	0.0	0.0	1.8	26.0	50.0	24.1	40	100.0	35.0	10.0
Pliny township (Aitkin)	109	105	-3.7	102	100.0	0.0	0.0	0.0	0.0	24.5	52.0	23.5	43	88.4	65.1	0.0
Plummer city & MCD (Red Lake)	292	292	0.0	405	89.1	0.0	0.0	1.5	9.4	36.5	54.7	8.6	159	69.8	42.1	17.6
Plymouth city & MCD (Hennepin)	70,561	75,057	6.4	72,868	80.7	4.9	7.8	3.0	3.6	22.9	63.9	13.2	29,597	72.1	14.2	59.0
Pohlitz township (Roseau)	34	34	0.0	42	100.0	0.0	0.0	0.0	0.0	14.2	80.9	4.8	24	54.2	20.8	16.7
Pokegama township (Pine)	2,733	2,646	-3.2	2,685	92.7	0.3	0.9	3.5	2.6	22.8	57.7	19.4	1,005	88.6	50.6	13.6
Polk Centre township (Pennington)	87	199	128.7	92	96.7	3.3	0.0	0.0	0.0	20.6	66.3	13.0	42	95.2	40.5	45.2
Polonia township (Roseau)	34	34	0.0	26	100.0	0.0	0.0	0.0	0.0	11.5	57.6	30.8	13	100.0	53.8	0.0
Pomme de Terre township (Grant)	133	132	-0.8	98	98.0	0.0	0.0	0.0	2.0	12.3	63.3	24.5	42	78.6	33.3	31.0
Pomroy township (Itasca)	39	39	0.0	34	100.0	0.0	0.0	0.0	0.0	50.0	41.1	8.8	11	100.0	18.2	54.5
Pomroy township (Kanabec)	425	415	-2.4	351	96.6	0.0	0.0	3.1	0.3	21.3	55.4	23.4	149	93.3	51.7	6.0
Ponemah CDP	724	NA	NA	673	1.3	0.0	0.0	91.8	6.8	41.9	50.9	7.3	159	32.7	88.1	0.0
Ponto Lake township (Cass)	481	483	0.4	522	96.0	0.6	1.7	0.4	1.3	9.9	53.9	36.2	268	91.0	43.3	15.7
Poplar township (Cass)	170	168	-1.2	151	98.7	0.0	0.0	1.3	0.0	17.9	73.5	8.6	69	91.3	55.1	5.8
Poplar Grove township (Roseau)	82	83	1.2	59	100.0	0.0	0.0	0.0	0.0	32.2	40.8	27.1	21	100.0	23.8	33.3
Poplar River township (Red Lake)	107	106	-0.9	75	94.7	0.0	0.0	4.0	1.3	24.1	61.3	14.7	31	87.1	51.6	12.9
Popple township (Clearwater)	531	530	-0.2	579	86.0	0.0	0.0	9.8	4.1	32.1	57.2	10.7	193	95.3	49.2	19.2
Popple Grove township (Mahnomen)	139	142	2.2	127	85.0	0.0	0.0	11.0	3.9	29.1	62.2	8.7	46	91.3	41.3	19.6
Poppleton township (Kittson)	120	117	-2.5	115	97.4	0.0	2.6	0.0	0.0	23.4	54.7	21.7	45	100.0	35.6	20.0
Portage township (St. Louis)	170	171	0.6	196	87.8	0.0	0.0	12.2	0.0	17.3	63.0	19.9	89	92.1	55.1	7.9
Porter city & MCD (Yellow Medicine)	183	183	0.0	182	96.2	0.0	0.5	0.5	2.7	23.6	57.0	19.2	76	75.0	56.6	6.6
Port Hope township (Beltrami)	673	676	0.4	693	93.2	0.0	0.0	6.8	0.0	18.4	69.8	12.0	268	89.2	20.1	28.4
Posen township (Yellow Medicine)	219	213	-2.7	245	100.0	0.0	0.0	0.0	0.0	28.2	61.6	10.2	89	79.8	47.2	9.0
Potamo township (Lake of the Woods)	107	NA	NA	329	98.2	0.0	0.0	1.8	0.0	19.8	75.4	4.9	87	100.0	20.7	8.0
Potshot Lake UT (St. Louis)	74	74	0.0	28	100.0	0.0	0.0	0.0	0.0	10.7	78.5	10.7	12	100.0	50.0	25.0
Powers township (Cass)	715	719	0.6	755	93.2	1.1	0.5	4.4	0.8	15.5	55.5	29.0	363	97.8	48.8	13.5
Prairie Lake township (St. Louis)	50	50	0.0	35	100.0	0.0	0.0	0.0	0.0	25.7	42.8	31.4	17	100.0	58.8	5.9
Prairie View township (Wilkin)	196	194	-1.0	184	100.0	0.0	0.0	0.0	0.0	26.1	65.6	8.2	74	98.6	27.0	17.6
Prairieville township (Brown)	255	251	-1.6	208	100.0	0.0	0.0	0.0	0.0	17.7	68.9	13.5	92	84.8	54.3	6.5
Preble township (Fillmore)	209	212	1.4	261	100.0	0.0	0.0	0.0	0.0	19.2	69.0	11.9	96	93.8	62.5	9.4
Prescott township (Faribault)	163	160	-1.8	179	99.4	0.0	0.0	0.0	0.6	15.6	52.7	31.8	74	90.5	48.6	16.2
Preston city & MCD (Fillmore)	1,325	1,294	-2.3	1,239	99.4	0.0	0.6	0.0	0.1	22.4	52.3	25.3	564	77.7	46.3	19.5
Preston township (Fillmore)	359	365	1.7	391	100.0	0.0	0.0	0.0	0.0	26.4	59.3	14.3	128	90.6	56.3	14.1

1 May be of any race.

Table A. All Places — **Population and Housing**

STATE City, town, township, borough, or CDP (county if applicable)	2010 census total population	2014 estimated population	Percent change 2010–2014	ACS total population estimate 2010–2014	White alone, not Hispanic or Latino	Black alone, not Hispanic or Latino	Asian alone, not Hispanic or Latino	All other races or 2 or more races, not Hispanic or Latino	Hispanic or Latino[1]	Under 18 years old	Age 18 to 64 years old	Age 65 years and older	Total occupied housing units	Percent owner occupied	High school diploma or less	Bachelor's degree or more
	1	2	3	4	5	6	7	8	9	10	11	12	13	14	15	16
MINNESOTA—Con.																
Preston Lake township (Renville)...........	271	260	-4.1	256	100.0	0.0	0.0	0.0	0.0	16.0	57.6	26.6	107	91.6	62.6	19.6
Princeton city................	4,745	4,696	-1.0	4,725	93.6	0.5	1.0	3.7	1.2	26.9	53.5	19.5	1,987	53.7	44.2	21.5
Princeton city (Mille Lacs)	4,695	4,645	-1.1	4,647	93.5	0.5	1.0	3.8	1.2	27.4	54.1	18.4	1,939	52.6	43.4	22.0
Princeton city (Sherburne)	50	51	2.0	78	100.0	0.0	0.0	0.0	0.0	0.0	12.8	87.2	48	100.0	77.1	0.0
Princeton township (Mille Lacs).............	2,209	2,188	-1.0	2,222	95.8	0.0	0.0	2.1	2.1	19.1	66.7	14.1	857	88.9	42.5	12.7
Prinsburg city & MCD (Kandiyohi)...........	497	494	-0.6	505	94.5	1.0	1.2	0.0	3.4	23.6	57.1	19.2	206	89.8	35.4	25.2
Prior township (Big Stone)	247	244	-1.2	159	96.9	0.0	0.0	3.1	0.0	19.5	49.9	30.8	66	83.3	56.1	13.6
Prior Lake city & MCD (Scott)...............	22,908	25,039	9.3	23,956	88.8	2.0	3.8	3.6	1.8	28.9	60.7	10.4	8,773	83.4	22.3	43.0
Proctor city & MCD (St. Louis)................	3,058	3,081	0.8	3,066	96.8	0.7	2.1	0.4	0.0	20.3	61.9	17.9	1,291	71.7	39.2	22.1
Prosper township (Lake of the Woods).........	164	NA	NA	196	95.9	0.0	0.0	4.1	0.0	0.0	43.4	56.6	93	100.0	21.5	62.4
Providence township (Lac qui Parle)............	169	161	-4.7	134	100.0	0.0	0.0	0.0	0.0	25.4	55.2	19.4	56	92.9	50.0	17.9
Pulaski township (Morrison)...............	300	299	-0.3	393	98.7	0.0	0.0	0.0	1.3	30.2	57.3	12.5	144	89.6	56.3	16.0
Quamba city & MCD (Kanabec).............	123	129	4.9	124	74.2	0.0	0.0	12.1	13.7	16.1	66.8	16.9	46	67.4	69.6	4.3
Queen township (Polk)	214	216	0.9	170	100.0	0.0	0.0	0.0	0.0	16.5	51.1	32.4	86	82.6	47.7	15.1
Quincy township (Olmsted)...............	339	351	3.5	337	95.5	2.4	2.1	0.0	0.0	27.9	61.4	10.7	117	76.1	51.3	22.2
Quiring township (Beltrami)................	70	71	1.4	81	86.4	4.9	0.0	8.6	0.0	34.6	58.0	7.4	27	88.9	40.7	33.3
Rabbit Lake township (Crow Wing).............	319	324	1.6	303	95.0	0.0	0.0	0.0	5.0	20.1	67.4	12.5	108	93.5	40.7	20.4
Racine city & MCD (Mower)................	442	498	12.7	424	96.5	0.0	2.8	0.7	0.0	30.4	59.0	10.6	139	98.6	33.1	18.0
Racine township (Mower) .	455	460	1.1	491	92.3	1.8	0.0	5.9	0.0	25.0	59.6	15.3	175	85.7	43.4	16.0
Rainy Lake UT (Koochiching).............	4,048	NA	NA	3,603	96.7	0.0	0.0	3.3	0.0	19.4	60.5	20.2	1,567	96.9	47.4	19.5
Ramsey city & MCD (Anoka)...............	23,668	25,598	8.2	24,441	89.4	2.0	4.2	2.3	2.1	27.3	64.5	8.2	8,245	90.6	28.5	30.0
Randall city & MCD (Morrison)...............	650	629	-3.2	589	96.3	0.0	0.5	0.0	3.2	24.7	57.9	17.3	260	73.8	48.1	16.9
Randolph city & MCD (Dakota)...............	436	442	1.4	373	99.5	0.0	0.0	0.5	0.0	23.3	68.6	8.0	145	75.9	41.4	18.6
Randolph township (Dakota)...............	659	685	3.9	574	96.5	0.0	0.0	2.6	0.9	18.9	60.7	20.2	223	91.5	42.6	22.0
Ranier city & MCD (Koochiching).............	612	588	-3.9	524	97.1	0.0	0.0	2.5	0.4	14.1	53.4	32.4	254	81.9	41.7	22.8
Ransom township (Nobles)................	230	232	0.9	191	96.3	0.0	1.6	2.1	0.0	11.0	53.4	35.6	85	77.6	56.5	14.1
Rapidan township (Blue Earth).................	1,101	1,108	0.6	979	97.1	0.0	1.9	0.0	0.9	11.0	69.2	19.6	406	90.1	36.5	32.8
Rapid River township (Lake of the Woods)......	12	NA	NA	0	0.0	0.0	0.0	0.0	0.0	0.0	0.0	0.0	0	0.0	0.0	0.0
Ravenna township (Dakota)...............	2,336	2,382	2.0	2,393	97.0	0.4	0.8	1.1	0.7	24.9	64.9	10.3	845	93.3	27.6	28.6
Raymond city & MCD (Kandiyohi)...........	764	751	-1.7	656	90.2	0.0	0.0	2.7	7.0	28.9	52.3	18.9	276	81.2	48.9	11.6
Raymond township (Stearns)...............	259	269	3.9	340	99.4	0.0	0.0	0.0	0.6	42.6	47.9	9.4	88	81.8	62.5	6.8
Redby CDP..................	1,334	NA	NA	1,321	2.4	1.1	0.0	86.1	10.4	42.8	52.4	4.8	377	55.7	65.5	13.3
Red Eye township (Wadena)...............	490	483	-1.4	484	94.6	0.8	0.4	1.0	3.1	31.2	58.2	10.5	182	84.6	51.6	11.0
Red Lake CDP...............	1,731	NA	NA	1,497	4.0	0.9	0.0	92.2	2.9	37.5	54.1	8.5	465	39.1	52.0	3.2
Red Lake Falls city & MCD (Red Lake)..........	1,427	1,404	-1.6	1,344	93.7	1.4	0.0	3.0	1.9	25.6	55.6	19.0	571	73.7	52.2	19.3
Red Lake Falls township (Red Lake)...............	201	200	-0.5	194	94.3	0.0	0.0	0.0	5.7	15.5	58.2	26.3	87	86.2	33.3	25.3
Redpath township (Traverse)...............	48	46	-4.2	50	100.0	0.0	0.0	0.0	0.0	36.0	46.0	18.0	18	100.0	33.3	38.9
Red Rock township (Mower)................	733	742	1.2	820	99.0	0.4	0.0	0.6	0.0	23.9	59.3	16.5	332	91.6	49.1	17.5
Red Wing city & MCD (Goodhue)...............	16,459	16,470	0.1	16,502	90.3	1.9	0.5	3.7	3.6	21.1	59.0	19.8	6,892	69.0	37.4	24.4
Redwood Falls city...........	5,254	5,059	-3.7	5,174	88.0	1.4	0.3	8.9	1.4	22.6	54.5	22.8	2,248	73.3	43.3	19.1
Redwood Falls city (Redwood)...............	5,254	5,059	-3.7	5,174	88.0	1.4	0.3	8.9	1.4	22.6	54.5	22.8	2,248	73.3	43.3	19.1
Redwood Falls city (Renville)...............	0	0	0.0	0	0.0	0.0	0.0	0.0	0.0	0.0	0.0	0.0	0	0.0	0.0	0.0
Redwood Falls township (Redwood)...............	181	175	-3.3	182	97.8	0.0	0.0	2.2	0.0	17.0	61.3	21.4	78	83.3	34.6	15.4
Regal city & MCD (Kandiyohi)...........	34	34	0.0	45	91.1	0.0	0.0	0.0	8.9	11.1	73.3	15.6	21	81.0	57.1	14.3
Reine township (Roseau) .	94	95	1.1	90	100.0	0.0	0.0	0.0	0.0	16.6	74.5	8.9	38	89.5	63.2	7.9
Reiner township (Pennington)............	87	87	0.0	102	97.1	0.0	0.0	2.9	0.0	6.9	55.8	37.3	42	97.6	45.2	0.0
Reis township (Polk).........	79	79	0.0	62	100.0	0.0	0.0	0.0	0.0	24.2	56.4	19.4	26	84.6	46.2	19.2
Remer city & MCD (Cass)	370	363	-1.9	400	91.0	0.0	0.0	6.0	3.0	27.6	53.7	19.0	198	58.1	56.6	6.6
Remer township (Cass)....	189	187	-1.1	153	92.2	7.8	0.0	0.0	0.0	15.0	57.6	27.5	57	96.5	61.4	22.8
Rendsville township (Stevens)................	161	160	-0.6	184	96.2	0.0	3.8	0.0	0.0	22.2	58.6	19.0	71	80.3	36.6	21.1
Reno township (Pope)	397	396	-0.3	372	97.3	0.8	0.0	1.9	0.0	19.1	61.9	19.1	145	95.2	35.2	18.6
Renville city & MCD (Renville)................	1,287	1,225	-4.8	1,384	76.7	0.0	2.7	0.4	20.2	21.3	55.9	23.0	567	69.8	48.0	20.8

1 May be of any race.

Table A. All Places — **Population and Housing**

STATE City, town, township, borough, or CDP (county if applicable)	2010 census total population	2014 estimated population	Percent change 2010–2014	ACS total population estimate 2010–2014	White alone, not Hispanic or Latino	Black alone, not Hispanic or Latino	Asian alone, not Hispanic or Latino	All other races or 2 or more races, not Hispanic or Latino	Hispanic or Latino[1]	Under 18 years old	Age 18 to 64 years old	Age 65 years and older	Total occupied housing units	Percent owner occupied	High school diploma or less	Bachelor's degree or more
	1	2	3	4	5	6	7	8	9	10	11	12	13	14	15	16
MINNESOTA—Con.																
Revere city & MCD (Redwood)	95	92	-3.2	85	92.9	3.5	1.2	2.4	0.0	20.1	63.7	16.5	28	82.1	50.0	10.7
Reynolds township (Todd)	662	651	-1.7	612	96.1	0.0	0.0	3.9	0.0	27.5	58.8	13.9	225	84.4	53.8	10.7
Rheiderland township (Chippewa)	269	265	-1.5	226	100.0	0.0	0.0	0.0	0.0	20.4	67.9	11.9	81	82.7	39.5	23.5
Rhinehart township (Polk)	139	138	-0.7	122	100.0	0.0	0.0	0.0	0.0	23.0	72.2	4.9	43	88.4	18.6	37.2
Rice city & MCD (Benton)	1,275	1,344	5.4	1,485	95.6	0.7	0.0	2.6	1.0	30.7	64.6	4.7	544	92.6	30.9	21.3
Rice township (Clearwater)	158	160	1.3	173	44.5	0.0	0.0	53.2	2.3	26.0	54.3	19.7	68	92.6	55.9	1.5
Rice Lake CDP	235	NA	NA	246	13.4	0.0	0.0	83.7	2.8	42.3	52.1	5.7	84	57.1	54.8	0.0
Rice Lake township (St. Louis)	4,094	4,124	0.7	4,101	97.8	0.7	0.0	1.5	0.0	18.8	67.8	13.4	1,693	92.3	31.7	20.6
Riceland township (Freeborn)	434	429	-1.2	433	89.6	0.0	0.0	0.0	10.4	24.6	55.2	20.1	160	88.8	49.4	12.5
Rice River township (Aitkin)	136	132	-2.9	142	100.0	0.0	0.0	0.0	0.0	18.3	64.7	16.9	75	90.7	45.3	13.3
Riceville township (Becker)	83	83	0.0	108	89.8	0.0	0.0	9.3	0.9	30.5	53.7	15.7	38	97.4	50.0	10.5
Richardson township (Morrison)	536	535	-0.2	474	97.9	0.0	0.0	2.1	0.0	10.0	54.8	35.2	223	96.9	58.3	14.3
Richardville township (Kittson)	102	100	-2.0	110	92.7	1.8	0.0	5.5	0.0	26.3	52.6	20.9	43	81.4	44.2	14.0
Richfield city & MCD (Hennepin)	35,228	36,179	2.7	35,877	59.3	10.3	6.4	4.5	19.4	20.9	65.0	14.1	14,689	63.5	33.0	33.6
Richland township (Rice)	416	421	1.2	425	97.2	0.0	0.0	2.8	0.0	24.8	62.0	13.4	166	81.3	49.4	18.7
Richmond city & MCD (Stearns)	1,422	1,422	0.0	1,466	97.3	0.0	0.0	0.5	2.2	24.3	56.1	19.7	612	80.2	51.5	11.4
Richmond township (Winona)	699	697	-0.3	566	97.2	2.8	0.0	0.0	0.0	11.5	72.5	16.1	257	92.2	40.9	14.8
Rich Valley township (McLeod)	698	685	-1.9	730	96.2	0.0	0.0	0.0	3.8	25.8	57.4	16.8	269	93.7	58.7	13.0
Richville city & MCD (Otter Tail)	96	96	0.0	84	100.0	0.0	0.0	0.0	0.0	13.1	58.5	28.6	38	81.6	50.0	5.3
Richwood township (Becker)	662	675	2.0	662	79.6	1.8	1.2	14.7	2.7	22.9	62.0	15.1	252	92.5	47.6	24.6
Ridgely township (Nicollet)	115	113	-1.7	87	94.3	0.0	0.0	0.0	5.7	18.3	60.7	20.7	33	93.9	30.3	30.3
Ripley township (Dodge)	195	197	1.0	209	87.6	0.0	0.0	0.0	12.4	23.4	62.2	14.4	83	83.1	62.7	13.3
Ripley township (Morrison)	729	722	0.0	781	94.9	0.5	1.4	1.0	2.2	24.1	65.9	10.0	297	94.9	45.1	15.5
River township (Red Lake)	65	65	0.0	117	100.0	0.0	0.0	0.0	0.0	29.1	59.0	12.0	36	97.2	47.2	27.8
Riverdale township (Watonwan)	294	291	-1.0	251	93.2	0.0	0.0	4.4	2.4	18.4	56.2	25.5	102	94.1	40.2	18.6
River Falls township (Pennington)	178	177	-0.6	185	97.3	0.0	0.5	1.1	1.1	21.7	65.8	12.4	70	91.4	30.0	28.6
Riverland CDP	276	NA	NA	219	10.5	0.0	2.7	78.1	8.7	57.0	38.3	4.6	55	0.0	54.5	1.8
Riverside township (Lac qui Parle)	310	295	-4.8	277	100.0	0.0	0.0	0.0	0.0	21.7	55.6	22.7	115	89.6	38.3	25.2
Riverton township (Clay)	446	460	3.1	434	94.7	0.0	0.7	1.4	3.2	29.3	55.2	15.4	156	93.6	37.8	29.5
Riverton city & MCD (Crow Wing)	117	117	0.0	111	87.4	4.5	0.0	8.1	0.0	13.5	72.9	13.5	49	87.8	30.6	18.4
Robbinsdale city & MCD (Hennepin)	13,951	14,320	2.6	14,196	77.3	14.3	1.6	3.6	3.1	22.1	64.2	13.7	5,977	67.3	27.9	39.5
Roberts township (Wilkin)	110	109	-0.9	127	100.0	0.0	0.0	0.0	0.0	26.8	51.1	22.0	44	93.2	29.5	43.2
Rochester city & MCD (Olmsted)	106,748	111,402	4.4	109,252	78.1	6.6	7.1	2.9	5.4	24.4	62.1	13.3	43,651	69.6	24.3	44.1
Rochester township (Olmsted)	1,634	1,781	9.0	1,618	91.2	0.0	5.4	1.5	1.9	22.9	64.6	12.4	589	98.1	13.4	72.0
Rock township (Pipestone)	182	178	-2.2	153	93.5	0.0	0.0	4.6	2.0	26.2	58.1	15.7	67	86.6	64.2	9.0
Rock Creek city & MCD (Pine)	1,628	1,602	-1.6	1,778	94.2	2.3	1.2	1.9	0.4	22.1	67.5	10.5	629	91.1	47.4	14.0
Rock Dell township (Olmsted)	645	664	2.9	604	98.8	0.8	0.0	0.3	0.0	24.8	50.5	24.7	226	88.1	45.6	13.7
Rockford city	4,316	4,366	1.2	4,214	92.3	2.2	0.6	1.2	3.6	27.6	66.8	5.5	1,526	78.8	30.1	30.7
Rockford city (Hennepin)	426	430	0.9	286	100.0	0.0	0.0	0.0	0.0	23.1	63.4	13.3	110	40.0	42.7	21.8
Rockford city (Wright)	3,890	3,936	1.2	3,928	91.8	2.4	0.7	1.3	3.9	28.0	67.1	4.9	1,416	81.8	29.1	31.4
Rockford township (Wright)	3,194	3,299	3.3	3,250	95.1	0.1	0.5	1.6	2.7	20.1	62.5	17.4	1,258	93.5	31.3	30.2
Rock Lake township (Lyon)	265	264	-0.4	283	92.6	0.0	0.0	0.0	7.4	20.5	64.9	14.5	111	91.0	43.2	12.6
Rocksbury township (Pennington)	1,202	1,185	-1.4	1,195	92.2	0.0	1.0	1.8	5.0	28.2	62.2	9.6	414	84.8	36.7	21.5
Rockville city & MCD (Stearns)	2,448	2,486	1.6	2,499	88.3	0.9	0.4	0.0	10.5	27.8	61.4	10.9	906	87.0	43.6	19.8
Rockwell township (Norman)	61	59	-3.3	78	100.0	0.0	0.0	0.0	0.0	14.1	44.9	41.0	35	77.1	42.9	11.4
Rockwood township (Hubbard)	430	429	-0.2	440	93.0	0.0	0.7	6.4	0.0	20.2	62.4	17.3	166	94.0	36.1	31.9
Rockwood township (Wadena)	390	385	-1.3	373	87.7	7.5	0.5	1.6	2.7	29.0	53.5	17.7	132	93.2	51.5	16.7
Rogers township (Cass)	63	63	0.0	69	94.2	0.0	0.0	5.8	0.0	4.3	41.9	53.6	42	100.0	47.6	19.0
Rogers city & MCD (Hennepin)	11,200	12,393	10.7	11,747	93.4	2.0	1.8	1.9	0.9	31.3	57.9	10.8	3,876	80.4	28.7	35.1
Rolling Forks township (Pope)	151	151	0.0	161	100.0	0.0	0.0	0.0	0.0	30.3	45.3	24.2	58	89.7	56.9	19.0
Rolling Green township (Martin)	266	259	-2.6	224	94.2	0.0	2.7	3.1	0.0	22.8	56.2	21.0	89	94.4	36.0	13.5
Rollingstone city & MCD (Winona)	664	660	-0.6	615	95.0	0.5	3.9	0.0	0.7	24.5	61.1	14.5	234	88.0	37.2	20.5
Rollingstone township (Winona)	701	698	-0.4	822	71.0	0.0	28.5	0.0	0.5	20.4	67.7	11.9	264	87.1	50.4	21.6
Rollis township (Marshall)	115	115	0.0	96	100.0	0.0	0.0	0.0	0.0	16.7	44.7	38.5	48	97.9	41.7	18.8

1 May be of any race.

Table A. All Places — **Population and Housing**

STATE City, town, township, borough, or CDP (county if applicable)	2010 census total population	2014 estimated population	Percent change 2010–2014	ACS total population estimate 2010–2014	White alone, not Hispanic or Latino	Black alone, not Hispanic or Latino	Asian alone, not Hispanic or Latino	All other races or 2 or more races, not Hispanic or Latino	Hispanic or Latino[1]	Under 18 years old	Age 18 to 64 years old	Age 65 years and older	Total occupied housing units	Percent owner occupied	High school diploma or less	Bachelor's degree or more
	1	2	3	4	5	6	7	8	9	10	11	12	13	14	15	16
MINNESOTA—Con.																
Rome township (Faribault)	143	140	-2.1	104	100.0	0.0	0.0	0.0	0.0	9.6	61.6	28.8	50	92.0	32.0	16.0
Ronneby CDP	67	NA	NA	35	100.0	0.0	0.0	0.0	0.0	11.4	71.4	17.1	16	100.0	56.3	12.5
Roome township (Polk)	177	176	-0.6	136	90.4	0.0	0.0	0.7	8.8	18.4	57.3	24.3	57	86.0	38.6	22.8
Roosevelt township (Beltrami)	225	229	1.8	232	84.5	0.0	0.0	15.5	0.0	25.8	62.9	11.2	92	96.7	40.2	23.9
Roosevelt township (Crow Wing)	601	612	1.8	638	86.7	0.0	0.0	13.3	0.0	16.1	48.1	35.6	318	89.6	49.7	11.3
Roosevelt city	151	153	1.3	74	100.0	0.0	0.0	0.0	0.0	6.8	66.4	27.0	40	75.0	77.5	0.0
Roosevelt city (Lake of the Woods)	7	7	0.0	0	0.0	0.0	0.0	0.0	0.0	0.0	0.0	0.0	0	0.0	0.0	0.0
Roosevelt city (Roseau)	144	146	1.4	74	100.0	0.0	0.0	0.0	0.0	6.8	66.4	27.0	40	75.0	77.5	0.0
Roscoe township (Goodhue)	732	739	1.0	690	98.7	0.0	0.7	0.0	0.6	23.1	63.3	13.5	247	96.0	34.8	32.0
Roscoe city & MCD (Stearns)	102	102	0.0	94	100.0	0.0	0.0	0.0	0.0	23.4	56.3	20.2	43	90.7	69.8	0.0
Roseau city & MCD (Roseau)	2,631	2,652	0.8	2,620	93.2	0.9	2.3	2.0	1.6	26.1	58.5	15.3	1,043	63.9	36.3	30.5
Rosebud township (Polk)	351	357	1.7	311	99.7	0.0	0.0	0.3	0.0	25.7	56.6	17.7	117	87.2	56.4	18.8
Rose Creek city & MCD (Mower)	394	401	1.8	434	99.3	0.0	0.0	0.7	0.0	28.1	54.4	17.5	178	82.0	47.8	14.0
Rosedale township (Mahnomen)	135	138	2.2	143	84.6	0.0	0.0	15.4	0.0	29.4	45.5	25.2	58	82.8	55.2	27.6
Rose Dell township (Rock)	206	203	-1.5	196	96.9	0.0	0.0	1.5	1.5	21.4	62.3	16.3	77	90.9	49.4	11.7
Rose Hill township (Cottonwood)	166	165	-0.6	134	100.0	0.0	0.0	0.0	0.0	22.4	59.0	18.7	57	80.7	42.1	14.0
Roseland township (Kandiyohi)	371	371	0.0	416	100.0	0.0	0.0	0.0	0.0	20.9	66.4	12.7	149	87.9	41.6	12.1
Rosemount city & MCD (Dakota)	21,874	22,998	5.1	22,469	83.4	5.5	4.9	1.8	4.5	30.4	60.1	9.4	7,759	86.8	21.5	46.0
Rosendale township (Watonwan)	300	297	-1.0	294	99.0	0.0	1.0	0.0	0.0	14.6	57.5	27.9	124	91.1	57.3	15.3
Roseville township (Grant)	124	123	-0.8	164	99.4	0.0	0.0	0.6	0.0	15.9	66.3	17.7	66	100.0	65.2	12.1
Roseville township (Kandiyohi)	622	621	-0.2	564	94.1	0.0	0.0	5.3	0.5	21.3	58.3	20.6	220	93.2	50.9	16.8
Roseville city & MCD (Ramsey)	33,660	35,319	4.9	34,554	77.0	6.4	8.0	2.7	5.8	17.6	61.3	21.3	14,797	64.4	24.5	47.5
Rosewood township (Chippewa)	348	342	-1.7	350	95.7	0.0	0.0	3.7	0.6	30.3	61.5	8.3	124	81.5	42.7	13.7
Rosing township (Morrison)	146	144	-1.4	118	96.6	0.0	0.0	3.4	0.0	21.2	59.3	19.5	51	92.2	51.0	7.8
Ross township (Roseau)	429	429	0.0	387	97.9	0.0	0.0	2.1	0.0	25.4	60.3	14.5	156	93.6	46.2	14.1
Ross Lake township (Crow Wing)	165	169	2.4	226	100.0	0.0	0.0	0.0	0.0	8.4	55.3	36.3	109	91.7	44.0	13.8
Rost township (Jackson)	211	211	0.0	237	96.6	0.0	0.0	3.4	0.0	23.7	63.8	12.7	86	80.2	46.5	16.3
Rothsay city	493	488	-0.9	435	98.6	0.0	0.0	1.4	0.0	21.8	59.5	18.6	198	82.3	41.4	24.2
Rothsay city (Otter Tail)	219	217	-0.9	196	100.0	0.0	0.0	0.0	0.0	22.4	58.2	19.4	86	84.9	44.2	24.4
Rothsay city (Wilkin)	274	271	-1.1	239	97.5	0.0	0.0	2.5	0.0	21.3	60.8	18.0	112	80.4	39.3	24.1
Round Grove township (McLeod)	251	246	-2.0	270	96.7	0.0	0.0	2.2	1.1	20.3	64.8	14.8	110	77.3	55.5	18.2
Round Lake township (Becker)	183	187	2.2	212	46.7	0.0	0.0	53.3	0.0	17.5	70.4	12.3	90	86.7	57.8	13.3
Round Lake township (Jackson)	166	166	0.0	168	95.8	0.0	0.0	0.0	4.2	22.7	49.0	28.6	65	93.8	27.7	12.3
Round Lake city & MCD (Nobles)	376	372	-1.1	399	95.0	0.0	1.0	1.3	2.8	18.1	64.9	17.0	188	70.5	56.9	10.6
Round Prairie township (Todd)	706	693	-1.8	715	97.9	0.0	0.0	2.1	0.0	24.5	57.1	18.6	268	90.7	62.7	12.3
Royal township (Lincoln)	178	178	0.0	175	100.0	0.0	0.0	0.0	0.0	11.4	47.4	41.1	91	87.9	78.0	5.5
Royalton city	1,239	1,218	-1.7	1,158	93.4	0.4	1.2	1.8	3.1	29.0	59.4	11.6	478	73.8	38.7	14.6
Royalton city (Benton)	0	0	0.0	0	0.0	0.0	0.0	0.0	0.0	0.0	0.0	0.0	0	0.0	0.0	0.0
Royalton city (Morrison)	1,239	1,218	-1.7	1,158	93.4	0.4	1.2	1.8	3.1	29.0	59.4	11.6	478	73.8	38.7	14.6
Royalton township (Pine)	1,163	1,147	-1.4	1,174	97.3	1.6	0.0	0.4	0.7	20.4	63.6	15.8	472	92.6	57.4	17.4
Roy Lake CDP	12	NA	NA	20	85.0	0.0	0.0	15.0	0.0	0.0	70.0	30.0	17	100.0	64.7	5.9
Rulien township (Lake of the Woods)	0	0	0.0	0	0.0	0.0	0.0	0.0	0.0	0.0	0.0	0.0	0	0.0	0.0	0.0
Runeberg township (Becker)	486	495	1.9	501	96.8	0.0	0.0	2.0	1.2	43.2	45.6	11.4	146	95.2	57.5	13.0
Rush City city & MCD (Chisago)	3,079	3,063	-0.5	3,074	79.3	11.5	0.3	6.3	2.6	16.0	70.0	14.0	916	64.2	51.2	12.1
Rushford city & MCD (Fillmore)	1,731	1,712	-1.1	2,102	97.1	1.0	0.3	0.2	1.3	29.0	50.7	20.3	781	65.2	42.9	17.3
Rushford Village city & MCD (Fillmore)	808	809	0.1	947	96.5	0.0	0.0	3.3	0.2	26.6	56.0	17.4	346	93.4	34.4	28.0
Rush Lake township (Otter Tail)	970	969	-0.1	948	99.1	0.0	0.0	0.9	0.0	18.2	61.4	20.4	408	86.3	37.0	19.9
Rushmore city & MCD (Nobles)	342	337	-1.5	281	91.8	1.4	0.0	0.7	6.0	21.7	55.0	23.1	142	76.8	64.1	7.7
Rushseba township (Chisago)	804	810	0.7	868	93.2	1.3	1.0	4.1	0.3	29.5	59.0	11.5	290	87.2	52.4	14.5
Russell city & MCD (Lyon)	338	333	-1.5	404	97.3	0.0	0.0	0.5	2.2	31.5	57.4	11.1	159	82.4	47.8	11.3
Russia township (Polk)	27	27	0.0	42	100.0	0.0	0.0	0.0	0.0	19.0	66.6	14.3	17	76.5	52.9	29.4
Ruthton city & MCD (Pipestone)	241	233	-3.3	270	80.7	0.0	0.0	0.0	19.3	25.2	63.7	11.1	125	75.2	74.4	6.4
Rutland township (Martin)	437	426	-2.5	480	99.0	0.0	0.0	0.8	0.2	27.5	56.6	15.8	174	81.6	35.6	19.5
Rutledge city & MCD (Pine)	229	221	-3.5	249	98.0	0.0	0.0	2.0	0.0	18.8	68.0	12.9	107	87.9	54.2	8.4
Sabin city & MCD (Clay)	522	552	5.7	577	97.9	0.0	0.0	0.7	1.4	32.3	63.5	4.3	184	96.7	31.5	23.9
Sacred Heart city & MCD (Renville)	548	520	-5.1	592	86.1	0.0	0.0	0.5	13.3	33.9	44.3	21.8	231	79.2	61.9	10.4
Sacred Heart township (Renville)	270	259	-4.1	264	99.6	0.0	0.4	0.0	0.0	18.2	68.2	13.6	118	76.3	39.0	9.3

1 May be of any race.

Table A. All Places — **Population and Housing**

STATE City, town, township, borough, or CDP (county if applicable)	2010 census total population	2014 estimated population	Percent change 2010–2014	ACS total population estimate 2010–2014	White alone, not Hispanic or Latino	Black alone, not Hispanic or Latino	Asian alone, not Hispanic or Latino	All other races or 2 or more races, not Hispanic or Latino	Hispanic or Latino[1]	Under 18 years old	Age 18 to 64 years old	Age 65 years and older	Total occupied housing units	Percent owner occupied	High school diploma or less	Bachelor's degree or more
	1	2	3	4	5	6	7	8	9	10	11	12	13	14	15	16
MINNESOTA—Con.																
Sago township (Itasca)	176	177	0.6	168	97.6	0.0	0.0	2.4	0.0	22.1	51.3	26.8	70	100.0	42.9	17.1
St. Anthony city (Hennepin and Ramsey)	8,226	8,960	8.9	8,501	79.4	6.8	5.5	4.6	3.8	18.9	60.8	20.4	3,678	58.2	24.3	47.4
St. Anthony city (Hennepin)	5,156	5,582	8.3	5,323	86.0	2.2	5.1	5.2	1.5	21.5	58.3	20.2	2,171	77.1	23.4	49.4
St. Anthony city (Ramsey)	3,070	3,378	10.0	3,178	68.4	14.4	6.1	3.6	7.5	14.5	64.8	20.8	1,507	31.1	25.5	44.5
St. Anthony city & MCD (Stearns)	86	86	0.0	98	100.0	0.0	0.0	0.0	0.0	35.7	51.1	13.3	35	85.7	34.3	17.1
St. Augusta city & MCD (Stearns)	3,317	3,545	6.9	3,434	97.7	0.0	1.2	0.4	0.7	27.2	62.0	10.7	1,182	93.1	34.5	27.0
St. Bonifacius city & MCD (Hennepin)	2,257	2,317	2.7	2,425	94.1	1.1	1.2	0.5	3.2	25.1	65.6	9.2	833	86.9	31.3	31.6
St. Charles city & MCD (Winona)	3,740	3,697	-1.1	3,716	78.2	0.3	5.5	1.6	14.4	28.6	56.8	14.6	1,333	71.3	42.6	25.9
St. Charles township (Winona)	624	624	0.0	688	90.6	0.0	1.0	3.1	5.4	35.5	50.6	14.0	217	94.9	36.9	25.3
St. Clair city & MCD (Blue Earth)	868	853	-1.7	846	81.9	0.0	0.0	3.5	14.5	35.1	56.1	8.7	277	83.0	39.7	22.7
St. Cloud city	65,946	66,389	0.7	66,038	83.2	8.5	2.6	3.3	2.4	19.2	70.2	10.8	25,279	53.4	27.7	27.1
St. Cloud city (Benton)	6,515	6,627	1.7	6,563	84.4	9.9	0.8	2.8	2.1	21.8	68.9	9.3	2,835	40.9	43.2	18.8
St. Cloud city (Sherburne)	6,785	6,954	2.5	6,865	75.2	15.4	1.0	3.8	4.6	17.3	68.3	14.4	2,287	41.6	19.0	28.4
St. Cloud city (Stearns)	52,646	52,808	0.3	52,610	84.1	7.4	3.1	3.3	2.1	19.1	70.6	10.5	20,157	56.5	26.5	28.1
St. Francis city	7,218	7,359	2.0	7,297	94.7	0.3	1.5	2.9	0.7	27.5	64.7	7.9	2,596	82.0	43.6	12.9
St. Francis city (Anoka)	7,218	7,359	2.0	7,297	94.7	0.3	1.5	2.9	0.7	27.5	64.7	7.9	2,596	82.0	43.6	12.9
St. Francis city (Isanti)	0	0	0.0	0	0.0	0.0	0.0	0.0	0.0	0.0	0.0	0.0	0	0.0	0.0	0.0
St. George township (Benton)	1,153	1,181	2.4	1,157	98.7	0.4	0.0	0.4	0.4	27.7	56.9	15.5	409	93.6	48.2	18.3
St. Hilaire city & MCD (Pennington)	279	276	-1.1	264	100.0	0.0	0.0	0.0	0.0	16.3	67.0	16.7	126	83.3	57.9	9.5
St. James city & MCD (Watonwan)	4,604	4,524	-1.7	4,565	63.6	0.0	0.0	0.9	35.5	28.2	56.6	15.2	1,831	62.1	57.2	14.5
St. James township (Watonwan)	261	258	-1.1	292	94.2	0.7	0.0	1.7	3.4	23.6	53.2	22.9	115	93.9	48.7	19.1
St. Johns township (Kandiyohi)	411	409	-0.5	400	96.5	0.0	1.0	0.5	2.0	27.3	54.7	18.3	147	87.1	37.4	15.6
St. Joseph township (Kittson)	56	55	-1.8	14	100.0	0.0	0.0	0.0	0.0	0.0	50.0	50.0	10	90.0	70.0	0.0
St. Joseph city & MCD (Stearns)	6,534	6,820	4.4	6,694	93.0	2.3	2.2	1.3	1.2	14.2	78.1	7.9	1,791	77.8	21.3	31.7
St. Joseph township (Stearns)	1,298	1,309	0.8	1,302	98.3	0.0	0.5	0.8	0.4	19.1	64.6	16.4	505	86.1	36.6	26.3
St. Lawrence township (Scott)	483	507	5.0	511	98.6	0.0	0.0	1.0	0.4	17.5	72.8	9.6	156	96.2	35.3	32.1
St. Leo city & MCD (Yellow Medicine)	100	97	-3.0	123	73.2	0.0	0.0	1.6	25.2	23.6	46.5	30.1	50	70.0	74.0	8.0
St. Louis Park city & MCD (Hennepin)	45,241	47,502	5.0	46,466	79.7	7.2	3.9	4.8	4.4	18.8	67.4	13.7	22,056	57.2	17.2	57.3
St. Martin city & MCD (Stearns)	308	309	0.3	331	93.7	0.0	0.0	0.0	6.3	33.2	56.1	10.6	120	95.0	60.8	5.8
St. Martin township (Stearns)	545	556	2.0	494	97.8	0.0	0.0	0.0	2.2	35.2	56.3	8.5	162	86.4	66.0	6.8
St. Mary township (Waseca)	460	465	1.1	427	96.7	0.0	0.5	0.0	2.8	22.9	61.3	15.7	166	92.2	45.2	21.7
St. Marys Point city & MCD (Washington)	370	379	2.4	404	99.0	0.0	0.0	0.5	0.5	28.2	53.3	18.6	156	84.6	30.1	35.9
St. Mathias township (Crow Wing)	622	632	1.6	746	96.2	0.0	0.7	0.0	3.1	34.7	56.6	8.7	269	73.6	39.4	17.8
St. Michael city & MCD (Wright)	16,399	17,087	4.2	16,767	93.4	1.9	1.7	2.3	0.7	30.6	61.4	8.1	5,498	90.7	22.0	39.1
St. Olaf township (Otter Tail)	352	347	-1.4	369	98.4	0.0	0.8	0.8	0.0	22.7	63.6	13.6	135	93.3	25.2	22.2
St. Paul city & MCD (Ramsey)	285,068	297,640	4.4	291,728	54.8	15.1	15.9	4.7	9.5	25.2	65.7	9.0	112,407	49.4	31.5	40.7
St. Paul Park city & MCD (Washington)	5,268	5,366	1.9	5,327	90.8	0.2	2.7	3.2	3.1	25.9	64.2	9.9	2,023	82.6	41.6	22.0
St. Peter city & MCD (Nicollet)	11,196	11,570	3.3	11,403	86.3	1.9	2.2	3.2	6.4	20.3	68.2	11.5	3,550	61.8	32.2	36.7
St. Rosa city & MCD (Stearns)	68	68	0.0	54	100.0	0.0	0.0	0.0	0.0	20.4	72.4	7.4	23	91.3	39.1	0.0
St. Stephen city & MCD (Stearns)	851	853	0.2	885	96.2	0.0	0.0	2.4	1.5	26.5	63.6	9.8	313	93.6	44.4	14.4
St. Vincent city & MCD (Kittson)	64	62	-3.1	40	92.5	5.0	0.0	2.5	0.0	2.5	70.0	27.5	27	81.5	44.4	29.6
St. Vincent township (Kittson)	58	57	-1.7	52	100.0	0.0	0.0	0.0	0.0	9.6	65.4	25.0	23	95.7	39.1	30.4
St. Wendel township (Stearns)	2,150	2,221	3.3	2,230	98.0	0.0	0.3	1.5	0.2	21.5	66.3	12.2	815	98.4	38.5	26.9
Salem township (Cass)	95	94	-1.1	103	91.3	0.0	1.9	6.8	0.0	27.2	60.2	12.6	42	76.2	31.0	19.0
Salem township (Olmsted)	1,086	1,119	3.0	1,157	91.3	6.2	0.6	1.4	0.5	24.5	59.2	16.2	407	85.0	40.8	34.9
Salo township (Aitkin)	102	98	-3.9	95	100.0	0.0	0.0	0.0	0.0	5.3	64.4	30.5	57	82.5	84.2	0.0
Sanborn city & MCD (Redwood)	339	321	-5.3	350	97.4	0.0	0.0	0.0	2.6	13.7	60.7	25.4	165	86.7	67.3	4.8
Sand Creek township (Scott)	1,521	1,588	4.4	1,574	92.6	0.1	0.5	0.8	6.0	26.3	60.0	13.5	522	86.6	42.1	24.3
Sanders township (Pennington)	298	307	3.0	322	99.1	0.0	0.0	0.0	0.9	31.7	55.4	12.7	118	97.5	47.5	11.9
Sand Lake township (Itasca)	146	147	0.7	147	87.1	0.0	0.0	12.9	0.0	12.2	45.0	42.9	74	95.9	36.5	32.4
Sand Lake UT (St. Louis)	1,066	1,074	0.8	878	95.9	0.2	2.1	0.0	1.8	19.1	60.1	20.7	390	100.0	37.4	26.4
Sandnes township (Yellow Medicine)	199	193	-3.0	199	98.5	0.0	0.0	0.0	1.5	20.1	69.2	10.6	86	90.7	43.0	20.9

1 May be of any race.

Table A. All Places — **Population and Housing**

STATE City, town, township, borough, or CDP (county if applicable)	Population 2010 census total population	2014 estimated population	Percent change 2010–2014	ACS total population estimate 2010–2014	Race and Hispanic or Latino origin (percent), 2010–2014 White alone, not Hispanic or Latino	Black alone, not Hispanic or Latino	Asian alone, not Hispanic or Latino	All other races or 2 or more races, not Hispanic or Latino	Hispanic or Latino[1]	Age (percent), 2010–2014 Under 18 years old	Age 18 to 64 years old	Age 65 years and older	Households, 2010–2014 Total occupied housing units	Percent owner occupied	Householders by level of education (percent) High school diploma or less	Bachelor's degree or more
	1	2	3	4	5	6	7	8	9	10	11	12	13	14	15	16
MINNESOTA—Con.																
Sandstone city & MCD (Pine)	2,849	2,741	-3.8	2,786	66.2	11.9	0.0	7.4	14.5	15.7	74.1	10.3	668	49.0	47.2	14.7
Sandstone township (Pine)	824	801	-2.8	854	90.3	0.8	0.0	7.8	1.1	20.0	62.2	17.8	360	98.3	61.4	7.2
Sandsville township (Polk)	67	67	0.0	29	100.0	0.0	0.0	0.0	0.0	6.8	75.8	17.2	13	92.3	23.1	7.7
Sandy township (St. Louis)	356	357	0.3	352	97.2	0.0	0.0	2.0	0.9	13.1	70.8	16.2	165	93.9	41.2	16.4
Sanford township (Grant)..	153	152	-0.7	138	100.0	0.0	0.0	0.0	0.0	16.6	57.8	25.4	59	93.2	49.2	16.9
San Francisco township (Carver)	832	849	2.0	760	97.9	0.0	0.3	1.4	0.4	22.3	61.8	15.8	276	96.0	54.7	17.8
Santiago township (Sherburne)	1,895	1,942	2.5	1,823	97.0	0.0	0.4	1.8	0.8	33.4	59.6	7.1	567	93.3	36.5	20.5
Saratoga township (Winona)	618	603	-2.4	792	96.7	0.0	1.4	0.6	1.3	39.6	53.4	6.9	202	85.1	54.0	13.9
Sargeant city & MCD (Mower)	61	61	0.0	79	98.7	0.0	0.0	0.0	1.3	10.1	78.5	11.4	47	95.7	57.4	2.1
Sargeant township (Mower)	310	312	0.6	301	94.7	0.0	0.0	0.0	5.3	34.9	49.5	15.6	92	82.6	52.2	14.1
Sartell city	15,951	16,523	3.6	16,123	92.0	1.6	2.8	1.6	1.9	30.6	58.0	11.5	6,063	70.3	23.0	41.8
Sartell city (Benton)	2,248	2,313	2.9	2,149	93.3	0.4	2.6	1.6	2.1	18.5	48.2	33.4	1,031	52.2	42.7	18.6
Sartell city (Stearns)	13,703	14,210	3.7	13,974	91.8	1.8	2.8	1.7	1.9	32.5	59.4	8.2	5,032	74.0	19.0	46.6
Sauk Centre city & MCD (Stearns)	4,311	4,324	0.3	4,317	86.7	0.0	0.0	0.0	13.3	23.4	56.3	20.3	1,822	62.1	48.0	22.3
Sauk Centre township (Stearns)	1,094	1,106	1.1	1,252	99.0	0.0	0.0	1.0	0.0	25.8	60.5	13.6	481	91.5	52.8	14.1
Sauk Rapids city & MCD (Benton)	12,836	13,348	4.0	13,079	92.2	1.6	2.2	1.7	2.4	26.4	63.7	10.0	5,090	64.2	28.3	26.8
Sauk Rapids township (Benton)	519	532	2.5	464	94.8	0.0	0.9	0.4	3.9	11.0	65.7	23.3	207	88.9	42.0	23.7
Savage city & MCD (Scott)	26,911	29,208	8.5	28,055	81.4	4.5	7.5	3.9	2.7	30.3	62.8	6.9	9,316	87.9	20.5	45.2
Savannah township (Becker)	163	169	3.7	110	99.1	0.0	0.0	0.9	0.0	11.8	61.9	26.4	52	92.3	50.0	26.9
Scambler township (Otter Tail)	476	470	-1.3	489	98.2	1.0	0.0	0.0	0.8	11.1	66.0	22.9	233	89.7	34.3	29.6
Scandia township (Polk) ...	74	74	0.0	53	100.0	0.0	0.0	0.0	0.0	13.2	64.2	22.6	23	82.6	26.1	34.8
Scandia city & MCD (Washington)	3,929	4,025	2.4	3,976	92.2	0.6	0.0	0.7	6.6	17.7	64.6	17.5	1,500	88.6	27.3	34.1
Scandia Valley township (Morrison)	1,191	1,185	-0.5	1,258	98.6	0.0	0.0	0.0	1.4	17.2	53.2	29.7	590	90.7	38.8	30.3
Scanlon city & MCD (Carlton)	991	981	-1.0	1,139	84.5	6.1	0.3	4.1	4.9	24.5	56.5	19.1	455	82.4	43.5	17.6
Schoolcraft township (Hubbard)	103	104	1.0	84	100.0	0.0	0.0	0.0	0.0	16.6	68.0	15.5	39	94.9	53.8	10.3
Schroeder township (Cook)	205	209	2.0	240	87.9	0.0	0.0	0.0	12.1	6.2	74.7	19.2	125	86.4	28.8	21.6
Sciota township (Dakota)..	414	431	4.1	422	93.6	0.5	0.0	5.9	0.0	25.6	61.5	12.8	136	96.3	44.1	25.0
Scott township (Stevens) ..	144	143	-0.7	115	100.0	0.0	0.0	0.0	0.0	27.7	47.8	24.3	43	100.0	48.8	11.6
Seaforth city & MCD (Redwood)	86	83	-3.5	82	86.6	0.0	0.0	0.0	13.4	30.4	50.0	19.5	28	92.9	60.7	14.3
Searles CDP	171	NA	NA	230	100.0	0.0	0.0	0.0	0.0	23.1	67.0	10.0	90	95.6	51.1	10.0
Seavey township (Aitkin) ..	61	59	-3.3	37	100.0	0.0	0.0	0.0	0.0	0.0	45.9	54.1	24	91.7	70.8	16.7
Sebeka city & MCD (Wadena)	711	690	-3.0	672	94.3	4.5	0.0	0.0	1.2	27.0	50.7	22.3	301	75.4	48.2	15.9
Second Assessment UT (Crow Wing)	117	118	0.9	106	100.0	0.0	0.0	0.0	0.0	21.7	47.2	31.1	54	81.5	31.5	24.1
Sedan city & MCD (Pope).	45	44	-2.2	30	100.0	0.0	0.0	0.0	0.0	6.7	83.3	10.0	18	100.0	55.6	0.0
Seely township (Faribault)	193	189	-2.1	158	96.8	1.3	0.0	1.3	0.6	10.8	59.0	30.4	77	77.9	58.4	14.3
Selma township (Cottonwood)	193	192	-0.5	194	91.2	0.0	7.2	1.5	0.0	25.8	58.9	15.5	77	89.6	64.9	3.9
Severance township (Sibley)	253	249	-1.6	237	92.8	0.0	0.0	3.0	4.2	18.2	61.3	20.7	99	88.9	52.5	23.2
Seward township (Nobles)	208	210	1.0	179	100.0	0.0	0.0	0.0	0.0	15.7	60.9	23.5	75	96.0	46.7	17.3
Shafer city & MCD (Chisago)	1,045	1,043	-0.2	936	97.9	0.0	0.0	1.5	0.6	32.3	60.5	7.2	358	84.1	34.1	16.8
Shafer township (Chisago)	1,048	1,061	1.2	1,021	95.1	0.4	0.2	4.3	0.0	20.9	69.6	9.6	362	93.6	33.7	20.2
Shakopee city & MCD (Scott)	37,073	39,677	7.0	38,613	70.6	4.7	11.2	4.2	9.3	29.8	63.3	7.0	12,981	77.1	30.8	40.3
Shamrock township (Aitkin)	1,272	1,244	-2.2	1,121	90.2	0.0	0.0	5.0	4.8	10.1	47.7	42.4	599	90.3	47.7	16.9
Shaokatan township (Lincoln)	178	176	-1.1	221	95.5	0.0	0.0	0.0	4.5	25.8	63.8	10.4	81	96.3	43.2	23.5
Sharon township (Le Sueur)	636	644	1.3	677	95.9	0.0	0.4	2.2	1.5	19.3	64.3	16.5	276	94.6	33.3	29.7
Shelburne township (Lyon)	178	176	-1.1	155	97.4	0.0	0.0	0.6	1.9	33.5	55.4	11.0	54	88.9	35.2	7.4
Shelby township (Blue Earth)	265	264	-0.4	302	95.0	0.0	1.0	2.3	1.7	26.8	57.3	15.9	111	89.2	36.9	23.4
Sheldon township (Houston)	266	261	-1.9	316	89.2	0.0	0.0	9.8	0.9	28.8	57.3	13.9	111	91.9	43.2	20.7
Shell Lake township (Becker)	293	299	2.0	258	88.4	0.0	0.0	11.6	0.0	11.7	62.5	26.0	123	96.7	39.8	19.5
Shell River township (Wadena)	233	229	-1.7	180	97.2	0.0	0.0	2.8	0.0	18.8	65.0	16.1	78	91.0	55.1	14.1
Shell Rock township (Freeborn)	427	422	-1.2	441	91.8	0.0	0.0	0.5	7.7	25.2	55.9	18.8	167	85.6	59.3	4.8
Shelly city & MCD (Norman)	191	185	-3.1	223	73.1	0.0	0.0	9.4	17.5	21.9	54.7	23.3	89	86.5	40.4	18.0
Shelly township (Norman)	115	112	-2.6	96	100.0	0.0	0.0	0.0	0.0	20.9	57.2	21.9	47	93.6	70.2	8.5
Sherburn city & MCD (Martin)	1,137	1,101	-3.2	1,018	98.8	1.1	0.0	0.1	0.0	24.3	56.1	19.7	420	76.0	53.8	17.4

1   May be of any race.

STATE City, town, township, borough, or CDP (county if applicable)	2010 census total population	2014 estimated population	Percent change 2010–2014	ACS total population estimate 2010–2014	White alone, not Hispanic or Latino	Black alone, not Hispanic or Latino	Asian alone, not Hispanic or Latino	All other races or 2 or more races, not Hispanic or Latino	Hispanic or Latino[1]	Under 18 years old	Age 18 to 64 years old	Age 65 years and older	Total occupied housing units	Percent owner occupied	High school diploma or less	Bachelor's degree or more
	1	2	3	4	5	6	7	8	9	10	11	12	13	14	15	16
MINNESOTA—Con.																
Sheridan township (Redwood)	197	191	-3.0	149	100.0	0.0	0.0	0.0	0.0	28.2	49.6	22.1	58	87.9	48.3	13.8
Sherman township (Redwood)	370	361	-2.4	388	50.5	2.1	0.0	40.5	7.0	32.8	56.4	10.8	128	84.4	50.0	11.7
Shetek township (Murray).	296	291	-1.7	289	94.1	2.1	0.0	0.0	3.8	19.0	52.0	29.1	126	85.7	26.2	23.8
Shevlin city & MCD (Clearwater)	176	178	1.1	172	79.7	0.0	5.2	15.1	0.0	25.0	58.7	16.3	69	71.0	60.9	5.8
Shevlin township (Clearwater)	452	452	0.0	421	90.3	0.0	1.0	4.8	4.0	26.7	58.2	15.2	165	94.5	60.0	18.2
Shible township (Swift)	124	120	-3.2	97	94.8	0.0	5.2	0.0	0.0	11.4	49.5	39.2	44	84.1	50.0	11.4
Shieldsville township (Rice)	1,137	1,153	1.4	1,102	96.1	0.0	1.2	1.3	1.5	20.6	63.5	16.0	433	86.1	34.4	15.0
Shingobee township (Cass)	1,518	1,527	0.6	1,710	72.8	0.6	1.0	22.5	3.1	20.8	54.5	24.8	761	83.7	35.3	30.5
Shooks township (Beltrami)	189	192	1.6	168	100.0	0.0	0.0	0.0	0.0	29.1	52.9	17.9	63	81.0	66.7	9.5
Shoreview city & MCD (Ramsey)	25,043	26,194	4.6	25,673	85.6	2.1	7.9	2.1	2.3	20.9	63.1	16.0	10,910	81.7	17.5	54.8
Shorewood city & MCD (Hennepin)	7,287	7,557	3.7	7,438	95.0	0.5	0.7	1.8	1.9	26.9	60.2	12.9	2,743	89.1	12.6	63.7
Shotley township (Beltrami)	35	36	2.9	24	83.3	0.0	0.0	16.7	0.0	0.0	37.5	62.5	12	100.0	25.0	58.3
Shotley Brook UT (Beltrami)	25	25	0.0	0	0.0	0.0	0.0	0.0	0.0	0.0	0.0	0.0	0	0.0	0.0	0.0
Sibley township (Sibley)....	255	251	-1.6	297	97.6	0.0	1.3	1.0	0.0	16.2	66.9	16.8	139	79.1	64.7	5.0
Sigel township (Brown).....	344	337	-2.0	395	97.5	0.0	1.0	1.5	0.0	15.2	67.8	17.0	163	93.9	59.5	11.0
Silver township (Carlton) ..	457	461	0.9	604	97.4	0.0	0.3	2.0	0.3	23.3	65.8	10.9	205	80.0	34.1	17.6
Silver Bay city & MCD (Lake)	1,887	1,829	-3.1	1,752	97.1	0.0	0.0	1.8	1.0	15.9	53.8	30.2	845	85.6	47.2	17.2
Silver Brook township (Carlton)	648	655	1.1	581	94.0	3.3	0.9	1.9	0.0	27.3	62.8	10.0	226	96.9	41.6	20.4
Silver Creek township (Lake)	1,138	1,141	0.3	1,161	92.1	0.0	0.0	3.9	4.0	14.2	59.7	26.0	572	87.9	35.0	28.5
Silver Creek CDP	256	NA	NA	209	100.0	0.0	0.0	0.0	0.0	20.6	62.2	17.2	81	90.1	43.2	23.5
Silver Creek township (Wright)	2,335	2,411	3.3	2,344	91.0	0.2	0.3	1.0	7.6	20.0	67.2	12.9	850	92.1	35.1	33.2
Silver Lake city & MCD (McLeod)	837	813	-2.9	890	95.2	0.2	0.4	0.3	3.8	29.1	59.8	11.1	364	67.6	60.7	8.2
Silver Lake township (Martin)	519	508	-2.1	490	96.1	0.2	0.0	0.2	3.5	17.6	60.3	22.2	189	95.2	46.6	21.2
Silver Leaf township (Becker)	534	545	2.1	655	96.9	0.5	0.6	2.0	0.0	31.0	56.5	12.5	221	89.1	57.0	7.2
Silverton township (Pennington).................	187	186	-0.5	154	96.8	0.0	0.0	1.3	1.9	22.1	55.2	22.7	63	76.2	36.5	19.0
Sinclair township (Clearwater)	164	166	1.2	114	98.2	0.0	0.0	1.8	0.0	15.8	52.5	31.6	57	77.2	38.6	7.0
Sinnott township (Marshall)	24	24	0.0	12	100.0	0.0	0.0	0.0	0.0	25.0	75.1	0.0	3	100.0	66.7	33.3
Sioux Agency township (Yellow Medicine)	226	219	-3.1	218	98.6	0.0	0.5	0.9	0.0	20.6	57.8	21.6	90	91.1	33.3	18.9
Sioux Valley township (Jackson).....................	192	192	0.0	190	100.0	0.0	0.0	0.0	0.0	26.4	57.4	16.3	73	93.2	39.7	17.8
Six Mile Grove township (Swift)	171	165	-3.5	121	96.7	0.0	0.0	0.0	3.3	24.0	59.4	16.5	53	86.8	41.5	7.5
Skagen township (Roseau)	235	237	0.9	179	98.3	0.0	0.0	1.7	0.0	25.7	48.7	25.7	76	86.8	53.9	6.6
Skandia township (Murray)....................	172	166	-3.5	139	100.0	0.0	0.0	0.0	0.0	19.4	59.9	20.9	54	79.6	33.3	24.1
Skane township (Kittson)..	46	45	-2.2	39	100.0	0.0	0.0	0.0	0.0	41.0	51.3	7.7	14	92.9	14.3	50.0
Skelton township (Carlton)	414	416	0.5	460	99.8	0.0	0.0	0.2	0.0	27.4	61.3	11.3	177	92.1	44.6	23.7
Skree township (Clay).......	159	162	1.9	214	95.3	0.0	0.9	0.9	2.8	29.4	56.9	13.6	75	92.0	58.7	8.0
Skyline city & MCD (Blue Earth)	295	294	-0.3	368	97.0	0.0	0.3	1.4	1.4	12.5	59.5	28.0	151	88.1	29.1	51.7
Slater township (Cass)	215	216	0.5	208	97.1	0.0	0.0	1.0	1.9	14.9	60.6	24.5	94	98.9	56.4	20.2
Slayton city & MCD (Murray).......................	2,153	2,078	-3.5	2,149	94.9	0.0	0.0	2.1	2.9	20.6	51.8	27.7	1,010	76.9	43.3	21.0
Slayton township (Murray)	295	293	-0.7	255	100.0	0.0	0.0	0.0	0.0	16.9	56.5	26.7	103	95.1	41.7	25.2
Sleepy Eye city & MCD (Brown)	3,599	3,460	-3.9	3,530	81.0	1.0	0.0	0.9	17.0	28.3	53.4	18.3	1,371	70.8	48.4	18.4
Sletten township (Polk)	177	176	-0.6	219	100.0	0.0	0.0	0.0	0.0	48.5	41.5	10.0	59	88.1	40.7	33.9
Smiley township (Pennington).................	580	567	-2.2	573	92.3	0.0	0.0	0.7	7.0	30.7	57.1	12.2	198	82.3	43.4	20.7
Smoky Hollow township (Cass)	70	71	1.4	50	98.0	0.0	0.0	2.0	0.0	4.0	56.0	40.0	28	96.4	42.9	14.3
Sobieski city & MCD (Morrison)...................	195	191	-2.1	197	99.0	0.0	0.0	1.0	0.0	26.5	59.9	13.7	82	82.9	56.1	4.9
Sodus township (Lyon)	283	282	-0.4	275	99.6	0.0	0.0	0.4	0.0	30.6	60.8	8.7	99	93.9	38.4	18.2
Solem township (Douglas)	233	234	0.4	216	98.6	0.0	0.0	1.4	0.0	20.8	61.6	17.6	89	94.4	41.6	14.6
Soler township (Roseau) ..	95	96	1.1	103	97.1	0.0	0.0	2.9	0.0	31.0	47.6	21.4	36	94.4	47.2	8.3
Solway city & MCD (Beltrami)	96	98	2.1	84	100.0	0.0	0.0	0.0	0.0	39.3	43.0	17.9	26	96.2	53.8	19.2
Solway township (St. Louis)	1,944	1,953	0.5	2,000	97.5	0.0	0.6	1.0	1.0	19.0	67.3	14.0	798	90.0	41.4	19.8
Somerset township (Steele)	732	733	0.1	674	99.3	0.0	0.0	0.4	0.0	17.2	65.8	16.9	271	94.5	52.0	13.7
Soudan CDP.....................	446	NA	NA	447	98.7	0.0	0.0	1.3	0.0	21.5	65.1	13.4	195	90.3	16.9	25.6
South Bend township (Blue Earth)	1,682	1,690	0.5	1,778	87.5	3.9	0.0	2.0	6.6	27.0	58.4	14.8	615	71.4	39.5	25.2
South Branch township (Watonwan)..................	282	279	-1.1	241	99.6	0.0	0.0	0.0	0.4	15.0	60.6	24.5	102	86.3	48.0	20.6

1 May be of any race.

Table A. All Places — **Population and Housing**

STATE City, town, township, borough, or CDP (county if applicable)	Population				Race and Hispanic or Latino origin (percent), 2010–2014					Age (percent), 2010–2014			Households, 2010–2014			
	2010 census total population	2014 estimated population	Percent change 2010–2014	ACS total population estimate 2010–2014	White alone, not Hispanic or Latino	Black alone, not Hispanic or Latino	Asian alone, not Hispanic or Latino	All other races or 2 or more races, not Hispanic or Latino	Hispanic or Latino[1]	Under 18 years old	Age 18 to 64 years old	Age 65 years and older	Total occupied housing units	Percent owner occupied	Householders by level of education (percent)	
															High school diploma or less	Bachelor's degree or more
	1	2	3	4	5	6	7	8	9	10	11	12	13	14	15	16
MINNESOTA—Con.																
Southbrook township (Cottonwood)	79	79	0.0	96	100.0	0.0	0.0	0.0	0.0	18.7	68.9	12.5	41	82.9	46.3	29.3
South Clearwater UT (Clearwater)	10	10	0.0	0	0.0	0.0	0.0	0.0	0.0	0.0	0.0	0.0	0	0.0	0.0	0.0
Southeast Roseau UT (Roseau)	231	233	0.9	157	100.0	0.0	0.0	0.0	0.0	16.6	75.2	8.3	79	100.0	19.0	27.8
South End CDP	0	NA	NA	55	0.0	0.0	0.0	100.0	0.0	43.6	41.7	14.5	20	95.0	90.0	0.0
South Fork township (Kanabec)	789	778	-1.4	806	97.1	0.4	0.0	0.4	2.1	26.6	63.8	9.7	273	94.1	41.4	13.6
South Harbor township (Mille Lacs)	798	791	-0.9	794	89.7	0.0	0.0	9.3	1.0	16.8	63.0	20.2	367	72.2	48.0	20.2
South Haven city & MCD (Wright)	187	191	2.1	198	94.9	0.0	0.0	1.0	4.0	38.4	54.5	7.1	59	81.4	54.2	15.3
South Koochiching UT (Koochiching)	189	NA	NA	126	92.9	0.0	0.0	7.1	0.0	4.8	62.8	32.5	78	79.5	37.2	16.7
South Red River township (Kittson)	19	19	0.0	57	100.0	0.0	0.0	0.0	0.0	28.1	42.0	29.8	19	100.0	10.5	10.5
South St. Paul city & MCD (Dakota)	20,158	20,487	1.6	20,368	77.8	4.7	1.7	3.0	12.7	23.8	64.3	12.0	8,380	66.6	34.6	21.8
Southside township (Wright)	1,521	1,568	3.1	1,468	99.5	0.2	0.0	0.0	0.3	17.8	59.8	22.5	600	96.3	43.3	28.5
Spalding township (Aitkin)	329	322	-2.1	380	43.4	0.0	0.0	46.6	10.0	29.5	57.4	13.2	170	67.6	44.7	13.5
Spang township (Itasca) ...	264	266	0.8	315	98.4	0.6	0.3	0.6	0.0	19.1	63.8	17.1	124	87.1	42.7	19.4
Sparta township (Chippewa)	748	736	-1.6	746	97.3	0.0	0.0	2.7	0.0	19.9	62.2	18.0	301	92.4	36.2	22.6
Spencer township (Aitkin).	518	506	-2.3	554	98.9	0.0	1.1	0.0	0.0	14.2	68.3	17.5	232	96.1	38.8	21.1
Spencer Brook township (Isanti)	1,589	1,610	1.3	1,577	96.3	0.3	0.4	1.0	2.0	22.7	60.5	16.8	522	95.6	51.0	17.6
Spicer city & MCD (Kandiyohi)	1,173	1,187	1.2	1,317	93.4	0.2	0.0	1.1	5.2	26.6	58.5	15.0	507	69.8	34.5	30.8
Splithand township (Itasca)	250	252	0.8	264	92.4	0.4	0.0	7.2	0.0	17.8	60.6	21.6	122	96.7	54.9	14.8
Split Rock township (Carlton)	166	168	1.2	159	98.1	0.0	0.6	1.3	0.0	23.3	54.6	22.0	68	89.7	55.9	14.7
Spooner township (Lake of the Woods)	190	NA	NA	104	82.7	0.0	0.0	17.3	0.0	17.3	66.2	16.3	60	100.0	68.3	11.7
Spring Brook township (Kittson)	52	51	-1.9	52	84.6	0.0	0.0	0.0	15.4	13.4	51.8	34.6	25	96.0	68.0	8.0
Spring Creek township (Becker)	114	115	0.9	124	75.8	0.0	0.0	24.2	0.0	36.2	57.3	6.5	39	97.4	38.5	17.9
Spring Creek township (Norman)	81	79	-2.5	78	65.4	0.0	0.0	0.0	34.6	11.5	78.2	10.3	25	92.0	48.0	0.0
Springdale township (Redwood)	217	210	-3.2	185	87.6	0.0	0.0	0.5	11.9	20.1	55.1	24.9	78	82.1	51.3	21.8
Springfield city & MCD (Brown)	2,152	2,078	-3.4	2,030	93.8	1.2	0.8	1.0	3.1	24.6	46.7	28.7	875	75.9	52.1	11.8
Springfield township (Cottonwood)	120	120	0.0	122	100.0	0.0	0.0	0.0	0.0	20.5	55.0	24.6	53	79.2	56.6	7.5
Spring Grove city & MCD (Houston)	1,330	1,296	-2.6	1,262	96.9	0.7	0.0	0.4	2.0	21.4	48.6	30.0	569	75.7	53.8	15.1
Spring Grove township (Houston)	402	399	-0.7	426	97.4	0.0	0.2	1.9	0.5	21.1	52.9	26.1	167	79.0	49.7	20.4
Spring Hill city & MCD (Stearns)	85	85	0.0	70	100.0	0.0	0.0	0.0	0.0	18.5	48.7	32.9	32	90.6	62.5	3.1
Spring Hill township (Stearns)	368	378	2.7	358	100.0	0.0	0.0	0.0	0.0	25.4	56.9	17.6	123	89.4	75.6	4.9
Spring Lake township (Scott)	3,522	3,703	5.1	3,603	89.0	0.0	4.2	1.5	5.4	24.5	60.4	15.1	1,258	99.0	33.1	36.2
Spring Lake Park city	6,412	6,464	0.8	6,503	78.7	4.5	5.6	4.3	6.9	21.3	60.9	17.8	2,659	70.1	42.8	17.8
Spring Lake Park city (Anoka)	6,234	6,278	0.7	6,254	79.6	4.7	4.0	4.5	7.2	21.5	60.8	17.6	2,561	69.7	43.7	17.3
Spring Lake Park city (Ramsey)	178	186	4.5	249	55.8	0.0	44.2	0.0	0.0	18.0	58.9	22.9	98	80.6	17.3	30.6
Spring Park city & MCD (Hennepin)	1,669	1,701	1.9	1,762	93.0	3.3	1.8	1.4	0.6	9.6	58.8	31.8	964	23.8	25.3	42.2
Spring Prairie township (Clay)	368	376	2.2	309	88.7	0.0	0.0	11.3	0.0	29.7	63.6	6.8	97	89.7	52.6	22.7
Springvale township (Isanti)	1,447	1,464	1.2	1,549	95.7	0.0	1.7	0.5	2.1	21.1	66.3	12.7	526	91.8	47.5	18.4
Spring Valley city & MCD (Fillmore)	2,479	2,416	-2.5	2,555	97.7	0.4	1.1	0.7	0.2	24.2	55.7	19.9	1,035	73.1	50.0	15.9
Spring Valley township (Fillmore)	518	527	1.7	530	97.5	0.0	0.0	1.7	0.8	17.2	64.4	18.5	231	98.3	41.6	19.9
Springwater township (Rock)	252	248	-1.6	229	100.0	0.0	0.0	0.0	0.0	27.1	59.9	13.1	81	88.9	35.8	32.1
Spruce township (Roseau)	568	565	-0.5	535	98.3	0.7	0.6	0.4	0.0	23.0	55.6	21.5	232	90.9	55.2	11.6
Spruce Grove township (Becker)	405	414	2.2	358	93.3	0.0	0.0	6.7	0.0	38.3	47.6	14.2	113	80.5	53.1	17.7
Spruce Grove township (Beltrami)	55	56	1.8	58	100.0	0.0	0.0	0.0	0.0	22.4	68.8	8.6	25	96.0	32.0	12.0
Spruce Hill township (Douglas)	441	443	0.5	472	97.9	0.0	1.1	1.1	0.0	28.2	57.4	14.6	172	92.4	54.1	9.3
Spruce Valley township (Marshall)	242	242	0.0	213	97.7	0.0	0.0	2.3	0.0	19.3	59.6	21.1	99	88.9	64.6	11.1
Squaw Lake city & MCD (Itasca)	107	108	0.9	123	30.1	0.0	0.0	69.9	0.0	42.3	46.3	11.4	38	50.0	55.3	28.9
Stacy city & MCD (Chisago)	1,450	1,472	1.5	1,539	97.7	0.0	0.0	1.3	1.0	23.9	69.7	6.4	575	84.0	51.8	12.2
Stafford township (Roseau)	284	287	1.1	276	95.7	0.0	1.1	0.4	2.9	25.3	56.7	17.8	105	97.1	43.8	23.8

1   May be of any race.

Table A. All Places — **Population and Housing**

STATE City, town, township, borough, or CDP (county if applicable)	Population				Race and Hispanic or Latino origin (percent), 2010–2014					Age (percent), 2010–2014			Households, 2010–2014			
	2010 census total population	2014 estimated population	Percent change 2010–2014	ACS total population estimate 2010–2014	White alone, not Hispanic or Latino	Black alone, not Hispanic or Latino	Asian alone, not Hispanic or Latino	All other races or 2 or more races, not Hispanic or Latino	Hispanic or Latino[1]	Under 18 years old	Age 18 to 64 years old	Age 65 years and older	Total occupied housing units	Percent owner occupied	High school diploma or less	Bachelor's degree or more
	1	2	3	4	5	6	7	8	9	10	11	12	13	14	15	16
MINNESOTA—Con.																
Stanchfield township (Isanti)	1,209	1,224	1.2	1,110	95.7	1.4	0.4	1.4	1.1	24.3	59.9	15.6	435	91.3	48.7	14.3
Stanchfield CDP	118	NA	NA	120	92.5	0.0	0.0	0.0	7.5	24.2	65.8	10.0	39	69.2	46.2	10.3
Stanford township (Isanti)	2,267	2,295	1.2	2,237	93.5	0.6	1.5	2.2	2.1	23.4	63.3	13.5	745	96.8	43.4	16.5
Stanley township (Lyon)	238	237	-0.4	241	96.7	0.0	1.2	2.1	0.0	29.5	57.0	13.3	85	92.9	45.9	16.5
Stanton township (Goodhue)	1,130	1,142	1.1	936	93.6	0.0	0.4	1.8	4.2	18.0	68.4	13.7	356	96.6	36.5	23.0
Staples city	2,981	2,891	-3.0	2,545	97.7	0.1	0.6	1.7	0.0	22.6	54.0	23.5	1,129	58.7	41.8	19.0
Staples city (Todd)	2,110	2,032	-3.7	1,939	97.7	0.1	0.0	2.2	0.0	20.9	58.1	20.8	965	54.6	46.2	12.0
Staples city (Wadena)	871	859	-1.4	606	97.5	0.0	2.5	0.0	0.0	28.1	40.3	31.8	164	82.9	15.9	59.8
Staples township (Todd)	627	615	-1.9	534	90.6	0.0	0.0	4.7	4.7	20.4	61.1	18.5	224	93.3	46.9	6.7
Star township (Pennington)	120	120	0.0	114	93.0	0.0	0.0	0.0	7.0	21.9	61.5	16.7	56	94.6	62.5	1.8
Starbuck city & MCD (Pope)	1,302	1,268	-2.6	1,239	94.4	0.1	0.0	1.7	3.9	20.0	54.5	25.6	560	77.7	42.9	13.6
Stark township (Brown)	348	341	-2.0	314	99.4	0.0	0.0	0.0	0.6	14.6	66.3	19.1	129	96.1	72.1	12.4
Star Lake township (Otter Tail)	415	410	-1.2	496	99.0	0.0	0.0	1.0	0.0	19.7	56.4	23.8	202	92.6	38.1	31.2
Stately township (Brown)	165	162	-1.8	234	100.0	0.0	0.0	0.0	0.0	32.5	58.0	9.4	75	84.0	41.3	21.3
Steamboat River township (Hubbard)	126	127	0.8	126	100.0	0.0	0.0	0.0	0.0	23.0	49.1	27.8	51	94.1	27.5	35.3
Steen city & MCD (Rock)	180	177	-1.7	208	84.6	7.7	0.0	7.2	0.5	31.3	57.2	11.5	76	84.2	53.9	13.2
Steenerson township (Beltrami)	23	23	0.0	50	72.0	0.0	0.0	26.0	2.0	0.0	78.0	22.0	22	100.0	50.0	31.8
Stephen city & MCD (Marshall)	658	657	-0.2	741	87.3	0.7	0.0	0.4	11.6	21.1	57.1	21.9	323	76.8	52.3	21.1
Sterling township (Blue Earth)	296	295	-0.3	350	92.3	0.6	7.1	0.0	0.0	25.7	60.4	13.7	118	97.5	44.9	34.7
Stevens township (Stevens)	77	77	0.0	52	100.0	0.0	0.0	0.0	0.0	28.9	55.8	15.4	20	100.0	55.0	25.0
Stewart city & MCD (McLeod)	571	552	-3.3	535	97.0	0.0	0.0	0.9	2.1	25.8	62.2	12.0	223	69.5	64.6	14.3
Stewartville city & MCD (Olmsted)	5,914	6,046	2.2	5,990	93.0	0.3	0.0	2.8	3.9	29.9	56.9	13.2	2,331	79.3	28.6	26.7
Stillwater city & MCD (Washington)	18,246	18,800	3.0	18,541	90.6	2.9	1.6	2.5	2.5	26.1	61.0	13.0	7,138	72.9	19.0	46.6
Stillwater township (Washington)	2,348	2,380	1.4	2,338	93.7	1.6	1.7	2.1	0.9	16.5	65.3	18.4	861	96.5	17.9	60.0
Stockholm township (Wright)	959	977	1.9	949	96.3	2.0	0.0	1.3	0.4	35.9	50.9	13.1	313	91.1	46.3	12.8
Stockton city & MCD (Winona)	697	724	3.9	710	92.8	0.3	3.1	1.8	2.0	26.5	65.4	8.0	262	93.9	41.6	17.2
Stokes township (Itasca)	230	231	0.4	294	91.5	0.0	5.4	0.3	2.7	21.8	54.7	23.5	118	94.9	40.7	31.4
Stokes township (Roseau)	215	217	0.9	175	98.9	0.0	0.0	1.1	0.0	22.3	62.9	14.9	83	94.0	59.0	7.2
Stoneham township (Chippewa)	241	238	-1.2	261	90.4	0.0	1.1	0.0	8.4	14.2	66.5	19.2	90	81.1	50.0	8.9
Stoney Brook township (St. Louis)	334	335	0.3	306	63.1	0.0	3.6	33.3	0.0	25.4	64.7	9.8	107	90.7	53.3	9.3
Stony Brook township (Grant)	133	132	-0.8	153	100.0	0.0	0.0	0.0	0.0	19.6	68.7	11.8	64	96.9	35.9	25.0
Stony River township (Lake)	173	174	0.6	122	82.8	0.0	0.0	17.2	0.0	12.3	56.6	31.1	63	92.1	60.3	11.1
Stony Run township (Yellow Medicine)	432	422	-2.3	479	95.0	1.0	0.0	0.8	3.1	23.0	63.0	14.0	173	89.0	45.1	27.7
Storden city & MCD (Cottonwood)	219	218	-0.5	235	96.6	0.0	0.0	0.0	3.4	21.7	52.3	26.0	111	77.5	44.1	22.5
Storden township (Cottonwood)	165	164	-0.6	150	100.0	0.0	0.0	0.0	0.0	18.6	62.0	19.3	66	68.2	51.5	13.6
Stowe Prairie township (Todd)	454	441	-2.9	426	96.5	0.0	0.0	1.6	1.9	21.1	68.6	10.3	181	94.5	47.0	11.0
Straight River township (Hubbard)	726	724	-0.3	793	94.1	4.7	0.0	1.3	0.0	24.6	58.2	17.3	324	84.3	42.6	19.8
Strand township (Norman)	99	96	-3.0	95	92.6	0.0	0.0	4.2	3.2	10.6	64.2	25.3	42	92.9	54.8	21.4
Strandquist city & MCD (Marshall)	69	69	0.0	84	100.0	0.0	0.0	0.0	0.0	19.1	72.7	8.3	34	79.4	64.7	8.8
Strathcona city & MCD (Roseau)	44	44	0.0	42	100.0	0.0	0.0	0.0	0.0	0.0	80.9	19.0	17	100.0	94.1	5.9
Sturgeon township (St. Louis)	140	140	0.0	139	89.9	0.0	0.0	2.9	7.2	0.0	16.5	69.1	14.4	65	96.9	53.8	9.2
Sturgeon Lake city & MCD (Pine)	439	425	-3.2	557	88.5	5.0	0.0	1.4	5.0	27.4	61.9	10.6	206	68.9	50.0	8.3
Sturgeon Lake township (Pine)	508	509	0.2	375	82.7	5.3	1.3	2.1	8.5	9.6	70.5	20.0	130	85.4	55.4	5.4
Sugar Bush township (Becker)	504	512	1.6	468	78.2	3.4	0.0	17.7	0.6	21.8	57.3	20.9	201	89.1	57.7	13.4
Sugar Bush township (Beltrami)	243	247	1.6	270	68.5	0.0	0.4	29.6	1.5	30.0	61.9	8.1	101	77.2	37.6	26.7
Sullivan township (Polk)	173	172	-0.6	182	92.3	0.0	0.0	0.0	7.7	21.3	64.1	14.3	65	93.8	35.4	9.2
Summit township (Beltrami)	252	256	1.6	236	97.0	0.0	0.0	3.0	0.0	21.6	65.6	12.7	92	96.7	40.2	31.5
Summit township (Steele)	466	467	0.2	464	100.0	0.0	0.0	0.0	0.0	30.2	56.5	13.4	145	91.0	49.0	14.5
Summit Lake township (Nobles)	323	326	0.9	356	92.7	0.0	0.0	0.0	7.3	24.7	63.4	11.8	129	92.2	44.2	13.2
Sumner township (Fillmore)	458	463	1.1	362	99.4	0.0	0.0	0.6	0.0	24.3	55.5	20.2	138	96.4	34.1	20.3
Sumter township (McLeod)	535	525	-1.9	489	95.9	0.0	0.4	0.8	2.9	24.9	59.3	15.7	182	92.9	49.5	8.8
Sunburg city & MCD (Kandiyohi)	100	99	-1.0	101	100.0	0.0	0.0	0.0	0.0	15.8	64.5	19.8	45	71.1	57.8	2.2
Sundal township (Norman)	157	152	-3.2	115	87.8	3.5	0.0	8.7	0.0	27.0	52.2	20.9	44	88.6	61.4	9.1

1 May be of any race.

Table A. All Places — **Population and Housing**

STATE City, town, township, borough, or CDP (county if applicable)	2010 census total population	2014 estimated population	Percent change 2010–2014	ACS total population estimate 2010–2014	White alone, not Hispanic or Latino	Black alone, not Hispanic or Latino	Asian alone, not Hispanic or Latino	All other races or 2 or more races, not Hispanic or Latino	Hispanic or Latino[1]	Under 18 years old	Age 18 to 64 years old	Age 65 years and older	Total occupied housing units	Percent owner occupied	High school diploma or less	Bachelor's degree or more
	1	2	3	4	5	6	7	8	9	10	11	12	13	14	15	16
MINNESOTA—Con.																
Sundown township (Redwood)	185	179	-3.2	198	90.9	0.0	7.6	1.5	0.0	18.7	63.3	18.2	82	89.0	69.5	7.3
Sunfish Lake city & MCD (Dakota)	521	536	2.9	509	91.0	0.2	2.4	1.4	5.1	22.4	53.5	24.2	196	95.4	8.7	68.4
Sunnyside township (Wilkin)	136	135	-0.7	138	96.4	0.0	0.0	3.6	0.0	16.7	72.4	10.9	53	100.0	45.3	7.5
Sunrise township (Chisago)	1,997	2,020	1.2	2,278	96.8	1.0	0.5	1.1	0.6	26.9	66.3	6.9	733	92.0	31.5	23.6
Svea township (Kittson)	49	48	-2.0	62	100.0	0.0	0.0	0.0	0.0	38.7	50.0	11.3	20	100.0	10.0	30.0
Sverdrup township (Otter Tail)	621	618	-0.5	639	99.7	0.0	0.0	0.3	0.0	21.3	58.3	20.3	270	93.7	36.7	30.7
Swan Lake township (Stevens)	194	195	0.5	192	100.0	0.0	0.0	0.0	0.0	22.9	54.2	22.9	73	95.9	34.2	27.4
Swan River township (Morrison)	743	739	-0.5	704	97.6	0.0	0.4	1.0	1.0	26.5	63.2	10.5	256	94.9	52.7	18.4
Swanville city	350	343	-2.0	310	97.4	0.0	0.0	1.3	1.3	25.1	59.7	15.2	130	77.7	59.2	8.5
Swanville city (Morrison)	348	341	-2.0	308	97.4	0.0	0.0	1.3	1.3	25.4	59.3	15.3	129	77.5	58.9	8.5
Swanville city (Todd)	2	2	0.0	2	100.0	0.0	0.0	0.0	0.0	0.0	100.0	0.0	1	100.0	100.0	0.0
Swanville township (Morrison)	517	515	-0.4	521	99.8	0.0	0.0	0.0	0.2	28.6	56.3	15.2	172	95.9	54.1	17.4
Swede Grove township (Meeker)	400	395	-1.3	331	92.4	0.0	0.9	0.0	6.6	27.5	58.8	13.6	115	89.6	53.0	9.6
Swede Prairie township (Yellow Medicine)	170	165	-2.9	125	100.0	0.0	0.0	0.0	0.0	28.0	57.6	14.4	55	92.7	34.5	20.0
Swedes Forest township (Redwood)	121	117	-3.3	139	95.7	0.0	0.0	4.3	0.0	23.0	60.4	16.5	52	92.3	36.5	21.2
Sweet township (Pipestone)	324	320	-1.2	333	97.9	0.6	0.0	1.2	0.3	30.9	58.5	10.5	130	86.2	37.7	25.4
Swenoda township (Swift)	140	136	-2.9	109	97.2	0.0	0.0	2.8	0.0	16.5	58.0	25.7	48	87.5	47.9	18.8
Swiftwater township (Lake of the Woods)	60	NA	NA	60	100.0	0.0	0.0	0.0	0.0	0.0	23.3	76.7	41	100.0	82.9	0.0
Sylvan township (Cass)	2,702	2,713	0.4	2,703	98.7	0.0	0.2	0.7	0.4	22.7	60.3	16.9	1,149	84.9	38.1	18.5
Synnes township (Stevens)	118	118	0.0	96	63.5	0.0	5.2	0.0	31.3	12.5	73.0	14.6	25	68.0	52.0	12.0
Tabor township (Polk)	113	112	-0.9	140	100.0	0.0	0.0	0.0	0.0	36.4	47.1	16.4	47	95.7	44.7	19.1
Taconite city	649	647	-0.3	688	89.7	0.3	0.7	4.8	4.5	27.2	59.0	13.8	278	80.6	36.7	11.2
Tamarac township (Marshall)	71	71	0.0	47	100.0	0.0	0.0	0.0	0.0	12.9	51.0	36.2	23	91.3	78.3	0.0
Tamarack city & MCD (Aitkin)	94	90	-4.3	57	100.0	0.0	0.0	0.0	0.0	3.5	79.1	17.5	32	68.8	50.0	28.1
Tanberg township (Wilkin)	69	68	-1.4	90	92.2	7.8	0.0	0.0	0.0	23.3	63.3	13.3	29	62.1	34.5	0.0
Tansem township (Clay)	259	264	1.9	272	91.9	2.9	1.8	2.6	0.7	23.2	63.6	13.2	93	96.8	33.3	38.7
Taopi city & MCD (Mower)	58	58	0.0	66	100.0	0.0	0.0	0.0	0.0	24.2	56.1	19.7	30	73.3	60.0	6.7
Tara township (Swift)	88	85	-3.4	110	99.1	0.0	0.0	0.0	0.9	23.6	61.9	14.5	36	94.4	63.9	16.7
Tara township (Traverse)	92	88	-4.3	139	100.0	0.0	0.0	0.0	0.0	28.1	58.9	12.9	48	79.2	31.3	25.0
Taunton city & MCD (Lyon)	139	137	-1.4	193	90.7	3.6	0.0	3.1	2.6	31.6	51.9	16.6	64	68.8	53.1	10.9
Taylor township (Beltrami)	107	109	1.9	126	97.6	2.4	0.0	0.0	0.0	26.3	53.1	20.6	51	92.2	31.4	39.2
Taylor township (Traverse)	105	100	-4.8	76	96.1	0.0	0.0	2.6	1.3	17.1	52.7	30.3	33	69.7	51.5	6.1
Taylors Falls city & MCD (Chisago)	976	967	-0.9	1,029	98.0	0.0	0.0	0.4	1.7	25.8	60.0	14.3	425	73.6	29.6	21.9
Tegner township (Kittson)	48	47	-2.1	43	100.0	0.0	0.0	0.0	0.0	9.3	55.9	34.9	22	95.5	18.2	22.7
Teien township (Kittson)	73	71	-2.7	61	91.8	8.2	0.0	0.0	0.0	13.2	63.9	23.0	29	75.9	41.4	17.2
Tenhassen township (Martin)	260	253	-2.7	244	99.2	0.0	0.0	0.0	0.8	12.7	63.7	23.8	114	82.5	45.6	18.4
Ten Lake township (Beltrami)	1,027	1,052	2.4	1,056	31.1	0.0	1.8	64.4	2.7	34.3	52.6	13.1	327	70.0	33.9	25.7
Ten Mile Lake township (Lac qui Parle)	153	146	-4.6	168	98.8	0.0	0.0	1.2	0.0	23.9	56.5	19.6	65	95.4	47.7	16.9
Tenstrike city & MCD (Beltrami)	203	206	1.5	185	91.9	0.0	0.0	8.1	0.0	26.5	58.0	15.7	76	94.7	40.8	25.0
Terrebonne township (Red Lake)	147	146	-0.7	146	91.8	0.0	0.0	8.2	0.0	18.5	69.9	11.6	81	93.8	30.9	30.9
The Lakes CDP	667	NA	NA	669	97.6	0.9	0.0	0.4	1.0	16.7	49.5	33.6	316	93.7	40.5	25.9
The Ranch CDP	9	NA	NA	31	0.0	0.0	0.0	100.0	0.0	0.0	77.4	22.6	9	100.0	22.2	0.0
Thief Lake township (Marshall)	37	37	0.0	40	95.0	5.0	0.0	0.0	0.0	20.0	50.0	30.0	16	100.0	56.3	6.3
Thief River Falls city & MCD (Pennington)	8,612	8,656	0.5	8,662	89.9	2.3	0.3	4.7	2.8	22.2	60.6	17.1	3,820	67.4	40.3	15.4
Third River township (Itasca)	50	50	0.0	39	94.9	0.0	0.0	0.0	5.1	0.0	43.6	56.4	22	100.0	59.1	27.3
Thomastown township (Wadena)	819	813	-0.7	749	91.7	0.0	0.3	0.0	8.0	20.5	63.6	15.9	307	97.1	25.7	23.5
Thompson township (Kittson)	152	148	-2.6	162	100.0	0.0	0.0	0.0	0.0	23.4	60.4	16.0	66	95.5	50.0	7.6
Thomson city & MCD (Carlton)	159	158	-0.6	169	98.2	0.0	0.0	1.8	0.0	20.8	62.2	17.2	69	95.7	43.5	24.6
Thomson township (Carlton)	5,003	5,044	0.8	5,013	96.4	0.1	0.0	3.0	0.5	26.1	60.7	13.3	1,790	92.2	33.0	32.2
Thorpe township (Hubbard)	45	46	2.2	44	100.0	0.0	0.0	0.0	0.0	9.1	34.0	56.8	22	100.0	22.7	45.5
Three Lakes township (Redwood)	194	188	-3.1	152	100.0	0.0	0.0	0.0	0.0	28.3	57.2	14.5	52	98.1	46.2	1.9
Thunder Lake township (Cass)	272	275	1.1	217	95.4	0.0	0.5	4.1	0.0	8.7	38.1	53.0	118	99.2	44.9	17.8
Timothy township (Crow Wing)	162	167	3.1	140	98.6	0.0	0.0	0.0	1.4	10.0	54.4	35.7	60	93.3	40.0	21.7
Tintah city & MCD (Traverse)	63	60	-4.8	55	78.2	0.0	0.0	18.2	3.6	40.0	45.5	14.5	21	71.4	38.1	4.8
Tintah township (Traverse)	33	31	-6.1	22	100.0	0.0	0.0	0.0	0.0	22.7	72.7	4.5	7	100.0	57.1	0.0

1 May be of any race.

Table A. All Places — **Population and Housing**

STATE City, town, township, borough, or CDP (county if applicable)	2010 census total population	2014 estimated population	Percent change 2010–2014	ACS total population estimate 2010–2014	White alone, not Hispanic or Latino	Black alone, not Hispanic or Latino	Asian alone, not Hispanic or Latino	All other races or 2 or more races, not Hispanic or Latino	Hispanic or Latino[1]	Under 18 years old	Age 18 to 64 years old	Age 65 years and older	Total occupied housing units	Percent owner occupied	High school diploma or less	Bachelor's degree or more
	1	2	3	4	5	6	7	8	9	10	11	12	13	14	15	16
MINNESOTA—Con.																
Toad Lake township (Becker)	539	548	1.7	485	98.8	0.0	0.0	0.8	0.4	30.9	47.5	21.6	181	95.6	50.3	17.1
Todd township (Hubbard)	1,393	1,385	-0.6	1,364	93.0	0.0	0.0	2.6	4.5	21.7	57.9	20.4	575	94.6	36.0	28.5
Tofte township (Cook)	249	254	2.0	258	86.4	0.0	0.0	5.8	7.8	5.8	64.1	30.2	147	68.7	44.9	11.6
Toivola township (St. Louis)	170	171	0.6	193	99.0	0.0	0.0	1.0	0.0	24.9	53.8	21.2	79	91.1	45.6	12.7
Tonka Bay city & MCD (Hennepin)	1,475	1,531	3.8	1,351	98.4	0.0	0.7	0.2	0.7	23.1	59.8	17.0	561	88.4	17.6	60.8
Toqua township (Big Stone)	53	51	-3.8	38	100.0	0.0	0.0	0.0	0.0	34.2	60.6	5.3	15	100.0	73.3	0.0
Tordenskjold township (Otter Tail)	551	547	-0.7	489	99.0	0.0	0.0	1.0	0.0	17.9	57.2	24.7	221	88.2	43.4	16.3
Torning township (Swift)	440	426	-3.2	402	99.5	0.0	0.0	0.0	0.5	28.1	60.1	11.7	150	94.0	37.3	21.3
Torrey township (Cass)	155	156	0.6	167	91.6	0.0	0.0	8.4	0.0	14.4	42.6	43.1	87	92.0	40.2	25.3
Tower city & MCD (St. Louis)	500	500	0.0	360	100.0	0.0	0.0	0.0	0.0	20.2	59.0	20.8	196	60.7	46.4	18.4
Township 157-30 (Lake of the Woods)	1	NA	NA	0	0.0	0.0	0.0	0.0	0.0	0.0	0.0	0.0	0	0.0	0.0	0.0
Township 158-30 (Lake of the Woods)	36	NA	NA	69	72.5	0.0	20.3	7.2	0.0	60.9	39.0	0.0	11	72.7	0.0	0.0
Tracy city & MCD (Lyon)	2,165	2,118	-2.2	2,076	82.4	0.7	16.4	0.5	0.0	25.9	52.2	22.1	864	71.2	54.6	18.9
Trail city & MCD (Polk)	46	46	0.0	67	71.6	0.0	0.0	16.4	11.9	17.9	56.7	25.4	35	57.1	71.4	11.4
Transit township (Sibley)	276	272	-1.4	319	100.0	0.0	0.0	0.0	0.0	18.2	58.3	23.5	132	84.8	56.8	13.6
Traverse township (Nicollet)	334	329	-1.5	284	100.0	0.0	0.0	0.0	0.0	16.2	63.4	20.4	117	92.3	35.9	23.1
Trelipe township (Cass)	150	151	0.7	108	88.9	0.0	0.0	7.4	3.7	9.3	49.0	41.7	59	84.7	76.3	11.9
Trimont city & MCD (Martin)	749	723	-3.5	760	93.4	0.7	0.0	4.9	1.1	23.5	51.7	24.9	315	80.3	46.7	14.9
Trommald city & MCD (Crow Wing)	98	101	3.1	103	87.4	0.0	0.0	8.7	3.9	23.3	70.9	5.8	44	72.7	43.2	2.3
Trondhjem township (Otter Tail)	192	192	0.0	124	87.1	0.0	3.2	0.0	9.7	18.5	55.4	25.8	49	89.8	46.9	20.4
Trosky city & MCD (Pipestone)	86	83	-3.5	112	100.0	0.0	0.0	0.0	0.0	24.1	61.6	14.3	47	100.0	29.8	14.9
Trout Lake township (Itasca)	1,087	1,098	1.0	1,055	98.8	0.6	0.0	0.7	0.0	20.8	64.0	15.2	439	92.7	30.8	25.7
Troy township (Pipestone)	289	282	-2.4	267	96.6	0.0	0.0	0.0	3.4	34.1	54.0	12.0	94	89.4	51.1	18.1
Troy township (Renville)	284	272	-4.2	301	100.0	0.0	0.0	0.0	0.0	20.6	63.1	16.3	124	85.5	44.4	13.7
Truman city & MCD (Martin)	1,115	1,080	-3.1	1,084	98.2	0.2	0.7	0.0	0.8	18.7	52.2	29.1	471	71.3	45.2	20.4
Tumuli township (Otter Tail)	449	443	-1.3	495	99.6	0.0	0.0	0.0	0.4	20.0	55.7	24.2	194	100.0	29.4	25.8
Tunsberg township (Chippewa)	208	203	-2.4	229	100.0	0.0	0.0	0.0	0.0	24.4	59.0	16.6	90	88.9	51.1	13.3
Turner township (Aitkin)	208	203	-2.4	216	77.8	4.2	0.0	18.1	0.0	21.3	46.3	32.4	97	76.3	49.5	22.7
Turtle Creek township (Todd)	295	289	-2.0	221	93.7	0.0	0.0	2.7	3.6	9.9	63.7	26.2	98	95.9	53.1	9.2
Turtle Lake township (Beltrami)	1,195	1,210	1.3	1,260	96.4	0.2	0.6	1.1	1.7	21.8	63.4	14.8	466	93.3	17.8	52.8
Turtle Lake township (Cass)	679	682	0.4	730	55.1	0.0	0.0	43.7	1.2	22.9	54.4	22.7	347	74.6	36.3	15.3
Turtle River city & MCD (Beltrami)	77	78	1.3	86	100.0	0.0	0.0	0.0	0.0	26.8	62.8	10.5	29	96.6	27.6	41.4
Turtle River township (Beltrami)	1,091	1,123	2.9	1,201	92.5	0.0	1.8	5.7	0.0	18.9	68.2	12.9	477	89.7	11.1	45.1
Twin Lakes township (Carlton)	2,108	2,136	1.3	2,075	90.9	2.3	0.0	2.9	3.9	21.3	67.4	11.2	795	90.4	34.5	31.7
Twin Lakes city & MCD (Freeborn)	151	149	-1.3	198	86.9	0.0	0.0	0.0	13.1	20.7	68.3	11.1	88	72.7	46.6	5.7
Twin Lakes CDP	149	NA	NA	182	35.2	3.3	0.0	59.9	1.6	31.2	58.1	10.4	72	80.6	52.8	5.6
Twin Lakes township (Mahnomen)	823	843	2.4	762	7.7	0.0	0.4	89.0	2.9	46.2	45.0	8.8	225	56.0	68.4	0.4
Twin Valley city & MCD (Norman)	821	795	-3.2	771	91.1	0.3	0.3	6.2	2.2	25.6	41.5	33.1	337	64.4	52.2	8.6
Two Harbors city & MCD (Lake)	3,745	3,611	-3.6	3,672	95.3	0.3	0.0	3.3	1.1	22.3	56.6	21.1	1,672	64.7	43.2	17.3
Two Inlets township (Becker)	213	219	2.8	311	98.7	0.0	0.0	1.0	0.3	24.5	58.5	17.0	123	96.7	26.8	37.4
Two Rivers township (Morrison)	689	683	-0.9	757	96.3	0.0	1.3	0.4	2.0	27.0	64.4	8.5	268	92.2	50.0	15.7
Tyler city & MCD (Lincoln)	1,143	1,116	-2.4	1,210	96.8	1.2	0.0	0.0	2.0	24.2	48.3	27.4	476	77.3	44.7	22.1
Tynsid township (Polk)	64	64	0.0	43	100.0	0.0	0.0	0.0	0.0	18.6	60.5	20.9	17	76.5	17.6	35.3
Tyro township (Yellow Medicine)	181	176	-2.8	201	99.5	0.0	0.0	0.0	0.5	26.4	60.7	12.9	66	89.4	30.3	28.8
Tyrone township (Le Sueur)	562	570	1.4	533	95.5	0.0	0.2	1.5	2.8	18.0	68.5	13.5	211	91.9	44.1	29.9
Udolpho township (Mower)	448	456	1.8	494	97.0	1.0	0.0	1.2	0.8	23.3	63.8	13.0	173	94.2	37.0	16.8
Ulen city & MCD (Clay)	547	553	1.1	573	93.2	0.0	0.7	5.6	0.5	19.2	46.9	34.0	249	69.9	58.2	12.4
Ulen township (Clay)	174	177	1.7	255	98.8	1.2	0.0	0.0	0.0	31.0	54.2	14.9	84	90.5	52.4	11.9
Underwood city & MCD (Otter Tail)	341	338	-0.9	381	82.2	0.5	0.0	17.3	0.0	30.6	47.6	21.5	151	80.8	41.1	22.5
Underwood township (Redwood)	206	199	-3.4	163	100.0	0.0	0.0	0.0	0.0	15.3	65.7	19.0	64	81.3	48.4	10.9
Union township (Houston)	370	368	-0.5	317	99.7	0.0	0.0	0.3	0.0	17.6	68.5	13.9	132	86.4	47.7	22.7
Union Grove township (Meeker)	633	630	-0.5	576	96.4	0.0	1.6	0.7	1.4	22.9	57.5	19.6	249	71.5	54.6	13.3
Upper Red Lake UT (Beltrami)	14	14	0.0	8	100.0	0.0	0.0	0.0	0.0	0.0	100.0	0.0	8	100.0	62.5	37.5
Upsala city & MCD (Morrison)	427	427	0.0	494	97.8	0.0	0.0	0.0	2.2	33.5	49.1	17.6	208	69.2	51.4	16.3

1 May be of any race.

Table A. All Places — **Population and Housing**

STATE City, town, township, borough, or CDP (county if applicable)	2010 census total population	2014 estimated population	Percent change 2010–2014	ACS total population estimate 2010–2014	White alone, not Hispanic or Latino	Black alone, not Hispanic or Latino	Asian alone, not Hispanic or Latino	All other races or 2 or more races, not Hispanic or Latino	Hispanic or Latino[1]	Under 18 years old	Age 18 to 64 years old	Age 65 years and older	Total occupied housing units	Percent owner occupied	High school diploma or less	Bachelor's degree or more
	1	2	3	4	5	6	7	8	9	10	11	12	13	14	15	16
MINNESOTA—Con.																
Urbank city & MCD (Otter Tail)	54	54	0.0	59	100.0	0.0	0.0	0.0	0.0	25.4	44.2	30.5	23	87.0	65.2	4.3
Urness township (Douglas)	243	246	1.2	199	99.5	0.0	0.0	0.5	0.0	11.5	64.2	24.1	101	99.0	35.6	15.8
Utica city & MCD (Winona)	291	287	-1.4	285	87.0	0.0	0.0	0.0	13.0	30.6	61.9	7.7	102	84.3	45.1	10.8
Utica township (Winona)	639	638	-0.2	514	95.7	0.0	0.0	0.8	3.5	30.2	54.0	15.8	174	85.1	39.1	14.9
Vadnais Heights city & MCD (Ramsey)	12,302	13,143	6.8	12,770	79.8	3.3	10.9	1.0	5.0	21.5	63.4	15.0	5,492	83.3	26.6	43.1
Vail township (Redwood)	229	221	-3.5	201	98.0	0.0	0.0	2.0	0.0	19.9	58.9	21.4	83	85.5	44.6	19.3
Vallers township (Lyon)	214	213	-0.5	177	100.0	0.0	0.0	0.0	0.0	34.5	60.4	5.1	57	87.7	42.1	8.8
Valley township (Marshall)	149	149	0.0	134	89.6	0.0	0.0	6.0	4.5	23.1	53.8	23.1	60	96.7	48.3	23.3
Van Buren township (St. Louis)	189	190	0.5	171	100.0	0.0	0.0	0.0	0.0	12.8	65.0	22.2	74	93.2	36.5	25.7
Vasa township (Goodhue)	910	918	0.9	934	99.4	0.6	0.0	0.0	0.0	18.6	67.5	13.9	353	96.0	46.5	21.2
Vega township (Marshall)	125	125	0.0	148	95.3	0.0	0.0	1.4	3.4	16.9	63.0	20.3	72	91.7	23.6	36.1
Veldt township (Marshall)	30	30	0.0	50	100.0	0.0	0.0	0.0	0.0	30.0	28.0	42.0	23	87.0	47.8	30.4
Verdi township (Lincoln)	206	204	-1.0	201	98.0	0.0	2.0	0.0	0.0	20.4	59.4	20.4	75	81.3	70.7	6.7
Verdon township (Aitkin)	45	43	-4.4	43	100.0	0.0	0.0	0.0	0.0	0.0	76.7	23.3	24	100.0	62.5	16.7
Vergas city & MCD (Otter Tail)	331	340	2.7	273	100.0	0.0	0.0	0.0	0.0	15.5	53.4	31.1	149	67.8	51.7	16.1
Vermilion Lake township (St. Louis)	278	279	0.4	274	97.4	0.0	1.8	0.0	0.7	12.5	61.0	26.6	146	95.2	33.6	24.0
Vermillion city & MCD (Dakota)	419	425	1.4	483	98.8	0.0	0.8	0.4	0.0	18.8	71.5	9.7	174	87.4	45.4	14.4
Vermillion township (Dakota)	1,192	1,232	3.4	1,186	93.3	0.0	3.0	3.7	0.0	26.4	62.3	11.1	421	94.3	42.5	22.1
Verndale city & MCD (Wadena)	602	582	-3.3	617	95.1	1.0	0.5	3.4	0.0	22.4	52.8	24.8	252	79.8	42.9	10.3
Vernon township (Dodge)	665	673	1.2	662	98.9	0.0	0.0	1.1	0.0	26.9	60.4	12.5	242	92.1	36.4	27.7
Vernon Center city & MCD (Blue Earth)	332	330	-0.6	330	97.3	0.0	0.0	0.0	2.7	28.2	57.2	14.8	140	87.9	42.9	26.4
Vernon Center township (Blue Earth)	262	261	-0.4	296	99.7	0.0	0.0	0.3	0.0	31.7	52.7	15.5	107	73.8	31.8	15.0
Verona township (Faribault)	364	361	-0.8	444	98.4	0.0	0.0	0.0	1.6	26.8	56.4	16.9	168	85.7	35.1	27.4
Vesta city & MCD (Redwood)	319	309	-3.1	306	95.8	0.0	0.0	4.2	0.0	25.5	52.5	21.9	121	75.2	60.3	8.3
Vesta township (Redwood)	192	186	-3.1	169	100.0	0.0	0.0	0.0	0.0	23.7	64.1	12.4	58	94.8	43.1	32.8
Victor township (Wright)	1,032	1,062	2.9	1,185	96.4	0.0	0.0	0.0	3.6	25.4	64.3	10.2	419	94.3	38.9	27.0
Victoria city & MCD (Carver)	7,379	8,374	13.5	7,845	94.0	0.1	2.4	1.1	2.4	32.3	58.9	8.8	2,516	91.4	10.7	62.1
Victory township (Lake of the Woods)	7	NA	NA	0	0.0	0.0	0.0	0.0	0.0	0.0	0.0	0.0	0	0.0	0.0	0.0
Viding township (Clay)	103	103	0.0	103	97.1	0.0	2.9	0.0	0.0	24.2	67.9	7.8	35	88.6	42.9	22.9
Vienna township (Rock)	156	153	-1.9	140	98.6	0.0	0.0	1.4	0.0	27.9	56.4	15.7	52	92.3	51.9	9.6
Viking city & MCD (Marshall)	104	104	0.0	120	95.8	0.0	0.0	0.0	4.2	44.2	40.8	15.0	41	92.7	36.6	26.8
Viking township (Marshall)	156	156	0.0	168	95.2	0.0	0.0	0.0	4.8	26.8	63.6	9.5	67	71.6	46.3	19.4
Villard city & MCD (Pope)	254	250	-1.6	288	91.3	0.0	0.0	7.3	1.4	20.2	65.3	14.6	131	71.0	61.1	4.6
Villard township (Todd)	656	642	-2.1	705	91.2	1.1	1.0	4.4	2.3	19.1	59.2	21.7	277	90.6	41.5	14.8
Vineland CDP	1,001	NA	NA	1,008	8.7	2.8	0.7	86.2	1.6	37.6	55.2	7.3	297	47.5	57.9	3.7
Vineland township (Polk)	87	87	0.0	125	88.0	0.0	0.0	8.8	3.2	20.0	71.2	8.8	53	94.3	60.4	7.5
Vining city & MCD (Otter Tail)	78	78	0.0	49	75.5	0.0	0.0	14.3	10.2	18.3	61.2	20.4	20	100.0	60.0	10.0
Viola township (Olmsted)	589	596	1.2	521	99.4	0.0	0.0	0.0	0.6	23.4	68.1	8.4	208	86.1	33.7	19.7
Virginia city & MCD (St. Louis)	8,712	8,649	-0.7	8,671	88.5	1.0	0.1	9.9	0.5	21.9	59.7	18.4	4,088	60.3	33.2	18.2
Vivian township (Waseca)	259	257	-0.8	227	99.6	0.0	0.0	0.0	0.4	16.7	59.3	23.8	100	88.0	50.0	15.0
Waasa township (St. Louis)	249	250	0.4	239	97.5	0.0	0.0	2.1	0.4	16.8	62.4	20.9	104	95.2	52.9	10.6
Wabana township (Itasca)	537	543	1.1	570	85.8	0.0	0.0	13.9	0.4	23.2	55.3	21.6	210	95.2	25.7	40.0
Wabanica township (Lake of the Woods)	237	NA	NA	153	92.2	0.0	0.0	7.8	0.0	22.2	77.7	0.0	73	86.3	24.7	19.2
Wabasha city & MCD (Wabasha)	2,521	2,482	-1.5	2,693	91.3	2.3	0.0	1.4	5.1	16.7	56.0	27.3	1,286	69.0	53.7	21.8
Wabasso city & MCD (Redwood)	696	675	-3.0	641	98.6	1.4	0.0	0.0	0.0	25.3	54.9	19.8	271	83.8	50.2	19.6
Wabedo township (Cass)	341	343	0.6	405	99.5	0.0	0.0	0.5	0.0	6.4	43.9	49.6	217	91.2	36.4	30.4
Waconia city & MCD (Carver)	10,697	11,774	10.1	11,230	93.7	0.6	0.0	2.8	2.9	30.0	57.4	12.6	4,115	80.7	24.7	45.7
Waconia township (Carver)	1,228	1,248	1.6	1,253	98.6	0.0	0.0	0.6	0.9	22.9	59.8	17.2	472	93.4	41.3	29.7
Wacouta township (Goodhue)	386	390	1.0	377	94.4	2.4	0.3	2.1	0.8	17.5	68.4	14.1	170	88.2	30.6	35.3
Wadena city	4,088	4,103	0.4	4,033	95.8	0.1	0.0	2.7	1.3	23.6	54.8	21.7	1,822	58.1	40.5	9.1
Wadena city (Otter Tail)	66	66	0.0	4	100.0	0.0	0.0	0.0	0.0	0.0	0.0	100.0	2	100.0	0.0	0.0
Wadena city (Wadena)	4,022	4,037	0.4	4,029	95.8	0.1	0.0	2.7	1.3	23.7	54.8	21.6	1,820	58.1	40.5	9.1
Wadena township (Wadena)	871	862	-1.0	870	99.0	0.0	0.0	0.0	1.0	20.6	57.5	22.1	365	93.7	44.7	11.0
Wagner township (Aitkin)	332	325	-2.1	332	96.1	0.0	0.0	3.6	0.3	12.3	55.2	32.2	174	93.7	55.7	14.9
Wahkon city & MCD (Mille Lacs)	206	209	1.5	209	77.5	15.3	0.0	6.2	1.0	15.4	60.7	23.9	116	69.0	68.1	6.0
Wahnena UT (Cass)	180	178	-1.1	90	97.8	0.0	0.0	2.2	0.0	13.4	65.5	21.1	40	100.0	47.5	0.0
Waite Park city & MCD (Stearns)	7,356	7,469	1.5	7,391	76.6	11.5	3.1	2.5	6.3	22.9	60.0	16.9	3,329	44.5	39.2	21.9
Wakefield township (Stearns)	2,756	2,790	1.2	2,766	99.1	0.0	0.6	0.1	0.1	25.5	57.0	17.5	1,005	97.0	36.7	27.1
Walcott township (Rice)	953	965	1.3	1,032	97.6	0.0	0.8	1.6	0.1	21.3	68.7	10.0	375	94.4	44.8	25.9
Walden township (Cass)	500	502	0.4	435	100.0	0.0	0.0	0.0	0.0	27.8	55.8	16.3	173	94.2	48.0	11.0

1 May be of any race.

Table A.   All Places — **Population and Housing**

	Population				Race and Hispanic or Latino origin (percent), 2010–2014					Age (percent), 2010–2014			Households, 2010–2014			
								All other races or 2 or more races, not Hispanic or Latino							Householders by level of education (percent)	
STATE City, town, township, borough, or CDP (county if applicable)	2010 census total population	2014 estimated population	Percent change 2010–2014	ACS total population estimate 2010–2014	White alone, not Hispanic or Latino	Black alone, not Hispanic or Latino	Asian alone, not Hispanic or Latino		Hispanic or Latino[1]	Under 18 years old	Age 18 to 64 years old	Age 65 years and older	Total occupied housing units	Percent owner occupied	High school diploma or less	Bachelor's degree or more
	1	2	3	4	5	6	7	8	9	10	11	12	13	14	15	16
MINNESOTA—Con.																
Walden township (Pope)...	169	171	1.2	186	98.9	0.0	0.0	1.1	0.0	22.1	64.1	14.0	72	77.8	34.7	12.5
Waldorf city & MCD (Waseca)	229	227	-0.9	156	100.0	0.0	0.0	0.0	0.0	19.9	55.1	25.0	72	70.8	45.8	22.2
Walhalla township (Lake of the Woods)	131	NA	NA	169	84.0	0.0	3.6	12.4	0.0	41.4	56.9	1.8	70	100.0	58.6	0.0
Walker city & MCD (Cass)	941	926	-1.6	985	91.3	0.0	0.0	6.0	2.7	19.9	57.6	22.3	451	51.0	33.9	29.7
Walls township (Traverse).	65	62	-4.6	54	94.4	0.0	0.0	5.6	0.0	9.3	55.6	35.2	32	96.9	40.6	6.3
Walnut Grove city & MCD (Redwood)	871	834	-4.2	997	49.8	0.0	47.0	0.4	2.7	37.0	45.1	17.8	334	56.0	73.4	10.5
Walnut Lake township (Faribault)	214	210	-1.9	241	99.6	0.0	0.0	0.0	0.4	15.8	69.7	14.5	96	92.7	62.5	13.5
Walter township (Lac qui Parle)	148	141	-4.7	160	99.4	0.0	0.0	0.6	0.0	24.4	56.9	18.8	70	87.1	41.4	14.3
Walters city & MCD (Faribault)	73	72	-1.4	139	98.6	0.0	0.0	0.0	1.4	25.2	64.1	10.8	50	78.0	48.0	0.0
Waltham city & MCD (Mower)	151	152	0.7	152	91.4	0.0	0.0	0.0	8.6	21.8	70.3	7.9	66	90.9	57.6	0.0
Waltham township (Mower)	339	343	1.2	355	96.6	0.0	1.1	2.3	0.0	20.0	64.5	15.5	144	90.3	44.4	22.9
Walworth township (Becker)	87	87	0.0	109	71.6	0.0	3.7	6.4	18.3	26.6	40.5	33.0	47	59.6	59.6	6.4
Wanamingo city & MCD (Goodhue)	1,086	1,084	-0.2	1,081	90.6	7.4	0.3	0.6	1.1	28.2	53.9	17.9	441	71.0	44.9	19.3
Wanamingo township (Goodhue)	456	459	0.7	433	96.5	0.0	1.2	0.7	1.6	19.7	65.5	14.8	170	91.2	45.3	20.6
Wanda city & MCD (Redwood)	84	81	-3.6	69	100.0	0.0	0.0	0.0	0.0	15.8	66.6	17.4	30	100.0	63.3	6.7
Wang township (Renville).	249	239	-4.0	240	95.8	0.0	0.0	0.0	4.2	25.0	59.8	15.4	94	85.1	41.5	11.7
Wanger township (Marshall)	75	75	0.0	100	100.0	0.0	0.0	0.0	0.0	13.0	61.0	26.0	47	91.5	53.2	2.1
Warba city & MCD (Itasca)	181	182	0.6	134	95.5	0.0	4.5	0.0	0.0	22.4	66.3	11.2	50	88.0	54.0	14.0
Ward township (Todd).......	447	438	-2.0	490	99.2	0.0	0.4	0.0	0.4	15.6	60.5	23.9	231	93.5	52.8	13.9
Warren city & MCD (Marshall)	1,563	1,562	-0.1	1,584	91.9	0.8	0.8	1.1	5.4	23.9	55.6	20.5	690	65.9	46.8	21.4
Warren township (Winona)	651	639	-1.8	682	97.2	1.8	0.6	0.4	0.0	30.6	59.8	9.7	215	81.9	44.7	28.8
Warrenton township (Marshall)	103	103	0.0	101	100.0	0.0	0.0	0.0	0.0	24.8	64.4	10.9	40	100.0	37.5	10.0
Warroad city & MCD (Roseau)	1,781	1,791	0.6	1,751	84.0	1.1	9.0	5.9	0.0	26.2	57.7	16.1	805	46.7	40.1	20.6
Warsaw township (Goodhue)	607	613	1.0	735	96.7	0.5	0.4	0.8	1.5	27.0	64.0	9.0	263	92.0	24.3	16.7
Warsaw CDP	627	NA	NA	747	94.0	0.0	0.8	3.9	1.3	20.2	57.5	22.4	313	93.0	36.1	21.1
Warsaw township (Rice) ...	1,320	1,339	1.4	1,349	96.1	0.0	1.0	2.1	0.7	19.1	61.7	19.1	576	88.9	39.9	21.2
Waseca city & MCD (Waseca)	9,415	9,272	-1.5	9,370	85.1	3.9	0.4	2.5	8.0	23.8	63.0	13.2	3,570	68.6	40.8	17.7
Washington township (Le Sueur)	713	722	1.3	707	98.9	0.0	0.4	0.0	0.7	16.8	57.8	25.5	314	95.5	19.7	48.7
Washington Lake township (Sibley)	498	490	-1.6	444	99.1	0.0	0.2	0.7	0.0	22.5	58.7	18.9	161	91.3	55.9	15.5
Wasioja township (Dodge)	913	927	1.5	970	83.2	1.0	2.5	1.9	11.4	21.5	63.7	14.7	379	84.2	51.7	20.3
Waskish township (Beltrami)	118	118	0.0	112	100.0	0.0	0.0	0.0	0.0	11.6	31.3	57.1	66	95.5	69.7	10.6
Watab township (Benton) .	3,093	3,153	1.9	3,124	98.9	0.0	0.0	0.4	0.7	23.7	62.4	13.9	1,234	94.7	35.7	22.8
Waterbury township (Redwood)	196	190	-3.1	197	100.0	0.0	0.0	0.0	0.0	18.8	54.4	26.9	84	88.1	48.8	20.2
Waterford township (Dakota)	497	501	0.8	435	94.3	2.5	0.5	1.8	0.9	19.0	64.5	16.3	165	87.9	46.1	29.1
Watertown city & MCD (Carver)	4,205	4,260	1.3	4,243	94.3	0.8	0.6	1.4	2.9	26.9	62.7	10.4	1,674	80.4	35.8	30.0
Watertown township (Carver)	1,243	1,270	2.2	1,449	98.3	0.3	0.5	0.9	0.0	19.0	69.0	12.0	533	93.8	38.3	24.2
Waterville city & MCD (Le Sueur)	1,868	1,864	-0.2	1,843	94.9	0.0	0.2	1.4	3.6	21.8	57.5	20.6	780	71.3	52.8	19.0
Waterville township (Le Sueur)	716	722	0.8	770	99.0	0.0	0.0	0.0	1.0	24.1	58.2	17.5	315	85.4	34.6	30.5
Watkins city & MCD (Meeker)	962	945	-1.8	897	99.0	0.0	0.0	1.0	0.0	27.0	54.4	18.5	369	76.4	58.0	5.7
Watopa township (Wabasha)	247	242	-2.0	250	99.2	0.0	0.0	0.0	0.8	24.4	59.6	16.0	95	91.6	46.3	22.1
Watson city & MCD (Chippewa)	205	200	-2.4	212	94.3	0.9	2.4	2.4	0.0	25.4	58.1	16.5	89	82.0	59.6	15.7
Waubun city & MCD (Mahnomen)	400	401	0.3	504	32.7	0.0	0.4	65.1	1.8	28.4	56.8	14.9	190	52.6	60.0	9.5
Waukenabo township (Aitkin)	316	310	-1.9	298	99.3	0.0	0.0	0.7	0.0	17.4	51.1	31.2	139	96.4	59.7	7.2
Waukon township (Norman)	114	111	-2.6	85	95.3	0.0	0.0	4.7	0.0	4.7	62.5	32.9	50	74.0	48.0	2.0
Waverly township (Martin)	208	203	-2.4	246	100.0	0.0	0.0	0.0	0.0	21.6	56.1	22.4	98	82.7	36.7	16.3
Waverly city & MCD (Wright)	1,358	1,387	2.1	1,416	95.0	0.7	0.9	1.1	2.3	25.8	64.1	10.1	529	85.6	34.8	26.3
Wawina township (Itasca).	77	78	1.3	74	100.0	0.0	0.0	0.0	0.0	12.2	75.8	12.2	32	68.8	25.0	9.4
Wayzata city & MCD (Hennepin)	3,700	4,449	20.2	3,991	90.0	3.5	2.4	1.6	2.5	14.5	63.5	21.9	2,019	59.9	19.1	52.4
Wealthwood township (Aitkin)	268	262	-2.2	251	96.8	0.0	0.0	0.8	2.4	6.8	40.8	52.6	129	98.4	41.9	9.3
Webster township (Rice)...	1,768	1,801	1.9	1,749	97.5	1.0	0.5	0.8	0.2	24.2	57.6	18.1	693	88.9	40.5	35.4
Weimer township (Jackson)	142	142	0.0	152	94.7	0.0	0.0	0.0	5.3	26.3	48.0	25.7	53	88.7	50.9	18.9
Welch township (Goodhue)	754	761	0.9	802	88.9	0.0	2.5	8.6	0.0	18.6	68.6	12.8	304	88.5	38.2	17.8

1   May be of any race.

Table A. All Places — Population and Housing

STATE City, town, township, borough, or CDP (county if applicable)	Population 2010 census total population	2014 estimated population	Percent change 2010–2014	ACS total population estimate 2010–2014	Race and Hispanic or Latino origin (percent), 2010–2014 White alone, not Hispanic or Latino	Black alone, not Hispanic or Latino	Asian alone, not Hispanic or Latino	All other races or 2 or more races, not Hispanic or Latino	Hispanic or Latino[1]	Age (percent), 2010–2014 Under 18 years old	Age 18 to 64 years old	Age 65 years and older	Households, 2010–2014 Total occupied housing units	Percent owner occupied	Householders by level of education (percent) High school diploma or less	Bachelor's degree or more
	1	2	3	4	5	6	7	8	9	10	11	12	13	14	15	16
MINNESOTA—Con.																
Welcome city & MCD (Martin)	686	666	-2.9	720	91.7	0.3	0.0	1.5	6.5	25.7	53.1	21.3	302	83.4	55.3	8.3
Wellington township (Renville)	185	177	-4.3	169	79.9	0.0	0.0	1.2	18.9	17.2	62.6	20.1	70	82.9	47.1	4.3
Wells city & MCD (Faribault)	2,343	2,272	-3.0	2,451	87.1	0.0	0.0	1.3	11.6	22.6	56.0	21.5	1,096	70.3	57.3	16.1
Wells township (Rice)	1,594	1,616	1.4	1,774	89.9	0.8	0.1	0.8	8.3	23.3	57.6	19.0	727	90.4	37.4	21.9
Wendell city & MCD (Grant)	167	166	-0.6	121	100.0	0.0	0.0	0.0	0.0	6.6	57.7	35.5	64	98.4	67.2	15.6
Wergeland township (Yellow Medicine)	153	149	-2.6	182	98.9	0.0	0.0	0.0	1.1	20.2	64.1	15.4	68	83.8	57.4	17.6
West Albany township (Wabasha)	398	395	-0.8	372	99.5	0.0	0.0	0.5	0.0	26.6	60.5	12.9	150	88.0	52.0	16.7
West Bank township (Swift)	150	145	-3.3	151	98.7	0.0	0.0	0.0	1.3	19.2	59.7	21.2	63	84.1	66.7	14.3
Westbrook city & MCD (Cottonwood)	739	730	-1.2	708	95.5	1.1	0.0	0.1	3.2	17.9	48.2	33.6	311	78.8	49.8	16.1
Westbrook township (Cottonwood)	216	215	-0.5	222	99.1	0.0	0.0	0.9	0.0	22.5	55.6	22.1	88	88.6	40.9	17.0
West Concord city & MCD (Dodge)	782	779	-0.4	821	85.9	1.8	0.0	0.6	11.7	29.5	54.7	16.0	314	78.7	50.3	16.6
West Cook UT (Cook)	1,617	1,647	1.9	1,549	97.4	0.1	0.6	1.4	0.6	16.4	62.0	21.6	718	92.6	18.7	46.9
Westerheim township (Lyon)	235	234	-0.4	312	100.0	0.0	0.0	0.0	0.0	28.2	59.6	12.2	108	87.0	26.9	23.1
Western township (Otter Tail)	129	137	6.2	157	94.9	0.0	0.0	5.1	0.0	31.2	50.8	17.8	51	82.4	11.8	5.9
Westfield township (Dodge)	451	459	1.8	463	98.9	0.6	0.0	0.0	0.4	23.5	64.8	11.7	160	90.6	36.9	16.9
Westford township (Martin)	295	287	-2.7	274	99.3	0.0	0.0	0.4	0.4	16.4	70.4	13.1	121	86.8	33.1	22.3
West Heron Lake township (Jackson)	181	181	0.0	143	99.3	0.0	0.0	0.0	0.7	21.7	62.3	16.1	58	94.8	24.1	27.6
West Lakeland township (Washington)	4,052	4,157	2.6	4,113	92.1	0.3	6.6	0.0	1.0	30.7	59.3	10.0	1,193	96.2	17.7	54.7
Westline township (Redwood)	178	172	-3.4	155	96.8	0.0	0.0	3.2	0.0	21.9	55.6	22.6	59	91.5	57.6	6.8
West Newton township (Nicollet)	423	416	-1.7	417	99.0	0.0	0.0	0.0	1.0	19.0	63.9	17.3	192	91.7	51.0	16.7
Westport city & MCD (Pope)	57	56	-1.8	37	100.0	0.0	0.0	0.0	0.0	35.1	48.6	16.2	15	100.0	53.3	20.0
Westport township (Pope)	278	276	-0.7	330	93.9	0.0	0.0	3.3	2.7	39.1	52.4	8.5	95	83.2	53.7	8.4
West Roy Lake CDP	74	NA	NA	34	5.9	0.0	0.0	94.1	0.0	32.4	41.1	26.5	17	100.0	47.1	0.0
West St. Paul city & MCD (Dakota)	19,540	19,806	1.4	19,690	67.8	6.8	3.3	4.3	17.8	23.7	57.8	18.6	8,508	57.7	35.9	26.8
Westside township (Nobles)	218	220	0.9	212	98.1	1.9	0.0	0.0	0.0	29.7	57.9	12.3	80	87.5	41.3	23.8
West Union city & MCD (Todd)	111	123	10.8	100	100.0	0.0	0.0	0.0	0.0	26.0	74.0	0.0	37	100.0	54.1	27.0
West Union township (Todd)	268	263	-1.9	334	97.0	0.0	0.0	0.9	2.1	25.2	64.2	10.8	133	87.2	43.6	12.8
West Valley township (Marshall)	132	132	0.0	175	98.3	0.0	0.0	0.0	1.7	27.4	62.8	9.7	69	91.3	53.6	18.8
Whalan city & MCD (Fillmore)	63	67	6.3	81	85.2	9.9	0.0	0.0	4.9	18.5	58.0	23.5	40	95.0	57.5	25.0
Wheatland township (Rice)	1,237	1,258	1.7	1,223	98.4	0.0	0.0	1.3	0.3	24.0	61.5	14.5	443	92.1	58.2	11.7
Wheaton city & MCD (Traverse)	1,424	1,355	-4.8	1,517	95.9	0.3	0.0	1.9	1.8	21.8	50.2	27.9	681	79.9	49.2	19.5
Wheeler township (Lake of the Woods)	281	NA	NA	272	100.0	0.0	0.0	0.0	0.0	8.1	48.9	43.0	118	89.8	62.7	17.8
Wheeling township (Rice)	551	558	1.3	538	98.1	0.0	0.7	0.6	0.6	28.4	63.1	8.6	188	94.7	30.3	28.2
Whipholt CDP	99	NA	NA	96	100.0	0.0	0.0	0.0	0.0	27.1	60.3	12.5	36	94.4	33.3	36.1
White township (St. Louis)	3,229	3,226	-0.1	3,228	98.5	0.0	0.0	1.4	0.0	17.6	60.6	21.8	1,463	85.6	51.9	10.7
White Bear township (Ramsey)	10,949	11,503	5.1	11,239	95.7	0.1	1.1	1.4	1.6	19.8	65.3	14.9	4,500	94.7	20.3	49.9
White Bear Lake township (Pope)	431	426	-1.2	418	97.6	0.0	0.0	0.0	2.4	14.4	63.1	22.5	176	94.9	40.9	25.0
White Bear Lake city	23,781	24,986	5.1	24,398	86.8	2.3	5.9	2.8	2.1	23.0	58.5	18.7	10,226	70.1	27.9	34.1
White Bear Lake city (Ramsey)	23,394	24,591	5.1	23,984	86.6	2.3	6.0	2.8	2.2	23.3	58.6	18.1	9,954	71.1	27.2	34.4
White Bear Lake city (Washington)	387	395	2.1	414	95.9	0.0	1.7	2.4	0.0	8.9	42.9	48.1	272	33.1	53.7	23.2
Whited township (Kanabec)	928	909	-2.0	923	97.8	0.0	0.0	1.0	1.2	26.7	55.7	17.7	347	93.9	55.9	12.4
White Earth CDP	580	NA	NA	559	5.0	0.0	0.0	95.0	0.0	34.8	53.2	11.8	230	38.7	66.1	5.2
White Earth township (Becker)	828	845	2.1	892	22.2	0.0	0.0	75.9	1.9	35.1	54.9	10.1	358	57.8	58.1	7.5
Whiteface Reservoir UT (St. Louis)	473	477	0.8	332	100.0	0.0	0.0	0.0	0.0	0.0	44.6	55.4	184	93.5	26.1	39.7
Whitefield township (Kandiyohi)	525	525	0.0	480	97.5	0.0	0.0	0.4	2.1	30.4	56.9	12.7	171	84.2	36.8	14.0
Whiteford township (Marshall)	46	46	0.0	38	100.0	0.0	0.0	0.0	0.0	18.4	52.5	28.9	17	88.2	64.7	17.6
White Oak township (Hubbard)	475	475	0.0	480	96.7	0.0	0.2	3.1	0.0	19.2	57.5	23.3	188	93.6	45.7	25.5
White Pine township (Aitkin)	34	33	-2.9	24	100.0	0.0	0.0	0.0	0.0	4.2	33.4	62.5	14	92.9	57.1	14.3
Whitewater township (Winona)	198	195	-1.5	170	100.0	0.0	0.0	0.0	0.0	17.1	67.7	15.3	79	78.5	43.0	22.8
Wilder city & MCD (Jackson)	60	62	3.3	42	100.0	0.0	0.0	0.0	0.0	14.3	38.2	47.6	23	95.7	78.3	8.7

1 May be of any race.

Table A. All Places — Population and Housing

STATE City, town, township, borough, or CDP (county if applicable)	2010 census total population	2014 estimated population	Percent change 2010–2014	ACS total population estimate 2010–2014	White alone, not Hispanic or Latino	Black alone, not Hispanic or Latino	Asian alone, not Hispanic or Latino	All other races or 2 or more races, not Hispanic or Latino	Hispanic or Latino[1]	Under 18 years old	Age 18 to 64 years old	Age 65 years and older	Total occupied housing units	Percent owner occupied	High school diploma or less	Bachelor's degree or more
	1	2	3	4	5	6	7	8	9	10	11	12	13	14	15	16
MINNESOTA—Con.																
Wild Rice township (Norman)	256	250	-2.3	238	87.0	1.7	0.0	7.1	4.2	21.0	64.8	14.3	97	86.6	47.4	12.4
Wildwood township (Itasca)	193	194	0.5	169	97.6	0.0	0.0	2.4	0.0	14.2	54.6	31.4	72	88.9	33.3	27.8
Wilkinson township (Cass)	401	402	0.2	422	42.4	0.0	0.5	54.5	2.6	28.9	50.9	20.1	174	71.3	35.6	11.5
Willernie city & MCD (Washington)	491	492	0.2	574	88.5	1.7	0.0	3.1	6.6	28.5	62.3	9.1	224	79.9	33.9	27.7
Williams township (Aitkin)	144	139	-3.5	155	95.5	0.0	0.0	4.5	0.0	9.7	56.1	34.2	78	96.2	64.1	5.1
Williams city & MCD (Lake of the Woods)	191	185	-3.1	233	94.0	5.2	0.0	0.9	0.0	27.9	56.2	15.9	87	89.7	62.1	19.5
Willmar city & MCD (Kandiyohi)	19,610	19,570	-0.2	19,626	71.4	5.7	0.2	1.9	20.8	25.1	59.1	15.9	7,811	58.5	40.2	22.2
Willmar township (Kandiyohi)	513	515	0.4	463	87.3	10.2	0.4	1.1	1.1	29.3	55.9	14.7	169	87.6	35.5	24.3
Willow Lake township (Redwood)	222	215	-3.2	255	100.0	0.0	0.0	0.0	0.0	32.5	51.4	16.1	84	88.1	34.5	8.3
Willow River city & MCD (Pine)	415	399	-3.9	352	99.4	0.0	0.0	0.3	0.3	27.3	62.0	10.8	153	81.0	37.3	23.5
Willow Valley township (St. Louis)	126	126	0.0	122	78.7	0.0	4.1	17.2	0.0	10.7	66.4	23.0	65	95.4	52.3	10.8
Wilma township (Pine)	65	64	-1.5	77	62.3	35.1	0.0	2.6	0.0	3.9	65.0	31.2	41	95.1	48.8	31.7
Wilmington township (Houston)	434	430	-0.9	441	97.1	0.0	0.0	2.7	0.2	23.8	64.1	12.2	165	72.7	43.0	23.0
Wilmont city & MCD (Nobles)	339	344	1.5	362	91.2	0.0	3.0	1.1	4.7	28.4	55.8	15.7	152	75.0	53.9	9.2
Wilmont township (Nobles)	184	185	0.5	153	98.0	0.0	0.0	2.0	0.0	15.1	66.8	18.3	65	90.8	55.4	7.7
Wilson township (Cass)	645	645	0.0	502	95.8	0.2	0.0	4.0	0.0	22.2	64.1	13.9	219	82.6	51.1	23.3
Wilson township (Winona)	1,174	1,167	-0.6	1,214	97.9	0.0	0.0	1.0	1.2	23.3	62.3	14.4	431	94.7	41.8	33.2
Wilton city & MCD (Beltrami)	210	269	28.1	177	88.1	0.0	0.0	5.1	6.8	23.2	64.8	11.9	75	82.7	25.3	37.3
Wilton township (Waseca)	365	370	1.4	400	94.8	0.0	0.0	0.8	4.5	24.1	56.8	19.5	152	78.9	48.7	12.5
Winchester township (Norman)	56	54	-3.6	62	100.0	0.0	0.0	0.0	0.0	12.9	58.1	29.0	27	92.6	59.3	11.1
Windemere township (Pine)	1,708	1,679	-1.7	1,602	96.1	0.0	1.4	1.9	0.6	18.4	57.2	24.4	684	84.9	41.5	28.4
Windom city & MCD (Cottonwood)	4,635	4,583	-1.1	4,616	85.7	1.2	0.3	3.1	9.6	22.4	53.1	24.4	2,024	70.0	50.3	15.9
Windom township (Mower)	606	615	1.5	697	80.8	0.0	0.4	0.0	18.8	31.3	54.1	14.5	238	83.6	45.4	11.8
Windsor township (Traverse)	66	63	-4.5	42	100.0	0.0	0.0	0.0	0.0	19.0	57.2	23.8	23	73.9	52.2	8.7
Winfield township (Renville)	224	215	-4.0	166	98.8	0.0	0.0	1.2	0.0	21.0	65.6	13.3	64	79.7	57.8	10.9
Winger city & MCD (Polk)	220	219	-0.5	258	81.4	0.0	0.0	18.6	0.0	39.2	51.0	9.7	92	78.3	30.4	17.4
Winger township (Polk)	206	208	1.0	165	99.4	0.0	0.0	0.6	0.0	26.6	54.6	18.8	60	100.0	55.0	15.0
Wing River township (Wadena)	468	461	-1.5	490	97.6	0.0	0.6	1.8	0.0	19.0	56.6	24.5	214	93.5	54.2	7.5
Winnebago city & MCD (Faribault)	1,437	1,394	-3.0	1,405	91.2	0.0	0.6	0.4	7.8	19.1	56.7	24.1	644	73.3	55.0	13.8
Winnebago township (Houston)	240	235	-2.1	259	100.0	0.0	0.0	0.0	0.0	27.8	60.8	11.2	92	89.1	56.5	12.0
Winnebago City township (Faribault)	201	197	-2.0	175	93.7	0.0	0.0	0.0	6.3	23.5	50.9	25.7	69	82.6	40.6	26.1
Winona city & MCD (Winona)	27,595	27,384	-0.8	27,526	93.3	2.0	2.6	1.4	0.6	13.3	72.1	14.6	10,219	61.7	32.4	29.1
Winsor township (Clearwater)	90	91	1.1	105	100.0	0.0	0.0	0.0	0.0	31.4	50.6	18.1	45	95.6	48.9	8.9
Winsted city & MCD (McLeod)	2,355	2,298	-2.4	2,325	95.7	1.4	1.2	1.5	0.2	25.6	57.9	16.6	949	74.3	43.5	19.9
Winsted township (McLeod)	968	950	-1.9	843	100.0	0.0	0.0	0.0	0.0	15.5	66.9	17.6	341	95.9	49.6	11.1
Winthrop city & MCD (Sibley)	1,403	1,368	-2.5	1,380	77.8	0.0	0.2	0.9	21.1	28.0	53.0	19.1	549	69.8	55.6	16.6
Winton city & MCD (St. Louis)	172	173	0.6	168	100.0	0.0	0.0	0.0	0.0	26.1	64.9	8.9	79	60.8	59.5	8.9
Wirt township (Itasca)	106	107	0.9	93	95.7	0.0	0.0	4.3	0.0	6.5	47.4	46.2	57	89.5	64.9	24.6
Wisconsin township (Jackson)	221	221	0.0	255	100.0	0.0	0.0	0.0	0.0	26.3	60.0	13.7	98	83.7	44.9	25.5
Wiscoy township (Winona)	361	360	-0.3	351	83.5	0.0	2.0	0.9	13.7	21.4	64.7	14.0	135	85.9	47.4	30.4
Wolf Lake city & MCD (Becker)	57	57	0.0	67	97.0	3.0	0.0	0.0	0.0	34.4	56.8	9.0	31	51.6	45.2	16.1
Wolf Lake township (Becker)	242	243	0.4	220	98.2	0.0	0.0	0.5	1.4	40.0	50.5	9.5	73	89.0	35.6	6.8
Wolford township (Crow Wing)	379	386	1.8	398	98.5	0.0	0.0	1.5	0.0	26.1	50.1	23.9	152	100.0	37.5	25.7
Wolverton city & MCD (Wilkin)	142	140	-1.4	79	100.0	0.0	0.0	0.0	0.0	13.9	53.2	32.9	44	81.8	36.4	40.9
Wolverton township (Wilkin)	128	127	-0.8	109	100.0	0.0	0.0	0.0	0.0	21.1	62.5	16.5	50	90.0	20.0	20.0
Woodbury city & MCD (Washington)	61,965	66,807	7.8	64,544	77.6	5.5	8.9	3.4	4.6	28.4	62.0	9.6	23,659	77.9	13.7	59.4
Wood Lake city & MCD (Yellow Medicine)	439	417	-5.0	397	97.0	0.0	0.0	1.8	1.3	23.7	60.5	15.6	181	81.8	42.0	14.9
Wood Lake township (Yellow Medicine)	231	224	-3.0	250	94.0	6.0	0.0	0.0	0.0	31.2	55.2	13.6	90	85.6	42.2	18.9
Woodland city & MCD (Hennepin)	432	452	4.6	422	95.0	0.0	0.0	0.7	4.3	23.8	56.3	20.1	167	92.8	2.4	72.5
Woodland township (Wright)	1,082	1,114	3.0	950	99.1	0.0	0.3	0.5	0.1	20.0	63.1	16.8	356	93.0	58.4	11.0
Woodrow township (Beltrami)	73	74	1.4	69	100.0	0.0	0.0	0.0	0.0	14.5	63.6	21.7	31	90.3	48.4	22.6

1 May be of any race.

Table A. All Places — **Population and Housing**

STATE City, town, township, borough, or CDP (county if applicable)	2010 census total population	2014 estimated population	Percent change 2010–2014	ACS total population estimate 2010–2014	White alone, not Hispanic or Latino	Black alone, not Hispanic or Latino	Asian alone, not Hispanic or Latino	All other races or 2 or more races, not Hispanic or Latino	Hispanic or Latino[1]	Under 18 years old	Age 18 to 64 years old	Age 65 years and older	Total occupied housing units	Percent owner occupied	High school diploma or less	Bachelor's degree or more
	1	2	3	4	5	6	7	8	9	10	11	12	13	14	15	16
MINNESOTA—Con.																
Woodrow township (Cass)	611	616	0.8	635	98.3	0.0	0.3	1.4	0.0	8.7	51.8	39.5	339	95.0	32.7	29.5
Woods township (Chippewa)	227	221	-2.6	216	76.4	13.0	0.0	0.0	10.6	24.1	62.1	13.9	66	77.3	48.5	15.2
Woodside township (Otter Tail)	277	277	0.0	330	99.4	0.0	0.0	0.0	0.6	28.8	55.0	16.4	117	89.7	59.8	11.1
Woodside township (Polk)	505	513	1.6	501	99.4	0.0	0.0	0.0	0.6	14.0	66.5	19.6	235	96.6	30.2	27.7
Woodstock city & MCD (Pipestone)	124	120	-3.2	172	95.9	0.0	0.0	4.1	0.0	25.0	59.4	15.7	78	57.7	41.0	6.4
Woodville township (Waseca)	1,327	1,340	1.0	1,503	93.7	0.0	0.8	0.0	5.5	25.9	58.7	15.4	545	92.8	27.0	34.5
Workman township (Aitkin)	207	202	-2.4	204	93.1	0.0	2.9	3.9	0.0	15.1	49.6	35.3	102	93.1	54.9	12.7
Worthington city & MCD (Nobles)	12,764	12,932	1.3	12,920	42.9	6.3	8.4	3.5	38.9	28.0	59.0	13.0	4,335	61.6	55.2	16.1
Worthington township (Nobles)	328	331	0.9	363	98.3	0.0	0.0	0.6	1.1	24.4	56.8	18.7	145	70.3	37.9	29.0
Wrenshall city & MCD (Carlton)	399	399	0.0	517	95.0	0.0	0.0	2.5	2.5	23.5	61.5	14.9	189	90.5	40.7	10.1
Wrenshall township (Carlton)	382	387	1.3	363	93.9	0.0	0.0	5.5	0.6	29.2	59.8	11.0	137	92.0	40.1	29.9
Wright city & MCD (Carlton)	127	126	-0.8	141	83.0	11.3	0.0	1.4	4.3	34.7	56.0	9.2	55	76.4	56.4	7.3
Wright township (Marshall)	116	116	0.0	88	97.7	0.0	0.0	2.3	0.0	19.3	48.9	31.8	40	95.0	70.0	0.0
Wuori township (St. Louis)	572	574	0.3	578	94.8	0.0	0.0	2.6	2.6	20.0	67.4	12.5	245	94.7	29.0	16.7
Wyandotte township (Pennington)	130	130	0.0	86	98.8	0.0	0.0	1.2	0.0	25.6	54.8	19.8	31	93.5	74.2	9.7
Wyanett township (Isanti)	1,729	1,751	1.3	1,749	92.4	0.0	0.7	1.8	5.1	24.8	57.5	17.7	589	94.6	38.0	22.6
Wykeham township (Todd)	409	400	-2.2	464	97.6	0.0	0.4	1.5	0.4	28.4	58.2	13.4	157	91.7	62.4	10.2
Wykoff city & MCD (Fillmore)	444	433	-2.5	459	99.8	0.0	0.0	0.2	0.0	20.1	64.0	15.9	201	71.6	59.2	7.5
Wylie township (Red Lake)	65	65	0.0	63	90.5	0.0	0.0	0.0	9.5	34.8	58.7	6.3	20	95.0	55.0	0.0
Wyoming city & MCD (Chisago)	7,796	7,781	-0.2	7,764	93.6	0.0	1.8	2.6	2.1	26.1	63.3	10.6	2,795	87.0	33.8	25.4
Yellow Bank township (Lac qui Parle)	159	151	-5.0	159	100.0	0.0	0.0	0.0	0.0	34.6	53.6	11.9	55	89.1	41.8	36.4
York township (Fillmore)	368	373	1.4	308	99.0	1.0	0.0	0.0	0.0	19.1	64.9	15.9	142	83.1	54.2	21.1
Young America township (Carver)	695	705	1.4	666	98.5	0.0	0.9	0.0	0.6	18.7	67.7	13.8	251	98.8	48.6	17.1
Yucatan township (Houston)	323	321	-0.6	264	98.1	0.0	0.0	1.9	0.0	11.3	65.2	23.5	117	94.9	40.2	14.5
Zemple city & MCD (Itasca)	93	94	1.1	75	70.7	0.0	0.0	29.3	0.0	26.6	57.3	16.0	25	80.0	24.0	24.0
Zimmerman city & MCD (Sherburne)	5,228	5,297	1.3	5,268	96.5	0.3	0.0	0.0	3.2	35.0	57.8	7.1	1,749	69.9	31.0	21.8
Zion township (Stearns)	335	341	1.8	305	98.4	0.0	0.0	0.7	1.0	25.2	63.9	10.8	111	91.0	64.0	9.9
Zippel township (Lake of the Woods)	118	NA	NA	137	100.0	0.0	0.0	0.0	0.0	0.0	77.4	22.6	74	87.8	51.4	10.8
Zumbro township (Wabasha)	724	721	-0.4	696	96.8	0.0	0.0	1.9	1.3	22.9	60.6	16.5	293	87.0	39.2	27.6
Zumbro Falls city & MCD (Wabasha)	207	244	17.9	151	90.7	2.6	2.6	4.0	0.0	23.9	65.7	10.6	67	94.0	29.9	10.4
Zumbrota city & MCD (Goodhue)	3,263	3,349	2.6	3,308	95.5	0.0	0.7	1.8	2.0	32.0	52.2	15.8	1,364	64.1	39.2	28.5
Zumbrota township (Goodhue)	586	592	1.0	663	96.5	0.0	0.6	2.3	0.6	24.5	60.5	14.9	240	95.8	40.8	23.8
MISSISSIPPI	2,968,103	2,994,079	0.9	2,984,345	57.6	37.2	0.9	1.5	2.8	25.0	61.6	13.5	1,092,627	68.9	44.8	21.7
Abbeville town	419	438	4.5	512	93.4	5.1	0.0	1.4	0.2	25.8	62.3	11.9	184	58.7	49.5	22.3
Aberdeen city	5,612	5,432	-3.2	5,492	26.0	71.8	0.1	1.2	0.9	22.6	60.8	16.5	2,086	65.8	51.4	19.6
Ackerman town	1,532	1,484	-3.1	1,816	53.1	46.1	0.4	0.0	0.3	25.6	54.7	19.6	798	48.1	49.6	23.3
Alcorn State University CDP	1,017	NA	NA	703	19.2	78.1	0.0	1.0	1.7	4.3	91.7	4.0	63	100.0	58.7	41.3
Algoma town	590	605	2.5	606	79.2	19.1	0.0	1.7	0.0	21.1	62.6	16.3	231	77.9	50.6	16.0
Alligator town	208	202	-2.9	382	32.2	67.8	0.0	0.0	0.0	42.9	50.2	6.8	111	58.6	59.5	3.6
Amory city	7,316	7,107	-2.9	7,197	67.1	31.3	0.0	1.3	0.3	24.2	57.6	18.3	2,680	68.5	43.8	21.0
Anguilla town	725	675	-6.9	566	43.3	53.7	3.0	0.0	0.0	23.4	58.6	18.2	254	73.6	46.9	21.3
Arcola town	368	362	-1.6	337	18.4	81.6	0.0	0.0	0.0	21.4	63.2	15.4	132	62.9	65.2	6.8
Arnold Line CDP	1,719	NA	NA	2,533	51.3	46.5	0.0	1.8	0.4	27.7	62.6	9.8	893	66.4	16.8	53.1
Artesia town	441	433	-1.8	398	5.3	91.0	0.0	0.3	3.5	24.9	66.2	9.0	142	74.6	70.4	4.2
Ashland town	569	543	-4.6	493	90.9	6.3	0.0	2.0	0.8	23.1	46.5	30.4	171	80.7	45.0	11.7
Baldwyn city	3,297	3,334	1.1	3,198	40.2	55.7	0.0	3.0	1.0	19.4	60.7	20.0	1,310	54.0	63.2	13.5
Bassfield town	244	231	-5.3	232	46.1	52.6	0.0	1.3	0.0	19.4	64.1	16.4	94	58.5	41.5	35.1
Batesville city	7,463	7,439	-0.3	7,436	59.0	40.8	0.0	0.0	0.2	29.8	52.9	17.3	2,693	67.7	34.7	31.7
Bay St. Louis city	9,262	11,388	23.0	10,313	80.5	15.2	1.6	1.5	1.1	22.7	59.7	17.5	4,336	59.8	33.7	33.9
Bay Springs city	1,794	1,743	-2.8	1,828	45.7	54.2	0.1	0.0	0.1	17.2	60.9	21.9	812	61.2	57.9	15.1
Beaumont town	951	941	-1.1	1,225	41.6	57.1	0.0	1.4	0.0	23.2	60.7	16.1	374	77.0	62.3	6.1
Beauregard village	332	327	-1.5	485	49.3	32.6	0.0	0.0	18.1	32.5	58.5	8.9	177	86.4	50.3	10.7
Beechwood CDP	3,426	NA	NA	4,299	61.3	30.5	1.6	0.2	6.4	27.0	58.4	14.5	1,534	73.6	34.4	25.9
Belmont town	2,037	2,024	-0.6	2,247	86.2	0.0	0.0	0.8	13.0	34.3	55.6	10.1	795	53.6	63.5	10.9
Belzoni city	2,235	2,088	-6.6	2,471	15.4	81.6	0.0	0.2	2.8	27.5	62.9	9.6	807	57.9	58.9	18.2
Benoit town	480	465	-3.1	488	19.5	80.3	0.0	0.2	0.0	29.9	53.2	16.8	167	61.1	54.5	29.9
Bentonia town	440	429	-2.5	556	63.8	36.2	0.0	0.0	0.0	24.2	61.8	14.2	191	51.3	54.5	18.3
Beulah town	348	337	-3.2	374	6.4	92.8	0.8	0.0	0.0	32.8	62.6	4.5	122	63.9	41.8	11.5
Big Creek village	154	152	-1.3	182	94.5	2.7	0.0	0.0	2.7	39.5	54.3	6.0	67	58.2	68.7	0.0
Big Point CDP	611	NA	NA	875	85.3	11.8	0.0	3.0	0.0	27.1	60.8	12.0	280	80.0	34.6	5.4
Biloxi city	44,054	44,984	2.1	44,527	60.9	21.3	4.7	5.8	7.3	22.3	65.3	12.5	17,619	46.9	35.5	25.1
Blue Mountain town	920	918	-0.2	828	64.4	21.9	1.2	1.2	11.4	21.4	71.0	7.6	228	58.3	49.6	18.9
Blue Springs village	228	231	1.3	254	82.3	16.5	0.0	0.0	1.2	18.5	71.2	10.2	91	54.9	44.0	20.9

1 May be of any race.

Table A. All Places — **Population and Housing**

STATE City, town, township, borough, or CDP (county if applicable)	Population: 2010 census total population	Population: 2014 estimated population	Population: Percent change 2010–2014	Population: ACS total population estimate 2010–2014	Race and Hispanic or Latino origin (percent), 2010–2014: White alone, not Hispanic or Latino	Black alone, not Hispanic or Latino	Asian alone, not Hispanic or Latino	All other races or 2 or more races, not Hispanic or Latino	Hispanic or Latino[1]	Age (percent), 2010–2014: Under 18 years old	Age 18 to 64 years old	Age 65 years and older	Households, 2010–2014: Total occupied housing units	Percent owner occupied	Householders by level of education (percent): High school diploma or less	Bachelor's degree or more
	1	2	3	4	5	6	7	8	9	10	11	12	13	14	15	16
MISSISSIPPI—Con.																
Bogue Chitto CDP (Kemper and Neshoba).	887	NA	NA	501	4.6	0.0	0.0	88.8	6.6	14.6	76.8	8.8	172	57.0	100.0	0.0
Bogue Chitto CDP (Lincoln)	522	NA	NA	479	2.5	97.5	0.0	0.0	0.0	20.9	63.4	15.7	162	91.4	72.2	0.0
Bolton town	567	554	-2.3	504	23.6	75.8	0.0	0.0	0.6	18.8	63.1	17.9	212	63.2	43.4	11.8
Booneville city	8,743	8,804	0.7	8,775	77.3	21.1	0.0	1.4	0.3	27.0	58.0	14.8	2,986	60.1	57.5	15.8
Boyle town	650	633	-2.6	916	42.4	55.1	0.0	2.5	0.0	33.7	61.1	5.2	292	44.2	45.5	19.5
Brandon city	22,066	23,156	4.9	22,616	77.2	17.2	1.6	1.2	2.8	25.2	62.5	12.5	8,067	78.4	25.0	41.0
Braxton village	183	183	0.0	266	86.5	0.4	0.0	13.2	0.0	26.0	63.8	10.2	83	71.1	59.0	1.2
Bridgetown CDP	1,742	NA	NA	1,745	94.4	0.7	1.0	3.8	0.0	18.1	71.2	10.7	654	90.1	41.6	23.4
Brookhaven city	12,513	12,470	-0.3	12,499	43.7	55.3	0.1	0.3	0.6	30.9	55.1	14.0	4,499	55.7	45.1	20.0
Brooksville town	1,223	1,178	-3.7	866	14.0	84.6	0.0	0.8	0.6	29.5	54.7	15.7	378	56.6	58.5	4.8
Bruce town	1,939	1,912	-1.4	1,675	52.9	44.5	0.0	0.0	2.6	21.1	60.3	18.6	813	55.8	59.0	15.3
Buckatunna CDP	516	NA	NA	458	8.1	91.9	0.0	0.0	0.0	30.4	62.6	7.0	163	100.0	47.9	17.8
Bude town	1,063	1,025	-3.6	990	37.7	62.3	0.0	0.0	0.0	28.1	56.9	14.8	440	46.8	45.2	22.0
Burnsville town	936	926	-1.1	1,152	97.9	0.6	1.5	0.0	0.0	28.3	58.1	13.5	402	55.5	70.9	6.0
Byhalia town	1,298	1,271	-2.1	1,342	26.4	70.3	0.0	3.4	0.0	32.4	53.0	14.5	530	55.3	53.6	9.2
Byram city	11,491	11,556	0.6	11,609	42.2	55.6	1.0	0.7	0.5	27.2	66.3	6.4	4,236	75.8	24.8	39.6
Caledonia town	1,041	1,022	-1.8	1,247	93.4	1.8	0.4	0.2	4.1	29.5	60.3	10.3	415	68.4	42.2	14.9
Calhoun City town	1,774	1,746	-1.6	1,755	51.5	39.4	0.0	1.8	7.4	28.6	49.2	22.3	664	62.7	58.3	16.4
Canton city	13,195	13,713	3.9	13,321	16.5	75.2	1.7	0.5	6.1	25.3	61.2	13.4	4,464	54.9	52.5	20.8
Carrollton town	190	183	-3.7	255	56.9	43.1	0.0	0.0	0.0	24.7	54.1	21.2	86	82.6	57.0	22.1
Carthage city	5,073	4,956	-2.3	4,995	36.8	48.3	0.0	2.5	12.4	33.0	53.0	14.0	1,645	50.8	54.2	15.0
Cary town	311	290	-6.8	419	33.9	64.4	0.0	0.0	1.7	24.1	66.9	9.1	172	41.9	68.0	7.6
Centreville town	1,684	1,578	-6.3	1,760	28.5	71.3	0.0	0.2	0.0	26.5	55.0	18.5	672	65.8	60.6	15.5
Charleston city	2,187	2,087	-4.6	1,801	23.1	75.2	0.6	1.2	0.0	33.9	49.9	16.3	743	56.4	60.6	15.3
Chunky town	326	329	0.9	406	80.8	0.0	0.0	0.0	19.2	23.2	66.6	10.3	173	78.6	41.0	12.7
Clara CDP	410	NA	NA	298	100.0	0.0	0.0	0.0	0.0	30.2	69.7	0.0	91	53.8	65.9	0.0
Clarksdale city	17,960	17,011	-5.3	17,497	19.6	78.9	0.8	0.6	0.1	30.5	56.7	12.7	6,239	49.7	44.3	21.7
Cleary CDP	1,544	NA	NA	1,070	87.2	6.0	1.1	0.0	5.7	15.2	61.2	23.6	471	79.4	33.8	16.6
Cleveland city	12,334	12,412	0.6	12,318	47.5	49.8	1.4	0.2	1.1	22.4	65.3	12.3	4,622	56.4	34.9	33.9
Clinton city	25,215	25,411	0.8	25,486	52.0	39.5	4.1	1.4	3.0	23.4	63.2	13.5	9,092	70.2	20.9	44.1
Cloverdale CDP	645	NA	NA	652	34.2	65.8	0.0	0.0	0.0	18.9	56.7	24.4	252	66.7	48.4	9.5
Coahoma town	377	359	-4.8	408	2.2	95.8	1.2	0.7	0.0	27.4	67.2	5.4	138	63.8	55.8	5.8
Coffeeville town	904	863	-4.5	966	41.3	58.2	0.0	0.5	0.0	28.9	60.0	11.4	349	59.3	55.3	22.3
Coldwater town	1,677	1,606	-4.2	1,167	25.0	71.4	0.0	0.0	3.6	25.8	63.5	10.6	448	59.4	50.7	12.7
Collins city	2,586	2,565	-0.8	2,568	45.4	45.6	1.1	3.7	4.2	24.3	55.5	20.1	802	70.2	49.5	23.8
Collinsville CDP	1,948	NA	NA	1,699	78.6	17.7	3.8	0.0	0.0	23.0	60.2	16.8	686	92.9	41.5	16.3
Columbia city	6,582	6,319	-4.0	6,446	57.7	40.8	0.0	0.2	1.3	26.0	54.2	19.7	2,354	60.7	46.9	17.8
Columbus city	23,640	23,248	-1.7	23,483	36.4	61.2	1.0	0.2	1.1	21.4	61.7	16.9	9,592	49.3	47.2	22.3
Columbus AFB CDP	1,373	NA	NA	1,478	69.1	11.6	5.5	5.5	8.3	27.3	72.2	0.5	575	2.6	10.6	69.4
Como town	1,279	1,259	-1.6	1,689	18.2	80.4	0.0	1.4	0.0	16.1	61.8	22.1	544	52.9	72.6	10.8
Conehatta CDP	1,342	NA	NA	1,177	8.6	4.6	0.0	80.3	6.5	40.2	55.8	3.9	349	78.2	43.0	0.0
Corinth city	14,573	14,865	2.0	14,797	68.4	23.5	0.2	2.9	5.0	23.3	59.0	17.8	6,111	57.6	50.9	22.1
Courtland town	511	514	0.6	562	46.4	47.2	0.0	4.4	2.0	35.1	56.2	8.7	179	64.2	55.9	14.5
Crawford town	641	629	-1.9	640	6.1	92.5	0.0	1.4	0.0	32.1	60.5	7.5	240	77.5	69.6	5.4
Crenshaw town	888	868	-2.3	895	19.3	79.0	1.7	0.0	0.0	23.7	60.8	15.5	308	74.0	75.3	4.9
Crosby town	318	299	-6.0	440	5.9	92.3	0.0	1.8	0.0	26.4	63.4	10.2	138	64.5	76.1	1.4
Crowder town	713	681	-4.5	570	44.9	55.1	0.0	0.0	0.0	27.6	51.2	21.2	260	71.5	67.7	0.0
Cruger town	386	364	-5.7	389	21.6	78.4	0.0	0.0	0.0	31.7	55.1	13.4	139	74.8	54.0	19.4
Crystal Springs city	5,044	4,958	-1.7	4,983	40.4	52.8	0.0	0.4	6.4	27.2	62.0	10.8	1,562	70.7	48.4	16.0
Darling CDP	226	NA	NA	239	0.0	100.0	0.0	0.0	0.0	25.5	59.0	15.5	101	66.3	79.2	3.0
Decatur town	1,841	1,804	-2.0	2,130	73.4	25.8	0.0	0.7	0.1	20.9	69.8	9.2	628	53.0	18.3	33.6
De Kalb town	1,154	1,095	-5.1	1,346	35.1	64.9	0.0	0.0	0.0	26.7	53.9	19.5	442	68.8	41.9	18.6
DeLisle CDP	1,147	NA	NA	996	56.7	39.8	0.0	3.5	0.0	22.9	55.1	21.8	333	92.8	40.8	35.4
Derma town	1,025	1,009	-1.6	1,086	25.6	69.1	0.0	0.0	5.3	23.5	61.8	14.8	433	66.7	70.7	2.3
Diamondhead city	8,378	8,180	-2.4	8,275	92.5	1.0	0.9	0.5	5.1	20.1	49.9	30.0	3,496	83.6	16.8	48.2
D'Iberville city	9,486	10,962	15.6	10,161	64.2	14.9	9.7	4.5	6.7	26.3	61.8	11.7	3,994	48.1	47.0	15.6
D'Lo town	452	451	-0.2	463	76.0	23.8	0.0	0.2	0.0	27.4	62.8	9.7	178	70.2	59.6	19.7
Doddsville town	98	92	-6.1	245	9.4	89.8	0.0	0.8	0.0	25.3	71.9	2.9	63	69.8	41.3	3.2
Drew city	1,927	1,801	-6.5	1,869	18.7	80.7	0.2	0.5	0.0	31.8	52.8	15.2	630	51.1	60.8	8.9
Duck Hill town	732	1,092	49.2	923	38.8	61.2	0.0	0.0	0.0	22.7	53.1	24.3	354	63.8	57.1	12.7
Dumas town	470	465	-1.1	451	99.1	0.4	0.2	0.0	0.2	22.6	55.3	22.0	161	85.7	59.6	14.9
Duncan town	423	414	-2.1	418	14.6	68.4	0.0	0.0	17.0	25.6	60.6	13.6	131	51.9	69.5	11.5
Durant city	2,673	2,510	-6.1	2,598	8.8	90.6	0.0	0.6	0.0	32.8	56.5	10.7	840	55.6	56.3	7.9
Ecru town	895	969	8.3	1,050	71.0	13.6	0.0	0.6	14.8	25.0	61.8	13.1	370	66.5	44.6	15.7
Eden village	103	100	-2.9	100	36.0	64.0	0.0	0.0	0.0	20.0	73.0	7.0	36	55.6	63.9	0.0
Edwards town	1,039	1,028	-1.1	1,444	15.4	79.8	1.8	1.4	1.5	29.3	62.2	8.4	436	77.8	51.1	10.8
Elliott CDP	990	NA	NA	1,170	84.9	15.1	0.0	0.0	0.0	34.2	58.4	7.4	353	73.7	73.7	2.3
Ellisville city	4,445	4,577	3.0	4,540	61.3	37.8	0.0	0.8	0.1	18.0	65.9	16.1	1,345	54.9	42.6	18.1
Enterprise town	526	513	-2.5	653	81.3	18.7	0.0	0.0	0.0	31.9	44.9	23.3	259	88.4	37.5	18.1
Escatawpa CDP	3,722	NA	NA	3,848	77.2	20.1	0.0	1.3	1.3	18.6	62.8	18.6	1,468	76.1	46.2	5.8
Ethel town	418	410	-1.9	610	68.4	31.6	0.0	0.0	0.0	20.8	73.4	5.7	185	76.2	68.6	4.9
Eupora city	2,194	2,128	-3.0	2,163	59.8	34.8	0.0	4.1	1.2	23.2	60.2	16.4	890	53.0	51.2	20.7
Falcon town	167	155	-7.2	303	0.0	100.0	0.0	0.0	0.0	34.3	58.5	7.3	95	61.1	73.7	2.1
Falkner town	514	508	-1.2	466	94.2	0.4	0.0	0.0	5.4	18.4	54.2	27.3	231	68.0	66.7	9.1
Farmington town	2,186	2,192	0.3	2,573	98.3	0.0	0.2	0.7	0.8	27.8	57.9	14.5	926	71.3	37.4	9.8
Farrell CDP	218	NA	NA	412	2.2	94.2	0.0	2.4	1.2	19.7	70.3	10.2	186	75.3	54.8	7.5
Fayette city	1,591	1,612	1.3	1,799	2.0	96.4	1.6	0.0	0.0	24.1	60.8	15.1	636	48.9	52.2	25.6
Flora town	1,886	1,888	0.1	1,862	48.1	51.8	0.0	0.2	0.0	30.7	57.9	11.5	650	56.9	49.7	15.5
Florence city	4,138	4,306	4.1	4,249	78.7	20.8	0.0	0.3	0.2	30.9	63.7	5.4	1,559	63.8	40.2	16.9
Flowood city	7,836	8,556	9.2	8,218	72.5	15.7	6.3	2.5	3.0	20.1	69.4	10.5	3,669	49.0	17.9	48.0
Forest city	5,684	5,744	1.1	5,719	31.1	44.6	3.1	0.0	21.3	27.2	60.2	12.5	1,982	48.3	53.5	18.3
Foxworth CDP	603	NA	NA	409	69.7	30.3	0.0	0.0	0.0	23.2	69.4	7.3	159	73.0	53.5	0.0
French Camp town	174	170	-2.3	211	82.9	3.3	0.9	8.5	4.3	28.9	46.4	24.6	36	33.3	2.8	50.0
Friars Point town	1,200	1,132	-5.7	924	6.6	90.6	0.0	2.8	0.0	33.5	55.1	11.5	383	49.9	46.2	15.9
Fulton city	3,955	4,030	1.9	3,988	76.6	21.1	0.9	0.3	1.2	22.1	59.9	18.0	1,174	57.5	38.9	23.2
Gattman village	90	88	-2.2	123	100.0	0.0	0.0	0.0	0.0	3.3	54.6	42.3	68	92.6	92.6	0.0
Gautier city	18,572	18,596	0.1	18,581	51.7	32.4	3.8	1.6	10.5	28.0	60.8	11.3	6,696	68.9	36.6	23.0
Georgetown town	289	285	-1.4	312	59.9	39.7	0.0	0.3	0.0	21.4	65.7	12.8	118	63.6	72.9	5.1
Glen town	412	411	-0.2	442	98.4	0.0	0.5	0.7	0.5	28.1	58.5	13.6	167	76.6	50.3	16.2

1 May be of any race.

Table A. All Places — **Population and Housing**

STATE City, town, township, borough, or CDP (county if applicable)	Population				Race and Hispanic or Latino origin (percent), 2010–2014					Age (percent), 2010–2014			Households, 2010–2014			
	2010 census total population	2014 estimated population	Percent change 2010–2014	ACS total population estimate 2010–2014	White alone, not Hispanic or Latino	Black alone, not Hispanic or Latino	Asian alone, not Hispanic or Latino	All other races or 2 or more races, not Hispanic or Latino	Hispanic or Latino[1]	Under 18 years old	Age 18 to 64 years old	Age 65 years and older	Total occupied housing units	Percent owner occupied	Householders by level of education (percent): High school diploma or less	Householders by level of education (percent): Bachelor's degree or more
	1	2	3	4	5	6	7	8	9	10	11	12	13	14	15	16
MISSISSIPPI—Con.																
Glendale CDP	1,657	NA	NA	1,428	35.6	61.5	1.2	0.0	1.7	29.7	51.3	18.9	583	81.0	53.5	11.1
Glendora village	151	143	-5.3	155	0.0	100.0	0.0	0.0	0.0	48.4	44.6	7.1	35	77.1	88.6	0.0
Gloster town	960	916	-4.6	1,026	39.2	60.8	0.0	0.0	0.0	23.6	56.2	20.2	408	64.0	65.0	8.1
Golden town	191	189	-1.0	175	86.3	7.4	0.0	0.0	6.3	27.9	46.2	25.7	88	68.2	58.0	17.0
Goodman town	1,386	1,331	-4.0	1,436	23.4	75.1	0.0	0.7	0.8	22.6	71.9	5.5	324	54.0	63.6	12.0
Greenville city	34,403	32,704	-4.9	33,518	19.9	77.6	0.7	0.8	1.1	26.9	60.5	12.6	12,228	52.9	47.8	21.3
Greenwood city	16,087	15,730	-2.2	15,873	27.5	68.0	1.3	1.3	1.9	28.5	59.9	11.7	5,510	48.0	53.8	26.4
Grenada city	13,092	12,956	-1.0	12,951	44.8	53.4	0.8	0.7	0.2	23.9	60.4	15.7	4,454	69.7	48.2	17.1
Gulf Hills CDP	7,144	NA	NA	8,398	76.8	13.2	3.0	3.0	3.9	25.2	61.3	13.5	2,918	68.3	29.8	27.7
Gulf Park Estates CDP	5,719	NA	NA	5,571	74.5	10.4	1.7	4.0	9.3	30.2	58.9	10.9	2,037	77.1	20.4	33.7
Gulfport city	67,786	71,750	5.8	69,913	54.3	35.6	1.2	2.9	5.9	24.6	62.9	12.5	27,335	51.6	41.1	20.7
Gunnison town	452	438	-3.1	260	15.4	84.2	0.0	0.4	0.0	31.9	55.4	12.7	106	52.8	56.6	9.4
Guntown town	2,083	2,508	20.4	2,306	70.9	20.9	2.9	4.0	1.4	31.6	60.3	8.3	793	74.3	42.9	26.1
Hamilton CDP	457	NA	NA	540	100.0	0.0	0.0	0.0	0.0	19.1	64.6	16.5	219	97.3	63.9	22.8
Hatley town	482	469	-2.7	409	99.5	0.0	0.0	0.5	0.0	22.3	51.0	26.7	177	82.5	56.5	16.4
Hattiesburg city	45,767	47,016	2.7	46,629	41.0	52.8	2.0	1.3	2.9	20.2	68.6	11.2	18,033	37.3	30.5	32.8
Hazlehurst city	4,009	3,934	-1.9	3,949	20.8	73.0	1.6	0.0	4.6	23.8	62.8	13.5	1,326	51.4	50.8	16.4
Heidelberg town	713	687	-3.6	769	12.9	86.7	0.0	0.4	0.0	20.7	60.7	18.6	346	76.6	55.8	11.8
Helena CDP	1,184	NA	NA	1,000	92.8	0.0	7.2	0.0	0.0	10.8	72.5	16.7	396	75.0	80.6	0.0
Henderson Point CDP	170	NA	NA	98	100.0	0.0	0.0	0.0	0.0	0.0	38.8	61.2	68	100.0	11.8	42.6
Hernando city	14,060	15,290	8.7	14,723	84.0	11.0	0.8	1.4	2.8	28.6	58.7	12.7	5,186	80.7	32.5	28.4
Hickory town	530	534	0.8	573	39.6	60.4	0.0	0.0	0.0	25.3	60.4	14.3	210	81.0	51.9	7.1
Hickory Flat town	601	565	-6.0	763	76.1	18.0	0.0	0.8	5.1	19.7	67.2	13.1	213	50.7	44.1	10.8
Hide-A-Way Lake CDP	1,859	NA	NA	1,132	93.2	0.0	0.0	0.0	6.8	13.9	54.8	31.2	524	95.0	13.9	35.7
Hillsboro CDP	1,130	NA	NA	1,401	50.2	44.8	0.0	0.0	5.0	29.2	58.4	12.5	463	79.9	41.7	13.8
Holcomb CDP	600	NA	NA	427	66.5	33.5	0.0	0.0	0.0	20.4	59.3	20.4	120	55.0	58.3	0.0
Hollandale city	2,704	2,584	-4.4	2,647	12.4	87.6	0.0	0.1	0.0	32.2	54.9	13.0	954	60.5	53.2	18.9
Holly Springs city	7,699	7,574	-1.6	7,585	18.5	79.1	0.1	1.0	1.4	21.7	66.9	11.4	2,375	57.3	53.3	17.3
Horn Lake city	26,068	26,766	2.7	26,486	54.7	34.9	1.1	2.8	6.5	30.6	61.4	8.0	9,225	62.4	46.4	12.7
Houston city	3,623	3,543	-2.2	3,577	40.5	44.1	0.9	1.5	13.0	25.7	58.3	16.0	1,318	64.8	59.9	12.7
Hurley CDP	1,551	NA	NA	1,538	98.6	0.0	1.2	0.3	0.0	24.0	57.9	18.1	556	82.9	35.3	17.8
Indianola city	10,683	10,078	-5.7	10,426	15.3	82.2	0.3	0.6	1.7	26.1	62.6	11.3	3,644	61.3	48.1	20.0
Inverness town	1,019	957	-6.1	875	51.1	47.4	0.5	0.0	1.0	24.1	61.1	14.7	320	64.1	46.6	25.6
Isola town	713	668	-6.3	884	17.1	80.5	0.0	0.0	2.4	35.9	55.1	9.2	246	52.8	70.7	12.6
Itta Bena city	2,048	1,999	-2.4	2,159	8.1	91.8	0.1	0.0	0.0	27.7	57.9	14.5	732	55.1	56.7	22.3
Iuka city	3,028	2,987	-1.4	3,013	93.9	3.8	0.0	2.3	0.0	24.6	51.7	23.6	1,187	53.7	57.9	12.5
Jackson city	173,593	171,155	-1.4	173,631	17.6	79.7	0.3	0.8	1.6	27.0	62.4	10.6	62,417	52.4	37.6	27.8
Jonestown town	1,300	1,226	-5.7	1,381	3.0	97.0	0.0	0.0	0.0	32.9	60.4	6.9	442	46.2	55.7	5.0
Jumpertown town	485	487	0.4	513	91.0	4.9	0.0	0.0	4.1	29.5	58.9	11.7	185	64.9	51.9	4.9
Kearney Park CDP	1,054	NA	NA	1,057	14.3	85.7	0.0	0.0	0.0	30.7	61.9	7.3	306	68.3	48.7	16.7
Kilmichael town	699	629	-10.0	944	23.1	76.9	0.0	0.0	0.0	21.6	64.5	14.0	378	62.4	72.2	9.8
Kiln CDP	2,238	NA	NA	1,709	89.1	2.3	0.0	5.7	2.9	14.7	62.8	22.6	803	79.3	38.2	26.8
Kosciusko city	7,399	7,237	-2.2	7,302	45.5	50.7	0.5	1.3	2.0	31.1	52.9	16.0	2,678	54.9	49.1	23.3
Kossuth village	209	209	0.0	220	91.4	0.0	0.0	0.0	8.6	15.4	66.9	17.7	90	90.0	55.6	7.8
Lake town	324	326	0.6	441	59.2	40.1	0.0	0.7	0.0	31.9	53.6	14.5	153	71.9	52.3	9.8
Lambert town	1,638	1,524	-7.0	1,132	6.8	93.2	0.0	0.0	0.0	24.6	66.4	9.0	508	57.1	66.3	7.9
Latimer CDP	6,079	NA	NA	7,066	85.3	9.0	2.9	2.0	0.8	27.5	63.6	9.0	2,183	82.4	40.4	15.9
Lauderdale CDP	442	NA	NA	522	73.8	26.2	0.0	0.0	0.0	18.3	66.6	14.9	216	100.0	75.5	0.0
Laurel city	18,543	18,868	1.8	18,720	31.0	59.9	0.9	0.6	7.6	27.4	58.6	14.1	6,738	56.7	48.5	18.3
Leakesville town	898	887	-1.2	786	72.8	20.4	0.0	1.3	5.6	23.0	56.5	20.6	280	68.2	54.3	23.2
Learned town	94	95	1.1	46	100.0	0.0	0.0	0.0	0.0	4.3	76.1	19.6	22	77.3	50.0	31.8
Leland city	4,481	4,262	-4.9	4,373	28.0	69.8	1.2	0.5	0.4	23.8	63.1	13.2	1,793	54.5	51.8	20.9
Lena town	148	143	-3.4	178	87.6	11.8	0.0	0.6	0.0	12.3	56.3	31.5	97	89.7	54.6	21.6
Lexington city	1,731	1,622	-6.3	2,113	23.6	73.5	2.9	0.0	0.0	23.1	63.3	13.7	766	68.4	56.9	19.7
Liberty town	725	694	-4.3	809	64.0	35.1	0.0	0.5	0.4	24.6	51.7	23.6	253	79.4	55.3	13.4
Long Beach city	14,792	15,448	4.4	15,224	86.0	6.4	3.1	0.8	3.7	24.8	62.4	12.7	5,837	62.6	32.9	25.9
Louin town	277	269	-2.9	267	77.2	22.8	0.0	0.0	0.0	25.5	51.5	22.8	126	81.7	53.2	11.9
Louise town	199	187	-6.0	155	48.4	43.9	7.7	0.0	0.0	5.2	57.5	37.4	68	83.8	36.8	8.8
Louisville city	6,631	6,325	-4.6	6,498	39.7	57.4	1.1	0.2	1.6	29.4	56.0	14.7	2,589	55.1	50.8	17.3
Lucedale city	2,923	3,016	3.2	2,978	65.7	28.0	0.6	4.3	1.4	25.5	58.0	16.6	859	63.7	54.2	15.0
Lula town	298	283	-5.0	348	12.4	87.6	0.0	0.0	0.0	22.9	55.9	21.0	132	59.8	62.1	10.6
Lumberton city	2,080	2,209	6.2	2,148	25.4	71.7	0.0	2.9	0.0	32.7	54.4	12.9	810	47.8	59.0	10.5
Lyman CDP	1,277	NA	NA	2,187	91.7	7.8	0.0	0.0	0.5	16.0	71.4	12.6	845	88.9	34.1	24.1
Lynchburg CDP	2,437	NA	NA	2,113	68.2	24.5	3.1	3.0	1.2	22.0	64.2	13.8	837	93.2	33.9	21.0
Lyon town	350	333	-4.9	308	82.5	16.6	0.0	0.0	1.0	14.2	63.2	22.4	144	67.4	27.8	43.1
Maben town	877	877	0.0	666	28.7	68.3	0.0	0.2	2.9	26.0	62.3	12.0	272	47.8	74.3	5.9
McComb city	12,790	12,703	-0.7	12,771	27.3	68.8	0.6	0.8	2.5	23.3	60.5	16.2	5,090	49.5	55.1	17.1
McCool town	135	132	-2.2	188	89.9	10.1	0.0	0.0	0.0	22.8	49.5	27.7	63	90.5	49.2	14.3
McLain town	441	436	-1.1	384	52.9	46.6	0.0	0.5	0.0	21.6	68.8	9.6	180	85.6	68.9	8.9
Macon city	2,757	2,647	-4.0	2,687	20.6	76.9	0.0	1.4	1.2	25.5	62.3	12.1	1,027	50.4	60.7	8.6
Madison city	24,149	25,455	5.4	24,871	85.9	8.9	3.4	1.2	0.6	29.4	58.8	12.0	8,870	92.5	10.5	65.9
Magee city	4,427	4,413	-0.3	4,418	48.1	47.5	0.0	0.1	4.3	34.3	53.6	12.2	1,407	62.8	48.7	18.5
Magnolia city	2,420	2,379	-1.7	1,926	31.6	66.6	0.2	1.3	0.3	24.7	57.9	17.3	653	67.8	53.1	14.2
Mantachie town	1,144	1,139	-0.4	1,318	94.9	2.1	0.0	2.7	0.3	25.3	53.6	21.0	554	59.6	57.2	15.5
Mantee village	232	226	-2.6	279	99.3	0.0	0.0	0.0	0.7	27.6	46.3	26.2	105	84.8	46.7	31.4
Marietta town	256	257	0.4	360	98.1	0.0	1.9	0.0	0.0	24.8	60.8	14.4	154	79.9	61.0	13.6
Marion town	1,479	1,584	7.1	1,596	40.3	53.8	3.7	0.4	1.8	24.3	66.8	8.8	611	41.2	37.6	15.7
Marks city	1,735	1,616	-6.9	1,755	40.6	57.7	0.0	1.7	0.0	24.6	53.8	21.5	690	66.5	38.4	24.3
Mathiston town	696	677	-2.7	764	80.4	17.7	1.3	0.7	0.0	20.3	61.1	18.7	311	76.2	51.4	17.4
Mayersville town	547	586	7.1	659	7.7	92.1	0.0	0.0	0.2	16.5	69.4	14.1	139	54.7	91.4	2.9
Meadville town	449	435	-3.1	440	76.1	23.4	0.0	0.0	0.5	17.0	56.4	26.6	168	75.0	32.7	28.0
Mendenhall city	2,504	2,502	-0.1	2,492	72.7	24.7	0.0	0.6	2.1	25.1	54.9	20.0	940	56.6	47.1	21.8
Meridian city	41,148	40,196	-2.3	40,809	34.7	60.7	0.9	1.7	2.0	25.5	60.9	13.6	15,959	51.6	38.7	23.5
Meridian Station CDP	1,090	NA	NA	649	50.8	25.4	0.2	6.6	16.9	5.2	94.7	0.0	45	0.0	0.0	28.9
Merigold town	439	425	-3.2	475	46.9	42.3	0.0	0.0	10.7	24.2	62.3	13.5	181	74.6	33.1	34.3
Metcalfe town	1,067	1,029	-3.6	1,183	0.5	99.5	0.0	0.0	0.0	35.2	54.6	10.2	416	53.8	54.3	17.8
Mississippi State CDP	4,005	NA	NA	3,637	66.3	29.3	1.1	1.6	1.6	1.3	98.6	0.0	76	19.7	0.0	72.4
Mississippi Valley State University CDP	1,182	NA	NA	1,315	11.2	74.4	0.0	11.6	2.8	12.2	86.8	0.9	173	6.9	3.5	63.6
Mize town	340	333	-2.1	276	97.5	0.0	0.0	2.5	0.0	37.0	49.0	14.1	97	84.5	61.9	5.2
Monticello town	1,570	1,525	-2.9	1,627	58.6	40.5	0.0	0.2	0.7	30.5	50.4	19.1	695	58.7	49.1	19.0

1 May be of any race.

Table A. All Places — **Population and Housing**

STATE City, town, township, borough, or CDP (county if applicable)	Population: 2010 census total population	Population: 2014 estimated population	Population: Percent change 2010–2014	Population: ACS total population estimate 2010–2014	Race and Hispanic or Latino origin (percent), 2010–2014: White alone, not Hispanic or Latino	Black alone, not Hispanic or Latino	Asian alone, not Hispanic or Latino	All other races or 2 or more races, not Hispanic or Latino	Hispanic or Latino[1]	Age (percent), 2010–2014: Under 18 years old	Age 18 to 64 years old	Age 65 years and older	Households, 2010–2014: Total occupied housing units	Percent owner occupied	Householders by level of education (percent): High school diploma or less	Householders by level of education (percent): Bachelor's degree or more
	1	2	3	4	5	6	7	8	9	10	11	12	13	14	15	16
MISSISSIPPI—Con.																
Montrose town	140	136	-2.9	102	67.6	26.5	0.0	5.9	0.0	26.5	52.1	21.6	41	90.2	73.2	12.2
Mooreville CDP	650	NA	NA	643	69.8	13.1	0.0	0.0	17.1	29.7	60.8	9.5	210	83.3	33.3	12.9
Moorhead city	2,405	2,301	-4.3	2,206	11.8	87.9	0.3	0.0	0.0	25.0	65.1	9.9	634	52.5	59.1	6.8
Morgan City town	255	250	-2.0	292	15.1	84.9	0.0	0.0	0.0	36.3	59.6	4.1	78	59.0	66.7	10.3
Morgantown CDP	1,412	NA	NA	1,799	24.2	74.6	0.0	1.2	0.0	36.0	52.2	11.9	575	84.9	51.1	16.2
Morton city	3,462	3,461	0.0	3,444	38.7	37.1	0.0	1.2	22.9	25.5	63.8	10.8	1,161	68.9	74.1	7.5
Moss Point city	13,704	13,671	-0.2	13,690	23.6	73.6	0.0	0.5	2.4	19.1	63.3	17.6	5,209	67.2	53.0	14.3
Mound Bayou city	1,533	1,497	-2.3	1,871	0.2	97.3	0.0	2.5	0.0	37.7	53.1	9.1	634	44.5	39.3	24.0
Mount Olive town	982	970	-1.2	1,019	56.1	38.7	0.0	0.0	5.2	32.5	55.4	12.2	364	54.7	41.8	25.0
Myrtle town	490	496	1.2	412	80.8	18.4	0.7	0.0	0.0	30.2	52.5	17.5	173	68.8	66.5	20.8
Natchez city	15,792	15,269	-3.3	15,563	37.9	59.7	0.4	0.6	1.4	21.5	60.3	18.4	6,493	55.4	45.2	23.3
Nellieburg CDP	1,414	NA	NA	1,432	82.3	17.5	0.0	0.2	0.0	15.2	62.0	22.8	578	78.5	48.6	19.4
Nettleton city	1,992	1,965	-1.4	1,634	61.6	34.0	1.8	1.9	0.7	17.2	58.3	24.4	724	63.1	64.4	9.8
New Albany city	8,034	8,708	8.4	8,291	59.8	26.0	2.3	3.2	8.8	27.3	57.3	15.4	2,995	57.3	41.2	21.4
New Augusta town	642	638	-0.6	763	52.9	47.1	0.0	0.0	0.0	37.0	53.9	9.2	248	64.9	50.4	6.5
New Hamilton CDP	553	NA	NA	472	97.9	0.0	0.0	2.1	0.0	23.4	68.0	8.5	172	91.3	45.3	16.3
New Hebron town	447	433	-3.1	586	90.1	5.6	0.0	0.3	3.9	29.9	51.3	18.9	198	76.8	42.9	14.6
New Hope CDP	3,193	NA	NA	3,524	77.8	18.2	0.0	0.0	4.0	27.8	63.7	8.5	1,287	83.8	38.5	19.0
New Houlka town	626	613	-2.1	731	78.0	17.5	0.0	0.0	4.5	24.6	60.1	15.2	284	62.7	62.0	3.5
Newton city	3,373	3,374	0.0	3,358	37.8	59.2	0.0	0.7	2.2	21.0	58.5	20.4	1,395	63.3	45.4	21.6
Nicholson CDP	3,092	NA	NA	2,904	84.9	10.1	1.4	0.4	3.2	24.4	68.3	7.3	1,135	56.9	55.2	4.6
North Carrollton town	474	455	-4.0	509	48.5	49.1	0.0	2.4	0.0	25.3	63.0	11.6	166	69.9	47.0	17.5
North Tunica CDP	1,035	NA	NA	1,096	4.3	95.5	0.0	0.0	0.2	28.1	63.6	8.4	313	61.7	46.3	3.5
Noxapater town	475	456	-4.0	408	51.0	49.0	0.0	0.0	0.0	27.1	58.9	13.7	153	45.1	62.7	20.3
Oakland town	527	508	-3.6	739	13.4	75.8	0.0	0.0	10.8	39.4	49.0	11.5	223	70.0	59.6	10.8
Ocean Springs city	17,442	17,530	0.5	17,446	79.7	10.6	1.2	2.6	5.9	22.8	60.7	16.4	6,608	71.6	25.0	40.7
Okolona city	2,712	2,641	-2.6	2,669	23.2	73.3	0.0	0.1	3.4	23.3	60.0	16.7	1,076	57.6	61.2	5.9
Olive Branch city	33,486	35,457	5.9	34,543	66.6	25.7	1.5	1.4	4.8	25.8	61.9	12.2	12,844	76.1	35.9	29.5
Osyka town	440	435	-1.1	375	38.9	51.2	1.1	7.7	1.1	35.8	47.0	17.3	120	58.3	61.7	9.2
Oxford city	18,877	21,757	15.3	20,200	72.6	18.9	4.4	0.5	3.5	16.0	73.9	10.0	7,504	38.1	15.9	46.9
Pace town	274	266	-2.9	140	6.4	80.7	12.1	0.7	0.0	10.7	67.8	21.4	51	74.5	51.0	11.8
Pachuta town	261	254	-2.7	333	76.6	22.5	0.0	0.9	0.0	16.2	58.2	25.5	154	61.7	51.9	14.9
Paden village	116	115	-0.9	128	96.9	0.0	3.1	0.0	0.0	20.3	61.7	18.0	52	92.3	51.9	3.8
Pascagoula city	22,392	22,224	-0.8	22,239	56.2	30.4	1.2	2.6	9.6	23.2	63.6	13.0	8,329	54.1	44.8	16.0
Pass Christian city	4,613	5,308	15.1	4,957	64.5	29.6	3.4	1.3	1.1	22.9	56.6	20.5	1,869	77.6	35.2	34.9
Pearl city	25,700	26,388	2.7	26,105	69.3	22.6	1.3	1.0	5.9	24.2	63.4	12.3	10,179	61.2	38.4	19.0
Pearlington CDP	1,332	NA	NA	1,504	49.9	43.4	0.0	0.0	6.7	23.4	66.5	10.0	572	91.3	56.1	6.1
Pearl River CDP	3,601	NA	NA	3,935	14.4	3.0	0.6	80.3	1.8	37.1	56.9	6.1	1,019	70.2	52.7	6.9
Pelahatchie town	1,334	1,358	1.8	1,431	55.8	41.6	0.0	2.1	0.6	29.4	52.0	18.6	521	74.9	66.8	10.9
Petal city	10,454	10,727	2.6	10,675	77.3	10.1	0.5	3.8	8.3	29.2	56.8	14.1	3,863	70.7	38.6	31.0
Philadelphia city	7,477	7,402	-1.0	7,446	45.4	51.1	0.7	1.7	1.1	28.3	56.5	15.2	2,877	62.4	38.3	21.1
Picayune city	10,877	10,749	-1.2	10,838	63.4	33.9	0.0	0.7	2.0	27.4	58.5	14.0	4,112	58.6	41.5	18.9
Pickens town	1,157	1,085	-6.2	850	6.6	93.4	0.0	0.0	0.0	26.9	59.4	13.6	331	67.4	50.8	13.9
Pittsboro village	202	199	-1.5	174	68.4	27.6	0.0	0.6	3.4	17.7	68.3	13.8	57	93.0	56.1	7.0
Plantersville town	1,155	1,166	1.0	933	36.2	63.6	0.0	0.2	0.0	16.6	62.5	20.8	397	58.7	52.9	9.1
Polkville town	833	817	-1.9	621	95.8	1.0	0.5	0.0	2.7	21.9	59.8	18.4	242	77.7	61.6	11.6
Pontotoc city	5,625	5,919	5.2	5,754	60.3	16.3	2.9	0.0	20.5	30.6	54.5	14.7	1,741	61.3	46.8	29.1
Pope village	213	211	-0.9	183	91.3	8.7	0.0	0.0	0.0	22.9	51.9	25.1	93	89.2	60.2	14.0
Poplarville city	2,894	2,899	0.2	2,874	66.1	22.7	0.4	8.7	2.1	26.6	59.8	13.8	739	67.7	20.0	29.8
Port Gibson city	1,567	1,443	-7.9	1,716	9.6	88.9	0.0	0.6	0.9	22.5	62.2	15.2	650	62.6	35.8	32.9
Potts Camp town	523	505	-3.4	417	62.8	30.2	1.9	1.2	3.8	19.5	70.0	10.6	164	67.1	56.1	18.3
Prentiss town	1,081	1,017	-5.9	1,099	64.5	33.3	0.0	1.0	1.2	16.0	59.2	24.7	418	68.9	45.9	14.1
Puckett village	316	324	2.5	309	94.8	5.2	0.0	0.0	0.0	35.3	54.9	9.7	112	74.1	48.2	17.0
Purvis city	2,173	2,322	6.9	1,990	69.3	25.1	0.0	2.5	3.1	21.4	64.4	14.1	674	73.1	48.4	15.6
Quitman city	2,323	2,254	-3.0	2,127	62.8	36.2	0.4	0.4	0.3	19.5	55.8	24.9	907	67.7	46.6	21.3
Raleigh town	1,458	1,441	-1.2	1,405	67.8	32.0	0.0	0.3	0.0	27.4	53.2	19.4	549	76.5	54.6	13.7
Rawls Springs CDP	1,254	NA	NA	1,084	36.9	63.1	0.0	0.0	0.0	27.7	52.0	20.5	418	53.1	70.3	19.1
Raymond city	1,937	2,177	12.4	2,160	49.1	48.4	0.4	1.7	0.3	8.2	80.5	11.3	499	54.3	25.5	40.5
Redwater CDP	633	NA	NA	643	16.0	25.2	0.0	58.8	0.0	20.7	66.1	13.2	247	73.7	47.8	9.3
Renova town	668	721	7.9	772	1.7	98.3	0.0	0.0	0.0	27.0	60.3	12.8	315	52.4	39.7	30.2
Richland city	6,913	7,071	2.3	7,012	79.8	15.5	2.4	0.9	1.4	27.8	59.6	12.6	2,632	61.9	46.2	15.3
Richton town	1,068	1,063	-0.5	964	76.3	21.9	0.0	1.8	0.0	21.7	54.6	23.7	338	68.6	38.5	23.1
Ridgeland city	24,040	24,221	0.8	24,209	54.9	35.5	4.3	1.3	4.0	23.7	65.3	10.9	10,523	44.8	15.9	53.1
Rienzi town	317	316	-0.3	425	62.4	36.2	0.0	0.0	1.4	24.2	52.2	23.5	181	77.3	52.5	7.2
Ripley city	5,395	5,349	-0.9	5,349	62.5	20.8	0.0	5.6	11.1	24.1	60.1	15.6	2,061	56.0	53.9	16.0
Robinhood CDP	1,605	NA	NA	1,405	94.4	0.3	1.0	0.8	3.5	27.8	59.6	12.7	520	76.2	59.4	12.5
Rolling Fork city	2,143	2,064	-3.7	2,474	23.4	74.9	0.0	0.0	1.7	20.1	64.0	16.0	897	61.8	65.3	13.4
Rosedale city	1,873	1,796	-4.1	1,852	8.1	91.5	0.0	0.1	0.3	28.1	62.1	9.8	674	39.3	55.3	11.7
Roxie town	497	479	-3.6	568	41.9	56.9	0.0	1.2	0.0	29.6	59.5	10.9	210	67.1	47.6	5.7
Ruleville city	3,007	2,831	-5.9	2,934	15.5	84.0	0.0	0.1	0.4	29.2	56.2	14.8	919	49.8	52.1	17.6
St. Martin CDP	7,730	NA	NA	7,627	70.3	12.3	12.0	3.6	1.9	25.4	63.2	11.5	2,571	57.5	39.9	20.0
Sallis town	134	131	-2.2	134	64.9	35.1	0.0	0.0	0.0	14.2	49.2	36.6	69	92.8	43.5	26.1
Saltillo city	4,752	5,004	5.3	4,916	93.1	3.7	2.7	0.5	0.0	21.2	65.9	12.9	1,945	69.3	26.9	19.8
Sandersville town	731	723	-1.1	795	95.8	2.8	0.0	0.9	0.5	18.2	64.4	17.4	323	87.9	60.4	17.6
Sardis town	1,702	1,678	-1.4	2,038	35.3	64.2	0.0	0.5	0.0	25.0	54.6	20.4	681	53.6	65.3	16.7
Satartia village	55	54	-1.8	35	28.6	65.7	0.0	0.0	5.7	34.3	48.6	17.1	13	100.0	53.8	7.7
Saucier CDP	1,342	NA	NA	1,190	82.5	13.4	0.0	4.0	0.0	30.3	57.7	12.1	393	61.1	62.8	3.1
Schlater town	310	304	-1.9	378	24.6	75.4	0.0	0.0	0.0	30.7	51.7	17.7	109	73.4	63.3	17.4
Scooba town	732	708	-3.3	995	26.6	72.8	0.6	0.0	0.0	22.9	64.4	12.6	258	49.2	55.4	19.0
Sebastopol town	279	281	0.7	252	81.7	1.2	0.0	0.0	17.1	26.6	53.3	20.2	92	82.6	39.1	25.0
Seminary town	314	312	-0.6	396	97.5	0.0	0.0	0.0	2.5	24.8	63.8	11.4	143	74.1	49.0	21.7
Senatobia city	8,165	7,928	-2.9	8,063	60.6	33.4	1.1	1.7	3.1	22.1	63.1	14.8	2,796	55.9	32.2	29.0
Shannon town	1,753	1,772	1.1	1,831	46.0	53.2	0.0	0.8	0.0	31.8	60.5	7.8	674	64.7	50.0	12.9
Sharon CDP	1,406	NA	NA	1,357	93.2	4.3	0.0	2.4	0.0	18.3	59.8	21.8	439	79.3	56.0	9.3
Shaw city	1,947	1,878	-3.5	1,801	10.8	89.2	0.0	0.0	0.0	26.4	59.4	14.1	670	51.2	54.6	12.1
Shelby city	2,229	2,158	-3.2	2,224	5.9	94.1	0.0	0.0	0.0	28.0	54.9	17.1	735	50.9	66.5	11.0
Sherman town	647	675	4.3	629	63.9	36.1	0.0	0.0	0.0	36.7	55.7	7.8	206	36.9	59.7	10.7
Shubuta town	441	430	-2.5	409	10.3	89.7	0.0	0.0	0.0	16.9	67.2	15.9	179	78.2	78.2	8.4
Shuqualak town	501	484	-3.4	492	8.7	91.3	0.0	0.0	0.0	23.9	63.3	12.8	203	70.0	56.2	13.3
Sidon town	509	499	-2.0	442	1.4	98.6	0.0	0.0	0.0	30.1	68.1	1.8	135	52.6	75.6	9.6
Silver City town	322	302	-6.2	263	24.3	75.7	0.0	0.0	0.0	27.0	61.8	11.0	98	75.5	65.3	15.3

1 May be of any race.

Table A. All Places — **Population and Housing**

STATE City, town, township, borough, or CDP (county if applicable)	Population: 2010 census total population	Population: 2014 estimated population	Population: Percent change 2010–2014	Population: ACS total population estimate 2010–2014	Race and Hispanic or Latino origin (percent), 2010–2014: White alone, not Hispanic or Latino	Black alone, not Hispanic or Latino	Asian alone, not Hispanic or Latino	All other races or 2 or more races, not Hispanic or Latino	Hispanic or Latino[1]	Age (percent), 2010–2014: Under 18 years old	Age 18 to 64 years old	Age 65 years and older	Households, 2010–2014: Total occupied housing units	Percent owner occupied	Householders by level of education (percent): High school diploma or less	Bachelor's degree or more
	1	2	3	4	5	6	7	8	9	10	11	12	13	14	15	16
MISSISSIPPI—Con.																
Silver Creek town	210	202	-3.8	223	59.2	40.8	0.0	0.0	0.0	27.4	52.8	19.7	77	74.0	68.8	0.0
Slate Springs village	110	108	-1.8	136	95.6	3.7	0.0	0.0	0.7	18.3	70.5	11.0	57	78.9	68.4	15.8
Sledge town	545	530	-2.8	482	7.1	91.3	0.0	1.7	0.0	31.9	57.9	10.2	185	81.1	45.4	10.8
Smithville town	942	917	-2.7	854	97.5	0.0	0.0	2.2	0.2	22.5	64.9	12.5	330	68.8	53.0	4.8
Snow Lake Shores town	315	301	-4.4	474	97.9	1.1	0.0	0.8	0.2	7.8	60.5	31.6	200	87.0	41.5	22.5
Soso town	404	404	0.0	459	85.6	14.4	0.0	0.0	0.0	27.7	61.2	11.1	163	82.8	41.1	24.5
Southaven city	48,976	51,824	5.8	50,389	66.9	24.0	1.9	2.1	5.1	28.6	61.1	10.3	17,986	68.8	33.2	23.5
Standing Pine CDP	504	NA	NA	287	29.6	0.0	0.0	70.4	0.0	53.7	39.7	6.6	92	76.1	29.3	18.5
Starkville city	23,909	24,886	4.1	24,457	58.7	34.4	3.3	1.6	2.0	19.1	70.6	10.2	9,845	41.6	18.4	44.5
State Line town	565	558	-1.2	541	47.3	47.9	0.0	0.0	4.8	23.3	57.8	19.0	246	69.9	64.6	4.1
Stonewall town	1,088	1,052	-3.3	1,348	71.9	27.3	0.0	0.0	0.8	30.3	51.6	18.1	547	74.0	60.1	8.4
Sturgis town	264	268	1.5	486	95.9	1.0	0.0	0.0	3.1	38.8	52.1	9.1	126	77.0	40.5	41.3
Summit town	1,705	1,684	-1.2	2,108	18.1	76.8	3.8	0.0	1.3	32.4	56.9	10.6	698	62.6	46.3	23.4
Sumner town	318	306	-3.8	317	65.6	33.1	0.0	1.3	0.0	16.1	65.1	18.9	102	86.3	32.4	21.6
Sumrall town	1,417	1,702	20.1	1,580	83.7	13.5	0.5	2.2	0.2	33.4	53.0	13.5	619	75.9	50.7	26.8
Sunflower town	1,159	1,089	-6.0	1,055	13.1	85.0	0.0	1.2	0.7	34.1	57.9	8.0	367	52.0	53.1	15.0
Sylvarena village	109	107	-1.8	120	97.5	0.8	0.0	0.0	1.7	13.3	55.0	31.7	48	100.0	43.8	8.3
Taylor village	322	343	6.5	265	87.2	10.9	0.0	1.9	0.0	22.6	65.6	11.7	118	56.8	32.2	27.1
Taylorsville town	1,353	1,319	-2.5	1,356	71.7	26.3	0.0	1.5	0.5	22.6	61.7	15.7	549	70.3	53.4	16.6
Tchula town	2,096	2,005	-4.3	2,023	1.2	98.6	0.0	0.2	0.0	32.9	56.4	10.6	687	46.7	71.2	11.4
Terry town	1,063	1,108	4.2	1,400	37.1	61.5	0.0	0.5	0.9	26.6	65.4	8.1	463	83.4	36.7	26.6
Thaxton town	643	659	2.5	906	92.2	0.0	0.0	0.0	7.8	29.3	58.2	12.6	272	87.1	58.8	12.5
Tillatoba town	91	NA	NA	251	100.0	0.0	0.0	0.0	0.0	72.5	27.4	0.0	34	100.0	100.0	0.0
Tishomingo town	339	335	-1.2	442	86.4	13.6	0.0	0.0	0.0	31.0	55.4	13.6	181	54.7	72.9	4.4
Toccopola town	246	252	2.4	210	80.0	11.9	0.0	2.9	5.2	11.9	72.9	15.2	83	78.3	66.3	3.6
Toomsuba CDP	773	NA	NA	1,020	40.8	59.2	0.0	0.0	0.0	46.6	45.3	8.1	330	67.0	44.5	0.0
Tremont town	465	465	0.0	445	98.2	0.0	0.0	1.1	0.7	28.8	60.6	10.6	144	50.7	53.5	9.7
Tucker CDP	662	NA	NA	762	1.3	3.7	6.7	88.3	0.0	46.1	52.0	1.8	201	71.6	43.8	0.0
Tunica town	1,033	1,009	-2.3	1,145	58.1	35.5	0.2	1.1	5.2	20.8	61.0	18.2	510	55.1	46.9	24.7
Tunica Resorts CDP	1,910	NA	NA	1,526	41.2	45.4	5.2	5.2	2.9	16.8	77.1	6.2	875	10.2	22.4	36.5
Tupelo city	34,546	35,688	3.3	35,345	55.0	38.5	0.8	2.0	3.7	28.1	57.0	14.8	13,261	61.8	35.8	29.7
Tutwiler town	3,550	3,507	-1.2	3,530	11.2	53.2	3.1	1.1	31.4	15.6	78.2	6.2	527	64.1	54.3	21.8
Tylertown town	1,609	1,544	-4.0	1,652	59.4	35.5	2.4	0.8	1.8	23.5	48.7	28.0	662	62.8	62.8	19.6
Union town	1,988	1,995	0.4	2,024	64.4	33.3	0.1	0.0	2.1	29.3	50.5	20.2	785	62.9	48.2	20.9
University CDP	4,202	NA	NA	4,331	82.3	14.5	0.7	1.1	1.3	0.5	99.4	0.2	61	0.0	100.0	0.0
Utica town	820	852	3.9	772	24.0	70.6	0.0	0.0	5.4	28.9	63.5	7.5	312	71.2	50.0	10.6
Vaiden town	731	756	3.4	1,120	21.7	78.3	0.0	0.0	0.0	29.1	60.9	10.0	285	62.5	69.1	14.7
Vancleave CDP	5,886	NA	NA	6,147	93.2	3.5	1.1	1.9	0.4	31.6	58.2	10.3	1,909	89.9	44.4	17.8
Vardaman town	1,316	1,297	-1.4	1,199	47.3	20.3	0.0	7.2	25.3	25.5	64.3	10.1	451	59.4	55.7	12.0
Verona city	3,006	3,060	1.8	3,052	15.2	81.0	0.0	2.0	1.7	26.0	65.6	8.4	1,224	43.5	55.1	4.1
Vicksburg city	23,856	23,392	-1.9	23,559	27.6	69.8	1.0	0.4	1.2	26.2	59.2	14.6	9,083	52.8	45.1	25.6
Wade CDP	1,074	NA	NA	821	100.0	0.0	0.0	0.0	0.0	38.2	47.7	14.0	301	88.4	57.1	4.7
Walls town	1,164	1,263	8.5	1,099	37.9	57.3	1.5	1.4	1.9	33.5	56.6	10.0	376	48.1	50.3	12.5
Walnut town	771	763	-1.0	772	83.7	13.2	0.0	0.0	3.1	25.9	53.4	20.7	319	53.3	71.5	7.2
Walnut Grove town	1,910	1,921	0.6	645	29.6	66.0	0.6	0.2	3.6	23.2	70.5	6.2	162	46.9	63.6	6.8
Walthall village	144	140	-2.8	215	94.0	6.0	0.0	0.0	0.0	24.2	72.1	3.7	95	42.1	23.2	47.4
Water Valley city	3,392	3,326	-1.9	3,345	55.5	41.3	0.2	0.8	2.1	23.2	59.7	17.2	1,289	56.9	59.0	7.1
Waveland city	6,433	6,419	-0.2	6,463	77.9	17.4	0.8	1.5	2.4	22.8	65.3	12.0	2,637	54.4	49.6	11.1
Waynesboro city	5,043	4,962	-1.6	4,998	36.4	63.0	0.0	0.0	0.6	30.6	57.8	11.4	1,892	62.8	59.9	12.8
Webb town	565	536	-5.1	293	22.9	77.1	0.0	0.0	0.0	22.9	63.8	13.3	149	67.8	57.0	5.4
Weir town	459	445	-3.1	528	51.1	48.1	0.0	0.8	0.0	27.2	60.6	12.5	204	75.0	43.1	23.0
Wesson town	1,925	1,915	-0.5	1,990	75.8	23.0	0.3	0.9	0.1	23.2	64.5	12.3	521	81.6	47.0	24.0
West town	185	174	-5.9	195	92.8	7.2	0.0	0.0	0.0	23.1	57.4	19.5	67	79.1	67.2	20.9
West Hattiesburg CDP	5,909	NA	NA	6,853	51.1	40.5	2.1	0.7	5.6	27.5	63.4	9.0	2,499	47.7	18.9	27.0
West Point city	11,318	11,093	-2.0	11,200	38.1	60.5	0.0	0.6	0.8	25.9	57.2	16.8	4,362	60.0	53.1	18.4
White Oak CDP	692	NA	NA	922	0.7	99.3	0.0	0.0	0.0	37.1	56.4	6.4	263	85.9	84.0	0.0
Wiggins city	4,390	4,496	2.4	4,463	64.4	32.0	0.0	0.6	3.0	20.9	64.8	14.3	1,247	54.3	47.6	12.9
Winona city	5,043	4,622	-8.3	4,832	46.2	53.0	0.0	0.8	0.0	28.0	53.7	18.4	1,812	67.5	56.3	20.0
Winstonville town	191	185	-3.1	207	0.5	99.5	0.0	0.0	0.0	10.1	67.2	22.7	88	61.4	44.3	14.8
Woodland village	125	122	-2.4	121	27.3	69.4	0.0	3.3	0.0	32.2	58.7	9.1	51	74.5	68.6	3.9
Woodville town	1,074	1,004	-6.5	1,133	21.6	78.4	0.0	0.0	0.0	23.8	62.4	13.9	481	61.5	47.6	26.2
Yazoo City city	11,403	11,366	-0.3	11,462	13.3	85.3	0.0	0.8	0.7	30.7	56.7	12.5	3,733	43.5	57.0	13.3
MISSOURI	5,988,923	6,063,589	1.2	6,028,076	80.5	11.4	1.7	2.6	3.8	23.4	62.0	14.6	2,361,232	67.9	39.9	28.0
Adrian city	1,677	1,637	-2.4	2,098	97.5	0.1	0.0	0.9	1.5	30.0	53.9	16.1	788	63.1	54.4	13.8
Advance city	1,347	1,364	1.3	1,465	99.0	0.0	0.0	0.1	1.0	28.4	44.6	27.0	568	75.7	53.0	16.7
Affton CDP	20,307	NA	NA	21,358	92.6	1.7	1.4	1.4	2.9	20.0	63.9	16.1	9,370	78.9	35.6	32.7
Agency village	683	675	-1.2	840	91.5	0.0	0.2	6.5	1.7	22.5	67.6	9.9	273	84.2	48.0	18.7
Airport Drive village	698	836	19.8	835	94.1	0.0	0.5	2.6	2.8	22.1	65.2	12.7	313	65.8	31.9	33.9
Alba city	555	540	-2.7	561	95.4	0.4	0.0	2.7	1.6	26.2	59.0	14.8	229	76.4	59.4	8.7
Albany city	1,730	1,745	0.9	2,125	94.6	2.1	1.0	0.9	1.4	23.7	56.5	19.7	823	75.3	49.8	21.3
Aldrich village	80	80	0.0	75	92.0	0.0	0.0	8.0	0.0	24.1	62.5	13.3	33	54.5	54.5	9.1
Alexandria city	159	155	-2.5	136	86.0	8.8	2.9	2.2	0.0	19.1	64.7	16.2	62	88.7	77.4	3.2
Allendale village	53	51	-3.8	94	100.0	0.0	0.0	0.0	0.0	36.2	46.8	17.0	39	82.1	53.8	17.9
Allenville village	116	118	1.7	76	100.0	0.0	0.0	0.0	0.0	14.4	73.6	11.8	31	87.1	67.7	16.1
Alma city	402	394	-2.0	375	98.1	0.0	0.0	0.0	1.9	19.5	52.3	28.3	165	90.9	48.5	33.9
Altamont village	204	201	-1.5	200	95.5	0.0	0.0	4.5	0.0	30.0	57.5	12.5	81	77.8	49.4	12.3
Altenburg city	349	352	0.9	466	100.0	0.0	0.0	0.0	0.0	32.9	58.8	8.6	167	88.6	68.3	19.8
Alton city	871	874	0.3	1,173	95.4	0.3	0.0	2.6	1.8	28.8	51.1	19.9	402	49.0	61.7	10.0
Amazonia village	312	308	-1.3	270	99.3	0.0	0.0	0.4	0.4	20.0	60.5	19.3	111	78.4	82.9	2.7
Amity town	54	54	0.0	24	100.0	0.0	0.0	0.0	0.0	4.2	66.6	29.2	12	100.0	66.7	0.0
Amoret city	190	186	-2.1	195	83.6	0.0	0.0	0.0	16.4	35.4	49.8	14.9	71	80.3	71.8	0.0
Amsterdam city	242	236	-2.5	237	93.2	0.0	0.0	6.8	0.0	28.3	52.3	19.4	87	88.5	75.9	3.4
Anderson city	1,989	1,993	0.2	2,508	63.7	0.9	2.5	14.6	18.3	30.0	55.6	14.4	838	58.0	59.7	12.2
Annada village	29	29	0.0	52	94.2	0.0	0.0	5.8	0.0	24.9	69.2	5.8	26	61.5	80.8	19.2
Annapolis city	358	349	-2.5	420	96.2	1.9	0.0	1.9	0.0	23.5	57.8	18.6	178	47.8	65.7	3.4
Anniston town	232	230	-0.9	219	99.5	0.0	0.0	0.5	0.0	14.5	54.3	31.1	105	65.7	85.7	1.0
Appleton City city	1,127	1,094	-2.9	1,334	90.4	2.3	0.6	2.6	4.0	23.4	52.7	23.8	531	63.5	60.6	15.6
Arbela town	41	42	2.4	22	100.0	0.0	0.0	0.0	0.0	13.6	45.3	40.9	14	71.4	92.9	0.0
Arbyrd city	509	494	-2.9	533	86.1	0.0	0.0	0.4	13.5	29.8	57.2	12.9	201	77.1	67.2	9.5

1 May be of any race.

Table A. All Places — **Population and Housing**

STATE City, town, township, borough, or CDP (county if applicable)	Population: 2010 census total population	Population: 2014 estimated population	Population: Percent change 2010–2014	Population: ACS total population estimate 2010–2014	Race and Hispanic or Latino origin (percent), 2010–2014: White alone, not Hispanic or Latino	Black alone, not Hispanic or Latino	Asian alone, not Hispanic or Latino	All other races or 2 or more races, not Hispanic or Latino	Hispanic or Latino[1]	Age (percent), 2010–2014: Under 18 years old	Age 18 to 64 years old	Age 65 years and older	Households, 2010–2014: Total occupied housing units	Percent owner occupied	Householders by level of education (percent): High school diploma or less	Bachelor's degree or more
	1	2	3	4	5	6	7	8	9	10	11	12	13	14	15	16
MISSOURI—Con.																
Arcadia city	606	583	-3.8	773	98.1	0.3	0.0	1.4	0.3	24.6	52.2	23.2	320	69.4	45.3	19.1
Archie city	1,170	1,180	0.9	1,339	94.7	0.0	0.0	2.8	2.5	32.7	55.5	11.9	488	69.3	50.0	12.1
Arcola village	55	54	-1.8	45	100.0	0.0	0.0	0.0	0.0	22.2	39.9	37.8	20	85.0	50.0	15.0
Argyle town	162	161	-0.6	135	100.0	0.0	0.0	0.0	0.0	20.0	53.4	26.7	60	85.0	66.7	10.0
Arkoe town	68	66	-2.9	84	100.0	0.0	0.0	0.0	0.0	44.1	52.4	3.6	23	82.6	34.8	8.7
Armstrong city	284	287	1.1	318	95.3	2.5	0.6	1.6	0.0	28.6	60.4	11.0	118	78.8	55.1	11.0
Arnold city	20,808	21,243	2.1	21,020	94.3	0.1	0.6	2.1	3.0	21.9	62.4	15.8	8,204	79.7	42.4	20.3
Arrow Point village	86	88	2.3	136	87.5	0.0	0.0	5.1	7.4	20.6	63.9	15.4	64	67.2	26.6	32.8
Arrow Rock town	56	57	1.8	38	100.0	0.0	0.0	0.0	0.0	0.0	44.7	55.3	23	95.7	26.1	52.2
Asbury city	207	205	-1.0	152	93.4	0.0	0.0	3.3	3.3	11.2	61.2	27.6	70	88.6	58.6	4.3
Ashburn town	52	NA	NA	32	100.0	0.0	0.0	0.0	0.0	0.0	53.2	46.9	18	100.0	100.0	0.0
Ash Grove city	1,472	1,471	-0.1	1,421	93.3	0.9	0.0	1.5	4.3	21.1	55.8	23.2	566	61.5	49.8	15.5
Ashland city	3,707	3,848	3.8	3,796	97.6	0.4	0.0	1.7	0.3	26.3	60.5	13.4	1,481	67.3	31.7	38.6
Ashley CDP	90	NA	NA	86	100.0	0.0	0.0	0.0	0.0	0.0	58.2	41.9	45	80.0	80.0	0.0
Atlanta city	385	377	-2.1	394	94.9	0.5	0.3	2.8	1.5	31.8	50.1	18.3	172	77.9	50.6	18.0
Augusta town	253	255	0.8	289	97.9	0.0	0.0	0.0	2.1	26.6	52.1	21.1	121	79.3	27.3	43.8
Aullville village	100	98	-2.0	116	91.4	0.0	0.0	7.8	0.9	29.3	56.9	13.8	33	69.7	66.7	3.0
Aurora city	7,508	7,450	-0.8	7,475	88.1	0.0	0.1	3.6	8.2	25.1	57.9	17.0	2,925	63.3	56.2	11.7
Auxvasse city	983	988	0.5	1,009	92.2	0.0	0.0	5.6	2.2	25.8	56.2	18.0	402	60.4	56.0	20.1
Ava city	2,995	2,970	-0.8	2,973	96.3	0.0	0.0	1.8	1.9	25.3	52.2	22.5	1,252	55.8	63.7	6.8
Avilla town	125	124	-0.8	120	92.5	0.0	0.0	7.5	0.0	36.6	45.0	18.3	38	57.9	71.1	0.0
Avondale city	440	458	4.1	493	87.2	3.4	0.0	2.6	6.7	17.8	70.0	12.2	220	58.2	27.3	33.6
Bagnell town	93	95	2.2	88	97.7	0.0	0.0	2.3	0.0	9.1	72.7	18.2	62	14.5	32.3	0.0
Baker village	3	NA	NA	0	0.0	0.0	0.0	0.0	0.0	0.0	0.0	0.0	0	0.0	0.0	0.0
Bakersfield village	246	238	-3.3	255	100.0	0.0	0.0	0.0	0.0	20.8	63.9	15.3	131	60.3	71.0	6.9
Baldwin Park village	92	92	0.0	84	89.3	0.0	0.0	3.6	7.1	14.3	78.5	7.1	39	82.1	89.7	0.0
Ballwin city	30,411	30,505	0.3	30,478	87.4	2.2	5.7	2.9	1.8	23.1	60.7	16.2	11,498	80.0	16.0	56.1
Baring city	132	129	-2.3	174	96.6	3.4	0.0	0.0	0.0	24.7	60.2	14.9	83	78.3	67.5	6.0
Barnard city	221	215	-2.7	276	93.8	1.8	0.0	3.6	0.7	31.5	55.8	12.7	105	76.2	69.5	5.7
Barnett city	203	202	-0.5	201	98.0	0.0	0.0	0.5	1.5	10.0	70.7	19.4	97	81.4	73.2	1.0
Barnhart CDP	5,682	NA	NA	5,746	96.3	1.1	0.0	0.3	2.3	25.0	70.0	5.1	1,976	91.7	36.2	23.2
Bates City city	224	220	-1.8	243	100.0	0.0	0.0	0.0	0.0	29.2	57.1	13.6	86	72.1	50.0	23.3
Battlefield city	5,595	5,925	5.9	5,759	90.3	1.5	0.2	5.1	2.8	27.6	60.1	12.1	2,185	85.3	21.3	37.3
Bella Villa city	746	739	-0.9	822	92.3	1.9	0.0	1.1	4.6	19.5	65.0	15.5	361	88.6	43.5	22.4
Bell City city	448	439	-2.0	456	96.7	0.2	0.0	3.1	0.0	23.9	68.0	8.1	174	63.2	71.3	6.9
Belle city	1,545	1,535	-0.6	1,777	97.2	0.7	0.3	0.0	1.8	28.7	58.0	13.2	703	50.2	61.6	11.9
Bellefontaine Neighbors city	10,852	10,807	-0.4	10,823	22.1	74.9	0.1	1.8	1.2	25.6	62.1	12.3	4,136	69.7	38.9	18.2
Bellerive village	188	188	0.0	203	49.3	49.3	0.0	1.5	0.0	15.2	49.6	35.0	82	91.5	6.1	70.7
Bellflower city	393	370	-5.9	347	96.3	0.0	0.0	2.9	0.9	24.5	66.3	9.2	144	70.1	70.8	3.5
Bel-Nor village	1,499	1,486	-0.9	1,522	48.9	47.1	1.6	2.2	0.3	14.0	70.9	15.2	690	87.0	11.9	61.2
Bel-Ridge village	2,737	2,724	-0.5	2,715	9.9	84.6	2.1	1.9	1.5	32.9	59.2	7.9	1,104	40.9	44.4	12.8
Belton city	23,116	23,165	0.2	23,197	81.1	6.2	1.7	2.9	8.0	28.2	60.7	11.2	8,327	65.8	38.7	22.0
Bennett Springs CDP	130	NA	NA	156	94.9	0.0	0.0	0.0	5.1	0.0	39.8	60.3	77	100.0	55.8	10.4
Benton city	865	860	-0.6	853	91.7	2.2	1.4	0.5	4.2	25.8	61.6	12.8	305	70.8	52.8	21.3
Benton City village	104	105	1.0	147	93.9	0.0	0.0	0.0	6.1	30.0	53.8	16.3	54	79.6	70.4	3.7
Berger city	221	220	-0.5	203	98.5	0.0	0.0	0.0	1.5	33.5	54.1	12.3	81	74.1	58.0	11.1
Berkeley city	9,127	9,084	-0.5	9,120	14.5	79.8	0.1	3.0	2.6	26.2	62.0	11.8	3,698	49.7	47.5	11.3
Bernie city	1,958	1,951	-0.4	2,071	87.2	5.5	0.0	4.9	2.5	26.5	55.4	18.0	893	53.6	64.2	5.6
Bertrand city	821	804	-2.1	908	90.9	1.7	0.0	7.5	0.0	17.5	58.6	23.8	425	64.2	71.3	3.8
Bethany city	3,292	3,158	-4.1	3,186	91.7	1.8	0.0	2.2	4.3	20.7	56.1	23.2	1,342	61.8	59.8	15.1
Bethel village	122	118	-3.3	121	99.2	0.0	0.0	0.8	0.0	20.7	60.4	19.0	60	48.3	56.7	11.7
Beverly Hills city	574	568	-1.0	440	9.1	88.9	0.0	2.0	0.0	13.9	66.2	19.8	205	60.5	50.7	6.8
Bevier city	718	711	-1.0	600	97.7	1.7	0.2	0.5	0.0	18.4	60.2	21.5	289	78.9	65.4	9.0
Biehle CDP	48	NA	NA	0	0.0	0.0	0.0	0.0	0.0	0.0	0.0	0.0	0	0.0	0.0	0.0
Bigelow village	27	25	-7.4	12	100.0	0.0	0.0	0.0	0.0	0.0	16.7	83.3	9	66.7	100.0	0.0
Big Lake village	159	146	-8.2	134	97.0	0.0	0.0	3.0	0.0	10.5	55.9	33.6	62	91.9	59.7	19.4
Big Spring CDP	167	NA	NA	59	50.8	0.0	0.0	49.2	0.0	0.0	84.6	15.3	45	100.0	75.6	0.0
Billings city	1,035	1,073	3.7	937	99.5	0.5	0.0	0.0	0.0	18.2	62.7	19.2	428	77.8	53.0	17.5
Birch Tree city	679	669	-1.5	639	88.7	0.0	0.0	0.3	11.0	23.9	57.2	18.9	264	60.2	70.5	6.1
Birmingham village	183	191	4.4	233	96.1	0.0	0.0	0.4	3.4	21.0	65.7	13.3	93	92.5	57.0	7.5
Bismarck city	1,546	1,493	-3.4	1,296	97.1	0.0	0.0	2.1	0.8	22.6	59.6	17.8	593	64.4	60.5	7.4
Blackburn city	249	251	0.8	281	91.5	7.5	0.0	0.4	0.7	23.8	56.2	19.9	113	67.3	58.4	14.2
Black Jack city	6,925	6,935	0.1	6,924	17.5	78.4	1.6	2.6	0.0	22.5	59.0	18.4	2,507	66.0	25.6	30.7
Blackwater city	162	162	0.0	147	99.3	0.0	0.0	0.0	0.7	37.4	52.5	10.2	54	88.9	57.4	7.4
Blairstown city	97	96	-1.0	140	80.7	0.0	0.0	10.7	8.6	27.9	59.2	12.9	52	61.5	90.4	0.0
Blanchard CDP	22	NA	NA	39	100.0	0.0	0.0	0.0	0.0	12.8	87.2	0.0	15	60.0	26.7	0.0
Bland city	539	523	-3.0	557	96.9	0.0	0.0	3.1	0.0	15.0	68.5	16.3	230	65.2	70.9	7.8
Blodgett village	213	211	-0.9	188	84.6	0.0	0.0	0.0	15.4	36.2	55.2	8.5	65	30.8	38.5	18.5
Bloomfield city	1,932	1,907	-1.3	1,924	97.5	1.5	0.1	0.5	0.6	15.7	63.4	20.8	775	69.4	65.8	8.3
Bloomsdale city	521	523	0.4	563	96.4	1.6	0.0	1.4	0.5	20.6	60.9	18.5	251	74.5	49.4	13.9
Blue Eye town	167	157	-6.0	188	95.7	0.0	0.0	2.7	1.6	22.9	60.2	17.0	78	39.7	39.7	15.4
Blue Springs city	52,637	53,573	1.8	53,053	83.1	7.2	1.5	4.0	4.2	27.3	61.7	10.9	19,353	68.0	32.3	31.1
Blythedale village	193	187	-3.1	185	98.9	0.0	0.0	1.1	0.0	32.5	49.7	17.8	77	84.4	51.9	13.0
Bogard city	164	160	-2.4	161	99.4	0.0	0.0	0.0	0.6	27.3	47.2	25.5	70	88.6	61.4	4.3
Bolckow city	187	189	1.1	253	90.9	0.0	0.0	6.3	2.8	23.3	67.1	9.5	88	88.6	58.0	2.3
Bolivar city	10,325	10,572	2.4	10,443	92.2	1.9	0.4	2.4	3.1	19.9	63.6	16.4	4,142	43.3	41.5	22.8
Bonne Terre city	6,864	7,031	2.4	7,025	70.0	25.1	0.1	3.9	1.0	13.7	78.0	8.3	1,394	53.7	44.7	11.0
Boonville city	8,315	8,374	0.7	8,320	81.3	11.5	0.1	4.7	2.4	19.2	64.6	16.1	2,977	59.7	44.9	21.5
Bosworth city	305	298	-2.3	249	98.0	0.0	0.0	1.6	0.4	22.8	61.2	15.7	101	76.2	73.3	6.9
Bourbon city	1,632	1,627	-0.3	1,659	95.8	0.8	0.0	2.0	1.3	23.9	63.5	12.6	662	58.6	62.1	8.3
Bowling Green city	5,334	5,505	3.2	5,452	85.0	10.1	0.4	2.5	2.1	21.7	61.7	16.6	1,822	60.3	64.3	10.1
Bragg City town	149	145	-2.7	149	100.0	0.0	0.0	0.0	0.0	28.1	57.6	14.1	45	84.4	73.3	6.7
Brandsville city	161	160	-0.6	132	96.2	0.0	0.0	3.8	0.0	26.6	56.1	17.4	62	66.1	41.9	25.8
Branson city	10,547	11,340	7.5	10,942	85.4	1.9	0.0	3.1	9.6	16.7	64.1	19.2	4,822	38.2	36.4	26.4
Branson West city	478	452	-5.4	655	84.0	0.0	0.0	2.3	13.7	29.2	51.0	19.8	221	50.2	62.4	11.3
Brashear city	273	271	-0.7	239	97.1	0.0	1.3	1.7	0.0	21.3	63.2	15.5	117	74.4	62.4	10.3
Braymer city	878	849	-3.3	749	96.7	0.9	0.0	0.7	1.7	25.3	56.2	18.4	351	62.7	65.8	13.1
Breckenridge city	383	360	-6.0	263	89.0	3.4	1.9	4.6	1.1	25.5	61.6	12.9	121	64.5	55.4	11.6
Breckenridge Hills city	4,746	4,720	-0.5	4,728	50.7	37.3	0.0	2.9	9.1	27.1	66.0	7.0	1,886	44.0	60.4	9.5
Brentwood city	8,055	8,043	-0.1	8,048	86.2	3.3	7.0	1.0	2.5	18.7	69.4	11.8	3,791	64.9	13.2	68.4

1 May be of any race.

Table A. All Places — **Population and Housing**

STATE City, town, township, borough, or CDP (county if applicable)	Population: 2010 census total population	Population: 2014 estimated population	Population: Percent change 2010–2014	Population: ACS total population estimate 2010–2014	Race and Hispanic or Latino origin (percent), 2010–2014: White alone, not Hispanic or Latino	Black alone, not Hispanic or Latino	Asian alone, not Hispanic or Latino	All other races or 2 or more races, not Hispanic or Latino	Hispanic or Latino[1]	Age (percent), 2010–2014: Under 18 years old	Age 18 to 64 years old	Age 65 years and older	Households, 2010–2014: Total occupied housing units	Percent owner occupied	Householders by level of education (percent): High school diploma or less	Bachelor's degree or more
	1	2	3	4	5	6	7	8	9	10	11	12	13	14	15	16
MISSOURI—Con.																
Brewer CDP	374	NA	NA	452	100.0	0.0	0.0	0.0	0.0	29.2	60.0	10.8	157	68.8	74.5	0.0
Bridgeton city	11,550	11,782	2.0	11,654	70.3	20.2	2.4	2.8	4.3	21.9	60.3	17.9	4,658	64.3	35.6	31.1
Brimson village	63	63	0.0	60	98.3	0.0	0.0	1.7	0.0	18.3	60.0	21.7	33	72.7	81.8	0.0
Bronaugh city	249	249	0.0	266	100.0	0.0	0.0	0.0	0.0	38.4	50.1	11.7	91	59.3	61.5	8.8
Brookfield city	4,542	4,364	-3.9	4,462	92.6	0.7	0.6	4.2	1.9	24.4	53.0	22.4	1,825	70.4	65.2	10.8
Brooklyn Heights town	100	99	-1.0	118	96.6	0.8	0.0	2.5	0.0	17.0	65.3	17.8	49	63.3	71.4	8.2
Browning city	265	256	-3.4	223	97.3	0.0	0.0	0.4	2.2	23.2	66.8	9.9	93	65.6	77.4	2.2
Brownington town	107	106	-0.9	88	98.9	0.0	0.0	1.1	0.0	9.1	72.7	18.2	46	91.3	87.0	0.0
Brumley town	91	93	2.2	195	84.6	0.0	0.0	10.8	4.6	32.9	49.8	17.4	49	100.0	61.2	14.3
Brunswick city	858	842	-1.9	914	88.2	7.8	0.0	2.6	1.4	26.3	51.5	22.1	347	60.5	59.1	13.3
Bucklin city	467	447	-4.3	554	96.4	0.9	0.2	0.4	2.2	19.8	57.7	22.4	204	75.0	65.2	6.9
Buckner city	3,076	3,071	-0.2	3,071	92.8	0.2	0.0	3.8	3.2	26.8	62.3	10.9	1,195	66.2	60.8	9.8
Buffalo city	3,089	3,039	-1.6	3,073	93.5	0.1	0.0	3.4	3.1	24.7	57.4	17.8	1,251	57.3	56.6	14.2
Bull Creek village	603	596	-1.2	506	80.6	0.8	0.0	3.2	15.4	46.4	48.4	5.1	174	27.6	57.5	1.7
Bunceton city	354	347	-2.0	350	94.6	2.6	1.4	0.9	0.6	27.9	56.8	15.1	147	72.8	53.1	9.5
Bunker city	406	404	-0.5	432	91.2	3.0	0.9	4.9	0.0	28.2	59.6	12.3	150	61.3	81.3	2.7
Burgess town	57	56	-1.8	60	85.0	0.0	0.0	15.0	0.0	16.7	66.6	16.7	28	78.6	67.9	21.4
Burlington Junction city	537	514	-4.3	554	95.1	0.7	0.0	0.9	3.2	30.6	56.9	12.5	232	65.9	68.5	9.9
Butler city	4,219	4,127	-2.2	4,112	95.1	2.6	0.0	0.7	1.7	23.5	55.4	21.2	1,801	55.5	63.5	11.2
Butterfield village	470	464	-1.3	524	66.8	0.0	0.0	1.5	31.7	26.2	64.6	9.4	155	83.9	64.5	5.2
Byrnes Mill city	2,781	2,832	1.8	2,795	98.0	0.0	1.2	0.4	0.4	21.2	64.0	14.7	1,111	78.0	41.8	21.1
Cabool city	2,146	2,126	-0.9	2,410	91.4	0.8	0.2	4.7	2.8	23.0	53.1	24.0	924	53.9	55.1	18.7
Cainsville city	290	281	-3.1	253	98.4	0.0	0.0	0.0	1.6	23.4	50.8	25.7	117	89.7	60.7	6.8
Cairo village	292	289	-1.0	322	94.1	0.0	0.0	0.3	5.6	35.1	52.2	12.7	93	82.8	43.0	2.2
Caledonia village	130	131	0.8	196	100.0	0.0	0.0	0.0	0.0	33.7	56.3	10.2	68	80.9	55.9	0.0
Calhoun city	469	455	-3.0	373	98.4	0.0	0.0	1.6	0.0	28.9	57.4	13.7	145	68.3	66.2	7.6
California city	4,297	4,364	1.6	4,342	86.9	1.3	0.0	0.7	11.1	27.0	55.1	17.9	1,864	58.2	57.9	20.9
Callao city	293	285	-2.7	351	100.0	0.0	0.0	0.0	0.0	35.9	56.1	8.0	103	86.4	69.9	8.7
Calverton Park village	1,293	1,287	-0.5	1,220	62.0	28.8	2.0	5.8	1.4	18.9	67.0	14.0	495	73.5	47.3	13.9
Camden city	191	187	-2.1	237	99.6	0.0	0.0	0.4	0.0	24.5	56.2	19.4	89	91.0	73.0	4.5
Camden Point city	474	522	10.1	482	97.7	0.0	0.0	0.6	1.7	27.0	61.2	11.8	165	91.5	40.6	26.7
Camdenton city	3,720	3,844	3.3	3,786	89.7	0.9	2.2	1.5	5.7	30.3	58.8	10.9	1,199	52.1	47.5	20.1
Cameron city	9,933	9,762	-1.7	10,008	78.7	14.1	1.3	3.7	2.2	18.6	67.0	14.4	2,644	45.6	48.2	16.5
Campbell city	1,992	1,949	-2.2	1,929	97.0	0.4	0.0	0.4	2.2	27.7	49.7	22.7	800	61.5	65.0	11.1
Canalou city	338	315	-6.8	339	99.1	0.0	0.0	0.0	0.9	42.1	48.6	9.1	93	75.3	75.3	0.0
Canton city	2,377	2,368	-0.4	2,544	93.0	2.6	0.4	3.9	0.2	23.2	61.5	15.3	848	59.2	56.5	16.5
Cape Girardeau city	37,995	39,167	3.1	38,665	79.6	13.0	2.2	2.8	2.4	18.7	66.2	15.2	15,279	54.3	35.5	33.4
Cardwell city	713	698	-2.1	598	95.2	0.0	1.0	2.2	1.7	18.4	59.0	22.6	290	58.6	73.4	7.2
Carl Junction city	7,445	7,660	2.9	7,511	94.2	0.6	0.4	3.0	1.8	31.2	56.3	12.6	2,744	76.1	32.9	38.9
Carrollton city	3,784	3,664	-3.2	3,652	96.3	1.6	0.0	1.2	0.9	21.8	56.4	21.7	1,539	64.3	57.9	18.1
Carterville city	1,891	1,852	-2.1	1,806	89.0	0.2	0.7	3.2	6.8	26.8	59.3	13.8	682	79.5	59.1	13.0
Carthage city	14,378	14,271	-0.7	14,281	63.6	2.0	0.0	3.0	31.4	29.3	55.2	15.5	5,083	54.7	59.4	17.7
Caruthersville city	6,168	5,975	-3.1	6,086	61.5	34.7	0.0	1.4	2.4	25.9	58.4	15.9	2,544	49.4	66.1	10.1
Carytown city	271	268	-1.1	226	87.6	0.0	0.0	1.3	11.1	30.1	54.9	15.0	76	84.2	59.2	27.6
Cassville city	3,266	3,287	0.6	3,275	88.1	0.3	2.0	1.6	7.9	21.5	56.6	21.8	1,379	60.0	47.3	23.5
Castle Point CDP	3,962	NA	NA	3,680	2.9	91.7	0.0	5.4	0.0	36.1	55.2	8.7	1,152	61.3	48.1	10.1
Catron town	67	64	-4.5	71	64.8	9.9	12.7	0.0	12.7	18.3	67.7	14.1	25	84.0	52.0	12.0
Cave town	5	5	0.0	1	100.0	0.0	0.0	0.0	0.0	0.0	0.0	100.0	1	0.0	100.0	0.0
Cedar Hill CDP	1,721	NA	NA	1,758	98.4	0.0	0.0	1.6	0.0	31.8	55.1	13.3	591	90.2	46.4	14.9
Cedar Hill Lakes village	237	238	0.4	191	95.3	1.0	0.0	2.1	1.6	14.1	71.2	14.7	83	90.4	56.6	15.7
Center city	508	509	0.2	379	100.0	0.0	0.0	0.0	0.0	19.7	63.4	16.9	140	65.7	73.6	4.3
Centertown town	278	275	-1.1	282	94.3	0.0	1.8	2.5	1.4	23.8	60.6	15.6	129	82.9	54.3	13.2
Centerview city	267	273	2.2	283	90.5	0.0	0.0	0.4	9.2	43.8	50.1	6.0	89	49.4	55.1	4.5
Centerville city	194	192	-1.0	248	94.4	4.0	0.0	1.6	0.0	13.7	59.6	26.6	78	57.7	60.3	12.8
Centralia city	4,027	4,175	3.7	4,125	96.0	2.1	0.0	1.7	0.2	23.8	60.0	16.2	1,769	62.8	45.3	16.8
Chaffee city	2,955	2,929	-0.9	2,958	94.3	0.2	0.8	2.0	2.7	25.9	57.0	17.1	1,177	59.8	60.9	6.5
Chain of Rocks village	93	96	3.2	128	100.0	0.0	0.0	0.0	0.0	32.8	62.5	4.7	37	94.6	48.6	5.4
Chain-O-Lakes village	128	131	2.3	175	98.3	0.0	0.0	1.7	0.0	22.8	59.9	17.1	72	86.1	38.9	9.7
Chamois city	396	387	-2.3	360	98.1	0.0	0.0	1.1	0.8	25.5	52.5	21.9	156	77.6	58.3	15.4
Champ village	13	13	0.0	11	100.0	0.0	0.0	0.0	0.0	0.0	0.0	100.0	5	0.0	20.0	0.0
Charlack city	1,367	1,371	0.3	1,274	50.9	43.1	2.4	3.7	0.0	20.2	70.6	9.3	547	50.3	32.2	18.8
Charleston city	5,947	5,907	-0.7	5,905	45.7	50.6	0.1	2.1	1.5	18.0	70.6	11.4	1,819	58.6	69.7	14.1
Charmwood town	32	32	0.0	0	0.0	0.0	0.0	0.0	0.0	0.0	0.0	0.0	0	0.0	0.0	0.0
Cherokee Pass CDP	235	NA	NA	250	100.0	0.0	0.0	0.0	0.0	12.0	62.4	25.6	110	92.7	82.7	0.0
Chesapeake CDP	49	NA	NA	49	100.0	0.0	0.0	0.0	0.0	0.0	100.0	0.0	33	100.0	100.0	0.0
Chesterfield city	47,484	47,777	0.6	47,651	82.4	3.5	9.3	1.2	3.5	22.1	56.0	22.1	19,196	77.0	10.3	66.8
Chilhowee town	325	332	2.2	231	88.7	0.0	0.0	11.3	0.0	21.3	59.0	19.9	117	64.1	62.4	17.1
Chillicothe city	9,515	9,504	-0.1	8,528	94.0	2.5	0.5	1.3	1.6	21.1	59.8	19.1	3,430	61.5	55.5	19.6
Chula city	210	203	-3.3	245	76.3	0.0	0.0	7.3	16.3	41.6	50.5	7.8	68	85.3	57.4	2.9
Clarence city	813	778	-4.3	886	96.7	0.7	0.0	1.1	1.5	27.5	51.2	21.3	364	73.1	64.0	8.5
Clark city	298	295	-1.0	344	98.5	0.9	0.0	0.6	0.0	22.0	64.5	13.4	114	64.9	72.8	2.6
Clarksburg city	334	331	-0.9	268	79.1	0.0	0.0	0.7	20.1	33.2	54.1	12.7	93	62.4	62.4	3.2
Clarksdale city	271	268	-1.1	307	98.7	0.0	0.0	0.3	1.0	23.2	53.7	23.1	130	67.7	43.8	7.7
Clarkson Valley city	2,632	2,648	0.6	2,638	89.2	0.8	3.8	1.9	4.2	23.7	59.4	16.9	884	99.5	7.4	81.3
Clarksville city	442	435	-1.6	409	96.3	2.7	0.0	0.7	0.2	9.3	65.2	25.4	234	62.4	47.0	26.5
Clarkton city	1,288	1,252	-2.8	1,141	69.6	18.2	0.0	1.5	10.7	30.6	58.9	10.4	422	53.8	77.0	5.2
Claycomo village	1,430	1,470	2.8	1,345	87.3	0.4	1.0	1.4	9.9	16.3	61.9	21.9	613	60.8	57.3	10.4
Clayton city	15,939	15,882	-0.4	15,912	75.3	8.7	10.4	2.6	3.1	16.7	69.4	13.9	5,900	57.6	3.2	86.1
Clearmont city	170	165	-2.9	200	96.0	0.0	0.0	4.0	0.0	13.5	48.0	38.5	106	65.1	73.6	11.3
Cleveland city	661	663	0.3	643	93.0	0.0	2.6	3.1	1.2	20.0	66.3	13.5	253	79.8	35.2	24.1
Clever city	2,139	2,434	13.8	2,185	94.4	1.8	0.0	1.2	2.6	28.9	60.7	10.4	817	79.6	38.3	26.2
Cliff Village village	40	40	0.0	34	100.0	0.0	0.0	0.0	0.0	38.2	58.8	2.9	11	100.0	36.4	9.1
Clifton Hill city	114	113	-0.9	89	100.0	0.0	0.0	0.0	0.0	22.4	57.2	20.2	32	90.6	75.0	9.4
Climax Springs village	120	120	0.0	114	98.2	1.8	0.0	0.0	0.0	28.0	68.4	3.5	30	66.7	56.7	13.3
Clinton city	9,008	9,015	0.1	9,014	93.7	2.4	0.2	2.1	1.6	23.5	56.3	20.3	3,951	58.1	51.0	15.9
Clyde village	82	80	-2.4	123	99.2	0.0	0.0	0.0	0.8	15.4	58.5	26.0	36	86.1	52.8	16.7
Cobalt village	226	230	1.8	224	96.4	0.0	0.0	3.6	0.0	31.3	63.1	5.8	72	58.3	79.2	1.4
Coffey city	166	164	-1.2	133	93.2	0.0	0.0	0.0	6.8	29.3	56.5	14.3	47	55.3	68.1	0.0
Cole Camp city	1,121	1,113	-0.7	1,567	97.9	0.0	0.0	0.1	2.0	25.7	53.2	21.2	588	71.1	47.6	20.9
Collins village	159	155	-2.5	141	96.5	0.0	0.0	0.7	2.8	13.5	60.9	25.5	68	69.1	76.5	13.2
Columbia city	108,835	116,906	7.4	113,155	76.5	10.5	5.4	4.2	3.4	19.0	72.0	8.9	44,378	48.3	17.0	52.6

1 May be of any race.

Table A. All Places — Population and Housing

STATE City, town, township, borough, or CDP (county if applicable)	Population: 2010 census total population	Population: 2014 estimated population	Population: Percent change 2010–2014	Population: ACS total population estimate 2010–2014	Race and Hispanic or Latino origin (percent), 2010–2014: White alone, not Hispanic or Latino	Black alone, not Hispanic or Latino	Asian alone, not Hispanic or Latino	All other races or 2 or more races, not Hispanic or Latino	Hispanic or Latino[1]	Age (percent), 2010–2014: Under 18 years old	Age 18 to 64 years old	Age 65 years and older	Households, 2010–2014: Total occupied housing units	Percent owner occupied	Householders by level of education (percent): High school diploma or less	Bachelor's degree or more
	1	2	3	4	5	6	7	8	9	10	11	12	13	14	15	16
MISSOURI—Con.																
Commerce village	67	66	-1.5	42	85.7	14.3	0.0	0.0	0.0	26.1	52.3	21.4	22	68.2	81.8	9.1
Conception CDP	210	NA	NA	231	89.2	1.3	2.2	3.5	3.9	14.3	75.8	10.0	38	92.1	60.5	5.3
Conception Junction town	198	193	-2.5	239	92.9	0.0	2.5	2.9	1.7	33.4	57.7	8.8	87	67.8	49.4	18.4
Concord CDP	16,421	NA	NA	16,645	97.3	0.1	0.9	0.6	1.1	19.2	56.9	23.9	7,057	87.8	29.1	40.2
Concordia city	2,450	2,389	-2.5	2,434	95.8	0.0	0.0	2.2	1.9	23.3	57.5	19.2	989	73.2	54.1	24.2
Coney Island village	75	72	-4.0	71	87.3	0.0	0.0	12.7	0.0	0.0	32.3	67.6	37	78.4	62.2	16.2
Conway city	788	778	-1.3	1,139	83.5	3.1	0.0	12.7	0.7	36.6	53.7	9.8	332	64.8	64.8	7.5
Cool Valley city	1,196	1,189	-0.6	1,133	15.1	77.0	2.3	2.8	2.8	17.1	62.6	20.4	421	72.7	50.4	15.9
Cooter city	469	446	-4.9	442	94.3	0.0	0.0	1.1	4.5	25.4	65.4	9.3	153	53.6	65.4	6.5
Corder city	407	397	-2.5	366	95.4	0.0	0.0	1.4	3.3	25.7	60.2	14.2	149	85.2	57.0	14.1
Corning town	15	14	-6.7	4	100.0	0.0	0.0	0.0	0.0	0.0	75.0	25.0	3	100.0	100.0	0.0
Cosby village	124	125	0.8	132	100.0	0.0	0.0	0.0	0.0	27.3	56.7	15.9	42	85.7	50.0	11.9
Cottleville city	3,065	3,877	26.5	3,492	91.2	4.2	2.7	0.5	1.4	28.4	59.6	12.0	1,255	92.0	18.2	44.8
Country Club village	2,449	2,475	1.1	2,797	89.2	2.1	0.3	2.6	5.8	23.9	60.1	15.7	1,105	72.2	32.9	33.2
Country Club Hills city	1,277	1,271	-0.5	1,415	5.1	90.5	0.0	4.4	0.0	40.3	55.4	4.3	494	41.7	60.1	9.5
Country Life Acres village	74	74	0.0	128	88.3	0.0	2.3	3.9	5.5	29.7	49.9	20.3	43	100.0	2.3	74.4
Cowgill city	188	180	-4.3	153	98.7	0.0	0.0	1.3	0.0	16.3	60.8	22.9	75	64.0	70.7	12.0
Craig city	248	230	-7.3	199	95.5	0.5	2.5	1.0	0.5	18.1	54.1	27.6	97	55.7	76.3	7.2
Crane city	1,462	1,390	-4.9	1,828	92.7	0.0	0.0	2.6	4.8	26.8	54.0	19.3	641	60.7	72.1	8.6
Creighton city	349	343	-1.7	336	82.7	2.7	0.0	9.8	4.8	28.5	53.9	17.6	133	76.7	65.4	5.3
Crestwood city	11,912	11,951	0.3	11,934	89.7	2.5	2.7	1.2	3.9	21.4	57.8	20.7	4,941	87.5	21.1	53.1
Creve Coeur city	17,835	17,868	0.2	17,841	74.4	7.5	12.0	3.5	2.7	21.0	57.9	21.2	7,414	70.4	8.2	73.7
Crocker city	1,110	1,081	-2.6	910	93.6	0.3	0.0	1.3	4.7	30.2	54.8	15.1	352	59.7	49.4	15.9
Cross Timbers city	216	210	-2.8	242	94.6	0.0	0.0	0.0	5.4	30.1	61.8	8.3	94	57.4	50.0	12.8
Crystal City city	4,855	4,839	-0.3	4,841	89.6	2.3	0.2	6.6	1.3	24.3	61.2	14.4	1,789	67.5	40.1	18.8
Crystal Lake Park city	470	499	6.2	582	84.7	3.4	6.0	4.6	1.2	28.2	53.9	17.9	220	97.7	5.9	76.4
Crystal Lakes city	358	350	-2.2	406	96.6	0.5	0.7	0.7	1.5	18.7	69.2	12.1	161	93.2	47.8	10.6
Cuba city	3,356	3,383	0.8	3,372	97.2	0.1	0.0	0.0	2.8	29.1	58.1	12.8	1,145	58.1	59.1	12.7
Curryville city	225	227	0.9	181	94.5	2.8	0.0	2.8	0.0	24.3	60.3	15.5	76	64.5	71.1	6.6
Dadeville village	234	228	-2.6	258	90.7	0.0	0.0	5.8	3.5	26.0	64.9	9.3	97	80.4	55.7	17.5
Dalton town	17	17	0.0	20	50.0	50.0	0.0	0.0	0.0	35.0	35.0	30.0	8	62.5	75.0	0.0
Danville CDP	34	NA	NA	44	100.0	0.0	0.0	0.0	0.0	43.2	31.8	25.0	25	44.0	100.0	0.0
Dardenne Prairie city	11,505	12,783	11.1	12,116	89.9	4.6	2.1	0.6	2.7	29.8	55.8	14.3	4,040	97.0	20.4	52.1
Darlington village	121	123	1.7	114	95.6	0.0	0.0	4.4	0.0	27.2	40.4	32.5	34	91.2	64.7	2.9
Dawn CDP	128	NA	NA	75	100.0	0.0	0.0	0.0	0.0	22.7	56.0	21.3	34	82.4	70.6	29.4
Dearborn city	496	506	2.0	480	86.9	0.6	0.0	5.8	6.7	26.9	54.0	19.0	194	64.4	47.9	20.1
Deepwater city	433	422	-2.5	367	90.5	1.1	0.0	0.8	7.6	26.9	55.3	17.7	160	80.6	67.5	7.5
Deerfield village	81	81	0.0	68	100.0	0.0	0.0	0.0	0.0	29.4	58.9	11.8	23	47.8	56.5	17.4
Defiance CDP	155	NA	NA	147	100.0	0.0	0.0	0.0	0.0	13.6	57.7	28.6	74	67.6	58.1	28.4
De Kalb town	220	221	0.5	205	96.1	0.0	0.0	3.9	0.0	20.5	67.8	11.7	71	87.3	62.0	14.1
Dellwood city	5,025	5,005	-0.4	5,010	16.6	80.7	0.0	2.7	0.0	32.8	58.0	9.1	1,612	72.8	40.6	17.6
Delta city	438	438	0.0	478	98.3	0.0	0.0	1.7	0.0	20.7	60.8	18.6	180	56.1	75.6	8.3
Dennis Acres village	76	77	1.3	61	100.0	0.0	0.0	0.0	0.0	45.9	46.0	8.2	22	36.4	68.2	0.0
Denver village	39	38	-2.6	59	100.0	0.0	0.0	0.0	0.0	23.7	55.9	20.3	25	92.0	68.0	8.0
Des Arc village	172	168	-2.3	208	100.0	0.0	0.0	0.0	0.0	23.0	66.8	10.1	82	57.3	69.5	0.0
Desloge city	5,054	4,920	-2.7	4,969	97.7	0.8	0.5	0.9	0.0	19.9	65.0	15.2	2,244	62.6	47.1	10.6
De Soto city	6,400	6,471	1.1	6,449	94.5	2.2	0.1	1.7	1.6	24.4	54.2	21.2	2,755	55.3	51.8	12.7
Des Peres city	8,376	8,534	1.9	8,443	96.0	1.0	1.9	0.2	0.8	22.9	59.1	18.0	3,014	91.8	8.9	73.6
De Witt city	124	121	-2.4	78	96.2	0.0	0.0	3.8	0.0	19.3	70.3	10.3	27	85.2	88.9	0.0
Dexter city	7,864	7,969	1.3	7,902	96.9	0.1	0.0	1.8	1.2	21.8	58.4	19.8	3,357	57.7	52.5	16.8
Diamond town	902	923	2.3	900	95.4	0.0	0.2	4.3	0.0	21.2	61.3	17.6	402	78.6	55.7	8.7
Diehlstadt village	161	160	-0.6	193	99.0	1.0	0.0	0.0	0.0	25.4	64.7	9.8	64	85.9	67.2	6.3
Diggins village	299	304	1.7	274	97.1	0.4	0.0	2.6	0.0	15.7	66.8	17.5	117	70.1	65.0	8.5
Dixon city	1,549	1,514	-2.3	1,452	85.7	0.1	1.6	5.0	7.6	29.0	50.0	21.1	556	52.5	48.6	11.5
Doe Run CDP	915	NA	NA	962	100.0	0.0	0.0	0.0	0.0	25.3	52.1	22.6	464	77.8	61.9	2.8
Doniphan city	1,997	2,002	0.3	2,546	96.3	0.0	0.4	1.9	1.4	24.1	60.2	15.6	979	52.6	54.1	13.1
Doolittle city	630	610	-3.2	640	96.6	0.3	0.0	3.1	0.0	22.1	64.3	13.6	235	81.3	50.2	6.4
Dover town	103	101	-1.9	99	87.9	0.0	0.0	0.0	12.1	19.2	59.7	21.2	42	78.6	59.5	9.5
Downing city	335	331	-1.2	262	99.2	0.0	0.0	0.4	0.4	13.4	61.0	25.6	140	72.9	60.0	5.0
Drexel city	965	956	-0.9	962	91.0	0.0	0.3	4.6	4.2	24.4	57.3	18.3	413	63.9	61.3	11.1
Dudley city	232	231	-0.4	154	94.2	0.0	0.0	0.0	5.8	16.2	60.8	22.7	84	58.3	71.4	4.8
Duenweg city	1,336	1,308	-2.1	1,083	93.4	0.0	0.0	4.8	1.8	29.8	57.1	13.1	452	69.5	50.9	21.9
Duquesne village	1,763	1,735	-1.6	1,721	86.6	4.1	1.3	4.2	3.8	20.0	68.1	12.0	726	54.5	39.4	23.4
Dutchtown village	94	96	2.1	40	100.0	0.0	0.0	0.0	0.0	17.5	47.5	35.0	16	50.0	62.5	12.5
Eagle Rock CDP	199	NA	NA	116	100.0	0.0	0.0	0.0	0.0	0.0	75.0	25.0	59	100.0	76.3	23.7
Eagleville town	316	305	-3.5	243	97.5	0.0	0.0	1.2	1.2	25.5	48.9	25.5	120	78.3	50.8	23.3
East Lynne city	303	304	0.3	277	92.1	0.0	0.0	5.8	2.2	36.4	50.0	13.4	103	73.8	58.3	5.8
Easton city	236	239	1.3	263	89.4	0.0	0.4	3.4	6.8	16.0	72.2	11.8	86	68.6	44.2	18.6
East Prairie city	3,176	3,184	0.3	3,191	87.4	6.5	0.0	0.7	5.4	33.8	50.2	16.0	1,206	57.3	74.5	9.0
Edgar Springs city	208	204	-1.9	244	100.0	0.0	0.0	0.0	0.0	24.1	58.1	17.6	91	67.0	69.2	5.5
Edgerton city	546	568	4.0	620	95.6	0.0	2.3	2.1	0.0	24.5	57.8	17.7	237	85.2	54.0	12.2
Edina city	1,176	1,134	-3.6	1,142	94.8	0.8	0.0	3.3	1.1	24.8	54.2	21.1	526	67.5	58.4	14.8
Edinburg CDP	92	NA	NA	93	100.0	0.0	0.0	0.0	0.0	28.0	54.9	17.2	39	100.0	61.5	0.0
Edmundson city	834	836	0.2	951	44.5	25.1	5.0	5.5	19.9	29.1	61.2	9.8	374	54.3	46.3	17.1
Eldon city	4,567	4,649	1.8	4,601	95.1	0.0	0.0	2.9	2.1	31.2	53.5	15.4	1,833	63.2	60.1	15.5
El Dorado Springs city	3,591	3,573	-0.5	3,562	97.1	0.1	1.5	1.3	0.0	24.7	53.4	21.7	1,586	54.5	68.8	13.3
Ellington city	987	979	-0.8	1,089	97.4	0.3	0.3	0.6	1.4	25.0	51.9	23.2	431	54.8	77.3	7.7
Ellisville city	9,133	9,253	1.3	9,162	91.1	2.4	1.7	1.2	3.6	23.3	57.1	19.6	3,421	86.4	29.8	48.9
Ellsinore city	453	449	-0.9	583	97.9	0.0	0.0	0.2	1.9	35.3	42.3	22.5	214	51.4	62.6	10.3
Elmer city	80	80	0.0	68	100.0	0.0	0.0	0.0	0.0	33.8	52.9	13.2	22	100.0	68.2	13.6
Elmira village	50	49	-2.0	65	100.0	0.0	0.0	0.0	0.0	29.2	57.0	13.8	24	70.8	50.0	8.3
Elmo city	168	163	-3.0	184	87.0	0.0	4.9	6.5	1.6	28.3	62.4	9.2	75	70.7	26.7	21.3
Elsberry city	1,934	1,975	2.1	1,850	92.5	4.1	0.0	0.2	3.2	24.1	56.6	19.4	726	63.6	64.6	11.8
Emerald Beach village	230	229	-0.4	358	88.5	0.0	0.0	5.0	6.4	16.5	44.7	38.8	142	95.8	59.9	13.4
Eminence city	599	591	-1.3	543	98.3	1.7	0.0	0.0	0.0	16.9	62.0	21.2	251	61.4	53.8	10.8
Emma city	240	239	-0.4	270	100.0	0.0	0.0	0.0	0.0	25.9	58.2	15.9	97	64.9	45.4	24.7
Eolia village	522	514	-1.5	434	86.9	9.9	0.0	1.4	1.8	26.5	60.7	12.9	176	75.6	52.8	13.1
Essex city	472	462	-2.1	603	92.5	0.0	0.7	0.0	6.8	20.6	65.4	14.1	250	76.0	75.2	4.4
Ethel town	62	62	0.0	51	86.3	0.0	0.0	13.7	0.0	9.9	45.1	45.1	31	77.4	77.4	6.5
Eureka city	10,194	10,543	3.4	10,375	88.0	4.1	3.0	3.0	1.9	29.7	60.0	10.4	3,051	83.9	21.1	45.8
Evergreen village	28	28	0.0	32	100.0	0.0	0.0	0.0	0.0	15.7	78.1	6.3	13	23.1	61.5	23.1

1 May be of any race.

Table A. All Places — **Population and Housing**

STATE City, town, township, borough, or CDP (county if applicable)	Population: 2010 census total population	Population: 2014 estimated population	Population: Percent change 2010–2014	Population: ACS total population estimate 2010–2014	Race and Hispanic or Latino origin (percent), 2010–2014: White alone, not Hispanic or Latino	Black alone, not Hispanic or Latino	Asian alone, not Hispanic or Latino	All other races or 2 or more races, not Hispanic or Latino	Hispanic or Latino[1]	Age (percent), 2010–2014: Under 18 years old	Age 18 to 64 years old	Age 65 years and older	Households, 2010–2014: Total occupied housing units	Percent owner occupied	Householders by level of education (percent): High school diploma or less	Bachelor's degree or more
	1	2	3	4	5	6	7	8	9	10	11	12	13	14	15	16
MISSOURI—Con.																
Everton city	319	303	-5.0	467	80.1	0.0	0.0	6.4	13.5	34.7	53.7	11.6	153	76.5	76.5	11.1
Ewing city	458	450	-1.7	370	99.5	0.0	0.0	0.5	0.0	27.8	45.1	27.0	168	59.5	67.9	0.6
Excello CDP	49	NA	NA	105	56.2	0.0	0.0	43.8	0.0	9.5	68.6	21.9	52	13.5	13.5	0.0
Excelsior Estates village	147	137	-6.8	165	95.8	0.0	3.0	0.0	1.2	27.9	68.1	4.2	57	75.4	66.7	0.0
Excelsior Springs city	11,084	11,488	3.6	11,391	89.7	3.5	2.8	1.6	2.4	26.2	60.9	12.8	3,984	67.3	48.7	14.9
Exeter city	772	770	-0.3	867	90.8	0.0	0.1	2.5	6.6	27.3	56.4	16.1	317	63.1	71.0	6.3
Fairdealing CDP	676	NA	NA	902	83.6	0.0	0.0	16.4	0.0	27.2	54.7	18.1	302	72.2	52.3	18.5
Fairfax city	638	601	-5.8	652	97.2	0.5	0.3	1.7	0.3	22.1	55.8	22.1	289	65.1	59.2	16.6
Fair Grove city	1,393	1,439	3.3	1,684	98.2	1.0	0.0	0.0	0.8	33.5	54.1	12.4	609	72.9	48.3	14.9
Fair Play city	475	465	-2.1	547	88.5	0.0	0.0	11.5	0.0	40.1	48.8	11.2	193	66.3	67.9	5.2
Fairview town	383	382	-0.3	364	83.8	3.3	2.7	1.6	8.5	31.9	54.6	13.5	129	82.2	70.5	7.0
Farber city	322	317	-1.6	422	93.6	0.5	0.0	4.0	1.9	18.0	60.5	21.3	191	73.3	69.1	4.2
Farley village	269	283	5.2	225	99.6	0.0	0.0	0.4	0.0	23.9	54.1	21.8	85	89.4	38.8	36.5
Farmington city	16,307	17,915	9.9	17,213	88.6	6.2	0.8	1.9	2.4	17.9	66.0	16.0	6,187	56.5	42.2	19.5
Fayette city	2,688	2,707	0.7	2,707	83.5	13.2	0.0	3.3	0.0	16.7	65.6	17.7	906	64.5	41.6	31.7
Fenton city	4,022	4,045	0.6	4,037	95.2	2.2	0.9	0.9	0.7	23.5	62.0	14.3	1,473	83.8	26.5	34.1
Ferguson city	21,203	21,086	-0.6	21,151	30.3	65.6	0.2	2.5	1.3	27.6	61.9	10.4	8,557	56.3	38.8	22.6
Ferrelview village	451	462	2.4	474	78.3	9.5	0.0	7.2	5.1	16.7	74.7	8.6	241	38.6	61.4	14.9
Festus city	11,602	11,885	2.4	11,740	91.3	4.2	0.2	3.5	0.7	28.3	58.0	13.7	4,471	69.2	45.9	20.0
Fidelity town	257	256	-0.4	237	89.9	0.0	1.3	7.2	1.7	21.5	62.1	16.5	93	57.0	64.5	6.5
Fillmore city	184	186	1.1	208	100.0	0.0	0.0	0.0	0.0	21.6	71.1	7.2	93	78.5	40.9	15.1
Fisk city	342	339	-0.9	459	98.0	0.0	0.0	2.0	0.0	27.3	59.3	13.5	186	68.8	62.4	12.4
Fleming city	128	125	-2.3	111	91.9	0.0	0.0	5.4	2.7	24.3	66.6	9.0	44	77.3	63.6	4.5
Flemington village	148	147	-0.7	93	97.8	0.0	0.0	2.2	0.0	37.6	53.8	8.6	36	55.6	75.0	0.0
Flint Hill city	499	514	3.0	574	99.7	0.0	0.0	0.3	0.0	30.2	56.6	13.4	200	90.5	33.5	39.5
Flordell Hills city	822	816	-0.7	839	6.0	93.1	0.0	0.5	0.5	27.5	64.5	8.0	335	52.5	61.8	10.4
Florida village	0	0	0.0	0	0.0	0.0	0.0	0.0	0.0	0.0	0.0	0.0	0	0.0	0.0	0.0
Florissant city	52,291	52,303	0.0	52,353	65.1	28.3	1.0	4.2	1.4	23.9	60.4	15.7	21,305	71.9	35.4	25.6
Foley city	161	166	3.1	108	100.0	0.0	0.0	0.0	0.0	17.6	73.1	9.3	35	85.7	62.9	5.7
Fordland city	800	803	0.4	935	95.2	0.4	0.0	4.1	0.3	35.0	53.0	12.0	327	59.3	59.6	12.8
Forest City city	275	254	-7.6	258	97.7	0.0	0.4	1.9	0.0	20.1	59.4	20.5	120	69.2	69.2	10.0
Foristell city	505	514	1.8	439	94.5	0.7	0.5	0.2	4.1	22.1	59.5	18.5	169	80.5	33.7	18.3
Forsyth city	2,346	2,419	3.1	1,874	90.3	2.6	0.0	3.7	3.4	14.0	55.3	30.9	808	72.3	37.9	24.1
Fortescue town	32	30	-6.3	8	75.0	0.0	25.0	0.0	0.0	0.0	75.0	25.0	6	66.7	16.7	83.3
Fort Leonard Wood CDP	15,061	NA	NA	17,061	56.9	15.5	2.6	7.0	18.1	19.3	80.7	0.0	2,293	0.3	33.5	20.0
Foster village	117	114	-2.6	112	96.4	0.0	0.0	3.6	0.0	18.8	57.1	24.1	48	83.3	62.5	10.4
Fountain N' Lakes village	165	160	-3.0	302	77.8	4.0	0.0	15.6	2.6	36.4	54.3	9.3	86	48.8	82.6	5.8
Frankclay CDP	221	NA	NA	93	100.0	0.0	0.0	0.0	0.0	0.0	38.7	61.3	56	73.2	62.5	0.0
Frankford city	323	322	-0.3	317	95.3	4.7	0.0	0.0	0.0	19.9	65.8	14.2	142	60.6	63.4	14.1
Franklin city	95	96	1.1	73	91.8	0.0	0.0	0.0	8.2	8.2	65.7	26.0	36	69.4	66.7	0.0
Fredericktown city	3,985	4,058	1.8	4,043	94.2	0.5	0.0	0.5	4.8	23.3	52.8	23.9	1,586	69.0	57.6	11.7
Freeburg village	437	430	-1.6	395	98.0	0.0	0.0	1.0	1.0	19.8	63.5	16.7	172	71.5	54.7	11.0
Freeman city	482	481	-0.2	529	93.6	0.0	0.0	1.9	4.5	30.8	59.4	9.6	206	78.6	40.3	8.3
Freistatt village	163	161	-1.2	191	90.6	0.0	0.0	2.6	6.8	13.6	65.5	20.9	91	56.0	79.1	7.7
Fremont CDP	129	NA	NA	38	100.0	0.0	0.0	0.0	0.0	0.0	71.1	28.9	18	100.0	100.0	0.0
Fremont Hills city	826	856	3.6	787	99.5	0.0	0.0	0.0	0.5	17.7	55.3	26.9	318	93.4	11.3	61.9
Frohna city	254	258	1.6	270	100.0	0.0	0.0	0.0	0.0	25.2	59.9	14.8	103	91.3	57.3	12.6
Frontenac city	3,482	3,539	1.6	3,512	92.2	3.8	2.5	1.0	0.5	21.8	55.6	22.7	1,374	88.8	5.2	84.1
Fulton city	12,790	12,864	0.6	12,791	82.1	10.1	1.4	3.8	2.5	17.3	69.9	12.6	4,161	52.6	43.5	24.5
Gainesville city	771	767	-0.5	733	96.9	0.0	0.0	0.8	2.3	21.4	59.2	19.5	396	42.2	57.6	10.6
Galena city	440	414	-5.9	629	85.1	1.0	0.0	2.5	11.4	35.7	51.6	12.6	214	64.5	62.6	7.9
Gallatin city	1,786	1,755	-1.7	1,715	97.5	0.1	0.5	0.7	1.2	24.5	52.0	23.4	739	66.4	55.5	20.3
Galt city	253	252	-0.4	264	97.3	0.0	1.5	0.0	1.1	20.1	55.7	24.2	140	70.7	62.1	3.6
Garden City city	1,642	1,628	-0.9	1,618	94.6	0.0	0.0	1.7	3.8	27.9	60.3	11.7	641	64.0	59.8	11.4
Gasconade city	223	215	-3.6	245	98.8	0.0	0.0	1.2	0.0	13.0	61.2	25.7	123	86.2	70.7	7.3
Gentry village	72	73	1.4	75	100.0	0.0	0.0	0.0	0.0	20.0	66.7	13.3	30	93.3	93.3	0.0
Gerald city	1,345	1,323	-1.6	1,358	96.8	1.5	0.0	0.0	1.6	30.9	53.9	15.1	502	64.9	58.6	15.1
Gerster town	25	24	-4.0	24	100.0	0.0	0.0	0.0	0.0	4.2	70.8	25.0	13	100.0	69.2	0.0
Gibbs village	107	106	-0.9	161	100.0	0.0	0.0	0.0	0.0	29.8	46.6	23.6	58	69.0	89.7	3.4
Gideon city	1,093	1,046	-4.3	1,021	99.3	0.3	0.0	0.0	0.4	26.0	54.3	19.7	373	61.7	64.9	14.7
Gilliam city	197	199	1.0	214	92.1	2.3	0.0	0.0	5.6	29.5	56.0	14.5	87	72.4	52.9	4.6
Gilman City city	383	365	-4.7	388	97.9	0.3	0.0	1.0	0.8	23.2	56.1	20.9	170	75.9	55.9	14.7
Ginger Blue village	61	61	0.0	40	97.5	0.0	0.0	0.0	2.5	0.0	87.5	12.5	26	53.8	76.9	11.5
Gladstone city	25,410	26,800	5.5	26,032	85.1	4.5	0.9	3.0	6.4	20.6	61.7	17.7	10,848	68.3	38.7	27.9
Glasgow city	1,103	1,105	0.2	1,346	90.8	2.7	0.0	4.2	2.4	28.3	54.4	17.2	474	81.2	55.5	22.8
Glasgow Village CDP	5,429	NA	NA	4,895	13.7	85.0	0.0	1.3	0.0	35.3	57.3	7.6	1,778	43.4	43.9	9.1
Glenaire city	545	577	5.9	551	94.4	0.0	1.5	1.1	3.1	27.0	56.1	16.7	225	91.1	45.8	20.9
Glen Allen town	85	86	1.2	84	100.0	0.0	0.0	0.0	0.0	26.2	62.0	11.9	31	51.6	71.0	0.0
Glendale city	5,925	5,925	0.0	5,926	95.9	0.3	1.6	1.4	0.8	30.1	56.7	13.3	2,159	97.0	4.0	79.0
Glen Echo Park village	160	160	0.0	122	11.5	83.6	0.0	0.0	4.9	27.1	51.5	21.3	44	95.5	15.9	43.2
Glenwood village	196	194	-1.0	204	100.0	0.0	0.0	0.0	0.0	26.5	59.1	14.7	80	67.5	53.8	6.3
Golden CDP	280	NA	NA	687	97.5	0.0	0.0	2.5	0.0	18.0	64.6	17.5	260	100.0	49.6	17.3
Golden City city	765	741	-3.1	689	92.7	0.3	0.0	3.2	3.8	24.3	56.1	19.7	349	57.3	58.5	7.4
Goodman town	1,249	1,244	-0.4	1,299	86.2	0.5	0.0	9.3	4.0	26.5	56.7	16.9	462	75.1	64.1	7.6
Goodnight village	18	18	0.0	4	100.0	0.0	0.0	0.0	0.0	0.0	0.0	100.0	2	100.0	100.0	0.0
Gordonville village	391	399	2.0	384	97.9	1.3	0.0	0.0	0.8	9.3	75.6	14.8	156	92.3	45.5	25.0
Goss town	0	0	0.0	0	0.0	0.0	0.0	0.0	0.0	0.0	0.0	0.0	0	0.0	0.0	0.0
Gower city	1,526	1,484	-2.8	1,598	94.4	1.9	0.0	2.3	1.4	28.8	54.8	16.3	558	78.1	43.7	24.7
Graham town	171	166	-2.9	191	97.4	0.0	0.0	2.6	0.0	29.8	43.8	26.2	73	83.6	64.4	5.5
Grain Valley city	12,853	13,236	3.0	13,037	88.6	1.9	0.0	2.9	6.6	34.1	58.2	7.8	4,438	62.7	37.8	24.4
Granby city	2,134	2,133	0.0	2,328	94.5	0.3	0.2	4.3	0.7	30.8	54.2	15.0	841	67.8	43.9	7.1
Grand Falls Plaza town	114	115	0.9	111	81.1	0.0	1.8	6.3	10.8	17.1	60.3	22.5	50	86.0	24.0	56.0
Grandin city	243	285	17.3	169	95.9	0.0	0.0	4.1	0.0	34.3	57.4	8.3	72	48.6	45.8	0.0
Grand Pass village	66	67	1.5	39	100.0	0.0	0.0	0.0	0.0	12.8	74.4	12.8	15	93.3	20.0	26.7
Grandview city	24,475	25,290	3.3	24,860	46.7	35.6	0.7	4.9	12.1	25.5	63.2	11.4	9,534	57.7	38.1	21.4
Granger village	34	34	0.0	14	100.0	0.0	0.0	0.0	0.0	14.3	35.7	50.0	8	100.0	50.0	0.0
Grant City town	859	818	-4.8	896	99.0	0.0	0.0	0.7	0.3	17.2	55.5	27.2	384	69.0	53.6	14.6
Grantwood Village town	863	865	0.2	881	96.8	0.3	0.9	0.0	1.9	22.0	56.9	20.9	350	94.6	14.3	63.1
Gravois Mills town	144	143	-0.7	164	100.0	0.0	0.0	0.0	0.0	35.4	53.5	11.0	51	58.8	90.2	0.0
Grayhawk CDP	525	NA	NA	748	93.6	0.0	0.0	0.0	6.4	19.5	67.3	13.1	275	100.0	42.5	2.5
Grayridge CDP	127	NA	NA	64	100.0	0.0	0.0	0.0	0.0	12.5	61.0	26.6	26	100.0	65.4	0.0

1 May be of any race.

Table A. All Places — **Population and Housing**

STATE City, town, township, borough, or CDP (county if applicable)	Population: 2010 census total population	Population: 2014 estimated population	Population: Percent change 2010–2014	Population: ACS total population estimate 2010–2014	Race and Hispanic or Latino origin (percent), 2010–2014: White alone, not Hispanic or Latino	Black alone, not Hispanic or Latino	Asian alone, not Hispanic or Latino	All other races or 2 or more races, not Hispanic or Latino	Hispanic or Latino[1]	Age (percent), 2010–2014: Under 18 years old	Age 18 to 64 years old	Age 65 years and older	Households, 2010–2014: Total occupied housing units	Percent owner occupied	Householders by level of education (percent): High school diploma or less	Bachelor's degree or more
	1	2	3	4	5	6	7	8	9	10	11	12	13	14	15	16
MISSOURI—Con.																
Gray Summit CDP	2,701	NA	NA	3,300	96.5	1.4	0.0	1.6	0.5	30.6	59.7	9.8	1,103	78.4	49.4	7.1
Greencastle city	275	257	-6.5	312	100.0	0.0	0.0	0.0	0.0	17.3	66.0	16.7	126	55.6	85.7	4.8
Green City city	657	625	-4.9	708	97.7	0.0	0.0	0.3	2.0	18.7	54.7	26.7	340	58.8	66.2	9.4
Greendale city	651	653	0.3	725	21.8	63.7	2.1	12.4	0.0	16.7	67.5	15.7	307	83.4	27.4	51.8
Greenfield city	1,371	1,323	-3.5	1,281	94.5	1.3	0.2	2.1	2.0	21.7	50.9	27.5	573	63.2	58.6	13.3
Green Park city	2,622	2,636	0.5	2,626	86.3	4.5	4.3	2.7	2.3	19.4	58.9	21.8	990	83.6	37.2	29.4
Green Ridge city	476	490	2.9	505	98.2	1.4	0.0	0.0	0.4	27.5	63.7	8.7	172	72.7	48.3	14.5
Greentop city	442	438	-0.9	453	96.5	0.9	1.8	0.2	0.7	27.2	49.9	23.2	188	67.6	55.9	13.3
Greenville city	495	491	-0.8	507	97.2	1.0	0.0	1.8	0.0	24.7	51.8	23.5	188	67.6	67.0	5.9
Greenwood city	5,218	5,476	4.9	5,322	87.8	2.2	2.8	4.2	3.0	32.5	61.0	6.6	1,823	89.1	29.3	35.2
Guilford town	85	83	-2.4	54	100.0	0.0	0.0	0.0	0.0	13.0	77.8	9.3	30	83.3	46.7	16.7
Gunn City village	118	118	0.0	85	92.9	7.1	0.0	0.0	0.0	37.6	60.0	2.4	22	72.7	81.8	4.5
Hale city	419	409	-2.4	463	92.2	1.3	0.0	5.4	1.1	27.1	57.3	15.8	176	71.6	58.0	13.1
Halfway village	173	172	-0.6	107	99.1	0.0	0.0	0.9	0.0	3.7	67.3	29.0	55	80.0	58.2	9.1
Hallsville city	1,491	1,543	3.5	1,678	96.5	0.4	0.2	1.0	1.8	33.2	54.0	12.9	645	76.4	43.6	26.8
Halltown village	173	171	-1.2	126	98.4	0.0	0.0	1.6	0.0	24.6	65.9	9.5	54	51.9	68.5	9.3
Hamilton city	1,809	1,717	-5.1	1,776	93.8	0.3	0.0	0.7	5.2	24.5	51.4	24.2	759	59.9	62.5	9.4
Hanley Hills village	2,119	2,124	0.2	2,109	8.4	90.4	0.0	1.2	0.0	21.3	68.6	10.1	952	57.4	44.7	12.2
Hannibal city	17,916	17,893	-0.1	17,779	86.8	8.1	1.0	1.8	2.3	22.4	61.3	16.1	7,060	60.8	49.0	20.9
Hardin city	569	548	-3.7	609	89.7	0.0	0.0	1.5	8.9	24.0	66.5	9.4	225	74.2	60.9	9.3
Harris town	61	59	-3.3	49	98.0	0.0	0.0	0.0	2.0	2.0	63.3	34.7	35	57.1	51.4	0.0
Harrisburg town	266	274	3.0	293	100.0	0.0	0.0	0.0	0.0	32.7	55.2	11.9	122	63.9	31.1	18.9
Harrisonville city	10,019	9,983	-0.4	10,019	93.8	1.4	0.0	1.2	3.5	26.1	57.1	16.8	4,012	58.8	45.2	20.9
Hartsburg town	103	104	1.0	114	96.5	0.0	0.0	0.9	2.6	15.8	60.5	23.7	69	59.4	33.3	27.5
Hartville city	613	598	-2.4	727	88.7	8.0	0.0	1.8	1.5	25.2	57.2	17.6	255	62.4	60.8	18.0
Hartwell CDP	16	NA	NA	0	0.0	0.0	0.0	0.0	0.0	0.0	0.0	0.0	0	0.0	0.0	0.0
Harviell CDP	106	NA	NA	342	100.0	0.0	0.0	0.0	0.0	55.9	44.1	0.0	125	16.8	83.2	16.8
Harwood village	47	47	0.0	103	100.0	0.0	0.0	0.0	0.0	28.1	65.1	6.8	33	72.7	54.5	6.1
Hawk Point city	669	679	1.5	729	75.2	1.8	6.7	5.8	10.6	37.7	54.1	8.2	208	56.3	55.8	10.6
Hayti city	2,939	2,818	-4.1	2,883	45.2	51.4	0.0	1.7	1.8	29.0	55.6	15.4	1,147	45.9	66.2	8.8
Hayti Heights city	626	597	-4.6	544	1.1	98.2	0.0	0.6	0.2	36.6	50.4	13.1	218	42.2	78.9	0.9
Hayward CDP	131	NA	NA	105	100.0	0.0	0.0	0.0	0.0	19.0	78.0	2.9	44	54.5	47.7	0.0
Haywood City village	206	204	-1.0	148	0.7	91.2	0.0	8.1	0.0	21.0	64.3	14.9	50	64.0	82.0	12.0
Hazelwood city	25,700	25,666	-0.1	25,671	58.1	32.9	2.4	3.4	3.1	23.0	65.0	12.2	10,799	63.1	34.7	25.9
Henrietta city	369	363	-1.6	352	84.1	9.4	0.0	1.4	5.1	15.3	63.9	20.7	109	74.3	74.3	4.6
Herculaneum city	3,468	3,843	10.8	3,684	88.5	4.9	0.9	5.1	0.6	28.1	56.1	15.9	1,281	78.6	45.7	13.4
Hermann city	2,431	2,378	-2.2	2,400	96.5	2.7	0.5	0.0	0.4	19.4	56.0	24.7	1,067	60.7	52.3	22.4
Hermitage city	469	458	-2.3	695	94.8	3.5	0.0	1.2	0.6	21.9	55.8	22.4	254	52.4	58.3	13.8
Higbee city	568	554	-2.5	572	98.6	0.0	0.0	0.5	0.9	23.2	59.9	16.8	239	85.4	49.0	6.7
Higginsville city	4,786	4,670	-2.4	4,740	93.5	2.4	0.0	0.7	3.4	24.3	51.6	24.2	1,909	65.0	53.9	22.4
High Hill city	195	188	-3.6	238	95.4	0.0	0.0	0.0	4.6	23.6	58.5	18.1	106	78.3	56.6	10.4
Highlandville city	912	934	2.4	1,114	99.2	0.0	0.0	0.8	0.0	29.0	63.5	7.5	396	87.6	45.7	22.2
High Ridge CDP	4,305	NA	NA	3,849	96.7	0.0	0.2	1.5	1.6	21.6	66.5	12.0	1,580	86.1	51.3	16.7
Hillsboro city	2,834	3,021	6.6	2,940	88.8	1.6	0.4	8.1	1.2	30.5	61.1	8.3	927	60.1	33.7	15.9
Hillsdale village	1,478	1,516	2.6	1,337	4.0	95.2	0.0	0.7	0.0	29.5	61.4	9.1	467	49.5	54.2	8.8
Hoberg village	56	56	0.0	46	95.7	0.0	0.0	4.3	0.0	17.4	80.4	2.2	17	100.0	76.5	0.0
Holcomb city	635	617	-2.8	790	98.1	0.0	0.0	0.0	1.9	33.6	50.6	15.6	275	62.5	65.5	11.3
Holden city	2,252	2,291	1.7	2,482	91.5	2.7	0.0	0.0	5.8	24.0	61.5	14.5	943	65.0	49.2	14.0
Holland town	229	222	-3.1	235	95.7	0.0	0.0	0.0	4.3	21.7	64.6	13.6	81	79.0	67.9	2.5
Holliday village	137	134	-2.2	97	95.9	0.0	4.1	0.0	0.0	23.7	55.7	20.6	41	87.8	68.3	14.6
Hollister city	4,426	4,481	1.2	4,436	88.1	0.0	0.0	5.0	6.9	22.9	57.5	19.6	1,736	47.8	59.7	13.2
Holt city	456	470	3.1	481	94.8	0.0	0.0	4.0	1.2	28.9	53.0	18.1	193	61.7	56.5	6.7
Holts Summit city	3,247	3,522	8.5	3,381	93.0	1.0	1.5	4.4	0.0	24.4	65.2	10.4	1,345	65.2	43.3	28.7
Homestead village	185	186	0.5	157	91.7	0.0	0.0	1.3	7.0	21.0	61.9	17.2	64	78.1	60.9	4.7
Homestown city	151	146	-3.3	126	0.0	100.0	0.0	0.0	0.0	19.9	64.3	15.9	38	89.5	76.3	10.5
Hopkins city	532	509	-4.3	471	97.0	0.0	0.0	3.0	0.0	29.5	58.7	11.9	205	62.9	62.4	14.6
Horine CDP	821	NA	NA	1,566	98.4	0.0	0.0	0.0	1.6	30.8	62.2	7.0	440	69.1	66.4	5.2
Hornersville city	663	645	-2.7	844	89.9	0.0	0.5	2.5	7.1	33.8	57.5	8.9	292	59.6	63.0	3.4
Houston city	2,081	2,078	-0.1	2,208	89.4	2.0	0.0	5.9	2.7	27.1	54.6	18.3	833	55.5	45.9	17.8
Houstonia city	220	221	0.5	216	100.0	0.0	0.0	0.0	0.0	23.6	62.6	13.9	83	75.9	60.2	12.0
Houston Lake city	235	243	3.4	290	90.3	0.7	1.0	1.7	6.2	16.8	66.9	16.2	109	81.7	32.1	21.1
Howardville city	383	369	-3.7	353	3.7	91.2	0.0	4.0	1.1	28.8	55.2	15.9	157	38.9	72.6	4.5
Hughesville village	183	184	0.5	176	98.9	0.0	1.1	0.0	0.0	28.4	59.7	11.9	69	82.6	60.9	4.3
Humansville city	1,048	1,037	-1.0	1,208	93.2	3.4	0.0	2.9	0.5	24.4	52.3	23.3	377	61.3	72.9	8.2
Hume town	336	328	-2.4	335	86.3	0.0	0.9	6.0	6.9	30.5	59.6	10.1	113	74.3	69.9	12.4
Humphreys village	118	114	-3.4	93	100.0	0.0	0.0	0.0	0.0	30.1	49.6	20.4	45	68.9	75.6	2.2
Hunnewell city	184	178	-3.3	120	95.0	0.0	0.0	5.0	0.0	5.0	63.4	31.7	67	65.7	64.2	0.0
Hunter CDP	168	NA	NA	95	100.0	0.0	0.0	0.0	0.0	45.3	50.5	4.2	33	84.8	51.5	0.0
Huntleigh city	334	335	0.3	468	88.0	7.1	4.7	0.0	0.2	29.3	55.7	15.2	147	98.0	6.8	74.1
Huntsdale town	31	32	3.2	30	90.0	0.0	0.0	10.0	0.0	0.0	83.2	16.7	13	61.5	46.2	23.1
Huntsville city	1,565	1,525	-2.6	1,598	85.3	4.1	0.1	2.7	7.9	30.1	56.2	13.6	550	64.0	60.4	15.3
Hurdland city	163	159	-2.5	166	94.0	0.0	0.0	6.0	0.0	27.1	51.6	21.1	68	85.3	60.3	22.1
Hurley city	178	171	-3.9	189	95.2	0.0	0.0	4.8	0.0	31.7	60.9	7.4	63	63.5	69.8	3.2
Iatan village	45	47	4.4	36	100.0	0.0	0.0	0.0	0.0	11.1	64.0	25.0	16	68.8	100.0	0.0
Iberia city	736	745	1.2	605	94.9	0.0	0.0	4.8	0.3	20.4	56.0	23.6	304	62.8	67.4	16.8
Imperial CDP	4,709	NA	NA	4,630	96.2	0.0	0.1	1.8	2.0	21.9	63.3	15.0	1,742	87.8	48.0	20.6
Independence city	116,828	117,494	0.6	117,160	80.0	7.0	1.2	3.1	8.8	22.4	60.8	16.8	48,170	64.7	47.3	19.1
Indian Point village	528	516	-2.3	555	94.2	0.0	0.0	0.4	5.4	21.4	49.4	29.2	223	78.5	41.3	21.5
Innsbrook village	552	575	4.2	611	98.0	0.7	0.0	1.3	0.0	8.0	41.3	50.6	275	97.1	19.3	61.5
Ionia town	88	87	-1.1	111	100.0	0.0	0.0	0.0	0.0	11.7	72.9	15.3	51	62.7	88.2	0.0
Irena village	18	17	-5.6	17	100.0	0.0	0.0	0.0	0.0	0.0	76.4	23.5	9	100.0	55.6	22.2
Irondale city	445	449	0.9	559	99.3	0.0	0.0	0.7	0.0	41.1	49.5	9.3	162	77.2	67.3	0.0
Iron Mountain Lake city	737	713	-3.3	838	98.7	0.0	0.0	0.6	0.7	27.9	56.7	15.4	321	78.2	69.5	6.5
Ironton city	1,462	1,412	-3.4	1,513	95.0	3.2	0.0	0.6	1.2	21.0	63.7	15.3	582	61.7	51.9	14.1
Irwin CDP	69	NA	NA	18	100.0	0.0	0.0	0.0	0.0	0.0	100.0	0.0	10	100.0	100.0	0.0
Jackson city	13,748	14,677	6.8	14,221	94.8	1.0	0.4	1.6	2.1	25.6	59.6	14.8	5,531	66.4	45.4	24.9
Jacksonville village	150	149	-0.7	167	92.8	3.0	0.0	4.2	0.0	18.6	72.6	9.0	61	85.2	50.8	4.9
Jameson town	133	131	-1.5	153	100.0	0.0	0.0	0.0	0.0	19.6	69.2	11.1	70	61.4	61.4	24.3
Jamesport city	524	511	-2.5	528	96.8	0.0	0.0	0.0	3.2	29.4	58.3	12.3	214	55.1	65.0	7.0
Jamestown town	386	388	0.5	377	95.5	0.0	0.0	4.5	0.0	28.4	55.7	15.9	152	69.7	68.4	17.1
Jane town	309	300	-2.9	422	62.6	0.0	0.0	3.6	33.9	33.4	45.7	20.9	155	80.6	69.7	11.0

1 May be of any race.

Table A. All Places — **Population and Housing**

STATE City, town, township, borough, or CDP (county if applicable)	Population				Race and Hispanic or Latino origin (percent), 2010–2014					Age (percent), 2010–2014			Households, 2010–2014			
	2010 census total population	2014 estimated population	Percent change 2010–2014	ACS total population estimate 2010–2014	White alone, not Hispanic or Latino	Black alone, not Hispanic or Latino	Asian alone, not Hispanic or Latino	All other races or 2 or more races, not Hispanic or Latino	Hispanic or Latino[1]	Under 18 years old	Age 18 to 64 years old	Age 65 years and older	Total occupied housing units	Percent owner occupied	Householders by level of education (percent): High school diploma or less	Householders by level of education (percent): Bachelor's degree or more
	1	2	3	4	5	6	7	8	9	10	11	12	13	14	15	16
MISSOURI—Con.																
Jasper city	931	921	-1.1	997	93.9	0.0	1.2	4.2	0.7	25.5	62.7	11.5	403	64.5	65.0	18.4
Jefferson City city	43,088	43,132	0.1	43,184	75.3	17.0	1.5	4.2	2.0	21.5	65.2	13.3	16,829	59.0	28.3	39.3
Jennings city	14,743	14,737	0.0	14,730	6.1	92.6	0.1	0.5	0.7	24.9	62.0	13.0	6,183	54.9	49.3	12.3
Jerico Springs village	228	229	0.4	223	78.5	0.0	1.8	13.0	6.7	18.8	60.1	21.1	98	88.8	56.1	1.0
Jonesburg city	765	739	-3.4	796	88.2	0.0	0.0	3.4	8.4	20.2	53.3	26.4	304	60.9	62.8	13.5
Joplin city	50,788	51,316	1.0	50,900	85.3	3.8	1.4	5.7	3.8	21.9	63.2	14.7	20,914	57.2	39.9	24.1
Josephville village	376	384	2.1	386	95.1	1.0	0.0	2.6	1.3	18.9	60.0	21.0	161	93.2	49.1	25.5
Junction City village	327	326	-0.3	435	94.7	0.0	0.0	1.6	3.7	27.3	54.7	17.9	170	18.2	51.8	5.3
Kahoka city	2,082	2,050	-1.5	1,885	98.2	0.5	0.0	1.3	0.0	24.3	56.7	18.9	815	58.5	50.2	9.7
Kansas City city	459,787	470,800	2.4	465,005	55.1	28.9	2.4	3.4	10.1	23.8	64.7	11.5	192,799	55.4	34.4	33.5
Kearney city	8,370	9,261	10.6	8,845	92.9	0.2	0.0	3.3	3.6	31.0	60.0	8.9	3,118	71.1	31.4	35.2
Kelso village	586	593	1.2	508	98.8	0.0	0.0	0.0	1.2	18.5	67.6	14.0	219	91.3	49.3	27.4
Kennett city	10,932	10,796	-1.2	11,002	79.2	13.7	0.0	1.7	5.3	25.5	58.1	16.4	4,389	53.9	64.0	13.4
Keytesville city	471	461	-2.1	532	99.2	0.2	0.0	0.2	0.4	17.9	59.5	22.6	240	62.5	65.0	14.6
Kidder city	323	310	-4.0	276	96.0	0.0	0.0	1.1	2.9	23.2	57.9	18.8	117	68.4	60.7	10.3
Kimberling City city	2,445	2,335	-4.5	2,573	97.2	0.0	0.0	0.0	2.8	12.8	50.6	36.6	1,145	73.4	35.8	27.1
Kimmswick city	157	158	0.6	159	99.4	0.6	0.0	0.0	0.0	28.3	60.9	10.7	54	92.6	27.8	18.5
King City city	1,013	1,028	1.5	949	98.2	0.1	0.5	1.2	0.0	28.5	51.9	19.8	380	67.9	58.7	20.8
Kingdom City village	128	130	1.6	108	99.1	0.0	0.9	0.0	0.0	8.3	72.3	19.4	45	86.7	66.7	6.7
Kingston city	348	339	-2.6	322	95.7	4.3	0.0	0.0	0.0	12.7	70.2	17.1	111	51.4	61.3	6.3
Kingsville city	269	275	2.2	306	97.4	0.0	0.0	2.0	0.7	23.8	52.1	24.2	128	62.5	60.2	9.4
Kinloch city	298	299	0.3	234	5.6	93.6	0.0	0.9	0.0	22.2	64.9	12.8	112	19.6	75.0	0.0
Kirbyville village	207	212	2.4	247	97.2	0.0	0.0	2.8	0.0	27.9	62.5	9.3	91	41.8	60.4	24.2
Kirksville city	17,505	17,633	0.7	17,578	88.9	3.0	3.0	1.7	3.4	15.7	72.7	11.5	6,470	46.3	32.7	31.9
Kirkwood city	27,540	27,660	0.4	27,587	88.1	6.8	1.3	1.6	2.3	22.0	59.9	18.2	12,011	77.0	14.8	62.0
Kissee Mills CDP	1,109	NA	NA	1,172	98.6	0.0	0.0	1.4	0.0	18.0	62.5	19.3	536	74.8	65.9	19.8
Knob Noster city	2,712	2,792	2.9	2,761	73.9	9.1	1.2	9.5	6.3	22.0	69.8	8.3	1,183	44.5	31.9	10.6
Knox City city	216	211	-2.3	211	100.0	0.0	0.0	0.0	0.0	18.6	66.9	14.7	113	70.8	67.3	0.9
Koshkonong town	209	212	1.4	248	86.7	0.0	0.0	13.3	0.0	20.6	62.8	16.5	104	54.8	63.5	7.7
LaBarque Creek CDP	1,558	NA	NA	1,758	98.4	0.0	0.0	1.5	0.1	22.4	68.2	9.2	616	97.7	15.6	47.2
La Belle city	660	653	-1.1	593	91.9	6.2	0.0	0.0	1.9	20.9	54.8	24.3	267	66.3	70.4	4.5
Laclede city	345	328	-4.9	294	100.0	0.0	0.0	0.0	0.0	17.3	54.2	28.6	137	73.7	75.9	2.9
Laddonia city	513	511	-0.4	517	97.1	1.4	0.0	1.5	0.0	24.9	60.6	14.5	222	76.6	65.3	4.1
La Due village	28	NA	NA	30	100.0	0.0	0.0	0.0	0.0	6.7	83.4	10.0	13	100.0	100.0	0.0
Ladue city	8,521	8,576	0.6	8,549	90.0	1.7	5.6	0.4	2.2	25.8	55.5	18.8	2,972	95.7	2.8	89.2
La Grange city	931	932	0.1	1,021	75.9	13.8	0.0	9.9	0.4	25.0	60.7	14.3	415	63.9	58.8	8.4
Lake Annette city	100	100	0.0	111	100.0	0.0	0.0	0.0	0.0	18.0	66.6	15.3	49	55.1	65.3	4.1
Lake Lafayette city	327	323	-1.2	372	88.7	7.3	0.0	4.0	0.0	21.5	65.6	12.9	138	84.1	59.4	6.5
Lake Lotawana city	1,939	1,984	2.3	2,138	99.0	0.0	0.0	1.0	0.0	20.3	64.0	15.7	886	81.2	23.1	44.2
Lake Mykee Town village	350	355	1.4	486	98.8	0.0	0.4	0.0	0.8	22.4	61.9	15.6	163	92.6	25.2	44.8
Lake Ozark city	1,586	1,676	5.7	1,588	96.0	0.0	1.3	1.8	0.8	18.6	57.8	23.7	668	75.3	36.1	27.5
Lake St. Louis city	14,558	15,014	3.1	14,759	88.5	4.2	1.9	1.2	4.1	23.8	59.5	16.7	5,767	73.5	23.4	43.9
Lakeshire city	1,432	1,429	-0.2	1,690	86.9	2.7	0.0	1.5	8.8	21.2	64.5	14.4	812	31.3	32.9	31.3
Lakeside city	0	0	0.0	0	0.0	0.0	0.0	0.0	0.0	0.0	0.0	0.0	0	0.0	0.0	0.0
Lake Tapawingo city	730	726	-0.5	632	96.0	0.3	0.5	2.1	1.1	8.7	65.7	25.6	315	88.3	21.3	48.6
Lake Tekakwitha village	254	255	0.4	232	92.7	0.0	0.4	0.9	6.0	17.2	72.8	9.9	97	89.7	44.3	8.2
Lake Viking CDP	483	NA	NA	368	94.6	0.3	0.0	1.9	3.3	4.4	43.2	52.4	206	95.6	49.0	12.6
Lake Waukomis city	870	897	3.1	936	97.1	0.0	0.3	1.5	1.1	14.0	63.1	22.9	439	93.2	18.0	43.1
Lake Winnebago city	1,131	1,136	0.4	1,297	98.8	0.0	0.3	0.0	0.8	23.3	56.2	20.5	491	96.9	10.6	59.9
Lamar city	4,532	4,426	-2.3	4,499	91.6	0.6	2.8	4.1	1.0	27.2	53.5	19.4	1,835	69.0	54.1	19.0
Lamar Heights city	178	174	-2.2	182	96.7	0.0	0.0	3.3	0.0	21.3	61.9	16.5	89	56.2	64.0	20.2
Lambert village	0	0	0.0	0	0.0	0.0	0.0	0.0	0.0	0.0	0.0	0.0	0	0.0	0.0	0.0
La Monte city	1,140	1,135	-0.4	1,376	49.9	1.5	0.0	0.5	48.1	33.2	58.1	8.8	452	55.8	63.3	10.8
Lanagan town	423	414	-2.1	498	79.3	3.0	0.0	6.6	11.0	28.7	63.0	8.0	175	38.9	66.3	3.4
Lancaster city	728	714	-1.9	751	96.1	3.6	0.0	0.3	0.0	25.2	55.5	19.4	344	61.0	54.7	12.5
La Plata city	1,366	1,350	-1.2	1,446	99.5	0.0	0.0	0.3	0.1	23.2	54.9	21.8	587	65.1	50.6	10.7
Laredo city	198	197	-0.5	215	96.7	0.0	1.9	1.4	0.0	22.3	57.2	20.5	90	81.1	55.6	10.0
La Russell city	114	113	-0.9	292	55.1	0.0	0.0	44.9	0.0	45.9	51.6	2.4	59	81.4	72.9	1.7
Lathrop city	2,086	2,019	-3.2	2,166	92.2	2.5	0.5	1.6	3.2	27.9	58.4	13.7	856	58.9	47.1	15.2
La Tour CDP	62	NA	NA	65	100.0	0.0	0.0	0.0	0.0	0.0	80.0	20.0	35	80.0	100.0	0.0
Laurie city	945	932	-1.4	931	97.2	1.7	0.0	0.0	1.1	8.4	45.3	46.4	454	54.2	55.5	7.5
Lawson city	2,473	2,423	-2.0	2,296	94.4	0.0	0.6	1.4	3.6	27.3	59.5	13.2	880	70.7	58.9	12.5
Leadington city	422	434	2.8	541	93.0	0.0	2.2	0.0	4.8	24.7	64.7	10.7	215	51.6	60.0	8.8
Leadwood city	1,282	1,234	-3.7	1,557	98.8	0.0	0.0	0.2	1.0	31.9	58.7	9.4	570	54.7	60.9	6.1
Leasburg village	338	336	-0.6	483	96.9	2.7	0.0	0.4	0.0	31.4	58.6	9.9	174	66.1	60.9	13.2
Leawood village	678	676	-0.3	719	90.4	1.1	1.7	2.6	4.2	29.0	55.2	15.7	251	83.3	35.1	35.1
Lebanon city	14,474	14,650	1.2	14,595	92.9	0.7	1.2	3.3	1.9	25.1	57.9	17.0	6,007	53.7	56.9	11.7
Lee's Summit city	91,388	93,864	2.7	92,813	81.9	8.7	2.3	3.2	3.9	27.7	60.2	12.1	33,785	76.0	21.9	44.1
Leeton city	566	571	0.9	764	91.0	2.0	0.5	3.1	3.4	29.7	56.5	13.7	287	70.7	51.6	10.1
Leisure Lake CDP	160	NA	NA	189	97.4	0.0	0.0	2.6	0.0	20.6	53.3	25.9	88	83.0	52.3	9.1
Lemay CDP	16,645	NA	NA	16,239	90.9	2.6	1.4	3.0	2.1	21.2	62.0	16.5	6,533	75.3	53.5	17.8
Leonard village	61	59	-3.3	54	100.0	0.0	0.0	0.0	0.0	26.0	38.9	35.2	24	100.0	62.5	16.7
Leslie village	170	169	-0.6	172	100.0	0.0	0.0	0.0	0.0	40.1	54.6	5.2	62	46.8	67.7	8.1
Levasy city	83	83	0.0	87	95.4	0.0	0.0	4.6	0.0	22.9	55.1	21.8	31	77.4	48.4	25.8
Lewis and Clark Village town	132	132	0.0	123	95.9	0.0	0.0	4.1	0.0	31.7	59.4	8.9	41	70.7	43.9	9.8
Lewistown town	534	527	-1.3	542	99.1	0.0	0.0	0.9	0.0	27.4	54.1	18.6	228	73.7	73.7	5.7
Lexington city	4,727	4,604	-2.6	4,676	83.7	8.2	0.6	4.2	3.3	17.7	61.9	20.4	2,082	73.3	46.5	22.4
Liberal city	759	733	-3.4	744	98.8	0.0	0.0	0.7	0.5	24.1	57.7	18.1	323	59.4	60.4	7.4
Liberty city	29,155	30,376	4.2	29,806	89.5	4.0	0.6	2.3	3.4	24.5	63.4	12.1	10,779	75.5	29.8	38.5
Licking city	3,124	3,109	-0.5	2,992	75.8	17.4	0.0	3.7	3.0	14.9	74.0	11.2	714	44.0	56.6	13.2
Lilbourn city	1,195	1,142	-4.4	1,055	57.4	41.2	0.0	0.4	0.9	23.3	60.0	16.7	436	64.0	63.8	8.9
Lincoln city	1,190	1,181	-0.8	1,171	98.7	0.6	0.0	0.7	0.0	22.7	54.7	22.5	475	63.6	62.5	8.0
Linn city	1,459	1,439	-1.4	1,701	96.8	0.1	0.0	2.7	0.4	25.4	64.2	10.2	666	55.4	45.6	13.7
Linn Creek city	244	244	0.0	257	86.4	0.0	0.0	6.6	7.0	12.1	72.4	15.6	102	81.4	28.4	20.6
Linneus city	278	270	-2.9	326	98.2	0.0	0.0	0.0	1.8	19.3	70.2	10.4	154	53.9	75.3	10.4
Lithium village	89	NA	NA	101	100.0	0.0	0.0	0.0	0.0	29.8	64.3	5.9	38	100.0	100.0	0.0
Livonia village	74	72	-2.7	94	94.7	0.0	0.0	4.3	1.1	22.3	62.8	14.9	46	69.6	76.1	0.0
Loch Lloyd village	600	679	13.2	722	93.4	4.2	0.6	0.0	1.9	15.1	56.1	28.7	324	95.4	8.3	68.8
Lock Springs village	57	56	-1.8	61	90.2	0.0	0.0	9.8	0.0	40.9	57.3	1.6	15	93.3	53.3	13.3
Lockwood city	936	910	-2.8	1,062	93.4	0.6	0.0	6.0	0.0	24.6	54.4	21.0	404	76.5	53.7	18.1

1 May be of any race.

Table A. All Places — **Population and Housing**

STATE City, town, township, borough, or CDP (county if applicable)	Population: 2010 census total population	Population: 2014 estimated population	Population: Percent change 2010–2014	Population: ACS total population estimate 2010–2014	Race and Hispanic or Latino origin (percent), 2010–2014: White alone, not Hispanic or Latino	Black alone, not Hispanic or Latino	Asian alone, not Hispanic or Latino	All other races or 2 or more races, not Hispanic or Latino	Hispanic or Latino[1]	Age (percent), 2010–2014: Under 18 years old	Age 18 to 64 years old	Age 65 years and older	Households, 2010–2014: Total occupied housing units	Percent owner occupied	Householders by level of education (percent): High school diploma or less	Bachelor's degree or more
	1	2	3	4	5	6	7	8	9	10	11	12	13	14	15	16
MISSOURI—Con.																
Lohman city	163	162	-0.6	174	90.2	0.0	0.6	1.1	8.0	22.9	64.8	12.1	65	86.2	55.4	18.5
Loma Linda town	725	764	5.4	800	88.8	1.3	0.9	7.1	2.0	16.0	61.1	23.1	328	80.8	23.8	48.8
Lone Jack city	1,050	1,081	3.0	983	91.8	2.3	1.5	1.0	3.4	33.6	58.2	8.2	327	70.6	40.4	20.5
Longtown town	102	103	1.0	116	92.2	0.0	0.0	0.0	7.8	29.3	63.0	7.8	39	89.7	46.2	2.6
Louisburg village	122	121	-0.8	143	71.3	0.0	0.0	24.5	4.2	31.5	50.4	18.2	62	93.5	43.5	1.6
Louisiana city	3,364	3,319	-1.3	3,340	87.2	1.6	0.0	6.5	4.8	25.9	57.4	16.6	1,352	59.3	66.9	11.1
Lowry City city	642	624	-2.8	458	97.6	2.0	0.0	0.0	0.4	15.2	50.2	34.5	206	69.4	71.8	8.7
Lucerne village	85	83	-2.4	110	100.0	0.0	0.0	0.0	0.0	19.1	45.5	35.5	54	100.0	81.5	0.0
Ludlow town	137	133	-2.9	145	100.0	0.0	0.0	0.0	0.0	15.8	71.0	13.1	66	51.5	90.9	1.5
Lupus town	33	34	3.0	27	100.0	0.0	0.0	0.0	0.0	3.7	88.9	7.4	15	100.0	26.7	66.7
Luray village	99	96	-3.0	66	100.0	0.0	0.0	0.0	0.0	21.2	72.6	6.1	24	75.0	66.7	0.0
McBaine town	10	10	0.0	8	75.0	0.0	0.0	25.0	0.0	0.0	100.0	0.0	8	62.5	0.0	37.5
McCord Bend village	297	277	-6.7	284	92.6	0.0	0.0	4.2	3.2	12.7	66.2	21.1	115	67.0	67.0	8.7
McFall city	93	95	2.2	121	95.0	0.0	0.0	4.1	0.8	29.0	59.4	11.6	48	52.1	62.5	18.8
Mackenzie village	133	133	0.0	122	100.0	0.0	0.0	0.0	0.0	9.0	74.5	16.4	60	91.7	26.7	43.3
McKittrick town	61	59	-3.3	60	100.0	0.0	0.0	0.0	0.0	11.6	63.4	25.0	34	67.6	64.7	5.9
Macks Creek CDP	244	NA	NA	426	85.0	0.0	0.0	12.7	2.3	28.7	60.1	11.3	144	64.6	54.2	7.6
Macon city	5,471	5,482	0.2	5,476	90.0	7.0	0.6	1.2	1.2	24.9	53.3	21.6	2,127	63.6	56.2	19.6
Madison city	554	536	-3.2	655	96.3	0.0	0.0	2.3	1.4	30.9	52.0	16.9	267	71.9	64.8	4.1
Maitland city	344	311	-9.6	354	98.9	0.0	0.0	0.6	0.6	25.4	63.0	11.6	150	60.0	56.0	3.3
Malden city	4,275	4,184	-2.1	4,425	62.7	30.2	0.1	4.5	2.4	28.4	56.0	15.7	1,761	54.6	68.3	10.3
Malta Bend town	250	252	0.8	348	95.7	4.3	0.0	0.0	0.0	29.6	62.2	8.0	116	87.1	67.2	5.2
Manchester city	18,095	18,197	0.6	18,125	81.7	5.0	8.4	1.8	3.1	22.9	65.0	12.0	6,921	76.4	16.1	53.7
Mansfield city	1,296	1,262	-2.6	1,185	94.7	0.0	0.0	4.5	0.8	24.3	60.4	15.4	532	52.8	63.3	11.1
Maplewood city	8,019	7,959	-0.7	7,987	74.9	16.8	2.1	4.2	2.0	13.8	77.5	8.6	4,509	40.6	26.2	39.2
Marble Hill city	1,492	1,509	1.1	1,698	88.3	1.8	4.1	0.5	5.2	28.4	55.3	16.1	614	52.9	63.0	8.5
Marceline city	2,233	2,154	-3.5	2,239	97.5	0.0	0.0	0.2	2.2	27.6	55.7	16.7	847	65.6	63.2	14.4
Marionville city	2,230	2,184	-2.1	2,242	94.5	0.5	0.0	5.0	0.0	24.6	51.7	23.7	895	62.1	59.3	12.2
Marlborough village	2,179	2,188	0.4	2,206	83.3	6.0	6.6	0.0	4.1	8.8	80.8	10.4	1,404	12.0	16.0	41.1
Marquand city	203	207	2.0	325	97.2	0.0	0.0	2.8	0.0	29.2	62.2	8.6	109	69.7	52.3	3.7
Marshall city	13,061	13,042	-0.1	13,059	75.6	6.7	0.5	3.9	13.3	23.6	61.7	14.8	4,784	59.4	54.8	19.1
Marshfield city	6,679	6,977	4.5	6,789	90.9	1.6	0.7	3.2	3.5	31.0	54.2	14.8	2,661	50.2	49.6	15.9
Marston city	503	480	-4.6	527	69.8	23.5	0.0	6.6	0.0	31.3	61.4	7.2	180	37.8	73.9	0.0
Marthasville city	1,136	1,145	0.8	1,416	97.1	0.0	0.0	1.1	1.8	36.5	56.6	6.9	514	68.3	38.9	18.3
Martinsburg town	304	307	1.0	355	97.7	1.4	0.0	0.0	0.8	25.4	58.6	16.1	141	70.2	54.6	17.0
Maryland Heights city	27,473	27,405	-0.2	27,420	67.2	11.3	10.3	4.6	6.6	20.9	67.3	11.8	11,641	57.3	21.4	44.4
Maryville city	11,999	12,007	0.1	12,018	91.6	3.5	2.3	1.2	1.5	11.3	77.1	11.6	4,547	37.5	34.0	24.0
Matthews city	628	631	0.5	745	95.6	0.0	0.0	0.0	4.4	24.1	48.9	27.0	267	63.7	77.2	3.4
Maysville city	1,114	1,094	-1.8	1,040	95.7	1.3	0.0	1.7	1.3	20.5	58.5	21.3	426	59.4	54.7	18.1
Mayview city	212	208	-1.9	363	64.2	7.2	0.0	27.3	1.4	41.8	49.5	8.8	118	86.4	78.8	2.5
Meadville city	462	449	-2.8	448	95.3	0.0	0.0	1.1	3.6	28.4	56.2	15.4	151	82.1	56.3	19.9
Mehlville CDP	28,380	NA	NA	29,413	88.1	3.0	2.3	3.4	3.1	18.8	62.6	18.5	12,973	65.0	39.1	26.6
Memphis city	1,822	1,835	0.7	1,913	98.5	1.0	0.0	0.0	0.4	26.7	49.4	23.8	838	66.9	48.3	14.0
Mendon city	171	169	-1.2	168	97.0	1.2	0.0	0.6	1.2	28.7	47.7	23.8	65	80.0	58.5	18.5
Mercer town	317	314	-0.9	461	93.7	1.5	0.7	4.1	0.0	22.4	54.2	23.4	208	75.0	60.1	8.2
Merriam Woods village	1,761	1,763	0.1	1,812	91.2	0.0	0.4	5.6	2.8	26.0	60.9	13.1	705	67.8	51.1	11.6
Merwin village	58	57	-1.7	42	100.0	0.0	0.0	0.0	0.0	11.9	78.5	9.5	22	95.5	81.8	4.5
Meta city	229	228	-0.4	208	100.0	0.0	0.0	0.0	0.0	22.7	62.6	14.9	90	80.0	70.0	8.9
Metz town	49	49	0.0	42	92.9	0.0	0.0	7.1	0.0	28.5	50.0	21.4	18	94.4	66.7	0.0
Mexico city	11,543	11,664	1.0	11,555	85.9	7.3	0.2	3.6	3.0	26.7	56.5	16.8	4,478	64.0	58.6	14.3
Miami city	175	177	1.1	194	81.4	4.6	0.0	13.9	0.0	30.4	48.3	21.1	63	85.7	42.9	3.2
Middletown town	167	161	-3.6	177	97.2	0.0	0.0	2.8	0.0	22.6	53.7	23.7	86	74.4	82.6	0.0
Milan city	1,960	1,870	-4.6	2,142	56.1	2.2	0.2	0.7	40.8	26.0	61.5	12.3	760	55.3	67.4	7.4
Milford village	26	25	-3.8	25	100.0	0.0	0.0	0.0	0.0	0.0	72.0	28.0	16	56.3	93.8	0.0
Millard village	89	88	-1.1	107	96.3	0.0	0.0	3.7	0.0	25.1	66.3	8.4	35	94.3	62.9	0.0
Miller city	699	685	-2.0	664	91.7	0.0	0.0	8.3	0.0	25.3	63.2	11.4	291	62.2	45.4	8.6
Mill Spring village	182	184	1.1	154	89.6	0.0	0.0	3.9	6.5	22.7	68.6	8.4	65	66.2	96.9	0.0
Milo village	90	90	0.0	123	97.6	0.0	0.0	0.0	2.4	40.7	52.0	7.3	37	94.6	54.1	27.0
Mindenmines city	365	350	-4.1	272	88.2	0.0	0.0	8.5	3.3	17.6	62.1	20.2	134	70.1	58.2	7.5
Mine La Motte CDP	348	NA	NA	295	92.9	0.0	0.0	0.0	7.1	15.3	59.3	25.4	113	100.0	55.8	21.2
Miner city	984	962	-2.2	886	92.6	3.0	3.2	0.0	1.2	14.7	64.6	20.7	381	84.8	73.5	9.4
Mineral Point town	358	351	-2.0	373	97.6	0.5	0.0	1.9	0.0	28.9	56.3	14.7	123	67.5	86.2	0.0
Miramiguoa Park village	120	119	-0.8	99	97.0	0.0	3.0	0.0	0.0	28.2	61.8	10.1	44	97.7	40.9	6.8
Missouri City city	270	281	4.1	265	86.4	3.8	0.0	7.2	2.6	19.6	69.9	10.6	99	76.8	64.6	7.1
Moberly city	13,986	13,890	-0.7	13,898	85.7	9.3	0.7	3.0	1.2	22.2	64.7	13.2	4,481	62.9	44.9	19.4
Mokane city	185	187	1.1	184	78.8	0.0	0.0	21.2	0.0	32.1	47.2	20.7	62	59.7	56.5	14.5
Moline Acres city	2,446	2,434	-0.5	2,299	5.8	91.0	0.0	3.2	0.0	25.0	58.7	16.4	860	64.4	43.1	17.4
Monett city	8,870	8,934	0.7	8,935	74.3	0.0	0.3	1.7	23.7	27.6	57.6	14.8	3,155	62.0	54.8	20.7
Monroe City city	2,531	2,477	-2.1	2,474	86.3	9.3	0.6	2.9	0.9	22.8	59.9	17.5	1,023	61.7	57.0	19.3
Montgomery City city	2,834	2,769	-2.3	2,804	94.4	1.7	0.6	0.8	2.4	28.9	57.9	13.3	1,157	58.3	59.7	14.2
Monticello village	98	98	0.0	143	89.5	10.5	0.0	0.0	0.0	4.9	83.3	11.9	53	94.3	66.0	11.3
Montier CDP	98	NA	NA	65	100.0	0.0	0.0	0.0	0.0	0.0	87.7	12.3	57	43.9	12.3	31.6
Montrose city	384	375	-2.3	386	97.7	0.5	0.0	1.8	0.0	12.5	67.0	20.7	205	69.8	64.4	14.1
Mooresville village	91	88	-3.3	79	100.0	0.0	0.0	0.0	0.0	26.6	63.3	10.1	31	67.7	71.0	19.4
Morehouse city	973	929	-4.5	754	96.3	2.1	0.0	1.2	0.4	20.4	62.7	16.8	337	52.2	77.2	2.7
Morley city	697	689	-1.1	683	86.1	1.8	0.0	7.8	4.4	28.0	57.7	14.2	276	80.1	66.3	14.1
Morrison city	139	137	-1.4	93	94.6	0.0	0.0	5.4	0.0	9.8	74.3	16.1	51	60.8	58.8	11.8
Morrisville town	388	384	-1.0	391	91.3	1.0	0.0	7.7	0.0	29.7	58.0	12.3	150	60.7	52.0	16.0
Mosby city	190	198	4.2	223	94.6	2.2	0.0	1.3	1.8	18.3	72.6	9.0	91	68.1	65.9	4.4
Moscow Mills city	2,458	2,544	3.5	2,508	80.1	10.2	0.0	6.3	3.3	36.9	56.9	6.4	752	66.1	51.7	8.2
Mound City city	1,159	1,068	-7.9	1,208	95.8	0.0	0.3	3.5	0.4	20.9	56.3	22.7	561	63.3	45.5	17.1
Moundville town	124	124	0.0	162	98.1	1.9	0.0	0.0	0.0	20.4	59.3	20.4	58	89.7	51.7	6.9
Mountain Grove city	4,789	4,682	-2.2	4,704	96.2	0.3	0.0	1.6	1.8	25.9	52.9	21.3	2,011	55.8	64.7	11.3
Mountain View city	2,719	2,680	-1.4	2,719	96.0	0.0	0.0	1.9	2.1	28.0	51.5	20.4	1,148	49.7	62.3	8.1
Mount Leonard town	87	88	1.1	74	86.5	0.0	1.4	12.2	0.0	32.5	52.9	14.9	25	68.0	56.0	16.0
Mount Moriah town	87	84	-3.4	134	100.0	0.0	0.0	0.0	0.0	32.8	48.5	18.7	57	73.7	86.0	1.8
Mount Vernon city	4,575	4,504	-1.6	4,539	87.1	0.5	0.0	1.8	10.7	24.5	56.2	19.4	1,772	50.3	61.9	11.9
Murphy CDP	8,690	NA	NA	8,418	90.7	0.6	0.7	3.0	5.1	22.4	65.3	12.4	3,360	78.9	43.3	16.6
Napoleon city	222	218	-1.8	257	97.3	0.0	1.6	1.2	0.0	25.3	62.6	12.1	95	74.7	57.9	8.4
Naylor city	632	624	-1.3	679	90.6	0.3	0.0	9.1	0.0	28.4	55.2	16.5	263	64.3	60.5	3.4
Neck City city	186	184	-1.1	223	96.4	0.0	2.2	1.3	0.0	11.1	79.3	9.4	66	81.8	81.8	9.1

1 May be of any race.

Table A. All Places — **Population and Housing**

STATE City, town, township, borough, or CDP (county if applicable)	Population				Race and Hispanic or Latino origin (percent), 2010–2014					Age (percent), 2010–2014			Households, 2010–2014		Householders by level of education (percent)	
	2010 census total population	2014 estimated population	Percent change 2010–2014	ACS total population estimate 2010–2014	White alone, not Hispanic or Latino	Black alone, not Hispanic or Latino	Asian alone, not Hispanic or Latino	All other races or 2 or more races, not Hispanic or Latino	Hispanic or Latino[1]	Under 18 years old	Age 18 to 64 years old	Age 65 years and older	Total occupied housing units	Percent owner occupied	High school diploma or less	Bachelor's degree or more
	1	2	3	4	5	6	7	8	9	10	11	12	13	14	15	16
MISSOURI—Con.																
Neelyville city	483	478	-1.0	513	69.0	25.0	0.0	6.0	0.0	35.5	56.7	7.8	179	56.4	68.7	5.6
Nelson city	192	194	1.0	210	85.7	12.4	0.0	1.9	0.0	22.9	64.8	12.4	81	92.6	80.2	0.0
Neosho city	11,835	12,134	2.5	12,038	78.7	2.7	0.9	5.9	11.9	27.2	58.4	14.4	4,666	60.1	48.7	17.1
Nevada city	8,384	8,295	-1.1	8,318	90.8	1.4	1.0	2.8	4.0	25.5	55.3	19.1	3,326	48.8	51.3	14.9
Newark village	94	92	-2.1	101	96.0	0.0	0.0	0.0	4.0	6.0	80.3	13.9	61	50.8	57.4	4.9
New Bloomfield city	672	679	1.0	830	87.8	2.5	0.0	6.5	3.1	26.5	64.6	8.9	297	62.3	55.6	17.2
Newburg city	470	455	-3.2	559	89.8	0.0	0.0	4.3	5.9	26.1	54.1	19.7	224	58.0	67.9	10.7
New Cambria city	195	195	0.0	172	97.7	0.0	0.0	1.7	0.6	12.8	69.7	17.4	80	81.3	41.3	13.8
New Florence city	769	736	-4.3	750	95.7	1.1	0.0	3.2	0.0	18.5	59.1	22.3	298	58.7	63.8	16.1
New Franklin city	1,089	1,086	-0.3	1,229	94.0	2.9	0.0	0.7	2.4	19.8	63.0	17.2	574	60.8	66.7	13.2
New Hampton city	291	282	-3.1	258	99.2	0.0	0.0	0.0	0.8	29.5	46.6	24.0	117	66.7	63.2	4.3
New Haven city	2,087	2,092	0.2	2,063	88.5	0.4	0.3	2.1	8.7	31.1	56.9	11.9	746	70.0	51.9	7.1
New London city	974	977	0.3	1,020	96.6	3.0	0.0	0.4	0.0	27.8	58.7	13.4	386	55.7	63.0	8.3
New Madrid city	3,131	3,018	-3.6	3,063	78.6	17.5	0.0	3.7	0.2	18.3	65.7	16.1	1,212	55.5	52.7	18.0
New Melle city	481	487	1.2	380	97.6	0.0	0.5	0.0	1.8	17.4	50.1	32.4	156	90.4	31.4	45.5
Newtonia town	199	201	1.0	210	93.3	0.0	0.0	3.3	3.3	25.2	58.9	15.7	76	80.3	60.5	13.2
Newtown town	183	176	-3.8	180	84.4	0.0	1.7	5.6	8.3	15.6	69.9	14.4	68	55.9	70.6	8.8
Niangua city	405	405	0.0	491	97.8	0.0	0.0	1.6	0.6	19.9	70.6	9.4	171	69.6	65.5	4.7
Nixa city	19,026	20,570	8.1	19,821	91.3	0.4	0.9	3.6	3.8	30.1	58.0	12.0	7,268	63.9	35.7	24.6
Noel city	1,835	1,831	-0.2	2,012	34.0	11.8	2.3	2.1	49.8	38.3	57.4	4.3	607	32.0	66.9	6.6
Norborne city	708	684	-3.4	723	92.4	2.1	0.0	2.1	3.5	22.9	58.1	19.1	300	84.7	54.3	15.7
Normandy city	5,008	4,983	-0.5	4,990	13.7	79.3	3.6	2.3	1.0	22.6	64.0	13.3	1,989	40.3	47.0	17.5
North Kansas City city	4,208	4,361	3.6	4,280	63.2	4.3	14.2	3.8	14.4	13.8	70.1	16.1	2,381	28.9	34.7	20.7
North Lilbourn village	49	47	-4.1	90	3.3	91.1	0.0	5.6	0.0	22.3	62.2	15.6	23	69.6	100.0	0.0
Northmoor city	325	328	0.9	394	94.4	2.0	0.0	1.3	2.3	23.1	66.7	10.2	143	66.4	55.9	12.6
Northwoods city	4,227	4,199	-0.7	4,213	5.1	93.2	1.2	0.0	0.6	21.1	56.2	22.7	1,736	72.9	47.4	27.4
Norwood city	665	643	-3.3	636	88.2	1.4	0.0	6.9	3.5	32.6	58.3	9.3	246	43.5	72.0	2.0
Norwood Court town	959	961	0.2	923	4.8	93.0	0.0	1.3	1.0	18.6	73.3	8.0	494	8.7	34.6	15.8
Novelty village	139	135	-2.9	163	90.8	0.0	0.0	9.2	0.0	20.8	63.3	16.0	67	83.6	76.1	4.5
Novinger city	456	446	-2.2	495	98.0	0.0	2.0	0.0	0.0	19.4	66.1	14.5	204	78.9	78.9	4.4
Oak Grove city	7,795	7,873	1.0	7,747	87.9	0.9	0.3	1.1	9.8	32.2	56.2	11.5	2,591	63.6	44.8	14.4
Oak Grove Village village	509	492	-3.3	392	96.2	1.5	0.0	2.3	0.0	22.7	62.3	15.1	169	53.3	59.8	3.6
Oakland city	1,381	1,379	-0.1	1,377	95.0	1.6	1.7	0.9	0.7	17.9	51.1	30.9	468	80.1	8.3	65.6
Oak Ridge town	243	248	2.1	231	98.3	0.0	0.0	0.9	0.9	26.9	52.6	20.8	84	86.9	57.1	13.1
Oaks village	129	134	3.9	128	71.9	0.0	2.3	3.1	22.7	32.1	54.7	13.3	50	76.0	20.0	46.0
Oakview village	375	391	4.3	475	93.5	0.0	0.4	2.3	3.8	24.0	68.6	7.4	169	87.0	30.2	23.1
Oakville CDP	36,143	NA	NA	36,776	94.0	1.6	1.5	1.2	1.7	21.7	62.5	15.8	14,015	85.4	26.5	38.7
Oakwood village	185	195	5.4	168	97.0	0.6	0.6	0.0	1.8	18.5	45.4	36.3	76	98.7	27.6	44.7
Oakwood Park village	188	196	4.3	172	87.2	0.0	3.5	4.1	5.2	12.8	68.7	18.6	79	87.3	34.2	41.8
Odessa city	5,300	5,173	-2.4	5,237	93.6	0.0	0.8	2.3	3.3	33.4	54.1	12.4	1,865	68.0	53.2	14.4
O'Fallon city	79,588	84,009	5.6	81,978	88.6	4.3	3.5	1.7	2.0	29.3	60.8	9.8	29,130	80.4	26.8	38.6
Old Appleton town	85	87	2.4	20	100.0	0.0	0.0	0.0	0.0	0.0	90.0	10.0	11	100.0	36.4	36.4
Old Jamestown CDP	19,184	NA	NA	19,745	40.5	52.5	0.7	3.5	2.8	22.5	62.6	14.7	7,108	93.2	24.1	42.5
Old Monroe city	265	280	5.7	268	98.5	0.0	0.0	0.0	1.5	19.8	70.7	9.7	119	83.2	44.5	5.0
Olean town	128	131	2.3	119	68.9	0.0	0.0	11.8	19.3	16.8	67.2	16.0	56	66.1	60.7	10.7
Olivette city	7,752	7,845	1.2	7,809	61.3	21.7	9.8	3.6	3.6	24.6	58.6	16.7	3,101	79.1	15.1	64.4
Olympian Village city	774	766	-1.0	565	98.1	0.0	0.0	1.2	0.7	22.8	67.4	9.9	205	82.4	57.6	5.9
Oran city	1,287	1,275	-0.9	1,217	96.2	0.2	0.0	0.6	3.0	22.0	62.1	15.9	487	68.0	59.8	13.6
Oregon city	848	781	-7.9	905	94.3	2.5	0.2	2.7	0.3	19.4	62.2	18.5	384	75.5	60.2	16.9
Oronogo city	2,381	2,398	0.7	2,673	95.9	0.4	0.5	2.0	1.3	33.4	60.5	6.2	810	86.3	36.0	33.2
Orrick city	837	812	-3.0	703	95.2	1.4	0.0	0.6	2.8	27.2	64.3	8.5	274	65.0	51.8	11.3
Osage Beach city	4,351	4,395	1.0	4,395	88.3	0.2	3.0	3.4	5.1	20.6	50.9	28.6	1,932	63.2	40.5	27.7
Osborn city	423	410	-3.1	452	96.7	0.0	0.4	2.7	0.2	17.1	62.6	20.4	198	73.7	58.6	6.6
Osceola city	946	915	-3.3	986	84.6	4.6	0.0	8.5	2.3	14.7	60.7	24.5	437	57.9	61.1	11.9
Osgood village	48	46	-4.2	14	92.9	0.0	0.0	0.0	7.1	42.9	42.8	14.3	6	50.0	16.7	50.0
Otterville city	454	449	-1.1	535	97.4	0.6	0.0	1.9	0.2	29.1	57.5	13.5	199	63.8	53.8	7.0
Overland city	16,062	15,985	-0.5	16,043	71.2	17.2	1.6	2.7	7.4	22.6	66.0	11.5	6,518	64.5	46.9	17.7
Owensville city	2,676	2,626	-1.9	2,658	97.3	0.6	0.2	1.2	0.7	27.4	52.7	19.9	1,069	59.8	55.8	14.9
Oxly CDP	200	NA	NA	80	92.5	0.0	0.0	7.5	0.0	7.5	71.4	21.3	46	63.0	67.4	17.4
Ozark city	17,820	18,871	5.9	18,369	92.4	1.3	0.4	2.1	3.9	26.3	59.9	13.9	6,894	62.6	35.0	30.1
Ozora CDP	183	NA	NA	127	99.2	0.8	0.0	0.0	0.0	10.2	52.8	37.0	52	69.2	69.2	0.0
Pacific city	7,007	7,113	1.5	6,047	88.2	8.4	0.3	2.6	0.4	25.2	62.9	11.8	2,502	56.6	43.8	13.1
Pagedale city	3,310	3,310	0.0	3,313	3.5	93.2	0.0	3.4	0.0	27.4	57.6	15.0	1,239	54.7	54.1	7.3
Palmyra city	3,612	3,612	0.0	3,630	95.2	1.8	0.0	2.9	0.1	27.5	55.9	16.6	1,364	69.9	59.6	17.2
Paris city	1,228	1,193	-2.9	1,184	96.4	2.7	0.0	0.9	0.0	22.0	50.8	27.3	480	75.4	56.0	20.2
Parkdale village	170	171	0.6	215	98.6	0.0	0.0	0.5	0.9	21.4	58.1	20.5	77	93.5	51.9	13.0
Park Hills city	8,757	8,618	-1.6	8,714	97.1	1.0	0.2	0.6	1.1	25.8	63.0	11.3	3,546	52.8	47.2	11.8
Parkville city	5,554	6,098	9.8	5,811	90.2	4.5	1.5	1.3	2.5	23.7	64.3	12.1	2,127	71.9	17.5	58.6
Parkway village	439	437	-0.5	356	99.2	0.0	0.8	0.0	0.0	24.8	59.2	16.0	152	77.0	56.6	10.5
Parma city	701	669	-4.6	670	68.2	30.6	0.0	1.2	0.0	27.3	53.2	19.6	275	45.5	78.2	1.1
Parnell city	191	186	-2.6	108	100.0	0.0	0.0	0.0	0.0	31.4	55.6	13.0	49	73.5	61.2	10.2
Pasadena Hills city	930	924	-0.6	964	33.2	64.7	0.0	1.8	0.3	11.9	68.3	19.9	490	78.6	17.1	54.7
Pasadena Park village	470	463	-1.5	527	27.7	66.0	4.2	1.3	0.8	20.2	66.1	13.7	253	92.5	13.0	53.8
Pascola village	108	105	-2.8	145	95.9	0.0	0.0	1.4	2.8	24.8	69.7	5.5	41	58.5	95.1	0.0
Passaic town	34	33	-2.9	34	88.2	0.0	0.0	11.8	0.0	2.9	94.1	2.9	16	68.8	75.0	0.0
Pattonsburg city	348	345	-0.9	354	81.4	14.4	0.0	2.0	2.3	17.2	68.0	14.7	92	77.2	68.5	5.4
Paynesville village	77	77	0.0	46	84.8	15.2	0.0	0.0	0.0	15.2	58.7	26.1	25	72.0	72.0	24.0
Peaceful Village village	9	9	0.0	5	100.0	0.0	0.0	0.0	0.0	0.0	40.0	60.0	1	100.0	100.0	0.0
Peculiar city	4,608	4,795	4.1	4,747	91.8	0.7	0.0	5.5	2.0	27.6	61.9	10.4	1,763	73.1	30.9	21.1
Pendleton village	43	43	0.0	23	100.0	0.0	0.0	0.0	0.0	21.6	56.3	21.7	7	57.1	100.0	0.0
Penermon village	64	64	0.0	64	12.5	75.0	0.0	12.5	0.0	14.1	67.2	18.8	42	45.2	45.2	2.4
Perry city	693	700	1.0	664	91.9	0.9	0.0	0.3	6.9	16.7	59.5	23.8	312	69.9	56.1	8.7
Perryville city	8,226	8,394	2.0	8,280	94.7	0.5	0.2	1.1	3.5	26.1	57.4	16.6	3,378	65.0	57.8	16.7
Pevely city	5,484	5,617	2.4	5,566	97.4	0.6	0.0	1.4	0.7	20.5	66.9	12.6	2,404	65.9	43.8	15.8
Phelps City CDP	24	NA	NA	7	100.0	0.0	0.0	0.0	0.0	0.0	100.0	0.0	3	100.0	100.0	0.0
Phillipsburg village	202	201	-0.5	207	97.1	0.0	0.0	2.9	0.0	22.2	64.7	13.0	80	45.0	60.0	11.3
Pickering town	160	156	-2.5	188	100.0	0.0	0.0	0.0	0.0	29.3	50.0	20.7	78	85.9	69.2	6.4
Piedmont city	1,983	1,983	0.0	2,230	95.2	0.7	0.0	2.2	1.8	20.6	55.8	23.4	973	54.7	70.2	4.6
Pierce City city	1,293	1,270	-1.8	1,283	86.6	0.0	0.0	6.7	6.7	27.5	53.0	19.6	532	63.5	61.5	7.9
Pierpont village	76	77	1.3	84	94.0	1.2	4.8	0.0	0.0	28.6	46.5	25.0	29	96.6	17.2	72.4
Pilot Grove city	768	761	-0.9	866	98.0	0.3	0.0	1.6	0.0	23.1	47.5	29.2	329	65.7	65.0	13.1

1 May be of any race.

Table A. All Places — **Population and Housing**

STATE City, town, township, borough, or CDP (county if applicable)	Population: 2010 census total population	Population: 2014 estimated population	Population: Percent change 2010–2014	Population: ACS total population estimate 2010–2014	Race and Hispanic or Latino origin (percent), 2010–2014: White alone, not Hispanic or Latino	Black alone, not Hispanic or Latino	Asian alone, not Hispanic or Latino	All other races or 2 or more races, not Hispanic or Latino	Hispanic or Latino[1]	Age (percent), 2010–2014: Under 18 years old	Age 18 to 64 years old	Age 65 years and older	Households, 2010–2014: Total occupied housing units	Percent owner occupied	Householders by level of education (percent): High school diploma or less	Bachelor's degree or more
	1	2	3	4	5	6	7	8	9	10	11	12	13	14	15	16
MISSOURI—Con.																
Pilot Knob city	746	725	-2.8	704	95.2	0.1	0.0	3.7	1.0	16.2	56.3	27.6	337	59.3	58.8	5.6
Pine Lawn city	3,286	3,425	4.2	3,335	0.7	97.7	0.0	1.6	0.1	26.6	61.0	12.3	1,298	50.6	52.0	5.7
Pineville city	796	790	-0.8	958	86.5	0.3	0.9	7.3	4.9	26.2	59.5	14.2	375	61.1	48.3	14.9
Pinhook village	30	NA	NA	20	0.0	100.0	0.0	0.0	0.0	0.0	60.0	40.0	15	46.7	80.0	13.3
Plato village	109	108	-0.9	131	82.4	0.0	0.0	4.6	13.0	37.4	45.9	16.8	50	74.0	32.0	24.0
Platte City city	4,691	4,824	2.8	4,775	86.3	5.5	1.8	2.8	3.6	26.7	63.9	9.6	1,997	43.8	27.5	29.9
Platte Woods city	385	399	3.6	437	95.4	0.0	1.4	0.7	2.5	16.2	62.0	21.7	190	89.5	11.6	54.2
Plattsburg city	2,319	2,258	-2.6	2,428	81.2	9.0	0.0	4.3	5.6	27.4	54.6	17.9	934	68.3	50.6	18.4
Pleasant Hill city	8,113	8,250	1.7	8,173	91.9	0.2	0.1	3.9	3.8	29.1	59.8	11.1	3,049	66.8	46.4	20.1
Pleasant Hope city	614	611	-0.5	619	92.4	0.0	0.0	6.3	1.3	27.1	63.1	9.7	264	69.3	55.7	14.4
Pleasant Valley city	2,961	3,056	3.2	3,013	88.3	0.2	0.0	8.3	3.3	18.7	63.4	18.1	1,138	62.3	34.9	18.5
Plevna CDP	21	NA	NA	40	100.0	0.0	0.0	0.0	0.0	0.0	25.0	75.0	29	65.5	65.5	34.5
Pocahontas town	114	116	1.8	111	100.0	0.0	0.0	0.0	0.0	47.7	45.0	7.2	31	71.0	58.1	12.9
Pollock village	89	86	-3.4	66	100.0	0.0	0.0	0.0	0.0	9.1	74.2	16.7	36	52.8	52.8	5.6
Polo city	575	543	-5.6	590	84.6	1.2	0.0	14.2	0.0	30.1	55.5	14.4	225	57.8	53.3	8.9
Pomona CDP	511	NA	NA	389	95.9	0.0	0.0	4.1	0.0	2.6	52.1	45.5	171	84.2	79.5	0.0
Pontiac CDP	175	NA	NA	262	100.0	0.0	0.0	0.0	0.0	22.2	61.8	16.0	119	78.2	40.3	10.1
Poplar Bluff city	17,050	17,242	1.1	17,190	83.6	10.5	0.8	3.3	1.8	23.0	59.7	17.2	7,125	48.8	49.6	14.2
Portage Des Sioux city	328	331	0.9	314	94.3	0.0	1.0	1.9	2.9	19.4	65.4	15.3	139	80.6	47.5	5.8
Portageville city	3,228	3,154	-2.3	3,184	75.1	22.7	0.0	1.3	0.9	30.0	55.2	14.9	1,239	52.1	62.6	12.9
Potosi city	2,659	2,669	0.4	2,666	94.1	2.9	0.0	1.8	1.2	26.8	53.4	19.9	1,071	41.0	55.8	14.5
Powersville village	60	58	-3.3	57	100.0	0.0	0.0	0.0	0.0	7.0	42.2	50.9	36	91.7	41.7	11.1
Prairie Home city	280	280	0.0	314	93.6	0.0	0.6	5.7	0.0	33.5	49.3	17.2	125	65.6	41.6	12.8
Prathersville village	124	131	5.6	141	97.2	0.0	2.1	0.7	0.0	8.5	58.3	33.3	68	88.2	45.6	11.8
Preston village	223	217	-2.7	264	96.6	0.0	0.0	2.3	1.1	20.5	62.5	17.0	97	68.0	68.0	0.0
Princeton city	1,165	1,142	-2.0	1,157	95.2	0.3	0.6	1.7	2.1	22.0	57.8	20.2	507	60.0	56.4	13.4
Purcell city	408	396	-2.9	447	94.6	2.5	0.0	2.0	0.9	32.8	58.0	9.2	152	84.2	57.9	5.3
Purdin city	190	184	-3.2	183	92.3	0.0	0.0	1.1	6.6	26.2	49.1	24.6	71	63.4	73.2	4.2
Purdy city	1,098	1,099	0.1	1,253	69.8	0.0	0.2	1.8	28.2	29.4	55.5	15.2	432	56.9	65.7	4.6
Puxico city	881	871	-1.1	796	97.1	0.5	0.0	0.4	2.0	23.7	55.9	20.2	311	65.3	54.7	17.0
Queen City city	598	587	-1.8	618	98.7	0.0	0.0	0.6	0.6	17.8	53.4	28.8	256	74.6	71.1	4.3
Quitman town	45	44	-2.2	57	86.0	0.0	0.0	14.0	0.0	29.8	47.5	22.8	30	96.7	76.7	10.0
Qulin city	458	455	-0.7	652	98.5	0.0	0.0	0.9	0.6	29.3	61.5	9.2	209	60.8	79.9	6.2
Randolph village	52	54	3.8	26	92.3	0.0	7.7	0.0	0.0	19.2	61.4	19.2	10	100.0	80.0	20.0
Ravanna CDP	98	NA	NA	40	100.0	0.0	0.0	0.0	0.0	0.0	50.0	50.0	33	87.9	87.9	0.0
Ravenwood town	440	420	-4.5	438	97.3	0.5	0.5	1.8	0.0	23.7	58.0	18.3	190	68.4	51.1	11.1
Raymondville town	363	361	-0.6	363	98.1	0.0	0.6	0.8	0.6	22.9	57.2	19.8	124	83.1	69.4	11.3
Raymore city	19,205	19,963	3.9	19,576	85.6	9.1	0.6	2.1	2.5	26.5	58.2	15.3	7,182	81.9	31.7	34.4
Raytown city	29,526	29,481	-0.2	29,520	61.7	28.7	0.9	2.4	6.2	25.7	58.9	15.7	11,513	68.3	38.6	24.8
Rayville CDP	223	NA	NA	247	96.0	0.0	0.0	4.0	0.0	20.6	64.9	14.6	94	77.7	87.2	5.3
Rea city	50	50	0.0	37	100.0	0.0	0.0	0.0	0.0	21.6	43.2	35.1	18	77.8	61.1	11.1
Redings Mill village	151	152	0.7	178	94.9	0.0	0.6	2.8	1.7	18.5	62.9	18.5	93	88.2	25.8	39.8
Reeds town	95	94	-1.1	76	96.1	0.0	0.0	0.0	3.9	9.2	78.9	11.8	32	87.5	34.4	6.3
Reeds Spring city	913	879	-3.7	1,063	96.7	0.0	0.0	0.8	2.4	33.9	55.8	10.3	384	57.0	45.6	12.8
Renick village	172	171	-0.6	150	100.0	0.0	0.0	0.0	0.0	17.3	64.7	18.0	65	86.2	50.8	0.0
Rensselaer village	228	232	1.8	218	99.1	0.9	0.0	0.0	0.0	28.5	63.3	8.3	66	90.9	40.9	9.1
Republic city	14,755	15,680	6.3	15,222	96.1	0.1	0.4	1.4	2.1	29.0	60.5	10.8	5,820	61.7	34.3	21.2
Revere town	79	77	-2.5	61	93.4	0.0	0.0	6.6	0.0	11.4	57.5	31.1	30	100.0	73.3	0.0
Rhineland town	142	137	-3.5	208	88.9	0.0	0.0	11.1	0.0	29.4	59.7	11.1	76	88.2	52.6	17.1
Richards town	97	97	0.0	124	87.1	0.0	0.0	12.9	0.0	33.8	46.8	19.4	46	93.5	41.3	4.3
Rich Hill city	1,396	1,348	-3.4	1,460	97.2	0.1	0.0	2.7	0.0	29.9	53.0	17.1	577	72.3	67.6	9.2
Richland city	1,863	1,839	-1.3	1,853	88.2	3.0	1.5	2.8	4.5	24.3	54.6	21.2	723	49.5	47.4	16.6
Richmond city	5,797	5,638	-2.7	5,702	90.7	4.7	0.0	1.9	2.8	23.4	58.2	18.3	2,304	53.9	59.5	15.4
Richmond Heights city	8,563	8,495	-0.8	8,526	78.4	11.9	4.7	2.2	2.8	18.7	67.2	14.1	4,032	55.2	12.8	66.5
Ridgely village	104	110	5.8	98	99.0	0.0	0.0	0.0	1.0	24.5	66.3	9.2	35	91.4	51.4	14.3
Ridgeway city	464	450	-3.0	504	98.6	0.0	0.4	0.8	0.2	28.3	51.4	20.2	213	68.1	70.0	10.3
Risco city	346	331	-4.3	320	100.0	0.0	0.0	0.0	0.0	15.6	70.2	14.4	132	87.9	66.7	3.8
Ritchey town	82	83	1.2	68	91.2	0.0	0.0	0.0	8.8	20.5	48.7	30.9	27	77.8	48.1	0.0
River Bend village	10	10	0.0	6	100.0	0.0	0.0	0.0	0.0	0.0	66.7	33.3	3	100.0	100.0	0.0
Riverside city	2,937	3,095	5.4	3,023	72.2	14.1	4.0	5.4	4.3	18.6	64.2	17.2	1,213	30.6	43.1	27.5
Riverview village	2,859	2,839	-0.7	2,854	24.7	71.2	0.8	2.3	1.1	30.8	59.5	9.8	1,068	53.1	41.5	6.7
Riverview Estates village	82	82	0.0	121	94.2	0.0	0.0	4.1	1.7	27.3	58.0	14.9	42	100.0	42.9	40.5
Rives town	63	62	-1.6	62	100.0	0.0	0.0	0.0	0.0	6.4	67.7	25.8	26	50.0	92.3	0.0
Rocheport city	239	248	3.8	214	98.6	0.0	0.5	0.9	0.0	13.1	64.0	22.9	106	64.2	24.5	34.0
Rockaway Beach city	841	862	2.5	929	84.3	0.6	0.0	12.1	3.0	25.7	60.4	13.9	367	56.7	42.5	7.9
Rock Hill city	4,635	4,643	0.2	4,635	77.1	15.0	4.6	1.9	1.5	20.6	66.9	12.4	2,029	83.3	14.6	53.9
Rock Port city	1,318	1,250	-5.2	1,384	97.5	0.2	0.0	1.1	1.2	19.3	55.9	24.9	642	66.4	48.4	24.6
Rockville city	166	162	-2.4	137	95.6	2.9	0.0	0.0	1.5	30.6	56.2	13.1	47	66.0	76.6	4.3
Rogersville city	3,073	3,308	7.6	3,529	96.5	0.1	0.0	2.9	0.5	34.9	58.1	6.7	1,212	54.9	23.9	29.6
Rolla city	19,561	19,926	1.9	19,808	80.9	4.0	7.4	3.3	4.4	18.4	69.7	11.8	7,136	41.1	33.7	30.8
Roscoe village	124	121	-2.4	139	100.0	0.0	0.0	0.0	0.0	28.7	51.1	20.1	57	80.7	66.7	0.0
Rosebud city	409	407	-0.5	378	95.5	0.0	1.1	0.5	2.9	20.9	51.9	27.2	171	87.1	71.9	12.3
Rosendale city	143	144	0.7	149	100.0	0.0	0.0	0.0	0.0	37.6	47.6	14.8	50	96.0	64.0	2.0
Rothville village	99	98	-1.0	105	90.5	0.0	0.0	8.6	1.0	48.5	47.7	3.8	38	63.2	44.7	13.2
Rush Hill village	151	153	1.3	131	100.0	0.0	0.0	0.0	0.0	23.7	56.5	19.8	59	81.4	79.7	5.1
Rushville town	277	278	0.4	305	100.0	0.0	0.0	0.0	0.0	26.5	62.4	11.1	98	78.6	64.3	8.2
Russellville city	807	800	-0.9	788	98.1	0.0	0.0	1.4	0.5	35.0	54.8	10.3	293	60.8	49.1	22.9
Rutledge town	109	111	1.8	120	96.7	0.0	0.0	3.3	0.0	39.1	41.7	19.2	42	69.0	88.1	0.0
Saddlebrooke village	202	231	14.4	319	77.4	0.0	2.8	6.9	12.9	23.8	62.7	13.5	112	100.0	35.7	39.3
Saginaw village	297	308	3.7	351	94.0	1.7	1.4	1.7	1.1	21.9	59.8	18.2	172	68.6	50.6	9.9
St. Ann city	13,020	12,955	-0.5	12,988	66.4	23.7	2.4	2.9	4.6	20.2	66.5	13.2	6,177	55.0	46.0	15.4
St. Charles city	65,846	68,090	3.4	66,900	84.1	6.9	2.1	2.5	4.3	19.8	66.9	13.3	26,604	64.3	31.6	36.8
St. Clair city	4,724	4,701	-0.5	4,708	93.7	2.1	2.8	1.4	0.0	23.3	62.2	14.4	1,890	55.7	55.9	9.9
St. Clement CDP	78	NA	NA	101	100.0	0.0	0.0	0.0	0.0	11.9	75.3	12.9	32	100.0	0.0	34.4
St. Cloud village	41	41	0.0	75	100.0	0.0	0.0	0.0	0.0	34.7	53.5	12.0	21	52.4	61.9	9.5
Ste. Genevieve city	4,410	4,471	1.4	4,413	90.4	0.9	0.0	8.0	0.7	26.2	54.7	19.0	1,758	60.4	57.6	14.5
St. Elizabeth village	336	342	1.8	359	99.4	0.0	0.0	0.0	0.6	25.9	47.8	26.2	126	82.5	51.6	31.0
St. Francisville CDP	179	NA	NA	94	100.0	0.0	0.0	0.0	0.0	20.2	59.5	20.2	46	78.3	80.4	8.7
St. James city	4,217	4,153	-1.5	4,184	93.5	0.4	0.0	5.9	0.2	28.2	53.5	18.2	1,519	55.5	55.1	18.2
St. John city	6,517	6,475	-0.6	6,486	63.8	26.5	0.5	2.1	7.1	22.1	63.2	14.9	2,727	75.5	46.0	22.4
St. Joseph city	76,807	76,967	0.2	77,040	83.5	5.5	1.0	3.9	6.2	23.5	62.8	13.8	28,825	60.0	46.3	21.2

1 May be of any race.

Table A. All Places — **Population and Housing**

STATE City, town, township, borough, or CDP (county if applicable)	Population				Race and Hispanic or Latino origin (percent), 2010–2014					Age (percent), 2010–2014			Households, 2010–2014			
	2010 census total population	2014 estimated population	Percent change 2010–2014	ACS total population estimate 2010–2014	White alone, not Hispanic or Latino	Black alone, not Hispanic or Latino	Asian alone, not Hispanic or Latino	All other races or 2 or more races, not Hispanic or Latino	Hispanic or Latino[1]	Under 18 years old	Age 18 to 64 years old	Age 65 years and older	Total occupied housing units	Percent owner occupied	Householders by level of education (percent): High school diploma or less	Householders by level of education (percent): Bachelor's degree or more
	1	2	3	4	5	6	7	8	9	10	11	12	13	14	15	16
MISSOURI—Con.																
St. Louis city	319,365	317,419	-0.6	318,727	42.8	47.9	2.8	2.8	3.7	20.6	68.3	11.1	139,594	44.2	36.3	32.5
St. Martins city	1,145	1,168	2.0	1,100	93.9	3.6	0.3	1.5	0.7	27.1	60.0	12.9	421	82.7	41.1	35.2
St. Mary city	362	350	-3.3	397	94.7	4.5	0.0	0.0	0.8	29.4	57.0	13.6	155	67.1	56.1	14.8
St. Paul city	1,802	1,847	2.5	1,995	98.2	0.7	0.0	1.1	0.0	18.8	67.8	13.5	702	92.0	35.2	33.0
St. Peters city	52,626	56,076	6.6	54,236	88.8	4.5	2.0	1.1	3.6	22.8	64.8	12.4	21,539	81.1	29.6	35.5
St. Robert city	4,340	5,747	32.4	4,882	49.0	14.4	10.3	11.5	14.7	30.1	64.1	5.7	1,862	35.0	21.4	34.7
St. Thomas town	267	270	1.1	225	100.0	0.0	0.0	0.0	0.0	30.3	57.9	12.0	79	97.5	50.6	30.4
Salem city	4,945	5,005	1.2	4,979	96.1	1.5	0.8	0.5	1.0	21.6	56.2	22.0	1,982	54.4	55.8	6.2
Salisbury city	1,618	1,586	-2.0	1,738	92.3	4.7	0.3	1.7	0.9	27.5	52.9	19.6	647	75.3	58.9	20.4
Sappington CDP	7,580	NA	NA	7,342	90.8	2.3	2.4	2.2	2.3	20.8	52.7	26.4	3,359	71.9	29.8	35.8
Sarcoxie city	1,334	1,303	-2.3	1,224	95.7	0.0	0.0	3.3	1.1	30.3	51.9	17.9	476	59.7	58.2	9.7
Savannah city	5,057	5,129	1.4	5,101	94.8	1.1	0.4	1.3	2.4	25.8	54.8	19.4	2,053	60.5	59.5	20.2
Schell City city	249	249	0.0	208	88.0	0.0	0.0	5.3	6.7	24.5	56.7	18.8	101	60.4	63.4	1.0
Scotsdale town	222	223	0.5	216	96.3	0.0	0.0	2.3	1.4	21.2	65.7	13.0	75	92.0	33.3	28.0
Scott City city	4,561	4,504	-1.2	4,551	92.8	0.8	2.0	2.0	2.5	27.4	57.7	15.0	1,759	71.9	62.5	9.8
Sedalia city	21,385	21,492	0.5	21,429	81.7	4.0	0.3	3.4	10.7	24.9	60.0	15.1	8,875	57.9	47.5	15.7
Sedgewickville village	173	175	1.2	213	100.0	0.0	0.0	0.0	0.0	27.7	66.7	5.6	58	96.6	75.9	6.9
Seligman city	851	841	-1.2	1,099	86.4	0.0	0.0	10.7	2.9	25.1	59.5	15.2	390	64.1	71.5	5.4
Senath city	1,767	1,735	-1.8	1,905	65.5	0.0	0.0	0.0	34.5	33.0	49.3	17.5	649	63.9	69.8	10.0
Seneca city	2,336	2,393	2.4	2,137	84.1	0.6	0.2	14.6	0.5	29.2	52.7	18.0	822	64.2	45.5	19.1
Seymour city	1,921	1,943	1.1	1,696	92.3	0.4	0.0	3.9	3.5	20.9	57.0	22.1	688	63.1	62.2	9.4
Shelbina city	1,704	1,634	-4.1	1,444	97.6	0.7	0.0	0.1	1.5	20.8	54.7	24.4	633	66.2	59.6	12.0
Shelbyville city	552	525	-4.9	602	97.5	0.8	0.0	0.2	1.5	18.8	64.3	16.9	251	72.5	58.2	13.5
Sheldon city	543	537	-1.1	729	99.0	0.4	0.0	0.5	0.0	27.9	63.2	8.9	260	73.8	60.4	11.2
Shell Knob CDP	1,379	NA	NA	1,568	98.1	0.0	0.0	1.9	0.0	18.4	54.2	27.4	643	93.8	47.4	24.3
Sheridan town	195	187	-4.1	205	100.0	0.0	0.0	0.0	0.0	15.6	56.7	27.8	108	72.2	52.8	15.7
Shoal Creek Drive village	337	340	0.9	288	87.8	0.3	0.3	3.5	8.0	21.5	56.6	21.9	129	88.4	34.9	29.5
Shoal Creek Estates village	96	97	1.0	128	92.2	3.9	0.0	0.0	3.9	27.4	62.5	10.2	48	100.0	4.2	52.1
Shrewsbury city	6,231	6,205	-0.4	6,217	83.9	3.3	7.0	2.0	3.8	16.1	58.2	25.7	3,115	59.9	16.3	55.0
Sibley village	357	359	0.6	342	96.5	0.0	0.0	1.2	2.3	23.4	58.7	17.8	118	78.8	62.7	8.5
Sikeston city	16,322	16,370	0.3	16,642	67.5	27.3	0.2	2.6	2.4	25.0	57.2	17.8	6,609	57.2	53.2	16.8
Silex village	187	281	50.3	84	100.0	0.0	0.0	0.0	0.0	3.6	77.5	19.0	21	85.7	42.9	19.0
Skidmore city	284	276	-2.8	337	92.3	0.9	5.0	0.9	0.9	33.2	49.5	17.2	135	68.9	62.2	14.1
Slater city	1,856	1,849	-0.4	2,150	83.7	9.2	0.0	2.0	5.1	22.7	60.4	16.9	841	76.7	58.5	13.9
Smithton city	570	563	-1.2	475	92.8	1.1	0.0	6.1	0.0	25.7	64.5	9.7	193	83.4	34.2	4.7
Smithville city	8,411	9,107	8.3	8,791	92.3	0.0	0.8	2.4	4.5	27.2	61.7	11.1	3,400	83.2	35.2	29.8
South Fork CDP	241	NA	NA	149	100.0	0.0	0.0	0.0	0.0	14.1	61.8	24.2	67	100.0	40.3	17.9
South Gifford village	50	50	0.0	41	100.0	0.0	0.0	0.0	0.0	14.6	75.7	9.8	22	95.5	68.2	0.0
South Gorin town	91	92	1.1	124	97.6	0.0	0.0	0.8	1.6	16.9	56.3	26.6	53	60.4	86.8	0.0
South Greenfield village	90	88	-2.2	114	88.6	0.0	0.0	5.3	6.1	7.1	71.0	21.9	56	75.0	69.6	0.0
South Lineville town	28	28	0.0	33	100.0	0.0	0.0	0.0	0.0	24.3	57.6	18.2	21	81.0	57.1	0.0
Southwest City town	970	965	-0.5	977	41.5	1.2	0.0	2.5	54.9	33.8	57.1	9.2	324	45.4	64.8	12.3
Spanish Lake CDP	19,650	NA	NA	19,652	19.7	73.7	0.6	4.6	1.5	32.3	55.5	12.3	7,536	50.0	38.8	16.1
Sparta city	1,756	1,787	1.8	1,927	95.5	0.5	0.0	2.5	1.6	28.7	61.8	9.3	736	59.9	51.6	14.5
Spickard city	254	253	-0.4	291	95.5	0.7	0.3	3.1	0.3	30.7	53.6	15.8	121	66.9	57.9	6.6
Spokane CDP	177	NA	NA	450	100.0	0.0	0.0	0.0	0.0	47.8	40.6	11.6	120	100.0	71.7	10.8
Springfield city	159,500	165,378	3.7	162,333	86.3	4.1	1.9	3.6	4.1	18.1	67.0	14.8	70,788	47.2	35.7	27.6
Stanberry city	1,185	1,204	1.6	1,276	97.7	0.1	0.0	0.4	1.8	27.2	52.0	20.7	503	64.4	49.9	13.1
Stark City town	139	140	0.7	141	98.6	0.0	0.0	0.7	0.7	4.9	75.1	19.9	58	75.9	53.4	1.7
Steele city	2,172	2,125	-2.2	2,290	78.7	15.7	0.0	2.4	3.1	29.7	54.1	16.2	753	43.4	50.7	10.9
Steelville city	1,642	1,709	4.1	1,943	93.4	0.6	0.0	4.7	1.3	27.5	55.6	16.9	654	62.2	59.0	15.9
Stella town	158	159	0.6	137	75.2	0.0	0.0	24.8	0.0	21.2	70.1	8.8	54	87.0	66.7	7.4
Stewartsville city	750	735	-2.0	772	97.2	2.3	0.0	0.0	0.5	26.1	59.5	14.4	276	69.2	51.1	16.3
Stockton city	1,815	1,852	2.0	1,942	91.7	1.6	0.7	4.1	1.9	22.7	56.5	20.9	798	60.2	51.9	18.4
Stotesbury town	18	18	0.0	18	100.0	0.0	0.0	0.0	0.0	0.0	61.1	38.9	9	66.7	100.0	0.0
Stotts City city	220	218	-0.9	144	83.3	0.7	0.0	1.4	14.6	18.1	60.4	21.5	71	73.2	63.4	11.3
Stoutland city	192	192	0.0	185	85.4	0.0	0.0	0.0	14.6	12.4	67.1	20.5	73	68.5	54.8	13.7
Stoutsville village	47	46	-2.1	39	100.0	0.0	0.0	0.0	0.0	20.5	61.6	17.9	19	42.1	68.4	0.0
Stover city	1,094	1,078	-1.5	1,116	83.4	0.4	0.0	11.2	5.0	26.4	54.6	18.9	415	75.4	63.9	7.0
Strafford city	2,338	2,366	1.2	2,247	95.6	1.4	0.1	2.1	0.8	29.2	58.6	12.2	842	63.7	46.9	14.8
Strasburg city	141	142	0.7	120	97.5	0.0	0.0	1.7	0.8	30.0	62.5	7.5	45	66.7	44.4	20.0
Sturgeon city	872	903	3.6	774	98.3	0.5	0.8	0.4	0.0	22.8	56.3	21.1	316	67.4	47.5	21.2
Sugar Creek city	3,345	3,334	-0.3	3,344	88.6	0.8	0.0	5.2	5.4	23.5	62.8	13.5	1,479	59.0	57.2	13.7
Sullivan city	7,092	7,054	-0.5	7,058	97.9	0.3	0.3	0.6	0.9	26.1	59.4	14.6	2,859	51.2	54.7	11.6
Summersville city	502	499	-0.6	515	92.8	0.0	0.0	6.4	0.8	28.2	54.2	17.7	210	71.9	55.7	7.6
Sumner town	102	101	-1.0	124	100.0	0.0	0.0	0.0	0.0	34.7	58.9	6.5	47	74.5	68.1	0.0
Sundown CDP	48	NA	NA	32	100.0	0.0	0.0	0.0	0.0	0.0	34.4	65.6	18	83.3	61.1	22.2
Sunrise Beach village	432	428	-0.9	416	96.6	0.0	0.0	2.2	1.2	18.6	49.0	32.5	179	84.9	66.5	10.6
Sunset Hills city	8,494	8,527	0.4	8,523	93.6	1.1	2.4	0.6	2.2	23.6	52.7	23.7	3,138	80.9	19.1	50.1
Sweet Springs city	1,484	1,481	-0.2	1,571	89.8	5.1	1.3	3.2	0.6	22.7	59.6	17.9	607	69.5	54.0	12.9
Sycamore Hills village	668	670	0.3	566	83.7	9.5	0.4	1.8	4.6	13.6	69.9	16.4	261	83.5	37.9	31.4
Syracuse city	172	171	-0.6	192	98.4	0.0	0.0	0.0	1.6	21.8	61.5	16.7	74	93.2	70.3	4.1
Tallapoosa city	168	162	-3.6	240	97.5	0.0	0.4	0.0	2.1	33.8	58.0	8.3	82	57.3	80.5	2.4
Taneyville village	396	396	0.0	334	80.5	0.0	0.0	14.4	5.1	22.8	63.6	13.8	125	67.2	56.0	8.0
Taos city	1,121	1,136	1.3	1,168	98.7	0.0	0.0	0.7	0.6	28.3	58.0	13.8	437	85.6	41.2	22.9
Tarkio city	1,583	1,499	-5.3	1,429	96.0	1.6	0.5	1.1	0.8	16.5	57.5	26.0	682	68.5	51.8	20.7
Tarrants village	0	0	0.0	0	0.0	0.0	0.0	0.0	0.0	0.0	0.0	0.0	0	0.0	0.0	0.0
Terre du Lac CDP	0	NA	NA	2,418	95.7	0.0	0.0	3.5	0.8	21.9	57.7	20.2	1,037	89.6	32.9	27.8
Thayer city	2,221	2,235	0.6	2,157	92.8	0.7	0.3	3.7	2.4	20.1	61.2	18.6	920	58.2	59.6	10.1
Theodosia village	243	256	5.3	217	94.5	0.0	0.0	5.5	0.0	19.3	56.6	24.0	94	74.5	71.3	12.8
Thomasville CDP	68	NA	NA	39	100.0	0.0	0.0	0.0	0.0	0.0	43.6	56.4	30	100.0	100.0	0.0
Three Creeks village	6	6	0.0	3	100.0	0.0	0.0	0.0	0.0	0.0	100.0	0.0	1	100.0	100.0	0.0
Tightwad village	69	68	-1.4	67	98.5	0.0	0.0	1.5	0.0	15.0	65.7	19.4	24	70.8	58.3	8.3
Tina village	157	153	-2.5	84	100.0	0.0	0.0	0.0	0.0	14.3	58.5	27.4	48	91.7	81.3	10.4
Tindall town	77	77	0.0	73	100.0	0.0	0.0	0.0	0.0	37.0	43.7	19.2	31	83.9	41.9	12.9
Tipton city	3,262	3,357	2.9	3,290	83.9	13.8	0.0	1.5	0.9	15.7	70.4	13.9	862	73.5	51.6	19.4
Town and Country city	10,848	10,975	1.2	10,890	84.6	3.0	8.2	2.5	1.7	20.5	53.4	26.2	3,658	91.4	5.7	80.7
Tracy city	208	220	5.8	202	82.2	4.0	0.0	6.9	6.9	22.3	56.9	20.8	87	81.6	43.7	19.5
Trenton city	6,001	5,955	-0.8	6,058	94.5	1.0	0.6	2.7	1.2	21.1	56.0	23.1	2,497	59.4	47.1	18.7
Trimble city	646	631	-2.3	637	94.7	0.0	0.0	1.4	3.9	26.4	62.1	11.5	263	63.9	47.1	11.4

1 May be of any race.

Table A. All Places — Population and Housing

STATE City, town, township, borough, or CDP (county if applicable)	2010 census total population	2014 estimated population	Percent change 2010–2014	ACS total population estimate 2010–2014	White alone, not Hispanic or Latino	Black alone, not Hispanic or Latino	Asian alone, not Hispanic or Latino	All other races or 2 or more races, not Hispanic or Latino	Hispanic or Latino[1]	Under 18 years old	Age 18 to 64 years old	Age 65 years and older	Total occupied housing units	Percent owner occupied	High school diploma or less	Bachelor's degree or more
	1	2	3	4	5	6	7	8	9	10	11	12	13	14	15	16
MISSOURI—Con.																
Triplett city	41	40	-2.4	21	100.0	0.0	0.0	0.0	0.0	0.0	52.3	47.6	13	92.3	53.8	30.8
Troy city	10,590	11,355	7.2	11,015	93.1	2.1	0.7	1.6	2.5	31.2	56.6	12.3	3,996	66.1	50.0	21.1
Truesdale city	732	728	-0.5	935	80.2	3.6	0.7	7.9	7.5	36.8	57.4	5.9	305	47.9	64.6	5.9
Truxton village	91	94	3.3	68	100.0	0.0	0.0	0.0	0.0	38.2	52.9	8.8	22	54.5	68.2	9.1
Turney village	148	145	-2.0	148	94.6	3.4	0.0	2.0	0.0	23.0	66.3	10.8	67	77.6	74.6	7.5
Tuscumbia town	203	206	1.5	237	87.3	6.8	0.0	3.8	2.1	14.8	74.2	11.0	70	87.1	35.7	25.7
Twin Oaks village	392	393	0.3	317	94.6	0.0	1.6	2.8	0.9	19.2	54.2	26.5	148	98.0	19.6	56.8
Umber View Heights village	48	48	0.0	62	100.0	0.0	0.0	0.0	0.0	12.9	64.6	22.6	26	100.0	34.6	26.9
Union city	10,295	10,859	5.5	10,517	98.0	0.2	0.7	0.3	0.8	24.4	64.6	11.0	4,134	62.6	36.2	18.3
Union Star town	437	424	-3.0	362	99.2	0.0	0.0	0.8	0.0	18.5	61.4	20.2	179	70.9	67.0	10.1
Unionville city	1,865	1,806	-3.2	1,960	94.9	0.9	1.0	1.0	2.2	21.6	60.3	18.2	901	54.2	59.2	9.3
Unity Village village	80	80	0.0	102	82.4	11.8	0.0	0.0	5.9	10.7	81.4	7.8	36	0.0	2.8	41.7
University City city	35,364	35,115	-0.7	35,226	51.8	37.2	3.3	3.3	4.4	18.2	63.9	17.8	15,837	57.0	18.3	54.6
Uplands Park village	445	446	0.2	391	0.5	99.0	0.0	0.5	0.0	16.6	54.8	28.4	163	77.9	48.5	18.4
Urbana city	417	406	-2.6	416	99.0	0.0	0.0	1.0	0.0	32.0	48.1	20.0	168	71.4	66.7	4.2
Urich city	505	492	-2.6	514	89.3	0.0	0.0	3.5	7.2	23.2	62.8	14.0	237	76.8	50.2	13.5
Utica village	269	256	-4.8	265	81.5	0.0	0.0	15.1	3.4	25.3	63.5	11.3	102	80.4	86.3	5.9
Valley Park city	6,986	6,976	-0.1	6,980	82.8	5.0	7.9	3.6	0.7	19.2	64.5	16.3	3,176	62.6	27.1	37.2
Van Buren town	820	831	1.3	1,077	95.3	0.4	0.0	0.8	3.5	31.6	48.1	20.4	477	61.6	45.0	16.2
Vandalia city	3,899	4,133	6.0	4,019	78.6	13.9	0.6	4.8	2.2	16.2	72.3	11.5	1,167	68.3	71.4	8.7
Vandiver village	71	72	1.4	110	82.7	0.0	0.0	0.0	17.3	41.8	43.6	14.5	37	91.9	67.6	13.5
Vanduser village	267	274	2.6	194	88.1	0.0	0.0	5.2	6.7	18.0	66.0	16.0	92	52.2	51.1	3.3
Velda City city	1,420	1,406	-1.0	1,252	6.3	89.9	0.0	0.2	3.6	24.9	58.4	16.7	539	62.2	50.1	11.7
Velda Village Hills village	1,055	1,058	0.3	917	1.7	96.3	0.0	2.0	0.0	23.2	52.7	24.0	396	65.4	50.0	12.6
Verona town	619	603	-2.6	630	64.9	0.0	0.0	2.2	32.9	30.8	60.9	8.3	217	71.0	65.9	6.9
Versailles city	2,482	2,444	-1.5	2,496	88.7	5.0	0.0	3.7	2.6	20.5	60.1	19.3	995	53.6	67.6	13.9
Viburnum city	693	670	-3.3	731	87.1	0.0	0.0	0.4	12.4	16.1	64.7	19.3	285	68.8	51.9	22.1
Vienna city	610	599	-1.8	788	93.7	0.0	0.0	6.3	0.0	23.0	53.4	23.6	301	57.5	46.8	15.0
Village of Four Seasons village	2,217	2,222	0.2	2,067	98.0	0.0	0.0	1.5	0.5	26.4	51.9	21.6	801	86.4	20.6	41.2
Villa Ridge CDP	2,636	NA	NA	2,630	98.9	0.6	0.0	0.5	0.0	27.8	58.8	13.3	1,000	85.0	49.8	16.4
Vinita Park city	1,880	1,885	0.3	1,776	28.5	56.9	0.8	6.0	7.7	24.4	67.0	8.6	764	48.8	47.9	23.0
Vinita Terrace village	277	278	0.4	230	17.8	76.1	0.0	5.2	0.9	14.7	69.8	15.2	90	81.1	18.9	45.6
Vista village	54	53	-1.9	40	92.5	0.0	0.0	7.5	0.0	17.5	57.5	25.0	20	100.0	90.0	10.0
Waco city	87	86	-1.1	59	79.7	0.0	0.0	20.3	0.0	23.8	62.9	13.6	21	81.0	61.9	4.8
Walker city	270	270	0.0	304	97.7	0.3	0.3	1.0	0.7	22.3	63.7	13.8	112	66.1	59.8	6.3
Walnut Grove city	665	740	11.3	709	95.9	0.0	0.0	2.0	2.1	27.0	56.4	16.5	284	63.4	56.7	14.8
Wardell town	427	408	-4.4	390	96.9	0.5	2.1	0.5	0.0	25.9	55.6	18.5	157	68.2	68.2	4.5
Wardsville village	1,506	1,538	2.1	1,654	94.9	0.0	0.5	4.3	0.3	36.6	56.0	7.3	543	78.1	31.1	37.2
Warrensburg city	18,848	19,963	5.9	19,548	83.3	6.6	2.8	4.5	2.9	19.1	72.4	8.4	6,913	42.3	21.6	35.9
Warrenton city	7,891	8,068	2.2	7,974	90.1	1.6	0.8	2.2	5.3	32.5	55.9	11.6	2,742	67.2	53.4	16.6
Warsaw city	2,127	2,115	-0.6	2,124	96.8	0.9	0.0	0.9	1.5	18.0	54.8	27.1	1,067	50.4	57.5	11.2
Warson Woods city	1,962	1,957	-0.3	1,865	98.1	0.1	0.5	0.9	0.4	25.7	49.6	24.6	723	98.5	4.4	79.5
Washburn city	435	433	-0.5	622	91.5	0.0	0.0	2.3	6.3	21.4	65.3	13.3	215	46.5	67.0	4.2
Washington city	13,982	14,020	0.3	13,982	92.1	2.0	1.3	1.5	3.0	24.0	58.9	17.1	5,847	67.6	35.5	27.3
Wasola CDP	113	NA	NA	45	100.0	0.0	0.0	0.0	0.0	0.0	62.2	37.8	35	48.6	100.0	0.0
Watson village	100	95	-5.0	86	100.0	0.0	0.0	0.0	0.0	31.4	59.3	9.3	27	92.6	88.9	3.7
Waverly city	849	826	-2.7	947	84.2	9.7	0.0	4.4	1.7	31.7	49.5	19.0	354	55.4	71.8	7.3
Wayland city	533	510	-4.3	531	98.9	0.0	0.0	1.1	0.0	24.7	52.1	23.2	231	58.4	64.1	6.9
Waynesville city	4,830	5,365	11.1	5,147	73.4	13.4	0.7	7.1	5.5	29.7	64.6	5.6	1,959	63.2	37.1	29.5
Weatherby town	107	106	-0.9	96	96.9	1.0	0.0	2.1	0.0	29.2	60.4	10.4	36	91.7	75.0	0.0
Weatherby Lake city	1,723	1,808	4.9	1,853	94.5	0.1	1.7	1.1	2.6	18.2	56.7	25.0	723	94.2	13.4	56.4
Weaubleau city	418	399	-4.5	430	93.0	0.0	0.0	6.5	0.5	22.5	59.0	18.4	191	65.4	52.9	11.0
Webb City city	10,996	11,075	0.7	10,985	87.0	1.6	0.0	3.5	7.9	26.5	60.0	13.5	4,483	60.2	52.4	16.3
Webster Groves city	22,995	23,186	0.8	23,084	87.1	7.3	0.8	2.1	2.7	24.1	60.7	15.2	9,141	81.4	10.6	65.6
Weingarten CDP	133	NA	NA	107	100.0	0.0	0.0	0.0	0.0	16.8	36.5	46.7	61	100.0	72.1	11.5
Weldon Spring city	5,445	5,553	2.0	5,496	95.9	0.5	1.6	1.3	0.6	20.4	55.0	24.7	2,199	86.6	16.4	57.0
Weldon Spring Heights town	91	92	1.1	77	96.1	0.0	3.9	0.0	0.0	9.1	46.8	44.2	32	100.0	43.8	37.5
Wellington city	812	789	-2.8	801	95.4	0.6	0.0	4.0	0.0	25.1	55.8	19.1	341	75.1	66.9	12.0
Wellston city	2,306	2,326	0.9	2,010	3.0	94.4	1.4	0.8	0.3	42.9	49.3	7.7	645	31.5	70.2	7.1
Wellsville city	1,217	1,166	-4.2	1,156	95.5	0.2	1.4	1.2	1.7	27.1	51.8	21.2	458	75.8	65.7	9.6
Wentworth village	147	148	0.7	105	96.2	0.0	0.0	0.0	3.8	12.4	71.4	16.2	47	89.4	70.2	6.4
Wentzville city	29,347	33,914	15.6	31,591	90.1	4.6	0.2	2.8	2.3	32.9	58.1	9.2	10,557	85.7	28.2	33.1
West Alton city	522	528	1.1	591	96.8	2.0	0.0	1.2	0.0	15.7	63.6	20.6	259	74.5	66.0	14.3
Westboro city	141	135	-4.3	183	95.6	0.5	0.0	1.1	2.7	37.2	57.9	4.9	65	72.3	70.8	18.5
West Line village	97	97	0.0	79	96.2	0.0	0.0	3.8	0.0	21.6	71.0	7.6	28	82.1	57.1	10.7
Weston city	1,641	1,714	4.4	1,735	96.0	0.0	0.0	2.4	1.6	27.5	56.5	15.9	709	61.8	34.1	33.7
Westphalia city	392	390	-0.5	353	99.2	0.3	0.0	0.3	0.3	15.3	61.4	23.2	155	66.5	52.9	16.8
West Plains city	11,986	12,275	2.4	12,176	91.8	0.6	1.3	3.1	3.1	24.9	56.5	18.7	5,194	50.7	48.1	15.9
West Sullivan town	119	119	0.0	50	100.0	0.0	0.0	0.0	0.0	30.0	54.0	16.0	15	53.3	53.3	13.3
Westwood village	278	279	0.4	327	86.9	0.0	9.8	0.0	3.4	16.2	58.4	25.4	156	96.2	7.7	84.0
Wheatland city	373	356	-4.6	351	95.7	0.0	0.0	2.6	1.7	25.1	51.9	23.1	153	56.2	84.3	3.3
Wheaton city	696	696	0.0	725	78.9	0.8	0.8	10.1	9.4	28.9	63.6	7.3	284	50.0	50.7	14.4
Wheeling city	271	265	-2.2	393	80.4	5.9	0.0	13.7	0.0	31.8	55.2	13.0	125	77.6	64.0	14.4
Whiteman AFB CDP	2,556	NA	NA	3,962	73.0	8.9	2.0	6.3	9.8	29.3	70.7	0.0	874	1.1	21.7	13.4
Whiteside village	75	77	2.7	75	100.0	0.0	0.0	0.0	0.0	17.3	53.3	29.3	33	84.8	78.8	0.0
Whitewater town	125	128	2.4	80	90.0	0.0	0.0	10.0	0.0	17.6	47.6	35.0	36	83.3	80.6	5.6
Wilbur Park village	475	476	0.2	517	98.6	1.4	0.0	0.0	0.0	17.8	71.2	11.0	221	86.9	37.6	35.7
Wildwood city	35,533	35,820	0.8	35,701	90.7	1.7	3.6	1.5	2.4	29.4	60.1	10.4	12,082	91.9	9.0	68.9
Willard city	5,288	5,454	3.1	5,395	90.3	2.2	0.0	1.6	5.8	32.0	57.3	10.8	2,054	65.9	43.5	21.9
Williamsville city	350	347	-0.9	384	99.5	0.0	0.0	0.5	0.0	19.8	63.7	16.4	152	71.7	62.5	3.3
Willow Springs city	2,184	2,154	-1.4	2,176	92.6	0.7	3.6	1.4	1.7	27.2	52.7	20.0	846	48.0	56.9	16.5
Wilson City village	115	118	2.6	58	0.0	100.0	0.0	0.0	0.0	0.0	60.3	39.7	41	36.6	73.2	4.9
Winchester city	1,547	1,541	-0.4	1,583	86.4	3.5	1.3	2.6	6.2	20.4	60.3	19.5	582	73.2	39.2	22.9
Windsor city	2,901	2,847	-1.9	2,896	94.8	3.9	0.0	1.3	0.0	21.4	59.5	19.2	1,303	75.7	49.7	15.1
Windsor Place village	330	330	0.0	394	93.1	1.5	2.8	2.3	0.3	25.7	63.2	11.2	154	62.3	29.9	22.1
Winfield city	1,404	1,425	1.5	1,721	92.5	0.3	0.5	1.7	5.0	34.3	55.6	10.0	602	60.8	58.0	11.3
Winigan CDP	44	NA	NA	59	74.6	0.0	0.0	0.0	25.4	20.4	47.5	32.2	16	100.0	43.8	25.0
Winona city	1,335	1,321	-1.0	1,344	94.9	0.9	0.0	3.1	1.0	24.2	59.1	16.7	550	62.7	66.7	3.8

1 May be of any race.

Table A. All Places — **Population and Housing**

STATE City, town, township, borough, or CDP (county if applicable)	2010 census total population	2014 estimated population	Percent change 2010–2014	ACS total population estimate 2010–2014	White alone, not Hispanic or Latino	Black alone, not Hispanic or Latino	Asian alone, not Hispanic or Latino	All other races or 2 or more races, not Hispanic or Latino	Hispanic or Latino[1]	Under 18 years old	Age 18 to 64 years old	Age 65 years and older	Total occupied housing units	Percent owner occupied	High school diploma or less	Bachelor's degree or more
	1	2	3	4	5	6	7	8	9	10	11	12	13	14	15	16
MISSOURI—Con.																
Winston village	259	256	-1.2	200	91.5	0.0	0.0	2.5	6.0	24.5	60.0	15.5	82	59.8	62.2	2.4
Wood Heights city	716	703	-1.8	724	97.5	0.0	0.0	0.7	1.8	28.0	52.8	19.1	269	88.5	58.7	11.2
Woodson Terrace city	4,063	4,060	0.1	4,070	62.9	20.2	2.7	8.5	5.7	20.7	62.8	16.5	1,784	73.4	48.7	18.2
Wooldridge village	61	61	0.0	29	96.6	0.0	0.0	3.4	0.0	13.8	86.1	0.0	12	100.0	50.0	8.3
Worth village	63	61	-3.2	70	100.0	0.0	0.0	0.0	0.0	17.1	72.9	10.0	29	96.6	86.2	0.0
Wortham CDP	275	NA	NA	222	91.9	0.0	0.0	0.0	8.1	8.1	91.9	0.0	65	55.4	49.2	16.9
Worthington village	81	79	-2.5	142	93.7	0.0	0.0	3.5	2.8	21.8	78.1	0.0	64	34.4	71.9	15.6
Wright City city	3,119	3,405	9.2	3,297	87.8	6.2	0.0	3.8	2.2	32.2	59.3	8.4	1,313	70.6	47.1	17.0
Wyaconda city	227	215	-5.3	241	100.0	0.0	0.0	0.0	0.0	34.4	51.5	14.1	109	78.9	74.3	5.5
Wyatt city	319	316	-0.9	471	92.4	7.2	0.0	0.4	0.0	26.2	55.3	18.5	189	63.0	66.1	8.5
Zalma village	90	91	1.1	142	100.0	0.0	0.0	0.0	0.0	26.0	63.8	9.9	69	62.3	79.7	10.1
MONTANA	989,417	1,023,579	3.5	1,006,370	87.2	0.4	0.6	8.5	3.2	22.3	62.1	15.7	407,797	67.7	34.8	30.1
Absarokee CDP	1,150	NA	NA	1,074	93.8	0.0	0.5	0.6	5.2	14.2	61.0	24.9	508	68.1	37.4	17.9
Alberton town	420	423	0.7	476	100.0	0.0	0.0	0.0	0.0	20.6	60.0	19.5	179	72.1	48.6	30.7
Alder CDP	103	NA	NA	109	100.0	0.0	0.0	0.0	0.0	28.4	54.1	17.4	47	34.0	80.9	0.0
Alzada CDP	29	NA	NA	37	100.0	0.0	0.0	0.0	0.0	18.9	70.2	10.8	15	66.7	60.0	0.0
Amsterdam CDP	180	NA	NA	207	92.3	0.0	6.3	0.0	1.4	34.3	60.7	4.8	60	46.7	38.3	13.3
Anaconda-Deer Lodge County	9,294	9,150	-1.5	9,243	91.2	1.2	0.5	4.1	3.0	18.1	62.6	19.4	3,909	73.0	43.5	19.1
Antelope CDP	51	NA	NA	23	100.0	0.0	0.0	0.0	0.0	0.0	34.8	65.2	19	100.0	100.0	0.0
Arlee CDP	636	NA	NA	610	37.7	0.0	1.1	60.3	0.8	30.2	58.1	11.8	263	65.0	30.4	26.2
Ashland CDP	824	NA	NA	851	37.7	0.0	0.0	60.9	1.4	39.9	48.7	11.3	266	44.4	35.3	30.8
Augusta CDP	309	NA	NA	243	88.5	0.0	0.0	6.2	5.3	12.4	59.1	28.4	127	71.7	48.8	28.3
Avon CDP	111	NA	NA	81	93.8	0.0	0.0	6.2	0.0	29.7	50.7	19.8	38	55.3	47.4	26.3
Azure CDP	286	NA	NA	176	0.0	0.0	0.0	100.0	0.0	43.7	52.4	4.0	52	40.4	30.8	13.5
Babb CDP	174	NA	NA	113	18.6	0.0	0.0	81.4	0.0	18.6	81.3	0.0	36	86.1	55.6	44.4
Bainville town	208	299	43.8	208	92.3	0.0	0.0	7.7	0.0	26.4	59.1	14.4	75	58.7	33.3	32.0
Baker city	1,742	1,911	9.7	1,843	95.9	1.8	0.4	0.8	1.2	22.6	63.2	14.2	767	64.8	52.7	13.0
Ballantine CDP	320	NA	NA	208	94.7	0.0	0.0	0.0	5.3	0.0	42.7	57.2	152	75.0	86.2	13.8
Basin CDP	212	NA	NA	210	93.8	0.0	0.5	4.8	1.0	25.2	59.7	15.2	94	76.6	28.7	26.6
Batavia CDP	385	NA	NA	353	93.5	0.0	0.0	4.0	2.5	34.0	54.6	11.3	119	71.4	43.7	14.3
Bearcreek town	79	83	5.1	129	97.7	0.0	0.0	2.3	0.0	19.4	51.3	29.5	47	70.2	29.8	19.1
Bear Dance CDP	275	NA	NA	273	90.8	0.0	0.0	9.2	0.0	0.0	59.4	40.7	159	81.1	28.3	55.3
Beaver Creek CDP	271	NA	NA	396	86.9	0.0	0.0	9.1	4.0	20.5	76.0	3.5	144	70.1	25.7	11.8
Belfry CDP	218	NA	NA	161	90.1	0.0	0.0	5.0	5.0	15.5	59.6	24.8	83	79.5	38.6	13.3
Belgrade city	7,463	7,798	4.5	7,625	93.5	0.0	0.0	2.4	4.0	28.6	65.5	6.0	3,034	56.2	33.2	27.4
Belknap CDP	158	NA	NA	221	100.0	0.0	0.0	0.0	0.0	0.0	57.5	42.5	120	100.0	75.0	0.0
Belt town	597	604	1.2	639	80.6	1.6	0.3	15.8	1.7	24.4	55.8	19.7	264	70.8	52.7	17.4
Biddle CDP	41	NA	NA	22	100.0	0.0	0.0	0.0	0.0	27.3	40.8	31.8	7	57.1	14.3	28.6
Big Arm CDP	177	NA	NA	260	50.4	0.0	0.0	49.6	0.0	23.1	33.9	43.1	82	96.3	82.9	0.0
Bigfork CDP	4,270	NA	NA	4,375	94.5	0.0	0.0	1.6	3.9	21.2	54.3	24.5	1,888	76.3	22.7	36.9
Big Sandy town	598	607	1.5	664	89.6	0.0	1.2	8.0	1.2	23.4	58.4	18.1	278	64.4	39.9	23.7
Big Sky CDP	2,308	NA	NA	2,694	92.4	0.6	0.0	1.3	5.8	19.2	73.0	7.8	1,054	60.8	16.8	56.0
Big Timber city	1,641	1,650	0.5	1,460	89.5	0.0	1.5	3.6	5.4	25.5	52.8	21.8	601	70.2	40.4	30.0
Billings city	104,224	108,869	4.5	106,979	86.8	0.8	0.9	6.1	5.5	23.0	62.0	14.9	44,208	63.0	34.1	31.6
Birney CDP	137	NA	NA	119	0.0	0.0	0.0	100.0	0.0	51.3	48.7	0.0	24	50.0	12.5	33.3
Black Eagle CDP	904	NA	NA	1,233	88.2	0.0	0.0	6.0	5.8	22.6	57.9	19.6	579	60.1	57.5	9.0
Boneau CDP	380	NA	NA	321	0.0	0.0	0.0	96.0	4.0	47.4	52.5	0.0	85	11.8	50.6	0.0
Bonner-West Riverside CDP	1,663	NA	NA	1,717	86.5	0.0	0.0	10.0	3.4	24.6	66.1	9.4	738	63.8	47.3	21.3
Boulder city	1,183	1,202	1.6	1,281	88.8	0.0	0.0	5.4	5.9	21.9	60.6	17.5	503	81.1	37.4	21.3
Box Elder CDP	87	NA	NA	84	33.3	0.0	0.0	44.0	22.6	40.5	50.1	9.5	29	75.9	17.2	37.9
Boyd CDP	35	NA	NA	23	100.0	0.0	0.0	0.0	0.0	0.0	100.0	0.0	6	100.0	0.0	0.0
Bozeman city	37,284	41,660	11.7	39,123	90.4	0.5	2.1	3.9	3.0	14.8	77.0	8.1	16,073	45.5	11.0	49.8
Brady CDP	140	NA	NA	133	100.0	0.0	0.0	0.0	0.0	6.0	76.7	17.3	78	92.3	35.9	20.5
Bridger town	708	732	3.4	1,034	88.4	0.0	0.8	2.9	7.9	25.6	57.6	16.7	343	72.0	42.9	16.6
Bridger CDP	30	NA	NA	67	43.3	0.0	0.0	0.0	56.7	32.8	67.2	0.0	22	100.0	0.0	100.0
Broadus town	466	482	3.4	586	85.7	0.0	0.0	9.6	4.8	31.7	45.1	23.2	223	61.0	36.8	21.5
Broadview town	192	195	1.6	179	97.8	0.0	0.0	1.1	1.1	26.8	52.5	20.7	65	81.5	30.8	18.5
Brockton town	255	277	8.6	274	10.6	0.0	0.0	89.4	0.0	39.0	54.4	6.6	61	45.9	57.4	16.4
Browning town	1,008	1,032	2.4	1,088	5.2	0.0	1.2	93.3	0.3	28.1	56.2	15.9	398	53.0	55.8	12.8
Busby CDP	745	NA	NA	726	4.3	0.0	0.0	95.7	0.0	51.2	41.7	7.0	149	45.6	59.1	4.0
Butte-Silver Bow	34,204	34,680	1.4	34,462	91.6	0.4	0.6	3.5	3.9	20.7	62.8	16.4	15,275	64.0	45.5	22.7
Butte-Silver Bow (balance)	33,502	33,980	1.4	33,481	91.9	0.4	0.6	3.2	3.9	20.4	62.9	16.7	14,905	63.7	45.4	22.8
Bynum CDP	31	NA	NA	40	100.0	0.0	0.0	0.0	0.0	0.0	85.0	15.0	18	38.9	50.0	16.7
Camas CDP	58	NA	NA	44	47.7	0.0	0.0	31.8	20.5	18.2	65.9	15.9	26	76.9	23.1	15.4
Camp Three CDP	173	NA	NA	210	99.0	0.0	0.0	1.0	0.0	30.5	47.2	22.4	75	57.3	48.0	4.0
Cardwell CDP	50	NA	NA	48	77.1	0.0	0.0	22.9	0.0	29.2	56.4	14.6	20	85.0	30.0	25.0
Carlton CDP	694	NA	NA	646	100.0	0.0	0.0	0.0	0.0	25.7	56.2	18.1	264	68.9	35.6	35.6
Carter CDP	58	NA	NA	64	90.6	0.0	0.0	9.4	0.0	26.5	54.7	18.8	27	77.8	40.7	0.0
Cascade town	685	705	2.9	632	98.7	0.0	0.0	1.3	0.0	20.6	62.2	17.2	256	64.8	46.5	23.4
Charlo CDP	379	NA	NA	345	76.8	0.0	0.0	19.1	4.1	29.6	58.8	11.6	137	58.4	46.0	10.9
Charlos Heights CDP	120	NA	NA	163	100.0	0.0	0.0	0.0	0.0	20.2	79.8	0.0	75	0.0	73.3	0.0
Chester town	847	860	1.5	834	99.0	0.7	0.0	0.2	0.0	19.0	48.9	32.3	379	65.4	34.8	29.0
Chinook city	1,203	1,230	2.2	1,165	89.9	0.7	0.0	4.8	4.6	19.6	53.9	26.6	544	67.6	58.1	13.2
Choteau city	1,686	1,698	0.7	1,616	95.1	0.1	0.0	4.2	0.6	19.2	55.7	25.1	719	64.7	50.9	23.9
Churchill CDP	902	NA	NA	989	96.6	0.0	0.3	2.1	1.0	30.9	50.9	18.3	348	81.3	30.5	29.6
Circle town	615	609	-1.0	614	99.5	0.0	0.0	0.5	0.0	17.7	56.2	25.9	286	76.9	56.3	16.4
Clancy CDP	1,661	NA	NA	1,099	96.1	0.0	0.5	1.5	1.8	18.2	68.5	13.4	681	88.1	26.9	47.6
Clinton CDP	1,052	NA	NA	1,028	98.1	0.0	0.0	1.9	0.0	22.6	69.1	8.3	422	76.5	53.6	22.7
Clyde Park town	289	295	2.1	254	100.0	0.0	0.0	0.0	0.0	18.5	62.1	19.3	109	81.7	47.7	17.4
Colstrip city	2,214	2,316	4.6	2,243	76.9	0.5	1.8	16.8	4.1	30.6	64.5	5.0	811	83.1	21.6	41.2
Columbia Falls city	4,688	4,922	5.0	4,765	95.8	0.0	1.4	1.6	1.2	27.0	59.1	13.7	1,850	59.4	32.9	17.7
Columbus town	1,893	1,996	5.4	2,250	94.4	1.4	0.1	1.9	2.1	23.9	57.0	19.0	900	77.6	46.0	13.9
Condon CDP	343	NA	NA	431	97.9	0.0	1.2	0.0	0.9	14.9	64.1	20.9	194	88.7	42.8	28.9
Conner CDP	216	NA	NA	67	100.0	0.0	0.0	0.0	0.0	31.3	43.3	25.4	31	100.0	71.0	0.0
Conrad city	2,570	2,604	1.3	2,600	90.4	1.0	0.7	5.1	2.9	27.8	46.8	25.3	1,002	66.2	45.4	21.4
Cooke City CDP	75	NA	NA	21	100.0	0.0	0.0	0.0	0.0	0.0	100.0	0.0	9	77.8	66.7	0.0
Coram CDP	539	NA	NA	560	92.5	0.0	0.0	7.5	0.0	13.4	76.9	9.8	259	44.8	43.2	22.4

1 May be of any race.

Table A. All Places — **Population and Housing**

STATE City, town, township, borough, or CDP (county if applicable)	2010 census total population	2014 estimated population	Percent change 2010–2014	ACS total population estimate 2010–2014	White alone, not Hispanic or Latino	Black alone, not Hispanic or Latino	Asian alone, not Hispanic or Latino	All other races or 2 or more races, not Hispanic or Latino	Hispanic or Latino[1]	Under 18 years old	Age 18 to 64 years old	Age 65 years and older	Total occupied housing units	Percent owner occupied	High school diploma or less	Bachelor's degree or more
	1	2	3	4	5	6	7	8	9	10	11	12	13	14	15	16
MONTANA—Con.																
Corvallis CDP	976	NA	NA	921	96.3	0.0	0.0	0.0	3.7	25.2	60.7	14.1	430	36.3	40.7	13.0
Corwin Springs CDP	109	NA	NA	102	92.2	0.0	0.0	7.8	0.0	2.0	53.9	44.1	48	60.4	14.6	41.7
Craig CDP	43	NA	NA	32	84.4	0.0	0.0	15.6	0.0	15.6	43.8	40.6	20	75.0	35.0	40.0
Crane CDP	102	NA	NA	205	100.0	0.0	0.0	0.0	0.0	31.7	58.4	9.8	83	55.4	19.3	16.9
Crow Agency CDP	1,616	NA	NA	1,821	4.4	0.0	0.0	94.0	1.6	33.8	59.7	6.4	334	48.8	49.7	8.4
Culbertson town	714	794	11.2	774	78.6	0.0	0.0	15.2	6.2	33.7	49.2	17.2	266	73.3	38.3	16.2
Custer CDP	159	NA	NA	163	100.0	0.0	0.0	0.0	0.0	23.4	55.2	21.5	79	82.3	41.8	32.9
Cut Bank city	2,869	2,996	4.4	2,947	71.6	0.0	0.7	24.3	3.4	35.8	51.6	12.5	996	62.6	48.4	27.1
Darby town	720	737	2.4	604	89.1	0.0	2.8	5.0	3.1	13.2	71.9	14.7	281	62.6	69.0	8.2
Dayton CDP	84	NA	NA	84	100.0	0.0	0.0	0.0	0.0	10.8	50.2	39.3	44	63.6	59.1	31.8
De Borgia CDP	78	NA	NA	21	100.0	0.0	0.0	0.0	0.0	0.0	47.6	52.4	16	68.8	31.3	0.0
Deer Lodge city	3,111	3,017	-3.0	3,085	96.5	0.0	0.9	2.1	0.5	24.4	56.1	19.6	1,278	67.2	38.7	22.9
Denton town	255	248	-2.7	231	84.8	4.3	0.0	2.2	8.7	26.0	49.0	25.1	93	84.9	32.3	24.7
Dillon city	4,136	4,223	2.1	4,181	88.7	0.0	2.9	3.3	5.1	19.9	65.7	14.4	1,757	51.3	34.8	29.9
Dixon CDP	203	NA	NA	255	56.1	0.4	0.0	37.6	5.9	29.8	58.8	11.4	106	65.1	28.3	22.6
Dodson town	124	123	-0.8	151	37.1	0.0	0.0	62.9	0.0	34.4	33.2	32.5	59	78.0	37.3	33.9
Drummond town	315	334	6.0	395	91.1	0.0	0.0	8.1	0.8	25.1	46.8	28.1	179	72.1	54.2	14.5
Dupuyer CDP	86	NA	NA	79	92.4	0.0	0.0	7.6	0.0	0.0	41.8	58.2	41	80.5	41.5	9.8
Dutton town	316	311	-1.6	384	91.1	0.0	0.0	7.0	1.8	20.9	55.9	23.4	157	85.4	44.6	28.7
East Glacier Park Village CDP	363	NA	NA	517	49.3	0.0	0.0	36.6	14.1	22.1	58.6	19.3	196	68.4	25.0	45.9
East Helena city	2,011	2,060	2.4	2,497	89.7	0.1	0.0	6.8	3.3	28.7	62.9	8.3	1,000	60.1	32.7	31.2
East Missoula CDP	2,157	NA	NA	2,597	93.0	0.5	1.5	2.6	2.4	16.4	74.4	9.3	923	71.2	24.5	26.3
Edgar CDP	114	NA	NA	144	93.8	0.0	0.0	6.3	0.0	13.2	64.5	22.2	57	91.2	61.4	10.5
Ekalaka town	332	343	3.3	342	98.2	0.0	0.0	0.6	1.2	14.3	47.5	38.3	162	80.2	35.8	21.6
Elkhorn CDP	10	NA	NA	18	100.0	0.0	0.0	0.0	0.0	0.0	50.0	50.0	9	100.0	0.0	100.0
Elliston CDP	219	NA	NA	299	97.7	0.0	0.3	2.0	0.0	19.1	60.1	20.7	122	75.4	23.0	28.7
Elmo CDP	180	NA	NA	177	42.4	0.0	0.0	57.6	0.0	33.9	49.1	16.9	68	64.7	30.9	26.5
Emigrant CDP	488	NA	NA	370	85.9	0.0	0.0	14.1	0.0	11.7	55.7	32.7	180	66.1	35.0	33.9
Ennis town	836	871	4.2	843	96.3	0.0	0.0	3.7	0.0	13.3	58.3	28.2	381	72.4	38.3	26.8
Eureka town	1,034	1,082	4.6	1,036	94.3	0.0	0.6	1.2	4.0	22.7	46.5	30.7	516	69.0	43.2	15.9
Evaro CDP	322	NA	NA	398	51.0	0.0	0.0	47.7	1.3	21.7	65.9	12.6	131	92.4	39.7	45.0
Evergreen CDP	7,616	NA	NA	6,711	93.0	0.0	0.2	3.0	3.7	27.1	59.1	13.8	2,571	71.4	49.4	11.5
Fairfield town	708	724	2.3	690	89.9	0.0	0.6	4.6	4.9	28.9	45.6	25.4	290	69.7	42.4	18.3
Fairview town	840	964	14.8	868	86.4	5.4	0.0	3.2	5.0	25.0	59.1	16.0	366	57.9	56.8	12.3
Fallon CDP	164	NA	NA	175	100.0	0.0	0.0	0.0	0.0	19.4	69.7	10.9	62	95.2	32.3	4.8
Finley Point CDP	480	NA	NA	744	85.2	0.0	0.0	14.0	0.8	0.0	38.9	61.2	395	90.9	18.5	61.3
Flaxville town	71	72	1.4	116	94.0	0.0	0.0	6.0	0.0	23.3	68.1	8.6	58	72.4	51.7	17.2
Florence CDP	765	NA	NA	798	100.0	0.0	0.0	0.0	0.0	13.0	74.6	12.4	294	81.6	35.0	37.8
Forest Hill Village CDP	206	NA	NA	235	100.0	0.0	0.0	0.0	0.0	17.0	83.0	0.0	127	67.7	74.0	0.0
Forsyth city	1,856	1,874	1.0	1,831	92.0	0.0	2.1	3.7	2.2	20.3	56.8	22.9	821	67.0	42.5	21.1
Fort Belknap Agency CDP	1,293	NA	NA	1,331	1.0	0.0	0.0	96.1	2.9	35.7	57.9	6.5	331	35.6	36.6	11.8
Fort Benton city	1,464	1,490	1.8	1,364	99.0	0.0	0.0	1.0	0.0	15.8	54.9	29.3	672	72.5	42.0	30.5
Fortine CDP	325	NA	NA	462	92.4	0.6	0.0	6.9	0.0	20.5	58.7	20.6	197	69.5	46.7	5.6
Fort Peck town	233	250	7.3	208	98.1	0.0	0.0	1.9	0.0	12.5	64.9	22.6	93	90.3	33.3	34.4
Fort Shaw CDP	280	NA	NA	278	100.0	0.0	0.0	0.0	0.0	16.2	68.7	15.1	120	100.0	44.2	19.2
Fort Smith CDP	161	NA	NA	47	72.3	0.0	0.0	27.7	0.0	17.0	53.2	29.8	39	69.2	82.1	0.0
Four Corners CDP	3,146	NA	NA	3,264	96.2	0.0	0.7	1.8	1.3	26.9	61.9	11.1	1,251	78.3	25.9	48.0
Fox Lake CDP	158	NA	NA	99	100.0	0.0	0.0	0.0	0.0	35.3	50.4	14.1	37	67.6	40.5	18.9
Frazer CDP	362	NA	NA	306	9.5	0.0	0.0	88.2	2.3	31.7	59.3	8.8	90	33.3	44.4	17.8
Frenchtown CDP	1,825	NA	NA	1,802	98.7	0.0	0.0	0.0	1.3	25.1	67.3	7.6	646	74.0	54.8	18.7
Froid town	185	203	9.7	131	99.2	0.0	0.0	0.8	0.0	9.2	61.9	29.0	59	79.7	40.7	33.9
Fromberg town	438	444	1.4	365	92.3	0.0	0.0	2.5	5.2	19.8	59.7	20.5	170	74.7	45.9	14.1
Gallatin Gateway CDP	856	NA	NA	866	97.3	0.8	0.0	0.0	1.8	19.8	67.4	12.8	340	79.4	35.0	34.7
Gallatin River Ranch CDP	69	NA	NA	45	100.0	0.0	0.0	0.0	0.0	8.9	31.1	60.0	21	100.0	23.8	52.4
Gardiner CDP	875	NA	NA	1,229	89.3	0.0	0.0	1.4	9.3	24.9	64.3	10.8	517	69.2	34.2	32.7
Garrison CDP	96	NA	NA	63	93.7	0.0	0.0	3.2	3.2	6.4	68.3	25.4	31	80.6	61.3	19.4
Geraldine town	261	271	3.8	268	100.0	0.0	0.0	0.0	0.0	33.2	37.4	29.5	118	73.7	50.0	20.3
Geyser CDP	87	NA	NA	55	100.0	0.0	0.0	0.0	0.0	16.4	54.7	29.1	29	65.5	62.1	3.4
Gibson Flats CDP	199	NA	NA	139	100.0	0.0	0.0	0.0	0.0	27.3	72.6	0.0	37	100.0	48.6	0.0
Gildford CDP	179	NA	NA	99	97.0	0.0	0.0	3.0	0.0	34.3	41.4	24.2	43	95.3	23.3	27.9
Glasgow city	3,250	3,380	4.0	3,327	88.2	0.0	0.0	10.9	0.8	21.9	55.8	22.4	1,471	59.2	42.3	20.1
Glendive city	4,935	5,399	9.4	5,167	89.7	1.1	0.8	4.5	3.9	20.2	63.6	16.3	2,195	58.1	43.5	19.1
Grass Range town	110	109	-0.9	137	96.4	0.0	0.0	3.6	0.0	19.7	66.3	13.9	57	63.2	61.4	7.0
Great Falls city	58,631	59,152	0.9	59,017	85.2	1.2	1.0	8.6	4.0	22.1	61.1	16.8	25,127	61.8	34.5	27.8
Greycliff CDP	112	NA	NA	63	100.0	0.0	0.0	0.0	0.0	23.8	58.7	17.5	27	74.1	44.4	7.4
Hamilton city	4,350	4,594	5.6	4,486	93.2	0.8	1.1	2.7	2.1	19.7	51.5	28.6	2,299	48.7	42.6	20.3
Happys Inn CDP	164	NA	NA	50	100.0	0.0	0.0	0.0	0.0	0.0	0.0	100.0	38	100.0	100.0	0.0
Hardin city	3,653	3,796	3.9	3,720	43.3	0.0	0.6	44.1	12.0	31.3	54.0	14.8	1,245	54.6	40.2	19.4
Harlem city	808	830	2.7	849	46.4	0.0	0.0	52.3	1.3	34.6	52.2	13.2	303	62.0	29.4	30.0
Harlowton city	997	974	-2.3	926	96.5	0.0	0.0	2.1	1.4	8.8	48.8	42.5	450	74.9	63.6	13.1
Harrison CDP	137	NA	NA	191	100.0	0.0	0.0	0.0	0.0	6.3	56.9	36.6	57	78.9	49.1	0.0
Havre city	9,442	9,792	3.7	9,668	85.1	0.6	0.6	10.7	3.0	24.2	60.9	14.9	3,906	66.9	29.6	27.4
Havre North CDP	716	NA	NA	785	61.0	0.0	0.0	31.1	7.9	27.9	59.9	12.1	314	51.0	44.9	10.5
Hays CDP	843	NA	NA	962	2.4	0.0	0.0	97.5	0.1	38.6	54.5	7.0	250	51.2	30.8	16.4
Heart Butte CDP	582	NA	NA	543	2.6	0.0	0.0	92.8	4.6	39.6	56.7	3.7	125	43.2	36.8	15.2
Hebgen Lake Estates CDP	70	NA	NA	106	100.0	0.0	0.0	0.0	0.0	43.4	56.6	0.0	37	100.0	40.5	18.9
Helena city	28,212	29,943	6.1	29,142	91.6	0.5	0.6	4.9	2.4	18.2	65.4	16.5	12,881	56.6	24.0	43.6
Helena Flats CDP	1,043	NA	NA	988	93.5	0.0	0.0	4.9	1.6	27.8	57.5	14.7	334	76.3	37.1	23.1
Helena Valley Northeast CDP	2,995	NA	NA	2,731	97.2	0.0	0.6	0.7	1.4	28.0	53.5	18.5	1,069	85.4	26.8	38.7
Helena Valley Northwest CDP	3,482	NA	NA	3,939	95.2	0.0	0.3	2.6	1.9	27.8	63.7	8.5	1,356	91.0	19.4	38.9
Helena Valley Southeast CDP	8,227	NA	NA	7,340	91.4	0.0	0.9	3.3	4.5	28.8	63.7	7.4	2,762	89.2	37.4	25.2
Helena Valley West Central CDP	7,883	NA	NA	8,502	92.6	1.1	0.4	5.1	0.9	27.0	58.8	14.3	3,154	86.8	28.9	34.0
Helena West Side CDP	1,637	NA	NA	1,324	94.5	0.2	0.0	5.4	0.0	7.2	82.8	9.8	665	86.3	32.9	47.2
Heron CDP	282	NA	NA	245	100.0	0.0	0.0	0.0	0.0	3.7	79.7	16.7	110	80.9	54.5	20.9
Herron CDP	116	NA	NA	53	100.0	0.0	0.0	0.0	0.0	0.0	84.9	15.1	35	100.0	11.4	0.0

1 May be of any race.

Table A. All Places — **Population and Housing**

STATE City, town, township, borough, or CDP (county if applicable)	Population: 2010 census total population	Population: 2014 estimated population	Population: Percent change 2010–2014	Population: ACS total population estimate 2010–2014	Race and Hispanic or Latino origin (percent), 2010–2014: White alone, not Hispanic or Latino	Black alone, not Hispanic or Latino	Asian alone, not Hispanic or Latino	All other races or 2 or more races, not Hispanic or Latino	Hispanic or Latino[1]	Age (percent), 2010–2014: Under 18 years old	Age 18 to 64 years old	Age 65 years and older	Households, 2010–2014: Total occupied housing units	Percent owner occupied	Householders by level of education (percent): High school diploma or less	Bachelor's degree or more
	1	2	3	4	5	6	7	8	9	10	11	12	13	14	15	16
MONTANA—Con.																
Highwood CDP	176	NA	NA	211	97.6	0.0	0.0	2.4	0.0	22.3	69.3	8.5	79	73.4	40.5	27.8
Hingham town	118	122	3.4	86	96.5	0.0	1.2	2.3	0.0	9.3	68.6	22.1	47	93.6	34.0	23.4
Hinsdale CDP	217	NA	NA	172	87.8	0.0	1.2	11.0	0.0	16.3	63.9	19.8	83	88.0	55.4	14.5
Hobson city	215	219	1.9	274	96.4	0.0	0.0	2.9	0.7	31.3	49.1	19.3	99	75.8	45.5	29.3
Hot Springs town	544	551	1.3	589	78.8	0.8	0.0	16.1	4.2	14.4	59.6	26.0	332	60.5	51.2	19.6
Hungry Horse CDP	826	NA	NA	898	98.0	0.0	0.0	0.0	2.0	20.9	65.0	14.0	413	60.5	69.7	7.5
Huntley CDP	446	NA	NA	461	97.2	0.0	0.0	0.0	2.8	21.7	66.1	12.1	224	81.3	33.9	30.4
Huson CDP	210	NA	NA	7	100.0	0.0	0.0	0.0	0.0	0.0	100.0	0.0	7	100.0	100.0	0.0
Hysham town	312	302	-3.2	329	87.5	0.0	0.0	7.3	5.2	19.8	54.4	25.8	136	81.6	44.9	12.5
Indian Springs CDP	31	NA	NA	139	100.0	0.0	0.0	0.0	0.0	0.0	90.6	9.4	70	100.0	0.0	18.6
Inverness CDP	55	NA	NA	115	100.0	0.0	0.0	0.0	0.0	27.8	42.6	29.6	46	100.0	47.8	15.2
Ismay town	19	21	10.5	32	100.0	0.0	0.0	0.0	0.0	40.7	53.1	6.3	11	45.5	27.3	18.2
Jardine CDP	57	NA	NA	47	91.5	0.0	0.0	8.5	0.0	42.6	57.5	0.0	19	68.4	21.1	47.4
Jefferson City CDP	472	NA	NA	681	81.6	0.0	1.6	10.7	6.0	40.8	51.2	8.1	187	74.9	35.8	30.5
Jette CDP	253	NA	NA	322	100.0	0.0	0.0	0.0	0.0	21.7	68.4	9.9	153	59.5	17.6	46.4
Joliet town	591	649	9.8	578	93.6	0.0	0.0	2.1	4.3	13.1	55.4	31.5	263	86.3	40.3	24.3
Joplin CDP	157	NA	NA	201	96.5	0.0	0.0	3.5	0.0	9.0	45.9	45.3	107	85.0	43.9	20.6
Jordan town	341	386	13.2	374	95.2	0.0	0.0	3.7	1.1	23.9	54.3	21.9	158	77.2	48.7	7.6
Judith Gap city	126	124	-1.6	79	100.0	0.0	0.0	0.0	0.0	11.4	49.5	39.2	50	92.0	46.0	32.0
Kalispell city	19,907	21,518	8.1	20,629	93.2	0.2	0.9	2.6	3.1	25.5	59.5	15.1	8,476	53.5	32.1	27.8
Kerr CDP	251	NA	NA	246	89.4	0.0	0.0	10.6	0.0	9.8	62.7	27.6	81	100.0	6.2	35.8
Kevin town	154	147	-4.5	107	100.0	0.0	0.0	0.0	0.0	23.4	45.8	30.8	54	77.8	44.4	0.0
Kicking Horse CDP	286	NA	NA	174	75.3	0.0	0.0	14.4	10.3	17.2	64.4	18.4	47	100.0	40.4	14.9
Kila CDP	392	NA	NA	478	99.4	0.0	0.0	0.6	0.0	17.2	69.2	13.6	200	72.5	25.0	29.0
King Arthur Park CDP	738	NA	NA	852	93.5	0.0	0.0	6.5	0.0	24.1	63.3	12.6	337	83.7	22.3	48.1
Kings Point CDP	151	NA	NA	69	100.0	0.0	0.0	0.0	0.0	0.0	62.3	37.7	56	100.0	28.6	33.9
Klein CDP	168	NA	NA	336	100.0	0.0	0.0	0.0	0.0	23.6	50.6	25.9	140	93.6	69.3	6.4
Kremlin CDP	98	NA	NA	84	100.0	0.0	0.0	0.0	0.0	20.3	57.1	22.6	43	86.0	41.9	11.6
Lake Mary Ronan CDP	65	NA	NA	90	100.0	0.0	0.0	0.0	0.0	30.0	41.1	28.9	43	67.4	16.3	55.8
Lakeside CDP	2,669	NA	NA	2,755	94.5	0.0	0.0	3.6	1.9	21.1	56.2	22.7	1,175	73.6	25.4	50.0
Lame Deer CDP	2,052	NA	NA	2,131	5.4	0.8	0.0	90.9	2.9	35.3	57.6	7.0	564	45.9	49.1	16.1
Laurel city	6,718	6,936	3.2	6,887	92.2	0.0	0.0	3.6	4.2	24.5	59.4	16.0	2,904	70.6	47.4	20.9
Lavina town	187	178	-4.8	200	88.5	0.0	0.0	11.5	0.0	25.0	53.0	22.0	82	67.1	46.3	22.0
Lewistown city	5,909	5,867	-0.7	5,879	93.3	0.0	2.1	2.1	2.5	15.1	62.8	22.2	2,880	68.1	44.4	30.2
Lewistown Heights CDP	407	NA	NA	849	100.0	0.0	0.0	0.0	0.0	46.0	41.6	12.2	239	77.4	46.0	12.6
Libby city	2,627	2,656	1.1	2,667	96.0	0.0	1.3	1.6	1.1	21.7	54.7	23.5	1,282	57.3	44.5	19.7
Lima town	221	224	1.4	201	89.1	0.0	0.0	4.5	6.5	14.0	50.3	35.8	112	95.5	53.6	20.5
Lincoln CDP	1,013	NA	NA	862	94.2	0.0	0.0	0.9	4.9	18.6	59.5	21.9	388	82.2	35.8	13.7
Lindisfarne CDP	284	NA	NA	265	80.8	0.0	0.0	0.0	19.2	6.0	53.6	40.4	119	89.1	50.4	0.0
Little Bitterroot Lake CDP	194	NA	NA	205	67.8	0.0	0.0	0.0	32.2	0.0	77.7	22.4	94	70.2	26.6	28.7
Little Browning CDP	206	NA	NA	256	0.0	0.0	6.6	80.9	12.5	53.5	42.9	3.5	57	59.6	35.1	29.8
Livingston city	7,037	7,245	3.0	7,086	93.9	0.4	0.0	3.2	2.4	19.9	62.4	17.7	2,901	70.0	34.4	32.7
Lockwood CDP	6,797	NA	NA	6,943	88.7	0.0	0.2	7.8	3.3	27.3	61.2	11.6	2,634	81.6	53.9	16.3
Lodge Grass town	428	445	4.0	278	10.4	0.0	0.0	89.6	0.0	37.0	46.9	16.2	79	74.7	38.0	20.3
Lodge Pole CDP	265	NA	NA	356	2.8	0.0	0.0	97.2	0.0	33.7	61.5	4.8	96	63.5	42.7	22.9
Logan CDP	99	NA	NA	58	100.0	0.0	0.0	0.0	0.0	0.0	75.8	24.1	30	100.0	66.7	33.3
Lolo CDP	3,892	NA	NA	3,994	97.1	0.0	0.0	2.7	0.3	22.5	69.5	8.0	1,455	85.6	34.8	27.2
Loma CDP	85	NA	NA	37	100.0	0.0	0.0	0.0	0.0	0.0	45.9	54.1	30	66.7	66.7	33.3
Lonepine CDP	162	NA	NA	172	75.6	0.0	0.0	10.5	14.0	30.2	55.8	14.0	65	81.5	63.1	6.2
Malmstrom AFB CDP	3,472	NA	NA	3,625	74.6	9.3	1.4	4.3	10.4	33.8	66.2	0.0	971	0.9	13.3	28.8
Malta city	1,994	1,970	-1.2	1,818	92.6	0.0	0.0	7.4	0.0	17.0	52.1	30.8	894	77.9	43.1	22.1
Manhattan town	1,520	1,571	3.4	1,267	98.3	0.0	0.0	0.9	0.7	21.8	61.5	16.7	553	67.3	32.7	32.7
Marion CDP	886	NA	NA	869	94.7	1.0	0.0	2.5	1.7	18.9	68.6	12.5	315	79.4	67.9	12.1
Martin City CDP	500	NA	NA	468	72.2	0.0	0.0	27.8	0.0	28.2	64.3	7.5	131	60.3	89.3	10.7
Martinsdale CDP	64	NA	NA	85	100.0	0.0	0.0	0.0	0.0	9.4	63.5	27.1	44	79.5	34.1	18.2
Marysville CDP	80	NA	NA	114	100.0	0.0	0.0	0.0	0.0	7.9	78.1	14.0	58	100.0	17.2	51.7
Maxville CDP	130	NA	NA	117	100.0	0.0	0.0	0.0	0.0	10.3	45.3	44.4	56	44.6	58.9	14.3
Medicine Lake town	225	245	8.9	289	94.8	0.0	0.0	4.8	0.3	23.5	57.5	19.0	136	80.9	26.5	31.6
Melstone town	96	106	10.4	61	96.7	0.0	0.0	3.3	0.0	1.6	54.1	44.3	45	91.1	73.3	11.1
Midvale CDP	393	NA	NA	411	100.0	0.0	0.0	0.0	0.0	52.8	43.3	3.9	121	100.0	42.1	26.4
Miles City city	8,393	8,758	4.3	8,553	93.4	0.3	0.5	3.6	2.3	22.5	60.3	17.2	3,592	68.1	38.0	19.4
Missoula city	66,877	69,821	4.4	68,377	89.4	0.6	1.3	5.4	3.3	18.1	70.2	11.8	29,266	48.1	21.5	42.6
Montana City CDP	2,715	NA	NA	2,683	96.0	0.1	0.0	2.9	1.0	25.9	59.6	14.4	1,015	92.0	20.9	50.0
Moore town	193	193	0.0	197	92.9	0.0	0.0	2.5	4.6	21.8	60.4	17.8	83	72.3	44.6	13.3
Muddy CDP	617	NA	NA	563	3.2	0.0	0.0	88.1	8.7	46.0	49.4	4.6	124	52.4	62.1	4.0
Musselshell CDP	60	NA	NA	63	92.1	0.0	0.0	0.0	7.9	0.0	65.0	34.9	37	73.0	51.4	0.0
Nashua town	290	296	2.1	284	95.8	0.0	0.0	4.2	0.0	17.0	59.4	23.9	132	82.6	59.1	9.8
Neihart town	51	51	0.0	53	81.1	0.0	0.0	18.9	0.0	0.0	54.7	45.3	33	63.6	66.7	21.2
Niarada CDP	27	NA	NA	11	27.3	0.0	0.0	72.7	0.0	0.0	0.0	100.0	7	100.0	42.9	57.1
North Browning CDP	2,408	NA	NA	2,363	4.3	0.0	0.0	95.1	0.6	35.6	57.1	7.2	653	33.8	44.7	6.3
Noxon CDP	218	NA	NA	243	81.1	0.0	0.0	18.9	0.0	27.2	58.4	14.4	98	100.0	44.9	21.4
Old Agency CDP	107	NA	NA	129	23.3	0.0	0.0	72.9	3.9	40.4	55.1	4.7	48	68.8	39.6	4.2
Olney CDP	191	NA	NA	198	66.2	0.0	0.0	24.7	9.1	24.8	64.6	10.6	84	85.7	57.1	0.0
Opheim town	85	89	4.7	110	69.1	0.0	0.0	2.7	28.2	35.4	34.5	30.0	47	74.5	34.0	23.4
Orchard Homes CDP	5,197	NA	NA	5,410	90.1	0.5	1.1	5.8	2.5	20.4	62.3	17.5	2,076	64.5	19.1	44.2
Outlook town	47	53	12.8	81	90.1	0.0	0.0	6.2	3.7	32.1	55.6	12.3	29	93.1	34.5	10.3
Ovando CDP	81	NA	NA	80	92.5	7.5	0.0	0.0	0.0	5.0	77.6	17.5	43	67.4	23.3	16.3
Pablo CDP	2,254	NA	NA	2,616	35.4	0.0	1.3	57.3	6.0	30.4	62.0	7.5	909	47.6	42.7	4.7
Paradise CDP	163	NA	NA	183	80.3	0.0	0.0	3.8	15.8	13.0	62.2	24.6	83	79.5	43.4	13.3
Park City CDP	983	NA	NA	1,072	88.4	0.0	0.0	10.5	1.0	32.2	55.8	12.0	367	78.2	52.0	11.7
Parker School CDP	340	NA	NA	656	0.9	0.0	0.0	99.1	0.0	38.6	55.7	5.8	176	73.9	23.9	27.8
Philipsburg town	840	869	3.5	725	96.3	0.0	0.0	2.1	1.7	12.0	53.2	34.9	350	69.1	38.0	23.7
Piltzville CDP	395	NA	NA	364	96.4	0.0	0.0	2.7	0.8	9.6	76.3	14.0	147	80.3	35.4	15.6
Pinesdale town	917	933	1.7	999	90.1	0.0	0.0	0.0	9.9	45.9	47.7	6.3	196	64.3	65.3	7.7
Pioneer Junction CDP	959	NA	NA	755	90.3	0.0	0.0	4.4	5.3	18.3	52.4	29.4	356	82.3	40.4	18.3
Plains town	1,048	1,068	1.9	766	89.9	0.0	0.0	3.9	6.1	14.9	57.8	27.3	408	57.6	63.5	13.2
Plentywood city	1,734	1,918	10.6	1,752	91.7	0.0	0.2	5.9	2.2	20.3	53.6	26.1	821	71.3	42.8	21.2
Plevna town	162	181	11.7	126	97.6	0.0	2.4	0.0	0.0	28.6	46.1	25.4	56	85.7	46.4	23.2
Polson city	4,497	4,607	2.4	4,580	70.4	0.0	0.5	22.9	6.2	24.4	58.8	16.8	1,989	53.0	42.0	29.0
Ponderosa Pines CDP	336	NA	NA	482	100.0	0.0	0.0	0.0	0.0	30.4	62.7	6.6	191	96.3	58.6	28.3
Pony CDP	118	NA	NA	144	100.0	0.0	0.0	0.0	0.0	7.7	59.0	33.3	75	84.0	46.7	21.3

1 May be of any race.

Table A. All Places — Population and Housing

	Population				Race and Hispanic or Latino origin (percent), 2010–2014					Age (percent), 2010–2014			Households, 2010–2014			
STATE City, town, township, borough, or CDP (county if applicable)	2010 census total population	2014 estimated population	Percent change 2010–2014	ACS total population estimate 2010–2014	White alone, not Hispanic or Latino	Black alone, not Hispanic or Latino	Asian alone, not Hispanic or Latino	All other races or 2 or more races, not Hispanic or Latino	Hispanic or Latino[1]	Under 18 years old	Age 18 to 64 years old	Age 65 years and older	Total occupied housing units	Percent owner occupied	High school diploma or less	Bachelor's degree or more
	1	2	3	4	5	6	7	8	9	10	11	12	13	14	15	16
MONTANA—Con.																
Poplar city	812	876	7.9	901	12.4	0.0	0.1	86.3	1.1	35.4	55.7	8.9	277	50.2	58.5	9.7
Power CDP	179	NA	NA	176	94.3	0.0	0.0	5.7	0.0	21.6	57.9	20.5	70	87.1	40.0	18.6
Pray CDP	681	NA	NA	572	94.8	0.0	0.0	2.4	2.8	12.6	65.1	22.4	280	80.0	26.8	55.4
Pryor CDP	618	NA	NA	665	17.9	0.0	0.0	81.8	0.3	37.0	55.1	8.0	149	67.1	26.8	16.1
Rader Creek CDP	363	NA	NA	188	86.7	0.0	0.0	0.0	13.3	17.5	48.9	33.5	81	100.0	27.2	37.0
Radersburg CDP	66	NA	NA	203	100.0	0.0	0.0	0.0	0.0	14.8	52.2	33.0	88	47.7	100.0	0.0
Ravalli CDP	76	NA	NA	77	44.2	0.0	0.0	55.8	0.0	0.0	85.7	14.3	57	50.9	12.3	0.0
Red Lodge city	2,123	2,215	4.3	2,337	94.6	0.0	0.0	2.9	2.5	18.2	62.1	19.7	1,034	66.5	23.5	44.9
Reed Point CDP	193	NA	NA	219	90.0	0.0	0.0	7.3	2.7	8.3	65.4	26.5	111	74.8	46.8	31.5
Reserve CDP	23	NA	NA	30	76.7	0.0	0.0	23.3	0.0	26.7	36.6	36.7	14	78.6	42.9	14.3
Rexford town	103	147	42.7	83	95.2	0.0	0.0	4.8	0.0	0.0	56.7	43.4	53	100.0	26.4	3.8
Richey town	177	189	6.8	155	100.0	0.0	0.0	0.0	0.0	18.6	63.9	17.4	74	63.5	27.0	35.1
Riverbend CDP	484	NA	NA	390	100.0	0.0	0.0	0.0	0.0	12.3	61.1	26.7	139	82.0	65.5	24.5
Roberts CDP	361	NA	NA	277	99.3	0.0	0.7	0.0	0.0	17.3	49.9	32.9	133	70.7	36.1	22.6
Rocky Boy's Agency CDP	355	NA	NA	501	8.2	0.0	0.0	91.8	0.0	41.6	53.4	5.2	119	43.7	20.2	44.5
Rocky Boy West CDP	890	NA	NA	992	1.0	0.0	0.0	93.5	5.4	37.8	56.4	5.8	266	12.4	42.5	9.4
Rocky Point CDP	97	NA	NA	85	100.0	0.0	0.0	0.0	0.0	0.0	87.1	12.9	54	75.9	24.1	20.4
Rollins CDP	209	NA	NA	181	82.9	0.0	0.0	3.3	13.8	6.6	60.9	32.6	83	65.1	27.7	34.9
Ronan city	1,871	1,930	3.2	1,906	59.4	0.2	0.8	33.3	6.3	28.4	59.7	11.9	768	58.3	40.6	18.0
Roscoe CDP	15	NA	NA	43	100.0	0.0	0.0	0.0	0.0	0.0	90.7	9.3	21	100.0	0.0	81.0
Rosebud CDP	111	NA	NA	121	100.0	0.0	0.0	0.0	0.0	22.3	57.0	20.7	50	90.0	60.0	14.0
Roundup city	1,788	1,839	2.9	1,740	94.4	0.5	1.3	1.7	2.1	20.3	58.9	20.7	780	63.8	50.6	17.1
Roy CDP	108	NA	NA	138	97.1	0.0	0.0	2.9	0.0	39.8	39.7	20.3	50	58.0	52.0	6.0
Rudyard CDP	258	NA	NA	260	96.5	0.0	0.0	3.5	0.0	30.0	46.5	23.5	107	90.7	35.5	22.4
Ryegate town	245	243	-0.8	212	96.7	0.0	0.0	1.9	1.4	8.0	59.4	32.5	99	82.8	70.7	15.2
Saco town	196	199	1.5	238	79.4	0.0	0.0	19.3	1.3	27.7	59.2	13.0	108	66.7	65.7	9.3
Saddle Butte CDP	128	NA	NA	172	75.6	0.0	0.0	24.4	0.0	56.4	43.6	0.0	30	100.0	13.3	26.7
St. Ignatius town	842	852	1.2	946	45.5	0.0	0.0	52.3	2.2	33.4	53.0	13.5	357	68.9	35.9	27.5
St. Marie CDP	264	NA	NA	454	91.2	1.3	0.0	0.0	7.5	26.5	47.5	26.0	192	68.8	49.0	10.9
St. Pierre CDP	350	NA	NA	402	0.7	0.0	0.0	94.5	4.7	36.6	56.6	6.7	88	56.8	21.6	20.5
St. Regis CDP	319	NA	NA	239	91.2	0.0	0.0	0.0	8.8	35.2	56.5	8.4	91	54.9	51.6	13.2
St. Xavier town	83	NA	NA	6	100.0	0.0	0.0	0.0	0.0	0.0	100.0	0.0	6	100.0	100.0	0.0
Sand Coulee CDP	212	NA	NA	243	84.8	0.0	0.0	15.2	0.0	20.6	70.0	9.5	102	78.4	45.1	14.7
Sangrey CDP	306	NA	NA	493	1.2	0.0	0.0	94.3	4.5	38.6	52.3	9.1	129	50.4	22.5	14.0
Santa Rita CDP	113	NA	NA	0	0.0	0.0	0.0	0.0	0.0	0.0	0.0	0.0	0	0.0	0.0	0.0
Savage CDP	0	NA	NA	290	75.5	0.0	12.4	2.4	9.7	21.7	65.1	13.1	110	56.4	50.0	32.7
Scobey city	1,019	1,052	3.2	1,096	96.1	0.0	0.1	1.5	2.4	19.0	52.7	28.1	537	77.7	31.7	19.4
Sedan CDP	99	NA	NA	174	100.0	0.0	0.0	0.0	0.0	20.6	69.5	9.8	63	82.5	31.7	41.3
Seeley Lake CDP	1,659	NA	NA	1,174	87.3	0.0	0.0	8.3	4.4	22.4	58.8	18.6	565	81.9	38.6	36.8
Shawmut CDP	42	NA	NA	33	100.0	0.0	0.0	0.0	0.0	12.1	51.6	36.4	18	100.0	61.1	5.6
Shelby city	3,382	3,301	-2.4	3,096	85.9	0.3	0.7	10.3	2.8	18.9	65.2	16.0	1,197	56.0	48.7	16.3
Shepherd CDP	516	NA	NA	766	99.6	0.0	0.0	0.0	0.4	22.1	71.1	6.8	256	81.3	34.0	15.6
Sheridan town	644	659	2.3	685	98.0	0.0	0.3	1.0	0.7	20.1	56.6	23.2	285	75.4	40.0	29.8
Sidney city	5,266	6,473	22.9	5,888	93.4	0.0	0.0	3.0	3.7	22.1	64.2	13.7	2,459	63.8	42.0	15.0
Silesia CDP	96	NA	NA	101	86.1	0.0	0.0	8.9	5.0	15.9	64.4	19.8	34	44.1	35.3	20.6
Silver Gate CDP	20	NA	NA	21	95.2	0.0	0.0	4.8	0.0	0.0	71.3	28.6	7	100.0	28.6	57.1
Simms CDP	354	NA	NA	367	100.0	0.0	0.0	0.0	0.0	21.3	60.8	18.0	148	64.2	58.8	19.6
Somers CDP	1,109	NA	NA	1,248	91.0	8.1	0.0	0.9	0.0	29.4	65.1	5.4	428	72.9	10.5	42.3
South Browning CDP	1,785	NA	NA	2,045	0.0	0.5	0.0	99.5	0.0	39.1	55.6	5.4	506	34.0	58.5	4.0
South Glastonbury CDP	0	NA	NA	406	100.0	0.0	0.0	0.0	0.0	26.6	73.5	0.0	105	100.0	41.9	41.0
South Hills CDP	517	NA	NA	426	97.4	0.0	0.0	0.0	2.6	32.4	61.3	6.3	148	93.2	12.8	68.9
Spokane Creek CDP	355	NA	NA	318	100.0	0.0	0.0	0.0	0.0	10.4	80.2	9.4	151	81.5	15.2	60.3
Springdale CDP	42	NA	NA	82	100.0	0.0	0.0	0.0	0.0	45.1	51.2	3.7	22	59.1	81.8	0.0
Springhill CDP	130	NA	NA	57	86.0	0.0	0.0	14.0	0.0	31.6	57.8	10.5	19	100.0	0.0	73.7
Stanford town	401	387	-3.5	419	98.6	0.0	0.0	1.4	0.0	18.7	57.2	24.1	197	76.6	35.5	33.5
Starr School CDP	252	NA	NA	140	0.0	0.0	0.0	100.0	0.0	35.8	59.4	5.0	66	54.5	27.3	0.0
Stevensville town	1,822	1,907	4.7	1,944	92.5	0.2	0.0	3.1	4.2	22.4	53.8	23.8	819	50.7	44.2	15.3
Stockett CDP	169	NA	NA	256	83.6	0.0	0.0	16.4	0.0	36.3	57.8	5.9	74	82.4	36.5	13.5
Stryker CDP	26	NA	NA	35	91.4	0.0	0.0	8.6	0.0	0.0	80.0	20.0	18	94.4	66.7	5.6
Sula CDP	37	NA	NA	61	59.0	0.0	0.0	0.0	41.0	16.4	64.0	19.7	22	36.4	63.6	18.2
Sunburst town	385	367	-4.7	320	93.4	0.0	0.0	0.6	5.9	25.7	65.3	9.1	110	77.3	34.5	11.8
Sun Prairie CDP	1,630	NA	NA	1,290	88.3	0.0	0.4	10.7	0.6	22.6	63.8	13.5	558	87.1	52.9	10.6
Sun River CDP	124	NA	NA	125	88.8	0.0	0.0	11.2	0.0	4.8	44.8	50.4	61	90.2	75.4	14.8
Superior town	811	848	4.6	864	92.2	4.1	0.7	2.2	0.8	30.8	51.2	18.2	317	50.8	45.7	15.5
Swan Lake CDP	113	NA	NA	85	100.0	0.0	0.0	0.0	0.0	15.3	55.4	29.4	46	100.0	23.9	41.3
Sweet Grass CDP	58	NA	NA	94	100.0	0.0	0.0	0.0	0.0	13.8	64.8	21.3	45	44.4	31.1	24.4
Sylvanite CDP	103	NA	NA	110	98.2	0.0	0.0	0.0	1.8	25.4	53.7	20.9	48	85.4	27.1	27.1
Terry town	605	591	-2.3	686	92.1	0.0	0.0	7.4	0.4	24.1	45.5	30.5	279	81.7	55.9	14.7
The Silos CDP	506	NA	NA	512	95.3	0.0	0.0	4.7	0.0	16.8	63.4	19.7	267	80.9	49.8	37.1
Thompson Falls city	1,317	1,340	1.7	1,080	95.2	0.0	0.3	3.0	1.6	19.9	51.4	28.6	477	74.4	61.4	15.9
Three Forks city	1,866	1,903	2.0	1,837	92.0	0.0	0.2	4.9	2.9	21.0	55.8	23.2	791	71.2	51.2	18.8
Toston CDP	108	NA	NA	204	100.0	0.0	0.0	0.0	0.0	27.5	64.8	7.8	86	100.0	93.0	7.0
Townsend city	1,878	1,942	3.4	2,033	88.8	0.0	3.2	5.0	3.0	29.3	53.4	17.4	808	72.4	59.5	17.9
Trego CDP	541	NA	NA	714	100.0	0.0	0.0	0.0	0.0	33.4	57.2	9.2	269	81.0	47.2	17.5
Trout Creek CDP	242	NA	NA	181	92.3	0.0	0.0	7.7	0.0	12.7	50.9	36.5	95	52.6	47.4	22.1
Troy city	932	941	1.0	924	95.5	0.0	0.3	1.4	2.8	13.6	67.1	19.2	502	70.7	38.4	19.3
Turah CDP	306	NA	NA	361	89.8	2.5	0.0	7.8	0.0	28.5	60.2	11.4	130	65.4	30.8	22.3
Turner CDP	61	NA	NA	99	100.0	0.0	0.0	0.0	0.0	21.2	69.7	9.1	37	73.0	40.5	27.0
Turtle Lake CDP	209	NA	NA	18	0.0	0.0	0.0	100.0	0.0	0.0	0.0	100.0	18	100.0	0.0	0.0
Twin Bridges town	375	386	2.9	299	91.6	0.0	0.7	5.4	2.3	20.8	55.5	23.7	145	84.1	35.2	37.2
Ulm CDP	738	NA	NA	541	96.5	0.0	0.0	2.2	1.3	20.4	55.5	24.2	204	100.0	38.7	15.2
Valier town	509	511	0.4	573	85.9	0.0	0.7	12.6	0.9	25.1	48.2	26.7	261	86.6	45.6	18.4
Vaughn CDP	658	NA	NA	804	86.1	0.6	0.0	9.8	3.5	26.4	58.8	14.7	293	79.9	54.9	16.4
Victor CDP	745	NA	NA	903	100.0	0.0	0.0	0.0	0.0	26.7	62.7	10.5	318	55.0	51.9	24.8
Virginia City town	189	198	4.8	209	95.7	0.0	0.0	2.4	1.9	6.2	69.5	24.4	89	77.5	31.5	33.7
Walkerville town	702	700	-0.3	981	80.9	0.0	0.0	13.4	5.7	28.9	63.5	7.6	370	78.4	49.5	17.8
Weeksville CDP	83	NA	NA	101	100.0	0.0	0.0	0.0	0.0	17.8	26.8	55.4	44	100.0	72.7	0.0
Westby town	163	183	12.3	168	94.0	0.0	1.8	3.0	1.2	18.5	54.1	27.4	88	50.0	53.4	10.2
West Glacier CDP	227	NA	NA	327	96.0	0.0	0.0	0.0	4.0	18.3	71.3	10.4	138	64.5	25.4	49.3
West Glendive CDP	1,948	NA	NA	1,972	98.4	0.0	0.0	1.1	0.5	23.4	56.1	20.6	814	89.4	40.0	21.3
West Havre CDP	316	NA	NA	81	100.0	0.0	0.0	0.0	0.0	12.3	87.7	0.0	28	100.0	35.7	35.7

1 May be of any race.

Table A. All Places — **Population and Housing**

STATE City, town, township, borough, or CDP (county if applicable)	Population: 2010 census total population	Population: 2014 estimated population	Population: Percent change 2010–2014	Population: ACS total population estimate 2010–2014	Race and Hispanic or Latino origin (percent), 2010–2014: White alone, not Hispanic or Latino	Black alone, not Hispanic or Latino	Asian alone, not Hispanic or Latino	All other races or 2 or more races, not Hispanic or Latino	Hispanic or Latino[1]	Age (percent), 2010–2014: Under 18 years old	Age 18 to 64 years old	Age 65 years and older	Households, 2010–2014: Total occupied housing units	Percent owner occupied	Householders by level of education (percent): High school diploma or less	Bachelor's degree or more
	1	2	3	4	5	6	7	8	9	10	11	12	13	14	15	16
MONTANA—Con.																
West Kootenai CDP	365	NA	NA	121	100.0	0.0	0.0	0.0	0.0	0.0	52.1	47.9	93	89.2	44.1	39.8
West Yellowstone town	1,271	1,322	4.0	1,434	89.3	3.3	0.0	1.0	6.5	21.8	67.0	11.2	665	38.8	38.6	29.2
Wheatland CDP	568	NA	NA	478	100.0	0.0	0.0	0.0	0.0	21.3	70.8	7.9	182	100.0	24.2	33.0
Whitefish city	6,363	6,864	7.9	6,542	96.8	0.0	0.2	1.0	2.0	15.8	68.0	16.3	2,986	56.3	22.7	48.3
Whitehall town	1,036	1,079	4.2	962	94.7	0.0	0.9	3.3	1.0	19.4	56.4	24.1	484	62.8	31.8	20.9
White Haven CDP	577	NA	NA	706	92.2	0.0	0.0	5.1	2.7	32.5	47.8	19.7	252	55.2	50.8	9.5
White Sulphur Springs city	939	925	-1.5	1,151	97.3	0.0	0.3	0.2	2.2	23.6	55.8	20.6	452	80.3	58.0	13.1
Whitewater CDP	64	NA	NA	34	100.0	0.0	0.0	0.0	0.0	29.4	55.8	14.7	15	60.0	80.0	6.7
Wibaux town	589	655	11.2	513	97.5	0.0	0.0	0.0	2.5	21.4	53.6	25.0	234	67.5	61.5	13.2
Willow Creek CDP	210	NA	NA	278	100.0	0.0	0.0	0.0	0.0	40.3	55.2	4.7	90	53.3	48.9	27.8
Wilsall CDP	178	NA	NA	102	96.1	0.0	0.0	3.9	0.0	13.7	48.1	38.2	55	85.5	21.8	56.4
Wineglass CDP	256	NA	NA	289	100.0	0.0	0.0	0.0	0.0	25.2	62.2	12.5	102	73.5	18.6	45.1
Winifred town	208	208	0.0	187	86.6	1.1	1.1	0.0	11.2	21.4	64.6	13.9	76	80.3	47.4	22.4
Winnett town	178	183	2.8	235	90.2	7.2	0.0	0.0	2.6	23.8	56.1	20.0	104	78.8	62.5	15.4
Winston CDP	147	NA	NA	0	0.0	0.0	0.0	0.0	0.0	0.0	0.0	0.0	0	0.0	0.0	0.0
Wisdom CDP	98	NA	NA	108	94.4	0.0	0.0	2.8	2.8	11.1	68.6	20.4	65	67.7	47.7	20.0
Wolf Point city	2,621	2,835	8.2	2,730	40.9	0.0	0.6	57.4	1.1	33.6	55.6	10.8	804	62.4	50.7	15.5
Woods Bay CDP	661	NA	NA	578	96.2	0.0	0.0	2.1	1.7	13.7	50.9	35.5	295	90.2	18.0	36.9
Worden CDP	577	NA	NA	573	85.3	0.0	0.0	14.7	0.0	21.4	58.0	20.4	208	91.8	46.6	14.9
Wye CDP	511	NA	NA	318	98.1	0.0	0.0	1.9	0.0	18.9	70.4	10.7	140	81.4	39.3	11.4
Wyola CDP	215	NA	NA	159	5.0	0.0	0.0	95.0	0.0	23.9	59.7	16.4	41	48.8	34.1	31.7
Yaak CDP	248	NA	NA	251	93.6	0.0	0.0	1.6	4.8	6.0	55.9	38.2	132	91.7	50.0	26.5
Zortman CDP	69	NA	NA	16	100.0	0.0	0.0	0.0	0.0	0.0	100.0	0.0	8	100.0	0.0	100.0
NEBRASKA	1,826,341	1,881,503	3.0	1,855,617	81.2	4.5	1.9	2.6	9.7	24.9	61.2	13.9	731,347	66.5	34.4	29.7
Abie village	69	68	-1.4	110	100.0	0.0	0.0	0.0	0.0	16.3	80.9	2.7	48	100.0	41.7	16.7
Adams village	583	588	0.9	560	97.0	0.0	0.0	0.4	2.7	30.0	46.4	23.6	196	69.4	40.8	20.9
Ainsworth city	1,728	1,621	-6.2	1,786	97.5	0.1	0.4	1.8	0.1	23.4	52.8	23.6	919	62.2	55.6	19.3
Albion city	1,650	1,607	-2.6	1,721	98.4	0.1	0.4	0.0	1.2	21.4	48.5	30.1	710	77.0	49.3	14.1
Alda village	642	656	2.2	635	79.4	0.0	0.0	4.3	16.4	25.5	63.5	11.0	236	77.5	58.1	4.7
Alexandria village	177	177	0.0	162	93.8	0.0	0.0	6.2	0.0	24.7	58.7	16.7	74	90.5	67.6	8.1
Allen village	377	362	-4.0	316	92.4	0.9	0.0	6.0	0.6	22.4	54.1	23.4	127	75.6	40.2	11.8
Alliance city	8,491	8,519	0.3	8,501	79.0	0.1	0.0	6.4	14.4	26.3	58.1	15.8	3,660	58.2	40.2	15.4
Alma city	1,133	1,157	2.1	1,159	94.6	0.3	0.0	1.0	4.1	18.5	48.9	32.8	529	76.9	42.9	14.4
Alvo village	132	132	0.0	155	92.9	7.1	0.0	0.0	0.0	31.6	58.1	10.3	64	81.3	32.8	12.5
Ames CDP	24	NA	NA	75	100.0	0.0	0.0	0.0	0.0	32.0	60.0	8.0	25	100.0	88.0	0.0
Amherst village	248	251	1.2	240	98.3	0.0	0.0	1.3	0.4	20.8	64.6	14.6	107	85.0	34.6	26.2
Anoka village	6	6	0.0	15	100.0	0.0	0.0	0.0	0.0	0.0	60.0	40.0	5	100.0	20.0	0.0
Anselmo village	145	143	-1.4	147	95.9	0.7	0.0	3.4	0.0	27.2	49.5	23.1	65	72.3	32.3	13.8
Ansley village	441	427	-3.2	398	95.2	0.0	1.5	0.0	3.3	19.1	55.2	25.6	194	82.5	39.2	22.2
Arapahoe city	1,026	1,018	-0.8	908	97.0	0.0	0.0	1.3	1.7	20.4	51.7	28.0	441	72.3	59.9	12.2
Arcadia village	311	307	-1.3	360	95.6	0.0	0.0	2.8	1.7	27.8	52.8	19.4	150	76.0	49.3	16.7
Archer CDP	81	NA	NA	62	100.0	0.0	0.0	0.0	0.0	0.0	100.0	0.0	28	100.0	100.0	0.0
Arlington village	1,243	1,246	0.2	1,187	98.1	0.0	0.0	1.0	0.9	28.9	59.1	12.0	450	77.8	39.3	24.7
Arnold village	597	580	-2.8	550	92.5	0.0	0.2	5.8	1.5	15.2	56.6	28.2	309	64.4	40.1	14.2
Arthur village	117	116	-0.9	167	100.0	0.0	0.0	0.0	0.0	36.0	50.4	13.8	72	56.9	25.0	25.0
Ashland city	2,453	2,540	3.5	2,479	93.1	0.0	0.3	3.5	3.1	22.3	58.8	19.1	1,010	65.7	36.8	30.0
Ashton village	194	189	-2.6	186	100.0	0.0	0.0	0.0	0.0	16.7	58.1	25.3	93	87.1	58.1	6.5
Aten CDP	112	NA	NA	58	100.0	0.0	0.0	0.0	0.0	0.0	56.9	43.1	21	52.4	81.0	0.0
Atkinson city	1,245	1,257	1.0	1,299	97.7	0.0	0.0	0.0	2.3	29.2	51.4	19.3	520	76.0	40.4	21.2
Atlanta village	131	130	-0.8	109	100.0	0.0	0.0	0.0	0.0	32.1	54.4	13.8	39	79.5	41.0	7.7
Auburn city	3,460	3,382	-2.3	3,426	97.0	1.1	0.6	1.0	0.4	22.5	59.4	18.4	1,399	63.0	37.0	23.9
Aurora city	4,479	4,472	-0.2	4,461	95.2	0.3	0.2	1.3	3.0	26.0	54.4	19.7	1,779	71.7	34.7	24.3
Avoca village	242	242	0.0	180	96.7	0.0	1.1	0.0	2.2	20.6	66.7	12.8	77	70.1	61.0	7.8
Axtell village	726	743	2.3	622	97.4	0.3	0.0	0.0	2.3	17.3	61.6	21.1	282	84.8	48.6	22.3
Ayr village	94	94	0.0	75	100.0	0.0	0.0	0.0	0.0	34.7	58.8	6.7	28	82.1	21.4	28.6
Bancroft village	495	482	-2.6	492	89.6	0.0	0.0	9.6	0.8	23.2	60.3	16.5	214	74.3	47.2	17.8
Barada village	24	24	0.0	9	100.0	0.0	0.0	0.0	0.0	0.0	99.9	0.0	5	100.0	100.0	0.0
Barneston village	116	113	-2.6	92	94.6	0.0	0.0	3.3	2.2	8.8	72.9	18.5	49	71.4	63.3	2.0
Bartlett village	117	111	-5.1	141	100.0	0.0	0.0	0.0	0.0	23.4	61.1	15.6	75	70.7	38.7	45.3
Bartley village	283	277	-2.1	269	96.7	0.0	0.0	3.3	0.0	21.5	56.0	22.3	127	85.8	41.7	15.0
Bassett city	619	582	-6.0	559	96.1	0.0	0.5	3.4	0.0	14.4	56.3	29.2	313	81.8	48.9	17.3
Battle Creek city	1,207	1,196	-0.9	1,103	98.6	0.0	0.0	0.0	1.4	23.3	57.2	19.4	454	83.9	27.3	18.1
Bayard city	1,209	1,154	-4.5	1,097	79.9	1.0	0.0	3.1	16.0	26.0	52.2	22.0	440	79.1	42.0	15.9
Bazile Mills village	29	28	-3.4	25	100.0	0.0	0.0	0.0	0.0	32.0	56.0	12.0	8	100.0	50.0	25.0
Beatrice city	12,437	12,055	-3.1	12,183	94.6	0.1	0.6	2.4	2.3	22.3	57.5	20.3	5,297	63.3	44.8	19.8
Beaver City city	609	596	-2.1	662	95.8	0.2	0.0	3.0	1.1	24.3	50.1	25.5	295	75.9	55.3	16.3
Beaver Crossing village	403	398	-1.2	391	96.2	1.3	0.0	2.6	0.0	18.9	66.8	14.3	160	78.8	54.4	13.8
Bee village	191	192	0.5	196	100.0	0.0	0.0	0.0	0.0	20.4	59.1	20.4	81	91.4	40.7	16.0
Beemer village	678	665	-1.9	579	86.7	0.9	3.8	3.8	4.8	17.2	45.3	37.3	270	66.3	54.8	14.4
Belden village	115	112	-2.6	93	95.7	0.0	1.1	3.2	0.0	16.1	68.9	15.1	38	97.4	47.4	7.9
Belgrade village	126	118	-6.3	150	98.7	0.0	0.0	0.0	1.3	22.0	61.3	16.7	65	67.7	75.4	0.0
Bellevue city	51,022	53,936	5.7	52,690	74.1	6.5	2.0	4.0	13.4	25.9	61.9	12.2	20,105	66.9	29.5	30.8
Bellwood village	435	419	-3.7	388	97.9	0.5	0.0	0.8	0.8	26.6	55.1	18.3	166	75.3	57.8	7.2
Belmar CDP	216	NA	NA	110	85.5	0.0	0.0	14.5	0.0	9.1	67.3	23.6	85	88.2	38.8	12.9
Belvidere village	48	48	0.0	38	100.0	0.0	0.0	0.0	0.0	23.7	58.0	18.4	14	78.6	50.0	0.0
Benedict village	234	236	0.9	214	100.0	0.0	0.0	0.0	0.0	25.2	63.1	11.7	81	81.5	44.4	11.1
Benkelman city	953	888	-6.8	974	96.1	0.1	1.5	0.5	1.7	21.9	51.9	26.2	470	67.7	24.9	23.2
Bennet village	719	835	16.1	896	98.2	0.0	0.0	1.2	0.6	28.7	59.1	12.2	328	89.6	25.3	28.7
Bennington city	1,458	1,482	1.6	1,357	91.5	2.5	0.2	2.3	3.5	26.3	57.7	16.1	513	68.4	31.8	32.6
Berea CDP	41	NA	NA	19	100.0	0.0	0.0	0.0	0.0	0.0	100.0	0.0	10	100.0	0.0	0.0
Bertrand village	750	732	-2.4	780	88.8	0.0	0.0	1.4	9.7	26.7	50.7	22.7	342	69.0	40.1	19.0
Berwyn village	83	82	-1.2	113	94.7	0.0	0.0	5.3	0.0	14.2	67.3	18.6	50	100.0	52.0	2.0
Big Springs village	400	397	-0.8	563	75.7	0.0	0.0	1.1	23.3	32.9	52.6	14.6	206	64.6	57.3	9.2
Bladen village	238	229	-3.8	251	90.4	0.0	0.0	1.2	8.4	26.4	59.6	14.3	98	83.7	45.9	13.3
Blair city	7,990	7,986	-0.1	7,990	93.6	1.4	0.1	2.8	2.2	24.0	61.0	15.1	3,138	69.9	43.4	26.6
Bloomfield city	1,028	985	-4.2	940	94.9	0.0	0.0	1.7	3.4	18.8	47.6	33.6	475	68.6	51.2	20.6
Bloomington village	103	99	-3.9	162	94.4	0.0	0.0	0.6	4.9	29.6	58.7	11.7	56	78.6	46.4	5.4
Blue Hill city	936	901	-3.7	876	92.9	0.0	5.7	0.2	1.1	24.2	51.5	24.3	356	71.6	36.0	25.3
Blue Springs city	331	320	-3.3	372	90.9	0.0	0.0	9.1	0.0	23.9	59.3	16.7	149	79.2	55.7	6.0

1 May be of any race.

Table A. All Places — **Population and Housing**

STATE City, town, township, borough, or CDP (county if applicable)	Population: 2010 census total population	Population: 2014 estimated population	Population: Percent change 2010–2014	Population: ACS total population estimate 2010–2014	Race and Hispanic or Latino origin (percent), 2010–2014: White alone, not Hispanic or Latino	Black alone, not Hispanic or Latino	Asian alone, not Hispanic or Latino	All other races or 2 or more races, not Hispanic or Latino	Hispanic or Latino[1]	Age (percent), 2010–2014: Under 18 years old	Age 18 to 64 years old	Age 65 years and older	Households, 2010–2014: Total occupied housing units	Percent owner occupied	Householders by level of education (percent): High school diploma or less	Bachelor's degree or more
	1	2	3	4	5	6	7	8	9	10	11	12	13	14	15	16
NEBRASKA—Con.																
Bow Valley CDP	116	NA	NA	108	100.0	0.0	0.0	0.0	0.0	28.7	48.2	23.1	39	89.7	53.8	7.7
Boys Town village	745	649	-12.9	914	73.9	18.4	0.1	2.0	5.7	67.0	32.7	0.3	18	0.0	77.8	16.7
Bradshaw village	273	275	0.7	267	96.6	0.0	0.0	0.0	3.4	21.4	58.1	20.6	113	80.5	52.2	15.0
Brady village	428	420	-1.9	367	98.9	0.0	0.0	0.8	0.3	28.3	53.7	18.0	154	76.0	46.1	24.0
Brainard village	330	327	-0.9	303	100.0	0.0	0.0	0.0	0.0	22.5	55.1	22.4	141	65.2	53.2	12.8
Brewster village	17	18	5.9	5	100.0	0.0	0.0	0.0	0.0	0.0	80.0	20.0	4	100.0	100.0	0.0
Bridgeport city	1,545	1,513	-2.1	1,767	75.7	0.1	1.2	0.2	22.9	28.0	60.0	12.1	692	69.2	43.1	25.0
Bristow village	65	63	-3.1	30	100.0	0.0	0.0	0.0	0.0	0.0	56.7	43.3	23	91.3	69.6	21.7
Broadwater village	128	124	-3.1	173	84.4	0.0	0.6	1.2	13.9	19.0	62.9	17.9	79	82.3	51.9	8.9
Brock village	112	110	-1.8	130	98.5	0.0	0.0	1.5	0.0	7.7	63.9	28.5	64	79.7	60.9	3.1
Broken Bow city	3,564	3,482	-2.3	3,525	94.5	0.7	0.0	0.0	4.7	24.0	54.4	21.7	1,604	64.3	44.3	23.0
Brownlee CDP	15	NA	NA	6	100.0	0.0	0.0	0.0	0.0	0.0	66.6	33.3	3	100.0	33.3	0.0
Brownville village	132	130	-1.5	141	88.7	0.0	0.0	0.0	11.3	12.7	42.4	44.7	75	82.7	50.7	17.3
Brule village	326	313	-4.0	418	82.8	0.0	1.2	1.4	14.6	19.9	53.9	26.1	204	79.9	54.9	14.2
Bruning village	279	279	0.0	261	98.9	0.0	0.0	1.1	0.0	16.5	50.2	33.3	132	90.9	38.6	13.6
Bruno village	99	97	-2.0	136	100.0	0.0	0.0	0.0	0.0	24.2	52.0	23.5	58	87.9	60.3	5.2
Brunswick village	138	136	-1.4	158	100.0	0.0	0.0	0.0	0.0	18.3	49.9	31.6	72	81.9	52.8	19.4
Burchard village	82	79	-3.7	48	100.0	0.0	0.0	0.0	0.0	14.6	35.5	50.0	23	65.2	47.8	21.7
Burr village	57	57	0.0	26	100.0	0.0	0.0	0.0	0.0	7.6	61.5	30.8	15	86.7	73.3	6.7
Burton village	10	10	0.0	19	100.0	0.0	0.0	0.0	0.0	10.5	15.9	73.7	9	33.3	88.9	11.1
Burwell city	1,209	1,191	-1.5	1,216	98.9	0.0	0.0	0.4	0.7	23.3	54.4	22.1	537	74.7	50.5	11.9
Bushnell village	124	122	-1.6	158	99.4	0.0	0.0	0.0	0.6	22.8	34.2	43.0	73	89.0	58.9	9.6
Butte village	326	316	-3.1	346	94.2	0.0	0.0	3.2	2.6	15.1	58.9	26.3	180	67.8	40.6	20.0
Byron village	83	83	0.0	110	100.0	0.0	0.0	0.0	0.0	20.1	53.6	26.4	61	93.4	36.1	4.9
Cairo village	785	808	2.9	849	89.0	0.6	0.0	1.4	9.0	32.7	51.8	15.5	296	73.0	39.9	22.6
Callaway village	539	526	-2.4	682	96.2	0.9	0.0	1.0	1.9	27.7	52.2	20.1	290	79.3	32.8	19.0
Cambridge city	1,063	1,048	-1.4	1,179	97.9	0.0	0.7	0.0	1.4	21.8	49.9	28.3	558	64.0	44.3	19.7
Campbell village	347	332	-4.3	345	95.1	0.3	0.3	4.1	0.3	20.6	50.2	29.3	140	87.1	55.0	4.3
Carleton village	91	91	0.0	103	100.0	0.0	0.0	0.0	0.0	7.8	71.8	20.4	49	93.9	30.6	10.2
Carroll village	229	225	-1.7	163	96.3	0.0	0.0	0.0	3.7	20.9	48.4	30.7	71	88.7	57.7	7.0
Cedar Bluffs village	610	594	-2.6	511	99.0	0.0	0.0	0.0	1.0	16.8	61.5	21.5	269	74.7	68.0	7.4
Cedar Creek village	390	397	1.8	406	96.8	0.0	0.0	2.0	1.2	17.7	55.2	27.1	180	83.9	42.8	29.4
Cedar Rapids village	382	371	-2.9	409	96.8	0.0	0.0	0.0	3.2	25.2	54.4	20.5	179	91.6	58.7	5.0
Center village	94	92	-2.1	129	90.7	0.0	0.0	4.7	4.7	26.4	59.8	14.0	46	89.1	28.3	28.3
Central City city	2,934	2,890	-1.5	2,897	92.8	0.1	0.2	3.7	3.2	20.7	58.8	20.6	1,330	63.8	43.8	12.6
Ceresco village	889	899	1.1	936	96.7	0.0	0.2	2.9	0.2	30.0	58.6	11.5	336	80.1	36.3	17.9
Chadron city	5,851	5,767	-1.4	5,829	83.6	0.8	2.0	8.7	4.9	16.0	70.7	13.3	2,333	53.2	23.3	41.5
Chalco CDP	10,994	NA	NA	10,811	85.3	3.1	1.7	3.2	6.7	28.3	67.7	4.1	3,982	70.6	25.5	32.1
Chambers village	268	268	0.0	256	98.0	0.0	0.0	2.0	0.0	16.8	49.6	33.6	136	93.4	49.3	21.3
Champion CDP	103	NA	NA	78	100.0	0.0	0.0	0.0	0.0	17.9	49.9	32.1	35	100.0	60.0	0.0
Chapman village	287	284	-1.0	282	91.5	0.0	0.0	1.1	7.4	24.4	56.6	18.8	129	73.6	51.2	9.3
Chappell city	929	930	0.1	870	95.1	0.0	0.0	1.7	3.2	23.7	51.6	24.6	389	78.9	40.1	26.7
Chester village	232	232	0.0	238	100.0	0.0	0.0	0.0	0.0	15.1	54.2	30.7	117	83.8	54.7	12.8
Clarks village	369	355	-3.8	366	93.2	0.0	2.7	0.0	4.1	24.6	61.2	14.2	150	74.0	44.7	6.0
Clarkson city	657	633	-3.7	817	94.9	2.2	0.6	0.6	1.7	18.1	61.1	20.9	353	81.6	39.4	12.5
Clatonia village	231	225	-2.6	300	92.0	0.0	0.0	0.0	8.0	33.7	57.5	8.7	122	85.2	45.9	5.7
Clay Center city	760	732	-3.7	800	86.8	0.1	1.5	0.9	10.8	21.8	60.2	18.0	363	76.0	35.0	14.0
Clearwater village	419	400	-4.5	351	87.5	0.0	0.0	0.0	12.5	30.5	48.0	21.4	147	83.0	37.4	13.6
Clinton village	41	40	-2.4	42	83.3	4.8	0.0	11.9	0.0	2.4	66.7	31.0	23	95.7	30.4	0.0
Cody village	154	155	0.6	112	98.2	0.0	0.0	1.8	0.0	24.1	60.8	15.2	50	82.0	36.0	16.0
Coleridge village	473	456	-3.6	565	99.5	0.0	0.0	0.5	0.0	28.5	47.4	24.1	235	70.2	34.5	10.6
Colon village	110	108	-1.8	122	99.2	0.0	0.0	0.0	0.8	27.1	49.1	23.8	47	78.7	51.1	17.0
Columbus city	22,184	22,630	2.0	22,436	77.9	0.3	0.7	1.3	19.8	26.2	58.4	15.4	8,928	67.3	39.3	23.5
Comstock village	93	91	-2.2	105	100.0	0.0	0.0	0.0	0.0	35.3	53.3	11.4	39	66.7	53.8	0.0
Concord village	166	159	-4.2	158	100.0	0.0	0.0	0.0	0.0	27.9	55.1	17.1	63	82.5	34.9	31.7
Cook village	321	315	-1.9	341	88.0	0.0	5.6	0.0	6.5	18.2	62.7	19.1	176	73.9	40.9	25.6
Cordova village	137	138	0.7	103	100.0	0.0	0.0	0.0	0.0	15.5	47.6	36.9	65	92.3	63.1	3.1
Cornlea village	36	36	0.0	65	100.0	0.0	0.0	0.0	0.0	38.4	58.5	3.1	16	100.0	81.3	0.0
Cortland village	482	465	-3.5	588	95.2	0.5	0.0	1.4	2.9	27.3	55.6	17.0	236	92.4	37.3	16.1
Cotesfield village	46	46	0.0	48	93.8	0.0	0.0	6.3	0.0	8.4	62.6	29.2	32	90.6	34.4	6.3
Cowles village	30	29	-3.3	16	100.0	0.0	0.0	0.0	0.0	12.6	31.3	56.3	8	75.0	87.5	12.5
Cozad city	3,977	3,912	-1.6	3,942	84.1	3.4	0.0	1.0	11.5	27.0	53.9	19.0	1,610	69.9	46.8	22.4
Crab Orchard village	38	37	-2.6	42	100.0	0.0	0.0	0.0	0.0	23.8	35.6	40.5	21	100.0	38.1	4.8
Craig village	199	191	-4.0	238	82.8	6.7	0.0	8.4	2.1	22.3	62.4	15.1	103	90.3	54.4	3.9
Crawford city	997	969	-2.8	956	95.2	0.4	0.3	1.0	3.0	21.9	51.0	27.0	464	77.8	46.8	18.8
Creighton city	1,154	1,098	-4.9	1,127	97.2	0.0	0.0	2.0	0.7	24.1	45.4	30.3	520	79.2	51.3	19.2
Creston village	203	203	0.0	174	97.7	0.0	0.0	1.7	0.6	26.4	57.9	15.5	82	72.0	43.9	11.0
Crete city	6,960	7,034	1.1	7,055	59.8	1.3	4.7	0.6	33.6	22.6	65.9	11.4	2,373	56.0	57.2	17.3
Crofton city	726	689	-5.1	741	97.6	0.0	0.0	2.4	0.0	30.1	50.2	19.8	307	72.6	41.0	12.7
Crookston village	69	69	0.0	24	41.7	0.0	0.0	58.3	0.0	37.5	33.4	29.2	12	100.0	41.7	8.3
Culbertson village	595	593	-0.3	672	99.1	0.0	0.0	0.0	0.9	21.2	56.4	22.6	319	82.1	34.5	14.1
Curtis city	939	920	-2.0	876	97.4	0.0	0.0	2.2	0.5	20.5	64.0	15.8	335	69.3	34.9	22.7
Cushing village	32	32	0.0	62	90.3	0.0	0.0	0.0	9.7	35.5	59.5	4.8	26	88.5	76.9	0.0
Dakota City city	1,919	1,904	-0.8	2,204	62.7	0.5	3.4	2.0	31.4	29.0	64.1	6.9	693	76.2	62.9	14.3
Dalton village	315	315	0.0	311	93.2	0.0	0.0	6.8	0.0	31.5	49.9	18.6	129	81.4	45.7	14.7
Danbury village	101	99	-2.0	79	92.4	0.0	0.0	0.0	7.6	16.4	55.8	27.8	44	84.1	31.8	25.0
Dannebrog village	303	305	0.7	347	91.4	0.0	0.0	5.5	3.2	19.5	65.4	15.0	160	75.0	60.6	17.5
Davenport village	294	295	0.3	258	100.0	0.0	0.0	0.0	0.0	21.0	47.0	32.2	119	89.1	47.1	21.8
Davey village	154	158	2.6	110	96.4	0.0	0.0	2.7	0.9	19.0	52.6	28.2	54	88.9	37.0	20.4
David City city	2,913	2,887	-0.9	2,886	92.9	1.7	0.0	0.6	4.8	26.0	53.4	20.5	1,156	64.4	46.0	14.0
Dawson village	146	143	-2.1	116	100.0	0.0	0.0	0.0	0.0	13.0	67.1	19.8	55	81.8	54.5	23.6
Daykin village	166	164	-1.2	202	92.6	0.0	0.0	0.0	7.4	30.2	51.0	18.8	82	96.3	50.0	22.0
Decatur village	481	469	-2.5	446	88.6	0.0	0.0	7.8	3.6	15.7	47.1	37.2	235	80.0	58.7	6.8
Denton village	190	195	2.6	251	93.2	0.0	2.0	1.2	3.6	23.2	62.0	15.1	97	68.0	30.9	4.1
Deshler city	747	762	2.0	670	95.7	0.0	0.0	3.6	0.7	25.2	55.9	19.0	291	68.4	32.6	16.5
Deweese village	67	65	-3.0	48	85.4	0.0	0.0	0.0	14.6	2.1	64.7	33.3	35	68.6	94.3	0.0
De Witt village	513	503	-1.9	442	91.6	0.0	0.0	0.7	7.7	20.6	56.9	22.4	186	81.2	49.5	14.0
Diller village	260	253	-2.7	200	98.5	0.0	0.0	0.0	1.5	21.5	60.5	18.0	96	93.8	49.0	13.5
Dix village	255	251	-1.6	322	95.3	0.0	0.9	0.0	3.7	26.7	61.5	11.8	115	80.0	58.3	8.7
Dixon village	87	83	-4.6	69	100.0	0.0	0.0	0.0	0.0	26.0	42.0	31.9	36	72.2	52.8	22.2
Dodge village	612	601	-1.8	620	93.9	0.8	0.3	0.0	5.0	23.0	50.7	26.5	272	90.4	52.6	9.6

1 May be of any race.

Table A. All Places — **Population and Housing**

STATE City, town, township, borough, or CDP (county if applicable)	Population				Race and Hispanic or Latino origin (percent), 2010–2014					Age (percent), 2010–2014			Households, 2010–2014			
	2010 census total population	2014 estimated population	Percent change 2010–2014	ACS total population estimate 2010–2014	White alone, not Hispanic or Latino	Black alone, not Hispanic or Latino	Asian alone, not Hispanic or Latino	All other races or 2 or more races, not Hispanic or Latino	Hispanic or Latino[1]	Under 18 years old	Age 18 to 64 years old	Age 65 years and older	Total occupied housing units	Percent owner occupied	Householders by level of education (percent): High school diploma or less	Householders by level of education (percent): Bachelor's degree or more
	1	2	3	4	5	6	7	8	9	10	11	12	13	14	15	16
NEBRASKA—Con.																
Doniphan village	829	850	2.5	935	93.6	0.9	0.0	0.5	5.0	31.9	55.4	12.7	351	75.2	39.0	13.4
Dorchester village	586	575	-1.9	598	89.6	0.0	0.2	1.2	9.0	26.8	58.1	15.2	235	76.2	46.4	13.6
Douglas village	173	173	0.0	194	100.0	0.0	0.0	0.0	0.0	22.7	72.5	4.6	88	79.5	36.4	12.5
Du Bois village	147	144	-2.0	151	92.1	0.0	0.0	1.3	6.6	17.9	56.8	25.2	67	85.1	67.2	4.5
Dunbar village	187	186	-0.5	176	96.6	0.0	0.0	0.0	3.4	23.9	66.3	9.7	68	73.5	52.9	10.3
Duncan village	351	365	4.0	381	97.1	0.0	0.0	0.0	2.9	24.1	63.7	12.1	148	84.5	48.6	7.4
Dunning village	103	110	6.8	87	97.7	0.0	0.0	2.3	0.0	12.6	68.8	18.4	46	67.4	47.8	15.2
Dwight village	204	200	-2.0	185	95.1	0.0	0.0	0.0	4.9	21.0	55.4	23.2	80	85.0	40.0	8.8
Eagle village	1,024	1,043	1.9	1,098	98.5	0.0	0.0	1.2	0.3	25.4	66.3	8.3	402	86.8	39.3	24.6
Eddyville village	97	96	-1.0	147	79.6	0.0	0.0	0.0	20.4	31.9	57.8	10.2	58	62.1	69.0	6.9
Edgar city	498	481	-3.4	482	98.1	0.0	1.0	0.8	0.0	17.5	50.4	32.0	214	81.3	39.7	17.3
Edison village	133	132	-0.8	156	94.9	0.0	0.0	5.1	0.0	27.6	52.7	19.9	68	83.8	45.6	8.8
Elba village	215	216	0.5	284	93.3	0.0	0.0	0.7	6.0	28.8	56.1	15.1	112	68.8	37.5	8.9
Elgin city	659	632	-4.1	524	98.7	0.0	0.0	1.3	0.0	18.7	46.1	35.3	267	83.1	47.6	19.9
Elk Creek village	98	96	-2.0	115	95.7	0.0	0.0	1.7	2.6	13.1	60.0	27.0	70	75.7	71.4	11.4
Elm Creek village	901	955	6.0	881	95.3	0.0	1.1	0.8	2.7	34.2	53.8	12.0	346	68.8	42.2	22.3
Elmwood village	634	638	0.6	550	93.3	1.6	0.2	0.7	4.2	29.6	55.9	14.5	207	79.7	34.8	29.0
Elsie village	106	104	-1.9	123	75.6	0.0	0.0	4.1	20.3	26.9	69.2	4.1	53	84.9	34.0	24.5
Elwood village	707	681	-3.7	732	94.7	0.0	0.0	0.3	5.1	28.7	48.8	22.5	247	77.7	48.2	15.8
Elyria village	51	50	-2.0	37	100.0	0.0	0.0	0.0	0.0	35.1	54.0	10.8	13	69.2	61.5	30.8
Emerson village	840	818	-2.6	800	93.6	0.0	0.0	3.6	2.8	23.4	51.0	25.8	339	71.7	48.4	14.5
Emmet village	48	48	0.0	27	88.9	0.0	7.4	3.7	0.0	11.1	62.9	25.9	14	100.0	14.3	42.9
Enders CDP	42	NA	NA	40	100.0	0.0	0.0	0.0	0.0	20.0	32.5	47.5	15	100.0	0.0	33.3
Endicott village	132	129	-2.3	123	100.0	0.0	0.0	0.0	0.0	12.1	65.9	22.0	62	87.1	40.3	3.2
Ericson village	94	88	-6.4	112	100.0	0.0	0.0	0.0	0.0	8.0	28.7	63.4	66	87.9	47.0	16.7
Eustis village	401	387	-3.5	420	97.6	0.0	0.0	1.0	1.4	20.2	53.9	26.0	193	86.0	46.1	20.2
Ewing village	387	383	-1.0	492	97.4	0.0	0.0	0.4	2.2	31.9	52.5	15.7	189	77.2	41.3	12.2
Exeter village	591	560	-5.2	638	100.0	0.0	0.0	0.0	0.0	20.3	57.5	22.1	260	80.0	38.5	20.4
Fairbury city	3,942	3,803	-3.5	3,902	94.7	0.0	0.5	1.3	3.4	22.0	52.0	26.0	1,817	73.1	55.8	9.9
Fairfield city	387	373	-3.6	380	97.4	0.0	0.0	2.6	0.0	31.1	51.1	17.9	153	86.9	45.8	13.1
Fairmont village	560	539	-3.8	524	97.7	0.0	0.0	1.0	1.3	13.0	61.8	25.2	235	77.4	57.9	13.6
Falls City city	4,325	4,216	-2.5	4,270	91.2	0.0	0.5	6.1	2.2	24.7	56.1	19.1	1,920	70.7	46.2	22.4
Farnam village	171	169	-1.2	233	95.7	0.0	0.0	4.3	0.0	20.1	54.6	25.3	97	77.3	43.3	17.5
Farwell village	122	121	-0.8	121	98.3	0.0	0.0	0.0	1.7	18.2	59.6	22.3	61	83.6	65.6	0.0
Filley village	132	128	-3.0	100	100.0	0.0	0.0	0.0	0.0	11.0	54.0	35.0	44	90.9	68.2	9.1
Firth village	590	585	-0.8	613	70.8	0.0	0.0	2.9	26.3	35.4	48.4	16.3	199	62.8	38.2	15.6
Fontanelle CDP	54	NA	NA	61	100.0	0.0	0.0	0.0	0.0	0.0	26.2	73.8	32	100.0	100.0	0.0
Fordyce village	139	136	-2.2	132	89.4	0.0	0.0	0.0	10.6	25.0	56.9	18.2	58	79.3	81.0	1.7
Fort Calhoun city	912	917	0.5	753	90.3	0.0	0.4	1.1	8.2	23.7	62.6	13.8	341	72.4	30.2	27.6
Foster village	51	50	-2.0	40	90.0	0.0	5.0	0.0	5.0	22.5	57.5	20.0	20	85.0	65.0	10.0
Franklin city	1,000	949	-5.1	970	95.9	0.7	0.7	1.3	1.3	19.8	50.9	29.2	444	81.3	41.2	12.4
Fremont city	26,413	26,500	0.3	26,483	83.4	0.4	0.8	1.7	13.7	24.4	59.0	16.5	10,668	60.7	47.6	19.5
Friend city	1,027	1,019	-0.8	1,162	94.6	1.0	0.0	0.7	3.7	25.2	52.9	22.0	403	87.1	25.3	26.6
Fullerton city	1,307	1,249	-4.4	1,375	96.1	0.2	0.0	0.4	3.3	20.8	57.8	21.2	626	72.5	43.1	18.1
Funk village	194	192	-1.0	180	96.1	0.6	0.0	0.6	2.8	27.9	54.4	17.8	68	95.6	50.0	17.6
Gandy village	32	31	-3.1	27	100.0	0.0	0.0	0.0	0.0	0.0	74.0	25.9	19	63.2	36.8	10.5
Garland village	216	219	1.4	263	98.1	0.4	0.4	0.0	1.1	23.9	55.3	20.5	118	79.7	49.2	9.3
Garrison village	54	53	-1.9	45	100.0	0.0	0.0	0.0	0.0	24.4	57.8	17.8	20	80.0	80.0	5.0
Geneva city	2,217	2,141	-3.4	2,103	94.7	1.3	0.0	0.6	3.3	23.4	53.2	23.4	888	70.7	44.6	19.3
Genoa city	1,003	952	-5.1	973	95.6	0.0	0.2	0.3	3.9	21.0	57.8	21.2	392	80.6	41.8	21.9
Gering city	8,500	8,372	-1.5	8,463	79.0	0.4	0.3	2.0	18.3	24.9	57.4	17.9	3,355	73.1	37.0	22.6
Gibbon city	1,833	1,885	2.8	1,747	66.3	0.5	0.0	0.6	32.6	31.3	52.7	16.1	639	67.1	56.3	22.5
Gilead village	39	39	0.0	43	100.0	0.0	0.0	0.0	0.0	34.9	58.2	7.0	12	100.0	58.3	16.7
Giltner village	352	340	-3.4	398	98.7	0.0	0.0	0.3	1.0	29.9	59.9	10.3	141	92.9	29.1	20.6
Glenvil village	310	298	-3.9	334	92.8	0.0	0.0	1.8	5.4	28.2	59.4	12.6	126	88.9	44.4	12.7
Glenwood CDP	466	NA	NA	930	100.0	0.0	0.0	0.0	0.0	35.7	63.0	1.1	230	97.0	10.9	68.7
Goehner village	154	155	0.6	89	92.1	0.0	0.0	0.0	7.9	17.9	55.0	27.0	43	74.4	44.2	18.6
Gordon city	1,612	1,542	-4.3	1,616	72.0	0.4	1.4	19.8	6.4	30.8	49.7	19.5	673	64.3	40.1	19.0
Gothenburg city	3,574	3,542	-0.9	3,555	94.8	0.3	0.0	1.5	3.4	26.1	54.5	19.3	1,432	78.4	48.0	19.8
Grafton village	126	121	-4.0	128	96.1	0.0	0.0	0.8	3.1	17.1	59.4	23.4	64	93.8	54.7	4.7
Grand Island city	48,645	51,236	5.3	50,059	66.9	2.4	1.3	1.5	28.0	27.3	59.6	13.2	18,702	60.8	46.1	17.8
Grant city	1,161	1,119	-3.6	1,218	95.9	0.0	0.0	0.7	3.4	23.6	53.9	22.3	545	68.4	33.9	22.9
Greeley Center village	466	455	-2.4	341	92.1	0.0	0.0	2.6	5.3	15.5	46.1	38.4	167	71.3	52.1	9.6
Greenwood village	568	573	0.9	625	93.9	0.0	3.8	0.0	2.2	28.9	54.0	17.1	230	91.3	41.7	20.4
Gresham village	223	225	0.9	251	98.8	0.0	1.2	0.0	0.0	36.3	49.6	14.3	83	68.7	65.1	8.4
Gretna city	4,936	5,890	19.3	5,416	94.6	1.8	0.2	0.5	3.0	29.9	57.9	12.2	1,929	68.1	27.0	38.5
Gross village	2	2	0.0	4	100.0	0.0	0.0	0.0	0.0	0.0	100.0	0.0	2	100.0	0.0	0.0
Guide Rock village	225	213	-5.3	238	86.6	0.0	0.0	0.0	13.4	26.5	55.8	17.6	98	87.8	45.9	12.2
Gurley village	214	214	0.0	193	68.9	0.0	0.0	17.1	14.0	19.7	57.4	22.8	91	72.5	38.5	9.9
Hadar village	293	295	0.7	342	97.7	0.0	0.6	0.6	1.2	25.2	58.3	16.4	126	85.7	39.7	23.0
Haigler village	162	154	-4.9	137	98.5	0.0	0.0	0.0	1.5	18.2	57.6	24.1	72	72.2	72.2	4.2
Hallam village	213	218	2.3	228	99.1	0.0	0.0	0.9	0.0	26.8	62.8	10.5	85	74.1	42.4	20.0
Halsey village	74	79	6.8	73	86.3	0.0	11.0	0.0	2.7	11.0	72.5	16.4	35	80.0	60.0	8.6
Hamlet village	57	55	-3.5	75	96.0	0.0	0.0	1.3	2.7	14.6	54.7	30.7	37	62.2	67.6	0.0
Hampton village	423	429	1.4	417	97.8	0.0	0.0	0.0	2.2	24.0	58.9	17.3	169	89.3	37.9	11.8
Harbine village	49	48	-2.0	55	100.0	0.0	0.0	0.0	0.0	20.0	74.6	5.5	19	100.0	63.2	5.3
Hardy village	159	155	-2.5	146	95.2	0.0	0.0	0.0	4.8	17.2	63.7	19.2	66	89.4	45.5	18.2
Harrisburg CDP	100	NA	NA	56	100.0	0.0	0.0	0.0	0.0	16.1	53.5	30.4	28	64.3	35.7	21.4
Harrison village	251	246	-2.0	283	98.2	0.0	0.0	0.0	1.8	20.1	51.5	28.3	141	83.7	34.8	32.6
Hartington city	1,554	1,513	-2.6	1,572	96.1	0.6	0.2	1.3	1.8	26.1	46.6	27.3	668	79.0	46.9	14.4
Harvard city	1,013	979	-3.4	876	70.4	3.7	0.0	1.7	24.2	27.2	56.7	16.0	353	68.8	53.0	11.6
Hastings city	25,222	24,915	-1.2	25,030	85.9	0.7	1.6	1.7	10.1	23.7	60.4	15.8	10,187	67.8	42.0	20.7
Hayes Center village	214	207	-3.3	295	87.5	0.0	0.0	0.0	12.5	21.4	46.0	32.5	134	74.6	44.0	19.4
Hay Springs village	570	551	-3.3	555	90.5	0.9	0.4	1.6	6.7	13.1	51.9	35.0	277	66.4	41.9	24.2
Hazard village	70	68	-2.9	61	96.7	0.0	0.0	0.0	3.3	11.5	47.7	41.0	35	97.1	60.0	31.4
Heartwell village	71	72	1.4	64	100.0	0.0	0.0	0.0	0.0	14.1	65.7	20.3	32	100.0	68.8	28.1
Hebron city	1,579	1,563	-1.0	1,608	91.5	0.0	0.0	7.2	1.3	18.8	52.6	28.7	737	63.0	44.9	15.1
Hemingford village	803	808	0.6	759	96.3	0.1	0.0	2.1	1.4	26.1	56.5	17.4	317	72.9	50.5	15.1
Henderson city	991	1,003	1.2	927	95.1	0.4	0.0	0.0	4.4	19.6	43.2	37.1	409	80.0	40.8	21.3
Hendley village	24	24	0.0	20	100.0	0.0	0.0	0.0	0.0	0.0	65.0	35.0	15	93.3	20.0	6.7
Henry village	106	105	-0.9	124	64.5	0.8	0.0	34.7	0.0	26.6	68.5	4.8	61	68.9	27.9	16.4

1 May be of any race.

Table A. All Places — **Population and Housing**

STATE City, town, township, borough, or CDP (county if applicable)	Population: 2010 census total population	Population: 2014 estimated population	Population: Percent change 2010–2014	Population: ACS total population estimate 2010–2014	Race and Hispanic or Latino origin (percent), 2010–2014: White alone, not Hispanic or Latino	Black alone, not Hispanic or Latino	Asian alone, not Hispanic or Latino	All other races or 2 or more races, not Hispanic or Latino	Hispanic or Latino[1]	Age (percent), 2010–2014: Under 18 years old	Age 18 to 64 years old	Age 65 years and older	Households, 2010–2014: Total occupied housing units	Percent owner occupied	Householders by level of education (percent): High school diploma or less	Bachelor's degree or more
	1	2	3	4	5	6	7	8	9	10	11	12	13	14	15	16
NEBRASKA—Con.																
Herman village	268	267	-0.4	259	96.9	0.0	0.8	0.8	1.5	22.4	60.6	17.0	109	86.2	51.4	10.1
Hershey village	665	663	-0.3	638	87.1	0.3	0.0	1.6	11.0	28.5	59.8	11.8	226	88.1	45.1	13.3
Hickman city	1,659	1,972	18.9	1,850	95.3	0.5	0.2	1.7	2.3	37.0	53.9	9.0	614	73.5	27.4	33.6
Hildreth village	378	355	-6.1	444	95.3	0.0	0.0	0.2	4.5	23.9	54.1	22.1	193	86.0	33.7	14.5
Holbrook village	207	203	-1.9	141	90.8	0.0	0.0	9.2	0.0	15.5	67.4	17.0	67	82.1	58.2	3.0
Holdrege city	5,495	5,508	0.2	5,506	93.2	0.1	0.1	1.4	5.2	22.9	56.0	21.0	2,384	70.3	34.6	24.9
Holmesville CDP	51	NA	NA	49	100.0	0.0	0.0	0.0	0.0	0.0	48.9	51.0	33	100.0	69.7	12.1
Holstein village	214	227	6.1	231	97.4	0.0	0.0	1.3	1.3	19.5	63.4	17.3	109	78.0	52.3	5.5
Homer village	549	546	-0.5	551	98.4	0.0	0.0	0.9	0.7	26.4	55.1	18.5	214	79.4	44.4	12.1
Hooper city	830	830	0.0	826	98.8	0.0	0.0	0.7	0.5	20.0	53.7	26.3	366	76.8	41.8	25.7
Hordville village	144	146	1.4	184	96.7	0.0	0.0	3.3	0.0	22.3	64.2	13.6	79	73.4	41.8	19.0
Hoskins village	285	290	1.8	203	81.8	0.0	1.5	16.7	0.0	15.3	69.9	14.8	92	95.7	35.9	14.1
Howard City village	189	190	0.5	201	92.5	0.0	1.0	5.5	1.0	14.9	65.7	19.4	104	76.9	62.5	9.6
Howells village	561	550	-2.0	598	95.0	0.0	0.0	1.2	3.8	21.3	58.2	20.6	271	86.3	41.0	19.2
Hubbard village	236	236	0.0	234	97.4	1.3	0.0	1.3	0.0	22.2	67.5	10.3	92	72.8	45.7	18.5
Hubbell village	68	68	0.0	54	92.6	0.0	0.0	0.0	7.4	20.5	59.5	20.4	26	80.8	34.6	0.0
Humboldt city	877	851	-3.0	925	95.1	0.0	0.0	2.8	2.1	23.4	44.8	31.9	409	67.7	49.4	14.2
Humphrey city	760	791	4.1	782	99.7	0.0	0.0	0.3	0.0	26.5	53.6	19.9	331	80.1	40.2	19.3
Huntley village	44	45	2.3	49	100.0	0.0	0.0	0.0	0.0	44.9	49.0	6.1	14	100.0	57.1	0.0
Hyannis village	182	184	1.1	166	97.6	0.0	0.0	0.0	2.4	6.6	53.0	40.4	90	91.1	38.9	15.6
Imperial city	2,071	2,073	0.1	2,130	80.0	0.0	0.0	1.8	18.2	23.2	57.3	19.5	950	78.8	46.8	20.9
Inavale CDP	117	NA	NA	63	100.0	0.0	0.0	0.0	0.0	0.0	50.9	49.2	25	88.0	56.0	8.0
Indianola city	584	566	-3.1	662	99.4	0.0	0.0	0.6	0.0	24.9	54.5	20.5	265	78.1	40.4	13.2
Inglewood village	325	322	-0.9	355	91.8	0.0	0.8	0.8	6.5	22.6	53.3	24.2	159	69.2	59.1	6.3
Inland CDP	0	NA	NA	140	100.0	0.0	0.0	0.0	0.0	35.7	64.3	0.0	39	76.9	25.6	0.0
Inman village	129	129	0.0	111	100.0	0.0	0.0	0.0	0.0	26.1	54.9	18.9	46	89.1	47.8	13.0
Ithaca village	148	151	2.0	156	88.5	0.0	0.0	9.0	2.6	24.4	64.7	10.9	56	91.1	33.9	16.1
Jackson village	223	218	-2.2	196	94.4	0.0	0.0	0.0	5.6	22.5	54.5	23.0	80	86.3	53.8	12.5
Jansen village	118	115	-2.5	140	97.9	0.0	0.0	2.1	0.0	20.7	68.7	10.7	62	83.9	59.7	8.1
Johnson village	328	334	1.8	357	91.9	0.0	0.0	0.6	7.6	25.3	50.6	24.1	167	89.8	47.3	21.0
Johnstown village	64	61	-4.7	72	100.0	0.0	0.0	0.0	0.0	26.4	45.9	27.8	34	79.4	44.1	2.9
Julian village	59	58	-1.7	66	75.8	0.0	0.0	0.0	24.2	19.7	68.1	12.1	34	88.2	29.4	41.2
Juniata village	755	805	6.6	774	92.5	4.8	0.0	0.8	1.9	23.1	66.6	10.3	325	82.8	38.8	17.2
Kearney city	30,803	32,469	5.4	31,759	87.1	1.1	1.7	2.0	8.1	21.2	67.1	11.7	12,351	57.8	25.7	33.7
Kenesaw village	880	931	5.8	1,020	97.5	0.0	0.0	1.1	1.4	24.2	54.8	21.2	387	90.4	31.8	22.2
Kennard village	361	357	-1.1	367	96.5	0.0	0.0	0.5	3.0	30.0	52.3	17.7	146	91.8	47.3	13.7
Keystone CDP	59	NA	NA	109	100.0	0.0	0.0	0.0	0.0	40.3	52.3	7.3	31	100.0	22.6	77.4
Kilgore village	77	78	1.3	42	83.3	0.0	0.0	16.7	0.0	26.1	64.4	9.5	17	94.1	35.3	11.8
Kimball city	2,496	2,422	-3.0	2,474	86.8	0.6	0.8	1.5	10.1	22.6	49.5	27.9	1,071	59.2	45.3	16.2
King Lake CDP	280	NA	NA	96	100.0	0.0	0.0	0.0	0.0	0.0	91.8	8.3	85	58.8	18.8	7.1
Lakeview CDP	317	NA	NA	280	97.5	0.0	0.0	0.0	2.5	27.2	57.1	15.7	112	100.0	23.2	37.5
Lamar village	23	23	0.0	25	100.0	0.0	0.0	0.0	0.0	0.0	76.0	24.0	12	100.0	33.3	8.3
La Platte CDP	114	NA	NA	92	52.2	0.0	0.0	0.0	47.8	21.7	78.3	0.0	45	100.0	0.0	31.1
Laurel city	964	942	-2.3	1,217	97.6	0.0	0.0	2.1	0.2	28.6	47.5	23.9	486	75.9	44.2	19.8
La Vista city	15,997	17,636	10.2	17,125	81.5	4.2	3.0	2.8	8.5	25.6	65.7	8.6	7,221	54.3	25.3	38.1
Lawrence village	304	297	-2.3	320	88.1	0.0	0.0	0.0	11.9	18.1	55.7	26.3	166	81.9	46.4	20.5
Lebanon village	80	78	-2.5	29	100.0	0.0	0.0	0.0	0.0	0.0	72.3	27.6	21	81.0	52.4	0.0
Leigh village	403	398	-1.2	473	96.8	0.0	0.0	3.2	0.0	17.1	62.8	20.1	238	66.0	36.6	21.0
Lemoyne CDP	82	NA	NA	37	100.0	0.0	0.0	0.0	0.0	0.0	0.0	100.0	18	100.0	55.6	0.0
Leshara village	112	110	-1.8	93	79.6	0.0	0.0	1.1	19.4	21.5	57.2	21.5	37	70.3	56.8	8.1
Lewellen village	228	209	-8.3	179	99.4	0.0	0.0	0.6	0.0	9.5	45.8	44.7	91	76.9	47.3	15.4
Lewiston village	68	66	-2.9	77	100.0	0.0	0.0	0.0	0.0	31.2	49.4	19.5	29	86.2	41.4	31.0
Lexington city	10,230	10,146	-0.8	10,189	27.0	8.1	0.0	0.4	64.5	33.4	57.9	8.8	2,994	59.0	63.3	10.5
Liberty village	76	74	-2.6	72	100.0	0.0	0.0	0.0	0.0	26.4	64.0	9.7	27	81.5	77.8	3.7
Lincoln city	258,468	272,996	5.6	265,811	82.3	4.0	4.2	2.7	6.7	22.7	65.9	11.3	106,512	56.8	25.9	36.6
Lindsay village	255	254	-0.4	251	95.2	0.0	0.0	0.0	4.8	30.7	44.0	25.5	98	78.6	41.8	25.5
Lindy CDP	13	NA	NA	15	100.0	0.0	0.0	0.0	0.0	13.3	33.3	53.3	8	62.5	75.0	0.0
Linwood village	88	86	-2.3	111	85.6	0.0	0.0	10.8	3.6	6.3	81.9	11.7	52	92.3	55.8	3.8
Lisco CDP	64	NA	NA	32	100.0	0.0	0.0	0.0	0.0	0.0	34.4	65.6	21	71.4	66.7	0.0
Litchfield village	262	256	-2.3	288	97.2	0.0	0.0	0.0	2.8	13.2	55.2	31.6	125	84.0	50.4	10.4
Lodgepole village	318	318	0.0	264	93.2	0.0	0.0	0.0	6.8	14.0	55.8	30.3	133	89.5	33.1	11.3
Long Pine city	307	286	-6.8	288	95.8	0.0	0.0	0.0	4.2	26.1	53.4	20.5	121	86.0	62.8	13.2
Loomis village	382	381	-0.3	424	99.8	0.0	0.0	0.2	0.0	23.5	63.2	13.2	166	79.5	48.2	13.3
Lorenzo CDP	58	NA	NA	79	100.0	0.0	0.0	0.0	0.0	17.7	82.3	0.0	21	100.0	0.0	0.0
Loretto CDP	42	NA	NA	88	100.0	0.0	0.0	0.0	0.0	27.3	72.7	0.0	47	55.3	57.4	0.0
Lorton village	41	41	0.0	62	83.9	0.0	0.0	6.5	9.7	22.6	72.6	4.8	20	95.0	75.0	20.0
Louisville city	1,106	1,149	3.9	1,074	96.6	0.0	0.0	2.0	1.4	27.1	53.9	19.0	506	62.3	51.2	17.2
Loup City city	1,030	1,006	-2.3	989	95.9	0.2	0.0	0.1	3.8	22.4	46.6	30.8	440	70.2	46.4	19.1
Lushton village	30	30	0.0	36	100.0	0.0	0.0	0.0	0.0	8.3	55.5	36.1	21	81.0	23.8	9.5
Lyman village	341	330	-3.2	459	54.0	0.7	0.0	0.9	44.4	37.0	52.2	10.9	172	70.9	52.9	11.0
Lynch village	245	234	-4.5	244	95.5	0.8	0.0	3.7	0.0	26.6	38.7	34.4	129	80.6	55.0	8.5
Lyons city	851	814	-4.3	838	97.3	0.0	0.0	1.3	1.4	13.8	54.1	32.1	409	74.1	53.5	13.7
McCook city	7,698	7,611	-1.1	7,670	91.9	0.6	0.3	1.1	6.0	22.2	57.7	20.1	3,332	69.1	45.1	17.8
McCool Junction village	409	412	0.7	394	89.6	0.0	0.8	7.4	2.3	30.0	55.4	14.7	152	80.3	30.9	30.9
McGrew village	105	104	-1.0	46	80.4	0.0	0.0	13.0	6.5	8.7	45.7	45.7	29	65.5	89.7	6.9
McLean village	36	36	0.0	27	100.0	0.0	0.0	0.0	0.0	0.0	40.7	59.3	15	73.3	46.7	13.3
Macy CDP	1,023	NA	NA	941	1.8	0.0	0.0	97.2	1.0	43.7	52.1	4.3	198	23.2	52.0	0.0
Madison city	2,402	2,380	-0.9	2,717	50.5	0.5	1.0	0.4	47.7	28.2	58.3	13.3	877	69.3	45.2	16.2
Madrid village	231	230	-0.4	352	90.1	1.1	0.0	2.6	6.3	31.2	47.2	21.6	139	85.6	59.0	15.8
Magnet village	57	56	-1.8	35	97.1	0.0	0.0	2.9	0.0	22.8	57.2	20.0	18	83.3	66.7	16.7
Malcolm village	382	398	4.2	352	98.3	0.0	0.0	1.7	0.0	23.2	69.6	7.1	145	74.5	40.7	18.6
Malmo village	120	118	-1.7	231	98.3	0.0	0.0	0.9	0.9	26.4	64.5	9.1	54	85.2	51.9	11.1
Manley village	164	164	0.0	158	98.1	0.0	0.0	1.9	0.0	19.1	58.3	22.8	64	87.5	45.3	26.6
Marquette village	229	230	0.4	232	97.4	0.0	0.0	0.9	1.7	23.7	63.3	12.9	86	88.4	39.5	15.1
Martin CDP	92	NA	NA	144	100.0	0.0	0.0	0.0	0.0	0.0	42.4	57.6	73	65.8	100.0	0.0
Martinsburg village	94	90	-4.3	56	98.2	0.0	0.0	0.0	1.8	19.7	57.2	23.2	30	86.7	70.0	13.3
Maskell village	76	73	-3.9	111	97.3	0.0	0.0	2.7	0.0	32.4	55.8	11.7	36	75.0	52.8	5.6
Mason City village	171	168	-1.8	188	100.0	0.0	0.0	0.0	0.0	26.1	59.1	14.9	77	84.4	37.7	28.6
Max CDP	57	NA	NA	43	100.0	0.0	0.0	0.0	0.0	41.9	32.5	25.6	13	100.0	76.9	0.0
Maxwell village	312	308	-1.3	307	98.4	0.0	0.0	1.0	0.7	15.9	69.6	14.3	138	74.6	33.3	12.3
Maywood village	261	259	-0.8	269	97.4	0.0	0.0	2.2	0.4	24.1	52.5	23.4	113	80.5	46.0	13.3

1 May be of any race.

Table A. All Places — **Population and Housing**

STATE City, town, township, borough, or CDP (county if applicable)	Population: 2010 census total population	Population: 2014 estimated population	Population: Percent change 2010–2014	Population: ACS total population estimate 2010–2014	Race and Hispanic or Latino origin (percent), 2010–2014: White alone, not Hispanic or Latino	Black alone, not Hispanic or Latino	Asian alone, not Hispanic or Latino	All other races or 2 or more races, not Hispanic or Latino	Hispanic or Latino[1]	Age (percent), 2010–2014: Under 18 years old	Age 18 to 64 years old	Age 65 years and older	Households, 2010–2014: Total occupied housing units	Percent owner occupied	Householders by level of education (percent): High school diploma or less	Bachelor's degree or more
	1	2	3	4	5	6	7	8	9	10	11	12	13	14	15	16
NEBRASKA—Con.																
Mead village	569	558	-1.9	634	97.5	0.0	0.0	0.6	1.9	27.5	57.7	15.0	220	84.5	43.2	13.6
Meadow Grove village	301	301	0.0	306	85.9	0.0	0.0	5.6	8.5	22.6	56.9	20.6	135	88.9	41.5	19.3
Melbeta village	112	111	-0.9	138	80.4	0.0	0.0	0.0	19.6	25.4	63.0	11.6	49	95.9	57.1	12.2
Memphis village	114	114	0.0	101	96.0	0.0	0.0	0.0	4.0	23.7	60.4	15.8	36	86.1	50.0	5.6
Merna village	363	359	-1.1	374	91.2	0.0	0.0	7.0	1.9	25.9	57.2	16.8	170	70.6	56.5	15.3
Merriman village	128	129	0.8	111	45.0	0.0	0.0	12.6	42.3	9.9	79.2	10.8	76	46.1	93.4	1.3
Milford city	2,090	2,194	5.0	2,351	94.9	0.3	0.7	1.2	3.0	21.4	65.1	13.4	827	66.7	38.1	19.1
Miller village	136	138	1.5	150	83.3	0.0	0.0	0.0	16.7	38.0	48.1	14.0	64	71.9	31.3	9.4
Milligan village	285	272	-4.6	369	98.6	0.0	0.0	0.0	1.4	23.0	56.1	20.9	168	82.7	53.6	10.1
Minatare city	816	804	-1.5	907	73.3	0.0	1.0	2.8	22.9	25.5	59.4	15.1	338	70.4	43.2	8.0
Minden city	2,923	3,029	3.6	3,103	93.7	0.1	0.0	1.7	4.4	24.1	55.5	20.6	1,258	63.7	42.8	20.0
Mitchell city	1,702	1,678	-1.4	1,768	66.0	0.0	1.4	5.8	26.8	20.1	61.1	18.8	664	71.4	43.7	14.8
Monowi village	1	1	0.0	0	0.0	0.0	0.0	0.0	0.0	0.0	0.0	0.0	0	0.0	0.0	0.0
Monroe village	284	288	1.4	304	100.0	0.0	0.0	0.0	0.0	29.0	56.0	15.1	121	81.0	43.8	2.5
Moorefield village	32	31	-3.1	26	100.0	0.0	0.0	0.0	0.0	0.0	96.1	3.8	14	92.9	64.3	21.4
Morrill village	921	917	-0.4	852	77.0	0.2	1.2	4.7	16.9	18.6	60.4	20.9	406	73.6	29.1	13.8
Morse Bluff village	135	135	0.0	161	98.1	0.0	0.0	0.0	1.9	30.4	54.1	15.5	67	82.1	41.8	11.9
Mullen village	509	501	-1.6	398	96.2	0.0	0.8	1.0	2.0	15.6	41.1	43.5	196	80.1	44.4	21.9
Murdock village	236	236	0.0	284	98.9	0.0	0.0	1.1	0.0	25.7	59.1	15.1	112	93.8	39.3	16.1
Murray village	463	472	1.9	423	88.7	0.0	0.5	3.5	7.3	21.3	57.0	21.7	181	80.1	37.0	20.4
Naper village	84	82	-2.4	96	100.0	0.0	0.0	0.0	0.0	13.6	56.3	30.2	43	72.1	48.8	16.3
Naponee village	106	102	-3.8	89	98.9	0.0	1.1	0.0	0.0	12.3	46.0	41.6	53	75.5	47.2	13.2
Nebraska City city	7,293	7,265	-0.4	7,279	83.0	0.2	1.2	2.6	13.0	23.9	55.8	20.4	3,103	67.4	50.1	19.0
Nehawka village	204	204	0.0	340	88.2	0.0	0.0	9.4	2.4	35.9	52.6	11.5	116	88.8	41.4	20.7
Neligh city	1,601	1,523	-4.9	1,547	93.1	0.3	0.0	2.4	4.1	23.3	52.7	24.2	686	71.6	37.5	26.1
Nelson city	488	471	-3.5	502	93.2	0.2	0.0	3.2	3.4	17.3	55.8	27.1	259	76.4	39.8	11.2
Nemaha village	149	146	-2.0	155	90.3	0.0	0.0	9.7	0.0	9.6	65.9	24.5	84	85.7	65.5	2.4
Nenzel village	20	20	0.0	26	100.0	0.0	0.0	0.0	0.0	23.1	69.1	7.7	9	66.7	11.1	33.3
Newcastle village	325	318	-2.2	293	92.8	0.0	0.0	2.4	4.8	22.2	53.5	24.2	139	82.7	51.8	12.9
Newman Grove city	721	732	1.5	599	89.8	6.2	2.0	0.0	2.0	14.5	50.5	35.1	292	80.1	44.9	22.3
Newport village	97	92	-5.2	117	83.8	0.0	0.0	16.2	0.0	21.4	63.2	15.4	64	100.0	62.5	9.4
Nickerson village	369	358	-3.0	331	64.4	0.0	0.0	9.4	26.3	23.2	67.9	8.8	147	76.2	72.8	0.7
Niobrara village	370	351	-5.1	344	76.7	0.0	0.0	23.3	0.0	16.4	51.7	32.0	181	66.9	53.0	22.7
Nora village	21	21	0.0	19	52.6	0.0	47.4	0.0	0.0	5.3	73.8	21.1	14	57.1	28.6	28.6
Norfolk city	24,210	24,444	1.0	24,364	81.3	1.5	0.6	3.2	13.4	25.0	60.4	14.4	9,897	58.1	38.9	21.6
Norman village	43	43	0.0	57	98.2	0.0	0.0	0.0	1.8	38.6	45.7	15.8	23	100.0	39.1	13.0
North Bend city	1,177	1,234	4.8	1,266	97.9	0.0	0.0	1.1	0.9	30.9	47.7	21.7	483	70.4	47.4	13.7
North Loup village	297	293	-1.3	280	90.4	0.0	0.0	4.3	5.4	15.6	53.2	31.1	146	74.7	41.8	8.9
North Platte city	24,736	24,327	-1.7	24,532	87.8	1.1	0.5	1.4	9.2	25.3	59.4	15.6	10,431	61.4	42.5	18.7
Oak village	66	65	-1.5	40	100.0	0.0	0.0	0.0	0.0	15.0	62.5	22.5	24	100.0	62.5	20.8
Oakdale village	322	300	-6.8	354	98.6	0.0	0.0	0.8	0.6	28.5	57.9	13.6	140	80.0	61.4	7.1
Oakland city	1,244	1,198	-3.7	1,232	92.1	1.7	0.9	5.3	0.0	22.1	50.1	27.6	550	79.6	32.5	17.8
Obert village	23	22	-4.3	28	75.0	0.0	0.0	0.0	25.0	21.4	46.4	32.1	11	90.9	90.9	0.0
Oconto village	151	149	-1.3	121	93.4	0.0	0.0	2.5	4.1	20.7	53.7	25.6	64	98.4	48.4	21.9
Octavia village	127	124	-2.4	160	61.3	0.0	0.0	1.3	37.5	21.9	69.5	8.8	78	80.8	62.8	2.6
Odell village	307	299	-2.6	340	100.0	0.0	0.0	0.0	0.0	28.3	54.4	17.4	132	83.3	55.3	11.4
Odessa CDP	130	NA	NA	48	100.0	0.0	0.0	0.0	0.0	14.6	68.9	16.7	25	100.0	72.0	0.0
Offutt AFB CDP	4,644	NA	NA	4,678	71.0	7.0	1.9	9.2	10.9	33.0	67.0	0.0	1,611	0.0	17.7	20.0
Ogallala city	4,737	4,594	-3.0	4,644	91.9	0.1	0.0	2.5	5.4	21.5	57.8	20.7	2,163	64.7	39.9	22.7
Ohiowa village	115	110	-4.3	131	54.2	0.0	0.0	0.0	45.8	32.8	46.5	20.6	48	81.3	64.6	4.2
Omaha city	423,327	446,599	5.5	435,454	68.2	12.7	2.7	3.2	13.3	25.2	63.4	11.5	172,034	58.1	31.0	35.5
O'Neill city	3,705	3,663	-1.1	3,686	90.3	0.1	0.0	2.3	7.3	22.0	52.9	25.1	1,650	67.6	43.6	21.0
Ong village	63	61	-3.2	62	100.0	0.0	0.0	0.0	0.0	17.7	69.4	12.9	31	100.0	29.0	16.1
Orchard village	379	355	-6.3	434	87.6	0.0	0.7	3.7	8.1	20.7	52.5	26.7	193	80.8	54.4	14.5
Ord city	2,112	2,084	-1.3	2,364	96.7	0.0	0.0	1.6	1.7	22.7	52.2	25.3	1,052	68.7	55.6	15.1
Orleans village	386	390	1.0	425	97.2	0.0	0.2	0.0	2.6	22.1	56.5	21.4	181	82.9	58.0	8.3
Osceola city	880	855	-2.8	874	93.9	0.0	0.0	4.7	1.4	22.1	57.3	20.5	380	69.7	25.3	28.7
Oshkosh city	883	825	-6.6	951	96.0	0.0	0.0	2.6	1.4	14.2	57.9	28.1	432	79.2	35.4	23.4
Osmond city	783	768	-1.9	752	94.3	0.7	0.0	2.0	3.1	25.8	56.1	18.4	312	72.8	48.7	21.8
Otoe village	171	171	0.0	131	100.0	0.0	0.0	0.0	0.0	27.4	50.5	22.1	50	92.0	62.0	8.0
Overland CDP	153	NA	NA	177	88.7	0.0	0.0	0.0	11.3	21.0	68.8	10.2	71	100.0	23.9	31.0
Overton village	594	581	-2.2	714	94.1	0.0	0.6	0.3	5.0	26.7	64.1	9.2	264	73.5	60.2	6.4
Oxford village	776	769	-0.9	834	97.8	0.6	0.0	0.0	1.6	20.7	60.9	18.2	415	77.1	44.6	12.3
Page village	166	166	0.0	281	100.0	0.0	0.0	0.0	0.0	29.1	53.6	17.1	114	71.1	50.0	8.8
Palisade village	351	353	0.6	459	93.7	0.9	0.0	5.2	0.2	23.8	59.4	16.8	183	75.4	34.4	8.2
Palmer village	472	470	-0.4	615	94.1	2.0	1.3	0.8	1.8	23.1	59.2	17.6	249	75.5	48.6	18.5
Palmyra village	545	551	1.1	627	97.9	0.0	0.0	1.4	0.6	27.0	61.9	11.2	256	82.4	49.6	9.8
Panama village	256	281	9.8	272	99.6	0.0	0.4	0.0	0.0	21.7	71.0	7.4	122	69.7	36.9	13.1
Papillion city	19,223	23,270	21.1	21,100	88.8	2.8	1.6	2.7	4.2	25.8	62.5	11.6	7,918	67.3	22.5	39.2
Parks CDP	23	NA	NA	12	100.0	0.0	0.0	0.0	0.0	0.0	41.7	58.3	5	100.0	0.0	100.0
Pawnee City city	878	843	-4.0	874	97.9	0.0	0.0	2.1	0.0	18.7	48.3	32.8	459	64.5	47.7	18.7
Paxton village	523	505	-3.4	609	93.1	0.0	4.1	1.0	1.8	26.2	57.7	16.1	253	70.4	31.2	19.8
Pender village	1,002	1,035	3.3	1,200	89.8	1.8	0.3	0.1	8.0	21.9	56.0	22.2	488	77.9	45.3	22.1
Peru city	773	837	8.3	874	85.7	5.5	0.0	5.0	3.8	14.4	79.0	6.6	250	52.8	26.0	33.2
Petersburg village	333	323	-3.0	355	99.4	0.0	0.3	0.3	0.0	22.8	55.5	21.7	154	87.0	56.5	7.1
Phillips village	287	286	-0.3	235	96.6	0.0	0.0	0.0	3.4	28.9	55.9	15.3	94	96.8	61.7	4.3
Pickrell village	199	194	-2.5	219	98.2	0.0	1.8	0.0	0.0	26.0	54.0	20.1	98	88.8	39.8	12.2
Pierce city	1,767	1,741	-1.5	1,916	94.9	0.1	0.2	1.8	3.0	26.1	53.4	20.4	743	83.3	39.4	24.8
Pilger village	352	340	-3.4	298	98.0	0.0	0.0	0.0	2.0	14.0	54.7	31.2	148	87.2	51.4	11.5
Plainview city	1,246	1,226	-1.6	967	98.4	0.0	0.2	0.6	0.7	16.4	51.1	32.6	470	81.1	42.3	17.4
Platte Center village	336	338	0.6	417	98.1	0.0	1.0	1.0	0.0	28.5	52.8	18.7	152	90.8	52.6	5.3
Plattsmouth city	6,502	6,487	-0.2	6,473	94.2	1.5	0.0	1.5	2.8	25.7	60.4	14.0	2,562	65.1	40.8	20.1
Pleasant Dale village	205	212	3.4	236	94.9	0.8	4.2	0.0	0.0	16.1	74.9	8.9	109	83.5	42.2	27.5
Pleasanton village	341	345	1.2	280	96.8	0.0	0.0	3.2	0.0	25.0	52.5	22.5	116	80.2	44.0	29.3
Plymouth village	409	393	-3.9	442	94.6	0.0	0.0	2.0	3.4	22.9	56.7	20.4	190	85.8	38.4	11.6
Polk village	322	309	-4.0	332	99.7	0.0	0.0	0.3	0.0	15.3	64.6	19.9	158	81.0	48.7	20.3
Ponca city	961	935	-2.7	1,092	94.9	0.0	0.0	1.9	3.2	24.0	54.7	21.3	427	80.3	45.2	18.0
Poole CDP	19	NA	NA	18	100.0	0.0	0.0	0.0	0.0	0.0	0.0	100.0	9	100.0	0.0	0.0
Potter village	337	333	-1.2	332	75.0	4.5	0.0	1.8	18.7	23.1	59.5	17.2	134	77.6	36.6	23.1
Prague village	303	298	-1.7	315	94.9	0.6	0.0	1.3	3.2	27.4	55.3	17.5	146	77.4	61.6	12.3
Preston village	28	27	-3.6	49	57.1	0.0	0.0	30.6	12.2	30.6	38.8	30.6	19	57.9	84.2	0.0

1 May be of any race.

Table A. All Places — **Population and Housing**

STATE City, town, township, borough, or CDP (county if applicable)	Population				Race and Hispanic or Latino origin (percent), 2010–2014					Age (percent), 2010–2014			Households, 2010–2014			
	2010 census total population	2014 estimated population	Percent change 2010–2014	ACS total population estimate 2010–2014	White alone, not Hispanic or Latino	Black alone, not Hispanic or Latino	Asian alone, not Hispanic or Latino	All other races or 2 or more races, not Hispanic or Latino	Hispanic or Latino[1]	Under 18 years old	Age 18 to 64 years old	Age 65 years and older	Total occupied housing units	Percent owner occupied	Householders by level of education (percent): High school diploma or less	Householders by level of education (percent): Bachelor's degree or more
	1	2	3	4	5	6	7	8	9	10	11	12	13	14	15	16
NEBRASKA—Con.																
Primrose village	61	59	-3.3	78	100.0	0.0	0.0	0.0	0.0	28.3	59.0	12.8	35	97.1	60.0	5.7
Prosser village	66	70	6.1	86	100.0	0.0	0.0	0.0	0.0	24.4	65.1	10.5	35	80.0	54.3	14.3
Raeville CDP	22	NA	NA	0	0.0	0.0	0.0	0.0	0.0	0.0	0.0	0.0	0	0.0	0.0	0.0
Ragan village	38	39	2.6	58	100.0	0.0	0.0	0.0	0.0	12.1	46.5	41.4	23	78.3	65.2	34.8
Ralston city	5,943	7,216	21.4	6,826	77.9	0.4	3.5	0.9	17.3	17.8	66.8	15.5	2,945	64.7	39.3	29.6
Randolph city	944	919	-2.6	823	97.0	0.0	0.0	0.6	2.4	23.1	44.9	32.1	359	89.1	59.3	16.7
Ravenna city	1,360	1,364	0.3	1,374	94.8	0.0	0.4	0.6	4.1	28.0	54.1	18.0	537	68.3	38.7	20.9
Raymond village	167	185	10.8	148	100.0	0.0	0.0	0.0	0.0	18.2	68.9	12.8	68	95.6	45.6	20.6
Red Cloud city	1,020	968	-5.1	1,120	87.9	0.4	0.4	3.7	7.7	23.3	53.2	23.7	486	71.6	50.4	15.4
Republican City village	150	156	4.0	158	100.0	0.0	0.0	0.0	0.0	15.3	44.8	39.9	84	83.3	71.4	4.8
Reynolds village	69	67	-2.9	54	92.6	0.0	0.0	7.4	0.0	7.4	66.7	25.9	30	76.7	53.3	0.0
Richfield CDP	43	NA	NA	166	100.0	0.0	0.0	0.0	0.0	54.2	45.8	0.0	46	67.4	0.0	0.0
Richland village	73	72	-1.4	61	93.4	0.0	0.0	3.3	3.3	23.0	60.6	16.4	27	81.5	59.3	14.8
Rising City village	374	367	-1.9	307	100.0	0.0	0.0	0.0	0.0	19.2	55.3	25.4	142	93.0	46.5	11.3
Riverdale village	182	184	1.1	159	92.5	0.0	0.0	0.0	7.5	17.0	68.6	14.5	67	92.5	41.8	25.4
Riverton village	89	85	-4.5	114	97.4	0.0	0.9	0.0	1.8	17.6	49.8	32.5	62	88.7	71.0	1.6
Roca village	220	258	17.3	200	99.5	0.0	0.0	0.5	0.0	21.5	70.5	8.0	73	79.5	19.2	26.0
Rockville village	106	104	-1.9	107	98.1	0.0	0.0	1.9	0.0	26.1	64.5	9.3	49	75.5	38.8	8.2
Rogers village	95	94	-1.1	62	87.1	0.0	0.0	8.1	4.8	14.5	61.4	24.2	28	92.9	60.7	17.9
Rosalie village	160	161	0.6	208	60.6	0.0	1.0	30.3	8.2	34.2	49.5	16.3	73	80.8	43.8	19.2
Roscoe CDP	63	NA	NA	15	100.0	0.0	0.0	0.0	0.0	0.0	100.0	0.0	7	100.0	0.0	0.0
Roseland village	235	249	6.0	244	95.1	0.0	0.0	1.2	3.7	24.6	61.6	13.9	98	90.8	53.1	21.4
Royal village	63	60	-4.8	92	58.7	0.0	6.5	0.0	34.8	6.6	78.2	15.2	47	59.6	61.7	4.3
Rulo village	172	167	-2.9	183	61.2	1.1	1.6	36.1	0.0	23.4	54.5	21.9	82	95.1	67.1	1.2
Rushville city	890	858	-3.6	818	74.9	0.0	0.7	24.2	0.1	18.7	51.1	30.2	412	65.8	40.5	24.3
Ruskin village	123	120	-2.4	98	95.9	0.0	0.0	0.0	4.1	16.4	52.0	31.6	55	89.1	56.4	12.7
St. Edward city	705	687	-2.6	683	96.3	0.0	0.0	0.0	3.7	23.2	46.7	30.3	260	76.5	51.2	15.0
St. Helena village	96	94	-2.1	92	100.0	0.0	0.0	0.0	0.0	17.4	56.5	26.1	37	100.0	89.2	10.8
St. Libory CDP	264	NA	NA	312	95.8	0.0	0.0	0.0	4.2	32.3	61.9	5.8	105	97.1	63.8	9.5
St. Paul city	2,307	2,335	1.2	2,289	98.3	0.3	0.2	0.9	0.3	25.6	53.2	21.1	958	63.7	49.3	20.6
Salem village	112	109	-2.7	102	100.0	0.0	0.0	0.0	0.0	18.6	59.8	21.6	55	87.3	60.0	14.5
Santee village	339	342	0.9	355	3.9	0.0	3.4	81.1	11.5	49.3	47.5	3.4	116	19.0	63.8	2.6
Sarben CDP	31	NA	NA	12	100.0	0.0	0.0	0.0	0.0	0.0	0.0	100.0	6	100.0	100.0	0.0
Sargent city	525	510	-2.9	570	96.3	1.6	0.0	0.0	2.1	19.9	58.0	22.1	270	82.2	48.9	14.1
Saronville village	47	45	-4.3	50	100.0	0.0	0.0	0.0	0.0	28.0	68.0	4.0	22	81.8	31.8	45.5
Schuyler city	6,212	6,169	-0.7	6,195	27.7	2.3	0.0	0.1	69.9	34.7	55.6	10.0	1,857	66.8	70.8	8.8
Scotia village	318	305	-4.1	397	96.2	1.3	0.8	1.5	0.3	20.7	56.4	22.9	163	79.1	55.2	12.9
Scottsbluff city	15,039	14,875	-1.1	14,998	65.8	1.1	1.1	2.5	29.6	25.9	57.2	16.9	6,028	59.3	42.2	23.7
Scribner city	857	844	-1.5	1,043	92.2	2.8	0.0	4.4	0.6	26.4	48.7	25.1	398	78.4	48.0	21.4
Seneca village	33	35	6.1	52	96.2	0.0	0.0	0.0	3.8	23.1	40.3	36.5	27	74.1	59.3	18.5
Seward city	6,964	7,128	2.4	7,050	95.1	0.4	0.5	1.6	2.4	23.4	60.7	15.8	2,487	67.9	29.6	31.3
Shelby village	714	694	-2.8	851	88.2	0.0	0.2	0.2	11.3	28.4	52.6	19.0	353	66.3	41.9	10.5
Shelton village	1,059	1,063	0.4	1,182	76.6	1.6	0.0	0.9	20.8	26.8	60.0	13.2	427	78.0	52.7	16.4
Shickley village	341	329	-3.5	349	88.8	1.7	0.0	0.6	8.9	19.3	57.0	23.8	152	78.9	27.6	31.6
Sholes village	21	21	0.0	17	100.0	0.0	0.0	0.0	0.0	11.8	53.0	35.3	7	71.4	85.7	0.0
Shubert village	150	146	-2.7	141	95.7	0.0	0.0	0.0	4.3	10.6	61.8	27.7	71	90.1	64.8	9.9
Sidney city	6,758	6,914	2.3	6,801	90.0	0.2	2.0	0.4	7.4	23.8	61.0	15.3	3,064	62.0	34.3	27.5
Silver Creek village	359	357	-0.6	422	91.7	0.0	0.0	1.9	6.4	27.5	53.6	19.0	206	81.6	54.4	5.8
Smithfield village	54	51	-5.6	36	94.4	0.0	0.0	0.0	5.6	0.0	86.2	13.9	13	92.3	61.5	0.0
Snyder village	300	298	-0.7	357	97.8	0.0	0.0	0.8	1.4	35.3	49.5	15.1	134	65.7	52.2	3.7
South Bend village	99	99	0.0	88	94.3	0.0	0.0	0.0	5.7	11.3	67.1	21.6	41	90.2	56.1	29.3
South Sioux City city	13,353	13,360	0.1	13,375	39.4	6.5	3.0	3.6	47.5	32.8	56.3	11.0	4,550	55.0	61.6	11.1
Spalding village	487	467	-4.1	537	97.8	1.1	0.6	0.0	0.6	24.2	50.3	25.5	227	90.3	46.7	18.9
Spencer village	455	439	-3.5	480	94.6	2.3	0.0	2.5	0.6	20.6	48.5	31.0	235	82.6	43.4	26.0
Sprague village	142	145	2.1	133	98.5	0.0	0.0	0.0	1.5	21.9	53.5	24.8	60	86.7	50.0	11.7
Springfield city	1,558	1,621	4.0	1,288	94.8	0.5	0.0	3.6	1.0	24.6	61.6	13.9	535	86.0	33.5	25.8
Springview village	242	237	-2.1	228	98.2	0.0	1.3	0.4	0.0	16.7	65.4	18.0	119	72.3	34.5	15.1
Stamford village	183	187	2.2	218	85.3	0.0	2.3	7.3	5.0	32.1	46.8	21.1	92	92.4	57.6	14.1
Stanton city	1,577	1,557	-1.3	1,684	93.2	1.0	0.5	2.1	3.1	29.4	47.4	23.2	673	74.6	48.0	14.3
Staplehurst village	242	243	0.4	240	95.0	0.0	0.0	3.8	1.3	21.3	65.1	13.8	93	78.5	62.4	14.0
Stapleton village	305	300	-1.6	267	94.4	0.7	0.0	2.6	2.2	19.5	43.7	36.7	133	78.2	35.3	24.8
Steele City village	61	59	-3.3	105	97.1	0.0	0.0	0.0	2.9	37.1	46.6	16.2	45	80.0	51.1	20.0
Steinauer village	75	72	-4.0	56	94.6	0.0	0.0	5.4	0.0	30.4	41.2	28.6	24	100.0	62.5	4.2
Stella village	152	148	-2.6	154	96.8	0.0	2.6	0.6	0.0	7.1	57.0	35.7	80	90.0	42.5	36.3
Sterling village	476	460	-3.4	450	96.7	0.4	0.0	1.3	1.6	25.5	57.1	17.3	232	64.2	53.4	10.3
Stockham village	44	43	-2.3	80	100.0	0.0	0.0	0.0	0.0	37.6	52.8	10.0	20	100.0	55.0	5.0
Stockville village	25	25	0.0	16	75.0	0.0	0.0	25.0	0.0	0.0	87.7	12.5	9	55.6	22.2	44.4
Strang village	29	28	-3.4	24	100.0	0.0	0.0	0.0	0.0	16.6	66.7	16.7	14	50.0	28.6	42.9
Stratton village	343	341	-0.6	389	85.1	0.0	2.1	0.5	12.3	23.5	51.4	25.2	174	68.4	43.7	21.8
Stromsburg city	1,171	1,152	-1.6	1,191	92.2	0.3	0.3	1.3	6.0	28.6	51.0	20.5	447	64.0	39.8	26.2
Stuart village	590	601	1.9	624	97.6	0.0	0.0	0.0	2.4	26.7	52.8	20.8	247	70.0	37.2	25.5
Sumner village	236	234	-0.8	286	80.1	3.8	0.0	12.2	3.8	29.0	52.2	18.5	112	64.3	33.0	18.8
Sunol CDP	73	NA	NA	84	100.0	0.0	0.0	0.0	0.0	15.4	54.8	29.8	40	55.0	25.0	10.0
Superior city	1,957	1,901	-2.9	1,965	96.5	0.1	0.6	1.7	1.1	17.2	53.8	28.8	950	69.5	46.8	18.6
Surprise village	43	42	-2.3	42	100.0	0.0	0.0	0.0	0.0	26.2	47.6	26.2	16	87.5	31.3	6.3
Sutherland village	1,370	1,344	-1.9	1,549	87.7	0.0	0.5	3.9	7.9	28.5	52.2	19.3	580	75.3	36.4	18.6
Sutton city	1,502	1,445	-3.8	1,578	86.2	0.0	0.0	0.5	13.3	26.7	52.9	20.3	601	72.9	54.2	18.6
Swanton village	94	94	0.0	95	86.3	0.0	0.0	3.2	10.5	32.6	52.8	14.7	36	88.9	38.9	11.1
Syracuse city	1,942	1,960	0.9	1,887	97.4	0.0	0.0	2.4	0.2	21.7	50.4	27.9	808	70.7	37.1	22.9
Table Rock village	269	260	-3.3	252	97.2	0.0	0.0	0.4	2.4	20.3	55.2	24.6	129	86.8	42.6	22.5
Talmage village	233	234	0.4	232	92.7	0.0	0.0	0.4	6.9	22.0	61.3	16.8	97	73.2	63.9	8.2
Tamora CDP	58	NA	NA	90	100.0	0.0	0.0	0.0	0.0	12.2	70.0	17.8	34	100.0	61.8	20.6
Tarnov village	46	46	0.0	84	100.0	0.0	0.0	0.0	0.0	31.0	65.7	3.6	32	81.3	37.5	9.4
Taylor village	190	178	-6.3	193	100.0	0.0	0.0	0.0	0.0	25.3	55.5	19.2	80	85.0	65.0	12.5
Tecumseh city	1,677	1,629	-2.9	1,655	79.2	0.0	3.4	1.9	15.6	25.4	51.5	23.0	776	69.2	53.2	12.1
Tekamah city	1,827	1,738	-4.9	1,616	95.6	1.1	0.0	1.6	1.7	23.6	52.3	24.0	698	73.6	43.7	15.5
Terrytown city	1,197	1,181	-1.3	981	59.7	0.4	0.2	0.4	39.2	26.8	65.6	7.5	365	70.7	53.2	15.1
Thayer village	62	63	1.6	56	100.0	0.0	0.0	0.0	0.0	23.2	67.9	8.9	21	81.0	33.3	33.3
Thedford village	188	200	6.4	166	96.4	0.0	1.2	2.4	0.0	14.4	55.3	30.1	88	72.7	33.0	35.2
Thurston village	132	132	0.0	110	100.0	0.0	0.0	0.0	0.0	27.2	48.9	23.6	43	86.0	74.4	9.3
Tilden city	953	944	-0.9	1,126	95.4	0.0	0.0	0.0	4.6	25.3	53.1	21.6	491	64.8	41.1	14.3

1 May be of any race.

Table A. All Places — **Population and Housing**

STATE City, town, township, borough, or CDP (county if applicable)	Population				Race and Hispanic or Latino origin (percent), 2010–2014					Age (percent), 2010–2014			Households, 2010–2014		Householders by level of education (percent)	
	2010 census total population	2014 estimated population	Percent change 2010–2014	ACS total population estimate 2010–2014	White alone, not Hispanic or Latino	Black alone, not Hispanic or Latino	Asian alone, not Hispanic or Latino	All other races or 2 or more races, not Hispanic or Latino	Hispanic or Latino[1]	Under 18 years old	Age 18 to 64 years old	Age 65 years and older	Total occupied housing units	Percent owner occupied	High school diploma or less	Bachelor's degree or more
	1	2	3	4	5	6	7	8	9	10	11	12	13	14	15	16
NEBRASKA—Con.																
Tobias village	106	106	0.0	121	98.3	0.0	0.0	0.0	1.7	15.7	52.1	32.2	59	91.5	72.9	6.8
Trenton village	560	563	0.5	610	97.5	0.3	0.0	0.2	2.0	27.7	51.7	20.8	253	66.8	45.8	13.0
Trumbull village	205	199	-2.9	226	95.6	0.0	0.0	4.4	0.0	31.0	56.1	12.8	78	84.6	39.7	6.4
Tryon CDP	157	NA	NA	88	100.0	0.0	0.0	0.0	0.0	4.6	51.1	44.3	52	61.5	34.6	11.5
Uehling village	230	228	-0.9	300	92.0	0.0	0.0	7.3	0.7	19.3	59.0	21.7	133	85.7	48.9	19.5
Ulysses village	171	168	-1.8	211	97.6	0.0	1.9	0.0	0.5	23.8	57.3	19.0	93	79.6	49.5	21.5
Unadilla village	311	314	1.0	310	96.8	0.6	0.0	0.3	2.3	17.7	63.9	18.4	138	88.4	45.7	10.9
Union village	233	233	0.0	202	85.1	0.0	1.0	2.5	11.4	24.3	58.4	17.3	90	83.3	56.7	5.6
Upland village	143	137	-4.2	183	100.0	0.0	0.0	0.0	0.0	23.5	70.0	6.6	66	93.9	53.0	22.7
Utica village	861	852	-1.0	851	98.1	0.0	0.4	0.9	0.6	23.4	60.0	16.7	368	68.8	40.5	24.2
Valentine city	2,737	2,785	1.8	2,763	85.9	0.1	0.8	13.2	0.1	19.7	53.0	27.2	1,253	70.6	46.9	25.5
Valley city	1,875	2,071	10.5	1,909	92.6	2.7	0.0	1.8	2.9	21.9	59.3	18.9	860	57.0	45.7	20.3
Valparaiso village	570	554	-2.8	735	96.5	0.0	0.3	2.7	0.5	28.2	58.3	13.6	291	73.5	40.9	16.2
Venango village	167	164	-1.8	138	93.5	0.0	0.0	0.0	6.5	13.0	56.4	30.4	66	83.3	36.4	13.6
Venice CDP	75	NA	NA	63	100.0	0.0	0.0	0.0	0.0	0.0	100.0	0.0	57	87.7	73.7	10.5
Verdel village	30	30	0.0	53	96.2	0.0	0.0	3.8	0.0	18.9	79.2	1.9	31	96.8	48.4	3.2
Verdigre village	575	549	-4.5	525	94.7	0.0	0.0	3.8	1.5	14.5	44.3	41.3	260	61.9	45.0	18.5
Verdon village	172	168	-2.3	207	98.6	0.0	0.0	1.0	0.5	18.3	56.9	24.6	88	86.4	42.0	1.1
Virginia village	60	58	-3.3	55	94.5	0.0	0.0	5.5	0.0	16.4	56.4	27.3	25	88.0	60.0	0.0
Waco village	236	246	4.2	269	84.4	0.0	1.1	1.5	13.0	21.6	55.7	22.7	118	80.5	58.5	18.6
Wahoo city	4,508	4,485	-0.5	4,500	94.6	0.1	0.7	1.3	3.3	27.0	55.6	17.3	1,786	66.4	39.4	29.2
Wakefield city	1,451	1,408	-3.0	1,637	55.3	5.1	0.0	0.7	39.0	26.0	57.4	16.5	629	67.4	59.0	16.4
Wallace village	366	361	-1.4	338	69.8	1.2	2.4	0.9	25.7	25.5	63.6	10.9	133	65.4	32.3	25.6
Walthill village	780	769	-1.4	778	16.2	0.0	0.0	81.0	2.8	37.0	51.8	11.2	210	70.0	31.9	13.8
Walton CDP	306	NA	NA	374	94.1	5.9	0.0	0.0	0.0	7.0	58.1	35.0	192	75.0	25.0	47.9
Wann CDP	86	NA	NA	131	100.0	0.0	0.0	0.0	0.0	62.6	37.4	0.0	49	73.5	0.0	73.5
Washington village	150	148	-1.3	125	89.6	0.0	0.0	0.0	10.4	13.6	69.6	16.8	43	100.0	23.3	34.9
Waterbury village	73	70	-4.1	60	93.3	0.0	0.0	0.0	6.7	9.9	75.1	15.0	23	69.6	73.9	17.4
Waterloo village	848	868	2.4	937	95.7	0.1	0.0	0.9	3.3	37.0	53.8	9.2	319	53.3	38.6	23.2
Wauneta village	577	577	0.0	770	86.5	0.0	0.0	2.7	10.8	32.8	45.1	22.1	270	82.2	50.4	13.0
Wausa village	634	603	-4.9	683	96.2	0.0	0.6	2.8	0.4	23.8	45.7	30.5	277	79.8	32.9	22.7
Waverly city	3,277	3,709	13.2	3,528	95.6	0.0	0.3	2.3	1.8	32.0	56.4	11.5	1,216	77.2	24.8	35.9
Wayne city	5,664	5,577	-1.5	5,578	90.5	2.4	0.1	0.4	6.6	16.5	70.4	13.1	2,019	50.9	18.8	40.5
Weeping Water city	1,050	1,058	0.8	1,175	98.9	0.0	0.0	0.9	0.3	26.7	61.3	12.0	474	78.3	39.2	11.2
Wellfleet village	78	77	-1.3	70	72.9	0.0	0.0	17.1	10.0	22.9	58.6	18.6	39	82.1	56.4	10.3
Western village	235	234	-0.4	326	95.7	0.0	0.0	0.9	3.4	20.6	64.7	14.7	126	72.2	54.8	17.5
Westerville CDP	39	NA	NA	42	88.1	0.0	0.0	0.0	11.9	35.7	40.4	23.8	16	68.8	0.0	31.3
Weston village	324	324	0.0	328	91.5	0.0	0.0	0.0	8.5	36.3	53.0	10.7	109	74.3	48.6	12.8
West Point city	3,364	3,330	-1.0	3,340	80.0	0.0	0.0	0.0	20.0	24.3	53.4	22.5	1,486	66.9	45.5	21.4
White Clay CDP	10	NA	NA	0	0.0	0.0	0.0	0.0	0.0	0.0	0.0	0.0	0	0.0	0.0	0.0
Whitney village	77	76	-1.3	41	100.0	0.0	0.0	0.0	0.0	2.4	61.0	36.6	26	61.5	42.3	26.9
Wilber city	1,855	1,862	0.4	1,692	90.3	0.4	0.0	0.9	8.5	23.7	60.0	16.4	672	63.5	39.9	15.3
Wilcox village	358	361	0.8	431	95.1	0.0	0.2	3.7	0.9	22.8	61.4	15.8	165	72.7	55.2	15.2
Willow Island CDP	26	NA	NA	11	100.0	0.0	0.0	0.0	0.0	0.0	100.0	0.0	6	100.0	100.0	0.0
Wilsonville village	93	92	-1.1	119	86.6	0.0	6.7	2.5	4.2	12.6	62.2	25.2	59	100.0	55.9	10.2
Winnebago village	774	776	0.3	955	2.3	0.2	0.0	94.6	2.9	44.2	50.4	5.4	208	32.7	34.6	13.0
Winnetoon village	68	65	-4.4	56	100.0	0.0	0.0	0.0	0.0	16.1	75.0	8.9	25	100.0	36.0	8.0
Winside village	427	414	-3.0	437	89.2	0.5	2.1	7.3	0.9	26.5	60.8	12.8	184	75.0	33.2	26.1
Winslow village	107	106	-0.9	83	100.0	0.0	0.0	0.0	0.0	25.3	68.6	6.0	34	94.1	64.7	5.9
Wisner city	1,170	1,168	-0.2	1,331	95.8	0.0	0.2	3.2	0.8	21.3	55.5	23.1	586	67.4	43.2	15.7
Wolbach village	281	269	-4.3	289	89.6	0.7	0.3	1.0	8.3	24.2	58.1	17.6	133	83.5	50.4	18.8
Wood Lake village	63	63	0.0	72	91.7	0.0	0.0	8.3	0.0	8.4	77.8	13.9	42	33.3	54.8	14.3
Woodland Hills CDP	215	NA	NA	141	100.0	0.0	0.0	0.0	0.0	13.4	67.3	19.1	65	100.0	13.8	70.8
Woodland Park CDP	1,866	NA	NA	1,979	85.8	0.6	0.0	1.4	12.2	31.8	61.8	6.4	639	90.1	39.9	19.9
Wood River city	1,325	1,369	3.3	1,429	75.1	2.2	0.0	0.2	22.5	28.3	54.6	17.1	463	78.2	49.0	18.6
Wymore city	1,457	1,400	-3.9	1,399	93.2	1.0	0.0	5.4	0.4	21.0	51.4	27.6	604	73.2	51.2	10.4
Wynot village	166	171	3.0	165	100.0	0.0	0.0	0.0	0.0	16.3	56.9	26.7	73	94.5	49.3	8.2
Yankee Hill CDP	292	NA	NA	270	100.0	0.0	0.0	0.0	0.0	37.4	55.2	7.4	89	93.3	32.6	11.2
York city	7,766	7,957	2.5	7,878	92.6	0.1	0.0	3.0	4.3	20.4	62.0	17.7	3,347	59.2	37.3	24.7
Yutan city	1,186	1,195	0.8	1,253	95.9	1.6	0.0	1.4	1.1	29.3	59.8	10.8	474	82.7	39.7	17.9
NEVADA	2,700,692	2,839,099	5.1	2,761,584	52.7	8.0	7.4	4.7	27.2	23.9	62.9	13.1	1,005,958	55.7	37.9	25.2
Alamo CDP	1,080	NA	NA	939	93.6	0.0	0.0	0.0	6.4	42.3	42.8	14.9	372	75.5	39.0	0.0
Austin CDP	192	NA	NA	74	100.0	0.0	0.0	0.0	0.0	8.1	24.4	67.6	55	100.0	100.0	0.0
Baker CDP	68	NA	NA	23	100.0	0.0	0.0	0.0	0.0	0.0	30.4	69.6	19	84.2	84.2	0.0
Battle Mountain CDP	3,635	NA	NA	3,253	68.0	0.1	0.8	5.2	25.9	22.4	59.6	17.9	1,190	79.1	52.2	11.6
Beatty CDP	1,010	NA	NA	1,021	84.6	0.0	0.0	2.3	13.1	13.6	59.6	26.9	460	55.2	49.6	13.7
Beaverdam CDP	44	NA	NA	17	100.0	0.0	0.0	0.0	0.0	58.8	41.2	0.0	4	100.0	100.0	0.0
Bennett Springs CDP	132	NA	NA	161	100.0	0.0	0.0	0.0	0.0	3.7	55.3	41.0	65	100.0	86.2	0.0
Blue Diamond CDP	290	NA	NA	274	96.7	0.0	1.8	0.0	1.5	16.8	54.1	29.2	102	100.0	31.4	52.0
Boulder City city	15,027	15,386	2.4	15,162	86.3	0.6	2.0	2.2	8.9	16.9	56.1	27.0	6,360	70.6	32.4	26.3
Bunkerville CDP	1,303	NA	NA	1,431	65.3	0.0	0.0	3.1	31.5	31.7	57.4	11.0	352	73.9	45.7	17.6
Caliente city	1,196	1,141	-4.6	1,140	75.6	0.4	0.0	4.2	19.8	32.1	50.9	17.1	420	56.2	40.5	18.8
Cal-Nev-Ari CDP	244	NA	NA	125	91.2	0.0	0.0	8.8	0.0	0.0	14.4	85.6	96	86.5	61.5	0.0
Carlin city	2,366	2,363	-0.1	2,409	88.9	0.7	0.0	0.2	10.3	22.3	62.7	14.9	799	76.2	57.3	5.9
Carson City	55,274	54,522	-1.4	54,634	69.4	1.5	2.1	4.7	22.2	21.4	60.7	17.8	21,225	58.2	36.3	22.2
Carter Springs CDP	553	NA	NA	511	71.4	2.0	0.8	6.1	19.8	18.8	67.0	14.3	210	67.6	36.7	9.5
Cold Springs CDP	8,544	NA	NA	8,606	76.8	2.9	1.7	8.6	10.0	28.3	61.8	9.7	3,087	87.8	34.2	14.0
Crescent Valley CDP	392	NA	NA	388	100.0	0.0	0.0	0.0	0.0	30.2	53.5	16.5	165	85.5	72.1	8.5
Crystal Bay CDP	305	NA	NA	193	100.0	0.0	0.0	0.0	0.0	0.0	71.1	29.0	100	80.0	0.0	47.0
Dayton CDP	8,964	NA	NA	8,972	79.1	0.6	0.2	4.6	15.4	25.6	56.7	17.7	3,423	77.4	28.2	20.9
Denio CDP	47	NA	NA	44	100.0	0.0	0.0	0.0	0.0	0.0	0.0	100.0	26	100.0	0.0	0.0
Double Spring CDP	158	NA	NA	117	93.2	0.0	5.1	0.0	1.7	10.3	69.1	20.5	62	83.9	38.7	16.1
Dry Valley CDP	78	NA	NA	43	100.0	0.0	0.0	0.0	0.0	0.0	0.0	100.0	23	100.0	69.6	0.0
Dyer CDP	259	NA	NA	149	63.8	0.0	0.0	24.2	12.1	0.0	65.2	34.9	92	58.7	50.0	13.0
East Valley CDP	1,474	NA	NA	1,478	96.4	0.0	0.0	1.3	2.3	17.2	63.7	19.2	562	89.1	27.8	36.7
Elko city	18,317	20,300	10.8	19,308	63.0	2.1	1.0	4.3	29.5	27.2	64.3	8.5	6,717	64.7	40.7	23.8
Ely city	4,255	4,221	-0.8	4,250	71.9	1.2	0.8	8.1	18.0	24.8	56.6	18.6	1,633	69.3	42.3	23.2
Empire CDP	217	NA	NA	41	100.0	0.0	0.0	0.0	0.0	0.0	100.0	0.0	21	0.0	0.0	0.0
Enterprise CDP	108,481	NA	NA	124,564	44.4	8.6	22.2	6.5	18.2	25.3	67.2	7.5	43,024	56.1	28.0	35.5

1 May be of any race.

Table A. All Places — **Population and Housing**

STATE City, town, township, borough, or CDP (county if applicable)	Population: 2010 census total population	Population: 2014 estimated population	Population: Percent change 2010–2014	Population: ACS total population estimate 2010–2014	Race and Hispanic or Latino origin (percent), 2010–2014: White alone, not Hispanic or Latino	Black alone, not Hispanic or Latino	Asian alone, not Hispanic or Latino	All other races or 2 or more races, not Hispanic or Latino	Hispanic or Latino[1]	Age (percent), 2010–2014: Under 18 years old	Age 18 to 64 years old	Age 65 years and older	Households, 2010–2014: Total occupied housing units	Percent owner occupied	Householders by level of education (percent): High school diploma or less	Bachelor's degree or more
	1	2	3	4	5	6	7	8	9	10	11	12	13	14	15	16
NEVADA—Con.																
Eureka CDP	610	NA	NA	423	89.1	2.1	0.0	8.3	0.5	14.0	65.4	20.8	239	42.7	38.5	31.8
Fallon city	8,606	8,349	-3.0	8,451	74.7	5.1	5.3	4.2	10.6	25.0	60.2	14.8	3,452	35.2	46.7	13.9
Fallon Station CDP	705	NA	NA	748	52.8	1.6	14.6	7.5	23.5	47.1	53.0	0.0	229	6.1	29.7	5.2
Fernley city	19,368	19,204	-0.8	19,184	75.8	1.4	2.2	5.3	15.5	25.7	59.9	14.4	6,928	64.7	40.6	15.2
Fish Springs CDP	648	NA	NA	784	96.2	0.0	1.1	0.3	2.4	23.5	53.2	23.3	268	92.2	26.9	45.1
Fort McDermitt CDP	341	NA	NA	573	3.8	0.0	0.7	92.3	3.1	42.9	50.5	6.5	136	78.7	72.1	3.7
Gabbs CDP	269	NA	NA	109	80.7	0.0	0.0	11.0	8.3	0.0	70.6	29.4	75	100.0	60.0	0.0
Gardnerville CDP	5,656	NA	NA	5,761	71.5	1.5	1.5	6.0	19.4	22.5	57.0	20.4	2,504	55.3	44.4	19.4
Gardnerville Ranchos CDP	11,312	NA	NA	11,040	79.9	0.6	1.0	7.5	11.0	22.0	60.3	17.7	4,471	66.2	33.5	20.6
Genoa CDP	939	NA	NA	1,104	96.6	0.0	0.0	0.0	3.4	20.8	49.0	30.3	436	96.1	18.3	56.0
Gerlach CDP	206	NA	NA	168	100.0	0.0	0.0	0.0	0.0	6.0	61.9	32.1	108	100.0	41.7	32.4
Glenbrook CDP	215	NA	NA	215	97.2	0.0	0.0	0.0	2.8	0.0	37.7	62.3	110	85.5	9.1	76.4
Golconda CDP	214	NA	NA	271	95.2	0.0	1.5	3.3	0.0	14.4	65.2	20.3	146	65.1	54.1	5.5
Golden Valley CDP	1,556	NA	NA	1,993	91.3	1.7	0.0	0.1	7.0	17.1	63.1	19.9	580	89.0	34.5	25.5
Goldfield CDP	268	NA	NA	412	95.4	0.0	0.0	1.9	2.7	25.9	45.8	28.2	171	74.9	49.7	16.4
Goodsprings CDP	229	NA	NA	102	100.0	0.0	0.0	0.0	0.0	0.0	0.0	100.0	39	100.0	100.0	0.0
Grass Valley CDP	1,161	NA	NA	927	80.6	0.0	0.0	0.0	19.4	28.4	64.3	7.3	395	76.2	50.6	15.9
Hawthorne CDP	3,269	NA	NA	3,272	67.7	2.4	5.4	10.1	14.3	20.3	61.1	18.6	1,333	66.2	41.8	13.7
Henderson city	257,354	277,440	7.8	266,245	67.8	5.6	7.8	3.8	14.9	22.2	61.9	16.0	102,051	62.0	28.3	33.9
Hiko CDP	119	NA	NA	105	100.0	0.0	0.0	0.0	0.0	31.4	68.6	0.0	51	78.4	56.9	43.1
Humboldt River Ranch CDP	119	NA	NA	29	100.0	0.0	0.0	0.0	0.0	0.0	0.0	100.0	14	100.0	0.0	100.0
Imlay CDP	171	NA	NA	80	100.0	0.0	0.0	0.0	0.0	0.0	87.6	12.5	52	69.2	50.0	0.0
Incline Village CDP	8,777	NA	NA	8,389	78.6	0.2	1.9	2.5	16.7	13.4	67.4	19.3	3,767	66.1	17.3	54.3
Indian Hills CDP	5,627	NA	NA	6,007	76.1	0.1	3.0	3.7	17.1	20.6	60.9	18.5	2,367	71.0	29.0	21.7
Indian Springs CDP	991	NA	NA	785	86.4	0.0	0.0	0.0	13.6	26.4	67.1	6.6	337	57.0	51.9	4.7
Jackpot CDP	1,195	NA	NA	1,490	36.1	0.0	0.0	0.0	63.9	30.4	69.4	0.3	490	40.6	74.5	0.0
Johnson Lane CDP	6,490	NA	NA	6,319	90.8	0.0	0.6	2.2	6.5	20.9	50.5	28.4	2,374	87.5	23.9	33.5
Kingsbury CDP	2,152	NA	NA	2,027	81.8	0.0	1.8	3.1	13.4	11.3	75.6	13.1	1,025	62.6	20.8	32.7
Kingston CDP	113	NA	NA	190	100.0	0.0	0.0	0.0	0.0	4.2	28.5	67.4	130	100.0	46.9	0.0
Lakeridge CDP	371	NA	NA	217	97.2	0.0	0.0	0.0	2.8	2.8	62.7	34.6	101	57.4	15.8	45.5
Lamoille CDP	105	NA	NA	115	100.0	0.0	0.0	0.0	0.0	0.0	100.0	0.0	93	100.0	0.0	0.0
Las Vegas city	584,240	613,599	5.0	597,353	46.3	11.0	6.2	4.3	32.2	24.6	62.2	13.3	213,037	52.5	39.6	24.7
Laughlin CDP	7,323	NA	NA	7,567	77.7	3.6	1.6	5.6	11.6	17.0	50.7	32.4	3,591	40.2	45.5	19.2
Lemmon Valley CDP	5,040	NA	NA	5,585	79.5	0.0	2.3	1.9	16.3	17.9	70.1	12.1	1,851	73.4	42.4	15.6
Logan Creek CDP	26	NA	NA	38	100.0	0.0	0.0	0.0	0.0	0.0	0.0	100.0	18	100.0	0.0	61.1
Lovelock city	1,891	1,900	0.5	2,319	68.2	0.7	0.0	14.0	17.1	29.4	57.2	13.5	938	45.0	56.5	7.2
Lund CDP	282	NA	NA	203	100.0	0.0	0.0	0.0	0.0	23.6	68.5	7.9	44	100.0	50.0	0.0
McDermitt CDP	172	NA	NA	183	100.0	0.0	0.0	0.0	0.0	33.9	66.2	0.0	61	68.9	26.2	0.0
McGill CDP	1,148	NA	NA	1,590	92.6	0.0	0.0	3.2	4.2	23.4	58.7	17.7	547	83.7	38.8	17.0
Mesquite city	15,277	16,970	11.1	16,072	70.9	0.9	0.9	2.1	25.2	18.9	50.0	31.0	6,800	66.0	41.6	20.4
Mina CDP	155	NA	NA	33	100.0	0.0	0.0	0.0	0.0	0.0	0.0	100.0	23	100.0	60.9	0.0
Minden CDP	3,001	NA	NA	3,408	84.7	0.6	0.8	4.6	9.3	14.9	52.9	32.1	1,547	69.9	24.0	38.5
Moapa Town CDP	1,025	NA	NA	1,087	73.7	0.0	0.0	1.0	25.3	34.6	58.3	7.2	309	84.8	56.6	8.1
Moapa Valley CDP	6,924	NA	NA	6,772	86.8	3.3	0.3	2.2	7.4	31.6	51.1	17.3	2,210	77.9	39.3	18.1
Mogul CDP	1,290	NA	NA	1,649	90.4	0.0	3.3	0.0	6.3	28.1	62.1	9.9	564	88.8	23.0	32.1
Montello CDP	84	NA	NA	83	100.0	0.0	0.0	0.0	0.0	0.0	90.4	9.6	63	28.6	34.9	0.0
Mount Charleston CDP	357	NA	NA	317	84.2	0.0	0.0	1.3	14.5	9.5	77.3	13.2	166	74.1	7.8	42.8
Mount Wilson CDP	33	NA	NA	27	100.0	0.0	0.0	0.0	0.0	0.0	100.0	0.0	18	100.0	100.0	0.0
Nellis AFB CDP	3,187	NA	NA	3,620	48.0	22.9	6.1	5.4	17.5	39.1	60.4	0.5	878	5.8	15.0	29.5
Nelson CDP	37	NA	NA	94	100.0	0.0	0.0	0.0	0.0	0.0	55.3	44.7	33	78.8	72.7	0.0
Nixon CDP	374	NA	NA	336	6.3	0.0	0.0	83.9	9.8	25.6	62.6	11.9	123	65.0	54.5	9.8
North Las Vegas city	216,700	230,788	6.5	223,336	30.1	19.7	5.9	5.3	38.9	30.6	61.3	7.9	68,001	55.2	44.9	16.8
Oasis CDP	29	NA	NA	0	0.0	0.0	0.0	0.0	0.0	0.0	0.0	0.0	0	0.0	0.0	0.0
Orovada CDP	155	NA	NA	151	100.0	0.0	0.0	0.0	0.0	0.0	0.0	100.0	74	100.0	87.8	0.0
Osino CDP	709	NA	NA	754	86.2	0.0	6.4	0.0	7.4	47.3	49.2	3.4	193	83.4	55.4	0.0
Owyhee CDP	953	NA	NA	1,276	8.5	0.0	2.7	82.9	5.9	26.9	59.4	13.6	460	54.3	47.6	11.1
Pahrump CDP	36,441	NA	NA	35,009	78.5	3.1	2.0	2.7	13.6	18.1	53.2	28.7	14,747	73.2	44.6	15.4
Panaca CDP	963	NA	NA	1,477	94.6	0.0	0.0	5.4	0.0	25.0	62.4	12.5	545	47.3	26.8	39.4
Paradise CDP	223,167	NA	NA	223,182	45.4	8.7	8.8	5.0	32.1	21.6	66.5	11.8	87,757	40.7	40.9	22.8
Paradise Valley CDP	109	NA	NA	147	87.1	0.7	0.0	0.0	12.2	6.1	93.8	0.0	109	100.0	22.0	11.9
Pioche CDP	1,002	NA	NA	909	59.0	13.6	0.2	16.4	10.8	14.1	68.8	17.3	254	82.7	30.3	19.3
Preston CDP	78	NA	NA	72	100.0	0.0	0.0	0.0	0.0	73.6	26.4	0.0	8	100.0	0.0	0.0
Rachel CDP	54	NA	NA	0	0.0	0.0	0.0	0.0	0.0	0.0	0.0	0.0	0	0.0	0.0	0.0
Reno city	226,012	236,995	4.9	231,103	61.9	2.7	6.3	4.4	24.7	22.8	64.6	12.6	91,133	46.6	31.9	31.9
Round Hill Village CDP	759	NA	NA	745	91.7	0.0	3.9	0.8	3.6	6.9	61.1	31.9	397	65.2	9.3	51.1
Ruhenstroth CDP	1,293	NA	NA	971	94.5	0.0	0.0	4.6	0.8	7.7	63.7	28.5	532	88.0	22.2	29.9
Ruth CDP	440	NA	NA	500	95.8	0.0	0.0	4.2	0.0	28.6	63.8	7.6	170	47.1	60.6	0.0
Sandy Valley CDP	2,051	NA	NA	1,354	91.9	0.0	0.0	0.0	8.1	6.3	63.5	30.3	645	87.4	48.7	19.5
Schurz CDP	658	NA	NA	728	15.0	0.0	2.1	76.4	6.6	22.5	61.9	15.5	266	56.8	48.5	1.5
Searchlight CDP	539	NA	NA	431	91.4	0.0	0.0	3.7	4.9	14.2	59.7	26.2	201	54.2	43.8	23.4
Silver City CDP	0	NA	NA	219	100.0	0.0	0.0	0.0	0.0	10.0	78.5	11.4	84	100.0	0.0	46.4
Silver Peak CDP	107	NA	NA	91	100.0	0.0	0.0	0.0	0.0	0.0	55.0	45.1	63	68.3	42.9	22.2
Silver Springs CDP	5,296	NA	NA	5,605	81.4	1.4	2.0	4.5	10.7	19.3	61.8	18.9	2,114	78.3	47.9	11.0
Skyland CDP	376	NA	NA	245	100.0	0.0	0.0	0.0	0.0	7.3	62.0	30.6	92	100.0	10.9	68.5
Smith Valley CDP	1,603	NA	NA	1,339	76.1	0.0	0.0	1.9	22.0	25.9	47.3	26.7	526	76.8	26.4	26.8
Spanish Springs CDP	15,064	NA	NA	15,322	78.2	1.4	1.3	5.4	13.7	23.9	63.1	12.8	5,328	83.0	31.3	25.2
Sparks city	90,258	94,708	4.9	92,236	59.5	2.0	5.6	4.7	28.2	24.3	62.8	12.8	34,750	58.1	36.9	24.2
Spring Creek CDP	12,361	NA	NA	14,012	87.9	0.0	0.8	3.2	8.0	30.0	62.2	7.9	4,658	85.9	35.1	22.0
Spring Valley CDP	178,395	NA	NA	183,937	45.5	9.5	18.2	5.0	21.8	19.9	67.6	12.5	70,360	46.7	36.1	26.3
Stagecoach CDP	1,874	NA	NA	1,581	85.8	0.0	4.2	3.5	6.5	20.5	57.7	21.8	640	86.1	43.0	11.1
Stateline CDP	842	NA	NA	1,017	48.7	0.0	1.0	7.9	42.5	27.6	67.5	5.0	420	19.5	29.5	19.5
Summerlin South CDP	24,085	NA	NA	25,315	70.5	3.3	10.8	2.4	13.0	21.2	60.1	18.5	10,494	64.7	18.3	50.8
Sunrise Manor CDP	189,372	NA	NA	187,647	28.9	11.4	5.9	3.8	50.0	28.8	61.7	9.6	59,862	51.0	56.1	11.1
Sun Valley CDP	19,299	NA	NA	18,778	58.0	1.7	3.6	2.4	34.3	27.4	60.8	11.8	6,191	71.7	53.9	8.6
Sutcliffe CDP	253	NA	NA	257	29.2	0.0	4.3	58.8	7.8	21.4	57.2	21.4	88	80.7	42.0	13.6
Tonopah CDP	2,478	NA	NA	2,557	84.8	1.4	0.0	2.7	11.1	20.9	65.8	13.3	1,066	46.4	40.6	20.9
Topaz Lake CDP	157	NA	NA	240	96.3	0.0	0.0	0.8	2.9	32.0	44.2	23.8	88	53.4	22.7	12.5

1 May be of any race.

Table A. All Places — **Population and Housing**

STATE City, town, township, borough, or CDP (county if applicable)	2010 census total population	2014 estimated population	Percent change 2010–2014	ACS total population estimate 2010–2014	White alone, not Hispanic or Latino	Black alone, not Hispanic or Latino	Asian alone, not Hispanic or Latino	All other races or 2 or more races, not Hispanic or Latino	Hispanic or Latino[1]	Under 18 years old	Age 18 to 64 years old	Age 65 years and older	Total occupied housing units	Percent owner occupied	High school diploma or less	Bachelor's degree or more
	1	2	3	4	5	6	7	8	9	10	11	12	13	14	15	16
NEVADA—Con.																
Topaz Ranch Estates CDP	1,501	NA	NA	1,703	86.4	0.4	0.2	3.7	9.3	12.6	61.5	26.0	753	79.0	40.8	10.8
Unionville CDP	0	NA	NA	14	100.0	0.0	0.0	0.0	0.0	0.0	0.0	100.0	14	100.0	0.0	100.0
Ursine CDP	91	NA	NA	135	100.0	0.0	0.0	0.0	0.0	0.0	47.4	52.6	59	100.0	28.8	0.0
Valmy CDP	37	NA	NA	7	100.0	0.0	0.0	0.0	0.0	0.0	100.0	0.0	7	100.0	100.0	0.0
Verdi CDP	1,415	NA	NA	1,509	92.0	0.0	0.0	0.0	8.0	12.1	75.5	12.5	693	61.6	13.6	43.1
Virginia City CDP	855	NA	NA	673	96.3	1.9	0.1	0.3	1.3	4.5	71.6	23.9	379	91.6	29.8	25.9
Wadsworth CDP	834	NA	NA	927	23.2	0.3	0.0	69.1	7.3	37.1	53.5	9.5	305	67.9	60.3	2.3
Walker Lake CDP	0	NA	NA	327	91.1	0.0	0.0	0.9	8.0	7.3	43.4	49.2	170	96.5	16.5	30.0
Washoe Valley CDP	3,019	NA	NA	3,434	92.5	0.0	2.4	2.5	2.5	15.8	71.8	12.3	1,236	87.5	22.7	30.8
Wells city	1,292	1,303	0.9	1,269	61.3	0.0	0.0	5.0	33.6	28.0	59.6	12.3	542	66.1	45.9	15.3
West Wendover city	4,410	4,442	0.7	4,448	34.3	0.0	1.9	4.0	59.9	41.3	52.2	6.4	1,348	57.6	70.8	10.3
Whitney CDP	38,585	NA	NA	39,458	36.1	9.9	11.1	4.7	38.1	23.5	65.6	10.9	13,698	56.5	45.1	19.2
Winchester CDP	27,978	NA	NA	28,111	36.6	7.0	5.5	3.0	47.8	21.1	65.1	13.8	10,802	36.5	50.2	20.9
Winnemucca city	7,408	8,001	8.0	7,736	67.7	0.2	0.0	2.9	29.2	29.3	61.6	9.1	2,860	66.9	46.7	19.8
Yerington city	3,046	3,031	-0.5	3,030	65.8	0.3	0.1	11.7	22.1	19.1	57.1	23.8	1,461	55.4	60.1	14.6
Zephyr Cove CDP	565	NA	NA	440	93.0	1.1	2.5	1.1	2.3	14.1	70.7	15.2	217	70.5	14.3	46.1
NEW HAMPSHIRE	1,316,466	1,326,813	0.8	1,321,069	91.7	1.1	2.3	1.9	3.1	20.8	64.6	14.7	519,580	71.0	33.8	36.1
Acworth town (Sullivan)	891	889	-0.2	923	97.2	0.0	1.7	1.1	0.0	22.5	61.3	16.5	347	79.0	50.1	25.4
Albany town (Carroll)	737	722	-2.0	800	95.9	1.6	0.0	2.5	0.0	26.9	56.5	16.5	308	85.4	47.1	25.6
Alexandria town (Grafton)	1,613	1,629	1.0	1,829	92.9	4.0	0.2	1.4	1.5	26.6	57.0	16.3	632	83.9	49.4	19.0
Allenstown town (Merrimack)	4,322	4,285	-0.9	4,303	96.5	0.8	0.4	0.4	1.8	19.8	66.7	13.4	1,787	70.1	49.8	14.5
Alstead town (Cheshire)	1,937	1,926	-0.6	1,922	97.5	0.2	0.4	0.4	1.5	23.4	60.5	16.0	770	80.1	28.8	43.0
Alton CDP	501	NA	NA	397	100.0	0.0	0.0	0.0	0.0	21.4	59.1	19.4	256	37.1	6.3	33.6
Alton town (Belknap)	5,251	5,294	0.8	5,270	93.5	1.8	1.8	2.6	0.3	17.8	64.9	17.4	2,193	80.3	27.0	27.7
Amherst CDP	613	NA	NA	490	100.0	0.0	0.0	0.0	0.0	25.5	52.2	22.2	202	90.1	5.4	89.6
Amherst town (Hillsborough)	11,201	11,266	0.6	11,234	93.0	0.4	1.0	2.9	2.8	27.6	58.6	13.8	3,931	91.1	11.5	69.0
Andover town (Merrimack)	2,371	2,360	-0.5	2,428	95.2	0.2	1.5	2.3	0.7	17.3	61.5	21.2	975	86.1	39.6	31.7
Antrim CDP	1,397	NA	NA	1,384	97.0	0.0	0.0	2.3	0.7	25.6	56.4	17.8	573	65.4	39.4	17.8
Antrim town (Hillsborough)	2,637	2,655	0.7	2,640	97.0	0.5	0.0	1.6	0.9	21.3	60.7	18.0	1,045	76.5	44.8	21.4
Ashland CDP	1,244	NA	NA	1,359	97.7	0.0	0.4	1.2	0.7	18.1	62.3	19.6	613	48.0	45.8	22.7
Ashland town (Grafton)	2,072	2,075	0.1	2,066	98.5	0.0	0.2	0.8	0.5	18.9	61.4	19.7	899	59.0	40.2	29.5
Atkinson town (Rockingham)	6,751	6,828	1.1	6,788	96.5	0.0	0.0	0.3	3.2	21.0	62.1	16.7	2,597	92.2	21.6	38.9
Atkinson and Gilmanton Academy grant (Coos)	0	0	0.0	0	0.0	0.0	0.0	0.0	0.0	0.0	0.0	0.0	0	0.0	0.0	0.0
Auburn town (Rockingham)	4,953	5,228	5.6	5,078	95.9	0.3	0.9	2.0	0.9	23.0	67.7	9.4	1,830	90.7	28.2	37.0
Barnstead town (Belknap)	4,595	4,593	0.0	4,605	99.9	0.0	0.0	0.1	0.0	18.8	66.0	15.4	1,824	90.8	39.4	26.3
Barrington town (Strafford)	8,576	8,768	2.2	8,691	97.9	0.0	0.3	1.1	0.7	22.0	67.0	11.0	3,307	89.1	31.1	41.3
Bartlett CDP	373	NA	NA	198	98.0	1.0	0.0	0.0	1.0	7.6	62.6	29.8	138	85.5	0.0	39.1
Bartlett town (Carroll)	2,788	2,759	-1.0	2,767	97.1	0.1	0.0	2.8	0.1	13.0	64.1	22.8	1,567	73.7	27.8	45.1
Bath town (Grafton)	1,077	1,091	1.3	872	97.2	0.2	0.9	0.6	1.0	14.9	54.7	30.5	397	84.1	42.3	32.7
Beans grant (Coos)	0	0	0.0	0	0.0	0.0	0.0	0.0	0.0	0.0	0.0	0.0	0	0.0	0.0	0.0
Beans purchase (Coos)	0	0	0.0	0	0.0	0.0	0.0	0.0	0.0	0.0	0.0	0.0	0	0.0	0.0	0.0
Bedford town (Hillsborough)	21,203	21,689	2.3	21,449	94.8	1.3	2.2	0.3	1.5	27.5	58.0	14.6	7,188	85.7	17.7	60.6
Belmont CDP	1,301	NA	NA	2,066	79.8	9.2	0.0	9.1	1.9	32.4	58.3	9.3	600	80.7	70.5	10.2
Belmont town (Belknap)	7,354	7,291	-0.9	7,319	87.7	3.7	0.3	2.8	5.5	25.4	62.3	12.4	2,672	78.0	44.3	18.0
Bennington CDP	381	NA	NA	286	98.3	0.0	0.0	1.7	0.0	29.4	59.0	11.5	119	58.0	44.5	14.3
Bennington town (Hillsborough)	1,476	1,475	-0.1	1,357	93.7	0.3	0.0	4.1	1.9	27.2	60.6	12.2	520	72.5	39.2	26.3
Benton town (Grafton)	364	372	2.2	482	97.9	0.0	0.2	1.7	0.2	25.9	49.5	24.5	125	88.8	72.0	9.6
Berlin city & MCD (Coos)	10,051	9,501	-5.5	9,710	92.6	2.9	0.2	1.9	2.4	16.7	62.8	20.6	4,185	60.5	57.1	10.2
Bethlehem CDP	972	NA	NA	979	88.8	0.0	0.0	11.2	0.0	30.7	60.5	9.0	388	58.8	22.9	38.7
Bethlehem town (Grafton)	2,526	2,558	1.3	2,537	92.1	0.0	0.0	7.6	0.3	24.5	62.1	13.5	1,079	63.1	29.2	37.3
Blodgett Landing CDP	101	NA	NA	89	100.0	0.0	0.0	0.0	0.0	0.0	44.9	55.1	45	100.0	48.9	13.3
Boscawen town (Merrimack)	3,965	3,940	-0.6	3,962	97.4	0.2	0.0	1.1	1.3	21.3	58.3	20.5	1,270	69.6	43.9	15.0
Bow town (Merrimack)	7,519	7,671	2.0	7,611	95.4	0.0	1.3	1.6	1.6	25.0	60.7	14.1	2,777	88.6	22.1	53.4
Bradford CDP	356	NA	NA	388	91.2	0.0	7.7	1.0	0.0	30.1	58.4	11.3	142	78.2	30.3	28.9
Bradford town (Merrimack)	1,650	1,657	0.4	1,706	96.0	0.2	1.9	0.9	0.9	18.6	65.8	15.5	684	88.5	31.4	39.6
Brentwood town (Rockingham)	4,486	4,728	5.4	4,598	95.4	0.3	0.3	1.8	2.2	26.2	63.0	10.6	1,400	82.0	25.1	52.6
Bridgewater town (Grafton)	1,083	1,090	0.6	1,092	98.4	0.0	0.0	0.4	1.2	11.6	63.3	25.0	488	86.9	44.9	31.6
Bristol CDP	1,688	NA	NA	1,562	96.7	0.0	1.8	1.5	0.0	26.1	57.2	16.7	702	61.0	48.9	22.5
Bristol town (Grafton)	3,054	3,068	0.5	3,054	98.1	0.0	1.1	0.8	0.0	23.0	57.2	19.8	1,288	72.9	42.8	22.3
Brookfield town (Carroll)	708	693	-2.1	786	97.5	0.4	0.0	2.2	0.0	24.0	53.3	22.8	298	97.0	30.2	40.9
Brookline town (Hillsborough)	4,991	5,152	3.2	5,051	96.4	0.0	0.9	2.5	0.3	27.1	65.2	7.5	1,709	88.9	25.2	48.2
Cambridge township (Coos)	8	8	0.0	17	100.0	0.0	0.0	0.0	0.0	0.0	70.6	29.4	8	100.0	50.0	50.0
Campton town (Grafton)	3,333	3,327	-0.2	3,317	94.8	0.4	1.6	3.2	0.0	15.2	66.0	18.8	1,416	86.1	34.2	40.5
Canaan CDP	524	NA	NA	613	100.0	0.0	0.0	0.0	0.0	18.7	63.0	18.1	233	64.8	26.6	36.9
Canaan town (Grafton)	3,911	3,914	0.1	3,910	97.4	0.0	0.0	2.2	0.4	20.5	64.4	15.1	1,480	79.8	39.3	32.7
Candia town (Rockingham)	3,909	3,920	0.3	3,920	95.5	0.0	2.7	0.6	1.2	20.0	67.8	12.3	1,466	97.3	32.3	38.0
Canterbury town (Merrimack)	2,352	2,382	1.3	2,291	97.9	0.5	0.0	0.0	1.5	20.1	64.0	15.8	894	95.5	18.5	54.4
Carroll town (Coos)	763	754	-1.2	991	97.1	0.5	2.1	0.0	0.3	21.5	58.0	20.4	362	73.8	38.4	26.2
Center Harbor town (Belknap)	1,096	1,099	0.3	1,012	96.5	0.0	1.6	1.5	0.4	13.8	64.9	21.0	446	83.6	24.7	46.4
Center Ossipee CDP	561	NA	NA	488	100.0	0.0	0.0	0.0	0.0	26.3	63.8	10.0	175	81.1	80.6	4.0
Center Sandwich CDP	123	NA	NA	74	100.0	0.0	0.0	0.0	0.0	9.5	50.1	40.5	42	73.8	31.0	59.5

1 May be of any race.

STATE City, town, township, borough, or CDP (county if applicable)	2010 census total population	2014 estimated population	Percent change 2010–2014	ACS total population estimate 2010–2014	White alone, not Hispanic or Latino	Black alone, not Hispanic or Latino	Asian alone, not Hispanic or Latino	All other races or 2 or more races, not Hispanic or Latino	Hispanic or Latino[1]	Under 18 years old	Age 18 to 64 years old	Age 65 years and older	Total occupied housing units	Percent owner occupied	High school diploma or less	Bachelor's degree or more
	1	2	3	4	5	6	7	8	9	10	11	12	13	14	15	16
NEW HAMPSHIRE—Con.																
Chandlers purchase (Coos)	0	0	0.0	0	0.0	0.0	0.0	0.0	0.0	0.0	0.0	0.0	0	0.0	0.0	0.0
Charlestown CDP............	1,152	NA	NA	1,129	95.0	0.0	0.0	5.0	0.0	23.0	60.6	16.5	469	74.8	28.1	17.9
Charlestown town (Sullivan)	5,114	5,014	-2.0	5,047	95.8	1.2	0.6	2.3	0.2	17.8	63.9	18.5	2,185	78.8	55.8	11.6
Chatham town (Carroll) ...	339	337	-0.6	393	92.1	0.0	0.0	7.9	0.0	21.4	62.6	16.0	161	83.2	54.7	29.2
Chester town (Rockingham).............	4,768	4,874	2.2	4,802	95.6	0.2	0.2	1.5	2.5	24.9	65.3	9.7	1,612	92.2	24.1	39.8
Chesterfield town (Cheshire)	3,604	3,587	-0.5	3,601	97.5	0.0	0.5	1.4	0.6	19.7	60.6	19.6	1,510	85.3	29.9	49.8
Chichester town (Merrimack)..................	2,523	2,567	1.7	2,552	97.0	0.0	0.2	2.3	0.5	18.6	67.8	13.6	996	90.2	31.2	38.4
Claremont city & MCD (Sullivan)	13,355	13,074	-2.1	13,169	96.5	0.4	0.3	1.2	1.6	22.9	61.3	15.9	5,418	64.3	53.4	21.1
Clarksville town (Coos)....	266	254	-4.5	315	95.6	0.0	0.0	0.0	4.4	16.9	57.5	25.7	152	88.8	56.6	11.2
Colebrook CDP...............	1,394	NA	NA	1,404	96.9	0.0	0.0	0.4	2.8	20.7	60.0	19.3	693	58.0	50.9	17.2
Colebrook town (Coos).....	2,301	2,212	-3.9	2,340	94.8	0.3	1.8	1.5	1.7	17.1	61.4	21.7	1,101	67.8	52.6	20.7
Columbia town (Coos)......	757	737	-2.6	726	99.3	0.0	0.0	0.1	0.6	18.0	59.4	22.6	315	80.6	53.7	17.5
Concord city & MCD (Merrimack)..................	42,692	42,444	-0.6	42,514	90.3	2.3	3.3	2.3	1.9	20.4	66.0	13.8	17,141	54.7	27.9	37.9
Contoocook CDP............	1,444	NA	NA	1,851	94.3	1.6	2.4	0.9	0.8	27.4	64.4	8.0	662	74.9	12.7	74.8
Conway CDP.................	1,823	NA	NA	1,232	86.9	0.0	8.1	5.0	0.0	11.2	67.4	21.4	601	54.2	51.2	18.6
Conway town (Carroll)	10,115	9,984	-1.3	10,054	93.7	0.6	1.8	2.6	1.2	20.0	62.7	17.5	4,365	67.9	37.7	27.5
Cornish town (Sullivan)....	1,640	1,625	-0.9	1,601	96.9	0.0	1.6	1.0	0.4	20.9	66.8	12.2	644	85.4	28.6	39.6
Crawfords purchase (Coos)	0	0	0.0	0	0.0	0.0	0.0	0.0	0.0	0.0	0.0	0.0	0	0.0	0.0	0.0
Croydon town (Sullivan)...	764	751	-1.7	651	94.0	0.0	0.0	6.0	0.0	19.2	68.1	12.6	257	82.9	50.6	20.6
Cutts grant (Coos)...........	0	0	0.0	0	0.0	0.0	0.0	0.0	0.0	0.0	0.0	0.0	0	0.0	0.0	0.0
Dalton town (Coos)..........	979	930	-5.0	933	94.4	0.2	0.9	1.6	2.9	14.8	58.9	26.3	414	80.9	57.2	13.5
Danbury town (Merrimack)..................	1,164	1,175	0.9	1,243	98.7	0.3	0.0	1.0	0.0	21.0	64.9	14.0	533	82.2	46.5	18.0
Danville town (Rockingham)...............	4,387	4,463	1.7	4,423	97.0	0.0	0.8	1.2	1.0	26.1	64.0	9.8	1,537	87.2	34.5	36.0
Deerfield town (Rockingham)...............	4,280	4,389	2.5	4,330	98.8	0.1	0.3	0.1	0.6	23.6	66.0	10.4	1,540	92.9	33.5	34.9
Deering town (Hillsborough)...............	1,912	1,924	0.6	1,772	96.4	0.2	0.0	2.4	1.0	16.9	70.1	13.0	682	85.2	36.1	27.1
Derry CDP...................	22,015	NA	NA	22,129	93.3	1.9	2.2	0.5	2.1	21.8	66.4	11.7	9,109	55.0	37.7	28.3
Derry town (Rockingham)	33,109	33,307	0.6	33,180	94.1	1.3	1.6	0.7	2.3	22.5	67.1	10.4	12,934	63.7	35.6	29.1
Dixs grant (Coos)............	1	1	0.0	0	0.0	0.0	0.0	0.0	0.0	0.0	0.0	0.0	0	0.0	0.0	0.0
Dixville township (Coos) ..	12	12	0.0	22	100.0	0.0	0.0	0.0	0.0	0.0	58.9	40.9	4	0.0	0.0	100.0
Dorchester town (Grafton)	355	356	0.3	318	95.9	1.3	1.6	1.3	0.0	7.2	71.7	21.1	129	88.4	44.2	17.8
Dover city & MCD (Strafford)	29,983	30,665	2.3	30,332	90.2	1.0	4.1	3.1	1.6	20.5	66.0	13.5	12,586	50.7	26.6	42.4
Dublin town (Cheshire)	1,597	1,567	-1.9	1,642	98.5	0.0	0.4	0.2	0.9	19.1	61.9	19.0	620	79.4	40.0	40.0
Dummer town (Coos)	304	292	-3.9	348	94.0	0.0	0.0	6.0	0.0	21.5	54.8	23.6	141	90.8	67.4	13.5
Dunbarton town (Merrimack)..................	2,758	2,786	1.0	2,779	95.6	0.4	0.6	2.7	0.7	21.5	68.0	10.4	1,053	87.1	27.2	35.8
Durham CDP	10,345	NA	NA	10,288	87.9	0.8	5.9	3.5	2.0	7.6	87.8	4.5	1,560	46.6	7.4	53.5
Durham town (Strafford) ..	14,638	15,759	7.7	15,180	89.6	0.5	5.0	2.9	1.9	11.0	82.0	7.0	3,073	61.6	6.9	59.6
East Kingston town (Rockingham)...............	2,357	2,406	2.1	2,453	98.0	0.0	0.5	0.6	0.9	22.5	59.7	17.9	882	91.2	30.2	38.1
East Merrimack CDP	4,197	NA	NA	3,784	96.3	0.0	2.9	0.3	0.5	13.0	65.0	22.1	1,929	61.6	40.1	31.7
Easton town (Grafton)	254	265	4.3	243	96.3	0.0	0.0	0.8	2.9	12.4	60.4	27.2	111	85.6	10.8	59.5
Eaton town (Carroll)........	393	393	0.0	348	95.4	0.0	1.4	2.9	0.3	8.0	63.8	28.2	176	83.0	27.3	43.8
Effingham town (Carroll)..	1,465	1,536	4.8	1,362	99.7	0.3	0.0	0.0	0.0	16.0	66.5	17.4	553	83.4	48.5	15.9
Ellsworth town (Grafton) ..	83	83	0.0	61	100.0	0.0	0.0	0.0	0.0	6.6	65.7	27.9	33	87.9	48.5	39.4
Enfield CDP...................	1,540	NA	NA	967	100.0	0.0	0.0	0.0	0.0	6.1	65.7	28.2	512	54.9	37.9	36.1
Enfield town (Grafton)......	4,580	4,578	0.0	4,565	96.6	1.2	0.6	0.1	1.2	17.3	62.0	20.6	1,945	79.3	34.3	42.9
Epping CDP....................	1,681	NA	NA	1,690	88.2	0.0	0.0	11.8	0.0	20.4	58.5	21.2	765	60.1	59.6	16.2
Epping town (Rockingham)...............	6,408	6,782	5.8	6,587	96.6	0.0	0.0	3.3	0.2	22.1	64.6	13.2	2,604	85.9	33.7	27.4
Epsom town (Merrimack).	4,566	4,628	1.4	4,597	99.1	0.0	0.0	0.9	0.0	19.6	63.7	16.7	1,809	84.2	41.8	23.4
Errol town (Coos)............	291	278	-4.5	301	98.7	0.0	0.0	1.3	0.0	6.7	61.7	31.6	186	80.1	58.6	13.4
Ervings location (Coos) ...	0	0	0.0	0	0.0	0.0	0.0	0.0	0.0	0.0	0.0	0.0	0	0.0	0.0	0.0
Exeter CDP....................	9,242	NA	NA	9,303	96.5	0.2	0.8	1.2	1.4	21.8	63.1	15.0	4,109	64.3	28.3	45.8
Exeter town (Rockingham)...............	14,306	14,543	1.7	14,434	96.4	0.1	0.7	1.7	1.1	23.1	58.1	18.9	6,248	68.2	26.8	49.2
Farmington CDP.............	3,885	NA	NA	3,562	95.5	0.0	1.5	1.7	1.3	20.2	67.9	11.9	1,485	67.6	48.1	17.8
Farmington town (Strafford)	6,786	6,832	0.7	6,824	97.4	0.0	1.1	0.9	0.7	21.1	67.1	11.8	2,625	70.6	46.7	19.6
Fitzwilliam town (Cheshire)	2,396	2,366	-1.3	2,454	93.3	0.0	0.6	6.1	0.0	19.1	64.2	16.7	1,036	90.7	47.5	23.6
Francestown town (Hillsborough)...............	1,562	1,568	0.4	1,551	95.6	0.3	0.0	1.8	2.3	16.5	69.3	14.2	605	89.1	17.2	44.0
Franconia town (Grafton).	1,104	1,122	1.6	1,168	96.1	0.9	0.0	2.6	0.4	13.4	56.7	30.0	496	80.4	19.2	62.3
Franklin city & MCD (Merrimack)..................	8,477	8,428	-0.6	8,462	93.3	1.9	1.1	1.5	2.3	23.3	61.5	15.2	3,379	59.6	50.3	18.2
Freedom town (Carroll)....	1,492	1,488	-0.3	1,195	97.4	0.3	0.3	1.7	0.3	17.5	50.7	31.8	532	83.1	41.0	27.6
Fremont town (Rockingham)...............	4,283	4,508	5.3	4,375	94.3	1.9	0.8	0.5	2.6	22.7	63.8	13.4	1,608	88.1	31.5	32.8
Gilford town (Belknap)	7,126	7,140	0.2	7,142	96.5	0.0	1.8	1.0	0.8	18.6	60.8	20.6	3,054	84.8	29.5	46.7
Gilmanton town (Belknap)	3,776	3,768	-0.2	3,778	94.1	0.0	3.3	1.7	0.8	21.7	61.2	17.3	1,427	95.0	32.1	35.7
Gilsum town (Cheshire) ...	813	809	-0.5	610	94.6	0.0	0.5	3.1	1.8	9.8	75.4	14.8	290	88.3	49.7	21.7
Goffstown CDP..............	3,196	NA	NA	3,197	97.8	0.0	0.0	1.5	0.7	21.5	62.4	16.2	1,366	62.1	27.3	38.9
Goffstown town (Hillsborough)...............	17,651	17,972	1.8	17,765	96.3	0.7	0.2	1.1	1.7	17.8	68.2	13.9	6,290	76.9	36.2	32.5
Gorham CDP.................	1,600	NA	NA	1,522	99.4	0.0	0.0	0.0	0.6	19.5	62.8	17.7	715	67.8	38.5	18.2
Gorham town (Coos)	2,848	2,706	-5.0	2,765	97.8	0.0	0.0	1.1	1.1	20.6	62.5	17.1	1,240	70.7	43.0	24.9
Goshen town (Sullivan)....	810	800	-1.2	821	97.1	0.5	0.0	2.4	0.0	17.0	65.8	17.3	320	79.4	42.8	29.1
Grafton town (Grafton).....	1,340	1,348	0.6	1,278	97.7	0.0	0.4	0.9	0.9	19.7	65.0	15.4	545	82.4	50.8	22.8

1 May be of any race.

Table A. All Places — Population and Housing

STATE City, town, township, borough, or CDP (county if applicable)	Population 2010 census total population	2014 estimated population	Percent change 2010–2014	ACS total population estimate 2010–2014	Race and Hispanic or Latino origin (percent), 2010–2014 White alone, not Hispanic or Latino	Black alone, not Hispanic or Latino	Asian alone, not Hispanic or Latino	All other races or 2 or more races, not Hispanic or Latino	Hispanic or Latino[1]	Age (percent), 2010–2014 Under 18 years old	Age 18 to 64 years old	Age 65 years and older	Households, 2010–2014 Total occupied housing units	Percent owner occupied	Householders by level of education (percent) High school diploma or less	Bachelor's degree or more
	1	2	3	4	5	6	7	8	9	10	11	12	13	14	15	16
NEW HAMPSHIRE—Con.																
Grantham town (Sullivan)	2,985	2,961	-0.8	2,970	97.9	0.4	0.4	0.3	1.0	23.5	56.7	19.9	1,084	91.4	18.9	63.7
Greenfield town (Hillsborough)	1,749	1,808	3.4	1,477	92.5	0.1	1.4	4.2	1.8	19.7	65.6	15.0	538	85.5	32.2	37.4
Greenland town (Rockingham)	3,549	3,811	7.4	3,668	97.5	0.0	1.2	0.0	1.3	24.0	60.4	15.7	1,397	86.3	17.2	54.0
Greens grant (Coos)	1	1	0.0	8	100.0	0.0	0.0	0.0	0.0	0.0	100.0	0.0	0	0.0	0.0	0.0
Greenville CDP	1,108	NA	NA	1,360	97.5	0.0	0.7	1.8	0.0	23.6	67.7	8.8	493	60.4	51.9	15.0
Greenville town (Hillsborough)	2,105	2,083	-1.0	2,374	96.6	0.0	0.4	2.9	0.1	22.4	66.1	11.5	892	73.7	51.6	12.3
Groton town (Grafton)	593	597	0.7	637	95.4	0.0	0.8	0.0	3.8	12.8	71.2	16.0	305	81.3	64.9	17.0
Groveton CDP	1,118	NA	NA	1,159	99.7	0.0	0.0	0.0	0.3	18.7	62.2	18.9	496	60.5	62.1	9.3
Hadleys purchase (Coos)	0	0	0.0	0	0.0	0.0	0.0	0.0	0.0	0.0	0.0	0.0	0	0.0	0.0	0.0
Hale's location (Carroll)	120	120	0.0	137	97.1	0.7	0.0	2.2	0.0	2.2	29.1	68.6	67	100.0	19.4	61.2
Hampstead town (Rockingham)	8,521	8,587	0.8	8,543	94.7	0.3	1.3	2.0	1.7	21.6	62.1	16.4	3,447	80.0	31.9	34.5
Hampton CDP	9,656	NA	NA	9,417	93.6	1.1	3.6	1.0	0.7	21.6	61.1	17.3	3,837	71.7	24.8	51.2
Hampton town (Rockingham)	14,976	15,208	1.5	15,073	93.8	0.8	2.8	1.2	1.3	18.4	61.6	20.1	6,618	70.9	26.1	48.5
Hampton Beach CDP	2,275	NA	NA	1,941	94.1	0.8	0.0	0.9	4.2	8.8	67.7	23.5	1,099	57.3	35.4	33.7
Hampton Falls town (Rockingham)	2,236	2,298	2.8	2,307	92.8	0.3	1.8	5.1	0.0	22.9	61.7	15.4	902	86.0	19.0	57.0
Hancock CDP	204	NA	NA	209	94.7	0.0	5.3	0.0	0.0	19.6	52.2	28.2	94	86.2	13.8	68.1
Hancock town (Hillsborough)	1,654	1,642	-0.7	1,805	96.4	0.2	0.7	1.1	1.6	21.1	56.7	22.3	717	89.1	13.0	63.9
Hanover CDP	8,636	NA	NA	8,411	79.8	3.7	11.7	2.0	2.9	8.3	80.5	11.4	1,936	44.2	4.2	83.7
Hanover town (Grafton)	11,260	11,379	1.1	11,311	83.4	2.7	9.6	1.7	2.6	12.8	75.5	11.9	2,958	59.0	6.3	80.7
Harrisville town (Cheshire)	961	949	-1.2	911	96.5	0.0	0.0	1.4	2.1	14.1	62.0	24.0	450	85.3	18.2	57.6
Hart's Location town (Carroll)	41	42	2.4	41	92.7	0.0	0.0	7.3	0.0	7.3	80.5	12.2	26	38.5	23.1	69.2
Haverhill town (Grafton)	4,697	4,656	-0.9	4,665	96.2	0.3	0.9	1.8	0.8	17.6	64.4	18.1	1,763	70.7	49.1	19.2
Hebron town (Grafton)	602	618	2.7	578	96.7	0.5	1.2	0.9	0.7	16.6	58.6	24.7	212	74.5	15.1	51.4
Henniker CDP	1,747	NA	NA	1,842	94.0	0.7	0.5	0.3	4.5	17.0	77.4	5.6	490	59.4	21.0	39.4
Henniker town (Merrimack)	4,836	4,850	0.3	4,822	96.1	0.5	0.2	0.7	2.4	24.2	69.6	6.2	1,598	67.0	26.7	43.9
Hill town (Merrimack)	1,089	1,092	0.3	1,164	98.3	0.0	0.0	1.7	0.0	21.6	64.8	13.7	445	92.8	58.9	16.4
Hillsborough CDP	1,976	NA	NA	2,058	98.5	0.0	0.0	0.8	0.7	34.6	51.9	13.5	642	65.0	42.7	22.0
Hillsborough town (Hillsborough)	6,011	5,990	-0.3	5,994	96.1	0.0	0.6	2.1	1.2	27.6	58.9	13.5	2,261	81.4	35.1	28.3
Hinsdale CDP	1,548	NA	NA	1,732	99.1	0.0	0.0	0.0	0.9	17.7	57.4	24.9	808	51.2	46.0	17.8
Hinsdale town (Cheshire)	4,046	3,954	-2.3	3,995	98.6	0.5	0.2	0.3	0.4	19.0	61.8	19.2	1,794	68.4	52.3	12.4
Holderness town (Grafton)	2,108	2,107	0.0	2,093	95.4	1.9	0.0	2.1	0.6	20.2	65.0	14.7	822	78.2	26.5	53.0
Hollis town (Hillsborough)	7,684	7,770	1.1	7,721	94.4	0.0	1.8	1.7	2.1	23.0	61.9	15.2	2,850	91.8	18.2	62.4
Hooksett CDP	4,147	NA	NA	4,112	88.7	1.2	6.0	1.6	2.5	14.8	67.7	17.6	1,818	84.2	28.7	37.6
Hooksett town (Merrimack)	13,451	13,771	2.4	13,669	91.8	0.6	1.9	1.2	4.5	19.1	68.0	13.0	5,216	85.8	31.4	36.8
Hopkinton town (Merrimack)	5,589	5,602	0.2	5,591	96.1	0.5	0.8	2.1	0.5	22.5	60.1	17.3	2,122	87.0	18.2	58.4
Hudson CDP	7,336	NA	NA	7,725	86.9	2.2	1.6	2.0	7.3	21.5	64.5	13.9	2,941	72.0	37.3	25.2
Hudson town (Hillsborough)	24,467	24,775	1.3	24,584	91.1	1.3	3.7	1.0	3.0	24.3	63.5	12.3	8,751	82.2	29.5	35.7
Jackson town (Carroll)	816	812	-0.5	1,032	95.9	0.0	1.6	0.9	1.6	17.7	47.7	34.6	444	81.8	8.6	55.2
Jaffrey CDP	2,757	NA	NA	2,421	96.4	0.0	0.0	3.0	0.6	19.7	61.8	18.6	1,169	46.9	53.9	14.7
Jaffrey town (Cheshire)	5,457	5,363	-1.7	5,416	96.9	0.0	1.3	1.5	0.3	21.7	58.0	20.2	2,246	68.7	39.4	22.0
Jefferson town (Coos)	1,107	1,063	-4.0	902	98.9	0.0	0.9	0.2	0.0	13.9	65.7	20.3	423	85.1	44.2	29.8
Keene city & MCD (Cheshire)	23,409	23,034	-1.6	23,281	93.7	0.9	1.6	2.0	1.9	15.6	69.5	15.0	9,208	55.4	30.7	39.7
Kensington town (Rockingham)	2,124	2,135	0.5	2,055	96.5	0.4	1.2	0.5	1.4	23.6	64.0	12.4	746	92.8	25.7	43.7
Kilkenny township (Coos)	0	0	0.0	0	0.0	0.0	0.0	0.0	0.0	0.0	0.0	0.0	0	0.0	0.0	0.0
Kingston town (Rockingham)	6,025	6,104	1.3	6,060	96.0	0.0	0.3	1.9	1.8	20.3	64.8	15.0	2,442	84.6	37.2	32.2
Laconia city & MCD (Belknap)	15,947	16,067	0.8	16,007	96.0	0.1	1.0	2.0	0.9	20.7	61.5	17.7	6,911	56.6	44.8	24.5
Lancaster CDP	1,725	NA	NA	1,514	94.6	0.6	0.0	4.4	0.4	21.8	65.0	13.2	704	59.2	42.2	32.2
Lancaster town (Coos)	3,507	3,408	-2.8	3,437	97.2	0.6	0.0	1.9	0.2	22.0	59.4	18.4	1,537	69.0	41.5	26.5
Landaff town (Grafton)	415	419	1.0	416	93.3	0.0	0.0	6.3	0.5	14.9	63.1	21.9	192	92.7	41.1	24.0
Langdon town (Sullivan)	688	681	-1.0	787	95.0	0.0	0.0	1.3	3.2	23.0	61.2	16.0	284	89.8	43.3	34.2
Lebanon city & MCD (Grafton)	13,151	13,589	3.3	13,474	81.1	0.6	8.1	5.2	5.0	19.3	65.2	15.5	6,224	49.3	31.3	47.3
Lee town (Strafford)	4,333	4,394	1.4	4,357	92.6	0.0	4.7	0.1	2.5	22.2	62.8	15.0	1,774	83.8	11.3	56.5
Lempster town (Sullivan)	1,154	1,151	-0.3	1,089	96.7	0.0	0.3	0.4	2.7	20.5	65.1	14.5	425	88.2	52.0	22.8
Lincoln CDP	993	NA	NA	754	99.5	0.0	0.0	0.5	0.0	11.7	61.9	26.4	420	50.5	63.6	9.0
Lincoln town (Grafton)	1,662	1,664	0.1	1,309	96.2	0.0	3.5	0.3	0.0	21.1	59.1	19.8	614	57.8	56.5	14.8
Lisbon CDP	980	NA	NA	960	91.4	0.0	0.5	2.3	5.8	25.7	64.3	10.1	343	67.9	48.4	18.4
Lisbon town (Grafton)	1,595	1,587	-0.5	1,557	93.6	0.0	0.3	2.4	3.6	20.6	66.5	12.8	619	72.5	51.1	17.1
Litchfield town (Hillsborough)	8,265	8,418	1.9	8,329	95.4	0.5	0.8	0.7	2.5	27.5	62.3	10.3	2,786	83.6	28.5	32.3
Littleton CDP	4,412	NA	NA	4,576	93.8	0.3	1.5	2.3	2.0	21.8	62.6	15.7	2,063	49.3	52.8	21.5
Littleton town (Grafton)	5,928	5,959	0.5	5,942	94.4	0.3	1.2	1.8	2.4	19.8	61.1	19.2	2,613	54.9	49.7	21.8
Livermore town (Grafton)	0	0	0.0	0	0.0	0.0	0.0	0.0	0.0	0.0	0.0	0.0	0	0.0	0.0	0.0
Londonderry CDP	11,037	NA	NA	10,637	95.8	0.6	0.4	0.9	2.4	21.9	64.5	13.7	3,985	84.9	28.1	42.9
Londonderry town (Rockingham)	24,129	24,403	1.1	24,247	94.8	0.8	1.0	0.8	2.6	24.6	64.6	10.8	8,750	86.8	26.4	43.9
Loudon CDP	559	NA	NA	585	100.0	0.0	0.0	0.0	0.0	20.0	42.7	37.3	267	63.7	44.6	31.1
Loudon town (Merrimack)	5,317	5,376	1.1	5,343	95.9	0.0	0.0	3.8	0.4	22.0	64.5	13.4	2,013	84.1	51.0	27.1
Low and Burbanks grant (Coos)	0	0	0.0	0	0.0	0.0	0.0	0.0	0.0	0.0	0.0	0.0	0	0.0	0.0	0.0
Lyman town (Grafton)	533	536	0.6	608	99.5	0.0	0.5	0.0	0.0	17.4	64.5	18.1	255	87.5	42.0	27.8
Lyme town (Grafton)	1,716	1,697	-1.1	1,733	93.4	0.0	2.1	2.5	1.9	22.8	57.6	19.6	680	88.7	11.0	68.2

1 May be of any race.

Table A. All Places — **Population and Housing**

STATE City, town, township, borough, or CDP (county if applicable)	2010 census total population	2014 estimated population	Percent change 2010–2014	ACS total population estimate 2010–2014	White alone, not Hispanic or Latino	Black alone, not Hispanic or Latino	Asian alone, not Hispanic or Latino	All other races or 2 or more races, not Hispanic or Latino	Hispanic or Latino[1]	Under 18 years old	Age 18 to 64 years old	Age 65 years and older	Total occupied housing units	Percent owner occupied	High school diploma or less	Bachelor's degree or more
	1	2	3	4	5	6	7	8	9	10	11	12	13	14	15	16
NEW HAMPSHIRE—Con.																
Lyndeborough town (Hillsborough).............	1,683	1,694	0.7	1,633	95.5	0.2	0.8	2.3	1.2	21.4	62.3	16.3	637	84.9	31.4	39.2
Madbury town (Strafford).	1,775	1,798	1.3	2,003	89.5	0.3	6.4	3.5	0.3	28.3	62.6	8.9	655	78.9	22.3	53.7
Madison town (Carroll)	2,500	2,516	0.6	2,507	99.4	0.6	0.0	0.0	0.0	17.7	65.5	16.8	1,133	86.5	40.3	33.7
Manchester city & MCD (Hillsborough).............	109,571	110,448	0.8	110,065	80.5	4.3	4.9	2.3	8.1	20.3	67.0	12.6	44,973	48.5	40.7	28.7
Marlborough CDP...........	1,094	NA	NA	986	95.5	4.5	0.0	0.0	0.0	18.9	65.3	15.6	459	47.3	51.6	20.9
Marlborough town (Cheshire)	2,063	2,088	1.2	1,840	96.2	2.4	0.0	0.6	0.8	19.5	63.4	17.0	840	66.5	43.9	27.9
Marlow town (Cheshire)...	742	738	-0.5	753	97.3	0.1	0.0	1.1	1.5	21.9	58.4	19.7	298	89.9	42.3	25.5
Martins location (Coos) ...	0	0	0.0	0	0.0	0.0	0.0	0.0	0.0	0.0	0.0	0.0	0	0.0	0.0	0.0
Mason town (Hillsborough).............	1,382	1,402	1.4	1,329	97.3	0.0	0.2	2.0	0.5	26.7	63.5	9.9	495	94.7	28.3	42.6
Melvin Village CDP	241	NA	NA	129	100.0	0.0	0.0	0.0	0.0	12.4	38.8	48.8	78	80.8	32.1	17.9
Meredith CDP	1,718	NA	NA	1,631	100.0	0.0	0.0	0.0	0.0	24.7	53.1	22.4	792	54.2	29.9	28.2
Meredith town (Belknap)..	6,245	6,314	1.1	6,303	97.4	0.6	1.3	0.2	0.6	21.3	53.8	24.8	2,832	72.2	31.5	37.7
Merrimack town (Hillsborough).............	25,494	25,659	0.6	25,563	93.9	0.1	2.0	1.4	2.6	22.0	65.8	12.1	9,606	86.3	27.5	46.6
Middleton town (Strafford)	1,783	1,783	0.0	1,567	96.4	0.5	0.0	2.0	1.1	23.2	65.3	11.5	553	87.3	44.7	13.0
Milan town (Coos)...........	1,337	1,284	-4.0	1,307	95.9	0.2	0.0	0.8	3.1	15.9	67.4	16.8	589	86.9	46.2	20.5
Milford CDP	8,835	NA	NA	8,970	88.5	0.5	2.8	4.8	3.5	23.0	60.9	16.3	3,850	51.8	35.9	32.4
Milford town (Hillsborough).............	15,115	15,153	0.3	15,133	91.0	0.3	2.4	3.2	3.1	23.4	62.5	14.0	6,013	64.9	33.1	37.1
Millsfield township (Coos)	23	22	-4.3	20	100.0	0.0	0.0	0.0	0.0	35.0	65.0	0.0	9	100.0	0.0	22.2
Milton CDP	575	NA	NA	801	100.0	0.0	0.0	0.0	0.0	22.1	72.1	5.7	267	62.9	62.9	4.1
Milton town (Strafford)	4,598	4,591	-0.2	4,592	98.7	0.3	0.0	0.8	0.2	22.7	63.8	13.5	1,656	84.3	51.1	19.0
Milton Mills CDP	299	NA	NA	358	92.5	0.0	0.0	7.5	0.0	30.2	63.2	6.7	87	93.1	0.0	46.0
Monroe town (Grafton)	788	784	-0.5	906	90.5	2.0	0.2	7.2	0.1	21.9	59.5	18.8	343	93.9	46.6	23.3
Mont Vernon town (Hillsborough).............	2,409	2,456	2.0	2,508	98.2	0.0	0.3	0.6	0.9	27.2	58.9	13.7	842	95.1	20.2	56.2
Moultonborough town (Carroll)	4,044	4,016	-0.7	4,032	99.6	0.0	0.0	0.0	0.4	15.6	58.6	25.9	1,762	90.3	23.2	48.9
Mountain Lakes CDP.......	488	NA	NA	400	97.0	0.0	0.0	0.0	3.0	10.3	69.9	20.0	178	70.2	57.9	19.1
Nashua city & MCD (Hillsborough).............	86,494	87,259	0.9	86,799	76.6	2.1	6.6	3.5	11.1	22.0	64.9	13.0	34,403	56.7	33.2	36.6
Nelson town (Cheshire) ...	729	726	-0.4	606	97.5	0.0	0.3	1.7	0.5	16.7	66.4	17.0	246	76.4	19.9	50.8
New Boston town (Hillsborough).............	5,321	5,453	2.5	5,390	96.0	0.4	0.0	2.4	1.1	24.0	68.5	7.6	1,866	91.5	26.0	41.8
Newbury town (Merrimack)	2,072	2,157	4.1	1,749	97.1	0.0	0.0	2.2	0.7	18.0	58.5	23.5	756	94.7	24.3	43.1
New Castle town (Rockingham)..............	968	976	0.8	980	91.7	0.0	1.4	0.5	6.3	12.3	54.2	33.5	451	76.9	5.1	61.6
New Durham town (Strafford)	2,638	2,658	0.8	2,648	99.2	0.0	0.0	0.5	0.4	23.1	63.6	13.3	1,001	88.7	31.7	33.2
Newfields CDP	301	NA	NA	239	91.2	0.0	0.0	4.2	4.6	26.0	61.9	12.1	102	72.5	39.2	48.0
Newfields town (Rockingham)..............	1,680	1,698	1.1	1,625	94.4	0.2	0.2	2.0	3.1	27.3	62.1	10.6	574	91.1	21.6	52.8
New Hampton CDP	351	NA	NA	357	100.0	0.0	0.0	0.0	0.0	16.3	57.0	26.6	119	84.0	35.3	43.7
New Hampton town (Belknap).....................	2,169	2,196	1.2	2,266	94.4	0.5	1.1	3.5	0.5	20.1	64.0	16.0	885	87.2	30.5	34.7
Newington town (Rockingham)..............	753	763	1.3	800	95.3	0.0	1.6	1.0	2.1	12.4	69.3	18.4	314	70.7	28.7	42.4
New Ipswich town (Hillsborough).............	5,099	5,147	0.9	5,123	98.4	0.0	0.0	0.2	1.4	29.7	60.4	9.8	1,829	87.0	32.3	37.2
New London CDP	1,415	NA	NA	1,470	86.0	3.5	3.3	2.1	5.2	0.0	84.2	15.8	329	40.1	30.4	59.0
New London town (Merrimack)	4,397	4,648	5.7	4,539	93.3	1.1	1.3	1.7	2.6	9.0	56.9	34.0	1,734	78.7	12.3	66.1
Newmarket CDP	5,297	NA	NA	5,589	81.1	2.0	7.8	2.9	6.2	18.5	73.2	8.3	2,469	39.2	27.9	42.9
Newmarket town (Rockingham)..............	8,936	8,938	0.0	8,928	87.4	1.2	5.1	1.8	4.5	21.2	68.7	10.1	3,816	53.4	25.9	45.4
Newport CDP.................	4,769	NA	NA	4,818	90.3	0.0	2.2	6.3	1.3	18.4	64.7	17.0	2,136	62.9	46.6	22.5
Newport town (Sullivan)...	6,507	6,394	-1.7	6,434	91.6	0.0	2.6	4.8	0.9	18.1	63.4	18.5	2,806	66.2	47.1	24.6
Newton town (Rockingham)..............	4,603	4,812	4.5	4,717	92.9	1.1	0.1	0.7	5.2	26.2	64.8	9.0	1,747	79.4	29.9	28.9
North Conway CDP	2,349	NA	NA	2,347	93.1	0.0	1.7	1.5	3.6	18.0	68.1	13.9	1,169	44.6	32.8	19.8
Northfield town (Merrimack)	4,829	4,802	-0.6	4,823	93.4	0.6	2.7	1.3	1.9	24.6	63.9	11.5	1,729	75.9	43.4	24.1
North Hampton town (Rockingham)..............	4,301	4,409	2.5	4,344	95.3	1.3	0.9	1.4	1.0	20.0	61.3	18.7	1,735	91.1	20.2	49.9
North Haverhill CDP	0	NA	NA	730	94.9	0.7	0.0	3.2	1.2	10.2	60.7	29.0	211	77.7	33.2	19.0
Northumberland town (Coos)	2,288	2,203	-3.7	2,179	98.9	0.6	0.0	0.0	0.5	21.0	62.3	16.7	904	72.7	59.4	12.6
North Walpole CDP	828	NA	NA	1,074	90.0	0.0	0.0	4.5	5.5	29.9	57.3	12.8	413	48.9	52.5	4.6
Northwood town (Rockingham)..............	4,241	4,287	1.1	4,269	93.6	0.0	1.5	2.2	2.8	21.5	63.8	14.8	1,676	87.1	33.4	36.6
North Woodstock CDP.....	528	NA	NA	299	91.6	0.0	0.0	5.7	2.7	23.8	53.7	22.7	129	61.2	34.9	19.4
Nottingham town (Rockingham)..............	4,785	4,911	2.6	4,855	97.2	0.7	0.0	1.6	0.5	21.4	69.1	9.3	1,824	95.8	24.7	44.1
Odell township (Coos)	4	4	0.0	0	0.0	0.0	0.0	0.0	0.0	0.0	0.0	0.0	0	0.0	0.0	0.0
Orange town (Grafton).....	331	332	0.3	308	99.4	0.0	0.0	0.6	0.0	17.2	60.3	22.4	134	90.3	36.6	28.4
Orford town (Grafton).......	1,237	1,247	0.8	1,572	96.8	0.0	0.1	2.0	1.0	22.0	60.7	17.3	585	74.4	32.8	45.0
Ossipee town (Carroll)....	4,342	4,265	-1.8	4,301	97.8	0.0	0.0	1.2	1.0	22.1	58.0	20.0	1,761	84.3	56.3	17.4
Pelham town (Hillsborough).............	12,897	13,219	2.5	13,032	94.8	0.5	0.5	2.2	2.0	25.1	63.8	11.2	4,439	86.1	38.3	30.8
Pembroke town (Merrimack)	7,115	7,112	0.0	7,121	95.3	0.0	2.0	0.3	2.4	22.4	66.3	11.4	2,787	71.3	39.0	27.1
Peterborough CDP	3,103	NA	NA	2,993	95.8	0.6	3.5	0.2	0.0	14.1	53.5	32.3	1,537	52.5	20.5	51.0
Peterborough town (Hillsborough).............	6,284	6,474	3.0	6,387	96.9	0.5	1.9	0.1	0.6	15.4	61.1	23.5	2,981	67.8	21.0	58.2
Piermont town (Grafton) ..	790	782		754	97.7	0.4	1.7	0.1	0.0	17.1	60.8	22.1	323	86.1	34.7	36.8
Pinardville CDP	4,780	NA	NA	4,601	95.2	0.5	0.1	0.3	3.9	16.4	68.7	14.9	2,018	69.5	42.8	27.4

1 May be of any race.

Table A. All Places — **Population and Housing**

STATE City, town, township, borough, or CDP (county if applicable)	Population				Race and Hispanic or Latino origin (percent), 2010–2014					Age (percent), 2010–2014			Households, 2010–2014			
	2010 census total population	2014 estimated population	Percent change 2010–2014	ACS total population estimate 2010–2014	White alone, not Hispanic or Latino	Black alone, not Hispanic or Latino	Asian alone, not Hispanic or Latino	All other races or 2 or more races, not Hispanic or Latino	Hispanic or Latino[1]	Under 18 years old	Age 18 to 64 years old	Age 65 years and older	Total occupied housing units	Percent owner occupied	High school diploma or less	Bachelor's degree or more
	1	2	3	4	5	6	7	8	9	10	11	12	13	14	15	16
NEW HAMPSHIRE—Con.																
Pinkhams grant (Coos)....	9	9	0.0	8	100.0	0.0	0.0	0.0	0.0	0.0	100.0	0.0	0	0.0	0.0	0.0
Pittsburg town (Coos)	869	840	-3.3	875	96.2	0.3	0.0	1.1	2.3	9.4	63.3	27.3	452	79.9	45.4	21.9
Pittsfield CDP	1,576	NA	NA	1,733	92.2	0.0	5.9	1.0	0.8	26.3	63.2	10.6	717	31.9	64.2	10.7
Pittsfield town (Merrimack).................	4,106	4,069	-0.9	4,082	93.4	1.5	2.5	1.0	1.5	23.0	65.1	11.9	1,525	59.1	49.4	20.2
Plainfield CDP	205	NA	NA	308	100.0	0.0	0.0	0.0	0.0	26.3	69.2	4.5	85	85.9	37.6	48.2
Plainfield town (Sullivan)..	2,364	2,347	-0.7	2,518	93.2	0.7	0.9	2.9	2.3	21.8	62.4	15.7	933	87.4	24.9	50.5
Plaistow town (Rockingham).................	7,609	7,628	0.2	7,614	97.9	0.0	0.2	0.9	1.0	21.9	64.4	13.6	2,949	77.3	38.9	25.0
Plymouth CDP	4,456	NA	NA	3,807	88.1	0.4	3.4	4.8	3.3	6.5	91.5	2.1	933	35.3	9.9	46.3
Plymouth town (Grafton)..	6,990	6,804	-2.7	6,902	90.1	0.2	1.9	3.3	4.4	11.9	79.2	8.9	2,157	49.8	26.9	35.5
Portsmouth city & MCD (Rockingham).................	21,233	21,598	1.7	21,366	88.1	2.0	4.1	2.6	3.2	15.9	67.5	16.6	10,325	52.8	20.4	56.4
Randolph town (Coos).....	310	296	-4.5	424	91.5	0.0	7.1	0.5	0.9	13.9	56.2	30.0	197	88.8	23.9	50.8
Raymond CDP	2,855	NA	NA	2,789	83.7	5.7	3.8	1.6	5.1	20.1	66.4	13.4	1,184	66.0	41.6	35.0
Raymond town (Rockingham).................	10,138	10,280	1.4	10,202	91.7	1.7	1.2	1.7	3.8	24.2	65.8	10.0	3,864	76.4	44.1	28.9
Richmond town (Cheshire)	1,155	1,152	-0.3	1,089	95.1	1.1	1.0	0.7	2.0	18.8	68.5	12.5	408	94.9	31.9	38.5
Rindge town (Cheshire) ..	6,014	5,956	-1.0	5,958	93.5	2.1	1.8	1.8	0.8	20.6	68.6	10.7	1,858	76.5	40.7	25.4
Rochester city & MCD (Strafford)....................	29,752	29,991	0.8	29,883	94.6	0.4	1.0	2.3	1.7	19.4	64.5	16.1	12,715	64.0	46.7	21.9
Rollinsford town (Strafford)....................	2,527	2,526	0.0	2,528	92.2	0.8	1.0	2.4	3.6	26.5	60.6	12.8	1,024	74.7	30.6	40.0
Roxbury town (Cheshire) .	229	227	-0.9	236	99.6	0.0	0.4	0.0	0.0	19.1	64.4	16.5	93	83.9	33.3	29.0
Rumney town (Grafton) ...	1,480	1,494	0.9	1,676	97.3	0.0	0.5	1.7	0.4	19.9	64.3	16.1	648	79.8	41.7	30.2
Rye town (Rockingham) ..	5,298	5,325	0.5	5,315	98.0	0.3	0.2	0.5	1.0	14.8	61.1	24.0	2,315	84.2	20.0	50.9
Salem town (Rockingham).................	28,776	29,005	0.8	28,841	88.0	0.5	3.7	2.0	5.8	20.0	64.5	15.5	11,093	76.2	37.6	32.9
Salisbury town (Merrimack).................	1,382	1,397	1.1	1,406	94.7	0.6	0.0	4.2	0.4	20.5	68.0	11.6	553	92.6	34.7	26.9
Sanbornton town (Belknap).................	2,966	2,972	0.2	2,977	96.3	0.1	0.0	0.3	3.4	17.1	64.1	18.7	1,235	93.7	24.0	44.5
Sanbornville CDP	1,056	NA	NA	916	89.7	0.0	0.4	2.5	7.3	9.5	72.1	18.3	444	80.9	30.9	16.9
Sandown town (Rockingham).................	5,988	6,243	4.3	6,133	97.5	0.2	0.0	1.6	0.7	24.1	66.9	9.0	2,130	91.8	34.9	28.5
Sandwich town (Carroll) ..	1,326	1,313	-1.0	1,484	98.5	0.4	0.0	0.3	0.7	22.0	53.2	24.9	645	77.7	17.1	61.9
Sargents purchase (Coos)	3	3	0.0	9	100.0	0.0	0.0	0.0	0.0	0.0	100.0	0.0	5	0.0	0.0	0.0
Seabrook town (Rockingham).................	8,693	8,796	1.2	8,747	94.5	0.1	2.7	0.8	1.8	15.0	64.9	20.1	3,837	63.0	42.8	15.0
Seabrook Beach CDP	992	NA	NA	826	99.3	0.0	0.7	0.0	0.0	9.7	51.0	39.3	409	71.1	24.2	42.3
Second College grant (Coos)	0	0	0.0	0	0.0	0.0	0.0	0.0	0.0	0.0	0.0	0.0	0	0.0	0.0	0.0
Sharon town (Hillsborough).................	352	361	2.6	320	97.5	0.0	1.9	0.6	0.0	10.3	66.7	23.1	145	86.9	18.6	67.6
Shelburne town (Coos)....	372	356	-4.3	358	99.4	0.0	0.0	0.3	0.3	15.3	60.1	24.6	165	85.5	39.4	30.9
Somersworth city & MCD (Strafford)....................	11,766	11,777	0.1	11,765	82.7	3.3	6.0	3.2	4.8	22.8	65.7	11.5	4,492	56.5	37.6	27.6
South Hampton town (Rockingham).................	814	814	0.0	799	94.6	0.4	1.0	0.9	3.1	18.7	64.7	16.8	306	83.0	30.1	40.8
South Hooksett CDP	5,418	NA	NA	5,378	94.2	0.5	0.2	0.3	4.7	17.8	70.6	11.6	1,825	85.0	37.5	30.9
Springfield town (Sullivan)	1,311	1,316	0.4	1,313	98.4	0.0	0.7	0.4	0.5	24.8	62.5	12.6	482	85.1	36.5	32.6
Stark town (Coos)...........	553	527	-4.7	490	96.9	0.0	0.0	3.1	0.0	19.2	58.5	22.4	217	83.4	46.5	19.8
Stewartstown town (Coos)	1,003	971	-3.2	811	95.9	0.7	0.0	3.3	0.0	10.5	52.8	36.7	373	72.9	57.9	13.9
Stoddard town (Cheshire)	1,232	1,244	1.0	1,124	95.9	3.3	0.3	0.3	0.3	20.1	61.0	18.7	484	91.3	30.6	36.8
Strafford town (Strafford) .	3,991	4,062	1.8	4,017	89.8	0.9	0.0	2.5	6.8	23.6	62.7	13.7	1,430	91.8	18.7	37.5
Stratford town (Coos).......	746	710	-4.8	710	99.2	0.4	0.0	0.4	0.0	22.7	53.8	23.5	332	81.6	66.6	9.9
Stratham town (Rockingham).................	7,255	7,366	1.5	7,303	96.6	0.0	0.5	2.0	0.9	23.5	64.3	12.1	2,781	92.9	13.2	61.8
Success township (Coos)	0	0	0.0	0	0.0	0.0	0.0	0.0	0.0	0.0	0.0	0.0	0	0.0	0.0	0.0
Sugar Hill town (Grafton) .	563	572	1.6	618	97.4	0.0	1.0	0.0	1.6	17.8	61.3	20.9	296	89.2	16.9	45.6
Suissevale CDP	249	NA	NA	86	100.0	0.0	0.0	0.0	0.0	0.0	60.5	39.5	63	90.5	9.5	77.8
Sullivan town (Cheshire)..	677	674	-0.4	741	96.9	0.0	0.0	0.0	3.1	20.8	63.7	15.4	294	79.6	45.9	37.4
Sunapee town (Sullivan)..	3,365	3,373	0.2	3,363	95.8	0.0	0.6	0.8	2.8	17.0	58.9	24.1	1,496	71.4	17.9	57.8
Suncook CDP	5,379	NA	NA	5,017	94.2	0.2	2.6	0.6	2.4	25.3	61.0	13.7	2,126	56.1	45.0	20.4
Surry town (Cheshire)......	732	731	-0.1	828	95.7	0.0	0.7	2.4	1.2	9.9	69.0	21.0	375	93.9	33.1	41.3
Sutton town (Merrimack) .	1,837	1,850	0.7	2,014	95.7	0.5	1.2	2.1	0.4	23.3	55.8	21.2	786	88.3	17.0	53.6
Swanzey town (Cheshire)	7,230	7,246	0.2	7,255	92.5	0.0	2.1	0.7	4.7	19.2	67.8	13.1	2,919	75.7	46.9	26.9
Tamworth town (Carroll) ..	2,856	2,846	-0.4	2,851	97.4	0.6	0.0	2.0	0.0	6.8	73.1	20.2	1,512	69.2	55.2	24.7
Temple town (Hillsborough).................	1,366	1,382	1.2	1,594	96.4	0.0	0.4	0.7	2.6	21.1	62.7	16.1	573	85.3	41.5	30.4
Thompson and Meserves purchase (Coos)	0	0	0.0	0	0.0	0.0	0.0	0.0	0.0	0.0	0.0	0.0	0	0.0	0.0	0.0
Thornton town (Grafton) ..	2,490	2,508	0.7	2,490	97.9	0.9	0.4	0.8	0.0	14.0	67.7	18.4	1,064	83.9	29.0	50.6
Tilton town (Belknap).......	3,567	3,571	0.1	3,573	97.7	0.0	0.2	0.3	1.8	18.2	61.8	19.9	1,531	66.8	38.3	27.0
Tilton Northfield CDP.......	3,075	NA	NA	3,919	94.2	0.8	3.4	0.0	1.7	25.9	59.2	15.0	1,369	49.4	39.4	23.2
Troy CDP	1,221	NA	NA	1,454	88.5	9.2	0.4	1.3	0.6	18.9	67.2	13.8	584	55.8	40.1	22.3
Troy town (Cheshire).......	2,145	2,110	-1.6	2,262	89.9	5.9	1.4	2.1	0.8	20.8	65.7	13.5	893	69.8	42.4	22.6
Tuftonboro town (Carroll).	2,387	2,347	-1.7	2,256	99.8	0.0	0.0	0.2	0.0	23.0	54.5	22.5	975	82.6	25.8	39.9
Union CDP	204	NA	NA	244	100.0	0.0	0.0	0.0	0.0	35.2	56.9	7.8	89	100.0	42.7	57.3
Unity town (Sullivan)........	1,671	1,615	-3.4	1,592	97.8	0.0	0.3	0.9	1.0	12.0	68.4	19.6	529	97.0	54.4	14.9
Wakefield town (Carroll) ..	5,081	4,985	-1.9	5,046	94.5	0.0	0.7	2.0	2.8	14.1	65.9	19.9	2,260	89.3	41.3	19.2
Walpole CDP	605	NA	NA	344	100.0	0.0	0.0	0.0	0.0	12.8	52.0	35.2	217	74.7	0.0	59.9
Walpole town (Cheshire) .	3,734	3,685	-1.3	3,704	94.5	0.0	0.5	2.1	3.0	25.0	59.4	15.5	1,548	72.2	37.9	30.4
Warner CDP	444	NA	NA	484	93.8	0.0	0.0	6.2	0.0	15.1	55.8	29.1	205	70.2	39.5	38.5
Warner town (Merrimack).	2,833	2,853	0.7	2,851	97.1	0.0	0.0	1.2	1.7	18.7	64.6	16.8	1,123	77.6	28.0	38.2
Warren town (Grafton)	904	896	-0.9	726	98.8	0.0	0.1	1.0	0.1	18.4	64.1	17.5	316	80.7	52.8	21.5
Washington town (Sullivan)	1,123	1,112	-1.0	1,013	95.3	0.9	0.0	1.3	2.6	14.4	61.1	24.4	449	93.1	36.7	29.0

1 May be of any race.

Table A. All Places — **Population and Housing**

STATE City, town, township, borough, or CDP (county if applicable)	Population				Race and Hispanic or Latino origin (percent), 2010–2014					Age (percent), 2010–2014			Households, 2010–2014			
	2010 census total population	2014 estimated population	Percent change 2010–2014	ACS total population estimate 2010–2014	White alone, not Hispanic or Latino	Black alone, not Hispanic or Latino	Asian alone, not Hispanic or Latino	All other races or 2 or more races, not Hispanic or Latino	Hispanic or Latino[1]	Under 18 years old	Age 18 to 64 years old	Age 65 years and older	Total occupied housing units	Percent owner occupied	High school diploma or less	Bachelor's degree or more
	1	2	3	4	5	6	7	8	9	10	11	12	13	14	15	16
NEW HAMPSHIRE—Con.																
Waterville Valley town (Grafton)	247	248	0.4	260	97.3	0.0	1.9	0.0	0.8	18.9	55.8	25.4	117	100.0	19.7	62.4
Weare town (Hillsborough)	8,785	8,922	1.6	8,849	96.9	0.2	0.0	1.7	1.3	27.1	66.6	6.2	3,126	89.8	31.3	31.9
Webster town (Merrimack)	1,872	1,893	1.1	1,891	96.5	0.0	0.0	3.2	0.3	22.9	64.9	12.4	767	87.4	32.3	31.0
Wentworth town (Grafton)	911	921	1.1	896	95.3	0.4	0.9	2.3	1.0	16.1	61.8	22.2	336	89.0	49.4	18.8
Wentworth location (Coos)	33	32	-3.0	62	83.9	0.0	0.0	0.0	16.1	6.5	71.1	22.6	37	54.1	35.1	27.0
Westmoreland town (Cheshire)	1,874	1,725	-8.0	2,066	98.0	0.3	1.5	0.1	0.1	23.0	56.5	20.6	691	86.7	26.3	50.8
West Stewartstown CDP	386	NA	NA	283	97.9	2.1	0.0	0.0	0.0	0.0	58.3	41.7	112	55.4	70.5	5.4
West Swanzey CDP	1,308	NA	NA	1,353	87.8	0.0	2.4	0.0	9.8	33.2	59.4	7.3	569	52.7	46.7	37.8
Whitefield CDP	1,142	NA	NA	1,032	92.1	0.0	0.0	6.2	1.7	22.6	58.9	18.5	468	48.7	52.1	12.8
Whitefield town (Coos)	2,306	2,239	-2.9	2,134	96.1	0.1	0.0	3.0	0.8	17.2	64.6	18.2	1,047	63.7	45.2	18.6
Wilmot town (Merrimack)	1,358	1,376	1.3	1,367	97.3	0.5	1.2	1.0	0.0	18.5	59.3	22.4	588	81.3	21.9	44.6
Wilton CDP	1,163	NA	NA	1,123	95.4	0.0	0.0	2.6	2.0	21.9	64.8	13.3	470	62.8	47.2	19.1
Wilton town (Hillsborough)	3,677	3,685	0.2	3,679	96.4	0.4	0.7	1.3	1.3	22.6	63.8	13.8	1,433	76.3	29.1	28.7
Winchester CDP	1,733	NA	NA	1,683	98.5	0.0	1.5	0.0	0.0	19.1	66.5	14.5	721	62.8	65.5	23.7
Winchester town (Cheshire)	4,341	4,258	-1.9	4,302	96.2	0.0	0.6	2.7	0.5	23.1	62.5	14.4	1,788	71.3	62.0	16.2
Windham town (Rockingham)	13,592	14,250	4.8	13,943	93.3	0.5	4.0	1.9	0.3	25.8	61.0	13.1	4,987	92.5	23.8	55.9
Windsor town (Hillsborough)	224	283	26.3	269	93.3	1.1	0.0	5.6	0.0	17.5	69.8	12.6	110	85.5	54.5	18.2
Wolfeboro CDP	2,838	NA	NA	2,679	88.2	0.0	0.5	2.7	8.6	10.7	54.2	35.1	1,223	78.1	17.0	49.4
Wolfeboro town (Carroll)	6,270	6,225	-0.7	6,231	94.9	0.0	0.2	1.2	3.7	16.6	50.6	32.7	2,734	81.0	21.9	42.6
Woodstock town (Grafton)	1,374	1,386	0.9	1,137	95.7	0.0	1.6	2.0	0.7	18.1	65.4	16.4	488	75.2	41.6	25.6
Woodsville CDP	1,126	NA	NA	1,420	99.3	0.0	0.0	0.7	0.0	26.5	62.5	10.9	504	47.8	62.9	10.3
NEW JERSEY	8,791,936	8,938,175	1.7	8,874,374	57.8	12.8	8.7	2.1	18.6	22.9	62.9	14.1	3,188,498	65.0	36.8	38.5
Aberdeen township (Monmouth)	18,209	18,292	0.5	18,216	66.6	12.3	7.1	2.3	11.7	22.1	65.8	12.0	6,818	76.3	27.7	41.1
Absecon city & MCD (Atlantic)	8,411	8,376	-0.4	8,400	75.4	5.0	7.0	2.3	10.3	20.1	61.7	18.3	3,247	83.4	36.5	30.0
Alexandria township (Hunterdon)	4,938	4,893	-0.9	4,909	96.1	0.0	1.3	0.0	2.6	23.0	63.6	13.4	1,651	97.5	21.6	52.1
Allamuchy CDP	78	NA	NA	100	100.0	0.0	0.0	0.0	0.0	34.0	66.0	0.0	32	100.0	0.0	100.0
Allamuchy township (Warren)	4,323	4,558	5.4	4,470	89.6	0.3	3.8	0.9	5.4	18.8	63.8	17.5	2,017	92.4	19.0	57.2
Allendale borough & MCD (Bergen)	6,505	6,789	4.4	6,666	79.6	1.6	14.1	0.3	4.5	28.9	56.3	14.8	2,214	88.8	13.3	68.2
Allenhurst borough & MCD (Monmouth)	496	489	-1.4	486	90.1	0.0	2.3	4.1	3.5	18.8	62.0	19.1	213	60.6	12.7	65.3
Allentown borough & MCD (Monmouth)	1,828	1,807	-1.1	1,828	89.2	4.1	0.4	2.8	3.4	24.3	64.2	11.5	677	77.3	28.2	43.3
Allenwood CDP	925	NA	NA	1,022	98.5	0.0	0.0	0.0	1.5	23.3	68.3	8.1	337	100.0	22.6	55.2
Alloway CDP	1,402	NA	NA	1,710	97.0	1.9	0.0	0.8	0.3	31.2	58.5	10.3	530	86.0	32.1	29.2
Alloway township (Salem)	3,467	3,418	-1.4	3,444	92.7	3.7	0.2	1.0	2.4	26.6	62.1	11.4	1,200	87.6	41.2	23.3
Alpha borough & MCD (Warren)	2,369	2,312	-2.4	2,320	89.7	5.4	0.0	0.5	4.3	22.8	61.1	16.1	966	70.5	57.6	15.7
Alpine borough & MCD (Bergen)	1,863	1,894	1.7	1,710	58.1	6.9	28.3	1.6	5.1	18.8	55.3	25.8	595	87.7	18.5	71.3
Anderson CDP	342	NA	NA	252	52.8	13.9	7.1	16.3	9.9	9.6	85.6	4.8	104	85.6	33.7	41.3
Andover borough & MCD (Sussex)	606	587	-3.1	677	84.6	1.5	0.4	2.7	10.8	17.6	68.9	13.6	260	73.8	29.6	34.2
Andover township (Sussex)	6,245	6,135	-1.8	6,207	88.2	3.1	2.2	0.4	6.0	21.1	60.6	18.3	1,997	87.3	23.3	45.8
Annandale CDP	1,695	NA	NA	1,404	90.6	3.2	4.8	0.4	0.9	24.6	69.6	5.8	533	65.3	25.0	61.2
Asbury CDP	273	NA	NA	225	100.0	0.0	0.0	0.0	0.0	4.9	86.7	8.4	100	90.0	49.0	17.0
Asbury Park city & MCD (Monmouth)	16,116	15,778	-2.1	15,933	23.4	43.3	0.5	2.7	30.2	23.7	65.7	10.6	6,622	20.0	52.8	19.6
Ashland CDP	8,302	NA	NA	8,260	76.2	4.3	13.4	2.1	4.0	20.2	60.7	19.1	2,980	93.5	18.8	54.3
Atlantic City city & MCD (Atlantic)	39,558	39,415	-0.4	39,521	19.0	37.3	15.9	2.7	25.1	24.8	62.0	13.1	15,847	29.6	61.5	15.8
Atlantic Highlands borough & MCD (Monmouth)	4,382	4,336	-1.0	4,357	89.2	1.6	1.2	3.4	4.6	21.6	64.3	14.2	1,797	79.4	20.5	51.4
Audubon borough & MCD (Camden)	8,819	8,710	-1.2	8,763	94.8	0.9	0.3	1.6	2.5	20.2	67.0	12.9	3,585	75.4	35.3	34.2
Audubon Park borough & MCD (Camden)	1,023	1,009	-1.4	1,051	95.2	0.0	0.0	1.4	3.3	7.5	60.4	32.1	520	17.5	68.7	9.4
Avalon borough & MCD (Cape May)	1,334	1,297	-2.8	1,852	97.0	0.1	0.9	0.0	2.1	8.4	50.4	41.3	933	91.3	22.2	60.6
Avenel CDP	17,011	NA	NA	17,952	37.6	24.0	21.1	1.2	16.1	17.0	73.7	9.5	5,139	52.0	37.2	36.6
Avon-by-the-Sea borough & MCD (Monmouth)	1,901	1,795	-5.6	1,810	95.1	0.1	0.1	2.0	2.7	15.8	55.8	28.6	924	60.9	13.3	65.3
Barclay CDP	4,428	NA	NA	4,321	91.2	1.9	1.9	1.2	3.7	23.9	57.5	18.5	1,527	98.4	10.6	68.3
Barnegat CDP	2,817	NA	NA	3,502	91.2	1.2	0.6	2.8	4.3	25.5	65.6	8.8	1,170	67.6	37.7	37.4
Barnegat township (Ocean)	20,936	22,303	6.5	21,584	84.4	3.9	2.1	1.7	8.0	20.2	55.3	24.4	8,374	87.3	42.2	29.3
Barnegat Light borough & MCD (Ocean)	574	580	1.0	592	96.8	0.0	0.0	0.0	3.2	7.3	51.6	41.0	293	88.7	22.5	45.1
Barrington borough & MCD (Camden)	6,980	6,826	-2.2	6,904	92.1	2.5	0.2	0.9	4.3	19.6	62.6	17.9	2,818	62.4	37.9	28.9
Bass River township (Burlington)	1,445	1,442	-0.2	1,481	91.1	0.6	0.7	1.3	6.3	18.4	68.8	12.8	548	85.2	60.0	14.8
Bay Head borough & MCD (Ocean)	968	1,001	3.4	997	96.5	0.0	0.6	2.2	0.7	15.7	49.8	34.3	459	85.6	13.5	62.7
Bayonne city & MCD (Hudson)	63,010	65,975	4.7	64,763	59.0	9.0	8.5	2.5	21.0	21.7	65.4	12.8	25,292	37.5	45.8	31.1

1   May be of any race.

Table A. All Places — **Population and Housing**

STATE City, town, township, borough, or CDP (county if applicable)	2010 census total population	2014 estimated population	Percent change 2010–2014	ACS total population estimate 2010–2014	White alone, not Hispanic or Latino	Black alone, not Hispanic or Latino	Asian alone, not Hispanic or Latino	All other races or 2 or more races, not Hispanic or Latino	Hispanic or Latino[1]	Under 18 years old	Age 18 to 64 years old	Age 65 years and older	Total occupied housing units	Percent owner occupied	High school diploma or less	Bachelor's degree or more
	1	2	3	4	5	6	7	8	9	10	11	12	13	14	15	16
NEW JERSEY—Con.																
Beach Haven borough & MCD (Ocean)	1,173	1,180	0.6	1,048	98.8	0.7	0.0	0.1	0.5	13.1	48.4	38.6	540	80.7	21.9	51.9
Beach Haven West CDP	3,896	NA	NA	4,140	96.7	0.0	1.3	0.0	2.1	8.4	60.4	31.2	1,866	87.5	35.1	44.6
Beachwood borough & MCD (Ocean)	11,045	11,253	1.9	11,127	87.2	1.0	1.5	2.0	8.2	24.9	65.2	9.9	3,748	85.6	42.2	23.0
Beattystown CDP	4,554	NA	NA	4,583	70.1	3.9	7.5	3.5	14.9	21.5	67.3	11.2	1,985	41.2	39.7	24.7
Beckett CDP	4,847	NA	NA	4,771	76.4	11.4	1.3	3.4	7.4	24.1	71.1	4.6	1,686	99.2	36.7	40.9
Bedminster township (Somerset)	8,165	8,213	0.6	8,221	82.9	1.5	6.9	2.3	6.3	15.0	67.1	17.7	4,125	81.1	14.7	66.6
Belford CDP	1,768	NA	NA	1,434	86.9	2.2	0.0	5.0	5.9	24.5	66.3	9.2	459	84.5	30.7	43.6
Belle Mead CDP	216	NA	NA	171	79.5	0.0	10.5	9.9	0.0	19.9	64.3	15.8	50	86.0	0.0	60.0
Belleplain CDP	597	NA	NA	559	81.4	0.0	0.0	11.6	7.0	33.8	54.0	12.3	186	77.4	65.1	12.4
Belleville township (Essex)	35,928	36,396	1.3	36,201	34.8	8.0	11.4	1.6	44.2	19.4	68.0	12.6	13,233	53.3	44.4	27.8
Bellmawr borough & MCD (Camden)	11,583	11,454	-1.1	11,538	81.5	1.7	5.6	2.1	9.1	19.2	62.8	17.9	4,531	65.4	56.2	14.3
Belmar borough & MCD (Monmouth)	5,794	5,719	-1.3	5,760	76.0	3.3	0.8	1.2	18.7	14.0	68.7	17.1	2,871	49.2	32.4	44.1
Belvidere town & MCD (Warren)	2,681	2,616	-2.4	2,647	93.1	1.2	0.5	2.1	3.2	21.1	63.9	15.0	1,106	64.6	46.1	30.1
Bergenfield borough & MCD (Bergen)	26,764	27,406	2.4	27,157	38.2	5.5	23.5	2.4	30.3	21.7	62.5	15.8	9,112	67.8	37.5	38.5
Berkeley township (Ocean)	41,254	41,950	1.7	41,591	89.8	2.3	1.0	0.8	6.2	13.1	44.4	42.5	20,597	89.1	57.6	17.3
Berkeley Heights township (Union)	13,183	13,542	2.7	13,379	81.0	1.2	10.0	0.5	7.3	25.9	57.1	17.1	4,342	92.2	20.1	66.0
Berlin borough & MCD (Camden)	7,588	7,546	-0.6	7,587	86.2	5.6	1.2	2.4	4.6	22.0	61.5	16.4	2,572	79.2	43.3	31.6
Berlin township (Camden)	5,357	5,362	0.1	5,360	73.2	11.7	7.3	1.5	6.4	21.1	63.5	15.4	1,861	68.9	55.2	22.2
Bernards township (Somerset)	26,654	26,857	0.8	26,849	76.6	1.9	13.9	2.8	4.9	28.1	58.4	13.3	9,618	84.3	10.0	75.8
Bernardsville borough & MCD (Somerset)	7,717	7,756	0.5	7,766	83.1	0.3	3.7	0.9	12.0	26.3	59.6	14.1	2,767	83.7	15.0	70.5
Bethlehem township (Hunterdon)	3,979	3,913	-1.7	3,941	91.3	0.2	2.6	1.6	4.3	24.5	64.5	10.9	1,325	93.1	21.6	58.9
Beverly city & MCD (Burlington)	2,577	2,554	-0.9	2,573	55.9	27.9	0.0	12.3	3.9	23.4	65.1	11.5	950	70.3	38.0	18.3
Blackwells Mills CDP	803	NA	NA	513	57.1	5.5	28.8	8.6	0.0	31.8	65.1	3.1	166	100.0	0.0	80.1
Blackwood CDP	4,545	NA	NA	4,645	90.3	3.2	1.1	1.7	3.8	22.7	64.9	12.5	1,564	73.7	52.8	14.2
Blairstown CDP	515	NA	NA	505	95.8	3.0	0.0	0.0	1.2	37.8	46.5	15.6	181	55.8	61.3	0.0
Blairstown township (Warren)	5,967	5,834	-2.2	5,892	89.8	0.3	0.7	2.1	7.0	23.8	60.7	15.4	2,068	86.7	37.7	27.4
Blawenburg CDP	280	NA	NA	515	65.4	0.0	30.9	0.0	3.7	30.6	45.5	23.9	138	93.5	0.0	93.5
Bloomfield township (Essex)	47,347	47,929	1.2	47,616	44.0	17.5	9.4	2.9	26.2	20.6	67.4	12.0	17,243	55.9	32.1	40.6
Bloomingdale borough & MCD (Passaic)	7,656	8,178	6.8	7,808	84.2	0.1	3.8	0.3	11.6	17.8	64.7	17.7	2,829	66.0	40.3	29.2
Bloomsbury borough & MCD (Hunterdon)	870	856	-1.6	769	88.8	0.7	0.8	2.5	7.3	27.7	65.4	6.8	304	80.9	34.9	37.2
Bogota borough & MCD (Bergen)	8,187	8,332	1.8	8,277	42.0	4.0	12.3	2.5	39.3	22.7	67.3	9.8	2,720	67.7	44.5	27.7
Boonton town & MCD (Morris)	8,347	8,412	0.8	8,424	69.4	4.5	9.6	1.6	14.9	20.3	65.9	13.9	3,117	64.2	27.7	44.8
Boonton township (Morris)	4,270	4,353	1.9	4,328	89.1	3.4	5.4	0.4	1.8	24.7	55.6	19.7	1,558	88.8	21.2	60.0
Bordentown city & MCD (Burlington)	3,924	3,900	-0.6	3,912	76.9	10.4	4.6	2.7	5.4	22.7	63.4	13.8	1,768	53.8	31.5	43.2
Bordentown township (Burlington)	11,367	11,604	2.1	11,444	71.1	9.6	9.7	2.6	7.1	25.6	62.7	11.7	4,284	75.7	31.1	41.4
Bound Brook borough & MCD (Somerset)	10,402	11,116	6.9	10,607	41.4	6.0	2.3	2.1	48.3	22.7	68.9	8.4	3,470	53.3	55.9	23.2
Bradley Beach borough & MCD (Monmouth)	4,298	4,270	-0.7	4,290	78.3	3.2	2.3	3.7	12.5	21.6	63.3	15.2	2,152	43.4	31.8	38.8
Bradley Gardens CDP	14,206	NA	NA	13,902	58.1	1.1	32.6	1.0	7.2	28.8	62.1	9.2	4,584	90.9	18.2	66.8
Brainards CDP	202	NA	NA	233	100.0	0.0	0.0	0.0	0.0	26.2	72.6	1.3	82	93.9	46.3	25.6
Branchburg township (Somerset)	14,459	14,552	0.6	14,547	78.8	5.3	10.1	0.6	5.2	24.6	63.7	11.8	5,101	88.9	16.5	63.9
Branchville borough & MCD (Sussex)	841	812	-3.4	826	95.3	0.0	2.9	1.0	0.8	26.0	56.5	17.7	319	63.3	47.3	21.3
Brass Castle CDP	1,555	NA	NA	1,346	94.5	1.0	0.0	0.0	4.5	20.5	55.0	24.5	532	100.0	35.9	39.5
Brick township (Ocean)	75,072	75,911	1.1	75,479	87.1	2.4	1.8	1.6	7.1	20.3	61.3	18.2	30,079	83.1	42.1	27.7
Bridgeton city & MCD (Cumberland)	25,349	25,347	0.0	25,252	15.5	33.1	0.3	2.3	48.7	28.0	65.2	6.7	5,937	40.2	67.3	9.1
Bridgeville CDP	106	NA	NA	99	100.0	0.0	0.0	0.0	0.0	30.4	43.4	26.3	28	100.0	100.0	0.0
Bridgewater township (Somerset)	44,462	44,903	1.0	44,855	66.1	2.8	19.5	1.6	10.0	24.3	61.3	14.3	15,276	84.8	20.0	61.2
Brielle borough & MCD (Monmouth)	4,774	4,759	-0.3	4,772	90.6	3.1	0.8	0.8	4.7	24.2	56.7	19.3	1,879	92.4	14.3	62.5
Brigantine city & MCD (Atlantic)	9,450	9,336	-1.2	9,420	84.1	2.2	3.9	1.9	8.0	14.3	61.3	24.5	4,379	68.8	32.7	35.9
Broadway CDP	244	NA	NA	241	82.6	0.0	0.0	0.0	17.4	23.7	58.9	17.4	103	71.8	55.3	35.9
Brookdale CDP	9,239	NA	NA	9,706	70.2	5.1	11.1	0.3	13.4	22.6	61.6	15.7	3,354	84.4	24.7	52.1
Brookfield CDP	675	NA	NA	744	100.0	0.0	0.0	0.0	0.0	0.0	2.8	97.2	500	80.0	44.4	15.6
Brooklawn borough & MCD (Camden)	1,955	1,929	-1.3	1,879	81.2	6.5	0.0	4.2	8.1	21.1	67.6	11.2	724	80.1	51.9	19.2
Browns Mills CDP	11,223	NA	NA	10,973	60.8	16.0	2.2	8.2	12.7	22.8	66.5	10.7	4,054	72.4	55.1	12.7
Brownville CDP	2,383	NA	NA	2,924	76.1	2.3	9.9	0.0	11.7	20.8	67.8	11.5	1,183	81.2	29.8	30.6
Budd Lake CDP	8,968	NA	NA	8,234	70.5	5.4	11.2	1.4	11.5	25.4	65.3	9.3	3,106	68.2	32.5	43.3
Buena borough & MCD (Atlantic)	4,603	4,610	0.2	4,623	65.1	2.6	0.2	0.9	31.2	22.5	64.5	13.2	1,751	60.0	52.0	13.6

1 May be of any race.

Table A. All Places — Population and Housing

STATE City, town, township, borough, or CDP (county if applicable)	2010 census total population	2014 estimated population	Percent change 2010–2014	ACS total population estimate 2010–2014	White alone, not Hispanic or Latino	Black alone, not Hispanic or Latino	Asian alone, not Hispanic or Latino	All other races or 2 or more races, not Hispanic or Latino	Hispanic or Latino[1]	Under 18 years old	Age 18 to 64 years old	Age 65 years and older	Total occupied housing units	Percent owner occupied	High school diploma or less	Bachelor's degree or more
	1	2	3	4	5	6	7	8	9	10	11	12	13	14	15	16
NEW JERSEY—Con.																
Buena Vista township (Atlantic)	7,570	7,586	0.2	7,587	71.5	10.6	3.5	1.8	12.6	21.5	58.8	19.6	2,987	82.2	58.3	17.0
Burleigh CDP	725	NA	NA	619	46.5	12.9	35.7	4.8	0.0	19.9	58.5	21.6	208	61.5	66.8	16.3
Burlington city & MCD (Burlington)	9,920	9,799	-1.2	9,865	49.6	32.8	2.8	7.0	7.8	20.7	64.5	14.6	4,062	63.3	49.2	17.5
Burlington township (Burlington)	22,598	22,673	0.3	22,613	53.6	28.0	4.2	5.2	8.9	26.4	62.5	11.1	7,596	78.2	35.2	34.6
Butler borough & MCD (Morris)	7,539	7,690	2.0	7,636	79.0	0.3	3.6	1.8	15.3	19.4	67.9	12.5	2,762	70.9	34.3	38.6
Buttzville CDP	146	NA	NA	194	100.0	0.0	0.0	0.0	0.0	0.0	80.9	19.1	74	100.0	50.0	0.0
Byram township (Sussex)	8,350	8,096	-3.0	8,220	94.1	0.3	1.6	1.0	3.0	25.5	63.1	11.3	2,914	93.9	27.1	41.8
Byram Center CDP	90	NA	NA	50	54.0	46.0	0.0	0.0	0.0	14.0	86.0	0.0	28	71.4	46.4	28.6
Caldwell borough & MCD (Essex)	7,817	7,898	1.0	7,864	83.7	3.4	5.1	2.9	4.9	16.5	65.1	18.3	3,428	49.9	25.5	50.5
Califon borough & MCD (Hunterdon)	1,076	1,087	1.0	1,245	96.7	0.0	1.1	0.9	1.3	25.5	64.1	10.5	440	87.0	15.2	61.6
Camden city & MCD (Camden)	77,346	77,332	0.0	77,294	4.9	43.0	2.3	1.9	48.0	31.5	60.2	8.2	25,189	39.3	66.9	8.4
Cape May city & MCD (Cape May)	3,607	3,535	-2.0	3,576	84.0	2.1	1.1	5.0	7.7	10.8	52.4	36.9	1,552	61.7	39.3	41.7
Cape May Court House CDP	5,338	NA	NA	5,664	82.9	9.8	1.2	0.9	5.2	19.6	56.6	23.7	2,396	71.3	49.1	30.9
Cape May Point borough & MCD (Cape May)	291	284	-2.4	200	99.0	0.5	0.0	0.5	0.0	0.5	36.0	63.5	115	87.8	16.5	63.5
Carlstadt borough & MCD (Bergen)	6,127	6,248	2.0	6,189	63.9	0.4	10.7	1.9	23.0	18.7	68.4	13.0	2,147	55.9	43.6	33.9
Carneys Point CDP	7,382	NA	NA	7,268	69.7	17.8	0.8	1.5	10.2	19.3	61.3	19.3	2,862	64.3	52.4	19.2
Carneys Point township (Salem)	8,049	7,929	-1.5	8,003	68.6	17.3	0.8	1.3	11.9	18.5	62.7	18.7	3,085	65.8	53.3	18.2
Carteret borough & MCD (Middlesex)	22,844	24,114	5.6	23,770	34.2	11.2	22.2	1.5	30.9	24.2	64.9	10.9	7,664	58.5	48.4	21.8
Cedar Glen Lakes CDP	1,421	NA	NA	1,527	94.3	1.1	1.0	2.4	1.1	0.0	18.4	81.7	1,086	100.0	56.0	13.5
Cedar Glen West CDP	1,267	NA	NA	955	100.0	0.0	0.0	0.0	0.0	0.0	40.5	59.5	653	93.0	60.6	2.6
Cedar Grove township (Essex)	12,411	12,542	1.1	12,499	82.5	4.6	6.5	0.9	5.5	19.6	56.1	24.1	4,214	78.8	24.2	57.3
Cedarville CDP	776	NA	NA	642	83.3	4.2	0.0	5.0	7.5	14.6	69.2	16.2	251	77.3	54.6	10.4
Chatham borough & MCD (Morris)	8,954	9,022	0.8	9,000	85.8	0.6	4.4	2.3	6.9	32.3	57.9	9.8	2,895	78.5	11.2	77.6
Chatham township (Morris)	10,452	10,615	1.6	10,593	86.1	2.5	7.4	1.1	2.9	27.4	56.2	16.3	3,923	84.5	12.5	72.0
Cherry Hill township (Camden)	70,876	71,417	0.8	71,152	72.3	5.9	14.2	2.0	5.5	22.5	60.0	17.4	26,041	79.9	22.5	55.4
Cherry Hill Mall CDP	14,171	NA	NA	13,950	64.9	9.4	16.2	0.7	8.8	22.2	64.0	13.8	5,220	68.7	22.4	50.7
Chesilhurst borough & MCD (Camden)	1,634	1,626	-0.5	1,675	37.2	37.8	1.5	4.3	19.2	15.3	63.5	21.1	571	84.4	50.4	18.2
Chester borough & MCD (Morris)	1,649	1,674	1.5	1,557	86.2	0.0	2.2	0.3	11.4	28.0	52.1	19.9	570	77.4	28.1	53.9
Chester township (Morris)	7,861	7,945	1.1	7,924	90.0	0.3	2.6	4.2	2.8	29.2	56.2	14.6	2,476	97.4	16.2	71.5
Chesterfield township (Burlington)	7,699	7,693	-0.1	7,725	62.4	17.6	7.9	1.2	11.0	25.4	67.1	7.5	1,803	93.2	22.3	57.3
Cinnaminson township (Burlington)	15,569	16,840	8.2	16,296	85.5	4.7	2.6	1.6	5.6	20.2	61.1	18.5	5,926	89.9	31.8	41.3
City of Orange township (Essex)	30,252	30,934	2.3	30,478	2.8	72.7	0.9	2.1	21.4	26.2	62.1	11.5	11,390	20.3	52.9	18.6
Clark township (Union)	14,756	15,460	4.8	15,056	85.7	0.9	1.8	1.3	10.2	21.2	61.7	17.2	5,475	81.0	32.7	43.9
Clayton borough & MCD (Gloucester)	8,183	8,307	1.5	8,225	72.1	14.2	1.9	6.2	5.6	28.0	61.9	10.1	2,853	74.2	54.5	23.0
Clearbrook Park CDP	2,667	NA	NA	2,489	88.1	4.3	2.8	0.5	4.2	0.0	16.7	83.3	1,761	88.9	44.9	30.9
Clementon borough & MCD (Camden)	5,000	4,940	-1.2	4,972	69.7	16.5	0.0	2.5	11.3	21.4	66.6	12.0	2,139	69.2	43.7	21.8
Cliffside Park borough & MCD (Bergen)	23,596	25,503	8.1	24,532	52.9	1.9	13.1	2.2	29.9	17.2	64.4	18.5	10,682	49.9	41.5	42.9
Cliffwood Beach CDP	3,194	NA	NA	3,331	56.4	12.8	5.6	2.6	22.6	21.3	67.0	11.6	1,143	96.3	40.5	23.3
Clifton city & MCD (Passaic)	84,136	85,927	2.1	85,138	50.1	4.3	8.9	2.0	34.7	22.6	64.2	13.1	28,652	61.8	41.0	32.4
Clinton town & MCD (Hunterdon)	2,719	2,684	-1.3	2,701	82.1	0.5	3.0	4.7	9.7	25.0	63.1	11.8	1,020	72.9	26.2	55.7
Clinton township (Hunterdon)	13,478	13,158	-2.4	13,319	75.4	9.3	4.1	1.5	9.7	20.0	69.5	10.6	4,176	85.8	15.9	61.9
Closter borough & MCD (Bergen)	8,373	8,592	2.6	8,519	57.4	2.0	33.4	0.7	6.5	26.6	59.9	13.3	2,697	83.6	18.7	62.1
Clyde CDP	213	NA	NA	290	24.1	11.0	16.9	0.0	47.9	37.6	57.5	4.8	64	76.6	23.4	53.1
Collings Lakes CDP	1,706	NA	NA	1,205	89.5	2.2	0.0	2.8	5.4	19.4	62.7	17.8	453	96.0	52.1	13.0
Collingswood borough & MCD (Camden)	13,933	13,962	0.2	13,929	78.5	8.6	2.0	2.1	8.9	19.3	67.7	13.1	6,025	56.7	29.9	46.0
Colonia CDP	17,795	NA	NA	17,530	71.8	3.5	11.1	1.9	11.7	22.0	62.6	15.3	5,868	89.1	37.9	33.7
Colts Neck township (Monmouth)	10,142	10,065	-0.8	10,103	89.7	0.8	4.3	1.2	4.1	24.3	60.0	15.7	3,335	91.9	15.7	61.3
Columbia CDP	229	NA	NA	353	92.6	0.0	1.7	5.7	0.0	34.0	57.4	8.5	107	57.9	50.5	17.8
Commercial township (Cumberland)	5,178	5,157	-0.4	5,166	72.8	11.3	1.3	2.9	11.7	28.6	62.0	9.5	1,869	72.4	63.4	4.5
Concordia CDP	3,092	NA	NA	3,092	92.7	2.2	1.8	0.7	2.7	0.1	22.4	77.4	2,046	87.6	31.9	39.1
Corbin City city & MCD (Atlantic)	492	494	0.4	596	95.8	0.3	0.2	1.5	2.2	17.4	70.4	12.4	234	77.4	59.4	20.1
Country Lake Estates CDP	3,943	NA	NA	3,484	64.5	22.0	3.7	1.9	7.9	22.1	65.8	12.1	1,216	85.0	41.0	17.6
Cranbury CDP	2,181	NA	NA	2,347	75.1	6.6	16.1	0.3	1.9	27.2	58.6	14.1	758	86.8	12.0	68.9
Cranbury township (Middlesex)	3,857	3,931	1.9	3,705	78.2	4.9	13.9	0.5	2.6	26.0	56.3	17.6	1,271	86.4	14.3	67.3
Crandon Lakes CDP	1,178	NA	NA	1,422	97.9	0.0	0.9	0.6	0.6	22.2	63.0	15.0	523	92.4	37.7	22.0
Cranford township (Union)	22,625	23,907	5.7	23,150	85.3	3.6	2.6	1.8	6.7	23.4	60.3	16.5	8,345	80.3	24.6	52.7

1 May be of any race.

Table A. All Places — **Population and Housing**

STATE City, town, township, borough, or CDP (county if applicable)	2010 census total population	2014 estimated population	Percent change 2010–2014	ACS total population estimate 2010–2014	White alone, not Hispanic or Latino	Black alone, not Hispanic or Latino	Asian alone, not Hispanic or Latino	All other races or 2 or more races, not Hispanic or Latino	Hispanic or Latino[1]	Under 18 years old	Age 18 to 64 years old	Age 65 years and older	Total occupied housing units	Percent owner occupied	High school diploma or less	Bachelor's degree or more
	1	2	3	4	5	6	7	8	9	10	11	12	13	14	15	16
NEW JERSEY—Con.																
Cresskill borough & MCD (Bergen)	8,559	8,763	2.4	8,669	64.2	0.4	24.4	1.0	10.0	26.3	55.0	18.8	3,007	85.7	20.4	61.4
Crestwood Village CDP	7,907	NA	NA	7,703	93.0	0.9	1.2	0.3	4.6	0.0	20.6	79.5	5,446	91.4	67.0	12.8
Dayton CDP	7,063	NA	NA	7,690	35.9	12.3	46.7	0.2	5.0	29.7	62.2	8.0	2,329	85.9	15.5	67.5
Deal borough & MCD (Monmouth)	750	737	-1.7	769	94.4	0.4	0.0	0.0	5.2	8.2	54.0	37.7	330	70.9	42.4	32.4
Deerfield township (Cumberland)	3,119	3,123	0.1	3,128	66.3	12.4	0.4	1.8	19.2	19.1	69.3	11.4	1,012	88.0	50.8	15.9
Delanco township (Burlington)	4,283	4,546	6.1	4,544	79.0	13.6	1.8	1.2	4.4	18.3	64.3	17.4	1,750	81.2	42.9	30.5
Delaware township (Hunterdon)	4,563	4,530	-0.7	4,536	97.1	0.1	0.6	1.7	0.5	17.4	63.2	19.6	1,888	89.2	24.1	55.5
Delaware CDP	150	NA	NA	86	80.2	0.0	0.0	0.0	19.8	27.9	72.1	0.0	27	40.7	0.0	0.0
Delaware Park CDP	700	NA	NA	769	89.9	0.0	0.0	0.0	10.1	23.3	71.2	5.3	278	100.0	51.4	30.6
Delran township (Burlington)	16,896	16,775	-0.7	16,856	77.0	8.4	8.6	3.0	3.1	23.6	63.0	13.3	5,887	77.4	35.1	40.1
Demarest borough & MCD (Bergen)	4,881	4,973	1.9	4,929	66.7	0.2	28.5	1.1	3.4	25.0	59.9	15.2	1,660	89.2	10.1	77.6
Dennis township (Cape May)	6,467	6,319	-2.3	6,397	95.7	0.3	0.0	2.2	1.8	22.9	60.9	16.0	2,475	86.5	46.6	24.6
Denville township (Morris)	16,680	16,829	0.9	16,814	84.3	1.2	7.3	1.3	5.9	21.6	62.4	16.0	6,569	86.8	23.7	51.2
Deptford township (Gloucester)	30,573	30,483	-0.3	30,568	72.8	13.6	4.8	2.6	6.2	20.6	63.9	15.4	11,561	75.7	49.5	24.3
Diamond Beach CDP	136	NA	NA	145	100.0	0.0	0.0	0.0	0.0	0.0	57.9	42.1	83	90.4	30.1	42.2
Dover town & MCD (Morris)	18,143	18,313	0.9	18,298	18.2	4.2	3.3	3.8	70.4	22.5	68.5	9.2	5,184	47.3	62.1	17.9
Dover Beaches North CDP	1,239	NA	NA	990	98.3	0.0	0.0	0.0	1.7	0.5	44.0	55.4	645	91.5	41.2	37.7
Dover Beaches South CDP	1,209	NA	NA	1,215	98.0	0.0	0.0	0.5	1.5	8.4	46.0	45.7	705	77.4	29.5	49.2
Downe township (Cumberland)	1,585	1,552	-2.1	1,411	89.1	3.5	0.6	2.3	4.6	17.5	60.6	21.7	598	83.6	62.7	12.9
Dumont borough & MCD (Bergen)	17,479	17,863	2.2	17,706	64.4	2.8	17.2	0.8	14.9	23.0	62.3	14.7	6,349	69.9	37.0	40.1
Dunellen borough & MCD (Middlesex)	7,227	7,417	2.6	7,317	55.8	9.2	3.8	2.6	28.6	24.0	65.7	10.2	2,530	74.5	40.9	31.6
Eaglewood township (Ocean)	1,603	1,617	0.9	1,551	92.7	0.2	0.7	4.1	2.3	23.4	61.9	14.6	601	89.5	46.6	23.8
Eastampton township (Burlington)	6,069	6,049	-0.3	6,065	70.7	11.2	5.6	8.0	4.5	21.4	67.8	10.9	2,295	66.4	31.7	35.8
East Amwell township (Hunterdon)	4,013	3,958	-1.4	3,980	89.0	0.6	2.8	1.2	6.4	19.1	62.8	18.1	1,468	89.9	33.7	44.0
East Brunswick township (Middlesex)	47,512	48,474	2.0	48,003	62.2	4.7	24.4	1.5	7.2	22.8	62.4	14.7	16,750	83.7	23.4	55.9
East Franklin CDP	8,669	NA	NA	7,647	19.1	41.4	6.9	3.6	29.0	29.2	60.8	9.9	2,415	58.2	60.7	18.1
East Freehold CDP	4,894	NA	NA	5,429	77.3	4.2	10.5	0.6	7.5	25.7	64.6	9.9	1,659	93.6	21.7	53.3
East Greenwich township (Gloucester)	9,555	10,292	7.7	10,018	81.1	8.0	5.2	2.0	3.7	29.0	59.5	11.4	3,334	91.1	31.5	47.7
East Hanover township (Morris)	11,156	11,289	1.2	11,256	76.7	0.6	13.8	0.7	8.2	20.4	59.7	19.8	3,906	91.1	38.7	40.3
East Millstone CDP	579	NA	NA	507	68.8	19.3	11.8	0.0	0.0	17.2	69.2	13.6	244	82.0	5.3	77.0
East Newark borough & MCD (Hudson)	2,406	2,835	17.8	2,551	22.4	0.9	7.7	4.8	64.1	22.8	71.1	6.0	760	25.4	58.7	16.3
East Orange city & MCD (Essex)	64,107	65,078	1.5	64,538	2.2	87.1	0.7	1.7	8.2	23.0	64.0	12.9	25,594	26.8	48.2	16.2
East Rocky Hill CDP	469	NA	NA	213	68.5	0.0	17.4	14.1	0.0	22.1	55.5	22.5	91	73.6	0.0	70.3
East Rutherford borough & MCD (Bergen)	8,913	9,798	9.9	9,298	55.5	1.5	17.7	1.3	23.9	17.0	68.5	14.5	3,976	40.7	33.6	44.8
East Windsor township (Mercer)	27,190	27,536	1.3	27,389	49.3	5.9	19.5	2.6	22.7	22.5	65.2	12.4	9,790	63.9	23.2	52.8
Eatontown borough & MCD (Monmouth)	12,709	12,257	-3.6	12,323	61.0	9.0	12.1	2.1	15.9	18.1	68.1	13.7	5,274	53.2	34.2	37.6
Echelon CDP	10,743	NA	NA	10,831	61.0	11.6	20.3	2.8	4.3	17.1	64.9	18.1	5,023	40.2	35.5	41.3
Edgewater borough & MCD (Bergen)	11,511	12,343	7.2	11,969	42.6	7.5	34.4	2.2	13.2	20.9	67.1	11.9	5,744	34.3	14.6	70.4
Edgewater Park township (Burlington)	8,881	8,806	-0.8	8,854	55.2	26.4	4.4	2.5	11.4	21.1	63.9	15.2	3,540	61.9	48.8	18.4
Edison township (Middlesex)	99,971	101,970	2.0	101,051	36.0	5.8	46.6	2.6	8.9	22.7	64.5	13.0	34,420	63.5	25.0	55.7
Egg Harbor township (Atlantic)	43,323	43,851	1.2	43,699	60.6	9.0	11.0	3.2	16.2	26.3	63.0	10.6	14,854	86.6	37.1	30.3
Egg Harbor City city & MCD (Atlantic)	4,243	4,264	0.5	4,253	46.8	18.8	3.8	1.5	29.1	27.6	63.0	9.5	1,408	62.0	55.6	16.1
Elizabeth city & MCD (Union)	124,969	128,705	3.0	126,964	15.5	16.9	2.1	2.8	62.8	27.2	63.3	9.4	39,273	27.1	62.4	13.2
Elk township (Gloucester)	4,216	4,234	0.4	4,243	78.0	15.1	0.5	0.3	6.2	22.2	64.9	12.9	1,493	89.8	46.3	29.8
Ellisburg CDP	4,413	NA	NA	4,684	74.6	3.1	13.5	4.6	4.4	22.5	56.5	20.9	1,831	56.1	34.7	37.2
Elmer borough & MCD (Salem)	1,395	1,355	-2.9	1,375	90.0	3.1	1.0	4.8	1.1	24.1	61.2	14.7	499	69.5	42.9	23.2
Elmwood Park borough & MCD (Bergen)	19,403	20,374	5.0	19,921	58.8	4.5	8.4	2.5	25.8	21.9	61.4	16.7	7,086	57.7	46.7	26.2
Elsinboro township (Salem)	1,036	1,009	-2.6	1,082	90.5	4.0	0.0	1.9	3.6	16.7	62.8	20.4	504	81.5	49.8	17.3
Elwood CDP	1,437	NA	NA	1,613	36.1	21.0	0.7	3.6	38.6	26.4	60.2	13.3	479	89.8	73.9	12.5
Emerson borough & MCD (Bergen)	7,401	7,617	2.9	7,538	74.5	1.9	6.5	3.3	13.8	23.3	58.5	18.1	2,412	81.4	24.3	43.2
Englewood city & MCD (Bergen)	27,127	27,670	2.0	27,435	31.8	33.1	10.9	3.2	21.0	21.7	63.5	15.0	10,462	51.3	31.6	51.2
Englewood Cliffs borough & MCD (Bergen)	5,281	5,385	2.0	5,346	51.1	1.7	39.2	2.4	5.6	23.3	52.3	24.4	1,796	88.3	24.3	64.5

1 May be of any race.

Table A. All Places — Population and Housing

STATE City, town, township, borough, or CDP (county if applicable)	2010 census total population	2014 estimated population	Percent change 2010–2014	ACS total population estimate 2010–2014	White alone, not Hispanic or Latino	Black alone, not Hispanic or Latino	Asian alone, not Hispanic or Latino	All other races or 2 or more races, not Hispanic or Latino	Hispanic or Latino[1]	Under 18 years old	Age 18 to 64 years old	Age 65 years and older	Total occupied housing units	Percent owner occupied	High school diploma or less	Bachelor's degree or more
	1	2	3	4	5	6	7	8	9	10	11	12	13	14	15	16
NEW JERSEY—Con.																
Englishtown borough & MCD (Monmouth)	1,847	1,962	6.2	2,101	83.5	0.5	5.7	1.8	8.5	25.6	61.8	12.8	703	63.0	35.3	29.7
Erma CDP	2,134	NA	NA	2,082	88.8	0.5	2.7	2.3	5.7	20.7	65.5	13.8	858	90.3	43.6	30.3
Essex Fells borough & MCD (Essex)	2,114	2,095	-0.9	2,140	90.8	0.4	3.5	2.9	2.5	29.0	56.0	15.0	719	94.0	14.6	76.8
Estell Manor city & MCD (Atlantic)	1,735	1,736	0.1	1,684	94.1	1.0	0.2	1.2	3.4	20.5	70.1	9.5	590	95.8	43.6	23.6
Evesham township (Burlington)	45,530	45,613	0.2	45,669	83.8	4.9	6.0	1.6	3.7	22.5	63.4	14.1	17,145	76.1	22.5	51.7
Ewing township (Mercer)	35,790	36,546	2.1	36,270	57.9	29.4	4.0	1.4	7.2	16.0	69.7	14.4	12,661	70.6	28.9	38.0
Fairfield township (Cumberland)	6,295	6,481	3.0	6,504	31.1	46.7	0.6	7.3	14.4	19.1	68.7	12.2	1,738	77.2	65.3	12.4
Fairfield township (Essex)	7,466	7,551	1.1	7,475	93.6	1.8	1.7	0.4	2.5	22.7	57.3	19.9	2,551	87.7	33.8	38.1
Fair Haven borough & MCD (Monmouth)	6,121	6,048	-1.2	6,093	91.8	3.0	1.2	1.2	2.7	30.8	57.7	11.4	2,084	93.3	13.2	71.7
Fair Lawn borough & MCD (Bergen)	32,457	33,549	3.4	32,962	71.1	1.5	13.0	1.0	13.5	22.5	62.2	15.4	11,807	78.2	22.2	55.3
Fairton CDP	1,264	NA	NA	1,182	62.4	11.9	0.6	7.1	17.9	26.8	57.8	15.4	449	77.7	72.8	8.0
Fairview borough & MCD (Bergen)	13,835	14,317	3.5	14,126	39.9	2.0	4.7	4.3	49.1	14.9	70.2	15.0	5,263	38.7	58.0	22.8
Fairview CDP	3,806	NA	NA	4,004	86.9	0.0	3.9	2.6	6.5	25.7	62.3	11.9	1,342	91.0	17.3	55.4
Fanwood borough & MCD (Union)	7,318	7,657	4.6	7,475	74.8	5.5	6.9	3.8	9.0	28.0	58.7	13.4	2,521	94.9	16.7	64.6
Far Hills borough & MCD (Somerset)	919	926	0.8	1,101	80.7	4.1	5.6	0.4	9.2	23.4	62.5	14.1	396	81.3	15.2	64.6
Farmingdale borough & MCD (Monmouth)	1,329	1,298	-2.3	1,396	81.9	8.6	5.3	0.2	4.0	23.3	66.4	10.2	560	50.9	36.1	33.8
Fieldsboro borough & MCD (Burlington)	540	530	-1.9	603	74.0	11.1	1.2	11.1	2.7	21.5	67.1	11.4	197	87.8	28.4	31.0
Finderne CDP	5,600	NA	NA	6,205	49.2	7.3	14.1	3.6	25.8	19.1	66.2	14.6	2,135	63.6	26.0	45.3
Finesville CDP	175	NA	NA	97	91.8	0.0	8.2	0.0	0.0	20.6	79.3	0.0	40	100.0	57.5	20.0
Flemington borough & MCD (Hunterdon)	4,581	4,683	2.2	4,688	52.3	3.1	13.5	4.8	26.3	22.9	62.8	14.2	1,972	36.2	45.6	32.8
Florence CDP	0	NA	NA	4,298	74.5	18.3	2.4	1.5	3.3	18.1	68.3	13.6	1,824	75.3	51.4	18.9
Florence township (Burlington)	12,109	12,357	2.0	12,287	74.2	12.7	5.3	2.4	5.3	20.7	64.7	14.7	4,809	85.4	39.8	32.9
Florham Park borough & MCD (Morris)	11,734	11,829	0.8	11,820	75.7	5.8	9.6	1.1	7.8	17.9	62.9	19.4	3,974	73.4	21.9	62.4
Folsom borough & MCD (Atlantic)	1,885	1,870	-0.8	1,799	79.6	10.7	0.5	1.1	8.2	22.4	63.7	13.8	612	87.1	52.8	17.5
Fords CDP	15,187	NA	NA	15,028	47.7	12.0	21.0	2.0	17.3	20.5	65.6	13.9	5,284	75.4	39.1	38.2
Forked River CDP	5,244	NA	NA	5,199	93.1	0.9	2.5	0.0	3.6	22.2	59.9	18.0	2,131	87.0	38.2	26.7
Fort Dix CDP	7,716	NA	NA	7,948	42.5	27.1	2.1	4.0	24.4	15.1	82.9	1.9	897	0.4	17.7	21.1
Fort Lee borough & MCD (Bergen)	35,336	37,026	4.8	36,048	43.2	1.3	40.0	2.6	12.9	16.9	61.1	22.0	16,604	57.6	25.0	56.6
Frankford township (Sussex)	5,565	5,466	-1.8	5,506	91.6	1.2	0.9	0.6	5.7	19.5	62.3	18.1	2,036	87.5	32.8	36.9
Franklin township (Gloucester)	16,820	16,702	-0.7	16,754	82.6	6.5	2.1	2.2	6.6	23.2	65.2	11.5	5,708	88.8	48.0	20.2
Franklin township (Hunterdon)	3,195	3,236	1.3	3,250	95.8	0.1	1.0	0.0	3.1	23.6	58.2	18.3	1,215	88.6	26.3	54.9
Franklin township (Somerset)	62,300	65,938	5.8	64,243	38.1	25.2	22.2	3.3	11.2	21.3	63.3	15.5	23,749	71.6	24.1	55.3
Franklin borough & MCD (Sussex)	5,066	4,906	-3.2	4,994	87.0	2.1	1.3	0.0	9.6	21.1	64.6	14.2	2,036	70.7	47.6	19.8
Franklin township (Warren)	3,176	3,112	-2.0	3,142	94.0	0.0	2.5	0.5	2.9	23.2	63.9	13.0	1,166	87.8	40.3	38.0
Franklin Center CDP	4,460	NA	NA	4,227	73.5	6.6	16.1	0.5	3.4	10.4	46.8	42.7	1,916	88.6	19.1	59.1
Franklin Lakes borough & MCD (Bergen)	10,590	10,837	2.3	10,726	80.9	0.4	9.3	2.0	7.4	26.1	56.2	17.8	3,599	86.8	15.0	72.6
Franklin Park CDP	13,295	NA	NA	14,815	27.7	27.3	32.4	3.7	8.9	23.9	67.3	8.9	5,648	58.0	16.9	62.7
Fredon township (Sussex)	3,398	3,293	-3.1	3,345	93.7	0.9	1.8	1.9	1.7	23.0	58.7	18.2	1,258	90.5	22.5	46.3
Freehold borough & MCD (Monmouth)	12,052	11,973	-0.7	12,018	40.5	13.5	3.6	0.3	42.1	26.5	63.6	9.9	3,972	51.1	50.6	21.7
Freehold township (Monmouth)	36,184	35,812	-1.0	35,995	77.4	5.3	7.8	1.1	8.4	22.1	63.5	14.2	12,529	85.1	26.1	49.4
Frelinghuysen township (Warren)	2,230	2,188	-1.9	2,445	89.9	1.5	0.7	1.8	6.1	22.6	58.5	18.8	830	87.5	36.5	40.2
Frenchtown borough & MCD (Hunterdon)	1,375	1,394	1.4	1,486	92.9	0.3	1.5	2.2	3.0	15.7	71.5	12.9	624	67.0	36.9	37.8
Galloway township (Atlantic)	37,349	37,583	0.6	37,471	62.8	12.2	9.9	2.4	12.7	20.7	65.2	14.1	12,132	75.0	38.6	27.8
Garfield city & MCD (Bergen)	30,487	31,486	3.3	30,996	57.8	4.8	2.4	0.9	34.0	23.0	66.6	10.4	10,673	35.7	55.7	20.5
Garwood borough & MCD (Union)	4,226	4,483	6.1	4,323	81.3	0.5	0.4	0.0	17.8	21.3	66.2	12.7	1,641	63.6	37.7	36.8
Gibbsboro borough & MCD (Camden)	2,270	2,240	-1.3	2,324	91.9	2.7	0.5	2.3	2.5	21.2	61.8	17.0	785	91.7	38.5	35.0
Gibbstown CDP	3,739	NA	NA	3,594	96.0	1.2	0.1	1.1	1.7	16.1	67.0	16.8	1,534	85.5	48.4	20.5
Glassboro borough & MCD (Gloucester)	18,579	19,007	2.3	18,798	73.4	16.9	2.7	1.4	5.5	19.4	70.0	10.7	5,925	68.6	33.7	31.4
Glendora CDP	4,750	NA	NA	4,557	95.5	0.0	2.1	0.3	2.0	20.3	60.0	19.4	1,785	77.9	52.1	16.4
Glen Gardner borough & MCD (Hunterdon)	1,704	1,676	-1.6	1,533	89.2	1.8	4.6	1.2	3.2	14.8	74.8	10.2	728	68.4	29.7	40.1
Glen Ridge borough & MCD (Essex)	7,527	7,681	2.0	7,606	80.4	4.2	3.1	1.8	10.4	33.3	57.1	9.6	2,411	89.8	12.1	79.9
Glen Rock borough & MCD (Bergen)	11,601	11,901	2.6	11,784	81.9	1.7	10.5	1.3	4.7	29.3	58.5	12.3	3,730	92.7	12.1	71.8
Gloucester township (Camden)	64,634	64,029	-0.9	64,356	71.9	16.1	3.8	2.4	5.8	23.0	64.9	12.1	23,085	74.1	36.7	30.4

1 May be of any race.

Table A. All Places — Population and Housing

STATE City, town, township, borough, or CDP (county if applicable)	2010 census total population	2014 estimated population	Percent change 2010–2014	ACS total population estimate 2010–2014	White alone, not Hispanic or Latino	Black alone, not Hispanic or Latino	Asian alone, not Hispanic or Latino	All other races or 2 or more races, not Hispanic or Latino	Hispanic or Latino[1]	Under 18 years old	Age 18 to 64 years old	Age 65 years and older	Total occupied housing units	Percent owner occupied	High school diploma or less	Bachelor's degree or more
	1	2	3	4	5	6	7	8	9	10	11	12	13	14	15	16
NEW JERSEY—Con.																
Gloucester City city & MCD (Camden)	11,458	11,317	-1.2	11,392	80.5	3.4	3.3	1.5	11.3	26.1	62.5	11.3	4,053	66.0	64.1	17.0
Golden Triangle CDP	4,145	NA	NA	3,751	70.7	10.6	5.6	0.8	12.4	18.5	63.8	17.5	1,377	72.4	42.9	34.5
Great Meadows CDP	303	NA	NA	288	99.3	0.3	0.0	0.3	0.0	48.3	37.1	14.6	81	100.0	34.6	0.0
Green township (Sussex)	3,601	3,512	-2.5	3,552	91.2	0.0	0.2	1.5	7.1	22.4	65.0	12.5	1,190	96.9	32.1	43.7
Green Brook township (Somerset)	7,203	7,252	0.7	7,183	66.5	2.2	23.5	0.9	6.8	23.9	59.7	16.3	2,318	91.5	16.8	59.2
Green Knoll CDP	6,200	NA	NA	5,954	67.0	4.2	20.0	1.1	7.7	23.1	57.7	19.2	2,295	68.9	22.9	57.3
Greentree CDP	11,367	NA	NA	11,529	63.8	7.1	24.0	2.1	3.0	24.5	59.8	15.6	3,966	86.0	17.1	66.1
Greenwich township (Cumberland)	804	802	-0.2	953	86.3	2.5	0.2	5.7	5.4	18.5	61.8	19.7	369	86.4	34.4	29.8
Greenwich township (Gloucester)	4,899	4,842	-1.2	4,874	94.5	1.7	0.1	1.5	2.2	18.1	64.6	17.4	2,017	85.8	49.2	21.3
Greenwich CDP	2,755	NA	NA	2,666	75.4	9.3	11.5	1.6	2.3	35.1	61.4	3.7	753	93.4	9.6	73.3
Greenwich township (Warren)	5,712	5,572	-2.5	5,626	84.3	5.7	5.7	1.5	2.9	30.3	61.5	8.1	1,755	89.5	17.9	58.7
Griggstown CDP	819	NA	NA	1,011	69.1	0.0	19.5	0.0	11.4	25.6	62.6	11.8	327	90.5	34.6	42.2
Groveville CDP	2,945	NA	NA	2,924	84.6	3.4	5.2	0.5	6.3	19.9	68.9	11.4	1,014	82.2	40.3	34.3
Guttenberg town & MCD (Hudson)	11,176	11,481	2.7	11,397	16.2	4.2	9.1	1.2	69.4	19.3	68.7	12.0	4,524	32.2	41.9	32.9
Hackensack city & MCD (Bergen)	43,010	44,519	3.5	43,903	31.7	21.6	10.4	2.4	33.9	18.2	68.8	13.0	18,345	35.5	39.9	37.1
Hackettstown town & MCD (Warren)	9,724	9,551	-1.8	9,633	74.0	2.9	3.0	1.2	18.9	20.8	66.1	13.2	3,469	55.9	44.9	26.9
Haddon township (Camden)	14,707	14,519	-1.3	14,611	91.3	3.1	2.9	0.6	2.1	20.7	62.5	16.8	5,933	72.3	28.7	41.1
Haddonfield borough & MCD (Camden)	11,593	11,411	-1.6	11,521	91.7	0.7	1.9	2.4	3.3	27.7	54.7	17.6	4,250	84.2	8.4	75.8
Haddon Heights borough & MCD (Camden)	7,473	7,375	-1.3	7,425	91.8	3.2	1.4	1.1	2.5	22.3	61.7	16.0	2,832	80.3	24.1	53.4
Hainesburg CDP	91	NA	NA	94	89.4	0.0	0.0	10.6	0.0	10.7	73.3	16.0	49	100.0	89.8	10.2
Hainesport township (Burlington)	6,110	6,092	-0.3	6,118	74.1	11.8	5.1	4.7	4.3	23.6	61.6	14.7	2,319	94.0	31.1	38.2
Haledon borough & MCD (Passaic)	8,326	8,471	1.7	8,397	38.0	8.5	6.6	3.6	43.4	23.1	63.5	13.2	2,582	50.2	43.8	27.2
Hamburg borough & MCD (Sussex)	3,277	3,178	-3.0	3,225	84.6	3.2	2.6	0.6	9.0	21.3	64.9	13.6	1,484	87.1	33.4	36.9
Hamilton township (Atlantic)	26,503	26,647	0.5	26,684	57.4	15.4	8.2	1.5	17.5	23.6	65.8	10.7	9,211	71.3	35.6	28.0
Hamilton township (Mercer)	88,464	89,136	0.8	88,809	70.5	12.1	3.5	1.5	12.4	20.4	62.8	16.8	33,734	74.2	40.3	29.5
Hamilton Square CDP	12,784	NA	NA	12,870	88.1	1.1	4.1	2.5	4.1	20.7	63.7	15.7	4,417	95.9	29.7	45.8
Hammonton town & MCD (Atlantic)	14,791	14,765	-0.2	14,796	74.9	3.2	2.3	0.2	19.4	19.5	62.7	17.9	5,437	70.6	49.4	23.4
Hampton borough & MCD (Hunterdon)	1,401	1,373	-2.0	1,174	90.9	1.4	6.0	0.4	1.3	18.5	66.3	15.2	475	69.3	33.3	32.8
Hampton township (Sussex)	5,189	5,035	-3.0	5,106	90.1	0.0	1.3	1.3	7.2	18.7	63.2	18.1	2,038	93.7	33.1	33.5
Hancocks Bridge CDP	254	NA	NA	196	72.4	27.6	0.0	0.0	0.0	47.0	42.0	11.2	68	67.6	57.4	7.4
Hanover township (Morris)	13,712	14,659	6.9	14,103	78.8	1.4	13.1	0.4	6.2	22.6	59.8	17.5	5,238	84.8	23.8	51.8
Harding township (Morris)	3,828	3,866	1.0	3,862	86.0	2.3	7.3	2.2	2.3	23.4	55.9	20.6	1,446	87.3	4.9	72.6
Hardwick township (Warren)	1,696	1,665	-1.8	1,560	94.0	0.1	1.5	0.5	3.8	24.6	63.2	12.1	528	90.9	38.3	37.9
Hardyston township (Sussex)	8,220	8,023	-2.4	8,126	95.0	1.2	1.6	0.2	2.1	18.8	63.5	17.7	3,334	85.9	35.0	34.8
Harlingen CDP	297	NA	NA	252	57.9	0.0	12.7	0.0	29.4	19.8	53.5	26.6	110	100.0	0.0	35.5
Harmony CDP	441	NA	NA	363	98.9	0.0	0.0	0.0	1.1	24.9	55.5	19.6	141	83.7	62.4	19.1
Harmony township (Warren)	2,667	2,565	-3.8	2,623	97.4	0.8	0.8	0.4	0.6	21.9	63.0	15.1	947	92.5	47.9	28.9
Harrington Park borough & MCD (Bergen)	4,664	4,781	2.5	4,736	77.7	1.0	15.8	1.4	4.1	28.3	57.4	14.4	1,570	93.1	14.3	64.5
Harrison township (Gloucester)	12,417	12,818	3.2	12,616	88.4	4.2	2.3	1.6	3.5	28.6	61.9	9.4	3,961	89.0	21.5	51.3
Harrison town & MCD (Hudson)	13,619	15,376	12.9	14,436	31.0	0.7	19.0	2.6	46.7	19.3	70.8	10.0	5,172	29.7	51.2	33.8
Harvey Cedars borough & MCD (Ocean)	340	344	1.2	479	98.7	0.4	0.0	0.8	0.0	8.1	42.1	49.9	252	94.8	16.7	71.0
Hasbrouck Heights borough & MCD (Bergen)	11,842	12,147	2.6	11,989	78.0	1.6	7.6	0.6	12.2	21.2	61.9	16.9	4,539	66.9	33.8	41.0
Haworth borough & MCD (Bergen)	3,382	3,448	2.0	3,419	81.1	1.7	13.5	2.0	1.7	27.5	57.4	15.1	1,162	93.8	10.8	73.4
Hawthorne borough & MCD (Passaic)	18,791	19,048	1.4	18,944	80.2	1.3	1.1	0.5	16.8	22.9	63.0	14.1	6,991	66.2	43.2	34.1
Hazlet township (Monmouth)	20,334	20,166	-0.8	20,253	85.6	2.0	4.9	0.2	7.3	19.8	64.6	15.6	7,128	90.0	42.3	27.2
Heathcote CDP	5,821	NA	NA	5,668	40.0	11.9	44.3	2.9	0.8	24.6	64.8	10.5	2,350	78.5	10.4	76.6
Helmetta borough & MCD (Middlesex)	2,178	2,218	1.8	2,390	76.0	1.7	11.3	0.9	10.1	21.7	67.5	10.7	879	85.7	24.3	35.7
High Bridge borough & MCD (Hunterdon)	3,648	3,588	-1.6	3,621	91.4	0.7	3.1	0.2	4.6	25.2	65.0	9.6	1,446	86.5	21.7	49.1
Highland Lakes CDP	0	NA	NA	4,944	89.3	0.3	0.2	1.5	8.7	21.7	69.7	8.6	1,861	84.4	30.4	33.6
Highland Park borough & MCD (Middlesex)	13,982	14,436	3.2	14,224	64.8	6.2	14.2	1.8	13.0	26.1	64.7	9.2	5,645	41.5	19.1	67.3
Highlands borough & MCD (Monmouth)	5,021	4,926	-1.9	4,985	87.7	1.2	0.8	1.3	9.1	16.1	72.2	11.7	2,395	66.4	31.1	43.9
Hightstown borough & MCD (Mercer)	5,494	5,567	1.3	5,557	49.2	5.8	1.7	1.7	41.6	21.6	64.8	13.6	2,071	62.0	35.2	42.8
Hillsborough township (Somerset)	38,303	39,544	3.2	39,064	71.2	5.4	13.3	1.9	8.2	24.6	65.2	10.2	13,294	86.8	20.9	57.5

1 May be of any race.

Table A. All Places — **Population and Housing**

STATE City, town, township, borough, or CDP (county if applicable)	2010 census total population	2014 estimated population	Percent change 2010–2014	ACS total population estimate 2010–2014	White alone, not Hispanic or Latino	Black alone, not Hispanic or Latino	Asian alone, not Hispanic or Latino	All other races or 2 or more races, not Hispanic or Latino	Hispanic or Latino[1]	Under 18 years old	Age 18 to 64 years old	Age 65 years and older	Total occupied housing units	Percent owner occupied	High school diploma or less	Bachelor's degree or more
	1	2	3	4	5	6	7	8	9	10	11	12	13	14	15	16
NEW JERSEY—Con.																
Hillsdale borough & MCD (Bergen)	10,223	10,482	2.5	10,381	81.8	0.9	7.1	0.3	9.9	26.2	58.3	15.5	3,494	86.5	20.3	56.8
Hillside township (Union)	21,404	21,919	2.4	21,676	20.3	58.7	2.3	2.7	16.1	23.2	64.4	12.3	7,204	69.1	40.8	22.6
Hi-Nella borough & MCD (Camden)	870	858	-1.4	817	70.5	11.4	2.7	8.8	6.6	20.6	67.3	12.1	345	27.2	37.7	19.4
Hoboken city & MCD (Hudson)	50,006	53,312	6.6	51,979	70.4	2.4	8.0	2.2	17.0	13.3	80.5	6.4	24,330	31.0	16.3	73.5
Ho-Ho-Kus borough & MCD (Bergen)	4,078	4,171	2.3	4,125	83.5	0.2	3.6	3.0	9.7	27.4	53.2	19.4	1,406	89.8	10.1	75.8
Holiday City-Berkeley CDP	12,831	NA	NA	12,013	94.8	1.2	0.3	0.4	3.2	0.1	25.7	74.1	7,832	91.8	66.9	11.6
Holiday City South CDP	3,689	NA	NA	3,609	80.8	8.0	0.6	0.2	10.4	4.7	32.2	62.9	2,172	87.7	57.3	12.7
Holiday Heights CDP	2,099	NA	NA	2,205	90.4	0.0	2.3	0.3	7.0	0.0	15.7	84.4	1,358	96.1	71.9	14.5
Holland township (Hunterdon)	5,291	5,204	-1.6	5,243	93.7	2.2	0.0	1.2	2.9	20.5	62.0	17.6	2,113	91.8	33.3	43.0
Holmdel township (Monmouth)	16,773	16,694	-0.5	16,722	71.6	1.6	19.8	1.9	5.0	25.5	58.1	16.5	5,427	87.3	17.3	67.8
Hopatcong borough & MCD (Sussex)	15,147	14,684	-3.1	14,921	84.3	1.5	2.6	1.3	10.4	20.9	68.1	11.1	5,540	91.5	34.0	32.7
Hope CDP	195	NA	NA	189	87.3	9.0	0.0	0.0	3.7	14.3	64.6	21.2	82	75.6	26.8	36.6
Hope township (Warren)	1,952	1,916	-1.8	1,861	92.4	0.9	2.1	0.0	4.6	21.2	59.6	19.2	688	87.8	28.9	35.9
Hopewell township (Cumberland)	4,571	4,506	-1.4	4,541	80.8	7.9	1.3	6.0	4.0	17.6	60.1	22.2	1,559	86.3	52.0	19.2
Hopewell borough & MCD (Mercer)	1,922	1,919	-0.2	1,891	93.5	1.6	1.1	2.0	1.9	22.5	64.5	13.0	771	73.9	11.8	70.3
Hopewell township (Mercer)	18,301	18,400	0.5	18,311	83.1	3.5	7.8	1.8	3.8	24.4	60.9	14.7	6,672	94.5	14.1	71.1
Howell township (Monmouth)	51,075	51,897	1.6	51,389	81.7	2.5	5.2	2.0	8.7	25.1	63.7	11.0	17,527	90.0	32.1	36.2
Hutchinson CDP	135	NA	NA	125	92.0	0.0	0.0	8.0	0.0	22.4	68.8	8.8	45	88.9	48.9	22.2
Independence township (Warren)	5,662	5,541	-2.1	5,594	92.4	0.3	3.4	1.6	2.3	21.4	66.7	11.9	2,328	80.4	27.0	38.3
Interlaken borough & MCD (Monmouth)	820	817	-0.4	826	97.0	0.0	1.5	0.2	1.3	15.4	56.1	28.6	364	96.2	15.1	68.4
Irvington township (Essex)	53,933	54,512	1.1	54,268	2.4	84.5	1.6	1.5	10.0	24.9	64.7	10.5	20,414	33.4	51.3	14.5
Iselin CDP	18,695	NA	NA	18,457	32.5	8.8	46.5	4.9	7.3	19.8	65.6	14.6	6,180	64.6	35.4	44.1
Island Heights borough & MCD (Ocean)	1,670	1,693	1.4	1,710	91.1	1.2	1.3	3.2	3.1	17.0	59.0	23.9	701	88.4	15.5	57.6
Jackson township (Ocean)	54,862	56,449	2.9	55,716	80.7	5.9	2.9	1.5	9.0	23.3	60.0	16.7	19,865	86.0	34.9	33.6
Jamesburg borough & MCD (Middlesex)	5,915	6,021	1.8	5,963	71.6	5.2	5.1	0.7	17.5	28.5	63.4	8.2	2,233	58.9	55.3	20.6
Jefferson township (Morris)	21,311	21,483	0.8	21,443	85.7	1.5	3.6	1.2	8.0	23.6	64.8	11.6	7,835	91.9	28.8	43.8
Jersey City city & MCD (Hudson)	247,643	262,146	5.9	255,861	21.5	23.6	24.7	2.8	27.4	20.9	69.9	9.3	96,634	29.9	36.1	44.0
Johnsonburg CDP	101	NA	NA	83	57.8	0.0	0.0	0.0	42.2	30.0	69.8	0.0	33	51.5	57.6	42.4
Juliustown CDP	429	NA	NA	284	90.1	0.0	1.8	4.9	3.2	13.1	67.0	20.1	113	92.9	72.6	4.4
Keansburg borough & MCD (Monmouth)	10,105	9,872	-2.3	10,011	72.8	5.2	2.3	4.0	15.7	19.7	68.1	12.1	4,162	53.1	52.3	17.2
Kearny town & MCD (Hudson)	40,684	41,837	2.8	41,538	43.9	2.3	4.5	4.3	44.9	22.8	66.0	11.1	13,691	45.7	52.6	23.7
Kendall Park CDP	9,339	NA	NA	10,331	55.6	5.4	29.6	2.6	6.9	25.4	62.4	12.2	3,376	87.4	27.5	49.6
Kenilworth borough & MCD (Union)	7,914	8,153	3.0	8,045	75.7	4.3	6.8	0.7	12.6	21.0	64.5	14.5	2,679	81.9	45.3	21.9
Kenvil CDP	3,009	NA	NA	2,694	71.9	4.4	8.8	1.5	13.3	20.2	60.1	19.6	945	79.9	34.3	42.9
Keyport borough & MCD (Monmouth)	7,240	7,162	-1.1	7,213	70.6	5.6	3.1	2.0	18.8	19.3	63.1	17.6	3,142	51.2	47.5	24.4
Kingston CDP	1,493	NA	NA	1,259	68.4	3.8	24.6	3.2	0.0	16.8	66.1	17.1	596	70.6	19.5	69.1
Kingston Estates CDP	5,685	NA	NA	6,161	68.4	5.4	15.1	4.1	6.9	22.9	57.9	19.3	2,328	73.3	29.3	43.9
Kingwood township (Hunterdon)	3,843	3,806	-1.0	3,829	96.1	0.3	1.6	1.0	1.1	22.0	60.8	17.0	1,340	89.9	33.2	40.7
Kinnelon borough & MCD (Morris)	10,248	10,381	1.3	10,349	89.0	0.4	4.3	0.1	6.3	25.9	60.8	13.4	3,610	87.0	16.4	67.5
Knowlton township (Warren)	3,055	2,996	-1.9	3,026	93.0	0.3	1.6	2.6	2.5	23.5	62.4	14.2	1,092	89.5	45.9	24.4
Lacey township (Ocean)	27,644	28,211	2.1	27,889	94.2	0.7	0.7	0.3	4.2	20.9	62.7	16.3	10,788	89.9	41.2	27.6
Lafayette township (Sussex)	2,525	2,462	-2.5	2,423	89.4	0.6	2.6	0.5	7.0	18.9	67.4	13.6	856	90.7	35.2	35.2
Lake Como borough & MCD (Monmouth)	1,759	1,714	-2.6	1,647	59.4	13.7	6.3	2.3	18.3	20.2	67.8	11.8	727	55.8	32.6	39.6
Lakehurst borough & MCD (Ocean)	2,654	2,713	2.2	2,676	69.4	6.5	1.4	3.0	19.7	29.2	63.1	7.6	846	71.0	50.0	11.9
Lake Mohawk CDP	9,916	NA	NA	9,568	92.2	0.6	2.0	1.1	4.0	25.0	62.1	12.9	3,609	89.9	17.9	56.4
Lake Telemark CDP	1,255	NA	NA	1,267	92.7	0.0	0.0	2.7	4.6	24.0	68.8	7.3	420	93.3	36.9	43.6
Lakewood township (Ocean)	92,837	95,177	2.5	93,473	78.1	4.0	0.5	0.9	16.5	44.9	44.0	11.0	23,688	50.3	44.0	29.5
Lakewood CDP	53,805	NA	NA	51,944	80.8	3.5	0.3	0.5	14.9	50.0	45.6	4.3	10,051	34.9	40.7	32.1
Lambertville city & MCD (Hunterdon)	3,911	3,856	-1.4	3,876	88.5	1.4	0.6	0.2	9.3	14.7	66.6	18.8	2,043	65.6	20.0	57.7
Laurel Lake CDP	2,989	NA	NA	2,965	75.2	0.6	1.7	2.3	20.2	33.0	60.8	6.3	1,086	60.7	68.7	5.7
Laurel Springs borough & MCD (Camden)	1,908	1,880	-1.5	1,910	87.6	3.0	2.5	0.5	6.5	20.9	65.0	14.1	680	78.2	39.1	29.7
Laurence Harbor CDP	6,536	NA	NA	6,845	68.9	9.9	10.2	2.0	9.0	20.0	69.8	10.1	2,634	76.7	42.4	27.0
Lavallette borough & MCD (Ocean)	1,875	1,833	-2.2	2,029	99.6	0.0	0.0	0.2	0.2	11.2	43.8	45.0	921	84.6	28.4	45.9
Lawnside borough & MCD (Camden)	2,948	2,909	-1.3	2,919	1.7	86.3	4.1	2.0	5.9	23.5	57.0	19.5	1,089	78.1	37.5	37.6
Lawrence township (Cumberland)	3,290	3,273	-0.5	3,301	70.7	12.4	0.0	2.8	14.1	24.3	65.1	10.7	1,101	85.6	56.0	13.3

1 May be of any race.

Table A. All Places — **Population and Housing**

STATE City, town, township, borough, or CDP (county if applicable)	2010 census total population	2014 estimated population	Percent change 2010–2014	ACS total population estimate 2010–2014	White alone, not Hispanic or Latino	Black alone, not Hispanic or Latino	Asian alone, not Hispanic or Latino	All other races or 2 or more races, not Hispanic or Latino	Hispanic or Latino[1]	Under 18 years old	Age 18 to 64 years old	Age 65 years and older	Total occupied housing units	Percent owner occupied	High school diploma or less	Bachelor's degree or more
	1	2	3	4	5	6	7	8	9	10	11	12	13	14	15	16
NEW JERSEY—Con.																
Lawrence township (Mercer)	33,472	33,130	-1.0	33,252	62.6	11.1	14.9	2.2	9.3	20.3	64.6	15.1	12,410	69.9	20.3	57.5
Lawrenceville CDP	3,887	NA	NA	3,538	88.8	1.7	5.1	1.1	3.3	15.8	67.0	17.1	1,711	92.4	11.7	69.4
Lebanon borough & MCD (Hunterdon)	1,358	1,388	2.2	1,765	86.8	0.5	2.7	3.2	6.8	24.1	63.7	12.2	720	55.8	21.9	52.5
Lebanon township (Hunterdon)	6,588	6,453	-2.0	6,507	93.1	0.7	0.7	0.9	4.6	22.6	62.0	15.4	2,257	86.6	34.1	41.9
Leisure Knoll CDP	2,490	NA	NA	2,453	92.2	1.1	0.0	1.6	5.1	0.0	23.5	76.4	1,485	96.4	65.1	14.9
Leisuretowne CDP	3,582	NA	NA	3,633	93.6	3.5	0.0	1.9	1.0	4.7	35.2	60.3	2,090	93.9	60.5	16.3
Leisure Village CDP	4,400	NA	NA	4,201	69.1	6.4	0.3	0.5	23.8	8.7	39.6	51.8	2,531	62.2	65.7	11.8
Leisure Village East CDP	4,217	NA	NA	3,689	95.5	1.0	1.5	0.0	2.0	0.4	20.9	78.8	2,522	92.2	53.6	22.1
Leisure Village West CDP	0	NA	NA	3,291	95.7	1.5	0.0	0.0	2.9	0.2	22.1	77.6	2,333	89.8	52.1	18.8
Leonardo CDP	2,757	NA	NA	2,236	94.1	0.0	0.9	1.4	3.7	16.2	73.5	10.2	946	83.7	30.8	32.2
Leonia borough & MCD (Bergen)	8,946	9,139	2.2	9,051	38.2	1.8	40.1	4.4	15.5	22.4	61.8	15.8	3,362	61.0	21.0	61.1
Liberty township (Warren)	2,942	2,869	-2.5	2,898	85.6	1.4	3.5	3.6	5.9	20.5	68.2	11.3	1,106	81.9	34.1	35.0
Lincoln Park borough & MCD (Morris)	10,521	10,482	-0.4	10,515	81.2	3.2	6.7	2.0	7.0	17.9	65.8	16.2	3,862	75.9	30.2	43.2
Lincroft CDP	6,135	NA	NA	6,436	86.5	1.6	8.2	0.5	3.3	27.2	55.6	17.2	2,114	88.4	21.1	60.5
Linden city & MCD (Union)	40,499	41,651	2.8	41,054	40.8	26.5	2.3	2.4	27.9	20.1	66.8	12.9	14,400	57.8	52.9	19.3
Lindenwold borough & MCD (Camden)	17,613	17,417	-1.1	17,512	40.0	29.2	1.8	4.3	24.7	20.7	68.0	11.3	7,344	39.5	47.6	18.6
Linwood city & MCD (Atlantic)	7,092	7,052	-0.6	7,071	91.6	0.7	1.4	2.1	4.2	24.2	56.8	19.0	2,537	86.0	23.4	48.1
Little Egg Harbor township (Ocean)	20,063	20,396	1.7	20,339	90.8	0.9	0.6	2.5	5.3	20.0	55.7	24.2	8,165	84.5	39.4	20.6
Little Falls township (Passaic)	14,432	14,516	0.6	14,510	70.8	4.0	8.9	4.2	12.0	17.3	64.3	18.4	5,339	66.1	41.4	39.1
Little Ferry borough & MCD (Bergen)	10,632	10,866	2.2	10,773	43.9	2.9	29.3	1.5	22.3	19.8	68.4	11.8	4,160	42.6	41.0	31.3
Little Silver borough & MCD (Monmouth)	5,950	5,918	-0.5	5,920	92.2	0.3	1.4	1.4	4.7	29.1	55.0	16.0	2,113	94.6	9.7	67.3
Livingston township (Essex)	29,361	29,931	1.9	29,617	71.5	1.3	21.1	1.7	4.4	26.4	56.7	17.0	9,517	92.0	14.5	72.0
Loch Arbour village & MCD (Monmouth)	194	190	-2.1	198	87.4	0.0	2.5	3.5	6.6	21.2	62.4	16.7	73	75.3	20.5	63.0
Lodi borough & MCD (Bergen)	24,136	24,654	2.1	24,428	46.3	6.7	6.9	1.6	38.5	22.2	65.2	12.5	9,240	37.1	45.7	24.1
Logan township (Gloucester)	6,042	5,971	-1.2	6,000	79.4	9.3	1.3	2.7	7.3	25.3	68.6	6.1	2,173	96.7	41.3	34.7
Long Beach township (Ocean)	3,048	3,060	0.4	3,040	97.3	0.7	0.4	0.3	1.4	9.3	40.0	50.6	1,494	94.6	24.8	54.8
Long Branch city & MCD (Monmouth)	30,719	30,522	-0.6	30,590	53.6	11.1	2.8	2.9	29.6	23.0	64.4	12.5	11,883	41.4	46.0	30.2
Long Hill township (Morris)	8,702	8,791	1.0	8,769	79.3	1.3	10.0	1.4	8.0	22.5	61.9	15.5	3,065	87.1	18.9	57.4
Longport borough & MCD (Atlantic)	895	880	-1.7	949	98.1	1.5	0.0	0.4	0.0	6.1	46.6	47.3	504	87.7	30.4	42.7
Long Valley CDP	1,879	NA	NA	1,682	92.2	0.0	2.9	1.4	3.5	24.7	57.6	17.8	586	94.0	16.6	45.2
Lopatcong township (Warren)	8,014	8,074	0.7	8,027	80.9	6.3	5.6	1.4	5.9	25.6	58.3	16.3	2,917	73.4	40.5	35.6
Lopatcong Overlook CDP	734	NA	NA	455	81.8	14.9	0.0	0.0	3.3	18.7	68.3	13.2	245	57.1	12.2	48.2
Lower township (Cape May)	22,866	22,262	-2.6	22,572	89.7	1.9	0.7	1.5	6.2	19.1	60.9	20.0	9,582	77.1	51.6	20.7
Lower Alloways Creek township (Salem)	1,770	1,732	-2.1	1,715	89.2	4.5	0.0	4.3	2.0	25.2	58.3	16.6	605	79.7	51.7	16.2
Lumberton township (Burlington)	12,559	12,447	-0.9	12,511	64.1	18.2	2.8	2.6	12.3	26.0	62.3	11.5	4,430	70.9	32.1	36.3
Lyndhurst township (Bergen)	20,554	22,079	7.4	21,207	68.9	0.9	7.2	1.6	21.4	20.3	62.7	17.1	8,062	53.0	45.2	30.2
McGuire AFB CDP	3,710	NA	NA	4,932	60.0	14.2	3.5	11.2	11.1	40.5	59.6	0.0	1,244	0.2	22.4	25.9
Madison borough & MCD (Morris)	15,819	16,122	1.9	16,043	83.7	2.4	5.2	2.4	6.4	23.7	61.3	15.0	5,532	69.7	21.0	66.2
Madison Park CDP	7,144	NA	NA	6,616	38.9	14.7	27.9	2.2	16.3	19.0	71.6	9.4	2,619	28.4	41.1	30.9
Magnolia borough & MCD (Camden)	4,341	4,288	-1.2	4,329	72.6	13.0	1.2	6.5	6.8	19.5	68.6	11.9	1,655	67.6	47.1	18.1
Mahwah township (Bergen)	25,890	26,500	2.4	26,242	78.1	3.7	9.5	2.6	6.2	19.0	66.7	14.1	9,426	84.2	17.7	58.3
Manahawkin CDP	2,303	NA	NA	2,608	70.4	0.3	3.0	4.2	22.1	21.9	67.0	11.2	949	61.7	41.7	36.5
Manalapan township (Monmouth)	38,872	39,987	2.9	39,543	84.2	2.6	7.2	1.2	4.7	24.3	62.4	13.4	13,233	91.1	26.6	49.4
Manasquan borough & MCD (Monmouth)	5,897	5,764	-2.3	5,841	94.9	0.0	0.0	0.0	5.0	19.5	60.8	19.6	2,452	74.0	23.8	55.9
Manchester township (Ocean)	43,070	43,555	1.1	43,222	86.3	5.2	2.3	1.4	4.9	10.1	40.8	48.8	22,659	89.4	56.7	17.1
Mannington township (Salem)	1,806	1,777	-1.6	1,680	66.0	21.1	0.0	1.0	11.9	14.5	67.1	18.3	474	86.7	51.9	23.4
Mansfield township (Burlington)	8,544	8,563	0.2	8,554	73.4	10.0	10.9	1.7	3.6	19.0	53.7	27.4	3,228	98.3	27.1	46.7
Mansfield township (Warren)	7,725	7,535	-2.5	7,614	78.2	3.1	5.0	2.7	11.1	20.6	64.9	14.4	3,083	57.3	36.1	29.7
Mantoloking borough & MCD (Ocean)	296	258	-12.8	356	88.2	3.1	7.6	0.0	1.1	9.0	38.3	52.8	174	95.4	4.0	85.6
Mantua township (Gloucester)	15,217	15,150	-0.4	15,170	90.1	5.1	1.1	0.6	3.0	23.2	62.4	14.3	5,796	88.1	33.8	29.2
Manville borough & MCD (Somerset)	10,344	10,388	0.4	10,426	73.4	3.3	2.5	0.1	20.7	19.6	64.6	15.6	3,874	64.9	57.5	15.2
Maple Shade township (Burlington)	19,131	18,979	-0.8	19,075	73.2	9.0	6.9	2.5	8.5	19.9	66.6	13.7	8,090	49.2	43.4	27.8

1 May be of any race.

Table A. All Places — Population and Housing

STATE City, town, township, borough, or CDP (county if applicable)	2010 census total population	2014 estimated population	Percent change 2010–2014	ACS total population estimate 2010–2014	White alone, not Hispanic or Latino	Black alone, not Hispanic or Latino	Asian alone, not Hispanic or Latino	All other races or 2 or more races, not Hispanic or Latino	Hispanic or Latino[1]	Under 18 years old	Age 18 to 64 years old	Age 65 years and older	Total occupied housing units	Percent owner occupied	High school diploma or less	Bachelor's degree or more
	1	2	3	4	5	6	7	8	9	10	11	12	13	14	15	16
NEW JERSEY—Con.																
Maplewood township (Essex)	23,869	24,657	3.3	24,233	54.0	29.9	3.2	3.4	9.5	29.7	59.6	10.5	8,034	77.8	17.2	66.3
Margate City city & MCD (Atlantic)	6,354	6,333	-0.3	6,343	94.5	1.2	1.4	0.2	2.7	10.9	52.3	36.7	3,272	76.2	30.1	40.6
Marksboro CDP	82	NA	NA	57	100.0	0.0	0.0	0.0	0.0	7.0	54.5	38.6	25	88.0	28.0	48.0
Marlboro township (Monmouth)	40,191	41,000	2.0	40,370	76.0	1.5	17.0	1.3	4.1	26.7	60.9	12.4	12,929	95.5	19.6	61.0
Marlton CDP	10,133	NA	NA	10,397	89.4	1.8	4.6	1.1	3.0	18.6	66.0	15.4	4,105	70.0	32.4	41.0
Martinsville CDP	11,980	NA	NA	11,914	80.1	2.4	10.7	2.0	4.7	21.7	60.8	17.6	4,080	97.2	18.2	64.0
Matawan borough & MCD (Monmouth)	8,809	8,718	-1.0	8,759	71.9	7.3	7.1	4.1	9.6	22.7	64.3	12.9	3,415	65.3	29.0	40.3
Maurice River township (Cumberland)	7,976	7,923	-0.7	7,985	49.0	32.5	3.2	1.0	14.3	8.8	84.4	7.0	1,337	80.6	62.0	14.5
Mays Landing CDP	2,135	NA	NA	1,714	86.9	5.7	0.6	1.6	5.1	19.9	70.5	9.7	735	82.6	29.0	35.1
Maywood borough & MCD (Bergen)	9,555	9,746	2.0	9,651	66.0	4.5	10.0	1.6	17.9	20.5	63.6	15.9	3,610	65.7	31.2	37.0
Medford township (Burlington)	23,033	23,357	1.4	23,215	89.1	2.4	2.2	1.6	4.8	23.5	60.3	16.3	8,275	84.9	19.1	56.4
Medford Lakes borough & MCD (Burlington)	4,146	4,110	-0.9	4,138	97.4	0.6	0.0	1.4	0.6	24.6	61.0	14.6	1,536	90.7	17.8	59.3
Mendham borough & MCD (Morris)	4,981	4,999	0.4	5,008	91.2	1.3	2.8	1.2	3.5	29.3	50.8	20.0	1,702	84.9	12.3	67.6
Mendham township (Morris)	5,853	5,882	0.5	5,877	87.6	0.5	5.0	3.2	3.8	29.3	54.4	16.5	1,940	95.0	9.5	75.5
Mercerville CDP	13,230	NA	NA	13,048	81.4	8.1	4.0	0.8	5.8	20.0	60.5	19.6	4,894	82.8	36.5	33.7
Merchantville borough & MCD (Camden)	3,821	3,777	-1.2	3,803	62.6	13.2	2.0	0.5	21.7	22.1	64.0	13.7	1,527	56.8	39.8	27.5
Metuchen borough & MCD (Middlesex)	13,574	13,826	1.9	13,707	71.6	4.9	14.0	2.9	6.6	23.5	61.7	14.6	5,149	79.8	17.2	64.1
Middle township (Cape May)	18,911	18,883	-0.1	18,882	79.7	10.6	2.6	1.0	6.1	19.5	59.9	20.4	7,442	80.6	48.1	28.1
Middlebush CDP	2,326	NA	NA	2,341	62.4	4.6	13.5	0.5	19.0	19.2	61.8	18.8	849	75.9	40.0	43.9
Middlesex borough & MCD (Middlesex)	13,635	13,888	1.9	13,766	72.7	5.2	5.8	1.6	14.8	22.7	64.2	13.2	4,902	78.2	38.5	31.1
Middletown township (Monmouth)	66,509	66,017	-0.7	66,290	89.5	0.8	2.8	1.0	5.9	23.4	61.5	15.0	23,896	85.3	27.2	46.9
Midland Park borough & MCD (Bergen)	7,128	7,305	2.5	7,229	81.9	0.5	2.7	2.4	12.5	24.9	61.1	13.9	2,811	68.2	28.4	57.7
Milford borough & MCD (Hunterdon)	1,233	1,211	-1.8	1,065	91.9	0.5	0.8	0.9	5.9	17.2	64.0	18.8	462	66.7	37.2	37.4
Millburn township (Essex)	20,120	20,401	1.4	20,200	75.8	1.9	15.7	1.6	5.0	32.7	55.5	11.7	6,560	80.1	7.5	85.0
Millstone township (Monmouth)	10,566	10,448	-1.1	10,509	84.7	5.0	4.1	2.8	3.3	26.2	63.0	10.8	3,379	95.9	17.7	55.1
Millstone borough & MCD (Somerset)	418	420	0.5	461	88.5	0.7	5.4	3.7	1.7	27.9	53.2	18.7	173	85.5	38.7	40.5
Milltown borough & MCD (Middlesex)	6,893	7,032	2.0	6,974	83.8	4.7	3.1	1.8	6.6	19.4	66.6	14.0	2,602	79.5	28.6	43.0
Millville city & MCD (Cumberland)	28,400	28,497	0.3	28,603	61.5	19.5	0.7	2.1	16.3	24.7	61.2	14.1	10,258	63.6	52.3	18.4
Mine Hill township (Morris)	3,643	3,657	0.4	3,664	72.1	3.3	4.5	1.2	19.0	26.2	61.1	12.8	1,194	89.4	43.3	27.9
Monmouth Beach borough & MCD (Monmouth)	3,279	3,256	-0.7	3,278	89.6	0.0	1.1	2.8	6.5	20.6	57.0	22.5	1,526	81.5	20.1	58.8
Monmouth Junction CDP	2,887	NA	NA	2,973	52.0	1.6	34.9	2.7	8.8	30.8	56.3	12.8	983	92.8	20.0	67.2
Monroe township (Gloucester)	36,125	37,379	3.5	36,700	75.5	14.1	3.0	1.9	5.5	24.9	60.7	14.3	13,130	83.0	45.0	25.6
Monroe township (Middlesex)	39,132	42,810	9.4	40,961	75.1	3.9	16.0	1.4	3.6	18.4	46.7	34.9	17,137	91.6	30.5	44.5
Montague township (Sussex)	3,872	3,770	-2.6	3,813	88.5	1.6	0.8	2.9	6.2	19.5	66.7	13.8	1,512	63.2	41.8	17.2
Montclair township (Essex)	37,676	38,142	1.2	37,934	59.1	24.4	3.7	4.3	8.5	25.6	62.0	12.4	14,472	57.7	14.7	69.8
Montgomery township (Somerset)	22,257	22,746	2.2	22,529	62.5	1.9	28.5	2.2	4.9	30.3	58.4	11.3	7,408	84.0	8.3	80.2
Montvale borough & MCD (Bergen)	7,844	8,148	3.9	8,000	73.8	0.0	13.3	1.5	11.5	25.8	58.5	15.9	2,733	83.1	20.6	59.2
Montville township (Morris)	21,524	21,842	1.5	21,730	73.3	0.6	17.4	1.9	6.7	25.1	60.2	14.8	7,421	84.3	18.6	63.1
Moonachie borough & MCD (Bergen)	2,702	2,783	3.0	2,741	64.2	0.0	7.9	0.9	27.0	17.8	65.0	17.2	1,013	80.7	61.8	18.2
Moorestown township (Burlington)	20,726	20,594	-0.6	20,686	82.8	5.9	6.3	2.9	2.1	25.6	57.3	17.1	7,245	84.0	16.9	62.1
Moorestown-Lenola CDP	14,217	NA	NA	14,436	84.2	8.1	2.5	2.4	2.8	24.6	58.6	16.8	5,233	80.8	17.1	57.2
Morganville CDP	5,040	NA	NA	5,052	73.1	2.7	15.8	2.7	5.8	28.4	60.6	11.1	1,585	99.7	21.1	52.9
Morris township (Morris)	22,434	22,573	0.6	22,549	82.0	5.2	4.6	2.3	6.0	21.8	60.0	18.2	8,247	86.3	15.6	73.5
Morris Plains borough & MCD (Morris)	5,532	5,733	3.6	5,635	82.7	3.2	3.9	1.0	9.2	21.6	60.3	18.0	2,100	85.1	20.5	58.3
Morristown town & MCD (Morris)	18,324	19,085	4.2	18,580	49.8	12.7	4.3	0.7	32.5	16.8	69.9	13.3	7,841	39.3	32.8	51.7
Mountain Lake CDP	575	NA	NA	676	95.6	0.7	1.6	1.0	1.0	11.4	66.8	21.7	320	78.1	30.3	32.8
Mountain Lakes borough & MCD (Morris)	4,160	4,262	2.5	4,235	84.8	0.2	10.6	2.0	2.3	31.6	57.0	11.3	1,296	92.8	4.0	90.0
Mountainside borough & MCD (Union)	6,685	6,837	2.3	6,765	82.6	5.0	4.6	2.7	5.1	25.1	53.8	21.0	2,322	90.6	19.0	61.8
Mount Arlington borough & MCD (Morris)	5,050	5,211	3.2	5,140	91.0	0.9	2.4	0.0	5.7	16.8	61.1	22.4	2,344	78.0	34.8	39.0
Mount Ephraim borough & MCD (Camden)	4,674	4,632	-0.9	4,669	90.8	4.6	0.5	0.9	3.2	20.6	67.2	12.2	1,799	81.0	52.9	17.7
Mount Hermon CDP	141	NA	NA	130	93.8	0.0	0.0	0.0	6.2	20.8	69.2	10.0	43	79.1	25.6	20.9

1 May be of any race.

Table A. All Places — **Population and Housing**

STATE City, town, township, borough, or CDP (county if applicable)	2010 census total population	2014 estimated population	Percent change 2010–2014	ACS total population estimate 2010–2014	White alone, not Hispanic or Latino	Black alone, not Hispanic or Latino	Asian alone, not Hispanic or Latino	All other races or 2 or more races, not Hispanic or Latino	Hispanic or Latino[1]	Under 18 years old	Age 18 to 64 years old	Age 65 years and older	Total occupied housing units	Percent owner occupied	High school diploma or less	Bachelor's degree or more
	1	2	3	4	5	6	7	8	9	10	11	12	13	14	15	16
NEW JERSEY—Con.																
Mount Holly township (Burlington)	9,536	9,490	-0.5	9,448	60.6	25.0	1.6	3.6	9.1	21.4	66.9	11.7	3,422	65.3	41.5	27.3
Mount Laurel township (Burlington)	41,864	41,743	-0.3	41,813	76.1	8.2	8.2	2.7	4.8	22.1	60.7	17.3	17,501	82.4	21.2	52.8
Mount Olive township (Morris)	28,109	28,921	2.9	28,530	72.2	5.3	7.0	1.1	14.3	26.3	63.4	10.3	10,777	55.7	30.0	42.2
Mullica township (Atlantic)	6,147	6,155	0.1	6,154	71.7	6.0	0.4	2.1	19.8	21.6	63.8	14.7	2,111	95.4	57.1	16.6
Mullica Hill CDP	3,982	NA	NA	4,437	85.5	6.4	3.8	0.6	3.7	18.0	65.7	16.2	1,591	81.4	33.1	33.0
Mystic Island CDP	8,493	NA	NA	7,792	89.5	1.4	0.2	1.3	7.6	17.5	57.3	24.9	3,181	87.7	47.4	15.2
National Park borough & MCD (Gloucester)	3,036	2,995	-1.4	3,018	93.2	1.4	1.1	1.9	2.4	24.8	63.6	11.7	1,041	84.2	52.0	13.5
Navesink CDP	2,020	NA	NA	1,638	87.3	5.4	0.0	0.9	6.5	33.1	60.0	7.0	538	97.6	24.9	48.9
Neptune township (Monmouth)	27,935	27,721	-0.8	27,880	49.2	35.9	2.1	3.2	9.5	20.6	62.7	16.8	11,019	66.7	34.3	30.8
Neptune City borough & MCD (Monmouth)	4,869	4,827	-0.9	4,849	63.7	20.7	4.4	1.7	9.6	22.1	63.2	14.7	1,981	56.7	42.6	28.2
Netcong borough & MCD (Morris)	3,232	3,254	0.7	3,248	69.9	1.2	4.5	1.1	23.3	20.9	65.1	13.9	1,429	49.3	48.3	23.0
Newark city & MCD (Essex)	277,149	280,579	1.2	278,750	11.1	49.0	1.8	3.3	34.8	25.7	65.9	8.5	91,771	22.3	60.0	13.9
New Brunswick city & MCD (Middlesex)	54,578	57,080	4.6	55,804	22.4	12.6	8.0	1.4	55.6	23.0	72.2	4.6	13,866	21.0	53.0	24.8
New Egypt CDP	2,512	NA	NA	2,138	87.3	0.0	1.9	0.7	10.1	23.1	62.3	14.5	795	70.8	51.3	16.5
Newfield borough & MCD (Gloucester)	1,553	1,531	-1.4	1,681	88.8	3.0	0.1	2.1	5.9	22.4	64.4	13.1	592	79.1	47.0	17.6
New Hanover township (Burlington)	7,385	7,258	-1.7	7,674	41.9	26.6	3.0	5.1	23.3	9.6	87.1	3.3	641	39.0	18.4	41.8
New Milford borough & MCD (Bergen)	16,341	16,678	2.1	16,524	60.6	4.9	17.5	2.4	14.7	21.3	62.2	16.6	6,175	61.6	35.9	42.3
New Providence borough & MCD (Union)	12,171	12,422	2.1	12,314	81.4	1.2	11.3	1.6	4.5	26.4	58.8	14.7	4,441	78.2	18.0	66.2
Newton town & MCD (Sussex)	8,130	7,878	-3.1	7,999	74.6	9.3	0.9	1.2	14.1	22.3	58.9	18.8	3,170	49.5	51.8	26.3
New Village CDP	421	NA	NA	362	94.8	0.0	1.7	0.0	3.6	13.3	70.5	16.3	171	81.3	67.3	9.4
North Arlington borough & MCD (Bergen)	15,392	15,723	2.2	15,587	66.7	1.2	7.7	1.1	23.2	19.9	63.1	16.9	6,155	51.6	44.8	33.1
North Beach Haven CDP	2,235	NA	NA	2,096	98.5	0.0	0.5	0.0	1.0	7.0	40.6	52.4	1,045	94.3	28.9	52.2
North Bergen township (Hudson)	60,772	62,602	3.0	62,114	17.2	1.6	6.2	1.6	73.4	21.4	65.1	13.7	21,968	42.9	45.4	26.7
North Brunswick township (Middlesex)	41,348	42,488	2.8	41,920	37.8	16.7	25.0	1.7	18.8	22.6	67.7	9.6	14,761	58.7	31.4	47.4
North Caldwell borough & MCD (Essex)	6,156	6,783	10.2	6,407	90.4	0.0	2.8	0.5	6.4	28.9	56.9	14.3	2,061	96.5	13.1	77.8
North Cape May CDP	3,226	NA	NA	2,860	92.0	0.7	0.0	0.0	7.3	16.1	61.1	23.1	1,322	77.5	60.6	18.8
Northfield city & MCD (Atlantic)	8,624	8,604	-0.2	8,616	82.4	1.0	6.1	1.1	9.3	26.0	57.4	16.6	3,089	90.4	35.8	31.2
North Haledon borough & MCD (Passaic)	8,417	8,512	1.1	8,478	79.0	4.7	4.8	1.3	10.2	21.3	61.5	17.3	2,969	90.6	35.9	44.1
North Hanover township (Burlington)	7,678	7,647	-0.4	7,655	69.4	14.3	2.1	6.1	8.1	32.7	60.4	7.1	2,542	45.9	41.8	21.1
North Middletown CDP	3,295	NA	NA	3,231	88.3	3.2	2.0	0.0	6.5	25.4	67.1	7.5	1,064	69.8	43.9	30.3
North Plainfield borough & MCD (Somerset)	21,936	22,029	0.4	22,056	30.3	16.7	5.8	1.6	45.6	24.5	67.6	7.8	7,255	58.1	45.3	29.6
Northvale borough & MCD (Bergen)	4,640	4,771	2.8	4,725	70.3	1.1	22.7	1.3	4.6	22.9	62.4	14.8	1,618	84.5	30.6	41.5
North Wildwood city & MCD (Cape May)	4,041	3,934	-2.6	3,995	99.3	0.4	0.0	0.0	0.4	18.1	54.5	27.6	1,944	74.5	49.1	29.6
Norwood borough & MCD (Bergen)	5,711	5,826	2.0	5,769	57.7	1.7	34.5	0.0	6.1	21.0	57.4	21.7	1,942	85.1	30.5	51.5
Nutley township (Essex)	28,370	28,700	1.2	28,551	72.2	2.6	10.8	2.5	12.0	19.1	64.9	16.1	11,225	68.1	34.0	46.9
Oakhurst CDP	3,995	NA	NA	3,904	93.4	0.3	2.2	0.6	3.5	25.0	61.2	13.9	1,312	91.5	20.8	48.6
Oakland borough & MCD (Bergen)	12,755	13,046	2.3	12,914	87.1	0.7	4.5	0.6	7.1	25.2	60.8	13.8	4,275	92.9	22.9	51.3
Oaklyn borough & MCD (Camden)	4,038	3,984	-1.3	4,022	88.7	3.5	2.3	0.3	5.1	17.2	67.8	15.0	1,688	69.5	41.4	30.2
Oak Valley CDP	3,483	NA	NA	3,414	97.0	1.1	0.2	1.1	0.6	20.5	64.0	15.4	1,224	96.0	62.3	8.5
Ocean township (Monmouth)	27,291	27,200	-0.3	27,241	71.3	7.8	6.3	2.9	11.7	23.7	59.7	16.5	10,363	64.0	29.2	44.2
Ocean township (Ocean)	8,332	8,658	3.9	8,539	92.5	0.2	0.4	1.6	5.3	14.7	54.4	31.0	3,541	92.5	43.2	31.9
Ocean Acres CDP	16,142	NA	NA	16,187	92.8	0.8	0.4	0.0	6.0	25.9	60.9	13.2	5,573	94.4	47.4	24.4
Ocean City city & MCD (Cape May)	11,701	11,374	-2.8	11,520	88.4	1.3	1.4	1.6	7.2	14.5	55.9	29.5	5,659	62.8	22.9	49.0
Ocean Gate borough & MCD (Ocean)	2,016	2,031	0.7	2,072	91.8	3.8	0.0	0.0	4.4	20.5	66.0	13.5	818	67.7	43.6	23.1
Ocean Grove CDP	3,342	NA	NA	3,134	85.8	2.0	2.4	1.7	8.1	9.0	64.6	26.3	1,771	53.9	20.0	52.2
Oceanport borough & MCD (Monmouth)	5,832	5,838	0.1	5,834	90.2	2.6	2.2	1.8	3.1	24.0	60.0	16.1	2,093	85.7	29.6	47.2
Ogdensburg borough & MCD (Sussex)	2,386	2,310	-3.2	2,348	94.0	0.0	1.0	0.5	4.5	25.3	62.9	11.9	823	83.0	39.6	23.8
Old Bridge CDP	23,753	NA	NA	23,572	73.6	2.9	12.2	2.3	9.1	22.2	63.9	14.0	7,808	84.5	32.2	38.4
Old Bridge township (Middlesex)	65,377	67,010	2.5	66,272	65.9	5.9	15.6	1.9	10.7	20.8	66.0	13.1	24,374	69.2	32.9	37.2
Oldmans township (Salem)	1,773	1,849	4.3	1,917	88.6	4.7	0.4	2.6	3.7	22.1	62.5	15.4	705	90.4	42.7	24.7
Old Tappan borough & MCD (Bergen)	5,750	5,943	3.4	5,835	72.8	3.2	19.5	1.4	3.2	24.9	56.1	18.9	1,949	92.9	21.7	56.4
Olivet CDP	1,408	NA	NA	1,423	92.3	0.0	4.4	2.3	1.1	22.9	64.6	12.6	524	96.2	27.5	47.3
Oradell borough & MCD (Bergen)	7,978	8,161	2.3	8,080	84.0	0.6	8.8	2.6	3.9	26.8	56.4	16.8	2,628	90.2	13.4	68.5
Oxford CDP	1,090	NA	NA	1,082	95.9	1.7	0.0	0.0	2.4	17.4	63.8	18.8	482	85.3	71.2	11.0
Oxford township (Warren)	2,514	2,467	-1.9	2,438	91.3	3.2	0.0	0.0	5.4	22.5	65.1	12.3	998	86.4	51.2	30.8

1 May be of any race.

Table A. All Places — Population and Housing

STATE City, town, township, borough, or CDP (county if applicable)	2010 census total population	2014 estimated population	Percent change 2010–2014	ACS total population estimate 2010–2014	White alone, not Hispanic or Latino	Black alone, not Hispanic or Latino	Asian alone, not Hispanic or Latino	All other races or 2 or more races, not Hispanic or Latino	Hispanic or Latino[1]	Under 18 years old	Age 18 to 64 years old	Age 65 years and older	Total occupied housing units	Percent owner occupied	High school diploma or less	Bachelor's degree or more
	1	2	3	4	5	6	7	8	9	10	11	12	13	14	15	16
NEW JERSEY—Con.																
Palisades Park borough & MCD (Bergen)	19,622	20,471	4.3	20,066	19.4	2.3	54.6	2.8	20.9	14.1	73.3	12.5	7,412	31.2	43.9	37.3
Palmyra borough & MCD (Burlington)	7,398	7,333	-0.9	7,372	77.3	10.3	1.9	3.0	7.5	17.8	66.3	15.9	3,272	80.1	44.7	30.2
Panther Valley CDP	3,327	NA	NA	3,376	89.4	0.4	5.1	1.2	3.9	16.5	67.3	16.2	1,638	91.5	16.5	56.5
Paramus borough & MCD (Bergen)	26,342	26,832	1.9	26,612	62.8	1.7	25.5	1.7	8.3	19.7	57.4	23.0	8,435	87.9	24.5	54.5
Park Ridge borough & MCD (Bergen)	8,648	8,841	2.2	8,763	77.3	2.7	6.5	2.4	11.2	25.4	55.4	19.2	3,225	77.9	22.1	56.1
Parsippany-Troy Hills township (Morris)	53,207	53,679	0.9	53,583	53.7	3.4	31.2	3.3	8.5	19.9	65.2	14.9	19,888	64.2	24.1	57.7
Passaic city & MCD (Passaic)	69,781	71,509	2.5	70,651	16.7	7.5	2.8	1.4	71.7	32.8	59.3	7.9	20,044	24.1	68.3	15.2
Paterson city & MCD (Passaic)	146,199	146,753	0.4	146,341	8.4	28.6	3.7	0.8	58.4	27.3	63.4	9.4	43,462	27.3	64.2	11.1
Paulsboro borough & MCD (Gloucester)	6,097	5,992	-1.7	6,041	50.5	34.0	0.0	5.2	10.2	32.1	57.3	10.6	2,216	62.7	65.3	11.4
Peapack and Gladstone borough & MCD (Somerset)	2,566	2,594	1.1	2,580	82.9	4.3	1.2	0.2	11.4	23.2	61.7	15.3	939	76.9	12.8	71.4
Pedricktown CDP	524	NA	NA	537	96.5	0.0	0.0	2.2	1.3	26.7	59.4	14.2	211	76.8	45.0	13.3
Pemberton borough & MCD (Burlington)	1,409	1,386	-1.6	1,467	57.7	10.2	1.4	4.8	26.0	17.6	68.2	14.1	608	67.6	36.3	26.5
Pemberton township (Burlington)	27,912	27,822	-0.3	27,925	60.8	18.3	2.0	6.1	12.8	23.0	64.7	12.3	10,144	67.9	47.8	15.4
Pemberton Heights CDP	2,423	NA	NA	2,598	41.1	38.9	2.7	4.3	13.1	16.1	65.6	18.2	1,216	47.4	42.8	15.6
Pennington borough & MCD (Mercer)	2,585	2,584	0.0	2,588	89.8	1.6	3.5	0.9	4.2	23.2	55.9	20.8	1,038	81.0	14.7	71.4
Pennsauken township (Camden)	35,885	35,561	-0.9	35,757	36.8	25.9	6.1	2.4	28.8	22.1	64.4	13.5	12,259	77.7	48.2	21.3
Penns Grove borough & MCD (Salem)	5,147	5,007	-2.7	5,082	24.5	42.7	0.0	2.2	30.7	32.7	58.9	8.4	1,841	31.2	70.7	4.2
Pennsville CDP	11,888	NA	NA	11,864	91.6	1.6	1.6	1.6	3.5	20.5	61.2	18.2	4,881	74.2	54.4	18.1
Pennsville township (Salem)	13,409	13,005	-3.0	13,229	91.8	1.8	1.6	1.5	3.3	20.1	61.7	18.2	5,495	73.4	51.9	19.7
Pequannock township (Morris)	15,540	15,567	0.2	15,577	90.2	0.4	1.3	2.1	6.0	20.1	55.8	24.2	6,321	80.7	29.7	43.8
Perth Amboy city & MCD (Middlesex)	50,814	52,328	3.0	51,727	10.1	7.3	1.7	0.9	80.0	27.2	62.1	10.5	16,306	33.6	61.2	15.6
Phillipsburg town & MCD (Warren)	14,950	14,570	-2.5	14,717	74.5	9.7	2.4	1.7	11.6	22.8	62.5	14.7	6,101	53.6	61.4	14.4
Pilesgrove township (Salem)	4,016	3,967	-1.2	3,996	87.0	5.7	0.6	1.2	5.6	23.4	56.7	20.0	1,485	80.8	41.2	32.1
Pine Beach borough & MCD (Ocean)	2,127	2,165	1.8	2,239	95.2	0.1	1.5	0.5	2.7	22.5	59.9	17.6	818	93.2	33.3	36.8
Pine Hill borough & MCD (Camden)	10,233	10,464	2.3	10,383	60.7	25.7	3.6	2.4	7.6	24.7	64.9	10.3	3,968	63.2	42.2	18.4
Pine Lake Park CDP	8,707	NA	NA	9,295	76.9	6.5	5.2	1.7	9.7	25.9	63.2	11.0	2,995	91.5	48.0	19.9
Pine Ridge at Crestwood CDP	2,369	NA	NA	2,239	91.1	2.1	2.1	0.5	4.2	0.0	35.3	64.6	1,439	89.4	59.8	12.2
Pine Valley borough & MCD (Camden)	12	12	0.0	2	100.0	0.0	0.0	0.0	0.0	0.0	100.0	0.0	1	100.0	0.0	100.0
Piscataway township (Middlesex)	56,042	58,982	5.2	57,636	32.2	18.9	35.6	2.8	10.4	19.4	70.1	10.4	17,206	67.2	25.9	51.7
Pitman borough & MCD (Gloucester)	9,011	8,895	-1.3	8,959	94.4	1.0	1.3	2.6	0.8	22.8	60.5	16.7	3,492	73.3	39.0	36.9
Pittsgrove township (Salem)	9,393	9,169	-2.4	9,287	84.0	8.5	1.8	1.4	4.3	21.9	63.4	14.7	3,331	89.5	44.7	24.5
Plainfield city & MCD (Union)	49,808	50,955	2.3	50,423	8.9	41.5	1.8	8.9	38.9	23.9	66.0	10.2	14,518	48.5	53.6	20.1
Plainsboro township (Middlesex)	22,999	23,429	1.9	23,224	37.0	6.6	46.2	4.6	5.5	23.7	68.1	8.3	9,539	47.6	9.0	74.3
Plainsboro Center CDP	2,712	NA	NA	2,904	50.0	6.3	41.3	0.4	1.9	18.4	71.5	10.0	1,440	41.2	4.9	71.0
Pleasant Plains CDP	922	NA	NA	732	16.3	10.7	37.6	18.0	17.5	18.6	74.5	6.8	186	76.9	0.0	57.0
Pleasantville city & MCD (Atlantic)	20,249	20,467	1.1	20,436	17.2	37.1	2.8	2.8	40.1	26.4	61.7	11.8	6,645	55.9	57.1	12.2
Plumsted township (Ocean)	8,421	8,584	1.9	8,490	88.3	3.2	0.5	1.0	7.0	27.0	60.3	12.8	2,970	85.3	49.1	20.0
Pohatcong township (Warren)	3,339	3,259	-2.4	3,290	92.8	2.0	0.6	1.6	3.0	21.9	64.2	14.0	1,176	87.3	42.8	26.2
Point Pleasant borough & MCD (Ocean)	18,392	18,665	1.5	18,481	95.2	0.4	0.2	0.7	3.5	21.2	64.6	14.1	7,199	82.3	31.9	42.9
Point Pleasant Beach borough & MCD (Ocean)	4,665	4,640	-0.5	4,664	86.0	0.0	0.0	4.0	10.1	22.1	61.8	16.1	1,882	61.8	28.6	45.4
Pomona CDP	7,124	NA	NA	7,164	44.9	7.9	25.3	4.7	17.2	26.5	58.8	14.7	1,974	82.0	39.5	33.5
Pompton Lakes borough & MCD (Passaic)	11,097	11,166	0.6	11,162	77.7	0.0	6.8	0.9	14.6	22.5	62.8	14.7	4,151	78.3	40.0	40.2
Port Colden CDP	122	NA	NA	112	90.2	0.0	9.8	0.0	0.0	10.7	80.4	8.9	43	100.0	76.7	23.3
Port Monmouth CDP	3,818	NA	NA	3,915	86.4	0.3	0.5	0.2	12.6	22.9	67.4	9.7	1,387	74.5	37.8	22.1
Port Murray CDP	129	NA	NA	90	100.0	0.0	0.0	0.0	0.0	0.0	83.4	16.7	58	27.6	100.0	0.0
Port Norris CDP	1,377	NA	NA	1,574	63.0	30.3	1.0	5.2	0.4	29.8	58.3	11.8	510	90.0	57.3	4.5
Port Reading CDP	3,728	NA	NA	3,836	68.2	7.9	3.6	0.0	20.3	27.8	58.5	13.7	1,279	76.2	56.5	20.3
Port Republic city & MCD (Atlantic)	1,115	1,121	0.5	1,093	81.3	0.7	14.1	0.4	3.5	21.4	60.5	18.0	377	89.1	37.7	31.3
Presidential Lakes Estates CDP	2,365	NA	NA	2,306	76.3	12.0	1.9	2.9	7.0	20.3	64.2	15.4	774	98.4	37.7	23.8
Princeton & MCD (Mercer)	28,573	30,108	5.4	28,940	68.5	6.3	15.5	3.3	6.4	17.5	68.5	14.0	9,528	58.2	8.4	82.7
Princeton Junction CDP	2,465	NA	NA	2,444	66.7	0.1	18.2	0.7	14.3	24.1	59.3	16.6	910	72.2	12.0	71.3
Princeton Meadows CDP	13,834	NA	NA	13,631	33.4	9.0	46.0	6.6	5.0	24.1	71.2	4.7	5,785	37.2	11.0	72.2

1 May be of any race.

Table A. All Places — Population and Housing

STATE City, town, township, borough, or CDP (county if applicable)	2010 census total population	2014 estimated population	Percent change 2010–2014	ACS total population estimate 2010–2014	White alone, not Hispanic or Latino	Black alone, not Hispanic or Latino	Asian alone, not Hispanic or Latino	All other races or 2 or more races, not Hispanic or Latino	Hispanic or Latino[1]	Under 18 years old	Age 18 to 64 years old	Age 65 years and older	Total occupied housing units	Percent owner occupied	High school diploma or less	Bachelor's degree or more
	1	2	3	4	5	6	7	8	9	10	11	12	13	14	15	16
NEW JERSEY—Con.																
Prospect Park borough & MCD (Passaic)	5,865	5,931	1.1	5,915	20.0	21.7	3.2	0.6	54.4	26.2	66.4	7.5	1,759	47.6	56.1	14.4
Quinton CDP	588	NA	NA	606	95.7	1.8	2.5	0.0	0.0	18.4	61.8	19.8	246	78.5	64.6	13.8
Quinton township (Salem)	2,666	2,621	-1.7	2,655	83.0	9.9	0.6	5.7	0.8	20.8	59.5	19.7	994	81.5	64.9	14.8
Rahway city & MCD (Union)	27,346	28,528	4.3	27,994	36.1	30.6	3.8	3.7	25.8	22.0	65.5	12.6	10,577	58.8	43.5	29.0
Ramblewood CDP	5,907	NA	NA	5,999	84.2	3.9	7.7	0.5	3.8	21.7	60.2	18.3	2,286	70.3	23.2	54.6
Ramsey borough & MCD (Bergen)	14,473	14,800	2.3	14,650	85.7	0.1	7.7	0.3	6.1	24.9	59.3	15.6	5,342	87.7	16.3	65.7
Ramtown CDP	6,242	NA	NA	5,886	82.5	0.3	6.4	3.7	7.0	25.2	69.8	4.9	1,780	95.4	30.0	39.8
Randolph township (Morris)	25,688	25,964	1.1	25,877	74.7	3.0	11.1	1.8	9.3	26.2	63.2	10.5	9,233	73.2	15.6	67.2
Raritan township (Hunterdon)	22,177	22,061	-0.5	22,106	89.4	0.8	6.0	0.4	3.4	25.4	62.0	12.7	8,204	87.9	24.2	52.4
Raritan borough & MCD (Somerset)	6,881	8,098	17.7	7,318	59.6	3.4	13.4	3.9	19.7	25.9	60.4	13.6	2,695	64.0	42.4	33.2
Readington township (Hunterdon)	16,126	16,040	-0.5	16,093	90.5	0.7	3.3	1.0	4.5	23.0	61.6	15.3	5,981	88.4	21.6	54.7
Red Bank borough & MCD (Monmouth)	12,206	12,445	2.0	12,250	54.8	13.4	1.2	0.3	30.3	21.0	65.7	13.3	5,193	46.7	36.2	43.5
Richwood CDP	3,459	NA	NA	3,104	92.3	1.1	1.3	4.1	1.3	30.8	63.1	6.1	983	91.0	17.7	67.3
Ridgefield borough & MCD (Bergen)	11,032	11,289	2.3	11,191	38.6	0.9	34.8	2.1	23.6	18.8	66.8	14.5	4,005	53.6	40.6	40.8
Ridgefield Park village & MCD (Bergen)	12,729	12,996	2.1	12,875	44.0	2.7	12.0	2.6	38.8	23.5	64.7	11.8	4,639	56.0	38.0	37.5
Ridgewood village & MCD (Bergen)	24,958	25,496	2.2	25,270	72.9	2.1	15.3	2.6	7.1	30.6	56.9	12.6	8,262	78.9	9.1	79.0
Ringwood borough & MCD (Passaic)	12,228	12,377	1.2	12,320	90.0	0.8	2.7	2.2	4.3	25.8	62.0	12.1	3,746	95.4	26.5	42.7
Rio Grande CDP	2,670	NA	NA	2,353	86.6	1.1	0.0	2.5	9.8	13.4	66.5	20.2	1,086	86.3	44.9	21.3
Riverdale borough & MCD (Morris)	3,559	4,046	13.7	3,906	92.1	0.0	3.4	0.2	4.3	13.3	71.2	15.5	1,821	77.0	28.6	50.8
River Edge borough & MCD (Bergen)	11,340	11,579	2.1	11,483	64.7	1.1	22.0	2.6	9.6	23.9	60.8	15.3	4,009	74.1	22.1	61.5
Riverside township (Burlington)	8,079	8,019	-0.7	8,051	78.4	8.7	0.6	5.1	7.2	22.2	67.2	10.6	2,839	65.8	58.7	11.4
Riverton borough & MCD (Burlington)	2,779	2,758	-0.8	2,766	91.9	1.6	1.2	0.3	5.0	20.7	61.3	17.9	1,048	77.9	24.1	49.0
River Vale township (Bergen)	9,659	10,021	3.7	9,841	77.5	1.1	11.8	3.4	6.2	27.1	56.8	16.0	3,319	89.5	17.1	65.1
Robbinsville CDP	3,041	NA	NA	3,333	66.2	5.2	22.7	4.4	1.6	27.5	58.4	14.2	1,374	68.6	28.5	56.3
Robbinsville township (Mercer)	13,642	14,112	3.4	13,952	79.6	2.8	12.4	2.0	3.1	27.7	63.3	9.0	5,138	84.1	21.2	57.3
Robertsville CDP	11,297	NA	NA	11,055	84.4	0.4	8.3	0.5	6.4	23.9	61.3	14.8	3,663	93.0	21.0	55.8
Rochelle Park township (Bergen)	5,530	5,781	4.5	5,644	67.2	0.2	12.0	0.3	20.3	18.5	63.1	18.4	1,965	72.4	41.3	34.7
Rockaway borough & MCD (Morris)	6,438	6,483	0.7	6,480	70.9	6.8	7.3	0.2	14.8	25.5	62.4	12.1	2,587	66.2	36.8	37.3
Rockaway township (Morris)	24,161	24,441	1.2	24,353	73.2	2.5	8.5	2.9	12.9	23.3	61.7	14.9	8,809	85.0	24.9	49.9
Rockleigh borough & MCD (Bergen)	531	537	1.1	508	83.5	8.5	1.6	0.8	5.7	15.6	31.5	52.8	69	87.0	29.0	52.2
Rocky Hill borough & MCD (Somerset)	682	685	0.4	554	92.8	1.3	1.1	1.1	3.8	22.8	55.6	21.7	234	82.5	11.1	68.8
Roebling CDP	3,715	NA	NA	3,861	84.1	5.7	0.5	5.0	4.7	22.7	63.8	13.5	1,467	84.7	43.7	26.7
Roosevelt borough & MCD (Monmouth)	882	872	-1.1	744	82.3	1.7	5.8	3.6	6.6	28.1	57.5	14.2	260	83.1	21.5	50.0
Roseland borough & MCD (Essex)	5,815	5,826	0.2	5,835	80.4	0.7	7.2	1.8	9.9	23.9	54.7	21.5	2,404	82.1	25.8	58.3
Roselle borough & MCD (Union)	21,085	21,551	2.2	21,348	13.6	51.2	3.9	1.8	29.5	23.6	62.9	13.5	8,234	51.1	46.2	18.2
Roselle Park borough & MCD (Union)	13,297	13,595	2.2	13,465	51.7	7.7	8.5	2.9	29.3	24.1	65.1	10.8	5,043	62.3	39.5	28.1
Rosenhayn CDP	1,098	NA	NA	1,202	51.5	29.3	0.9	0.8	17.5	14.4	71.7	14.1	396	87.6	67.4	12.4
Ross Corner CDP	13	NA	NA	0	0.0	0.0	0.0	0.0	0.0	0.0	0.0	0.0	0	0.0	diploma	degree
Rossmoor CDP	2,666	NA	NA	2,814	84.3	6.4	2.8	0.5	6.1	0.0	21.2	78.7	2,046	88.5	41.7	30.3
Roxbury township (Morris)	23,324	23,524	0.9	23,485	80.0	2.8	5.4	1.6	10.3	23.9	62.1	14.2	7,974	88.0	28.7	46.0
Rumson borough & MCD (Monmouth)	7,122	6,978	-2.0	7,045	94.7	0.5	0.9	0.7	3.2	30.6	58.3	11.1	2,358	89.6	10.9	73.1
Runnemede borough & MCD (Camden)	8,468	8,376	-1.1	8,435	77.4	6.9	2.5	3.6	9.6	22.6	63.4	14.0	3,140	73.0	52.0	17.1
Rutherford borough & MCD (Bergen)	18,061	18,464	2.2	18,297	66.3	3.3	13.9	1.5	15.0	20.8	67.3	11.8	6,856	60.5	21.9	52.9
Saddle Brook township (Bergen)	13,659	13,984	2.4	13,841	79.4	0.7	6.2	0.8	13.0	18.4	64.2	17.4	5,184	66.4	36.9	32.2
Saddle River borough & MCD (Bergen)	3,152	3,210	1.8	3,176	73.3	2.9	8.2	0.0	15.6	22.9	53.7	23.6	1,047	78.0	26.1	59.2
Salem city & MCD (Salem)	5,146	4,971	-3.4	5,045	33.1	53.3	0.2	2.3	11.1	30.1	58.6	11.4	1,927	33.7	66.5	11.4
Sandyston township (Sussex)	1,073	1,914	-3.0	1,903	87.8	3.1	3.4	1.9	3.8	19.0	65.5	15.3	768	89.6	45.2	31.0
Sayreville borough & MCD (Middlesex)	42,702	45,262	6.0	43,962	56.4	11.7	18.0	1.1	12.7	21.7	64.3	13.9	15,811	68.4	35.9	34.7
Scotch Plains township (Union)	23,510	24,086	2.5	23,845	71.0	12.2	9.3	0.8	6.8	24.0	61.2	14.8	8,475	78.6	20.7	54.5
Sea Bright borough & MCD (Monmouth)	1,412	1,348	-4.5	1,349	85.0	0.3	0.2	1.7	12.8	12.7	73.5	13.9	703	60.9	23.9	44.7
Seabrook Farms CDP	1,484	NA	NA	995	23.6	44.9	2.2	8.6	20.6	35.1	52.7	12.2	394	32.2	67.5	12.2
Sea Girt borough & MCD (Monmouth)	1,828	1,814	-0.8	1,844	98.3	0.1	0.4	0.0	1.2	20.0	48.6	31.6	756	90.9	16.9	67.7

1 May be of any race.

Table A. All Places — **Population and Housing**

STATE City, town, township, borough, or CDP (county if applicable)	2010 census total population	2014 estimated population	Percent change 2010–2014	ACS total population estimate 2010–2014	White alone, not Hispanic or Latino	Black alone, not Hispanic or Latino	Asian alone, not Hispanic or Latino	All other races or 2 or more races, not Hispanic or Latino	Hispanic or Latino[1]	Under 18 years old	Age 18 to 64 years old	Age 65 years and older	Total occupied housing units	Percent owner occupied	High school diploma or less	Bachelor's degree or more
	1	2	3	4	5	6	7	8	9	10	11	12	13	14	15	16
NEW JERSEY—Con.																
Sea Isle City city & MCD (Cape May)	2,114	2,083	-1.5	1,824	98.0	0.1	0.0	1.0	0.9	6.4	49.4	44.1	964	76.7	32.4	40.7
Seaside Heights borough & MCD (Ocean)	2,887	2,914	0.9	2,899	61.8	1.0	1.9	2.2	33.1	19.6	68.0	12.3	1,178	26.0	72.2	11.5
Seaside Park borough & MCD (Ocean)............	1,579	1,579	0.0	1,406	97.3	1.5	0.0	0.9	0.3	9.0	57.2	33.9	798	69.7	31.3	43.5
Secaucus town & MCD (Hudson)	16,260	18,416	13.3	17,614	48.3	4.9	24.1	4.6	18.0	19.4	64.1	16.5	6,546	60.1	34.9	46.3
Sewaren CDP	2,756	NA	NA	2,341	64.7	14.7	5.0	0.5	15.2	14.2	72.8	13.3	837	85.5	45.2	21.5
Shamong township (Burlington)	6,461	6,432	-0.4	6,461	94.8	0.3	1.7	0.4	2.8	23.8	63.2	13.0	2,234	96.6	30.8	42.6
Shark River Hills CDP	3,697	NA	NA	3,770	94.6	1.4	0.0	2.5	1.5	15.7	67.5	16.7	1,525	95.0	23.7	44.1
Shiloh borough & MCD (Cumberland)	516	509	-1.4	579	77.4	0.0	1.4	6.7	14.5	18.6	67.5	13.8	217	77.0	55.3	21.2
Ship Bottom borough & MCD (Ocean)............	1,153	1,148	-0.4	1,025	94.4	1.3	1.0	0.8	2.5	9.7	58.5	32.0	496	86.1	25.6	44.2
Short Hills CDP	13,165	NA	NA	12,729	79.4	0.2	15.3	2.1	3.1	34.5	52.7	13.0	3,975	92.4	4.2	92.5
Shrewsbury borough & MCD (Monmouth)	3,809	4,125	8.3	3,899	92.5	0.1	0.5	0.9	6.1	28.1	55.6	16.3	1,353	95.9	18.9	63.4
Shrewsbury township (Monmouth).................	1,141	1,119	-1.9	1,130	58.0	11.9	3.4	2.0	24.7	24.5	63.2	12.2	532	51.1	36.3	22.2
Silver Lake CDP (Essex) .	4,243	NA	NA	3,594	34.9	9.2	8.3	0.4	47.2	20.1	69.3	10.7	1,448	26.9	56.0	14.7
Silver Lake CDP (Warren)	368	NA	NA	300	95.7	0.0	2.7	0.0	1.7	26.7	60.0	13.3	115	87.0	26.1	25.2
Silver Ridge CDP	1,133	NA	NA	1,447	94.1	2.6	0.0	0.6	2.8	0.5	31.9	67.7	916	94.0	54.8	21.8
Singac CDP	3,618	NA	NA	4,928	59.6	0.3	9.9	9.5	20.7	22.4	63.4	14.2	1,776	61.0	44.5	37.7
Six Mile Run CDP...........	3,184	NA	NA	3,106	26.3	30.6	26.9	5.0	11.2	18.5	70.9	10.8	1,100	73.2	21.5	59.6
Skillman CDP	242	NA	NA	115	72.2	0.0	0.0	27.8	0.0	16.5	77.5	6.1	43	100.0	16.3	53.5
Smithville CDP	7,242	NA	NA	6,950	71.6	11.8	6.3	2.3	8.0	17.5	54.5	28.0	2,919	77.0	28.4	31.4
Society Hill CDP	3,829	NA	NA	3,555	28.7	11.3	52.7	0.9	6.4	20.2	69.4	10.4	1,136	81.6	11.8	72.7
Somerdale borough & MCD (Camden)............	5,151	5,339	3.6	5,246	66.3	20.5	4.1	3.0	6.1	18.5	66.0	15.5	2,135	69.6	45.7	20.0
Somerset CDP	22,083	NA	NA	24,375	40.2	27.1	20.8	2.9	9.0	20.2	64.7	15.2	8,846	74.9	19.7	58.7
Somers Point city & MCD (Atlantic)...................	10,795	10,756	-0.4	10,783	69.7	14.8	3.9	1.0	10.7	22.8	62.0	15.3	4,601	55.6	42.4	24.1
Somerville borough & MCD (Somerset)	12,098	12,153	0.5	12,175	58.0	10.2	9.8	1.9	20.1	22.3	64.6	13.1	4,590	57.0	38.5	36.9
South Amboy city & MCD (Middlesex)	8,633	8,853	2.5	8,749	77.1	3.3	2.7	1.3	15.7	20.8	64.9	14.3	3,732	61.6	50.8	22.1
Southampton township (Burlington)	10,464	10,362	-1.0	10,420	92.6	3.2	0.6	1.2	2.5	14.0	53.3	32.8	4,620	92.9	50.4	24.8
South Bound Brook borough & MCD (Somerset)	4,563	4,587	0.5	4,585	46.0	8.0	5.6	8.5	31.9	21.0	69.5	9.6	1,575	64.6	39.8	24.6
South Brunswick township (Middlesex)	43,417	45,163	4.0	44,355	46.1	7.4	39.7	2.0	4.9	25.9	63.1	11.1	15,230	76.9	18.3	63.3
South Hackensack township (Bergen)........	2,378	2,470	3.9	2,652	52.1	6.9	4.0	2.8	34.2	20.6	64.2	15.1	973	48.9	58.4	20.8
South Harrison township (Gloucester)	3,162	3,226	2.0	3,195	82.4	8.6	0.2	2.6	6.1	30.0	59.9	10.1	1,005	93.6	27.0	49.1
South Orange Village township (Essex)..........	16,198	16,362	1.0	16,290	60.2	25.5	6.0	2.6	5.8	22.1	66.9	10.9	5,233	69.4	13.9	70.6
South Plainfield borough & MCD (Middlesex)	23,385	23,960	2.5	23,686	56.8	11.0	15.4	2.5	14.3	20.8	64.6	14.7	8,035	81.5	37.5	39.7
South River borough & MCD (Middlesex)	16,008	16,334	2.0	16,177	59.7	9.3	5.1	1.8	24.1	23.9	64.1	12.0	5,366	67.9	48.9	23.4
South Toms River borough & MCD (Ocean).......................	3,684	3,762	2.1	3,722	52.9	19.7	0.0	4.8	22.6	33.1	59.8	7.1	993	75.9	61.4	14.1
Sparta township (Sussex)	19,723	19,333	-2.0	19,547	88.3	2.2	2.7	1.6	5.1	28.5	60.8	10.7	6,498	89.9	17.5	60.1
Spotswood borough & MCD (Middlesex)	8,257	8,447	2.3	8,359	88.9	1.7	2.1	1.1	6.2	20.0	62.2	17.8	3,217	85.8	49.6	25.0
Springdale CDP..............	14,518	NA	NA	14,402	79.1	3.5	13.7	1.2	2.5	22.7	57.1	20.2	5,228	90.6	15.3	70.5
Springfield township (Burlington)	3,414	3,387	-0.8	3,412	84.5	1.9	1.9	2.8	8.8	22.5	65.5	12.2	1,174	92.4	36.8	33.3
Springfield township (Union)	15,817	17,193	8.7	16,729	76.3	6.2	8.5	1.0	8.1	18.4	61.7	19.6	7,045	64.6	23.5	59.3
Spring Lake borough & MCD (Monmouth)	2,993	2,992	0.0	2,999	95.3	0.6	0.7	0.5	3.0	19.9	46.5	33.4	1,194	83.0	18.8	67.5
Spring Lake Heights borough & MCD (Monmouth).................	4,713	4,664	-1.0	4,691	93.7	1.9	0.0	0.8	3.6	14.2	61.4	24.2	2,332	53.7	16.5	65.6
Stafford township (Ocean)	26,535	26,809	1.0	26,796	89.4	0.4	0.9	1.1	8.2	21.0	59.9	19.0	10,035	87.6	43.6	29.6
Stanhope borough & MCD (Sussex)...................	3,610	3,494	-3.2	3,543	84.2	1.1	3.0	4.7	7.1	21.8	65.5	12.7	1,404	85.8	30.4	35.4
Stewartsville CDP...........	349	NA	NA	173	80.9	13.3	0.0	0.0	5.8	16.7	62.4	20.8	75	76.0	88.0	0.0
Stillwater township (Sussex)	4,099	3,975	-3.0	4,036	95.2	0.0	1.9	1.4	1.5	18.6	71.4	10.0	1,678	88.5	35.2	22.7
Stockton borough & MCD (Hunterdon)	538	529	-1.7	516	96.5	0.4	0.8	0.8	1.6	19.5	64.7	15.9	198	70.7	14.6	57.1
Stone Harbor borough & MCD (Cape May)	866	844	-2.5	775	98.3	1.2	0.5	0.0	0.0	9.2	50.2	40.6	423	81.8	22.7	57.2
Stow Creek township (Cumberland)...............	1,431	1,430	-0.1	1,373	90.7	1.5	0.6	4.9	2.3	16.7	63.1	20.2	563	82.9	53.8	15.8
Stratford borough & MCD (Camden)...................	7,040	6,944	-1.4	6,997	79.0	10.8	4.8	1.7	3.8	21.3	64.0	14.6	2,627	76.9	40.2	26.6
Strathmere CDP	158	NA	NA	106	100.0	0.0	0.0	0.0	0.0	0.0	84.9	15.1	54	100.0	14.8	85.2
Strathmore CDP	7,258	NA	NA	6,975	80.1	5.2	7.0	1.3	6.4	22.9	61.6	15.5	2,498	90.0	17.9	54.4
Succasunna CDP	9,152	NA	NA	9,047	86.4	2.1	3.4	1.1	7.1	23.3	64.5	12.3	2,909	97.5	18.6	56.2
Summit city & MCD (Union)	21,457	22,071	2.9	21,826	71.9	4.0	8.6	2.8	12.7	28.1	59.9	12.0	7,804	71.2	14.4	73.6

1 May be of any race.

Table A. All Places — **Population and Housing**

	Population				Race and Hispanic or Latino origin (percent), 2010–2014					Age (percent), 2010–2014			Households, 2010–2014			
STATE City, town, township, borough, or CDP (county if applicable)	2010 census total population	2014 estimated population	Percent change 2010–2014	ACS total population estimate 2010–2014	White alone, not Hispanic or Latino	Black alone, not Hispanic or Latino	Asian alone, not Hispanic or Latino	All other races or 2 or more races, not Hispanic or Latino	Hispanic or Latino[1]	Under 18 years old	Age 18 to 64 years old	Age 65 years and older	Total occupied housing units	Percent owner occupied	High school diploma or less	Bachelor's degree or more
	1	2	3	4	5	6	7	8	9	10	11	12	13	14	15	16
NEW JERSEY—Con.																
Surf City borough & MCD (Ocean)	1,205	1,216	0.9	1,148	97.6	0.0	0.5	0.0	1.8	5.0	49.0	46.0	612	81.7	30.6	51.1
Sussex borough & MCD (Sussex)	2,130	2,078	-2.4	2,070	84.2	1.0	6.5	0.0	8.4	23.9	62.5	13.6	834	42.6	54.9	21.2
Swedesboro borough & MCD (Gloucester)	2,584	2,623	1.5	2,627	66.2	15.9	1.3	2.7	13.9	27.0	61.1	11.6	944	71.2	38.2	24.3
Tabernacle township (Burlington)	6,978	6,954	-0.3	6,983	89.2	1.0	0.4	1.1	8.2	24.2	62.3	13.3	2,348	92.6	35.1	31.7
Tavistock borough & MCD (Camden)	5	5	0.0	9	77.8	0.0	22.2	0.0	0.0	22.2	33.3	44.4	3	66.7	0.0	66.7
Teaneck township (Bergen)	39,796	40,587	2.0	40,261	44.4	27.3	7.3	2.4	18.7	23.9	60.6	15.5	13,278	76.9	22.5	60.4
Tenafly borough & MCD (Bergen)	14,488	14,816	2.3	14,672	61.5	0.8	27.7	2.7	7.3	31.4	54.9	13.5	4,748	74.8	13.6	74.8
Ten Mile Run CDP	1,959	NA	NA	1,774	30.8	5.4	49.4	6.7	7.7	19.2	71.7	9.1	671	88.7	9.2	83.3
Teterboro borough & MCD (Bergen)	67	71	6.0	56	55.4	0.0	0.0	5.4	39.3	17.8	67.9	14.3	29	3.4	48.3	31.0
Tewksbury township (Hunterdon)	5,993	5,925	-1.1	5,942	89.0	0.8	3.9	1.0	5.3	21.1	56.9	22.0	2,172	93.8	13.2	65.8
Tinton Falls CDP	17,892	17,898	0.0	17,933	77.8	7.8	3.3	4.1	7.0	18.5	56.1	25.4	7,984	74.2	26.5	44.4
Tinton Falls borough & MCD (Monmouth)																
Toms River CDP	88,791	NA	NA	89,459	83.6	2.2	4.4	1.3	8.5	21.0	61.6	17.4	33,475	81.1	40.6	31.2
Toms River township (Ocean)	91,238	91,250	0.0	91,664	84.0	2.1	4.3	1.3	8.3	20.7	61.2	18.2	34,825	81.2	40.4	31.7
Totowa borough & MCD (Passaic)	10,804	10,937	1.2	10,872	73.2	3.1	5.0	1.8	16.9	17.8	62.5	19.8	3,457	79.8	42.5	38.9
Trenton city & MCD (Mercer)	84,910	84,034	-1.0	84,459	13.8	49.4	1.1	1.8	34.0	25.5	65.8	8.7	27,998	38.0	62.1	12.6
Tuckerton borough & MCD (Ocean)	3,347	3,396	1.5	3,370	92.2	1.0	2.3	0.2	4.4	21.2	61.3	17.7	1,311	69.0	51.6	24.9
Turnersville CDP	3,742	NA	NA	3,506	96.3	0.9	1.2	0.5	1.1	19.6	66.1	14.2	1,186	97.0	23.9	43.0
Twin Rivers CDP	7,443	NA	NA	7,402	47.3	7.0	10.2	2.7	32.7	20.3	68.6	11.1	2,336	80.1	28.3	50.5
Union township (Hunterdon)	5,908	5,765	-2.4	5,837	78.6	10.2	2.8	1.0	7.4	23.2	64.3	12.5	1,831	88.8	15.9	62.0
Union township (Union)	56,642	57,832	2.1	57,285	41.7	28.5	9.5	2.9	17.4	20.1	65.1	14.8	20,334	73.4	38.5	33.4
Union Beach borough & MCD (Monmouth)	6,245	5,700	-8.7	6,040	81.7	4.7	0.1	1.6	11.8	19.4	70.3	10.3	1,991	84.6	49.5	19.0
Union City city & MCD (Hudson)	66,439	68,668	3.4	68,001	10.3	1.2	2.9	0.5	85.0	23.1	66.7	10.1	22,786	18.7	57.5	20.7
Upper township (Cape May)	12,373	12,113	-2.1	12,231	93.7	1.1	0.4	2.0	2.8	22.5	61.0	16.6	4,611	92.2	35.0	36.5
Upper Deerfield township (Cumberland)	7,660	7,618	-0.5	7,648	69.7	14.4	7.1	1.5	7.3	23.6	56.3	19.9	2,875	77.1	42.5	27.0
Upper Freehold township (Monmouth)	6,902	6,889	-0.2	6,898	91.6	1.1	4.3	1.1	1.9	28.2	57.4	14.5	2,309	96.9	20.5	56.4
Upper Montclair CDP	11,565	NA	NA	11,637	84.3	3.9	3.7	2.6	5.5	30.4	58.3	11.3	4,125	82.5	4.2	88.3
Upper Pittsgrove township (Salem)	3,505	3,452	-1.5	3,494	91.0	2.3	1.9	0.7	4.1	20.1	62.9	16.9	1,176	81.6	50.2	28.3
Upper Pohatcong CDP	1,781	NA	NA	1,588	87.7	4.2	0.4	2.2	5.5	23.2	58.2	18.6	563	89.0	55.2	15.1
Upper Saddle River borough & MCD (Bergen)	8,208	8,356	1.8	8,304	78.1	1.7	14.6	1.8	3.7	30.5	57.8	11.6	2,561	90.5	10.1	71.4
Upper Stewartsville CDP	212	NA	NA	210	100.0	0.0	0.0	0.0	0.0	6.2	77.2	16.7	89	55.1	50.6	4.5
Ventnor City city & MCD (Atlantic)	10,650	10,597	-0.5	10,632	64.4	1.4	12.8	1.7	19.7	16.4	62.8	20.8	4,170	58.5	39.0	30.0
Vernon township (Sussex)	23,542	22,799	-3.2	23,168	86.1	1.6	1.0	1.7	9.5	22.7	67.3	10.1	8,209	84.5	34.7	30.1
Vernon Center CDP	1,713	NA	NA	2,011	68.4	2.2	0.0	1.3	28.1	20.1	69.3	10.5	930	47.1	33.4	25.7
Vernon Valley CDP	1,626	NA	NA	1,416	87.6	0.8	1.2	2.0	8.3	19.4	63.6	17.1	520	90.0	51.7	9.6
Verona township (Essex)	13,338	13,701	2.7	13,508	85.9	1.2	3.9	1.8	7.1	21.8	58.2	19.9	5,169	77.2	22.6	57.6
Victory Gardens borough & MCD (Morris)	1,520	1,531	0.7	1,646	15.7	17.3	3.8	8.5	54.7	27.6	63.0	9.2	560	34.8	66.8	12.1
Victory Lakes CDP	2,111	NA	NA	1,833	91.3	1.4	0.0	1.5	5.9	18.8	63.9	17.2	701	98.1	57.1	17.5
Vienna CDP	981	NA	NA	754	91.1	0.0	7.2	0.0	1.7	20.8	67.4	11.8	315	87.9	15.6	32.4
Villas CDP	9,483	NA	NA	9,199	90.7	1.9	0.4	1.3	5.7	22.2	61.8	16.0	3,899	73.2	60.3	13.4
Vineland city & MCD (Cumberland)	60,724	61,171	0.7	60,985	47.2	12.1	1.1	2.4	37.2	24.9	60.4	14.6	20,966	66.9	56.7	17.3
Vista Center CDP	2,095	NA	NA	2,127	84.4	3.4	0.0	1.2	11.0	6.9	49.8	43.3	879	97.6	22.4	57.2
Voorhees township (Camden)	29,316	29,023	-1.0	29,227	67.4	9.4	16.9	2.8	3.7	20.8	61.0	18.1	11,077	66.0	25.1	52.1
Voorhees CDP	976	NA	NA	775	9.4	71.0	17.4	0.0	2.2	31.8	63.8	4.5	258	54.7	46.1	38.0
Waldwick borough & MCD (Bergen)	9,638	9,947	3.2	9,808	82.7	2.1	6.0	1.1	8.0	24.6	60.7	14.7	3,419	86.1	23.0	50.9
Wall township (Monmouth)	26,164	26,032	-0.5	26,091	93.2	2.5	1.5	0.7	2.1	22.2	59.4	18.3	10,124	79.7	24.4	52.4
Wallington borough & MCD (Bergen)	11,335	11,626	2.6	11,487	76.1	2.9	5.7	2.3	13.1	18.4	69.2	12.4	4,589	38.4	50.1	24.8
Walpack township (Sussex)	16	15	-6.3	9	100.0	0.0	0.0	0.0	0.0	0.0	0.0	100.0	7	100.0	57.1	0.0
Wanamassa CDP	4,532	NA	NA	4,477	85.1	2.3	5.7	1.1	5.7	25.9	61.9	12.1	1,654	80.3	31.8	44.6
Wanaque borough & MCD (Passaic)	11,115	11,447	3.0	11,243	79.3	1.6	4.5	3.3	11.3	15.1	60.3	24.6	4,156	83.2	37.2	34.9
Wantage township (Sussex)	11,358	11,154	-1.8	11,244	90.3	1.3	0.9	2.8	4.7	23.9	62.1	13.9	4,083	88.6	36.5	27.5
Waretown CDP	1,569	NA	NA	1,421	94.6	0.0	0.0	2.0	3.4	15.1	57.1	27.7	630	97.5	53.5	20.2
Warren township (Somerset)	15,311	15,948	4.2	15,729	72.5	0.9	16.0	1.3	9.3	26.5	58.3	15.2	4,999	91.6	19.4	64.7
Washington township (Bergen)	9,102	9,308	2.3	9,220	87.3	0.4	4.3	0.7	7.3	21.1	58.0	20.9	3,241	92.6	24.6	52.4
Washington township (Burlington)	687	673	-2.0	827	81.7	0.8	0.5	0.5	16.4	16.5	68.6	14.9	284	78.9	53.9	24.6

1 May be of any race.

Table A.   All Places — **Population and Housing**

STATE City, town, township, borough, or CDP (county if applicable)	2010 census total population	2014 estimated population	Percent change 2010–2014	ACS total population estimate 2010–2014	White alone, not Hispanic or Latino	Black alone, not Hispanic or Latino	Asian alone, not Hispanic or Latino	All other races or 2 or more races, not Hispanic or Latino	Hispanic or Latino[1]	Under 18 years old	Age 18 to 64 years old	Age 65 years and older	Total occupied housing units	Percent owner occupied	High school diploma or less	Bachelor's degree or more
	1	2	3	4	5	6	7	8	9	10	11	12	13	14	15	16
NEW JERSEY—Con.																
Washington township (Gloucester)	48,547	47,841	-1.5	48,216	84.5	5.6	3.5	1.4	5.0	22.4	63.4	14.3	17,133	82.7	34.4	32.8
Washington township (Morris)	18,537	18,706	0.9	18,680	87.2	2.7	3.6	1.3	5.1	25.0	62.8	12.2	6,509	88.7	18.4	57.7
Washington borough & MCD (Warren)	6,461	6,466	0.1	6,439	79.3	3.7	2.5	0.9	13.6	26.4	65.7	7.9	2,521	51.4	49.6	20.9
Washington township (Warren)	6,651	6,482	-2.5	6,547	83.6	10.6	0.9	0.0	4.9	20.1	63.0	17.0	2,428	96.1	32.9	44.9
Watchung borough & MCD (Somerset)	5,801	5,863	1.1	5,855	75.9	1.8	13.9	1.2	7.2	20.1	57.8	22.2	2,085	85.8	17.8	64.0
Waterford township (Camden)	10,649	10,732	0.8	10,683	87.5	2.6	0.2	4.2	5.5	23.2	64.9	11.9	3,564	87.0	44.8	25.6
Wayne township (Passaic)	54,709	55,049	0.6	55,003	79.1	2.0	9.0	0.9	9.0	19.8	63.1	17.0	18,247	80.5	27.6	54.3
Weehawken township (Hudson)	12,554	13,870	10.5	13,113	44.5	4.9	8.6	3.1	38.9	14.6	72.6	12.6	5,398	34.7	25.3	55.0
Wenonah borough & MCD (Gloucester)	2,278	2,250	-1.2	2,115	92.8	0.8	2.1	3.3	1.1	21.9	63.3	14.8	763	86.9	22.5	53.1
Westampton township (Burlington)	8,813	8,741	-0.8	8,792	57.7	21.6	3.8	5.4	11.5	24.1	63.6	12.1	3,062	88.3	17.5	48.2
West Amwell township (Hunterdon)	2,845	2,800	-1.6	2,815	80.2	11.0	2.5	1.3	4.9	15.9	70.7	13.3	898	89.3	23.6	54.9
West Belmar CDP	2,493	NA	NA	2,517	87.4	0.6	2.5	2.2	7.3	18.8	69.3	12.1	1,049	72.7	35.7	41.5
West Caldwell township (Essex)	10,794	11,030	2.2	10,903	86.6	0.4	7.5	0.3	5.2	21.8	57.2	21.1	3,858	85.3	21.9	54.4
West Cape May borough & MCD (Cape May)......	1,024	1,015	-0.9	855	73.9	9.7	4.1	1.6	10.6	11.9	57.0	31.0	420	76.9	35.5	36.0
West Deptford township (Gloucester)	21,677	21,382	-1.4	21,537	85.9	7.1	2.2	1.3	3.5	20.0	63.3	16.8	9,004	70.6	40.7	30.9
Westfield town & MCD (Union)	30,316	30,890	1.9	30,647	82.2	3.4	5.6	1.7	7.0	28.4	58.6	13.0	10,327	79.9	14.2	70.0
West Freehold CDP	13,613	NA	NA	13,922	81.3	2.1	6.5	1.2	8.9	23.1	61.0	15.8	5,237	89.1	22.2	51.4
West Long Branch borough & MCD (Monmouth)	8,097	8,352	3.1	8,391	89.9	1.3	2.3	0.9	5.6	17.8	65.9	16.2	2,674	79.7	29.1	42.4
West Milford township (Passaic)	26,249	26,632	1.5	26,492	89.7	0.4	0.9	1.3	7.6	21.2	64.9	13.8	9,358	87.3	38.9	34.8
West New York town & MCD (Hudson)	49,708	52,597	5.8	51,511	13.8	1.7	4.8	1.2	78.5	20.9	67.2	11.9	19,034	20.3	52.4	28.2
Weston CDP	1,235	NA	NA	1,655	78.7	8.4	7.9	5.1	0.0	3.2	37.8	59.0	851	93.3	31.5	46.4
West Orange township (Essex)	46,239	46,995	1.6	46,703	46.6	25.7	6.9	1.9	19.0	22.8	61.2	16.0	16,244	68.4	27.7	53.2
Westville borough & MCD (Gloucester)	4,288	4,224	-1.5	4,263	87.3	1.2	4.0	0.9	6.6	20.6	66.9	12.6	1,761	71.5	52.9	19.2
West Wildwood borough & MCD (Cape May)......	603	579	-4.0	522	97.7	1.1	0.0	0.0	1.1	7.2	55.6	37.2	264	72.7	54.2	12.1
West Windsor township (Mercer)	27,165	28,465	4.8	28,108	46.3	2.4	41.7	3.5	6.0	28.2	60.4	11.5	9,664	74.9	7.2	81.7
Westwood borough & MCD (Bergen)	10,908	11,149	2.2	11,056	74.1	7.1	5.2	0.6	13.0	22.6	59.6	17.6	4,230	64.7	31.7	49.1
Weymouth township (Atlantic)	2,715	2,711	-0.1	2,715	89.2	3.0	2.0	1.1	4.7	16.4	53.8	29.7	1,171	91.1	54.7	20.8
Wharton borough & MCD (Morris)	6,537	6,612	1.1	6,586	42.8	2.5	3.1	5.9	45.7	22.8	66.2	11.1	2,261	59.9	54.1	25.3
White township (Warren) .	4,882	4,769	-2.3	4,815	90.9	2.7	0.3	1.1	5.1	11.7	52.7	35.6	2,258	79.7	52.2	14.3
White Horse CDP	9,494	NA	NA	8,422	80.6	4.1	4.7	0.1	10.5	16.8	62.4	20.7	3,721	84.0	43.2	24.9
White House Station CDP	2,089	NA	NA	1,831	90.1	0.0	0.8	0.0	9.1	16.7	61.9	21.5	909	77.3	23.3	49.3
White Meadow Lake CDP	8,836	NA	NA	8,734	74.5	1.6	9.6	1.9	12.3	25.3	62.7	12.0	2,918	96.6	18.2	57.7
Whitesboro CDP	0	NA	NA	2,070	41.5	47.4	0.7	0.0	10.3	22.1	53.6	24.4	832	98.9	70.1	22.1
Whittingham CDP	2,476	NA	NA	2,423	96.9	0.4	0.0	0.7	2.0	3.2	16.7	79.9	1,393	97.8	27.0	38.9
Wildwood city & MCD (Cape May)	5,325	5,185	-2.6	5,255	60.5	10.6	1.5	0.4	27.0	20.2	64.2	15.7	2,396	44.1	61.6	16.1
Wildwood Crest borough & MCD (Cape May)......	3,270	3,198	-2.2	3,225	94.4	0.1	0.6	1.0	4.0	15.5	49.8	34.6	1,511	77.2	33.1	34.9
Williamstown CDP	15,567	NA	NA	15,425	78.0	11.6	1.8	1.7	6.9	24.9	59.4	15.9	5,676	73.5	50.5	22.2
Willingboro township (Burlington)	31,625	31,804	0.6	31,735	12.8	70.4	2.3	4.6	9.8	21.9	61.5	16.6	10,466	84.5	36.9	25.9
Winfield township (Union)	1,471	1,502	2.1	1,473	88.3	2.8	0.0	2.0	6.9	16.5	68.5	15.1	688	23.3	56.4	15.0
Winslow township (Camden)	39,499	38,895	-1.5	39,207	51.3	32.8	3.0	3.4	9.4	25.7	62.2	12.1	13,820	78.7	36.8	28.2
Woodbine borough & MCD (Cape May)	2,472	2,439	-1.3	2,605	43.8	28.5	0.0	2.0	25.6	21.7	68.4	10.0	778	53.3	62.1	9.3
Woodbridge CDP	19,265	NA	NA	20,434	46.0	8.6	22.8	2.3	20.3	24.2	65.5	10.3	7,278	58.1	32.1	43.6
Woodbridge township (Middlesex)	99,580	100,824	1.2	100,344	47.3	11.3	22.6	2.3	16.5	21.0	66.4	12.5	33,557	67.3	38.6	37.4
Woodbury city & MCD (Gloucester)	10,174	10,016	-1.6	10,098	63.4	22.9	0.8	2.8	10.2	21.2	65.4	13.2	3,918	61.9	38.6	27.9
Woodbury Heights borough & MCD (Gloucester)	3,055	3,008	-1.5	3,028	90.6	2.6	1.0	1.9	3.9	17.9	66.6	15.7	1,103	92.0	39.6	26.4
Woodcliff Lake borough & MCD (Bergen)	5,723	5,870	2.6	5,785	87.1	0.1	7.2	1.4	4.1	25.1	57.8	17.1	2,077	89.1	13.0	74.0
Woodland township (Burlington)	1,788	1,795	0.4	1,386	94.2	1.2	0.2	0.9	3.5	20.6	64.5	15.0	505	85.1	44.6	20.4
Woodland Park borough & MCD (Passaic).........	11,819	12,403	4.9	12,129	67.6	1.9	5.1	1.1	24.3	20.6	61.0	18.4	4,355	61.1	44.2	33.8
Woodlynne borough & MCD (Camden)...........	2,978	2,938	-1.3	2,972	13.8	23.0	13.6	0.6	49.0	27.9	66.3	5.8	886	54.0	59.3	11.3
Wood-Ridge borough & MCD (Bergen)..............	7,626	8,450	10.8	8,249	75.8	1.0	12.1	1.8	9.3	18.9	66.9	14.3	3,019	78.2	29.8	38.8
Woodstown borough & MCD (Salem)	3,505	3,454	-1.5	3,497	81.1	13.6	0.1	0.7	4.4	23.6	60.8	15.7	1,344	66.9	30.6	43.3

1 May be of any race.

Table A. All Places — **Population and Housing**

STATE City, town, township, borough, or CDP (county if applicable)	2010 census total population	2014 estimated population	Percent change 2010–2014	ACS total population estimate 2010–2014	White alone, not Hispanic or Latino	Black alone, not Hispanic or Latino	Asian alone, not Hispanic or Latino	All other races or 2 or more races, not Hispanic or Latino	Hispanic or Latino[1]	Under 18 years old	Age 18 to 64 years old	Age 65 years and older	Total occupied housing units	Percent owner occupied	High school diploma or less	Bachelor's degree or more
	1	2	3	4	5	6	7	8	9	10	11	12	13	14	15	16
NEW JERSEY—Con.																
Woolwich township (Gloucester)	10,200	11,783	15.5	10,961	77.4	8.1	8.5	1.9	4.2	33.8	58.7	7.4	3,512	83.4	17.8	55.5
Wrightstown borough & MCD (Burlington)	802	795	-0.9	884	42.3	19.3	9.3	7.0	22.1	22.8	68.4	8.7	343	34.1	53.1	12.0
Wyckoff township (Bergen)	16,683	17,039	2.1	16,877	88.6	0.2	5.9	0.7	4.6	26.3	57.1	16.7	5,728	91.4	13.5	69.4
Yardville CDP	7,186	NA	NA	6,825	92.5	1.6	1.3	1.1	3.4	18.9	63.1	18.1	2,564	80.7	41.2	24.8
Yorketown CDP	6,535	NA	NA	6,598	90.0	0.8	3.3	0.3	5.7	26.2	64.0	9.8	1,963	94.7	27.1	43.5
Zarephath CDP	37	NA	NA	0	0.0	0.0	0.0	0.0	0.0	0.0	0.0	0.0	0	0.0	0.0	0.0
NEW MEXICO	2,059,192	2,085,572	1.3	2,080,085	39.6	1.8	1.3	10.2	47.0	24.6	61.2	14.2	764,684	68.2	37.4	28.9
Abeytas CDP	56	NA	NA	60	63.3	0.0	0.0	0.0	36.7	0.0	100.0	0.0	33	100.0	66.7	33.3
Abiquiu CDP	231	NA	NA	57	0.0	0.0	0.0	0.0	100.0	26.3	22.8	50.9	13	100.0	0.0	0.0
Acomita Lake CDP	416	NA	NA	377	1.6	0.0	0.0	94.7	3.7	22.0	72.1	5.8	88	95.5	68.2	0.0
Adelino CDP	823	NA	NA	809	15.0	0.0	0.0	8.2	76.9	7.5	60.7	31.6	351	100.0	42.5	0.0
Agua Fria CDP	2,800	NA	NA	3,255	10.4	0.0	0.0	0.2	89.5	34.7	57.0	8.4	1,151	57.4	63.7	13.5
Alamillo CDP	102	NA	NA	162	45.1	0.0	0.0	0.0	54.9	0.0	67.3	32.7	39	100.0	38.5	43.6
Alamo CDP	1,085	NA	NA	707	2.0	0.0	0.0	96.0	2.0	30.3	59.6	10.0	132	59.8	71.2	15.2
Alamogordo city	30,415	31,060	2.1	31,224	55.7	5.4	1.8	3.4	33.6	22.7	60.0	17.1	12,470	58.3	37.4	20.4
Albuquerque city	546,360	557,169	2.0	553,576	41.3	2.9	2.5	5.9	47.3	23.6	63.5	12.8	222,868	59.3	30.2	35.2
Alcalde CDP	285	NA	NA	300	2.3	0.0	0.0	14.7	83.0	18.6	76.7	4.7	109	92.7	39.4	3.7
Algodones CDP	814	NA	NA	896	27.5	0.0	0.0	16.6	55.9	23.0	60.4	16.3	317	89.9	49.5	25.2
Angel Fire village	1,216	1,141	-6.2	1,161	79.5	0.0	0.9	1.5	18.1	14.3	59.7	26.1	547	73.7	13.2	46.8
Animas CDP	237	NA	NA	148	92.6	0.0	0.0	0.0	7.4	10.8	47.3	41.9	80	70.0	47.5	18.8
Anthony city	9,500	9,318	-1.9	9,462	1.4	0.0	0.0	0.4	98.2	32.1	58.9	8.8	2,830	63.6	75.0	2.0
Anton Chico CDP	188	NA	NA	55	0.0	0.0	0.0	0.0	100.0	0.0	41.8	58.2	38	100.0	52.6	47.4
Anzac Village CDP	54	NA	NA	140	0.0	0.0	0.0	100.0	0.0	20.7	79.3	0.0	26	100.0	42.3	19.2
Apache Creek CDP	67	NA	NA	63	92.1	0.0	0.0	0.0	7.9	0.0	65.0	34.9	46	100.0	13.0	0.0
Aragon CDP	94	NA	NA	13	0.0	0.0	0.0	0.0	100.0	0.0	100.0	0.0	13	100.0	0.0	0.0
Arenas Valley CDP	1,522	NA	NA	1,025	55.4	0.0	1.0	0.0	43.6	19.4	68.3	12.2	492	72.4	15.4	29.7
Arrey CDP	232	NA	NA	393	0.0	0.0	0.0	0.0	100.0	28.3	56.2	15.5	90	100.0	100.0	0.0
Arroyo Hondo CDP	474	NA	NA	303	28.4	0.0	0.0	0.0	71.6	24.1	53.9	22.1	98	86.7	67.3	19.4
Arroyo Seco CDP	1,785	NA	NA	1,408	61.0	0.0	0.0	0.0	39.0	3.8	72.5	23.7	564	87.1	23.6	61.0
Artesia city	11,321	11,842	4.6	11,494	45.0	0.3	1.4	3.5	49.7	29.8	56.8	13.4	4,140	71.1	50.9	13.1
Atoka CDP	1,077	NA	NA	633	44.2	0.0	0.0	6.3	49.4	4.6	73.5	21.8	331	86.4	61.6	18.7
Aztec city	6,757	6,419	-5.0	6,619	66.0	0.0	0.3	7.8	26.0	23.7	61.3	14.9	2,658	61.3	44.3	16.7
Bayard city	2,337	2,304	-1.4	2,640	11.1	0.0	0.0	1.3	87.7	25.8	54.3	20.1	1,032	67.0	60.4	10.4
Beclabito CDP	317	NA	NA	294	0.0	0.0	0.0	100.0	0.0	25.9	62.9	11.2	59	93.2	49.2	3.4
Belen city	7,272	7,175	-1.3	7,249	27.0	0.1	0.2	2.8	69.8	29.0	54.3	16.8	2,703	61.2	49.7	14.8
Bent CDP	119	NA	NA	135	100.0	0.0	0.0	0.0	0.0	0.0	42.3	57.8	83	71.1	45.8	16.9
Berino CDP	1,441	NA	NA	1,674	0.0	0.0	0.0	0.0	100.0	39.9	51.7	8.6	375	75.5	78.9	3.2
Bernalillo town	8,320	8,564	2.9	8,400	23.5	0.3	0.4	6.9	69.0	20.4	64.0	15.6	3,065	73.8	50.7	20.4
Bibo CDP	140	NA	NA	156	0.0	0.0	0.0	0.0	100.0	29.5	60.9	9.6	52	100.0	28.8	71.2
Black Rock CDP	1,323	NA	NA	1,325	6.8	0.5	3.3	88.7	0.8	36.2	60.9	3.0	313	17.6	37.7	25.9
Blanco CDP	388	NA	NA	166	74.7	0.0	0.0	0.0	25.3	31.9	49.5	18.7	76	100.0	38.2	14.5
Bloomfield city	8,112	7,638	-5.8	7,877	37.7	0.7	0.0	34.5	27.2	32.6	56.5	10.9	2,419	60.8	49.2	17.5
Bluewater Acres CDP	206	NA	NA	752	23.3	0.0	0.0	10.9	65.8	29.7	49.1	21.1	191	71.7	91.1	0.0
Bluewater Village CDP	628	NA	NA	446	75.6	0.0	0.0	0.0	24.4	40.6	29.7	29.6	184	82.1	39.7	25.5
Boles Acres CDP	1,638	NA	NA	2,329	83.7	2.7	0.0	3.0	10.5	15.9	64.1	20.0	979	84.8	23.4	19.0
Bosque Farms village	3,907	3,850	-1.5	3,886	56.3	0.0	0.1	3.2	40.3	21.8	58.3	19.9	1,484	90.6	32.3	32.7
Brazos CDP	44	NA	NA	27	0.0	0.0	0.0	0.0	100.0	0.0	100.0	0.0	15	100.0	0.0	0.0
Brimhall Nizhoni CDP	199	NA	NA	370	0.0	0.0	0.0	95.1	4.9	16.7	75.3	7.8	82	92.7	68.3	7.3
Buckhorn CDP	200	NA	NA	198	84.8	0.0	0.0	0.0	15.2	21.7	61.1	17.2	118	61.0	23.7	38.1
Caballo CDP	112	NA	NA	25	100.0	0.0	0.0	0.0	0.0	0.0	0.0	100.0	14	100.0	0.0	0.0
Cañada de los Alamos CDP	434	NA	NA	340	70.3	0.0	0.0	0.0	29.7	2.9	80.5	16.5	160	55.0	42.5	49.4
Canjilon CDP	256	NA	NA	251	0.0	0.0	0.0	0.0	100.0	4.0	52.2	43.8	104	77.9	48.1	8.7
Cannon AFB CDP	2,245	NA	NA	2,591	60.9	9.7	3.9	3.0	22.5	26.5	73.1	0.4	743	0.3	9.7	15.2
Cañon CDP	327	NA	NA	211	39.3	0.0	0.0	3.3	57.3	29.3	42.7	28.0	114	90.4	52.6	29.8
Cañones CDP	118	NA	NA	93	2.2	0.0	0.0	0.0	97.8	11.8	46.2	41.9	30	100.0	90.0	0.0
Canova CDP	118	NA	NA	0	0.0	0.0	0.0	0.0	0.0	0.0	0.0	0.0	0	0.0	0.0	0.0
Capitan village	1,495	1,418	-5.2	1,261	65.6	3.9	0.0	1.9	28.6	13.3	62.5	24.3	584	86.5	49.5	12.5
Capulin CDP	66	NA	NA	127	54.3	0.0	0.0	0.0	45.7	23.6	53.4	22.8	51	66.7	60.8	7.8
Carlsbad city	26,200	28,103	7.3	26,996	51.9	2.0	0.5	1.3	44.3	27.3	58.0	14.8	10,068	70.0	47.4	18.6
Carnuel CDP	1,232	NA	NA	1,303	35.8	0.0	0.0	0.0	64.2	15.7	57.5	26.7	537	79.1	41.7	19.6
Carrizozo town	996	955	-4.1	866	46.2	0.7	0.5	6.8	45.8	10.5	71.2	18.2	366	84.2	52.7	17.8
Casa Colorada CDP	272	NA	NA	149	23.5	0.0	0.0	0.0	76.5	10.7	48.3	40.9	78	88.5	50.0	6.4
Causey village	104	100	-3.8	60	76.7	0.0	1.7	0.0	21.7	11.7	60.1	28.3	25	88.0	28.0	20.0
Cedar Crest CDP	958	NA	NA	958	47.4	0.0	0.0	2.5	50.1	17.3	73.3	9.3	347	95.4	21.3	49.6
Cedar Grove CDP	747	NA	NA	754	91.9	0.0	1.1	0.0	7.0	14.4	71.3	14.3	321	100.0	7.2	45.2
Cedar Hill CDP	847	NA	NA	973	95.7	0.0	0.5	1.0	2.8	23.1	62.8	14.0	373	84.2	29.5	33.0
Cedro CDP	430	NA	NA	288	84.4	0.0	5.2	4.2	6.3	8.3	68.8	22.9	191	95.8	32.5	48.2
Chama village	1,022	1,012	-1.0	876	34.9	0.7	0.0	0.0	64.4	24.1	58.0	17.9	333	65.8	40.8	29.7
Chamberino CDP	919	NA	NA	855	7.6	0.0	0.0	0.0	92.4	23.6	66.0	10.2	237	87.8	60.3	21.1
Chamisal CDP	310	NA	NA	322	3.1	0.0	0.0	4.0	92.9	10.6	64.5	24.8	135	88.1	54.1	15.6
Chamita CDP	870	NA	NA	1,037	3.2	0.0	0.0	7.9	88.9	25.8	58.7	15.5	332	86.4	58.7	6.9
Chamizal CDP	101	NA	NA	48	31.3	0.0	0.0	0.0	68.8	0.0	58.4	41.7	25	100.0	48.0	52.0
Chaparral CDP	14,631	NA	NA	13,905	14.2	0.2	0.0	0.5	85.1	36.0	54.8	9.2	3,825	79.3	70.1	6.2
Chical CDP	107	NA	NA	139	0.0	0.0	0.0	100.0	0.0	12.2	84.1	3.6	52	75.0	15.4	0.0
Chili CDP	654	NA	NA	953	0.0	0.0	0.0	0.0	100.0	22.7	70.1	7.2	145	91.7	55.9	20.7
Chilili CDP	137	NA	NA	39	0.0	0.0	0.0	0.0	100.0	0.0	99.9	0.0	21	100.0	100.0	0.0
Chimayo CDP	3,177	NA	NA	2,572	10.6	0.0	0.0	2.0	87.4	17.3	72.2	10.4	1,032	70.3	62.2	7.7
Chupadero CDP	362	NA	NA	221	58.4	0.0	0.0	0.0	41.6	7.7	74.7	17.6	117	65.0	13.7	70.1
Church Rock CDP	1,128	NA	NA	1,058	0.6	0.0	0.0	96.7	2.7	35.6	55.7	8.9	218	68.3	60.6	3.7
Cimarron village	1,019	933	-8.4	1,003	43.3	0.0	0.0	0.0	56.7	15.2	60.1	24.9	425	82.1	53.9	20.0
City of the Sun CDP	31	NA	NA	37	100.0	0.0	0.0	0.0	0.0	0.0	0.0	100.0	20	100.0	0.0	0.0
Clayton town	2,982	2,832	-5.0	2,387	46.8	2.6	0.2	1.3	49.1	22.7	58.0	19.4	971	58.5	56.0	16.0
Cliff CDP	293	NA	NA	365	85.8	0.0	0.0	8.2	6.0	17.8	58.2	23.8	174	100.0	39.1	22.4
Cloudcroft village	673	690	2.5	577	89.9	0.0	0.0	2.3	7.8	10.1	60.4	29.6	310	71.0	16.8	44.8
Clovis city	37,790	39,860	5.5	39,204	48.1	6.2	1.4	3.0	41.3	26.7	61.7	11.5	14,618	60.4	40.8	20.5

1 May be of any race.

Table A. All Places — **Population and Housing**

STATE City, town, township, borough, or CDP (county if applicable)	2010 census total population	2014 estimated population	Percent change 2010–2014	ACS total population estimate 2010–2014	White alone, not Hispanic or Latino	Black alone, not Hispanic or Latino	Asian alone, not Hispanic or Latino	All other races or 2 or more races, not Hispanic or Latino	Hispanic or Latino[1]	Under 18 years old	Age 18 to 64 years old	Age 65 years and older	Total occupied housing units	Percent owner occupied	High school diploma or less	Bachelor's degree or more
	1	2	3	4	5	6	7	8	9	10	11	12	13	14	15	16
NEW MEXICO—Con.																
Cobre CDP	39	NA	NA	21	0.0	0.0	0.0	0.0	100.0	0.0	0.0	100.0	21	100.0	0.0	100.0
Cochiti CDP	528	NA	NA	498	0.0	0.0	0.0	86.5	13.5	28.7	55.8	15.3	142	88.0	48.6	5.6
Cochiti Lake CDP	569	NA	NA	534	55.8	1.5	0.6	27.7	14.4	12.0	61.7	26.4	255	91.0	15.3	49.8
Columbus village	1,664	1,634	-1.8	1,278	13.1	0.0	0.0	0.0	86.9	27.5	44.3	28.2	482	68.0	70.7	21.8
Conchas Dam CDP	186	NA	NA	65	84.6	0.0	0.0	0.0	15.4	36.9	47.7	15.4	19	100.0	52.6	0.0
Cordova CDP	414	NA	NA	304	3.9	0.0	0.0	0.0	96.1	0.0	43.7	56.3	131	72.5	69.5	21.4
Corona village	172	164	-4.7	147	74.1	0.0	0.0	6.1	19.7	4.1	53.7	42.2	80	87.5	42.5	20.0
Corrales village	8,333	8,374	0.5	8,426	63.4	0.3	1.8	3.7	30.7	17.1	59.3	23.5	3,394	90.1	21.4	58.1
Costilla CDP	205	NA	NA	73	20.5	0.0	0.0	0.0	79.5	13.7	75.3	11.0	55	43.6	16.4	27.3
Cotton City CDP	388	NA	NA	270	44.8	0.0	0.0	0.0	55.2	18.9	54.0	27.0	107	89.7	72.9	7.5
Coyote CDP	128	NA	NA	147	0.0	0.0	0.0	6.8	93.2	10.9	62.0	27.2	64	92.2	81.3	0.0
Crownpoint CDP	2,278	NA	NA	2,502	5.2	2.6	1.7	88.8	1.7	28.4	65.4	6.3	571	41.9	42.2	19.4
Cruzville CDP	72	NA	NA	169	81.7	0.0	0.0	0.0	18.3	56.2	24.8	18.9	33	100.0	36.4	63.6
Crystal CDP	311	NA	NA	359	0.6	2.2	1.1	91.4	4.7	29.7	54.5	15.6	100	89.0	48.0	17.0
Cuartelez CDP	469	NA	NA	433	0.0	0.0	0.0	6.0	94.0	22.7	56.9	20.3	166	84.3	26.5	24.1
Cuba village	731	731	0.0	617	6.8	0.0	0.0	37.1	56.1	33.2	51.8	14.9	234	64.5	70.9	9.4
Cubero CDP	289	NA	NA	125	16.8	0.0	0.0	0.0	83.2	0.0	57.6	42.4	97	100.0	78.4	21.6
Cundiyo CDP	72	NA	NA	8	100.0	0.0	0.0	0.0	0.0	0.0	100.0	0.0	8	0.0	100.0	0.0
Cuyamungue CDP	479	NA	NA	568	16.0	0.5	1.6	4.9	76.9	22.0	60.8	17.3	227	75.8	43.2	19.8
Cuyamungue Grant CDP	226	NA	NA	203	36.5	0.0	0.0	0.0	63.5	5.9	69.4	24.6	98	79.6	41.8	30.6
Datil CDP	54	NA	NA	99	27.3	0.0	0.0	0.0	72.7	0.0	72.7	27.3	52	100.0	19.2	0.0
Deming city	14,848	14,605	-1.6	14,760	26.2	1.4	0.5	1.8	70.1	27.3	53.8	18.9	5,437	58.2	65.2	14.7
Des Moines village	141	132	-6.4	190	66.3	0.0	0.0	0.0	33.7	29.4	47.3	23.2	67	56.7	86.6	6.0
Dexter town	1,266	1,274	0.6	1,510	15.8	0.0	0.0	0.0	84.2	36.9	52.4	10.7	442	74.0	58.8	12.9
Dixon CDP	926	NA	NA	870	28.9	0.0	0.0	0.0	71.1	17.9	51.3	30.7	410	72.4	33.7	22.0
Doña Ana CDP	1,211	NA	NA	1,796	7.4	0.0	0.0	0.0	92.6	36.9	54.8	8.3	552	69.7	62.5	17.6
Dora village	133	129	-3.0	41	92.7	0.0	0.0	0.0	7.3	9.8	75.6	14.6	24	58.3	45.8	37.5
Dulce CDP	2,743	NA	NA	2,537	2.0	0.6	2.1	88.8	6.5	32.0	58.7	9.3	758	66.1	58.2	7.8
Duran CDP	35	NA	NA	2	0.0	0.0	0.0	0.0	100.0	0.0	0.0	100.0	2	100.0	0.0	0.0
Eagle Nest village	290	267	-7.9	319	77.1	0.0	0.0	2.8	20.1	21.9	62.0	16.0	122	82.0	19.7	32.0
East Pecos CDP	757	NA	NA	499	0.0	0.0	0.0	0.0	100.0	34.7	65.2	0.0	237	47.7	81.4	0.0
Edgewood town	3,733	3,805	1.9	3,763	76.1	0.2	2.3	3.5	17.9	25.1	60.9	14.1	1,482	90.1	27.8	39.4
Edith Endave CDP	211	NA	NA	240	40.8	0.0	1.7	11.3	46.3	23.7	66.0	10.4	94	76.6	46.8	27.7
El Cerro CDP	2,953	NA	NA	2,962	45.0	0.0	0.0	3.1	51.9	22.4	61.4	16.2	998	96.3	42.8	22.4
El Cerro Mission CDP	4,657	NA	NA	4,519	20.9	0.0	0.0	1.8	77.3	30.6	62.9	6.4	1,358	78.0	59.3	4.3
Eldorado at Santa Fe CDP	6,130	NA	NA	5,990	83.1	0.8	1.5	1.4	13.3	10.8	63.5	25.8	2,986	84.7	6.6	74.4
El Duende CDP	707	NA	NA	1,010	4.4	0.0	0.0	0.0	95.6	40.8	54.1	5.0	299	67.9	70.9	15.7
Elephant Butte city	1,431	1,356	-5.2	1,562	78.2	0.0	0.0	1.5	20.3	13.1	44.5	42.4	513	86.2	39.2	19.3
Elida town	197	190	-3.6	236	62.7	0.0	0.0	0.0	37.3	18.6	61.5	19.9	98	73.5	43.9	20.4
El Rancho CDP	1,199	NA	NA	1,180	22.3	0.0	0.0	5.0	72.7	24.2	61.0	14.7	481	80.9	43.9	26.8
El Rito CDP	808	NA	NA	710	12.8	0.0	0.0	0.1	87.0	14.5	67.2	18.2	324	75.0	65.4	4.0
El Valle de Arroyo Seco CDP	1,440	NA	NA	1,414	15.3	0.0	1.6	0.0	83.1	29.6	60.7	9.8	467	65.7	66.2	7.5
Encinal CDP	210	NA	NA	127	0.0	0.0	0.0	95.3	4.7	23.6	49.6	26.8	57	89.5	61.4	14.0
Encino village	82	78	-4.9	46	19.6	0.0	0.0	6.5	73.9	13.0	47.7	39.1	28	100.0	100.0	0.0
Ensenada CDP	107	NA	NA	154	0.0	0.0	0.0	0.0	100.0	14.9	29.2	55.8	55	100.0	30.9	0.0
Escondida CDP	47	NA	NA	18	0.0	0.0	0.0	0.0	100.0	0.0	100.0	0.0	18	100.0	100.0	0.0
Escudilla Bonita CDP	119	NA	NA	27	100.0	0.0	0.0	0.0	0.0	0.0	66.7	33.3	27	100.0	0.0	0.0
Española city	10,234	10,130	-1.0	10,216	8.9	0.8	1.5	3.4	85.5	24.9	60.9	14.1	3,936	63.3	52.9	14.7
Estancia town	1,655	1,606	-3.0	1,394	28.3	0.0	0.0	2.7	69.0	21.0	67.6	11.5	362	61.3	65.7	5.0
Eunice city	2,922	3,147	7.7	3,006	50.1	0.0	0.0	0.7	49.2	25.0	60.9	14.3	1,126	77.4	51.6	10.7
Fairacres CDP	824	NA	NA	892	16.0	0.0	3.9	0.0	80.0	26.6	60.0	13.6	346	66.5	22.3	38.7
Farmington city	45,886	44,445	-3.1	45,383	49.7	0.9	0.6	25.6	23.2	28.5	59.8	11.7	15,255	68.4	37.3	23.1
Faywood CDP	33	NA	NA	62	66.1	0.0	0.0	0.0	33.9	0.0	58.1	41.9	38	100.0	78.9	0.0
Fence Lake CDP	42	NA	NA	0	0.0	0.0	0.0	0.0	0.0	0.0	0.0	0.0	0	0.0	0.0	0.0
Flora Vista CDP	2,191	NA	NA	2,115	62.7	0.0	0.0	8.7	28.6	21.4	59.4	19.2	821	87.3	46.9	15.5
Floyd village	121	117	-3.3	112	79.5	0.0	0.0	0.0	20.5	26.0	54.5	19.6	32	59.4	46.9	25.0
Folsom village	59	55	-6.8	85	80.0	0.0	0.0	9.4	10.6	24.7	48.1	27.1	27	85.2	59.3	11.1
Fort Sumner village	1,031	931	-9.7	1,099	54.1	0.0	0.0	7.4	38.5	14.3	67.0	18.7	319	74.3	61.4	5.0
Galisteo CDP	253	NA	NA	209	80.9	0.0	0.0	2.4	16.7	33.5	54.2	12.4	124	39.5	9.7	39.5
Gallina CDP	0	NA	NA	266	8.3	0.0	0.0	0.0	91.7	8.3	81.8	9.8	110	91.8	69.1	17.3
Gallup city	21,788	22,469	3.1	22,189	23.7	1.0	2.0	38.2	35.0	35.2	53.9	10.9	6,072	62.0	46.8	24.6
Garfield CDP	137	NA	NA	43	30.2	0.0	0.0	44.2	25.6	0.0	83.7	16.3	18	100.0	61.1	38.9
Gila CDP	314	NA	NA	463	76.5	0.0	0.0	7.3	16.2	31.4	61.3	7.6	177	83.1	39.0	25.4
Glen Acres CDP	208	NA	NA	384	24.2	0.0	0.0	0.0	75.8	28.6	64.1	7.3	131	84.7	72.5	5.3
Glenwood CDP	143	NA	NA	16	100.0	0.0	0.0	0.0	0.0	0.0	100.0	0.0	16	100.0	0.0	100.0
Glorieta CDP	430	NA	NA	282	21.6	0.0	0.0	0.0	78.4	2.1	77.7	20.2	140	73.6	38.6	47.1
Golden CDP	37	NA	NA	66	43.9	0.0	0.0	0.0	56.1	10.6	66.7	22.7	45	100.0	66.7	33.3
Grady village	107	108	0.9	70	78.6	0.0	0.0	0.0	21.4	25.6	46.0	28.6	32	78.1	37.5	25.0
Grants city	9,177	9,241	0.7	9,245	27.8	1.6	0.9	15.7	54.1	25.2	61.1	13.9	3,156	63.1	43.1	19.1
Grenville village	38	36	-5.3	17	88.2	0.0	0.0	0.0	11.8	35.3	58.8	5.9	7	57.1	0.0	14.3
Hachita CDP	49	NA	NA	50	84.0	0.0	0.0	0.0	16.0	0.0	24.0	76.0	46	50.0	23.9	50.0
Hagerman town	1,251	1,258	0.6	1,158	25.2	0.0	0.0	0.0	74.8	29.9	54.4	15.8	378	61.4	54.0	4.2
Hanover CDP	167	NA	NA	147	13.6	0.0	0.0	32.0	54.4	62.6	37.4	0.0	55	100.0	45.5	18.2
Happy Valley CDP	519	NA	NA	930	63.3	0.0	4.3	0.0	32.4	30.5	55.0	14.6	325	89.5	57.8	0.0
Hatch village	1,618	1,601	-1.1	1,830	14.1	0.0	0.3	0.4	85.1	31.6	56.9	11.4	520	73.7	75.2	6.3
Hernandez CDP	946	NA	NA	1,156	5.5	0.0	0.0	0.7	93.8	30.6	49.7	19.6	386	78.2	73.8	2.3
Highland Meadows CDP	624	NA	NA	676	65.2	0.0	0.0	18.9	15.8	30.2	63.5	6.2	282	65.6	40.4	6.4
High Rolls CDP	834	NA	NA	591	89.8	0.0	0.0	3.7	6.4	10.8	62.0	27.2	290	86.2	9.3	34.5
Hillsboro CDP	124	NA	NA	103	100.0	0.0	0.0	0.0	0.0	0.0	100.1	0.0	72	100.0	47.2	0.0
Hobbs city	34,133	37,118	8.7	35,343	38.6	4.7	0.3	3.1	53.3	30.4	60.0	9.6	11,128	66.8	55.6	15.1
Holloman AFB CDP	3,054	NA	NA	3,813	64.6	14.4	2.5	4.8	13.7	34.8	65.2	0.0	983	0.0	4.1	20.8
Homestead CDP	47	NA	NA	47	100.0	0.0	0.0	0.0	0.0	0.0	66.0	34.0	32	100.0	0.0	100.0
Hope village	105	106	1.0	120	64.2	0.0	0.0	10.8	25.0	10.8	55.9	33.3	43	93.0	58.1	27.9
Hot Springs Landing CDP	110	NA	NA	134	32.8	0.0	0.0	67.2	0.0	0.0	0.0	100.0	66	30.3	69.7	0.0
House village	68	64	-5.9	71	90.1	0.0	0.0	0.0	9.9	0.0	67.6	32.4	25	100.0	44.0	12.0
Hurley town	1,297	1,278	-1.5	1,232	40.5	0.0	0.0	1.9	57.5	17.8	49.0	33.4	562	77.6	42.7	22.1
Indian Hills CDP	892	NA	NA	1,216	73.3	2.8	0.0	0.5	23.4	20.4	74.6	4.9	345	81.4	54.8	5.2
Isleta Village Proper CDP	491	NA	NA	374	0.0	0.0	0.0	93.3	6.7	14.7	48.8	36.4	175	85.7	58.3	18.3
Jacona CDP	412	NA	NA	437	31.4	0.0	1.6	3.4	63.6	26.8	53.8	19.5	178	72.5	36.5	33.1

1 May be of any race.

Table A. All Places — **Population and Housing**

STATE City, town, township, borough, or CDP (county if applicable)	Population				Race and Hispanic or Latino origin (percent), 2010–2014					Age (percent), 2010–2014			Households, 2010–2014		Householders by level of education (percent)	
	2010 census total population	2014 estimated population	Percent change 2010–2014	ACS total population estimate 2010–2014	White alone, not Hispanic or Latino	Black alone, not Hispanic or Latino	Asian alone, not Hispanic or Latino	All other races or 2 or more races, not Hispanic or Latino	Hispanic or Latino[1]	Under 18 years old	Age 18 to 64 years old	Age 65 years and older	Total occupied housing units	Percent owner occupied	High school diploma or less	Bachelor's degree or more
	1	2	3	4	5	6	7	8	9	10	11	12	13	14	15	16
NEW MEXICO—Con.																
Jaconita CDP	332	NA	NA	503	29.0	0.0	0.6	2.2	68.2	23.7	71.0	5.4	207	63.3	26.1	47.8
Jal city	2,047	2,209	7.9	2,130	48.9	0.6	0.0	2.4	48.1	26.5	57.0	16.6	718	72.4	55.0	10.7
Jarales CDP	2,475	NA	NA	2,022	27.6	0.0	0.3	1.5	70.5	20.6	58.8	20.5	776	81.7	47.7	8.6
Jemez Pueblo CDP	1,788	NA	NA	1,894	0.7	0.4	0.4	98.3	0.2	24.9	64.8	10.3	444	96.2	45.3	8.8
Jemez Springs village	250	251	0.4	232	42.7	0.0	1.3	3.0	53.0	13.4	47.1	39.7	88	81.8	31.8	35.2
Keeler Farm CDP	1,305	NA	NA	2,131	34.4	2.1	0.0	1.5	62.1	37.4	46.3	16.3	599	78.6	63.9	4.0
Kingston CDP	32	NA	NA	96	100.0	0.0	0.0	0.0	0.0	32.3	59.4	8.3	23	100.0	34.8	0.0
Kirtland CDP	7,875	NA	NA	6,189	35.3	1.1	0.1	52.3	11.1	23.2	64.3	12.4	1,875	76.6	35.0	24.7
La Cienega CDP	3,819	NA	NA	3,004	21.5	0.7	0.0	2.4	75.4	25.3	62.4	12.3	1,039	76.7	37.9	22.6
La Cueva CDP	168	NA	NA	124	100.0	0.0	0.0	0.0	0.0	0.0	84.0	16.1	72	90.3	0.0	23.6
Laguna CDP	1,241	NA	NA	1,309	0.3	0.0	0.0	96.2	3.5	26.2	59.4	14.5	354	86.7	52.0	10.2
La Hacienda CDP	725	NA	NA	402	2.5	0.0	0.0	0.0	97.5	27.2	68.6	4.2	97	100.0	87.6	0.0
La Huerta CDP	1,246	NA	NA	1,467	66.3	10.0	0.0	3.3	20.3	28.7	56.5	14.7	542	81.0	29.5	26.2
La Jara CDP	207	NA	NA	151	2.6	0.0	0.0	9.9	87.4	9.9	56.3	33.8	85	82.4	61.2	5.9
La Joya CDP	82	NA	NA	0	0.0	0.0	0.0	0.0	0.0	0.0	0.0	0.0	0	0.0	0.0	0.0
Lake Arthur town	436	438	0.5	424	27.4	0.0	0.0	0.0	72.6	24.8	63.5	11.8	136	89.0	65.4	5.9
Lake Roberts CDP	53	NA	NA	14	100.0	0.0	0.0	0.0	0.0	0.0	0.0	100.0	14	100.0	100.0	0.0
Lake Roberts Heights CDP	32	NA	NA	0	0.0	0.0	0.0	0.0	0.0	0.0	0.0	0.0	0	0.0	0.0	0.0
Lake Sumner CDP	143	NA	NA	126	67.5	0.0	0.0	0.0	32.5	25.4	51.8	23.0	50	84.0	46.0	24.0
Lake Valley CDP	64	NA	NA	61	0.0	0.0	0.0	100.0	0.0	18.1	70.5	11.5	18	100.0	72.2	0.0
La Luz CDP	1,697	NA	NA	1,611	84.0	0.0	0.0	1.9	14.1	24.3	57.3	18.3	573	77.8	47.8	12.2
La Madera CDP	154	NA	NA	151	58.3	0.0	0.0	0.0	41.7	0.0	64.9	35.1	107	100.0	37.4	41.1
La Mesa CDP	728	NA	NA	973	7.9	0.0	0.0	0.0	92.1	30.1	57.2	12.7	300	67.0	41.0	11.3
La Mesilla CDP	1,772	NA	NA	2,039	25.0	0.1	0.3	4.1	70.5	19.3	67.3	13.5	794	89.5	30.4	35.5
Lamy CDP	218	NA	NA	173	75.1	0.0	0.0	8.1	16.8	27.7	72.3	0.0	92	100.0	31.5	45.7
La Plata CDP	612	NA	NA	956	78.3	0.0	0.0	0.0	21.7	38.4	52.2	9.4	253	73.9	35.6	13.8
La Puebla CDP	1,186	NA	NA	996	17.4	0.0	0.0	0.0	82.6	17.4	56.4	25.9	401	68.6	61.6	23.9
Las Cruces city	97,636	101,408	3.9	100,360	37.1	1.9	1.7	2.6	56.7	24.0	62.6	13.6	38,670	56.0	27.6	34.6
Las Maravillas CDP	1,628	NA	NA	1,925	34.0	0.9	0.5	3.5	61.1	29.0	62.4	8.6	614	86.6	31.3	21.3
Las Nutrias CDP	149	NA	NA	237	34.2	0.0	0.0	0.0	65.8	21.0	53.3	25.7	98	100.0	36.7	13.3
Las Palomas CDP	173	NA	NA	230	88.7	0.0	0.0	0.0	11.3	18.7	68.2	13.0	61	100.0	29.5	42.6
Las Vegas city	14,055	13,518	-3.8	13,833	19.0	2.3	1.0	2.5	75.2	22.8	60.2	16.9	5,319	63.5	38.5	25.1
La Union CDP	1,106	NA	NA	1,259	2.3	0.0	0.0	0.0	97.7	40.9	45.5	13.6	331	72.2	71.3	8.5
La Villita CDP	957	NA	NA	980	4.4	0.0	0.0	0.5	95.1	25.6	65.4	9.0	311	77.5	63.0	0.0
Lee Acres CDP	5,858	NA	NA	6,164	39.2	0.0	0.0	24.1	36.8	30.0	58.0	12.0	1,718	76.7	52.8	9.4
Lemitar CDP	330	NA	NA	245	29.0	0.0	0.0	0.0	71.0	24.5	66.9	8.6	78	100.0	47.4	0.0
Livingston Wheeler CDP	609	NA	NA	444	23.9	0.0	0.0	0.0	76.1	19.1	62.4	18.5	141	100.0	44.7	45.4
Llano del Medio CDP	118	NA	NA	45	0.0	0.0	0.0	0.0	100.0	0.0	0.0	100.0	41	100.0	61.0	39.0
Loco Hills CDP	126	NA	NA	33	100.0	0.0	0.0	0.0	0.0	0.0	100.0	0.0	33	0.0	100.0	0.0
Logan village	1,042	973	-6.6	1,089	77.6	0.0	0.0	1.9	20.5	13.1	62.8	24.2	470	83.0	62.1	14.9
Lordsburg city	2,797	2,609	-6.7	2,831	25.5	0.5	0.0	0.2	73.9	27.6	54.9	17.4	1,047	61.6	61.9	7.9
Los Alamos CDP	12,019	NA	NA	11,843	72.7	0.4	8.3	2.6	16.1	21.8	62.4	15.9	5,230	68.6	11.3	70.2
Los Cerrillos CDP	321	NA	NA	301	94.4	0.0	0.0	2.3	3.3	16.3	56.2	27.6	131	59.5	24.4	32.8
Los Chaves CDP	5,446	NA	NA	4,375	40.7	0.0	0.2	5.0	54.1	25.2	62.8	12.1	1,696	76.3	46.4	17.9
Los Luceros CDP	906	NA	NA	573	7.3	0.0	0.0	0.0	92.7	18.8	40.6	40.5	225	100.0	16.0	9.8
Los Lunas village	14,935	15,206	1.8	15,203	35.0	2.0	1.0	4.2	57.9	27.3	59.7	12.9	5,618	78.5	34.4	20.9
Los Ojos CDP	125	NA	NA	177	14.1	0.0	0.0	0.0	85.9	10.7	53.7	35.6	85	63.5	31.8	30.6
Los Ranchos de Albuquerque village	6,024	6,063	0.6	6,074	63.9	0.6	0.7	3.8	31.0	18.8	61.8	19.2	2,756	68.1	25.3	43.4
Loving village	1,384	1,399	1.1	1,524	14.4	0.0	0.0	2.9	82.7	22.8	62.9	14.4	535	78.1	74.4	4.7
Lovington city	11,009	11,840	7.5	11,364	23.7	1.9	0.0	1.0	73.5	34.6	56.2	9.2	3,378	67.7	68.6	7.6
Lower Frisco CDP	31	NA	NA	0	0.0	0.0	0.0	0.0	0.0	0.0	0.0	0.0	0	0.0	0.0	0.0
Luis Lopez CDP	107	NA	NA	265	90.9	0.0	0.0	0.0	9.1	20.4	52.9	26.8	84	100.0	81.0	19.0
Lumberton CDP	73	NA	NA	101	18.8	0.0	2.0	64.4	14.9	0.0	59.5	40.6	34	44.1	100.0	0.0
Luna CDP	158	NA	NA	156	92.9	0.0	0.0	0.0	7.1	0.0	26.9	73.1	118	100.0	0.0	44.1
Lyden CDP	245	NA	NA	400	6.8	0.0	0.0	0.0	93.3	22.5	70.9	6.8	115	100.0	19.1	36.5
McCartys Village CDP	48	NA	NA	130	0.0	0.0	0.0	100.0	0.0	10.0	63.9	26.2	25	100.0	48.0	0.0
McIntosh CDP	1,484	NA	NA	1,181	68.2	0.0	0.0	0.0	31.8	24.9	50.1	25.0	371	86.3	41.2	19.7
Madrid CDP	204	NA	NA	191	88.0	0.0	0.0	0.0	12.0	0.0	55.0	45.0	136	65.4	0.0	41.9
Madrone CDP	707	NA	NA	710	28.3	4.5	0.0	10.4	56.8	35.1	56.2	8.9	194	79.4	88.7	0.0
Magdalena village	940	913	-2.9	657	36.2	0.0	0.6	11.3	51.9	18.9	47.6	33.5	218	84.9	39.0	22.9
Malaga CDP	147	NA	NA	63	9.5	0.0	0.0	15.9	74.6	0.0	34.9	65.1	41	70.7	85.4	0.0
Manzano CDP	29	NA	NA	14	0.0	100.0	0.0	0.0	0.0	0.0	100.0	0.0	14	100.0	0.0	100.0
Manzano Springs CDP	137	NA	NA	190	100.0	0.0	0.0	0.0	0.0	20.0	64.2	15.8	87	100.0	12.6	35.6
Maxwell village	253	233	-7.9	156	24.4	0.0	0.0	0.0	75.6	21.9	45.4	32.7	94	55.3	56.4	10.6
Mayhill CDP	75	NA	NA	219	67.6	0.0	0.0	0.5	32.0	16.0	51.6	32.4	44	100.0	20.5	79.5
Meadow Lake CDP	4,708	NA	NA	5,626	19.3	2.4	0.0	2.3	76.1	36.7	57.8	5.3	1,421	75.2	73.8	4.6
Melrose village	653	657	0.6	727	93.5	0.4	0.0	1.5	4.5	29.0	54.4	16.6	327	63.0	46.2	12.8
Mescalero CDP	1,338	NA	NA	1,601	2.9	0.5	0.0	87.6	8.9	34.2	60.6	5.2	312	57.7	57.7	9.6
Mesilla town	1,895	1,880	-0.8	2,364	44.4	0.2	0.2	0.7	54.5	14.0	64.3	21.8	930	61.4	26.9	52.8
Mesita CDP	804	NA	NA	941	2.0	0.0	0.0	94.9	3.1	28.6	62.4	8.9	187	93.6	42.8	20.9
Mesquite CDP	1,112	NA	NA	639	0.0	0.0	0.0	0.0	100.0	40.0	51.8	8.3	217	62.7	77.0	9.2
Middle Frisco CDP	77	NA	NA	180	81.7	0.0	0.0	6.1	12.2	12.2	63.8	23.9	34	100.0	67.6	0.0
Midway CDP	971	NA	NA	904	63.2	0.0	0.0	0.0	36.8	39.3	49.3	11.5	289	82.4	60.6	0.0
Milan village	3,243	3,255	0.4	3,261	21.9	0.5	0.5	7.0	70.2	17.7	70.9	11.4	864	77.8	47.2	15.9
Mimbres CDP	667	NA	NA	659	88.8	0.0	0.0	6.8	4.4	21.1	48.8	30.0	330	88.5	22.4	13.3
Monterey Park CDP	1,567	NA	NA	1,415	6.7	0.0	0.0	0.0	93.3	29.6	68.5	1.8	300	78.0	86.7	5.0
Monument CDP	206	NA	NA	244	85.2	0.0	0.0	0.0	14.8	0.0	93.4	6.6	86	72.1	60.5	18.6
Moquino CDP	37	NA	NA	0	0.0	0.0	0.0	0.0	0.0	0.0	0.0	0.0	0	0.0	0.0	0.0
Mora CDP	656	NA	NA	874	20.0	0.0	0.0	0.0	80.0	22.0	66.5	11.6	164	51.8	64.6	0.0
Moriarty city	1,910	1,821	-4.7	2,075	48.9	1.0	0.0	10.3	39.8	27.0	57.1	15.8	807	64.2	48.7	7.8
Morningside CDP	367	NA	NA	468	0.0	0.0	0.0	0.0	100.0	59.0	31.4	9.6	109	83.5	100.0	0.0
Mosquero village	93	91	-2.2	63	36.5	0.0	1.6	0.0	61.9	22.2	50.7	27.0	34	88.2	52.9	17.6
Mountainair town	928	885	-4.6	1,045	30.1	0.9	0.6	6.4	62.0	32.5	54.2	13.4	404	70.8	56.2	11.1
Mountain View CDP	122	NA	NA	37	100.0	0.0	0.0	0.0	0.0	0.0	0.0	100.0	37	100.0	0.0	0.0
Nadine CDP	376	NA	NA	297	61.3	0.0	0.0	0.0	38.7	22.9	72.1	5.1	101	88.1	67.3	5.0
Nageezi CDP	286	NA	NA	360	4.4	0.0	0.0	94.2	1.4	35.9	46.7	17.5	118	78.8	87.3	0.0
Nakaibito CDP	466	NA	NA	472	0.4	0.0	0.0	97.7	1.9	25.7	65.8	8.7	125	85.6	56.0	13.6
Nambe CDP	1,818	NA	NA	2,150	21.2	0.3	0.6	19.0	58.9	24.0	60.1	15.7	831	78.8	36.6	32.1
Napi Headquarters CDP	727	NA	NA	732	0.0	0.0	0.0	100.0	0.0	41.4	53.7	4.9	156	35.3	70.5	2.6

1 May be of any race.

STATE City, town, township, borough, or CDP (county if applicable)	Population				Race and Hispanic or Latino origin (percent), 2010–2014					Age (percent), 2010–2014			Households, 2010–2014			
	2010 census total population	2014 estimated population	Percent change 2010–2014	ACS total population estimate 2010–2014	White alone, not Hispanic or Latino	Black alone, not Hispanic or Latino	Asian alone, not Hispanic or Latino	All other races or 2 or more races, not Hispanic or Latino	Hispanic or Latino[1]	Under 18 years old	Age 18 to 64 years old	Age 65 years and older	Total occupied housing units	Percent owner occupied	High school diploma or less	Bachelor's degree or more
	1	2	3	4	5	6	7	8	9	10	11	12	13	14	15	16
NEW MEXICO—Con.																
Nara Visa CDP	95	NA	NA	45	100.0	0.0	0.0	0.0	0.0	0.0	26.7	73.3	37	100.0	32.4	13.5
Naschitti CDP	301	NA	NA	208	2.4	0.0	0.0	93.8	3.8	15.4	68.8	15.9	79	79.7	44.3	13.9
Navajo CDP	1,645	NA	NA	2,142	0.7	0.4	2.1	95.8	1.0	42.6	52.4	4.9	398	7.8	63.8	10.3
Navajo Dam CDP	281	NA	NA	100	67.0	0.0	0.0	0.0	33.0	14.0	53.0	33.0	86	86.0	38.4	32.6
Nenahnezad CDP	688	NA	NA	700	0.0	0.0	0.3	97.3	2.4	26.7	67.5	5.9	188	86.2	57.4	2.7
Newcomb CDP	339	NA	NA	268	4.5	1.1	3.7	90.7	0.0	18.3	69.4	12.3	96	75.0	45.8	32.3
Newkirk CDP	7	NA	NA	0	0.0	0.0	0.0	0.0	0.0	0.0	0.0	0.0	0	0.0	0.0	0.0
Nogal CDP	96	NA	NA	80	61.3	0.0	0.0	0.0	38.8	7.5	61.4	31.3	30	90.0	0.0	86.7
North Acomita Village CDP	303	NA	NA	248	3.6	0.0	0.0	91.9	4.4	25.4	64.9	9.7	59	69.5	23.7	33.9
North Hobbs CDP	5,391	NA	NA	5,869	59.4	2.6	0.2	6.6	31.1	26.0	62.2	12.0	2,002	82.6	44.9	16.2
North Hurley CDP	300	NA	NA	310	2.9	2.6	0.0	50.3	44.2	49.1	38.4	12.6	113	70.8	55.8	7.1
North Light Plant CDP	414	NA	NA	474	45.1	0.0	0.0	42.8	12.0	45.2	47.9	7.0	103	54.4	45.6	45.6
North San Ysidro CDP	159	NA	NA	150	0.0	0.0	0.0	0.0	100.0	14.0	67.4	18.7	85	100.0	35.3	36.5
North Valley CDP	11,333	NA	NA	11,189	37.3	0.0	0.8	5.9	56.0	20.8	60.2	19.0	4,317	81.5	42.3	31.2
Oasis CDP	149	NA	NA	183	100.0	0.0	0.0	0.0	0.0	0.0	75.4	24.6	36	100.0	72.2	0.0
Ohkay Owingeh CDP	1,143	NA	NA	1,549	4.5	0.0	0.0	72.1	23.4	27.9	60.7	11.2	421	80.8	48.5	9.3
Ojo Amarillo CDP	766	NA	NA	768	0.0	0.0	0.0	91.8	8.2	32.0	63.5	4.6	164	22.6	67.7	4.3
Organ CDP	323	NA	NA	116	62.1	0.0	0.0	0.0	37.9	0.0	75.0	25.0	57	100.0	28.1	0.0
Orogrande CDP	52	NA	NA	65	100.0	0.0	0.0	0.0	0.0	29.2	60.0	10.8	26	100.0	0.0	0.0
Paguate CDP	421	NA	NA	301	3.3	0.0	0.0	96.7	0.0	3.7	81.6	15.0	133	92.5	45.1	20.3
Pajarito Mesa CDP	579	NA	NA	317	0.0	0.0	0.0	0.0	100.0	41.0	59.0	0.0	69	17.4	100.0	0.0
Paradise Hills CDP	4,256	NA	NA	4,593	60.7	0.1	0.8	3.4	35.0	23.5	58.2	18.3	1,636	79.8	25.7	30.6
Paraje CDP	777	NA	NA	787	0.5	0.0	0.0	98.5	1.0	23.6	59.3	17.2	184	79.3	62.0	10.3
Pastura CDP	23	NA	NA	7	71.4	0.0	0.0	0.0	28.6	0.0	28.6	71.4	5	100.0	100.0	0.0
Peak Place CDP	377	NA	NA	340	10.3	0.0	1.5	3.2	85.0	36.7	58.3	5.0	106	82.1	76.4	5.7
Pecan Park CDP	75	NA	NA	66	86.4	0.0	0.0	0.0	13.6	0.0	48.5	51.5	45	100.0	0.0	0.0
Pecos village	1,392	1,336	-4.0	1,431	11.2	0.0	0.0	0.0	88.8	22.2	63.7	14.2	619	69.0	47.2	20.2
Peña Blanca CDP	709	NA	NA	544	13.8	1.3	0.0	9.2	75.7	22.7	62.6	14.5	202	87.1	35.6	17.8
Peñasco CDP	589	NA	NA	507	11.4	0.0	0.0	1.0	87.6	19.7	58.3	21.9	206	77.7	51.9	20.4
Peralta town	3,660	3,597	-1.7	3,636	42.8	1.5	1.7	4.4	49.6	20.1	59.7	20.1	1,305	79.8	42.5	22.3
Picuris Pueblo CDP	68	NA	NA	40	0.0	0.0	0.0	97.5	2.5	7.5	72.5	20.0	18	94.4	94.4	0.0
Pie Town CDP	186	NA	NA	61	88.5	0.0	0.0	0.0	11.5	0.0	100.0	0.0	48	100.0	52.1	20.8
Pinehill CDP	88	NA	NA	77	0.0	0.0	0.0	100.0	0.0	7.8	74.1	18.2	24	100.0	50.0	0.0
Pinon CDP	25	NA	NA	44	100.0	0.0	0.0	0.0	0.0	0.0	52.3	47.7	34	100.0	61.8	0.0
Pinos Altos CDP	198	NA	NA	22	100.0	0.0	0.0	0.0	0.0	0.0	100.0	0.0	6	100.0	0.0	100.0
Placitas CDP (Doña Ana)	576	NA	NA	646	9.6	0.0	0.0	0.0	90.4	44.9	55.0	0.0	182	35.2	57.7	0.0
Placitas CDP (Sandoval)	4,977	NA	NA	5,145	76.1	0.4	0.7	3.0	19.7	11.1	65.2	23.8	2,442	93.5	11.7	53.8
Playas CDP	74	NA	NA	197	82.2	0.0	0.0	8.6	9.1	33.0	67.1	0.0	52	0.0	0.0	26.9
Pleasanton CDP	106	NA	NA	45	60.0	0.0	0.0	0.0	40.0	0.0	84.4	15.6	34	52.9	20.6	0.0
Pojoaque CDP	1,907	NA	NA	2,257	16.5	0.4	0.7	12.4	70.0	27.3	60.5	12.2	861	66.9	40.0	23.5
Polvadera CDP	269	NA	NA	535	58.5	0.0	0.0	0.0	41.5	23.6	59.8	16.6	150	100.0	24.7	22.0
Ponderosa CDP	387	NA	NA	446	33.0	0.0	2.2	39.2	25.6	40.1	46.0	13.9	193	79.8	25.4	24.4
Ponderosa Pine CDP	1,195	NA	NA	1,037	81.7	0.0	0.0	0.0	18.3	14.4	59.3	26.3	533	96.1	13.3	59.1
Portales city	12,265	12,233	-0.3	12,481	49.0	3.6	0.7	2.9	43.8	26.1	64.0	10.0	4,387	52.5	29.5	27.1
Pueblito CDP	91	NA	NA	77	0.0	0.0	0.0	0.0	74.0	26.0	68.9	26.0	26	100.0	30.8	11.5
Pueblitos CDP	794	NA	NA	795	50.7	0.0	0.0	0.0	49.3	16.2	61.2	22.5	294	75.5	39.8	16.0
Pueblo CDP	0	NA	NA	12	0.0	0.0	0.0	0.0	100.0	0.0	100.0	0.0	12	100.0	100.0	0.0
Pueblo of Sandia Village CDP	369	NA	NA	338	1.2	0.0	1.2	88.5	9.2	28.7	60.7	10.7	116	83.6	28.4	24.1
Pueblo Pintado CDP	192	NA	NA	260	2.7	0.0	0.0	93.8	3.5	43.1	51.9	5.0	54	61.1	61.1	27.8
Puerto de Luna CDP	141	NA	NA	166	0.0	0.0	0.0	0.0	100.0	34.3	59.7	6.0	14	100.0	100.0	0.0
Pulpotio Bareas CDP	120	NA	NA	243	16.5	0.0	0.0	0.0	83.5	30.1	69.9	0.0	36	41.7	100.0	0.0
Quemado CDP	228	NA	NA	257	64.2	0.0	0.0	25.3	10.5	18.7	76.7	4.7	67	65.7	52.2	0.0
Questa village	1,770	1,769	-0.1	1,779	11.2	0.6	0.0	0.0	88.2	24.0	56.9	18.9	715	68.7	53.3	7.3
Radium Springs CDP	1,699	NA	NA	1,292	56.5	0.0	0.0	0.0	43.5	17.0	62.2	20.8	484	88.6	40.9	36.8
Ramah CDP	370	NA	NA	186	69.4	0.0	0.0	29.6	1.1	25.9	50.6	23.7	60	53.3	76.7	0.0
Rancho Grande CDP	142	NA	NA	254	94.1	0.0	3.5	0.0	2.4	0.0	87.8	12.2	89	100.0	71.9	11.2
Ranchos de Taos CDP	2,518	NA	NA	2,285	49.1	2.9	0.5	3.1	44.4	22.9	53.8	23.3	849	72.7	42.6	26.6
Raton city	6,885	6,326	-8.1	6,627	38.0	0.4	0.2	1.8	59.6	20.6	57.9	21.5	2,761	63.0	48.5	15.6
Red River town	477	480	0.6	383	85.1	0.0	0.0	3.7	11.2	11.9	67.6	20.4	198	45.5	29.3	34.3
Regina CDP	105	NA	NA	5	100.0	0.0	0.0	0.0	0.0	0.0	0.0	100.0	5	100.0	0.0	100.0
Reserve village	292	279	-4.5	620	64.2	0.2	0.0	1.3	34.4	16.5	61.3	22.1	177	71.2	57.1	7.3
Ribera CDP	416	NA	NA	610	10.0	0.0	2.5	4.9	82.6	21.3	66.1	12.6	152	92.8	78.9	10.5
Rincon CDP	271	NA	NA	52	0.0	0.0	0.0	0.0	100.0	71.2	28.9	0.0	8	100.0	100.0	0.0
Rio Communities CDP	4,723	NA	NA	5,476	48.4	3.5	0.0	2.9	45.2	26.3	53.0	20.6	2,077	80.7	34.8	17.9
Rio en Medio CDP	143	NA	NA	239	0.0	0.0	0.0	48.5	51.5	7.1	86.6	6.3	87	89.7	62.1	0.0
Rio Lucio CDP	389	NA	NA	385	1.8	0.0	0.0	0.5	97.7	16.8	63.2	20.0	140	88.6	45.0	15.7
Rio Rancho city	87,394	93,820	7.4	90,627	52.1	2.8	1.7	4.4	38.9	27.2	60.7	12.1	32,574	78.6	25.9	31.2
Rivers CDP	28	NA	NA	0	0.0	0.0	0.0	0.0	0.0	0.0	0.0	0.0	0	0.0	0.0	0.0
Rock Springs CDP	567	NA	NA	277	0.0	0.0	0.0	95.3	4.7	53.7	36.9	9.4	55	98.2	65.5	0.0
Rodeo CDP	101	NA	NA	95	46.3	0.0	0.0	0.0	53.7	23.2	52.7	24.2	39	89.7	71.8	10.3
Rodey CDP	388	NA	NA	163	0.0	0.0	0.0	0.0	100.0	40.5	45.4	14.1	45	51.1	100.0	0.0
Rosedale CDP	394	NA	NA	249	68.3	0.0	0.0	0.0	31.7	0.0	40.6	59.4	138	76.8	63.0	37.0
Roswell city	48,411	48,608	0.4	48,568	39.3	2.1	1.1	1.8	55.7	28.1	57.4	14.5	17,731	61.5	45.2	19.5
Rowe CDP	415	NA	NA	294	31.3	0.0	0.0	0.0	68.7	4.1	75.3	20.7	137	89.8	73.7	7.3
Roy village	234	230	-1.7	256	35.2	0.0	0.0	0.0	64.8	11.0	61.7	27.3	81	84.0	56.8	16.0
Ruidoso village	8,027	7,824	-2.5	7,954	69.0	0.5	0.4	7.5	22.6	20.1	52.6	27.1	3,576	73.1	28.1	38.3
Ruidoso Downs city	2,792	2,635	-5.6	2,722	42.0	0.0	0.0	1.8	56.2	26.1	59.1	14.7	1,029	64.0	52.0	12.1
Sacramento CDP	58	NA	NA	74	86.5	0.0	0.0	0.0	13.5	0.0	100.0	0.0	31	54.8	45.2	0.0
Salem CDP	942	NA	NA	957	0.0	0.0	0.0	0.0	100.0	44.2	53.0	2.7	251	78.1	79.3	10.0
San Acacia CDP	44	NA	NA	254	29.5	0.0	0.0	0.0	70.5	27.2	36.2	36.6	51	100.0	74.5	0.0
San Antonio CDP	165	NA	NA	24	100.0	0.0	0.0	0.0	0.0	0.0	100.0	0.0	24	100.0	0.0	100.0
San Antonio CDP (Bernalillo)	985	NA	NA	888	73.1	0.0	5.1	0.0	21.8	19.1	59.6	21.3	417	96.4	28.1	51.6
San Antonio CDP (Socorro)	94	NA	NA	87	56.3	0.0	0.0	0.0	43.7	0.0	75.9	24.1	44	100.0	63.6	36.4
San Cristobal CDP	273	NA	NA	232	53.9	0.0	0.0	0.0	46.1	0.0	63.7	36.2	85	100.0	31.8	15.3
Sandia Heights CDP	3,193	NA	NA	3,239	89.7	0.0	1.9	3.6	4.8	8.5	54.3	37.2	1,552	90.3	3.5	74.9
Sandia Knolls CDP	1,208	NA	NA	1,526	90.2	0.0	0.0	0.0	9.8	19.2	62.6	18.1	609	83.3	11.5	54.2
Sandia Park CDP	237	NA	NA	236	44.5	0.0	0.0	0.0	55.5	28.8	57.6	13.6	96	100.0	67.7	25.0

1 May be of any race.

Table A. All Places — **Population and Housing**

STATE City, town, township, borough, or CDP (county if applicable)	Population: 2010 census total population	Population: 2014 estimated population	Population: Percent change 2010–2014	Population: ACS total population estimate 2010–2014	Race and Hispanic or Latino origin (percent), 2010–2014: White alone, not Hispanic or Latino	Black alone, not Hispanic or Latino	Asian alone, not Hispanic or Latino	All other races or 2 or more races, not Hispanic or Latino	Hispanic or Latino[1]	Age (percent), 2010–2014: Under 18 years old	Age 18 to 64 years old	Age 65 years and older	Households, 2010–2014: Total occupied housing units	Percent owner occupied	Householders by level of education (percent): High school diploma or less	Bachelor's degree or more
	1	2	3	4	5	6	7	8	9	10	11	12	13	14	15	16
NEW MEXICO—Con.																
San Felipe Pueblo CDP	2,404	NA	NA	3,027	0.0	0.0	0.0	99.4	0.6	32.6	61.2	6.1	505	93.7	56.8	7.1
San Fidel CDP	138	NA	NA	143	2.1	0.0	0.7	0.7	96.5	22.4	77.0	0.7	69	100.0	100.0	0.0
San Ildefonso Pueblo CDP	524	NA	NA	677	6.5	0.0	0.0	66.9	26.6	20.5	67.1	12.4	229	88.2	46.3	17.5
San Jon village	216	204	-5.6	163	73.0	0.0	0.0	4.3	22.7	34.4	36.8	28.8	66	77.3	51.5	12.1
San Jose CDP (Rio Arriba)	695	NA	NA	695	2.0	1.3	0.0	2.3	94.4	23.1	57.8	19.1	265	84.5	49.4	10.9
San Jose CDP (San Miguel)	137	NA	NA	102	0.0	0.0	0.0	0.0	100.0	0.0	49.0	51.0	39	100.0	17.9	28.2
San Lorenzo CDP	97	NA	NA	38	0.0	0.0	0.0	0.0	100.0	0.0	100.0	0.0	18	100.0	100.0	0.0
San Luis CDP	59	NA	NA	0	0.0	0.0	0.0	0.0	0.0	0.0	0.0	0.0	0	0.0	0.0	0.0
San Mateo CDP	161	NA	NA	190	50.0	0.0	32.1	0.0	17.9	14.8	20.5	64.7	72	100.0	18.1	58.3
San Miguel CDP	1,153	NA	NA	1,426	11.4	0.0	0.0	0.0	88.6	35.4	51.5	13.1	446	73.1	74.2	10.8
Sanostee CDP	371	NA	NA	361	0.0	0.0	0.0	100.0	0.0	31.5	61.7	6.6	119	81.5	65.5	7.6
San Pablo CDP	806	NA	NA	1,007	23.8	0.0	1.3	0.0	74.9	30.6	55.1	14.4	335	89.9	51.0	29.9
San Pedro CDP	184	NA	NA	157	94.9	0.0	0.0	0.0	5.1	0.0	95.5	4.5	75	100.0	24.0	61.3
San Rafael CDP	933	NA	NA	860	24.0	0.0	0.0	7.2	68.8	21.3	69.8	8.8	279	92.5	59.9	0.0
Santa Ana Pueblo CDP	610	NA	NA	684	0.0	0.0	0.3	97.2	2.5	29.9	58.4	11.7	183	94.0	41.0	12.6
Santa Clara village	1,691	1,665	-1.5	1,474	12.6	0.0	0.0	1.8	85.6	22.7	52.2	25.0	571	66.4	53.6	11.6
Santa Clara Pueblo CDP	1,018	NA	NA	989	1.1	0.0	0.0	72.7	26.2	22.4	64.2	13.5	362	88.1	42.0	16.9
Santa Cruz CDP	368	NA	NA	345	5.8	0.0	0.0	0.0	94.2	38.0	46.7	15.4	126	38.9	54.0	9.5
Santa Fe city	67,968	70,297	3.4	69,245	45.4	0.9	1.6	3.5	48.6	19.0	61.6	19.6	31,498	61.0	24.8	48.9
Santa Rosa city	2,850	2,729	-4.2	2,965	19.0	3.6	0.0	4.5	72.8	17.3	64.8	17.7	749	69.3	57.4	12.1
Santa Teresa CDP	4,258	NA	NA	4,271	22.5	1.5	0.0	1.1	74.9	31.7	57.0	11.5	1,584	57.4	32.3	35.9
Santo Domingo Pueblo CDP	2,456	NA	NA	2,517	0.0	0.0	0.0	99.7	0.3	31.0	58.4	10.6	417	89.0	65.0	7.2
San Ysidro CDP	2,090	NA	NA	2,335	34.0	0.3	0.5	4.2	61.0	26.7	51.3	22.1	722	94.6	37.5	26.2
San Ysidro village	193	194	0.5	150	26.0	0.0	2.7	10.0	61.3	16.6	65.9	17.3	63	82.5	38.1	31.7
Sausal CDP	1,056	NA	NA	966	44.3	0.0	0.0	2.3	53.4	20.1	63.6	16.3	358	71.8	49.7	18.2
Seama CDP	465	NA	NA	302	0.0	0.0	0.0	75.5	24.5	24.2	54.5	21.2	87	95.4	49.4	0.0
Seboyeta CDP	179	NA	NA	201	9.5	0.0	0.0	5.5	85.1	16.4	63.2	20.4	100	73.0	81.0	19.0
Sedillo CDP	802	NA	NA	715	46.7	0.0	2.9	0.0	50.3	17.9	74.4	7.7	287	95.8	16.0	59.2
Sena CDP	129	NA	NA	162	0.0	0.0	0.0	0.0	100.0	0.0	100.0	0.0	91	100.0	69.2	0.0
Sheep Springs CDP	245	NA	NA	236	0.0	0.0	0.0	91.5	8.5	33.5	60.7	5.9	73	46.6	58.9	11.0
Shiprock CDP	8,295	NA	NA	9,004	3.3	0.2	1.0	93.9	1.6	33.0	59.9	7.2	2,269	54.6	47.0	12.1
Silver City town	10,315	10,172	-1.4	10,245	39.6	0.5	0.2	2.8	56.9	22.1	60.2	17.8	4,146	66.6	30.5	36.5
Skyline-Ganipa CDP	1,224	NA	NA	1,234	2.2	0.0	0.0	97.8	0.0	30.1	63.7	6.3	266	83.8	55.3	6.4
Socorro city	9,043	8,751	-3.2	8,898	37.0	1.5	0.5	5.2	55.8	25.5	59.9	14.6	2,681	61.5	51.5	26.8
Soham CDP	210	NA	NA	144	0.0	0.0	0.0	0.0	100.0	14.6	85.5	0.0	100	100.0	100.0	0.0
Sombrillo CDP	351	NA	NA	561	45.1	0.0	0.0	0.0	54.9	13.7	63.1	23.4	275	85.1	25.5	41.1
South Acomita Village CDP	105	NA	NA	136	0.0	0.0	0.0	100.0	0.0	10.3	62.4	27.2	28	85.7	53.6	0.0
South Valley CDP	40,976	NA	NA	41,760	16.2	0.8	0.2	1.7	81.0	24.4	61.8	13.7	13,413	74.6	59.0	14.6
Spencerville CDP	1,258	NA	NA	1,419	59.8	0.0	0.8	8.2	31.3	28.4	55.3	16.1	520	93.7	59.4	8.5
Springer town	1,047	963	-8.0	1,188	30.0	0.7	0.0	1.9	67.4	27.0	56.3	16.7	452	63.1	46.5	11.1
Sunland Park city	14,140	15,400	8.9	14,794	3.7	0.3	0.0	0.0	95.9	32.7	58.3	9.0	3,855	67.5	72.4	9.4
Sunshine CDP	420	NA	NA	312	63.8	0.0	0.0	1.6	34.6	17.9	68.5	13.5	139	74.8	40.3	30.2
Tajique CDP	130	NA	NA	42	0.0	0.0	0.0	0.0	100.0	0.0	0.0	100.0	21	100.0	100.0	0.0
Talpa CDP	778	NA	NA	1,065	19.7	0.0	0.0	0.0	80.3	21.5	66.0	12.3	355	89.9	27.9	34.9
Taos town	5,720	5,766	0.8	5,713	43.9	0.3	0.6	7.6	47.6	18.8	62.7	18.7	2,491	49.8	30.1	35.1
Taos Pueblo CDP	1,135	NA	NA	1,006	0.4	0.0	0.0	94.0	5.6	15.8	63.1	21.3	385	88.6	30.9	22.3
Taos Ski Valley village	69	69	0.0	91	72.5	0.0	0.0	3.3	24.2	17.6	82.5	0.0	27	22.2	14.8	63.0
Tatum town	798	859	7.6	652	55.1	0.0	0.0	3.7	41.3	27.0	54.3	18.7	244	81.1	64.8	6.1
Tecolote CDP	298	NA	NA	97	0.0	0.0	0.0	0.0	100.0	0.0	31.0	69.1	85	89.4	89.4	0.0
Tecolotito CDP	232	NA	NA	122	0.0	0.0	0.0	0.0	100.0	41.0	52.5	6.6	37	100.0	100.0	0.0
Tesuque CDP	925	NA	NA	867	77.3	0.0	0.0	1.5	21.2	8.3	70.6	21.1	528	69.5	15.0	61.9
Tesuque Pueblo CDP	233	NA	NA	176	1.7	0.0	0.0	85.2	13.1	30.6	56.3	13.1	50	80.0	52.0	16.0
Texico city	1,130	1,137	0.6	1,230	32.2	7.4	0.0	3.3	57.2	30.8	58.9	10.2	429	61.3	56.9	7.0
Thoreau CDP	1,865	NA	NA	1,514	6.1	0.0	0.0	76.2	17.7	32.7	56.4	11.0	388	75.8	60.8	26.3
Tierra Amarilla CDP	382	NA	NA	362	1.1	0.0	0.0	2.5	96.4	13.0	66.3	20.7	103	100.0	24.3	0.0
Tijeras village	542	545	0.6	418	41.1	2.9	0.7	2.4	52.9	11.8	74.6	13.6	146	82.9	38.4	33.6
Timberon CDP	348	NA	NA	238	88.2	0.0	0.0	3.8	8.0	26.9	58.8	14.3	143	88.8	65.0	0.0
Tohatchi CDP	808	NA	NA	978	5.6	0.0	2.5	91.2	0.7	29.6	56.7	13.8	256	53.5	39.8	30.1
Tome CDP	1,867	NA	NA	1,578	17.9	0.0	0.0	0.0	82.1	11.7	75.6	12.7	702	71.9	38.5	16.2
Torreon CDP (Sandoval)	326	NA	NA	409	3.4	0.0	0.0	91.2	5.4	28.1	63.7	8.3	82	76.8	79.3	8.5
Torreon CDP (Torrance)	237	NA	NA	369	36.0	0.0	0.0	0.0	64.0	0.0	54.5	45.5	179	100.0	89.4	0.0
Trout Valley CDP	16	NA	NA	0	0.0	0.0	0.0	0.0	0.0	0.0	0.0	0.0	0	0.0	0.0	0.0
Truchas CDP	560	NA	NA	915	31.4	0.0	0.0	0.0	68.6	17.3	45.7	36.9	407	97.1	42.0	45.7
Truth or Consequences city	6,474	6,103	-5.7	6,337	64.5	0.4	1.8	1.8	31.5	14.0	54.8	31.1	2,815	70.5	47.5	20.9
Tse Bonito CDP	299	NA	NA	227	18.5	0.0	0.0	23.3	58.1	44.5	46.6	8.8	76	100.0	34.2	0.0
Tucumcari city	5,363	5,051	-5.8	5,237	42.6	0.8	0.0	0.4	56.2	25.4	55.8	18.9	1,849	67.9	53.4	16.6
Tularosa village	2,843	2,894	1.8	2,916	34.5	0.0	1.4	5.6	58.5	19.0	57.7	23.3	1,345	72.3	35.0	27.7
Twin Forks CDP	196	NA	NA	99	100.0	0.0	0.0	0.0	0.0	0.0	0.0	100.0	51	100.0	0.0	49.0
Twin Lakes CDP	1,052	NA	NA	895	2.9	0.0	0.0	97.1	0.0	24.3	63.4	12.3	218	81.2	72.9	2.8
Tyrone CDP	637	NA	NA	721	66.4	0.0	0.0	0.0	33.6	27.6	43.1	29.3	331	78.2	19.6	32.3
University Park CDP	4,192	NA	NA	3,179	34.2	7.4	12.4	5.3	40.6	12.4	87.4	0.2	634	0.0	4.4	29.5
Upper Fruitland CDP	1,662	NA	NA	1,623	1.4	0.0	0.0	97.5	1.1	27.8	65.4	6.9	430	90.9	59.3	7.7
Ute Park CDP	71	NA	NA	112	100.0	0.0	0.0	0.0	0.0	0.0	51.8	48.2	91	100.0	0.0	100.0
Vadito CDP	270	NA	NA	279	5.7	0.0	0.0	0.7	93.5	22.3	62.7	15.1	93	91.4	41.9	14.0
Vado CDP	3,194	NA	NA	2,781	8.1	0.7	0.0	0.0	91.2	32.2	51.8	16.0	798	80.1	87.5	1.1
Valencia CDP	2,192	NA	NA	2,258	46.6	0.0	0.8	0.0	52.7	13.5	69.9	16.4	956	84.5	54.2	18.1
Vaughn town	446	423	-5.2	509	19.1	0.6	0.0	0.0	80.4	28.8	58.7	12.6	173	76.9	58.4	8.1
Veguita CDP	232	NA	NA	219	9.1	0.0	0.0	0.0	90.9	23.3	57.0	19.6	71	100.0	74.6	0.0
Velarde CDP	502	NA	NA	251	39.0	0.0	0.0	0.0	61.0	27.1	61.0	12.0	109	100.0	26.6	36.7
Ventura CDP	468	NA	NA	285	83.2	0.0	0.0	0.0	16.8	7.4	42.4	50.2	155	100.0	49.0	6.5
Villanueva CDP	229	NA	NA	252	19.0	0.0	0.0	0.0	81.0	18.6	58.3	23.0	75	100.0	56.0	14.7
Virden village	151	141	-6.6	128	93.8	0.0	0.0	0.0	6.3	18.0	65.6	16.4	55	83.6	27.3	40.0
Wagon Mound village	314	296	-5.7	603	22.4	0.5	0.0	0.0	77.1	11.2	60.7	28.2	225	63.1	46.2	28.9
Waterflow CDP	1,670	NA	NA	1,673	61.1	0.0	0.0	26.7	12.3	25.2	65.3	9.6	471	84.1	41.8	28.0
Watrous CDP	135	NA	NA	0	0.0	0.0	0.0	0.0	0.0	0.0	0.0	0.0	0	0.0	0.0	0.0

1 May be of any race.

Table A. All Places — **Population and Housing**

STATE City, town, township, borough, or CDP (county if applicable)	Population				Race and Hispanic or Latino origin (percent), 2010–2014					Age (percent), 2010–2014			Households, 2010–2014		Householders by level of education (percent)	
	2010 census total population	2014 estimated population	Percent change 2010–2014	ACS total population estimate 2010–2014	White alone, not Hispanic or Latino	Black alone, not Hispanic or Latino	Asian alone, not Hispanic or Latino	All other races or 2 or more races, not Hispanic or Latino	Hispanic or Latino[1]	Under 18 years old	Age 18 to 64 years old	Age 65 years and older	Total occupied housing units	Percent owner occupied	High school diploma or less	Bachelor's degree or more
	1	2	3	4	5	6	7	8	9	10	11	12	13	14	15	16
NEW MEXICO—Con.																
Weed CDP	63	NA	NA	37	100.0	0.0	0.0	0.0	0.0	0.0	32.4	67.6	25	56.0	44.0	56.0
West Hammond CDP	2,790	NA	NA	2,829	55.4	0.0	0.6	11.6	32.4	20.2	71.3	8.4	905	90.2	42.9	13.5
White Rock CDP	5,725	NA	NA	5,977	79.9	0.7	2.5	3.4	13.5	26.8	57.4	15.7	2,221	90.7	5.0	63.8
White Sands CDP	1,651	NA	NA	1,670	55.4	22.5	1.7	4.5	15.9	34.7	64.2	1.1	482	0.0	37.3	16.0
Whites City CDP	7	NA	NA	118	100.0	0.0	0.0	0.0	0.0	0.0	100.0	0.0	31	0.0	100.0	0.0
White Signal CDP	181	NA	NA	208	88.9	0.0	0.0	3.8	7.2	9.6	57.2	33.2	103	100.0	20.4	44.7
Willard village	253	242	-4.3	194	2.6	0.0	0.0	0.0	97.4	29.9	49.4	20.6	71	81.7	74.6	2.8
Williamsburg village	450	427	-5.1	525	87.0	0.0	0.0	0.0	13.0	15.5	50.1	34.5	231	70.6	42.0	3.9
Windmill CDP	43	NA	NA	55	81.8	0.0	0.0	0.0	18.2	25.5	59.9	14.5	23	78.3	17.4	21.7
Winston CDP	61	NA	NA	0	0.0	0.0	0.0	0.0	0.0	0.0	0.0	0.0	0	0.0	0.0	0.0
Yah-ta-hey CDP	590	NA	NA	407	0.0	0.0	0.0	100.0	0.0	40.8	57.7	1.5	102	100.0	91.2	0.0
Young Place CDP	187	NA	NA	65	100.0	0.0	0.0	0.0	0.0	0.0	100.0	0.0	65	100.0	0.0	0.0
Youngsville CDP	56	NA	NA	58	36.2	0.0	0.0	0.0	63.8	0.0	93.1	6.9	28	67.9	89.3	0.0
Zia Pueblo CDP	737	NA	NA	886	0.6	0.0	0.0	96.8	2.6	30.6	60.8	8.6	202	91.6	57.4	7.4
Zuni Pueblo CDP	6,302	NA	NA	9,504	0.5	0.0	0.3	96.3	2.9	22.1	69.9	8.1	1,524	94.4	57.9	10.0
NEW YORK	19,378,112	19,746,227	1.9	19,594,330	57.3	14.4	7.7	2.4	18.2	21.9	64.1	14.1	7,255,528	53.8	37.6	36.1
Accord CDP	562	NA	NA	765	79.2	2.5	0.0	15.3	3.0	41.3	54.4	4.2	187	77.5	18.2	26.2
Adams village	1,782	1,839	3.2	1,612	91.7	1.1	2.1	1.9	3.2	25.1	60.4	14.6	719	58.1	41.2	22.8
Adams town (Jefferson)	5,145	5,302	3.1	5,272	95.1	0.5	1.0	1.6	1.8	21.5	63.7	14.9	2,052	70.1	43.9	24.4
Adams Center CDP	1,568	NA	NA	1,996	94.6	0.0	0.9	2.7	1.8	17.3	70.2	12.7	804	71.8	51.5	19.7
Addison village	1,763	1,730	-1.9	1,809	98.2	0.2	0.1	1.1	0.4	28.0	56.5	15.4	745	71.1	47.7	18.0
Addison town (Steuben)	2,595	2,560	-1.3	2,583	98.5	0.2	0.3	0.7	0.3	27.6	58.0	14.4	1,052	70.4	46.1	15.7
Afton village	832	818	-1.7	1,082	97.0	0.2	0.0	1.8	1.1	25.0	55.7	19.1	437	70.3	54.5	18.3
Afton town (Chenango)	2,857	2,811	-1.6	2,827	97.7	0.1	0.5	1.3	0.4	20.0	58.1	21.9	1,135	79.7	56.2	16.4
Airmont village	8,628	8,878	2.9	8,770	84.3	2.3	4.1	2.6	6.7	27.6	55.4	17.1	2,711	76.9	32.6	43.5
Akron village	2,873	2,855	-0.6	2,850	90.8	1.0	1.2	5.1	1.9	22.2	62.5	15.2	1,228	59.4	43.3	25.1
Alabama town (Genesee)	1,863	1,826	-2.0	1,713	93.2	1.3	0.6	4.2	0.7	19.2	63.9	16.9	682	80.5	56.5	12.9
Albany city & MCD (Albany)	97,856	98,566	0.7	98,287	51.7	29.3	6.2	3.6	9.2	17.6	70.1	12.2	39,903	38.1	32.3	39.6
Albertson CDP	5,182	NA	NA	5,154	66.9	0.0	24.4	1.9	6.7	18.9	61.4	19.6	1,773	96.6	23.9	53.4
Albion village	6,056	6,007	-0.8	5,799	78.7	11.1	0.5	0.7	9.0	21.7	64.3	14.2	2,332	58.8	63.2	8.0
Albion town (Orleans)	8,468	8,431	-0.4	8,442	68.6	17.8	0.4	2.6	10.5	16.3	72.4	11.5	2,343	62.5	59.0	13.2
Albion town (Oswego)	2,073	2,137	3.1	2,087	96.1	0.0	0.8	2.0	1.1	27.2	62.0	11.0	730	85.9	54.2	10.7
Alden village	2,605	2,599	-0.2	2,606	97.7	0.1	0.0	0.8	1.5	22.6	62.6	14.8	1,191	61.5	38.0	22.7
Alden town (Erie)	10,865	10,629	-2.2	10,717	86.7	7.9	0.1	2.3	2.9	19.0	65.7	15.4	3,409	78.7	41.5	23.2
Alexander village	509	500	-1.8	528	97.3	2.3	0.4	0.0	0.0	32.4	56.9	10.8	188	67.6	31.4	15.4
Alexander town (Genesee)	2,534	2,495	-1.5	2,631	98.2	0.7	0.7	0.0	0.4	23.1	64.1	12.7	964	87.7	48.5	13.3
Alexandria town (Jefferson)	4,057	4,180	3.0	4,157	96.9	0.7	0.3	1.1	1.1	24.4	61.1	14.5	1,693	75.1	44.9	17.4
Alexandria Bay village	1,067	1,101	3.2	1,001	92.2	2.8	1.1	2.9	1.0	20.9	64.1	15.1	451	50.3	43.5	22.6
Alfred village	4,175	4,028	-3.5	4,278	77.2	10.1	5.3	2.0	5.4	3.9	94.2	1.8	394	27.9	6.6	59.9
Alfred town (Allegany)	5,238	5,068	-3.2	5,127	80.8	8.4	4.4	1.9	4.5	7.2	88.5	4.3	783	48.8	18.6	57.0
Allegany village	1,816	1,767	-2.7	1,868	93.5	0.9	1.9	2.4	1.2	15.7	69.5	14.8	718	62.8	22.7	40.5
Allegany town (Cattaraugus)	8,004	7,763	-3.0	7,860	93.1	1.6	1.6	1.4	2.2	15.1	68.7	16.3	2,699	75.1	40.3	25.0
Allegany Reservation (Cattaraugus)	1,004	994	-1.0	932	27.0	1.1	6.1	65.1	0.6	27.6	58.9	13.5	373	70.5	59.2	4.8
Allen town (Allegany)	448	446	-0.4	581	100.0	0.0	0.0	0.0	0.0	40.0	45.2	15.0	192	92.2	67.7	8.3
Alma town (Allegany)	842	845	0.4	905	98.1	0.0	0.0	0.0	1.9	27.3	59.5	13.4	347	80.1	62.8	9.2
Almond village	466	451	-3.2	535	94.4	0.0	3.4	1.1	1.1	26.8	60.2	13.1	208	71.6	21.6	32.2
Almond town (Allegany)	1,633	1,587	-2.8	1,706	94.7	0.0	3.6	1.0	0.7	26.0	60.5	13.6	661	85.0	34.8	33.1
Altamont village	1,720	1,725	0.3	1,609	94.0	0.1	0.0	0.7	5.1	19.9	65.8	14.2	670	69.4	25.2	38.4
Altmar village	407	393	-3.4	372	94.1	0.0	1.9	1.6	2.4	29.0	63.2	7.8	143	58.0	60.1	3.5
Altona CDP	730	NA	NA	832	53.5	32.1	0.2	0.7	13.5	9.5	78.6	11.9	157	73.2	73.9	5.7
Altona town (Clinton)	2,887	2,944	2.0	2,913	84.1	9.4	0.6	1.7	4.2	19.2	71.0	9.9	973	81.8	61.6	8.6
Amagansett CDP	1,165	NA	NA	1,355	92.5	2.1	0.5	0.0	4.9	18.9	44.9	36.2	502	81.5	28.7	61.4
Amboy town (Oswego)	1,263	1,300	2.9	1,350	95.3	0.0	0.0	3.9	0.8	24.4	66.0	9.5	492	91.1	56.1	12.6
Amenia CDP	955	NA	NA	1,222	68.5	1.7	0.0	0.3	29.5	29.8	67.1	3.0	445	54.6	57.8	8.3
Amenia town (Dutchess)	4,436	4,353	-1.9	4,399	82.2	4.5	1.1	0.8	11.5	20.4	64.2	15.4	1,692	66.7	41.8	19.6
Ames village	145	143	-1.4	176	96.6	0.6	0.0	0.0	2.8	25.5	53.4	21.0	64	85.9	42.2	18.8
Amherst town (Erie)	122,366	124,837	2.0	123,542	81.0	5.6	7.7	2.4	3.3	19.4	61.6	18.7	49,174	71.0	19.5	55.1
Amity town (Allegany)	2,308	2,242	-2.9	2,401	95.7	1.0	0.1	2.2	1.0	22.0	58.9	18.9	965	74.3	48.3	17.9
Amityville village	9,523	9,522	0.0	9,551	67.3	9.4	1.8	2.7	18.8	20.0	61.6	18.5	3,449	65.9	33.7	37.7
Amsterdam city & MCD (Montgomery)	18,627	18,135	-2.6	18,348	66.6	2.7	0.5	2.4	27.7	24.0	59.9	16.2	7,584	49.7	52.0	14.6
Amsterdam town (Montgomery)	5,559	6,000	7.9	5,801	94.3	0.2	0.0	0.3	5.2	14.3	60.2	25.5	2,448	84.8	43.7	22.1
Ancram town (Columbia)	1,571	1,534	-2.4	1,606	87.8	6.0	1.8	1.2	3.2	18.1	58.6	23.0	633	75.2	48.3	34.9
Andes CDP	252	NA	NA	219	89.0	0.0	1.8	0.0	9.1	32.9	48.9	18.3	96	64.6	42.7	36.5
Andes town (Delaware)	1,301	1,268	-2.5	1,133	95.6	0.5	0.9	0.5	2.5	17.4	54.8	27.7	525	88.2	42.5	25.9
Andover village	1,041	1,017	-2.3	860	97.2	0.8	1.6	0.0	0.3	20.3	60.1	19.5	379	71.2	39.6	23.7
Andover town (Allegany)	1,829	1,785	-2.4	1,695	97.1	0.4	0.8	0.0	1.7	23.7	57.3	19.1	701	74.2	46.1	17.0
Angelica village	869	845	-2.8	894	98.8	0.0	0.4	0.6	0.2	23.1	57.2	19.8	369	74.8	47.4	15.2
Angelica town (Allegany)	1,403	1,376	-1.9	1,376	99.1	0.1	0.3	0.4	0.1	24.2	57.8	18.1	569	79.8	48.9	16.5
Angola village	2,127	2,120	-0.3	1,813	92.5	0.0	0.3	4.5	2.7	23.9	59.7	16.3	765	74.2	41.7	18.8
Angola on the Lake CDP	1,675	NA	NA	1,720	97.8	0.1	1.1	0.5	0.4	16.1	62.2	21.6	770	81.3	54.3	12.3
Annsville town (Oneida)	3,012	2,978	-1.1	2,985	95.8	0.2	0.0	1.0	3.0	27.4	61.4	11.1	1,091	77.1	60.9	11.3
Antwerp village	680	700	2.9	540	91.1	0.0	2.8	1.7	4.4	22.8	62.5	14.6	207	72.9	51.7	13.0
Antwerp town (Jefferson)	1,846	1,899	2.9	1,627	94.8	0.1	1.8	1.1	2.3	24.7	62.1	13.2	605	78.5	61.3	12.1
Apalachin CDP	1,131	NA	NA	1,448	95.6	0.3	0.7	0.4	2.9	22.8	61.7	15.7	492	59.1	58.3	11.8
Aquebogue CDP	2,438	NA	NA	2,012	74.4	9.3	0.0	0.0	16.3	18.2	69.7	11.9	751	69.6	44.2	33.7
Arcade village	2,065	2,003	-3.0	2,187	98.1	0.0	1.1	0.2	0.5	26.7	64.7	8.6	931	60.9	42.9	18.9
Arcade town (Wyoming)	4,199	4,136	-1.5	4,177	97.2	0.0	1.6	0.6	0.6	20.8	61.0	18.1	1,837	72.9	47.6	17.3
Arcadia town (Wayne)	14,240	13,915	-2.3	14,078	87.4	4.7	0.8	1.4	5.6	20.7	62.6	16.7	5,784	67.8	50.1	17.0
Ardsley village	4,452	4,555	2.3	4,519	61.9	3.9	21.7	1.1	11.4	23.7	57.2	19.1	1,535	80.8	11.3	70.4
Argyle village	303	297	-2.0	318	99.7	0.0	0.0	0.3	0.0	22.9	60.1	17.0	133	61.7	57.1	24.1
Argyle town (Washington)	3,782	3,727	-1.5	3,758	97.5	0.4	1.7	0.4	0.0	18.5	64.0	17.3	1,449	88.6	48.1	20.8
Arietta town (Hamilton)	304	294	-3.3	230	98.7	0.0	0.0	0.0	1.3	6.5	79.1	14.3	63	95.2	34.9	31.7

1 May be of any race.

Table A. All Places — **Population and Housing**

STATE City, town, township, borough, or CDP (county if applicable)	Population: 2010 census total population	Population: 2014 estimated population	Population: Percent change 2010–2014	Population: ACS total population estimate 2010–2014	Race and Hispanic or Latino origin (percent), 2010–2014: White alone, not Hispanic or Latino	Race: Black alone, not Hispanic or Latino	Race: Asian alone, not Hispanic or Latino	Race: All other races or 2 or more races, not Hispanic or Latino	Race: Hispanic or Latino[1]	Age (percent), 2010–2014: Under 18 years old	Age: Age 18 to 64 years old	Age: Age 65 years and older	Households, 2010–2014: Total occupied housing units	Households: Percent owner occupied	Households: Householders by level of education (percent): High school diploma or less	Households: Householders by level of education (percent): Bachelor's degree or more
	1	2	3	4	5	6	7	8	9	10	11	12	13	14	15	16
NEW YORK—Con.																
Arkport village	844	829	-1.8	785	96.8	0.0	0.0	0.0	3.2	26.4	55.6	18.1	338	75.7	42.9	14.2
Arkwright town (Chautauqua)	1,061	1,049	-1.1	975	96.8	0.3	0.4	1.6	0.8	16.1	65.2	18.7	399	93.5	55.4	21.8
Arlington CDP	4,061	NA	NA	4,033	51.8	19.4	11.8	3.8	13.3	19.8	67.1	13.1	1,369	30.6	38.1	29.6
Armonk CDP	4,330	NA	NA	4,535	88.3	0.9	2.2	0.8	7.8	34.5	52.7	12.8	1,375	88.9	13.7	76.1
Asharoken village	654	654	0.0	552	96.6	0.0	1.6	0.7	1.1	15.4	62.1	22.5	215	84.7	15.3	55.8
Ashford town (Cattaraugus)	2,132	2,095	-1.7	2,101	95.3	0.2	0.3	2.7	1.5	21.1	60.5	18.3	860	81.3	50.5	14.9
Ashland town (Chemung)	1,695	1,653	-2.5	1,541	96.2	0.7	0.0	2.7	0.4	21.5	60.7	17.8	647	79.8	57.0	12.7
Ashland town (Greene)	790	773	-2.2	769	92.5	0.7	0.0	2.0	4.9	14.5	53.9	31.6	347	88.5	46.7	22.8
Athens village	1,677	1,620	-3.4	1,432	88.8	2.0	2.3	0.9	6.0	14.5	61.2	24.3	602	65.9	49.0	20.9
Athens town (Greene)	4,090	3,965	-3.1	4,034	85.6	1.5	2.1	3.6	7.3	17.3	65.6	17.1	1,488	80.4	43.0	23.3
Atlantic Beach village	1,891	1,910	1.0	1,613	93.5	0.0	1.3	0.2	5.0	15.9	58.9	25.1	688	83.7	13.2	62.8
Attica village	2,547	2,493	-2.1	2,609	95.5	0.0	1.3	2.1	1.1	24.8	63.0	12.2	1,080	57.7	40.5	18.0
Attica town (Wyoming)	7,702	7,477	-2.9	7,564	59.3	27.7	0.7	2.4	9.8	11.5	80.9	7.8	1,656	66.2	41.2	18.6
Auburn city & MCD (Cayuga)	27,688	27,019	-2.4	27,369	83.3	8.8	0.9	3.3	3.7	20.2	63.8	16.0	11,119	47.8	45.0	19.2
Augusta town (Oneida)	2,020	2,053	1.6	2,366	96.5	0.6	0.0	1.1	1.7	27.0	59.7	13.2	936	77.0	53.0	19.6
Aurelius town (Cayuga)	2,792	2,745	-1.7	2,780	99.3	0.3	0.0	0.4	0.0	17.9	62.0	20.0	1,133	87.8	42.4	20.3
Aurora village	724	773	6.8	734	84.1	3.8	0.5	1.6	9.9	5.0	83.6	11.6	146	68.5	21.9	47.9
Aurora town (Erie)	13,782	13,839	0.4	13,818	95.5	0.4	1.0	0.8	2.3	22.8	60.7	16.4	5,431	80.8	26.5	49.0
Au Sable town (Clinton)	3,146	3,129	-0.5	3,141	96.1	0.9	1.5	0.8	0.8	20.2	63.2	16.7	1,342	72.6	61.3	14.4
Au Sable Forks CDP	559	NA	NA	393	100.0	0.0	0.0	0.0	0.0	20.3	60.6	19.1	181	69.1	56.4	18.2
Austerlitz town (Columbia)	1,663	1,649	-0.8	1,503	96.5	2.1	0.5	0.1	0.7	21.0	61.5	17.5	642	83.6	29.1	45.8
Ava town (Oneida)	676	697	3.1	589	86.4	3.1	0.2	5.3	5.1	21.8	65.0	13.2	233	90.6	62.2	6.0
Averill Park CDP	1,693	NA	NA	1,781	92.6	4.8	0.0	0.0	2.5	25.8	63.1	11.3	682	83.0	28.6	40.2
Avoca village	946	930	-1.7	957	95.4	0.6	0.0	1.1	2.8	22.5	62.1	15.4	380	78.2	41.6	11.8
Avoca town (Steuben)	2,264	2,223	-1.8	2,271	96.3	0.6	0.0	1.4	1.8	21.1	60.8	18.1	939	75.0	48.2	18.7
Avon village	3,391	3,318	-2.2	3,357	94.0	0.5	2.4	1.1	1.8	23.2	61.2	15.4	1,322	66.1	31.5	34.7
Avon town (Livingston)	7,161	7,024	-1.9	7,103	95.0	1.4	1.2	1.6	0.9	25.3	59.8	14.9	2,828	75.5	33.1	27.9
Babylon village	12,166	12,172	0.0	12,177	82.6	1.1	4.4	3.4	8.5	20.5	66.7	13.0	4,510	75.0	24.2	45.7
Babylon town (Suffolk)	213,603	214,191	0.3	214,194	60.3	15.8	3.1	1.9	18.9	21.9	64.9	13.3	69,634	74.4	43.2	26.7
Bainbridge village	1,355	1,337	-1.3	1,337	93.0	0.3	0.2	2.5	4.0	22.6	57.8	19.7	573	60.0	39.8	25.8
Bainbridge town (Chenango)	3,308	3,257	-1.5	3,282	95.4	0.1	0.8	1.0	2.7	22.5	59.6	17.8	1,348	72.5	53.4	21.1
Baiting Hollow CDP	1,642	NA	NA	1,508	97.9	0.9	0.3	0.0	0.8	14.6	63.4	22.0	644	92.4	32.3	29.8
Baldwin town (Chemung)	832	822	-1.2	850	98.1	0.0	0.5	1.4	0.0	14.3	69.9	15.8	382	88.2	57.6	12.0
Baldwin CDP	24,033	NA	NA	24,897	39.0	30.5	3.0	1.9	25.6	25.0	63.6	11.4	7,587	80.4	27.0	45.8
Baldwin Harbor CDP	8,102	NA	NA	7,799	51.4	27.6	3.6	2.4	15.1	22.2	62.8	15.2	2,577	89.1	26.4	43.9
Baldwinsville village	7,595	7,681	1.1	7,655	90.0	1.3	0.8	3.9	4.0	23.7	55.4	21.0	3,156	62.0	35.0	32.3
Ballston town (Saratoga)	9,765	10,411	6.6	10,034	95.4	0.7	0.8	0.9	2.2	23.8	59.5	16.7	3,620	76.6	23.0	44.2
Ballston Spa village	5,416	5,393	-0.4	5,298	90.4	1.8	0.8	2.5	4.6	17.3	64.1	18.5	2,499	50.6	31.5	31.7
Balmville CDP	3,178	NA	NA	3,072	56.5	10.1	6.9	0.6	25.8	22.0	59.0	19.1	1,150	76.1	38.3	35.2
Bangor town (Franklin)	2,224	2,254	1.3	2,532	98.4	0.0	0.0	0.9	0.7	25.5	63.4	11.1	926	79.2	48.6	21.4
Bardonia CDP	4,108	NA	NA	3,721	77.3	2.3	11.9	1.9	6.6	19.6	56.5	24.1	1,331	86.9	25.6	52.7
Barker town (Broome)	2,732	2,696	-1.3	2,710	97.6	0.0	0.2	0.4	1.7	23.4	64.3	12.3	1,000	90.6	53.0	15.2
Barker village	533	516	-3.2	705	74.2	0.0	0.0	0.9	25.0	36.8	53.9	9.4	211	60.7	58.3	14.2
Barneveld village	284	283	-0.4	225	88.9	0.0	0.0	8.0	3.1	16.9	54.2	28.9	104	76.0	32.7	37.5
Barnum Island CDP	2,414	NA	NA	2,489	71.3	1.2	3.1	1.6	22.8	21.2	62.2	16.6	844	80.3	33.3	33.4
Barre town (Orleans)	2,025	1,954	-3.5	2,052	93.0	0.0	0.1	0.7	6.1	23.3	62.2	14.6	742	87.9	56.3	17.0
Barrington town (Yates)	1,681	1,700	1.1	1,445	97.0	1.5	0.0	0.6	1.0	20.1	61.1	18.8	575	91.1	52.9	27.3
Barton town (Tioga)	8,858	8,663	-2.2	8,751	97.4	1.9	0.1	0.1	0.5	24.0	61.6	14.4	3,553	66.7	46.7	17.5
Batavia city & MCD (Genesee)	15,447	15,077	-2.4	15,274	85.2	6.8	0.8	3.2	4.0	20.1	61.5	18.7	6,432	52.1	45.4	20.0
Batavia town (Genesee)	6,809	6,870	0.9	6,870	95.3	0.4	0.1	0.2	3.9	21.1	61.3	17.5	2,949	85.0	42.3	20.2
Bath village	5,786	5,687	-1.7	5,747	94.2	2.9	0.1	0.6	2.1	19.5	59.1	21.3	2,810	53.8	53.8	16.7
Bath town (Steuben)	12,379	12,184	-1.6	12,306	93.1	3.5	0.5	0.8	2.0	19.8	59.9	20.2	5,234	64.2	57.1	16.0
Baxter Estates village	999	1,012	1.3	955	75.7	0.0	12.6	2.5	9.2	23.6	61.1	15.3	389	70.7	14.7	74.6
Bay Park CDP	2,212	NA	NA	1,637	96.8	0.0	0.0	0.0	3.2	19.8	58.5	21.7	711	97.7	24.2	29.4
Bayport CDP	8,896	NA	NA	8,355	90.2	0.9	1.4	1.4	6.0	24.0	59.3	16.6	3,131	65.9	24.3	39.3
Bay Shore CDP	26,337	NA	NA	28,883	39.3	19.6	3.9	1.2	36.1	23.3	65.5	11.2	9,598	56.8	46.4	27.0
Bayville village	6,669	6,748	1.2	6,724	93.3	0.7	1.2	0.9	4.0	19.9	59.7	20.5	2,482	82.1	29.7	43.2
Baywood CDP	7,350	NA	NA	7,681	43.3	13.9	1.3	2.6	38.8	26.0	64.4	9.7	2,201	82.4	41.3	22.4
Beacon city & MCD (Dutchess)	14,604	14,238	-2.5	14,437	56.9	17.3	1.6	4.0	20.2	19.7	65.4	14.8	5,452	51.0	41.0	32.6
Beaver Dam Lake CDP	0	NA	NA	2,493	81.5	2.0	0.0	0.0	16.5	28.7	61.4	9.7	832	97.0	24.2	37.3
Bedford CDP	1,834	NA	NA	2,248	86.4	1.6	1.5	1.3	9.2	30.4	55.5	14.1	748	84.0	22.2	68.9
Bedford town (Westchester)	17,335	17,910	3.3	17,643	73.9	6.6	2.9	1.9	14.8	26.2	61.2	12.6	5,467	73.3	19.6	64.6
Bedford Hills CDP	3,001	NA	NA	3,146	48.7	8.6	0.9	0.0	41.9	27.7	61.5	10.6	1,171	42.1	39.9	35.4
Beekman town (Dutchess)	14,587	14,473	-0.8	14,557	77.4	9.1	2.1	0.9	10.6	21.6	67.3	11.0	4,324	92.1	33.8	36.6
Beekmantown town (Clinton)	5,545	5,538	-0.1	5,545	96.1	0.5	1.2	2.2	0.1	22.1	63.8	14.2	2,317	78.4	46.9	28.2
Belfast CDP	837	NA	NA	917	95.1	0.0	0.0	0.4	4.5	26.9	54.5	18.5	425	52.0	56.7	11.5
Belfast town (Allegany)	1,665	1,633	-1.9	1,792	97.0	0.0	0.0	0.2	2.8	25.4	57.4	17.4	749	70.6	60.2	13.0
Bellerose village	1,193	1,201	0.7	1,072	74.1	1.5	8.8	5.8	9.9	24.0	60.9	15.0	346	95.4	14.5	65.0
Bellerose Terrace CDP	2,198	NA	NA	1,975	37.6	0.4	32.4	9.0	20.7	24.4	65.9	9.6	588	86.6	28.9	29.8
Belle Terre village	792	795	0.4	834	91.8	0.0	4.3	1.4	2.4	29.6	52.6	17.7	286	96.9	12.6	74.1
Belleville CDP	226	NA	NA	346	86.4	0.0	0.0	0.0	13.6	50.0	44.1	5.8	102	41.2	69.6	7.8
Bellmont town (Franklin)	1,434	1,438	0.3	1,535	96.0	0.0	0.6	1.7	1.8	21.2	59.2	19.6	606	86.0	46.9	18.5
Bellmore CDP	16,218	NA	NA	16,260	87.5	0.3	5.3	1.3	5.5	22.7	62.6	14.6	5,533	90.5	27.7	44.8
Bellport village	2,084	2,083	0.0	1,970	94.1	1.0	0.9	1.0	3.0	14.9	57.9	27.2	967	80.4	15.7	60.9
Belmont village	969	947	-2.3	1,031	95.5	0.3	0.0	3.7	0.5	25.0	57.7	17.5	433	64.9	43.9	23.3
Bemus Point village	364	360	-1.1	212	100.0	0.0	0.0	0.0	0.0	17.0	42.5	40.6	100	56.0	35.0	30.0
Bennington town (Wyoming)	3,359	3,298	-1.8	3,338	97.2	0.0	0.4	0.0	2.4	25.0	60.3	14.6	1,234	86.5	48.9	20.6
Benson town (Hamilton)	192	188	-2.1	185	100.0	0.0	0.0	0.0	0.0	16.8	65.4	17.8	87	93.1	34.5	21.8
Benton town (Yates)	2,836	2,839	0.1	2,842	98.2	0.9	0.0	0.8	0.1	30.6	49.1	20.4	912	82.8	57.7	16.9
Bergen village	1,176	1,150	-2.2	1,305	94.4	1.4	0.8	0.8	2.5	28.4	60.3	11.3	450	78.0	34.0	23.3
Bergen town (Genesee)	3,120	3,063	-1.8	3,096	93.3	0.6	1.6	1.6	2.9	24.2	58.9	17.0	1,192	79.9	35.3	28.9

1 May be of any race.

Table A. All Places — **Population and Housing**

STATE City, town, township, borough, or CDP (county if applicable)	Population: 2010 census total population	Population: 2014 estimated population	Population: Percent change 2010–2014	Population: ACS total population estimate 2010–2014	Race: White alone, not Hispanic or Latino	Race: Black alone, not Hispanic or Latino	Race: Asian alone, not Hispanic or Latino	Race: All other races or 2 or more races, not Hispanic or Latino	Race: Hispanic or Latino[1]	Age: Under 18 years old	Age: Age 18 to 64 years old	Age: Age 65 years and older	Households: Total occupied housing units	Households: Percent owner occupied	Householders by level of education: High school diploma or less	Householders by level of education: Bachelor's degree or more
	1	2	3	4	5	6	7	8	9	10	11	12	13	14	15	16
NEW YORK—Con.																
Berkshire town (Tioga)	1,412	1,382	-2.1	1,526	97.0	0.0	0.5	2.1	0.4	27.7	55.0	17.5	566	90.8	55.5	12.7
Berlin town (Rensselaer)	1,880	1,864	-0.9	1,853	98.7	0.0	0.0	1.0	0.3	22.1	60.2	17.8	745	82.1	48.7	24.3
Berne town (Albany)	2,794	2,826	1.1	2,809	97.1	0.7	0.4	1.5	0.3	17.5	64.7	17.9	1,214	91.3	30.7	33.4
Bethany town (Genesee)	1,765	1,742	-1.3	1,625	95.8	0.8	0.5	2.0	1.0	19.1	64.3	16.3	692	80.1	44.8	20.8
Bethel town (Sullivan)	4,255	4,175	-1.9	4,221	79.5	4.4	2.7	4.4	9.0	15.3	64.8	19.9	1,749	68.7	35.7	32.0
Bethlehem town (Albany)	33,658	34,685	3.1	34,163	88.8	2.5	4.3	1.8	2.6	24.1	60.5	15.2	13,178	77.0	16.6	58.4
Bethpage CDP	16,429	NA	NA	16,337	84.7	0.2	6.6	1.7	6.8	19.3	58.2	22.5	5,769	90.6	39.2	38.7
Big Flats CDP	5,277	NA	NA	5,247	92.2	0.7	3.8	1.7	1.5	24.6	56.9	18.5	2,138	84.4	24.9	42.3
Big Flats town (Chemung)	7,731	7,770	0.5	7,775	93.2	1.8	2.6	1.4	1.0	21.9	60.4	17.8	3,315	83.7	26.8	38.6
Billington Heights CDP	1,685	NA	NA	1,445	96.9	0.0	0.0	0.0	3.1	20.2	61.4	18.3	575	72.3	19.8	47.8
Binghamton city & MCD (Broome)	47,376	46,299	-2.3	46,771	72.7	11.3	5.0	4.2	6.8	19.4	64.8	16.0	19,902	46.6	41.1	25.4
Binghamton town (Broome)	4,942	4,857	-1.7	4,893	94.2	0.8	0.5	2.8	1.7	21.1	61.8	17.0	1,872	90.8	24.0	33.7
Binghamton University CDP	6,177	NA	NA	6,172	55.7	10.3	21.0	3.2	9.8	1.6	98.5	0.0	0	0.0	0.0	0.0
Birdsall town (Allegany)	221	222	0.5	177	98.9	0.0	0.0	0.0	1.1	7.3	59.4	33.3	89	93.3	66.3	11.2
Black Brook town (Clinton)	1,497	1,485	-0.8	1,446	98.3	1.0	0.0	0.6	0.1	15.6	68.0	16.5	625	79.0	57.1	22.7
Black River village	1,350	1,361	0.8	1,374	80.9	3.3	1.5	8.6	5.6	26.9	59.6	13.4	522	69.9	32.8	26.8
Blasdell village	2,553	2,590	1.4	2,565	92.9	1.6	0.1	3.3	2.1	21.3	66.6	11.9	1,086	51.9	51.3	10.8
Blauvelt CDP	5,689	NA	NA	5,868	79.4	1.9	7.1	0.8	10.8	26.2	58.3	15.7	1,715	95.9	21.6	59.2
Bleecker town (Fulton)	533	514	-3.6	642	96.7	0.0	0.5	2.8	0.0	15.1	63.3	21.7	260	86.5	56.5	29.2
Blenheim town (Schoharie)	377	371	-1.6	382	93.5	3.1	0.0	1.0	2.4	16.9	55.8	27.2	155	85.2	55.5	21.9
Bliss CDP	527	NA	NA	557	99.5	0.5	0.0	0.0	0.0	25.1	61.0	14.0	216	90.7	48.1	10.2
Blodgett Mills CDP	303	NA	NA	307	100.0	0.0	0.0	0.0	0.0	21.8	68.8	9.4	99	71.7	61.6	0.0
Bloomfield village	1,356	1,335	-1.5	1,581	97.4	0.1	1.7	0.2	0.6	24.7	63.1	12.1	633	67.3	31.6	26.7
Bloomingburg village	425	420	-1.2	453	76.6	10.2	0.0	5.7	7.5	25.1	59.7	15.0	165	32.7	55.2	11.5
Blooming Grove town (Orange)	18,027	17,750	-1.5	17,876	76.3	3.4	1.0	1.9	17.4	22.5	64.2	13.1	6,146	84.1	34.9	30.3
Bloomville CDP	213	NA	NA	205	100.0	0.0	0.0	0.0	0.0	7.3	67.9	24.9	95	94.7	70.5	8.4
Blue Point CDP	4,773	NA	NA	4,602	94.7	0.0	0.7	0.1	4.5	23.7	59.6	16.7	1,639	86.2	31.3	39.4
Bohemia CDP	10,180	NA	NA	10,275	88.6	0.6	1.5	0.2	9.1	24.7	59.0	16.2	3,569	76.4	38.6	28.9
Bolivar village	1,047	1,015	-3.1	1,136	97.4	0.4	0.0	2.2	0.0	24.9	63.2	11.8	495	60.4	58.6	16.8
Bolivar town (Allegany)	2,189	2,126	-2.9	2,273	98.4	0.4	0.0	1.1	0.2	27.2	58.6	14.1	932	73.0	55.6	14.8
Bolton town (Warren)	2,326	2,307	-0.8	2,394	90.9	3.8	0.8	0.0	4.4	13.4	62.3	24.5	1,069	73.0	36.9	35.7
Bolton Landing CDP	513	NA	NA	620	71.8	11.8	0.0	0.0	16.5	17.8	58.7	23.5	266	55.6	40.2	33.5
Bombay town (Franklin)	1,357	1,343	-1.0	1,274	64.1	0.1	1.0	32.9	1.9	30.0	59.6	10.4	491	71.1	59.3	13.4
Boonville village	2,072	2,053	-0.9	2,120	96.5	0.0	1.4	0.9	1.2	22.2	54.0	23.7	873	53.6	53.7	18.3
Boonville town (Oneida)	4,555	4,550	-0.1	4,561	96.8	0.0	1.4	1.1	0.7	20.0	62.1	17.9	1,764	70.5	49.5	22.1
Boston town (Erie)	8,023	8,042	0.2	8,025	98.7	0.1	0.0	0.1	1.1	21.0	60.4	18.6	3,265	82.9	33.0	37.4
Bovina town (Delaware)	633	612	-3.3	574	96.0	0.0	0.9	1.6	1.6	23.2	55.0	21.8	227	78.9	27.8	37.9
Boylston town (Oswego)	549	554	0.9	526	94.9	0.0	0.0	2.5	2.7	22.7	61.9	15.6	195	82.6	52.3	20.0
Bradford town (Steuben)	855	840	-1.8	759	98.9	0.0	0.0	0.3	0.8	22.0	63.3	14.8	291	85.2	60.8	12.7
Brandon town (Franklin)	577	569	-1.4	743	96.2	3.1	0.5	0.0	0.1	18.1	71.0	10.9	280	97.1	71.4	6.1
Brant town (Erie)	2,065	2,067	0.1	2,058	90.1	0.1	0.2	4.7	4.9	18.7	60.9	20.3	845	79.5	42.8	25.4
Brasher town (St. Lawrence)	2,512	2,472	-1.6	2,129	90.5	0.1	1.1	6.6	1.6	24.3	63.9	11.7	852	77.9	52.6	14.8
Brasher Falls CDP	669	NA	NA	449	99.6	0.0	0.0	0.0	0.4	26.3	49.6	24.1	215	59.5	50.7	21.4
Breesport CDP	626	NA	NA	913	96.4	0.0	1.5	2.1	0.0	33.3	53.9	12.9	312	100.0	34.9	14.1
Brentwood CDP	60,664	NA	NA	59,436	14.7	13.2	2.5	1.8	67.9	26.8	64.6	8.5	13,882	70.1	64.5	14.6
Brewerton CDP	4,029	NA	NA	4,289	94.8	0.0	0.9	3.1	1.2	25.9	63.3	10.7	1,694	60.5	40.3	21.9
Brewster village	2,390	2,347	-1.8	2,350	35.6	1.1	2.0	3.1	58.2	20.3	70.1	9.4	869	20.3	62.4	12.3
Brewster Hill CDP	2,089	NA	NA	1,381	84.4	0.0	0.0	6.9	8.8	27.9	55.6	16.4	474	96.8	36.7	21.3
Briarcliff Manor village	7,836	7,991	2.0	7,783	75.1	2.9	11.9	4.2	5.9	22.5	59.2	18.3	2,599	83.8	16.5	70.2
Bridgehampton CDP	1,756	NA	NA	1,416	79.0	1.8	0.6	0.0	18.6	18.4	59.9	21.6	599	83.3	36.1	47.4
Bridgeport CDP	1,490	NA	NA	1,583	91.7	0.1	0.0	2.0	6.3	23.0	60.5	16.4	678	64.6	54.1	5.5
Bridgewater village	470	458	-2.6	522	93.5	0.0	0.0	0.6	5.9	32.9	55.9	11.1	175	72.0	62.3	8.6
Bridgewater town (Oneida)	1,522	1,500	-1.4	1,518	93.8	2.7	0.0	1.4	2.0	25.1	63.3	11.6	543	81.6	53.4	11.0
Brighton town (Franklin)	1,435	1,436	0.1	1,379	91.9	3.8	1.5	2.5	0.4	8.5	82.8	8.7	348	80.7	10.1	46.3
Brighton CDP & town (Monroe)	36,632	36,941	0.8	36,870	76.1	6.3	12.0	2.9	2.7	18.4	63.0	18.4	15,762	55.7	11.5	66.3
Brightwaters village	3,103	3,101	-0.1	3,117	87.1	0.6	3.7	1.0	7.6	23.5	63.8	12.6	1,069	90.2	18.1	57.0
Brinckerhoff CDP	2,900	NA	NA	2,940	78.1	10.4	2.3	2.0	7.1	19.2	64.7	16.0	981	89.1	24.9	37.5
Bristol town (Ontario)	2,322	2,302	-0.9	2,294	97.1	0.0	0.0	1.1	1.8	21.5	67.6	10.9	889	93.3	32.8	28.5
Broadalbin village	1,355	1,309	-3.4	1,649	91.2	0.0	0.0	1.2	7.6	27.5	57.9	14.6	617	63.5	28.0	28.4
Broadalbin town (Fulton)	5,260	5,169	-1.7	5,234	95.5	0.0	0.0	1.0	3.6	20.6	63.8	15.6	2,180	83.6	41.7	18.7
Brockport village	8,366	8,377	0.1	8,398	86.1	3.1	2.8	4.4	3.6	12.4	77.5	10.2	2,414	47.1	26.7	33.6
Brocton village	1,486	1,445	-2.8	1,553	96.8	0.6	0.0	1.8	0.8	25.4	58.7	15.9	676	58.1	49.3	10.9
Bronx borough (Bronx)	1,385,108	1,438,159	3.8	1,413,566	10.5	29.8	3.5	1.8	54.3	26.0	63.3	10.9	480,323	19.1	53.7	19.9
Bronxville village	6,323	6,418	1.5	6,378	84.8	0.6	5.3	2.4	6.9	29.8	56.2	14.0	2,204	78.4	10.8	77.6
Brookfield town (Madison)	2,545	2,482	-2.5	2,489	98.0	0.0	0.0	1.9	0.2	27.1	59.9	13.0	942	84.9	49.6	15.7
Brookhaven CDP	3,451	NA	NA	3,337	80.3	7.0	0.0	1.6	11.0	22.1	56.0	21.8	1,086	82.0	26.5	46.9
Brookhaven town (Suffolk)	486,040	489,403	0.7	488,485	75.1	5.1	4.3	1.8	13.7	23.3	63.6	13.0	162,015	79.4	36.3	33.5
Brooklyn borough (Kings)	2,504,709	2,621,793	0.0	2,570,801	35.7	31.6	11.1	1.9	19.7	23.6	64.6	11.8	925,371	29.5	44.0	34.1
Brookville village	3,465	3,547	2.4	3,518	74.4	7.3	9.8	2.2	6.2	21.4	66.9	11.7	756	94.6	7.1	85.2
Broome town (Schoharie)	973	955	-1.8	890	97.8	0.4	0.6	0.2	1.0	13.9	60.5	25.5	413	89.3	64.2	15.0
Brownville village	1,113	1,150	3.3	922	95.4	2.3	0.0	0.8	1.5	22.0	59.2	18.7	385	61.3	43.4	23.4
Brownville town (Jefferson)	6,243	6,475	3.7	6,438	95.5	0.9	0.9	1.0	1.6	24.2	62.0	13.8	2,448	79.5	45.3	18.3
Brunswick town (Rensselaer)	11,941	12,265	2.7	12,124	92.2	1.0	3.8	1.8	1.2	17.1	66.0	17.0	5,151	79.8	27.0	37.8
Brushton village	474	465	-1.9	546	92.1	0.9	0.0	4.6	2.4	31.7	57.9	10.4	216	58.3	51.9	10.2
Brutus town (Cayuga)	4,464	4,374	-2.0	4,437	96.2	0.4	0.5	1.1	1.8	21.2	64.7	14.2	1,882	80.7	42.7	18.2
Buchanan village	2,223	2,262	1.8	2,330	74.2	4.5	1.7	4.5	15.1	21.4	65.6	13.0	862	76.6	38.6	30.5
Buffalo city & MCD (Erie)	261,325	258,703	-1.0	259,959	45.6	36.8	4.2	3.3	10.0	22.9	65.3	11.8	111,444	41.6	42.7	24.7
Burdett village	340	330	-2.9	332	99.4	0.0	0.0	0.6	0.0	17.1	60.3	22.3	161	84.5	50.9	18.6
Burke village	211	213	0.9	166	97.6	0.0	0.0	1.2	1.2	22.9	57.7	19.3	71	85.9	54.9	15.5
Burke town (Franklin)	1,465	1,494	2.0	1,257	95.9	0.0	0.9	1.9	1.3	20.4	65.5	14.2	550	92.0	60.7	12.0

1 May be of any race.

Table A. All Places — Population and Housing

STATE City, town, township, borough, or CDP (county if applicable)	2010 census total population	2014 estimated population	Percent change 2010–2014	ACS total population estimate 2010–2014	White alone, not Hispanic or Latino	Black alone, not Hispanic or Latino	Asian alone, not Hispanic or Latino	All other races or 2 or more races, not Hispanic or Latino	Hispanic or Latino[1]	Under 18 years old	Age 18 to 64 years old	Age 65 years and older	Total occupied housing units	Percent owner occupied	High school diploma or less	Bachelor's degree or more
	1	2	3	4	5	6	7	8	9	10	11	12	13	14	15	16
NEW YORK—Con.																
Burlington town (Otsego).	1,140	1,112	-2.5	1,154	97.7	0.2	0.0	0.3	1.8	18.4	64.7	17.1	453	93.6	56.7	8.6
Burns town (Allegany)	1,180	1,146	-2.9	1,551	93.8	0.0	2.1	2.0	2.1	31.9	55.8	12.4	591	71.9	54.8	10.8
Busti CDP......................	391	NA	NA	514	95.9	0.0	4.1	0.0	0.0	31.5	61.1	7.4	139	79.9	55.4	15.8
Busti town (Chautauqua).	7,351	7,243	-1.5	7,302	94.5	0.6	2.3	0.7	1.8	21.7	58.7	19.8	3,089	78.4	34.1	30.0
Butler town (Wayne)	2,064	1,955	-5.3	2,003	93.1	3.2	0.0	0.0	3.7	23.3	59.0	17.7	734	78.1	72.1	9.1
Butternuts town (Otsego).	1,786	1,740	-2.6	1,991	95.4	0.3	1.2	0.5	2.6	18.5	63.5	18.0	852	82.3	48.0	21.2
Byersville CDP................	47	NA	NA	123	100.0	0.0	0.0	0.0	0.0	42.3	55.3	2.4	24	58.3	87.5	0.0
Byron town (Genesee).....	2,369	2,323	-1.9	2,292	97.8	0.3	0.0	1.9	0.0	18.9	66.8	14.5	891	86.6	35.8	18.9
Cairo CDP......................	1,402	NA	NA	1,341	99.9	0.1	0.0	0.0	0.0	13.7	70.2	16.0	564	60.3	65.6	9.8
Cairo town (Greene)	6,667	6,501	-2.5	6,576	95.1	1.5	1.9	0.1	1.4	20.5	60.1	19.5	2,684	71.1	50.8	16.1
Calcium CDP...................	3,491	NA	NA	3,540	52.7	13.8	4.4	4.9	24.2	22.9	73.2	3.8	1,601	16.1	25.5	27.0
Caledonia village	2,201	2,145	-2.5	2,219	92.1	3.7	1.5	1.4	1.3	19.3	64.2	16.6	989	67.3	41.4	21.8
Caledonia town (Livingston)	4,255	4,183	-1.7	4,219	94.8	2.8	0.8	0.9	0.7	18.7	65.6	15.5	1,761	79.5	38.9	27.4
Callicoon CDP.................	167	NA	NA	143	88.8	0.0	0.0	0.0	11.2	21.7	78.4	0.0	81	49.4	45.7	32.1
Callicoon town (Sullivan) .	3,057	2,976	-2.6	3,023	94.1	0.4	1.1	0.4	3.9	23.4	55.4	21.4	1,225	71.7	54.8	29.5
Calverton CDP.................	6,510	NA	NA	6,372	81.9	9.1	1.6	1.6	5.8	12.0	54.8	33.2	2,953	86.0	44.8	23.7
Cambria town (Niagara) ..	5,838	5,814	-0.4	5,836	87.6	2.3	0.0	5.2	4.9	20.0	65.7	14.2	2,213	92.8	37.3	21.8
Cambridge village...........	1,870	1,835	-1.9	1,602	94.4	0.2	0.1	0.0	5.2	20.1	62.6	17.3	730	60.8	44.2	24.5
Cambridge town (Washington)	2,021	1,972	-2.4	1,974	93.4	0.2	0.5	5.9	0.0	20.6	58.1	21.2	844	83.5	37.6	40.0
Camden village...............	2,231	2,208	-1.0	2,398	93.5	1.5	1.1	2.8	1.1	23.9	55.8	20.2	1,021	52.5	58.1	17.0
Camden town (Oneida) ...	4,934	4,917	-0.3	4,942	95.4	0.7	1.0	1.4	1.5	23.3	61.4	15.3	1,998	71.6	56.6	19.3
Cameron town (Steuben)	945	948	0.3	931	98.8	0.0	0.0	1.0	0.2	28.2	57.7	14.1	343	75.2	63.6	5.2
Camillus village..............	1,261	1,235	-2.1	1,235	96.3	1.0	0.0	0.6	2.2	25.2	55.2	19.6	572	49.8	32.2	32.3
Camillus town (Onondaga).	24,173	24,285	0.5	24,259	93.4	0.6	1.3	1.8	2.9	21.6	60.5	17.8	9,783	81.1	26.5	39.3
Campbell CDP.................	713	NA	NA	763	95.9	2.5	0.0	0.0	1.6	22.6	65.7	11.7	305	70.5	50.8	5.9
Campbell town (Steuben).	3,406	3,347	-1.7	3,378	98.1	0.6	0.0	0.1	1.1	22.5	60.1	17.3	1,422	81.3	52.4	13.6
Canaan town (Columbia).	1,708	1,683	-1.5	1,614	86.1	4.5	1.9	3.4	4.1	24.0	55.2	21.0	623	82.3	20.4	50.4
Canadice town (Ontario)..	1,755	1,722	-1.9	1,680	99.3	0.0	0.0	0.2	0.4	15.1	70.1	14.8	777	81.2	39.4	27.8
Canajoharie village.........	2,231	2,173	-2.6	2,192	93.3	2.2	0.7	1.9	1.8	25.6	55.4	18.9	767	63.1	36.5	27.6
Canajoharie town (Montgomery)	3,730	3,645	-2.3	3,678	92.4	1.8	0.4	2.0	3.4	24.4	58.3	17.3	1,313	70.4	37.1	24.0
Canandaigua city & MCD (Ontario)	10,591	10,488	-1.0	10,532	93.9	0.9	1.8	1.7	1.6	19.7	61.6	18.7	4,846	53.6	33.6	32.2
Canandaigua town (Ontario).	9,962	10,518	5.6	10,285	94.1	1.8	0.8	1.3	1.9	20.4	59.4	20.2	4,362	71.0	29.8	41.6
Canaseraga village..........	546	529	-3.1	671	93.0	0.0	4.8	0.0	2.2	31.9	53.6	14.5	258	64.7	59.3	7.8
Canastota village............	4,787	4,705	-1.7	4,741	94.7	3.1	0.0	1.5	0.7	23.6	62.7	13.7	1,996	58.0	36.9	34.4
Candor village.................	851	822	-3.4	722	95.7	0.0	0.0	0.7	3.6	26.3	61.2	12.5	283	72.8	47.0	19.1
Candor town (Tioga)........	5,305	5,152	-2.9	5,215	94.5	0.6	0.0	2.5	2.5	25.6	55.9	18.5	1,995	85.2	53.8	16.0
Caneadea town (Allegany)..................	2,540	2,351	-7.4	2,602	90.4	4.0	2.9	0.5	2.4	14.8	70.7	14.5	624	72.1	27.6	41.0
Canisteo village	2,270	2,224	-2.0	2,304	96.6	1.6	0.3	0.1	1.4	29.4	54.1	16.6	890	67.6	53.6	17.2
Canisteo town (Steuben).	3,391	3,328	-1.9	3,364	95.9	1.1	0.2	1.2	1.6	24.8	59.3	15.9	1,320	74.3	54.2	13.6
Canton village.................	6,314	6,601	4.5	6,600	81.9	5.0	2.8	3.5	6.6	10.8	80.6	8.6	1,683	46.3	28.2	48.3
Canton town (St. Lawrence).....	10,995	11,214	2.0	11,233	88.5	3.1	1.7	2.4	4.3	15.9	72.1	11.7	3,437	63.6	35.3	38.2
Cape Vincent village........	723	746	3.2	647	95.7	1.1	0.0	2.9	0.3	15.9	47.0	36.9	344	68.3	37.8	34.0
Cape Vincent town (Jefferson).................	2,777	2,886	3.9	2,856	73.5	15.4	0.1	2.4	8.6	11.0	68.0	20.9	962	81.2	42.3	26.3
Carle Place CDP.............	4,981	NA	NA	5,377	71.7	4.1	13.3	0.8	10.1	23.0	63.3	13.7	1,829	68.3	30.0	44.0
Carlisle town (Schoharie)	1,950	1,888	-3.2	1,848	90.5	2.3	3.5	0.7	3.0	20.2	66.9	12.9	693	81.2	46.3	23.2
Carlton town (Orleans)	2,994	2,945	-1.6	2,981	90.1	3.7	0.2	3.9	2.1	18.7	62.6	18.6	1,254	95.1	42.2	20.6
Carmel town (Putnam).....	34,305	34,387	0.2	34,392	83.0	1.1	2.9	1.3	11.6	22.6	64.5	12.9	11,327	84.8	30.0	41.8
Carmel Hamlet CDP........	6,817	NA	NA	6,824	81.6	1.8	6.7	0.7	9.3	25.5	58.4	16.0	2,227	77.0	37.3	36.1
Caroga town (Fulton).......	1,205	1,169	-3.0	1,223	96.6	0.0	0.0	2.8	0.7	18.7	61.0	20.4	518	87.5	45.0	20.3
Caroga Lake CDP	518	NA	NA	576	100.0	0.0	0.0	0.0	0.0	15.6	63.8	20.5	254	90.2	45.7	20.5
Caroline town (Tompkins)	3,292	3,371	2.4	3,327	93.2	2.6	0.5	3.1	0.6	16.1	69.5	14.4	1,451	80.0	30.3	49.6
Carroll town (Chautauqua).............	3,524	3,447	-2.2	3,495	97.5	0.8	0.0	0.9	0.9	16.1	60.7	23.1	1,542	80.3	46.3	19.8
Carrollton town (Cattaraugus).............	1,300	1,263	-2.8	1,242	96.2	0.2	0.2	1.7	1.8	24.9	59.3	15.9	517	75.8	67.3	7.9
Carthage village.............	3,656	3,655	0.0	3,689	93.6	0.1	0.7	1.7	3.9	31.5	58.6	9.7	1,449	49.8	48.7	11.1
Cassadaga village...........	634	616	-2.8	600	98.2	0.0	0.0	0.5	1.3	22.7	54.4	22.8	235	71.1	49.8	19.1
Castile village.................	1,015	989	-2.6	969	99.0	0.0	0.0	0.0	1.0	18.2	66.6	15.3	403	67.5	47.6	18.4
Castile town (Wyoming)...	2,906	2,843	-2.2	2,873	94.8	0.4	0.2	1.2	3.3	20.7	60.1	19.2	1,203	83.4	43.6	23.4
Castleton-on-Hudson village......................	1,473	1,462	-0.7	1,337	94.5	1.1	0.4	1.9	2.0	22.9	61.5	15.8	501	80.0	23.6	35.1
Castorland village............	351	352	0.3	401	95.5	0.0	0.0	0.0	4.5	27.7	40.0	32.2	122	54.9	58.2	18.9
Catharine town (Schuyler)	1,762	1,737	-1.4	1,763	97.3	0.4	0.0	1.1	1.2	24.1	59.8	16.0	718	79.8	49.9	18.2
Catlin town (Chemung)....	2,618	2,586	-1.2	2,614	96.5	2.3	0.1	0.5	0.6	21.4	66.4	12.3	1,096	82.9	48.9	15.3
Cato village....................	532	526	-1.1	665	90.4	0.0	0.0	9.2	0.5	31.3	57.9	11.0	238	58.0	59.2	5.9
Cato town (Cayuga).........	2,540	2,521	-0.7	2,530	96.6	1.2	0.3	1.2	0.8	20.1	66.6	13.2	1,006	83.8	50.5	20.8
Caton town (Steuben)......	2,179	2,166	-0.6	2,108	97.7	0.5	0.0	0.7	1.2	19.9	62.4	17.6	828	88.8	44.6	20.2
Catskill village................	4,069	3,898	-4.2	3,989	78.3	14.9	0.0	3.8	3.0	22.2	64.5	13.3	1,491	43.8	39.2	21.4
Catskill town (Greene)	11,776	11,454	-2.7	11,627	82.2	7.5	0.9	4.4	4.9	20.3	61.0	18.5	4,466	62.7	43.2	16.7
Cattaraugus village..........	1,001	978	-2.3	1,042	92.6	0.1	0.0	1.0	6.3	21.7	60.9	17.5	450	71.1	45.3	18.2
Cattaraugus Reservation (Cattaraugus)	314	309	-1.6	334	3.3	0.0	16.2	80.5	0.0	41.7	46.5	12.0	112	62.5	81.3	4.5
Cattaraugus Reservation (Chautauqua)	38	37	-2.6	139	0.0	0.0	0.0	100.0	0.0	64.8	28.8	6.5	27	22.2	100.0	0.0
Cattaraugus Reservation (Erie)	1,838	1,850	0.7	1,868	4.0	0.2	3.4	82.9	9.5	31.4	55.1	13.5	716	77.7	50.3	16.2
Cayuga village.................	549	534	-2.7	523	99.4	0.2	0.0	0.4	0.0	20.1	55.8	24.3	216	78.2	29.6	30.6
Cayuga Heights village.....	3,730	3,788	1.6	3,756	73.6	1.1	18.5	2.2	4.6	13.4	64.9	21.7	1,571	46.1	1.8	89.6
Cayuta town (Schuyler) ...	556	546	-1.8	407	93.1	1.7	0.0	3.7	1.5	20.6	64.8	14.5	155	82.6	61.3	10.3
Cazenovia village	2,833	2,826	-0.2	2,808	91.0	3.9	0.6	0.4	4.2	11.7	69.3	18.9	981	55.5	22.7	46.6
Cazenovia town (Madison).................	7,090	7,063	-0.4	7,063	94.8	1.5	0.7	0.6	2.4	21.9	59.5	18.5	2,460	75.0	23.0	50.2

1 May be of any race.

Table A. All Places — **Population and Housing**

	Population				Race and Hispanic or Latino origin (percent), 2010–2014					Age (percent), 2010–2014			Households, 2010–2014			
STATE City, town, township, borough, or CDP (county if applicable)	2010 census total population	2014 estimated population	Percent change 2010–2014	ACS total population estimate 2010–2014	White alone, not Hispanic or Latino	Black alone, not Hispanic or Latino	Asian alone, not Hispanic or Latino	All other races or 2 or more races, not Hispanic or Latino	Hispanic or Latino[1]	Under 18 years old	Age 18 to 64 years old	Age 65 years and older	Total occupied housing units	Percent owner occupied	High school diploma or less	Bachelor's degree or more
	1	2	3	4	5	6	7	8	9	10	11	12	13	14	15	16
NEW YORK—Con.																
Cedarhurst village............	6,592	6,672	1.2	6,631	75.0	0.0	2.5	0.0	22.6	28.3	59.7	11.9	1,932	58.6	21.1	53.3
Celoron village................	1,112	1,082	-2.7	1,078	94.2	0.0	0.2	1.6	4.0	18.5	62.3	19.4	509	62.9	46.6	10.2
Centereach CDP............	31,578	NA	NA	32,270	76.7	3.2	5.9	2.0	12.2	22.4	64.8	12.8	9,888	85.7	36.2	31.4
Center Moriches CDP......	7,580	NA	NA	8,363	89.6	0.7	0.9	0.5	8.3	25.0	64.4	10.6	2,818	81.0	40.3	28.0
Centerport CDP..............	5,508	NA	NA	5,717	95.0	0.5	2.5	0.6	1.4	28.4	58.3	13.3	1,943	91.9	13.0	61.9
Centerville town (Allegany)................	822	820	-0.2	816	97.9	0.0	0.0	2.1	0.0	28.4	60.5	11.2	287	86.4	72.5	8.4
Central Bridge CDP........	593	NA	NA	405	97.0	0.0	0.0	3.0	0.0	12.8	49.2	38.0	218	50.5	46.3	6.0
Central Islip CDP............	34,450	NA	NA	36,233	18.0	22.6	3.6	1.9	53.9	26.5	64.3	9.1	9,728	63.3	54.1	18.4
Central Square village.........	1,848	1,823	-1.4	1,944	99.6	0.0	0.0	0.3	0.1	22.0	62.3	15.6	783	61.0	50.1	14.6
Centre Island village........	410	410	0.0	418	91.4	0.0	4.8	0.0	3.8	17.5	59.3	23.2	162	92.6	13.6	70.4
Chadwicks CDP..............	1,506	NA	NA	2,087	97.4	0.0	0.0	0.0	2.6	27.8	56.1	16.1	699	45.1	43.9	24.2
Champion town (Jefferson)................	4,494	4,639	3.2	4,612	83.8	4.0	1.7	1.5	8.9	25.5	62.6	11.9	1,703	63.5	43.5	25.7
Champlain village............	1,101	1,082	-1.7	1,107	96.0	0.5	0.4	2.7	0.4	25.2	63.1	11.7	477	56.8	57.4	20.3
Champlain town (Clinton)	5,754	5,695	-1.0	5,732	96.4	0.9	0.1	1.8	0.7	19.5	65.3	15.1	2,484	69.9	48.8	20.5
Chappaqua CDP	1,436	NA	NA	1,170	78.7	7.1	4.4	2.7	7.1	18.7	59.3	21.9	497	74.6	15.3	80.7
Charleston town (Montgomery)	1,373	1,349	-1.7	1,293	90.4	1.7	1.5	2.7	3.7	26.7	60.4	13.0	479	83.9	47.4	15.2
Charlotte town (Chautauqua)................	1,729	1,708	-1.2	1,832	98.6	0.0	0.1	0.7	0.5	27.2	58.1	14.6	701	83.6	55.9	13.4
Charlton town (Saratoga)	4,142	4,189	1.1	4,162	95.3	0.3	0.0	4.2	0.2	21.7	58.7	19.5	1,604	94.9	28.0	32.4
Chateaugay village...........	833	824	-1.1	639	98.1	0.6	0.8	0.2	0.3	18.3	63.8	18.0	291	66.3	43.0	24.1
Chateaugay town (Franklin)	2,155	2,063	-4.3	2,026	88.1	6.6	0.2	0.8	4.2	18.4	69.3	12.5	721	71.4	58.9	14.0
Chatham village..............	1,773	1,717	-3.2	1,490	95.2	3.0	0.7	0.3	0.9	16.0	66.6	17.4	648	45.7	40.6	25.0
Chatham town (Columbia)	4,126	4,040	-2.1	4,079	93.8	0.7	0.7	1.2	3.6	20.8	60.8	18.4	1,670	78.9	35.4	39.8
Chaumont village............	626	625	-0.2	701	94.0	0.9	1.4	3.1	0.6	22.1	60.8	17.0	270	65.2	45.2	14.8
Chautauqua CDP............	191	NA	NA	559	93.7	1.8	2.7	0.0	1.8	5.4	52.2	42.4	188	91.5	17.6	82.4
Chautauqua town (Chautauqua)................	4,464	4,403	-1.4	4,433	91.9	2.0	2.1	1.7	2.2	14.2	65.5	20.2	1,701	83.4	32.0	36.9
Chautauqua Lake UT (Chautauqua)................	0	0	0.0	0	0.0	0.0	0.0	0.0	0.0	0.0	0.0	0.0	0	0.0	0.0	0.0
Chazy CDP....................	565	NA	NA	533	97.0	0.0	3.0	0.0	0.0	33.8	50.5	15.8	169	92.3	27.2	36.7
Chazy town (Clinton)	4,284	4,249	-0.8	4,251	95.9	0.9	1.1	0.0	2.2	21.8	62.0	16.3	1,769	75.6	46.2	24.6
Cheektowaga CDP..........	75,178	NA	NA	74,967	83.3	9.8	1.6	1.9	3.3	17.9	63.0	19.3	33,252	69.9	43.1	22.6
Cheektowaga town (Erie)	88,226	87,840	-0.4	87,959	85.0	8.5	1.5	1.8	3.2	18.0	62.6	19.4	38,959	70.7	44.1	21.5
Chemung town (Chemung).................	2,563	2,523	-1.6	2,555	97.9	0.6	0.2	0.7	0.6	19.6	61.8	18.5	982	86.6	52.9	14.3
Chenango town (Broome)	11,252	11,045	-1.8	11,134	96.2	0.4	1.0	0.7	1.7	20.3	62.1	17.6	4,478	84.5	34.9	31.2
Chenango Bridge CDP....	2,883	NA	NA	2,903	99.5	0.0	0.0	0.1	0.4	19.2	61.3	19.4	1,127	91.9	28.4	42.1
Cherry Creek village.......	461	445	-3.5	480	99.8	0.0	0.0	0.0	0.2	26.1	58.4	15.6	184	65.2	54.3	16.8
Cherry Creek town (Chautauqua)................	1,118	1,084	-3.0	1,020	99.0	0.0	0.3	0.3	0.4	24.8	58.3	16.7	382	79.8	56.0	18.8
Cherry Valley village........	520	509	-2.1	537	90.9	0.2	4.1	1.5	3.4	13.5	63.6	23.1	257	68.1	43.2	19.1
Cherry Valley town (Otsego)...................	1,223	1,200	-1.9	1,282	93.4	0.1	2.5	1.1	3.0	15.2	63.0	22.0	582	77.0	47.8	23.4
Chester village...............	3,969	3,915	-1.4	3,943	51.5	19.9	6.2	2.6	19.8	17.9	72.0	10.2	1,665	67.0	31.9	28.4
Chester town (Orange)....	11,981	11,872	-0.9	11,938	67.2	10.2	4.0	1.5	17.2	21.5	66.0	12.5	4,161	80.3	26.5	41.5
Chester town (Warren).....	3,355	3,321		3,335	99.0	0.0	0.4	0.5	0.1	24.7	58.4	16.8	1,210	82.5	50.5	21.2
Chesterfield town (Essex)	2,445	2,400	-1.8	2,715	95.7	0.1	0.4	2.0	1.7	17.2	67.0	15.6	1,095	80.5	40.4	25.2
Chestertown CDP............	677	NA	NA	1,033	99.7	0.0	0.0	0.0	0.3	34.3	56.5	9.2	368	79.3	57.9	13.6
Chestnut Ridge village......	7,916	8,140	2.8	8,035	61.1	17.9	7.8	1.5	11.7	22.6	57.8	19.5	2,551	82.8	24.7	50.5
Chili town (Monroe)	28,623	28,766	0.5	28,726	82.9	9.8	1.9	1.2	4.2	22.4	62.5	15.1	11,130	76.3	26.5	38.0
Chittenango village..........	5,082	5,016	-1.3	5,052	96.2	0.0	0.2	1.0	2.7	27.0	58.7	14.1	1,941	77.8	36.5	35.7
Churchville village...........	1,963	1,988	1.3	1,997	93.1	1.1	0.4	0.6	4.9	22.6	62.8	14.8	822	83.5	28.0	36.5
Cicero town (Onondaga) .	31,632	31,608	-0.1	31,672	92.9	1.7	1.5	2.1	1.7	24.6	63.1	12.4	12,334	78.7	32.3	30.3
Cincinnatus town (Cortland).................	1,056	1,036	-1.9	920	99.1	0.4	0.0	0.0	0.4	25.4	55.3	19.2	357	75.4	61.3	12.6
Clare town (St. Lawrence)	105	106	1.0	121	98.3	0.0	0.0	1.7	0.0	30.6	47.9	21.5	43	79.1	60.5	11.6
Clarence CDP................	2,646	NA	NA	2,811	92.0	1.5	2.0	0.1	4.3	20.5	52.0	27.6	1,044	72.8	23.3	40.2
Clarence town (Erie).......	30,673	31,769	3.6	31,048	90.9	0.9	5.2	1.1	1.9	25.1	58.6	16.1	11,371	84.4	21.6	51.3
Clarence Center CDP......	2,257	NA	NA	2,069	95.3	0.0	4.0	0.8	0.0	27.7	64.5	7.9	750	90.7	12.7	61.5
Clarendon town (Orleans)	3,648	3,586	-1.7	3,645	95.1	1.5	0.0	1.5	1.9	19.3	64.7	16.1	1,518	89.5	51.6	20.2
Clark Mills CDP	1,905	NA	NA	2,105	98.4	0.0	0.5	0.0	1.0	22.9	58.9	18.1	1,037	49.3	30.6	26.8
Clarkson CDP................	4,358	NA	NA	4,546	95.3	0.0	0.6	1.1	3.0	26.2	58.2	15.6	1,641	76.3	46.7	27.4
Clarkson town (Monroe) ..	6,736	6,813	1.1	6,796	92.8	0.1	0.4	0.8	6.0	23.5	61.3	15.2	2,296	77.4	48.0	27.9
Clarkstown town (Rockland).................	84,187	87,059	3.4	85,801	64.6	9.2	10.7	2.0	13.4	22.0	60.3	17.6	29,238	78.8	24.3	52.3
Clarksville town (Allegany)................	1,161	1,129	-2.8	846	94.8	0.5	1.9	0.0	2.8	14.1	64.6	21.3	402	87.3	60.0	10.0
Claverack town (Columbia)	6,010	5,906	-1.7	5,953	92.0	2.1	0.2	2.2	3.5	17.1	58.1	24.9	2,584	72.1	47.0	25.6
Claverack-Red Mills CDP	913	NA	NA	776	100.0	0.0	0.0	0.0	0.0	9.5	66.6	24.0	412	64.1	11.9	60.9
Clay town (Onondaga).....	58,206	59,806	2.7	58,945	89.5	3.3	2.1	2.2	2.8	22.6	64.0	13.3	23,468	74.8	32.7	35.0
Clayton village...............	1,976	1,994	0.9	1,891	98.9	0.4	0.0	0.6	0.1	24.2	56.1	19.6	795	46.4	38.0	30.1
Clayton town (Jefferson)..	5,160	5,203	0.8	5,263	98.8	0.1	0.0	0.2	0.9	28.0	57.0	15.0	2,027	73.7	39.9	21.4
Clayville village..............	351	341	-2.8	387	95.1	0.8	0.0	4.1	0.0	18.4	72.9	8.8	179	62.6	70.4	8.4
Clermont town (Columbia)	1,970	1,946	-1.2	1,893	88.6	0.3	2.7	2.5	5.9	20.6	67.1	12.3	681	80.2	41.3	33.9
Cleveland village............	750	742	-1.1	813	97.4	0.0	0.0	1.8	0.7	22.5	62.0	15.6	308	79.9	60.4	7.5
Clifton town (St. Lawrence)................	751	746	-0.7	865	95.8	0.0	0.5	2.5	1.2	16.2	55.9	27.9	352	77.8	52.6	15.3
Clifton Park town (Saratoga).................	36,734	37,030	0.8	36,955	89.9	2.0	3.7	1.7	2.7	24.3	61.1	14.6	14,537	80.5	12.7	59.7
Clifton Springs village......	2,126	2,102	-1.1	2,293	87.6	4.8	4.4	1.1	2.1	26.8	52.2	21.0	840	58.8	45.8	23.8
Clinton town (Clinton)	737	733	-0.5	696	98.3	0.0	0.0	1.6	0.1	18.6	63.1	18.4	270	84.1	71.1	4.8
Clinton town (Dutchess) ..	4,308	4,281	-0.6	4,306	91.6	1.5	1.3	2.1	3.5	23.7	61.7	14.7	1,569	78.6	23.7	43.2
Clinton village................	1,942	1,908	-1.8	1,979	88.9	1.3	2.7	3.0	4.1	19.5	63.3	17.1	903	58.8	18.3	51.7
Clintondale CDP.............	1,452	NA	NA	1,152	81.6	3.6	3.3	8.9	2.6	12.4	64.0	23.6	540	50.9	45.7	20.2
Clyde village..................	2,093	2,017	-3.6	1,987	90.6	3.9	1.1	2.1	2.3	29.8	57.4	12.6	660	72.4	55.5	16.1

1 May be of any race.

Table A. All Places — **Population and Housing**

STATE City, town, township, borough, or CDP (county if applicable)	2010 census total population	2014 estimated population	Percent change 2010–2014	ACS total population estimate 2010–2014	White alone, not Hispanic or Latino	Black alone, not Hispanic or Latino	Asian alone, not Hispanic or Latino	All other races or 2 or more races, not Hispanic or Latino	Hispanic or Latino[1]	Under 18 years old	Age 18 to 64 years old	Age 65 years and older	Total occupied housing units	Percent owner occupied	High school diploma or less	Bachelor's degree or more
	1	2	3	4	5	6	7	8	9	10	11	12	13	14	15	16
NEW YORK—Con.																
Clymer town (Chautauqua)	1,698	1,677	-1.2	1,630	98.5	0.2	0.4	0.9	0.0	32.0	51.4	16.7	554	81.8	57.9	12.3
Cobleskill village	4,682	4,533	-3.2	4,489	86.6	5.4	0.7	1.7	5.6	11.5	74.0	14.3	1,579	41.9	48.1	24.2
Cobleskill town (Schoharie)	6,649	6,440	-3.1	6,525	89.7	3.7	0.5	1.5	4.6	14.3	69.3	16.5	2,387	54.7	47.9	21.4
Cochecton town (Sullivan)	1,373	1,340	-2.4	1,350	89.9	0.5	0.7	2.1	6.8	16.1	60.4	23.4	593	84.0	45.4	22.8
Coeymans town (Albany)	7,418	7,439	0.3	7,437	90.9	5.2	0.6	0.6	2.7	21.6	62.7	15.6	3,017	71.5	44.6	18.0
Cohocton village	838	825	-1.6	1,094	97.2	0.0	0.0	2.8	0.0	29.2	56.6	14.2	368	72.3	46.7	10.9
Cohocton town (Steuben)	2,561	2,538	-0.9	2,567	97.4	0.2	0.0	1.8	0.6	25.7	57.4	16.9	974	77.7	50.1	13.0
Cohoes city & MCD (Albany)	16,168	16,212	0.3	16,195	86.9	3.5	1.3	3.3	5.0	17.9	64.6	17.5	7,139	44.0	46.1	20.2
Colchester town (Delaware)	2,077	2,049	-1.3	1,984	95.6	0.2	0.9	0.9	2.4	21.2	57.1	21.7	843	79.6	51.0	20.2
Cold Brook village	329	326	-0.9	383	88.8	0.0	0.0	0.0	11.2	26.4	64.6	9.1	144	63.9	56.9	9.7
Colden town (Erie)	3,265	3,277	0.4	3,268	98.8	0.1	0.3	0.8	0.0	22.4	63.0	14.6	1,295	87.5	34.7	29.7
Coldspring town (Cattaraugus)	663	650	-2.0	628	96.8	0.0	0.0	2.2	1.0	20.1	63.8	16.1	260	80.4	48.8	12.3
Cold Spring village	2,013	1,977	-1.8	1,831	86.3	0.4	1.5	3.6	8.2	17.8	60.0	22.3	891	58.2	23.7	48.6
Cold Spring Harbor CDP	5,070	NA	NA	5,041	92.0	0.0	2.4	1.1	4.5	25.7	57.5	16.7	1,733	93.4	12.9	72.4
Colesville town (Broome)	5,232	5,144	-1.7	5,184	98.4	0.8	0.0	0.0	0.8	22.7	61.8	15.4	1,901	82.2	57.7	13.4
Colonie village	7,793	7,913	1.5	7,869	84.0	1.3	7.0	2.6	5.1	18.9	61.4	19.6	3,254	76.3	27.8	35.7
Colonie town (Albany)	81,591	83,015	1.7	82,197	82.0	4.8	7.0	2.1	4.1	19.0	64.6	16.3	31,941	71.8	29.4	41.3
Colton CDP	345	NA	NA	394	95.7	0.0	1.3	2.3	0.8	21.6	65.4	12.9	181	67.4	23.2	27.1
Colton town (St. Lawrence)	1,451	1,452	0.1	1,618	94.3	1.5	1.1	1.6	1.5	17.6	55.7	26.6	765	77.9	37.1	26.3
Columbia town (Herkimer)	1,572	1,567	-0.3	1,546	96.1	0.8	0.2	0.7	2.3	24.9	60.3	14.9	590	94.1	42.4	19.8
Columbus town (Chenango)	975	958	-1.7	936	98.6	0.0	0.0	0.0	1.4	24.1	60.7	15.2	357	85.7	63.9	16.2
Commack CDP	36,124	NA	NA	35,487	86.3	1.4	4.6	2.0	5.7	24.5	58.1	17.3	11,770	91.3	23.8	49.9
Concord town (Erie)	8,494	8,576	1.0	8,534	96.3	0.9	0.5	1.2	1.2	21.8	58.7	19.4	3,601	74.0	44.8	20.5
Conesus town (Livingston)	2,473	2,432	-1.7	2,413	98.1	0.2	0.0	1.4	0.3	20.8	66.7	12.4	976	90.8	41.2	26.5
Conesus Hamlet CDP	308	NA	NA	397	100.0	0.0	0.0	0.0	0.0	37.0	58.2	4.8	136	63.2	29.4	19.9
Conesus Lake CDP	2,584	NA	NA	2,415	97.5	0.2	0.0	0.3	2.0	6.9	60.9	32.2	1,233	85.2	22.8	45.5
Conesville town (Schoharie)	734	710	-3.3	785	93.1	0.8	0.0	1.7	4.5	16.8	57.6	25.7	329	89.1	48.0	17.3
Conewango town (Cattaraugus)	1,860	1,838	-1.2	1,973	97.2	0.0	0.0	2.0	0.8	39.7	50.5	9.9	561	79.9	63.6	11.9
Congers CDP	8,363	NA	NA	8,496	72.0	2.4	9.5	1.5	14.5	22.4	62.0	15.7	2,867	83.4	27.2	48.0
Conklin town (Broome)	5,441	5,313	-2.4	5,368	97.9	0.8	0.0	0.4	1.0	20.2	63.4	16.4	2,035	89.2	40.2	23.3
Conquest town (Cayuga)	1,819	1,780	-2.1	1,554	98.4	0.0	0.0	1.2	0.5	21.6	62.0	16.3	612	91.7	60.6	10.8
Constable town (Franklin)	1,566	1,607	2.6	1,405	94.8	1.7	0.1	2.1	1.3	21.3	68.1	10.7	516	85.1	55.8	10.9
Constableville village	242	242	0.0	239	92.9	0.0	0.0	7.1	0.0	21.7	67.8	10.5	112	79.5	39.3	18.8
Constantia CDP	1,182	NA	NA	972	100.0	0.0	0.0	0.0	0.0	11.3	75.7	13.1	396	75.0	50.0	17.4
Constantia town (Oswego)	4,973	4,934	-0.8	4,961	95.8	0.0	0.3	1.6	2.4	22.2	64.7	13.1	1,874	79.8	56.3	16.2
Coopers Plains CDP	598	NA	NA	429	100.0	0.0	0.0	0.0	0.0	9.3	63.9	26.8	231	73.6	39.4	16.5
Cooperstown village	1,852	1,812	-2.2	2,133	90.7	0.7	5.3	2.0	1.3	12.4	65.8	21.9	1,014	59.1	26.5	51.1
Copake town (Columbia)	3,620	3,565	-1.5	3,589	94.7	0.1	0.2	1.8	3.3	16.0	62.7	21.4	1,354	77.8	31.6	31.3
Copake Falls CDP	0	NA	NA	122	55.7	0.0	0.0	44.3	0.0	17.3	68.1	14.8	77	58.4	44.2	9.1
Copake Hamlet CDP	0	NA	NA	386	100.0	0.0	0.0	0.0	0.0	17.4	63.4	19.2	143	74.1	28.7	15.4
Copake Lake CDP	823	NA	NA	593	100.0	0.0	0.0	0.0	0.0	26.8	47.1	26.1	228	91.7	24.1	34.6
Copenhagen village	801	807	0.7	547	94.3	1.5	0.0	0.5	3.7	13.2	65.6	21.2	244	44.3	46.3	9.0
Copiague CDP	22,993	NA	NA	22,527	58.0	7.4	1.9	0.3	32.5	20.1	68.4	11.6	7,495	70.2	50.0	18.3
Coram CDP	39,113	NA	NA	40,637	68.4	8.8	5.9	2.0	14.8	22.2	64.4	13.5	14,844	66.9	35.1	35.9
Corfu village	709	723	2.0	792	98.4	1.6	0.0	0.0	0.0	22.3	57.0	20.8	348	70.1	45.7	22.4
Corinth village	2,567	2,521	-1.8	2,554	94.0	0.4	0.4	3.4	1.8	27.9	59.1	12.9	970	64.4	56.7	12.6
Corinth town (Saratoga)	6,531	6,472	-0.9	6,518	92.8	2.2	0.2	2.1	2.8	23.8	62.3	13.8	2,397	79.3	50.5	21.7
Corning city & MCD (Steuben)	11,183	10,993	-1.7	11,108	90.3	2.4	2.3	3.1	1.9	21.9	63.3	14.9	5,239	49.0	32.8	31.4
Corning town (Steuben)	6,270	6,393	2.0	6,323	94.9	1.8	2.1	0.8	0.5	22.0	60.7	17.2	2,535	81.9	38.9	29.7
Cornwall town (Orange)	12,646	12,508	-1.1	12,565	82.6	1.3	1.9	4.2	10.1	25.5	61.0	13.5	4,714	72.5	23.0	51.5
Cornwall-on-Hudson village	3,018	2,972	-1.5	2,998	90.0	0.0	1.4	3.7	4.9	23.1	62.3	14.5	1,171	72.3	17.5	56.2
Cortland city & MCD (Cortland)	19,192	19,164	-0.1	19,218	90.0	3.1	0.5	2.7	3.7	16.3	72.0	11.6	6,732	46.3	39.9	23.0
Cortlandt town (Westchester)	41,592	42,714	2.7	42,247	72.6	6.5	3.5	2.8	14.6	23.2	60.7	16.2	15,196	77.0	25.2	47.5
Cortlandville town (Cortland)	8,488	8,399	-1.0	8,440	95.8	0.4	0.9	1.4	1.6	19.2	58.5	22.3	3,310	77.2	41.9	27.9
Cortland West CDP	1,356	NA	NA	1,350	98.6	0.1	0.0	0.0	1.3	21.7	51.7	26.7	541	98.3	24.0	48.6
Country Knolls CDP	2,224	NA	NA	2,186	89.3	3.9	3.8	0.5	2.5	25.5	54.3	20.1	773	96.2	3.4	75.0
Cove Neck village	286	297	3.8	271	86.7	0.0	4.8	0.0	8.5	21.7	52.1	26.2	105	83.8	2.9	74.3
Coventry town (Chenango)	1,649	1,621	-1.7	1,598	93.2	0.3	0.8	1.2	4.6	22.3	63.2	14.7	581	87.8	59.6	15.5
Covert town (Seneca)	2,151	2,150	0.0	2,213	96.9	0.0	0.6	1.1	1.4	18.6	58.8	22.5	934	78.2	34.6	26.6
Covington town (Wyoming)	1,232	1,210	-1.8	1,120	99.6	0.0	0.0	0.4	0.0	18.6	67.2	14.1	436	84.9	48.9	19.3
Coxsackie village	2,816	2,720	-3.4	2,767	87.4	9.9	0.0	0.0	2.7	23.0	60.8	16.1	992	61.9	55.7	15.6
Coxsackie town (Greene)	8,929	8,720	-2.3	8,815	66.9	19.4	0.3	0.9	12.6	16.7	72.5	11.0	2,365	74.0	47.7	23.6
Cragsmoor CDP	449	NA	NA	658	95.1	0.0	0.0	0.0	4.9	13.8	52.8	33.3	289	85.8	37.7	40.8
Cranberry Lake CDP	200	NA	NA	205	100.0	0.0	0.0	0.0	0.0	9.8	42.9	47.3	89	96.6	42.7	43.8
Crawford town (Orange)	9,316	9,236	-0.9	9,291	83.6	3.3	0.5	1.4	11.1	25.3	62.9	11.8	3,142	84.2	33.3	31.0
Croghan village	618	623	0.8	691	96.1	0.4	0.0	0.6	2.9	27.0	54.6	18.5	291	55.7	60.1	12.4
Croghan town (Lewis)	3,092	3,126	1.1	3,117	95.9	0.3	0.0	0.0	3.8	20.2	62.4	17.5	1,273	81.2	62.0	12.2
Crompond CDP	2,292	NA	NA	2,364	78.8	4.5	3.4	3.8	9.3	21.8	55.7	22.3	804	95.5	15.7	55.0
Croton-on-Hudson village	8,070	8,235	2.0	8,168	74.4	5.6	3.8	4.7	11.6	26.2	60.1	13.7	2,934	76.0	14.0	61.2
Crown Heights CDP	2,840	NA	NA	2,737	66.1	6.1	4.2	8.1	15.6	22.0	61.3	16.7	1,051	83.2	39.3	33.7
Crown Point town (Essex)	2,024	1,969	-2.7	1,843	96.6	0.2	2.6	0.7	0.0	20.8	61.0	18.0	767	76.9	52.3	12.3
Crugers CDP	1,534	NA	NA	1,781	70.5	5.2	0.0	0.0	24.3	8.2	46.0	45.8	834	20.5	40.6	36.2

1 May be of any race.

Table A.   All Places — **Population and Housing**

STATE City, town, township, borough, or CDP (county if applicable)	2010 census total population	2014 estimated population	Percent change 2010–2014	ACS total population estimate 2010–2014	White alone, not Hispanic or Latino	Black alone, not Hispanic or Latino	Asian alone, not Hispanic or Latino	All other races or 2 or more races, not Hispanic or Latino	Hispanic or Latino[1]	Under 18 years old	Age 18 to 64 years old	Age 65 years and older	Total occupied housing units	Percent owner occupied	High school diploma or less	Bachelor's degree or more
	1	2	3	4	5	6	7	8	9	10	11	12	13	14	15	16
Crystal Beach CDP	644	NA	NA	643	92.2	0.0	7.8	0.0	0.0	10.2	52.4	37.3	326	67.5	62.3	8.0
Cuba village	1,571	1,538	-2.1	1,648	95.6	0.6	1.1	2.2	0.5	19.9	61.8	18.1	680	65.0	38.5	26.0
Cuba town (Allegany)	3,243	3,195	-1.5	3,231	96.8	0.3	1.0	1.1	0.7	21.1	60.2	18.6	1,362	80.6	36.3	24.6
Cumberland Head CDP	1,627	NA	NA	1,578	98.5	0.8	0.0	0.5	0.1	17.4	57.0	25.6	697	89.4	29.6	35.3
Cumminsville CDP	183	NA	NA	135	100.0	0.0	0.0	0.0	0.0	0.0	60.7	39.3	81	100.0	100.0	0.0
Cutchogue CDP	3,349	NA	NA	3,202	91.8	4.7	1.8	0.0	1.6	18.2	54.8	27.0	1,253	86.6	25.1	48.2
Cuyler town (Cortland)	980	954	-2.7	757	96.3	0.0	0.0	2.8	0.9	25.2	58.1	16.8	273	71.1	62.6	9.9
Cuylerville CDP	297	NA	NA	332	92.8	0.0	0.0	0.0	7.2	19.6	66.4	13.9	148	60.8	45.3	27.7
Dalton CDP	362	NA	NA	363	100.0	0.0	0.0	0.0	0.0	23.7	53.7	22.6	129	83.7	52.7	10.9
Danby town (Tompkins)	3,327	3,495	5.0	3,417	94.4	1.3	0.4	1.7	2.0	16.4	65.9	17.8	1,462	89.1	18.7	31.3
Dannemora village	3,952	3,822	-3.3	3,785	40.5	43.1	0.1	0.6	15.8	5.0	90.4	4.8	380	64.2	40.5	16.3
Dannemora town (Clinton)	4,898	4,767	-2.7	4,802	49.6	36.2	0.1	0.8	13.3	6.2	86.1	7.7	737	71.6	48.3	17.9
Dansville village	4,715	4,573	-3.0	4,618	97.3	0.1	0.0	0.3	2.4	20.7	61.6	17.8	2,080	65.3	53.8	24.3
Dansville town (Steuben)	1,842	1,825	-0.9	1,566	98.3	0.6	0.2	0.0	1.0	18.9	66.3	14.9	664	78.6	49.7	15.2
Danube town (Herkimer)	1,039	1,032	-0.7	1,059	97.2	0.0	0.0	2.5	0.3	20.1	63.7	16.2	419	83.5	59.4	11.9
Darien town (Genesee)	3,158	3,108	-1.6	3,134	97.4	0.2	0.0	0.4	1.9	23.5	60.7	15.8	1,165	86.9	50.3	15.3
Davenport town (Delaware)	2,971	2,874	-3.3	2,923	95.7	0.3	2.5	0.3	1.3	17.5	61.0	21.5	1,213	79.3	57.1	20.1
Davenport Center CDP	349	NA	NA	405	96.8	1.0	0.0	1.0	1.2	10.9	70.6	18.5	181	78.5	72.4	8.8
Day town (Saratoga)	856	851	-0.6	887	97.9	0.8	0.0	0.9	0.5	14.6	61.9	23.6	397	83.1	49.9	20.4
Dayton town (Cattaraugus)	1,893	1,856	-2.0	2,108	97.7	0.0	0.0	1.2	1.0	27.2	57.8	14.9	795	78.2	60.6	8.1
Decatur town (Otsego)	353	347	-1.7	321	90.0	0.0	5.9	2.2	1.9	17.1	61.5	21.5	142	83.1	51.4	17.6
Deerfield town (Oneida)	4,273	4,272	0.0	4,295	97.1	0.6	0.4	0.8	1.0	20.8	63.7	15.5	1,612	91.6	27.2	32.3
Deerpark town (Orange)	7,902	7,789	-1.4	7,843	86.2	2.6	0.5	2.4	8.3	23.4	59.5	17.1	3,122	78.0	56.8	16.0
Deer Park CDP	27,745	NA	NA	27,290	66.5	12.5	8.0	1.3	11.7	22.8	61.8	15.5	9,345	83.0	41.8	28.2
Deferiet village	294	297	1.0	273	88.6	5.9	0.7	3.7	1.1	19.4	67.0	13.6	111	59.5	53.2	14.4
De Kalb town (St. Lawrence)	2,434	2,423	-0.5	2,182	96.5	0.4	0.2	1.0	2.0	27.1	60.5	12.4	786	84.0	49.1	16.8
DeKalb Junction CDP	519	NA	NA	398	95.5	0.0	0.0	0.0	4.5	18.6	75.9	5.5	139	85.6	55.4	23.7
Delanson village	377	380	0.8	367	98.6	0.0	0.5	0.3	0.5	23.4	58.5	18.0	131	84.7	29.0	23.7
Delaware town (Sullivan)	2,669	2,610	-2.2	2,638	88.2	2.8	2.8	1.9	4.3	16.5	64.9	18.6	1,067	74.3	42.6	25.3
Delevan village	1,089	1,065	-2.2	1,115	96.3	0.0	0.9	2.8	0.0	26.6	63.3	10.0	444	60.8	53.6	11.0
Delhi village	3,087	3,074	-0.4	3,023	75.9	11.3	1.5	1.6	9.8	10.7	79.3	10.0	688	54.2	30.2	32.0
Delhi town (Delaware)	5,117	4,900	-4.2	4,978	84.4	7.3	0.9	1.0	6.4	11.7	72.8	15.5	1,446	71.4	29.0	31.7
Denmark town (Lewis)	2,860	2,884	0.8	2,873	95.7	1.3	0.0	0.4	2.6	25.3	58.5	16.1	1,059	76.7	53.9	13.3
Denning town (Ulster)	551	547	-0.7	712	97.6	0.0	1.0	0.0	1.4	27.9	52.0	19.9	242	78.1	29.8	29.3
Depauville CDP	577	NA	NA	959	99.5	0.0	0.0	0.0	0.5	44.9	55.0	0.0	282	83.3	33.0	1.1
Depew village	15,304	15,205	-0.6	15,262	94.9	0.3	0.7	1.1	3.0	20.6	61.5	18.0	6,588	72.8	46.6	19.8
De Peyster town (St. Lawrence)	998	1,028	3.0	1,215	97.9	0.2	0.2	0.8	0.9	34.9	57.1	7.9	334	86.8	60.8	10.8
Deposit village	1,663	1,614	-2.9	1,815	90.6	4.7	0.0	0.9	3.8	21.4	59.1	19.7	765	59.5	58.8	12.3
Deposit town (Delaware)	1,712	1,659	-3.1	1,806	91.4	4.7	0.2	0.9	2.8	20.4	56.3	23.3	750	67.3	59.2	13.9
Dering Harbor village	11	11	0.0	5	100.0	0.0	0.0	0.0	0.0	0.0	40.0	60.0	3	66.7	0.0	100.0
DeRuyter village	558	545	-2.3	532	96.8	0.0	3.2	0.0	0.0	21.5	56.8	21.6	231	56.7	49.4	21.6
DeRuyter town (Madison)	1,585	1,571	-0.9	1,725	95.9	2.4	1.0	0.6	0.0	20.9	60.9	18.1	685	78.5	44.2	20.6
De Witt town (Onondaga)	25,812	25,735	-0.3	25,786	81.9	7.6	4.9	2.6	3.0	21.4	62.0	16.6	10,095	71.1	28.1	46.9
Dexter village	1,040	1,102	6.0	1,397	96.5	0.1	0.0	0.6	2.8	27.6	58.8	13.5	530	63.0	43.0	16.4
Diana town (Lewis)	1,709	1,723	0.8	1,552	98.1	0.5	0.0	1.2	0.3	25.5	61.5	13.0	616	71.4	56.8	12.8
Dickinson town (Broome)	5,278	5,223	-1.0	5,251	84.9	4.7	4.5	2.1	3.7	16.4	65.6	18.1	1,932	67.4	31.7	26.2
Dickinson town (Franklin)	823	816	-0.9	988	96.6	0.4	0.0	1.5	1.5	27.6	58.2	14.4	357	90.5	58.0	11.5
Dix town (Schuyler)	3,864	3,933	1.8	3,904	96.2	0.5	0.4	1.2	1.7	19.7	59.6	20.6	1,669	72.0	52.0	17.0
Dix Hills CDP	26,892	NA	NA	26,969	77.3	4.6	10.9	1.9	5.3	24.6	61.5	13.9	8,270	92.1	17.5	63.0
Dobbs Ferry village	10,875	11,098	2.1	11,001	73.9	5.2	6.8	3.2	10.9	21.6	62.8	15.5	3,717	61.5	19.8	64.6
Dolgeville village	2,203	2,155	-2.2	2,086	97.7	0.6	0.0	0.0	1.8	27.2	54.4	18.2	847	69.7	47.2	15.6
Dover town (Dutchess)	8,703	8,550	-1.8	8,638	80.4	2.8	2.5	2.2	12.0	21.1	68.8	10.0	3,107	71.0	52.3	15.8
Dover Plains CDP	1,323	NA	NA	1,190	82.9	0.6	0.0	0.0	16.5	11.9	66.2	21.8	613	43.6	74.7	10.0
Downsville CDP	617	NA	NA	633	98.4	0.0	0.0	0.9	0.6	32.4	52.3	15.3	263	51.7	57.4	11.0
Dresden town (Washington)	652	645	-1.1	545	93.0	0.0	0.4	2.6	4.0	18.4	52.8	29.0	240	80.4	48.8	17.1
Dresden village	308	302	-1.9	442	74.2	0.0	0.0	5.0	20.8	24.0	65.4	10.6	147	66.0	44.2	23.8
Dryden village	1,891	2,095	10.8	2,100	87.6	0.0	1.2	3.0	8.2	25.0	63.1	12.0	889	62.3	23.4	42.0
Dryden town (Tompkins)	14,436	14,978	3.8	14,723	91.8	3.0	1.4	2.0	1.8	22.1	65.3	12.6	6,120	66.8	25.0	43.6
Duane town (Franklin)	174	180	3.4	146	97.9	0.0	0.0	2.1	0.0	5.5	66.3	28.1	73	91.8	23.3	34.2
Duane Lake CDP	323	NA	NA	392	85.7	4.3	0.0	0.0	9.9	16.1	66.8	17.1	185	100.0	23.2	48.1
Duanesburg CDP	391	NA	NA	448	90.2	0.0	0.0	0.0	9.8	19.8	73.5	6.7	120	72.5	0.0	19.2
Duanesburg town (Schenectady)	6,122	6,309	3.1	6,218	94.3	0.3	2.1	2.0	1.4	17.2	70.0	12.8	2,159	88.4	23.3	29.6
Dundee village	1,725	1,679	-2.7	1,508	95.4	0.6	0.5	1.1	2.5	22.1	62.5	15.5	706	54.4	52.7	17.8
Dunkirk city & MCD (Chautauqua)	12,563	12,216	-2.8	12,386	65.3	5.0	0.3	1.4	28.0	22.0	62.9	15.2	5,504	60.6	51.0	17.5
Dunkirk town (Chautauqua)	1,318	1,296	-1.7	1,263	84.7	1.3	1.7	0.6	11.8	12.2	56.1	31.7	497	79.7	42.9	24.9
Durham town (Greene)	2,723	2,676	-1.7	2,706	98.6	0.3	0.7	0.3	0.0	17.0	62.7	20.2	1,090	86.5	48.6	21.7
Durhamville CDP	584	NA	NA	842	100.0	0.0	0.0	0.0	0.0	47.1	40.9	12.0	281	32.0	41.3	0.0
Eagle town (Wyoming)	1,192	1,180	-1.0	1,194	96.4	0.3	0.0	0.0	3.4	22.6	61.9	15.5	470	90.2	47.9	11.5
Earlville village	872	843	-3.3	984	89.5	1.0	2.4	5.8	1.2	29.7	58.8	11.5	374	65.0	35.6	31.0
East Atlantic Beach CDP	2,049	NA	NA	2,229	89.7	3.0	0.4	0.5	6.4	15.1	64.7	20.2	880	79.4	15.6	51.9
East Aurora village	6,236	6,264	0.4	6,255	96.3	0.7	0.8	0.7	1.4	23.3	58.6	18.0	2,538	70.6	22.1	50.9
East Avon CDP	608	NA	NA	555	86.8	0.0	0.0	13.2	0.0	38.7	49.7	11.5	226	43.8	59.3	11.9
East Bloomfield town (Ontario)	3,631	3,617	-0.4	3,618	98.9	0.1	0.7	0.1	0.2	22.0	60.0	18.0	1,460	80.0	29.9	32.7
Eastchester CDP	19,554	NA	NA	19,800	83.4	1.9	6.8	2.1	5.8	21.8	58.7	19.4	7,813	83.3	22.9	56.6
Eastchester town (Westchester)	32,362	33,030	2.1	32,737	79.4	4.3	6.4	2.6	7.3	23.1	59.5	17.3	12,786	74.7	20.4	59.2
East Farmingdale CDP	6,484	NA	NA	6,389	51.0	11.2	5.4	3.7	28.7	20.8	67.9	11.2	2,003	66.8	45.2	31.4
East Fishkill town (Dutchess)	29,033	29,332	1.0	29,241	84.3	2.0	3.5	2.4	7.8	25.3	62.8	12.0	9,483	92.9	27.3	43.3
East Garden City CDP	6,208	NA	NA	6,249	66.0	16.9	5.8	3.1	8.1	3.9	76.8	19.4	1,336	65.3	16.3	55.8
East Glenville CDP	6,616	NA	NA	6,772	91.3	1.0	2.2	2.3	3.2	22.2	58.1	19.7	2,607	76.5	22.6	43.0
East Greenbush CDP	4,487	NA	NA	4,641	83.4	1.8	2.6	5.1	7.0	23.3	64.0	12.7	1,808	69.1	16.5	61.6

1   May be of any race.

Table A. All Places — **Population and Housing**

STATE City, town, township, borough, or CDP (county if applicable)	Population				Race and Hispanic or Latino origin (percent), 2010–2014					Age (percent), 2010–2014			Households, 2010–2014			
	2010 census total population	2014 estimated population	Percent change 2010–2014	ACS total population estimate 2010–2014	White alone, not Hispanic or Latino	Black alone, not Hispanic or Latino	Asian alone, not Hispanic or Latino	All other races or 2 or more races, not Hispanic or Latino	Hispanic or Latino[1]	Under 18 years old	Age 18 to 64 years old	Age 65 years and older	Total occupied housing units	Percent owner occupied	High school diploma or less	Bachelor's degree or more
	1	2	3	4	5	6	7	8	9	10	11	12	13	14	15	16

NEW YORK—Con.

STATE City, town, township, borough, or CDP (county if applicable)	1	2	3	4	5	6	7	8	9	10	11	12	13	14	15	16
East Greenbush town (Rensselaer)	16,473	16,434	-0.2	16,437	89.1	1.0	3.9	1.7	4.4	21.8	63.6	14.7	6,617	76.4	24.9	43.5
East Hampton village	1,083	1,113	2.8	1,159	90.3	0.0	0.5	0.3	8.9	11.4	43.5	45.0	590	71.9	19.5	63.4
East Hampton town (Suffolk)	21,457	21,927	2.2	21,726	74.0	3.1	2.4	1.6	18.8	18.9	59.3	21.9	9,207	77.7	24.0	49.3
East Hampton North CDP	4,142	NA	NA	4,201	56.5	5.6	0.0	0.6	37.3	23.3	63.0	13.8	1,637	63.9	30.3	36.2
East Hills village	6,955	7,093	2.0	7,025	88.5	0.1	6.8	1.4	3.1	30.9	53.0	16.2	2,289	98.3	9.1	79.2
East Islip CDP	14,475	NA	NA	13,989	90.6	0.5	0.5	1.0	7.4	25.5	62.2	12.3	4,407	89.7	30.1	39.8
East Ithaca CDP	2,231	NA	NA	2,441	59.9	5.2	32.9	0.5	1.6	14.0	76.0	10.1	1,194	40.9	9.9	77.8
East Kingston CDP	276	NA	NA	277	89.5	0.0	0.0	0.0	10.5	30.0	57.1	13.0	87	59.8	62.1	9.2
East Marion CDP	926	NA	NA	932	89.6	0.0	0.3	3.1	7.0	9.6	51.3	39.3	450	89.8	36.4	36.9
East Massapequa CDP	19,069	NA	NA	19,891	70.3	11.2	1.6	1.4	15.5	20.6	62.2	17.1	6,517	83.7	36.2	36.2
East Meadow CDP	38,132	NA	NA	37,513	71.6	4.3	10.8	1.1	12.2	19.0	63.5	17.6	12,386	86.4	33.8	37.7
East Moriches CDP	5,249	NA	NA	5,074	90.7	2.2	0.4	0.4	6.3	18.5	66.4	15.1	1,892	73.9	38.0	37.4
East Nassau village	587	575	-2.0	636	83.3	1.6	0.6	9.3	5.2	27.3	59.0	13.7	241	75.9	44.8	21.6
East Northport CDP	20,217	NA	NA	19,708	87.8	1.1	2.2	1.0	7.8	23.3	62.5	14.3	6,990	84.5	24.9	48.4
East Norwich CDP	2,709	NA	NA	2,677	90.2	0.0	3.4	0.3	6.1	23.8	59.6	16.5	937	96.4	23.9	54.2
Easton town (Washington)	2,336	2,286	-2.1	2,375	96.8	0.0	0.8	0.0	2.4	24.6	57.6	17.7	926	87.9	41.7	38.2
East Otto town (Cattaraugus)	1,062	1,066	0.4	949	98.3	0.0	0.3	1.3	0.1	20.8	70.1	9.1	400	87.8	45.3	11.3
East Patchogue CDP	22,469	NA	NA	22,203	75.5	4.5	2.6	1.7	15.7	21.1	62.5	16.6	8,429	62.2	43.7	24.4
Eastport CDP	1,831	NA	NA	1,679	86.5	0.0	3.0	0.0	10.4	11.4	62.9	25.7	675	71.0	35.9	36.3
East Quogue CDP	4,757	NA	NA	4,355	92.2	0.2	0.5	2.8	4.2	23.4	57.2	19.3	1,699	87.6	24.4	40.0
East Randolph CDP	620	NA	NA	573	89.2	1.2	0.0	4.7	4.9	35.1	46.2	18.8	181	60.8	39.8	14.4
East Rochester village & town (Monroe)	6,606	6,699	1.4	6,687	83.4	7.9	1.3	1.0	6.3	24.7	63.7	11.7	2,889	62.3	36.2	29.6
East Rockaway village	9,818	9,896	0.8	9,861	86.1	0.1	1.0	0.4	12.4	21.0	64.4	14.5	3,608	74.6	34.2	42.7
East Shoreham CDP	6,666	NA	NA	6,636	86.3	0.1	1.9	1.9	9.8	27.1	60.9	11.9	2,033	93.3	22.1	47.4
East Syracuse village	3,084	3,025	-1.9	3,051	89.7	2.8	0.6	2.5	4.4	23.2	65.9	11.1	1,419	42.1	49.2	17.8
East Williston village	2,556	2,577	0.8	2,569	90.9	0.0	4.2	0.0	4.9	27.5	56.6	15.7	836	95.9	11.4	70.3
Eaton town (Madison)	5,257	4,901	-6.8	5,004	83.5	8.6	1.3	1.3	5.4	14.1	74.3	11.6	1,270	82.0	40.2	21.5
Eatons Neck CDP	1,406	NA	NA	1,374	88.4	0.3	4.0	2.5	4.7	21.6	54.3	24.2	529	97.7	9.5	66.9
Eden CDP	3,516	NA	NA	3,214	98.7	0.1	0.1	0.0	1.2	24.3	59.3	16.3	1,220	88.7	30.6	31.0
Eden town (Erie)	7,688	7,703	0.2	7,704	98.8	0.0	0.0	0.0	1.1	19.6	61.5	18.9	3,019	89.5	39.9	27.9
Edinburg town (Saratoga)	1,214	1,218	0.3	1,427	99.1	0.2	0.0	0.0	0.7	15.2	55.3	29.6	661	94.7	48.6	27.5
Edmeston CDP	657	NA	NA	809	96.7	0.0	1.1	1.1	1.1	30.0	64.0	5.9	297	64.0	43.8	15.2
Edmeston town (Otsego)	1,826	1,785	-2.2	1,874	95.7	2.5	0.5	0.6	0.7	23.7	63.5	13.0	702	73.1	51.1	12.7
Edwards CDP	439	NA	NA	311	93.2	0.3	1.6	1.0	3.9	18.4	58.0	23.8	142	69.7	47.9	14.1
Edwards town (St. Lawrence)	1,156	1,140	-1.4	827	94.1	0.4	0.6	2.1	2.9	19.1	63.3	17.5	357	71.7	51.5	12.3
Eggertsville CDP	15,019	NA	NA	15,357	78.6	11.9	6.3	2.0	1.1	22.2	61.6	16.1	6,503	75.3	17.9	51.7
Elba village	676	664	-1.8	644	89.0	0.9	0.0	5.9	4.2	21.3	67.2	11.5	242	81.4	35.1	26.0
Elba town (Genesee)	2,370	2,329	-1.7	2,463	81.5	1.0	2.6	1.6	13.3	20.4	70.3	9.3	858	80.2	39.3	25.8
Elbridge village	1,058	1,040	-1.7	1,001	93.9	0.0	0.3	4.1	1.7	21.0	63.6	15.5	359	80.5	27.6	26.5
Elbridge town (Onondaga)	5,922	5,839	-1.4	5,881	97.0	0.0	0.3	1.7	1.0	20.5	66.3	13.2	2,246	85.1	45.2	23.6
Elizabethtown CDP	754	NA	NA	792	95.2	3.2	0.8	0.9	0.0	14.4	58.1	27.3	325	69.5	32.6	36.6
Elizabethtown town (Essex)	1,163	1,135	-2.4	1,125	96.2	2.2	0.5	0.8	0.3	13.2	61.9	25.0	502	75.3	29.5	38.0
Ellenburg town (Clinton)	1,743	1,732	-0.6	1,811	95.4	0.2	3.0	0.4	1.0	24.0	61.7	14.4	702	79.6	69.4	13.4
Ellenville village	4,133	4,096	-0.9	4,126	55.7	10.0	3.0	4.1	27.2	31.0	56.6	12.5	1,490	57.0	48.6	19.6
Ellery town (Chautauqua)	4,528	4,458	-1.5	4,497	99.2	0.8	0.0	0.0	0.0	17.8	55.7	26.4	1,990	84.5	33.1	28.6
Elliott town (Chautauqua)	8,714	8,566	-1.7	8,634	94.0	0.8	0.4	2.8	2.0	20.7	59.4	19.9	3,698	74.6	38.9	19.5
Ellicottville village	376	387	2.9	239	100.0	0.0	0.0	0.0	0.0	9.3	55.7	35.1	142	78.2	21.8	31.0
Ellicottville town (Cattaraugus)	1,602	1,607	0.3	1,424	94.4	1.3	0.0	0.0	4.4	23.0	51.1	25.9	634	80.4	35.5	31.2
Ellington town (Chautauqua)	1,643	1,604	-2.4	1,651	94.7	0.1	0.0	1.8	3.5	27.0	63.5	9.8	634	88.8	60.1	9.3
Ellisburg village	244	249	2.0	271	95.9	0.4	0.0	2.2	1.5	24.8	61.9	13.3	101	70.3	59.4	20.8
Ellisburg town (Jefferson)	3,474	3,581	3.1	3,569	95.9	1.6	0.0	1.0	1.4	24.5	64.4	11.1	1,358	78.1	51.8	16.9
Elma town (Erie)	11,317	11,720	3.6	11,518	98.7	0.0	0.5	0.0	0.7	18.0	60.6	21.3	4,599	90.8	32.0	36.7
Elma Center CDP	2,571	NA	NA	2,606	100.0	0.0	0.0	0.0	0.0	16.4	57.7	25.9	1,046	96.7	40.7	34.3
Elmira city & MCD (Chemung)	29,200	28,647	-1.9	29,046	76.4	13.2	0.4	5.2	4.8	23.0	65.6	11.5	10,826	46.6	48.3	16.6
Elmira town (Chemung)	6,934	6,803	-1.9	6,896	91.9	2.1	1.6	4.3	0.2	23.8	57.0	19.2	2,888	82.7	24.2	44.9
Elmira Heights village	4,097	4,008	-2.2	4,111	90.2	1.6	2.7	5.2	0.3	26.7	60.4	12.8	1,658	51.9	51.2	13.7
Elmont CDP	33,198	NA	NA	36,762	16.2	46.1	14.4	3.9	19.4	21.1	68.0	10.9	9,837	79.3	37.7	29.2
Elmsford village	4,664	4,776	2.4	4,719	37.5	20.0	9.4	2.5	30.6	21.3	69.7	9.2	1,491	49.2	35.9	37.1
Elwood CDP	11,177	NA	NA	10,833	76.2	6.9	7.7	1.4	7.9	26.9	57.6	15.6	3,543	93.8	22.7	50.9
Endicott village	13,392	13,083	-2.3	13,216	85.0	4.0	2.1	3.2	5.6	19.3	64.0	16.9	5,985	42.4	43.6	20.8
Endwell CDP	11,446	NA	NA	11,315	90.0	1.5	2.1	1.7	4.7	21.4	59.7	18.9	4,942	72.1	28.2	36.7
Enfield town (Tompkins)	3,512	3,627	3.3	3,593	91.0	3.3	0.0	4.0	1.6	19.8	66.2	14.0	1,507	73.5	48.6	21.6
Ephratah town (Fulton)	1,682	1,622	-3.6	1,555	98.3	0.0	0.2	0.8	0.7	21.3	65.7	13.1	600	91.3	57.7	14.8
Erin CDP	483	NA	NA	384	97.1	0.8	0.0	2.1	0.0	11.5	73.2	15.4	187	95.7	57.8	7.5
Erin town (Chemung)	1,962	1,933	-1.5	2,043	94.0	0.3	0.0	0.7	5.0	21.3	63.3	15.3	801	93.6	52.6	11.5
Erwin town (Steuben)	8,037	8,454	5.2	8,303	82.9	3.4	9.9	0.6	3.1	22.9	60.4	16.7	3,531	64.2	27.6	39.3
Esopus town (Ulster)	9,041	8,918	-1.4	8,984	92.2	2.4	0.9	1.6	3.0	19.3	65.0	15.7	3,294	74.2	38.9	31.2
Esperance village	345	334	-3.2	393	90.6	5.3	1.5	0.0	2.5	32.1	57.7	10.2	134	88.8	53.0	14.2
Esperance town (Schoharie)	2,076	2,012	-3.1	2,005	95.3	1.3	0.3	0.8	2.2	23.0	62.5	14.3	775	89.7	45.8	18.3
Essex town (Essex)	671	653	-2.7	577	97.7	0.2	1.4	0.3	0.3	11.1	63.1	25.6	253	87.0	34.8	36.4
Evans town (Erie)	16,356	16,300	-0.3	16,334	95.1	0.4	0.6	2.3	1.6	19.8	63.7	16.4	6,581	83.2	43.8	21.8
Evans Mills village	611	611	0.0	477	93.1	1.7	0.6	1.5	3.1	20.7	64.0	15.3	210	61.4	31.9	27.6
Exeter town (Otsego)	987	966	-2.1	943	90.7	0.3	1.1	4.2	3.7	22.2	59.9	17.8	363	84.3	54.0	17.1
Fabius village	352	349	-0.9	368	98.6	0.0	0.0	0.8	0.5	27.9	56.9	15.2	149	78.5	41.6	31.5
Fabius town (Onondaga)	1,964	1,957	-0.4	2,206	89.0	0.7	1.5	1.5	7.4	23.7	63.8	12.4	774	85.5	30.7	30.2
Fairfield town (Herkimer)	1,627	1,591	-2.2	1,455	96.6	1.4	0.0	0.8	1.2	21.5	63.1	15.4	557	85.6	48.7	16.7
Fair Haven village	745	736	-1.2	746	94.1	1.1	0.8	1.6	2.4	16.0	59.0	25.2	332	71.4	46.1	29.8
Fairmount CDP	10,224	NA	NA	10,120	92.8	1.1	1.2	1.3	3.6	20.6	60.6	18.7	4,092	80.6	30.0	30.4
Fairport village	5,353	5,372	0.4	5,364	93.5	0.1	3.6	1.3	1.5	16.2	65.4	18.3	2,480	72.5	20.5	51.4
Fairview CDP (Dutchess)	5,515	NA	NA	5,554	72.8	13.4	0.4	2.1	11.3	23.0	67.3	9.7	1,730	72.5	40.9	24.9

1 May be of any race.

Table A. All Places — **Population and Housing**

STATE City, town, township, borough, or CDP (county if applicable)	2010 census total population	2014 estimated population	Percent change 2010–2014	ACS total population estimate 2010–2014	White alone, not Hispanic or Latino	Black alone, not Hispanic or Latino	Asian alone, not Hispanic or Latino	All other races or 2 or more races, not Hispanic or Latino	Hispanic or Latino[1]	Under 18 years old	Age 18 to 64 years old	Age 65 years and older	Total occupied housing units	Percent owner occupied	High school diploma or less	Bachelor's degree or more
	1	2	3	4	5	6	7	8	9	10	11	12	13	14	15	16
NEW YORK—Con.																
Fairview CDP (Westchester)...............	3,099	NA	NA	2,978	7.2	49.8	3.9	6.9	32.2	23.1	65.1	11.7	933	40.1	47.9	22.6
Falconer village	2,420	2,348	-3.0	2,594	93.1	0.5	0.8	1.7	3.9	25.0	58.7	16.4	1,080	58.1	43.2	17.4
Fallsburg town (Sullivan)..	12,870	12,845	-0.2	12,900	58.0	12.6	3.7	2.1	23.5	25.2	63.9	10.8	3,786	55.2	47.3	25.3
Farmersville town (Cattaraugus).............	1,090	1,074	-1.5	904	97.8	0.0	0.0	0.6	1.7	15.7	62.8	21.5	407	86.7	70.3	8.8
Farmingdale village	8,189	8,619	5.3	8,306	72.6	2.0	8.0	1.3	16.1	16.6	65.1	18.1	3,266	68.2	34.1	38.5
Farmington town (Ontario)	11,829	12,904	9.1	12,501	86.9	2.4	1.9	2.4	6.4	28.8	60.7	10.6	4,755	74.9	29.6	34.6
Farmingville CDP...........	15,481	NA	NA	16,097	78.5	1.9	3.0	1.3	15.3	22.7	66.7	10.5	4,782	85.6	41.9	24.2
Farnham village.............	382	373	-2.4	374	91.2	0.8	0.0	5.9	2.1	18.4	70.8	10.7	143	75.5	38.5	11.9
Fayette town (Seneca).....	3,931	3,881	-1.3	3,928	96.3	0.3	0.6	2.5	0.3	24.2	60.0	16.0	1,487	84.8	38.0	25.9
Fayetteville village.........	4,373	4,324	-1.1	4,342	93.0	2.0	1.7	1.3	2.0	18.8	60.8	20.5	2,038	69.4	9.5	54.5
Felts Mills CDP	372	NA	NA	290	77.6	17.6	4.8	0.0	0.0	23.1	64.0	12.8	138	67.4	60.9	5.1
Fenner town (Madison)....	1,726	1,714	-0.7	1,803	92.8	0.0	0.0	5.8	1.4	22.6	64.4	13.2	660	83.8	44.2	24.1
Fenton town (Broome)......	6,674	6,532	-2.1	6,595	96.1	0.3	0.3	3.4	0.0	22.0	60.3	17.7	2,691	85.1	45.9	22.1
Fillmore CDP	603	NA	NA	621	98.7	0.3	0.0	1.0	0.0	30.1	56.4	13.5	285	50.5	32.3	22.5
Fine town (St. Lawrence).	1,511	1,501	-0.7	1,506	92.5	1.4	1.7	2.3	2.1	19.1	62.7	18.1	556	85.1	60.4	14.7
Fire Island CDP	292	NA	NA	319	70.5	2.5	3.8	2.5	20.7	23.8	61.2	15.0	103	78.6	28.2	31.1
Firthcliffe CDP	4,949	NA	NA	4,957	83.4	0.0	1.5	1.5	13.6	23.1	62.1	14.8	1,962	57.3	27.8	42.1
Fishers Island CDP........	236	NA	NA	296	100.0	0.0	0.0	0.0	0.0	14.2	67.9	17.9	132	84.1	14.4	61.4
Fishers Landing CDP	89	NA	NA	49	100.0	0.0	0.0	0.0	0.0	0.0	0.0	100.0	33	100.0	15.2	0.0
Fishkill village	2,169	2,143	-1.2	1,923	72.0	3.7	11.2	0.5	12.7	23.0	61.6	15.3	937	31.2	40.0	43.0
Fishkill town (Dutchess) ..	23,003	23,596	2.6	23,392	68.5	10.5	5.9	3.3	11.8	18.4	65.9	15.7	8,653	65.1	30.3	42.4
Flanders CDP	4,472	NA	NA	4,851	39.2	9.0	3.9	2.4	45.5	30.6	59.7	9.6	1,402	83.0	45.2	28.2
Fleischmanns village	348	335	-3.7	328	67.4	4.0	0.0	4.6	24.1	32.0	54.1	13.7	113	73.5	41.6	20.4
Fleming town (Cayuga)....	2,636	2,612	-0.9	2,627	93.3	0.2	1.4	2.4	2.7	21.5	58.5	20.1	1,069	86.2	30.4	28.7
Floral Park village..........	15,863	15,967	0.7	16,190	77.7	3.0	7.0	1.8	10.5	22.3	62.1	15.6	5,589	80.0	29.4	43.5
Florence town (Oneida) ...	1,025	1,026	0.1	1,026	97.9	0.3	0.0	0.2	1.7	20.5	65.3	14.2	385	78.7	66.2	8.6
Florida town (Montgomery).............	2,696	2,700	0.1	2,689	94.1	0.6	0.4	2.8	2.2	18.2	66.1	15.8	1,100	82.2	44.8	22.6
Florida village	2,833	2,888	1.9	2,842	76.5	7.5	1.7	2.1	12.2	22.1	63.2	14.6	1,069	75.8	38.1	31.2
Flower Hill village...........	4,665	4,803	3.0	4,741	78.0	0.6	12.5	0.8	8.1	32.9	52.9	14.1	1,396	91.4	13.7	77.5
Floyd town (Oneida)	3,819	3,793	-0.7	3,799	95.7	0.3	0.3	2.5	1.2	20.4	64.4	15.5	1,455	95.6	34.6	21.9
Fonda village.................	795	776	-2.4	704	80.4	7.2	4.8	0.9	6.7	23.7	61.9	14.3	277	50.5	54.5	11.2
Forestburgh town (Sullivan)...................	819	803	-2.0	868	96.0	0.1	0.9	0.3	2.6	17.9	64.1	18.1	368	82.3	31.5	38.3
Forest Home CDP	572	NA	NA	575	28.7	2.8	56.5	0.0	12.0	14.3	75.7	9.9	298	17.1	2.7	95.6
Forestport town (Oneida).	1,535	1,546	0.7	1,481	98.0	0.0	0.0	1.6	0.4	11.4	62.3	26.4	681	82.5	49.6	17.9
Forestville village	697	677	-2.9	791	92.9	0.0	0.3	3.3	3.5	30.7	56.1	13.1	287	66.6	46.3	15.3
Fort Ann village.............	484	477	-1.4	571	92.3	0.7	0.4	1.8	4.9	28.6	59.0	12.6	195	73.3	47.7	15.4
Fort Ann town (Washington)...............	6,190	6,152	-0.6	6,175	65.4	23.0	0.5	2.9	8.1	11.8	77.1	10.9	1,447	85.6	53.8	18.7
Fort Covington town (Franklin)...................	1,676	1,650	-1.6	1,942	69.3	1.9	0.3	27.2	1.2	27.6	60.8	11.4	775	68.6	42.1	13.3
Fort Covington Hamlet CDP	1,308	NA	NA	1,542	65.2	0.3	0.4	32.7	1.3	28.0	60.4	11.6	605	66.3	41.2	14.7
Fort Drum CDP..............	12,955	NA	NA	14,057	59.4	11.6	2.1	7.6	19.3	31.8	67.9	0.3	3,760	0.7	35.8	19.3
Fort Edward village.........	3,369	3,280	-2.6	3,326	95.7	0.9	0.0	0.9	2.6	21.5	64.2	14.3	1,353	69.1	55.7	19.3
Fort Edward town (Washington)...............	6,350	6,193	-2.5	6,275	94.6	1.8	0.1	1.6	1.9	21.2	62.8	16.0	2,337	65.3	53.4	15.1
Fort Johnson village	490	474	-3.3	533	89.3	1.1	0.0	0.8	8.8	20.1	64.0	15.9	198	84.3	51.0	19.2
Fort Montgomery CDP	1,571	NA	NA	1,385	82.1	5.4	1.1	3.6	7.8	17.3	69.4	13.4	537	71.7	26.3	40.2
Fort Plain village	2,339	2,272	-2.9	2,027	94.8	0.0	2.1	2.3	0.9	22.6	59.1	18.3	862	60.4	55.2	15.8
Fort Salonga CDP	10,008	NA	NA	9,895	91.2	0.4	3.3	0.5	4.6	25.0	58.0	17.0	3,303	90.5	20.1	54.9
Fowler town (St. Lawrence).................	2,202	2,164	-1.7	2,162	98.0	0.8	0.8	0.0	0.4	24.3	61.3	14.4	802	90.3	50.1	13.5
Fowlerville CDP	227	NA	NA	249	93.2	6.8	0.0	0.0	0.0	23.7	54.1	22.1	96	59.4	60.4	30.2
Frankfort village	2,595	2,534	-2.4	2,577	92.0	1.6	0.2	2.9	3.2	25.0	62.1	12.9	1,046	61.5	35.9	21.4
Frankfort town (Herkimer)	7,633	7,533	-1.3	7,598	96.2	0.9	0.1	1.1	1.6	19.6	62.5	17.9	3,127	76.9	39.4	25.1
Franklin village..............	374	357	-4.5	346	96.5	3.5	0.0	0.0	0.0	27.5	60.7	11.8	155	52.3	31.0	26.5
Franklin town (Delaware).	2,411	2,355	-2.3	2,225	97.6	1.7	0.3	0.2	0.3	24.7	57.7	17.6	933	84.2	42.6	30.3
Franklin town (Franklin) ...	1,140	1,146	0.5	1,076	97.8	0.1	0.0	0.7	1.5	16.9	62.1	21.0	512	93.2	38.1	30.7
Franklin Square CDP	29,320	NA	NA	31,291	67.9	3.4	10.0	2.5	16.2	21.0	62.3	16.5	9,859	82.1	44.0	30.8
Franklinville village.........	1,740	1,696	-2.5	1,794	90.7	1.7	1.3	2.0	4.3	29.7	57.9	12.4	708	61.2	52.7	16.1
Franklinville town (Cattaraugus).............	2,990	2,923	-2.2	2,960	93.3	1.0	0.8	1.2	3.7	26.8	59.4	13.8	1,187	71.6	53.7	17.7
Fredonia village	11,230	10,792	-3.9	10,988	91.1	2.2	2.1	0.6	3.9	12.5	74.3	13.4	3,862	61.2	31.4	37.3
Freedom town (Cattaraugus).............	2,399	2,348	-2.1	2,434	98.7	0.8	0.0	0.0	0.5	21.7	62.8	15.4	983	86.7	66.6	11.0
Freedom Plains CDP.......	421	NA	NA	496	96.6	0.0	0.0	0.0	3.4	14.1	50.8	35.1	254	74.4	33.9	26.0
Freeport village..............	42,860	43,304	1.0	43,168	22.1	30.4	1.9	3.0	42.5	23.1	62.5	14.4	13,557	66.2	45.4	28.9
Freetown town (Cortland)	757	760	0.4	626	99.5	0.0	0.0	0.5	0.0	18.9	71.0	10.2	265	80.8	49.8	14.7
Freeville village	520	523	0.6	558	95.0	2.7	0.0	2.3	0.0	19.2	71.5	9.3	237	58.6	21.9	50.6
Fremont town (Steuben)..	1,008	986	-2.2	1,012	96.1	0.0	0.0	1.0	2.9	20.1	60.9	18.8	440	84.1	49.8	18.6
Fremont town (Sullivan)...	1,381	1,353	-2.0	1,530	94.8	1.4	0.8	1.0	2.0	17.0	60.9	22.0	619	81.6	52.8	27.3
French Creek town (Chautauqua).............	906	896	-1.1	848	97.4	0.0	0.0	1.9	0.7	22.4	59.7	17.8	337	80.4	57.0	16.0
Frewsburg CDP.............	1,906	NA	NA	2,183	100.0	0.0	0.0	0.0	0.0	14.7	61.4	23.9	941	70.8	40.6	21.6
Friendship CDP	1,218	NA	NA	1,138	98.2	0.0	0.0	1.8	0.0	27.4	61.6	11.0	443	59.6	58.5	19.9
Friendship town (Allegany)..................	2,004	1,947	-2.8	2,003	98.8	0.0	0.0	1.2	0.0	27.2	56.6	15.9	823	68.5	57.0	15.4
Fulton city & MCD (Oswego).................	11,896	11,648	-2.1	11,786	92.5	0.3	0.7	0.8	5.7	26.7	61.1	12.3	4,532	53.1	54.8	17.1
Fulton town (Schoharie) ..	1,437	1,279	-11.0	1,191	92.4	2.8	1.3	3.0	0.6	20.6	62.8	16.5	514	88.3	49.6	21.0
Fultonville village	784	789	0.6	662	92.6	0.0	2.1	5.1	0.2	25.6	65.1	9.2	253	68.0	46.6	9.5
Gaines town (Orleans).....	3,378	3,288	-2.7	3,345	96.2	2.9	0.4	0.1	0.4	18.3	63.1	18.5	1,412	77.9	47.7	20.3
Gainesville village	229	223	-2.6	228	100.0	0.0	0.0	0.0	0.0	19.8	61.7	18.4	103	77.7	55.3	15.5
Gainesville town (Wyoming).................	2,180	2,131	-2.2	2,267	96.6	0.0	0.3	0.9	2.2	21.6	64.6	13.8	846	83.1	55.2	15.7
Galen town (Wayne)	4,290	4,205	-2.0	4,223	88.7	2.0	1.3	1.6	6.4	26.8	57.5	15.7	1,458	82.7	58.8	11.6
Galeville CDP	4,617	NA	NA	4,676	82.2	8.1	7.1	1.5	1.2	20.2	54.2	25.6	2,112	68.9	46.3	15.3

1 May be of any race.

Table A.   All Places — **Population and Housing**

STATE City, town, township, borough, or CDP (county if applicable)	2010 census total population	2014 estimated population	Percent change 2010–2014	ACS total population estimate 2010–2014	White alone, not Hispanic or Latino	Black alone, not Hispanic or Latino	Asian alone, not Hispanic or Latino	All other races or 2 or more races, not Hispanic or Latino	Hispanic or Latino[1]	Under 18 years old	Age 18 to 64 years old	Age 65 years and older	Total occupied housing units	Percent owner occupied	High school diploma or less	Bachelor's degree or more
	1	2	3	4	5	6	7	8	9	10	11	12	13	14	15	16
NEW YORK—Con.																
Gallatin town (Columbia)	1,668	1,648	-1.2	1,790	95.0	0.3	0.6	2.4	1.8	14.1	64.3	21.7	742	86.1	37.7	36.3
Galway village	200	198	-1.0	243	95.5	0.0	0.0	2.1	2.5	28.4	60.5	11.1	76	75.0	46.1	25.0
Galway town (Saratoga)	3,545	3,531	-0.4	3,550	98.5	0.0	0.3	1.0	0.2	22.0	58.8	19.3	1,460	90.1	33.1	24.4
Gang Mills CDP	4,185	NA	NA	4,399	71.4	5.3	17.7	0.8	4.8	25.8	60.1	14.1	1,764	56.6	21.7	47.8
Garden City village	22,362	22,616	1.1	22,543	89.7	0.5	2.6	2.6	4.6	25.6	57.4	17.1	7,403	95.0	13.7	69.6
Garden City Park CDP	7,806	NA	NA	7,807	45.5	2.0	36.4	2.3	13.8	21.8	60.2	18.1	2,546	81.7	29.9	41.5
Garden City South CDP	4,024	NA	NA	3,985	76.3	1.0	10.5	2.2	10.0	20.1	61.4	18.3	1,317	90.6	26.8	44.3
Gardiner CDP	950	NA	NA	691	94.8	0.0	0.0	0.0	5.2	13.3	68.6	18.1	301	70.4	18.3	54.2
Gardiner town (Ulster)	5,713	5,681	-0.6	5,703	89.9	2.7	0.5	0.7	6.3	21.5	62.8	15.8	2,124	77.0	20.3	54.9
Gardnertown CDP	4,373	NA	NA	4,498	63.6	22.9	1.2	2.7	9.7	20.7	64.7	14.4	1,653	88.1	36.2	30.9
Gasport CDP	1,248	NA	NA	994	96.8	1.6	0.0	1.6	0.0	23.6	62.7	13.7	393	66.2	36.1	0.0
Gates town (Monroe)	28,400	28,592	0.7	28,506	78.8	9.4	3.4	2.3	6.0	19.0	61.4	19.6	12,054	74.3	44.2	26.6
Gates CDP	4,910	NA	NA	5,049	77.2	10.4	3.2	3.4	5.7	19.5	59.6	20.9	2,051	91.3	48.2	24.2
Geddes town (Onondaga)	17,118	16,875	-1.4	17,003	93.2	0.6	0.3	1.6	4.3	18.4	61.3	20.2	7,116	74.5	37.5	32.1
Genesee town (Allegany)	1,693	1,659	-2.0	1,298	96.9	0.0	1.0	0.5	1.6	17.5	62.8	19.6	572	84.3	53.1	14.3
Genesee Falls town (Wyoming)	438	434	-0.9	395	94.2	0.0	1.8	0.0	4.1	12.2	69.8	18.0	202	79.2	53.5	11.4
Geneseo village	8,045	8,114	0.9	8,043	81.6	2.9	6.3	3.8	5.4	9.7	82.7	7.6	1,850	39.0	25.2	36.1
Geneseo town (Livingston)	10,483	10,663	1.7	10,535	85.2	2.3	4.8	3.0	4.7	10.6	77.7	11.6	3,005	49.6	27.2	36.4
Geneva city	13,272	13,160	-0.8	13,202	73.8	8.0	1.5	3.7	13.0	17.5	69.1	13.3	4,767	50.0	39.4	27.4
Geneva city (Ontario)	13,272	13,160	-0.8	13,202	73.8	8.0	1.5	3.7	13.0	17.5	69.1	13.3	4,767	50.0	39.4	27.4
Geneva city (Seneca)	0	0	0.0	0	0.0	0.0	0.0	0.0	0.0	0.0	0.0	0.0	0	0.0	0.0	0.0
Geneva town (Ontario)	3,285	3,244	-1.2	3,252	83.9	3.3	0.0	1.4	11.4	17.3	61.6	21.2	1,441	69.6	29.8	39.6
Genoa town (Cayuga)	1,935	1,931	-0.2	1,847	92.6	0.1	0.0	0.9	6.4	23.1	60.6	16.4	732	76.8	49.7	23.8
Georgetown town (Madison)	974	828	-15.0	603	88.9	5.5	0.0	1.3	4.3	11.9	70.4	17.6	208	92.8	44.7	19.7
German town (Chenango)	370	364	-1.6	347	96.8	0.0	0.0	1.7	1.4	17.6	62.7	19.6	150	87.3	68.0	7.3
German Flatts town (Herkimer)	13,253	13,013	-1.8	13,180	96.0	0.4	0.2	1.5	1.9	22.6	60.1	17.4	5,638	61.3	42.8	23.7
Germantown CDP	845	NA	NA	973	86.0	1.6	1.0	3.7	7.6	25.4	63.5	11.1	334	74.0	35.0	25.7
Germantown town (Columbia)	1,949	1,906	-2.2	2,075	91.2	0.8	0.8	3.2	4.0	21.4	57.8	20.7	844	71.8	32.9	31.9
Gerry town (Chautauqua)	1,905	1,868	-1.9	2,229	96.4	0.6	0.3	2.1	0.6	22.4	56.7	21.0	787	78.9	45.0	17.3
Ghent CDP	564	NA	NA	430	100.0	0.0	0.0	0.0	0.0	28.2	68.6	3.3	163	83.4	8.6	53.4
Ghent town (Columbia)	5,407	5,276	-2.4	5,348	95.2	2.6	0.9	0.1	1.1	16.3	62.0	21.6	2,031	81.3	34.2	25.7
Gilbertsville village	399	384	-3.8	354	97.7	0.0	2.3	0.0	0.0	22.6	51.9	25.4	157	70.1	55.4	15.9
Gilboa town (Schoharie)	1,320	1,277	-3.3	1,342	95.8	0.4	0.5	1.3	2.1	21.4	61.0	17.6	506	87.2	42.9	22.7
Gilgo CDP	131	NA	NA	264	100.0	0.0	0.0	0.0	0.0	25.0	59.0	15.9	96	100.0	0.0	74.0
Glasco CDP	2,099	NA	NA	2,465	86.0	5.2	2.7	2.0	4.1	22.8	56.1	21.1	953	74.1	42.4	22.6
Glen town (Montgomery)	2,504	2,476	-1.1	2,544	93.0	1.7	0.6	1.5	3.3	19.7	66.8	13.4	805	75.5	49.4	17.3
Glen Aubrey CDP	485	NA	NA	351	100.0	0.0	0.0	0.0	0.0	13.0	60.3	26.5	162	61.1	50.0	14.8
Glen Cove city & MCD (Nassau)	26,964	27,314	1.3	27,161	55.7	6.2	3.7	3.8	30.6	21.1	60.8	18.0	9,531	52.1	40.5	38.1
Glen Head CDP	4,697	NA	NA	4,575	84.6	0.1	1.7	1.4	12.2	23.8	59.2	17.0	1,636	86.6	29.5	49.6
Glen Park village	502	519	3.4	505	89.7	2.4	0.4	2.4	5.1	27.4	63.6	9.1	175	79.4	42.3	14.3
Glens Falls city & MCD (Warren)	14,700	14,428	-1.9	14,574	91.9	1.8	0.8	2.1	3.4	17.5	69.3	13.2	6,747	50.1	40.5	27.2
Glens Falls North CDP	8,443	NA	NA	8,645	93.5	0.7	2.9	1.2	1.8	21.8	57.9	20.4	3,737	63.2	33.4	35.6
Glenville town (Schenectady)	29,478	29,666	0.6	29,560	92.8	1.4	1.1	1.9	2.7	21.4	60.4	18.2	11,368	76.8	28.3	35.2
Glenwood Landing CDP	3,779	NA	NA	3,955	89.9	0.4	3.3	1.8	4.6	24.7	60.0	15.0	1,386	81.1	20.0	62.0
Gloversville city & MCD (Fulton)	15,640	15,122	-3.3	15,395	90.5	2.4	0.4	2.4	4.3	23.9	60.9	15.2	6,277	47.5	53.6	14.4
Golden's Bridge CDP	1,630	NA	NA	1,559	86.6	0.0	5.3	0.8	6.8	28.7	60.2	11.0	601	94.8	10.8	72.0
Gordon Heights CDP	4,042	NA	NA	3,918	21.6	47.7	1.9	5.0	23.9	30.3	62.0	7.7	1,173	65.7	41.1	17.9
Gorham CDP	617	NA	NA	710	100.0	0.0	0.0	0.0	0.0	29.0	64.7	6.2	237	65.0	27.4	25.7
Gorham town (Ontario)	4,250	4,269	0.4	4,258	95.7	0.1	1.2	1.9	1.1	18.4	61.4	20.2	1,799	82.0	40.9	29.9
Goshen village	5,454	5,384	-1.3	5,417	72.4	4.4	4.3	2.5	16.3	25.9	57.1	17.0	2,080	52.5	25.0	44.0
Goshen town (Orange)	13,687	13,733	0.3	13,671	73.5	6.5	6.2	1.7	12.1	22.4	60.7	17.0	4,561	68.4	29.9	37.6
Gouverneur village	3,949	3,866	-2.1	3,915	96.8	0.8	0.1	0.9	1.4	21.9	63.9	14.1	1,620	47.6	46.9	16.7
Gouverneur town (St. Lawrence)	7,085	6,990	-1.3	7,021	87.4	7.5	0.0	1.7	3.4	21.2	66.5	12.3	2,415	57.6	45.1	16.2
Gowanda village	2,709	2,648	-2.3	2,679	86.3	4.9	3.0	5.7	0.0	19.1	62.6	18.2	1,104	57.6	44.7	17.0
Grafton town (Rensselaer)	2,130	2,141	0.5	1,958	95.9	1.5	1.0	1.5	0.1	13.5	70.7	15.8	854	89.9	38.3	26.2
Granby town (Oswego)	6,821	6,699	-1.8	6,760	97.5	0.8	0.0	0.4	1.2	22.5	64.9	12.4	2,387	81.9	53.5	19.5
Grand Island town (Erie)	20,374	20,734	1.8	20,580	91.9	1.5	1.7	1.6	3.3	22.6	62.0	15.3	7,946	79.4	24.0	46.0
Grand View-on-Hudson village	285	296	3.9	317	94.6	0.0	1.3	1.3	2.8	18.6	60.1	21.1	136	75.7	10.3	67.6
Grandyle Village CDP	4,629	NA	NA	4,766	92.4	1.2	0.8	1.2	4.4	25.8	59.6	14.7	1,877	82.8	27.8	35.3
Granger town (Allegany)	538	528	-1.9	585	100.0	0.0	0.0	0.0	0.0	22.0	63.6	14.4	238	83.6	77.7	10.1
Granville village	2,542	2,471	-2.8	2,544	94.8	0.0	0.7	1.3	3.1	24.2	54.7	21.1	1,079	52.5	63.2	10.4
Granville town (Washington)	6,669	6,528	-2.1	6,604	96.5	0.6	0.5	0.7	1.8	20.9	59.1	20.0	2,502	68.7	60.8	11.6
Great Bend CDP	843	NA	NA	1,073	76.0	0.0	0.7	0.0	23.4	28.2	56.4	15.4	373	68.4	45.0	38.6
Great Neck village	9,975	10,118	1.4	10,052	81.6	1.3	8.5	2.1	6.5	27.6	55.2	17.2	3,306	74.3	24.1	54.6
Great Neck Estates village	2,761	2,813	1.9	2,791	86.5	0.8	9.3	1.9	1.5	26.6	56.6	17.0	915	89.6	9.1	77.3
Great Neck Gardens CDP	1,186	NA	NA	1,119	67.6	0.0	16.0	16.4	0.0	27.1	58.9	13.9	320	100.0	20.9	73.8
Great Neck Plaza village	6,707	6,918	3.1	6,823	73.8	1.1	12.1	2.7	10.3	16.1	53.8	30.3	3,482	48.0	23.1	57.7
Great River CDP	1,489	NA	NA	1,636	93.0	0.1	4.3	0.0	2.7	25.2	59.5	15.3	541	92.8	15.7	47.1
Great Valley town (Cattaraugus)	1,983	1,963	-1.0	2,281	97.6	0.6	0.0	1.4	0.4	24.8	57.5	17.8	894	83.9	51.6	21.5
Greece CDP	14,519	NA	NA	14,482	89.4	2.8	1.4	1.6	4.8	19.2	61.5	19.3	6,214	75.5	35.8	28.1
Greece town (Monroe)	96,095	97,084	1.0	96,606	85.5	5.7	1.7	1.8	5.2	19.8	62.6	17.6	39,741	73.9	35.7	28.4
Greenburgh town (Westchester)	88,400	91,388	3.4	90,135	61.2	12.3	9.3	2.9	14.3	22.5	60.4	17.0	32,922	73.9	17.5	64.0
Greene village	1,580	1,530	-3.2	1,750	95.1	1.7	0.2	1.0	2.0	25.8	57.1	17.3	717	56.1	42.8	21.9
Greene town (Chenango)	5,604	5,428	-3.1	5,512	95.9	1.6	0.3	1.0	1.1	22.4	60.6	17.2	2,114	78.1	44.3	21.5

1   May be of any race.

Table A. All Places — Population and Housing

STATE City, town, township, borough, or CDP (county if applicable)	Population				Race and Hispanic or Latino origin (percent), 2010–2014					Age (percent), 2010–2014			Households, 2010–2014		Householders by level of education (percent)	
	2010 census total population	2014 estimated population	Percent change 2010–2014	ACS total population estimate 2010–2014	White alone, not Hispanic or Latino	Black alone, not Hispanic or Latino	Asian alone, not Hispanic or Latino	All other races or 2 or more races, not Hispanic or Latino	Hispanic or Latino[1]	Under 18 years old	Age 18 to 64 years old	Age 65 years and older	Total occupied housing units	Percent owner occupied	High school diploma or less	Bachelor's degree or more
	1	2	3	4	5	6	7	8	9	10	11	12	13	14	15	16
NEW YORK—Con.																
Greenfield town (Saratoga)	7,777	7,770	-0.1	7,780	96.0	1.0	1.0	2.0	0.0	21.7	60.3	18.0	3,228	82.0	35.9	35.6
Green Island village & town (Albany)	2,620	2,618	-0.1	2,612	86.7	1.0	3.9	4.5	3.9	19.2	69.3	11.4	1,058	30.2	38.6	19.9
Greenlawn CDP	13,742	NA	NA	14,189	63.7	17.2	2.5	2.6	14.0	26.8	55.8	17.6	4,528	80.1	28.6	42.6
Greenport town (Columbia)	4,164	4,127	-0.9	4,110	80.9	5.2	3.2	6.6	4.2	18.9	59.8	21.4	1,814	68.5	53.0	15.3
Greenport village	2,197	2,212	0.7	2,369	56.1	10.4	0.4	3.2	30.3	19.9	64.3	15.9	906	48.3	39.7	42.1
Greenport West CDP	2,124	NA	NA	1,936	91.5	1.5	0.0	0.0	7.0	12.1	41.8	46.0	929	78.7	33.7	36.7
Greenvale CDP	1,094	NA	NA	765	72.4	0.0	19.2	1.0	7.3	13.4	62.4	24.2	319	70.8	30.1	58.6
Greenville CDP (Greene)	688	NA	NA	573	100.0	0.0	0.0	0.0	0.0	22.2	53.9	23.9	241	76.3	58.1	13.3
Greenville town (Greene)	3,734	3,618	-3.1	3,683	98.0	0.0	0.0	0.9	1.1	19.2	60.7	20.3	1,433	77.0	44.6	20.2
Greenville town (Orange)	4,616	4,674	1.3	4,637	80.6	3.4	0.9	2.9	12.2	23.7	62.6	13.8	1,505	93.5	42.6	24.3
Greenville CDP (Westchester)	7,116	NA	NA	7,138	74.6	2.6	16.4	2.9	3.6	29.6	55.4	15.0	2,314	93.3	7.5	81.3
Greenwich village	1,772	1,747	-1.4	1,947	96.7	0.7	0.4	0.3	2.0	23.9	63.1	13.0	779	53.5	38.1	24.4
Greenwich town (Washington)	4,944	4,887	-1.2	4,929	96.2	0.3	1.9	0.7	1.0	19.9	64.4	15.8	2,018	72.8	41.1	29.1
Greenwood town (Steuben)	801	792	-1.1	758	98.7	0.0	0.4	0.3	0.7	25.5	56.2	18.3	304	79.3	44.4	16.8
Greenwood Lake village	3,154	3,112	-1.3	3,129	74.4	0.6	0.0	0.3	24.7	23.6	67.8	8.6	1,159	77.3	42.8	21.2
Greig town (Lewis)	1,199	1,215	1.3	1,343	96.8	2.5	0.0	0.4	0.2	20.3	59.4	20.3	562	73.5	47.5	17.3
Greigsville CDP	209	NA	NA	239	100.0	0.0	0.0	0.0	0.0	20.1	72.0	7.9	85	100.0	10.6	15.3
Groton village	2,362	2,413	2.2	2,469	95.5	0.8	0.4	2.1	1.2	19.7	65.5	14.8	1,033	65.4	44.2	20.7
Groton town (Tompkins)	5,977	6,136	2.7	6,067	96.8	0.3	0.2	1.1	1.7	20.0	64.5	15.4	2,540	72.4	51.1	21.2
Grove town (Allegany)	548	538	-1.8	489	98.6	0.0	0.0	1.0	0.4	18.4	64.2	17.4	217	82.5	61.3	12.9
Groveland town (Livingston)	3,249	3,342	2.9	3,299	60.8	25.6	0.8	1.6	11.2	7.8	84.1	8.3	575	72.7	39.8	27.8
Groveland Station CDP	281	NA	NA	280	100.0	0.0	0.0	0.0	0.0	32.8	59.6	7.5	101	86.1	51.5	11.9
Guilderland town (Albany)	35,303	35,818	1.5	35,511	84.9	3.1	7.0	1.6	3.4	19.0	66.2	14.8	14,304	68.8	20.0	54.5
Guilford CDP	362	NA	NA	308	85.7	0.0	0.0	1.6	12.7	10.4	67.9	21.8	141	70.2	40.4	18.4
Guilford town (Chenango)	2,924	2,874	-1.7	2,889	94.9	0.6	0.0	1.1	3.4	16.8	63.6	19.6	1,241	83.8	52.2	23.0
Hadley CDP	1,009	NA	NA	857	97.1	0.0	0.0	2.5	0.5	13.5	67.8	18.9	424	72.9	55.0	11.3
Hadley town (Saratoga)	2,048	2,059	0.5	1,714	98.0	0.0	0.0	1.6	0.5	19.2	66.0	14.8	769	81.4	48.2	16.3
Hagaman village	1,285	1,294	0.7	1,284	93.0	0.5	0.0	1.1	5.5	11.3	65.4	23.3	524	86.1	41.4	19.5
Hague town (Warren)	699	692	-1.0	809	96.5	0.2	1.2	1.4	0.6	18.3	49.3	32.3	373	89.3	39.9	34.0
Hailesboro CDP	624	NA	NA	590	99.5	0.3	0.0	0.0	0.2	23.4	63.1	13.6	233	80.7	42.9	17.2
Halcott town (Greene)	256	250	-2.3	252	87.7	0.0	0.0	4.8	7.5	20.7	51.8	27.8	109	84.4	40.4	29.4
Halesite CDP	2,498	NA	NA	2,773	94.7	0.0	0.8	0.3	4.2	20.7	63.6	15.5	1,075	86.9	16.7	62.0
Halfmoon town (Saratoga)	21,517	23,369	8.6	22,416	86.1	1.2	6.3	2.0	4.4	21.2	64.4	14.4	9,487	61.8	25.6	43.0
Hall CDP	216	NA	NA	176	100.0	0.0	0.0	0.0	0.0	15.3	66.4	18.2	74	94.6	37.8	16.2
Hamburg village	9,413	9,565	1.6	9,482	93.6	0.3	0.1	1.0	4.8	23.6	59.8	16.7	4,069	70.5	26.9	43.5
Hamburg town (Erie)	56,936	57,904	1.7	57,441	94.2	1.5	0.2	1.7	2.5	21.0	62.8	16.1	23,926	73.5	32.1	31.9
Hamden town (Delaware)	1,325	1,280	-3.4	1,240	91.8	2.6	0.0	1.2	4.4	19.8	55.9	24.2	518	81.5	46.9	18.7
Hamilton village	4,235	4,199	-0.9	4,070	80.2	8.4	6.2	1.9	3.3	9.9	81.7	8.4	762	60.0	17.5	59.1
Hamilton town (Madison)	6,688	6,610	-1.2	6,638	86.6	5.3	4.2	1.6	2.3	16.4	73.6	10.1	1,739	67.4	25.2	49.5
Hamlin CDP	5,521	NA	NA	5,508	94.7	3.7	0.4	0.6	0.6	26.8	63.2	9.9	1,940	84.2	41.5	18.1
Hamlin town (Monroe)	9,045	9,105	0.7	9,090	95.2	2.8	1.0	0.6	0.4	23.9	65.0	11.3	3,299	83.9	38.2	22.2
Hammond village	280	277	-1.1	377	94.4	0.0	0.5	1.1	4.0	32.6	52.2	15.1	135	61.5	41.5	19.3
Hammond town (St. Lawrence)	1,191	1,185	-0.5	1,551	96.1	0.5	0.7	1.5	1.1	29.5	57.4	13.2	598	77.1	42.5	23.1
Hammondsport village	661	650	-1.7	708	93.4	6.4	0.0	0.3	0.0	17.3	58.9	23.7	357	60.5	21.3	44.8
Hampton town (Washington)	938	929	-1.0	969	92.5	1.2	0.0	0.6	5.7	22.1	65.0	13.0	382	80.6	59.4	17.5
Hampton Bays CDP	13,603	NA	NA	12,712	68.3	1.1	0.8	0.7	29.2	18.8	63.4	17.9	5,085	72.0	35.9	35.0
Hamptonburgh town (Orange)	5,561	5,522	-0.7	5,546	82.3	4.8	8.1	1.6	3.1	23.4	64.3	12.4	1,624	93.5	29.8	36.8
Hampton Manor CDP	2,417	NA	NA	2,129	92.8	0.0	3.3	0.0	3.9	21.5	66.6	11.8	999	84.3	32.5	15.5
Hancock village	1,031	993	-3.7	950	91.6	1.1	2.5	2.8	2.0	17.7	63.8	18.5	436	59.9	53.7	16.3
Hancock town (Delaware)	3,224	3,130	-2.9	3,174	94.3	1.6	1.0	1.2	1.9	19.2	61.3	19.4	1,249	77.0	55.6	14.5
Hannawa Falls CDP	1,042	NA	NA	980	93.6	0.0	2.9	0.0	3.6	19.8	51.5	28.7	446	79.1	25.6	39.7
Hannibal village	555	539	-2.9	632	95.9	0.0	0.0	0.0	4.1	21.7	55.9	22.5	250	76.4	49.2	18.0
Hannibal town (Oswego)	4,854	4,732	-2.5	4,805	92.9	1.1	1.4	2.3	2.2	23.0	66.5	10.6	1,890	81.5	58.9	9.1
Hanover town (Chautauqua)	7,127	6,970	-2.2	7,034	93.5	0.5	0.0	2.6	3.3	21.2	59.6	19.1	2,886	78.3	47.5	19.5
Harbor Hills CDP	575	NA	NA	535	76.4	0.0	16.6	1.3	5.6	21.7	53.2	25.2	165	100.0	0.0	71.5
Harbor Isle CDP	1,301	NA	NA	1,471	87.9	0.0	1.4	2.7	8.0	23.9	58.5	17.6	468	97.6	23.7	43.8
Hardenburgh town (Ulster)	237	231	-2.5	175	96.6	0.0	0.0	0.0	3.4	9.7	58.3	32.0	94	73.4	45.7	27.7
Harford town (Cortland)	943	942	-0.1	708	96.2	0.0	0.0	3.7	0.1	20.2	61.0	18.8	309	79.3	52.4	16.8
Harmony town (Chautauqua)	2,206	2,146	-2.7	2,136	97.3	0.0	0.0	2.5	0.2	22.7	59.7	17.5	855	85.8	45.4	16.1
Harpersfield town (Delaware)	1,577	1,532	-2.9	1,677	94.7	0.5	0.5	2.5	1.8	18.4	54.4	27.3	655	75.3	48.4	23.4
Harrietstown town (Franklin)	5,707	5,665	-0.7	5,679	95.7	1.4	0.1	2.4	0.4	19.2	65.0	15.8	2,662	54.4	29.9	31.7
Harriman village	2,424	2,468	1.8	2,771	51.2	16.0	2.4	2.9	27.5	21.7	70.1	8.1	1,052	58.4	34.6	28.3
Harrisburg town (Lewis)	437	442	1.1	415	96.6	0.0	0.7	2.7	0.0	22.7	65.1	12.3	149	96.6	63.8	10.1
Harris Hill CDP	5,508	NA	NA	5,380	88.5	2.4	4.3	1.7	3.0	22.4	57.5	20.1	2,182	83.9	25.5	49.0
Harrison village & town (Westchester)	27,471	28,151	2.5	27,822	71.9	3.2	7.1	1.3	16.6	22.3	64.4	13.3	8,299	64.4	25.8	53.6
Harrisville village	628	631	0.5	562	96.6	0.0	0.0	2.5	0.9	29.1	57.1	13.9	210	70.5	51.0	21.9
Hartford town (Washington)	2,267	2,244	-1.0	2,337	98.2	0.0	0.3	1.4	0.1	19.8	67.9	12.1	889	81.3	52.4	12.5
Hartland town (Niagara)	4,115	4,047	-1.7	4,078	95.9	0.0	0.2	2.1	1.9	20.8	63.6	15.4	1,616	81.2	53.2	16.1
Hartsdale CDP	5,293	NA	NA	5,346	60.3	4.6	21.3	2.7	11.2	16.7	60.7	22.6	2,571	72.3	18.0	65.0
Hartsville town (Steuben)	609	603	-1.0	579	98.1	0.0	0.0	1.7	0.2	14.3	64.2	21.6	259	93.4	41.3	16.6
Hartwick CDP	629	NA	NA	583	98.6	0.0	0.0	1.4	0.0	19.4	71.3	9.4	254	67.7	38.2	37.8
Hartwick town (Otsego)	2,110	2,064	-2.2	1,958	97.7	0.0	0.0	0.9	1.5	21.7	60.0	18.3	807	82.8	33.5	35.2
Hastings town (Oswego)	9,469	9,401	-0.7	9,438	97.6	0.0	0.6	1.3	0.5	23.6	63.3	13.3	3,390	79.9	58.5	12.4

1 May be of any race.

Table A. All Places — **Population and Housing**

STATE City, town, township, borough, or CDP (county if applicable)	Population 2010 census total population	2014 estimated population	Percent change 2010–2014	ACS total population estimate 2010–2014	Race and Hispanic or Latino origin (percent), 2010–2014 White alone, not Hispanic or Latino	Black alone, not Hispanic or Latino	Asian alone, not Hispanic or Latino	All other races or 2 or more races, not Hispanic or Latino	Hispanic or Latino[1]	Age (percent), 2010–2014 Under 18 years old	Age 18 to 64 years old	Age 65 years and older	Households, 2010–2014 Total occupied housing units	Percent owner occupied	Householders by level of education (percent) High school diploma or less	Bachelor's degree or more
	1	2	3	4	5	6	7	8	9	10	11	12	13	14	15	16
NEW YORK—Con.																
Hastings-on-Hudson village	7,849	7,975	1.6	7,905	85.6	3.4	2.8	1.5	6.8	24.4	55.2	20.3	2,964	70.1	13.8	71.2
Hauppauge CDP	20,882	NA	NA	20,617	86.5	1.5	3.7	1.3	7.0	22.6	59.7	17.6	7,117	84.8	25.0	47.5
Haverstraw village	11,910	12,172	2.2	12,060	21.8	11.7	1.9	1.0	63.6	25.2	63.2	11.5	3,647	44.3	48.5	23.1
Haverstraw town (Rockland)	36,634	37,530	2.4	37,138	39.7	11.5	3.7	1.5	43.5	23.7	64.2	12.1	11,842	62.0	39.0	31.3
Haviland CDP	3,634	NA	NA	3,516	88.5	5.9	0.0	0.8	4.8	17.9	61.4	20.6	1,430	89.2	21.2	36.0
Hawthorne CDP	4,586	NA	NA	4,545	87.0	1.3	4.9	1.0	5.9	19.6	64.1	16.1	1,526	85.3	31.5	40.6
Head of the Harbor village	1,472	1,480	0.5	1,286	91.5	0.0	3.0	1.7	3.8	19.7	61.2	19.2	475	88.2	16.6	64.2
Hebron town (Washington)	1,853	1,831	-1.2	1,713	94.9	1.8	0.2	1.9	1.2	20.8	64.0	15.1	746	86.2	49.2	23.7
Hector town (Schuyler)	4,940	5,015	1.5	4,968	95.4	0.0	0.6	2.2	1.7	18.0	66.5	15.4	2,136	87.1	40.7	22.8
Hemlock CDP	557	NA	NA	483	100.0	0.0	0.0	0.0	0.0	18.0	74.4	7.7	215	93.0	49.8	14.0
Hempstead village	53,891	55,527	3.0	54,801	7.4	47.7	1.9	1.8	41.2	25.4	64.6	10.2	16,233	42.7	55.1	17.6
Hempstead town (Nassau)	759,933	770,116	1.3	765,852	57.7	16.2	6.0	1.9	18.2	22.9	62.5	14.6	242,294	80.4	32.9	40.7
Henderson CDP	224	NA	NA	184	100.0	0.0	0.0	0.0	0.0	26.1	47.9	26.1	75	64.0	57.3	18.7
Henderson town (Jefferson)	1,360	1,404	3.2	1,610	98.4	0.0	0.0	1.3	0.2	19.4	53.4	27.3	674	81.3	32.6	27.2
Henrietta town (Monroe)	42,581	43,639	2.5	43,291	76.3	8.8	7.0	3.4	4.5	18.0	69.9	12.2	15,054	71.0	25.7	38.8
Heritage Hills CDP	3,975	NA	NA	4,174	93.1	0.4	1.8	0.7	3.9	5.3	31.2	63.4	2,429	86.3	22.9	49.8
Herkimer village	7,737	7,592	-1.9	7,752	90.4	3.0	1.5	2.3	2.9	18.3	61.3	20.3	3,330	42.7	40.7	21.0
Herkimer town (Herkimer)	10,169	10,001	-1.7	10,118	91.9	2.4	1.1	2.3	2.2	18.3	61.7	20.1	4,294	52.5	42.5	20.4
Hermon village	420	409	-2.6	393	93.9	1.8	0.0	2.0	2.3	23.4	59.2	17.3	170	71.8	46.5	22.4
Hermon town (St. Lawrence)	1,106	1,091	-1.4	1,082	97.6	0.8	0.0	0.7	0.8	26.0	59.6	14.4	418	78.0	42.8	22.5
Herricks CDP	4,295	NA	NA	4,309	47.8	1.1	39.8	5.2	6.1	22.8	61.8	15.4	1,276	96.2	32.4	52.3
Herrings village	90	91	1.1	85	85.9	1.2	0.0	0.0	12.9	18.9	61.3	20.0	30	96.7	63.3	13.3
Heuvelton village	717	718	0.1	743	95.2	0.8	0.0	1.3	2.7	23.5	61.8	14.5	287	72.1	40.4	25.4
Hewlett CDP	6,819	NA	NA	6,481	88.1	0.1	7.9	0.4	3.3	23.2	56.9	19.9	2,257	88.4	25.1	53.9
Hewlett Bay Park village	404	428	5.9	397	83.1	0.5	4.0	1.0	11.3	16.7	63.4	20.2	140	98.6	5.0	83.6
Hewlett Harbor village	1,263	1,274	0.9	1,259	93.6	0.3	2.2	0.2	3.6	29.2	52.4	18.5	405	98.3	6.2	79.3
Hewlett Neck village	445	473	6.3	366	90.2	5.2	2.5	0.0	2.2	27.9	52.2	19.9	122	99.2	8.2	78.7
Hicksville CDP	41,547	NA	NA	41,784	62.1	2.4	19.3	2.7	13.4	18.7	64.6	16.6	13,368	84.3	34.4	35.9
High Falls CDP	627	NA	NA	738	93.0	0.0	0.0	0.0	7.0	11.5	60.1	28.3	364	67.3	20.1	39.8
Highland town (Sullivan)	2,530	2,473	-2.3	2,400	89.6	3.2	1.3	2.4	3.4	16.0	66.9	17.3	1,065	71.0	34.6	26.1
Highland CDP	5,647	NA	NA	5,315	77.7	4.5	2.4	3.3	12.1	23.2	61.1	15.6	2,228	59.6	26.4	38.9
Highland Falls village	3,900	3,841	-1.5	3,852	57.8	16.4	6.6	4.1	15.0	20.1	67.6	12.3	1,715	41.1	31.0	32.6
Highlands town (Orange)	12,492	12,201	-2.3	12,327	69.0	7.7	4.1	5.2	14.0	19.5	74.7	5.7	3,111	38.1	23.6	44.7
Hillburn village	951	979	2.9	878	39.9	26.5	0.5	14.5	18.7	24.7	63.0	12.3	292	75.0	35.6	27.4
Hillcrest CDP	7,558	NA	NA	7,566	14.9	56.7	10.5	3.3	14.7	21.0	63.7	15.5	1,900	89.2	27.7	29.6
Hillsdale town (Columbia)	1,923	1,886	-1.9	1,726	89.2	7.5	0.6	1.0	1.7	17.9	57.8	24.3	670	80.9	33.9	47.0
Hillside CDP	877	NA	NA	845	99.1	0.9	0.0	0.0	0.0	21.2	59.2	19.6	310	98.1	15.5	52.6
Hillside Lake CDP	1,084	NA	NA	1,089	82.3	0.0	1.2	3.8	12.8	23.0	62.1	14.8	387	88.9	46.8	19.9
Hilton village	5,886	5,952	1.1	5,954	94.0	0.0	0.6	0.7	4.7	23.5	62.2	14.3	2,268	64.9	38.0	22.3
Hinsdale town (Cattaraugus)	2,168	2,102	-3.0	1,987	96.5	2.3	0.0	1.0	0.3	26.3	58.6	15.1	750	85.9	57.6	14.4
Hobart village	441	421	-4.5	515	88.7	7.8	1.9	1.0	0.6	22.3	63.2	14.6	201	59.2	32.3	33.8
Holbrook CDP	27,195	NA	NA	27,765	83.0	1.0	3.1	1.1	11.9	22.9	63.4	13.6	9,151	78.2	35.9	32.7
Holland CDP	1,206	NA	NA	1,253	93.4	0.1	0.0	1.7	4.9	26.2	60.0	13.7	467	75.4	50.1	17.6
Holland town (Erie)	3,401	3,397	-0.1	3,395	97.6	0.0	0.0	0.6	1.8	21.2	64.4	14.4	1,378	85.3	45.2	20.2
Holland Patent village	458	456	-0.4	376	99.5	0.0	0.0	0.5	0.0	18.9	58.3	22.9	153	76.5	34.0	26.8
Holley village	1,811	1,756	-3.0	2,011	95.2	0.3	0.8	1.4	2.3	27.0	60.7	12.4	876	55.7	60.0	13.1
Holtsville CDP	19,714	NA	NA	20,054	78.6	3.5	3.3	1.3	13.3	22.9	65.2	11.8	6,754	81.2	36.0	29.9
Homer village	3,291	3,223	-2.1	3,250	87.0	0.9	1.4	4.8	6.0	25.1	60.4	14.5	1,292	66.3	35.2	34.5
Homer town (Cortland)	6,405	6,406	0.0	6,424	93.4	0.4	0.7	2.4	3.1	23.6	62.4	14.0	2,543	72.9	37.4	28.3
Honeoye CDP	579	NA	NA	631	97.0	0.0	0.0	3.0	0.0	15.5	64.9	19.7	286	81.1	39.2	32.2
Honeoye Falls village	2,674	2,704	1.1	2,707	98.0	0.4	0.0	0.7	0.9	26.4	56.3	17.3	1,236	63.8	24.1	41.7
Hoosick town (Rensselaer)	6,924	6,835	-1.3	6,865	95.8	0.4	0.4	2.2	1.2	21.4	61.5	17.1	2,767	68.7	40.7	20.7
Hoosick Falls village	3,501	3,427	-2.1	3,459	96.5	0.8	0.4	1.6	0.7	22.3	59.1	18.6	1,405	60.4	40.0	24.1
Hope town (Hamilton)	403	387	-4.0	583	98.6	0.0	0.0	0.0	1.4	20.8	65.3	14.1	145	78.6	46.9	22.8
Hopewell town (Ontario)	3,753	3,732	-0.6	3,732	91.2	3.5	0.0	1.7	3.5	20.3	63.0	16.8	1,301	92.3	42.7	12.8
Hopewell Junction CDP	376	NA	NA	611	83.6	1.5	0.0	3.9	11.0	21.6	67.8	10.6	213	90.1	36.2	16.9
Hopkinton town (St. Lawrence)	1,077	1,065	-1.1	1,007	98.4	0.0	0.7	0.9	0.0	26.4	57.5	16.0	410	84.1	52.0	22.0
Horicon town (Warren)	1,389	1,375	-1.0	1,724	91.6	0.0	0.0	7.5	0.2	14.0	56.5	29.5	763	90.0	46.4	30.1
Hornby town (Steuben)	1,706	1,694	-0.7	1,687	97.0	1.1	0.6	0.8	0.5	24.2	62.1	13.6	651	90.3	46.7	16.6
Hornell city & MCD (Steuben)	8,563	8,404	-1.9	8,508	92.8	3.0	0.6	2.2	1.7	23.5	62.6	14.0	3,621	52.2	49.0	17.2
Hornellsville town (Steuben)	4,151	4,113	-0.9	4,134	95.8	0.0	1.1	1.0	2.2	19.0	58.9	22.1	1,922	75.9	47.2	18.9
Horseheads village	6,461	6,678	3.4	6,593	91.4	0.2	3.4	2.4	2.6	20.4	56.7	23.1	2,975	59.5	37.5	28.5
Horseheads town (Chemung)	19,485	19,613	0.7	19,618	91.2	1.0	3.9	2.1	1.8	22.1	58.0	19.8	8,148	68.0	36.5	29.0
Horseheads North CDP	2,843	NA	NA	2,658	92.8	0.6	1.9	0.0	4.7	16.5	66.0	17.5	1,130	81.5	18.1	44.2
Hortonville CDP	218	NA	NA	322	100.0	0.0	0.0	0.0	0.0	27.7	62.4	9.9	107	39.3	64.5	0.0
Houghton CDP	1,693	NA	NA	1,763	87.0	5.8	4.3	0.3	2.6	12.4	77.2	10.4	270	62.6	8.5	70.4
Hounsfield town (Jefferson)	3,470	3,582	3.2	3,547	94.5	0.4	1.1	2.0	1.9	27.2	58.2	14.6	1,442	62.5	24.6	36.0
Howard town (Steuben)	1,467	1,442	-1.7	1,391	98.3	0.0	0.0	0.2	0.6	25.2	60.7	14.2	542	79.2	50.9	16.6
Hudson city & MCD (Columbia)	6,712	6,576	-2.0	6,658	55.5	18.9	7.0	8.4	10.2	22.7	64.8	12.6	2,821	34.3	43.6	25.3
Hudson Falls village	7,295	7,225	-1.0	7,266	95.6	0.0	0.0	2.1	2.3	23.9	63.2	12.8	2,851	57.5	50.6	13.8
Hume town (Allegany)	2,071	2,030	-2.0	1,825	98.7	0.3	0.0	0.7	0.3	21.4	63.8	14.8	866	62.7	56.4	15.6
Humphrey town (Cattaraugus)	687	669	-2.6	694	96.1	0.3	0.0	3.0	0.6	20.7	64.2	15.0	289	90.3	57.1	9.0
Hunt CDP	78	NA	NA	62	100.0	0.0	0.0	0.0	0.0	11.3	43.6	45.2	26	100.0	61.5	0.0
Hunter village	500	487	-2.6	531	98.5	0.8	0.0	0.8	0.0	10.0	63.2	26.7	232	66.4	34.1	35.3
Hunter town (Greene)	2,732	2,662	-2.6	2,699	92.2	0.5	0.1	1.1	6.1	19.5	58.3	22.2	1,073	73.7	47.7	25.6
Huntington CDP	18,046	NA	NA	18,378	87.9	1.2	2.3	0.7	8.0	20.8	62.8	16.4	7,019	82.3	15.1	67.9

1 May be of any race.

Table A. All Places — **Population and Housing**

STATE City, town, township, borough, or CDP (county if applicable)	2010 census total population	2014 estimated population	Percent change 2010–2014	ACS total population estimate 2010–2014	White alone, not Hispanic or Latino	Black alone, not Hispanic or Latino	Asian alone, not Hispanic or Latino	All other races or 2 or more races, not Hispanic or Latino	Hispanic or Latino[1]	Under 18 years old	Age 18 to 64 years old	Age 65 years and older	Total occupied housing units	Percent owner occupied	High school diploma or less	Bachelor's degree or more
	1	2	3	4	5	6	7	8	9	10	11	12	13	14	15	16
NEW YORK—Con.																
Huntington town (Suffolk)	203,260	204,673	0.7	204,088	77.9	4.3	4.8	1.2	11.8	23.9	60.0	16.2	69,026	84.3	22.9	54.0
Huntington Bay village	1,425	1,433	0.6	1,441	92.3	0.0	3.4	1.5	2.8	16.5	62.6	20.9	572	97.2	9.3	78.0
Huntington Station CDP ..	33,029	NA	NA	34,005	50.4	7.6	2.9	1.2	37.9	25.4	63.2	11.5	10,364	69.9	44.2	31.1
Hurley CDP	3,458	NA	NA	3,407	91.4	1.4	2.4	1.5	3.2	20.1	60.5	19.4	1,370	90.0	25.8	41.1
Hurley town (Ulster)	6,314	6,202	-1.8	6,256	90.9	2.2	0.6	3.2	3.1	18.3	59.9	21.8	2,659	91.1	26.7	47.4
Huron town (Wayne)	2,118	2,070	-2.3	2,280	91.5	0.0	2.2	2.1	4.1	19.5	61.0	19.4	862	82.6	48.5	19.8
Hyde Park CDP	1,908	NA	NA	2,314	91.3	2.9	0.6	1.6	3.5	21.9	64.5	13.7	842	75.2	26.5	41.4
Hyde Park town (Dutchess)	21,581	21,309	-1.3	21,474	85.4	5.7	2.4	2.1	4.4	18.3	65.5	16.3	7,805	74.1	30.8	32.2
Ilion village	8,048	7,890	-2.0	7,968	96.2	0.5	0.3	2.1	0.8	23.8	59.8	16.4	3,471	55.1	39.8	26.3
Independence town (Allegany)	1,167	1,176	0.8	1,193	95.7	0.0	3.6	0.0	0.7	24.5	59.7	15.8	476	80.3	68.1	5.9
Indian Lake town (Hamilton)	1,352	1,324	-2.1	1,114	95.1	0.2	0.1	4.4	0.3	22.2	46.5	31.2	410	75.9	49.0	31.0
Inlet town (Hamilton)	333	324	-2.7	487	99.8	0.2	0.0	0.0	0.0	17.9	54.6	27.5	183	80.3	27.9	35.0
Interlaken village	605	621	2.6	638	97.3	0.2	1.3	0.8	0.5	21.3	61.2	17.4	248	69.0	37.5	27.8
Inwood CDP	9,792	NA	NA	9,609	25.8	22.4	4.7	3.1	44.0	28.5	60.1	11.3	2,945	48.2	55.6	17.0
Ira town (Cayuga)	2,203	2,239	1.6	2,310	94.8	0.4	0.0	2.9	1.9	30.0	57.6	12.3	838	89.4	43.6	22.7
Irondequoit CDP & town (Monroe)	51,692	51,462	-0.4	51,594	81.8	8.1	1.8	1.5	6.8	20.0	61.3	18.7	22,315	78.1	33.2	35.7
Irvington village	6,420	6,581	2.5	6,506	78.3	1.3	8.7	2.1	9.7	25.3	59.5	15.1	2,462	78.2	17.1	71.7
Ischua town (Cattaraugus)	859	833	-3.0	937	98.9	0.0	0.0	0.0	1.1	24.7	59.8	15.5	364	83.0	59.3	20.9
Islandia village	3,335	3,384	1.5	3,346	44.9	15.6	10.3	4.1	25.1	20.5	65.5	13.7	1,012	89.6	29.6	32.9
Island Park village	4,655	4,736	1.7	4,686	64.7	0.4	6.3	1.9	26.7	17.9	63.6	18.5	1,798	65.6	41.2	24.1
Islip CDP	18,689	NA	NA	18,229	77.7	5.5	2.4	1.4	13.0	20.9	64.9	14.0	6,292	83.0	35.0	32.5
Islip town (Suffolk)	335,543	336,793	0.4	336,758	56.3	8.9	2.8	1.6	30.4	24.3	63.5	12.2	102,716	76.1	41.0	29.5
Islip Terrace CDP	5,389	NA	NA	5,132	83.1	1.3	2.1	1.1	12.3	22.7	64.5	12.8	1,679	88.4	43.1	30.0
Italy town (Yates)	1,141	1,155	1.2	1,160	97.7	0.1	0.0	1.8	0.4	20.9	62.1	17.0	519	90.9	51.6	25.6
Ithaca city & MCD (Tompkins)	30,020	30,720	2.3	30,399	64.6	6.3	17.5	3.6	8.0	8.7	86.1	5.1	9,489	27.5	15.3	55.1
Ithaca town (Tompkins)	19,920	20,515	3.0	20,141	70.5	5.2	15.0	3.5	5.9	13.5	73.1	13.3	6,994	49.2	12.0	73.4
Jackson town (Washington)	1,800	1,780	-1.1	1,799	97.1	0.4	0.1	1.1	1.4	19.4	58.3	22.2	790	79.6	38.4	29.4
Jamesport CDP	1,710	NA	NA	1,573	83.6	2.7	0.0	0.0	13.7	12.6	73.1	14.3	564	87.8	21.5	42.4
Jamestown city & MCD (Chautauqua)	31,146	30,429	-2.3	30,799	82.8	4.3	0.5	3.4	9.0	25.0	60.4	14.7	13,108	50.8	46.2	18.6
Jamestown West CDP	2,408	NA	NA	2,146	92.5	2.6	0.0	4.1	0.7	15.6	61.6	22.9	920	88.6	31.0	36.4
Jasper town (Steuben)	1,424	1,428	0.3	1,301	99.1	0.2	0.0	0.8	0.0	36.0	53.3	10.8	417	76.7	65.2	7.0
Java town (Wyoming)	2,057	2,014	-2.1	1,958	98.5	0.2	0.0	1.3	0.0	19.8	67.7	12.6	791	86.7	55.4	16.7
Jay town (Essex)	2,506	2,473	-1.3	2,726	98.0	0.2	0.1	1.5	0.3	18.5	62.1	19.3	1,096	76.7	41.5	27.1
Jefferson town (Schoharie)	1,402	1,377	-1.8	1,573	95.0	0.4	0.5	2.0	2.0	21.5	59.8	18.8	635	82.7	43.3	23.8
Jefferson Heights CDP	1,094	NA	NA	1,019	65.1	2.8	3.8	10.7	17.6	19.9	44.4	35.6	304	52.0	32.9	24.0
Jefferson Valley-Yorktown CDP	14,142	NA	NA	14,682	83.7	3.3	2.5	1.7	8.8	24.6	56.1	19.3	5,252	90.5	28.2	43.3
Jeffersonville village	359	345	-3.9	334	85.9	1.8	4.2	1.5	6.6	16.5	58.8	24.9	139	64.7	22.3	41.0
Jericho CDP	13,567	NA	NA	13,445	66.2	2.0	28.7	1.5	1.5	24.0	60.6	15.5	4,676	81.0	11.0	71.3
Jerusalem town (Yates) ...	4,469	4,474	0.1	4,487	96.7	1.0	1.3	0.9	0.1	14.7	66.8	18.5	1,569	80.8	38.6	31.4
Jewett town (Greene)	953	942	-1.2	788	96.3	0.0	1.1	0.0	2.5	8.5	54.9	36.7	433	86.4	38.6	29.1
Johnsburg town (Warren)	2,395	2,373	-0.9	1,773	98.5	0.0	0.4	0.6	0.5	18.6	53.4	28.0	743	81.4	52.8	22.5
Johnson City village	15,174	14,832	-2.3	14,977	79.4	5.4	5.2	5.1	4.9	21.2	61.1	17.7	6,545	53.7	42.2	24.1
Johnstown city & MCD (Fulton)	8,657	8,389	-3.1	8,552	92.2	1.9	2.2	1.9	1.9	19.9	62.0	18.1	3,780	55.8	41.6	16.9
Johnstown town (Fulton) .	7,209	7,233	0.3	7,177	91.9	2.4	1.0	1.0	3.7	20.7	62.6	16.5	2,583	91.9	48.5	15.8
Jordan village	1,368	1,341	-2.0	1,390	98.7	0.0	0.2	1.1	0.0	23.7	65.8	10.4	511	71.0	41.7	25.4
Junius town (Seneca)	1,471	1,461	-0.7	1,408	94.3	0.0	0.0	1.4	4.3	30.2	56.6	13.2	543	86.0	58.9	14.5
Kaser village	4,724	5,015	6.2	4,919	99.2	0.0	0.4	0.1	0.3	59.8	39.3	1.0	949	5.3	74.8	8.9
Katonah CDP	1,679	NA	NA	1,781	68.4	6.6	6.7	5.6	12.6	26.5	61.9	11.4	581	68.2	13.1	66.4
Keene town (Essex)	1,105	1,099	-0.5	998	96.1	0.0	0.3	1.1	2.5	18.7	54.9	26.3	443	77.0	17.8	51.0
Keeseville village	1,815	1,784	-1.7	1,986	92.1	1.7	2.3	2.7	1.2	20.8	64.4	14.7	808	61.8	52.7	15.1
Kendall town (Orleans)	2,724	2,672	-1.9	2,695	93.9	0.4	0.0	2.3	3.4	23.9	59.9	16.2	1,060	84.2	42.5	17.8
Kenmore village	15,423	15,236	-1.2	15,334	88.4	4.0	0.3	3.1	4.1	19.4	64.7	15.8	6,900	66.1	27.7	32.5
Kennedy CDP	465	NA	NA	466	96.8	0.0	0.0	3.2	0.0	15.2	70.0	14.8	188	73.9	58.5	12.2
Kensington village	1,161	1,184	2.0	1,116	88.9	0.0	8.5	2.2	0.4	21.9	54.4	23.6	404	96.8	13.4	74.8
Kent town (Putnam)	13,533	13,399	-1.0	13,460	79.3	4.4	0.7	2.0	13.5	22.2	63.5	14.3	4,583	87.2	34.1	35.9
Kerhonkson CDP	1,684	NA	NA	2,002	94.7	0.7	0.0	0.3	4.3	27.4	59.3	13.1	651	78.8	53.8	24.0
Keuka Park CDP	1,137	NA	NA	934	85.7	4.2	5.2	4.3	0.6	2.1	87.0	11.0	72	73.6	29.2	44.4
Kiantone town (Chautauqua)	1,350	1,341	-0.7	1,462	96.9	1.0	0.0	0.9	1.3	24.7	62.0	13.3	560	86.8	43.8	27.9
Kinderhook village	1,210	1,192	-1.5	1,463	96.6	1.7	0.0	0.8	1.0	22.4	61.8	15.8	611	83.1	27.3	46.3
Kinderhook town (Columbia)	8,497	8,503	0.1	8,464	94.6	1.1	0.9	0.6	2.8	22.0	59.1	19.0	3,197	79.9	25.9	44.5
Kingsbury town (Washington)	12,692	12,619	-0.6	12,696	95.9	0.1	0.0	1.4	2.6	22.4	64.3	13.4	5,078	61.5	52.6	14.9
Kings Park CDP	17,282	NA	NA	17,694	91.1	0.6	3.0	0.7	4.6	21.4	59.6	19.0	6,099	82.8	30.9	41.1
Kings Point village	5,038	5,122	1.7	5,076	92.3	2.2	2.0	1.3	2.4	25.3	58.4	16.3	1,356	92.5	21.1	65.5
Kingston city & MCD (Ulster)	23,881	23,557	-1.4	23,707	63.2	14.7	1.7	5.2	15.2	21.2	63.2	15.4	9,834	44.5	44.4	23.7
Kingston town (Ulster)	889	896	0.8	982	88.4	0.7	4.6	3.9	2.4	19.0	68.5	12.6	435	91.0	45.7	30.6
Kirkland town (Oneida)	10,315	10,263	-0.5	10,274	91.1	2.1	2.9	1.0	2.9	16.7	66.7	16.7	3,548	62.1	19.9	47.1
Kirkwood town (Broome) .	5,857	5,761	-1.6	5,800	95.4	0.3	0.4	2.2	1.6	17.9	61.3	20.8	2,371	73.4	51.1	18.1
Kiryas Joel village	20,175	22,246	10.3	21,201	97.4	0.1	0.1	0.3	2.1	62.0	36.6	1.2	3,772	35.0	71.2	9.4
Knox town (Albany)	2,692	2,728	1.3	2,618	96.3	0.3	0.2	1.1	2.1	22.7	62.2	14.9	970	86.3	42.7	29.4
Kortright town (Delaware)	1,675	1,632	-2.6	1,460	88.2	1.6	4.5	1.8	3.8	23.3	51.5	25.3	544	91.4	44.7	18.8
Kysorville CDP	110	NA	NA	150	94.7	0.0	0.0	0.0	5.3	30.0	64.0	6.0	53	94.3	50.9	13.2
Lackawanna city & MCD (Erie)	18,141	17,955	-1.0	18,037	79.2	8.0	0.5	3.1	9.3	23.1	60.6	16.5	7,661	57.1	52.1	16.3
Lacona village	582	567	-2.6	621	95.5	0.2	1.4	2.6	0.3	23.5	66.1	10.5	243	69.5	41.6	22.2
La Fargeville CDP	608	NA	NA	381	95.8	0.0	0.0	1.3	2.9	21.3	53.3	25.5	165	80.6	47.9	21.8

1 May be of any race.

Table A. All Places — **Population and Housing**

STATE City, town, township, borough, or CDP (county if applicable)	2010 census total population	2014 estimated population	Percent change 2010–2014	ACS total population estimate 2010–2014	White alone, not Hispanic or Latino	Black alone, not Hispanic or Latino	Asian alone, not Hispanic or Latino	All other races or 2 or more races, not Hispanic or Latino	Hispanic or Latino[1]	Under 18 years old	Age 18 to 64 years old	Age 65 years and older	Total occupied housing units	Percent owner occupied	High school diploma or less	Bachelor's degree or more
	1	2	3	4	5	6	7	8	9	10	11	12	13	14	15	16
LaFayette town (Onondaga)	4,952	4,932	-0.4	4,943	91.3	2.6	2.2	4.0	0.0	24.5	60.8	14.7	1,956	82.9	32.5	34.7
La Grange town (Dutchess)	15,721	15,750	0.2	15,763	83.1	3.0	3.7	1.8	8.3	25.0	62.1	12.9	5,287	92.4	22.8	40.4
Lake Carmel CDP	8,282	NA	NA	8,127	75.4	4.0	0.7	2.2	17.7	23.4	64.5	12.0	2,798	88.0	37.0	27.7
Lake Erie Beach CDP	3,872	NA	NA	4,068	96.2	0.0	0.5	2.1	1.1	17.7	65.6	16.7	1,650	85.8	42.7	20.1
Lake George village	906	896	-1.1	932	95.9	0.2	1.0	1.6	1.3	15.2	70.5	14.3	418	51.7	34.4	29.7
Lake George town (Warren)	3,515	3,486	-0.8	3,500	97.8	0.1	0.3	0.6	1.2	15.8	62.0	22.2	1,555	72.2	25.0	33.8
Lake Grove village	11,191	11,241	0.4	11,235	78.9	0.8	4.5	3.8	12.0	22.8	64.0	13.1	3,695	80.5	30.1	38.7
Lake Katrine CDP	2,397	NA	NA	2,374	86.3	1.7	0.8	8.4	2.8	13.2	55.0	31.8	824	56.9	47.1	14.1
Lakeland CDP	2,786	NA	NA	2,580	96.5	0.0	0.4	0.3	2.8	13.7	62.2	24.2	1,088	89.6	49.5	22.8
Lake Luzerne CDP	0	NA	NA	1,142	98.2	1.3	0.0	0.0	0.5	22.1	64.2	13.7	410	76.8	49.0	15.9
Lake Luzerne town (Warren)	3,347	3,311	-1.1	3,342	97.7	0.4	0.4	0.0	1.4	18.3	63.5	18.2	1,285	80.8	49.5	11.5
Lake Mohegan CDP	6,010	NA	NA	5,514	65.2	4.5	3.0	0.3	26.9	22.5	61.3	16.3	2,023	74.7	25.2	40.1
Lake Placid village	2,521	2,465	-2.2	2,356	90.4	1.1	0.5	1.4	6.6	21.7	60.8	17.6	1,196	37.3	31.2	44.0
Lake Pleasant town (Hamilton)	781	763	-2.3	815	91.2	1.1	0.2	6.6	0.9	14.5	57.7	27.9	254	85.8	38.6	30.3
Lake Ronkonkoma CDP	20,155	NA	NA	19,933	82.7	1.9	3.4	1.0	11.0	22.7	63.2	14.1	6,782	75.5	38.7	32.6
Lake Success village	2,934	3,036	3.5	2,985	56.4	7.0	31.7	1.5	3.4	19.5	46.9	33.5	802	96.8	6.4	80.3
Lakeview CDP	5,615	NA	NA	6,357	2.4	70.2	0.5	5.2	21.6	24.8	64.9	10.1	1,489	83.7	39.7	36.6
Lakeville CDP	756	NA	NA	1,097	94.3	0.0	5.7	0.0	0.0	36.2	60.8	3.0	271	49.4	50.9	7.0
Lakewood village	3,002	2,944	-1.9	2,978	93.5	0.8	3.8	0.3	1.6	21.5	55.0	23.5	1,365	67.5	20.6	37.7
Lancaster village	10,364	10,294	-0.7	10,314	94.6	0.0	0.7	3.6	1.1	20.1	65.5	14.3	4,306	70.9	32.2	27.7
Lancaster town (Erie)	41,617	42,748	2.7	42,221	95.2	0.6	0.4	1.6	2.1	23.0	63.0	14.3	16,596	76.9	34.2	32.9
Lansing village	3,547	3,653	3.0	3,614	57.9	3.6	29.9	1.0	7.6	17.5	70.2	12.1	1,684	30.8	5.9	77.0
Lansing town (Tompkins)	11,027	11,444	3.8	11,259	77.6	2.0	12.8	3.8	3.8	21.1	65.0	14.0	4,745	62.5	16.3	65.3
Lapeer town (Cortland)	767	759	-1.0	806	99.3	0.0	0.0	0.0	0.7	32.6	55.2	12.3	245	96.7	51.0	15.5
Larchmont village	5,864	6,111	4.2	5,952	86.0	1.8	2.8	4.9	4.6	31.1	56.2	12.6	2,125	73.3	4.2	84.2
Lattingtown village	1,739	1,777	2.2	1,594	87.5	1.6	6.0	0.4	4.5	23.8	53.8	22.6	575	84.7	17.4	68.7
Laurel CDP	1,394	NA	NA	1,242	97.4	0.0	0.0	0.0	2.6	12.1	59.0	28.7	481	93.3	20.8	47.6
Laurel Hollow village	1,952	2,013	3.1	1,720	85.3	2.0	7.4	1.1	4.1	28.1	57.2	14.8	536	99.4	8.6	80.2
Laurens village	265	260	-1.9	237	93.7	0.0	0.0	0.4	5.9	14.3	74.6	11.0	104	63.5	32.7	21.2
Laurens town (Otsego)	2,424	2,372	-2.1	2,721	93.5	0.2	0.6	0.3	5.4	22.3	58.6	19.3	1,119	82.7	42.6	24.7
Lawrence village	6,456	6,553	1.5	6,511	96.1	0.3	0.7	0.0	2.9	27.4	53.0	19.7	2,126	83.9	7.7	79.4
Lawrence town (St. Lawrence)	1,826	1,824	-0.1	2,028	94.1	1.2	1.3	3.0	0.3	28.7	56.0	15.2	674	84.7	54.7	17.8
Lebanon town (Madison)	1,330	1,324	-0.5	1,360	98.2	0.0	0.0	1.3	0.4	27.1	56.8	16.1	486	84.0	54.3	17.1
Ledyard town (Cayuga)	1,886	1,934	2.5	1,810	92.3	1.7	0.7	0.8	4.5	13.1	72.0	14.9	578	81.5	37.0	38.6
Lee town (Oneida)	6,488	6,456	-0.5	6,476	93.9	1.7	0.4	0.5	3.6	21.6	60.0	18.3	2,499	86.2	39.8	26.9
Leeds CDP	377	NA	NA	550	94.2	0.0	0.0	5.8	0.0	24.8	75.2	0.0	130	74.6	26.9	13.1
Leicester village	466	457	-1.9	498	95.8	0.0	1.0	2.8	0.4	21.0	56.4	22.3	198	74.2	42.9	17.7
Leicester town (Livingston)	2,200	2,153	-2.1	2,183	90.7	1.1	0.7	1.9	5.6	17.2	65.8	17.0	923	77.5	48.0	16.5
Lenox town (Madison)	9,119	9,022	-1.1	9,060	94.2	2.4	0.0	3.1	0.3	20.9	62.5	16.6	3,794	69.1	46.0	23.8
Leon town (Cattaraugus)	1,358	1,336	-1.6	1,252	96.0	0.2	0.0	3.5	0.2	39.4	53.4	7.3	352	74.1	66.2	13.4
Le Ray town (Jefferson)	21,782	22,416	2.9	22,280	61.4	11.0	2.6	7.2	17.8	29.6	67.8	2.7	6,964	18.9	33.7	21.9
Le Roy village	4,386	4,304	-1.9	4,348	90.8	3.9	0.0	2.5	2.9	24.1	59.3	16.7	1,668	63.8	45.2	24.6
Le Roy town (Genesee)	7,636	7,509	-1.7	7,579	90.5	3.6	0.2	3.3	2.4	22.6	59.4	17.8	3,055	70.0	44.9	24.3
Levittown CDP	51,881	NA	NA	52,485	78.8	0.6	7.3	1.4	11.8	22.4	63.0	14.6	16,604	90.9	34.9	33.5
Lewis town (Essex)	1,382	1,357	-1.8	1,503	94.2	1.3	0.5	1.1	2.8	22.7	62.0	15.2	537	84.4	54.4	11.5
Lewis town (Lewis)	854	841	-1.5	760	96.8	3.0	0.0	0.1	0.0	22.0	68.6	9.3	295	83.4	52.2	10.8
Lewisboro town (Westchester)	12,411	12,724	2.5	12,576	89.0	2.3	2.6	1.4	4.7	25.3	61.0	13.6	4,432	91.3	8.7	76.7
Lewiston village	2,701	2,694	-0.3	2,702	97.7	0.0	0.7	0.9	0.7	15.9	57.2	27.0	1,357	76.3	21.7	47.0
Lewiston town (Niagara)	16,262	16,110	-0.9	16,188	95.3	0.8	1.1	1.0	1.9	15.9	62.5	21.7	6,318	82.3	30.6	40.1
Lexington town (Greene)	803	783	-2.5	1,069	94.9	0.0	0.0	0.0	5.1	11.3	62.5	26.2	449	89.8	46.1	24.9
Leyden town (Lewis)	1,785	1,782	-0.2	1,881	98.9	0.4	0.0	0.5	0.2	29.4	58.6	11.9	745	75.0	58.4	8.1
Liberty village	4,371	4,200	-3.9	4,281	57.1	5.4	1.3	2.5	33.7	24.7	60.8	14.6	1,589	34.6	51.4	14.8
Liberty town (Sullivan)	9,887	9,538	-3.5	9,719	71.1	3.3	1.5	2.3	21.8	23.7	61.2	15.2	3,567	57.8	50.9	18.6
Lido Beach CDP	2,897	NA	NA	2,505	91.5	0.1	0.0	0.0	8.3	21.1	56.8	22.1	993	94.7	12.8	71.0
Lima village	2,139	2,107	-1.5	2,487	86.8	0.2	2.3	9.0	1.7	21.4	64.5	14.2	992	64.2	36.1	27.5
Lima town (Livingston)	4,264	4,200	-1.5	4,224	91.9	0.1	1.7	5.3	1.0	20.1	63.3	16.5	1,718	73.2	34.7	29.5
Lime Lake CDP	867	NA	NA	725	97.0	2.5	0.0	0.6	0.0	23.9	45.6	30.6	230	79.6	48.7	18.7
Limestone CDP	389	NA	NA	411	98.3	0.5	0.0	0.5	0.7	28.7	60.2	10.9	149	57.7	55.7	4.7
Lincklaen town (Chenango)	396	390	-1.5	383	93.5	0.0	2.9	2.3	1.3	22.6	58.0	19.3	156	87.2	59.6	7.7
Lincoln town (Madison)	2,009	1,992	-0.8	1,952	93.3	0.0	0.0	5.1	1.4	26.9	62.3	10.9	707	90.2	50.2	23.3
Lincolndale CDP	1,521	NA	NA	1,629	92.5	0.0	0.9	0.0	6.6	25.2	64.3	10.6	489	86.3	36.0	49.1
Lincoln Park CDP	2,366	NA	NA	2,275	92.1	1.4	4.2	0.6	1.7	20.7	54.8	24.3	1,075	45.2	49.5	18.6
Lindenhurst village	27,253	27,321	0.2	27,303	82.3	1.8	1.8	0.9	13.1	19.5	67.3	13.3	9,012	79.1	44.3	24.4
Lindley town (Steuben)	1,967	1,972	0.3	2,064	96.6	0.0	0.0	2.2	1.2	26.8	60.0	13.1	783	81.7	61.6	14.6
Linwood CDP	74	NA	NA	64	90.6	9.4	0.0	0.0	0.0	50.0	40.6	9.4	32	100.0	46.9	53.1
Lisbon town (St. Lawrence)	4,102	4,090	-0.3	4,095	97.3	0.0	0.7	2.0	0.0	27.6	57.6	14.9	1,540	86.9	45.3	19.6
Lisle village	320	309	-3.4	266	94.7	0.0	0.0	1.1	4.1	20.0	64.9	15.0	129	74.4	34.9	23.3
Lisle town (Broome)	2,751	2,697	-2.0	2,716	97.1	0.0	0.0	2.0	1.0	24.3	62.5	13.3	1,014	83.5	56.7	15.6
Litchfield town (Herkimer)	1,513	1,512	-0.1	1,516	96.1	0.0	0.6	2.5	0.8	20.8	64.1	15.2	606	86.5	42.9	27.4
Little Falls city & MCD (Herkimer)	4,946	4,846	-2.0	4,909	94.8	0.0	1.2	2.4	0.8	20.8	58.9	20.4	2,200	53.5	46.6	21.3
Little Falls town (Herkimer)	1,587	1,558	-1.8	1,603	94.8	1.4	0.5	3.2	0.2	20.8	62.8	16.4	632	86.7	42.6	16.8
Little Valley village	1,143	1,112	-2.7	1,203	85.0	4.6	0.0	4.0	6.5	27.7	57.7	14.5	409	65.0	63.8	8.3
Little Valley town (Cattaraugus)	1,740	1,694	-2.6	1,773	88.2	3.1	0.2	4.1	4.4	26.6	57.6	15.8	643	73.9	57.7	12.9
Liverpool village	2,347	2,305	-1.8	2,240	90.3	2.3	0.4	1.1	5.9	14.2	65.5	20.5	1,132	64.4	22.1	40.2
Livingston town (Columbia)	3,648	3,596	-1.4	3,624	81.0	2.8	0.9	2.2	13.2	17.9	62.2	20.0	1,265	64.0	45.6	16.5
Livingston Manor CDP	1,221	NA	NA	967	73.0	0.0	0.6	3.7	22.6	16.9	65.8	17.2	440	56.4	65.2	11.1
Livonia village	1,409	1,395	-1.0	1,322	96.7	0.2	1.0	1.4	0.7	26.1	64.2	9.8	564	63.5	38.7	24.5

1 May be of any race.

Table A. All Places — **Population and Housing**

STATE City, town, township, borough, or CDP (county if applicable)	2010 census total population	2014 estimated population	Percent change 2010–2014	ACS total population estimate 2010–2014	White alone, not Hispanic or Latino	Black alone, not Hispanic or Latino	Asian alone, not Hispanic or Latino	All other races or 2 or more races, not Hispanic or Latino	Hispanic or Latino[1]	Under 18 years old	Age 18 to 64 years old	Age 65 years and older	Total occupied housing units	Percent owner occupied	High school diploma or less	Bachelor's degree or more
	1	2	3	4	5	6	7	8	9	10	11	12	13	14	15	16
NEW YORK—Con.																
Livonia town (Livingston) .	7,804	7,676	-1.6	7,737	97.6	0.3	1.0	0.7	0.5	25.7	61.5	12.8	2,934	82.2	32.0	27.9
Livonia Center CDP........	421	NA	NA	300	100.0	0.0	0.0	0.0	0.0	27.6	69.1	3.3	104	74.0	0.0	37.5
Lloyd town (Ulster)..........	10,863	10,620	-2.2	10,742	81.0	6.2	1.3	2.6	8.9	23.0	61.4	15.5	4,182	68.5	30.3	37.6
Lloyd Harbor village........	3,660	3,686	0.7	3,684	92.9	0.0	3.3	0.8	3.0	31.3	53.0	15.6	1,147	92.5	3.1	80.5
Loch Sheldrake CDP.......	0	NA	NA	1,083	56.8	15.4	1.4	0.7	25.7	15.8	71.5	12.8	295	73.9	40.3	14.9
Locke town (Cayuga).......	1,951	1,921	-1.5	1,797	97.9	0.4	0.3	1.2	0.2	21.9	61.3	16.9	719	86.5	49.8	18.1
Lockport city & MCD (Niagara).................	21,179	20,743	-2.1	20,957	84.6	6.8	1.1	2.9	4.5	22.2	62.1	15.6	9,016	57.7	45.8	20.9
Lockport town (Niagara) ..	20,526	20,260	-1.3	20,380	90.0	3.7	1.6	1.2	3.4	21.0	63.0	16.0	8,212	78.8	38.5	27.6
Locust Valley CDP	3,406	NA	NA	3,241	82.8	2.3	0.4	0.6	14.0	20.7	63.4	15.9	1,251	72.3	25.5	43.5
Lodi village..................	291	297	2.1	418	98.8	0.0	0.0	0.7	0.5	18.9	69.1	12.0	163	83.4	59.5	14.7
Lodi town (Seneca).........	1,550	1,541	-0.6	1,686	94.1	2.6	0.0	2.2	1.2	22.7	61.9	15.4	649	87.2	51.2	23.1
Long Beach city & MCD (Nassau)	33,275	33,664	1.2	33,522	69.9	5.3	3.8	2.3	18.7	15.9	68.0	16.2	14,418	55.2	24.4	49.6
Long Lake CDP	547	NA	NA	323	94.4	1.5	0.3	0.0	3.7	16.6	58.3	25.1	132	80.3	21.2	33.3
Long Lake town (Hamilton)	711	690	-3.0	482	93.6	1.0	0.2	0.0	5.2	11.2	62.8	25.9	185	81.6	28.1	28.6
Lorenz Park CDP............	2,053	NA	NA	2,253	78.0	5.1	2.8	11.9	2.2	24.9	53.3	21.7	998	68.3	53.4	8.9
Lorraine CDP.................	174	NA	NA	123	100.0	0.0	0.0	0.0	0.0	14.6	65.9	19.5	50	90.0	38.0	20.0
Lorraine town (Jefferson) .	1,037	1,067	2.9	1,062	97.3	0.0	0.6	0.4	1.8	25.4	64.4	10.1	369	81.0	58.0	12.2
Louisville town (St. Lawrence)	3,145	3,126	-0.6	3,141	88.7	0.0	1.3	6.4	3.6	20.4	62.8	16.7	1,348	77.7	49.8	21.0
Lowville village..............	3,470	3,451	-0.5	3,646	94.3	0.4	2.1	1.8	1.3	20.3	59.0	20.7	1,679	55.7	52.3	18.2
Lowville town (Lewis).......	4,982	4,959	-0.5	4,958	94.3	1.2	1.9	1.6	1.0	22.4	56.2	21.2	2,155	61.1	50.8	19.6
Lumberland town (Sullivan)	2,468	2,420	-1.9	2,555	87.6	0.9	3.0	0.2	8.3	24.5	56.6	19.0	988	86.8	38.0	24.0
Lyme town (Jefferson)	2,192	2,242	2.3	2,370	95.4	0.3	0.8	2.7	0.8	24.5	58.4	17.2	904	80.6	42.0	18.4
Lynbrook village..............	19,423	19,558	0.7	19,517	77.0	2.7	5.4	1.0	13.8	21.1	62.0	17.0	7,201	73.1	30.1	42.9
Lyncourt CDP.................	4,250	NA	NA	4,267	84.4	4.6	2.5	5.0	3.5	18.1	63.6	18.4	1,868	78.2	50.2	18.3
Lyndon town (Cattaraugus)	707	688	-2.7	738	97.4	0.0	0.0	0.8	1.8	22.9	57.4	19.8	327	84.4	52.3	11.3
Lyndonville village..........	838	812	-3.1	797	96.5	0.5	1.1	1.9	0.0	25.7	60.6	13.6	317	77.3	50.2	16.1
Lyon Mountain CDP........	423	NA	NA	342	98.5	0.0	0.0	1.5	0.0	8.8	59.3	31.9	188	84.0	61.2	8.5
Lyons village.................	3,619	3,520	-2.7	3,343	83.2	11.5	0.0	2.8	2.5	21.6	60.2	18.3	1,525	59.2	51.3	15.5
Lyons town (Wayne)........	5,682	5,527	-2.7	5,596	86.5	8.2	0.0	2.3	3.0	18.2	61.4	20.4	2,300	67.8	49.2	17.1
Lyonsdale town (Lewis) ...	1,227	1,238	0.9	1,251	96.9	0.1	0.3	1.5	1.2	23.2	63.6	13.2	494	79.4	70.4	6.9
Lyons Falls village..........	566	569	0.5	761	89.4	7.2	0.0	0.8	2.6	26.3	52.4	21.2	308	69.8	59.4	14.9
Lysander town (Onondaga)	21,759	22,413	3.0	22,175	92.3	0.7	1.5	2.4	3.1	24.8	60.0	15.1	8,579	80.2	24.5	49.1
McDonough town (Chenango)	886	870	-1.8	721	92.9	0.0	0.6	1.0	5.5	11.6	66.8	21.6	324	89.8	59.6	13.6
Macedon village.............	1,523	1,492	-2.0	1,648	93.5	0.8	0.0	1.0	4.7	24.3	66.6	9.0	581	83.0	28.6	42.2
Macedon town (Wayne)...	9,148	9,004	-1.6	9,085	94.6	0.3	0.1	1.4	3.6	24.3	63.2	12.7	3,426	78.9	35.3	32.0
McGraw village	1,053	1,032	-2.0	1,097	91.2	0.2	0.0	0.7	7.8	23.9	54.5	21.5	418	61.5	55.7	14.1
Machias CDP.................	471	NA	NA	553	94.8	0.0	0.0	5.2	0.0	21.9	62.0	16.1	214	68.2	69.2	2.8
Machias town (Cattaraugus)	2,375	2,344	-1.3	2,403	96.6	0.7	0.0	2.2	0.5	24.6	57.6	17.9	817	84.2	56.7	13.6
Macomb town (St. Lawrence)	906	902	-0.4	843	96.6	0.1	1.3	2.0	0.0	24.3	64.0	11.6	312	85.3	56.1	13.5
Madison village..............	305	302		299	97.3	0.0	0.7	2.0	0.0	17.3	69.3	13.4	139	66.9	66.2	5.0
Madison town (Madison) .	3,008	2,980	-0.9	2,996	95.8	0.3	0.1	1.2	2.7	14.3	64.7	21.0	1,188	88.6	46.0	32.2
Madrid CDP..................	757	NA	NA	715	91.0	1.3	1.3	4.3	2.1	23.6	48.2	28.3	259	73.0	52.5	18.5
Madrid town (St. Lawrence)	1,735	1,708	-1.6	1,708	93.2	0.5	2.4	2.3	1.5	23.0	57.1	20.0	664	80.7	48.0	19.7
Mahopac CDP	8,369	NA	NA	7,755	78.1	0.0	2.7	1.9	17.3	17.7	69.9	12.3	2,852	74.5	30.3	41.9
Maine town (Broome)......	5,377	5,283	-1.7	5,332	97.9	0.0	0.8	1.3	0.1	25.8	57.8	16.4	1,833	78.3	50.0	19.0
Malden-on-Hudson CDP .	405	NA	NA	417	95.7	0.0	0.0	0.0	4.3	15.9	62.5	21.6	145	85.5	75.2	13.8
Malone village...............	5,918	5,824	-1.6	5,866	94.0	2.3	0.0	1.6	2.2	21.5	61.8	16.6	2,458	55.7	44.9	17.3
Malone town (Franklin)	14,545	14,377	-1.2	14,511	74.0	16.0	0.4	1.9	7.6	15.7	73.0	11.4	4,261	67.3	41.8	22.6
Malta town (Saratoga)	14,765	14,873	0.7	14,851	94.0	0.7	1.0	1.7	2.6	19.6	66.0	14.4	6,353	67.7	25.4	45.9
Malverne village.............	8,518	8,570	0.6	8,544	88.9	2.3	4.5	0.3	4.0	19.7	62.6	17.6	3,157	92.6	25.8	53.1
Malverne Park Oaks CDP	505	NA	NA	476	67.2	7.1	8.0	0.0	17.6	14.9	64.6	20.4	180	100.0	8.3	77.2
Mamakating town (Sullivan)	12,083	11,700	-3.2	11,909	83.9	3.2	0.7	2.2	9.9	21.0	66.2	12.9	4,475	76.4	46.6	17.2
Mamaroneck village........	18,930	19,302	2.0	19,133	67.8	5.6	5.4	2.9	18.3	23.0	61.3	15.7	7,380	58.9	28.6	51.6
Mamaroneck town (Westchester)..............	29,156	29,860	2.4	29,501	76.3	3.7	5.0	3.1	12.0	25.8	58.0	16.1	11,019	69.6	16.9	68.3
Manchester village..........	1,694	1,678	-0.9	1,691	91.7	1.2	0.0	3.1	4.0	20.2	61.5	18.2	789	79.0	50.3	14.3
Manchester town (Ontario)..................	9,389	9,429	0.4	9,439	93.8	1.6	1.0	1.5	2.0	23.1	58.5	18.3	3,827	78.4	52.9	15.9
Manhasset CDP	8,080	NA	NA	7,929	67.5	8.3	8.8	2.1	13.3	25.8	53.4	20.8	2,642	74.0	17.0	67.9
Manhasset Hills CDP.......	3,592	NA	NA	3,697	42.4	1.8	36.1	6.2	13.6	24.0	52.5	23.5	1,218	92.2	16.1	69.0
Manhattan borough (New York)......................	1,585,873	1,636,268	3.2	1,618,398	47.4	12.8	11.3	2.8	25.7	14.6	71.4	13.9	745,089	22.6	22.3	63.3
Manheim town (Herkimer)	3,331	3,283	-1.4	3,328	98.5	0.4	0.0	0.0	1.1	28.1	54.8	17.1	1,315	76.2	55.2	14.8
Manlius village...............	4,704	4,649	-1.2	4,691	87.5	3.0	3.9	3.0	2.5	26.7	56.5	16.7	1,886	67.8	20.9	53.9
Manlius town (Onondaga)	32,370	32,405	0.1	32,391	90.3	3.0	3.7	1.7	1.3	23.2	58.7	18.1	13,241	79.2	18.9	54.4
Mannsville village...........	354	367	3.7	332	89.8	8.7	0.0	1.5	0.0	30.4	58.2	11.1	119	84.9	39.5	16.0
Manorhaven village.........	6,556	6,700	2.2	6,638	58.1	0.5	14.7	1.5	25.2	21.6	65.7	12.9	2,397	37.8	23.4	51.4
Manorville CDP	14,314	NA	NA	14,169	91.7	1.5	0.5	1.8	4.5	26.5	62.3	11.2	4,729	85.6	25.4	39.9
Mansfield town (Cattaraugus)	808	818	1.2	898	98.9	0.0	0.0	0.4	0.7	17.8	60.6	21.6	376	91.8	45.7	28.7
Marathon village	919	903	-1.7	1,081	84.9	0.0	10.5	2.6	2.0	22.0	63.4	14.4	430	57.7	44.4	14.9
Marathon town (Cortland)	1,967	1,940	-1.4	2,077	88.3	1.0	5.4	2.3	3.0	23.9	62.7	13.4	799	75.7	49.8	16.8
Marbletown town (Ulster).	5,602	5,550	-0.9	5,581	93.3	0.8	3.5	1.4	1.1	18.2	64.3	17.6	2,466	83.7	24.5	49.8
Marcellus village............	1,813	1,781	-1.8	1,700	96.1	0.0	3.6	0.3	0.0	22.8	56.0	21.1	739	58.1	25.0	43.8
Marcellus town (Onondaga)	6,210	6,186	-0.4	6,210	95.1	0.5	1.1	2.2	1.1	24.2	59.1	16.5	2,423	82.6	24.8	44.1
Marcy town (Oneida).......	8,982	9,299	3.5	9,121	68.9	13.8	2.3	5.4	9.6	15.9	75.0	9.4	2,146	84.8	23.7	37.5
Margaretville village........	596	584	-2.0	539	95.4	1.1	0.0	2.8	0.7	3.8	52.9	43.2	258	48.8	39.1	19.8
Mariaville Lake CDP........	722	NA	NA	727	100.0	0.0	0.0	0.0	0.0	12.9	77.5	9.5	237	100.0	27.0	35.4

1 May be of any race.

Table A. All Places — **Population and Housing**

STATE City, town, township, borough, or CDP (county if applicable)	2010 census total population	2014 estimated population	Percent change 2010-2014	ACS total population estimate 2010-2014	White alone, not Hispanic or Latino	Black alone, not Hispanic or Latino	Asian alone, not Hispanic or Latino	All other races or 2 or more races, not Hispanic or Latino	Hispanic or Latino[1]	Under 18 years old	Age 18 to 64 years old	Age 65 years and older	Total occupied housing units	Percent owner occupied	High school diploma or less	Bachelor's degree or more
	1	2	3	4	5	6	7	8	9	10	11	12	13	14	15	16
NEW YORK—Con.																
Marilla town (Erie)	5,327	5,359	0.6	5,341	97.2	0.0	0.0	0.0	2.8	24.0	61.1	15.0	1,960	88.4	37.8	27.9
Marion CDP	1,511	NA	NA	1,522	96.1	3.4	0.0	0.0	0.5	29.2	52.1	18.7	656	62.8	54.4	18.1
Marion town (Wayne)	4,746	4,672	-1.6	4,702	94.8	2.2	1.7	0.9	0.4	22.8	62.3	14.9	1,930	84.2	47.4	21.6
Marlboro CDP	3,669	NA	NA	3,373	86.2	7.9	1.5	0.0	4.4	27.3	54.5	18.2	1,375	62.3	42.5	27.3
Marlborough town (Ulster)	8,808	8,714	-1.1	8,788	83.6	3.9	1.0	3.2	8.2	22.9	62.7	14.4	3,383	65.9	41.1	29.9
Marshall town (Oneida)	2,131	2,128	-0.1	2,074	98.1	0.0	0.2	0.2	1.4	21.1	64.3	14.6	781	85.3	40.8	28.4
Martinsburg town (Lewis)	1,433	1,448	1.0	1,358	93.8	0.2	0.2	0.3	5.4	20.0	67.6	12.3	504	69.6	62.1	11.1
Maryland town (Otsego)	1,893	1,851	-2.2	1,854	96.9	0.5	0.0	1.3	1.2	19.5	63.3	17.4	762	78.1	55.2	18.1
Masonville town (Delaware)	1,320	1,297	-1.7	1,598	95.2	1.1	0.9	1.3	1.6	25.9	57.6	16.7	586	87.9	55.6	13.7
Massapequa CDP	21,685	NA	NA	22,323	92.8	0.4	1.7	0.5	4.6	23.6	60.8	15.6	7,235	92.4	28.8	45.3
Massapequa Park village	17,008	17,206	1.2	17,137	91.6	0.3	1.2	0.4	6.6	23.9	60.6	15.5	5,479	97.2	28.6	40.1
Massena village	10,936	10,723	-1.9	10,937	95.7	0.3	1.4	2.0	0.6	21.3	62.0	16.7	4,933	57.2	45.7	20.4
Massena town (St. Lawrence)	12,883	12,652	-1.8	12,794	94.7	0.4	1.2	3.1	0.7	19.3	61.7	19.0	5,848	59.6	46.2	18.7
Mastic CDP	15,481	NA	NA	16,274	66.5	8.1	4.1	1.1	20.1	28.6	63.9	7.7	5,024	77.9	55.6	13.2
Mastic Beach village	14,841	14,874	0.2	14,880	66.8	12.7	1.1	3.0	16.4	28.3	64.3	7.3	4,786	70.7	56.6	12.2
Matinecock village	810	817	0.9	886	89.2	0.0	4.7	0.8	5.3	27.3	56.7	15.9	279	80.6	10.4	82.8
Mattituck CDP	4,219	NA	NA	4,391	93.4	1.8	0.8	0.9	3.1	23.6	55.2	21.2	1,860	81.2	36.6	36.1
Mattydale CDP	6,446	NA	NA	6,741	84.4	6.0	1.3	3.9	4.4	27.3	60.1	12.7	2,621	65.2	59.1	10.6
Maybrook village	2,958	3,113	5.2	3,022	60.4	11.3	1.4	6.5	20.4	23.0	66.2	10.9	1,124	57.3	43.0	26.0
Mayfield village	840	808	-3.8	795	98.1	0.3	0.0	0.4	1.3	13.8	71.3	15.0	328	85.1	43.9	14.9
Mayfield town (Fulton)	6,495	6,307	-2.9	6,412	97.4	0.0	0.1	1.6	0.9	18.5	63.8	17.8	2,712	78.2	53.2	15.4
Mayville village	1,711	1,691	-1.2	1,386	88.3	4.7	0.2	3.2	3.5	14.7	69.9	15.4	524	68.5	33.2	28.4
Mechanicstown CDP	6,858	NA	NA	7,030	42.3	25.9	3.1	1.8	26.8	20.0	60.7	19.3	2,738	45.1	43.3	20.2
Mechanicville city & MCD (Saratoga)	5,199	5,172	-0.5	5,207	93.1	0.9	1.5	1.8	2.7	22.4	65.8	11.7	2,272	34.2	45.2	17.2
Medford CDP	24,142	NA	NA	24,535	70.6	5.3	3.8	1.8	18.5	23.4	64.0	12.5	7,823	85.7	41.1	26.0
Medina village	6,065	5,864	-3.3	5,962	82.1	8.0	0.9	5.0	4.1	26.3	55.8	17.7	2,407	55.1	45.7	24.1
Melrose Park CDP	2,294	NA	NA	2,026	99.1	0.0	0.0	0.2	0.6	18.4	65.5	16.1	802	92.5	21.9	41.5
Melville CDP	18,985	NA	NA	19,228	80.7	4.7	7.9	1.0	5.6	22.2	53.6	24.1	6,883	86.5	17.7	62.6
Menands village	3,992	4,004	0.3	4,004	66.3	4.5	20.8	3.7	4.7	19.7	68.7	11.6	1,701	37.3	24.6	56.1
Mendon town (Monroe)	9,148	9,263	1.3	9,245	95.2	0.4	1.8	1.1	1.5	28.3	58.6	13.2	3,648	85.1	16.4	62.9
Mentz town (Cayuga)	2,380	2,328	-2.2	2,542	97.1	0.4	0.0	1.7	0.8	21.6	62.2	16.3	965	80.6	56.0	11.4
Meredith town (Delaware)	1,529	1,487	-2.7	1,641	90.7	0.2	2.9	0.8	5.4	13.1	69.6	17.4	662	79.0	30.7	33.8
Meridian village	309	306	-1.0	267	86.9	0.0	0.0	6.0	7.1	24.0	64.1	12.0	96	83.3	42.7	13.5
Merrick CDP	22,097	NA	NA	21,293	87.2	1.9	2.8	0.3	7.7	23.8	62.7	13.6	6,961	94.9	18.5	61.8
Merritt Park CDP	1,256	NA	NA	1,446	48.1	6.4	32.6	0.5	12.5	25.1	61.7	13.2	521	89.3	20.3	66.0
Mexico village	1,624	1,592	-2.0	1,765	95.6	0.0	0.3	2.4	1.6	31.8	58.4	9.7	693	59.2	30.6	28.6
Mexico town (Oswego)	5,197	5,177	-0.4	5,192	95.4	0.0	0.3	3.6	0.8	23.8	62.3	14.0	1,989	79.4	46.4	19.1
Middleburgh town (Schoharie)	3,746	3,607	-3.7	3,685	96.2	0.4	0.2	0.4	2.8	20.5	61.7	17.7	1,499	79.1	51.2	17.3
Middleburgh village	1,504	1,455	-3.3	1,458	95.3	0.6	0.5	1.0	2.6	18.6	65.7	15.8	630	63.3	48.9	17.1
Middlebury town (Wyoming)	1,441	1,407	-2.4	1,437	96.9	1.0	0.0	0.2	1.9	19.1	65.0	15.9	587	81.4	43.6	18.7
Middlefield town (Otsego)	2,114	2,075	-1.8	1,965	92.5	1.6	2.8	0.3	2.8	14.3	63.4	22.2	858	78.1	32.3	44.3
Middle Island CDP	10,483	NA	NA	10,030	74.0	11.6	4.1	2.1	8.2	20.7	60.0	19.3	4,120	76.5	36.0	28.4
Middleport village	1,840	1,798	-2.3	1,706	99.0	0.0	0.4	0.3	0.4	26.8	58.2	15.2	686	66.0	46.4	13.6
Middlesex town (Yates)	1,495	1,488	-0.5	1,334	96.9	0.9	0.3	0.5	1.3	15.6	68.6	15.4	574	89.7	33.1	25.6
Middletown town (Delaware)	3,751	3,644	-2.9	3,699	84.0	0.8	0.2	3.5	11.5	13.4	62.6	24.2	1,700	73.6	33.6	24.6
Middletown city & MCD (Orange)	28,086	27,728	-1.3	27,904	35.7	20.4	3.4	2.0	38.5	24.6	63.6	11.8	9,976	51.1	45.4	22.4
Middleville village	512	505	-1.4	550	98.4	0.0	0.0	1.6	0.0	21.5	59.5	18.9	213	81.7	46.5	9.4
Milan town (Dutchess)	2,367	2,362	-0.2	2,254	85.8	3.0	4.2	2.6	4.3	20.5	64.8	14.7	946	80.5	29.2	41.9
Milford village	414	407	-1.7	420	96.4	0.5	2.1	0.0	1.0	13.2	66.6	20.2	197	74.1	57.4	20.8
Milford town (Otsego)	3,044	2,978	-2.2	3,027	99.0	0.4	0.3	0.0	0.2	16.7	60.9	22.2	1,337	80.6	46.1	23.3
Millbrook village	1,455	1,434	-1.4	1,510	88.9	0.5	2.9	2.2	5.6	18.1	55.1	26.9	718	43.5	32.2	35.2
Miller Place CDP	12,339	NA	NA	11,783	92.9	0.8	2.4	0.8	3.1	28.8	59.5	11.8	3,929	95.1	27.3	45.4
Millerton village	960	946	-1.5	764	72.9	3.5	5.2	2.9	15.4	19.1	65.2	15.7	333	57.4	41.7	23.4
Mill Neck village	997	1,010	1.3	986	88.9	0.0	5.6	0.0	5.5	18.9	59.9	21.1	368	88.9	13.6	65.8
Millport village	312	299	-4.2	398	96.7	0.0	0.0	2.8	0.5	28.6	62.9	8.3	133	82.7	69.9	7.5
Milo town (Yates)	7,011	6,903	-1.5	6,924	95.6	1.1	0.8	1.2	1.2	25.7	56.9	17.3	2,886	68.4	47.3	28.0
Milton town (Saratoga)	18,568	18,968	2.2	18,784	95.0	0.8	0.5	1.9	1.7	23.9	65.2	11.0	7,374	74.3	35.6	32.7
Milton CDP (Saratoga)	3,087	NA	NA	3,340	97.4	0.0	0.7	0.0	1.8	22.7	63.5	13.7	1,214	85.4	26.3	39.0
Milton CDP (Ulster)	1,403	NA	NA	1,529	88.4	0.1	1.9	1.3	8.3	17.5	70.1	12.3	549	67.6	34.8	32.1
Mina town (Chautauqua)	1,106	1,091	-1.4	971	100.0	0.0	0.0	0.0	0.0	19.7	65.5	14.8	394	83.5	50.5	18.8
Minden town (Montgomery)	4,314	4,193	-2.8	4,240	96.9	0.0	1.0	1.4	0.7	25.6	58.7	15.8	1,657	77.1	60.3	13.4
Mineola village	18,799	19,028	1.2	18,918	68.6	0.9	8.3	0.3	22.0	19.8	63.8	16.7	7,291	65.8	35.4	41.4
Minerva town (Essex)	809	797	-1.5	591	99.0	0.2	0.2	0.3	0.3	15.5	50.1	34.3	262	84.7	44.3	23.7
Minetto CDP	1,069	NA	NA	979	96.3	0.3	1.7	0.5	1.1	23.5	59.1	17.5	405	81.5	34.1	29.1
Minetto town (Oswego)	1,659	1,627	-1.9	1,599	95.5	1.4	1.4	0.7	0.9	22.8	59.7	17.3	653	81.2	36.1	32.2
Mineville CDP	1,269	NA	NA	1,238	88.0	7.4	0.0	2.2	2.4	15.2	72.3	12.4	304	88.2	65.8	5.9
Minisink town (Orange)	4,490	4,517	0.6	4,507	91.3	1.9	0.1	2.8	3.9	29.8	64.3	5.9	1,450	88.6	35.7	26.8
Minoa village	3,442	3,529	2.5	3,492	95.8	1.2	0.0	1.9	1.1	22.0	63.2	14.9	1,467	80.9	26.6	37.5
Mohawk village	2,731	2,670	-2.2	2,632	96.0	0.2	0.1	1.1	2.6	19.8	63.2	17.2	1,098	61.7	46.7	19.4
Mohawk town (Montgomery)	3,847	3,793	-1.4	3,809	91.4	1.3	1.9	1.7	3.7	24.6	61.5	13.9	1,449	78.2	42.1	16.1
Moira town (Franklin)	2,934	2,881	-1.8	2,901	94.7	0.2	0.0	1.9	3.2	19.8	59.4	20.9	1,248	71.6	54.5	12.6
Monroe village	8,364	8,562	2.4	8,493	74.3	1.9	6.5	0.9	16.7	26.8	61.1	12.0	2,692	82.8	25.2	46.3
Monroe town (Orange)	39,912	42,280	5.9	41,159	85.3	2.1	2.4	1.0	9.2	44.7	49.8	5.4	10,172	64.3	41.7	33.5
Monsey CDP	18,412	NA	NA	20,171	94.2	2.2	0.3	0.6	2.8	53.1	41.6	5.4	3,733	39.3	64.7	14.5
Montague town (Lewis)	78	79	1.3	89	100.0	0.0	0.0	0.0	0.0	31.5	60.6	7.9	32	93.8	71.9	9.4
Montauk CDP	3,326	NA	NA	3,471	87.7	3.5	2.4	0.4	5.9	11.5	63.6	25.0	1,742	79.0	32.7	40.4
Montebello village	4,526	4,646	2.7	4,588	69.6	11.5	6.0	4.1	8.8	24.6	55.3	20.1	1,499	84.8	24.8	63.9
Montezuma town (Cayuga)	1,277	1,254	-1.8	1,182	97.6	0.0	0.7	0.5	1.2	17.0	69.7	13.5	471	85.1	63.9	7.4
Montgomery village	3,814	4,617	21.1	4,159	78.7	4.3	0.6	1.2	15.2	28.8	57.5	13.6	1,429	67.0	34.5	28.9
Montgomery town (Orange)	22,606	23,523	4.1	22,993	75.5	4.8	0.7	3.3	15.6	24.9	62.9	12.2	8,013	71.0	40.2	27.0

1 May be of any race.

Table A. All Places — **Population and Housing**

	Population				Race and Hispanic or Latino origin (percent), 2010–2014					Age (percent), 2010–2014			Households, 2010–2014			
STATE City, town, township, borough, or CDP (county if applicable)	2010 census total population	2014 estimated population	Percent change 2010–2014	ACS total population estimate 2010–2014	White alone, not Hispanic or Latino	Black alone, not Hispanic or Latino	Asian alone, not Hispanic or Latino	All other races or 2 or more races, not Hispanic or Latino	Hispanic or Latino[1]	Under 18 years old	Age 18 to 64 years old	Age 65 years and older	Total occupied housing units	Percent owner occupied	High school diploma or less	Bachelor's degree or more
	1	2	3	4	5	6	7	8	9	10	11	12	13	14	15	16
NEW YORK—Con.																
Monticello village	6,869	6,651	-3.2	6,780	31.8	34.0	0.4	6.6	27.3	25.0	62.4	12.5	2,785	23.9	56.6	12.6
Montour town (Schuyler) .	2,308	2,302	-0.3	2,398	97.9	0.0	0.3	1.0	0.9	20.3	58.8	21.0	1,105	60.8	50.4	16.6
Montour Falls village.......	1,711	1,694	-1.0	1,932	96.6	0.6	0.6	0.8	1.3	20.5	54.5	24.9	824	51.1	55.0	14.6
Montrose CDP................	2,731	NA	NA	2,681	80.0	0.0	4.3	1.8	14.0	17.5	65.7	16.8	1,069	84.1	28.3	36.9
Mooers CDP..................	442	NA	NA	161	91.3	0.0	0.0	0.0	8.7	8.7	78.9	12.4	132	61.4	70.5	15.2
Mooers town (Clinton)	3,592	3,600	0.2	3,597	96.3	0.6	0.6	1.7	0.8	20.9	68.3	10.7	1,512	80.2	66.1	14.6
Moravia village...............	1,280	1,251	-2.3	1,512	97.4	0.0	1.0	1.2	0.4	20.1	60.4	19.5	594	68.2	49.7	18.2
Moravia town (Cayuga)....	3,624	3,508	-3.2	3,550	82.8	11.0	0.5	1.4	4.4	16.8	69.5	13.7	1,075	77.0	50.0	15.8
Moreau town (Saratoga)..	14,739	15,350	4.1	15,049	93.8	2.5	0.5	0.7	2.5	20.3	66.5	13.3	5,834	74.4	43.0	18.3
Morehouse town (Hamilton)	86	83	-3.5	31	100.0	0.0	0.0	0.0	0.0	0.0	61.4	38.7	14	78.6	50.0	0.0
Moriah town (Essex)........	4,798	4,729	-1.4	4,791	94.6	2.2	0.0	2.2	1.0	22.4	62.6	15.0	1,685	76.0	53.1	14.8
Moriches CDP................	2,838	NA	NA	2,254	80.0	7.5	7.4	1.5	3.5	18.9	59.5	21.6	1,129	49.4	31.4	36.7
Morris village	583	571	-2.1	387	92.0	0.0	0.0	3.4	4.7	11.7	61.8	26.6	212	75.9	27.4	33.0
Morris town (Otsego)	1,878	1,836	-2.2	1,551	96.3	0.0	0.8	1.7	1.2	16.8	58.6	24.5	671	82.4	44.6	20.0
Morrisonville CDP...........	1,545	NA	NA	1,730	95.3	1.7	0.9	0.3	1.8	24.5	59.3	16.3	724	69.9	37.6	29.3
Morristown village............	395	389	-1.5	428	95.6	2.1	0.2	1.6	0.5	15.7	65.7	18.5	179	81.6	40.2	24.6
Morristown town (St. Lawrence)	1,977	1,944	-1.7	2,242	97.5	0.4	0.0	1.9	0.1	21.1	58.0	21.0	869	81.4	49.0	23.1
Morrisville village............	2,166	1,819	-16.0	2,053	70.2	19.1	2.7	0.9	7.1	7.8	81.4	10.7	257	60.3	32.7	27.2
Mountain Lodge Park CDP	1,588	NA	NA	1,983	81.0	3.2	0.0	6.5	9.3	20.8	73.0	6.5	701	93.2	54.8	17.8
Mount Hope town (Orange)..................	7,018	7,079	0.9	7,043	65.0	15.5	1.4	2.4	15.6	18.5	73.2	8.3	1,761	86.4	28.1	30.2
Mount Ivy CDP...............	6,878	NA	NA	6,926	53.8	7.8	5.1	3.1	30.1	23.0	66.2	10.7	2,706	62.2	37.3	34.7
Mount Kisco village & town (Westchester)	10,877	11,103	2.1	11,016	49.1	3.9	4.1	1.2	41.7	22.6	64.6	12.7	4,085	52.8	32.4	45.4
Mount Morris village	2,985	2,905	-2.7	2,610	83.8	2.4	0.0	1.8	12.0	27.7	57.9	14.4	1,045	48.1	57.6	12.8
Mount Morris town (Livingston)	4,464	4,371	-2.1	4,411	83.5	1.7	0.1	1.1	13.6	24.7	56.6	18.7	1,538	59.2	61.2	12.3
Mount Pleasant town (Westchester)..............	43,727	44,638	2.1	44,249	70.3	4.5	5.3	1.8	18.0	23.6	63.0	13.5	14,069	69.8	26.2	54.3
Mount Sinai CDP............	12,118	NA	NA	12,620	83.0	1.7	3.6	1.4	10.3	25.8	57.8	16.4	4,251	94.2	27.3	43.2
Mount Vernon city & MCD (Westchester)..............	67,290	68,458	1.7	67,962	17.7	62.2	2.1	3.3	14.7	23.2	63.0	13.7	25,750	38.8	42.7	29.3
Munnsville village	486	472	-2.9	473	94.7	0.0	0.6	3.8	0.8	28.8	63.1	8.2	153	63.4	54.9	11.1
Munsey Park village.........	2,693	2,715	0.8	2,712	91.0	0.0	3.5	1.7	3.8	32.5	55.3	12.1	780	100.0	5.1	89.6
Munsons Corners CDP ...	2,728	NA	NA	2,333	94.9	0.6	0.3	4.0	0.3	16.4	55.6	27.9	968	52.4	44.1	21.9
Murray town (Orleans).....	4,988	4,839	-3.0	4,917	95.8	1.2	0.3	1.4	1.3	21.1	63.7	15.4	2,081	76.5	55.5	14.5
Muttontown village	3,497	3,657	4.6	3,581	66.5	7.5	21.0	0.5	4.6	23.7	61.1	15.2	1,077	95.5	13.6	72.0
Myers Corner CDP	6,790	NA	NA	6,927	74.3	3.9	12.5	2.0	7.4	23.4	60.5	16.0	2,331	96.9	24.1	48.6
Nanticoke town (Broome).	1,672	1,626	-2.8	1,568	98.1	0.6	0.0	0.7	0.6	20.7	62.8	16.6	592	77.4	52.7	14.0
Nanuet CDP...................	17,882	NA	NA	18,366	56.1	14.3	11.7	1.2	16.6	19.8	62.8	17.3	6,698	67.1	29.9	43.5
Napanoch CDP...............	1,174	NA	NA	1,079	76.6	0.7	3.2	0.0	19.6	19.5	68.0	12.4	465	76.1	45.2	19.4
Napeague CDP	200	NA	NA	172	100.0	0.0	0.0	0.0	0.0	11.0	58.0	30.8	95	77.9	48.4	47.4
Naples village	1,044	1,025	-1.8	1,187	99.3	0.0	0.0	0.4	0.3	21.6	61.7	16.5	444	66.4	31.1	30.6
Naples town (Ontario)......	2,506	2,493	-0.5	2,505	99.1	0.1	0.0	0.5	0.2	20.3	61.6	18.0	998	78.3	44.0	25.6
Napoli town (Cattaraugus)	1,248	1,290	3.4	1,311	97.6	0.2	0.0	2.1	0.2	36.0	53.0	11.1	404	91.1	55.9	15.1
Narrowsburg CDP............	431	NA	NA	422	89.6	6.2	0.0	0.5	3.8	12.0	60.7	27.3	204	67.6	31.4	36.3
Nassau village	1,133	1,123	-0.9	1,103	89.6	1.6	0.0	4.8	4.0	19.8	63.4	16.9	508	63.8	38.2	25.0
Nassau town (Rensselaer)	4,789	4,800	0.2	4,804	87.3	2.9	2.3	4.1	3.4	20.8	62.5	16.9	2,043	77.5	42.0	24.6
Natural Bridge CDP.........	365	NA	NA	734	100.0	0.0	0.0	0.0	0.0	45.0	54.7	0.0	161	58.4	92.5	0.0
Nedrow CDP..................	2,244	NA	NA	2,267	74.0	7.1	0.0	15.8	3.2	19.9	68.3	12.0	893	85.7	44.6	11.5
Nelliston village..............	596	579	-2.9	583	97.9	0.0	0.5	0.3	1.2	16.0	61.6	22.3	266	75.6	69.2	6.4
Nelson town (Madison)....	1,980	1,973	-0.4	1,954	98.4	0.0	0.5	0.7	0.5	22.8	59.4	18.0	777	88.2	35.0	42.3
Nelsonville village	628	625	-0.5	804	85.9	0.9	2.7	0.0	10.4	31.3	60.6	8.1	253	66.8	25.3	47.8
Nesconset CDP..............	13,387	NA	NA	14,080	88.1	1.5	6.0	0.2	4.1	25.4	60.5	14.2	4,474	83.6	25.4	46.6
Neversink town (Sullivan).	3,557	3,472	-2.4	3,530	88.0	1.8	0.0	2.7	7.5	22.5	59.6	18.1	1,467	81.3	34.2	22.1
New Albion town (Cattaraugus)...............	1,972	1,933	-2.0	1,871	93.9	0.1	0.0	2.2	3.9	17.6	63.7	18.7	830	73.0	47.6	13.3
Newark village	9,145	8,902	-2.7	9,019	83.2	6.6	0.5	2.0	7.6	21.1	63.8	15.1	3,793	54.9	50.8	18.5
Newark Valley village.......	997	964	-3.3	1,093	91.2	0.5	0.2	4.9	3.2	28.4	56.2	15.6	449	71.9	40.1	25.2
Newark Valley town (Tioga).....................	3,946	3,838	-2.7	3,892	97.1	0.1	0.1	1.8	0.9	19.0	61.3	19.8	1,692	81.4	47.8	24.1
New Baltimore town (Greene)..................	3,366	3,271	-2.8	3,315	97.2	0.6	0.0	0.9	1.2	18.1	65.6	16.4	1,181	94.6	43.1	19.5
New Berlin village	1,028	990	-3.7	1,240	93.8	0.0	0.0	2.7	3.5	19.1	51.8	29.0	502	61.8	60.4	12.5
New Berlin town (Chenango)...............	2,682	2,585	-3.6	2,636	95.6	0.0	0.4	2.4	1.7	16.3	55.7	28.0	1,148	77.0	53.7	14.4
New Bremen town (Lewis)	2,707	2,730	0.8	2,723	98.1	0.5	0.1	0.1	1.1	33.3	55.6	11.2	904	80.5	61.3	8.5
Newburgh city & MCD (Orange)..................	28,866	28,358	-1.8	28,614	19.7	27.9	0.6	2.5	49.3	31.9	59.9	8.3	8,762	32.0	66.8	10.3
Newburgh town (Orange)	29,801	30,584	2.6	30,485	65.4	10.5	2.9	1.8	19.4	22.9	62.5	14.6	10,826	81.4	34.8	34.6
New Cassel CDP............	14,059	NA	NA	13,988	6.4	36.5	1.5	5.6	49.9	31.3	59.5	9.1	3,086	57.5	57.8	17.7
New Castle town (Westchester)..............	17,547	17,967	2.4	17,786	83.7	1.4	7.3	2.5	5.1	30.3	58.1	11.5	5,815	92.2	6.0	86.6
New City CDP................	33,559	NA	NA	33,874	71.7	6.8	10.2	3.3	8.1	22.4	59.6	17.8	11,005	90.1	18.3	59.3
Newcomb town (Essex) ...	436	424	-2.8	493	99.8	0.0	0.0	0.0	0.2	13.4	49.8	36.7	208	91.3	45.2	28.4
Newfane CDP................	3,822	NA	NA	3,600	98.2	0.4	0.0	1.4	0.0	23.1	54.3	22.6	1,399	80.1	47.7	17.9
Newfane town (Niagara)..	9,666	9,466	-2.1	9,560	97.9	0.2	0.0	1.3	0.5	20.7	61.5	17.8	3,746	81.2	48.2	16.0
Newfield town (Tompkins)	5,181	5,322	2.7	5,258	93.8	1.4	1.6	1.2	2.0	24.1	62.2	13.6	2,025	74.6	38.5	32.5
Newfield Hamlet CDP......	759	NA	NA	659	97.9	0.0	0.0	0.0	2.1	7.5	67.4	25.0	333	81.7	54.4	33.0
New Hartford village	1,847	1,848	0.1	1,767	95.3	1.6	0.0	0.0	3.1	23.0	55.4	21.5	830	64.1	22.3	46.0
New Hartford town (Oneida)...................	22,166	22,150	-0.1	22,080	93.0	1.3	3.4	1.1	1.2	18.8	56.6	24.7	9,367	71.1	24.9	43.2
New Haven town (Oswego).................	2,856	2,873	0.6	2,867	97.9	0.1	0.0	2.0	0.0	23.3	64.9	11.7	1,059	82.3	57.5	16.5
New Hempstead village...	5,132	5,306	3.4	5,240	61.7	12.4	7.0	0.7	18.2	33.8	57.3	8.8	1,169	97.4	22.7	55.8
New Hudson town (Allegany).................	781	773	-1.0	773	96.5	0.0	0.8	2.3	0.4	27.0	58.2	14.7	305	83.3	56.1	16.4

1 May be of any race.

Table A. All Places — Population and Housing

STATE City, town, township, borough, or CDP (county if applicable)	2010 census total population	2014 estimated population	Percent change 2010–2014	ACS total population estimate 2010–2014	White alone, not Hispanic or Latino	Black alone, not Hispanic or Latino	Asian alone, not Hispanic or Latino	All other races or 2 or more races, not Hispanic or Latino	Hispanic or Latino[1]	Under 18 years old	Age 18 to 64 years old	Age 65 years and older	Total occupied housing units	Percent owner occupied	High school diploma or less	Bachelor's degree or more
	1	2	3	4	5	6	7	8	9	10	11	12	13	14	15	16
NEW YORK—Con.																
New Hyde Park village.....	9,712	9,799	0.9	9,764	51.1	0.3	29.1	3.0	16.5	21.4	64.0	14.7	3,071	81.9	25.0	43.8
New Lebanon town (Columbia)	2,306	2,250	-2.4	2,406	89.7	3.0	3.4	2.1	1.8	18.7	62.2	19.0	1,056	78.1	39.4	29.7
New Lisbon town (Otsego).....................	1,114	1,089	-2.2	918	98.0	0.0	0.4	0.8	0.8	17.0	62.4	20.9	407	90.4	54.3	17.7
New Paltz village	6,823	6,966	2.1	6,945	74.8	3.0	5.7	3.4	13.2	8.2	82.9	9.0	1,994	28.2	12.3	46.1
New Paltz town (Ulster) ...	14,003	14,096	0.7	14,092	78.1	2.5	4.3	2.6	12.5	13.7	73.3	12.9	4,480	53.6	16.8	51.3
Newport village	640	627	-2.0	512	92.4	3.5	0.0	3.9	0.2	30.4	56.9	12.7	217	49.8	29.0	22.1
Newport town (Herkimer) .	2,302	2,288	-0.6	2,302	94.5	1.1	0.0	2.1	2.3	26.2	58.8	14.9	849	80.6	40.4	15.5
New Rochelle city & MCD (Westchester)............	77,062	79,637	3.3	78,476	47.8	18.5	4.0	2.8	26.9	22.1	63.2	14.6	28,251	49.8	35.3	42.1
New Scotland town (Albany)....................	8,648	8,787	1.6	8,725	93.7	0.2	1.0	1.9	3.3	21.9	63.0	15.0	3,358	84.3	26.8	44.5
New Square village.........	6,956	7,691	10.6	7,328	98.0	0.0	0.0	0.9	1.1	61.5	38.3	0.4	1,228	15.4	87.4	3.1
Newstead town (Erie)	8,605	8,662	0.7	8,624	95.4	1.4	0.8	1.7	0.6	18.4	63.5	18.1	3,569	79.3	48.4	22.7
New Suffolk CDP	349	NA	NA	298	91.3	0.0	0.0	0.0	8.7	2.0	57.0	40.9	161	73.3	28.0	47.8
New Windsor CDP..........	8,922	NA	NA	8,520	60.3	8.5	1.0	3.8	26.4	19.7	64.6	15.8	3,358	72.6	39.8	24.9
New Windsor town (Orange)....................	25,244	26,265	4.0	25,717	63.1	11.1	3.6	2.3	19.8	22.8	64.3	12.8	9,272	74.3	34.0	29.0
New York city	8,174,959	8,491,079	3.9	8,354,889	32.7	22.6	13.2	2.7	28.8	21.3	66.1	12.5	3,095,931	31.9	39.6	38.6
New York Mills village	3,327	3,307	-0.6	3,001	96.1	1.1	0.6	2.1	0.0	26.1	46.5	27.4	1,507	44.1	35.7	9.7
Niagara town (Niagara)....	8,399	8,179	-2.6	8,278	91.9	3.5	0.1	3.1	1.4	17.4	66.7	16.1	3,575	76.7	50.4	12.8
Niagara Falls city & MCD (Niagara)...................	50,172	49,219	-1.9	49,679	70.3	23.0	0.9	3.6	2.2	21.9	63.3	14.9	21,300	56.3	51.3	15.9
Nichols village..............	512	491	-4.1	484	97.7	0.0	0.0	1.2	1.2	22.1	65.5	12.6	172	73.3	48.3	19.2
Nichols town (Tioga)........	2,525	2,512	-0.5	2,519	94.5	0.4	0.5	1.2	3.4	25.2	58.6	16.2	931	80.8	51.0	15.6
Niles town (Cayuga)	1,194	1,180	-1.2	1,159	96.6	0.9	0.0	1.4	1.0	18.8	58.0	23.3	471	91.5	50.7	26.3
Niskayuna CDP	0	NA	NA	5,129	88.2	0.6	8.0	1.1	2.1	28.6	58.5	12.8	1,806	92.9	8.2	70.2
Niskayuna town (Schenectady)............	21,778	22,277	2.3	22,022	84.5	2.5	8.1	2.2	2.7	24.4	57.4	18.0	7,904	83.7	16.2	63.2
Nissequogue village	1,749	1,761	0.7	1,692	94.7	1.9	0.9	1.4	1.2	25.0	56.3	18.7	560	93.6	10.0	63.0
Niverville CDP	1,662	NA	NA	1,688	97.7	0.0	1.7	0.0	0.6	16.3	58.6	25.1	660	89.7	34.2	47.9
Norfolk CDP	1,327	NA	NA	1,417	95.0	0.2	0.0	3.0	1.8	25.3	64.3	10.2	583	57.8	58.8	8.2
Norfolk town (St. Lawrence)	4,668	4,632	-0.8	4,651	96.8	0.3	0.0	2.1	0.6	26.5	61.4	12.1	1,839	72.0	53.0	12.0
North Amityville CDP	17,862	NA	NA	19,608	7.6	52.2	1.9	2.2	36.1	25.1	62.8	12.0	5,378	60.7	52.9	20.3
Northampton town (Fulton)...................	2,670	2,605	-2.4	2,654	98.0	0.0	0.0	1.4	0.6	19.7	61.5	18.8	1,101	77.2	39.8	23.8
Northampton CDP	570	NA	NA	548	31.2	26.3	0.5	1.5	40.5	6.2	81.0	12.8	244	45.5	47.5	0.0
North Babylon CDP	17,509	NA	NA	17,262	75.4	6.9	2.3	1.3	14.2	22.0	64.3	13.7	5,972	81.4	38.4	28.7
North Ballston Spa CDP ..	1,338	NA	NA	1,489	90.3	0.1	0.0	9.2	0.4	24.1	60.9	14.9	558	84.4	36.4	28.3
North Bay Shore CDP	18,944	NA	NA	19,995	12.2	21.5	2.5	4.7	59.2	27.2	65.3	7.4	4,740	71.9	52.9	14.1
North Bellmore CDP	19,941	NA	NA	20,483	80.9	0.7	6.7	2.0	9.7	22.3	63.0	14.7	6,511	90.1	30.2	44.5
North Bellport CDP	11,545	NA	NA	11,680	34.9	24.7	4.4	3.7	32.3	29.8	63.7	6.5	3,490	58.1	45.0	21.2
North Boston CDP	2,521	NA	NA	2,487	99.6	0.0	0.0	0.4	0.0	14.5	58.5	27.1	1,082	76.2	43.7	27.2
North Castle town (Westchester)............	11,860	12,225	3.1	12,054	84.4	2.3	3.7	1.7	7.8	30.1	57.0	12.9	3,805	87.4	14.7	69.0
North Collins village.........	1,232	1,228	-0.3	1,284	97.7	0.0	0.0	2.3	0.0	29.9	60.2	10.0	446	72.2	45.7	25.3
North Collins town (Erie) .	3,523	3,514	-0.3	3,519	98.1	0.1	0.0	1.4	0.3	23.5	63.5	13.0	1,280	83.0	44.3	24.1
North Creek CDP	616	NA	NA	406	97.8	0.0	0.0	0.0	2.2	15.3	46.8	37.9	184	59.8	45.1	10.3
North Dansville town (Livingston)	5,538	5,398	-2.5	5,461	97.7	0.1	0.0	0.2	2.0	18.7	62.0	19.5	2,536	66.4	57.7	21.1
North East town (Dutchess)................	3,033	3,003	-1.0	3,022	82.1	2.6	3.1	0.7	11.4	16.6	65.5	17.8	1,207	71.1	39.3	29.4
Northeast Ithaca CDP	2,641	NA	NA	3,092	58.7	8.0	26.9	3.3	3.1	24.1	68.1	7.9	1,167	49.4	3.9	82.4
North Elba town (Essex)..	8,957	8,628	-3.7	8,782	78.9	9.9	0.6	1.5	9.0	14.0	70.6	15.2	3,181	54.8	28.1	43.9
North Gates CDP	9,512	NA	NA	9,956	72.3	7.8	6.2	2.6	11.1	19.1	63.0	18.0	4,304	57.8	53.3	19.5
North Great River CDP....	4,001	NA	NA	4,133	83.6	0.4	4.6	0.6	10.8	20.2	65.3	14.4	1,290	87.5	38.6	20.6
North Greenbush town (Rensselaer)..............	12,075	12,120	0.4	12,078	93.3	1.9	0.7	2.0	2.1	22.2	58.5	19.2	4,693	77.1	27.5	38.6
North Harmony town (Chautauqua).............	2,267	2,236	-1.4	2,208	94.9	0.0	0.3	2.1	2.6	21.4	59.5	19.2	917	84.7	48.6	25.4
North Haven village	833	864	3.7	924	97.7	0.0	0.3	0.3	1.6	19.9	59.0	21.1	381	86.9	18.9	63.5
North Hempstead town (Nassau)..................	226,319	229,637	1.5	228,245	63.7	5.3	15.2	2.3	13.5	23.7	58.5	17.7	76,868	78.4	23.3	57.0
North Hills village...........	5,073	5,167	1.9	5,122	73.7	0.3	24.2	1.1	0.7	14.9	48.6	36.5	2,287	91.2	12.3	66.7
North Hornell village........	778	775	-0.4	748	98.3	0.0	1.1	0.3	0.4	21.9	54.2	23.8	338	86.7	33.1	40.5
North Hudson town (Essex)....................	240	240	0.0	172	99.4	0.0	0.0	0.6	0.0	8.1	66.4	25.6	78	88.5	53.8	14.1
North Lindenhurst CDP	11,652	NA	NA	11,334	70.9	3.9	3.4	2.5	19.3	24.4	63.4	12.1	3,678	66.8	50.1	21.8
North Lynbrook CDP	793	NA	NA	556	73.0	0.0	0.0	1.3	25.7	13.9	60.5	25.7	169	91.1	62.1	14.2
North Massapequa CDP .	17,886	NA	NA	18,970	91.5	0.6	2.6	0.3	5.0	22.8	61.3	15.9	6,270	93.3	35.5	32.4
North Merrick CDP	12,272	NA	NA	11,772	85.0	1.2	5.6	0.6	7.7	23.5	62.0	14.4	3,817	93.2	26.6	43.0
North New Hyde Park CDP	14,899	NA	NA	15,230	55.7	1.5	31.2	3.3	8.2	22.2	59.2	18.6	4,698	97.7	25.8	49.2
North Norwich town (Chenango)..............	1,783	1,754	-1.6	1,698	96.5	0.0	0.6	1.8	1.1	23.6	65.5	10.8	634	84.9	46.1	17.8
North Patchogue CDP	7,246	NA	NA	6,735	74.8	3.5	1.7	0.7	19.2	24.4	64.1	11.7	2,267	89.3	45.7	24.0
Northport village	7,401	7,411	0.1	7,417	93.1	0.1	3.8	1.2	1.8	21.4	61.3	17.4	2,933	73.1	9.9	69.3
North Rose CDP	636	NA	NA	694	73.6	14.3	0.0	0.0	12.1	22.4	64.6	12.8	291	87.6	37.5	12.0
North Salem town (Westchester)............	5,104	5,198	1.8	5,162	88.2	1.6	1.0	1.8	7.4	19.8	59.0	21.2	1,858	82.8	22.4	55.8
North Sea CDP	4,458	NA	NA	4,134	88.2	0.2	2.2	0.0	9.4	16.4	58.7	24.9	1,708	77.4	28.5	47.6
North Syracuse village	6,800	6,882	1.2	6,659	93.5	1.1	0.0	2.7	2.7	17.8	61.7	20.3	3,171	64.5	40.6	23.1
North Tonawanda city & MCD (Niagara)	31,568	30,929	-2.0	31,245	94.2	1.8	1.0	1.2	1.9	18.7	64.7	16.7	13,939	66.8	40.5	25.8
Northumberland town (Saratoga)................	5,103	5,140	0.7	5,147	96.6	0.5	0.2	1.3	1.4	25.4	64.6	10.0	1,888	82.5	40.4	18.6
North Valley Stream CDP	16,628	NA	NA	17,247	19.5	50.8	12.9	3.7	13.1	21.9	63.8	14.3	5,121	89.7	28.8	41.4
Northville village	1,099	1,073	-2.4	1,112	97.0	0.0	0.1	2.9	0.0	24.5	55.9	19.5	441	73.7	46.5	22.4
Northville CDP...............	1,340	NA	NA	1,574	90.5	0.0	0.0	0.0	9.5	17.8	55.7	26.4	670	84.0	31.6	35.2

1 May be of any race.

Table A. All Places — Population and Housing

STATE City, town, township, borough, or CDP (county if applicable)	2010 census total population	2014 estimated population	Percent change 2010–2014	ACS total population estimate 2010–2014	White alone, not Hispanic or Latino	Black alone, not Hispanic or Latino	Asian alone, not Hispanic or Latino	All other races or 2 or more races, not Hispanic or Latino	Hispanic or Latino[1]	Under 18 years old	Age 18 to 64 years old	Age 65 years and older	Total occupied housing units	Percent owner occupied	High school diploma or less	Bachelor's degree or more
	1	2	3	4	5	6	7	8	9	10	11	12	13	14	15	16
NEW YORK—Con.																
North Wantagh CDP.......	11,960	NA	NA	11,773	89.4	0.2	2.5	1.0	6.9	23.1	58.2	18.5	4,104	94.3	31.5	40.4
Northwest Harbor CDP....	3,317	NA	NA	3,909	77.2	1.4	10.8	0.5	10.1	21.6	60.3	18.1	1,669	85.2	15.3	57.9
Northwest Ithaca CDP.....	1,413	NA	NA	1,156	83.8	5.4	0.0	0.0	10.7	12.9	57.1	30.0	498	44.0	28.7	58.8
Norway town (Herkimer)..	762	781	2.5	944	98.3	0.4	0.0	0.0	1.3	21.3	68.8	9.9	355	86.2	52.7	14.1
Norwich city & MCD (Chenango)	7,190	7,009	-2.5	7,080	92.8	1.2	1.0	2.7	2.3	25.5	56.2	18.3	2,854	50.6	39.0	28.4
Norwich town (Chenango)	3,998	3,906	-2.3	3,935	98.0	1.0	0.0	0.7	0.3	18.9	66.2	14.9	1,435	80.9	48.4	21.2
Norwood village..............	1,657	1,627	-1.8	1,498	90.5	0.3	1.6	4.3	3.3	23.8	57.4	18.8	637	63.0	33.3	27.8
Noyack CDP...................	3,568	NA	NA	3,908	73.8	0.0	5.2	0.0	20.9	19.8	63.9	16.3	1,621	79.7	19.1	59.8
Nunda village..................	1,367	1,331	-2.6	1,479	96.6	0.3	0.6	1.6	0.8	21.0	52.9	26.0	614	55.4	56.0	12.1
Nunda town (Livingston)..	3,064	2,989	-2.4	3,026	96.8	0.2	0.3	0.9	1.8	20.2	60.5	19.3	1,275	73.4	56.2	15.8
Nyack village.................	6,765	7,002	3.5	6,857	57.0	19.9	2.6	2.9	17.5	20.7	65.4	13.8	3,295	31.7	22.5	52.6
Oak Beach-Captree CDP	286	NA	NA	363	100.0	0.0	0.0	0.0	0.0	10.5	71.5	17.9	181	100.0	2.8	52.5
Oakdale CDP.................	7,974	NA	NA	7,551	87.4	1.2	3.8	0.6	6.9	19.2	63.8	16.8	2,852	85.5	28.6	34.6
Oakfield village..............	1,813	1,770	-2.4	1,797	92.2	2.6	0.2	1.3	3.7	25.0	62.5	12.5	689	65.5	41.9	16.0
Oakfield town (Genesee)..	3,250	3,178	-2.2	3,221	95.3	1.4	0.1	0.7	2.4	24.3	64.2	11.6	1,246	72.6	47.2	15.7
Ocean Beach village........	79	80	1.3	59	100.0	0.0	0.0	0.0	0.0	10.2	39.1	50.8	32	100.0	15.6	56.3
Oceanside CDP..............	32,109	NA	NA	30,329	87.4	0.6	2.3	0.4	9.3	19.8	63.7	16.7	10,743	87.9	30.6	46.5
Odessa village...............	591	578	-2.2	666	96.8	1.1	0.0	0.6	1.5	19.8	64.9	15.6	281	69.8	45.6	17.4
Ogden town (Monroe)......	19,856	20,225	1.9	20,059	90.5	2.5	1.5	2.1	3.4	23.0	64.2	12.7	7,275	79.8	28.4	39.2
Ogdensburg city & MCD (St. Lawrence)	11,128	10,895	-2.1	11,029	85.7	7.1	0.4	2.9	3.9	20.0	67.2	12.9	4,170	62.3	42.4	20.4
Ohio town (Herkimer)	1,002	1,006	0.4	1,071	96.1	0.0	0.0	2.9	1.0	19.9	65.5	14.6	436	84.2	58.9	10.8
Oil Springs Reservation (Allegany)................	1	1	0.0	15	0.0	0.0	0.0	100.0	0.0	0.0	100.0	0.0	6	0.0	0.0	100.0
Oil Springs Reservation (Cattaraugus)...............	0	0	0.0	0	0.0	0.0	0.0	0.0	0.0	0.0	0.0	0.0	0	0.0	0.0	0.0
Olcott CDP....................	1,241	NA	NA	1,188	97.5	0.1	0.1	0.3	2.0	16.7	65.0	18.4	560	71.4	40.2	21.4
Old Bethpage CDP.........	5,523	NA	NA	5,501	92.5	0.0	5.2	0.6	1.7	24.9	57.3	17.7	1,835	90.1	18.6	62.5
Old Brookville village	2,134	2,196	2.9	2,585	76.0	0.9	14.6	2.3	6.2	29.2	56.1	14.7	783	90.5	12.9	67.2
Old Field village.............	918	917	-0.1	919	84.1	0.0	12.4	0.7	2.8	20.4	61.3	18.3	329	93.6	7.0	82.4
Old Forge CDP...............	756	NA	NA	529	98.5	0.4	0.0	0.6	0.6	6.6	72.0	21.4	293	61.4	27.3	10.9
Old Westbury village........	4,671	4,613	-1.2	4,599	61.9	8.0	18.6	4.2	7.3	16.5	73.8	9.7	982	89.1	11.2	72.9
Olean city & MCD (Cattaraugus)...............	14,452	14,043	-2.8	14,232	91.0	3.4	1.7	2.9	1.1	22.5	62.6	14.9	6,222	54.5	44.0	29.3
Olean town (Cattaraugus)	1,963	1,925	-1.9	1,828	96.9	0.1	1.6	0.4	1.0	18.2	63.4	18.5	794	80.7	37.3	23.4
Olive town (Ulster).........	4,419	4,347	-1.6	4,389	87.9	1.8	1.2	2.9	6.3	16.0	62.5	21.7	2,147	80.4	28.5	35.8
Oneida city & MCD (Madison)................	11,406	11,192	-1.9	11,290	92.9	0.8	1.0	2.2	3.1	21.5	64.5	14.1	4,340	59.1	41.2	25.2
Oneida Castle village.......	625	620	-0.8	698	96.4	0.0	0.9	2.0	0.7	20.5	63.3	16.3	297	67.0	34.7	22.9
Oneonta city & MCD (Otsego).................	13,901	13,838	-0.5	13,906	85.5	3.4	1.6	3.4	6.1	11.2	78.8	9.9	4,105	45.4	24.7	37.8
Oneonta town (Otsego) ...	5,227	5,123	-2.0	5,176	83.3	7.6	1.0	2.0	6.1	21.0	62.3	17.0	1,985	85.0	37.0	35.7
Onondaga town (Onondaga)................	23,101	23,082	-0.1	23,111	88.0	3.1	2.0	3.3	3.6	21.3	61.5	17.3	8,607	79.5	28.0	39.9
Onondaga Nation Reservation (Onondaga)................	468	473	1.1	184	0.0	0.0	0.0	0.0	100.0	0.0	40.2	59.8	43	100.0	100.0	0.0
Ontario CDP..................	2,160	NA	NA	2,188	92.0	0.0	0.0	0.0	8.0	17.0	67.2	15.9	1,006	73.2	53.8	24.0
Ontario town (Wayne)......	10,136	10,097	-0.4	10,129	91.2	2.8	1.3	1.2	3.5	21.7	62.7	15.5	4,218	82.6	35.7	29.5
Oppenheim town (Fulton)	1,924	1,880	-2.3	1,895	95.8	1.6	0.0	2.5	0.2	24.5	58.8	16.7	727	91.1	71.4	9.4
Orange town (Schuyler)...	1,609	1,618	0.6	1,796	90.4	3.9	1.3	2.6	1.7	20.9	67.2	11.9	637	85.4	55.4	11.3
Orangeburg CDP............	4,568	NA	NA	4,129	68.7	2.3	16.6	1.4	11.1	16.7	52.0	31.3	1,368	65.7	38.7	44.7
Orange Lake CDP	6,982	NA	NA	7,606	55.1	9.3	4.0	1.3	30.3	22.1	59.4	18.5	2,600	84.0	35.0	34.0
Orangetown town (Rockland)................	49,212	50,463	2.5	49,905	74.8	5.8	8.6	1.8	8.9	22.6	59.7	17.6	17,914	73.0	22.6	54.4
Orangeville town (Wyoming)................	1,355	1,341	-1.0	1,573	98.7	0.0	0.3	0.2	0.8	19.3	66.7	14.2	602	88.0	46.3	22.9
Orchard Park village	3,246	3,219	-0.8	3,230	95.5	1.8	0.0	0.7	2.0	23.6	57.5	18.8	1,383	68.2	17.1	59.1
Orchard Park town (Erie).	29,054	29,545	1.7	29,351	96.0	0.8	0.7	0.7	1.9	21.8	60.0	18.3	11,499	79.1	24.8	46.6
Orient CDP...................	743	NA	NA	713	97.5	0.3	0.1	0.0	2.1	5.9	48.1	45.9	359	91.9	23.4	54.3
Oriskany village	1,400	1,378	-1.6	1,263	97.5	0.0	0.0	0.4	2.1	18.5	55.5	26.0	512	68.2	39.1	22.1
Oriskany Falls village.......	732	720	-1.6	836	98.3	0.5	0.0	0.8	0.4	28.6	55.3	16.0	333	62.5	59.5	16.8
Orleans town (Jefferson) .	2,790	2,876	3.1	2,858	93.6	1.9	0.0	2.6	2.0	22.0	59.5	18.5	1,110	84.5	48.1	20.0
Orwell town (Oswego)......	1,165	1,194	2.5	1,307	94.0	1.5	0.0	1.4	3.1	28.0	55.8	16.1	414	89.4	51.4	15.0
Osceola town (Lewis)	229	232	1.3	210	97.1	0.0	0.0	0.0	2.9	11.0	71.0	18.1	105	95.2	49.5	11.4
Ossian town (Livingston) .	789	776	-1.6	773	96.6	0.4	0.0	2.1	0.9	22.4	61.9	15.8	310	93.2	48.1	14.2
Ossining village	25,071	25,359	1.1	25,232	31.7	12.8	4.2	2.1	49.1	23.0	68.0	9.1	7,449	47.4	43.3	36.2
Ossining town (Westchester).............	37,674	38,214	1.4	37,998	47.2	9.5	5.7	2.3	35.4	22.3	64.8	13.1	11,818	61.6	33.8	48.2
Oswegatchie town (St. Lawrence)	4,395	4,397	0.0	4,421	96.5	1.2	1.0	0.8	0.5	24.5	55.8	19.5	1,502	91.3	46.9	20.8
Oswego city & MCD (Oswego).................	18,142	17,988	-0.8	18,119	89.9	1.9	1.0	2.9	4.2	19.6	64.7	15.7	7,669	51.3	41.7	25.3
Oswego town (Oswego)...	7,984	7,920	-0.8	7,904	89.3	3.6	1.3	1.1	4.6	10.6	81.2	8.2	1,590	88.6	43.5	35.8
Otego village..................	1,010	984	-2.6	1,179	89.2	0.0	1.4	8.8	0.6	22.3	61.8	15.8	457	76.4	42.9	35.0
Otego town (Otsego)	3,115	3,032	-2.7	3,073	95.3	0.3	0.5	3.6	0.2	15.9	64.3	19.9	1,273	76.6	46.5	31.0
Otisco town (Onondaga)..	2,541	2,555	0.6	2,556	98.4	0.0	0.0	1.0	0.6	24.0	62.8	13.3	1,031	86.5	35.2	24.8
Otisville village...............	1,068	1,049	-1.8	1,245	74.5	5.4	2.5	1.7	16.0	23.1	66.0	10.9	429	77.2	37.3	22.6
Otsego town (Otsego)	3,897	3,822	-1.9	3,867	95.1	0.5	2.3	1.5	0.6	15.0	60.6	24.2	1,613	69.8	30.8	48.9
Otselic town (Chenango) .	1,054	1,036	-1.7	910	94.6	0.0	0.0	1.9	3.5	25.8	58.0	16.2	370	73.2	54.6	12.2
Otto town (Cattaraugus) ..	808	789	-2.4	834	87.8	1.6	0.0	0.0	10.7	24.7	59.5	15.9	316	82.3	54.4	19.3
Ovid village...................	611	626	2.5	620	81.5	9.4	3.4	4.0	1.8	24.7	60.3	15.0	286	61.5	58.7	17.1
Ovid town (Seneca)........	2,311	2,347	1.6	2,226	91.2	4.1	1.2	2.2	1.2	19.4	61.1	19.6	922	74.9	50.2	20.9
Owasco town (Cayuga) ...	3,793	3,744	-1.3	3,761	98.9	0.0	0.1	0.6	0.3	20.3	63.0	16.8	1,506	94.2	21.9	39.9
Owego village................	3,896	3,774	-3.1	3,819	91.1	2.3	1.8	1.0	3.8	18.2	67.2	14.6	1,699	56.9	44.3	35.8
Owego town (Tioga)	19,883	19,340	-2.7	19,595	94.4	0.8	1.0	2.0	1.7	21.9	61.0	17.0	7,665	80.8	33.2	38.1
Oxbow CDP...................	108	NA	NA	85	100.0	0.0	0.0	0.0	0.0	15.3	55.3	29.4	40	95.0	95.0	5.0
Oxford village................	1,450	1,425	-1.7	1,565	95.4	0.0	0.0	1.2	3.5	24.6	60.8	14.6	571	76.7	37.7	21.0
Oxford town (Chenango) .	3,899	3,852	-1.2	3,870	95.4	0.0	0.0	0.8	3.7	18.8	60.8	20.2	1,475	86.8	43.2	13.8
Oyster Bay CDP	6,707	NA	NA	6,548	71.8	5.0	4.1	3.9	15.2	21.5	58.5	20.1	2,669	61.0	29.0	49.3

1 May be of any race.

Table A. All Places — **Population and Housing**

STATE City, town, township, borough, or CDP (county if applicable)	Population				Race and Hispanic or Latino origin (percent), 2010–2014					Age (percent), 2010–2014			Households, 2010–2014			
	2010 census total population	2014 estimated population	Percent change 2010–2014	ACS total population estimate 2010–2014	White alone, not Hispanic or Latino	Black alone, not Hispanic or Latino	Asian alone, not Hispanic or Latino	All other races or 2 or more races, not Hispanic or Latino	Hispanic or Latino[1]	Under 18 years old	Age 18 to 64 years old	Age 65 years and older	Total occupied housing units	Percent owner occupied	Householders by level of education (percent): High school diploma or less	Bachelor's degree or more
	1	2	3	4	5	6	7	8	9	10	11	12	13	14	15	16
NEW YORK—Con.																
Oyster Bay town (Nassau)	293,219	297,896	1.6	295,821	79.1	2.2	9.4	1.4	7.9	21.9	60.9	17.2	98,801	87.5	27.1	48.8
Oyster Bay Cove village ..	2,197	2,245	2.2	2,165	86.9	1.8	7.5	1.6	2.3	25.2	60.5	14.4	681	92.4	14.5	71.4
Painted Post village	1,809	2,016	11.4	1,732	94.2	1.2	2.8	0.9	0.9	19.4	57.0	23.6	811	61.7	31.1	36.1
Palatine town (Montgomery)	3,240	3,227	-0.4	3,244	95.8	0.4	0.1	2.8	1.0	24.0	56.0	20.1	1,307	78.0	56.6	15.8
Palatine Bridge village	737	762	3.4	806	97.6	0.1	0.0	0.9	1.4	17.5	50.1	32.3	327	65.1	51.7	18.3
Palenville CDP	1,037	NA	NA	797	98.1	1.9	0.0	0.0	0.0	13.3	65.2	21.5	395	75.9	38.0	11.1
Palermo town (Oswego) ..	3,664	3,651	-0.4	3,670	99.3	0.2	0.0	0.2	0.3	22.9	64.9	12.2	1,348	74.3	54.5	7.4
Palmyra village	3,536	3,436	-2.8	3,473	93.3	0.1	0.9	2.4	4.2	20.5	65.8	13.8	1,426	53.0	48.0	19.6
Palmyra town (Wayne).....	7,969	7,746	-2.8	7,845	94.0	0.3	0.9	1.9	3.0	21.3	63.3	15.3	3,217	66.7	45.9	18.4
Pamelia town (Jefferson) .	3,153	3,166	0.4	3,203	82.9	3.2	0.8	8.1	5.0	25.8	60.1	14.3	1,155	75.7	45.4	18.2
Pamelia Center CDP	264	NA	NA	294	81.6	10.9	1.4	6.1	0.0	7.1	63.3	29.6	133	86.5	19.5	54.9
Panama village	479	462	-3.5	492	99.0	0.0	0.0	0.2	0.8	28.3	52.1	19.7	200	73.5	42.5	18.5
Parc CDP.......................	254	NA	NA	175	69.7	4.6	5.7	0.0	20.0	0.0	100.1	0.0	10	50.0	50.0	50.0
Paris town (Oneida)	4,411	4,346	-1.5	4,393	94.0	1.3	0.3	1.6	2.8	17.6	66.3	16.1	1,798	82.5	35.2	29.0
Parish village	450	441	-2.0	529	97.2	0.0	0.0	1.9	0.9	25.4	62.0	12.7	197	67.5	58.9	18.3
Parish town (Oswego)	2,558	2,501	-2.2	2,530	98.5	0.0	0.0	1.1	0.4	26.4	61.0	12.5	913	86.5	56.6	14.9
Parishville CDP	647	NA	NA	750	98.3	0.0	0.8	0.3	0.7	19.1	59.7	21.2	331	79.5	50.5	15.7
Parishville town (St. Lawrence)	2,153	2,115	-1.8	2,068	97.9	0.0	0.5	1.4	0.2	20.3	59.7	20.0	886	75.6	40.2	27.0
Parma town (Monroe)......	15,633	15,863	1.5	15,783	93.7	1.2	1.0	0.7	3.4	23.5	62.2	14.5	5,825	80.0	33.7	24.7
Patchogue village	11,798	12,364	4.8	12,045	60.5	6.2	0.1	2.0	31.1	23.1	66.5	10.4	4,616	56.8	40.3	31.3
Patterson town (Putnam) .	12,035	12,011	-0.2	12,032	78.4	3.0	4.1	1.5	13.0	22.0	67.3	10.7	3,835	80.4	32.1	36.9
Paul Smiths CDP.............	671	NA	NA	615	89.9	3.3	2.8	3.4	0.7	0.5	99.5	0.0	0	0.0	0.0	0.0
Pavilion CDP...................	646	NA	NA	517	100.0	0.0	0.0	0.0	0.0	25.2	56.0	18.8	201	89.1	55.2	26.4
Pavilion town (Genesee)..	2,495	2,464	-1.2	2,605	98.5	0.9	0.0	0.5	0.0	24.5	63.0	12.4	942	86.2	49.4	19.1
Pawling village	2,317	2,309	-0.3	2,297	71.5	3.0	0.4	1.3	23.7	22.7	62.7	14.6	887	57.0	43.1	32.6
Pawling town (Dutchess) .	8,447	8,374	-0.9	8,420	82.8	2.8	2.0	1.1	11.3	22.5	62.5	15.0	2,995	75.2	33.4	42.2
Peach Lake CDP	1,629	NA	NA	1,665	95.1	0.0	0.4	0.0	4.5	19.6	66.2	14.2	631	86.7	23.5	52.8
Pearl River CDP	15,876	NA	NA	15,901	86.6	1.1	6.4	1.0	4.9	24.6	59.1	16.2	5,628	81.6	25.1	47.8
Peconic CDP	683	NA	NA	452	100.0	0.0	0.0	0.0	0.0	2.2	51.8	46.0	262	96.2	31.3	58.4
Peekskill city & MCD (Westchester)	23,583	24,058	2.0	23,875	34.0	21.5	3.8	3.6	37.1	22.1	64.0	13.9	9,088	50.3	47.4	28.5
Pelham village	6,910	7,025	1.7	6,984	65.6	10.9	6.5	4.8	12.3	28.3	61.0	10.6	2,186	70.7	26.0	58.7
Pelham town (Westchester)	12,396	12,607	1.7	12,523	74.8	8.0	4.9	3.6	8.7	28.8	58.9	12.4	3,945	80.5	21.6	66.6
Pelham Manor village	5,486	5,582	1.7	5,539	86.4	4.4	2.8	2.1	4.3	29.1	56.0	14.7	1,759	92.6	16.1	76.5
Pembroke town (Genesee)	4,292	4,288	-0.1	4,314	96.0	0.6	1.6	0.3	1.4	19.0	65.8	15.3	1,681	80.5	50.6	22.0
Pendleton town (Niagara) .	6,397	6,557	2.5	6,483	99.5	0.0	0.0	0.4	0.0	23.0	61.3	15.6	2,318	95.0	37.1	31.5
Penfield town (Monroe)....	36,262	37,189	2.6	36,751	90.9	1.6	2.6	1.5	3.5	23.1	58.4	18.4	14,519	83.9	20.5	52.6
Penn Yan village..............	5,164	5,061	-2.0	5,011	92.9	2.1	1.1	2.2	1.8	24.4	55.0	20.5	2,078	55.5	52.4	24.6
Perinton town (Monroe) ...	46,462	46,658	0.4	46,569	92.6	1.4	2.8	1.5	1.6	22.2	60.2	17.6	19,125	77.4	16.7	57.1
Perry village	3,673	3,542	-3.6	3,383	99.0	0.1	0.0	0.6	0.3	27.7	55.6	16.7	1,433	62.0	42.4	18.6
Perry town (Wyoming)	4,616	4,458	-3.4	4,534	99.7	0.1	0.0	0.0	0.2	26.0	59.3	14.6	1,858	69.4	43.3	17.4
Perrysburg CDP...............	401	NA	NA	308	95.8	0.0	0.3	2.6	1.3	22.4	63.6	14.0	135	68.9	49.6	20.7
Perrysburg town (Cattaraugus)	1,626	1,609	-1.0	1,522	89.2	0.0	1.1	6.2	3.5	20.8	62.5	16.7	662	80.5	37.9	20.4
Persia town (Cattaraugus)	2,404	2,335	-2.9	2,377	90.2	5.6	1.3	2.9	0.0	18.0	62.3	19.5	951	65.5	44.8	13.7
Perth town (Fulton)	3,646	3,502	-3.9	3,572	94.2	2.5	1.3	0.7	1.3	22.6	57.4	19.9	1,450	80.3	41.2	22.5
Peru CDP	1,591	NA	NA	1,233	99.1	0.0	0.0	0.0	0.9	22.0	54.6	23.5	481	77.8	20.0	39.1
Peru town (Clinton)..........	6,998	7,029	0.4	7,007	93.4	2.6	1.1	0.9	2.0	23.6	61.4	14.9	2,733	83.4	36.6	32.2
Petersburgh town (Rensselaer)	1,525	1,507	-1.2	1,711	97.9	0.0	0.0	1.3	0.8	19.3	60.7	20.1	661	89.9	43.9	20.4
Pharsalia town (Chenango)	593	584	-1.5	573	95.6	1.2	0.0	3.1	0.0	18.5	59.3	22.2	223	85.2	58.3	12.6
Phelps village	1,986	1,958	-1.4	2,008	91.2	0.4	0.3	1.3	6.8	21.4	62.6	15.9	912	63.9	40.0	21.5
Phelps town (Ontario)......	7,085	7,018	-0.9	7,039	94.1	1.8	0.2	1.9	2.0	21.4	62.1	16.6	3,002	76.1	45.7	19.1
Philadelphia village	1,234	1,246	1.0	1,138	81.7	4.5	1.1	4.7	8.0	30.9	57.8	11.3	437	36.2	39.6	16.9
Philadelphia town (Jefferson)	1,947	1,980	1.7	1,799	87.4	3.1	0.7	3.4	5.3	26.8	62.1	11.3	707	50.1	42.4	19.4
Philipstown town (Putnam)	9,664	9,720	0.6	9,698	87.9	1.6	2.1	3.0	5.4	20.7	59.9	19.5	3,681	78.1	22.1	57.3
Philmont village	1,371	1,331	-2.9	1,364	90.2	2.5	0.7	5.5	1.1	19.9	66.1	13.9	592	51.5	49.0	14.7
Phoenicia CDP	309	NA	NA	305	100.0	0.0	0.0	0.0	0.0	2.6	58.7	38.7	204	56.9	41.7	29.4
Phoenix village	2,382	2,332	-2.1	2,497	91.3	0.5	1.1	2.6	4.4	28.5	61.6	9.9	968	47.8	42.7	12.2
Piercefield town (St. Lawrence)	310	304	-1.9	330	97.9	0.0	0.0	0.0	2.1	17.6	64.8	17.6	136	90.4	40.4	30.9
Piermont village	2,510	2,571	2.4	2,541	75.9	3.7	9.0	5.0	6.5	15.7	63.9	20.3	1,258	68.0	16.8	68.2
Pierrepont town (St. Lawrence)	2,589	2,578	-0.4	2,580	96.4	0.0	1.6	0.7	1.4	20.9	61.9	17.2	1,035	85.6	33.3	30.2
Pierrepont Manor CDP	228	NA	NA	135	100.0	0.0	0.0	0.0	0.0	18.5	55.6	25.9	66	59.1	18.2	81.8
Piffard CDP....................	220	NA	NA	190	94.2	0.0	0.0	0.0	5.8	5.3	73.2	21.6	100	67.0	20.0	17.0
Pike CDP	371	NA	NA	330	98.5	0.0	0.0	1.5	0.0	24.6	65.0	10.3	122	77.9	68.9	5.7
Pike town (Wyoming).......	1,112	1,098	-1.3	1,088	92.1	0.0	3.1	1.8	2.9	25.6	65.2	9.3	415	85.1	55.9	9.6
Pinckney town (Lewis)	329	332	0.9	257	100.0	0.0	0.0	0.0	0.0	15.5	77.4	7.0	98	94.9	58.2	14.3
Pine Bush CDP................	1,780	NA	NA	1,564	69.6	3.9	0.0	5.3	21.2	12.2	59.5	28.1	683	53.9	41.6	26.5
Pine Hill CDP..................	275	NA	NA	205	100.0	0.0	0.0	0.0	0.0	10.2	69.7	20.0	105	58.1	50.5	4.8
Pine Plains CDP	1,353	NA	NA	1,481	90.8	0.0	0.0	1.4	7.8	22.7	58.9	18.5	565	68.1	42.7	20.0
Pine Plains town (Dutchess)	2,473	2,456	-0.7	2,576	91.2	0.2	0.0	0.8	7.8	19.8	61.7	18.8	987	75.1	36.4	22.3
Pine Valley CDP	813	NA	NA	829	93.7	6.3	0.0	0.0	0.0	13.4	75.4	11.2	423	67.6	62.4	14.4
Pitcairn town (St. Lawrence)	846	827	-2.2	730	94.5	0.0	1.6	1.5	2.3	29.2	57.8	12.9	268	91.0	54.9	13.1
Pitcher town (Chenango).	803	790	-1.6	622	99.2	0.0	0.0	0.0	0.8	20.5	66.2	13.3	259	88.0	49.4	10.8
Pittsfield town (Otsego) ...	1,366	1,334	-2.3	1,295	98.2	0.0	0.7	0.2	0.8	22.0	61.3	16.6	500	84.0	57.0	8.0
Pittsford village	1,355	1,349	-0.4	1,507	93.8	1.9	1.1	0.9	2.3	22.9	58.6	18.4	643	73.7	11.0	74.7
Pittsford town (Monroe) ...	29,396	29,570	0.6	29,577	86.1	2.7	6.6	2.2	2.4	23.2	58.3	18.4	10,173	86.1	8.3	75.8
Pittstown town (Rensselaer)	5,735	5,713	-0.4	5,731	98.4	1.0	0.0	0.2	0.4	21.6	64.3	14.0	2,256	89.4	43.9	21.9
Plainedge CDP................	8,817	NA	NA	9,234	83.5	0.2	6.5	1.8	8.1	22.3	63.5	14.4	2,878	92.1	34.0	33.2

1 May be of any race.

Table A. All Places — **Population and Housing**

STATE City, town, township, borough, or CDP (county if applicable)	Population				Race and Hispanic or Latino origin (percent), 2010–2014					Age (percent), 2010–2014			Households, 2010–2014			
								All other races or 2 or more races, not Hispanic or Latino							Householders by level of education (percent)	
	2010 census total population	2014 estimated population	Percent change 2010–2014	ACS total population estimate 2010–2014	White alone, not Hispanic or Latino	Black alone, not Hispanic or Latino	Asian alone, not Hispanic or Latino		Hispanic or Latino[1]	Under 18 years old	Age 18 to 64 years old	Age 65 years and older	Total occupied housing units	Percent owner occupied	High school diploma or less	Bachelor's degree or more
	1	2	3	4	5	6	7	8	9	10	11	12	13	14	15	16
NEW YORK—Con.																
Plainfield town (Otsego) ..	915	891	-2.6	902	96.3	0.0	0.6	2.1	1.0	23.1	57.8	19.3	347	82.7	54.8	17.3
Plainview CDP	26,217	NA	NA	26,206	82.0	0.6	11.8	0.9	4.7	23.4	58.0	18.7	9,009	93.4	19.5	62.4
Plandome village	1,349	1,383	2.5	1,430	91.4	0.0	5.6	2.0	1.0	31.7	55.0	13.4	416	92.5	3.4	85.1
Plandome Heights village	1,005	1,026	2.1	956	78.1	0.0	15.0	1.7	5.2	27.8	55.4	16.7	308	94.8	5.5	83.8
Plandome Manor village ..	872	875	0.3	827	84.8	0.0	9.2	1.1	5.0	26.4	53.4	20.2	295	92.9	14.9	70.2
Plattekill CDP	1,260	NA	NA	1,463	48.5	29.2	1.5	1.8	19.0	23.2	68.1	8.7	497	52.1	47.3	20.7
Plattekill town (Ulster)	10,499	10,336	-1.6	10,390	72.8	5.9	1.8	2.7	16.8	20.6	65.8	13.7	3,965	70.2	46.3	21.2
Plattsburgh city & MCD (Clinton)	19,989	19,740	-1.2	19,840	88.0	3.2	2.3	2.8	3.6	14.1	71.4	14.5	8,005	38.3	34.8	26.9
Plattsburgh town (Clinton)	11,870	11,839	-0.3	11,861	93.2	2.0	1.8	0.9	2.0	20.1	62.4	17.5	4,858	76.1	41.3	28.1
Plattsburgh West CDP	1,364	NA	NA	1,462	94.0	1.3	1.1	0.5	3.1	21.4	65.2	13.4	613	68.0	60.8	13.5
Pleasant Valley CDP	1,145	NA	NA	1,308	88.1	3.1	4.2	0.0	4.7	24.2	60.7	15.1	562	36.8	35.4	37.2
Pleasant Valley town (Dutchess)	9,677	9,769	1.0	9,708	86.3	3.4	1.6	2.2	6.5	20.3	66.6	13.1	3,809	71.6	38.3	27.1
Pleasantville village	7,007	7,154	2.1	7,090	83.6	4.8	2.9	0.9	7.8	24.3	60.7	15.0	2,586	72.7	16.5	62.4
Plessis CDP	164	NA	NA	116	100.0	0.0	0.0	0.0	0.0	6.0	81.0	12.9	47	100.0	14.9	14.9
Plymouth town (Chenango)	1,804	1,777	-1.5	2,135	94.0	0.0	0.1	3.5	2.4	23.1	61.1	15.8	717	87.6	48.5	12.4
Poestenkill CDP	1,061	NA	NA	969	100.0	0.0	0.0	0.0	0.0	27.1	54.5	18.4	385	89.6	50.1	28.1
Poestenkill town (Rensselaer)	4,530	4,528	0.0	4,531	96.1	0.0	0.0	2.9	1.0	24.9	63.1	12.0	1,632	83.3	30.3	33.0
Point Lookout CDP	1,219	NA	NA	1,246	94.9	0.0	0.0	0.0	5.1	19.2	55.2	25.7	522	74.7	19.7	57.9
Poland town (Chautauqua)	2,356	2,290	-2.8	2,319	96.9	0.3	0.2	0.9	1.6	19.1	63.3	17.7	924	89.9	50.5	11.9
Poland village	508	504	-0.8	407	89.4	0.2	0.0	6.6	3.7	22.3	65.7	12.0	150	82.0	38.0	26.7
Pomfret town (Chautauqua)	14,965	14,471	-3.3	14,698	88.9	3.0	1.6	1.0	5.5	14.2	71.2	14.8	5,302	68.1	34.4	34.3
Pomona village	3,103	3,205	3.3	3,060	59.2	18.7	9.4	2.6	10.1	20.6	64.3	15.1	928	93.0	15.5	70.7
Pompey town (Onondaga)	7,080	7,328	3.5	7,223	90.3	0.8	4.1	1.7	3.2	25.3	60.7	14.3	2,533	89.8	23.3	49.1
Poospatuck Reservation (Suffolk)	324	326	0.6	488	18.9	10.0	0.0	66.0	5.1	24.4	61.3	14.3	146	80.8	70.5	6.8
Poquott village	953	950	-0.3	958	83.4	0.0	8.7	4.2	3.8	22.8	61.1	15.9	361	83.7	10.2	67.3
Portage town (Livingston)	884	860	-2.7	855	98.7	0.0	0.0	0.0	1.3	20.2	63.2	16.7	366	79.2	66.4	5.7
Port Byron village	1,292	1,259	-2.6	1,387	97.5	0.8	0.0	0.3	1.4	26.2	59.9	13.7	494	69.8	49.2	9.1
Port Chester village	28,968	29,522	1.9	29,275	29.8	6.2	1.6	1.1	61.3	22.4	67.1	10.7	9,251	43.6	53.6	23.6
Port Dickinson village	1,641	1,603	-2.3	1,639	94.8	1.7	0.2	1.2	2.1	22.2	65.6	12.1	700	64.6	39.9	25.9
Porter town (Niagara)	6,771	6,650	-1.8	6,708	93.6	0.9	0.2	2.1	3.2	19.5	61.6	18.9	2,707	86.5	36.8	30.0
Port Ewen CDP	3,546	NA	NA	3,393	86.4	5.3	2.3	3.9	2.1	17.1	61.8	21.2	1,528	71.3	45.9	27.8
Port Gibson CDP	453	NA	NA	482	97.7	1.2	0.0	1.0	0.0	17.2	39.1	43.6	203	87.7	73.4	7.9
Port Henry village	1,194	1,154	-3.4	1,042	95.9	1.2	0.2	2.0	0.7	25.5	58.1	16.4	436	64.9	53.0	17.0
Port Jefferson village	7,750	7,835	1.1	7,789	84.3	1.5	5.3	1.0	7.9	19.8	60.5	19.7	3,044	73.1	15.0	66.3
Port Jefferson Station CDP	7,838	NA	NA	8,828	73.1	1.5	4.7	1.9	18.9	21.7	64.9	13.3	2,820	74.9	38.3	37.4
Port Jervis city & MCD (Orange)	8,828	8,638	-2.2	8,736	73.3	9.9	2.9	5.7	8.3	27.1	58.6	14.3	3,413	49.8	54.3	18.3
Portland town (Chautauqua)	4,827	4,858	0.6	4,910	85.1	6.5	0.6	1.7	6.0	16.4	65.9	17.7	1,698	74.7	47.9	14.8
Port Leyden village	672	673	0.1	774	97.8	1.0	0.0	0.8	0.4	32.4	57.4	10.2	285	62.8	59.6	13.7
Portville village	1,014	989	-2.5	1,135	95.0	0.4	0.0	3.6	1.0	29.5	53.0	17.5	444	74.5	37.8	20.3
Portville town (Cattaraugus)	3,730	3,644	-2.3	3,692	96.9	0.6	0.0	1.1	1.4	17.6	59.6	22.7	1,547	76.9	49.5	17.8
Port Washington CDP	15,846	NA	NA	15,847	75.8	2.7	6.2	2.0	13.3	24.6	56.4	18.8	5,709	71.7	18.8	66.9
Port Washington North village	3,154	3,203	1.6	3,186	82.0	6.0	6.7	1.1	4.2	23.2	53.4	23.4	1,310	71.1	8.8	70.2
Potsdam village	9,428	9,617	2.0	9,577	87.0	3.4	2.6	2.7	4.4	7.2	85.3	7.3	2,425	33.0	27.4	47.3
Potsdam town (St. Lawrence)	16,041	16,190	0.9	16,172	88.9	2.1	2.6	3.0	3.3	14.5	76.3	9.5	4,931	55.4	32.9	39.8
Potter town (Yates)	1,864	1,861	-0.2	2,018	93.7	0.7	0.1	0.6	4.9	24.8	63.2	12.1	732	85.5	47.5	12.3
Pottersville CDP	424	NA	NA	485	94.0	0.2	2.5	3.3	0.0	25.8	65.6	8.7	84	29.8	85.7	8.3
Poughkeepsie city & MCD (Dutchess)	30,900	30,513	-1.3	30,716	38.6	34.3	2.3	3.3	21.4	23.0	63.3	13.8	12,018	38.7	44.8	26.2
Poughkeepsie town (Dutchess)	45,170	44,640	-1.2	44,944	69.2	10.4	6.7	2.7	11.0	20.6	65.2	14.3	15,118	67.9	33.4	37.5
Pound Ridge town (Westchester)	5,104	5,228	2.4	5,170	89.6	0.8	6.4	0.0	3.2	24.9	56.6	18.5	1,908	87.4	12.2	71.6
Prattsburgh CDP	656	NA	NA	800	92.5	0.0	0.0	0.0	7.5	24.6	59.3	16.3	310	57.7	56.5	11.3
Prattsburgh town (Steuben)	2,084	2,044	-1.9	2,389	94.1	0.0	0.2	1.0	4.7	20.8	64.6	14.5	953	80.6	52.2	15.4
Prattsville CDP	355	NA	NA	279	100.0	0.0	0.0	0.0	0.0	22.9	52.9	24.0	102	72.5	77.5	5.9
Prattsville town (Greene)	702	682	-2.8	630	100.0	0.0	0.0	0.0	0.0	14.8	66.0	19.4	283	81.3	61.8	19.1
Preble town (Cortland)	1,393	1,362	-2.2	1,483	99.1	0.0	0.3	0.0	0.7	26.7	62.4	10.8	538	84.2	42.4	20.8
Preston town (Chenango)	1,044	1,025	-1.8	1,111	98.5	0.0	0.4	1.2	0.0	25.5	63.7	10.9	423	87.2	63.4	11.8
Preston-Potter Hollow CDP	366	NA	NA	354	98.6	0.0	0.6	0.8	0.0	18.6	50.5	30.8	146	89.7	63.0	13.0
Princetown town (Schenectady)	2,115	2,136	1.0	2,124	98.9	0.3	0.0	0.0	0.8	16.7	68.0	15.3	749	87.4	42.2	39.1
Prospect village	291	290	-0.3	232	94.0	0.0	0.0	4.7	0.9	25.1	55.6	19.4	94	75.5	45.7	12.8
Providence town (Saratoga)	1,995	2,029	1.7	2,120	94.0	0.2	0.0	3.2	2.5	18.9	69.0	12.0	813	89.5	47.0	20.5
Pulaski village	2,365	2,329	-1.5	2,200	97.9	0.0	0.3	1.0	0.8	29.4	55.2	15.6	943	45.2	46.0	17.7
Pulteney town (Steuben)	1,285	1,285	0.0	1,303	98.2	0.2	0.3	1.3	0.0	22.9	54.9	22.0	553	90.1	47.0	28.2
Pultneyville CDP	698	NA	NA	598	100.0	0.0	0.0	0.0	0.0	25.9	52.9	21.1	236	97.5	28.0	40.7
Putnam town (Washington)	609	594	-2.5	698	100.0	0.0	0.0	0.0	0.0	19.2	55.6	25.2	304	86.2	42.8	27.6
Putnam Lake CDP	3,844	NA	NA	4,010	82.1	4.4	0.4	1.4	11.6	22.5	66.4	11.2	1,474	84.9	38.4	23.7
Putnam Valley town (Putnam)	11,809	11,722	-0.7	11,780	86.2	0.7	1.2	1.4	10.5	23.4	61.1	15.5	4,188	90.4	24.5	43.3
Queens borough (Queens)	2,230,539	2,321,580	4.1	2,280,602	26.5	17.5	23.8	4.3	27.8	20.5	66.2	13.2	780,069	43.8	42.1	33.6
Queensbury town (Warren)	27,899	27,675	-0.8	27,793	94.8	1.1	1.5	0.9	1.7	21.5	59.5	19.1	11,412	73.7	33.2	34.1

1 May be of any race.

Table A. All Places — **Population and Housing**

STATE City, town, township, borough, or CDP (county if applicable)	Population: 2010 census total population	Population: 2014 estimated population	Population: Percent change 2010–2014	Population: ACS total population estimate 2010–2014	Race and Hispanic or Latino origin (percent), 2010–2014: White alone, not Hispanic or Latino	Black alone, not Hispanic or Latino	Asian alone, not Hispanic or Latino	All other races or 2 or more races, not Hispanic or Latino	Hispanic or Latino[1]	Age (percent), 2010–2014: Under 18 years old	Age 18 to 64 years old	Age 65 years and older	Households, 2010–2014: Total occupied housing units	Percent owner occupied	Householders by level of education (percent): High school diploma or less	Bachelor's degree or more
	1	2	3	4	5	6	7	8	9	10	11	12	13	14	15	16
NEW YORK—Con.																
Quiogue CDP	0	NA	NA	651	80.6	0.0	0.0	0.0	19.4	19.9	64.2	16.0	236	83.5	29.7	46.2
Quogue village	967	986	2.0	888	88.5	6.0	1.4	2.6	1.6	14.8	56.7	28.5	404	83.9	22.5	56.2
Ramapo town (Rockland)	126,595	133,351	5.3	130,064	65.4	15.8	3.5	1.8	13.5	35.5	53.4	11.0	34,365	58.7	40.4	34.2
Randolph CDP	1,286	NA	NA	1,215	93.6	0.0	0.0	1.6	4.9	27.6	55.2	17.2	518	61.8	48.1	12.9
Randolph town (Cattaraugus)	2,599	2,551	-1.8	2,570	93.5	0.7	0.3	2.3	3.3	27.6	54.8	17.7	995	72.3	50.1	13.7
Ransomville CDP	1,419	NA	NA	1,421	86.0	0.0	0.4	6.7	6.9	19.2	65.1	15.6	572	89.7	48.6	7.9
Rapids CDP	1,636	NA	NA	1,648	98.1	0.0	0.0	0.5	1.4	25.5	62.5	12.0	644	91.9	34.6	30.7
Rathbone town (Steuben)	1,126	1,111	-1.3	1,195	98.7	0.5	0.0	0.4	0.3	31.8	57.2	11.0	383	86.9	63.7	6.3
Ravena village	3,266	3,274	0.2	3,275	85.1	9.3	0.5	1.2	3.9	23.1	63.0	13.8	1,387	62.9	44.1	15.0
Reading town (Schuyler)	1,707	1,714	0.4	1,578	93.3	1.0	0.5	1.8	3.5	22.3	56.1	21.5	648	87.3	45.1	20.5
Red Creek village	532	519	-2.4	629	94.8	4.1	0.0	0.0	1.1	38.1	48.9	13.0	222	81.5	45.9	20.3
Redfield town (Oswego)	547	576	5.3	534	98.5	0.0	0.0	0.0	1.5	22.6	53.3	24.2	214	93.5	60.7	11.7
Redford CDP	477	NA	NA	544	100.0	0.0	0.0	0.0	0.0	23.3	73.4	3.3	146	100.0	56.8	20.5
Red Hook village	1,956	1,977	1.1	1,760	86.5	0.7	3.7	3.5	5.7	19.3	60.9	19.9	838	54.1	32.5	36.0
Red Hook town (Dutchess)	11,319	11,263	-0.5	11,298	86.2	1.3	3.5	3.3	5.6	19.2	67.0	13.8	3,810	73.7	22.9	44.8
Red House town (Cattaraugus)	38	40	5.3	45	100.0	0.0	0.0	0.0	0.0	40.0	42.2	17.8	14	64.3	64.3	28.6
Red Oaks Mill CDP	3,613	NA	NA	4,128	73.1	10.4	0.2	1.8	14.6	23.4	62.4	14.3	1,458	87.9	31.1	35.7
Redwood CDP	605	NA	NA	529	94.5	0.0	0.0	2.1	3.4	37.6	53.3	9.1	186	52.2	40.9	0.0
Remsen village	508	499	-1.8	534	88.8	0.4	1.1	4.5	5.2	33.4	54.1	12.5	202	62.9	60.4	5.0
Remsen town (Oneida)	1,928	1,915	-0.7	1,961	95.9	0.4	0.5	1.4	1.8	21.0	66.0	13.2	806	85.4	44.2	19.9
Remsenburg-Speonk CDP	2,642	NA	NA	2,317	79.0	2.1	4.4	1.6	12.9	25.1	60.0	14.9	914	81.6	26.8	46.1
Rensselaer city & MCD (Rensselaer)	9,392	9,471	0.8	9,476	80.1	3.3	2.2	9.6	4.9	20.4	67.6	12.0	4,279	41.6	40.6	21.4
Rensselaer Falls village	332	329	-0.9	390	98.7	0.0	0.0	0.3	1.0	29.9	60.1	9.7	143	77.6	35.7	21.7
Rensselaerville town (Albany)	1,845	1,853	0.4	1,942	96.4	1.2	0.3	2.1	0.1	20.6	58.9	20.5	754	85.4	51.3	23.3
Retsof CDP	340	NA	NA	225	100.0	0.0	0.0	0.0	0.0	26.7	69.2	4.0	74	100.0	41.9	23.0
Rhinebeck village	2,656	2,629	-1.0	2,642	89.3	2.8	2.0	1.2	4.7	19.7	54.7	25.7	1,158	58.9	18.8	50.4
Rhinebeck town (Dutchess)	7,557	7,838	3.7	7,641	92.2	2.2	1.3	0.6	3.7	15.8	55.7	28.5	3,213	69.5	21.8	51.0
Rhinecliff CDP	425	NA	NA	464	89.7	1.5	1.1	0.4	7.3	17.2	52.8	30.0	206	80.1	14.1	56.8
Richburg village	450	443	-1.6	670	99.7	0.0	0.0	0.0	0.3	30.5	59.2	10.3	252	72.6	69.8	6.3
Richfield town (Otsego)	2,391	2,338	-2.2	2,304	95.2	1.0	2.2	1.2	0.4	15.3	63.3	21.2	997	73.8	50.4	22.1
Richfield Springs village	1,264	1,238	-2.1	1,193	92.3	1.8	3.4	1.7	0.8	16.8	65.1	17.9	560	62.0	54.6	22.0
Richford town (Tioga)	1,172	1,145	-2.3	1,033	97.1	0.0	0.0	2.2	0.7	14.7	70.8	14.3	480	85.4	59.4	12.5
Richland town (Oswego)	5,718	5,686	-0.6	5,723	98.1	0.2	0.1	0.6	1.1	30.6	55.6	13.7	2,171	64.1	48.9	17.9
Richmond town (Ontario)	3,368	3,315	-1.6	3,333	94.5	0.0	0.0	4.9	0.6	13.5	67.4	19.1	1,484	94.0	40.4	26.4
Richmondville village	918	881	-4.0	996	89.3	0.0	1.2	2.6	6.9	27.5	57.2	15.1	360	56.7	63.3	15.3
Richmondville town (Schoharie)	2,610	2,513	-3.7	2,554	92.6	1.3	1.2	1.0	3.9	23.6	62.9	13.5	1,023	71.5	48.6	25.5
Richville village	323	322	-0.3	413	94.4	0.7	1.0	2.2	1.7	34.4	58.8	6.8	129	82.9	51.2	17.1
Ridge CDP	13,336	NA	NA	12,921	86.6	4.7	2.4	1.0	5.2	18.2	54.5	27.2	5,372	85.1	38.8	27.5
Ridgeway town (Orleans)	6,780	6,596	-2.7	6,687	87.2	2.7	0.6	4.8	4.8	25.5	60.0	14.6	2,586	70.4	47.5	20.3
Rifton CDP	456	NA	NA	873	100.0	0.0	0.0	0.0	0.0	37.6	57.7	4.6	278	62.2	23.0	47.1
Riga town (Monroe)	5,592	5,615	0.4	5,612	92.0	1.7	0.5	1.3	4.5	18.7	64.0	17.3	2,282	92.4	33.7	34.2
Ripley CDP	872	NA	NA	826	97.9	1.5	0.0	0.0	0.6	22.1	64.7	13.1	351	71.8	46.7	8.5
Ripley town (Chautauqua)	2,415	2,368	-1.9	2,080	95.5	0.6	0.0	0.2	3.7	21.2	62.0	16.8	853	80.7	54.3	10.9
Riverhead CDP	13,299	NA	NA	14,354	54.7	15.3	1.9	2.5	25.7	20.9	60.2	18.9	4,927	57.3	48.9	21.1
Riverhead town (Suffolk)	33,505	33,777	0.8	33,715	73.6	7.8	1.3	1.5	15.8	19.5	60.3	20.2	12,685	76.5	40.0	29.1
Riverside village	497	489	-1.6	631	92.1	2.2	4.6	1.0	0.2	29.5	56.6	13.9	238	84.5	51.7	18.1
Riverside CDP	2,911	NA	NA	4,995	45.0	33.7	0.0	0.7	20.7	8.5	82.2	9.2	773	70.8	66.6	8.2
Rochester city & MCD (Monroe)	210,512	209,983	-0.3	210,461	36.6	38.9	3.4	3.8	17.2	24.1	66.0	9.7	86,025	38.2	44.3	25.8
Rochester town (Ulster)	7,313	7,238		7,275	90.6	0.3	0.2	4.4	4.5	22.7	63.1	14.2	2,741	82.6	37.6	30.5
Rock Hill CDP	1,742	NA	NA	1,347	78.2	3.3	5.3	3.0	10.1	19.6	62.5	17.6	536	84.7	22.6	50.4
Rockland town (Sullivan)	3,773	3,668	-2.8	3,722	87.9	3.1	0.2	1.8	7.0	20.4	61.2	18.5	1,544	67.9	44.4	20.5
Rockville Centre village	24,023	24,191	0.7	24,128	83.0	4.2	1.3	1.9	9.6	23.9	57.9	18.3	9,187	70.8	22.8	60.0
Rocky Point CDP	14,014	NA	NA	14,145	89.5	0.0	0.2	1.5	8.9	25.7	64.8	9.5	4,737	87.5	30.9	37.3
Rodman CDP	153	NA	NA	246	93.1	0.0	1.2	0.0	5.7	32.5	52.9	14.6	66	81.8	59.1	16.7
Rodman town (Jefferson)	1,176	1,215	3.3	1,333	87.1	0.0	0.7	8.5	3.8	30.3	59.5	10.4	438	80.6	47.7	17.1
Rome city & MCD (Oneida)	33,725	32,645	-3.2	33,161	84.7	5.2	1.2	2.7	6.1	20.0	63.1	17.1	13,249	56.7	43.5	21.4
Romulus CDP	409	NA	NA	619	93.9	0.2	0.0	0.0	6.0	29.3	58.5	12.3	191	83.8	63.9	6.3
Romulus town (Seneca)	4,316	4,353	0.9	4,353	58.1	26.5	0.1	2.6	12.7	11.3	78.4	10.6	831	72.1	41.9	25.0
Ronkonkoma CDP	19,082	NA	NA	18,978	82.9	2.1	4.3	1.3	9.4	22.6	65.4	12.1	6,342	78.6	37.0	27.5
Roosevelt CDP	16,258	NA	NA	16,554	1.8	61.9	0.8	3.1	32.4	26.3	63.9	9.7	4,219	66.6	56.2	16.4
Root town (Montgomery)	1,715	1,695	-1.2	1,724	95.8	2.3	0.5	0.6	0.8	25.9	63.7	10.4	620	87.3	51.9	15.3
Roscoe CDP	541	NA	NA	652	99.1	0.9	0.0	0.0	0.0	16.6	64.6	18.9	295	66.4	33.2	20.3
Rose town (Wayne)	2,369	2,322	-2.0	2,540	91.8	3.9	0.0	1.0	3.3	24.0	62.4	13.5	925	84.9	44.6	17.9
Roseboom town (Otsego)	711	696	-2.1	619	98.5	0.3	0.0	0.8	0.3	16.6	60.8	22.6	288	84.7	54.2	21.5
Rosendale town (Ulster)	6,080	5,980	-1.6	6,043	88.9	1.9	0.2	1.1	7.8	18.8	64.4	16.8	2,457	73.6	35.0	36.3
Rosendale Hamlet CDP	1,349	NA	NA	1,495	87.2	0.1	0.0	0.0	12.7	24.0	57.7	18.3	609	65.4	34.6	37.6
Roslyn village	2,770	2,810	1.4	2,798	81.3	1.3	10.4	2.5	4.5	17.7	54.4	27.8	1,143	65.8	17.6	70.9
Roslyn Estates village	1,251	1,264	1.0	1,194	88.2	1.3	9.5	0.9	0.0	30.5	50.9	18.6	388	95.1	6.7	85.8
Roslyn Harbor village	1,051	1,075	2.3	946	83.5	1.2	11.2	1.9	2.2	22.7	56.3	21.1	354	91.0	6.8	79.9
Roslyn Heights CDP	6,577	NA	NA	7,243	62.2	3.6	21.4	4.1	8.7	26.4	59.4	14.5	2,173	87.8	16.0	63.6
Rossie town (St. Lawrence)	877	863	-1.6	787	98.2	0.0	0.0	0.3	1.5	24.5	59.3	16.3	314	91.1	64.3	20.1
Rotterdam CDP	20,652	NA	NA	20,956	91.0	2.5	1.5	2.2	2.7	20.1	61.8	18.0	7,959	81.9	37.3	22.2
Rotterdam town (Schenectady)	29,098	29,411	1.1	29,199	92.3	2.0	1.5	1.8	2.4	20.3	62.1	17.3	11,109	80.2	37.6	26.0
Round Lake village	623	614	-1.4	576	91.1	0.0	1.4	3.0	4.5	16.0	69.1	14.9	260	74.2	11.2	55.4
Rouses Point village	2,209	2,183	-1.2	2,336	96.9	2.0	0.2	0.2	0.8	18.8	65.1	16.1	1,076	54.9	40.2	25.9
Roxbury town (Delaware)	2,504	2,427	-3.1	2,345	91.6	3.5	0.3	2.2	2.5	18.8	58.3	23.0	1,002	73.2	46.4	21.3
Royalton town (Niagara)	7,659	7,572	-1.1	7,597	94.5	0.4	0.5	4.5	0.1	23.7	61.3	14.9	2,667	81.5	47.0	14.2
Rush town (Monroe)	3,478	3,479	0.0	3,473	94.3	1.6	0.6	0.1	3.4	21.6	60.9	17.5	1,384	91.4	21.7	48.3
Rushford CDP	363	NA	NA	307	96.1	3.9	0.0	0.0	0.0	14.0	65.5	20.5	136	66.9	65.4	19.9

1 May be of any race.

Table A. All Places — Population and Housing

STATE City, town, township, borough, or CDP (county if applicable)	Population — 2010 census total population	2014 estimated population	Percent change 2010–2014	ACS total population estimate 2010–2014	Race and Hispanic or Latino origin (percent), 2010–2014 — White alone, not Hispanic or Latino	Black alone, not Hispanic or Latino	Asian alone, not Hispanic or Latino	All other races or 2 or more races, not Hispanic or Latino	Hispanic or Latino[1]	Age (percent), 2010–2014 — Under 18 years old	Age 18 to 64 years old	Age 65 years and older	Households, 2010–2014 — Total occupied housing units	Percent owner occupied	Householders by level of education (percent) — High school diploma or less	Bachelor's degree or more
	1	2	3	4	5	6	7	8	9	10	11	12	13	14	15	16
NEW YORK—Con.																
Rushford town (Allegany)	1,150	1,134	-1.4	1,045	98.1	1.1	0.8	0.0	0.0	15.0	60.7	24.3	494	82.4	59.1	24.1
Rushville village	678	666	-1.8	692	90.5	0.7	0.0	1.4	7.4	20.8	67.1	12.0	270	66.7	35.2	8.5
Russell town (St. Lawrence)	1,858	1,844	-0.8	1,869	97.2	0.2	0.1	2.3	0.2	19.8	65.1	15.2	768	81.9	56.1	13.3
Russell Gardens village	945	951	0.6	880	71.0	1.0	23.6	0.9	3.4	23.9	57.9	18.3	333	71.2	9.0	82.9
Russia town (Herkimer)	2,588	2,573	-0.6	2,584	93.6	0.7	0.0	3.4	2.3	24.0	61.9	14.2	1,045	82.0	38.4	30.9
Rutland town (Jefferson)	3,066	3,147	2.6	3,152	84.1	4.3	1.3	4.4	6.0	23.8	63.4	12.8	1,265	75.0	50.0	14.1
Rye city & MCD (Westchester)	15,720	16,000	1.8	15,892	85.4	1.0	5.5	2.2	6.0	32.1	52.9	15.1	5,460	74.3	10.7	73.8
Rye town (Westchester)	45,930	46,837	2.0	46,423	48.8	4.8	2.7	1.3	42.5	23.3	63.6	12.9	15,488	56.4	41.9	38.0
Rye Brook village	9,347	9,553	2.2	9,456	81.9	2.2	5.4	0.6	9.9	25.0	54.4	20.6	3,444	81.6	20.6	66.3
Sackets Harbor village	1,452	1,500	3.3	1,434	88.0	1.0	1.2	5.0	4.8	23.7	64.5	11.7	668	40.3	23.7	51.0
Saddle Rock village	830	866	4.3	1,043	90.2	0.3	6.8	1.3	1.3	32.6	50.6	16.8	283	88.3	21.9	61.5
Saddle Rock Estates CDP	466	NA	NA	387	98.4	0.0	1.6	0.0	0.0	22.5	57.4	20.2	126	100.0	0.0	93.7
Sagaponack village	313	323	3.2	232	94.8	5.2	0.0	0.0	0.0	19.8	48.7	31.5	111	96.4	20.7	74.8
Sag Harbor village	2,169	2,268	4.6	1,954	69.5	10.2	1.3	3.1	15.9	17.7	57.1	25.3	841	73.5	24.7	49.9
St. Armand town (Essex)	1,550	1,521	-1.9	1,717	98.9	0.2	0.0	0.3	0.6	20.3	59.6	20.2	727	76.1	29.2	34.4
St. Bonaventure CDP	2,044	NA	NA	1,975	83.0	5.3	1.6	2.5	7.6	3.6	85.4	11.0	266	75.2	38.3	45.9
St. James CDP	13,338	NA	NA	13,274	93.4	0.8	1.6	1.2	3.0	22.6	58.1	19.1	4,535	90.8	27.5	46.3
St. Johnsville village	1,732	1,688	-2.5	1,655	95.3	0.5	0.0	0.7	3.4	26.7	54.0	19.3	605	51.9	56.9	12.7
St. Johnsville town (Montgomery)	2,631	2,566	-2.5	2,581	96.9	0.3	0.0	0.6	2.2	29.9	53.0	17.1	893	63.9	60.1	11.0
St. Regis Falls CDP	464	NA	NA	384	99.0	0.0	0.0	0.0	1.0	21.4	62.5	16.1	201	76.6	60.2	3.5
St. Regis Mohawk Reservation (Franklin)	3,228	3,248	0.6	3,244	7.1	0.1	1.9	88.6	2.3	30.3	56.4	13.3	1,202	73.4	41.2	18.1
Salamanca city & MCD (Cattaraugus)	5,815	5,652	-2.8	5,717	71.0	1.7	0.6	22.2	4.5	27.6	57.5	14.8	2,384	52.7	56.6	12.8
Salamanca town (Cattaraugus)	481	467	-2.9	515	93.0	0.0	0.0	6.6	0.4	22.1	58.2	19.6	212	96.2	48.1	22.2
Salem village	946	934	-1.3	833	95.7	0.4	0.0	0.5	3.5	21.6	57.8	20.5	368	71.2	37.5	25.5
Salem town (Washington)	2,715	2,683	-1.2	2,708	94.8	0.6	0.5	0.8	3.3	20.9	58.6	20.6	1,155	82.2	40.3	29.4
Salina town (Onondaga)	33,710	33,450	-0.8	33,673	87.0	4.6	2.2	3.0	3.3	19.5	61.8	18.6	14,872	67.7	39.7	25.5
Salisbury town (Herkimer)	1,958	1,921	-1.9	2,057	94.7	0.7	2.0	2.4	0.2	24.3	65.2	10.5	766	83.9	57.4	8.1
Salisbury CDP	12,093	NA	NA	12,154	66.5	3.0	15.9	1.1	13.5	20.0	64.5	15.6	3,911	90.8	27.2	38.6
Salisbury Mills CDP	536	NA	NA	328	91.5	0.0	0.0	8.5	0.0	16.5	75.3	8.2	103	81.6	44.7	44.7
Saltaire village	37	37	0.0	81	76.5	7.4	2.5	0.0	13.6	30.8	38.2	30.9	33	81.8	6.1	81.8
Salt Point CDP	190	NA	NA	244	99.2	0.0	0.0	0.8	0.0	26.3	62.7	11.1	85	100.0	18.8	56.5
Sanborn CDP	1,645	NA	NA	1,235	86.5	9.2	3.8	0.0	0.5	11.7	68.9	19.4	544	86.6	52.9	17.6
Sand Lake town (Rensselaer)	8,530	8,515	-0.2	8,532	95.0	1.3	0.7	1.6	1.5	22.0	65.2	12.7	3,266	90.3	29.0	39.5
Sand Ridge CDP	849	NA	NA	845	96.6	0.0	0.0	3.4	0.0	13.5	71.2	15.3	393	89.1	69.0	4.8
Sands Point village	2,675	2,739	2.4	2,718	89.6	1.7	5.3	1.4	2.1	24.5	54.2	21.3	910	95.1	6.5	79.0
Sandy Creek village	769	751	-2.3	799	90.5	0.0	7.4	0.5	1.6	30.6	58.4	11.0	264	65.9	46.2	20.8
Sandy Creek town (Oswego)	3,939	3,872	-1.7	3,913	96.7	0.0	2.1	0.5	0.7	21.5	59.0	19.6	1,565	75.8	52.1	17.6
Sanford town (Broome)	2,407	2,381	-1.1	2,478	94.5	0.5	0.3	3.5	1.3	19.5	59.7	20.8	1,070	74.6	57.8	14.2
Sangerfield town (Oneida)	2,561	2,512	-1.9	2,537	98.9	0.2	0.0	0.4	0.6	18.9	60.6	20.4	1,025	65.3	51.3	19.8
Santa Clara town (Franklin)	345	342	-0.9	461	91.5	2.6	0.0	1.1	4.8	3.9	71.7	24.3	175	78.3	16.6	61.7
Saranac town (Clinton)	4,007	3,990	-0.4	4,013	98.7	0.0	0.3	0.2	0.8	22.6	65.0	12.5	1,668	86.6	46.6	24.5
Saranac Lake village	5,406	5,318	-1.6	6,055	95.7	1.4	0.4	2.5	0.0	20.8	65.2	14.2	2,749	47.8	26.6	33.9
Saratoga town (Saratoga)	5,668	5,661	-0.1	5,676	90.6	2.1	0.7	1.3	5.4	24.2	61.7	14.2	2,283	79.4	35.5	33.4
Saratoga Springs city & MCD (Saratoga)	26,565	27,436	3.3	26,998	89.3	2.1	2.4	2.2	4.0	16.0	65.7	18.2	11,590	54.1	21.2	51.4
Sardinia town (Erie)	2,775	2,789	0.5	2,788	98.5	0.0	0.0	0.6	1.0	22.1	64.2	13.5	1,018	91.3	43.5	20.8
Saugerties village	3,971	3,900	-1.8	3,930	85.1	0.7	0.0	1.6	12.6	18.5	67.0	14.4	1,683	50.3	44.7	26.8
Saugerties town (Ulster)	19,482	19,235	-1.3	19,362	87.8	2.0	1.4	2.8	6.0	19.7	64.8	15.5	7,444	76.2	39.0	26.9
Saugerties South CDP	2,218	NA	NA	1,977	89.1	2.0	5.2	1.7	2.0	19.8	63.0	17.0	777	82.1	32.4	23.2
Savannah CDP	558	NA	NA	426	94.6	2.8	0.0	2.6	0.0	23.8	58.4	17.8	194	80.4	50.0	11.9
Savannah town (Wayne)	1,730	1,692	-2.2	1,340	89.9	2.7	0.0	3.3	4.2	24.8	57.4	17.8	575	81.6	57.7	9.9
Savona village	827	816	-1.3	748	94.8	0.8	0.8	2.4	1.2	25.1	61.4	13.6	295	69.2	55.9	9.8
Sayville CDP	16,853	NA	NA	16,311	92.3	0.5	1.1	1.0	5.2	23.5	59.1	17.4	5,759	80.2	29.0	48.0
Scarsdale village & town (Westchester)	17,166	17,729	3.3	17,471	79.4	1.1	13.4	2.0	4.1	33.6	52.7	13.7	5,394	88.5	4.6	91.1
Schaghticoke village	592	587	-0.8	608	95.6	0.0	0.0	3.1	1.3	31.4	57.8	10.9	225	65.3	49.3	24.9
Schaghticoke town (Rensselaer)	7,677	7,658	-0.2	7,662	92.2	2.6	0.3	2.8	2.1	23.4	60.8	15.7	2,785	86.5	44.9	23.3
Schenectady city & MCD (Schenectady)	66,134	65,936	-0.3	66,055	55.6	19.6	5.4	8.2	11.2	23.9	64.0	12.1	24,557	47.9	47.4	21.9
Schenevus CDP	551	NA	NA	361	100.0	0.0	0.0	0.0	0.0	16.9	73.6	9.4	145	50.3	66.2	13.1
Schodack town (Rensselaer)	12,794	13,123	2.6	12,984	95.6	1.0	0.5	1.7	1.2	21.6	61.8	16.8	5,097	83.1	36.2	32.5
Schoharie village	920	848	-7.8	855	92.3	2.3	0.0	0.7	4.7	10.5	63.8	25.6	421	48.2	52.0	26.1
Schoharie town (Schoharie)	3,203	3,073	-4.1	3,126	97.5	0.6	0.0	0.6	1.3	16.9	58.6	24.6	1,420	72.4	43.5	21.0
Schroeppel town (Oswego)	8,482	8,371	-1.3	8,447	95.8	0.4	0.3	1.9	1.6	21.8	64.3	14.0	3,259	80.0	45.3	14.8
Schroon town (Essex)	1,654	1,621	-2.0	1,348	94.7	1.2	2.6	0.3	1.2	13.0	53.7	33.2	605	86.9	40.7	19.0
Schroon Lake CDP	833	NA	NA	569	90.7	1.6	4.7	0.5	2.5	15.2	55.8	29.0	286	72.7	36.4	22.0
Schuyler town (Herkimer)	3,420	3,420	0.0	3,436	97.5	0.0	0.0	0.2	2.3	21.5	57.3	21.2	1,415	85.0	36.7	29.8
Schuyler Falls town (Clinton)	5,181	5,162	-0.4	5,174	97.1	0.1	1.1	0.5	1.1	25.3	63.2	11.4	1,981	83.9	43.9	24.9
Schuylerville village	1,390	1,376	-1.0	1,667	89.5	6.1	0.7	1.8	1.9	24.7	64.1	11.2	666	58.9	42.9	24.5
Scio CDP	609	NA	NA	460	97.6	0.0	0.0	1.1	1.3	15.2	68.6	16.1	216	81.9	37.0	20.8
Scio town (Allegany)	1,833	1,784	-2.7	1,577	98.8	0.4	0.0	0.4	0.4	19.4	61.1	19.5	697	84.8	50.2	16.8
Scipio town (Cayuga)	1,713	1,674	-2.3	1,872	98.3	0.3	0.0	0.2	1.2	23.3	64.8	11.9	650	84.8	51.5	19.2
Scotchtown CDP	9,212	NA	NA	9,132	44.5	19.1	6.7	4.5	25.1	25.2	62.2	12.5	3,151	64.6	35.3	29.5
Scotia village	7,723	7,803	1.0	7,742	90.9	2.5	0.8	2.1	3.7	24.3	62.6	13.2	2,946	68.9	34.6	26.1
Scott town (Cortland)	1,176	1,163	-1.1	1,137	99.5	0.0	0.0	0.0	0.5	24.6	63.1	12.2	391	85.7	52.9	16.9
Scottsburg CDP	117	NA	NA	118	100.0	0.0	0.0	0.0	0.0	10.1	78.0	11.9	53	92.5	35.8	20.8

1 May be of any race.

Table A. All Places — **Population and Housing**

STATE City, town, township, borough, or CDP (county if applicable)	Population				Race and Hispanic or Latino origin (percent), 2010–2014					Age (percent), 2010–2014			Households, 2010–2014			
	2010 census total population	2014 estimated population	Percent change 2010–2014	ACS total population estimate 2010–2014	White alone, not Hispanic or Latino	Black alone, not Hispanic or Latino	Asian alone, not Hispanic or Latino	All other races or 2 or more races, not Hispanic or Latino	Hispanic or Latino[1]	Under 18 years old	Age 18 to 64 years old	Age 65 years and older	Total occupied housing units	Percent owner occupied	High school diploma or less	Bachelor's degree or more
	1	2	3	4	5	6	7	8	9	10	11	12	13	14	15	16

NEW YORK—Con.																
Scotts Corners CDP	711	NA	NA	740	96.5	0.0	0.0	0.0	3.5	9.7	55.6	34.6	320	82.8	15.0	54.1
Scottsville village	2,001	1,974	-1.3	2,446	85.1	7.1	0.9	1.9	5.0	25.7	61.4	12.9	914	69.3	29.9	31.7
Scriba town (Oswego)	6,840	6,726	-1.7	6,792	96.4	0.6	1.1	0.5	1.4	20.6	66.8	12.6	2,818	73.2	46.1	16.7
Sea Cliff village	4,995	5,024	0.6	5,012	84.9	4.7	1.8	3.2	5.4	21.7	62.5	15.8	1,980	73.3	14.6	70.9
Seaford CDP	15,294	NA	NA	15,405	93.4	0.0	1.1	0.8	4.7	22.6	61.5	16.0	5,232	88.8	26.9	39.8
Searingtown CDP	4,915	NA	NA	4,495	52.6	0.2	43.8	1.5	1.8	24.7	60.3	15.0	1,441	98.5	10.8	67.6
Selden CDP	19,851	NA	NA	20,390	71.8	2.7	4.2	2.0	19.3	23.2	66.0	10.9	6,316	79.7	38.2	29.5
Sempronius town (Cayuga)	895	936	4.6	925	97.2	0.0	0.5	1.8	0.4	23.1	63.4	13.6	363	89.3	55.9	15.2
Seneca town (Ontario)	2,729	2,742	0.5	2,742	97.0	0.1	0.0	0.7	2.2	21.3	64.0	14.6	1,005	82.7	48.3	20.6
Seneca Falls CDP	6,681	NA	NA	6,533	93.0	1.4	1.2	3.0	1.4	19.4	63.4	17.1	2,895	64.6	41.6	28.4
Seneca Falls town (Seneca)	9,043	8,860	-2.0	8,986	92.5	1.1	1.7	2.5	2.3	18.7	63.9	17.3	3,929	64.0	41.2	26.9
Seneca Knolls CDP	2,011	NA	NA	1,936	95.3	1.2	0.0	2.7	0.7	14.4	66.8	18.7	858	96.4	46.5	11.5
Sennett town (Cayuga)	3,595	3,575	-0.6	3,581	95.0	3.1	1.1	0.0	0.8	24.5	59.0	16.4	1,222	89.2	31.2	39.2
Setauket-East Setauket CDP	15,477	NA	NA	14,293	83.9	1.6	7.4	2.8	4.3	23.8	58.8	17.4	5,089	94.6	15.4	61.1
Seward town (Schoharie)	1,737	1,692	-2.6	1,600	95.9	1.3	0.0	1.1	1.8	19.9	66.2	13.8	600	92.8	39.7	24.8
Shandaken town (Ulster)	3,085	3,016	-2.2	2,866	88.1	0.2	4.3	5.6	1.8	10.7	67.3	22.1	1,497	80.2	33.0	34.2
Sharon town (Schoharie)	1,846	1,784	-3.4	1,744	97.4	0.2	1.3	0.3	0.8	20.7	64.7	14.6	693	67.0	50.1	17.6
Sharon Springs village	558	534	-4.3	477	95.4	0.0	3.1	0.6	0.8	17.8	70.2	11.9	213	48.8	36.6	24.4
Shawangunk town (Ulster)	14,332	14,174	-1.1	14,224	80.0	6.8	1.3	2.4	9.4	18.3	70.5	11.3	3,730	81.0	32.8	28.7
Shelby town (Orleans)	5,319	5,181	-2.6	5,260	85.1	7.1	2.1	2.1	3.6	22.6	58.5	18.8	1,993	66.8	56.8	18.6
Sheldon town (Wyoming)	2,409	2,347	-2.6	2,328	94.9	2.8	0.3	0.6	1.3	18.7	63.3	17.9	973	73.6	55.2	10.4
Shelter Island CDP	1,333	NA	NA	1,270	82.3	0.0	0.0	3.9	13.9	20.1	59.3	20.4	524	84.5	18.3	54.4
Shelter Island town (Suffolk)	2,390	2,414	1.0	2,669	91.3	0.1	0.2	1.8	6.6	21.4	51.0	27.7	1,063	88.5	14.4	53.9
Shelter Island Heights CDP	1,048	NA	NA	1,394	99.4	0.1	0.4	0.0	0.0	22.6	43.2	34.3	536	92.5	10.6	53.2
Shenorock CDP	1,898	NA	NA	1,589	79.7	3.1	8.7	0.0	8.4	20.9	65.4	13.7	628	92.7	27.1	44.4
Sherburne village	1,367	1,345	-1.6	1,371	95.2	2.2	0.0	0.0	2.6	25.5	55.1	19.1	630	48.9	42.5	20.2
Sherburne town (Chenango)	4,050	3,973	-1.9	4,005	96.2	0.7	0.0	1.1	1.9	24.9	59.5	15.4	1,585	67.4	43.3	21.2
Sheridan town (Chautauqua)	2,673	2,619	-2.0	2,655	92.0	0.5	1.2	0.9	5.4	20.3	64.4	15.3	1,099	86.6	38.1	17.7
Sherman village	730	709	-2.9	701	96.7	0.0	0.0	1.4	1.9	30.5	57.5	12.1	280	73.6	47.5	18.9
Sherman town (Chautauqua)	1,653	1,622	-1.9	1,953	98.8	0.0	0.0	0.5	0.7	38.2	52.4	9.6	586	79.0	62.1	11.1
Sherrill city & MCD (Oneida)	3,071	3,076	0.2	3,072	93.5	2.5	0.4	0.0	3.6	20.7	60.0	19.2	1,342	73.8	33.8	27.7
Shinnecock Hills CDP	2,188	NA	NA	2,019	59.9	1.5	8.5	4.9	25.2	17.4	61.7	20.8	736	59.5	26.2	54.1
Shinnecock Reservation (Suffolk)	662	677	2.3	244	2.5	2.5	4.1	91.0	0.0	30.8	58.5	10.7	68	88.2	38.2	4.4
Shirley CDP	27,854	NA	NA	25,931	65.8	7.4	4.2	3.2	19.5	23.8	68.3	7.8	7,778	83.2	54.1	16.1
Shokan CDP	1,183	NA	NA	941	69.3	4.0	0.0	10.3	16.4	12.7	64.9	22.3	491	82.9	44.8	22.2
Shoreham village	531	535	0.8	468	91.2	0.0	1.7	0.4	6.6	13.8	47.1	39.1	188	98.4	9.6	78.2
Shortsville village	1,432	1,437	0.3	1,387	94.1	0.6	0.0	4.4	0.9	20.6	63.2	16.2	578	76.8	50.9	19.6
Shrub Oak CDP	2,011	NA	NA	2,044	74.8	0.0	0.2	1.1	23.9	14.7	61.9	23.3	864	76.3	29.3	39.8
Sidney village	3,900	3,818	-2.1	3,900	95.2	0.0	1.0	0.3	3.5	22.4	61.2	16.3	1,836	58.2	59.2	23.5
Sidney town (Delaware)	5,774	5,642	-2.3	5,694	96.2	0.0	0.7	0.7	2.4	20.2	60.1	19.7	2,599	68.8	56.6	20.3
Silver Creek village	2,656	2,574	-3.1	2,607	96.7	0.6	0.0	1.0	1.7	26.2	62.4	11.4	1,065	72.9	43.2	22.2
Silver Springs village	776	756	-2.6	787	96.3	0.1	0.8	1.9	0.9	18.9	64.9	16.3	320	71.3	65.6	8.8
Sinclairville village	588	572	-2.7	587	98.1	0.0	0.0	1.2	0.7	32.2	50.2	17.7	217	75.6	54.8	4.1
Skaneateles village	2,450	2,459	0.4	2,513	96.3	0.0	1.1	0.4	2.2	20.4	50.5	29.2	1,181	66.6	12.6	67.2
Skaneateles town (Onondaga)	7,209	7,224	0.2	7,216	98.1	0.0	0.6	0.5	0.9	21.8	55.5	22.6	3,061	81.3	17.0	57.0
Sleepy Hollow village	9,870	10,208	3.4	10,002	42.5	4.6	4.1	1.9	46.9	24.5	60.5	15.1	3,662	38.8	43.2	43.0
Sloan village	3,661	3,619	-1.1	3,642	95.6	2.5	0.0	1.1	0.9	18.5	63.7	17.7	1,725	69.0	56.9	3.4
Sloatsburg village	3,039	3,133	3.1	3,086	80.9	3.7	2.8	1.2	11.4	23.0	65.4	11.7	1,075	74.1	42.0	14.1
Smallwood CDP	580	NA	NA	152	65.1	0.0	0.0	0.0	34.9	10.5	65.2	24.3	92	54.3	22.8	14.1
Smithfield town (Madison)	1,290	1,267	-1.8	1,084	97.3	0.0	0.0	1.3	1.4	17.0	69.8	13.4	422	85.5	54.0	15.2
Smithtown CDP	26,470	NA	NA	26,408	89.3	1.1	3.9	1.0	4.7	24.5	57.8	17.6	8,649	86.8	23.7	47.7
Smithtown town (Suffolk)	117,801	118,446	0.5	118,337	89.1	1.2	3.7	1.3	4.7	24.0	59.0	17.0	39,431	88.4	25.2	47.6
Smithville town (Chenango)	1,330	1,306	-1.8	1,659	84.4	2.8	3.3	6.8	2.6	25.2	62.4	12.4	578	77.0	50.3	17.0
Smithville Flats CDP	351	NA	NA	530	85.7	1.3	0.0	13.0	0.0	29.4	62.4	8.1	189	74.6	46.6	13.2
Smyrna village	213	208	-2.3	183	100.0	0.0	0.0	0.0	0.0	32.3	49.3	18.6	66	69.7	57.6	21.2
Smyrna town (Chenango)	1,280	1,256	-1.9	1,139	98.8	0.0	0.0	1.2	0.0	20.8	61.9	17.2	453	80.4	64.6	15.2
Sodus village	1,819	1,767	-2.9	2,226	72.2	12.5	0.8	2.3	12.2	29.7	61.1	9.2	818	60.3	57.1	17.0
Sodus town (Wayne)	8,384	8,220	-2.0	8,306	84.3	6.4	0.5	3.1	5.7	23.0	61.0	15.9	3,256	79.0	55.1	19.3
Sodus Point village	900	879	-2.3	1,093	90.4	3.4	0.2	3.3	2.7	21.2	57.8	20.8	446	82.7	39.2	31.6
Solon town (Cortland)	1,079	1,079	0.0	1,067	93.7	0.0	0.0	3.7	2.6	22.2	66.4	11.4	377	84.9	50.1	14.3
Solvay village	6,584	6,455	-2.0	6,514	88.1	1.2	0.4	2.9	7.3	18.1	65.8	16.1	2,981	49.5	47.2	20.4
Somers town (Westchester)	20,434	21,280	4.1	20,876	88.2	1.1	4.1	0.9	5.7	24.1	52.0	23.9	7,668	91.9	18.6	58.9
Somerset town (Niagara)	2,662	2,598	-2.4	2,718	90.4	0.3	0.0	2.8	6.5	27.6	57.2	15.2	967	80.4	55.0	11.2
Sound Beach CDP	7,612	NA	NA	7,480	86.3	0.1	2.0	0.5	11.1	28.3	63.4	8.5	2,488	87.7	25.7	37.4
Southampton village	3,109	3,205	3.1	3,154	73.7	16.6	2.9	1.2	5.6	15.7	55.1	29.2	1,260	72.1	22.6	56.7
Southampton town (Suffolk)	56,792	58,093	2.3	57,515	71.3	6.0	2.2	1.2	19.2	18.8	61.9	19.3	21,378	77.2	30.9	43.8
South Blooming Grove village	3,234	3,189	-1.4	3,212	74.8	5.2	1.7	3.2	15.0	23.5	62.2	14.3	1,143	84.7	32.5	24.1
South Bristol town (Ontario)	1,588	1,598	0.6	1,643	96.9	0.0	0.0	2.4	0.7	18.5	57.6	23.7	722	89.5	19.5	50.1
South Corning village	1,145	1,130	-1.3	1,029	86.5	7.3	3.8	2.0	0.4	16.3	62.3	21.4	464	74.4	38.4	23.5
South Dayton village	620	601	-3.1	816	97.4	0.0	0.0	0.4	2.2	32.9	55.3	11.6	318	69.2	61.9	6.0
Southeast town (Putnam)	18,404	18,248	-0.8	18,335	76.7	1.9	1.6	2.5	17.3	23.2	65.0	12.0	6,550	74.7	33.3	41.2
South Fallsburg CDP	2,870	NA	NA	3,131	49.4	7.1	2.5	0.4	40.7	43.4	50.9	5.9	806	27.7	58.3	21.8
South Farmingdale CDP	14,486	NA	NA	14,576	83.1	2.0	4.3	0.5	10.1	22.5	62.2	15.3	4,702	92.6	36.2	33.9
South Floral Park village	1,764	1,783	1.1	2,017	6.8	57.9	4.8	8.5	22.0	21.9	66.7	11.3	618	69.4	29.6	34.8

1 May be of any race.

Table A. All Places — **Population and Housing**

STATE City, town, township, borough, or CDP (county if applicable)	Population				Race and Hispanic or Latino origin (percent), 2010–2014					Age (percent), 2010–2014			Households, 2010–2014			
	2010 census total population	2014 estimated population	Percent change 2010–2014	ACS total population estimate 2010–2014	White alone, not Hispanic or Latino	Black alone, not Hispanic or Latino	Asian alone, not Hispanic or Latino	All other races or 2 or more races, not Hispanic or Latino	Hispanic or Latino[1]	Under 18 years old	Age 18 to 64 years old	Age 65 years and older	Total occupied housing units	Percent owner occupied	Householders by level of education (percent) High school diploma or less	Householders by level of education (percent) Bachelor's degree or more
	1	2	3	4	5	6	7	8	9	10	11	12	13	14	15	16
NEW YORK—Con.																
South Glens Falls village .	3,512	3,580	1.9	3,575	92.8	2.2	0.8	0.3	3.9	18.4	67.4	14.3	1,672	53.2	46.9	14.7
South Hempstead CDP ...	3,243	NA	NA	3,181	62.4	14.1	3.0	0.6	19.9	25.8	59.7	14.5	1,003	87.6	20.3	54.8
South Hill CDP..............	6,673	NA	NA	6,380	81.2	4.2	3.3	3.7	7.5	7.1	86.2	6.7	1,022	66.9	22.5	54.8
South Huntington CDP	9,422	NA	NA	9,462	82.0	2.2	6.4	0.8	8.6	19.0	62.9	18.0	3,359	84.3	25.0	44.6
South Lima CDP..............	240	NA	NA	229	100.0	0.0	0.0	0.0	0.0	16.6	41.9	41.5	115	65.2	37.4	27.8
South Lockport CDP........	8,324	NA	NA	8,255	86.5	4.7	2.8	1.3	4.6	21.3	61.1	17.4	3,647	66.7	46.4	19.5
South Nyack village	3,510	3,577	1.9	3,554	66.6	15.0	6.2	4.8	7.3	18.5	69.8	11.6	1,267	58.6	11.5	65.4
Southold CDP..............	5,748	NA	NA	6,323	94.1	0.0	0.6	3.8	1.5	16.2	55.2	28.6	2,618	89.2	32.4	38.2
Southold town (Suffolk)....	21,969	22,248	1.3	22,154	89.6	2.3	0.6	1.7	5.7	16.7	54.9	28.4	9,411	82.5	32.0	41.4
Southport CDP..............	7,238	NA	NA	7,145	88.3	0.6	0.6	6.3	4.3	21.8	60.4	17.6	3,188	72.1	53.7	13.4
Southport town (Chemung)	10,940	10,620	-2.9	10,848	86.5	4.6	0.4	4.2	4.4	20.1	63.2	16.9	4,367	76.9	49.6	16.7
South Valley town (Cattaraugus)	264	266	0.8	202	98.0	0.0	0.0	2.0	0.0	5.0	62.9	32.2	113	94.7	41.6	28.3
South Valley Stream CDP	5,962	NA	NA	6,293	38.9	30.6	15.1	2.7	12.8	19.5	65.1	15.6	2,003	78.0	32.3	53.2
Spackenkill CDP	4,123	NA	NA	3,800	84.3	3.5	5.8	2.5	3.9	20.4	61.4	18.2	1,340	95.9	14.3	59.3
Spafford town (Onondaga)	1,686	1,669	-1.0	1,719	97.1	0.0	0.7	1.0	1.2	20.0	61.8	18.1	688	92.3	30.1	48.4
Sparkill CDP.................	1,565	NA	NA	1,439	67.5	8.5	10.7	0.0	13.3	29.5	57.8	12.7	503	89.3	21.7	59.4
Sparta town (Livingston)..	1,624	1,599	-1.5	1,678	98.1	0.0	0.0	0.6	1.3	25.5	58.1	16.3	619	93.9	47.2	19.5
Speculator village	324	317	-2.2	360	89.4	1.1	0.6	8.1	0.8	8.3	64.8	26.9	87	82.8	36.8	40.2
Spencer village	759	734	-3.3	981	98.0	1.2	0.6	0.0	0.2	28.3	57.4	14.3	391	58.1	48.8	23.8
Spencer town (Tioga)	3,153	3,053	-3.2	3,102	96.5	0.5	0.6	0.1	2.4	24.7	61.9	13.3	1,262	72.3	58.6	15.8
Spencerport village..........	3,601	3,615	0.4	3,606	92.7	2.2	0.2	1.3	3.6	23.4	61.5	15.2	1,422	69.8	26.2	36.4
Springfield town (Otsego)	1,358	1,328	-2.2	1,397	97.3	0.0	0.0	1.6	1.1	24.1	54.7	21.0	555	72.8	42.5	25.2
Springport town (Cayuga)	2,366	2,337	-1.2	2,492	88.5	1.3	0.4	4.3	5.5	20.8	60.2	19.1	941	76.5	33.6	27.7
Springs CDP..................	6,592	NA	NA	5,855	69.0	1.1	0.0	3.6	26.2	20.7	59.3	20.0	2,314	82.0	18.6	51.4
Spring Valley village.........	31,275	32,510	3.9	32,007	26.9	38.1	3.5	1.8	29.7	33.8	58.2	7.8	8,604	29.7	51.4	18.7
Springville village...........	4,296	4,360	1.5	4,318	94.2	1.6	0.0	1.8	2.3	22.5	56.7	20.9	1,893	62.4	45.2	20.2
Springwater town (Livingston)	2,346	2,304	-1.8	2,265	96.2	0.8	0.0	2.0	0.9	19.4	68.0	12.5	945	90.9	44.3	16.0
Springwater Hamlet CDP	549	NA	NA	520	98.7	0.0	0.0	1.3	0.0	23.9	69.1	7.1	217	81.6	51.6	5.5
Staatsburg CDP..............	377	NA	NA	470	88.3	4.9	1.5	1.9	3.4	32.1	48.7	19.1	149	85.2	22.1	77.9
Stafford town (Genesee)..	2,459	2,414	-1.8	2,342	95.6	0.3	0.3	3.2	0.7	19.9	61.3	18.8	954	87.8	40.5	18.2
Stamford village.............	1,119	1,090	-2.6	1,303	91.3	0.5	0.5	1.4	6.4	19.7	54.7	25.6	578	55.0	41.5	31.1
Stamford town (Delaware)	2,267	2,201	-2.9	2,583	94.5	2.0	0.4	0.5	2.6	18.0	61.6	20.3	1,021	69.0	41.5	24.8
Stanford town (Dutchess)	3,817	3,796	-0.6	3,819	81.2	6.9	0.0	2.0	9.8	16.8	69.0	14.2	1,387	69.5	32.2	39.2
Stannards CDP..............	798	NA	NA	912	99.2	0.0	0.0	0.0	0.8	17.4	63.7	18.8	430	63.0	62.6	16.3
Stark town (Herkimer).....	757	741	-2.1	730	99.7	0.0	0.1	0.1	0.0	21.7	61.7	16.6	301	84.1	48.2	28.2
Starkey town (Yates)........	3,573	3,524	-1.4	3,548	94.1	0.8	0.2	0.5	4.5	29.2	53.2	17.6	1,310	63.7	40.2	31.1
Star Lake CDP................	809	NA	NA	921	93.2	1.0	2.8	2.7	0.3	19.2	64.4	16.4	314	79.9	52.2	18.5
Staten Island borough (Richmond)	468,730	473,279	1.0	471,522	63.2	9.6	7.9	1.6	17.7	22.7	63.6	13.6	165,079	68.8	40.9	31.2
Stephentown town (Rensselaer)	2,903	2,890	-0.4	2,889	97.0	0.0	0.6	0.7	1.8	19.6	63.0	17.1	1,187	85.6	43.0	19.0
Sterling town (Cayuga) ...	3,040	3,040	0.0	3,053	98.4	0.3	0.2	0.5	0.6	22.9	58.1	18.8	1,245	86.4	50.0	23.0
Steuben town (Oneida)....	1,100	1,115	1.4	966	99.7	0.1	0.0	0.0	0.2	20.6	61.1	18.3	400	90.5	52.5	16.3
Stewart Manor village......	1,905	1,914	0.5	2,112	85.2	1.8	5.2	1.2	6.6	24.8	56.7	18.4	745	88.7	20.1	59.1
Stillwater village.............	1,737	1,724	-0.7	1,880	92.8	0.9	1.4	1.1	3.8	28.2	58.5	13.3	651	69.1	43.6	20.1
Stillwater town (Saratoga)	8,308	8,401	1.1	8,357	94.5	1.0	0.4	0.2	3.8	25.8	59.2	14.8	3,063	81.2	41.6	22.3
Stockbridge town (Madison)	2,094	2,064	-1.4	2,365	92.3	0.0	0.1	7.0	0.5	23.0	66.1	10.9	816	78.8	53.8	12.1
Stockholm town (St. Lawrence)	3,665	3,668	0.1	3,678	98.6	0.5	0.0	0.2	0.7	28.5	55.8	15.7	1,454	84.9	44.1	20.7
Stockport town (Columbia)	2,815	2,750	-2.3	2,771	97.5	1.9	0.0	0.0	0.6	18.1	65.6	16.3	1,138	75.4	48.1	15.9
Stockton town (Chautauqua)	2,248	2,179	-3.1	2,219	99.3	0.0	0.0	0.3	0.4	28.7	54.4	16.9	797	70.5	52.9	14.3
Stone Ridge CDP	1,173	NA	NA	1,454	87.6	0.2	11.8	0.4	0.0	21.1	65.9	12.9	451	80.7	29.9	33.0
Stony Brook CDP	13,740	NA	NA	13,936	84.3	1.4	8.8	0.6	4.8	23.6	58.6	17.7	4,846	90.8	12.3	70.1
Stony Brook University CDP	9,216	NA	NA	8,997	37.7	8.9	38.8	4.4	10.2	2.8	92.6	4.4	44	93.2	13.6	59.1
Stony Creek town (Warren).....................	767	757	-1.3	850	95.8	0.2	2.0	1.2	0.8	19.3	58.0	22.7	349	86.0	51.9	16.3
Stony Point CDP.............	12,147	NA	NA	12,854	73.9	4.3	2.1	0.9	18.7	21.5	63.1	15.3	4,182	84.6	35.6	32.3
Stony Point town (Rockland)	15,059	15,463	2.7	15,278	76.7	3.9	1.8	0.9	16.7	22.0	62.4	15.6	5,035	85.2	33.0	33.7
Stottville CDP	1,375	NA	NA	1,388	95.5	4.1	0.0	0.4	0.0	21.1	58.7	20.3	584	63.2	57.7	10.8
Stratford town (Fulton)	610	593	-2.8	559	99.1	0.0	0.0	0.9	0.0	18.5	61.9	19.9	252	92.1	55.2	20.6
Strykersville CDP............	647	NA	NA	621	97.9	2.1	0.0	0.0	0.0	24.4	61.9	13.5	239	74.9	49.8	11.3
Stuyvesant town (Columbia)	2,028	1,978	-2.5	2,052	94.2	1.1	0.2	3.3	1.2	20.2	66.7	13.2	824	77.7	27.7	26.8
Suffern village................	10,723	10,991	2.5	10,864	69.2	5.0	4.2	2.2	19.3	20.8	61.2	18.1	4,334	69.5	28.9	41.6
Sullivan town (Madison)...	15,339	15,386	0.3	15,345	97.7	0.0	0.4	0.3	1.5	23.4	60.9	15.5	5,913	82.1	38.1	30.1
Summerhill town (Cayuga)	1,217	1,193	-2.0	1,250	97.4	0.7	0.6	0.3	1.0	28.6	60.5	11.0	404	90.8	54.7	18.1
Summit town (Schoharie)	1,148	1,107	-3.6	1,130	91.0	0.0	0.6	2.5	5.9	24.3	60.7	15.0	454	91.6	52.6	14.5
Sunset Bay CDP.............	660	NA	NA	750	86.7	2.9	0.0	6.4	4.0	11.9	57.9	30.4	294	71.4	33.7	27.6
SUNY Oswego CDP.........	3,676	NA	NA	3,733	80.3	6.7	2.6	2.4	8.1	1.0	98.9	0.0	17	0.0	52.9	47.1
Sweden town (Monroe) ...	14,175	14,259	0.6	14,210	89.3	2.7	2.3	3.1	2.6	15.7	73.3	11.1	4,899	58.8	28.8	34.7
Sylvan Beach village	897	894	-0.3	863	99.3	0.0	0.0	0.7	0.0	15.0	60.6	24.3	416	76.7	58.4	8.2
Syosset CDP..................	18,829	NA	NA	18,872	69.9	0.8	22.1	1.6	5.6	25.5	58.9	15.5	6,172	91.5	14.7	67.4
Syracuse city & MCD (Onondaga)	145,196	144,263	-0.6	144,648	51.8	28.6	6.4	5.2	8.0	22.8	66.2	10.9	55,279	38.5	42.6	27.3
Taconic Shores CDP	0	NA	NA	603	98.5	0.0	0.0	1.5	0.0	13.3	64.3	22.4	253	93.7	37.5	34.8
Taghkanic town (Columbia)	1,311	1,303	-0.6	1,264	96.1	0.1	0.2	0.4	3.2	15.4	59.9	24.8	506	84.2	43.5	30.6
Tannersville village	537	517	-3.7	596	66.6	1.5	0.0	4.2	27.7	36.9	50.6	12.4	223	45.3	37.2	18.4
Tappan CDP	6,613	NA	NA	7,071	67.9	4.5	17.5	1.0	9.1	25.7	56.1	18.2	2,284	96.1	18.5	62.1
Tarrytown village.............	11,277	11,537	2.3	11,423	64.2	5.4	5.2	3.5	21.6	22.1	61.2	16.7	4,471	63.7	24.3	59.2
Taylor town (Cortland)	523	509	-2.7	465	92.3	1.5	0.9	0.4	4.9	23.8	62.3	13.8	159	71.7	57.9	15.7

1 May be of any race.

Table A. All Places — **Population and Housing**

Items 1–16

STATE City, town, township, borough, or CDP (county if applicable)	2010 census total population	2014 estimated population	Percent change 2010–2014	ACS total population estimate 2010–2014	White alone, not Hispanic or Latino	Black alone, not Hispanic or Latino	Asian alone, not Hispanic or Latino	All other races or 2 or more races, not Hispanic or Latino	Hispanic or Latino[1]	Under 18 years old	Age 18 to 64 years old	Age 65 years and older	Total occupied housing units	Percent owner occupied	High school diploma or less	Bachelor's degree or more
	1	2	3	4	5	6	7	8	9	10	11	12	13	14	15	16
NEW YORK—Con.																
Terryville CDP	11,849	NA	NA	11,686	78.7	1.3	1.2	1.7	17.0	24.7	58.9	16.4	3,684	78.9	36.8	34.0
Thendara CDP	0	NA	NA	214	100.0	0.0	0.0	0.0	0.0	20.1	79.8	0.0	85	100.0	20.0	34.1
Theresa village	863	863	0.0	844	89.2	1.2	0.6	2.4	6.6	28.4	58.9	12.7	329	67.8	53.8	14.3
Theresa town (Jefferson)	2,911	2,974	2.2	2,984	93.6	1.1	0.4	1.9	2.9	26.7	61.6	11.5	1,114	76.9	48.5	13.7
Thiells CDP	5,032	NA	NA	5,295	66.5	6.7	5.2	0.0	21.6	21.6	61.7	16.7	1,588	88.7	21.7	47.5
Thomaston village	2,617	2,640	0.9	2,630	66.8	0.8	21.5	1.2	9.7	26.1	56.0	17.9	984	83.6	17.1	69.6
Thompson town (Sullivan)	15,308	15,066	-1.6	15,202	55.9	19.8	1.0	3.4	19.9	24.1	60.8	15.1	5,827	47.8	49.2	18.2
Thornwood CDP	3,759	NA	NA	4,248	85.1	0.1	2.2	0.8	11.7	23.1	64.0	13.0	1,306	68.3	32.2	41.7
Thousand Island Park CDP	31	NA	NA	78	100.0	0.0	0.0	0.0	0.0	0.0	0.0	100.0	48	100.0	0.0	100.0
Three Mile Bay CDP	227	NA	NA	182	70.3	0.0	0.0	20.9	8.8	26.9	46.6	26.4	74	60.8	63.5	23.0
Throop town (Cayuga)	1,989	1,988	-0.1	2,041	94.9	1.2	0.3	1.0	2.6	21.8	59.9	18.3	748	93.2	52.0	13.6
Thurman town (Warren)	1,219	1,205	-1.1	1,223	93.9	2.2	0.4	1.0	2.5	22.1	61.1	16.8	480	87.7	66.0	12.3
Thurston town (Steuben)	1,350	1,324	-1.9	1,266	99.5	0.0	0.0	0.0	0.5	20.3	67.9	11.9	491	81.9	52.5	12.6
Ticonderoga CDP	3,382	NA	NA	3,335	97.9	0.1	0.1	1.8	0.1	18.8	61.2	20.1	1,413	69.8	44.4	15.1
Ticonderoga town (Essex)	5,042	5,002	-0.8	5,020	97.6	0.6	0.1	1.7	0.1	19.7	58.5	21.8	2,220	71.2	43.2	17.2
Tillson CDP	1,586	NA	NA	1,604	90.2	6.4	0.6	1.4	1.4	16.1	66.8	17.3	638	78.2	28.2	40.4
Tioga town (Tioga)	4,871	4,785	-1.8	4,831	96.2	0.0	1.3	1.6	0.9	17.9	63.5	18.6	2,034	79.3	50.5	22.5
Titusville CDP	811	NA	NA	548	84.1	0.0	1.1	0.9	13.9	12.6	61.4	25.9	236	100.0	8.5	60.6
Tivoli village	1,118	1,105	-1.2	1,091	84.0	0.4	0.8	1.3	13.6	16.4	67.9	15.8	460	48.5	28.7	31.1
Tompkins town (Delaware)	1,245	1,199	-3.7	1,005	97.2	2.5	0.0	0.3	0.0	21.0	57.4	21.9	431	82.6	65.9	8.1
Tonawanda city & MCD (Erie)	15,130	14,976	-1.0	15,048	95.4	0.0	0.1	3.3	1.2	19.0	64.0	17.1	6,728	71.8	39.7	23.5
Tonawanda CDP	58,144	NA	NA	58,204	89.1	2.7	3.0	2.1	3.1	18.8	61.8	19.6	25,694	73.3	34.3	33.8
Tonawanda town (Erie)	73,567	73,281	-0.4	73,538	89.0	3.0	2.4	2.3	3.3	19.0	62.1	18.8	32,594	71.8	32.9	33.5
Tonawanda Reservation (Erie)	34	34	0.0	17	0.0	0.0	0.0	100.0	0.0	58.8	41.2	0.0	3	100.0	100.0	0.0
Tonawanda Reservation (Genesee)	483	476	-1.4	543	4.6	0.0	10.9	84.5	0.0	10.6	67.2	22.3	264	89.8	45.8	16.7
Tonawanda Reservation (Niagara)	0	0	0.0	0	0.0	0.0	0.0	0.0	0.0	0.0	0.0	0.0	0	0.0	0.0	0.0
Torrey town (Yates)	1,282	1,264	-1.4	1,523	90.6	0.0	0.0	3.0	6.4	23.9	61.5	14.6	565	86.0	38.1	32.0
Town Line CDP	2,367	NA	NA	2,491	94.9	1.5	0.0	2.7	0.9	19.0	64.0	17.1	948	89.0	39.5	26.6
Trenton town (Oneida)	4,498	4,470	-0.6	4,480	97.9	0.0	0.6	1.1	0.4	23.4	59.8	16.8	1,735	81.6	31.9	32.1
Triangle town (Broome)	2,946	2,885	-2.1	2,915	96.2	0.8	0.0	0.8	2.3	25.0	58.4	16.6	1,107	78.0	45.3	19.5
Tribes Hill CDP	1,003	NA	NA	1,110	98.3	0.0	0.0	0.6	1.1	18.5	62.5	19.0	466	97.2	28.5	18.9
Troupsburg town (Steuben)	1,291	1,301	0.8	1,333	97.8	0.6	0.3	1.3	0.0	35.7	49.4	15.1	416	86.1	58.4	15.6
Troy city & MCD (Rensselaer)	50,129	49,910	-0.4	49,965	68.7	13.0	3.7	6.1	8.5	19.7	69.3	11.1	19,962	38.6	38.9	27.2
Trumansburg village	1,787	1,829	2.4	1,723	99.0	0.0	0.4	0.0	0.6	20.1	59.2	20.7	709	58.8	26.8	41.5
Truxton town (Cortland)	1,133	1,121	-1.1	1,168	96.5	0.9	0.0	2.3	0.3	22.7	63.0	14.3	432	77.3	41.7	20.8
Tuckahoe CDP	1,373	NA	NA	1,426	57.6	17.2	4.0	1.8	19.4	16.2	60.5	23.4	518	76.3	27.4	46.7
Tuckahoe village	6,485	6,623	2.1	6,559	61.9	15.4	6.1	4.1	12.5	20.6	65.1	14.2	2,769	47.5	20.7	51.7
Tully village	873	870	-0.3	1,037	87.5	0.1	1.9	6.9	3.6	24.9	58.4	16.7	435	50.6	30.6	25.7
Tully town (Onondaga)	2,738	2,739	0.0	2,743	93.2	0.7	1.1	3.1	2.0	23.9	60.8	15.3	1,102	74.8	21.4	40.4
Tupper Lake village	3,667	3,619	-1.3	3,533	97.5	1.1	0.1	1.3	0.0	24.7	60.5	14.9	1,496	56.5	59.0	13.5
Tupper Lake town (Franklin)	5,971	5,917	-0.9	5,941	95.4	3.0	0.1	0.8	0.8	22.2	61.5	16.4	2,335	67.9	50.4	20.0
Turin village	232	233	0.4	137	100.0	0.0	0.0	0.0	0.0	17.5	45.2	37.2	69	95.7	58.0	21.7
Turin town (Lewis)	761	767	0.8	550	100.0	0.0	0.0	0.0	0.0	12.9	62.3	24.7	252	95.2	68.7	10.3
Tuscarora CDP	74	NA	NA	0	0.0	0.0	0.0	0.0	0.0	0.0	0.0	0.0	0	0.0	0.0	0.0
Tuscarora town (Steuben)	1,473	1,471	-0.1	1,413	93.7	0.0	0.6	5.5	0.2	24.4	62.4	13.2	573	79.6	62.0	11.2
Tuscarora Nation Reservation (Niagara)	1,152	1,149	-0.3	1,061	8.1	0.0	9.2	80.9	1.8	27.0	62.4	10.6	407	88.5	50.4	16.0
Tusten town (Sullivan)	1,515	1,504	-0.7	1,325	84.5	5.5	0.0	6.7	3.3	14.3	60.1	25.6	614	76.1	36.6	32.2
Tuxedo town (Orange)	3,624	3,590	-0.9	3,602	85.5	1.5	5.7	1.8	5.5	21.4	58.3	20.2	1,560	77.4	18.2	52.9
Tuxedo Park village	623	610	-2.1	538	76.6	0.0	13.9	6.5	3.0	22.9	50.9	26.2	222	88.7	12.6	71.2
Tyre town (Seneca)	978	979	0.1	923	100.0	0.0	0.0	0.0	0.0	25.9	63.5	10.7	373	86.1	56.8	12.9
Tyrone town (Schuyler)	1,598	1,614	1.0	1,644	98.8	0.0	0.0	1.0	0.2	22.3	56.2	21.5	691	74.0	53.1	14.3
Ulster town (Ulster)	12,339	12,151	-1.7	12,245	86.6	2.1	3.9	2.7	4.6	17.1	62.4	20.7	4,840	68.6	40.2	21.3
Ulysses town (Tompkins)	4,903	5,083	3.7	4,995	93.4	0.2	1.5	4.0	1.0	20.5	62.3	17.2	2,007	73.6	23.0	43.4
Unadilla village	1,128	1,100	-2.5	975	92.8	0.0	0.0	0.7	6.5	20.6	60.6	18.9	428	72.4	48.4	24.3
Unadilla town (Otsego)	4,392	4,289	-2.3	4,343	96.2	0.5	0.0	1.0	2.3	23.7	57.6	18.7	1,753	79.3	48.1	15.6
Union town (Broome)	56,346	55,202	-2.0	55,700	86.4	3.6	2.9	3.2	3.8	20.6	61.3	18.1	24,367	59.9	34.9	30.3
Uniondale CDP	24,759	NA	NA	24,787	9.8	48.8	1.8	3.1	36.5	24.3	63.3	12.3	5,890	76.7	47.9	23.6
Union Springs village	1,196	1,188	-0.7	1,330	81.9	2.2	0.7	5.6	9.7	22.5	60.3	17.4	475	70.9	39.4	23.4
Union Vale town (Dutchess)	4,863	4,849	-0.3	4,864	92.7	0.5	1.2	1.2	4.4	21.4	62.0	16.6	1,850	78.3	23.2	44.4
Unionville village	612	596	-2.6	613	84.2	5.5	0.0	0.0	10.3	27.0	60.2	12.9	230	90.0	51.7	24.8
University at Buffalo CDP	6,066	NA	NA	6,058	55.0	10.1	23.4	2.7	8.8	1.2	98.9	0.0	106	0.0	0.0	97.2
University Gardens CDP	4,226	NA	NA	4,059	56.1	6.2	30.0	2.4	5.3	21.9	62.9	15.3	1,550	89.7	15.8	71.5
Upper Brookville village	1,698	1,742	2.6	1,447	78.0	0.9	16.0	2.1	3.0	13.4	60.8	25.8	479	93.9	14.8	63.7
Upper Nyack village	2,063	2,149	4.2	2,020	83.2	6.5	3.5	1.5	5.3	23.2	56.3	20.4	741	87.2	11.2	63.0
Urbana town (Steuben)	2,343	2,309	-1.5	2,234	95.3	3.0	0.0	0.9	0.8	14.8	60.1	25.0	996	76.4	32.4	33.6
Utica city & MCD (Oneida)	62,235	61,332	-1.5	61,852	61.8	14.4	9.2	4.1	10.5	25.0	59.8	15.3	23,828	47.2	48.5	17.8
Vails Gate CDP	3,369	NA	NA	3,477	42.2	21.0	12.4	0.4	24.0	19.3	62.7	18.0	1,486	46.7	50.2	18.2
Valatie village	1,819	1,914	5.2	1,791	89.7	1.3	3.3	0.7	4.9	25.7	49.7	24.6	564	59.8	29.8	29.8
Valhalla CDP	3,162	NA	NA	3,219	75.6	0.8	9.2	2.3	12.1	23.3	61.8	15.0	1,118	76.6	20.8	53.8
Valley Cottage CDP	9,107	NA	NA	10,185	65.1	5.1	16.2	0.7	12.9	20.0	60.0	19.9	3,485	77.8	22.9	55.1
Valley Falls village	466	459	-1.5	502	97.8	0.0	1.2	0.0	1.0	21.9	61.6	16.7	191	75.9	45.0	31.9
Valley Stream village	37,559	37,832	0.7	37,764	36.8	16.1	14.5	2.5	30.1	23.5	63.8	12.7	11,422	79.0	36.4	36.2
Van Buren town (Onondaga)	13,184	13,372	1.4	13,302	92.2	1.4	1.3	2.6	2.5	19.4	60.7	19.9	5,858	70.1	39.5	26.9
Van Etten village	537	526	-2.0	558	95.0	1.1	0.0	2.9	1.1	27.3	63.7	9.3	223	75.8	39.5	16.1
Van Etten town (Chemung)	1,557	1,523	-2.2	1,592	97.1	0.4	0.0	1.6	0.9	21.5	65.2	13.5	620	84.2	49.7	16.1
Varick town (Seneca)	1,857	1,815	-2.3	1,914	94.8	1.3	0.2	1.6	2.1	26.6	54.7	18.6	699	82.3	50.4	26.3
Venice town (Cayuga)	1,368	1,367	-0.1	1,350	87.7	1.9	0.0	1.6	8.8	22.9	60.8	16.4	485	81.4	52.4	16.1

1 May be of any race.

NY(Terryville CDP)—NY(Venice town (Cayuga)) 313

Table A. All Places — **Population and Housing**

STATE City, town, township, borough, or CDP (county if applicable)	Population				Race and Hispanic or Latino origin (percent), 2010–2014					Age (percent), 2010–2014			Households, 2010–2014		Householders by level of education (percent)	
	2010 census total population	2014 estimated population	Percent change 2010–2014	ACS total population estimate 2010–2014	White alone, not Hispanic or Latino	Black alone, not Hispanic or Latino	Asian alone, not Hispanic or Latino	All other races or 2 or more races, not Hispanic or Latino	Hispanic or Latino[1]	Under 18 years old	Age 18 to 64 years old	Age 65 years and older	Total occupied housing units	Percent owner occupied	High school diploma or less	Bachelor's degree or more
	1	2	3	4	5	6	7	8	9	10	11	12	13	14	15	16
NEW YORK—Con.																
Vernon village	1,172	1,160	-1.0	1,079	95.5	0.3	0.9	2.0	1.3	16.0	66.2	17.7	496	43.8	40.7	21.6
Vernon town (Oneida)	5,408	5,413	0.1	5,421	95.2	0.1	0.3	1.0	3.4	20.3	65.4	14.4	2,132	74.8	40.8	19.9
Verona CDP	852	NA	NA	576	100.0	0.0	0.0	0.0	0.0	18.6	52.1	29.3	248	100.0	59.7	15.3
Verona town (Oneida)	6,293	6,274	-0.3	6,291	99.1	0.0	0.0	0.5	0.4	27.4	59.6	13.1	2,334	74.0	42.6	15.9
Verplanck CDP	1,729	NA	NA	1,634	73.4	1.7	2.4	4.5	18.0	25.1	64.0	11.0	637	49.8	44.6	9.6
Vestal town (Broome)	28,043	28,242	0.7	28,170	79.2	4.1	11.1	1.8	3.7	15.7	68.2	16.2	8,915	80.5	22.7	45.0
Veteran town (Chemung)	3,313	3,277	-1.1	3,303	96.8	0.2	2.0	0.9	0.1	21.4	60.6	17.9	1,318	88.9	39.3	29.7
Victor village	2,771	2,837	2.4	2,798	96.5	0.0	1.1	0.4	1.9	29.8	58.6	11.5	995	74.8	19.8	49.2
Victor town (Ontario)	14,272	14,616	2.4	14,387	94.3	0.5	2.7	0.5	2.1	26.1	57.4	16.6	5,688	79.0	19.4	55.7
Victory town (Cayuga)	1,660	1,623	-2.2	1,662	98.3	0.0	0.0	1.7	0.0	21.3	59.5	19.3	673	90.8	54.5	16.8
Victory village	603	591	-2.0	499	96.8	1.8	0.0	1.4	0.0	25.2	62.6	12.0	190	80.0	47.9	19.5
Vienna town (Oneida)	5,440	5,476	0.7	5,475	98.5	0.0	0.3	1.3	0.0	21.7	61.4	17.0	2,366	81.8	59.1	12.0
Village Green CDP	3,891	NA	NA	3,722	92.1	2.1	3.0	2.5	0.3	17.9	61.1	21.0	1,919	57.5	40.1	37.1
Village of the Branch village	1,807	1,814	0.4	1,965	87.1	1.6	3.2	1.5	6.7	33.1	54.3	12.6	591	93.7	12.4	68.0
Villenova town (Chautauqua)	1,110	1,089	-1.9	940	97.0	0.0	0.0	2.8	0.2	18.5	61.8	19.6	382	91.1	51.6	15.2
Viola CDP	6,868	NA	NA	6,558	95.2	1.1	0.0	0.0	3.7	37.9	49.2	12.8	1,690	63.5	32.6	43.4
Virgil CDP	0	NA	NA	335	100.0	0.0	0.0	0.0	0.0	30.5	47.4	22.4	128	92.2	49.2	30.5
Virgil town (Cortland)	2,401	2,411	0.4	2,659	89.2	1.2	0.0	8.8	0.8	21.1	67.1	11.8	897	81.5	37.2	32.0
Volney town (Oswego)	5,926	5,843	-1.4	5,884	97.7	0.0	0.0	1.2	1.1	19.9	64.0	16.2	2,136	80.2	53.1	23.9
Voorheesville village	2,789	2,837	1.7	2,813	88.3	0.6	2.1	2.8	6.3	24.4	59.5	16.2	1,092	81.7	15.6	55.7
Waddington village	972	969	-0.3	813	91.8	3.0	0.0	3.2	2.1	18.2	56.6	25.3	384	67.2	41.1	29.9
Waddington town (St. Lawrence)	2,266	2,264	-0.1	2,330	93.2	1.0	0.0	5.0	0.7	25.4	59.5	15.2	896	71.3	44.0	24.9
Wading River CDP	7,719	NA	NA	7,694	89.8	1.1	0.7	0.6	7.7	25.7	62.2	12.1	2,707	93.6	26.4	41.7
Wadsworth CDP	190	NA	NA	218	100.0	0.0	0.0	0.0	0.0	17.9	76.7	5.5	75	100.0	14.7	36.0
Wainscott CDP	650	NA	NA	719	83.6	0.6	0.4	0.8	14.6	14.1	63.0	22.9	301	74.1	24.3	53.8
Walden village	6,978	6,855	-1.8	6,919	66.4	4.8	1.5	3.5	23.9	24.0	66.5	9.3	2,458	65.9	43.9	22.5
Wales town (Erie)	3,005	3,033	0.9	3,021	96.0	0.0	0.2	1.2	2.7	25.0	61.0	14.1	1,228	88.8	30.4	27.0
Walker Valley CDP	853	NA	NA	606	88.1	0.0	0.0	8.7	3.1	37.5	46.8	15.8	260	83.1	19.2	30.0
Wallkill town (Orange)	27,426	28,176	2.7	27,832	55.8	15.2	4.2	3.0	21.9	23.1	63.3	13.7	9,962	68.2	39.8	26.9
Wallkill CDP	2,288	NA	NA	2,254	87.7	0.0	2.8	0.3	9.2	31.0	58.1	10.9	835	60.1	34.1	30.4
Walton village	3,088	2,976	-3.6	3,043	96.9	0.2	0.0	0.5	2.3	19.1	59.1	22.0	1,415	50.2	67.1	13.8
Walton town (Delaware)	5,576	5,393	-3.3	5,484	96.7	0.1	0.0	1.2	2.0	22.3	58.7	19.1	2,466	61.9	62.3	18.7
Walton Park CDP	2,669	NA	NA	2,669	72.3	6.3	6.6	0.4	14.4	25.8	68.1	6.0	762	95.3	17.6	50.9
Walworth town (Wayne)	9,449	9,384	-0.7	9,415	95.5	0.9	0.3	1.7	1.6	27.6	61.3	11.2	3,432	91.4	24.0	40.0
Wampsville village	537	555	3.4	513	100.0	0.0	0.0	0.0	0.0	12.3	66.1	21.6	221	95.0	41.6	11.3
Wanakah CDP	3,199	NA	NA	3,107	98.9	0.0	0.0	1.1	0.0	15.5	65.1	19.4	1,254	87.2	32.2	27.4
Wantagh CDP	18,871	NA	NA	19,074	90.5	0.3	3.5	0.6	5.0	25.4	60.2	14.5	5,957	96.2	24.3	46.9
Wappinger town (Dutchess)	27,111	27,137	0.1	27,194	68.9	6.6	7.9	2.0	14.6	20.8	65.0	14.4	10,251	67.6	31.6	35.8
Wappingers Falls village	5,483	5,591	2.0	5,377	51.4	7.1	14.3	0.6	26.5	18.2	66.7	15.2	2,154	33.1	44.8	23.1
Ward town (Allegany)	368	361	-1.9	286	96.2	0.7	0.0	1.7	1.4	20.9	62.8	16.1	103	88.3	47.6	23.3
Warren town (Herkimer)	1,151	1,129	-1.9	1,075	92.6	3.3	0.7	1.1	2.4	24.2	61.8	13.9	387	73.9	40.3	27.1
Warrensburg CDP	3,103	NA	NA	3,226	97.0	0.2	0.0	0.3	2.4	23.4	61.7	14.9	1,321	74.9	48.7	24.9
Warrensburg town (Warren)	4,094	4,043	-1.2	4,071	97.5	0.2	0.0	0.2	2.1	20.9	63.1	16.1	1,713	76.9	47.5	24.6
Warsaw village	3,471	3,383	-2.5	3,591	93.0	2.4	0.0	2.0	2.6	19.0	57.9	23.0	1,613	51.8	53.9	8.2
Warsaw town (Wyoming)	5,062	4,944	-2.3	4,987	95.0	1.7	0.0	1.4	1.9	18.3	60.4	21.2	2,259	56.9	50.8	10.4
Warwick village	6,731	6,785	0.8	6,783	89.8	3.6	0.0	0.8	5.8	23.1	51.9	25.1	2,856	66.2	29.7	37.1
Warwick town (Orange)	32,065	31,293	-2.4	31,581	79.4	5.2	0.9	2.3	12.2	22.9	62.3	14.9	11,727	79.9	31.8	36.3
Washington town (Dutchess)	4,738	4,697	-0.9	4,725	91.9	2.3	1.1	1.3	3.5	21.6	58.5	20.0	1,935	60.7	27.5	36.2
Washington Heights CDP	1,689	NA	NA	2,218	50.7	15.6	0.0	4.1	29.7	16.8	74.5	8.7	732	81.8	43.9	24.7
Washington Mills CDP	1,183	NA	NA	1,191	88.8	0.0	2.5	6.2	2.4	11.6	72.2	16.2	455	42.6	2.4	64.6
Washingtonville village	5,898	5,794	-1.8	5,837	62.3	5.1	2.1	1.6	29.0	20.2	63.9	15.6	2,111	79.8	29.6	27.3
Watchtower CDP	2,381	NA	NA	2,566	65.6	11.1	3.9	1.6	17.8	2.2	89.8	8.0	0	0.0	0.0	0.0
Waterford village	1,998	1,966	-1.6	2,344	85.4	1.5	4.9	4.1	4.2	17.6	66.5	15.8	1,034	47.9	38.6	19.0
Waterford town (Saratoga)	8,420	8,353	-0.8	8,418	91.1	1.3	1.9	4.3	1.4	18.0	69.1	12.9	3,737	57.9	36.8	21.7
Waterloo village	5,163	5,048	-2.2	5,178	96.9	1.2	0.0	1.2	0.7	23.9	55.5	20.6	2,011	68.8	37.9	22.8
Waterloo town (Seneca)	7,636	7,497	-1.8	7,595	95.3	2.7	0.0	0.6	1.4	20.7	61.2	17.9	3,118	68.5	45.6	15.9
Water Mill CDP	1,559	NA	NA	2,217	88.7	0.0	4.7	1.8	4.8	14.3	58.9	26.9	959	94.0	17.4	66.1
Watertown city & MCD (Jefferson)	27,031	27,590	2.1	27,590	82.6	5.8	2.1	3.7	5.7	23.7	63.7	12.6	11,865	39.7	39.4	22.0
Watertown town (Jefferson)	4,460	4,601	3.2	4,581	78.4	9.5	1.8	4.9	5.5	19.6	68.2	12.1	1,594	80.1	37.2	28.5
Waterville village	1,583	1,548	-2.2	1,618	98.8	0.2	0.0	0.4	0.6	18.5	61.2	20.3	627	57.4	49.6	21.7
Watervliet city & MCD (Albany)	10,254	10,233	-0.2	10,250	83.9	8.1	1.6	3.1	3.3	21.5	66.0	12.4	4,740	39.7	41.1	19.1
Watkins Glen village	1,859	1,883	1.3	1,847	93.6	1.2	0.5	2.4	2.2	18.9	58.1	23.0	864	59.0	46.4	30.3
Watson town (Lewis)	1,881	1,887	0.3	1,903	95.7	1.6	0.0	1.7	0.9	19.0	66.4	14.9	747	86.7	53.3	17.0
Waverly town (Franklin)	1,022	1,017	-0.5	826	98.4	0.1	0.0	0.5	1.0	19.7	58.1	22.2	417	75.1	62.6	7.7
Waverly village	4,444	4,300	-3.2	4,362	96.1	3.1	0.1	0.2	0.4	22.7	60.7	16.6	1,885	55.5	43.7	20.5
Wawarsing town (Ulster)	13,159	13,100	-0.4	13,189	64.3	10.1	2.3	2.8	20.5	20.2	64.3	15.6	4,370	67.7	46.8	23.0
Wawayanda town (Orange)	7,266	7,287	0.3	7,263	83.0	1.8	1.6	1.2	12.5	25.4	65.8	8.7	2,335	79.5	34.7	28.2
Wayland village	1,865	1,834	-1.7	1,806	96.0	0.5	0.6	1.6	1.4	24.1	61.4	14.5	812	57.1	52.0	13.7
Wayland town (Steuben)	4,102	4,032	-1.7	4,077	95.4	1.1	0.7	1.8	1.0	21.7	63.8	14.5	1,795	71.7	51.8	10.5
Wayne town (Steuben)	1,040	1,028	-1.2	1,042	97.5	0.3	1.2	0.3	0.8	16.9	58.4	24.9	477	89.3	28.1	34.8
Webb town (Herkimer)	1,807	1,821	0.8	1,729	95.3	0.1	0.0	0.2	4.5	11.7	57.9	30.4	855	83.5	24.4	27.8
Webster village	5,399	5,577	3.3	5,528	75.2	3.1	10.3	6.4	5.0	23.5	61.5	14.9	2,493	38.0	40.8	34.2
Webster town (Monroe)	42,641	43,892	2.9	43,402	90.7	1.7	3.3	1.8	2.6	23.5	59.5	16.9	17,145	76.4	25.7	44.0
Websters Crossing CDP	69	NA	NA	11	100.0	0.0	0.0	0.0	0.0	0.0	100.0	0.0	6	100.0	100.0	0.0
Weedsport village	1,815	1,782	-1.8	1,910	95.2	0.8	1.2	1.7	1.0	19.4	64.1	16.4	791	69.2	35.5	23.9
Wells CDP	0	NA	NA	768	99.3	0.3	0.0	0.3	0.1	17.0	61.6	21.4	263	81.0	41.1	24.0
Wells town (Hamilton)	674	662	-1.8	856	98.1	0.4	0.1	0.2	1.2	16.1	61.9	22.0	298	83.2	40.3	24.5
Wellsburg village	580	564	-2.8	558	96.6	1.3	0.0	2.2	0.0	20.8	65.6	13.6	227	74.4	54.2	13.2
Wellsville village	4,679	4,558	-2.6	4,621	96.2	0.5	0.0	1.0	2.4	21.3	61.2	17.7	1,980	53.7	37.5	26.5
Wellsville town (Allegany)	7,397	7,213	-2.5	7,306	96.0	0.3	0.4	1.3	1.9	20.3	59.6	19.9	3,177	61.0	41.3	20.6

1 May be of any race.

Table A. All Places — Population and Housing

STATE City, town, township, borough, or CDP (county if applicable)	2010 census total population	2014 estimated population	Percent change 2010–2014	ACS total population estimate 2010–2014	White alone, not Hispanic or Latino	Black alone, not Hispanic or Latino	Asian alone, not Hispanic or Latino	All other races or 2 or more races, not Hispanic or Latino	Hispanic or Latino[1]	Under 18 years old	Age 18 to 64 years old	Age 65 years and older	Total occupied housing units	Percent owner occupied	High school diploma or less	Bachelor's degree or more
	1	2	3	4	5	6	7	8	9	10	11	12	13	14	15	16
NEW YORK—Con.																
Wesley Hills village.........	5,628	5,905	4.9	5,779	93.9	1.0	0.0	1.8	3.2	35.9	51.0	13.1	1,639	88.5	18.7	63.1
West Almond town (Allegany)..................	334	332	-0.6	373	88.5	0.0	2.9	7.2	1.3	29.4	54.2	16.4	128	92.2	49.2	21.1
West Babylon CDP.........	43,213	NA	NA	43,725	70.2	9.7	2.3	2.7	15.1	21.5	64.5	14.3	14,039	76.7	45.5	23.2
West Bay Shore CDP	4,648	NA	NA	4,571	73.2	2.4	3.0	2.0	19.4	23.3	56.9	19.8	1,652	94.6	19.3	45.3
West Bloomfield town (Ontario).................	2,518	2,540	0.9	2,533	98.3	0.0	0.6	0.5	0.7	20.4	62.6	17.2	1,075	85.5	44.0	23.5
Westbury village	15,040	15,329	1.9	15,201	42.5	21.3	6.1	1.6	28.4	21.0	63.2	15.8	4,950	76.0	34.3	42.5
West Carthage village	2,012	2,079	3.3	1,897	79.4	7.2	2.5	3.7	7.1	23.0	63.8	13.1	780	41.8	42.6	21.4
West Chazy CDP............	529	NA	NA	893	100.0	0.0	0.0	0.0	0.0	36.7	55.1	8.2	319	72.7	54.9	6.6
West Elmira CDP............	4,967	NA	NA	5,077	90.9	2.8	1.9	4.4	0.0	23.9	55.5	20.7	2,155	82.9	18.6	52.5
West End CDP	1,940	NA	NA	1,555	90.4	2.4	3.4	0.0	3.8	12.9	56.4	30.7	768	81.0	33.6	35.2
Westerlo town (Albany)....	3,361	3,391	0.9	3,378	97.2	0.6	1.9	0.0	0.3	21.0	61.1	17.7	1,369	91.7	51.6	25.1
Western town (Oneida)....	1,951	1,953	0.1	1,959	93.8	1.5	0.0	2.1	2.7	19.5	62.3	18.1	806	83.6	45.8	25.7
Westfield village............	3,224	3,134	-2.8	3,571	96.3	0.3	0.0	0.0	3.4	22.8	56.9	20.2	1,414	73.0	39.1	27.9
Westfield town (Chautauqua)	4,896	4,792	-2.1	4,838	96.6	0.2	0.0	0.0	3.2	20.6	57.4	21.9	2,023	74.8	43.4	23.2
Westford town (Otsego)...	868	851	-2.0	914	94.4	0.9	0.7	2.2	1.9	25.5	61.3	13.0	349	85.1	45.8	27.2
West Glens Falls CDP	7,071	NA	NA	7,359	96.0	0.5	2.3	0.5	0.7	25.6	61.1	13.3	2,843	75.5	44.2	22.0
Westhampton CDP..........	3,079	NA	NA	2,978	87.4	1.7	0.4	1.1	9.4	21.5	55.4	22.9	1,107	80.7	30.0	48.2
Westhampton Beach village....................	1,721	1,763	2.4	1,817	88.5	1.6	1.5	1.1	7.3	14.9	47.5	37.6	849	73.9	25.6	55.6
West Hampton Dunes village....................	55	58	5.5	47	87.2	0.0	0.0	4.3	8.5	6.4	42.5	51.1	25	92.0	0.0	84.0
West Haverstraw village ..	10,165	10,417	2.5	10,308	32.8	13.1	3.1	1.7	49.3	25.1	65.6	9.4	2,963	63.9	42.5	21.2
West Hempstead CDP	18,862	NA	NA	18,801	62.7	11.3	8.6	1.9	15.5	23.7	61.3	14.8	5,868	85.7	30.5	46.2
West Hills CDP	5,592	NA	NA	5,124	89.0	0.4	5.6	0.6	4.5	21.2	60.9	17.8	1,952	90.7	15.1	57.5
West Hurley CDP............	1,939	NA	NA	1,915	91.7	0.9	0.0	1.9	5.4	13.2	59.7	27.4	913	92.3	28.5	52.6
West Islip CDP	28,335	NA	NA	27,545	91.1	0.2	1.6	0.7	6.4	23.4	61.6	15.0	8,855	93.9	32.2	34.9
Westmere CDP	7,284	NA	NA	7,066	75.0	4.5	13.5	1.8	5.3	17.7	65.1	17.2	3,215	56.2	20.8	52.5
West Monroe town (Oswego)...............	4,252	4,222	-0.7	4,242	95.8	0.3	0.0	3.6	0.4	24.2	63.6	12.1	1,596	83.7	48.4	14.5
Westmoreland CDP........	427	NA	NA	323	70.0	0.0	15.2	14.9	0.0	14.9	62.9	22.3	150	80.7	59.3	11.3
Westmoreland town (Oneida)..................	6,138	6,106	-0.5	6,118	91.1	0.3	3.7	1.8	3.1	22.7	61.5	16.0	2,450	91.6	41.6	23.5
West Nyack CDP	3,439	NA	NA	3,385	76.5	2.7	8.9	1.4	10.4	24.3	54.8	20.9	1,241	94.2	22.8	59.8
Weston Mills CDP...........	1,472	NA	NA	1,346	94.8	0.1	2.0	0.0	3.1	13.5	57.5	28.8	581	73.5	54.9	23.6
West Point CDP.............	6,763	NA	NA	6,892	72.3	3.6	3.4	6.3	14.5	20.0	79.8	0.2	777	1.7	3.6	75.4
Westport CDP...............	518	NA	NA	393	94.1	0.5	0.0	4.8	0.5	17.3	56.5	26.2	152	80.9	52.6	18.4
Westport town (Essex).....	1,312	1,306	-0.5	1,476	92.1	0.1	0.1	2.4	5.3	22.1	58.0	19.7	527	87.9	49.3	23.9
West Sand Lake CDP.......	2,660	NA	NA	2,791	94.2	0.9	2.1	1.5	1.3	23.9	64.8	11.4	1,010	91.7	26.4	51.3
West Sayville CDP..........	5,011	NA	NA	4,685	90.6	0.0	1.7	2.4	5.3	21.2	62.8	16.1	1,596	86.8	29.5	39.3
West Seneca CDP & town (Erie)...................	44,696	45,219	1.2	44,902	95.2	1.5	0.4	1.1	1.8	20.1	59.5	20.4	19,051	77.2	37.5	26.6
West Sparta town (Livingston).............	1,255	1,291	2.9	1,332	98.0	0.0	0.0	1.1	1.0	23.7	62.3	13.9	502	83.1	64.5	11.4
West Turin town (Lewis)...	1,524	1,535	0.7	1,924	94.2	3.0	0.0	1.5	1.2	26.9	57.9	15.3	736	79.5	52.9	17.7
West Union town (Steuben)	312	307	-1.6	375	98.9	0.0	0.3	0.8	0.0	21.4	62.9	15.7	157	77.1	60.5	12.7
Westvale CDP	4,963	NA	NA	5,111	98.1	0.0	0.2	1.0	0.7	20.2	60.6	19.3	2,075	96.1	17.7	53.6
West Valley CDP............	518	NA	NA	488	100.0	0.0	0.0	0.0	0.0	26.7	55.7	17.6	196	67.3	32.1	13.8
Westville town (Franklin)..	1,819	1,819	0.0	1,642	97.5	0.4	0.0	1.2	0.9	22.8	58.5	18.6	676	84.5	61.5	10.4
West Winfield village........	826	882	6.8	787	89.6	0.0	0.0	4.6	5.8	23.3	52.1	24.5	348	67.2	39.9	28.4
Wethersfield town (Wyoming)...............	883	870	-1.5	846	97.0	0.0	0.0	0.5	2.5	26.9	63.7	9.3	322	79.2	47.8	16.1
Wheatfield town (Niagara)	18,117	18,320	1.1	18,249	90.5	2.8	3.3	0.6	2.8	22.7	57.9	19.4	6,968	77.5	35.2	32.2
Wheatland town (Monroe)	4,775	4,760	-0.3	4,768	87.9	6.8	0.5	1.4	3.4	19.1	67.2	13.7	2,075	66.7	29.1	28.3
Wheatley Heights CDP	5,130	NA	NA	5,211	23.1	59.6	5.5	1.8	9.9	25.5	64.5	9.8	1,435	79.0	23.9	51.8
Wheeler town (Steuben)..	1,260	1,260	0.0	1,186	95.6	1.9	0.0	0.9	1.5	24.2	59.2	16.6	470	83.8	59.4	11.7
White Creek town (Washington)..............	3,356	3,313	-1.3	3,342	95.8	0.0	1.3	0.4	2.5	23.8	57.7	18.6	1,393	81.0	46.3	25.5
Whitehall village............	2,617	2,585	-1.2	2,791	97.0	0.5	0.0	0.9	1.6	23.4	62.9	13.7	1,180	47.0	62.7	14.2
Whitehall town (Washington)..............	4,042	3,989	-1.3	4,013	97.5	0.4	0.0	1.0	1.1	22.3	61.0	16.7	1,665	62.5	66.5	11.5
White Plains city & MCD (Westchester)..........	56,853	58,035	2.1	57,505	45.2	11.3	6.7	2.8	34.0	20.2	64.2	15.6	22,033	51.5	27.6	53.2
Whitesboro village	3,772	3,713	-1.6	3,749	99.5	0.5	0.0	0.0	0.1	21.2	60.7	18.1	1,679	55.7	38.0	18.8
Whitestown town (Oneida)..................	18,667	18,610	-0.3	18,671	96.5	1.2	0.2	0.6	1.5	20.5	60.8	18.7	7,511	75.5	34.2	28.3
Whitney Point village	964	945	-2.0	1,016	92.9	1.5	0.0	1.3	4.3	29.7	51.6	18.7	407	61.4	41.3	25.1
Willet town (Cortland)	1,043	1,019	-2.3	1,276	96.9	0.0	0.0	2.0	1.2	31.4	60.0	8.5	418	86.6	61.7	12.2
Williamson CDP.............	2,495	NA	NA	2,252	96.8	1.5	0.6	0.0	1.1	17.2	66.2	16.6	961	70.4	46.7	22.1
Williamson town (Wayne)	6,984	6,857	-1.8	6,918	87.2	5.0	0.4	1.7	5.7	22.3	60.8	16.8	2,585	84.6	43.4	25.8
Williamstown town (Oswego)...............	1,280	1,281	0.1	1,223	94.7	0.0	0.0	5.2	0.2	22.0	67.8	10.1	416	87.0	56.3	3.8
Williamsville village	5,303	5,283	-0.4	5,286	91.1	2.5	2.2	1.1	3.2	14.7	61.3	24.1	2,566	61.1	16.7	56.4
Willing town (Allegany) ...	1,228	1,205	-1.9	1,458	98.4	0.3	0.0	0.8	0.5	23.8	56.1	20.0	610	73.8	52.0	16.7
Williston Park village........	7,287	7,327	0.5	7,319	73.5	0.0	11.7	3.8	11.0	22.0	61.6	16.4	2,567	79.9	24.9	52.1
Willsboro CDP	753	NA	NA	676	96.6	0.0	0.0	3.4	0.0	17.2	62.9	20.0	332	67.8	51.8	18.7
Willsboro town (Essex)	2,025	2,063	1.9	1,890	97.6	0.1	0.0	1.7	0.6	16.9	52.0	31.1	854	83.0	52.2	18.3
Wilmington CDP	937	NA	NA	955	99.9	0.0	0.0	0.0	0.1	22.0	65.2	12.9	381	73.2	37.8	26.8
Wilmington town (Essex) .	1,253	1,262	0.7	1,305	98.5	0.1	0.0	0.1	1.3	22.3	62.6	15.1	531	77.8	39.0	30.5
Wilna town (Jefferson)	6,427	6,439	0.2	6,507	90.8	2.1	0.6	2.9	3.6	30.5	59.2	10.4	2,288	55.6	55.4	10.3
Wilson village................	1,264	1,239	-2.0	1,202	99.3	0.1	0.0	0.7	0.0	21.2	59.8	18.7	512	70.7	36.1	20.7
Wilson town (Niagara)	5,994	5,912	-1.4	5,956	97.2	0.5	0.0	1.0	1.3	22.7	61.9	15.4	2,283	87.3	37.8	24.9
Wilton town (Saratoga)	16,154	16,638	3.0	16,462	92.5	2.2	1.6	1.2	2.5	25.1	62.6	12.3	6,509	75.0	23.5	44.5
Windham CDP...............	367	NA	NA	436	100.0	0.0	0.0	0.0	0.0	3.2	54.0	42.9	205	77.1	40.5	32.7
Windham town (Greene) .	1,699	1,670	-1.7	1,655	94.0	0.0	0.0	1.9	4.1	10.9	51.9	37.3	701	84.0	41.2	30.7
Windsor village..............	916	901	-1.6	1,005	97.4	0.7	0.9	0.4	0.6	23.9	62.0	14.3	373	72.1	45.3	20.9
Windsor town (Broome)...	6,274	6,163	-1.8	6,212	97.5	0.9	0.1	0.8	0.6	22.5	62.7	14.8	2,358	84.4	53.3	17.6
Winfield town (Herkimer) .	2,086	2,128	2.0	2,089	90.5	0.5	0.3	2.5	6.2	24.4	57.1	18.5	796	76.8	44.0	24.9

1 May be of any race.

Table A. All Places — **Population and Housing**

STATE City, town, township, borough, or CDP (county if applicable)	Population: 2010 census total population	Population: 2014 estimated population	Population: Percent change 2010–2014	Population: ACS total population estimate 2010–2014	Race and Hispanic or Latino origin (percent), 2010–2014: White alone, not Hispanic or Latino	Black alone, not Hispanic or Latino	Asian alone, not Hispanic or Latino	All other races or 2 or more races, not Hispanic or Latino	Hispanic or Latino[1]	Age (percent), 2010–2014: Under 18 years old	Age 18 to 64 years old	Age 65 years and older	Households, 2010–2014: Total occupied housing units	Percent owner occupied	Householders by level of education (percent): High school diploma or less	Bachelor's degree or more
	1	2	3	4	5	6	7	8	9	10	11	12	13	14	15	16
NEW YORK—Con.																
Winthrop CDP	510	NA	NA	301	100.0	0.0	0.0	0.0	0.0	18.2	58.8	22.9	149	89.9	56.4	18.1
Wirt town (Allegany)	1,111	1,084	-2.4	1,082	97.9	0.0	1.7	0.3	0.2	24.3	60.9	14.9	441	83.9	68.3	6.3
Witherbee CDP	347	NA	NA	384	90.6	0.0	0.0	9.4	0.0	28.7	51.2	20.3	171	53.2	71.3	0.0
Wolcott village	1,701	1,652	-2.9	1,698	89.5	4.4	0.0	1.9	4.2	23.8	61.6	14.7	750	60.8	62.1	14.5
Wolcott town (Wayne)	4,453	4,385	-1.5	4,427	91.5	4.2	0.0	1.2	3.0	23.5	62.0	14.3	1,777	77.7	58.9	12.3
Woodbury CDP	8,907	NA	NA	8,553	86.1	2.4	8.9	0.8	1.8	19.5	52.7	27.9	3,018	87.4	16.6	72.0
Woodbury village	10,686	10,814	1.2	10,638	79.0	2.3	3.3	1.4	14.1	27.7	60.4	11.9	3,358	88.0	21.0	46.1
Woodbury town (Orange)	11,353	11,496	1.3	11,388	76.9	2.7	3.3	1.3	15.8	28.0	60.5	11.4	3,586	86.4	20.0	45.5
Woodhull town (Steuben)	1,719	1,689	-1.7	2,103	98.9	0.0	0.0	0.9	0.3	33.3	53.1	13.6	710	84.1	59.6	13.9
Woodmere CDP	17,121	NA	NA	17,067	85.2	3.2	3.3	2.4	5.9	31.2	53.7	15.0	5,042	89.7	15.9	64.0
Woodridge village	821	794	-3.3	831	52.9	6.0	3.5	2.2	35.4	24.0	63.0	13.0	303	29.4	53.1	22.4
Woodsburgh village	778	781	0.4	728	96.8	0.0	1.4	0.7	1.1	24.7	58.4	17.0	264	93.9	9.8	70.8
Woodstock CDP	2,088	NA	NA	1,922	80.9	2.0	0.6	10.2	6.3	4.7	59.7	35.5	1,104	75.1	14.0	63.0
Woodstock town (Ulster)	5,884	5,876	-0.1	5,893	89.2	1.1	1.1	4.8	3.8	13.6	59.2	27.2	3,004	79.9	12.0	62.9
Woodsville CDP	80	NA	NA	64	100.0	0.0	0.0	0.0	0.0	21.9	62.6	15.6	24	66.7	83.3	16.7
Worcester CDP	1,113	NA	NA	1,223	94.8	1.4	0.0	0.0	3.8	19.1	54.5	26.6	458	85.4	41.5	26.9
Worcester town (Otsego)	2,220	2,171	-2.2	2,423	88.1	0.8	0.0	0.9	10.2	19.1	58.6	22.4	978	82.1	41.9	23.0
Worth town (Jefferson)	231	239	3.5	215	98.6	0.0	0.0	1.4	0.0	27.0	61.8	11.2	85	77.6	62.4	17.6
Wright town (Schoharie)	1,539	1,481	-3.8	1,773	92.9	0.5	1.9	0.7	4.1	22.7	63.4	13.8	643	87.7	43.4	25.5
Wurtsboro village	1,240	1,195	-3.6	1,086	81.1	5.8	0.0	3.2	9.9	17.4	63.2	19.3	506	59.3	44.9	17.4
Wyandanch CDP	11,647	NA	NA	11,187	5.0	65.8	0.3	2.7	26.3	25.1	66.6	8.2	3,040	62.3	50.8	20.4
Wynantskill CDP	3,276	NA	NA	2,946	90.4	4.3	0.3	2.9	2.1	20.3	62.2	17.4	1,220	91.5	29.9	36.6
Wyoming village	434	430	-0.9	386	99.7	0.0	0.0	0.0	0.3	24.7	57.5	17.9	159	76.1	43.4	20.1
Yaphank CDP	5,945	NA	NA	5,906	77.6	5.4	1.3	2.2	13.4	18.9	67.8	13.2	1,771	92.4	36.7	35.9
Yates town (Orleans)	2,559	2,492	-2.6	2,468	95.8	1.9	0.5	0.6	1.2	26.7	60.6	12.7	905	85.5	48.8	14.0
Yonkers city & MCD (Westchester)	195,979	200,667	2.4	198,654	41.0	14.8	6.9	1.7	35.6	22.3	62.4	15.4	73,357	48.4	42.0	32.8
York town (Livingston)	3,397	3,325	-2.1	3,353	94.5	0.8	0.4	4.0	0.4	19.5	65.6	15.0	1,431	85.5	44.0	21.0
York Hamlet CDP	544	NA	NA	643	80.1	0.0	0.0	19.9	0.0	27.2	67.6	5.1	293	88.4	45.4	9.6
Yorkshire CDP	1,180	NA	NA	1,103	96.7	0.0	0.0	2.5	0.7	9.0	67.3	23.7	635	74.8	73.5	6.9
Yorkshire town (Cattaraugus)	3,919	3,823	-2.4	3,869	96.5	0.0	0.3	1.5	1.7	20.1	66.3	13.6	1,754	71.6	63.1	9.2
Yorktown town (Westchester)	36,081	36,976	2.5	36,566	79.7	3.3	3.2	1.4	12.4	23.1	58.9	18.0	13,043	85.1	24.7	48.7
Yorktown Heights CDP	1,781	NA	NA	2,290	81.8	8.0	4.7	1.5	4.0	21.2	66.7	12.1	698	76.1	26.6	51.3
Yorkville village	2,689	2,649	-1.5	2,677	95.3	0.0	0.8	0.4	3.4	17.9	66.4	15.6	1,081	72.2	43.9	20.0
Youngstown village	1,935	1,896	-2.0	2,002	96.7	0.2	0.0	0.5	2.6	24.6	53.4	21.8	807	80.5	27.3	38.5
Zena CDP	1,031	NA	NA	1,264	93.6	0.0	1.2	4.4	0.9	24.2	58.2	17.5	479	90.8	16.7	56.2
NORTH CAROLINA	9,535,691	9,943,964	4.3	9,750,405	64.6	21.2	2.4	3.2	8.7	23.4	62.8	13.8	3,742,514	65.8	37.5	29.7
Aberdeen town	6,363	7,131	12.1	6,702	64.7	21.2	4.2	6.2	3.7	25.0	58.5	16.6	2,837	50.3	29.5	31.1
Advance CDP	1,138	NA	NA	1,145	96.9	2.1	0.0	0.0	1.0	23.9	69.3	7.0	406	89.2	29.1	40.1
Ahoskie town	5,061	4,973	-1.7	5,017	29.8	64.4	1.9	2.8	1.2	24.8	53.9	21.4	1,986	42.9	50.6	16.7
Alamance village	951	978	2.8	786	95.5	4.5	0.0	0.0	0.0	20.9	66.3	12.8	332	86.4	29.8	31.6
Albemarle city	15,902	15,976	0.5	15,924	68.3	22.4	3.1	3.1	3.0	23.4	58.6	17.9	6,524	57.0	48.1	18.5
Alliance town	776	761	-1.9	802	82.0	15.2	0.2	0.5	2.0	25.4	46.4	28.2	290	68.3	39.0	17.2
Altamahaw CDP	347	NA	NA	376	76.9	0.0	0.0	0.0	23.1	8.3	64.0	27.7	126	78.6	61.9	0.0
Andrews town	1,787	1,762	-1.4	1,959	82.6	1.8	0.0	3.8	11.7	29.6	52.4	18.0	670	58.7	47.8	15.7
Angier town	4,348	4,836	11.2	4,760	61.6	19.8	0.0	5.0	13.6	25.2	63.2	11.6	1,753	64.9	37.3	16.7
Ansonville town	631	606	-4.0	650	20.5	79.5	0.0	0.0	0.0	18.8	62.6	18.8	282	77.3	59.2	6.0
Apex town	37,501	43,907	17.1	40,631	75.1	8.1	6.7	2.4	7.6	32.5	61.7	5.8	13,811	71.2	8.8	61.4
Aquadale CDP	397	NA	NA	353	100.0	0.0	0.0	0.0	0.0	15.0	65.7	19.3	157	90.4	38.2	8.9
Arapahoe town	556	546	-1.8	494	82.2	12.1	0.0	4.0	1.6	15.1	62.2	22.7	203	84.7	54.2	17.7
Archdale city	11,403	11,539	1.2	11,322	85.1	4.6	5.2	2.0	3.1	22.5	61.2	16.3	4,386	72.4	44.2	17.7
Archer Lodge town	4,279	4,594	7.4	4,441	62.6	11.5	3.6	2.0	20.2	29.1	68.4	2.5	1,441	92.3	42.8	12.1
Asheboro city	25,195	25,886	2.7	25,573	59.5	11.2	1.0	2.5	25.8	27.2	58.8	13.8	10,012	52.0	53.5	18.8
Asheville city	83,417	87,882	5.4	85,783	77.7	12.4	1.8	2.1	6.1	19.0	64.2	16.7	37,709	50.8	25.2	46.5
Ashley Heights CDP	380	NA	NA	337	51.6	15.1	0.0	22.8	10.4	45.7	32.9	21.4	77	100.0	53.2	0.0
Askewville town	244	231	-5.3	224	100.0	0.0	0.0	0.0	0.0	16.5	62.6	21.0	98	79.6	61.2	9.2
Atkinson town	299	320	7.0	319	83.7	7.8	0.0	0.0	8.5	21.0	58.6	20.4	124	84.7	53.2	10.5
Atlantic CDP	543	NA	NA	405	94.1	0.0	0.0	0.0	5.9	6.5	51.9	41.7	226	77.4	66.4	18.6
Atlantic Beach town	1,495	1,506	0.7	1,618	95.6	0.6	2.6	1.3	0.0	9.7	66.3	23.9	891	55.3	27.4	32.8
Aulander town	895	843	-5.8	806	30.9	67.5	0.0	0.2	1.4	30.4	48.5	21.2	330	56.4	62.4	8.2
Aurora town	520	520	0.0	545	49.0	41.8	0.0	7.2	2.0	24.1	54.1	21.8	219	57.1	58.4	5.0
Autryville town	200	203	1.5	405	96.0	0.0	0.0	0.0	4.0	30.4	60.0	9.6	154	41.6	68.2	7.8
Avery Creek CDP	1,950	NA	NA	2,605	87.9	0.0	0.7	2.9	8.5	25.7	63.3	11.0	969	72.0	15.9	49.9
Avon CDP	776	NA	NA	949	93.7	0.0	0.0	0.0	6.3	12.7	70.7	16.8	491	77.8	57.2	20.4
Ayden town	4,912	5,059	3.0	5,018	39.7	50.2	0.1	1.1	8.9	27.5	56.4	16.0	1,984	43.5	47.8	11.7
Badin town	1,974	1,976	0.1	1,608	56.2	32.3	0.2	3.7	7.6	11.5	75.5	12.9	516	70.0	39.1	25.8
Bailey town	569	567	-0.4	494	54.5	36.8	0.0	2.6	6.1	22.7	59.4	17.8	200	72.5	59.0	11.5
Bakersville town	464	455	-1.9	391	95.4	1.8	1.3	0.3	1.3	27.9	57.3	15.1	166	30.7	65.7	8.4
Bald Head Island village	158	168	6.3	179	100.0	0.0	0.0	0.0	0.0	1.1	58.1	40.8	90	100.0	7.8	74.4
Balfour CDP	1,187	NA	NA	1,453	78.3	0.1	0.0	15.2	6.4	18.1	66.0	15.9	607	79.6	49.6	12.5
Banner Elk town	1,028	1,113	8.3	1,078	79.9	12.2	2.8	1.9	3.2	8.0	81.1	10.9	264	54.5	14.8	42.4
Barker Heights CDP	1,254	NA	NA	1,652	56.8	4.7	4.8	1.6	32.0	25.4	64.9	9.7	637	74.9	43.0	9.1
Barker Ten Mile CDP	952	NA	NA	895	69.5	18.5	0.6	11.4	0.0	18.2	59.3	22.5	358	88.0	24.9	38.3
Bath town	249	249	0.0	244	98.4	1.6	0.0	0.0	0.0	8.2	53.9	37.7	113	85.8	26.5	39.8
Bayboro town	1,263	1,252	-0.9	1,393	30.7	60.9	0.9	4.7	2.9	18.0	74.4	7.8	343	62.4	50.7	12.8
Bayshore CDP	3,393	NA	NA	3,390	93.9	3.5	0.4	1.7	0.5	17.9	58.4	23.7	1,584	65.7	28.1	40.6
Bayview CDP	346	NA	NA	260	96.5	3.5	0.0	0.0	0.0	10.8	36.2	53.1	134	83.6	40.3	25.4
Bear Grass town	73	71	-2.7	138	100.0	0.0	0.0	0.0	0.0	36.3	49.3	14.5	45	64.4	62.2	20.0
Beaufort town	4,039	4,195	3.9	4,119	71.9	17.6	0.0	6.5	4.1	20.0	63.5	16.5	1,963	46.0	32.9	23.9
Beech Mountain town	320	319	-0.3	561	97.0	0.0	0.0	1.6	1.4	7.3	46.7	46.0	287	94.8	6.6	62.4
Belhaven town	1,688	1,612	-4.5	1,787	42.0	53.0	0.0	0.6	4.4	20.0	55.9	24.3	772	55.4	61.0	10.5
Bell Arthur CDP	466	NA	NA	430	17.7	29.1	0.0	0.0	53.3	35.9	43.2	20.9	139	84.9	51.1	0.0
Belmont city	10,243	10,456	2.1	10,346	83.8	7.0	4.4	1.2	3.5	21.9	65.3	12.6	4,012	68.7	34.9	32.2
Belville town	1,938	2,059	6.2	2,166	76.4	16.9	0.4	2.2	4.2	31.4	60.6	8.1	754	86.7	15.3	46.3
Belvoir CDP	307	NA	NA	340	79.7	20.3	0.0	0.0	0.0	16.8	65.9	17.4	143	88.8	86.0	14.0
Belwood town	950	934	-1.7	1,040	81.2	2.1	0.4	3.2	13.2	28.4	55.9	15.7	366	83.6	53.8	14.2
Bennett CDP	282	NA	NA	133	100.0	0.0	0.0	0.0	0.0	0.0	57.1	42.9	88	100.0	79.5	0.0

1 May be of any race.

Table A. All Places — **Population and Housing**

STATE City, town, township, borough, or CDP (county if applicable)	Population: 2010 census total population	Population: 2014 estimated population	Population: Percent change 2010–2014	Population: ACS total population estimate 2010–2014	Race and Hispanic or Latino origin (percent), 2010–2014: White alone, not Hispanic or Latino	Black alone, not Hispanic or Latino	Asian alone, not Hispanic or Latino	All other races or 2 or more races, not Hispanic or Latino	Hispanic or Latino[1]	Age (percent), 2010–2014: Under 18 years old	Age 18 to 64 years old	Age 65 years and older	Households, 2010–2014: Total occupied housing units	Percent owner occupied	Householders by level of education (percent): High school diploma or less	Bachelor's degree or more
	1	2	3	4	5	6	7	8	9	10	11	12	13	14	15	16
NORTH CAROLINA—Con.																
Benson town	3,311	3,536	6.8	3,435	52.0	16.1	1.4	0.3	30.2	28.1	56.6	15.4	1,271	48.9	28.6	30.1
Bent Creek CDP	1,287	NA	NA	1,509	87.4	0.8	1.5	0.9	9.5	17.4	64.5	18.2	664	83.0	7.7	46.7
Bermuda Run town	2,508	2,538	1.2	2,532	91.4	4.7	1.2	2.3	0.5	8.0	43.2	48.9	1,406	91.6	15.6	67.0
Bessemer City city	5,340	5,484	2.7	5,410	83.5	11.2	0.0	1.1	4.2	24.7	63.8	11.5	1,924	65.4	58.8	6.2
Bethania town	328	342	4.3	311	87.5	8.7	0.0	1.6	2.3	6.4	58.5	35.0	136	81.6	30.1	29.4
Bethel town	1,577	1,622	2.9	1,834	37.7	62.2	0.0	0.2	0.0	24.2	57.7	18.1	757	60.2	51.1	20.9
Bethlehem CDP	4,214	NA	NA	4,493	93.5	4.1	0.0	1.1	1.3	18.5	64.1	17.5	1,824	88.0	34.8	40.2
Beulaville town	1,298	1,342	3.4	1,632	69.1	24.8	0.2	1.2	4.7	21.6	53.9	24.7	739	48.7	48.6	18.7
Biltmore Forest town	1,343	1,422	5.9	1,459	96.4	0.0	0.0	0.5	3.0	20.5	48.7	30.6	592	94.6	3.9	84.3
Biscoe town	1,700	1,685	-0.9	1,753	37.3	17.2	1.3	1.5	42.8	31.5	53.9	14.5	553	55.9	60.2	6.3
Black Creek town	769	765	-0.5	788	60.0	27.9	0.0	1.4	10.7	39.3	53.5	7.0	293	66.2	51.2	11.3
Black Mountain town	7,840	8,145	3.9	7,977	89.0	5.7	0.7	2.4	2.2	15.8	60.6	23.6	3,637	55.5	28.0	41.3
Bladenboro town	1,750	1,733	-1.0	1,938	62.1	21.7	0.0	3.2	13.0	28.5	51.2	20.2	839	41.7	54.7	16.3
Blowing Rock town	1,241	1,233	-0.6	1,175	96.3	0.0	0.0	1.4	2.4	7.6	51.4	40.9	588	68.0	16.3	64.6
Blue Clay Farms CDP	33	NA	NA	11	100.0	0.0	0.0	0.0	0.0	0.0	0.0	100.0	11	100.0	0.0	100.0
Boardman town	157	155	-1.3	147	70.7	26.5	0.0	0.0	2.7	18.3	61.8	19.7	70	74.3	64.3	2.9
Bogue town	684	701	2.5	771	84.7	4.8	0.0	0.8	9.7	17.8	67.8	14.4	272	79.8	25.4	21.3
Boiling Spring Lakes city	5,372	5,689	5.9	5,529	90.6	4.1	1.0	1.7	2.6	18.6	64.2	17.1	2,278	84.0	38.5	18.8
Boiling Springs town	4,644	4,588	-1.2	4,619	88.6	6.9	2.1	0.8	1.6	22.2	69.2	8.3	1,248	70.4	28.7	45.4
Bolivia town	143	150	4.9	292	99.7	0.0	0.0	0.3	0.0	49.6	37.0	13.4	77	68.8	44.2	10.4
Bolton town	695	677	-2.6	726	36.1	57.2	0.0	5.0	1.8	25.5	59.5	15.0	294	74.1	56.8	0.7
Bonnetsville CDP	443	NA	NA	666	57.5	9.3	0.0	0.0	33.2	44.0	51.3	4.8	153	33.3	86.3	2.0
Boone town	17,123	18,130	5.9	17,802	90.0	2.2	1.6	3.0	3.2	4.6	91.2	4.1	5,766	20.2	12.8	33.3
Boonville town	1,222	1,212	-0.8	1,547	89.3	4.0	0.0	1.4	5.4	28.8	48.5	22.6	634	73.3	54.4	12.0
Bostic town	386	379	-1.8	388	88.9	5.4	4.9	0.8	0.0	15.8	64.8	19.6	175	70.9	40.0	14.3
Bowmore CDP	103	NA	NA	35	0.0	100.0	0.0	0.0	0.0	0.0	40.0	60.0	17	100.0	100.0	0.0
Brevard city	7,683	7,692	0.1	7,651	76.5	9.7	1.0	8.8	4.0	22.7	51.7	25.7	3,140	55.2	30.6	34.1
Brices Creek CDP	3,073	NA	NA	3,593	79.1	17.5	3.0	0.0	0.4	31.5	54.3	14.1	1,246	84.1	14.1	40.0
Bridgeton town	454	447	-1.5	371	96.0	1.1	0.0	0.0	3.0	15.6	63.0	21.3	146	63.0	40.4	21.9
Broad Creek CDP	2,334	NA	NA	2,248	94.6	1.3	0.0	1.5	2.6	24.7	62.2	13.1	931	78.8	36.4	27.8
Broadway town	1,229	1,264	2.8	1,291	67.9	12.5	2.4	1.9	15.4	21.2	58.0	20.8	483	86.1	38.1	25.1
Brogden CDP	2,633	NA	NA	2,499	28.3	50.5	0.2	5.8	15.1	26.9	57.7	15.2	897	72.7	47.8	13.6
Brookford town	382	376	-1.6	415	79.8	7.2	0.0	0.5	12.5	24.3	53.3	22.4	160	43.1	70.6	8.8
Brunswick town	1,140	1,115	-2.2	492	25.4	69.7	0.0	3.9	1.0	24.0	60.3	15.7	177	44.6	59.9	6.2
Bryson City town	1,419	1,436	1.2	1,585	84.1	0.5	0.8	13.7	0.9	26.2	54.4	19.4	543	49.7	52.5	15.1
Buies Creek CDP	2,942	NA	NA	2,772	73.3	8.4	10.4	2.9	5.0	6.6	88.2	5.2	478	26.6	12.3	59.2
Bunn town	344	357	3.8	383	65.3	22.2	1.0	2.9	8.6	21.4	60.0	18.5	180	52.8	59.4	6.7
Bunnlevel CDP	552	NA	NA	820	54.1	31.0	0.0	5.1	9.8	24.8	67.2	7.9	267	62.2	61.4	13.1
Burgaw town	3,868	4,060	5.0	3,960	55.2	36.8	0.2	2.7	5.2	18.1	60.6	21.3	1,203	50.7	34.3	36.2
Burlington city	50,922	51,812	1.7	51,740	53.0	28.2	2.5	3.4	13.0	22.5	60.9	16.7	21,873	55.8	42.8	22.4
Burnsville town	1,695	1,673	-1.3	1,702	88.1	3.2	0.6	2.3	5.9	12.5	60.7	26.7	788	42.3	48.0	18.5
Butner town	7,591	7,718	1.7	7,661	45.3	34.3	0.7	5.1	14.6	21.6	66.8	11.4	2,125	67.1	40.3	13.9
Butters CDP	294	NA	NA	148	68.2	31.8	0.0	0.0	0.0	0.0	89.8	10.1	78	100.0	85.9	0.0
Buxton CDP	1,273	NA	NA	1,259	78.6	0.0	0.0	0.0	21.4	30.0	54.4	15.6	458	78.6	38.4	15.1
Cajah's Mountain town	2,800	2,757	-1.5	2,781	91.6	0.8	0.0	1.1	6.5	17.9	61.8	20.3	1,024	73.6	53.0	21.2
Calabash town	1,786	2,092	17.1	1,738	77.6	5.4	0.7	2.2	14.0	15.7	54.8	29.5	825	76.6	46.5	20.7
Calypso town	538	555	3.2	538	55.6	15.2	0.0	0.4	28.8	25.7	63.5	10.8	174	60.9	57.5	6.3
Camden CDP	599	NA	NA	634	91.3	8.7	0.0	0.0	0.0	30.4	62.3	7.3	210	49.5	24.8	14.8
Cameron town	283	292	3.2	356	89.3	10.7	0.0	0.0	0.0	20.2	66.7	13.2	137	71.5	50.4	21.9
Candor town	840	833	-0.8	775	41.3	10.1	0.0	0.0	48.6	24.3	60.8	15.0	264	66.3	63.6	17.0
Canton town	4,212	4,159	-1.3	4,160	86.6	0.9	0.3	4.4	7.8	19.1	59.2	21.7	1,840	68.2	43.1	18.0
Cape Carteret town	1,992	2,058	3.3	2,237	97.5	0.2	0.3	0.6	1.4	22.2	54.3	23.7	892	80.7	19.1	41.9
Caroleen CDP	652	NA	NA	438	80.1	11.0	0.0	8.9	0.0	19.9	62.1	18.0	166	83.1	30.7	0.0
Carolina Beach town	5,706	6,042	5.9	5,888	92.9	1.9	0.2	3.2	1.8	20.0	63.6	16.5	2,469	49.5	18.5	34.5
Carolina Shores town	3,328	3,609	8.4	3,461	96.3	0.4	0.5	1.6	1.1	5.2	44.4	50.4	1,868	86.9	28.9	25.9
Carrboro town	19,589	20,984	7.1	20,337	61.7	9.3	8.1	4.4	16.5	22.9	71.4	5.5	8,673	37.4	14.7	69.8
Carthage town	2,274	2,369	4.2	2,238	71.8	25.3	0.0	0.0	2.9	28.4	55.2	16.5	787	63.2	45.9	18.3
Cary town	135,276	155,227	14.7	146,041	66.2	7.7	14.0	3.2	8.9	26.9	63.9	9.1	53,975	68.7	12.9	65.6
Casar town	297	295	-0.7	306	100.0	0.0	0.0	0.0	0.0	28.7	53.0	18.3	128	70.3	59.4	3.1
Cashiers CDP	157	NA	NA	87	100.0	0.0	0.0	0.0	0.0	0.0	68.9	31.0	60	100.0	18.3	16.7
Castalia town	268	264	-1.5	285	50.9	34.0	0.0	1.8	13.3	19.0	58.7	22.5	104	74.0	65.4	7.7
Castle Hayne CDP	1,202	NA	NA	967	79.4	11.9	0.0	0.0	8.7	26.2	61.1	12.7	408	66.4	41.4	24.8
Caswell Beach town	392	416	6.1	450	89.6	0.0	6.2	1.8	2.4	9.6	46.1	44.2	215	90.2	9.3	57.2
Catawba town	613	615	0.3	706	72.7	16.6	0.0	1.4	9.3	30.7	52.1	17.1	247	77.3	57.5	14.2
Cedar Point town	1,279	1,305	2.0	1,480	92.2	0.0	3.3	2.6	2.0	22.0	55.8	22.2	610	76.9	30.7	44.8
Cedar Rock village	300	295	-1.7	299	96.7	1.0	0.0	1.0	1.3	11.4	53.8	34.8	121	97.5	9.1	53.7
Centerville town	89	91	2.2	36	100.0	0.0	0.0	0.0	0.0	8.4	77.9	13.9	16	87.5	56.3	0.0
Cerro Gordo town	212	203	-4.2	201	76.1	10.4	0.0	2.5	10.9	32.3	59.4	8.5	78	84.6	42.3	14.1
Chadbourn town	1,842	1,801	-2.2	2,141	33.2	58.7	0.0	4.7	3.5	30.8	53.9	15.4	859	53.8	43.7	15.1
Chapel Hill town	57,233	59,376	3.7	58,379	70.0	8.4	12.7	3.1	5.9	16.6	73.4	10.0	20,271	48.6	8.8	70.8
Charlotte city	735,758	809,958	10.1	774,807	43.9	34.4	5.5	2.7	13.4	24.8	66.2	9.0	298,815	55.4	26.4	43.4
Cherokee CDP	2,138	NA	NA	2,710	9.9	0.7	1.4	82.3	5.8	25.4	56.7	17.9	961	76.1	60.5	12.9
Cherryville city	5,760	5,906	2.5	5,826	80.0	12.8	0.0	3.6	3.7	19.8	59.0	21.4	2,404	72.8	48.8	17.3
Chimney Rock Village village	110	109	-0.9	111	91.9	0.0	0.0	8.1	0.0	11.7	65.7	22.5	55	85.5	18.2	21.8
China Grove town	4,162	4,172	0.2	4,155	67.0	14.6	4.5	3.1	10.9	27.9	61.3	10.9	1,535	55.0	47.9	12.5
Chocowinity town	820	818	-0.2	966	61.0	31.4	0.3	2.7	4.7	21.7	59.1	19.0	381	63.3	57.2	12.3
Claremont city	1,352	1,360	0.6	1,546	76.7	6.7	1.6	3.0	12.0	28.4	59.7	12.0	633	73.8	43.3	23.2
Clarkton town	837	822	-1.8	723	57.7	38.0	0.0	2.9	1.4	12.3	58.0	29.9	358	61.7	44.1	15.4
Clayton town	16,208	18,445	13.8	17,274	71.0	19.4	0.6	2.2	6.8	27.9	61.5	10.6	6,594	68.2	25.7	31.8
Clemmons village	18,623	19,522	4.8	19,101	79.3	6.5	4.7	2.5	7.0	25.7	59.1	15.3	7,508	74.1	24.1	47.2
Cleveland town	868	870	0.2	822	58.8	29.1	2.4	1.5	8.3	23.4	64.6	11.9	322	73.3	41.6	16.8
Cliffside CDP	611	NA	NA	338	100.0	0.0	0.0	0.0	0.0	23.6	55.2	21.0	120	74.2	74.2	11.7
Clinton city	8,640	8,787	1.7	8,729	48.0	38.8	0.8	2.6	9.7	22.9	54.8	22.3	3,421	49.7	45.7	21.7
Clyde town	1,225	1,235	0.8	1,362	76.0	1.0	0.0	1.0	22.0	20.3	67.1	12.6	645	67.0	48.2	16.7
Coats town	2,112	2,376	12.5	2,405	64.0	10.2	0.5	1.2	24.1	18.5	68.2	13.3	882	50.8	39.0	19.3
Cofield village	412	402	-2.4	295	12.5	83.7	0.0	3.7	0.0	18.3	68.4	13.2	138	73.9	41.3	8.7
Coinjock CDP	335	NA	NA	190	96.3	0.0	0.0	3.7	0.0	23.1	60.0	16.8	83	32.5	66.3	7.2
Colerain town	204	193	-5.4	188	97.3	2.1	0.0	0.0	0.5	13.8	61.3	25.0	95	72.6	29.5	23.2
Columbia town	878	843	-4.0	850	39.1	27.1	1.6	1.8	30.5	25.0	55.8	19.2	348	56.6	69.8	8.6
Columbus town	999	992	-0.7	1,506	77.4	3.9	0.0	0.3	18.4	19.0	62.8	18.3	642	50.3	41.0	18.7

1 May be of any race.

Table A. All Places — **Population and Housing**

STATE City, town, township, borough, or CDP (county if applicable)	Population				Race and Hispanic or Latino origin (percent), 2010–2014					Age (percent), 2010–2014			Households, 2010–2014			
															Householders by level of education (percent)	
	2010 census total population	2014 estimated population	Percent change 2010–2014	ACS total population estimate 2010–2014	White alone, not Hispanic or Latino	Black alone, not Hispanic or Latino	Asian alone, not Hispanic or Latino	All other races or 2 or more races, not Hispanic or Latino	Hispanic or Latino[1]	Under 18 years old	Age 18 to 64 years old	Age 65 years and older	Total occupied housing units	Percent owner occupied	High school diploma or less	Bachelor's degree or more
	1	2	3	4	5	6	7	8	9	10	11	12	13	14	15	16
NORTH CAROLINA—Con.																
Como town	91	90	-1.1	75	68.0	32.0	0.0	0.0	0.0	18.6	73.3	8.0	25	88.0	32.0	8.0
Concord city	79,195	85,560	8.0	82,266	63.9	18.5	3.5	1.7	12.4	27.7	61.7	10.8	29,228	67.3	32.3	32.6
Conetoe town	294	284	-3.4	416	36.1	62.0	0.0	1.2	0.7	23.3	63.6	13.2	162	69.8	37.0	3.1
Connelly Springs town	1,666	1,635	-1.9	1,643	82.8	0.3	13.9	0.2	2.8	26.8	59.8	13.4	533	72.0	57.2	9.9
Conover city	8,183	8,215	0.4	8,200	68.5	8.4	2.0	3.5	17.6	25.3	57.2	17.4	3,232	64.1	40.2	27.8
Conway town	836	778	-6.9	799	55.1	41.9	0.0	2.0	1.0	32.6	51.4	16.1	311	65.0	55.3	16.1
Cooleemee town	963	965	0.2	750	76.7	15.2	0.0	1.9	6.3	21.7	57.0	21.3	309	78.6	66.3	10.0
Cordova CDP	1,775	NA	NA	1,748	80.1	19.9	0.0	0.0	0.0	19.0	66.8	14.2	791	60.9	53.7	16.1
Cornelius town	24,894	27,481	10.4	26,246	84.0	4.8	2.8	1.3	7.2	25.1	63.8	11.2	10,735	66.1	17.9	54.7
Cove City town	399	401	0.5	437	38.7	59.7	0.0	1.1	0.5	18.8	63.3	17.8	163	73.0	45.4	6.7
Cove Creek CDP	1,171	NA	NA	1,018	95.2	0.0	0.4	2.8	1.6	16.4	61.1	22.6	428	75.9	46.0	31.8
Cramerton town	4,165	4,279	2.7	4,212	88.6	4.7	2.8	2.4	1.5	20.3	67.2	12.6	1,688	73.2	25.1	37.1
Creedmoor city	4,107	4,373	6.5	4,228	59.3	32.3	0.0	5.7	2.8	27.4	62.5	10.2	1,402	68.6	30.7	25.7
Creswell town	276	265	-4.0	370	49.2	45.7	0.0	0.0	5.1	29.0	52.8	18.1	134	56.0	50.0	18.7
Cricket CDP	1,855	NA	NA	1,813	80.7	1.0	0.0	3.9	14.5	22.1	57.2	20.8	790	75.9	55.1	15.6
Crossnore town	192	202	5.2	278	81.3	5.0	0.0	11.9	1.8	33.8	58.4	7.9	113	45.1	41.6	30.1
Cullowhee CDP	6,228	NA	NA	5,531	78.6	7.3	1.1	2.5	10.5	6.9	90.7	2.4	1,252	18.2	22.0	22.6
Dallas town	4,453	4,570	2.6	4,508	68.3	25.7	0.5	1.6	3.9	20.8	65.2	14.1	1,881	54.7	37.8	18.5
Dana CDP	3,329	NA	NA	2,466	86.3	0.0	4.5	0.0	9.2	20.0	66.4	13.6	1,098	84.2	33.6	25.7
Danbury town	189	187	-1.1	190	75.3	17.9	2.6	0.0	4.2	6.4	75.9	17.9	52	63.5	51.9	38.5
Davidson town	10,933	11,981	9.6	11,492	79.6	10.5	2.0	2.1	5.8	22.9	66.8	10.2	3,975	75.8	10.4	67.2
Davis CDP	422	NA	NA	378	100.0	0.0	0.0	0.0	0.0	15.1	44.2	40.7	143	100.0	62.9	28.7
Deercroft CDP	411	NA	NA	337	96.7	0.0	0.0	0.0	3.3	11.3	59.5	29.1	191	84.3	20.4	56.0
Delco CDP	348	NA	NA	266	98.5	0.0	0.0	1.5	0.0	4.1	50.8	45.1	125	100.0	32.8	28.8
Dellview town	13	NA	NA	5	100.0	0.0	0.0	0.0	0.0	0.0	100.0	0.0	5	100.0	0.0	0.0
Delway CDP	203	NA	NA	85	100.0	0.0	0.0	0.0	0.0	0.0	20.0	80.0	60	75.0	100.0	0.0
Denton town	1,638	1,651	0.8	1,682	98.2	0.2	0.0	1.1	0.5	20.3	62.3	17.5	705	57.9	61.4	6.2
Denver CDP	2,309	NA	NA	1,837	99.2	0.0	0.0	0.0	0.8	20.6	60.8	18.6	869	63.5	43.5	27.2
Dillsboro town	232	237	2.2	319	93.7	1.9	0.0	1.6	2.8	8.1	72.4	19.4	146	63.0	17.8	37.0
Dobbins Heights town	860	845	-1.7	786	15.9	79.6	0.0	0.4	4.1	22.5	60.5	17.0	363	48.5	59.2	8.3
Dobson town	1,586	1,577	-0.6	1,550	69.9	4.6	0.0	1.0	24.5	20.6	65.4	14.1	554	46.6	55.1	20.8
Dortches town	937	932	-0.5	1,096	69.6	22.5	0.4	2.3	5.2	25.0	58.9	16.3	384	78.1	46.1	25.3
Dover town	401	403	0.5	426	36.4	63.1	0.0	0.0	0.5	22.5	59.2	18.3	195	65.6	56.4	3.6
Drexel town	1,878	1,866	-0.6	1,662	87.3	3.1	5.7	0.9	3.1	20.0	59.0	20.9	670	66.6	34.5	24.3
Dublin town	338	335	-0.9	315	60.3	24.1	0.0	1.0	14.6	33.7	52.8	13.7	116	53.4	31.9	22.4
Duck town	369	378	2.4	497	98.4	0.4	0.0	0.0	1.2	5.8	51.4	42.7	250	81.6	15.6	58.8
Dundarrach CDP	41	NA	NA	68	55.9	0.0	0.0	44.1	0.0	0.0	99.9	0.0	39	23.1	76.9	0.0
Dunn city	9,266	9,710	4.8	9,570	47.2	39.7	0.3	3.3	9.6	21.8	59.0	19.3	3,843	54.3	48.9	18.4
Durham city	228,404	251,893	10.3	240,107	38.3	39.9	4.7	3.2	13.9	22.6	68.0	9.5	98,318	49.9	24.5	50.3
Earl town	260	258	-0.8	326	92.0	6.4	0.0	1.5	0.0	32.8	62.8	4.3	97	80.4	42.3	16.5
East Arcadia town	492	480	-2.4	483	1.9	87.6	2.9	7.7	0.0	34.6	55.6	9.7	159	69.8	56.0	7.5
East Bend town	612	602	-1.6	511	74.6	1.6	0.0	0.0	23.9	18.0	57.8	24.3	242	72.7	62.8	11.6
East Flat Rock CDP	4,995	NA	NA	3,917	67.2	3.3	0.3	2.3	26.9	24.0	63.8	12.4	1,707	65.3	59.5	12.6
East Laurinburg town	300	290	-3.3	320	60.6	12.8	0.0	25.9	0.6	17.2	64.2	18.8	110	70.0	66.4	0.9
Eastover town	3,628	3,687	1.6	3,679	80.0	14.9	1.7	3.3	0.0	23.3	57.2	19.4	1,483	71.3	43.3	16.5
East Rockingham CDP	3,736	NA	NA	4,069	53.5	15.7	0.0	7.5	23.3	26.9	61.3	11.8	1,613	49.0	57.2	15.8
East Spencer town	1,537	1,545	0.5	1,520	8.2	84.7	0.0	0.3	6.8	33.3	55.1	11.7	571	40.8	59.7	7.0
Eden city	15,704	15,407	-1.9	15,543	65.5	24.7	0.9	3.9	5.0	23.2	57.9	18.7	6,471	56.9	52.5	13.7
Edenton town	5,004	4,915	-1.8	4,979	45.3	54.3	0.0	0.3	0.1	27.0	51.0	21.9	2,009	41.9	44.0	22.2
Edneyville CDP	2,367	NA	NA	2,255	68.3	2.7	0.0	2.7	26.3	28.7	62.9	8.4	721	53.1	44.1	22.5
Efland CDP	734	NA	NA	815	73.6	23.2	0.0	1.5	1.7	22.2	60.3	17.5	333	93.4	44.7	30.3
Elizabeth City city	18,635	18,047	-3.2	18,343	36.7	55.3	0.7	1.2	6.1	21.6	64.4	13.9	6,691	43.3	40.7	20.9
Elizabethtown town	3,634	3,608	-0.7	3,611	41.2	48.9	0.0	4.9	5.1	23.7	57.2	19.0	1,585	50.1	48.1	16.7
Elkin town	4,023	4,001	-0.5	4,198	62.8	6.1	0.3	2.3	28.5	25.6	54.3	20.2	1,564	54.3	46.0	20.7
Elk Park town	452	445	-1.5	337	90.2	0.0	0.0	5.3	4.5	17.8	60.5	21.7	170	61.8	60.6	5.3
Ellenboro town	873	858	-1.7	1,321	84.3	12.3	0.0	3.5	0.0	39.4	52.2	8.3	392	48.0	55.1	9.7
Ellerbe town	1,027	1,012	-1.5	1,554	36.3	42.3	0.0	3.1	18.3	36.7	54.0	9.2	518	59.1	54.2	7.9
Elm City town	1,298	1,345	3.6	1,766	34.1	52.2	0.5	6.2	7.1	25.0	63.1	11.9	633	60.2	55.6	11.4
Elon town	9,407	9,630	2.4	9,516	81.4	12.2	2.5	1.9	1.9	11.5	70.6	18.0	2,889	48.3	20.6	36.4
Elrod CDP	417	NA	NA	508	16.5	2.0	0.0	81.5	0.0	29.3	64.4	6.3	145	62.1	74.5	0.0
Elroy CDP	3,869	NA	NA	3,698	54.2	26.6	2.1	4.7	12.5	17.8	66.8	15.3	1,712	69.2	54.8	7.2
Emerald Isle town	3,655	3,717	1.7	3,689	94.9	0.1	0.1	0.6	4.2	17.4	56.8	25.8	1,786	67.9	25.1	48.7
Enfield town	2,532	2,448	-3.3	2,282	7.6	91.2	0.0	1.2	0.0	21.2	62.0	16.8	873	43.1	71.0	9.2
Engelhard CDP	445	NA	NA	545	58.7	41.3	0.0	0.0	0.0	9.5	80.8	9.7	253	82.6	41.9	21.7
Enochville CDP	2,925	NA	NA	2,664	95.7	0.0	0.0	0.0	4.3	17.6	63.3	19.2	1,122	85.0	51.1	13.5
Erwin town	4,405	4,614	4.7	4,551	71.8	17.8	0.1	1.8	8.5	25.1	58.2	16.6	1,783	67.9	53.2	18.8
Etowah CDP	6,944	NA	NA	6,862	95.1	0.8	1.3	0.9	1.8	17.7	55.4	27.0	3,060	89.5	32.6	28.4
Eureka town	197	200	1.5	178	82.6	14.0	0.0	2.2	1.1	13.4	60.0	26.4	88	80.7	51.1	12.5
Everetts town	164	159	-3.0	133	51.9	48.1	0.0	0.0	0.0	12.8	70.7	16.5	58	62.1	58.6	5.2
Evergreen CDP	420	NA	NA	351	88.6	11.4	0.0	0.0	0.0	14.6	73.6	12.0	155	63.9	51.6	10.3
Fair Bluff town	948	920	-3.0	1,029	32.3	66.3	0.0	1.5	0.0	19.8	54.4	25.8	457	52.5	62.1	10.7
Fairfield CDP	258	NA	NA	363	68.6	31.4	0.0	0.0	0.0	3.0	32.2	64.7	149	75.8	65.1	0.0
Fairfield Harbour CDP	2,952	NA	NA	2,969	96.9	1.2	0.0	0.0	1.9	10.0	42.5	47.7	1,458	87.2	19.8	48.8
Fairmont town	2,663	2,700	1.4	2,699	25.4	58.0	0.0	8.6	7.9	24.3	57.0	18.8	1,084	50.3	60.1	16.8
Fairplains CDP	2,120	NA	NA	2,229	79.3	11.3	0.0	1.1	8.3	23.7	62.0	14.2	871	62.0	59.7	8.5
Fairview CDP	2,678	NA	NA	2,882	83.8	3.3	0.0	2.7	10.2	25.3	60.1	14.5	1,096	75.5	37.0	36.2
Fairview town	3,340	3,612	8.1	3,480	96.7	1.4	0.3	1.6	0.0	24.4	65.4	10.1	1,201	78.6	49.8	21.1
Faison town	961	992	3.2	1,184	50.8	14.2	0.0	0.7	34.4	21.6	62.7	15.7	431	56.6	47.1	10.4
Faith town	804	808	0.5	911	94.8	5.2	0.0	0.0	0.0	25.6	50.6	23.7	337	84.0	47.2	27.0
Falcon town	265	269	1.5	274	85.0	3.6	9.5	0.0	1.8	28.5	57.3	14.2	81	85.2	29.6	18.5
Falkland town	96	98	2.1	43	53.5	46.5	0.0	0.0	0.0	27.9	65.3	7.0	14	50.0	71.4	28.6
Fallston town	607	602	-0.8	653	87.3	12.6	0.0	0.2	0.0	22.5	63.1	14.4	232	80.6	51.7	18.5
Farmville town	4,654	4,771	2.5	4,716	51.5	42.0	0.0	2.6	4.0	24.7	55.8	19.4	1,984	50.6	45.2	14.6
Fayetteville city	200,582	203,948	1.7	202,421	40.7	40.1	2.9	5.4	10.9	24.8	64.8	10.5	77,935	48.6	30.4	25.9
Fearrington Village CDP	2,339	NA	NA	2,772	95.7	2.9	1.4	0.0	0.0	2.8	25.3	71.9	1,656	74.8	11.7	74.4
Five Points CDP	689	NA	NA	1,090	45.1	19.4	0.0	3.0	32.4	26.9	57.2	15.9	322	81.7	33.5	30.4
Flat Rock village	3,113	3,264	4.9	3,181	96.1	0.8	0.5	0.5	2.0	8.4	46.2	45.4	1,515	89.4	12.1	68.1
Flat Rock CDP	1,556	NA	NA	1,424	84.8	4.6	4.6	5.1	0.8	13.2	72.1	14.8	688	66.7	58.4	5.4
Fletcher town	7,192	7,487	4.1	7,320	90.3	2.1	4.0	1.7	1.9	21.3	61.6	17.0	3,170	81.2	28.5	34.5
Fontana Dam town	7	7	0.0	0	0.0	0.0	0.0	0.0	0.0	0.0	0.0	0.0	0	0.0	0.0	0.0
Forest City town	7,476	7,324	-2.0	7,387	59.5	28.2	0.1	1.3	10.9	29.0	54.2	16.9	2,998	41.8	51.9	13.6

1 May be of any race.

Table A. All Places — **Population and Housing**

STATE City, town, township, borough, or CDP (county if applicable)	Population				Race and Hispanic or Latino origin (percent), 2010–2014					Age (percent), 2010–2014			Households, 2010–2014			
															Householders by level of education (percent)	
	2010 census total population	2014 estimated population	Percent change 2010–2014	ACS total population estimate 2010–2014	White alone, not Hispanic or Latino	Black alone, not Hispanic or Latino	Asian alone, not Hispanic or Latino	All other races or 2 or more races, not Hispanic or Latino	Hispanic or Latino[1]	Under 18 years old	Age 18 to 64 years old	Age 65 years and older	Total occupied housing units	Percent owner occupied	High school diploma or less	Bachelor's degree or more
	1	2	3	4	5	6	7	8	9	10	11	12	13	14	15	16
NORTH CAROLINA—Con.																
Forest Hills village	365	369	1.1	454	97.8	0.0	2.2	0.0	0.0	11.4	76.7	11.9	183	47.5	0.5	51.9
Forest Oaks CDP	3,890	NA	NA	3,378	81.9	7.8	1.4	5.9	3.0	16.5	63.2	20.3	1,327	98.7	22.2	45.9
Foscoe CDP	1,370	NA	NA	1,153	88.6	0.7	2.7	3.3	4.7	14.4	65.9	19.7	578	64.2	16.4	54.7
Fountain town	427	437	2.3	459	63.2	32.7	0.0	3.5	0.7	25.9	51.1	22.9	193	51.3	57.0	7.3
Four Oaks town	1,923	2,030	5.6	2,068	51.0	18.4	2.8	0.5	27.3	27.8	61.0	11.1	776	52.1	53.5	17.9
Foxfire village	910	960	5.5	1,130	92.2	5.8	0.3	0.0	1.7	20.0	48.5	31.5	486	76.3	19.8	40.3
Franklin town	3,902	3,900	-0.1	3,893	76.2	0.1	0.7	1.6	21.4	15.9	56.1	28.0	1,891	57.3	44.3	26.0
Franklinton town	2,021	2,105	4.2	1,823	55.9	38.0	0.0	0.8	5.3	24.1	54.6	21.4	764	64.4	52.9	15.7
Franklinville town	1,168	1,160	-0.7	987	61.6	10.5	0.0	1.4	26.4	27.8	62.1	10.2	373	61.7	61.4	8.8
Fremont town	1,255	1,280	2.0	1,271	46.4	44.1	0.3	4.9	4.3	24.8	47.5	27.6	535	58.3	52.0	11.6
Frisco CDP	200	NA	NA	116	100.0	0.0	0.0	0.0	0.0	0.0	49.2	50.9	79	100.0	17.7	11.4
Fruitland CDP	2,031	NA	NA	2,443	77.1	2.7	0.3	1.5	18.5	15.6	60.5	23.8	1,144	67.9	50.4	15.7
Fuquay-Varina town	17,985	22,644	25.9	20,246	65.4	19.8	2.0	2.0	10.8	27.7	61.9	10.6	7,357	72.0	26.0	36.6
Gamewell town	4,053	3,969	-2.1	3,996	94.0	3.2	0.8	2.0	0.0	17.5	64.2	18.4	1,792	64.9	66.5	10.9
Garland town	625	635	1.6	699	53.1	41.2	2.3	0.0	3.4	23.7	52.1	24.2	254	59.1	61.0	12.6
Garner town	25,758	27,814	8.0	26,723	51.5	37.4	1.6	1.9	7.5	23.8	63.6	12.5	10,322	64.2	27.4	36.3
Garysburg town	1,057	984	-6.9	1,101	1.2	96.7	0.4	1.3	0.5	24.7	61.9	13.3	469	51.8	53.5	6.8
Gaston town	1,155	1,076	-6.8	962	61.9	31.5	0.0	1.1	5.5	19.4	66.1	14.6	398	53.0	66.8	8.5
Gastonia city	71,741	73,698	2.7	72,664	58.0	26.7	1.6	3.0	10.7	26.5	60.5	13.0	26,895	55.4	41.8	22.8
Gatesville town	321	305	-5.0	562	88.3	8.0	0.9	2.7	0.2	25.6	59.1	15.3	180	70.0	23.9	35.6
Germanton CDP	827	NA	NA	872	83.8	12.4	0.0	3.8	0.0	14.1	67.9	18.0	370	73.0	68.1	7.0
Gerton CDP	254	NA	NA	268	100.0	0.0	0.0	0.0	0.0	20.5	57.0	22.4	107	89.7	18.7	41.1
Gibson town	540	522	-3.3	544	32.9	46.5	0.0	20.2	0.4	34.7	51.9	13.4	203	37.9	62.1	5.9
Gibsonville town	6,421	6,697	4.3	6,565	76.7	11.9	0.7	4.3	6.4	25.7	64.5	9.8	2,525	75.6	32.3	34.6
Glen Alpine town	1,517	1,499	-1.2	1,511	77.6	9.3	9.0	2.4	1.7	21.7	62.4	15.9	621	80.4	35.7	21.6
Glen Raven CDP	2,750	NA	NA	2,621	80.4	2.4	0.0	5.0	12.2	23.8	63.7	12.4	978	72.1	45.5	37.8
Glenville CDP	110	NA	NA	60	100.0	0.0	0.0	0.0	0.0	0.0	90.0	10.0	45	80.0	26.7	0.0
Gloucester CDP	537	NA	NA	514	92.2	0.0	0.0	7.8	0.0	21.5	56.4	22.2	217	83.9	42.4	22.6
Godwin town	139	144	3.6	123	58.5	31.7	1.6	6.5	1.6	28.4	50.6	21.1	45	71.1	33.3	26.7
Goldsboro city	35,524	35,947	1.2	35,908	36.1	54.6	1.3	3.0	5.0	24.7	60.5	15.0	14,095	38.0	40.0	20.5
Goldston town	268	290	8.2	242	88.0	4.1	0.8	6.2	0.8	15.7	54.9	29.3	108	79.6	42.6	15.7
Gorman CDP	1,011	NA	NA	1,115	53.5	5.8	3.9	0.0	36.8	17.5	69.9	12.6	394	86.5	68.5	7.6
Graham city	14,305	14,479	1.2	14,384	58.3	17.9	0.4	3.9	19.5	28.5	56.4	15.1	5,796	55.2	48.3	17.8
Grandfather village	25	25	0.0	70	100.0	0.0	0.0	0.0	0.0	2.9	37.2	60.0	41	100.0	2.4	95.1
Granite Falls town	4,720	4,673	-1.0	4,694	92.2	0.8	1.2	1.6	4.3	23.5	61.0	15.4	1,735	63.2	38.7	18.3
Granite Quarry town	2,962	2,984	0.7	2,971	87.8	4.6	0.7	3.2	3.6	31.4	55.4	13.3	1,107	70.0	35.0	27.3
Grantsboro town	688	673	-2.2	804	73.5	12.1	0.7	11.8	1.9	23.7	59.4	17.0	305	72.8	50.8	8.5
Greenevers town	634	656	3.5	813	9.0	74.8	0.0	0.5	15.7	35.7	50.7	13.7	263	56.7	55.5	12.9
Green Level town	2,100	2,135	1.7	2,078	8.8	57.8	0.0	2.7	30.7	29.5	60.7	9.6	757	64.5	63.5	6.1
Greensboro city	268,877	282,586	5.1	276,225	45.4	40.2	3.9	3.0	7.4	22.1	65.5	12.2	113,232	51.8	29.3	38.9
Greenville city	84,573	89,852	6.2	87,546	54.0	36.6	2.8	2.4	4.3	18.3	73.4	8.2	34,741	37.1	23.8	36.5
Grifton town	2,615	2,679	2.4	2,608	56.3	41.4	0.0	0.2	2.1	29.6	49.2	21.3	1,014	52.2	38.9	21.7
Grimesland town	436	446	2.3	453	51.4	42.8	0.7	0.0	5.1	20.5	63.1	16.3	188	56.4	59.0	5.3
Grover town	708	703	-0.7	1,092	61.0	22.4	4.9	0.5	11.3	31.6	56.5	11.8	347	56.2	54.8	14.4
Gulf CDP	144	NA	NA	283	100.0	0.0	0.0	0.0	0.0	0.0	94.0	6.0	120	100.0	73.3	0.0
Half Moon CDP	8,352	NA	NA	8,655	61.8	25.5	0.8	4.5	7.4	27.7	66.8	5.3	2,859	63.3	42.0	17.2
Halifax town	233	227	-2.6	279	73.1	15.1	0.0	9.7	2.2	15.8	68.4	15.8	113	69.0	36.3	39.8
Hallsboro CDP	465	NA	NA	446	43.7	56.3	0.0	0.0	0.0	16.4	65.7	17.9	216	73.6	54.6	8.8
Hamilton town	404	386	-4.5	337	42.4	50.1	0.0	0.0	7.4	19.6	46.5	34.1	143	74.8	64.3	5.6
Hamlet city	6,574	6,513	-0.9	6,566	53.3	34.4	0.0	8.1	4.2	30.0	56.2	13.8	2,334	56.6	45.7	12.0
Hampstead CDP	4,083	NA	NA	4,247	95.3	2.4	0.0	1.5	0.8	29.3	56.7	14.0	1,628	85.0	45.9	35.3
Harkers Island CDP	1,207	NA	NA	1,671	98.8	0.0	0.2	0.5	0.4	16.2	64.2	19.6	597	86.1	54.3	6.9
Harmony town	531	552	4.0	564	93.1	5.3	0.0	0.0	1.6	18.7	63.8	17.4	225	67.6	60.0	13.3
Harrells town	202	206	2.0	156	58.3	37.8	0.0	0.6	3.2	13.4	47.4	39.1	71	85.9	53.5	19.7
Harrellsville town	107	106	-0.9	107	72.9	24.3	0.0	2.8	0.0	27.1	60.8	12.1	39	71.8	53.8	10.3
Harrisburg town	13,044	14,132	8.3	13,549	73.1	16.5	4.6	1.7	4.1	33.2	57.6	9.3	4,333	88.5	20.9	46.9
Hassell town	84	82	-2.4	34	64.7	35.3	0.0	0.0	0.0	8.8	47.1	44.1	18	83.3	44.4	0.0
Hatteras CDP	504	NA	NA	388	99.5	0.0	0.3	0.0	0.3	12.4	62.3	25.3	181	84.5	53.6	26.0
Havelock city	20,735	20,706	-0.1	20,850	61.6	15.0	2.3	7.2	13.9	28.0	67.4	4.6	6,564	41.0	36.0	11.1
Haw River town	2,313	2,373	2.6	2,380	65.3	12.9	0.0	2.4	19.4	25.9	60.1	14.0	941	66.0	52.7	9.4
Hayesville town	343	348	1.5	393	95.7	3.3	0.0	1.0	0.0	9.1	47.1	43.8	188	60.6	46.3	24.5
Hays CDP	1,851	NA	NA	1,866	93.9	0.0	0.0	0.0	6.1	31.6	55.4	13.0	710	80.0	61.5	10.6
Hemby Bridge town	1,520	1,645	8.2	1,341	95.8	1.3	0.6	0.7	1.5	19.3	67.3	13.3	510	83.5	52.9	14.5
Henderson city	15,415	15,265	-1.0	15,325	26.5	60.3	0.4	1.8	11.0	28.5	55.9	15.5	5,604	44.3	60.7	13.9
Hendersonville city	13,109	13,650	4.1	13,350	73.0	11.4	0.1	2.3	13.2	21.5	50.6	28.1	5,920	46.6	32.2	32.8
Henrietta CDP	461	NA	NA	509	100.0	0.0	0.0	0.0	0.0	18.0	73.6	8.3	183	56.8	69.9	0.0
Hertford town	2,143	2,140	-0.1	2,353	46.5	46.4	0.0	2.8	4.3	25.6	56.7	17.6	944	52.3	52.4	20.0
Hickory city	40,065	40,143	0.2	40,108	69.3	13.8	3.2	1.9	11.9	23.1	61.5	15.6	15,991	53.5	35.9	34.0
Hiddenite CDP	536	NA	NA	785	88.3	0.0	0.0	0.0	11.7	12.5	73.0	14.5	363	95.9	45.7	27.8
Highlands town	924	926	0.2	1,082	92.1	2.3	4.2	1.1	0.3	13.6	44.5	42.0	555	75.1	16.0	53.3
High Point city	104,387	108,629	4.1	106,797	48.1	33.4	7.5	2.4	8.6	25.0	62.8	12.0	40,988	56.5	35.6	31.7
High Shoals city	696	713	2.4	559	81.9	7.0	0.0	1.1	10.0	22.2	65.9	12.0	222	74.8	62.6	4.5
Hightsville CDP	739	NA	NA	700	54.6	43.7	0.0	0.0	1.7	0.0	89.2	10.7	120	100.0	63.3	16.7
Hildebran town	2,023	2,000	-1.1	2,006	90.1	4.1	0.5	3.1	2.1	21.8	61.2	16.9	764	61.4	50.0	15.7
Hillsborough town	6,095	6,388	4.8	6,256	56.9	33.6	1.6	4.2	3.7	28.2	59.6	12.5	2,274	59.6	32.0	40.7
Hobgood town	348	338	-2.9	416	60.3	37.0	0.5	0.7	1.4	10.2	59.9	29.8	177	67.8	61.0	16.9
Hobucken CDP	129	NA	NA	113	100.0	0.0	0.0	0.0	0.0	30.9	51.3	17.7	44	54.5	79.5	0.0
Hoffman town	590	578	-2.0	548	28.5	60.9	0.0	9.9	0.7	17.1	60.9	21.9	215	73.0	73.0	2.8
Holden Beach town	575	619	7.7	880	95.3	3.1	0.3	0.0	1.3	10.7	49.8	39.7	433	92.6	13.6	60.7
Hollister CDP	674	NA	NA	1,166	4.2	14.7	0.7	72.4	8.1	33.7	60.0	6.2	314	63.7	57.0	7.0
Holly Ridge town	1,278	1,944	52.1	1,553	89.5	6.6	0.0	1.9	1.9	16.2	71.6	12.2	645	62.5	34.4	29.3
Holly Springs town	24,676	30,157	22.2	27,339	75.8	13.6	3.9	2.8	3.8	33.8	59.4	6.9	9,040	86.6	16.9	56.4
Hookerton town	408	403	-1.2	391	67.5	27.4	0.0	0.0	5.1	17.9	49.6	32.5	194	60.3	60.8	4.1
Hoopers Creek CDP	1,056	NA	NA	1,197	98.2	1.3	0.4	0.0	0.0	26.0	55.9	18.1	487	71.9	26.5	20.3
Hope Mills town	15,540	16,301	4.9	16,024	52.5	28.7	1.8	6.9	10.2	32.0	59.5	8.5	5,756	56.9	34.8	23.3
Horse Shoe CDP	2,351	NA	NA	2,832	97.2	2.2	0.0	0.2	0.4	22.8	58.1	19.2	1,058	89.2	30.7	32.6
Hot Springs town	560	563	0.5	686	94.0	0.1	0.0	0.7	5.1	16.4	59.2	24.5	335	49.9	66.9	12.2
Hudson town	3,776	3,727	-1.3	3,744	97.9	0.2	0.0	0.8	1.1	26.3	54.8	18.9	1,359	79.0	41.4	20.1
Huntersville town	46,774	51,567	10.2	49,279	81.1	9.2	1.8	2.8	5.1	27.8	64.4	7.8	18,181	74.4	15.2	58.4
Icard CDP	2,664	NA	NA	3,194	89.6	0.5	0.0	1.6	8.4	16.4	67.5	16.1	1,211	71.8	46.4	7.5
Indian Beach town	114	116	1.8	222	97.7	1.8	0.0	0.0	0.5	9.5	50.5	40.1	104	90.4	22.1	60.6

1 May be of any race.

Table A. All Places — **Population and Housing**

STATE City, town, township, borough, or CDP (county if applicable)	Population				Race and Hispanic or Latino origin (percent), 2010–2014					Age (percent), 2010–2014			Households, 2010–2014			
	2010 census total population	2014 estimated population	Percent change 2010–2014	ACS total population estimate 2010–2014	White alone, not Hispanic or Latino	Black alone, not Hispanic or Latino	Asian alone, not Hispanic or Latino	All other races or 2 or more races, not Hispanic or Latino	Hispanic or Latino[1]	Under 18 years old	Age 18 to 64 years old	Age 65 years and older	Total occupied housing units	Percent owner occupied	Householders by level of education (percent): High school diploma or less	Householders by level of education (percent): Bachelor's degree or more
	1	2	3	4	5	6	7	8	9	10	11	12	13	14	15	16
NORTH CAROLINA—Con.																
Indian Trail town	33,608	36,360	8.2	34,950	73.0	14.0	1.8	1.4	9.8	31.7	60.2	8.0	11,209	83.7	26.8	38.9
Ingold CDP	471	NA	NA	557	18.5	17.4	0.0	0.0	64.1	40.3	48.7	11.1	193	68.9	65.3	26.9
Iron Station CDP	755	NA	NA	737	77.3	19.1	0.0	3.5	0.0	16.0	52.1	31.9	339	87.3	50.7	12.4
Ivanhoe CDP	264	NA	NA	264	67.8	26.9	0.0	5.3	0.0	17.0	76.8	6.1	87	70.1	19.5	31.0
JAARS CDP	597	NA	NA	430	100.0	0.0	0.0	0.0	0.0	21.9	52.8	25.3	163	39.9	16.0	61.3
Jackson town	513	483	-5.8	583	60.0	38.6	0.0	1.4	0.0	6.2	64.8	29.0	259	90.7	40.2	18.9
Jackson Heights CDP	1,141	NA	NA	837	90.9	7.5	0.0	1.6	0.0	19.4	47.7	33.0	346	88.2	59.0	0.0
Jacksonville city	70,145	69,047	-1.6	69,300	56.6	21.6	2.9	4.3	14.7	24.6	69.2	6.4	21,112	35.0	33.7	20.8
James City CDP	5,899	NA	NA	5,635	74.1	16.4	0.0	2.3	7.2	17.7	64.6	17.6	2,300	74.4	38.1	21.3
Jamestown town	3,384	3,663	8.2	3,549	75.1	13.0	1.5	2.4	7.9	21.4	57.6	21.2	1,324	80.2	23.7	50.1
Jamesville town	491	470	-4.3	535	53.8	18.9	4.9	1.3	21.1	21.2	55.5	23.4	202	63.4	58.4	5.9
Jefferson town	1,611	1,600	-0.7	1,493	85.9	5.9	1.0	1.9	5.3	20.4	47.6	32.1	539	54.2	45.8	19.1
Jonesville town	2,285	2,266	-0.8	2,405	74.5	8.0	0.0	3.6	13.9	24.7	62.1	13.2	1,000	49.2	62.5	8.0
Kannapolis city	42,615	45,245	6.2	43,865	65.0	20.2	1.4	1.9	11.5	25.7	62.0	12.2	16,020	58.5	44.3	18.3
Keener CDP	567	NA	NA	897	41.7	25.5	0.0	0.0	32.8	41.5	46.5	12.0	244	52.0	73.0	0.0
Kelford town	251	238	-5.2	184	28.8	70.1	1.1	0.0	0.0	26.1	45.8	28.3	86	59.3	72.1	5.8
Kelly CDP	544	NA	NA	631	62.0	38.0	0.0	0.0	0.0	23.5	55.7	20.9	311	79.7	31.5	0.0
Kenansville town	855	876	2.5	1,022	48.3	43.8	0.9	1.9	5.1	16.2	56.7	27.1	372	43.0	44.1	17.5
Kenly town	1,339	1,420	6.0	1,563	47.4	42.0	0.0	1.0	9.5	28.7	57.7	13.6	617	40.2	56.9	11.3
Kernersville town	23,121	23,739	2.7	23,522	74.6	12.5	4.0	1.5	7.4	23.6	62.3	14.2	9,892	55.5	36.1	32.1
Kill Devil Hills town	6,683	6,931	3.7	6,810	91.0	0.4	0.0	1.0	7.6	21.7	68.1	10.2	3,020	57.2	32.2	30.8
King city	6,901	6,887	-0.2	6,732	90.8	4.5	1.3	2.3	1.0	22.7	58.6	18.7	2,620	81.4	43.8	27.3
Kings Grant CDP	8,113	NA	NA	8,504	75.0	10.2	2.0	3.8	9.0	19.7	68.1	12.3	3,310	65.4	35.4	29.7
Kings Mountain city	10,595	10,644	0.5	10,743	73.5	19.2	0.4	4.2	2.7	25.4	59.2	15.5	4,144	54.0	51.8	12.6
Kingstown town	681	676	-0.7	726	7.4	88.6	0.0	4.0	0.0	18.9	66.9	14.2	283	74.6	70.0	9.9
Kinston city	21,677	21,392	-1.3	21,589	26.4	67.6	0.8	2.2	3.0	23.3	58.1	18.6	9,050	44.0	50.6	15.0
Kittrell town	467	471	0.9	239	47.3	36.8	0.0	15.9	0.0	34.7	49.7	15.5	78	74.4	56.4	6.4
Kitty Hawk town	3,272	3,395	3.8	3,338	98.0	0.0	0.7	0.7	0.6	18.1	66.2	15.7	1,557	72.2	26.1	28.6
Knightdale town	11,406	13,871	21.6	12,692	43.0	35.3	3.7	3.7	14.3	28.5	63.6	7.8	4,654	66.6	24.6	48.3
Kure Beach town	2,012	2,081	3.4	2,388	88.1	0.4	3.8	7.2	0.5	16.3	57.3	26.4	1,013	71.4	18.7	50.6
La Grange town	2,877	2,827	-1.7	2,856	46.6	52.7	0.0	0.0	0.8	19.4	53.9	26.6	1,525	61.4	52.5	15.5
Lake Junaluska CDP	2,734	NA	NA	2,472	99.6	0.0	0.0	0.0	0.4	13.4	55.0	31.8	1,175	68.9	22.4	54.6
Lake Lure town	1,195	1,186	-0.8	1,375	97.0	0.6	2.4	0.0	0.0	11.9	50.3	37.8	639	74.0	16.6	47.3
Lake Norman of Catawba CDP	7,411	NA	NA	7,331	97.1	1.4	0.0	0.5	1.0	21.2	59.4	19.4	2,991	84.3	33.1	35.6
Lake Park village	3,422	3,720	8.7	3,572	77.7	11.1	2.8	2.7	5.7	27.1	56.6	16.3	1,255	88.4	15.9	40.0
Lake Royale CDP	2,506	NA	NA	3,280	72.8	19.6	0.0	5.6	2.0	21.5	52.2	26.4	1,246	80.5	31.7	38.5
Lake Santeetlah town	45	44	-2.2	40	100.0	0.0	0.0	0.0	0.0	5.0	47.5	47.5	24	91.7	16.7	54.2
Lake Waccamaw town	1,471	1,472	0.1	1,390	86.5	6.7	0.0	5.6	1.2	20.4	45.2	34.5	508	73.0	25.4	42.5
Landis town	3,095	3,108	0.4	3,104	79.1	5.9	1.0	0.7	13.3	19.9	61.7	18.2	1,307	70.0	46.5	20.8
Lansing town	158	156	-1.3	197	95.9	3.0	0.0	0.0	1.0	28.5	58.4	13.2	70	64.3	55.7	14.3
Lasker town	122	115	-5.7	106	79.2	6.6	0.0	11.3	2.8	8.5	52.0	39.6	53	84.9	73.6	3.8
Lattimore town	488	486	-0.4	406	89.4	6.4	0.0	0.2	3.9	10.4	76.9	12.6	109	79.8	49.5	23.9
Laurel Hill CDP	1,254	NA	NA	974	56.9	29.3	0.0	10.3	3.6	17.5	69.3	13.3	389	82.3	72.8	13.4
Laurel Park town	2,178	2,278	4.6	2,696	95.8	0.6	1.2	0.9	1.5	16.1	42.5	41.4	1,188	80.4	13.0	57.3
Laurinburg city	15,962	15,593	-2.3	15,799	42.2	46.7	1.3	7.5	2.4	24.8	58.1	17.2	6,104	52.1	50.3	22.1
Lawndale town	606	595	-1.8	689	74.6	13.1	0.0	0.3	12.0	24.8	54.6	20.6	285	71.9	67.4	6.7
Leggett town	60	59	-1.7	50	38.0	62.0	0.0	0.0	0.0	24.0	60.0	16.0	14	64.3	42.9	0.0
Leland town	13,673	17,015	24.4	15,316	84.1	3.9	1.6	4.4	5.9	20.6	60.6	18.8	6,609	73.1	20.2	44.3
Lenoir city	18,234	17,920	-1.7	18,061	74.5	11.6	1.1	2.1	10.8	22.4	58.2	19.4	6,941	62.6	51.7	17.0
Lewiston Woodville town	549	514	-6.4	893	5.5	90.3	0.7	2.9	0.7	38.2	55.1	6.7	274	61.7	49.6	14.6
Lewisville town	12,710	13,342	5.0	13,037	87.8	7.3	1.1	1.2	2.5	23.4	61.4	15.1	5,001	89.6	26.0	39.9
Lexington city	18,931	19,257	1.7	19,029	49.1	28.0	4.6	3.4	14.9	26.4	59.0	14.4	7,359	42.1	59.2	15.1
Liberty town	2,656	2,680	0.9	2,666	69.9	13.7	0.0	3.0	13.4	25.4	59.9	14.7	1,041	69.3	45.1	19.3
Light Oak CDP	691	NA	NA	798	47.9	42.7	0.0	0.0	9.4	21.6	67.5	10.9	357	68.3	43.4	15.7
Lilesville town	536	514	-4.1	540	48.5	51.5	0.0	0.0	0.0	28.9	47.3	23.9	224	71.9	60.7	9.8
Lillington town	3,187	3,449	8.2	3,334	50.3	40.3	0.9	3.4	5.1	15.0	69.0	16.0	997	39.8	39.4	22.8
Lincolnton city	10,484	10,732	2.4	10,601	63.7	15.6	0.3	5.4	15.0	25.3	58.5	16.3	4,064	50.6	45.4	17.9
Linden town	130	134	3.1	156	91.0	4.5	0.0	3.2	1.3	26.9	44.2	28.8	58	65.5	60.3	6.9
Littleton town	672	652	-3.0	557	39.3	35.7	0.0	25.0	0.0	22.6	55.6	21.7	258	60.9	57.4	17.8
Locust city	2,930	2,955	0.9	2,997	87.5	3.2	1.1	3.0	5.1	23.8	59.4	16.7	1,202	85.1	45.6	15.6
Long View town	4,871	4,879	0.2	4,966	61.9	14.8	4.5	4.8	14.0	26.3	58.7	14.9	1,893	58.2	57.4	9.2
Louisburg town	3,400	3,547	4.3	3,474	42.7	47.9	1.9	0.5	7.1	22.2	56.7	21.2	1,104	56.3	46.8	25.5
Love Valley town	95	98	3.2	95	78.9	0.0	0.0	0.0	21.1	31.6	50.5	17.9	34	79.4	61.8	8.8
Lowell city	3,526	3,613	2.5	3,561	79.7	7.9	0.0	2.1	10.2	18.2	65.4	16.4	1,342	62.7	49.9	16.8
Lowesville CDP	2,945	NA	NA	3,159	93.9	1.9	1.0	3.0	0.2	22.5	60.3	17.3	1,168	75.9	26.2	33.4
Lowgap CDP	324	NA	NA	230	97.4	0.0	0.0	0.0	2.6	14.3	85.5	0.0	100	90.0	48.0	0.0
Lucama town	1,136	1,129	-0.6	1,019	48.6	27.8	0.0	1.0	22.7	23.7	66.6	9.7	399	52.4	58.4	2.3
Lumber Bridge town	92	93	1.1	89	59.6	21.3	0.0	14.6	4.5	9.0	81.9	9.0	45	86.7	46.7	11.1
Lumberton city	21,548	21,716	0.8	21,707	38.4	33.6	1.3	15.6	11.0	25.6	60.5	14.1	7,403	49.8	45.3	21.4
McAdenville town	651	667	2.5	617	98.7	0.8	0.0	0.0	0.5	19.0	60.9	19.9	266	78.9	41.0	36.8
Macclesfield town	471	457	-3.0	443	70.0	28.2	1.1	0.7	0.0	12.2	59.8	28.0	227	63.4	61.7	17.6
McDonald town	113	114	0.9	111	33.3	27.9	0.0	38.7	0.0	14.4	70.2	15.3	44	56.8	54.5	11.4
McFarlan town	117	113	-3.4	173	74.0	2.3	0.0	0.0	23.7	17.9	65.9	16.2	60	81.7	75.0	13.3
McLeansville CDP	1,021	NA	NA	934	99.5	0.5	0.0	0.0	0.0	17.3	67.9	14.8	401	80.5	44.6	20.4
Macon town	119	116	-2.5	118	83.9	16.1	0.0	0.0	0.0	3.4	71.1	25.4	53	79.2	52.8	24.5
Madison town	2,246	2,194	-2.3	2,240	61.2	37.0	0.4	1.0	0.5	17.5	58.5	24.1	941	66.1	53.9	17.0
Maggie Valley town	1,149	1,247	8.5	1,411	90.9	1.1	3.8	1.4	2.8	16.5	54.7	28.8	650	78.9	30.5	32.2
Magnolia town	935	959	2.6	1,301	15.6	45.2	0.5	2.6	36.0	31.7	52.5	15.8	442	58.4	49.5	7.0
Maiden town	3,320	3,354	1.0	3,339	81.5	8.7	3.8	2.0	4.0	29.7	56.6	13.7	1,127	79.5	48.3	5.1
Mamers CDP	826	NA	NA	1,135	77.9	19.6	0.0	2.5	0.0	35.1	51.3	13.7	341	63.3	28.7	19.9
Manns Harbor CDP	821	NA	NA	1,212	67.6	0.4	0.0	12.9	19.1	30.2	61.2	8.6	438	54.3	63.7	11.6
Manteo town	1,321	1,366	3.4	1,472	79.6	7.3	0.4	2.0	10.7	18.5	62.0	19.5	685	44.8	26.3	40.9
Marble CDP	321	NA	NA	249	98.4	0.0	0.0	1.6	0.0	28.0	42.8	28.9	95	95.8	60.0	20.0
Marietta town	175	177	1.1	149	50.3	44.3	0.0	2.0	3.4	22.8	59.8	17.4	64	70.3	56.3	14.1
Marion city	8,027	7,885	-1.8	7,948	77.9	7.2	0.3	2.5	12.2	21.6	61.7	16.8	2,817	53.3	50.4	14.1
Mar-Mac CDP	3,615	NA	NA	3,894	45.1	24.3	2.6	3.0	24.9	29.8	58.9	11.3	1,613	52.4	49.7	9.3
Marshall town	874	877	0.3	897	83.9	2.3	0.0	6.1	7.6	21.4	61.7	16.9	403	49.9	50.4	25.8
Marshallberg CDP	403	NA	NA	238	100.0	0.0	0.0	0.0	0.0	9.7	55.0	35.3	112	100.0	41.1	9.8
Mars Hill town	1,962	2,228	13.6	2,168	86.4	10.7	0.6	1.0	1.4	15.5	74.1	10.4	613	55.6	21.2	44.4
Marshville town	2,410	2,596	7.7	2,493	35.9	56.9	0.4	0.7	6.1	22.8	64.6	12.4	865	56.4	71.7	8.4

1 May be of any race.

Table A. All Places — **Population and Housing**

STATE City, town, township, borough, or CDP (county if applicable)	Population: 2010 census total population	Population: 2014 estimated population	Population: Percent change 2010–2014	Population: ACS total population estimate 2010–2014	Race and Hispanic or Latino origin (percent), 2010–2014: White alone, not Hispanic or Latino	Black alone, not Hispanic or Latino	Asian alone, not Hispanic or Latino	All other races or 2 or more races, not Hispanic or Latino	Hispanic or Latino[1]	Age (percent), 2010–2014: Under 18 years old	Age 18 to 64 years old	Age 65 years and older	Households, 2010–2014: Total occupied housing units	Percent owner occupied	Householders by level of education (percent): High school diploma or less	Bachelor's degree or more
	1	2	3	4	5	6	7	8	9	10	11	12	13	14	15	16
NORTH CAROLINA—Con.																
Marvin village	5,583	6,060	8.5	5,806	83.9	2.5	9.2	2.7	1.7	39.0	54.7	6.1	1,690	96.6	4.3	73.6
Matthews town	27,196	30,008	10.3	28,677	79.4	10.4	3.5	1.7	5.0	24.7	60.3	14.9	10,907	73.9	16.4	54.3
Maury CDP	1,685	NA	NA	1,228	26.5	61.9	0.0	4.2	7.4	22.9	73.8	3.3	204	41.2	45.1	0.0
Maxton town	2,429	2,455	1.1	2,431	15.8	70.0	0.1	12.7	1.4	26.3	57.3	16.4	986	46.8	56.0	12.2
Mayodan town	2,478	2,464	-0.6	2,756	88.3	9.7	0.1	1.2	0.7	25.4	56.3	18.3	1,200	48.2	66.8	9.6
Maysville town	1,019	1,011	-0.8	1,098	45.6	40.2	0.8	11.2	2.2	23.3	64.2	12.7	425	64.9	47.3	7.3
Mebane city	11,366	13,277	16.8	12,509	65.7	21.8	1.4	4.2	6.9	24.1	63.1	12.7	5,331	59.2	29.8	33.4
Mesic town	220	215	-2.3	303	26.1	71.9	0.0	1.3	0.7	16.6	56.7	26.7	133	80.5	42.9	1.5
Micro town	441	473	7.3	468	81.4	10.3	0.0	0.0	8.3	15.2	56.3	28.6	214	70.1	47.7	10.3
Middleburg town	133	131	-1.5	177	52.0	48.0	0.0	0.0	0.0	28.3	53.6	18.1	75	58.7	62.7	5.3
Middlesex town	822	816	-0.7	1,084	37.5	27.7	0.0	0.1	34.8	31.9	52.7	15.3	390	53.8	62.8	4.4
Midland town	3,075	3,302	7.4	3,183	86.8	7.2	0.0	1.7	4.3	18.1	60.4	21.5	1,255	88.8	57.5	14.8
Midway town	4,694	4,724	0.6	4,717	94.7	4.6	0.0	0.5	0.2	19.9	58.4	21.8	1,993	92.3	46.3	21.6
Millers Creek CDP	2,112	NA	NA	1,849	94.8	0.0	0.0	0.6	4.6	20.6	59.2	20.3	780	72.4	61.3	4.5
Millingport CDP	599	NA	NA	651	99.7	0.3	0.0	0.0	0.0	29.4	60.9	9.7	244	90.6	57.4	11.1
Mills River town	6,804	7,085	4.1	6,917	90.3	2.5	0.2	4.3	2.7	18.1	59.5	22.4	2,769	85.9	29.5	26.8
Milton town	166	161	-3.0	171	42.7	56.7	0.0	0.6	0.0	16.9	53.2	29.8	85	67.1	57.6	15.3
Mineral Springs town	2,639	2,851	8.0	2,752	75.9	10.8	0.0	0.8	12.6	20.9	69.2	10.0	963	84.3	43.5	18.5
Minnesott Beach town	440	435	-1.1	375	94.7	1.6	0.5	1.1	2.1	3.7	61.5	34.7	193	86.5	26.4	43.0
Mint Hill town	22,763	25,076	10.2	23,934	75.3	12.5	2.5	2.6	7.1	22.4	61.6	16.1	8,909	79.8	25.9	37.5
Misenheimer village	728	684	-6.0	583	83.9	12.7	0.5	0.9	2.1	6.9	89.6	3.6	114	53.5	32.5	37.7
Mocksville town	5,051	5,104	1.0	5,086	66.5	20.8	0.3	2.0	10.4	22.5	57.2	20.3	1,991	64.1	50.8	23.0
Momeyer town	224	221	-1.3	391	89.3	6.4	0.8	1.5	2.0	27.4	59.6	13.0	127	71.7	56.7	13.4
Moncure CDP	711	NA	NA	455	76.7	15.4	0.0	0.0	7.9	26.0	51.2	22.9	228	86.8	58.8	14.5
Monroe city	32,797	34,331	4.7	33,588	43.8	23.8	1.8	2.0	28.6	30.2	59.4	10.5	11,069	58.1	51.6	19.1
Montreat town	723	699	-3.3	668	84.6	6.0	2.7	6.3	0.4	4.3	69.3	26.2	176	78.4	4.5	75.6
Mooresboro town	311	309	-0.6	387	95.1	4.1	0.5	0.0	0.3	24.6	58.2	17.3	158	80.4	58.9	15.2
Mooresville town	33,651	35,300	4.9	34,466	77.1	10.9	3.6	2.4	6.0	27.7	62.7	9.5	12,237	67.6	26.8	33.2
Moravian Falls CDP	1,901	NA	NA	1,554	69.5	4.9	6.0	2.0	17.6	28.1	57.0	14.9	679	59.8	50.4	10.0
Morehead City town	8,667	9,258	6.8	9,030	77.9	12.4	2.4	2.2	5.1	20.5	58.6	21.0	4,247	50.1	32.1	30.2
Morganton city	16,918	16,690	-1.3	16,816	66.3	11.4	1.0	4.4	16.9	22.4	58.7	18.9	6,590	57.3	42.8	26.3
Morrisville town	18,576	22,772	22.6	20,728	42.5	15.2	33.6	3.8	4.9	29.0	67.0	4.0	7,905	50.4	8.5	67.4
Morven town	509	484	-4.9	435	10.3	87.6	0.0	0.0	2.1	25.9	59.3	14.7	172	58.7	66.3	18.0
Mountain Home CDP	3,622	NA	NA	3,345	89.6	4.1	0.0	0.0	6.2	17.3	59.0	23.9	1,387	65.8	43.8	22.9
Mountain View CDP	3,552	NA	NA	3,010	86.6	10.0	0.0	0.0	3.3	14.7	61.5	23.8	1,259	87.8	42.7	20.4
Mount Airy city	10,394	10,383	-0.1	10,411	80.7	10.8	0.2	0.6	7.7	22.8	55.4	21.6	4,659	59.0	42.4	26.9
Mount Gilead town	1,183	1,173	-0.8	1,456	48.8	44.8	4.1	2.3	0.0	23.5	58.9	17.7	544	64.3	53.1	9.7
Mount Holly city	13,646	14,016	2.7	13,815	68.5	19.8	3.0	2.0	6.7	24.4	62.3	13.3	5,712	64.4	34.3	28.0
Mount Olive town	4,589	4,713	2.7	4,693	35.1	51.1	0.0	0.6	13.1	19.5	61.5	19.0	1,626	57.1	56.2	12.9
Mount Pleasant town	1,652	1,779	7.7	1,864	94.8	3.8	0.0	1.4	0.0	24.6	62.7	12.7	623	75.1	40.9	20.5
Moyock CDP	3,759	NA	NA	3,390	88.9	2.7	0.1	3.4	4.9	30.8	61.1	8.2	1,111	85.9	26.2	15.8
Mulberry CDP	2,332	NA	NA	1,956	90.5	2.8	0.0	0.0	6.7	18.2	61.6	20.3	748	87.2	56.4	15.2
Murfreesboro town	2,835	2,880	1.6	2,847	41.3	55.2	0.6	1.2	1.7	14.2	72.8	13.0	976	53.1	43.9	29.2
Murphy town	1,627	1,613	-0.9	2,100	80.2	8.6	0.4	5.2	5.6	25.1	50.7	24.1	762	56.8	39.9	18.8
Murraysville CDP	14,215	NA	NA	14,305	80.8	11.7	2.2	1.1	4.1	21.8	66.4	11.7	6,141	77.1	25.3	34.5
Myrtle Grove CDP	8,875	NA	NA	9,030	90.0	2.8	2.3	0.8	4.0	21.1	62.1	17.0	3,625	86.4	26.5	44.0
Nags Head town	2,757	2,840	3.0	2,798	93.7	1.5	1.7	0.0	3.0	12.4	67.9	19.7	1,227	66.5	14.3	51.4
Nashville town	5,460	5,464	0.1	5,469	55.8	42.0	0.0	2.2	0.0	21.0	63.3	15.9	2,267	70.0	38.4	17.6
Navassa town	1,480	1,542	4.2	1,919	20.4	54.2	0.0	19.4	6.0	27.5	62.6	9.8	630	82.4	47.0	12.4
Neuse Forest CDP	2,005	NA	NA	2,508	76.5	16.4	0.6	0.6	5.9	27.5	63.1	9.4	775	81.4	30.8	32.8
New Bern city	29,547	30,291	2.5	30,171	54.8	31.1	4.8	4.2	5.1	25.1	57.6	17.2	12,320	50.9	38.9	26.4
Newland town	698	692	-0.9	725	68.6	1.8	1.2	7.7	20.7	20.8	64.9	14.2	337	57.9	43.9	18.7
New London town	606	604	-0.3	546	80.4	17.6	2.0	0.0	0.0	21.6	60.7	17.6	213	82.6	39.0	25.4
Newport town	4,170	4,694	12.6	4,487	79.5	9.0	3.2	5.0	3.3	19.9	62.9	17.1	1,785	59.5	27.2	15.6
Newton city	12,968	13,005	0.3	12,998	68.8	13.3	4.4	1.6	12.0	22.7	60.1	17.1	5,018	58.7	55.5	15.2
Newton Grove town	569	578	1.6	649	78.4	11.2	0.6	7.6	2.2	14.5	61.1	24.5	266	53.8	42.9	16.9
Norlina town	1,118	1,086	-2.9	968	49.2	47.5	0.0	3.3	0.0	20.6	58.9	20.6	454	48.5	66.5	13.0
Norman town	138	134	-2.9	149	49.0	32.9	0.0	0.0	18.1	36.2	52.5	11.4	58	22.4	70.7	8.6
Northchase CDP	3,747	NA	NA	3,328	74.7	19.1	2.5	2.3	1.4	20.3	62.9	16.7	1,468	53.9	14.8	34.5
Northlakes CDP	1,534	NA	NA	1,423	96.6	0.0	0.0	1.8	1.7	20.0	56.4	23.8	573	93.9	13.6	44.5
North Topsail Beach town	743	735	-1.1	1,145	90.9	3.6	1.2	3.9	0.3	11.2	72.3	16.6	573	45.4	9.2	54.5
Northwest city	735	764	3.9	881	26.0	67.4	0.0	4.1	2.5	19.2	60.5	20.4	341	84.8	58.1	14.1
North Wilkesboro town	4,290	4,242	-1.1	4,262	72.2	14.1	0.0	2.9	10.8	24.5	57.4	18.1	1,501	39.0	57.9	20.5
Norwood town	2,379	2,389	0.4	2,727	76.4	21.6	0.0	1.6	0.4	21.8	59.1	19.1	1,041	67.8	50.5	13.4
Oakboro town	1,861	1,870	0.5	1,885	75.3	15.8	2.0	0.4	6.5	22.9	58.3	18.9	758	75.6	42.9	23.5
Oak City town	317	302	-4.7	314	34.1	63.1	0.0	0.0	2.9	22.0	56.0	22.0	124	65.3	64.5	4.8
Oak Island town	6,806	7,345	7.9	7,051	94.2	1.1	0.0	2.2	2.5	14.3	60.3	25.6	3,437	66.7	30.8	30.8
Oak Ridge town	6,274	6,604	5.3	6,435	87.4	4.9	3.2	2.1	2.3	29.0	60.4	10.6	2,198	92.9	20.4	53.9
Ocean Isle Beach town	541	582	7.6	659	95.1	0.0	1.4	0.0	3.5	5.7	53.7	40.7	360	86.4	18.3	52.8
Ocracoke CDP	948	NA	NA	556	97.3	2.5	0.0	0.2	0.0	12.9	59.3	27.7	261	68.2	39.8	21.1
Ogden CDP	6,766	NA	NA	6,653	95.3	0.0	0.5	1.5	2.7	23.4	61.9	14.6	2,612	89.2	18.6	50.2
Old Fort town	909	911	0.2	965	87.5	8.8	0.0	0.6	3.1	11.7	68.4	19.8	374	55.6	62.6	7.2
Old Hundred CDP	287	NA	NA	276	42.0	0.0	0.0	58.0	0.0	39.9	43.5	16.7	96	100.0	70.8	0.0
Oriental town	900	895	-0.6	969	91.4	5.2	0.0	3.3	0.1	11.7	52.7	35.7	448	76.8	17.9	50.4
Orrum town	91	92	1.1	60	55.0	8.3	0.0	21.7	15.0	25.0	56.6	18.3	26	76.9	65.4	19.2
Ossipee town	543	555	2.2	631	88.1	4.6	0.0	2.9	4.4	17.7	74.2	8.1	205	74.6	37.1	15.1
Oxford city	8,465	8,713	2.9	8,585	42.0	52.0	0.8	2.1	3.1	19.3	63.5	17.1	3,135	48.4	45.4	20.6
Pantego town	179	177	-1.1	196	76.5	18.9	0.0	0.0	4.6	25.0	53.1	21.9	76	78.9	28.9	23.7
Parkton town	435	440	1.1	597	70.0	16.8	0.0	2.2	11.1	25.4	62.2	12.4	203	67.0	43.8	12.3
Parmele town	278	264	-5.0	324	8.3	91.4	0.0	0.3	0.0	16.1	63.5	20.7	119	72.3	57.1	11.8
Patterson Springs town	622	608	-2.3	644	79.8	12.7	0.0	1.1	6.4	26.7	65.3	8.1	223	62.3	59.6	7.6
Peachland town	437	421	-3.7	442	60.0	39.1	0.2	0.0	0.7	24.0	61.1	14.9	163	61.3	63.8	16.6
Peletier town	644	654	1.6	879	96.7	1.0	0.3	1.3	0.7	20.6	68.2	11.3	340	73.2	43.2	17.1
Pembroke town	2,973	3,011	1.3	3,005	14.7	25.4	0.2	58.8	0.9	20.3	65.7	14.0	1,131	21.7	40.5	14.2
Pikeville town	678	693	2.2	716	90.4	3.2	0.0	2.7	3.8	19.4	63.9	16.8	304	68.1	39.5	15.8
Pilot Mountain town	1,477	1,469	-0.5	1,752	86.2	5.0	1.1	1.8	5.9	28.7	57.4	13.9	682	53.1	46.2	21.4
Pinebluff town	1,298	1,416	9.1	1,342	85.1	7.9	1.1	4.1	1.8	21.1	66.7	12.0	520	75.8	31.5	25.2
Pinehurst village	14,669	15,434	5.2	15,052	92.7	1.9	1.0	1.0	3.4	13.7	45.1	41.2	6,959	85.5	15.3	61.5
Pine Knoll Shores town	1,339	1,366	2.0	1,549	93.5	0.3	0.3	1.7	4.3	12.6	47.6	40.0	755	91.5	15.5	57.4
Pine Level town	1,700	1,818	6.9	2,000	66.5	15.9	0.3	0.6	16.9	27.3	58.7	14.3	792	64.8	43.4	17.3
Pinetops town	1,374	1,338	-2.6	1,277	39.6	60.4	0.0	0.0	0.0	26.8	53.1	20.2	560	49.5	66.1	9.6

1 May be of any race.

Table A. All Places — **Population and Housing**

STATE City, town, township, borough, or CDP (county if applicable)	Population: 2010 census total population	Population: 2014 estimated population	Population: Percent change 2010–2014	Population: ACS total population estimate 2010–2014	Race and Hispanic or Latino origin (percent), 2010–2014: White alone, not Hispanic or Latino	Black alone, not Hispanic or Latino	Asian alone, not Hispanic or Latino	All other races or 2 or more races, not Hispanic or Latino	Hispanic or Latino[1]	Age (percent), 2010–2014: Under 18 years old	Age 18 to 64 years old	Age 65 years and older	Households, 2010–2014: Total occupied housing units	Percent owner occupied	Householders by level of education (percent): High school diploma or less	Bachelor's degree or more
	1	2	3	4	5	6	7	8	9	10	11	12	13	14	15	16
NORTH CAROLINA—Con.																
Pinetown CDP	155	NA	NA	93	100.0	0.0	0.0	0.0	0.0	0.0	88.3	11.8	32	100.0	34.4	0.0
Pineville town	7,479	8,236	10.1	7,855	48.7	18.7	5.8	1.4	25.3	23.9	59.5	16.5	3,617	33.4	33.6	30.1
Piney Green CDP	13,293	NA	NA	13,701	57.1	20.2	4.0	4.8	13.9	28.0	63.9	7.9	4,752	54.8	36.7	15.0
Pink Hill town	552	542	-1.8	377	56.2	25.7	0.0	0.5	17.5	12.7	66.6	20.7	174	62.1	60.9	20.7
Pinnacle CDP	894	NA	NA	656	98.0	2.0	0.0	0.0	0.0	23.0	55.7	21.3	264	92.0	67.0	12.9
Pittsboro town	3,766	4,063	7.9	3,912	56.3	24.0	0.4	4.1	15.1	15.9	62.2	21.9	1,518	70.4	32.5	48.3
Plain View CDP	1,961	NA	NA	2,183	85.7	9.1	0.0	0.0	5.2	22.2	61.5	16.4	993	78.2	63.6	13.3
Pleasant Garden town	4,489	4,683	4.3	4,585	82.8	7.5	0.0	5.0	4.7	21.5	55.6	22.9	1,628	85.8	41.1	23.6
Pleasant Hill CDP	878	NA	NA	760	89.3	4.1	0.0	0.0	6.6	19.6	54.3	26.1	309	40.8	81.6	4.5
Plymouth town	3,878	3,711	-4.3	3,782	27.2	70.2	0.0	0.3	2.3	27.5	51.1	21.3	1,466	52.9	61.8	10.6
Polkton town	3,372	3,157	-6.4	3,268	30.2	63.2	0.5	3.2	2.9	16.8	78.2	5.1	488	50.4	61.3	7.8
Polkville city	545	539	-1.1	492	88.4	8.9	0.4	0.6	1.6	16.2	57.1	26.6	217	80.6	52.1	16.1
Pollocksville town	311	309	-0.6	476	43.1	56.5	0.0	0.0	0.4	33.8	50.7	15.5	186	45.7	33.9	15.1
Porters Neck CDP	6,204	NA	NA	6,476	86.9	10.3	0.4	0.2	2.2	20.4	53.7	25.9	2,536	74.0	8.9	72.9
Potters Hill CDP	481	NA	NA	529	100.0	0.0	0.0	0.0	0.0	12.7	74.5	12.9	175	85.7	52.0	0.0
Powellsville town	276	262	-5.1	259	35.1	64.9	0.0	0.0	0.0	22.0	61.6	16.2	101	65.3	78.2	4.0
Princeton town	1,196	1,259	5.3	1,401	68.2	22.1	0.0	2.1	7.5	26.5	54.0	19.5	472	51.9	46.0	8.5
Princeville town	2,082	2,021	-2.9	2,373	2.6	96.2	0.0	0.8	0.5	28.1	59.7	12.0	794	60.3	48.1	7.6
Proctorville town	117	119	1.7	176	60.8	26.1	1.7	5.1	6.3	17.6	59.2	23.3	59	86.4	52.5	20.3
Prospect CDP	981	NA	NA	855	5.5	0.0	4.8	89.7	0.0	14.5	59.5	26.1	340	76.8	59.7	12.4
Pumpkin Center CDP	2,222	NA	NA	1,952	63.8	14.2	5.0	3.1	13.9	15.9	67.5	16.8	760	76.8	30.5	11.1
Raeford city	4,611	4,797	4.0	4,783	36.0	44.8	1.8	4.9	12.5	30.7	55.3	14.0	1,804	47.4	41.2	16.9
Raemon CDP	282	NA	NA	144	27.8	15.3	0.0	56.9	0.0	36.8	48.7	14.6	54	66.7	88.9	0.0
Raleigh city	403,971	439,896	8.9	423,287	54.0	28.5	4.3	2.3	10.9	22.8	68.5	8.9	166,316	53.2	20.2	51.3
Ramseur town	1,692	1,705	0.8	2,080	64.7	12.0	3.1	2.5	17.6	29.2	50.7	20.1	724	62.4	57.7	10.5
Randleman city	4,116	4,149	0.8	4,143	89.0	3.6	0.4	5.9	1.0	22.8	58.6	18.5	1,829	54.1	62.1	6.9
Ranlo town	3,434	3,517	2.4	3,471	67.8	18.1	1.9	3.4	8.8	26.4	61.8	12.0	1,353	73.3	37.8	17.7
Raynham town	72	73	1.4	66	60.6	9.1	0.0	30.3	0.0	27.3	62.2	10.6	27	96.3	37.0	7.4
Red Cross town	740	741	0.1	690	87.5	1.2	1.2	0.4	9.7	20.8	56.0	23.2	306	81.0	58.2	7.2
Red Oak town	3,430	3,430	0.0	3,440	90.1	9.0	0.0	0.0	0.9	21.8	66.4	11.8	1,304	93.6	27.5	25.8
Red Springs town	3,428	3,452	0.7	3,445	26.5	48.4	0.7	13.3	11.1	33.6	49.7	16.7	1,305	47.9	53.3	19.5
Reidsville city	14,449	14,073	-2.6	14,249	52.4	41.0	1.2	2.5	2.9	21.6	60.5	17.9	6,061	53.9	48.8	17.4
Rennert town	383	379	-1.0	344	5.2	31.7	0.0	55.8	7.3	25.2	66.1	8.7	98	70.4	55.1	14.3
Rex CDP	55	NA	NA	79	100.0	0.0	0.0	0.0	0.0	0.0	63.3	36.7	29	55.2	55.2	44.8
Rhodhiss town	1,066	1,049	-1.6	988	87.0	0.0	3.0	1.8	8.1	25.6	61.3	13.4	358	77.4	66.8	5.3
Richfield town	613	611	-0.3	774	80.1	13.6	2.5	1.3	2.6	15.9	74.4	9.7	227	67.8	55.9	11.0
Richlands town	1,526	1,674	9.7	2,470	70.7	12.0	1.9	4.2	11.1	37.4	54.7	7.8	821	63.3	39.5	16.1
Rich Square town	958	908	-5.2	1,013	42.3	53.7	0.0	4.0	0.0	16.4	53.2	30.4	397	67.0	61.2	12.6
Riegelwood CDP	579	NA	NA	228	60.5	39.5	0.0	0.0	0.0	13.1	38.1	48.7	148	91.2	72.3	0.0
River Bend town	3,119	3,171	1.7	3,151	94.7	2.3	0.0	0.3	2.6	11.6	49.7	38.6	1,390	84.8	30.0	36.6
River Road CDP	4,394	NA	NA	3,797	60.2	14.5	0.0	0.0	25.3	14.5	62.3	23.1	1,773	78.6	48.5	28.5
Roanoke Rapids city	15,754	15,495	-1.6	15,653	65.6	28.8	1.5	1.1	3.0	27.2	57.0	15.6	6,242	53.6	42.3	17.9
Robbins town	1,125	1,174	4.4	1,026	44.9	2.0	0.0	1.9	51.2	29.2	53.8	16.9	343	57.4	59.2	16.0
Robbinsville town	620	600	-3.2	653	70.9	0.5	0.0	3.8	24.8	20.0	67.3	12.7	254	49.2	68.5	1.6
Robersonville town	1,488	1,430	-3.9	1,351	27.5	70.7	0.0	0.1	1.7	16.6	61.2	22.1	600	53.2	64.3	11.5
Rockfish CDP	3,298	NA	NA	3,738	64.7	21.4	4.4	5.4	4.2	32.0	63.6	4.5	1,228	78.1	19.4	25.3
Rockingham city	9,558	9,276	-3.0	9,444	56.5	31.7	2.1	3.8	5.9	22.6	61.3	16.0	3,835	57.4	45.7	19.1
Rockwell town	2,124	2,136	0.6	1,801	98.3	0.3	0.2	0.8	0.3	19.1	63.1	17.8	751	66.2	37.3	16.9
Rocky Mount city	57,719	56,325	-2.4	57,071	30.7	62.4	1.2	2.4	3.3	23.9	60.3	15.9	22,614	53.6	47.9	20.5
Rocky Point CDP	1,602	NA	NA	1,901	46.0	20.7	0.0	2.9	30.3	21.0	60.7	18.3	620	69.7	58.2	8.9
Rodanthe CDP	261	NA	NA	282	100.0	0.0	0.0	0.0	0.0	20.2	63.5	16.3	137	29.2	0.0	40.1
Rolesville town	3,786	5,785	52.8	4,530	74.0	10.9	1.7	3.1	10.4	29.5	62.3	8.0	1,528	88.7	20.8	49.1
Ronda town	417	414	-0.7	418	94.7	0.7	0.0	2.2	2.4	21.7	59.6	18.7	175	72.6	65.7	2.9
Roper town	611	579	-5.2	598	12.2	78.8	0.0	1.2	7.9	40.5	46.6	12.9	219	41.1	68.9	14.2
Roseboro town	1,188	1,207	1.6	1,374	57.1	40.3	0.0	2.3	0.3	27.9	54.7	17.5	539	63.6	39.9	17.1
Rose Hill town	1,625	1,680	3.4	1,523	41.8	32.4	2.3	0.0	23.5	24.0	55.8	20.2	642	61.2	45.0	9.7
Rosman town	576	570	-1.0	723	82.3	1.1	0.7	5.3	10.7	18.6	60.5	20.9	314	49.7	73.2	10.8
Rougemont CDP	978	NA	NA	876	92.5	5.3	0.0	1.1	1.1	16.9	62.8	20.3	366	97.3	24.9	44.3
Rowland town	1,037	1,052	1.4	1,204	19.1	65.6	0.2	13.8	1.2	21.2	62.3	16.4	456	54.2	48.5	13.2
Roxboro city	8,355	8,304	-0.6	8,330	40.3	47.3	0.2	2.0	10.2	22.2	59.6	18.1	3,039	36.5	52.7	14.0
Roxobel town	240	227	-5.4	325	33.5	66.5	0.0	0.0	0.0	15.6	68.1	16.3	120	60.8	70.8	6.7
Royal Pines CDP	4,272	NA	NA	5,124	87.6	2.6	0.3	1.0	8.6	26.7	59.3	14.0	1,909	79.8	14.0	55.6
Ruffin CDP	368	NA	NA	384	100.0	0.0	0.0	0.0	0.0	27.4	62.2	10.4	170	82.4	31.2	28.2
Rural Hall town	2,939	3,077	4.7	3,014	76.1	8.3	2.8	1.3	11.6	18.9	65.6	15.4	1,381	62.1	47.5	16.9
Ruth town	440	430	-2.3	416	84.9	3.6	0.0	2.2	9.4	14.7	67.0	18.3	164	76.8	64.6	12.2
Rutherford College town	1,341	1,324	-1.3	1,092	93.7	0.3	5.5	0.5	0.0	18.0	57.4	24.6	470	72.1	50.2	18.5
Rutherfordton town	4,230	4,172	-1.4	4,208	80.5	11.4	0.8	3.4	3.9	14.6	60.3	25.1	1,837	69.2	27.8	27.5
St. Helena village	389	407	4.6	362	67.7	32.3	0.0	0.0	0.0	27.6	58.0	14.4	147	78.9	29.9	28.6
St. James town	3,175	4,409	38.9	3,704	97.7	0.9	0.7	0.0	0.6	0.9	42.6	56.5	1,860	90.2	13.6	67.8
St. Pauls town	2,402	2,424	0.9	2,147	49.9	20.3	0.7	9.8	19.3	22.5	55.4	22.1	890	52.9	70.0	9.3
St. Stephens CDP	8,759	NA	NA	9,052	76.8	4.0	5.6	3.6	10.0	25.3	59.0	15.9	3,202	78.9	41.1	16.7
Salem CDP	2,218	NA	NA	2,349	87.1	0.6	2.3	1.0	8.9	17.3	63.5	19.2	904	73.9	55.2	16.3
Salemburg town	430	436	1.4	473	81.2	10.8	0.0	3.6	4.4	19.1	49.3	31.9	220	75.5	30.5	20.5
Salisbury city	33,524	33,710	0.6	33,524	49.4	37.9	1.5	3.1	8.2	22.9	60.3	17.0	12,428	50.0	40.4	26.3
Saluda city	717	706	-1.5	596	92.3	3.0	0.0	1.7	3.0	13.2	45.5	41.3	240	70.0	26.7	53.3
Salvo CDP	229	NA	NA	248	93.5	0.0	0.0	6.5	0.0	44.4	45.9	9.7	88	71.6	14.8	61.4
Sandy Creek town	260	267	2.7	319	92.8	1.9	0.0	4.1	1.3	29.1	57.3	13.5	108	64.8	56.5	5.6
Sandyfield town	443	428	-3.4	501	7.6	82.6	0.0	6.6	3.2	26.0	66.0	8.2	157	78.3	52.9	5.1
Sanford city	28,135	29,116	3.5	28,798	47.8	24.9	1.3	2.5	23.4	27.8	60.5	11.8	10,029	53.9	43.0	25.1
Saratoga town	408	407	-0.2	436	51.6	48.4	0.0	0.0	0.0	26.6	54.0	19.5	174	70.1	70.7	13.2
Sawmills town	5,240	5,122	-2.3	5,164	89.4	0.6	2.3	2.7	5.0	20.7	64.6	14.8	1,808	66.5	52.3	12.1
Saxapahaw CDP	1,648	NA	NA	1,329	61.6	25.4	0.0	2.0	11.1	16.5	65.8	17.7	559	71.2	39.4	30.1
Scotch Meadows CDP	580	NA	NA	538	60.6	19.3	0.0	18.4	1.7	22.3	58.2	19.5	189	100.0	32.3	47.6
Scotland Neck town	2,059	1,990	-3.4	1,711	29.9	57.9	0.0	0.4	11.9	13.5	56.6	29.9	778	47.4	69.0	10.9
Seaboard town	632	591	-6.5	756	24.5	74.3	0.0	0.0	1.2	21.7	54.5	23.8	318	55.0	45.6	16.4
Sea Breeze CDP	1,969	NA	NA	2,178	75.8	16.9	0.0	7.4	0.0	23.0	57.9	19.1	860	80.7	27.3	43.1
Seagrove town	228	229	0.4	249	94.0	1.2	0.0	0.4	4.4	27.6	54.1	18.1	102	60.8	63.7	7.8
Sedalia town	623	652	4.7	610	15.1	80.8	0.0	0.8	3.3	11.7	64.6	23.8	244	84.4	49.6	14.3
Selma town	6,073	6,257	3.0	6,172	23.6	26.6	0.0	0.6	49.2	28.6	61.7	9.6	2,087	34.2	65.7	9.9
Seven Devils town	196	198	1.0	228	96.9	0.4	0.4	1.3	0.9	9.6	47.0	43.4	122	92.6	20.5	54.1
Seven Lakes CDP	4,888	NA	NA	4,719	94.8	4.0	0.3	0.6	0.3	22.6	49.4	28.1	2,008	95.5	22.1	45.3

1 May be of any race.

Table A. All Places — **Population and Housing**

STATE City, town, township, borough, or CDP (county if applicable)	Population: 2010 census total population	Population: 2014 estimated population	Population: Percent change 2010–2014	Population: ACS total population estimate 2010–2014	Race and Hispanic or Latino origin (percent), 2010–2014: White alone, not Hispanic or Latino	Black alone, not Hispanic or Latino	Asian alone, not Hispanic or Latino	All other races or 2 or more races, not Hispanic or Latino	Hispanic or Latino[1]	Age (percent), 2010–2014: Under 18 years old	Age 18 to 64 years old	Age 65 years and older	Households, 2010–2014: Total occupied housing units	Percent owner occupied	Householders by level of education (percent): High school diploma or less	Bachelor's degree or more
	1	2	3	4	5	6	7	8	9	10	11	12	13	14	15	16
NORTH CAROLINA—Con.																
Seven Springs town	110	111	0.9	118	96.6	3.4	0.0	0.0	0.0	22.8	55.0	22.0	53	52.8	35.8	22.6
Severn town	276	259	-6.2	243	81.1	18.1	0.0	0.8	0.0	21.0	38.9	39.9	107	71.0	67.3	13.1
Shallotte town	3,507	3,766	7.4	3,639	75.6	12.0	1.9	4.4	6.1	17.9	57.2	25.0	1,621	56.6	38.5	22.0
Shannon CDP	283	NA	NA	232	9.9	9.1	0.0	76.7	4.3	34.0	61.2	4.7	81	74.1	54.3	0.0
Sharpsburg town	2,024	2,009	-0.7	1,956	36.9	49.8	0.0	9.4	3.9	31.6	54.9	13.4	779	49.0	44.5	9.8
Shelby city	20,326	20,276	-0.2	20,283	51.4	41.3	2.4	1.1	3.9	22.9	59.4	17.8	8,070	52.4	49.8	21.0
Siler City town	7,880	8,273	5.0	8,109	28.3	21.2	0.5	2.3	47.8	29.9	58.2	11.9	2,582	52.6	61.5	14.6
Silver City CDP	882	NA	NA	977	11.0	77.2	0.0	11.9	0.0	13.2	64.0	22.7	338	63.6	62.7	6.8
Silver Lake CDP	5,598	NA	NA	6,024	76.2	7.3	0.0	5.2	11.3	26.5	65.1	8.5	2,176	68.6	33.1	18.3
Simpson village	416	426	2.4	413	73.1	26.4	0.0	0.0	0.5	24.1	57.4	18.4	181	79.6	38.7	26.0
Sims town	282	281	-0.4	300	73.3	13.3	0.0	2.7	10.7	24.9	65.0	10.0	123	78.0	46.3	22.8
Skippers Corner CDP	2,785	NA	NA	2,750	65.6	16.1	0.0	3.9	14.4	21.0	68.8	10.3	838	72.8	33.1	45.3
Smithfield town	10,960	11,735	7.1	11,357	55.8	26.4	2.4	2.4	12.9	20.4	56.9	22.6	4,155	52.3	47.9	21.0
Sneads Ferry CDP	2,646	NA	NA	3,830	87.9	0.6	0.0	3.1	8.5	28.0	61.9	10.1	1,359	53.1	33.2	24.7
Snow Hill town	1,590	1,582	-0.5	1,878	43.8	44.6	0.2	0.5	10.9	23.8	55.2	21.0	808	46.7	49.5	14.0
Southern Pines town	12,352	13,235	7.1	12,782	71.0	21.1	0.9	2.8	4.3	18.9	53.1	27.9	5,757	60.7	25.8	44.4
Southern Shores town	2,714	2,818	3.8	2,759	92.4	0.0	0.4	4.0	3.2	15.8	53.8	30.4	1,182	87.3	12.7	58.5
South Henderson CDP	1,213	NA	NA	941	28.1	50.4	0.0	5.0	16.6	22.0	68.2	9.8	337	54.6	70.3	1.8
South Mills CDP	454	NA	NA	245	93.5	0.0	0.0	6.5	0.0	16.7	64.1	19.2	135	57.0	12.6	0.0
Southmont CDP	1,470	NA	NA	1,316	99.1	0.0	0.0	0.9	0.0	8.6	85.7	5.5	471	91.1	52.7	20.0
Southport city	2,836	3,267	15.2	3,032	81.7	13.6	0.0	4.7	0.0	21.0	54.3	24.5	1,271	55.1	27.5	37.8
South Rosemary CDP	2,836	NA	NA	2,898	35.7	49.8	0.0	12.1	2.4	26.3	58.7	15.0	1,281	59.6	63.5	8.3
South Weldon CDP	705	NA	NA	825	9.9	85.9	0.0	4.1	0.0	34.7	54.3	10.9	305	29.8	50.8	11.8
Sparta town	1,770	1,732	-2.1	2,089	79.6	4.0	1.3	5.3	9.9	19.1	57.0	23.9	937	51.4	64.4	11.5
Speed town	80	79	-1.3	91	18.7	81.3	0.0	0.0	0.0	9.9	55.0	35.2	40	72.5	67.5	0.0
Spencer town	3,267	3,285	0.6	3,267	60.5	25.0	0.7	5.2	8.5	21.2	63.2	15.6	1,381	60.3	52.3	12.3
Spencer Mountain town	37	37	0.0	28	35.7	10.7	0.0	10.7	42.9	28.5	53.6	17.9	6	33.3	83.3	0.0
Spindale town	4,321	4,274	-1.1	4,296	64.4	31.2	0.0	1.3	3.1	16.4	64.7	18.9	1,774	58.2	57.0	11.3
Spivey's Corner CDP	506	NA	NA	357	53.8	46.2	0.0	0.0	0.0	15.7	76.7	7.6	137	81.8	34.3	56.2
Spring Hope town	1,320	1,316	-0.3	1,205	45.5	46.9	0.0	2.5	5.1	18.3	51.7	29.8	584	37.8	58.0	14.2
Spring Lake town	12,007	13,370	11.4	13,101	38.5	34.9	3.1	7.4	16.1	36.1	59.8	4.1	4,516	20.4	33.2	15.5
Spruce Pine town	2,154	2,123	-1.4	2,257	85.1	0.9	0.4	0.5	13.2	25.4	57.9	16.7	865	57.7	47.1	20.9
Staley town	393	395	0.5	521	51.8	11.1	0.0	3.5	33.6	41.4	48.5	10.2	150	72.7	65.3	10.7
Stallings town	13,797	14,968	8.5	14,185	83.1	5.1	1.6	4.2	6.0	27.2	59.4	13.4	5,147	86.8	20.7	46.0
Stanfield town	1,486	1,488	0.1	1,732	97.0	0.4	0.0	0.9	1.7	25.7	64.5	9.8	595	80.5	41.7	17.3
Stanley town	3,552	3,641	2.5	3,591	92.6	3.5	0.3	3.5	0.0	19.5	56.4	24.1	1,392	74.0	53.4	12.6
Stantonsburg town	786	787	0.1	649	54.7	42.2	0.0	0.0	3.1	21.4	57.3	21.3	291	66.3	56.4	16.8
Star town	876	868	-0.9	856	74.5	5.1	0.0	0.9	19.4	16.7	67.4	16.0	335	73.4	44.8	20.0
Statesville city	24,541	25,722	4.8	25,132	49.4	35.6	1.0	1.5	12.5	26.5	58.7	14.9	9,527	48.4	41.5	23.0
Stedman town	1,025	1,046	2.0	1,134	74.6	13.8	1.2	7.9	2.4	28.7	60.6	10.6	405	78.0	39.8	22.5
Stem town	463	470	1.5	737	50.6	35.4	0.0	3.0	11.0	29.9	63.6	6.4	239	84.9	38.1	20.9
Stokes CDP	376	NA	NA	357	78.4	21.6	0.0	0.0	0.0	0.0	79.7	20.2	209	100.0	66.5	0.0
Stokesdale town	5,047	5,289	4.8	5,177	77.4	7.0	1.9	1.8	11.9	27.2	62.5	10.4	1,763	81.5	37.8	34.4
Stoneville town	1,057	1,037	-1.9	1,177	77.7	12.1	1.2	0.6	8.3	18.6	60.9	20.5	541	66.0	55.6	16.1
Stonewall town	281	275	-2.1	214	77.6	8.4	0.5	7.9	5.6	43.0	43.9	13.1	82	61.0	70.7	6.1
Stony Point CDP	1,317	NA	NA	1,674	78.0	0.0	0.0	5.4	16.7	28.2	63.9	7.9	582	59.8	70.8	2.6
Stovall town	418	429	2.6	327	40.4	59.6	0.0	0.0	0.0	24.5	53.6	22.0	119	69.7	50.4	20.2
Sugar Mountain village	198	198	0.0	508	87.6	0.0	0.4	12.0	0.0	18.9	58.9	22.2	234	53.4	10.7	44.0
Summerfield town	10,232	10,753	5.1	10,477	90.6	3.7	2.5	2.2	1.1	25.6	61.4	12.9	3,836	88.9	22.5	55.5
Sunbury CDP	289	NA	NA	236	78.0	17.8	0.0	0.0	4.2	23.7	61.6	14.8	79	60.8	45.6	22.8
Sunset Beach town	3,571	3,752	5.1	3,654	97.8	0.0	0.0	0.0	2.2	3.5	40.7	55.9	1,792	91.2	20.6	46.9
Surf City town	1,900	2,126	11.9	2,498	97.5	0.0	0.4	1.6	0.5	12.4	67.9	19.6	1,175	66.1	18.9	54.5
Swannanoa CDP	4,576	NA	NA	4,444	85.6	5.7	0.0	1.0	7.7	19.6	68.7	11.7	1,798	60.7	57.6	13.2
Swan Quarter CDP	324	NA	NA	239	44.4	29.7	0.0	0.0	25.9	14.7	66.5	18.8	105	79.0	63.8	0.0
Swansboro town	2,661	3,074	15.5	2,869	84.6	3.4	2.1	2.0	8.0	19.5	66.0	14.6	1,182	62.9	25.5	33.1
Swepsonville town	1,154	1,187	2.9	1,114	89.9	7.2	0.0	0.4	2.5	18.2	63.1	18.5	486	79.2	39.5	24.7
Sylva town	2,584	2,602	0.7	2,581	80.6	4.6	2.8	7.6	4.5	22.8	63.4	13.9	1,082	46.2	34.8	33.4
Tabor City town	4,021	3,912	-2.7	3,970	58.8	35.1	0.0	3.8	2.2	22.6	57.9	19.5	1,695	49.4	53.3	15.6
Tarboro town	11,413	11,310	-0.9	11,323	44.3	48.0	0.0	2.6	5.1	20.9	57.4	21.8	4,420	53.1	44.2	17.4
Tar Heel town	148	147	-0.7	160	77.5	12.5	0.0	0.0	10.0	16.2	55.7	28.1	65	64.6	29.2	18.5
Taylorsville town	2,077	2,086	0.4	2,062	79.9	11.7	1.0	6.6	0.8	27.0	52.2	20.8	747	45.5	55.3	13.9
Taylortown town	772	807	4.5	1,142	27.8	62.4	0.0	9.7	0.0	27.8	61.1	11.2	380	70.5	40.0	14.2
Teachey town	426	441	3.5	341	47.5	36.1	0.0	0.0	16.4	32.0	58.3	9.7	123	69.9	47.2	13.8
Thomasville city	26,772	27,002	0.9	27,042	62.6	20.8	0.6	1.4	14.6	26.2	58.6	15.2	10,593	59.9	53.6	12.2
Toast CDP	1,450	NA	NA	1,330	80.1	1.7	7.1	0.0	11.1	17.6	58.8	23.5	556	78.4	66.5	15.1
Tobaccoville village	2,434	2,545	4.6	2,492	86.3	9.4	0.2	1.4	2.7	28.3	53.1	18.5	970	82.9	47.6	20.8
Topsail Beach town	368	399	8.4	428	96.5	0.0	0.0	1.6	1.9	7.5	60.6	31.8	233	81.1	19.7	48.9
Trenton town	294	293	-0.3	346	45.7	41.3	0.0	8.1	4.9	24.3	60.7	15.0	126	69.0	46.8	17.5
Trent Woods town	4,155	4,221	1.6	4,210	97.8	0.0	0.0	0.0	2.2	15.5	56.5	28.0	1,853	88.5	13.3	54.0
Trinity city	6,612	6,662	0.8	6,648	91.1	3.0	0.7	2.2	3.0	24.3	60.9	14.8	2,635	83.1	50.9	14.0
Troutman town	2,383	2,496	4.7	2,379	74.4	13.7	0.0	6.1	5.8	27.6	60.1	12.4	848	76.8	38.0	19.7
Troy town	3,513	3,399	-3.2	3,458	47.1	39.6	0.2	4.7	8.4	20.6	66.8	12.6	1,196	52.1	40.5	20.2
Tryon town	1,643	1,632	-0.7	1,681	80.4	19.6	0.0	0.0	0.0	13.3	49.1	37.7	853	63.8	28.6	41.6
Turkey town	292	296	1.4	397	56.7	24.4	0.0	4.3	14.6	14.1	70.1	15.9	147	63.3	68.0	2.7
Tyro CDP	3,879	NA	NA	3,555	94.6	3.5	0.0	0.2	1.7	24.1	59.5	16.4	1,416	78.6	59.7	13.9
Unionville town	5,959	6,442	8.1	6,180	94.0	2.0	2.6	1.1	0.3	24.9	62.6	12.5	2,218	80.5	40.8	19.7
Valdese town	4,489	4,455	-0.8	4,468	87.1	3.9	3.1	2.3	3.6	19.6	55.2	25.1	1,817	65.8	46.6	22.9
Valle Crucis CDP	412	NA	NA	360	84.7	0.0	15.3	0.0	0.0	27.5	58.8	13.6	162	48.1	22.8	50.0
Valley Hill CDP	2,070	NA	NA	2,316	80.7	0.4	0.0	0.0	18.9	17.4	53.9	28.5	1,134	58.9	42.7	18.1
Vanceboro town	1,005	1,011	0.6	1,092	69.4	25.9	0.0	2.8	1.8	26.5	57.9	15.6	405	50.9	52.3	8.9
Vandemere town	254	248	-2.4	291	49.1	50.9	0.0	0.0	0.0	18.9	62.2	18.9	130	86.2	56.9	7.7
Vander CDP	1,146	NA	NA	1,070	73.0	20.7	0.9	0.7	4.6	15.8	56.1	28.0	538	64.7	53.3	9.5
Vann Crossroads CDP	336	NA	NA	324	83.0	10.2	0.0	6.8	0.0	21.3	45.6	33.0	129	75.2	68.2	15.5
Varnamtown town	541	568	5.0	556	98.0	0.0	0.5	1.1	0.4	20.1	58.7	21.2	213	78.4	41.8	21.6
Vass town	711	742	4.4	604	57.8	11.6	0.0	4.3	26.3	24.7	59.7	15.7	279	62.7	59.1	9.3
Waco town	321	319	-0.6	294	89.1	9.9	0.0	1.0	0.0	18.0	72.0	9.9	111	76.6	64.9	6.3
Wade town	556	561	0.9	477	79.7	15.5	0.2	4.6	0.0	25.4	52.7	22.0	213	51.2	54.0	14.6
Wadesboro town	5,817	5,620	-3.4	5,711	34.3	56.7	1.1	1.6	6.4	22.7	56.8	20.5	2,276	56.7	57.6	15.2
Wagram town	840	813	-3.2	804	40.3	47.4	0.0	11.2	1.1	20.5	61.2	18.4	312	78.5	56.1	14.1
Wake Forest town	30,096	36,693	21.9	33,319	72.3	16.3	2.9	2.1	6.4	31.2	58.4	10.4	11,510	73.7	17.7	52.1
Wakulla CDP	105	NA	NA	147	28.6	0.0	0.0	71.4	0.0	28.6	71.4	0.0	54	100.0	0.0	0.0

1 May be of any race.

Table A. All Places — **Population and Housing**

STATE City, town, township, borough, or CDP (county if applicable)	Population				Race and Hispanic or Latino origin (percent), 2010–2014					Age (percent), 2010–2014			Households, 2010–2014			
	2010 census total population	2014 estimated population	Percent change 2010–2014	ACS total population estimate 2010–2014	White alone, not Hispanic or Latino	Black alone, not Hispanic or Latino	Asian alone, not Hispanic or Latino	All other races or 2 or more races, not Hispanic or Latino	Hispanic or Latino[1]	Under 18 years old	Age 18 to 64 years old	Age 65 years and older	Total occupied housing units	Percent owner occupied	Householders by level of education (percent): High school diploma or less	Householders by level of education (percent): Bachelor's degree or more
	1	2	3	4	5	6	7	8	9	10	11	12	13	14	15	16
NORTH CAROLINA—Con.																
Walkertown town	4,682	4,889	4.4	4,790	77.1	17.9	0.3	0.3	4.4	19.7	60.8	19.6	1,981	67.6	45.8	18.6
Wallace town	3,879	4,001	3.1	3,953	62.4	14.3	0.0	0.0	23.3	14.1	62.3	23.8	1,811	47.9	73.4	8.9
Wallburg town	3,044	3,066	0.7	3,056	96.0	0.3	0.5	0.2	3.0	17.1	67.7	15.2	1,212	79.2	55.3	16.9
Walnut Cove town	1,425	1,409	-1.1	1,599	71.9	19.2	3.1	0.7	5.1	22.8	55.7	21.7	629	51.0	51.7	11.1
Walnut Creek village	835	859	2.9	962	93.1	2.4	3.1	0.2	1.1	19.8	53.3	26.7	399	100.0	9.0	70.2
Walstonburg town	219	218	-0.5	320	79.7	15.0	0.0	4.4	0.9	21.2	68.2	10.6	118	82.2	46.6	19.5
Wanchese CDP	1,642	NA	NA	1,753	93.1	0.0	0.0	1.1	5.8	24.1	51.3	24.4	717	66.7	47.7	5.4
Warrenton town	895	869	-2.9	883	41.2	48.1	0.0	3.3	7.4	22.0	53.1	24.9	442	53.6	44.1	24.0
Warsaw town	3,085	3,196	3.6	3,162	28.8	55.5	0.0	5.2	10.5	26.3	51.1	22.7	1,432	38.6	49.0	5.7
Washington city	9,742	9,789	0.5	9,768	46.0	46.2	0.0	2.2	5.6	24.3	54.3	21.2	3,951	47.3	40.8	24.5
Washington Park town	451	451	0.0	503	95.0	0.6	0.0	0.0	4.4	25.7	55.1	19.3	194	82.0	8.2	59.3
Watha town	192	228	18.8	275	86.5	7.6	0.0	1.1	4.7	21.1	64.7	14.2	108	76.9	47.2	1.9
Waves CDP	134	NA	NA	65	100.0	0.0	0.0	0.0	0.0	0.0	100.0	0.0	41	100.0	0.0	100.0
Waxhaw town	9,860	12,750	29.3	10,878	76.1	11.5	3.5	2.3	6.6	33.4	57.2	9.3	3,522	86.5	17.9	53.5
Waynesville town	9,863	9,761	-1.0	9,770	92.4	2.8	0.2	1.3	3.3	15.5	62.1	22.3	4,690	59.0	43.2	23.0
Weaverville town	3,677	3,898	6.0	3,783	96.3	0.2	0.0	1.1	2.3	22.2	48.2	29.8	1,520	81.6	18.2	50.3
Webster town	363	373	2.8	391	92.1	1.3	0.0	4.9	1.8	25.0	63.5	11.5	168	67.3	12.5	48.2
Weddington town	9,508	10,322	8.6	9,906	90.0	1.9	1.8	2.5	3.7	24.1	64.6	11.4	3,295	98.2	8.7	68.3
Welcome CDP	4,162	NA	NA	4,891	82.9	2.6	7.0	0.3	7.2	23.5	61.9	14.8	1,805	79.5	53.3	14.8
Weldon town	1,652	1,593	-3.6	1,644	28.0	70.9	0.0	0.6	0.5	21.6	51.0	27.4	671	66.6	47.2	23.1
Wendell town	5,845	6,182	5.8	6,085	61.6	19.9	3.1	2.7	12.8	29.2	55.6	15.1	2,537	67.5	34.9	33.9
Wentworth town	2,807	2,759	-1.7	2,782	80.2	16.0	0.3	1.0	2.6	21.3	63.8	15.0	1,012	80.5	46.8	17.0
Wesley Chapel village	7,573	8,192	8.2	7,882	91.7	1.2	1.0	1.5	4.5	31.6	59.1	9.0	2,416	97.5	22.2	48.3
West Canton CDP	1,247	NA	NA	1,223	90.2	0.0	0.0	0.4	9.4	19.1	59.8	21.0	488	73.0	54.7	6.8
West Jefferson town	1,304	1,311	0.5	1,508	95.1	1.0	0.0	0.4	3.5	25.9	51.3	22.8	652	47.5	50.9	17.9
West Marion CDP	1,348	NA	NA	1,503	93.6	3.7	0.0	1.0	1.7	27.9	54.8	17.4	626	73.5	47.8	14.7
Westport CDP	4,026	NA	NA	3,794	93.4	0.7	0.2	4.0	1.8	24.7	63.6	11.7	1,482	96.4	9.2	58.6
Whispering Pines village	2,949	3,112	5.5	3,023	83.8	0.0	2.0	9.5	4.7	26.1	46.0	27.9	1,172	88.5	13.7	42.1
Whitakers town	744	731	-1.7	916	21.4	69.1	0.4	8.5	0.5	21.1	62.0	16.9	327	59.6	58.7	8.6
White Lake town	802	788	-1.7	933	84.4	7.9	0.0	3.2	4.5	13.2	73.3	13.5	466	59.9	28.1	35.6
White Oak CDP	338	NA	NA	336	25.6	70.8	0.0	0.0	3.6	11.4	77.6	11.3	129	65.1	54.3	14.0
White Plains CDP	1,074	NA	NA	1,115	84.6	1.2	0.0	3.9	10.3	10.9	61.6	27.6	550	71.1	41.6	17.6
Whiteville city	5,377	5,601	4.2	5,465	45.4	42.3	2.5	4.4	5.3	21.6	55.9	22.5	2,522	51.8	44.1	21.7
Whitsett town	590	618	4.7	770	86.6	1.9	1.6	0.8	9.1	19.3	64.1	16.5	290	74.1	42.4	19.7
Wilkesboro town	3,555	3,556	0.0	3,559	80.9	7.8	0.9	5.5	5.0	22.2	53.3	24.4	1,498	51.7	31.6	23.1
Williamston town	5,524	5,322	-3.7	5,410	31.0	67.8	0.0	0.2	1.0	26.3	52.4	21.3	2,159	56.2	51.5	13.4
Wilmington city	106,478	113,657	6.7	110,100	71.9	19.3	1.4	1.6	5.8	17.8	67.9	14.2	47,528	45.1	26.5	38.9
Wilson city	49,159	49,395	0.5	49,389	40.8	46.8	1.2	2.3	8.8	24.4	60.2	15.5	19,581	50.9	46.5	24.5
Wilson's Mills town	2,277	2,430	6.7	2,823	38.7	37.7	0.0	1.5	22.2	35.2	59.9	4.8	816	64.3	52.3	8.7
Windsor town	3,634	3,512	-3.4	3,546	30.2	65.6	1.9	1.4	0.9	19.3	65.1	15.6	1,128	60.5	50.4	19.3
Winfall town	599	602	0.5	643	52.4	41.2	0.3	0.9	5.1	24.9	52.3	22.9	243	65.4	44.4	19.3
Wingate town	3,491	3,906	11.9	3,708	47.9	37.7	0.8	0.9	12.8	18.9	70.8	10.4	1,078	63.5	42.5	21.7
Winston-Salem city	229,634	239,269	4.2	234,469	46.5	34.2	2.0	2.0	15.3	24.4	62.9	12.8	92,567	55.7	34.4	35.8
Winterville town	9,242	9,511	2.9	9,424	57.1	36.9	1.8	1.3	2.9	29.1	60.6	10.3	3,341	84.2	24.0	36.4
Winton town	769	753	-2.1	893	30.2	66.0	0.0	3.5	0.3	23.2	56.7	20.2	359	56.3	51.5	10.0
Woodfin town	6,037	6,283	4.1	6,167	82.8	5.3	1.9	2.2	7.8	16.0	68.8	15.1	2,414	47.7	37.4	32.3
Woodland town	806	750	-6.9	911	37.3	58.2	0.0	3.1	1.4	16.7	60.1	23.2	400	40.8	76.8	5.8
Woodlawn CDP	900	NA	NA	915	73.1	23.4	0.0	0.0	3.5	24.2	64.9	10.9	342	76.9	49.1	28.9
Wrightsboro CDP	4,896	NA	NA	5,780	56.9	28.9	0.5	5.0	8.6	24.7	62.3	13.0	2,163	74.6	52.8	12.1
Wrightsville Beach town	2,475	2,549	3.0	2,525	97.3	0.0	0.1	0.9	1.6	15.6	70.9	13.4	1,084	53.8	8.9	66.1
Yadkinville town	2,962	2,930	-1.1	2,946	67.5	5.1	1.5	1.8	24.1	20.9	57.1	22.2	1,068	58.1	50.8	16.7
Yanceyville town	2,039	2,002	-1.8	2,025	36.7	52.8	2.8	4.2	3.6	15.1	64.0	20.9	648	37.7	65.3	4.9
Youngsville town	1,157	1,200	3.7	1,366	62.4	28.8	0.2	1.0	7.6	26.8	63.4	9.9	637	33.9	41.6	22.1
Zebulon town	4,433	4,750	7.2	4,590	33.6	34.7	1.3	2.2	28.3	29.7	59.4	11.0	1,382	61.7	54.4	21.1
NORTH DAKOTA	672,591	739,482	9.9	704,925	87.7	1.5	1.1	7.1	2.6	22.4	63.3	14.3	292,616	65.1	34.3	27.2
Abercrombie city	259	260	0.4	251	82.9	0.0	0.0	17.1	0.0	31.9	56.7	11.6	103	82.5	32.0	13.6
Adams city	127	125	-1.6	138	82.6	0.0	0.0	17.4	0.0	15.2	61.5	23.2	78	71.8	43.6	19.2
Alamo city	57	52	-8.8	62	95.2	0.0	0.0	4.8	0.0	29.0	59.8	11.3	27	96.3	29.6	7.4
Alexander city	223	331	48.4	272	88.2	0.0	0.0	0.0	11.8	26.1	65.6	8.5	92	89.1	43.5	4.3
Alice city	40	40	0.0	35	100.0	0.0	0.0	0.0	0.0	8.6	59.9	31.4	18	100.0	66.7	0.0
Almont city	122	115	-5.7	122	99.2	0.0	0.0	0.8	0.0	41.1	53.2	5.7	47	85.1	70.2	2.1
Alsen city	35	34	-2.9	55	100.0	0.0	0.0	0.0	0.0	38.1	50.8	10.9	18	100.0	11.1	11.1
Ambrose city	26	27	3.8	26	100.0	0.0	0.0	0.0	0.0	0.0	76.8	23.1	21	85.7	19.0	23.8
Amenia city	94	95	1.1	125	97.6	0.0	0.0	2.4	0.0	26.4	64.8	8.8	42	90.5	47.6	23.8
Amidon city	20	21	5.0	32	100.0	0.0	0.0	0.0	0.0	0.0	68.7	31.3	17	100.0	41.2	58.8
Anamoose city	227	252	11.0	265	100.0	0.0	0.0	0.0	0.0	17.7	53.9	28.3	138	89.9	46.4	22.5
Aneta city	222	215	-3.2	278	99.3	0.0	0.0	0.7	0.0	12.2	59.0	28.8	145	75.2	55.2	9.0
Antler city	27	28	3.7	9	100.0	0.0	0.0	0.0	0.0	0.0	22.2	77.8	9	77.8	55.6	44.4
Ardoch city	67	67	0.0	79	16.5	0.0	0.0	2.5	81.0	41.8	57.0	1.3	25	100.0	100.0	0.0
Argusville city	475	481	1.3	394	98.0	0.0	0.0	1.5	0.5	38.3	57.6	4.1	137	94.2	25.5	42.3
Arnegard city	115	166	44.3	245	62.0	0.0	0.0	2.9	35.1	24.4	69.7	5.7	61	82.0	47.5	8.2
Arthur city	337	352	4.5	362	98.1	0.8	0.0	0.6	0.6	27.6	47.7	24.6	142	62.7	14.8	34.5
Ashley city	749	756	0.9	744	92.7	0.0	0.5	6.3	0.4	13.4	35.8	50.8	385	79.2	48.6	19.7
Auburn CDP	48	NA	NA	8	100.0	0.0	0.0	0.0	0.0	50.0	50.0	0.0	4	100.0	0.0	0.0
Ayr city	17	17	0.0	20	100.0	0.0	0.0	0.0	0.0	0.0	90.0	10.0	16	12.5	37.5	50.0
Balfour city	26	28	7.7	13	100.0	0.0	0.0	0.0	0.0	0.0	92.3	7.7	8	87.5	50.0	12.5
Balta city	65	65	0.0	94	100.0	0.0	0.0	0.0	0.0	40.3	51.0	8.5	33	78.8	84.8	0.0
Bantry city	14	15	7.1	17	100.0	0.0	0.0	0.0	0.0	29.5	52.9	17.6	7	85.7	14.3	14.3
Barney city	52	51	-1.9	56	100.0	0.0	0.0	0.0	0.0	16.1	73.2	10.7	25	88.0	60.0	4.0
Barton CDP	20	NA	NA	8	100.0	0.0	0.0	0.0	0.0	0.0	0.0	100.0	4	100.0	0.0	0.0
Bathgate city	43	41	-4.7	35	100.0	0.0	0.0	0.0	0.0	5.7	85.8	8.6	15	100.0	20.0	53.3
Beach city	1,021	1,107	8.4	964	97.7	0.0	0.0	1.6	0.7	22.5	52.1	25.4	474	70.0	31.9	20.0
Belcourt CDP	2,078	NA	NA	1,721	0.9	0.3	0.0	93.6	5.2	33.9	53.8	12.3	627	46.9	38.0	21.1
Belfield city	800	1,026	28.3	958	97.6	0.0	0.1	2.2	0.1	24.3	59.4	16.4	395	68.6	44.1	11.1
Benedict city	66	67	1.5	77	96.1	0.0	0.0	3.9	0.0	36.4	48.1	15.6	23	100.0	69.6	0.0
Bergen city	7	7	0.0	6	66.7	0.0	0.0	0.0	33.3	0.0	0.0	100.0	3	100.0	33.3	0.0
Berlin city	34	35	2.9	26	100.0	0.0	0.0	0.0	0.0	26.9	30.7	42.3	13	100.0	76.9	0.0
Berthold city	454	496	9.3	394	98.5	1.5	0.0	0.0	0.0	30.8	55.3	14.0	142	85.9	33.8	18.3
Beulah city	3,121	3,356	7.5	3,231	98.4	0.0	0.0	0.0	1.6	22.6	60.9	16.3	1,383	76.9	33.8	18.0

1 May be of any race.

Table A. All Places — **Population and Housing**

STATE City, town, township, borough, or CDP (county if applicable)	Population 2010 census total population	2014 estimated population	Percent change 2010–2014	ACS total population estimate 2010–2014	White alone, not Hispanic or Latino	Black alone, not Hispanic or Latino	Asian alone, not Hispanic or Latino	All other races or 2 or more races, not Hispanic or Latino	Hispanic or Latino[1]	Under 18 years old	Age 18 to 64 years old	Age 65 years and older	Total occupied housing units	Percent owner occupied	High school diploma or less	Bachelor's degree or more
	1	2	3	4	5	6	7	8	9	10	11	12	13	14	15	16

NORTH DAKOTA—Con.

STATE City, town, township, borough, or CDP (county if applicable)	1	2	3	4	5	6	7	8	9	10	11	12	13	14	15	16
Binford city	183	175	-4.4	167	95.2	2.4	0.0	1.2	1.2	13.2	48.6	38.3	91	72.5	53.8	20.9
Bisbee city	126	130	3.2	121	90.9	0.0	0.0	9.1	0.0	19.8	61.0	19.0	60	88.3	45.0	6.7
Bismarck city	61,264	68,896	12.5	65,123	90.9	0.8	0.7	6.0	1.7	21.6	63.0	15.4	28,550	64.8	30.7	34.0
Blanchard CDP	26	NA	NA	10	100.0	0.0	0.0	0.0	0.0	0.0	50.0	50.0	5	100.0	0.0	0.0
Bottineau city	2,211	2,305	4.3	2,294	87.5	1.4	0.2	7.9	3.0	18.7	58.5	22.9	1,033	62.1	38.2	19.3
Bowbells city	336	365	8.6	394	93.1	0.0	0.0	6.9	0.0	19.8	66.9	13.2	197	60.4	49.2	14.7
Bowdon city	131	133	1.5	119	93.3	0.0	0.0	0.0	6.7	9.3	39.4	51.3	65	93.8	61.5	12.3
Bowman city	1,651	1,706	3.3	1,649	93.8	0.0	0.0	1.0	5.2	22.3	54.6	23.2	742	70.4	51.3	22.2
Braddock city	21	21	0.0	9	100.0	0.0	0.0	0.0	0.0	0.0	0.0	100.0	5	100.0	40.0	60.0
Briarwood city	73	76	4.1	61	100.0	0.0	0.0	0.0	0.0	36.1	57.3	6.6	20	100.0	5.0	80.0
Brinsmade city	35	35	0.0	71	100.0	0.0	0.0	0.0	0.0	56.3	42.3	1.4	17	100.0	47.1	11.8
Brocket city	57	56	-1.8	93	100.0	0.0	0.0	0.0	0.0	25.9	51.6	22.6	35	88.6	37.1	31.4
Brooktree Park CDP	80	NA	NA	30	100.0	0.0	0.0	0.0	0.0	0.0	23.3	76.7	16	100.0	0.0	0.0
Buchanan city	90	109	21.1	81	91.4	0.0	0.0	8.6	0.0	22.2	77.8	0.0	27	100.0	18.5	48.1
Bucyrus city	27	27	0.0	14	78.6	0.0	0.0	21.4	0.0	0.0	57.1	42.9	10	100.0	50.0	0.0
Buffalo city	188	195	3.7	163	99.4	0.0	0.0	0.6	0.0	15.9	68.6	15.3	81	76.5	33.3	11.1
Burlington city	1,060	1,044	-1.5	1,315	83.0	0.0	8.7	5.4	3.0	23.9	68.3	7.6	454	77.3	41.6	17.0
Butte city	68	69	1.5	64	100.0	0.0	0.0	0.0	0.0	20.3	36.0	43.8	35	85.7	68.6	5.7
Buxton city	323	319	-1.2	384	90.6	0.0	0.0	9.4	0.0	30.2	57.9	12.0	149	81.2	44.3	15.4
Caledonia CDP	39	NA	NA	10	100.0	0.0	0.0	0.0	0.0	0.0	100.0	0.0	5	100.0	0.0	0.0
Calio city	22	21	-4.5	4	100.0	0.0	0.0	0.0	0.0	0.0	0.0	100.0	3	100.0	66.7	33.3
Calvin city	20	19	-5.0	19	100.0	0.0	0.0	0.0	0.0	10.5	31.7	57.9	13	100.0	0.0	84.6
Cando city	1,115	1,142	2.4	1,132	92.0	0.0	0.3	6.8	1.0	24.8	51.9	23.2	511	65.4	36.2	21.7
Cannon Ball CDP	875	NA	NA	949	8.6	0.0	0.0	90.9	0.4	40.2	54.2	5.7	204	32.8	46.6	14.2
Canton City city	45	43	-4.4	24	100.0	0.0	0.0	0.0	0.0	0.0	75.0	25.0	17	100.0	47.1	23.5
Carpio city	157	149	-5.1	124	97.6	0.0	0.0	2.4	0.0	29.8	50.7	19.4	51	74.5	52.9	5.9
Carrington city	2,065	2,074	0.4	1,944	95.4	0.0	0.8	1.3	2.5	18.6	57.1	24.2	992	69.0	42.4	20.3
Carson city	293	287	-2.0	246	95.9	0.0	0.0	3.7	0.4	15.9	57.3	26.8	139	69.1	50.4	15.1
Casselton city	2,329	2,523	8.3	2,434	96.8	0.0	0.0	2.9	0.2	28.6	57.8	13.6	940	76.9	30.9	35.2
Cathay city	43	43	0.0	46	71.7	0.0	0.0	28.3	0.0	21.7	52.2	26.1	18	77.8	38.9	22.2
Cavalier city	1,302	1,249	-4.1	1,272	90.6	0.4	0.0	5.6	3.4	19.6	52.8	27.5	613	66.6	45.8	18.3
Cayuga city	27	27	0.0	35	100.0	0.0	0.0	0.0	0.0	0.0	82.9	17.1	21	100.0	66.7	4.8
Center city	571	569	-0.4	566	85.2	0.0	0.0	9.5	5.3	15.9	56.5	27.7	280	74.6	49.6	18.6
Christine city	150	152	1.3	139	100.0	0.0	0.0	0.0	0.0	26.0	64.8	9.4	64	92.2	31.3	17.2
Churchs Ferry city	12	12	0.0	7	100.0	0.0	0.0	0.0	0.0	0.0	100.0	0.0	3	100.0	0.0	0.0
Cleveland city	83	82	-1.2	105	88.6	0.0	0.0	11.4	0.0	35.2	49.6	15.2	42	88.1	42.9	28.6
Clifford city	44	44	0.0	13	100.0	0.0	0.0	0.0	0.0	0.0	38.5	61.5	9	88.9	0.0	11.1
Cogswell city	99	100	1.0	90	95.6	0.0	0.0	3.3	1.1	3.3	80.0	16.7	60	90.0	71.7	5.0
Coleharbor city	79	85	7.6	62	96.8	0.0	0.0	0.0	3.2	8.0	67.7	24.2	37	94.6	35.1	5.4
Colfax city	121	136	12.4	127	100.0	0.0	0.0	0.0	0.0	27.5	59.1	13.4	54	98.1	9.3	29.6
Columbus city	133	150	12.8	183	68.9	4.4	1.1	1.1	24.6	31.7	60.7	7.7	73	50.7	42.5	13.7
Conway city	23	22	-4.3	9	88.9	0.0	0.0	11.1	0.0	11.1	55.5	33.3	6	100.0	66.7	33.3
Cooperstown city	984	946	-3.9	1,082	99.0	0.8	0.0	0.0	0.2	18.6	50.4	31.0	476	66.0	48.5	16.6
Courtenay city	45	44	-2.2	49	100.0	0.0	0.0	0.0	0.0	32.6	65.2	2.0	20	100.0	35.0	30.0
Crary city	142	142	0.0	145	80.7	0.0	0.0	6.9	12.4	18.5	71.0	10.3	59	69.5	67.8	16.9
Crosby city	1,070	1,383	29.3	1,064	98.9	0.0	0.0	1.1	0.0	10.8	56.7	32.4	565	81.6	49.7	23.5
Crystal city	138	132	-4.3	140	95.7	0.0	0.0	4.3	0.0	17.1	68.6	14.3	74	93.2	52.7	16.2
Dahlen CDP	18	NA	NA	70	100.0	0.0	0.0	0.0	0.0	27.1	72.9	0.0	39	38.5	0.0	38.5
Davenport city	252	256	1.6	203	92.6	0.0	0.0	2.0	5.4	26.5	60.6	12.8	82	87.8	42.7	18.3
Dawson city	61	61	0.0	56	100.0	0.0	0.0	0.0	0.0	16.1	66.0	17.9	27	81.5	77.8	11.1
Dazey city	104	103	-1.0	125	100.0	0.0	0.0	0.0	0.0	34.4	56.8	8.8	46	78.3	50.0	21.7
Deering city	98	115	17.3	109	98.2	0.0	0.0	1.8	0.0	26.6	65.1	8.3	46	93.5	43.5	34.8
De Lamere CDP	30	NA	NA	17	100.0	0.0	0.0	0.0	0.0	0.0	17.6	82.4	10	100.0	70.0	30.0
Denhoff CDP	20	NA	NA	23	100.0	0.0	0.0	0.0	0.0	0.0	82.6	17.4	14	100.0	14.3	21.4
Des Lacs city	204	203	-0.5	223	99.1	0.0	0.0	0.0	0.9	21.9	61.0	17.0	84	96.4	47.6	36.9
Devils Lake city	7,141	7,288	2.1	7,218	83.1	1.3	0.6	14.7	0.3	21.1	58.4	20.4	3,299	52.2	46.2	19.1
Dickey city	42	42	0.0	31	100.0	0.0	0.0	0.0	0.0	13.0	71.0	16.1	18	88.9	66.7	33.3
Dickinson city	17,866	22,322	24.9	19,920	90.9	1.3	1.7	2.1	4.0	22.2	64.1	13.6	8,135	66.4	37.8	26.5
Dodge city	87	105	20.7	123	96.7	0.0	0.0	3.3	0.0	27.6	56.0	16.3	47	74.5	70.2	10.6
Donnybrook city	58	55	-5.2	88	84.1	0.0	0.0	0.0	15.9	31.8	42.0	26.1	36	100.0	55.6	11.1
Douglas city	64	61	-4.7	71	91.5	0.0	0.0	7.0	1.4	22.6	49.3	28.2	26	100.0	61.5	7.7
Drake city	275	291	5.8	321	95.0	0.0	0.0	3.4	1.6	23.1	46.9	29.9	162	80.9	63.6	5.6
Drayton city	824	789	-4.2	759	97.6	0.0	0.0	1.7	0.7	21.1	54.8	24.0	370	66.5	52.2	14.3
Driscoll CDP	82	NA	NA	62	91.9	0.0	0.0	8.1	0.0	24.1	45.1	30.6	31	80.6	54.8	0.0
Dunn Center city	146	196	34.2	199	97.0	0.0	3.0	0.0	0.0	17.0	59.6	23.1	95	77.9	53.7	15.8
Dunseith city	773	795	2.8	838	14.0	0.0	0.0	83.2	2.0	32.6	54.0	13.2	294	54.8	31.3	16.3
Dwight city	82	81	-1.2	88	73.9	0.0	0.0	0.0	26.1	25.0	67.0	8.0	33	81.8	27.3	6.1
East Dunseith CDP	500	NA	NA	496	0.0	0.0	0.0	90.7	9.3	47.5	49.7	2.6	124	62.9	37.1	4.0
East Fairview CDP	76	NA	NA	119	100.0	0.0	0.0	0.0	0.0	37.0	50.5	12.6	38	100.0	26.3	5.3
Edgeley city	563	554	-1.6	572	98.4	0.0	0.0	0.0	1.6	19.1	57.1	23.8	277	70.8	35.0	23.5
Edinburg city	196	191	-2.6	168	97.0	1.8	0.0	1.2	0.0	7.2	60.1	32.7	102	86.3	42.2	24.5
Edmore city	182	177	-2.7	201	93.0	0.0	0.0	5.0	2.0	13.5	49.0	37.8	96	64.6	28.1	32.3
Egeland city	28	29	3.6	15	100.0	0.0	0.0	0.0	0.0	0.0	33.3	66.7	13	100.0	46.2	0.0
Elgin city	642	624	-2.8	588	98.8	0.0	0.0	1.2	0.0	15.1	50.5	34.4	311	70.1	51.8	14.8
Ellendale city	1,394	1,348	-3.3	1,506	92.3	2.7	0.1	3.6	1.3	19.6	58.0	22.3	622	61.4	35.4	24.1
Elliott city	25	25	0.0	16	100.0	0.0	0.0	0.0	0.0	0.0	62.5	37.5	9	100.0	44.4	11.1
Embden CDP	59	NA	NA	63	100.0	0.0	0.0	0.0	0.0	22.2	69.8	7.9	27	88.9	55.6	0.0
Emerado city	414	435	5.1	331	76.7	6.3	2.1	9.1	5.7	9.9	79.4	10.6	167	41.3	53.9	9.6
Enderlin city	886	878	-0.9	865	94.2	1.6	1.2	2.5	0.5	15.5	57.2	27.3	414	57.0	51.9	9.7
Englevale CDP	40	NA	NA	155	100.0	0.0	0.0	0.0	0.0	23.9	67.7	8.4	33	100.0	87.9	0.0
Epping city	96	88	-8.3	107	77.6	0.0	0.0	22.4	0.0	34.6	62.6	2.8	39	87.2	28.2	0.0
Erie CDP	50	NA	NA	140	100.0	0.0	0.0	0.0	0.0	42.9	46.4	10.7	44	79.5	54.5	34.1
Esmond city	100	101	1.0	108	100.0	0.0	0.0	0.0	0.0	13.0	33.5	53.7	60	85.0	65.0	5.0
Fairdale city	38	37	-2.6	23	100.0	0.0	0.0	0.0	0.0	8.7	52.2	39.1	13	69.2	76.9	15.4
Fairmount city	367	364	-0.8	384	96.1	0.0	0.3	1.8	1.8	27.1	60.2	12.8	160	82.5	50.0	10.0
Fargo city	105,549	115,863	9.8	110,725	87.9	3.0	3.1	3.2	2.8	19.6	70.1	10.3	48,958	44.3	22.9	36.4
Fessenden city	479	477	-0.4	539	92.2	0.0	0.0	7.8	0.0	23.1	52.4	24.7	255	80.4	38.0	24.7
Fingal city	97	96	-1.0	133	90.2	0.0	0.0	9.8	0.0	27.1	61.7	11.3	63	68.3	44.4	7.9
Finley city	445	439	-1.3	445	99.6	0.0	0.0	0.0	0.4	20.2	53.4	26.3	231	61.9	52.4	6.9
Flasher city	232	221	-4.7	295	82.4	0.0	0.0	4.4	13.2	28.5	55.1	16.3	129	84.5	35.7	22.5
Flaxton city	66	71	7.6	58	70.7	0.0	0.0	10.3	19.0	18.9	44.8	36.2	28	60.7	35.7	28.6

1 May be of any race.

Table A. All Places — **Population and Housing**

STATE City, town, township, borough, or CDP (county if applicable)	2010 census total population	2014 estimated population	Percent change 2010–2014	ACS total population estimate 2010–2014	White alone, not Hispanic or Latino	Black alone, not Hispanic or Latino	Asian alone, not Hispanic or Latino	All other races or 2 or more races, not Hispanic or Latino	Hispanic or Latino[1]	Under 18 years old	Age 18 to 64 years old	Age 65 years and older	Total occupied housing units	Percent owner occupied	High school diploma or less	Bachelor's degree or more
	1	2	3	4	5	6	7	8	9	10	11	12	13	14	15	16
NORTH DAKOTA—Con.																
Forbes city	53	53	0.0	49	100.0	0.0	0.0	0.0	0.0	20.3	51.1	28.6	25	84.0	68.0	0.0
Fordville city	212	208	-1.9	241	96.7	0.0	0.0	0.0	3.3	17.9	55.1	27.0	127	96.9	40.2	11.8
Forest River city	125	121	-3.2	121	78.5	0.0	0.0	1.7	19.8	17.3	64.5	18.2	52	90.4	32.7	15.4
Forman city	504	518	2.8	542	90.6	0.4	1.3	0.6	7.2	19.6	54.0	26.6	238	55.0	34.5	9.7
Fort Ransom city	77	78	1.3	77	94.8	0.0	5.2	0.0	0.0	1.3	58.5	40.3	45	77.8	55.6	20.0
Fort Totten CDP	1,243	NA	NA	1,269	0.9	0.0	0.6	97.3	1.2	49.8	46.5	3.8	310	15.5	53.2	5.8
Fortuna city	22	23	4.5	51	100.0	0.0	0.0	0.0	0.0	47.1	47.0	5.9	19	89.5	31.6	31.6
Fort Yates city	182	194	6.6	229	4.8	0.0	0.0	95.2	0.0	38.9	57.3	3.9	58	70.7	34.5	29.3
Four Bears Village CDP	517	NA	NA	567	1.1	0.0	0.0	96.3	2.6	38.2	60.1	1.6	115	2.6	32.2	20.0
Foxholm CDP	75	NA	NA	88	100.0	0.0	0.0	0.0	0.0	23.8	57.9	18.2	38	100.0	50.0	15.8
Fredonia city	46	44	-4.3	51	100.0	0.0	0.0	0.0	0.0	15.6	64.7	19.6	25	92.0	64.0	4.0
Frontier city	214	215	0.5	208	99.0	0.5	0.0	0.5	0.0	14.9	78.4	6.7	77	97.4	19.5	36.4
Fullerton city	54	52	-3.7	60	100.0	0.0	0.0	0.0	0.0	16.7	51.7	31.7	33	97.0	42.4	12.1
Gackle city	310	297	-4.2	390	91.0	1.8	0.0	0.0	7.2	22.4	51.7	25.9	164	77.4	49.4	5.5
Galesburg city	108	107	-0.9	114	82.5	0.0	0.0	3.5	14.0	10.5	73.7	15.8	64	92.2	34.4	17.2
Gardena city	29	30	3.4	12	100.0	0.0	0.0	0.0	0.0	0.0	66.7	33.3	9	100.0	44.4	0.0
Gardner city	74	77	4.1	82	89.0	0.0	0.0	11.0	0.0	32.9	65.8	1.2	26	100.0	61.5	11.5
Garrison city	1,453	1,542	6.1	1,414	92.9	0.0	0.0	5.8	1.3	19.5	51.1	29.5	639	72.6	50.4	16.7
Gascoyne city	16	16	0.0	9	100.0	0.0	0.0	0.0	0.0	0.0	0.0	100.0	6	83.3	33.3	16.7
Gilby city	237	236	-0.4	279	90.3	0.0	0.0	9.0	0.7	28.7	60.6	10.8	123	79.7	34.1	17.9
Gladstone city	239	338	41.4	314	92.0	0.0	1.0	4.5	2.5	22.0	65.3	12.7	136	75.7	51.5	4.4
Glenburn city	413	448	8.5	468	94.2	0.0	1.7	4.1	0.0	33.6	59.3	7.1	184	70.7	28.3	15.2
Glenfield city	91	92	1.1	101	88.1	3.0	1.0	0.0	7.9	18.9	62.4	18.8	55	69.1	16.4	36.4
Glen Ullin city	807	759	-5.9	681	95.2	0.0	0.0	2.1	2.8	18.5	59.0	22.5	358	83.5	65.1	14.0
Golden Valley city	182	182	0.0	232	96.1	0.0	0.9	2.2	0.9	18.1	66.0	15.9	119	79.8	52.9	11.8
Golva city	61	68	11.5	118	100.0	0.0	0.0	0.0	0.0	6.8	77.9	15.3	49	61.2	40.8	14.3
Goodrich city	98	97	-1.0	115	93.0	0.0	0.0	3.5	3.5	14.8	53.1	32.2	59	88.1	45.8	10.2
Grace City city	63	63	0.0	62	100.0	0.0	0.0	0.0	0.0	17.7	72.6	9.7	28	75.0	46.4	0.0
Grafton city	4,284	4,268	-0.4	4,291	80.1	0.0	0.7	5.5	13.7	23.6	57.3	19.0	1,897	62.2	53.0	15.8
Grand Forks city	52,876	56,057	6.0	54,095	86.6	2.6	2.6	5.4	2.8	18.5	70.8	10.6	22,844	46.7	27.4	33.2
Grand Forks AFB CDP	2,367	NA	NA	2,387	66.6	10.6	2.6	7.6	12.7	31.7	68.5	0.0	573	1.2	22.2	22.0
Grandin city	173	176	1.7	196	91.3	0.0	0.0	8.2	0.5	23.5	66.8	9.7	78	78.2	48.7	16.7
Grano city	7	7	0.0	3	100.0	0.0	0.0	0.0	0.0	0.0	100.0	0.0	1	100.0	100.0	0.0
Granville city	241	272	12.9	246	88.6	0.0	0.8	2.8	7.7	23.2	56.0	20.7	116	62.9	55.2	19.8
Great Bend city	60	59	-1.7	58	100.0	0.0	0.0	0.0	0.0	12.0	65.5	22.4	31	96.8	61.3	9.7
Green Acres CDP	575	NA	NA	667	0.0	0.0	0.0	100.0	0.0	55.0	44.8	0.0	187	0.0	52.9	0.0
Grenora city	244	257	5.3	187	95.7	4.3	0.0	0.0	0.0	28.3	62.2	9.6	84	66.7	44.0	25.0
Gwinner city	753	822	9.2	814	94.8	0.0	1.0	1.4	2.8	25.2	63.2	11.5	356	68.0	39.9	21.6
Hague city	71	67	-5.6	64	100.0	0.0	0.0	0.0	0.0	14.1	42.2	43.8	34	100.0	50.0	0.0
Halliday city	188	222	18.1	279	84.9	0.7	0.4	14.0	0.0	26.1	59.5	14.3	105	74.3	53.3	13.3
Hamberg city	21	21	0.0	13	100.0	0.0	0.0	0.0	0.0	0.0	61.6	38.5	10	90.0	80.0	20.0
Hamilton city	61	60	-1.6	59	100.0	0.0	0.0	0.0	0.0	5.1	66.2	28.8	31	100.0	48.4	3.2
Hampden city	48	47	-2.1	39	100.0	0.0	0.0	0.0	0.0	18.0	59.0	23.1	19	63.2	47.4	0.0
Hankinson city	919	912	-0.8	951	95.0	0.0	0.1	3.8	1.2	20.4	50.0	29.4	408	80.1	54.7	10.5
Hannaford city	131	125	-4.6	107	93.5	0.0	0.0	6.5	0.0	0.0	51.5	48.6	64	85.9	59.4	15.6
Hannah city	15	14	-6.7	11	100.0	0.0	0.0	0.0	0.0	9.1	81.9	9.1	8	100.0	87.5	0.0
Hansboro city	12	12	0.0	19	100.0	0.0	0.0	0.0	0.0	10.6	79.1	10.5	13	92.3	23.1	61.5
Harmon CDP	145	NA	NA	216	100.0	0.0	0.0	0.0	0.0	37.5	51.9	10.6	68	100.0	0.0	47.1
Harvey city	1,783	1,777	-0.3	1,830	99.3	0.0	0.0	0.7	0.0	20.5	48.4	31.1	877	66.2	54.3	17.1
Harwood city	718	760	5.8	845	98.2	0.0	0.0	0.9	0.8	30.7	64.2	5.1	279	92.1	19.0	32.6
Hatton city	777	771	-0.8	761	95.8	0.0	0.0	4.2	0.0	23.2	42.2	34.4	350	76.3	42.3	20.6
Havana city	71	72	1.4	72	97.2	0.0	0.0	0.0	2.8	2.8	41.7	55.6	40	85.0	47.5	15.0
Haynes city	23	23	0.0	15	100.0	0.0	0.0	0.0	0.0	0.0	73.4	26.7	9	77.8	88.9	0.0
Hazelton city	235	225	-4.3	253	100.0	0.0	0.0	0.0	0.0	27.3	50.6	22.1	131	64.9	38.2	16.0
Hazen city	2,411	2,450	1.6	2,607	92.3	1.0	0.3	3.3	3.0	22.3	64.2	13.6	1,070	80.8	33.7	26.3
Hebron city	747	703	-5.9	848	82.3	1.8	0.0	0.0	15.9	29.0	54.2	16.7	319	89.7	56.7	25.7
Heil CDP	15	NA	NA	16	100.0	0.0	0.0	0.0	0.0	0.0	37.5	62.5	9	33.3	66.7	33.3
Heimdal CDP	27	NA	NA	5	100.0	0.0	0.0	0.0	0.0	0.0	0.0	100.0	5	100.0	100.0	0.0
Hettinger city	1,226	1,256	2.4	1,219	92.0	0.5	1.6	4.7	1.1	17.9	59.8	22.2	549	60.8	40.3	26.6
Hillsboro city	1,603	1,591	-0.7	1,692	88.8	0.4	0.4	0.7	9.6	25.0	56.8	18.3	702	69.2	40.9	26.8
Hoople city	242	235	-2.9	318	67.9	0.0	0.0	0.3	31.8	34.9	57.5	7.5	119	84.0	47.9	10.9
Hope city	258	258	0.0	351	100.0	0.0	0.0	0.0	0.0	20.4	60.1	19.4	167	73.1	52.1	10.8
Horace city	2,430	2,548	4.9	2,502	97.5	0.0	0.3	0.5	1.7	31.7	60.8	7.5	836	95.6	28.1	44.5
Hunter city	261	270	3.4	369	98.1	0.0	0.0	1.9	0.0	33.1	56.5	10.6	134	79.9	41.8	16.4
Hurdsfield city	84	83	-1.2	57	96.5	0.0	0.0	0.0	3.5	17.6	57.9	24.6	32	71.9	68.8	18.8
Inkster city	50	49	-2.0	30	90.0	0.0	0.0	10.0	0.0	20.0	63.3	16.7	15	80.0	73.3	6.7
Jamestown city	15,427	15,446	0.1	15,407	92.7	0.7	0.5	3.7	2.4	19.1	63.7	17.0	6,791	60.4	50.1	24.0
Jessie CDP	25	NA	NA	30	100.0	0.0	0.0	0.0	0.0	20.0	73.4	6.7	12	100.0	50.0	0.0
Jud city	72	73	1.4	66	90.9	1.5	0.0	6.1	1.5	18.1	42.2	39.4	31	90.3	64.5	6.5
Karlsruhe city	82	87	6.1	87	100.0	0.0	0.0	0.0	0.0	16.0	65.5	18.4	41	78.0	73.2	7.3
Kathryn city	52	52	0.0	64	100.0	0.0	0.0	0.0	0.0	4.7	42.1	53.1	40	87.5	57.5	2.5
Kenmare city	1,096	1,089	-0.6	1,027	84.4	0.3	0.0	5.3	10.0	24.0	50.6	25.5	406	75.4	47.8	13.5
Kensal city	163	160	-1.8	189	88.9	0.0	0.0	11.1	0.0	17.5	57.6	24.9	90	88.9	53.3	10.0
Kief city	13	14	7.7	16	100.0	0.0	0.0	0.0	0.0	0.0	93.9	6.3	9	66.7	66.7	0.0
Killdeer city	751	1,026	36.6	914	91.0	0.2	0.9	4.3	3.6	23.6	57.4	18.8	335	82.1	34.0	34.0
Kindred city	692	735	6.2	656	95.7	0.0	0.5	1.4	2.4	31.7	56.7	11.7	248	77.0	27.8	29.4
Knox city	25	25	0.0	36	100.0	0.0	0.0	0.0	0.0	0.0	69.6	30.6	22	100.0	86.4	0.0
Kramer city	29	30	3.4	30	96.7	0.0	0.0	3.3	0.0	13.4	66.6	20.0	17	76.5	35.3	0.0
Kulm city	354	344	-2.8	305	99.3	0.0	0.0	0.0	0.7	20.6	39.8	39.3	161	83.2	50.3	23.6
Lakota city	672	661	-1.6	570	91.2	0.0	0.0	4.2	4.6	19.3	56.2	24.4	291	73.2	35.4	28.2
LaMoure city	889	935	5.2	946	99.6	0.0	0.0	0.0	0.4	25.6	52.6	21.9	401	64.1	39.2	20.2
Landa city	38	39	2.6	72	100.0	0.0	0.0	0.0	0.0	23.6	66.6	9.7	34	73.5	91.2	0.0
Langdon city	1,878	1,806	-3.8	1,878	96.9	0.0	0.0	0.7	2.4	19.7	52.7	27.6	871	83.1	40.1	17.9
Lankin city	98	95	-3.1	143	97.9	0.0	0.0	1.4	0.7	27.3	56.7	16.1	69	87.0	40.6	15.9
Lansford city	245	253	3.3	272	97.4	1.5	0.0	0.0	1.1	16.6	75.9	7.4	135	75.6	15.6	15.6
Larimore city	1,346	1,351	0.4	1,527	85.7	0.7	0.0	4.7	8.8	30.5	52.4	17.3	582	65.6	40.2	19.8
Larson CDP	12	NA	NA	0	0.0	0.0	0.0	0.0	0.0	0.0	0.0	0.0	0	0.0	0.0	0.0
Lawton city	30	30	0.0	24	100.0	0.0	0.0	0.0	0.0	0.0	58.4	41.7	17	100.0	35.3	35.3
Leal city	20	20	0.0	29	100.0	0.0	0.0	0.0	0.0	37.9	58.5	3.4	11	100.0	45.5	27.3
Leeds city	427	438	2.6	421	98.3	0.0	0.0	1.7	0.0	26.7	53.9	19.5	195	74.4	37.9	23.1
Lehr city	80	79	-1.3	88	100.0	0.0	0.0	0.0	0.0	0.0	48.8	51.1	61	75.4	73.8	1.6

1 May be of any race.

Table A. All Places — **Population and Housing**

STATE City, town, township, borough, or CDP (county if applicable)	Population: 2010 census total population	Population: 2014 estimated population	Population: Percent change 2010–2014	Population: ACS total population estimate 2010–2014	Race and Hispanic or Latino origin (percent), 2010–2014: White alone, not Hispanic or Latino	Black alone, not Hispanic or Latino	Asian alone, not Hispanic or Latino	All other races or 2 or more races, not Hispanic or Latino	Hispanic or Latino[1]	Age (percent), 2010–2014: Under 18 years old	Age 18 to 64 years old	Age 65 years and older	Households, 2010–2014: Total occupied housing units	Percent owner occupied	Householders by level of education (percent): High school diploma or less	Bachelor's degree or more
	1	2	3	4	5	6	7	8	9	10	11	12	13	14	15	16
NORTH DAKOTA—Con.																
Leith city	16	16	0.0	25	96.0	4.0	0.0	0.0	0.0	32.0	52.0	16.0	11	81.8	54.5	0.0
Leonard city	223	228	2.2	302	98.7	0.0	0.0	0.7	0.7	24.9	58.9	16.2	121	78.5	48.8	19.8
Lidgerwood city	652	635	-2.6	713	95.2	0.0	0.0	1.0	3.8	21.9	45.9	32.3	333	70.6	50.5	15.3
Lignite city	155	248	60.0	81	92.6	2.5	0.0	4.9	0.0	6.2	61.6	32.1	52	51.9	51.9	9.6
Lincoln city	2,406	3,351	39.3	2,864	94.3	0.0	0.0	3.5	2.2	31.3	61.0	7.9	1,002	99.6	35.6	19.2
Linton city	1,097	1,047	-4.6	1,114	99.5	0.0	0.3	0.3	0.0	14.6	52.7	32.6	619	70.8	62.8	10.3
Lisbon city	2,154	2,139	-0.7	2,074	94.8	0.0	0.0	2.6	2.6	26.7	53.4	20.0	915	63.4	49.8	21.1
Litchville city	172	171	-0.6	148	95.3	0.0	0.0	3.4	1.4	9.5	56.8	33.8	80	93.8	65.0	13.8
Logan CDP	194	NA	NA	203	100.0	0.0	0.0	0.0	0.0	19.8	63.6	16.7	70	85.7	34.3	8.6
Loma city	16	15	-6.3	19	100.0	0.0	0.0	0.0	0.0	42.1	57.9	0.0	4	100.0	0.0	25.0
Loraine city	9	9	0.0	0	0.0	0.0	0.0	0.0	0.0	0.0	0.0	0.0	0	0.0	0.0	0.0
Ludden city	23	22	-4.3	42	95.2	0.0	0.0	0.0	4.8	19.0	47.6	33.3	19	84.2	89.5	10.5
Luverne city	31	31	0.0	51	98.0	0.0	0.0	0.0	2.0	0.0	96.1	3.9	31	96.8	87.1	0.0
McClusky city	380	380	0.0	284	100.0	0.0	0.0	0.0	0.0	11.3	53.9	34.9	160	74.4	57.5	21.3
McHenry city	56	56	0.0	108	98.1	0.0	0.0	0.0	1.9	37.1	33.5	29.6	38	84.2	55.3	7.9
McLeod CDP	27	NA	NA	16	100.0	0.0	0.0	0.0	0.0	0.0	100.0	0.0	11	100.0	45.5	0.0
McVille city	349	345	-1.1	325	96.0	0.0	0.0	4.0	0.0	10.8	46.1	43.1	180	82.2	29.4	18.9
Maddock city	382	387	1.3	362	98.9	0.0	0.0	0.3	0.8	19.9	55.3	24.9	177	71.2	43.5	15.8
Makoti city	154	148	-3.9	199	68.3	0.0	0.0	29.6	2.0	33.2	54.6	12.1	77	67.5	39.0	11.7
Mandan city	18,425	20,820	13.0	19,381	91.1	0.8	0.3	6.4	1.4	23.7	61.8	14.6	8,219	72.8	36.6	28.0
Mandaree CDP	596	NA	NA	829	4.7	1.6	0.0	80.7	13.0	48.5	48.4	3.1	168	11.3	39.3	13.7
Manning CDP	74	NA	NA	35	100.0	0.0	0.0	0.0	0.0	14.3	77.1	8.6	18	100.0	77.8	22.2
Mantador city	64	63	-1.6	79	100.0	0.0	0.0	0.0	0.0	10.1	84.8	5.1	29	100.0	65.5	0.0
Manvel city	360	380	5.6	408	95.8	0.0	0.0	1.2	2.9	28.4	63.5	8.1	158	89.2	31.6	17.1
Mapleton city	762	868	13.9	815	86.6	8.3	0.0	3.9	1.1	33.5	62.9	3.8	259	95.8	32.0	23.9
Marion city	133	133	0.0	171	100.0	0.0	0.0	0.0	0.0	16.3	66.6	17.0	81	74.1	30.9	32.1
Marmarth city	136	143	5.1	137	95.6	1.5	0.0	0.7	2.2	26.3	56.3	17.5	59	89.8	81.4	1.7
Martin city	78	78	0.0	106	91.5	8.5	0.0	0.0	0.0	17.9	65.2	17.0	41	97.6	51.2	9.8
Max city	334	344	3.0	364	94.0	0.0	0.0	4.9	1.1	28.3	58.8	12.9	151	76.8	53.6	9.3
Maxbass city	84	86	2.4	61	98.4	0.0	0.0	1.6	0.0	34.4	55.7	9.8	24	54.2	33.3	16.7
Mayville city	1,858	1,843	-0.8	1,808	94.0	2.6	0.0	2.3	1.1	13.6	64.1	22.4	769	53.8	24.7	35.8
Medina city	308	304	-1.3	342	95.9	0.0	0.0	1.2	2.9	30.4	50.2	19.3	143	81.1	55.2	14.0
Medora city	112	132	17.9	161	77.6	2.5	16.1	3.1	0.6	8.1	80.5	11.2	63	46.0	19.0	47.6
Menoken CDP	70	NA	NA	71	93.0	0.0	0.0	7.0	0.0	22.6	64.9	12.7	31	93.5	35.5	19.4
Mercer city	94	98	4.3	67	88.1	3.0	0.0	4.5	4.5	14.9	50.8	34.3	35	94.3	45.7	14.3
Michigan City city	294	285	-3.1	199	100.0	0.0	0.0	0.0	0.0	14.5	63.3	22.1	105	86.7	39.0	13.3
Milnor city	653	662	1.4	545	95.4	0.0	0.0	1.8	2.8	21.5	63.8	14.9	244	77.0	35.2	16.8
Milton city	58	56	-3.4	52	84.6	0.0	0.0	15.4	0.0	7.6	53.8	38.5	25	100.0	52.0	12.0
Minnewaukan city	224	227	1.3	214	87.4	0.0	0.0	12.6	0.0	19.5	66.3	14.0	114	38.6	36.0	47.4
Minot city	40,962	47,997	17.2	44,533	87.5	2.9	1.0	5.2	3.4	22.3	64.2	13.4	18,226	60.7	32.6	26.2
Minot AFB CDP	5,521	NA	NA	5,813	66.4	10.5	2.0	6.4	14.7	30.1	69.9	0.0	1,558	1.3	22.0	18.0
Minto city	604	613	1.5	728	80.2	0.4	0.0	0.0	19.4	31.0	56.2	12.9	276	90.2	58.3	14.5
Mohall city	783	818	4.5	759	96.8	0.8	1.1	0.8	0.5	18.8	60.3	20.9	309	76.1	41.1	13.6
Monango city	36	35	-2.8	41	87.8	12.2	0.0	0.0	0.0	51.2	26.8	22.0	12	100.0	33.3	33.3
Montpelier city	87	87	0.0	98	95.9	0.0	0.0	4.1	0.0	26.5	59.2	14.3	37	89.2	56.8	0.0
Mooreton city	197	195	-1.0	207	92.8	0.0	0.0	6.8	0.5	30.9	59.9	9.2	88	92.0	28.4	18.2
Mott city	721	786	9.0	782	94.8	0.0	0.0	5.2	0.0	26.5	46.8	26.5	326	78.5	49.4	19.6
Mountain city	92	88	-4.3	86	100.0	0.0	0.0	0.0	0.0	8.1	41.9	50.0	24	87.5	75.0	16.7
Munich city	210	205	-2.4	261	93.1	1.1	0.0	5.7	0.0	23.4	48.5	28.0	114	85.1	46.5	15.8
Mylo city	20	20	0.0	8	100.0	0.0	0.0	0.0	0.0	0.0	62.5	37.5	6	100.0	66.7	0.0
Napoleon city	792	784	-1.0	774	97.0	0.0	0.8	2.2	0.0	21.9	46.2	31.9	357	79.3	58.0	14.6
Nash CDP	32	NA	NA	8	100.0	0.0	0.0	0.0	0.0	0.0	50.0	50.0	6	100.0	66.7	33.3
Neche city	371	361	-2.7	349	95.7	0.6	0.0	2.6	1.1	23.3	59.0	17.8	144	83.3	56.9	15.3
Nekoma city	50	48	-4.0	37	100.0	0.0	0.0	0.0	0.0	21.6	67.5	10.8	15	100.0	33.3	60.0
Newburg city	110	114	3.6	163	89.0	0.0	0.0	2.5	8.6	24.6	49.7	25.8	75	57.3	50.7	5.3
New England city	600	635	5.8	587	91.7	2.9	0.0	5.5	0.0	11.3	69.3	19.4	256	81.6	53.9	13.7
New Leipzig city	221	216	-2.3	230	96.5	3.0	0.0	0.0	0.4	11.2	55.1	33.5	128	89.1	47.7	22.7
New Rockford city	1,391	1,390	-0.1	1,376	92.3	0.0	0.0	3.4	4.3	21.7	52.1	26.2	632	67.2	44.0	17.7
New Salem city	946	897	-5.2	864	94.8	0.0	0.1	5.1	0.0	20.0	54.5	25.5	372	74.7	42.7	22.6
New Town city	1,925	2,401	24.7	2,210	22.1	1.0	0.6	69.5	6.8	28.1	65.4	6.5	657	52.7	40.9	23.0
Niagara city	53	52	-1.9	44	70.5	0.0	0.0	29.5	0.0	29.5	43.2	27.3	24	87.5	41.7	25.0
Nome city	62	62	0.0	60	96.7	0.0	0.0	3.3	0.0	41.7	45.1	13.3	16	100.0	18.8	12.5
Noonan city	121	127	5.0	195	88.2	4.1	4.1	3.6	0.0	27.2	57.9	14.9	81	65.4	58.0	2.5
North River city	56	56	0.0	59	100.0	0.0	0.0	0.0	0.0	25.5	67.9	6.8	19	94.7	10.5	63.2
Northwood city	945	918	-2.9	750	97.1	0.0	0.0	0.7	2.3	21.7	45.7	32.7	341	63.3	54.3	17.0
Oakes city	1,856	1,801	-3.0	1,937	91.5	1.3	0.4	0.8	6.0	23.1	55.7	21.2	819	62.9	43.8	26.5
Oberon city	105	106	1.0	163	27.6	0.0	0.0	30.7	41.7	44.8	44.8	10.4	53	69.8	56.6	3.8
Oriska city	118	121	2.5	83	85.5	0.0	0.0	9.6	4.8	32.5	60.1	7.2	32	68.8	59.4	6.3
Orrin CDP	22	NA	NA	0	0.0	0.0	0.0	0.0	0.0	0.0	0.0	0.0	0	0.0	0.0	0.0
Osnabrock city	134	119	-11.2	113	91.2	0.9	0.0	8.0	0.0	3.6	54.0	42.5	53	83.0	58.5	0.0
Overly city	18	18	0.0	24	54.2	0.0	0.0	45.8	0.0	37.5	45.9	16.7	9	66.7	44.4	0.0
Oxbow city	305	307	0.7	343	97.7	1.2	0.6	0.6	0.0	38.2	56.9	5.0	102	97.1	14.7	59.8
Page city	232	234	0.9	314	97.5	0.0	0.0	0.0	2.5	41.1	52.2	6.7	98	78.6	40.8	8.2
Palermo city	74	82	10.8	85	96.5	0.0	3.5	0.0	0.0	10.6	70.5	18.8	42	69.0	81.0	0.0
Park River city	1,403	1,379	-1.7	1,424	91.9	0.8	1.1	1.8	4.5	18.2	55.1	26.8	655	67.8	41.5	17.4
Parshall city	903	1,220	35.1	1,028	34.9	0.8	0.5	58.2	5.6	31.1	56.1	12.8	368	56.5	31.8	16.3
Pekin city	70	68	-2.9	108	83.3	3.7	0.0	0.0	13.0	23.1	61.1	15.7	41	68.3	29.3	22.0
Pembina city	592	567	-4.2	602	96.2	0.3	0.7	1.2	1.7	31.0	55.2	13.6	251	72.9	43.8	18.7
Perth city	9	9	0.0	10	100.0	0.0	0.0	0.0	0.0	20.0	80.0	0.0	6	33.3	33.3	66.7
Petersburg city	192	185	-3.6	188	79.8	13.8	0.0	2.7	3.7	27.7	49.9	22.3	83	79.5	34.9	13.3
Pettibone city	70	69	-1.4	61	100.0	0.0	0.0	0.0	0.0	14.7	54.1	31.1	31	77.4	58.1	6.5
Pick City city	123	135	9.8	145	85.5	0.0	0.0	14.5	0.0	8.2	61.4	30.3	75	98.7	69.3	14.7
Pillsbury city	12	12	0.0	21	100.0	0.0	0.0	0.0	0.0	0.0	38.1	61.9	13	92.3	84.6	0.0
Pingree city	60	59	-1.7	70	88.6	0.0	0.0	0.0	11.4	27.1	65.7	7.1	34	79.4	50.0	5.9
Pisek city	106	103	-2.8	89	100.0	0.0	0.0	0.0	0.0	10.1	60.7	29.2	54	72.2	59.3	14.8
Plaza city	171	188	9.9	235	77.9	0.0	0.0	14.5	7.7	36.6	53.9	9.4	87	62.1	48.3	8.0
Porcupine CDP	146	NA	NA	144	0.0	0.0	0.0	100.0	0.0	51.4	48.8	0.0	22	54.5	40.9	9.1
Portal city	126	154	22.2	119	92.4	0.0	0.0	7.6	0.0	27.8	55.4	16.8	54	79.6	46.3	27.8
Portland city	606	599	-1.2	660	93.5	0.6	0.0	4.5	1.4	26.3	58.4	15.2	277	69.7	30.0	31.0
Powers Lake city	280	301	7.5	411	94.4	0.0	0.2	0.0	5.4	30.2	53.7	16.1	172	51.7	48.3	17.4
Prairie Rose city	73	73	0.0	118	99.2	0.0	0.8	0.0	0.0	39.0	56.7	4.2	40	100.0	17.5	67.5

1 May be of any race.

Table A. All Places — **Population and Housing**

STATE City, town, township, borough, or CDP (county if applicable)	Population				Race and Hispanic or Latino origin (percent), 2010–2014					Age (percent), 2010–2014			Households, 2010–2014			
	2010 census total population	2014 estimated population	Percent change 2010–2014	ACS total population estimate 2010–2014	White alone, not Hispanic or Latino	Black alone, not Hispanic or Latino	Asian alone, not Hispanic or Latino	All other races or 2 or more races, not Hispanic or Latino	Hispanic or Latino[1]	Under 18 years old	Age 18 to 64 years old	Age 65 years and older	Total occupied housing units	Percent owner occupied	Householders by level of education (percent): High school diploma or less	Householders by level of education (percent): Bachelor's degree or more
	1	2	3	4	5	6	7	8	9	10	11	12	13	14	15	16
NORTH DAKOTA—Con.																
Raleigh CDP	12	NA	NA	8	100.0	0.0	0.0	0.0	0.0	0.0	100.0	0.0	6	100.0	66.7	33.3
Ray city	592	751	26.9	651	85.3	0.0	0.0	14.6	0.2	22.1	66.4	11.4	289	80.6	24.2	11.1
Reeder city	162	163	0.6	154	94.2	1.3	0.0	3.2	1.3	12.2	53.8	33.8	86	70.9	47.7	19.8
Regan city	43	44	2.3	58	53.4	0.0	0.0	0.0	46.6	37.9	44.7	17.2	27	70.4	37.0	14.8
Regent city	160	171	6.9	220	100.0	0.0	0.0	0.0	0.0	26.8	52.8	20.5	101	68.3	54.5	8.9
Reile's Acres city	513	583	13.6	618	97.9	0.3	0.0	1.3	0.5	37.5	60.8	1.6	168	100.0	13.7	47.0
Reynolds city	301	305	1.3	313	96.5	0.0	1.0	2.6	0.0	21.4	62.6	16.0	140	86.4	35.0	19.3
Rhame city	169	176	4.1	199	93.5	0.0	0.0	0.0	6.5	20.1	73.4	6.5	90	74.4	46.7	14.4
Richardton city	530	548	3.4	526	95.6	0.0	0.0	1.3	3.0	17.3	62.6	20.2	268	78.4	40.7	25.4
Riverdale city	205	221	7.8	207	99.0	0.0	0.5	0.5	0.0	16.9	68.1	15.0	95	97.9	47.4	17.9
Robinson city	37	37	0.0	34	100.0	0.0	0.0	0.0	0.0	8.8	44.1	47.1	22	86.4	31.8	36.4
Rocklake city	101	105	4.0	155	83.2	0.0	0.0	15.5	1.3	25.2	54.9	20.0	74	70.3	32.4	24.3
Rogers city	46	46	0.0	59	100.0	0.0	0.0	0.0	0.0	27.1	69.5	3.4	26	76.9	15.4	7.7
Rolette city	594	608	2.4	656	64.2	0.2	0.0	32.6	3.0	29.0	44.5	26.5	239	60.3	37.2	25.9
Rolla city	1,280	1,332	4.1	1,280	48.9	2.3	0.0	48.8	0.0	31.1	56.4	12.5	497	58.1	35.0	23.5
Ross city	97	108	11.3	92	90.2	0.0	0.0	9.8	0.0	11.9	83.8	4.3	45	71.1	48.9	15.6
Rugby city	2,876	2,911	1.2	2,989	91.4	0.3	0.0	6.5	1.8	19.3	55.4	25.2	1,356	66.1	43.7	14.5
Ruso city	4	4	0.0	8	100.0	0.0	0.0	0.0	0.0	75.0	25.0	0.0	1	0.0	100.0	0.0
Ruthville CDP	191	NA	NA	206	45.6	14.6	0.0	39.8	0.0	35.9	59.2	4.9	76	68.4	19.7	15.8
Rutland city	163	164	0.6	176	98.3	0.0	0.0	1.7	0.0	16.4	68.8	14.8	89	79.8	50.6	15.7
Ryder city	85	82	-3.5	99	100.0	0.0	0.0	0.0	0.0	33.4	56.7	10.1	34	73.5	58.8	0.0
St. John city	341	360	5.6	361	26.6	0.0	0.0	73.4	0.0	32.4	53.2	14.4	145	73.8	44.8	24.1
St. Thomas city	331	318	-3.9	330	83.6	0.0	0.0	0.0	16.4	21.2	65.3	13.6	144	75.0	37.5	22.2
Sanborn city	192	193	0.5	173	100.0	0.0	0.0	0.0	0.0	26.6	64.6	8.7	79	84.8	65.8	8.9
Sarles city	28	27	-3.6	12	100.0	0.0	0.0	0.0	0.0	0.0	25.0	75.0	8	100.0	0.0	25.0
Sawyer city	357	345	-3.4	305	98.0	0.0	1.3	0.7	0.0	17.4	67.6	15.1	125	90.4	47.2	14.4
Scranton city	281	286	1.8	270	92.6	1.1	0.0	6.3	0.0	23.3	54.4	22.2	120	63.3	35.8	11.7
Selfridge city	160	170	6.3	189	47.1	0.0	0.0	52.9	0.0	40.7	42.8	16.4	64	79.7	37.5	28.1
Selz CDP	46	NA	NA	19	100.0	0.0	0.0	0.0	0.0	0.0	0.0	100.0	13	100.0	46.2	0.0
Sentinel Butte city	56	62	10.7	91	100.0	0.0	0.0	0.0	0.0	35.2	50.6	14.3	33	87.9	21.2	39.4
Sharon city	96	95	-1.0	95	96.8	0.0	0.0	0.0	3.2	11.6	66.4	22.1	57	56.1	57.9	14.0
Sheldon city	116	121	4.3	94	100.0	0.0	0.0	0.0	0.0	18.1	66.1	16.0	40	92.5	50.0	17.5
Shell Valley CDP	1,197	NA	NA	1,365	1.1	0.0	0.0	96.5	2.4	40.6	56.3	3.0	350	76.9	18.3	38.6
Sherwood city	242	252	4.1	233	100.0	0.0	0.0	0.0	0.0	22.8	53.5	23.6	117	74.4	46.2	25.6
Sheyenne city	204	202	-1.0	206	77.7	0.0	0.0	22.3	0.0	12.6	69.8	17.5	118	73.7	44.9	21.2
Sibley city	30	30	0.0	25	100.0	0.0	0.0	0.0	0.0	24.0	52.0	24.0	14	78.6	50.0	0.0
Solen city	83	89	7.2	75	20.0	0.0	0.0	80.0	0.0	8.0	85.4	6.7	26	88.5	61.5	11.5
Souris city	58	59	1.7	72	86.1	0.0	0.0	13.9	0.0	38.9	47.2	13.9	26	76.9	46.2	0.0
South Heart city	301	403	33.9	287	94.4	0.0	0.0	4.5	1.0	28.9	57.1	13.9	114	89.5	42.1	40.4
Spiritwood CDP	18	NA	NA	9	100.0	0.0	0.0	0.0	0.0	0.0	100.0	0.0	5	100.0	100.0	0.0
Spiritwood Lake city	90	96	6.7	114	100.0	0.0	0.0	0.0	0.0	17.6	49.0	33.3	49	89.8	30.6	38.8
Springbrook city	27	25	-7.4	11	81.8	0.0	0.0	18.2	0.0	27.3	72.8	0.0	5	100.0	40.0	20.0
Stanley city	1,458	2,427	66.5	1,944	88.8	0.1	0.0	4.5	6.6	23.7	60.1	16.2	763	73.8	29.6	20.7
Stanton city	366	367	0.3	426	94.1	0.0	0.0	5.2	0.7	24.0	56.1	20.0	192	80.7	48.4	10.9
Starkweather city	117	117	0.0	182	69.8	0.0	0.0	24.7	5.5	38.4	58.1	3.3	64	51.6	45.3	28.1
Steele city	715	711	-0.6	722	94.6	0.0	0.0	0.0	5.4	25.8	50.4	23.8	320	70.6	39.4	33.4
Strasburg city	409	392	-4.2	511	98.4	0.0	0.0	1.6	0.0	22.1	44.2	33.7	212	91.0	39.2	28.3
Streeter city	170	167	-1.8	80	92.5	0.0	0.0	7.5	0.0	5.0	55.2	40.0	53	64.2	54.7	13.2
Surrey city	934	1,211	29.7	1,027	86.5	0.0	1.9	3.1	8.5	16.6	73.2	10.3	372	87.9	49.7	14.8
Sutton CDP	17	NA	NA	25	100.0	0.0	0.0	0.0	0.0	0.0	40.0	60.0	21	100.0	38.1	0.0
Sykeston city	117	116	-0.9	102	100.0	0.0	0.0	0.0	0.0	16.7	66.7	16.7	53	71.7	35.8	22.6
Tappen city	197	200	1.5	272	88.6	0.0	0.0	1.5	9.9	30.5	56.6	12.9	101	93.1	62.4	16.8
Taylor city	148	175	18.2	190	95.8	0.0	0.5	2.6	1.1	22.7	60.1	17.4	88	79.5	31.8	17.0
Thompson city	986	1,009	2.3	1,163	96.4	0.0	0.0	1.7	1.9	31.7	61.7	6.4	385	93.8	30.4	29.9
Tioga city	1,236	1,603	29.7	1,097	85.7	0.0	1.6	2.6	10.1	17.7	55.4	26.8	538	57.2	52.4	14.5
Tolley city	47	49	4.3	34	100.0	0.0	0.0	0.0	0.0	8.8	64.8	26.5	25	80.0	68.0	0.0
Tolna city	166	160	-3.6	179	100.0	0.0	0.0	0.0	0.0	12.8	61.9	25.1	98	69.4	42.9	13.3
Tower City city	253	261	3.2	240	100.0	0.0	0.0	0.0	0.0	17.9	65.4	16.7	120	75.8	36.7	15.8
Towner city	533	571	7.1	525	82.9	0.4	0.0	7.0	9.7	17.8	57.4	24.8	285	72.3	42.1	22.1
Turtle Lake city	581	593	2.1	488	96.7	0.0	0.6	2.5	0.2	14.5	56.2	29.3	277	72.6	60.6	14.4
Tuttle city	80	80	0.0	80	100.0	0.0	0.0	0.0	0.0	0.0	45.1	55.0	52	75.0	61.5	15.4
Underwood city	778	774	-0.5	746	96.2	0.0	0.0	2.1	1.6	17.4	58.9	23.7	299	78.3	55.9	16.4
Upham city	130	144	10.8	249	98.0	0.0	0.4	1.6	0.0	23.2	64.6	12.0	107	62.6	54.2	0.9
Valley City city	6,617	6,676	0.9	6,636	92.9	1.0	2.7	1.9	1.5	17.0	60.0	22.8	3,078	58.8	43.4	25.0
Velva city	1,102	1,267	15.0	1,008	97.8	0.0	0.0	0.3	1.9	26.6	52.8	20.7	458	67.7	47.4	17.7
Venturia city	13	13	0.0	27	100.0	0.0	0.0	0.0	0.0	48.1	40.7	11.1	12	100.0	100.0	0.0
Verona city	85	86	1.2	74	100.0	0.0	0.0	0.0	0.0	10.9	70.3	18.9	40	82.5	70.0	10.0
Voltaire city	40	42	5.0	54	100.0	0.0	0.0	0.0	0.0	20.5	55.8	24.1	30	100.0	50.0	3.3
Wahpeton city	7,766	7,903	1.8	7,804	90.3	1.2	1.1	4.0	3.4	18.5	69.2	12.2	3,132	58.7	29.3	21.9
Walcott city	235	235	0.0	216	100.0	0.0	0.0	0.0	0.0	27.4	59.8	13.0	95	77.9	44.2	15.8
Wales city	31	30	-3.2	23	100.0	0.0	0.0	0.0	0.0	21.7	43.4	34.8	14	100.0	57.1	42.9
Walhalla city	996	960	-3.6	1,104	83.4	0.0	0.0	11.6	5.0	25.5	46.4	28.1	502	72.5	60.2	14.5
Warwick city	65	66	1.5	90	72.2	0.0	0.0	27.8	0.0	26.7	61.2	12.2	33	75.8	48.5	36.4
Washburn city	1,246	1,312	5.3	1,296	95.9	0.0	0.0	2.4	1.7	22.6	62.0	15.4	576	73.6	34.9	18.8
Watford City city	1,744	4,206	141.2	2,738	93.7	0.2	0.7	1.6	3.8	26.2	58.3	15.4	1,030	67.0	41.3	22.6
West Fargo city	25,830	31,771	23.0	28,371	90.2	3.8	1.8	3.2	1.0	26.9	64.1	9.0	11,125	68.6	24.7	35.7
Westhope city	429	426	-0.7	506	93.9	2.0	0.4	0.8	3.0	13.1	62.2	24.7	243	67.5	59.3	8.2
Wheatland CDP	68	NA	NA	53	100.0	0.0	0.0	0.0	0.0	0.0	52.9	47.2	36	75.0	55.6	25.0
White Earth city	80	90	12.5	89	97.8	0.0	0.0	2.2	0.0	41.7	54.0	4.5	35	68.6	31.4	22.9
White Shield CDP	336	NA	NA	429	1.9	0.0	0.0	96.7	1.4	38.0	55.8	6.3	160	20.6	41.3	5.0
Wildrose city	110	101	-8.2	90	83.3	0.0	0.0	3.3	13.3	22.2	67.8	10.0	43	74.4	41.9	18.6
Williston city	15,910	24,562	54.4	19,849	89.2	1.2	0.5	5.4	3.7	23.5	65.6	10.9	8,293	64.5	39.3	19.5
Willow City city	163	167	2.5	204	93.6	0.0	0.0	6.4	0.0	24.0	56.9	19.1	98	78.6	52.0	5.1
Wilton city	711	726	2.1	977	97.7	0.1	0.0	2.1	0.0	25.8	59.5	14.5	360	73.6	41.9	20.6
Wimbledon city	216	215	-0.5	251	96.0	0.0	0.8	0.0	3.2	30.3	63.5	6.4	106	90.6	41.5	21.7
Wing city	152	156	2.6	138	98.6	0.0	0.0	1.4	0.0	25.3	48.4	26.1	61	75.4	45.9	27.9
Wishek city	1,002	992	-1.0	957	95.5	0.0	1.7	2.3	0.5	16.8	45.8	37.5	446	76.2	51.6	20.4
Wolford city	36	36	0.0	33	100.0	0.0	0.0	0.0	0.0	30.3	45.4	24.2	18	94.4	94.4	0.0
Woodworth city	50	49	-2.0	28	100.0	0.0	0.0	0.0	0.0	0.0	49.9	50.0	21	66.7	76.2	9.5
Wyndmere city	429	421	-1.9	497	94.8	0.0	0.0	2.2	3.0	24.9	49.2	25.6	229	83.8	57.2	18.3
York city	23	23	0.0	41	92.7	0.0	0.0	0.0	7.3	4.8	83.0	12.2	27	100.0	74.1	0.0

1 May be of any race.

Table A. All Places — **Population and Housing**

STATE City, town, township, borough, or CDP (county if applicable)	Population: 2010 census total population	Population: 2014 estimated population	Population: Percent change 2010–2014	Population: ACS total population estimate 2010–2014	Race and Hispanic or Latino origin (percent), 2010–2014: White alone, not Hispanic or Latino	Black alone, not Hispanic or Latino	Asian alone, not Hispanic or Latino	All other races or 2 or more races, not Hispanic or Latino	Hispanic or Latino[1]	Age (percent), 2010–2014: Under 18 years old	Age 18 to 64 years old	Age 65 years and older	Households, 2010–2014: Total occupied housing units	Percent owner occupied	Householders by level of education (percent): High school diploma or less	Bachelor's degree or more
	1	2	3	4	5	6	7	8	9	10	11	12	13	14	15	16
NORTH DAKOTA—Con.																
Ypsilanti CDP	104	NA	NA	149	100.0	0.0	0.0	0.0	0.0	24.8	64.4	10.7	72	81.9	58.3	23.6
Zap city	237	245	3.4	211	93.4	1.4	1.9	2.4	0.9	19.0	56.3	24.6	108	93.5	74.1	6.5
Zeeland city	86	85	-1.2	85	100.0	0.0	0.0	0.0	0.0	17.6	57.7	24.7	46	78.3	30.4	17.4
OHIO	11,536,725	11,594,163	0.5	11,560,380	80.5	12.0	1.8	2.4	3.3	23.2	62.1	14.7	4,570,015	66.9	42.5	26.8
Aberdeen village	1,638	1,618	-1.2	1,617	94.8	1.1	0.0	3.0	1.1	19.0	63.4	17.6	741	56.1	70.7	7.8
Ada village	5,959	5,832	-2.1	6,112	92.9	1.8	3.1	1.1	1.1	17.4	74.2	8.4	1,667	48.2	37.4	25.1
Adamsville village	114	115	0.9	126	94.4	0.0	5.6	0.0	0.0	29.4	60.4	10.3	45	48.9	53.3	6.7
Addyston village	938	934	-0.4	970	90.3	6.3	0.0	2.4	1.0	25.0	64.8	10.1	373	35.7	72.7	5.6
Adelphi village	380	373	-1.8	399	98.5	0.0	0.0	1.5	0.0	27.6	55.7	16.8	144	72.9	78.5	3.5
Adena village	759	735	-3.2	689	98.1	1.5	0.0	0.4	0.0	15.3	56.8	28.0	300	84.0	60.0	11.3
Akron city	199,092	197,859	-0.6	198,492	60.7	30.1	2.7	4.3	2.1	22.3	64.6	13.0	83,021	53.3	44.7	21.3
Albany village	844	896	6.2	1,202	96.8	1.7	0.3	0.9	0.2	20.3	65.1	14.7	487	65.7	46.0	22.8
Alexandria village	514	518	0.8	572	97.4	1.0	0.0	1.0	0.5	21.4	65.2	13.1	190	73.2	45.3	17.9
Alger village	860	849	-1.3	910	98.6	0.3	0.0	0.0	1.1	23.5	64.9	11.4	332	70.2	84.6	3.6
Alliance city	22,322	22,078	-1.1	22,196	83.0	10.1	0.2	3.7	2.9	21.4	62.0	16.6	8,706	54.6	56.6	14.8
Alvordton CDP	217	NA	NA	195	88.7	3.6	6.7	0.0	1.0	10.3	72.6	16.9	82	62.2	50.0	30.5
Amanda village	737	748	1.5	670	92.7	0.4	0.0	6.9	0.0	29.8	54.2	16.1	254	69.3	53.9	5.5
Amberley village	3,585	3,598	0.4	3,585	88.1	8.4	0.2	1.0	2.3	26.7	52.6	20.9	1,316	93.9	7.5	76.1
Amelia village	4,801	4,920	2.5	5,323	95.2	1.3	0.4	2.8	0.3	31.3	63.2	5.4	1,961	61.7	36.4	19.8
Amesville village	156	158	1.3	153	91.5	0.0	0.0	0.0	8.5	37.8	54.9	7.2	46	71.7	37.0	17.4
Amherst city	12,021	12,143	1.0	12,080	92.1	1.7	1.3	1.2	3.7	23.1	59.7	17.2	4,568	83.7	38.1	27.4
Amsterdam village	511	491	-3.9	538	98.9	0.0	0.0	1.1	0.0	23.9	58.8	17.1	217	64.5	61.3	11.5
Andersonville CDP	779	NA	NA	886	95.5	4.5	0.0	0.0	0.0	23.7	65.4	10.9	315	86.7	40.6	25.4
Andover village	1,145	1,124	-1.8	1,029	96.7	0.0	0.0	0.4	2.9	19.6	56.2	24.2	390	52.3	65.9	9.2
Anna village	1,572	1,547	-1.6	1,444	93.8	0.8	0.8	4.2	0.5	32.1	58.3	9.6	515	74.2	40.8	15.1
Ansonia village	1,174	1,154	-1.7	962	97.3	0.6	0.0	0.1	2.0	24.2	58.8	16.9	399	62.2	64.9	6.8
Antioch village	86	86	0.0	119	93.3	1.7	0.0	5.0	0.0	18.5	75.6	5.9	42	78.6	59.5	9.5
Antwerp village	1,736	1,689	-2.7	1,583	91.7	0.2	0.3	2.7	5.1	25.7	54.2	20.0	712	66.0	61.7	13.1
Apple Creek village	1,173	1,180	0.6	1,168	94.4	0.0	0.3	2.5	2.8	23.3	64.3	12.5	444	74.5	51.4	17.6
Apple Valley CDP	5,058	NA	NA	5,465	97.8	0.4	0.5	1.1	0.2	23.0	54.0	23.1	2,195	90.2	25.7	37.7
Aquilla village	340	342	0.6	336	100.0	0.0	0.0	0.0	0.0	25.1	62.7	12.2	140	67.9	56.4	4.3
Arcadia village	590	586	-0.7	639	95.6	0.0	0.0	4.1	0.3	27.9	57.5	14.7	267	68.9	56.9	19.5
Arcanum village	2,122	2,092	-1.4	2,309	98.2	0.0	0.0	0.7	1.1	24.9	61.6	13.4	993	65.7	50.3	18.6
Archbold village	4,346	4,344	0.0	4,374	81.9	0.6	0.0	0.6	17.0	30.1	51.9	18.0	1,681	67.6	47.1	26.3
Arlington village	1,455	1,453	-0.1	1,467	94.5	1.2	0.0	3.0	1.2	23.6	59.7	16.8	586	70.3	41.8	28.8
Arlington Heights village	745	743	-0.3	985	79.8	16.2	0.0	3.6	0.4	30.1	62.3	7.7	375	49.1	67.2	1.6
Ashland city	20,362	20,218	-0.7	20,421	94.6	1.4	1.3	1.6	1.1	20.4	62.3	17.3	8,145	58.8	47.7	29.1
Ashley village	1,330	1,354	1.8	1,152	97.7	0.0	0.1	0.0	2.2	23.7	60.2	16.1	456	64.0	68.2	12.5
Ashtabula city	19,124	18,508	-3.2	18,819	78.0	9.0	0.2	4.3	8.5	25.2	59.3	15.6	7,801	49.9	60.1	9.5
Ashville village	4,097	4,149	1.3	4,130	90.8	0.0	0.0	5.4	3.8	34.4	58.9	6.9	1,398	54.7	57.1	16.0
Athalia village	373	371	-0.5	356	91.9	1.7	0.0	6.2	0.3	22.4	62.0	15.4	134	76.9	52.2	20.1
Athens city	23,838	24,024	0.8	24,151	83.1	3.6	7.3	3.1	2.8	6.5	88.8	4.8	6,772	28.3	11.2	45.3
Attica village	899	880	-2.1	980	96.4	0.0	0.0	3.0	0.6	24.0	57.4	18.7	413	66.6	58.4	13.3
Atwater CDP	758	NA	NA	677	97.8	0.0	0.0	0.0	2.2	22.0	67.2	10.6	220	87.7	62.3	4.1
Aurora city	15,546	15,734	1.2	15,568	88.4	5.0	3.5	1.7	1.3	23.4	57.5	19.1	6,181	78.7	21.5	51.2
Austinburg CDP	516	NA	NA	350	90.3	2.9	0.6	0.0	6.3	7.7	46.0	46.3	127	74.0	31.5	8.7
Austintown CDP	29,677	NA	NA	29,034	89.1	7.0	0.7	1.2	2.1	20.1	60.1	19.9	12,904	66.4	47.8	20.4
Avon city	21,191	22,302	5.2	21,783	86.4	6.4	2.1	1.2	3.9	29.9	54.5	15.7	7,953	79.2	20.8	53.3
Avon Lake city	22,581	23,204	2.8	22,881	93.4	1.3	0.8	1.8	2.7	26.6	57.9	15.5	9,000	80.0	21.9	52.5
Bailey Lakes village	371	376	1.3	531	98.7	1.1	0.0	0.0	0.2	30.3	56.8	13.0	197	59.9	55.3	9.6
Bainbridge CDP	3,267	NA	NA	2,728	95.7	2.0	0.0	1.0	1.4	17.9	64.2	17.7	1,227	92.9	13.4	62.7
Bainbridge village	860	852	-0.9	772	90.9	3.2	0.0	3.8	2.1	18.4	61.7	19.7	362	64.9	57.2	11.9
Bairdstown village	130	132	1.5	206	93.2	0.0	0.5	6.3	0.0	22.8	62.1	15.0	78	71.8	66.7	2.6
Ballville CDP	2,976	NA	NA	2,940	89.0	5.4	0.0	0.2	5.4	16.5	58.5	25.0	1,330	89.7	40.2	25.1
Baltic village	785	783	-0.3	709	89.8	2.7	0.3	2.1	5.1	22.3	54.2	23.4	244	75.8	76.2	7.0
Baltimore village	2,966	2,962	-0.1	2,970	95.9	0.0	0.1	0.7	3.3	34.8	52.6	12.6	1,085	50.9	47.9	10.9
Bannock CDP	211	NA	NA	268	100.0	0.0	0.0	0.0	0.0	3.7	94.0	2.2	84	91.7	48.8	10.7
Barberton city	26,570	26,302	-1.0	26,375	88.6	6.7	0.3	2.7	1.7	23.9	59.6	16.2	10,603	63.2	60.6	12.6
Barnesville village	4,193	4,139	-1.3	4,115	95.5	1.3	0.9	2.2	0.1	20.4	60.6	19.0	1,705	66.0	54.7	12.6
Barnhill village	396	389	-1.8	384	100.0	0.0	0.0	0.0	0.0	29.5	57.8	12.8	134	69.4	84.3	3.0
Bascom CDP	390	NA	NA	377	89.9	0.0	10.1	0.0	0.0	27.6	53.1	19.1	152	84.9	28.9	14.5
Batavia village	1,613	1,645	2.0	2,008	91.8	5.4	0.0	0.9	1.8	17.1	65.5	17.5	677	66.5	39.0	25.6
Batesville village	101	98	-3.0	95	93.7	0.0	0.0	5.3	1.1	17.9	61.1	21.1	32	87.5	71.9	9.4
Bay View village	632	616	-2.5	511	95.3	0.0	0.4	2.3	2.0	10.9	65.5	23.5	250	84.4	58.4	13.2
Bay Village city	15,651	15,435	-1.4	15,508	96.6	0.6	0.6	1.3	0.9	24.4	58.4	17.3	6,043	91.8	13.9	60.1
Beach City village	1,033	1,013	-1.9	943	99.3	0.0	0.0	0.0	0.7	20.2	59.1	20.7	387	72.9	75.7	4.9
Beachwood city	11,953	11,797	-1.3	11,855	78.2	10.0	9.7	0.7	1.3	19.2	50.2	30.7	4,857	61.3	16.8	62.1
Beallsville village	409	407	-0.5	418	99.5	0.0	0.0	0.5	0.0	21.3	63.9	14.8	176	67.0	64.2	8.5
Beaver village	449	439	-2.2	439	98.6	0.0	0.0	0.0	1.4	29.2	54.9	15.9	182	37.9	77.5	10.4
Beavercreek city	45,193	45,934	1.6	45,738	86.8	2.7	5.1	2.5	3.0	20.6	63.6	15.8	18,423	71.7	18.4	56.0
Beaverdam village	385	373	-3.1	442	98.4	0.0	0.0	0.0	1.6	20.6	66.0	13.3	176	72.2	58.0	6.3
Beckett Ridge CDP	9,187	NA	NA	8,693	82.8	5.9	5.4	1.0	4.9	24.6	65.1	10.2	3,438	76.7	16.1	54.8
Bedford city	13,074	12,805	-2.1	12,927	42.2	50.3	0.8	3.4	3.4	22.8	62.2	14.8	5,826	52.1	42.0	22.8
Bedford Heights city	10,757	10,675	-0.8	10,680	18.7	73.1	1.6	4.5	2.1	20.9	62.6	16.5	4,883	51.1	41.4	18.3
Beechwood Trails CDP	3,020	NA	NA	3,058	96.0	1.7	0.0	1.4	0.9	19.3	70.6	10.2	1,166	100.0	27.0	47.3
Bellaire village	4,279	4,207	-1.7	4,239	94.9	4.4	0.5	0.0	0.2	20.7	64.1	15.3	1,804	57.3	63.5	8.6
Bellbrook city	6,943	7,031	1.3	7,035	96.4	0.3	1.0	1.5	0.8	25.6	61.5	12.8	2,827	83.0	21.5	49.9
Belle Center village	813	801	-1.5	820	95.4	0.2	0.0	3.5	0.9	26.0	61.1	12.9	318	88.4	61.0	5.3
Bellefontaine city	13,370	13,167	-1.5	13,141	88.4	3.8	0.9	4.6	2.3	26.5	60.0	13.6	5,447	55.4	60.2	17.3
Belle Valley village	223	217	-2.7	271	95.6	0.0	0.0	2.6	1.8	17.4	57.4	25.5	111	73.0	73.0	9.9
Bellevue city	8,203	8,059	-1.8	8,157	95.8	0.2	0.1	1.6	2.3	24.0	61.8	14.2	3,203	69.6	51.2	14.2
Bellville village	1,918	1,878	-2.1	1,692	94.7	1.5	0.0	0.4	3.4	21.7	56.6	21.7	736	81.4	50.5	17.8
Belmont village	452	446	-1.3	478	100.0	0.0	0.0	0.0	0.0	11.8	72.9	15.3	205	83.9	55.6	8.3
Belmore village	143	141	-1.4	117	84.6	0.0	0.0	8.5	6.8	30.8	42.6	26.5	46	100.0	60.9	13.0
Beloit village	978	946	-3.3	1,045	98.9	0.3	0.0	0.4	0.5	20.7	54.1	25.0	450	64.0	63.3	9.3
Belpre city	6,441	6,436	-0.1	6,431	92.5	4.0	0.6	1.4	1.4	16.7	61.1	22.3	2,938	60.5	51.3	12.4
Bentleyville village	864	859	-0.6	882	95.6	0.2	1.1	0.8	2.3	27.0	59.7	13.4	300	96.3	9.3	77.3
Benton Ridge village	299	303	1.3	360	98.9	0.0	0.0	1.1	0.0	16.9	69.5	13.6	159	78.0	51.6	12.6
Bentonville CDP	287	NA	NA	114	100.0	0.0	0.0	0.0	0.0	18.4	59.6	21.9	46	67.4	21.7	0.0

1 May be of any race.

Table A. All Places — **Population and Housing**

STATE City, town, township, borough, or CDP (county if applicable)	Population: 2010 census total population	Population: 2014 estimated population	Population: Percent change 2010–2014	Population: ACS total population estimate 2010–2014	Race and Hispanic or Latino origin (percent), 2010–2014: White alone, not Hispanic or Latino	Black alone, not Hispanic or Latino	Asian alone, not Hispanic or Latino	All other races or 2 or more races, not Hispanic or Latino	Hispanic or Latino[1]	Age (percent), 2010–2014: Under 18 years old	Age 18 to 64 years old	Age 65 years and older	Households, 2010–2014: Total occupied housing units	Percent owner occupied	Householders by level of education (percent): High school diploma or less	Bachelor's degree or more
	1	2	3	4	5	6	7	8	9	10	11	12	13	14	15	16
OHIO—Con.																
Berea city	19,093	18,986	-0.6	19,044	87.1	6.6	1.5	2.0	2.9	15.4	68.9	15.7	7,447	70.4	29.0	33.4
Bergholz village	664	641	-3.5	768	97.7	1.0	0.0	1.3	0.0	27.2	62.8	10.2	260	75.0	62.7	14.2
Berkey village	237	236	-0.4	360	98.9	0.3	0.0	0.8	0.0	26.7	57.0	16.4	143	79.0	37.1	25.9
Berlin CDP	898	NA	NA	1,346	98.8	0.0	0.0	0.0	1.2	15.6	74.6	9.7	443	70.2	70.0	5.2
Berlin Heights village	714	695	-2.7	571	94.6	1.2	0.0	3.5	0.7	17.2	58.5	24.3	238	84.9	46.2	23.5
Bethel village	2,713	2,766	2.0	2,734	97.4	0.0	0.0	1.0	1.5	21.8	62.2	16.1	1,027	49.3	69.6	10.5
Bethesda village	1,256	1,251	-0.4	1,536	91.2	0.0	0.0	8.8	0.0	28.3	62.6	9.2	558	62.2	48.6	10.0
Bettsville village	661	643	-2.7	666	93.8	0.9	0.0	1.7	3.6	21.5	57.3	21.5	307	77.9	66.8	8.1
Beulah Beach CDP	53	NA	NA	63	100.0	0.0	0.0	0.0	0.0	0.0	23.8	76.2	31	67.7	19.4	25.8
Beverly village	1,313	1,297	-1.2	1,072	97.0	0.0	0.0	2.5	0.5	18.1	57.4	24.4	495	70.3	50.7	15.4
Bexley city	13,054	13,517	3.5	13,286	89.3	5.5	1.0	2.1	2.1	25.8	64.2	10.0	4,532	75.1	9.8	72.8
Blacklick Estates CDP	8,682	NA	NA	8,580	69.6	22.8	0.1	4.3	3.1	28.4	59.8	11.8	3,096	66.8	54.0	14.0
Bladensburg CDP	191	NA	NA	155	100.0	0.0	0.0	0.0	0.0	30.3	65.1	4.5	56	44.6	92.9	0.0
Blakeslee village	96	96	0.0	63	98.4	1.6	0.0	0.0	0.0	15.9	63.4	20.6	37	51.4	32.4	2.7
Blanchester village	4,243	4,241	0.0	4,182	96.3	0.4	0.4	2.9	0.0	26.4	57.2	16.5	1,651	59.4	63.7	9.1
Bloomdale village	678	687	1.3	759	97.8	0.0	0.0	1.7	0.5	29.2	57.8	13.0	267	83.5	50.9	19.5
Bloomingburg village	938	924	-1.5	1,246	88.3	1.8	0.0	0.8	9.1	35.4	56.2	8.3	435	60.5	61.8	8.0
Bloomingdale village	202	197	-2.5	147	100.0	0.0	0.0	0.0	0.0	19.1	62.6	18.4	55	90.9	43.6	10.9
Bloomville village	957	934	-2.4	982	97.4	0.0	0.4	0.5	1.7	25.5	57.4	17.2	391	60.9	68.5	9.0
Blue Ash city	12,114	12,149	0.3	12,124	76.1	8.3	10.9	1.9	2.8	19.3	62.7	17.9	5,299	68.7	20.8	58.5
Blue Jay CDP	959	NA	NA	1,003	94.1	5.9	0.0	0.0	0.0	23.3	55.1	21.8	363	96.1	38.3	28.7
Bluffton village	4,199	4,202	0.1	4,157	93.2	1.9	1.0	0.4	3.5	20.8	58.7	20.5	1,566	69.3	28.4	47.9
Boardman CDP	35,376	NA	NA	34,835	86.9	6.3	1.1	1.3	4.5	18.8	62.7	18.6	15,576	64.1	37.6	28.6
Bolindale CDP	2,089	NA	NA	1,997	88.1	5.7	0.0	4.8	1.4	14.6	64.1	21.5	936	74.1	61.6	2.8
Bolivar village	994	992	-0.2	1,006	98.8	0.6	0.0	0.6	0.0	20.4	56.2	23.7	377	82.2	44.8	13.8
Boston Heights village	1,300	1,293	-0.5	1,302	94.7	1.0	2.4	1.6	0.3	23.3	63.9	13.0	464	92.2	25.0	42.2
Botkins village	1,168	1,155	-1.1	1,494	99.3	0.0	0.5	0.0	0.2	30.0	57.8	12.2	583	73.9	53.9	17.5
Bourneville CDP	199	NA	NA	285	52.3	0.0	0.0	21.8	26.0	31.2	68.8	0.0	108	69.4	56.5	13.0
Bowerston village	398	394	-1.0	393	91.1	5.9	0.0	2.8	0.3	21.6	52.3	26.2	160	47.5	70.0	4.4
Bowersville village	312	312	0.0	291	84.9	0.0	9.6	5.5	0.0	37.5	53.2	9.3	97	60.8	59.8	2.1
Bowling Green city	30,048	31,591	5.1	31,366	85.2	5.2	1.4	1.9	6.2	13.1	77.8	9.1	11,007	41.1	24.3	38.2
Bradford village	1,842	1,847	0.3	1,708	98.0	0.0	0.7	0.2	1.1	25.0	57.6	17.5	620	76.8	66.9	6.3
Bradner village	985	1,011	2.6	1,040	86.3	0.2	0.4	4.1	8.9	27.9	63.2	8.9	413	65.9	58.4	9.7
Brady Lake village	466	464	-0.4	405	94.8	0.0	0.0	5.2	0.0	17.3	67.9	14.8	170	71.8	41.8	24.1
Bratenahl village	1,197	1,175	-1.8	1,169	82.5	12.0	3.3	1.9	0.3	7.5	56.0	36.5	660	83.5	6.5	74.5
Brecksville city	13,659	13,469	-1.4	13,543	95.2	1.5	2.5	0.3	0.5	21.3	58.7	19.9	5,240	83.4	15.0	56.1
Brecon CDP	244	NA	NA	256	30.9	0.0	0.0	0.0	69.1	15.2	67.2	17.6	95	100.0	100.0	0.0
Bremen village	1,425	1,436	0.8	1,494	97.0	0.7	0.0	0.9	1.4	26.3	60.4	13.3	544	71.9	47.8	14.7
Brewster village	2,169	2,170	0.0	2,500	94.6	0.3	1.0	3.2	0.9	18.7	64.8	16.6	923	70.6	64.0	8.1
Brice village	116	120	3.4	152	89.5	7.2	0.0	3.3	0.0	16.5	76.8	6.6	90	32.2	25.6	56.7
Bridgeport village	1,834	1,803	-1.7	1,858	84.3	11.3	0.4	3.1	0.9	21.2	64.4	14.6	744	61.0	55.8	10.6
Bridgetown CDP	14,407	NA	NA	14,412	97.6	1.0	0.2	0.4	0.7	23.9	57.3	18.9	5,783	85.5	44.6	25.2
Brilliant CDP	1,482	NA	NA	1,623	99.5	0.5	0.0	0.0	0.0	19.9	62.7	17.4	628	58.9	46.3	7.5
Brimfield CDP	3,343	NA	NA	3,691	91.3	3.0	0.0	3.1	2.7	28.5	60.0	11.6	1,270	72.4	42.6	23.0
Broadview Heights city	19,397	19,254	-0.7	19,309	85.4	2.5	7.8	2.4	1.9	23.4	61.4	15.1	7,572	82.6	21.8	48.3
Brookfield Center CDP	1,207	NA	NA	1,206	94.3	5.7	0.0	0.0	0.0	14.6	66.7	18.7	456	84.2	49.1	21.5
Brooklyn city	11,169	10,947	-2.0	11,047	78.3	4.4	5.4	1.3	10.6	19.6	62.1	18.3	4,851	58.6	54.6	13.4
Brooklyn Heights village	1,543	1,532	-0.7	1,518	96.2	0.3	0.0	1.1	2.5	21.8	62.2	16.0	564	85.6	42.4	20.4
Brook Park city	19,212	18,886	-1.7	19,027	87.2	3.2	1.4	2.4	5.9	21.2	59.6	19.3	7,687	77.8	53.0	14.3
Brookside village	629	617	-1.9	745	97.3	0.9	0.0	1.6	0.1	21.8	61.4	17.0	300	83.0	46.7	15.3
Brookville city	5,884	5,894	0.2	6,351	96.9	0.6	0.2	1.1	1.1	22.5	53.0	24.5	2,911	67.0	46.0	11.4
Broughton village	120	117	-2.5	98	98.0	0.0	0.0	0.0	2.0	20.5	66.3	13.3	44	100.0	84.1	9.1
Brownsville CDP	220	NA	NA	135	100.0	0.0	0.0	0.0	0.0	0.0	54.1	45.9	78	100.0	100.0	0.0
Brunswick city	34,274	34,604	1.0	34,438	94.5	0.7	0.6	1.3	2.8	23.2	63.8	13.0	13,351	74.0	42.2	21.1
Bryan city	8,549	8,473	-0.9	8,523	92.5	0.2	0.3	1.9	5.2	24.8	58.9	16.4	3,630	60.9	55.0	14.5
Buchtel village	557	555	-0.4	524	98.1	0.4	0.0	0.0	1.5	17.9	62.8	19.3	197	80.2	45.2	22.3
Buckeye Lake village	2,744	2,737	-0.3	2,707	92.3	0.0	0.0	2.6	5.1	23.4	59.5	17.2	1,234	59.5	66.1	10.5
Buckland village	233	232	-0.4	268	94.8	0.4	0.0	4.9	0.0	33.9	53.6	12.3	107	57.0	54.2	3.7
Bucyrus city	12,362	11,973	-3.1	12,140	94.5	1.1	0.7	1.7	2.0	21.7	57.8	20.4	5,293	61.0	55.4	12.5
Buffalo CDP	401	NA	NA	304	100.0	0.0	0.0	0.0	0.0	19.1	67.2	13.8	139	72.7	66.9	0.0
Buford CDP	352	NA	NA	415	100.0	0.0	0.0	0.0	0.0	29.4	59.9	10.8	140	95.0	59.3	12.9
Burbank village	207	208	0.5	210	98.6	0.0	0.0	0.0	1.4	23.8	54.8	21.4	87	66.7	80.5	3.4
Burgoon village	172	171	-0.6	146	100.0	0.0	0.0	0.0	0.0	28.1	58.3	13.7	48	95.8	58.3	10.4
Burkettsville village	244	247	1.2	216	100.0	0.0	0.0	0.0	0.0	21.8	58.9	19.4	105	87.6	68.6	11.4
Burlington CDP	2,676	NA	NA	2,614	92.4	2.2	0.0	5.4	0.0	16.4	53.9	29.6	1,034	67.2	58.1	12.2
Burton village	1,452	1,463	0.8	1,224	96.2	0.0	0.1	1.1	2.6	21.8	54.7	23.5	529	49.9	34.4	31.4
Butler village	938	916	-2.3	1,026	95.6	0.0	0.0	3.6	0.8	23.1	58.5	18.5	435	75.4	51.7	9.4
Butlerville village	165	166	0.6	113	98.2	0.9	0.0	0.0	0.9	24.7	60.2	15.0	52	88.5	71.2	0.0
Byesville village	2,438	2,400	-1.6	2,504	99.4	0.0	0.4	0.2	0.0	23.6	59.2	17.2	967	64.6	64.1	4.0
Cadiz village	3,353	3,289	-1.9	3,261	95.1	4.2	0.0	0.3	0.4	21.7	58.8	19.4	1,288	70.0	47.1	15.8
Cairo village	549	536	-2.4	492	93.9	4.5	0.2	0.0	1.4	21.3	62.0	16.7	201	91.5	49.8	8.5
Calcutta CDP	3,742	NA	NA	3,815	96.5	0.3	0.8	2.4	0.0	21.6	54.0	24.4	1,508	70.6	49.2	18.1
Caldwell village	1,748	1,695	-3.0	1,577	98.2	0.3	0.0	0.5	1.0	14.3	52.4	33.2	773	60.3	61.1	19.5
Caledonia village	582	561	-3.6	742	99.1	0.0	0.3	0.7	0.0	18.9	59.8	21.3	312	81.1	59.0	8.3
Cambridge city	10,635	10,485	-1.4	10,558	92.3	2.6	0.4	3.0	1.6	24.4	55.5	20.1	4,511	58.9	54.6	16.9
Camden village	2,044	1,984	-2.9	2,264	95.2	1.1	0.0	2.3	1.4	23.4	60.3	16.3	888	62.2	68.2	4.4
Campbell city	8,235	8,033	-2.5	8,127	59.2	24.4	0.0	3.1	13.4	22.9	58.7	18.4	3,311	67.8	60.4	7.5
Camp Dennison CDP	375	NA	NA	276	84.8	15.2	0.0	0.0	0.0	7.2	75.4	17.4	113	77.0	56.6	34.5
Canal Fulton city	5,479	5,493	0.3	5,479	96.5	0.6	0.0	2.4	0.5	24.4	55.0	20.7	2,344	65.6	48.7	24.1
Canal Lewisville CDP	320	NA	NA	336	100.0	0.0	0.0	0.0	0.0	20.0	66.7	13.4	137	62.8	75.2	6.6
Canal Winchester city	7,100	7,704	8.5	7,334	90.1	5.0	3.4	1.5	0.0	24.3	57.2	18.6	2,738	89.2	32.8	37.0
Candlewood Lake CDP	1,147	NA	NA	1,176	93.5	0.0	0.0	0.0	6.5	18.4	61.1	20.6	489	97.8	30.9	24.5
Canfield city	7,530	7,390	-1.9	7,443	93.4	0.0	4.2	1.7	0.6	19.7	61.2	19.1	3,182	75.0	33.7	40.1
Canton city	73,017	72,297	-1.0	72,668	66.8	23.0	0.5	7.1	2.6	25.7	60.6	13.7	29,874	51.5	51.3	14.5
Carbon Hill CDP	233	NA	NA	187	100.0	0.0	0.0	0.0	0.0	17.1	39.5	43.3	85	72.9	88.2	11.8
Cardington village	2,046	2,054	0.4	2,192	98.1	0.1	0.0	1.5	0.2	31.9	59.0	9.3	762	60.8	63.5	12.3
Carey village	3,674	3,608	-1.8	3,587	95.6	0.6	1.4	1.2	1.1	23.0	61.5	15.6	1,597	61.4	61.7	11.8
Carlisle village	4,939	5,200	5.3	5,001	97.5	0.0	0.4	1.8	0.3	23.9	61.0	15.2	1,810	78.0	60.3	9.7
Carroll village	524	521	-0.6	403	98.0	0.0	0.0	2.0	0.0	16.1	64.2	19.6	173	64.7	60.1	4.0
Carrollton village	3,247	3,180	-2.1	3,085	96.2	1.3	0.9	0.6	1.0	20.1	59.1	20.8	1,228	58.0	52.7	15.8
Casstown village	267	271	1.5	266	99.2	0.0	0.0	0.8	0.0	33.0	52.7	14.3	92	82.6	40.2	16.3

1 May be of any race.

Table A. All Places — **Population and Housing**

STATE City, town, township, borough, or CDP (county if applicable)	Population: 2010 census total population	Population: 2014 estimated population	Population: Percent change 2010–2014	Population: ACS total population estimate 2010–2014	Race and Hispanic or Latino origin (percent), 2010–2014: White alone, not Hispanic or Latino	Black alone, not Hispanic or Latino	Asian alone, not Hispanic or Latino	All other races or 2 or more races, not Hispanic or Latino	Hispanic or Latino[1]	Age (percent), 2010–2014: Under 18 years old	Age 18 to 64 years old	Age 65 years and older	Households, 2010–2014: Total occupied housing units	Percent owner occupied	Householders by level of education (percent): High school diploma or less	Bachelor's degree or more
	1	2	3	4	5	6	7	8	9	10	11	12	13	14	15	16
OHIO—Con.																
Castalia village	850	835	-1.8	887	94.1	0.5	0.0	0.2	5.2	22.4	64.5	13.2	365	66.8	50.1	25.8
Castine village	130	128	-1.5	197	98.5	0.0	0.0	1.0	0.5	26.4	59.8	13.7	58	58.6	75.9	1.7
Catawba village	268	266	-0.7	386	100.0	0.0	0.0	0.0	0.0	33.7	51.7	14.5	133	60.2	63.9	2.3
Cecil village	188	185	-1.6	205	92.7	0.0	0.0	1.0	6.3	22.5	66.9	10.7	72	83.3	72.2	6.9
Cedarville village	3,984	4,140	3.9	3,758	83.2	10.4	0.5	3.7	2.3	7.8	83.3	8.8	743	45.9	35.1	34.5
Celeryville CDP	210	NA	NA	352	95.7	0.0	0.0	0.0	4.3	42.3	44.5	13.1	128	60.2	38.3	16.4
Celina city	10,407	10,373	-0.3	10,374	93.6	1.2	0.6	3.0	1.6	23.0	61.5	15.5	4,468	63.5	57.3	14.4
Centerburg village	1,773	1,989	12.2	1,854	93.6	5.1	0.0	1.2	0.2	32.0	56.6	11.5	599	45.7	52.3	12.0
Centerville village	103	102	-1.0	127	90.6	0.0	0.0	9.4	0.0	29.1	60.6	10.2	47	100.0	29.8	38.3
Centerville city	23,994	23,915	-0.3	23,986	85.1	6.3	3.7	2.8	2.1	20.6	53.8	25.5	10,755	70.2	20.4	48.1
Chagrin Falls village	4,104	4,039	-1.6	4,099	97.5	0.3	0.0	1.6	0.5	23.2	54.1	22.8	1,983	63.6	12.7	62.0
Champion Heights CDP	6,498	NA	NA	6,626	95.4	1.4	0.0	2.0	1.3	22.5	57.5	20.2	2,706	77.4	52.4	15.4
Chardon city	5,148	5,186	0.7	5,161	90.0	2.8	2.0	1.6	3.6	23.7	60.4	16.0	2,185	57.1	30.6	28.1
Chatfield village	189	189	0.0	184	98.4	0.0	0.0	0.0	1.6	18.5	69.0	12.5	68	97.1	73.5	1.5
Chauncey village	1,038	1,034	-0.4	1,258	94.4	1.0	0.3	4.2	0.0	25.7	58.8	15.7	466	49.4	57.3	7.9
Cherry Fork village	155	155	0.0	137	100.0	0.0	0.0	0.0	0.0	19.0	44.5	36.5	62	87.1	46.8	12.9
Cherry Grove CDP	4,378	NA	NA	4,493	92.6	0.3	5.1	0.9	1.1	28.4	60.4	11.3	1,492	88.2	15.3	47.7
Chesapeake village	745	733	-1.6	891	93.7	0.0	0.0	1.3	4.9	23.0	63.3	13.8	368	61.4	51.1	11.1
Cheshire village	132	131	-0.8	234	99.1	0.0	0.0	0.0	0.9	22.7	62.3	15.0	106	73.6	76.4	0.0
Chesterhill village	289	285	-1.4	319	65.2	20.4	0.0	11.9	2.5	25.1	56.3	18.5	130	73.1	61.5	5.4
Chesterland CDP	2,521	NA	NA	2,257	98.3	0.1	0.0	1.6	0.0	14.7	56.8	28.5	1,069	92.3	30.5	35.2
Chesterville village	228	231	1.3	216	94.0	1.9	0.0	2.8	1.4	37.0	44.1	19.0	68	94.1	57.4	17.6
Cheviot city	8,375	8,325	-0.6	8,330	83.2	12.0	0.4	1.5	2.9	18.5	66.4	15.2	3,961	55.0	44.5	24.0
Chickasaw village	290	298	2.8	347	100.0	0.0	0.0	0.0	0.0	18.1	59.2	22.8	158	74.7	62.7	20.3
Chillicothe city	21,901	21,738	-0.7	21,802	86.6	7.0	0.6	4.7	1.1	19.9	60.8	19.3	9,281	58.1	49.0	21.4
Chilo village	63	63	0.0	69	97.1	0.0	0.0	2.9	0.0	20.2	56.4	23.2	30	76.7	93.3	6.7
Chippewa Lake village	710	724	2.0	746	92.2	2.3	0.3	4.7	0.5	18.6	66.2	15.0	312	67.0	52.9	20.2
Chippewa Park CDP	891	NA	NA	945	99.3	0.0	0.0	0.0	0.7	12.6	59.1	28.1	471	87.3	71.5	4.7
Choctaw Lake CDP	1,546	NA	NA	1,148	94.8	0.0	1.2	2.3	1.7	19.8	61.0	19.3	453	93.2	17.9	53.4
Christiansburg village	526	507	-3.6	500	96.2	2.0	0.0	1.8	0.0	25.4	57.6	17.0	188	83.0	59.6	6.9
Churchill CDP	2,149	NA	NA	2,108	82.0	16.0	0.0	2.0	0.0	13.9	61.3	24.8	976	73.0	61.0	8.7
Cincinnati city	296,950	298,165	0.4	297,117	48.8	43.3	1.9	3.1	3.0	22.0	67.0	11.2	131,160	39.4	37.6	32.8
Cinnamon Lake CDP	1,243	NA	NA	888	100.0	0.0	0.0	0.0	0.0	19.8	55.6	24.4	401	88.8	56.6	21.7
Circleville city	13,316	13,455	1.0	13,395	93.4	2.7	0.0	2.2	1.6	22.7	59.0	18.4	5,290	54.9	57.5	16.6
Clarington village	384	380	-1.0	412	94.4	0.0	0.0	3.4	2.2	23.1	60.7	16.3	173	76.9	56.6	11.6
Clarksburg village	455	458	0.7	574	97.0	0.5	0.0	2.1	0.3	31.1	57.9	11.0	211	64.0	69.7	9.0
Clarksville village	548	546	-0.4	457	99.6	0.0	0.0	0.4	0.0	27.9	63.1	9.0	193	52.8	60.6	16.1
Clarktown CDP	958	NA	NA	804	100.0	0.0	0.0	0.0	0.0	17.8	55.7	26.6	377	88.9	53.3	4.0
Clay Center village	276	282	2.2	291	85.9	0.0	0.0	2.4	11.7	28.6	58.2	13.4	120	85.8	65.8	9.2
Clayton city	13,209	13,170	-0.3	13,212	75.2	19.7	1.7	2.1	1.3	23.5	61.8	14.8	5,123	84.5	30.6	34.2
Cleveland city	396,697	389,521	-1.8	392,114	34.3	51.3	1.7	2.7	10.0	23.5	64.1	12.4	166,650	43.5	52.1	16.3
Cleveland Heights city	46,238	45,181	-2.3	45,657	49.7	41.3	4.3	2.9	1.9	22.4	63.7	14.0	19,530	56.9	18.6	53.9
Cleves village	3,289	3,365	2.3	3,354	96.7	0.4	0.0	1.7	1.2	33.7	59.1	7.2	1,117	69.8	53.1	20.2
Clifton village	152	152	0.0	145	83.4	1.4	0.0	2.8	12.4	21.4	63.4	15.2	75	61.3	54.7	25.3
Clinton village	1,214	1,217	0.2	1,149	97.2	0.0	0.9	0.6	1.3	20.8	64.7	14.4	462	87.0	52.6	18.0
Cloverdale village	168	166	-1.2	176	97.7	0.0	0.0	2.3	0.0	29.6	60.8	9.7	59	94.9	74.6	6.8
Clyde city	6,404	6,312	-1.4	6,350	89.4	0.0	0.7	2.8	7.1	24.0	63.2	12.8	2,568	71.2	46.0	16.7
Coal Grove village	2,165	2,155	-0.5	2,127	99.2	0.0	0.3	0.0	0.6	19.3	61.6	19.0	809	69.1	61.4	11.6
Coalton village	479	467	-2.5	604	97.7	0.5	0.0	1.8	0.0	29.8	62.8	7.5	220	62.3	63.2	5.5
Coldstream CDP	1,173	NA	NA	1,316	96.4	0.0	0.4	1.6	1.6	27.4	56.2	16.5	428	97.9	10.0	77.3
Coldwater village	4,427	4,451	0.5	4,452	96.7	0.1	0.0	2.2	1.0	25.4	56.3	18.4	1,734	75.1	63.7	17.2
College Corner village	407	407	0.0	355	99.2	0.0	0.3	0.6	0.0	14.9	70.7	14.4	177	59.9	59.9	7.9
Collins CDP	631	NA	NA	539	91.3	0.0	0.0	0.0	8.7	22.7	57.3	20.0	236	96.6	53.0	16.5
Columbiana city	6,397	6,329	-1.1	6,341	98.4	0.2	0.3	0.0	1.2	17.5	55.0	27.5	2,856	65.8	50.5	23.1
Columbus city	788,654	835,957	6.0	811,943	58.4	27.4	4.4	4.0	5.7	23.1	68.0	9.0	329,994	45.9	32.9	35.8
Columbus Grove village	2,123	2,080	-2.0	1,915	90.4	0.0	0.0	2.4	7.2	25.1	55.0	19.7	825	78.4	56.1	12.7
Commercial Point village	1,582	1,599	1.1	1,591	94.2	0.3	0.5	2.8	2.3	33.8	58.0	8.4	544	84.0	34.7	24.6
Concorde Hills CDP	663	NA	NA	570	91.8	0.0	8.2	0.0	0.0	18.2	59.3	22.5	204	88.2	11.3	76.5
Conesville village	347	345	-0.6	277	100.0	0.0	0.0	0.0	0.0	17.0	63.3	19.9	122	83.6	54.9	8.2
Congress village	185	186	0.5	227	99.1	0.0	0.0	0.9	0.0	33.0	54.0	12.8	70	60.0	80.0	0.0
Conneaut city	12,841	12,813	-0.2	12,836	87.4	8.2	0.2	2.1	2.1	19.3	64.7	15.9	4,731	68.5	59.2	12.2
Connorville CDP	0	NA	NA	153	100.0	0.0	0.0	0.0	0.0	18.9	60.1	20.9	72	94.4	52.8	16.7
Continental village	1,153	1,129	-2.1	965	96.7	0.0	0.0	0.8	2.5	21.9	64.9	13.4	409	83.4	69.2	11.2
Convoy village	1,085	1,064	-1.9	1,213	93.3	0.0	2.9	2.1	1.7	30.3	56.4	13.4	428	80.6	54.7	9.8
Coolville village	494	490	-0.8	579	98.8	0.0	0.0	1.2	0.0	31.2	57.5	11.2	197	89.8	80.2	6.1
Corning village	582	573	-1.5	641	94.9	0.0	0.0	2.0	3.1	26.2	62.9	10.8	221	58.8	56.6	5.4
Cortland city	7,104	6,963	-2.0	7,050	98.8	0.7	0.0	0.2	0.2	20.1	58.8	21.3	3,162	71.1	37.9	32.8
Corwin village	416	437	5.0	559	98.0	0.7	0.0	0.4	0.9	22.8	54.8	22.5	231	84.4	41.6	26.0
Coshocton city	11,216	11,107	-1.0	11,179	93.2	1.7	0.7	2.8	1.7	20.3	59.4	20.3	4,917	60.5	60.8	15.7
Covedale CDP	6,447	NA	NA	6,660	93.9	4.6	0.9	0.6	0.0	21.7	61.7	16.6	2,471	91.7	32.2	39.4
Covington village	2,584	2,616	1.2	2,598	98.0	0.0	0.0	1.5	0.5	26.9	55.5	17.6	950	63.1	63.8	9.5
Craig Beach village	1,173	1,149	-2.0	1,049	96.3	0.0	0.0	2.6	1.1	20.3	63.5	16.2	464	62.9	60.8	9.5
Crestline village	4,626	4,463	-3.5	4,516	95.7	1.2	0.1	2.8	0.2	20.6	61.8	17.5	1,876	67.8	62.4	12.3
Creston village	2,164	2,174	0.5	2,239	98.6	0.0	0.0	0.5	0.8	28.5	59.1	12.5	854	77.8	67.1	8.7
Cridersville village	1,852	1,833	-1.0	1,807	96.2	0.0	0.0	0.3	3.4	24.1	52.8	23.1	773	63.6	58.5	14.9
Crooksville village	2,534	2,493	-1.6	2,463	95.9	0.0	0.8	3.2	0.2	23.1	60.7	16.3	1,030	57.6	62.1	8.1
Crown City village	413	404	-2.2	367	98.4	0.0	1.6	0.0	0.0	15.0	69.9	15.3	160	66.9	77.5	9.4
Crystal Lakes CDP	1,483	NA	NA	1,398	77.1	0.0	0.0	6.7	16.2	29.1	59.5	11.2	557	78.3	45.8	10.2
Crystal Rock CDP	176	NA	NA	109	100.0	0.0	0.0	0.0	0.0	10.1	78.9	11.0	37	62.2	70.3	29.7
Cumberland village	367	362	-1.4	367	96.7	0.0	0.0	1.9	1.4	24.6	61.7	13.9	129	89.1	60.5	7.8
Curtice CDP	1,526	NA	NA	1,732	99.1	0.0	0.0	0.9	0.0	20.5	68.0	11.3	713	90.0	51.6	20.1
Custar village	179	182	1.7	130	93.1	0.0	0.0	0.0	6.9	4.6	83.1	12.3	62	67.7	72.6	0.0
Cuyahoga Falls city	49,583	49,210	-0.8	49,316	91.8	2.9	1.0	1.8	2.5	21.0	63.5	15.4	21,811	61.0	35.3	32.6
Cuyahoga Heights village	638	621	-2.7	577	92.0	1.4	1.6	3.1	1.9	26.3	57.1	16.5	229	69.4	61.1	12.2
Cygnet village	597	613	2.7	688	91.6	0.3	3.2	2.8	2.2	32.6	55.4	12.1	224	82.1	55.4	14.7
Cynthiana CDP	68	NA	NA	23	100.0	0.0	0.0	0.0	0.0	0.0	0.0	100.0	11	100.0	100.0	0.0
Dalton village	1,830	1,843	0.7	1,864	96.3	1.9	0.0	0.6	1.2	21.3	56.1	22.6	766	67.9	56.8	21.5
Damascus CDP	443	NA	NA	422	100.0	0.0	0.0	0.0	0.0	19.9	63.7	16.4	162	83.3	71.0	11.7
Danville village	1,044	1,024	-1.9	1,090	93.0	0.6	0.0	2.4	3.9	23.5	58.4	18.3	490	46.7	67.6	9.6
Darbydale CDP	793	NA	NA	921	98.5	0.0	1.5	0.0	0.0	32.6	52.6	14.9	297	92.3	64.0	4.7
Darbyville village	222	226	1.8	206	100.0	0.0	0.0	0.0	0.0	27.2	60.8	12.1	82	63.4	73.2	11.0

1 May be of any race.

Table A. All Places — **Population and Housing**

STATE City, town, township, borough, or CDP (county if applicable)	Population				Race and Hispanic or Latino origin (percent), 2010–2014					Age (percent), 2010–2014			Households, 2010–2014		Householders by level of education (percent)	
	2010 census total population	2014 estimated population	Percent change 2010–2014	ACS total population estimate 2010–2014	White alone, not Hispanic or Latino	Black alone, not Hispanic or Latino	Asian alone, not Hispanic or Latino	All other races or 2 or more races, not Hispanic or Latino	Hispanic or Latino[1]	Under 18 years old	Age 18 to 64 years old	Age 65 years and older	Total occupied housing units	Percent owner occupied	High school diploma or less	Bachelor's degree or more
	1	2	3	4	5	6	7	8	9	10	11	12	13	14	15	16
OHIO—Con.																
Darrtown CDP	516	NA	NA	364	100.0	0.0	0.0	0.0	0.0	18.7	61.4	19.8	146	100.0	25.3	31.5
Day Heights CDP	2,620	NA	NA	2,349	98.5	1.0	0.0	0.0	0.6	29.6	56.4	14.1	860	90.5	36.4	30.9
Dayton city	141,761	141,003	-0.5	141,776	51.4	41.0	1.1	3.1	3.4	21.4	66.5	12.1	57,367	49.3	46.0	17.2
Deer Park city	5,736	5,703	-0.6	5,720	89.8	5.1	1.3	2.2	1.6	18.9	66.2	15.0	2,493	68.5	38.2	32.1
Deersville village	79	78	-1.3	52	100.0	0.0	0.0	0.0	0.0	19.2	55.7	25.0	33	100.0	48.5	0.0
Defiance city	16,995	16,776	-1.3	16,646	79.8	3.3	0.1	2.2	14.7	22.6	60.7	16.7	6,917	64.9	46.4	21.4
De Graff village	1,287	1,268	-1.5	1,468	89.4	0.0	2.9	7.8	0.0	34.7	54.3	11.0	535	72.3	56.3	11.6
Delaware city	34,756	37,372	7.5	36,188	91.0	4.4	0.7	2.4	1.5	25.0	63.3	11.8	13,858	62.3	34.7	35.2
Delhi Hills CDP	5,259	NA	NA	5,032	95.7	0.7	2.2	1.3	0.0	22.9	65.8	11.4	1,687	91.0	39.9	25.7
Dellroy village	356	351	-1.4	314	95.5	0.0	0.0	0.0	4.5	32.8	52.8	14.3	110	60.0	52.7	4.5
Delphos city	7,099	7,036	-0.9	7,267	96.9	1.3	0.1	0.6	1.1	24.6	59.8	15.5	2,862	67.7	50.9	16.1
Delshire CDP	3,180	NA	NA	2,831	93.5	0.4	0.0	1.6	4.5	26.4	62.1	11.7	922	80.7	44.3	23.5
Delta village	3,103	3,114	0.4	3,464	85.3	1.2	2.7	0.2	10.7	29.2	56.0	14.8	1,336	78.4	52.1	18.3
Dennison village	2,655	2,640	-0.6	2,749	94.3	3.5	0.4	0.6	1.2	28.6	59.4	11.9	1,080	55.9	60.6	10.6
Dent CDP	10,497	NA	NA	10,930	95.0	1.6	1.4	1.1	1.0	21.4	63.1	15.5	4,463	78.3	30.2	35.9
Derby CDP	408	NA	NA	428	100.0	0.0	0.0	0.0	0.0	32.3	57.7	10.0	153	51.0	93.5	0.0
Deshler village	1,799	1,788	-0.6	1,758	91.0	0.5	0.6	1.2	6.8	26.3	56.5	17.3	673	78.5	66.3	10.1
Devola CDP	2,652	NA	NA	2,612	92.9	0.5	1.7	2.1	2.9	23.1	53.9	23.0	974	90.2	27.4	33.5
Dexter City village	129	126	-2.3	132	100.0	0.0	0.0	0.0	0.0	22.7	73.7	3.8	46	50.0	84.8	13.0
Dillonvale CDP	3,474	NA	NA	3,685	93.6	2.3	1.6	0.9	1.5	23.1	61.2	15.7	1,472	82.9	36.1	29.3
Dillonvale village	665	643	-3.3	774	94.1	1.2	0.0	3.9	0.9	20.7	58.0	21.4	323	83.3	62.5	7.1
Dola CDP	140	NA	NA	74	83.8	0.0	0.0	16.2	0.0	10.8	59.5	29.7	34	100.0	100.0	0.0
Donnelsville village	304	301	-1.0	428	98.4	0.0	0.0	0.7	0.9	29.2	61.5	9.1	159	70.4	35.8	24.5
Dover city	12,826	12,857	0.2	12,839	92.1	1.3	0.1	1.3	5.2	22.2	53.1	24.7	5,230	72.7	54.1	22.4
Doylestown village	3,051	3,075	0.8	3,061	92.8	2.8	1.0	0.0	3.4	18.9	58.8	22.2	1,368	67.4	51.6	24.8
Dresden village	1,563	1,697	8.6	1,641	97.9	0.3	0.0	1.2	0.7	25.7	60.8	13.5	671	58.1	53.4	11.8
Drexel CDP	2,076	NA	NA	1,872	47.0	48.6	0.0	4.4	0.0	33.1	56.0	11.0	744	45.3	42.3	6.2
Dry Ridge CDP	2,782	NA	NA	2,451	87.2	3.4	7.7	1.3	0.4	14.3	61.0	24.7	1,035	94.8	30.0	40.2
Dry Run CDP	7,281	NA	NA	7,446	93.5	0.3	3.6	0.2	2.3	32.5	59.0	8.6	2,343	98.0	8.8	75.9
Dublin city	41,345	44,214	6.9	42,378	75.7	2.1	15.8	1.9	4.5	29.9	61.0	9.0	15,068	79.1	6.9	76.9
Duncan Falls CDP	880	NA	NA	885	100.0	0.0	0.0	0.0	0.0	20.7	59.6	19.5	348	82.2	37.9	8.6
Dundee CDP	297	NA	NA	651	97.5	0.0	0.0	0.0	2.5	21.5	77.3	1.2	216	68.5	89.8	0.0
Dunkirk village	875	866	-1.0	1,054	93.6	1.0	0.1	4.2	1.0	32.9	56.9	10.2	366	81.1	68.0	9.8
Dunlap CDP	1,719	NA	NA	2,227	88.4	9.5	0.0	0.3	1.8	18.6	75.4	5.9	735	91.3	38.1	33.5
Dupont village	318	312	-1.9	237	100.0	0.0	0.0	0.0	0.0	28.7	58.2	13.1	99	84.8	50.5	17.2
East Canton village	1,591	1,600	0.6	1,460	96.2	1.8	0.0	1.4	0.6	23.1	63.9	12.7	589	73.7	47.0	10.5
East Cleveland city	17,844	17,432	-2.3	17,619	5.5	90.6	0.2	1.4	2.4	23.4	57.2	19.2	7,982	35.2	54.4	10.4
East Fultonham CDP	335	NA	NA	303	100.0	0.0	0.0	0.0	0.0	34.4	57.4	8.3	106	69.8	72.6	8.5
Eastlake city	18,577	18,321	-1.4	18,448	94.7	1.7	1.1	0.8	1.6	19.4	63.9	16.5	7,896	74.6	48.0	17.5
East Liberty CDP	366	NA	NA	238	78.6	0.0	0.0	0.0	21.4	17.7	76.2	6.3	102	100.0	87.3	0.0
East Liverpool city	11,212	10,951	-2.3	11,065	88.9	6.5	0.0	3.5	1.0	23.9	61.3	14.7	4,826	51.7	63.1	7.1
East Palestine village	4,718	4,621	-2.1	4,663	93.9	0.0	0.6	2.9	2.6	25.6	58.4	15.9	1,833	66.6	57.1	6.2
East Rochester CDP	231	NA	NA	203	100.0	0.0	0.0	0.0	0.0	28.6	56.7	14.8	83	68.7	67.5	32.5
East Sparta village	819	808	-1.3	888	99.0	0.0	0.5	0.6	0.0	24.9	60.8	14.4	300	77.3	61.7	5.7
East Springfield CDP	0	NA	NA	507	100.0	0.0	0.0	0.0	0.0	23.8	69.3	6.9	144	70.1	26.4	23.6
Eaton city	8,409	8,261	-1.8	8,334	96.1	0.7	1.2	1.4	0.5	26.4	55.7	18.0	3,289	58.5	52.6	13.2
Eaton Estates CDP	1,222	NA	NA	776	97.4	0.0	0.0	0.5	2.1	25.4	61.9	12.8	285	84.9	63.9	10.5
Edgerton village	2,012	1,985	-1.3	2,168	91.6	0.6	0.0	0.4	7.4	20.8	58.1	20.9	880	77.8	58.9	14.2
Edgewood CDP	4,432	NA	NA	4,328	94.4	0.5	0.0	2.4	2.7	21.3	60.5	18.3	1,774	70.6	63.0	9.6
Edison village	437	438	0.2	399	82.7	0.3	0.0	7.3	9.8	23.5	61.9	14.5	149	63.8	65.8	8.1
Edon village	834	823	-1.3	924	96.6	0.0	0.2	2.5	0.6	29.8	49.0	21.1	373	76.9	56.0	13.9
Eldorado village	509	502	-1.4	662	98.6	0.0	0.0	1.4	0.0	23.4	66.8	9.8	255	65.5	51.8	17.3
Elgin village	57	56	-1.8	40	97.5	0.0	0.0	2.5	0.0	25.0	45.0	30.0	17	100.0	47.1	11.8
Elida village	1,889	1,866	-1.2	1,783	92.3	3.0	0.8	2.6	1.3	24.2	63.4	12.3	665	86.2	41.5	17.6
Elizabethtown CDP	350	NA	NA	302	88.4	0.0	0.0	7.0	4.6	21.9	69.8	8.3	120	67.5	91.7	0.0
Elmore village	1,410	1,401	-0.6	1,390	88.6	0.0	0.0	1.4	10.1	27.4	57.9	14.9	562	77.4	40.0	20.1
Elmwood Place village	2,188	2,173	-0.7	1,887	79.7	15.9	0.0	1.7	2.7	23.6	66.1	10.4	789	41.8	68.7	6.0
Elyria city	54,533	53,972	-1.0	54,216	75.4	13.7	0.6	5.2	5.1	22.6	63.2	14.2	22,646	60.4	45.6	14.7
Empire village	299	284	-5.0	288	99.7	0.0	0.0	0.3	0.0	30.9	58.0	11.1	123	63.4	61.0	11.4
Englewood city	13,465	13,457	-0.1	13,468	80.3	10.2	3.7	5.4	0.4	22.1	57.6	20.3	5,580	68.7	35.6	30.3
Enon village	2,415	2,400	-0.6	2,810	94.3	0.0	1.5	3.3	0.9	17.1	59.7	23.1	1,278	71.5	38.3	26.8
Etna CDP	1,215	NA	NA	1,070	97.7	2.3	0.0	0.0	0.0	25.1	70.0	4.9	402	81.6	44.0	26.1
Euclid city	48,905	47,893	-2.1	48,313	39.5	56.4	0.4	2.3	1.5	23.4	62.1	14.6	22,191	50.4	43.1	19.5
Evendale village	2,767	2,773	0.2	2,768	85.5	7.4	5.6	1.4	0.0	20.2	58.3	21.4	1,067	94.5	22.3	58.8
Fairborn city	32,763	33,329	1.7	33,039	80.7	8.5	4.1	3.5	3.2	20.6	65.8	13.6	14,149	48.9	35.9	28.3
Fairfax village	1,699	1,703	0.2	1,666	92.1	4.7	1.9	0.2	1.0	23.1	66.4	10.5	679	73.3	41.2	28.3
Fairfield city	42,503	42,770	0.6	42,643	76.6	14.1	1.3	2.2	5.8	21.2	64.9	14.0	17,315	62.7	36.7	29.0
Fairfield Beach CDP	1,292	NA	NA	951	99.2	0.0	0.0	0.0	0.8	19.0	64.7	16.4	411	76.6	54.0	9.7
Fairlawn city	7,459	7,426	-0.4	7,430	77.8	12.7	6.9	1.7	0.9	15.9	55.5	28.5	3,411	71.0	18.8	55.9
Fairport Harbor village	3,113	3,094	-0.6	3,110	92.9	0.4	0.0	0.3	6.4	24.4	61.1	14.6	1,379	69.5	45.5	22.3
Fairview village	83	82	-1.2	96	100.0	0.0	0.0	0.0	0.0	12.6	57.2	30.2	38	86.8	55.3	0.0
Fairview Park city	16,826	16,481	-2.1	16,625	88.9	2.0	2.0	2.3	4.8	20.9	61.9	17.3	7,531	73.6	29.5	39.3
Farmersville village	1,009	1,007	-0.2	1,051	99.1	0.0	0.0	0.5	0.4	26.2	61.6	12.0	383	81.2	53.8	9.9
Fayette village	1,283	1,272	-0.9	1,372	93.4	0.0	1.1	1.1	4.4	26.2	62.0	11.8	598	59.2	59.9	9.0
Fayetteville village	330	323	-2.1	313	97.8	0.0	1.0	0.0	1.3	19.5	59.7	20.8	126	65.9	65.9	11.1
Felicity village	818	828	1.2	872	88.2	1.4	0.0	4.7	5.7	25.3	59.3	15.5	400	40.0	79.8	4.8
Findlay city	41,186	41,098	-0.2	41,297	87.1	2.2	2.5	1.9	6.3	21.4	63.0	15.8	17,451	61.2	40.7	27.4
Finneytown CDP	12,741	NA	NA	12,907	55.1	35.0	2.1	4.9	3.0	22.6	61.5	15.8	5,006	74.2	26.6	34.8
Five Points CDP	1,824	NA	NA	1,775	100.0	0.0	0.0	0.0	0.0	22.1	60.3	17.6	683	100.0	16.0	50.1
Flat Rock CDP	233	NA	NA	50	96.0	4.0	0.0	0.0	0.0	34.0	26.0	40.0	11	100.0	100.0	0.0
Fletcher village	472	479	1.5	448	93.1	0.2	0.0	0.0	6.7	25.2	56.6	18.1	165	84.8	63.0	7.9
Florida village	232	231	-0.4	279	87.8	1.1	0.7	1.8	8.6	28.3	57.8	14.0	104	72.1	65.4	10.6
Flushing village	879	866	-1.5	775	98.2	0.3	0.0	1.4	0.1	17.4	58.2	24.3	367	72.2	61.3	8.2
Forest village	1,461	1,444	-1.2	1,688	97.5	0.7	0.0	0.7	1.1	28.8	60.4	10.7	572	70.5	65.4	14.0
Forest Park city	18,720	18,723	0.0	18,685	21.0	67.7	1.6	2.6	7.1	23.8	63.4	12.7	7,139	56.8	34.9	28.6
Forestville CDP	10,532	NA	NA	10,595	91.2	2.4	4.9	1.4	0.2	24.6	54.8	20.7	4,346	73.0	23.1	51.8
Fort Jennings village	485	481	-0.8	436	97.9	0.7	0.0	1.4	0.0	25.4	52.9	21.6	191	85.3	47.1	22.0
Fort Loramie village	1,483	1,490	0.5	1,334	99.0	0.0	0.0	0.1	0.8	28.2	56.1	15.7	497	76.1	52.7	22.1
Fort Recovery village	1,428	1,420	-0.6	1,487	94.4	0.0	0.0	1.9	3.8	27.0	57.5	15.5	593	74.2	58.9	12.1
Fort Seneca CDP	254	NA	NA	316	91.5	0.0	0.0	0.0	8.5	11.7	65.7	22.5	129	83.7	65.1	6.2
Fort Shawnee CDP	3,726	NA	NA	6,040	91.1	5.7	1.1	1.1	1.1	18.1	64.1	17.7	2,568	88.4	39.9	25.7

1 May be of any race.

Table A. All Places — **Population and Housing**

STATE City, town, township, borough, or CDP (county if applicable)	Population: 2010 census total population	Population: 2014 estimated population	Population: Percent change 2010–2014	Population: ACS total population estimate 2010–2014	Race and Hispanic or Latino origin (percent), 2010–2014: White alone, not Hispanic or Latino	Black alone, not Hispanic or Latino	Asian alone, not Hispanic or Latino	All other races or 2 or more races, not Hispanic or Latino	Hispanic or Latino[1]	Age (percent), 2010–2014: Under 18 years old	Age 18 to 64 years old	Age 65 years and older	Households, 2010–2014: Total occupied housing units	Percent owner occupied	Householders by level of education (percent): High school diploma or less	Bachelor's degree or more
	1	2	3	4	5	6	7	8	9	10	11	12	13	14	15	16
OHIO—Con.																
Fostoria city	13,441	13,182	-1.9	13,003	81.0	5.3	0.2	4.2	9.3	26.6	56.2	17.2	5,453	69.2	61.1	9.8
Four Bridges CDP	2,919	NA	NA	3,168	90.5	2.6	4.0	1.5	1.5	29.6	50.8	19.6	1,217	63.8	9.3	63.4
Frankfort village	1,064	1,062	-0.2	829	95.2	1.6	0.0	2.5	0.7	19.3	57.2	23.5	366	68.9	52.2	13.7
Franklin city	11,769	11,811	0.4	11,817	94.3	0.9	1.0	2.4	1.3	26.7	59.6	13.6	4,613	56.2	52.4	11.8
Franklin Furnace CDP	1,660	NA	NA	1,639	84.6	8.7	0.0	4.1	2.6	27.4	54.7	17.8	476	72.5	67.0	18.1
Frazeysburg village	1,326	1,317	-0.7	1,629	97.3	0.0	0.9	1.8	0.0	27.8	62.8	9.3	617	53.3	55.1	6.6
Fredericksburg village	423	422	-0.2	424	100.0	0.0	0.0	0.0	0.0	25.9	56.8	17.2	179	70.9	57.0	17.3
Fredericktown village	2,493	2,501	0.3	2,487	97.0	0.2	0.7	0.9	1.2	26.2	59.7	14.3	995	64.7	46.0	18.7
Freeport village	369	359	-2.7	367	96.7	0.0	1.9	0.8	0.5	19.1	61.2	19.6	178	70.8	61.8	10.1
Fremont city	16,734	16,448	-1.7	16,555	69.3	8.6	0.0	2.9	19.2	27.4	58.5	14.0	6,525	57.8	54.7	12.0
Fresno CDP	140	NA	NA	93	100.0	0.0	0.0	0.0	0.0	19.4	73.2	7.5	51	100.0	88.2	0.0
Friendship CDP	351	NA	NA	344	86.0	0.0	0.0	0.0	14.0	12.5	59.0	28.5	124	100.0	92.7	0.0
Fruit Hill CDP	3,755	NA	NA	3,431	92.8	2.9	4.0	0.3	0.0	24.2	57.5	18.3	1,350	92.2	14.1	47.6
Fulton village	258	261	1.2	276	93.5	0.0	0.0	6.5	0.0	33.7	57.3	9.1	97	70.1	69.1	4.1
Fultonham village	176	177	0.6	122	100.0	0.0	0.0	0.0	0.0	29.5	59.1	11.5	48	68.8	75.0	2.1
Gahanna city	33,233	34,257	3.1	33,786	81.9	12.5	2.6	1.6	1.4	24.0	63.6	12.5	12,931	73.4	23.0	48.6
Galena village	650	684	5.2	820	91.5	0.0	2.3	4.1	2.1	31.2	61.1	7.7	262	76.7	29.0	36.3
Galion city	10,510	10,175	-3.2	10,314	95.9	0.7	0.1	1.6	1.6	26.2	57.5	16.4	4,267	58.5	59.3	10.3
Gallipolis village	3,641	3,607	-0.9	3,325	90.0	4.8	0.5	3.4	1.3	22.2	58.7	19.3	1,347	52.6	50.9	20.3
Gambier village	2,391	2,473	3.4	2,266	89.1	3.5	2.9	2.0	2.6	4.3	89.9	5.8	319	54.2	17.6	63.6
Gann village	125	124	-0.8	164	100.0	0.0	0.0	0.0	0.0	23.1	66.4	10.4	63	52.4	69.8	9.5
Garfield Heights city	28,849	28,229	-2.1	28,492	54.8	39.3	0.7	2.6	2.6	23.9	59.8	16.3	11,422	70.0	50.3	13.9
Garrettsville village	2,338	2,329	-0.4	2,801	91.3	0.6	1.1	2.8	4.2	30.8	58.3	10.9	1,042	61.2	43.1	19.6
Gates Mills village	2,270	2,245	-1.1	2,250	93.2	1.7	1.8	1.3	2.0	16.5	58.0	25.5	905	95.1	13.0	68.1
Geneva city	6,215	6,079	-2.2	6,158	87.7	0.5	1.4	1.9	8.6	26.0	57.3	16.8	2,298	72.0	47.9	15.8
Geneva-on-the-Lake village	1,254	1,220	-2.7	1,462	93.8	0.1	0.3	1.0	4.9	24.6	60.3	15.0	648	50.2	45.7	17.1
Genoa village	2,336	2,321	-0.6	2,588	90.7	0.2	2.5	3.5	3.1	29.4	55.0	15.5	984	75.7	30.1	22.9
Georgetown village	4,493	4,469	-0.5	4,706	93.1	4.3	1.5	0.8	0.3	25.1	60.6	14.5	1,811	56.7	62.0	11.0
Germantown city	5,535	5,505	-0.5	5,545	95.5	0.0	2.4	0.7	1.4	26.0	57.8	16.2	2,072	71.6	33.8	21.4
Gettysburg village	513	506	-1.4	591	98.6	0.0	0.0	0.0	1.4	31.0	60.4	8.6	196	71.4	65.3	4.6
Gibsonburg village	2,581	2,588	0.3	2,679	88.8	0.3	0.0	4.2	6.6	31.8	53.4	14.7	910	72.2	42.7	9.9
Gilboa village	190	187	-1.6	174	83.9	2.3	0.0	0.0	13.8	32.7	61.5	5.7	64	76.6	54.7	20.3
Girard city	9,958	9,673	-2.9	9,799	88.9	3.4	1.9	2.5	3.3	23.3	60.2	16.6	4,216	61.3	52.6	19.2
Glandorf village	995	1,001	0.6	1,049	98.7	0.0	0.2	0.0	1.1	29.7	57.5	12.6	342	96.8	44.2	29.5
Glencoe CDP	310	NA	NA	229	100.0	0.0	0.0	0.0	0.0	38.8	51.9	9.2	76	89.5	78.9	9.2
Glendale village	2,155	2,157	0.1	2,219	83.2	10.1	2.7	2.4	1.5	20.5	59.8	19.7	951	87.3	14.1	68.2
Glenford village	173	176	1.7	242	96.3	0.0	0.0	3.7	0.0	36.0	55.8	8.3	71	69.0	46.5	14.1
Glenmont village	272	283	4.0	226	99.1	0.0	0.0	0.9	0.0	20.4	58.7	20.8	98	93.9	77.6	5.1
Glenmoor CDP	1,987	NA	NA	1,872	97.6	0.0	0.0	1.4	1.0	25.1	59.4	15.5	778	76.0	70.4	2.1
Glenwillow village	923	926	0.3	1,085	45.0	30.9	19.7	4.1	0.3	29.4	53.5	17.1	363	92.3	38.3	46.3
Gloria Glens Park village	425	433	1.9	409	97.1	0.0	1.0	0.0	2.0	18.8	70.1	11.0	173	82.1	50.9	17.3
Glouster village	1,793	1,788	-0.3	1,745	92.1	1.8	3.3	2.0	0.7	30.1	59.6	10.3	616	63.0	60.6	5.7
Gnadenhutten village	1,288	1,289	0.1	1,473	99.6	0.1	0.0	0.3	0.0	27.5	58.9	13.6	536	77.6	52.6	14.2
Golf Manor village	3,611	3,595	-0.4	3,601	19.8	74.2	1.0	4.7	0.3	28.1	60.9	11.0	1,539	49.1	36.0	28.7
Good Hope CDP	234	NA	NA	327	95.7	0.0	0.0	4.3	0.0	36.1	46.8	17.1	122	66.4	73.8	15.6
Gordon village	212	209	-1.4	189	94.7	1.1	0.0	2.6	1.6	15.4	68.8	15.9	77	80.5	68.8	5.2
Goshen CDP	0	NA	NA	673	96.3	0.0	0.0	0.0	3.7	21.6	59.6	18.9	265	62.6	39.6	12.5
Grafton village	6,636	6,077	-8.4	6,145	76.6	18.3	0.5	2.7	1.9	13.4	76.7	9.6	1,428	80.5	53.6	12.6
Grand Rapids village	967	992	2.6	1,086	95.6	0.5	0.2	0.4	3.4	28.1	54.5	17.4	411	76.6	31.9	23.8
Grand River village	399	396	-0.8	369	95.7	2.2	1.4	0.0	0.8	23.7	64.3	11.9	134	64.2	59.0	6.7
Grandview CDP	1,466	NA	NA	1,501	100.0	0.0	0.0	0.0	0.0	33.9	62.8	3.3	453	83.4	42.4	36.4
Grandview Heights city	6,518	7,244	11.1	6,836	93.5	0.3	2.3	1.6	2.3	21.6	69.8	8.7	2,732	64.0	7.4	72.6
Granville village	5,667	5,723	1.0	5,689	88.7	4.5	2.6	1.8	2.5	18.5	71.2	10.3	1,466	73.1	10.2	62.8
Granville South CDP	1,410	NA	NA	1,483	93.9	0.0	6.1	0.0	0.0	35.0	47.4	17.7	476	87.8	21.6	58.6
Gratiot village	221	223	0.9	333	94.3	0.0	0.0	5.7	0.0	33.9	56.7	9.3	119	74.8	64.7	5.9
Gratis village	881	864	-1.9	925	98.6	0.9	0.0	0.5	0.0	18.6	67.3	14.3	330	78.5	60.6	3.6
Graysville village	76	76	0.0	81	92.6	7.4	0.0	0.0	0.0	32.1	54.3	13.6	27	74.1	44.4	0.0
Green city	25,744	25,917	0.7	25,835	94.0	2.0	0.7	2.3	1.0	20.6	63.0	16.3	10,411	77.4	36.7	34.2
Green Camp village	374	366	-2.1	326	96.6	0.0	0.0	1.2	2.1	26.4	57.2	16.6	128	61.7	62.5	10.2
Greenfield village	4,639	4,575	-1.4	4,666	98.4	0.8	0.0	0.8	0.0	26.7	57.8	15.7	1,913	47.4	67.3	9.2
Greenhills village	3,615	3,596	-0.5	3,597	89.5	3.4	0.0	2.6	4.5	22.1	63.1	14.8	1,412	71.7	28.6	35.7
Green Meadows CDP	2,327	NA	NA	2,513	95.2	1.2	1.7	0.8	1.1	23.6	58.9	17.7	1,077	77.3	36.3	18.9
Green Springs village	1,368	1,339	-2.1	1,392	95.3	0.0	1.1	0.7	2.9	29.6	50.1	20.3	453	64.7	49.4	9.1
Greentown CDP	3,804	NA	NA	4,368	96.2	0.8	0.6	2.1	0.2	23.6	65.1	11.2	1,538	79.5	28.2	43.6
Greenville city	13,227	13,037	-1.4	13,121	95.2	1.6	0.3	2.0	0.8	21.2	56.5	22.4	6,121	52.9	62.3	12.8
Greenwich village	1,476	1,439	-2.5	1,316	93.7	0.2	0.0	5.2	0.9	28.2	56.0	15.8	564	70.2	63.7	10.1
Groesbeck CDP	6,788	NA	NA	6,688	73.7	13.8	0.7	7.0	4.7	25.8	60.8	13.3	2,536	76.1	49.5	24.1
Grove City city	35,578	38,519	8.3	36,981	92.0	2.2	1.4	2.3	2.0	24.2	63.4	12.3	14,233	69.3	34.8	30.1
Groveport city	5,362	5,672	5.8	5,535	77.8	19.2	0.8	1.6	0.7	19.8	64.1	16.0	2,338	72.4	40.5	25.8
Grover Hill village	402	383	-4.7	387	94.6	0.3	0.0	1.0	4.1	25.8	58.9	15.2	154	81.2	64.9	6.5
Hamden village	879	869	-1.1	936	98.9	0.0	0.0	1.1	0.0	20.2	61.1	18.8	400	70.8	72.3	3.5
Hamersville village	546	538	-1.5	612	98.0	0.0	0.0	2.0	0.0	26.6	65.4	8.0	205	60.0	60.5	8.8
Hamilton city	62,272	62,486	0.3	62,366	83.0	8.5	0.6	2.5	5.5	25.0	61.6	13.4	24,168	56.4	55.2	16.6
Hamler village	576	572	-0.7	674	85.2	0.0	0.0	0.4	14.4	30.3	53.2	16.5	245	80.0	64.9	10.6
Hanging Rock village	221	220	-0.5	184	96.7	0.0	0.0	3.3	0.0	15.3	66.3	18.5	83	73.5	66.3	7.2
Hannibal CDP	411	NA	NA	415	100.0	0.0	0.0	0.0	0.0	16.0	68.7	15.4	164	61.0	61.0	23.8
Hanover village	913	1,103	20.8	1,045	98.7	0.5	0.4	0.5	0.0	28.4	59.7	12.0	378	77.2	43.9	19.3
Hanoverton village	408	403	-1.2	357	93.8	0.0	0.8	5.3	0.0	16.8	63.3	19.9	148	74.3	78.4	6.1
Harbor Hills CDP	1,509	NA	NA	1,574	100.0	0.0	0.0	0.0	0.0	16.1	52.0	31.7	654	80.1	53.7	19.9
Harbor View village	101	100	-1.0	145	58.6	0.0	0.0	41.4	0.0	49.6	44.8	5.5	39	51.3	41.0	0.0
Harpster village	204	202	-1.0	225	89.8	0.0	0.0	0.9	9.3	25.3	59.1	15.6	88	65.9	75.0	1.1
Harrisburg village	321	331	3.1	377	98.7	1.3	0.0	0.0	0.0	23.9	63.2	12.7	150	60.0	56.0	12.7
Harrison city	9,920	10,479	5.6	10,212	98.0	0.1	0.1	1.0	0.9	27.8	63.3	8.9	3,761	75.4	40.8	24.6
Harrisville village	235	233	-0.9	287	100.0	0.0	0.0	0.0	0.0	21.3	66.3	12.5	132	86.4	78.0	8.3
Harrod village	418	413	-1.2	403	100.0	0.0	0.0	0.0	0.0	24.8	63.9	11.4	142	85.9	42.3	6.3
Hartford village	397	400	0.8	505	97.6	2.4	0.0	0.0	0.0	25.9	63.7	10.5	173	79.8	38.2	11.0
Hartville village	2,944	2,962	0.6	2,941	94.7	1.5	0.0	3.4	0.4	24.0	55.4	20.5	1,177	65.6	41.3	26.1
Harveysburg village	547	552	0.9	646	99.7	0.0	0.0	0.3	0.0	28.1	65.2	6.7	252	75.0	46.4	14.3
Haskins village	1,188	1,223	2.9	1,251	95.1	0.0	0.7	1.3	2.9	33.0	59.9	7.3	432	87.7	28.5	30.8
Haviland village	215	212	-1.4	130	97.7	0.0	0.0	0.0	2.3	30.8	54.6	14.6	51	78.4	76.5	9.8

1 May be of any race.

Table A. All Places — **Population and Housing**

STATE City, town, township, borough, or CDP (county if applicable)	Population				Race and Hispanic or Latino origin (percent), 2010–2014					Age (percent), 2010–2014			Households, 2010–2014			
															Householders by level of education (percent)	
	2010 census total population	2014 estimated population	Percent change 2010–2014	ACS total population estimate 2010–2014	White alone, not Hispanic or Latino	Black alone, not Hispanic or Latino	Asian alone, not Hispanic or Latino	All other races or 2 or more races, not Hispanic or Latino	Hispanic or Latino[1]	Under 18 years old	Age 18 to 64 years old	Age 65 years and older	Total occupied housing units	Percent owner occupied	High school diploma or less	Bachelor's degree or more
	1	2	3	4	5	6	7	8	9	10	11	12	13	14	15	16
OHIO—Con.																
Haydenville CDP	381	NA	NA	150	100.0	0.0	0.0	0.0	0.0	20.0	56.7	23.3	69	87.0	78.3	21.7
Hayesville village	451	461	2.2	393	95.2	0.0	0.3	0.5	4.1	19.4	58.0	22.6	179	89.9	61.5	17.3
Heath city	10,282	10,456	1.7	10,381	91.5	2.3	2.1	3.3	0.8	22.1	59.3	18.7	4,367	66.2	45.9	20.7
Hebron village	2,336	2,386	2.1	2,338	98.4	0.0	0.0	0.3	1.3	20.4	60.5	19.0	1,032	53.3	67.6	8.3
Helena village	224	222	-0.9	264	98.5	0.0	0.0	1.5	0.0	32.2	49.2	18.6	98	79.6	49.0	10.2
Hemlock village	155	155	0.0	196	96.4	0.0	0.0	3.6	0.0	21.0	69.5	9.7	72	70.8	62.5	12.5
Hessville CDP	214	NA	NA	225	77.8	0.0	3.6	4.9	13.8	19.1	59.6	21.3	79	91.1	38.0	0.0
Hicksville village	3,554	3,468	-2.4	3,300	90.4	0.0	0.3	1.2	8.0	24.9	56.7	18.5	1,398	64.9	70.9	10.0
Hide-A-Way Hills CDP	794	NA	NA	660	93.5	0.0	0.0	6.5	0.0	0.0	77.4	22.6	348	100.0	4.0	32.8
Higginsport village	251	246	-2.0	317	100.0	0.0	0.0	0.0	0.0	21.4	57.8	20.8	148	64.2	48.6	15.5
Highland village	254	253	-0.4	255	90.2	0.0	1.6	3.5	4.7	41.2	47.4	11.4	83	61.4	48.2	7.2
Highland Heights city	8,345	8,366	0.3	8,324	90.5	1.5	3.8	1.6	2.5	20.3	60.0	19.8	3,170	91.9	22.6	59.0
Highland Hills village	1,130	992	-12.2	999	19.3	75.8	0.0	1.3	3.6	16.2	64.4	19.3	235	36.2	43.4	11.1
Highland Holiday CDP	550	NA	NA	407	100.0	0.0	0.0	0.0	0.0	18.0	50.9	31.2	183	80.3	78.7	9.8
Highpoint CDP	1,503	NA	NA	1,438	91.6	1.7	1.0	0.0	5.7	24.3	57.0	18.6	522	91.2	39.7	36.2
Hilliard city	28,225	32,465	15.0	30,815	87.6	2.8	5.8	1.9	1.9	29.9	59.9	10.2	10,937	77.7	22.1	52.2
Hills and Dales village	221	221	0.0	323	94.1	0.0	2.8	0.0	3.1	33.2	44.8	22.0	102	100.0	6.9	63.7
Hillsboro city	6,607	6,550	-0.9	6,570	87.5	5.2	0.9	5.1	1.3	22.9	59.1	18.0	2,732	54.9	54.0	14.4
Hilltop CDP	532	NA	NA	325	100.0	0.0	0.0	0.0	0.0	14.2	71.6	14.5	141	83.7	61.0	11.3
Hiram village	1,406	1,299	-7.6	1,338	84.2	7.5	5.5	1.6	1.2	11.6	84.4	4.0	218	56.0	10.6	57.3
Hockingport CDP	212	NA	NA	130	100.0	0.0	0.0	0.0	0.0	22.3	47.7	30.0	41	100.0	36.6	22.0
Holgate village	1,109	1,100	-0.8	1,210	65.7	0.3	0.4	0.2	33.3	26.4	54.8	18.8	487	78.9	58.7	7.0
Holiday City village	52	52	0.0	46	91.3	0.0	0.0	0.0	8.7	26.0	49.9	23.9	19	73.7	52.6	10.5
Holiday Lakes CDP	749	NA	NA	623	100.0	0.0	0.0	0.0	0.0	14.6	65.1	20.2	275	96.7	52.7	16.0
Holiday Valley CDP	1,510	NA	NA	1,320	93.9	2.2	0.7	1.7	1.5	14.5	59.8	25.5	509	84.7	27.3	30.8
Holland village	1,704	1,702	-0.1	1,895	75.8	7.1	7.8	7.4	2.0	26.2	52.6	21.3	747	58.9	47.9	21.8
Hollansburg village	227	224	-1.3	312	99.4	0.0	0.0	0.6	0.0	32.6	56.6	10.9	118	60.2	71.2	5.1
Holloway village	338	327	-3.3	251	98.4	0.0	0.0	1.2	0.4	27.9	53.2	19.1	109	76.1	72.5	0.0
Holmesville village	372	388	4.3	414	100.0	0.0	0.0	0.0	0.0	25.8	64.2	9.9	151	71.5	78.1	2.0
Homeworth CDP	481	NA	NA	266	100.0	0.0	0.0	0.0	0.0	13.5	77.9	8.6	113	85.0	84.1	8.8
Hooven CDP	534	NA	NA	548	100.0	0.0	0.0	0.0	0.0	22.6	66.5	10.8	199	41.2	60.3	0.0
Hopedale village	950	933	-1.8	982	94.8	2.3	0.0	2.3	0.5	20.9	59.5	19.6	396	71.0	51.3	10.9
Howard CDP	242	NA	NA	197	100.0	0.0	0.0	0.0	0.0	21.9	62.9	15.2	92	41.3	80.4	0.0
Howland Center CDP	6,351	NA	NA	6,670	96.3	1.2	0.5	0.7	1.4	21.6	55.9	22.5	2,748	76.5	42.7	29.0
Hoytville village	303	300	-1.0	284	72.5	2.5	1.1	5.6	18.3	27.8	57.3	14.8	88	79.5	75.0	0.0
Hubbard city	7,874	7,695	-2.3	7,787	94.9	0.5	0.0	2.9	1.7	23.3	56.8	20.0	3,494	73.2	45.2	21.3
Huber Heights city	38,102	38,162	0.2	38,484	76.5	12.5	1.9	5.5	3.6	24.4	61.1	14.4	15,159	70.5	33.2	25.9
Huber Ridge CDP	4,604	NA	NA	4,816	74.3	13.8	0.3	9.4	2.2	30.3	60.5	9.3	1,728	65.0	36.0	24.0
Hudson city	22,262	22,448	0.8	22,351	91.2	1.4	4.7	1.0	1.7	28.3	57.6	14.2	7,670	86.2	9.5	76.0
Hunter CDP	2,100	NA	NA	2,386	96.5	1.2	0.0	0.8	1.5	15.3	60.9	23.7	989	88.7	57.4	10.4
Hunting Valley village	707	714	1.0	750	94.4	0.7	1.9	0.9	2.1	25.3	48.8	26.0	272	89.7	2.6	88.2
Huntsville village	431	430	-0.2	432	95.4	0.0	0.2	1.9	2.5	32.6	57.3	10.2	154	73.4	74.7	0.6
Huron city	7,148	7,045	-1.4	7,095	94.0	1.0	0.5	3.2	1.4	19.4	61.3	19.2	3,138	71.0	34.2	33.0
Iberia CDP	452	NA	NA	421	100.0	0.0	0.0	0.0	0.0	26.9	47.9	25.4	162	82.1	37.0	0.0
Independence city	7,125	7,136	0.2	7,136	97.5	0.4	0.4	0.5	1.2	22.7	58.4	18.8	2,688	94.3	38.4	34.9
Irondale village	384	368	-4.2	348	98.9	0.0	0.6	0.6	0.0	31.3	52.3	16.4	144	81.9	72.9	5.6
Ironton city	11,129	10,995	-1.2	11,190	89.9	7.3	0.1	1.9	0.9	21.7	59.5	18.7	4,468	61.6	52.9	18.6
Ithaca village	136	134	-1.5	150	97.3	0.0	0.0	2.0	0.7	36.0	57.9	6.0	50	58.0	60.0	4.0
Jackson city	6,397	6,284	-1.8	6,343	96.3	0.5	0.1	1.0	2.1	21.8	61.6	16.8	2,848	62.1	53.3	25.3
Jacksonburg village	63	64	1.6	67	100.0	0.0	0.0	0.0	0.0	22.4	71.7	6.0	33	90.9	93.9	3.0
Jackson Center village	1,462	1,455	-0.5	1,770	97.9	0.1	0.0	1.0	1.1	29.7	55.5	14.6	643	76.8	59.1	12.8
Jacksonville village	484	481	-0.6	611	99.5	0.5	0.0	0.0	0.0	21.0	66.2	12.6	190	75.8	58.9	12.6
Jamestown village	1,993	2,014	1.1	1,852	95.5	1.4	0.1	2.3	0.8	30.5	55.7	13.8	706	60.8	53.7	11.6
Jefferson village	3,120	3,053	-2.1	2,998	97.9	1.2	0.5	0.0	0.4	15.8	58.9	25.3	1,320	67.8	50.1	18.5
Jeffersonville village	1,203	1,197	-0.5	1,147	92.7	1.0	0.0	2.8	3.6	21.8	60.4	17.9	496	57.5	75.8	9.7
Jenera village	221	222	0.5	212	82.1	0.0	0.0	16.5	1.4	40.1	54.2	5.7	64	78.1	34.4	26.6
Jeromesville village	561	561	0.0	639	99.4	0.0	0.0	0.0	0.6	29.0	63.0	8.1	219	56.2	50.2	11.4
Jerry City village	427	435	1.9	477	89.3	0.0	0.0	0.0	10.7	27.5	62.2	10.5	179	77.1	75.4	10.1
Jerusalem village	161	161	0.0	163	100.0	0.0	0.0	0.0	0.0	20.2	57.7	22.1	78	78.2	61.5	7.7
Jewett village	692	676	-2.3	650	93.5	0.5	0.8	5.2	0.0	27.2	61.6	11.1	250	69.2	67.2	1.6
Johnstown village	4,644	4,870	4.9	5,154	91.2	1.0	0.0	0.9	6.8	27.4	62.6	10.1	1,912	63.8	48.2	27.2
Junction City village	819	809	-1.2	843	92.8	0.0	0.0	5.5	1.8	26.9	58.7	14.2	315	60.0	67.9	1.0
Kalida village	1,542	1,558	1.0	1,449	99.4	0.3	0.2	0.0	0.0	22.7	60.5	16.9	554	83.0	42.1	34.3
Kanauga CDP	175	NA	NA	145	100.0	0.0	0.0	0.0	0.0	40.7	59.3	0.0	61	29.5	100.0	0.0
Kansas CDP	179	NA	NA	114	100.0	0.0	0.0	0.0	0.0	0.0	92.1	7.9	57	61.4	45.6	0.0
Kelleys Island village	312	312	0.0	171	88.9	5.8	0.0	0.0	5.3	0.0	64.4	35.7	99	74.7	29.3	23.2
Kent city	28,906	29,639	2.5	29,367	79.2	10.2	5.4	3.5	1.8	15.2	77.2	7.3	9,839	38.5	23.9	37.8
Kenton city	8,262	8,242	-0.2	7,783	93.8	0.9	0.0	1.6	3.6	23.3	62.1	14.5	3,151	55.3	66.2	8.4
Kenwood CDP	6,981	NA	NA	6,852	80.9	8.3	6.7	2.0	2.1	21.4	53.8	24.6	3,049	62.4	13.9	60.6
Kettering city	56,161	55,705	-0.8	56,138	91.4	2.6	1.8	2.1	2.2	21.4	60.6	18.1	25,340	61.6	29.4	32.9
Kettlersville village	179	177	-1.1	188	98.9	0.0	0.0	1.1	0.0	33.5	57.4	9.0	62	82.3	43.5	21.0
Kidron CDP	944	NA	NA	1,058	99.6	0.4	0.0	0.0	0.0	39.6	49.2	11.2	321	83.8	59.2	30.8
Kilbourne CDP	139	NA	NA	138	100.0	0.0	0.0	0.0	0.0	13.8	50.0	36.2	62	54.8	61.3	0.0
Killbuck village	817	844	3.3	869	96.5	0.5	0.9	1.2	0.9	25.0	58.0	17.1	355	57.2	74.6	5.6
Kimbolton CDP	144	NA	NA	129	100.0	0.0	0.0	0.0	0.0	38.8	50.4	10.9	44	84.1	100.0	0.0
Kings Mills CDP	1,319	NA	NA	1,100	99.1	0.0	0.0	0.9	0.0	22.4	73.6	3.8	376	80.1	23.1	48.4
Kingston village	1,032	1,023	-0.9	1,237	98.5	0.0	0.0	1.2	0.2	18.9	64.4	16.7	499	61.5	55.1	9.2
Kinsman Center CDP	616	NA	NA	522	93.3	0.0	6.7	0.0	0.0	15.0	69.5	15.5	204	86.3	50.5	16.2
Kipton village	243	242	-0.4	260	99.6	0.0	0.0	0.4	0.0	31.5	59.3	9.2	103	81.6	51.5	4.9
Kirby village	118	116	-1.7	106	99.1	0.0	0.0	0.0	0.9	14.1	66.9	18.9	54	79.6	88.9	3.7
Kirkersville village	525	536	2.1	612	99.5	0.0	0.5	0.0	0.0	21.2	64.9	13.7	235	69.4	55.7	15.7
Kirtland city	6,861	6,819	-0.6	6,838	97.6	0.4	0.2	0.4	1.5	22.1	56.5	21.4	2,540	85.0	27.1	41.0
Kirtland Hills village	646	643	-0.5	690	97.2	0.0	0.0	0.0	2.8	22.6	58.5	18.8	251	93.2	26.3	50.6
Kunkle CDP	246	NA	NA	142	100.0	0.0	0.0	0.0	0.0	0.0	100.1	0.0	97	29.9	60.8	13.4
La Croft CDP	1,144	NA	NA	986	99.7	0.0	0.0	0.3	0.0	25.0	62.3	12.9	421	75.5	48.7	17.1
Lafayette village	445	432	-2.9	385	99.0	0.0	0.0	0.5	0.5	22.1	61.7	16.4	150	70.7	47.3	12.0
Lafayette CDP	202	NA	NA	334	100.0	0.0	0.0	0.0	0.0	22.2	62.1	15.9	122	82.0	62.3	31.1
Lafferty CDP	304	NA	NA	427	100.0	0.0	0.0	0.0	0.0	8.7	70.6	20.6	221	46.2	52.9	0.0
LaGrange village	2,103	2,120	0.8	2,303	94.1	0.7	0.1	0.6	4.5	23.5	62.0	14.7	843	77.0	43.7	16.8
Lake Buckhorn CDP	601	NA	NA	622	100.0	0.0	0.0	0.0	0.0	14.4	66.9	18.6	296	100.0	62.5	24.7
Lake Darby CDP	4,592	NA	NA	4,639	89.5	0.6	3.6	5.1	1.2	30.3	64.8	4.9	1,570	95.0	26.4	38.7

1 May be of any race.

Table A. All Places — **Population and Housing**

STATE City, town, township, borough, or CDP (county if applicable)	Population				Race and Hispanic or Latino origin (percent), 2010–2014					Age (percent), 2010–2014			Households, 2010–2014			
	2010 census total population	2014 estimated population	Percent change 2010–2014	ACS total population estimate 2010–2014	White alone, not Hispanic or Latino	Black alone, not Hispanic or Latino	Asian alone, not Hispanic or Latino	All other races or 2 or more races, not Hispanic or Latino	Hispanic or Latino[1]	Under 18 years old	Age 18 to 64 years old	Age 65 years and older	Total occupied housing units	Percent owner occupied	Householders by level of education (percent): High school diploma or less	Householders by level of education (percent): Bachelor's degree or more
	1	2	3	4	5	6	7	8	9	10	11	12	13	14	15	16
OHIO—Con.																
Lake Lakengren CDP	3,383	NA	NA	3,369	99.6	0.0	0.4	0.0	0.0	27.1	61.4	11.4	1,173	81.4	33.6	24.2
Lakeline village	226	224	-0.9	269	98.1	1.1	0.0	0.7	0.0	22.3	65.1	12.6	105	91.4	39.0	24.8
Lake Lorelei CDP	1,170	NA	NA	1,053	98.7	0.0	0.0	0.0	1.3	24.8	46.5	28.7	431	84.9	38.1	33.9
Lake Milton CDP	0	NA	NA	687	95.5	0.0	0.0	0.0	4.5	15.8	68.3	15.9	266	68.4	61.7	12.0
Lake Mohawk CDP	1,652	NA	NA	1,558	99.0	0.0	0.0	1.0	0.0	14.7	62.7	22.5	642	94.9	24.1	38.6
Lakemore village	3,058	3,052	-0.2	3,056	90.0	6.4	0.0	3.0	0.6	19.4	60.8	19.7	1,199	73.9	56.2	13.1
Lake Seneca CDP	465	NA	NA	668	100.0	0.0	0.0	0.0	0.0	29.9	54.7	15.3	247	94.3	34.0	24.3
Lakeside CDP	694	NA	NA	608	97.7	0.0	0.0	2.3	0.0	0.0	31.3	68.8	424	61.3	53.5	39.9
Lake Tomahawk CDP	485	NA	NA	640	100.0	0.0	0.0	0.0	0.0	16.7	54.4	29.1	256	100.0	32.8	54.7
Lakeview village	1,072	1,054	-1.7	1,084	95.1	0.2	0.7	3.4	0.6	20.7	60.0	19.4	483	70.8	64.6	4.6
Lake Waynoka CDP	1,173	NA	NA	902	87.1	0.0	0.0	12.9	0.0	19.7	60.3	19.8	420	100.0	40.7	23.6
Lakewood city	52,131	50,926	-2.3	51,434	84.0	6.8	1.4	3.8	4.1	19.2	70.0	10.8	24,573	44.2	26.4	43.2
Lancaster city	38,781	39,595	2.1	39,105	95.0	1.2	0.9	1.3	1.6	23.1	60.9	15.9	16,186	54.4	53.0	16.8
Landen CDP	6,782	NA	NA	7,171	92.9	1.1	4.2	1.5	0.3	29.1	62.5	8.3	2,693	70.7	14.8	51.7
Lansing CDP	634	NA	NA	718	100.0	0.0	0.0	0.0	0.0	26.1	63.0	10.9	289	67.1	77.2	0.0
La Rue village	747	722	-3.3	606	77.2	0.2	0.0	2.3	20.3	28.8	52.0	19.3	273	52.0	66.3	4.4
Latty village	193	188	-2.6	182	87.4	2.7	0.0	5.5	4.4	21.9	69.6	8.2	76	84.2	61.8	17.1
Laura village	474	470	-0.8	379	97.9	0.5	0.0	1.6	0.0	22.6	63.1	14.2	154	80.5	53.2	6.5
Laurelville village	527	521	-1.1	404	100.0	0.0	0.0	0.0	0.0	20.5	61.5	17.8	219	32.4	77.6	6.8
Leavittsburg CDP	1,973	NA	NA	1,625	95.0	1.4	0.7	1.9	1.0	19.7	63.4	16.9	671	83.6	72.4	8.3
Lebanon city	20,032	20,434	2.0	20,338	90.5	5.4	0.9	1.0	2.1	29.6	60.8	9.7	7,088	61.3	32.2	32.6
Leesburg village	1,317	1,297	-1.5	1,371	99.7	0.0	0.0	0.3	0.0	26.0	62.0	12.0	487	60.8	65.7	11.7
Leesville village	158	156	-1.3	122	100.0	0.0	0.0	0.0	0.0	9.0	64.7	26.2	59	83.1	59.3	0.0
Leetonia village	1,959	1,922	-1.9	2,020	96.7	0.4	0.0	1.5	1.3	22.8	62.0	15.3	805	72.5	58.4	9.7
Leipsic village	2,092	2,048	-2.1	2,145	70.8	0.4	0.0	1.4	27.4	22.1	57.6	20.3	898	67.6	68.3	13.0
Lewisburg village	1,820	1,783	-2.0	1,611	96.3	0.4	2.7	0.6	0.0	26.5	57.7	15.8	604	70.9	55.8	8.4
Lewistown CDP	222	NA	NA	121	100.0	0.0	0.0	0.0	0.0	6.6	71.9	21.5	67	100.0	68.7	0.0
Lewisville village	176	176	0.0	217	97.7	2.3	0.0	0.0	0.0	18.5	61.0	20.7	89	88.8	62.9	15.7
Lexington village	4,822	4,743	-1.6	5,706	94.4	0.2	1.0	3.2	1.2	28.4	56.8	14.9	2,208	67.9	33.0	27.4
Liberty Center village	1,180	1,160	-1.7	1,133	92.7	0.0	0.0	2.1	5.2	22.2	64.9	13.0	479	76.6	66.0	10.2
Lima city	38,761	38,265	-1.3	38,432	65.7	26.5	0.4	4.6	2.9	26.5	62.4	11.1	14,125	44.8	52.6	11.5
Limaville village	151	151	0.0	300	99.0	0.0	0.3	0.0	0.7	43.7	49.0	7.3	94	83.0	46.8	8.5
Lincoln Heights village	3,286	3,368	2.5	3,348	0.9	95.3	0.0	2.6	1.2	25.3	61.1	13.6	1,413	32.6	61.2	4.3
Lincoln Village CDP	9,032	NA	NA	8,994	81.2	8.5	0.3	1.7	8.4	20.0	65.3	14.6	3,738	64.2	56.5	11.9
Lindsey village	446	435	-2.5	552	85.1	2.4	0.0	0.5	12.0	17.9	68.5	13.8	200	88.0	37.0	22.5
Linndale village	179	177	-1.1	190	64.7	5.3	0.0	3.2	26.8	36.8	56.3	6.8	63	41.3	42.9	11.1
Lisbon village	2,819	2,753	-2.3	2,782	96.8	1.2	0.0	0.4	1.5	21.9	64.3	13.8	1,063	60.4	57.4	12.9
Lithopolis village	1,118	1,290	15.4	1,350	82.5	14.0	0.4	2.5	0.5	23.9	57.1	19.1	515	81.0	43.3	21.7
Little Hocking CDP	263	NA	NA	253	100.0	0.0	0.0	0.0	0.0	0.0	86.2	13.8	148	53.4	62.8	37.2
Lockbourne village	238	245	2.9	259	94.2	0.0	0.0	5.0	0.8	30.9	55.2	13.9	100	45.0	78.0	7.0
Lockington village	141	139	-1.4	141	85.8	0.0	0.0	14.2	0.0	22.7	61.0	16.3	57	70.2	82.5	3.5
Lockland village	3,449	3,432	-0.5	3,444	44.7	37.4	0.0	0.6	17.4	23.6	66.6	9.8	1,322	46.2	70.0	3.9
Lodi village	2,753	2,790	1.3	2,777	94.9	2.1	0.9	0.4	1.7	21.2	61.7	17.3	1,148	61.4	66.5	8.9
Logan city	7,149	7,154	0.1	7,314	95.2	0.8	0.4	1.9	1.6	24.8	57.1	18.0	3,069	59.9	53.5	12.3
Logan Elm Village CDP	1,118	NA	NA	1,202	91.7	0.5	7.2	0.7	0.0	24.1	49.8	26.1	442	54.5	60.0	9.7
London city	9,906	10,056	1.5	9,924	87.0	4.4	2.5	3.3	2.8	24.4	61.2	14.4	3,944	52.6	52.1	19.1
Lorain city	64,097	63,776	-0.5	63,885	54.6	14.6	1.1	3.1	26.7	25.6	59.6	14.6	25,562	58.2	53.3	12.2
Lordstown village	3,422	3,322	-2.9	3,374	97.2	0.4	0.7	1.2	0.4	18.0	60.2	21.8	1,524	77.2	60.4	15.4
Lore City village	325	322	-0.9	289	98.3	0.0	0.0	1.0	0.7	15.6	63.2	21.5	117	82.9	71.8	8.5
Loudonville village	2,645	2,626	-0.7	2,777	99.2	0.3	0.4	0.0	0.1	19.5	59.7	20.7	1,096	64.4	62.2	12.9
Louisville city	9,186	9,147	-0.4	9,151	97.1	0.0	0.1	1.6	1.2	22.8	59.5	17.8	3,812	64.0	47.2	20.0
Loveland city	12,063	12,405	2.8	12,425	93.0	2.9	1.0	1.1	1.9	25.2	61.6	13.1	4,720	77.5	27.2	44.2
Loveland Park CDP	1,523	NA	NA	1,311	98.4	0.0	0.0	0.0	1.6	22.1	60.8	16.9	542	92.3	61.4	13.8
Lowell village	549	550	0.2	478	88.3	1.3	0.0	9.2	1.3	27.0	50.9	22.0	203	82.8	55.7	14.3
Lowellville village	1,155	1,115	-3.5	1,132	94.5	0.3	0.0	0.9	4.3	27.1	58.0	14.8	440	69.1	49.8	12.7
Lower Salem village	86	86	0.0	40	100.0	0.0	0.0	0.0	0.0	27.5	67.5	5.0	16	56.3	68.8	0.0
Lucas village	615	605	-1.6	561	98.8	0.0	0.0	0.4	0.9	30.6	55.1	14.1	213	58.2	54.9	7.5
Lucasville CDP	2,757	NA	NA	2,626	81.8	15.5	0.0	2.7	0.0	15.8	72.4	11.8	680	70.4	46.6	24.1
Luckey village	1,012	1,043	3.1	988	93.7	0.0	0.0	0.0	6.3	27.5	59.2	13.4	400	80.5	46.3	26.0
Ludlow Falls village	208	211	1.4	285	97.5	0.0	0.0	0.0	2.5	30.6	64.2	5.3	113	43.4	62.8	9.7
Lynchburg village	1,499	1,485	-0.9	1,290	98.7	0.0	0.0	0.9	0.5	37.4	52.5	10.2	432	60.9	55.3	6.9
Lyndhurst city	14,001	13,733	-1.9	13,856	88.3	9.0	1.2	0.5	1.0	18.1	58.6	23.3	5,985	81.1	21.0	50.7
Lyons village	562	553	-1.6	467	94.4	0.0	0.0	0.0	5.6	22.1	62.8	15.4	190	74.7	53.7	15.8
McArthur village	1,705	1,687	-1.1	1,883	94.6	0.0	0.1	4.6	0.6	26.8	60.1	13.1	748	61.6	55.3	11.1
McClure village	725	714	-1.5	759	92.5	0.3	0.5	1.1	5.7	25.7	58.5	15.9	308	83.1	57.8	10.4
McComb village	1,648	1,644	-0.2	1,729	87.2	0.0	0.6	1.1	11.1	28.4	60.5	11.2	639	73.7	63.7	10.5
McConnelsville village	1,784	1,797	0.7	1,889	87.6	7.5	2.4	2.5	0.0	20.0	54.4	25.6	848	53.5	59.7	13.9
McCutchenville CDP	400	NA	NA	440	100.0	0.0	0.0	0.0	0.0	28.1	58.7	13.0	142	82.4	64.1	6.3
McDermott CDP	434	NA	NA	539	100.0	0.0	0.0	0.0	0.0	33.2	52.3	14.5	193	40.4	94.3	0.0
McDonald village	3,263	3,174	-2.7	3,219	96.6	0.7	0.0	0.0	2.7	24.1	59.4	16.5	1,311	75.8	51.9	19.3
Macedonia city	11,133	11,579	4.0	11,364	83.0	10.2	2.7	2.1	2.0	20.7	63.2	16.0	4,434	91.2	34.5	39.5
McGuffey village	501	492	-1.8	509	92.3	0.0	0.2	1.6	5.9	21.1	64.2	14.7	173	68.8	68.8	3.5
Mack CDP	11,585	NA	NA	10,919	97.4	0.0	0.7	1.1	0.7	21.8	61.8	16.4	3,941	97.9	30.8	39.9
McKinley Heights CDP	1,060	NA	NA	906	99.7	0.0	0.0	0.0	0.3	19.4	68.6	12.0	342	88.6	23.1	21.3
Macksburg village	186	186	0.0	133	97.7	0.0	0.0	2.3	0.0	13.5	67.0	19.5	67	79.1	85.1	0.0
Madeira city	8,726	8,936	2.4	8,801	94.3	0.7	1.3	1.4	2.4	26.8	57.4	16.0	3,223	86.5	17.2	58.3
Madison village	3,184	3,176	-0.3	3,173	98.1	0.3	0.8	0.4	0.4	24.4	60.4	15.3	1,245	78.6	37.6	26.1
Magnetic Springs village	268	273	1.9	250	100.0	0.0	0.0	0.0	0.0	28.8	61.6	9.6	91	57.1	70.3	9.9
Magnolia village	978	975	-0.3	1,079	99.2	0.0	0.0	0.0	0.8	28.6	57.2	14.2	391	80.6	47.1	16.6
Maineville village	912	969	6.3	915	95.5	0.2	0.2	1.1	3.0	22.5	67.3	10.2	361	76.2	39.9	31.6
Malinta village	265	266	0.4	251	80.1	0.0	0.0	0.8	19.1	25.2	49.9	25.1	113	75.2	47.8	3.5
Malta village	671	661	-1.5	891	90.7	3.5	0.0	5.8	0.0	36.5	52.0	11.6	298	75.5	63.4	10.1
Malvern village	1,191	1,171	-1.7	1,145	93.8	2.2	0.3	3.1	0.7	21.0	59.5	19.5	491	54.0	57.6	11.0
Manchester village	2,023	1,984	-1.9	2,127	95.7	0.0	0.0	1.8	2.4	24.7	61.2	14.1	787	55.0	70.4	9.8
Mansfield city	47,821	46,824	-2.1	47,150	71.6	20.2	0.3	5.6	2.2	20.5	63.4	16.3	18,179	54.7	53.1	15.3
Mantua village	1,030	1,023	-0.7	1,295	96.1	0.0	0.0	1.3	2.5	21.0	65.5	13.6	529	53.9	46.1	19.3
Maple Heights city	23,138	22,735	-1.7	22,880	26.4	68.9	1.0	2.3	1.3	21.9	64.9	13.1	9,758	66.5	47.9	15.4
Maple Ridge CDP	761	NA	NA	866	97.2	0.0	0.0	2.8	0.0	34.5	45.7	20.0	325	76.0	68.3	0.0
Maplewood Park CDP	280	NA	NA	340	48.8	35.6	0.0	0.0	15.6	3.3	74.3	22.4	160	73.1	69.4	2.5
Marble Cliff village	569	581	2.1	605	92.9	1.0	1.7	2.8	1.7	15.8	64.9	19.3	291	56.0	13.1	75.3
Marblehead village	903	894	-1.0	961	97.3	0.0	0.2	0.8	1.7	9.3	55.2	35.5	481	84.8	33.5	28.3

1 May be of any race.

Table A. All Places — **Population and Housing**

STATE City, town, township, borough, or CDP (county if applicable)	Population: 2010 census total population	Population: 2014 estimated population	Population: Percent change 2010–2014	Population: ACS total population estimate 2010–2014	Race and Hispanic or Latino origin (percent), 2010–2014: White alone, not Hispanic or Latino	Black alone, not Hispanic or Latino	Asian alone, not Hispanic or Latino	All other races or 2 or more races, not Hispanic or Latino	Hispanic or Latino[1]	Age (percent), 2010–2014: Under 18 years old	Age 18 to 64 years old	Age 65 years and older	Households, 2010–2014: Total occupied housing units	Percent owner occupied	Householders by level of education (percent): High school diploma or less	Bachelor's degree or more
	1	2	3	4	5	6	7	8	9	10	11	12	13	14	15	16
OHIO—Con.																
Marengo village	342	346	1.2	291	96.9	0.0	0.0	3.1	0.0	32.7	56.7	10.7	115	46.1	70.4	15.7
Mariemont village	3,403	3,386	-0.5	3,384	92.9	0.9	0.0	2.9	3.4	31.6	53.5	14.9	1,303	67.5	11.3	75.4
Marietta city	14,085	13,954	-0.9	14,029	93.9	1.5	1.8	2.0	0.9	17.2	62.9	20.1	6,047	58.6	46.1	25.6
Marion city	36,828	36,620	-0.6	36,791	84.1	9.9	0.5	2.2	3.2	21.7	66.1	12.2	12,536	58.4	58.2	10.7
Marlboro CDP	0	NA	NA	239	100.0	0.0	0.0	0.0	0.0	24.6	51.0	24.3	81	100.0	60.5	0.0
Marne CDP	783	NA	NA	668	95.2	2.1	0.0	2.7	0.0	29.4	56.5	13.8	241	89.6	58.9	20.3
Marseilles village	112	111	-0.9	156	100.0	0.0	0.0	0.0	0.0	32.7	58.9	8.3	62	90.3	45.2	9.7
Marshallville village	756	759	0.4	729	99.0	0.0	1.0	0.0	0.0	24.1	60.2	15.5	284	73.2	71.1	9.2
Martinsburg village	237	232	-2.1	229	98.3	0.0	0.0	1.7	0.0	20.5	62.9	16.6	91	56.0	70.3	6.6
Martins Ferry city	6,915	6,814	-1.5	6,850	87.9	4.2	0.0	6.8	1.1	21.1	64.1	14.9	2,882	63.4	50.0	13.2
Martinsville village	463	463	0.0	398	98.2	0.0	0.0	0.8	1.0	33.5	56.5	10.1	128	66.4	56.3	9.4
Marysville city	22,098	22,708	2.8	22,773	89.4	3.0	2.6	3.4	1.5	24.9	66.6	8.5	7,531	60.5	39.8	27.8
Mason city	30,857	31,613	2.5	31,289	79.3	3.9	10.3	1.9	4.6	30.0	58.2	12.0	11,112	81.0	20.9	57.3
Massillon city	32,199	32,274	0.2	32,224	85.9	8.4	0.1	3.1	2.4	22.4	60.8	16.7	13,127	65.5	50.5	16.6
Masury CDP	2,064	NA	NA	2,213	95.5	0.7	0.0	2.4	1.4	21.8	63.2	14.9	964	66.6	59.0	8.7
Matamoras village	896	886	-1.1	822	97.4	0.0	0.0	0.5	2.1	18.9	60.7	20.4	359	54.9	62.7	11.1
Maumee city	14,286	14,036	-1.7	14,148	91.1	2.4	1.8	1.3	3.4	22.2	62.2	15.6	5,899	70.3	32.0	34.5
Mayfield village	3,460	3,413	-1.4	3,432	87.4	3.1	6.8	2.5	0.2	16.8	60.0	23.2	1,410	73.7	18.6	58.1
Mayfield Heights city	19,155	18,849	-1.6	18,973	78.1	11.1	5.9	2.5	2.3	20.1	57.8	22.2	9,318	52.1	31.3	40.4
Mechanicsburg village	1,644	1,605	-2.4	1,823	91.1	4.3	0.0	3.8	0.8	29.6	59.0	11.5	656	53.2	59.9	11.9
Medina city	26,666	26,523	-0.5	26,544	90.8	4.5	0.8	2.2	1.7	28.2	60.1	11.7	10,266	65.1	36.6	31.7
Melmore CDP	153	NA	NA	133	100.0	0.0	0.0	0.0	0.0	32.3	60.9	6.8	53	100.0	15.1	18.9
Melrose village	275	268	-2.5	173	98.3	1.2	0.0	0.6	0.0	26.6	64.8	8.7	65	78.5	75.4	10.8
Mendon village	662	651	-1.7	587	98.6	0.0	0.0	0.9	0.5	24.8	56.9	18.2	241	74.7	64.7	3.7
Mentor city	47,159	46,870	-0.6	47,008	95.5	1.6	1.4	0.6	1.0	20.1	62.3	17.5	19,230	85.1	31.0	33.6
Mentor-on-the-Lake city	7,443	7,412	-0.4	7,430	95.2	1.3	0.6	1.9	1.0	19.1	65.0	15.8	3,301	61.4	51.8	10.5
Metamora village	627	616	-1.8	574	98.6	0.0	0.3	0.7	0.3	26.1	60.9	12.9	217	76.5	37.8	23.0
Meyers Lake village	569	572	0.5	647	94.6	2.5	0.0	0.0	2.9	4.6	60.4	34.9	332	80.1	26.8	47.9
Miami Heights CDP	4,731	NA	NA	4,796	94.6	0.1	0.7	1.9	2.7	28.5	59.2	12.3	1,657	96.2	31.4	34.8
Miamisburg city	20,181	20,092	-0.4	20,168	93.1	2.9	0.9	1.5	1.6	24.0	58.1	18.0	8,219	72.0	40.8	22.5
Miamitown CDP	1,259	NA	NA	1,113	90.2	3.3	0.0	6.5	0.0	25.7	67.5	6.7	469	8.5	39.7	14.3
Miamiville CDP	242	NA	NA	288	100.0	0.0	0.0	0.0	0.0	38.2	43.4	18.4	88	50.0	20.5	14.8
Middleburg Heights city	15,946	15,751	-1.2	15,823	83.3	2.0	9.4	1.4	3.9	19.0	58.1	22.9	6,764	71.7	32.0	36.0
Middlefield village	2,690	2,707	0.6	2,707	93.1	0.2	0.7	1.8	4.1	21.1	56.5	22.5	1,127	56.5	49.1	16.8
Middle Point village	576	565	-1.9	538	97.2	0.0	0.0	0.0	2.8	26.6	61.5	11.9	214	85.5	71.0	9.3
Middleport village	2,529	2,484	-1.8	2,320	94.9	1.5	0.6	3.1	0.0	19.3	59.9	20.8	1,002	63.1	57.9	11.4
Middletown city	48,678	48,791	0.2	48,256	79.6	11.3	1.5	3.4	4.3	24.0	61.2	15.0	19,631	55.8	58.2	15.8
Midland village	315	315	0.0	441	99.5	0.0	0.0	0.5	0.0	39.7	56.4	3.9	136	47.8	69.1	1.5
Midvale village	754	749	-0.7	944	96.3	0.4	0.0	0.0	3.3	27.8	64.2	8.1	319	58.9	67.4	8.5
Midway village	322	327	1.6	227	98.7	0.0	0.0	1.3	0.0	31.3	49.4	19.4	72	79.2	72.2	8.3
Mifflin village	137	137	0.0	113	100.0	0.0	0.0	0.0	0.0	24.8	66.5	8.8	50	74.0	64.0	4.0
Milan village	1,367	1,346	-1.5	1,382	93.0	1.1	2.3	0.7	2.9	24.4	59.6	15.8	494	75.5	41.9	28.1
Milford city	6,709	6,892	2.7	6,748	92.7	3.4	0.5	3.1	0.2	25.2	54.7	20.0	2,919	49.5	42.7	27.3
Milford Center village	792	813	2.7	771	97.0	0.3	0.4	0.9	1.4	26.8	59.8	13.4	274	68.2	66.1	7.7
Millbury village	1,200	1,241	3.4	1,219	92.2	0.0	1.0	1.3	5.5	21.2	62.1	16.7	500	78.4	52.0	16.8
Milledgeville village	114	113	-0.9	174	87.9	0.0	0.0	12.1	0.0	43.7	44.2	12.1	58	60.3	62.1	0.0
Miller City village	137	139	1.5	111	99.1	0.0	0.0	0.0	0.9	9.0	67.5	23.4	62	83.9	51.6	11.3
Millersburg village	3,035	3,146	3.7	3,088	95.1	0.0	0.0	1.6	3.3	23.1	60.2	16.8	1,230	55.4	61.6	13.7
Millersport village	1,044	1,048	0.4	1,338	98.5	0.0	0.0	1.1	0.4	30.0	59.1	10.8	486	68.7	56.2	15.4
Millfield CDP	341	NA	NA	252	100.0	0.0	0.0	0.0	0.0	7.9	72.5	19.4	130	100.0	86.9	0.0
Millville village	708	716	1.1	847	99.5	0.0	0.0	0.5	0.0	22.9	64.0	13.1	336	81.3	56.3	12.8
Milton Center village	144	147	2.1	140	87.9	0.7	0.0	0.0	11.4	32.9	55.8	11.4	52	90.4	50.0	5.8
Miltonsburg village	43	43	0.0	50	74.0	26.0	0.0	0.0	0.0	20.0	66.0	14.0	22	100.0	63.6	0.0
Mineral City village	727	724	-0.4	719	97.2	0.0	2.8	0.0	0.0	16.3	73.1	10.6	301	74.8	62.1	7.0
Mineral Ridge CDP	3,892	NA	NA	3,744	97.3	2.1	0.0	0.0	0.6	22.9	61.2	15.8	1,376	74.4	52.5	19.7
Minerva village	3,720	3,698	-0.6	3,793	94.8	1.7	0.0	1.6	1.8	23.1	59.1	17.9	1,499	68.4	51.8	10.9
Minerva Park village	1,272	1,306	2.7	1,626	81.9	11.4	0.7	4.7	1.4	27.4	58.2	14.2	606	89.4	20.0	51.8
Minford CDP	693	NA	NA	553	96.9	0.0	0.0	3.1	0.0	12.7	53.9	33.5	275	70.5	78.2	6.5
Mingo Junction village	3,454	3,344	-3.2	3,125	91.6	3.6	0.0	4.8	0.0	19.2	59.4	21.4	1,323	74.5	57.7	13.5
Minster village	2,807	2,830	0.8	2,933	98.9	0.1	0.2	0.2	0.6	27.6	56.1	16.4	1,068	79.5	37.2	29.6
Mitiwanga CDP	0	NA	NA	163	93.3	0.0	0.0	6.7	0.0	14.1	74.2	11.7	87	100.0	17.2	55.2
Mogadore village	3,860	3,893	0.9	3,925	97.9	0.0	0.5	1.0	0.7	27.9	60.4	11.6	1,343	83.8	44.6	18.8
Monfort Heights CDP	11,948	NA	NA	11,965	93.3	4.5	1.3	0.6	0.2	21.6	59.1	19.2	4,665	82.4	31.1	42.4
Monroe city	12,453	13,279	6.6	13,633	89.7	2.8	2.0	2.3	3.2	28.4	57.3	14.3	4,799	75.5	34.9	31.1
Monroeville village	1,400	1,377	-1.6	1,192	97.1	0.0	0.0	1.8	1.1	25.9	64.0	10.2	490	61.4	49.0	10.6
Montezuma village	161	161	0.0	187	100.0	0.0	0.0	0.0	0.0	20.3	68.5	11.2	89	65.2	57.3	2.2
Montgomery city	10,251	10,440	1.8	10,332	89.0	2.0	5.4	1.7	1.9	25.8	53.2	20.9	3,858	87.2	8.6	72.9
Montpelier village	4,072	4,020	-1.3	4,049	94.5	0.1	1.2	1.7	2.4	24.0	61.2	14.7	1,637	56.9	55.8	13.9
Montrose-Ghent CDP	5,177	NA	NA	4,876	88.6	3.3	4.9	1.9	1.3	22.0	54.6	23.5	2,022	93.7	12.7	71.0
Moraine city	6,307	6,365	0.9	6,333	84.4	12.5	0.8	0.8	1.4	27.0	61.3	11.7	2,369	58.4	53.7	14.1
Moreland Hills village	3,320	3,306	-0.4	3,305	89.6	1.2	3.9	1.3	4.1	23.5	56.9	19.6	1,279	90.9	7.6	76.4
Morgandale CDP	1,224	NA	NA	998	93.2	4.6	0.0	2.2	0.0	18.5	67.6	13.7	503	74.8	67.0	9.5
Morral village	399	386	-3.3	477	97.3	0.6	0.0	2.1	0.0	26.4	66.6	6.9	188	86.7	58.5	4.8
Morristown village	304	302	-0.7	225	92.9	1.8	0.0	4.4	0.9	23.5	62.3	14.2	95	89.5	34.7	13.7
Morrow village	1,197	1,261	5.3	1,412	95.4	0.4	0.0	1.6	2.7	28.5	59.5	12.0	523	60.8	50.9	14.1
Moscow village	185	186	0.5	125	100.0	0.0	0.0	0.0	0.0	5.6	72.8	21.6	60	80.0	76.7	8.3
Mount Blanchard village	492	485	-1.4	502	92.8	2.2	0.0	1.8	3.2	30.9	53.8	15.5	190	67.9	43.2	24.2
Mount Carmel CDP	4,741	NA	NA	4,654	97.0	0.3	0.0	1.5	1.2	22.4	62.9	14.7	1,847	55.9	46.3	14.9
Mount Cory village	204	205	0.5	248	94.0	0.0	0.0	2.4	3.6	40.3	42.3	17.3	80	78.8	63.8	6.3
Mount Eaton village	241	242	0.4	231	98.3	0.0	0.9	0.9	0.0	25.1	58.2	16.9	99	72.7	65.7	17.2
Mount Gilead village	3,660	3,662	0.1	3,583	96.9	1.2	0.0	0.7	1.3	19.4	60.8	19.9	1,418	57.3	54.7	18.3
Mount Healthy city	6,098	6,061	-0.6	6,061	56.1	34.7	1.9	5.5	1.8	23.6	56.2	20.1	2,920	44.0	42.3	21.8
Mount Healthy Heights CDP	3,264	NA	NA	3,556	54.1	41.5	0.0	3.7	0.7	31.5	58.9	9.5	1,285	59.8	59.4	7.0
Mount Orab village	3,686	3,657	-0.8	3,819	94.7	2.3	0.0	0.2	2.9	37.1	51.3	11.7	1,377	60.9	64.5	7.6
Mount Pleasant village	478	459	-4.0	491	99.8	0.2	0.0	0.0	0.0	21.3	60.3	18.3	195	86.7	62.1	11.8
Mount Repose CDP	4,672	NA	NA	4,481	93.0	1.7	0.4	0.8	4.1	28.4	56.7	14.9	1,677	82.8	41.6	25.9
Mount Sterling village	1,728	1,748	1.2	1,726	97.9	0.2	0.1	1.6	0.3	28.4	60.8	10.8	672	46.3	55.7	8.6
Mount Vernon city	16,990	16,788	-1.2	16,919	96.3	0.9	0.1	2.0	0.7	20.5	62.7	16.7	6,910	51.1	54.5	21.0
Mount Victory village	627	624	-0.5	629	89.3	1.0	2.2	7.5	0.0	22.3	63.9	14.0	242	76.0	57.0	10.7
Mowrystown village	360	358	-0.6	296	97.6	0.0	0.0	1.7	0.7	23.7	56.7	19.6	118	74.6	61.9	11.9

1 May be of any race.

Table A. All Places — **Population and Housing**

STATE City, town, township, borough, or CDP (county if applicable)	Population: 2010 census total population	Population: 2014 estimated population	Population: Percent change 2010–2014	Population: ACS total population estimate 2010–2014	Race and Hispanic or Latino origin (percent), 2010–2014: White alone, not Hispanic or Latino	Black alone, not Hispanic or Latino	Asian alone, not Hispanic or Latino	All other races or 2 or more races, not Hispanic or Latino	Hispanic or Latino[1]	Age (percent), 2010–2014: Under 18 years old	Age 18 to 64 years old	Age 65 years and older	Households, 2010–2014: Total occupied housing units	Percent owner occupied	Householders by level of education (percent): High school diploma or less	Bachelor's degree or more
	1	2	3	4	5	6	7	8	9	10	11	12	13	14	15	16
OHIO—Con.																
Mulberry CDP	3,323	NA	NA	3,385	94.9	3.3	0.7	0.7	0.4	14.8	54.0	31.2	1,421	76.1	30.8	44.8
Munroe Falls city	5,056	5,022	-0.7	5,037	92.2	1.7	4.0	1.0	1.1	19.0	62.0	19.0	2,115	77.6	34.8	42.4
Murray City village	449	440	-2.0	399	98.5	0.0	0.0	0.0	1.5	21.8	61.3	17.0	165	63.0	68.5	4.8
Mutual village	104	102	-1.9	132	100.0	0.0	0.0	0.0	0.0	25.0	52.2	22.7	56	62.5	50.0	3.6
Napoleon city	8,777	8,646	-1.5	8,940	89.9	0.2	0.8	1.8	7.3	23.0	58.4	18.6	3,857	66.1	54.0	14.7
Nashville village	197	206	4.6	232	98.7	0.0	0.0	1.3	0.0	31.1	49.1	19.8	90	77.8	77.8	5.6
Navarre village	1,957	1,931	-1.3	2,013	95.7	0.3	3.0	0.2	0.6	19.6	55.8	24.7	863	66.9	54.2	17.8
Neapolis CDP	423	NA	NA	383	94.5	0.0	0.0	0.0	5.5	19.8	45.8	34.2	133	92.5	69.9	9.0
Neffs CDP	993	NA	NA	1,027	100.0	0.0	0.0	0.0	0.0	12.9	71.1	15.9	408	94.1	58.3	11.3
Negley CDP	281	NA	NA	186	88.2	0.0	0.0	0.0	11.8	21.0	52.2	26.9	86	88.4	89.5	0.0
Nellie village	131	131	0.0	128	100.0	0.0	0.0	0.0	0.0	29.8	53.0	17.2	49	83.7	69.4	12.2
Nelsonville city	5,394	5,214	-3.3	5,596	91.3	3.9	0.7	2.5	1.6	18.8	72.1	9.0	1,794	43.9	49.8	9.0
Nettle Lake CDP	0	NA	NA	392	96.9	0.0	0.0	0.0	3.1	15.5	64.4	20.2	138	92.0	44.9	6.5
Nevada village	760	745	-2.0	753	91.5	0.8	0.0	1.2	6.5	30.6	57.9	11.6	291	66.0	55.0	12.0
Neville village	100	100	0.0	94	90.4	1.1	0.0	6.4	2.1	24.4	67.0	8.5	38	65.8	42.1	26.3
New Albany city	7,738	9,202	18.9	8,169	81.8	1.8	7.3	7.3	1.8	36.5	55.5	7.8	2,594	93.0	9.7	72.9
New Alexandria village	272	265	-2.6	203	99.0	0.0	0.0	1.0	0.0	17.3	54.1	28.6	83	75.9	65.1	7.2
Newark city	47,574	47,839	0.6	47,744	91.0	3.6	0.4	3.7	1.3	24.8	60.1	15.1	19,719	54.1	51.1	17.0
New Athens village	328	323	-1.5	236	100.0	0.0	0.0	0.0	0.0	14.4	52.6	33.1	107	83.2	64.5	13.1
New Baltimore CDP	661	NA	NA	523	100.0	0.0	0.0	0.0	0.0	26.3	60.7	12.8	241	86.3	66.4	5.4
New Bavaria village	99	98	-1.0	127	97.6	0.0	2.4	0.0	0.0	26.7	67.8	5.5	50	80.0	56.0	30.0
New Bloomington village	520	501	-3.7	422	91.7	0.0	0.0	0.2	8.1	25.3	60.9	13.7	184	65.8	83.2	0.0
New Boston village	2,272	2,198	-3.3	2,255	96.5	0.8	2.1	0.4	0.3	22.7	56.3	20.9	962	36.1	68.9	6.4
New Bremen village	2,978	2,969	-0.3	3,063	97.0	0.0	0.4	0.8	1.8	24.9	62.1	13.1	1,261	77.0	44.8	29.1
Newburgh Heights village	2,167	2,109	-2.7	2,000	75.1	18.7	2.3	2.4	1.6	25.2	63.1	12.1	883	52.3	53.7	13.3
New Burlington CDP	5,069	NA	NA	5,071	50.6	42.6	0.0	4.3	2.5	26.0	54.1	20.0	1,700	69.1	41.0	18.8
New California CDP	1,411	NA	NA	1,581	90.3	9.7	0.0	0.0	0.0	34.0	58.4	7.6	446	100.0	3.1	63.2
New Carlisle city	5,785	5,714	-1.2	5,732	82.9	0.2	0.2	1.0	15.8	27.3	58.1	14.6	2,082	62.0	51.2	8.9
Newcomerstown village	3,822	3,797	-0.7	3,871	88.4	6.8	0.9	1.7	2.2	25.0	56.4	18.5	1,447	63.0	60.1	10.5
New Concord village	2,491	2,334	-6.3	2,728	90.1	2.5	2.2	1.8	3.4	10.5	76.2	13.3	690	50.9	28.1	40.7
New Franklin city	14,222	14,292	0.5	14,245	97.4	0.4	0.4	1.5	0.4	19.5	60.6	19.9	5,511	89.7	46.6	25.3
New Hampshire CDP	174	NA	NA	161	100.0	0.0	0.0	0.0	0.0	41.0	42.8	16.1	46	32.6	10.9	54.3
New Haven CDP (Hamilton)	583	NA	NA	813	99.0	0.0	0.0	1.0	0.0	23.9	67.5	8.6	309	100.0	44.3	12.3
New Haven CDP (Huron)	399	NA	NA	382	78.3	9.4	0.0	12.3	0.0	11.5	44.3	44.2	158	94.3	56.3	28.5
New Holland village	801	832	3.9	663	97.6	0.0	0.3	0.5	1.7	23.3	61.5	15.2	267	70.0	70.4	6.4
New Knoxville village	879	870	-1.0	844	95.4	0.0	0.0	4.4	0.2	29.3	59.0	11.8	336	72.3	34.5	26.5
New Lebanon village	3,995	3,989	-0.2	4,021	98.7	0.5	0.0	0.0	0.8	25.5	58.9	15.7	1,533	56.6	68.7	7.9
New Lexington village	4,758	4,717	-0.9	4,889	94.4	0.6	0.0	3.8	1.1	29.4	59.6	10.8	1,684	50.5	53.7	13.5
New London village	2,461	2,395	-2.7	2,589	90.4	5.2	0.3	1.5	2.6	31.4	58.0	10.5	866	59.7	68.2	11.1
New Madison village	892	881	-1.2	869	91.4	1.6	0.7	4.6	1.7	23.8	60.8	15.4	368	66.3	68.5	10.6
New Marshfield CDP	326	NA	NA	276	100.0	0.0	0.0	0.0	0.0	6.2	67.0	26.8	116	55.2	56.9	28.4
New Miami village	2,249	2,293	2.0	2,107	91.4	3.7	0.0	2.7	2.2	26.9	61.0	12.1	742	62.7	75.7	4.9
New Middletown village	1,621	1,584	-2.3	1,661	98.4	0.0	0.0	0.4	1.2	17.2	54.7	28.1	753	81.7	55.4	18.5
New Paris village	1,629	1,592	-2.3	1,702	93.1	1.4	0.0	2.9	2.6	29.4	56.1	14.3	707	60.1	68.7	6.6
New Philadelphia city	17,283	17,438	0.9	17,334	90.7	1.8	0.8	2.3	4.4	22.7	62.1	15.4	6,987	62.5	56.0	15.6
New Pittsburg CDP	388	NA	NA	260	100.0	0.0	0.0	0.0	0.0	11.9	65.8	22.3	71	81.7	63.4	0.0
Newport CDP (Shelby)	198	NA	NA	125	100.0	0.0	0.0	0.0	0.0	17.6	58.4	24.0	73	100.0	47.9	0.0
Newport CDP (Washington)	1,003	NA	NA	1,048	100.0	0.0	0.0	0.0	0.0	25.7	56.9	17.3	423	92.2	57.2	26.5
New Richmond village	2,582	2,630	1.9	2,606	96.7	2.3	0.0	0.8	0.2	27.0	57.3	15.6	967	66.5	54.8	17.7
New Riegel village	249	245	-1.6	248	96.8	0.8	0.0	0.0	2.4	24.5	61.8	13.7	101	61.4	67.3	11.9
New Straitsville village	722	713	-1.2	686	96.5	1.3	0.0	1.5	0.7	22.5	63.5	14.1	287	63.8	65.5	3.1
Newton Falls village	4,795	4,682	-2.4	4,740	96.4	0.3	0.8	0.7	1.9	17.4	63.9	18.7	2,275	49.4	66.3	7.0
Newtonsville village	392	394	0.5	417	91.6	0.0	0.0	2.2	6.2	29.7	65.0	5.3	126	69.8	68.3	9.5
Newtown village	2,672	2,672	0.0	2,670	93.2	0.8	2.1	0.6	3.3	25.5	60.7	13.7	1,080	67.4	31.6	46.5
New Vienna village	1,224	1,205	-1.6	1,475	98.4	0.0	0.3	1.2	0.1	29.2	62.4	8.5	522	43.1	66.7	4.8
New Washington village	967	939	-2.9	1,029	96.7	0.0	0.0	2.7	0.6	27.1	55.5	17.5	408	80.6	53.7	16.9
New Waterford village	1,238	1,210	-2.3	1,340	96.2	0.8	0.2	2.4	0.4	26.6	60.3	13.0	516	77.7	70.0	6.0
New Weston village	136	134	-1.5	74	91.9	0.0	0.0	4.1	4.1	21.7	59.6	18.9	29	44.8	55.2	6.9
Ney village	354	354	0.0	355	88.7	0.8	0.0	1.7	8.7	24.5	65.8	9.6	133	75.2	56.4	7.5
Niles city	19,266	18,778	-2.5	19,028	91.5	3.9	0.6	3.0	1.0	23.0	59.0	18.0	8,197	59.2	56.4	15.6
North Baltimore village	3,432	3,524	2.7	3,577	93.3	0.0	0.7	0.2	5.8	28.3	58.3	13.5	1,335	60.0	49.4	10.4
North Bend village	857	861	0.5	886	98.8	0.0	0.0	1.2	0.0	16.6	59.1	24.3	377	80.1	28.6	39.0
Northbrook CDP	10,668	NA	NA	10,384	64.1	26.5	0.1	6.2	3.1	29.6	59.5	10.8	3,894	66.3	53.4	12.0
North Canton city	17,486	17,490	0.0	17,437	93.4	1.3	0.8	1.9	2.7	16.5	62.0	21.5	7,383	66.3	31.3	36.3
North College Hill city	9,397	9,362	-0.4	9,366	49.3	46.7	0.1	1.7	2.1	22.5	65.3	12.2	4,134	53.4	44.4	15.7
North Fairfield village	560	542	-3.2	690	91.2	0.0	0.9	3.0	4.9	32.5	57.2	10.3	225	83.6	63.1	8.4
Northfield village	3,677	3,643	-0.9	3,658	77.1	2.0	11.3	7.5	2.1	19.6	62.1	18.2	1,528	60.6	52.7	18.0
Northgate CDP	7,377	NA	NA	7,332	79.8	16.1	0.7	2.8	0.7	22.6	61.8	15.6	2,644	77.8	44.1	19.5
North Hampton village	478	474	-0.8	529	97.9	0.8	0.4	0.6	0.4	35.2	55.8	8.9	169	63.9	37.9	14.2
North Kingsville village	2,923	2,855	-2.3	2,892	90.3	1.9	1.2	2.2	4.4	21.1	63.6	15.2	1,225	87.5	45.1	19.9
North Lawrence CDP	268	NA	NA	225	92.9	0.0	7.1	0.0	0.0	16.0	66.2	17.8	124	100.0	76.6	0.0
North Lewisburg village	1,490	1,451	-2.6	1,461	94.0	0.2	0.0	3.8	2.1	25.9	62.5	11.6	614	63.7	56.2	12.5
North Madison CDP	8,547	NA	NA	8,952	97.9	0.1	0.1	1.8	0.2	28.8	59.7	11.5	3,245	74.1	45.0	17.2
North Olmsted city	32,713	32,130	-1.8	32,374	89.3	2.2	2.9	1.6	4.0	19.1	61.8	19.1	13,462	76.7	30.8	34.9
North Perry village	893	891	-0.2	753	99.9	0.0	0.0	0.0	0.1	18.2	63.9	17.9	311	80.1	44.4	24.1
North Randall village	1,027	1,011	-1.6	954	11.6	86.4	0.3	0.5	1.2	15.5	55.0	29.6	455	24.0	49.5	9.0
Northridge CDP	7,572	NA	NA	7,404	96.6	0.0	1.3	1.4	0.6	21.3	56.8	21.9	3,235	78.7	45.3	18.4
North Ridgeville city	29,466	31,871	8.2	30,680	92.6	1.3	1.4	1.0	3.7	23.0	60.0	16.9	11,954	85.6	35.9	29.6
North Robinson village	205	201	-2.0	188	98.4	0.0	0.0	0.0	1.6	7.5	67.1	25.5	95	92.6	74.7	6.3
North Royalton city	30,444	30,327	-0.4	30,353	91.5	1.7	3.3	1.6	1.9	19.8	63.6	16.5	12,511	71.8	31.4	38.9
North Star village	236	233	-1.3	275	100.0	0.0	0.0	0.0	0.0	28.7	54.9	16.4	97	86.6	43.3	29.9
Northwood city	5,221	5,341	2.3	5,285	91.7	0.0	0.6	2.0	5.7	20.5	68.4	11.0	2,216	84.7	40.4	20.6
North Zanesville CDP	2,816	NA	NA	3,007	83.7	7.7	0.9	7.2	0.5	22.4	57.2	20.4	1,208	88.1	31.7	40.7
Norton city	12,090	12,042	-0.4	12,052	96.0	1.7	0.1	0.4	1.8	22.5	61.0	16.3	4,712	85.9	41.2	25.1
Norwalk city	17,013	16,898	-0.7	16,927	88.2	1.7	0.2	2.5	7.5	26.2	57.8	16.0	6,725	64.4	54.7	16.2
Norwich village	102	103	1.0	93	96.8	0.0	0.0	2.2	1.1	10.8	62.4	26.9	40	85.0	62.5	22.5
Norwood city	19,207	19,405	1.0	19,170	84.9	7.9	0.2	3.0	4.1	18.8	69.5	11.7	8,681	47.1	47.1	25.2
Oak Harbor village	2,759	2,736	-0.8	2,750	94.3	0.0	0.1	0.0	5.6	22.7	61.6	15.6	1,190	65.0	40.8	19.3
Oak Hill village	1,551	1,514	-2.4	1,777	95.1	0.1	0.1	4.7	0.0	28.7	59.1	12.5	723	48.3	54.9	14.7

1 May be of any race.

Table A. All Places — **Population and Housing**

STATE City, town, township, borough, or CDP (county if applicable)	Population: 2010 census total population	Population: 2014 estimated population	Population: Percent change 2010–2014	Population: ACS total population estimate 2010–2014	Race and Hispanic or Latino origin (percent), 2010–2014: White alone, not Hispanic or Latino	Race: Black alone, not Hispanic or Latino	Race: Asian alone, not Hispanic or Latino	Race: All other races or 2 or more races, not Hispanic or Latino	Race: Hispanic or Latino[1]	Age (percent), 2010–2014: Under 18 years old	Age: Age 18 to 64 years old	Age: Age 65 years and older	Households, 2010–2014: Total occupied housing units	Households: Percent owner occupied	Households: Householders by level of education (percent): High school diploma or less	Households: Householders by level of education (percent): Bachelor's degree or more
	1	2	3	4	5	6	7	8	9	10	11	12	13	14	15	16
OHIO—Con.																
Oakwood village (Cuyahoga)	3,661	3,696	1.0	3,678	26.1	65.5	0.0	1.3	7.1	18.4	63.9	17.7	1,403	70.2	42.1	21.0
Oakwood city	9,202	9,083	-1.3	9,150	95.6	0.5	0.7	2.5	0.7	30.0	56.0	14.0	3,417	79.9	4.9	75.5
Oakwood village (Paulding)	611	586	-4.1	611	94.4	0.0	0.0	0.3	5.2	25.0	57.6	17.3	236	79.2	66.9	7.2
Oberlin city	8,286	8,251	-0.4	8,368	66.6	17.1	3.7	8.2	4.5	13.6	72.0	14.4	2,524	58.3	26.7	41.3
Obetz village	4,542	4,706	3.6	4,521	84.6	11.0	0.0	1.2	3.1	28.1	62.3	9.6	1,605	68.8	55.8	11.8
Oceola CDP	190	NA	NA	125	100.0	0.0	0.0	0.0	0.0	39.2	55.2	5.6	35	20.0	100.0	0.0
Octa village	59	59	0.0	54	100.0	0.0	0.0	0.0	0.0	22.2	42.7	35.2	24	75.0	100.0	0.0
Ohio City village	705	688	-2.4	738	95.9	0.0	0.0	2.0	2.0	24.9	60.5	14.6	309	86.7	69.9	7.4
Olde West Chester CDP	240	NA	NA	135	100.0	0.0	0.0	0.0	0.0	30.4	62.3	7.4	60	43.3	16.7	68.3
Old Fort CDP	186	NA	NA	104	100.0	0.0	0.0	0.0	0.0	4.8	71.3	24.0	49	89.8	57.1	10.2
Old Washington village	279	277	-0.7	321	98.1	0.0	0.0	1.9	0.0	18.4	57.0	24.6	128	71.1	60.9	4.7
Olmsted Falls city	9,024	8,883	-1.6	8,943	95.4	0.7	0.3	1.5	2.1	25.2	60.7	14.1	3,486	82.0	21.2	37.9
Ontario city	6,225	6,127	-1.6	6,160	85.9	3.4	7.2	0.9	2.6	16.8	62.1	21.2	2,588	70.8	40.6	21.8
Orange village	3,323	3,280	-1.3	3,292	75.1	10.4	9.3	1.6	3.6	21.9	56.4	21.5	1,334	88.5	10.9	74.1
Orangeville village	197	193	-2.0	232	100.0	0.0	0.0	0.0	0.0	37.1	51.3	11.6	77	79.2	57.1	31.2
Oregon city	20,313	20,196	-0.6	20,282	87.4	0.9	1.6	1.2	8.9	21.0	60.8	18.2	8,459	69.7	44.1	17.4
Orient village	270	275	1.9	299	94.6	3.0	0.0	2.3	0.0	23.7	66.6	9.7	88	77.3	60.2	9.1
Orrville city	8,380	8,456	0.9	8,389	92.5	1.9	2.1	2.1	1.5	24.7	58.4	17.0	3,516	63.9	50.2	19.4
Orwell village	1,660	1,617	-2.6	1,624	98.2	0.7	0.2	0.2	0.7	26.0	59.2	15.0	636	52.2	59.7	10.2
Osgood village	302	298	-1.3	275	98.5	1.1	0.0	0.0	0.4	21.4	56.0	22.5	104	93.3	64.4	12.5
Ostrander village	640	674	5.3	856	90.5	0.0	0.0	0.8	8.6	35.4	57.3	7.2	274	83.6	46.7	35.8
Ottawa village	4,465	4,420	-1.0	4,426	84.5	0.2	0.3	0.7	14.3	23.6	57.3	19.0	1,949	67.9	41.5	27.6
Ottawa Hills village	4,517	4,473	-1.0	4,508	91.1	1.9	6.3	0.4	0.3	27.4	58.3	14.3	1,645	82.6	9.9	72.6
Ottoville village	984	975	-0.9	892	99.3	0.0	0.0	0.2	0.4	27.4	57.4	15.2	361	80.9	39.9	20.5
Otway village	87	85	-2.3	104	98.1	0.0	0.0	1.9	0.0	40.4	46.1	13.5	40	50.0	62.5	17.5
Owensville village	794	812	2.3	890	99.1	0.0	0.0	0.0	0.9	28.7	53.7	17.8	410	23.9	65.9	10.2
Oxford city	21,376	21,782	1.9	21,552	87.7	3.1	5.6	1.3	2.3	5.9	87.7	6.4	5,561	31.5	18.3	47.0
Painesville city	19,559	19,840	1.4	19,689	57.3	13.4	0.7	3.7	25.0	27.2	62.9	10.0	7,147	47.4	53.4	16.4
Palestine village	200	197	-1.5	181	100.0	0.0	0.0	0.0	0.0	23.2	49.2	27.6	75	73.3	58.7	0.0
Pancoastburg CDP	87	NA	NA	122	88.5	0.0	0.0	11.5	0.0	0.0	81.2	18.9	55	41.8	74.5	0.0
Pandora village	1,167	1,154	-1.1	1,163	96.6	0.0	0.0	2.3	1.1	23.8	58.6	17.4	468	75.6	45.1	21.2
Park Layne CDP	4,343	NA	NA	4,747	89.2	0.5	0.3	5.8	4.2	29.5	61.5	9.1	1,462	64.0	55.4	8.6
Parkman CDP	0	NA	NA	224	75.4	0.0	0.0	5.4	19.2	21.9	53.6	24.6	130	82.3	21.5	24.6
Parma city	81,601	80,015	-1.9	80,699	88.8	2.4	1.8	1.9	5.1	20.0	62.2	17.9	33,400	74.6	45.3	21.0
Parma Heights city	20,718	20,330	-1.9	20,490	88.6	2.7	3.5	1.8	3.4	20.9	60.7	18.4	8,936	56.0	42.1	21.9
Parral village	218	220	0.9	223	98.7	0.0	0.0	1.3	0.0	16.1	65.1	18.8	101	76.2	62.4	9.9
Pataskala city	14,924	15,192	1.8	15,069	92.8	3.9	1.2	2.0	0.2	24.8	62.6	12.4	5,595	75.7	38.8	30.0
Patterson village	139	138	-0.7	148	100.0	0.0	0.0	0.0	0.0	27.7	58.2	14.2	52	63.5	69.2	5.8
Paulding village	3,605	3,494	-3.1	3,631	85.0	1.1	2.4	2.3	9.1	25.9	57.5	16.6	1,550	61.0	63.0	12.6
Payne village	1,194	1,157	-3.1	1,098	91.3	1.3	0.5	1.9	4.9	23.4	59.0	17.5	480	64.8	62.9	7.5
Peebles village	1,791	1,770	-1.2	1,907	93.3	0.8	0.2	3.5	2.3	27.1	57.6	15.2	749	50.3	69.6	6.0
Pemberville village	1,373	1,414	3.0	1,521	92.0	0.0	0.5	0.3	7.3	30.3	52.7	16.9	566	79.0	40.1	26.0
Peninsula village	565	569	0.7	595	96.0	0.0	0.3	1.3	2.4	20.5	62.8	16.6	236	84.7	22.5	52.5
Pepper Pike city	5,979	6,205	3.8	6,079	84.0	4.2	5.3	3.5	3.1	24.4	50.1	25.5	2,167	95.3	10.2	75.0
Perry village	1,633	1,625	-0.5	1,615	96.7	0.1	2.1	0.5	0.6	28.5	57.6	13.7	588	90.8	37.9	32.8
Perry Heights CDP	8,441	NA	NA	8,434	96.3	2.2	0.1	0.4	1.0	19.8	63.6	16.6	3,475	69.3	51.3	15.2
Perrysburg city	20,796	21,368	2.8	21,122	89.3	2.4	3.7	1.2	3.4	25.1	60.9	14.0	8,581	69.3	17.7	51.9
Perrysville village	728	722	-0.8	710	96.9	0.7	0.0	2.4	0.0	25.4	62.9	11.7	262	66.4	61.5	4.6
Pettisville CDP	498	NA	NA	530	81.1	4.3	0.0	0.0	14.5	26.5	52.9	20.8	203	86.2	46.3	15.8
Pheasant Run CDP	1,397	NA	NA	1,576	100.0	0.0	0.0	0.0	0.0	35.6	54.9	9.3	552	75.2	49.5	17.9
Phillipsburg village	557	555	-0.4	542	93.9	1.3	0.0	3.1	1.7	17.5	58.4	24.0	255	71.8	54.9	12.5
Philo village	733	729	-0.5	764	93.7	0.0	0.0	1.6	4.7	27.7	64.1	8.1	260	81.5	63.5	8.5
Pickerington city	18,278	19,408	6.2	19,014	77.2	13.8	3.7	2.4	2.9	30.5	61.4	8.0	6,564	74.8	25.3	41.6
Pigeon Creek CDP	882	NA	NA	996	93.6	0.0	1.1	1.4	3.9	27.7	55.4	16.7	365	100.0	23.0	47.9
Piketon village	2,182	2,146	-1.6	2,028	94.3	0.0	0.0	3.5	2.2	26.8	59.8	13.4	751	51.8	54.6	10.9
Pioneer village	1,380	1,407	2.0	1,648	91.3	0.4	0.1	2.5	5.6	27.3	61.8	10.7	661	65.1	47.8	13.5
Piqua city	20,523	20,759	1.1	20,649	90.3	4.6	1.1	3.1	1.0	24.7	60.2	15.1	8,489	60.5	56.1	10.0
Pitsburg village	388	383	-1.3	479	95.8	0.0	0.8	2.5	0.8	24.9	56.7	18.4	186	81.2	66.1	6.5
Plain City village	4,228	4,295	1.6	4,210	96.5	0.0	0.0	0.7	2.8	28.7	54.9	16.5	1,723	68.7	37.4	26.6
Plainfield village	157	165	5.1	169	96.4	0.0	0.0	2.4	1.2	24.3	64.0	11.8	66	83.3	66.7	9.1
Plainville CDP	87	NA	NA	11	100.0	0.0	0.0	0.0	0.0	0.0	0.0	100.0	11	100.0	0.0	0.0
Pleasant City village	447	439	-1.8	446	95.1	0.0	0.0	4.9	0.0	19.1	69.7	11.2	159	73.6	62.3	12.6
Pleasant Grove CDP	1,742	NA	NA	2,039	94.7	0.7	0.9	2.9	0.8	26.7	57.0	16.4	938	50.3	33.7	24.4
Pleasant Hill village	1,200	1,216	1.3	1,163	100.0	0.0	0.0	0.0	0.0	25.3	59.8	14.7	456	79.2	53.5	13.8
Pleasant Hills CDP	606	NA	NA	467	34.0	66.0	0.0	0.0	0.0	19.9	48.6	31.5	229	94.8	33.2	27.1
Pleasant Plain village	149	155	4.0	131	98.5	0.0	0.0	1.5	0.0	11.5	75.7	13.0	52	57.7	51.9	5.8
Pleasant Run CDP	4,953	NA	NA	4,914	73.3	18.5	2.1	3.7	2.4	23.8	65.9	10.3	1,687	82.9	40.5	22.3
Pleasant Run Farm CDP	4,654	NA	NA	4,453	58.7	34.9	0.3	5.3	0.7	27.2	59.5	13.3	1,537	82.5	40.2	31.9
Pleasantville village	960	958	-0.2	1,201	96.3	0.2	0.0	3.2	0.2	35.3	56.6	8.0	414	52.4	60.4	7.0
Plumwood CDP	319	NA	NA	228	100.0	0.0	0.0	0.0	0.0	28.5	66.1	5.3	84	56.0	70.2	15.5
Plymouth village	1,857	1,812	-2.4	1,772	95.3	0.0	0.0	1.9	2.8	22.9	58.4	18.8	742	65.6	57.0	13.2
Poland village	2,555	2,497	-2.3	2,728	98.4	0.0	0.6	0.2	0.9	22.9	58.4	18.6	1,067	85.1	24.9	47.2
Polk village	336	339	0.9	300	96.0	0.0	0.0	0.0	4.0	19.9	65.6	14.3	115	82.6	65.2	13.0
Pomeroy village	1,852	1,827	-1.3	1,705	93.1	4.1	0.0	2.4	0.4	26.9	61.3	12.0	750	49.9	66.7	10.9
Portage village	438	448	2.3	410	89.5	0.0	1.0	2.9	6.6	26.2	64.1	9.8	167	64.1	43.1	33.5
Portage Lakes CDP	6,968	NA	NA	6,978	96.4	1.1	1.4	0.3	0.7	15.8	69.0	15.2	3,183	62.5	42.7	26.2
Port Clinton city	6,056	6,009	-0.8	6,038	87.3	2.7	0.0	2.1	7.9	23.1	61.7	15.4	2,608	72.0	46.4	21.9
Port Jefferson village	368	359	-2.4	537	99.4	0.0	0.6	0.0	0.0	35.6	56.0	8.2	202	74.3	70.3	4.5
Portsmouth city	20,226	20,326	0.5	20,320	89.1	5.5	0.8	2.7	1.9	19.2	64.6	16.2	7,992	52.1	47.6	17.5
Port Washington village	569	569	0.0	556	100.0	0.0	0.0	0.0	0.0	26.0	63.2	10.8	209	69.9	77.0	6.7
Port William village	254	254	0.0	290	91.0	3.8	0.0	5.2	0.0	32.8	60.1	7.2	96	60.4	72.9	12.5
Potsdam village	288	292	1.4	275	99.3	0.0	0.0	0.7	0.0	28.4	58.5	13.1	101	67.3	51.5	12.9
Pottery Addition CDP	293	NA	NA	316	100.0	0.0	0.0	0.0	0.0	45.9	42.4	11.7	83	51.8	47.0	0.0
Powell city	11,498	12,511	8.8	12,012	86.8	2.6	9.0	0.7	0.8	34.5	55.5	10.0	3,923	94.1	6.1	77.2
Powhatan Point village	1,592	1,577	-0.9	1,550	98.9	0.0	0.0	1.1	0.0	20.2	61.9	17.7	680	77.8	65.6	9.4
Proctorville village	574	563	-1.9	535	96.4	0.0	0.0	3.0	0.6	26.9	41.8	31.2	246	67.1	72.4	5.7
Prospect village	1,109	1,076	-3.0	1,113	95.1	0.0	0.0	3.6	1.3	27.3	58.6	14.1	442	62.9	54.3	20.6
Pulaski CDP	132	NA	NA	67	100.0	0.0	0.0	0.0	0.0	17.9	82.1	0.0	33	100.0	100.0	0.0
Put-in-Bay village	138	138	0.0	114	68.4	0.0	0.0	0.0	31.6	3.5	67.6	28.9	84	44.0	7.1	26.2

1 May be of any race.

Table A. All Places — **Population and Housing**

STATE City, town, township, borough, or CDP (county if applicable)	Population: 2010 census total population	Population: 2014 estimated population	Population: Percent change 2010–2014	Population: ACS total population estimate 2010–2014	Race and Hispanic or Latino origin (percent), 2010–2014: White alone, not Hispanic or Latino	Black alone, not Hispanic or Latino	Asian alone, not Hispanic or Latino	All other races or 2 or more races, not Hispanic or Latino	Hispanic or Latino[1]	Age (percent), 2010–2014: Under 18 years old	Age 18 to 64 years old	Age 65 years and older	Households, 2010–2014: Total occupied housing units	Percent owner occupied	Householders by level of education (percent): High school diploma or less	Bachelor's degree or more
	1	2	3	4	5	6	7	8	9	10	11	12	13	14	15	16
OHIO—Con.																
Quaker City village	502	494	-1.6	501	96.8	0.0	0.0	3.2	0.0	18.4	61.2	20.6	201	68.7	72.1	2.0
Quincy village	706	691	-2.1	612	94.4	0.7	0.0	2.5	2.5	30.4	53.8	15.7	226	63.3	70.4	7.5
Racine village	675	664	-1.6	625	100.0	0.0	0.0	0.0	0.0	22.3	59.8	18.2	259	64.9	50.6	9.3
Radnor CDP	201	NA	NA	220	100.0	0.0	0.0	0.0	0.0	18.2	81.8	0.0	99	65.7	87.9	0.0
Rarden village	159	155	-2.5	156	100.0	0.0	0.0	0.0	0.0	4.5	80.9	14.7	54	87.0	77.8	7.4
Ravenna city	11,723	11,643	-0.7	11,635	90.9	2.6	0.2	4.5	1.8	19.9	65.3	14.8	5,036	50.3	54.5	13.8
Rawson village	570	573	0.5	519	94.6	0.0	0.4	1.9	3.1	36.8	54.0	9.2	176	72.2	52.3	11.4
Rayland village	417	405	-2.9	390	98.5	0.5	0.0	0.0	1.0	24.3	56.3	19.2	172	83.7	57.0	14.0
Raymond CDP	257	NA	NA	77	100.0	0.0	0.0	0.0	0.0	29.9	70.2	0.0	30	100.0	53.3	0.0
Reading city	10,385	10,354	-0.3	10,357	87.4	9.2	0.5	1.9	1.0	20.3	64.3	15.3	4,489	59.6	52.0	17.6
Reminderville village	3,404	3,852	13.2	3,630	84.9	10.1	1.8	3.1	0.0	28.4	59.4	12.3	1,307	86.2	25.6	38.8
Remington CDP	328	NA	NA	125	100.0	0.0	0.0	0.0	0.0	0.0	69.6	30.4	87	80.5	19.5	80.5
Rendville village	36	36	0.0	96	83.3	7.3	0.0	9.4	0.0	53.2	39.6	7.3	30	73.3	60.0	3.3
Reno CDP	1,293	NA	NA	1,127	93.9	0.1	0.0	6.0	0.0	24.9	56.5	18.6	535	57.0	53.1	8.6
Republic village	549	537	-2.2	557	98.9	0.0	0.0	1.1	0.0	19.5	70.3	10.2	250	71.2	55.2	13.6
Reynoldsburg city	35,900	36,711	2.3	36,439	65.3	23.2	2.9	4.1	4.5	24.9	62.3	12.6	14,216	59.9	31.3	31.5
Richfield village	3,648	3,690	1.2	3,661	95.4	2.2	0.2	1.0	1.2	22.3	60.4	17.1	1,396	90.1	31.6	49.2
Richmond village	481	466	-3.1	438	96.6	0.0	0.7	1.1	1.6	16.6	63.4	19.9	161	77.0	61.5	5.6
Richmond Dale CDP	377	NA	NA	387	87.3	8.0	0.0	4.7	0.0	29.9	56.9	13.2	168	66.7	92.9	0.0
Richmond Heights city	10,557	10,495	-0.6	10,508	47.2	43.4	4.9	2.1	2.4	15.3	63.8	20.8	4,848	64.2	23.9	38.3
Richville CDP	3,324	NA	NA	3,385	93.8	2.1	0.7	2.8	0.6	21.7	63.5	14.8	1,265	82.8	53.8	13.8
Richwood village	2,232	2,251	0.9	2,248	94.8	0.1	0.0	3.6	1.6	33.7	54.6	11.6	806	61.2	65.0	7.2
Ridgeville Corners CDP	435	NA	NA	309	98.4	0.0	0.0	1.6	0.0	18.5	64.8	16.8	135	80.7	62.2	2.2
Ridgeway village	338	336	-0.6	320	97.5	1.6	0.0	0.9	0.0	32.5	58.6	9.1	104	91.3	67.3	8.7
Rio Grande village	834	837	0.4	1,066	84.4	10.6	0.3	2.8	1.9	24.7	74.3	1.0	241	21.6	56.8	10.8
Ripley village	1,750	1,733	-1.0	1,923	92.3	6.0	0.0	1.8	0.0	22.7	60.7	16.5	839	68.9	61.9	13.5
Risingsun village	606	624	3.0	610	92.0	0.0	0.0	0.8	7.2	31.8	57.1	11.1	206	71.8	59.2	6.8
Rittman city	6,494	6,554	0.9	6,457	96.3	0.5	0.6	2.6	0.0	26.4	59.1	14.7	2,489	73.1	59.4	15.9
Riverlea village	547	564	3.1	613	96.1	0.5	0.5	2.9	0.0	29.8	56.7	13.7	250	80.0	6.4	79.6
Riverside city	25,201	25,040	-0.6	25,143	86.1	5.6	1.6	3.2	3.5	23.0	62.6	14.4	10,213	54.5	42.7	16.9
Roaming Shores village	1,508	1,482	-1.7	1,804	97.2	0.0	0.0	0.3	2.5	26.9	59.3	13.9	666	97.4	38.7	35.0
Robertsville CDP	331	NA	NA	363	99.2	0.0	0.0	0.0	0.8	28.9	68.0	3.0	146	85.6	62.3	21.2
Rochester village	182	181	-0.5	251	97.6	0.0	0.0	1.2	1.2	24.8	58.3	17.1	86	81.4	59.3	9.3
Rockbridge CDP	182	NA	NA	226	100.0	0.0	0.0	0.0	0.0	37.6	56.6	5.8	92	55.4	81.5	0.0
Rock Creek village	529	518	-2.1	462	100.0	0.0	0.0	0.0	0.0	19.9	70.4	9.7	201	55.7	58.7	2.5
Rockford village	1,120	1,108	-1.1	1,275	99.3	0.5	0.0	0.2	0.0	26.7	60.2	13.1	477	74.2	60.0	12.2
Rocky Fork Point CDP	639	NA	NA	578	90.3	3.3	0.0	6.4	0.0	18.4	68.1	13.5	259	86.5	90.3	0.0
Rocky Ridge village	417	412	-1.2	395	97.5	0.0	0.0	0.0	2.5	25.8	63.5	10.6	153	72.5	58.2	3.9
Rocky River city	20,213	20,433	1.1	20,145	95.5	1.5	1.1	0.5	1.4	21.4	54.6	24.0	8,822	73.5	19.4	58.0
Rogers village	237	234	-1.3	213	99.1	0.0	0.0	0.9	0.0	18.3	67.5	14.1	81	82.7	77.8	11.1
Rome village	94	94	0.0	80	95.0	0.0	5.0	0.0	0.0	23.8	58.9	17.5	30	86.7	86.7	0.0
Rose Farm CDP	0	NA	NA	246	100.0	0.0	0.0	0.0	0.0	13.8	61.8	24.4	63	100.0	100.0	0.0
Rosemount CDP	2,112	NA	NA	2,081	96.0	0.0	0.0	0.0	4.0	19.3	56.2	24.5	773	70.8	35.6	30.3
Roseville village	1,860	1,846	-0.8	2,283	97.4	0.0	0.3	2.1	0.2	33.9	56.4	9.7	825	67.3	73.7	3.3
Rosewood CDP	257	NA	NA	332	96.7	0.0	0.0	3.3	0.0	43.0	37.0	19.9	104	83.7	77.9	0.0
Ross CDP	3,417	NA	NA	3,856	98.6	0.0	0.0	0.8	0.6	28.3	60.2	11.3	1,333	76.8	34.6	18.9
Rossburg village	201	198	-1.5	195	94.4	2.1	0.5	3.1	0.0	15.4	68.8	15.9	82	80.5	64.6	11.0
Rossford city	6,337	6,499	2.6	6,434	92.0	2.4	0.4	1.1	4.1	22.6	62.9	14.7	2,675	71.7	29.6	22.3
Rossmoyne CDP	2,230	NA	NA	2,301	65.3	25.8	6.3	1.7	0.9	26.8	66.0	7.3	899	58.0	52.5	17.9
Roswell village	219	221	0.9	217	99.5	0.0	0.0	0.5	0.0	25.9	64.1	10.1	88	67.0	78.4	5.7
Rudolph CDP	458	NA	NA	333	88.0	0.0	0.0	0.0	12.0	21.0	59.4	19.5	157	71.3	41.4	3.8
Rushsylvania village	516	503	-2.5	517	96.3	0.0	0.0	3.7	0.0	27.9	61.3	10.8	206	77.2	65.0	6.3
Rushville village	302	304	0.7	375	97.6	0.0	0.0	2.4	0.0	33.9	60.8	5.3	119	58.0	41.2	13.4
Russells Point village	1,391	1,366	-1.8	1,140	92.9	3.9	0.0	2.7	0.5	31.5	52.9	15.4	475	46.3	64.8	3.4
Russellville village	561	547	-2.5	623	98.9	0.0	0.0	0.0	1.1	17.4	66.6	16.1	249	67.5	79.1	9.6
Russia village	640	654	2.2	648	97.2	0.0	0.9	1.9	0.0	37.6	50.1	12.2	215	80.9	37.2	27.0
Rutland village	393	383	-2.5	615	100.0	0.0	0.0	0.0	0.0	23.6	62.3	14.1	222	76.6	51.8	1.8
Sabina village	2,564	2,540	-0.9	2,327	95.9	0.1	0.7	1.9	1.4	23.7	58.3	17.9	922	66.4	59.1	11.6
St. Bernard village	4,368	4,361	-0.2	4,358	75.0	20.1	1.1	2.7	1.0	25.2	60.9	13.8	1,802	53.3	46.3	14.0
St. Clairsville city	5,184	5,122	-1.2	5,151	95.5	3.0	0.9	0.3	0.2	18.7	54.7	26.6	2,200	65.0	32.8	27.7
St. Henry village	2,427	2,488	2.5	2,603	95.9	0.2	0.4	0.1	3.4	30.2	58.1	11.8	862	80.6	49.1	23.4
St. Johns CDP	185	NA	NA	212	97.6	0.0	0.0	2.4	0.0	33.5	63.6	2.8	81	58.0	79.0	0.0
St. Louisville village	371	374	0.8	364	97.8	0.0	0.0	0.5	1.6	20.7	63.2	16.2	150	82.0	70.0	13.3
St. Martin CDP	129	NA	NA	315	99.4	0.0	0.3	0.3	0.0	17.1	68.2	14.6	112	89.3	74.1	9.8
St. Marys city	8,332	8,259	-0.9	8,193	95.9	0.5	1.1	1.5	1.0	24.8	58.5	16.6	3,412	62.7	49.6	13.5
St. Paris village	2,084	2,033	-2.4	2,141	98.5	0.3	0.0	1.0	0.3	30.4	56.3	13.3	758	68.9	54.2	13.3
Salem city	12,295	12,087	-1.7	12,214	95.3	0.7	0.1	1.4	2.6	21.0	60.5	18.5	5,136	61.4	52.1	15.4
Salem Heights CDP	3,839	NA	NA	3,479	97.3	1.2	0.0	1.5	0.0	24.1	58.2	17.7	1,331	92.1	25.8	40.6
Salesville village	129	128	-0.8	125	100.0	0.0	0.0	0.0	0.0	23.2	64.8	12.0	44	72.7	77.3	0.0
Salineville village	1,310	1,284	-2.0	1,221	96.9	0.1	0.0	2.7	0.3	29.0	56.6	14.5	477	62.1	69.0	4.2
Sandusky city	25,919	25,346	-2.2	25,626	67.5	21.4	0.3	5.2	5.6	22.8	60.5	16.8	11,432	52.2	54.5	14.4
Sandyville CDP	368	NA	NA	207	100.0	0.0	0.0	0.0	0.0	6.3	36.3	57.5	133	100.0	28.6	9.8
Sarahsville village	171	167	-2.3	168	100.0	0.0	0.0	0.0	0.0	14.9	65.0	20.2	68	85.3	70.6	2.9
Sardinia village	982	965	-1.7	1,223	98.5	0.0	0.0	1.5	0.0	35.9	55.9	8.2	397	54.9	66.5	3.5
Sardis CDP	559	NA	NA	492	93.9	0.0	0.0	6.1	0.0	19.3	43.3	37.4	244	74.2	73.8	0.0
Savannah village	413	408	-1.2	471	99.2	0.0	0.0	0.8	0.0	34.8	58.0	7.0	147	62.6	64.6	12.9
Sawyerwood CDP	1,540	NA	NA	1,215	95.9	0.0	1.0	1.0	2.1	19.0	68.9	12.3	522	62.5	62.5	7.9
Scio village	763	747	-2.1	804	88.6	0.0	0.0	2.0	9.5	21.4	67.7	11.1	356	58.7	61.0	7.9
Sciotodale CDP	1,081	NA	NA	1,012	100.0	0.0	0.0	0.0	0.0	16.8	63.3	20.0	398	82.7	53.3	13.3
Scott village	286	280	-2.1	289	99.0	0.0	0.0	0.0	1.0	29.1	61.1	10.0	119	84.0	63.0	4.2
Seaman village	944	928	-1.7	894	95.1	0.0	0.0	0.7	4.3	31.0	53.0	16.0	327	60.6	57.5	13.5
Sebring village	4,420	4,300	-2.7	4,360	94.9	0.4	0.0	0.0	4.7	18.5	53.7	27.8	1,983	50.7	51.2	19.2
Senecaville village	457	449	-1.8	428	94.6	0.0	1.9	2.3	1.2	22.9	59.3	17.8	166	73.5	57.8	13.3
Seven Hills city	11,812	11,702	-0.9	11,735	95.9	0.5	1.3	1.1	1.2	16.1	57.9	25.9	4,879	94.2	36.8	34.2
Seven Mile village	751	759	1.1	777	98.3	0.0	0.9	0.8	0.0	24.5	61.5	14.0	324	64.8	56.8	16.7
Seville village	2,305	2,353	2.1	2,270	97.6	0.7	0.6	0.5	0.5	17.2	62.2	20.6	966	82.5	52.2	21.8
Shadyside village	3,785	3,729	-1.5	3,812	97.8	0.2	0.3	1.7	0.0	17.3	60.4	22.5	1,673	73.5	46.3	21.1
Shaker Heights city	28,448	27,790	-2.3	28,071	53.5	33.6	6.5	3.9	2.5	25.6	57.4	16.9	11,447	62.8	14.2	66.6
Sharonville city	13,560	13,581	0.2	13,836	72.6	13.1	4.6	3.2	6.5	23.3	59.7	16.9	6,134	62.0	32.9	37.6
Shawnee CDP	724	NA	NA	891	92.3	0.0	0.0	7.7	0.0	14.0	64.7	21.1	335	89.3	54.3	23.6
Shawnee village	655	645	-1.5	587	100.0	0.0	0.0	0.0	0.0	23.0	63.9	13.1	247	76.5	66.8	3.6

1 May be of any race.

Table A. All Places — **Population and Housing**

STATE City, town, township, borough, or CDP (county if applicable)	Population: 2010 census total population	Population: 2014 estimated population	Population: Percent change 2010–2014	Population: ACS total population estimate 2010–2014	Race and Hispanic or Latino origin (percent), 2010–2014: White alone, not Hispanic or Latino	Black alone, not Hispanic or Latino	Asian alone, not Hispanic or Latino	All other races or 2 or more races, not Hispanic or Latino	Hispanic or Latino[1]	Age (percent), 2010–2014: Under 18 years old	Age 18 to 64 years old	Age 65 years and older	Households, 2010–2014: Total occupied housing units	Percent owner occupied	Householders by level of education (percent): High school diploma or less	Bachelor's degree or more
	1	2	3	4	5	6	7	8	9	10	11	12	13	14	15	16
OHIO—Con.																
Shawnee Hills village	677	729	7.7	844	90.4	1.2	2.1	3.3	3.0	28.9	62.3	9.0	325	87.1	19.7	54.8
Shawnee Hills CDP	2,171	NA	NA	2,251	98.5	0.0	0.0	0.0	1.5	27.1	60.5	12.5	847	93.9	39.3	15.2
Sheffield village	3,983	4,038	1.4	4,004	84.9	4.0	1.9	0.4	8.8	19.0	62.7	18.3	1,597	78.3	36.3	25.5
Sheffield Lake city	9,137	9,058	-0.9	9,090	92.1	0.6	0.3	1.6	5.5	21.6	64.7	13.8	3,867	71.6	46.2	16.6
Shelby city	9,317	9,088	-2.5	9,149	97.7	0.0	0.2	0.3	1.8	23.9	58.5	17.5	3,904	59.9	52.0	17.3
Sherrodsville village	304	299	-1.6	270	96.3	0.0	0.0	1.1	2.6	27.5	63.7	8.9	89	75.3	61.8	3.4
Sherwood village	834	823	-1.3	802	93.8	0.0	0.7	2.7	2.7	27.6	58.4	14.1	308	72.7	56.2	15.9
Sherwood CDP	3,719	NA	NA	3,640	94.9	0.9	0.0	3.7	0.5	23.1	65.1	12.0	1,389	94.2	22.6	46.4
Shiloh village	649	634	-2.3	629	96.5	0.0	0.6	2.2	0.6	24.2	63.1	12.7	229	83.0	66.8	5.7
Shreve village	1,514	1,499	-1.0	1,476	95.0	0.2	1.8	2.3	0.7	27.5	61.2	11.4	557	64.3	70.7	10.4
Sidney city	21,225	20,905	-1.5	21,126	88.1	5.1	1.2	2.9	2.7	26.1	60.5	13.2	8,456	60.4	58.0	13.8
Silver Lake village	2,519	2,525	0.2	2,520	97.1	0.0	0.6	1.8	0.5	18.7	59.1	22.0	1,037	92.7	16.4	59.6
Silverton village	4,781	4,779	0.0	4,781	42.7	49.6	0.0	5.4	2.2	17.7	66.1	16.1	2,456	59.0	26.0	37.5
Sinking Spring village	133	132	-0.8	157	100.0	0.0	0.0	0.0	0.0	15.3	58.1	26.8	57	91.2	86.0	14.0
Sixteen Mile Stand CDP	2,928	NA	NA	3,601	70.9	11.2	9.3	3.2	5.3	18.1	75.8	6.1	1,377	43.2	12.2	60.2
Skyline Acres CDP	1,717	NA	NA	1,931	9.2	90.4	0.0	0.4	0.0	29.1	57.5	13.4	622	64.5	48.6	8.2
Smithfield village	867	840	-3.1	796	90.8	5.7	0.5	0.4	2.6	16.0	60.9	23.0	339	70.2	66.4	9.4
Smithville village	1,252	1,263	0.9	1,184	95.7	1.9	0.0	0.3	2.0	23.1	63.5	13.6	479	65.8	47.8	23.4
Solon city	23,348	23,075	-1.2	23,177	71.8	11.7	11.7	2.5	2.4	27.6	57.3	15.2	8,262	85.3	17.6	61.0
Somerset village	1,481	1,461	-1.4	1,488	100.0	0.0	0.0	0.0	0.0	32.7	51.6	15.8	533	56.8	55.0	11.8
Somerville village	281	283	0.7	268	100.0	0.0	0.0	0.0	0.0	21.2	62.4	16.4	92	67.4	69.6	14.1
South Amherst village	1,688	1,674	-0.8	1,779	96.2	0.1	0.2	1.3	2.2	17.2	65.4	17.4	701	86.9	54.6	11.7
South Bloomfield village	1,744	1,812	3.9	2,275	93.8	1.5	0.0	3.1	1.5	27.5	61.0	11.5	804	80.7	52.6	13.4
South Canal CDP	1,100	NA	NA	1,274	96.6	0.0	0.0	3.4	0.0	14.6	69.8	15.5	487	85.4	64.7	15.4
South Charleston village	1,693	1,668	-1.5	1,785	97.1	0.0	0.0	2.7	0.2	27.9	61.6	10.8	703	50.5	50.9	12.2
South Euclid city	22,295	21,869	-1.9	22,052	49.4	43.7	2.3	2.5	2.1	22.0	64.9	13.2	8,925	78.6	24.8	43.3
South Lebanon village	4,094	4,303	5.1	5,215	96.6	1.3	1.3	0.5	0.3	28.0	62.0	10.1	1,890	68.1	43.1	38.0
South Point village	3,958	3,958	0.0	3,738	91.8	2.1	0.0	1.6	4.6	23.5	62.8	13.6	1,532	69.8	47.8	15.1
South Russell village	3,822	3,841	0.5	3,840	98.8	0.0	0.0	0.7	0.5	28.4	56.1	15.6	1,461	93.7	10.3	75.4
South Salem village	204	208	2.0	247	99.6	0.4	0.0	0.0	0.0	28.8	56.3	15.0	87	69.0	71.3	13.8
South Solon village	355	361	1.7	369	100.0	0.0	0.0	0.0	0.0	16.0	73.4	10.6	139	76.3	69.1	6.5
South Vienna village	384	380	-1.0	363	98.3	0.0	0.0	0.0	1.7	16.6	65.7	17.6	150	68.7	45.3	14.0
South Webster village	866	838	-3.2	730	98.8	0.0	0.7	0.0	0.5	24.1	55.1	20.8	276	77.5	56.5	26.4
South Zanesville village	1,989	1,968	-1.1	2,181	86.5	5.9	0.0	6.5	1.1	27.5	60.4	12.2	843	71.4	66.2	6.9
Sparta village	161	163	1.2	135	100.0	0.0	0.0	0.0	0.0	31.8	61.4	6.7	49	61.2	69.4	6.1
Spencer village	753	768	2.0	673	100.0	0.0	0.0	0.0	0.0	19.9	63.6	16.3	253	64.0	67.2	6.7
Spencerville village	2,225	2,211	-0.6	2,064	95.1	2.4	0.0	2.1	0.3	29.3	55.6	15.1	764	69.1	65.2	7.1
Springboro city	17,334	18,017	3.9	17,499	88.2	2.5	5.2	2.7	1.5	30.8	57.8	11.5	5,951	84.4	21.0	53.0
Springdale city	11,223	11,212	-0.1	11,201	43.5	30.4	5.7	1.3	19.1	30.1	52.6	17.4	3,883	54.7	37.6	30.0
Springfield city	60,608	59,956	-1.1	60,216	73.5	18.0	0.7	4.6	3.2	24.6	60.1	15.2	24,449	49.8	51.6	15.9
Spring Valley village	479	482	0.6	474	100.0	0.0	0.0	0.0	0.0	16.5	69.4	14.1	193	86.0	46.6	25.4
Stafford village	81	81	0.0	98	92.9	0.0	0.0	7.1	0.0	12.2	64.1	23.5	44	61.4	56.8	0.0
Sterling CDP	457	NA	NA	631	98.7	1.3	0.0	0.0	0.0	21.5	69.7	8.9	209	65.1	70.8	2.4
Steubenville city	18,659	18,303	-1.9	18,437	77.6	15.2	0.5	4.0	2.7	18.2	63.0	18.9	7,441	55.6	45.2	22.5
Stewart CDP	247	NA	NA	230	100.0	0.0	0.0	0.0	0.0	13.5	77.9	8.7	130	63.8	50.8	13.1
Stockdale CDP	135	NA	NA	84	100.0	0.0	0.0	0.0	0.0	45.2	54.8	0.0	31	41.9	58.1	41.9
Stockport village	503	492	-2.2	518	83.6	6.6	0.0	9.8	0.0	27.8	55.2	17.0	202	67.8	50.5	7.4
Stone Creek village	177	178	0.6	171	100.0	0.0	0.0	0.0	0.0	30.3	56.1	13.5	65	90.8	76.9	4.6
Stony Prairie CDP	1,284	NA	NA	1,219	93.3	0.0	0.0	0.0	6.7	20.7	61.0	18.3	525	77.7	43.8	7.4
Stony Ridge CDP	411	NA	NA	311	77.8	0.0	0.0	2.6	19.6	8.1	82.0	10.0	118	71.2	48.3	28.8
Stoutsville village	560	564	0.7	554	98.6	0.0	0.0	0.5	0.9	24.4	62.5	13.2	212	75.0	53.8	14.2
Stow city	34,837	34,773	-0.2	34,741	92.8	2.3	1.8	1.9	1.2	22.0	62.7	15.2	13,978	71.0	27.0	45.1
Strasburg village	2,608	2,658	1.9	2,726	98.6	0.0	0.0	0.7	0.7	17.7	58.7	23.5	1,204	65.3	56.0	20.3
Stratton village	294	280	-4.8	248	100.0	0.0	0.0	0.0	0.0	20.9	61.6	17.3	123	67.5	62.6	6.5
Streetsboro city	16,029	16,238	1.3	16,152	87.0	6.4	1.7	2.2	2.8	22.0	64.5	13.5	6,603	66.8	42.5	27.4
Strongsville city	44,750	44,654	-0.2	44,649	88.2	3.1	4.8	1.3	2.6	22.3	60.1	17.8	17,403	80.6	25.0	46.9
Struthers city	10,713	10,441	-2.5	10,574	92.0	1.8	0.1	1.9	4.2	22.5	59.1	18.4	4,287	67.8	59.7	13.3
Stryker village	1,335	1,319	-1.2	1,271	87.3	0.4	0.5	1.3	10.5	30.0	57.5	12.7	495	66.3	51.7	9.9
Sugar Bush Knolls village	175	174	-0.6	158	93.7	0.6	3.8	1.9	0.0	12.7	65.2	22.2	62	88.7	14.5	74.2
Sugarcreek village	2,220	2,233	0.6	2,372	99.3	0.0	0.7	0.0	0.0	22.1	59.3	18.6	968	80.2	59.8	17.7
Sugar Grove village	426	429	0.7	411	99.8	0.0	0.0	0.2	0.0	21.4	69.2	9.2	149	47.7	66.4	10.1
Sulphur Springs CDP	194	NA	NA	142	94.4	0.0	0.0	5.6	0.0	0.0	93.6	6.3	78	100.0	38.5	0.0
Summerfield village	254	243	-4.3	235	94.5	0.0	0.0	5.5	0.0	14.1	54.4	31.5	97	75.3	58.8	7.2
Summerside CDP	5,083	NA	NA	5,380	96.9	1.0	0.0	0.4	1.6	26.2	60.2	13.5	2,110	76.5	46.2	22.4
Summitville village	135	133	-1.5	111	100.0	0.0	0.0	0.0	0.0	26.1	45.9	27.9	39	94.9	59.0	17.9
Sunbury village	4,395	4,909	11.7	4,639	91.2	2.0	1.0	2.5	3.3	26.0	60.0	14.0	1,796	73.9	39.6	38.6
Swanton village	3,878	3,894	0.4	3,899	94.7	1.1	0.0	0.2	4.1	23.5	61.4	15.0	1,563	69.2	44.8	20.4
Sycamore village	861	842	-2.2	1,126	98.0	0.0	0.0	0.0	2.0	30.6	54.2	15.5	435	80.0	56.8	12.6
Sylvania city	18,971	18,965	0.0	18,923	88.9	4.1	2.4	2.0	2.7	23.1	58.7	18.1	7,482	69.4	23.0	44.5
Syracuse village	826	817	-1.1	803	97.4	2.5	0.0	0.0	0.1	21.0	52.6	26.5	319	68.3	57.4	10.0
Tallmadge city	17,572	17,527	-0.3	17,463	91.6	4.5	1.1	1.9	0.8	21.7	57.7	20.6	6,830	77.6	35.4	29.4
Tarlton village	282	288	2.1	305	93.8	3.3	0.0	0.0	3.0	20.6	66.9	12.5	102	88.2	67.6	6.9
Taylor Creek CDP	3,062	NA	NA	3,534	93.2	1.2	0.8	4.7	0.0	20.8	65.9	13.3	1,289	82.2	33.7	20.6
Tedrow CDP	173	NA	NA	212	58.0	14.2	0.0	0.0	27.8	16.5	73.1	10.4	73	64.4	57.5	6.8
Terrace Park village	2,251	2,254	0.1	2,249	98.4	0.0	0.7	0.4	0.6	33.7	56.5	9.7	759	94.6	5.0	80.0
The Plains CDP	3,080	NA	NA	3,030	84.5	3.5	1.6	5.0	5.5	29.5	48.0	22.5	1,216	44.5	44.6	34.9
The Village of Indian Hill city	5,785	5,808	0.4	5,802	87.9	0.9	7.3	2.6	1.4	28.6	54.5	17.0	2,055	94.1	4.2	90.2
Thornport CDP	1,004	NA	NA	1,216	100.0	0.0	0.0	0.0	0.0	17.9	69.0	13.2	601	51.9	51.4	20.6
Thornville village	995	992	-0.3	1,203	100.0	0.0	0.0	0.0	0.0	28.1	58.3	13.5	446	64.6	47.5	17.0
Thurston village	604	609	0.8	512	97.7	0.0	0.2	0.4	1.8	26.4	62.3	11.1	189	61.9	65.1	10.1
Tiffin city	17,963	17,739	-1.2	17,835	90.1	2.9	1.1	1.2	4.6	21.1	63.5	15.4	6,635	58.9	51.0	18.2
Tiltonsville village	1,372	1,325	-3.4	1,356	98.6	0.2	0.0	1.2	0.0	17.5	64.1	18.4	603	68.3	45.1	13.9
Timberlake village	675	663	-1.8	772	96.9	0.0	0.8	2.3	0.0	19.4	56.0	24.6	311	91.0	34.1	28.9
Tipp City city	9,693	9,858	1.7	9,778	97.8	0.5	0.8	0.3	0.6	25.2	59.7	15.0	3,903	64.2	35.5	29.3
Tippecanoe CDP	121	NA	NA	122	100.0	0.0	0.0	0.0	0.0	42.6	37.0	20.5	48	70.8	77.1	0.0
Tiro village	280	274	-2.1	195	84.1	0.5	0.0	4.1	11.3	22.6	59.4	17.9	73	80.8	69.9	9.6
Toledo city	287,206	281,031	-2.2	283,932	61.3	26.2	1.2	3.8	7.6	23.4	63.8	12.7	117,785	54.6	45.4	18.4
Tontogany village	367	378	3.0	439	93.2	0.9	0.0	1.8	4.1	21.0	67.7	11.4	181	80.7	53.6	14.9
Toronto city	5,091	4,911	-3.5	4,961	95.2	1.1	0.0	2.1	1.6	19.1	61.7	19.1	2,238	66.8	55.5	8.5
Tremont City village	375	371	-1.1	468	96.6	0.6	0.0	1.9	0.9	20.1	67.2	12.8	169	67.5	64.5	5.9

1 May be of any race.

Table A. All Places — **Population and Housing**

STATE City, town, township, borough, or CDP (county if applicable)	Population				Race and Hispanic or Latino origin (percent), 2010–2014					Age (percent), 2010–2014			Households, 2010–2014		Householders by level of education (percent)	
	2010 census total population	2014 estimated population	Percent change 2010–2014	ACS total population estimate 2010–2014	White alone, not Hispanic or Latino	Black alone, not Hispanic or Latino	Asian alone, not Hispanic or Latino	All other races or 2 or more races, not Hispanic or Latino	Hispanic or Latino[1]	Under 18 years old	Age 18 to 64 years old	Age 65 years and older	Total occupied housing units	Percent owner occupied	High school diploma or less	Bachelor's degree or more
	1	2	3	4	5	6	7	8	9	10	11	12	13	14	15	16
OHIO—Con.																
Trenton city	11,869	12,260	3.3	12,091	93.2	1.0	0.0	2.7	3.1	30.3	60.2	9.4	4,267	70.4	61.1	13.9
Trimble village	401	396	-1.2	413	95.6	0.0	0.0	2.2	2.2	23.5	66.8	9.9	155	65.8	65.2	9.7
Trinway CDP	365	NA	NA	238	100.0	0.0	0.0	0.0	0.0	20.6	60.9	18.5	75	86.7	69.3	0.0
Trotwood city	24,432	24,171	-1.1	24,322	27.4	67.7	0.4	2.7	1.8	23.0	58.8	18.2	10,130	55.0	44.1	17.4
Troy city	25,235	25,564	1.3	25,334	88.4	4.3	2.6	2.7	2.1	22.8	61.9	15.4	10,415	60.7	45.8	23.7
Tuppers Plains CDP	465	NA	NA	451	78.7	7.3	0.0	0.0	14.0	33.5	59.0	7.5	151	43.7	72.8	6.0
Turpin Hills CDP	5,099	NA	NA	4,998	93.5	0.0	0.7	0.9	5.0	30.9	56.7	12.2	1,759	87.3	9.2	67.9
Tuscarawas village	1,056	1,056	0.0	1,365	98.1	0.0	0.9	1.0	0.0	26.7	63.5	10.0	507	76.1	62.5	17.8
Twinsburg city	18,796	18,837	0.2	18,784	74.4	15.6	5.8	1.9	2.3	23.8	59.8	16.4	7,465	74.0	30.2	44.4
Twinsburg Heights CDP	925	NA	NA	939	15.3	66.9	0.0	17.8	0.0	43.2	55.1	1.7	280	59.3	29.6	12.5
Uhrichsville city	5,413	5,403	-0.2	5,408	98.6	0.2	0.0	0.8	0.4	24.9	59.7	15.3	2,183	55.4	69.9	6.6
Union city	6,427	6,391	-0.6	6,425	97.5	0.0	0.0	0.0	2.5	28.2	58.2	13.6	2,439	81.3	41.3	16.5
Union City village	1,666	1,641	-1.5	1,709	88.4	1.5	0.0	0.6	9.5	26.7	55.6	17.6	655	51.3	74.2	3.1
Uniontown CDP	3,309	NA	NA	3,469	98.9	0.3	0.3	0.5	0.0	26.0	55.3	18.6	1,313	90.3	35.7	29.4
Unionville Center village	233	236	1.3	266	94.7	0.8	0.0	1.5	3.0	27.1	65.3	7.5	93	84.9	69.9	11.8
Uniopolis village	222	221	-0.5	221	97.7	0.0	0.9	1.4	0.0	16.3	65.2	18.6	116	53.4	41.4	6.9
University Heights city	13,539	13,203	-2.5	13,404	74.8	18.1	1.6	1.8	3.7	23.1	65.7	11.2	4,666	66.5	13.3	61.1
Upper Arlington city	33,682	34,609	2.8	34,191	89.8	1.1	4.4	1.9	2.8	26.1	57.4	16.5	13,369	82.4	8.0	77.4
Upper Sandusky city	6,596	6,561	-0.5	6,792	92.5	0.3	3.2	0.5	3.6	21.8	57.5	20.8	3,054	57.0	61.5	11.4
Urbana city	11,790	11,524	-2.3	11,587	88.3	5.4	0.6	3.8	1.8	24.6	59.7	15.9	4,744	55.4	57.0	16.8
Urbancrest village	960	1,011	5.3	1,024	25.7	61.7	4.9	2.1	5.7	28.9	65.8	5.5	393	44.3	76.3	3.6
Utica village	2,145	2,176	1.4	2,388	91.6	0.1	0.8	0.1	7.3	25.9	60.6	13.5	898	63.7	60.6	12.4
Valley City CDP	0	NA	NA	578	99.0	0.0	0.0	0.0	1.0	10.6	75.3	14.2	246	81.7	37.0	39.8
Valley Hi village	212	209	-1.4	302	84.8	12.9	0.0	1.3	1.0	35.4	56.6	7.9	120	25.8	58.3	5.8
Valley View village	2,034	2,014	-1.0	1,975	95.2	2.1	0.0	1.7	1.0	19.2	62.4	18.6	711	87.8	41.1	27.1
Valleyview village	616	630	2.3	805	91.9	4.1	1.2	2.1	0.6	24.7	64.2	11.1	291	75.3	52.6	14.8
Van Buren village	330	363	10.0	504	85.9	0.0	1.0	4.4	8.7	28.6	62.7	8.7	150	93.3	40.0	24.0
Vandalia city	15,246	15,139	-0.7	15,220	87.1	6.3	0.8	4.4	1.3	23.3	61.1	15.6	6,292	63.5	37.0	21.0
Vanlue village	359	361	0.6	396	89.1	1.8	0.0	0.0	9.1	30.3	58.0	11.6	153	75.2	47.1	17.0
Van Wert city	10,846	10,768	-0.7	10,859	92.4	1.9	0.1	1.2	4.4	23.5	57.1	19.3	4,423	64.0	54.7	15.1
Vaughnsville CDP	262	NA	NA	231	100.0	0.0	0.0	0.0	0.0	32.0	68.0	0.0	66	90.9	53.0	33.3
Venedocia village	124	122	-1.6	140	97.9	0.0	0.0	2.1	0.0	24.3	57.9	17.9	52	71.2	55.8	5.8
Vermilion city	10,586	10,478	-1.0	10,415	95.7	0.0	0.4	0.7	3.2	18.1	59.8	22.0	4,283	76.4	52.0	17.5
Verona village	494	488	-1.2	473	96.4	0.0	0.8	2.7	0.0	30.5	60.2	9.3	168	78.0	63.7	6.0
Versailles village	2,687	2,648	-1.5	2,685	97.9	0.0	0.0	1.6	0.6	27.3	53.4	19.2	1,059	70.7	47.8	19.5
Vickery CDP	121	NA	NA	159	100.0	0.0	0.0	0.0	0.0	27.7	64.1	8.2	72	45.8	52.8	19.4
Vienna Center CDP	650	NA	NA	803	97.9	0.0	0.0	0.0	2.1	23.4	65.2	11.6	327	79.5	41.9	23.5
Vincent CDP	339	NA	NA	365	100.0	0.0	0.0	0.0	0.0	31.8	60.2	7.9	133	100.0	57.1	0.0
Vinton village	222	220	-0.9	252	96.8	1.2	0.0	1.2	0.8	39.3	50.3	10.3	85	81.2	61.2	10.6
Wadsworth city	21,538	21,893	1.6	21,752	93.7	1.3	1.5	2.1	1.4	27.0	56.8	16.1	8,464	69.0	34.1	34.8
Waite Hill village	471	467	-0.8	441	97.7	0.0	0.9	0.7	0.7	12.7	58.3	29.0	192	85.4	13.5	70.3
Wakeman village	1,047	1,038	-0.9	949	95.0	0.0	0.0	3.8	1.2	20.8	66.6	12.8	394	69.8	52.0	11.9
Walbridge village	3,019	3,091	2.4	3,056	97.4	0.0	0.0	0.3	2.3	15.1	57.2	27.6	1,455	74.4	55.9	7.0
Waldo village	339	327	-3.5	356	98.9	0.0	0.3	0.8	0.0	23.1	55.9	21.1	151	78.8	56.3	8.6
Walnut Creek CDP	878	NA	NA	943	97.5	2.5	0.0	0.0	0.0	23.9	48.1	27.8	240	66.7	72.5	11.7
Walton Hills village	2,281	2,249	-1.4	2,272	90.9	7.1	0.0	2.0	0.0	9.7	59.3	30.9	909	97.8	36.9	24.8
Wapakoneta city	9,867	9,818	-0.5	9,853	93.9	1.1	0.3	2.3	2.4	25.7	57.8	16.5	3,942	65.1	50.9	16.0
Warren city	41,557	40,633	-2.2	40,925	63.5	30.0	0.2	3.7	2.6	24.6	59.3	16.1	16,991	53.3	60.8	12.6
Warrensville Heights city	13,542	13,286	-1.9	13,387	4.7	93.0	0.6	1.3	0.4	21.2	60.2	18.6	6,097	44.2	39.8	16.2
Warsaw village	682	674	-1.2	770	88.8	8.2	0.3	2.7	0.0	25.6	65.3	9.1	284	74.3	54.2	11.3
Washington Court House city	14,192	14,085	-0.8	14,123	92.8	3.2	1.1	1.6	1.2	23.8	60.2	15.9	5,838	52.0	59.1	15.6
Washingtonville village	801	782	-2.4	859	91.3	2.4	1.6	2.3	2.3	22.4	63.8	13.9	345	52.8	64.9	11.6
Waterford CDP	450	NA	NA	364	100.0	0.0	0.0	0.0	0.0	38.8	51.6	9.6	129	65.9	60.5	31.0
Waterville city	5,523	5,516	-0.1	5,499	92.2	1.7	3.1	1.1	1.9	29.5	57.1	13.5	1,970	81.7	23.0	32.8
Wauseon city	7,332	7,322	-0.1	6,953	79.3	0.2	0.0	3.2	17.3	27.5	57.9	14.7	2,636	66.8	45.9	18.6
Waverly village	4,406	4,290	-2.6	4,353	94.6	1.6	1.2	0.6	2.0	18.7	54.1	27.2	2,057	47.9	50.9	22.7
Wayne village	887	898	1.2	1,103	88.8	0.0	0.2	0.9	10.2	36.2	55.2	8.5	381	60.4	59.3	5.2
Wayne Lakes village	718	709	-1.3	699	96.7	0.0	0.0	3.0	0.3	17.7	57.6	24.6	319	75.9	55.5	15.7
Waynesburg village	923	924	0.1	962	92.9	2.2	0.3	3.5	1.0	20.8	61.6	17.6	416	74.8	69.0	10.8
Waynesfield village	847	850	0.4	787	89.6	0.1	0.0	3.4	6.9	23.7	67.2	9.0	290	76.9	58.6	15.9
Waynesville village	2,813	2,968	5.5	2,896	94.2	0.0	0.0	1.5	4.4	26.6	55.9	17.4	1,008	61.9	48.3	26.0
Wellington village	4,807	4,846	0.8	5,004	95.0	1.9	0.1	1.4	1.6	28.8	55.5	15.7	1,815	57.7	51.7	10.8
Wellston city	5,663	5,535	-2.3	5,590	94.7	0.2	0.0	5.1	0.0	20.4	62.5	17.2	2,415	61.9	58.0	14.5
Wellsville village	3,541	3,446	-2.7	3,493	89.2	3.2	0.0	6.6	1.0	29.5	59.1	11.5	1,248	55.5	67.5	4.5
West Alexandria village	1,379	1,348	-2.2	1,799	93.7	0.2	2.3	3.3	0.4	26.8	63.6	9.6	727	64.1	45.0	17.6
West Carrollton city	13,143	13,018	-1.0	13,087	79.8	13.6	0.8	3.0	2.8	21.7	61.9	16.3	6,120	56.7	39.8	16.1
West Elkton village	197	194	-1.5	201	82.1	0.0	3.0	11.9	3.0	23.4	62.9	13.9	79	73.4	84.8	5.1
Westerville city	36,116	37,667	4.3	37,101	84.8	7.2	2.3	3.7	2.0	22.2	63.3	14.5	13,827	75.3	19.5	57.3
West Farmington village	499	490	-1.8	574	96.9	0.0	0.3	1.4	1.4	36.9	59.7	3.5	164	66.5	71.3	6.1
Westfield Center village	1,116	1,140	2.2	1,212	99.1	0.0	0.0	0.4	0.5	20.2	56.2	23.5	509	84.5	29.3	36.7
West Hill CDP	2,273	NA	NA	2,122	90.3	9.0	0.7	0.0	0.0	24.1	60.2	15.8	898	52.1	62.4	11.5
West Jefferson village	4,227	4,272	1.1	4,223	95.7	0.5	0.0	3.4	0.4	24.8	60.4	14.7	1,602	64.5	59.6	7.6
West Lafayette village	2,320	2,285	-1.5	2,239	96.5	0.1	0.0	1.7	1.8	24.0	57.5	18.5	878	70.5	60.9	15.6
Westlake city	32,729	32,424	-0.9	32,513	87.1	2.1	5.5	1.9	3.4	21.6	58.4	19.9	13,547	74.5	16.1	57.5
West Leipsic village	206	203	-1.5	266	53.8	0.0	0.0	1.9	44.4	32.0	60.9	7.1	90	68.9	52.2	2.2
West Liberty village	1,805	1,781	-1.3	1,695	91.6	3.0	0.2	2.7	2.5	21.0	51.6	27.4	702	68.1	59.0	16.4
West Manchester village	474	467	-1.5	580	97.6	0.0	0.0	2.4	0.0	23.8	65.8	10.3	194	61.9	52.6	5.2
West Mansfield village	682	671	-1.6	732	93.3	0.3	1.0	4.8	0.7	26.8	55.2	18.2	285	71.2	61.4	12.6
West Millgrove village	174	177	1.7	154	89.6	0.0	0.0	0.0	10.4	31.8	62.3	5.8	55	78.2	49.1	27.3
West Milton village	4,630	4,700	1.5	4,659	95.7	0.0	0.6	2.7	1.0	20.7	60.3	18.9	2,087	65.5	36.1	17.1
Westminster CDP	0	NA	NA	326	96.9	0.0	0.0	3.1	0.0	27.9	61.1	11.0	142	73.9	82.4	0.0
Weston village	1,590	1,630	2.5	1,662	79.7	0.4	0.0	2.1	17.8	23.9	61.5	14.7	649	76.4	56.2	10.2
West Portsmouth CDP	3,149	NA	NA	2,794	93.9	0.0	0.2	5.9	0.0	23.5	60.9	15.7	1,121	73.7	64.3	7.6
West Rushville village	134	135	0.7	187	85.6	14.4	0.0	0.0	0.0	30.5	61.5	8.0	73	64.4	60.3	2.7
West Salem village	1,468	1,480	0.8	1,557	95.5	2.8	0.0	0.8	1.0	26.8	61.8	11.4	600	70.8	74.3	3.5
West Union village	3,241	3,196	-1.4	3,184	98.3	1.4	0.0	0.0	0.3	21.0	60.5	18.7	1,289	52.4	63.1	9.1
West Unity village	1,678	1,656	-1.3	1,783	94.3	0.0	0.8	1.2	3.6	24.6	64.1	11.2	699	73.2	50.6	12.2
Wetherington CDP	1,302	NA	NA	1,313	86.8	2.6	5.6	0.0	5.0	11.9	65.0	23.3	569	93.7	20.0	57.1
Wharton village	358	354	-1.1	465	100.0	0.0	0.0	0.0	0.0	30.6	60.0	9.5	172	67.4	67.4	4.7
Wheelersburg CDP	6,437	NA	NA	6,283	93.8	1.0	1.0	2.5	1.7	20.4	62.4	17.1	2,539	67.9	42.7	24.6

1 May be of any race.

Table A. All Places — **Population and Housing**

STATE City, town, township, borough, or CDP (county if applicable)	Population				Race and Hispanic or Latino origin (percent), 2010–2014					Age (percent), 2010–2014			Households, 2010–2014			
	2010 census total population	2014 estimated population	Percent change 2010–2014	ACS total population estimate 2010–2014	White alone, not Hispanic or Latino	Black alone, not Hispanic or Latino	Asian alone, not Hispanic or Latino	All other races or 2 or more races, not Hispanic or Latino	Hispanic or Latino[1]	Under 18 years old	Age 18 to 64 years old	Age 65 years and older	Total occupied housing units	Percent owner occupied	Householders by level of education (percent): High school diploma or less	Householders by level of education (percent): Bachelor's degree or more
	1	2	3	4	5	6	7	8	9	10	11	12	13	14	15	16
OKLAHOMA—Con.																
Whitehall city	18,135	18,558	2.3	18,383	52.2	29.1	0.9	3.9	13.8	26.8	63.2	10.0	7,359	37.7	56.4	10.2
Whitehouse village	4,149	4,406	6.2	4,391	95.3	0.8	0.3	0.3	3.4	28.1	57.2	14.8	1,570	78.3	24.1	29.1
White Oak CDP	19,167	NA	NA	18,814	83.5	11.4	2.8	1.1	1.1	23.0	61.0	16.1	7,724	69.9	38.2	27.4
Whites Landing CDP	375	NA	NA	405	100.0	0.0	0.0	0.0	0.0	15.1	80.4	4.4	141	53.2	44.0	10.6
Wickliffe city	12,747	12,584	-1.3	12,671	91.6	4.5	0.6	2.5	0.9	21.0	58.2	20.9	5,467	81.1	44.3	22.0
Wightmans Grove CDP	72	NA	NA	10	100.0	0.0	0.0	0.0	0.0	0.0	100.0	0.0	10	0.0	100.0	0.0
Wilberforce CDP	2,271	NA	NA	2,166	32.3	64.3	0.6	2.2	0.5	9.3	89.6	1.2	161	62.1	39.1	51.6
Wilkesville village	149	149	0.0	121	100.0	0.0	0.0	0.0	0.0	19.8	67.8	12.4	59	89.8	67.8	5.1
Willard city	6,236	6,094	-2.3	6,163	75.9	0.2	0.4	2.8	20.7	28.4	58.3	13.2	2,188	50.8	60.6	11.6
Williamsburg village	2,487	2,538	2.1	2,512	96.9	1.8	0.0	0.8	0.6	30.3	60.9	8.8	797	47.9	60.1	10.9
Williamsdale CDP	581	NA	NA	665	100.0	0.0	0.0	0.0	0.0	28.8	61.8	9.5	258	55.8	80.6	3.1
Williamsport village	1,023	1,043	2.0	1,209	98.0	0.0	0.0	1.4	0.6	34.4	57.8	8.0	341	63.6	60.1	6.5
Williston CDP	487	NA	NA	607	74.6	1.6	0.0	3.3	20.4	19.8	66.1	14.2	171	45.0	47.4	9.9
Willoughby city	22,268	22,453	0.8	22,361	90.8	4.2	2.5	1.0	1.6	18.2	62.0	19.8	10,491	60.0	38.2	31.9
Willoughby Hills city	9,486	9,405	-0.9	9,446	75.4	16.8	5.2	1.6	1.0	17.8	64.3	17.9	4,338	48.2	28.8	38.9
Willowick city	14,175	14,009	-1.2	14,084	93.2	1.5	1.3	1.8	2.2	21.1	60.8	18.1	6,026	80.8	46.1	22.5
Willshire village	397	387	-2.5	466	100.0	0.0	0.0	0.0	0.0	19.5	62.1	18.5	192	83.9	63.5	4.7
Wilmington city	12,520	12,375	-1.2	12,424	86.1	7.5	0.0	3.2	3.2	23.2	61.5	15.5	5,196	43.8	54.4	14.8
Wilmot village	304	304	0.0	256	97.3	0.0	0.4	0.0	2.3	23.8	59.2	16.8	103	68.0	68.9	8.7
Wilson village	125	125	0.0	155	92.9	0.0	0.0	0.0	7.1	21.3	58.7	20.0	51	98.0	56.9	11.8
Winchester village	1,051	1,039	-1.1	1,127	91.3	0.0	0.0	8.7	0.0	33.1	54.3	12.7	365	56.7	68.2	6.8
Windham village	2,223	2,206	-0.8	1,998	92.9	3.6	0.0	3.0	0.5	27.5	64.7	8.1	697	40.9	70.4	4.3
Winesburg CDP	352	NA	NA	368	100.0	0.0	0.0	0.0	0.0	16.6	54.1	29.3	162	55.6	88.9	11.1
Wintersville village	3,924	3,815	-2.8	3,930	88.7	7.5	1.5	1.4	1.0	15.7	59.7	24.6	1,778	59.6	48.5	17.9
Withamsville CDP	7,021	NA	NA	6,841	98.1	0.2	1.2	0.0	0.5	17.4	68.1	14.3	3,058	55.6	41.1	22.2
Wolfhurst CDP	1,239	NA	NA	1,458	91.8	1.6	0.0	6.6	0.0	17.9	53.4	28.6	664	67.2	70.8	7.5
Woodlawn village	3,294	3,300	0.2	3,303	31.3	62.0	2.3	3.0	1.4	24.1	61.8	14.0	1,410	45.0	30.6	37.6
Woodmere village	884	868	-1.8	1,004	13.8	69.4	6.5	5.6	4.7	30.6	60.1	9.6	417	39.3	24.0	34.5
Woodsfield village	2,384	2,356	-1.2	2,349	96.7	1.5	0.0	1.7	0.0	21.9	52.0	25.9	1,037	66.0	58.8	11.5
Woodstock village	305	302	-1.0	330	95.5	0.0	0.0	0.6	3.9	29.4	62.9	7.6	113	74.3	46.9	6.2
Woodville village	2,135	2,102	-1.5	2,036	88.8	0.0	0.2	1.6	9.5	22.2	62.6	15.2	870	74.3	41.6	19.3
Wooster city	26,119	26,540	1.6	26,353	88.5	3.9	2.5	2.7	2.5	19.7	63.2	17.3	10,639	57.6	45.3	28.4
Worthington city	13,567	14,384	6.0	13,727	92.8	0.9	1.8	2.5	2.1	24.4	56.7	18.9	5,674	78.9	9.6	67.8
Wren village	194	191	-1.5	200	92.5	0.0	0.0	7.5	0.0	11.0	75.5	13.5	94	90.4	38.3	0.0
Wright-Patterson AFB CDP	1,821	NA	NA	2,456	72.2	12.9	1.3	1.7	11.8	22.8	75.9	1.3	620	0.0	4.5	50.6
Wyoming city	8,437	8,427	-0.1	8,404	76.1	12.0	4.5	5.1	2.4	29.6	54.5	15.8	2,934	84.6	13.2	71.7
Xenia city	25,658	25,911	1.0	25,903	79.7	14.9	0.6	3.4	1.5	25.1	58.6	16.4	10,588	62.0	43.6	20.0
Yankee Lake village	79	78	-1.3	87	100.0	0.0	0.0	0.0	0.0	16.1	67.6	16.1	38	65.8	42.1	34.2
Yellow Springs village	3,487	3,529	1.2	3,549	80.7	12.6	1.8	2.0	2.9	14.4	62.6	23.0	1,702	67.3	6.5	67.1
Yorkshire village	96	95	-1.0	79	100.0	0.0	0.0	0.0	0.0	24.1	59.7	16.5	32	93.8	90.6	0.0
Yorkville village	1,079	1,050	-2.7	1,125	99.5	0.5	0.0	0.0	0.0	15.6	62.8	21.6	496	62.1	53.8	16.1
Youngstown city	66,982	65,062	-2.9	66,013	43.0	42.6	0.6	3.7	10.0	22.3	61.9	16.0	26,477	57.7	55.3	11.6
Zaleski village	278	270	-2.9	403	99.0	0.0	0.0	1.0	0.0	22.4	53.9	23.8	160	72.5	79.4	0.0
Zanesfield village	197	196	-0.5	288	96.2	0.0	2.4	1.4	0.0	32.2	47.9	19.8	114	76.3	38.6	22.8
Zanesville city	25,484	25,372	-0.4	25,444	85.5	7.3	0.1	6.1	1.0	24.6	59.1	16.3	10,830	44.5	56.6	12.5
Zoar village	169	178	5.3	195	95.4	0.5	0.0	4.1	0.0	9.8	69.3	21.0	93	78.5	33.3	51.6
OKLAHOMA	3,751,616	3,878,051	3.4	3,818,851	67.8	7.1	1.8	13.9	9.4	24.6	61.3	14.0	1,450,117	66.5	41.0	25.4
Achille town	491	507	3.3	493	71.0	2.4	0.0	25.4	1.2	23.2	64.0	13.0	198	80.8	70.2	9.6
Ada city	16,827	17,130	1.8	17,061	63.1	4.0	0.6	26.4	6.0	21.1	63.7	15.2	7,065	49.1	41.5	29.4
Adair town	827	818	-1.1	738	74.4	0.0	0.0	23.3	2.3	26.2	62.4	11.1	296	65.2	44.6	9.8
Addington town	113	109	-3.5	110	87.3	0.9	0.0	10.9	0.9	22.6	47.2	30.0	46	82.6	71.7	8.7
Afton town	1,045	1,054	0.9	930	67.8	0.0	2.2	25.8	4.2	30.8	52.6	16.7	374	59.9	59.1	13.1
Agra town	339	342	0.9	314	74.5	3.5	0.0	13.7	8.3	26.1	55.4	18.5	115	67.0	69.6	14.8
Akins CDP	493	NA	NA	481	68.4	0.0	0.0	31.6	0.0	19.8	54.2	26.0	167	83.8	61.7	10.8
Albany CDP	143	NA	NA	115	90.4	0.0	0.0	9.6	0.0	17.4	35.7	47.0	55	69.1	80.0	0.0
Albion town	106	102	-3.8	83	67.5	0.0	0.0	27.7	4.8	18.1	62.6	19.3	38	60.5	34.2	2.6
Alderson town	304	292	-3.9	300	65.0	1.7	1.7	30.0	1.7	26.9	53.9	19.0	119	77.3	62.2	18.5
Alex town	550	550	0.0	547	79.3	0.0	0.0	11.7	9.0	29.3	50.0	20.8	225	74.7	61.3	16.4
Aline town	207	215	3.9	234	90.2	0.0	0.0	9.8	0.0	24.4	62.4	13.2	97	82.5	45.4	20.6
Allen town	932	935	0.3	990	76.4	0.7	0.0	18.1	4.8	22.8	57.2	20.0	338	78.4	60.1	15.7
Altus city	19,813	19,531	-1.4	19,716	60.5	9.1	1.3	4.5	24.5	25.3	61.9	12.7	7,708	53.1	43.7	19.2
Alva city	4,945	5,174	4.6	4,990	85.2	2.8	0.3	7.0	4.7	20.5	63.5	16.1	2,030	59.6	37.7	28.9
Amber town	419	444	6.0	352	82.4	0.3	0.0	11.6	5.7	29.6	57.5	13.1	130	72.3	60.0	10.8
Ames town	239	247	3.3	254	95.7	0.0	0.0	4.3	0.0	15.4	60.2	24.4	126	76.2	54.0	17.5
Amorita town	37	38	2.7	1	100.0	0.0	0.0	0.0	0.0	0.0	0.0	100.0	1	100.0	0.0	100.0
Anadarko city	6,761	6,723	-0.6	6,786	32.4	4.8	0.8	47.0	15.0	29.0	60.2	10.7	2,166	56.8	49.8	15.0
Antlers city	2,444	2,346	-4.0	2,437	72.5	2.8	0.2	20.8	3.6	28.0	53.0	19.0	1,021	51.4	52.1	17.7
Apache town	1,448	1,429	-1.3	1,315	55.7	1.9	0.2	36.7	5.4	27.8	59.7	12.5	539	55.5	61.4	20.2
Arapaho town	796	824	3.5	483	77.0	4.6	0.0	13.7	4.8	11.0	75.9	13.0	187	74.9	61.5	11.8
Arcadia town	247	255	3.2	145	16.6	74.5	0.0	9.0	0.0	13.2	64.7	22.1	67	52.2	59.7	10.4
Ardmore city	24,446	25,226	3.2	24,877	63.3	10.5	1.5	15.8	8.9	26.1	58.1	15.7	9,101	61.6	47.3	23.5
Arkoma town	1,989	1,941	-2.4	1,954	85.5	0.4	0.4	12.6	1.1	20.7	58.4	21.0	789	70.0	68.9	9.4
Armstrong town	105	109	3.8	193	79.3	1.0	0.0	19.7	0.0	27.0	58.9	14.0	65	60.0	78.5	3.1
Arnett town	524	523	-0.2	504	86.7	1.6	0.0	5.2	6.5	18.9	62.5	18.7	220	90.0	44.1	29.5
Arpelar CDP	272	NA	NA	276	73.6	4.3	0.0	22.1	0.0	20.3	57.7	22.1	129	77.5	34.9	38.8
Asher town	393	416	5.9	409	80.2	0.0	0.0	13.2	6.6	24.7	54.0	21.3	144	67.4	72.9	3.5
Ashland town	66	63	-4.5	24	79.2	0.0	0.0	20.8	0.0	0.0	62.6	37.5	12	75.0	58.3	8.3
Atoka city	3,114	3,067	-1.5	3,093	66.5	8.0	1.9	17.1	6.5	25.0	59.2	15.8	1,323	57.3	57.8	9.6
Atwood town	74	72	-2.7	76	85.5	0.0	0.0	14.5	0.0	21.0	38.3	40.8	36	88.9	72.2	5.6
Avant town	320	319	-0.3	369	74.0	0.0	3.0	21.7	1.4	32.0	49.4	18.7	154	83.8	76.0	1.9
Badger Lee CDP	76	NA	NA	102	47.1	0.0	0.0	52.9	0.0	57.8	42.2	0.0	24	0.0	100.0	0.0
Ballou CDP	176	NA	NA	63	73.0	0.0	0.0	27.0	0.0	17.5	65.1	17.5	31	100.0	48.4	25.8
Barnsdall city	1,243	1,221	-1.8	1,244	64.6	0.0	0.0	32.3	3.1	28.5	55.1	16.5	512	71.9	57.2	10.0
Bartlesville city	35,752	36,498	2.1	36,193	75.6	3.4	2.0	13.1	5.9	23.4	58.5	18.0	15,057	69.0	35.8	32.0
Bearden town	133	133	0.0	159	80.5	4.4	0.0	10.7	4.4	33.9	57.3	8.8	54	79.6	44.4	3.7
Beaver town	1,515	1,470	-3.0	1,511	71.8	0.7	0.5	3.4	23.5	24.4	57.5	18.0	618	66.7	51.5	17.2
Bee CDP	140	NA	NA	111	99.1	0.0	0.0	0.9	0.0	7.2	63.0	29.7	56	76.8	100.0	0.0
Beggs city	1,269	1,243	-2.0	1,127	65.2	9.2	0.0	23.9	1.7	29.4	57.7	13.0	418	67.7	58.4	9.8

1 May be of any race.

Table A. All Places — **Population and Housing**

STATE City, town, township, borough, or CDP (county if applicable)	2010 census total population	2014 estimated population	Percent change 2010–2014	ACS total population estimate 2010–2014	White alone, not Hispanic or Latino	Black alone, not Hispanic or Latino	Asian alone, not Hispanic or Latino	All other races or 2 or more races, not Hispanic or Latino	Hispanic or Latino[1]	Under 18 years old	Age 18 to 64 years old	Age 65 years and older	Total occupied housing units	Percent owner occupied	High school diploma or less	Bachelor's degree or more
	1	2	3	4	5	6	7	8	9	10	11	12	13	14	15	16
OKLAHOMA—Con.																
Belfonte CDP	394	NA	NA	390	44.6	0.0	0.0	44.4	11.0	17.5	48.8	33.6	136	95.6	48.5	37.5
Bell CDP	535	NA	NA	522	32.8	0.0	1.3	65.9	0.0	28.5	68.2	3.3	155	80.6	78.7	0.0
Bennington town	334	345	3.3	285	69.1	0.0	0.0	30.9	0.0	30.9	56.0	13.3	112	63.4	65.2	17.9
Bernice town	565	563	-0.4	499	77.4	0.0	0.0	22.2	0.4	12.4	48.8	38.7	253	85.8	55.3	11.5
Bessie town	181	180	-0.6	186	90.3	0.0	0.0	3.2	6.5	19.4	69.4	11.3	79	65.8	58.2	11.4
Bethany city	19,051	19,580	2.8	19,390	69.2	6.9	0.6	10.1	13.2	25.8	58.7	15.6	7,134	59.9	38.6	25.8
Bethel Acres town	2,895	3,073	6.1	2,970	81.7	1.5	1.7	13.0	2.0	22.5	59.8	17.7	1,062	84.8	43.7	20.6
Big Cabin town	265	257	-3.0	290	61.7	0.0	1.0	33.1	4.1	30.7	49.7	19.7	112	71.4	66.1	9.8
Billings town	509	508	-0.2	487	84.8	6.4	0.0	6.2	2.7	13.8	70.8	15.4	175	66.3	41.1	8.6
Binger town	672	656	-2.4	606	71.6	3.5	0.0	21.6	3.3	22.8	52.2	25.1	214	76.6	60.3	10.3
Bison CDP	65	NA	NA	88	100.0	0.0	0.0	0.0	0.0	38.6	50.1	11.4	34	100.0	55.9	38.2
Bixby city	20,910	24,008	14.8	22,480	83.3	1.3	2.0	9.8	3.6	31.3	57.3	11.5	7,872	79.6	24.4	41.8
Blackburn town	108	107	-0.9	77	61.0	0.0	0.0	29.9	9.1	19.5	58.5	22.1	32	81.3	62.5	12.5
Blackgum CDP	51	NA	NA	71	28.2	0.0	0.0	23.9	47.9	35.3	64.8	0.0	22	100.0	31.8	68.2
Blackwell city	7,092	6,917	-2.5	6,957	77.9	0.1	0.0	10.0	12.0	20.8	61.2	18.0	2,965	69.2	49.2	18.6
Blair town	818	791	-3.3	606	77.1	0.0	1.0	9.4	12.5	24.9	58.1	17.0	263	70.0	51.0	12.5
Blanchard city	7,391	8,049	8.9	7,625	83.8	0.7	0.8	11.9	2.8	26.9	62.6	10.6	2,732	81.6	40.3	24.2
Blue CDP	195	NA	NA	302	97.0	0.0	0.0	3.0	0.0	22.5	65.3	12.3	115	46.1	75.7	8.7
Bluejacket town	339	330	-2.7	319	69.9	0.0	0.0	30.1	0.0	21.6	65.2	13.2	97	76.3	41.2	8.2
Boise City city	1,264	1,168	-7.6	1,162	70.0	1.0	0.5	0.3	28.2	27.1	55.1	17.7	464	72.6	55.8	12.9
Bokchito town	632	653	3.3	583	74.6	0.0	0.0	25.4	0.0	23.5	51.7	24.9	245	71.0	70.6	9.8
Bokoshe town	509	497	-2.4	487	71.9	1.0	0.0	25.7	1.4	23.0	63.2	13.8	192	64.6	63.0	6.8
Boley town	1,184	1,183	-0.1	1,078	51.9	35.3	0.6	6.3	5.9	3.4	89.8	6.8	90	70.0	46.7	16.7
Boswell town	709	707	-0.3	729	44.3	12.6	0.0	34.2	8.9	22.4	63.4	14.4	310	53.2	64.5	7.4
Bowlegs town	405	403	-0.5	431	70.5	0.0	0.0	28.3	1.2	22.3	64.9	12.8	156	81.4	52.6	9.6
Box CDP	224	NA	NA	129	69.8	0.0	0.0	17.8	12.4	0.0	98.5	1.6	62	100.0	54.8	0.0
Boynton town	248	244	-1.6	167	25.1	52.7	0.0	21.0	1.2	24.6	51.6	24.0	75	86.7	57.3	4.0
Bradley town	128	130	1.6	113	72.6	0.0	0.0	23.9	3.5	17.7	75.3	7.1	42	90.5	52.4	7.1
Braggs town	259	255	-1.5	196	59.7	0.0	0.0	39.8	0.5	26.0	54.6	19.4	86	82.6	31.4	17.4
Braman town	217	213	-1.8	174	83.9	0.0	0.0	13.8	2.3	21.2	56.1	22.4	75	80.0	49.3	22.7
Bray town	1,208	1,191	-1.4	1,252	85.9	0.0	0.2	12.2	1.6	27.4	57.2	15.3	458	80.1	54.8	10.5
Breckenridge town	245	256	4.5	280	76.8	0.0	0.0	23.2	0.0	32.9	54.6	12.5	105	78.1	46.7	27.6
Brent CDP	716	NA	NA	647	69.1	0.5	0.0	19.2	11.3	25.5	64.0	10.4	236	89.8	55.9	11.4
Bridge Creek town	327	332	1.5	227	84.6	0.0	0.0	2.6	12.8	26.4	64.4	9.3	80	86.3	43.8	17.5
Bridgeport city	116	114	-1.7	170	58.2	0.0	0.0	30.6	11.2	21.8	68.8	9.4	43	86.0	83.7	4.7
Briggs CDP	303	NA	NA	287	40.4	8.7	0.0	42.5	8.4	43.9	43.2	12.9	83	79.5	57.8	6.0
Bristow city	4,222	4,221	0.0	4,251	71.1	9.5	0.0	17.6	1.9	27.5	53.1	19.2	1,722	55.9	60.2	13.4
Broken Arrow city	98,832	104,726	6.0	101,917	74.0	4.0	3.2	11.8	6.9	26.7	61.9	11.3	36,731	77.1	27.3	34.5
Broken Bow city	4,120	4,132	0.3	4,141	60.9	3.9	0.0	26.4	8.8	30.2	54.1	15.6	1,519	43.7	49.4	14.8
Bromide town	167	168	0.6	184	72.8	0.0	0.0	7.1	20.1	21.2	61.4	17.4	74	93.2	63.5	10.8
Brooksville town	59	60	1.7	71	29.6	49.3	0.0	21.1	0.0	25.4	60.6	14.1	33	78.8	57.6	18.2
Brush Creek CDP	35	NA	NA	60	0.0	0.0	0.0	100.0	0.0	35.0	65.0	0.0	18	100.0	0.0	100.0
Brushy CDP	900	NA	NA	865	59.9	0.0	0.0	36.3	3.8	18.4	62.0	19.7	324	83.3	52.8	20.7
Buffalo town	1,294	1,332	2.9	1,397	71.3	0.1	0.2	0.3	28.1	25.9	54.4	19.6	596	73.8	68.6	10.7
Bull Hollow CDP	67	NA	NA	34	0.0	0.0	0.0	70.6	29.4	29.4	70.6	0.0	15	100.0	100.0	0.0
Burbank town	141	140	-0.7	146	72.6	0.0	0.0	27.4	0.0	23.3	64.4	12.3	57	75.4	73.7	7.0
Burlington town	152	158	3.9	213	88.7	0.0	0.0	11.3	0.0	38.0	44.7	17.4	69	71.0	55.1	17.4
Burns Flat town	2,057	2,031	-1.3	2,357	68.8	4.0	0.0	10.5	16.8	36.2	56.7	7.1	756	41.0	48.9	12.2
Bushyhead CDP	1,314	NA	NA	1,178	76.2	0.3	0.0	21.8	1.6	26.0	64.7	9.4	423	84.6	43.7	11.3
Butler town	287	303	5.6	301	87.4	0.0	0.0	9.0	3.7	22.7	55.5	21.9	125	87.2	68.8	8.8
Butler CDP	117	NA	NA	169	52.1	0.0	0.0	47.9	0.0	21.3	77.6	1.2	72	65.3	58.3	18.1
Byars town	255	261	2.4	179	69.8	0.0	0.0	23.5	6.7	18.4	52.5	29.1	79	77.2	70.9	13.9
Byng town	1,180	1,191	0.9	1,297	68.0	3.9	0.0	21.4	6.6	23.2	66.1	10.6	448	81.9	43.8	21.2
Byron town	35	36	2.9	37	100.0	0.0	0.0	0.0	0.0	0.0	45.9	54.1	20	95.0	60.0	15.0
Cache city	2,796	2,942	5.2	2,922	73.4	2.8	0.0	19.4	4.4	25.5	61.6	12.7	1,104	63.3	48.5	17.8
Caddo town	1,009	1,043	3.4	1,203	74.1	1.3	0.0	21.9	2.7	25.1	59.8	15.1	480	61.7	51.5	23.1
Calera town	2,164	2,235	3.3	2,686	66.5	2.3	0.4	27.9	2.9	30.1	57.8	12.4	943	55.9	43.8	15.7
Calumet town	507	553	9.1	687	86.3	2.6	0.0	7.7	3.3	29.7	58.1	12.2	229	80.3	35.4	26.2
Calvin town	294	287	-2.4	260	80.0	0.4	0.0	12.7	6.9	32.3	49.6	18.1	96	67.7	54.2	7.3
Camargo town	178	182	2.2	204	77.0	0.0	0.0	2.9	20.1	36.2	51.5	12.3	58	58.6	65.5	13.8
Cameron town	302	295	-2.3	291	88.3	0.0	0.0	11.0	0.7	26.1	65.1	8.9	91	71.4	60.4	14.3
Canadian town	220	211	-4.1	219	68.5	0.0	0.0	28.8	2.7	18.2	63.0	18.7	77	75.3	64.9	5.2
Caney town	205	198	-3.4	258	69.0	0.0	0.0	29.1	1.9	29.0	56.3	14.7	99	56.6	55.6	5.1
Canton town	625	622	-0.5	600	81.5	0.0	0.0	10.3	8.2	32.4	47.0	20.7	259	67.2	57.5	13.9
Canute town	541	539	-0.4	385	89.9	0.0	0.0	2.6	7.5	22.9	55.1	22.1	167	86.2	53.9	13.2
Capron town	23	NA	NA	3	100.0	0.0	0.0	0.0	0.0	0.0	33.3	66.7	3	100.0	100.0	0.0
Carlisle town	606	NA	NA	649	67.2	0.0	0.0	32.8	0.0	23.0	65.3	11.7	213	93.4	81.2	15.5
Carlton Landing town	0	0	0.0	0	0.0	0.0	0.0	0.0	0.0	0.0	0.0	0.0	0	0.0	0.0	0.0
Carmen town	355	362	2.0	501	86.8	1.2	0.0	7.2	4.8	31.2	48.4	20.6	209	76.1	48.8	23.0
Carnegie town	1,721	1,699	-1.3	2,021	48.8	0.9	0.0	30.8	19.5	29.6	58.1	12.3	710	60.7	51.7	12.7
Carney town	647	653	0.9	712	88.8	0.0	0.0	11.2	0.0	31.0	58.0	11.1	252	86.9	73.0	6.7
Carrier town	85	89	4.7	69	71.0	0.0	0.0	29.0	0.0	28.9	68.0	2.9	22	100.0	31.8	40.9
Carter town	256	266	3.9	275	70.2	0.0	0.0	6.2	23.6	41.1	53.9	5.1	91	59.3	67.0	11.0
Cartwright CDP	609	NA	NA	637	78.5	0.0	2.0	13.8	5.7	29.9	58.0	12.1	233	61.8	74.7	6.4
Cashion town	797	836	4.9	704	90.2	0.0	0.0	9.4	0.4	28.7	62.5	8.8	270	78.5	41.1	22.6
Castle town	106	106	0.0	124	54.0	4.8	0.0	41.1	0.0	29.8	61.3	8.9	38	76.3	65.8	0.0
Catoosa city	7,151	7,114	-0.5	7,407	64.6	1.2	2.0	22.0	10.2	27.4	61.6	11.0	2,684	64.8	43.1	19.4
Cayuga CDP	140	NA	NA	232	77.2	0.0	0.0	21.1	1.7	56.0	31.1	12.9	59	78.0	66.1	8.5
Cedar Crest CDP	312	NA	NA	240	51.3	0.0	0.0	45.8	2.9	11.3	71.7	17.1	95	92.6	68.4	0.0
Cedar Valley city	288	312	8.3	336	78.0	0.0	1.2	8.0	12.8	14.3	53.7	32.1	156	94.2	30.1	37.2
Cement town	501	494	-1.4	550	72.7	2.4	0.0	15.1	9.8	25.4	50.4	18.2	225	60.9	73.3	6.2
Centrahoma city	97	95	-2.1	84	77.4	0.0	0.0	19.0	3.6	25.0	68.0	7.1	36	94.4	61.1	5.6
Central High town	1,197	1,180	-1.4	1,173	83.1	0.0	0.2	15.1	1.6	23.7	58.0	18.4	451	81.2	38.6	23.3
Chandler city	3,101	3,139	1.2	3,113	81.8	6.8	0.0	10.3	1.1	22.2	59.4	18.6	1,295	61.0	50.0	10.5
Chattanooga town	461	457	-0.9	422	84.8	1.4	0.0	5.9	7.8	26.3	57.8	15.9	174	73.0	53.4	15.5
Checotah city	3,335	3,285	-1.5	3,343	67.9	8.6	0.0	19.1	4.4	24.5	56.6	19.1	1,178	62.0	61.5	8.0
Chelsea town	1,964	1,956	-0.4	1,892	61.6	0.2	0.5	32.9	4.8	22.8	61.7	15.5	777	56.0	58.2	3.7
Cherokee city	1,498	1,538	2.7	1,557	81.2	0.0	0.0	13.0	5.8	19.5	60.6	19.8	675	77.6	37.6	22.5
Cherry Tree CDP	883	NA	NA	970	17.5	0.0	3.0	66.1	13.4	30.3	58.9	10.8	287	86.1	66.9	7.7
Chester CDP	117	NA	NA	162	78.4	0.0	0.0	17.3	4.3	34.6	48.9	16.7	62	53.2	46.8	27.4
Chewey CDP	135	NA	NA	98	33.7	0.0	0.0	61.2	5.1	21.4	62.2	16.3	35	51.4	85.7	14.3

1 May be of any race.

Table A. All Places — **Population and Housing**

STATE City, town, township, borough, or CDP (county if applicable)	Population				Race and Hispanic or Latino origin (percent), 2010–2014					Age (percent), 2010–2014			Households, 2010–2014			
	2010 census total population	2014 estimated population	Percent change 2010–2014	ACS total population estimate 2010–2014	White alone, not Hispanic or Latino	Black alone, not Hispanic or Latino	Asian alone, not Hispanic or Latino	All other races or 2 or more races, not Hispanic or Latino	Hispanic or Latino[1]	Under 18 years old	Age 18 to 64 years old	Age 65 years and older	Total occupied housing units	Percent owner occupied	Householders by level of education (percent): High school diploma or less	Householders by level of education (percent): Bachelor's degree or more
	1	2	3	4	5	6	7	8	9	10	11	12	13	14	15	16
OKLAHOMA—Con.																
Cheyenne town	799	818	2.4	961	86.2	0.1	0.0	5.6	8.1	30.1	57.6	12.2	321	59.8	50.2	18.7
Chickasha city	16,038	16,334	1.8	16,195	77.3	4.7	0.5	9.8	7.6	22.6	61.7	15.8	6,392	59.6	46.9	21.4
Choctaw city	11,146	11,992	7.6	11,619	85.5	1.4	1.3	9.4	2.3	25.7	60.0	14.3	4,272	84.0	39.4	26.6
Chouteau town	2,113	2,085	-1.3	2,060	73.3	1.7	0.4	23.6	1.0	23.7	57.8	18.4	786	72.6	47.8	22.5
Christie CDP	218	NA	NA	192	28.1	0.0	0.0	71.9	0.0	18.2	43.3	38.5	73	100.0	71.2	0.0
Cimarron City town	150	162	8.0	176	90.3	2.3	1.1	6.3	0.0	19.4	61.9	18.8	67	95.5	35.8	38.8
Claremore city	18,581	18,971	2.1	18,849	67.3	2.0	0.2	24.9	5.5	22.9	59.4	17.7	7,769	55.0	40.2	19.1
Clayton town	823	790	-4.0	729	63.9	0.0	0.0	29.5	6.6	18.5	62.5	19.1	347	53.6	70.9	6.3
Clearview town	48	48	0.0	32	0.0	90.6	0.0	0.0	9.4	21.9	43.9	34.4	17	88.2	58.8	0.0
Cleora CDP	1,463	NA	NA	1,429	75.7	0.6	0.0	21.2	2.4	14.0	49.4	36.5	690	82.0	46.8	25.5
Cleo Springs town	338	349	3.3	354	94.6	0.0	0.0	5.4	0.0	29.6	47.9	22.3	144	84.7	70.1	6.9
Cleveland city	3,251	3,212	-1.2	3,238	83.6	0.3	1.0	14.1	1.1	26.1	56.2	17.8	1,224	56.5	58.4	13.0
Clinton city	9,033	9,505	5.2	9,281	54.9	3.5	2.0	9.0	30.5	27.7	56.6	15.7	3,223	58.4	59.7	19.1
Cloud Creek CDP	121	NA	NA	84	47.6	0.0	0.0	52.4	0.0	20.2	79.7	0.0	25	40.0	100.0	0.0
Coalgate city	1,968	1,920	-2.4	1,920	72.4	0.7	0.3	21.1	5.4	23.8	54.9	21.1	807	51.2	60.1	13.3
Colbert town	1,140	1,177	3.2	1,496	63.0	17.2	0.0	18.0	1.8	26.8	55.2	17.9	525	61.9	52.0	13.5
Colcord town	819	816	-0.4	924	57.3	0.3	2.2	36.4	3.9	30.4	63.1	6.5	333	61.9	65.8	14.1
Cole town	555	568	2.3	603	80.4	0.0	0.0	16.3	3.3	26.7	59.0	14.4	187	85.6	61.5	13.9
Collinsville city	5,642	6,334	12.3	5,970	76.5	2.9	0.2	16.9	3.4	29.3	57.5	13.2	2,200	67.2	35.7	26.7
Colony town	136	136	0.0	134	72.4	0.0	0.0	11.2	16.4	23.8	55.1	20.9	66	80.3	51.5	12.1
Comanche city	1,660	1,627	-2.0	1,655	82.5	1.1	0.0	14.1	2.3	24.9	59.4	15.8	696	61.4	57.6	11.6
Commerce city	2,471	2,492	0.8	2,520	56.0	0.4	0.2	21.8	21.7	27.8	54.6	17.6	918	67.1	64.4	7.5
Cooperton town	16	16	0.0	0	0.0	0.0	0.0	0.0	0.0	0.0	0.0	0.0	0	0.0	0.0	0.0
Copan town	733	741	1.1	769	80.6	0.0	0.0	17.7	1.7	23.1	55.3	21.8	314	84.4	63.7	7.0
Copeland CDP	1,629	NA	NA	1,288	82.9	0.0	0.0	16.8	0.2	15.7	62.8	21.7	599	81.8	44.9	11.2
Corn town	503	501	-0.4	504	90.3	0.0	0.0	1.2	8.5	19.3	41.5	39.5	178	75.3	44.9	26.4
Cornish town	163	158	-3.1	198	67.2	1.0	0.0	20.2	11.6	29.3	61.3	9.6	49	81.6	81.6	6.1
Council Hill town	158	156	-1.3	129	82.9	3.9	0.0	13.2	0.0	21.0	59.1	20.2	50	78.0	48.0	4.0
Covington town	527	550	4.4	499	95.2	0.0	0.0	0.6	4.2	30.0	54.6	15.2	198	73.2	46.0	17.7
Coweta city	9,379	9,511	1.4	9,483	76.0	3.7	0.2	15.1	4.9	28.0	60.6	11.3	3,319	71.8	46.4	18.4
Cowlington town	155	151	-2.6	172	95.9	0.0	0.0	4.1	0.0	19.2	70.9	9.9	66	84.8	63.6	13.6
Coyle town	325	352	8.3	310	63.5	24.8	0.0	4.2	7.4	22.3	73.0	4.8	154	57.8	46.8	39.0
Crescent city	1,411	1,508	6.9	1,384	86.7	3.5	0.4	5.6	3.8	22.8	51.0	26.2	578	66.6	48.6	15.7
Cromwell town	287	286	-0.3	307	61.6	0.0	0.3	34.9	3.3	26.7	58.0	15.3	106	75.5	58.5	11.3
Crowder town	430	413	-4.0	397	76.3	0.0	0.0	21.9	1.8	20.1	64.3	15.6	164	78.0	54.3	18.3
Cushing city	7,826	7,868	0.5	7,870	79.8	1.6	0.1	12.0	6.5	25.4	59.5	15.0	2,933	60.4	56.4	14.9
Custer City town	375	396	5.6	314	78.0	0.0	0.0	19.7	2.2	20.7	54.5	24.8	148	62.8	53.4	8.1
Cyril town	1,059	1,045	-1.3	1,080	77.8	0.0	0.0	22.2	0.0	26.6	52.6	20.7	398	69.8	51.8	16.1
Dacoma town	107	113	5.6	126	96.0	0.0	0.0	1.6	2.4	5.6	55.7	38.9	52	90.4	30.8	30.8
Dale CDP	181	NA	NA	151	58.3	0.0	0.0	41.7	0.0	35.0	45.6	19.2	61	52.5	49.2	42.6
Davenport town	814	813	-0.1	808	83.5	1.7	0.0	10.4	4.3	27.7	57.8	14.5	306	73.5	75.8	3.3
Davidson town	315	302	-4.1	374	66.0	2.9	0.3	3.7	27.0	31.8	52.8	15.2	157	73.2	79.6	5.7
Davis city	2,683	2,761	2.9	2,723	72.5	4.7	0.7	17.3	4.8	27.7	54.9	17.4	1,012	66.2	54.7	18.2
Deer Creek town	132	131	-0.8	145	95.9	0.0	0.0	4.1	0.0	32.5	46.1	21.4	59	91.5	57.6	15.3
Deer Lick CDP	46	NA	NA	22	100.0	0.0	0.0	0.0	0.0	0.0	59.1	40.9	9	100.0	0.0	0.0
Delaware town	417	417	0.0	285	76.1	0.0	0.0	23.9	0.0	17.6	62.5	20.0	130	79.2	71.5	2.3
Del City city	21,332	22,008	3.2	21,756	59.3	20.4	1.7	8.8	9.7	27.8	58.2	14.0	8,563	61.6	43.3	12.4
Dennis CDP	195	NA	NA	79	51.9	0.0	0.0	48.1	0.0	6.3	54.5	39.2	36	66.7	38.9	0.0
Depew town	476	483	1.5	484	72.1	5.2	0.0	15.9	6.8	33.1	50.7	16.1	179	65.4	64.2	14.0
Devol town	151	150	-0.7	154	94.2	0.0	0.0	5.8	0.0	29.8	54.9	14.9	62	71.0	61.3	6.5
Dewar town	900	871	-3.2	960	58.1	3.0	0.0	37.4	1.5	28.6	57.8	13.5	335	76.7	58.5	5.1
Dewey city	3,434	3,506	2.1	3,476	62.0	1.4	2.3	24.5	9.9	29.4	51.7	19.1	1,392	77.1	58.8	3.4
Dibble town	810	829	2.3	979	80.5	0.0	0.0	9.9	9.6	27.9	61.6	10.5	328	86.6	68.6	6.4
Dickson town	1,211	1,258	3.9	1,524	79.1	0.5	0.0	17.5	2.9	27.1	61.1	11.9	458	84.5	47.6	16.8
Dill City town	562	560	-0.4	607	83.2	0.0	0.2	5.9	10.7	32.5	55.1	12.5	210	91.9	65.2	8.6
Disney town	311	303	-2.6	168	72.6	0.0	0.0	26.8	0.6	9.5	58.3	32.1	95	78.9	41.1	10.5
Dodge CDP	115	NA	NA	101	61.4	0.0	0.0	38.6	0.0	18.8	81.1	0.0	50	86.0	58.0	42.0
Dotyville CDP	101	NA	NA	95	85.3	0.0	0.0	14.7	0.0	23.2	66.4	10.5	32	100.0	50.0	25.0
Dougherty town	215	219	1.9	256	71.1	3.9	0.0	22.3	2.7	27.8	55.5	16.8	86	75.6	70.9	7.0
Douglas town	32	33	3.1	18	72.2	0.0	5.6	22.2	0.0	33.4	66.8	0.0	6	83.3	33.3	16.7
Dover town	464	473	1.9	341	62.2	4.1	0.0	5.0	28.7	35.7	55.9	8.2	109	65.1	64.2	16.5
Dripping Springs CDP	50	NA	NA	21	47.6	0.0	0.0	52.4	0.0	52.4	28.6	19.0	8	100.0	62.5	37.5
Drowning Creek CDP	155	NA	NA	207	69.1	0.0	0.0	30.9	0.0	20.3	44.4	35.3	115	61.7	41.7	7.8
Drummond town	455	470	3.3	460	59.3	0.0	0.0	12.6	28.0	31.9	51.2	17.0	178	75.8	61.8	6.7
Drumright city	2,907	2,883	-0.8	2,926	81.4	0.5	0.0	16.6	1.5	27.0	57.9	15.1	1,079	64.2	57.9	11.4
Dry Creek CDP	227	NA	NA	256	73.4	0.0	0.0	26.6	0.0	13.7	43.0	43.4	126	98.4	49.2	7.9
Duchess Landing CDP	114	NA	NA	219	43.8	0.0	0.0	56.2	0.0	43.4	42.1	14.6	71	60.6	71.8	0.0
Duncan city	23,423	23,173	-1.1	23,364	77.8	3.8	0.9	7.7	9.7	24.1	57.9	17.9	9,536	63.5	48.9	20.6
Durant city	15,861	17,041	7.4	16,507	69.4	2.4	0.4	20.4	7.4	22.2	63.2	14.6	6,305	44.8	42.3	22.4
Dustin town	391	381	-2.6	339	51.9	0.0	0.0	44.0	4.1	18.3	58.3	23.3	134	83.6	62.7	3.0
Dwight Mission CDP	55	NA	NA	0	0.0	0.0	0.0	0.0	0.0	0.0	0.0	0.0	0	0.0	0.0	0.0
Eagletown CDP	528	NA	NA	664	75.0	5.0	0.0	18.5	1.5	31.2	57.5	11.3	242	80.2	72.7	4.1
Eakly town	338	334	-1.2	344	55.2	0.9	0.0	9.9	34.0	31.7	50.8	17.4	117	72.6	66.7	12.8
Earlsboro town	628	640	1.9	574	73.9	4.7	1.6	17.1	2.8	29.4	51.3	19.3	188	84.0	56.9	7.4
East Duke town	424	412	-2.8	332	81.0	0.0	0.0	6.0	13.0	25.6	47.1	27.1	153	71.9	43.1	22.9
Edmond city	81,399	88,605	8.9	85,084	78.6	5.9	3.5	7.0	5.0	24.8	63.3	12.1	31,792	69.6	16.9	53.4
Eldon CDP	368	NA	NA	268	37.7	0.0	10.1	50.0	2.2	15.3	76.2	8.6	111	82.9	36.9	40.5
Eldorado town	446	435	-2.5	466	77.7	4.7	0.0	7.9	9.7	27.4	51.4	21.2	234	67.9	50.0	17.5
Elgin city	2,151	2,901	34.9	2,560	70.2	3.9	2.0	15.7	8.2	28.2	60.6	11.1	932	72.5	33.8	27.1
Elk City city	11,706	12,680	8.3	12,198	79.7	1.5	0.1	6.0	12.7	27.6	60.5	11.8	4,308	61.0	49.0	19.8
Elmer town	96	94	-2.1	111	91.0	2.7	0.0	2.7	3.6	29.7	55.8	14.4	46	89.1	28.3	8.7
Elm Grove CDP	198	NA	NA	194	57.2	0.0	0.0	42.8	0.0	14.9	84.9	0.0	73	89.0	38.4	24.7
Elmore City town	701	702	0.1	730	76.0	1.5	0.4	11.2	10.8	25.6	58.6	15.8	282	68.4	61.0	8.2
El Reno city	16,749	18,153	8.4	17,515	63.9	7.1	0.9	14.3	13.9	24.3	62.5	13.1	5,632	65.4	48.8	14.1
Empire City town	935	922	-1.4	833	85.0	1.2	0.1	5.8	7.9	24.2	57.7	18.0	310	88.7	43.9	15.2
Enid city	49,379	51,386	4.1	50,232	76.4	3.8	0.9	7.4	11.5	25.0	59.9	15.1	19,445	61.9	45.4	22.5
Erick city	1,052	1,091	3.7	921	92.0	0.0	0.1	4.5	3.5	26.5	53.7	19.8	321	58.9	70.1	10.3
Erin Springs town	87	NA	NA	167	100.0	0.0	0.0	0.0	0.0	7.2	86.9	6.0	72	100.0	41.7	6.9
Etowah town	92	92	0.0	96	83.3	0.0	0.0	16.7	0.0	15.7	67.8	16.7	36	69.4	33.3	19.4
Eufaula city	2,812	2,909	3.4	2,881	53.5	4.8	0.5	38.3	2.9	21.7	53.1	25.3	1,148	58.8	48.9	9.4
Evening Shade CDP	359	NA	NA	233	72.5	0.0	0.0	9.4	18.0	12.0	55.5	32.6	141	93.6	64.5	22.0

1 May be of any race.

Table A. All Places — **Population and Housing**

STATE City, town, township, borough, or CDP (county if applicable)	Population				Race and Hispanic or Latino origin (percent), 2010–2014					Age (percent), 2010–2014			Households, 2010–2014			
	2010 census total population	2014 estimated population	Percent change 2010–2014	ACS total population estimate 2010–2014	White alone, not Hispanic or Latino	Black alone, not Hispanic or Latino	Asian alone, not Hispanic or Latino	All other races or 2 or more races, not Hispanic or Latino	Hispanic or Latino[1]	Under 18 years old	Age 18 to 64 years old	Age 65 years and older	Total occupied housing units	Percent owner occupied	Householders by level of education (percent): High school diploma or less	Householders by level of education (percent): Bachelor's degree or more
	1	2	3	4	5	6	7	8	9	10	11	12	13	14	15	16
OKLAHOMA—Con.																
Fairfax town	1,380	1,361	-1.4	1,639	60.4	2.9	0.0	36.1	0.5	29.3	50.3	20.4	626	79.1	63.9	8.3
Fairfield CDP	584	NA	NA	490	32.7	0.0	0.0	61.8	5.5	33.0	54.4	12.7	170	80.6	57.1	15.3
Fairland town	1,057	1,066	0.9	1,028	69.2	1.5	0.1	28.8	0.5	26.9	55.2	17.8	397	59.2	45.8	12.8
Fairmont town	134	140	4.5	160	98.8	1.3	0.0	0.0	0.0	13.1	66.3	20.6	76	100.0	53.9	27.6
Fair Oaks town	91	91	0.0	49	75.5	0.0	0.0	22.4	2.0	12.3	81.6	6.1	30	83.3	43.3	16.7
Fairview city	2,579	2,646	2.6	2,613	89.9	1.2	0.0	4.9	4.0	23.2	58.7	18.2	1,134	65.2	45.0	14.2
Fallis town	27	27	0.0	33	100.0	0.0	0.0	0.0	0.0	24.2	63.6	12.1	15	100.0	46.7	33.3
Fanshawe town	419	409	-2.4	410	64.6	0.0	12.2	20.7	2.4	27.3	58.5	14.1	133	77.4	57.1	12.0
Fargo town	366	367	0.3	354	89.3	0.0	0.0	1.4	9.3	28.3	56.0	15.8	140	65.7	58.6	12.1
Faxon town	136	135	-0.7	73	94.5	0.0	0.0	2.7	2.7	13.7	56.1	30.1	32	90.6	75.0	12.5
Felt CDP	93	NA	NA	88	56.8	0.0	0.0	9.1	34.1	34.1	35.1	30.7	32	68.8	34.4	31.3
Fitzhugh town	230	232	0.9	273	78.4	0.0	0.0	20.9	0.7	28.3	59.8	12.1	96	81.3	33.3	22.9
Fletcher town	1,177	1,174	-0.3	1,059	87.2	0.6	0.4	9.1	2.8	29.7	58.7	11.6	362	74.3	44.8	22.9
Flint Creek CDP	732	NA	NA	703	72.3	0.0	0.0	17.1	10.7	13.1	69.3	17.6	249	95.6	60.2	12.9
Flute Springs CDP	130	NA	NA	51	25.5	0.0	0.0	74.5	0.0	27.5	54.9	17.6	20	80.0	90.0	0.0
Foraker town	19	19	0.0	6	66.7	0.0	0.0	0.0	33.3	0.0	66.7	33.3	5	60.0	100.0	0.0
Forest Park town	998	1,059	6.1	1,179	14.8	72.3	2.0	9.2	1.8	13.3	57.1	29.6	475	95.8	24.0	37.9
Forgan town	547	534	-2.4	484	65.1	0.0	0.0	2.5	32.4	34.6	52.7	12.8	169	78.7	58.0	13.6
Fort Cobb town	644	629	-2.3	638	79.2	0.5	0.0	17.2	3.1	28.1	51.3	20.5	251	69.3	48.6	20.3
Fort Coffee town	426	416	-2.3	485	14.6	64.3	0.0	18.6	2.5	24.2	50.0	25.8	226	81.4	55.8	15.9
Fort Gibson town	4,154	4,104	-1.2	4,129	60.5	4.0	0.5	28.5	6.5	22.6	60.5	16.8	1,677	73.2	47.8	22.5
Fort Supply town	330	352	6.7	519	85.0	0.4	0.0	3.3	11.4	38.7	48.0	13.3	167	80.2	65.3	10.2
Fort Towson town	506	505	-0.2	669	80.6	3.0	0.0	13.6	2.8	21.5	52.8	25.7	271	70.8	64.6	11.8
Foss town	151	150	-0.7	194	80.4	0.0	0.0	9.8	9.8	23.7	59.6	16.5	79	82.3	58.2	15.2
Foster town	161	161	0.0	120	90.8	0.0	0.0	9.2	0.0	10.0	64.2	25.8	49	85.7	46.9	38.8
Foyil town	344	344	0.0	285	68.1	6.7	1.1	23.5	0.7	34.0	55.2	10.9	101	70.3	56.4	12.9
Francis town	315	318	1.0	300	75.0	0.0	0.0	16.0	9.0	28.0	62.3	9.7	99	67.7	66.7	13.1
Frederick city	3,940	3,748	-4.9	3,837	56.0	5.3	0.2	4.2	34.3	25.0	58.6	16.3	1,483	71.5	70.1	14.4
Freedom town	289	306	5.9	275	86.9	0.0	0.7	2.2	10.2	26.2	59.8	14.2	106	74.5	39.6	14.2
Friendship town	24	23	-4.2	26	65.4	0.0	34.6	0.0	0.0	3.8	73.1	23.1	18	61.1	22.2	22.2
Gage town	442	436	-1.4	445	88.5	0.0	0.2	4.7	6.5	23.6	51.4	24.9	197	84.3	44.2	20.8
Gans town	316	305	-3.5	337	59.9	2.1	0.0	34.7	3.3	26.5	63.5	10.1	121	61.2	69.4	5.0
Garber city	822	849	3.3	720	90.6	0.0	0.0	8.9	0.6	25.4	60.3	14.3	301	69.1	38.9	15.9
Garvin town	253	251	-0.8	197	75.1	0.0	0.0	21.8	3.0	31.5	51.4	17.3	76	84.2	75.0	5.3
Gate town	93	91	-2.2	91	62.6	0.0	0.0	0.0	37.4	30.8	63.8	5.5	35	74.3	65.7	11.4
Geary city	1,280	1,309	2.3	1,197	53.1	4.3	0.0	32.0	10.5	24.7	58.9	16.5	534	57.3	60.9	12.9
Gene Autry town	158	159	0.6	169	85.2	3.6	0.0	10.1	1.2	15.5	68.0	16.6	53	92.5	84.9	3.8
Geronimo town	1,264	1,242	-1.7	989	64.1	2.4	0.0	33.2	0.3	26.9	57.9	15.3	352	76.1	44.3	19.6
Gerty town	118	115	-2.5	84	83.3	0.0	0.0	13.1	3.6	25.0	60.8	14.3	30	93.3	63.3	6.7
Gideon CDP	49	NA	NA	17	0.0	29.4	0.0	70.6	0.0	23.5	76.4	0.0	3	0.0	100.0	0.0
Glencoe town	601	605	0.7	519	82.3	0.0	0.0	17.1	0.6	36.4	47.1	16.6	173	76.9	54.9	10.4
Glenpool city	10,791	11,855	9.9	11,398	73.8	1.7	0.7	18.8	5.1	28.8	62.1	9.2	3,845	74.9	29.8	22.2
Goldsby town	1,804	2,007	11.3	2,246	73.6	0.1	1.0	15.0	10.3	26.2	58.5	15.4	775	90.2	34.5	27.1
Goltry town	249	259	4.0	163	84.0	0.6	0.0	15.3	0.0	13.5	49.7	36.8	85	82.4	56.5	14.1
Goodwell town	1,293	1,341	3.7	1,498	67.6	11.1	0.8	7.6	12.8	22.3	73.2	4.4	371	39.6	18.3	46.9
Gore town	976	951	-2.6	1,026	65.0	5.0	0.4	24.3	5.4	22.5	61.3	16.4	388	59.8	42.3	22.7
Gotebo town	226	225	-0.4	171	96.5	0.0	0.0	2.3	1.2	11.1	55.5	33.3	102	86.3	39.2	14.7
Gould town	141	135	-4.3	181	70.2	0.0	0.0	0.0	29.8	20.5	69.2	10.5	77	70.1	41.6	28.6
Gracemont town	318	314	-1.3	222	62.2	0.0	0.0	27.0	10.8	26.7	54.8	18.9	95	63.2	64.2	7.4
Grainola town	31	31	0.0	27	70.4	0.0	0.0	29.6	0.0	11.1	55.5	33.3	13	100.0	30.8	15.4
Grandfield city	1,038	988	-4.8	1,018	54.8	21.1	0.0	4.4	19.6	30.6	48.3	21.2	415	68.2	56.9	15.4
Grand Lake Towne town	74	73	-1.4	151	73.5	0.0	0.0	23.2	3.3	11.8	69.4	18.5	67	97.0	25.4	47.8
Grandview CDP	394	NA	NA	323	53.6	0.0	0.0	46.4	0.0	8.7	87.9	3.4	107	76.6	43.0	29.0
Granite town	2,065	2,048	-0.8	1,911	69.3	17.2	0.2	7.6	5.7	13.2	75.0	11.8	442	66.5	49.5	16.1
Grant CDP	289	NA	NA	226	59.7	12.4	0.9	19.0	8.0	19.9	61.5	18.6	103	86.4	72.8	2.9
Grayson town	159	155	-2.5	154	1.3	40.9	0.0	41.6	16.2	33.8	47.2	18.8	65	83.1	53.8	21.5
Greasy CDP	372	NA	NA	300	49.3	0.7	0.0	49.3	0.7	27.3	49.4	23.3	115	75.7	66.1	13.9
Greenfield town	93	94	1.1	97	93.8	0.0	0.0	6.2	0.0	21.7	51.5	26.8	45	64.4	73.3	11.1
Gregory CDP	171	NA	NA	138	42.0	0.0	0.0	6.5	51.4	26.8	73.2	0.0	42	100.0	61.9	16.7
Grove city	6,625	6,717	1.4	6,658	81.8	0.0	2.5	14.5	1.2	18.2	49.9	32.0	3,166	69.3	37.3	27.0
Guthrie city	10,191	11,096	8.9	10,668	70.3	17.0	0.2	9.5	3.0	24.1	60.2	15.7	3,837	54.0	39.0	24.1
Guymon city	11,446	12,128	6.0	11,921	38.9	1.4	2.1	2.1	55.6	28.2	63.0	9.0	4,018	57.4	57.5	19.1
Haileyville city	813	781	-3.9	698	67.6	3.9	0.0	24.1	4.4	24.6	60.5	14.8	326	66.9	55.5	10.1
Hallett town	125	124	-0.8	111	89.2	0.0	0.0	9.0	1.8	26.1	63.9	9.9	41	75.6	68.3	0.0
Hammon town	568	588	3.5	534	61.2	0.2	0.2	26.2	12.2	28.1	59.9	12.0	131	66.4	43.5	16.0
Hanna town	138	136	-1.4	135	43.0	0.0	0.0	57.0	0.0	35.5	51.7	12.6	45	73.3	88.9	0.0
Hardesty town	212	226	6.6	243	49.8	0.0	0.0	0.0	50.2	31.7	63.0	5.3	77	72.7	71.4	7.8
Harrah city	5,095	5,724	12.3	5,412	79.2	2.2	1.1	12.3	5.1	29.9	52.1	18.1	2,043	73.7	40.4	20.4
Hartshorne city	2,125	2,027	-4.6	1,969	66.0	1.4	0.0	28.4	4.2	24.3	60.3	15.5	835	69.9	50.1	13.5
Haskell town	2,005	1,993	-0.6	1,760	73.5	6.6	0.0	18.7	1.1	23.3	59.4	17.3	686	66.9	64.3	13.8
Hastings town	143	139	-2.8	61	93.4	0.0	0.0	6.6	0.0	0.0	49.2	50.8	35	100.0	85.7	0.0
Haworth town	297	295	-0.7	261	76.6	0.0	0.0	10.0	13.4	23.8	60.1	16.1	107	56.1	72.0	8.4
Headrick town	94	92	-2.1	147	66.0	0.0	0.0	1.4	32.7	43.5	41.5	15.0	53	73.6	37.7	20.8
Healdton city	2,788	2,792	0.1	2,779	89.7	0.0	0.0	8.6	1.7	24.1	56.3	19.5	1,059	75.6	63.1	16.4
Heavener city	3,414	3,368	-1.3	3,397	53.8	0.1	0.5	11.4	34.1	29.7	59.8	10.4	1,103	56.3	64.2	8.1
Helena town	1,403	1,419	1.1	1,458	54.4	8.5	0.1	26.5	10.5	8.3	79.1	12.5	214	58.9	49.5	20.6
Hendrix town	79	82	3.8	67	46.3	20.9	0.0	32.8	0.0	23.9	53.8	22.4	27	59.3	74.1	11.1
Hennessey town	2,131	2,194	3.0	2,508	68.3	0.0	0.0	0.4	31.3	32.2	55.2	12.5	847	66.8	58.1	13.2
Henryetta city	5,927	5,759	-2.8	5,848	71.2	0.9	1.1	23.4	3.4	25.3	54.2	20.5	2,139	65.3	55.5	10.2
Hickory town	71	72	1.4	64	60.9	0.0	0.0	23.4	15.6	25.0	56.3	18.8	23	65.2	56.5	17.4
Hillsdale town	121	126	4.1	138	97.8	0.0	0.0	2.2	0.0	24.6	67.2	8.0	54	88.9	33.3	25.9
Hinton town	3,198	3,220	0.7	3,199	53.8	9.3	0.6	15.0	21.4	18.7	71.2	10.1	767	70.4	53.3	11.7
Hitchcock town	121	122	0.8	103	92.2	0.0	0.0	1.0	6.8	30.1	59.0	10.7	48	100.0	81.3	6.3
Hitchita town	88	87	-1.1	125	72.8	0.0	0.0	27.2	0.0	16.0	68.8	15.2	38	65.8	81.6	10.5
Hobart city	3,756	3,700	-1.5	3,729	71.8	6.7	0.3	8.8	12.4	26.6	57.3	16.2	1,529	56.4	48.8	17.1
Hoffman town	127	124	-2.4	140	56.4	7.9	0.0	25.7	10.0	21.5	75.7	2.9	49	57.1	67.3	8.2
Holdenville city	5,771	5,780	0.2	5,768	60.0	11.6	0.0	21.2	7.2	20.4	65.8	13.9	1,658	69.4	58.7	10.7
Hollis city	2,060	1,974	-4.2	2,110	56.2	8.7	1.3	4.4	29.4	25.7	56.3	18.1	863	64.2	53.8	16.2
Hollister town	50	48	-4.0	33	87.9	0.0	3.0	0.0	9.1	30.3	54.6	15.2	13	100.0	61.5	0.0
Hominy city	3,567	3,532	-1.0	3,548	49.1	12.5	0.2	33.5	4.8	18.2	69.8	12.1	942	65.0	62.6	12.4
Hooker city	1,919	2,030	5.8	2,082	59.0	0.0	1.5	2.1	37.4	29.9	59.2	10.9	709	83.5	52.8	19.6

1 May be of any race.

Table A. All Places — **Population and Housing**

STATE City, town, township, borough, or CDP (county if applicable)	2010 census total population	2014 estimated population	Percent change 2010–2014	ACS total population estimate 2010–2014	White alone, not Hispanic or Latino	Black alone, not Hispanic or Latino	Asian alone, not Hispanic or Latino	All other races or 2 or more races, not Hispanic or Latino	Hispanic or Latino[1]	Under 18 years old	Age 18 to 64 years old	Age 65 years and older	Total occupied housing units	Percent owner occupied	High school diploma or less	Bachelor's degree or more
	1	2	3	4	5	6	7	8	9	10	11	12	13	14	15	16
OKLAHOMA—Con.																
Hoot Owl town	4	4	0.0	0	0.0	0.0	0.0	0.0	0.0	0.0	0.0	0.0	0	0.0	0.0	0.0
Horntown town	97	95	-2.1	107	69.2	0.0	0.0	29.9	0.9	30.8	49.6	19.6	37	89.2	56.8	16.2
Howe town	812	795	-2.1	758	78.9	0.5	0.3	16.1	4.2	20.2	63.5	16.4	289	64.4	54.0	6.2
Hugo city	5,311	5,287	-0.5	5,294	53.9	23.9	0.2	18.2	3.8	26.9	53.9	19.1	2,125	49.6	66.8	12.1
Hulbert town	590	601	1.9	624	32.2	0.6	0.0	65.1	2.1	33.6	56.2	10.3	206	49.0	53.4	16.0
Hunter town	165	172	4.2	155	87.7	0.0	0.0	11.0	1.3	24.5	56.8	18.7	59	89.8	88.1	5.1
Hydro town	969	962	-0.7	1,029	86.2	0.3	0.0	7.4	6.1	26.4	55.3	18.3	386	69.7	55.4	21.2
Idabel city	7,009	7,010	0.0	7,015	51.0	22.9	0.0	18.7	7.4	27.4	58.0	14.7	2,854	46.4	48.4	22.6
Indiahoma town	344	343	-0.3	329	66.6	0.9	0.0	22.2	10.3	21.0	71.4	7.6	126	79.4	50.0	10.3
Indianola CDP	48	NA	NA	0	0.0	0.0	0.0	0.0	0.0	0.0	0.0	0.0	0	0.0	0.0	0.0
Indianola town	162	156	-3.7	198	83.8	0.0	0.0	14.1	2.0	34.8	50.0	15.2	61	77.0	68.9	8.2
Inola town	1,787	1,824	2.1	1,838	69.7	0.9	0.2	26.2	3.1	25.2	58.4	16.5	688	73.8	45.9	11.9
Iron Post CDP	92	NA	NA	69	92.8	0.0	0.0	7.2	0.0	0.0	99.9	0.0	27	100.0	100.0	0.0
Isabella CDP	136	NA	NA	186	41.9	0.0	0.0	0.0	58.1	43.1	51.1	5.9	51	39.2	100.0	0.0
IXL town	51	51	0.0	38	15.8	68.4	0.0	15.8	0.0	2.6	52.6	44.7	24	70.8	83.3	12.5
Jay city	2,498	2,472	-1.0	2,481	44.8	0.0	0.4	48.5	6.3	26.8	59.9	13.4	887	59.6	65.1	12.1
Jefferson town	12	12	0.0	24	91.7	0.0	0.0	8.3	0.0	0.0	75.1	25.0	12	100.0	91.7	0.0
Jenks city	16,928	19,951	17.9	18,312	79.7	3.0	3.1	9.3	4.9	31.0	59.7	9.2	6,246	81.1	17.7	48.7
Jennings town	360	357	-0.8	304	81.9	0.0	0.0	17.1	1.0	21.4	60.4	18.1	127	71.7	79.5	3.1
Jet town	213	221	3.8	160	90.6	0.0	0.0	9.4	0.0	18.2	48.3	33.8	81	87.7	38.3	25.9
Johnson town	247	252	2.0	251	64.5	2.8	0.0	27.1	5.6	19.2	60.3	20.7	90	87.8	42.2	24.4
Jones town	2,691	2,873	6.8	2,773	79.9	3.1	0.0	12.5	4.5	26.6	60.5	13.1	991	76.6	56.2	12.5
Justice CDP	1,324	NA	NA	1,183	78.1	0.0	0.0	21.9	0.0	23.0	58.4	18.8	436	86.7	34.6	24.1
Kansas town	787	784	-0.4	857	32.4	0.7	2.2	59.3	5.4	28.6	57.7	13.7	252	61.5	63.5	11.9
Katie town	349	349	0.0	251	88.4	1.2	0.0	7.2	3.2	20.4	56.8	23.1	105	81.0	61.0	15.2
Kaw City city	376	380	1.1	277	76.9	0.0	0.0	20.2	2.9	17.3	46.4	36.1	139	86.3	53.2	5.0
Kellyville town	1,144	1,145	0.1	1,429	67.6	0.0	0.2	30.1	2.1	34.0	55.5	10.4	441	70.7	50.3	6.3
Kemp town	133	137	3.0	154	72.1	1.3	0.0	26.6	0.0	20.8	60.3	18.8	76	80.3	61.8	14.5
Kendrick town	139	140	0.7	125	76.8	1.6	0.0	21.6	0.0	39.2	39.2	21.6	41	85.4	73.2	0.0
Kenefic town	196	203	3.6	214	72.9	0.0	0.0	21.0	6.1	35.5	57.7	6.5	61	72.1	60.7	4.9
Kenton CDP	17	NA	NA	69	79.7	0.0	0.0	0.0	20.3	14.5	39.0	46.4	25	76.0	56.0	0.0
Kenwood CDP	1,224	NA	NA	1,003	27.7	0.0	0.4	70.4	1.5	22.2	70.2	7.9	366	84.2	63.4	10.9
Keota town	564	568	0.7	602	78.7	0.0	0.0	19.4	1.8	34.4	54.4	11.3	201	53.2	75.6	5.0
Ketchum town	443	431	-2.7	464	63.4	0.2	0.2	30.6	5.6	30.6	54.5	14.9	170	68.8	48.2	13.5
Keyes town	324	298	-8.0	260	85.4	0.0	0.0	3.1	11.5	18.5	60.0	21.5	119	84.0	58.8	10.9
Keys CDP	565	NA	NA	707	65.8	0.0	0.0	30.8	3.4	31.3	59.2	9.6	266	62.0	25.9	20.3
Kiefer town	1,685	1,896	12.5	2,005	72.8	0.6	0.1	18.9	7.6	27.4	61.9	10.5	703	80.5	45.2	18.6
Kildare town	100	98	-2.0	71	78.9	0.0	0.0	21.1	0.0	12.7	67.6	19.7	31	100.0	48.4	12.9
Kingfisher city	4,633	4,828	4.2	4,707	81.2	0.6	0.0	10.5	7.7	26.8	54.8	18.5	1,901	72.4	44.7	22.4
Kingston town	1,601	1,627	1.6	1,658	73.1	0.0	0.0	21.4	5.5	21.9	55.7	22.4	665	61.7	52.3	10.4
Kinta town	297	299	0.7	257	75.5	0.0	0.0	23.3	1.2	34.6	49.0	16.3	97	62.9	44.3	14.4
Kiowa town	731	699	-4.4	536	78.2	0.0	0.0	20.0	1.9	21.3	54.2	24.4	227	85.5	64.3	9.7
Knowles town	11	11	0.0	26	57.7	0.0	0.0	0.0	42.3	0.0	84.6	15.4	15	46.7	26.7	20.0
Konawa city	1,298	1,285	-1.0	1,398	63.6	0.4	0.9	33.7	1.4	18.8	63.6	17.7	501	57.1	54.7	14.2
Krebs city	2,053	1,981	-3.5	2,384	69.5	1.4	0.8	24.8	3.5	25.8	60.4	13.8	979	58.9	40.2	13.9
Kremlin town	255	266	4.3	264	92.4	0.0	0.0	3.8	3.8	27.7	58.2	14.0	101	79.2	32.7	20.8
Lahoma town	611	647	5.9	665	70.7	0.3	0.3	25.1	3.6	42.1	46.6	11.4	215	82.8	46.5	18.6
Lake Aluma town	88	91	3.4	91	94.5	0.0	0.0	5.5	0.0	13.2	56.1	30.8	39	97.4	12.8	74.4
Lamar town	158	154	-2.5	181	81.2	0.0	0.0	18.8	0.0	24.4	64.8	11.0	63	88.9	68.3	7.9
Lambert town	6	6	0.0	6	33.3	0.0	0.0	66.7	0.0	0.0	66.7	33.3	5	20.0	0.0	0.0
Lamont town	417	412	-1.2	318	92.8	0.0	0.0	7.2	0.0	31.4	48.4	20.1	123	73.2	42.3	17.9
Lane CDP	414	NA	NA	340	80.0	0.0	0.0	15.6	4.4	23.2	53.1	23.5	149	82.6	61.7	17.4
Langley town	829	820	-1.1	759	65.5	0.5	0.0	31.9	2.1	22.2	52.5	25.2	320	72.5	52.2	12.2
Langston town	1,748	1,811	3.6	1,457	1.6	92.7	0.7	4.6	0.3	8.6	84.7	6.8	223	40.8	13.9	44.4
Laverne town	1,344	1,388	3.3	1,206	70.1	0.0	0.2	3.3	26.4	30.6	59.9	9.4	436	74.8	46.3	17.0
Lawrence Creek town	149	149	0.0	220	88.6	0.0	0.0	10.9	0.5	34.1	64.1	1.8	55	89.1	34.5	7.3
Lawton city	96,867	97,017	0.2	97,788	52.7	19.8	2.3	11.2	14.0	24.8	65.3	9.9	34,320	49.2	38.6	21.8
Leach CDP	237	NA	NA	231	39.8	0.0	0.0	58.9	1.3	23.9	60.4	16.0	87	78.2	43.7	21.8
Lebanon CDP	303	NA	NA	208	72.6	0.0	0.0	27.4	0.0	23.6	33.7	42.8	87	66.7	49.4	10.3
Leedey town	435	446	2.5	438	75.3	0.0	0.2	16.4	8.0	32.8	44.7	22.4	163	66.3	54.0	23.9
Le Flore town	181	177	-2.2	197	67.0	0.0	0.0	33.0	0.0	25.5	58.8	15.7	76	78.9	52.6	21.1
Lehigh city	356	350	-1.7	357	69.5	1.1	0.0	26.3	3.1	35.8	56.7	7.6	115	86.1	81.7	2.6
Lenapah town	293	293	0.0	240	69.6	0.4	0.0	30.0	0.0	33.3	58.8	7.9	78	67.9	57.7	3.8
Leon town	91	95	4.4	114	90.4	0.0	0.0	7.0	2.6	14.9	57.1	28.1	47	55.3	78.7	8.5
Lexington city	2,152	2,165	0.6	2,339	75.7	1.4	0.0	11.4	11.5	27.4	55.1	17.6	794	65.6	69.4	7.9
Liberty CDP	0	NA	NA	274	63.9	0.0	0.0	31.0	5.1	17.2	60.0	23.0	98	100.0	58.2	8.2
Liberty town	219	218	-0.5	189	84.7	0.0	0.0	15.3	0.0	22.1	58.2	19.6	72	75.0	61.1	23.6
Lima town	53	53	0.0	78	24.4	44.9	0.0	16.7	14.1	20.5	62.8	16.7	29	89.7	69.0	10.3
Limestone CDP	629	NA	NA	697	82.9	0.0	0.0	14.6	2.4	12.4	61.1	26.7	277	89.9	42.2	19.9
Lindsay city	2,840	2,821	-0.7	2,822	85.2	0.0	0.0	9.2	5.6	24.0	57.2	18.7	1,225	67.8	58.1	13.5
Loco town	122	120	-1.6	130	95.4	0.0	0.0	4.6	0.0	14.6	66.9	18.5	53	98.1	79.2	7.5
Locust Grove town	1,420	1,404	-1.1	1,307	60.3	0.0	0.5	34.9	4.3	26.1	56.3	17.5	559	66.4	69.8	8.1
Lone Grove city	5,054	5,211	3.1	5,142	77.4	3.0	1.2	14.0	4.3	28.4	60.1	11.6	1,815	72.8	59.3	13.6
Lone Wolf town	438	429	-2.1	405	81.5	4.0	0.0	8.4	6.2	18.6	56.7	24.9	192	63.5	45.3	22.9
Long CDP	370	NA	NA	335	53.7	0.0	0.0	46.3	0.0	32.3	61.1	6.9	144	89.6	68.1	4.2
Longdale town	262	264	0.8	302	81.1	0.0	0.0	18.9	0.0	28.7	55.0	16.2	131	67.2	87.0	0.0
Longtown CDP	2,739	NA	NA	3,100	86.3	2.0	0.0	10.5	1.2	13.4	53.2	33.3	1,415	89.8	51.4	12.5
Lookeba town	166	164	-1.2	146	50.7	0.0	0.0	8.9	40.4	36.9	49.3	13.7	50	92.0	78.0	10.0
Lost City CDP	770	NA	NA	821	34.0	1.2	0.0	64.3	0.5	25.8	63.0	11.1	244	93.0	54.9	14.3
Lotsee town	2	2	0.0	3	66.7	0.0	0.0	33.3	0.0	0.0	100.0	0.0	1	100.0	0.0	100.0
Loveland town	13	13	0.0	7	100.0	0.0	0.0	0.0	0.0	0.0	42.9	57.1	2	100.0	100.0	0.0
Loyal town	79	81	2.5	92	76.1	0.0	0.0	23.9	0.0	21.7	64.0	14.1	34	85.3	58.8	14.7
Lucien CDP	88	NA	NA	100	100.0	0.0	0.0	0.0	0.0	48.0	52.0	0.0	28	100.0	7.1	67.9
Luther town	1,221	1,464	19.9	1,170	70.5	2.6	0.2	13.8	12.9	28.6	62.3	9.1	435	73.6	47.8	32.6
Lyons Switch CDP	288	NA	NA	329	44.1	0.0	0.0	43.2	12.8	25.5	60.8	13.7	122	70.5	60.7	16.4
McAlester city	18,383	18,247	-0.7	18,354	65.6	7.2	0.9	20.0	6.3	23.4	61.5	15.1	7,102	61.1	46.1	18.5
McCord CDP	1,440	NA	NA	1,594	86.8	0.2	1.5	10.3	1.2	17.8	55.4	26.8	684	93.1	49.7	14.5
McCurtain town	516	520	0.8	450	64.7	0.0	0.0	33.8	1.6	31.3	54.8	14.0	156	65.4	62.8	7.1
McLoud city	4,501	4,597	2.1	4,557	64.3	4.2	0.8	22.7	8.0	19.4	66.5	13.9	1,170	70.1	47.8	13.4
Macomb town	32	33	3.1	32	84.4	0.0	0.0	15.6	0.0	37.6	56.3	6.3	10	60.0	90.0	10.0
Madill city	3,758	3,905	3.9	3,810	52.3	5.1	0.0	8.6	34.0	24.2	60.1	15.7	1,385	71.3	56.6	13.0

1 May be of any race.

Table A. All Places — **Population and Housing**

STATE City, town, township, borough, or CDP (county if applicable)	Population: 2010 census total population	Population: 2014 estimated population	Population: Percent change 2010–2014	Population: ACS total population estimate 2010–2014	Race and Hispanic or Latino origin (percent), 2010–2014: White alone, not Hispanic or Latino	Black alone, not Hispanic or Latino	Asian alone, not Hispanic or Latino	All other races or 2 or more races, not Hispanic or Latino	Hispanic or Latino[1]	Age (percent), 2010–2014: Under 18 years old	Age 18 to 64 years old	Age 65 years and older	Households, 2010–2014: Total occupied housing units	Percent owner occupied	Householders by level of education (percent): High school diploma or less	Bachelor's degree or more
	1	2	3	4	5	6	7	8	9	10	11	12	13	14	15	16
OKLAHOMA—Con.																
Manchester town	103	103	0.0	86	87.2	0.0	0.0	10.5	2.3	32.6	55.8	11.6	36	77.8	41.7	5.6
Mangum city	3,010	2,957	-1.8	2,947	77.5	2.2	0.0	6.2	14.1	24.5	55.0	20.4	1,167	62.8	45.4	19.0
Manitou town	181	174	-3.9	195	86.2	0.0	0.0	7.7	6.2	26.6	55.4	17.9	72	68.1	51.4	4.2
Mannford town	3,067	3,113	1.5	3,214	86.0	0.0	0.0	13.2	0.8	25.7	58.6	15.6	1,225	69.5	46.0	16.2
Mannsville town	863	863	0.0	899	68.3	0.2	1.8	22.1	7.6	27.2	60.0	12.9	307	72.0	58.6	15.3
Maramec town	91	90	-1.1	104	77.9	0.0	2.9	17.3	1.9	28.0	44.2	27.9	39	79.5	66.7	7.7
Marble City town	263	254	-3.4	235	28.5	1.3	0.0	58.7	11.5	20.8	65.1	14.0	77	76.6	68.8	9.1
Marietta CDP	106	NA	NA	132	34.1	0.0	0.0	59.8	6.1	18.1	72.0	9.8	40	80.0	65.0	15.0
Marietta city	2,626	2,707	3.1	2,659	52.6	3.4	0.0	10.5	33.6	32.9	52.7	14.5	867	51.2	61.9	11.5
Marland town	225	225	0.0	266	35.7	1.1	0.0	38.0	25.2	22.6	66.6	10.9	94	72.3	77.7	0.0
Marlow city	4,662	4,590	-1.5	4,635	88.0	0.9	0.0	9.1	1.9	23.1	60.3	16.7	1,859	60.2	56.1	16.3
Marshall town	272	294	8.1	347	85.3	6.6	0.0	3.7	4.3	20.8	66.6	12.7	121	81.0	61.2	17.4
Martha town	164	160	-2.4	140	55.7	0.0	0.0	19.3	25.0	25.0	52.9	22.1	69	65.2	59.4	20.3
Maud city	1,048	1,060	1.1	1,046	77.2	0.0	3.1	16.9	2.8	29.0	57.9	13.1	371	70.4	65.5	3.5
May town	39	41	5.1	49	100.0	0.0	0.0	0.0	0.0	4.1	42.9	53.1	21	100.0	61.9	28.6
Maysville town	1,219	1,227	0.7	1,322	80.9	0.0	1.3	12.3	5.5	27.7	56.0	16.2	466	67.0	66.5	15.7
Mazie CDP	91	NA	NA	175	92.6	0.0	0.0	7.4	0.0	0.0	78.2	21.7	88	100.0	60.2	0.0
Mead town	122	126	3.3	72	59.7	4.2	0.0	36.1	0.0	12.5	68.0	19.4	36	75.0	33.3	16.7
Medford city	996	986	-1.0	1,008	87.9	0.3	0.3	3.3	8.2	18.4	53.6	28.1	477	74.0	48.0	30.2
Medicine Park town	384	430	12.0	212	94.8	1.9	0.0	1.4	1.9	12.2	75.8	11.8	113	71.7	32.7	23.9
Meeker town	1,144	1,159	1.3	1,135	78.0	0.3	0.4	13.7	7.8	28.3	53.5	18.0	425	67.3	55.3	11.1
Meno town	235	243	3.4	247	70.9	0.0	0.0	1.6	27.5	23.1	64.7	12.1	80	81.3	43.8	33.8
Meridian town	38	41	7.9	45	0.0	100.0	0.0	0.0	0.0	24.4	33.3	42.2	30	90.0	50.0	26.7
Meridian CDP	1,493	NA	NA	1,108	91.5	0.0	1.2	6.3	1.0	18.9	64.2	16.9	476	78.6	55.0	15.1
Miami city	13,574	13,671	0.7	13,669	65.7	1.3	0.4	27.7	4.9	24.3	58.6	17.2	5,148	62.8	47.1	17.5
Midwest City city	54,371	57,039	4.9	55,964	62.7	19.7	1.7	9.2	6.7	24.8	61.7	13.5	22,812	59.9	35.8	21.9
Milburn town	317	320	0.9	313	84.3	0.0	0.0	15.0	0.6	23.3	56.7	20.1	113	75.2	48.7	10.6
Mill Creek town	319	323	1.3	365	74.2	0.0	0.0	23.0	2.7	36.4	49.3	14.2	129	65.1	50.4	3.9
Millerton town	319	317	-0.6	325	68.6	2.5	0.0	28.0	0.9	21.8	58.1	20.0	124	85.5	65.3	14.5
Minco city	1,630	1,644	0.9	1,423	88.2	0.0	0.9	5.2	5.7	24.4	58.5	17.1	564	72.0	53.5	17.0
Moffett town	128	123	-3.9	122	52.5	23.0	0.0	24.6	0.0	26.3	65.6	8.2	42	33.3	78.6	4.8
Moore city	55,081	59,196	7.5	57,563	71.3	3.5	2.4	12.4	10.4	26.7	63.9	9.3	21,226	72.0	36.4	24.9
Mooreland town	1,212	1,284	5.9	1,590	92.5	0.0	0.0	3.5	4.0	30.4	56.1	13.5	571	73.6	43.3	18.2
Morris city	1,479	1,460	-1.3	1,606	56.6	1.8	0.7	27.3	13.6	28.1	61.4	10.3	571	58.5	37.7	13.5
Morrison town	733	731	-0.3	846	89.4	1.1	0.0	7.7	1.9	32.4	57.3	10.4	322	79.2	40.4	22.7
Mounds town	1,149	1,174	2.2	1,169	65.4	1.1	0.0	26.4	7.1	27.6	57.3	15.1	422	60.0	57.6	9.5
Mountain Park town	409	407	-0.5	436	85.6	0.5	0.0	5.5	8.5	22.7	60.5	16.7	197	67.0	64.5	9.1
Mountain View town	795	784	-1.4	832	92.4	0.0	0.0	7.6	0.0	20.6	58.5	20.9	369	74.3	54.2	20.3
Mulberry CDP	138	NA	NA	119	60.5	0.0	0.0	36.1	3.4	36.1	53.8	10.1	40	67.5	47.5	40.0
Muldrow town	3,460	3,314	-4.2	3,375	65.1	1.2	0.8	28.2	4.6	29.7	62.3	7.9	1,204	62.4	59.1	15.5
Mulhall town	225	244	8.4	195	87.7	6.2	0.0	2.1	4.1	20.5	60.5	19.0	80	78.8	42.5	18.8
Murphy CDP	219	NA	NA	168	92.9	0.0	0.0	7.1	0.0	8.4	70.1	21.4	67	79.1	62.7	0.0
Muskogee city	39,222	38,616	-1.5	38,937	55.1	15.7	1.0	20.8	7.4	26.3	58.4	15.4	15,083	58.4	44.6	21.3
Mustang city	17,395	19,638	12.9	18,575	84.6	0.3	0.8	7.5	6.9	27.1	61.3	11.6	6,547	75.3	35.0	22.8
Mutual town	61	65	6.6	115	75.7	0.0	0.0	0.0	24.3	17.4	65.1	17.4	47	48.9	66.0	21.3
Narcissa CDP	99	NA	NA	49	77.6	0.0	0.0	22.4	0.0	0.0	46.9	53.1	29	100.0	44.8	20.7
Nardin CDP	52	NA	NA	84	100.0	0.0	0.0	0.0	0.0	0.0	100.0	0.0	42	100.0	83.3	16.7
Nash town	204	203	-0.5	214	97.2	0.0	0.0	2.8	0.0	14.0	51.8	34.1	102	92.2	47.1	17.6
Nescatunga CDP	70	NA	NA	87	78.2	0.0	0.0	21.8	0.0	18.4	42.5	39.1	39	76.9	100.0	0.0
New Alluwe town	90	90	0.0	83	73.5	0.0	0.0	22.9	3.6	14.4	64.9	20.5	38	89.5	65.8	10.5
Newcastle city	7,682	9,155	19.2	8,383	83.8	0.7	0.7	9.8	5.0	26.5	60.9	12.9	3,044	84.0	33.8	27.0
New Cordell city	2,921	2,892	-1.0	2,917	88.4	0.0	0.4	4.9	6.2	22.7	58.3	18.9	1,254	66.7	53.4	13.9
New Eucha CDP	405	NA	NA	528	39.4	0.0	0.0	60.6	0.0	28.6	58.9	12.3	133	59.4	42.9	9.0
Newkirk city	2,317	2,264	-2.3	2,297	79.7	0.8	0.3	15.2	3.9	27.6	55.2	17.2	843	67.9	48.2	11.3
New Woodville town	132	NA	NA	106	18.9	0.0	0.0	81.1	0.0	46.2	44.3	9.4	25	100.0	60.0	0.0
Nichols Hills city	3,710	3,870	4.3	3,797	90.3	1.5	1.2	4.8	2.2	21.3	61.1	17.6	1,664	83.7	5.0	80.7
Nicoma Park city	2,393	2,467	3.1	2,480	86.4	3.2	0.0	6.3	4.1	31.0	53.1	15.9	889	73.1	41.2	16.4
Nicut CDP	360	NA	NA	225	43.6	0.0	0.0	56.4	0.0	20.0	57.7	22.2	83	85.5	74.7	10.8
Ninnekah town	1,002	1,021	1.9	990	80.0	0.4	0.3	17.5	1.8	23.7	57.8	18.5	397	82.1	53.4	15.1
Noble city	6,481	6,583	1.6	6,602	82.3	0.3	0.0	11.6	5.8	29.7	57.6	12.8	2,129	76.1	44.7	18.8
Norge town	145	147	1.4	129	78.3	2.3	0.0	3.9	15.5	25.6	54.3	20.2	44	81.8	75.0	0.0
Norman city	110,925	118,040	6.4	115,521	76.3	4.1	4.1	9.1	6.5	19.4	69.5	11.1	44,637	55.6	24.2	42.8
North Enid town	860	908	5.6	950	73.7	0.0	12.0	11.7	2.6	25.2	55.2	19.6	326	85.0	41.7	26.4
North Miami town	374	382	2.1	340	62.1	0.0	1.5	27.6	8.8	16.4	58.4	25.0	123	83.7	64.2	6.5
Notchietown CDP	373	NA	NA	301	59.8	0.0	0.0	40.2	0.0	23.0	65.6	11.6	121	100.0	74.4	3.3
Nowata city	3,731	3,726	-0.1	3,734	63.7	3.9	0.6	29.4	2.4	25.4	51.4	23.3	1,509	69.8	58.1	16.8
Oak Grove town	18	NA	NA	11	100.0	0.0	0.0	0.0	0.0	0.0	100.0	0.0	6	100.0	100.0	0.0
Oakhurst CDP	2,185	NA	NA	2,448	72.5	1.1	0.3	21.0	5.1	23.2	61.6	15.3	1,010	82.6	58.4	7.5
Oakland town	1,057	1,073	1.5	1,085	35.0	1.0	0.0	10.9	53.1	32.8	58.2	8.9	359	70.8	72.7	8.1
Oaks town	288	287	-0.3	316	19.6	0.6	1.6	76.9	1.3	34.5	56.3	9.2	87	70.1	62.1	14.9
Oakwood town	65	67	3.1	58	69.0	0.0	0.0	13.8	17.2	37.9	51.6	10.3	17	82.4	52.9	11.8
Ochelata town	424	429	1.2	335	75.5	0.0	1.8	20.3	2.4	17.7	57.8	24.8	154	76.6	54.5	7.1
Oilton city	1,013	1,014	0.1	1,188	86.6	0.0	0.0	10.6	2.8	29.8	58.1	12.3	395	66.1	57.2	11.1
Okarche town	1,215	1,301	7.1	998	85.6	3.8	0.0	5.3	5.3	20.8	58.0	21.0	423	80.4	35.9	23.2
Okay town	616	616	0.0	566	54.6	1.8	0.0	38.2	5.5	25.9	61.9	12.2	241	66.8	59.8	5.4
Okeene town	1,204	1,214	0.8	1,108	85.4	0.5	0.0	4.5	9.7	20.9	53.2	25.7	523	69.0	49.7	13.4
Okemah city	3,223	3,252	0.9	3,263	61.2	3.4	0.3	30.3	4.8	28.7	56.3	15.0	1,088	50.2	57.4	16.2
Oklahoma City city	580,008	620,602	7.0	600,729	55.7	14.4	4.2	7.8	18.0	25.6	63.0	11.4	230,517	58.8	35.9	30.8
Okmulgee city	12,574	12,227	-2.8	12,398	52.5	18.4	0.2	25.7	3.2	22.9	60.7	16.4	4,943	52.6	45.5	15.3
Oktaha town	390	384	-1.5	392	62.0	1.0	0.0	36.2	0.8	33.4	56.3	10.2	130	70.0	59.2	4.6
Old Eucha CDP	52	NA	NA	3	0.0	0.0	0.0	100.0	0.0	0.0	100.0	0.0	2	100.0	100.0	0.0
Old Green CDP	315	NA	NA	520	46.9	0.0	0.0	49.2	3.8	45.2	43.3	11.5	139	93.5	38.1	8.6
Olustee town	607	593	-2.3	450	49.8	0.0	0.0	8.9	41.3	33.8	50.0	16.2	156	73.7	60.3	7.7
Oologah town	1,149	1,177	2.4	1,054	79.3	0.0	1.1	16.0	3.5	28.7	59.5	11.8	417	72.4	42.2	22.5
Optima town	356	379	6.5	516	31.4	1.9	0.2	3.3	63.2	35.8	61.4	2.7	142	60.6	73.9	1.4
Orlando town	148	160	8.1	200	90.5	0.0	0.0	9.5	0.0	26.5	54.5	19.0	90	73.3	66.7	2.2
Osage town	156	155	-0.6	121	90.9	0.0	0.0	9.1	0.0	7.4	71.2	21.5	63	90.5	90.5	0.0
Owasso city	29,720	33,773	13.6	31,738	74.2	2.4	2.7	13.9	6.7	28.1	62.5	9.1	11,630	67.2	29.4	32.9
Paden town	461	459	-0.4	602	71.9	0.0	0.0	23.1	5.0	31.2	54.6	14.3	239	61.5	58.6	5.4
Panama town	1,412	1,379	-2.3	1,457	75.1	0.8	1.2	18.1	4.9	21.9	60.4	17.6	560	65.9	67.1	7.3
Paoli town	610	611	0.2	588	74.5	0.0	0.0	14.6	10.9	27.1	61.9	11.1	211	68.7	58.3	12.8

1 May be of any race.

Table A. All Places — **Population and Housing**

STATE City, town, township, borough, or CDP (county if applicable)	Population				Race and Hispanic or Latino origin (percent), 2010–2014					Age (percent), 2010–2014			Households, 2010–2014			
	2010 census total population	2014 estimated population	Percent change 2010–2014	ACS total population estimate 2010–2014	White alone, not Hispanic or Latino	Black alone, not Hispanic or Latino	Asian alone, not Hispanic or Latino	All other races or 2 or more races, not Hispanic or Latino	Hispanic or Latino[1]	Under 18 years old	Age 18 to 64 years old	Age 65 years and older	Total occupied housing units	Percent owner occupied	High school diploma or less	Bachelor's degree or more
	1	2	3	4	5	6	7	8	9	10	11	12	13	14	15	16
OKLAHOMA—Con.																
Paradise Hill town	85	83	-2.4	40	72.5	0.0	0.0	27.5	0.0	7.5	67.5	25.0	16	100.0	31.3	62.5
Park Hill CDP	3,909	NA	NA	3,887	43.8	1.0	0.2	47.4	7.6	33.3	56.6	10.2	1,250	54.2	48.1	21.1
Pauls Valley city	6,104	6,070	-0.6	6,054	64.1	6.5	0.4	12.3	16.8	21.5	63.2	15.2	2,337	56.4	57.3	16.4
Pawhuska city	3,689	3,636	-1.4	3,679	58.7	2.7	0.0	33.3	5.3	22.9	57.5	19.7	1,662	65.3	57.3	4.9
Pawnee city	2,196	2,159	-1.7	2,247	58.7	3.6	0.0	33.5	4.2	23.5	58.3	18.3	901	61.6	50.3	18.2
Peavine CDP	423	NA	NA	403	49.1	0.0	0.0	50.9	0.0	27.7	58.7	13.4	124	87.1	61.3	16.1
Peggs CDP	813	NA	NA	739	70.2	1.1	0.0	27.6	1.1	18.6	66.9	14.3	284	91.9	60.2	19.4
Pensacola town	125	124	-0.8	188	66.0	0.0	1.1	33.0	0.0	28.8	67.5	3.7	45	88.9	64.4	4.4
Peoria town	132	133	0.8	102	69.6	0.0	0.0	30.4	0.0	23.5	48.0	28.4	47	85.1	87.2	4.3
Perkins city	2,831	2,852	0.7	2,851	76.4	4.0	0.0	16.2	3.4	29.2	59.3	11.4	1,098	57.4	56.9	24.0
Perry city	5,126	5,075	-1.0	5,087	83.9	2.9	0.0	10.6	2.6	25.4	57.9	16.6	2,036	65.0	54.9	20.0
Pettit CDP	954	NA	NA	888	58.0	0.0	0.0	38.0	4.1	21.3	54.8	23.9	360	86.7	31.1	40.3
Phillips town	135	133	-1.5	134	63.4	0.0	0.0	31.3	5.2	26.1	61.8	11.9	54	94.4	75.9	3.7
Piedmont city	5,720	6,734	17.7	6,232	86.3	1.6	0.4	8.3	3.4	30.4	60.5	9.1	2,168	92.6	17.4	44.7
Piney CDP	115	NA	NA	244	24.2	0.0	0.0	75.8	0.0	31.9	53.3	14.8	80	90.0	55.0	45.0
Pinhook Corner CDP	171	NA	NA	192	33.9	0.0	0.0	66.1	0.0	32.8	62.0	5.2	69	52.2	30.4	10.1
Pink town	2,058	2,097	1.9	2,282	83.9	0.9	0.7	10.1	4.4	23.5	60.3	16.0	840	86.5	45.2	13.7
Pin Oak Acres CDP	421	NA	NA	574	71.4	0.0	0.0	28.6	0.0	21.3	68.8	9.9	227	75.8	57.3	11.9
Pittsburg town	207	199	-3.9	172	67.4	0.0	0.0	31.4	1.2	17.5	69.1	13.4	75	78.7	62.7	1.3
Pocasset town	199	202	1.5	130	82.3	0.0	3.1	13.1	1.5	31.5	52.4	16.2	50	82.0	56.0	8.0
Pocola town	4,048	4,030	-0.4	4,043	82.6	1.6	0.8	14.1	0.8	23.7	59.5	16.8	1,582	80.7	60.0	8.9
Ponca City city	25,401	24,766	-2.5	24,951	74.8	3.2	1.0	13.9	7.0	26.0	56.2	17.8	10,114	66.5	42.3	22.8
Pond Creek city	856	853	-0.4	847	84.3	0.0	0.7	5.9	9.1	28.2	54.8	16.9	348	81.9	49.4	18.4
Porter town	558	578	3.6	572	59.4	14.0	0.5	23.4	2.6	25.6	61.6	12.6	228	78.9	55.7	4.8
Porum town	727	716	-1.5	590	46.8	0.5	0.0	51.9	0.8	28.4	58.5	13.1	253	61.3	66.4	4.7
Poteau city	8,512	8,665	1.8	8,563	68.9	3.8	0.1	13.2	14.1	24.4	61.6	13.8	2,973	63.6	43.7	18.6
Prague city	2,386	2,428	1.8	2,671	81.1	2.2	0.0	11.0	5.7	30.8	52.1	17.0	902	61.0	57.6	10.9
Proctor CDP	231	NA	NA	152	6.6	0.0	0.0	86.8	6.6	31.6	42.8	25.7	69	68.1	53.6	0.0
Prue town	466	464	-0.4	451	92.5	0.2	0.0	7.3	0.0	26.8	55.1	18.2	167	86.2	74.3	9.6
Pryor Creek city	9,536	9,445	-1.0	9,479	65.0	0.5	0.9	27.3	6.4	25.4	58.1	16.5	3,738	59.4	47.7	21.5
Pump Back CDP	175	NA	NA	192	82.8	0.0	0.0	17.2	0.0	21.9	50.6	27.6	90	100.0	42.2	35.6
Purcell city	6,168	6,340	2.8	6,259	73.7	3.1	0.8	8.6	13.8	24.8	60.7	14.5	2,493	71.3	53.8	14.2
Putnam town	29	30	3.4	5	100.0	0.0	0.0	0.0	0.0	0.0	20.0	80.0	3	100.0	100.0	0.0
Quapaw town	904	907	0.3	920	60.8	1.1	0.0	36.5	1.6	30.4	56.6	12.9	299	62.2	53.5	7.4
Quinton town	1,051	1,011	-3.8	1,027	66.5	0.9	0.0	22.3	10.3	26.6	55.9	17.6	418	63.9	56.5	6.9
Ralston town	330	327	-0.9	324	88.9	0.0	0.0	11.1	0.0	23.5	62.5	14.2	129	79.1	58.9	17.1
Ramona town	539	545	1.1	503	72.2	0.0	0.0	27.8	0.0	27.3	59.3	13.5	233	63.9	71.2	9.9
Randlett town	438	436	-0.5	410	88.5	0.0	0.0	4.4	7.1	15.1	58.8	26.1	195	80.0	60.5	14.4
Ratliff City town	120	121	0.8	109	49.5	28.4	0.0	14.7	7.3	21.1	56.9	22.0	40	65.0	90.0	0.0
Rattan town	310	298	-3.9	291	63.6	0.0	0.0	30.6	5.8	25.4	54.7	19.9	109	70.6	64.2	12.8
Ravia town	528	529	0.2	476	75.6	0.0	0.0	14.3	10.1	23.6	62.0	14.5	186	81.7	68.8	4.8
Redbird town	137	141	2.9	92	4.3	71.7	0.0	23.9	0.0	30.4	51.1	18.5	36	69.4	69.4	13.9
Redbird Smith CDP	465	NA	NA	282	94.7	0.0	0.0	5.3	0.0	5.3	54.9	39.7	145	79.3	53.8	11.0
Red Oak town	549	518	-5.6	564	59.9	0.0	0.0	36.0	4.1	24.5	54.4	21.1	219	68.5	53.4	10.5
Red Rock town	283	282	-0.4	256	16.4	0.0	7.4	71.5	4.7	32.0	59.6	8.6	79	70.9	43.0	2.5
Remy CDP	562	NA	NA	465	59.8	0.0	0.9	37.0	2.4	18.7	62.9	18.5	183	80.9	29.5	18.6
Renfrow town	12	12	0.0	15	86.7	0.0	0.0	13.3	0.0	0.0	60.0	40.0	13	100.0	100.0	0.0
Rentiesville town	128	126	-1.6	116	29.3	55.2	0.0	13.8	1.7	6.0	62.9	31.0	54	87.0	66.7	3.7
Reydon town	210	217	3.3	202	73.8	0.0	0.0	5.4	20.8	33.7	48.6	17.8	76	61.8	64.5	14.5
Ringling town	1,037	1,005	-3.1	960	75.4	0.0	0.0	18.8	5.8	27.2	57.5	15.3	387	65.9	68.7	6.5
Ringwood town	497	513	3.2	475	50.9	0.0	0.0	3.4	45.7	27.3	58.2	14.3	138	83.3	59.4	6.5
Ripley town	403	406	0.7	369	85.4	0.0	0.0	10.3	4.3	30.4	56.3	13.3	144	68.1	41.7	18.1
River Bottom CDP	154	NA	NA	134	67.2	0.0	0.0	32.8	0.0	9.7	63.5	26.9	59	81.4	52.5	10.2
Rock Island town	655	639	-2.4	735	79.5	1.4	0.0	17.8	1.4	24.0	63.6	12.5	278	80.9	65.5	6.5
Rocky town	162	161	-0.6	169	95.3	0.0	0.6	4.1	0.0	16.0	62.7	21.3	69	71.0	71.0	11.6
Rocky Ford CDP	61	NA	NA	62	50.0	0.0	30.6	19.4	0.0	27.4	54.8	17.7	20	100.0	75.0	0.0
Rocky Mountain CDP	420	NA	NA	448	45.1	0.0	0.0	54.0	0.9	29.9	58.0	12.1	177	64.4	71.8	11.3
Roff town	725	723	-0.3	809	74.4	0.0	0.0	21.8	3.8	36.5	54.5	8.9	247	74.9	63.2	11.7
Roland town	3,160	3,439	8.8	3,284	65.3	4.8	1.3	24.1	4.5	30.6	58.8	10.5	1,276	48.4	51.8	6.7
Roosevelt town	248	247	-0.4	263	76.4	8.7	1.9	11.0	1.9	16.3	62.3	21.3	124	77.4	54.8	10.5
Rose CDP	285	NA	NA	142	35.2	0.0	0.0	64.8	0.0	36.6	40.1	23.2	46	80.4	58.7	0.0
Rosedale town	68	69	1.5	65	35.4	0.0	0.0	55.4	9.2	21.5	58.3	20.0	22	77.3	54.5	0.0
Rosston town	31	32	3.2	31	80.6	0.0	0.0	9.7	9.7	0.0	58.1	41.9	16	100.0	56.3	0.0
Rush Springs town	1,234	1,262	2.3	1,301	85.7	1.5	0.0	10.9	1.8	27.5	59.5	13.0	465	58.7	66.2	11.6
Ryan town	816	791	-3.1	765	66.0	0.3	0.0	10.1	23.7	27.3	51.1	21.4	304	70.1	66.4	11.5
St. Louis town	158	161	1.9	167	78.4	0.0	0.0	21.6	0.0	16.8	55.8	27.5	69	89.9	71.0	4.3
Salem CDP	112	NA	NA	126	65.9	0.0	0.0	34.1	0.0	11.9	88.1	0.0	34	67.6	67.6	32.4
Salina town	1,399	1,382	-1.2	1,331	52.2	0.0	0.2	43.6	4.0	26.1	57.5	16.5	510	58.2	62.2	16.3
Sallisaw city	8,932	8,650	-3.2	8,761	64.9	1.0	1.0	28.2	4.9	24.4	59.4	16.2	3,295	51.9	59.2	12.9
Sams Corner CDP	137	NA	NA	172	66.9	0.0	0.0	33.1	0.0	18.6	59.8	21.5	61	77.0	41.0	39.3
Sand Hill CDP	395	NA	NA	317	71.0	0.0	0.0	29.0	0.0	16.7	57.7	25.6	135	88.9	50.4	20.0
Sand Springs city	18,833	19,553	3.8	19,277	77.9	2.1	0.6	16.0	3.4	27.2	59.0	13.7	7,332	68.9	42.9	21.4
Sapulpa city	20,076	20,432	1.8	20,308	75.3	2.6	1.1	15.8	5.1	24.2	58.9	16.8	7,632	65.8	46.5	18.7
Sasakwa town	145	144	-0.7	122	39.3	1.6	0.0	56.6	2.5	34.4	58.2	7.4	34	61.8	52.9	5.9
Savanna town	686	659	-3.9	636	77.7	2.2	0.9	16.8	2.4	24.3	57.9	17.8	281	76.2	47.3	13.5
Sawyer town	321	320	-0.3	373	75.6	0.3	0.0	19.0	5.1	15.2	64.1	20.6	139	80.6	49.6	18.7
Sayre city	4,375	4,746	8.5	4,524	70.2	7.1	0.8	6.1	15.8	20.9	69.2	9.7	1,429	56.8	47.8	21.1
Schulter town	509	498	-2.2	464	68.1	0.0	0.0	30.6	1.3	28.4	59.4	12.1	192	87.0	52.6	9.9
Scraper CDP	191	NA	NA	178	93.3	0.0	0.0	6.7	0.0	30.4	51.1	18.5	90	54.4	0.0	28.9
Seiling city	856	868	1.4	869	81.1	0.0	0.0	12.7	6.2	30.7	47.1	22.2	335	69.0	49.0	14.3
Seminole city	7,483	7,486	0.0	7,493	67.4	5.4	0.3	21.7	5.3	28.9	56.3	14.9	2,760	65.7	49.0	16.8
Sentinel town	901	898	-0.3	972	72.0	0.0	0.0	1.5	26.4	28.5	58.7	12.6	365	74.8	55.1	15.6
Sequoyah CDP	698	NA	NA	571	72.9	0.0	0.0	27.1	0.0	14.2	60.7	25.2	248	85.5	64.9	10.1
Shady Grove CDP (Cherokee)	556	NA	NA	484	49.4	0.0	1.4	48.6	0.6	28.5	59.3	12.2	166	77.7	57.8	20.5
Shady Grove CDP (McIntosh)	194	NA	NA	300	70.0	0.0	0.0	18.3	11.7	15.7	61.4	23.0	118	88.1	51.7	0.0
Shady Point town	1,028	1,004	-2.3	1,143	82.6	0.0	0.3	15.2	1.9	21.3	63.0	15.7	441	67.8	56.5	13.4
Shamrock town	101	NA	NA	51	70.6	0.0	0.0	13.7	15.7	19.6	78.4	2.0	16	62.5	56.3	0.0
Sharon town	135	144	6.7	61	54.1	0.0	0.0	0.0	45.9	29.5	58.9	11.5	18	61.1	83.3	11.1
Shattuck town	1,356	1,359	0.2	1,281	85.7	0.0	0.9	3.1	10.2	28.2	52.4	19.4	534	71.0	53.0	22.5

1 May be of any race.

Table A. All Places — **Population and Housing**

STATE City, town, township, borough, or CDP (county if applicable)	2010 census total population	2014 estimated population	Percent change 2010–2014	ACS total population estimate 2010–2014	White alone, not Hispanic or Latino	Black alone, not Hispanic or Latino	Asian alone, not Hispanic or Latino	All other races or 2 or more races, not Hispanic or Latino	Hispanic or Latino[1]	Under 18 years old	Age 18 to 64 years old	Age 65 years and older	Total occupied housing units	Percent owner occupied	High school diploma or less	Bachelor's degree or more
	1	2	3	4	5	6	7	8	9	10	11	12	13	14	15	16
OKLAHOMA—Con.																
Shawnee city	29,857	31,254	4.7	30,609	69.9	4.0	0.7	19.6	5.9	24.8	61.0	14.2	11,858	56.7	43.0	23.1
Shidler city	441	439	-0.5	402	69.7	0.0	0.0	25.6	4.7	28.1	56.8	15.2	174	81.6	75.3	10.3
Short CDP	293	NA	NA	373	61.1	0.0	0.0	23.1	15.8	33.0	63.3	3.8	101	68.3	40.6	2.0
Silo town	335	346	3.3	291	74.6	0.0	0.0	25.4	0.0	21.6	60.4	17.9	110	82.7	39.1	24.5
Simms CDP	325	NA	NA	247	54.3	3.2	0.0	42.5	0.0	13.4	55.1	31.6	103	87.4	73.8	1.9
Skedee town	51	51	0.0	41	68.3	0.0	7.3	24.4	0.0	14.6	78.2	7.3	16	68.8	62.5	12.5
Skiatook town	7,257	7,788	7.3	7,571	79.9	1.1	0.0	17.5	1.4	27.1	59.6	13.1	2,770	66.4	53.1	11.8
Slaughterville town	4,146	4,210	1.5	4,223	84.8	0.0	0.0	13.0	2.2	28.5	59.1	12.5	1,431	76.9	52.5	6.4
Slick town	131	131	0.0	148	60.8	26.4	0.0	12.8	0.0	25.6	65.5	8.8	46	89.1	84.8	0.0
Smith Village town	66	68	3.0	63	77.8	4.8	0.0	17.5	0.0	9.6	69.8	20.6	28	60.7	64.3	0.0
Smithville town	113	NA	NA	123	48.0	0.0	0.0	47.2	4.9	34.9	49.6	15.4	59	45.8	67.8	10.2
Snake Creek CDP	257	NA	NA	121	54.5	0.0	0.0	45.5	0.0	21.4	71.8	6.6	55	83.6	52.7	0.0
Snyder city	1,394	1,373	-1.5	1,564	69.6	5.9	0.0	8.7	15.9	28.1	55.3	16.6	611	59.7	49.9	12.6
Soper town	261	260	-0.4	248	64.1	0.0	0.8	35.1	0.0	22.2	52.7	25.0	100	77.0	64.0	12.0
Sour John CDP	60	NA	NA	37	64.9	0.0	0.0	35.1	0.0	0.0	48.6	51.4	27	48.1	88.9	0.0
South Coffeyville town	781	774	-0.9	787	73.3	1.1	0.0	22.5	3.0	21.4	62.0	16.4	334	80.8	46.1	7.5
Sparks town	169	171	1.2	166	89.2	0.0	0.0	10.8	0.0	22.9	60.2	16.9	67	83.6	86.6	3.0
Spaulding town	178	174	-2.2	212	65.1	0.0	0.0	31.6	3.3	33.5	54.1	12.3	75	90.7	54.7	0.0
Spavinaw town	437	432	-1.1	372	54.3	0.0	0.5	39.8	5.4	18.0	65.3	16.7	176	79.5	61.9	5.1
Spencer city	3,912	4,024	2.9	3,979	32.2	60.2	1.2	4.4	2.0	21.4	65.9	12.6	1,560	75.5	46.7	14.1
Sperry town	1,204	1,246	3.5	1,040	78.2	2.5	0.5	16.2	2.7	23.4	59.7	17.1	427	68.4	63.2	10.5
Spiro town	2,164	2,178	0.6	2,502	71.9	4.2	0.4	19.3	4.2	24.3	56.1	19.7	952	65.1	62.4	9.8
Sportsmen Acres town	317	314	-0.9	390	73.3	0.0	0.0	24.4	2.3	33.3	60.1	6.4	157	34.4	60.5	8.3
Springer town	700	705	0.7	548	61.9	3.5	0.0	33.0	1.6	20.3	54.3	25.5	190	78.4	61.6	10.5
Steely Hollow CDP	206	NA	NA	105	56.2	0.0	0.0	43.8	0.0	3.8	70.4	25.7	61	49.2	21.3	31.1
Sterling town	793	806	1.6	630	78.7	0.5	0.3	12.1	8.4	25.2	55.4	19.4	256	76.2	54.3	15.6
Stidham town	20	20	0.0	50	36.0	34.0	0.0	30.0	0.0	28.0	40.0	32.0	23	82.6	34.8	0.0
Stigler city	2,691	2,741	1.9	2,704	76.2	0.0	0.7	18.8	4.3	24.8	57.1	18.1	1,068	57.2	56.8	13.8
Stillwater city	45,688	48,406	5.9	46,851	75.3	4.6	6.3	9.3	4.6	15.6	76.1	8.3	18,202	38.1	17.5	41.7
Stilwell city	3,960	4,008	1.2	3,974	27.3	0.7	1.1	53.6	17.3	29.8	56.5	13.8	1,484	45.1	59.2	10.4
Stonewall town	470	474	0.9	348	77.6	1.7	0.0	19.3	1.4	13.8	57.2	29.0	133	80.5	65.4	7.5
Stoney Point CDP	238	NA	NA	271	70.8	0.0	0.0	29.2	0.0	30.9	40.6	28.4	84	95.2	72.6	19.0
Strang town	89	88	-1.1	58	58.6	0.0	0.0	41.4	0.0	15.5	75.7	8.6	25	84.0	56.0	4.0
Stratford town	1,525	1,526	0.1	1,478	68.4	0.0	0.0	28.2	3.4	28.9	58.2	12.9	573	54.8	60.6	11.7
Stringtown town	417	403	-3.4	320	67.2	4.1	0.0	26.3	2.5	20.3	59.4	20.3	144	79.9	64.6	13.9
Strong City town	47	49	4.3	70	97.1	0.0	0.0	2.9	0.0	7.1	75.6	17.1	19	100.0	57.9	21.1
Stroud city	2,690	2,721	1.2	2,696	76.2	1.2	0.0	19.2	3.3	24.9	57.5	17.5	1,249	56.0	53.6	12.7
Stuart town	180	175	-2.8	202	82.2	0.0	0.0	16.3	1.5	27.2	60.0	12.9	62	72.6	59.7	24.2
Sugden town	43	42	-2.3	45	64.4	0.0	0.0	28.9	6.7	24.4	57.7	17.8	19	100.0	42.1	0.0
Sulphur city	4,929	5,052	2.5	4,996	69.1	0.8	0.0	20.4	9.8	25.8	56.4	17.7	1,723	58.2	56.4	13.5
Summit town	139	137	-1.4	176	19.3	75.6	0.0	5.1	0.0	28.4	58.7	13.1	54	98.1	68.5	3.7
Sweetwater town	87	90	3.4	134	76.1	0.0	0.0	3.7	20.1	29.9	47.0	23.1	48	50.0	31.3	29.2
Swink CDP	66	NA	NA	86	84.9	0.0	0.0	15.1	0.0	14.0	61.8	24.4	41	58.5	51.2	12.2
Sycamore CDP	177	NA	NA	294	20.4	0.0	0.0	79.6	0.0	23.8	66.9	9.2	88	85.2	86.4	0.0
Taft town	250	246	-1.6	240	8.3	63.3	0.0	28.3	0.0	23.0	58.4	18.8	96	55.2	64.6	11.5
Tagg Flats CDP	13	NA	NA	112	29.5	0.0	0.0	70.5	0.0	47.4	52.7	0.0	35	71.4	51.4	0.0
Tahlequah city	15,739	16,496	4.8	16,190	47.5	1.8	0.3	39.6	10.8	21.5	63.9	14.5	5,806	44.4	31.3	29.9
Talala town	270	276	2.2	398	83.9	0.0	0.0	10.6	5.5	40.0	49.6	10.3	127	78.7	54.3	13.4
Talihina town	1,129	1,103	-2.3	1,230	46.8	2.9	0.0	41.3	8.9	26.0	55.6	18.6	474	59.7	55.9	11.4
Taloga town	302	309	2.3	325	92.6	0.0	2.2	3.4	1.8	23.3	61.1	15.4	131	76.3	47.3	27.5
Tamaha town	176	177	0.6	126	69.0	0.0	0.0	24.6	6.3	19.1	54.0	27.0	61	83.6	72.1	6.6
Tatums town	151	152	0.7	74	0.0	100.0	0.0	0.0	0.0	12.2	58.2	29.7	34	67.6	85.3	2.9
Tecumseh city	6,457	6,631	2.7	6,556	67.4	1.6	0.1	29.1	2.0	29.2	57.0	13.7	2,402	68.0	49.1	8.1
Temple town	1,002	993	-0.9	1,208	71.0	6.7	1.4	8.8	12.1	30.3	52.0	17.9	414	84.1	71.0	7.5
Tenkiller CDP	633	NA	NA	591	47.7	0.7	0.0	43.3	8.3	11.5	65.5	23.0	204	90.2	61.8	5.4
Teresita CDP	159	NA	NA	142	64.8	0.0	0.0	31.7	3.5	18.2	76.7	4.9	51	72.5	56.9	7.8
Terlton CDP	111	110	-0.9	107	65.4	0.0	0.0	34.6	0.0	17.8	65.3	16.8	41	78.0	41.5	0.0
Terral town	382	404	5.8	372	72.0	0.0	0.0	11.0	16.9	26.1	52.9	21.0	144	80.6	77.8	10.4
Texanna CDP	2,261	NA	NA	2,355	78.6	0.7	1.8	18.3	0.6	19.4	61.6	19.1	1,002	86.6	61.9	11.1
Texhoma town	926	986	6.5	894	54.3	0.0	0.0	0.0	45.7	35.2	56.0	8.6	314	68.8	54.1	23.6
Texola town	36	37	2.8	43	100.0	0.0	0.0	0.0	0.0	0.0	93.1	7.0	14	100.0	35.7	21.4
Thackerville town	445	462	3.8	424	71.9	0.5	0.0	15.8	11.8	18.6	66.0	15.3	143	73.4	69.9	0.7
The Village city	8,929	9,324	4.4	9,147	72.9	11.3	2.0	7.1	6.8	20.2	62.6	17.1	4,371	68.9	26.2	42.8
Thomas city	1,181	1,238	4.8	1,278	76.4	0.0	0.3	13.1	10.2	21.9	59.4	18.5	516	79.8	41.9	27.5
Tiawah CDP	189	NA	NA	213	92.5	0.0	0.0	7.5	0.0	22.5	75.2	2.3	68	64.7	54.4	33.8
Tipton town	847	807	-4.7	950	59.2	12.3	0.0	7.8	20.7	23.0	54.9	22.1	385	75.3	62.6	10.6
Tishomingo city	3,034	3,101	2.2	3,063	65.1	3.6	2.0	23.7	5.6	23.0	59.7	17.4	1,228	46.3	44.0	13.6
Titanic CDP	356	NA	NA	189	59.8	0.0	0.0	40.2	0.0	13.8	64.6	21.7	78	87.2	67.9	12.8
Tonkawa city	3,214	3,143	-2.2	3,144	77.1	0.4	0.2	14.1	8.2	26.0	58.7	15.3	1,192	65.7	43.6	19.6
Tribbey town	393	400	1.8	402	88.8	0.0	0.0	6.5	4.7	23.6	58.6	17.9	152	87.5	73.7	4.6
Tryon town	491	496	1.0	471	82.6	1.3	0.0	11.7	4.5	29.7	55.0	15.3	183	68.3	67.2	10.9
Tullahassee town	101	105	4.0	266	9.8	86.5	0.0	2.3	1.5	12.0	79.3	8.6	60	86.7	71.7	3.3
Tulsa city	391,922	399,682	2.0	395,599	57.0	15.0	2.6	10.7	14.8	24.6	62.6	12.8	163,519	52.9	35.0	31.5
Tupelo city	329	323	-1.8	330	60.0	0.0	0.3	39.7	0.0	29.7	54.6	15.8	120	68.3	65.0	5.0
Turley CDP	2,756	NA	NA	2,516	55.4	17.6	0.0	18.6	8.4	19.3	65.7	15.0	889	78.3	65.1	3.7
Turpin CDP	467	NA	NA	584	65.1	0.0	0.0	1.5	33.4	29.2	63.5	7.4	164	65.2	53.7	21.3
Tushka town	312	302	-3.2	321	67.0	0.0	0.0	30.8	2.2	24.9	58.1	16.8	128	60.9	39.8	21.1
Tuskahoma CDP	151	NA	NA	138	74.6	0.0	0.0	25.4	0.0	18.8	49.1	31.9	77	85.7	58.4	23.4
Tuttle city	5,997	6,542	9.1	6,252	81.9	0.2	0.1	13.1	4.6	25.5	61.5	13.1	2,153	83.7	37.5	16.2
Twin Oaks CDP	198	NA	NA	401	69.8	0.0	0.0	28.4	1.7	32.2	55.1	12.7	107	91.6	67.3	0.0
Tyrone town	762	802	5.2	812	62.8	3.3	0.0	1.8	32.0	39.2	54.6	6.3	243	71.2	59.3	2.9
Union City town	1,645	1,887	14.7	1,647	82.6	6.7	0.0	4.3	6.4	18.5	68.9	12.6	487	82.8	40.7	20.5
Valley Brook town	765	782	2.2	677	67.2	1.3	2.1	16.4	13.0	25.6	64.9	9.6	244	42.6	63.9	2.9
Valley Park town	70	70	0.0	30	76.7	0.0	0.0	20.0	3.3	26.7	66.6	6.7	12	66.7	66.7	33.3
Valliant town	754	745	-1.2	834	67.4	10.3	0.0	19.4	2.9	29.4	56.8	13.8	300	61.0	54.0	13.0
Velma town	620	612	-1.3	727	89.1	0.0	0.0	9.2	1.7	27.6	61.8	10.7	263	73.4	64.3	12.5
Vera town	244	247	1.2	130	69.2	0.0	0.0	30.8	0.0	27.8	55.4	16.9	59	83.1	72.9	6.8
Verden town	530	529	-0.2	184	79.8	0.0	0.0	11.1	9.1	25.5	59.1	15.4	184	76.6	62.0	9.8
Verdigris town	3,988	4,237	6.2	4,117	80.1	0.2	1.2	15.9	2.6	22.7	62.2	15.1	1,585	88.6	33.8	21.2
Vian town	1,466	1,409	-3.9	1,510	54.7	9.0	0.0	33.8	2.5	29.2	55.8	14.9	507	46.9	56.4	6.9
Vici town	699	715	2.3	859	80.7	0.0	0.2	9.5	9.5	26.7	53.2	20.0	329	61.4	59.6	24.3

1 May be of any race.

Table A. All Places — **Population and Housing**

STATE City, town, township, borough, or CDP (county if applicable)	Population: 2010 census total population	Population: 2014 estimated population	Population: Percent change 2010–2014	Population: ACS total population estimate 2010–2014	Race and Hispanic or Latino origin (percent), 2010–2014: White alone, not Hispanic or Latino	Black alone, not Hispanic or Latino	Asian alone, not Hispanic or Latino	All other races or 2 or more races, not Hispanic or Latino	Hispanic or Latino[1]	Age (percent), 2010–2014: Under 18 years old	Age 18 to 64 years old	Age 65 years and older	Households, 2010–2014: Total occupied housing units	Percent owner occupied	Householders by level of education (percent): High school diploma or less	Bachelor's degree or more
	1	2	3	4	5	6	7	8	9	10	11	12	13	14	15	16
OKLAHOMA—Con.																
Vinita city	5,743	5,554	-3.3	5,637	62.6	4.6	1.0	29.5	2.3	22.3	57.0	20.6	2,299	67.6	53.1	14.3
Wagoner city	8,317	8,612	3.5	8,499	66.6	6.9	0.2	23.0	3.3	26.3	57.9	15.8	3,258	58.6	54.8	13.8
Wainwright town	165	162	-1.8	163	72.4	0.0	0.0	27.6	0.0	31.3	55.9	12.9	49	69.4	87.8	0.0
Wakita town	344	343	-0.3	335	83.6	7.8	0.0	7.8	0.9	10.2	65.5	24.5	148	74.3	63.5	10.8
Walters city	2,590	2,569	-0.8	2,564	72.3	1.3	0.0	21.1	5.3	28.1	60.0	11.8	890	67.1	56.4	14.8
Wanette town	350	356	1.7	295	86.1	0.3	0.0	11.2	2.4	28.1	60.0	11.9	114	79.8	57.0	9.6
Wann town	125	125	0.0	192	66.7	0.0	0.0	27.1	6.3	26.1	59.8	14.1	61	91.8	65.6	23.0
Wapanucka town	438	443	1.1	389	54.0	0.0	0.0	36.5	9.5	30.9	56.8	12.3	149	75.8	62.4	4.0
Warner town	1,641	1,619	-1.3	1,763	63.1	3.7	0.0	28.7	4.4	22.5	64.8	12.5	569	55.7	44.3	14.2
Warr Acres city	10,043	10,408	3.6	10,268	58.1	7.4	4.4	9.5	20.6	23.2	62.7	14.1	3,866	64.0	43.3	21.3
Warwick town	148	150	1.4	125	88.8	0.0	0.0	11.2	0.0	19.2	66.4	14.4	56	76.8	76.8	5.4
Washington town	618	632	2.3	613	84.3	0.5	2.0	10.1	3.1	33.2	56.9	9.8	195	69.2	37.9	17.9
Watonga city	5,111	3,040	-40.5	2,993	57.0	16.9	0.4	10.1	15.6	12.8	77.4	9.9	760	70.9	57.1	17.1
Watts town	324	314	-3.1	293	52.6	0.0	0.3	42.0	5.1	25.6	63.7	10.6	98	64.3	71.4	9.2
Wauhillau CDP	345	NA	NA	341	30.8	0.0	0.0	67.7	1.5	35.3	59.2	5.6	116	94.8	57.8	27.6
Waukomis town	1,286	1,355	5.4	1,505	91.8	0.8	0.5	2.4	4.6	31.4	52.5	16.0	536	72.9	58.6	16.4
Waurika city	2,071	1,993	-3.8	1,856	84.0	1.8	0.4	5.1	8.7	23.1	58.9	18.0	740	65.5	59.9	15.4
Wayne town	688	704	2.3	646	75.9	0.0	0.3	18.3	5.6	27.6	61.0	11.1	243	44.9	52.7	13.6
Waynoka city	927	966	4.2	1,081	83.3	0.5	0.0	5.5	10.8	25.7	59.1	15.3	421	60.3	61.8	16.9
Weatherford city	10,835	11,989	10.7	11,410	75.6	4.3	1.6	8.8	9.8	22.3	69.9	7.9	4,056	45.4	27.0	34.3
Webb City town	62	62	0.0	85	88.2	0.0	0.0	11.8	0.0	40.0	47.2	12.9	33	78.8	60.6	0.0
Webbers Falls town	618	605	-2.1	482	64.5	6.2	0.0	24.9	4.4	27.0	51.1	22.0	213	72.3	53.1	10.8
Welch town	619	601	-2.9	588	68.9	0.0	0.7	22.8	7.7	24.7	52.8	22.4	246	80.1	52.4	15.4
Weleetka town	998	988	-1.0	997	47.3	9.6	1.2	35.5	6.3	20.2	64.0	15.5	382	59.7	59.4	9.2
Welling CDP	771	NA	NA	874	57.4	0.0	0.0	42.6	0.0	31.4	53.8	14.8	261	90.4	65.1	15.7
Wellston town	784	787	0.4	797	83.3	4.9	0.0	11.4	0.4	24.5	65.0	10.5	327	66.7	57.5	15.3
West Peavine CDP	218	NA	NA	267	38.6	0.0	1.1	60.3	0.0	27.0	53.6	19.5	89	75.3	69.7	19.1
Westport town	303	300	-1.0	343	92.7	0.6	0.0	5.2	1.5	21.3	55.8	23.0	135	95.6	33.3	29.6
West Siloam Springs town	846	843	-0.4	988	57.6	0.4	1.0	36.8	4.1	22.3	59.6	18.0	271	59.0	58.3	11.4
Westville town	1,632	1,584	-2.9	1,860	49.8	1.4	0.0	42.8	6.0	30.8	57.3	11.8	660	47.9	63.5	8.6
Wetumka city	1,282	1,251	-2.4	1,231	47.4	5.0	0.0	45.5	2.0	26.3	55.5	18.0	409	57.7	63.8	4.6
Wewoka city	3,430	3,434	0.1	3,444	48.8	17.9	0.0	30.1	3.2	30.1	50.1	19.9	1,256	55.4	61.8	11.1
Whitefield town	391	394	0.8	484	68.4	3.9	0.0	10.5	17.1	27.8	63.2	8.9	175	61.7	54.3	27.4
White Oak CDP	263	NA	NA	214	35.0	0.0	0.0	59.8	5.1	26.6	53.2	20.1	70	84.3	55.7	20.0
Whitesboro CDP	250	NA	NA	193	51.3	0.0	0.0	46.1	2.6	33.6	41.5	24.9	73	64.4	45.2	23.3
White Water CDP	80	NA	NA	17	100.0	0.0	0.0	0.0	0.0	0.0	47.1	52.9	8	100.0	0.0	0.0
Wickliffe CDP	75	NA	NA	28	78.6	0.0	0.0	21.4	0.0	0.0	57.1	42.9	18	100.0	66.7	0.0
Wilburton city	2,845	2,734	-3.9	2,797	69.8	0.9	1.3	22.7	5.3	20.3	65.3	14.4	998	55.1	44.7	13.4
Willow town	149	147	-1.3	216	66.2	0.0	0.0	0.9	32.9	13.9	48.8	37.5	124	78.2	44.4	2.4
Wilson city	1,726	1,738	0.7	1,611	90.1	0.0	0.0	7.0	3.0	21.8	56.6	21.5	584	65.6	67.5	10.1
Winchester town	516	505	-2.1	478	74.7	0.6	0.0	18.8	5.9	19.3	68.9	11.9	183	92.3	57.4	10.9
Wister town	1,102	1,076	-2.4	1,147	75.9	0.0	0.0	20.7	3.4	28.5	54.4	17.3	452	67.0	55.3	9.5
Woodall CDP	823	NA	NA	949	38.3	0.0	0.5	58.8	2.4	27.5	60.5	12.0	294	86.7	52.4	10.5
Woodlawn Park town	153	158	3.3	155	97.4	0.0	0.0	2.6	0.0	9.6	58.7	31.6	77	79.2	28.6	41.6
Woodward city	11,972	12,963	8.3	12,389	78.8	0.1	0.1	6.0	15.1	27.1	60.4	12.4	4,478	64.8	49.9	20.3
Wright City town	762	748	-1.8	629	36.9	7.2	0.0	55.5	0.5	31.5	54.2	14.3	224	70.5	59.8	11.6
Wyandotte town	331	334	0.9	329	57.8	0.0	1.2	37.4	3.6	28.0	59.8	12.5	115	70.4	53.0	8.7
Wynnewood city	2,211	2,213	0.1	2,343	74.6	8.6	0.0	13.4	3.4	23.9	55.2	20.8	901	59.8	61.4	12.5
Wynona town	437	435	-0.5	431	76.6	0.0	0.0	23.0	0.5	22.8	61.3	15.8	177	85.9	65.0	6.8
Yale city	1,227	1,224	-0.2	1,169	87.4	0.0	0.2	10.6	1.8	27.4	55.7	16.9	471	69.2	67.7	5.9
Yeager town	75	73	-2.7	76	82.9	0.0	0.0	15.8	1.3	22.3	60.5	17.1	34	97.1	52.9	0.0
Yukon city	22,709	25,349	11.6	24,127	85.5	1.2	2.0	5.3	6.0	25.9	58.9	15.2	8,631	77.4	32.6	26.5
Zeb CDP	497	NA	NA	565	58.8	0.0	0.0	38.1	3.2	17.4	69.5	13.1	236	87.7	48.7	16.5
Zena CDP	122	NA	NA	58	100.0	0.0	0.0	0.0	0.0	0.0	86.2	13.8	42	54.8	42.9	19.0
Zion CDP	41	NA	NA	15	46.7	0.0	0.0	53.3	0.0	0.0	66.7	33.3	8	100.0	37.5	50.0
OREGON	3,831,073	3,970,239	3.6	3,900,343	77.6	1.7	3.8	4.7	12.1	22.0	63.1	14.9	1,522,988	61.5	30.5	32.2
Adair Village city	827	815	-1.5	881	87.5	1.2	2.3	4.4	4.5	36.9	57.1	6.1	267	68.2	17.2	42.3
Adams city	350	348	-0.6	356	92.4	0.0	0.0	4.2	3.4	13.0	65.9	21.1	148	89.2	31.1	16.2
Adrian city	177	172	-2.8	163	68.1	0.0	3.1	0.6	28.2	19.0	65.8	15.3	70	52.9	32.9	20.0
Albany city	50,158	51,980	3.6	51,210	80.8	0.7	2.3	4.3	12.0	25.5	61.3	13.3	19,512	59.0	31.7	23.3
Aloha CDP	49,425	NA	NA	52,902	60.1	3.1	8.8	4.8	23.2	28.7	63.9	7.3	17,239	64.5	31.1	29.4
Alpine CDP	171	NA	NA	136	92.6	0.0	0.0	7.4	0.0	17.6	65.4	16.9	59	76.3	42.4	23.7
Alsea CDP	164	NA	NA	142	94.4	0.0	0.0	0.0	5.6	31.7	58.3	9.9	49	65.3	57.1	0.0
Altamont CDP	19,257	NA	NA	19,278	79.8	0.5	1.0	5.7	13.0	25.2	57.8	17.0	7,627	70.7	40.7	21.1
Amity city	1,614	1,631	1.1	1,568	77.6	0.0	0.3	5.1	17.0	25.5	63.1	11.4	544	62.9	34.7	13.2
Annex CDP	235	NA	NA	317	64.7	0.0	0.6	0.9	33.8	24.0	64.1	12.0	100	62.0	63.0	9.0
Antelope city	46	47	2.2	8	100.0	0.0	0.0	0.0	0.0	0.0	75.0	25.0	7	28.6	57.1	14.3
Arlington city	586	604	3.1	563	89.7	0.4	0.0	0.0	9.9	29.2	58.6	12.1	214	66.4	48.6	22.4
Ashland city	20,078	20,684	3.0	20,412	87.7	2.2	2.2	3.6	4.3	17.3	63.7	19.1	9,324	54.6	11.0	58.0
Astoria city	9,477	9,521	0.5	9,503	82.9	1.4	2.7	4.0	9.0	18.9	63.2	18.0	4,233	50.3	24.4	32.3
Athena city	1,132	1,134	0.2	1,053	90.5	0.6	0.1	8.5	0.3	27.8	50.6	21.7	387	70.8	31.0	17.8
Aumsville city	3,589	3,923	9.3	3,740	88.3	0.0	0.7	3.2	7.8	31.9	58.3	9.8	1,248	71.0	44.2	10.2
Aurora city	918	957	4.2	998	89.2	0.0	0.0	1.2	9.6	22.0	65.6	12.2	399	83.0	25.8	42.1
Baker City city	9,828	9,801	-0.3	9,774	92.1	0.1	0.8	4.0	3.0	23.3	56.1	20.7	4,254	59.2	41.9	19.3
Bandon city	3,066	3,037	-0.9	3,055	95.0	1.4	0.8	1.3	1.5	12.5	57.1	30.4	1,585	63.5	24.6	29.5
Banks city	1,777	1,885	6.1	1,699	88.9	0.0	1.2	2.4	7.4	33.8	62.5	3.6	536	76.5	31.7	28.5
Barlow city	135	138	2.2	170	47.1	0.0	0.0	7.6	45.3	24.7	67.6	7.6	57	84.2	49.1	17.5
Barview CDP	1,844	NA	NA	1,698	93.6	1.4	1.1	1.6	2.2	18.5	57.5	24.0	755	71.8	49.3	8.5
Bay City city	1,286	1,292	0.5	1,428	91.1	0.0	2.4	0.3	6.2	21.2	60.1	18.8	539	82.0	48.4	15.2
Bayside Gardens CDP	880	NA	NA	750	94.5	0.0	1.6	3.9	0.0	9.5	62.2	28.3	359	73.5	39.3	23.7
Beatty CDP	0	NA	NA	39	0.0	0.0	0.0	100.0	0.0	0.0	100.0	0.0	19	100.0	0.0	0.0
Beaver CDP	122	NA	NA	202	100.0	0.0	0.0	0.0	0.0	42.0	30.7	27.2	75	44.0	70.7	12.0
Beavercreek CDP	4,485	NA	NA	4,129	92.6	0.2	0.2	5.9	1.1	22.4	60.7	16.8	1,462	91.5	26.6	23.3
Beaverton city	89,779	95,109	5.9	92,593	65.2	2.3	12.1	4.5	15.8	23.0	66.4	10.5	37,028	47.8	22.0	46.0
Bellfountain CDP	75	NA	NA	95	100.0	0.0	0.0	0.0	0.0	64.2	25.2	10.5	22	100.0	45.5	54.5
Bend city	76,639	84,080	9.7	79,698	87.1	0.5	1.9	2.3	8.2	22.8	62.9	14.3	32,442	58.3	20.1	41.5
Bethany CDP	20,646	NA	NA	21,658	53.3	1.5	33.9	5.2	6.0	31.8	58.6	9.7	7,529	78.7	10.1	69.9
Biggs Junction CDP	22	NA	NA	33	100.0	0.0	0.0	0.0	0.0	0.0	100.0	0.0	9	0.0	0.0	100.0
Black Butte Ranch CDP	366	NA	NA	262	100.0	0.0	0.0	0.0	0.0	0.0	23.2	76.7	135	100.0	9.6	79.3

1 May be of any race.

Table A. All Places — **Population and Housing**

STATE City, town, township, borough, or CDP (county if applicable)	Population: 2010 census total population	Population: 2014 estimated population	Population: Percent change 2010–2014	Population: ACS total population estimate 2010–2014	Race and Hispanic or Latino origin (percent), 2010–2014: White alone, not Hispanic or Latino	Black alone, not Hispanic or Latino	Asian alone, not Hispanic or Latino	All other races or 2 or more races, not Hispanic or Latino	Hispanic or Latino[1]	Age (percent), 2010–2014: Under 18 years old	Age 18 to 64 years old	Age 65 years and older	Households, 2010–2014: Total occupied housing units	Percent owner occupied	Householders by level of education (percent): High school diploma or less	Bachelor's degree or more
	1	2	3	4	5	6	7	8	9	10	11	12	13	14	15	16
OREGON—Con.																
Blodgett CDP	58	NA	NA	36	100.0	0.0	0.0	0.0	0.0	0.0	47.2	52.8	18	100.0	100.0	0.0
Boardman city	3,228	3,329	3.1	3,305	30.4	0.0	0.0	1.8	67.8	34.0	58.6	7.3	961	61.1	73.9	4.4
Bonanza town	415	409	-1.4	469	80.4	0.0	0.9	6.8	11.9	30.1	56.4	13.4	164	61.0	59.8	19.5
Brogan CDP	90	NA	NA	221	100.0	0.0	0.0	0.0	0.0	24.9	58.3	16.7	70	55.7	28.6	15.7
Brookings city	6,336	6,407	1.1	6,350	85.1	0.0	0.5	7.0	7.4	12.9	60.0	27.1	3,164	51.4	29.9	29.4
Brooks CDP	398	NA	NA	997	60.8	0.0	0.0	22.7	16.5	27.8	68.7	3.3	268	72.8	32.5	19.8
Brownsville city	1,668	1,693	1.5	1,474	92.3	1.1	0.4	2.8	3.4	18.8	64.6	16.6	618	77.5	44.3	12.5
Bull Mountain CDP	9,133	NA	NA	8,977	75.5	0.3	13.5	7.2	3.6	26.9	65.9	7.1	3,010	82.6	8.5	62.3
Bunker Hill CDP	1,444	NA	NA	909	84.8	0.0	4.3	7.7	3.2	31.2	58.6	10.1	393	59.8	56.2	3.3
Burns city	2,806	2,722	-3.0	2,753	88.7	0.4	0.3	5.5	5.2	17.4	59.0	23.5	1,184	68.6	49.7	18.4
Butte Falls town	423	433	2.4	438	92.0	0.0	0.0	7.3	0.7	27.8	63.0	9.1	141	56.0	30.5	9.9
Butteville CDP	265	NA	NA	123	82.9	0.0	0.0	0.0	17.1	12.2	51.2	36.6	57	100.0	12.3	57.9
Camp Sherman CDP	233	NA	NA	370	90.3	0.0	1.6	4.9	3.2	9.9	58.2	31.6	143	77.6	14.0	71.3
Canby city	16,649	17,010	2.2	16,821	75.6	0.0	2.2	1.4	20.8	27.0	59.8	13.3	5,795	66.8	33.9	24.3
Cannon Beach city	1,690	1,694	0.2	1,542	81.3	0.1	0.0	7.6	11.0	11.1	67.2	21.7	722	54.2	25.5	42.5
Canyon City town	703	671	-4.6	800	91.9	0.6	0.1	3.8	3.6	20.9	54.7	24.4	323	83.3	36.2	13.3
Canyonville city	1,884	1,898	0.7	2,276	83.7	0.0	2.0	10.5	3.9	26.8	50.7	22.5	888	53.5	52.1	10.5
Cape Meares CDP	99	NA	NA	136	100.0	0.0	0.0	0.0	0.0	0.0	37.5	62.5	78	76.9	28.2	26.9
Carlton city	2,007	2,043	1.8	1,850	88.3	0.0	0.3	4.6	6.8	29.8	60.6	9.6	643	74.8	37.5	14.5
Cascade Locks city	1,144	1,157	1.1	1,108	88.7	0.0	0.5	8.8	1.9	21.9	64.4	13.7	465	65.6	54.8	16.3
Cascadia CDP	147	NA	NA	110	42.7	0.0	0.0	0.0	57.3	40.0	60.0	0.0	44	52.3	47.7	0.0
Cave Junction city	1,880	1,886	0.3	2,059	85.2	5.1	1.5	2.8	5.4	20.2	53.1	26.4	897	65.7	45.3	14.6
Cayuse CDP	68	NA	NA	64	57.8	0.0	0.0	42.2	0.0	39.1	54.8	6.3	14	78.6	42.9	21.4
Cedar Hills CDP	8,300	NA	NA	8,757	80.3	1.4	3.9	2.5	11.9	21.7	66.4	11.7	3,537	62.7	19.8	52.7
Cedar Mill CDP	14,546	NA	NA	15,482	76.2	1.3	13.6	4.2	4.6	25.8	62.7	11.5	5,932	75.5	8.8	62.3
Central Point city	17,174	17,724	3.2	17,443	85.9	0.1	0.3	4.7	8.9	26.4	55.5	17.9	6,637	61.8	37.7	21.3
Chenoweth CDP	1,855	NA	NA	1,601	80.0	0.0	1.0	1.1	18.0	18.5	63.4	18.2	636	83.3	41.7	9.3
Chiloquin city	734	716	-2.5	780	32.4	1.3	0.9	64.4	1.0	28.7	57.2	14.1	318	50.0	40.9	23.0
Clatskanie city	1,747	1,746	-0.1	1,949	79.5	0.0	0.0	7.7	12.7	21.7	60.3	18.2	733	65.8	46.2	12.0
Cloverdale CDP	250	NA	NA	272	72.8	0.0	0.0	0.0	27.2	35.6	37.2	27.2	86	76.7	33.7	25.6
Coburg city	1,035	1,040	0.5	1,021	85.6	1.6	2.9	5.0	4.9	21.7	63.4	14.9	437	74.6	19.9	28.8
Columbia City city	1,946	1,953	0.4	2,351	95.1	0.0	0.2	1.4	3.4	20.4	56.9	22.8	866	81.2	28.1	27.8
Condon city	682	705	3.4	606	95.7	1.5	0.0	0.8	2.0	15.4	45.5	39.3	324	66.4	44.8	13.9
Coos Bay city	15,973	16,039	0.4	16,022	79.9	1.2	2.1	7.2	9.6	20.6	58.4	21.0	6,608	55.3	39.0	24.0
Coquille city	3,866	3,806	-1.6	3,831	86.3	0.0	0.2	6.5	7.0	20.2	57.4	22.4	1,491	67.3	34.5	24.2
Cornelius city	11,869	12,185	2.7	12,068	45.1	0.8	1.2	3.3	49.5	30.3	61.2	8.6	3,247	78.9	47.7	12.4
Corvallis city	54,488	54,953	0.9	54,735	79.5	1.0	8.6	3.2	7.7	14.7	74.3	10.7	21,251	44.3	12.0	51.3
Cottage Grove city	9,685	9,845	1.7	9,772	83.7	0.0	0.4	6.3	9.5	25.7	57.4	16.9	3,957	55.8	46.7	14.4
Cove city	552	554	0.4	604	93.4	0.0	0.0	6.6	0.0	22.5	57.1	20.4	250	80.0	48.0	16.0
Crabtree CDP	391	NA	NA	319	97.2	0.0	0.0	0.0	2.8	24.5	38.5	37.0	116	100.0	82.8	0.0
Crane CDP	129	NA	NA	191	100.0	0.0	0.0	0.0	0.0	27.7	63.3	8.9	58	65.5	34.5	3.4
Crawfordsville CDP	332	NA	NA	285	97.5	0.0	0.0	2.5	0.0	21.4	58.6	20.0	112	68.8	64.3	0.0
Creswell city	5,031	5,102	1.4	5,065	87.3	0.0	0.8	5.4	6.5	26.5	57.2	16.2	1,931	76.3	25.0	19.6
Culver city	1,357	1,392	2.6	1,755	62.8	1.9	0.1	4.9	30.2	36.0	59.4	4.8	524	57.1	44.7	8.0
Dallas city	14,583	15,102	3.6	14,788	91.5	0.2	0.8	3.2	4.4	25.9	56.2	17.8	5,694	61.8	40.5	19.3
Damascus city	10,547	10,893	3.3	10,711	88.5	0.4	4.1	3.1	4.0	20.3	64.2	15.4	3,677	89.5	34.0	28.1
Days Creek CDP	272	NA	NA	324	81.5	0.0	0.0	1.5	17.0	12.9	62.6	24.4	141	83.7	55.3	9.9
Dayton city	2,534	2,572	1.5	2,545	53.2	0.4	0.7	5.2	40.4	33.5	54.5	12.0	822	69.7	49.0	18.5
Dayville town	149	145	-2.7	146	95.9	0.0	0.0	4.1	0.0	18.5	55.5	26.0	70	71.4	41.4	27.1
Deer Island CDP	294	NA	NA	421	93.8	0.0	0.0	6.2	0.0	12.8	76.7	10.5	208	83.2	72.6	3.4
Depoe Bay city	1,398	1,400	0.1	1,622	90.1	0.0	1.4	2.3	6.3	8.2	62.5	29.3	826	65.1	25.9	37.9
Deschutes River Woods CDP	5,077	NA	NA	5,358	90.6	0.0	0.5	0.8	8.2	25.2	65.3	9.5	1,928	71.1	36.0	12.2
Detroit city	202	210	4.0	151	87.4	0.0	0.0	2.6	9.9	6.6	66.2	27.2	70	71.4	20.0	38.6
Dillard CDP	478	NA	NA	392	88.3	0.0	0.0	0.0	11.7	31.7	58.7	9.7	144	36.1	41.7	0.0
Donald city	979	979	0.0	1,068	78.6	3.7	0.0	2.0	15.8	22.5	63.3	14.2	395	87.1	37.0	25.6
Drain city	1,151	1,141	-0.9	1,146	90.4	0.0	2.0	4.3	3.3	19.2	59.5	21.4	430	66.3	57.9	6.3
Dufur city	604	607	0.5	532	96.8	0.0	0.0	2.8	0.4	31.7	50.9	17.3	210	84.3	45.7	6.2
Dundee city	3,162	3,197	1.1	3,181	78.5	0.2	1.8	2.7	16.9	22.4	65.2	12.5	1,069	78.9	26.8	26.0
Dunes City city	1,303	1,327	1.8	1,267	92.4	0.6	0.3	5.6	1.0	13.0	50.1	37.0	562	88.3	26.7	22.8
Durham city	1,351	1,924	42.4	1,327	80.3	2.8	2.3	3.4	11.2	21.1	62.8	16.1	551	61.0	14.3	44.5
Eagle Crest CDP	1,696	NA	NA	1,436	94.6	0.0	0.0	4.0	1.4	8.7	40.0	51.4	711	86.9	11.1	45.6
Eagle Point city	8,469	8,753	3.4	8,599	87.3	0.0	1.2	6.4	5.1	27.0	59.2	13.7	3,105	60.5	36.9	11.5
Echo city	699	704	0.7	690	79.3	0.0	0.0	9.4	11.3	22.2	61.7	16.1	228	70.2	52.6	15.8
Elgin city	1,711	1,713	0.1	1,699	91.0	0.0	0.0	5.0	4.0	24.9	60.4	14.7	653	60.9	50.2	8.3
Elkton city	195	194	-0.5	224	90.2	0.0	0.0	8.0	1.8	30.8	41.6	27.7	91	74.7	35.2	18.7
Enterprise city	1,940	1,886	-2.8	1,978	94.3	1.0	0.0	1.7	3.0	22.1	53.7	24.0	800	65.0	40.5	24.8
Eola CDP	45	NA	NA	0	0.0	0.0	0.0	0.0	0.0	0.0	0.0	0.0	0	0.0	0.0	0.0
Estacada city	2,695	2,999	11.3	2,860	84.2	0.0	0.9	2.8	12.1	22.2	62.6	15.2	1,166	59.2	52.5	11.3
Eugene city	156,358	160,561	2.7	158,131	80.6	1.4	4.1	5.5	8.4	18.0	68.4	13.6	65,924	48.9	20.9	38.7
Fair Oaks CDP	278	NA	NA	275	100.0	0.0	0.0	0.0	0.0	10.5	64.7	24.7	105	100.0	15.2	0.0
Fairview city	8,920	9,218	3.3	9,094	75.9	4.7	3.0	2.9	13.4	22.4	65.2	12.5	3,856	51.4	31.6	22.7
Falls City city	947	960	1.4	916	87.6	0.0	0.2	9.9	2.3	18.7	62.2	19.3	350	81.7	45.1	14.9
Florence city	8,466	8,506	0.5	8,498	92.3	0.7	1.4	3.9	1.7	12.5	50.6	36.7	4,344	62.2	29.7	27.3
Foots Creek CDP	799	NA	NA	708	92.7	0.0	0.0	4.7	2.7	5.2	45.8	48.9	302	95.7	48.7	15.9
Forest Grove city	21,088	23,096	9.5	22,070	70.6	0.5	2.6	4.0	22.3	26.5	60.2	13.4	7,686	58.7	40.9	24.2
Fort Hill CDP	129	NA	NA	142	97.9	0.0	0.0	0.7	1.4	0.0	99.3	0.7	128	97.7	88.3	0.0
Fossil city	473	449	-5.1	435	91.3	0.0	0.0	7.8	0.9	8.5	56.4	35.2	251	67.3	34.3	17.5
Four Corners CDP	15,947	NA	NA	17,202	51.3	2.0	1.1	4.5	41.2	28.6	60.0	11.3	5,429	56.3	48.2	12.0
Fruitdale CDP	1,177	NA	NA	1,057	89.0	1.3	0.0	0.0	9.6	19.5	67.9	12.6	401	62.6	34.4	23.7
Garden Home-Whitford CDP	6,674	NA	NA	6,019	87.2	0.8	1.2	3.7	7.1	15.6	65.4	19.0	2,791	65.4	15.6	53.6
Gardiner CDP	248	NA	NA	195	90.3	0.0	0.0	9.7	0.0	14.4	58.5	27.2	99	78.8	45.5	0.0
Garibaldi city	779	768	-1.4	805	94.7	1.0	0.0	1.1	3.2	17.3	60.7	22.2	351	68.1	34.8	14.5
Gaston city	637	673	5.7	703	85.3	0.0	1.6	7.7	5.4	18.5	75.2	6.4	259	65.3	48.6	10.8
Gates city	471	477	1.3	580	95.5	0.0	0.3	4.1	0.0	19.3	58.7	21.9	252	65.1	54.0	8.7
Gearhart city	1,462	1,506	3.0	1,592	92.9	1.1	1.0	0.6	4.4	22.8	57.1	20.2	691	83.1	28.4	37.8
Gervais city	2,464	2,575	4.5	2,527	33.9	0.1	0.3	2.9	62.8	35.4	60.7	3.8	633	83.1	52.6	12.8
Gladstone city	11,497	11,888	3.4	11,668	82.8	1.5	3.0	2.8	10.0	22.2	62.7	15.2	4,578	56.6	37.1	20.9
Glasgow CDP	763	NA	NA	957	61.3	0.0	3.8	32.2	2.7	15.3	71.2	13.4	406	77.6	47.3	21.7
Glendale city	874	866	-0.9	783	86.3	0.0	0.0	5.2	8.4	20.4	58.1	21.6	346	56.1	52.9	4.3

1 May be of any race.

Table A. All Places — **Population and Housing**

STATE City, town, township, borough, or CDP (county if applicable)	Population: 2010 census total population	Population: 2014 estimated population	Population: Percent change 2010–2014	Population: ACS total population estimate 2010–2014	Race and Hispanic or Latino origin (percent), 2010–2014: White alone, not Hispanic or Latino	Black alone, not Hispanic or Latino	Asian alone, not Hispanic or Latino	All other races or 2 or more races, not Hispanic or Latino	Hispanic or Latino[1]	Age (percent), 2010–2014: Under 18 years old	Age 18 to 64 years old	Age 65 years and older	Households, 2010–2014: Total occupied housing units	Percent owner occupied	Householders by level of education (percent): High school diploma or less	Bachelor's degree or more
	1	2	3	4	5	6	7	8	9	10	11	12	13	14	15	16
OREGON—Con.																
Glide CDP	1,795	NA	NA	1,933	81.4	2.4	0.0	12.5	3.7	27.6	57.7	14.6	690	79.0	44.3	26.8
Gold Beach city	2,253	2,247	-0.3	2,263	90.7	0.0	2.4	4.2	2.7	14.6	62.6	22.8	1,012	68.2	36.0	26.8
Gold Hill city	1,220	1,254	2.8	1,054	91.6	0.3	0.3	4.5	3.4	21.9	63.1	15.1	451	71.2	36.4	14.6
Gopher Flats CDP	379	NA	NA	364	87.4	0.0	0.0	9.1	3.6	12.4	51.1	36.5	154	58.4	36.4	14.3
Government Camp CDP	193	NA	NA	81	100.0	0.0	0.0	0.0	0.0	0.0	49.4	50.6	40	100.0	0.0	35.0
Grand Ronde CDP	1,661	NA	NA	1,516	54.0	0.0	1.0	35.9	9.0	22.0	58.5	19.5	626	61.8	55.1	12.8
Granite city	38	37	-2.6	20	95.0	0.0	0.0	5.0	0.0	0.0	60.0	40.0	14	100.0	50.0	0.0
Grants Pass city	34,654	35,272	1.8	34,916	84.2	0.2	0.7	5.0	9.8	25.3	54.1	20.5	13,943	50.1	39.1	17.3
Grass Valley city	164	161	-1.8	164	85.4	1.2	0.6	3.0	9.8	17.0	59.2	23.8	68	73.5	33.8	29.4
Green CDP	7,515	NA	NA	7,954	87.7	0.0	0.4	4.0	8.0	24.3	60.9	14.9	2,954	76.6	48.1	8.9
Greenhorn city	0	0	0.0	10	100.0	0.0	0.0	0.0	0.0	0.0	0.0	100.0	5	100.0	0.0	0.0
Gresham city	105,590	109,892	4.1	108,250	67.5	3.6	4.1	5.7	19.0	25.5	62.7	11.8	38,556	52.3	40.2	19.9
Haines city	416	413	-0.7	426	90.1	0.0	0.0	4.9	4.9	16.8	60.3	22.8	184	60.9	44.6	10.9
Halfway city	290	288	-0.7	350	88.9	0.0	0.0	10.0	1.1	20.3	61.0	18.6	179	55.3	53.1	14.5
Halsey city	904	922	2.0	1,114	84.2	0.0	0.0	4.7	11.1	34.6	55.9	9.4	348	62.1	23.9	15.8
Happy Valley city	14,283	17,319	21.3	15,693	69.5	1.4	16.9	6.4	5.8	29.7	62.4	7.8	4,877	86.2	14.6	53.3
Harbor CDP	2,391	NA	NA	1,956	89.4	0.1	0.0	9.5	1.0	7.6	58.5	34.0	1,091	59.2	36.9	22.5
Harper CDP	109	NA	NA	109	99.1	0.0	0.0	0.9	0.0	26.6	40.5	33.0	51	80.4	56.9	11.8
Harrisburg city	3,567	3,641	2.1	3,618	89.1	0.0	0.0	2.5	8.4	27.8	66.1	6.1	1,191	73.2	47.2	16.5
Hayesville CDP	19,936	NA	NA	18,611	44.7	1.8	3.8	7.5	42.2	31.2	57.4	11.4	6,327	50.4	46.3	16.3
Hebo CDP	232	NA	NA	203	82.8	0.0	0.0	9.9	7.4	2.0	36.0	62.1	121	52.9	85.1	0.0
Helix city	184	186	1.1	196	92.9	0.0	0.0	6.1	1.0	32.2	56.2	11.7	71	76.1	22.5	16.9
Heppner city	1,291	1,284	-0.5	1,268	90.3	0.0	2.1	3.2	4.4	28.2	53.3	18.5	551	64.6	43.7	22.0
Hermiston city	16,751	17,137	2.3	17,031	64.4	0.2	0.8	1.6	32.9	32.2	57.1	10.7	6,224	55.4	47.2	16.8
Hillsboro city	92,149	99,393	7.9	95,765	60.2	1.4	8.7	5.6	24.1	27.0	64.8	8.4	33,559	53.5	26.9	37.2
Hines city	1,566	1,500	-4.2	1,691	90.7	1.3	0.0	1.7	6.3	29.3	55.7	15.1	723	58.9	41.9	11.3
Holley CDP	378	NA	NA	331	100.0	0.0	0.0	0.0	0.0	18.5	49.5	32.0	124	85.5	65.3	16.9
Hood River city	7,133	7,476	4.8	7,311	68.9	0.0	2.2	1.9	27.1	24.9	63.0	12.1	3,062	48.6	34.9	37.6
Hubbard city	3,173	3,221	1.5	3,206	63.7	0.0	0.0	1.3	35.0	37.4	58.1	4.6	975	75.4	52.2	13.2
Huntington city	440	437	-0.7	349	86.8	0.0	4.3	4.9	4.0	11.1	55.2	33.5	182	73.1	49.5	2.7
Idanha city	134	137	2.2	145	88.3	0.0	0.0	4.1	7.6	11.8	58.5	29.7	68	66.2	44.1	11.8
Idaville CDP	337	NA	NA	461	82.6	0.0	0.0	9.3	8.0	18.1	63.5	18.4	133	73.7	60.9	0.0
Imbler city	306	306	0.0	277	90.6	0.0	0.0	6.1	3.2	26.4	57.4	16.2	115	96.5	33.0	26.1
Independence city	8,601	8,768	1.9	8,654	59.4	0.4	1.6	5.0	33.5	28.4	63.7	7.7	3,008	56.7	40.0	17.4
Ione city	329	328	-0.3	296	94.6	0.0	0.0	0.0	5.4	17.6	62.8	19.6	116	81.9	36.2	25.0
Irrigon city	1,826	1,791	-1.9	2,065	61.7	0.0	0.0	2.9	35.4	36.0	53.1	10.9	593	74.0	51.8	11.1
Island City city	993	994	0.1	1,028	95.5	0.0	0.0	1.8	2.6	22.3	52.6	25.0	375	77.3	38.9	20.0
Jacksonville city	2,785	2,847	2.2	2,816	94.1	0.9	3.1	1.9	0.0	11.3	48.7	39.9	1,510	68.5	24.4	44.0
Jeffers Gardens CDP	0	NA	NA	363	98.9	0.0	0.0	1.1	0.0	14.1	78.5	7.4	152	88.2	26.3	18.4
Jefferson city	3,102	3,202	3.2	3,152	76.2	0.0	1.4	4.3	18.1	34.3	56.1	9.6	983	72.0	45.8	10.2
Jennings Lodge CDP	7,315	NA	NA	7,416	76.6	2.2	4.2	4.7	12.4	22.3	63.8	14.0	3,001	56.1	37.8	21.2
John Day city	1,746	1,680	-3.8	1,663	93.1	1.1	0.2	2.5	3.0	22.0	56.9	21.1	747	59.4	40.3	24.0
Johnson City city	566	569	0.5	573	73.1	1.2	6.5	0.3	18.8	21.9	58.8	19.4	278	95.7	53.2	12.2
Jordan Valley city	181	175	-3.3	158	96.8	0.0	0.0	0.0	3.2	11.4	54.4	34.2	80	86.3	60.0	15.0
Joseph city	1,081	1,052	-2.7	1,000	81.8	0.9	1.6	8.3	7.4	20.4	58.0	21.6	500	60.4	31.8	25.6
Junction City city	5,379	5,708	6.1	5,566	90.0	0.1	0.2	2.0	7.7	24.1	58.2	17.7	2,107	58.2	39.8	12.7
Juntura CDP	57	NA	NA	41	92.7	0.0	0.0	7.3	0.0	31.7	48.8	19.5	20	60.0	55.0	0.0
Keizer city	36,485	37,303	2.2	36,875	73.0	0.8	1.4	4.5	20.4	26.2	59.4	14.5	13,830	60.4	33.3	27.2
Kerby CDP	595	NA	NA	311	100.0	0.0	0.0	0.0	0.0	18.3	58.2	23.5	136	50.0	24.3	55.1
King City city	3,111	3,641	17.0	3,351	91.5	0.0	2.1	2.6	3.8	13.5	42.1	44.6	1,927	76.9	40.4	21.0
Kings Valley CDP	65	NA	NA	57	36.8	0.0	0.0	63.2	0.0	0.0	0.0	100.0	46	78.3	78.3	21.7
Kirkpatrick CDP	179	NA	NA	147	55.1	0.0	2.7	34.0	8.2	27.8	61.9	10.2	50	92.0	22.0	20.0
Klamath Falls city	20,991	21,119	0.6	21,165	76.8	1.5	1.3	8.6	11.9	21.1	65.6	13.1	9,108	46.4	39.9	21.2
Labish Village CDP	412	NA	NA	172	14.5	0.0	0.0	0.0	85.5	50.6	49.5	0.0	49	100.0	32.7	44.9
Lacomb CDP	546	NA	NA	557	92.3	0.0	0.0	5.0	2.7	32.6	50.0	17.2	163	62.6	26.4	16.0
Lafayette city	3,742	3,835	2.5	3,770	75.9	0.0	0.3	0.5	23.3	32.6	58.0	9.4	1,027	83.2	45.6	17.0
La Grande city	13,090	13,026	-0.5	13,090	89.9	1.0	1.2	4.7	3.2	19.5	64.7	15.7	5,481	52.2	33.6	27.0
Lake Oswego city	36,654	37,999	3.7	37,310	86.0	0.6	6.6	2.8	4.0	22.1	60.4	17.5	16,004	67.2	9.3	67.8
Lakeside city	1,699	1,686	-0.8	1,715	92.0	0.5	0.5	2.4	4.7	15.3	44.4	40.4	818	82.4	29.1	14.9
Lakeview town	2,294	2,298	0.2	2,796	90.2	0.0	1.5	3.1	5.1	22.0	60.8	17.1	1,320	57.4	35.6	23.7
Langlois CDP	177	NA	NA	237	91.6	0.0	0.0	0.0	8.4	21.9	59.9	18.1	99	100.0	53.5	37.4
La Pine city	1,653	1,742	5.4	1,714	88.2	0.0	1.8	3.4	6.7	22.0	61.0	17.0	734	51.6	50.5	14.7
Lebanon city	15,517	15,982	3.0	15,761	91.0	0.8	0.2	5.3	2.8	23.7	58.9	17.4	6,255	56.8	41.0	16.0
Lexington town	238	238	0.0	232	94.8	0.0	0.0	3.4	1.7	25.1	54.8	20.3	85	95.3	43.5	4.7
Lincoln Beach CDP	2,045	NA	NA	1,760	76.4	0.0	1.2	1.6	20.7	8.9	63.0	28.2	853	68.6	36.3	31.4
Lincoln City city	7,930	8,036	1.3	7,977	78.0	0.1	3.2	5.1	13.5	23.3	57.8	18.9	3,566	46.2	44.5	23.1
Lonerock city	21	22	4.8	19	100.0	0.0	0.0	0.0	0.0	0.0	26.3	73.7	13	76.9	84.6	0.0
Long Creek city	197	192	-2.5	195	95.9	0.0	0.0	4.1	0.0	19.5	62.6	17.9	79	73.4	55.7	2.5
Lookingglass CDP	855	NA	NA	1,018	100.0	0.0	0.0	0.0	0.0	23.3	52.8	23.9	388	85.8	33.5	16.0
Lostine city	213	209	-1.9	285	87.7	0.0	3.2	3.9	5.3	29.8	58.0	12.3	92	73.9	33.7	21.7
Lowell city	1,045	1,068	2.2	1,138	90.3	0.0	0.8	2.6	6.2	28.3	59.2	12.5	409	70.2	40.8	16.9
Lyons city	1,161	1,170	0.8	1,083	96.0	0.3	0.0	1.3	2.4	24.0	59.5	16.5	398	74.4	60.3	6.8
McMinnville city	32,187	33,393	3.7	32,839	70.5	1.5	1.9	4.3	21.8	25.4	58.9	15.5	11,644	55.9	42.4	21.8
Madras city	6,319	6,533	3.4	6,419	49.2	0.5	2.0	11.3	37.0	29.7	60.8	9.5	2,363	42.8	47.8	15.4
Malin city	805	789	-2.0	712	30.8	0.0	1.0	0.3	68.0	28.9	54.8	16.3	217	68.7	70.5	12.4
Manzanita city	598	613	2.5	413	83.1	0.0	8.7	1.5	6.8	16.9	49.6	33.7	184	72.8	21.2	60.9
Marion CDP	313	NA	NA	175	100.0	0.0	0.0	0.0	0.0	0.0	81.0	18.9	79	100.0	32.9	0.0
Maupin city	418	423	1.2	503	92.4	0.2	0.0	6.8	0.6	13.5	48.0	38.8	232	62.5	43.1	17.2
Maywood Park city	752	772	2.7	894	84.2	7.6	1.7	3.8	2.7	19.9	64.4	15.7	369	87.8	15.7	42.0
Medford city	74,943	78,557	4.8	76,648	79.8	0.9	1.3	4.7	13.4	23.4	60.5	16.1	29,695	51.2	35.9	26.2
Mehama CDP	292	NA	NA	200	88.0	0.0	0.0	12.0	0.0	22.5	71.5	6.0	80	63.8	51.3	0.0
Melrose CDP	735	NA	NA	749	93.5	0.0	1.5	3.6	1.5	11.7	62.1	26.0	276	100.0	37.7	29.3
Merlin CDP	1,615	NA	NA	1,594	87.6	0.0	1.6	10.7	0.2	13.2	71.0	15.7	675	69.6	27.3	6.8
Merrill city	844	824	-2.4	843	46.4	0.0	0.0	1.4	52.2	37.7	53.1	9.0	298	58.4	62.1	6.7
Metolius city	710	723	1.8	862	58.4	0.9	0.2	5.8	34.7	34.9	53.6	11.4	292	62.0	57.9	14.0
Metzger CDP	3,765	NA	NA	3,541	77.9	1.9	5.7	4.6	9.9	15.8	70.5	13.7	1,637	51.6	32.9	40.5
Mill City city	1,855	1,869	0.8	1,665	83.4	0.0	0.4	2.6	13.6	26.2	54.7	19.1	609	74.9	48.3	11.0
Millersburg city	1,329	1,410	6.1	1,771	74.0	0.0	0.5	3.7	21.8	29.9	57.4	12.4	600	78.8	38.5	24.8
Milton-Freewater city	7,050	7,088	0.5	7,094	42.8	0.3	1.2	1.0	54.7	32.2	56.7	11.1	2,495	51.8	49.2	13.1
Milwaukie city	20,291	20,640	1.7	20,449	83.6	2.5	3.6	4.7	5.5	19.1	66.3	14.5	8,652	58.5	28.4	28.7
Mission CDP	1,037	NA	NA	934	15.8	0.0	0.2	75.1	8.9	43.0	49.3	7.6	285	42.5	41.1	12.6

1 May be of any race.

Table A. All Places — **Population and Housing**

STATE City, town, township, borough, or CDP (county if applicable)	Population				Race and Hispanic or Latino origin (percent), 2010–2014					Age (percent), 2010–2014			Households, 2010–2014		Householders by level of education (percent)	
	2010 census total population	2014 estimated population	Percent change 2010–2014	ACS total population estimate 2010–2014	White alone, not Hispanic or Latino	Black alone, not Hispanic or Latino	Asian alone, not Hispanic or Latino	All other races or 2 or more races, not Hispanic or Latino	Hispanic or Latino[1]	Under 18 years old	Age 18 to 64 years old	Age 65 years and older	Total occupied housing units	Percent owner occupied	High school diploma or less	Bachelor's degree or more
	1	2	3	4	5	6	7	8	9	10	11	12	13	14	15	16
OREGON—Con.																
Mitchell city	130	125	-3.8	131	96.2	0.0	0.0	3.8	0.0	13.0	51.9	35.1	66	63.6	59.1	1.5
Molalla city	8,106	8,422	3.9	8,247	88.9	0.0	0.4	1.6	9.2	28.7	60.9	10.3	3,057	69.3	32.5	14.8
Monmouth city	9,534	9,950	4.4	9,769	79.0	0.8	2.9	6.1	11.1	19.5	71.5	8.9	3,344	49.0	25.1	31.0
Monroe city	617	615	-0.3	746	80.3	0.0	0.0	5.8	13.9	14.4	71.2	14.3	294	59.5	47.3	6.1
Monument city	128	125	-2.3	120	91.7	1.7	1.7	5.0	0.0	24.1	60.8	15.0	58	81.0	34.5	6.9
Moro city	324	312	-3.7	329	90.3	0.6	0.0	5.2	4.0	21.0	57.5	21.6	162	62.3	44.4	12.3
Mosier city	433	435	0.5	456	73.9	0.0	2.0	2.2	21.9	18.7	64.5	16.9	201	53.2	28.4	24.9
Mount Angel city	3,379	3,407	0.8	3,389	70.6	0.4	0.6	1.0	27.4	23.5	52.0	24.3	1,197	62.7	50.1	9.9
Mount Hood CDP	286	NA	NA	262	96.2	0.0	0.0	0.0	3.8	27.9	56.5	15.6	90	94.4	33.3	11.1
Mount Hood Village CDP	4,864	NA	NA	5,417	92.7	0.0	0.4	0.7	6.2	16.3	62.4	21.3	2,300	76.8	28.3	29.4
Mount Vernon city	527	506	-4.0	629	93.6	0.0	0.0	4.6	1.7	22.0	59.4	18.8	281	66.5	57.3	6.8
Mulino CDP	2,103	NA	NA	2,314	91.8	0.0	0.7	5.4	2.1	26.7	58.1	15.2	749	83.0	29.8	18.7
Myrtle Creek city	3,424	3,414	-0.3	3,413	82.6	0.0	0.0	6.4	11.0	19.0	65.0	16.1	1,345	48.4	47.5	11.4
Myrtle Point city	2,514	2,482	-1.3	2,416	87.5	0.0	0.7	7.3	4.5	21.1	57.0	21.9	953	64.8	47.8	16.6
Neahkahnie CDP	0	NA	NA	103	100.0	0.0	0.0	0.0	0.0	0.0	29.1	70.9	75	60.0	17.3	42.7
Nehalem city	271	266	-1.8	263	98.9	0.0	0.0	0.4	0.8	14.4	53.5	31.9	100	86.0	44.0	30.0
Nesika Beach CDP	463	NA	NA	404	85.9	0.0	0.0	0.0	14.1	0.0	66.8	33.2	220	67.3	36.8	8.2
Neskowin CDP	134	NA	NA	147	87.1	0.0	0.0	0.0	12.9	3.4	51.0	45.6	83	100.0	0.0	59.0
Netarts CDP	748	NA	NA	934	88.3	0.0	2.1	0.0	9.5	10.6	55.9	33.5	434	55.1	32.0	31.3
Newberg city	22,123	22,692	2.6	22,451	79.5	0.6	1.6	3.5	14.7	23.6	65.3	11.2	7,331	61.2	34.2	25.4
New Hope CDP	1,515	NA	NA	1,443	98.7	0.0	0.0	0.0	1.3	14.9	68.7	16.4	671	77.5	38.6	19.2
New Pine Creek CDP	120	NA	NA	108	69.4	0.0	0.0	30.6	0.0	14.8	46.4	38.9	43	46.5	93.0	0.0
Newport city	9,989	10,116	1.3	10,045	79.1	0.8	1.0	7.9	11.3	19.6	60.4	20.1	4,570	52.5	32.5	29.4
North Bend city	9,695	9,543	-1.6	9,591	83.8	0.3	1.2	8.3	6.5	23.2	57.6	19.3	3,697	57.7	33.3	25.1
North Plains city	1,947	2,058	5.7	1,868	84.8	0.0	0.3	5.0	9.9	22.4	66.5	11.1	746	77.7	40.2	22.1
North Powder city	435	434	-0.2	526	86.7	0.0	1.0	4.9	7.4	34.8	43.3	22.1	191	70.2	47.1	15.2
Nyssa city	3,267	3,167	-3.1	3,221	34.5	0.0	0.4	0.7	64.4	33.4	53.6	12.9	991	62.1	64.7	6.3
Oak Grove CDP	16,629	NA	NA	17,202	82.8	1.6	0.8	4.6	10.1	22.2	58.7	19.2	7,145	59.6	28.6	26.4
Oak Hills CDP	11,333	NA	NA	11,946	68.9	1.6	19.6	4.6	5.4	26.9	65.0	8.1	4,346	55.9	16.2	57.8
Oakland city	927	920	-0.8	732	97.1	0.0	0.0	1.2	1.6	15.3	64.8	19.9	343	65.6	41.4	19.0
Oakridge city	3,206	3,201	-0.2	3,205	96.7	0.0	0.0	1.8	1.6	14.6	57.8	27.5	1,565	79.0	49.9	11.4
Oatfield CDP	13,415	NA	NA	13,618	90.2	0.7	1.4	3.4	4.3	17.7	60.8	21.3	5,311	76.8	28.4	27.3
O'Brien CDP	504	NA	NA	112	100.0	0.0	0.0	0.0	0.0	0.0	70.6	29.5	79	44.3	20.3	0.0
Oceanside CDP	361	NA	NA	199	88.4	0.0	0.0	2.0	9.5	9.0	52.4	38.7	127	88.2	6.3	49.6
Odell CDP	2,255	NA	NA	2,301	32.8	0.2	0.0	3.8	63.3	39.9	52.4	7.6	649	92.1	66.9	6.9
Ontario city	11,366	10,982	-3.4	11,148	55.1	0.6	2.3	1.8	40.2	28.7	55.3	16.1	4,343	50.8	46.8	13.8
Oregon City city	32,628	35,266	8.1	33,834	85.5	0.7	1.6	3.0	9.2	25.0	64.0	10.9	12,639	65.4	29.7	24.9
Pacific City CDP	1,035	NA	NA	905	92.4	1.5	0.0	2.5	3.5	5.4	47.6	47.0	454	94.9	28.0	30.8
Paisley city	243	237	-2.5	254	97.6	0.0	2.0	0.0	0.4	12.2	54.2	33.5	141	58.2	41.8	13.5
Parkdale CDP	311	NA	NA	286	6.6	0.0	10.1	0.0	83.2	28.3	61.5	10.1	60	18.3	68.3	31.7
Pendleton city	16,612	16,904	1.8	16,830	81.0	1.7	1.2	7.7	8.4	23.6	62.7	13.7	6,213	55.3	28.2	22.0
Peoria CDP	94	NA	NA	84	100.0	0.0	0.0	0.0	0.0	15.5	84.6	0.0	35	100.0	80.0	20.0
Philomath city	4,586	4,563	-0.5	4,577	84.0	0.7	1.4	4.0	9.9	24.2	65.9	9.7	1,732	70.8	24.2	44.5
Phoenix city	4,428	4,514	1.9	4,465	80.9	0.4	0.3	8.7	9.7	18.8	57.7	23.5	2,034	67.9	49.5	21.8
Pilot Rock city	1,502	1,510	0.5	1,607	87.5	0.0	0.0	9.2	3.3	28.2	60.7	11.0	566	71.7	51.8	7.1
Pine Grove CDP	148	NA	NA	76	100.0	0.0	0.0	0.0	0.0	0.0	42.1	57.9	46	73.9	60.9	19.6
Pine Hollow CDP	494	NA	NA	445	89.7	0.0	1.1	2.0	7.2	8.7	52.2	39.1	219	73.1	37.9	9.1
Pistol River CDP	84	NA	NA	26	100.0	0.0	0.0	0.0	0.0	0.0	0.0	100.0	12	100.0	100.0	0.0
Plush CDP	57	NA	NA	43	95.3	0.0	0.0	4.7	0.0	4.7	65.2	30.2	26	46.2	30.8	53.8
Portland city	583,789	619,360	6.1	602,568	71.8	5.9	7.4	5.2	9.6	18.8	70.3	11.0	252,185	52.8	22.1	47.0
Port Orford city	1,133	1,133	0.0	1,263	94.5	0.0	0.2	1.2	4.1	17.8	52.8	29.4	593	60.4	32.2	27.8
Powers city	689	678	-1.6	862	81.9	0.0	0.0	11.8	6.3	21.5	51.7	26.8	336	69.9	47.0	9.2
Prairie City city	909	879	-3.3	887	96.3	0.0	0.0	2.6	1.1	26.0	49.7	24.4	341	63.9	39.9	17.3
Prescott city	58	58	0.0	44	93.2	0.0	0.0	0.0	6.8	2.3	77.3	20.5	23	95.7	43.5	52.2
Prineville city	9,253	9,258	0.1	9,184	86.5	0.4	0.3	3.3	9.6	22.3	59.0	18.7	4,105	52.4	58.9	12.5
Pronghorn CDP	34	NA	NA	19	100.0	0.0	0.0	0.0	0.0	0.0	68.4	31.6	12	100.0	0.0	50.0
Prospect CDP	455	NA	NA	468	83.1	0.0	0.0	13.2	3.6	14.6	64.9	20.5	222	68.5	57.2	16.2
Rainier city	1,916	1,913	-0.2	1,908	85.7	1.9	1.2	6.6	4.7	20.4	63.0	16.7	774	59.0	45.6	18.2
Raleigh Hills CDP	5,896	NA	NA	6,197	83.1	4.2	7.1	3.6	2.0	17.5	59.2	23.0	2,867	56.5	12.1	64.2
Redmond city	26,215	27,941	6.6	27,002	82.0	0.5	0.9	3.5	13.1	27.6	58.5	13.9	10,156	54.2	34.7	20.4
Redwood CDP	2,627	NA	NA	2,661	95.1	0.0	0.5	1.2	3.2	12.0	48.4	39.6	1,174	80.6	47.7	20.4
Reedsport city	4,154	4,085	-1.7	4,107	83.7	0.0	2.0	5.6	8.7	18.5	53.9	27.7	1,867	63.8	43.0	18.2
Richland city	164	163	-0.6	129	89.9	0.0	0.0	10.1	0.0	10.1	37.2	52.7	77	67.5	50.6	23.4
Rickreall CDP	77	NA	NA	44	100.0	0.0	0.0	0.0	0.0	47.7	52.3	0.0	13	100.0	100.0	0.0
Riddle city	1,185	1,177	-0.7	1,128	83.9	0.0	0.0	10.5	5.6	17.8	61.8	20.5	488	64.5	53.1	6.4
Rivergrove city	289	299	3.5	322	80.4	0.0	8.1	5.9	5.6	26.8	59.0	14.3	118	85.6	10.2	60.2
Riverside CDP	199	NA	NA	152	77.6	0.0	1.3	6.6	14.5	15.8	65.1	19.1	63	90.5	25.4	30.2
Rockaway Beach city	1,312	1,310	-0.2	1,197	90.1	0.1	0.0	5.5	4.3	14.0	55.5	30.4	562	66.5	36.3	21.9
Rockcreek CDP	9,316	NA	NA	9,261	67.2	3.1	12.5	5.0	12.1	22.4	66.6	10.9	3,624	66.7	15.3	51.4
Rogue River city	2,131	2,178	2.2	2,173	83.8	0.3	0.0	5.8	10.2	19.1	51.8	29.1	1,065	46.9	44.5	9.7
Roseburg city	21,884	21,903	0.1	21,858	89.2	0.6	0.5	4.9	4.9	19.4	58.4	22.4	9,669	55.8	33.8	21.9
Roseburg North CDP	5,912	NA	NA	6,140	90.4	0.0	0.6	4.6	4.5	24.8	54.3	20.8	2,543	66.5	39.2	11.5
Rose Lodge CDP	1,894	NA	NA	1,924	96.3	0.0	1.2	2.0	0.5	16.6	61.7	21.8	799	81.5	54.3	16.9
Rowena CDP	187	NA	NA	195	93.3	0.0	0.0	3.1	3.6	12.8	71.2	15.9	89	75.3	51.7	32.6
Ruch CDP	840	NA	NA	847	94.7	0.0	0.0	0.0	5.3	29.7	62.6	7.9	293	86.3	27.3	35.5
Rufus city	249	239	-4.0	234	75.2	0.0	0.0	10.3	14.5	11.5	51.6	36.8	113	60.2	57.5	4.4
St. Helens city	13,028	13,061	0.3	13,017	84.4	0.1	1.7	6.9	6.9	27.0	62.7	10.2	4,669	63.0	39.9	16.1
St. Paul city	421	430	2.1	353	76.8	0.0	2.3	1.7	19.3	27.2	55.5	17.3	129	86.0	38.8	32.6
Salem city	154,742	161,637	4.5	157,967	68.5	1.3	2.9	6.0	21.3	24.8	62.4	12.8	57,925	53.5	34.2	30.1
Sandy city	9,600	10,309	7.4	9,945	87.8	0.2	0.9	3.6	7.5	28.4	59.7	12.1	3,813	62.4	39.2	18.0
Scappoose city	6,694	6,856	2.4	6,778	89.8	0.0	1.8	4.2	4.2	25.7	58.6	15.5	2,522	71.1	32.9	21.9
Scio city	838	852	1.7	901	97.7	0.9	0.0	0.8	0.7	30.1	57.8	12.1	301	77.4	42.9	17.3
Scotts Mills city	357	365	2.2	457	88.2	0.0	0.0	1.8	10.1	28.5	65.5	6.1	159	74.2	41.5	18.2
Seaside city	6,457	6,492	0.5	6,481	82.7	0.1	0.7	3.8	12.7	20.1	59.5	20.4	2,838	47.1	36.0	24.4
Selma CDP	695	NA	NA	653	70.3	0.2	2.0	10.9	16.7	13.5	51.0	35.5	307	63.2	31.3	18.9
Seneca city	199	194	-2.5	148	92.6	0.0	0.0	1.4	6.1	4.1	65.0	31.1	74	94.6	51.4	8.1
Seventh Mountain CDP	187	NA	NA	238	100.0	0.0	0.0	0.0	0.0	0.0	47.9	52.1	109	100.0	0.0	100.0
Shady Cove city	2,904	2,973	2.4	2,936	90.1	0.0	0.0	2.0	8.0	16.0	57.1	26.8	1,380	72.0	41.1	19.6
Shaniko city	36	37	2.8	7	100.0	0.0	0.0	0.0	0.0	0.0	28.6	71.4	5	100.0	100.0	0.0
Shedd CDP	204	NA	NA	280	74.6	0.0	0.0	15.4	10.0	20.7	73.0	6.4	91	86.8	87.9	0.0
Sheridan city	6,136	6,065	-1.2	6,081	75.8	4.6	0.4	6.9	12.3	16.9	74.4	8.6	1,662	59.0	51.7	11.2

1 May be of any race.

Table A. All Places — **Population and Housing**

STATE City, town, township, borough, or CDP (county if applicable)	2010 census total population	2014 estimated population	Percent change 2010–2014	ACS total population estimate 2010–2014	White alone, not Hispanic or Latino	Black alone, not Hispanic or Latino	Asian alone, not Hispanic or Latino	All other races or 2 or more races, not Hispanic or Latino	Hispanic or Latino[1]	Under 18 years old	Age 18 to 64 years old	Age 65 years and older	Total occupied housing units	Percent owner occupied	High school diploma or less	Bachelor's degree or more
	1	2	3	4	5	6	7	8	9	10	11	12	13	14	15	16
OREGON—Con.																
Sherwood city	18,194	18,978	4.3	18,687	85.1	0.1	4.3	4.0	6.5	32.5	59.4	8.1	6,532	74.8	17.9	44.6
Siletz city	1,210	1,193	-1.4	1,684	66.4	1.7	0.1	29.7	2.1	28.7	57.8	13.5	591	71.1	51.8	8.0
Silver Lake CDP	149	NA	NA	50	100.0	0.0	0.0	0.0	0.0	16.0	78.0	6.0	39	10.3	79.5	20.5
Silverton city	9,222	9,493	2.9	9,342	89.9	0.1	2.2	2.1	5.8	28.4	57.5	14.2	3,468	64.1	29.6	29.3
Sisters city	2,038	2,224	9.1	2,227	87.4	0.1	1.0	3.0	8.5	26.2	56.6	17.2	882	48.1	27.9	36.1
Sodaville city	308	312	1.3	452	85.6	0.4	0.9	10.8	2.2	24.6	68.1	7.3	164	77.4	46.3	14.6
South Lebanon CDP	1,005	NA	NA	1,164	98.9	0.0	0.0	0.0	1.1	22.5	57.0	20.6	464	78.9	52.6	6.7
Spray town	159	153	-3.8	118	90.7	0.0	1.7	0.8	6.8	9.3	51.7	39.0	50	80.0	74.0	4.0
Springfield city	59,361	60,263	1.5	59,882	81.0	0.7	1.3	5.2	11.8	23.3	65.3	11.4	23,648	52.5	40.7	15.6
Stafford CDP	1,577	NA	NA	2,073	74.5	0.0	7.5	3.8	14.3	27.1	61.6	11.2	709	77.6	10.9	46.1
Stanfield city	2,043	2,044	0.0	2,148	64.9	0.0	0.5	5.0	29.7	24.1	63.7	12.1	807	64.4	46.2	12.3
Stayton city	7,644	7,846	2.6	7,719	76.2	0.0	0.3	5.3	18.2	28.8	59.3	11.9	2,897	52.4	50.6	13.8
Sublimity city	2,681	2,834	5.7	2,764	94.7	0.0	0.7	1.2	3.4	19.8	50.3	29.9	1,158	66.1	31.5	35.0
Summerville town	135	135	0.0	78	93.6	0.0	0.0	6.4	0.0	28.2	39.8	32.1	34	79.4	41.2	5.9
Summit CDP	82	NA	NA	90	61.1	0.0	0.0	38.9	0.0	0.0	27.8	72.2	47	78.7	21.3	78.7
Sumpter city	204	203	-0.5	171	94.7	0.0	0.0	5.3	0.0	5.9	42.2	52.0	111	91.0	31.5	21.6
Sunriver CDP	1,393	NA	NA	1,008	96.4	0.0	0.0	3.6	0.0	4.5	48.0	47.6	533	64.9	16.7	64.5
Sutherlin city	7,815	7,762	-0.7	7,776	90.5	0.8	1.3	3.5	3.9	27.3	53.6	19.1	2,893	66.0	43.1	11.0
Sweet Home city	8,925	9,074	1.7	9,042	94.6	0.2	0.5	1.7	3.0	26.0	56.0	18.1	3,476	60.8	49.5	10.5
Takilma CDP	378	NA	NA	266	100.0	0.0	0.0	0.0	0.0	22.5	70.3	7.1	119	100.0	8.4	31.1
Talent city	6,056	6,323	4.4	6,164	85.1	0.0	1.0	3.0	10.9	24.5	57.8	17.8	2,691	60.9	28.2	28.9
Tangent city	1,164	1,183	1.6	1,097	79.0	0.9	0.0	1.8	18.2	26.5	61.7	11.9	398	71.6	26.4	18.6
Terrebonne CDP	1,257	NA	NA	1,257	100.0	0.0	0.0	0.0	0.0	24.3	58.2	17.6	509	71.7	54.2	11.8
Tetherow CDP	45	NA	NA	84	100.0	0.0	0.0	0.0	0.0	0.0	71.4	28.6	28	100.0	0.0	100.0
The Dalles city	14,944	15,162	1.5	15,068	78.4	0.3	0.7	3.5	17.1	25.4	55.0	19.4	6,010	61.2	35.6	19.4
Three Rivers CDP	3,014	NA	NA	3,981	92.8	0.4	0.0	3.7	3.0	17.4	67.8	14.7	1,592	67.6	21.5	32.3
Tigard city	48,085	50,787	5.6	49,633	76.6	1.3	6.2	4.7	11.3	21.5	64.8	13.7	19,694	61.1	21.2	42.9
Tillamook city	4,971	4,940	-0.6	4,957	84.4	0.0	0.5	4.3	10.7	25.3	61.7	12.9	1,953	39.6	42.4	18.8
Toledo city	3,465	3,459	-0.2	3,449	90.3	0.0	0.0	3.9	5.8	25.3	62.0	12.8	1,242	50.6	44.3	11.4
Trail CDP	702	NA	NA	430	91.4	0.0	0.0	0.0	8.6	12.8	40.9	46.3	243	69.5	38.7	28.4
Tri-City CDP	3,931	NA	NA	3,737	82.7	0.0	1.6	5.8	9.9	16.4	66.8	16.8	1,364	74.7	51.0	10.0
Troutdale city	15,962	16,552	3.7	16,339	77.2	2.6	8.0	2.7	9.6	27.5	64.0	8.4	5,784	63.9	33.2	21.8
Tualatin city	26,049	26,907	3.3	26,604	73.3	1.4	2.2	4.6	18.5	23.6	67.3	9.1	10,677	56.2	22.7	43.7
Tumalo CDP	488	NA	NA	387	100.0	0.0	0.0	0.0	0.0	0.0	76.3	23.8	199	53.3	46.7	47.2
Turner city	1,854	1,937	4.5	2,272	87.3	0.0	0.7	4.3	7.7	23.0	59.5	17.6	842	71.6	42.5	19.2
Tutuilla CDP	487	NA	NA	490	63.1	0.0	0.0	30.6	6.3	23.9	62.8	13.3	175	81.7	36.6	24.0
Tygh Valley CDP	206	NA	NA	165	95.2	3.0	0.0	1.8	0.0	3.6	79.4	17.0	93	95.7	19.4	15.1
Ukiah city	186	191	2.7	196	89.3	0.0	2.0	3.1	5.6	16.9	64.2	18.9	70	61.4	44.3	15.7
Umapine CDP	315	NA	NA	270	91.5	0.0	0.0	0.0	8.5	17.7	65.5	16.7	109	66.1	26.6	8.3
Umatilla city	6,906	7,005	1.4	6,998	55.6	1.7	0.9	5.6	36.3	21.0	73.1	5.8	1,556	52.7	63.3	10.0
Union city	2,121	2,112	-0.4	1,795	92.9	0.4	0.9	3.7	2.1	22.8	57.7	19.6	714	75.9	53.8	10.8
Unity city	71	70	-1.4	49	93.9	0.0	0.0	0.0	6.1	4.1	67.3	28.6	29	69.0	69.0	6.9
Vale city	1,874	1,817	-3.0	1,812	75.2	0.7	0.3	1.1	22.7	30.2	52.5	17.3	635	63.6	49.6	12.1
Veneta city	4,561	4,722	3.5	4,633	83.5	0.2	3.1	4.4	8.7	29.7	55.9	14.3	1,672	65.6	33.1	22.5
Vernonia city	2,165	2,157	-0.4	2,052	94.2	1.0	0.0	1.9	2.8	24.3	58.9	16.9	770	80.0	46.2	11.4
Waldport city	2,063	2,087	1.2	1,922	90.5	0.4	1.1	5.0	3.0	13.5	57.0	29.5	904	64.7	35.7	17.0
Wallowa city	808	790	-2.2	828	94.3	0.0	0.0	4.2	1.4	22.1	59.1	18.7	360	57.5	40.8	15.0
Wallowa Lake CDP	62	NA	NA	82	100.0	0.0	0.0	0.0	0.0	0.0	58.5	41.5	41	39.0	39.0	0.0
Wamic CDP	85	NA	NA	29	100.0	0.0	0.0	0.0	0.0	0.0	48.3	51.7	19	47.4	26.3	0.0
Warm Springs CDP	2,945	NA	NA	3,148	6.0	0.0	0.2	84.2	9.5	34.8	58.1	7.2	757	63.5	43.5	9.0
Warren CDP	1,787	NA	NA	1,949	95.4	0.0	0.5	0.5	3.6	21.5	61.0	17.5	749	74.1	26.2	24.3
Warrenton city	4,989	5,173	3.7	5,089	87.6	0.0	1.0	3.4	7.6	29.2	59.1	11.8	1,950	54.6	27.3	21.9
Wasco city	410	397	-3.2	458	87.6	0.4	0.0	4.6	7.4	19.2	56.1	24.7	209	67.9	47.4	11.0
Waterloo town	229	232	1.3	272	82.7	0.0	0.0	0.7	16.5	23.1	61.0	15.8	92	82.6	41.3	20.7
Westfir city	253	256	1.2	273	93.8	0.0	0.0	4.0	2.2	25.3	59.5	15.4	129	82.2	24.0	9.3
West Haven-Sylvan CDP	8,001	NA	NA	7,861	84.7	1.0	7.5	4.3	2.5	14.2	70.6	15.1	3,712	62.1	7.7	66.0
West Linn city	25,107	26,289	4.7	25,710	86.5	0.6	5.0	3.4	4.6	22.8	63.0	14.2	9,902	76.3	10.8	58.4
Weston city	667	666	-0.1	631	87.6	0.0	1.1	4.8	6.5	17.6	62.9	19.7	247	78.9	40.5	10.1
Westport CDP	321	NA	NA	283	98.2	0.0	0.0	0.0	1.8	7.4	77.7	14.8	143	56.6	21.0	0.0
West Scio CDP	120	NA	NA	109	39.4	0.0	0.0	0.0	60.6	45.0	34.8	20.2	43	93.0	0.0	41.9
West Slope CDP	6,554	NA	NA	7,240	80.0	5.9	3.0	6.0	5.1	24.4	63.1	12.7	3,037	52.5	21.7	50.7
Wheeler city	414	414	0.0	349	94.6	0.0	0.0	0.0	5.4	15.2	50.0	35.0	145	64.8	51.0	23.4
White City CDP	7,975	NA	NA	8,355	61.7	0.2	0.3	5.8	32.0	24.7	66.9	8.5	2,378	73.8	47.9	11.4
Willamina city	2,021	2,087	3.3	1,766	83.4	0.0	0.2	12.9	3.6	23.1	62.1	14.8	626	65.3	46.8	11.8
Williams CDP	1,072	NA	NA	1,142	81.9	2.1	0.0	5.2	10.9	19.5	52.9	27.7	485	82.5	31.3	29.3
Wilsonville city	19,509	22,026	12.9	20,335	76.8	0.7	3.0	5.4	14.0	22.4	63.4	14.1	8,090	47.2	20.5	42.7
Wimer CDP	678	NA	NA	534	96.8	0.0	0.0	0.2	3.0	7.3	68.0	24.7	292	75.0	26.7	20.2
Winchester Bay CDP	382	NA	NA	313	96.5	0.0	0.0	3.2	0.3	0.3	37.3	62.3	135	76.3	31.1	38.5
Winston city	5,380	5,342	-0.7	5,356	86.3	0.0	2.1	4.1	7.6	27.8	56.4	15.7	1,876	59.8	35.8	10.7
Woodburn city	24,069	24,734	2.8	24,282	40.3	0.2	1.0	2.5	56.0	29.3	55.1	15.5	7,874	57.4	55.6	14.1
Wood Village city	3,878	3,966	2.3	3,946	51.4	1.7	4.0	10.3	32.6	30.7	61.5	7.8	1,294	58.0	46.3	19.9
Yachats city	690	706	2.3	743	76.7	1.1	0.0	8.3	13.9	8.8	51.7	39.6	375	70.7	19.2	47.2
Yamhill city	1,024	1,056	3.1	1,492	96.8	0.0	0.8	0.9	1.4	43.6	48.3	8.1	357	77.3	35.3	14.6
Yoncalla city	1,047	1,037	-1.0	1,117	88.2	0.0	0.0	5.6	6.2	16.0	59.4	24.5	468	73.9	50.0	4.9
PENNSYLVANIA	12,702,884	12,787,209	0.7	12,758,729	78.5	10.5	2.9	1.9	6.1	21.5	62.5	16.0	4,957,736	69.5	44.6	29.7
Aaronsburg CDP (Centre)	613	NA	NA	687	99.4	0.0	0.0	0.0	0.6	23.2	60.4	16.2	247	82.2	72.5	14.6
Aaronsburg CDP (Washington)	259	NA	NA	266	100.0	0.0	0.0	0.0	0.0	12.0	67.7	20.3	106	88.7	66.0	15.1
Abbott township (Potter)	242	238	-1.7	182	98.9	0.0	0.0	1.1	0.0	12.6	59.1	28.0	88	86.4	58.0	11.4
Abbottstown borough & MCD (Adams)	1,011	1,013	0.2	917	89.4	0.0	1.2	1.5	7.9	25.7	63.3	11.0	332	75.0	62.3	8.1
Abington township (Montgomery)	55,343	55,682	0.6	55,559	76.2	11.8	5.3	2.5	4.2	21.5	60.6	17.8	20,822	79.1	27.8	47.7
Ackermanville CDP	610	NA	NA	687	100.0	0.0	0.0	0.0	0.0	29.6	56.0	14.6	243	72.4	49.0	16.0
Adams township (Butler)	11,652	12,930	11.0	12,335	92.5	0.4	4.2	0.9	2.0	25.4	61.5	13.1	4,871	86.8	20.8	59.8
Adams township (Cambria)	5,972	5,798	-2.9	5,877	98.0	0.0	0.0	0.1	1.9	17.4	57.2	25.3	2,432	83.5	58.4	15.7
Adams township (Snyder)	907	919	1.3	897	97.2	0.8	0.0	0.0	2.0	24.7	60.5	14.8	325	78.2	71.4	11.4

1 May be of any race.

Table A. All Places — **Population and Housing**

STATE City, town, township, borough, or CDP (county if applicable)	2010 census total population	2014 estimated population	Percent change 2010–2014	ACS total population estimate 2010–2014	White alone, not Hispanic or Latino	Black alone, not Hispanic or Latino	Asian alone, not Hispanic or Latino	All other races or 2 or more races, not Hispanic or Latino	Hispanic or Latino[1]	Under 18 years old	Age 18 to 64 years old	Age 65 years and older	Total occupied housing units	Percent owner occupied	High school diploma or less	Bachelor's degree or more
	1	2	3	4	5	6	7	8	9	10	11	12	13	14	15	16
PENNSYLVANIA—Con.																
Adamsburg borough & MCD (Westmoreland) ..	172	169	-1.7	259	91.5	0.0	0.0	0.8	7.7	19.3	64.4	16.2	93	89.2	62.4	9.7
Adamstown borough........	1,789	1,837	2.7	1,733	87.0	5.8	2.0	1.7	3.5	25.6	64.4	10.2	697	67.9	38.2	31.0
Adamstown borough (Berks)	14	14	0.0	6	100.0	0.0	0.0	0.0	0.0	0.0	0.0	100.0	3	100.0	0.0	100.0
Adamstown borough (Lancaster)...............	1,775	1,823	2.7	1,727	87.0	5.8	2.0	1.7	3.5	25.6	64.6	9.9	694	67.7	38.3	30.7
Adamsville CDP..............	67	NA	NA	62	82.3	0.0	0.0	17.7	0.0	14.5	51.6	33.9	33	100.0	84.8	0.0
Addison borough & MCD (Somerset)	207	202	-2.4	198	99.0	0.0	0.0	1.0	0.0	21.2	59.1	19.7	79	78.5	59.5	16.5
Addison township (Somerset)	974	947	-2.8	975	98.2	0.0	0.0	0.1	1.7	20.6	52.5	26.9	411	83.7	62.8	11.9
Akron borough & MCD (Lancaster)...............	3,883	3,978	2.4	3,923	94.7	0.1	0.4	1.2	3.5	21.4	61.5	17.0	1,652	68.2	48.1	22.9
Alba borough & MCD (Bradford)	157	154	-1.9	103	100.0	0.0	0.0	0.0	0.0	12.7	70.9	16.5	45	77.8	60.0	8.9
Albany township (Berks)..	1,724	1,730	0.3	1,561	97.8	0.3	0.0	0.8	1.2	17.4	61.6	21.1	659	80.4	46.1	29.1
Albany township (Bradford)	911	896	-1.6	814	93.7	0.0	0.4	4.3	1.6	20.3	56.1	23.7	336	80.7	69.3	8.9
Albion borough & MCD (Erie)	1,516	1,478	-2.5	1,526	94.5	1.4	0.4	1.7	2.0	19.0	63.6	17.4	652	64.0	58.9	13.2
Albrightsville CDP...........	202	NA	NA	154	90.9	9.1	0.0	0.0	0.0	42.2	38.2	19.5	41	100.0	17.1	0.0
Alburtis borough & MCD (Lehigh)..................	2,361	2,402	1.7	2,372	90.6	2.2	0.3	1.2	5.7	29.8	60.7	9.4	853	84.2	44.2	30.7
Aldan borough & MCD (Delaware).................	4,152	4,166	0.3	4,164	76.2	22.9	0.0	0.3	0.6	20.7	63.9	15.2	1,632	77.9	46.8	27.5
Aleppo township (Allegheny)	1,916	1,912	-0.2	1,713	97.5	0.8	0.9	0.8	0.1	10.2	35.8	54.2	973	50.9	26.1	48.7
Aleppo township (Greene)	502	502	0.0	434	100.0	0.0	0.0	0.0	0.0	22.4	62.6	15.0	190	77.9	66.3	12.1
Alexandria borough & MCD (Huntingdon).......	346	333	-3.8	401	99.8	0.0	0.0	0.2	0.0	21.9	55.1	22.9	164	70.7	51.2	19.5
Alfarata CDP..................	149	NA	NA	199	95.0	0.0	5.0	0.0	0.0	37.7	46.1	16.1	57	87.7	91.2	8.8
Aliquippa city & MCD (Beaver)	9,438	9,244	-2.1	9,356	55.8	39.3	0.6	3.3	1.0	19.9	61.2	19.1	4,219	60.5	54.0	17.0
Allegany township (Potter)	422	415	-1.7	414	98.6	0.0	0.5	1.0	0.0	22.0	63.3	14.7	161	85.1	56.5	11.8
Allegheny township (Blair)	6,735	6,660	-1.1	6,714	98.0	0.3	0.0	1.8	0.0	17.8	58.6	23.6	2,680	78.7	58.8	17.2
Allegheny township (Butler)	641	639	-0.3	617	87.2	8.9	0.0	3.1	0.0	23.9	59.7	16.4	243	79.0	66.7	8.6
Allegheny township (Cambria)	2,851	2,842	-0.3	2,869	69.7	18.3	1.2	1.8	9.0	11.5	79.8	9.0	540	85.6	53.3	26.7
Allegheny township (Somerset)	698	686	-1.7	734	99.6	0.4	0.0	0.0	0.0	19.7	58.1	22.1	289	82.4	65.7	12.1
Allegheny township (Venango)	276	268	-2.9	252	97.6	0.0	0.0	1.6	0.8	23.0	53.0	24.2	108	87.0	63.0	25.0
Allegheny township (Westmoreland)	8,164	8,242	1.0	8,256	96.5	2.0	0.1	0.6	0.8	21.2	61.5	17.4	3,213	83.9	46.7	26.5
Alleghenyville CDP.........	1,134	NA	NA	1,199	96.2	0.7	0.6	2.6	0.0	26.3	60.1	13.7	407	98.3	39.8	46.9
Allen township (Northampton)..............	4,269	4,541	6.4	4,410	91.9	3.0	3.1	0.1	2.0	22.3	58.7	19.0	1,679	92.9	36.7	35.0
Allenport CDP................	648	NA	NA	592	99.3	0.0	0.0	0.7	0.0	23.6	58.6	17.7	239	73.6	74.5	7.1
Allenport borough & MCD (Washington)	537	530	-1.3	461	99.3	0.0	0.0	0.7	0.0	21.0	62.9	16.1	184	77.7	57.6	31.5
Allensville CDP..............	503	NA	NA	452	99.8	0.0	0.0	0.0	0.2	32.9	55.7	11.3	156	76.3	90.4	5.1
Allentown city & MCD (Lehigh)..................	118,161	119,104	0.8	118,793	40.0	9.7	1.7	2.6	46.0	26.1	62.1	11.8	41,537	46.2	54.6	17.0
Allenwood CDP	321	NA	NA	513	94.0	0.0	0.4	1.0	4.7	25.3	56.5	18.1	189	79.4	64.0	10.6
Allison township (Clinton)	193	196	1.6	244	94.3	1.2	0.0	2.0	2.5	29.1	57.4	13.5	79	93.7	48.1	34.2
Allison CDP....................	625	NA	NA	564	84.9	15.1	0.0	0.0	0.0	12.2	59.3	28.4	248	86.3	91.1	0.0
Allison Park CDP............	21,552	NA	NA	20,867	93.6	0.8	3.9	0.6	1.0	20.0	60.8	19.3	8,401	81.4	25.0	51.8
Allport CDP....................	264	NA	NA	367	100.0	0.0	0.0	0.0	0.0	43.0	54.3	2.7	110	62.7	92.7	7.3
Almedia CDP..................	1,078	NA	NA	1,014	100.0	0.0	0.0	0.0	0.0	14.9	56.9	28.1	473	77.8	52.0	14.8
Alsace township (Berks)..	3,751	3,740	-0.3	3,745	96.8	1.5	0.5	0.6	0.6	22.5	58.5	18.9	1,470	96.6	54.7	25.9
Alsace Manor CDP..........	478	NA	NA	285	100.0	0.0	0.0	0.0	0.0	18.3	54.1	27.7	137	100.0	83.9	0.0
Altamont CDP................	602	NA	NA	710	92.0	0.0	0.0	2.3	5.8	17.9	63.4	18.7	321	94.4	53.0	10.9
Altoona city & MCD (Blair)	46,321	45,558	-1.6	45,987	93.0	2.9	1.0	2.1	1.0	23.1	60.8	16.2	18,755	66.3	56.3	17.3
Ambler borough & MCD (Montgomery)	6,417	6,506	1.4	6,481	71.9	14.7	3.8	2.3	7.3	19.5	64.9	15.6	2,598	56.6	29.7	42.1
Ambridge borough & MCD (Beaver)	7,050	6,895	-2.2	6,973	68.8	17.2	1.0	8.8	4.2	21.9	63.1	14.9	3,233	42.1	47.3	17.6
Amity township (Berks)....	12,583	12,784	1.6	12,699	89.3	4.6	1.9	1.9	2.3	28.5	59.3	12.1	4,378	77.5	37.3	40.9
Amity township (Erie)......	1,073	1,076	0.3	1,066	97.7	0.4	0.2	1.7	0.0	21.5	59.3	19.1	397	89.7	56.7	20.4
Amity Gardens CDP	3,402	NA	NA	3,290	93.6	2.7	0.0	3.0	0.6	23.8	61.4	14.8	1,211	67.2	35.7	36.7
Amwell township (Washington)	3,751	3,725	-0.7	3,731	98.7	0.0	0.0	1.1	0.2	15.3	69.3	15.4	1,496	88.2	61.8	18.2
Ancient Oaks CDP..........	6,661	NA	NA	7,312	80.5	4.3	8.5	2.2	4.5	28.2	55.8	16.0	2,779	84.9	21.6	56.0
Annin township (McKean)	694	688	-0.9	634	97.2	0.0	2.1	0.2	0.6	19.0	57.2	23.8	286	72.4	58.7	23.4
Annville CDP & township (Lebanon).................	4,767	4,860	2.0	4,826	88.8	3.0	3.9	1.4	2.9	13.1	73.8	12.9	1,338	60.4	46.0	24.8
Anthony township (Lycoming)	865	882	2.0	886	100.0	0.0	0.0	0.0	0.0	17.5	69.1	13.4	340	90.9	56.2	21.2
Anthony township (Montour)	1,501	1,551	3.3	1,617	99.4	0.4	0.0	0.0	0.1	26.4	61.0	12.6	579	89.5	64.4	15.7
Antis township (Blair).......	6,484	6,433	-0.8	6,463	96.4	2.0	1.5	0.1	0.0	20.9	63.1	16.0	2,462	84.0	55.8	13.1
Antrim township (Franklin)	14,890	15,356	3.1	15,135	93.2	1.4	0.4	1.2	3.8	24.7	61.6	13.7	5,476	83.0	55.3	17.5
Apolacon township (Susquehanna)	500	495	-1.0	519	98.3	0.0	1.0	0.8	0.0	18.5	63.6	17.9	224	85.7	47.8	16.1
Apollo borough & MCD (Armstrong)	1,647	1,607	-2.4	1,534	96.4	1.1	0.7	1.5	0.3	23.9	60.0	16.2	677	51.6	60.7	12.9
Applewold borough & MCD (Armstrong)........	310	300	-3.2	307	95.8	1.3	0.0	2.9	0.0	17.9	57.6	24.4	132	56.8	57.6	22.0

1 May be of any race.

Table A. All Places — **Population and Housing**

STATE City, town, township, borough, or CDP (county if applicable)	2010 census total population	2014 estimated population	Percent change 2010–2014	ACS total population estimate 2010–2014	White alone, not Hispanic or Latino	Black alone, not Hispanic or Latino	Asian alone, not Hispanic or Latino	All other races or 2 or more races, not Hispanic or Latino	Hispanic or Latino[1]	Under 18 years old	Age 18 to 64 years old	Age 65 years and older	Total occupied housing units	Percent owner occupied	High school diploma or less	Bachelor's degree or more
	1	2	3	4	5	6	7	8	9	10	11	12	13	14	15	16
PENNSYLVANIA—Con.																
Ararat township (Susquehanna)	563	545	-3.2	430	96.3	0.0	2.1	0.7	0.9	9.8	55.1	35.1	222	89.6	52.7	24.3
Arcadia University CDP ...	595	NA	NA	623	71.1	2.6	15.9	2.9	7.5	1.8	98.2	0.0	0	0.0	0.0	0.0
Archbald borough & MCD (Lackawanna)...............	6,984	7,075	1.3	7,053	96.8	0.0	0.7	0.4	2.1	20.4	61.1	18.4	2,919	82.4	39.3	27.9
Ardmore CDP	12,455	NA	NA	12,867	73.4	12.1	4.3	2.0	8.1	19.3	64.4	16.1	5,454	64.5	17.1	66.4
Arendtsville borough & MCD (Adams)	952	954	0.2	994	77.8	0.9	0.2	2.7	18.4	31.4	57.4	11.0	346	61.6	57.2	25.4
Aristes CDP....................	311	NA	NA	319	100.0	0.0	0.0	0.0	0.0	21.0	62.4	16.6	123	91.1	87.0	4.9
Arlington Heights CDP.....	6,333	NA	NA	5,392	70.0	12.8	7.0	0.6	9.6	17.7	65.0	17.3	2,085	77.9	39.9	31.3
Armagh borough & MCD (Indiana)....................	122	119	-2.5	102	98.0	0.0	0.0	2.0	0.0	7.8	67.6	24.5	46	82.6	60.9	13.0
Armagh township (Mifflin)	3,863	3,833	-0.8	3,860	98.5	0.2	0.8	0.3	0.2	21.5	60.2	18.2	1,499	80.9	69.5	13.7
Armenia township (Bradford).................	184	182	-1.1	294	98.6	0.0	0.0	1.4	0.0	21.8	52.6	25.5	97	71.1	80.4	6.2
Armstrong township (Indiana)....................	2,997	2,915	-2.7	2,961	90.2	0.0	9.8	0.0	0.0	22.5	62.7	14.8	1,142	89.2	37.0	38.0
Armstrong township (Lycoming).................	681	691	1.5	693	97.5	1.6	0.0	0.6	0.3	24.1	63.6	12.3	269	84.8	58.4	20.4
Arnold city & MCD (Westmoreland)	5,157	5,022	-2.6	5,090	71.0	19.4	0.0	5.5	4.0	23.5	58.2	18.3	2,498	40.0	54.3	8.6
Arnold City CDP	498	NA	NA	609	88.7	7.1	0.0	4.3	0.0	21.0	60.4	18.6	263	36.5	53.6	10.3
Arnot CDP......................	332	NA	NA	400	98.3	1.8	0.0	0.0	0.0	21.1	64.5	14.8	155	92.3	70.3	14.2
Arona borough & MCD (Westmoreland)	370	356	-3.8	368	94.6	0.0	5.4	0.0	0.0	22.6	65.0	12.5	134	72.4	71.6	8.2
Ashland township (Clarion)....................	1,114	1,101	-1.2	1,104	97.2	2.0	0.0	0.8	0.0	25.5	58.2	16.2	392	87.8	61.5	20.7
Ashland borough	2,817	2,757	-2.1	2,780	97.4	0.0	0.0	0.3	2.3	12.2	68.1	19.7	1,410	61.3	63.8	18.5
Ashland borough (Columbia)	0	0	0.0	0	0.0	0.0	0.0	0.0	0.0	0.0	0.0	0.0	0	0.0	0.0	0.0
Ashland borough (Schuylkill).................	2,817	2,757	-2.1	2,780	97.4	0.0	0.0	0.3	2.3	12.2	68.1	19.7	1,410	61.3	63.8	18.5
Ashley borough & MCD (Luzerne)..................	2,790	2,741	-1.8	2,765	97.1	1.1	0.3	0.8	0.7	18.6	63.4	18.1	1,190	74.4	51.9	16.2
Ashville borough & MCD (Cambria)...................	227	221	-2.6	182	90.7	1.1	0.0	8.2	0.0	26.9	52.1	20.9	81	74.1	51.9	7.4
Aspers CDP....................	350	NA	NA	404	95.0	0.0	0.0	0.0	5.0	21.5	61.9	16.6	149	94.6	63.1	8.1
Aspinwall borough & MCD (Allegheny).........	2,801	2,779	-0.8	2,794	94.0	0.4	4.0	0.2	1.3	21.1	64.1	14.7	1,340	40.7	18.9	60.7
Aston township (Delaware).................	16,592	16,863	1.6	16,787	95.3	2.2	1.0	1.0	0.5	21.7	62.4	15.9	5,980	86.8	43.9	27.3
Asylum township (Bradford).................	1,058	1,063	0.5	991	98.7	0.0	0.0	1.3	0.0	14.7	69.2	16.1	413	83.1	57.9	15.3
Atglen borough & MCD (Chester)...................	1,406	1,410	0.3	1,507	80.6	6.3	0.0	3.1	10.0	33.2	60.8	6.0	451	71.4	50.6	24.4
Athens borough & MCD (Bradford).................	3,367	3,287	-2.4	3,344	95.8	0.4	0.4	1.0	2.4	24.6	56.5	18.6	1,315	63.7	63.2	15.8
Athens township (Bradford).................	5,253	5,136	-2.2	5,220	97.4	1.5	0.0	1.1	0.0	20.5	58.8	20.8	2,019	86.0	48.8	29.5
Athens township (Crawford)................	734	734	0.0	651	98.5	0.0	0.0	0.0	1.5	21.4	61.8	16.9	248	88.3	58.9	13.7
Atkinson Mills CDP..........	174	NA	NA	243	100.0	0.0	0.0	0.0	0.0	27.2	69.9	2.9	79	93.7	78.5	6.3
Atlantic CDP...................	77	NA	NA	36	100.0	0.0	0.0	0.0	0.0	25.0	52.7	22.2	14	100.0	57.1	0.0
Atlas CDP......................	809	NA	NA	932	99.8	0.2	0.0	0.0	0.0	14.1	58.4	27.5	449	71.9	76.2	3.8
Atlasburg CDP................	401	NA	NA	258	100.0	0.0	0.0	0.0	0.0	22.9	67.9	9.3	116	75.9	28.4	23.3
Atwood borough & MCD (Armstrong)...............	107	106	-0.9	110	96.4	0.0	1.8	1.8	0.0	14.6	71.8	13.6	42	88.1	76.2	16.7
Auburn borough & MCD (Schuylkill).................	738	724	-1.9	879	98.9	0.0	0.0	0.6	0.6	24.6	56.8	18.5	348	73.6	72.1	6.3
Auburn township (Susquehanna)	1,939	1,884	-2.8	1,850	98.4	0.2	0.0	0.4	1.0	24.0	59.6	16.4	734	89.4	59.5	19.2
Audubon CDP..................	8,433	NA	NA	8,483	72.3	6.3	19.4	0.7	1.4	25.3	53.7	21.0	3,220	62.4	24.4	57.8
Austin borough & MCD (Potter)...................	564	554	-1.8	545	97.6	0.0	0.0	0.4	2.0	20.7	65.0	14.3	207	72.0	70.0	7.7
Avalon borough & MCD (Allegheny)...............	4,705	4,667	-0.8	4,704	84.8	7.3	1.5	6.4	0.0	16.7	63.8	19.6	2,462	51.4	37.2	28.1
Avella CDP.....................	804	NA	NA	933	96.1	1.2	0.0	1.5	1.2	24.1	61.8	14.3	324	75.3	57.7	17.3
Avis borough & MCD (Clinton)...................	1,484	1,515	2.1	1,732	96.8	1.2	0.4	0.1	1.4	26.0	61.5	12.6	658	73.9	56.7	12.6
Avoca borough & MCD (Luzerne)...................	2,661	2,652	-0.3	2,663	97.5	0.0	1.8	0.2	0.5	20.3	61.8	17.9	1,088	75.5	47.4	16.6
Avon CDP.......................	1,667	NA	NA	1,681	91.4	0.0	1.4	0.0	7.2	21.7	61.4	16.9	603	82.1	72.8	7.5
Avondale borough & MCD (Chester)..........	1,265	1,402	10.8	1,587	23.4	6.5	4.3	0.2	65.6	30.2	64.9	4.9	389	53.2	59.9	20.1
Avonia CDP....................	1,205	NA	NA	1,086	100.0	0.0	0.0	0.0	0.0	23.2	58.2	18.5	440	93.4	21.6	58.6
Avonmore borough & MCD (Westmoreland) ..	1,011	988	-2.3	961	90.4	0.9	0.0	2.2	6.5	20.4	52.1	27.6	424	79.0	63.4	9.9
Ayr township (Fulton).......	2,085	2,048	-1.8	2,068	98.4	0.8	0.0	0.8	0.0	23.0	58.7	18.6	828	79.6	63.2	15.1
Baden borough & MCD (Beaver)...................	4,135	4,056	-1.9	4,089	92.2	3.7	1.2	2.9	0.0	14.0	58.4	27.6	1,850	66.2	55.4	17.2
Baidland CDP..................	1,563	NA	NA	1,697	98.4	0.0	0.0	0.9	0.8	17.2	62.8	20.0	625	88.6	55.0	18.6
Baileyville CDP...............	201	NA	NA	310	100.0	0.0	0.0	0.0	0.0	20.6	46.5	32.9	112	86.6	78.6	21.4
Bainbridge CDP...............	1,355	NA	NA	1,689	99.3	0.0	0.7	0.0	0.0	29.3	61.1	9.7	598	84.8	70.6	18.1
Bairdford CDP	698	NA	NA	1,096	99.9	0.1	0.0	0.0	0.0	22.9	54.4	22.7	419	79.2	69.7	23.6
Bakerstown CDP.............	1,761	NA	NA	2,277	98.3	0.0	0.0	0.9	0.8	27.8	53.0	19.3	820	72.1	20.4	56.8
Bald Eagle township (Clinton)...................	2,065	2,090	1.2	2,210	96.2	0.3	0.4	2.6	0.5	23.7	61.8	14.7	830	84.5	54.1	22.2
Baldwin borough & MCD (Allegheny)...............	19,765	19,740	-0.1	19,791	89.9	6.0	2.9	0.4	0.7	20.7	59.9	19.5	8,281	78.6	45.7	24.1
Baldwin township (Allegheny).................	1,992	1,977	-0.8	1,987	97.8	0.0	0.2	1.5	0.6	18.9	64.2	17.0	838	89.7	36.8	31.0

1 May be of any race.

Table A. All Places — Population and Housing

STATE City, town, township, borough, or CDP (county if applicable)	Population 2010 census total population	2014 estimated population	Percent change 2010– 2014	ACS total population estimate 2010–2014	Race and Hispanic or Latino origin (percent), 2010–2014 White alone, not Hispanic or Latino	Black alone, not Hispanic or Latino	Asian alone, not Hispanic or Latino	All other races or 2 or more races, not Hispanic or Latino	Hispanic or Latino[1]	Age (percent), 2010–2014 Under 18 years old	Age 18 to 64 years old	Age 65 years and older	Households, 2010–2014 Total occupied housing units	Percent owner occupied	Householders by level of education (percent) High school diploma or less	Bachelor's degree or more
	1	2	3	4	5	6	7	8	9	10	11	12	13	14	15	16
PENNSYLVANIA—Con.																
Bally borough & MCD (Berks)	1,090	1,099	0.8	1,247	93.6	0.4	0.0	3.5	2.5	20.8	62.0	17.2	480	81.9	58.8	19.8
Bangor borough & MCD (Northampton)	5,273	5,233	-0.8	5,256	98.8	0.0	0.0	1.2	0.0	24.4	58.3	17.3	2,058	54.7	56.7	14.0
Banks township (Carbon)	1,262	1,229	-2.6	1,218	93.6	1.2	0.0	1.1	4.0	18.6	57.5	23.9	526	72.4	61.4	8.2
Banks township (Indiana)	1,018	980	-3.7	1,020	100.0	0.0	0.0	0.0	0.0	24.7	61.6	13.7	335	86.0	74.6	7.5
Barkeyville borough & MCD (Venango)	207	205	-1.0	270	90.4	0.7	0.0	4.4	4.4	22.2	60.1	17.8	99	82.8	60.6	19.2
Barnett township (Forest)	361	349	-3.3	385	97.1	0.0	0.0	1.0	1.8	11.5	55.5	33.0	206	86.9	50.0	13.6
Barnett township (Jefferson)	254	251	-1.2	196	95.4	1.0	0.0	3.6	0.0	6.6	61.3	32.1	96	80.2	55.2	13.5
Barr township (Cambria)	2,056	2,021	-1.7	1,840	99.0	0.3	0.0	0.8	0.0	22.9	60.2	16.8	696	91.8	63.4	17.4
Barree township (Huntingdon)	477	473	-0.8	416	99.0	0.0	0.0	0.7	0.2	19.7	64.4	15.9	176	84.7	47.7	22.7
Barrett township (Monroe)	4,226	4,094	-3.1	4,159	87.4	4.8	0.3	3.1	4.3	18.9	66.4	14.7	1,658	78.2	47.5	16.2
Barrville CDP	160	NA	NA	192	100.0	0.0	0.0	0.0	0.0	35.5	50.6	14.1	66	77.3	71.2	12.1
Barry township (Schuylkill)	932	913	-2.0	908	100.0	0.0	0.0	0.0	0.0	14.6	64.3	21.3	377	85.7	58.9	15.6
Bart township (Lancaster)	3,094	3,274	5.8	3,186	94.7	0.4	0.0	0.1	4.8	38.4	52.8	8.9	835	72.6	81.0	11.0
Bastress township (Lycoming)	546	564	3.3	501	99.8	0.0	0.0	0.0	0.2	18.0	64.0	18.2	189	91.5	58.7	10.1
Bath borough & MCD (Northampton)	2,693	2,680	-0.5	2,684	87.1	3.6	0.2	1.0	8.0	30.1	55.6	14.2	999	60.4	50.9	23.5
Baumstown CDP	422	NA	NA	465	97.0	3.0	0.0	0.0	0.0	30.3	60.5	9.5	155	60.0	50.3	0.0
Beale township (Juniata)	830	840	1.2	850	90.4	1.9	5.2	2.6	0.0	28.3	56.5	15.1	296	88.2	68.9	18.2
Beallsville borough & MCD (Washington)	466	453	-2.8	555	100.0	0.0	0.0	0.0	0.0	18.5	63.0	18.6	215	90.7	43.7	16.3
Bear Creek township (Luzerne)	2,774	2,767	-0.3	2,788	98.3	0.1	1.3	0.0	0.3	17.4	62.2	20.4	1,214	90.9	38.2	29.5
Bear Creek Village borough & MCD (Luzerne)	257	256	-0.4	312	95.5	0.0	1.9	0.0	2.6	23.6	49.0	27.2	119	89.1	18.5	49.6
Bear Lake borough & MCD (Warren)	164	161	-1.8	168	93.5	0.0	5.4	1.2	0.0	26.8	55.4	17.9	65	93.8	78.5	4.6
Bear Rocks CDP	1,048	NA	NA	968	96.4	0.0	1.5	0.0	2.1	20.1	66.8	13.0	432	98.1	43.3	22.7
Beaver borough & MCD (Beaver)	4,531	4,440	-2.0	4,479	93.7	2.2	1.1	1.3	1.8	18.6	59.1	22.4	2,090	63.2	33.0	38.8
Beaver township (Clarion)	1,757	1,738	-1.1	1,754	99.0	0.4	0.0	0.2	0.5	21.1	58.0	21.0	742	85.4	67.9	10.5
Beaver township (Columbia)	917	920	0.3	857	95.7	0.0	0.0	3.6	0.7	18.8	62.0	19.4	348	90.5	60.9	16.1
Beaver township (Crawford)	900	875	-2.8	911	97.9	0.4	0.0	1.3	0.3	27.6	60.3	12.1	296	87.2	74.7	5.1
Beaver township (Jefferson)	498	492	-1.2	441	98.2	0.0	0.2	0.0	1.6	20.4	59.8	19.7	198	88.9	49.0	34.8
Beaver township (Snyder)	525	526	0.2	535	100.0	0.0	0.0	0.0	0.0	21.9	61.1	17.0	193	87.6	70.5	15.0
Beaverdale CDP	1,035	NA	NA	1,174	100.0	0.0	0.0	0.0	0.0	26.3	57.8	15.9	488	85.9	55.7	16.0
Beaver Falls city & MCD (Beaver)	8,987	8,740	-2.7	8,842	79.2	13.2	0.7	5.5	1.4	21.0	63.0	15.9	3,304	49.5	57.1	15.0
Beaver Meadows borough & MCD (Carbon)	869	850	-2.2	713	97.6	2.4	0.0	0.0	0.0	18.5	57.4	24.1	328	69.2	72.0	7.3
Beaver Springs CDP	674	NA	NA	695	98.1	0.0	0.0	0.3	1.6	27.2	53.7	19.0	258	72.1	64.3	10.5
Beavertown borough & MCD (Snyder)	965	973	0.8	965	98.0	0.0	0.0	0.6	1.3	19.3	64.8	15.9	355	75.5	70.4	11.5
Beccaria township (Clearfield)	1,782	1,754	-1.6	1,844	98.5	0.3	0.0	0.6	0.4	20.5	62.4	17.1	685	85.5	66.1	11.7
Bechtelsville borough & MCD (Berks)	942	940	-0.2	828	97.5	0.0	0.2	1.1	1.2	20.9	68.9	10.3	322	71.7	55.3	17.4
Bedford borough & MCD (Bedford)	2,841	2,768	-2.6	2,804	97.5	0.0	0.0	0.7	1.8	20.1	52.8	27.2	1,421	50.7	58.3	22.2
Bedford township (Bedford)	5,395	5,272	-2.3	5,325	94.0	1.8	1.1	0.9	2.3	19.7	58.8	21.4	2,094	84.6	55.8	16.3
Bedminster township (Bucks)	6,574	7,005	6.6	6,847	94.4	0.0	1.7	1.8	2.0	22.2	64.9	13.0	2,508	85.6	34.1	39.8
Beech Creek borough & MCD (Clinton)	701	703	0.3	716	95.9	0.0	0.0	0.0	4.1	14.8	67.4	17.7	310	72.9	70.0	11.6
Beech Creek township (Clinton)	1,015	1,021	0.6	816	98.3	1.7	0.0	0.0	0.0	21.2	62.4	16.4	315	85.1	63.5	11.1
Beech Mountain Lakes CDP	2,022	NA	NA	1,948	98.6	0.3	0.0	0.0	1.1	21.5	62.5	16.0	890	96.2	40.8	35.6
Belfast township (Fulton)	1,448	1,439	-0.6	1,153	97.8	0.0	0.0	1.3	0.9	23.2	56.0	20.7	475	82.9	60.2	16.6
Belfast CDP	1,257	NA	NA	1,133	98.4	0.0	0.0	1.6	0.0	24.6	62.0	13.3	400	83.5	30.5	21.5
Bell township (Clearfield)	760	751	-1.2	717	99.3	0.0	0.6	0.1	0.0	16.5	66.8	16.6	308	84.4	68.2	6.8
Bell township (Jefferson)	2,050	2,030	-1.0	2,085	98.0	0.0	0.7	1.2	0.2	17.7	65.8	16.4	880	86.8	59.0	18.6
Bell township (Westmoreland)	2,348	2,314	-1.4	2,657	97.1	2.1	0.0	0.6	0.2	20.3	62.8	16.6	1,032	86.6	54.6	18.1
Bell Acres borough & MCD (Allegheny)	1,390	1,401	0.8	1,428	91.5	4.8	0.4	2.6	0.8	23.3	60.5	16.3	557	91.0	28.9	51.5
Bellefonte borough & MCD (Centre)	6,187	6,227	0.6	6,250	94.1	3.5	0.2	0.5	1.7	18.9	64.4	16.7	2,704	49.4	41.1	33.0
Belle Vernon borough & MCD (Fayette)	1,093	1,073	-1.8	1,165	83.6	4.5	2.6	6.8	2.6	14.5	62.9	22.4	568	37.8	69.8	7.8
Delleville CDP	1,827	NA	NA	1,913	96.8	0.9	0.0	0.9	1.4	19.5	50.0	30.5	815	74.2	58.9	18.4
Bellevue borough & MCD (Allegheny)	8,370	8,300	-0.8	8,338	85.3	7.3	1.4	4.3	1.8	16.3	71.0	12.6	4,143	36.2	37.7	30.4
Bellwood borough & MCD (Blair)	1,824	1,794	-1.6	1,810	97.0	0.2	0.7	0.3	1.8	25.5	56.8	17.6	738	72.6	61.8	10.2
Belmont CDP	2,784	NA	NA	3,045	94.8	0.5	1.1	1.8	1.7	17.4	53.3	29.4	1,286	65.9	43.6	30.3
Ben Avon borough & MCD (Allegheny)	1,781	1,786	0.3	1,755	95.7	2.1	0.2	1.4	0.6	25.4	62.4	12.2	708	84.5	15.0	66.7

1 May be of any race.

Table A. All Places — Population and Housing

STATE City, town, township, borough, or CDP (county if applicable)	2010 census total population	2014 estimated population	Percent change 2010–2014	ACS total population estimate 2010–2014	White alone, not Hispanic or Latino	Black alone, not Hispanic or Latino	Asian alone, not Hispanic or Latino	All other races or 2 or more races, not Hispanic or Latino	Hispanic or Latino[1]	Under 18 years old	Age 18 to 64 years old	Age 65 years and older	Total occupied housing units	Percent owner occupied	High school diploma or less	Bachelor's degree or more
	1	2	3	4	5	6	7	8	9	10	11	12	13	14	15	16
PENNSYLVANIA—Con.																
Ben Avon Heights borough & MCD (Allegheny)	371	372	0.3	362	96.4	0.0	0.8	0.0	2.8	29.0	57.5	13.5	138	98.6	8.0	91.3
Bendersville borough & MCD (Adams)	641	641	0.0	741	67.2	0.0	0.0	0.0	32.8	31.0	57.5	11.5	255	75.3	64.7	18.8
Benezette township (Elk)	207	200	-3.4	236	99.6	0.0	0.4	0.0	0.0	14.0	57.3	28.8	107	93.5	52.3	18.7
Benner township (Centre)	6,177	8,908	44.2	7,430	79.0	14.1	1.0	1.6	4.3	15.6	72.5	11.8	2,205	94.7	45.3	30.0
Bensalem township (Bucks)	60,427	60,420	0.0	60,425	72.6	6.9	11.3	2.3	6.9	20.3	65.4	14.1	23,612	59.6	41.6	26.8
Benson borough & MCD (Somerset)	191	187	-2.1	212	100.0	0.0	0.0	0.0	0.0	18.8	74.9	6.1	81	74.1	82.7	2.5
Bentleyville borough & MCD (Washington)	2,581	2,531	-1.9	2,554	94.0	0.3	2.1	2.8	0.8	24.2	59.2	16.7	1,057	58.1	52.2	16.6
Benton borough & MCD (Columbia)	824	831	0.8	1,005	97.4	0.5	0.7	1.4	0.0	28.8	54.0	17.5	396	64.1	61.4	19.4
Benton township (Columbia)	1,245	1,253	0.6	1,149	98.8	0.0	0.0	0.0	1.2	17.8	61.5	20.8	491	84.7	62.1	15.9
Benton township (Lackawanna)	1,908	1,903	-0.3	1,808	99.0	0.6	0.2	0.0	0.2	25.5	60.4	14.2	638	88.1	43.1	34.3
Berlin borough & MCD (Somerset)	2,104	2,039	-3.1	2,036	96.8	0.2	0.0	1.7	1.2	18.4	53.2	28.4	853	70.5	69.1	9.6
Berlin township (Wayne)	2,562	2,468	-3.7	2,648	91.1	0.2	1.4	2.3	5.0	24.0	60.1	15.9	978	79.1	41.2	22.6
Bern township (Berks)	6,797	6,896	1.5	6,848	80.8	4.6	0.0	1.7	12.9	14.6	65.6	20.0	1,781	83.4	47.7	30.8
Bernville borough & MCD (Berks)	955	951	-0.4	812	91.7	0.2	0.0	0.4	7.6	21.0	64.5	14.7	331	66.5	56.8	14.5
Berrysburg borough & MCD (Dauphin)	368	370	0.5	404	100.0	0.0	0.0	0.0	0.0	18.8	67.1	14.1	170	75.3	69.4	14.1
Berwick township (Adams)	2,389	2,388	0.0	2,202	91.9	1.8	0.2	0.4	5.7	18.9	61.9	19.2	864	88.0	62.5	16.1
Berwick borough & MCD (Columbia)	10,475	10,316	-1.5	10,398	93.6	0.9	2.0	1.0	2.4	23.5	60.4	16.1	4,253	56.6	61.5	15.9
Berwyn CDP	3,631	NA	NA	3,222	84.1	7.2	3.5	2.8	2.4	24.4	51.5	24.1	1,329	69.5	30.8	55.2
Bessemer borough & MCD (Lawrence)	1,111	1,081	-2.7	1,220	97.7	0.0	0.4	0.7	1.1	19.2	64.8	16.0	477	69.2	53.2	17.4
Bethany borough & MCD (Wayne)	245	236	-3.7	299	99.3	0.0	0.0	0.7	0.0	25.4	57.8	16.7	122	78.7	45.1	39.3
Bethel township (Armstrong)	1,188	1,178	-0.8	1,259	98.0	0.0	0.0	2.0	0.0	20.9	61.6	17.3	510	87.6	54.7	18.4
Bethel CDP	499	NA	NA	751	98.1	0.0	0.0	1.9	0.0	25.4	58.9	15.7	267	50.9	78.7	16.5
Bethel township (Berks)	4,112	4,121	0.2	4,112	96.0	2.7	1.0	0.3	0.0	23.2	57.8	19.2	1,508	80.9	80.7	5.2
Bethel township (Delaware)	8,791	9,119	3.7	8,986	89.0	2.2	6.1	2.0	0.7	24.1	61.4	14.6	3,064	97.6	23.6	54.9
Bethel township (Fulton)	1,508	1,493		1,559	97.5	0.2	0.3	0.9	1.2	21.0	63.1	16.0	633	81.4	58.5	13.9
Bethel township (Lebanon)	5,018	5,116	2.0	5,086	97.1	0.9	0.5	0.4	1.1	23.0	59.1	18.0	1,914	87.4	64.4	11.9
Bethel Park municipality & MCD (Allegheny)	32,315	32,257	-0.2	32,338	94.1	1.6	1.4	1.9	0.9	20.4	60.1	19.6	13,198	78.7	28.4	47.5
Bethlehem city (Lehigh)	74,982	75,135	0.2	75,050	63.0	6.1	2.8	2.6	25.5	19.4	65.4	15.2	29,359	51.0	42.8	28.9
Bethlehem city (Lehigh)	19,343	19,634	1.5	19,524	74.4	4.3	1.2	2.2	17.8	17.7	62.5	19.9	8,656	54.4	42.8	27.1
Bethlehem city (Northampton)	55,639	55,501	-0.2	55,526	58.9	6.8	3.3	2.8	28.2	20.1	66.4	13.6	20,703	49.5	42.8	29.6
Bethlehem township (Northampton)	23,820	23,885	0.3	23,842	79.8	4.6	4.8	1.7	9.2	20.0	61.1	19.0	8,674	86.6	31.8	38.0
Beurys Lake CDP	124	NA	NA	133	100.0	0.0	0.0	0.0	0.0	8.3	77.4	14.3	72	83.3	61.1	25.0
Big Bass Lake CDP	1,270	NA	NA	1,556	90.0	3.5	1.3	0.7	4.5	17.7	62.0	20.4	616	91.2	37.5	26.5
Big Beaver borough & MCD (Beaver)	1,970	1,934	-1.8	2,005	96.9	2.3	0.4	0.4	0.0	13.5	62.2	24.3	822	89.8	46.8	24.1
Bigler CDP	398	NA	NA	381	100.0	0.0	0.0	0.0	0.0	32.5	52.5	15.0	158	72.8	66.5	3.8
Bigler township (Clearfield)	1,289	1,261	-2.2	1,181	99.7	0.0	0.3	0.1	0.0	22.4	61.4	16.3	447	87.0	67.3	9.8
Biglerville borough & MCD (Adams)	1,200	1,202	0.2	1,107	79.0	0.0	0.0	0.0	21.0	23.9	56.6	19.6	444	60.1	54.3	21.6
Big Run borough & MCD (Jefferson)	624	616	-1.3	625	96.5	0.0	0.0	0.0	3.5	24.6	58.1	17.1	240	66.3	66.3	14.6
Bingham township (Potter)	684	681	-0.4	657	97.3	0.9	0.0	0.0	1.8	24.7	60.0	15.4	232	87.9	58.6	17.2
Birchwood Lakes CDP	1,386	NA	NA	1,695	92.3	0.0	4.9	1.6	1.2	29.1	61.1	9.7	540	90.9	51.5	11.1
Bird-in-Hand CDP	402	NA	NA	493	100.0	0.0	0.0	0.0	0.0	31.6	63.8	4.5	163	52.8	59.5	17.2
Birdsboro borough & MCD (Berks)	5,163	5,150	-0.3	5,158	92.4	1.5	0.5	3.6	1.9	22.0	65.4	12.8	1,989	79.6	50.0	18.8
Birmingham township (Chester)	4,208	4,257	1.2	4,242	87.5	2.1	8.0	0.0	2.3	28.8	57.4	13.8	1,433	97.2	7.7	81.1
Birmingham borough & MCD (Huntingdon)	90	89	-1.1	105	95.2	0.0	4.8	0.0	0.0	27.7	56.3	16.2	35	68.6	31.4	28.6
Black township (Somerset)	926	901	-2.7	814	99.1	0.0	0.0	0.7	0.1	17.0	61.3	21.6	352	89.5	81.8	6.8
Black Creek township (Luzerne)	2,016	2,058	2.1	2,051	97.5	0.0	0.0	0.0	2.5	17.7	63.2	19.1	878	76.5	60.4	17.5
Blacklick township (Cambria)	2,013	1,958	-2.7	2,101	100.0	0.0	0.0	0.0	0.0	18.5	63.7	17.7	879	86.6	65.3	15.5
Black Lick CDP	1,462	NA	NA	1,489	92.5	2.1	2.2	3.2	0.0	25.7	52.5	21.9	603	56.9	70.1	3.3
Black Lick township (Indiana)	1,237	1,197	-3.2	1,114	99.4	0.0	0.0	0.0	0.6	14.5	69.0	16.5	505	84.8	54.3	15.4
Blain borough & MCD (Perry)	263	260	-1.1	240	95.8	0.0	0.0	4.2	0.0	28.4	63.1	8.8	84	63.1	72.6	7.1
Blaine township (Washington)	690	676	-2.0	805	99.9	0.0	0.0	0.1	0.0	31.6	59.6	8.7	248	89.1	58.5	24.2
Blair township (Blair)	4,495	4,544	1.1	4,537	92.5	1.9	2.7	2.9	0.0	17.5	60.5	22.1	1,857	78.4	61.3	25.1
Blairsville borough & MCD (Indiana)	3,412	3,327	-2.5	3,385	93.5	1.9	2.3	0.3	1.9	22.8	57.6	19.7	1,450	71.2	42.3	24.6

1 May be of any race.

Table A. All Places — Population and Housing

STATE City, town, township, borough, or CDP (county if applicable)	2010 census total population	2014 estimated population	Percent change 2010–2014	ACS total population estimate 2010–2014	White alone, not Hispanic or Latino	Black alone, not Hispanic or Latino	Asian alone, not Hispanic or Latino	All other races or 2 or more races, not Hispanic or Latino	Hispanic or Latino[1]	Under 18 years old	Age 18 to 64 years old	Age 65 years and older	Total occupied housing units	Percent owner occupied	High school diploma or less	Bachelor's degree or more
	1	2	3	4	5	6	7	8	9	10	11	12	13	14	15	16
PENNSYLVANIA—Con.																
Blakely borough & MCD (Lackawanna)..............	6,564	6,475	-1.4	6,534	91.6	0.2	2.9	2.5	2.8	14.9	57.0	28.2	2,826	71.4	39.5	21.4
Blanchard CDP.............	740	NA	NA	660	100.0	0.0	0.0	0.0	0.0	18.5	60.9	20.6	292	75.7	67.1	6.2
Blandburg CDP.............	402	NA	NA	371	96.0	4.0	0.0	0.0	0.0	27.2	60.9	11.9	165	95.2	76.4	0.0
Blandon CDP................	7,152	NA	NA	7,139	92.2	2.4	0.2	0.8	4.4	27.0	62.9	10.1	2,580	84.1	45.8	24.6
Blawnox borough & MCD (Allegheny)............	1,432	1,423	-0.6	1,512	85.6	2.2	9.9	0.6	1.7	19.0	64.1	16.9	807	36.8	45.8	27.8
Bloom township (Clearfield)	414	407	-1.7	408	99.3	0.0	0.0	0.2	0.5	14.2	62.4	23.3	178	86.0	65.7	9.6
Bloomfield township (Bedford)	1,016	1,004	-1.2	937	98.3	0.0	0.0	0.0	1.7	23.9	61.6	14.5	333	91.0	62.2	16.5
Bloomfield township (Crawford)	1,919	1,881	-2.0	1,852	99.4	0.3	0.0	0.3	0.0	21.8	62.7	15.4	750	91.7	65.3	15.1
Bloomfield borough & MCD (Perry).............	1,249	1,246	-0.2	1,346	92.3	2.4	0.0	1.3	4.1	21.1	57.1	21.8	477	60.8	41.3	29.1
Blooming Grove township (Pike)...................	4,814	4,705	-2.3	4,772	80.2	7.6	1.5	1.4	9.3	18.7	59.4	21.8	1,671	83.4	38.7	28.5
Blooming Valley borough & MCD (Crawford)	337	333	-1.2	373	98.7	0.8	0.3	0.3	0.0	18.7	60.2	21.2	157	88.5	64.3	16.6
Bloomsburg town & MCD (Columbia)	14,855	14,727	-0.9	14,699	86.3	6.1	2.0	0.7	4.9	10.7	80.3	8.9	4,881	37.3	36.0	25.8
Bloss township (Tioga)	353	348	-1.4	436	98.4	1.6	0.0	0.0	0.0	21.0	63.2	15.8	168	92.9	67.3	18.5
Blossburg borough & MCD (Tioga).................	1,534	1,534	0.0	1,595	94.7	0.4	0.9	3.7	0.3	26.5	53.9	19.6	617	68.7	53.0	24.3
Blue Ball CDP................	1,031	NA	NA	1,097	72.8	0.0	27.2	0.0	0.0	19.3	75.6	5.0	375	67.2	82.9	6.9
Blue Bell CDP................	6,067	NA	NA	6,049	87.3	1.8	9.1	0.8	1.0	19.9	58.8	21.3	2,377	88.6	10.9	71.6
Blue Ridge Summit CDP .	891	NA	NA	1,243	87.7	4.8	5.6	1.9	0.0	25.4	58.2	16.5	511	62.2	59.3	11.7
Blythe township (Schuylkill)................	924	911	-1.4	987	98.4	0.0	0.0	1.1	0.5	24.7	58.6	16.9	381	83.5	62.7	13.6
Boalsburg CDP..............	3,722	NA	NA	3,896	89.8	1.1	2.0	3.2	3.9	28.4	55.3	16.2	1,423	72.1	19.9	54.1
Bobtown CDP................	757	NA	NA	798	92.4	0.0	0.0	6.6	1.0	20.7	56.0	23.6	349	84.5	68.5	15.2
Boggs township (Armstrong).............	936	949	1.4	859	99.4	0.0	0.3	0.2	0.0	22.4	62.4	15.1	338	84.3	56.5	16.0
Boggs township (Centre) .	2,987	2,939	-1.6	2,971	96.5	0.0	0.0	0.6	2.9	18.6	69.0	12.5	1,135	80.8	62.1	10.7
Boggs township (Clearfield)	1,751	1,760	0.5	1,533	98.6	0.0	1.4	0.0	0.0	18.4	65.1	16.3	617	90.0	61.9	10.9
Boiling Springs CDP........	3,225	NA	NA	2,822	95.1	0.0	0.9	1.6	2.4	20.5	62.0	17.6	1,109	85.1	41.8	37.9
Bolivar borough & MCD (Westmoreland)	465	450	-3.2	431	96.3	1.9	0.7	0.7	0.5	17.1	61.7	21.1	172	87.2	61.6	10.5
Bonneauville borough & MCD (Adams)............	1,800	1,813	0.7	1,937	88.4	1.3	0.0	1.7	8.6	27.8	58.6	13.6	687	69.0	63.5	11.2
Boothwyn CDP	4,933	NA	NA	4,889	80.9	10.4	1.2	2.6	4.9	20.3	66.0	13.7	2,012	64.5	45.2	14.9
Boston CDP	545	NA	NA	366	100.0	0.0	0.0	0.0	0.0	9.8	66.7	23.5	195	69.2	70.3	29.7
Boswell borough & MCD (Somerset)	1,277	1,238	-3.1	1,317	94.4	1.7	0.0	2.0	2.0	19.4	59.5	21.1	589	59.8	71.5	9.8
Bowers CDP	326	NA	NA	251	100.0	0.0	0.0	0.0	0.0	13.6	32.7	53.8	130	100.0	71.5	21.5
Bowmanstown borough & MCD (Carbon).............	906	892	-1.5	1,085	94.0	0.0	0.0	1.5	4.5	21.4	60.3	18.3	409	77.0	61.1	13.7
Bowmansville CDP	2,077	NA	NA	2,170	93.5	0.0	4.0	0.9	1.6	28.8	61.1	10.0	732	84.6	49.7	29.6
Boyertown borough & MCD (Berks)	4,055	4,037	-0.4	4,048	94.4	0.8	0.3	1.9	2.7	20.4	55.6	23.8	1,953	44.1	62.7	14.4
Brackenridge borough & MCD (Allegheny).........	3,260	3,229	-1.0	3,256	90.2	4.8	1.5	3.5	0.0	20.7	59.6	19.7	1,424	64.6	44.9	27.0
Braddock borough & MCD (Allegheny).........	2,159	2,140	-0.9	2,030	30.4	64.2	0.0	4.0	1.3	19.5	60.7	20.1	789	45.5	66.0	8.7
Braddock Hills borough & MCD (Allegheny).........	1,880	1,870	-0.5	1,713	69.5	27.6	0.0	2.7	0.2	12.3	61.7	26.0	984	50.3	48.3	20.8
Bradenville CDP	545	NA	NA	753	100.0	0.0	0.0	0.0	0.0	38.8	41.6	19.5	248	50.8	69.4	0.0
Bradford township (Clearfield)	3,034	3,005	-1.0	3,030	99.4	0.0	0.6	0.0	0.0	23.1	57.5	19.3	1,249	89.3	68.9	9.3
Bradford city & MCD (McKean).................	8,770	8,552	-2.5	8,665	97.4	0.8	0.0	1.1	0.8	25.4	60.9	13.7	3,747	51.2	53.5	17.6
Bradford township (McKean).................	4,805	4,754	-1.1	4,798	95.1	0.7	2.5	0.6	1.2	15.2	67.0	17.6	1,693	89.3	53.7	18.5
Bradford Woods borough & MCD (Allegheny).........	1,171	1,174	0.3	1,249	97.9	0.0	1.2	0.1	0.8	21.4	57.4	21.1	507	96.6	11.0	75.9
Brady township (Butler) ...	1,310	1,273	-2.8	1,177	97.9	0.3	0.0	0.8	1.0	22.7	64.4	12.9	465	81.3	52.9	22.4
Brady township (Clarion) .	55	56	1.8	54	100.0	0.0	0.0	0.0	0.0	14.9	81.6	3.7	27	63.0	51.9	18.5
Brady township (Clearfield)	2,000	1,982	-0.9	2,093	96.5	0.0	0.2	0.3	3.0	24.6	60.4	14.9	738	90.5	66.3	16.8
Brady township (Huntingdon)	1,177	1,150	-2.3	1,114	98.3	0.0	0.0	1.7	0.0	25.6	56.3	18.0	406	84.2	70.4	11.3
Brady township (Lycoming)	521	540	3.6	583	97.3	0.0	0.3	2.2	0.2	21.3	69.5	9.1	190	86.8	52.6	18.4
Bradys Bend township (Armstrong)	770	751	-2.5	873	97.7	0.0	0.0	0.9	1.4	19.9	65.0	15.0	345	78.6	60.6	13.3
Braintrim township (Wyoming)	502	501	-0.2	440	93.9	0.0	0.5	1.4	4.3	24.2	62.0	13.9	161	73.9	59.6	10.6
Branch township (Schuylkill)................	1,840	1,799	-2.2	1,606	98.9	0.7	0.0	0.0	0.4	14.8	63.5	21.7	725	91.3	59.0	12.7
Branchdale CDP	388	NA	NA	397	100.0	0.0	0.0	0.0	0.0	20.2	71.2	8.6	163	81.0	74.2	3.7
Brandonville CDP	197	NA	NA	155	100.0	0.0	0.0	0.0	0.0	12.3	69.7	18.1	69	100.0	73.9	0.0
Bratton township (Mifflin) .	1,319	1,308	-0.8	1,341	98.5	0.3	0.0	0.0	1.2	21.0	60.1	18.8	504	80.6	71.0	6.9
Brave CDP	201	NA	NA	198	100.0	0.0	0.0	0.0	0.0	33.3	57.0	9.6	74	70.3	73.0	9.5
Brecknock township (Berks)	4,585	4,613	0.6	4,599	91.6	0.2	5.6	1.5	1.2	23.1	62.6	14.4	1,640	92.8	45.5	31.4
Brecknock township (Lancaster)................	7,199	7,375	2.4	7,303	95.6	0.0	1.5	0.9	2.0	27.3	59.2	13.5	2,385	84.0	64.6	19.2
Breinigsville CDP............	4,138	NA	NA	4,651	65.5	6.9	13.1	3.7	10.9	31.6	59.1	9.3	1,693	91.5	26.3	53.8
Brentwood borough & MCD (Allegheny).........	9,643	9,563	-0.8	9,625	89.4	2.4	2.7	3.6	1.9	19.6	65.8	14.5	4,276	63.7	40.2	24.5

1 May be of any race.

Table A. All Places — **Population and Housing**

STATE City, town, township, borough, or CDP (county if applicable)	2010 census total population (1)	2014 estimated population (2)	Percent change 2010–2014 (3)	ACS total population estimate 2010–2014 (4)	White alone, not Hispanic or Latino (5)	Black alone, not Hispanic or Latino (6)	Asian alone, not Hispanic or Latino (7)	All other races or 2 or more races, not Hispanic or Latino (8)	Hispanic or Latino[1] (9)	Under 18 years old (10)	Age 18 to 64 years old (11)	Age 65 years and older (12)	Total occupied housing units (13)	Percent owner occupied (14)	High school diploma or less (15)	Bachelor's degree or more (16)
PENNSYLVANIA—Con.																
Bressler CDP	1,437	NA	NA	1,390	83.2	12.9	0.0	0.0	4.0	13.6	67.9	18.3	570	94.4	42.5	25.8
Briar Creek borough & MCD (Columbia)	662	688	3.9	761	96.1	0.7	0.0	3.0	0.3	19.7	50.6	29.8	333	53.2	74.2	9.3
Briar Creek township (Columbia)	3,016	3,022	0.2	3,022	94.8	0.0	0.0	0.5	4.8	17.8	59.8	22.3	1,282	89.9	53.0	15.8
Brickerville CDP	1,309	NA	NA	1,646	95.9	0.0	0.6	3.5	0.0	27.3	62.5	10.1	560	78.9	62.1	14.3
Bridgeport borough & MCD (Montgomery)	4,554	4,578	0.5	4,573	76.1	11.9	5.0	1.5	5.5	14.1	75.2	10.6	2,098	44.7	51.0	25.7
Bridgeton township (Bucks)	1,277	1,285	0.6	1,296	94.4	0.9	1.0	0.8	2.9	17.0	64.0	19.2	529	74.5	54.3	25.1
Bridgeville borough & MCD (Allegheny)	5,148	5,116	-0.6	5,142	94.2	1.2	1.8	2.1	0.7	18.6	59.1	22.3	2,484	62.0	47.7	23.4
Bridgewater borough & MCD (Beaver)	709	697	-1.7	690	89.1	3.5	0.0	5.4	2.0	16.3	64.8	18.8	319	62.1	43.6	30.7
Bridgewater township (Susquehanna)	2,842	2,820	-0.8	2,809	97.5	0.5	0.0	0.5	1.5	16.8	65.6	17.6	1,188	77.6	50.3	20.5
Brighton township (Beaver)	8,227	8,338	1.3	8,255	97.2	1.1	0.1	0.6	1.0	22.1	57.1	20.8	3,168	86.9	28.1	40.8
Brisbin borough & MCD (Clearfield)	411	400	-2.7	333	98.8	0.0	0.0	1.2	0.0	23.7	59.7	16.5	140	86.4	57.1	11.4
Bristol borough & MCD (Bucks)	9,726	9,595	-1.3	9,657	69.2	13.3	0.2	2.4	15.0	22.2	64.1	13.7	3,700	54.7	57.8	12.2
Bristol township (Bucks)	54,582	54,160	-0.8	54,431	76.8	10.6	2.7	2.3	7.5	20.8	66.3	12.8	19,695	76.5	55.4	13.0
Brittany Farms-The Highlands CDP	3,695	NA	NA	3,862	93.3	0.6	4.3	1.0	0.8	24.3	58.1	17.7	1,534	80.9	28.1	51.3
Broad Top township (Bedford)	1,687	1,647	-2.4	1,723	95.8	0.0	2.3	0.7	1.2	18.7	58.4	23.0	724	80.0	73.5	7.0
Broad Top City borough & MCD (Huntingdon)	452	444	-1.8	381	99.7	0.0	0.0	0.3	0.0	12.3	60.9	26.8	166	85.5	67.5	4.8
Brockway borough & MCD (Jefferson)	2,072	2,048	-1.2	2,066	97.9	1.1	0.0	0.4	0.6	19.9	57.2	22.9	955	57.1	59.9	13.5
Brodheadsville CDP	1,800	NA	NA	1,746	79.2	0.0	0.0	0.0	20.8	17.5	61.7	20.7	665	86.6	35.3	21.5
Brokenstraw township (Warren)	1,884	1,831	-2.8	1,755	96.2	0.8	0.0	2.5	0.5	19.5	47.3	33.3	716	75.1	62.0	14.7
Brookfield township (Tioga)	421	418	-0.7	409	99.3	0.0	0.7	0.0	0.0	22.7	59.7	17.6	167	79.0	70.7	10.2
Brookhaven borough & MCD (Delaware)	8,006	8,073	0.8	8,045	91.6	3.3	1.4	1.4	2.3	16.8	63.8	19.3	3,481	85.7	43.1	29.8
Brooklyn township (Susquehanna)	961	933	-2.9	960	97.1	0.0	0.0	0.7	2.2	15.4	65.4	19.2	409	88.0	64.5	16.1
Brookville borough & MCD (Jefferson)	3,932	3,884	-1.2	3,906	97.6	0.0	0.8	1.0	0.6	19.9	57.7	22.5	1,862	66.7	49.4	22.8
Broomall CDP	10,789	NA	NA	10,312	85.7	4.7	7.2	1.5	0.8	18.7	62.3	18.9	4,008	78.5	41.5	36.0
Brothersvalley township (Somerset)	2,398	2,352	-1.9	2,389	99.1	0.0	0.0	0.1	0.8	23.8	62.7	13.4	921	84.6	61.7	13.0
Brown township (Lycoming)	96	97	1.0	77	100.0	0.0	0.0	0.0	0.0	2.6	62.4	35.1	45	86.7	71.1	15.6
Brown township (Mifflin)	4,053	4,074	0.5	4,076	98.6	0.0	0.3	1.2	0.0	23.2	56.1	20.8	1,585	83.0	56.8	21.5
Brownstown borough & MCD (Cambria)	744	716	-3.8	711	99.7	0.3	0.0	0.0	0.0	23.7	54.7	21.7	300	80.0	60.3	20.0
Brownstown CDP	2,816	NA	NA	2,559	90.9	0.0	8.1	0.7	0.4	27.5	59.6	12.9	864	88.4	52.7	29.4
Brownsville borough & MCD (Fayette)	2,331	2,292	-1.7	2,378	77.0	11.5	0.0	8.7	2.8	22.1	58.9	19.0	1,075	49.8	64.9	14.0
Brownsville township (Fayette)	683	671	-1.8	803	76.5	16.8	0.0	5.1	1.6	29.8	52.5	17.7	300	75.7	63.7	17.7
Browntown CDP	1,418	NA	NA	1,375	97.2	1.0	0.0	1.7	0.0	15.2	62.2	22.6	571	70.8	56.9	16.3
Bruin borough & MCD (Butler)	528	509	-3.6	482	98.8	0.2	0.0	0.0	1.0	21.9	64.2	13.7	182	76.9	69.8	9.9
Brush Creek township (Fulton)	819	799	-2.4	873	91.2	1.0	0.6	1.8	5.4	23.8	54.9	21.3	344	85.5	64.5	7.6
Brush Valley township (Indiana)	1,858	1,801	-3.1	1,724	99.5	0.0	0.0	0.0	0.5	22.1	62.8	15.2	681	86.6	62.4	19.2
Bryn Athyn borough & MCD (Montgomery)	1,369	1,396	2.0	1,348	89.5	2.9	2.6	2.5	2.4	18.2	68.5	13.2	455	62.4	16.9	55.6
Bryn Mawr CDP	3,779	NA	NA	3,507	66.7	11.6	13.7	3.2	4.9	9.3	78.0	12.9	1,065	41.4	9.9	70.1
Buck township (Luzerne)	435	433	-0.5	410	94.4	0.7	1.5	2.7	0.7	14.9	68.8	16.1	189	75.7	50.3	12.2
Buckhorn CDP	318	NA	NA	397	90.2	0.8	2.3	0.0	6.8	24.4	59.3	16.4	146	89.7	52.1	21.9
Buckingham township (Bucks)	20,075	20,386	1.5	20,268	89.5	0.4	5.9	1.5	2.7	27.5	57.6	14.8	7,192	92.3	16.8	60.3
Buckingham township (Wayne)	520	504	-3.1	491	98.6	0.0	0.0	1.4	0.0	11.6	57.8	30.8	248	94.0	56.9	19.4
Buck Run CDP	176	NA	NA	112	100.0	0.0	0.0	0.0	0.0	15.2	55.5	29.5	53	90.6	71.7	15.1
Buffalo township (Butler)	7,307	7,246	-0.8	7,303	96.1	0.4	0.0	0.6	2.9	20.8	62.4	16.9	2,988	90.7	42.3	32.5
Buffalo township (Perry)	1,219	1,212	-0.6	1,221	98.4	0.5	0.0	0.8	0.3	21.7	65.0	13.5	485	86.8	56.9	15.9
Buffalo township (Union)	3,537	3,583	1.3	3,550	89.4	5.5	0.7	1.1	3.3	23.4	58.3	18.4	1,361	68.4	50.3	18.4
Buffalo township (Washington)	2,069	2,065	-0.2	2,149	98.1	0.3	0.0	0.4	1.3	20.9	61.9	17.1	815	84.7	58.4	23.6
Buffington CDP	292	NA	NA	353	73.1	26.9	0.0	0.0	0.0	0.3	61.1	38.5	140	92.9	66.4	0.0
Buffington township (Indiana)	1,328	1,297	-2.3	1,232	99.0	0.0	0.2	0.0	0.7	24.5	56.8	18.7	476	92.4	73.5	8.0
Bulger CDP	407	NA	NA	476	100.0	0.0	0.0	0.0	0.0	21.1	62.4	16.6	204	91.7	69.1	8.8
Bullskin township (Fayette)	6,970	6,840	-1.9	6,902	99.3	0.0	0.4	0.0	0.3	18.9	62.3	18.7	2,785	88.3	60.6	13.1
Burgettstown borough & MCD (Washington)	1,388	1,360	-2.0	1,385	96.2	1.3	0.0	0.4	2.1	21.3	59.1	19.7	585	66.8	53.0	20.3
Burlington borough & MCD (Bradford)	156	153	-1.9	161	82.6	0.0	0.0	0.0	17.4	41.6	42.8	15.5	50	74.0	56.0	20.0
Burlington township (Bradford)	791	789	-0.3	877	91.8	3.2	0.0	1.8	3.2	20.9	59.8	19.2	342	79.2	57.3	20.8
Burnham borough & MCD (Mifflin)	2,054	2,027	-1.3	1,995	98.2	0.1	0.0	0.7	1.1	22.8	59.2	18.0	855	75.7	60.9	15.2

1 May be of any race.

Table A. All Places — **Population and Housing**

STATE City, town, township, borough, or CDP (county if applicable)	Population 2010 census total population	2014 estimated population	Percent change 2010–2014	ACS total population estimate 2010–2014	Race and Hispanic or Latino origin (percent), 2010–2014 White alone, not Hispanic or Latino	Black alone, not Hispanic or Latino	Asian alone, not Hispanic or Latino	All other races or 2 or more races, not Hispanic or Latino	Hispanic or Latino[1]	Age (percent), 2010–2014 Under 18 years old	Age 18 to 64 years old	Age 65 years and older	Households, 2010–2014 Total occupied housing units	Percent owner occupied	Householders by level of education (percent) High school diploma or less	Bachelor's degree or more
	1	2	3	4	5	6	7	8	9	10	11	12	13	14	15	16
PENNSYLVANIA—Con.																
Burnside township (Centre)	439	430	-2.1	493	99.6	0.0	0.0	0.0	0.4	24.5	55.7	19.7	200	91.5	66.0	13.5
Burnside borough & MCD (Clearfield)	234	231	-1.3	258	93.0	0.0	0.0	0.0	7.0	20.2	63.2	16.7	84	79.8	84.5	1.2
Burnside township (Clearfield)	1,074	1,055	-1.8	1,018	99.3	0.0	0.0	0.7	0.0	21.9	60.7	17.4	380	86.1	66.8	12.6
Burrell township (Armstrong)	689	699	1.5	617	98.2	0.0	0.0	1.8	0.0	17.2	61.8	21.1	256	88.7	66.0	11.3
Burrell township (Indiana)	4,393	4,249	-3.3	4,327	91.0	3.4	0.8	3.4	1.4	18.2	60.7	21.1	1,665	73.5	65.6	10.5
Bushkill township (Northampton)	8,178	8,384	2.5	8,288	96.7	0.2	1.0	1.3	0.8	22.8	62.3	15.0	2,858	93.2	38.2	35.5
Butler township (Adams)	2,567	2,565	-0.1	2,556	90.2	0.2	0.0	0.1	9.4	15.2	67.3	17.7	1,024	79.9	58.0	16.9
Butler city & MCD (Butler)	13,757	13,369	-2.8	13,609	92.0	3.9	0.3	1.7	2.0	22.3	64.4	13.2	5,968	43.7	49.4	15.4
Butler township (Butler)	17,248	16,877	-2.2	17,113	96.0	1.2	0.5	1.2	1.1	18.7	59.8	21.7	7,462	77.6	38.7	29.7
Butler township (Luzerne)	9,224	9,493	2.9	9,379	92.9	2.8	2.1	0.5	1.7	18.4	63.7	17.8	3,791	88.3	39.9	28.6
Butler township (Schuylkill)	5,224	5,196	-0.5	5,217	76.8	13.1	0.5	1.4	8.2	10.4	72.1	17.4	1,687	90.0	54.3	22.2
Byrnedale CDP	427	NA	NA	565	96.3	1.2	0.9	1.6	0.0	30.5	63.4	6.2	179	83.2	54.7	4.5
Cadogan township (Armstrong)	344	331	-3.8	288	99.0	1.0	0.0	0.0	0.0	10.4	60.7	28.8	141	87.9	69.5	4.3
Caernarvon township (Berks)	4,014	4,025	0.3	4,017	93.8	0.6	3.4	1.8	0.4	28.7	60.5	10.8	1,484	81.9	34.8	37.2
Caernarvon township (Lancaster)	4,748	4,783	0.7	4,777	98.2	0.5	0.5	0.5	0.3	32.8	51.6	15.6	1,404	81.7	76.3	12.0
Cairnbrook CDP	520	NA	NA	477	96.6	0.0	0.0	0.0	3.4	12.8	57.5	29.8	251	83.7	68.9	13.1
California borough & MCD (Washington)	6,795	6,678	-1.7	6,703	87.3	5.2	1.5	3.9	2.1	10.1	73.8	16.1	2,462	57.4	43.6	22.1
Callensburg borough & MCD (Clarion)	207	204	-1.4	184	100.0	0.0	0.0	0.0	0.0	29.9	47.3	22.8	82	65.9	74.4	0.0
Callery borough & MCD (Butler)	394	389	-1.3	465	96.6	0.0	0.4	1.9	1.1	26.7	66.3	7.1	164	67.7	51.2	16.5
Callimont borough & MCD (Somerset)	41	40	-2.4	47	100.0	0.0	0.0	0.0	0.0	2.1	66.0	31.9	20	90.0	65.0	10.0
Caln CDP	1,519	NA	NA	1,441	57.3	37.3	0.0	4.4	1.1	26.5	66.4	7.1	532	74.6	47.0	32.1
Caln township (Chester)	13,815	14,168	2.6	14,025	70.2	17.8	5.8	1.3	4.9	19.3	67.7	12.9	5,588	67.3	38.0	36.7
Calumet CDP	1,241	NA	NA	1,079	93.5	0.0	0.0	0.0	6.5	14.1	62.5	23.4	502	76.7	51.8	9.8
Cambria township (Cambria)	6,102	5,967	-2.2	6,040	94.0	4.0	1.3	0.3	0.4	20.4	62.7	16.9	2,074	81.4	44.7	30.4
Cambridge township (Crawford)	1,563	1,530	-2.1	1,510	97.2	0.9	0.8	0.6	0.5	24.5	62.8	12.7	602	94.5	53.8	21.9
Cambridge Springs borough & MCD (Crawford)	2,595	2,528	-2.6	2,530	84.6	8.8	0.1	3.0	3.4	15.9	72.3	11.9	647	51.3	41.1	24.6
Campbelltown CDP	3,616	NA	NA	3,978	89.8	3.3	3.8	0.6	2.4	28.2	55.5	16.3	1,390	78.8	30.4	43.2
Camp Hill borough & MCD (Cumberland)	7,888	7,892	0.1	7,891	88.4	2.4	5.3	1.3	2.7	21.9	60.9	17.4	3,360	69.5	19.6	53.4
Canaan township (Wayne)	3,963	4,001	1.0	3,964	56.1	26.9	0.0	3.0	13.1	6.1	87.1	6.9	335	74.0	59.4	17.0
Canadohta Lake CDP	516	NA	NA	524	100.0	0.0	0.0	0.0	0.0	15.0	62.6	22.5	266	88.3	60.2	16.2
Canal township (Venango)	1,015	984	-3.1	995	99.1	0.0	0.3	0.4	0.2	20.3	60.8	18.6	405	85.7	71.4	17.3
Canoe township (Indiana)	1,511	1,457	-3.6	1,493	98.9	0.9	0.0	0.2	0.0	18.6	67.2	14.2	557	79.0	69.1	5.6
Canonsburg borough & MCD (Washington)	8,992	8,924	-0.8	8,973	86.1	5.7	1.3	4.6	2.2	21.4	59.4	19.1	4,114	55.8	44.0	30.0
Canton borough & MCD (Bradford)	1,974	1,941	-1.7	2,065	99.2	0.5	0.0	0.0	0.2	24.7	60.7	14.4	848	47.4	59.9	13.1
Canton township (Bradford)	2,143	2,107	-1.7	2,128	97.6	0.1	0.2	1.6	0.5	25.1	56.3	18.5	758	78.9	66.6	13.1
Canton township (Washington)	8,375	8,242	-1.6	8,324	94.1	3.8	0.0	1.1	1.0	18.6	62.1	19.2	3,494	85.5	57.4	16.0
Carbon township (Huntingdon)	372	366	-1.6	362	99.4	0.0	0.0	0.6	0.0	19.1	59.8	21.0	156	84.0	69.9	14.1
Carbondale city & MCD (Lackawanna)	8,891	8,758	-1.5	8,843	91.4	1.5	0.5	2.2	4.4	22.4	56.0	21.8	3,757	57.3	59.6	15.4
Carbondale township (Lackawanna)	1,115	1,127	1.1	1,215	90.0	0.0	0.0	0.0	10.0	21.2	61.4	17.4	454	76.0	53.1	19.8
Carlisle borough & MCD (Cumberland)	18,682	18,916	1.3	18,877	80.3	8.8	4.2	3.5	3.2	19.1	65.7	15.1	7,384	50.0	37.6	36.7
Carmichaels borough & MCD (Greene)	483	468	-3.1	393	97.5	0.0	0.0	1.8	0.8	24.4	57.8	17.6	186	57.0	57.0	22.0
Carnegie borough & MCD (Allegheny)	7,972	7,912	-0.8	7,960	81.8	11.8	0.5	5.1	0.7	20.7	63.9	15.4	3,709	46.0	44.6	24.6
Carnot-Moon CDP	11,372	NA	NA	12,081	84.3	5.5	4.7	1.8	3.8	15.6	71.0	13.5	5,001	54.8	27.8	44.5
Carroll township (Perry)	5,265	5,228	-0.7	5,246	96.7	0.0	0.0	1.7	1.6	22.7	65.7	11.6	2,101	85.4	51.1	16.4
Carroll township (Washington)	5,640	5,574	-1.2	5,603	95.0	1.6	0.0	1.1	2.4	16.9	61.0	22.1	2,217	89.2	47.6	24.5
Carroll township (York)	5,936	6,171	4.0	6,069	92.6	0.9	2.9	2.7	0.8	27.0	63.6	9.3	2,116	82.3	41.5	36.1
Carrolltown borough & MCD (Cambria)	853	826	-3.2	828	95.0	0.0	0.0	1.0	4.0	17.3	63.3	19.4	374	78.9	68.2	9.1
Carroll Valley borough & MCD (Adams)	3,876	3,910	0.9	3,894	95.1	0.0	0.4	0.3	4.2	24.5	64.3	11.2	1,342	94.6	37.9	34.0
Cascade township (Lycoming)	412	414	0.5	491	99.0	0.0	0.8	0.2	0.0	27.1	60.9	12.0	192	83.3	48.4	15.1
Cashtown CDP	459	NA	NA	453	91.2	0.0	0.0	0.0	8.8	29.8	61.0	9.3	199	60.3	81.9	18.1
Cass township (Huntingdon)	1,117	1,099	-1.6	909	99.2	0.0	0.0	0.1	0.7	25.5	57.7	17.1	365	81.6	79.7	4.4
Cass township (Schuylkill)	1,958	1,910	-2.5	1,793	97.2	0.4	1.2	0.1	1.1	19.7	62.0	18.3	757	86.3	69.6	4.4
Cassandra borough & MCD (Cambria)	147	143	-2.7	121	99.2	0.0	0.0	0.8	0.0	18.1	62.0	19.8	51	86.3	58.8	11.8
Casselman borough & MCD (Somerset)	94	94	0.0	86	100.0	0.0	0.0	0.0	0.0	30.2	59.4	10.5	28	89.3	89.3	0.0

1 May be of any race.

Table A. All Places — **Population and Housing**

	Population				Race and Hispanic or Latino origin (percent), 2010–2014					Age (percent), 2010–2014			Households, 2010–2014			
								All other races or 2 or more races, not Hispanic or Latino							Householders by level of education (percent)	
STATE City, town, township, borough, or CDP (county if applicable)	2010 census total population	2014 estimated population	Percent change 2010–2014	ACS total population estimate 2010–2014	White alone, not Hispanic or Latino	Black alone, not Hispanic or Latino	Asian alone, not Hispanic or Latino		Hispanic or Latino[1]	Under 18 years old	Age 18 to 64 years old	Age 65 years and older	Total occupied housing units	Percent owner occupied	High school diploma or less	Bachelor's degree or more
	1	2	3	4	5	6	7	8	9	10	11	12	13	14	15	16
PENNSYLVANIA—Con.																
Cassville borough & MCD (Huntingdon)	143	141	-1.4	128	99.2	0.0	0.0	0.8	0.0	26.6	51.7	21.9	53	88.7	83.0	3.8
Castanea township (Clinton)	1,185	1,191	0.5	1,160	98.0	0.0	0.0	0.4	1.6	13.8	62.1	24.1	528	79.9	57.8	14.6
Castanea CDP	1,125	NA	NA	1,145	98.0	0.0	0.0	0.4	1.6	14.0	62.2	23.8	519	80.2	58.2	14.3
Castle Shannon borough & MCD (Allegheny)	8,316	8,273	-0.5	8,317	88.8	1.3	5.6	2.0	2.3	15.5	67.0	17.6	3,882	58.8	38.3	28.8
Catasauqua borough & MCD (Lehigh)	6,436	6,512	1.2	6,477	88.5	2.5	0.8	2.3	5.9	20.9	64.9	14.1	2,545	55.8	54.9	20.6
Catawissa borough & MCD (Columbia)	1,552	1,527	-1.6	1,530	92.1	4.1	0.1	1.9	1.8	25.1	57.8	17.1	684	61.3	51.8	20.0
Catawissa township (Columbia)	932	942	1.1	908	99.8	0.0	0.1	0.1	0.0	16.6	60.7	22.6	394	90.4	47.0	25.1
Catharine township (Blair)	724	720	-0.6	742	98.2	0.0	0.0	0.9	0.8	22.7	64.2	13.2	284	79.9	68.3	13.0
Cecil township (Washington)	11,271	11,884	5.4	11,584	95.2	0.7	1.6	1.3	1.1	22.2	63.3	14.3	4,522	85.6	33.7	40.2
Cecil-Bishop CDP	2,476	NA	NA	2,581	98.5	0.0	0.3	0.3	0.9	20.2	67.6	12.1	975	92.9	34.3	35.8
Cedar Crest CDP	195	NA	NA	226	100.0	0.0	0.0	0.0	0.0	22.1	58.9	19.0	80	80.0	87.5	3.8
Cementon CDP	1,538	NA	NA	1,551	85.7	0.0	3.5	0.0	10.8	19.7	68.5	11.7	637	86.7	50.9	15.9
Center township (Beaver)	11,795	11,783	-0.1	11,774	92.7	4.1	0.5	1.2	1.5	20.6	61.2	18.2	4,512	81.5	34.9	36.6
Center township (Butler)	7,898	7,827	-0.9	7,855	97.7	0.5	0.7	0.6	0.5	19.4	57.1	23.7	3,445	80.1	41.5	27.5
Center township (Greene)	1,269	1,233	-2.8	1,297	99.5	0.0	0.3	0.0	0.2	22.2	60.9	16.8	522	75.5	60.2	19.9
Center township (Indiana)	4,768	4,611	-3.3	4,698	97.5	0.0	0.0	0.0	2.5	20.0	59.5	20.6	1,849	79.2	59.1	13.6
Center township (Snyder)	2,458	2,466	0.3	2,228	95.4	0.8	0.0	2.7	1.1	23.8	63.6	12.6	831	74.6	71.1	10.0
Centerport borough & MCD (Berks)	387	397	2.6	368	96.2	0.0	0.0	0.8	3.0	29.6	55.5	14.9	138	68.8	55.8	21.7
Centerville borough & MCD (Crawford)	218	215	-1.4	211	95.3	0.0	0.5	0.0	4.3	28.9	56.4	14.7	83	88.0	65.1	14.5
Centerville borough & MCD (Washington)	3,263	3,206	-1.7	3,236	97.8	0.7	0.0	1.3	0.2	21.0	60.4	18.6	1,319	79.7	54.1	17.7
Central City borough & MCD (Somerset)	1,124	1,084	-3.6	1,000	98.4	0.6	0.0	0.7	0.3	19.3	61.2	19.5	393	84.7	71.0	14.5
Centralia borough & MCD (Columbia)	10	10	0.0	2	100.0	0.0	0.0	0.0	0.0	0.0	100.0	0.0	2	100.0	0.0	0.0
Centre township (Berks)	4,036	4,055	0.5	4,041	96.1	0.0	0.0	0.3	3.6	19.7	68.4	11.9	1,586	87.8	58.0	20.5
Centre township (Perry)	2,489	2,479	-0.4	2,664	98.8	0.5	0.0	0.1	0.7	27.1	59.4	13.6	930	89.9	59.9	16.5
Centre Hall borough & MCD (Centre)	1,265	1,238	-2.1	1,146	99.3	0.0	0.7	0.0	0.0	24.1	55.2	20.8	468	73.7	49.1	28.4
Ceres township (McKean)	905	886	-2.1	936	99.9	0.0	0.0	0.0	0.1	21.5	56.9	21.7	411	83.9	64.2	9.5
Cetronia CDP	0	NA	NA	1,774	87.1	6.4	0.0	4.8	1.6	10.8	62.0	27.2	755	89.9	36.3	29.4
Chadds Ford township (Delaware)	3,640	3,737	2.7	3,705	83.2	1.4	9.7	2.7	3.0	21.5	59.8	18.9	1,526	90.8	14.4	70.6
Chalfant borough & MCD (Allegheny)	800	795	-0.6	956	87.2	8.6	0.0	3.8	0.4	11.5	70.6	17.8	455	73.4	29.2	31.4
Chalfont borough & MCD (Bucks)	4,009	4,077	1.7	4,052	93.2	1.9	2.5	0.0	2.4	25.8	63.8	10.4	1,460	87.1	26.6	42.0
Chalkhill CDP	141	NA	NA	113	100.0	0.0	0.0	0.0	0.0	9.7	36.2	54.0	48	100.0	60.4	20.8
Chambersburg borough & MCD (Franklin)	20,268	20,602	1.6	20,430	67.9	8.2	1.4	3.7	18.8	23.8	58.4	17.7	7,966	50.2	53.0	21.6
Chanceford township (York)	6,111	6,132	0.3	6,120	97.2	0.5	0.0	1.0	1.3	23.6	66.3	10.2	2,246	83.7	56.7	12.0
Chapman township (Clinton)	848	857	1.1	832	98.6	1.4	0.0	0.0	0.0	17.4	58.7	24.0	369	87.5	66.4	10.3
Chapman borough & MCD (Northampton)	199	199	0.0	177	97.7	0.0	0.0	1.1	1.1	24.3	62.2	13.6	70	64.3	48.6	34.3
Chapman township (Snyder)	1,554	1,596	2.7	1,530	96.6	0.0	0.0	0.0	3.4	34.1	53.6	12.3	401	87.5	79.8	6.7
Charleroi borough & MCD (Washington)	4,120	4,035	-2.1	4,069	96.1	3.4	0.2	0.1	0.1	21.8	59.0	19.2	1,769	52.6	58.2	14.6
Charleston township (Tioga)	3,356	3,467	3.3	3,429	95.9	1.7	0.5	1.3	0.7	22.7	55.9	21.1	1,276	84.4	47.8	23.8
Charlestown township (Chester)	5,671	5,634	-0.7	5,659	79.6	5.3	8.9	4.6	1.7	26.2	61.1	12.6	1,804	96.3	8.5	75.8
Chartiers township (Washington)	7,818	7,910	1.2	7,879	93.7	3.2	0.0	0.8	2.3	20.3	57.6	22.2	2,995	90.0	48.9	25.1
Chase CDP	978	NA	NA	859	97.9	0.0	2.1	0.0	0.0	20.4	59.5	20.0	331	91.8	39.3	30.5
Chatham township (Tioga)	589	594	0.8	535	97.2	0.0	0.2	1.5	1.1	16.0	52.5	31.6	238	96.2	54.2	18.5
Cheltenham township (Montgomery)	36,756	37,024	0.7	36,912	51.8	32.8	7.6	3.1	4.8	20.4	62.9	16.6	14,287	62.6	19.4	55.0
Cherry township (Butler)	1,106	1,087	-1.7	1,077	96.5	0.9	0.3	0.6	1.8	19.9	68.6	11.5	426	82.4	56.3	11.3
Cherry township (Sullivan)	1,704	1,674	-1.8	1,761	97.2	0.0	0.0	0.0	2.8	17.1	57.3	25.5	691	91.5	60.8	11.4
Cherry Grove township (Warren)	216	211	-2.3	160	96.3	0.0	0.0	1.3	2.5	8.1	63.7	28.1	81	84.0	79.0	9.9
Cherryhill township (Indiana)	2,767	2,698	-2.5	2,731	97.0	0.9	0.6	0.5	0.9	20.5	63.2	16.5	1,057	82.0	55.9	20.7
Cherry Ridge township (Wayne)	1,898	1,856	-2.2	1,872	95.9	0.0	0.0	0.2	3.9	19.8	61.2	19.0	771	79.8	55.1	18.0
Cherry Tree borough & MCD (Indiana)	364	352	-3.3	358	100.0	0.0	0.0	0.0	0.0	19.3	50.0	30.7	124	85.5	71.8	12.9
Cherrytree township (Venango)	1,540	1,500	-2.6	1,484	98.6	0.0	0.9	0.5	0.0	21.0	60.9	18.1	575	83.5	62.3	12.0
Cherry Valley borough & MCD (Butler)	66	65	-1.5	43	100.0	0.0	0.0	0.0	0.0	9.4	53.6	37.2	27	70.4	37.0	18.5
Cherryville CDP	1,580	NA	NA	1,433	89.2	0.0	4.0	0.0	6.8	14.8	72.2	12.8	598	87.3	29.3	33.9
Chest township (Cambria)	349	355	1.7	338	97.9	0.0	0.0	2.1	0.0	14.0	62.4	23.7	133	94.7	51.1	23.3
Chest township (Clearfield)	515	505	-1.9	519	94.2	0.0	0.0	4.6	1.2	16.7	62.8	20.4	212	94.8	73.1	5.2
Chester city & MCD (Delaware)	33,972	34,133	0.5	34,007	15.2	72.2	0.6	2.0	10.1	23.5	64.3	12.1	12,068	39.7	61.9	10.5

1 May be of any race.

Table A. All Places — **Population and Housing**

STATE City, town, township, borough, or CDP (county if applicable)	2010 census total population	2014 estimated population	Percent change 2010–2014	ACS total population estimate 2010–2014	White alone, not Hispanic or Latino	Black alone, not Hispanic or Latino	Asian alone, not Hispanic or Latino	All other races or 2 or more races, not Hispanic or Latino	Hispanic or Latino[1]	Under 18 years old	Age 18 to 64 years old	Age 65 years and older	Total occupied housing units	Percent owner occupied	High school diploma or less	Bachelor's degree or more
	1	2	3	4	5	6	7	8	9	10	11	12	13	14	15	16
PENNSYLVANIA—Con.																
Chester township (Delaware)	3,940	4,102	4.1	4,069	17.9	74.7	0.0	4.2	3.2	29.3	61.5	9.2	1,361	52.0	55.1	13.2
Chesterbrook CDP	4,589	NA	NA	4,483	74.7	4.2	15.8	3.1	2.1	17.9	65.7	16.3	2,281	81.9	6.8	80.2
Chester Heights borough & MCD (Delaware)	2,531	2,622	3.6	2,568	86.1	5.5	4.0	1.6	2.7	21.6	58.6	19.7	1,095	71.8	21.6	52.1
Chester Hill borough & MCD (Clearfield)	883	864	-2.2	981	96.1	0.0	0.3	2.4	1.1	26.4	60.3	13.3	402	60.4	60.4	14.7
Chestnuthill township (Monroe)	17,164	16,732	-2.5	16,976	75.0	7.8	1.3	1.4	14.4	23.1	63.8	13.0	5,705	88.3	46.5	24.0
Chest Springs borough & MCD (Cambria)	149	145	-2.7	194	99.0	1.0	0.0	0.0	0.0	33.0	52.6	14.4	71	73.2	64.8	12.7
Cheswick borough & MCD (Allegheny)	1,746	1,735	-0.6	1,723	99.7	0.1	0.0	0.2	0.0	16.0	57.4	26.5	809	90.7	37.1	32.9
Chevy Chase Heights CDP	1,502	NA	NA	1,511	86.2	8.2	2.9	2.6	0.0	20.1	58.4	21.6	677	67.4	38.6	34.4
Chewton CDP	488	NA	NA	499	100.0	0.0	0.0	0.0	0.0	24.6	51.0	24.2	200	82.0	66.5	14.0
Cheyney University CDP	988	NA	NA	929	34.8	59.8	3.2	1.1	1.1	0.0	100.0	0.0	8	0.0	0.0	100.0
Chicora borough & MCD (Butler)	1,043	1,012	-3.0	983	98.9	0.0	0.0	0.6	0.5	23.9	55.9	20.2	410	70.7	56.8	19.0
Chinchilla CDP	2,098	NA	NA	2,066	99.2	0.0	0.0	0.0	0.8	19.7	64.0	16.5	1,004	80.0	33.8	47.8
Chippewa township (Beaver)	7,620	7,800	2.4	7,729	96.9	0.1	0.6	1.3	1.1	20.9	57.3	21.8	3,167	78.3	30.0	33.5
Choconut township (Susquehanna)	713	686	-3.8	681	97.9	0.0	0.6	1.0	0.4	15.7	66.0	18.4	292	82.2	50.0	21.9
Christiana borough & MCD (Lancaster)	1,168	1,170	0.2	1,026	79.9	9.6	0.4	4.3	5.8	24.8	50.9	24.4	325	55.4	51.7	20.6
Church Hill CDP	1,627	NA	NA	1,440	99.2	0.0	0.8	0.0	0.0	13.7	63.8	22.5	669	91.8	42.8	38.9
Churchill borough & MCD (Allegheny)	3,011	2,992	-0.6	3,006	75.5	14.3	2.7	4.8	2.7	18.7	56.5	24.8	1,285	89.9	14.4	63.7
Churchtown CDP	470	NA	NA	434	98.2	0.0	0.0	1.8	0.0	33.8	62.1	3.9	152	71.1	57.9	28.9
Churchville CDP	4,128	NA	NA	3,843	95.4	0.9	1.4	1.7	0.6	25.7	60.6	13.9	1,230	99.4	24.1	51.3
Clairton city & MCD (Allegheny)	6,786	6,720	-1.0	6,752	54.0	38.9	0.0	4.2	2.9	17.7	66.0	16.2	3,143	57.0	53.2	14.7
Clara township (Potter)	197	196	-0.5	202	100.0	0.0	0.0	0.0	0.0	24.2	55.0	20.8	74	91.9	63.5	18.9
Clarence CDP	626	NA	NA	594	99.7	0.0	0.0	0.0	0.3	19.2	61.3	19.4	232	97.4	68.1	8.2
Clarendon borough & MCD (Warren)	450	443	-1.6	519	97.1	1.2	0.6	1.2	0.0	28.7	59.3	11.9	194	72.7	65.5	10.8
Clarion borough & MCD (Clarion)	5,276	4,817	-8.7	5,000	90.7	2.6	3.7	2.3	0.7	10.1	77.9	12.0	1,789	34.9	28.8	37.2
Clarion township (Clarion)	4,121	4,016	-2.5	4,075	95.1	3.9	0.0	0.3	0.8	14.1	74.6	11.2	1,707	42.6	49.7	11.5
Clark borough & MCD (Mercer)	640	633	-1.1	629	99.0	0.0	0.5	0.0	0.5	12.6	64.0	23.4	241	91.3	52.3	28.2
Clarks Green borough & MCD (Lackawanna)	1,476	1,460	-1.1	1,387	95.7	0.3	2.4	0.1	1.5	21.3	56.3	22.4	576	89.6	18.2	61.3
Clarks Summit borough & MCD (Lackawanna)	5,116	5,063	-1.0	5,101	97.1	0.0	0.0	2.5	0.4	19.7	60.0	20.3	2,409	75.9	19.2	48.3
Clarksville borough & MCD (Greene)	230	230	0.0	254	92.9	0.0	1.2	2.0	3.9	17.7	70.8	11.4	85	77.6	65.9	21.2
Clay township (Butler)	2,703	2,657	-1.7	2,688	99.0	0.0	0.0	0.0	1.0	15.4	69.9	14.6	1,106	88.5	56.6	14.7
Clay township (Huntingdon)	922	910	-1.3	863	98.7	0.2	0.0	0.1	0.9	22.4	59.4	18.3	376	81.6	77.4	7.4
Clay CDP	1,559	NA	NA	1,886	95.2	0.0	1.0	0.5	3.3	27.2	54.1	18.7	683	82.9	67.8	18.4
Clay township (Lancaster)	6,308	6,712	6.4	6,520	94.5	1.0	0.7	0.6	3.2	25.9	57.3	17.0	2,305	86.3	68.5	16.2
Claysburg CDP	1,625	NA	NA	1,808	96.3	2.0	0.0	1.2	0.5	32.9	57.5	9.6	631	67.5	66.1	7.9
Claysville borough & MCD (Washington)	829	814	-1.8	769	96.7	2.3	0.0	0.9	0.0	21.7	60.8	17.6	279	51.3	60.2	12.9
Clearfield township (Butler)	2,645	2,605	-1.5	2,633	97.3	0.0	0.0	0.7	2.0	24.9	59.9	15.2	955	80.8	59.0	14.5
Clearfield township (Cambria)	1,604	1,565	-2.4	1,532	97.6	0.8	0.4	0.2	1.0	23.0	65.0	12.0	572	90.6	59.3	18.7
Clearfield borough & MCD (Clearfield)	6,215	6,064	-2.4	6,143	96.1	0.1	0.0	1.4	2.4	20.2	63.0	16.6	2,878	54.8	51.7	18.4
Cleona borough & MCD (Lebanon)	2,080	2,121	2.0	2,248	91.8	0.6	0.0	0.4	7.2	20.5	65.5	13.9	962	75.6	54.3	14.4
Cleveland township (Columbia)	1,110	1,092	-1.6	1,068	95.5	0.6	0.0	2.0	2.0	16.0	65.7	18.4	434	92.2	51.4	19.8
Clifford township (Susquehanna)	2,408	2,348	-2.5	2,125	98.6	0.1	0.0	0.0	1.3	19.4	66.3	14.1	909	77.0	51.4	22.2
Clifton township (Lackawanna)	1,480	1,482	0.1	1,711	91.0	3.2	1.2	0.6	4.0	17.5	61.2	21.2	673	89.2	42.2	21.2
Clifton Heights borough & MCD (Delaware)	6,652	6,668	0.2	6,656	70.0	18.3	6.1	2.5	3.1	27.2	61.3	11.5	2,502	58.8	51.0	18.9
Clinton CDP	434	NA	NA	367	100.0	0.0	0.0	0.0	0.0	10.6	76.1	13.4	174	71.8	58.6	0.0
Clinton township (Butler)	2,867	2,849	-0.6	2,857	97.0	0.0	0.6	1.2	1.2	20.8	65.5	13.9	1,142	87.7	49.7	23.0
Clinton township (Lycoming)	3,708	3,720	0.3	3,729	80.0	11.6	0.9	3.4	4.2	13.6	75.9	10.5	844	75.5	52.4	14.8
Clinton township (Venango)	854	829	-2.9	893	96.9	0.7	0.0	0.3	2.1	21.5	54.4	24.2	350	87.4	64.0	8.6
Clinton township (Wayne)	2,053	2,004	-2.4	2,272	99.3	0.0	0.1	0.5	0.0	17.9	64.5	17.7	853	83.2	58.0	19.5
Clinton township (Wyoming)	1,323	1,302	-1.6	1,406	98.5	0.4	0.1	0.1	0.8	20.6	65.4	14.2	537	87.2	50.5	23.8
Clintonville borough & MCD (Venango)	508	492	-3.1	411	99.3	0.0	0.0	0.7	0.0	27.0	58.5	14.6	179	66.5	72.6	12.8
Clover township (Jefferson)	448	443	-1.1	441	100.0	0.0	0.0	0.0	0.0	18.1	64.9	17.0	185	84.3	56.8	15.1
Clymer borough & MCD (Indiana)	1,357	1,318	-2.9	1,275	96.5	0.0	0.0	2.2	1.3	22.8	60.7	16.6	545	63.9	62.4	18.2
Clymer township (Tioga)	581	581	0.0	589	94.1	0.5	0.5	0.8	4.1	20.2	52.5	27.2	252	88.9	77.4	9.5
Coal township (Northumberland)	10,383	10,517	1.3	10,491	76.6	15.5	0.3	2.6	4.9	13.9	68.5	17.6	3,220	77.9	64.9	14.2

1 May be of any race.

Table A. All Places — **Population and Housing**

STATE City, town, township, borough, or CDP (county if applicable)	Population				Race and Hispanic or Latino origin (percent), 2010–2014					Age (percent), 2010–2014			Households, 2010–2014			
	2010 census total population	2014 estimated population	Percent change 2010–2014	ACS total population estimate 2010–2014	White alone, not Hispanic or Latino	Black alone, not Hispanic or Latino	Asian alone, not Hispanic or Latino	All other races or 2 or more races, not Hispanic or Latino	Hispanic or Latino[1]	Under 18 years old	Age 18 to 64 years old	Age 65 years and older	Total occupied housing units	Percent owner occupied	High school diploma or less	Bachelor's degree or more
	1	2	3	4	5	6	7	8	9	10	11	12	13	14	15	16
PENNSYLVANIA—Con.																
Coal Center borough & MCD (Washington).......	139	138	-0.7	75	97.3	0.0	0.0	2.7	0.0	2.7	66.6	30.7	34	50.0	29.4	20.6
Coaldale borough & MCD (Bedford)	161	160	-0.6	156	100.0	0.0	0.0	0.0	0.0	29.5	51.9	18.6	50	60.0	64.0	8.0
Coaldale borough & MCD (Schuylkill)	2,281	2,220	-2.7	2,274	93.6	0.0	0.4	0.2	5.8	21.8	60.3	17.9	1,052	71.1	57.3	13.4
Coalmont borough & MCD (Huntingdon)	106	105	-0.9	85	94.1	0.0	0.0	3.5	2.4	25.9	51.8	22.4	33	63.6	72.7	0.0
Coalport borough & MCD (Clearfield)	523	508	-2.9	536	97.2	0.4	0.0	0.6	1.9	19.9	54.4	25.6	231	68.4	72.7	2.6
Coatesville city & MCD (Chester)	13,102	13,164	0.5	13,130	25.6	48.0	0.7	4.2	21.5	33.7	58.0	8.4	4,406	36.7	64.1	11.9
Coburn CDP	236	NA	NA	109	100.0	0.0	0.0	0.0	0.0	21.1	44.2	34.9	41	92.7	61.0	22.0
Cochranton borough & MCD (Crawford)	1,136	1,118	-1.6	1,265	93.3	1.0	0.3	3.0	2.4	29.2	55.6	15.3	466	72.3	45.9	19.3
Cochranville CDP	668	NA	NA	646	95.0	0.0	0.0	0.0	5.0	19.4	65.8	14.9	263	79.5	55.5	13.3
Codorus township (York) .	3,800	3,865	1.7	3,843	96.7	0.7	1.5	0.4	0.6	22.2	58.5	19.2	1,478	90.4	57.8	25.1
Cogan House township (Lycoming)	953	948	-0.5	917	99.7	0.2	0.0	0.0	0.1	23.8	58.0	18.3	342	86.8	62.9	13.2
Cokeburg borough & MCD (Washington).......	630	621	-1.4	593	96.5	0.0	0.3	1.9	1.3	16.4	53.3	30.2	268	69.8	56.3	12.3
Cold Spring township (Lebanon)	53	54	1.9	45	100.0	0.0	0.0	0.0	0.0	13.3	68.9	17.8	22	100.0	63.6	0.0
Colebrook township (Clinton)	199	202	1.5	213	100.0	0.0	0.0	0.0	0.0	36.1	52.1	11.7	66	69.7	62.1	7.6
Colebrookdale township (Berks)	5,078	5,074	-0.1	5,080	97.9	0.0	0.0	0.7	1.3	17.2	66.7	16.1	2,009	90.1	58.8	21.6
Colerain township (Bedford)	1,192	1,182	-0.8	1,279	99.5	0.0	0.0	0.0	0.5	23.2	57.0	19.8	491	82.3	68.6	14.3
Colerain township (Lancaster)	3,635	3,747	3.1	3,686	98.2	0.7	0.0	0.6	0.5	35.2	51.8	13.1	1,086	82.1	66.4	17.3
College township (Centre)	9,521	10,153	6.6	9,706	91.9	1.8	3.2	1.8	1.2	18.2	65.5	16.4	3,706	75.3	16.7	63.8
Collegeville borough & MCD (Montgomery)	5,089	5,322	4.6	5,263	81.6	6.4	6.3	3.2	2.5	16.8	73.0	10.1	1,257	77.0	19.9	55.1
Colley township (Sullivan)	695	692	-0.4	768	82.6	13.5	0.7	1.2	2.1	11.4	70.8	17.7	206	90.3	59.7	13.6
Collier township (Allegheny)	7,080	7,817	10.4	7,450	93.0	0.8	3.3	1.2	1.8	17.1	64.2	18.7	3,341	81.1	35.8	39.9
Collingdale borough & MCD (Delaware)	8,783	8,797	0.2	8,778	55.0	38.6	2.1	1.6	2.7	28.3	61.3	10.4	3,148	66.1	50.0	16.1
Collinsburg CDP	1,125	NA	NA	1,138	97.3	0.0	0.0	1.1	1.7	16.4	71.6	12.0	428	97.4	52.3	13.6
Colonial Park CDP..........	13,229	NA	NA	13,124	67.8	13.0	6.3	4.0	9.8	19.3	62.6	18.1	5,851	47.6	36.2	32.4
Colony Park CDP............	1,076	NA	NA	1,093	93.5	0.0	0.0	0.8	5.7	22.9	63.7	13.4	413	98.1	28.8	45.5
Columbia township (Bradford)	1,198	1,180	-1.5	1,144	91.7	2.0	0.7	4.5	1.1	25.9	58.4	15.9	384	75.8	62.5	14.1
Columbia borough & MCD (Lancaster)..........	10,400	10,383	-0.2	10,399	80.4	5.3	1.1	2.7	10.4	24.7	59.8	15.4	4,133	59.3	65.7	10.6
Columbus CDP	824	NA	NA	754	94.2	0.0	0.0	3.2	2.7	20.1	60.9	18.8	264	88.3	60.6	18.2
Columbus township (Warren)	2,034	1,985	-2.4	1,950	94.5	0.1	0.2	2.2	3.0	21.1	62.8	16.1	679	86.7	58.6	15.3
Colver CDP	959	NA	NA	746	100.0	0.0	0.0	0.0	0.0	19.8	60.5	19.8	366	81.7	41.3	17.5
Colwyn borough & MCD (Delaware)	2,546	2,553	0.3	2,542	14.3	80.8	1.2	2.4	1.3	28.3	65.7	5.9	818	61.1	48.7	20.3
Commodore CDP	331	NA	NA	238	87.4	0.0	0.0	0.0	12.6	10.5	73.5	16.0	135	54.8	64.4	6.7
Conashaugh Lakes CDP .	1,294	NA	NA	1,340	64.7	1.0	0.0	5.5	28.7	29.2	66.5	4.4	406	100.0	53.0	36.2
Concord township (Butler)	1,505	1,467	-2.5	1,641	97.0	0.2	0.0	1.3	1.6	25.5	59.9	14.6	631	82.1	68.6	8.6
Concord township (Delaware).............	17,231	17,533	1.8	17,372	84.3	8.1	4.5	1.9	1.3	20.7	55.6	23.6	6,282	71.0	24.0	55.8
Concord township (Erie)..	1,344	1,313	-2.3	1,409	96.0	0.0	1.2	2.1	0.6	19.8	64.9	15.4	495	83.0	59.2	13.1
Conemaugh township (Cambria)	2,012	1,944	-3.4	2,019	95.9	2.2	0.0	1.2	0.7	16.3	58.3	25.3	869	91.5	65.0	12.4
Conemaugh township (Indiana)	2,303	2,223	-3.5	2,449	95.3	0.0	0.0	0.0	4.7	17.7	62.9	19.3	988	83.6	53.5	15.6
Conemaugh township (Somerset)	7,279	7,094	-2.5	7,203	97.8	0.7	0.0	1.1	0.4	17.3	61.2	21.5	3,027	84.1	58.3	18.1
Conestoga CDP	1,258	NA	NA	1,103	94.2	0.0	4.5	1.3	0.0	19.7	65.0	15.3	441	77.8	57.4	19.5
Conestoga township (Lancaster)	3,776	3,827	1.4	3,799	93.3	0.0	2.4	1.2	3.1	23.1	63.8	13.0	1,434	81.1	60.1	25.3
Conewago township (Adams)	7,091	7,128	0.5	7,111	94.0	0.5	1.1	1.6	2.8	21.3	60.2	18.5	2,796	81.4	52.0	22.1
Conewago township (Dauphin)	2,997	3,004	0.2	3,000	95.1	1.6	0.4	0.7	2.3	23.5	63.6	12.8	1,045	88.9	40.3	44.1
Conewago township (York)	7,510	7,896	5.1	7,739	83.8	5.6	0.0	1.5	9.0	25.5	62.7	11.8	2,905	83.8	54.5	24.6
Conewango township (Warren)	3,594	3,498	-2.7	3,539	96.9	0.7	1.0	0.6	0.7	17.4	61.7	20.8	1,383	83.7	54.4	22.4
Confluence borough & MCD (Somerset)	780	755	-3.2	769	98.8	0.0	0.0	0.7	0.5	17.0	59.3	23.7	326	52.8	59.5	17.5
Conneaut township (Crawford)	1,476	1,438	-2.6	1,427	97.9	0.0	0.3	1.6	0.2	22.4	59.7	17.9	538	89.0	64.1	12.8
Conneaut township (Erie)	4,290	4,355	1.5	4,348	70.8	21.1	0.0	1.1	6.9	9.8	81.1	9.1	798	85.0	67.4	17.5
Conneaut Lake borough & MCD (Crawford)	656	641	-2.3	563	94.3	0.9	0.0	2.1	2.7	17.5	56.0	26.5	279	65.6	49.1	19.4
Conneaut Lakeshore CDP	2,395	NA	NA	2,840	96.7	0.5	0.9	1.9	0.0	18.2	58.0	23.7	1,344	81.3	42.5	35.6
Conneautville borough & MCD (Crawford)	774	756	-2.3	948	97.9	0.0	0.6	0.7	0.7	31.0	50.3	18.7	376	54.3	54.5	18.1
Connellsville city & MCD (Fayette)	7,636	7,514	-1.6	7,578	94.2	1.7	0.5	2.4	1.1	22.7	61.5	15.6	3,231	51.3	60.4	11.7
Connellsville township (Fayette)	2,392	2,325	-2.8	2,531	96.8	0.5	0.0	1.5	1.3	19.4	64.2	16.4	1,043	80.5	68.3	9.2

1 May be of any race.

Table A. All Places — **Population and Housing**

STATE City, town, township, borough, or CDP (county if applicable)	2010 census total population	2014 estimated population	Percent change 2010–2014	ACS total population estimate 2010–2014	White alone, not Hispanic or Latino	Black alone, not Hispanic or Latino	Asian alone, not Hispanic or Latino	All other races or 2 or more races, not Hispanic or Latino	Hispanic or Latino[1]	Under 18 years old	Age 18 to 64 years old	Age 65 years and older	Total occupied housing units	Percent owner occupied	High school diploma or less	Bachelor's degree or more
	1	2	3	4	5	6	7	8	9	10	11	12	13	14	15	16
PENNSYLVANIA—Con.																
Connoquenessing borough & MCD (Butler)	528	602	14.0	611	99.2	0.0	0.2	0.7	0.0	24.9	57.2	17.8	226	83.2	45.6	22.1
Connoquenessing township (Butler)	4,170	4,044	-3.0	4,115	92.3	1.1	1.7	0.6	4.4	18.8	63.3	17.9	1,723	86.7	48.5	28.2
Conoy township (Lancaster)	3,194	3,396	6.3	3,325	99.7	0.0	0.3	0.0	0.0	21.4	67.0	11.5	1,289	90.5	58.3	17.0
Conshohocken borough & MCD (Montgomery)	7,833	7,895	0.8	7,864	88.9	4.0	2.3	1.1	3.8	14.8	73.7	11.6	3,845	51.1	29.2	56.7
Conway borough & MCD (Beaver)	2,176	2,155	-1.0	2,166	94.6	1.0	0.0	3.5	0.8	20.4	55.7	23.9	948	80.3	55.7	19.6
Conyngham township (Columbia)	756	759	0.4	728	97.9	0.0	0.0	0.0	2.1	18.0	63.8	18.3	313	91.4	74.1	12.5
Conyngham borough & MCD (Luzerne)	1,914	1,888	-1.4	1,917	98.2	0.0	1.8	0.0	0.0	15.9	58.5	25.6	840	78.2	22.6	49.3
Conyngham township (Luzerne)	1,453	1,443	-0.7	1,320	96.2	0.5	0.5	0.5	2.3	15.2	63.8	21.0	573	75.9	64.6	14.3
Cook township (Westmoreland)	2,246	2,224	-1.0	2,181	95.0	0.0	0.0	1.1	3.9	16.2	62.8	20.8	913	86.9	52.6	20.0
Cooke township (Cumberland)	179	184	2.8	187	96.3	1.1	2.7	0.0	0.0	20.8	65.7	13.4	75	97.3	41.3	33.3
Coolbaugh township (Monroe)	20,564	20,257	-1.5	20,450	46.9	30.3	1.8	2.5	18.5	23.3	64.7	11.9	6,323	80.2	43.1	19.0
Coolspring township (Mercer)	2,278	2,260	-0.8	2,268	98.8	0.8	0.0	0.2	0.2	20.3	51.5	28.1	905	82.9	52.2	22.7
Cooper township (Clearfield)	2,709	2,677	-1.2	2,699	97.0	0.0	0.2	1.6	1.2	20.5	59.3	20.2	996	90.8	76.1	10.4
Cooper township (Montour)	932	953	2.3	1,021	97.3	0.0	0.2	0.0	2.5	15.0	61.8	23.3	428	90.4	53.5	22.0
Coopersburg borough & MCD (Lehigh)	2,386	2,406	0.8	2,286	95.1	0.3	0.2	1.4	3.0	25.2	52.5	22.3	890	67.4	48.4	24.2
Cooperstown borough & MCD (Venango)	460	441	-4.1	491	99.4	0.0	0.0	0.2	0.4	18.7	64.2	17.1	209	93.3	56.5	12.9
Coplay borough & MCD (Lehigh)	3,192	3,222	0.9	3,214	88.1	1.1	0.0	1.5	9.3	20.7	57.2	22.1	1,431	71.3	54.9	12.2
Coral CDP	325	NA	NA	562	100.0	0.0	0.0	0.0	0.0	21.0	51.9	27.2	243	46.9	41.2	7.4
Coraopolis borough & MCD (Allegheny)	5,677	5,624	-0.9	5,655	76.0	11.8	0.4	7.4	4.4	17.8	63.8	18.4	2,686	49.5	49.1	23.0
Cornplanter township (Venango)	2,420	2,364	-2.3	2,425	97.4	0.2	0.8	1.2	0.5	16.8	60.3	22.8	998	86.5	49.9	22.5
Cornwall borough & MCD (Lebanon)	4,112	4,198	2.1	4,166	95.2	0.0	3.3	0.8	0.7	15.4	54.7	29.9	1,720	77.8	35.1	43.1
Cornwells Heights CDP	1,391	NA	NA	1,445	89.1	2.6	1.3	3.1	3.9	16.3	71.2	12.7	462	71.2	46.3	17.3
Corry city & MCD (Erie)	6,605	6,457	-2.2	6,546	94.6	0.7	0.4	4.1	0.2	24.3	59.4	16.3	2,534	53.1	56.3	15.6
Corsica borough & MCD (Jefferson)	357	353	-1.1	332	96.1	0.0	0.0	3.6	0.3	29.5	54.0	16.3	138	61.6	58.7	9.4
Corydon township (McKean)	275	271	-1.5	304	97.4	0.0	0.0	1.6	1.0	11.9	68.5	19.7	135	94.1	64.4	18.5
Coudersport borough & MCD (Potter)	2,546	2,496	-2.0	2,439	95.1	0.7	1.4	2.1	0.7	22.3	59.4	18.5	998	66.7	44.6	32.4
Courtdale borough & MCD (Luzerne)	732	731	-0.1	678	99.7	0.0	0.0	0.0	0.3	13.7	62.8	23.5	304	84.5	56.6	6.6
Covington township (Clearfield)	526	515	-2.1	837	79.1	12.3	0.0	2.6	6.0	11.7	79.1	9.3	218	88.1	72.9	2.3
Covington township (Lackawanna)	2,289	2,316	1.2	1,838	96.6	0.0	0.0	0.0	3.4	23.3	62.7	13.9	652	86.7	44.0	33.0
Covington township (Tioga)	1,029	1,030	0.1	889	96.0	0.0	0.0	1.8	2.2	15.9	58.8	25.0	357	87.1	66.7	11.8
Cowanshannock township (Armstrong)	2,895	2,864	-1.1	2,881	99.0	0.0	0.5	0.6	0.0	23.1	60.2	16.7	1,153	86.7	66.7	9.8
Crabtree CDP	277	NA	NA	282	85.1	0.0	0.0	14.9	0.0	25.2	63.5	11.3	118	74.6	82.2	4.2
Crafton borough & MCD (Allegheny)	5,951	5,908	-0.7	5,931	89.6	6.6	0.0	2.8	1.0	18.0	69.1	13.0	2,731	53.5	35.0	36.3
Cranberry township (Butler)	28,098	30,170	7.4	29,023	94.0	0.8	2.3	1.9	1.0	28.4	62.2	9.4	10,581	83.8	19.0	59.3
Cranberry township (Venango)	6,685	6,546	-2.1	6,620	98.2	0.0	0.1	1.5	0.2	20.3	58.7	20.8	2,814	77.3	57.1	19.4
Cranesville borough & MCD (Erie)	638	619	-3.0	544	95.0	0.0	1.3	3.3	0.4	21.6	66.1	12.1	205	85.4	64.4	13.2
Crawford township (Clinton)	939	948	1.0	859	98.1	0.0	0.2	0.3	1.3	19.2	62.8	17.9	342	90.6	67.3	11.7
Creekside borough & MCD (Indiana)	309	301	-2.6	365	100.0	0.0	0.0	0.0	0.0	19.7	66.9	13.4	148	77.0	62.8	9.5
Crenshaw CDP	468	NA	NA	524	99.2	0.0	0.0	0.0	0.8	21.8	63.0	15.3	213	65.3	56.3	16.9
Crescent township (Allegheny)	2,640	2,622	-0.7	2,637	94.9	2.9	0.9	0.6	0.6	20.2	58.6	21.0	1,074	82.2	36.2	29.0
Cresson borough & MCD (Cambria)	1,711	1,650	-3.6	1,626	96.3	0.0	0.9	2.1	0.7	19.7	66.0	14.2	734	62.9	46.9	19.3
Cresson township (Cambria)	4,336	2,791	-35.6	3,695	75.3	17.6	1.0	2.3	3.7	12.3	77.3	10.3	819	71.9	55.3	21.0
Cressona borough & MCD (Schuylkill)	1,651	1,635	-1.0	1,815	90.9	1.1	1.8	0.6	5.6	22.3	64.7	13.1	743	70.0	51.5	17.9
Cromwell township (Huntingdon)	1,622	1,596	-1.6	1,669	96.3	0.2	0.0	0.0	3.2	24.0	59.5	16.7	687	84.6	75.1	5.4
Cross Creek township (Washington)	1,556	1,534	-1.4	1,537	94.9	0.3	1.2	2.4	1.3	18.2	65.2	16.7	610	77.9	55.7	16.6
Cross Creek CDP	137	NA	NA	104	96.2	0.0	0.0	3.8	0.0	21.2	67.2	11.5	37	81.1	37.8	18.9
Cross Roads borough & MCD (York)	512	513	0.2	604	91.7	6.0	0.5	0.3	1.5	20.7	67.2	12.3	191	92.7	51.8	21.5
Crown CDP	183	NA	NA	218	99.5	0.5	0.0	0.0	0.0	11.5	68.4	20.2	70	64.3	74.3	25.7
Croydon CDP	9,950	NA	NA	10,017	80.4	5.5	3.1	3.5	7.6	18.8	69.7	11.6	3,693	74.8	61.2	11.0

1 May be of any race.

Table A. All Places — **Population and Housing**

STATE City, town, township, borough, or CDP (county if applicable)	2010 census total population	2014 estimated population	Percent change 2010–2014	ACS total population estimate 2010–2014	White alone, not Hispanic or Latino	Black alone, not Hispanic or Latino	Asian alone, not Hispanic or Latino	All other races or 2 or more races, not Hispanic or Latino	Hispanic or Latino[1]	Under 18 years old	Age 18 to 64 years old	Age 65 years and older	Total occupied housing units	Percent owner occupied	High school diploma or less	Bachelor's degree or more
	1	2	3	4	5	6	7	8	9	10	11	12	13	14	15	16
PENNSYLVANIA—Con.																
Croyle township (Cambria)	2,339	2,300	-1.7	2,239	99.3	0.0	0.4	0.1	0.1	20.4	61.9	17.6	859	87.2	64.4	17.7
Crucible CDP	725	NA	NA	971	100.0	0.0	0.0	0.0	0.0	38.1	54.5	7.3	326	63.5	42.0	32.8
Cumberland township (Adams)	6,177	6,195	0.3	6,184	87.8	4.8	1.3	1.9	4.2	17.2	56.2	26.6	2,458	81.1	41.0	36.4
Cumberland township (Greene)	6,623	6,461	-2.4	6,530	96.7	0.2	0.3	2.4	0.4	27.6	53.7	18.6	2,800	71.8	48.4	22.4
Cumberland Valley township (Bedford)	1,600	1,575	-1.6	1,489	99.8	0.0	0.0	0.0	0.2	20.8	60.1	19.1	580	84.7	52.2	13.4
Cumbola CDP	443	NA	NA	419	97.6	0.0	0.0	1.2	1.2	25.9	55.1	18.9	175	67.4	60.6	10.3
Cummings township (Lycoming)	270	270	0.0	252	99.2	0.0	0.0	0.0	0.8	14.7	58.0	27.4	121	86.0	55.4	19.0
Cumru township (Berks)	15,147	15,192	0.3	15,180	84.7	1.7	2.4	1.3	9.8	19.4	58.8	21.8	6,497	65.2	36.8	36.6
Curtin township (Centre)	618	604	-2.3	604	100.0	0.0	0.0	0.0	0.0	16.6	66.6	16.7	230	86.1	71.7	10.0
Curtisville CDP	1,064	NA	NA	926	95.0	0.0	0.0	0.0	5.0	23.6	68.6	7.9	409	85.6	59.2	12.2
Curwensville borough & MCD (Clearfield)	2,543	2,486	-2.2	2,493	99.4	0.0	0.0	0.0	0.6	19.6	58.4	22.1	1,032	72.0	57.2	16.4
Cussewago township (Crawford)	1,555	1,555	0.0	1,360	96.8	0.8	0.4	1.4	0.6	20.3	63.9	15.7	570	86.8	57.2	26.3
Daisytown borough & MCD (Cambria)	326	317	-2.8	371	98.9	0.0	0.0	1.1	0.0	28.6	52.3	19.1	147	90.5	59.2	21.1
Dale borough & MCD (Cambria)	1,234	1,187	-3.8	1,213	89.0	5.4	0.7	4.0	0.9	27.2	57.1	15.7	541	43.8	65.2	7.6
Dallas borough & MCD (Luzerne)	2,804	2,788	-0.6	2,806	93.5	0.0	1.4	2.7	2.4	19.3	64.1	16.5	1,125	80.8	19.3	48.1
Dallas township (Luzerne)	8,994	9,235	2.7	9,138	97.1	0.4	0.7	0.0	1.8	18.4	60.4	21.2	3,346	74.7	32.1	40.9
Dallastown borough & MCD (York)	4,049	4,016	-0.8	4,029	96.0	0.2	0.0	0.5	3.2	28.0	59.4	12.7	1,626	53.1	61.4	11.7
Dalmatia CDP	488	NA	NA	519	99.0	0.0	0.0	1.0	0.0	20.7	61.7	17.5	240	72.1	74.6	5.8
Dalton borough & MCD (Lackawanna)	1,234	1,234	0.0	1,265	96.4	0.0	0.2	1.6	1.8	20.4	59.7	19.8	506	85.4	16.8	55.9
Damascus township (Wayne)	3,661	3,586	-2.0	3,618	97.2	0.0	0.0	1.1	1.7	17.6	59.0	23.5	1,600	89.1	53.3	21.6
Danville borough & MCD (Montour)	4,699	4,726	0.6	4,703	91.5	1.3	2.1	0.9	4.1	20.6	63.3	16.2	2,164	49.5	50.2	26.8
Darby borough & MCD (Delaware)	10,690	10,695	0.0	10,689	13.6	80.0	0.2	0.8	5.5	36.5	54.2	9.3	3,080	45.2	53.0	10.3
Darby township (Delaware)	9,264	9,315	0.6	9,293	60.1	35.8	0.7	1.9	1.5	22.9	61.6	15.6	3,653	73.0	51.9	16.2
Darlington borough & MCD (Beaver)	254	252	-0.8	379	98.2	0.5	0.0	1.3	0.0	45.1	46.1	8.7	106	65.1	76.4	11.3
Darlington township (Beaver)	1,962	1,939	-1.2	1,846	97.6	0.3	0.0	0.8	1.3	15.2	67.4	17.5	800	82.3	64.6	10.8
Dauberville CDP	848	NA	NA	861	97.6	0.0	0.0	0.0	2.4	28.1	63.5	8.5	307	87.6	48.9	25.1
Daugherty township (Beaver)	3,187	3,146	-1.3	3,170	97.7	0.1	0.5	1.6	0.0	15.2	62.5	22.3	1,263	85.1	46.3	20.0
Dauphin borough & MCD (Dauphin)	791	785	-0.8	981	94.1	0.9	0.2	1.0	3.8	28.4	58.0	13.8	346	74.9	49.4	17.9
Davidson township (Sullivan)	573	558	-2.6	543	90.1	0.0	0.0	9.9	0.0	11.0	64.9	24.1	215	87.4	72.1	6.5
Davidsville CDP	1,130	NA	NA	1,306	96.9	0.0	0.0	2.1	0.9	22.1	52.3	25.7	539	94.8	55.1	35.1
Dawson borough & MCD (Fayette)	367	359	-2.2	390	90.5	9.0	0.0	0.5	0.0	17.2	64.1	18.7	154	70.1	57.8	14.3
Dayton borough & MCD (Armstrong)	553	537	-2.9	464	99.1	0.0	0.0	0.9	0.0	24.8	60.2	15.1	194	64.4	75.8	12.4
Dean township (Cambria)	391	379	-3.1	439	99.5	0.0	0.0	0.0	0.5	21.0	57.0	22.1	175	90.3	70.9	8.0
Decatur township (Clearfield)	4,548	4,810	5.8	4,651	72.6	5.9	1.1	3.2	17.2	12.9	73.2	13.8	1,490	78.4	82.0	3.8
Decatur township (Mifflin)	3,137	3,112	-0.8	3,127	97.6	0.7	0.3	0.7	0.8	22.1	61.2	16.8	1,117	88.3	73.2	9.1
Deemston borough & MCD (Washington)	722	714	-1.1	755	98.8	0.5	0.3	0.0	0.4	19.6	64.0	16.4	299	89.6	48.2	24.4
Deer Creek township (Mercer)	502	492	-2.0	497	98.8	0.0	0.0	0.2	1.0	17.7	57.8	24.3	192	94.3	78.6	8.3
Deerfield township (Tioga)	662	669	1.1	582	96.4	0.5	0.0	0.0	3.1	18.4	57.9	23.7	243	82.3	55.1	11.5
Deerfield township (Warren)	339	330	-2.7	225	98.7	0.4	0.0	0.9	0.0	10.2	65.3	24.4	106	84.9	66.0	15.1
Deer Lake CDP	495	NA	NA	584	100.0	0.0	0.0	0.0	0.0	29.7	66.2	4.1	199	100.0	33.7	23.1
Deer Lake borough & MCD (Schuylkill)	687	680	-1.0	686	96.1	0.0	2.8	0.0	1.2	24.3	64.1	11.7	256	93.8	33.6	32.0
Defiance CDP	239	NA	NA	274	100.0	0.0	0.0	0.0	0.0	32.4	47.1	20.4	93	96.8	57.0	16.1
Delano CDP	342	NA	NA	389	97.9	0.0	2.1	0.0	0.0	18.0	62.2	19.8	170	100.0	52.4	10.0
Delano township (Schuylkill)	445	432	-2.9	436	98.2	0.0	1.8	0.0	0.0	17.4	61.9	20.6	196	94.4	53.6	10.2
Delaware township (Juniata)	1,560	1,569	0.6	1,684	98.5	0.1	0.1	0.4	1.0	22.5	61.3	16.2	628	86.3	71.3	7.5
Delaware township (Mercer)	2,291	2,260	-1.4	2,241	97.6	0.0	0.1	0.0	2.3	18.5	63.1	18.3	839	94.2	57.2	13.7
Delaware township (Northumberland)	4,489	4,474	-0.3	4,476	95.4	2.4	0.7	0.1	1.4	21.0	63.8	15.2	1,697	80.0	61.8	17.4
Delaware township (Pike)	7,396	7,220	-2.4	7,320	90.9	1.6	1.9	1.8	3.7	24.2	61.3	14.4	2,566	88.2	44.7	16.6
Delaware Water Gap borough & MCD (Monroe)	743	717	-3.5	704	79.3	10.8	2.1	0.0	7.8	16.9	70.0	13.2	331	39.3	26.6	44.4
Delmar township (Tioga)	2,858	2,884	0.9	2,885	96.5	0.0	0.7	2.7	0.1	19.4	61.6	19.0	1,166	86.2	52.3	19.6
Delmont borough & MCD (Westmoreland)	2,686	2,651	-1.3	2,668	96.9	0.6	1.5	0.6	0.4	23.7	61.9	14.4	1,137	68.6	38.3	36.0
Delta borough & MCD (York)	728	724	-0.5	636	92.8	2.7	1.1	0.6	2.8	25.8	62.6	11.5	265	58.1	47.5	10.6
Dennison township (Luzerne)	1,125	1,120	-0.4	1,124	96.7	0.0	0.3	1.4	1.6	16.5	63.2	20.3	446	94.2	44.6	19.5

1 May be of any race.

Table A. All Places — **Population and Housing**

STATE City, town, township, borough, or CDP (county if applicable)	2010 census total population	2014 estimated population	Percent change 2010–2014	ACS total population estimate 2010–2014	White alone, not Hispanic or Latino	Black alone, not Hispanic or Latino	Asian alone, not Hispanic or Latino	All other races or 2 or more races, not Hispanic or Latino	Hispanic or Latino[1]	Under 18 years old	Age 18 to 64 years old	Age 65 years and older	Total occupied housing units	Percent owner occupied	High school diploma or less	Bachelor's degree or more
	1	2	3	4	5	6	7	8	9	10	11	12	13	14	15	16
PENNSYLVANIA—Con.																
Denver borough & MCD (Lancaster)	3,861	3,869	0.2	3,862	91.2	0.6	0.2	3.3	4.7	20.9	64.2	15.0	1,536	71.4	49.0	22.9
Derry township (Dauphin)	24,679	24,881	0.8	24,779	83.1	3.7	6.1	2.1	5.0	19.9	64.3	15.7	9,870	63.2	24.9	56.3
Derry township (Mifflin)	7,339	7,315	-0.3	7,338	98.5	0.5	0.0	0.1	1.0	20.2	53.9	25.9	3,149	82.0	61.6	14.8
Derry township (Montour)	1,130	1,148	1.6	1,022	98.3	0.8	0.4	0.5	0.0	19.6	61.4	18.8	435	81.4	77.9	9.7
Derry borough & MCD (Westmoreland)	2,688	2,613	-2.8	2,649	97.0	0.0	0.3	2.2	0.5	23.0	61.0	16.2	1,137	67.5	51.7	22.3
Derry township (Westmoreland)	14,504	14,340	-1.1	14,435	95.6	1.3	0.1	2.3	0.7	18.4	59.4	22.1	6,050	75.3	58.2	14.1
DeSales University CDP	953	NA	NA	863	84.1	7.4	0.9	1.3	6.3	2.1	97.7	0.2	0	0.0	0.0	0.0
Devon CDP	1,515	NA	NA	1,790	83.2	1.1	5.7	2.8	7.2	32.1	55.3	12.7	627	88.0	4.3	88.4
Dewart CDP	1,471	NA	NA	1,509	90.8	7.0	2.2	0.0	0.0	21.7	61.8	16.4	559	89.4	60.5	12.3
Dickinson township (Cumberland)	5,223	5,311	1.7	5,273	97.0	0.2	0.9	1.9	0.0	19.8	65.4	15.0	1,942	90.9	51.0	34.2
Dickson City borough & MCD (Lackawanna)	6,070	6,006	-1.1	6,049	93.6	1.0	2.0	1.0	2.4	20.9	60.8	18.4	2,605	65.2	48.6	22.6
Dicksonville CDP	467	NA	NA	311	100.0	0.0	0.0	0.0	0.0	14.8	66.7	18.3	149	89.9	65.1	4.7
Dillsburg borough & MCD (York)	2,568	2,569	0.0	2,573	94.4	0.5	0.7	1.4	2.9	20.7	61.2	18.2	1,116	66.9	42.6	30.0
Dimock township (Susquehanna)	1,497	1,456	-2.7	1,483	97.6	0.5	0.0	1.6	0.3	27.7	57.6	14.6	511	88.5	49.5	25.0
Dingman township (Pike)	11,928	11,699	-1.9	11,834	82.8	3.6	1.2	2.8	9.7	24.2	62.7	13.0	4,027	91.3	39.7	25.6
District township (Berks)	1,386	1,404	1.3	1,438	98.7	0.6	0.8	0.0	0.0	18.2	65.0	16.8	554	78.9	62.1	18.4
Donaldson CDP	328	NA	NA	338	99.7	0.0	0.0	0.3	0.0	21.6	64.0	14.2	128	86.7	68.0	0.8
Donegal township (Butler)	1,864	1,842	-1.2	1,934	99.2	0.3	0.0	0.2	0.3	21.3	60.3	18.5	680	86.6	57.1	11.8
Donegal township (Washington)	2,465	2,441	-1.0	2,386	98.0	0.0	0.0	0.9	1.1	20.9	60.2	18.7	980	73.2	65.9	12.8
Donegal borough & MCD (Westmoreland)	120	120	0.0	178	100.0	0.0	0.0	0.0	0.0	12.4	50.0	37.6	75	73.3	68.0	14.7
Donegal township (Westmoreland)	2,403	2,376	-1.1	2,153	100.0	0.0	0.0	0.0	0.0	15.3	66.5	18.4	903	85.0	63.0	13.8
Donora borough & MCD (Washington)	4,781	4,684	-2.0	4,733	77.9	12.9	2.2	5.5	1.6	20.7	59.4	19.8	1,968	69.0	61.7	16.2
Dormont borough & MCD (Allegheny)	8,593	8,515	-0.9	8,565	92.5	0.8	1.0	2.1	3.5	16.1	71.3	12.8	3,940	55.4	28.7	40.3
Dorneyville CDP	4,406	NA	NA	4,782	81.5	5.8	3.5	0.0	9.2	18.9	57.9	23.0	1,789	88.7	24.0	49.8
Dorrance township (Luzerne)	2,191	2,214	1.0	2,159	100.0	0.0	0.0	0.0	0.0	19.6	66.6	13.9	878	89.9	42.9	21.0
Douglass township (Berks)	3,446	3,518	2.1	3,474	93.1	3.9	0.8	1.6	0.5	20.1	60.2	19.7	1,400	86.5	61.6	13.6
Douglass township (Montgomery)	10,195	10,401	2.0	10,313	95.1	2.4	0.5	0.6	1.4	23.7	61.7	14.6	3,755	83.6	42.9	30.5
Douglassville CDP	448	NA	NA	784	84.8	0.0	13.6	1.5	0.0	16.8	52.1	31.1	322	8.1	54.7	41.3
Dover borough & MCD (York)	2,007	1,991	-0.8	1,878	92.3	2.8	1.3	1.7	2.0	23.6	64.2	12.2	789	58.6	56.9	17.1
Dover township (York)	21,078	21,286	1.0	21,179	90.2	3.1	0.5	3.5	2.8	22.1	62.7	15.4	8,431	80.8	55.2	17.8
Downingtown borough & MCD (Chester)	7,891	7,936	0.6	7,921	73.5	13.5	4.1	2.4	6.4	19.6	67.1	13.5	3,425	56.7	43.4	31.1
Doylestown borough & MCD (Bucks)	8,380	8,307	-0.9	8,353	93.4	1.9	1.5	1.3	1.9	16.0	55.8	28.1	3,808	48.5	28.3	45.9
Doylestown township (Bucks)	17,680	17,506	-1.0	17,603	91.8	3.3	0.7	1.5	2.6	18.7	62.5	18.9	5,846	81.1	19.8	60.2
Dravosburg borough & MCD (Allegheny)	1,792	1,774	-1.0	1,821	94.9	2.0	0.0	1.1	1.9	15.3	62.6	22.1	883	63.6	52.3	19.4
Dreher township (Wayne)	1,412	1,359	-3.8	1,334	95.1	2.7	0.5	0.4	1.3	17.3	62.0	20.7	481	86.7	54.9	22.2
Drexel Hill CDP	28,043	NA	NA	28,262	79.6	9.5	4.6	2.7	3.6	23.7	62.8	13.7	11,016	67.8	33.6	39.5
Driftwood borough & MCD (Cameron)	67	64	-4.5	100	100.0	0.0	0.0	0.0	0.0	14.0	51.0	35.0	40	100.0	87.5	0.0
Drumore township (Lancaster)	2,560	2,600	1.6	2,586	99.8	0.0	0.2	0.0	0.0	31.8	55.6	12.5	804	82.6	70.3	17.5
Dry Tavern CDP	697	NA	NA	605	100.0	0.0	0.0	0.0	0.0	16.5	68.0	15.4	262	81.3	46.9	28.2
Dryville CDP	398	NA	NA	729	97.0	3.0	0.0	0.0	0.0	19.2	65.9	15.0	220	91.8	57.7	20.9
Dublin borough & MCD (Bucks)	2,158	2,148	-0.5	2,158	79.2	0.4	0.8	3.7	15.9	22.1	69.2	8.7	851	43.1	42.3	35.4
Dublin township (Fulton)	1,264	1,232	-2.5	1,334	97.7	0.0	0.0	0.7	1.6	18.7	58.8	22.3	552	81.7	71.6	8.7
Dublin township (Huntingdon)	1,290	1,278	-0.9	1,153	98.5	0.0	0.0	0.7	0.8	22.6	61.3	16.3	453	91.2	68.9	14.3
DuBois city & MCD (Clearfield)	7,794	7,632	-2.1	7,718	91.3	0.5	1.0	0.9	6.2	21.4	61.6	16.8	3,508	56.4	50.7	17.5
Duboistown borough & MCD (Lycoming)	1,205	1,213	0.7	1,243	99.3	0.1	0.0	0.6	0.1	16.7	61.8	21.4	528	80.5	47.0	24.6
Dudley borough & MCD (Huntingdon)	187	185	-1.1	105	100.0	0.0	0.0	0.0	0.0	10.5	62.8	26.7	48	81.3	62.5	4.2
Dunbar borough & MCD (Fayette)	1,039	1,019	-1.9	1,083	98.9	0.3	0.0	0.0	0.8	20.2	64.2	15.7	460	70.0	68.7	12.2
Dunbar township (Fayette)	7,129	6,995	-1.9	7,063	97.0	1.7	0.0	0.8	0.5	20.0	61.7	18.3	2,888	82.8	63.1	9.7
Duncan township (Tioga)	210	211	0.5	226	99.1	0.0	0.0	0.4	0.4	19.0	59.3	21.7	102	83.3	61.8	3.9
Duncannon borough & MCD (Perry)	1,522	1,493	-1.9	1,681	91.4	1.2	5.8	0.8	0.8	23.5	63.0	13.6	712	55.8	44.4	21.5
Duncansville borough & MCD (Blair)	1,233	1,210	-1.9	1,433	94.6	0.2	1.0	0.9	3.3	23.3	54.5	22.1	654	59.6	59.9	18.7
Dunkard township (Greene)	2,379	2,336	-1.8	2,138	96.7	0.0	0.0	2.9	0.4	18.2	60.7	21.1	938	86.9	72.0	10.6
Dunlevy borough & MCD (Washington)	381	382	0.3	400	97.5	0.3	0.0	0.0	2.3	18.8	56.0	25.5	164	77.4	58.5	18.3
Dunlo CDP	342	NA	NA	127	100.0	0.0	0.0	0.0	0.0	14.2	66.1	19.7	57	80.7	100.0	0.0
Dunmore borough & MCD (Lackawanna)	14,057	13,791	-1.9	13,974	91.2	1.0	1.7	1.6	4.6	18.1	63.4	18.6	5,726	57.8	39.9	31.7
Dunnstable township (Clinton)	1,010	1,019	0.9	1,053	97.9	0.0	0.0	1.7	0.4	21.2	58.9	19.8	415	87.5	54.7	24.8

1 May be of any race.

Table A. All Places — **Population and Housing**

STATE City, town, township, borough, or CDP (county if applicable)	2010 census total population	2014 estimated population	Percent change 2010–2014	ACS total population estimate 2010–2014	White alone, not Hispanic or Latino	Black alone, not Hispanic or Latino	Asian alone, not Hispanic or Latino	All other races or 2 or more races, not Hispanic or Latino	Hispanic or Latino[1]	Under 18 years old	Age 18 to 64 years old	Age 65 years and older	Total occupied housing units	Percent owner occupied	High school diploma or less	Bachelor's degree or more
	1	2	3	4	5	6	7	8	9	10	11	12	13	14	15	16
PENNSYLVANIA—Con.																
Dunnstown CDP............	1,360	NA	NA	1,220	96.1	0.0	0.0	2.6	1.3	15.6	61.3	23.1	553	80.5	44.1	27.1
Dupont borough & MCD (Luzerne).....................	2,711	2,704	-0.3	2,708	94.2	0.0	0.0	5.8	0.0	19.3	55.2	25.4	1,211	69.6	42.0	25.5
Duquesne city & MCD (Allegheny)..................	5,565	5,521	-0.8	5,558	34.9	51.9	0.6	11.4	1.2	28.7	56.2	15.0	2,369	41.5	63.5	7.8
Durham township (Bucks)	1,144	1,136	-0.7	1,147	95.8	0.0	2.0	1.3	0.9	17.4	61.0	21.5	452	95.1	28.1	45.1
Duryea borough & MCD (Luzerne).....................	4,922	4,914	-0.2	4,918	92.2	0.5	1.4	2.9	3.0	21.7	61.2	17.3	2,104	78.3	43.9	29.2
Dushore borough & MCD (Sullivan)....................	608	595	-2.1	644	100.0	0.0	0.0	0.0	0.0	15.2	64.3	20.5	329	42.2	62.0	12.2
Dyberry township (Wayne)......................	1,407	1,388	-1.4	1,289	92.6	0.0	0.0	1.9	5.5	17.6	67.3	15.0	462	80.1	53.7	23.2
Eagle Lake CDP............	12	NA	NA	0	0.0	0.0	0.0	0.0	0.0	0.0	0.0	0.0	0	0.0	0.0	0.0
Eagles Mere borough & MCD (Sullivan).............	120	118	-1.7	101	97.0	0.0	3.0	0.0	0.0	7.0	34.7	58.4	52	98.1	9.6	76.9
Eagleview CDP.............	1,644	NA	NA	2,052	94.5	2.8	0.0	0.9	1.7	20.4	65.0	14.6	885	64.3	17.4	64.1
Eagleville CDP (Centre) ..	324	NA	NA	292	100.0	0.0	0.0	0.0	0.0	16.8	78.7	4.5	113	100.0	86.7	13.3
Eagleville CDP (Montgomery)	4,800	NA	NA	4,768	63.9	22.2	9.4	2.0	2.5	14.7	77.1	8.3	1,170	60.2	31.5	41.3
Earl township (Berks)	3,195	3,214	0.6	3,206	99.5	0.0	0.0	0.2	0.3	13.3	72.4	14.3	1,316	85.9	49.9	28.0
Earl township (Lancaster)	7,024	7,149	1.8	7,113	94.0	0.0	4.7	0.0	1.3	26.4	48.2	25.5	2,365	62.0	72.6	12.6
Earlston CDP................	1,122	NA	NA	813	100.0	0.0	0.0	0.0	0.0	8.5	67.0	24.5	438	90.0	76.0	7.1
East Allen township (Northampton).............	4,903	4,890	-0.3	4,901	91.4	2.1	0.5	3.5	2.4	18.2	60.4	21.3	1,787	93.5	44.4	27.5
East Bangor borough & MCD (Northampton)	1,172	1,517	29.4	1,233	90.3	0.2	0.3	1.9	7.1	25.2	64.6	10.1	396	72.0	53.0	16.2
East Berlin borough & MCD (Adams)	1,521	1,524	0.2	1,380	97.0	0.2	0.4	2.2	0.2	23.7	58.4	18.0	569	67.7	65.6	13.9
East Berwick CDP	2,007	NA	NA	1,858	91.0	0.0	1.1	0.0	8.0	13.8	62.5	23.7	851	87.8	52.4	19.5
East Bethlehem township (Washington).............	2,354	2,311	-1.8	2,298	96.4	0.9	0.0	2.0	0.8	22.5	62.6	14.9	873	85.0	54.5	21.1
East Bradford township (Chester).................	9,942	10,038	1.0	9,996	91.0	3.0	1.8	1.2	3.0	21.0	65.2	13.8	3,420	86.6	11.5	69.6
East Brady borough & MCD (Clarion)	942	927	-1.6	1,068	97.3	0.0	0.0	1.8	0.9	21.0	58.3	20.8	454	63.2	69.4	10.8
East Brandywine township (Chester).......	6,742	8,033	19.1	7,328	95.4	0.0	1.3	0.7	2.7	26.2	62.3	11.6	2,518	94.0	24.1	56.6
East Brunswick township (Schuylkill)...............	1,793	1,755	-2.1	1,923	96.3	0.7	0.8	0.4	1.7	23.1	61.7	15.4	732	85.9	49.6	27.5
East Buffalo township (Union)	6,409	6,466	0.9	6,426	91.5	0.3	4.3	0.7	3.3	17.3	64.8	17.8	2,123	84.0	16.5	63.8
East Butler borough & MCD (Butler)...............	732	710	-3.0	701	96.6	2.0	0.0	0.7	0.7	21.4	60.4	18.3	331	78.2	52.0	14.8
East Caln township (Chester).................	4,838	4,877	0.8	4,860	80.4	5.1	11.4	0.6	2.5	23.4	60.7	16.0	2,094	60.2	23.3	63.8
East Cameron township (Northumberland).........	748	746	-0.3	653	98.8	0.0	0.0	1.1	0.2	16.8	60.7	22.7	291	93.5	63.9	13.1
East Carroll township (Cambria)..................	1,654	1,620	-2.1	1,613	99.3	0.2	0.0	0.2	0.4	20.7	61.7	17.6	625	88.2	57.1	18.1
East Chillisquaque township (Northumberland).........	668	657	-1.6	826	98.2	0.0	0.0	0.7	1.1	23.0	59.0	18.0	328	82.9	67.4	19.8
East Cocalico township (Lancaster)................	10,310	10,435	1.2	10,375	91.0	0.0	0.8	0.8	7.4	25.1	59.2	15.5	3,683	82.2	54.1	21.5
East Conemaugh borough & MCD (Cambria)	1,220	1,172	-3.9	1,153	98.5	0.8	0.0	0.5	0.2	25.6	55.6	18.8	492	60.4	67.1	6.5
East Coventry township (Chester).................	6,636	6,753	1.8	6,734	92.0	1.0	2.2	1.5	3.2	23.7	59.8	16.6	2,514	80.4	31.9	43.6
East Deer township (Allegheny)...............	1,500	1,488	-0.8	1,337	93.3	2.7	0.0	3.2	0.7	19.2	68.4	12.4	608	67.4	34.9	21.4
East Donegal township (Lancaster)................	7,755	8,145	5.0	7,972	94.8	1.2	0.4	1.7	1.8	25.0	62.2	12.8	2,858	84.4	47.0	24.5
East Drumore township (Lancaster)................	3,791	3,845	1.4	3,820	93.3	1.0	0.0	0.5	5.1	24.0	54.4	21.6	1,289	77.2	70.8	16.1
East Earl CDP..............	1,144	NA	NA	1,088	94.4	0.0	1.0	0.0	4.6	34.2	54.6	11.4	300	90.3	67.7	18.3
East Earl township (Lancaster)................	6,507	6,743	3.6	6,625	88.8	0.0	5.8	0.3	5.1	30.5	56.9	12.7	1,980	74.0	78.1	8.7
East Fairfield township (Crawford)	922	899	-2.5	948	99.9	0.0	0.1	0.0	0.0	24.6	56.0	19.3	357	93.0	65.3	14.0
East Fallowfield township (Chester).................	7,449	7,567	1.6	7,522	82.6	9.2	1.7	2.1	4.5	23.9	66.1	9.9	2,716	90.1	35.6	39.3
East Fallowfield township (Crawford)	1,620	1,598	-1.4	1,536	98.4	0.0	0.1	0.7	0.8	31.0	54.3	14.7	498	81.9	75.1	8.0
East Finley township (Washington).............	1,392	1,370	-1.6	1,437	99.0	0.1	0.0	0.9	0.0	19.1	67.8	13.0	501	75.0	64.1	19.0
East Franklin township (Armstrong)...............	4,082	4,013	-1.7	4,043	100.0	0.0	0.0	0.0	0.0	17.0	62.9	20.0	1,626	83.6	54.9	21.2
East Freedom CDP..........	972	NA	NA	1,000	100.0	0.0	0.0	0.0	0.0	22.9	57.0	20.1	362	71.5	59.1	4.4
East Goshen township (Chester).................	18,026	18,198	1.0	18,139	94.0	2.0	1.9	0.4	1.5	17.1	57.6	25.2	8,145	72.2	17.1	60.1
East Greenville borough & MCD (Montgomery)..	2,951	2,962	0.4	2,957	93.9	1.4	0.4	1.9	2.5	26.6	65.0	8.3	1,072	71.8	53.2	19.9
East Hanover township (Dauphin).................	5,718	5,868	2.6	5,809	94.5	2.2	0.5	0.5	2.2	22.7	64.5	12.6	2,188	90.9	45.1	30.3
East Hanover township (Lebanon).................	2,801	2,859	2.1	2,833	98.4	0.1	0.4	0.3	0.8	18.6	64.8	16.6	1,175	81.0	62.2	19.3
East Hempfield township (Lancaster)................	23,522	24,139	2.6	23,829	85.9	2.3	4.4	1.1	6.2	23.0	57.5	19.5	9,626	75.8	31.6	43.5
East Hopewell township (York).....................	2,416	2,419	0.1	2,447	96.2	0.0	0.2	0.2	3.4	20.7	65.6	13.6	872	94.2	46.4	17.0

1 May be of any race.

Table A. All Places — **Population and Housing**

STATE City, town, township, borough, or CDP (county if applicable)	Population				Race and Hispanic or Latino origin (percent), 2010–2014					Age (percent), 2010–2014			Households, 2010–2014			
	2010 census total population	2014 estimated population	Percent change 2010–2014	ACS total population estimate 2010–2014	White alone, not Hispanic or Latino	Black alone, not Hispanic or Latino	Asian alone, not Hispanic or Latino	All other races or 2 or more races, not Hispanic or Latino	Hispanic or Latino[1]	Under 18 years old	Age 18 to 64 years old	Age 65 years and older	Total occupied housing units	Percent owner occupied	High school diploma or less	Bachelor's degree or more
	1	2	3	4	5	6	7	8	9	10	11	12	13	14	15	16
PENNSYLVANIA—Con.																
East Huntingdon township (Westmoreland)	7,960	7,817	-1.8	7,895	94.0	0.7	2.7	1.5	1.2	17.7	63.1	19.2	3,288	77.2	56.8	16.8
East Keating township (Clinton)	11	11	0.0	10	100.0	0.0	0.0	0.0	0.0	0.0	60.0	40.0	6	100.0	16.7	33.3
East Lackawannock township (Mercer)	1,682	1,660	-1.3	1,617	97.9	0.6	0.0	1.5	0.0	17.1	60.5	22.4	651	90.5	52.5	20.9
East Lampeter township (Lancaster).............	16,453	16,909	2.8	16,691	76.5	8.5	3.3	3.1	8.6	24.3	61.3	14.3	6,255	58.7	48.2	26.4
East Lansdowne borough & MCD (Delaware).......	2,668	2,668	0.0	2,670	32.3	47.7	13.4	1.2	5.4	22.7	67.4	10.0	948	62.7	41.1	24.1
Eastlawn Gardens CDP...	3,307	NA	NA	2,963	93.6	0.0	0.0	0.0	6.4	23.9	64.9	11.2	1,113	86.8	31.4	34.4
East McKeesport borough & MCD (Allegheny)	2,138	2,120	-0.8	2,233	88.4	4.5	1.3	4.6	1.2	20.6	62.1	17.3	1,051	57.6	51.2	17.2
East Mahoning township (Indiana)...............	1,077	1,041	-3.3	1,085	98.9	0.0	0.0	1.1	0.0	26.1	60.7	13.2	403	90.8	67.5	17.1
East Manchester township (York)	7,264	7,383	1.6	7,325	88.7	4.1	1.3	1.9	4.1	24.6	61.6	13.9	2,606	89.8	47.2	23.4
East Marlborough township (Chester).......	7,026	7,247	3.1	7,152	91.5	1.6	3.6	0.9	2.4	20.7	62.3	16.8	2,628	86.7	14.3	67.3
East Mead township (Crawford)	1,498	1,464	-2.3	1,541	95.7	0.6	0.7	2.7	0.2	24.2	61.5	14.2	609	87.0	58.9	15.1
East Nantmeal township (Chester)	1,803	1,838	1.9	1,779	92.7	1.6	0.3	2.5	2.9	17.4	64.8	17.7	646	88.5	29.1	53.6
East Norriton township (Montgomery)	13,590	14,103	3.8	13,941	80.8	9.8	6.4	0.5	2.5	16.7	60.5	22.8	5,788	75.3	30.5	42.5
East Norwegian township (Schuylkill)	861	843	-2.1	956	94.9	0.3	0.0	0.0	4.8	23.3	58.6	18.1	374	87.2	56.7	15.5
East Nottingham township (Chester)	8,650	8,864	2.5	8,777	87.5	2.1	0.8	0.8	8.8	33.0	58.8	8.2	2,839	85.4	38.6	33.8
Easton city & MCD (Northampton).............	26,800	27,052	0.9	26,977	55.7	14.5	2.7	5.5	21.7	22.1	66.7	11.3	9,513	47.6	51.4	17.7
East Penn township (Carbon)...................	2,881	2,825	-1.9	2,849	94.4	0.2	0.3	2.7	2.4	20.6	65.6	13.7	1,109	87.5	51.4	17.9
East Pennsboro township (Cumberland)	20,625	21,384	3.7	20,926	85.5	2.7	4.6	3.5	3.8	21.2	64.4	14.5	8,367	69.6	40.5	27.8
East Petersburg borough & MCD (Lancaster)......	4,506	4,518	0.3	4,504	83.6	1.3	1.2	0.8	13.1	20.2	66.6	13.3	1,672	86.5	49.3	29.5
East Pikeland township (Chester)	7,079	7,358	3.9	7,230	91.2	0.4	2.2	0.7	5.6	20.6	59.9	19.5	3,075	82.2	27.2	50.9
East Pittsburgh borough & MCD (Allegheny)	1,822	1,804	-1.0	1,910	44.5	46.3	5.4	1.9	1.8	30.0	58.0	12.0	790	34.4	51.1	12.0
East Prospect borough & MCD (York)	905	936	3.4	1,140	86.1	4.3	0.0	0.2	9.5	32.8	61.7	5.7	407	83.3	50.6	14.5
East Providence township (Bedford)	1,854	1,855	0.1	1,784	97.0	1.1	0.0	0.0	1.8	21.4	61.8	17.0	767	80.7	67.1	8.7
East Rochester borough & MCD (Beaver)..........	567	553	-2.5	568	91.0	2.3	0.0	4.6	2.1	18.6	54.8	26.6	258	51.6	52.3	11.6
East Rockhill township (Bucks)...................	5,706	5,740	0.6	5,719	97.5	0.5	0.3	1.0	0.8	22.9	63.7	13.5	1,989	82.6	41.0	29.9
East St. Clair township (Bedford)	3,048	2,976	-2.4	3,012	97.3	1.2	0.0	1.5	0.0	20.8	60.0	19.3	1,284	80.5	64.5	13.2
East Salem CDP.............	186	NA	NA	177	92.1	1.1	0.0	0.0	6.8	27.7	67.7	4.5	78	59.0	65.4	2.6
East Side borough & MCD (Carbon).............	317	307	-3.2	247	96.8	0.0	0.8	1.6	0.8	12.9	66.0	21.1	115	81.7	59.1	13.0
East Stroudsburg borough & MCD (Monroe).........	9,840	9,624	-2.2	9,773	65.4	12.2	2.5	4.1	15.9	17.8	69.7	12.4	2,987	54.2	38.2	29.0
East Taylor township (Cambria)	2,726	2,629	-3.6	2,681	97.6	0.4	0.0	0.8	1.2	20.2	61.3	18.6	1,051	91.2	58.5	17.7
Easttown township (Chester)	10,497	10,608	1.1	10,562	86.3	2.7	5.9	2.4	2.7	28.7	52.2	19.2	3,830	86.1	13.8	76.4
East Union township (Schuylkill)	1,606	1,610	0.2	1,432	90.6	1.1	0.3	2.5	5.4	16.6	62.2	21.2	623	87.5	59.6	8.8
East Uniontown CDP.......	2,419	NA	NA	2,433	87.3	4.6	0.0	8.2	0.0	17.5	60.6	21.9	1,090	60.7	63.4	15.1
Eastvale borough & MCD (Beaver)................	225	223	-0.9	231	99.1	0.0	0.4	0.0	0.4	25.5	60.3	14.3	88	75.0	73.9	10.2
East Vandergrift borough & MCD (Westmoreland)	674	657	-2.5	705	95.2	2.4	0.0	2.0	0.4	21.0	62.9	16.2	323	70.9	61.9	14.2
East Vincent township (Chester)	6,821	6,859	0.6	6,849	86.3	6.9	1.2	3.3	2.4	29.5	53.5	17.1	2,378	80.8	32.0	46.0
East Washington borough & MCD (Washington) ...	2,002	1,972	-1.5	2,076	89.8	3.1	3.0	0.5	3.7	13.3	72.7	13.9	837	52.0	19.6	60.8
East Waterford CDP	0	NA	NA	186	98.9	0.5	0.0	0.5	0.0	20.0	59.7	20.4	72	54.2	83.3	0.0
East Wheatfield township (Indiana)...............	2,369	2,290	-3.3	2,370	98.1	0.0	0.0	0.8	1.1	20.2	56.9	23.0	990	82.7	56.7	16.9
East Whiteland township (Chester)	10,650	10,750	0.9	10,681	75.4	4.2	10.1	2.4	7.9	23.3	65.4	11.3	3,561	68.4	23.1	59.9
East York CDP	8,777	NA	NA	8,504	84.2	2.8	3.8	2.0	7.2	19.5	57.8	22.7	3,513	72.6	34.6	34.5
Eaton township (Wyoming)	1,514	1,525	0.7	1,568	98.6	0.0	0.1	0.6	0.7	18.5	56.1	25.3	643	79.8	50.7	27.2
Eau Claire borough & MCD (Butler)...............	316	302	-4.4	341	100.0	0.0	0.0	0.0	0.0	20.5	63.9	15.5	134	50.7	70.1	3.7
Ebensburg borough & MCD (Cambria)	3,351	3,237	-3.4	3,295	98.9	0.1	0.0	0.0	1.0	19.3	61.9	18.8	1,560	53.8	36.1	33.0
Economy borough & MCD (Beaver)	8,972	9,294	3.6	9,133	94.9	1.3	1.1	0.6	2.0	18.1	63.9	18.0	3,581	95.6	38.8	30.8
Eddington CDP...............	1,906	NA	NA	2,000	96.8	0.0	0.0	0.0	3.3	24.3	59.7	16.4	755	87.5	46.1	15.9
Eddystone borough & MCD (Delaware)	2,410	2,409	0.0	2,572	77.2	11.3	1.4	7.6	2.5	32.1	59.5	8.4	874	55.5	57.3	9.7
Eden township (Lancaster).............	2,094	2,133	1.9	2,280	94.6	2.2	0.1	0.2	2.9	31.6	57.3	11.1	710	76.3	71.5	12.3
Edenborn CDP	294	NA	NA	283	84.5	12.4	0.0	3.2	0.0	21.5	73.3	5.3	107	85.0	34.6	0.0

1 May be of any race.

Table A. All Places — Population and Housing

STATE City, town, township, borough, or CDP (county if applicable)	Population				Race and Hispanic or Latino origin (percent), 2010–2014					Age (percent), 2010–2014			Households, 2010–2014			
	2010 census total population	2014 estimated population	Percent change 2010–2014	ACS total population estimate 2010–2014	White alone, not Hispanic or Latino	Black alone, not Hispanic or Latino	Asian alone, not Hispanic or Latino	All other races or 2 or more races, not Hispanic or Latino	Hispanic or Latino[1]	Under 18 years old	Age 18 to 64 years old	Age 65 years and older	Total occupied housing units	Percent owner occupied	High school diploma or less	Bachelor's degree or more
	1	2	3	4	5	6	7	8	9	10	11	12	13	14	15	16

PENNSYLVANIA—Con.

STATE City, town, township, borough, or CDP (county if applicable)	1	2	3	4	5	6	7	8	9	10	11	12	13	14	15	16
Edenburg CDP	681	NA	NA	809	92.8	0.0	0.7	3.8	2.6	24.4	57.3	18.4	338	86.1	63.3	19.5
Edgewood borough & MCD (Allegheny)	3,118	3,087	-1.0	3,109	83.4	8.0	4.3	0.7	3.5	18.2	68.7	13.1	1,507	68.0	9.8	72.5
Edgewood CDP	2,384	NA	NA	2,148	90.1	0.5	0.0	8.8	0.7	22.7	55.5	21.8	1,005	66.1	61.4	17.0
Edgeworth borough & MCD (Allegheny)	1,680	1,674	-0.4	1,650	93.9	0.4	0.7	1.7	3.3	28.9	54.4	16.8	604	91.9	7.5	85.4
Edgmont township (Delaware)	3,987	4,061	1.9	4,011	92.9	1.1	5.2	0.3	0.4	20.2	51.6	28.1	1,691	77.7	16.1	62.6
Edie CDP	83	NA	NA	36	100.0	0.0	0.0	0.0	0.0	0.0	72.2	27.8	20	100.0	65.0	35.0
Edinboro borough & MCD (Erie)	6,438	6,437	0.0	6,484	91.9	2.0	2.0	0.1	4.0	14.8	76.2	9.1	2,349	39.0	27.4	36.2
Edwardsville borough & MCD (Luzerne)	4,816	4,750	-1.4	4,792	90.4	8.5	0.6	0.4	0.2	27.6	54.1	18.2	2,082	34.1	61.2	16.9
Effort CDP	2,269	NA	NA	2,402	84.7	0.9	0.0	0.0	14.4	40.9	53.7	5.5	781	75.2	31.2	21.0
Egypt CDP	2,391	NA	NA	2,429	82.9	0.8	2.1	1.6	12.6	18.5	72.2	9.3	888	81.2	39.4	23.4
Ehrenfeld borough & MCD (Cambria)	228	222	-2.6	205	100.0	0.0	0.0	0.0	0.0	28.3	60.6	11.2	71	91.5	78.9	4.2
Eighty Four CDP	657	NA	NA	742	92.9	1.6	0.0	5.5	0.0	18.5	55.8	25.6	313	87.9	59.7	12.5
Elco borough & MCD (Washington)	323	320	-0.9	321	98.1	0.0	0.0	1.9	0.0	18.4	53.6	28.0	124	73.4	70.2	6.5
Elder township (Cambria)	1,038	1,008	-2.9	1,018	99.0	0.0	0.0	0.0	1.0	21.2	54.0	24.6	377	91.0	65.3	8.0
Elderton borough & MCD (Armstrong)	356	351	-1.4	295	100.0	0.0	0.0	0.0	0.0	9.5	58.2	32.5	146	59.6	65.1	20.5
Eldred township (Jefferson)	1,226	1,210	-1.3	1,242	99.0	0.0	0.0	0.3	0.7	19.7	59.4	20.9	519	92.3	59.9	20.2
Eldred township (Lycoming)	2,122	2,150	1.3	2,089	96.0	2.4	0.4	0.4	0.8	20.2	60.6	19.2	823	96.7	46.4	24.5
Eldred borough & MCD (McKean)	825	813	-1.5	744	96.0	0.7	0.0	2.0	1.3	24.6	56.0	19.4	326	66.6	64.1	10.7
Eldred township (McKean)	1,592	1,562	-1.9	1,689	95.6	1.2	0.5	2.5	0.1	24.4	57.7	17.7	678	84.2	60.8	13.9
Eldred township (Monroe)	2,914	2,843	-2.4	2,912	90.5	2.3	0.6	1.6	5.0	18.0	65.7	16.3	1,050	87.9	56.1	21.2
Eldred township (Schuylkill)	758	746	-1.6	754	97.5	0.1	0.8	1.6	0.0	25.1	57.0	18.0	269	85.1	62.8	14.1
Eldred township (Warren)	650	632	-2.8	572	99.5	0.2	0.0	0.3	0.0	21.0	58.6	20.3	242	81.4	73.1	9.9
Elgin borough & MCD (Erie)	218	215	-1.4	257	100.0	0.0	0.0	0.0	0.0	31.5	52.3	16.3	80	80.0	72.5	3.8
Elim CDP	3,727	NA	NA	3,859	96.4	1.2	1.0	0.9	0.4	15.5	61.1	23.5	1,532	75.1	40.9	32.6
Elizabeth borough & MCD (Allegheny)	1,493	1,497	0.3	1,397	92.3	1.1	0.0	3.9	2.6	20.2	62.0	17.8	655	54.7	53.7	13.6
Elizabeth township (Allegheny)	13,271	13,277	0.0	13,297	97.6	0.9	0.1	0.9	0.4	19.3	59.1	21.6	5,434	86.0	43.8	27.2
Elizabeth township (Lancaster)	3,886	3,970	2.2	3,933	97.4	0.3	0.3	2.0	0.0	24.1	61.8	14.1	1,445	85.0	64.3	19.1
Elizabethtown borough & MCD (Lancaster)	11,545	11,611	0.6	11,602	93.1	1.3	1.5	1.3	2.8	19.6	67.9	12.6	3,980	58.3	40.4	35.1
Elizabethville borough & MCD (Dauphin)	1,510	1,494	-1.1	1,751	95.0	2.5	0.0	2.3	0.3	26.6	57.1	16.3	646	57.6	61.9	7.7
Elk township (Chester)	1,681	1,697	1.0	1,682	87.3	2.4	1.2	5.3	3.9	26.0	63.1	10.9	591	87.6	35.2	40.3
Elk township (Clarion)	1,491	1,458	-2.2	1,313	98.2	0.2	0.0	1.6	0.0	16.1	61.8	22.2	559	82.3	61.0	17.7
Elk township (Tioga)	49	49	0.0	21	100.0	0.0	0.0	0.0	0.0	14.3	61.9	23.8	11	100.0	45.5	54.5
Elk township (Warren)	520	510	-1.9	418	98.8	0.0	0.7	0.5	0.0	12.2	67.0	20.8	194	95.4	47.9	20.1
Elk Creek township (Erie)	1,798	1,787	-0.6	1,773	96.2	1.6	0.0	0.9	1.4	19.9	62.7	17.4	706	94.1	56.2	19.4
Elkland township (Sullivan)	577	565	-2.1	438	95.7	0.0	3.2	0.0	1.1	11.0	54.7	34.2	162	80.9	60.5	21.0
Elkland borough & MCD (Tioga)	1,821	1,800	-1.2	1,850	97.4	0.4	0.0	1.2	1.0	19.5	64.5	16.0	824	69.9	58.5	11.8
Elk Lick township (Somerset)	2,241	2,177	-2.9	2,199	98.0	0.0	0.0	0.3	1.8	23.8	60.2	16.0	775	82.6	70.3	14.3
Ellport borough & MCD (Lawrence)	1,180	1,148	-2.7	1,167	96.8	0.3	0.6	1.7	0.6	18.4	62.5	19.1	494	83.0	51.0	17.8
Ellsworth borough & MCD (Washington)	1,027	1,002	-2.4	778	94.6	2.3	0.0	3.1	0.0	15.6	62.4	22.0	351	69.8	67.0	15.1
Ellwood City borough	7,921	7,682	-3.0	7,743	94.8	1.1	0.4	2.2	1.5	20.2	61.3	18.4	3,363	67.8	49.3	25.1
Ellwood City borough (Beaver)	632	618	-2.2	565	99.5	0.0	0.0	0.0	0.5	33.6	44.0	22.5	225	56.4	52.0	23.1
Ellwood City borough (Lawrence)	7,289	7,064	-3.1	7,178	94.4	1.2	0.4	2.4	1.5	19.3	62.6	18.1	3,138	68.6	49.1	25.2
Elmhurst township (Lackawanna)	894	879	-1.7	1,052	94.7	0.0	0.0	2.2	3.1	19.8	50.6	29.6	332	82.5	38.6	37.0
Elrama CDP	307	NA	NA	345	94.2	0.0	0.0	0.0	5.8	26.6	50.1	23.2	148	51.4	64.9	0.0
Elverson borough & MCD (Chester)	1,225	1,307	6.7	1,332	96.8	0.0	0.4	2.0	0.8	17.0	44.8	38.3	635	74.6	41.9	32.1
Elysburg CDP	2,194	NA	NA	2,182	96.6	0.0	0.0	1.6	1.7	20.2	58.0	21.8	1,005	69.4	44.3	36.7
Emerald Lakes CDP	2,886	NA	NA	3,283	53.2	15.5	1.4	6.0	23.9	27.9	59.5	12.6	952	81.0	44.4	27.7
Emigsville CDP	2,672	NA	NA	2,967	92.2	2.0	0.3	2.1	3.4	27.7	57.9	14.3	1,105	72.6	64.3	14.9
Emlenton borough	625	605	-3.2	705	90.4	0.0	1.0	3.4	5.2	26.4	55.5	18.2	277	64.6	62.5	18.1
Emlenton borough (Clarion)	8	8	0.0	11	100.0	0.0	0.0	0.0	0.0	0.0	100.0	0.0	2	100.0	100.0	0.0
Emlenton borough (Venango)	617	597	-3.2	694	90.2	0.0	1.0	3.5	5.3	26.8	54.7	18.4	275	64.4	62.2	18.2
Emmaus borough & MCD (Lehigh)	11,215	11,335	1.1	11,291	89.4	0.8	2.0	3.5	4.3	20.1	63.9	16.0	4,883	62.8	41.3	33.1
Emporium borough & MCD (Cameron)	2,073	1,963	-5.3	1,886	97.3	1.4	0.0	0.3	1.0	18.8	59.5	21.7	886	49.1	64.2	10.9
Emsworth borough & MCD (Allegheny)	2,449	2,432	-0.7	2,471	93.7	3.2	0.0	2.0	1.2	19.7	68.2	12.0	1,103	60.0	31.1	35.4
Englewood CDP	532	NA	NA	792	100.0	0.0	0.0	0.0	0.0	28.9	48.7	22.5	317	76.7	47.6	32.2
Enhaut CDP	1,007	NA	NA	906	64.3	12.0	0.0	0.0	23.6	21.3	47.0	31.7	344	63.1	49.1	7.6
Enlow CDP	1,013	NA	NA	1,040	96.3	0.0	0.9	0.0	2.8	27.6	57.0	15.4	402	87.8	45.5	15.9
Enola CDP	6,111	NA	NA	6,053	82.3	6.1	4.3	2.3	5.1	23.0	67.7	9.3	2,549	55.6	50.0	13.9

1 May be of any race.

Table A. All Places — **Population and Housing**

STATE City, town, township, borough, or CDP (county if applicable)	2010 census total population	2014 estimated population	Percent change 2010–2014	ACS total population estimate 2010–2014	White alone, not Hispanic or Latino	Black alone, not Hispanic or Latino	Asian alone, not Hispanic or Latino	All other races or 2 or more races, not Hispanic or Latino	Hispanic or Latino[1]	Under 18 years old	Age 18 to 64 years old	Age 65 years and older	Total occupied housing units	Percent owner occupied	High school diploma or less	Bachelor's degree or more
	1	2	3	4	5	6	7	8	9	10	11	12	13	14	15	16
PENNSYLVANIA—Con.																
Enon Valley borough & MCD (Lawrence)	306	300	-2.0	361	99.2	0.0	0.0	0.0	0.8	16.0	58.6	25.2	149	79.9	54.4	14.8
Ephrata borough & MCD (Lancaster)	13,392	13,837	3.3	13,529	91.4	1.4	2.0	1.8	3.4	21.9	66.6	11.6	5,657	62.6	54.7	19.6
Ephrata township (Lancaster)	9,395	10,109	7.6	9,859	91.6	1.7	2.7	0.7	3.2	26.4	58.7	14.6	3,433	69.8	55.6	23.2
Erie city & MCD (Erie)	101,784	99,452	-2.3	100,832	71.6	15.6	2.4	3.8	6.7	23.2	63.6	13.1	40,825	51.4	52.2	22.0
Ernest borough & MCD (Indiana)	462	450	-2.6	343	98.8	0.0	0.0	0.3	0.9	21.6	68.3	10.2	147	72.1	51.7	15.0
Espy CDP	1,642	NA	NA	1,577	99.9	0.1	0.0	0.1	0.0	16.9	65.5	17.7	739	74.7	45.7	31.1
Etna borough & MCD (Allegheny)	3,451	3,421	-0.9	3,446	95.0	1.4	0.0	1.5	2.0	19.3	68.8	11.8	1,619	54.1	46.9	19.9
Eulalia township (Potter)	893	883	-1.1	922	94.6	1.0	0.8	0.7	3.0	16.1	55.1	28.5	320	87.5	44.1	35.3
Evansburg CDP	2,129	NA	NA	2,287	81.1	0.7	16.5	1.7	0.0	26.8	64.8	8.7	795	85.0	18.1	49.8
Evans City borough & MCD (Butler)	1,833	1,783	-2.7	1,788	98.4	0.0	0.0	1.6	0.0	21.0	64.3	14.7	822	62.0	43.2	25.5
Everett borough & MCD (Bedford)	1,834	1,776	-3.2	1,969	95.5	2.7	0.0	0.6	1.1	27.6	56.7	15.8	872	54.5	63.6	9.1
Everson borough & MCD (Fayette)	793	779	-1.8	752	96.8	2.7	0.0	0.5	0.0	18.7	67.9	13.4	316	69.6	61.4	9.2
Exeter township (Berks)	25,550	25,768	0.9	25,684	88.3	5.1	1.8	1.9	2.9	24.9	60.5	14.6	9,602	87.1	33.8	36.6
Exeter borough & MCD (Luzerne)	5,654	5,604	-0.9	5,633	87.8	2.1	0.4	0.6	9.0	22.5	57.1	20.5	2,342	74.3	39.8	31.0
Exeter township (Luzerne)	2,376	2,364	-0.5	2,238	97.7	0.0	0.3	0.9	1.1	13.9	72.9	13.1	867	91.2	44.2	23.5
Exeter township (Wyoming)	690	681	-1.3	699	98.0	0.0	0.1	0.0	1.9	11.6	66.2	22.2	317	79.5	60.6	23.7
Export borough & MCD (Westmoreland)	917	890	-2.9	1,054	96.3	0.0	1.0	2.1	0.6	25.5	58.6	15.8	455	59.3	44.2	16.0
Exton CDP	4,842	NA	NA	4,609	72.7	6.1	19.5	0.3	1.4	19.8	67.5	12.6	2,123	39.7	20.2	66.1
Eyers Grove CDP	105	NA	NA	131	100.0	0.0	0.0	0.0	0.0	10.6	71.8	17.6	53	75.5	56.6	32.1
Factoryville borough & MCD (Wyoming)	1,201	1,214	1.1	1,010	87.3	2.8	4.2	2.0	3.8	15.3	76.7	8.2	285	66.0	34.7	31.2
Fairchance borough & MCD (Fayette)	1,969	1,933	-1.8	1,910	92.3	0.3	0.3	6.6	0.6	25.6	59.5	14.9	709	69.1	56.1	16.9
Fairdale CDP	2,059	NA	NA	1,812	93.5	0.7	0.9	4.8	0.0	22.2	54.4	23.3	834	61.2	59.8	17.3
Fairfield borough & MCD (Adams)	507	506	-0.2	587	95.9	1.9	0.3	0.7	1.2	15.0	57.4	27.6	243	78.2	53.1	27.6
Fairfield township (Crawford)	1,019	999	-2.0	1,069	96.4	0.5	0.0	0.7	2.3	26.6	57.4	16.1	401	84.5	68.3	8.0
Fairfield township (Lycoming)	2,792	2,805	0.5	2,804	96.7	0.9	0.7	1.1	0.6	19.8	63.4	16.8	1,211	88.9	46.1	22.0
Fairfield township (Westmoreland)	2,428	2,405	-0.9	2,339	96.8	0.7	0.3	1.4	0.9	20.5	60.8	18.6	912	86.1	57.3	20.2
Fairhope CDP	1,151	NA	NA	1,289	99.3	0.7	0.0	0.0	0.0	22.0	65.3	12.6	495	85.3	41.0	16.0
Fairhope township (Somerset)	134	131	-2.2	101	100.0	0.0	0.0	0.0	0.0	12.9	68.4	18.8	46	91.3	84.8	4.3
Fairless Hills CDP	8,466	NA	NA	9,289	83.9	4.3	4.1	3.6	4.1	22.7	65.1	12.1	3,429	71.5	49.7	16.3
Fairmount township (Luzerne)	1,276	1,267	-0.7	1,418	97.7	1.3	0.4	0.7	0.0	21.8	62.5	15.7	540	88.3	50.0	20.4
Fairview borough & MCD (Butler)	198	197	-0.5	243	92.6	5.8	0.0	1.6	0.0	35.4	52.8	11.9	70	90.0	62.9	12.9
Fairview township (Butler)	2,080	2,043	-1.8	2,157	99.4	0.3	0.0	0.4	0.0	21.8	63.1	15.1	838	86.6	55.7	10.4
Fairview CDP	2,348	NA	NA	2,870	92.4	0.9	0.2	1.0	5.4	21.1	60.3	18.6	967	78.3	36.6	29.9
Fairview township (Erie)	10,102	10,184	0.8	10,187	95.1	0.9	0.1	1.2	2.8	20.5	58.2	21.2	3,800	86.4	28.6	46.6
Fairview township (Luzerne)	4,520	4,494	-0.6	4,503	91.8	1.3	2.7	2.0	2.3	23.3	60.6	16.1	1,669	83.3	28.6	42.4
Fairview township (Mercer)	1,085	1,077	-0.7	1,020	97.0	0.4	0.0	0.9	1.8	29.4	56.6	14.1	347	84.7	74.6	12.1
Fairview township (York)	16,668	17,039	2.2	16,863	94.0	0.7	0.6	1.0	3.7	23.6	63.5	13.0	6,313	85.0	36.1	36.9
Fairview-Ferndale CDP	2,139	NA	NA	1,768	99.7	0.1	0.0	0.0	0.2	13.6	66.7	19.7	816	83.1	61.3	14.3
Fallowfield township (Washington)	4,321	4,266	-1.3	4,302	93.0	4.3	0.2	1.8	0.8	19.0	61.3	19.8	1,643	92.1	47.8	15.8
Falls township (Bucks)	34,300	33,968	-1.0	34,172	83.2	5.2	2.8	2.8	5.9	21.3	64.9	13.6	12,828	72.1	45.7	21.3
Falls township (Wyoming)	1,990	1,976	-0.7	1,812	96.4	0.6	0.0	0.6	2.4	25.4	58.1	16.5	663	79.8	49.2	14.5
Falls Creek borough	1,037	1,024	-1.3	1,193	95.4	0.2	0.0	2.3	2.1	24.3	61.4	14.1	498	63.3	53.8	8.8
Falls Creek borough (Clearfield)	48	47	-2.1	29	100.0	0.0	0.0	0.0	0.0	6.9	34.5	58.6	18	27.8	72.2	0.0
Falls Creek borough (Jefferson)	989	977	-1.2	1,164	95.3	0.2	0.0	2.4	2.1	24.7	62.3	13.0	480	64.6	53.1	9.2
Fallston borough & MCD (Beaver)	261	259	-0.8	197	95.9	1.0	0.0	3.0	0.0	12.8	70.6	16.8	89	68.5	59.6	14.6
Falmouth CDP	420	NA	NA	334	100.0	0.0	0.0	0.0	0.0	16.2	64.8	19.2	155	97.4	61.3	6.5
Fannett township (Franklin)	2,548	2,588	1.6	2,561	99.3	0.1	0.1	0.5	0.0	32.5	53.9	13.5	847	81.7	71.9	11.6
Farmersville CDP	991	NA	NA	1,185	100.0	0.0	0.0	0.0	0.0	27.5	35.4	37.2	356	58.1	78.1	14.9
Farmington township (Clarion)	1,933	1,894	-2.0	1,881	99.7	0.3	0.0	0.0	0.0	18.1	62.3	19.7	812	90.4	60.6	20.9
Farmington CDP	767	NA	NA	866	99.8	0.0	0.0	0.2	0.0	22.8	50.9	26.4	110	77.3	54.5	17.3
Farmington township (Tioga)	652	670	2.8	532	97.9	0.0	0.9	0.0	1.1	16.7	56.6	26.7	237	88.2	59.1	18.1
Farmington township (Warren)	1,266	1,234	-2.5	1,262	98.6	0.0	0.5	0.0	1.0	22.4	63.0	14.6	484	87.4	65.9	11.4
Farrell city & MCD (Mercer)	4,954	4,829	-2.5	4,883	44.8	45.5	1.6	5.7	2.4	26.4	54.9	18.7	2,023	65.6	50.2	13.8
Fawn township (Allegheny)	2,376	2,362	-0.6	2,354	96.7	0.8	0.6	0.3	1.6	16.1	65.0	19.0	1,011	77.0	54.8	15.1
Fawn township (York)	3,099	3,111	0.4	3,104	95.2	0.4	0.6	2.7	1.1	23.3	63.1	13.6	1,127	90.1	46.0	16.8
Fawn Grove borough & MCD (York)	452	455	0.7	402	97.8	0.2	0.0	2.0	0.0	22.1	60.9	16.9	154	72.1	54.5	24.7
Fawn Lake Forest CDP	755	NA	NA	778	94.7	0.0	0.0	0.8	4.5	16.7	53.5	29.8	371	100.0	53.4	21.6
Faxon CDP	1,395	NA	NA	1,350	95.5	0.0	1.0	0.7	2.8	18.2	53.6	28.1	669	74.9	36.5	40.5

1 May be of any race.

Table A. All Places — **Population and Housing**

STATE City, town, township, borough, or CDP (county if applicable)	2010 census total population	2014 estimated population	Percent change 2010–2014	ACS total population estimate 2010–2014	White alone, not Hispanic or Latino	Black alone, not Hispanic or Latino	Asian alone, not Hispanic or Latino	All other races or 2 or more races, not Hispanic or Latino	Hispanic or Latino[1]	Under 18 years old	Age 18 to 64 years old	Age 65 years and older	Total occupied housing units	Percent owner occupied	High school diploma or less	Bachelor's degree or more
	1	2	3	4	5	6	7	8	9	10	11	12	13	14	15	16
PENNSYLVANIA—Con.																
Fayette township (Juniata)	3,478	3,510	0.9	3,495	100.0	0.0	0.0	0.0	0.0	22.0	57.3	20.8	1,228	82.3	74.3	14.6
Fayette City borough & MCD (Fayette)	596	586	-1.7	560	100.0	0.0	0.0	0.0	0.0	31.5	54.0	14.5	196	79.1	55.1	13.8
Fayetteville CDP	3,128	NA	NA	3,139	91.4	6.6	0.0	1.0	1.0	21.6	60.6	17.7	1,266	71.8	46.7	25.4
Feasterville CDP	3,074	NA	NA	3,656	89.8	3.1	2.5	0.0	4.7	26.6	63.3	9.9	1,369	42.3	33.2	21.0
Fell township (Lackawanna)	2,170	2,144	-1.2	2,167	97.6	0.0	0.0	0.1	2.3	20.1	61.6	18.4	928	67.3	55.7	13.3
Fellsburg CDP	1,180	NA	NA	1,174	97.7	0.6	0.0	1.7	0.0	11.6	60.1	28.2	479	89.1	45.7	17.7
Felton borough & MCD (York)	506	507	0.2	590	94.9	1.0	0.3	2.0	1.7	27.6	59.0	13.4	209	80.9	58.4	16.3
Ferguson township (Centre)	17,690	18,310	3.5	17,962	78.4	2.7	13.4	2.2	3.3	18.8	68.1	13.1	7,398	61.3	18.4	57.7
Ferguson township (Clearfield)	444	447	0.7	465	100.0	0.0	0.0	0.0	0.0	17.2	53.1	29.7	183	90.2	73.8	11.5
Fermanagh township (Juniata)	2,811	2,849	1.4	2,839	92.9	1.3	0.0	0.0	5.7	23.0	52.4	24.5	1,102	74.2	59.8	20.1
Ferndale borough & MCD (Cambria)	1,636	1,575	-3.7	1,559	94.0	1.4	0.5	1.0	3.1	22.2	62.0	15.9	722	68.1	54.0	16.1
Fernville CDP	556	NA	NA	455	95.6	0.0	3.5	0.0	0.9	18.5	58.0	23.5	205	87.3	58.0	23.9
Findlay township (Allegheny)	5,078	5,424	6.8	5,199	92.6	3.8	0.0	2.1	1.5	25.2	60.1	14.7	2,133	80.3	37.0	34.3
Findley township (Mercer)	2,910	2,898	-0.4	2,898	67.6	27.3	0.1	1.9	3.2	7.5	82.2	10.2	501	82.6	56.1	17.2
Finleyville borough & MCD (Washington)	461	450	-2.4	467	97.9	1.5	0.6	0.0	0.0	13.9	72.2	13.9	266	38.0	47.0	14.7
Fishing Creek township (Columbia)	1,416	1,418	0.1	1,445	98.5	0.8	0.4	0.1	0.2	17.6	66.0	16.5	557	87.1	62.1	13.8
Fivepointville CDP	1,156	NA	NA	1,181	98.0	0.0	0.0	2.0	0.0	25.0	59.4	15.5	444	77.0	57.9	27.0
Fleetwood borough & MCD (Berks)	4,085	4,078	-0.2	4,084	87.4	0.9	0.2	1.7	9.8	20.7	61.4	17.9	1,677	77.6	46.8	23.3
Flemington borough & MCD (Clinton)	1,330	1,341	0.8	1,306	94.0	0.5	0.0	3.9	1.7	19.0	60.1	20.8	590	75.8	50.5	21.0
Flora Dale CDP	38	NA	NA	0	0.0	0.0	0.0	0.0	0.0	0.0	0.0	0.0	0	0.0	0.0	0.0
Flourtown CDP	4,538	NA	NA	4,802	86.7	4.5	2.9	0.8	5.0	23.5	59.7	17.0	1,754	83.2	15.6	61.6
Flying Hills CDP	2,568	NA	NA	2,628	87.7	1.0	0.5	0.0	10.8	12.9	61.7	25.4	1,543	43.4	23.5	54.2
Folcroft borough & MCD (Delaware)	6,606	6,636	0.5	6,615	63.1	27.9	3.4	0.7	4.8	28.1	62.7	9.3	2,380	77.9	50.1	17.6
Folsom CDP	8,323	NA	NA	8,282	88.6	1.4	4.4	3.0	2.6	21.8	66.3	11.8	3,064	77.7	46.6	24.9
Foot of Ten CDP	672	NA	NA	734	100.0	0.0	0.0	0.0	0.0	9.8	78.2	12.0	316	93.4	76.3	1.3
Force CDP	253	NA	NA	283	99.3	0.0	0.7	0.0	0.0	30.8	46.9	22.3	98	87.8	73.5	7.1
Ford City borough & MCD (Armstrong)	2,991	2,914	-2.6	2,945	89.8	4.0	0.0	0.7	5.5	22.1	58.3	19.6	1,287	52.5	60.2	10.6
Ford Cliff borough & MCD (Armstrong)	371	366	-1.3	451	98.7	0.0	0.0	0.0	1.3	16.5	62.2	21.5	193	88.6	61.7	8.8
Forest City borough & MCD (Susquehanna)	1,911	1,824	-4.6	2,068	95.7	0.0	0.7	2.0	1.6	18.7	54.1	27.1	797	59.2	55.2	19.9
Forest Hills borough & MCD (Allegheny)	6,518	6,477	-0.6	6,501	82.6	13.3	1.5	1.1	1.5	18.6	60.6	20.8	3,040	77.4	26.1	49.5
Forest Lake township (Susquehanna)	1,193	1,145	-4.0	1,214	97.6	0.0	0.0	0.3	2.1	14.2	62.4	23.3	499	83.0	57.9	17.6
Forestville CDP	435	NA	NA	339	100.0	0.0	0.0	0.0	0.0	6.2	64.1	29.8	169	84.6	58.6	5.9
Forks township (Northampton)	14,721	15,230	3.5	15,037	77.3	5.4	4.2	1.4	11.7	24.1	59.8	16.1	5,489	90.8	30.1	42.0
Forks township (Sullivan)	377	376	-0.3	455	89.9	0.0	2.0	8.1	0.0	11.4	63.3	25.3	154	90.9	48.1	18.2
Forkston township (Wyoming)	396	389	-1.8	319	99.7	0.3	0.0	0.0	0.0	18.0	65.9	16.3	128	83.6	53.1	16.4
Forksville borough & MCD (Sullivan)	145	145	0.0	71	100.0	0.0	0.0	0.0	0.0	2.8	64.8	32.4	52	61.5	55.8	15.4
Fort Indiantown Gap CDP	143	NA	NA	76	100.0	0.0	0.0	0.0	0.0	0.0	88.1	11.8	49	38.8	63.3	0.0
Fort Loudon CDP	886	NA	NA	968	100.0	0.0	0.0	0.0	0.0	21.5	56.1	22.3	391	62.1	74.2	5.6
Fort Washington CDP	5,446	NA	NA	5,619	85.0	4.4	5.6	2.0	3.0	26.2	57.9	16.0	2,006	89.2	11.7	71.9
Forty Fort borough & MCD (Luzerne)	4,214	4,144	-1.7	4,184	99.6	0.4	0.0	0.0	0.0	18.5	64.6	16.9	1,791	67.5	30.9	38.9
Forward township (Allegheny)	3,376	3,361	-0.4	3,369	92.6	4.1	0.0	0.0	3.3	18.2	59.5	22.4	1,554	81.4	55.1	16.9
Forward township (Butler)	2,531	2,565	1.3	2,534	98.9	0.5	0.0	0.6	0.0	19.6	63.6	16.6	1,002	87.2	49.9	19.4
Foster township (Luzerne)	3,467	3,448	-0.5	3,460	96.8	0.5	1.4	1.1	0.3	14.9	65.5	19.6	1,489	86.2	63.9	12.3
Foster township (McKean)	4,316	4,230	-2.0	4,278	97.2	0.3	0.0	0.3	2.2	19.5	60.5	19.9	1,841	84.8	56.3	17.1
Foster township (Schuylkill)	251	253	0.8	188	100.0	0.0	0.0	0.0	0.0	19.2	53.8	27.1	86	87.2	70.9	14.0
Foster Brook CDP	1,251	NA	NA	1,150	96.2	0.0	0.0	0.0	3.8	22.8	62.8	14.3	479	85.8	47.4	21.9
Foundryville CDP	256	NA	NA	60	76.7	0.0	0.0	23.3	0.0	0.0	88.4	11.7	36	100.0	80.6	19.4
Fountain Hill borough & MCD (Lehigh)	4,597	4,622	0.5	4,610	69.8	7.3	0.3	2.6	20.0	18.1	63.2	18.7	1,990	62.0	39.6	30.5
Fountain Springs CDP	278	NA	NA	346	98.8	1.2	0.0	0.0	0.0	11.2	68.9	19.9	151	82.8	90.7	0.0
Fox township (Elk)	3,630	3,557	-2.0	3,593	98.6	0.4	0.5	0.5	0.0	20.1	63.6	16.1	1,473	87.5	65.4	20.4
Fox township (Sullivan)	358	349	-2.5	261	93.1	0.0	0.0	6.1	0.8	16.1	54.7	29.1	111	89.2	65.8	15.3
Foxburg borough & MCD (Clarion)	183	182	-0.5	242	100.0	0.0	0.0	0.0	0.0	22.0	58.2	19.8	97	77.3	56.7	18.6
Fox Chapel borough & MCD (Allegheny)	5,386	5,401	0.3	5,397	90.2	0.0	5.2	2.9	1.8	29.0	54.4	16.6	1,959	96.2	6.1	84.4
Fox Chase CDP	1,622	NA	NA	1,340	78.9	5.1	9.8	5.2	1.0	15.4	59.0	25.4	530	97.2	38.7	19.1
Frackville borough & MCD (Schuylkill)	3,805	3,739	-1.7	3,775	96.4	0.3	0.3	0.5	2.5	25.2	53.0	21.7	1,555	74.4	57.9	14.5
Frailey township (Schuylkill)	429	417	-2.8	458	99.8	0.0	0.0	0.2	0.0	22.9	65.1	12.0	168	89.3	69.0	1.8
Franconia township (Montgomery)	13,064	13,260	1.5	13,193	91.4	1.4	4.0	0.8	2.5	24.0	55.0	20.8	4,642	80.4	35.7	40.3
Frankfort Springs borough & MCD (Beaver)	130	129	-0.8	115	100.0	0.0	0.0	0.0	0.0	17.4	56.4	26.1	46	91.3	43.5	8.7
Franklin township (Adams)	4,877	4,883	0.1	4,878	90.1	0.0	0.0	1.7	8.2	18.7	65.5	15.9	1,869	75.7	50.9	26.6

1 May be of any race.

Table A. All Places — **Population and Housing**

STATE City, town, township, borough, or CDP (county if applicable)	2010 census total population	2014 estimated population	Percent change 2010–2014	ACS total population estimate 2010–2014	White alone, not Hispanic or Latino	Black alone, not Hispanic or Latino	Asian alone, not Hispanic or Latino	All other races or 2 or more races, not Hispanic or Latino	Hispanic or Latino[1]	Under 18 years old	Age 18 to 64 years old	Age 65 years and older	Total occupied housing units	Percent owner occupied	High school diploma or less	Bachelor's degree or more
	1	2	3	4	5	6	7	8	9	10	11	12	13	14	15	16
PENNSYLVANIA—Con.																
Franklin township (Beaver)	4,052	4,000	-1.3	4,036	98.6	0.3	1.1	0.0	0.0	20.3	61.2	18.6	1,590	81.6	56.7	23.5
Franklin township (Bradford)	723	720	-0.4	709	100.0	0.0	0.0	0.0	0.0	21.8	67.4	10.7	271	72.0	68.6	4.8
Franklin township (Butler)	2,620	2,676	2.1	2,661	97.0	0.0	0.5	1.2	1.2	16.5	59.7	23.8	1,174	89.4	44.2	23.4
Franklin borough & MCD (Cambria)	323	308	-4.6	293	84.0	14.7	0.0	1.4	0.0	16.4	63.3	20.5	135	76.3	64.4	20.7
Franklin township (Carbon)	4,262	4,193	-1.6	4,228	95.0	1.8	0.0	0.0	3.2	17.6	66.5	15.9	1,579	87.7	59.5	16.0
Franklin township (Chester)	4,352	4,468	2.7	4,415	89.7	0.3	1.4	1.6	7.0	28.4	62.7	8.9	1,459	89.4	23.6	51.2
Franklin township (Columbia)	596	588	-1.3	552	96.9	0.0	0.0	0.0	3.1	19.5	65.6	14.9	233	88.4	57.5	17.2
Franklin township (Erie)	1,633	1,636	0.2	1,573	96.6	0.2	1.1	0.7	1.4	18.6	65.6	15.7	611	92.8	48.3	27.7
Franklin township (Fayette)	2,528	2,478	-2.0	2,576	94.5	0.6	0.0	4.1	0.8	19.6	58.3	21.9	941	92.1	62.8	14.0
Franklin township (Greene)	7,278	7,126	-2.1	7,156	68.1	23.2	0.2	3.3	5.2	9.4	75.0	15.6	1,719	69.7	47.2	24.3
Franklin township (Huntingdon)	466	467	0.2	493	92.1	0.0	0.0	0.0	7.9	21.9	63.3	14.8	202	78.7	42.6	28.2
Franklin township (Luzerne)	1,757	1,757	0.0	1,801	96.1	0.5	0.6	1.5	1.3	21.0	61.5	17.6	710	91.4	41.0	24.8
Franklin township (Lycoming)	933	952	2.0	966	99.1	0.0	0.0	0.9	0.0	23.3	62.3	14.5	371	81.7	59.8	19.7
Franklin township (Snyder)	2,259	2,277	0.8	1,997	99.5	0.2	0.0	0.3	0.0	15.5	66.4	18.5	874	80.7	72.8	7.2
Franklin township (Susquehanna)	936	908	-3.0	918	97.9	0.0	0.9	0.7	0.5	20.9	60.1	19.0	354	84.2	59.6	17.2
Franklin city & MCD (Venango)	6,545	6,350	-3.0	6,448	93.0	1.6	0.0	1.9	3.5	20.6	60.3	19.1	2,839	57.4	52.1	22.8
Franklin township (York)	4,678	4,885	4.4	4,834	94.5	0.0	0.7	0.7	4.0	19.0	67.5	13.5	1,964	79.9	45.5	25.6
Franklin Park borough & MCD (Allegheny)	13,467	14,269	6.0	13,882	86.2	1.2	9.4	2.4	0.7	28.9	59.1	12.1	4,807	95.7	14.2	70.4
Franklintown borough & MCD (York)	486	487	0.2	498	82.1	1.8	0.0	2.0	14.1	27.9	65.3	6.6	201	47.3	46.3	12.9
Frankstown township (Blair)	7,381	7,435	0.7	7,409	97.3	0.0	1.3	0.6	0.8	20.9	61.7	17.4	2,810	88.0	38.4	41.7
Frazer township (Allegheny)	1,157	1,156	-0.1	1,111	98.2	0.0	0.6	1.2	0.0	18.1	63.4	18.5	487	89.7	63.2	12.3
Fredericksburg CDP (Crawford)	733	NA	NA	545	100.0	0.0	0.0	0.0	0.0	9.0	52.9	38.2	298	70.1	49.3	8.1
Fredericksburg CDP (Lebanon)	1,357	NA	NA	1,475	94.8	0.7	1.7	1.3	1.4	21.9	58.1	19.9	607	82.7	61.3	18.9
Fredericktown CDP	403	NA	NA	505	96.4	0.0	0.0	0.0	3.6	20.4	69.0	10.7	188	76.6	68.1	16.5
Fredonia borough & MCD (Mercer)	502	487	-3.0	440	92.0	0.0	0.0	1.1	6.8	20.0	64.1	15.9	198	70.7	74.7	1.0
Freeburg borough & MCD (Snyder)	575	574	-0.2	632	91.3	0.0	0.0	0.0	8.7	19.6	65.3	15.0	262	69.1	51.5	12.6
Freedom township (Adams)	831	835	0.5	831	97.7	0.2	0.0	0.4	1.7	15.3	62.4	22.1	349	83.4	41.0	38.7
Freedom borough & MCD (Beaver)	1,569	1,537	-2.0	1,634	87.1	6.3	0.6	3.7	2.3	27.6	58.5	13.9	639	68.7	51.2	9.1
Freedom township (Blair)	3,457	3,436	-0.6	3,445	98.8	0.8	0.0	0.3	0.2	21.8	62.0	16.1	1,383	77.7	60.8	12.9
Freehold township (Warren)	1,510	1,475	-2.3	1,425	97.1	0.1	0.0	0.1	2.7	33.0	50.8	16.1	480	84.6	66.9	7.1
Freeland borough & MCD (Luzerne)	3,531	3,472	-1.7	3,509	96.4	0.1	0.0	0.7	2.8	22.9	60.1	16.8	1,449	66.5	57.3	17.5
Freemansburg borough & MCD (Northampton)	2,636	2,624	-0.5	2,631	61.2	7.6	1.9	2.8	26.6	23.6	66.4	10.1	910	70.2	48.7	19.7
Freeport borough & MCD (Armstrong)	1,813	1,766	-2.6	1,796	98.6	0.0	0.0	0.3	1.1	24.5	61.4	14.4	772	55.8	45.6	18.5
Freeport township (Greene)	310	301	-2.9	273	99.3	0.0	0.7	0.0	0.0	22.3	64.5	13.2	104	70.2	68.3	16.3
French Creek township (Mercer)	771	758	-1.7	787	96.3	0.0	0.3	1.5	1.9	24.5	62.7	12.8	293	82.9	56.0	17.1
Frenchcreek township (Venango)	1,542	1,496	-3.0	1,538	99.0	0.0	0.0	0.3	0.7	16.1	65.6	18.4	672	82.3	64.4	15.6
Friedens CDP	1,523	NA	NA	1,684	97.9	0.0	0.5	1.6	0.0	23.2	63.0	13.9	643	89.1	69.8	13.4
Friedensburg CDP	858	NA	NA	765	96.6	0.0	0.0	3.4	0.0	7.9	65.0	27.2	396	65.2	77.0	11.6
Friendsville borough & MCD (Susquehanna)	111	107	-3.6	186	100.0	0.0	0.0	0.0	0.0	24.3	56.1	19.9	78	87.2	65.4	10.3
Frizzleburg CDP	602	NA	NA	478	91.2	1.5	0.0	7.3	0.0	3.6	78.4	18.0	278	89.6	82.0	7.6
Frystown CDP	380	NA	NA	137	100.0	0.0	0.0	0.0	0.0	20.4	79.5	0.0	57	77.2	100.0	0.0
Fullerton CDP	14,925	NA	NA	15,529	64.0	8.4	8.3	1.8	17.5	24.3	60.1	15.7	6,490	49.9	39.5	25.6
Fulton township (Lancaster)	3,074	3,136	2.0	3,114	96.0	0.0	0.0	0.3	3.8	27.3	57.5	15.3	1,059	71.9	76.6	10.2
Gaines township (Tioga)	542	549	1.3	693	94.9	0.0	0.0	4.3	0.7	21.0	62.2	16.6	276	77.2	59.1	11.6
Galeton borough & MCD (Potter)	1,150	1,133	-1.5	1,240	99.1	0.5	0.0	0.3	0.1	21.0	59.1	19.9	490	62.9	61.4	10.2
Gallagher township (Clinton)	384	387	0.8	326	97.5	0.0	1.2	1.2	0.0	16.9	59.8	23.3	130	89.2	57.7	18.5
Gallitzin borough & MCD (Cambria)	1,668	1,622	-2.8	1,616	96.8	0.5	0.0	0.6	2.2	22.6	62.9	14.4	682	75.1	68.5	10.3
Gallitzin township (Cambria)	1,324	1,296	-2.1	1,269	99.3	0.0	0.0	0.3	0.4	19.1	68.2	12.8	486	94.9	60.5	14.2
Gamble township (Lycoming)	756	761	0.7	793	99.6	0.0	0.0	0.4	0.0	19.7	65.9	14.5	309	95.5	50.5	19.7
Gap CDP	1,931	NA	NA	1,966	94.2	0.9	0.8	0.8	3.4	31.0	59.5	9.7	633	72.5	61.1	26.1
Garden View CDP	2,503	NA	NA	2,539	96.4	1.7	0.7	0.6	0.6	14.5	59.5	26.0	1,233	71.6	53.1	16.2
Gardners CDP	150	NA	NA	142	95.8	0.0	4.2	0.0	0.0	9.1	66.9	23.9	61	90.2	91.8	8.2

1 May be of any race.

Table A. All Places — **Population and Housing**

STATE City, town, township, borough, or CDP (county if applicable)	Population				Race and Hispanic or Latino origin (percent), 2010–2014					Age (percent), 2010–2014			Households, 2010–2014			
	2010 census total population	2014 estimated population	Percent change 2010–2014	ACS total population estimate 2010–2014	White alone, not Hispanic or Latino	Black alone, not Hispanic or Latino	Asian alone, not Hispanic or Latino	All other races or 2 or more races, not Hispanic or Latino	Hispanic or Latino[1]	Under 18 years old	Age 18 to 64 years old	Age 65 years and older	Total occupied housing units	Percent owner occupied	High school diploma or less	Bachelor's degree or more
	1	2	3	4	5	6	7	8	9	10	11	12	13	14	15	16
PENNSYLVANIA—Con.																
Garrett borough & MCD (Somerset)	456	441	-3.3	401	100.0	0.0	0.0	0.0	0.0	22.4	64.6	13.0	154	93.5	84.4	4.5
Gaskill township (Jefferson)	708	700	-1.1	793	97.7	0.5	0.0	1.3	0.5	25.9	59.8	14.4	263	79.5	59.7	17.5
Gastonville CDP	2,818	NA	NA	2,919	98.7	0.1	0.0	0.8	0.4	17.7	59.4	22.9	1,274	89.3	54.4	19.7
Geistown borough & MCD (Cambria)	2,467	2,390	-3.1	2,426	96.0	1.0	1.5	0.7	0.7	20.2	58.9	20.8	1,133	70.5	40.9	27.4
Genesee township (Potter)	799	787	-1.5	985	96.0	0.0	0.0	2.9	1.0	31.4	53.8	14.8	378	62.4	65.1	9.5
Geneva CDP	109	NA	NA	116	100.0	0.0	0.0	0.0	0.0	15.5	64.8	19.8	50	92.0	70.0	14.0
Georges township (Fayette)	6,618	6,478	-2.1	6,548	95.9	2.6	0.0	1.2	0.2	20.1	64.3	15.7	2,543	78.9	69.2	9.4
Georgetown borough & MCD (Beaver)	174	172	-1.1	155	94.8	0.0	0.0	3.9	1.3	30.3	52.3	17.4	64	81.3	37.5	20.3
Georgetown CDP (Lancaster)	1,022	NA	NA	965	99.4	0.0	0.0	0.0	0.6	33.6	54.1	12.3	294	72.4	78.2	13.6
Georgetown CDP (Luzerne)	1,640	NA	NA	1,671	88.6	0.2	0.0	0.0	11.2	20.2	64.5	15.4	640	65.6	44.7	16.4
German township (Fayette)	5,097	4,995	-2.0	5,048	95.3	4.0	0.0	0.2	0.6	20.7	61.6	17.5	1,999	79.5	53.3	14.5
Germany township (Adams)	2,700	2,711	0.4	2,703	99.3	0.0	0.7	0.0	0.0	23.7	62.3	14.2	966	91.9	53.9	17.7
Gettysburg borough & MCD (Adams)	7,605	7,633	0.4	7,632	74.2	6.9	2.8	4.8	11.3	17.7	70.6	11.6	2,235	38.5	46.9	30.1
Gibraltar CDP	680	NA	NA	560	88.0	0.0	12.0	0.0	0.0	4.3	80.4	15.4	243	96.7	57.6	10.7
Gibson township (Cameron)	164	154	-6.1	127	98.4	0.0	0.0	1.6	0.0	2.4	68.6	29.1	67	91.0	71.6	3.0
Gibson township (Susquehanna)	1,224	1,199	-2.0	988	92.2	2.5	1.0	4.1	0.1	20.2	62.0	17.8	393	82.4	50.9	16.8
Gibsonia CDP	2,733	NA	NA	2,987	94.1	0.6	3.5	0.0	1.7	26.1	59.4	14.5	1,075	90.4	26.7	31.9
Gilberton borough & MCD (Schuylkill)	768	754	-1.8	749	97.2	0.0	0.0	0.3	2.5	22.3	61.9	15.8	287	85.7	70.4	4.9
Gilbertsville CDP	4,832	NA	NA	4,780	96.4	1.3	0.0	1.2	1.2	20.9	60.9	18.0	1,902	77.0	46.3	26.0
Gilmore township (Greene)	260	247	-5.0	247	98.8	0.0	0.0	0.8	0.4	21.0	67.1	11.7	101	76.2	74.3	9.9
Gilpin township (Armstrong)	2,506	2,463	-1.7	2,476	98.4	0.1	0.2	1.0	0.3	17.9	60.1	22.1	1,052	90.5	58.6	19.6
Girard township (Clearfield)	534	522	-2.2	525	98.9	0.0	0.0	0.0	1.1	16.6	69.9	13.5	209	91.4	77.0	5.7
Girard borough & MCD (Erie)	3,104	3,041	-2.0	3,078	95.9	1.4	1.1	1.6	0.0	20.9	61.4	17.6	1,297	66.4	53.3	23.9
Girard township (Erie)	5,102	5,011	-1.8	5,068	99.3	0.0	0.0	0.2	0.6	20.4	62.2	17.2	1,962	85.4	60.7	19.3
Girardville borough & MCD (Schuylkill)	1,519	1,490	-1.9	1,356	98.5	0.0	0.0	0.5	1.0	21.3	60.6	18.0	558	80.1	71.3	8.8
Glade township (Warren)	2,308	2,252	-2.4	2,313	98.4	0.0	0.8	0.3	0.5	18.9	58.1	22.8	978	76.5	55.8	18.9
Glasgow borough & MCD (Beaver)	60	59	-1.7	63	95.2	0.0	0.0	4.8	0.0	25.4	58.6	15.9	23	82.6	60.9	8.7
Glassport borough & MCD (Allegheny)	4,483	4,444	-0.9	4,485	95.2	1.4	0.6	2.2	0.4	19.6	63.7	16.6	1,967	63.1	55.3	15.7
Glenburn CDP	953	NA	NA	1,058	90.3	0.0	0.9	1.9	7.0	32.4	55.6	11.9	365	95.1	18.9	58.1
Glenburn township (Lackawanna)	1,246	1,246	0.0	1,306	91.2	0.0	0.7	1.7	6.4	28.6	56.9	14.5	473	93.9	24.7	50.7
Glen Campbell borough & MCD (Indiana)	245	238	-2.9	242	98.8	0.0	0.0	0.0	1.2	26.8	55.8	17.4	96	84.4	69.8	14.6
Glendon borough & MCD (Northampton)	440	441	0.2	340	88.2	2.4	2.1	5.3	2.1	14.7	70.3	15.0	131	79.4	53.4	13.7
Glenfield borough & MCD (Allegheny)	205	214	4.4	202	90.6	3.5	0.0	4.0	2.0	21.8	60.5	17.8	84	83.3	54.8	21.4
Glen Hope borough & MCD (Clearfield)	142	140	-1.4	150	100.0	0.0	0.0	0.0	0.0	12.6	62.0	25.3	63	92.1	71.4	3.2
Glen Lyon CDP	1,873	NA	NA	1,719	98.0	0.0	0.0	0.0	2.0	24.4	62.6	12.9	729	47.6	74.5	2.3
Glenolden borough & MCD (Delaware)	7,153	7,174	0.3	7,150	81.9	8.4	2.6	5.0	2.1	20.0	64.5	15.5	2,943	65.1	46.4	23.7
Glen Osborne borough & MCD (Allegheny)	547	541	-1.1	563	95.4	1.4	0.0	3.2	0.0	23.3	57.4	19.2	215	96.7	17.7	64.2
Glen Rock borough & MCD (York)	2,026	2,019	-0.3	1,738	97.7	0.5	0.0	0.7	1.1	22.6	67.6	9.7	702	65.1	44.7	27.8
Glenshaw CDP	8,981	NA	NA	8,908	97.6	0.0	0.9	0.1	1.4	17.5	62.3	20.3	3,638	95.3	34.4	43.4
Glenside CDP	8,384	NA	NA	7,614	83.6	8.7	2.4	3.3	2.0	23.8	62.7	13.6	2,766	74.6	20.1	53.1
Gold Key Lake CDP	1,830	NA	NA	1,686	78.9	9.7	0.0	5.9	5.4	26.5	53.2	20.2	648	91.7	52.5	10.2
Goldsboro borough & MCD (York)	948	939	-0.9	953	94.8	0.3	0.5	3.9	0.5	28.6	60.2	11.0	335	88.4	40.6	20.9
Goodville CDP	482	NA	NA	554	85.6	0.0	0.0	0.0	14.4	46.2	48.5	5.2	147	32.0	82.3	8.2
Gordon borough & MCD (Schuylkill)	763	748	-2.0	841	97.7	0.0	0.0	0.0	2.3	28.7	59.7	11.5	332	83.1	52.4	20.2
Gordonville CDP	508	NA	NA	671	90.2	2.2	0.0	2.7	4.9	29.8	51.3	18.8	205	62.9	67.8	10.7
Goshen township (Clearfield)	435	433	-0.5	507	99.0	0.0	0.0	0.8	0.2	23.3	62.5	14.2	196	83.2	68.9	5.1
Gouglersville CDP	548	NA	NA	380	97.9	0.0	0.0	2.1	0.0	7.1	70.1	22.9	213	73.7	50.7	12.7
Gouldsboro CDP	890	NA	NA	658	98.6	0.0	0.0	0.0	1.4	18.2	57.2	24.6	299	81.3	55.9	19.4
Graceton CDP	257	NA	NA	238	100.0	0.0	0.0	0.0	0.0	31.5	58.0	10.5	117	70.9	61.5	0.0
Graham township (Clearfield)	1,383	1,364	-1.4	1,459	96.2	0.0	0.6	0.1	3.2	21.0	63.9	15.2	552	90.6	66.3	12.3
Grampian borough & MCD (Clearfield)	356	343	-3.7	412	96.1	1.7	0.0	2.2	0.0	31.8	56.4	11.9	144	72.9	59.7	15.3
Grant township (Indiana)	741	715	-3.5	686	97.7	0.0	0.6	0.0	1.7	22.1	63.6	14.3	279	83.2	60.9	9.3
Grantley CDP	3,628	NA	NA	3,742	83.2	6.3	1.1	2.0	7.5	14.6	75.9	9.4	719	82.1	13.2	65.8
Granville township (Bradford)	950	935	-1.6	932	97.1	0.9	0.1	0.4	1.5	20.7	56.6	22.7	351	80.1	61.5	16.8
Granville CDP	440	NA	NA	477	100.0	0.0	0.0	0.0	0.0	24.5	53.2	22.2	192	63.0	65.6	7.8

1 May be of any race.

Table A. All Places — **Population and Housing**

STATE City, town, township, borough, or CDP (county if applicable)	2010 census total population	2014 estimated population	Percent change 2010–2014	ACS total population estimate 2010–2014	White alone, not Hispanic or Latino	Black alone, not Hispanic or Latino	Asian alone, not Hispanic or Latino	All other races or 2 or more races, not Hispanic or Latino	Hispanic or Latino[1]	Under 18 years old	Age 18 to 64 years old	Age 65 years and older	Total occupied housing units	Percent owner occupied	High school diploma or less	Bachelor's degree or more
	1	2	3	4	5	6	7	8	9	10	11	12	13	14	15	16
PENNSYLVANIA—Con.																
Granville township (Mifflin)	5,103	5,069	-0.7	5,093	99.3	0.3	0.0	0.0	0.4	16.8	61.5	21.8	2,261	71.3	69.0	10.2
Grapeville CDP	538	NA	NA	714	100.0	0.0	0.0	0.0	0.0	37.5	57.0	5.5	239	69.9	54.4	12.1
Grassflat CDP	511	NA	NA	477	90.6	0.0	0.0	2.7	6.7	19.3	62.0	18.7	175	97.1	61.7	8.6
Gratz borough & MCD (Dauphin)	763	755	-1.0	834	94.2	0.0	0.0	4.8	1.0	28.1	52.9	18.9	330	71.8	70.9	7.9
Gray township (Greene)	219	219	0.0	226	100.0	0.0	0.0	0.0	0.0	28.8	59.3	11.9	87	60.9	72.4	6.9
Grazierville CDP	665	NA	NA	603	100.0	0.0	0.0	0.0	0.0	8.3	80.6	11.1	281	80.8	70.8	13.5
Great Bend borough & MCD (Susquehanna)	734	700	-4.6	749	100.0	0.0	0.0	0.0	0.0	12.5	60.2	27.1	362	62.2	71.3	11.9
Great Bend township (Susquehanna)	1,951	1,877	-3.8	2,038	100.0	0.0	0.0	0.0	0.0	20.8	66.0	13.2	869	70.2	58.7	10.4
Green township (Forest)	522	502	-3.8	274	95.6	0.0	2.2	0.0	2.2	9.8	55.3	34.7	124	89.5	75.8	11.3
Green township (Indiana)	3,839	3,700	-3.6	3,775	94.0	2.0	0.0	2.2	1.7	20.9	62.8	16.3	1,496	84.4	71.1	8.6
Greencastle borough & MCD (Franklin)	3,996	4,042	1.2	4,023	88.2	9.1	0.0	1.7	1.0	23.4	56.7	19.9	1,819	56.1	50.0	25.2
Greene township (Beaver)	2,356	2,380	1.0	2,394	91.1	1.7	0.0	5.1	2.2	26.8	60.3	12.9	861	91.8	42.9	12.4
Greene township (Clinton)	1,695	1,728	1.9	1,797	97.7	0.7	0.0	0.6	1.1	33.9	57.6	8.6	532	83.1	56.0	15.2
Greene township (Erie)	4,706	4,658	-1.0	4,688	97.2	0.9	0.2	0.5	1.2	20.2	63.6	16.2	1,809	92.0	49.1	24.0
Greene township (Franklin)	16,700	17,401	4.2	17,184	90.8	4.0	0.9	1.0	3.3	23.0	57.6	19.4	6,615	80.5	48.4	27.3
Greene township (Greene)	445	427	-4.0	588	99.7	0.0	0.0	0.3	0.0	24.0	65.8	10.2	228	76.8	57.0	17.1
Greene township (Mercer)	1,091	1,073	-1.6	1,295	98.6	0.0	0.0	0.8	0.5	21.2	63.4	15.4	453	90.7	53.6	13.2
Greene township (Pike)	3,947	3,852	-2.4	3,911	94.5	0.2	1.5	0.2	3.6	14.5	61.7	23.7	1,575	83.2	51.5	23.5
Greenfield township (Blair)	4,161	4,107	-1.3	4,142	98.2	1.1	0.0	0.5	0.2	23.1	62.3	14.4	1,592	72.3	71.3	9.7
Greenfield township (Erie)	1,933	1,937	0.2	1,869	97.8	0.4	0.0	1.1	0.7	21.1	66.1	12.8	743	89.1	61.6	12.5
Greenfield township (Lackawanna)	2,113	2,072	-1.9	2,286	99.7	0.0	0.0	0.3	0.0	19.5	61.9	18.4	872	88.5	51.4	27.5
Greenfields CDP	1,170	NA	NA	1,033	77.3	0.0	0.0	5.5	17.2	9.5	66.1	24.4	445	73.7	42.7	30.6
Green Hills borough & MCD (Washington)	29	29	0.0	47	100.0	0.0	0.0	0.0	0.0	25.6	61.8	12.8	17	88.2	5.9	11.8
Green Lane borough & MCD (Montgomery)	508	506	-0.4	431	98.1	0.0	0.0	0.0	1.9	25.5	63.6	10.7	175	66.9	52.0	27.4
Greenock CDP	2,195	NA	NA	1,852	98.2	0.0	0.0	0.4	1.4	18.1	54.1	27.7	854	78.0	53.0	13.7
Greensboro borough & MCD (Greene)	260	258	-0.8	216	99.5	0.5	0.0	0.0	0.0	14.8	70.0	15.3	94	86.2	47.9	24.5
Greensburg city & MCD (Westmoreland)	14,892	14,571	-2.2	14,726	87.4	5.1	1.4	4.1	2.0	16.7	63.7	19.7	6,823	48.1	38.9	32.0
Greens Landing CDP	894	NA	NA	839	98.5	0.0	0.0	1.5	0.0	25.4	60.6	14.1	278	91.4	62.2	12.9
Green Tree borough & MCD (Allegheny)	4,432	4,991	12.6	4,542	93.1	2.0	4.7	0.2	0.0	15.6	64.1	20.2	1,967	91.9	24.4	45.4
Greenville borough & MCD (Mercer)	5,955	5,870	-1.4	5,919	94.1	2.9	0.2	0.9	1.8	21.5	64.5	13.9	2,232	55.1	50.2	21.6
Greenville township (Somerset)	668	658	-1.5	782	100.0	0.0	0.0	0.0	0.0	29.4	58.2	12.3	266	78.9	62.4	17.3
Greenwich township (Berks)	3,725	3,721	-0.1	3,729	96.3	0.8	0.0	0.0	2.9	23.3	62.2	14.6	1,490	77.1	56.8	22.6
Greenwood CDP	2,458	NA	NA	2,506	100.0	0.0	0.0	0.0	0.0	17.4	69.4	13.3	1,078	65.0	62.4	5.4
Greenwood township (Clearfield)	372	370	-0.5	361	100.0	0.0	0.0	0.0	0.0	22.7	58.5	18.8	142	83.8	72.5	9.2
Greenwood township (Columbia)	1,952	1,931	-1.1	2,076	97.8	0.0	0.0	0.1	2.1	21.7	62.2	16.0	813	79.7	60.5	20.9
Greenwood township (Crawford)	1,457	1,435	-1.5	1,503	98.9	0.1	0.3	0.7	0.0	17.9	66.6	15.6	572	90.2	66.6	13.5
Greenwood township (Juniata)	619	621	0.3	681	94.4	0.6	0.0	2.2	2.8	23.9	58.3	17.9	237	89.5	67.5	9.7
Greenwood township (Perry)	994	990	-0.4	886	98.6	0.3	0.5	0.2	0.3	17.7	65.3	16.9	368	90.8	58.4	17.9
Gregg township (Centre)	2,405	2,395	-0.4	3,107	98.2	0.4	0.7	0.1	0.6	28.3	58.8	12.9	1,065	74.2	62.2	20.4
Gregg township (Union)	4,984	4,850	-2.7	4,916	42.7	30.8	0.7	4.3	21.4	5.8	86.9	7.4	535	70.8	66.9	12.0
Grier City CDP	241	NA	NA	360	100.0	0.0	0.0	0.0	0.0	36.1	58.6	5.3	111	100.0	8.1	30.6
Grill CDP	1,468	NA	NA	1,470	79.9	2.4	4.4	9.3	3.9	23.3	60.7	16.0	586	90.4	35.7	37.4
Grindstone CDP	498	NA	NA	488	92.6	1.6	0.0	5.3	0.4	31.8	49.6	18.9	193	87.0	75.6	3.1
Grove township (Cameron)	183	173	-5.5	77	94.8	0.0	0.0	5.2	0.0	29.9	70.1	17.4	46	95.7	76.1	17.4
Grove City borough & MCD (Mercer)	8,321	8,215	-1.3	8,242	94.9	1.0	1.5	1.5	1.1	15.2	71.2	13.7	2,683	54.8	36.2	34.8
Grugan township (Clinton)	51	52	2.0	91	94.5	0.0	0.0	5.5	0.0	34.1	42.9	23.1	37	75.7	40.5	13.5
Guilford CDP	2,138	NA	NA	2,257	73.4	17.7	4.1	0.0	4.8	24.2	61.0	15.0	835	89.6	47.1	44.1
Guilford township (Franklin)	14,531	14,700	1.2	14,619	90.7	4.1	2.1	1.0	2.1	19.3	56.9	23.9	5,821	80.4	48.1	30.9
Gulich township (Clearfield)	1,235	1,229	-0.5	1,181	99.9	0.0	0.0	0.1	0.0	18.0	59.2	22.7	491	86.2	67.4	9.2
Guys Mills CDP	124	NA	NA	130	100.0	0.0	0.0	0.0	0.0	17.7	79.2	3.1	25	100.0	44.0	16.0
Haines township (Centre)	1,564	1,561	-0.2	1,650	99.8	0.0	0.0	0.0	0.2	26.2	58.9	15.2	563	81.0	69.6	13.1
Halfmoon township (Centre)	2,667	2,708	1.5	2,700	95.9	0.6	0.4	2.0	1.2	26.7	65.6	7.8	924	91.2	19.5	62.6
Halfway House CDP	2,881	NA	NA	2,996	87.0	7.5	0.8	0.3	4.3	28.4	62.4	9.1	990	89.2	35.6	41.0
Halifax borough & MCD (Dauphin)	841	833	-1.0	910	93.1	3.3	1.0	1.4	1.2	28.1	60.4	11.5	358	57.0	71.8	7.0
Halifax township (Dauphin)	3,483	3,542	1.7	3,551	97.8	0.0	0.6	1.0	0.5	17.7	62.4	19.8	1,534	75.0	70.7	12.6
Hallam borough & MCD (York)	2,681	2,664	-0.6	2,674	93.5	1.6	0.7	1.9	2.2	16.7	69.9	13.3	1,322	52.1	43.9	20.3
Hallstead borough & MCD (Susquehanna)	1,304	1,257	-3.6	1,254	96.7	1.8	0.0	0.1	1.4	21.1	59.2	19.5	558	55.2	65.8	10.2
Hamburg borough & MCD (Berks)	4,289	4,338	1.1	4,293	96.2	0.2	0.3	0.0	3.4	16.8	64.0	19.1	1,960	65.4	60.6	13.6

1 May be of any race.

Table A. All Places — **Population and Housing**

	Population				Race and Hispanic or Latino origin (percent), 2010–2014					Age (percent), 2010–2014			Households, 2010–2014			
STATE City, town, township, borough, or CDP (county if applicable)	2010 census total population	2014 estimated population	Percent change 2010–2014	ACS total population estimate 2010–2014	White alone, not Hispanic or Latino	Black alone, not Hispanic or Latino	Asian alone, not Hispanic or Latino	All other races or 2 or more races, not Hispanic or Latino	Hispanic or Latino[1]	Under 18 years old	Age 18 to 64 years old	Age 65 years and older	Total occupied housing units	Percent owner occupied	High school diploma or less	Bachelor's degree or more
	1	2	3	4	5	6	7	8	9	10	11	12	13	14	15	16

PENNSYLVANIA—Con.

	1	2	3	4	5	6	7	8	9	10	11	12	13	14	15	16
Hamilton township (Adams)	2,530	2,542	0.5	2,538	90.7	5.1	0.0	0.2	4.1	25.3	60.5	14.2	897	92.9	49.2	25.4
Hamilton township (Franklin)	10,791	11,054	2.4	10,962	92.9	1.1	0.4	1.2	4.4	22.8	61.5	15.8	4,268	77.7	50.1	14.1
Hamilton township (McKean)	543	528	-2.8	521	99.0	0.0	0.0	0.2	0.8	20.1	59.5	20.3	259	88.0	63.7	12.7
Hamilton township (Monroe)	9,087	8,840	-2.7	8,958	90.5	3.6	0.4	2.4	3.1	20.5	62.5	17.2	3,017	85.4	43.8	28.4
Hamilton township (Tioga)	499	507	1.6	680	97.9	0.0	1.2	0.9	0.0	32.4	58.9	8.8	230	71.3	57.0	10.9
Hamiltonban township (Adams)	2,372	2,375	0.1	2,310	95.3	0.8	0.5	2.0	1.4	15.9	61.7	22.4	911	86.3	60.7	20.9
Hamlin township (McKean)	734	714	-2.7	659	99.4	0.0	0.0	0.6	0.0	18.2	59.9	21.9	273	86.8	68.9	11.0
Hampden township (Cumberland)	27,647	28,940	4.7	28,291	86.4	1.5	8.0	1.9	2.3	22.3	61.3	16.5	11,871	78.0	26.0	50.8
Hampton CDP	632	NA	NA	656	96.2	0.0	0.0	0.0	3.8	29.2	63.6	7.3	209	61.7	74.2	4.8
Hampton township (Allegheny)	18,363	18,478	0.6	18,444	95.5	0.4	2.6	0.5	1.0	23.0	59.9	17.1	7,231	86.4	25.0	49.2
Hannasville CDP	176	NA	NA	163	99.4	0.0	0.0	0.6	0.0	21.4	58.1	20.2	66	75.8	74.2	15.2
Hanover township (Beaver)	3,690	3,650	-1.1	3,674	94.4	0.7	0.5	2.3	2.1	21.1	64.6	14.3	1,392	89.4	48.6	18.1
Hanover township (Lehigh)	1,571	1,581	0.6	1,701	81.1	4.8	3.5	2.3	8.3	20.6	60.8	18.5	758	48.0	44.9	25.1
Hanover township (Luzerne)	11,076	10,976	-0.9	11,059	94.9	1.5	0.3	1.3	2.1	18.4	62.3	19.4	4,876	67.9	50.9	21.1
Hanover township (Northampton)	10,866	11,380	4.7	11,121	78.2	2.4	6.3	2.1	11.0	21.4	56.4	22.1	4,156	81.6	28.8	47.9
Hanover township (Washington)	2,673	2,645	-1.0	2,664	96.8	0.3	0.0	2.3	0.6	20.4	64.0	15.5	1,082	84.8	60.5	14.0
Hanover borough & MCD (York)	15,277	15,454	1.2	15,365	87.6	1.2	1.4	1.4	8.4	20.9	60.4	18.9	6,645	54.6	57.0	16.7
Harborcreek township (Erie)	17,234	17,578	2.0	17,336	93.9	1.8	1.1	1.1	2.1	18.5	65.8	15.7	5,944	79.4	42.4	28.3
Harford township (Susquehanna)	1,427	1,383	-3.1	1,464	92.9	2.0	0.0	0.3	4.8	17.0	56.6	26.2	602	79.2	57.5	18.3
Harleigh CDP	1,104	NA	NA	936	100.0	0.0	0.0	0.0	0.0	14.9	44.5	40.7	375	95.7	41.9	31.5
Harleysville CDP	9,286	NA	NA	9,348	87.2	5.0	5.2	1.6	1.0	23.3	60.8	15.9	3,549	66.4	28.5	47.9
Harmar township (Allegheny)	2,921	3,082	5.5	2,991	96.2	1.4	1.4	0.5	0.5	14.3	52.2	33.4	1,325	78.1	39.5	30.7
Harmonsburg CDP	401	NA	NA	152	100.0	0.0	0.0	0.0	0.0	11.2	54.6	34.2	78	100.0	55.1	5.1
Harmony township (Beaver)	3,197	3,130	-2.1	3,169	97.4	1.8	0.0	0.0	0.8	19.0	63.9	17.2	1,350	82.7	45.1	24.1
Harmony borough & MCD (Butler)	890	868	-2.5	797	98.5	0.0	0.0	1.5	0.0	21.6	59.7	18.6	338	77.2	34.9	34.9
Harmony township (Forest)	666	639	-4.1	469	100.0	0.0	0.0	0.0	0.0	14.9	56.3	28.8	228	91.7	67.1	5.3
Harmony township (Susquehanna)	525	508	-3.2	419	91.4	1.7	0.0	1.2	5.7	21.0	62.0	16.9	156	87.2	56.4	16.7
Harris township (Centre)	4,873	5,198	6.7	5,041	92.1	0.9	1.5	2.4	3.0	24.8	55.8	19.4	1,940	74.3	19.5	56.9
Harrisburg city & MCD (Dauphin)	49,528	49,082	-0.9	49,297	24.8	47.9	4.1	3.7	19.5	27.5	62.9	9.6	20,346	38.6	53.3	21.0
Harrison township (Allegheny)	10,461	10,472	0.1	10,462	93.3	2.4	0.3	3.5	0.4	18.2	64.1	17.6	4,376	68.2	47.1	25.0
Harrison township (Bedford)	972	942	-3.1	878	96.6	0.0	0.0	1.6	1.8	17.7	54.8	27.3	380	75.3	58.4	15.3
Harrison township (Potter)	1,037	1,023	-1.4	1,284	95.3	1.6	0.1	0.9	2.1	23.7	60.4	16.0	478	81.2	67.6	7.9
Harrison City CDP	134	NA	NA	144	100.0	0.0	0.0	0.0	0.0	0.0	63.2	36.8	102	43.1	40.2	20.6
Harrisville borough & MCD (Butler)	897	885	-1.3	953	96.3	2.1	0.0	1.6	0.0	21.0	61.7	17.5	341	71.3	49.0	22.3
Hartleton borough & MCD (Union)	285	285	0.0	281	94.3	3.6	0.0	2.1	0.0	31.6	57.6	10.7	92	81.5	75.0	5.4
Hartley township (Union)	1,820	1,824	0.2	1,860	96.5	0.0	0.4	0.2	2.9	25.3	55.6	19.2	703	83.2	70.4	10.5
Hartstown CDP	201	NA	NA	175	92.6	4.6	0.0	0.0	2.9	29.7	52.0	18.3	70	94.3	60.0	24.3
Harveys Lake borough & MCD (Luzerne)	2,792	2,777	-0.5	2,795	92.5	0.0	1.4	5.2	0.8	15.4	64.9	19.6	1,245	82.5	42.8	27.1
Harwick CDP	899	NA	NA	935	99.1	0.0	0.0	0.9	0.0	11.2	63.5	25.2	485	69.1	47.0	21.0
Hasson Heights CDP	1,351	NA	NA	1,390	98.1	0.4	0.7	0.4	0.4	18.8	63.4	17.9	592	85.3	48.8	24.2
Hastings borough & MCD (Cambria)	1,278	1,238	-3.1	1,284	99.6	0.0	0.0	0.0	0.4	21.0	58.3	20.6	562	74.7	56.4	18.3
Hatboro borough & MCD (Montgomery)	7,360	7,426	0.9	7,403	85.5	1.2	3.4	1.5	8.4	21.2	64.9	13.9	2,960	63.1	30.9	33.2
Hatfield borough & MCD (Montgomery)	3,290	3,314	0.7	3,299	62.7	1.7	23.7	1.6	10.3	18.7	71.3	10.0	1,303	51.2	43.0	31.3
Hatfield township (Montgomery)	17,249	17,589	2.0	17,460	69.8	5.4	17.3	2.4	5.1	20.5	64.6	14.9	6,571	65.2	35.6	39.6
Haverford township (Delaware)	48,484	48,909	0.9	48,698	90.4	2.7	4.1	1.5	1.3	23.2	60.7	15.9	17,577	85.1	21.2	58.5
Haverford College CDP	1,331	NA	NA	1,311	70.6	12.7	8.7	4.6	3.5	5.2	93.3	1.4	74	13.5	0.0	100.0
Hawk Run CDP	534	NA	NA	632	100.0	0.0	0.0	0.0	0.0	24.3	52.3	23.4	241	84.2	77.2	4.6
Hawley borough & MCD (Wayne)	1,212	1,163	-4.0	1,282	92.4	2.3	0.0	0.0	5.4	18.3	66.8	14.9	526	53.8	52.5	20.7
Hawthorn borough & MCD (Clarion)	494	479	-3.0	540	99.4	0.0	0.0	0.6	0.0	29.7	52.5	17.6	195	68.2	76.9	5.1
Haycock township (Bucks)	2,225	2,219	-0.3	1,999	98.2	0.0	0.5	0.0	1.3	16.5	66.4	17.4	821	84.9	39.0	30.5
Hayfield township (Crawford)	2,944	2,893	-1.7	2,914	98.4	0.9	0.6	0.1	0.0	17.2	63.9	18.7	1,278	85.6	61.7	19.3
Haysville borough & MCD (Allegheny)	70	70	0.0	87	90.8	0.0	0.0	2.3	6.9	11.5	57.3	31.0	43	74.4	32.6	20.9
Hazle township (Luzerne)	9,544	9,563	0.2	9,568	86.6	0.3	0.1	0.1	12.8	19.2	58.9	22.1	3,942	73.2	60.1	14.9
Hazleton city & MCD (Luzerne)	25,340	24,932	-1.6	25,179	49.6	2.4	0.4	1.3	46.2	26.1	58.8	15.0	9,068	50.7	63.1	11.1

1 May be of any race.

Table A. All Places — **Population and Housing**

STATE City, town, township, borough, or CDP (county if applicable)	2010 census total population	2014 estimated population	Percent change 2010–2014	ACS total population estimate 2010–2014	White alone, not Hispanic or Latino	Black alone, not Hispanic or Latino	Asian alone, not Hispanic or Latino	All other races or 2 or more races, not Hispanic or Latino	Hispanic or Latino[1]	Under 18 years old	Age 18 to 64 years old	Age 65 years and older	Total occupied housing units	Percent owner occupied	High school diploma or less	Bachelor's degree or more
	1	2	3	4	5	6	7	8	9	10	11	12	13	14	15	16
PENNSYLVANIA—Con.																
Heath township (Jefferson)	124	122	-1.6	135	98.5	0.0	0.0	1.5	0.0	8.2	55.5	36.3	79	84.8	62.0	16.5
Hebron CDP	1,305	NA	NA	1,037	84.6	2.9	0.5	0.9	11.2	13.9	50.7	35.4	203	57.1	71.4	2.5
Hebron township (Potter)	589	586	-0.5	714	98.2	1.3	0.0	0.6	0.0	31.8	49.5	18.8	253	85.0	58.1	13.8
Heckscherville CDP	220	NA	NA	154	100.0	0.0	0.0	0.0	0.0	14.3	66.2	19.5	60	100.0	61.7	11.7
Hector township (Potter)	386	382	-1.0	429	93.5	0.0	0.0	1.2	5.4	31.2	49.1	19.8	159	81.1	69.8	12.6
Hegins CDP	812	NA	NA	821	100.0	0.0	0.0	0.0	0.0	18.9	61.8	19.4	372	76.3	54.0	15.6
Hegins township (Schuylkill)	3,516	3,484	-0.9	3,504	97.9	0.0	0.2	1.7	0.3	19.0	62.7	18.3	1,456	75.8	63.6	14.0
Heidelberg borough & MCD (Allegheny)	1,244	1,238	-0.5	1,321	96.3	0.9	0.0	0.0	2.8	15.6	66.8	17.5	625	63.4	60.8	17.6
Heidelberg township (Berks)	1,722	1,730	0.5	1,806	92.7	3.0	1.9	0.3	2.1	21.0	60.4	18.4	628	86.5	48.9	22.9
Heidelberg township (Lebanon)	4,069	4,148	1.9	4,105	95.1	4.1	0.0	0.1	0.6	30.2	52.2	17.6	1,381	82.7	75.2	13.6
Heidelberg township (Lehigh)	3,416	3,468	1.5	3,453	95.3	0.0	0.0	0.6	4.0	24.3	61.5	14.2	1,291	87.2	41.9	24.4
Heidelberg township (York)	3,078	3,072	-0.2	3,075	99.3	0.3	0.4	0.0	0.0	21.5	62.0	16.7	1,100	85.5	60.5	21.8
Heidlersburg CDP	707	NA	NA	680	85.9	0.0	0.0	1.9	12.2	26.0	62.0	12.1	253	85.8	44.7	9.5
Heilwood CDP	711	NA	NA	607	99.0	0.8	0.0	0.0	0.2	15.6	64.1	20.3	243	85.6	80.2	6.2
Hellam township (York)	6,027	6,002	-0.4	6,006	97.1	0.3	0.2	1.0	1.4	19.5	62.3	18.4	2,608	78.1	52.5	20.2
Hellertown borough & MCD (Northampton)	5,898	5,858	-0.7	5,881	93.6	0.3	0.4	0.5	5.2	20.5	62.4	17.0	2,390	70.0	44.2	24.6
Hemlock township (Columbia)	2,249	2,272	1.0	2,244	94.9	0.1	1.3	0.9	2.7	25.0	58.3	16.8	903	86.0	47.1	31.7
Hemlock Farms CDP	3,271	NA	NA	3,448	84.3	5.4	0.3	1.0	9.0	19.1	54.0	26.9	1,255	85.9	30.8	29.6
Hempfield township (Mercer)	3,741	3,733	-0.2	3,753	97.0	0.0	0.0	1.1	1.7	17.8	52.1	30.1	1,621	80.9	48.6	36.0
Hempfield township (Westmoreland)	43,247	41,733	-3.5	42,605	94.9	2.3	0.7	1.0	1.1	17.6	61.8	20.4	16,855	81.4	38.2	34.6
Henderson township (Huntingdon)	928	908	-2.2	942	98.1	0.0	1.7	0.2	0.0	18.6	58.6	22.6	396	81.1	77.0	9.1
Henderson township (Jefferson)	1,816	1,791	-1.4	1,781	99.6	0.0	0.0	0.4	0.0	32.5	54.0	13.5	570	92.5	78.1	7.2
Hendersonville CDP	325	NA	NA	327	98.2	1.8	0.0	0.0	0.0	35.8	55.7	8.6	122	66.4	22.1	33.6
Henry Clay township (Fayette)	2,066	2,029	-1.8	1,581	100.0	0.0	0.0	0.0	0.0	15.7	66.4	17.8	663	70.9	66.2	10.4
Hepburn township (Lycoming)	2,762	2,761	0.0	2,767	93.1	0.2	3.3	1.0	2.3	16.4	64.7	18.9	1,078	91.9	51.8	21.2
Hereford CDP	930	NA	NA	709	75.6	0.0	0.0	0.0	24.4	10.3	64.8	24.8	322	97.8	63.4	4.7
Hereford township (Berks)	2,941	2,923	-0.6	2,929	93.8	0.0	0.0	0.0	6.2	19.6	59.8	20.6	1,072	89.4	50.0	20.0
Herminie CDP	789	NA	NA	836	98.7	0.0	0.0	0.0	1.3	25.9	67.8	6.2	311	70.1	72.0	19.3
Hermitage city & MCD (Mercer)	16,375	16,118	-1.6	16,237	93.5	3.2	0.3	1.3	1.8	18.5	56.9	24.6	7,088	73.4	38.5	32.4
Herndon borough & MCD (Northumberland)	324	314	-3.1	359	98.3	1.7	0.0	0.0	0.0	30.4	55.1	14.5	130	73.8	76.2	12.3
Herrick township (Bradford)	752	749	-0.4	620	92.7	0.3	0.0	0.5	6.5	21.9	58.7	19.4	244	87.3	65.6	14.3
Herrick township (Susquehanna)	716	700	-2.2	774	99.6	0.0	0.4	0.0	0.0	25.3	60.4	14.2	293	80.2	54.6	24.2
Hershey CDP	14,257	NA	NA	14,172	79.9	4.7	5.7	2.4	7.3	16.7	66.1	17.3	5,627	53.4	25.5	53.4
Hickory township (Forest)	558	536	-3.9	472	96.8	0.0	3.2	0.0	0.0	10.4	52.4	37.3	239	84.9	72.0	13.4
Hickory township (Lawrence)	2,470	2,438	-1.3	2,464	96.6	0.0	0.0	2.0	1.4	20.9	58.9	20.3	1,009	88.3	46.8	21.9
Hickory CDP	740	NA	NA	793	100.0	0.0	0.0	0.0	0.0	22.8	63.8	13.4	288	72.6	49.3	16.3
Hickory Hills CDP	562	NA	NA	621	92.4	1.9	0.0	4.2	1.4	22.1	72.7	5.3	246	74.4	61.4	10.2
Highland township (Adams)	943	947	0.4	917	91.7	2.6	0.0	3.5	2.2	19.9	59.0	21.2	365	90.4	36.7	45.2
Highland township (Chester)	1,272	1,286	1.1	1,272	91.5	2.9	0.4	1.4	3.8	22.3	59.4	18.3	483	75.6	59.4	21.3
Highland township (Clarion)	525	515	-1.9	509	100.0	0.0	0.0	0.0	0.0	14.6	64.4	21.0	225	90.7	59.6	20.4
Highland township (Elk)	492	484	-1.6	418	99.3	0.0	0.0	0.7	0.0	9.0	71.0	19.9	184	95.1	67.4	11.4
Highland Park CDP	1,380	NA	NA	1,289	95.6	0.0	0.0	0.0	4.4	23.1	38.4	38.5	532	77.6	63.3	24.8
Highspire borough & MCD (Dauphin)	2,399	2,378	-0.9	2,438	69.5	7.1	1.0	5.3	17.1	21.0	66.6	12.5	1,117	61.2	52.6	16.5
Hilldale CDP	1,246	NA	NA	939	95.8	0.0	4.2	0.0	0.0	5.0	57.1	37.7	476	91.4	27.3	26.3
Hiller CDP	1,155	NA	NA	1,080	96.5	3.5	0.0	0.0	0.0	10.1	65.2	24.7	480	76.7	73.5	12.5
Hillsgrove township (Sullivan)	287	287	0.0	206	99.5	0.0	0.0	0.0	0.5	19.4	56.3	24.3	83	89.2	63.9	14.5
Hilltown township (Bucks)	15,030	15,190	1.1	15,122	89.1	1.7	2.6	1.8	4.8	24.8	59.8	15.3	5,503	82.0	32.3	39.4
Hokendauqua CDP	3,378	NA	NA	3,368	86.6	3.0	6.2	2.6	1.7	18.8	61.6	19.6	1,414	80.1	40.7	29.0
Holiday Pocono CDP	476	NA	NA	538	81.6	0.0	0.0	0.0	18.4	18.6	66.3	15.2	234	81.2	43.2	14.1
Hollenback township (Luzerne)	1,195	1,200	0.4	1,145	96.8	0.5	0.0	1.3	1.4	20.6	62.8	16.6	444	83.1	57.7	20.9
Hollidaysburg borough & MCD (Blair)	5,790	5,779	-0.2	5,792	93.2	0.4	0.2	1.3	4.9	17.6	58.1	24.4	2,682	53.7	37.0	38.0
Homeacre-Lyndora CDP	6,906	NA	NA	6,966	95.8	1.2	0.1	2.0	0.9	18.9	59.6	21.5	3,119	69.1	44.0	24.2
Homer township (Potter)	433	424	-2.1	488	95.9	0.0	0.6	1.6	1.8	31.2	63.1	5.7	156	94.9	41.0	30.8
Homer City borough & MCD (Indiana)	1,704	1,656	-2.8	1,674	97.8	0.4	0.2	0.5	1.0	20.5	60.3	19.2	744	70.6	49.6	26.9
Homestead borough & MCD (Allegheny)	3,165	3,133	-1.0	3,157	25.2	70.6	1.3	2.9	0.0	24.8	57.7	17.6	1,472	40.0	52.6	15.8
Hometown CDP	1,349	NA	NA	1,395	93.4	0.0	1.7	1.6	3.2	20.5	56.3	23.3	581	97.1	36.3	39.9
Homewood borough & MCD (Beaver)	109	108	-0.9	107	100.0	0.0	0.0	0.0	0.0	5.6	68.1	26.2	57	87.7	57.9	15.8
Honesdale borough & MCD (Wayne)	4,476	4,269	-4.6	4,364	97.6	0.2	0.0	0.5	1.7	21.2	56.8	22.0	2,033	47.1	47.1	21.7
Honey Brook borough & MCD (Chester)	1,713	1,761	2.8	1,681	93.8	1.1	0.2	3.6	1.3	26.2	63.5	10.3	647	69.6	51.8	20.2

1 May be of any race.

Table A. All Places — **Population and Housing**

	Population				Race and Hispanic or Latino origin (percent), 2010–2014					Age (percent), 2010–2014			Households, 2010–2014			
STATE City, town, township, borough, or CDP (county if applicable)	2010 census total population	2014 estimated population	Percent change 2010–2014	ACS total population estimate 2010–2014	White alone, not Hispanic or Latino	Black alone, not Hispanic or Latino	Asian alone, not Hispanic or Latino	All other races or 2 or more races, not Hispanic or Latino	Hispanic or Latino[1]	Under 18 years old	Age 18 to 64 years old	Age 65 years and older	Total occupied housing units	Percent owner occupied	High school diploma or less	Bachelor's degree or more
	1	2	3	4	5	6	7	8	9	10	11	12	13	14	15	16
PENNSYLVANIA—Con.																
Honey Brook township (Chester)	7,639	8,080	5.8	7,858	97.3	0.7	0.3	1.5	0.3	29.4	55.3	15.2	2,531	76.1	51.9	17.8
Hookstown borough & MCD (Beaver)	147	146	-0.7	150	98.7	0.0	0.0	0.0	1.3	18.7	65.3	16.0	62	67.7	69.4	6.5
Hooversville borough & MCD (Somerset)	645	625	-3.1	651	100.0	0.0	0.0	0.0	0.0	17.3	59.1	23.7	266	72.2	72.9	12.8
Hop Bottom borough & MCD (Susquehanna)	337	316	-6.2	326	95.4	0.0	0.0	0.0	4.6	21.2	63.5	15.3	135	65.2	64.4	3.7
Hopeland CDP	738	NA	NA	638	98.4	0.0	1.6	0.0	0.0	18.8	66.5	14.6	262	78.6	86.3	7.6
Hopewell township (Beaver)	12,593	12,529	-0.5	12,571	94.3	2.1	0.3	0.7	2.6	19.7	59.8	20.6	5,132	80.0	43.5	24.2
Hopewell borough & MCD (Bedford)	230	247	7.4	268	100.0	0.0	0.0	0.0	0.0	36.5	53.6	9.7	95	78.9	50.5	21.1
Hopewell township (Bedford)	2,010	1,977	-1.6	2,106	95.9	0.8	0.0	1.4	1.9	22.1	63.0	15.1	786	86.1	71.1	6.7
Hopewell township (Cumberland)	2,329	2,385	2.4	2,401	97.9	1.0	0.0	0.2	0.8	26.5	60.0	13.5	772	87.4	70.9	18.1
Hopewell township (Huntingdon)	587	590	0.5	607	99.7	0.0	0.0	0.3	0.0	20.1	54.6	25.4	262	83.6	63.4	7.3
Hopewell township (Washington)	957	939	-1.9	939	97.9	0.0	0.4	0.5	1.2	21.9	61.6	16.5	359	90.5	53.5	23.7
Hopewell township (York)	5,435	5,445	0.2	5,432	97.8	0.0	0.5	0.0	1.7	24.8	63.2	12.0	1,910	95.7	42.6	30.6
Hopwood CDP	2,090	NA	NA	1,834	97.1	0.0	0.0	0.0	2.9	19.3	60.5	20.2	753	66.5	58.6	16.6
Horsham CDP	14,842	NA	NA	14,936	86.9	4.0	3.9	2.2	3.0	20.7	65.7	13.6	5,822	75.0	31.0	36.8
Horsham township (Montgomery)	26,147	26,557	1.6	26,353	86.5	3.0	5.3	2.1	3.2	23.1	64.5	12.4	9,580	77.5	25.9	47.5
Horton township (Elk)	1,452	1,428	-1.7	1,481	98.2	0.3	0.7	0.7	0.0	17.3	67.5	15.1	633	83.9	67.0	11.2
Hostetter CDP	740	NA	NA	842	94.3	0.5	0.0	3.3	1.9	13.4	60.2	26.2	368	69.3	61.4	10.1
Houserville CDP	1,814	NA	NA	1,905	90.7	0.5	2.3	3.1	3.4	19.7	70.3	10.0	778	86.4	16.1	68.1
Houston borough & MCD (Washington)	1,296	1,273	-1.8	1,239	91.8	5.3	1.1	0.5	1.3	17.0	62.1	20.7	573	54.1	60.7	17.3
Houtzdale borough & MCD (Clearfield)	797	779	-2.3	817	98.9	0.4	0.0	0.7	0.0	21.4	63.4	15.3	304	77.6	66.8	13.5
Hovey township (Armstrong)	98	97	-1.0	75	100.0	0.0	0.0	0.0	0.0	1.3	70.7	28.0	37	81.1	29.7	18.9
Howard borough & MCD (Centre)	720	718	-0.3	847	99.3	0.0	0.0	0.4	0.4	20.9	61.7	17.2	340	75.6	49.7	13.5
Howard township (Centre)	964	950	-1.5	826	97.2	1.0	0.0	0.6	1.2	16.9	64.9	18.0	321	86.9	65.7	15.6
Howe township (Forest)	405	401	-1.0	371	67.1	20.8	0.0	1.3	10.8	36.4	45.8	17.8	74	82.4	58.1	9.5
Howe township (Perry)	393	389	-1.0	353	98.0	0.0	0.0	0.0	2.0	11.9	69.1	19.0	159	86.8	44.0	27.0
Hublersburg CDP	104	NA	NA	17	100.0	0.0	0.0	0.0	0.0	0.0	0.0	100.0	17	100.0	100.0	0.0
Hubley township (Schuylkill)	854	844	-1.2	680	99.4	0.0	0.0	0.0	0.6	18.8	60.3	20.9	300	78.7	61.0	14.7
Hudson CDP	1,443	NA	NA	1,502	100.0	0.0	0.0	0.0	0.0	14.7	61.1	24.2	723	75.8	47.3	19.2
Hughestown borough & MCD (Luzerne)	1,392	1,391	-0.1	1,436	98.2	0.0	0.0	1.3	0.5	15.7	61.2	23.0	572	81.1	50.7	19.1
Hughesville borough & MCD (Lycoming)	2,128	2,118	-0.5	1,860	96.3	0.3	0.2	1.2	1.9	22.1	60.4	17.7	822	61.2	50.6	21.5
Hulmeville borough & MCD (Bucks)	1,003	999	-0.4	966	95.7	1.8	0.9	1.2	0.4	19.8	66.2	14.2	330	69.7	46.4	20.6
Hummelstown borough & MCD (Dauphin)	4,538	4,554	0.4	4,544	91.0	0.0	0.9	3.6	4.5	26.9	57.8	15.1	1,876	58.0	46.7	29.3
Hummels Wharf CDP	1,353	NA	NA	1,503	100.0	0.0	0.0	0.0	0.0	21.6	64.9	13.6	633	77.6	49.3	28.8
Hunker borough & MCD (Westmoreland)	291	287	-1.4	331	96.4	0.0	1.2	0.0	2.4	16.0	62.6	21.5	131	98.5	61.1	13.7
Hunlock township (Luzerne)	2,443	2,430	-0.5	2,566	97.2	0.0	0.2	2.7	0.0	21.7	62.7	15.7	926	87.0	58.2	14.0
Hunterstown CDP	547	NA	NA	642	60.3	0.0	7.3	2.6	29.8	32.3	50.3	17.4	230	78.7	84.8	11.3
Huntingdon borough & MCD (Huntingdon)	7,093	7,037	-0.8	7,069	94.3	1.9	0.7	1.8	1.3	16.4	67.0	16.7	2,703	54.7	50.1	29.3
Huntington township (Adams)	2,369	2,368	0.0	2,323	91.2	0.8	1.4	3.7	3.0	22.5	60.3	17.3	932	84.2	57.5	14.2
Huntington township (Luzerne)	2,244	2,233	-0.5	2,093	97.8	0.0	0.0	0.0	2.2	22.0	57.1	21.0	739	88.6	56.0	20.4
Huston township (Blair)	1,337	1,342	0.4	1,310	100.0	0.0	0.0	0.0	0.0	26.8	58.5	14.7	443	85.6	69.8	14.7
Huston township (Centre)	1,360	1,356	-0.3	1,382	98.3	0.3	0.6	0.4	0.4	18.1	64.7	17.1	535	87.1	50.8	26.4
Huston township (Clearfield)	1,433	1,394	-2.7	1,294	95.8	0.0	3.0	1.2	0.0	20.4	60.9	18.7	516	84.3	70.0	7.0
Hyde CDP	1,399	NA	NA	1,392	99.7	0.0	0.0	0.3	0.0	31.2	49.9	18.7	539	63.1	60.7	6.5
Hyde Park CDP	2,528	NA	NA	2,649	66.6	1.0	1.4	1.4	29.6	26.5	61.2	12.4	941	79.7	56.6	22.6
Hyde Park borough & MCD (Westmoreland)	500	484	-3.2	486	99.6	0.0	0.0	0.4	0.0	16.7	57.0	26.3	220	73.6	65.5	8.6
Hydetown borough & MCD (Crawford)	535	523	-2.2	458	99.6	0.0	0.0	0.4	0.0	18.6	47.9	33.4	199	83.4	72.9	8.0
Hyndman borough & MCD (Bedford)	910	886	-2.6	862	94.0	0.0	0.0	4.5	1.5	21.2	55.4	23.3	384	75.0	69.5	6.3
Idaville CDP	177	NA	NA	152	92.8	7.2	0.0	0.0	0.0	7.2	71.1	21.7	67	92.5	64.2	7.5
Imperial CDP	2,541	NA	NA	2,917	93.8	0.5	0.0	3.1	2.6	26.6	64.2	9.1	1,195	60.3	40.2	29.3
Independence township (Beaver)	2,503	2,463	-1.6	2,477	97.1	1.3	0.0	1.0	0.6	17.1	68.4	14.6	992	90.6	45.9	21.0
Independence township (Washington)	1,557	1,528	-1.9	1,667	98.8	0.7	0.0	0.5	0.0	21.2	64.6	14.2	612	85.6	57.5	17.6
Indiana township (Allegheny)	7,253	7,309	0.8	7,297	90.6	1.4	2.2	3.0	2.7	23.5	59.3	17.0	2,590	81.0	26.9	51.1
Indiana borough & MCD (Indiana)	13,975	14,194	1.6	14,025	88.5	6.3	1.4	1.7	2.2	8.9	83.5	7.7	4,823	39.2	23.0	30.9
Indian Lake borough & MCD (Somerset)	394	392	-0.5	413	97.8	0.7	0.0	1.5	0.0	6.3	57.1	36.6	204	98.0	26.5	50.5
Indian Mountain Lake CDP	4,372	NA	NA	4,411	49.0	18.8	0.0	0.0	32.1	28.4	61.4	10.1	1,432	92.7	40.2	23.0

1 May be of any race.

Table A. All Places — **Population and Housing**

STATE City, town, township, borough, or CDP (county if applicable)	2010 census total population	2014 estimated population	Percent change 2010–2014	ACS total population estimate 2010–2014	White alone, not Hispanic or Latino	Black alone, not Hispanic or Latino	Asian alone, not Hispanic or Latino	All other races or 2 or more races, not Hispanic or Latino	Hispanic or Latino[1]	Under 18 years old	Age 18 to 64 years old	Age 65 years and older	Total occupied housing units	Percent owner occupied	High school diploma or less	Bachelor's degree or more
	1	2	3	4	5	6	7	8	9	10	11	12	13	14	15	16
PENNSYLVANIA—Con.																
Industry borough & MCD (Beaver)	1,835	1,800	-1.9	1,914	96.9	0.4	0.3	0.3	2.2	20.0	62.0	17.9	745	90.2	43.8	16.0
Ingram borough & MCD (Allegheny)	3,330	3,300	-0.9	3,310	91.4	5.2	1.7	1.3	0.5	21.3	64.7	14.2	1,471	64.6	35.9	30.5
Inkerman CDP	1,819	NA	NA	1,872	98.6	1.4	0.0	0.0	0.0	12.7	37.6	49.8	805	53.4	40.7	18.9
Intercourse CDP	1,274	NA	NA	1,300	96.6	0.0	0.0	0.0	3.4	29.6	48.1	22.2	529	58.2	66.4	20.6
Iola CDP	144	NA	NA	262	93.9	0.0	0.0	0.0	6.1	27.5	64.2	8.4	96	39.6	61.5	3.1
Irvona borough & MCD (Clearfield)	647	629	-2.8	805	99.1	0.0	0.0	0.0	0.9	20.4	65.2	14.4	284	83.8	71.8	5.6
Irwin township (Venango)	1,391	1,342	-3.5	1,522	97.2	0.3	0.7	0.8	1.0	25.0	64.9	10.1	584	87.5	58.0	14.2
Irwin borough & MCD (Westmoreland)	3,971	3,883	-2.2	3,924	98.9	0.8	0.0	0.0	0.3	17.5	68.7	13.8	1,924	42.2	31.4	28.5
Ivyland borough & MCD (Bucks)	1,041	1,051	1.0	1,016	81.8	1.1	11.0	0.7	5.4	26.5	57.8	15.7	320	90.3	31.6	38.8
Jackson township (Butler)	3,657	3,593	-1.8	3,637	99.3	0.4	0.2	0.0	0.0	18.8	59.6	21.7	1,594	77.9	39.0	32.0
Jackson township (Cambria)	4,389	4,249	-3.2	4,314	99.4	0.0	0.0	0.1	0.4	17.6	63.9	18.8	1,769	88.8	54.2	18.7
Jackson township (Columbia)	626	636	1.6	636	89.6	8.8	0.0	1.6	0.0	18.5	58.7	22.8	239	88.7	64.9	12.1
Jackson township (Dauphin)	1,941	1,949	0.4	1,985	97.2	0.2	0.4	0.8	1.4	19.8	63.4	16.7	731	93.7	61.6	16.7
Jackson township (Greene)	487	474	-2.7	454	98.2	0.0	0.2	1.5	0.0	22.9	60.7	16.3	176	74.4	74.4	11.4
Jackson township (Huntingdon)	864	858	-0.7	768	96.4	2.5	0.0	0.5	0.7	21.0	57.0	22.0	302	78.8	52.6	23.5
Jackson township (Lebanon)	8,157	8,478	3.9	8,314	96.5	0.6	0.7	0.4	1.7	24.1	51.3	24.6	3,172	87.2	53.9	21.0
Jackson township (Luzerne)	4,646	4,639	-0.2	4,628	66.1	25.5	0.5	0.6	7.3	10.8	77.4	11.7	932	91.2	29.9	43.1
Jackson township (Lycoming)	396	395	-0.3	396	99.7	0.0	0.0	0.3	0.0	23.9	60.6	15.4	157	91.1	60.5	17.2
Jackson township (Mercer)	1,273	1,272	-0.1	1,202	97.9	0.7	0.0	1.3	0.0	17.7	62.1	20.4	482	85.1	54.4	25.9
Jackson township (Monroe)	7,020	6,849	-2.4	6,946	70.4	7.9	3.2	1.5	17.0	17.7	66.8	15.5	2,510	82.0	39.9	30.6
Jackson township (Northumberland)	875	887	1.4	1,047	94.7	0.0	0.0	0.3	5.0	23.5	59.6	16.9	405	86.7	70.1	7.7
Jackson township (Perry)	547	541	-1.1	520	95.4	1.2	0.0	0.2	3.3	34.5	53.6	11.9	172	77.3	80.8	1.2
Jackson township (Snyder)	1,382	1,424	3.0	1,840	96.2	2.2	0.0	0.5	1.1	36.5	52.8	10.7	563	75.0	65.0	13.9
Jackson township (Susquehanna)	853	816	-4.3	769	96.1	1.6	0.5	1.0	0.8	15.8	59.7	24.3	345	84.9	58.0	19.7
Jackson township (Tioga)	1,873	1,899	1.4	1,968	98.2	0.8	0.0	0.2	0.9	17.5	63.4	19.1	774	88.1	56.1	11.0
Jackson township (Venango)	1,147	1,150	0.3	938	99.3	0.1	0.0	0.6	0.0	17.3	61.7	21.0	397	83.1	65.2	13.1
Jackson township (York)	7,494	7,784	3.9	7,604	92.8	4.7	0.4	1.0	1.1	23.3	62.3	14.4	2,819	90.6	56.5	26.5
Jackson Center borough & MCD (Mercer)	224	221	-1.3	215	100.0	0.0	0.0	0.0	0.0	23.3	64.2	12.6	83	84.3	61.4	8.4
Jacksonville CDP (Centre)	0	NA	NA	108	100.0	0.0	0.0	0.0	0.0	29.7	59.3	11.1	31	93.5	77.4	16.1
Jacksonville CDP (Indiana)	637	NA	NA	665	96.2	0.9	0.0	2.9	0.0	18.0	65.1	17.0	333	64.6	61.3	12.9
Jacksonwald CDP	3,393	NA	NA	3,223	89.9	6.0	0.0	0.0	4.1	27.9	62.3	9.8	1,111	97.9	28.4	45.8
Jacobus borough & MCD (York)	1,838	1,843	0.3	1,896	89.7	1.4	2.8	4.1	1.9	26.1	61.4	12.4	676	87.3	40.1	34.6
James City CDP	287	NA	NA	264	100.0	0.0	0.0	0.0	0.0	11.7	68.6	19.7	109	100.0	73.4	10.1
Jamestown borough & MCD (Mercer)	617	600	-2.8	622	99.5	0.0	0.0	0.5	0.0	21.9	52.5	25.6	268	70.1	63.1	10.4
Jamison City CDP	134	NA	NA	111	100.0	0.0	0.0	0.0	0.0	19.8	38.7	41.4	53	96.2	56.6	5.7
Jay township (Elk)	2,072	2,005	-3.2	2,336	97.2	0.3	0.4	1.0	1.1	25.2	57.3	17.5	869	86.9	64.2	10.2
Jeannette city & MCD (Westmoreland)	9,654	9,400	-2.6	9,522	90.9	4.0	0.8	3.8	0.5	18.3	64.0	17.7	4,394	61.8	52.1	18.4
Jeddo borough & MCD (Luzerne)	98	98	0.0	120	96.7	0.0	0.0	0.0	3.3	13.3	79.3	7.5	57	77.2	71.9	3.5
Jefferson township (Berks)	1,977	2,005	1.4	1,762	95.6	0.8	0.8	2.8	0.0	22.7	59.8	17.5	685	92.0	49.8	28.3
Jefferson township (Butler)	5,504	5,384	-2.2	5,456	99.0	0.0	0.2	0.4	0.4	18.8	58.1	23.3	2,132	77.5	59.5	18.3
Jefferson township (Dauphin)	362	366	1.1	318	98.1	0.0	0.0	0.6	1.3	16.1	65.3	18.6	131	83.2	61.1	19.1
Jefferson township (Fayette)	2,016	1,981	-1.7	2,116	97.0	0.4	0.0	1.2	1.4	22.1	59.9	18.0	805	88.9	60.4	16.0
Jefferson borough & MCD (Greene)	266	260	-2.3	255	99.2	0.0	0.0	0.0	0.0	17.3	65.5	17.3	111	74.8	55.9	27.9
Jefferson township (Greene)	2,357	2,305	-2.2	2,486	90.2	8.4	0.0	0.2	1.2	14.5	66.4	19.2	1,109	80.3	62.1	15.8
Jefferson township (Lackawanna)	3,730	3,763	0.9	3,760	98.2	0.0	0.9	0.9	0.0	18.3	66.0	15.8	1,512	91.6	52.6	16.8
Jefferson township (Mercer)	1,880	1,883	0.2	1,777	97.1	0.2	1.1	1.2	0.5	16.7	63.0	20.3	741	92.4	56.3	20.5
Jefferson township (Somerset)	1,423	1,388	-2.5	1,277	98.8	0.0	0.0	0.0	1.2	15.9	66.3	17.5	466	83.0	50.6	20.2
Jefferson township (Washington)	1,162	1,159	-0.3	1,320	95.8	0.0	0.0	1.0	3.2	19.2	56.7	24.1	511	93.9	53.6	12.5
Jefferson borough & MCD (York)	729	737	1.1	639	96.1	0.0	0.0	3.9	0.0	27.9	60.0	12.1	233	77.3	58.8	10.7
Jefferson Hills borough & MCD (Allegheny)	10,629	11,232	5.7	10,984	95.6	2.1	0.8	0.8	0.7	20.7	62.3	17.0	4,442	81.6	32.4	46.2
Jenkins township (Luzerne)	4,442	4,453	0.2	4,458	97.4	0.6	0.0	0.0	2.0	16.7	53.0	30.3	1,777	74.2	45.2	21.3
Jenkintown borough & MCD (Montgomery)	4,422	4,445	0.5	4,441	88.0	6.1	0.0	2.3	3.6	21.3	55.6	23.4	2,024	70.1	17.1	59.5

1 May be of any race.

Table A. All Places — Population and Housing

STATE City, town, township, borough, or CDP (county if applicable)	2010 census total population	2014 estimated population	Percent change 2010–2014	ACS total population estimate 2010–2014	White alone, not Hispanic or Latino	Black alone, not Hispanic or Latino	Asian alone, not Hispanic or Latino	All other races or 2 or more races, not Hispanic or Latino	Hispanic or Latino[1]	Under 18 years old	Age 18 to 64 years old	Age 65 years and older	Total occupied housing units	Percent owner occupied	High school diploma or less	Bachelor's degree or more
	1	2	3	4	5	6	7	8	9	10	11	12	13	14	15	16
PENNSYLVANIA—Con.																
Jenks township (Forest)...	3,629	3,577	-1.4	4,303	50.2	38.5	0.3	3.2	7.8	4.7	84.6	10.8	538	76.8	53.3	24.7
Jenner township (Somerset)	4,122	3,993	-3.1	4,047	99.4	0.0	0.0	0.6	0.0	22.5	59.6	18.2	1,467	88.3	65.6	11.9
Jennerstown borough & MCD (Somerset)	695	676	-2.7	681	98.2	0.3	0.0	1.3	0.1	20.2	60.0	20.0	299	92.0	47.8	26.8
Jermyn borough & MCD (Lackawanna)	2,169	2,147	-1.0	2,236	93.0	2.1	0.0	1.5	3.4	21.6	58.0	20.4	939	64.1	53.5	16.9
Jerome CDP	1,017	NA	NA	1,055	98.8	0.0	0.0	1.2	0.0	16.2	64.9	19.0	480	80.8	77.3	5.0
Jersey Shore borough & MCD (Lycoming)	4,361	4,315	-1.1	4,339	97.5	1.5	0.0	0.6	0.4	28.8	59.6	11.6	1,531	55.3	57.8	10.8
Jerseytown CDP	184	NA	NA	110	100.0	0.0	0.0	0.0	0.0	24.6	59.0	16.4	49	71.4	65.3	20.4
Jessup borough & MCD (Lackawanna)	4,676	4,600	-1.6	4,650	95.2	0.0	0.0	0.4	4.4	26.9	57.8	15.3	1,735	72.6	49.3	29.9
Jessup township (Susquehanna)	536	521	-2.8	554	95.7	0.5	0.0	0.0	3.8	27.4	61.5	11.2	196	82.1	53.6	27.0
Jim Thorpe borough & MCD (Carbon)	4,781	4,683	-2.0	4,730	94.1	1.5	0.0	1.3	3.1	21.1	61.9	17.0	1,757	71.8	46.4	20.9
Joffre CDP	536	NA	NA	659	100.0	0.0	0.0	0.0	0.0	26.7	61.1	12.1	275	85.8	56.7	11.3
Johnsonburg borough & MCD (Elk)	2,483	2,405	-3.1	2,451	97.6	0.0	0.0	1.3	1.1	23.7	56.3	20.0	1,153	74.6	71.3	6.0
Johnstown city & MCD (Cambria)	20,975	20,184	-3.8	20,576	78.5	12.9	0.3	5.8	2.4	21.3	59.6	18.9	9,850	50.2	61.0	11.3
Jones township (Elk)	1,624	1,596	-1.7	1,565	97.6	1.0	0.0	0.0	1.4	18.3	62.2	19.5	678	85.7	60.2	17.6
Jonestown CDP	64	NA	NA	79	100.0	0.0	0.0	0.0	0.0	40.5	54.4	5.1	31	71.0	54.8	25.8
Jonestown borough & MCD (Lebanon)	1,905	1,945	2.1	1,603	87.8	1.0	0.0	1.9	9.4	28.3	61.0	10.7	596	75.8	51.8	16.3
Jordan township (Clearfield)	461	457	-0.9	563	99.8	0.0	0.2	0.0	0.0	14.2	65.7	20.1	210	91.0	76.7	6.2
Jordan township (Lycoming)	863	870	0.8	858	99.3	0.0	0.0	0.2	0.5	25.3	58.0	16.4	308	79.5	64.0	17.2
Jordan township (Northumberland)	794	787	-0.9	795	97.6	0.0	0.0	0.9	1.5	20.1	61.5	18.4	318	85.2	74.2	10.4
Julian CDP	152	NA	NA	145	100.0	0.0	0.0	0.0	0.0	16.6	66.3	17.2	66	75.8	60.6	15.2
Juniata township (Bedford)	948	938	-1.1	865	95.1	0.6	0.0	1.4	2.9	17.8	60.1	22.3	388	85.8	68.0	8.5
Juniata township (Blair)	1,112	1,103	-0.8	1,086	100.0	0.0	0.0	0.0	0.0	16.9	63.1	20.1	428	92.8	72.0	11.0
Juniata township (Huntingdon)	547	545	-0.4	594	99.5	0.0	0.0	0.5	0.0	22.2	57.6	20.2	253	80.2	59.7	18.6
Juniata township (Perry)	1,410	1,402	-0.6	1,389	95.5	0.0	0.2	0.9	3.3	19.0	66.9	14.2	564	93.6	55.0	20.0
Juniata Terrace borough & MCD (Mifflin)	542	543	0.2	802	81.4	1.1	1.4	11.2	4.9	34.9	55.9	9.1	312	55.8	58.0	4.2
Kane borough & MCD (McKean)	3,730	3,632	-2.6	3,679	91.7	0.0	1.1	4.4	2.7	23.2	56.1	20.5	1,574	62.8	57.4	12.6
Kapp Heights CDP	863	NA	NA	875	92.7	0.0	0.0	0.0	7.3	15.9	62.3	21.8	326	70.9	60.4	9.8
Karns City borough & MCD (Butler)	209	210	0.5	197	90.4	0.0	0.0	9.6	0.0	21.2	54.8	23.9	82	75.6	68.3	4.9
Karthaus township (Clearfield)	811	904	11.5	451	97.6	1.6	0.0	0.0	0.9	12.9	66.3	20.8	190	85.3	75.3	8.9
Keating township (McKean)	3,021	2,964	-1.9	2,996	94.0	2.6	0.0	0.4	2.9	18.3	61.5	20.0	1,050	86.1	62.1	10.6
Keating township (Potter)	312	307	-1.6	228	100.0	0.0	0.0	0.0	0.0	12.8	61.8	25.4	101	96.0	74.3	8.9
Kelayres CDP	533	NA	NA	513	84.2	0.0	0.0	0.0	15.8	22.1	63.3	14.6	252	62.7	45.6	7.9
Kelly township (Union)	5,376	5,239	-2.5	5,355	67.8	16.0	0.2	7.3	8.7	19.1	62.6	18.3	1,461	56.5	48.5	31.6
Kempton CDP	169	NA	NA	126	100.0	0.0	0.0	0.0	0.0	7.1	78.4	14.3	51	84.3	41.2	33.3
Kenhorst borough & MCD (Berks)	2,877	2,864	-0.5	2,868	83.8	6.5	0.0	0.5	9.2	19.3	62.6	18.1	1,208	82.9	52.1	19.4
Kenilworth CDP	1,907	NA	NA	1,858	94.2	1.4	3.0	0.8	0.7	21.0	64.7	14.3	758	77.0	45.1	31.1
Kenmar CDP	4,124	NA	NA	4,337	90.2	3.3	0.8	4.0	1.7	20.2	52.4	27.4	2,065	71.2	47.8	26.4
Kennedy township (Allegheny)	7,671	8,032	4.7	7,839	92.4	3.1	2.9	1.3	0.3	17.5	60.7	21.8	3,264	84.6	37.5	32.6
Kennerdell CDP	247	NA	NA	184	99.5	0.0	0.0	0.5	0.0	10.9	47.3	41.8	88	76.1	47.7	10.2
Kennett township (Chester)	7,556	7,982	5.6	7,754	87.0	2.0	2.6	0.6	7.8	20.8	58.6	20.5	3,203	78.2	19.0	62.0
Kennett Square borough & MCD (Chester)	6,077	6,151	1.2	6,123	41.9	5.5	0.3	2.7	49.7	25.9	62.5	11.5	2,024	54.6	50.8	27.7
Kerrtown CDP	305	NA	NA	402	100.0	0.0	0.0	0.0	0.0	14.2	78.9	7.0	169	51.5	100.0	0.0
Kersey CDP	937	NA	NA	927	100.0	0.0	0.0	0.0	0.0	16.3	71.2	12.4	412	74.5	76.9	11.9
Kidder township (Carbon)	1,935	1,940	0.3	1,736	90.1	1.6	2.1	0.3	5.9	20.8	57.5	21.9	734	85.1	30.1	34.7
Kilbuck township (Allegheny)	697	694	-0.4	715	90.8	2.8	1.1	4.9	0.4	27.2	53.8	19.2	295	93.6	24.4	51.5
Kimmel township (Bedford)	1,629	1,592	-2.3	1,703	98.9	0.4	0.0	0.8	0.0	18.2	65.0	16.8	723	82.0	75.2	7.9
King township (Bedford)	1,238	1,216	-1.8	1,295	99.8	0.0	0.0	0.0	0.2	24.3	61.5	14.2	511	82.2	66.7	11.5
King of Prussia CDP	19,936	NA	NA	19,919	67.0	4.5	22.3	2.8	3.3	20.0	63.0	16.9	8,547	59.5	23.7	57.1
Kingsley township (Forest)	363	348	-4.1	318	100.0	0.0	0.0	0.0	0.0	16.9	45.5	37.7	149	84.6	60.4	17.4
Kingston borough & MCD (Luzerne)	13,182	12,994	-1.4	13,105	85.3	5.8	2.1	2.8	4.0	16.3	62.3	21.3	5,782	50.2	32.9	32.4
Kingston township (Luzerne)	6,999	6,977	-0.3	7,010	96.0	0.8	0.2	1.3	1.8	20.6	64.4	15.1	2,809	80.8	30.8	37.7
Kirkwood CDP	396	NA	NA	305	100.0	0.0	0.0	0.0	0.0	35.7	44.3	20.0	104	76.0	84.6	5.8
Kiskimere CDP	136	NA	NA	57	89.5	10.5	0.0	0.0	0.0	15.8	33.3	50.9	32	100.0	81.3	18.8
Kiskiminetas township (Armstrong)	4,800	4,702	-2.0	4,737	98.1	1.3	0.1	0.0	0.5	20.0	62.0	18.0	2,017	87.6	62.9	9.4
Kistler borough & MCD (Mifflin)	320	321	0.3	380	81.6	0.5	1.1	8.9	7.9	24.2	61.8	13.9	166	74.7	71.1	9.6
Kittanning borough & MCD (Armstrong)	4,026	3,933	-2.3	3,977	96.8	0.8	0.0	2.3	0.1	20.2	61.5	18.4	1,917	49.6	55.0	20.1
Kittanning township (Armstrong)	2,265	2,250	-0.7	2,322	98.4	0.6	0.5	0.4	0.1	22.1	56.3	21.5	879	78.7	60.8	15.9
Kline township (Schuylkill)	1,438	1,408	-2.1	1,539	91.9	0.0	0.0	0.5	7.7	15.6	59.2	25.2	702	78.9	54.4	12.3

1 May be of any race.

Table A. All Places — Population and Housing

STATE City, town, township, borough, or CDP (county if applicable)	Population 2010 census total population	2014 estimated population	Percent change 2010–2014	ACS total population estimate 2010–2014	Race and Hispanic or Latino origin (percent), 2010–2014 White alone, not Hispanic or Latino	Black alone, not Hispanic or Latino	Asian alone, not Hispanic or Latino	All other races or 2 or more races, not Hispanic or Latino	Hispanic or Latino[1]	Age (percent), 2010–2014 Under 18 years old	Age 18 to 64 years old	Age 65 years and older	Households, 2010–2014 Total occupied housing units	Percent owner occupied	Householders by level of education (percent) High school diploma or less	Bachelor's degree or more
	1	2	3	4	5	6	7	8	9	10	11	12	13	14	15	16
PENNSYLVANIA—Con.																
Klingerstown CDP	127	NA	NA	88	100.0	0.0	0.0	0.0	0.0	18.2	57.9	23.9	42	66.7	50.0	19.0
Knox borough & MCD (Clarion)	1,150	1,122	-2.4	1,098	95.5	0.1	0.6	0.0	3.7	18.2	60.5	21.3	467	69.8	52.5	21.4
Knox township (Clarion)	1,036	1,024	-1.2	1,062	96.6	0.1	0.0	2.9	0.4	17.7	67.6	14.7	460	80.0	60.7	12.6
Knox township (Clearfield)	647	633	-2.2	494	99.2	0.0	0.6	0.2	0.0	16.7	60.5	22.9	218	93.1	79.8	0.9
Knox township (Jefferson)	1,042	1,027	-1.4	887	98.4	0.0	0.0	1.4	0.2	20.0	62.2	17.7	391	80.1	70.3	8.7
Knoxville borough & MCD (Tioga)	629	630	0.2	571	98.9	0.0	0.0	1.1	0.0	22.5	61.9	15.8	232	74.1	56.0	4.7
Koppel borough & MCD (Beaver)	762	747	-2.0	638	91.1	0.9	0.0	3.0	5.0	23.5	51.7	24.8	313	70.6	51.4	18.8
Kratzerville CDP	383	NA	NA	474	96.8	0.0	0.0	1.3	1.9	13.1	67.7	19.2	190	74.2	59.5	11.1
Kreamer CDP	822	NA	NA	796	98.4	0.0	0.0	1.6	0.0	13.0	73.7	13.4	348	88.8	47.7	30.5
Kulpmont borough & MCD (Northumberland)	2,924	2,878	-1.6	2,904	97.8	0.2	0.0	0.0	2.0	20.4	57.6	22.1	1,297	78.5	66.1	17.3
Kulpsville CDP	8,194	NA	NA	8,401	75.9	7.8	11.8	2.2	2.4	22.0	59.0	19.0	3,405	78.1	24.8	50.4
Kutztown borough & MCD (Berks)	5,002	5,013	0.2	5,016	86.7	2.1	1.7	0.3	9.2	14.9	66.9	18.3	1,891	56.5	41.2	24.4
Kutztown University CDP	2,918	NA	NA	2,016	80.5	8.9	2.0	4.8	3.9	0.3	99.7	0.0	0	0.0	0.0	0.0
Kylertown CDP	340	NA	NA	406	97.3	0.0	0.0	2.7	0.0	14.3	48.0	37.9	171	90.1	100.0	0.0
Laceyville borough & MCD (Wyoming)	379	371	-2.1	426	88.3	0.0	0.0	1.4	10.3	20.8	60.6	18.3	169	64.5	73.4	7.7
Lack township (Juniata)	785	781	-0.5	608	96.9	0.2	0.0	1.6	1.3	16.3	57.8	25.8	276	71.0	78.6	6.9
Lackawannock township (Mercer)	2,662	2,635	-1.0	2,657	99.4	0.4	0.1	0.0	0.2	27.8	57.4	14.8	1,012	87.5	71.0	11.1
Lackawaxen township (Pike)	4,997	5,033	0.7	5,037	86.1	4.5	0.1	4.2	5.0	14.9	50.7	34.3	2,148	91.5	39.4	24.8
Lafayette township (McKean)	2,350	2,327	-1.0	2,188	44.5	34.9	1.0	3.8	15.9	5.3	86.1	8.5	399	93.0	53.6	25.1
Laflin borough & MCD (Luzerne)	1,487	1,472	-1.0	1,577	91.5	0.1	5.8	1.3	1.4	18.7	57.5	23.8	615	92.8	28.6	47.3
Lake township (Luzerne)	2,058	2,045	-0.6	2,090	98.6	0.0	0.0	0.8	0.7	20.7	65.4	13.8	811	84.8	58.2	20.6
Lake township (Mercer)	780	776	-0.5	835	98.0	0.0	0.0	1.9	0.1	41.4	48.2	10.5	260	83.5	61.2	13.5
Lake township (Wayne)	5,275	5,161	-2.2	5,218	90.2	6.6	0.5	0.6	2.2	18.1	60.4	21.5	1,865	87.9	49.5	29.1
Lake Arthur Estates CDP	594	NA	NA	613	95.3	0.0	0.0	1.0	3.8	16.8	61.5	21.7	333	85.9	66.4	4.5
Lake City borough & MCD (Erie)	3,031	2,974	-1.9	3,008	95.0	0.0	0.0	1.1	4.0	29.1	60.0	11.2	1,096	74.9	49.2	19.0
Lake Heritage CDP	1,333	NA	NA	1,560	96.5	1.3	0.0	0.0	2.2	13.2	61.3	25.6	624	100.0	33.2	44.7
Lake Latonka CDP	1,012	NA	NA	845	98.8	0.7	0.0	0.5	0.0	17.7	55.2	27.0	368	92.9	17.4	49.7
Lake Meade CDP	2,563	NA	NA	2,624	97.5	0.0	1.0	0.6	0.9	19.6	69.7	10.7	980	96.0	27.1	43.8
Lakemont CDP	1,868	NA	NA	2,461	98.9	0.0	1.1	0.0	0.0	19.4	64.3	16.3	1,025	74.9	49.0	16.9
Lake Winola CDP	748	NA	NA	688	95.8	0.0	0.0	4.2	0.0	17.0	52.4	30.7	304	79.3	44.4	20.4
Lake Wynonah CDP	2,640	NA	NA	2,569	93.3	0.0	0.0	0.5	6.2	23.4	62.6	14.0	1,073	93.0	34.1	28.4
Lamar CDP	562	NA	NA	623	100.0	0.0	0.0	0.0	0.0	17.3	55.2	27.4	270	80.4	69.3	7.8
Lamar township (Clinton)	2,517	2,569	2.1	2,539	96.4	1.1	0.5	0.3	1.7	23.2	60.5	16.2	948	85.8	26.2	26.2
Lampeter CDP	1,669	NA	NA	1,628	94.8	0.0	0.0	4.3	0.9	33.3	62.0	4.7	534	73.6	14.4	57.7
Lancaster township (Butler)	2,532	2,514	-0.7	2,525	99.3	0.2	0.0	0.5	0.1	20.2	62.1	17.8	909	89.2	37.8	34.4
Lancaster city & MCD (Lancaster)	59,322	59,302	0.0	59,368	41.2	13.6	3.1	2.5	39.7	25.3	65.6	9.2	21,825	42.9	56.8	20.0
Lancaster township (Lancaster)	16,121	17,002	5.5	16,677	64.9	6.7	1.4	2.0	25.1	22.2	60.4	17.4	6,435	58.4	46.9	30.7
Landingville borough & MCD (Schuylkill)	159	156	-1.9	104	95.2	0.0	4.8	0.0	0.0	9.7	77.0	13.5	49	89.8	65.3	20.4
Landisburg borough & MCD (Perry)	221	218	-1.4	219	89.5	0.0	0.0	9.6	0.9	23.7	61.2	15.1	92	63.0	76.1	7.6
Landisville CDP	1,893	NA	NA	1,844	89.6	4.2	3.6	1.5	1.1	27.3	59.0	13.7	623	89.1	31.0	42.5
Lanesboro borough & MCD (Susquehanna)	506	484	-4.3	489	96.7	0.0	0.8	1.8	0.6	24.7	56.2	19.0	216	64.4	58.8	14.4
Langeloth CDP	717	NA	NA	587	95.9	0.0	0.0	0.9	3.2	11.0	74.4	14.7	273	67.8	66.7	11.4
Langhorne borough & MCD (Bucks)	1,622	1,603	-1.2	1,503	86.9	9.2	1.1	1.9	0.8	16.3	65.8	18.0	547	65.4	30.5	37.1
Langhorne Manor borough & MCD (Bucks)	1,442	1,434	-0.6	1,446	92.5	3.6	1.2	1.6	1.1	11.3	72.8	16.0	322	80.4	24.2	48.8
Lansdale borough & MCD (Montgomery)	16,269	16,487	1.3	16,382	72.9	9.0	11.3	2.6	4.2	21.2	65.2	13.7	6,524	55.0	36.7	32.5
Lansdowne borough & MCD (Delaware)	10,620	10,641	0.2	10,618	40.8	49.8	4.4	3.4	1.6	20.9	65.2	14.0	4,369	62.2	30.0	35.7
Lansford borough & MCD (Carbon)	3,941	3,836	-2.7	3,891	88.6	2.5	0.0	2.5	6.4	20.9	61.6	17.4	1,717	69.3	64.6	9.3
La Plume township (Lackawanna)	602	589	-2.2	625	96.5	2.7	0.0	0.8	0.0	12.9	69.1	17.9	257	87.2	62.6	16.3
Laporte borough & MCD (Sullivan)	314	308	-1.9	369	98.6	0.0	0.0	0.0	1.4	7.3	54.7	37.9	117	86.3	44.4	28.2
Laporte township (Sullivan)	351	354	0.9	391	100.0	0.0	0.0	0.0	0.0	17.2	56.1	26.6	146	99.3	46.6	30.8
Larimer township (Somerset)	595	582	-2.2	528	98.9	0.9	0.0	0.2	0.0	14.5	66.1	19.5	228	86.4	75.4	6.6
Larksville borough & MCD (Luzerne)	4,480	4,430	-1.1	4,462	95.5	0.0	0.0	1.5	3.0	17.9	64.8	17.3	1,906	78.9	46.2	26.0
Lathrop township (Susquehanna)	841	815	-3.1	832	96.0	0.8	0.4	1.9	0.8	19.5	61.5	19.0	309	74.1	59.9	14.2
Latimore township (Adams)	2,580	2,588	0.3	2,589	95.4	0.8	0.0	0.2	3.6	20.1	64.9	14.9	952	83.7	47.7	24.4
Latrobe city & MCD (Westmoreland)	8,338	8,129	-2.5	8,237	97.3	0.9	0.4	1.1	0.3	21.8	58.0	20.2	3,718	64.0	44.2	21.0
Lattimer CDP	554	NA	NA	569	100.0	0.0	0.0	0.0	0.0	15.8	74.6	9.7	237	82.7	40.5	26.2
Laureldale borough & MCD (Berks)	3,911	3,895	-0.4	3,905	81.4	0.9	0.0	0.7	17.0	18.8	61.5	19.8	1,607	82.1	57.4	14.9
Laurel Mountain borough & MCD (Westmoreland)	167	165	-1.2	197	98.0	0.0	0.0	0.0	2.0	23.9	52.7	23.4	82	95.1	9.8	28.0

1 May be of any race.

Table A. All Places — **Population and Housing**

	Population				Race and Hispanic or Latino origin (percent), 2010–2014					Age (percent), 2010–2014			Households, 2010–2014			
STATE City, town, township, borough, or CDP (county if applicable)	2010 census total population	2014 estimated population	Percent change 2010–2014	ACS total population estimate 2010–2014	White alone, not Hispanic or Latino	Black alone, not Hispanic or Latino	Asian alone, not Hispanic or Latino	All other races or 2 or more races, not Hispanic or Latino	Hispanic or Latino[1]	Under 18 years old	Age 18 to 64 years old	Age 65 years and older	Total occupied housing units	Percent owner occupied	High school diploma or less	Bachelor's degree or more
	1	2	3	4	5	6	7	8	9	10	11	12	13	14	15	16
PENNSYLVANIA—Con.																
Laurel Run borough & MCD (Luzerne)	500	508	1.6	515	96.9	0.0	0.6	0.6	1.9	15.9	66.4	17.7	230	85.7	60.0	20.0
Laurelton CDP	221	NA	NA	226	96.5	0.0	3.5	0.0	0.0	25.2	61.8	12.8	89	78.7	73.0	3.4
Laurys Station CDP	1,243	NA	NA	1,236	98.2	0.0	0.0	0.6	1.1	21.1	67.0	11.9	445	98.0	52.6	26.1
Lausanne township (Carbon)	233	232	-0.4	295	96.6	0.0	1.4	1.4	0.7	29.2	60.7	10.2	101	99.0	54.5	7.9
Lavelle CDP	742	NA	NA	627	91.9	0.0	0.0	0.0	8.1	7.5	58.7	34.0	273	91.9	41.8	27.8
Lawton CDP	3,813	NA	NA	3,685	68.0	20.0	4.6	2.9	4.5	20.9	63.5	15.6	1,552	65.5	44.5	26.4
Lawrence township (Clearfield)	7,681	7,538	-1.9	7,603	96.6	0.8	1.5	0.7	0.4	18.5	58.0	23.3	3,146	75.8	54.8	15.7
Lawrence township (Tioga)	1,726	1,725	-0.1	1,706	97.2	0.6	0.0	2.1	0.1	17.3	63.2	19.3	673	79.6	59.4	18.6
Lawrence CDP	540	NA	NA	381	100.0	0.0	0.0	0.0	0.0	13.7	75.0	11.3	210	31.4	44.8	20.0
Lawrence Park CDP & township (Erie)	3,982	3,881	-2.5	3,930	93.7	0.1	0.7	0.2	5.3	24.0	56.9	18.9	1,466	82.5	41.7	28.2
Lawrenceville borough & MCD (Tioga)	578	620	7.3	525	98.3	0.0	0.0	1.3	0.4	19.8	66.6	13.5	234	57.7	56.8	17.1
Lawson Heights CDP	2,194	NA	NA	1,980	98.3	1.7	0.0	0.0	0.0	9.2	53.0	37.8	973	80.3	47.3	22.6
Leacock township (Lancaster)	5,220	5,401	3.5	5,307	97.5	0.3	0.0	0.3	1.9	34.7	51.0	14.3	1,566	63.3	77.3	13.7
Lebanon city & MCD (Lebanon)	25,477	25,573	0.4	25,553	56.0	2.8	0.6	2.6	38.1	27.2	59.3	13.4	9,956	44.3	66.5	10.7
Lebanon township (Wayne)	684	664	-2.9	753	94.0	0.0	0.0	2.4	3.6	15.9	59.0	25.1	283	89.0	52.7	19.8
Lebanon South CDP	2,270	NA	NA	2,428	96.5	0.6	0.4	0.0	2.6	20.0	56.5	23.5	996	82.6	51.8	20.8
LeBoeuf township (Erie)	1,698	1,677	-1.2	1,838	97.9	0.7	0.7	0.5	0.2	21.7	63.3	15.1	699	87.1	53.1	25.2
Leechburg borough & MCD (Armstrong)	2,147	2,095	-2.4	2,137	96.4	1.5	1.5	0.6	0.0	22.8	58.7	18.5	994	63.1	51.1	18.3
Leeper CDP	158	NA	NA	162	100.0	0.0	0.0	0.0	0.0	6.2	52.5	41.4	91	94.5	79.1	20.9
Leesport borough & MCD (Berks)	1,918	1,910	-0.4	2,000	88.1	3.5	0.0	2.0	6.4	25.4	63.2	11.6	769	80.8	51.2	22.8
Leet township (Allegheny)	1,632	1,626	-0.4	1,592	88.8	0.6	7.5	2.0	1.1	25.9	60.6	13.5	601	89.9	22.3	49.3
Leetsdale borough & MCD (Allegheny)	1,218	1,206	-1.0	1,253	87.6	4.5	1.8	4.4	1.7	23.2	59.4	17.6	554	59.4	36.5	31.6
Lehigh township (Carbon)	483	477	-1.2	514	97.5	0.0	0.0	2.5	0.0	5.7	69.2	25.3	244	91.0	63.5	13.1
Lehigh township (Northampton)	10,526	10,439	-0.8	10,486	94.9	1.4	0.9	0.7	2.1	18.9	63.8	17.3	4,094	90.8	49.6	25.0
Lehigh township (Wayne)	1,881	1,802	-4.2	1,728	91.1	3.2	0.0	2.0	3.6	14.1	67.0	18.8	751	82.6	52.7	23.0
Lehighton borough & MCD (Carbon)	5,500	5,365	-2.5	5,427	96.1	0.0	0.0	2.6	1.3	20.8	60.1	19.0	2,310	53.1	60.0	18.0
Lehman township (Luzerne)	3,498	3,492	-0.2	3,499	98.4	0.0	0.6	1.0	0.0	22.4	59.5	17.9	1,352	83.2	37.6	35.8
Lehman township (Pike)	10,663	10,427	-2.2	10,571	57.2	16.1	0.8	2.1	23.9	24.1	62.9	13.1	3,606	82.2	39.9	22.5
Leidy township (Clinton)	180	180	0.0	117	100.0	0.0	0.0	0.0	0.0	2.6	55.6	41.9	64	81.3	59.4	3.1
Leith-Hatfield CDP	2,546	NA	NA	2,748	96.0	0.1	0.0	3.9	0.0	17.9	53.6	28.5	1,170	84.2	46.9	32.4
Lemon township (Wyoming)	1,241	1,232	-0.7	1,412	99.1	0.0	0.2	0.2	0.5	22.3	66.0	11.8	590	77.1	54.2	18.3
Lemont CDP	2,270	NA	NA	2,706	97.1	0.0	0.8	2.1	0.0	25.8	70.6	3.7	988	75.5	12.1	67.3
Lemont Furnace CDP	827	NA	NA	747	96.0	4.0	0.0	0.0	0.0	17.4	69.4	13.1	275	72.7	75.3	2.5
Lemoyne borough & MCD (Cumberland)	4,553	4,622	1.5	4,592	84.0	1.5	1.0	8.4	5.2	27.2	58.4	14.3	2,054	55.5	36.6	30.7
Lenape Heights CDP	1,167	NA	NA	1,082	100.0	0.0	0.0	0.0	0.0	12.1	70.6	17.4	513	69.0	56.7	18.5
Lenhartsville borough & MCD (Berks)	165	166	0.6	168	93.5	3.6	0.0	0.0	3.0	31.0	49.4	19.6	69	43.5	63.8	13.0
Lenkerville CDP	550	NA	NA	481	100.0	0.0	0.0	0.0	0.0	2.9	78.1	19.1	244	82.8	64.8	9.0
Lenox township (Susquehanna)	1,934	1,870	-3.3	1,870	98.7	0.2	1.0	0.2	0.0	20.0	62.4	17.6	756	84.1	67.6	16.5
Leola CDP	0	NA	NA	7,088	82.8	2.1	6.5	1.3	7.3	27.1	58.1	14.8	2,527	66.0	50.5	27.5
Le Raysville borough & MCD (Bradford)	290	285	-1.7	328	97.9	0.0	2.1	0.0	0.0	32.9	56.0	11.0	106	82.1	61.3	14.2
Leroy township (Bradford)	720	707	-1.8	873	99.3	0.0	0.0	0.7	0.0	30.4	50.9	18.9	308	77.3	59.4	14.3
Letterkenny township (Franklin)	2,318	2,351	1.4	2,491	94.8	0.2	0.7	1.2	3.1	27.8	58.5	13.7	901	83.7	60.9	7.9
Level Green CDP	4,020	NA	NA	3,840	97.6	2.1	0.0	0.2	0.0	24.1	54.8	21.1	1,497	93.6	36.1	33.8
Levittown CDP	52,983	NA	NA	51,326	88.6	3.4	1.2	1.2	5.6	20.6	65.2	14.2	18,066	85.7	48.2	18.5
Lewis township (Lycoming)	987	977	-1.0	1,059	98.3	0.6	0.0	0.4	0.8	18.4	64.8	16.9	424	77.6	57.8	11.1
Lewis township (Northumberland)	1,915	1,935	1.0	2,018	98.3	0.7	0.0	0.3	0.7	29.5	57.0	13.5	702	87.0	60.7	10.4
Lewis township (Union)	1,480	1,482	0.1	1,299	99.7	0.0	0.0	0.3	0.0	21.0	63.5	15.6	518	74.7	74.5	5.4
Lewisberry borough & MCD (York)	362	363	0.3	402	91.3	0.0	0.0	4.2	4.5	16.7	70.8	12.4	178	66.9	49.4	18.5
Lewisburg borough & MCD (Union)	5,792	5,775	-0.3	5,781	87.9	3.0	2.8	1.7	4.7	8.9	78.6	12.4	1,842	35.6	34.8	34.5
Lewis Run borough & MCD (McKean)	617	600	-2.8	600	98.5	0.0	0.0	0.0	1.5	18.7	57.7	23.7	297	72.4	57.2	14.8
Lewistown borough & MCD (Mifflin)	8,338	8,297	-0.5	8,341	91.8	2.1	1.4	1.7	3.0	22.9	63.3	13.9	3,558	44.8	64.5	13.5
Liberty borough & MCD (Adams)	1,237	1,241	0.3	1,254	97.5	0.0	0.0	1.5	1.0	17.5	63.0	19.2	508	83.9	40.7	26.0
Liberty borough & MCD (Allegheny)	2,551	2,532	-0.7	2,536	95.3	2.4	1.3	0.3	0.7	16.8	63.3	19.8	1,042	86.0	51.6	17.9
Liberty township (Bedford)	1,368	1,323	-3.3	1,514	99.3	0.0	0.0	0.0	0.7	21.9	60.0	18.1	598	88.0	54.7	22.4
Liberty township (Centre)	2,117	2,087	-1.4	1,880	99.6	0.2	0.1	0.0	0.1	16.5	67.2	16.3	770	85.3	74.3	7.5
Liberty township (McKean)	1,612	1,574	-2.4	1,701	98.0	0.6	0.2	1.1	0.1	20.0	63.5	16.4	693	84.3	61.2	12.8
Liberty township (Mercer)	1,414	1,393	-1.5	1,296	98.5	0.0	0.0	1.4	0.2	20.9	60.2	18.8	501	93.8	46.3	32.9
Liberty township (Montour)	1,584	1,631	3.0	1,720	94.5	4.8	0.3	0.0	0.3	19.9	64.6	15.5	608	88.7	59.9	22.7
Liberty township (Susquehanna)	1,290	1,234	-4.3	1,398	98.6	0.0	0.0	0.8	0.6	24.0	56.1	19.8	530	83.4	54.9	14.7

1 May be of any race.

Table A. All Places — **Population and Housing**

STATE City, town, township, borough, or CDP (county if applicable)	2010 census total population	2014 estimated population	Percent change 2010–2014	ACS total population estimate 2010–2014	White alone, not Hispanic or Latino	Black alone, not Hispanic or Latino	Asian alone, not Hispanic or Latino	All other races or 2 or more races, not Hispanic or Latino	Hispanic or Latino[1]	Under 18 years old	Age 18 to 64 years old	Age 65 years and older	Total occupied housing units	Percent owner occupied	High school diploma or less	Bachelor's degree or more
	1	2	3	4	5	6	7	8	9	10	11	12	13	14	15	16
PENNSYLVANIA—Con.																
Liberty borough & MCD (Tioga)	248	249	0.4	186	87.6	0.0	0.0	8.6	3.8	28.5	53.8	17.7	68	67.6	60.3	8.8
Liberty township (Tioga)	1,032	1,037	0.5	1,090	97.8	0.0	0.4	0.6	1.2	31.7	51.3	17.2	369	74.8	51.8	21.1
Licking township (Clarion)	536	547	2.1	561	96.8	0.7	0.9	1.1	0.5	34.2	52.1	13.7	183	84.2	57.9	20.8
Licking Creek township (Fulton)	1,703	1,687	-0.9	1,701	99.7	0.0	0.1	0.2	0.0	24.6	62.9	12.5	663	73.2	70.0	8.7
Lightstreet CDP	1,093	NA	NA	889	96.0	0.0	4.0	0.0	0.0	15.6	55.6	28.7	446	82.3	47.5	21.5
Ligonier borough & MCD (Westmoreland)	1,573	1,549	-1.5	1,460	99.2	0.1	0.0	0.0	0.8	11.5	57.0	31.5	774	57.0	29.8	39.5
Ligonier township (Westmoreland)	6,603	6,553	-0.8	6,573	97.8	0.0	0.0	1.0	1.2	16.7	57.0	26.1	2,899	83.1	43.8	26.5
Lilly borough & MCD (Cambria)	968	938	-3.1	846	95.3	0.0	0.6	1.2	3.0	15.6	62.0	22.5	385	80.3	72.5	11.2
Lima CDP	2,735	NA	NA	2,345	85.2	9.3	1.9	0.4	3.1	9.0	30.9	60.0	1,043	54.3	38.3	45.6
Limerick township (Montgomery)	18,074	18,756	3.8	18,474	86.8	3.7	4.1	2.0	3.4	25.9	60.8	13.3	6,923	78.4	24.3	44.6
Lime Ridge CDP	890	NA	NA	1,000	90.1	0.0	0.8	2.2	6.9	25.5	56.7	17.8	431	75.2	76.8	12.3
Limestone township (Clarion)	1,858	1,822	-1.9	1,666	99.0	0.0	0.0	0.8	0.2	22.5	61.5	15.9	692	86.1	55.6	19.1
Limestone township (Lycoming)	2,019	2,024	0.2	1,954	98.6	0.0	0.0	0.8	0.6	25.9	60.3	13.8	699	86.3	51.5	19.6
Limestone township (Montour)	1,066	1,129	5.9	1,091	97.1	1.6	0.5	0.0	0.0	29.6	56.0	14.4	347	94.5	57.9	20.2
Limestone township (Union)	1,723	1,747	1.4	1,940	91.2	0.3	0.0	0.9	7.6	30.8	59.4	9.7	692	79.6	56.8	20.2
Limestone township (Warren)	403	389	-3.5	265	95.8	0.0	0.0	1.9	2.3	15.9	64.5	19.6	121	73.6	39.7	17.4
Lincoln borough & MCD (Allegheny)	1,072	1,066	-0.6	1,000	92.6	0.8	0.0	0.6	6.0	17.7	61.4	20.9	419	87.4	59.9	10.7
Lincoln township (Bedford)	425	410	-3.5	377	93.1	0.0	0.0	5.6	1.3	29.7	56.3	14.1	128	91.4	71.1	7.8
Lincoln township (Huntingdon)	338	336	-0.6	300	97.7	0.0	1.7	0.7	0.0	27.3	54.4	18.3	112	87.5	53.6	17.9
Lincoln township (Somerset)	1,519	1,492	-1.8	1,599	99.7	0.0	0.0	0.3	0.0	22.4	61.9	15.7	623	84.9	62.1	12.4
Lincoln Park CDP	1,615	NA	NA	1,428	86.3	2.4	6.5	1.8	3.0	26.4	59.9	13.5	621	63.3	38.2	44.0
Lincoln University CDP	1,726	NA	NA	1,771	27.7	63.6	0.8	2.8	5.0	2.3	97.6	0.0	6	100.0	0.0	0.0
Lincolnville CDP	96	NA	NA	116	100.0	0.0	0.0	0.0	0.0	15.5	71.7	12.9	47	93.6	51.1	17.0
Linesville borough & MCD (Crawford)	1,036	1,008	-2.7	940	99.4	0.0	0.0	0.2	0.4	17.7	62.8	19.7	432	56.5	49.3	18.5
Linglestown CDP	6,334	NA	NA	6,482	94.9	0.5	1.7	0.8	2.1	21.2	61.6	17.1	2,620	86.7	38.2	35.8
Linntown CDP	1,489	NA	NA	1,649	96.4	0.0	1.2	0.0	2.4	19.3	62.7	17.9	750	80.3	15.1	61.6
Linwood CDP	3,281	NA	NA	3,394	80.2	14.6	0.6	3.6	1.1	27.8	63.6	8.6	1,132	57.2	62.5	9.3
Lionville CDP	0	NA	NA	6,334	83.7	4.8	7.3	1.3	2.8	20.9	65.7	13.5	2,560	62.6	24.7	50.6
Litchfield township (Bradford)	1,318	1,333	1.1	1,219	99.0	0.0	0.0	0.5	0.5	12.2	68.8	18.9	520	90.8	54.0	13.5
Lititz borough & MCD (Lancaster)	9,369	9,397	0.3	9,386	89.4	1.0	3.4	1.0	5.1	23.4	55.4	21.2	3,747	61.7	40.4	33.3
Little Beaver township (Lawrence)	1,414	1,377	-2.6	1,243	95.9	1.8	0.0	1.4	0.9	20.5	61.1	18.3	470	81.7	70.6	12.6
Little Britain CDP	372	NA	NA	83	100.0	0.0	0.0	0.0	0.0	0.0	22.9	77.1	53	100.0	56.6	43.4
Little Britain township (Lancaster)	4,106	4,203	2.4	4,163	98.1	0.0	0.0	0.0	1.9	28.1	60.3	11.6	1,397	91.0	57.6	15.9
Little Mahanoy township (Northumberland)	479	466	-2.7	400	96.0	3.3	0.0	0.3	0.5	24.1	62.5	13.8	136	74.3	68.4	17.6
Little Meadows borough & MCD (Susquehanna)	273	263	-3.7	240	100.0	0.0	0.0	0.0	0.0	8.3	60.0	31.7	125	87.2	50.4	17.6
Littlestown borough & MCD (Adams)	4,434	4,448	0.3	4,438	96.1	0.0	0.2	2.2	1.5	23.9	61.5	14.5	1,800	62.5	52.8	21.9
Liverpool borough & MCD (Perry)	959	957	-0.2	796	96.1	0.0	0.5	2.1	1.3	19.7	59.1	21.2	368	50.5	51.9	18.5
Liverpool township (Perry)	1,053	1,048	-0.5	1,172	96.3	0.2	0.0	2.0	1.5	23.8	65.3	10.9	424	89.4	55.2	17.9
Lock Haven city & MCD (Clinton)	9,772	9,862	0.9	9,860	92.3	3.4	1.1	1.8	1.5	16.4	73.3	10.3	3,194	37.1	47.8	16.3
Locust township (Columbia)	1,406	1,418	0.9	1,281	99.1	0.1	0.0	0.3	0.5	16.2	60.9	23.0	549	89.4	55.9	20.4
Locustdale CDP	177	NA	NA	178	100.0	0.0	0.0	0.0	0.0	6.2	76.5	17.4	103	100.0	68.9	5.8
Logan township (Blair)	12,303	12,319	0.1	12,338	96.0	1.5	0.9	0.4	1.1	14.1	65.7	20.0	4,822	80.4	54.7	17.7
Logan township (Clinton)	817	822	0.6	895	95.6	0.7	1.1	2.1	0.4	30.3	52.4	17.3	282	81.9	64.5	14.5
Logan township (Huntingdon)	676	669	-1.0	702	98.9	0.0	1.0	0.0	0.1	23.0	55.6	21.2	288	75.7	57.6	18.8
Loganton borough & MCD (Clinton)	468	473	1.1	509	99.2	0.0	0.0	0.8	0.0	29.1	49.1	21.8	177	86.4	60.5	10.7
Loganville borough & MCD (York)	1,240	1,232	-0.6	1,226	95.4	0.0	1.5	1.9	1.2	28.0	58.2	13.8	461	82.4	50.8	21.3
London Britain township (Chester)	3,139	3,255	3.7	3,199	92.7	1.5	1.9	0.8	3.1	25.9	61.3	12.8	1,057	91.5	15.9	56.6
Londonderry township (Bedford)	1,856	1,820	-1.9	1,872	99.1	0.0	0.0	0.5	0.3	18.1	62.0	19.8	744	84.5	65.2	8.3
Londonderry township (Chester)	2,149	2,368	10.2	2,339	88.4	0.7	1.5	0.0	9.4	24.4	63.8	11.8	793	85.4	39.1	39.0
Londonderry township (Dauphin)	5,235	5,208	-0.5	5,222	99.8	0.1	0.0	0.0	0.1	22.2	61.7	15.9	2,060	88.2	61.3	13.5
London Grove township (Chester)	7,475	8,435	12.8	7,945	65.1	1.4	0.9	0.9	31.6	30.9	59.5	9.8	2,461	82.7	36.1	40.7
Long Branch borough & MCD (Washington)	447	437	-2.2	455	94.5	0.9	0.4	3.7	0.4	20.7	58.9	20.4	172	93.0	56.4	19.8
Longfellow CDP	215	NA	NA	208	100.0	0.0	0.0	0.0	0.0	14.5	65.4	20.2	90	82.2	70.0	12.2
Longswamp township (Berks)	5,680	5,684	0.1	5,687	96.2	0.9	0.6	0.2	2.1	17.5	63.4	19.3	2,261	73.7	62.2	13.9

1 May be of any race.

Table A. All Places — **Population and Housing**

	Population				Race and Hispanic or Latino origin (percent), 2010–2014					Age (percent), 2010–2014			Households, 2010–2014			
								All other races or 2 or more races, not Hispanic or Latino							Householders by level of education (percent)	
STATE City, town, township, borough, or CDP (county if applicable)	2010 census total population	2014 estimated population	Percent change 2010–2014	ACS total population estimate 2010–2014	White alone, not Hispanic or Latino	Black alone, not Hispanic or Latino	Asian alone, not Hispanic or Latino		Hispanic or Latino[1]	Under 18 years old	Age 18 to 64 years old	Age 65 years and older	Total occupied housing units	Percent owner occupied	High school diploma or less	Bachelor's degree or more
	1	2	3	4	5	6	7	8	9	10	11	12	13	14	15	16
PENNSYLVANIA—Con.																
Lorain borough & MCD (Cambria)	759	731	-3.7	875	99.4	0.1	0.3	0.1	0.0	31.7	57.7	10.6	330	86.1	63.9	11.2
Lorane CDP	4,236	NA	NA	3,868	87.0	3.9	2.0	1.1	5.9	17.1	64.8	18.2	1,638	78.1	45.4	25.0
Loretto borough & MCD (Cambria)	1,302	1,308	0.5	1,277	95.0	1.8	0.2	0.7	2.3	3.1	92.3	4.5	124	49.2	23.4	43.5
Lower Allen CDP	6,694	NA	NA	7,012	90.2	1.2	0.4	2.4	5.8	19.8	58.3	21.8	3,239	67.8	37.2	38.7
Lower Allen township (Cumberland)	17,980	18,949	5.4	18,335	78.1	10.7	3.1	2.3	5.8	14.5	64.9	20.6	7,170	63.9	44.2	34.9
Lower Alsace township (Berks)	4,475	4,465	-0.2	4,478	81.0	3.7	2.2	1.6	11.5	23.3	61.4	15.3	1,774	71.4	45.9	26.5
Lower Augusta township (Northumberland)	1,064	1,053	-1.0	935	99.9	0.0	0.0	0.0	0.1	13.2	65.0	21.8	425	86.1	69.4	12.0
Lower Burrell city & MCD (Westmoreland)	11,761	11,531	-2.0	11,653	97.6	0.5	0.5	0.3	1.1	19.3	59.5	21.3	4,915	77.9	43.5	29.3
Lower Chanceford township (York)	3,028	3,074	1.5	3,046	97.3	0.0	0.7	1.6	0.4	24.5	62.0	13.7	1,088	78.9	63.3	11.4
Lower Chichester township (Delaware)	3,468	3,478	0.3	3,466	80.4	14.3	0.6	3.5	1.3	28.0	63.5	8.4	1,158	57.0	61.7	9.1
Lower Frankford township (Cumberland)	1,732	1,734	0.1	1,788	96.7	0.3	0.4	1.4	1.2	18.8	66.5	14.8	733	81.3	65.8	16.4
Lower Frederick township (Montgomery)	4,840	4,896	1.2	4,880	91.8	2.3	1.2	0.0	4.8	22.7	66.9	10.6	1,831	85.9	42.5	29.3
Lower Gwynedd township (Montgomery)	11,405	11,553	1.3	11,500	79.1	8.7	7.9	3.1	1.2	20.7	54.7	24.6	4,577	70.4	18.1	63.1
Lower Heidelberg township (Berks)	5,513	5,843	6.0	5,633	90.2	2.0	3.1	0.3	4.4	26.7	59.1	14.2	1,987	83.8	31.8	45.4
Lower Macungie township (Lehigh)	30,629	31,639	3.3	31,226	82.9	3.2	5.2	2.7	6.0	24.2	57.6	18.3	11,894	89.0	25.7	50.6
Lower Mahanoy township (Northumberland)	1,701	1,693	-0.5	1,515	99.5	0.0	0.0	0.5	0.0	17.4	61.3	21.3	666	80.3	70.9	11.9
Lower Makefield township (Bucks)	32,559	32,687	0.4	32,622	87.9	1.8	6.9	1.8	1.6	25.2	60.4	14.3	11,920	88.2	13.5	70.8
Lower Merion township (Montgomery)	57,837	58,273	0.8	58,114	80.0	5.9	7.1	2.9	4.1	22.2	58.5	19.2	22,070	76.4	10.2	77.4
Lower Mifflin township (Cumberland)	1,783	1,777	-0.3	1,842	98.5	0.0	0.2	1.0	0.3	21.3	64.9	13.9	735	81.0	66.3	16.3
Lower Milford township (Lehigh)	3,775	3,839	1.7	3,819	98.2	0.0	0.0	0.0	1.8	21.6	60.9	17.4	1,354	93.7	40.8	33.5
Lower Moreland township (Montgomery)	12,988	13,215	1.7	13,133	87.6	0.9	9.2	1.2	1.1	22.7	56.3	21.0	4,628	85.7	25.8	57.9
Lower Mount Bethel township (Northampton)	3,101	3,081	-0.6	3,091	94.6	0.0	0.0	0.0	5.4	16.5	67.3	16.2	1,219	91.9	51.8	17.3
Lower Nazareth township (Northampton)	5,698	5,916	3.8	5,765	97.2	0.3	0.8	0.3	1.3	24.7	62.5	12.8	2,010	92.0	33.2	43.3
Lower Oxford township (Chester)	5,200	5,018	-3.5	5,095	55.0	24.0	0.7	2.2	18.1	19.4	73.2	7.2	1,104	79.3	57.2	18.6
Lower Paxton township (Dauphin)	47,360	48,086	1.5	47,705	76.9	10.7	4.2	3.1	5.1	20.9	63.9	15.2	20,053	65.6	30.3	40.8
Lower Pottsgrove township (Montgomery)	12,059	12,192	1.1	12,145	84.1	8.0	1.0	2.7	4.1	24.9	60.7	14.4	4,484	82.0	39.8	33.5
Lower Providence township (Montgomery)	25,436	25,694	1.0	25,603	77.0	6.9	12.6	1.2	2.3	23.5	61.6	14.8	8,572	75.1	26.9	49.7
Lower Salford township (Montgomery)	14,959	15,348	2.6	15,201	87.1	4.1	4.8	1.3	2.7	24.7	63.0	12.4	5,541	76.9	26.3	51.3
Lower Saucon township (Northampton)	10,772	10,794	0.2	10,788	93.5	0.2	1.1	0.5	4.7	20.5	59.7	19.8	4,196	88.5	32.9	44.7
Lower Southampton township (Bucks)	18,909	19,010	0.5	18,960	92.4	1.1	3.1	1.3	2.1	22.4	63.1	14.3	6,827	80.7	33.8	28.1
Lower Swatara township (Dauphin)	8,236	8,651	5.0	8,419	84.9	7.5	3.0	2.2	2.3	20.8	63.2	16.0	3,133	87.0	45.1	28.2
Lower Towamensing township (Carbon)	3,259	3,212	-1.4	3,244	98.0	0.0	1.0	0.0	1.0	20.6	62.8	16.6	1,159	90.3	58.0	13.2
Lower Turkeyfoot township (Somerset)	603	587	-2.7	749	98.4	0.8	0.0	0.5	0.3	16.7	51.8	31.4	267	84.6	67.8	12.7
Lower Tyrone township (Fayette)	1,123	1,102	-1.9	1,093	99.6	0.4	0.0	0.0	0.0	18.2	65.2	16.5	407	90.4	68.3	6.4
Lower Windsor township (York)	7,382	7,432	0.7	7,399	94.4	0.0	0.7	3.6	1.3	22.1	62.2	15.7	2,887	84.6	62.4	13.6
Lower Yoder township (Cambria)	2,699	2,604	-3.5	2,653	97.1	0.4	0.3	1.4	0.9	12.4	54.1	33.5	1,396	84.7	53.7	19.9
Lowhill township (Lehigh)	2,173	2,239	3.0	2,214	92.9	1.5	0.0	3.0	2.6	21.3	62.0	16.8	827	91.7	39.5	37.5
Loyalhanna CDP	3,428	NA	NA	3,351	94.7	0.4	0.0	3.8	1.2	15.9	55.7	28.5	1,512	78.4	55.9	15.7
Loyalhanna township (Westmoreland)	2,379	2,327	-2.2	2,027	97.7	0.3	0.0	0.0	2.0	16.2	66.6	17.2	767	86.3	52.2	19.4
Loyalsock township (Lycoming)	11,026	11,201	1.6	11,144	93.1	1.9	1.9	2.0	1.0	17.0	53.6	29.4	5,009	73.9	41.9	32.9
Lucerne Mines CDP	937	NA	NA	596	95.6	0.0	0.0	0.0	4.4	8.4	69.2	22.5	246	95.1	93.9	0.0
Lumber township (Cameron)	195	185	-5.1	201	99.0	0.0	0.0	0.0	1.0	19.9	58.8	21.4	81	91.4	49.4	19.8
Lumber City borough & MCD (Clearfield)	76	75	-1.3	100	100.0	0.0	0.0	0.0	0.0	8.0	76.0	16.0	37	89.2	56.8	2.7
Lumber City CDP	255	NA	NA	234	100.0	0.0	0.0	0.0	0.0	25.2	48.3	26.5	133	61.7	73.7	26.3
Lurgan township (Franklin)	2,151	2,172	1.0	2,155	99.0	0.0	0.0	0.6	0.5	25.7	57.8	16.5	762	80.1	72.8	10.9
Luzerne township (Fayette)	5,965	5,912	-0.9	5,948	75.2	18.0	0.0	2.2	4.6	10.4	71.8	17.7	1,667	85.8	67.5	17.9
Luzerne borough & MCD (Luzerne)	2,845	2,839	-0.2	2,843	94.1	0.9	1.7	1.5	1.9	17.5	68.1	14.6	1,328	53.1	48.3	19.5
Lycoming township (Lycoming)	1,480	1,498	1.2	1,483	95.5	2.8	0.0	1.3	0.3	16.6	64.5	18.9	601	88.2	59.4	8.8

1 May be of any race.

Table A. All Places — **Population and Housing**

Items 1–16

STATE City, town, township, borough, or CDP (county if applicable)	2010 census total population	2014 estimated population	Percent change 2010–2014	ACS total population estimate 2010–2014	White alone, not Hispanic or Latino	Black alone, not Hispanic or Latino	Asian alone, not Hispanic or Latino	All other races or 2 or more races, not Hispanic or Latino	Hispanic or Latino[1]	Under 18 years old	Age 18 to 64 years old	Age 65 years and older	Total occupied housing units	Percent owner occupied	High school diploma or less	Bachelor's degree or more
	1	2	3	4	5	6	7	8	9	10	11	12	13	14	15	16
PENNSYLVANIA—Con.																
Lykens borough & MCD (Dauphin)	1,779	1,761	-1.0	1,631	95.6	0.0	0.3	0.7	3.4	21.2	58.3	20.4	687	69.9	68.7	11.8
Lykens township (Dauphin)	1,620	1,633	0.8	1,675	100.0	0.0	0.0	0.0	0.0	38.9	51.8	9.3	447	81.2	74.5	5.8
Lynn township (Lehigh)	4,229	4,294	1.5	4,274	98.4	0.6	0.0	0.0	1.0	21.4	62.6	15.9	1,614	86.0	45.5	24.6
Lynnwood-Pricedale CDP	2,031	NA	NA	2,129	91.2	4.1	3.9	0.0	0.8	15.8	63.8	20.5	955	72.1	50.1	16.9
Lyons borough & MCD (Berks)	478	472	-1.3	479	87.3	7.5	0.0	3.3	1.9	10.2	63.3	26.5	202	53.5	62.4	7.9
McAdoo borough & MCD (Schuylkill)	2,300	2,230	-3.0	2,643	90.5	0.0	0.0	0.0	9.5	26.0	58.2	15.9	1,028	56.8	69.1	7.5
McAlisterville CDP	971	NA	NA	975	100.0	0.0	0.0	0.0	0.0	29.2	42.3	28.5	399	74.9	75.2	16.8
McCalmont township (Jefferson)	1,082	1,067	-1.4	942	98.8	0.0	0.0	1.2	0.0	26.3	56.5	17.4	369	81.3	62.1	14.9
McCandless township (Allegheny)	28,457	28,921	1.6	28,788	89.8	1.9	6.3	0.8	1.2	20.3	61.4	18.4	11,579	77.1	18.4	59.1
McClure borough & MCD (Snyder)	941	942	0.1	917	98.4	0.0	0.1	0.4	1.1	20.4	56.3	23.1	389	73.3	73.5	12.6
McConnellsburg borough & MCD (Fulton)	1,077	1,049	-2.6	1,015	90.6	5.4	1.2	2.7	0.1	19.8	60.4	19.8	485	42.7	68.0	20.6
McConnellstown CDP	1,194	NA	NA	1,286	98.3	0.0	0.7	0.8	0.2	21.8	58.5	19.8	513	89.5	49.3	29.0
McDonald borough	2,149	2,107	-2.0	2,121	94.3	1.7	0.0	0.6	3.3	21.3	60.0	18.7	887	65.4	62.2	18.2
McDonald borough (Allegheny)	383	378	-1.3	522	98.9	0.0	0.0	1.1	0.0	27.4	57.6	14.9	200	94.0	77.0	10.5
McDonald borough (Washington)	1,766	1,729	-2.1	1,599	92.9	2.3	0.0	0.4	4.4	19.4	60.8	19.9	687	57.1	57.9	20.4
McElhattan CDP	598	NA	NA	627	97.0	0.3	0.0	1.8	1.0	18.3	59.4	22.2	266	87.6	66.9	5.3
McEwensville borough & MCD (Northumberland)	279	280	0.4	339	100.0	0.0	0.0	0.0	0.0	18.0	66.7	15.3	132	64.4	60.6	9.1
McGovern CDP	2,742	NA	NA	2,687	92.4	7.6	0.0	0.0	0.0	22.2	55.4	22.4	1,128	89.7	36.5	27.4
McHenry township (Lycoming)	143	142	-0.7	167	98.8	0.0	0.0	1.2	0.0	22.2	51.6	26.3	64	85.9	73.4	3.1
McIntyre township (Lycoming)	521	515	-1.2	663	98.3	0.0	0.0	1.5	0.2	20.6	63.9	15.5	243	77.4	57.6	20.2
McKean borough & MCD (Erie)	388	385	-0.8	439	95.7	1.6	1.1	1.4	0.2	22.0	60.3	17.8	208	52.9	39.9	35.1
McKean township (Erie)	4,409	4,402	-0.2	4,418	97.9	0.6	0.1	0.9	0.5	20.6	64.7	14.8	1,709	96.3	59.6	19.1
McKeansburg CDP	163	NA	NA	137	96.4	0.0	0.0	0.0	3.6	21.8	54.0	24.1	58	63.8	65.5	20.7
McKeesport city & MCD (Allegheny)	19,731	19,561	-0.9	19,663	61.6	28.5	1.2	5.1	3.5	20.2	61.9	17.9	8,760	53.1	58.1	10.4
McKees Rocks borough & MCD (Allegheny)	6,104	6,046	-1.0	6,088	67.8	25.2	0.0	5.6	1.4	23.4	63.8	12.7	2,738	35.2	59.3	10.0
McKnightstown CDP	226	NA	NA	73	100.0	0.0	0.0	0.0	0.0	0.0	48.0	52.1	55	100.0	0.0	30.9
McMurray CDP	4,647	NA	NA	4,727	99.0	0.3	0.0	0.1	0.5	26.2	57.7	16.1	1,722	97.3	18.6	59.0
McNett township (Lycoming)	174	170	-2.3	149	100.0	0.0	0.0	0.0	0.0	15.5	51.0	33.6	66	84.8	53.0	7.6
McSherrystown borough & MCD (Adams)	3,038	3,048	0.3	3,050	95.6	0.0	0.0	1.2	3.1	28.1	54.1	17.8	1,231	49.9	76.8	6.7
Macungie borough & MCD (Lehigh)	3,074	3,116	1.4	3,106	86.4	1.0	1.7	1.1	9.8	18.0	68.1	14.1	1,407	57.5	41.2	35.2
McVeytown borough & MCD (Mifflin)	342	335	-2.0	317	98.1	0.0	0.0	1.6	0.3	15.1	63.4	21.5	154	79.9	64.3	16.2
Madison township (Armstrong)	820	800	-2.4	910	98.4	0.5	0.0	0.0	1.1	18.8	58.8	22.4	372	82.5	61.3	7.5
Madison township (Clarion)	1,212	1,185	-2.2	1,308	99.5	0.0	0.0	0.1	0.4	17.5	60.9	21.6	531	76.8	75.9	9.4
Madison township (Columbia)	1,605	1,617	0.7	1,544	97.9	0.1	0.0	0.1	1.9	20.4	61.7	17.9	614	84.5	60.7	23.0
Madison township (Lackawanna)	2,750	2,722	-1.0	2,748	98.2	0.1	0.9	0.4	0.3	18.9	67.1	14.0	1,087	93.9	55.8	15.5
Madison borough & MCD (Westmoreland)	397	383	-3.5	372	100.0	0.0	0.0	0.0	0.0	5.0	69.3	25.5	178	83.7	58.4	16.9
Madisonburg CDP	168	NA	NA	193	94.8	0.0	0.0	0.0	5.2	18.2	70.9	10.9	72	94.4	79.2	18.1
Mahaffey borough & MCD (Clearfield)	370	356	-3.8	351	98.9	0.0	0.0	1.1	0.0	28.2	57.5	14.2	124	83.9	62.9	6.5
Mahanoy township (Schuylkill)	3,152	3,341	6.0	3,254	48.5	40.4	0.4	3.2	7.5	3.4	90.7	5.9	354	88.1	70.6	5.9
Mahanoy City borough & MCD (Schuylkill)	4,162	4,083	-1.9	4,126	90.2	4.0	0.0	2.0	3.9	28.2	52.9	18.8	1,678	67.7	64.0	12.3
Mahoning township (Armstrong)	1,425	1,390	-2.5	1,470	96.3	0.3	0.5	2.7	0.1	24.1	57.6	18.5	595	77.3	76.6	9.9
Mahoning township (Carbon)	4,304	4,256	-1.1	4,284	96.7	2.6	0.7	0.0	0.0	17.9	58.0	24.1	1,630	86.7	50.1	14.2
Mahoning township (Lawrence)	3,083	2,990	-3.0	3,024	96.7	0.1	0.0	1.0	2.2	22.6	58.9	18.4	1,173	85.5	63.3	11.8
Mahoning township (Montour)	4,171	4,263	2.2	4,233	85.8	2.5	8.0	0.2	3.5	18.4	54.6	27.0	1,619	69.4	32.5	47.6
Maidencreek township (Berks)	9,130	9,412	3.1	9,284	92.6	1.8	0.4	0.6	4.5	25.3	63.4	11.1	3,364	85.0	45.7	25.0
Main township (Columbia)	1,236	1,296	4.9	1,370	96.8	0.1	0.9	0.7	1.5	21.8	61.8	16.3	498	83.5	44.4	30.3
Mainville CDP	132	NA	NA	105	100.0	0.0	0.0	0.0	0.0	17.1	68.5	14.3	34	82.4	50.0	11.8
Maitland CDP	357	NA	NA	212	100.0	0.0	0.0	0.0	0.0	13.2	63.1	23.6	102	74.5	64.7	0.0
Malvern borough & MCD (Chester)	2,998	3,434	14.5	3,179	79.3	5.9	4.0	1.2	9.6	24.1	59.5	16.4	1,416	59.0	20.6	58.6
Mammoth CDP	525	NA	NA	587	96.9	0.0	0.0	0.0	3.1	10.0	77.6	12.3	236	100.0	53.4	25.0
Manchester township (Wayne)	834	810	-2.9	827	96.3	0.0	0.5	1.2	2.1	16.1	54.8	29.1	335	86.9	72.8	9.3
Manchester borough & MCD (York)	2,763	2,753	-0.4	2,759	87.0	2.2	1.2	3.4	6.1	26.4	62.5	11.2	1,108	56.9	64.0	21.8
Manchester township (York)	18,161	18,439	1.5	18,304	81.9	8.3	2.8	3.3	3.7	26.8	59.3	13.9	6,814	87.5	38.0	35.2

1 May be of any race.

Table A. All Places — **Population and Housing**

STATE City, town, township, borough, or CDP (county if applicable)	2010 census total population	2014 estimated population	Percent change 2010–2014	ACS total population estimate 2010–2014	White alone, not Hispanic or Latino	Black alone, not Hispanic or Latino	Asian alone, not Hispanic or Latino	All other races or 2 or more races, not Hispanic or Latino	Hispanic or Latino[1]	Under 18 years old	Age 18 to 64 years old	Age 65 years and older	Total occupied housing units	Percent owner occupied	High school diploma or less	Bachelor's degree or more
	1	2	3	4	5	6	7	8	9	10	11	12	13	14	15	16
PENNSYLVANIA—Con.																
Manheim borough & MCD (Lancaster)	4,862	4,869	0.1	4,864	93.0	0.5	0.0	2.4	4.0	17.8	64.9	17.2	2,031	64.6	64.4	9.5
Manheim township (Lancaster)	38,167	39,341	3.1	38,770	83.2	2.4	3.9	2.2	8.4	22.9	55.6	21.5	15,275	72.8	32.7	46.4
Manheim township (York)	3,380	3,424	1.3	3,404	99.7	0.0	0.3	0.0	0.0	19.9	66.0	14.2	1,236	91.8	37.5	21.4
Mann township (Bedford)	500	490	-2.0	494	96.8	0.0	0.0	1.4	1.8	16.2	61.1	22.7	214	89.7	71.5	8.4
Manns Choice borough & MCD (Bedford)	300	298	-0.7	313	92.7	5.4	0.0	0.3	1.6	23.6	64.2	12.1	123	70.7	78.0	12.2
Manor township (Armstrong)	4,241	4,221	-0.5	4,245	99.0	1.0	0.0	0.0	0.0	17.0	58.7	24.3	1,838	75.3	58.0	20.1
Manor township (Lancaster)	19,612	20,423	4.1	20,006	86.2	3.9	1.2	1.2	7.5	20.9	63.7	15.6	8,131	76.3	46.1	27.3
Manor borough & MCD (Westmoreland)	3,239	3,308	2.1	3,261	100.0	0.0	0.0	0.0	0.0	21.3	66.0	12.5	1,331	86.7	38.0	35.2
Manorville borough & MCD (Armstrong)	410	400	-2.4	407	97.5	0.0	0.0	2.5	0.0	17.4	69.2	13.3	182	61.0	44.5	23.1
Mansfield borough & MCD (Tioga)	3,625	3,519	-2.9	3,582	92.7	1.3	1.2	1.5	3.4	12.6	72.3	15.2	1,406	47.2	32.0	38.8
Maple Glen CDP	6,742	NA	NA	6,767	89.0	1.4	7.4	0.4	1.8	22.8	64.0	13.4	2,359	92.3	17.6	59.2
Mapleton borough & MCD (Huntingdon)	444	429	-3.4	478	96.4	0.0	0.0	2.7	0.8	27.9	53.2	18.8	185	80.0	76.8	2.7
Mapletown CDP	130	NA	NA	158	100.0	0.0	0.0	0.0	0.0	27.9	58.3	13.9	47	100.0	59.6	19.1
Marcus Hook borough & MCD (Delaware)	2,397	2,399	0.1	2,430	77.0	16.6	0.0	2.5	3.8	32.9	56.8	10.5	810	42.0	62.3	9.6
Marianna borough & MCD (Washington)	494	482	-2.4	539	86.6	6.9	0.0	3.2	3.3	27.1	59.6	13.4	191	82.7	72.3	6.8
Marianne CDP	1,167	NA	NA	1,354	94.0	1.8	0.0	1.4	2.7	18.4	58.4	23.2	515	83.5	40.2	40.0
Marienville CDP	3,137	NA	NA	2,815	48.3	35.8	0.5	4.9	10.4	4.1	83.5	12.5	318	69.5	50.9	25.5
Marietta borough & MCD (Lancaster)	2,588	2,604	0.6	2,595	91.8	4.2	0.0	0.9	3.1	23.1	63.9	12.9	1,101	64.9	67.7	13.4
Marion township (Beaver)	913	904	-1.0	920	97.9	0.4	1.2	0.4	0.0	20.0	63.2	16.8	387	85.0	41.6	35.4
Marion township (Berks)	1,684	1,817	7.9	1,789	98.3	0.4	0.0	0.2	1.1	18.7	65.0	16.3	711	75.9	57.1	21.7
Marion township (Butler)	1,239	1,212	-2.2	1,333	95.8	0.2	0.0	3.6	0.5	22.5	64.2	13.5	505	79.8	68.1	10.1
Marion township (Centre)	1,224	1,220	-0.3	1,179	99.0	0.3	0.2	0.4	0.2	30.7	60.8	8.6	387	92.8	53.5	25.3
Marion CDP	953	NA	NA	1,050	82.4	0.0	0.0	0.0	17.6	26.8	62.6	10.5	365	68.2	57.8	12.1
Marion Center borough & MCD (Indiana)	451	430	-4.7	469	99.8	0.0	0.0	0.2	0.0	27.4	61.3	11.1	179	68.7	58.7	15.1
Marion Heights borough & MCD (Northumberland)	611	611	0.0	589	99.3	0.0	0.0	0.7	0.0	16.7	62.7	20.7	266	88.3	58.3	14.3
Marklesburg borough & MCD (Huntingdon)	204	203	-0.5	260	100.0	0.0	0.0	0.0	0.0	25.3	55.4	19.2	101	81.2	62.4	20.8
Markleysburg borough & MCD (Fayette)	284	279	-1.8	278	96.0	0.0	0.0	1.8	2.2	13.7	50.8	35.6	97	73.2	73.2	5.2
Marlborough township (Montgomery)	3,178	3,299	3.8	3,256	98.1	0.1	0.2	0.6	1.0	21.5	63.0	15.5	1,156	88.8	48.4	24.9
Marlin CDP	661	NA	NA	551	94.7	0.0	5.3	0.0	0.0	27.4	42.8	29.8	255	76.5	62.4	11.8
Marple township (Delaware)	23,428	23,708	1.2	23,551	87.5	3.1	6.0	1.0	2.4	19.3	59.6	21.1	8,403	83.9	34.5	42.9
Mars borough & MCD (Butler)	1,699	1,663	-2.1	1,460	93.7	1.5	0.7	3.2	0.9	17.8	57.6	24.5	654	51.7	34.6	25.7
Marshall township (Allegheny)	6,915	7,504	8.5	7,225	86.4	2.5	9.4	1.2	0.5	30.6	58.5	10.9	2,526	89.1	9.9	74.3
Marshallton CDP	1,441	NA	NA	1,340	99.9	0.0	0.0	0.0	0.1	19.3	59.1	21.6	559	79.8	66.2	14.3
Martic township (Lancaster)	5,190	5,207	0.3	5,206	97.2	0.2	0.0	0.4	2.2	22.6	63.9	13.4	1,845	86.7	62.0	16.7
Martinsburg borough & MCD (Blair)	1,956	1,921	-1.8	1,993	98.0	2.0	0.0	0.0	0.0	17.1	51.1	31.9	917	70.4	60.0	21.0
Martins Creek CDP	631	NA	NA	615	100.0	0.0	0.0	0.0	0.0	4.7	81.4	14.0	294	88.8	67.7	15.6
Marysville borough & MCD (Perry)	2,534	2,525	-0.4	2,536	91.1	0.6	0.0	3.3	5.0	20.0	62.9	17.2	1,176	69.3	50.9	19.0
Masontown borough & MCD (Fayette)	3,450	3,399	-1.5	3,420	83.1	5.8	0.0	7.7	3.4	26.4	57.2	16.4	1,286	62.4	64.0	16.0
Masthope CDP	685	NA	NA	769	70.6	5.9	0.9	11.7	10.9	26.8	41.4	31.6	291	74.9	33.7	38.5
Matamoras borough & MCD (Pike)	2,469	2,398	-2.9	2,337	88.1	0.5	0.0	3.5	7.9	25.2	59.1	15.7	893	68.3	49.7	27.1
Mather CDP	737	NA	NA	536	100.0	0.0	0.0	0.0	0.0	22.4	60.6	17.0	238	88.2	57.1	12.6
Mattawana CDP	276	NA	NA	325	99.4	0.0	0.0	0.0	0.6	25.6	64.0	10.5	111	62.2	71.2	4.5
Maxatawny township (Berks)	7,916	7,419	-6.3	7,707	86.5	5.8	1.1	3.2	3.3	9.6	81.2	9.3	1,378	81.9	53.0	30.5
Mayberry township (Montour)	250	257	2.8	224	100.0	0.0	0.0	0.0	0.0	13.4	71.8	14.7	106	85.8	37.7	34.0
Mayfield borough & MCD (Lackawanna)	1,807	1,778	-1.6	1,665	97.9	0.4	0.7	0.2	0.8	22.4	60.7	16.7	728	79.5	41.6	22.5
Maytown CDP	3,824	NA	NA	3,661	96.7	0.0	1.0	1.6	0.8	30.0	60.0	10.0	1,267	85.3	44.0	26.0
Mead township (Warren)	1,386	1,348	-2.7	1,462	98.6	0.7	0.0	0.8	0.0	17.8	63.2	18.9	606	89.4	64.0	13.4
Meadowlands CDP	822	NA	NA	755	100.0	0.0	0.0	0.0	0.0	19.2	52.4	28.3	286	95.5	72.7	16.1
Meadowood CDP	2,693	NA	NA	2,663	93.3	3.4	2.4	0.5	0.3	16.8	56.5	26.8	1,083	88.9	34.3	33.3
Meadville city & MCD (Crawford)	13,392	13,238	-1.1	13,307	89.4	5.4	1.0	2.6	1.6	19.5	65.5	15.0	5,282	46.3	42.4	29.0
Mechanicsburg borough & MCD (Cumberland)	8,975	8,969	-0.1	8,971	89.7	4.4	1.2	2.3	2.4	21.2	63.9	14.9	3,935	61.1	34.3	34.1
Mechanicsville borough & MCD (Schuylkill)	457	452	-1.1	509	98.2	0.4	0.0	0.0	1.4	13.0	70.6	16.5	206	82.5	65.5	15.0
Media borough & MCD (Delaware)	5,327	5,344	0.3	5,341	82.5	11.8	2.6	1.8	1.4	13.7	69.3	17.0	2,601	43.9	20.4	53.6
Mehoopany township (Wyoming)	897	907	1.1	810	97.4	0.0	0.5	0.5	1.6	16.7	66.6	16.7	346	81.8	50.9	10.7
Menallen township (Adams)	3,515	3,518	0.1	3,526	92.4	1.5	0.8	0.0	5.3	22.9	63.4	13.7	1,287	80.3	66.3	17.9
Menallen township (Fayette)	4,205	4,107	-2.3	4,160	91.2	3.5	0.0	5.0	0.3	15.8	63.5	20.8	1,717	78.7	61.4	18.5

1 May be of any race.

Table A. All Places — **Population and Housing**

STATE City, town, township, borough, or CDP (county if applicable)	Population				Race and Hispanic or Latino origin (percent), 2010–2014					Age (percent), 2010–2014			Households, 2010–2014			
	2010 census total population	2014 estimated population	Percent change 2010–2014	ACS total population estimate 2010–2014	White alone, not Hispanic or Latino	Black alone, not Hispanic or Latino	Asian alone, not Hispanic or Latino	All other races or 2 or more races, not Hispanic or Latino	Hispanic or Latino[1]	Under 18 years old	Age 18 to 64 years old	Age 65 years and older	Total occupied housing units	Percent owner occupied	High school diploma or less	Bachelor's degree or more
	1	2	3	4	5	6	7	8	9	10	11	12	13	14	15	16
PENNSYLVANIA—Con.																
Menno township (Mifflin)..	1,883	1,926	2.3	1,835	99.8	0.1	0.0	0.0	0.2	39.6	50.7	9.8	513	76.8	83.0	5.7
Mercer township (Butler) .	1,100	1,078	-2.0	1,137	99.6	0.0	0.2	0.3	0.0	16.9	62.3	20.9	501	88.6	56.9	20.6
Mercer borough & MCD (Mercer)	2,002	1,951	-2.5	2,024	97.7	0.9	0.3	1.0	0.0	21.2	65.1	13.7	832	59.0	50.0	23.1
Mercersburg borough & MCD (Franklin)..............	1,561	1,560	-0.1	1,478	86.4	6.3	0.0	2.8	4.5	17.3	64.5	18.3	674	47.8	58.3	23.6
Meridian CDP	3,881	NA	NA	3,541	99.0	0.3	0.2	0.1	0.4	20.3	59.5	20.2	1,527	94.2	36.3	32.3
Mertztown CDP	664	NA	NA	898	100.0	0.0	0.0	0.0	0.0	31.0	57.1	12.0	297	38.0	91.2	0.0
Meshoppen borough & MCD (Wyoming)..............	563	565	0.4	457	78.8	1.1	0.0	6.1	14.0	23.2	70.3	6.6	154	53.2	81.8	6.5
Meshoppen township (Wyoming).....................	1,073	1,050	-2.1	970	99.3	0.0	0.2	0.5	0.0	25.0	61.4	13.7	391	66.5	74.2	7.9
Messiah College CDP	2,215	NA	NA	2,305	84.0	4.5	4.1	3.0	4.4	0.2	99.8	0.0	0	0.0	0.0	0.0
Metal township (Franklin).	1,866	1,871	0.3	1,912	98.7	0.0	0.0	0.4	0.8	20.3	60.1	19.8	725	86.2	73.1	9.7
Mexico CDP	472	NA	NA	385	100.0	0.0	0.0	0.0	0.0	12.2	65.3	22.6	177	91.0	79.7	7.9
Meyersdale borough & MCD (Somerset)..........	2,184	2,107	-3.5	1,975	99.2	0.0	0.3	0.5	0.0	18.2	62.9	19.1	848	70.5	66.7	14.3
Middleburg borough & MCD (Snyder)	1,309	1,306	-0.2	1,362	94.6	3.6	0.0	1.5	0.3	27.5	56.2	16.2	543	45.3	64.6	9.9
Middlebury township (Tioga)..........................	1,299	1,316	1.3	1,390	97.4	0.0	0.2	1.7	0.6	23.9	59.6	16.7	542	87.1	59.2	17.3
Middlecreek township (Snyder).....................	2,110	2,152	2.0	2,239	99.2	0.0	0.0	0.0	0.8	19.7	65.6	14.7	863	89.3	57.1	16.5
Middlecreek township (Somerset)...................	875	854	-2.4	840	97.1	2.9	0.0	0.0	0.0	18.8	64.4	16.9	366	82.5	51.9	22.7
Middle Paxton township (Dauphin)....................	4,976	5,026	1.0	5,003	88.3	1.9	1.1	6.1	2.6	17.9	67.2	14.8	2,083	82.3	41.0	28.1
Middleport borough & MCD (Schuylkill)	405	397	-2.0	343	97.1	0.0	0.0	0.0	2.9	5.2	65.1	29.7	171	77.8	69.0	8.2
Middlesex township (Butler)	5,390	5,504	2.1	5,436	98.8	0.1	0.0	0.0	1.0	24.6	59.8	15.6	2,067	84.2	47.4	24.1
Middlesex township (Cumberland)..............	7,042	7,271	3.3	7,178	93.7	1.8	0.1	1.8	2.7	20.7	62.2	17.1	2,573	86.4	48.3	30.1
Middle Smithfield township (Monroe)	16,001	15,730	-1.7	15,884	64.3	13.8	2.9	1.5	17.5	23.6	64.4	11.9	5,385	85.3	38.5	26.9
Middle Taylor township (Cambria)...................	727	703	-3.3	739	94.5	0.0	0.0	4.2	1.4	22.7	54.7	22.5	310	90.0	61.9	19.7
Middletown township (Bucks)......................	45,436	45,332	-0.2	45,438	85.1	5.1	3.5	1.4	4.9	21.0	62.1	17.0	16,503	75.0	30.6	41.4
Middletown borough & MCD (Dauphin)...........	8,933	8,870	-0.7	8,909	78.4	10.9	1.6	2.3	6.8	22.0	62.1	16.0	3,817	48.7	53.6	16.4
Middletown township (Delaware).................	15,807	15,945	0.9	15,855	88.1	2.3	5.3	1.2	3.0	19.0	57.9	23.0	5,867	76.4	27.2	52.0
Middletown CDP..............	7,441	NA	NA	7,529	83.3	5.1	1.9	2.1	7.6	19.7	63.5	16.7	2,818	90.8	40.8	30.9
Middletown township (Susquehanna)	382	363	-5.0	322	96.3	0.0	0.0	2.8	0.9	19.6	58.3	22.0	128	82.0	66.4	10.9
Midland borough & MCD (Beaver)...................	2,635	2,579	-2.1	2,608	67.7	24.2	0.0	4.5	3.7	29.6	54.1	16.4	1,048	51.1	58.4	13.1
Midway CDP	2,125	NA	NA	1,912	89.5	1.6	3.2	0.7	4.9	13.4	62.6	24.0	855	68.8	68.7	16.0
Midway borough & MCD (Washington)...............	913	896	-1.9	898	99.0	0.0	0.0	0.4	0.6	27.0	55.2	17.8	324	67.3	63.0	9.0
Mifflin township (Columbia)..................	2,322	2,299	-1.0	2,457	98.7	0.0	0.0	0.5	0.8	19.5	61.5	18.9	961	89.3	61.5	18.5
Mifflin township (Dauphin)	784	787	0.4	691	97.5	0.4	0.0	0.9	1.2	25.3	58.3	16.4	224	87.1	73.2	9.8
Mifflin borough & MCD (Juniata)....................	640	632	-1.3	577	87.0	1.7	0.0	0.0	11.3	22.2	69.0	8.7	217	69.6	81.1	12.4
Mifflin township (Lycoming)	1,070	1,060	-0.9	1,081	96.0	0.0	0.0	2.6	1.4	20.5	65.9	13.6	434	88.5	55.3	14.5
Mifflinburg borough & MCD (Union)	3,540	3,531	-0.3	3,541	95.3	3.0	0.5	0.5	0.6	23.4	58.0	18.7	1,606	64.3	55.5	19.2
Mifflintown borough & MCD (Juniata)...........	936	931	-0.5	1,009	72.0	1.3	0.0	0.7	26.1	28.3	58.0	13.7	377	46.2	61.8	9.8
Mifflinville CDP	1,253	NA	NA	1,345	98.5	0.0	0.0	0.0	1.5	19.4	57.8	22.8	499	87.6	64.3	20.6
Miles township (Centre)...	1,983	1,976	-0.4	1,615	97.7	0.0	1.2	0.5	0.6	26.0	58.5	15.3	560	76.6	72.9	12.5
Milesburg borough & MCD (Centre)..............	1,123	1,095	-2.5	947	97.7	1.3	0.0	0.7	0.3	20.3	65.6	14.3	417	64.5	62.4	21.6
Milford township (Bucks)..	9,902	9,970	0.7	9,928	93.0	3.5	0.1	1.4	2.0	22.0	62.2	16.0	3,664	91.9	43.0	34.4
Milford township (Juniata)	2,090	2,104	0.7	2,070	95.5	0.6	0.0	0.6	3.3	16.7	56.4	26.9	838	74.5	62.4	14.7
Milford borough & MCD (Pike)........................	1,024	988	-3.5	1,039	94.9	1.3	0.0	1.1	2.7	15.2	61.7	23.0	487	52.2	32.4	33.1
Milford township (Pike)	1,525	1,489	-2.4	1,513	89.7	2.0	1.7	2.6	4.1	21.4	58.8	19.8	575	87.0	35.3	40.9
Milford township (Somerset)...................	1,553	1,532	-1.4	1,611	97.4	0.2	1.0	0.6	0.8	20.5	63.9	15.6	612	94.1	56.0	18.0
Milford Square CDP.........	897	NA	NA	1,055	81.3	0.0	0.0	6.9	11.8	17.8	80.0	2.2	409	72.6	31.5	33.7
Millbourne borough & MCD (Delaware)..........	1,159	1,162	0.3	1,291	12.8	26.7	37.9	10.8	11.9	28.7	66.2	5.2	388	24.2	56.2	23.2
Millcreek township (Clarion)...................	396	385	-2.8	379	99.2	0.3	0.0	0.0	0.5	15.8	62.7	21.6	166	83.1	59.0	19.9
Millcreek township (Erie) .	53,517	54,012	0.9	53,914	92.3	2.3	1.4	2.0	2.0	22.5	59.9	17.6	22,469	69.6	34.7	38.7
Mill Creek borough & MCD (Huntingdon).......	328	326	-0.6	386	97.4	0.0	0.0	2.6	0.0	27.4	51.5	21.0	153	70.6	71.2	3.9
Millcreek township (Lebanon)...................	3,892	3,980	2.3	3,944	96.0	0.0	0.0	0.2	3.8	28.9	59.9	11.4	1,386	78.7	66.3	17.3
Mill Creek township (Lycoming)	609	626	2.8	618	99.7	0.0	0.0	0.0	0.3	23.2	64.4	12.5	208	86.1	48.1	18.8
Mill Creek township (Mercer)	720	717	-0.4	719	97.2	0.0	0.3	1.9	0.6	16.3	67.4	16.3	314	93.3	55.4	10.2
Miller township (Huntingdon)	462	455	-1.5	399	98.0	0.5	0.0	1.5	0.0	14.6	64.4	21.1	167	86.2	55.1	23.4
Miller township (Perry).....	1,095	1,081	-1.3	945	95.3	0.0	0.0	0.0	4.7	23.4	67.3	9.4	378	86.5	58.5	13.8

1 May be of any race.

Table A. All Places — **Population and Housing**

STATE City, town, township, borough, or CDP (county if applicable)	Population				Race and Hispanic or Latino origin (percent), 2010–2014					Age (percent), 2010–2014			Households, 2010–2014			
								All other races or 2 or more races, not Hispanic or Latino							Householders by level of education (percent)	
	2010 census total population	2014 estimated population	Percent change 2010–2014	ACS total population estimate 2010–2014	White alone, not Hispanic or Latino	Black alone, not Hispanic or Latino	Asian alone, not Hispanic or Latino		Hispanic or Latino[1]	Under 18 years old	Age 18 to 64 years old	Age 65 years and older	Total occupied housing units	Percent owner occupied	High school diploma or less	Bachelor's degree or more
	1	2	3	4	5	6	7	8	9	10	11	12	13	14	15	16

PENNSYLVANIA—Con.

STATE City, town, township, borough, or CDP (county if applicable)	1	2	3	4	5	6	7	8	9	10	11	12	13	14	15	16
Millersburg borough & MCD (Dauphin)	2,557	2,534	-0.9	2,540	94.6	1.9	0.0	0.8	2.7	24.3	53.4	22.5	1,143	54.3	59.5	10.0
Millerstown borough & MCD (Perry)	673	670	-0.4	723	97.8	0.0	0.0	0.8	1.4	23.6	61.4	14.9	275	86.5	38.9	22.9
Millersville borough & MCD (Lancaster)	8,167	8,482	3.9	8,320	83.9	7.1	2.7	2.9	3.4	10.6	77.6	11.8	2,504	59.8	34.9	28.6
Millerton CDP	316	NA	NA	373	95.4	1.6	0.0	0.0	2.9	18.5	64.9	16.6	158	74.7	53.2	9.5
Mill Hall borough & MCD (Clinton)	1,613	1,622	0.6	1,631	97.7	0.6	0.3	0.9	0.5	20.4	59.6	20.3	705	70.5	59.4	18.4
Millheim borough & MCD (Centre)	904	886	-2.0	952	98.0	0.0	0.0	2.0	0.0	29.9	52.9	17.1	342	82.2	52.3	21.6
Millsboro CDP	666	NA	NA	496	100.0	0.0	0.0	0.0	0.0	14.1	66.6	19.2	237	91.6	27.4	30.4
Millstone township (Elk)	82	79	-3.7	58	94.8	0.0	0.0	5.2	0.0	10.3	29.3	60.3	30	90.0	70.0	6.7
Millvale borough & MCD (Allegheny)	3,744	3,710	-0.9	3,740	94.9	2.9	0.3	1.1	0.8	19.2	66.7	14.0	1,795	45.6	46.8	21.4
Mill Village borough & MCD (Erie)	412	396	-3.9	455	97.8	0.7	0.0	1.5	0.0	19.2	68.0	13.0	169	75.7	50.3	11.8
Millville borough & MCD (Columbia)	948	957	0.9	989	97.6	1.1	0.0	0.1	1.2	20.2	49.9	30.0	415	61.4	60.5	18.3
Millwood CDP	566	NA	NA	613	84.7	0.0	0.0	15.3	0.0	27.2	48.7	24.1	260	69.6	67.7	3.8
Milroy CDP	1,498	NA	NA	1,634	99.3	0.0	0.0	0.7	0.0	15.3	59.8	24.9	661	74.9	69.4	11.2
Milton borough & MCD (Northumberland)	7,042	6,982	-0.9	7,017	91.2	1.6	0.5	1.7	5.1	20.6	61.2	18.2	3,075	52.3	56.7	18.0
Mineral township (Venango)	538	527	-2.0	530	96.4	0.0	0.8	2.8	0.0	21.0	60.8	18.3	222	86.9	66.7	15.3
Minersville borough & MCD (Schuylkill)	4,397	4,269	-2.9	4,332	94.9	0.0	0.0	2.9	2.2	19.8	60.8	19.2	1,927	60.4	70.8	10.6
Mingoville CDP	503	NA	NA	494	100.0	0.0	0.0	0.0	0.0	22.7	66.8	10.5	212	90.6	33.0	7.5
Mocanaqua CDP	646	NA	NA	668	98.1	0.0	0.9	1.0	0.0	21.5	58.0	20.2	287	66.9	68.6	15.3
Modena borough & MCD (Chester)	535	530	-0.9	496	45.8	22.0	0.0	13.1	19.2	24.0	73.3	2.6	178	53.9	73.0	10.1
Mohnton borough & MCD (Berks)	3,043	3,033	-0.3	3,048	88.7	2.3	0.9	2.2	5.9	23.5	63.5	12.9	1,319	70.9	42.3	29.7
Mohrsville CDP	383	NA	NA	581	100.0	0.0	0.0	0.0	0.0	22.1	62.1	15.8	211	82.0	56.9	12.3
Monaca borough & MCD (Beaver)	5,737	5,676	-1.1	5,721	95.1	1.6	0.3	2.7	0.3	18.6	60.4	20.9	2,562	68.5	48.7	16.9
Monaghan township (York)	2,630	2,658	1.1	2,634	96.3	0.7	1.4	0.6	1.0	21.3	61.0	17.7	1,046	90.1	41.1	35.3
Monessen city & MCD (Westmoreland)	7,720	7,529	-2.5	7,630	78.2	15.2	0.4	4.1	2.0	15.9	59.5	24.5	3,667	65.7	57.8	16.3
Monongahela township (Greene)	1,572	1,538	-2.2	1,632	99.3	0.2	0.0	0.3	0.2	22.8	61.0	16.2	647	87.3	59.4	12.7
Monongahela city & MCD (Washington)	4,300	4,206	-2.2	4,260	92.6	4.4	0.0	1.5	1.5	18.3	61.5	20.2	1,812	64.1	53.0	12.9
Monroe township (Bedford)	1,327	1,307	-1.5	1,327	97.6	0.0	0.0	0.4	2.0	16.8	62.9	20.2	513	87.5	77.0	8.8
Monroe borough & MCD (Bradford)	554	534	-3.6	684	96.6	0.0	1.9	1.5	0.0	29.8	64.5	5.7	221	79.2	43.4	27.1
Monroe township (Bradford)	1,250	1,237	-1.0	1,187	96.7	0.8	0.0	1.9	0.7	25.6	60.4	14.1	442	77.4	68.1	7.2
Monroe township (Clarion)	1,544	1,516	-1.8	1,401	96.1	1.4	0.6	0.6	1.3	21.2	60.3	18.6	565	81.2	47.8	26.7
Monroe township (Cumberland)	5,823	5,987	2.8	5,907	97.2	0.1	0.2	0.4	2.1	18.5	64.0	17.6	2,363	92.0	35.5	35.0
Monroe township (Juniata)	2,237	2,230	-0.3	2,197	98.8	0.2	0.7	0.0	0.3	23.7	61.3	14.8	764	80.5	75.9	10.7
Monroe township (Snyder)	3,897	4,059	4.2	3,974	93.8	0.9	1.2	1.9	2.2	18.5	64.6	16.9	1,555	85.3	48.2	28.3
Monroe township (Wyoming)	1,652	1,639	-0.8	1,606	97.1	0.3	0.0	2.6	0.0	20.5	64.1	15.3	637	81.0	57.8	15.1
Monroeville municipality & MCD (Allegheny)	28,341	28,285	-0.2	28,365	77.8	12.3	5.2	3.3	1.4	17.6	60.8	21.4	12,594	65.4	29.6	42.4
Mont Alto borough & MCD (Franklin)	1,711	1,736	1.5	1,743	94.3	4.2	0.0	1.4	0.1	23.6	62.8	13.7	637	74.7	58.2	7.2
Montandon CDP	903	NA	NA	885	99.9	0.1	0.0	0.0	0.0	25.4	62.1	12.4	391	67.3	73.4	3.8
Montgomery township (Franklin)	6,118	6,153	0.6	6,138	97.9	1.7	0.0	0.0	0.4	25.7	59.7	14.5	2,031	82.5	67.1	14.4
Montgomery township (Indiana)	1,568	1,515	-3.4	1,588	98.7	0.6	0.5	0.2	0.0	18.9	61.8	19.5	611	74.6	72.0	11.6
Montgomery borough & MCD (Lycoming)	1,579	1,571	-0.5	1,501	96.5	0.3	0.3	1.5	1.4	26.7	61.6	11.6	556	59.4	54.5	14.9
Montgomery township (Montgomery)	24,790	25,946	4.7	25,397	72.1	5.2	18.3	2.3	2.1	24.0	61.9	14.0	9,201	89.5	19.1	57.9
Montgomeryville CDP	12,624	NA	NA	12,977	73.3	4.9	16.5	2.3	3.0	23.6	64.0	12.4	4,431	94.2	15.4	59.7
Montour township (Columbia)	1,344	1,330	-1.0	1,419	91.6	0.8	3.3	1.6	2.6	18.3	65.2	16.3	585	79.5	61.4	16.8
Montoursville borough & MCD (Lycoming)	4,615	4,584	-0.7	4,616	95.7	0.0	1.1	1.9	1.4	19.4	57.3	23.4	2,060	67.4	44.3	21.0
Montrose borough & MCD (Susquehanna)	1,619	1,541	-4.8	1,694	95.1	1.6	0.0	0.8	2.5	16.0	62.9	21.1	744	61.8	40.6	24.6
Montrose Manor CDP	604	NA	NA	556	80.0	1.3	0.0	1.4	17.3	20.7	49.2	30.0	240	92.1	42.9	45.0
Monument CDP	150	NA	NA	185	100.0	0.0	0.0	0.0	0.0	17.3	73.4	9.2	53	100.0	96.2	0.0
Moon township (Allegheny)	24,167	25,524	5.6	24,966	88.0	4.3	3.7	1.4	2.6	19.3	67.0	13.6	9,903	72.5	24.9	47.4
Moore township (Northampton)	9,198	9,248	0.5	9,225	95.6	1.9	0.1	0.1	2.3	21.5	58.8	19.9	3,475	87.7	59.6	17.5
Moosic borough & MCD (Lackawanna)	5,719	5,681	-0.7	5,712	99.7	0.0	0.0	0.0	0.3	18.7	61.9	19.3	2,328	80.2	42.7	24.5
Moreland township (Lycoming)	943	965	2.3	1,004	97.6	0.0	0.0	0.8	1.6	20.7	63.5	16.0	381	91.9	62.5	16.5

1 May be of any race.

Table A. All Places — **Population and Housing**

	Population				Race and Hispanic or Latino origin (percent), 2010–2014					Age (percent), 2010–2014			Households, 2010–2014			
STATE City, town, township, borough, or CDP (county if applicable)	2010 census total population	2014 estimated population	Percent change 2010–2014	ACS total population estimate 2010–2014	White alone, not Hispanic or Latino	Black alone, not Hispanic or Latino	Asian alone, not Hispanic or Latino	All other races or 2 or more races, not Hispanic or Latino	Hispanic or Latino[1]	Under 18 years old	Age 18 to 64 years old	Age 65 years and older	Total occupied housing units	Percent owner occupied	High school diploma or less	Bachelor's degree or more
	1	2	3	4	5	6	7	8	9	10	11	12	13	14	15	16

PENNSYLVANIA—Con.

STATE	1	2	3	4	5	6	7	8	9	10	11	12	13	14	15	16
Morgan township (Greene)	2,587	2,510	-3.0	2,544	99.5	0.0	0.3	0.2	0.0	23.2	59.2	17.6	1,059	82.4	55.8	16.8
Morgantown CDP	826	NA	NA	1,199	93.3	0.0	3.1	2.2	1.4	25.9	66.2	8.0	423	60.5	49.4	22.2
Morris township (Clearfield)	2,938	2,919	-0.6	2,927	100.0	0.0	0.0	0.0	0.0	24.9	57.6	17.5	1,134	82.0	73.2	9.0
Morris township (Greene)	818	811	-0.9	732	97.5	1.1	0.0	1.4	0.0	21.6	64.1	14.3	270	75.6	57.8	13.7
Morris township (Huntingdon)	410	417	1.7	420	94.5	0.0	1.0	2.4	2.1	24.0	56.8	19.0	155	75.5	61.9	14.2
Morris township (Tioga)	612	606	-1.0	596	95.3	1.7	0.5	2.5	0.0	17.3	65.7	17.1	252	76.6	52.8	15.1
Morris township (Washington)	1,105	1,103	-0.2	1,087	93.8	1.5	1.1	3.1	0.5	23.7	61.5	14.8	376	81.1	59.6	17.0
Morrisdale CDP	754	NA	NA	654	100.0	0.0	0.0	0.0	0.0	18.0	63.4	18.5	246	86.6	75.6	6.9
Morrisville borough & MCD (Bucks)	8,728	8,631	-1.1	8,689	64.0	18.5	1.7	5.7	10.1	27.0	63.1	10.0	3,360	63.1	35.4	29.0
Morrisville CDP	1,265	NA	NA	814	98.9	0.0	0.1	0.5	0.5	16.3	47.8	36.0	415	66.0	53.0	20.7
Morton borough & MCD (Delaware)	2,669	2,690	0.8	2,670	68.4	25.8	3.6	1.6	0.6	18.2	67.4	14.6	1,144	63.4	41.8	28.6
Moscow borough & MCD (Lackawanna)	2,026	2,003	-1.1	2,588	97.6	0.3	1.0	0.0	1.1	22.5	65.0	12.4	896	79.7	32.3	39.2
Moshannon CDP	281	NA	NA	233	100.0	0.0	0.0	0.0	0.0	14.2	70.8	15.0	95	76.8	63.2	5.3
Mount Aetna CDP	354	NA	NA	420	100.0	0.0	0.0	0.0	0.0	11.0	70.1	19.0	152	85.5	79.6	15.1
Mountainhome CDP	1,182	NA	NA	1,060	82.6	9.3	0.0	0.0	8.0	17.2	64.1	18.8	428	93.0	55.4	17.5
Mountain Top CDP	10,982	NA	NA	11,182	91.7	1.2	4.1	1.6	1.5	23.4	59.7	16.9	4,131	88.5	29.0	38.1
Mount Carbon borough & MCD (Schuylkill)	91	89	-2.2	95	100.0	0.0	0.0	0.0	0.0	10.6	70.5	18.9	49	61.2	49.0	10.2
Mount Carmel borough & MCD (Northumberland)	5,893	5,785	-1.8	5,833	95.6	0.5	0.0	0.9	2.9	19.8	61.2	18.9	2,878	69.8	60.5	18.5
Mount Carmel township (Northumberland)	3,139	3,096	-1.4	3,120	99.9	0.1	0.0	0.0	0.0	14.1	56.4	29.5	1,364	70.5	69.0	9.8
Mount Cobb CDP	1,799	NA	NA	1,545	97.9	0.0	2.1	0.0	0.0	23.3	60.4	16.2	597	93.1	50.1	21.9
Mount Eagle CDP	103	NA	NA	90	100.0	0.0	0.0	0.0	0.0	15.5	64.5	20.0	38	76.3	78.9	5.3
Mount Gretna borough & MCD (Lebanon)	198	196	-1.0	157	100.0	0.0	0.0	0.0	0.0	14.7	50.9	34.4	72	91.7	11.1	65.3
Mount Gretna Heights CDP	323	NA	NA	224	87.1	0.0	0.0	0.0	12.9	4.5	64.3	31.3	136	87.5	39.0	54.4
Mount Holly Springs borough & MCD (Cumberland)	2,032	2,033	0.0	1,828	93.4	2.4	0.0	0.0	4.2	20.6	62.2	17.2	817	67.0	57.3	8.8
Mount Jewett borough & MCD (McKean)	919	902	-1.8	949	99.1	0.0	0.0	0.9	0.0	23.2	63.2	13.6	404	72.3	52.5	24.0
Mount Joy township (Adams)	3,670	3,683	0.4	3,676	95.0	1.2	0.0	1.6	2.2	17.6	58.7	23.6	1,516	92.1	33.2	38.5
Mount Joy borough & MCD (Lancaster)	7,410	8,008	8.1	7,774	85.7	4.8	1.0	3.3	5.1	21.8	65.3	12.9	3,220	62.4	46.0	28.9
Mount Joy township (Lancaster)	9,873	10,724	8.6	10,279	93.6	0.3	1.8	0.5	3.7	25.0	62.3	12.7	3,968	70.6	40.9	30.2
Mount Lebanon township (Allegheny)	33,137	32,922	-0.6	33,085	91.2	1.1	3.9	1.5	2.2	23.5	57.0	19.4	13,963	73.7	15.2	65.7
Mount Morris CDP	737	NA	NA	837	98.4	1.1	0.0	0.5	0.0	15.6	60.8	23.7	365	75.9	60.8	14.0
Mount Oliver borough & MCD (Allegheny)	3,403	3,373	-0.9	3,400	53.1	36.2	7.1	2.7	0.9	32.3	58.8	8.9	1,351	44.0	57.7	6.7
Mount Penn borough & MCD (Berks)	3,106	3,164	1.9	3,150	78.3	1.0	2.6	2.4	15.7	24.5	64.0	11.3	1,261	65.5	48.7	24.1
Mount Pleasant township (Adams)	4,693	4,691	0.0	4,696	88.2	0.7	0.0	0.2	10.8	21.8	64.1	14.0	1,772	85.6	60.1	19.2
Mount Pleasant township (Columbia)	1,609	1,618	0.6	1,536	97.9	0.7	0.0	0.7	0.8	19.0	68.1	12.9	599	81.5	52.6	27.0
Mount Pleasant township (Washington)	3,515	3,513	-0.1	3,523	98.3	0.2	0.0	0.0	1.5	22.0	60.3	17.8	1,443	80.2	53.7	22.8
Mount Pleasant township (Wayne)	1,357	1,333	-1.8	1,441	93.7	0.3	0.8	1.3	4.0	20.4	60.0	19.5	576	81.6	56.8	18.4
Mount Pleasant borough & MCD (Westmoreland)	4,454	4,391	-1.4	4,431	96.4	0.4	2.0	0.9	0.2	19.5	55.8	24.6	2,011	59.0	49.2	23.6
Mount Pleasant township (Westmoreland)	10,911	10,680	-2.1	10,782	98.8	0.0	0.0	0.1	1.0	16.1	64.3	19.8	4,654	83.6	59.2	15.3
Mount Pleasant Mills CDP	464	NA	NA	487	98.4	0.0	0.0	1.6	0.0	25.4	54.3	20.1	200	61.5	66.0	9.5
Mount Pocono borough & MCD (Monroe)	3,170	3,077	-2.9	3,126	52.6	23.3	3.3	2.1	18.6	34.0	53.7	12.2	1,086	62.3	38.5	31.9
Mount Union borough & MCD (Huntingdon)	2,447	2,405	-1.7	2,621	87.3	9.1	0.0	2.3	1.3	25.7	58.1	16.2	1,210	51.2	65.7	11.4
Mountville borough & MCD (Lancaster)	2,802	2,849	1.7	2,831	84.8	0.8	7.9	2.1	4.4	14.3	66.5	19.0	1,374	71.3	46.1	22.3
Mount Wolf borough & MCD (York)	1,393	1,381	-0.9	1,648	95.4	1.9	0.0	0.3	2.4	19.1	61.6	19.2	657	71.5	59.7	15.4
Muddy Creek township (Butler)	2,254	2,198	-2.5	2,226	95.5	0.0	0.3	0.4	3.8	20.0	63.1	16.8	1,003	89.2	55.2	21.4
Muhlenberg township (Berks)	19,630	19,857	1.2	19,782	76.4	2.4	2.1	1.2	17.9	20.1	61.6	18.2	7,731	81.1	55.9	23.7
Muhlenberg Park CDP	1,420	NA	NA	2,028	78.4	3.4	4.2	0.7	13.4	17.6	55.6	26.7	785	85.0	49.3	24.6
Muir CDP	451	NA	NA	434	97.0	0.0	0.0	3.0	0.0	19.8	61.0	19.1	192	85.4	49.0	16.7
Muncy borough & MCD (Lycoming)	2,477	2,454	-0.9	2,590	94.6	0.0	0.5	3.5	1.5	22.9	63.6	13.4	1,100	63.4	42.1	35.0
Muncy township (Lycoming)	1,089	1,100	1.0	1,102	96.2	0.3	1.5	1.2	0.8	23.7	60.8	15.6	425	87.8	58.8	13.6
Muncy Creek township (Lycoming)	3,474	3,546	2.1	3,514	96.5	0.0	0.0	2.6	0.8	18.2	54.6	27.2	1,495	76.1	48.2	22.7
Mundys Corner CDP	1,651	NA	NA	1,919	99.7	0.0	0.0	0.3	0.0	22.2	61.6	16.2	722	85.2	60.1	16.9
Munhall borough & MCD (Allegheny)	11,406	11,305	-0.9	11,355	88.5	6.2	0.0	3.0	1.6	17.8	62.9	19.3	5,288	65.7	45.0	22.5
Munster township (Cambria)	690	687	-0.4	586	100.0	0.0	0.0	0.0	0.0	27.6	58.1	14.2	212	84.4	47.2	19.3

1 May be of any race.

Table A. All Places — **Population and Housing**

STATE City, town, township, borough, or CDP (county if applicable)	2010 census total population	2014 estimated population	Percent change 2010– 2014	ACS total population estimate 2010–2014	White alone, not Hispanic or Latino	Black alone, not Hispanic or Latino	Asian alone, not Hispanic or Latino	All other races or 2 or more races, not Hispanic or Latino	Hispanic or Latino[1]	Under 18 years old	Age 18 to 64 years old	Age 65 years and older	Total occupied housing units	Percent owner occupied	High school diploma or less	Bachelor's degree or more
	1	2	3	4	5	6	7	8	9	10	11	12	13	14	15	16
PENNSYLVANIA—Con.																
Murrysville municipality & MCD (Westmoreland) ..	20,079	20,162	0.4	20,171	93.0	0.6	4.4	0.4	1.6	20.5	57.9	21.5	7,956	89.4	24.1	53.6
Muse CDP	2,504	NA	NA	2,592	94.3	0.0	0.0	3.5	2.2	29.0	59.5	11.4	891	83.5	34.7	44.8
Myerstown borough & MCD (Lebanon)	3,062	3,122	2.0	3,098	86.2	0.3	0.4	0.3	12.9	25.0	58.3	16.8	1,121	52.7	67.1	14.2
Nanticoke city & MCD (Luzerne)......................	10,465	10,301	-1.6	10,395	93.6	2.0	0.9	0.7	2.8	19.7	59.0	21.3	4,551	53.8	54.7	15.1
Nanty-Glo borough & MCD (Cambria)...........	2,734	2,629	-3.8	2,675	99.3	0.0	0.6	0.0	0.1	23.4	55.4	21.3	1,162	80.7	66.4	15.5
Naomi CDP.....................	69	NA	NA	61	100.0	0.0	0.0	0.0	0.0	0.0	68.8	31.1	29	34.5	100.0	0.0
Napier township (Bedford)	2,198	2,155	-2.0	2,066	98.8	0.0	0.0	0.9	0.3	16.2	62.3	21.7	877	87.0	65.1	14.8
Narberth borough & MCD (Montgomery)	4,282	4,295	0.3	4,295	90.3	1.2	4.5	1.4	2.6	22.2	65.8	11.9	1,875	60.2	8.7	71.4
Nazareth borough & MCD (Northampton).............	5,746	5,714	-0.6	5,723	91.7	2.6	3.7	1.0	0.9	17.5	61.8	20.7	2,510	48.2	43.5	30.7
Needmore CDP	170	NA	NA	111	96.4	0.0	0.0	3.6	0.0	10.8	54.0	35.1	54	66.7	50.0	13.0
Nelson township (Tioga)..	568	570	0.4	602	95.5	0.0	0.0	4.5	0.0	26.2	55.3	18.4	233	73.8	48.5	16.7
Nemacolin CDP	937	NA	NA	539	85.5	0.0	0.0	9.3	5.2	14.1	40.5	45.3	353	73.4	36.8	33.4
Nescopeck borough & MCD (Luzerne)	1,583	1,558	-1.6	1,700	89.9	0.4	0.8	1.1	7.9	19.9	65.2	14.9	733	54.0	63.6	12.4
Nescopeck township (Luzerne)	1,155	1,160	0.4	1,225	95.4	0.0	0.0	4.6	0.0	20.1	61.9	17.9	494	89.7	73.7	10.5
Neshannock township (Lawrence)	9,609	9,429	-1.9	9,511	95.5	1.3	1.1	1.3	0.7	18.4	55.0	26.7	4,318	77.1	39.8	35.5
Nesquehoning borough & MCD (Carbon).............	3,349	3,279	-2.1	3,321	89.9	2.3	0.0	1.5	6.3	20.5	54.9	24.6	1,389	63.7	59.3	12.9
Nether Providence township (Delaware)	13,706	13,805	0.7	13,757	85.7	4.2	5.1	3.5	1.5	23.0	58.1	19.0	5,083	88.8	22.0	62.7
Neville township (Allegheny)	1,084	1,073	-1.0	1,088	95.1	0.4	0.8	2.3	1.4	13.5	65.1	21.5	574	51.0	57.5	16.2
New Albany borough & MCD (Bradford)	356	352	-1.1	375	90.9	0.0	0.0	0.3	8.8	30.7	56.3	13.1	131	62.6	71.8	0.8
New Alexandria borough & MCD (Westmoreland)	560	552	-1.4	579	93.6	2.1	0.0	4.3	0.0	12.3	55.5	32.1	253	78.7	50.6	19.8
New Baltimore borough & MCD (Somerset)	180	176	-2.2	169	100.0	0.0	0.0	0.0	0.0	24.8	59.4	16.0	58	81.0	77.6	3.4
New Beaver borough & MCD (Lawrence)..........	1,499	1,461	-2.5	1,583	97.1	0.5	0.0	0.5	1.9	18.6	66.1	15.1	668	82.5	65.7	12.1
New Bedford CDP	925	NA	NA	911	100.0	0.0	0.0	0.0	0.0	11.6	57.2	31.1	420	87.4	38.3	25.0
New Berlin borough & MCD (Union)	873	868	-0.6	937	93.0	0.0	0.3	0.0	6.7	22.0	63.6	14.4	378	81.2	46.0	24.1
New Berlinville CDP	1,368	NA	NA	1,453	100.0	0.0	0.0	0.0	0.0	12.2	79.4	8.3	654	87.8	57.0	17.1
Newberry township (York)	15,289	15,365	0.5	15,316	95.0	0.7	1.1	1.1	2.1	23.3	66.6	10.1	5,942	84.9	54.0	23.9
New Bethlehem borough & MCD (Clarion)	989	959	-3.0	902	97.8	0.2	0.0	0.3	1.7	15.2	55.0	29.8	484	48.8	63.6	20.2
New Brighton borough & MCD (Beaver)	6,022	5,915	-1.8	5,973	82.6	10.1	0.0	5.5	1.9	22.8	61.9	15.3	2,631	49.9	55.5	16.7
New Britain borough & MCD (Bucks)...............	3,037	3,025	-0.4	3,028	93.1	0.9	2.6	0.0	3.4	16.7	72.3	11.0	939	80.9	26.3	43.7
New Britain township (Bucks)	11,075	11,258	1.7	11,095	93.3	1.1	3.6	0.9	1.1	23.6	61.3	15.0	4,017	87.7	28.6	49.4
New Buffalo borough & MCD (Perry)	129	128	-0.8	105	99.0	0.0	0.0	1.0	0.0	14.3	57.2	28.6	54	64.8	75.9	0.0
Newburg borough & MCD (Clearfield)	92	91	-1.1	127	100.0	0.0	0.0	0.0	0.0	22.8	67.5	9.4	39	89.7	76.9	5.1
Newburg borough & MCD (Cumberland)	336	339	0.9	260	95.8	0.0	0.0	1.9	2.3	20.4	63.8	15.8	125	76.8	61.6	12.8
New Castle city & MCD (Lawrence)	23,273	22,575	-3.0	22,883	80.7	13.2	0.3	3.9	1.8	23.5	57.6	18.8	9,527	58.5	58.9	14.4
New Castle township (Schuylkill)	414	399	-3.6	465	99.6	0.0	0.0	0.0	0.4	22.1	55.7	22.2	190	77.9	67.9	13.7
New Castle Northwest CDP	1,413	NA	NA	1,126	94.9	1.8	0.0	0.0	3.3	9.4	48.9	41.8	569	75.0	63.1	24.3
New Centerville borough & MCD (Somerset).......	133	132	-0.8	168	100.0	0.0	0.0	0.0	0.0	26.2	47.2	26.8	67	85.1	71.6	13.4
New Columbia CDP.........	1,013	NA	NA	778	100.0	0.0	0.0	0.0	0.0	16.7	60.6	22.8	400	82.8	75.0	8.8
New Columbus borough & MCD (Luzerne)	227	226	-0.4	200	99.0	0.0	0.0	0.0	1.0	24.0	57.0	19.0	91	87.9	59.3	11.0
New Cumberland borough & MCD (Cumberland) ..	7,277	7,271	-0.1	7,276	92.1	1.4	1.1	2.3	3.1	20.7	61.9	17.3	3,295	69.0	38.0	33.9
New Eagle borough & MCD (Washington).......	2,184	2,137	-2.2	2,168	91.8	0.9	4.3	1.8	1.2	19.3	60.5	20.3	970	68.9	52.0	19.6
Newell borough & MCD (Fayette)	541	532	-1.7	566	99.3	0.0	0.0	0.7	0.0	24.6	59.8	15.5	224	78.1	55.8	12.9
New Florence borough & MCD (Westmoreland) ..	687	671	-2.3	774	96.4	1.6	0.0	0.6	1.4	21.1	59.7	19.1	321	60.7	64.2	8.1
New Freedom borough & MCD (York)	4,466	4,565	2.2	4,528	91.9	1.3	0.0	2.3	4.5	25.8	56.8	17.4	1,715	85.4	26.2	39.0
New Freeport CDP	112	NA	NA	116	100.0	0.0	0.0	0.0	0.0	24.2	63.8	12.1	44	54.5	79.5	20.5
New Galilee borough & MCD (Beaver)	379	367	-3.2	453	98.0	1.1	0.0	0.9	0.0	20.1	63.4	16.6	173	76.3	64.7	10.4
New Garden township (Chester)	11,988	12,098	0.9	12,079	69.6	1.5	2.4	1.4	25.1	27.7	63.8	8.4	3,750	72.3	31.4	54.3
New Hanover township (Montgomery)	10,939	12,227	11.8	11,684	90.8	0.8	1.6	3.3	3.5	26.0	60.4	13.5	4,041	93.9	31.8	42.9
New Holland borough & MCD (Lancaster).........	5,378	5,420	0.8	5,407	85.9	4.7	3.1	0.7	5.7	19.6	61.7	18.7	2,336	60.8	56.0	20.5
New Hope borough & MCD (Bucks)...............	2,528	2,508	-0.8	2,526	91.4	0.6	1.9	2.7	3.4	17.5	66.5	16.0	1,247	60.1	11.2	64.8
New Jerusalem CDP	649	NA	NA	839	93.1	1.3	0.0	3.2	2.4	35.5	50.1	14.4	288	72.6	46.5	47.2

1 May be of any race.

Table A. All Places — **Population and Housing**

STATE City, town, township, borough, or CDP (county if applicable)	2010 census total population	2014 estimated population	Percent change 2010–2014	ACS total population estimate 2010–2014	White alone, not Hispanic or Latino	Black alone, not Hispanic or Latino	Asian alone, not Hispanic or Latino	All other races or 2 or more races, not Hispanic or Latino	Hispanic or Latino[1]	Under 18 years old	Age 18 to 64 years old	Age 65 years and older	Total occupied housing units	Percent owner occupied	High school diploma or less	Bachelor's degree or more
	1	2	3	4	5	6	7	8	9	10	11	12	13	14	15	16
PENNSYLVANIA—Con.																
New Kensington city & MCD (Westmoreland) ..	13,116	12,796	-2.4	12,959	81.7	10.9	1.1	5.3	1.0	22.4	58.3	19.2	5,824	60.9	52.5	19.0
New Kingstown CDP	495	NA	NA	349	96.3	0.0	0.0	0.0	3.7	14.0	51.2	34.7	158	62.7	41.1	38.6
New Lebanon borough & MCD (Mercer)	189	181	-4.2	203	100.0	0.0	0.0	0.0	0.0	33.0	50.3	16.7	67	86.6	67.2	4.5
Newlin township (Chester)	1,285	1,350	5.1	1,317	95.7	0.3	0.0	0.6	3.3	26.0	57.8	16.2	479	84.8	24.0	58.0
New London township (Chester).................	5,631	5,915	5.0	5,776	88.1	1.0	0.0	4.3	6.6	32.1	62.4	5.5	1,849	93.1	30.4	46.9
Newmanstown CDP........	2,478	NA	NA	2,679	95.0	0.0	0.0	0.3	4.7	32.2	58.4	9.4	905	75.0	63.5	20.0
New Market CDP............	816	NA	NA	546	86.3	4.4	1.8	0.0	7.5	21.8	64.6	13.6	286	29.4	68.2	21.7
New Milford borough & MCD (Susquehanna) ...	868	873	0.6	913	94.1	4.1	0.0	0.4	1.4	29.7	59.1	11.2	345	66.1	55.9	15.9
New Milford township (Susquehanna)	2,042	1,963	-3.9	1,977	95.4	0.6	0.0	1.5	2.5	18.7	59.6	21.7	774	92.0	61.8	15.4
New Morgan borough & MCD (Berks)	71	71	0.0	55	23.6	38.2	0.0	0.0	38.2	41.8	50.9	7.3	6	0.0	100.0	0.0
New Oxford borough & MCD (Adams)	1,783	1,786	0.2	2,328	67.3	0.8	0.5	2.7	28.7	27.2	60.8	12.0	835	48.1	62.8	9.7
New Paris borough & MCD (Bedford)	186	182	-2.2	216	96.3	0.9	0.0	0.0	2.8	18.9	75.6	5.6	82	72.0	63.4	8.5
New Philadelphia borough & MCD (Schuylkill)	1,085	1,067	-1.7	1,070	97.7	0.0	0.0	1.5	0.8	20.6	60.6	19.0	492	82.9	70.5	9.8
Newport township (Luzerne)..................	5,374	5,422	0.9	5,420	84.4	11.1	0.0	0.9	3.6	17.3	67.3	15.5	1,801	67.3	64.6	12.0
Newport borough & MCD (Perry)	1,574	1,561	-0.8	1,517	89.6	4.6	0.5	3.1	2.2	27.0	63.5	9.6	650	38.9	59.2	16.8
New Ringgold borough & MCD (Schuylkill)	276	271	-1.8	282	97.9	0.0	0.0	1.1	1.1	20.6	67.4	12.1	127	77.2	66.1	6.3
Newry borough & MCD (Blair)	270	268	-0.7	290	89.7	0.0	0.0	10.3	0.0	25.5	61.8	12.8	111	69.4	63.1	14.4
New Salem CDP..............	579	NA	NA	366	91.3	0.0	0.0	8.5	0.3	13.1	72.9	13.9	158	86.1	26.6	56.3
New Salem borough & MCD (York)	724	777	7.3	814	92.9	3.9	0.0	0.0	3.2	18.2	58.6	23.1	314	88.2	50.0	20.7
New Schaefferstown CDP	223	NA	NA	282	100.0	0.0	0.0	0.0	0.0	27.4	59.6	13.1	99	81.8	66.7	21.2
New Sewickley township (Beaver)	7,358	7,466	1.5	7,455	97.9	0.9	1.0	0.3	0.0	17.6	61.3	21.2	3,214	78.1	48.0	23.1
New Stanton borough & MCD (Westmoreland) ..	2,173	2,141	-1.5	2,510	90.7	2.1	1.0	3.9	2.3	20.6	64.9	14.5	1,100	55.2	34.6	35.0
Newton township (Lackawanna)...............	2,846	2,848	0.1	2,838	96.4	0.8	0.4	1.2	1.3	21.1	63.2	15.9	1,064	91.0	45.5	30.4
Newton Hamilton borough & MCD (Mifflin)...........	205	205	0.0	187	90.4	9.6	0.0	0.0	0.0	26.7	46.1	27.3	79	78.5	77.2	13.9
Newtown borough & MCD (Bucks)	2,248	2,227	-0.9	2,240	98.3	0.4	0.0	0.8	0.5	20.1	63.0	16.8	978	73.9	16.2	67.4
Newtown township (Bucks)	19,299	19,668	1.9	19,459	84.6	0.4	9.0	3.0	3.0	23.1	64.1	12.9	7,317	86.0	13.5	66.7
Newtown township (Delaware)................	12,216	12,428	1.7	12,294	94.0	0.8	3.5	0.8	0.8	20.8	58.1	21.1	4,697	78.2	22.6	56.0
Newtown CDP	243	NA	NA	230	100.0	0.0	0.0	0.0	0.0	23.5	57.8	18.7	95	88.4	76.8	5.3
Newtown Grant CDP	3,620	NA	NA	3,764	84.5	0.0	12.4	0.3	2.7	21.4	69.0	9.7	1,555	87.1	13.4	63.9
New Tripoli CDP............	898	NA	NA	745	99.1	0.0	0.0	0.0	0.9	33.4	56.8	9.8	268	76.1	42.9	38.1
New Vernon township (Mercer)	504	507	0.6	443	99.3	0.0	0.7	0.0	0.0	16.7	59.9	23.5	187	88.8	69.5	9.6
Newville borough & MCD (Cumberland)..............	1,326	1,326	0.0	1,363	93.8	2.0	1.2	2.1	1.0	24.2	65.7	10.2	595	39.7	52.8	24.2
New Washington borough & MCD (Clearfield)........	59	58	-1.7	66	97.0	0.0	3.0	0.0	0.0	19.6	63.6	16.7	26	73.1	88.5	0.0
New Wilmington borough & MCD (Lawrence)	2,466	2,244	-9.0	2,472	96.5	1.5	0.2	0.5	1.3	10.2	72.8	17.3	561	51.2	18.9	54.7
Nicholson township (Fayette)...................	1,805	1,767	-2.1	1,605	98.1	0.5	0.0	0.5	0.9	19.5	66.3	14.2	613	80.6	68.4	6.9
Nicholson borough & MCD (Wyoming)...........	765	750	-2.0	904	95.7	1.1	0.0	0.3	2.9	24.6	58.7	16.7	357	65.8	57.4	18.2
Nicholson township (Wyoming)..............	1,388	1,363	-1.8	1,450	96.0	0.5	0.1	1.6	1.8	18.6	65.4	15.9	595	88.6	54.8	16.5
Nippenose township (Lycoming)...............	709	712	0.4	712	99.3	0.0	0.0	0.3	0.4	19.5	62.2	18.5	281	82.9	66.2	9.3
Nittany CDP..................	658	NA	NA	641	98.0	0.0	0.0	0.0	2.0	17.0	65.1	17.9	265	58.5	76.2	5.3
Nixon CDP....................	1,373	NA	NA	1,373	93.8	0.0	5.0	0.3	0.9	25.1	59.8	15.1	526	96.2	15.0	54.6
Noblestown CDP	575	NA	NA	391	100.0	0.0	0.0	0.0	0.0	22.0	68.6	9.5	141	87.2	14.9	41.1
Nockamixon township (Bucks)	3,441	3,420	-0.6	3,425	98.2	0.5	0.2	0.5	0.7	16.6	66.6	16.8	1,338	81.7	43.1	33.4
Norristown borough & MCD (Montgomery)	34,324	34,484	0.5	34,454	34.4	34.9	1.9	4.0	24.8	24.8	65.1	10.1	12,735	39.3	54.2	19.3
North Abington township (Lackawanna)..............	703	688	-2.1	629	93.0	1.4	0.5	1.0	4.1	19.6	64.3	16.2	226	91.2	15.5	53.5
Northampton township (Bucks)	39,726	39,577	-0.4	39,675	91.9	0.5	4.5	1.4	1.7	23.4	60.1	16.4	13,863	90.7	23.2	52.9
Northampton borough & MCD (Northampton)	9,926	9,915	-0.1	9,921	90.1	1.0	1.5	2.1	5.2	22.9	62.5	14.6	4,185	73.6	49.4	16.9
Northampton township (Somerset)	343	334	-2.6	335	100.0	0.0	0.0	0.0	0.0	17.7	59.1	23.3	127	91.3	74.0	9.4
North Annville township (Lebanon)..................	2,381	2,437	2.4	2,350	98.7	0.0	0.0	0.8	0.5	16.4	66.9	16.6	932	83.8	55.8	21.8
North Apollo borough & MCD (Armstrong).........	1,297	1,272	-1.9	1,423	97.5	2.5	0.0	0.0	0.0	21.3	61.9	16.8	545	83.3	56.7	20.2
North Beaver township (Lawrence)................	4,121	4,044	-1.9	4,077	97.4	0.0	0.0	1.4	1.2	20.6	63.2	16.4	1,572	93.8	49.7	27.4
North Belle Vernon borough & MCD (Westmoreland)	1,971	1,918	-2.7	1,880	96.3	0.3	0.3	0.4	2.7	18.0	65.7	16.3	813	62.1	46.1	22.6

1 May be of any race.

Table A. All Places — **Population and Housing**

STATE City, town, township, borough, or CDP (county if applicable)	Population				Race and Hispanic or Latino origin (percent), 2010–2014					Age (percent), 2010–2014			Households, 2010–2014			
	2010 census total population	2014 estimated population	Percent change 2010–2014	ACS total population estimate 2010–2014	White alone, not Hispanic or Latino	Black alone, not Hispanic or Latino	Asian alone, not Hispanic or Latino	All other races or 2 or more races, not Hispanic or Latino	Hispanic or Latino[1]	Under 18 years old	Age 18 to 64 years old	Age 65 years and older	Total occupied housing units	Percent owner occupied	Householders by level of education (percent) High school diploma or less	Householders by level of education (percent) Bachelor's degree or more
	1	2	3	4	5	6	7	8	9	10	11	12	13	14	15	16
PENNSYLVANIA—Con.																
North Bethlehem township (Washington).	1,631	1,606	-1.5	1,698	98.4	0.0	0.2	1.4	0.0	20.9	66.1	13.0	654	82.6	48.5	23.5
North Braddock borough & MCD (Allegheny)	4,857	4,815	-0.9	4,847	55.2	37.1	0.1	6.7	0.9	22.7	62.1	15.2	2,170	53.9	51.6	9.3
North Branch township (Wyoming)	208	212	1.9	212	100.0	0.0	0.0	0.0	0.0	15.6	56.9	27.4	88	87.5	69.3	8.0
North Buffalo township (Armstrong)	3,011	2,992	-0.6	2,994	99.9	0.0	0.0	0.0	0.1	14.3	63.8	21.7	1,309	82.8	63.3	17.2
North Catasauqua borough & MCD (Northampton)	2,849	2,844	-0.2	2,844	94.6	1.2	0.4	2.8	1.0	21.9	62.3	15.7	1,211	64.4	46.4	23.9
North Centre township (Columbia)	2,105	2,135	1.4	2,223	97.4	0.4	0.0	1.7	0.5	20.2	67.0	12.8	859	90.7	54.1	20.7
North Charleroi borough & MCD (Washington)	1,313	1,288	-1.9	1,255	88.1	6.3	0.0	4.1	1.4	18.5	61.6	19.9	577	61.2	52.3	18.0
North Codorus township (York)	8,941	9,018	0.9	8,966	93.2	2.8	0.7	0.3	2.9	22.8	64.5	12.7	3,241	82.5	54.1	17.4
North Cornwall township (Lebanon)	7,580	7,754	2.3	7,683	78.6	6.2	1.2	4.1	10.0	24.4	58.1	17.4	2,832	66.5	43.7	30.9
North Coventry township (Chester)	7,866	8,021	2.0	7,935	91.1	2.8	3.4	1.2	1.5	24.1	61.2	14.9	3,093	73.6	40.9	35.3
North East borough & MCD (Erie)	4,294	4,197	-2.3	4,253	95.5	0.4	0.0	0.4	3.7	29.6	58.2	12.3	1,626	53.4	47.8	21.5
North East township (Erie)	6,315	6,334	0.3	6,370	94.9	1.4	0.5	2.4	0.7	23.3	61.7	14.9	2,356	82.7	43.5	25.3
Northeast Madison township (Perry)	788	785	-0.4	893	97.6	0.3	0.7	0.4	0.9	25.1	62.4	12.4	313	82.7	66.1	9.6
Northern Cambria borough & MCD (Cambria)	3,835	3,694	-3.7	3,769	100.0	0.0	0.0	0.0	0.0	23.1	56.8	20.1	1,568	77.9	57.5	20.2
North Fayette township (Allegheny)	13,934	14,377	3.2	14,136	92.6	1.6	2.0	1.6	2.2	23.1	66.3	10.4	5,821	78.7	31.0	41.3
North Franklin township (Washington)	4,583	4,568	-0.3	4,573	94.0	0.7	0.1	0.9	4.4	19.6	56.3	24.2	1,704	76.5	49.9	31.0
North Heidelberg township (Berks)	1,216	1,221	0.4	1,119	94.5	1.5	0.0	0.9	3.1	15.8	63.8	20.6	439	89.1	55.8	21.2
North Hopewell township (York)	2,791	2,792	0.0	2,797	98.7	0.0	0.2	0.9	0.2	21.1	63.2	15.7	1,101	83.4	54.4	20.0
North Huntingdon township (Westmoreland)	30,611	30,748	0.4	30,738	96.7	0.5	1.2	0.6	1.0	21.9	58.9	19.2	12,168	90.4	37.8	34.7
North Irwin borough & MCD (Westmoreland)	846	825	-2.5	777	98.8	0.0	0.0	0.1	1.0	19.0	68.0	12.9	344	66.9	40.1	18.9
North Lebanon township (Lebanon)	11,429	11,686	2.2	11,571	90.3	0.6	1.9	1.3	5.8	20.0	62.9	17.1	4,595	86.0	57.5	18.2
North Londonderry township (Lebanon)	8,068	8,290	2.8	8,195	95.8	0.0	0.8	2.2	1.2	20.4	55.0	24.6	3,438	83.7	42.7	30.6
North Mahoning township (Indiana)	1,428	1,381	-3.3	1,583	94.8	1.1	0.0	2.5	1.6	33.4	53.5	13.0	492	84.1	76.4	10.4
North Manheim township (Schuylkill)	3,770	3,710	-1.6	3,748	97.2	0.4	1.3	0.5	0.6	22.5	59.1	18.4	1,362	86.6	52.1	20.6
North Middleton township (Cumberland)	11,143	11,383	2.2	11,280	92.7	1.4	1.1	1.0	3.8	24.4	60.5	15.2	4,450	73.9	48.5	24.9
Northmoreland township (Wyoming)	1,558	1,549	-0.6	1,564	98.3	0.2	0.3	1.2	0.0	22.1	62.8	14.9	578	88.8	53.6	21.6
North Newton township (Cumberland)	2,430	2,485	2.3	2,522	99.0	0.0	0.0	0.9	0.2	29.7	55.6	14.8	910	85.1	62.4	15.2
North Philipsburg CDP	660	NA	NA	781	94.9	0.0	0.0	0.0	5.1	14.8	54.6	30.6	343	63.3	50.1	6.7
North Sewickley township (Beaver)	5,488	5,530	0.8	5,547	96.2	1.0	1.3	1.6	0.0	24.0	59.9	16.2	2,083	81.1	46.0	24.5
North Shenango township (Crawford)	1,410	1,378	-2.3	1,362	99.0	0.4	0.2	0.1	0.2	13.9	57.1	29.0	656	88.6	60.7	10.8
North Strabane township (Washington)	13,408	14,076	5.0	13,756	91.9	3.0	1.7	1.8	1.6	20.6	61.3	18.1	5,432	85.7	26.8	49.1
North Towanda township (Bradford)	1,132	1,121	-1.0	1,117	95.5	0.7	0.0	0.6	3.1	15.6	49.1	35.4	530	44.9	62.1	17.7
Northumberland borough & MCD (Northumberland)	3,804	3,753	-1.3	3,772	98.0	0.0	0.0	0.4	1.6	15.4	62.7	21.8	1,889	65.1	51.1	23.5
North Union township (Fayette)	12,726	12,488	-1.9	12,607	93.7	1.9	0.6	3.5	0.3	19.1	60.3	20.6	5,234	66.5	62.8	13.8
North Union township (Schuylkill)	1,476	1,450	-1.8	1,432	97.1	0.7	1.0	0.0	1.2	19.0	64.2	16.8	576	86.5	52.6	21.7
North Vandergrift CDP	447	NA	NA	453	80.4	17.4	0.0	2.2	0.0	16.8	69.6	13.7	244	63.9	76.6	5.3
North Versailles township (Allegheny)	10,217	10,154	-0.6	10,200	78.1	19.4	0.5	1.8	0.3	20.3	62.3	17.5	4,691	69.4	49.5	17.0
North Wales borough & MCD (Montgomery)	3,229	3,238	0.3	3,227	88.0	2.7	4.6	4.0	0.7	22.0	66.6	11.2	1,395	69.2	38.4	32.5
North Warren CDP	1,934	NA	NA	1,900	94.6	1.4	1.9	0.8	1.3	16.3	59.7	24.0	780	80.1	44.2	32.7
Northwest Harborcreek CDP	8,949	NA	NA	9,492	94.4	1.7	0.8	1.2	1.9	21.4	62.0	16.7	3,581	76.7	45.1	28.1
North Whitehall township (Lehigh)	15,703	16,063	2.3	15,900	94.6	0.2	0.8	1.1	3.3	20.9	64.7	14.4	5,934	87.5	38.0	34.1
Northwood CDP	296	NA	NA	426	100.0	0.0	0.0	0.0	0.0	20.9	62.5	16.7	151	64.2	74.2	0.0
North Woodbury township (Blair)	2,643	2,670	1.0	2,680	98.4	1.0	0.0	0.6	0.0	19.5	50.8	29.7	1,080	71.7	59.4	19.8
North York borough & MCD (York)	1,914	1,974	3.1	1,712	84.1	6.8	0.0	4.2	4.9	19.3	70.8	9.9	695	53.5	60.0	12.8
Norvelt CDP	948	NA	NA	1,125	100.0	0.0	0.0	0.0	0.0	14.5	62.4	23.2	455	98.5	37.4	25.5
Norwegian township (Schuylkill)	2,310	2,274	-1.6	2,249	97.2	0.6	1.3	0.0	0.9	21.7	54.8	23.3	946	82.8	55.5	21.7

1 May be of any race.

Table A. All Places — **Population and Housing**

STATE City, town, township, borough, or CDP (county if applicable)	Population				Race and Hispanic or Latino origin (percent), 2010–2014					Age (percent), 2010–2014			Households, 2010–2014			
	2010 census total population	2014 estimated population	Percent change 2010–2014	ACS total population estimate 2010–2014	White alone, not Hispanic or Latino	Black alone, not Hispanic or Latino	Asian alone, not Hispanic or Latino	All other races or 2 or more races, not Hispanic or Latino	Hispanic or Latino[1]	Under 18 years old	Age 18 to 64 years old	Age 65 years and older	Total occupied housing units	Percent owner occupied	High school diploma or less	Bachelor's degree or more
	1	2	3	4	5	6	7	8	9	10	11	12	13	14	15	16
PENNSYLVANIA—Con.																
Norwich township (McKean)................	583	569	-2.4	512	99.4	0.0	0.0	0.6	0.0	19.4	68.7	11.9	224	84.4	54.9	13.4
Norwood borough & MCD (Delaware)................	5,890	5,901	0.2	5,897	91.8	3.2	1.5	2.1	1.4	21.5	67.4	11.2	2,192	77.8	53.1	16.0
Nottingham township (Washington)...............	3,036	3,033	-0.1	3,039	95.4	0.0	0.5	4.1	0.0	23.7	64.9	11.5	1,088	94.2	37.6	30.6
Noxen CDP.................	633	NA	NA	671	93.7	0.0	0.3	2.2	3.7	19.8	68.9	11.5	264	76.5	59.8	12.5
Noxen township (Wyoming)................	901	881	-2.2	957	95.6	0.0	0.2	1.6	2.6	19.8	66.3	14.0	366	81.7	65.3	9.0
Noyes township (Clinton).	356	359	0.8	325	100.0	0.0	0.0	0.0	0.0	15.0	59.8	25.2	156	97.4	61.5	14.1
Nuangola borough & MCD (Luzerne)	679	669	-1.5	852	97.4	0.1	2.5	0.0	0.0	19.1	57.7	23.2	330	92.4	37.6	31.8
Numidia CDP..............	244	NA	NA	248	100.0	0.0	0.0	0.0	0.0	24.5	62.1	13.3	89	95.5	52.8	9.0
Nuremberg CDP	434	NA	NA	366	97.8	0.0	2.2	0.0	0.0	19.9	59.0	21.0	149	65.1	81.2	4.0
Oakdale borough & MCD (Allegheny)...............	1,459	1,477	1.2	1,414	97.9	0.4	0.0	0.6	1.1	17.1	60.6	22.3	617	82.5	49.9	26.9
Oak Hills CDP.................	2,333	NA	NA	2,402	96.5	1.1	0.2	2.1	0.0	16.1	66.0	17.9	1,063	60.0	31.6	37.7
Oakland township (Butler)	2,987	2,924	-2.1	2,973	96.3	0.8	0.4	2.5	0.0	19.9	64.7	15.4	1,139	88.5	52.8	16.2
Oakland CDP (Cambria)..	1,578	NA	NA	1,414	93.4	2.1	2.8	1.8	0.0	3.3	63.0	33.6	701	88.9	61.8	15.4
Oakland CDP (Lawrence)	1,569	NA	NA	1,307	89.4	6.0	2.7	1.6	0.4	18.6	60.4	21.1	518	87.1	60.4	13.9
Oakland borough & MCD (Susquehanna)	616	587	-4.7	700	100.0	0.0	0.0	0.0	0.0	28.5	58.1	13.4	248	74.2	57.7	8.9
Oakland township (Susquehanna)	564	536	-5.0	527	90.7	0.0	0.0	4.2	5.1	18.7	67.0	14.4	212	80.2	67.9	13.2
Oakland township (Venango)	1,501	1,480	-1.4	1,499	95.7	0.5	0.6	2.7	0.5	18.1	64.6	17.4	597	89.9	56.6	17.9
Oakmont borough & MCD (Allegheny)...............	6,303	6,426	2.0	6,358	96.2	0.6	1.3	0.2	1.8	16.2	58.3	25.5	3,068	64.5	29.6	47.0
Oakwood CDP................	2,270	NA	NA	2,281	96.1	2.7	0.0	0.0	1.3	18.6	57.9	23.5	1,010	82.8	57.4	11.7
Oberlin CDP.................	588	NA	NA	467	78.2	4.9	0.0	7.3	9.6	30.9	45.6	23.6	162	87.0	69.8	16.0
Ogle township (Somerset)	501	488	-2.6	410	98.8	0.0	0.5	0.7	0.0	15.6	68.3	16.1	178	88.8	49.4	27.0
O'Hara township (Allegheny)...............	8,409	8,557	1.8	8,499	86.5	0.9	7.2	4.5	1.1	21.3	56.5	22.2	3,502	86.6	19.6	66.9
Ohio township (Allegheny)	4,760	5,858	23.1	5,493	89.2	4.8	2.9	2.1	1.0	26.2	65.1	8.8	2,015	74.2	16.1	69.4
Ohiopyle borough & MCD (Fayette)................	59	58	-1.7	41	100.0	0.0	0.0	0.0	0.0	12.2	65.9	22.0	22	81.8	63.6	27.3
Ohioville borough & MCD (Beaver)	3,533	3,482	-1.4	3,511	96.6	1.3	0.0	2.1	0.0	19.9	63.0	17.2	1,366	83.7	50.2	14.9
Oil City city & MCD (Venango)	10,557	10,227	-3.1	10,383	95.3	1.7	0.6	1.6	0.8	24.2	60.4	15.3	4,260	61.3	55.8	16.0
Oil Creek township (Crawford)	1,868	1,819	-2.6	1,986	98.8	0.0	0.0	0.9	0.3	20.8	64.1	15.1	812	80.3	56.7	21.7
Oil Creek township (Venango)	854	831	-2.7	855	99.6	0.0	0.0	0.4	0.0	13.7	64.2	22.2	341	88.0	71.8	7.3
Oklahoma CDP..............	782	NA	NA	1,150	92.3	0.0	3.7	4.0	0.0	28.1	53.6	18.4	404	67.1	56.2	8.4
Oklahoma borough & MCD (Westmoreland) ..	811	791	-2.5	735	95.9	0.5	0.0	0.4	3.1	11.3	63.8	25.0	349	80.2	56.2	13.8
Old Forge borough & MCD (Lackawanna)	8,313	8,216	-1.2	8,265	95.0	0.6	1.0	0.1	3.3	17.7	62.1	20.1	3,664	68.3	48.5	21.0
Old Lycoming township (Lycoming)...............	4,938	5,066	2.6	5,016	97.0	1.9	0.3	0.5	0.3	14.3	63.9	21.8	2,301	84.3	52.5	17.6
Old Orchard CDP	2,434	NA	NA	2,191	92.1	1.5	0.6	1.6	4.2	15.4	59.9	24.9	849	100.0	40.0	29.1
Oley CDP..................	1,282	NA	NA	1,282	97.1	0.0	0.0	0.0	2.9	25.3	65.9	8.7	492	77.4	40.2	36.2
Oley township (Berks)	3,620	3,677	1.6	3,655	97.9	0.0	0.6	0.0	1.4	17.4	67.2	15.5	1,424	73.7	44.8	24.3
Oliver CDP..................	2,535	NA	NA	2,964	90.1	2.9	1.3	5.5	0.2	22.9	64.5	12.5	1,196	53.7	61.1	15.6
Oliver township (Jefferson)..................	1,083	1,068	-1.4	971	97.5	0.5	0.4	1.5	0.0	22.6	59.9	17.5	392	88.8	63.0	17.1
Oliver township (Mifflin) ...	2,173	2,198	1.2	2,012	95.8	0.5	0.0	3.0	0.7	22.6	56.1	21.3	807	79.4	76.3	12.1
Oliver township (Perry)	1,934	1,926	-0.4	2,016	93.0	0.3	0.3	3.7	2.7	24.2	58.2	17.6	828	67.9	66.5	9.8
Olyphant borough & MCD (Lackawanna)..............	5,151	5,210	1.1	5,178	96.3	0.1	0.4	0.0	3.1	16.7	65.9	17.5	2,245	57.6	40.5	26.6
Oneida township (Huntingdon)	1,077	1,074	-0.3	1,114	95.7	0.0	3.1	1.2	0.0	19.9	57.1	23.0	473	85.4	58.6	23.9
Oneida CDP	200	NA	NA	162	100.0	0.0	0.0	0.0	0.0	14.2	77.9	8.0	75	69.3	54.7	17.3
Ontelaunee township (Berks)	1,646	1,787	8.6	1,774	75.2	2.3	2.9	4.6	15.0	24.8	59.1	16.2	680	88.4	55.4	21.3
Orange township (Columbia)	1,257	1,247	-0.8	1,236	99.2	0.0	0.2	0.0	0.6	21.9	62.6	15.6	486	95.3	53.5	26.3
Orangeville borough & MCD (Columbia)	508	506	-0.4	436	93.1	0.0	0.5	6.4	0.0	13.3	55.5	31.2	132	72.0	62.1	12.1
Orbisonia borough & MCD (Huntingdon)	428	417	-2.6	518	98.5	0.4	0.0	0.0	1.2	23.3	62.7	13.9	209	61.2	73.7	17.7
Orchard Hills CDP	1,952	NA	NA	1,851	96.7	3.3	0.0	0.0	0.0	17.7	61.5	20.9	840	77.4	63.3	1.8
Oregon township (Wayne)	776	760	-2.1	782	96.9	0.0	0.0	0.6	2.4	17.0	64.9	18.0	297	85.5	53.5	26.3
Oreland CDP	5,678	NA	NA	5,748	76.0	15.2	2.7	2.0	4.2	24.9	60.8	14.3	2,065	81.7	32.4	48.0
Orrstown borough & MCD (Franklin)	262	264	0.8	269	97.0	0.0	0.0	1.1	1.9	19.7	54.0	26.4	111	55.9	70.3	7.2
Orrtanna CDP.................	173	NA	NA	171	90.1	4.1	0.0	0.0	5.8	23.9	57.9	18.1	60	100.0	56.7	11.7
Orviston CDP	95	NA	NA	91	100.0	0.0	0.0	0.0	0.0	8.8	71.5	19.8	30	100.0	73.3	23.3
Orwell township (Bradford)................	1,159	1,146	-1.1	1,030	98.7	0.0	0.0	1.3	0.0	25.5	53.9	20.5	377	82.0	53.8	24.4
Orwigsburg borough & MCD (Schuylkill)	3,099	3,029	-2.3	3,053	90.7	1.4	5.4	1.6	0.9	18.2	58.7	23.0	1,214	69.3	36.0	35.6
Orwin CDP...................	314	NA	NA	291	98.6	0.0	0.0	1.4	0.0	15.4	72.2	12.4	99	100.0	66.7	23.2
Osceola township (Tioga)	659	655	-0.6	613	97.9	2.1	0.0	0.0	0.0	20.4	70.8	8.8	235	83.8	62.1	5.5
Osceola Mills borough & MCD (Clearfield)	1,141	1,112	-2.5	1,255	99.0	0.1	0.0	1.0	0.0	25.6	60.7	13.9	508	76.6	56.1	8.1
Oswayo borough & MCD (Potter)	139	138	-0.7	168	99.4	0.0	0.0	0.6	0.0	20.3	65.4	14.3	59	91.5	67.8	8.5
Oswayo township (Potter)	278	275	-1.1	232	95.3	0.0	0.0	1.3	3.4	19.4	63.1	17.7	91	84.6	71.4	13.2

1 May be of any race.

Table A. All Places — **Population and Housing**

STATE City, town, township, borough, or CDP (county if applicable)	Population				Race and Hispanic or Latino origin (percent), 2010–2014					Age (percent), 2010–2014			Households, 2010–2014			
								All other races or 2 or more races, not Hispanic or Latino							Householders by level of education (percent)	
	2010 census total population	2014 estimated population	Percent change 2010–2014	ACS total population estimate 2010–2014	White alone, not Hispanic or Latino	Black alone, not Hispanic or Latino	Asian alone, not Hispanic or Latino		Hispanic or Latino[1]	Under 18 years old	Age 18 to 64 years old	Age 65 years and older	Total occupied housing units	Percent owner occupied	High school diploma or less	Bachelor's degree or more
	1	2	3	4	5	6	7	8	9	10	11	12	13	14	15	16
PENNSYLVANIA—Con.																
Otter Creek township (Mercer)	589	580	-1.5	564	98.4	0.0	0.2	0.7	0.7	20.4	65.8	13.8	230	92.2	61.3	14.3
Otto township (McKean)	1,556	1,524	-2.1	1,514	96.6	0.3	0.0	2.1	0.9	23.6	58.7	17.7	607	81.1	61.3	15.8
Oval CDP	361	NA	NA	366	99.2	0.0	0.0	0.0	0.8	26.3	54.2	19.7	141	100.0	46.8	27.0
Overfield township (Wyoming)	1,664	1,653	-0.7	1,616	97.0	0.4	0.0	2.1	0.4	22.4	52.8	24.9	627	85.0	51.2	22.2
Overton township (Bradford)	247	240	-2.8	245	98.0	0.0	0.0	0.0	2.0	20.4	58.0	21.6	99	92.9	79.8	4.0
Oxford township (Adams)	5,517	5,552	0.6	5,529	93.0	1.3	0.0	1.5	4.2	23.3	54.7	21.8	1,979	76.5	57.9	21.7
Oxford borough & MCD (Chester)	5,077	5,126	1.0	5,100	66.7	6.1	0.0	0.8	26.4	33.0	51.4	15.6	1,781	40.1	53.8	21.6
Packer township (Carbon)	998	994	-0.4	1,029	97.8	0.3	0.0	1.2	0.8	21.7	60.3	18.0	403	93.1	62.3	11.7
Paint township (Clarion)	1,699	1,660	-2.3	1,792	94.1	1.5	0.0	2.3	2.1	17.6	59.6	22.9	713	82.6	47.7	32.1
Paint borough & MCD (Somerset)	1,002	977	-2.5	854	99.6	0.0	0.0	0.4	0.0	13.6	36.3	50.0	364	67.0	64.8	12.4
Paint township (Somerset)	3,149	3,118	-1.0	3,139	98.5	0.0	0.0	0.3	1.1	16.8	61.5	21.8	1,294	90.2	65.4	11.6
Palmdale CDP	1,308	NA	NA	1,343	97.2	0.6	1.6	0.0	0.7	28.0	57.0	14.9	496	66.7	44.2	41.7
Palmer township (Northampton)	20,634	20,930	1.4	20,768	80.6	6.8	5.8	1.8	5.1	20.8	58.4	20.6	8,077	83.6	37.1	32.9
Palmer Heights CDP	3,762	NA	NA	3,733	81.6	7.8	1.2	1.2	8.3	19.1	57.6	23.1	1,406	92.0	39.2	25.5
Palmerton borough & MCD (Carbon)	5,414	5,350	-1.2	5,382	90.9	0.0	0.0	3.4	5.6	18.8	64.3	17.0	2,354	72.2	62.7	11.0
Palmyra borough & MCD (Lebanon)	7,320	7,436	1.6	7,399	91.3	1.9	2.0	1.2	3.5	21.2	60.0	18.9	3,316	49.4	54.3	23.3
Palmyra township (Pike)	3,320	3,261	-1.8	3,297	98.0	0.0	0.6	0.7	0.7	19.3	55.9	24.9	1,447	87.6	40.0	31.4
Palmyra township (Wayne)	1,338	1,303	-2.6	1,115	90.5	0.0	5.5	1.3	2.8	15.2	60.4	24.5	501	85.4	48.1	23.8
Palo Alto borough & MCD (Schuylkill)	1,032	1,013	-1.8	1,066	93.2	0.0	0.5	4.0	2.3	18.3	64.8	16.9	429	71.1	64.3	5.4
Paoli CDP	5,575	NA	NA	5,616	81.2	4.7	10.1	2.4	1.6	19.9	57.2	22.8	2,344	65.5	22.8	60.1
Paradise CDP	1,129	NA	NA	1,024	91.5	3.3	0.6	3.9	0.7	23.6	67.5	9.0	327	74.6	70.3	15.3
Paradise township (Lancaster)	5,131	5,365	4.6	5,251	97.0	0.6	0.1	1.2	1.0	32.3	54.2	13.6	1,590	73.3	79.9	7.7
Paradise township (Monroe)	3,183	3,101	-2.6	3,150	71.4	3.4	0.4	0.2	24.6	22.3	62.1	15.5	1,092	76.0	37.8	29.9
Paradise township (York)	3,766	3,870	2.8	3,816	98.8	0.3	0.3	0.0	0.6	20.1	62.4	17.4	1,409	94.8	65.4	16.0
Pardeesville CDP	572	NA	NA	338	98.2	0.0	1.8	0.0	0.0	15.4	37.7	47.0	168	89.9	85.7	4.8
Paris CDP	732	NA	NA	781	91.2	0.0	0.0	6.8	2.0	13.1	61.7	25.2	313	80.8	71.6	11.5
Park Crest CDP	542	NA	NA	672	99.1	0.0	0.0	0.0	0.9	14.8	60.7	24.4	256	94.9	41.4	18.4
Parker city & MCD (Armstrong)	839	832	-0.8	745	99.1	0.9	0.0	0.0	0.0	24.3	57.5	18.1	331	57.1	73.7	6.6
Parker township (Butler)	635	624	-1.7	515	100.0	0.0	0.0	0.0	0.0	18.1	59.6	22.3	238	93.3	63.4	13.0
Parkesburg borough & MCD (Chester)	3,593	3,670	2.1	3,636	78.3	6.2	0.6	1.2	13.7	24.7	62.8	12.4	1,400	66.2	52.8	18.0
Park Forest Village CDP	9,660	NA	NA	9,276	80.4	1.1	12.8	5.0	0.8	15.3	73.1	11.5	3,846	50.6	12.7	56.2
Parks township (Armstrong)	2,741	2,678	-2.3	2,710	93.0	5.7	0.0	0.6	0.7	20.9	64.6	14.5	1,134	82.4	67.5	12.9
Parkside borough & MCD (Delaware)	2,328	2,334	0.3	2,192	74.4	14.6	3.5	2.9	4.7	26.9	64.5	8.6	795	78.4	49.2	23.9
Parkville CDP	6,706	NA	NA	6,949	90.6	0.0	1.1	3.7	4.6	23.9	64.3	11.7	2,605	67.7	62.8	11.2
Parryville borough & MCD (Carbon)	525	512	-2.5	604	100.0	0.0	0.0	0.0	0.0	19.9	64.2	15.9	234	79.5	55.6	12.8
Patterson township (Beaver)	3,029	2,988	-1.4	3,013	95.9	0.7	2.4	1.0	0.0	21.1	55.3	23.5	1,282	66.0	42.0	33.5
Patterson Heights borough & MCD (Beaver)	636	621	-2.4	630	96.8	0.5	0.0	0.8	1.9	19.0	63.1	18.1	251	90.8	17.9	53.4
Patton borough & MCD (Cambria)	1,769	1,700	-3.9	1,858	97.7	1.1	0.0	0.6	0.6	19.8	56.6	23.7	834	66.3	68.9	9.2
Patton township (Centre)	15,311	15,808	3.2	15,489	77.4	7.4	7.4	4.4	3.4	15.2	75.8	9.0	6,380	46.9	20.1	54.1
Paupack township (Wayne)	3,830	3,734	-2.5	3,766	97.5	0.0	1.4	0.3	0.8	17.4	55.4	27.1	1,537	90.2	43.3	22.4
Pavia township (Bedford)	295	283	-4.1	196	98.5	0.0	0.0	0.0	1.5	12.2	71.9	15.8	93	87.1	64.5	14.0
Paxtang borough & MCD (Dauphin)	1,561	1,542	-1.2	1,450	73.9	5.0	2.4	7.3	11.3	23.0	64.0	13.0	624	80.9	30.4	40.4
Paxtonia CDP	5,412	NA	NA	4,896	84.7	6.9	3.8	2.0	2.5	18.6	73.0	8.6	1,970	76.9	31.5	41.3
Paxtonville CDP	265	NA	NA	196	100.0	0.0	0.0	0.0	0.0	4.6	63.9	31.6	97	94.8	60.8	5.2
Peach Bottom township (York)	4,813	4,912	2.1	4,849	95.9	0.8	0.8	2.5	0.0	28.2	63.2	8.5	1,705	84.9	56.2	8.9
Pen Argyl borough & MCD (Northampton)	3,595	3,562	-0.9	3,576	95.5	1.0	0.0	1.7	1.8	25.5	63.9	10.6	1,333	58.6	50.8	20.0
Penbrook borough & MCD (Dauphin)	3,008	2,975	-1.1	2,997	52.3	24.6	8.8	5.8	8.5	28.8	62.5	8.6	1,200	50.2	47.6	22.7
Pen Mar CDP	929	NA	NA	1,093	88.7	7.4	1.4	0.0	2.5	27.8	61.3	10.8	442	85.7	62.2	15.6
Penn township (Berks)	1,949	1,993	2.3	2,077	94.4	0.1	0.0	2.4	3.1	19.8	64.6	15.6	753	95.1	48.9	26.0
Penn township (Butler)	5,067	4,970	-1.9	5,039	97.4	0.0	1.3	0.2	1.1	21.2	60.4	18.5	2,030	92.2	34.4	37.2
Penn township (Centre)	1,181	1,168	-1.1	1,094	97.4	0.0	0.5	0.7	1.3	27.8	57.9	14.2	392	84.9	61.0	21.7
Penn township (Chester)	5,364	5,471	2.0	5,441	85.3	1.9	3.7	1.3	7.8	23.0	48.4	28.7	2,317	76.5	37.0	44.9
Penn township (Clearfield)	1,264	1,240	-1.9	1,218	99.3	0.0	0.0	0.0	0.7	18.2	65.4	16.3	462	91.3	62.8	14.9
Penn township (Cumberland)	2,924	2,960	1.2	2,935	94.7	1.2	0.1	2.8	1.2	21.1	66.4	12.5	1,138	87.7	64.0	13.6
Penn township (Huntingdon)	1,084	1,081	-0.3	821	98.5	0.0	0.0	0.0	1.5	9.0	66.8	24.1	411	88.6	56.4	22.1
Penn township (Lancaster)	8,789	9,108	3.6	8,978	88.7	1.7	2.9	0.4	6.3	23.7	55.9	20.3	3,384	81.5	56.5	28.3
Penn township (Lycoming)	960	984	2.5	855	100.0	0.0	0.0	0.0	0.0	18.7	62.7	18.6	345	87.5	64.9	18.3
Penn township (Perry)	3,225	3,191	-1.1	3,206	97.8	0.1	0.0	2.2	0.0	16.9	64.0	19.1	1,275	78.7	50.9	11.9
Penn township (Snyder)	4,328	4,371	1.0	4,334	89.3	0.8	3.5	0.4	5.9	22.7	60.0	17.4	1,558	84.6	43.8	31.5
Penn borough & MCD (Westmoreland)	475	482	1.5	596	95.1	0.3	0.2	2.5	1.8	30.1	63.2	6.9	205	74.6	52.7	10.2

1 May be of any race.

Table A. All Places — **Population and Housing**

STATE City, town, township, borough, or CDP (county if applicable)	2010 census total population	2014 estimated population	Percent change 2010–2014	ACS total population estimate 2010–2014	White alone, not Hispanic or Latino	Black alone, not Hispanic or Latino	Asian alone, not Hispanic or Latino	All other races or 2 or more races, not Hispanic or Latino	Hispanic or Latino[1]	Under 18 years old	Age 18 to 64 years old	Age 65 years and older	Total occupied housing units	Percent owner occupied	High school diploma or less	Bachelor's degree or more
	1	2	3	4	5	6	7	8	9	10	11	12	13	14	15	16
PENNSYLVANIA—Con.																
Penn township (Westmoreland)	20,005	19,750	-1.3	19,886	98.9	0.5	0.1	0.4	0.0	21.6	61.7	16.6	7,551	90.2	32.7	38.4
Penn township (York).......	15,618	15,928	2.0	15,726	91.4	0.6	1.0	2.1	4.9	21.3	61.5	17.0	6,052	78.6	52.2	22.4
Penndel borough & MCD (Bucks)	2,328	2,249	-3.4	2,700	72.4	11.0	2.3	2.5	11.8	19.3	71.3	9.4	941	43.7	44.2	22.5
Penn Estates CDP.........	4,493	NA	NA	5,972	49.1	22.4	1.0	0.7	26.8	23.4	67.8	8.8	1,727	85.2	27.0	30.1
Penn Forest township (Carbon)	9,582	9,701	1.2	9,673	86.2	2.5	2.0	2.1	7.2	24.3	59.7	16.0	3,544	88.0	47.3	19.9
Penn Hills township (Allegheny)	42,331	42,109	-0.5	42,292	57.6	37.3	0.7	3.0	1.4	19.6	61.6	18.9	18,272	76.4	39.6	26.9
Penn Lake Park borough & MCD (Luzerne)........	308	308	0.0	304	100.0	0.0	0.0	0.0	0.0	6.9	75.0	18.1	142	89.4	26.8	34.5
Pennsburg borough & MCD (Montgomery)	3,843	3,876	0.9	3,870	93.0	1.6	0.0	2.4	2.9	26.7	60.4	12.9	1,278	68.9	50.8	24.2
Pennsbury township (Chester)	3,604	3,640	1.0	3,621	87.8	3.6	5.1	3.1	0.4	21.3	49.3	29.4	1,489	74.3	8.5	72.7
Pennsbury Village borough & MCD (Allegheny)	661	671	1.5	690	94.1	4.2	0.0	1.3	0.4	6.7	80.3	13.2	475	83.2	16.4	64.0
Penns Creek CDP	715	NA	NA	559	93.4	0.2	0.0	2.9	3.6	11.6	69.5	19.0	229	65.1	69.4	11.8
Pennside CDP	4,215	NA	NA	4,122	81.8	3.9	0.6	2.3	11.5	25.4	58.5	16.1	1,615	70.8	46.9	23.0
Penn State Erie (Behrend) CDP............	1,629	NA	NA	1,642	85.0	6.2	5.8	1.5	1.6	0.4	99.6	0.0	0	0.0	0.0	0.0
Pennville CDP................	1,947	NA	NA	1,968	96.3	0.5	0.8	0.0	2.4	14.6	62.5	22.9	862	79.2	48.5	32.4
Pennwyn CDP..............	780	NA	NA	794	99.6	0.0	0.0	0.4	0.0	20.5	60.7	18.8	301	87.0	40.9	25.9
Penn Wynne CDP...........	5,697	NA	NA	5,740	71.1	9.5	11.7	6.1	1.7	25.1	54.5	20.4	2,118	91.8	10.7	75.9
Penryn CDP..............	1,024	NA	NA	1,176	87.0	0.0	9.6	0.0	3.4	20.3	63.2	16.5	416	93.8	56.3	22.8
Pequea township (Lancaster)	4,605	4,689	1.8	4,642	92.0	2.6	1.6	0.7	3.0	20.6	62.7	16.6	1,871	81.0	51.3	21.8
Perkasie borough & MCD (Bucks)	8,511	8,484	-0.3	8,511	95.2	1.1	0.2	0.8	2.7	22.3	66.2	11.4	3,285	72.1	36.4	30.7
Perkiomen township (Montgomery)	9,139	9,250	1.2	9,196	82.5	6.9	6.4	0.3	3.9	32.8	58.9	8.4	3,092	87.8	25.5	51.9
Perry township (Armstrong)	355	345	-2.8	329	98.8	0.0	0.0	0.3	0.9	19.8	60.5	19.8	119	94.1	56.3	13.4
Perry township (Berks)	2,417	2,427	0.4	2,536	96.0	0.0	0.2	0.6	3.2	15.5	65.4	19.0	1,004	81.6	62.3	14.9
Perry township (Clarion) ..	947	932	-1.6	1,083	99.6	0.0	0.0	0.4	0.0	23.6	61.9	14.5	406	90.6	65.5	14.3
Perry township (Fayette)..	2,552	2,501	-2.0	2,525	92.7	3.1	0.0	3.0	1.3	18.0	61.6	20.5	1,016	83.1	63.7	17.9
Perry township (Greene)..	1,514	1,466	-3.2	1,598	98.8	0.6	0.0	0.6	0.1	16.5	61.3	22.1	678	79.1	67.0	12.7
Perry township (Jefferson)	1,226	1,209	-1.4	1,180	99.0	0.0	0.0	0.6	0.4	18.7	63.7	17.6	473	88.6	65.3	17.5
Perry township (Lawrence)	1,938	1,910	-1.4	1,800	95.5	0.0	1.2	2.8	0.5	18.9	61.7	19.4	744	90.3	51.5	15.9
Perry township (Mercer) ..	1,453	1,421	-2.2	1,482	98.6	0.0	0.0	1.3	0.1	17.9	62.3	19.9	640	93.1	65.2	14.2
Perry township (Snyder) ..	2,183	2,214	1.4	2,143	98.2	0.0	0.0	1.8	0.0	27.7	57.7	14.7	756	77.4	75.5	8.2
Perryopolis borough & MCD (Fayette).............	1,784	1,741	-2.4	1,877	99.1	0.0	0.0	0.7	0.2	20.6	55.7	23.8	819	80.6	46.4	24.5
Peters township (Franklin)	4,430	4,455	0.6	4,446	97.1	2.0	0.0	0.4	0.5	23.2	61.0	15.7	1,692	69.9	63.5	6.0
Peters township (Washington)	21,213	21,975	3.6	21,587	94.8	0.4	2.0	1.0	1.8	28.4	57.4	14.5	7,484	93.0	13.2	65.1
Petersburg borough & MCD (Huntingdon)	482	473	-1.9	552	96.0	0.0	0.0	0.0	4.0	30.2	59.1	10.5	204	69.1	70.1	3.4
Petrolia borough & MCD (Butler)	212	208	-1.9	254	96.9	2.4	0.0	0.8	0.0	28.3	62.7	9.1	90	80.0	60.0	1.1
Philadelphia city & MCD (Philadelphia).............	1,526,006	1,560,297	2.2	1,546,920	36.2	41.8	6.6	2.4	13.0	22.3	65.4	12.3	580,297	52.9	48.3	26.9
Philipsburg borough & MCD (Centre)..............	2,770	2,707	-2.3	2,736	96.0	0.7	2.0	0.3	1.0	16.8	62.6	20.6	1,349	65.3	53.2	16.2
Phoenixville borough & MCD (Chester)............	16,440	16,599	1.0	16,530	75.7	7.8	4.6	2.2	9.7	20.4	67.2	12.3	7,356	55.5	38.5	40.8
Piatt township (Lycoming)	1,180	1,170	-0.8	1,026	99.7	0.0	0.0	0.3	0.0	24.4	61.1	14.4	386	80.8	56.5	11.4
Picture Rocks borough & MCD (Lycoming)	678	669	-1.3	752	98.0	0.0	1.2	0.8	0.0	26.1	57.5	16.4	283	90.1	37.1	27.6
Pike township (Berks)......	1,723	1,746	1.3	1,821	96.0	1.1	0.4	0.9	1.6	22.0	62.4	15.7	630	93.2	43.8	22.5
Pike township (Bradford) .	671	677	0.9	706	95.6	0.0	1.3	2.0	1.1	24.4	62.0	13.5	272	83.1	62.5	7.4
Pike township (Clearfield)	2,310	2,311	0.0	2,277	97.0	0.0	0.0	0.3	2.7	16.5	58.6	24.8	938	84.8	64.7	12.4
Pike township (Potter).....	324	324	0.0	260	96.9	0.4	0.0	2.7	0.0	26.6	53.6	20.0	114	72.8	64.0	11.4
Pikes Creek CDP.............	269	NA	NA	250	100.0	0.0	0.0	0.0	0.0	24.0	59.2	16.8	94	75.5	68.1	10.6
Pillow borough & MCD (Dauphin)	298	300	0.7	267	77.2	9.4	0.0	1.9	11.6	31.1	57.2	11.6	97	93.8	57.7	24.7
Pine township (Allegheny)	11,497	12,531	9.0	11,975	92.4	2.3	3.4	0.5	1.4	29.1	62.8	8.1	3,993	86.1	11.7	68.3
Pine township (Armstrong)	412	399	-3.2	396	93.9	0.0	0.0	1.0	5.1	25.0	54.9	20.2	157	74.5	71.3	3.8
Pine township (Clearfield)	60	59	-1.7	62	100.0	0.0	0.0	0.0	0.0	9.7	82.4	8.1	27	74.1	25.9	22.2
Pine township (Columbia)	1,046	1,034	-1.1	949	98.4	0.0	0.4	0.3	0.8	16.5	64.5	19.1	411	91.2	58.9	16.8
Pine township (Crawford)	466	455	-2.4	452	99.6	0.0	0.0	0.2	0.2	12.8	65.2	21.9	180	90.0	65.6	10.0
Pine township (Indiana) ...	2,033	1,953	-3.9	1,819	99.5	0.3	0.2	0.0	0.1	18.4	64.9	16.7	728	87.1	68.8	14.0
Pine township (Lycoming)	294	299	1.7	292	98.3	0.0	0.0	1.7	0.0	20.9	55.8	23.3	112	86.6	59.8	10.7
Pine township (Mercer)....	5,151	5,102	-1.0	5,131	89.4	8.1	0.2	1.5	0.7	27.3	54.4	18.3	1,768	85.1	52.0	27.3
Pine Creek township (Clinton)	3,217	3,299	2.5	3,268	95.8	0.5	0.5	2.4	0.9	18.5	57.8	23.7	1,349	83.0	53.4	20.0
Pine Creek township (Jefferson)	1,353	1,338	-1.1	1,470	92.7	2.4	0.0	4.1	0.8	17.0	53.0	30.0	507	73.8	64.3	7.7
Pine Glen CDP	190	NA	NA	220	99.1	0.0	0.0	0.0	0.9	25.0	59.5	15.5	87	96.6	66.7	11.5
Pine Grove borough & MCD (Schuylkill)	2,186	2,148	-1.7	2,125	89.1	1.9	6.4	0.0	2.6	25.1	59.2	15.8	848	57.8	61.6	13.9
Pine Grove township (Schuylkill)................	4,123	4,088	-0.8	4,107	99.1	0.0	0.1	0.8	0.0	19.5	59.8	20.7	1,628	85.3	61.9	10.8
Pinegrove township (Venango)	1,353	1,312	-3.0	1,213	98.2	0.0	0.0	1.3	0.5	22.1	61.1	16.7	462	82.5	63.9	15.6
Pine Grove township (Warren)	2,695	2,627	-2.5	2,650	97.5	0.5	0.6	0.4	1.1	18.0	59.2	22.9	1,181	90.1	48.3	26.1

1 May be of any race.

Table A. All Places — **Population and Housing**

STATE City, town, township, borough, or CDP (county if applicable)	2010 census total population	2014 estimated population	Percent change 2010–2014	ACS total population estimate 2010–2014	White alone, not Hispanic or Latino	Black alone, not Hispanic or Latino	Asian alone, not Hispanic or Latino	All other races or 2 or more races, not Hispanic or Latino	Hispanic or Latino[1]	Under 18 years old	Age 18 to 64 years old	Age 65 years and older	Total occupied housing units	Percent owner occupied	High school diploma or less	Bachelor's degree or more
	1	2	3	4	5	6	7	8	9	10	11	12	13	14	15	16
Pine Grove Mills CDP	1,502	NA	NA	1,133	97.5	0.0	1.1	0.0	1.4	14.3	73.6	12.0	523	83.7	31.0	50.3
Pine Ridge CDP	2,707	NA	NA	2,887	64.7	18.4	0.8	4.7	11.4	18.3	67.5	14.2	899	85.7	51.1	13.3
Piney township (Clarion)	453	440	-2.9	380	87.6	7.6	1.3	2.1	1.3	17.4	45.3	37.4	118	87.3	56.8	17.8
Pitcairn borough & MCD (Allegheny)	3,294	3,264	-0.9	3,283	78.7	16.0	0.0	3.4	1.9	18.8	65.6	15.7	1,585	51.4	56.3	16.6
Pittsburgh city & MCD (Allegheny)	305,702	305,412	-0.1	306,045	65.1	24.3	4.8	3.1	2.7	16.2	69.7	14.0	132,379	48.8	33.3	39.5
Pittsfield township (Warren)	1,405	1,367	-2.7	1,491	98.3	0.3	0.0	1.2	0.1	15.6	65.5	19.0	574	90.6	50.7	11.5
Pittston city & MCD (Luzerne)	7,734	7,685	-0.6	7,702	95.2	0.3	0.0	1.1	3.4	20.7	61.6	17.8	3,356	57.5	53.0	18.6
Pittston township (Luzerne)	3,368	3,387	0.6	3,382	97.5	1.1	0.0	0.7	0.7	17.3	62.5	20.2	1,326	84.7	57.6	13.6
Plainfield CDP	399	NA	NA	238	70.6	0.0	0.0	0.0	29.4	18.1	37.8	44.1	143	67.1	24.5	18.9
Plainfield township (Northampton)	6,138	6,149	0.2	6,141	95.2	1.3	0.0	0.8	2.8	18.3	69.5	12.3	2,305	81.3	41.6	24.6
Plain Grove township (Lawrence)	813	799	-1.7	724	97.2	1.4	0.0	0.4	1.0	18.8	68.0	13.3	302	85.4	65.6	12.6
Plains CDP	4,335	NA	NA	4,020	95.5	0.5	2.2	0.8	1.0	13.3	56.5	30.0	2,042	63.5	59.9	20.2
Plains township (Luzerne)	9,943	9,814	-1.3	9,888	94.2	0.9	3.0	0.9	1.1	15.3	55.3	29.5	4,542	67.1	48.1	23.8
Platea borough & MCD (Erie)	430	415	-3.5	473	96.8	1.3	0.0	1.3	0.6	26.5	62.4	11.2	169	82.2	65.1	14.2
Pleasant township (Warren)	2,444	2,386	-2.4	2,482	97.9	0.8	0.7	0.7	0.0	16.1	55.9	28.0	1,095	84.6	50.2	27.5
Pleasant Gap CDP	2,879	NA	NA	2,852	90.7	7.4	0.0	0.9	1.0	18.0	65.3	16.5	1,238	70.9	46.4	28.8
Pleasant Hill CDP	2,643	NA	NA	2,620	69.5	8.7	0.6	4.9	16.2	29.7	60.9	9.3	1,005	57.0	46.9	26.9
Pleasant Hills borough & MCD (Allegheny)	8,268	8,284	0.2	8,291	94.8	2.8	1.6	0.2	0.5	19.4	58.6	22.0	3,482	78.0	24.2	45.1
Pleasant Valley township (Potter)	86	85	-1.2	97	99.0	0.0	1.0	0.0	0.0	31.0	50.5	18.6	30	80.0	30.0	46.7
Pleasant View CDP	780	NA	NA	950	99.4	0.0	0.0	0.0	0.6	24.6	65.2	10.1	402	83.1	66.7	18.4
Pleasantville borough & MCD (Bedford)	198	194	-2.0	197	91.9	0.0	0.0	8.1	0.0	22.3	54.8	22.8	73	75.3	68.5	11.0
Pleasantville borough & MCD (Venango)	892	865	-3.0	864	94.2	0.0	3.2	0.5	2.1	24.1	55.9	20.1	359	81.1	51.3	20.6
Plum borough & MCD (Allegheny)	27,124	27,532	1.5	27,386	93.4	3.0	0.8	1.3	1.5	21.7	59.5	18.7	10,867	81.5	35.0	36.2
Plum township (Venango)	1,056	1,024	-3.0	1,071	99.3	0.0	0.0	0.5	0.3	21.4	59.9	19.0	410	89.5	64.1	15.4
Plumcreek township (Armstrong)	2,375	2,321	-2.3	2,395	97.1	0.0	0.0	0.7	2.2	19.9	60.2	20.0	973	76.3	65.0	13.9
Plumstead township (Bucks)	12,442	13,208	6.2	12,730	92.2	0.9	1.7	1.3	3.9	28.9	62.2	8.8	4,445	86.9	25.9	52.2
Plumsteadville CDP	2,637	NA	NA	3,214	97.4	0.0	1.4	0.0	1.2	36.4	59.3	4.4	972	87.2	25.1	52.4
Plumville borough & MCD (Indiana)	307	299	-2.6	266	100.0	0.0	0.0	0.0	0.0	25.6	60.9	13.5	107	70.1	64.5	18.7
Plunketts Creek township (Lycoming)	684	695	1.6	596	98.5	0.2	0.5	0.5	0.3	22.5	60.8	16.8	247	88.3	44.9	19.8
Plymouth borough & MCD (Luzerne)	5,951	5,857	-1.6	5,905	92.3	1.7	0.8	2.7	2.6	22.6	61.4	16.0	2,567	53.1	53.8	14.7
Plymouth township (Luzerne)	1,812	1,792	-1.1	1,781	98.9	0.0	0.4	0.1	0.6	16.7	62.9	20.5	795	84.7	55.0	16.0
Plymouth township (Montgomery)	16,525	16,715	1.1	16,637	79.3	6.2	7.4	2.8	4.3	21.9	61.5	16.7	6,581	70.9	28.9	46.8
Plymouth Meeting CDP	6,177	NA	NA	5,721	81.6	3.6	10.1	1.0	3.7	19.8	64.3	15.9	2,414	70.7	20.9	55.4
Plymptonville CDP	981	NA	NA	902	95.8	0.2	3.1	0.9	0.0	12.1	72.2	15.6	413	81.1	49.2	15.5
Pocono township (Monroe)	11,070	10,820	-2.3	10,956	72.7	12.3	0.6	4.7	9.7	19.7	65.9	14.4	3,935	84.0	40.7	27.1
Pocono Mountain Lake Estates CDP	842	NA	NA	605	84.8	0.0	5.6	0.0	9.6	5.1	67.7	27.1	292	68.5	34.9	30.8
Pocono Pines CDP	1,409	NA	NA	1,203	83.4	2.4	0.0	2.7	11.5	18.6	50.3	31.1	504	77.2	16.1	43.5
Pocono Ranch Lands CDP	1,062	NA	NA	1,015	65.8	3.9	0.0	0.0	30.2	26.8	63.0	10.2	319	83.4	32.3	22.6
Pocono Springs CDP	926	NA	NA	1,131	87.6	5.8	0.0	1.8	4.8	8.9	73.1	17.8	490	87.3	55.3	20.2
Pocono Woodland Lakes CDP	3,209	NA	NA	2,880	86.8	0.4	0.0	3.6	9.1	21.6	69.2	9.3	1,009	95.8	35.9	18.6
Pocopson township (Chester)	4,582	4,848	5.8	4,713	80.0	9.1	4.1	0.7	6.1	18.1	66.3	15.5	1,118	90.4	9.1	75.1
Point township (Northumberland)	3,685	3,722	1.0	3,715	95.0	0.2	0.0	0.8	4.0	16.6	59.8	23.8	1,458	84.6	57.5	20.2
Point Marion borough & MCD (Fayette)	1,159	1,140	-1.6	1,020	96.5	0.2	0.0	2.7	0.6	12.0	66.7	21.2	449	67.9	64.8	15.1
Polk township (Jefferson)	265	262	-1.1	285	100.0	0.0	0.0	0.0	0.0	21.8	59.5	18.9	98	84.7	65.3	11.2
Polk township (Monroe)	7,869	7,679	-2.4	7,775	89.4	2.3	1.0	0.0	7.4	22.5	60.0	17.6	2,895	80.4	47.5	16.1
Polk borough & MCD (Venango)	816	799	-2.1	829	96.1	1.2	0.0	1.9	0.7	15.8	69.1	15.2	217	71.0	51.6	9.2
Pomeroy CDP	401	NA	NA	151	95.4	4.6	0.0	0.0	0.0	0.0	64.9	35.1	105	79.0	31.4	47.6
Portage borough & MCD (Cambria)	2,638	2,536	-3.9	2,594	97.7	0.9	0.0	1.2	0.2	24.0	58.3	17.7	1,071	70.3	60.0	16.1
Portage township (Cambria)	3,640	3,534	-2.9	3,578	98.7	0.0	0.0	0.1	1.1	21.1	59.6	19.3	1,392	82.0	60.1	16.6
Portage township (Cameron)	171	163	-4.7	205	99.0	0.0	0.0	1.0	0.0	25.4	64.9	9.8	80	81.3	73.8	7.5
Portage township (Potter)	226	224	-0.9	198	87.4	0.0	0.0	9.1	3.5	26.8	50.1	23.2	78	84.6	60.3	15.4
Port Allegany borough & MCD (McKean)	2,157	2,102	-2.5	2,120	98.8	0.0	0.0	0.2	0.9	24.7	59.1	16.1	900	64.2	55.0	18.9
Port Carbon borough & MCD (Schuylkill)	1,889	1,837	-2.8	1,884	97.2	1.0	0.0	1.6	0.3	20.9	62.2	16.9	808	76.6	63.4	13.4
Port Clinton borough & MCD (Schuylkill)	326	321	-1.5	215	95.8	0.0	0.0	0.0	4.2	20.0	65.2	14.9	94	73.4	66.0	2.1
Porter township (Clarion)	1,348	1,313	-2.6	1,220	98.4	0.3	0.0	0.3	1.0	20.6	60.7	18.8	497	82.5	72.8	15.1
Porter township (Clinton)	1,460	1,496	2.5	1,599	99.8	0.0	0.0	0.0	0.2	21.4	55.4	23.1	627	84.2	66.8	15.0

1 May be of any race.

Table A. All Places — **Population and Housing**

STATE City, town, township, borough, or CDP (county if applicable)	2010 census total population	2014 estimated population	Percent change 2010–2014	ACS total population estimate 2010–2014	White alone, not Hispanic or Latino	Black alone, not Hispanic or Latino	Asian alone, not Hispanic or Latino	All other races or 2 or more races, not Hispanic or Latino	Hispanic or Latino[1]	Under 18 years old	Age 18 to 64 years old	Age 65 years and older	Total occupied housing units	Percent owner occupied	High school diploma or less	Bachelor's degree or more
	1	2	3	4	5	6	7	8	9	10	11	12	13	14	15	16
PENNSYLVANIA—Con.																
Porter township (Huntingdon)	1,968	1,949	-1.0	1,970	99.5	0.0	0.0	0.0	0.5	18.8	62.7	18.5	808	88.0	64.7	13.1
Porter township (Jefferson)	305	301	-1.3	291	97.6	0.0	1.4	1.0	0.0	23.3	59.5	17.2	119	84.0	74.8	1.7
Porter township (Lycoming)	1,601	1,596	-0.3	1,890	95.8	1.4	0.4	1.4	1.0	20.2	58.3	21.3	754	74.1	63.1	12.6
Porter township (Pike)	485	472	-2.7	436	91.7	0.0	0.0	0.0	8.3	5.7	48.0	46.3	196	88.3	44.9	18.4
Porter township (Schuylkill)	2,177	2,133	-2.0	1,934	97.8	0.0	0.0	1.5	0.7	16.8	61.8	21.4	851	87.2	67.0	11.8
Portersville borough & MCD (Butler)	235	237	0.9	266	99.2	0.0	0.0	0.4	0.4	16.6	63.0	20.7	111	76.6	38.7	34.2
Portland borough & MCD (Northampton)	519	514	-1.0	523	79.5	6.1	3.4	3.8	7.1	21.8	60.7	17.6	216	75.9	36.1	23.6
Port Matilda borough & MCD (Centre)	606	596	-1.7	709	98.4	0.3	0.0	0.8	0.4	23.3	67.1	9.7	306	57.5	51.3	27.8
Port Royal borough & MCD (Juniata)	925	927	0.2	975	89.8	0.0	0.0	5.3	4.8	24.7	58.0	17.3	403	60.5	63.5	10.7
Port Trevorton CDP	769	NA	NA	668	100.0	0.0	0.0	0.0	0.0	28.5	56.2	15.3	237	67.5	74.3	10.5
Port Vue borough & MCD (Allegheny)	3,798	3,765	-0.9	3,784	96.4	0.0	0.0	3.1	0.6	18.2	61.9	19.9	1,785	76.9	49.1	12.4
Potlicker Flats CDP	172	NA	NA	163	100.0	0.0	0.0	0.0	0.0	26.4	58.3	15.3	71	62.0	69.0	8.5
Potter township (Beaver)	548	570	4.0	630	98.6	0.0	0.2	1.3	0.0	21.9	55.6	22.4	268	79.1	57.1	18.7
Potter township (Centre)	3,517	3,490	-0.8	3,523	99.4	0.0	0.6	0.0	0.0	14.1	61.9	24.0	1,610	90.8	53.5	26.9
Pottsgrove CDP	3,469	NA	NA	3,249	96.2	0.8	0.7	1.6	0.8	15.8	65.2	18.8	1,292	92.2	37.2	44.0
Pottstown borough & MCD (Montgomery)	22,377	22,684	1.4	22,519	71.4	17.6	0.3	3.7	6.9	23.6	63.2	13.1	9,504	58.1	51.6	19.0
Pottsville city & MCD (Schuylkill)	14,324	13,940	-2.7	14,136	88.8	3.5	0.7	3.5	3.5	21.6	60.0	18.4	5,932	55.2	57.2	17.7
President township (Venango)	540	525	-2.8	405	97.8	0.0	0.0	1.2	1.0	8.4	61.7	29.9	213	95.3	54.0	20.7
Preston township (Wayne)	1,014	991	-2.3	892	95.3	0.1	0.4	3.3	0.9	14.0	63.3	22.6	387	79.8	50.9	19.1
Price township (Monroe)	3,565	3,527	-1.1	3,556	70.9	17.8	2.7	1.1	7.5	23.0	63.6	13.4	1,276	85.6	48.0	29.5
Pringle borough & MCD (Luzerne)	979	966	-1.3	927	97.7	1.2	0.0	0.0	1.1	15.6	62.5	21.8	426	74.6	61.7	14.6
Progress CDP	9,765	NA	NA	9,717	61.0	27.7	1.7	2.1	7.5	20.4	65.1	14.4	4,239	57.7	35.7	29.5
Prompton borough & MCD (Wayne)	250	241	-3.6	246	93.9	0.0	0.0	0.0	6.1	26.8	57.8	15.4	94	78.7	46.8	24.5
Prospect borough & MCD (Butler)	1,169	1,144	-2.1	1,263	97.5	0.0	0.0	1.8	0.7	24.3	62.1	13.8	517	83.6	44.7	23.8
Prospect Park CDP	327	NA	NA	288	97.9	0.0	0.0	1.4	0.7	14.7	58.8	26.7	138	74.6	58.7	26.1
Prospect Park borough & MCD (Delaware)	6,454	6,484	0.5	6,464	87.8	5.0	1.7	2.8	2.7	24.8	63.6	11.6	2,416	59.0	42.7	21.5
Providence township (Lancaster)	6,897	6,945	0.7	6,933	94.7	0.0	0.0	2.6	2.7	24.3	60.4	15.1	2,716	80.7	66.5	14.1
Pulaski township (Beaver)	1,503	1,470	-2.2	1,356	90.6	4.7	0.0	2.6	2.1	17.0	66.4	16.5	624	61.1	63.5	7.1
Pulaski township (Lawrence)	3,452	3,354	-2.8	3,398	98.6	0.4	0.0	1.0	0.0	17.7	62.1	20.1	1,468	84.7	56.3	16.0
Punxsutawney borough & MCD (Jefferson)	5,962	5,887	-1.3	5,927	94.6	1.0	0.3	2.1	2.0	20.1	59.2	20.8	2,504	56.3	60.3	16.9
Putnam township (Tioga)	421	418	-0.7	609	98.7	0.0	0.0	1.3	0.0	33.0	57.7	9.4	200	73.0	35.5	17.5
Pymatuning township (Mercer)	3,281	3,205	-2.3	3,246	96.2	0.0	0.0	2.0	1.8	14.6	64.3	21.1	1,597	82.6	70.3	5.2
Pymatuning Central CDP	2,269	NA	NA	2,216	98.6	0.2	0.1	0.5	0.5	15.3	58.6	26.3	1,029	86.3	59.4	15.5
Pymatuning North CDP	311	NA	NA	266	100.0	0.0	0.0	0.0	0.0	12.5	57.9	29.7	132	84.8	64.4	16.7
Pymatuning South CDP	479	NA	NA	475	99.4	0.0	0.0	0.0	0.6	17.5	63.9	18.5	209	84.2	62.7	12.0
Quakertown borough & MCD (Bucks)	8,979	8,881	-1.1	8,939	91.9	1.7	0.9	0.9	4.7	21.4	64.0	14.5	3,536	54.8	47.4	24.8
Quarryville borough & MCD (Lancaster)	2,576	2,678	4.0	2,635	95.3	0.0	0.2	0.3	4.2	26.4	57.4	16.3	1,051	60.7	61.9	17.5
Queens Gate CDP	1,464	NA	NA	1,414	72.4	5.9	15.8	3.7	2.1	15.5	74.9	9.5	761	15.5	35.0	54.7
Quemahoning township (Somerset)	2,025	1,980	-2.2	1,976	99.5	0.0	0.0	0.5	0.0	22.3	61.4	16.3	731	92.1	69.8	8.1
Quentin CDP	594	NA	NA	454	89.6	0.0	3.1	4.2	3.1	17.9	67.6	14.5	192	84.9	31.3	24.5
Quincy township (Franklin)	5,535	5,520	-0.3	5,519	94.4	4.4	0.2	0.6	0.4	19.9	58.8	21.4	1,824	69.7	53.6	16.7
Raccoon township (Beaver)	3,064	3,018	-1.5	3,043	98.9	0.0	0.2	0.7	0.2	17.9	65.5	16.6	1,196	84.7	46.2	20.6
Radnor township (Delaware)	31,531	31,480	-0.2	31,474	80.6	6.0	7.6	1.8	3.9	19.4	68.7	11.8	9,710	64.9	12.8	73.3
Railroad borough & MCD (York)	278	278	0.0	218	97.2	0.0	0.0	2.3	0.5	13.7	74.8	11.5	83	63.9	55.4	8.4
Rainsburg borough & MCD (Bedford)	133	134	0.8	160	83.1	0.0	5.0	11.9	0.0	35.7	53.3	11.3	57	73.7	70.2	5.3
Ralpho township (Northumberland)	4,320	4,327	0.2	4,336	98.2	0.0	0.1	0.8	0.9	18.0	58.9	23.0	1,910	78.0	52.6	29.5
Ramblewood CDP	849	NA	NA	975	78.4	8.2	0.0	9.0	4.4	30.1	61.0	8.9	355	90.7	27.9	64.5
Ramey borough & MCD (Clearfield)	453	445	-1.8	491	99.4	0.0	0.0	0.6	0.0	15.7	67.4	16.9	200	85.0	55.0	15.5
Randolph township (Crawford)	1,782	1,748	-1.9	1,890	95.4	1.7	0.0	2.3	0.6	25.9	58.6	15.6	646	85.8	58.5	14.9
Rankin borough & MCD (Allegheny)	2,122	2,102	-0.9	2,142	24.1	70.4	0.0	2.1	3.4	29.1	57.4	13.4	890	35.6	57.9	7.8
Ranshaw CDP	510	NA	NA	431	100.0	0.0	0.0	0.0	0.0	13.0	52.2	34.8	211	82.9	63.5	13.3
Ransom township (Lackawanna)	1,420	1,412	-0.6	1,449	98.2	0.0	0.2	0.7	0.9	17.9	63.0	19.2	572	78.3	48.4	15.7
Rapho township (Lancaster)	10,438	11,443	9.6	10,936	93.7	0.7	0.1	0.5	5.0	21.9	60.4	17.6	4,213	82.7	55.7	24.7
Raubsville CDP	1,088	NA	NA	991	96.1	0.0	0.0	0.0	3.9	18.0	59.1	22.9	403	97.5	40.9	20.3
Rauchtown CDP	726	NA	NA	699	98.7	0.0	0.0	0.4	0.9	19.2	62.8	17.9	285	86.7	65.3	12.6
Ravine CDP	662	NA	NA	636	98.4	0.0	0.8	0.8	0.0	18.6	67.5	13.8	269	68.8	59.5	16.4

1 May be of any race.

Table A. All Places — **Population and Housing**

STATE City, town, township, borough, or CDP (county if applicable)	2010 census total population	2014 estimated population	Percent change 2010–2014	ACS total population estimate 2010–2014	White alone, not Hispanic or Latino	Black alone, not Hispanic or Latino	Asian alone, not Hispanic or Latino	All other races or 2 or more races, not Hispanic or Latino	Hispanic or Latino[1]	Under 18 years old	Age 18 to 64 years old	Age 65 years and older	Total occupied housing units	Percent owner occupied	High school diploma or less	Bachelor's degree or more
	1	2	3	4	5	6	7	8	9	10	11	12	13	14	15	16
PENNSYLVANIA—Con.																
Rayburn township (Armstrong)...............	1,907	1,859	-2.5	1,716	96.5	2.2	0.2	0.5	0.6	18.5	62.5	19.0	695	79.4	69.8	12.4
Rayne township (Indiana)	2,992	2,892	-3.3	2,947	99.6	0.3	0.0	0.1	0.0	20.5	60.4	18.9	1,085	80.4	54.5	17.1
Reade township (Cambria)...................	1,619	1,566	-3.3	1,674	97.7	0.9	0.4	1.0	0.0	23.1	61.9	15.1	661	84.3	73.8	3.3
Reading township (Adams)...................	5,780	5,805	0.4	5,792	95.9	0.0	0.4	0.5	3.1	21.1	65.3	13.6	2,194	89.1	52.5	25.5
Reading city & MCD (Berks)...................	88,080	87,812	-0.3	88,051	26.9	9.5	0.8	2.9	60.0	30.6	59.9	9.3	30,435	42.8	68.6	9.0
Reamstown CDP...........	3,361	NA	NA	3,929	83.5	0.0	0.4	0.0	16.2	22.6	61.5	15.8	1,248	74.7	47.2	24.1
Rebersburg CDP............	494	NA	NA	491	96.7	0.0	3.3	0.0	0.0	20.0	55.1	25.1	194	78.9	64.4	12.9
Redbank township (Armstrong)...............	1,064	1,039	-2.3	1,168	98.5	0.0	0.0	1.5	0.0	19.7	66.0	14.3	486	86.8	72.8	10.1
Redbank township (Clarion)...................	1,370	1,344	-1.9	1,479	100.0	0.0	0.0	0.0	0.0	23.1	58.9	18.1	572	87.1	73.4	9.6
Red Hill borough & MCD (Montgomery).............	2,383	2,389	0.3	2,499	90.2	1.4	1.2	2.9	4.3	19.9	55.8	24.2	1,087	65.0	56.0	21.0
Red Lion borough & MCD (York)...................	6,376	6,319	-0.9	6,343	94.3	1.1	0.0	1.2	3.5	23.5	60.3	16.3	2,685	56.7	59.0	17.2
Redstone township (Fayette)...................	5,566	5,468	-1.8	5,517	85.6	9.3	0.0	3.9	1.2	25.2	57.0	17.8	2,139	71.0	61.8	13.1
Reed township (Dauphin)	239	239	0.0	249	100.0	0.0	0.0	0.0	0.0	13.6	73.7	12.4	95	84.2	55.8	11.6
Reedsville CDP..............	641	NA	NA	481	90.0	0.0	0.0	10.0	0.0	18.2	53.8	28.1	185	73.0	57.8	5.9
Refton CDP...................	298	NA	NA	165	100.0	0.0	0.0	0.0	0.0	23.0	43.7	33.3	62	100.0	100.0	0.0
Rehrersburg CDP...........	319	NA	NA	405	62.5	0.0	0.0	3.2	34.3	33.5	57.5	8.9	128	46.9	68.0	10.2
Reiffton CDP.................	4,178	NA	NA	4,817	94.0	3.4	0.0	0.7	1.9	26.8	54.0	19.1	1,677	93.7	28.4	45.2
Reilly township (Schuylkill)...............	726	710	-2.2	754	100.0	0.0	0.0	0.0	0.0	18.9	68.6	12.6	318	86.8	69.2	6.0
Reinerton CDP...............	424	NA	NA	360	97.8	0.0	0.0	2.2	0.0	16.9	54.7	28.3	159	91.2	64.8	18.9
Reinholds CDP...............	1,803	NA	NA	1,821	95.6	2.4	2.0	0.0	0.0	26.8	64.4	8.8	573	92.0	40.0	24.1
Rennerdale CDP.............	1,150	NA	NA	741	98.9	0.0	0.0	0.0	1.1	18.6	66.7	14.7	342	95.9	26.3	44.4
Renningers CDP.............	574	NA	NA	379	100.0	0.0	0.0	0.0	0.0	22.4	46.3	31.4	165	83.0	52.1	39.4
Renovo borough & MCD (Clinton)...................	1,230	1,234	0.3	1,180	97.5	0.0	0.0	0.3	2.2	27.7	53.7	18.4	511	56.4	72.4	5.5
Republic CDP................	1,096	NA	NA	1,089	90.0	10.0	0.0	0.0	0.0	35.0	54.8	10.2	359	72.1	58.2	19.5
Reserve township (Allegheny)................	3,333	3,310	-0.7	3,325	95.8	3.4	0.0	0.8	0.0	16.1	65.7	18.3	1,426	86.3	48.7	28.5
Revloc CDP...................	570	NA	NA	685	93.0	7.0	0.0	0.0	0.0	23.7	68.0	8.3	295	54.9	60.3	9.5
Rew CDP......................	199	NA	NA	123	100.0	0.0	0.0	0.0	0.0	5.7	94.3	0.0	74	89.2	90.5	9.5
Reynolds Heights CDP....	2,061	NA	NA	1,808	93.2	0.0	0.0	3.5	3.3	19.5	61.7	18.8	895	70.8	69.4	5.7
Reynoldsville borough & MCD (Jefferson)..........	2,759	2,724	-1.3	2,746	98.8	0.7	0.0	0.0	0.5	20.0	63.3	16.8	1,192	62.5	60.6	16.5
Rheems CDP.................	1,598	NA	NA	1,647	96.4	0.4	0.8	2.4	0.0	37.2	48.8	14.1	536	73.5	39.2	37.9
Rice township (Luzerne)..	3,335	3,501	5.0	3,439	92.7	1.1	2.9	3.0	0.2	24.8	64.5	10.8	1,267	97.6	30.6	39.1
Rices Landing borough & MCD (Greene)	463	449	-3.0	463	99.1	0.0	0.0	0.9	0.0	21.4	56.5	22.0	179	86.0	44.1	23.5
Riceville CDP.................	68	NA	NA	50	100.0	0.0	0.0	0.0	0.0	0.0	80.0	20.0	25	100.0	52.0	0.0
Richboro CDP................	6,563	NA	NA	6,382	93.5	0.1	2.5	2.5	1.4	21.9	59.8	18.1	2,183	96.2	28.3	51.9
Richfield CDP................	549	NA	NA	496	94.4	2.2	2.8	0.0	0.6	11.9	59.2	28.8	209	75.1	70.8	13.4
Richhill township (Greene)...................	896	861	-3.9	826	100.0	0.0	0.0	0.0	0.0	25.4	58.9	15.6	312	70.2	76.6	8.0
Richland township (Allegheny)................	11,100	11,522	3.8	11,377	93.8	1.5	2.5	0.3	1.9	24.6	57.2	18.2	4,265	85.4	25.7	50.0
Richland township (Bucks)...................	13,052	13,100	0.4	13,081	86.3	1.5	2.7	2.4	7.2	24.5	61.6	13.8	4,774	86.6	45.5	29.3
Richland township (Cambria)...................	12,814	12,346	-3.7	12,581	93.8	1.0	1.1	1.2	2.9	16.6	61.2	22.3	4,836	68.2	45.5	30.5
Richland township (Clarion)...................	494	483	-2.2	423	95.7	0.0	0.0	2.8	1.4	14.8	62.4	22.7	184	94.0	59.2	11.4
Richland borough & MCD (Lebanon).................	1,519	1,549	2.0	1,758	97.8	0.0	0.0	1.5	0.7	21.3	60.2	18.5	683	77.2	66.9	11.3
Richland township (Venango).................	777	759	-2.3	690	98.6	0.0	0.0	1.2	0.3	17.3	62.6	20.1	297	87.9	52.9	22.2
Richlandtown borough & MCD (Bucks).............	1,327	1,316	-0.8	1,246	92.1	2.3	0.6	1.1	3.9	25.4	59.7	14.9	436	79.1	51.1	26.6
Richmond township (Berks)...................	3,395	3,450	1.6	3,418	97.1	1.4	0.3	0.0	1.1	18.5	64.7	16.8	1,491	65.7	56.9	16.5
Richmond township (Crawford)................	1,475	1,444	-2.1	1,467	99.1	0.0	0.0	0.9	0.0	25.8	59.4	14.9	556	87.6	59.0	16.4
Richmond township (Tioga)...................	2,371	2,419	2.0	2,541	96.1	2.3	0.4	0.4	0.9	17.4	66.5	16.1	869	79.7	47.8	21.2
Ridgebury township (Bradford).................	1,978	1,966	-0.6	1,927	98.9	0.0	0.0	0.3	0.8	22.5	59.3	18.4	726	84.8	60.3	12.9
Ridgway borough & MCD (Elk)...................	4,078	3,951	-3.1	4,024	98.5	0.5	0.4	0.3	0.2	20.1	64.5	15.4	1,822	69.9	44.7	20.9
Ridgway township (Elk) ...	2,523	2,469	-2.1	2,341	98.8	0.0	0.0	0.5	0.7	18.4	63.0	18.4	970	86.8	59.6	11.8
Ridley township (Delaware)................	30,767	31,047	0.9	30,921	85.4	5.3	3.8	2.9	2.6	22.0	64.2	13.9	11,903	69.8	48.0	24.9
Ridley Park borough & MCD (Delaware)	7,003	7,034	0.4	7,021	93.0	1.5	3.7	0.9	1.0	19.3	65.3	15.5	2,806	71.1	37.6	26.3
Riegelsville borough & MCD (Bucks)..............	868	860	-0.9	842	93.0	0.4	0.0	4.6	2.0	14.1	63.6	22.1	368	77.2	42.7	34.0
Rimersburg borough & MCD (Clarion)...........	946	929	-1.8	1,012	97.7	0.3	0.0	0.9	1.1	28.5	60.4	11.2	409	47.9	73.1	6.1
Ringgold township (Jefferson)................	741	732	-1.2	876	98.2	0.0	0.0	0.8	1.0	16.9	62.7	20.2	344	89.5	67.7	8.4
Ringtown borough & MCD (Schuylkill)...............	817	801	-2.0	654	99.5	0.5	0.0	0.0	0.0	14.1	63.2	22.8	280	83.6	53.9	20.7
Riverside CDP...............	381	NA	NA	286	98.3	1.4	0.0	0.0	0.3	23.0	43.2	33.6	154	89.0	38.3	14.3
Riverside borough & MCD (Northumberland)........	1,932	1,927	-0.3	1,991	92.5	1.8	2.3	2.6	0.9	21.7	63.2	15.1	818	82.9	37.3	37.9

1 May be of any race.

Table A. All Places — **Population and Housing**

STATE City, town, township, borough, or CDP (county if applicable)	2010 census total population	2014 estimated population	Percent change 2010–2014	ACS total population estimate 2010–2014	White alone, not Hispanic or Latino	Black alone, not Hispanic or Latino	Asian alone, not Hispanic or Latino	All other races or 2 or more races, not Hispanic or Latino	Hispanic or Latino[1]	Under 18 years old	Age 18 to 64 years old	Age 65 years and older	Total occupied housing units	Percent owner occupied	High school diploma or less	Bachelor's degree or more
	1	2	3	4	5	6	7	8	9	10	11	12	13	14	15	16
PENNSYLVANIA—Con.																
Riverview Park CDP	3,380	NA	NA	3,039	81.6	0.0	4.4	2.2	11.7	16.8	56.6	26.7	1,210	83.9	49.9	29.1
Roaring Brook township (Lackawanna)	1,907	1,965	3.0	1,752	96.9	0.2	1.1	0.6	1.3	23.5	56.1	20.5	652	94.2	29.3	35.7
Roaring Creek township (Columbia)	545	542	-0.6	528	96.6	0.0	0.0	0.6	2.8	19.3	63.6	17.0	221	90.0	53.8	20.4
Roaring Spring borough & MCD (Blair)	2,585	2,549	-1.4	2,572	95.8	0.7	2.2	1.0	0.3	24.1	58.8	17.1	1,058	72.5	63.1	13.0
Robeson township (Berks)	7,216	7,333	1.6	7,298	95.9	0.0	0.9	0.9	2.2	19.9	65.0	15.2	2,621	94.4	42.4	29.0
Robesonia borough & MCD (Berks)	2,061	2,062	0.0	1,998	89.5	0.9	0.4	1.4	7.8	17.0	65.3	17.9	836	78.6	61.5	16.0
Robinson township (Allegheny)	13,355	13,692	2.5	13,549	88.8	2.5	4.0	2.3	2.3	16.9	67.3	15.7	5,820	71.5	23.2	52.1
Robinson CDP	614	NA	NA	546	97.4	0.0	0.0	2.6	0.0	17.0	63.6	19.4	216	90.7	66.7	2.8
Robinson township (Washington)	1,931	1,912	-1.0	1,849	95.8	1.3	0.0	2.4	0.5	18.1	64.9	17.1	794	73.6	55.4	19.0
Rochester borough & MCD (Beaver)	3,657	3,587	-1.9	3,628	80.8	15.8	0.0	2.0	1.4	22.2	63.2	14.7	1,595	46.7	57.3	12.1
Rochester township (Beaver)	2,802	2,752	-1.8	2,779	96.1	2.6	0.0	0.7	0.6	11.4	68.3	20.4	1,199	84.7	48.5	20.4
Rockdale township (Crawford)	1,506	1,474	-2.1	1,394	99.3	0.0	0.0	0.2	0.5	27.7	58.6	13.8	487	83.6	59.1	17.7
Rockefeller township (Northumberland)	2,273	2,271	-0.1	2,418	98.9	0.0	0.0	0.3	0.8	19.8	64.0	16.3	946	87.6	64.5	11.1
Rockhill borough & MCD (Huntingdon)	371	364	-1.9	277	98.2	0.7	0.0	0.4	0.7	11.5	60.8	27.8	128	88.3	75.8	8.6
Rockland township (Berks)	3,776	3,791	0.4	3,791	96.3	0.9	0.0	0.7	2.1	19.2	66.1	14.7	1,414	93.1	46.9	37.3
Rockland township (Venango)	1,456	1,415	-2.8	1,382	94.0	0.4	1.6	3.6	0.4	16.8	58.8	24.5	613	86.6	64.4	12.1
Rockledge borough & MCD (Montgomery)	2,543	2,549	0.2	2,553	89.9	0.2	3.2	3.3	3.4	20.9	68.0	11.0	1,032	66.5	41.2	28.1
Rockwood borough & MCD (Somerset)	890	863	-3.0	879	98.4	0.0	0.0	1.5	0.1	22.2	61.8	15.9	348	60.6	68.7	8.0
Rogersville CDP	249	NA	NA	229	99.6	0.0	0.0	0.0	0.4	17.5	72.0	10.5	96	60.4	49.0	17.7
Rohrsburg CDP	145	NA	NA	125	100.0	0.0	0.0	0.0	0.0	16.8	60.0	23.2	56	82.1	55.4	26.8
Rome borough & MCD (Bradford)	441	424	-3.9	339	98.5	0.0	0.0	0.0	1.5	26.8	60.3	13.0	143	69.2	70.6	9.8
Rome township (Bradford)	1,191	1,246	4.6	1,201	95.1	0.1	0.2	4.3	0.2	28.8	57.2	14.0	412	89.1	66.3	12.4
Rome township (Crawford)	1,840	1,807	-1.8	2,346	96.0	0.7	0.0	2.6	0.8	41.7	49.7	8.7	609	76.5	72.4	10.8
Ronco CDP	256	NA	NA	62	100.0	0.0	0.0	0.0	0.0	0.0	0.0	100.0	45	100.0	100.0	0.0
Ronks CDP	362	NA	NA	231	100.0	0.0	0.0	0.0	0.0	0.0	99.9	0.0	103	39.8	88.3	0.0
Roscoe borough & MCD (Washington)	812	797	-1.8	706	98.6	0.0	0.0	1.4	0.0	14.6	53.4	31.9	325	78.2	52.6	21.2
Rose township (Jefferson)	1,249	1,232	-1.4	1,363	98.3	0.4	0.0	0.0	1.3	23.5	62.7	14.0	508	84.3	59.8	13.8
Roseto borough & MCD (Northampton)	1,567	1,559	-0.5	1,772	96.3	0.0	0.5	1.1	2.1	26.9	52.8	20.3	662	74.5	55.0	19.2
Rose Valley borough & MCD (Delaware)	913	949	3.9	885	85.4	1.0	10.3	1.7	1.6	20.9	55.1	24.0	343	99.1	7.0	85.1
Roseville borough & MCD (Tioga)	189	190	0.5	166	100.0	0.0	0.0	0.0	0.0	22.2	54.6	22.9	66	81.8	50.0	13.6
Ross township (Allegheny)	31,105	31,012	-0.3	31,108	91.6	2.5	3.2	1.5	1.3	17.0	61.8	21.4	13,982	74.8	31.5	44.9
Ross township (Luzerne)	2,938	2,924	-0.5	2,936	99.0	0.0	0.0	1.0	0.0	18.2	62.3	19.5	1,218	89.7	55.8	20.5
Ross township (Monroe)	5,937	5,781	-2.6	5,870	92.7	1.8	1.0	2.1	2.4	22.5	63.6	14.0	1,929	98.8	46.6	20.8
Rossiter CDP	646	NA	NA	565	97.5	2.5	0.0	0.0	0.0	17.6	67.5	14.9	209	71.8	68.4	7.7
Rosslyn Farms borough & MCD (Allegheny)	427	428	0.2	445	97.1	0.9	0.2	0.9	0.9	22.0	62.0	16.0	173	92.5	7.5	78.6
Rostraver township (Westmoreland)	11,363	11,212	-1.3	11,279	93.7	2.1	2.4	1.1	0.8	19.8	62.5	17.7	4,340	88.1	44.4	27.9
Rote CDP	507	NA	NA	648	99.2	0.0	0.0	0.0	0.8	25.3	60.7	14.0	250	93.2	57.6	12.4
Rothsville CDP	3,044	NA	NA	2,598	91.2	2.2	2.7	1.2	2.7	23.8	63.7	12.5	1,000	77.1	37.4	42.7
Roulette CDP	779	NA	NA	745	98.4	0.0	0.0	0.4	1.2	21.0	61.5	17.4	309	77.3	61.5	9.7
Roulette township (Potter)	1,197	1,175	-1.8	1,216	99.0	0.0	0.0	0.2	0.7	20.6	58.4	20.9	510	82.0	60.0	10.0
Rouseville borough & MCD (Venango)	523	503	-3.8	590	95.6	0.2	0.0	3.2	1.0	28.2	58.2	13.7	219	76.3	62.1	5.5
Rouzerville CDP	917	NA	NA	817	96.0	0.0	4.0	0.0	0.0	17.8	66.4	16.0	354	57.3	70.6	7.6
Rowes Run CDP	564	NA	NA	336	100.0	0.0	0.0	0.0	0.0	0.0	43.6	56.5	200	100.0	78.0	4.0
Royalton borough & MCD (Dauphin)	907	1,022	12.7	1,054	85.8	2.2	0.9	3.8	7.3	25.0	61.7	13.4	439	63.6	57.6	12.1
Royersford borough & MCD (Montgomery)	4,752	4,785	0.7	4,774	90.0	3.6	2.9	1.0	2.5	20.0	68.0	12.1	2,230	45.9	43.5	26.4
Rupert CDP	183	NA	NA	225	92.0	0.0	0.0	0.0	8.0	11.5	66.3	22.2	84	81.0	78.6	7.1
Rural Valley borough & MCD (Armstrong)	880	861	-2.2	843	97.4	0.0	0.0	0.7	1.9	22.0	61.9	16.1	359	75.8	53.8	18.9
Ruscombmanor township (Berks)	4,112	4,131	0.5	4,120	95.9	0.6	1.8	0.0	1.7	16.2	68.5	15.3	1,657	90.9	61.7	22.6
Rush township (Centre)	4,008	3,939	-1.7	3,988	97.5	0.0	0.2	1.0	1.3	16.9	61.4	21.9	1,686	87.5	56.7	12.8
Rush township (Dauphin)	231	231	0.0	224	100.0	0.0	0.0	0.0	0.0	30.3	47.3	22.3	75	97.3	60.0	14.7
Rush township (Northumberland)	1,122	1,122	0.0	1,225	96.6	0.6	0.5	0.5	1.9	27.3	55.4	17.3	440	86.6	58.6	22.0
Rush township (Schuylkill)	3,412	3,352	-1.8	3,382	97.3	0.0	0.7	0.7	1.3	15.7	56.7	27.6	1,369	96.4	38.8	37.3
Rush township (Susquehanna)	1,267	1,235	-2.5	1,128	90.6	0.7	0.0	1.8	6.9	17.0	63.5	19.4	459	75.8	62.7	10.7
Russell CDP	1,408	NA	NA	1,271	96.1	0.8	1.3	0.8	1.1	14.9	56.2	28.8	607	87.8	40.7	35.9
Russellton CDP	1,440	NA	NA	1,621	99.2	0.0	0.0	0.8	0.0	13.6	66.1	20.2	694	63.0	36.7	13.0
Rutherford CDP	4,303	NA	NA	4,651	61.7	17.7	7.4	8.9	4.3	28.5	59.2	12.3	1,709	79.5	44.4	18.8
Rutland township (Tioga)	820	836	2.0	752	97.1	0.0	0.0	1.3	1.6	19.5	59.6	21.0	297	79.1	60.9	19.2
Rutledge borough & MCD (Delaware)	784	797	1.7	753	88.4	4.9	5.8	0.0	0.8	20.6	67.9	11.6	279	76.0	21.1	61.6

1 May be of any race.

Table A. All Places — **Population and Housing**

PENNSYLVANIA—Con.

STATE City, town, township, borough, or CDP (county if applicable)	2010 census total population	2014 estimated population	Percent change 2010–2014	ACS total population estimate 2010–2014	White alone, not Hispanic or Latino	Black alone, not Hispanic or Latino	Asian alone, not Hispanic or Latino	All other races or 2 or more races, not Hispanic or Latino	Hispanic or Latino[1]	Under 18 years old	Age 18 to 64 years old	Age 65 years and older	Total occupied housing units	Percent owner occupied	High school diploma or less	Bachelor's degree or more
	1	2	3	4	5	6	7	8	9	10	11	12	13	14	15	16
Ryan township (Schuylkill)	2,459	2,540	3.3	2,510	69.4	24.3	0.2	2.0	4.1	9.0	80.2	10.7	516	93.8	46.3	23.3
Rye township (Perry)	2,364	2,331	-1.4	2,245	96.6	0.1	0.5	2.4	0.4	16.1	70.4	13.7	909	97.0	48.3	23.9
Sadsbury township (Chester)	3,570	3,768	5.5	3,674	81.4	8.2	0.3	4.2	5.9	24.3	63.7	12.0	1,337	82.0	30.7	40.6
Sadsbury township (Crawford)	2,930	2,894	-1.2	2,902	97.6	0.1	0.9	0.4	1.0	15.5	56.2	28.4	1,422	83.0	42.8	37.6
Sadsbury township (Lancaster)	3,395	3,455	1.8	3,416	96.9	0.2	0.1	2.1	0.7	34.3	52.6	13.2	939	88.8	64.2	19.7
Saegertown borough & MCD (Crawford)	997	980	-1.7	1,018	87.1	6.0	0.4	1.8	4.7	18.6	69.4	12.0	378	70.6	46.0	18.5
St. Clair borough & MCD (Schuylkill)..................	3,006	2,923	-2.8	2,976	97.1	2.3	0.6	0.0	0.0	22.1	60.3	17.6	1,254	65.5	68.4	9.1
St. Clair township (Westmoreland)	1,519	1,484	-2.3	1,397	98.3	0.7	0.3	0.7	0.0	19.4	62.4	18.3	613	77.2	64.1	10.1
St. Clairsville borough & MCD (Bedford)	78	77	-1.3	78	93.6	6.4	0.0	0.0	0.0	28.2	57.7	14.1	26	84.6	92.3	0.0
St. Lawrence borough & MCD (Berks)	1,809	1,810	0.1	1,863	84.3	1.2	1.7	1.8	11.1	21.2	64.2	14.6	768	70.8	50.1	22.9
St. Marys city & MCD (Elk)............................	13,070	12,793	-2.1	12,940	97.1	0.9	0.5	0.6	0.9	19.9	57.7	22.5	5,379	76.5	56.3	18.3
St. Michael CDP	408	NA	NA	425	100.0	0.0	0.0	0.0	0.0	0.0	17.9	82.1	117	88.9	100.0	0.0
St. Petersburg borough & MCD (Clarion)..............	400	385	-3.8	288	94.8	0.0	0.0	5.2	0.0	19.1	60.8	20.1	124	89.5	48.4	12.1
St. Thomas township (Franklin)	5,935	5,964	0.5	5,949	93.4	1.4	0.2	3.5	1.4	26.6	58.9	14.5	2,183	88.9	55.7	18.9
St. Vincent College CDP..	1,357	NA	NA	1,299	84.1	10.1	0.3	1.2	4.2	0.8	95.2	3.9	0	0.0	0.0	0.0
Salem township (Clarion)	881	863	-2.0	876	98.7	0.5	0.0	0.8	0.0	23.6	61.3	15.2	335	79.7	55.5	17.9
Salem township (Luzerne)	4,255	4,219	-0.8	4,243	94.5	0.6	0.5	0.1	4.4	16.3	60.6	23.1	1,757	85.4	58.8	17.0
Salem township (Mercer).	754	747	-0.9	744	99.1	0.0	0.9	0.0	0.0	22.5	61.7	15.9	280	91.1	62.1	13.2
Salem township (Wayne).	4,265	4,122	-3.4	4,180	89.6	0.2	0.4	0.2	9.6	18.2	58.5	23.2	1,672	77.0	43.6	24.3
Salem township (Westmoreland)	6,623	6,602	-0.3	6,605	95.6	1.0	1.1	1.9	0.3	14.9	60.5	24.7	2,940	80.3	57.6	22.7
Salford township (Montgomery)	2,504	2,935	17.2	2,673	97.6	0.0	0.9	1.2	0.2	22.9	63.9	13.1	987	87.9	37.8	40.5
Salisbury township (Lancaster).................	11,062	11,264	1.8	11,178	96.2	0.8	0.1	0.7	2.1	34.2	53.8	12.0	3,258	73.1	73.2	13.1
Salisbury township (Lehigh)	13,501	13,673	1.3	13,619	84.8	4.3	1.4	1.1	8.3	18.1	61.0	20.9	5,158	86.9	39.5	34.1
Salisbury borough & MCD (Somerset)	727	705	-3.0	776	97.8	0.3	0.0	1.0	0.9	19.0	55.7	25.3	347	70.0	57.9	15.9
Salix CDP	1,149	NA	NA	1,205	100.0	0.0	0.0	0.0	0.0	11.7	66.7	21.7	543	71.3	54.9	7.6
Salladasburg borough & MCD (Lycoming)	238	240	0.8	238	99.2	0.0	0.0	0.8	0.0	18.5	63.1	18.5	96	64.6	49.0	15.6
Saltillo borough & MCD (Huntingdon)	350	346	-1.1	314	99.0	0.0	0.0	1.0	0.0	25.6	57.8	16.9	128	89.8	68.8	14.8
Saltlick township (Fayette)	3,463	3,405	-1.7	3,433	98.3	0.0	0.0	1.7	0.0	16.8	65.7	17.4	1,608	79.4	60.2	19.9
Saltsburg borough & MCD (Indiana).............	864	839	-2.9	768	98.6	0.0	0.7	0.3	0.5	18.3	63.0	18.5	347	58.2	57.3	18.2
Salunga CDP..................	2,695	NA	NA	2,974	87.6	0.0	1.6	1.0	9.8	24.6	59.4	16.1	1,126	88.3	34.9	39.4
Sanatoga CDP................	8,378	NA	NA	8,581	79.1	11.0	1.2	3.1	5.5	27.4	59.6	12.9	3,104	77.9	41.5	29.2
Sand Hill CDP.................	2,496	NA	NA	2,246	89.1	0.0	1.9	0.4	8.7	18.8	70.7	10.5	953	91.0	57.0	18.9
Sandy CDP.....................	1,429	NA	NA	1,350	97.6	0.0	0.0	2.4	0.0	14.5	61.0	24.7	648	74.7	53.4	8.5
Sandy township (Clearfield)	10,623	10,617	-0.1	10,640	96.9	0.1	0.5	1.0	1.5	20.5	58.2	21.3	4,142	83.8	48.6	21.6
Sandy Creek township (Mercer)	795	781	-1.8	686	99.3	0.3	0.1	0.3	0.0	24.0	63.5	12.4	272	84.2	65.8	13.6
Sandycreek township (Venango)	2,260	2,217	-1.9	2,434	92.2	3.6	1.1	1.5	1.5	18.9	59.3	21.9	979	89.5	49.9	27.8
Sandy Lake borough & MCD (Mercer)	659	649	-1.5	636	98.3	0.3	0.6	0.3	0.5	20.2	61.4	18.2	277	63.2	64.6	13.4
Sandy Lake township (Mercer)	1,226	1,210	-1.3	1,195	97.2	0.0	0.1	1.5	1.3	21.4	57.1	21.7	467	86.3	60.8	14.1
Sandy Ridge CDP	407	NA	NA	64	100.0	0.0	0.0	0.0	0.0	14.1	85.9	0.0	36	100.0	77.8	0.0
Sankertown borough & MCD (Cambria)	675	653	-3.3	655	97.6	0.0	0.0	1.8	0.6	19.3	61.9	18.9	279	77.4	66.7	14.7
Saville township (Perry) ...	2,504	2,490	-0.6	2,427	97.2	0.8	0.0	0.5	1.5	25.6	61.7	12.5	857	81.9	58.9	17.2
Saw Creek CDP	4,016	NA	NA	3,711	49.8	12.7	0.0	1.3	36.2	28.1	57.4	14.3	1,300	82.7	36.1	29.5
Saxonburg borough & MCD (Butler)	1,522	1,498	-1.6	1,481	98.0	0.0	0.0	0.5	1.4	15.5	50.1	34.2	704	55.8	46.3	19.9
Saxton borough & MCD (Bedford)	735	713	-3.0	659	94.7	0.5	0.0	4.4	0.5	22.9	58.0	19.0	297	58.6	63.6	14.8
Saylorsburg CDP	1,126	NA	NA	616	100.0	0.0	0.0	0.0	0.0	15.9	70.1	14.0	266	72.2	44.4	21.8
Sayre borough & MCD (Bradford)	5,587	5,482	-1.9	5,553	98.5	0.3	0.6	0.2	0.4	22.8	60.2	17.0	2,459	57.3	54.0	26.3
Scalp Level borough & MCD (Cambria)...........	778	749	-3.7	808	96.9	0.0	0.0	1.1	2.0	19.6	60.0	20.4	356	75.8	66.0	17.1
Schaefferstown CDP	941	NA	NA	800	86.6	12.6	0.0	0.8	0.0	17.1	49.9	33.3	311	89.7	78.5	13.5
Schellsburg borough & MCD (Bedford)	338	336	-0.6	305	96.1	0.0	0.0	1.6	2.3	16.4	64.5	19.0	130	70.0	55.4	15.4
Schlusser CDP	5,265	NA	NA	4,988	92.4	2.0	1.1	1.3	3.2	20.6	61.7	17.7	2,138	75.1	51.2	20.8
Schnecksville CDP	2,935	NA	NA	2,614	97.0	0.0	2.1	0.5	0.4	22.7	61.6	15.7	1,059	75.3	24.3	42.3
Schoeneck CDP	1,056	NA	NA	817	94.9	0.0	0.0	0.0	5.1	28.4	63.9	7.8	294	84.4	77.9	8.8
Schubert CDP	249	NA	NA	129	89.1	0.0	10.9	0.0	0.0	0.0	46.6	53.5	78	79.5	100.0	0.0
Schuylkill township (Chester)	8,516	8,568	0.6	8,545	91.3	2.4	1.8	1.7	2.7	25.9	61.2	12.8	2,845	93.3	19.8	64.4
Schuylkill township (Schuylkill).................	1,129	1,103	-2.3	1,146	99.2	0.0	0.0	0.0	0.8	25.1	51.5	23.2	450	70.4	61.8	5.3
Schuylkill Haven borough & MCD (Schuylkill)	5,437	5,284	-2.8	5,368	99.2	0.0	0.2	0.0	0.6	24.3	58.2	17.4	2,291	69.6	58.5	16.4
Schwenksville borough & MCD (Montgomery)	1,385	1,398	0.9	1,415	90.0	1.0	0.6	1.4	7.1	20.0	61.9	18.2	658	54.9	40.3	24.5

1 May be of any race.

Table A. All Places — Population and Housing

STATE City, town, township, borough, or CDP (county if applicable)	2010 census total population	2014 estimated population	Percent change 2010–2014	ACS total population estimate 2010–2014	White alone, not Hispanic or Latino	Black alone, not Hispanic or Latino	Asian alone, not Hispanic or Latino	All other races or 2 or more races, not Hispanic or Latino	Hispanic or Latino[1]	Under 18 years old	Age 18 to 64 years old	Age 65 years and older	Total occupied housing units	Percent owner occupied	High school diploma or less	Bachelor's degree or more
	1	2	3	4	5	6	7	8	9	10	11	12	13	14	15	16
PENNSYLVANIA—Con.																
Scotland CDP	1,395	NA	NA	1,206	99.0	1.0	0.0	0.0	0.0	23.9	58.9	17.3	476	77.9	45.0	26.5
Scott township (Allegheny)	17,024	16,939	-0.5	17,017	83.8	4.4	8.5	2.2	1.2	16.6	61.7	21.5	7,723	65.5	28.0	47.1
Scott township (Columbia)	5,113	5,126	0.3	5,114	97.5	0.9	1.0	0.6	0.0	17.2	62.5	20.2	2,231	80.1	39.1	32.9
Scott township (Lackawanna)	4,905	4,929	0.5	4,925	97.3	0.0	1.0	0.3	1.4	16.1	62.6	21.3	2,126	89.1	42.3	30.2
Scott township (Lawrence)	2,344	2,303	-1.7	2,401	98.8	0.0	0.0	0.8	0.4	23.0	65.5	11.7	879	85.8	48.2	25.3
Scott township (Wayne)	593	574	-3.2	430	95.8	0.0	0.0	2.8	1.4	23.2	56.0	20.7	168	88.1	61.3	19.6
Scottdale borough & MCD (Westmoreland)	4,384	4,278	-2.4	4,336	93.2	5.5	0.0	1.0	0.3	19.7	61.6	18.7	1,967	69.4	52.6	15.1
Scranton city & MCD (Lackawanna)	76,089	75,281	-1.1	75,842	77.5	6.1	3.5	1.9	10.9	20.3	62.9	16.6	28,924	51.9	48.7	23.4
Scrubgrass township (Venango)	751	736	-2.0	851	96.4	0.1	0.0	2.8	0.7	19.8	62.1	18.0	356	77.5	55.9	9.8
Selinsgrove borough & MCD (Snyder)	5,654	5,790	2.4	5,698	92.7	2.4	0.5	0.9	3.4	14.1	70.9	15.0	1,770	49.9	45.1	25.9
Sellersville borough & MCD (Bucks)	4,249	4,222	-0.6	4,232	93.9	0.5	1.1	3.2	1.2	20.9	68.5	10.5	1,628	76.8	41.9	24.1
Seltzer CDP	350	NA	NA	251	100.0	0.0	0.0	0.0	0.0	7.2	49.5	43.4	135	69.6	89.6	10.4
Seneca CDP	1,065	NA	NA	1,335	100.0	0.0	0.0	0.0	0.0	27.3	55.3	17.5	495	90.5	58.8	23.4
Sergeant township (McKean)	141	138	-2.1	179	100.0	0.0	0.0	0.0	0.0	13.4	50.4	36.3	83	85.5	49.4	15.7
Seven Fields borough & MCD (Butler)	2,887	2,858	-1.0	2,886	91.1	2.0	4.2	1.4	1.3	27.3	66.6	6.1	1,163	73.8	8.7	76.9
Seven Springs borough (Somerset)	26	26	0.0	16	100.0	0.0	0.0	0.0	0.0	0.0	100.1	0.0	16	18.8	0.0	37.5
Seven Springs borough (Fayette)	15	15	0.0	13	100.0	0.0	0.0	0.0	0.0	0.0	100.1	0.0	13	0.0	0.0	30.8
Seven Springs borough (Somerset)	11	11	0.0	3	100.0	0.0	0.0	0.0	0.0	0.0	100.0	0.0	3	100.0	0.0	66.7
Seven Valleys borough & MCD (York)	517	508	-1.7	537	97.6	0.0	1.7	0.4	0.4	25.1	62.5	12.5	204	77.5	73.0	10.3
Seward borough & MCD (Westmoreland)	495	481	-2.8	415	97.6	0.0	0.0	1.0	1.4	17.1	55.4	27.7	202	79.7	66.3	7.9
Sewickley borough & MCD (Allegheny)	3,827	3,851	0.6	3,832	84.9	8.6	2.0	1.4	3.1	24.0	58.7	17.2	1,709	60.0	19.5	56.7
Sewickley township (Westmoreland)	5,996	5,877	-2.0	5,928	98.7	0.3	0.0	0.7	0.4	20.5	62.0	17.7	2,343	82.5	54.9	18.3
Sewickley Heights borough & MCD (Allegheny)	816	821	0.6	723	86.0	1.4	1.2	2.4	9.0	25.8	57.9	16.3	270	94.4	8.5	75.9
Sewickley Hills borough & MCD (Allegheny)	633	738	16.6	668	96.1	1.3	1.6	0.1	0.7	21.1	62.6	16.2	251	90.4	27.5	53.8
Shade township (Somerset)	2,774	2,688	-3.1	2,732	97.5	0.0	0.0	1.4	1.1	17.4	62.6	19.8	1,140	80.9	68.4	11.0
Shade Gap borough & MCD (Huntingdon)	105	104	-1.0	141	100.0	0.0	0.0	0.0	0.0	35.4	55.9	8.5	46	56.5	87.0	0.0
Shaler township (Allegheny)	28,757	28,641	-0.4	28,736	97.2	1.0	0.4	0.7	0.7	18.5	61.1	20.4	11,849	87.5	37.0	39.5
Shamokin city & MCD (Northumberland)	7,374	7,233	-1.9	7,295	98.0	0.1	0.0	1.4	0.6	23.2	59.3	17.5	3,348	54.8	75.9	5.9
Shamokin township (Northumberland)	2,407	2,434	1.1	2,490	99.0	0.0	0.4	0.4	0.2	21.4	62.2	16.2	1,011	92.2	53.6	21.4
Shamokin Dam borough & MCD (Snyder)	1,684	1,702	1.1	1,592	94.5	0.0	2.3	2.4	0.8	11.6	55.7	32.6	792	68.4	52.7	20.6
Shanksville borough & MCD (Somerset)	237	232	-2.1	218	94.5	0.0	3.2	1.4	0.9	17.5	67.0	15.6	81	77.8	63.0	22.2
Shanor-Northvue CDP	5,051	NA	NA	5,156	97.7	0.5	1.1	0.3	0.5	22.2	53.0	24.8	2,206	76.2	37.6	31.9
Sharon city & MCD (Mercer)	14,038	13,669	-2.6	13,845	76.6	14.1	3.0	5.2	1.1	23.3	59.5	17.2	6,165	56.4	56.6	15.7
Sharon township (Potter)	869	854	-1.7	786	98.1	0.6	0.0	1.3	0.0	19.9	55.2	24.9	294	91.8	77.9	8.5
Sharon Hill borough & MCD (Delaware)	5,697	5,706	0.2	5,685	29.9	62.3	5.6	1.6	0.6	29.4	59.2	11.5	2,010	69.3	50.2	22.3
Sharpsburg borough & MCD (Allegheny)	3,446	3,417	-0.8	3,436	76.5	13.6	2.4	2.6	4.9	20.6	64.0	15.5	1,579	40.2	51.8	16.3
Sharpsville borough & MCD (Mercer)	4,415	4,304	-2.5	4,353	96.5	2.2	0.1	0.1	1.1	26.5	58.2	15.2	1,785	63.0	42.9	23.4
Shartlesville CDP	455	NA	NA	430	100.0	0.0	0.0	0.0	0.0	10.9	67.8	21.2	229	75.5	69.4	5.7
Shavertown CDP	2,019	NA	NA	2,048	95.0	0.6	0.5	1.4	2.4	17.0	69.1	14.0	939	73.2	35.8	28.6
Sheakleyville borough & MCD (Mercer)	142	140	-1.4	160	100.0	0.0	0.0	0.0	0.0	21.3	66.3	12.5	63	66.7	66.7	20.6
Sheatown CDP	671	NA	NA	702	100.0	0.0	0.0	0.0	0.0	16.6	54.2	29.2	267	79.8	71.5	21.7
Sheffield CDP	1,132	NA	NA	1,202	99.6	0.4	0.0	0.0	0.0	17.6	60.7	21.7	475	72.0	64.8	22.7
Sheffield township (Warren)	2,121	2,063	-2.7	2,383	99.8	0.2	0.0	0.0	0.0	18.8	63.9	17.2	864	82.6	67.4	17.2
Shelocta borough & MCD (Indiana)	130	126	-3.1	141	100.0	0.0	0.0	0.0	0.0	23.4	68.7	7.8	57	36.8	80.7	5.3
Shenandoah borough & MCD (Schuylkill)	5,071	4,925	-2.9	5,002	76.9	1.4	0.0	1.7	20.0	19.3	60.9	19.7	2,070	56.1	78.5	6.1
Shenandoah Heights CDP	1,233	NA	NA	1,200	99.9	0.1	0.0	0.0	0.0	17.0	66.8	16.5	504	98.2	51.8	23.2
Shenango township (Lawrence)	7,511	7,407	-1.4	7,457	97.9	0.3	0.0	1.6	0.2	23.2	58.0	18.9	2,805	81.7	55.4	20.4
Shenango township (Mercer)	3,929	3,857	-1.8	3,886	98.1	0.2	0.2	0.7	0.7	25.5	53.8	20.5	1,452	79.1	69.5	14.3
Sheppton CDP	239	NA	NA	181	68.5	0.0	0.0	0.0	31.5	20.4	71.3	8.3	55	80.0	94.5	5.5
Sheshequin township (Bradford)	1,348	1,306	-3.1	1,271	97.8	0.6	1.1	0.6	0.0	22.1	62.3	15.4	521	87.7	64.7	10.9
Shickshinny borough & MCD (Luzerne)	837	826	-1.3	700	93.0	0.1	0.0	1.0	5.9	20.1	54.7	25.3	316	57.0	66.8	8.5

1 May be of any race.

Table A. All Places — **Population and Housing**

STATE City, town, township, borough, or CDP (county if applicable)	2010 census total population	2014 estimated population	Percent change 2010–2014	ACS total population estimate 2010–2014	White alone, not Hispanic or Latino	Black alone, not Hispanic or Latino	Asian alone, not Hispanic or Latino	All other races or 2 or more races, not Hispanic or Latino	Hispanic or Latino[1]	Under 18 years old	Age 18 to 64 years old	Age 65 years and older	Total occupied housing units	Percent owner occupied	High school diploma or less	Bachelor's degree or more
	1	2	3	4	5	6	7	8	9	10	11	12	13	14	15	16
PENNSYLVANIA—Con.																
Shillington borough & MCD (Berks)	5,273	5,259	-0.3	5,272	84.6	0.0	0.8	1.1	13.5	26.4	53.5	20.2	2,220	73.7	45.8	25.5
Shiloh CDP	11,218	NA	NA	11,493	87.8	2.9	2.3	0.1	6.8	18.4	58.3	23.3	4,647	79.2	46.2	28.9
Shinglehouse borough & MCD (Potter)	1,126	1,102	-2.1	979	100.0	0.0	0.0	0.0	0.0	16.8	57.9	25.2	457	68.9	61.1	15.1
Shippen township (Cameron)	2,232	2,103	-5.8	2,343	97.5	0.1	0.4	1.5	0.4	18.0	60.2	21.7	1,014	82.9	58.9	19.5
Shippen township (Tioga)	527	529	0.4	460	95.0	0.0	0.0	0.4	4.6	14.8	50.8	34.3	217	79.7	57.1	14.3
Shippensburg borough	5,492	5,542	0.9	5,479	86.4	2.0	0.4	3.9	7.2	17.5	65.8	16.8	2,580	35.0	52.2	17.2
Shippensburg borough (Cumberland)	4,416	4,457	0.9	4,434	84.2	2.5	0.5	4.9	8.0	18.0	68.8	13.1	2,044	24.4	54.0	14.1
Shippensburg borough (Franklin)	1,076	1,085	0.8	1,045	95.9	0.0	0.0	0.0	4.1	15.3	52.6	32.2	536	75.6	45.5	28.9
Shippensburg township (Cumberland)	5,429	5,457	0.5	5,466	86.2	7.9	1.0	2.2	2.7	5.0	89.1	5.8	1,386	42.4	34.6	15.2
Shippensburg University CDP	2,625	NA	NA	2,360	74.7	14.8	2.2	3.1	5.1	2.2	97.7	0.0	64	0.0	0.0	7.8
Shippenville borough & MCD (Clarion)	480	464	-3.3	613	96.2	0.2	0.8	0.7	2.1	25.7	60.4	13.7	262	82.1	53.1	21.8
Shippingport borough & MCD (Beaver)	214	212	-0.9	149	98.0	0.0	0.0	0.0	2.0	15.5	69.8	14.8	59	78.0	59.3	1.7
Shiremanstown borough & MCD (Cumberland) ..	1,569	1,573	0.3	1,606	91.5	1.2	0.8	1.2	5.3	19.9	65.9	14.2	684	59.8	32.5	34.5
Shirley township (Huntingdon)	2,524	2,498	-1.0	2,520	95.6	0.2	1.3	2.3	0.5	21.8	57.2	20.9	1,004	83.0	77.8	4.1
Shirleysburg borough & MCD (Huntingdon)	150	148	-1.3	116	99.1	0.0	0.0	0.0	0.9	15.5	49.1	35.3	53	77.4	73.6	20.8
Shoemakersville borough & MCD (Berks)	1,378	1,368	-0.7	1,431	95.0	0.0	0.9	0.0	4.1	21.4	59.1	19.4	585	65.6	60.3	12.5
Shohola township (Pike)..	2,475	2,375	-4.0	2,409	88.5	0.7	0.3	1.7	8.8	20.7	60.7	18.8	1,000	79.3	33.3	31.3
Shrewsbury township (Lycoming)	409	406	-0.7	414	99.5	0.0	0.0	0.5	0.0	20.8	61.2	17.9	171	76.6	71.3	12.3
Shrewsbury township (Sullivan)	319	318	-0.3	392	84.2	14.5	1.3	0.0	0.0	15.0	61.7	23.2	158	91.1	47.5	18.4
Shrewsbury borough & MCD (York)	3,823	3,842	0.5	3,827	94.0	2.3	1.5	0.7	1.5	22.8	57.2	20.0	1,407	83.2	54.4	22.8
Shrewsbury township (York)	6,447	6,683	3.7	6,594	93.6	2.1	2.2	0.9	1.2	19.4	59.5	21.0	2,521	86.1	42.1	28.5
Sidman CDP	431	NA	NA	383	100.0	0.0	0.0	0.0	0.0	23.4	34.8	41.8	169	91.1	59.8	24.9
Sierra View CDP	4,813	NA	NA	5,154	64.7	22.4	1.9	0.0	11.0	27.6	64.7	7.9	1,534	96.1	47.8	21.0
Siglerville CDP	106	NA	NA	96	66.7	0.0	33.3	0.0	0.0	12.5	87.5	0.0	42	76.2	100.0	0.0
Silkworth CDP	820	NA	NA	819	100.0	0.0	0.0	0.0	0.0	19.4	60.6	20.0	376	83.0	45.5	19.7
Silverdale borough & MCD (Bucks)	871	859	-1.4	963	96.2	2.2	0.5	0.3	0.8	17.0	70.1	12.9	349	79.9	39.5	30.1
Silver Lake township (Susquehanna)	1,716	1,656	-3.5	1,772	96.7	0.0	0.3	1.0	2.0	25.4	57.5	17.2	659	93.3	37.5	24.9
Silver Spring township (Cumberland)	13,666	15,728	15.1	14,629	88.5	1.6	3.4	1.4	5.1	22.0	59.2	18.9	6,024	83.0	37.2	38.7
Simpson CDP	1,275	NA	NA	1,350	98.1	0.0	0.0	0.0	1.9	18.8	62.2	19.2	613	58.6	52.2	11.7
Sinking Spring borough & MCD (Berks)	3,999	4,097	2.5	4,033	73.2	8.7	2.7	1.3	14.1	29.3	59.9	10.9	1,529	63.5	33.8	29.6
Skippack CDP	3,758	NA	NA	3,856	88.9	0.9	4.6	3.9	1.7	28.0	57.0	14.9	1,509	88.5	30.9	44.1
Skippack township (Montgomery)	13,715	15,204	10.9	14,433	76.1	13.6	3.1	2.6	4.6	21.8	65.6	12.6	4,149	87.4	25.5	48.2
Skyline View CDP............	4,003	NA	NA	3,439	92.4	4.9	2.3	0.0	0.4	21.0	60.4	18.5	1,453	94.6	31.2	45.6
Slabtown CDP	156	NA	NA	125	99.2	0.8	0.0	0.0	0.0	4.8	69.6	25.6	62	75.8	48.4	3.2
Slatedale CDP	455	NA	NA	303	76.6	0.0	0.0	11.9	11.6	6.6	68.7	24.8	126	72.2	72.2	0.0
Slatington borough & MCD (Lehigh)	4,232	4,267	0.8	4,258	91.2	1.0	0.4	0.8	6.6	23.6	62.9	13.6	1,732	56.2	58.6	13.3
Slickville CDP	388	NA	NA	354	100.0	0.0	0.0	0.0	0.0	2.8	69.7	27.4	204	71.1	81.4	6.9
Sligo borough & MCD (Clarion)	720	700	-2.8	663	98.5	0.0	0.8	0.8	0.0	20.1	63.6	16.4	279	74.6	56.3	16.5
Slippery Rock borough & MCD (Butler)	3,625	3,576	-1.4	3,646	87.8	2.7	6.6	2.3	0.6	7.4	82.9	9.7	1,202	36.4	21.3	35.0
Slippery Rock township (Butler)	5,614	6,401	14.0	5,749	90.3	5.3	0.3	1.8	2.2	9.0	84.8	6.2	1,645	53.7	20.5	29.4
Slippery Rock township (Lawrence)	3,286	3,207	-2.4	3,249	99.7	0.0	0.0	0.2	0.1	22.2	62.4	15.4	1,314	78.2	50.2	14.9
Slippery Rock University CDP	1,898	NA	NA	1,805	88.7	6.9	0.0	2.8	1.6	0.9	99.0	0.0	8	100.0	0.0	100.0
Slocum township (Luzerne)	1,115	1,101	-1.3	1,031	100.0	0.0	0.0	0.0	0.0	21.9	59.8	18.4	409	91.2	48.9	20.5
Slovan CDP	555	NA	NA	338	100.0	0.0	0.0	0.0	0.0	9.5	85.6	5.0	185	56.2	93.0	2.7
Smethport borough & MCD (McKean)	1,655	1,606	-3.0	1,668	98.6	0.0	0.2	1.1	0.1	20.0	54.4	25.5	735	68.4	49.5	19.9
Smicksburg borough & MCD (Indiana)	46	45	-2.2	46	100.0	0.0	0.0	0.0	0.0	13.1	49.9	37.0	20	90.0	65.0	0.0
Smith township (Washington)	4,476	4,431	-1.0	4,445	99.5	0.0	0.0	0.1	0.4	20.4	63.2	16.5	1,831	78.5	66.4	10.3
Smithfield township (Bradford)	1,498	1,477	-1.4	1,493	97.7	0.3	0.4	1.2	0.4	23.2	60.8	16.1	564	92.6	59.6	18.8
Smithfield borough & MCD (Fayette)	875	859	-1.8	1,010	100.0	0.0	0.0	0.0	0.0	25.1	62.3	12.6	372	65.9	57.0	16.7
Smithfield township (Huntingdon)	4,390	4,532	3.2	4,488	44.2	43.9	0.3	2.7	8.8	2.9	89.6	7.4	471	71.8	63.7	15.1
Smithfield township (Monroe)	7,364	7,297	-0.9	7,344	72.4	9.5	1.6	2.5	14.0	23.1	63.7	13.2	2,504	76.1	41.9	31.8
Smithton borough & MCD (Westmoreland)	399	385	-3.5	374	100.0	0.0	0.0	0.0	0.0	19.2	58.8	21.9	150	64.7	52.7	14.7
Smock CDP	583	NA	NA	557	83.8	2.7	0.0	11.1	2.3	10.4	59.0	30.3	275	77.8	66.2	8.7
Smoketown CDP	357	NA	NA	308	93.8	6.2	0.0	0.0	0.0	17.6	48.7	33.8	102	80.4	80.4	19.6

1 May be of any race.

Table A. All Places — **Population and Housing**

STATE / City, town, township, borough, or CDP (county if applicable)	2010 census total population	2014 estimated population	Percent change 2010–2014	ACS total population estimate 2010–2014	White alone, not Hispanic or Latino	Black alone, not Hispanic or Latino	Asian alone, not Hispanic or Latino	All other races or 2 or more races, not Hispanic or Latino	Hispanic or Latino[1]	Under 18 years old	Age 18 to 64 years old	Age 65 years and older	Total occupied housing units	Percent owner occupied	High school diploma or less	Bachelor's degree or more
	1	2	3	4	5	6	7	8	9	10	11	12	13	14	15	16
PENNSYLVANIA—Con.																
Snake Spring township (Bedford)	1,639	1,759	7.3	1,675	97.1	0.2	1.0	0.1	1.7	17.0	52.7	30.3	632	83.4	56.6	23.6
Snow Shoe borough & MCD (Centre).............	765	774	1.2	841	99.9	0.0	0.0	0.0	0.1	27.2	57.7	15.1	302	79.8	62.3	14.6
Snow Shoe township (Centre).................	1,746	1,721	-1.4	1,656	99.5	0.0	0.0	0.2	0.4	18.2	65.2	16.5	652	89.4	69.0	8.4
S.N.P.J. borough & MCD (Lawrence)................	19	19	0.0	16	87.5	0.0	0.0	12.5	0.0	12.5	62.6	25.0	5	80.0	60.0	40.0
Snyder township (Blair) ...	3,371	3,333	-1.1	3,358	99.7	0.3	0.0	0.0	0.0	18.5	65.4	16.1	1,347	87.6	66.4	14.1
Snyder township (Jefferson)...............	2,549	2,523	-1.0	2,530	99.0	0.4	0.0	0.3	0.3	24.2	62.7	12.9	997	80.2	58.9	16.2
Snydertown CDP	0	NA	NA	501	100.0	0.0	0.0	0.0	0.0	30.0	56.0	14.2	174	100.0	67.2	30.5
Snydertown borough & MCD (Northumberland)	335	333	-0.6	370	97.8	0.0	1.6	0.0	0.5	20.5	61.2	18.4	167	85.6	52.1	18.6
Solebury township (Bucks)....................	8,692	8,647	-0.5	8,674	91.4	0.4	3.5	0.7	4.0	19.7	62.5	17.8	3,533	89.1	10.0	66.7
Somerset borough & MCD (Somerset)	6,277	6,092	-2.9	6,185	95.3	0.6	0.7	1.4	1.9	20.1	60.5	19.4	2,733	48.2	47.9	27.1
Somerset township (Somerset)	12,122	12,306	1.5	12,219	80.8	13.7	0.3	1.4	3.9	13.9	70.0	16.2	3,495	81.1	65.2	16.5
Somerset township (Washington).............	2,684	2,668	-0.6	2,691	96.9	0.0	1.3	0.6	1.3	18.3	60.2	21.5	1,095	90.1	52.9	24.3
Soudersburg CDP	540	NA	NA	487	90.3	6.4	0.0	0.0	3.3	8.0	75.5	16.4	255	69.4	60.8	11.0
Souderton borough & MCD (Montgomery)	6,618	6,739	1.8	6,668	84.0	2.0	6.0	1.8	6.2	21.2	64.7	14.0	2,573	64.9	46.4	25.0
South Abington township (Lackawanna)............	9,073	9,063	-0.1	9,057	93.6	0.7	3.9	0.6	1.2	22.6	61.2	16.2	3,281	76.3	23.5	55.8
Southampton township (Bedford).................	976	952	-2.5	886	98.8	0.0	0.0	0.9	0.3	18.1	54.7	27.3	383	91.6	74.4	12.0
Southampton township (Cumberland).............	6,359	6,730	5.8	6,618	92.1	3.6	1.8	1.2	1.3	26.2	60.6	13.3	2,598	75.1	54.0	27.9
Southampton township (Franklin).................	7,987	8,429	5.5	8,226	94.0	3.1	0.0	0.6	2.3	29.8	59.0	11.3	3,025	76.6	60.7	13.9
Southampton township (Somerset)	630	622	-1.3	587	98.1	0.0	0.0	0.0	1.9	17.2	62.8	19.9	232	89.7	72.0	19.0
South Annville township (Lebanon).................	2,852	2,909	2.0	2,886	95.0	1.9	0.0	1.8	1.3	23.0	58.2	18.8	1,073	92.8	62.0	16.3
South Beaver township (Beaver).................	2,717	2,681	-1.3	2,697	96.0	1.4	0.7	0.1	1.7	16.5	59.8	23.8	1,056	92.1	49.4	23.3
South Bend township (Armstrong)..............	1,167	1,156	-0.9	1,005	97.7	1.1	0.0	1.2	0.0	17.7	60.5	22.1	426	82.4	68.8	13.8
South Bethlehem borough & MCD (Armstrong)	481	468	-2.7	505	94.5	0.0	0.0	3.0	2.6	19.6	58.7	21.6	212	76.4	65.6	10.8
South Buffalo township (Armstrong)..............	2,636	2,623	-0.5	2,626	99.2	0.0	0.0	0.6	0.3	19.9	63.8	16.3	1,023	85.1	46.0	20.2
South Canaan township (Wayne).................	1,766	1,726	-2.3	1,665	95.3	0.4	0.0	0.2	4.1	25.6	57.9	16.3	531	87.6	48.6	21.5
South Centre township (Columbia)	1,937	1,942	0.3	2,024	90.1	0.2	4.9	1.3	3.6	23.6	56.1	20.3	868	77.9	67.3	16.1
South Coatesville borough & MCD (Chester).................	1,303	1,439	10.4	1,581	41.4	44.0	0.0	7.8	6.8	30.4	59.2	10.4	548	74.8	45.6	31.0
South Connellsville borough & MCD (Fayette).................	1,970	1,936	-1.7	1,695	97.9	1.7	0.0	0.0	0.4	16.1	63.0	20.8	682	80.4	64.1	11.1
South Coventry township (Chester).................	2,604	2,616	0.5	2,612	96.6	2.2	0.8	0.0	0.4	25.4	60.0	14.6	1,001	89.4	29.5	43.7
South Creek township (Bradford).................	1,128	1,109	-1.7	1,324	96.2	0.0	1.0	1.5	1.3	25.7	55.1	19.3	508	76.0	69.5	10.6
South Fayette township (Allegheny)..................	14,416	15,311	6.2	14,898	91.0	1.2	5.8	1.0	1.0	23.9	60.6	15.5	5,770	81.2	27.3	50.4
South Fork borough & MCD (Cambria)...........	928	888	-4.3	1,009	97.2	0.0	0.0	0.8	2.0	23.0	64.1	13.0	417	75.8	65.2	9.6
South Franklin township (Washington)...............	3,310	3,270	-1.2	3,284	98.9	0.0	0.0	0.5	0.6	15.0	68.9	16.2	1,313	89.8	42.1	23.7
South Greensburg borough & MCD (Westmoreland)	2,117	2,068	-2.3	2,056	94.2	0.5	3.2	1.9	0.2	16.8	59.0	24.4	995	66.0	44.5	23.2
South Hanover township (Dauphin).................	6,248	6,632	6.1	6,465	84.3	4.1	5.5	1.7	4.4	21.1	66.2	12.8	2,379	74.6	25.9	49.6
South Heidelberg township (Berks)	7,271	7,318	0.6	7,310	87.6	2.7	2.2	1.2	6.3	21.1	62.9	16.0	2,560	86.2	42.0	24.9
South Heights borough & MCD (Beaver)	475	463	-2.5	414	98.6	1.2	0.0	0.2	0.0	18.1	62.0	19.8	195	76.9	66.7	13.3
South Huntingdon township (Westmoreland)	5,794	5,653	-2.4	5,713	97.7	0.4	0.5	0.1	1.3	16.3	66.0	17.7	2,370	80.4	61.7	15.4
South Lebanon township (Lebanon).................	9,461	9,673	2.2	9,601	91.2	1.0	0.4	0.7	6.7	22.2	56.1	21.8	3,398	81.9	52.9	24.3
South Londonderry township (Lebanon)	6,993	7,470	6.8	7,212	93.4	2.0	2.2	1.0	1.3	24.0	61.4	14.5	2,603	84.9	34.6	38.2
South Mahoning township (Indiana)................	1,841	1,775	-3.6	1,577	98.7	0.0	0.0	1.3	0.0	28.9	56.4	14.9	552	83.5	74.5	7.2
South Manheim township (Schuylkill)................	2,510	2,530	0.8	2,521	96.4	0.0	0.0	0.2	3.4	20.4	65.1	14.6	1,010	96.0	46.5	23.1
South Middleton township (Cumberland).............	14,661	15,066	2.8	14,864	92.3	1.2	2.3	1.1	3.1	21.8	58.3	20.0	5,856	83.6	43.0	34.2
Southmont borough & MCD (Cambria)...........	2,284	2,198	-3.8	2,251	93.0	0.6	2.9	2.2	1.3	21.5	56.7	21.6	1,002	73.0	31.5	42.1

1 May be of any race.

Table A. All Places — **Population and Housing**

STATE City, town, township, borough, or CDP (county if applicable)	Population				Race and Hispanic or Latino origin (percent), 2010–2014					Age (percent), 2010–2014			Households, 2010–2014			
	2010 census total population	2014 estimated population	Percent change 2010–2014	ACS total population estimate 2010–2014	White alone, not Hispanic or Latino	Black alone, not Hispanic or Latino	Asian alone, not Hispanic or Latino	All other races or 2 or more races, not Hispanic or Latino	Hispanic or Latino[1]	Under 18 years old	Age 18 to 64 years old	Age 65 years and older	Total occupied housing units	Percent owner occupied	Householders by level of education (percent) High school diploma or less	Bachelor's degree or more
	1	2	3	4	5	6	7	8	9	10	11	12	13	14	15	16

PENNSYLVANIA—Con.

STATE City, town, township, borough, or CDP (county if applicable)	1	2	3	4	5	6	7	8	9	10	11	12	13	14	15	16
South New Castle borough & MCD (Lawrence)	709	686	-3.2	634	96.7	0.9	0.0	0.5	1.9	19.2	64.0	16.7	275	84.0	65.8	5.1
South Newton township (Cumberland)	1,383	1,424	3.0	1,406	95.9	0.0	0.0	1.1	3.1	23.2	64.1	12.7	523	84.5	64.4	13.6
South Park CDP & township (Allegheny)	13,416	13,498	0.6	13,492	93.0	2.0	2.2	1.5	1.3	21.8	63.2	15.0	5,440	79.9	29.5	40.6
South Philipsburg CDP	410	NA	NA	428	100.0	0.0	0.0	0.0	0.0	20.7	58.6	20.6	187	91.4	54.5	9.1
South Pottstown CDP	2,081	NA	NA	1,759	77.0	11.0	6.3	2.1	3.6	24.5	62.0	13.5	829	48.6	47.4	23.8
South Pymatuning township (Mercer)	2,697	2,641	-2.1	2,669	98.0	0.0	1.8	0.2	0.0	22.1	58.4	19.3	1,107	87.0	55.6	20.3
South Renovo borough & MCD (Clinton)	438	438	0.0	416	98.3	0.2	0.5	0.5	0.5	14.0	58.1	27.9	180	86.7	66.7	13.3
South Shenango township (Crawford)	2,037	2,015	-1.1	1,910	98.4	0.0	0.0	1.2	0.5	17.6	57.1	25.3	852	81.9	62.8	16.0
South Strabane township (Washington)	9,346	9,510	1.8	9,475	97.0	2.2	0.2	0.4	0.2	16.8	57.2	26.0	4,305	69.6	44.3	28.8
South Temple CDP	1,424	NA	NA	1,596	74.6	1.3	0.0	0.0	24.1	18.2	67.0	15.0	636	88.5	61.9	24.2
South Union township (Fayette)	10,683	10,639	-0.4	10,693	95.1	2.1	0.0	1.5	1.3	19.6	57.9	22.4	4,362	73.8	50.8	23.9
South Uniontown CDP	1,360	NA	NA	1,116	95.0	5.0	0.0	0.0	0.0	18.7	64.9	16.4	502	87.5	46.4	18.7
South Versailles township (Allegheny)	351	352	0.3	470	94.7	0.0	3.0	0.4	1.9	19.3	59.6	21.1	174	86.2	55.7	14.4
Southview CDP	276	NA	NA	111	91.0	0.0	0.0	9.0	0.0	5.4	70.2	24.3	41	73.2	100.0	0.0
South Waverly borough & MCD (Bradford)	1,027	1,033	0.6	1,189	95.2	0.0	4.2	0.6	0.0	15.9	60.9	23.0	499	88.4	51.1	19.2
Southwest township (Warren)	527	512	-2.8	549	97.4	0.2	0.0	2.4	0.0	18.6	68.9	12.6	199	87.9	73.4	4.5
Southwest Greensburg borough & MCD (Westmoreland)	2,155	2,100	-2.6	2,130	98.1	1.3	0.0	0.0	0.6	22.0	60.7	17.4	970	55.6	35.7	30.2
Southwest Madison township (Perry)	992	988	-0.4	901	98.0	0.2	0.0	1.8	0.0	31.0	58.4	10.7	326	84.7	72.4	10.4
South Whitehall township (Lehigh)	19,180	19,602	2.2	19,442	83.8	2.0	6.6	1.3	6.3	18.9	58.0	23.1	7,724	80.8	31.7	43.4
South Williamsport borough & MCD (Lycoming)	6,379	6,330	-0.8	6,370	96.8	1.0	0.0	1.3	0.0	23.6	60.8	15.5	2,764	62.2	43.6	25.3
South Woodbury township (Bedford)	2,155	2,113	-1.9	1,986	99.6	0.0	0.0	0.4	0.0	26.5	58.3	15.2	745	85.0	61.9	15.2
Sparta township (Crawford)	1,832	1,799	-1.8	1,638	97.5	0.1	0.0	1.6	0.8	33.2	56.1	10.5	508	82.5	67.7	10.2
Spartansburg borough & MCD (Crawford)	305	301	-1.3	284	94.0	0.7	0.0	5.3	0.0	18.3	57.7	23.9	136	78.7	69.9	11.8
Speers borough & MCD (Washington)	1,154	1,136	-1.6	1,124	95.1	0.4	0.0	3.4	1.1	12.5	61.4	26.2	558	77.2	41.6	26.9
Spinnerstown CDP	1,826	NA	NA	1,796	93.2	6.8	0.0	0.0	0.0	27.0	65.9	7.1	556	96.2	30.8	46.2
Spring township (Berks)	27,128	27,443	1.2	27,313	84.2	3.7	2.8	1.4	8.0	20.8	61.6	17.7	10,545	77.4	37.9	38.3
Spring township (Centre)	7,470	7,587	1.6	7,579	94.4	2.9	1.3	0.3	1.1	18.9	63.5	17.7	3,221	71.4	49.9	28.2
Spring township (Crawford)	1,550	1,527	-1.5	1,562	97.3	1.0	0.0	0.4	1.3	21.1	63.2	15.7	592	80.7	64.2	13.3
Spring township (Perry)	2,213	2,206	-0.3	1,995	99.3	0.0	0.2	0.2	0.3	22.1	61.6	16.3	825	86.3	52.4	21.9
Spring township (Snyder)	1,616	1,632	1.0	1,649	97.2	0.0	0.0	2.1	0.7	25.7	58.2	16.1	567	76.2	72.1	8.6
Springboro borough & MCD (Crawford)	477	462	-3.1	430	95.3	1.6	1.6	1.4	0.0	26.5	58.3	15.1	158	69.6	67.1	14.6
Spring Brook township (Lackawanna)	2,763	2,761	-0.1	2,780	99.0	0.4	0.0	0.4	0.2	24.1	59.7	16.3	1,042	84.3	47.0	26.6
Spring City borough & MCD (Chester)	3,323	3,328	0.2	3,337	90.1	5.0	1.3	1.6	2.1	24.4	63.3	12.4	1,383	49.5	59.1	18.8
Spring Creek township (Elk)	233	227	-2.6	141	97.9	2.1	0.0	0.0	0.0	5.6	48.2	46.1	77	89.6	64.9	16.9
Spring Creek township (Warren)	852	824	-3.3	703	95.6	0.1	0.7	3.1	0.4	16.4	72.2	11.4	298	77.2	60.1	19.8
Springdale borough & MCD (Allegheny)	3,405	3,393	-0.4	3,400	94.5	0.6	1.4	1.4	2.1	20.5	64.0	15.5	1,508	66.1	49.2	24.3
Springdale township (Allegheny)	1,636	1,625	-0.7	1,639	99.3	0.0	0.0	0.7	0.0	11.9	64.7	23.6	793	77.9	49.9	21.6
Springettsbury township (York)	26,668	26,849	0.7	26,735	80.0	6.6	3.5	2.9	7.0	17.2	64.0	18.8	9,559	71.5	39.2	32.4
Springfield township (Bradford)	1,124	1,092	-2.8	1,054	96.3	0.6	1.2	0.4	1.5	25.0	52.8	22.2	400	86.0	53.8	17.3
Springfield township (Bucks)	5,035	5,028	-0.1	5,040	96.4	0.3	2.0	0.0	1.3	21.6	56.7	21.9	1,912	87.7	36.0	39.3
Springfield township (Delaware)	24,211	24,375	0.7	24,276	93.7	1.6	3.3	0.7	0.8	22.6	60.2	17.2	8,566	90.6	26.1	43.2
Springfield township (Erie)	3,425	3,373	-1.5	3,407	97.1	0.0	0.3	1.4	1.2	22.0	63.2	14.8	1,341	80.1	58.6	14.5
Springfield township (Fayette)	3,041	2,978	-2.1	3,013	99.6	0.0	0.0	0.2	0.1	22.9	60.9	16.2	1,138	82.6	71.8	9.0
Springfield township (Huntingdon)	655	645	-1.5	668	98.4	0.0	0.0	0.1	1.5	19.7	57.8	22.3	277	88.8	65.3	10.8
Springfield township (Mercer)	1,981	1,973	-0.4	2,096	98.1	0.4	0.0	1.4	0.1	26.9	59.4	13.8	771	88.8	55.3	19.1
Springfield township (Montgomery)	19,422	19,546	0.6	19,510	80.7	10.9	3.2	1.6	3.5	22.2	57.6	20.2	7,393	79.4	19.7	61.2
Springfield township (York)	5,155	5,410	4.9	5,285	90.2	4.9	1.5	2.3	1.1	23.7	62.4	13.9	2,010	91.0	38.6	35.9
Spring Garden township (York)	12,490	12,803	2.5	12,717	84.7	5.2	2.5	1.8	5.8	19.7	63.8	16.6	4,249	87.3	29.7	45.5
Spring Grove borough & MCD (York)	2,167	2,168	0.0	2,455	92.2	0.5	0.5	1.2	5.5	26.1	61.4	12.5	946	61.8	60.9	14.2

1 May be of any race.

Table A.   All Places — **Population and Housing**

	Population				Race and Hispanic or Latino origin (percent), 2010–2014					Age (percent), 2010–2014			Households, 2010–2014			
STATE City, town, township, borough, or CDP (county if applicable)	2010 census total population	2014 estimated population	Percent change 2010–2014	ACS total population estimate 2010–2014	White alone, not Hispanic or Latino	Black alone, not Hispanic or Latino	Asian alone, not Hispanic or Latino	All other races or 2 or more races, not Hispanic or Latino	Hispanic or Latino[1]	Under 18 years old	Age 18 to 64 years old	Age 65 years and older	Total occupied housing units	Percent owner occupied	High school diploma or less	Bachelor's degree or more
	1	2	3	4	5	6	7	8	9	10	11	12	13	14	15	16
PENNSYLVANIA—Con.																
Spring Hill CDP..............	839	NA	NA	820	99.5	0.0	0.0	0.0	0.5	19.4	59.9	20.6	350	81.7	50.0	26.9
Springhill township (Fayette)	2,907	2,846	-2.1	2,875	99.2	0.3	0.0	0.0	0.5	25.4	64.7	9.9	1,061	72.5	64.3	13.9
Springhill township (Greene),......................	349	340	-2.6	281	98.2	0.0	0.0	1.8	0.0	7.1	72.6	20.3	142	78.9	81.0	7.7
Spring House CDP	3,804	NA	NA	3,673	81.1	3.4	8.2	5.9	1.3	23.2	48.3	28.6	1,493	71.8	18.2	63.3
Spring Mills CDP	268	NA	NA	301	98.3	0.0	0.0	0.0	1.7	19.6	71.3	9.0	115	40.9	40.0	15.7
Springmont CDP.............	724	NA	NA	591	100.0	0.0	0.0	0.0	0.0	28.3	60.4	11.3	256	89.1	30.9	57.0
Spring Mount CDP..........	2,259	NA	NA	2,317	89.6	4.7	1.9	0.0	3.7	23.4	70.7	5.7	955	86.7	50.3	27.3
Spring Ridge CDP	1,003	NA	NA	912	100.0	0.0	0.0	0.0	0.0	14.0	41.2	45.0	521	97.5	26.9	52.8
Springville township (Susquehanna)	1,641	1,572	-4.2	1,616	99.5	0.0	0.0	0.1	0.4	25.6	56.5	17.9	595	73.9	60.8	16.3
Spruce Creek township (Huntingdon)	240	237	-1.3	268	97.0	1.5	0.0	1.5	0.0	18.6	61.2	20.1	117	90.6	44.4	26.5
Spruce Hill township (Juniata)	837	865	3.3	860	89.0	6.3	3.7	1.0	0.0	27.1	61.0	12.0	316	77.2	56.0	21.2
Spry CDP	4,891	NA	NA	4,664	92.9	4.0	0.7	0.0	2.4	18.6	66.4	14.8	2,018	65.9	38.6	37.6
Standing Stone township (Bradford)	644	654	1.6	666	97.6	0.0	0.0	2.1	0.3	31.4	52.0	16.8	237	82.3	70.5	18.1
Starbrick CDP.................	522	NA	NA	488	100.0	0.0	0.0	0.0	0.0	9.7	71.4	18.9	248	84.3	79.8	5.6
Star Junction CDP	616	NA	NA	544	100.0	0.0	0.0	0.0	0.0	12.0	56.9	31.3	230	78.3	81.7	9.6
Starrucca borough & MCD (Wayne)	173	168	-2.9	210	98.1	1.9	0.0	0.0	0.0	20.0	56.3	23.8	76	96.1	44.7	23.7
State College borough & MCD (Centre)...............	42,034	42,100	0.2	42,066	80.2	3.8	10.0	1.9	4.2	5.3	90.2	4.4	12,106	21.0	15.5	48.2
State Line CDP................	2,709	NA	NA	2,562	88.2	7.0	0.7	1.7	2.4	21.6	58.2	20.2	1,074	81.3	58.8	15.6
Steelton borough & MCD (Dauphin)	5,990	5,931	-1.0	5,959	41.2	40.7	0.1	6.3	11.8	32.5	57.1	10.5	2,026	50.1	54.3	13.5
Sterling township (Wayne)	1,450	1,411	-2.7	1,385	96.2	2.3	0.1	0.4	0.9	21.4	64.2	14.3	531	86.1	58.0	12.8
Steuben township (Crawford)	798	786	-1.5	848	99.2	0.0	0.0	0.8	0.0	23.1	61.2	15.7	336	83.6	64.9	7.4
Stevens township (Bradford)	437	439	0.5	404	99.0	0.0	0.0	0.5	0.5	20.0	56.6	23.3	154	89.6	60.4	22.7
Stevens CDP...................	612	NA	NA	632	96.5	0.0	1.6	1.9	0.0	17.1	61.7	21.2	284	79.2	62.3	2.8
Stewardson township (Potter)	74	73	-1.4	20	100.0	0.0	0.0	0.0	0.0	0.0	55.0	45.0	15	93.3	73.3	6.7
Stewart township (Fayette)	731	718	-1.8	724	97.7	0.0	0.0	1.1	1.2	23.5	65.0	11.5	269	84.8	62.5	21.9
Stewartstown borough & MCD (York)	2,089	2,304	10.3	2,130	91.0	5.8	1.4	0.2	1.6	23.0	59.9	17.0	908	72.4	45.2	25.0
Stiles CDP......................	1,113	NA	NA	969	92.0	0.0	5.1	3.0	0.0	22.3	60.3	17.5	341	81.5	24.9	42.5
Stillwater borough & MCD (Columbia)	209	212	1.4	178	100.0	0.0	0.0	0.0	0.0	13.0	74.1	12.9	77	83.1	61.0	31.2
Stockdale borough & MCD (Washington).......	502	508	1.2	438	100.0	0.0	0.0	0.0	0.0	15.7	65.5	18.7	217	67.3	44.2	16.1
Stockertown borough & MCD (Northampton)	927	921	-0.6	1,057	91.0	3.7	0.6	0.9	3.8	26.5	60.5	13.0	387	73.1	43.2	24.8
Stoneboro borough & MCD (Mercer)	1,051	1,024	-2.6	1,016	97.7	0.5	0.0	1.8	0.0	18.8	61.7	19.5	462	73.6	52.8	16.5
Stonerstown CDP	376	NA	NA	433	97.7	0.0	0.0	0.0	2.3	19.8	62.2	17.8	173	87.9	61.3	23.1
Stonybrook CDP.............	2,384	NA	NA	2,058	95.0	0.0	0.0	0.4	4.6	19.4	53.1	27.5	830	97.3	31.3	42.5
Stonycreek township (Cambria)....................	2,844	2,745	-3.5	2,795	93.1	1.5	2.6	2.8	0.0	11.8	62.2	26.0	1,341	79.7	53.2	14.6
Stonycreek township (Somerset)...................	2,237	2,178	-2.6	2,272	99.7	0.0	0.0	0.3	0.0	23.3	62.0	14.7	827	84.9	64.2	11.7
Stony Creek Mills CDP....	1,045	NA	NA	870	82.6	1.0	8.4	3.0	4.9	20.1	63.7	16.3	418	92.8	69.1	18.9
Stormstown CDP.............	2,366	NA	NA	2,384	95.3	0.7	0.4	2.2	1.3	28.2	64.6	7.2	790	91.6	19.4	62.7
Stouchsburg CDP............	600	NA	NA	531	98.5	0.8	0.0	0.8	0.0	13.9	67.7	18.3	228	64.9	57.0	11.8
Stowe township (Allegheny).................	6,362	6,303	-0.9	6,351	71.8	20.2	0.2	6.8	1.1	22.7	61.4	15.9	2,734	55.2	58.5	15.3
Stowe CDP......................	3,695	NA	NA	3,765	82.3	10.7	0.0	3.1	3.9	24.0	65.4	10.5	1,466	63.2	63.7	12.6
Stoystown borough & MCD (Somerset).........	355	340	-4.2	298	100.0	0.0	0.0	0.0	0.0	19.4	51.5	29.2	134	68.7	56.0	21.6
Straban township (Adams)......................	4,928	4,933	0.1	4,924	87.9	0.5	3.0	0.5	8.1	19.8	58.0	22.2	1,813	72.3	56.8	26.5
Strasburg borough & MCD (Lancaster)..........	2,809	2,872	2.2	2,843	92.5	0.0	3.5	0.0	4.0	27.3	58.8	13.8	1,063	73.3	41.9	31.2
Strasburg township (Lancaster).................	4,182	4,247	1.6	4,210	98.9	0.6	0.0	0.5	0.0	31.6	55.0	13.3	1,198	92.2	56.8	18.9
Strattanville borough & MCD (Clarion)..............	545	536	-1.7	620	92.7	2.1	0.0	4.5	0.6	14.3	73.2	12.6	272	52.9	68.4	14.7
Strausstown borough & MCD (Berks)	342	344	0.6	243	95.1	0.0	0.0	0.0	4.9	18.2	62.6	19.3	110	78.2	61.8	11.8
Strodes Mills CDP	757	NA	NA	543	99.1	0.0	0.0	0.9	0.0	20.1	67.3	12.7	241	79.3	64.7	10.8
Strong CDP....................	147	NA	NA	28	100.0	0.0	0.0	0.0	0.0	0.0	82.1	17.9	28	50.0	67.9	0.0
Stroud township (Monroe)	19,215	18,747	-2.4	19,013	64.4	15.3	4.9	1.1	14.3	22.2	64.5	13.5	6,546	82.3	31.8	35.1
Stroudsburg borough & MCD (Monroe)	5,567	5,466	-1.8	5,528	65.4	11.0	4.8	4.0	14.7	21.0	63.4	15.7	2,383	31.6	36.6	22.7
Sturgeon CDP.................	1,710	NA	NA	1,261	94.4	0.0	3.8	0.0	1.8	27.4	57.2	15.5	538	100.0	48.7	31.4
Sugarcreek township (Armstrong).................	1,539	1,513	-1.7	1,547	93.7	4.2	0.9	0.3	0.9	16.2	54.2	29.5	530	87.5	63.8	18.1
Sugarcreek borough & MCD (Venango)	5,303	5,162	-2.7	5,238	97.5	0.4	0.0	2.2	0.0	21.2	58.1	20.8	2,161	89.0	63.8	8.2
Sugar Grove township (Mercer)	971	954	-1.8	989	97.6	0.5	0.0	1.1	0.8	19.8	62.2	18.0	434	87.3	60.6	18.4
Sugar Grove borough & MCD (Warren).............	614	604	-1.6	601	96.2	0.0	1.5	0.7	1.7	22.7	51.7	25.8	236	81.4	55.9	26.7
Sugar Grove township (Warren)	1,716	1,687	-1.7	1,562	98.7	0.0	0.3	0.4	0.7	18.5	67.2	14.1	612	88.4	64.1	11.8
Sugarloaf township (Columbia)	913	911	-0.2	725	99.4	0.0	0.0	0.6	0.0	11.5	50.9	37.5	351	94.0	62.4	14.5

1   May be of any race.

Table A. All Places — **Population and Housing**

STATE City, town, township, borough, or CDP (county if applicable)	Population 2010 census total population	2014 estimated population	Percent change 2010-2014	ACS total population estimate 2010-2014	Race and Hispanic or Latino origin (percent), 2010–2014 White alone, not Hispanic or Latino	Black alone, not Hispanic or Latino	Asian alone, not Hispanic or Latino	All other races or 2 or more races, not Hispanic or Latino	Hispanic or Latino[1]	Age (percent), 2010–2014 Under 18 years old	Age 18 to 64 years old	Age 65 years and older	Households, 2010–2014 Total occupied housing units	Percent owner occupied	Householders by level of education (percent) High school diploma or less	Bachelor's degree or more
	1	2	3	4	5	6	7	8	9	10	11	12	13	14	15	16
PENNSYLVANIA—Con.																
Sugarloaf township (Luzerne).................	4,211	4,179	-0.8	4,207	95.2	0.9	0.3	0.4	3.2	17.4	64.1	18.3	1,531	90.9	34.4	31.0
Sugar Notch borough & MCD (Luzerne)............	989	976	-1.3	953	97.9	0.9	0.2	0.3	0.6	18.4	62.6	18.9	399	80.7	62.4	14.0
Sullivan township (Tioga)..	1,476	1,498	1.5	1,580	99.2	0.0	0.0	0.4	0.4	21.1	61.8	17.0	563	84.4	61.5	20.8
Summerhill borough & MCD (Cambria)............	490	471	-3.9	434	98.8	0.0	0.0	0.0	1.2	16.4	57.4	26.3	201	81.6	60.2	18.9
Summerhill township (Cambria).................	2,465	2,386	-3.2	2,470	99.8	0.0	0.0	0.0	0.2	23.0	59.8	17.3	976	91.0	59.4	19.2
Summerhill township (Crawford)................	1,234	1,219	-1.2	1,142	97.8	0.3	0.0	1.0	1.0	16.4	57.4	26.2	395	90.4	60.5	19.7
Summerville borough & MCD (Jefferson).........	528	522	-1.1	485	97.7	0.0	1.6	0.6	0.0	19.8	62.3	17.9	211	68.7	69.2	11.4
Summit township (Butler) .	4,884	4,773	-2.3	4,855	94.5	5.3	0.0	0.2	0.0	26.2	58.2	15.6	1,797	69.7	54.8	15.9
Summit township (Crawford)................	2,029	1,993	-1.8	1,896	96.5	0.6	0.0	2.2	0.7	19.4	66.1	14.3	837	85.3	51.6	15.5
Summit township (Erie)	6,603	6,786	2.8	6,730	96.7	1.0	0.0	1.6	0.7	20.0	58.1	21.8	2,811	87.9	46.5	24.9
Summit township (Potter) .	188	184	-2.1	202	92.1	0.0	0.0	1.0	6.9	24.3	51.4	24.3	78	88.5	43.6	15.4
Summit township (Somerset)	2,271	2,223	-2.1	2,351	97.4	0.4	0.0	0.9	1.2	19.0	59.3	21.6	828	82.5	71.1	12.8
Summit Hill borough & MCD (Carbon)............	3,034	2,976	-1.9	3,002	92.5	0.0	0.0	2.0	5.6	20.5	65.2	14.4	1,189	82.1	55.8	21.8
Summit Station CDP.........	174	NA	NA	142	100.0	0.0	0.0	0.0	0.0	0.0	16.9	83.1	82	100.0	87.8	12.2
Sunbury city & MCD (Northumberland).........	9,905	9,736	-1.7	9,817	89.5	1.6	0.3	1.7	6.9	24.1	59.0	16.9	4,164	48.6	67.6	8.7
Sunrise Lake CDP............	1,387	NA	NA	1,648	96.8	1.5	0.0	0.0	1.7	23.1	63.7	13.3	510	88.2	37.3	29.4
Sun Valley CDP	2,399	NA	NA	2,112	81.1	7.6	0.0	3.3	8.0	20.8	68.3	11.1	754	87.4	51.6	24.8
Susquehanna township (Cambria)	2,007	1,936	-3.5	1,972	99.3	0.0	0.0	0.6	0.1	22.4	61.5	16.0	826	85.1	60.8	14.0
Susquehanna township (Dauphin)	24,036	24,482	1.9	24,332	62.6	26.1	4.7	2.0	4.6	18.8	63.7	17.4	10,649	69.6	32.4	38.7
Susquehanna township (Juniata)	1,250	1,258	0.6	1,203	95.8	3.9	0.2	0.0	0.0	23.9	54.8	21.4	443	89.2	73.1	7.4
Susquehanna township (Lycoming)	1,000	995	-0.5	972	98.1	0.7	0.0	1.1	0.0	19.6	61.3	19.2	405	86.4	51.1	15.8
Susquehanna Depot borough & MCD (Susquehanna)	1,643	1,572	-4.3	1,523	92.4	1.0	0.0	3.5	3.2	23.2	57.5	19.2	555	56.4	66.7	9.5
Susquehanna Trails CDP..	2,264	NA	NA	2,906	97.3	0.8	0.8	1.1	0.0	32.6	63.0	4.5	912	95.6	49.9	10.1
Sutersville borough & MCD (Westmoreland) ...	605	588	-2.8	587	99.3	0.0	0.3	0.3	0.0	17.4	64.8	17.7	239	79.1	59.0	14.6
Swarthmore borough & MCD (Delaware)	6,194	6,202	0.1	6,198	79.9	4.6	5.3	2.5	7.7	20.6	66.2	13.1	1,888	74.7	8.7	77.8
Swartzville CDP	2,283	NA	NA	2,032	91.9	0.0	0.6	2.7	4.7	25.0	50.9	24.1	858	88.9	38.6	31.9
Swatara township (Dauphin)	23,362	24,474	4.8	23,934	62.7	18.4	4.0	4.5	10.4	22.0	63.1	14.8	8,819	70.7	41.0	25.1
Swatara township (Lebanon)	4,555	4,617	1.4	4,615	90.6	1.6	1.0	0.5	6.4	23.1	65.7	11.2	1,678	80.2	64.8	9.9
Sweden township (Potter).	872	861	-1.3	660	97.0	0.6	0.3	1.2	0.9	19.7	54.1	26.1	269	82.9	50.2	23.0
Sweden Valley CDP.........	223	NA	NA	157	100.0	0.0	0.0	0.0	0.0	24.1	52.9	22.9	57	91.2	49.1	12.3
Swissvale borough & MCD (Allegheny)..........	8,985	8,906	-0.9	8,963	59.4	33.7	2.1	2.4	2.4	15.2	69.3	15.5	4,683	51.4	34.7	35.1
Swoyersville borough & MCD (Luzerne)	5,062	5,000	-1.2	5,038	99.6	0.0	0.2	0.2	0.0	18.4	59.4	22.1	2,122	78.8	44.5	25.9
Sykesville borough & MCD (Jefferson)............	1,157	1,141	-1.4	1,233	100.0	0.0	0.0	0.0	0.0	23.4	60.9	15.7	562	64.9	60.3	8.9
Sylvania borough & MCD (Bradford)	219	217	-0.9	288	99.3	0.7	0.0	0.0	0.0	28.1	62.9	9.0	91	69.2	56.0	19.8
Sylvania township (Potter)	77	75	-2.6	64	84.4	0.0	0.0	0.0	15.6	12.5	65.7	21.9	26	100.0	53.8	7.7
Table Rock CDP	62	NA	NA	43	60.5	0.0	0.0	0.0	39.5	20.9	60.4	18.6	13	69.2	69.2	0.0
Tamaqua borough & MCD (Schuylkill).................	7,107	6,899	-2.9	6,994	94.6	0.5	0.0	0.3	4.7	21.1	61.0	17.9	2,968	60.9	56.2	14.9
Tarentum borough & MCD (Allegheny).................	4,530	4,489	-0.9	4,514	87.7	10.3	0.0	1.9	0.0	21.9	63.4	14.7	2,031	48.1	48.8	18.0
Tatamy borough & MCD (Northampton).............	1,146	1,138	-0.7	1,015	87.4	1.0	8.5	2.2	1.0	25.8	60.3	13.8	345	89.9	43.5	36.5
Taylor township (Blair).....	2,469	2,479	0.4	2,266	94.2	0.8	0.0	1.8	3.3	16.9	60.5	22.6	922	69.6	57.5	11.3
Taylor township (Centre)...	849	843	-0.7	792	97.3	0.0	0.6	0.9	1.1	22.9	65.5	11.6	331	93.1	59.8	18.1
Taylor township (Fulton)....	1,117	1,094	-2.1	1,012	99.0	0.0	0.0	1.0	0.0	22.4	53.6	23.7	401	85.3	65.6	14.0
Taylor borough & MCD (Lackawanna)...............	6,263	6,163	-1.6	6,230	88.7	1.4	0.4	1.4	8.1	21.1	58.9	20.0	2,518	66.7	59.3	14.6
Taylor township (Lawrence).................	1,052	1,024	-2.7	1,115	97.3	1.7	0.0	0.0	1.0	17.4	57.1	25.5	444	74.3	64.9	5.9
Taylorstown CDP	217	NA	NA	200	100.0	0.0	0.0	0.0	0.0	24.5	60.0	15.5	78	89.7	70.5	17.9
Telford borough...............	4,866	4,870	0.1	4,910	76.3	6.8	6.7	2.0	8.2	20.5	61.2	18.5	1,957	56.1	49.7	24.2
Telford borough (Bucks)....	2,207	2,196	-0.5	2,243	83.5	4.2	2.1	2.2	8.0	18.2	57.0	24.7	1,026	45.5	50.9	25.5
Telford borough (Montgomery)	2,659	2,674	0.6	2,667	70.3	9.0	10.6	1.7	8.4	22.3	64.3	13.2	931	67.8	48.3	22.7
Tell township (Huntingdon)	662	647	-2.3	609	98.9	0.7	0.0	0.0	0.5	20.3	60.3	19.4	250	81.6	58.0	11.2
Temple CDP	1,877	NA	NA	1,592	90.2	1.7	0.0	0.3	7.8	27.8	55.2	17.0	748	59.4	52.5	22.1
Templeton CDP	325	NA	NA	331	92.7	0.0	0.0	1.2	6.0	24.8	51.5	23.6	131	76.3	75.6	3.1
Terre Hill borough & MCD (Lancaster)..............	1,295	1,359	4.9	1,384	94.0	0.0	0.4	2.7	2.9	24.9	60.4	14.7	510	79.6	61.2	21.4
Terry township (Bradford) .	992	971	-2.1	1,048	98.8	0.0	0.0	0.2	1.0	25.2	58.6	16.0	396	87.6	65.7	12.4
Texas township (Wayne)...	2,589	2,479	-4.2	2,612	94.1	3.3	0.0	0.3	2.3	25.0	57.9	16.9	923	77.9	54.6	19.0
Tharptown (Uniontown) CDP	498	NA	NA	537	100.0	0.0	0.0	0.0	0.0	21.2	52.1	26.6	227	81.5	70.9	8.8
The Hideout CDP	3,013	NA	NA	3,000	86.1	8.2	0.4	0.0	5.3	14.4	57.6	28.0	1,272	81.5	47.1	34.7
Thompson township (Fulton).......................	1,098	1,084	-1.3	1,203	98.8	0.2	0.0	0.5	0.4	23.7	60.6	15.9	445	80.4	57.5	19.3

1 May be of any race.

Table A. All Places — **Population and Housing**

STATE City, town, township, borough, or CDP (county if applicable)	2010 census total population	2014 estimated population	Percent change 2010-2014	ACS total population estimate 2010-2014	White alone, not Hispanic or Latino	Black alone, not Hispanic or Latino	Asian alone, not Hispanic or Latino	All other races or 2 or more races, not Hispanic or Latino	Hispanic or Latino[1]	Under 18 years old	Age 18 to 64 years old	Age 65 years and older	Total occupied housing units	Percent owner occupied	High school diploma or less	Bachelor's degree or more
	1	2	3	4	5	6	7	8	9	10	11	12	13	14	15	16
PENNSYLVANIA—Con.																
Thompson borough & MCD (Susquehanna)	297	279	-6.1	332	97.0	0.0	0.9	2.1	0.0	27.0	59.4	13.3	132	61.4	56.8	6.8
Thompson township (Susquehanna)	412	401	-2.7	521	96.7	0.0	1.5	0.0	1.7	12.7	64.1	23.2	210	94.3	49.5	13.3
Thompsontown borough & MCD (Juniata)	689	684	-0.7	804	97.1	0.7	0.2	1.5	0.4	20.2	59.9	19.7	342	51.8	62.6	10.5
Thompsonville CDP..........	3,520	NA	NA	3,853	94.6	0.2	0.5	0.5	4.2	22.6	55.0	22.3	1,322	91.3	16.0	59.5
Thornburg borough & MCD (Allegheny)............	455	456	0.2	538	97.2	0.0	1.9	0.6	0.4	21.2	57.9	21.0	196	97.4	9.2	63.8
Thornbury township (Chester)......................	3,263	3,336	2.2	3,310	78.4	9.9	9.1	1.3	1.4	23.5	64.4	12.0	1,111	78.4	9.0	73.9
Thornbury township (Delaware)....................	7,782	7,844	0.8	7,833	77.1	11.5	6.1	1.5	3.8	27.7	61.9	10.5	2,258	92.3	15.4	66.8
Thorndale CDP...............	3,407	NA	NA	3,586	81.2	9.8	6.4	0.9	1.6	15.9	72.3	11.7	1,520	61.1	40.1	34.5
Thornhurst township (Lackawanna)	1,085	1,079	-0.6	1,026	93.3	0.9	0.0	2.9	2.9	19.6	63.4	17.1	398	88.7	43.2	15.8
Three Springs borough & MCD (Huntingdon)	444	436	-1.8	497	100.0	0.0	0.0	0.0	0.0	24.1	52.0	23.5	200	66.0	67.0	5.0
Throop borough & MCD (Lackawanna)...........	4,088	4,049	-1.0	4,077	92.1	3.5	0.0	1.7	2.7	18.4	60.7	20.7	1,825	71.7	42.5	25.7
Tidioute borough & MCD (Warren)..................	688	672	-2.3	812	99.8	0.0	0.0	0.2	0.0	20.4	55.4	24.3	347	66.3	65.7	6.3
Tilden township (Berks)....	3,597	3,586	-0.3	3,600	86.8	7.8	0.4	0.0	5.0	27.0	56.8	16.4	1,232	89.0	59.3	15.8
Timber Hills CDP.............	360	NA	NA	277	100.0	0.0	0.0	0.0	0.0	16.2	50.2	33.6	145	100.0	29.0	42.1
Timblin borough & MCD (Jefferson)................	157	155	-1.3	188	100.0	0.0	0.0	0.0	0.0	38.8	51.7	9.6	55	69.1	89.1	3.6
Tinicum township (Bucks).	3,995	3,969	-0.7	3,993	96.0	0.6	0.4	1.3	1.8	16.8	62.4	20.8	1,630	85.6	31.9	43.9
Tinicum township (Delaware)....................	4,091	4,105	0.3	4,103	94.5	0.2	0.5	1.9	2.8	23.0	63.9	13.3	1,586	63.7	51.6	13.2
Tioga borough & MCD (Tioga).....................	665	666	0.2	653	98.3	0.5	0.3	0.6	0.3	25.5	59.9	14.5	265	72.5	56.2	10.2
Tioga township (Tioga).....	961	967	0.6	973	97.8	0.0	0.9	0.0	1.2	25.2	58.0	16.8	373	71.8	66.0	12.1
Tionesta borough & MCD (Forest)...................	483	463	-4.1	497	95.2	0.0	2.6	0.6	1.6	13.0	51.2	35.6	275	66.2	56.0	17.8
Tionesta township (Forest)	729	703	-3.6	560	92.5	0.0	0.0	0.9	6.6	19.3	50.3	30.5	242	85.5	61.2	14.5
Tipton CDP......................	1,083	NA	NA	847	97.4	0.0	2.6	0.0	0.0	22.7	54.3	23.0	328	88.4	54.3	13.4
Titusville city & MCD (Crawford)	5,601	5,419	-3.2	5,479	94.8	1.4	0.1	2.6	1.2	22.0	58.3	19.5	2,258	45.7	56.5	19.1
Toboyne township (Perry) .	443	440	-0.7	506	97.4	1.2	0.0	1.0	0.0	25.1	51.3	23.5	210	83.8	81.4	3.8
Toby township (Clarion)....	991	972	-1.9	937	97.4	0.1	0.0	2.5	0.0	19.5	64.8	15.7	361	82.8	64.5	16.3
Tobyhanna township (Monroe)....................	8,554	8,438	-1.4	8,504	67.6	8.5	0.6	7.4	15.9	23.9	55.6	20.5	3,123	83.4	44.7	28.6
Todd township (Fulton)	1,527	1,524	-0.2	1,648	90.8	6.0	0.0	0.5	2.7	25.1	58.8	16.2	668	81.4	58.7	15.1
Todd township (Huntingdon)	952	947	-0.5	1,060	96.1	0.9	0.0	0.0	2.9	19.2	61.3	19.4	372	85.8	68.5	6.2
Toftrees CDP...................	2,053	NA	NA	2,786	81.6	0.9	13.3	1.5	2.8	5.4	76.1	18.4	1,392	25.9	14.2	71.1
Topton borough & MCD (Berks)....................	2,068	2,059	-0.4	2,275	97.4	0.0	0.0	0.8	1.7	21.0	60.2	18.8	885	73.9	49.6	20.1
Toughkenamon CDP	1,492	NA	NA	2,002	25.6	0.0	0.0	2.2	72.1	31.0	67.0	1.7	456	45.0	62.5	23.7
Towamencin township (Montgomery)	17,578	18,205	3.6	17,943	79.3	5.7	9.2	2.0	3.9	20.0	61.2	18.7	7,384	71.2	26.7	51.3
Towamensing township (Carbon)...................	4,478	4,455	-0.5	4,462	98.4	0.0	0.0	0.0	1.6	17.3	61.7	21.0	1,824	98.8	40.8	21.2
Towamensing Trails CDP..	2,292	NA	NA	1,675	79.0	0.0	0.0	1.1	19.9	19.1	66.7	14.4	728	77.9	26.1	29.9
Towanda borough & MCD (Bradford)	2,919	2,841	-2.7	2,899	91.6	0.0	4.2	0.3	3.9	24.2	62.4	13.3	1,172	58.1	44.5	31.4
Towanda township (Bradford)	1,149	1,128	-1.8	1,097	95.7	0.0	0.0	2.8	1.5	15.2	65.3	19.5	421	82.2	60.1	21.9
Tower City borough & MCD (Schuylkill)	1,346	1,320	-1.9	1,278	93.3	0.0	0.0	6.5	0.0	20.9	59.5	19.7	528	75.2	63.6	10.6
Townville borough & MCD (Crawford)	329	320	-2.7	385	97.1	0.0	0.8	2.1	0.0	20.6	55.8	23.6	163	73.0	54.6	14.1
Trafford borough	3,224	3,162	-1.9	3,339	97.4	1.5	0.5	0.6	0.0	16.9	62.0	21.3	1,459	70.3	46.7	24.7
Trafford borough (Allegheny)..................	111	111	0.0	256	91.8	0.0	0.0	8.2	0.0	16.0	76.9	7.0	79	25.3	73.4	0.0
Trafford borough (Westmoreland)	3,113	3,051	-2.0	3,083	97.9	1.6	0.5	0.0	0.0	16.9	60.5	22.5	1,380	72.8	45.2	26.2
Trainer borough & MCD (Delaware)................	1,828	1,846	1.0	1,752	76.1	18.1	0.6	0.9	4.3	31.0	55.7	13.5	588	72.6	62.4	8.5
Trappe borough & MCD (Montgomery)	3,509	3,556	1.3	3,533	81.4	4.6	6.8	3.3	3.8	27.6	60.7	11.7	1,414	79.7	30.8	48.0
Treasure Lake CDP	3,861	NA	NA	3,646	95.2	0.0	0.2	0.2	4.4	23.2	63.9	12.8	1,252	97.0	30.3	41.3
Tredyffrin township (Chester)...................	29,334	29,545	0.7	29,455	82.3	1.8	12.2	2.1	1.7	23.8	60.4	15.7	12,023	76.9	9.9	77.4
Tremont borough & MCD (Schuylkill)...............	1,752	1,722	-1.7	1,710	97.3	0.0	1.5	0.0	1.2	19.7	54.5	25.8	608	74.3	73.7	6.7
Tremont township (Schuylkill)................	280	275	-1.8	287	99.7	0.3	0.0	0.0	0.0	25.4	55.4	19.2	107	86.9	75.7	2.8
Trescow CDP..................	880	NA	NA	803	95.5	1.0	0.0	0.5	3.0	17.3	54.2	28.5	368	75.8	64.8	10.9
Trevorton CDP................	1,834	NA	NA	1,669	95.0	0.2	3.2	0.0	1.6	17.0	63.4	19.7	759	78.9	64.8	16.3
Trevose CDP...................	3,550	NA	NA	3,062	91.7	0.1	0.0	5.7	2.5	22.6	62.0	15.5	1,114	82.4	43.7	21.4
Trexlertown CDP.............	1,988	NA	NA	1,984	80.4	0.5	12.1	1.3	5.6	22.4	57.3	20.3	849	41.9	35.6	42.5
Triumph township (Warren)..................	316	307	-2.8	280	91.4	0.4	0.0	8.2	0.0	22.6	58.8	18.6	130	92.3	71.5	3.8
Trooper CDP...................	5,744	NA	NA	5,868	85.0	2.7	5.5	1.1	5.8	27.4	61.2	11.4	1,919	90.3	33.4	37.2
Troutville borough & MCD (Clearfield)	240	237	-1.3	184	100.0	0.0	0.0	0.0	0.0	14.7	65.3	20.1	69	82.6	56.5	15.9
Troxelville CDP...............	221	NA	NA	275	93.8	0.0	0.0	0.0	6.2	35.3	56.4	8.4	81	85.2	55.6	25.9
Troy borough & MCD (Bradford)	1,320	1,283	-2.8	1,407	97.7	0.1	1.0	1.1	0.2	19.5	58.9	21.4	514	52.3	58.6	17.9
Troy township (Bradford)...	1,675	1,663	-0.7	1,735	96.3	0.2	0.9	0.7	1.9	18.7	61.3	20.0	720	85.1	52.6	21.1

1 May be of any race.

Table A. All Places — **Population and Housing**

STATE City, town, township, borough, or CDP (county if applicable)	2010 census total population	2014 estimated population	Percent change 2010-2014	ACS total population estimate 2010-2014	White alone, not Hispanic or Latino	Black alone, not Hispanic or Latino	Asian alone, not Hispanic or Latino	All other races or 2 or more races, not Hispanic or Latino	Hispanic or Latino[1]	Under 18 years old	Age 18 to 64 years old	Age 65 years and older	Total occupied housing units	Percent owner occupied	High school diploma or less	Bachelor's degree or more
	1	2	3	4	5	6	7	8	9	10	11	12	13	14	15	16
PENNSYLVANIA—Con.																
Troy township (Crawford)..	1,235	1,205	-2.4	1,122	100.0	0.0	0.0	0.0	0.0	17.5	65.8	16.8	438	82.2	63.9	18.0
Trucksville CDP	2,152	NA	NA	2,023	95.1	2.0	0.0	0.7	2.2	17.1	65.8	17.0	850	77.3	32.1	33.2
Trumbauersville borough & MCD (Bucks)	974	962	-1.2	1,081	83.3	1.6	0.4	0.0	14.7	34.2	58.2	7.7	373	68.1	55.2	31.4
Tullytown borough & MCD (Bucks)	1,872	1,862	-0.5	1,781	94.0	1.2	1.2	2.2	1.3	18.9	61.9	19.1	704	65.3	63.8	13.4
Tulpehocken township (Berks)	3,278	3,280	0.1	3,278	88.0	1.8	0.5	2.1	7.6	25.8	61.1	13.2	981	81.8	68.6	12.0
Tunkhannock township (Monroe)	6,789	6,695	-1.4	6,758	58.1	16.5	0.0	0.0	25.3	30.8	60.4	8.8	1,926	90.0	49.0	19.5
Tunkhannock borough & MCD (Wyoming)...........	1,836	1,805	-1.7	2,041	92.2	3.3	2.1	0.8	1.7	20.7	59.0	20.4	829	52.8	51.6	31.5
Tunkhannock township (Wyoming)	4,282	4,343	1.4	4,314	96.5	0.7	0.4	1.9	0.4	18.3	63.1	18.6	1,631	82.2	54.1	16.4
Tunnelhill borough	363	356	-1.9	362	97.8	0.0	0.3	1.9	0.0	18.5	65.2	16.3	148	84.5	70.9	9.5
Tunnelhill borough (Blair)..	118	117	-0.8	117	93.2	0.0	0.9	6.0	0.0	8.5	74.2	17.1	48	95.8	77.1	6.3
Tunnelhill borough (Cambria)	245	239	-2.4	245	100.0	0.0	0.0	0.0	0.0	23.2	60.8	15.9	100	79.0	68.0	11.0
Turbett township (Juniata)	981	994	1.3	1,056	99.4	0.0	0.2	0.4	0.0	25.8	60.0	14.3	376	89.9	68.1	10.9
Turbot township (Northumberland).........	1,806	1,803	-0.2	1,735	96.5	0.5	0.0	0.1	3.0	22.4	50.8	26.7	705	93.5	55.2	22.7
Turbotville borough & MCD (Northumberland)	705	692	-1.8	694	100.0	0.0	0.0	0.0	0.0	28.8	60.3	10.8	275	70.9	52.4	22.5
Turtle Creek borough & MCD (Allegheny)...........	5,349	5,301	-0.9	5,335	78.8	17.6	0.0	0.9	2.7	22.7	58.6	18.7	2,465	38.0	52.7	12.0
Tuscarora township (Bradford)	1,131	1,127	-0.4	1,125	99.4	0.3	0.0	0.0	0.4	16.7	65.0	18.4	431	80.7	65.4	7.2
Tuscarora township (Juniata)	1,237	1,239	0.2	1,124	100.0	0.0	0.0	0.0	0.0	23.0	59.4	17.6	476	74.8	79.4	4.0
Tuscarora township (Perry)	1,191	1,184	-0.6	1,226	97.6	1.0	0.0	0.2	1.1	24.2	59.1	16.5	448	87.3	61.8	17.2
Tuscarora CDP	980	NA	NA	964	99.1	0.0	0.0	0.0	0.9	22.9	52.2	24.8	381	68.2	61.4	4.5
Twilight borough & MCD (Washington)................	233	231	-0.9	265	98.9	1.1	0.0	0.0	0.0	30.9	53.1	15.8	91	76.9	42.9	19.8
Tyler Run CDP	1,901	NA	NA	1,472	96.3	2.0	0.0	1.0	0.7	12.7	46.5	41.0	754	84.2	31.4	40.2
Tylersburg CDP	196	NA	NA	90	100.0	0.0	0.0	0.0	0.0	4.4	83.4	12.2	51	100.0	62.7	0.0
Tyrone township (Adams)..	2,298	2,289	-0.4	2,069	93.5	0.5	0.5	1.3	4.3	20.0	66.8	13.2	804	88.2	60.4	11.7
Tyrone borough & MCD (Blair)	5,477	5,380	-1.8	5,433	97.5	0.0	0.0	0.2	2.3	21.0	60.5	18.5	2,131	58.0	55.7	21.4
Tyrone township (Blair)....	1,885	1,893	0.4	1,670	93.2	0.3	0.0	2.3	4.1	25.9	55.8	18.3	619	89.3	57.0	23.3
Tyrone township (Perry)....	2,119	2,108	-0.5	2,098	96.5	2.7	0.0	0.0	0.8	30.9	52.2	16.9	728	75.1	69.8	8.9
Ulster township (Bradford)	1,337	1,321	-1.2	1,388	96.9	0.0	0.0	1.3	1.8	23.5	60.5	15.8	510	68.4	59.8	15.3
Ulysses borough & MCD (Potter)......................	621	608	-2.1	639	98.6	0.6	0.0	0.8	0.0	20.2	57.2	22.7	264	71.2	67.4	11.0
Ulysses township (Potter).	635	633	-0.3	739	98.8	0.0	0.1	1.1	0.0	15.9	56.9	27.1	258	79.1	72.5	10.1
Union township (Adams) ..	3,148	3,165	0.5	3,164	98.5	0.0	0.0	0.0	1.5	22.3	60.7	17.1	1,129	89.7	53.6	20.1
Union township (Berks)	3,503	3,514	0.3	3,514	91.3	5.2	0.0	0.6	2.9	17.4	62.6	20.0	1,420	87.2	52.9	17.4
Union township (Centre)...	1,390	1,405	1.1	1,578	99.1	0.1	0.0	0.6	0.1	20.4	66.7	12.8	589	91.2	54.7	21.6
Union township (Clearfield)	892	893	0.1	857	100.0	0.0	0.0	0.0	0.0	11.9	72.7	15.5	371	91.1	61.7	8.6
Union township (Crawford)	1,010	988	-2.2	958	95.0	1.0	0.0	2.0	2.0	23.2	56.6	20.1	409	86.1	56.2	23.0
Union township (Erie)	1,655	1,630	-1.5	1,655	96.9	0.6	0.1	1.0	1.5	20.1	62.2	17.6	610	90.0	57.7	18.7
Union township (Fulton)....	706	705	-0.1	652	98.2	0.5	0.0	1.4	0.0	19.1	60.9	20.1	266	90.6	59.0	15.8
Union township (Huntingdon)	1,028	1,023	-0.5	1,116	98.1	0.4	1.3	0.3	0.0	21.9	58.9	19.2	425	92.2	69.4	7.8
Union township (Jefferson)...................	855	843	-1.4	928	98.2	0.0	0.9	0.6	0.3	23.1	58.9	17.9	374	82.4	57.2	9.4
Union township (Lawrence)...................	5,190	5,060	-2.5	5,106	93.6	4.2	0.7	0.4	1.1	19.4	57.4	23.2	2,199	79.0	59.3	11.8
Union township (Lebanon)	3,098	3,114	0.5	3,104	96.0	0.0	1.0	1.4	1.7	20.4	65.3	14.3	1,243	75.8	65.2	15.2
Union township (Luzerne).	2,041	2,033	-0.4	2,085	98.8	0.5	0.0	0.2	0.4	19.4	62.4	18.3	805	90.8	52.4	18.0
Union township (Mifflin)	3,460	3,454	-0.2	3,456	97.9	0.5	0.3	0.5	0.8	28.4	47.0	24.5	1,266	70.4	65.0	14.6
Union township (Schuylkill)...................	1,273	1,248	-2.0	1,339	95.7	0.0	0.0	0.7	3.6	18.1	59.1	22.7	567	93.8	55.0	19.6
Union township (Snyder) ..	1,522	1,531	0.6	1,547	99.7	0.0	0.0	0.0	0.3	25.9	60.0	14.0	496	80.6	72.4	9.7
Union township (Tioga)....	1,005	1,013	0.8	896	97.4	0.0	0.3	1.0	1.2	21.1	61.1	17.9	351	86.0	54.1	13.7
Union township (Union)	1,594	1,601	0.4	1,490	90.6	7.2	0.0	0.3	1.9	18.7	61.3	20.3	616	85.4	58.1	24.0
Union township (Washington)................	5,700	5,729	0.5	5,730	98.4	0.0	0.0	0.5	1.0	15.3	59.0	25.7	2,628	89.0	60.3	14.2
Union City borough & MCD (Erie)	3,320	3,239	-2.4	3,271	96.7	0.6	0.7	1.1	0.9	25.9	58.2	16.1	1,241	63.6	66.4	13.8
Union Dale borough & MCD (Susquehanna)	264	248	-6.1	276	99.6	0.0	0.0	0.0	0.4	12.3	65.8	21.7	142	87.3	60.6	11.3
Union Deposit CDP	407	NA	NA	429	72.0	2.1	5.6	15.6	4.7	13.1	79.5	7.5	205	35.6	34.1	38.0
Uniontown city & MCD (Fayette)	10,372	10,064	-3.0	10,203	78.0	15.1	0.2	5.7	1.1	18.9	63.3	17.7	4,339	41.4	61.8	15.7
Unionville CDP	962	NA	NA	937	98.4	0.0	0.0	0.0	1.6	19.0	59.9	21.2	463	97.6	52.1	10.8
Unionville borough & MCD (Centre)....................	291	281	-3.4	258	98.1	1.9	0.0	0.0	0.0	20.6	68.4	10.9	113	76.1	52.2	27.4
Unity township (Westmoreland)	22,606	22,403	-0.9	22,527	96.1	1.3	0.5	1.2	1.0	19.3	62.7	17.9	8,546	81.4	39.5	31.4
University of Pittsburgh Johnstown CDP	1,572	NA	NA	1,396	92.0	1.9	1.6	2.6	2.0	0.0	100.0	0.0	0	0.0	0.0	0.0
Upland borough & MCD (Delaware).................	3,239	3,252	0.4	3,248	47.9	39.9	0.0	0.9	11.3	32.0	57.2	10.8	1,125	42.7	70.1	10.8
Upper Allen township (Cumberland)	18,056	19,193	6.3	18,516	90.1	3.2	2.7	2.8	1.2	18.3	64.4	17.5	6,865	72.9	32.0	45.0
Upper Augusta township (Northumberland)	2,588	2,582	-0.2	2,584	94.2	0.6	1.1	0.7	3.4	17.9	63.6	18.3	1,059	91.3	56.5	21.5
Upper Bern township (Berks)	1,736	1,737	0.1	1,488	98.3	0.0	0.0	0.7	1.1	16.6	64.1	19.2	668	84.7	68.3	9.1

1 May be of any race.

Table A. All Places — Population and Housing

STATE City, town, township, borough, or CDP (county if applicable)	2010 census total population	2014 estimated population	Percent change 2010-2014	ACS total population estimate 2010-2014	White alone, not Hispanic or Latino	Black alone, not Hispanic or Latino	Asian alone, not Hispanic or Latino	All other races or 2 or more races, not Hispanic or Latino	Hispanic or Latino[1]	Under 18 years old	Age 18 to 64 years old	Age 65 years and older	Total occupied housing units	Percent owner occupied	High school diploma or less	Bachelor's degree or more
	1	2	3	4	5	6	7	8	9	10	11	12	13	14	15	16
PENNSYLVANIA—Con.																
Upper Burrell township (Westmoreland)	2,326	2,285	-1.8	2,260	96.6	3.1	0.0	0.0	0.2	18.8	66.6	14.8	865	88.7	44.7	26.4
Upper Chichester township (Delaware)	16,739	16,987	1.5	16,867	78.6	12.7	2.4	2.3	4.0	18.3	65.5	16.2	6,719	71.5	44.4	25.6
Upper Darby township (Delaware)	82,795	82,927	0.2	82,804	51.6	28.5	11.9	2.6	5.4	24.3	65.0	10.8	30,455	59.1	40.0	29.8
Upper Dublin township (Montgomery)	25,569	26,218	2.5	26,042	83.2	5.9	7.3	1.4	2.1	24.4	58.9	16.7	9,513	87.8	14.6	67.9
Upper Exeter CDP	707	NA	NA	640	96.9	0.0	0.0	3.1	0.0	18.5	74.3	7.3	229	86.9	38.0	21.8
Upper Fairfield township (Lycoming)	1,818	1,820	0.1	1,763	97.2	0.8	0.4	0.7	0.9	17.7	63.6	18.7	726	90.8	47.7	27.3
Upper Frankford township (Cumberland)	2,005	2,033	1.4	2,072	99.3	0.0	0.2	0.0	0.4	24.1	59.8	16.1	879	83.6	67.6	8.1
Upper Frederick township (Montgomery)	3,523	3,563	1.1	3,550	93.9	2.1	1.3	1.4	1.4	19.8	60.9	19.4	1,348	83.0	39.2	37.1
Upper Gwynedd township (Montgomery)	15,552	15,944	2.5	15,784	80.4	2.8	13.2	1.0	2.6	20.0	59.5	20.5	6,317	73.8	20.2	56.1
Upper Hanover township (Montgomery)	6,464	7,124	10.2	6,750	98.2	1.0	0.1	0.4	0.3	25.1	60.1	14.7	2,514	91.4	32.9	31.8
Upper Leacock township (Lancaster)	8,708	8,840	1.5	8,811	88.4	1.7	2.0	1.5	6.4	32.3	54.7	13.1	2,855	63.4	57.7	22.4
Upper Macungie township (Lehigh)	20,067	22,404	11.6	21,461	77.6	2.8	10.8	3.2	5.6	26.0	61.4	12.6	7,844	82.4	25.5	52.5
Upper Mahanoy township (Northumberland)	796	787	-1.1	622	94.1	0.0	0.0	5.9	0.0	25.2	56.6	18.3	254	79.1	64.6	23.2
Upper Mahantongo township (Schuylkill)	655	640	-2.3	709	98.3	0.8	0.0	0.0	0.8	23.5	59.0	17.5	271	78.2	69.0	5.2
Upper Makefield township (Bucks)	8,190	8,231	0.5	8,222	87.4	0.8	6.2	1.8	3.8	22.8	61.9	15.5	2,841	94.5	10.5	73.5
Upper Merion township (Montgomery)	28,388	28,638	0.9	28,569	71.0	4.8	17.1	2.6	4.5	20.6	62.8	16.6	11,988	66.2	22.3	58.9
Upper Mifflin township (Cumberland)	1,304	1,335	2.4	1,255	95.5	0.0	0.0	3.0	1.4	23.1	64.2	12.7	475	82.7	70.7	10.7
Upper Milford township (Lehigh)	7,292	7,522	3.2	7,417	94.9	0.0	1.7	0.8	2.6	21.4	64.6	14.0	2,743	88.4	36.9	37.1
Upper Moreland township (Montgomery)	24,015	24,274	1.1	24,167	83.5	6.0	3.9	2.7	3.9	22.0	61.3	16.5	9,602	63.8	36.0	37.0
Upper Mount Bethel township (Northampton)	6,706	6,835	1.9	6,801	90.0	1.4	2.7	1.4	4.5	18.7	61.8	19.5	2,658	86.4	48.4	23.7
Upper Nazareth township (Northampton)	6,231	6,616	6.2	6,390	93.7	0.8	0.2	0.6	4.7	22.7	56.5	20.6	2,058	89.9	31.7	34.3
Upper Oxford township (Chester)	2,484	2,505	0.8	2,493	94.3	1.7	0.2	0.4	3.4	32.7	55.0	12.4	788	83.1	42.1	34.6
Upper Paxton township (Dauphin)	4,161	4,163	0.0	4,152	97.8	1.1	0.0	0.0	1.1	16.5	59.2	24.3	1,694	89.5	62.0	12.3
Upper Pottsgrove township (Montgomery)	5,315	5,421	2.0	5,382	90.0	5.1	0.8	0.9	3.2	24.1	64.8	11.1	1,831	90.3	38.1	37.5
Upper Providence township (Delaware)	10,142	10,332	1.9	10,246	85.7	3.5	6.9	2.0	1.9	20.2	64.4	15.4	3,898	71.4	16.3	60.7
Upper Providence township (Montgomery)	21,219	22,667	6.8	21,802	85.7	2.6	6.7	2.2	2.8	28.3	60.9	10.7	7,441	87.7	18.5	61.3
Upper St. Clair CDP & township (Allegheny)	19,229	19,335	0.6	19,303	89.2	0.2	6.3	1.9	2.3	26.6	56.6	16.7	6,973	90.9	10.9	72.1
Upper Salford township (Montgomery)	3,299	3,373	2.2	3,347	98.0	0.8	0.5	0.0	0.7	27.0	56.1	17.0	1,090	86.6	33.7	39.7
Upper Saucon township (Lehigh)	14,808	15,878	7.2	15,354	89.4	0.5	3.6	2.4	4.1	24.0	62.4	13.8	4,985	91.6	27.9	48.5
Upper Southampton township (Bucks)	15,152	15,152	0.0	15,171	93.9	0.4	2.5	0.2	3.0	17.4	59.1	23.7	5,767	84.2	32.0	36.0
Upper Tulpehocken township (Berks)	1,573	1,567	-0.4	1,615	97.1	0.1	0.3	0.0	2.5	23.2	62.6	14.2	583	80.1	59.0	17.2
Upper Turkeyfoot township (Somerset)	1,119	1,090	-2.6	1,214	99.1	0.0	0.0	0.9	0.0	19.3	57.9	22.7	471	88.1	61.8	10.6
Upper Tyrone township (Fayette)	2,056	2,013	-2.1	2,238	95.2	0.8	0.0	4.0	0.0	17.4	58.2	24.4	771	84.8	68.9	9.2
Upper Uwchlan township (Chester)	11,227	11,540	2.8	11,419	77.3	0.3	18.3	2.3	1.7	32.4	61.2	6.3	3,660	93.2	8.2	74.4
Upper Yoder township (Cambria)	5,449	5,296	-2.8	5,367	97.3	0.9	0.9	0.7	0.3	15.4	59.0	25.6	2,215	77.1	39.4	36.9
Ursina borough & MCD (Somerset)	225	213	-5.3	293	100.0	0.0	0.0	0.0	0.0	25.2	51.5	23.2	114	78.1	74.6	11.4
Utica borough & MCD (Venango)	189	185	-2.1	156	93.6	0.0	0.0	5.8	0.6	23.1	62.3	14.7	60	71.7	63.3	1.7
Uwchlan township (Chester)	18,088	18,618	2.9	18,325	89.2	3.4	4.6	1.2	1.6	25.6	64.2	10.2	6,629	79.6	17.3	61.6
Valencia borough & MCD (Butler)	551	574	4.2	617	99.7	0.0	0.0	0.0	0.3	7.1	30.5	62.2	322	21.4	33.9	44.1
Valley township (Armstrong)	656	652	-0.6	668	96.6	0.0	0.0	3.1	0.3	16.7	67.8	15.4	259	86.5	51.0	18.9
Valley township (Chester)	6,794	7,488	10.2	7,163	67.4	23.0	0.2	3.6	5.8	23.7	59.7	16.7	2,669	83.4	35.2	33.6
Valley township (Montour)	2,158	2,197	1.8	2,161	97.1	0.0	1.4	1.0	0.4	20.5	59.4	20.1	839	91.1	38.1	33.8
Valley Groen CDP	3,429	NA	NA	3,761	83.7	2.8	1.6	4.2	7.7	26.3	68.6	5.3	1,367	84.1	45.4	35.4
Valley-Hi borough & MCD (Fulton)	15	15	0.0	6	100.0	0.0	0.0	0.0	0.0	0.0	100.0	0.0	6	100.0	100.0	0.0
Valley View CDP (Schuylkill)	1,683	NA	NA	1,582	95.3	0.0	0.4	3.7	0.6	15.6	59.2	25.1	681	66.1	72.8	15.0
Valley View CDP (York)	2,817	NA	NA	2,670	82.9	1.5	3.7	0.5	11.4	21.5	59.2	19.2	1,138	89.5	41.9	41.8
Vanderbilt borough & MCD (Fayette)	476	468	-1.7	443	98.6	0.2	0.0	1.1	0.0	16.3	59.4	24.4	185	65.9	69.7	15.7
Vandergrift borough & MCD (Westmoreland)	5,205	5,067	-2.7	5,142	88.2	8.8	0.0	2.5	0.6	24.9	56.8	18.3	2,250	59.2	51.7	11.2

1 May be of any race.

Table A. All Places — **Population and Housing**

STATE City, town, township, borough, or CDP (county if applicable)	2010 census total population	2014 estimated population	Percent change 2010-2014	ACS total population estimate 2010-2014	White alone, not Hispanic or Latino	Black alone, not Hispanic or Latino	Asian alone, not Hispanic or Latino	All other races or 2 or more races, not Hispanic or Latino	Hispanic or Latino[1]	Under 18 years old	Age 18 to 64 years old	Age 65 years and older	Total occupied housing units	Percent owner occupied	High school diploma or less	Bachelor's degree or more
	1	2	3	4	5	6	7	8	9	10	11	12	13	14	15	16
PENNSYLVANIA—Con.																
Vandling borough & MCD (Lackawanna)	751	739	-1.6	717	95.4	1.1	0.0	1.0	2.5	20.9	56.8	22.3	291	75.6	56.0	24.4
Vanport township (Beaver)	1,321	1,304	-1.3	1,430	96.0	2.6	0.0	0.3	1.1	12.4	49.5	38.1	753	30.8	59.2	15.8
Van Voorhis CDP	166	NA	NA	139	100.0	0.0	0.0	0.0	0.0	0.0	84.8	15.1	87	85.1	39.1	16.1
Venango township (Butler)	868	853	-1.7	891	97.0	0.3	0.0	2.7	0.0	22.5	59.6	18.0	350	82.9	60.0	11.1
Venango borough & MCD (Crawford)	239	243	1.7	205	99.0	0.0	0.0	1.0	0.0	15.6	60.1	24.4	91	80.2	59.3	19.8
Venango township (Crawford)	997	990	-0.7	1,041	96.3	2.8	0.0	0.6	0.3	22.2	65.1	12.8	392	83.4	51.8	28.3
Venango township (Erie)	2,297	2,299	0.1	2,235	98.3	0.2	0.0	1.4	0.0	21.8	64.6	13.6	815	92.4	49.8	22.6
Vernon township (Crawford)	5,630	5,526	-1.8	5,568	94.0	1.5	1.3	0.6	2.6	17.9	59.3	22.8	2,472	79.0	50.8	22.8
Verona borough & MCD (Allegheny)	2,474	2,455	-0.8	2,502	87.6	7.7	0.0	1.8	2.9	23.0	63.2	13.9	1,146	39.9	52.6	14.8
Versailles borough & MCD (Allegheny)	1,515	1,504	-0.7	1,634	91.6	5.1	1.1	2.0	0.3	18.5	59.5	22.0	784	48.3	55.6	12.8
Vicksburg CDP	261	NA	NA	233	89.3	0.0	10.7	0.0	0.0	13.8	46.3	39.9	108	100.0	50.9	40.7
Victory township (Venango)	410	398	-2.9	294	98.6	0.0	0.0	0.3	1.0	11.6	68.6	19.7	142	90.8	64.8	7.7
Village Green-Green Ridge CDP	7,822	NA	NA	7,804	99.4	0.1	0.0	0.5	0.0	23.6	58.3	18.1	2,914	83.8	49.3	20.9
Village Shires CDP	3,949	NA	NA	4,069	95.6	1.2	2.6	0.3	0.3	24.1	53.3	22.6	1,744	65.7	22.8	45.9
Vinco CDP	1,305	NA	NA	1,175	99.8	0.1	0.0	0.0	0.1	16.3	64.2	19.7	508	90.7	46.3	21.1
Vintondale borough & MCD (Cambria)	414	396	-4.3	410	93.9	0.0	0.0	0.0	6.1	16.3	66.7	16.8	180	80.6	66.1	7.2
Virginville CDP	309	NA	NA	206	94.7	0.0	0.0	0.0	5.3	12.1	57.8	30.1	101	100.0	71.3	18.8
Volant borough & MCD (Lawrence)	168	165	-1.8	115	96.5	3.5	0.0	0.0	0.0	19.1	64.3	16.5	47	72.3	42.6	29.8
Vowinckel CDP	139	NA	NA	141	100.0	0.0	0.0	0.0	0.0	29.8	56.7	13.5	62	79.0	100.0	0.0
Wagner CDP	128	NA	NA	226	96.5	0.0	0.0	3.5	0.0	24.3	61.5	14.2	70	91.4	90.0	5.7
Wakefield CDP	609	NA	NA	757	100.0	0.0	0.0	0.0	0.0	34.1	56.4	9.5	209	67.9	81.8	8.1
Walker township (Centre)	4,433	4,548	2.6	4,509	95.4	0.0	0.0	0.2	4.4	25.5	62.5	11.9	1,737	87.0	47.5	25.2
Walker township (Huntingdon)	1,947	1,931	-0.8	2,187	98.5	0.0	0.4	0.5	0.6	23.4	58.3	18.2	847	88.7	51.0	28.3
Walker township (Juniata)	2,735	2,762	1.0	2,761	98.6	0.0	0.0	0.2	1.2	24.7	60.1	15.1	1,010	86.5	74.6	12.5
Walker township (Schuylkill)	1,054	1,034	-1.9	1,128	95.9	0.0	0.0	1.2	2.8	22.1	62.5	15.5	422	73.5	47.9	12.8
Wall borough & MCD (Allegheny)	580	575	-0.9	744	81.5	12.1	0.0	2.3	4.2	16.8	72.6	10.5	300	67.3	46.0	9.0
Wallace township (Chester)	3,458	3,686	6.6	3,581	93.3	3.6	1.4	0.0	1.7	31.0	59.3	9.9	1,127	89.5	18.5	58.6
Wallaceton borough & MCD (Clearfield)	313	312	-0.3	336	99.7	0.0	0.0	0.3	0.0	17.6	65.8	16.7	142	88.0	74.6	7.7
Wallenpaupack Lake Estates CDP	1,279	NA	NA	1,444	97.9	0.0	2.1	0.0	0.0	29.9	44.3	25.8	522	90.6	39.5	19.5
Waller CDP	48	NA	NA	105	100.0	0.0	0.0	0.0	0.0	8.6	72.4	19.0	41	92.7	65.9	4.9
Walnutport borough & MCD (Northampton)	2,070	2,063	-0.3	2,050	90.0	0.7	0.3	4.0	5.1	20.0	63.1	16.9	783	78.4	53.5	15.6
Walnuttown CDP	484	NA	NA	370	100.0	0.0	0.0	0.0	0.0	3.8	82.5	13.8	153	77.1	73.2	17.6
Wampum borough & MCD (Lawrence)	717	694	-3.2	657	97.7	0.6	0.0	1.7	0.0	16.4	62.9	20.7	275	64.7	68.0	9.5
Wanamie CDP	612	NA	NA	700	98.6	0.0	0.0	1.4	0.0	19.0	66.9	14.0	271	81.9	57.6	9.6
Ward township (Tioga)	166	180	8.4	138	92.8	0.0	2.9	2.9	1.4	13.7	62.3	23.9	56	91.1	64.3	16.1
Warminster township (Bucks)	32,682	32,659	-0.1	32,716	85.9	1.3	1.7	1.2	10.0	20.3	54.4	25.1	12,497	69.0	45.6	27.2
Warminster Heights CDP	4,124	NA	NA	4,335	57.5	6.6	0.3	2.8	32.8	27.6	58.7	13.6	1,537	24.6	71.9	6.7
Warren township (Bradford)	959	940	-2.0	1,138	96.7	0.0	0.4	3.0	0.0	25.8	53.9	20.3	420	77.1	57.4	16.0
Warren township (Franklin)	367	375	2.2	289	96.2	0.0	0.0	3.8	0.0	21.5	65.7	12.8	115	84.3	58.3	20.0
Warren city & MCD (Warren)	9,710	9,410	-3.1	9,543	96.9	1.3	0.4	0.4	1.1	22.5	59.6	18.0	4,254	58.4	42.9	26.6
Warrington township (Bucks)	23,418	23,743	1.4	23,541	84.8	2.3	7.8	1.7	3.4	27.0	59.2	13.9	8,140	82.8	24.7	53.3
Warrington township (York)	4,521	4,577	1.2	4,550	97.7	0.0	1.3	0.2	0.7	16.1	65.6	18.2	1,810	90.7	54.6	14.0
Warrior Run borough & MCD (Luzerne)	584	584	0.0	533	98.1	0.0	1.3	0.6	0.0	17.3	68.5	14.3	222	71.6	52.7	12.6
Warriors Mark township (Huntingdon)	1,796	1,806	0.6	1,721	96.9	0.6	0.6	1.9	0.0	20.3	63.5	16.3	722	83.8	52.4	22.4
Warsaw township (Jefferson)	1,424	1,405	-1.3	1,295	98.0	0.0	0.0	0.8	1.2	24.2	57.5	18.2	491	81.7	68.2	7.1
Warwick township (Bucks)	14,437	14,694	1.8	14,579	92.1	0.1	5.0	1.0	1.8	24.7	61.4	13.8	5,157	94.6	20.9	53.1
Warwick township (Chester)	2,507	2,541	1.4	2,516	96.8	0.0	1.5	1.0	0.7	20.6	63.1	16.4	992	85.5	33.3	39.8
Warwick township (Lancaster)	17,778	17,945	0.9	17,855	94.7	1.9	0.6	0.8	1.9	24.7	60.4	14.8	6,557	77.7	42.2	35.5
Washington township (Armstrong)	923	948	2.7	933	98.0	0.0	0.0	2.0	0.0	23.2	55.3	21.7	353	91.2	60.6	12.5
Washington township (Berks)	3,817	3,962	3.8	3,906	94.1	3.2	0.0	1.4	1.3	25.7	57.5	16.7	1,320	87.0	53.2	18.9
Washington township (Butler)	1,297	1,267	-2.3	1,295	98.1	0.0	0.0	1.8	0.0	19.0	62.1	18.9	546	80.4	65.4	7.9
Washington township (Cambria)	875	875	0.0	1,074	99.3	0.0	0.0	0.7	0.0	22.6	61.5	16.0	397	90.9	56.4	16.1
Washington township (Clarion)	1,888	1,845	-2.3	1,939	98.3	0.0	0.0	1.2	0.5	30.9	53.7	15.4	683	82.1	62.4	17.1
Washington township (Dauphin)	2,268	2,264	-0.2	2,033	96.3	0.5	0.7	1.3	1.2	25.3	54.3	20.3	800	87.3	52.1	16.8
Washington township (Erie)	4,432	4,524	2.1	4,467	94.4	0.0	0.0	1.0	4.6	28.2	61.7	10.1	1,574	88.1	27.8	45.2

1 May be of any race.

Table A. All Places — **Population and Housing**

STATE City, town, township, borough, or CDP (county if applicable)	2010 census total population	2014 estimated population	Percent change 2010-2014	ACS total population estimate 2010-2014	White alone, not Hispanic or Latino	Black alone, not Hispanic or Latino	Asian alone, not Hispanic or Latino	All other races or 2 or more races, not Hispanic or Latino	Hispanic or Latino[1]	Under 18 years old	Age 18 to 64 years old	Age 65 years and older	Total occupied housing units	Percent owner occupied	High school diploma or less	Bachelor's degree or more
	1	2	3	4	5	6	7	8	9	10	11	12	13	14	15	16
PENNSYLVANIA—Con.																
Washington township (Fayette)	3,901	3,790	-2.8	3,847	97.3	1.4	0.0	0.9	0.4	16.8	59.9	23.4	1,624	72.7	50.6	15.4
Washington township (Franklin)	14,009	14,454	3.2	14,270	93.2	1.5	2.4	0.7	2.3	22.1	59.1	18.7	5,731	80.9	49.7	25.2
Washington township (Greene)	1,098	1,069	-2.6	990	98.8	0.0	0.0	1.0	0.2	15.3	65.8	18.9	385	84.2	49.1	23.4
Washington township (Indiana)	1,808	1,743	-3.6	1,917	98.5	0.0	0.0	1.5	0.0	23.7	65.4	10.9	672	89.9	65.9	14.3
Washington township (Jefferson)	1,926	1,901	-1.3	1,780	96.7	1.7	0.0	1.6	0.0	19.1	59.0	21.7	745	83.1	65.5	14.8
Washington township (Lawrence)	799	788	-1.4	743	97.8	0.0	0.0	0.4	1.7	20.0	62.3	17.6	297	88.6	68.7	17.8
Washington township (Lehigh)	6,624	6,731	1.6	6,690	96.0	0.0	0.0	1.0	3.0	16.5	64.1	19.4	2,717	87.4	54.1	16.7
Washington township (Lycoming)	1,619	1,665	2.8	1,783	98.7	0.1	0.1	0.9	0.2	23.6	63.8	12.6	638	86.2	55.5	15.5
Washington township (Northampton)	5,122	5,171	1.0	5,154	96.1	0.5	0.5	0.0	2.9	19.9	60.3	19.7	1,937	82.4	53.7	17.2
Washington township (Northumberland)	746	749	0.4	775	98.3	0.0	0.0	0.0	1.7	29.0	54.6	16.5	286	89.2	72.7	11.9
Washington township (Schuylkill)	3,036	2,979	-1.9	3,005	95.8	2.2	0.1	0.9	1.0	22.3	62.6	15.1	1,124	86.7	62.3	19.6
Washington township (Snyder)	1,652	1,685	2.0	1,653	100.0	0.0	0.0	0.0	0.0	24.5	63.8	11.6	577	88.9	70.2	14.9
Washington city & MCD (Washington)	13,895	13,551	-2.5	13,715	76.7	16.5	0.2	5.3	1.2	18.1	67.9	14.1	5,660	43.6	53.1	17.3
Washington township (Westmoreland)	7,422	7,286	-1.8	7,357	99.5	0.1	0.0	0.1	0.3	17.1	58.0	24.9	3,053	81.7	47.5	24.7
Washington township (Wyoming)	1,412	1,387	-1.8	1,425	94.9	0.0	0.0	0.3	4.8	28.0	55.1	17.1	495	81.4	50.7	15.6
Washington township (York)	2,673	2,669	-0.1	2,679	98.7	0.0	0.0	0.4	0.8	22.3	63.5	14.0	940	82.1	63.4	15.7
Washington Boro CDP	729	NA	NA	640	96.9	0.0	0.0	2.2	0.9	22.3	65.3	12.3	279	90.3	65.9	24.7
Washingtonville borough & MCD (Montour)	273	277	1.5	198	100.0	0.0	0.0	0.0	0.0	20.7	64.2	15.2	82	61.0	78.0	11.0
Waterford borough & MCD (Erie)	1,517	1,543	1.7	1,414	98.8	0.0	0.2	0.2	0.8	24.3	56.1	19.5	598	69.2	53.0	22.9
Waterford township (Erie)	3,920	3,878	-1.1	3,928	97.3	1.0	0.0	1.3	0.4	23.3	64.5	12.2	1,466	94.1	59.9	15.6
Watson township (Lycoming)	537	541	0.7	576	99.8	0.2	0.0	0.0	0.0	20.1	63.5	16.3	241	93.4	41.9	24.5
Watson township (Warren)	274	267	-2.6	275	95.3	0.0	0.0	1.5	3.3	19.3	68.3	12.4	108	98.1	54.6	21.3
Watsontown borough & MCD (Northumberland)	2,351	2,342	-0.4	2,296	95.1	0.3	0.9	0.2	3.5	18.5	58.6	23.0	987	55.0	55.9	18.7
Watts township (Perry)	1,265	1,258	-0.6	1,402	95.7	0.0	1.1	0.6	2.6	18.7	71.5	9.8	564	73.8	57.4	12.4
Wattsburg borough & MCD (Erie)	403	388	-3.7	494	93.7	0.0	0.0	1.2	5.1	30.4	60.2	9.5	166	69.9	66.3	13.9
Waverly CDP	604	NA	NA	529	100.0	0.0	0.0	0.0	0.0	16.3	57.7	26.1	235	89.8	10.6	69.4
Waverly township (Lackawanna)	1,743	1,750	0.4	1,533	92.0	0.0	4.4	1.3	2.2	24.3	53.5	22.1	607	94.6	10.7	70.8
Waymart borough & MCD (Wayne)	1,341	1,288	-4.0	1,284	95.3	0.2	0.0	0.7	3.7	22.5	56.9	20.6	426	72.8	47.4	16.0
Wayne township (Armstrong)	1,200	1,166	-2.8	1,049	98.1	0.6	0.0	1.3	0.0	23.6	57.1	19.4	405	80.7	75.6	14.6
Wayne township (Clinton)	1,666	1,691	1.5	1,572	86.5	5.7	1.7	1.6	4.6	18.6	66.1	15.3	524	83.6	60.7	13.7
Wayne township (Crawford)	1,539	1,516	-1.5	1,523	97.1	0.0	0.4	1.6	0.9	25.2	63.8	11.2	527	84.1	55.0	15.7
Wayne township (Dauphin)	1,341	1,350	0.7	1,447	98.1	0.0	0.6	0.3	1.0	26.0	63.0	11.1	508	92.9	52.0	23.4
Wayne township (Erie)	1,659	1,627	-1.9	1,552	98.1	0.2	0.5	1.1	0.1	21.7	57.7	20.6	637	90.6	54.8	20.3
Wayne township (Greene)	1,197	1,179	-1.5	1,175	98.5	0.0	0.0	0.8	0.8	23.1	64.2	12.6	483	73.3	68.1	13.7
Wayne township (Lawrence)	2,606	2,547	-2.3	2,578	98.3	0.0	0.5	1.0	0.1	19.4	60.9	19.6	1,019	81.6	55.0	17.5
Wayne township (Mifflin)	2,552	2,535	-0.7	2,545	96.5	0.7	0.2	0.4	2.2	22.8	57.4	19.7	997	84.6	74.7	8.8
Wayne township (Schuylkill)	5,110	5,076	-0.7	5,097	96.8	0.0	0.0	0.8	2.3	18.6	62.2	19.1	2,074	82.1	52.8	19.7
Wayne Heights CDP	2,545	NA	NA	2,749	96.4	0.8	1.7	1.0	0.0	27.5	56.4	16.0	1,051	74.9	38.8	33.4
Waynesboro borough & MCD (Franklin)	10,568	10,760	1.8	10,673	89.3	4.8	1.2	1.1	3.6	22.1	61.9	16.0	4,539	52.2	57.0	16.9
Waynesburg borough & MCD (Greene)	4,175	4,131	-1.1	4,145	97.0	1.6	0.6	0.2	0.6	17.8	73.2	8.9	1,481	43.4	40.4	29.2
Weatherly borough & MCD (Carbon)	2,525	2,479	-1.8	2,535	96.8	0.0	0.5	0.9	1.8	15.6	56.0	28.2	940	83.9	59.3	11.8
Webster CDP	255	NA	NA	279	100.0	0.0	0.0	0.0	0.0	15.4	72.9	11.8	122	68.9	72.1	5.7
Weedville CDP	542	NA	NA	674	97.9	0.0	0.4	1.6	0.0	22.3	53.1	24.6	274	78.5	66.1	15.7
Weigelstown CDP	12,875	NA	NA	13,174	86.2	4.5	0.2	5.0	4.0	24.0	59.5	16.4	5,151	78.7	54.3	18.5
Weisenberg township (Lehigh)	4,923	5,056	2.7	5,011	93.7	0.0	2.4	1.6	2.3	22.4	65.1	12.5	1,854	93.6	33.1	37.4
Weissport borough & MCD (Carbon)	412	398	-3.4	405	92.3	3.5	0.7	1.0	2.5	25.2	62.9	11.9	169	43.2	71.6	3.0
Weissport East CDP	1,624	NA	NA	1,256	94.7	1.9	0.0	0.0	3.4	16.5	57.6	25.9	523	73.2	49.3	14.7
Wellersburg borough & MCD (Somerset)	181	177	-2.2	221	100.0	0.0	0.0	0.0	0.0	24.4	56.6	19.0	96	79.2	77.1	8.3
Wells township (Bradford)	814	818	0.5	645	97.4	0.2	0.0	2.0	0.5	24.4	57.1	18.6	235	83.4	63.4	17.4
Wells township (Fulton)	477	463	-2.9	523	99.6	0.0	0.0	0.4	0.0	14.9	62.8	22.4	215	92.1	79.1	6.0
Wellsboro borough & MCD (Tioga)	3,263	3,326	1.9	3,301	93.6	0.0	1.9	0.5	4.0	19.2	58.7	22.2	1,467	60.2	36.2	37.2
Wellsville borough & MCD (York)	253	257	1.6	287	97.9	0.0	0.0	2.1	0.0	21.3	69.4	9.4	129	53.5	66.7	11.6
Wernersville borough & MCD (Berks)	2,494	2,534	1.6	2,512	88.3	2.0	2.8	1.6	5.3	20.9	56.9	22.4	932	70.1	48.5	26.0
Wescosville CDP	5,872	NA	NA	5,951	83.1	2.2	5.1	2.1	7.5	23.6	58.3	18.1	2,255	88.2	29.4	44.3

1 May be of any race.

Table A. All Places — Population and Housing

STATE City, town, township, borough, or CDP (county if applicable)	Population				Race and Hispanic or Latino origin (percent), 2010–2014					Age (percent), 2010–2014			Households, 2010–2014			
	2010 census total population	2014 estimated population	Percent change 2010-2014	ACS total population estimate 2010-2014	White alone, not Hispanic or Latino	Black alone, not Hispanic or Latino	Asian alone, not Hispanic or Latino	All other races or 2 or more races, not Hispanic or Latino	Hispanic or Latino[1]	Under 18 years old	Age 18 to 64 years old	Age 65 years and older	Total occupied housing units	Percent owner occupied	High school diploma or less	Bachelor's degree or more
	1	2	3	4	5	6	7	8	9	10	11	12	13	14	15	16
PENNSYLVANIA—Con.																
Wesleyville borough & MCD (Erie)	3,341	3,249	-2.8	3,297	88.8	3.5	1.1	5.0	1.6	23.6	63.2	13.0	1,267	68.0	49.0	18.6
West township (Huntingdon)	571	564	-1.2	549	96.7	0.0	1.6	0.2	1.5	18.0	64.3	17.7	222	77.9	52.7	20.3
West Abington township (Lackawanna)	250	252	0.8	152	100.0	0.0	0.0	0.0	0.0	11.8	60.4	27.6	72	97.2	50.0	34.7
West Alexander CDP	604	NA	NA	731	94.1	0.0	0.0	2.2	3.7	34.9	51.3	13.8	268	56.3	66.8	7.5
West Beaver township (Snyder)	1,110	1,107	-0.3	1,198	100.0	0.0	0.0	0.0	0.0	25.0	61.5	13.6	380	89.7	79.7	5.0
West Bethlehem township (Washington)	1,460	1,447	-0.9	1,462	97.9	0.0	0.6	1.4	0.0	17.2	63.3	19.6	589	77.1	64.7	12.2
West Bradford township (Chester)	12,223	12,625	3.3	12,426	84.1	4.2	7.0	2.6	2.1	25.5	64.0	10.5	4,222	94.9	23.8	56.1
West Branch township (Potter)	393	393	0.0	370	98.6	0.0	0.0	1.4	0.0	13.0	49.8	37.3	159	89.9	69.8	17.0
West Brandywine township (Chester)	7,394	7,458	0.9	7,420	90.4	3.2	0.5	3.1	2.7	20.9	58.8	20.4	2,838	88.9	30.3	38.8
West Brownsville borough & MCD (Washington)	992	979	-1.3	909	98.6	0.0	0.3	0.0	1.1	13.0	63.5	23.7	404	76.5	65.1	17.8
West Brunswick township (Schuylkill)	3,327	3,287	-1.2	3,323	97.5	0.8	1.1	0.0	0.7	20.0	61.3	18.7	1,554	82.6	42.2	23.9
West Buffalo township (Union)	2,984	3,025	1.4	2,997	97.5	0.9	0.0	0.1	1.5	26.3	60.8	12.7	1,088	81.5	71.9	10.9
West Burlington township (Bradford)	696	679	-2.4	803	89.5	7.5	0.1	2.5	0.4	15.4	57.6	26.9	168	86.9	61.3	16.7
West Caln township (Chester)	9,014	9,085	0.8	9,055	86.8	5.7	1.9	1.0	4.6	22.7	62.0	15.2	3,207	92.6	45.4	23.5
West Cameron township (Northumberland)	541	547	1.1	564	98.4	0.5	0.0	0.4	0.7	21.3	69.4	9.4	224	93.8	72.8	8.0
West Carroll township (Cambria)	1,296	1,254	-3.2	1,136	97.7	0.9	0.0	0.1	1.3	17.8	57.0	25.2	509	96.5	66.4	11.6
West Chester borough & MCD (Chester)	18,461	19,189	3.9	18,860	73.1	10.7	0.8	2.3	13.1	11.7	79.7	8.5	6,539	36.4	26.4	42.2
West Chillisquaque township (Northumberland)	2,627	2,584	-1.6	2,609	98.0	0.0	0.0	0.0	1.9	20.8	60.0	19.2	1,140	83.7	71.7	9.5
West Cocalico township (Lancaster)	7,280	7,373	1.3	7,329	96.7	0.6	0.5	0.0	2.2	28.1	61.0	11.1	2,432	86.4	64.1	16.8
West Conshohocken borough & MCD (Montgomery)	1,320	1,381	4.6	1,322	87.1	1.9	4.1	2.3	4.6	8.6	76.8	14.6	589	71.1	17.7	65.9
West Cornwall township (Lebanon)	1,945	1,979	1.7	2,002	91.2	0.2	2.1	2.4	4.1	16.8	50.9	32.0	832	92.5	44.1	35.5
West Decatur CDP	533	NA	NA	487	98.6	0.0	1.4	0.0	0.0	22.7	64.1	13.3	200	79.0	62.0	11.5
West Deer township (Allegheny)	11,771	11,902	1.1	11,837	97.6	0.4	0.2	1.4	0.5	20.1	61.1	18.8	4,841	83.8	45.9	28.9
West Donegal township (Lancaster)	8,260	8,646	4.7	8,430	97.2	1.0	0.2	0.9	0.8	21.6	47.2	31.1	3,142	68.5	45.4	31.9
West Earl township (Lancaster)	7,868	8,098	2.9	7,975	87.9	0.6	7.9	0.5	3.1	27.6	52.3	20.1	2,687	78.3	58.6	25.9
West Easton borough & MCD (Northampton)	1,257	1,255	-0.2	1,315	79.5	7.3	4.0	1.0	8.3	20.9	67.0	12.0	530	61.9	57.0	14.5
West Elizabeth borough & MCD (Allegheny)	518	511	-1.4	636	91.0	0.9	0.0	3.0	5.0	25.5	60.2	14.3	253	65.6	59.7	10.3
West Fairview CDP	1,282	NA	NA	1,313	89.1	2.4	0.0	0.0	8.5	21.5	69.9	8.5	521	53.0	61.8	17.7
Westfall township (Pike)	2,323	2,272	-2.2	2,407	91.8	1.8	0.1	0.4	5.9	20.5	54.8	24.8	992	74.9	39.8	22.9
West Fallowfield township (Chester)	2,566	2,585	0.7	2,576	93.6	0.0	0.0	1.0	5.4	27.0	58.7	14.1	904	84.1	49.9	18.1
West Fallowfield township (Crawford)	605	590	-2.5	536	95.1	1.5	0.0	2.4	0.9	20.6	56.6	22.8	224	89.7	58.0	16.5
West Falls CDP	382	NA	NA	444	100.0	0.0	0.0	0.0	0.0	11.3	66.0	22.7	189	70.4	61.4	19.0
Westfield borough & MCD (Tioga)	1,073	1,063	-0.9	1,182	96.4	0.1	0.3	3.1	0.0	20.9	59.6	19.3	492	54.3	72.8	7.5
Westfield township (Tioga)	1,038	1,032	-0.6	927	98.5	0.4	0.0	0.8	0.3	20.3	59.1	20.5	404	79.2	68.6	13.1
West Finley township (Washington)	878	877	-0.1	935	98.8	0.3	0.7	0.1	0.0	18.9	65.3	15.7	331	87.0	57.1	15.1
West Franklin township (Armstrong)	1,853	1,809	-2.4	1,857	98.4	0.0	1.0	0.6	0.0	21.2	62.1	17.0	743	85.1	66.4	11.8
West Goshen township (Chester)	21,866	23,050	5.4	22,598	85.6	2.8	6.2	2.0	3.4	22.2	65.9	12.0	8,205	71.0	21.0	56.8
West Grove borough & MCD (Chester)	2,854	2,863	0.3	2,856	61.0	6.7	0.8	1.4	30.2	28.6	64.3	7.0	917	72.6	45.1	33.5
West Hamburg CDP	1,979	NA	NA	1,996	82.1	14.0	0.0	0.0	3.9	23.1	53.2	23.9	700	94.7	51.7	17.0
West Hanover township (Dauphin)	9,343	9,759	4.5	9,558	94.2	3.7	1.3	0.0	0.7	21.5	62.0	16.4	3,852	86.8	41.8	34.9
West Hazleton borough & MCD (Luzerne)	4,594	4,523	-1.5	4,565	51.5	1.3	0.0	0.2	46.9	28.3	58.6	13.3	1,764	52.3	61.1	12.1
West Hemlock township (Montour)	503	509	1.2	485	94.6	1.2	0.0	2.7	1.4	21.0	66.1	13.0	173	90.8	45.7	28.9
West Hempfield township (Lancaster)	16,153	16,411	1.6	16,287	85.6	2.3	1.8	1.4	8.9	22.1	65.2	12.7	6,205	83.9	50.0	28.2
West Hills CDP	1,263	NA	NA	1,403	100.0	0.0	0.0	0.0	0.0	19.0	55.7	25.5	530	89.1	47.4	33.8
West Homestead borough & MCD (Allegheny)	1,929	1,929	0.0	1,798	85.4	12.5	0.0	2.1	0.0	14.1	61.0	24.7	817	80.7	48.2	31.2
West Keating township (Clinton)	29	30	3.4	21	100.0	0.0	0.0	0.0	0.0	0.0	33.3	66.7	12	66.7	58.3	0.0
West Kittanning borough & MCD (Armstrong)	1,175	1,147	-2.4	1,287	97.9	0.5	0.3	1.3	0.0	19.9	55.4	24.9	582	72.5	51.4	19.9
West Lampeter township (Lancaster)	15,180	15,734	3.6	15,428	93.4	0.6	0.8	1.8	3.5	20.9	49.2	29.8	6,183	69.6	32.8	40.3
Westland CDP	167	NA	NA	88	43.2	0.0	0.0	0.0	56.8	30.7	57.9	11.4	33	30.3	0.0	0.0

1 May be of any race.

STATE City, town, township, borough, or CDP (county if applicable)	Population				Race and Hispanic or Latino origin (percent), 2010–2014					Age (percent), 2010–2014			Households, 2010–2014			
	2010 census total population	2014 estimated population	Percent change 2010-2014	ACS total population estimate 2010-2014	White alone, not Hispanic or Latino	Black alone, not Hispanic or Latino	Asian alone, not Hispanic or Latino	All other races or 2 or more races, not Hispanic or Latino	Hispanic or Latino[1]	Under 18 years old	Age 18 to 64 years old	Age 65 years and older	Total occupied housing units	Percent owner occupied	High school diploma or less	Bachelor's degree or more
	1	2	3	4	5	6	7	8	9	10	11	12	13	14	15	16

PENNSYLVANIA—Con.

STATE City, town, township, borough, or CDP (county if applicable)	1	2	3	4	5	6	7	8	9	10	11	12	13	14	15	16
West Lawn CDP	1,715	NA	NA	1,672	73.5	3.1	0.0	3.1	20.3	23.1	65.0	12.0	679	63.9	56.6	14.1
West Lebanon township (Lebanon)	781	795	1.8	830	88.8	0.0	0.4	1.7	0.2	25.2	60.9	14.0	355	73.5	60.8	9.0
West Leechburg borough & MCD (Westmoreland)	1,294	1,273	-1.6	1,345	97.5	0.3	0.0	2.1	0.1	20.3	57.2	22.5	573	75.9	49.7	21.6
West Liberty borough & MCD (Butler)	343	339	-1.2	342	95.3	0.0	1.8	2.9	0.0	21.6	58.8	19.6	133	88.0	51.9	21.1
West Mahanoy township (Schuylkill)	2,872	2,809	-2.2	2,832	95.7	0.0	1.6	0.8	1.8	14.7	61.6	23.8	1,226	96.4	54.8	19.2
West Mahoning township (Indiana)	1,357	1,314	-3.2	1,396	99.9	0.0	0.0	0.1	0.0	46.8	47.5	5.7	336	78.6	84.8	5.4
West Manchester township (York)	18,894	18,861	-0.2	18,859	84.7	5.2	2.5	1.6	5.9	18.7	59.9	21.4	7,845	79.8	50.1	25.2
West Manheim township (York)	7,744	8,178	5.6	7,954	94.6	0.6	2.5	1.7	0.6	27.1	60.5	12.5	2,719	85.4	43.1	30.0
West Marlborough township (Chester)	814	821	0.9	798	89.6	0.4	0.0	0.0	10.0	21.5	62.9	15.7	310	53.2	34.2	49.7
West Mayfield borough & MCD (Beaver)	1,239	1,218	-1.7	1,375	96.1	0.9	0.3	2.0	0.7	25.9	59.3	15.0	527	70.6	51.0	12.9
West Mead township (Crawford)	5,236	5,156	-1.5	5,188	95.1	1.6	0.1	2.2	1.0	23.7	58.6	17.8	2,214	74.3	41.1	32.4
West Middlesex borough & MCD (Mercer)	863	846	-2.0	863	96.4	0.0	0.6	0.7	2.3	22.0	58.0	19.8	344	73.5	50.9	19.2
West Middletown borough & MCD (Washington)	139	138	-0.7	108	91.7	6.5	0.0	0.9	0.9	12.0	69.4	18.5	44	84.1	65.9	22.7
West Mifflin borough & MCD (Allegheny)	20,313	20,175	-0.7	20,271	84.8	10.8	0.2	2.8	1.3	18.5	62.2	19.4	8,688	76.7	46.1	20.5
West Milton CDP	900	NA	NA	748	90.9	2.7	0.0	6.4	0.0	20.7	51.3	28.1	311	74.9	59.8	24.8
Westmont borough & MCD (Cambria)	5,181	4,990	-3.7	5,086	95.3	2.0	0.8	0.0	1.8	21.3	58.3	20.5	2,250	80.8	49.8	
West Nanticoke CDP	749	NA	NA	763	100.0	0.0	0.0	0.0	0.0	16.6	65.6	17.8	331	88.2	57.4	14.8
West Nantmeal township (Chester)	2,170	2,194	1.1	1,939	94.6	0.1	1.7	0.7	2.9	20.8	61.8	17.6	816	80.5	37.1	37.7
West Newton borough & MCD (Westmoreland)	2,633	2,562	-2.7	2,599	98.9	0.0	0.3	0.0	0.7	15.2	64.2	20.7	1,200	62.3	56.4	11.3
West Norriton township (Montgomery)	15,663	15,805	0.9	15,751	78.2	11.7	6.0	1.2	3.0	14.6	68.1	17.2	7,402	64.7	29.8	42.6
West Nottingham township (Chester)	2,722	2,710	-0.4	2,720	89.2	4.7	0.0	1.0	5.1	26.5	60.5	13.0	990	79.9	62.0	13.8
Weston CDP	321	NA	NA	328	100.0	0.0	0.0	0.0	0.0	21.6	53.0	25.3	156	91.7	40.4	19.2
Westover borough & MCD (Clearfield)	390	385	-1.3	377	97.1	0.0	2.4	0.0	0.5	15.1	71.2	13.8	141	74.5	64.5	10.6
West Penn township (Schuylkill)	4,442	4,375	-1.5	4,423	99.1	0.0	0.2	0.6	0.0	19.4	61.1	19.6	1,782	90.9	55.6	13.6
West Pennsboro township (Cumberland)	5,561	5,580	0.3	5,567	90.4	0.3	3.1	3.1	3.2	20.1	61.6	18.4	2,198	86.4	47.8	23.4
West Perry township (Snyder)	1,071	1,077	0.6	992	98.4	0.7	0.0	0.6	0.3	23.2	55.4	21.4	364	78.6	79.7	8.5
West Pikeland township (Chester)	4,024	4,073	1.2	4,047	92.2	0.3	1.5	2.1	3.9	27.1	61.6	11.3	1,427	93.7	8.2	72.6
West Pike Run township (Washington)	1,587	1,569	-1.1	1,770	91.3	6.7	0.2	1.2	0.6	20.0	61.6	18.5	702	83.3	58.7	23.2
West Pittsburg CDP	808	NA	NA	813	99.9	0.1	0.0	0.0	0.0	16.9	59.4	23.7	357	76.5	69.2	6.2
West Pittston borough & MCD (Luzerne)	4,868	4,793	-1.5	4,834	99.5	0.1	0.0	0.0	0.4	15.9	60.0	24.2	2,230	61.5	46.6	23.1
West Pottsgrove township (Montgomery)	3,874	3,895	0.5	3,886	82.8	10.4	0.0	3.0	3.7	24.2	65.5	10.3	1,510	63.2	64.4	12.5
West Providence township (Bedford)	3,219	3,144	-2.3	3,179	100.0	0.0	0.0	0.0	0.0	18.8	59.3	21.9	1,347	85.7	66.2	16.5
West Reading borough & MCD (Berks)	4,212	4,190	-0.5	4,204	69.5	10.6	0.5	0.5	18.9	23.5	54.5	21.9	1,692	60.2	47.3	22.0
West Rockhill township (Bucks)	5,256	5,275	0.4	5,275	92.3	4.1	2.2	0.0	1.3	15.5	55.5	28.9	2,221	74.7	46.4	28.1
West Sadsbury township (Chester)	2,444	2,480	1.5	2,238	85.6	8.0	0.4	0.0	5.7	22.5	63.9	13.8	774	85.8	64.6	13.7
West St. Clair township (Bedford)	1,730	1,713	-1.0	1,857	97.3	2.0	0.0	0.7	0.0	28.7	57.9	13.4	671	83.6	63.3	13.0
West Salem township (Mercer)	3,538	3,485	-1.5	3,509	97.2	1.1	0.0	1.3	0.4	17.1	52.5	30.4	1,450	86.3	65.0	14.6
West Shenango township (Crawford)	504	497	-1.4	486	99.2	0.0	0.0	0.0	0.8	16.5	63.6	20.0	206	86.4	64.1	10.2
West Sunbury borough & MCD (Butler)	192	189	-1.6	113	97.3	0.0	0.0	2.7	0.0	25.6	68.2	6.2	47	48.9	34.0	12.8
West Taylor township (Cambria)	795	771	-3.0	761	93.6	2.4	1.6	0.1	2.4	13.3	61.8	25.0	341	84.8	72.1	10.9
Westtown township (Chester)	10,827	10,919	0.8	10,874	90.5	3.3	3.0	1.6	1.6	21.7	64.5	13.8	3,985	79.1	12.7	68.2
West View borough & MCD (Allegheny)	6,771	6,717	-0.8	6,752	96.9	1.7	0.0	0.6	0.6	20.1	66.4	13.6	3,024	69.3	35.0	28.1
West Vincent township (Chester)	4,567	5,007	9.6	4,787	90.5	1.8	2.0	2.1	3.6	20.2	60.1	13.6	1,673	77.8	15.0	66.2
West Waynesburg CDP	446	NA	NA	329	100.0	0.0	0.0	0.0	0.0	24.0	61.4	14.6	135	47.4	48.9	0.0
West Wheatfield township (Indiana)	2,314	2,233	-3.5	2,578	96.7	0.2	0.0	3.1	0.0	24.6	60.9	14.7	912	95.6	57.6	6.3
West Whiteland township (Chester)	18,274	18,453	1.0	18,397	78.0	5.0	12.9	1.4	2.8	23.8	65.0	11.3	7,084	72.7	19.4	59.4
Westwood CDP	950	NA	NA	1,282	69.4	11.9	0.0	0.0	18.6	24.9	62.8	12.0	424	54.7	36.6	8.5
West Wyoming borough & MCD (Luzerne)	2,725	2,692	-1.2	2,702	97.8	0.0	0.0	0.0	2.2	18.8	61.8	19.5	1,103	83.2	51.9	19.0
West Wyomissing CDP	3,407	NA	NA	3,360	81.3	1.2	0.0	1.2	16.3	20.4	58.6	21.0	1,436	80.7	62.0	16.2

1 May be of any race.

Items 1–16

STATE City, town, township, borough, or CDP (county if applicable)	Population 2010 census total population	2014 estimated population	Percent change 2010-2014	ACS total population estimate 2010-2014	White alone, not Hispanic or Latino	Black alone, not Hispanic or Latino	Asian alone, not Hispanic or Latino	All other races or 2 or more races, not Hispanic or Latino	Hispanic or Latino[1]	Under 18 years old	Age 18 to 64 years old	Age 65 years and older	Total occupied housing units	Percent owner occupied	High school diploma or less	Bachelor's degree or more
	1	2	3	4	5	6	7	8	9	10	11	12	13	14	15	16
PENNSYLVANIA—Con.																
West York borough & MCD (York)	4,617	4,571	-1.0	4,594	70.0	9.6	0.8	7.9	11.8	27.3	63.5	8.9	1,937	62.9	51.9	10.3
Wetmore township (McKean)	1,650	1,618	-1.9	1,690	99.4	0.0	0.0	0.1	0.5	20.7	61.8	17.5	725	85.8	56.6	19.9
Wharton township (Fayette)	3,575	3,514	-1.7	3,548	99.5	0.0	0.0	0.5	0.0	20.9	59.3	19.8	1,199	79.7	58.0	12.2
Wharton township (Potter)	99	97	-2.0	92	100.0	0.0	0.0	0.0	0.0	0.0	54.3	45.7	51	96.1	78.4	0.0
Wheatfield township (Perry)	3,338	3,299	-1.2	3,314	98.9	0.1	0.0	0.5	0.5	21.0	65.2	13.9	1,325	92.5	52.8	13.8
Wheatland borough & MCD (Mercer)	632	616	-2.5	833	72.0	24.6	0.5	2.9	0.0	19.0	64.7	16.3	377	66.8	56.8	11.9
Whitaker borough & MCD (Allegheny)	1,271	1,262	-0.7	1,278	88.4	9.2	0.0	0.7	1.6	17.5	66.5	15.9	550	76.4	49.5	12.2
White township (Beaver)	1,394	1,373	-1.5	1,248	85.5	7.9	0.7	3.3	2.6	17.5	65.3	17.1	559	53.1	44.0	14.8
White township (Cambria)	836	813	-2.8	906	97.4	0.3	0.0	0.0	2.3	23.2	56.6	20.2	346	92.8	66.2	11.6
White township (Indiana)	15,821	16,322	3.2	16,027	89.1	5.5	2.2	1.9	1.4	14.1	65.1	20.8	7,019	63.3	35.0	44.6
White Deer township (Union)	4,552	4,598	1.0	4,582	100.0	0.0	0.0	0.0	0.0	18.6	63.9	17.6	2,043	95.3	72.1	12.4
Whitehall borough & MCD (Allegheny)	13,944	13,896	-0.3	13,931	86.5	4.9	7.4	0.5	0.8	19.3	57.7	22.9	6,112	71.6	42.0	36.2
Whitehall township (Lehigh)	26,738	27,214	1.8	27,025	72.6	6.2	6.6	1.8	12.8	21.8	60.8	17.4	11,063	61.5	40.9	26.5
White Haven borough & MCD (Luzerne)	1,097	1,103	0.5	1,169	93.8	0.0	1.2	1.2	3.8	20.7	63.4	16.1	463	74.3	54.0	15.1
Whiteley township (Greene)	649	642	-1.1	838	99.9	0.0	0.0	0.0	0.1	22.2	67.5	10.3	297	79.1	62.6	19.2
Whitemarsh township (Montgomery)	17,349	17,674	1.9	17,496	88.6	3.5	4.5	1.1	2.4	22.0	61.7	16.4	6,779	79.5	16.2	64.6
White Mills CDP	659	NA	NA	673	98.7	0.0	0.0	0.0	1.3	27.1	53.7	19.0	307	84.0	64.2	18.6
White Oak borough & MCD (Allegheny)	7,862	7,814	-0.6	7,851	94.4	4.4	0.6	0.2	0.4	11.4	62.6	26.0	3,789	75.9	42.9	23.1
Whitfield CDP	4,733	NA	NA	5,171	82.5	3.2	6.6	1.8	5.9	18.7	59.3	21.9	1,950	87.0	21.8	51.7
Whitpain township (Montgomery)	18,875	19,180	1.6	19,064	78.5	4.6	11.7	2.0	3.2	22.3	59.1	18.7	7,178	79.1	17.1	63.8
Wickerham Manor-Fisher CDP	1,728	NA	NA	2,009	91.5	1.6	0.0	1.3	5.5	13.1	57.8	29.1	823	92.0	41.7	30.1
Wiconisco CDP	921	NA	NA	793	94.5	0.0	0.0	1.1	4.4	19.8	61.5	18.7	377	80.1	71.4	8.8
Wiconisco township (Dauphin)	1,208	1,193	-1.2	1,148	93.4	0.0	0.0	0.8	5.8	22.5	60.7	16.7	506	79.2	65.2	11.5
Wilburton Number One CDP	196	NA	NA	184	98.9	0.0	0.0	0.0	1.1	13.1	73.9	13.0	77	100.0	76.6	13.0
Wilburton Number Two CDP	96	NA	NA	81	92.6	0.0	0.0	0.0	7.4	32.1	48.1	19.8	37	59.5	40.5	24.3
Wilcox CDP	383	NA	NA	441	100.0	0.0	0.0	0.0	0.0	21.6	56.4	22.0	184	67.9	69.6	3.3
Wilkes-Barre city & MCD (Luzerne)	41,498	40,814	-1.6	41,202	70.6	12.1	1.4	2.5	13.3	21.5	64.3	14.4	15,808	47.2	52.2	16.6
Wilkes-Barre township (Luzerne)	2,985	2,944	-1.4	2,969	76.4	3.6	5.9	5.1	9.0	19.3	64.0	16.6	1,294	47.8	36.9	24.7
Wilkins township (Allegheny)	6,357	6,324	-0.5	6,348	77.7	17.8	0.8	2.3	1.4	17.9	60.7	21.4	2,927	61.9	34.0	36.2
Wilkinsburg borough & MCD (Allegheny)	15,930	15,813	-0.7	15,894	30.5	61.7	1.2	5.3	1.3	18.8	65.5	15.8	8,014	35.5	37.5	32.4
Williams township (Dauphin)	1,114	1,110	-0.4	1,037	94.8	1.4	0.0	2.6	1.2	19.0	61.9	19.2	437	81.0	70.9	8.0
Williams township (Northampton)	5,884	6,032	2.5	5,940	90.9	4.1	3.1	1.2	0.7	18.4	58.5	23.1	2,373	88.1	42.9	34.0
Williamsburg borough & MCD (Blair)	1,254	1,229	-2.0	1,308	99.2	0.0	0.0	0.4	0.5	22.9	58.7	18.3	548	57.8	62.4	10.4
Williamsport city & MCD (Lycoming)	29,381	29,197	-0.6	29,377	77.6	14.5	0.6	3.5	3.8	22.3	66.7	11.1	10,756	43.7	47.6	18.8
Williamstown borough & MCD (Dauphin)	1,387	1,369	-1.3	1,244	97.5	0.6	0.0	0.9	1.0	24.5	59.4	16.2	492	71.1	65.2	8.7
Willistown township (Chester)	10,497	10,823	3.1	10,622	91.4	2.5	3.2	0.8	2.1	20.3	56.6	23.2	4,228	87.7	15.2	67.5
Willow Grove CDP	15,726	NA	NA	16,185	81.4	6.9	5.1	2.7	3.9	22.5	61.9	15.7	6,297	68.4	34.0	39.0
Willow Street CDP	7,578	NA	NA	7,485	94.5	1.8	1.3	0.4	2.0	13.7	43.1	43.2	3,484	53.5	34.3	39.0
Wilmerding borough & MCD (Allegheny)	2,185	2,167	-0.8	1,690	70.7	23.3	0.3	4.4	1.4	17.8	60.9	21.2	863	34.2	55.0	14.3
Wilmington township (Lawrence)	2,715	2,657	-2.1	2,683	98.0	0.0	0.0	0.6	1.5	24.3	60.7	15.0	987	83.3	53.8	31.6
Wilmington township (Mercer)	1,415	1,425	0.7	1,448	95.9	0.0	0.0	1.2	2.9	28.1	53.7	18.2	485	92.4	51.1	27.2
Wilmore borough & MCD (Cambria)	225	221	-1.8	214	100.0	0.0	0.0	0.0	0.0	24.8	63.0	12.1	80	86.3	53.8	21.3
Wilmot township (Bradford)	1,204	1,186	-1.5	1,166	95.5	0.3	0.0	1.2	3.0	22.9	58.2	18.8	432	86.3	61.6	15.7
Wilson borough & MCD (Northampton)	7,896	7,827	-0.9	7,852	76.7	3.7	1.9	2.0	15.6	23.4	64.3	12.3	3,164	61.2	40.1	15.6
Windber borough & MCD (Somerset)	4,159	4,019	-3.4	4,078	93.8	0.0	2.6	2.6	0.9	21.0	60.1	18.8	1,824	67.8	57.8	17.2
Wind Gap borough & MCD (Northampton)	2,720	2,716	-0.1	2,724	94.1	0.4	2.9	0.0	2.6	22.0	55.5	22.4	1,249	48.8	57.9	9.5
Windham township (Bradford)	933	938	0.5	1,045	94.1	0.0	1.6	2.0	2.3	22.5	54.8	22.7	402	84.3	55.0	9.7
Windham township (Wyoming)	841	836	-0.6	811	96.8	0.0	1.1	1.4	0.7	25.7	57.9	16.5	308	85.7	70.1	7.1
Wind Ridge CDP	215	NA	NA	217	100.0	0.0	0.0	0.0	0.0	26.7	55.9	17.5	95	67.4	85.3	10.5
Windsor township (Berks)	2,279	2,315	1.6	2,419	97.4	0.0	0.2	1.4	0.9	19.6	64.2	16.4	925	80.5	63.2	19.2
Windsor borough & MCD (York)	1,319	1,474	11.8	1,298	91.0	0.4	0.0	1.0	7.6	26.4	63.7	10.0	509	65.0	69.7	8.4
Windsor township (York)	17,504	17,853	2.0	17,695	91.5	4.2	1.0	1.1	2.1	22.5	62.3	15.2	6,644	84.4	45.1	26.0

1 May be of any race.

Table A. All Places — **Population and Housing**

	Population				Race and Hispanic or Latino origin (percent), 2010–2014					Age (percent), 2010–2014			Households, 2010–2014		Householders by level of education (percent)	
STATE City, town, township, borough, or CDP (county if applicable)	2010 census total population	2014 estimated population	Percent change 2010-2014	ACS total population estimate 2010-2014	White alone, not Hispanic or Latino	Black alone, not Hispanic or Latino	Asian alone, not Hispanic or Latino	All other races or 2 or more races, not Hispanic or Latino	Hispanic or Latino[1]	Under 18 years old	Age 18 to 64 years old	Age 65 years and older	Total occupied housing units	Percent owner occupied	High school diploma or less	Bachelor's degree or more
	1	2	3	4	5	6	7	8	9	10	11	12	13	14	15	16
PENNSYLVANIA—Con.																
Winfield township (Butler).	3,535	3,493	-1.2	3,516	99.0	0.0	0.2	0.8	0.0	18.6	56.8	24.8	1,446	78.5	59.9	16.9
Winfield CDP	900	NA	NA	784	95.8	0.0	0.0	0.6	3.6	19.2	58.0	23.0	334	87.1	56.9	24.0
Winslow township (Jefferson)	2,622	2,590	-1.2	2,598	99.4	0.0	0.0	0.6	0.0	19.5	60.9	19.5	1,046	86.4	69.7	10.6
Winterstown borough & MCD (York)	632	626	-0.9	596	99.3	0.0	0.0	0.7	0.0	14.3	63.4	22.5	254	73.2	61.4	19.3
Witmer CDP..................	492	NA	NA	626	99.7	0.0	0.0	0.3	0.0	32.6	60.1	7.2	188	62.2	59.0	4.3
Wolf township (Lycoming).	2,907	3,024	4.0	3,008	98.1	1.5	0.0	0.1	0.3	23.3	60.3	16.4	1,155	93.1	49.9	22.6
Wolf Creek township (Mercer)	832	851	2.3	868	97.0	0.0	0.3	0.2	2.4	15.2	62.4	22.5	332	87.3	55.4	18.4
Wolfdale CDP	2,888	NA	NA	3,020	95.9	1.8	0.0	2.4	0.0	16.2	62.3	21.5	1,321	95.3	59.4	15.2
Womelsdorf borough & MCD (Berks)	2,810	2,804	-0.2	2,812	74.6	9.5	9.9	2.1	3.9	31.4	54.9	13.8	962	76.0	49.3	22.8
Wood township (Huntingdon)	708	714	0.8	714	99.9	0.0	0.0	0.1	0.0	24.7	55.9	19.5	257	89.1	83.3	6.6
Woodbourne CDP	3,851	NA	NA	3,719	87.6	4.4	2.5	0.0	5.6	23.6	70.3	6.1	1,388	71.1	12.1	74.3
Woodbury borough & MCD (Bedford)	284	278	-2.1	217	96.8	0.0	0.0	2.8	0.5	9.6	66.7	23.5	95	88.4	64.2	13.7
Woodbury township (Bedford)	1,263	1,252	-0.9	1,303	98.6	0.0	0.0	0.7	0.7	28.2	57.8	14.1	434	87.8	64.5	19.1
Woodbury township (Blair)	1,693	1,676	-1.0	1,813	95.3	2.5	0.0	0.1	2.0	24.6	58.8	16.7	577	80.8	73.8	10.1
Woodcock borough & MCD (Crawford)..........	160	158	-1.3	142	100.0	0.0	0.0	0.0	0.0	18.3	62.5	19.0	53	88.7	69.8	13.2
Woodcock township (Crawford)	2,858	2,805	-1.9	2,824	98.5	0.2	0.0	0.1	1.1	24.2	56.4	19.3	1,066	93.2	61.9	15.9
Woodland Heights CDP....	1,261	NA	NA	1,167	95.6	0.0	0.8	3.6	0.0	23.5	59.8	16.8	507	69.6	47.9	21.1
Woodlyn CDP	9,485	NA	NA	10,131	79.2	10.4	1.8	4.4	4.2	23.5	61.0	15.4	3,873	66.7	49.7	20.0
Woodside CDP	2,425	NA	NA	2,714	89.6	0.0	5.7	4.1	0.6	28.7	58.1	13.2	894	97.2	7.4	86.1
Woodward CDP	110	NA	NA	132	100.0	0.0	0.0	0.0	0.0	28.8	53.0	18.2	57	84.2	26.3	31.6
Woodward township (Clearfield)	3,992	4,185	4.8	4,096	60.9	30.5	0.3	3.2	5.0	7.7	82.3	9.9	844	73.0	71.3	14.3
Woodward township (Clinton)	2,368	2,409	1.7	2,314	97.3	0.0	0.0	2.0	0.7	18.7	60.2	21.1	1,011	81.5	47.9	27.3
Woodward township (Lycoming)	2,200	2,200	0.0	2,147	95.5	0.5	0.6	3.0	0.4	15.2	65.5	19.2	912	84.1	63.0	11.2
Worcester township (Montgomery)	9,750	10,326	5.9	10,034	82.8	3.0	9.1	1.4	3.7	26.6	58.7	14.8	3,773	84.7	18.8	59.9
Wormleysburg borough & MCD (Cumberland).......	3,070	3,068	-0.1	3,064	78.0	3.9	9.4	4.9	3.7	16.5	68.7	14.7	1,639	37.6	29.2	47.8
Worth township (Butler)....	1,416	1,453	2.6	1,410	95.2	0.0	0.0	0.9	3.9	17.1	67.0	15.8	615	74.3	43.6	21.3
Worth township (Centre) ...	822	816	-0.7	734	99.3	0.0	0.0	0.4	0.3	18.4	64.2	17.3	299	92.6	56.9	21.7
Worth township (Mercer) ..	899	905	0.7	801	99.6	0.0	0.0	0.4	0.0	16.3	66.5	17.2	356	86.5	58.4	19.7
Worthington borough & MCD (Armstrong).........	639	622	-2.7	669	100.0	0.0	0.0	0.0	0.0	22.6	60.1	17.3	280	78.9	57.1	17.5
Worthville borough & MCD (Jefferson).............	67	66	-1.5	69	92.8	0.0	0.0	0.0	7.2	11.5	69.4	18.8	28	100.0	71.4	14.3
Woxall CDP	1,318	NA	NA	1,212	100.0	0.0	0.0	0.0	0.0	22.9	62.4	14.9	412	93.4	34.0	42.7
Wright township (Luzerne)	5,651	5,646	-0.1	5,659	91.8	0.6	5.9	0.6	1.1	22.7	58.1	19.2	2,103	90.0	28.3	35.8
Wrightstown township (Bucks)	2,995	3,112	3.9	3,056	93.1	0.6	4.9	1.4	0.0	24.7	59.5	16.0	1,059	89.0	25.3	55.1
Wrightsville borough & MCD (York)	2,316	2,291	-1.1	2,356	90.5	2.0	0.3	3.3	4.0	21.1	62.6	16.3	1,008	70.9	64.4	10.9
Wyalusing borough & MCD (Bradford).............	596	579	-2.9	425	95.1	2.4	0.5	2.1	0.0	18.3	59.7	21.9	204	53.9	57.8	28.4
Wyalusing township (Bradford)	1,240	1,246	0.5	1,253	89.9	0.0	1.1	3.2	5.7	18.8	60.2	21.0	504	80.8	62.5	20.0
Wyano CDP	484	NA	NA	405	100.0	0.0	0.0	0.0	0.0	15.7	55.0	29.1	172	93.6	76.7	6.4
Wylandville CDP	391	NA	NA	450	88.4	6.2	0.0	2.9	2.4	17.0	63.8	19.1	183	91.3	59.6	8.7
Wyncote CDP	3,044	NA	NA	3,307	86.8	6.4	1.0	0.7	5.0	21.4	53.7	25.1	1,135	65.0	15.0	66.9
Wyndmoor CDP	5,498	NA	NA	5,681	72.7	16.7	3.8	3.1	3.7	21.4	55.8	22.8	2,065	86.7	15.2	69.5
Wyoming borough & MCD (Luzerne)	3,073	3,033	-1.3	3,057	98.9	0.3	0.8	0.0	0.0	12.0	66.3	21.6	1,480	59.9	38.6	27.8
Wyomissing borough & MCD (Berks)	10,461	10,472	0.1	10,467	87.3	1.9	3.7	1.1	5.9	19.0	56.4	24.6	4,406	72.6	25.6	51.1
Wysox township (Bradford).................	1,721	1,695	-1.5	1,461	91.2	1.0	0.5	1.8	5.4	16.7	61.7	21.9	616	84.1	55.5	17.7
Yardley borough & MCD (Bucks)	2,434	2,434	0.0	2,324	86.9	4.3	4.0	0.9	4.0	21.8	64.0	14.2	1,051	65.8	17.0	59.7
Yatesville borough & MCD (Luzerne).................	607	607	0.0	567	98.4	0.9	0.7	0.0	0.0	14.0	57.9	28.0	244	89.3	42.2	32.0
Yeadon borough & MCD (Delaware).................	11,443	11,525	0.7	11,506	6.0	91.0	0.5	0.8	1.6	22.5	63.7	13.9	4,411	64.4	34.3	27.9
Yeagertown CDP	1,050	NA	NA	1,075	98.8	1.2	0.0	0.0	0.0	16.6	63.9	19.5	447	86.6	58.4	2.5
Yoe borough & MCD (York).................	1,018	1,011	-0.7	952	88.4	1.1	0.0	6.3	4.2	25.2	59.9	15.0	403	59.1	57.6	13.4
York city & MCD (York)	43,806	43,865	0.1	43,817	40.4	24.7	1.0	5.4	28.5	27.9	62.8	9.3	16,482	41.3	64.9	12.1
York township (York)	27,790	28,127	1.2	27,961	89.5	3.1	2.8	0.0	3.7	21.1	57.8	21.2	11,649	71.0	37.5	35.3
Yorkana borough & MCD (York).................	229	229	0.0	254	96.1	0.0	0.0	2.0	2.0	18.5	66.1	15.4	103	73.8	69.9	11.7
York Haven borough & MCD (York)	709	701	-1.1	758	69.8	2.4	0.4	8.0	19.4	34.4	59.6	6.1	250	44.4	49.4	28.2
Yorklyn CDP	1,912	NA	NA	1,809	78.8	15.5	1.4	2.4	1.8	16.5	68.9	14.4	732	68.2	48.4	9.8
York Springs borough & MCD (Adams)	833	834	0.1	789	49.0	0.0	0.0	1.6	49.3	28.1	64.8	6.8	252	45.2	78.2	9.1
Young township (Indiana) .	1,775	1,710	-3.7	1,745	98.1	0.3	0.0	1.5	0.0	21.0	63.9	15.1	735	79.7	66.8	8.0
Young township (Jefferson)	1,749	1,728	-1.2	1,684	97.3	0.2	0.7	1.7	0.1	22.2	60.4	17.2	712	83.3	55.6	17.1
Youngstown borough & MCD (Westmoreland) ...	326	317	-2.8	335	94.9	0.0	0.0	0.0	5.1	19.4	65.5	15.2	140	79.3	40.0	22.1
Youngsville borough & MCD (Warren).............	1,729	1,678	-2.9	1,854	96.1	0.2	0.0	2.6	1.1	21.4	59.3	19.3	802	75.6	52.1	15.5

1 May be of any race.

Table A. All Places — **Population and Housing**

STATE City, town, township, borough, or CDP (county if applicable)	2010 census total population	2014 estimated population	Percent change 2010-2014	ACS total population estimate 2010-2014	White alone, not Hispanic or Latino	Black alone, not Hispanic or Latino	Asian alone, not Hispanic or Latino	All other races or 2 or more races, not Hispanic or Latino	Hispanic or Latino[1]	Under 18 years old	Age 18 to 64 years old	Age 65 years and older	Total occupied housing units	Percent owner occupied	High school diploma or less	Bachelor's degree or more
	1	2	3	4	5	6	7	8	9	10	11	12	13	14	15	16
PENNSYLVANIA—Con.																
Youngwood borough & MCD (Westmoreland) ...	3,050	2,975	-2.5	3,018	98.1	0.0	0.0	0.7	1.2	22.9	60.2	17.0	1,367	65.5	59.2	17.0
Yukon CDP	677	NA	NA	605	97.4	0.0	2.6	0.0	0.0	10.6	65.4	24.1	269	73.2	70.6	13.4
Zelienople borough & MCD (Butler)	3,812	3,718	-2.5	3,780	98.7	0.0	0.3	0.6	0.5	18.0	59.3	22.6	1,851	51.7	32.1	36.7
Zerbe township (Northumberland).........	1,872	1,839	-1.8	1,669	95.0	0.2	3.2	0.0	1.6	17.0	63.4	19.7	759	78.9	64.8	16.3
Zion CDP	2,030	NA	NA	2,171	96.9	0.0	0.0	0.0	3.1	26.0	64.0	9.9	845	87.0	41.7	39.1
RHODE ISLAND	1,052,931	1,055,173	0.2	1,053,252	75.1	5.2	3.1	3.3	13.3	20.7	64.2	15.1	409,569	60.3	38.2	33.2
Ashaway CDP	1,485	NA	NA	1,307	95.5	0.0	4.5	0.0	0.0	14.5	69.6	15.9	530	95.5	33.8	22.3
Barrington town (Bristol) ...	16,314	16,236	-0.5	16,290	91.9	0.5	2.3	3.8	1.5	27.4	56.6	16.0	6,068	87.6	13.9	69.2
Bradford CDP	1,406	NA	NA	1,212	83.7	5.9	0.0	6.2	4.2	29.0	58.2	12.7	440	73.0	70.9	20.2
Bristol town (Bristol).........	22,955	22,332	-2.7	22,493	93.7	0.9	1.5	1.3	2.6	14.8	66.0	19.1	8,545	68.3	36.6	37.8
Burrillville town (Providence)	15,955	16,246	1.8	16,108	95.4	0.5	0.5	1.7	2.0	21.3	63.5	15.1	6,228	71.9	44.5	23.3
Carolina CDP	970	NA	NA	867	87.9	5.2	1.7	1.5	3.7	15.0	67.9	17.1	382	83.2	24.3	36.6
Central Falls city & MCD (Providence)	19,383	19,328	-0.3	19,406	23.0	8.6	0.0	3.3	65.1	29.9	62.2	7.8	6,415	27.5	69.5	9.4
Charlestown town (Washington)	7,827	7,782	-0.6	7,788	93.4	0.1	0.0	4.1	2.3	18.6	61.4	19.9	3,173	80.7	32.3	37.8
Chepachet CDP	1,675	NA	NA	1,510	97.7	0.0	0.0	0.0	2.3	15.8	67.9	16.3	546	80.8	38.8	38.8
Clayville CDP	300	NA	NA	119	100.0	0.0	0.0	0.0	0.0	0.0	62.1	37.8	52	100.0	30.8	55.8
Coventry town (Kent)	35,020	35,021	0.0	34,992	95.9	0.5	0.6	1.4	1.6	20.3	65.1	14.6	13,653	78.7	40.3	26.2
Cranston city & MCD (Providence)	80,386	81,037	0.8	80,680	75.6	4.6	5.0	3.4	11.5	19.3	64.8	15.6	30,536	65.5	38.4	32.5
Cumberland town (Providence)	33,506	34,301	2.4	33,930	90.3	0.7	1.9	1.8	5.2	22.0	61.0	17.1	13,553	73.9	33.1	38.8
Cumberland Hill CDP	7,934	NA	NA	8,194	93.3	0.0	1.5	2.4	2.7	24.0	59.9	16.0	3,332	81.4	33.3	37.9
East Greenwich town (Kent)	13,147	13,147	0.0	13,118	91.9	1.1	1.9	2.8	2.4	24.5	59.8	15.8	5,018	76.5	21.7	60.4
East Providence city & MCD (Providence)	47,033	47,331	0.6	47,166	80.0	5.7	2.2	6.8	5.3	20.6	61.6	17.7	19,896	55.6	44.1	27.2
Exeter town (Washington)	6,425	6,613	2.9	6,673	92.3	1.3	2.2	0.2	3.9	17.3	71.5	11.2	2,390	84.7	29.2	37.1
Foster town (Providence)..	4,608	4,681	1.6	4,642	95.3	1.4	0.1	3.3	0.0	17.3	68.5	14.2	1,631	85.8	34.9	29.6
Foster Center CDP	355	NA	NA	340	97.6	0.0	0.0	2.4	0.0	19.2	50.9	30.0	153	54.2	54.9	14.4
Glocester town (Providence)	9,746	9,931	1.9	9,844	97.0	0.3	0.3	1.0	1.3	18.4	68.4	13.1	3,599	91.6	35.9	34.6
Greene CDP	888	NA	NA	849	99.4	0.0	0.6	0.0	0.0	18.2	66.9	15.0	308	89.9	45.5	24.4
Greenville CDP	8,658	NA	NA	8,596	94.9	1.6	1.2	0.7	1.7	18.8	58.4	22.7	3,215	81.2	32.9	40.2
Harmony CDP	985	NA	NA	969	94.8	0.0	0.0	0.0	5.2	12.3	70.9	16.7	410	93.4	43.4	20.5
Harrisville CDP	1,605	NA	NA	1,965	96.2	0.8	0.0	2.4	0.6	25.7	52.2	22.0	927	38.6	48.9	18.3
Hope Valley CDP	1,612	NA	NA	1,696	100.0	0.0	0.0	0.0	0.0	25.8	65.8	8.5	623	68.7	34.3	29.7
Hopkinton town (Washington)	8,188	8,121	-0.8	8,144	93.6	3.1	0.9	0.9	1.5	17.1	67.5	15.5	3,398	78.7	34.6	31.5
Jamestown town (Newport)	5,405	5,474	1.3	5,444	94.3	0.4	0.0	3.0	2.3	16.3	63.6	20.1	2,438	79.9	12.6	67.2
Johnston town (Providence)	28,769	29,144	1.3	28,987	85.7	1.8	4.7	2.0	5.8	18.9	61.5	19.5	11,709	67.1	43.7	27.7
Kingston CDP	6,974	NA	NA	7,136	80.5	5.4	2.2	3.1	8.9	7.0	89.0	3.9	849	76.3	11.7	62.0
Lincoln town (Providence)	21,104	21,507	1.9	21,300	86.7	3.0	1.5	3.4	5.5	22.7	61.2	16.0	8,187	68.5	28.2	38.8
Little Compton town (Newport)	3,492	3,504	0.3	3,491	95.9	1.1	0.4	1.3	1.3	18.2	57.0	24.9	1,571	77.2	22.9	51.8
Melville CDP	1,320	NA	NA	1,611	44.1	24.7	4.2	13.0	14.0	45.5	54.4	0.0	495	0.0	16.2	31.7
Middletown town (Newport)	16,097	16,105	0.0	16,081	78.3	5.8	4.0	5.4	6.5	23.9	58.8	17.2	6,527	54.2	26.8	45.1
Misquamicut CDP	390	NA	NA	419	95.0	1.0	0.0	4.1	0.0	21.9	45.3	32.7	170	72.4	7.6	60.0
Narragansett town (Washington)	15,900	15,705	-1.2	15,786	95.9	0.4	0.1	1.2	2.4	14.1	67.4	18.4	7,004	68.7	14.2	54.5
Narragansett Pier CDP.....	3,409	NA	NA	3,749	93.6	0.0	0.2	0.6	5.5	14.6	65.6	19.8	1,872	59.3	16.1	53.3
Newport city & MCD (Newport)	24,974	24,089	-3.5	24,599	78.7	5.5	0.9	5.8	9.1	15.0	70.5	14.6	10,626	42.6	27.7	51.1
Newport East CDP	11,769	NA	NA	10,953	77.5	5.8	3.8	6.5	6.4	20.2	59.0	20.9	4,729	50.7	30.5	40.5
New Shoreham town (Washington)	1,051	1,045	-0.6	893	95.5	0.7	0.0	2.1	1.7	11.6	63.2	25.1	418	77.0	22.2	58.1
North Kingstown town (Washington)	26,601	26,291	-1.2	26,404	91.3	1.2	3.0	1.8	2.7	23.3	61.6	15.0	10,294	74.2	25.2	49.8
North Providence town (Providence)	32,084	32,366	0.9	32,208	82.5	6.7	2.0	1.8	7.0	16.1	63.1	20.5	14,082	62.1	37.4	30.6
North Smithfield town (Providence)	11,967	12,218	2.1	12,106	96.5	0.2	0.4	1.5	1.3	19.8	58.5	21.7	4,522	70.9	34.9	33.3
Pascoag CDP	4,577	NA	NA	4,310	94.2	0.6	0.4	2.2	2.6	22.7	60.2	17.1	1,630	57.5	47.7	17.7
Pawtucket city & MCD (Providence)	71,141	71,499	0.5	71,313	54.1	15.2	1.6	8.4	20.6	22.9	64.9	12.2	28,124	43.7	51.5	18.2
Portsmouth town (Newport)	17,393	17,373	-0.1	17,352	92.5	1.3	2.0	2.0	2.2	21.1	59.1	19.8	6,983	74.8	24.0	49.3
Providence city & MCD (Providence)	178,038	179,154	0.6	178,562	36.5	12.7	6.3	4.2	40.4	22.6	68.7	8.8	60,967	35.0	44.8	30.3
Quonochontaug CDP	333	NA	NA	483	100.0	0.0	0.0	0.0	0.0	10.6	36.3	53.2	230	85.7	30.0	50.0
Richmond town (Washington)................	7,708	7,615	-1.2	7,648	94.6	1.1	1.5	1.2	1.6	24.4	65.9	9.6	2,746	88.3	30.2	39.0
Scituate town (Providence)	10,327	10,496	1.6	10,414	96.9	0.0	0.2	2.0	0.9	20.1	63.3	16.7	4,018	85.7	38.8	37.9
Smithfield town (Providence)	21,430	21,507	0.4	21,478	92.0	1.7	2.4	1.5	2.4	17.1	64.9	17.9	7,204	79.0	28.9	39.5
South Kingstown town (Washington)	30,607	30,750	0.5	30,546	87.9	2.5	2.3	3.3	3.9	16.3	67.5	16.1	10,489	74.1	23.4	54.9
Tiverton CDP	7,557	NA	NA	7,300	96.0	1.1	0.5	1.2	1.3	16.9	61.5	21.6	3,265	75.8	43.3	32.3
Tiverton town (Newport) ...	15,780	15,813	0.2	15,805	97.1	0.5	0.3	1.2	0.9	18.7	60.6	20.5	6,688	79.8	37.6	34.5
Valley Falls CDP	11,547	NA	NA	12,108	87.2	0.9	1.3	1.8	8.8	20.6	64.0	15.4	4,663	70.3	38.2	27.2

1 May be of any race.

Table A. All Places — Population and Housing

STATE City, town, township, borough, or CDP (county if applicable)	2010 census total population	2014 estimated population	Percent change 2010-2014	ACS total population estimate 2010-2014	White alone, not Hispanic or Latino	Black alone, not Hispanic or Latino	Asian alone, not Hispanic or Latino	All other races or 2 or more races, not Hispanic or Latino	Hispanic or Latino[1]	Under 18 years old	Age 18 to 64 years old	Age 65 years and older	Total occupied housing units	Percent owner occupied	High school diploma or less	Bachelor's degree or more
	1	2	3	4	5	6	7	8	9	10	11	12	13	14	15	16
RHODE ISLAND—Con.																
Wakefield-Peacedale CDP	8,487	NA	NA	8,911	88.6	3.0	1.3	4.8	2.2	21.7	61.9	16.4	3,513	70.7	27.9	51.1
Warren town (Bristol)	10,606	10,492	-1.1	10,555	96.6	0.1	0.0	0.9	2.4	19.5	62.6	18.0	4,554	56.8	43.7	30.3
Warwick city & MCD (Kent)	82,670	81,963	-0.9	82,065	89.6	1.3	2.8	1.8	4.4	18.4	63.1	18.5	35,156	71.5	34.8	31.6
Watch Hill CDP	154	NA	NA	179	91.1	0.0	0.6	0.0	8.4	0.0	62.0	38.0	98	100.0	5.1	85.7
Weekapaug CDP	425	NA	NA	419	97.9	1.7	0.0	0.5	0.0	8.3	45.9	45.6	219	74.0	11.4	65.3
Westerly CDP	17,936	NA	NA	17,984	91.7	0.9	3.0	2.2	2.2	21.0	60.1	18.8	7,644	60.4	40.5	30.1
Westerly town (Washington)	22,787	22,731	-0.2	22,727	92.2	1.1	2.4	2.3	2.0	20.6	59.2	20.1	9,579	64.5	38.4	34.4
West Greenwich town (Kent)	6,136	6,117	-0.3	6,118	88.8	1.7	4.5	2.4	2.6	27.3	64.1	8.5	2,109	78.8	25.2	36.9
West Warwick town (Kent)	29,185	28,880	-1.0	28,960	86.9	2.3	2.9	2.8	5.2	20.1	64.6	15.3	12,492	53.5	40.8	21.3
Woonsocket city & MCD (Providence)	41,186	41,228	0.1	41,136	69.8	6.0	7.1	2.9	14.2	23.7	62.4	14.1	16,979	39.2	53.5	14.6
Wyoming CDP	270	NA	NA	156	100.0	0.0	0.0	0.0	0.0	9.6	80.1	10.3	55	100.0	70.9	0.0
SOUTH CAROLINA	4,625,401	4,832,482	4.5	4,727,273	63.9	27.4	1.3	2.1	5.3	22.9	62.4	14.7	1,795,715	68.6	41.3	27.2
Abbeville city	5,278	5,191	-1.6	5,207	44.0	54.2	0.0	1.8	0.0	24.8	58.0	17.2	2,155	62.1	59.3	10.7
Aiken city	29,553	30,258	2.4	29,980	62.8	29.0	2.4	1.0	4.8	19.8	57.2	22.9	12,374	69.3	28.8	46.4
Alcolu CDP	429	NA	NA	596	25.8	44.5	0.0	0.0	29.7	30.8	63.2	6.0	203	37.9	40.9	7.9
Allendale town	3,482	3,195	-8.2	3,328	10.0	90.0	0.0	0.0	0.0	23.2	63.9	12.9	1,247	60.2	59.5	11.9
Anderson city	26,387	27,181	3.0	26,798	58.0	35.4	1.0	1.6	4.0	22.8	58.4	18.8	10,851	50.0	46.5	21.3
Andrews town	2,861	2,862	0.0	2,839	33.7	64.2	0.0	0.2	1.9	29.3	60.2	10.5	979	53.5	60.4	7.3
Antreville CDP	140	NA	NA	120	73.3	26.7	0.0	0.0	0.0	0.0	41.7	58.3	62	100.0	79.0	0.0
Arcadia CDP	2,634	NA	NA	3,123	43.7	2.0	0.4	1.3	52.6	36.2	60.6	3.2	935	39.5	54.3	22.0
Arcadia Lakes town	861	871	1.2	876	83.7	8.2	4.2	1.3	2.6	16.7	51.5	31.7	415	83.4	10.1	63.1
Arial CDP	2,543	NA	NA	2,739	90.4	1.1	0.3	7.7	0.6	25.5	56.5	18.0	980	73.9	54.8	13.4
Atlantic Beach town	334	362	8.4	267	44.2	48.3	0.0	2.6	4.9	20.9	69.6	9.4	128	26.6	58.6	19.5
Awendaw town	1,294	1,356	4.8	1,408	36.4	58.7	0.0	2.3	2.6	25.0	61.5	13.6	515	81.6	44.7	16.1
Aynor town	560	640	14.3	748	82.4	15.8	0.0	1.6	0.3	26.2	49.3	24.6	314	62.4	52.9	17.8
Bamberg town	3,607	3,453	-4.3	3,542	47.8	50.6	0.0	0.0	1.6	18.3	61.7	20.1	1,340	75.7	36.3	29.3
Barnwell city	4,750	4,649	-2.1	4,717	44.2	50.5	0.0	2.8	2.5	34.7	50.6	14.6	1,767	59.0	46.6	16.4
Batesburg-Leesville town	5,360	5,423	1.2	5,242	45.0	49.0	1.2	1.4	3.4	24.6	56.0	19.3	2,071	62.2	58.5	17.0
Beaufort city	12,443	13,130	5.5	12,702	61.4	23.4	2.0	3.0	10.2	23.8	62.0	14.2	4,538	55.6	23.6	43.6
Belton city	4,149	4,289	3.4	4,211	83.7	10.7	0.0	1.0	4.6	22.1	59.7	18.3	1,889	65.3	55.8	19.6
Belvedere CDP	5,792	NA	NA	5,504	63.0	21.7	0.0	2.9	12.4	27.7	55.6	16.7	1,949	82.2	55.3	17.3
Bennettsville city	9,069	8,833	-2.6	8,928	30.0	65.8	0.7	1.8	1.6	23.1	60.4	16.5	3,092	51.8	64.2	13.7
Berea CDP	14,295	NA	NA	14,230	53.3	20.8	2.4	2.2	21.3	29.0	55.8	15.2	5,537	60.8	59.5	12.6
Bethune town	334	343	2.7	308	76.6	9.7	0.0	12.7	1.0	16.9	63.4	19.8	139	85.6	56.1	14.4
Bishopville city	3,471	3,300	-4.9	3,372	25.1	71.9	0.0	1.3	1.7	24.9	60.8	14.1	991	47.8	61.8	8.2
Blacksburg town	1,848	1,874	1.4	1,823	59.5	35.3	0.3	3.6	1.3	30.8	54.5	14.5	680	59.1	74.0	6.0
Blackville town	2,406	2,327	-3.3	2,324	18.4	74.2	5.0	0.0	2.4	17.7	65.7	16.5	983	63.3	64.6	8.5
Blenheim town	154	149	-3.2	144	47.2	45.1	0.0	7.6	0.0	10.4	69.5	20.1	55	80.0	89.1	7.3
Bluffton town	13,353	15,199	13.8	13,979	58.9	17.2	2.3	3.0	18.7	29.7	60.8	9.7	4,436	73.9	33.1	36.0
Blythewood town	2,054	2,485	21.0	2,113	61.1	32.9	2.4	3.3	0.2	26.4	59.9	13.8	747	93.0	20.7	53.1
Boiling Springs CDP	8,219	NA	NA	8,542	86.0	7.4	2.5	0.8	3.4	29.2	60.4	10.4	3,240	75.8	26.9	40.9
Bonneau town	487	507	4.1	387	83.2	16.3	0.0	0.0	0.5	20.7	62.6	16.8	173	67.6	57.2	8.1
Bonneau Beach CDP	1,929	NA	NA	2,195	95.2	2.2	0.0	2.6	0.0	27.0	54.3	18.7	715	81.8	59.7	2.4
Bowman town	968	943	-2.6	776	26.3	73.3	0.0	0.0	0.4	21.5	61.4	17.1	348	65.2	60.3	17.0
Boykin CDP	100	NA	NA	114	100.0	0.0	0.0	0.0	0.0	27.2	72.6	0.0	44	86.4	25.0	18.2
Bradley CDP	170	NA	NA	157	52.2	47.8	0.0	0.0	0.0	14.6	60.5	24.8	58	100.0	39.7	20.7
Branchville town	1,024	998	-2.5	1,179	66.8	31.4	0.3	1.4	0.0	23.0	62.1	14.9	412	72.6	56.1	11.9
Briarcliffe Acres town	457	510	11.6	466	98.1	0.6	0.6	0.2	0.4	13.7	55.3	30.9	212	93.4	12.7	69.8
Brookdale CDP	4,873	NA	NA	4,271	1.2	97.6	1.0	0.1	0.1	22.9	57.8	19.4	1,697	48.7	50.7	17.0
Brunson town	553	531	-4.0	479	62.4	33.4	0.0	0.0	4.2	18.2	57.5	24.4	213	79.8	46.9	8.5
Bucksport CDP	876	NA	NA	760	4.9	95.1	0.0	0.0	0.0	18.7	55.3	26.1	334	94.3	73.1	3.6
Buffalo CDP	1,266	NA	NA	1,359	81.4	14.6	0.0	4.0	0.0	18.2	68.5	13.3	580	63.8	63.4	7.8
Burnettown town	2,684	2,764	3.0	2,742	72.3	16.7	0.3	4.3	6.4	21.7	61.4	17.2	1,108	72.7	51.1	12.0
Burton CDP	6,976	NA	NA	6,173	46.6	35.1	0.5	5.2	12.6	23.9	64.6	11.4	2,408	58.5	40.0	19.7
Calhoun Falls town	2,004	1,966	-1.9	1,912	31.9	64.0	0.0	4.1	0.0	22.5	63.8	13.8	738	71.8	64.5	3.8
Camden city	6,836	7,030	2.8	6,931	63.6	30.1	0.3	1.0	5.0	19.9	56.8	23.1	2,984	70.8	27.0	35.3
Cameron town	424	418	-1.4	586	56.0	38.1	1.0	4.9	0.0	27.5	52.8	19.8	207	79.2	41.1	19.8
Campobello town	501	521	4.0	505	89.5	6.1	0.0	2.0	2.4	24.2	59.2	16.6	182	90.1	44.0	12.6
Cane Savannah CDP	1,117	NA	NA	1,118	40.6	51.3	0.0	5.7	2.4	20.4	59.7	19.9	408	81.9	39.2	12.3
Carlisle town	435	416	-4.4	498	1.2	98.2	0.0	0.6	0.0	24.5	54.8	20.5	194	78.4	64.4	3.1
Catawba CDP	1,343	NA	NA	1,438	80.3	12.4	0.0	5.3	1.9	29.6	61.7	8.7	552	45.1	68.7	12.7
Cayce city	12,522	12,951	3.4	12,944	69.0	19.4	2.8	2.1	6.8	18.3	67.3	14.3	5,353	61.6	37.1	27.6
Centerville CDP	6,586	NA	NA	6,749	80.4	13.2	1.3	1.5	3.5	21.1	61.7	17.0	2,681	80.7	48.4	16.2
Central town	5,183	5,149	-0.7	5,170	73.2	11.9	3.1	1.3	10.5	13.1	80.0	6.9	1,972	19.8	35.8	28.3
Central Pacolet town	215	221	2.8	210	93.8	0.0	0.0	6.2	0.0	38.1	52.0	10.0	77	55.8	87.0	0.0
Chapin town	1,435	1,528	6.5	1,459	78.5	7.1	1.9	4.0	8.4	25.6	56.7	17.8	617	83.1	30.8	34.5
Charleston city	120,246	130,113	8.2	125,458	69.7	24.2	1.3	2.0	2.8	18.4	69.0	12.8	52,150	52.5	21.1	50.0
Cheraw town	5,851	5,793	-1.0	5,809	33.0	64.6	0.0	0.2	2.2	22.6	52.5	24.9	2,493	43.4	56.4	15.6
Cherryvale CDP	2,496	NA	NA	2,316	53.8	33.9	0.0	1.3	11.0	27.6	62.8	9.6	829	46.4	56.1	6.4
Chesnee city	860	889	3.4	785	75.4	22.8	0.0	1.0	0.8	13.8	70.4	15.8	391	38.1	74.4	3.8
Chester city	5,607	5,494	-2.0	5,543	29.1	66.6	0.2	2.3	1.8	24.8	60.9	14.5	2,149	55.9	63.1	13.7
Chesterfield town	1,465	1,454	-0.8	1,364	58.6	39.0	0.0	1.8	0.7	21.8	61.0	17.2	524	57.3	47.1	26.3
City View CDP	1,345	NA	NA	1,467	28.1	22.8	0.0	0.0	49.1	32.9	60.0	7.1	486	10.5	80.7	8.2
Clarks Hill CDP	381	NA	NA	240	32.9	67.1	0.0	0.0	0.0	21.7	65.0	13.3	93	66.7	54.8	15.1
Clearwater CDP	4,370	NA	NA	4,470	82.3	8.4	0.6	0.3	8.4	22.9	64.9	12.2	1,908	56.9	67.2	7.7
Clemson city	13,962	15,072	8.0	14,254	77.2	7.9	9.3	3.3	2.3	15.1	74.3	10.5	5,620	44.2	10.2	50.9
Clifton CDP	541	NA	NA	325	100.0	0.0	0.0	0.0	0.0	12.0	72.8	15.1	152	86.8	77.6	0.0
Clinton city	8,490	8,619	1.5	8,525	54.1	42.2	0.8	0.9	2.0	24.9	59.1	16.1	2,453	41.9	56.1	19.4
Clio town	726	696	-4.1	633	32.7	63.0	0.6	3.2	0.5	15.8	67.4	16.6	225	71.6	68.0	12.0
Clover town	5,110	5,579	9.2	5,321	77.1	17.1	0.0	3.5	2.3	31.4	59.0	9.7	1,915	65.1	50.3	16.1
Cokesbury CDP	215	NA	NA	138	38.4	61.6	0.0	0.0	0.0	0.0	76.0	23.9	91	100.0	73.6	9.9
Columbia city	130,065	132,067	1.5	131,331	48.3	41.7	2.2	2.5	5.3	17.0	73.7	9.2	44,992	45.9	25.8	43.8
Converse CDP	608	NA	NA	835	89.5	2.4	0.0	0.0	8.1	25.2	53.4	21.4	303	67.7	53.1	23.4
Conway city	17,295	20,175	16.7	18,645	57.8	38.5	0.7	1.4	1.6	20.7	64.6	14.8	6,611	57.8	38.0	22.9
Cope town	77	76	-1.3	154	89.6	10.4	0.0	0.0	0.0	31.7	62.9	5.2	38	81.6	36.8	13.2

1 May be of any race.

Table A. All Places — **Population and Housing**

STATE City, town, township, borough, or CDP (county if applicable)	Population: 2010 census total population	Population: 2014 estimated population	Population: Percent change 2010-2014	Race and Hispanic or Latino origin (percent), 2010–2014: ACS total population estimate 2010-2014	White alone, not Hispanic or Latino	Black alone, not Hispanic or Latino	Asian alone, not Hispanic or Latino	All other races or 2 or more races, not Hispanic or Latino	Hispanic or Latino[1]	Age (percent), 2010–2014: Under 18 years old	Age 18 to 64 years old	Age 65 years and older	Households, 2010–2014: Total occupied housing units	Percent owner occupied	Householders by level of education (percent): High school diploma or less	Bachelor's degree or more
	1	2	3	4	5	6	7	8	9	10	11	12	13	14	15	16
SOUTH CAROLINA—Con.																
Cordova town	169	166	-1.8	217	90.8	0.5	0.0	7.4	1.4	32.7	50.2	17.1	79	67.1	31.6	17.7
Coronaca CDP	191	NA	NA	126	90.5	0.0	0.0	9.5	0.0	18.3	68.2	13.5	83	100.0	50.6	28.9
Cottageville town	765	740	-3.3	913	88.7	6.7	0.3	3.9	0.3	25.1	62.9	11.9	325	76.3	59.7	8.3
Coward town	755	755	0.0	515	81.7	17.3	0.0	1.0	0.0	24.3	56.3	19.4	232	65.5	68.1	1.3
Cowpens town	2,160	2,235	3.5	1,739	84.4	12.3	0.0	0.6	2.7	18.1	57.0	24.8	742	62.9	57.1	8.8
Cross Anchor CDP	126	NA	NA	211	87.2	12.8	0.0	0.0	0.0	21.4	78.7	0.0	47	100.0	59.6	0.0
Cross Hill town	504	497	-1.4	550	37.1	55.5	0.0	2.2	5.3	21.7	66.3	12.2	211	81.0	48.3	14.7
Dalzell CDP	3,059	NA	NA	4,504	42.3	46.5	1.5	9.6	0.0	35.6	58.8	5.6	1,436	55.2	49.3	17.3
Darlington city	6,288	6,206	-1.3	6,232	42.0	56.7	0.8	0.5	0.0	23.8	59.3	17.0	2,636	50.6	53.2	21.5
Denmark city	3,530	3,372	-4.5	3,467	5.3	93.5	0.4	0.8	0.0	22.2	66.1	11.6	1,111	55.5	41.2	21.3
Dentsville CDP	14,062	NA	NA	14,122	19.4	66.5	4.9	1.6	7.7	22.1	64.9	13.1	5,972	34.8	32.5	30.4
Dillon city	6,814	6,658	-2.3	6,731	34.3	53.6	0.0	5.9	6.2	30.3	51.9	17.9	2,472	48.5	66.7	9.2
Donalds town	348	344	-1.1	323	71.2	22.3	0.0	6.5	0.0	23.5	58.7	17.6	143	67.8	45.5	16.8
Due West town	1,247	1,254	0.6	1,120	76.1	21.8	0.0	1.8	0.4	10.6	72.1	17.4	239	69.0	31.4	47.7
Duncan town	3,153	3,269	3.7	3,214	66.5	24.0	4.4	0.5	4.6	26.7	60.8	12.7	1,323	42.1	51.6	16.1
Dunean CDP	3,671	NA	NA	3,906	47.4	37.1	0.6	0.0	14.8	24.7	58.2	17.2	1,560	53.2	65.6	11.0
Easley city	20,027	20,549	2.6	20,242	78.5	12.5	0.5	2.9	5.6	22.9	58.9	18.0	8,120	63.8	42.0	25.0
East Gaffney CDP	3,085	NA	NA	3,258	66.5	21.8	0.0	2.9	8.7	17.4	69.4	13.1	1,282	54.1	70.6	9.6
Eastover town	813	820	0.9	670	3.3	90.7	6.0	0.0	0.0	31.2	48.7	20.0	266	52.6	72.9	9.8
East Sumter CDP	1,343	NA	NA	1,275	43.8	38.2	0.0	0.0	18.0	22.3	55.8	21.8	514	71.2	74.9	6.8
Edgefield town	4,750	4,718	-0.7	4,719	38.2	45.9	0.7	2.3	12.8	15.7	72.4	11.9	1,114	50.4	63.7	11.9
Edisto CDP	2,559	NA	NA	2,329	29.5	63.1	0.0	0.0	7.4	30.2	52.0	17.8	892	44.5	59.2	12.4
Edisto Beach town	414	414	0.0	592	98.1	0.0	0.0	1.9	0.0	1.0	53.5	45.4	346	89.6	7.8	63.0
Ehrhardt town	548	518	-5.5	509	54.0	46.0	0.0	0.0	0.0	21.1	60.0	19.1	187	79.1	42.2	15.0
Elgin town	1,311	1,423	8.5	1,499	76.8	11.1	1.5	1.6	9.1	25.3	65.4	9.4	529	88.8	37.6	25.0
Elgin CDP	2,607	NA	NA	2,767	69.8	20.1	0.0	0.0	10.2	22.9	61.3	15.7	1,059	74.6	55.9	14.7
Elko town	193	189	-2.1	174	39.1	60.9	0.0	0.0	0.0	35.0	56.5	8.6	67	65.7	61.2	9.0
Elloree town	702	688	-2.0	821	48.7	45.3	0.9	3.7	1.5	19.1	62.0	18.9	307	76.9	54.7	19.9
Enoree CDP	665	NA	NA	823	99.1	0.0	0.0	0.9	0.0	31.8	53.0	15.2	277	61.7	49.8	10.1
Estill town	2,040	2,025	-0.7	2,357	12.9	73.4	0.0	0.0	13.6	28.4	58.6	12.9	821	67.1	62.0	12.9
Eureka Mill CDP	1,476	NA	NA	1,583	25.1	71.8	0.0	2.0	1.1	20.0	67.1	12.9	581	71.6	70.4	12.6
Eutawville town	314	308	-1.9	446	39.9	59.0	0.0	0.0	1.1	23.0	56.5	20.4	158	72.8	65.8	14.6
Fairfax town	2,025	1,897	-6.3	1,791	13.2	86.7	0.0	0.0	0.1	29.3	53.6	17.1	702	48.1	61.3	6.8
Fairforest CDP	1,693	NA	NA	1,728	54.3	23.7	0.0	3.8	18.2	25.9	64.8	9.4	672	50.0	56.3	11.0
Fair Play CDP	687	NA	NA	674	100.0	0.0	0.0	0.0	0.0	18.4	62.1	19.4	269	100.0	54.6	13.8
Fingerville CDP	134	NA	NA	36	100.0	0.0	0.0	0.0	0.0	0.0	69.4	30.6	23	52.2	100.0	0.0
Five Forks CDP	14,140	NA	NA	16,173	84.2	5.2	3.9	3.7	3.0	32.7	59.2	8.1	5,024	91.7	11.6	67.6
Florence city	37,023	37,961	2.5	37,512	48.9	46.4	1.2	1.3	2.1	25.0	60.9	14.0	14,870	59.2	37.8	31.2
Folly Beach city	2,617	2,739	4.7	2,679	92.5	0.0	0.0	3.9	3.5	10.1	78.1	11.6	1,276	56.2	7.9	62.0
Forest Acres city	10,401	10,603	1.9	10,533	72.5	22.2	2.2	1.9	1.2	21.3	58.2	20.4	4,921	70.1	15.2	55.8
Forestbrook CDP	4,612	NA	NA	4,539	86.2	6.5	1.7	0.9	4.6	21.1	63.4	15.6	1,801	81.1	34.5	15.2
Fort Lawn town	895	870	-2.8	818	43.8	53.2	0.0	1.6	1.5	26.4	60.2	13.3	301	71.4	64.1	8.3
Fort Mill town	11,283	13,087	16.0	12,068	76.0	12.5	2.5	2.2	6.7	29.4	59.3	11.3	4,827	62.0	31.2	34.6
Fountain Inn city	7,658	8,134	6.2	8,031	62.8	32.7	1.0	1.3	2.2	30.2	57.4	12.4	3,092	69.8	40.1	21.3
Furman town	237	231	-2.5	259	27.4	72.6	0.0	0.0	0.0	22.0	49.8	28.2	115	77.4	79.1	13.0
Gadsden CDP	1,632	NA	NA	1,696	5.5	85.1	0.0	8.0	1.5	21.0	64.7	14.3	637	63.7	75.7	10.0
Gaffney city	12,545	12,597	0.4	12,565	48.9	45.2	1.2	2.4	2.3	22.3	59.8	17.9	4,797	54.3	57.9	17.7
Gantt CDP	14,229	NA	NA	14,630	22.4	62.4	0.1	1.4	13.7	27.5	60.1	12.4	5,315	49.7	58.9	14.0
Garden City CDP	9,209	NA	NA	8,824	96.4	0.7	0.0	1.6	1.3	13.2	47.3	39.4	4,508	78.3	37.4	23.7
Gaston town	1,637	1,652	0.9	1,571	81.6	10.0	1.0	2.0	5.3	21.9	65.0	13.2	653	68.8	65.1	8.0
Gayle Mill CDP	913	NA	NA	833	45.0	55.0	0.0	0.0	0.0	29.4	49.7	21.0	377	37.9	68.4	2.4
Georgetown city	9,163	9,054	-1.2	9,110	36.2	58.2	0.0	1.2	4.4	22.6	59.4	17.9	3,442	62.0	50.1	16.2
Gifford town	287	276	-3.8	309	1.3	94.8	0.0	3.9	0.0	28.1	61.8	10.0	100	92.0	90.0	0.0
Gilbert town	565	596	5.5	688	76.7	1.7	0.0	0.3	21.2	29.2	63.2	7.6	252	73.8	47.2	15.9
Glendale CDP	307	NA	NA	159	96.2	3.8	0.0	0.0	0.0	0.0	78.0	22.0	96	74.0	58.3	6.3
Gloverville CDP	2,831	NA	NA	3,117	90.0	9.6	0.0	0.4	0.0	26.8	57.3	15.8	1,291	58.5	69.0	5.3
Golden Grove CDP	2,467	NA	NA	2,133	77.1	10.8	0.6	1.7	9.8	21.9	54.1	24.1	890	72.5	60.3	19.3
Goose Creek city	36,145	40,370	11.7	38,545	67.6	18.9	4.2	3.6	5.6	25.0	66.3	8.7	12,984	64.8	29.6	27.0
Govan town	65	62	-4.6	91	68.1	30.8	0.0	0.0	1.1	13.2	61.6	25.3	34	79.4	76.5	2.9
Gramling CDP	86	NA	NA	0	0.0	0.0	0.0	0.0	0.0	0.0	0.0	0.0	0	0.0	0.0	0.0
Graniteville CDP	2,614	NA	NA	2,725	50.0	44.6	0.0	0.6	4.8	27.4	60.2	12.4	1,052	48.8	50.9	9.9
Gray Court town	795	791	-0.5	834	36.8	55.2	0.0	1.8	6.2	19.8	65.0	15.2	318	69.2	57.5	10.1
Great Falls town	1,979	1,936	-2.2	1,627	70.3	27.2	0.4	1.5	0.6	25.8	57.1	17.1	652	70.4	62.9	14.0
Greeleyville town	431	409	-5.1	513	18.3	78.8	0.0	1.4	1.6	23.4	57.2	19.3	198	55.6	63.6	5.6
Greenville city	59,153	62,252	5.2	60,670	60.9	29.8	1.8	2.1	5.5	19.4	68.3	12.1	26,161	43.6	31.2	42.7
Greenwood city	23,285	23,236	-0.2	23,296	43.6	42.6	1.0	2.6	10.2	25.6	59.0	15.4	8,566	45.9	53.8	18.2
Greer city	25,595	27,676	8.1	26,626	60.0	17.8	2.4	2.5	17.4	24.8	64.6	10.6	10,067	57.2	37.3	32.8
Hampton town	2,808	2,702	-3.8	2,740	43.3	52.4	2.3	0.9	1.1	29.7	52.5	17.8	1,036	75.0	44.5	25.6
Hanahan city	17,994	19,865	10.4	18,999	69.1	14.5	4.3	3.2	9.0	25.0	64.7	10.3	7,424	58.8	37.1	26.9
Hardeeville city	3,060	4,789	56.5	3,914	45.4	22.8	1.8	5.1	24.9	26.2	63.1	10.7	1,374	42.3	37.3	32.9
Harleyville town	667	688	3.1	660	73.3	25.5	0.0	0.0	1.2	24.2	58.3	17.4	236	72.9	55.9	14.0
Hartsville city	7,776	7,852	1.0	7,857	49.8	46.5	0.8	2.0	1.0	22.7	58.6	18.7	3,286	50.5	45.3	27.7
Heath Springs town	790	867	9.7	873	39.4	59.8	0.0	0.0	0.8	25.8	62.7	11.5	312	67.6	57.7	7.4
Hemingway town	459	434	-5.4	516	49.8	47.5	0.0	2.7	0.0	24.1	56.8	19.0	200	67.5	68.0	10.0
Hickory Grove town	440	479	8.9	367	66.8	22.3	0.0	10.9	0.0	19.9	66.5	13.6	147	78.2	63.9	14.3
Hilda town	447	430	-3.8	503	89.3	9.1	0.0	1.6	0.0	20.9	64.3	14.9	184	84.8	63.0	4.3
Hilton Head Island town	37,096	40,039	7.9	38,497	76.1	8.5	0.7	0.6	14.1	15.2	52.5	32.3	16,805	72.4	22.4	51.9
Hodges town	155	154	-0.6	129	90.7	7.0	1.6	0.8	0.0	22.6	62.9	14.7	52	86.5	28.8	23.1
Holly Hill town	1,277	1,249	-2.2	1,247	40.2	50.4	3.5	1.8	4.2	24.7	49.2	26.1	492	61.8	63.2	20.1
Hollywood town	4,714	4,904	4.0	4,831	51.3	47.4	1.3	0.0	0.0	14.3	63.3	22.4	2,157	87.3	36.2	38.6
Homeland Park CDP	6,296	NA	NA	6,574	55.5	37.5	0.0	2.1	4.8	23.1	63.3	13.7	2,712	55.6	75.6	3.6
Honea Path town	3,560	3,670	3.1	3,610	79.6	17.1	0.0	0.9	2.4	20.2	58.7	21.2	1,562	70.4	60.8	11.9
Hopkins CDP	2,882	NA	NA	3,257	21.3	72.2	0.0	0.1	6.4	16.8	68.8	14.4	1,122	75.4	62.7	15.2
India Hook CDP	3,328	NA	NA	3,804	84.9	3.5	0.8	0.0	10.8	26.3	58.3	15.4	1,551	88.2	36.2	29.7
Inman city	2,167	2,225	2.7	2,345	65.0	23.4	5.3	4.7	1.6	27.3	57.1	15.5	938	52.7	54.3	12.6
Inman Mills CDP	1,050	NA	NA	2,058	75.2	6.4	0.8	1.7	15.9	33.2	49.9	17.0	440	50.2	58.9	5.5
Irmo town	11,118	11,893	7.0	11,518	62.2	28.3	1.9	1.1	6.6	26.5	61.8	11.7	4,382	79.9	26.7	41.5
Irwin CDP	1,405	NA	NA	1,354	56.1	24.9	0.0	0.4	18.6	22.0	57.4	20.5	509	86.1	87.8	3.3
Islandton CDP	70	NA	NA	52	100.0	0.0	0.0	0.0	0.0	46.1	46.1	7.7	18	100.0	22.2	77.8
Isle of Palms city	4,133	4,319	4.5	4,241	94.4	1.3	0.1	0.2	4.0	15.9	56.1	28.1	1,889	82.3	7.7	67.7
Iva town	1,230	1,265	2.8	1,107	90.8	9.2	0.0	0.0	0.0	18.8	58.1	22.9	459	58.6	66.2	3.9

1 May be of any race.

Table A. All Places — **Population and Housing**

STATE City, town, township, borough, or CDP (county if applicable)	Population				Race and Hispanic or Latino origin (percent), 2010–2014					Age (percent), 2010–2014			Households, 2010–2014			
	2010 census total population	2014 estimated population	Percent change 2010-2014	ACS total population estimate 2010-2014	White alone, not Hispanic or Latino	Black alone, not Hispanic or Latino	Asian alone, not Hispanic or Latino	All other races or 2 or more races, not Hispanic or Latino	Hispanic or Latino[1]	Under 18 years old	Age 18 to 64 years old	Age 65 years and older	Total occupied housing units	Percent owner occupied	Householders by level of education (percent): High school diploma or less	Householders by level of education (percent): Bachelor's degree or more
	1	2	3	4	5	6	7	8	9	10	11	12	13	14	15	16
SOUTH CAROLINA—Con.																
Jackson town	1,700	1,753	3.1	1,545	83.4	10.7	0.3	4.3	1.3	19.8	60.7	19.5	627	80.9	53.3	12.6
Jacksonboro CDP	478	NA	NA	493	32.3	67.7	0.0	0.0	0.0	27.0	65.1	7.9	149	61.7	47.0	12.8
James Island town	11,217	11,630	3.7	11,451	82.0	13.6	1.1	2.2	1.1	16.2	62.0	21.7	4,979	82.1	27.5	37.9
Jamestown town	72	76	5.6	145	42.1	55.2	0.0	2.8	0.0	13.8	80.0	6.2	46	82.6	52.2	23.9
Jefferson town	753	746	-0.9	959	50.2	40.6	1.7	7.6	0.0	30.5	54.7	14.7	377	58.9	61.3	17.8
Jenkinsville town	46	44	-4.3	47	0.0	100.0	0.0	0.0	0.0	21.2	63.8	14.9	17	76.5	88.2	0.0
Joanna CDP	1,539	NA	NA	1,369	65.7	27.0	0.3	7.0	0.0	18.5	66.4	15.0	631	69.3	50.1	14.3
Johnsonville city	1,480	1,508	1.9	1,602	77.0	16.2	1.7	1.2	3.9	27.3	58.1	14.8	604	69.4	47.5	21.7
Johnston town	2,362	2,337	-1.1	2,216	30.7	69.0	0.0	0.0	0.4	23.7	61.1	15.3	778	54.5	70.2	14.0
Jonesville town	911	873	-4.2	856	61.1	32.8	0.0	4.3	1.8	20.7	59.2	19.9	409	50.4	68.0	5.6
Judson CDP	2,050	NA	NA	2,028	21.6	62.6	0.5	1.9	13.3	23.3	65.2	11.4	811	50.8	72.1	6.9
Kershaw town	1,803	1,977	9.7	2,239	63.5	31.4	0.8	2.1	2.3	26.6	54.6	18.6	817	56.9	59.7	9.3
Kiawah Island town	1,626	1,725	6.1	1,311	98.8	0.6	0.0	0.0	0.6	1.4	42.0	56.7	708	94.4	4.2	86.0
Kingstree town	3,328	3,185	-4.3	3,254	25.1	69.5	1.3	0.0	4.0	27.8	55.3	16.9	1,128	46.6	41.7	26.6
Kline town	197	193	-2.0	273	55.3	33.3	0.0	0.0	11.4	30.4	60.9	8.8	88	70.5	58.0	13.6
Ladson CDP	13,790	NA	NA	15,369	56.5	28.2	2.7	5.1	7.5	27.4	64.3	8.2	4,994	72.5	47.5	17.3
Lake City city	6,672	6,732	0.9	6,720	22.3	73.9	0.2	0.3	3.4	25.1	57.0	18.1	2,525	51.9	63.0	11.2
Lake Murray of Richland CDP	5,484	NA	NA	5,475	91.4	3.8	0.2	1.3	3.3	19.8	58.4	21.9	1,935	87.8	16.1	58.8
Lake Secession CDP	1,083	NA	NA	1,388	97.6	1.0	0.0	0.6	0.8	15.7	61.6	22.7	539	83.7	54.0	11.1
Lake View town	807	789	-2.2	815	60.0	34.1	0.0	4.3	1.6	14.9	56.7	28.3	350	59.7	51.1	22.0
Lakewood CDP	3,032	NA	NA	2,942	60.1	39.5	0.0	0.4	0.0	29.8	60.1	10.0	1,054	66.3	55.3	14.9
Lake Wylie CDP	8,841	NA	NA	9,640	89.2	2.8	1.2	0.6	6.2	30.3	56.5	13.1	3,679	75.6	19.9	51.4
Lamar town	989	977	-1.2	899	51.3	40.2	8.3	0.2	0.0	17.0	55.4	27.6	406	82.0	62.6	19.5
Lancaster city	8,526	8,960	5.1	8,801	41.7	53.5	1.2	1.1	2.4	25.2	57.8	16.9	3,249	47.5	52.5	18.2
Landrum city	2,371	2,459	3.7	2,597	83.6	10.2	0.3	0.6	5.4	24.7	62.0	13.2	1,061	70.8	44.7	21.5
Lane town	508	480	-5.5	496	15.5	82.7	0.0	1.8	0.0	17.3	63.5	19.2	232	75.0	54.3	9.1
Langley CDP	1,447	NA	NA	1,118	90.3	7.2	0.0	2.6	0.0	12.9	68.7	18.4	566	68.4	69.4	4.8
Latta town	1,379	1,347	-2.3	1,237	56.2	40.8	0.0	1.9	1.1	24.6	56.4	19.1	554	68.6	59.2	20.0
Laurel Bay CDP	5,891	NA	NA	6,404	59.3	24.3	1.7	4.0	10.7	41.2	56.8	2.1	2,004	17.6	41.1	10.6
Laurens city	9,137	9,182	0.5	9,136	56.4	32.9	0.6	0.3	9.8	23.8	56.2	20.0	3,859	53.4	53.6	14.1
Lesslie CDP	3,112	NA	NA	2,408	93.2	3.4	0.0	1.6	1.7	25.9	63.2	11.0	843	75.8	43.3	9.3
Lexington town	17,887	19,893	11.2	19,007	75.7	13.5	4.3	2.6	3.8	23.3	65.8	10.9	7,565	60.5	20.9	45.5
Liberty city	3,269	3,235	-1.0	3,262	83.9	9.7	0.0	0.0	6.4	24.3	53.9	21.7	1,508	78.6	52.8	18.0
Lincolnville town	1,142	1,199	5.0	1,488	41.1	46.5	0.8	1.6	10.0	19.7	68.4	11.9	512	60.4	53.1	9.0
Little Mountain town	291	294	1.0	175	76.6	23.4	0.0	0.0	0.0	22.9	56.6	20.6	69	78.3	33.3	34.8
Little River CDP	8,960	NA	NA	9,273	84.9	6.3	1.3	3.0	4.4	10.8	63.0	26.2	4,721	70.8	34.2	29.9
Livingston town	136	134	-1.5	135	74.1	20.0	0.0	5.9	0.0	17.8	60.1	22.2	60	80.0	68.3	11.7
Lockhart town	488	475	-2.7	517	80.7	9.3	0.0	10.1	0.0	16.4	57.5	26.1	253	67.2	63.6	0.0
Lodge town	120	118	-1.7	100	95.0	5.0	0.0	0.0	0.0	7.0	69.0	24.0	65	58.5	61.5	16.9
Loris city	2,396	2,538	5.9	2,459	49.4	40.2	2.0	0.4	8.0	22.7	55.9	21.3	960	58.9	51.9	17.1
Lowndesville town	125	123	-1.6	167	90.4	9.6	0.0	0.0	0.0	36.0	52.8	11.4	67	49.3	83.6	0.0
Lowrys town	200	196	-2.0	202	64.4	25.7	0.0	0.5	9.4	25.2	58.4	16.3	69	82.6	46.4	17.4
Lugoff CDP	7,434	NA	NA	8,039	75.3	17.3	0.2	2.8	4.4	25.4	61.1	13.4	2,872	77.4	39.3	29.6
Luray town	127	124	-2.4	191	24.1	46.1	0.0	0.0	29.8	29.4	53.9	16.8	71	81.7	77.5	11.3
Lydia CDP	642	NA	NA	407	9.1	78.1	10.1	1.5	1.2	24.1	66.8	9.1	194	70.1	55.2	0.0
Lyman town	3,255	3,375	3.7	3,314	86.0	4.5	6.8	1.3	1.4	17.6	66.1	16.2	1,320	77.4	38.6	21.1
Lynchburg town	373	358	-4.0	385	5.7	94.3	0.0	0.0	0.0	15.4	66.0	18.7	182	67.6	55.5	13.2
McBee town	871	859	-1.4	696	50.1	46.6	0.0	1.3	2.0	25.2	60.8	14.1	270	76.7	61.1	16.7
McClellanville town	499	525	5.2	477	98.5	1.5	0.0	0.0	0.0	20.5	53.5	26.0	203	96.1	18.7	52.7
McColl town	2,174	2,091	-3.8	2,390	56.8	19.7	0.1	19.4	3.9	30.4	55.8	13.8	917	69.7	67.9	7.0
McConnells town	255	271	6.3	323	61.9	36.2	0.0	0.9	0.9	16.4	67.8	15.8	127	85.8	59.8	20.5
McCormick town	2,783	2,704	-2.8	2,744	30.0	66.7	0.0	1.1	2.2	13.1	76.0	10.9	714	50.4	61.9	16.5
Manning city	4,111	4,059	-1.3	4,075	32.2	65.7	0.0	1.2	0.8	25.4	57.4	17.0	1,553	52.4	59.9	16.2
Marion city	6,939	6,751	-2.7	6,833	18.9	78.8	2.0	0.1	0.3	30.7	54.1	15.1	2,413	48.1	49.8	19.2
Mauldin city	23,138	24,823	7.3	23,985	63.0	24.0	2.3	2.0	8.8	24.5	62.9	12.6	9,181	65.7	27.7	36.8
Mayesville town	731	731	0.0	571	15.4	83.2	0.0	0.0	1.4	22.3	60.7	17.2	220	72.3	65.5	19.5
Mayo CDP	1,592	NA	NA	1,234	94.5	0.0	0.0	5.5	0.0	16.7	64.7	18.6	479	79.7	44.1	14.2
Meggett town	1,230	1,298	5.5	1,416	88.1	8.7	0.2	1.4	1.6	15.7	61.1	23.3	597	90.3	36.3	32.7
Modoc CDP	218	NA	NA	210	88.6	0.0	0.0	8.1	3.3	0.0	60.9	39.0	112	95.5	30.4	14.3
Monarch Mill CDP	1,811	NA	NA	1,850	78.2	10.3	0.0	3.8	7.7	22.5	58.2	19.2	689	80.3	65.7	3.9
Moncks Corner town	7,910	9,460	19.6	8,711	61.4	27.5	1.3	4.2	5.6	23.1	66.9	10.0	3,197	65.7	45.0	14.8
Monetta town	231	233	0.9	233	79.0	12.0	0.0	4.7	4.3	26.6	55.8	17.6	87	72.4	57.5	19.5
Mount Carmel CDP	216	NA	NA	149	10.1	89.9	0.0	0.0	0.0	16.1	65.8	18.1	52	65.4	51.9	28.8
Mount Croghan town	195	194	-0.5	198	89.9	7.6	0.0	2.0	0.5	16.6	72.2	11.1	74	75.7	64.9	4.1
Mount Pleasant town	67,854	77,796	14.7	72,379	89.6	4.4	1.8	1.4	2.8	23.6	63.1	13.5	29,101	71.6	13.0	62.7
Mountville CDP	108	NA	NA	89	100.0	0.0	0.0	0.0	0.0	7.9	58.4	33.7	42	81.0	40.5	11.9
Mulberry CDP	529	NA	NA	453	35.3	64.7	0.0	0.0	0.0	37.2	40.5	22.1	153	77.8	73.2	10.5
Mullins city	4,672	4,534	-3.0	4,593	38.8	59.3	0.0	0.7	1.2	22.5	58.0	19.4	1,650	61.5	60.8	17.8
Murphys Estates CDP	1,441	NA	NA	1,635	85.0	10.2	0.0	0.0	4.8	38.9	49.7	11.5	481	93.8	45.3	22.9
Murrells Inlet CDP	7,547	NA	NA	8,027	93.1	5.6	0.4	0.8	0.1	15.2	53.8	31.0	3,506	80.2	33.7	34.3
Myrtle Beach city	27,105	29,992	10.7	28,455	69.9	12.4	1.4	3.1	13.3	17.8	64.6	17.6	12,222	51.8	39.0	29.9
Neeses town	374	363	-2.9	299	78.6	18.7	0.0	2.7	0.0	20.7	64.1	15.1	119	71.4	58.0	10.1
Newberry city	10,281	10,268	-0.1	10,259	42.0	42.7	1.7	1.4	12.1	25.6	59.6	14.7	3,590	47.6	58.4	24.9
New Ellenton town	2,056	2,110	2.6	2,712	60.5	35.2	0.0	0.8	3.5	30.1	55.8	14.3	1,071	75.1	54.0	12.5
Newport CDP	4,136	NA	NA	3,724	86.8	4.7	2.3	0.4	5.8	21.7	65.5	13.0	1,393	82.7	20.0	44.8
Newry CDP	172	NA	NA	71	100.0	0.0	0.0	0.0	0.0	11.3	26.8	62.0	53	100.0	15.1	0.0
Nichols town	368	359	-2.4	389	67.4	30.8	0.0	0.0	1.8	15.4	66.5	18.0	165	73.9	61.8	15.2
Ninety Six town	2,036	2,034	-0.1	1,972	71.8	23.3	0.0	1.2	3.8	23.6	58.1	18.3	798	70.8	54.9	13.7
Norris town	813	813	0.0	803	92.7	5.9	1.5	0.0	0.0	17.3	63.6	19.1	347	72.6	61.1	7.8
North town	769	750	-2.5	883	49.7	46.2	0.9	0.9	2.3	27.8	53.0	19.3	348	51.1	51.1	8.3
North Augusta city	21,327	22,300	4.6	21,832	72.4	18.4	0.8	2.9	5.4	22.4	62.2	15.4	8,802	66.8	29.1	35.9
North Charleston city	97,601	106,749	9.4	102,143	37.1	47.8	2.0	2.8	10.2	25.2	66.2	8.5	36,913	46.5	43.0	21.3
North Hartsville CDP	3,251	NA	NA	3,211	62.3	29.1	0.0	0.6	8.0	24.1	64.5	11.5	1,154	75.2	56.2	17.9
Northlake CDP	3,745	NA	NA	4,317	81.9	11.2	3.6	0.8	2.5	25.8	58.6	15.6	1,701	78.1	28.3	39.8
North Myrtle Beach city	13,802	15,174	9.9	14,485	89.9	2.6	1.5	0.6	5.3	8.0	59.2	32.8	7,582	70.2	31.4	34.0
Norway town	337	331	-1.8	359	45.7	54.3	0.0	0.0	0.0	10.3	72.3	17.3	153	68.0	48.4	22.9
Oak Grove CDP	10,291	NA	NA	10,344	74.7	18.2	0.2	2.2	4.7	25.9	61.0	13.0	4,143	71.0	37.0	25.9
Oakland CDP	1,232	NA	NA	1,267	50.2	43.8	2.6	0.0	3.4	26.9	52.0	21.3	569	46.7	27.6	19.0
Olanta town	563	572	1.6	707	60.4	36.8	0.0	2.8	0.0	25.2	52.0	22.9	258	64.3	46.1	16.3
Olar town	257	244	-5.1	249	47.8	50.6	0.0	0.0	1.6	15.6	54.1	30.1	108	75.9	47.2	17.6

1 May be of any race.

Table A. All Places — **Population and Housing**

STATE City, town, township, borough, or CDP (county if applicable)	Population: 2010 census total population	Population: 2014 estimated population	Population: Percent change 2010-2014	Population: ACS total population estimate 2010-2014	Race and Hispanic or Latino origin (percent), 2010–2014: White alone, not Hispanic or Latino	Black alone, not Hispanic or Latino	Asian alone, not Hispanic or Latino	All other races or 2 or more races, not Hispanic or Latino	Hispanic or Latino[1]	Age (percent), 2010–2014: Under 18 years old	Age 18 to 64 years old	Age 65 years and older	Households, 2010–2014: Total occupied housing units	Percent owner occupied	Householders by level of education (percent): High school diploma or less	Bachelor's degree or more
	1	2	3	4	5	6	7	8	9	10	11	12	13	14	15	16
SOUTH CAROLINA—Con.																
Orangeburg city	13,960	13,553	-2.9	13,790	16.3	79.0	1.5	1.7	1.5	21.3	64.7	14.2	4,755	43.7	39.2	33.9
Oswego CDP	84	NA	NA	62	100.0	0.0	0.0	0.0	0.0	0.0	61.2	38.7	35	100.0	65.7	34.3
Pacolet town	2,244	2,319	3.3	2,291	68.7	23.6	0.0	4.6	3.1	23.2	58.4	18.5	904	70.8	60.8	6.2
Pageland town	2,757	2,744	-0.5	2,739	49.9	29.0	0.7	3.4	16.9	17.3	63.5	19.2	1,214	55.6	67.7	10.5
Pamplico town	1,226	1,247	1.7	1,132	39.5	59.7	0.0	0.8	0.0	28.2	57.3	14.5	362	69.9	47.0	21.0
Parker CDP	11,431	NA	NA	11,987	54.6	22.4	0.1	2.0	20.9	26.8	61.8	11.5	3,985	51.4	66.1	9.1
Parksville town	117	112	-4.3	145	90.3	0.7	0.0	7.6	1.4	19.4	68.2	12.4	74	83.8	43.2	2.7
Patrick town	351	348	-0.9	390	75.6	20.0	0.0	1.3	3.1	21.9	54.6	23.6	179	68.7	72.1	4.5
Pawleys Island town	103	105	1.9	84	100.0	0.0	0.0	0.0	0.0	0.0	47.7	52.4	52	86.5	3.8	67.3
Paxville town	190	187	-1.6	210	41.0	59.0	0.0	0.0	0.0	29.0	61.0	10.0	65	63.1	56.9	10.8
Peak town	64	64	0.0	52	80.8	19.2	0.0	0.0	0.0	9.6	71.1	19.2	27	59.3	29.6	25.9
Pelion town	684	698	2.0	754	91.8	1.1	0.0	1.7	5.4	25.7	63.5	10.6	240	85.0	50.4	12.9
Pelzer town	89	91	2.2	44	70.5	11.4	0.0	11.4	6.8	22.7	52.3	25.0	20	75.0	45.0	25.0
Pendleton town	3,015	3,115	3.3	3,061	73.4	14.4	2.5	4.3	5.4	15.8	64.6	19.5	1,574	52.9	37.7	29.5
Perry town	233	236	1.3	300	61.7	29.0	2.3	7.0	0.0	26.3	62.2	11.3	112	80.4	75.0	0.9
Pickens city	3,126	3,149	0.7	3,137	85.8	13.9	0.0	0.2	0.0	24.7	59.3	16.0	1,179	49.4	47.5	10.5
Piedmont CDP	5,103	NA	NA	5,396	83.9	15.4	0.0	0.4	0.3	23.7	61.7	14.7	2,034	69.1	57.3	9.4
Pine Ridge town	2,066	2,194	6.2	2,142	88.9	7.1	1.6	0.0	2.3	22.1	61.4	16.4	785	84.3	41.5	22.2
Pinewood town	538	540	0.4	678	32.7	65.8	1.5	0.0	0.0	35.9	43.0	21.2	249	50.6	59.4	8.0
Pinopolis CDP	948	NA	NA	944	92.3	0.0	0.0	0.0	7.7	13.6	57.9	28.4	419	85.0	12.9	48.7
Plum Branch town	82	78	-4.9	126	97.6	2.4	0.0	0.0	0.0	17.5	65.1	17.5	63	95.2	44.4	36.5
Pomaria town	179	180	0.6	91	64.8	35.2	0.0	0.0	0.0	24.2	57.2	18.7	35	97.1	42.9	31.4
Port Royal town	10,689	11,870	11.0	11,264	58.3	25.0	1.6	4.0	11.1	20.4	74.4	5.3	2,722	34.3	30.3	37.5
Powdersville CDP	0	NA	NA	7,513	85.7	5.8	1.6	1.3	5.7	25.2	61.4	13.4	2,799	78.4	45.1	26.4
Princeton CDP	62	NA	NA	60	100.0	0.0	0.0	0.0	0.0	0.0	100.0	0.0	37	100.0	78.4	21.6
Privateer CDP	2,349	NA	NA	3,003	78.8	18.1	0.0	2.2	0.9	36.7	55.0	8.5	990	81.0	53.2	11.6
Promised Land CDP	511	NA	NA	702	0.0	100.0	0.0	0.0	0.0	2.3	71.4	26.4	245	93.9	80.0	12.7
Prosperity town	1,178	1,192	1.2	1,058	57.5	39.2	0.0	1.2	2.1	19.7	63.2	17.3	461	69.6	50.1	21.3
Quinby town	924	945	2.3	1,151	20.9	77.5	0.0	1.5	0.1	19.4	64.3	16.4	425	85.2	32.2	26.1
Ravenel town	2,465	2,571	4.3	2,525	41.3	57.3	0.8	0.7	0.0	29.0	57.1	14.0	921	86.9	53.3	10.4
Red Bank CDP	9,617	NA	NA	9,128	87.2	6.3	0.8	1.8	3.8	25.5	63.2	11.3	3,675	80.5	44.2	21.9
Red Hill CDP	13,223	NA	NA	14,565	75.5	11.2	1.4	3.1	8.7	17.8	62.9	19.3	5,803	68.5	41.0	24.9
Reevesville town	194	202	4.1	242	63.6	36.4	0.0	0.0	0.0	21.5	54.6	24.0	99	87.9	52.5	26.3
Reidville town	595	611	2.7	817	92.3	5.6	0.6	0.7	0.7	28.7	63.7	7.6	288	81.3	46.9	19.1
Rembert CDP	306	NA	NA	231	10.0	85.7	3.0	1.3	0.0	6.1	71.1	22.9	91	75.8	45.1	25.3
Richburg town	275	264	-4.0	343	42.6	57.4	0.0	0.0	0.0	26.5	61.2	12.2	116	66.4	60.3	18.1
Ridgeland town	4,030	4,076	1.1	4,051	33.3	46.4	1.6	0.3	18.4	23.3	67.7	9.1	1,292	53.3	51.3	10.4
Ridge Spring town	737	743	0.8	795	31.7	65.2	0.0	0.0	3.1	21.0	54.8	24.4	294	67.3	72.8	11.9
Ridgeville town	1,967	1,959	-0.4	1,790	31.7	63.7	0.3	1.9	2.3	3.6	88.2	8.3	215	80.9	64.2	6.5
Ridgeway town	319	313	-1.9	423	49.2	48.2	0.0	0.0	2.6	26.7	64.5	8.7	172	66.9	36.6	14.0
Riverview CDP	681	NA	NA	232	74.1	0.0	0.0	0.0	25.9	10.8	66.0	23.3	132	88.6	79.5	20.5
Rock Hill city	66,474	69,967	5.3	68,185	51.2	38.7	2.3	2.9	4.8	23.7	65.1	11.1	26,635	50.7	34.7	29.0
Rockville town	134	139	3.7	187	88.8	10.2	0.0	0.0	1.1	5.3	45.4	49.2	91	90.1	24.2	39.6
Roebuck CDP	2,200	NA	NA	2,065	68.7	21.1	3.4	2.0	4.7	22.2	61.1	16.8	746	85.9	41.4	19.8
Rowesville town	304	299	-1.6	359	58.8	39.0	0.0	1.7	0.6	33.4	55.2	11.4	126	73.8	59.5	2.4
Ruby town	358	355	-0.8	393	87.3	8.7	0.3	2.8	1.0	29.5	58.0	12.5	156	82.7	53.8	20.5
Russellville CDP	488	NA	NA	672	69.3	30.7	0.0	0.0	0.0	10.2	63.9	26.0	283	94.3	37.8	5.7
St. Andrews CDP	20,493	NA	NA	21,298	25.8	65.1	3.0	2.9	3.3	24.8	66.9	8.4	9,495	36.7	31.3	26.0
St. George town	2,067	2,137	3.4	2,291	51.3	44.6	0.0	1.0	3.0	24.7	57.1	18.2	807	58.1	49.4	18.2
St. Matthews town	2,024	1,992	-1.6	1,887	40.4	58.0	0.0	1.2	0.4	19.8	57.0	23.1	808	56.2	55.2	27.2
St. Stephen town	1,697	1,777	4.7	1,785	54.6	43.4	0.0	1.8	0.2	32.2	54.8	13.1	572	66.3	62.2	10.0
Salem town	147	147	0.0	126	100.0	0.0	0.0	0.0	0.0	8.0	69.8	22.2	54	66.7	57.4	14.8
Salley town	403	415	3.0	430	40.5	54.7	2.8	2.1	0.0	24.2	48.8	27.0	181	70.2	69.6	9.9
Saluda town	3,558	3,607	1.4	3,590	29.8	35.2	0.0	0.9	34.2	26.8	59.9	13.3	1,215	48.1	66.1	8.7
Sangaree CDP	8,220	NA	NA	8,782	67.1	24.9	1.1	3.0	3.9	25.9	67.2	7.0	2,992	71.7	29.9	19.3
Sans Souci CDP	7,869	NA	NA	7,743	54.9	17.6	2.2	1.4	24.0	24.3	63.1	12.7	3,220	48.8	56.1	17.0
Santee town	961	944	-1.8	1,004	18.5	59.0	2.3	20.2	0.0	26.8	58.9	14.5	376	47.6	60.6	17.8
Saxon CDP	3,424	NA	NA	3,603	41.7	45.8	0.7	3.0	8.8	24.3	66.3	9.4	1,125	42.0	65.3	5.8
Scotia town	215	210	-2.3	206	27.2	71.8	0.0	1.0	0.0	18.5	71.3	10.2	90	62.2	54.4	13.3
Scranton town	856	861	0.6	772	38.2	58.8	0.0	1.4	1.6	18.3	56.4	25.4	282	64.2	60.3	13.1
Seabrook Island town	1,714	1,819	6.1	1,711	97.1	0.5	0.3	0.0	2.0	3.6	41.6	54.8	910	91.2	6.6	80.7
Sellers town	219	214	-2.3	117	14.5	82.1	0.0	3.4	0.0	17.2	48.8	34.2	57	54.4	66.7	19.3
Seneca city	8,130	8,246	1.4	8,147	62.6	25.3	1.0	3.8	7.4	21.1	60.6	18.2	3,754	58.7	44.5	27.1
Seven Oaks CDP	15,144	NA	NA	15,906	58.4	30.9	2.7	4.3	3.6	24.4	59.8	15.8	6,650	57.6	24.4	43.1
Sharon town	499	544	9.0	460	91.5	6.3	0.0	1.7	0.4	25.6	57.1	17.4	186	70.4	53.8	8.1
Shell Point CDP	2,336	NA	NA	2,384	57.6	32.2	1.7	1.0	7.4	26.6	58.4	14.8	785	75.0	35.2	15.4
Shiloh CDP	214	NA	NA	126	18.3	78.6	0.0	0.0	3.2	3.2	84.2	12.7	48	85.4	54.2	10.4
Silverstreet town	162	163	0.6	204	85.8	14.2	0.0	0.0	0.0	19.2	67.1	13.7	92	82.6	30.4	26.1
Simpsonville city	18,401	20,125	9.4	19,219	67.9	18.6	2.0	0.7	10.7	21.5	67.2	11.4	7,471	65.4	34.3	31.4
Six Mile town	675	678	0.4	928	96.1	1.7	1.4	0.8	0.0	31.4	54.2	14.5	315	75.6	29.5	29.5
Slater-Marietta CDP	2,176	NA	NA	2,414	62.6	0.6	0.0	1.9	34.9	23.3	64.1	12.5	869	44.3	68.1	9.9
Smoaks town	126	124	-1.6	130	100.0	0.0	0.0	0.0	0.0	13.8	70.2	16.2	60	81.7	48.3	26.7
Smyrna town	45	46	2.2	47	100.0	0.0	0.0	0.0	0.0	6.4	70.2	23.4	20	95.0	65.0	10.0
Snelling town	274	262	-4.4	312	78.5	19.9	0.0	0.0	1.6	36.5	58.3	5.1	112	81.3	52.7	19.6
Socastee CDP	19,952	NA	NA	20,496	76.2	7.9	1.6	3.9	10.4	23.8	62.8	13.1	7,682	57.4	41.0	18.6
Society Hill town	563	552	-2.0	751	41.9	38.3	0.0	18.6	1.1	19.6	63.6	16.8	288	62.8	64.6	12.5
South Congaree town	2,306	2,376	3.0	2,475	84.6	7.7	1.1	3.8	2.9	26.9	62.8	10.4	947	67.6	42.7	14.8
Southern Shops CDP	3,767	NA	NA	4,394	29.8	15.9	0.0	0.9	53.3	31.8	61.6	6.5	1,144	34.6	78.1	2.4
South Sumter CDP	2,411	NA	NA	2,154	4.9	89.0	0.0	3.0	3.1	28.5	58.1	13.5	743	59.9	60.4	8.9
Spartanburg city	36,757	37,525	2.1	37,216	47.2	46.5	1.7	2.1	2.6	23.4	61.5	15.2	15,332	50.8	40.7	28.0
Springdale CDP	2,574	NA	NA	2,216	63.8	26.9	0.0	0.5	8.8	26.3	64.3	9.5	785	44.6	68.3	12.1
Springdale town	2,633	2,747	4.3	2,693	79.2	10.1	3.8	1.9	5.0	16.9	58.0	25.1	1,122	70.3	37.7	24.3
Springfield town	524	509	-2.9	496	63.1	33.1	0.0	3.8	0.0	24.6	51.2	24.2	189	84.7	48.7	18.0
Starr town	184	188	2.2	168	85.1	12.5	0.0	2.4	0.0	34.5	55.5	10.1	57	77.2	40.4	19.3
Startex CDP	859	NA	NA	1,100	57.1	0.0	0.0	0.0	42.9	46.0	43.9	10.0	326	58.9	64.4	0.0
Stateburg CDP	1,380	NA	NA	1,615	68.4	29.0	2.2	0.4	0.0	27.9	63.3	8.7	567	79.4	25.9	40.9
Stuckey town	245	235	-4.1	444	10.6	85.8	0.0	3.6	0.0	20.7	69.4	9.9	139	95.7	56.1	5.8
Sullivan's Island town	1,791	1,896	5.9	2,042	97.0	0.3	0.0	1.3	1.4	21.8	61.3	16.9	768	88.3	4.7	75.9
Summerton town	997	977	-2.0	1,029	31.0	68.7	0.0	0.0	0.3	20.1	54.6	25.4	478	42.1	60.0	11.7
Summerville town	42,590	46,974	10.3	44,717	73.2	18.7	1.1	2.7	4.3	26.4	62.0	11.6	16,542	63.2	29.3	33.5
Summit town	402	424	5.5	556	93.2	6.3	0.0	0.2	0.4	32.6	54.5	13.1	208	82.7	34.6	15.4

1 May be of any race.

Table A. All Places — **Population and Housing**

STATE City, town, township, borough, or CDP (county if applicable)	Population: 2010 census total population	Population: 2014 estimated population	Population: Percent change 2010-2014	Population: ACS total population estimate 2010-2014	Race and Hispanic or Latino origin (percent), 2010–2014: White alone, not Hispanic or Latino	Black alone, not Hispanic or Latino	Asian alone, not Hispanic or Latino	All other races or 2 or more races, not Hispanic or Latino	Hispanic or Latino[1]	Age (percent), 2010–2014: Under 18 years old	Age 18 to 64 years old	Age 65 years and older	Households, 2010–2014: Total occupied housing units	Percent owner occupied	Householders by level of education (percent): High school diploma or less	Bachelor's degree or more
	1	2	3	4	5	6	7	8	9	10	11	12	13	14	15	16
SOUTH CAROLINA—Con.																
Sumter city	40,524	40,929	1.0	40,819	44.6	47.8	1.6	1.9	4.1	24.4	61.4	14.5	16,001	51.7	38.0	26.2
Surfside Beach town	3,837	4,187	9.1	4,017	88.4	0.7	0.4	2.6	7.9	14.6	61.4	23.9	1,960	64.2	29.3	35.2
Swansea town	828	878	6.0	708	53.2	42.9	0.0	3.4	0.4	21.9	55.4	22.7	308	68.8	60.1	15.6
Sycamore town	180	167	-7.2	217	78.3	20.3	0.0	0.0	1.4	12.5	72.8	14.7	66	81.8	56.1	19.7
Tatum town	75	73	-2.7	115	91.3	8.7	0.0	0.0	0.0	13.0	80.8	6.1	38	81.6	42.1	13.2
Taylors CDP	21,617	NA	NA	23,490	76.9	12.2	2.5	1.8	6.7	23.0	62.4	14.8	8,607	69.8	33.1	30.3
Tega Cay city	7,716	9,120	18.2	8,224	88.5	4.9	1.4	1.4	3.8	28.8	61.4	9.7	2,818	92.1	10.0	64.1
Tigerville CDP	1,312	NA	NA	1,839	84.4	7.6	3.2	0.9	4.0	1.5	98.0	0.5	20	55.0	45.0	55.0
Timmonsville town	2,347	2,383	1.5	2,251	16.3	78.4	0.9	3.3	1.1	24.3	65.7	9.9	930	52.3	61.9	9.9
Travelers Rest city	4,597	4,916	6.9	4,768	78.9	12.3	0.2	2.0	6.6	28.5	59.8	11.8	1,715	65.0	41.5	18.7
Trenton town	196	191	-2.6	248	73.4	26.6	0.0	0.0	0.0	16.5	54.4	29.0	116	72.4	42.2	17.2
Troy town	93	93	0.0	85	81.2	17.6	0.0	0.0	1.2	18.9	63.7	17.6	36	97.2	52.8	19.4
Turbeville town	834	813	-2.5	1,098	46.1	52.9	0.0	0.5	0.5	31.9	57.4	10.7	391	59.8	63.2	17.6
Ulmer town	87	81	-6.9	52	76.9	19.2	0.0	3.8	0.0	19.2	61.6	19.2	25	72.0	28.0	44.0
Union city	8,390	8,041	-4.2	8,191	49.7	48.5	0.0	1.6	0.2	24.6	58.5	16.8	3,643	53.3	51.3	20.1
Utica CDP	1,489	NA	NA	1,247	74.2	17.6	0.0	1.4	6.7	27.4	58.9	13.7	493	60.0	55.8	8.5
Valley Falls CDP	6,299	NA	NA	5,886	67.9	20.7	4.4	1.0	6.0	14.7	72.2	13.2	2,180	41.2	31.7	23.2
Vance town	170	167	-1.8	107	8.4	89.7	0.0	1.9	0.0	33.6	53.3	13.1	40	62.5	40.0	17.5
Varnville town	2,162	2,093	-3.2	2,294	35.0	64.1	0.0	0.0	0.9	24.9	61.0	14.1	929	65.2	59.4	9.7
Wade Hampton CDP	20,622	NA	NA	19,586	78.1	9.0	3.9	1.2	7.8	20.1	59.5	20.3	8,660	61.3	29.4	39.3
Wagener town	797	817	2.5	696	26.7	71.4	1.4	0.0	0.4	19.6	60.2	20.3	278	56.5	59.4	7.2
Walhalla city	4,238	4,218	-0.5	4,231	59.0	9.3	0.0	3.9	27.8	35.6	49.4	15.0	1,480	54.5	64.5	12.2
Wallace CDP	892	NA	NA	878	47.6	40.9	0.0	11.5	0.0	16.3	77.5	6.4	398	61.6	75.6	8.8
Walterboro city	5,401	5,281	-2.2	5,339	39.3	59.5	0.0	1.0	0.1	26.6	52.7	20.6	2,181	48.8	53.6	20.4
Ward town	91	92	1.1	107	76.6	23.4	0.0	0.0	0.0	14.0	64.2	21.5	52	61.5	63.5	3.8
Ware Place CDP	228	NA	NA	83	100.0	0.0	0.0	0.0	0.0	10.8	71.1	18.1	52	100.0	100.0	0.0
Ware Shoals town	2,174	2,164	-0.5	2,092	67.5	22.3	0.3	3.4	6.5	26.9	56.6	16.6	816	56.1	59.9	14.6
Warrenville CDP	1,233	NA	NA	971	97.7	2.3	0.0	0.0	0.0	18.4	62.8	18.9	422	74.4	77.7	6.6
Waterloo town	159	159	0.0	222	18.0	82.0	0.0	0.0	0.0	11.3	70.4	18.5	96	59.4	80.2	7.3
Watts Mills CDP	1,635	NA	NA	1,736	49.3	36.1	1.3	0.5	12.8	35.2	54.7	10.1	562	50.0	65.7	10.0
Wedgefield CDP	1,615	NA	NA	1,337	57.5	35.7	4.7	0.8	1.3	29.3	59.3	11.3	513	78.8	53.2	11.3
Welcome CDP	6,668	NA	NA	5,972	57.5	28.0	0.0	0.6	14.0	21.3	59.5	19.2	2,469	66.9	57.3	13.1
Wellford city	2,438	2,519	3.3	2,472	49.6	37.4	3.6	1.4	8.0	22.8	64.3	12.9	930	63.4	61.6	10.4
West Columbia city	15,262	15,920	4.3	15,623	65.2	15.6	2.4	2.6	14.2	15.5	66.3	18.1	7,247	54.9	34.0	35.6
Westminster city	2,435	2,467	1.3	2,539	88.5	9.8	0.0	0.4	1.3	19.0	61.7	19.2	1,061	69.0	60.3	11.1
West Pelzer town	868	896	3.2	844	86.8	6.2	0.0	0.6	6.4	26.1	58.0	15.9	372	50.5	67.7	11.0
West Union town	308	311	1.0	321	74.5	1.6	0.0	1.2	22.7	25.3	57.3	17.4	152	60.5	63.2	7.2
Whitmire town	1,441	1,453	0.8	1,368	71.9	23.8	0.0	3.7	0.7	19.7	61.2	19.2	562	67.6	53.2	9.1
Wilkinson Heights CDP	2,493	NA	NA	2,514	0.7	96.9	0.0	0.0	2.4	13.2	68.0	18.7	980	65.2	49.0	16.6
Williams town	117	115	-1.7	109	51.4	48.6	0.0	0.0	0.0	14.6	56.0	29.4	35	80.0	74.3	17.1
Williamston town	3,934	4,072	3.5	4,003	86.8	4.2	0.0	0.5	8.5	28.8	57.6	13.5	1,513	72.2	44.2	20.2
Willington CDP	142	NA	NA	129	10.1	89.9	0.0	0.0	0.0	12.4	56.7	31.0	70	100.0	41.4	0.0
Williston town	3,139	3,054	-2.7	3,087	47.7	51.9	0.0	0.4	0.0	28.3	54.9	16.7	1,094	75.0	55.0	20.8
Windsor town	121	122	0.8	153	95.4	3.9	0.0	0.0	0.7	12.4	75.1	12.4	70	40.0	64.3	11.4
Winnsboro town	3,550	3,384	-4.7	3,456	24.6	66.9	0.0	0.9	7.6	22.6	65.2	12.0	1,483	44.2	55.4	13.8
Winnsboro Mills CDP	1,898	NA	NA	1,727	46.7	48.3	0.0	0.0	5.0	28.0	58.5	13.4	713	43.8	69.7	14.3
Woodfield CDP	9,303	NA	NA	9,484	23.1	51.4	6.1	1.2	18.3	22.1	63.9	14.0	3,514	53.0	40.2	18.0
Woodford town	185	182	-1.6	143	32.2	65.0	0.0	0.7	2.1	6.3	73.5	20.3	61	82.0	80.3	3.3
Woodruff city	4,085	4,111	0.6	4,101	67.3	23.0	0.0	7.0	2.7	22.1	50.4	27.4	1,409	45.3	80.8	9.7
Yemassee town	1,022	993	-2.8	819	59.1	35.0	0.0	4.0	1.8	29.2	65.2	5.6	326	63.2	39.3	14.1
York city	7,751	8,038	3.7	7,913	50.4	41.0	0.7	4.0	4.0	26.5	60.0	13.6	2,748	51.5	55.5	13.4
SOUTH DAKOTA	814,191	853,175	4.8	834,708	83.6	1.5	1.1	10.6	3.2	24.7	60.7	14.7	327,101	68.0	38.2	27.2
Aberdeen city	26,091	27,800	6.6	26,979	89.4	1.3	2.1	5.1	2.1	23.7	60.5	16.0	11,363	63.5	40.7	26.2
Agar town	76	78	2.6	58	93.1	0.0	0.0	0.0	6.9	8.6	32.7	58.6	39	97.4	66.7	5.1
Agency Village CDP	181	NA	NA	150	13.3	0.0	0.0	84.7	2.0	48.0	52.0	0.0	26	19.2	42.3	0.0
Akaska town	42	42	0.0	35	100.0	0.0	0.0	0.0	0.0	0.0	62.8	37.1	22	100.0	72.7	13.6
Albee town	16	16	0.0	7	100.0	0.0	0.0	0.0	0.0	0.0	71.5	28.6	5	40.0	100.0	0.0
Alcester city	807	788	-2.4	785	87.4	0.0	0.4	6.0	6.2	28.1	47.7	24.5	327	72.2	43.7	17.1
Alexandria city	615	631	2.6	740	96.1	1.1	0.4	0.0	2.4	35.9	53.0	11.1	240	83.8	38.8	23.3
Allen CDP	420	NA	NA	655	0.0	4.4	0.0	90.7	4.9	55.2	42.2	2.7	92	3.3	92.4	0.0
Alpena town	286	276	-3.5	296	72.3	0.0	0.0	9.8	17.9	27.8	56.7	15.5	122	68.9	63.1	10.7
Altamont town	34	33	-2.9	41	100.0	0.0	0.0	0.0	0.0	39.1	60.9	0.0	21	85.7	76.2	0.0
Anderson CDP	371	NA	NA	229	100.0	0.0	0.0	0.0	0.0	26.2	55.0	18.8	85	100.0	22.4	16.5
Andover town	91	88	-3.3	87	75.9	0.0	0.0	0.0	24.1	20.6	65.4	13.8	45	66.7	35.6	17.8
Antelope CDP	826	NA	NA	1,211	3.0	0.0	0.7	94.0	2.4	38.9	52.5	8.7	275	25.8	55.6	7.6
Arlington city	915	899	-1.7	1,010	92.6	0.0	0.4	0.2	6.8	29.4	52.9	17.4	449	64.4	52.8	17.1
Armour city	699	685	-2.0	902	95.1	0.0	0.0	4.9	0.0	24.4	47.1	28.4	368	75.8	47.8	23.6
Artas town	9	9	0.0	6	100.0	0.0	0.0	0.0	0.0	0.0	33.3	66.7	4	100.0	100.0	0.0
Artesian town	138	137	-0.7	124	85.5	0.0	0.0	0.0	14.5	11.3	73.4	15.3	68	61.8	57.4	17.6
Ashland Heights CDP	754	NA	NA	622	81.0	0.0	0.0	17.5	1.4	15.6	68.5	16.1	275	70.9	24.0	27.3
Ashton city	122	127	4.1	164	100.0	0.0	0.0	0.0	0.0	26.7	67.6	5.5	60	78.3	45.0	5.0
Astoria town	139	137	-1.4	161	98.8	0.0	0.0	0.0	1.2	24.9	62.1	13.0	72	81.9	47.2	18.1
Aurora town	532	621	16.7	704	98.2	0.0	0.0	1.7	0.1	20.0	69.9	10.1	330	77.9	47.9	27.6
Aurora Center CDP	12	NA	NA	56	82.1	0.0	0.0	17.9	0.0	42.8	53.7	3.6	22	100.0	86.4	13.6
Avon city	590	577	-2.2	618	99.4	0.0	0.0	0.0	0.6	31.6	47.1	21.4	239	87.0	41.4	31.0
Badger town	107	105	-1.9	70	100.0	0.0	0.0	0.0	0.0	11.4	35.8	52.9	35	97.1	54.3	22.9
Baltic city	1,083	1,135	4.8	1,000	93.0	0.0	0.7	2.8	3.5	29.0	63.1	7.9	365	87.1	37.8	27.7
Bancroft town	19	19	0.0	17	100.0	0.0	0.0	0.0	0.0	17.6	58.9	23.5	12	100.0	50.0	0.0
Batesland town	108	113	4.6	157	6.4	0.0	0.0	93.6	0.0	31.8	62.3	5.7	36	86.1	27.8	36.1
Bath CDP	172	NA	NA	252	100.0	0.0	0.0	0.0	0.0	35.3	61.5	3.2	80	100.0	45.0	0.0
Bath Corner CDP	49	NA	NA	63	100.0	0.0	0.0	0.0	0.0	0.0	80.9	19.0	51	100.0	23.5	0.0
Belle Fourche city	5,591	5,707	2.1	5,677	91.9	0.1	0.2	4.0	3.9	22.8	59.3	17.9	2,285	65.3	51.0	12.9
Belvidere town	49	53	8.2	51	100.0	0.0	0.0	0.0	0.0	25.4	60.7	13.7	24	83.3	45.8	0.0
Beresford city	2,005	2,025	1.0	2,411	96.4	0.3	0.6	1.0	1.7	28.0	58.1	14.0	976	78.0	45.5	25.7
Big Stone City city	467	460	-1.5	583	97.8	0.0	0.0	0.9	1.4	23.0	59.0	17.8	251	77.3	53.8	7.6
Bijou Hills CDP	6	NA	NA	0	0.0	0.0	0.0	0.0	0.0	0.0	0.0	0.0	0	0.0	0.0	0.0
Bison town	333	340	2.1	308	95.1	0.0	0.0	3.9	1.0	17.2	53.4	29.5	150	67.3	53.3	10.0
Blackhawk CDP	2,892	NA	NA	2,754	94.3	0.0	0.0	3.5	2.2	19.4	70.1	10.3	1,094	85.6	23.1	23.7
Blucksberg Mountain CDP	462	NA	NA	493	98.0	0.0	0.0	2.0	0.0	11.5	69.1	19.3	227	100.0	52.9	30.4

1 May be of any race.

Table A. All Places — **Population and Housing**

STATE City, town, township, borough, or CDP (county if applicable)	2010 census total population	2014 estimated population	Percent change 2010-2014	ACS total population estimate 2010-2014	White alone, not Hispanic or Latino	Black alone, not Hispanic or Latino	Asian alone, not Hispanic or Latino	All other races or 2 or more races, not Hispanic or Latino	Hispanic or Latino[1]	Under 18 years old	Age 18 to 64 years old	Age 65 years and older	Total occupied housing units	Percent owner occupied	High school diploma or less	Bachelor's degree or more
	1	2	3	4	5	6	7	8	9	10	11	12	13	14	15	16
SOUTH DAKOTA—Con.																
Blunt city	354	366	3.4	378	84.1	0.0	0.0	15.9	0.0	29.3	55.8	14.8	150	75.3	57.3	13.3
Bonesteel city	275	271	-1.5	276	67.4	0.0	0.0	32.2	0.4	17.1	50.8	32.2	144	68.8	56.3	19.4
Bowdle city	526	503	-4.4	491	99.4	0.0	0.4	0.0	0.2	27.2	43.4	29.3	212	69.8	53.3	13.7
Box Elder city	7,810	9,233	18.2	8,683	76.4	6.0	1.7	8.0	7.9	27.0	69.4	3.7	2,974	43.6	27.5	18.2
Bradley town	72	71	-1.4	101	100.0	0.0	0.0	0.0	0.0	27.7	57.5	14.9	39	79.5	71.8	17.9
Brandon city	8,899	9,779	9.9	9,350	97.2	0.5	0.4	1.1	0.7	33.5	57.5	9.0	3,264	73.1	27.1	33.4
Brandt town	107	105	-1.9	85	94.1	0.0	0.0	0.0	5.9	14.1	56.5	29.4	49	79.6	44.9	34.7
Brant Lake CDP	159	NA	NA	201	93.0	0.0	0.0	7.0	0.0	13.0	62.7	24.4	96	100.0	29.2	33.3
Brentford town	77	79	2.6	85	100.0	0.0	0.0	0.0	0.0	36.5	51.8	11.8	38	71.1	47.4	0.0
Bridgewater city	492	488	-0.8	517	87.2	1.5	0.0	1.4	9.9	27.1	49.8	23.2	199	70.4	36.2	13.6
Bristol city	341	332	-2.6	316	94.6	0.0	0.0	4.4	0.9	18.6	42.2	38.9	135	74.8	54.1	17.0
Britton city	1,241	1,226	-1.2	1,442	98.0	0.0	0.0	1.0	1.0	22.4	55.6	21.8	532	69.0	38.5	22.2
Broadland town	31	32	3.2	61	100.0	0.0	0.0	0.0	0.0	21.3	70.3	8.2	20	100.0	45.0	5.0
Brookings city	22,073	23,225	5.2	22,645	89.9	1.6	3.9	2.4	2.1	16.8	74.8	8.5	8,369	48.6	23.3	39.5
Bruce city	204	205	0.5	182	98.9	0.0	0.0	1.1	0.0	17.5	53.2	29.1	79	87.3	41.8	16.5
Bryant city	456	452	-0.9	401	99.8	0.2	0.0	0.0	0.0	25.7	45.5	28.7	167	62.9	71.9	6.6
Buffalo town	330	336	1.8	358	98.0	0.8	1.1	0.0	0.0	22.9	57.5	19.6	166	65.7	31.9	23.5
Buffalo Gap town	126	123	-2.4	151	86.1	0.0	0.0	9.3	4.6	25.8	54.5	19.9	73	90.4	31.5	34.2
Bullhead CDP	348	NA	NA	366	0.0	0.0	0.0	100.0	0.0	40.5	59.6	0.0	69	8.7	79.7	13.0
Burke city	604	594	-1.7	678	85.3	0.0	0.0	11.7	3.1	19.6	54.0	26.4	328	71.6	47.0	18.0
Bushnell town	65	65	0.0	92	90.2	0.0	0.0	9.8	0.0	22.8	70.8	6.5	36	61.1	55.6	11.1
Butler town	17	16	-5.9	21	100.0	0.0	0.0	0.0	0.0	0.0	100.1	0.0	9	100.0	100.0	0.0
Camp Crook town	63	64	1.6	84	100.0	0.0	0.0	0.0	0.0	11.9	76.2	11.9	35	85.7	51.4	20.0
Canistota city	656	652	-0.6	522	93.3	0.8	0.0	1.1	4.8	23.6	50.4	26.1	210	75.7	44.3	28.1
Canova town	105	100	-4.8	83	85.5	2.4	0.0	12.0	0.0	20.5	33.6	45.8	36	94.4	41.7	22.2
Canton city	3,085	3,317	7.5	3,218	90.7	2.2	0.2	3.2	3.6	21.0	64.0	15.0	1,314	66.1	30.6	26.4
Caputa CDP	0	NA	NA	0	0.0	0.0	0.0	0.0	0.0	0.0	0.0	0.0	0	0.0	0.0	0.0
Carthage city	144	137	-4.9	210	98.1	0.0	0.0	1.9	0.0	20.4	53.4	26.2	112	75.0	48.2	10.7
Castlewood city	628	624	-0.6	682	97.5	0.0	0.4	0.9	1.2	31.4	54.7	13.9	250	78.4	42.4	15.2
Cavour town	114	118	3.5	144	100.0	0.0	0.0	0.0	0.0	34.1	55.7	10.4	53	94.3	58.5	1.9
Centerville city	882	874	-0.9	758	92.1	1.3	0.3	0.4	5.9	24.4	52.6	23.0	341	77.7	43.7	17.3
Central City city	134	131	-2.2	126	100.0	0.0	0.0	0.0	0.0	17.5	62.8	19.8	65	67.7	69.2	1.5
Chamberlain city	2,387	2,402	0.6	2,660	78.8	0.0	0.0	19.0	2.2	25.7	56.2	18.0	1,008	58.2	42.4	24.6
Chancellor town	264	260	-1.5	305	87.2	5.6	0.0	1.6	5.6	26.6	62.5	10.8	126	81.0	57.1	9.5
Chelsea town	27	27	0.0	61	96.7	0.0	3.3	0.0	0.0	37.7	57.4	4.9	19	89.5	42.1	15.8
Chester CDP	261	NA	NA	302	100.0	0.0	0.0	0.0	0.0	27.1	54.6	18.2	120	86.7	45.8	10.0
Claire City town	76	77	1.3	78	96.2	0.0	0.0	3.8	0.0	20.5	61.5	17.9	30	86.7	53.3	0.0
Claremont town	127	128	0.8	168	94.0	0.0	0.0	0.0	6.0	26.8	53.1	20.2	68	100.0	47.1	14.7
Clark city	1,139	1,051	-7.7	1,039	98.4	0.0	0.0	0.8	0.9	16.4	51.5	32.2	545	70.1	47.9	15.6
Clear Lake city	1,273	1,248	-2.0	1,374	98.3	0.0	0.0	1.4	0.4	22.5	53.4	23.9	576	76.2	51.4	19.3
Colman city	594	573	-3.5	685	95.2	0.0	0.0	4.8	0.0	35.0	48.2	16.8	273	61.5	37.7	14.7
Colome city	296	288	-2.7	248	94.8	0.0	0.4	4.8	0.0	26.6	54.4	19.0	119	81.5	36.1	22.7
Colonial Pine Hills CDP	2,493	NA	NA	2,328	94.4	0.0	0.0	4.0	1.6	28.1	57.5	14.5	800	100.0	19.5	48.3
Colton city	687	695	1.2	749	96.9	0.0	0.0	2.4	0.7	27.5	61.5	10.8	284	79.2	47.9	13.7
Columbia city	136	137	0.7	148	100.0	0.0	0.0	0.0	0.0	12.2	64.1	23.6	85	78.8	50.6	20.0
Conde city	140	147	5.0	146	98.6	0.0	0.0	1.4	0.0	11.7	66.6	21.9	78	83.3	56.4	19.2
Corn Creek CDP	105	NA	NA	148	0.0	0.0	0.0	100.0	0.0	32.4	54.8	12.8	26	69.2	53.8	30.8
Corona town	109	111	1.8	106	100.0	0.0	0.0	0.0	0.0	23.6	61.3	15.1	43	95.3	44.2	27.9
Corsica city	592	594	0.3	599	96.8	0.0	0.2	2.3	0.7	20.5	48.4	31.1	246	85.4	60.6	11.8
Cottonwood town	9	10	11.1	3	100.0	0.0	0.0	0.0	0.0	0.0	0.0	100.0	1	100.0	100.0	0.0
Cow Creek CDP	30	NA	NA	41	87.8	0.0	0.0	12.2	0.0	14.6	70.8	14.6	20	100.0	0.0	55.0
Cresbard town	104	102	-1.9	126	100.0	0.0	0.0	0.0	0.0	8.7	58.7	33.3	70	72.9	38.6	15.7
Crocker CDP	19	NA	NA	0	0.0	0.0	0.0	0.0	0.0	0.0	0.0	0.0	0	0.0	0.0	0.0
Crooks city	1,269	1,330	4.8	1,547	93.9	0.3	0.0	4.5	1.2	29.6	64.1	6.1	489	94.9	38.0	24.7
Custer city	1,997	1,969	-1.4	1,918	88.9	0.0	0.0	7.9	3.2	20.1	60.2	19.5	898	64.7	29.0	30.8
Dakota Dunes CDP	2,540	NA	NA	2,895	89.3	2.3	5.1	1.0	2.3	27.7	60.9	11.4	1,187	59.1	21.3	52.7
Dallas town	120	123	2.5	97	88.7	0.0	0.0	11.3	0.0	11.4	66.1	22.7	50	82.0	54.0	4.0
Dante town	84	85	1.2	82	96.3	0.0	0.0	3.7	0.0	34.2	41.6	24.4	30	93.3	63.3	13.3
Davis town	85	83	-2.4	60	98.3	0.0	0.0	1.7	0.0	21.7	46.6	31.7	30	86.7	40.0	10.0
Deadwood city	1,272	1,261	-0.9	1,153	89.8	1.2	1.0	3.7	4.2	11.6	65.9	22.6	596	60.6	44.3	21.0
Dell Rapids city	3,633	3,700	1.8	3,687	94.2	0.0	0.5	1.9	3.3	28.5	56.0	15.6	1,430	76.2	38.5	29.0
Delmont city	234	231	-1.3	220	80.9	0.0	0.0	19.1	0.0	20.0	53.2	26.8	114	78.9	29.8	17.5
De Smet city	1,089	1,090	0.1	1,223	93.8	0.0	2.0	3.4	0.7	21.8	53.8	24.3	554	75.3	41.0	21.5
Dimock town	125	122	-2.4	174	98.9	0.0	1.1	0.0	0.0	37.3	48.2	14.4	67	83.6	37.3	26.9
Doland city	180	188	4.4	187	92.5	0.0	0.0	1.1	6.4	16.5	70.1	13.4	95	75.8	50.5	25.3
Dolton town	37	36	-2.7	37	59.5	0.0	0.0	0.0	40.5	18.9	81.0	0.0	13	92.3	92.3	0.0
Draper town	82	78	-4.9	80	100.0	0.0	0.0	0.0	0.0	15.0	71.4	13.8	45	84.4	57.8	13.3
Dupree city	525	531	1.1	582	31.3	1.5	0.0	60.0	7.2	45.4	48.6	6.0	161	54.7	49.1	19.3
Eagle Butte city	1,310	1,353	3.3	1,369	6.2	0.2	0.0	85.3	8.3	40.0	55.1	4.7	361	36.8	54.0	12.5
Eden town	89	90	1.1	90	97.8	0.0	0.0	2.2	0.0	11.1	50.0	38.9	58	74.1	43.1	27.6
Edgemont city	766	742	-3.1	859	94.5	0.0	0.0	5.5	0.0	16.0	65.3	18.7	440	79.5	55.0	14.5
Egan city	278	271	-2.5	329	92.7	0.0	0.0	7.3	0.0	33.4	54.0	12.5	129	81.4	54.3	12.4
Elk Point city	1,969	1,940	-1.5	2,075	94.6	2.3	0.2	2.1	0.9	29.8	59.4	11.0	771	75.1	43.7	29.4
Elkton city	736	729	-1.0	655	74.5	0.6	0.0	7.3	17.6	39.7	47.7	12.6	262	69.5	41.2	28.6
Emery city	447	462	3.4	509	96.7	0.0	0.8	2.6	0.0	39.7	47.7	12.6	175	78.3	52.6	16.0
Erwin town	45	44	-2.2	60	56.7	36.7	0.0	6.7	0.0	20.0	36.7	43.3	31	64.5	35.5	6.5
Estelline city	768	755	-1.7	818	86.7	0.0	0.0	0.6	12.7	24.9	49.0	26.2	310	70.3	57.4	10.3
Ethan town	331	324	-2.1	349	100.0	0.0	0.0	0.0	0.0	34.4	52.4	13.2	126	80.2	48.4	19.0
Eureka city	868	850	-2.1	879	100.0	0.0	0.0	0.0	0.0	17.5	40.0	42.3	417	86.3	52.8	21.8
Fairburn town	85	83	-2.4	63	92.1	0.0	4.8	0.0	3.2	15.9	69.9	14.3	30	86.7	50.0	33.3
Fairfax town	115	113	-1.7	100	99.0	0.0	0.0	1.0	0.0	8.0	61.0	31.0	64	79.7	57.8	21.9
Fairview town	60	65	8.3	50	100.0	0.0	0.0	0.0	0.0	18.0	70.0	12.0	24	87.5	62.5	4.2
Faith city	416	418	0.5	413	76.0	0.0	0.0	8.0	16.0	26.1	52.8	21.1	186	63.4	48.4	16.1
Farmer town	10	10	0.0	2	100.0	0.0	0.0	0.0	0.0	0.0	0.0	100.0	1	100.0	100.0	0.0
Faulkton city	736	744	1.1	744	98.4	0.0	0.0	0.4	1.2	21.7	48.1	30.5	357	64.4	47.6	18.8
Fedora CDP	37	NA	NA	24	100.0	0.0	0.0	0.0	0.0	0.0	37.5	62.5	19	100.0	47.4	52.6
Ferney CDP	43	NA	NA	28	100.0	0.0	0.0	0.0	0.0	0.0	0.0	100.0	28	100.0	100.0	0.0
Flandreau city	2,341	2,283	-2.5	2,088	57.1	0.0	3.4	32.9	6.6	24.7	57.5	17.8	983	52.3	44.3	25.9
Florence town	374	374	0.0	379	96.6	0.0	2.9	0.5	0.0	28.7	53.8	17.4	157	84.7	54.8	14.0
Forestburg CDP	73	NA	NA	123	100.0	0.0	0.0	0.0	0.0	8.9	87.8	3.3	61	75.4	50.8	9.8
Fort Pierre city	2,109	2,135	1.2	2,322	84.2	0.0	0.0	13.4	2.4	26.0	56.0	17.8	948	77.1	42.2	27.1

1 May be of any race.

STATE City, town, township, borough, or CDP (county if applicable)	2010 census total population	2014 estimated population	Percent change 2010-2014	ACS total population estimate 2010-2014	White alone, not Hispanic or Latino	Black alone, not Hispanic or Latino	Asian alone, not Hispanic or Latino	All other races or 2 or more races, not Hispanic or Latino	Hispanic or Latino[1]	Under 18 years old	Age 18 to 64 years old	Age 65 years and older	Total occupied housing units	Percent owner occupied	High school diploma or less	Bachelor's degree or more
	1	2	3	4	5	6	7	8	9	10	11	12	13	14	15	16
SOUTH DAKOTA—Con.																
Fort Thompson CDP	1,282	NA	NA	1,305	1.8	0.5	0.0	95.9	1.8	39.9	54.7	5.4	319	26.6	53.6	13.5
Frankfort city	149	156	4.7	144	100.0	0.0	0.0	0.0	0.0	36.2	37.6	26.4	57	94.7	75.4	3.5
Frederick town	199	200	0.5	320	97.2	0.0	0.0	1.9	0.9	31.8	46.3	21.9	133	75.2	42.9	13.5
Freeman city	1,306	1,274	-2.5	1,275	92.9	0.0	0.0	2.7	4.3	23.0	45.8	31.1	582	66.8	40.9	30.9
Fruitdale town	64	64	0.0	67	95.5	0.0	0.0	4.5	0.0	17.9	61.3	20.9	25	92.0	28.0	12.0
Fulton town	91	94	3.3	113	98.2	0.0	0.0	1.8	0.0	33.7	53.0	13.3	42	92.9	50.0	21.4
Gann Valley CDP	14	NA	NA	17	100.0	0.0	0.0	0.0	0.0	0.0	23.5	76.5	10	100.0	40.0	0.0
Garden City town	53	53	0.0	64	89.1	0.0	0.0	10.9	0.0	20.3	62.6	17.2	19	94.7	52.6	15.8
Garretson city	1,166	1,212	3.9	1,305	93.0	0.7	0.8	5.4	0.2	32.3	54.2	13.6	477	70.9	34.4	26.6
Gary city	227	229	0.9	236	97.5	0.0	0.0	0.0	2.5	11.4	55.8	32.6	140	57.9	70.7	5.0
Gayville town	405	411	1.5	339	90.0	0.0	0.3	4.7	5.0	19.4	64.6	15.9	149	72.5	49.7	22.8
Geddes city	210	212	1.0	209	100.0	0.0	0.0	0.0	0.0	12.0	57.8	30.1	132	85.6	50.0	23.5
Gettysburg city	1,162	1,172	0.9	1,225	91.9	0.0	1.1	6.3	0.7	19.6	55.7	24.6	560	74.1	39.6	27.9
Glenham town	105	107	1.9	91	100.0	0.0	0.0	0.0	0.0	9.9	64.9	25.3	46	80.4	71.7	17.4
Goodwill CDP	513	NA	NA	672	2.7	0.0	0.0	97.3	0.0	34.1	59.3	6.7	122	9.8	41.0	7.4
Goodwin town	146	144	-1.4	160	63.8	0.0	0.0	0.0	36.3	21.3	64.5	14.4	61	85.2	59.0	6.6
Green Grass CDP	35	NA	NA	14	0.0	0.0	0.0	100.0	0.0	28.6	71.4	0.0	5	100.0	0.0	100.0
Green Valley CDP	928	NA	NA	639	87.9	0.0	3.4	8.6	0.0	16.9	64.9	18.2	360	100.0	44.4	15.8
Gregory city	1,293	1,264	-2.2	1,448	90.7	0.0	0.0	8.8	0.4	23.9	48.4	27.7	707	65.3	50.9	18.1
Grenville town	54	52	-3.7	95	94.7	0.0	0.0	2.1	3.2	36.9	46.4	16.8	36	94.4	66.7	11.1
Groton city	1,458	1,495	2.5	1,817	92.6	0.3	0.0	2.3	4.8	30.2	56.6	13.4	670	81.3	38.8	22.1
Hamill CDP	11	NA	NA	0	0.0	0.0	0.0	0.0	0.0	0.0	0.0	0.0	0	0.0	0.0	0.0
Harrisburg city	4,096	5,190	26.7	4,678	91.7	2.9	0.8	2.5	2.0	39.2	58.4	2.4	1,444	84.9	21.7	38.2
Harrison CDP	52	NA	NA	111	100.0	0.0	0.0	0.0	0.0	35.1	45.9	18.9	45	73.3	17.8	55.6
Harrold town	124	126	1.6	139	88.5	0.0	0.0	11.5	0.0	8.6	60.3	30.9	69	81.2	55.1	7.2
Hartford city	2,539	2,983	17.5	2,781	97.9	0.3	0.2	1.0	0.6	31.0	59.2	9.8	958	75.8	32.9	28.0
Hayti town	381	380	-0.3	319	95.6	0.0	0.0	0.6	3.8	29.1	56.6	14.1	135	74.1	56.3	21.5
Hazel town	91	90	-1.1	69	94.2	5.8	0.0	0.0	0.0	37.6	57.9	4.3	26	96.2	50.0	7.7
Hecla city	227	228	0.4	189	100.0	0.0	0.0	0.0	0.0	7.9	36.1	56.1	117	87.2	44.4	19.7
Henry town	267	267	0.0	366	97.5	0.0	0.0	2.5	0.0	32.2	58.0	9.8	147	76.9	57.8	12.2
Hermosa town	400	398	-0.5	463	80.6	0.0	0.0	6.5	13.0	25.3	61.4	13.4	176	71.6	57.4	11.9
Herreid city	438	417	-4.8	514	89.5	0.0	0.0	10.5	0.0	32.4	43.3	24.1	222	76.6	55.9	12.2
Herrick town	105	104	-1.0	99	96.0	0.0	0.0	4.0	0.0	13.2	55.5	31.3	50	86.0	64.0	4.0
Hetland town	46	45	-2.2	36	100.0	0.0	0.0	0.0	0.0	58.3	36.1	5.6	10	100.0	90.0	0.0
Highmore city	795	779	-2.0	975	84.7	0.0	0.9	11.7	2.7	23.5	53.7	22.9	328	78.4	57.6	19.5
Hill City city	945	990	4.8	1,171	75.2	0.0	0.4	13.5	10.8	32.2	56.7	11.2	438	68.7	48.9	24.9
Hillsview town	3	3	0.0	0	0.0	0.0	0.0	0.0	0.0	0.0	0.0	0.0	0	0.0	0.0	0.0
Hitchcock town	91	94	3.3	102	100.0	0.0	0.0	0.0	0.0	22.5	57.8	19.6	47	63.8	25.5	36.2
Hosmer city	208	203	-2.4	231	100.0	0.0	0.0	0.0	0.0	19.1	53.4	27.7	88	67.0	54.5	10.2
Hot Springs city	3,650	3,503	-4.0	3,565	79.0	2.0	0.7	14.1	4.2	20.1	53.8	26.2	1,660	54.4	43.5	21.3
Hoven town	406	407	0.2	422	99.5	0.0	0.0	0.5	0.0	25.6	46.3	28.2	172	87.8	66.9	8.7
Howard city	858	819	-4.5	1,045	90.2	0.9	0.0	5.0	3.9	26.3	49.7	24.0	441	66.2	48.8	26.3
Hudson town	296	316	6.8	299	98.3	0.0	0.0	1.7	0.0	16.1	63.9	20.1	140	85.0	47.9	8.6
Humboldt town	589	590	0.2	597	97.3	0.0	0.0	1.3	1.3	15.7	64.8	19.4	251	86.5	39.4	23.1
Hurley city	415	403	-2.9	369	98.9	0.0	0.0	0.0	1.1	24.2	54.5	21.4	168	84.5	32.1	19.0
Huron city	12,592	13,163	4.5	12,982	77.3	0.7	7.5	2.7	11.8	26.1	58.6	15.3	5,416	59.9	47.8	22.0
Interior town	94	102	8.5	77	53.2	0.0	0.0	46.8	0.0	35.1	52.0	13.0	28	100.0	71.4	3.6
Ipswich city	954	950	-0.4	1,125	98.8	0.0	0.0	1.2	0.0	20.7	58.8	20.6	470	72.1	43.8	26.4
Irene city	420	412	-1.9	531	97.6	0.6	0.0	0.8	1.1	23.5	60.0	16.6	205	81.5	57.6	10.2
Iroquois city	266	266	0.0	254	98.0	0.0	0.0	1.6	0.4	20.9	63.7	15.4	130	85.4	59.2	9.2
Isabel town	135	144	6.7	175	80.0	0.0	0.0	20.0	0.0	38.3	48.2	13.7	69	76.8	49.3	26.1
Java town	129	131	1.6	176	84.7	9.7	0.0	5.7	0.0	29.6	44.3	26.1	82	76.8	59.8	13.4
Jefferson city	547	535	-2.2	570	91.2	0.0	0.0	1.1	7.7	25.0	62.4	12.5	246	76.8	56.9	13.8
Johnson Siding CDP	659	NA	NA	653	70.8	0.0	7.5	2.1	19.6	5.2	83.0	11.8	307	87.9	23.5	27.4
Kadoka city	654	699	6.9	670	85.1	0.0	0.1	14.8	0.0	25.1	50.1	24.9	260	80.0	35.8	32.7
Kaylor CDP	47	NA	NA	71	100.0	0.0	0.0	0.0	0.0	0.0	100.1	0.0	46	100.0	76.1	23.9
Kennebec town	240	252	5.0	346	88.4	0.0	0.0	11.6	0.0	33.8	48.8	17.3	140	74.3	54.3	12.9
Keystone town	337	344	2.1	365	71.5	0.5	9.6	8.2	10.1	17.8	70.2	11.8	155	51.0	40.6	12.3
Kidder CDP	57	NA	NA	0	0.0	0.0	0.0	0.0	0.0	0.0	0.0	0.0	0	0.0	0.0	0.0
Kimball city	703	697	-0.9	522	95.2	0.0	0.0	2.9	1.9	17.8	54.7	27.6	257	80.5	47.5	20.2
Kranzburg town	172	179	4.1	177	98.3	0.0	0.0	0.0	1.7	26.5	59.8	13.6	73	95.9	38.4	26.0
Kyle CDP	846	NA	NA	746	7.5	0.0	0.0	92.5	0.0	36.2	58.3	5.5	192	49.0	35.4	27.6
La Bolt town	68	66	-2.9	102	96.1	0.0	1.0	2.0	1.0	34.3	52.8	12.7	37	100.0	56.8	27.0
Lake Andes city	820	833	1.6	922	44.5	0.0	1.1	50.4	4.0	37.7	46.0	16.4	265	66.8	44.2	14.7
Lake City town	51	51	0.0	33	100.0	0.0	0.0	0.0	0.0	30.4	51.4	18.2	10	80.0	10.0	10.0
Lake Madison CDP	683	NA	NA	776	96.9	0.0	0.0	0.6	2.4	6.9	59.8	33.4	363	86.5	28.7	42.4
Lake Norden city	467	475	1.7	606	91.6	0.0	0.0	1.3	7.1	21.7	48.9	29.5	225	60.0	41.3	13.8
Lake Poinsett CDP	493	NA	NA	448	97.1	0.0	0.0	2.9	0.0	11.9	57.4	30.8	216	100.0	19.9	51.9
Lake Preston city	599	583	-2.7	662	96.7	0.0	0.0	0.6	2.7	20.7	61.3	18.1	318	62.6	53.1	13.5
Lane town	59	57	-3.4	101	100.0	0.0	0.0	0.0	0.0	28.7	69.3	2.0	33	84.8	72.7	24.2
Langford town	313	315	0.6	373	85.5	0.0	0.0	12.6	1.9	30.4	54.5	15.3	149	74.5	45.0	28.2
La Plant CDP	171	NA	NA	233	0.0	0.0	0.0	100.0	0.0	33.5	51.1	15.5	54	57.4	96.3	0.0
Lead city	3,124	3,030	-3.0	3,097	92.4	0.0	1.6	2.3	3.7	23.4	60.1	16.6	1,439	76.2	50.7	22.6
Lebanon town	47	47	0.0	35	80.0	0.0	0.0	20.0	0.0	34.4	48.6	17.1	19	89.5	78.9	0.0
Lemmon city	1,227	1,240	1.1	1,356	94.5	0.1	0.0	3.8	1.5	18.4	57.2	24.5	660	62.7	48.5	18.8
Lennox city	2,111	2,264	7.2	2,155	96.7	0.8	0.0	1.5	1.0	26.4	56.8	16.8	897	67.6	47.3	17.7
Leola city	457	444	-2.8	471	95.5	0.4	0.0	1.9	2.1	27.4	53.5	19.1	263	64.6	57.0	11.0
Lesterville town	127	127	0.0	138	100.0	0.0	0.0	0.0	0.0	11.5	68.1	20.3	73	74.0	61.6	17.8
Letcher town	173	172	-0.6	219	97.3	0.0	1.4	1.4	0.0	33.8	54.7	11.4	98	75.5	31.6	9.2
Lily town	4	4	0.0	3	100.0	0.0	0.0	0.0	0.0	0.0	0.0	100.0	3	100.0	100.0	0.0
Little Eagle CDP	319	NA	NA	281	0.0	0.0	3.6	96.4	0.0	40.2	58.6	1.1	57	29.8	49.1	5.3
Long Hollow CDP	192	NA	NA	314	20.1	0.0	0.0	76.4	3.5	38.2	53.0	8.9	91	25.3	26.4	9.9
Long Lake town	31	31	0.0	12	41.7	0.0	58.3	0.0	0.0	66.7	33.3	0.0	8	100.0	0.0	62.5
Loomis CDP	34	NA	NA	22	100.0	0.0	0.0	0.0	0.0	0.0	22.7	77.3	13	100.0	61.5	0.0
Lower Brule CDP	613	NA	NA	727	4.1	0.0	0.0	95.2	0.7	36.4	58.9	4.8	199	30.2	51.3	13.1
Lowry town	6	6	0.0	8	100.0	0.0	0.0	0.0	0.0	0.0	50.0	50.0	4	100.0	50.0	0.0
McIntosh city	168	174	3.6	184	89.1	0.0	0.0	10.9	0.0	27.7	47.2	25.0	76	63.2	50.0	0.0
McLaughlin city	660	677	2.6	574	28.4	0.0	0.0	70.4	1.2	26.7	62.4	10.8	207	54.6	42.0	19.8
Madison city	6,497	7,126	9.7	6,830	92.0	0.8	1.5	3.2	2.6	20.2	63.5	16.3	2,686	60.1	37.2	30.0
Manderson-White Horse Creek CDP	626	NA	NA	847	0.0	0.0	0.0	100.0	0.0	47.0	50.1	3.0	107	0.0	57.0	0.0

1 May be of any race.

Table A. All Places — **Population and Housing**

STATE City, town, township, borough, or CDP (county if applicable)	2010 census total population	2014 estimated population	Percent change 2010-2014	ACS total population estimate 2010-2014	White alone, not Hispanic or Latino	Black alone, not Hispanic or Latino	Asian alone, not Hispanic or Latino	All other races or 2 or more races, not Hispanic or Latino	Hispanic or Latino[1]	Under 18 years old	Age 18 to 64 years old	Age 65 years and older	Total occupied housing units	Percent owner occupied	High school diploma or less	Bachelor's degree or more
	1	2	3	4	5	6	7	8	9	10	11	12	13	14	15	16
SOUTH DAKOTA—Con.																
Mansfield CDP	93	NA	NA	65	92.3	0.0	0.0	0.0	7.7	13.9	60.0	26.2	34	85.3	35.3	23.5
Marion city	784	771	-1.7	730	94.9	0.0	0.0	3.7	1.4	20.5	46.7	32.9	334	64.7	50.6	17.1
Martin city	1,066	1,064	-0.2	981	38.5	0.0	0.0	60.1	1.3	24.4	53.7	21.9	418	59.6	42.3	19.1
Marty CDP	402	NA	NA	588	1.0	0.0	0.0	99.0	0.0	42.8	53.9	3.2	134	20.1	29.1	3.7
Marvin town	34	33	-2.9	89	96.6	0.0	0.0	3.4	0.0	9.0	87.6	3.4	21	100.0	66.7	0.0
Meadow View Addition CDP	538	NA	NA	397	97.5	0.0	2.5	0.0	0.0	1.8	76.5	21.7	196	89.8	49.5	15.8
Mellette city	210	221	5.2	164	100.0	0.0	0.0	0.0	0.0	25.0	60.9	14.0	70	95.7	31.4	12.9
Menno city	608	590	-3.0	577	98.1	0.0	0.0	1.9	0.0	13.3	43.1	43.5	308	84.4	59.4	21.8
Midland town	129	123	-4.7	178	98.3	0.0	0.0	1.7	0.0	25.8	53.4	20.8	81	85.2	48.1	8.6
Milbank city	3,353	3,269	-2.5	3,310	91.8	0.7	0.0	2.7	4.8	20.3	57.1	22.4	1,492	73.0	64.7	14.8
Miller city	1,490	1,440	-3.4	1,494	98.8	0.0	0.0	0.9	0.3	17.5	49.5	32.9	716	59.5	41.8	23.6
Milltown CDP	10	NA	NA	20	100.0	0.0	0.0	0.0	0.0	0.0	100.0	0.0	10	100.0	100.0	0.0
Mission city	1,182	1,208	2.2	880	11.4	1.0	1.7	78.8	7.2	35.9	55.7	8.4	322	48.4	32.0	28.6
Mission Hill town	177	177	0.0	247	85.0	0.0	0.0	10.1	4.9	34.0	54.3	11.7	81	79.0	63.0	18.5
Mitchell city	15,278	15,693	2.7	15,490	91.5	0.7	0.1	5.3	2.3	22.4	60.1	17.4	6,843	57.5	35.7	27.2
Mobridge city	3,462	3,515	1.5	3,293	73.3	0.0	3.6	21.9	1.2	18.8	56.9	24.2	1,543	54.4	45.4	28.3
Monroe town	160	156	-2.5	162	85.2	0.0	0.0	7.4	7.4	31.4	61.2	7.4	67	53.7	43.3	9.0
Montrose city	472	474	0.4	530	93.8	0.0	0.0	4.5	1.7	35.5	52.5	11.9	188	69.7	47.3	18.6
Morningside CDP	105	NA	NA	60	100.0	0.0	0.0	0.0	0.0	11.7	80.0	8.3	29	82.8	62.1	0.0
Morristown town	67	69	3.0	68	98.5	0.0	0.0	1.5	0.0	7.3	61.8	30.9	47	63.8	76.6	12.8
Mound City town	71	67	-5.6	62	100.0	0.0	0.0	0.0	0.0	0.0	45.1	54.8	44	79.5	65.9	25.0
Mount Vernon city	462	443	-4.1	558	91.6	0.0	0.0	2.3	6.1	36.7	55.1	8.2	197	73.1	37.6	13.7
Murdo city	488	482	-1.2	351	91.5	2.8	0.6	4.0	1.1	17.7	59.6	22.8	210	61.0	41.0	24.8
Naples town	41	38	-7.3	20	100.0	0.0	0.0	0.0	0.0	35.0	55.0	10.0	7	100.0	57.1	14.3
New Effington town	256	261	2.0	204	67.6	0.0	0.0	32.4	0.0	28.5	46.6	25.0	92	77.2	66.3	5.4
Newell city	600	600	0.0	726	86.5	0.0	0.0	2.5	11.0	25.3	55.4	19.1	277	74.7	61.0	14.8
New Holland CDP	76	NA	NA	49	100.0	0.0	0.0	0.0	0.0	0.0	0.0	100.0	20	80.0	100.0	0.0
New Underwood city	660	674	2.1	601	88.7	0.0	0.0	10.8	0.5	21.5	60.7	17.8	229	81.7	36.7	16.2
New Witten town	79	77	-2.5	42	100.0	0.0	0.0	0.0	0.0	0.0	76.1	23.8	29	82.8	44.8	20.7
Nisland town	235	240	2.1	339	90.9	0.0	0.0	5.0	4.1	28.3	56.1	15.6	128	78.1	57.0	7.8
Norris CDP	152	NA	NA	120	37.5	0.0	0.0	62.5	0.0	43.4	47.6	9.2	34	35.3	61.8	11.8
North Eagle Butte CDP	1,954	NA	NA	2,083	2.9	0.8	0.0	96.2	0.0	38.6	55.3	6.1	558	42.7	39.1	18.5
North Sioux City city	2,530	2,636	4.2	2,551	89.3	0.0	0.1	4.6	5.9	23.5	63.6	13.1	1,094	64.9	41.4	28.8
North Spearfish CDP	2,221	NA	NA	1,969	86.1	0.0	0.0	8.8	5.1	15.4	65.6	18.9	1,014	68.2	40.6	29.2
Northville town	143	148	3.5	145	100.0	0.0	0.0	0.0	0.0	48.2	47.6	4.1	41	100.0	24.4	56.1
Nunda town	43	47	9.3	52	96.2	0.0	0.0	3.8	0.0	23.1	30.7	46.2	21	100.0	52.4	38.1
Oacoma town	451	474	5.1	483	90.1	0.0	0.0	9.9	0.0	15.2	69.1	15.7	224	79.9	58.0	15.2
Oelrichs town	126	123	-2.4	148	85.1	0.0	0.0	12.8	2.0	16.2	60.1	23.6	73	78.1	57.5	11.0
Oglala CDP	1,290	NA	NA	1,321	2.4	1.4	0.0	96.2	0.0	39.7	56.0	4.2	248	60.1	40.7	16.9
Okaton CDP	36	NA	NA	6	100.0	0.0	0.0	0.0	0.0	0.0	100.0	0.0	3	100.0	100.0	0.0
Okreek CDP	269	NA	NA	380	2.9	0.0	0.0	92.9	4.2	37.1	59.2	3.7	94	51.1	53.2	37.2
Ola CDP	13	NA	NA	0	0.0	0.0	0.0	0.0	0.0	0.0	0.0	0.0	0	0.0	0.0	0.0
Oldham city	133	130	-2.3	135	99.3	0.0	0.0	0.7	0.0	21.4	61.4	17.0	68	57.4	60.3	14.7
Olivet town	74	72	-2.7	92	100.0	0.0	0.0	0.0	0.0	18.5	47.8	33.7	37	83.8	67.6	5.4
Onaka town	15	15	0.0	14	100.0	0.0	0.0	0.0	0.0	14.3	57.1	28.6	9	100.0	44.4	44.4
Onida city	658	675	2.6	757	97.6	0.0	0.0	1.8	0.5	26.5	61.2	12.3	282	66.7	37.2	24.5
Orient town	63	63	0.0	52	100.0	0.0	0.0	0.0	0.0	3.8	69.3	26.9	34	94.1	82.4	2.9
Ortley town	65	66	1.5	41	87.8	0.0	0.0	12.2	0.0	12.2	70.8	17.1	22	86.4	40.9	45.5
Parker city	1,022	1,001	-2.1	1,138	96.1	1.2	0.0	2.1	0.5	28.7	53.6	17.7	452	72.3	39.8	21.7
Parkston city	1,516	1,476	-2.6	1,781	97.9	0.0	0.0	2.1	0.0	28.0	48.2	23.7	685	72.3	35.8	22.6
Parmelee CDP	562	NA	NA	837	0.0	0.0	0.0	100.0	0.0	53.3	43.3	3.3	162	16.0	58.0	10.5
Peever town	168	171	1.8	221	49.8	0.0	0.0	50.2	0.0	30.8	62.8	6.3	71	56.3	59.2	18.3
Philip city	779	745	-4.4	773	95.1	0.0	0.0	3.4	1.6	24.7	52.5	23.2	359	81.3	56.5	13.1
Pickstown town	203	217	6.9	176	63.1	0.0	0.0	36.4	0.6	24.4	51.1	24.4	74	62.2	25.7	17.6
Piedmont city	826	835	1.1	878	89.6	0.0	0.0	6.6	3.8	42.1	51.1	6.8	280	88.6	46.4	21.8
Pierpont town	135	131	-3.0	125	100.0	0.0	0.0	0.0	0.0	29.6	48.0	22.4	54	85.2	72.2	9.3
Pierre city	13,646	14,054	3.0	13,885	82.4	0.7	0.9	13.1	2.9	22.9	62.1	15.0	5,834	59.8	31.6	36.1
Pine Lakes Addition CDP	314	NA	NA	307	100.0	0.0	0.0	0.0	0.0	38.4	52.2	9.4	79	100.0	17.7	50.6
Pine Ridge CDP	3,308	NA	NA	3,329	5.3	0.0	0.1	93.8	0.9	40.3	54.4	5.2	690	32.5	28.6	26.8
Plankinton city	707	718	1.6	716	87.0	0.0	0.0	0.0	13.0	25.4	54.7	20.0	305	78.4	50.2	22.6
Platte city	1,230	1,248	1.5	1,427	98.1	0.1	0.0	1.3	0.6	21.4	53.1	25.4	605	72.6	48.9	17.7
Pollock town	241	227	-5.8	172	99.4	0.0	0.0	0.0	0.6	11.6	44.8	43.6	114	78.1	62.3	6.1
Porcupine CDP	1,062	NA	NA	1,351	0.7	0.0	0.0	97.7	1.6	32.5	59.2	8.4	257	52.5	46.7	14.0
Prairie City CDP	23	NA	NA	6	100.0	0.0	0.0	0.0	0.0	0.0	33.3	66.7	6	66.7	66.7	33.3
Presho city	497	507	2.0	509	98.6	0.0	0.0	1.4	0.0	30.8	54.4	14.7	232	82.3	48.7	21.1
Pringle town	112	111	-0.9	192	78.1	1.6	0.0	9.4	10.9	18.8	52.4	28.6	102	71.6	56.9	10.8
Pukwana town	290	287	-1.0	250	68.8	0.0	0.0	19.6	11.6	26.8	58.8	14.4	97	75.3	62.9	9.3
Quinn town	56	58	3.6	93	87.1	0.0	3.2	7.5	2.2	22.5	58.1	19.4	43	90.7	48.8	4.7
Ramona town	174	191	9.8	164	81.1	0.0	0.0	1.2	17.7	22.6	42.0	35.4	83	67.5	73.5	8.4
Rapid City city	67,964	72,638	6.9	70,126	77.6	1.2	1.1	15.0	5.2	24.0	60.9	15.2	28,244	58.8	31.0	31.1
Rapid Valley CDP	8,260	NA	NA	8,619	89.7	1.1	1.0	6.5	1.6	27.9	65.0	7.1	3,029	91.8	34.3	17.6
Ravinia town	61	62	1.6	84	17.9	1.2	0.0	81.0	0.0	52.4	37.0	10.7	21	66.7	61.9	14.3
Raymond town	50	50	0.0	59	100.0	0.0	0.0	0.0	0.0	5.1	52.6	42.4	30	96.7	63.3	20.0
Redfield city	2,368	2,416	2.0	2,583	96.9	0.0	0.0	2.0	1.0	21.8	51.7	26.6	1,128	59.7	47.8	18.4
Ree Heights town	62	61	-1.6	68	100.0	0.0	0.0	0.0	0.0	19.1	54.3	26.5	25	96.0	60.0	0.0
Reliance town	191	209	9.4	228	84.6	0.0	0.0	13.6	1.8	36.9	44.3	18.9	78	92.3	46.2	24.4
Renner Corner CDP	305	NA	NA	250	100.0	0.0	0.0	0.0	0.0	8.8	79.6	11.6	125	91.2	33.6	9.6
Revillo town	119	116	-2.5	100	99.0	0.0	0.0	1.0	0.0	32.0	42.0	26.0	41	56.1	61.0	24.4
Richland CDP	89	NA	NA	76	100.0	0.0	0.0	0.0	0.0	0.0	46.1	53.9	50	80.0	86.0	14.0
Rockham town	33	32	-3.0	75	100.0	0.0	0.0	0.0	0.0	61.4	37.4	1.3	17	76.5	70.6	0.0
Roscoe city	329	316	-4.0	315	99.4	0.0	0.0	0.0	0.6	23.2	51.5	25.4	155	76.1	64.5	16.8
Rosebud CDP	1,587	NA	NA	1,682	6.9	1.5	0.0	87.3	4.3	41.8	54.4	3.8	450	34.9	49.8	23.8
Rosholt town	422	432	2.4	551	94.4	1.3	0.0	4.4	0.0	29.6	45.8	24.7	209	69.4	38.8	18.2
Roslyn town	183	178	-2.7	193	97.4	0.0	0.0	2.6	0.0	17.6	33.1	49.2	86	79.1	70.9	5.8
Roswell CDP	15	NA	NA	9	100.0	0.0	0.0	0.0	0.0	0.0	44.4	55.6	7	100.0	100.0	0.0
Running Water CDP	36	NA	NA	65	64.6	0.0	0.0	35.4	0.0	30.7	58.5	10.8	38	39.5	60.5	21.1
St. Charles CDP	11	NA	NA	22	100.0	0.0	0.0	0.0	0.0	13.6	63.7	22.7	10	70.0	50.0	0.0
St. Francis town	544	561	3.1	689	2.6	0.0	0.0	92.9	4.5	44.6	51.0	4.4	144	61.1	49.3	13.9
St. Lawrence town	198	197	-0.5	140	98.6	0.0	0.7	0.7	0.0	27.1	52.8	20.0	57	93.0	47.4	12.3
St. Onge CDP	191	NA	NA	26	100.0	0.0	0.0	0.0	0.0	0.0	50.0	50.0	13	100.0	0.0	0.0

1 May be of any race.

Table A. All Places — **Population and Housing**

	Population				Race and Hispanic or Latino origin (percent), 2010–2014					Age (percent), 2010–2014			Households, 2010–2014			
STATE City, town, township, borough, or CDP (county if applicable)	2010 census total population	2014 estimated population	Percent change 2010-2014	ACS total population estimate 2010-2014	White alone, not Hispanic or Latino	Black alone, not Hispanic or Latino	Asian alone, not Hispanic or Latino	All other races or 2 or more races, not Hispanic or Latino	Hispanic or Latino[1]	Under 18 years old	Age 18 to 64 years old	Age 65 years and older	Total occupied housing units	Percent owner occupied	Householders by level of education (percent) High school diploma or less	Householders by level of education (percent) Bachelor's degree or more
	1	2	3	4	5	6	7	8	9	10	11	12	13	14	15	16
SOUTH DAKOTA—Con.																
Salem city	1,351	1,350	-0.1	1,377	98.3	0.0	0.0	0.9	0.8	23.4	54.0	22.7	603	76.9	48.3	21.6
Scotland city	841	830	-1.3	871	91.6	0.0	0.5	0.5	7.5	25.8	49.7	24.6	386	75.6	56.5	24.4
Selby city	642	644	0.3	800	95.0	0.0	0.0	1.3	3.8	22.3	46.7	31.1	304	84.9	48.7	15.5
Seneca town	38	37	-2.6	50	100.0	0.0	0.0	0.0	0.0	26.0	68.0	6.0	17	100.0	76.5	5.9
Sherman town	78	82	5.1	103	99.0	0.0	0.0	0.0	1.0	37.8	62.1	0.0	36	91.7	66.7	11.1
Shindler CDP	584	NA	NA	684	100.0	0.0	0.0	0.0	0.0	25.0	69.6	5.4	174	100.0	32.8	44.3
Sinai town	120	119	-0.8	169	90.5	0.0	0.0	0.0	9.5	43.2	52.7	4.1	49	91.8	44.9	26.5
Sioux Falls city	153,897	168,586	9.5	160,964	83.8	4.5	2.2	4.7	4.8	24.8	63.8	11.4	64,197	60.8	34.0	33.4
Sisseton city	2,440	2,473	1.4	2,597	41.8	0.0	0.4	56.5	1.2	30.6	52.4	17.1	930	50.8	44.2	18.8
Soldier Creek CDP	227	NA	NA	87	0.0	0.0	0.0	100.0	0.0	11.5	74.7	13.8	36	100.0	33.3	0.0
South Shore town	225	227	0.9	193	92.7	0.0	0.0	3.1	4.1	23.8	53.9	22.3	97	80.4	57.7	15.5
Spearfish city	10,532	11,091	5.3	10,836	91.9	0.1	1.0	5.4	1.6	17.7	66.0	16.4	4,553	51.7	34.7	31.2
Spencer city	154	155	0.6	141	87.2	0.0	0.0	12.8	0.0	26.2	56.7	17.0	61	93.4	72.1	8.2
Spring Creek CDP	268	NA	NA	168	0.0	0.0	0.0	100.0	0.0	43.5	51.2	5.4	50	46.0	62.0	0.0
Springfield city	1,988	1,963	-1.3	1,926	72.5	1.9	0.0	18.2	7.4	11.2	74.2	14.4	347	76.9	43.8	22.2
Stickney town	284	286	0.7	238	100.0	0.0	0.0	0.0	0.0	18.5	49.9	31.5	122	74.6	35.2	23.0
Stockholm town	108	105	-2.8	103	98.1	0.0	0.0	1.9	0.0	19.4	68.0	12.6	44	68.2	65.9	4.5
Storla CDP	6	NA	NA	0	0.0	0.0	0.0	0.0	0.0	0.0	0.0	0.0	0	0.0	0.0	0.0
Strandburg town	72	70	-2.8	68	91.2	0.0	0.0	8.8	0.0	14.7	72.1	13.2	39	69.2	74.4	0.0
Stratford town	72	72	0.0	74	81.1	0.0	0.0	0.0	18.9	29.8	58.2	12.2	32	78.1	28.1	18.8
Sturgis city	6,637	6,741	1.6	6,652	93.1	0.0	0.0	5.8	1.0	24.7	56.5	18.9	2,966	56.9	47.2	15.7
Summerset city	1,825	2,118	16.1	2,240	86.4	1.5	0.6	6.9	4.6	33.3	61.9	4.7	734	77.7	24.5	31.2
Summit town	288	293	1.7	284	65.8	0.4	0.0	30.3	3.5	31.6	51.6	16.5	108	57.4	62.0	12.0
Tabor town	420	413	-1.7	379	96.6	0.0	1.3	2.1	0.0	22.8	53.7	23.5	170	76.5	44.1	18.2
Tea city	3,808	4,531	19.0	4,226	95.3	1.9	0.0	2.4	0.4	34.1	63.7	2.3	1,438	78.2	25.5	41.9
Timber Lake city	443	477	7.7	469	57.1	0.0	0.0	42.9	0.0	29.4	53.5	17.1	167	69.5	51.5	19.8
Tolstoy town	36	36	0.0	20	100.0	0.0	0.0	0.0	0.0	0.0	55.0	45.0	15	100.0	53.3	0.0
Toronto town	212	209	-1.4	234	84.6	13.7	0.0	0.9	0.9	33.7	45.3	20.9	99	76.8	54.5	24.2
Trent town	232	231	-0.4	278	94.2	0.0	0.0	4.7	1.1	19.1	63.0	18.0	138	72.5	47.1	8.7
Tripp city	647	627	-3.1	550	93.6	0.0	0.0	0.7	5.6	19.4	47.3	33.5	242	84.7	59.1	12.0
Tulare town	207	218	5.3	255	100.0	0.0	0.0	0.0	0.0	25.0	56.9	18.0	98	75.5	45.9	16.3
Turton town	48	49	2.1	42	100.0	0.0	0.0	0.0	0.0	23.8	47.7	28.6	23	60.9	43.5	21.7
Twin Brooks town	69	67	-2.9	60	100.0	0.0	0.0	0.0	0.0	30.0	56.6	13.3	22	100.0	63.6	0.0
Two Strike CDP	209	NA	NA	425	0.0	0.0	0.0	98.1	1.9	30.3	67.2	2.4	120	50.8	44.2	10.8
Tyndall city	1,067	1,059	-0.7	1,188	92.3	0.6	2.4	1.6	3.1	20.8	54.0	25.3	495	74.7	45.1	18.4
Utica town	65	65	0.0	52	48.1	42.3	3.8	0.0	5.8	19.2	61.4	19.2	34	35.3	23.5	8.8
Vale CDP	136	NA	NA	170	88.8	0.0	0.0	11.2	0.0	11.8	62.9	25.3	75	66.7	68.0	25.3
Valley Springs city	759	775	2.1	701	95.3	0.4	0.0	2.6	1.7	30.1	62.2	7.7	270	81.1	43.0	20.0
Veblen city	531	528	-0.6	436	34.4	0.5	0.0	31.0	34.2	25.9	58.3	15.8	168	48.2	64.3	13.7
Verdon town	5	5	0.0	2	100.0	0.0	0.0	0.0	0.0	0.0	100.0	0.0	2	0.0	100.0	0.0
Vermillion city	10,578	10,699	1.1	10,697	86.7	1.9	2.2	6.3	3.0	15.6	76.5	8.0	3,902	39.0	27.5	41.0
Viborg city	782	767	-1.9	862	96.3	0.0	0.0	3.7	0.0	18.4	50.0	31.6	396	65.7	55.8	18.4
Vienna town	45	44	-2.2	57	84.2	12.3	0.0	3.5	0.0	35.1	59.7	5.3	21	95.2	52.4	0.0
Vilas town	20	19	-5.0	10	100.0	0.0	0.0	0.0	0.0	0.0	100.0	0.0	5	100.0	40.0	0.0
Virgil town	16	17	6.3	13	100.0	0.0	0.0	0.0	0.0	0.0	38.5	61.5	8	100.0	75.0	0.0
Vivian CDP	119	NA	NA	76	88.2	0.0	0.0	11.8	0.0	9.2	46.0	44.7	44	63.6	47.7	31.8
Volga city	1,768	1,817	2.8	2,259	93.8	1.3	0.0	1.5	3.5	31.7	59.6	8.7	818	69.9	35.9	27.8
Volin town	161	161	0.0	152	98.7	0.0	0.0	1.3	0.0	24.3	62.6	13.2	56	78.6	55.4	7.1
Wagner city	1,565	1,576	0.7	1,633	55.3	0.0	0.2	38.2	6.2	25.8	51.9	22.2	652	60.3	52.8	18.1
Wakonda town	321	313	-2.5	340	94.7	0.3	0.0	4.1	0.9	19.4	59.4	21.2	137	68.6	42.3	17.5
Wall town	766	882	15.1	912	77.7	0.0	0.4	20.8	0.7	31.8	54.1	14.0	367	69.8	34.1	29.2
Wallace town	85	85	0.0	90	86.7	0.0	0.0	13.3	0.0	29.9	63.3	6.7	40	67.5	45.0	5.0
Wanblee CDP	725	NA	NA	680	4.4	0.7	2.2	86.6	6.0	33.9	61.0	5.1	201	5.5	44.8	14.9
Ward town	48	49	2.1	35	85.7	0.0	0.0	14.3	0.0	22.9	71.4	5.7	14	92.9	14.3	7.1
Warner town	457	480	5.0	478	97.9	0.0	0.0	1.3	0.8	21.3	70.8	7.9	194	91.2	42.3	26.3
Wasta town	80	82	2.5	55	100.0	0.0	0.0	0.0	0.0	7.3	60.0	32.7	29	72.4	24.1	37.9
Watertown city	21,517	22,057	2.5	21,795	93.4	0.1	0.5	4.2	1.7	23.9	60.5	15.5	9,335	64.4	45.3	19.2
Waubay city	576	574	-0.3	681	50.1	0.0	0.0	49.2	0.7	33.7	41.6	24.7	270	75.2	59.6	18.5
Waverly CDP	37	NA	NA	19	100.0	0.0	0.0	0.0	0.0	15.8	84.2	0.0	10	100.0	70.0	30.0
Webster city	1,886	1,833	-2.8	1,890	95.7	0.0	0.6	2.4	1.3	21.8	55.3	22.9	952	61.2	48.0	24.8
Wentworth village	171	189	10.5	139	97.1	0.0	0.0	1.4	1.4	14.4	66.9	18.7	66	98.5	48.5	16.7
Wessington town	170	180	5.9	231	99.1	0.0	0.0	0.0	0.9	29.0	51.9	19.0	101	76.2	63.4	4.0
Wessington Springs city	956	925	-3.2	846	98.1	0.0	0.0	1.1	0.8	16.3	49.4	34.3	420	74.8	39.5	17.4
Westport town	133	134	0.8	105	100.0	0.0	0.0	0.0	0.0	9.5	69.5	21.0	51	100.0	41.2	9.8
Wetonka town	8	8	0.0	7	100.0	0.0	0.0	0.0	0.0	28.6	71.5	0.0	2	100.0	100.0	0.0
White city	485	487	0.4	476	98.9	0.0	0.0	0.4	0.6	18.9	64.9	16.2	209	71.8	43.1	26.3
Whitehorse CDP	141	NA	NA	163	9.8	0.0	0.0	90.2	0.0	41.1	56.3	2.5	44	25.0	45.5	29.5
White Horse CDP	276	NA	NA	216	0.0	0.0	0.0	95.8	4.2	42.2	54.7	3.2	47	40.4	25.5	17.0
White Lake city	372	373	0.3	386	94.3	0.0	0.0	0.0	5.7	20.5	53.9	25.6	164	82.9	56.1	10.4
White River city	581	590	1.5	508	58.7	0.0	0.0	36.4	4.9	34.1	46.7	19.3	192	64.1	35.4	23.4
White Rock town	3	3	0.0	4	25.0	0.0	0.0	0.0	75.0	0.0	25.0	75.0	4	100.0	100.0	0.0
Whitewood city	930	923	-0.8	899	93.4	0.0	0.0	3.7	2.9	33.4	52.6	14.0	352	69.3	63.6	11.9
Willow Lake city	263	244	-7.2	380	87.9	0.0	0.0	3.7	8.4	30.8	54.7	14.5	158	74.7	66.5	10.8
Wilmot city	496	506	2.0	523	98.1	0.0	0.0	1.7	0.2	25.1	44.8	30.2	209	79.9	62.7	23.0
Winfred CDP	52	NA	NA	90	100.0	0.0	0.0	0.0	0.0	26.6	66.7	6.7	33	54.5	45.5	54.5
Winner city	2,931	2,862	-2.4	2,871	81.5	0.1	0.5	17.4	0.4	23.2	54.9	21.9	1,378	60.3	40.9	27.2
Wolsey town	376	393	4.5	519	99.2	0.0	0.0	0.0	0.8	26.1	58.6	15.2	222	67.1	52.7	14.0
Wood town	62	64	3.2	32	84.4	0.0	0.0	15.6	0.0	25.0	59.4	15.6	18	61.1	44.4	22.2
Woonsocket city	655	652	-0.5	588	98.6	0.0	0.0	1.4	0.0	16.6	50.1	33.3	298	66.4	66.4	14.8
Worthing city	877	942	7.4	937	92.0	0.0	0.0	6.9	1.1	31.5	64.9	3.8	348	89.7	29.0	22.1
Wounded Knee CDP	382	NA	NA	462	0.0	0.0	0.0	94.8	5.2	33.6	66.5	0.0	71	32.4	35.2	0.0
Yale town	108	112	3.7	95	97.9	0.0	0.0	2.1	0.0	20.0	65.2	14.7	47	93.6	66.0	0.0
Yankton city	14,454	14,552	0.7	14,513	87.3	2.6	1.0	4.9	4.2	21.9	60.5	17.6	5,874	63.2	39.4	29.1
TENNESSEE	6,346,275	6,549,352	3.2	6,451,365	75.0	16.7	1.5	2.0	4.8	23.1	62.6	14.2	2,487,349	67.1	44.4	26.0
Adams city	635	650	2.4	836	81.0	10.6	0.0	4.1	4.3	25.0	67.5	7.5	272	76.1	44.1	21.0
Adamsville town	2,207	2,258	2.3	1,909	96.3	2.4	0.0	1.4	0.0	16.6	55.1	28.3	786	68.7	64.9	19.2
Alamo town	2,490	2,498	0.3	2,423	70.4	16.3	0.0	2.6	10.6	26.9	52.9	20.2	879	58.5	59.5	9.2
Alcoa city	8,431	8,753	3.8	8,556	77.4	15.1	1.2	0.7	5.6	22.7	60.2	17.1	3,718	66.7	42.1	20.2
Alexandria town	966	985	2.0	1,184	96.6	3.1	0.3	0.0	0.0	23.2	60.8	15.9	421	66.0	59.1	11.9

1 May be of any race.

Table A. All Places — **Population and Housing**

STATE City, town, township, borough, or CDP (county if applicable)	Population: 2010 census total population	Population: 2014 estimated population	Population: Percent change 2010-2014	Population: ACS total population estimate 2010-2014	Race and Hispanic or Latino origin (percent), 2010–2014: White alone, not Hispanic or Latino	Black alone, not Hispanic or Latino	Asian alone, not Hispanic or Latino	All other races or 2 or more races, not Hispanic or Latino	Hispanic or Latino[1]	Age (percent), 2010–2014: Under 18 years old	Age 18 to 64 years old	Age 65 years and older	Households, 2010–2014: Total occupied housing units	Percent owner occupied	Householders by level of education (percent): High school diploma or less	Bachelor's degree or more
	1	2	3	4	5	6	7	8	9	10	11	12	13	14	15	16
TENNESSEE—Con.																
Algood city	3,495	3,596	2.9	3,538	89.6	5.2	0.0	2.1	3.1	24.5	57.3	18.4	1,328	61.7	55.4	17.8
Allardt city	634	630	-0.6	558	99.3	0.0	0.0	0.7	0.0	16.3	67.6	16.1	250	83.2	60.8	15.6
Altamont town	1,048	1,024	-2.3	1,070	73.5	0.7	0.0	25.8	0.0	19.0	60.6	20.4	390	81.0	84.6	4.4
Andersonville CDP	472	NA	NA	238	100.0	0.0	0.0	0.0	0.0	24.9	47.9	27.3	108	85.2	51.9	38.0
Apison CDP	2,469	NA	NA	2,617	95.0	2.5	0.0	0.0	2.5	22.7	65.4	12.0	988	72.8	31.6	26.2
Ardmore city	1,213	1,212	-0.1	1,182	80.3	7.6	2.5	6.3	3.3	21.5	60.3	18.2	463	68.5	57.5	11.4
Arlington town	11,517	11,634	1.0	11,623	82.6	10.0	3.4	2.7	1.3	36.8	57.9	5.2	3,340	90.3	18.7	43.7
Ashland City town	4,547	4,674	2.8	4,643	84.7	8.1	1.7	2.6	2.9	25.6	61.1	13.2	1,983	62.4	44.5	22.3
Athens city	13,563	13,664	0.7	13,603	81.2	7.1	0.7	2.7	8.3	23.7	60.8	15.5	5,500	52.9	47.3	23.5
Atoka town	8,379	8,935	6.6	8,727	78.6	8.8	1.0	8.2	3.4	27.1	61.0	11.8	3,100	84.0	37.6	25.0
Atwood town	938	929	-1.0	966	75.2	23.1	0.1	0.5	1.1	17.5	58.4	23.9	432	74.8	61.6	8.1
Auburntown town	269	268	-0.4	387	98.2	0.3	0.0	0.5	1.0	28.7	59.5	11.9	142	69.0	64.1	12.7
Baileyton town	431	428	-0.7	493	98.6	0.6	0.0	0.6	0.2	20.5	64.7	14.8	234	59.0	65.4	12.0
Baneberry city	482	504	4.6	491	98.0	0.0	0.0	0.8	1.2	11.6	54.1	34.2	228	76.8	29.4	28.9
Banner Hill CDP	1,497	NA	NA	1,470	87.2	5.1	0.0	0.0	7.7	10.0	48.0	42.0	646	80.3	73.2	8.4
Bartlett city	56,922	58,264	2.4	57,805	74.1	18.9	2.7	1.5	2.8	25.9	60.4	13.6	19,683	82.7	26.4	39.1
Baxter town	1,365	1,396	2.3	1,533	98.2	0.0	0.0	1.4	0.4	28.9	53.2	17.9	630	63.5	68.3	11.1
Bean Station city	3,075	3,084	0.3	3,072	93.9	0.0	0.0	0.2	5.9	20.1	58.9	21.0	1,343	81.6	62.2	8.0
Beersheba Springs town	477	469	-1.7	651	80.6	0.0	0.0	19.4	0.0	25.0	53.0	22.0	262	79.8	80.2	9.2
Bell Buckle town	500	512	2.4	409	85.6	5.4	2.7	2.0	4.4	18.4	69.3	12.2	136	69.1	33.1	36.0
Belle Meade city	2,912	3,017	3.6	2,930	97.9	0.5	0.2	0.4	1.0	31.2	51.3	17.5	1,019	93.3	2.0	87.4
Bells city	2,439	2,457	0.7	2,774	53.7	24.8	0.0	1.4	20.1	26.0	59.8	14.2	965	61.2	56.1	15.5
Benton town	1,385	1,309	-5.5	1,844	90.9	0.8	0.0	4.3	4.1	27.4	60.6	12.1	651	60.5	57.6	5.8
Berry Hill city	537	551	2.6	559	83.9	6.3	0.7	3.2	5.9	3.8	86.5	9.7	328	36.3	23.2	52.7
Bethel Springs town	718	719	0.1	847	82.4	14.0	0.0	1.9	1.7	30.6	52.7	16.9	290	69.0	63.4	13.4
Bethpage CDP	288	NA	NA	296	100.0	0.0	0.0	0.0	0.0	4.1	81.1	14.9	147	66.0	84.4	0.0
Big Sandy town	554	542	-2.2	593	99.2	0.0	0.0	0.5	0.3	14.5	61.2	24.1	274	70.1	73.4	2.9
Blaine city	1,851	1,870	1.0	1,786	99.2	0.7	0.0	0.0	0.2	18.5	65.3	16.2	708	83.8	64.8	13.3
Bloomingdale CDP	9,888	NA	NA	9,882	92.4	0.9	0.0	6.5	0.2	21.1	60.7	18.2	4,011	72.7	58.5	9.1
Blountville CDP	3,074	NA	NA	2,412	94.8	2.7	0.0	1.2	1.2	5.1	72.0	23.0	952	73.2	56.8	11.2
Bluff City city	1,733	1,734	0.1	1,791	90.3	2.3	0.4	6.9	0.0	26.0	61.4	12.5	733	73.9	42.3	14.1
Bolivar city	5,434	5,152	-5.2	5,275	40.3	59.0	0.6	0.0	0.1	23.9	58.0	18.2	1,775	62.7	61.6	11.0
Bon Aqua Junction CDP	1,230	NA	NA	863	88.4	2.0	0.0	3.2	6.4	16.8	66.6	16.5	474	55.7	68.1	5.7
Bowman CDP	302	NA	NA	254	100.0	0.0	0.0	0.0	0.0	14.2	85.8	0.0	84	65.5	69.0	0.0
Braden town	282	277	-1.8	204	70.1	15.7	0.5	4.4	9.3	11.9	61.8	26.5	92	87.0	47.8	21.7
Bradford town	1,048	1,017	-3.0	1,187	89.0	7.2	0.0	1.9	1.9	25.5	55.6	19.0	472	83.9	53.8	19.5
Bransford CDP	170	NA	NA	168	100.0	0.0	0.0	0.0	0.0	21.4	51.8	26.8	71	100.0	90.1	0.0
Brentwood city	37,060	40,982	10.6	39,059	85.0	4.1	5.5	2.9	2.6	30.6	58.2	11.5	12,486	91.5	11.0	72.4
Brighton town	2,883	2,942	2.0	2,931	77.6	14.7	3.5	1.2	3.0	35.1	58.9	5.9	904	70.1	40.2	20.2
Bristol city	26,709	26,729	0.1	26,705	93.8	2.7	0.5	0.9	2.2	20.1	61.8	18.1	11,292	68.7	48.2	23.7
Brownsville city	10,292	9,974	-3.1	10,079	29.7	65.2	0.0	2.7	2.4	27.4	58.0	14.7	3,945	49.0	64.4	13.7
Bruceton town	1,478	1,453	-1.7	1,779	91.1	3.9	0.1	4.0	1.0	29.1	51.6	19.2	568	67.4	53.5	18.1
Bulls Gap town	738	729	-1.2	606	100.0	0.0	0.0	0.0	0.0	22.4	57.0	20.6	267	72.7	70.8	13.1
Burlison town	419	418	-0.2	451	99.8	0.0	0.0	0.0	0.2	19.9	63.9	16.2	187	74.3	62.6	10.7
Burns town	1,464	1,457	-0.5	1,534	94.0	0.7	0.3	4.0	1.0	20.3	60.8	18.7	586	70.6	58.7	13.8
Byrdstown town	802	810	1.0	1,069	96.9	2.0	0.0	0.2	0.9	24.2	53.5	22.4	444	62.4	75.5	7.0
Calhoun town	490	495	1.0	530	91.9	3.8	0.0	3.4	0.9	16.6	56.5	27.0	185	83.8	58.4	11.9
Camden city	3,582	3,582	0.0	3,596	90.2	5.0	1.1	0.4	3.3	20.5	55.6	24.0	1,466	62.1	69.4	12.8
Carthage town	2,306	2,261	-2.0	2,042	88.8	8.8	0.2	1.4	0.8	19.3	61.4	19.3	832	49.8	67.5	9.1
Caryville town	2,297	2,223	-3.2	2,632	96.3	0.3	0.9	1.9	0.6	25.4	57.9	16.6	1,033	69.3	63.3	8.8
Castalian Springs CDP	556	NA	NA	965	100.0	0.0	0.0	0.0	0.0	24.4	73.8	1.8	235	75.7	60.0	24.3
Cedar Hill city	314	318	1.3	366	88.5	6.8	0.0	4.6	0.0	32.8	59.2	7.9	100	80.0	79.0	9.0
Celina city	1,495	1,485	-0.7	1,497	89.2	10.0	0.0	0.0	0.7	25.7	51.9	22.3	581	50.3	70.4	10.7
Centertown town	243	244	0.4	253	95.7	0.4	0.0	3.2	0.8	28.8	57.2	13.8	96	84.4	47.9	12.5
Centerville town	3,641	3,595	-1.3	3,586	81.9	7.3	0.0	0.8	10.1	15.8	58.5	25.5	1,559	72.5	61.3	21.0
Central CDP	2,279	NA	NA	2,060	98.1	0.0	0.9	0.4	0.6	17.4	62.9	19.7	914	63.5	70.5	6.7
Chapel Hill town	1,445	1,461	1.1	1,425	94.6	2.9	0.0	0.8	1.7	26.1	57.3	16.4	546	77.3	53.3	17.4
Charleston city	651	671	3.1	674	65.0	23.7	3.3	1.6	6.4	29.0	62.8	8.3	252	73.4	52.8	10.7
Charlotte town	1,491	1,494	0.2	1,610	88.4	5.9	0.0	4.1	1.6	21.7	63.0	15.4	593	61.4	67.3	8.9
Chattanooga city	168,828	173,778	2.9	171,863	56.6	33.8	2.1	1.9	5.5	21.0	63.9	15.0	69,890	53.3	38.3	28.6
Chesterfield CDP	469	NA	NA	378	100.0	0.0	0.0	0.0	0.0	27.5	61.7	10.8	135	84.4	67.4	9.6
Church Hill city	6,737	6,752	0.2	6,742	94.1	2.1	0.3	1.8	1.7	21.6	63.3	14.8	2,668	71.7	48.5	16.1
Clarkrange CDP	575	NA	NA	618	98.2	0.0	0.0	0.0	1.8	20.4	63.3	16.3	270	67.0	67.0	6.7
Clarksburg town	393	387	-1.5	475	92.2	2.5	0.8	1.5	2.9	22.5	57.4	20.0	160	81.3	71.9	10.0
Clarksville city	132,963	146,806	10.4	140,563	60.3	22.4	2.3	4.9	10.2	27.8	64.6	7.6	50,351	55.0	32.8	24.8
Cleveland city	41,285	43,182	4.6	42,331	78.8	8.4	1.7	2.3	8.8	22.7	63.1	14.2	15,671	49.2	40.6	25.4
Clifton city	2,694	2,673	-0.8	2,684	59.7	34.3	0.2	1.4	4.3	6.6	87.1	6.5	338	68.9	69.2	11.2
Clinton city	9,841	9,889	0.5	9,874	93.7	1.6	0.6	2.2	1.8	18.5	60.5	21.1	4,384	63.2	43.3	23.1
Coalfield CDP	2,463	NA	NA	2,475	96.6	0.2	0.0	2.8	0.3	26.8	58.7	14.5	897	85.1	56.5	12.4
Coalmont city	838	822	-1.9	619	83.0	0.0	0.0	17.0	0.0	19.6	58.3	22.0	263	76.4	82.9	6.8
Collegedale city	8,548	10,729	25.5	9,488	75.0	10.3	4.0	1.5	9.1	16.3	67.3	16.5	3,219	65.5	26.0	36.8
Collierville town	45,604	48,655	6.7	46,780	76.0	12.8	6.4	1.9	2.9	28.2	61.9	9.9	15,370	85.7	15.9	57.6
Collinwood city	982	986	0.4	941	97.3	0.2	0.3	0.9	1.3	22.4	59.4	18.3	384	76.6	60.9	14.3
Colonial Heights CDP	6,934	NA	NA	3,462	96.7	1.0	0.0	0.8	1.5	19.5	59.6	20.9	1,429	84.5	48.1	25.1
Columbia city	34,685	36,071	4.0	35,207	69.7	19.2	0.9	2.4	7.8	26.3	59.5	14.2	13,838	57.9	47.0	16.2
Cookeville city	30,557	31,335	2.5	31,004	85.4	4.3	1.8	2.3	6.2	17.6	69.3	13.2	12,738	42.5	41.3	26.4
Coopertown town	4,278	4,385	2.5	4,321	94.1	2.6	0.0	2.9	0.4	29.6	59.2	11.1	1,424	86.6	43.7	22.7
Copperhill city	354	333	-5.9	486	90.7	0.0	0.0	2.9	6.4	20.2	57.4	22.4	230	77.0	65.2	11.3
Cornersville town	1,194	1,210	1.3	1,161	90.3	3.1	0.0	2.4	4.2	24.7	55.0	20.4	465	74.2	50.1	9.5
Cottage Grove town	88	88	0.0	117	88.0	0.0	0.0	0.0	12.0	19.6	64.1	16.2	44	77.3	61.4	18.2
Cottontown CDP	367	NA	NA	427	96.3	0.0	0.0	0.0	3.7	10.3	81.2	8.4	153	94.8	48.4	7.2
Covington city	9,038	9,010	-0.3	9,033	40.3	56.0	0.1	0.6	2.9	19.6	64.4	15.9	3,489	49.8	56.8	10.2
Cowan city	1,737	1,717	-1.2	1,439	82.6	8.5	0.0	4.5	4.4	21.1	57.3	21.5	659	67.2	68.0	8.8
Crab Orchard city	752	763	1.5	759	96.8	0.0	0.0	2.5	0.7	22.2	62.5	15.2	303	89.1	78.5	3.6
Cross Plains city	1,714	1,728	0.8	1,909	96.7	1.2	0.0	1.4	0.7	26.8	62.3	10.9	675	72.0	50.5	17.3
Crossville city	10,832	11,330	4.6	11,125	91.7	0.7	0.2	1.1	6.3	25.1	53.3	21.6	4,398	48.5	51.8	20.9
Crump city	1,427	1,406	-1.5	1,256	94.3	0.3	1.1	2.2	2.1	16.6	61.4	22.1	537	80.3	66.3	5.0
Cumberland City town	311	304	-2.3	468	64.1	22.4	0.0	12.4	1.1	26.7	62.4	10.9	165	64.8	61.2	12.1
Cumberland Gap town	494	489	-1.0	410	83.7	10.2	3.2	0.5	2.4	4.9	87.8	7.3	160	26.3	22.5	63.8
Dandridge town	2,802	2,874	2.6	2,834	87.3	6.2	0.0	1.5	5.0	20.9	60.4	18.8	913	73.6	38.4	23.9
Darden CDP	399	NA	NA	480	100.0	0.0	0.0	0.0	0.0	40.4	54.5	5.2	131	100.0	32.1	7.6

1 May be of any race.

Table A. All Places — **Population and Housing**

STATE City, town, township, borough, or CDP (county if applicable)	Population: 2010 census total population	Population: 2014 estimated population	Population: Percent change 2010-2014	Race and Hispanic or Latino origin (percent), 2010–2014: ACS total population estimate 2010-2014	White alone, not Hispanic or Latino	Black alone, not Hispanic or Latino	Asian alone, not Hispanic or Latino	All other races or 2 or more races, not Hispanic or Latino	Hispanic or Latino[1]	Age (percent), 2010–2014: Under 18 years old	Age 18 to 64 years old	Age 65 years and older	Households, 2010–2014: Total occupied housing units	Percent owner occupied	Householders by level of education (percent): High school diploma or less	Householders by level of education (percent): Bachelor's degree or more
	1	2	3	4	5	6	7	8	9	10	11	12	13	14	15	16
TENNESSEE—Con.																
Dayton city	7,191	7,395	2.8	7,316	88.4	5.7	0.2	2.4	3.3	20.1	61.4	18.5	2,701	47.4	57.6	12.8
Decatur town	1,596	1,570	-1.6	1,503	98.1	1.3	0.0	0.2	0.4	22.1	55.5	22.4	587	65.9	61.2	7.5
Decaturville town	870	868	-0.2	949	87.0	11.9	0.0	0.8	0.2	20.9	53.6	25.7	348	61.2	74.1	8.6
Decherd city	2,362	2,437	3.2	2,424	71.5	11.1	0.2	9.3	7.9	24.1	57.8	18.2	955	67.3	60.0	10.3
Dickson city	14,658	14,993	2.3	14,814	83.0	8.9	1.2	3.4	3.5	25.5	59.1	15.3	5,679	56.9	59.4	14.3
Dodson Branch CDP	1,074	NA	NA	1,358	95.9	0.0	0.0	1.9	2.2	14.9	68.7	16.5	486	79.0	64.8	5.3
Dover city	1,417	1,430	0.9	1,696	87.0	2.4	1.5	1.7	7.4	19.8	55.5	24.8	720	68.8	55.3	24.0
Dowelltown town	355	364	2.5	359	95.8	1.9	0.0	0.0	2.2	21.7	67.5	10.9	134	88.1	57.5	12.7
Doyle town	537	543	1.1	585	74.2	0.0	0.0	17.6	8.2	31.6	54.5	13.8	193	75.1	77.2	8.8
Dresden town	2,996	2,908	-2.9	2,949	85.5	7.9	0.0	0.8	5.9	26.2	54.8	19.2	1,179	67.8	66.6	18.4
Ducktown city	475	457	-3.8	449	92.4	0.9	6.2	0.0	0.4	12.2	42.5	45.2	152	47.4	53.3	15.1
Dunlap city	4,815	5,068	5.3	4,953	83.3	0.2	0.0	9.8	6.6	21.0	57.9	21.1	2,023	59.6	56.3	13.3
Dyer city	2,337	2,281	-2.4	2,335	72.5	21.2	0.3	3.4	2.5	23.6	54.7	21.8	902	69.2	53.0	14.0
Dyersburg city	17,145	16,839	-1.8	16,998	68.0	25.6	0.4	2.6	3.4	23.2	60.1	16.8	7,165	49.3	51.1	22.0
Eagleton Village CDP	5,052	NA	NA	3,969	85.6	7.9	0.0	1.8	4.7	18.3	63.0	18.6	1,823	65.3	51.2	15.0
Eagleville city	602	629	4.5	684	96.9	0.0	0.0	3.1	0.0	18.3	63.4	18.3	267	83.1	58.8	22.8
East Cleveland CDP	1,608	NA	NA	1,622	88.2	8.6	0.0	3.2	0.0	21.7	67.6	10.7	657	51.0	76.4	5.8
East Ridge city	20,979	21,317	1.6	21,220	74.0	12.6	2.5	2.9	8.0	22.5	61.1	16.4	8,889	53.8	46.3	20.1
Eastview town	704	705	0.1	769	91.7	6.0	0.0	1.8	0.5	20.9	57.7	21.5	316	81.6	54.7	11.1
Elgin CDP	282	NA	NA	154	98.7	1.3	0.0	0.0	0.0	20.7	55.8	23.4	84	83.3	100.0	0.0
Elizabethton city	14,308	14,271	-0.3	14,322	91.9	3.2	0.3	2.4	2.2	17.7	59.4	22.9	6,084	61.4	44.9	23.5
Elkton city	578	565	-2.2	788	80.3	17.8	0.4	1.5	0.0	16.8	71.7	11.5	264	77.3	62.9	12.9
Englewood town	1,532	1,532	0.0	1,870	94.1	1.2	0.0	3.3	1.4	26.5	57.6	15.7	714	61.2	62.3	7.3
Enville town	189	190	0.5	226	93.4	2.7	0.0	4.0	0.0	20.8	55.7	23.5	87	86.2	62.1	5.7
Erin city	1,327	1,311	-1.2	1,451	82.1	7.9	0.0	7.2	2.8	24.7	53.7	21.6	549	51.2	62.5	14.2
Erwin town	6,097	6,021	-1.2	6,052	91.9	0.8	0.0	0.8	6.5	23.7	56.4	19.9	2,492	64.4	58.2	12.2
Estill Springs town	2,055	2,049	-0.3	2,120	90.7	2.5	0.5	3.5	2.9	21.0	60.1	18.9	808	85.6	49.4	18.2
Ethridge town	465	470	1.1	564	96.8	0.0	0.0	2.7	0.5	26.7	57.3	16.0	210	76.2	58.1	9.0
Etowah city	3,490	3,503	0.4	3,498	97.6	0.8	0.0	0.5	1.1	25.7	54.0	20.2	1,361	68.8	55.2	11.9
Eva CDP	293	NA	NA	234	100.0	0.0	0.0	0.0	0.0	23.9	56.0	20.1	108	92.6	66.7	13.0
Fairfield CDP	131	NA	NA	357	100.0	0.0	0.0	0.0	0.0	13.2	56.6	30.3	97	90.7	100.0	0.0
Fairfield Glade CDP	6,989	NA	NA	7,754	93.7	2.5	0.9	1.5	1.3	5.3	32.5	62.3	4,126	89.5	31.9	40.1
Fairgarden CDP	529	NA	NA	384	100.0	0.0	0.0	0.0	0.0	14.1	64.8	21.1	153	83.0	100.0	0.0
Fairmount CDP	2,825	NA	NA	2,535	96.1	0.0	0.6	1.8	1.6	33.7	59.0	7.4	842	86.8	21.7	56.3
Fairview city	7,730	8,224	6.4	8,020	93.2	0.3	1.3	2.4	2.8	27.6	62.5	9.9	2,924	77.1	36.6	28.0
Fall Branch CDP	1,291	NA	NA	1,396	100.0	0.0	0.0	0.0	0.0	25.9	62.5	11.5	532	74.1	52.1	18.6
Falling Water CDP	1,232	NA	NA	1,320	93.4	3.7	2.3	0.6	0.0	12.5	69.5	18.1	563	87.2	28.8	31.3
Farragut town	20,673	21,687	4.9	21,111	87.7	3.1	5.8	1.2	2.3	24.8	57.7	17.5	7,513	88.5	11.7	66.9
Fayetteville city	6,817	7,102	4.2	6,991	71.3	16.0	0.3	8.3	4.1	23.5	55.5	21.0	3,047	52.8	55.9	17.9
Fincastle CDP	1,618	NA	NA	1,343	97.2	0.0	2.8	0.0	0.0	18.8	57.7	23.4	567	85.5	57.3	9.9
Finger city	298	299	0.3	330	85.2	0.0	0.0	1.2	13.6	27.8	58.0	14.2	120	79.2	58.3	20.0
Flat Top Mountain CDP	422	NA	NA	369	100.0	0.0	0.0	0.0	0.0	7.8	69.5	22.8	156	87.2	39.1	21.2
Flintville CDP	627	NA	NA	411	94.9	0.0	1.0	4.1	0.0	16.5	55.1	28.2	209	89.5	87.6	3.3
Forest Hills city	4,812	5,027	4.5	4,911	94.8	0.0	1.3	2.8	1.1	23.9	56.5	19.6	1,723	98.5	4.9	82.0
Franklin city	62,601	70,612	12.8	66,596	81.4	5.5	4.6	1.7	6.7	26.5	62.6	10.8	25,740	68.3	17.1	58.3
Friendship city	668	672	0.6	858	70.5	3.3	0.9	2.1	23.2	34.6	56.1	9.3	276	53.6	62.0	9.1
Friendsville city	913	923	1.1	845	95.9	0.0	0.1	2.6	1.4	17.8	60.8	21.3	351	82.3	55.3	10.0
Gadsden town	470	468	-0.4	336	73.2	18.8	0.0	0.0	8.0	17.5	64.3	18.2	141	80.1	72.3	13.5
Gainesboro town	962	958	-0.4	1,037	87.1	3.8	0.4	3.0	5.8	26.3	52.2	21.6	338	61.2	61.8	9.2
Gallatin city	30,399	33,347	9.7	31,800	74.3	14.2	1.0	1.8	8.8	25.1	61.4	13.4	11,892	55.6	43.2	22.0
Gallaway city	680	665	-2.2	851	44.2	53.9	0.0	1.1	0.8	22.7	59.7	17.7	294	26.2	77.9	9.2
Garland town	310	309	-0.3	313	96.5	0.0	0.0	3.5	0.0	21.7	63.2	15.0	128	82.0	51.6	17.2
Gates town	647	635	-1.9	791	40.8	59.2	0.0	0.0	0.0	24.7	61.9	13.5	299	50.8	66.2	6.0
Gatlinburg city	3,944	4,158	5.4	4,059	96.8	0.1	0.9	0.5	1.7	11.5	55.8	32.9	2,016	63.2	45.9	14.1
Germantown city	38,844	39,267	1.1	39,207	84.7	5.0	6.2	1.2	3.0	23.9	58.7	17.4	14,585	86.7	8.3	70.2
Gibson town	396	378	-4.5	359	92.5	0.0	0.3	0.0	7.2	31.7	55.4	12.8	135	60.7	47.4	15.6
Gilt Edge city	477	476	-0.2	528	97.3	1.1	0.0	0.8	0.8	22.1	63.1	14.8	195	74.4	66.7	11.3
Gleason town	1,447	1,409	-2.6	1,365	99.4	0.0	0.6	0.0	0.0	19.6	62.5	17.9	568	62.7	57.6	14.1
Goodlettsville city	15,921	16,991	6.7	16,466	71.7	19.5	2.2	2.8	3.9	19.5	64.6	15.9	6,652	57.7	37.6	30.7
Gordonsville town	1,213	1,192	-1.7	1,463	95.3	1.2	2.5	0.1	1.0	25.2	64.6	10.3	568	68.7	63.2	12.5
Graball CDP	236	NA	NA	127	100.0	0.0	0.0	0.0	0.0	8.7	71.7	19.7	54	100.0	63.0	16.7
Grand Junction city	325	307	-5.5	415	49.6	49.9	0.0	0.5	0.0	21.7	63.3	14.9	165	83.0	67.3	10.9
Gray CDP	1,222	NA	NA	1,885	99.0	0.0	0.0	1.0	0.0	20.4	69.0	10.7	744	74.7	29.4	40.3
Graysville town	1,504	1,528	1.6	1,748	98.2	0.2	0.0	1.5	0.1	32.4	58.5	9.0	610	48.0	73.4	3.6
Greenback city	1,063	1,103	3.8	1,032	98.4	0.0	0.0	1.6	0.0	24.5	62.9	12.6	404	81.4	58.7	7.9
Greenbrier town	6,433	6,685	3.9	6,550	93.6	1.9	0.8	1.9	1.7	28.5	59.6	11.8	2,536	78.7	51.7	21.2
Greeneville town	15,062	15,035	-0.2	15,015	86.5	5.0	1.3	1.3	5.9	21.7	59.1	19.2	6,225	52.7	49.5	23.9
Greenfield city	2,182	2,125	-2.6	2,222	89.3	8.1	0.0	1.1	1.5	22.0	58.2	19.8	964	71.2	58.8	13.8
Green Hill CDP	6,618	NA	NA	6,667	91.5	4.3	0.2	1.2	2.8	21.2	62.7	16.2	2,481	94.0	31.1	35.3
Grimsley CDP	1,167	NA	NA	1,329	97.7	0.9	0.0	1.4	0.0	25.4	63.0	11.7	546	72.2	72.5	5.5
Gruetli-Laager city	1,817	1,775	-2.3	1,646	83.2	0.0	2.4	14.3	0.1	22.9	56.1	20.8	675	80.6	66.2	9.6
Guys town	466	468	0.4	630	58.4	22.7	0.0	1.3	17.6	25.8	60.9	13.3	217	62.2	69.1	12.0
Halls town	2,260	2,202	-2.6	2,621	69.5	26.0	0.0	3.2	1.2	30.3	52.0	17.7	1,006	52.3	62.9	6.7
Harriman city	6,380	6,219	-2.5	6,296	87.2	6.4	0.8	2.4	3.3	23.7	53.9	22.4	2,718	48.7	51.5	9.1
Harrison CDP	7,769	NA	NA	7,595	72.6	19.9	0.4	3.1	3.9	18.6	65.7	15.6	3,090	83.1	31.7	23.6
Harrogate city	4,389	4,365	-0.5	4,349	94.1	2.6	1.8	1.1	0.5	12.7	69.4	17.9	1,517	81.7	47.7	27.8
Hartsville/Trousdale County	7,870	8,002	1.7	7,859	85.7	11.3	2.5	0.4	0.1	23.6	62.2	14.3	2,928	75.1	66.8	10.9
Helenwood CDP	865	NA	NA	738	97.6	0.0	0.0	0.0	2.4	9.2	85.4	5.4	227	71.4	76.7	0.0
Henderson city	6,309	6,513	3.2	6,429	78.7	17.5	0.7	1.2	1.9	21.2	68.3	10.6	1,907	51.0	49.6	19.1
Hendersonville city	51,328	55,153	7.5	53,257	84.2	8.5	2.3	1.3	3.6	25.4	61.1	13.6	20,333	70.8	33.0	33.5
Henning town	945	921	-2.5	887	18.5	74.9	0.0	6.7	0.0	23.1	58.1	18.7	443	61.2	81.9	1.6
Henry town	464	470	1.3	480	66.7	10.0	0.0	0.6	22.7	26.7	65.1	8.3	176	70.5	80.1	10.2
Hickory Valley town	99	94	-5.1	165	55.8	44.2	0.0	0.0	0.0	6.0	85.4	8.5	76	77.6	89.5	7.9
Hillsboro CDP	450	NA	NA	403	75.9	0.0	0.0	24.1	0.0	26.1	62.9	10.9	165	64.2	44.2	30.3
Hohenwald city	3,757	3,679	-2.1	3,716	86.8	1.1	6.1	0.9	5.0	20.5	58.1	21.6	1,458	61.1	62.8	13.6
Hollow Rock town	718	706	-1.7	589	82.7	11.2	0.0	3.9	2.2	26.9	60.8	12.4	235	80.0	63.0	11.9
Hopewell CDP	1,874	NA	NA	1,871	98.9	1.1	0.0	0.0	0.0	14.7	59.0	26.3	742	86.3	33.7	22.9
Hornbeak town	424	412	-2.8	392	98.7	0.0	0.0	1.3	0.0	21.2	54.1	24.7	159	81.1	66.0	6.3
Hornsby town	300	284	-5.3	308	95.8	0.0	0.0	3.6	0.6	30.2	57.5	12.3	117	65.8	59.8	6.8
Humboldt city	8,452	8,348	-1.2	8,363	49.3	45.6	0.1	2.0	2.9	20.6	58.1	21.3	3,498	62.2	55.2	7.9

1 May be of any race.

Table A. All Places — **Population and Housing**

STATE City, town, township, borough, or CDP (county if applicable)	Population				Race and Hispanic or Latino origin (percent), 2010–2014					Age (percent), 2010–2014			Households, 2010–2014			
	2010 census total population	2014 estimated population	Percent change 2010-2014	ACS total population estimate 2010-2014	White alone, not Hispanic or Latino	Black alone, not Hispanic or Latino	Asian alone, not Hispanic or Latino	All other races or 2 or more races, not Hispanic or Latino	Hispanic or Latino[1]	Under 18 years old	Age 18 to 64 years old	Age 65 years and older	Total occupied housing units	Percent owner occupied	Householders by level of education (percent): High school diploma or less	Householders by level of education (percent): Bachelor's degree or more
	1	2	3	4	5	6	7	8	9	10	11	12	13	14	15	16
TENNESSEE—Con.																
Hunter CDP	1,854	NA	NA	1,757	99.1	0.0	0.0	0.9	0.0	18.9	66.6	14.6	772	70.3	56.5	19.6
Huntingdon town	3,985	3,970	-0.4	3,979	72.4	19.8	0.9	1.1	5.9	18.3	60.4	21.2	1,578	68.9	65.6	11.0
Huntland town	872	860	-1.4	749	91.5	2.8	0.0	4.8	0.9	22.1	54.0	23.8	337	84.0	70.9	9.5
Huntsville town	1,248	1,234	-1.1	1,405	94.0	3.0	0.0	3.0	0.1	23.2	56.1	20.7	505	40.0	69.3	11.7
Iron City CDP	328	NA	NA	245	100.0	0.0	0.0	0.0	0.0	25.8	62.3	11.8	97	73.2	68.0	16.5
Jacksboro town	2,020	1,968	-2.6	1,917	90.1	1.9	1.5	2.3	4.2	11.2	67.5	21.3	806	62.5	64.8	13.3
Jackson city	66,929	67,319	0.6	67,190	47.1	45.5	1.5	1.3	4.6	23.8	62.4	13.6	24,804	56.5	41.6	27.9
Jamestown city	1,959	1,940	-1.0	1,810	93.1	1.2	0.4	1.4	3.9	20.4	52.9	26.6	823	36.9	68.8	10.7
Jasper town	3,257	3,299	1.3	3,267	96.1	2.5	0.0	1.4	0.0	16.0	66.9	17.2	1,221	59.6	54.5	25.9
Jefferson City city	8,278	8,370	1.1	8,342	86.5	8.6	0.1	1.5	3.2	19.6	65.2	15.3	3,226	42.8	45.8	23.1
Jellico city	2,358	2,279	-3.4	2,444	91.6	5.5	0.0	1.6	1.3	17.0	58.4	24.6	1,014	62.0	72.0	8.1
Johnson City city	63,476	65,813	3.7	64,614	83.9	6.8	2.4	2.8	4.2	19.1	65.7	15.2	27,460	55.1	31.1	39.0
Jonesborough town	5,042	5,238	3.9	5,138	92.9	2.1	0.0	1.7	3.3	18.6	66.4	15.1	1,933	69.8	34.5	38.5
Kenton town	1,281	1,235	-3.6	1,090	82.9	12.9	0.6	3.5	0.0	17.8	59.0	23.5	519	63.8	72.1	7.3
Kimball town	1,417	1,399	-1.3	1,349	87.2	0.2	0.7	1.0	10.7	21.1	62.0	16.8	563	69.6	63.9	14.9
Kingsport city	52,777	53,028	0.5	52,835	89.9	3.2	1.1	3.1	2.7	20.5	57.6	22.0	23,497	64.2	45.6	25.8
Kingston city	5,966	5,835	-2.2	5,888	91.8	3.2	0.4	3.4	1.2	18.0	56.7	25.4	2,565	68.3	48.5	18.5
Kingston Springs town	2,756	2,790	1.2	2,759	95.3	0.8	0.1	1.6	2.2	25.1	63.4	11.5	1,076	83.5	33.8	30.6
Knoxville city	178,764	184,281	3.1	181,759	73.6	17.2	1.7	2.7	4.7	18.3	67.6	14.0	82,079	48.0	36.2	30.6
Lafayette city	4,526	4,962	9.6	4,731	93.2	0.2	0.0	0.7	5.9	24.0	55.9	20.2	2,040	52.6	70.0	6.8
La Follette city	7,460	7,131	-4.4	7,304	98.9	0.2	0.2	0.0	0.7	22.5	56.7	20.9	2,954	43.3	67.6	8.2
La Grange town	133	132	-0.8	104	89.4	6.7	0.0	0.0	3.8	4.8	60.6	34.6	57	82.5	52.6	31.6
Lake City city	1,781	1,771	-0.6	1,773	98.1	0.0	0.0	1.4	0.5	23.7	52.9	23.2	724	49.2	82.6	2.9
Lakeland city	12,430	12,564	1.1	12,549	79.1	8.9	9.4	1.0	1.6	28.3	59.8	11.9	4,619	79.6	24.0	47.3
Lakesite city	1,831	1,871	2.2	2,046	97.1	0.0	0.0	0.6	2.3	24.8	59.7	15.4	725	82.1	29.5	32.8
Lake Tansi CDP	3,803	NA	NA	3,934	99.1	0.0	0.0	0.4	0.5	21.4	49.7	28.9	1,640	83.8	44.4	19.3
Lakewood Park CDP	990	NA	NA	491	88.6	0.0	0.0	11.4	0.0	20.4	61.7	17.9	251	67.7	46.2	6.4
La Vergne city	32,588	34,274	5.2	33,637	56.1	20.1	2.5	2.0	19.3	31.9	62.3	5.8	10,651	75.6	48.3	20.5
Lawrenceburg city	10,407	10,498	0.9	10,440	85.2	6.4	1.2	2.0	5.3	22.3	58.9	18.7	4,467	51.4	58.2	9.2
Lebanon city	26,156	29,427	12.5	27,847	77.5	12.0	2.0	1.2	7.3	24.9	60.1	15.1	10,328	56.7	51.9	22.8
Lenoir City city	8,646	9,034	4.5	8,867	77.0	1.5	0.0	2.1	19.4	29.0	60.2	10.9	3,398	56.6	51.0	11.7
Lewisburg city	11,100	11,371	2.4	11,252	73.7	15.8	1.1	1.5	8.0	22.2	62.9	14.9	4,445	55.7	61.6	10.4
Lexington city	7,634	7,825	2.5	7,771	76.7	17.0	0.3	2.2	3.8	25.5	58.4	15.9	3,031	63.7	54.1	15.1
Liberty town	310	318	2.6	268	99.6	0.0	0.0	0.4	0.0	22.1	56.0	22.0	114	81.6	86.8	5.3
Linden town	908	897	-1.2	889	79.5	17.2	0.0	0.0	3.3	18.6	53.5	27.9	382	58.4	61.5	16.8
Livingston town	4,058	4,052	-0.1	4,060	89.4	3.4	0.0	2.8	4.4	21.5	57.8	20.8	1,717	57.0	55.8	14.0
Lobelville city	897	885	-1.3	879	94.2	0.0	0.0	4.6	1.3	26.1	58.7	15.2	376	62.5	67.8	12.8
Lone Oak CDP	1,206	NA	NA	1,000	90.3	0.0	0.0	9.7	0.0	16.6	57.2	26.2	453	80.8	48.6	24.9
Lookout Mountain town	1,866	1,893	1.4	1,878	93.1	2.3	1.9	0.4	2.3	24.7	53.6	21.6	722	87.1	4.6	83.0
Loretto city	1,715	1,735	1.2	1,911	96.0	1.4	0.0	1.9	0.6	17.0	57.3	25.6	792	77.9	57.6	14.3
Loudon town	5,380	5,715	6.2	5,606	71.3	4.5	0.2	1.2	22.6	31.2	50.0	18.6	2,049	55.7	60.3	10.3
Louisville city	2,438	2,470	1.3	2,434	91.7	1.7	0.7	2.6	3.2	16.8	68.6	14.5	986	85.2	32.3	39.0
Luttrell town	1,074	1,080	0.6	1,001	93.2	0.0	0.0	6.8	0.0	26.1	60.8	13.2	423	57.7	72.3	4.7
Lyles CDP	734	NA	NA	680	98.1	0.0	0.0	1.9	0.0	11.8	75.1	13.1	350	52.0	75.4	12.9
Lynchburg	6,362	6,319	-0.7	6,348	93.9	3.2	0.0	2.8	0.1	20.9	59.2	19.9	2,444	83.3	55.0	14.8
Lynnville town	287	282	-1.7	337	86.9	12.5	0.3	0.3	0.0	22.3	56.1	21.7	128	67.2	67.2	18.8
McEwen city	1,750	1,699	-2.9	1,823	98.8	0.2	0.0	0.4	0.6	22.0	56.1	21.8	763	75.0	57.3	14.9
McKenzie city	5,310	5,462	2.9	5,561	81.1	12.4	0.1	5.6	0.9	22.1	58.1	19.8	2,180	60.3	48.0	27.5
McLemoresville town	352	349	-0.9	288	93.4	2.1	0.3	0.0	4.2	24.3	55.9	19.8	112	76.8	50.0	9.8
McMinnville city	13,605	13,620	0.1	13,600	81.4	2.1	1.5	4.5	10.6	22.1	59.3	18.7	5,549	53.2	62.2	13.3
Madisonville city	4,577	4,735	3.5	4,703	87.6	3.1	0.8	2.4	6.0	24.9	55.6	19.7	1,950	51.6	60.2	8.8
Manchester city	10,113	10,349	2.3	10,223	82.7	3.7	2.3	2.7	8.5	22.3	60.6	17.2	4,116	48.7	55.6	19.0
Martin city	11,468	11,322	-1.3	11,396	76.0	20.0	0.2	1.6	2.1	16.0	73.4	10.5	4,079	43.5	30.2	24.4
Maryville city	27,466	28,329	3.1	27,824	91.5	2.3	1.6	1.9	2.6	24.2	59.7	16.0	10,572	64.5	32.0	37.7
Mascot CDP	2,411	NA	NA	2,592	95.6	3.7	0.0	0.7	0.0	23.1	61.1	15.6	1,026	68.1	58.3	12.7
Mason town	1,612	1,600	-0.7	1,357	25.5	68.8	0.0	0.3	5.4	22.0	73.1	5.0	350	64.6	60.9	9.1
Maury City town	674	679	0.7	638	60.7	22.6	1.3	1.7	13.8	26.3	54.7	19.0	257	56.0	70.0	7.0
Maynardville city	2,413	2,366	-1.9	2,374	95.5	0.8	0.4	1.3	2.1	24.6	58.7	16.8	906	54.5	67.5	8.9
Medina city	3,562	4,058	13.9	3,852	88.9	7.7	0.0	1.0	2.5	35.7	56.1	8.0	1,368	84.8	24.1	36.9
Medon city	178	174	-2.2	153	98.0	2.0	0.0	0.0	0.0	15.7	62.2	22.2	65	73.8	41.5	10.8
Memphis city	651,858	656,861	0.8	656,715	27.4	62.6	1.7	1.7	6.5	25.3	64.0	10.7	248,320	49.9	41.3	26.8
Michie town	591	593	0.3	639	94.2	0.0	0.0	5.8	0.0	13.9	52.4	33.6	303	70.6	71.9	7.9
Middleton city	706	669	-5.2	605	83.1	13.9	2.5	0.2	0.3	26.1	57.2	16.7	211	72.5	54.0	19.0
Middle Valley CDP	12,684	NA	NA	13,282	91.9	2.8	2.8	0.7	1.8	21.4	61.7	16.8	5,044	83.2	32.2	30.1
Midtown CDP	1,360	NA	NA	1,528	87.7	3.0	2.4	5.8	1.0	19.1	68.2	12.6	569	73.8	55.5	8.3
Milan city	7,851	7,834	-0.2	7,826	71.7	21.2	0.7	1.4	4.9	27.3	56.4	16.2	3,042	60.5	48.5	14.6
Milledgeville town	266	267	0.4	226	88.1	3.1	0.0	5.8	3.1	10.1	58.0	31.9	108	88.9	70.4	1.9
Millersville city	6,440	6,660	3.4	6,481	88.2	3.2	0.2	1.7	6.8	22.8	68.0	9.3	2,401	70.6	43.0	15.9
Millington city	11,149	11,080	-0.6	11,152	61.5	25.4	2.7	2.1	8.3	23.8	61.0	15.4	4,393	55.6	42.4	18.1
Minor Hill city	537	527	-1.9	633	98.9	0.0	0.3	0.3	0.5	32.0	58.0	10.0	211	61.1	65.4	13.7
Mitchellville city	190	198	4.2	151	89.4	2.0	0.0	2.0	6.6	12.6	71.0	16.6	72	59.7	75.0	4.2
Monteagle town	1,191	1,175	-1.3	1,591	87.2	2.6	0.0	9.5	0.7	18.9	56.4	24.6	613	59.9	48.6	24.5
Monterey town	2,850	2,860	0.4	2,851	69.5	0.5	0.0	0.1	29.8	26.7	54.5	18.8	1,063	48.2	77.4	8.1
Mooresburg CDP	941	NA	NA	1,124	100.0	0.0	0.0	0.0	0.0	22.1	61.3	16.7	441	81.9	72.3	2.3
Morrison town	694	691	-0.4	622	76.0	5.8	0.0	1.8	16.4	26.9	59.2	14.0	250	51.6	73.2	10.8
Morristown city	28,988	29,304	1.1	29,152	69.9	6.2	0.8	2.9	20.1	25.8	59.2	15.1	11,028	52.2	59.3	16.5
Moscow city	556	538	-3.2	584	38.0	59.8	0.0	2.2	0.0	19.9	66.3	14.0	200	58.5	66.0	11.5
Mosheim town	2,360	2,335	-1.1	2,604	94.4	3.7	0.0	0.6	1.4	22.5	63.2	14.3	1,045	63.1	62.2	8.1
Mountain City town	2,531	2,480	-2.0	2,611	95.2	2.0	0.1	0.7	2.1	14.4	59.8	25.9	1,202	56.9	61.9	12.1
Mount Carmel town	5,427	5,453	0.5	5,443	95.8	1.4	0.0	0.1	2.7	22.4	61.9	15.5	2,132	84.8	49.0	14.3
Mount Juliet city	24,760	29,387	18.7	27,053	82.8	8.5	2.4	3.0	3.3	28.6	61.1	10.2	9,775	78.4	26.3	35.6
Mount Pleasant city	4,561	4,709	3.2	4,604	67.6	18.5	0.0	8.5	5.5	25.7	58.5	15.9	1,916	59.9	59.6	12.5
Mowbray Mountain CDP	1,615	NA	NA	1,580	97.4	0.0	2.3	0.3	0.0	19.1	61.2	19.7	632	85.8	46.0	17.1
Munford city	5,961	6,055	1.6	6,001	84.3	8.7	0.2	4.8	2.0	27.3	63.0	9.8	2,061	59.2	40.9	14.9
Murfreesboro city	109,046	120,954	10.9	114,660	72.0	16.4	3.5	2.8	5.2	22.3	68.7	9.0	43,431	51.8	26.1	37.3
Nashville-Davidson metropolitan government	626,663	668,347	6.7	648,048	57.1	27.5	3.1	2.4	9.8	21.7	67.5	10.7	259,557	54.0	32.6	39.5
Nashville-Davidson metropolitan government (balance)	603,506	644,014	6.7	624,261	56.1	28.1	3.2	2.4	10.1	21.7	67.8	10.5	250,256	53.5	33.0	39.1

1 May be of any race.

Table A. All Places — **Population and Housing**

STATE City, town, township, borough, or CDP (county if applicable)	Population: 2010 census total population	Population: 2014 estimated population	Population: Percent change 2010-2014	Population: ACS total population estimate 2010-2014	Race and Hispanic or Latino origin (percent), 2010–2014: White alone, not Hispanic or Latino	Black alone, not Hispanic or Latino	Asian alone, not Hispanic or Latino	All other races or 2 or more races, not Hispanic or Latino	Hispanic or Latino[1]	Age (percent), 2010–2014: Under 18 years old	Age 18 to 64 years old	Age 65 years and older	Households, 2010–2014: Total occupied housing units	Percent owner occupied	Householders by level of education (percent): High school diploma or less	Bachelor's degree or more
	1	2	3	4	5	6	7	8	9	10	11	12	13	14	15	16
TENNESSEE—Con.																
Newbern town	3,313	3,324	0.3	3,317	93.8	3.6	0.0	0.2	2.4	27.4	61.6	10.9	1,202	59.1	61.5	10.5
New Deal CDP	368	NA	NA	393	100.0	0.0	0.0	0.0	0.0	23.6	59.2	17.0	169	88.2	69.8	8.3
New Hope city	1,082	1,070	-1.1	902	94.8	0.0	0.9	1.8	2.5	25.7	60.0	14.1	360	72.5	55.8	9.4
New Johnsonville city	1,951	1,894	-2.9	1,934	95.4	0.2	0.4	1.7	2.3	23.5	62.6	14.0	767	83.6	57.1	19.6
New Market town	1,334	1,354	1.5	1,214	90.3	3.5	0.0	0.3	5.8	20.5	60.5	19.2	516	83.7	52.7	12.4
Newport city	6,945	6,880	-0.9	6,890	91.9	2.8	0.0	1.6	3.7	21.4	56.7	21.9	3,096	49.1	63.7	7.9
New Tazewell town	3,026	2,968	-1.9	2,994	90.3	2.1	0.0	6.9	0.7	16.8	61.5	21.7	1,276	52.9	74.1	9.0
New Union CDP	1,431	NA	NA	1,688	98.8	0.0	0.0	0.8	0.4	22.3	65.6	12.1	596	89.1	45.8	20.8
Niota city	718	718	0.0	850	81.6	1.5	6.2	7.4	3.2	24.0	57.8	18.1	333	74.2	67.6	8.7
Nolensville town	5,869	6,423	9.4	6,131	82.3	8.3	4.9	0.8	3.7	37.0	57.9	5.3	1,889	92.4	16.6	63.5
Normandy town	141	147	4.3	92	100.0	0.0	0.0	0.0	0.0	14.2	81.6	4.3	46	93.5	54.3	15.2
Norris city	1,630	1,652	1.3	1,938	96.6	0.9	0.0	0.7	1.8	19.8	52.2	28.0	782	74.3	21.5	56.3
Oakdale town	212	222	4.7	230	96.5	0.0	0.0	2.6	0.9	30.9	60.9	8.3	82	53.7	68.3	6.1
Oak Grove CDP (Sumner)	231	NA	NA	178	100.0	0.0	0.0	0.0	0.0	20.3	44.4	35.4	52	100.0	28.8	15.4
Oak Grove CDP (Washington)	4,425	NA	NA	4,732	98.7	0.5	0.3	0.5	0.0	21.5	64.0	14.5	1,983	59.2	44.2	26.4
Oak Hill city	4,529	4,703	3.8	4,639	95.4	2.0	1.4	0.0	1.2	22.4	61.0	16.6	1,725	88.2	6.0	74.4
Oakland town	6,626	7,316	10.4	6,944	80.4	15.6	1.0	0.5	2.5	25.9	63.0	11.0	2,745	88.8	24.0	36.7
Oak Ridge city	29,330	29,303	-0.1	29,301	79.7	8.6	3.1	3.6	5.0	22.2	59.4	18.3	12,391	60.0	27.4	42.9
Obion town	1,119	1,086	-2.9	1,047	89.6	3.4	0.0	4.7	2.3	18.5	60.5	21.0	463	71.9	60.0	8.9
Oliver Springs town	3,231	3,232	0.0	3,063	95.8	3.3	0.0	0.9	0.0	21.7	61.3	17.0	1,248	71.4	59.1	15.0
Olivet CDP	1,350	NA	NA	1,279	92.3	0.2	1.2	6.3	0.0	16.8	62.1	21.3	508	92.9	63.4	10.8
Oneida town	3,746	3,715	-0.8	3,734	98.6	0.1	0.5	0.9	0.0	31.7	51.5	16.9	1,538	62.6	57.5	16.3
Ooltewah CDP	687	NA	NA	325	100.0	0.0	0.0	0.0	0.0	8.6	48.3	43.1	235	51.5	53.2	26.0
Orlinda city	859	881	2.6	1,080	88.8	4.9	0.3	5.5	0.6	27.2	60.5	12.3	371	74.1	62.5	12.7
Orme town	123	123	0.0	195	100.0	0.0	0.0	0.0	0.0	18.0	68.8	13.3	80	82.5	51.3	5.0
Palmer town	672	661	-1.6	738	76.8	0.0	0.0	23.2	0.0	21.0	60.4	18.6	295	92.2	82.4	3.1
Paris city	10,166	10,156	-0.1	10,165	74.3	19.4	0.2	4.3	1.8	23.8	57.9	18.2	4,153	56.1	62.6	13.7
Park City CDP	2,442	NA	NA	3,023	89.0	2.9	0.0	7.0	1.1	27.8	56.9	15.3	1,138	83.9	51.7	19.6
Parker's Crossroads city	330	332	0.6	327	86.9	13.1	0.0	0.0	0.0	18.3	60.5	21.1	130	87.7	48.5	11.5
Parrottsville town	263	262	-0.4	247	90.3	7.7	0.0	0.4	1.6	22.6	68.5	8.9	98	67.3	86.7	0.0
Parsons city	2,373	2,342	-1.3	2,445	89.2	4.0	0.9	2.2	3.6	21.8	53.1	25.1	1,005	65.1	55.8	10.1
Pegram town	2,093	2,114	1.0	2,225	96.0	2.7	0.4	0.6	0.4	23.0	61.3	15.9	775	89.3	40.5	24.1
Pelham CDP	403	NA	NA	396	85.6	0.0	0.0	14.4	0.0	20.7	50.9	28.3	166	68.7	62.7	7.8
Petersburg town	544	547	0.6	602	95.3	4.7	0.0	0.0	0.0	18.6	63.6	17.8	252	72.6	65.1	19.0
Petros CDP	583	NA	NA	556	100.0	0.0	0.0	0.0	0.0	21.3	60.9	18.0	269	84.4	82.9	0.0
Philadelphia city	656	683	4.1	901	90.3	4.1	0.0	0.0	5.5	23.7	62.3	14.0	286	72.4	70.3	8.7
Pigeon Forge city	5,872	6,132	4.4	6,004	90.4	1.1	2.9	1.0	4.6	17.9	61.8	20.5	2,574	45.6	55.9	17.6
Pikeville city	1,607	1,625	1.1	2,047	79.9	7.7	0.0	2.5	9.8	26.2	56.5	17.3	724	43.1	65.6	9.5
Pine Crest CDP	2,388	NA	NA	2,155	92.7	0.5	0.0	1.6	5.3	11.5	70.1	18.4	1,050	57.2	37.2	32.7
Piperton city	1,445	1,570	8.7	1,552	71.8	20.2	1.3	1.7	4.9	16.7	61.5	21.8	610	91.1	32.8	37.9
Pittman Center town	503	555	10.3	422	89.3	0.0	1.4	1.2	8.1	14.2	63.5	22.3	170	71.2	39.4	28.2
Plainview city	2,123	2,073	-2.4	2,061	96.5	1.8	0.0	0.7	1.0	20.6	62.9	16.4	770	80.8	71.7	10.6
Pleasant Hill town	563	566	0.5	493	98.6	0.6	0.0	0.8	0.0	8.7	25.7	65.5	227	76.2	52.4	27.8
Pleasant View city	4,149	4,251	2.5	4,187	94.2	1.2	0.9	0.5	3.2	25.1	67.0	7.9	1,437	86.9	37.2	36.2
Portland city	11,486	12,218	6.4	11,853	87.8	3.7	0.6	3.9	4.1	26.9	61.6	11.3	4,251	60.4	47.6	15.0
Powells Crossroads town	1,322	1,319	-0.2	1,645	95.5	0.1	0.0	2.7	1.7	26.2	57.2	16.7	638	87.5	58.6	13.0
Pulaski city	7,870	7,625	-3.1	7,734	65.4	26.3	1.1	3.7	3.4	21.5	59.6	19.0	3,197	48.7	59.1	17.1
Puryear city	671	670	-0.1	785	93.0	4.3	0.0	1.7	1.0	16.5	60.1	23.4	330	79.7	65.8	11.2
Ramer city	319	320	0.3	268	81.7	14.9	0.0	3.4	0.0	21.3	50.3	28.4	101	80.2	63.4	14.9
Red Bank city	11,653	11,784	1.1	11,759	81.5	6.3	1.3	2.5	8.4	17.1	70.2	12.8	5,249	50.0	37.1	28.9
Red Boiling Springs city	1,112	1,135	2.1	1,138	94.2	1.0	0.0	0.5	4.3	26.2	53.1	20.7	413	49.6	81.6	5.3
Riceville CDP	670	NA	NA	662	100.0	0.0	0.0	0.0	0.0	10.7	69.5	19.9	296	75.7	54.4	5.1
Ridgely town	1,795	1,732	-3.5	2,114	78.0	13.2	0.2	4.0	4.6	27.3	56.7	16.0	807	48.1	65.4	7.1
Ridgeside city	393	415	5.6	510	97.3	2.0	0.2	0.0	0.6	22.3	57.4	20.2	184	94.0	9.2	68.5
Ridgetop city	1,894	1,979	4.5	2,353	94.2	2.1	0.2	0.6	2.9	24.1	57.1	18.8	766	86.3	57.3	18.0
Ripley city	8,445	8,257	-2.2	8,350	41.1	54.1	1.3	1.3	2.2	27.2	59.9	12.9	3,341	41.5	60.1	16.1
Rives town	326	319	-2.1	269	90.3	5.6	0.0	1.5	2.6	20.9	63.6	15.6	90	63.3	83.3	2.2
Roan Mountain CDP	1,360	NA	NA	1,595	93.4	1.3	0.0	0.6	4.8	31.3	59.3	9.3	482	87.6	64.1	4.1
Robbins CDP	287	NA	NA	219	100.0	0.0	0.0	0.0	0.0	12.3	79.0	8.7	88	27.3	93.2	6.8
Rockford city	856	861	0.6	873	97.4	0.6	0.3	0.0	1.7	16.7	66.4	17.0	370	71.4	45.4	22.2
Rockwood city	5,562	5,427	-2.4	5,480	93.7	4.6	0.4	1.3	0.0	21.9	59.3	18.8	2,440	45.5	61.6	6.2
Rogersville town	4,424	4,406	-0.4	4,410	95.5	1.7	0.0	2.2	0.5	18.0	59.4	22.4	2,075	46.9	56.0	19.8
Rossville town	664	704	6.0	641	88.6	6.7	0.0	1.9	2.8	11.7	73.0	15.3	276	82.2	40.2	29.3
Rural Hill CDP	2,007	NA	NA	1,752	91.6	5.8	1.5	0.0	1.1	9.6	73.6	17.0	780	90.8	27.3	29.5
Rutherford town	1,151	1,116	-3.0	1,150	79.8	18.6	0.0	1.0	0.5	18.9	60.1	20.9	469	66.7	74.8	9.2
Rutledge town	1,124	1,166	3.7	1,393	94.3	2.6	0.3	0.0	2.8	18.0	56.6	25.7	568	57.0	68.1	9.3
St. Joseph city	778	785	0.9	878	98.6	0.0	0.0	1.4	0.0	16.4	60.8	23.0	357	70.3	67.5	8.4
Sale Creek CDP	2,845	NA	NA	2,564	99.6	0.0	0.0	0.4	0.0	14.6	66.6	18.7	1,057	80.1	59.7	9.7
Saltillo town	518	508	-1.9	521	74.5	20.0	0.0	3.5	2.1	16.9	52.2	30.9	235	80.9	65.1	11.5
Samburg town	217	212	-2.3	238	100.0	0.0	0.0	0.0	0.0	5.0	65.0	29.8	132	87.1	45.5	6.1
Sardis town	378	380	0.5	385	91.7	0.0	0.0	1.0	7.3	16.0	61.1	22.9	167	84.4	77.2	9.6
Saulsbury town	101	96	-5.0	160	61.9	38.1	0.0	0.0	0.0	15.7	62.1	22.5	62	38.7	88.7	8.1
Savannah city	6,982	7,053	1.0	7,029	84.4	12.6	0.7	1.1	1.3	22.3	58.9	18.6	2,661	59.8	57.0	13.7
Scotts Hill town	980	983	0.3	925	94.9	1.2	0.0	3.2	0.6	21.4	59.7	18.9	411	70.3	60.6	10.0
Selmer town	4,400	4,513	2.6	4,482	80.5	14.1	0.0	4.0	1.4	16.6	65.6	17.8	1,829	57.5	59.0	17.9
Sevierville city	14,788	16,355	10.6	15,592	78.5	1.3	4.2	2.6	13.4	21.0	62.6	16.4	5,968	47.9	52.8	19.3
Sewanee CDP	2,311	NA	NA	2,684	82.1	11.9	1.9	1.9	2.2	6.3	84.8	9.0	541	50.1	4.6	83.2
Seymour CDP	10,919	NA	NA	10,703	97.4	0.3	0.3	0.5	1.5	21.0	62.0	17.0	4,389	72.9	48.8	20.1
Shackle Island CDP	2,844	NA	NA	2,916	97.7	0.5	0.5	0.4	0.9	25.4	65.3	9.4	964	96.3	20.4	52.6
Sharon town	944	919	-2.6	1,026	86.3	11.7	0.9	1.0	0.2	19.7	55.6	25.0	452	68.8	60.8	11.1
Shelbyville city	20,334	21,037	3.5	20,616	61.2	10.3	1.2	5.4	21.8	29.8	58.0	11.9	7,283	49.6	68.6	7.1
Signal Mountain town	8,277	8,519	2.9	8,416	97.8	0.7	0.0	1.2	0.3	26.0	52.6	21.4	3,194	86.8	11.9	70.6
Silerton town	111	105	-5.4	87	86.2	3.4	0.0	10.3	0.0	31.0	52.7	16.1	33	57.6	48.5	30.3
Slayden town	178	179	0.6	178	100.0	0.0	0.0	0.0	0.0	15.7	58.9	25.3	72	73.6	90.3	2.8
Smithville city	4,530	4,661	2.9	4,587	84.8	3.8	3.4	0.0	8.0	18.7	63.6	17.5	1,767	47.7	65.5	12.5
Smyrna town	39,976	45,274	13.3	42,235	72.7	12.9	3.3	2.2	9.0	28.3	62.2	9.3	15,367	65.2	38.5	24.9
Sneedville town	1,390	1,361	-2.1	1,448	96.1	2.6	0.0	1.1	0.1	30.5	56.4	13.0	558	38.9	69.9	10.4
Soddy-Daisy city	12,934	13,190	2.0	13,109	97.4	0.5	0.0	1.1	1.0	20.1	60.4	19.5	5,138	72.0	51.5	19.1
Somerville town	3,094	3,104	0.3	3,113	49.2	47.7	0.3	1.6	1.2	22.8	52.9	24.4	1,378	40.9	58.5	20.3
South Carthage town	1,322	1,323	0.1	1,399	87.6	5.3	0.5	2.8	3.9	23.1	56.7	20.2	616	64.8	70.5	8.0

1 May be of any race.

Table A. All Places — **Population and Housing**

STATE City, town, township, borough, or CDP (county if applicable)	Population: 2010 census total population	Population: 2014 estimated population	Population: Percent change 2010-2014	Population: ACS total population estimate 2010-2014	Race and Hispanic or Latino origin (percent), 2010–2014: White alone, not Hispanic or Latino	Race: Black alone, not Hispanic or Latino	Race: Asian alone, not Hispanic or Latino	Race: All other races or 2 or more races, not Hispanic or Latino	Race: Hispanic or Latino[1]	Age (percent), 2010–2014: Under 18 years old	Age: Age 18 to 64 years old	Age: Age 65 years and older	Households, 2010–2014: Total occupied housing units	Households: Percent owner occupied	Householders by level of education (percent): High school diploma or less	Householders by level of education (percent): Bachelor's degree or more
	1	2	3	4	5	6	7	8	9	10	11	12	13	14	15	16
TENNESSEE—Con.																
South Cleveland CDP	6,912	NA	NA	5,951	93.2	0.6	3.4	1.1	1.7	22.4	61.5	16.0	2,339	85.4	53.8	12.3
South Fulton city	2,354	2,284	-3.0	2,352	78.8	18.6	0.5	1.5	0.6	19.9	58.8	21.3	972	65.2	59.0	15.4
South Pittsburg city	3,109	3,110	0.0	3,104	83.8	10.0	0.4	4.7	1.1	26.7	58.5	14.8	1,241	55.2	51.4	11.8
Sparta city	4,925	5,075	3.0	5,036	92.0	6.1	0.1	1.7	0.2	16.5	58.5	25.1	2,239	59.8	62.9	10.0
Spencer town	1,604	1,624	1.2	1,823	98.7	0.4	0.0	0.9	0.1	19.3	59.3	21.5	632	79.7	71.7	11.7
Spring City town	1,981	2,009	1.4	2,137	90.7	2.6	0.0	1.3	5.4	23.7	54.5	21.7	847	64.9	59.9	11.0
Springfield city	16,478	16,752	1.7	16,598	58.1	24.4	0.7	1.8	14.9	25.5	61.4	12.9	6,059	60.5	60.9	15.1
Spring Hill city	29,038	34,269	18.0	31,467	85.3	4.7	1.0	1.4	7.5	33.3	60.7	6.0	10,401	78.2	19.1	42.3
Spurgeon CDP	3,957	NA	NA	3,747	96.6	0.8	1.1	0.9	0.6	19.6	60.6	19.8	1,676	68.9	49.3	21.1
Stanton town	450	431	-4.2	338	15.7	73.4	0.0	5.0	5.9	21.8	71.0	7.1	110	34.5	82.7	0.9
Stantonville town	283	284	0.4	311	98.7	0.6	0.0	0.0	0.6	19.7	49.9	30.5	130	80.8	80.8	10.8
Summertown CDP	866	NA	NA	647	98.1	0.0	0.0	1.9	0.0	23.0	64.6	12.4	290	80.3	50.0	9.7
Sunbright city	552	547	-0.9	541	96.3	0.0	0.0	3.5	0.2	28.6	60.4	10.9	210	66.7	66.2	15.7
Surgoinsville town	1,800	1,799	-0.1	1,823	97.5	0.0	0.0	0.6	1.9	23.3	60.8	15.9	728	82.0	61.7	13.2
Sweetwater city	5,790	5,874	1.5	5,856	90.1	7.4	0.0	1.1	1.4	19.2	57.6	23.1	2,409	63.5	65.3	12.8
Tazewell town	2,223	2,181	-1.9	2,088	96.3	1.8	0.0	2.0	0.0	23.8	51.8	24.4	904	58.6	73.8	12.9
Telford CDP	921	NA	NA	852	96.1	0.0	0.0	3.9	0.0	30.4	56.7	12.9	312	94.9	54.8	0.0
Tellico Plains town	880	913	3.8	902	95.0	0.0	0.0	2.3	2.7	23.7	60.0	16.3	380	56.6	66.1	8.9
Tellico Village CDP	5,791	NA	NA	6,385	98.8	0.0	0.0	0.6	0.6	2.0	34.9	62.9	3,150	96.0	12.0	68.6
Tennessee Ridge town	1,368	1,347	-1.5	1,278	97.6	0.1	0.0	0.5	1.9	19.7	60.2	20.2	512	79.3	64.3	12.3
Thompson's Station town	2,204	3,180	44.3	2,552	95.3	2.6	2.0	0.2	0.0	26.1	65.9	7.9	811	89.3	26.0	49.7
Three Way city	1,709	1,692	-1.0	1,579	84.8	14.4	0.0	0.5	0.3	18.2	67.2	14.6	625	94.4	30.6	37.8
Tiptonville town	4,464	4,385	-1.8	4,425	55.5	39.0	0.2	1.4	3.8	10.7	77.4	11.9	816	53.1	71.8	14.8
Toone town	364	346	-4.9	417	63.5	36.5	0.0	0.0	0.0	21.4	61.4	17.3	142	66.9	77.5	9.2
Townsend city	448	451	0.7	470	93.8	0.0	0.4	1.9	3.8	8.3	58.5	33.2	228	90.4	37.3	22.8
Tracy City town	1,474	1,441	-2.2	1,697	84.4	0.2	0.5	14.3	0.5	23.9	58.7	17.4	724	74.2	71.1	8.3
Trenton city	4,264	4,157	-2.5	4,215	64.3	30.1	0.0	0.1	5.5	21.9	56.4	21.8	1,778	51.9	59.1	15.6
Trezevant town	859	851	-0.9	885	84.3	15.5	0.0	0.1	0.1	23.3	58.5	18.2	362	76.2	63.8	7.5
Trimble town	637	625	-1.9	608	89.8	3.0	0.0	3.1	4.1	22.6	60.8	16.6	263	63.5	52.1	13.7
Troy town	1,371	1,331	-2.9	1,451	96.3	0.2	0.0	1.7	1.9	22.4	64.7	12.9	573	58.5	61.8	13.3
Tullahoma city	18,655	18,899	1.3	18,900	87.4	3.6	0.6	4.9	3.5	22.1	58.5	19.3	8,161	59.7	45.4	24.9
Tusculum city	2,663	2,663	0.0	2,659	89.8	7.0	0.4	2.4	0.5	16.2	65.4	18.4	776	80.9	41.2	28.6
Unicoi town	3,632	3,574	-1.6	3,618	91.2	0.2	1.7	1.1	5.8	20.2	61.5	18.3	1,524	80.4	42.4	23.2
Union City city	10,912	10,666	-2.3	10,791	68.5	24.2	0.0	2.2	5.0	25.5	58.1	16.5	4,358	51.3	53.8	17.8
Unionville CDP	1,368	NA	NA	1,492	84.9	1.7	0.0	12.4	0.9	31.3	60.4	8.3	506	85.8	64.4	12.3
Vanleer town	395	398	0.8	387	98.2	0.0	0.0	1.0	0.8	21.4	62.6	16.0	150	70.0	65.3	6.0
Viola town	131	131	0.0	58	69.0	17.2	0.0	0.0	13.8	8.6	77.6	13.8	34	67.6	73.5	2.9
Vonore town	1,473	1,476	0.2	1,585	93.7	2.1	0.3	2.8	1.1	25.3	59.4	15.5	637	57.1	53.8	14.6
Walden town	1,907	2,031	6.5	2,002	95.5	0.5	1.1	0.5	2.3	24.3	56.2	19.3	715	80.6	18.6	60.3
Walland CDP	259	NA	NA	195	100.0	0.0	0.0	0.0	0.0	2.6	74.0	23.6	87	85.1	63.2	26.4
Walnut Grove CDP (Hardin)	396	NA	NA	318	91.2	0.0	3.1	5.7	0.0	11.0	53.1	35.8	137	65.7	71.5	12.4
Walnut Grove CDP (Sumner)	864	NA	NA	866	83.8	0.0	0.0	0.6	15.6	21.8	65.1	13.0	334	82.9	68.9	2.7
Walnut Hill CDP	2,394	NA	NA	2,375	97.0	0.0	1.9	0.6	0.5	18.0	58.5	23.6	1,015	84.3	50.7	12.9
Walterhill CDP	401	NA	NA	255	85.5	14.5	0.0	0.0	0.0	31.3	68.6	0.0	77	100.0	80.5	19.5
Wartburg city	918	906	-1.3	764	95.2	0.0	0.0	3.3	1.6	20.0	57.5	22.5	303	38.9	68.3	12.2
Wartrace town	651	658	1.1	604	75.0	5.8	11.9	2.6	4.6	24.0	56.9	19.0	255	78.8	71.0	14.9
Watauga city	458	445	-2.8	360	92.8	0.0	2.8	4.4	0.0	18.3	67.5	14.2	152	74.3	60.5	11.2
Watertown city	1,477	1,516	2.6	1,564	91.2	5.2	0.1	0.5	3.0	23.5	59.4	17.1	625	70.4	58.1	10.6
Waverly city	4,092	4,091	0.0	4,113	84.2	11.7	0.0	0.4	3.7	22.1	61.8	16.2	1,731	70.0	45.6	17.9
Waynesboro city	2,450	2,420	-1.2	2,649	93.8	2.4	0.0	1.7	2.0	20.8	54.3	24.9	1,142	67.9	62.6	11.0
Westmoreland town	2,206	2,282	3.4	1,945	98.0	1.0	0.0	0.2	0.8	30.3	55.9	13.8	667	59.7	58.8	13.8
White Bluff town	3,206	3,332	3.9	3,269	98.9	0.0	0.0	0.9	0.2	24.0	62.8	13.0	1,230	72.1	52.3	5.2
White House city	10,273	11,042	7.5	10,618	92.7	0.7	0.8	2.0	3.8	28.9	61.1	10.0	3,813	85.8	38.0	26.4
White Pine town	2,210	2,231	1.0	2,405	76.4	2.0	0.0	3.0	18.7	32.3	54.6	13.1	877	57.8	65.7	8.2
Whiteville town	4,636	4,550	-1.9	4,593	38.4	56.1	0.4	1.1	3.9	6.8	86.5	6.7	615	48.9	77.9	7.0
Whitwell city	1,698	1,716	1.1	2,139	90.7	0.6	0.0	2.6	6.0	22.5	55.1	22.3	858	61.4	76.2	5.2
Wildwood CDP	1,098	NA	NA	1,358	85.9	14.1	0.0	0.0	0.0	26.6	62.6	10.8	520	66.2	39.2	12.5
Wildwood Lake CDP	3,124	NA	NA	3,541	96.7	0.0	0.0	1.2	2.1	20.3	56.5	23.1	1,408	77.9	67.7	8.5
Williston city	395	387	-2.0	418	49.5	46.7	0.7	2.2	1.0	29.7	60.2	10.0	128	73.4	65.6	15.6
Winchester city	8,535	8,547	0.1	8,493	84.0	4.9	1.1	5.6	4.4	23.1	55.4	21.5	3,572	65.9	45.8	22.8
Winfield town	967	954	-1.3	789	93.4	0.0	0.0	5.4	1.1	21.9	61.1	17.0	342	57.6	64.9	12.6
Woodbury town	2,680	2,730	1.9	2,701	90.9	3.7	0.0	3.2	2.3	26.2	52.2	21.5	1,036	48.7	56.4	16.2
Woodland Mills city	378	369	-2.4	474	92.2	7.0	0.0	0.6	0.2	19.0	61.6	19.4	175	84.0	65.7	13.7
Wrigley CDP	281	NA	NA	162	53.1	46.9	0.0	0.0	0.0	17.9	74.1	8.0	91	85.7	78.0	22.0
Yorkville city	286	279	-2.4	382	96.6	0.0	1.0	0.8	1.6	29.8	59.9	10.2	127	81.1	52.8	32.3
TEXAS	25,146,104	26,956,958	7.2	26,092,033	44.3	11.6	4.0	1.9	38.2	26.8	62.2	10.9	9,013,582	62.7	38.6	29.9
Abbott city	361	358	-0.8	431	90.7	0.5	0.0	0.0	8.8	31.3	57.8	10.9	167	79.0	34.1	29.3
Abernathy city	2,815	2,750	-2.3	3,247	46.0	1.4	0.2	1.1	51.2	25.3	59.2	15.4	1,163	71.2	63.2	13.5
Abilene city	117,463	120,958	3.0	120,776	60.5	9.7	1.8	2.3	25.6	22.7	64.9	12.4	42,491	55.3	37.6	24.8
Abram CDP	2,067	NA	NA	1,927	0.0	0.0	0.0	0.0	100.0	32.2	51.0	16.8	558	88.2	86.6	11.3
Ackerly city	220	229	4.1	122	41.8	0.0	0.0	0.0	58.2	32.8	60.6	6.6	43	51.2	86.0	7.0
Addison town	13,056	15,457	18.4	14,594	54.0	9.8	9.0	2.0	25.3	14.8	76.8	8.7	8,202	22.8	15.3	58.8
Adrian city	166	167	0.6	218	83.5	0.0	0.0	0.5	16.1	25.6	59.6	14.7	85	78.8	28.2	40.0
Agua Dulce CDP	3,014	NA	NA	2,926	0.8	0.0	0.0	0.0	99.2	38.5	56.3	5.2	683	82.4	85.7	0.0
Agua Dulce city	812	825	1.6	722	32.1	2.9	0.0	1.0	64.0	24.4	62.3	13.4	275	80.7	50.9	8.7
Aguilares CDP	21	NA	NA	50	0.0	0.0	0.0	0.0	100.0	28.0	46.0	26.0	7	100.0	100.0	0.0
Airport Heights CDP	161	NA	NA	95	0.0	0.0	0.0	0.0	100.0	37.9	39.9	22.1	19	100.0	100.0	0.0
Airport Road Addition CDP	93	NA	NA	67	0.0	0.0	0.0	0.0	100.0	46.3	11.9	41.8	31	100.0	51.6	22.6
Alamo city	18,518	19,224	3.8	18,907	14.6	0.2	0.0	0.0	85.3	28.7	51.9	19.5	5,998	77.8	62.3	14.6
Alamo Heights city	7,031	7,806	11.0	7,397	71.3	1.5	0.9	3.9	22.3	23.8	59.9	16.3	3,116	79.5	6.7	77.2
Alba town	502	507	1.0	801	97.9	0.0	0.0	0.2	1.9	34.8	51.9	13.5	283	46.3	67.5	13.1
Albany city	2,034	2,011	-1.1	2,307	84.7	1.9	0.0	1.6	11.7	26.9	58.6	14.3	927	77.7	46.0	23.1
Aldine CDP	15,869	NA	NA	15,375	9.5	4.2	0.9	0.2	85.2	33.3	60.5	6.2	3,745	63.2	80.4	3.9
Aledo city	2,713	3,110	14.6	2,866	83.3	0.7	0.2	4.7	11.1	37.2	55.6	7.2	856	78.7	24.4	36.6
Alfred CDP	91	NA	NA	128	0.0	0.0	0.0	0.0	100.0	0.0	100.0	0.0	22	100.0	100.0	0.0
Alice city	19,109	19,395	1.5	19,358	12.7	0.6	0.8	0.9	85.0	30.0	57.5	12.4	6,313	62.7	53.0	14.9

1 May be of any race.

Table A. All Places — **Population and Housing**

STATE City, town, township, borough, or CDP (county if applicable)	Population: 2010 census total population	Population: 2014 estimated population	Population: Percent change 2010-2014	Population: ACS total population estimate 2010-2014	Race and Hispanic or Latino origin (percent), 2010–2014: White alone, not Hispanic or Latino	Black alone, not Hispanic or Latino	Asian alone, not Hispanic or Latino	All other races or 2 or more races, not Hispanic or Latino	Hispanic or Latino[1]	Age (percent), 2010–2014: Under 18 years old	Age 18 to 64 years old	Age 65 years and older	Households, 2010–2014: Total occupied housing units	Percent owner occupied	Householders by level of education (percent): High school diploma or less	Bachelor's degree or more
	1	2	3	4	5	6	7	8	9	10	11	12	13	14	15	16
TEXAS—Con.																
Alice Acres CDP	490	NA	NA	354	0.0	0.0	0.0	0.0	100.0	40.2	59.9	0.0	97	57.7	81.4	18.6
Allen city	84,290	94,179	11.7	89,845	64.4	7.9	13.2	3.7	10.8	30.9	62.7	6.3	29,344	76.8	13.0	57.3
Alma town	331	336	1.5	412	63.3	0.0	0.0	1.5	35.2	23.3	63.6	13.1	157	85.4	62.4	17.8
Alpine city	5,993	5,967	-0.4	6,026	44.7	2.8	0.0	0.9	51.6	22.5	63.5	13.9	2,512	52.9	36.9	31.6
Alto town	1,225	1,208	-1.4	1,323	42.6	36.8	5.4	0.8	14.5	23.5	59.9	16.5	524	44.5	53.8	8.0
Alto Bonito Heights CDP	342	NA	NA	415	0.0	0.0	0.0	0.0	100.0	0.0	72.0	28.0	98	100.0	100.0	0.0
Alton city	13,900	15,497	11.5	14,735	2.7	0.0	0.0	0.1	97.3	34.7	59.2	6.0	3,842	62.3	66.4	7.3
Alvarado city	3,798	3,911	3.0	3,832	77.9	3.5	0.0	3.5	15.0	26.5	59.9	13.5	1,432	62.4	51.0	9.0
Alvin city	24,223	25,525	5.4	24,938	59.5	3.9	0.6	0.9	35.1	25.2	62.7	12.2	8,679	58.1	42.6	17.9
Alvord town	1,334	1,377	3.2	1,523	92.6	0.0	0.0	1.6	5.8	30.0	63.2	6.8	545	65.5	57.6	12.1
Amada Acres CDP	92	NA	NA	115	0.0	0.0	0.0	0.0	100.0	60.9	39.1	0.0	20	0.0	0.0	0.0
Amargosa CDP	291	NA	NA	5	0.0	0.0	0.0	0.0	100.0	0.0	0.0	100.0	3	100.0	100.0	0.0
Amarillo city	190,672	197,254	3.5	194,930	57.8	6.3	3.4	2.6	30.0	27.1	60.6	12.3	74,457	61.3	38.5	22.9
Amaya CDP	93	NA	NA	31	25.8	0.0	0.0	0.0	74.2	29.0	45.2	25.8	17	100.0	64.7	0.0
Ames city	1,003	1,040	3.7	1,195	3.1	78.9	0.0	5.7	12.3	32.0	56.6	11.2	366	87.7	50.5	5.5
Amherst city	721	696	-3.5	949	33.7	3.9	0.0	3.8	58.6	32.6	52.5	15.0	265	83.8	56.6	6.0
Amistad CDP	53	NA	NA	14	100.0	0.0	0.0	0.0	0.0	0.0	0.0	100.0	10	100.0	30.0	60.0
Anacua CDP	12	NA	NA	0	0.0	0.0	0.0	0.0	0.0	0.0	0.0	0.0	0	0.0	0.0	0.0
Anahuac city	2,241	2,316	3.3	2,110	60.7	13.3	1.6	1.8	22.7	19.6	66.7	13.7	732	74.2	47.8	14.6
Anderson city	222	226	1.8	247	59.5	32.4	0.0	4.5	3.6	27.9	36.5	35.6	84	88.1	33.3	41.7
Andrews city	11,083	13,245	19.5	12,160	44.3	1.3	0.8	1.3	52.4	29.9	58.1	11.9	4,233	74.6	53.5	13.6
Angleton city	18,862	19,472	3.2	19,034	52.0	12.9	1.7	1.6	31.9	28.2	60.0	11.9	6,852	62.9	47.2	14.6
Angus city	414	412	-0.5	379	72.8	3.7	1.1	0.5	21.9	19.7	63.6	16.6	158	66.5	46.2	8.2
Anna city	8,282	10,571	27.6	9,108	61.6	8.5	0.4	2.8	26.7	31.5	60.8	7.8	3,022	81.0	35.8	30.4
Annetta town	1,288	1,383	7.4	1,509	88.7	0.0	0.4	2.2	8.7	27.7	56.9	15.4	483	91.9	13.7	45.3
Annetta North town	540	562	4.1	415	93.7	0.0	0.0	0.7	5.5	16.3	55.6	28.0	176	89.8	20.5	53.4
Annetta South town	526	548	4.2	537	92.0	0.0	0.0	1.3	6.7	20.5	53.0	26.4	214	87.4	10.7	52.8
Annona town	315	304	-3.5	348	39.1	27.0	1.7	4.3	27.9	26.7	53.3	20.1	113	71.7	56.6	10.6
Anson city	2,430	2,325	-4.3	2,069	53.9	3.6	0.0	1.3	41.2	36.3	47.5	16.1	755	67.3	60.0	17.0
Anthony town	5,011	5,423	8.2	5,218	13.3	6.2	0.5	1.3	78.7	24.1	69.2	6.7	1,062	57.8	58.3	8.8
Anton city	1,126	1,144	1.6	1,280	40.6	2.1	0.2	0.9	56.2	31.4	57.4	11.2	418	71.3	43.1	18.4
Appleby city	472	470	-0.4	577	79.7	6.4	2.4	0.7	10.7	26.9	63.9	9.0	195	82.6	41.5	23.6
Aquilla city	109	108	-0.9	77	100.0	0.0	0.0	0.0	0.0	2.6	76.7	20.8	39	76.9	59.0	5.1
Aransas Pass city	8,204	8,461	3.1	8,287	55.9	1.6	0.7	1.6	40.2	22.0	60.2	17.6	3,297	61.6	56.2	11.4
Archer City city	1,834	1,776	-3.2	1,619	89.5	2.8	2.1	3.4	2.2	25.6	56.8	17.7	689	70.4	59.1	10.6
Arcola city	1,609	1,660	3.2	1,964	23.0	23.3	0.0	0.9	52.9	35.9	57.4	6.7	517	72.9	61.5	22.6
Argyle city	3,229	3,717	15.1	3,449	88.5	0.0	1.1	1.2	9.1	25.6	60.9	13.6	1,185	88.9	15.0	61.5
Arlington city	365,361	383,204	4.9	375,305	42.9	19.3	7.0	2.2	28.7	27.1	64.1	8.8	133,601	56.7	33.7	30.7
Arp city	968	988	2.1	857	84.4	7.1	0.0	0.9	7.6	26.9	61.9	11.2	327	88.1	52.0	18.7
Arroyo Colorado Estates CDP	997	NA	NA	579	0.0	0.0	0.0	0.0	100.0	26.8	68.8	4.5	152	100.0	100.0	0.0
Arroyo Gardens CDP	456	NA	NA	415	3.1	0.0	0.0	0.0	96.9	22.9	69.9	7.2	92	100.0	32.6	0.0
Asherton city	1,046	1,153	10.2	1,254	7.0	0.1	0.0	0.0	92.9	28.9	50.8	20.2	434	70.7	66.6	8.5
Aspermont town	919	865	-5.9	976	67.2	6.7	0.0	1.0	25.1	36.1	41.0	22.7	356	75.3	64.9	8.7
Atascocita CDP	65,844	NA	NA	69,470	50.6	20.0	3.2	2.3	23.9	29.9	62.5	7.6	21,592	79.6	22.3	38.9
Athens city	12,708	12,819	0.9	12,782	51.0	17.0	1.2	0.1	30.7	27.7	58.1	14.3	4,436	54.6	45.7	17.4
Atlanta city	5,671	5,596	-1.3	5,638	69.7	26.7	0.6	0.5	2.5	25.4	57.1	17.3	2,023	68.7	53.9	12.8
Aubrey city	2,605	2,814	8.0	2,709	81.0	0.4	0.0	3.0	15.7	26.8	65.2	7.9	956	62.0	36.6	18.9
Aurora city	1,220	1,267	3.9	1,529	71.9	0.1	0.0	0.3	27.7	38.1	52.8	9.2	493	75.9	53.8	27.8
Austin city	811,458	912,791	12.5	864,218	48.7	7.5	6.5	2.5	34.8	21.9	70.7	7.3	344,289	44.8	23.5	49.3
Austwell city	147	150	2.0	157	27.4	3.8	0.0	0.6	68.2	13.3	49.6	36.9	69	79.7	55.1	18.8
Avery town	477	460	-3.6	395	94.7	0.0	0.0	1.0	4.3	24.8	57.7	17.5	169	78.1	60.9	14.2
Avinger town	444	440	-0.9	518	70.1	21.0	0.0	5.2	3.7	24.6	58.1	17.2	207	58.5	56.0	16.4
Azle city	10,947	11,530	5.3	10,744	89.7	0.7	0.6	1.2	7.8	22.0	60.8	17.2	4,199	66.0	40.1	20.3
Bacliff CDP	8,619	NA	NA	8,606	56.8	2.1	1.0	4.6	35.6	32.2	59.8	8.1	2,939	66.5	45.0	16.9
Bailey city	289	287	-0.7	230	87.4	0.0	0.0	12.6	0.0	22.6	63.4	13.9	72	73.6	80.6	0.0
Bailey's Prairie village	726	743	2.3	735	71.6	19.6	0.0	1.0	7.9	24.5	62.0	13.6	255	90.2	37.3	18.4
Baird city	1,496	1,479	-1.1	1,775	78.8	0.6	0.7	1.3	18.5	18.9	63.2	17.9	620	74.7	43.9	12.1
Balch Springs city	23,876	25,120	5.2	24,693	21.4	22.6	0.2	1.8	54.0	36.8	57.0	6.4	7,006	56.3	63.0	9.4
Balcones Heights city	2,748	2,898	5.5	2,825	18.9	6.5	0.2	0.8	73.6	25.7	67.1	7.2	1,246	11.9	51.8	11.9
Ballinger city	3,768	3,732	-1.0	3,744	63.6	1.0	0.0	0.0	35.4	28.5	51.0	20.4	1,252	74.7	63.2	11.3
Balmorhea city	479	506	5.6	552	12.3	0.0	0.0	0.0	87.7	35.0	52.5	12.5	168	60.7	58.3	13.1
B and E CDP	518	NA	NA	751	0.0	0.0	0.0	0.0	100.0	32.4	54.8	12.8	146	86.3	100.0	0.0
Bandera city	857	864	0.8	1,127	77.4	1.1	4.3	1.3	16.0	27.6	56.0	16.5	356	57.3	46.6	16.0
Bangs city	1,613	1,573	-2.5	1,703	78.4	6.6	0.0	0.2	14.9	28.0	53.9	18.1	649	65.6	49.5	9.9
Banquete CDP	726	NA	NA	837	3.9	0.0	3.9	12.5	79.6	18.1	76.8	5.1	227	62.1	60.4	15.0
Bardwell city	649	668	2.9	684	36.3	13.6	0.0	3.4	46.8	34.5	54.4	11.0	216	75.0	76.9	2.8
Barrera CDP	108	NA	NA	0	0.0	0.0	0.0	0.0	0.0	0.0	0.0	0.0	0	0.0	0.0	0.0
Barrett CDP	3,199	NA	NA	4,282	6.7	76.0	0.0	0.0	17.3	31.5	55.1	13.4	1,333	64.5	55.5	10.8
Barry city	242	241	-0.4	314	94.9	1.6	0.0	0.0	3.5	33.4	50.2	16.2	95	64.2	69.5	9.5
Barstow city	349	378	8.3	396	9.1	0.0	1.3	0.0	89.6	24.0	46.2	29.8	169	74.6	80.5	0.6
Bartlett city	2,684	2,751	2.5	2,068	30.2	19.9	1.2	0.8	47.9	21.1	67.6	11.2	440	81.6	60.9	12.5
Barton Creek CDP	3,077	NA	NA	3,483	85.0	0.0	2.1	0.0	12.9	20.6	49.1	30.4	1,461	66.1	2.8	83.4
Bartonville town	1,562	1,659	6.2	1,879	84.6	0.0	0.3	0.4	14.8	28.0	60.7	11.2	591	93.6	22.2	47.2
Bastrop city	7,216	7,856	8.9	7,469	64.2	13.7	0.8	2.2	19.1	19.8	60.7	19.5	2,713	58.3	39.8	22.5
Batesville CDP	1,068	NA	NA	1,123	3.2	0.0	0.0	0.0	96.8	23.4	70.0	6.5	332	81.3	87.7	0.0
Bay City city	17,618	17,368	-1.4	17,499	39.9	13.5	0.8	3.4	42.4	26.9	61.3	11.9	6,236	54.7	56.1	14.5
Bayou Vista city	1,534	1,568	2.2	1,970	87.5	0.4	1.0	2.0	9.1	9.3	68.1	22.4	999	80.8	24.0	35.3
Bayside town	325	330	1.5	419	64.2	2.9	0.0	6.9	26.0	17.2	52.5	30.3	194	83.0	38.1	16.5
Baytown city	72,024	76,127	5.7	74,157	36.8	16.8	1.0	1.8	43.7	29.8	59.8	10.3	24,771	60.0	47.5	14.0
Bayview town	377	389	3.2	540	57.0	0.0	0.0	0.0	43.0	19.1	57.4	23.5	155	94.2	40.0	32.3
Beach City city	2,273	2,524	11.0	2,406	88.4	0.8	0.0	0.2	10.6	27.7	58.9	13.3	861	76.5	32.3	30.0
Bear Creek village	382	381	-0.3	403	91.1	1.7	0.7	2.5	4.0	19.1	70.3	10.7	146	93.8	10.3	63.0
Beasley city	644	663	3.0	519	42.8	4.4	0.0	0.0	52.8	22.9	59.4	17.7	231	78.4	55.4	7.4
Beaumont city	117,267	117,585	0.3	117,543	33.6	47.8	3.2	1.5	13.8	24.6	62.5	13.2	45,301	57.8	42.5	24.3
Beckville city	847	843	-0.5	894	46.5	25.7	0.0	3.1	24.6	33.9	55.4	10.9	291	64.6	46.4	10.7
Bedford city	46,979	48,908	4.1	48,104	73.1	6.4	4.5	3.3	12.7	20.0	64.9	15.2	21,136	56.7	21.5	36.9
Bedias city	441	449	1.8	315	68.9	24.8	0.0	1.9	4.4	16.8	58.5	24.8	124	84.7	60.5	11.3
Bee Cave city	3,925	5,960	51.8	4,910	76.6	2.1	6.8	2.9	11.6	28.7	61.0	10.5	1,761	64.2	7.6	67.7
Beeville city	12,863	13,303	3.4	13,102	28.2	3.0	0.2	0.6	68.0	27.3	60.5	12.2	4,608	58.0	45.9	12.6
Bellaire city	16,855	18,252	8.3	17,533	67.7	0.8	18.1	3.2	10.2	29.2	59.0	11.7	6,017	87.5	6.1	80.5

1 May be of any race.

Table A. All Places — **Population and Housing**

STATE City, town, township, borough, or CDP (county if applicable)	Population: 2010 census total population	Population: 2014 estimated population	Population: Percent change 2010-2014	Population: ACS total population estimate 2010-2014	Race and Hispanic or Latino origin (percent), 2010–2014: White alone, not Hispanic or Latino	Black alone, not Hispanic or Latino	Asian alone, not Hispanic or Latino	All other races or 2 or more races, not Hispanic or Latino	Hispanic or Latino[1]	Age (percent), 2010–2014: Under 18 years old	Age 18 to 64 years old	Age 65 years and older	Households, 2010–2014: Total occupied housing units	Percent owner occupied	Householders by level of education (percent): High school diploma or less	Bachelor's degree or more
	1	2	3	4	5	6	7	8	9	10	11	12	13	14	15	16
TEXAS—Con.																
Bellevue city	362	349	-3.6	373	89.5	0.0	0.0	9.1	1.3	18.2	64.8	16.9	153	75.2	58.8	13.7
Bellmead city	9,901	10,184	2.9	10,052	41.6	18.1	0.0	3.1	37.2	33.4	59.0	7.5	3,262	55.6	57.4	7.1
Bells town	1,392	1,407	1.1	1,555	87.3	2.6	0.4	7.2	2.6	28.4	58.6	13.0	548	67.5	46.4	17.5
Bellville city	4,097	4,208	2.7	4,142	69.8	9.0	0.0	1.9	19.3	24.0	57.3	18.8	1,759	62.3	35.1	27.6
Belton city	18,223	20,128	10.5	19,292	55.6	8.7	1.9	2.1	31.7	24.3	63.6	12.1	5,894	54.5	38.2	29.8
Benavides city	1,362	1,331	-2.3	1,840	2.0	0.0	0.4	0.0	97.6	24.2	52.1	23.6	682	68.2	61.6	15.0
Benbrook city	21,234	22,419	5.6	21,898	77.1	6.3	2.1	2.6	12.0	21.2	60.5	18.2	9,380	68.7	25.5	36.9
Benjamin city	258	267	3.5	302	78.5	4.6	0.0	1.0	15.9	29.8	49.5	20.5	115	62.6	50.4	18.3
Benjamin Perez CDP	34	NA	NA	0	0.0	0.0	0.0	0.0	0.0	0.0	0.0	0.0	0	0.0	0.0	0.0
Berryville town	975	1,015	4.1	1,043	82.5	7.0	1.3	5.5	3.7	24.3	56.1	19.8	422	66.6	51.4	17.8
Bertram city	1,351	1,374	1.7	1,545	75.9	2.3	0.0	0.4	21.4	24.2	61.4	14.2	562	58.5	41.8	17.4
Beverly Hills city	2,024	2,041	0.8	1,579	35.1	9.1	0.4	1.3	54.1	22.7	61.9	15.5	610	59.7	58.0	5.1
Bevil Oaks city	1,274	1,244	-2.4	1,299	85.5	8.9	0.0	2.8	2.8	15.1	62.5	22.3	523	98.1	31.9	27.2
Bigfoot CDP	450	NA	NA	108	0.0	0.0	0.0	54.6	45.4	0.0	100.0	0.0	78	100.0	24.4	0.0
Big Lake city	2,936	3,277	11.6	3,162	28.6	3.5	0.0	0.4	67.5	30.6	57.3	12.2	1,079	72.0	68.6	12.3
Big Sandy town	1,343	1,370	2.0	1,863	71.7	16.4	4.2	2.6	5.2	35.7	52.0	12.1	654	56.1	50.3	14.4
Big Spring city	27,282	28,472	4.4	27,768	45.6	6.4	1.2	2.8	44.0	23.1	65.5	11.4	8,025	61.2	42.6	18.0
Big Thicket Lake Estates CDP	742	NA	NA	680	78.8	0.0	0.0	8.8	12.4	22.1	68.3	9.6	240	93.8	61.7	15.0
Big Wells city	697	771	10.6	533	7.7	0.0	0.0	0.0	92.3	21.1	56.7	22.3	189	83.1	77.2	5.8
Bishop city	3,134	3,170	1.1	3,162	26.2	0.0	0.8	0.2	72.9	26.8	56.8	16.4	1,112	77.9	56.3	12.0
Bishop Hills town	193	187	-3.1	277	84.1	0.0	0.0	0.4	15.5	31.1	48.7	20.2	95	87.4	20.0	53.7
Bixby CDP	504	NA	NA	410	7.6	0.0	0.0	0.0	92.4	29.0	62.9	8.0	110	100.0	100.0	0.0
Blackwell city	311	310	-0.3	366	93.2	0.0	0.0	0.0	6.8	22.2	57.7	20.2	138	74.6	54.3	21.7
Blanco city	1,774	1,876	5.7	2,215	62.3	3.2	1.9	1.2	31.5	31.6	55.0	13.5	772	63.1	50.8	20.7
Blanket town	390	381	-2.3	398	68.8	0.0	0.0	0.5	30.7	30.1	45.7	24.1	154	82.5	59.7	7.1
Blessing CDP	927	NA	NA	1,176	13.8	2.2	0.0	0.0	84.0	43.5	44.5	12.2	329	54.7	87.8	0.0
Bloomburg town	402	398	-1.0	307	83.7	13.7	0.0	0.0	2.6	22.4	59.4	18.2	121	71.1	63.6	7.4
Blooming Grove town	821	820	-0.1	833	84.8	5.9	0.0	1.6	7.8	24.9	63.5	11.6	307	76.9	46.9	11.7
Bloomington CDP	2,459	NA	NA	1,878	18.5	4.8	0.0	0.9	75.8	29.6	61.3	9.1	695	72.4	73.4	4.0
Blossom city	1,495	1,546	3.4	1,326	86.0	3.8	0.3	3.6	6.3	19.9	64.6	15.5	518	70.5	50.4	11.4
Blue Berry Hill CDP	866	NA	NA	624	21.2	0.0	0.0	0.0	78.8	16.8	61.9	21.3	252	72.2	76.2	0.0
Blue Mound city	2,394	2,475	3.4	2,835	39.6	0.5	0.2	1.7	57.9	25.9	62.1	12.0	835	84.3	68.6	6.7
Blue Ridge city	815	842	3.3	1,033	93.0	0.0	0.0	1.5	5.5	31.4	62.2	6.5	339	70.5	53.7	4.4
Bluetown CDP	356	NA	NA	319	8.2	0.0	0.0	0.0	91.8	35.1	47.3	17.6	132	60.6	92.4	0.0
Blum town	444	441	-0.7	502	94.0	0.0	0.0	0.4	5.6	27.3	61.9	11.0	176	60.8	74.4	8.0
Boerne city	10,603	12,835	21.1	11,674	72.5	1.5	0.6	2.2	23.2	25.2	56.5	18.3	4,492	49.3	30.9	39.0
Bogata city	1,154	1,114	-3.5	1,266	91.9	0.9	0.0	2.4	4.7	20.2	56.3	23.5	518	71.8	64.3	10.0
Boling CDP	1,122	NA	NA	952	44.5	0.0	0.0	0.0	55.5	12.0	73.6	14.5	374	83.7	63.4	6.4
Bolivar Peninsula CDP	2,417	NA	NA	1,959	93.3	0.0	0.0	1.8	4.9	20.1	58.0	21.9	858	86.5	36.9	27.6
Bonanza Hills CDP	37	NA	NA	43	0.0	0.0	0.0	0.0	100.0	48.9	51.1	0.0	9	100.0	0.0	0.0
Bonham city	10,127	10,058	-0.7	10,059	70.9	12.2	0.0	2.1	14.7	17.9	63.6	18.5	3,096	56.4	50.5	18.6
Bonney village	310	333	7.4	522	35.4	26.1	0.0	0.4	38.1	25.8	71.7	2.5	119	29.4	64.7	5.9
Booker town	1,516	1,621	6.9	1,494	48.5	0.1	0.9	1.9	48.7	28.4	61.6	10.0	476	67.4	54.4	20.6
Borger city	13,350	12,978	-2.8	13,121	63.3	3.6	0.6	4.1	28.4	27.7	58.6	13.8	5,043	71.3	44.6	15.0
Botines CDP	117	NA	NA	21	0.0	0.0	0.0	0.0	100.0	0.0	100.0	0.0	21	42.9	57.1	42.9
Bovina city	1,868	1,803	-3.5	1,784	15.1	3.3	0.0	0.0	81.6	32.8	57.8	9.4	546	56.8	70.9	5.7
Bowie city	5,218	5,153	-1.2	5,195	83.8	0.1	0.0	3.6	12.4	25.3	54.7	19.7	2,194	57.6	47.7	15.7
Box Canyon CDP	34	NA	NA	16	62.5	0.0	0.0	0.0	37.5	0.0	100.0	0.0	9	55.6	100.0	0.0
Boyd town	1,207	1,287	6.6	1,601	82.4	0.0	1.0	1.1	15.5	25.9	60.1	13.9	578	67.3	52.2	9.7
Boys Ranch CDP	282	NA	NA	77	92.2	1.3	0.0	2.6	3.9	26.0	74.1	0.0	27	0.0	0.0	77.8
Brackettville city	1,688	1,645	-2.5	2,070	17.1	1.7	0.0	0.6	80.6	25.7	59.3	14.8	610	78.2	69.3	6.9
Brady city	5,533	5,457	-1.4	5,515	59.4	1.9	0.0	1.8	36.9	28.9	54.2	16.8	1,927	72.5	56.6	16.5
Brazoria city	3,019	3,075	1.9	3,038	59.2	19.7	0.7	2.8	17.7	27.0	59.9	13.2	1,215	62.8	45.2	9.1
Brazos Bend city	306	316	3.3	352	90.1	0.0	4.8	0.0	5.1	14.0	50.9	35.2	136	100.0	19.1	42.6
Brazos Country city	469	478	1.9	609	87.4	2.0	0.0	2.3	8.4	22.0	60.8	17.2	212	95.3	16.0	49.5
Breckenridge city	5,780	5,545	-4.1	5,631	66.3	2.2	0.4	0.5	30.6	29.4	55.0	15.7	2,100	64.2	60.8	14.6
Bremond city	929	918	-1.2	954	69.8	19.1	1.3	1.6	8.3	17.8	61.9	20.3	379	60.7	64.9	9.8
Brenham city	15,716	16,297	3.7	16,029	59.6	20.3	3.4	0.5	16.2	20.8	60.9	18.3	5,127	63.0	43.8	25.2
Briar CDP	5,665	NA	NA	4,655	90.7	1.5	0.0	1.7	6.2	11.2	68.6	20.1	1,885	83.5	44.9	13.1
Briarcliff village	1,436	1,511	5.2	1,403	87.2	0.0	0.0	0.2	12.5	19.4	68.6	12.0	577	91.0	14.0	46.8
Briaroaks city	492	493	0.2	626	92.2	0.0	0.0	1.4	6.4	23.8	54.5	21.6	197	99.5	28.4	36.0
Bridge City city	7,840	7,924	1.1	7,898	86.2	0.1	2.4	2.6	8.7	28.9	60.0	11.1	2,783	78.8	47.6	16.6
Bridgeport city	5,982	6,239	4.3	6,099	47.7	4.7	0.2	1.9	45.5	28.4	63.5	8.2	1,799	58.2	48.5	16.1
Bristol CDP	668	NA	NA	343	100.0	0.0	0.0	0.0	0.0	13.4	59.8	26.8	151	65.6	38.4	25.8
Broaddus town	207	201	-2.9	198	87.4	0.0	0.0	0.0	12.6	20.8	56.0	23.2	75	61.3	69.3	2.7
Bronte town	999	974	-2.5	896	71.3	1.2	0.3	1.0	26.1	20.8	50.1	29.1	434	68.0	43.5	22.8
Brookshire city	4,702	4,946	5.2	4,804	16.6	36.5	0.4	6.5	40.0	36.7	53.7	9.7	1,568	38.3	69.3	5.5
Brookside Village city	1,515	1,569	3.6	1,784	50.2	12.1	0.8	1.8	35.0	23.3	67.9	8.8	569	83.3	42.2	16.9
Browndell city	199	197	-1.0	168	53.6	46.4	0.0	0.0	0.0	18.4	47.6	33.9	67	74.6	74.6	9.0
Brownfield city	9,657	9,719	0.6	9,678	39.1	5.7	0.0	0.6	54.6	26.4	59.3	14.5	2,977	69.7	56.3	13.0
Brownsboro city	1,044	1,065	2.0	1,172	65.6	3.5	0.0	8.5	22.4	35.7	55.5	9.0	370	65.7	55.4	9.7
Brownsville city	174,982	183,046	4.6	179,834	5.0	0.2	0.8	0.3	93.7	33.5	56.6	10.0	50,207	62.4	55.5	19.2
Brownwood city	19,287	18,972	-1.6	19,107	64.4	5.8	0.5	1.8	27.5	26.4	59.7	13.9	6,405	55.9	47.1	20.0
Bruceville-Eddy city	1,477	1,498	1.4	1,731	61.5	8.7	0.0	0.1	29.8	32.9	57.9	9.2	554	75.3	52.7	10.8
Brundage CDP	27	NA	NA	0	0.0	0.0	0.0	0.0	0.0	0.0	0.0	0.0	0	0.0	0.0	0.0
Bruni CDP	379	NA	NA	265	3.4	0.0	0.0	0.0	96.6	18.8	51.0	30.2	101	86.1	49.5	12.9
Brushy Creek CDP	21,764	NA	NA	22,537	70.0	4.7	10.1	3.4	11.7	32.5	61.1	6.3	7,164	76.7	11.2	58.1
Bryan city	76,218	80,913	6.2	78,368	41.3	17.1	2.1	1.4	38.1	24.2	66.1	9.8	28,265	47.6	41.9	28.4
Bryson city	539	528	-2.0	549	96.9	0.4	0.0	0.0	2.7	35.0	54.0	11.1	204	52.9	78.4	4.9
Buchanan Dam CDP	1,519	NA	NA	1,071	97.2	0.0	0.0	0.0	2.8	2.8	48.9	48.3	641	85.5	43.4	20.3
Buchanan Lake Village CDP	692	NA	NA	598	95.3	0.0	0.0	1.0	3.7	7.0	46.8	46.2	362	75.4	57.2	9.9
Buckholts town	515	504	-2.1	525	50.5	0.0	0.0	1.5	48.0	36.7	48.8	14.5	172	68.6	70.9	9.3
Buda city	7,343	11,461	56.1	9,443	57.4	2.2	1.6	0.8	38.0	33.1	59.0	7.9	3,399	78.6	25.3	38.3
Buena Vista CDP	102	NA	NA	249	0.0	0.0	0.0	0.0	100.0	62.3	37.7	0.0	52	100.0	100.0	0.0
Buffalo city	1,855	1,864	0.5	2,198	51.6	13.5	0.0	2.2	32.7	30.4	54.8	14.7	662	64.8	59.7	10.4
Buffalo Gap town	464	468	0.9	379	83.9	0.0	6.9	0.8	8.4	14.2	57.5	28.2	154	82.5	43.5	20.8
Buffalo Springs village	453	454	0.2	394	87.8	0.0	0.0	2.5	9.6	11.4	65.0	23.6	214	79.0	37.4	24.3
Bullard town	2,465	2,735	11.0	2,630	92.7	0.8	0.0	2.2	4.3	33.4	56.2	10.5	991	72.5	32.2	30.1
Bulverde city	4,550	4,847	6.5	4,706	65.2	3.6	1.4	3.0	26.8	20.6	63.6	15.8	1,652	94.4	25.4	31.4

1 May be of any race.

Table A. All Places — **Population and Housing**

STATE City, town, township, borough, or CDP (county if applicable)	Population: 2010 census total population	Population: 2014 estimated population	Population: Percent change 2010-2014	Population: ACS total population estimate 2010-2014	Race and Hispanic or Latino origin (percent), 2010–2014: White alone, not Hispanic or Latino	Black alone, not Hispanic or Latino	Asian alone, not Hispanic or Latino	All other races or 2 or more races, not Hispanic or Latino	Hispanic or Latino[1]	Age (percent), 2010–2014: Under 18 years old	Age 18 to 64 years old	Age 65 years and older	Households, 2010–2014: Total occupied housing units	Percent owner occupied	Householders by level of education (percent): High school diploma or less	Bachelor's degree or more
	1	2	3	4	5	6	7	8	9	10	11	12	13	14	15	16
TEXAS—Con.																
Buna CDP	2,142	NA	NA	2,354	90.1	3.4	2.6	3.9	0.0	32.9	52.4	14.7	771	65.9	51.8	5.8
Bunker Hill Village city	3,633	3,914	7.7	3,777	77.1	0.4	15.7	1.1	5.7	31.1	51.0	17.9	1,218	95.6	3.6	85.5
Burkburnett city	10,811	11,142	3.1	10,915	84.7	3.1	0.7	2.5	9.0	23.7	58.4	17.9	4,422	73.7	44.7	17.8
Burke city	737	732	-0.7	713	59.5	1.0	1.8	0.8	36.9	22.2	62.0	15.6	235	78.7	53.2	9.8
Burleson city	36,696	41,818	14.0	39,335	82.3	3.3	0.6	1.4	12.4	29.4	60.6	10.1	14,018	72.1	33.1	26.4
Burnet city	5,993	6,138	2.4	6,065	61.7	5.0	0.2	5.1	28.1	28.1	56.8	15.1	1,933	48.2	50.9	19.4
Burton city	300	302	0.7	473	93.2	6.8	0.0	0.0	0.0	28.9	48.0	23.0	172	68.6	30.2	40.1
Butterfield CDP	114	NA	NA	147	0.0	0.0	0.0	0.0	100.0	27.2	70.0	2.7	43	83.7	76.7	0.0
Byers city	496	478	-3.6	428	95.6	0.0	2.6	0.0	1.9	19.4	59.8	20.8	216	87.0	59.3	15.3
Bynum town	199	197	-1.0	219	89.5	3.7	2.3	0.0	4.6	18.2	76.7	5.0	86	90.7	25.6	39.5
Cactus city	3,179	3,179	0.0	3,197	4.8	5.6	21.1	0.0	68.5	32.9	65.4	1.7	780	50.3	75.3	7.8
Caddo Mills city	1,340	1,432	6.9	1,789	85.8	10.3	0.0	1.2	2.7	35.8	54.5	9.7	564	65.4	51.2	13.8
Caldwell city	4,104	4,217	2.8	4,179	59.1	17.1	0.0	0.9	22.9	22.9	56.9	20.1	1,505	69.8	50.0	19.6
Callender Lake CDP	1,039	NA	NA	1,286	93.4	0.0	0.0	2.9	3.7	4.4	55.0	40.4	546	93.4	41.9	23.3
Callisburg city	353	357	1.1	366	84.4	0.0	0.0	15.6	0.0	34.7	52.1	13.1	138	68.8	48.6	11.6
Calvert city	1,192	1,147	-3.8	1,200	22.3	61.2	0.0	7.0	9.6	32.5	53.3	14.4	425	48.2	67.5	9.2
Camargito CDP	388	NA	NA	434	0.0	0.0	0.0	0.0	100.0	30.2	56.5	13.4	127	80.3	88.2	0.0
Cameron city	5,552	5,398	-2.8	5,445	44.5	19.3	0.0	6.2	30.0	28.6	50.7	20.7	2,032	58.7	56.5	14.1
Cameron Park CDP	6,963	NA	NA	7,811	2.8	0.0	0.0	0.0	97.2	36.6	59.5	4.1	1,705	67.3	89.8	1.2
Campbell city	638	649	1.7	467	85.9	2.8	5.4	0.2	5.8	25.0	53.4	21.6	196	80.6	58.7	15.3
Campo Verde CDP	132	NA	NA	152	0.0	0.0	0.0	0.0	100.0	38.2	61.8	0.0	18	100.0	100.0	0.0
Camp Swift CDP	6,383	NA	NA	6,184	39.3	8.6	0.2	3.1	48.8	26.0	68.0	6.0	1,440	74.8	50.5	9.7
Camp Wood city	705	713	1.1	1,057	69.0	0.0	0.0	0.4	30.7	23.8	51.6	24.6	329	65.0	64.4	12.5
Canadian city	2,649	2,947	11.2	3,221	56.6	0.2	0.3	1.7	41.3	32.3	53.7	14.0	1,093	76.3	47.8	20.5
Caney City town	217	217	0.0	221	64.7	34.4	0.0	0.0	0.9	6.8	50.8	42.5	107	80.4	59.8	23.4
Canton city	3,570	3,578	0.2	3,565	85.9	3.3	2.2	3.8	4.8	19.3	63.2	17.6	1,355	63.2	54.5	10.6
Cantu Addition CDP	188	NA	NA	367	0.0	0.0	0.0	0.0	100.0	29.9	59.0	10.9	93	86.0	91.4	8.6
Canutillo CDP	6,321	NA	NA	6,091	8.7	7.5	0.0	1.0	82.9	26.2	60.0	13.8	1,673	69.2	65.4	11.4
Canyon city	13,312	14,432	8.4	13,882	75.7	2.7	1.1	1.6	19.0	21.8	68.5	9.9	5,354	48.0	21.6	36.1
Canyon Creek CDP	916	NA	NA	1,269	96.4	1.3	0.0	0.0	2.3	21.3	54.0	24.7	463	86.2	47.3	21.6
Canyon Lake CDP	21,262	NA	NA	21,469	81.5	0.7	0.2	2.1	15.4	17.4	60.2	22.4	9,113	81.5	29.9	33.7
Cape Royale CDP	670	NA	NA	519	91.5	0.0	0.0	0.0	8.5	0.0	27.4	72.6	267	95.5	13.1	53.2
Carbon town	272	266	-2.2	333	53.8	0.0	0.0	0.0	46.2	28.2	51.6	20.1	125	88.0	64.8	16.0
Carlsbad CDP	719	NA	NA	770	76.9	3.2	0.0	2.2	17.7	29.6	61.7	8.8	179	65.9	73.2	9.5
Carl's Corner town	173	172	-0.6	414	63.5	2.4	0.0	0.0	34.1	31.9	59.9	8.2	104	96.2	75.0	12.5
Carmine city	250	255	2.0	181	77.9	18.8	0.0	0.0	3.3	9.4	57.0	33.7	93	83.9	47.3	16.1
Carrizo Hill CDP	582	NA	NA	1,326	1.9	0.0	0.0	0.0	98.1	48.1	48.6	3.2	264	73.5	75.4	4.2
Carrizo Springs city	5,368	5,958	11.0	5,662	10.4	0.7	0.0	0.0	88.9	26.3	58.4	15.3	2,053	69.8	55.5	14.2
Carrollton city	119,100	128,353	7.8	124,501	42.6	8.7	13.8	2.5	32.4	24.9	66.0	9.1	44,394	61.6	28.1	40.1
Carthage city	6,779	6,822	0.6	6,835	64.1	27.0	0.1	0.7	8.1	26.2	56.1	17.8	2,506	64.8	48.5	10.3
Casa Blanca CDP	54	NA	NA	32	0.0	0.0	0.0	0.0	100.0	0.0	100.0	0.0	8	100.0	100.0	0.0
Casas CDP	39	NA	NA	25	0.0	0.0	0.0	0.0	100.0	68.0	32.0	0.0	8	100.0	100.0	0.0
Cashion Community city	348	347	-0.3	283	94.3	0.4	0.0	2.5	2.8	19.8	46.9	33.2	120	72.5	31.7	27.5
Castle Hills city	4,116	4,362	6.0	4,247	59.1	2.4	0.9	0.5	37.1	18.5	48.4	33.1	1,772	71.5	20.3	52.0
Castroville city	2,785	2,909	4.5	2,838	58.2	0.8	0.6	1.4	39.0	21.1	54.7	24.2	1,050	75.3	40.8	27.6
Catarina CDP	118	NA	NA	36	77.8	0.0	0.0	0.0	22.2	0.0	0.0	100.0	17	100.0	76.5	0.0
Cedar Hill city	45,030	48,084	6.8	46,414	22.6	51.9	2.7	2.7	20.0	29.2	63.1	7.4	15,833	71.5	28.1	32.4
Cedar Park city	51,743	63,574	22.9	58,088	68.0	5.6	7.5	2.9	16.0	29.2	62.7	8.0	19,667	69.1	16.0	47.2
Cedar Point CDP	630	NA	NA	823	95.3	0.0	2.3	0.0	2.4	11.9	69.5	18.6	386	87.0	58.5	17.6
Celeste city	814	826	1.5	845	91.6	5.8	0.0	0.4	2.2	29.4	56.8	13.8	287	60.6	49.5	12.5
Celina city	6,028	7,086	17.6	6,558	73.1	3.6	1.1	1.6	20.6	30.7	61.0	8.3	2,108	78.5	23.9	35.4
Center city	5,180	5,232	1.0	5,239	32.1	32.4	2.3	0.5	32.7	31.2	50.2	18.5	1,930	57.2	63.8	14.4
Centerville city	892	891	-0.1	1,027	82.3	5.6	0.0	2.0	10.0	22.2	54.7	23.3	371	59.0	58.0	11.9
Central Gardens CDP	4,347	NA	NA	4,026	83.6	0.4	3.6	0.0	12.4	17.3	62.2	20.4	1,685	74.1	31.5	28.2
C sar ChBvez CDP	1,929	NA	NA	1,764	10.5	0.0	0.0	0.0	89.5	36.8	48.4	14.7	542	81.0	62.2	18.5
Chandler city	2,734	2,861	4.6	2,783	75.0	13.7	1.9	1.4	8.0	24.8	56.0	19.3	987	74.0	29.9	29.6
Channelview CDP	38,289	NA	NA	38,980	19.8	15.4	0.6	2.1	62.1	34.0	60.2	5.7	11,392	68.2	56.7	10.6
Channing city	363	356	-1.9	191	86.9	0.0	0.0	2.6	10.5	18.8	53.9	27.2	98	57.1	48.0	7.1
Chaparrito CDP	114	NA	NA	8	0.0	0.0	0.0	0.0	100.0	0.0	100.0	0.0	8	0.0	100.0	0.0
Chapeno CDP	47	NA	NA	63	0.0	0.0	0.0	0.0	100.0	42.9	57.1	0.0	12	100.0	100.0	0.0
Charlotte city	1,715	1,796	4.7	1,971	16.2	0.6	0.0	0.0	83.2	29.4	54.8	15.8	653	77.0	79.9	6.4
Chester town	317	312	-1.6	341	93.8	0.6	0.6	0.0	5.0	29.5	48.1	22.3	133	82.7	55.6	12.0
Chico city	1,015	1,052	3.6	1,071	91.3	0.0	0.5	0.9	7.3	26.1	63.5	10.4	330	74.5	71.2	4.8
Childress city	6,105	6,092	-0.2	6,140	59.9	10.6	0.5	3.5	25.4	23.3	63.9	12.9	1,944	63.2	49.9	20.0
Chillicothe city	707	674	-4.7	686	71.6	1.5	0.0	0.4	26.5	12.2	68.1	19.8	295	72.9	53.9	15.3
Chilton CDP	911	NA	NA	851	29.0	10.2	0.0	0.0	60.8	39.4	47.3	13.4	215	75.3	75.8	5.1
China city	1,158	1,127	-2.7	955	82.9	12.8	0.0	1.9	2.4	18.5	62.3	19.2	441	85.5	52.6	11.3
China Grove town	1,180	1,273	7.9	1,152	62.7	7.8	0.3	0.9	28.3	11.0	71.4	17.7	405	95.6	36.8	24.2
China Spring CDP	1,281	NA	NA	1,533	80.7	0.0	0.0	0.0	19.3	23.7	67.9	8.4	538	55.0	41.8	22.9
Chireno city	386	385	-0.3	409	69.9	13.2	0.0	2.9	13.9	25.6	55.6	18.8	158	78.5	56.3	14.6
Christine town	390	410	5.1	350	22.9	3.1	0.0	0.0	74.0	27.5	68.0	4.6	111	84.7	64.9	4.5
Christoval CDP	504	NA	NA	276	93.8	0.0	0.0	4.3	1.8	27.5	56.9	15.6	142	88.0	62.7	8.5
Chula Vista CDP (Cameron)	288	NA	NA	236	0.0	0.0	0.0	0.0	100.0	30.1	69.9	0.0	63	52.4	100.0	0.0
Chula Vista CDP (Maverick)	3,818	NA	NA	3,474	0.5	0.0	0.0	0.7	98.7	36.3	51.8	11.9	1,054	80.9	73.7	4.3
Chula Vista CDP (Zavala)	450	NA	NA	436	5.3	0.0	0.0	0.0	94.7	50.9	49.1	0.0	72	36.1	69.4	0.0
Cibolo city	20,091	25,280	25.8	22,744	53.8	10.9	2.7	3.4	29.3	32.4	61.6	6.1	7,064	81.1	17.1	47.3
Cienegas Terrace CDP	3,424	NA	NA	3,270	0.3	2.1	0.0	0.0	97.6	35.1	57.2	7.7	744	84.8	92.6	3.6
Cinco Ranch CDP	18,274	NA	NA	18,028	58.2	5.8	17.2	3.9	14.9	29.7	61.4	8.7	6,124	76.2	8.8	71.4
Circle D-KC Estates CDP	2,393	NA	NA	2,144	79.5	0.0	1.5	0.0	19.0	18.3	66.1	15.7	862	89.9	44.9	25.5
Cisco city	3,902	3,777	-3.2	3,846	78.1	4.9	0.1	0.9	15.9	20.0	62.2	18.0	1,342	66.9	47.0	11.3
Citrus City CDP	2,321	NA	NA	3,853	0.0	0.0	0.3	0.0	99.7	50.6	47.9	1.5	723	70.1	83.8	6.2
Clarendon city	2,077	1,977	-4.8	2,015	82.0	8.2	0.7	0.7	8.3	21.9	62.0	16.4	630	71.0	44.6	19.0
Clarksville city	3,278	3,176	-3.1	3,220	42.0	44.2	0.0	0.5	13.4	26.8	49.0	24.1	1,268	55.0	58.1	15.5
Clarksville City city	865	875	1.2	820	91.8	1.5	0.1	1.6	5.0	21.8	63.3	14.9	300	83.0	41.3	14.7
Claude city	1,199	1,230	2.6	1,192	79.8	2.9	0.0	2.8	14.5	26.2	53.1	20.9	382	75.1	32.7	25.1
Clear Lake Shores city	1,063	1,138	7.1	1,295	90.3	0.0	1.2	2.5	6.1	17.6	64.8	17.6	555	71.7	7.9	56.6
Cleburne city	29,763	29,848	0.3	29,765	66.3	3.3	0.6	4.3	25.4	27.5	59.1	13.4	10,495	59.9	49.0	17.7
Cleveland city	7,675	7,745	0.9	7,684	48.7	21.8	0.3	0.6	28.7	27.2	62.9	10.0	2,508	58.3	63.1	15.1
Clifton city	3,440	3,353	-2.5	3,400	65.4	3.1	0.1	4.0	27.4	24.9	50.2	24.9	1,123	74.4	45.4	20.2

1 May be of any race.

Table A. All Places — **Population and Housing**

STATE City, town, township, borough, or CDP (county if applicable)	Population: 2010 census total population	Population: 2014 estimated population	Population: Percent change 2010-2014	Population: ACS total population estimate 2010-2014	Race and Hispanic or Latino origin (percent), 2010–2014: White alone, not Hispanic or Latino	Black alone, not Hispanic or Latino	Asian alone, not Hispanic or Latino	All other races or 2 or more races, not Hispanic or Latino	Hispanic or Latino[1]	Age (percent), 2010–2014: Under 18 years old	Age 18 to 64 years old	Age 65 years and older	Households, 2010–2014: Total occupied housing units	Percent owner occupied	Householders by level of education (percent): High school diploma or less	Bachelor's degree or more
	1	2	3	4	5	6	7	8	9	10	11	12	13	14	15	16
TEXAS—Con.																
Clint town	926	1,143	23.4	892	13.8	0.6	0.8	0.2	84.6	22.6	55.6	21.7	301	80.4	58.8	16.6
Cloverleaf CDP	22,942	NA	NA	23,732	15.8	9.7	0.7	0.9	72.9	34.4	58.3	7.3	6,584	59.6	65.2	10.8
Clute city	11,211	11,392	1.6	11,277	34.5	11.5	0.2	2.7	51.1	28.2	62.0	9.8	4,060	45.4	51.7	13.6
Clyde city	3,713	3,757	1.2	3,723	88.6	1.6	0.3	2.6	6.9	29.0	51.5	19.5	1,365	78.7	51.6	13.1
Coahoma town	817	867	6.1	748	68.0	0.0	0.0	0.5	31.4	25.5	56.0	18.4	305	80.7	53.4	12.1
Cockrell Hill city	4,193	4,306	2.7	4,267	9.6	3.7	0.3	1.2	85.3	33.3	60.1	6.7	1,051	56.4	79.0	3.4
Coffee City town	279	279	0.0	352	57.4	37.2	0.6	0.0	4.8	13.4	70.7	15.9	134	77.6	47.0	11.9
Coldspring city	867	890	2.7	996	63.3	25.3	0.0	0.0	11.4	30.3	57.3	12.1	343	55.1	59.8	10.5
Coleman city	4,709	4,449	-5.5	4,581	76.1	2.4	0.0	1.0	20.5	23.6	54.3	22.0	1,765	65.5	53.0	9.1
College Station city	94,061	103,483	10.0	98,505	67.5	6.6	9.2	2.3	14.3	15.9	79.1	5.1	35,032	34.3	13.2	44.9
Colleyville city	22,805	24,952	9.4	23,928	80.6	1.5	8.8	1.9	7.2	25.8	61.4	12.8	8,211	95.9	9.8	69.8
Collinsville town	1,624	1,650	1.6	1,694	89.0	0.3	0.1	3.7	6.9	29.1	57.9	12.9	619	65.4	38.1	17.4
Colmesneil city	596	585	-1.8	582	80.6	7.7	0.0	5.2	6.5	24.3	52.6	23.2	255	90.2	61.6	9.8
Colorado Acres CDP	296	NA	NA	100	0.0	0.0	0.0	0.0	100.0	44.0	40.0	16.0	26	65.4	69.2	0.0
Colorado City city	4,146	4,133	-0.3	4,118	52.1	4.8	0.0	0.3	42.8	26.9	54.8	18.4	1,473	65.4	56.3	8.8
Columbus city	3,655	3,655	0.0	3,658	55.5	18.9	0.0	0.0	25.5	21.9	52.7	25.3	1,310	67.9	58.2	19.5
Comanche city	4,335	4,242	-2.1	4,269	60.5	0.4	0.0	0.7	38.5	26.5	54.7	18.8	1,403	70.8	71.8	14.5
Combes town	2,895	3,042	5.1	2,991	15.7	0.0	0.0	0.0	84.3	25.5	56.8	17.6	898	87.2	69.3	6.9
Combine city	1,944	2,053	5.6	1,983	83.3	1.2	1.9	5.0	8.6	21.5	67.5	11.1	677	85.4	44.3	23.6
Comfort CDP	2,363	NA	NA	3,208	46.9	0.0	0.0	0.0	53.1	34.4	52.1	13.4	897	63.5	48.6	16.9
Commerce city	8,073	8,599	6.5	8,348	53.9	22.1	5.2	4.3	14.5	18.8	71.3	9.9	2,638	39.8	41.6	24.8
Como town	695	701	0.9	667	61.2	0.0	0.0	1.6	37.2	36.5	44.9	18.3	238	63.9	56.3	4.6
Concepcion CDP	62	NA	NA	30	0.0	0.0	0.0	0.0	100.0	0.0	0.0	100.0	22	100.0	100.0	0.0
Conroe city	56,992	65,871	15.6	61,268	50.7	10.0	1.0	0.6	37.7	26.7	62.8	10.4	21,234	48.8	45.2	21.4
Converse city	18,198	21,054	15.7	19,738	35.7	18.7	2.5	5.1	38.0	28.1	64.0	8.0	6,574	66.2	31.2	30.4
Cool city	157	163	3.8	212	87.7	0.0	0.0	0.0	12.3	19.4	63.5	17.0	71	67.6	62.0	9.9
Coolidge town	955	959	0.4	827	29.9	12.8	0.0	0.7	56.6	22.0	66.5	11.4	270	58.9	67.8	4.4
Cooper city	1,967	1,970	0.2	2,076	74.0	15.5	1.4	1.0	8.0	19.9	59.3	20.8	739	65.5	57.0	15.2
Coppell city	38,659	40,678	5.2	40,021	61.9	5.1	19.4	2.4	11.3	28.6	65.2	6.2	14,309	71.3	10.4	66.1
Copperas Cove city	32,169	32,943	2.4	33,023	60.2	17.3	2.1	5.3	15.2	29.2	61.4	9.3	11,323	59.2	25.5	21.3
Copper Canyon town	1,336	1,418	6.1	1,353	97.6	0.2	0.0	0.4	1.8	20.1	64.3	15.7	490	94.3	14.7	55.3
Corinth city	19,796	20,836	5.3	20,432	78.6	5.6	2.2	3.2	10.3	30.4	61.2	8.3	7,126	84.0	23.5	42.0
Corpus Christi city	305,215	320,434	5.0	312,680	32.0	4.0	1.8	1.3	60.8	25.5	62.3	12.2	113,376	56.7	42.5	23.2
Corral City town	27	28	3.7	31	80.6	6.5	0.0	12.9	0.0	19.4	80.7	0.0	12	50.0	8.3	0.0
Corrigan town	1,595	1,538	-3.6	1,629	38.7	29.6	0.8	1.0	29.9	26.2	62.9	11.0	617	48.1	53.0	3.2
Corsicana city	23,835	23,989	0.6	23,968	45.3	21.0	0.9	1.7	31.1	27.8	58.8	13.3	8,683	55.8	48.8	18.1
Cottonwood city	185	197	6.5	191	98.4	0.0	0.0	1.0	0.5	24.7	61.2	14.1	63	87.3	44.4	14.3
Cottonwood Shores city	1,123	1,136	1.2	1,408	70.7	0.8	0.0	1.5	27.1	27.6	65.4	7.1	478	63.8	61.7	11.5
Cotulla city	3,605	4,095	13.6	3,843	8.8	0.3	0.0	0.0	90.9	35.0	52.6	12.4	1,053	61.5	77.2	11.7
Country Acres CDP	185	NA	NA	197	69.5	0.0	0.0	0.0	30.5	48.2	51.8	0.0	50	100.0	70.0	0.0
Coupland city	277	298	7.6	186	95.7	0.0	0.0	1.6	2.7	24.7	62.9	12.4	65	83.1	63.1	23.1
Cove city	512	513	0.2	518	72.2	0.0	0.0	0.4	27.4	34.4	52.1	13.5	185	87.0	35.7	24.9
Covington city	269	269	0.0	233	97.0	0.0	0.0	0.0	3.0	18.9	61.3	19.7	86	79.1	59.3	2.3
Coyanosa CDP	163	NA	NA	168	0.0	0.0	0.0	0.0	100.0	19.0	66.0	14.9	57	78.9	100.0	0.0
Coyote Acres CDP	508	NA	NA	556	0.0	0.0	0.0	0.0	100.0	36.9	63.1	0.0	136	83.1	53.7	0.0
Coyote Flats city	312	313	0.3	380	94.5	0.0	0.0	0.0	5.5	8.6	49.1	42.4	126	85.7	58.7	22.2
Crandall city	2,847	3,119	9.6	2,979	86.7	1.8	0.0	1.9	9.5	29.0	63.4	7.7	986	82.9	46.6	17.0
Crane city	3,353	3,823	14.0	3,653	37.7	3.6	0.0	0.3	58.4	29.3	59.2	11.5	1,291	72.8	54.2	11.8
Cranfills Gap city	281	274	-2.5	281	68.0	0.0	0.0	1.1	31.0	19.3	60.6	20.3	129	69.0	56.6	14.7
Crawford town	717	738	2.9	716	88.0	3.9	0.0	0.6	7.5	30.2	55.7	14.1	260	68.5	43.5	13.1
Creedmoor city	202	221	9.4	187	36.9	0.0	0.0	0.0	63.1	11.3	65.3	23.5	74	52.7	64.9	20.3
Cresson city	741	772	4.2	733	88.0	0.0	2.2	0.0	9.8	18.9	73.2	7.8	283	83.0	35.0	22.6
Crockett city	6,950	6,564	-5.6	6,702	35.7	49.9	0.1	2.1	12.2	24.4	56.6	18.9	2,491	47.1	57.5	14.5
Crosby CDP	2,299	NA	NA	2,619	50.8	8.4	0.0	3.0	37.8	30.3	60.0	9.7	886	71.4	62.2	7.7
Crosbyton city	1,741	1,683	-3.3	1,720	30.8	8.4	0.0	0.0	60.8	24.9	53.8	21.5	688	64.5	62.8	10.5
Cross Mountain CDP	3,124	NA	NA	2,647	61.9	0.2	8.0	1.3	28.5	29.5	60.5	9.9	920	89.6	14.1	69.8
Cross Plains town	982	970	-1.2	1,360	80.5	0.0	0.8	5.2	13.5	32.6	52.1	15.1	427	68.1	67.2	9.4
Cross Roads town	807	841	4.2	870	86.7	4.6	2.5	0.9	5.3	22.9	63.6	13.6	304	90.8	16.4	53.6
Cross Timber town	268	271	1.1	276	92.4	0.0	0.0	0.0	7.6	21.7	59.5	18.8	96	79.2	43.8	22.9
Crowell city	948	905	-4.5	811	83.0	1.5	0.0	0.0	15.5	20.4	49.7	30.0	364	66.8	53.3	25.0
Crowley city	12,838	14,572	13.5	13,762	64.1	12.4	1.8	2.7	19.0	33.1	59.8	7.1	4,553	71.3	30.0	25.7
Crystal City city	7,135	7,513	5.3	7,353	2.0	0.1	0.0	0.0	97.9	33.0	54.4	12.6	2,278	67.2	68.7	10.1
Cuero city	6,879	7,063	2.7	6,979	37.5	17.4	0.0	0.9	44.2	27.8	58.2	14.0	2,030	61.2	54.7	12.5
Cuevitas CDP	40	NA	NA	16	0.0	0.0	0.0	0.0	100.0	0.0	100.0	0.0	16	100.0	100.0	0.0
Cumby city	777	784	0.9	725	93.7	0.0	0.0	0.0	6.3	20.4	60.1	19.4	284	72.9	63.0	16.2
Cumings CDP	981	NA	NA	762	22.4	46.7	0.0	0.0	30.8	25.3	67.9	6.8	312	100.0	50.6	49.4
Cuney town	140	139	-0.7	133	9.0	54.9	0.0	12.8	23.3	35.4	53.4	11.3	49	71.4	57.1	4.1
Cushing city	612	610	-0.3	613	91.7	0.0	1.5	0.3	6.5	20.9	66.1	13.1	236	69.9	64.0	18.6
Cut and Shoot city	1,062	1,103	3.9	1,455	84.0	0.5	0.1	0.8	14.6	27.5	60.7	11.8	451	85.1	64.5	8.9
Daingerfield city	2,558	2,500	-2.3	2,515	57.7	30.0	0.2	0.2	12.0	24.8	55.8	19.4	901	65.5	54.9	9.5
Daisetta city	966	979	1.3	852	95.0	0.9	0.0	1.5	2.6	29.7	58.7	11.6	291	70.1	66.7	11.7
Dalhart city	7,932	8,326	5.0	8,150	59.4	1.6	0.6	2.1	36.3	29.8	59.2	11.0	2,854	69.1	43.2	22.1
Dallas city	1,197,792	1,281,047	7.0	1,240,985	29.3	24.3	3.0	1.7	41.7	25.9	64.9	9.2	467,501	43.0	40.8	33.8
Dalworthington Gardens city	2,259	2,355	4.2	2,077	85.1	5.3	3.1	3.3	3.2	16.6	66.7	16.8	752	84.6	10.6	57.3
Damon CDP	552	NA	NA	477	50.9	0.0	0.0	0.0	49.1	33.5	52.6	13.8	163	73.0	54.6	0.0
Danbury city	1,718	1,757	2.3	1,486	84.9	0.3	0.0	0.2	14.6	25.9	61.7	12.4	550	78.2	39.1	18.2
Darrouzett town	350	384	9.7	376	79.5	0.5	0.8	5.9	13.3	23.9	62.7	13.3	149	70.5	53.7	20.8
Dawson town	807	796	-1.4	874	71.3	8.7	0.0	1.8	18.2	25.2	57.4	17.4	351	63.2	58.4	19.1
Dayton city	7,247	7,465	3.0	7,350	55.4	20.5	3.9	1.9	18.3	21.1	70.3	8.7	2,301	57.1	57.5	11.6
Dayton Lakes city	93	94	1.1	70	91.4	0.0	0.0	0.0	8.6	20.0	65.8	14.3	29	82.8	65.5	17.2
Dean city	493	476	-3.4	588	88.4	0.0	0.3	3.7	7.5	21.7	63.5	14.6	223	88.3	48.4	18.8
Decatur city	6,042	6,339	4.9	6,201	73.6	3.4	0.1	2.6	20.2	28.1	57.2	14.8	2,098	56.5	37.8	27.1
DeCordova city	2,683	2,787	3.9	2,731	100.0	0.0	0.0	0.0	0.0	16.0	47.0	37.0	1,327	96.9	19.3	50.0
Deer Park city	32,010	33,719	5.3	32,965	66.5	1.7	1.2	1.5	29.0	27.5	62.4	10.1	11,139	73.1	35.5	20.9
De Kalb city	1,679	1,664	-0.9	1,865	66.6	21.7	0.6	3.8	7.3	21.0	57.7	21.2	706	65.3	50.8	12.5
De Leon city	2,246	2,173	-3.3	2,332	73.8	0.0	0.0	2.6	23.6	28.7	51.4	20.0	853	75.1	58.4	11.6
Dell City city	365	336	-7.9	314	52.9	0.0	0.0	0.0	47.1	25.1	44.6	30.3	129	67.4	72.1	7.0
Del Mar Heights CDP	113	NA	NA	261	6.5	0.0	0.0	0.0	93.5	52.1	45.5	2.3	62	62.9	100.0	0.0
Delmita CDP	216	NA	NA	63	0.0	0.0	0.0	0.0	100.0	17.4	55.6	27.0	33	66.7	84.8	0.0
Del Rio city	35,926	36,079	0.4	36,081	13.9	0.8	0.6	0.6	84.1	29.8	56.3	13.8	11,368	64.5	57.4	18.7

1 May be of any race.

Table A. All Places — **Population and Housing**

STATE City, town, township, borough, or CDP (county if applicable)	Population: 2010 census total population	Population: 2014 estimated population	Population: Percent change 2010-2014	Population: ACS total population estimate 2010-2014	Race and Hispanic or Latino origin (percent), 2010–2014: White alone, not Hispanic or Latino	Race: Black alone, not Hispanic or Latino	Race: Asian alone, not Hispanic or Latino	Race: All other races or 2 or more races, not Hispanic or Latino	Race: Hispanic or Latino[1]	Age (percent), 2010–2014: Under 18 years old	Age: Age 18 to 64 years old	Age: Age 65 years and older	Households, 2010–2014: Total occupied housing units	Households: Percent owner occupied	Householders by level of education (percent): High school diploma or less	Householders by level of education (percent): Bachelor's degree or more
	1	2	3	4	5	6	7	8	9	10	11	12	13	14	15	16
TEXAS—Con.																
Del Sol CDP	239	NA	NA	457	19.9	0.0	0.0	0.0	80.1	28.5	64.6	7.0	122	100.0	54.1	19.7
Denison city	22,697	22,907	0.9	22,745	77.3	8.1	0.6	4.5	9.4	24.0	58.3	17.8	9,101	62.0	44.5	17.0
Denton city	116,207	128,205	10.3	122,742	59.5	10.6	4.4	3.3	22.2	20.4	70.8	8.7	42,961	48.5	22.8	39.0
Denver City town	4,479	4,707	5.1	4,577	30.9	1.1	1.5	1.0	65.5	29.2	57.8	13.0	1,515	75.8	68.3	10.2
Deport city	578	567	-1.9	472	86.9	2.3	0.0	2.8	8.1	18.4	61.8	19.7	205	63.4	52.7	7.8
DeSoto city	49,027	51,934	5.9	50,837	16.2	68.3	0.4	2.0	13.2	25.3	61.8	12.8	18,720	64.8	26.9	32.2
Detroit town	732	706	-3.6	738	71.1	20.3	0.0	7.0	1.5	22.6	65.7	11.5	283	59.4	52.3	12.7
Devers city	447	452	1.1	454	39.4	20.9	0.0	1.5	38.1	27.9	59.1	13.0	152	92.8	65.1	4.6
Devine city	4,348	4,582	5.4	4,471	38.6	0.5	0.2	0.0	60.7	33.9	51.0	15.2	1,422	65.8	38.4	12.1
Deweyville CDP	1,023	NA	NA	1,091	100.0	0.0	0.0	0.0	0.0	9.9	67.6	22.4	394	89.8	51.0	10.7
D'Hanis CDP	847	NA	NA	1,038	39.1	0.0	0.0	0.0	60.9	28.2	50.9	20.7	312	84.6	58.3	19.9
Diboll city	5,402	5,378	-0.4	5,377	36.8	16.7	0.1	1.2	45.2	29.8	60.7	9.5	1,572	65.0	50.3	6.9
Dickens city	286	256	-10.5	242	87.2	0.0	0.0	0.8	12.0	12.8	55.3	31.8	110	79.1	60.9	6.4
Dickinson city	18,679	19,595	4.9	19,135	53.8	12.8	3.1	1.1	29.3	25.6	63.4	11.0	6,407	69.7	39.4	25.6
Dilley city	3,894	4,158	6.8	4,029	17.6	9.3	0.3	0.1	72.6	23.8	67.5	8.8	775	65.9	73.2	5.8
Dimmitt city	4,393	4,263	-3.0	4,394	25.1	0.5	0.6	2.3	71.6	33.8	53.8	12.4	1,367	72.9	59.2	18.4
DISH town	201	349	73.6	227	83.3	1.3	2.6	0.0	12.8	19.5	70.9	9.7	95	78.9	47.4	18.9
Dodd City town	369	366	-0.8	360	93.6	0.3	0.0	6.1	0.0	32.8	54.8	12.5	120	77.5	58.3	16.7
Dodson town	109	108	-0.9	177	15.8	0.0	0.0	0.0	84.2	28.9	44.0	27.1	41	100.0	85.4	4.9
Doffing CDP	5,091	NA	NA	5,059	1.2	2.1	0.0	0.0	96.7	38.7	57.2	4.2	1,274	74.5	86.5	0.3
Domino town	78	77	-1.3	79	0.0	100.0	0.0	0.0	0.0	19.0	64.6	16.5	28	89.3	28.6	28.6
Donna city	15,759	16,448	4.4	16,169	8.3	0.3	0.4	0.0	91.0	35.3	53.0	11.7	4,570	61.7	69.5	9.9
Doolittle CDP	2,769	NA	NA	3,597	3.3	0.0	0.0	0.0	96.7	43.8	47.4	8.8	837	84.9	71.1	7.0
Dorchester city	87	88	1.1	73	71.2	0.0	0.0	0.0	28.8	24.7	49.2	26.0	31	58.1	25.8	29.0
Double Oak town	2,867	3,034	5.8	2,951	90.5	0.8	1.7	1.1	5.9	27.7	60.4	11.9	900	93.3	13.4	56.6
Douglassville town	229	227	-0.9	106	79.2	13.2	0.0	4.7	2.8	13.2	46.2	40.6	61	88.5	72.1	9.8
Doyle CDP	254	NA	NA	113	83.2	0.0	0.0	0.0	16.8	8.8	91.2	0.0	27	66.7	33.3	66.7
Driftwood CDP	144	NA	NA	84	100.0	0.0	0.0	0.0	0.0	0.0	90.4	9.5	55	45.5	25.5	74.5
Dripping Springs city	2,020	2,231	10.4	2,088	57.4	0.3	1.3	5.6	35.4	27.6	58.7	13.7	722	66.8	43.1	28.5
Driscoll city	745	757	1.6	744	23.0	0.0	0.0	0.0	77.0	30.8	53.9	15.3	238	79.8	66.4	8.4
Dublin city	3,654	3,623	-0.8	3,658	64.4	0.1	0.0	2.0	33.5	30.1	59.5	10.5	1,324	60.0	54.3	14.0
Dumas city	14,691	14,937	1.7	14,908	36.6	2.0	6.8	1.7	52.8	32.4	57.6	10.0	4,542	69.1	56.1	16.3
Duncanville city	38,544	39,707	3.0	39,315	30.4	30.6	1.4	1.2	36.5	26.8	60.0	13.1	13,812	67.4	36.7	30.6
Eagle Lake city	3,637	3,607	-0.8	3,611	22.8	26.4	0.0	0.0	50.8	27.5	59.3	13.2	1,289	61.2	70.4	10.0
Eagle Pass city	26,247	28,329	7.9	27,463	3.7	0.2	0.3	0.4	95.5	31.5	55.2	13.3	8,543	62.6	53.0	21.2
Early city	2,790	2,794	0.1	2,797	81.6	0.9	0.0	1.1	16.4	27.1	58.1	14.9	904	72.2	38.7	26.9
Earth city	1,065	1,029	-3.4	827	38.5	2.9	0.0	0.0	58.6	28.3	54.2	17.4	292	74.0	67.5	12.3
East Alto Bonito CDP	824	NA	NA	1,075	0.0	0.0	0.0	0.0	100.0	25.9	71.3	2.7	284	100.0	94.7	2.1
East Bernard city	2,271	2,280	0.4	2,745	68.5	6.7	0.3	0.3	24.3	28.2	58.0	13.8	992	73.4	46.3	17.8
Eastland city	3,956	3,862	-2.4	3,919	84.3	0.8	0.2	4.3	10.4	17.4	62.0	20.7	1,607	78.2	53.6	15.8
East Lopez CDP	166	NA	NA	117	0.0	0.0	0.0	0.0	100.0	35.9	64.2	0.0	39	100.0	41.0	0.0
East Mountain city	791	808	2.1	1,081	86.0	0.0	0.0	0.0	14.0	31.0	52.1	16.8	352	82.7	55.1	6.0
Easton city	510	499	-2.2	468	7.1	65.0	0.0	0.0	28.0	23.3	63.8	12.8	157	86.6	58.0	8.3
East Tawakoni city	878	889	1.3	935	86.3	0.0	4.0	6.5	3.2	19.5	58.0	22.6	346	88.4	48.3	13.0
Ector city	695	690	-0.7	847	87.7	1.3	4.0	4.7	2.2	29.7	58.2	11.9	288	64.2	43.4	13.9
Edcouch city	3,161	3,276	3.6	3,217	2.8	0.0	0.0	0.0	97.2	34.4	50.7	14.9	933	62.7	75.5	4.7
Eden city	2,762	2,766	0.1	2,578	27.8	1.3	0.4	0.2	70.3	10.8	76.8	12.6	370	68.9	52.4	17.8
Edgecliff Village town	2,776	2,953	6.4	2,883	48.8	14.1	2.2	1.2	33.7	22.0	58.7	19.3	952	85.1	34.8	27.3
Edgewater Estates CDP	72	NA	NA	127	8.7	0.0	0.0	0.0	91.3	44.9	46.5	8.7	38	71.1	100.0	0.0
Edgewood town	1,437	1,441	0.3	1,434	78.2	12.3	0.0	1.5	8.0	24.3	57.4	18.4	543	58.7	60.8	12.9
Edinburg city	74,565	83,014	11.3	79,002	7.2	1.5	2.7	0.5	88.2	31.1	61.1	7.8	23,575	55.6	40.2	29.4
Edmonson town	111	106	-4.5	92	34.8	0.0	0.0	4.3	60.9	30.5	64.2	5.4	40	62.5	40.0	20.0
Edna city	5,492	5,764	5.0	5,616	42.5	14.2	0.0	1.9	41.4	28.5	56.6	14.9	1,859	65.2	57.7	15.1
Edom city	373	375	0.5	249	76.7	0.0	0.0	0.0	23.3	27.7	56.5	15.7	87	87.4	40.2	18.4
Edroy CDP	331	NA	NA	187	0.0	0.0	0.0	7.0	93.0	11.2	76.5	12.3	84	69.0	69.0	0.0
Eidson Road CDP	8,960	NA	NA	10,643	1.0	0.0	0.0	0.0	99.0	36.1	57.0	6.8	2,659	79.0	81.4	2.0
Elbert CDP	30	NA	NA	63	100.0	0.0	0.0	0.0	0.0	33.3	38.1	28.6	22	59.1	63.6	18.2
El Brazil CDP	47	NA	NA	59	0.0	0.0	0.0	0.0	100.0	5.1	10.2	84.7	30	100.0	90.0	0.0
El Camino Angosto CDP	253	NA	NA	135	80.0	0.0	0.0	0.0	20.0	22.2	66.0	11.9	27	100.0	59.3	40.7
El Campo city	11,602	11,577	-0.2	11,549	38.3	11.6	0.1	0.0	50.0	28.8	55.1	16.1	3,831	69.8	62.0	16.1
El Castillo CDP	188	NA	NA	295	0.0	0.0	0.0	0.0	100.0	43.1	57.0	0.0	50	100.0	100.0	0.0
El Cenizo CDP	249	NA	NA	386	0.0	0.0	0.0	0.0	100.0	44.0	49.7	6.2	74	100.0	100.0	0.0
El Cenizo city	3,273	3,292	0.6	3,302	0.1	0.3	0.0	0.0	99.6	42.0	53.8	4.4	758	76.4	86.7	1.3
El Chaparral CDP	464	NA	NA	98	30.6	0.0	0.0	0.0	69.4	22.4	55.2	22.4	42	100.0	54.8	45.2
Eldorado city	1,951	1,784	-8.6	1,925	40.5	0.2	0.5	0.2	58.6	28.7	62.1	9.2	645	71.8	60.3	18.0
Electra city	2,791	2,748	-1.5	2,764	83.1	3.8	0.0	5.3	7.7	19.3	57.1	23.6	1,175	66.9	61.4	11.6
Elgin city	8,135	8,622	6.0	8,224	37.4	16.2	0.0	1.9	44.5	31.2	55.9	12.9	2,804	70.2	57.8	14.8
Elias-Fela Solis CDP	30	NA	NA	24	0.0	0.0	0.0	0.0	100.0	0.0	0.0	100.0	13	100.0	100.0	0.0
El Indio CDP	190	NA	NA	209	0.0	0.0	0.0	0.0	100.0	11.0	54.9	34.0	82	100.0	48.8	0.0
Elkhart town	1,371	1,335	-2.6	1,475	74.4	12.0	0.0	4.9	8.7	28.1	53.9	18.0	481	60.5	60.7	9.6
El Lago city	2,706	2,774	2.5	2,755	87.0	1.2	1.9	2.8	7.0	21.3	62.4	16.2	1,116	81.2	20.1	59.0
Elm Creek CDP	2,469	NA	NA	2,776	0.0	0.0	0.0	0.0	100.0	36.5	60.7	2.8	669	77.6	75.0	6.6
Elmendorf city	1,488	1,637	10.0	1,325	28.0	3.5	0.5	1.7	66.3	17.3	70.1	12.8	478	86.4	61.5	4.8
El Mesquite CDP	38	NA	NA	0	0.0	0.0	0.0	0.0	0.0	0.0	0.0	0.0	0	0.0	0.0	0.0
Elmo CDP	768	NA	NA	1,037	100.0	0.0	0.0	0.0	0.0	41.9	34.6	23.4	315	55.9	76.2	19.0
El Paso city	649,133	679,036	4.6	669,771	14.8	3.1	1.1	1.2	79.7	28.0	60.5	11.6	218,490	59.3	42.4	24.5
El Quiote CDP	208	NA	NA	204	0.0	0.0	0.0	0.0	100.0	35.3	64.7	0.0	49	77.6	77.6	22.4
El Rancho Vela CDP	274	NA	NA	218	0.0	0.0	0.0	0.0	100.0	33.4	65.3	1.4	61	100.0	49.2	21.3
El Refugio CDP	331	NA	NA	435	0.0	0.0	0.0	0.0	100.0	25.6	57.6	16.8	127	100.0	78.0	0.0
Elsa city	5,654	6,617	17.0	6,232	0.7	0.0	0.0	0.0	99.3	34.4	51.6	13.9	1,883	52.4	80.7	4.2
El Socio CDP	130	NA	NA	163	0.0	0.0	0.0	0.0	100.0	24.5	75.4	0.0	63	100.0	76.2	0.0
Emerald Bay CDP	1,047	NA	NA	943	96.1	3.1	0.0	0.0	0.8	8.4	28.7	62.9	449	90.0	15.8	37.4
Emhouse town	133	135	1.5	141	68.1	0.0	0.0	10.6	21.3	19.1	68.8	12.1	51	74.5	66.7	15.7
Emory city	1,231	1,238	0.6	1,160	77.6	5.3	0.1	0.7	16.4	20.4	58.4	21.1	461	46.4	50.8	12.6
Encantada-Ranchito-El Calaboz CDP	2,255	NA	NA	2,049	0.9	0.0	0.0	0.0	99.1	36.7	48.0	15.2	539	82.0	86.8	1.3
Enchanted Oaks town	326	333	2.1	296	91.6	0.3	0.0	3.0	5.1	7.4	40.0	52.4	136	97.8	31.6	36.0
Encinal city	559	580	3.8	874	2.2	0.0	0.0	0.0	97.8	25.4	57.1	17.4	285	74.4	87.0	1.1
Encino CDP	143	NA	NA	83	0.0	0.0	0.0	0.0	100.0	7.2	67.4	25.3	55	7.3	74.5	0.0
Ennis city	18,511	18,823	1.7	18,674	48.8	11.8	0.6	2.0	36.8	30.3	58.6	11.2	6,307	53.4	51.9	14.5
Escobares city	2,347	2,418	3.0	2,003	0.8	0.3	0.0	0.0	98.8	26.7	56.2	17.0	541	74.9	83.5	5.7

1 May be of any race.

Table A. All Places — **Population and Housing**

STATE City, town, township, borough, or CDP (county if applicable)	Population: 2010 census total population	Population: 2014 estimated population	Population: Percent change 2010-2014	Population: ACS total population estimate 2010-2014	Race and Hispanic or Latino origin (percent), 2010–2014: White alone, not Hispanic or Latino	Race: Black alone, not Hispanic or Latino	Race: Asian alone, not Hispanic or Latino	Race: All other races or 2 or more races, not Hispanic or Latino	Race: Hispanic or Latino[1]	Age (percent), 2010–2014: Under 18 years old	Age: Age 18 to 64 years old	Age: Age 65 years and older	Households, 2010–2014: Total occupied housing units	Households: Percent owner occupied	Householders by level of education (percent): High school diploma or less	Householders by level of education (percent): Bachelor's degree or more
	1	2	3	4	5	6	7	8	9	10	11	12	13	14	15	16
TEXAS—Con.																
Estelline town	145	137	-5.5	155	55.5	3.9	0.0	0.0	40.6	22.6	60.8	16.8	45	73.3	57.8	4.4
Eugenio Saenz CDP	159	NA	NA	151	0.0	0.0	0.0	0.0	100.0	46.4	53.7	0.0	33	100.0	100.0	0.0
Euless city	51,295	53,630	4.6	52,649	53.7	10.2	11.6	4.7	19.9	24.4	67.5	8.2	21,315	43.1	27.3	34.4
Eureka city	310	309	-0.3	314	87.6	0.6	0.0	6.4	5.4	21.4	60.2	18.5	137	75.2	32.8	33.6
Eustace city	996	988	-0.8	1,259	94.0	0.3	0.0	0.2	5.5	31.1	57.8	11.1	398	52.8	48.7	18.3
Evadale CDP	1,483	NA	NA	1,669	95.7	0.0	1.9	0.1	2.3	26.2	58.9	14.9	560	77.7	60.9	5.9
Evant town	426	412	-3.3	465	79.8	0.6	0.0	1.3	18.3	27.3	65.0	7.7	156	53.2	52.6	11.5
Evergreen CDP	73	NA	NA	0	0.0	0.0	0.0	0.0	0.0	0.0	0.0	0.0	0	0.0	0.0	0.0
Everman city	6,108	6,315	3.4	6,213	26.1	18.3	0.2	4.5	50.9	29.9	59.6	10.5	1,932	70.5	65.4	4.1
Fabens CDP	8,257	NA	NA	8,282	1.0	0.0	0.0	0.0	99.0	36.4	54.2	9.5	2,116	64.7	81.2	1.7
Fabrica CDP	923	NA	NA	945	2.4	0.0	0.0	0.0	97.6	34.6	48.5	16.9	220	76.4	63.6	23.6
Fairchilds village	785	969	23.4	746	58.3	0.0	0.0	0.0	41.7	30.9	60.8	8.3	259	92.3	60.6	11.2
Fairfield city	2,951	2,909	-1.4	2,909	57.6	24.5	0.7	0.9	16.3	25.3	59.0	15.9	1,119	67.2	43.8	15.8
Fair Oaks Ranch city	5,966	6,914	15.9	6,534	82.4	0.0	1.0	1.3	15.3	23.1	53.3	23.5	2,279	95.2	7.0	68.1
Fairview town	7,248	8,361	15.4	7,882	90.2	2.3	2.0	3.2	2.3	19.2	54.7	26.2	3,263	82.0	13.6	65.5
Falconaire CDP	132	NA	NA	58	0.0	0.0	0.0	0.0	100.0	48.3	51.7	0.0	17	100.0	0.0	0.0
Falcon Heights CDP	53	NA	NA	30	0.0	0.0	0.0	0.0	100.0	0.0	100.0	0.0	15	100.0	0.0	0.0
Falcon Lake Estates CDP	1,036	NA	NA	1,683	13.9	0.0	0.0	0.0	86.1	47.9	45.8	6.2	430	79.5	40.9	7.4
Falcon Mesa CDP	405	NA	NA	657	27.2	0.0	0.0	0.0	72.8	26.5	65.0	8.5	246	100.0	53.3	4.1
Falcon Village CDP	47	NA	NA	58	27.6	0.0	0.0	0.0	72.4	0.0	72.5	27.6	43	0.0	62.8	0.0
Falfurrias city	4,978	4,944	-0.7	4,683	9.6	0.1	1.3	0.0	89.0	23.7	58.5	17.7	1,532	56.3	70.0	12.3
Falls City city	611	655	7.2	485	85.2	0.0	0.0	0.4	14.4	15.7	68.1	16.3	214	83.2	42.5	27.1
Falman CDP	76	NA	NA	108	100.0	0.0	0.0	0.0	0.0	37.9	26.8	35.2	51	78.4	21.6	25.5
Fannett CDP	2,252	NA	NA	2,003	86.0	1.4	5.3	0.0	7.3	22.8	64.7	12.2	745	89.1	50.3	26.2
Farmers Branch city	28,616	32,560	13.8	30,261	48.4	3.3	5.3	2.1	40.8	24.9	61.6	13.4	11,091	59.1	34.6	37.7
Farmersville city	3,303	3,427	3.8	3,393	73.5	6.8	0.5	2.0	17.2	20.2	66.1	13.7	1,344	56.3	54.5	13.4
Farwell city	1,363	1,312	-3.7	1,741	63.1	4.5	0.0	0.1	32.3	27.4	55.9	16.8	633	84.0	56.4	16.1
Fate city	6,439	8,812	36.9	7,643	63.0	10.7	3.2	4.6	18.4	33.8	60.3	6.0	2,435	91.9	16.8	42.2
Fayetteville city	258	260	0.8	293	95.6	3.4	0.0	0.0	1.0	13.3	59.8	27.0	146	76.7	45.2	26.7
Faysville CDP	439	NA	NA	785	0.0	0.0	0.0	0.0	100.0	39.0	55.3	5.7	208	27.4	66.3	15.4
Fernando Salinas CDP	15	NA	NA	8	0.0	0.0	0.0	0.0	100.0	0.0	50.0	50.0	4	100.0	100.0	0.0
Ferris city	2,436	2,508	3.0	2,469	44.9	18.8	0.4	2.7	33.2	28.8	59.4	11.7	783	71.9	59.4	12.0
Fifth Street CDP	2,486	NA	NA	2,362	1.0	0.0	0.0	0.8	98.1	45.1	50.6	4.3	549	59.2	96.4	3.6
Flatonia town	1,385	1,386	0.1	1,575	38.0	7.6	1.6	0.0	52.8	24.8	56.0	19.2	567	72.8	61.7	11.3
Flor del Rio CDP	122	NA	NA	110	0.0	0.0	0.0	0.0	100.0	66.4	33.6	0.0	17	100.0	100.0	0.0
Florence city	1,137	1,219	7.2	918	59.3	0.0	1.7	0.0	39.0	21.2	65.4	13.5	338	59.2	53.0	11.2
Floresville city	6,448	7,149	10.9	6,813	37.2	1.8	0.1	0.7	60.2	23.0	57.6	19.4	2,476	66.7	55.0	9.8
Flowella CDP	118	NA	NA	74	0.0	0.0	0.0	0.0	100.0	24.3	55.5	20.3	41	82.9	65.9	17.1
Flower Mound town	64,685	69,650	7.7	67,630	76.2	3.8	9.1	2.3	8.5	30.3	63.2	6.3	21,952	89.3	10.0	63.7
Floydada city	3,038	2,806	-7.6	2,946	30.9	3.4	0.0	0.3	65.5	29.9	54.1	16.0	1,143	64.2	58.2	13.6
Follett city	459	493	7.4	567	72.8	0.0	1.1	5.8	20.3	27.7	58.6	13.8	178	80.9	51.7	19.7
Forest Hill city	12,355	12,795	3.6	12,612	10.4	47.9	0.4	1.3	40.0	31.0	57.7	11.2	3,943	73.6	52.6	10.8
Forney city	14,608	17,536	20.0	16,017	71.4	6.4	0.3	4.0	17.9	33.5	59.5	7.0	5,081	86.2	32.2	31.9
Forsan city	210	222	5.7	232	64.2	0.0	0.0	1.7	34.1	37.1	51.7	11.2	66	69.7	40.9	15.2
Fort Bliss CDP	8,591	NA	NA	8,450	45.4	23.4	3.8	6.0	21.4	27.1	72.7	0.2	1,245	0.5	20.2	28.8
Fort Clark Springs CDP	1,228	NA	NA	1,083	80.0	0.0	0.0	0.0	20.0	22.6	57.4	20.2	485	86.8	34.6	20.2
Fort Davis CDP	1,201	NA	NA	1,132	38.5	0.0	1.2	1.8	58.5	20.4	52.4	27.2	525	79.8	42.1	33.0
Fort Hancock CDP	1,750	NA	NA	1,590	2.1	0.0	0.8	0.0	97.2	33.8	51.9	14.5	493	89.7	83.4	6.5
Fort Hood CDP	29,589	NA	NA	32,177	50.5	19.6	2.0	6.2	21.6	33.2	66.7	0.1	5,682	0.7	27.8	13.5
Fort Stockton city	8,289	8,482	2.3	8,373	21.4	3.4	0.0	1.2	74.0	25.6	62.0	12.6	2,425	61.9	54.8	15.0
Fort Worth city	742,060	812,238	9.5	778,573	40.9	18.7	3.7	2.5	34.2	28.8	62.4	8.6	268,884	57.7	38.3	29.8
Four Corners CDP	12,382	NA	NA	13,973	7.7	21.6	34.4	2.2	34.1	31.6	63.0	5.5	3,295	77.0	36.3	30.5
Four Points CDP	18	NA	NA	0	0.0	0.0	0.0	0.0	0.0	0.0	0.0	0.0	0	0.0	0.0	0.0
Fowlerton CDP	55	NA	NA	135	100.0	0.0	0.0	0.0	0.0	60.8	39.3	0.0	26	100.0	100.0	0.0
Franklin city	1,613	1,608	-0.3	2,045	74.6	14.7	0.0	2.3	8.4	29.6	51.7	18.8	639	46.0	59.5	13.8
Frankston town	1,229	1,185	-3.6	1,106	78.5	17.6	0.0	0.7	3.2	21.0	57.1	21.9	432	67.1	50.5	24.1
Fredericksburg city	10,530	10,886	3.4	10,707	76.2	0.5	0.0	2.0	21.3	18.1	50.5	31.2	4,650	63.1	34.6	36.9
Freeport city	12,049	12,191	1.2	12,108	29.9	11.4	0.1	0.2	58.4	29.9	61.3	8.7	4,074	59.0	67.3	6.6
Freer city	2,818	2,760	-2.1	2,781	14.4	1.3	0.0	0.9	83.4	32.6	56.2	11.3	775	75.6	71.7	1.9
Fresno CDP	19,069	NA	NA	20,374	4.9	67.4	0.6	2.4	24.6	34.8	61.3	3.7	5,642	83.0	31.0	35.5
Friendswood city	35,803	38,248	6.8	37,001	75.8	3.0	4.8	1.6	14.9	25.7	60.6	13.8	13,032	79.9	15.7	53.0
Friona city	4,123	3,969	-3.7	4,059	21.6	0.7	0.0	0.3	77.4	29.5	59.0	11.6	1,188	69.0	67.6	13.6
Frisco city	117,084	145,035	23.9	130,499	64.1	7.5	11.6	3.7	13.1	32.6	60.8	6.6	43,491	74.8	10.9	62.4
Fritch city	2,113	2,076	-1.8	2,743	92.9	0.3	0.3	1.6	4.8	29.8	57.9	12.4	958	85.9	42.9	13.9
Fronton CDP	180	NA	NA	93	0.0	0.0	0.0	0.0	100.0	12.9	49.5	37.6	44	100.0	100.0	0.0
Fronton Ranchettes CDP	113	NA	NA	200	20.5	0.0	0.0	0.0	79.5	27.0	73.0	0.0	66	37.9	37.9	62.1
Frost city	643	645	0.3	729	59.4	2.9	0.0	0.0	37.7	32.9	56.4	10.6	245	84.1	55.5	15.5
Fruitvale city	408	410	0.5	561	85.4	2.3	0.0	3.7	8.6	34.8	55.6	9.6	173	57.8	76.9	2.9
Fulshear city	1,169	4,306	268.3	2,284	59.5	12.2	3.9	6.4	18.0	33.3	58.7	8.0	747	91.7	18.2	57.8
Fulton town	1,358	1,498	10.3	1,225	73.1	1.1	6.4	2.9	16.7	15.2	53.1	31.8	551	60.8	43.7	18.7
Gail CDP	231	NA	NA	301	81.4	0.0	0.0	1.0	17.6	32.6	48.8	18.6	105	58.1	43.8	38.1
Gainesville city	16,002	16,095	0.6	16,040	61.7	5.2	1.1	2.6	29.3	25.9	59.7	14.5	6,004	54.9	52.8	16.0
Galena Park city	10,916	11,178	2.4	11,093	14.3	5.9	0.0	0.0	79.7	30.5	60.9	8.5	3,005	67.4	61.9	6.4
Gallatin city	419	417	-0.5	283	91.9	1.8	0.0	0.0	6.4	11.0	77.4	11.7	129	78.3	62.0	17.1
Galveston city	47,745	49,608	3.9	48,513	44.7	19.5	4.2	1.5	30.0	19.1	66.5	14.2	20,401	45.1	38.1	33.0
Ganado city	1,994	2,082	4.4	1,888	45.2	5.9	0.0	3.7	45.2	30.1	51.9	18.1	654	67.4	69.6	8.4
Garceno CDP	420	NA	NA	499	0.0	0.0	0.0	0.0	100.0	38.0	61.8	0.0	108	92.6	84.3	15.7
Garciasville CDP	46	NA	NA	58	0.0	0.0	0.0	0.0	100.0	62.1	38.0	0.0	11	0.0	100.0	0.0
Garden City CDP	334	NA	NA	319	67.1	0.0	0.0	0.0	32.9	18.4	64.9	16.6	135	60.0	29.6	23.7
Gardendale CDP	1,574	NA	NA	1,084	73.1	11.3	2.9	3.9	8.9	22.0	58.3	19.8	432	77.3	39.8	15.5
Garden Ridge city	3,259	3,742	14.8	3,514	77.3	7.2	0.5	2.2	12.9	23.2	55.0	21.8	1,312	97.7	5.6	72.5
Garfield CDP	1,698	NA	NA	1,576	35.7	6.9	0.6	0.6	56.2	31.7	58.0	10.2	549	86.5	46.8	17.1
Garland city	226,871	235,501	3.8	232,305	32.1	12.8	10.6	4.4	40.1	28.6	61.5	10.0	74,989	63.9	43.1	24.0
Garrett town	802	814	1.5	950	29.2	3.2	1.7	0.9	65.1	38.8	56.1	4.9	277	55.2	63.5	4.0
Garrison city	895	896	0.1	837	55.4	20.7	4.8	3.8	15.3	29.4	45.9	24.7	327	50.2	47.1	12.5
Gary City town	308	306	-0.6	394	99.7	0.0	0.0	0.0	0.3	29.4	57.1	13.5	132	84.8	62.9	6.8
Garza-Salinas II CDP	719	NA	NA	694	0.0	0.0	0.0	0.0	100.0	32.6	60.2	7.2	154	83.8	87.7	0.0
Gatesville city	15,745	15,872	0.8	15,946	51.6	16.6	0.6	7.1	24.1	16.0	77.1	7.1	2,839	56.3	55.8	13.3
Georgetown city	47,455	59,102	24.5	53,007	70.6	3.2	0.7	1.5	24.0	22.2	50.6	27.3	20,769	71.4	23.5	48.1
George West city	2,439	2,590	6.2	2,500	36.5	0.9	3.0	2.3	57.3	31.1	52.6	16.4	649	73.8	62.7	10.2
Geronimo CDP	1,032	NA	NA	1,085	62.8	0.0	0.0	0.0	37.2	21.5	71.4	7.0	315	78.4	61.9	24.8

1 May be of any race.

Table A. All Places — **Population and Housing**

STATE City, town, township, borough, or CDP (county if applicable)	Population: 2010 census total population	Population: 2014 estimated population	Population: Percent change 2010-2014	Population: ACS total population estimate 2010-2014	Race and Hispanic or Latino origin (percent), 2010–2014: White alone, not Hispanic or Latino	Black alone, not Hispanic or Latino	Asian alone, not Hispanic or Latino	All other races or 2 or more races, not Hispanic or Latino	Hispanic or Latino[1]	Age (percent), 2010–2014: Under 18 years old	Age 18 to 64 years old	Age 65 years and older	Households, 2010–2014: Total occupied housing units	Percent owner occupied	Householders by level of education (percent): High school diploma or less	Bachelor's degree or more
	1	2	3	4	5	6	7	8	9	10	11	12	13	14	15	16
TEXAS—Con.																
Gholson city	1,061	1,076	1.4	864	90.5	0.1	2.0	0.3	7.1	16.2	63.5	20.6	373	77.7	46.1	16.6
Giddings city	4,881	5,042	3.3	4,942	40.6	15.7	0.1	0.5	43.0	29.8	56.1	14.1	1,496	62.4	63.4	18.1
Gilmer city	4,896	5,158	5.4	5,031	58.2	20.3	0.0	1.3	20.2	28.1	55.6	16.3	1,536	63.8	48.7	18.4
Girard CDP	50	NA	NA	49	83.7	0.0	0.0	0.0	16.3	28.6	44.9	26.5	22	100.0	86.4	0.0
Gladewater city	6,435	6,432	0.0	6,461	72.0	20.3	0.6	1.6	5.5	22.8	62.2	15.0	2,261	57.1	47.7	12.5
Glenn Heights city	11,278	11,915	5.6	11,671	24.7	55.6	0.7	3.7	15.2	31.6	60.5	7.8	3,801	70.9	32.2	27.4
Glen Rose city	2,444	2,544	4.1	2,506	77.6	0.3	0.0	2.4	19.8	22.6	56.3	21.1	962	52.5	33.5	37.5
Glidden CDP	661	NA	NA	367	54.2	18.5	0.0	2.5	24.8	26.4	50.7	22.9	130	66.9	43.8	13.1
Godley city	1,005	1,050	4.5	1,202	87.2	0.0	0.0	0.0	12.8	34.2	56.0	9.7	386	55.4	52.6	14.5
Goldsmith city	257	272	5.8	231	91.8	0.0	0.0	1.7	6.5	15.6	72.8	11.7	96	80.2	40.6	8.3
Goldthwaite city	1,878	1,851	-1.4	2,235	82.2	0.1	0.0	0.1	17.6	30.1	48.3	21.6	809	73.8	47.3	19.0
Goliad city	1,908	2,001	4.9	2,248	36.2	6.0	0.9	0.2	56.8	24.0	59.3	16.5	842	66.6	51.5	20.4
Golinda city	559	552	-1.3	440	68.0	30.0	0.0	0.0	2.0	24.3	59.8	15.9	163	70.6	35.6	11.7
Gonzales city	7,237	7,461	3.1	7,317	31.7	9.6	0.4	0.0	58.4	29.7	55.0	15.3	2,165	58.8	60.2	13.6
Goodlow city	200	199	-0.5	205	5.9	93.2	0.0	0.0	1.0	12.7	68.7	18.5	98	70.4	64.3	5.1
Goodrich city	273	262	-4.0	282	38.3	23.4	0.0	4.3	34.0	28.4	66.4	5.3	91	68.1	61.5	5.5
Gordon city	478	474	-0.8	479	92.5	0.0	0.0	0.6	6.9	24.0	52.2	23.8	191	87.4	48.2	26.7
Goree city	203	211	3.9	188	59.6	5.9	0.0	0.0	34.6	19.2	49.9	30.9	79	88.6	74.7	12.7
Gorman city	1,083	1,049	-3.1	850	75.9	0.9	0.0	0.4	22.8	25.4	47.6	26.8	359	77.4	60.2	12.0
Graford city	584	579	-0.9	746	80.6	0.0	0.0	1.2	18.2	31.9	58.4	9.7	215	75.8	61.4	1.4
Graham city	8,908	8,864	-0.5	8,840	74.4	1.7	0.4	0.0	23.5	26.6	56.8	16.5	3,384	64.2	53.1	17.6
Granbury city	7,978	9,052	13.5	8,496	85.7	2.2	0.4	1.8	9.9	19.4	52.2	28.5	3,721	38.1	40.6	23.9
Grand Acres CDP	49	NA	NA	0	0.0	0.0	0.0	0.0	0.0	0.0	0.0	0.0	0	0.0	0.0	0.0
Grandfalls town	360	390	8.3	374	25.1	0.0	0.0	0.8	74.1	34.8	50.0	15.2	115	57.4	76.5	9.6
Grand Prairie city	175,468	185,453	5.7	181,135	27.9	20.3	6.5	2.0	43.3	29.7	63.3	7.0	58,531	61.7	41.1	25.7
Grand Saline city	3,136	3,094	-1.3	3,109	67.4	0.3	0.0	4.4	27.9	28.0	56.7	15.2	967	59.2	61.7	12.1
Grandview city	1,561	1,584	1.5	1,463	72.8	4.5	0.0	0.1	22.6	29.7	57.7	12.6	521	60.8	51.8	15.2
Granger city	1,417	1,493	5.4	1,617	61.2	2.5	0.4	1.0	34.9	24.7	63.2	12.0	495	71.5	49.3	16.4
Granite Shoals city	4,910	4,996	1.8	4,954	56.7	0.0	0.0	0.6	42.6	29.5	53.0	17.5	1,620	77.8	54.6	15.6
Granjeno city	293	299	2.0	313	0.0	0.0	0.0	15.0	85.0	15.6	63.6	20.8	90	94.4	60.0	8.9
Grape Creek CDP	3,154	NA	NA	2,888	76.4	0.0	0.9	0.0	22.7	27.8	56.1	16.2	1,116	78.2	47.8	12.7
Grapeland city	1,489	1,422	-4.5	1,857	67.4	29.9	0.0	0.6	2.0	21.6	55.2	23.2	706	63.7	58.5	16.1
Grapevine city	46,334	50,844	9.7	48,671	70.9	1.9	4.1	3.5	19.6	24.7	66.3	9.2	19,349	57.9	22.0	48.3
Grays Prairie village	337	355	5.3	339	97.3	0.0	0.0	1.5	1.2	21.6	68.7	9.7	125	88.8	53.6	8.8
Greatwood CDP	11,538	NA	NA	12,657	68.2	3.4	8.4	3.7	16.2	32.7	53.5	13.9	4,067	93.4	8.7	69.4
Green Valley Farms CDP	1,272	NA	NA	892	0.0	0.0	0.0	0.0	100.0	16.3	80.0	3.6	188	91.0	73.4	0.0
Greenville city	25,557	26,180	2.4	25,892	56.7	15.3	1.8	2.1	24.1	25.5	59.9	14.6	9,575	53.7	47.7	20.2
Gregory city	1,907	1,972	3.4	2,096	5.1	0.0	3.6	0.0	91.3	29.8	59.5	10.7	635	64.7	70.7	8.8
Grey Forest city	483	503	4.1	499	77.8	0.0	5.4	2.2	14.6	23.4	51.4	25.1	195	77.9	13.8	50.8
Groesbeck city	4,320	4,321	0.0	4,325	57.5	13.0	1.1	1.1	27.3	28.7	58.0	13.2	1,254	70.7	51.0	15.2
Groom town	574	563	-1.9	456	88.4	0.0	0.7	3.7	7.2	22.2	60.8	17.1	208	85.1	28.8	18.8
Groves city	16,144	15,753	-2.4	15,911	69.5	5.5	2.6	1.9	20.4	23.5	59.6	16.9	6,283	74.4	45.8	13.2
Groveton city	1,057	1,017	-3.8	1,575	65.3	15.4	0.0	0.4	18.9	31.9	49.5	18.6	418	54.5	55.3	9.1
Gruver city	1,195	1,167	-2.3	1,097	57.7	0.0	2.0	1.4	38.9	26.9	59.0	14.0	417	73.4	48.2	24.0
Guadalupe Guerra CDP	37	NA	NA	19	0.0	0.0	0.0	0.0	100.0	36.9	47.4	15.8	3	100.0	100.0	0.0
Guerra CDP	6	NA	NA	0	0.0	0.0	0.0	0.0	0.0	0.0	0.0	0.0	0	0.0	0.0	0.0
Gun Barrel City city	5,667	5,956	5.1	5,805	91.0	1.6	0.0	2.3	5.1	17.6	59.3	23.0	2,437	70.7	53.3	15.6
Gunter city	1,498	1,486	-0.8	1,569	62.3	2.0	0.0	0.7	35.0	28.4	54.2	17.3	458	60.5	30.8	27.3
Gustine town	476	459	-3.6	490	46.3	0.0	0.0	0.0	53.7	22.5	64.6	12.9	153	79.7	65.4	18.3
Guthrie CDP	160	NA	NA	158	87.3	0.0	0.0	0.0	12.7	12.6	67.8	19.6	75	21.3	50.7	25.3
Gutierrez CDP	79	NA	NA	31	0.0	0.0	0.0	0.0	100.0	42.0	58.1	0.0	18	100.0	66.7	0.0
Hackberry town	968	1,000	3.3	1,370	28.6	7.2	7.8	0.4	56.1	28.9	66.7	4.5	405	80.5	44.4	33.8
Hale Center city	2,252	2,139	-5.0	2,711	30.3	2.2	0.0	1.1	66.4	33.1	48.9	18.0	923	73.1	65.9	10.1
Hallettsville city	2,550	2,598	1.9	2,569	69.8	15.8	0.3	0.6	13.5	25.2	52.1	22.7	1,033	59.5	55.2	17.0
Hallsburg city	507	518	2.2	487	91.8	0.0	0.0	0.2	8.0	24.3	60.8	15.0	182	87.9	36.3	14.3
Hallsville city	3,567	3,905	9.5	3,799	93.8	1.6	0.3	2.9	1.4	24.3	63.0	12.5	1,319	78.8	32.2	33.6
Haltom City city	42,409	43,913	3.5	43,259	45.0	5.6	6.6	2.0	40.9	27.7	61.4	10.8	15,049	55.9	57.3	12.6
Hamilton city	3,097	2,962	-4.4	3,018	83.5	1.1	0.3	1.1	14.1	19.1	53.9	26.9	1,126	69.4	55.3	12.6
Hamlin city	2,124	2,037	-4.1	1,773	70.0	6.0	0.0	1.9	22.1	29.2	50.6	20.1	789	74.0	59.1	14.7
Happy town	678	658	-2.9	764	64.9	0.1	0.0	1.8	33.1	32.5	51.8	15.8	247	83.0	46.6	25.1
Hardin city	829	853	2.9	819	86.0	1.1	9.9	2.6	0.5	23.7	50.2	26.0	348	65.5	60.9	15.2
Hargill CDP	877	NA	NA	295	0.0	0.0	0.0	0.0	100.0	29.9	43.9	26.4	127	82.7	92.9	0.0
Harker Heights city	26,718	28,526	6.8	27,757	52.5	14.7	4.4	6.7	21.8	30.0	62.7	7.2	8,901	60.9	22.4	33.9
Harlingen city	64,918	65,914	1.5	65,677	17.7	1.3	1.0	0.4	79.6	30.4	56.1	13.4	20,562	58.8	50.5	21.0
Harper CDP	1,192	NA	NA	1,056	93.0	0.0	0.0	1.0	6.0	22.1	59.2	18.8	467	79.2	49.3	26.8
Hart city	1,114	1,062	-4.7	1,279	15.7	0.5	0.0	2.4	81.3	22.0	60.9	17.0	337	71.5	78.6	6.2
Hartley CDP	540	NA	NA	512	50.2	0.6	0.0	0.0	49.2	36.6	54.8	8.8	175	54.9	63.4	19.4
Haskell city	3,322	3,246	-2.3	3,300	60.7	4.3	1.6	1.2	32.2	18.8	63.9	17.2	1,139	68.6	54.5	20.3
Haslet city	1,517	1,719	13.3	1,529	76.9	4.3	0.0	4.6	14.2	26.4	62.4	11.4	548	91.1	19.9	40.5
Havana CDP	407	NA	NA	500	12.0	0.0	0.0	0.0	88.0	35.8	59.2	5.0	135	42.2	54.8	28.9
Hawk Cove city	483	489	1.2	417	84.2	0.7	0.0	8.4	6.7	17.7	65.5	16.8	165	85.5	60.6	0.0
Hawkins city	1,264	1,285	1.7	1,764	69.5	15.8	0.0	4.3	10.5	31.9	54.5	13.5	436	73.4	39.7	15.6
Hawley city	632	611	-3.3	780	98.1	0.0	0.0	1.9	0.0	35.5	51.6	12.9	298	81.9	40.9	21.8
Hays city	217	217	0.0	335	68.7	0.0	0.6	0.3	30.4	20.0	67.3	12.8	109	82.6	39.4	39.4
H. Cuellar Estates CDP	20	NA	NA	27	0.0	0.0	0.0	0.0	100.0	22.2	77.7	0.0	6	100.0	0.0	100.0
Hearne city	4,458	4,416	-0.9	4,443	20.1	43.4	0.0	0.0	36.5	27.8	57.8	14.4	1,526	58.5	76.8	4.8
Heath city	7,311	7,999	9.4	7,620	95.1	0.5	1.1	0.1	3.1	24.5	59.8	15.8	2,583	98.1	9.0	64.6
Hebbronville CDP	4,558	NA	NA	4,627	3.3	2.3	0.0	0.8	93.5	24.0	56.6	19.4	1,570	73.4	62.2	12.5
Hebron town	390	404	3.6	581	70.9	6.9	10.0	0.5	11.7	31.2	58.6	10.2	193	94.8	8.8	67.4
Hedley city	329	312	-5.2	363	75.8	0.0	0.0	1.1	23.1	26.0	50.7	23.4	113	77.9	42.5	13.3
Hedwig Village city	2,557	2,677	4.7	2,635	66.1	1.6	16.5	3.4	12.4	29.1	57.1	13.7	959	65.3	14.6	68.2
Heidelberg CDP	1,725	NA	NA	2,311	2.9	0.0	0.0	0.0	97.1	40.7	57.1	2.1	496	66.9	59.9	16.3
Helotes city	7,341	8,364	13.9	7,880	58.6	3.4	4.4	3.4	30.1	27.4	55.7	16.7	2,658	90.4	17.0	52.4
Hemphill city	1,257	1,199	-4.6	1,248	85.3	8.3	0.0	0.0	6.5	28.8	49.4	21.8	394	75.1	60.2	5.6
Hempstead city	5,773	6,699	16.0	6,197	24.3	46.2	0.0	1.9	27.6	24.8	66.5	8.7	2,000	50.7	56.0	6.7
Henderson city	13,712	13,604	-0.8	13,723	52.0	26.7	1.4	1.0	19.0	20.9	65.3	13.7	3,947	67.2	46.1	20.1
Henrietta city	3,141	3,016	-4.0	3,074	95.4	0.2	0.3	2.7	1.4	28.6	53.0	18.4	1,069	76.8	44.6	18.1
Hereford city	15,370	15,216	-1.0	15,330	23.9	1.0	0.3	1.2	73.7	34.2	55.1	10.9	4,832	66.2	61.9	12.8
Hermleigh CDP	345	NA	NA	382	64.9	0.8	0.0	0.8	33.5	29.3	59.9	10.7	137	73.0	51.8	32.8
Hewitt city	13,548	14,166	4.6	13,905	71.3	6.7	4.3	4.0	13.8	22.5	65.3	12.2	5,135	70.4	24.8	39.1
Hickory Creek town	3,247	4,007	23.4	3,605	76.0	1.9	2.3	7.3	12.5	25.4	65.6	9.1	1,250	90.3	23.8	37.8

1 May be of any race.

Table A. All Places — **Population and Housing**

STATE City, town, township, borough, or CDP (county if applicable)	Population				Race and Hispanic or Latino origin (percent), 2010–2014					Age (percent), 2010–2014			Households, 2010–2014			
	2010 census total population	2014 estimated population	Percent change 2010-2014	ACS total population estimate 2010-2014	White alone, not Hispanic or Latino	Black alone, not Hispanic or Latino	Asian alone, not Hispanic or Latino	All other races or 2 or more races, not Hispanic or Latino	Hispanic or Latino[1]	Under 18 years old	Age 18 to 64 years old	Age 65 years and older	Total occupied housing units	Percent owner occupied	Householders by level of education (percent): High school diploma or less	Householders by level of education (percent): Bachelor's degree or more
	1	2	3	4	5	6	7	8	9	10	11	12	13	14	15	16
TEXAS—Con.																
Hico city	1,379	1,330	-3.6	1,707	82.7	0.8	0.5	0.5	15.6	25.7	53.7	20.8	585	53.8	46.3	16.6
Hidalgo city	12,522	13,497	7.8	13,063	1.0	0.0	0.2	0.0	98.8	37.9	54.6	7.5	2,872	73.5	61.0	22.5
Hideaway city	3,083	3,194	3.6	3,154	98.2	0.0	0.0	1.0	0.8	4.4	40.8	54.9	1,673	98.5	14.2	44.9
Higgins city	397	429	8.1	454	90.7	0.0	0.0	5.5	3.7	31.0	55.4	13.7	161	71.4	59.6	18.6
Highland Haven city	431	443	2.8	385	97.1	0.0	0.0	0.8	2.1	11.7	45.3	42.9	198	89.4	26.3	43.9
Highland Park town	8,564	8,950	4.5	8,796	88.8	0.0	2.3	2.3	6.6	28.6	54.9	16.5	3,414	81.7	3.5	84.5
Highlands CDP	7,522	NA	NA	7,775	65.5	3.9	0.3	0.4	29.9	29.7	59.4	10.8	2,618	72.9	48.7	9.5
Highland Village city	15,085	15,995	6.0	15,589	88.1	2.1	1.6	1.8	6.4	26.8	62.2	10.9	5,018	95.3	8.2	60.9
Hill Country Village city	985	1,050	6.6	874	80.9	1.8	2.4	0.5	14.4	16.7	61.8	21.6	297	97.0	5.7	75.8
Hillcrest village	730	739	1.2	776	87.2	0.0	0.0	0.8	12.0	15.3	54.6	30.0	301	94.7	16.6	46.8
Hillsboro city	8,437	8,350	-1.0	8,394	40.2	15.9	0.3	1.2	42.4	29.0	56.4	14.5	2,873	50.3	53.1	12.2
Hillside Acres CDP	30	NA	NA	0	0.0	0.0	0.0	0.0	0.0	0.0	0.0	0.0	0	0.0	0.0	0.0
Hilltop CDP (Frio)	287	NA	NA	120	0.0	0.0	0.0	0.0	100.0	0.0	92.5	7.5	69	100.0	72.5	0.0
Hilltop CDP (Starr)	77	NA	NA	30	0.0	0.0	0.0	0.0	100.0	0.0	100.0	0.0	19	100.0	100.0	0.0
Hilltop Lakes CDP	1,101	NA	NA	1,012	100.0	0.0	0.0	0.0	0.0	9.9	52.2	37.9	476	95.2	53.4	35.9
Hilshire Village city	746	796	6.7	606	79.9	0.0	8.3	5.3	6.6	23.8	51.6	24.6	255	93.7	9.8	77.6
Hitchcock city	6,961	7,442	6.9	7,206	45.0	29.7	0.3	1.2	23.8	26.2	58.6	15.4	2,741	64.8	51.3	9.2
Holiday Beach CDP	514	NA	NA	362	76.8	0.0	0.0	0.8	22.4	0.0	59.4	40.6	244	87.7	32.4	12.3
Holiday Lakes town	1,121	1,167	4.1	1,093	36.5	6.0	0.0	0.6	56.8	38.0	54.6	7.4	324	81.8	78.1	4.0
Holland town	1,121	1,123	0.2	1,018	67.6	6.6	0.0	1.5	24.4	30.2	60.1	9.8	295	71.9	60.3	6.4
Holliday city	1,760	1,728	-1.8	1,717	91.7	0.0	0.7	0.0	7.6	25.6	63.4	11.1	617	78.8	58.0	17.5
Holly Lake Ranch CDP	2,774	NA	NA	2,981	91.1	0.0	0.0	1.3	7.6	14.9	39.2	45.8	1,254	93.7	26.8	33.7
Hollywood Park town	3,091	3,258	5.4	3,179	82.8	0.0	2.0	4.2	11.0	16.7	46.5	36.9	1,334	86.3	13.6	59.5
Homestead Meadows North CDP	5,124	NA	NA	4,974	5.8	0.0	0.0	0.0	94.2	37.6	54.7	7.5	1,220	74.3	66.6	12.6
Homestead Meadows South CDP	7,247	NA	NA	5,831	0.6	0.0	0.0	0.0	99.4	29.6	66.9	3.5	1,582	81.9	77.1	3.2
Hondo city	8,803	9,056	2.9	8,929	27.7	9.2	0.0	1.0	62.1	21.2	68.2	10.5	2,145	57.7	56.0	16.6
Honey Grove city	1,668	1,666	-0.1	1,991	59.6	16.4	0.0	2.2	21.8	26.9	53.1	19.8	706	71.0	57.9	15.0
Hooks city	2,769	2,751	-0.7	2,762	68.6	13.4	0.0	4.0	14.0	29.5	56.6	13.9	1,072	44.9	62.6	9.4
Horizon City city	16,730	19,332	15.6	18,477	14.6	1.6	0.8	1.5	81.5	40.4	54.8	4.8	4,771	87.3	35.4	22.7
Hornsby Bend CDP	6,791	NA	NA	7,355	9.8	35.5	0.3	1.2	53.2	31.0	65.0	3.9	2,058	73.7	51.9	13.3
Horseshoe Bay city	3,418	3,471	1.6	3,487	93.1	3.6	0.0	0.9	2.4	12.4	38.6	48.8	1,747	88.8	22.7	43.0
Horseshoe Bend CDP	789	NA	NA	703	78.7	0.0	0.0	17.8	3.6	18.2	54.0	27.9	283	100.0	51.9	27.9
Houston city	2,096,661	2,239,558	6.8	2,167,988	25.5	22.8	6.3	1.5	43.9	25.3	65.3	9.5	792,763	44.5	40.5	33.7
Howardwick city	402	380	-5.5	475	87.6	0.0	0.4	1.7	10.3	19.6	44.9	35.6	191	95.3	65.4	10.5
Howe town	2,600	2,614	0.5	2,600	84.1	0.2	4.8	2.7	8.2	27.7	59.9	12.5	943	68.0	40.1	17.2
Hubbard city	1,423	1,395	-2.0	1,592	60.1	34.7	0.0	1.1	4.1	30.7	51.4	18.0	608	63.7	52.6	12.8
Hudson city	4,727	4,773	1.0	4,758	62.7	7.7	1.5	3.7	24.4	35.3	58.0	6.7	1,547	57.1	43.1	14.1
Hudson Bend CDP	2,981	NA	NA	2,878	69.4	0.4	7.9	1.7	20.7	23.5	65.3	11.1	1,224	78.3	17.2	52.8
Hudson Oaks city	1,674	1,974	17.9	1,952	89.9	1.6	0.2	1.1	7.2	20.4	65.7	13.9	714	94.4	20.6	43.4
Hughes Springs city	1,760	1,770	0.6	1,983	58.3	30.6	0.3	4.4	6.5	28.5	50.5	21.0	658	53.0	56.7	9.6
Hull CDP	669	NA	NA	540	100.0	0.0	0.0	0.0	0.0	12.0	48.9	39.1	296	100.0	81.1	0.0
Humble city	15,127	15,616	3.2	15,402	25.4	20.9	3.7	6.4	43.5	25.4	63.3	11.2	5,446	45.0	42.0	18.1
Hungerford CDP	347	NA	NA	93	20.4	79.6	0.0	0.0	0.0	0.0	79.6	20.4	39	0.0	100.0	0.0
Hunters Creek Village city	4,367	4,692	7.4	4,545	83.8	2.1	6.9	2.5	4.7	29.2	56.8	13.9	1,474	96.5	2.3	91.2
Huntington city	2,112	2,106	-0.3	2,169	88.1	5.1	0.0	1.7	5.1	30.2	54.1	15.6	817	63.2	51.5	7.0
Huntsville city	38,550	40,435	4.9	39,764	50.1	27.7	1.7	0.9	19.6	14.3	78.4	7.3	10,617	35.3	28.9	26.6
Hurst city	37,335	38,733	3.7	38,140	68.6	5.7	2.4	1.8	21.5	23.8	60.7	15.5	14,578	65.6	37.6	27.8
Hutchins city	5,338	5,430	1.7	5,410	23.8	36.3	0.0	2.1	37.8	25.1	67.1	7.7	1,444	77.4	62.0	9.6
Hutto city	16,459	21,170	28.6	18,839	47.2	13.5	0.3	2.4	36.5	31.9	62.7	5.4	5,789	88.3	27.1	26.4
Huxley city	375	375	0.0	336	100.0	0.0	0.0	0.0	0.0	22.4	39.4	38.4	144	93.1	55.6	5.6
Iago CDP	161	NA	NA	372	16.7	1.9	0.0	0.0	81.5	67.0	31.3	1.9	69	21.7	11.6	33.3
Idalou city	2,295	2,330	1.5	2,369	54.5	0.4	2.8	2.7	39.6	31.6	54.7	13.8	814	66.0	46.8	21.9
Iglesia Antigua CDP	413	NA	NA	370	0.0	0.0	0.0	0.0	100.0	22.4	73.7	3.8	86	94.2	93.0	0.0
Impact town	35	35	0.0	9	22.2	0.0	0.0	0.0	77.8	0.0	100.0	0.0	9	77.8	77.8	22.2
Imperial CDP	278	NA	NA	302	48.0	0.0	0.0	1.0	51.0	22.8	65.7	11.6	94	73.4	46.8	7.4
Indian Hills CDP	2,591	NA	NA	2,460	2.9	1.3	0.0	0.0	95.8	39.8	56.5	3.7	520	83.1	91.9	1.3
Indian Lake town	640	644	0.6	992	26.1	0.0	0.0	0.0	73.9	29.6	52.0	18.3	334	77.5	56.3	13.8
Indian Springs CDP	785	NA	NA	799	93.9	0.0	0.0	2.9	3.3	33.9	59.9	6.4	342	60.8	61.7	19.6
Indio CDP	50	NA	NA	0	0.0	0.0	0.0	0.0	0.0	0.0	0.0	0.0	0	0.0	0.0	0.0
Industry city	304	313	3.0	254	72.4	11.0	0.0	7.5	9.1	15.3	51.6	33.1	124	75.0	71.8	25.8
Inez CDP	2,098	NA	NA	2,260	85.4	0.0	0.0	1.2	13.5	26.7	61.8	11.5	743	76.2	38.4	23.3
Ingleside city	9,381	9,639	2.8	9,468	49.5	2.3	2.3	0.8	45.0	32.1	58.9	8.9	3,101	67.2	39.1	14.2
Ingleside on the Bay city	615	638	3.7	579	72.4	0.0	0.7	6.7	20.2	14.1	63.1	22.8	221	79.2	28.5	27.6
Ingram city	1,790	1,815	1.4	2,176	63.6	0.4	0.0	0.9	35.1	29.3	60.2	10.8	680	64.7	64.7	6.6
Iola city	401	408	1.7	603	69.3	0.8	0.0	7.6	22.2	36.1	51.3	12.6	197	73.6	69.0	8.6
Iowa Colony village	1,164	1,213	4.2	1,399	42.2	6.9	8.1	0.6	42.0	20.9	66.4	12.9	445	83.4	49.9	16.0
Iowa Park city	6,372	6,391	0.3	6,375	90.8	0.0	0.0	4.9	4.2	27.6	57.4	15.0	2,487	79.8	45.8	17.1
Iraan city	1,229	1,259	2.4	1,336	40.6	2.2	0.0	0.0	57.1	29.8	58.8	11.5	439	64.5	44.2	27.1
Iredell city	339	331	-2.4	368	79.6	0.0	0.0	2.7	17.7	19.3	60.9	19.8	155	89.0	54.2	21.3
Irving city	216,287	232,406	7.5	224,859	28.5	12.3	15.2	2.3	41.7	27.3	65.7	7.1	82,817	38.7	35.5	36.7
Italy town	1,857	1,883	1.4	1,888	70.0	10.6	0.0	0.0	19.4	29.5	55.1	15.4	709	75.2	55.1	8.5
Itasca city	1,644	1,621	-1.4	1,780	54.8	16.3	0.0	1.6	27.2	26.4	61.5	12.1	629	69.2	60.1	7.8
Ivanhoe city	1,427	1,404	-1.6	1,177	86.4	5.5	0.0	6.1	2.0	12.6	58.4	29.1	587	74.8	55.0	20.4
Jacinto City city	10,553	10,809	2.4	10,717	9.1	3.5	0.1	0.4	86.8	31.2	59.7	9.2	2,987	57.9	82.6	3.6
Jacksboro city	4,511	4,413	-2.2	4,481	68.2	7.8	0.2	1.2	22.6	21.5	67.1	11.3	1,169	60.9	54.7	14.1
Jacksonville city	14,537	14,675	0.9	14,654	39.5	21.9	0.5	1.3	36.9	31.1	56.9	12.1	4,794	54.1	57.5	12.9
Jamaica Beach city	983	1,030	4.8	991	84.4	0.9	0.0	2.2	12.5	12.4	64.7	22.7	495	73.7	21.4	30.5
Jardin de San Julian CDP	22	NA	NA	26	0.0	0.0	0.0	0.0	100.0	26.9	53.8	19.2	5	100.0	100.0	0.0
Jarrell city	994	1,097	10.4	899	72.3	2.3	0.0	0.8	24.6	23.9	63.2	12.8	312	76.0	51.0	20.2
Jasper city	7,603	7,637	0.4	7,688	31.7	50.2	0.3	1.7	16.1	31.4	54.8	13.8	2,272	51.5	65.3	11.0
Jayton city	534	515	-3.6	599	80.1	0.2	0.0	0.2	19.5	24.0	51.4	24.5	253	70.0	47.4	18.6
Jefferson city	2,106	2,045	-2.9	2,210	53.7	42.8	0.4	0.8	2.4	21.0	54.4	24.7	902	66.6	52.5	21.3
Jersey Village city	7,620	7,906	3.8	7,795	67.2	7.0	8.2	1.1	16.4	16.4	65.9	17.8	3,342	60.8	24.8	40.9
Jewett city	1,173	1,174	0.1	1,196	57.0	6.4	0.0	1.7	34.9	27.9	63.3	8.7	381	67.7	69.3	7.3
JF Villarreal CDP	104	NA	NA	33	0.0	0.0	0.0	0.0	100.0	0.0	36.4	63.6	12	100.0	100.0	0.0
Joaquin city	822	823	0.1	781	75.2	17.8	0.0	1.2	5.9	32.8	55.4	11.8	318	64.2	53.1	11.0
Johnson City city	1,667	1,860	11.6	1,716	60.5	0.1	0.0	1.5	37.9	28.5	56.6	14.9	666	62.5	41.0	25.2
Jolly city	172	166	-3.5	148	98.6	0.0	0.0	1.4	0.0	12.2	61.4	26.4	70	94.3	44.3	15.7
Jones Creek village	2,063	2,082	0.9	2,335	65.5	0.5	0.0	1.7	32.3	26.6	60.2	13.4	819	93.4	49.9	10.6

1 May be of any race.

Table A. All Places — **Population and Housing**

STATE City, town, township, borough, or CDP (county if applicable)	Population: 2010 census total population	Population: 2014 estimated population	Population: Percent change 2010-2014	Population: ACS total population estimate 2010-2014	Race and Hispanic or Latino origin (percent), 2010–2014: White alone, not Hispanic or Latino	Race and Hispanic or Latino origin (percent), 2010–2014: Black alone, not Hispanic or Latino	Race and Hispanic or Latino origin (percent), 2010–2014: Asian alone, not Hispanic or Latino	Race and Hispanic or Latino origin (percent), 2010–2014: All other races or 2 or more races, not Hispanic or Latino	Race and Hispanic or Latino origin (percent), 2010–2014: Hispanic or Latino[1]	Age (percent), 2010–2014: Under 18 years old	Age (percent), 2010–2014: Age 18 to 64 years old	Age (percent), 2010–2014: Age 65 years and older	Households, 2010–2014: Total occupied housing units	Households, 2010–2014: Percent owner occupied	Households, 2010–2014: Householders by level of education (percent): High school diploma or less	Households, 2010–2014: Householders by level of education (percent): Bachelor's degree or more
	1	2	3	4	5	6	7	8	9	10	11	12	13	14	15	16
TEXAS—Con.																
Jonestown city	1,833	2,021	10.3	2,115	77.3	1.5	2.2	2.5	16.5	16.6	71.5	11.8	896	81.7	25.6	30.2
Josephine city	812	1,117	37.6	791	82.7	2.7	0.5	1.5	12.6	23.3	64.4	12.1	265	87.2	49.4	19.2
Joshua city	5,887	6,002	2.0	5,935	81.7	1.8	0.3	3.2	13.0	32.3	54.6	13.1	2,181	75.3	49.9	16.6
Jourdanton city	3,871	4,191	8.3	4,034	47.8	0.3	0.0	0.1	51.7	24.2	57.6	18.3	1,547	77.0	66.8	6.9
Juarez CDP	1,017	NA	NA	260	0.0	0.0	0.0	0.0	100.0	0.0	85.4	14.6	136	100.0	100.0	0.0
Junction city	2,571	2,472	-3.9	2,766	68.9	0.0	0.0	0.7	30.3	21.9	58.8	19.3	1,227	68.9	58.7	11.2
Justin city	3,246	3,372	3.9	3,314	86.2	0.3	0.4	3.9	9.1	25.0	65.4	9.5	1,124	74.3	30.6	25.2
Karnes City city	3,041	3,315	9.0	3,162	23.3	4.3	0.5	0.0	71.9	25.6	62.0	12.5	969	65.2	60.5	10.7
Katy city	14,121	15,591	10.4	15,071	65.2	3.1	2.0	0.8	28.9	26.9	60.4	12.8	5,292	74.0	31.5	33.1
Kaufman city	6,703	6,982	4.2	6,837	58.8	9.6	0.5	2.7	28.4	30.2	57.2	12.6	2,362	51.1	51.0	15.6
K-Bar Ranch CDP	358	NA	NA	524	19.3	0.0	0.0	0.0	80.7	14.3	76.1	9.7	197	65.0	38.1	6.6
Keene city	6,086	6,153	1.1	6,089	39.1	7.6	0.9	6.3	46.1	31.8	57.0	11.1	1,828	49.6	45.5	22.5
Keller city	39,633	43,924	10.8	41,913	84.0	2.3	4.0	2.6	7.2	29.4	60.1	10.6	14,170	84.0	13.5	59.9
Kemah city	1,773	1,962	10.7	1,845	77.1	1.7	5.4	0.9	14.9	22.9	65.1	12.1	706	78.6	34.4	35.3
Kemp city	1,154	1,214	5.2	1,469	73.4	10.1	0.0	7.9	8.6	27.9	58.1	13.9	481	60.9	62.0	10.8
Kempner city	1,089	1,083	-0.6	1,133	69.0	4.0	1.3	7.3	18.4	23.5	68.0	8.6	442	69.7	37.8	9.7
Kendleton city	380	391	2.9	326	1.5	93.6	0.0	0.0	4.9	9.8	67.7	22.7	168	67.3	46.4	11.3
Kenedy city	3,312	3,432	3.6	3,385	24.1	2.6	0.8	0.5	71.9	25.9	58.6	15.4	1,226	68.7	56.0	16.3
Kenefick town	563	583	3.6	423	94.3	0.0	0.0	0.0	5.7	13.9	71.3	14.7	174	90.2	65.5	9.8
Kennard city	337	323	-4.2	432	71.3	22.2	0.0	3.0	3.5	29.6	48.3	22.2	175	79.4	49.7	14.3
Kennedale city	6,763	7,394	9.3	7,093	76.6	7.0	3.6	2.7	10.2	22.7	64.8	12.5	2,430	70.2	33.6	26.0
Kerens city	1,573	1,556	-1.1	1,895	66.0	23.2	0.6	3.7	6.5	32.9	50.8	16.1	720	63.1	54.7	10.3
Kermit city	5,708	6,286	10.1	5,894	38.0	2.2	0.0	0.0	59.8	30.6	57.7	11.7	2,129	81.1	54.0	12.2
Kerrville city	22,384	22,905	2.3	22,560	65.7	2.9	1.2	1.9	28.2	19.4	53.1	27.4	9,581	61.0	40.2	29.8
Kilgore city	13,478	14,948	10.9	14,178	65.1	14.0	4.2	1.3	15.4	24.2	62.0	13.9	5,047	63.1	35.8	25.4
Killeen city	127,911	138,154	8.0	134,030	33.4	31.9	3.2	7.1	24.4	30.1	64.4	5.4	45,383	48.4	30.8	18.6
Kingsbury CDP	782	NA	NA	881	78.3	0.0	0.0	0.0	21.7	23.0	53.6	23.4	342	81.0	51.8	31.9
Kingsland CDP	6,030	NA	NA	6,581	82.2	3.6	0.0	0.2	14.0	26.3	52.0	21.7	2,400	67.3	42.8	21.8
Kingsville city	26,213	26,529	1.2	26,348	19.4	4.5	2.4	0.6	73.2	25.7	62.7	11.5	9,195	46.7	40.3	25.5
Kirby city	8,000	8,442	5.5	8,221	28.1	13.3	4.4	3.6	50.6	25.1	61.5	13.5	2,840	67.9	41.8	13.1
Kirbyville city	2,145	2,129	-0.7	2,246	60.5	26.0	0.0	2.0	11.5	26.6	52.8	20.5	856	46.7	69.4	8.1
Kirvin town	129	128	-0.8	156	97.4	0.0	0.0	0.0	2.6	21.2	68.4	10.3	65	83.1	41.5	4.6
Knippa CDP	689	NA	NA	682	22.1	0.0	0.0	0.4	77.4	31.1	54.2	14.8	206	89.8	48.1	16.0
Knollwood city	432	436	0.9	364	86.5	1.9	3.6	3.3	4.7	11.3	69.9	19.0	189	41.8	29.1	15.3
Knox City town	1,130	1,180	4.4	1,144	65.1	1.7	0.0	0.3	33.0	31.4	48.7	19.8	440	69.3	55.0	12.5
Kosse town	464	466	0.4	478	72.6	14.0	0.0	2.9	10.5	16.5	68.0	15.5	196	55.6	73.5	4.6
Kountze city	2,123	2,097	-1.2	2,108	66.3	19.0	1.9	0.9	12.0	27.6	56.9	15.6	750	70.3	60.0	11.3
Kress city	715	691	-3.4	631	25.8	4.0	1.9	7.1	61.2	24.6	58.7	16.6	249	68.7	53.0	13.3
Krugerville city	1,580	1,651	4.5	1,603	88.6	0.5	0.0	1.8	9.1	27.2	60.2	12.7	538	91.3	20.6	43.3
Krum city	4,163	4,919	18.2	4,508	75.7	0.9	0.2	6.3	16.8	35.3	61.1	3.5	1,363	82.1	26.6	31.4
Kurten town	398	399	0.3	351	60.7	3.4	0.0	8.8	27.1	29.3	63.2	7.4	119	79.0	54.6	19.3
Kyle city	28,016	32,881	17.4	30,664	44.1	6.8	0.9	1.6	46.6	34.8	61.2	4.1	9,271	78.8	29.3	33.7
La Blanca CDP	2,488	NA	NA	2,759	0.0	0.0	0.0	0.0	100.0	28.9	61.1	9.9	719	80.8	71.1	9.3
La Carla CDP	70	NA	NA	137	0.0	0.0	0.0	0.0	100.0	46.7	53.2	0.0	20	80.0	100.0	0.0
La Casita CDP	128	NA	NA	0	0.0	0.0	0.0	0.0	0.0	0.0	0.0	0.0	0	0.0	0.0	0.0
La Chuparosa CDP	49	NA	NA	0	0.0	0.0	0.0	0.0	0.0	0.0	0.0	0.0	0	0.0	0.0	0.0
Lackland AFB CDP	9,918	NA	NA	7,926	63.4	11.5	2.2	8.0	14.8	9.6	90.5	0.0	362	0.0	5.8	22.7
La Coma CDP	48	NA	NA	0	0.0	0.0	0.0	0.0	0.0	0.0	0.0	0.0	0	0.0	0.0	0.0
LaCoste city	1,119	1,163	3.9	1,135	43.3	0.7	0.0	2.1	53.9	27.0	55.0	18.1	417	85.6	48.2	13.7
Lacy-Lakeview city	6,489	6,633	2.2	6,569	45.4	29.3	0.9	3.3	21.1	27.6	62.1	10.4	2,601	40.4	39.3	10.6
Ladonia town	612	608	-0.7	659	57.1	34.1	5.6	3.2	0.0	30.2	49.5	20.2	272	64.7	62.5	17.6
La Escondida CDP	153	NA	NA	25	0.0	0.0	0.0	0.0	100.0	36.0	64.0	0.0	5	100.0	100.0	0.0
La Esperanza CDP	229	NA	NA	17	0.0	0.0	0.0	0.0	100.0	0.0	100.0	0.0	9	100.0	100.0	0.0
La Feria city	7,269	7,308	0.5	7,301	12.8	0.0	2.8	0.0	84.3	29.8	53.3	16.7	2,231	63.2	62.9	11.3
La Feria North CDP	212	NA	NA	85	0.0	0.0	0.0	0.0	100.0	0.0	100.0	0.0	42	100.0	100.0	0.0
Lago CDP	204	NA	NA	148	0.0	0.0	0.0	0.0	100.0	50.0	38.5	11.5	36	100.0	100.0	0.0
Lago Vista city	6,083	6,478	6.5	6,349	85.7	1.3	0.2	1.6	11.3	19.5	59.8	20.7	2,543	78.8	19.1	45.1
Lago Vista CDP	115	NA	NA	184	35.9	0.0	0.0	0.0	64.1	39.7	60.3	0.0	39	84.6	64.1	35.9
La Grange city	4,641	4,670	0.6	4,658	56.4	7.8	0.0	0.3	35.5	31.5	50.6	18.1	1,712	63.3	58.4	9.4
La Grulla city	1,622	1,673	3.1	1,312	5.0	0.0	0.1	0.0	95.0	21.0	61.6	17.6	430	79.8	84.0	2.8
Laguna Heights CDP	3,488	NA	NA	3,075	3.0	0.0	0.0	0.0	97.0	42.4	49.8	7.8	842	53.6	83.4	3.2
Laguna Park CDP	1,276	NA	NA	1,478	88.8	0.0	0.0	0.0	11.2	15.2	56.7	28.1	619	80.0	51.5	15.2
Laguna Seca CDP	266	NA	NA	326	1.5	0.0	0.0	0.0	98.5	18.7	73.5	7.7	82	91.5	36.6	0.0
Laguna Vista town	3,142	3,213	2.3	3,197	52.7	0.0	0.9	0.0	46.4	22.8	56.6	20.7	1,314	78.0	34.9	38.5
La Homa CDP	11,985	NA	NA	13,535	4.0	0.0	0.1	0.2	95.6	39.2	54.7	6.2	3,204	77.3	74.2	5.1
La Joya city	3,980	4,219	6.0	4,115	0.9	0.0	0.0	0.0	99.1	36.7	52.8	10.5	1,233	66.7	73.4	8.4
Lake Bridgeport city	340	354	4.1	288	94.4	0.0	0.0	0.7	4.9	13.5	66.0	20.5	134	85.8	48.5	15.7
Lake Brownwood CDP	1,532	NA	NA	1,649	84.8	3.5	0.0	1.3	10.4	25.1	60.2	14.9	628	82.5	66.4	5.9
Lake Bryan CDP	1,728	NA	NA	2,211	43.0	2.7	0.0	0.0	54.3	36.1	53.5	10.5	669	87.9	67.7	5.2
Lake Cherokee CDP	3,071	NA	NA	2,711	86.5	1.9	0.0	0.2	11.4	14.7	62.7	22.5	1,171	84.6	34.5	38.3
Lake City town	509	518	1.8	487	64.3	0.0	1.2	0.0	34.5	25.2	59.5	15.2	184	75.5	42.9	7.6
Lake Colorado City CDP	588	NA	NA	664	86.6	2.6	0.0	3.3	7.5	19.6	63.3	17.0	305	82.3	30.2	18.0
Lake Dallas city	7,105	7,429	4.6	7,306	76.8	2.4	1.1	0.8	18.9	25.9	65.1	8.9	2,748	61.4	32.9	32.4
Lake Dunlap CDP	1,934	NA	NA	2,363	42.8	4.8	0.0	5.4	47.0	24.9	60.7	14.4	804	78.0	61.6	13.6
Lakehills CDP	5,150	NA	NA	5,363	74.6	1.2	0.8	2.8	20.5	19.4	61.9	18.7	2,206	79.6	30.9	20.6
Lake Jackson city	26,830	27,604	2.9	27,224	64.1	7.0	3.8	1.9	23.2	25.0	62.8	12.4	9,984	67.3	24.3	33.3
Lake Kiowa CDP	1,906	NA	NA	2,549	96.1	0.0	0.0	3.9	0.0	7.5	50.8	41.6	1,210	78.8	20.3	40.2
Lake Medina Shores CDP	1,235	NA	NA	926	68.9	0.0	0.0	5.4	25.7	19.5	70.6	9.9	497	78.1	57.9	7.6
Lake Meredith Estates CDP	437	NA	NA	158	100.0	0.0	0.0	0.0	0.0	0.0	64.6	35.4	100	100.0	86.0	0.0
Lakeport city	974	963	-1.1	1,021	29.4	60.1	0.0	1.8	8.7	26.5	59.2	14.2	394	87.8	38.6	14.2
Lakeshore Gardens-Hidden Acres CDP	504	NA	NA	947	35.2	0.0	0.0	0.0	64.8	19.3	57.2	23.7	295	71.9	51.2	6.4
Lakeside town (San Patricio)	312	316	1.3	283	50.5	0.0	0.0	1.8	47.7	23.3	50.3	26.5	111	91.0	63.1	13.5
Lakeside town (Tarrant)	1,307	1,372	5.0	1,418	85.3	2.3	0.4	5.9	6.1	13.8	60.0	26.2	571	94.9	28.2	34.3
Lakeside City town	998	982	-1.6	987	92.9	0.0	0.1	1.9	5.1	23.3	62.0	14.8	353	95.5	22.4	40.5
Lake Tanglewood village	803	858	6.8	721	95.3	0.0	0.7	0.1	3.9	13.6	58.7	27.7	323	98.1	16.7	49.2
Lakeview town	107	101	-5.6	132	22.0	17.4	0.0	0.0	60.6	17.5	62.1	20.5	45	93.3	80.0	4.4
Lake View CDP	199	NA	NA	81	100.0	0.0	0.0	0.0	0.0	0.0	43.2	56.8	49	100.0	16.3	26.5
Lakeway city	11,673	13,685	17.2	12,709	78.9	1.1	5.1	1.6	13.3	25.6	57.0	17.3	4,852	82.1	5.9	68.4

1 May be of any race.

Table A. All Places — **Population and Housing**

STATE City, town, township, borough, or CDP (county if applicable)	Population				Race and Hispanic or Latino origin (percent), 2010–2014					Age (percent), 2010–2014			Households, 2010–2014			
	2010 census total population	2014 estimated population	Percent change 2010-2014	ACS total population estimate 2010-2014	White alone, not Hispanic or Latino	Black alone, not Hispanic or Latino	Asian alone, not Hispanic or Latino	All other races or 2 or more races, not Hispanic or Latino	Hispanic or Latino[1]	Under 18 years old	Age 18 to 64 years old	Age 65 years and older	Total occupied housing units	Percent owner occupied	Householders by level of education (percent) High school diploma or less	Householders by level of education (percent) Bachelor's degree or more
	1	2	3	4	5	6	7	8	9	10	11	12	13	14	15	16
TEXAS—Con.																
Lakewood Village city	545	565	3.7	612	79.6	0.5	1.6	3.9	14.4	28.6	57.1	14.4	221	92.3	14.5	29.0
Lake Worth city	4,584	4,727	3.1	4,671	70.0	0.8	0.6	1.6	27.0	19.4	60.6	20.2	1,963	69.9	48.3	11.9
La Loma de Falcon CDP	95	NA	NA	149	12.8	0.0	0.0	0.0	87.2	36.2	51.0	12.8	50	78.0	78.0	0.0
Lamar CDP	636	NA	NA	848	85.0	3.3	0.0	3.8	7.9	8.3	49.6	42.1	378	65.9	45.0	25.9
La Marque city	14,511	15,521	7.0	14,981	34.7	37.4	1.3	2.3	24.2	27.3	58.6	14.0	5,489	72.8	42.4	16.3
Lamesa city	9,422	9,440	0.2	9,365	38.0	2.5	0.4	0.5	58.7	28.9	54.0	17.2	3,553	72.7	62.9	11.5
La Minita CDP	171	NA	NA	196	0.0	0.0	0.0	0.0	100.0	29.6	48.4	21.9	36	63.9	77.8	0.0
Lampasas city	6,704	7,223	7.7	6,885	65.9	5.0	0.7	2.7	25.7	24.1	55.8	20.0	2,646	60.1	48.3	18.8
Lancaster city	36,655	38,453	4.9	37,731	12.6	64.1	0.2	2.2	20.9	31.6	59.9	8.4	12,840	65.4	41.6	20.9
Lantana CDP	6,874	NA	NA	8,025	79.0	4.6	0.8	3.9	11.7	35.2	59.1	5.7	2,472	90.7	8.8	68.6
La Paloma CDP	2,903	NA	NA	3,128	2.2	0.0	0.0	0.0	97.8	40.5	51.5	8.0	692	92.3	57.5	3.8
La Paloma Addition CDP	330	NA	NA	168	0.0	0.0	0.0	0.0	100.0	15.5	74.4	10.1	54	100.0	100.0	0.0
La Paloma-Lost Creek CDP	408	NA	NA	624	11.7	0.0	0.0	0.0	88.3	31.5	58.0	10.4	173	91.3	62.4	5.2
La Paloma Ranchettes CDP	239	NA	NA	453	0.0	0.0	0.0	0.0	100.0	43.4	56.6	0.0	76	100.0	76.3	0.0
La Porte city	33,800	35,039	3.7	34,473	60.9	5.3	1.0	2.3	30.4	26.1	64.8	9.1	11,606	74.4	41.3	15.7
La Presa CDP	319	NA	NA	300	0.0	0.0	0.0	0.0	100.0	46.3	53.7	0.0	60	38.3	61.7	15.0
La Pryor CDP	1,643	NA	NA	1,562	6.5	0.0	0.0	0.4	93.1	29.5	56.8	13.8	513	79.1	61.2	5.1
La Puerta CDP	632	NA	NA	540	26.3	0.0	0.0	0.0	73.7	33.1	61.1	5.7	155	72.3	94.2	0.6
Laredo city	236,058	252,309	6.9	245,048	3.7	0.3	0.6	0.2	95.3	34.4	57.5	8.2	65,014	61.8	54.6	19.2
Laredo Ranchettes CDP	22	NA	NA	61	32.8	0.0	0.0	0.0	67.2	54.1	45.9	0.0	8	0.0	100.0	0.0
Laredo Ranchettes West CDP	0	NA	NA	0	0.0	0.0	0.0	0.0	100.0	20.3	79.7	0.0	13	100.0	0.0	100.0
La Rosita CDP	85	NA	NA	64	0.0	0.0	0.0	0.0	100.0	20.3	79.7	0.0	13	100.0	0.0	100.0
Lasana CDP	84	NA	NA	52	23.1	0.0	0.0	0.0	76.9	19.2	57.7	23.1	21	100.0	47.6	28.6
Lasara CDP	1,039	NA	NA	881	2.2	0.0	0.0	1.6	96.3	30.4	54.5	15.1	209	91.9	80.9	4.3
Las Haciendas CDP	7	NA	NA	0	0.0	0.0	0.0	0.0	0.0	0.0	0.0	0.0	0	0.0	0.0	0.0
Las Lomas CDP	3,147	NA	NA	3,906	0.0	0.0	0.0	0.0	100.0	37.2	59.1	3.6	764	71.5	91.5	3.0
Las Lomitas CDP	244	NA	NA	403	0.0	0.0	0.0	0.0	100.0	47.1	53.0	0.0	85	89.4	100.0	0.0
Las Palmas CDP	67	NA	NA	17	100.0	0.0	0.0	0.0	0.0	0.0	0.0	100.0	17	100.0	0.0	0.0
Las Palmas II CDP	1,605	NA	NA	1,437	1.3	0.0	0.0	0.0	98.7	33.0	61.9	5.1	350	54.9	80.6	0.0
Las Pilas CDP	28	NA	NA	0	0.0	0.0	0.0	0.0	0.0	0.0	0.0	0.0	0	0.0	0.0	0.0
Las Quintas Fronterizas CDP	3,290	NA	NA	2,489	0.0	0.0	0.0	0.0	100.0	30.5	61.6	8.0	676	81.8	51.5	10.4
Latexo city	322	309	-4.0	308	88.6	0.0	0.0	0.3	11.0	34.7	53.1	12.0	112	60.7	58.0	6.3
La Tina Ranch CDP	618	NA	NA	549	5.8	0.0	0.0	0.0	94.2	27.9	61.5	10.6	167	100.0	51.5	0.0
Laughlin AFB CDP	1,569	NA	NA	1,700	67.1	8.2	3.3	13.0	8.4	17.0	82.9	0.0	582	0.0	0.0	73.4
Laureles CDP	3,692	NA	NA	4,582	15.4	0.0	0.9	0.7	83.1	35.9	58.1	6.0	1,011	70.5	70.6	0.0
La Vernia city	1,031	1,208	17.2	1,471	68.3	0.3	0.0	2.2	29.2	28.2	52.7	19.2	514	74.7	39.1	19.6
La Victoria CDP	171	NA	NA	108	0.0	0.0	0.0	0.0	100.0	0.0	55.6	44.4	33	100.0	100.0	0.0
La Villa city	2,444	2,511	2.7	2,477	1.9	0.0	0.0	0.0	98.1	34.0	54.7	11.1	695	81.2	64.2	5.6
Lavon city	2,219	2,600	17.2	2,367	68.7	18.3	2.2	2.8	8.1	34.8	60.9	4.4	721	83.4	19.4	38.0
La Ward city	213	223	4.7	204	59.3	0.0	0.0	0.0	40.7	28.4	64.3	7.4	63	92.1	42.9	12.7
Lawn town	314	318	1.3	298	82.2	0.0	0.0	1.0	16.8	25.6	53.9	20.5	120	92.5	49.2	11.7
League City city	83,560	94,403	13.0	88,979	65.9	7.4	5.6	2.2	18.9	27.7	64.1	8.3	31,666	71.6	18.9	44.9
Leakey city	425	434	2.1	469	77.8	0.0	0.0	0.0	22.2	19.2	59.7	21.1	160	53.8	49.4	23.1
Leander city	26,262	34,172	30.1	30,040	60.7	3.6	2.4	2.9	30.3	33.0	61.3	5.7	9,122	77.9	26.8	31.8
Leary city	485	483	-0.4	690	90.1	1.2	0.0	3.2	5.5	22.5	68.2	9.3	284	75.0	55.6	14.4
Lefors town	497	512	3.0	330	90.3	0.3	0.0	4.5	4.8	19.7	66.1	14.2	149	68.5	52.3	14.1
Leming CDP	946	NA	NA	656	30.9	0.0	0.0	0.0	69.1	24.6	64.1	11.3	281	86.8	74.4	4.3
Leona city	175	175	0.0	204	94.6	5.4	0.0	0.0	0.0	29.9	63.4	6.9	59	74.6	39.0	30.5
Leonard city	1,978	1,975	-0.2	2,123	78.6	7.2	0.0	1.6	12.7	29.5	54.4	15.7	697	62.8	52.1	15.6
Leon Valley city	10,152	11,015	8.5	10,658	34.2	3.8	3.6	1.8	56.5	20.4	63.2	16.5	4,370	59.1	27.8	36.1
Leroy city	337	341	1.2	327	92.0	4.0	0.0	0.0	4.0	20.4	64.0	15.6	133	96.2	44.4	9.0
Levelland city	13,555	13,954	2.9	13,735	40.3	5.0	0.5	2.2	52.0	26.0	60.0	13.8	4,822	63.7	47.8	14.2
Lewisville city	95,309	102,889	8.0	99,039	49.3	8.5	7.8	4.1	30.2	25.5	66.8	7.8	38,272	44.6	29.8	34.3
Lexington town	1,174	1,169	-0.4	1,551	70.9	16.1	0.0	0.4	12.6	33.7	56.0	10.2	506	64.4	60.7	10.9
Liberty city	8,397	8,919	6.2	8,696	60.9	17.5	0.0	0.6	21.1	27.1	58.1	15.1	2,885	68.6	45.6	20.6
Liberty City CDP	2,351	NA	NA	2,206	79.8	10.4	0.0	1.3	8.5	23.8	62.2	14.0	881	79.2	42.2	10.6
Liberty Hill city	927	1,050	13.3	1,416	72.0	1.7	1.2	0.8	24.3	32.5	60.2	7.6	426	59.6	49.5	18.1
Lincoln Park town	308	321	4.2	288	80.6	1.4	0.0	1.7	16.3	16.3	69.7	13.9	125	57.6	53.6	11.2
Lindale city	4,823	5,502	14.1	5,169	89.1	5.0	0.0	3.2	2.7	32.6	52.8	14.5	1,868	47.3	41.3	25.9
Linden city	1,987	1,971	-0.8	2,466	73.8	14.6	1.0	3.3	7.4	27.0	50.5	22.6	951	46.1	60.5	13.1
Lindsay city	1,019	1,060	4.0	1,095	93.3	0.0	4.3	0.9	1.5	29.1	57.9	13.1	403	82.6	24.6	34.0
Lindsay CDP	271	NA	NA	406	2.5	0.0	0.0	0.0	97.5	25.1	51.7	23.2	99	100.0	100.0	0.0
Linn CDP	801	NA	NA	689	4.5	0.0	0.0	1.2	94.3	36.0	50.7	13.2	204	66.7	60.8	12.7
Lipan city	428	442	3.3	501	88.4	0.0	0.0	0.8	10.8	30.0	54.2	16.0	196	75.0	43.4	16.3
Lipscomb CDP	37	NA	NA	29	79.3	10.3	0.0	0.0	10.3	0.0	48.2	51.7	11	90.9	9.1	0.0
Little Elm city	25,896	35,414	36.8	30,213	54.5	15.4	2.5	4.0	23.7	34.4	60.9	4.7	9,378	80.3	25.0	37.3
Littlefield city	6,377	6,180	-3.1	6,325	37.8	7.0	0.0	1.0	54.3	29.3	55.7	15.0	2,102	68.6	62.4	15.1
Little River-Academy city	1,961	1,950	-0.6	1,940	79.0	0.9	1.9	2.1	16.1	27.3	58.9	13.8	657	78.5	49.2	13.5
Live Oak city	13,131	15,116	15.1	14,213	41.0	15.4	2.8	6.2	34.5	21.5	66.6	11.7	5,548	56.5	27.1	34.9
Liverpool city	486	500	2.9	493	63.7	0.0	0.0	0.0	36.3	31.4	55.5	13.0	176	89.8	46.6	14.2
Livingston town	5,343	5,169	-3.3	5,245	57.2	23.6	1.7	3.6	13.9	23.3	60.4	16.4	2,138	59.1	47.3	20.4
Llano city	3,265	3,324	1.8	3,300	85.1	0.2	0.0	0.4	14.4	18.3	51.7	30.0	1,443	66.7	44.7	29.0
Llano Grande CDP	3,008	NA	NA	2,938	10.1	0.0	0.0	0.0	89.9	26.7	57.4	15.8	766	83.2	64.1	16.1
Lockhart city	12,698	13,232	4.2	12,966	35.3	9.6	0.4	0.9	53.9	23.8	64.2	12.0	4,057	59.1	54.3	18.3
Lockney town	1,842	1,693	-8.1	1,878	38.8	2.6	0.0	3.8	54.8	28.6	51.0	20.6	723	73.9	51.2	12.6
Log Cabin city	714	715	0.1	663	93.4	0.0	0.5	1.1	5.1	10.4	66.5	23.1	290	83.8	61.4	10.3
Lolita CDP	555	NA	NA	480	69.4	0.0	0.0	0.8	29.8	22.5	64.1	13.3	240	72.1	58.8	15.8
Loma Grande CDP	107	NA	NA	19	0.0	0.0	0.0	0.0	100.0	0.0	47.4	52.6	19	100.0	100.0	0.0
Loma Linda CDP	122	NA	NA	55	0.0	0.0	0.0	0.0	100.0	38.2	61.8	0.0	18	100.0	0.0	0.0
Loma Linda East CDP (Jim Wells)	254	NA	NA	351	0.0	0.0	0.0	0.0	100.0	36.2	63.7	0.0	96	79.2	66.7	0.0
Loma Linda East CDP (Starr)	44	NA	NA	0	0.0	0.0	0.0	0.0	0.0	0.0	0.0	0.0	0	0.0	0.0	0.0
Loma Linda West CDP	114	NA	NA	31	0.0	0.0	0.0	0.0	100.0	77.4	22.6	0.0	7	100.0	100.0	0.0
Loma Vista CDP	160	NA	NA	196	0.0	0.0	0.0	16.8	83.2	0.0	79.6	20.4	35	100.0	100.0	0.0
Lometa city	860	854	-0.7	869	45.6	2.3	0.0	0.5	51.7	36.2	52.7	11.2	268	61.2	61.6	4.9
Lone Oak city	598	617	3.2	496	95.8	1.0	0.0	1.0	2.2	32.6	57.3	9.9	171	66.1	53.2	22.8

1 May be of any race.

STATE City, town, township, borough, or CDP (county if applicable)	Population: 2010 census total population	Population: 2014 estimated population	Population: Percent change 2010-2014	Population: ACS total population estimate 2010-2014	Race and Hispanic or Latino origin (percent), 2010–2014: White alone, not Hispanic or Latino	Black alone, not Hispanic or Latino	Asian alone, not Hispanic or Latino	All other races or 2 or more races, not Hispanic or Latino	Hispanic or Latino[1]	Age (percent), 2010–2014: Under 18 years old	Age 18 to 64 years old	Age 65 years and older	Households, 2010–2014: Total occupied housing units	Percent owner occupied	Householders by level of education (percent): High school diploma or less	Bachelor's degree or more
	1	2	3	4	5	6	7	8	9	10	11	12	13	14	15	16
TEXAS—Con.																
Lone Star city	1,581	1,557	-1.5	1,439	58.6	29.0	0.0	3.3	9.0	27.2	51.8	20.9	587	53.7	61.7	14.5
Longoria CDP	92	NA	NA	0	0.0	0.0	0.0	0.0	0.0	0.0	0.0	0.0	0	0.0	0.0	0.0
Longview city	80,455	81,593	1.4	82,030	55.8	22.1	1.2	1.7	19.2	25.7	60.5	13.7	30,535	56.5	38.5	21.8
Loop CDP	225	NA	NA	342	39.5	0.6	0.0	1.5	58.5	31.5	52.2	16.4	117	51.3	56.4	31.6
Lopeño CDP	174	NA	NA	0	0.0	0.0	0.0	0.0	0.0	0.0	0.0	0.0	0	0.0	0.0	0.0
Lopezville CDP	4,333	NA	NA	3,711	0.5	0.0	0.0	0.0	99.5	32.3	52.5	15.2	1,049	63.8	72.7	14.8
Loraine town	602	607	0.8	645	41.9	2.6	0.0	8.4	47.1	24.2	47.8	27.9	293	72.7	80.5	5.8
Lorena city	1,691	1,733	2.5	1,766	83.6	0.0	0.6	3.9	11.8	32.5	56.6	11.0	606	74.1	29.4	25.4
Lorenzo city	1,147	1,147	0.0	1,070	33.1	2.3	0.0	2.0	62.6	33.1	52.1	15.0	369	67.8	60.2	9.8
Los Altos CDP	140	NA	NA	26	0.0	0.0	0.0	0.0	100.0	0.0	38.5	61.5	26	100.0	100.0	0.0
Los Alvarez CDP	303	NA	NA	290	0.0	0.0	0.0	0.0	100.0	14.1	73.7	12.1	92	100.0	100.0	0.0
Los Angeles CDP	121	NA	NA	128	0.0	0.0	0.0	0.0	100.0	64.1	0.0	35.9	21	100.0	100.0	0.0
Los Arcos CDP	127	NA	NA	38	0.0	0.0	0.0	0.0	100.0	52.6	47.4	0.0	9	0.0	100.0	0.0
Los Arrieros CDP	91	NA	NA	53	0.0	0.0	0.0	0.0	100.0	7.5	47.2	45.3	23	100.0	100.0	0.0
Los Barreras CDP	288	NA	NA	269	27.1	0.0	0.0	0.0	72.9	46.0	41.6	12.3	72	100.0	26.4	73.6
Los Centenarios CDP	87	NA	NA	0	0.0	0.0	0.0	0.0	0.0	0.0	0.0	0.0	0	0.0	0.0	0.0
Los Corralitos CDP	35	NA	NA	112	0.0	0.0	0.0	0.0	100.0	0.0	41.1	58.9	79	41.8	100.0	0.0
Los Ebanos CDP (Hidalgo)	335	NA	NA	162	58.6	0.0	0.0	0.0	41.4	9.9	43.9	46.3	91	100.0	75.8	24.2
Los Ebanos CDP (Starr)	280	NA	NA	568	6.5	0.0	0.0	0.0	93.5	33.3	65.3	1.4	150	84.0	100.0	0.0
Los Fresnos city	5,930	6,447	8.7	6,164	8.8	0.0	0.0	0.0	91.1	29.5	59.7	10.8	1,651	74.3	59.4	17.0
Los Fresnos CDP	67	NA	NA	233	0.0	0.0	0.0	0.0	100.0	68.2	23.6	8.2	41	43.9	56.1	0.0
Los Huisaches CDP	17	NA	NA	28	0.0	0.0	0.0	0.0	100.0	32.1	67.9	0.0	10	100.0	0.0	100.0
Los Indios town	1,083	1,110	2.5	1,081	3.7	0.0	0.0	0.0	96.3	27.0	57.0	15.8	308	84.7	78.2	2.9
Los Lobos CDP	9	NA	NA	16	100.0	0.0	0.0	0.0	0.0	0.0	0.0	100.0	8	0.0	100.0	0.0
Los Minerales CDP	20	NA	NA	37	0.0	0.0	0.0	0.0	100.0	16.2	83.8	0.0	25	24.0	76.0	0.0
Los Nopalitos CDP	62	NA	NA	35	0.0	0.0	0.0	0.0	100.0	51.4	48.6	0.0	9	100.0	100.0	0.0
Lost Creek CDP	0	NA	NA	4,651	85.3	0.0	3.6	2.7	8.5	30.3	58.2	11.4	1,620	97.0	1.2	82.1
Los Veteranos I CDP	24	NA	NA	0	0.0	0.0	0.0	0.0	0.0	0.0	0.0	0.0	0	0.0	0.0	0.0
Los Veteranos II CDP	24	NA	NA	77	0.0	0.0	0.0	0.0	100.0	0.0	100.1	0.0	22	100.0	100.0	0.0
Los Ybanez city	19	19	0.0	4	100.0	0.0	0.0	0.0	0.0	0.0	100.0	0.0	4	0.0	100.0	0.0
Lott city	759	729	-4.0	851	64.2	17.4	0.4	3.3	14.8	23.9	58.5	17.6	290	52.4	46.9	13.4
Louise CDP	995	NA	NA	686	75.7	0.0	0.0	0.0	24.3	25.6	61.3	13.1	270	79.6	38.5	27.8
Lovelady city	647	621	-4.0	667	87.6	1.2	1.9	3.1	6.1	32.7	51.3	15.9	234	64.1	44.0	12.8
Lowry Crossing city	1,711	1,779	4.0	1,813	86.0	2.3	0.2	1.2	10.3	21.3	69.4	9.2	646	92.9	31.3	30.5
Lozano CDP	404	NA	NA	462	0.0	0.0	0.0	0.0	100.0	42.9	52.0	5.2	118	80.5	38.1	0.0
Lubbock city	229,399	243,839	6.3	236,868	54.8	7.5	2.3	2.1	33.2	23.5	65.4	11.3	90,394	53.6	31.8	30.4
Lucas city	5,221	6,554	25.5	5,928	92.8	0.0	1.3	0.6	5.3	31.1	59.5	9.3	1,819	85.5	14.1	50.4
Lueders city	346	334	-3.5	178	87.1	0.6	0.0	9.0	3.4	15.2	56.8	28.1	99	80.8	45.5	3.0
Lufkin city	35,064	36,141	3.1	35,754	46.0	28.0	1.2	0.9	23.8	25.2	59.6	15.4	13,252	53.5	43.4	22.8
Luling city	5,411	5,732	5.9	5,569	47.5	8.2	0.0	0.2	44.1	22.0	57.4	20.5	2,019	62.2	53.5	20.4
Lumberton city	11,972	12,312	2.8	12,153	93.8	0.8	0.9	0.6	3.9	26.2	59.5	14.2	4,576	71.7	42.6	18.5
Lyford city	2,611	2,589	-0.8	2,615	5.1	0.0	0.0	0.0	94.9	31.1	58.4	10.4	692	84.4	64.5	13.6
Lytle city	2,497	2,782	11.4	3,025	25.7	0.0	0.3	1.5	72.6	25.3	60.8	13.8	1,006	70.7	58.3	15.9
Mabank town	3,035	3,224	6.2	3,579	83.5	2.9	3.3	1.9	8.4	30.1	55.7	14.3	1,258	44.0	51.0	11.9
McAllen city	130,289	138,596	6.4	135,048	11.3	0.5	2.6	0.7	85.0	28.9	60.3	10.8	42,040	60.3	42.3	30.7
McCamey city	1,887	1,950	3.3	1,810	35.2	4.6	0.0	1.0	59.1	34.5	54.5	10.9	641	72.4	65.2	8.9
McDade CDP	685	NA	NA	874	58.8	0.0	0.0	0.5	40.7	24.1	67.1	8.8	299	79.6	58.2	16.4
Macdona CDP	559	NA	NA	353	39.4	0.0	0.0	0.0	60.6	5.1	68.4	26.3	131	71.0	75.6	6.9
McGregor city	4,987	5,041	1.1	5,041	59.7	9.8	0.0	1.1	29.3	30.1	52.6	17.3	1,590	61.2	49.1	12.8
McKinney city	131,025	156,767	19.6	144,066	62.6	11.2	4.6	2.3	19.3	31.3	60.7	7.8	47,490	68.7	20.6	48.0
McKinney Acres CDP	815	NA	NA	948	19.1	9.8	0.0	1.8	69.3	25.6	70.5	3.8	279	75.3	79.2	9.7
McLean town	778	808	3.9	858	92.7	0.7	0.0	2.0	4.7	29.0	50.8	20.2	299	75.6	56.5	9.7
McLendon-Chisholm city	1,373	1,877	36.7	1,801	83.0	2.3	1.8	3.8	9.1	27.8	56.3	15.9	606	90.8	24.9	38.9
McQueeney CDP	2,545	NA	NA	2,698	65.0	1.7	0.0	3.6	29.6	20.8	64.6	14.7	1,086	75.2	49.6	16.5
Madisonville city	4,396	4,555	3.6	4,479	53.8	21.2	0.0	3.5	21.4	28.9	49.6	21.3	1,683	60.7	61.6	7.7
Magnolia city	1,385	1,654	19.4	1,428	65.5	16.2	2.9	1.8	13.6	23.9	62.8	13.3	544	47.6	49.1	18.9
Malakoff city	2,324	2,312	-0.5	2,817	55.4	24.0	0.7	1.3	18.6	32.7	51.3	15.9	925	54.9	56.2	13.9
Malone town	269	267	-0.7	244	82.4	7.0	0.0	1.2	9.4	30.3	50.5	19.3	91	89.0	51.6	6.6
Manchaca CDP	1,133	NA	NA	1,448	67.5	0.3	0.0	0.0	32.3	16.6	72.1	11.2	493	78.9	35.9	49.7
Manor city	5,044	6,920	37.2	5,936	18.4	31.8	1.5	1.8	46.5	34.7	61.5	3.9	1,727	81.0	39.6	25.1
Mansfield city	56,373	62,246	10.4	59,757	64.5	15.3	4.3	2.5	13.4	30.5	61.4	8.2	19,744	79.0	22.5	43.9
Manuel Garcia CDP	203	NA	NA	246	0.0	0.0	0.0	0.0	100.0	36.6	63.5	0.0	53	100.0	100.0	0.0
Manuel Garcia II CDP	77	NA	NA	238	0.0	0.0	0.0	0.0	100.0	31.1	43.2	25.6	37	100.0	0.0	0.0
Manvel city	5,179	7,165	38.3	6,159	42.4	27.9	0.8	1.9	27.1	27.8	61.4	10.8	2,074	83.3	36.0	24.3
Marathon CDP	430	NA	NA	625	44.5	0.0	0.0	2.7	52.8	14.1	58.6	27.4	307	73.6	48.5	35.2
Marble Falls city	6,082	6,185	1.7	6,137	61.3	5.5	0.0	0.3	32.9	19.5	63.3	17.3	2,606	45.9	47.9	22.6
Marfa city	1,982	1,765	-10.9	2,124	34.6	0.9	0.1	0.0	64.5	20.2	59.9	19.9	851	68.6	47.2	26.3
Marietta town	134	133	-0.7	88	98.9	1.1	0.0	0.0	0.0	9.1	54.6	36.4	49	91.8	63.3	22.4
Marion city	1,066	1,105	3.7	987	52.8	5.3	0.2	3.2	38.5	28.1	60.6	11.4	312	78.2	55.8	12.5
Markham CDP	1,082	NA	NA	1,242	44.3	8.9	0.0	0.0	46.9	21.3	56.8	21.8	463	83.8	74.3	9.5
Marlin city	5,967	5,738	-3.8	5,867	27.9	44.5	0.0	0.5	27.1	23.3	60.0	16.7	1,983	58.4	60.6	14.5
Marquez city	262	262	0.0	270	63.7	0.0	0.0	0.0	36.3	21.5	61.5	17.0	92	90.2	62.0	14.1
Marshall city	23,523	24,701	5.0	24,424	40.0	40.1	0.9	0.5	18.6	25.6	60.6	13.8	8,473	61.8	49.1	22.3
Mart city	1,897	1,917	1.1	2,288	56.5	27.0	0.0	2.2	14.3	29.4	55.0	15.6	763	65.8	54.9	14.9
Martindale city	1,116	1,202	7.7	1,575	30.0	1.3	0.0	0.8	68.0	33.4	52.3	14.3	503	71.6	53.9	18.1
Martinez CDP	69	NA	NA	0	0.0	0.0	0.0	0.0	0.0	0.0	0.0	0.0	0	0.0	0.0	0.0
Mason city	2,113	2,158	2.1	1,907	55.1	0.0	6.4	0.5	37.9	17.3	51.6	31.1	834	79.9	55.8	23.0
Matador town	612	583	-4.7	542	85.2	0.7	0.0	1.3	12.7	27.5	50.9	21.6	207	71.5	40.1	11.6
Matagorda CDP	503	NA	NA	469	55.0	4.9	0.0	0.6	39.4	3.4	69.9	26.7	195	75.9	44.1	18.5
Mathis city	4,942	5,037	1.9	4,971	4.6	0.7	0.1	0.0	94.6	20.1	57.0	14.0	1,553	63.4	64.3	9.3
Maud city	1,056	1,064	0.8	1,056	89.8	5.3	0.0	4.9	0.0	36.3	47.1	16.5	376	66.2	48.1	15.4
Mauriceville CDP	3,252	NA	NA	3,130	82.4	0.0	0.0	4.7	12.9	29.7	62.3	8.1	1,112	87.9	44.2	19.6
Maypearl city	931	966	3.8	729	72.4	8.5	0.0	0.0	19.1	28.9	62.1	9.1	253	67.6	51.0	17.8
Meadow town	593	597	0.7	706	32.2	0.0	0.0	1.4	66.4	28.6	59.7	11.6	205	80.0	49.8	9.8
Meadowlakes city	1,777	1,838	3.4	2,050	92.9	0.0	0.0	1.0	6.1	21.5	35.9	42.5	879	87.8	16.3	53.4
Meadows Place city	4,638	4,752	2.5	4,701	51.0	10.4	20.0	0.9	17.7	23.4	58.6	18.1	1,693	86.5	15.7	48.4
Medina CDP	3,935	NA	NA	4,332	1.0	0.0	0.0	0.0	99.0	37.2	58.3	4.5	1,095	78.7	86.4	2.5
Megargel town	203	196	-3.4	246	94.3	0.0	0.0	1.6	4.1	11.4	58.2	30.5	105	90.5	54.3	0.0
Melissa city	4,684	6,703	43.1	5,675	68.9	14.5	3.7	0.1	12.7	33.8	63.4	2.5	1,671	89.5	22.1	40.1
Melvin town	178	177	-0.6	240	46.7	0.0	0.0	0.4	52.9	26.3	49.7	24.2	100	85.0	57.0	10.0

1 May be of any race.

Table A. All Places — **Population and Housing**

STATE City, town, township, borough, or CDP (county if applicable)	Population				Race and Hispanic or Latino origin (percent), 2010–2014					Age (percent), 2010–2014			Households, 2010–2014			
	2010 census total population	2014 estimated population	Percent change 2010-2014	ACS total population estimate 2010-2014	White alone, not Hispanic or Latino	Black alone, not Hispanic or Latino	Asian alone, not Hispanic or Latino	All other races or 2 or more races, not Hispanic or Latino	Hispanic or Latino[1]	Under 18 years old	Age 18 to 64 years old	Age 65 years and older	Total occupied housing units	Percent owner occupied	Householders by level of education (percent): High school diploma or less	Householders by level of education (percent): Bachelor's degree or more
	1	2	3	4	5	6	7	8	9	10	11	12	13	14	15	16
TEXAS—Con.																
Memphis city	2,290	2,146	-6.3	2,069	54.5	6.1	0.0	1.4	38.0	24.5	52.6	23.1	753	67.6	55.4	14.6
Menard city	1,471	1,410	-4.1	1,586	48.3	1.5	0.0	1.5	48.8	29.8	51.0	19.2	591	77.7	63.5	8.3
Mentone CDP	19	NA	NA	15	26.7	0.0	0.0	73.3	0.0	0.0	100.1	0.0	8	62.5	87.5	0.0
Mercedes city	15,677	16,591	5.8	16,271	6.3	0.0	0.0	0.1	93.6	37.8	48.8	13.3	4,695	60.9	64.8	12.0
Meridian city	1,492	1,445	-3.2	1,692	69.1	4.7	0.0	1.7	24.5	26.6	59.7	13.7	559	52.1	58.1	5.7
Merkel town	2,590	2,601	0.4	2,601	81.5	0.0	0.2	0.7	17.5	21.1	61.4	17.4	1,057	73.8	62.5	11.5
Mertens town	125	124	-0.8	119	62.2	2.5	4.2	18.5	12.6	28.5	40.4	31.1	48	83.3	43.8	4.2
Mertzon city	781	769	-1.5	778	56.6	0.0	0.0	3.5	40.0	28.9	58.2	12.9	276	76.8	62.7	13.4
Mesquite city	139,629	144,416	3.4	142,552	37.4	23.4	3.1	1.6	34.5	29.7	61.6	8.6	47,927	58.8	43.2	19.2
Mesquite CDP	505	NA	NA	454	0.0	0.0	0.0	0.0	100.0	28.0	67.6	4.4	109	75.2	100.0	0.0
Mexia city	7,446	7,501	0.7	7,502	34.7	34.7	0.3	1.0	29.3	29.3	58.5	12.2	2,241	64.6	49.0	15.7
Miami city	597	596	-0.2	566	97.9	0.0	0.4	0.7	1.1	21.7	54.8	23.5	224	93.8	41.1	42.4
Midland city	111,127	128,037	15.2	119,409	49.1	7.2	1.6	1.7	40.4	27.3	61.7	10.9	42,010	64.8	35.6	27.8
Midlothian city	18,311	20,934	14.3	19,590	83.0	4.2	0.2	0.8	11.7	31.4	58.8	9.7	6,678	74.9	31.8	30.9
Midway city	228	227	-0.4	410	96.3	0.7	0.0	1.2	1.7	34.7	55.8	9.5	124	67.7	53.2	22.6
Midway North CDP	4,752	NA	NA	5,159	2.2	0.0	0.0	0.0	97.8	35.1	56.4	8.5	1,051	82.8	75.0	7.4
Midway South CDP	2,239	NA	NA	2,994	6.1	0.0	0.0	0.0	93.9	38.4	58.3	3.4	585	86.5	76.1	5.8
Miguel Barrera CDP	128	NA	NA	425	0.0	0.0	0.0	0.0	100.0	47.1	40.8	12.2	84	100.0	61.9	0.0
Mikes CDP	910	NA	NA	554	0.0	0.0	0.0	0.0	100.0	54.5	45.4	0.0	118	100.0	83.9	16.1
Mila Doce CDP	6,222	NA	NA	5,386	3.3	0.0	0.0	0.0	96.7	44.9	48.8	6.5	1,215	85.1	81.2	3.0
Milam CDP	1,480	NA	NA	1,283	93.7	5.8	0.0	0.0	0.5	7.0	59.3	33.8	566	87.1	38.5	9.4
Milano city	428	417	-2.6	489	72.0	4.1	0.0	3.1	20.9	30.3	55.0	14.7	167	73.1	59.9	12.0
Mildred town	370	369	-0.3	515	89.3	0.6	0.6	0.4	9.1	14.4	57.8	27.8	191	95.8	57.1	7.9
Miles city	852	842	-1.2	1,090	44.6	0.0	0.0	0.0	55.4	23.1	56.9	19.8	355	76.6	67.6	8.5
Milford town	728	730	0.3	721	49.9	16.4	0.0	7.4	26.4	24.9	59.9	15.3	259	65.3	61.0	3.9
Miller's Cove town	149	149	0.0	178	10.1	0.0	0.0	0.0	89.9	39.8	54.5	5.6	35	45.7	88.6	5.7
Millican town	240	241	0.4	221	88.2	11.8	0.0	0.0	0.0	11.3	66.9	21.7	87	86.2	60.9	17.2
Millsap town	403	420	4.2	408	74.8	0.0	0.0	5.9	19.4	25.6	67.1	7.6	135	80.0	48.1	8.9
Mineola city	4,502	4,564	1.4	4,514	66.9	15.9	0.1	2.3	14.7	26.4	50.2	23.3	1,534	67.9	44.7	18.6
Mineral Wells city	16,790	15,362	-8.5	16,593	64.3	6.3	0.9	1.4	27.0	24.5	63.3	12.2	5,234	58.3	60.5	11.0
Mingus city	235	233	-0.9	285	84.6	0.0	0.0	3.9	11.6	17.9	60.6	21.4	115	84.3	71.3	1.7
Mi Ranchito Estate CDP	281	NA	NA	115	0.0	0.0	0.0	0.0	100.0	0.0	52.2	47.8	57	100.0	100.0	0.0
Mirando City CDP	375	NA	NA	290	0.0	0.0	0.0	0.0	100.0	31.0	59.0	10.0	80	70.0	70.0	0.0
Mission city	77,665	82,431	6.1	80,538	12.3	0.4	1.1	0.2	86.1	34.3	54.4	11.2	23,478	71.0	48.6	26.1
Mission Bend CDP	36,501	NA	NA	37,110	12.4	28.5	14.3	1.5	43.3	27.7	64.8	7.4	10,620	79.9	40.0	28.2
Missouri City city	66,825	71,710	7.3	69,152	22.3	42.8	15.4	2.3	17.2	25.4	63.9	10.5	22,430	84.3	20.6	48.2
Mobeetie city	101	107	5.9	195	94.9	0.0	0.5	3.6	1.0	30.8	58.6	10.8	83	65.1	45.8	14.5
Mobile City city	188	192	2.1	246	19.1	4.1	0.0	0.0	76.8	35.4	59.3	5.3	90	6.7	71.1	0.0
Monahans city	6,958	7,617	9.5	7,204	42.0	5.5	0.1	1.8	50.7	27.7	57.8	14.4	2,522	67.2	50.9	18.1
Montague CDP	304	NA	NA	288	86.1	0.0	0.0	0.0	13.9	14.9	55.9	29.2	127	76.4	65.4	11.0
Mont Belvieu city	3,834	4,847	26.4	4,343	74.2	8.0	0.0	2.4	15.4	32.2	59.5	8.4	1,290	76.2	33.5	23.7
Monte Alto CDP	1,924	NA	NA	1,807	1.4	0.0	0.0	0.0	98.6	38.4	47.5	14.0	498	81.5	70.9	7.4
Montgomery city	619	710	14.7	639	64.8	19.1	0.0	2.3	13.8	28.3	56.6	15.2	235	74.9	42.1	26.0
Moody city	1,371	1,384	0.9	1,614	65.6	6.9	0.0	0.9	26.6	19.0	63.3	17.5	585	73.7	51.8	8.7
Moore CDP	475	NA	NA	380	18.4	0.0	0.0	0.0	81.6	7.6	67.1	25.3	152	89.5	83.6	16.4
Moore Station city	199	199	0.0	233	6.9	92.3	0.0	0.0	0.9	17.2	58.4	24.5	92	88.0	73.9	3.3
Moraida CDP	212	NA	NA	202	0.0	0.0	0.0	0.0	100.0	33.8	66.3	0.0	51	100.0	100.0	0.0
Morales-Sanchez CDP	84	NA	NA	112	0.0	0.0	0.0	0.0	100.0	0.0	42.9	57.1	35	100.0	71.4	0.0
Moran city	270	267	-1.1	305	99.7	0.0	0.0	0.0	0.3	14.7	71.9	13.4	129	65.1	69.0	3.9
Morgan city	490	478	-2.4	543	52.7	0.0	0.0	0.9	46.4	31.8	56.5	11.8	156	67.9	75.6	0.0
Morgan Farm CDP	463	NA	NA	555	29.5	0.0	0.0	0.0	70.5	16.1	72.1	11.9	195	100.0	77.4	17.4
Morgan's Point city	339	353	4.1	315	64.4	17.5	0.0	2.9	15.2	29.6	58.5	12.1	114	86.0	14.0	46.5
Morgan's Point Resort city	4,170	4,210	1.0	4,208	81.3	0.3	0.0	1.4	17.1	31.9	54.8	13.2	1,379	85.4	37.0	26.4
Morning Glory CDP	651	NA	NA	443	2.0	0.0	0.0	4.3	93.7	33.1	59.9	6.8	130	83.8	93.1	0.0
Morse CDP	147	NA	NA	248	70.2	0.0	0.0	0.0	29.8	37.5	48.3	14.1	79	83.5	39.2	30.4
Morton city	2,006	1,880	-6.3	1,909	24.0	4.2	0.2	0.7	71.0	27.2	57.6	15.1	640	81.9	65.6	12.2
Moulton town	886	899	1.5	1,005	73.5	0.7	0.0	0.6	25.2	28.4	50.4	21.5	359	72.7	61.3	8.6
Mountain City city	648	647	-0.2	663	69.5	0.0	0.0	6.9	23.5	23.5	68.8	7.7	226	97.3	18.1	50.0
Mount Calm city	317	315	-0.6	292	72.3	6.2	0.0	0.0	21.6	24.0	60.3	15.8	115	73.0	41.7	21.7
Mount Enterprise city	447	446	-0.2	394	91.4	2.8	0.0	0.0	5.8	20.6	58.3	21.1	182	71.4	63.7	10.4
Mount Pleasant city	15,985	16,021	0.2	16,066	29.5	14.4	0.4	1.0	54.6	33.4	56.2	10.5	4,822	57.8	58.2	12.6
Mount Vernon town	2,778	2,747	-1.1	2,770	61.3	16.5	1.0	3.2	18.0	27.1	58.8	14.1	1,105	58.5	45.8	19.5
Muenster city	1,544	1,586	2.7	1,739	93.0	0.1	0.0	0.9	6.0	28.0	57.5	14.6	622	76.2	46.8	24.0
Muleshoe city	5,158	4,975	-3.5	5,161	36.0	2.3	0.5	0.2	61.1	34.1	52.9	12.9	1,696	63.9	67.7	9.0
Mullin town	177	174	-1.7	148	93.9	0.0	0.0	0.0	6.1	20.9	68.2	10.8	49	95.9	67.3	12.2
Munday city	1,300	1,340	3.1	1,411	41.6	12.9	0.0	0.1	45.4	26.9	54.9	18.0	521	67.9	63.1	10.9
Muniz CDP	1,370	NA	NA	1,423	0.0	0.0	0.0	0.0	100.0	23.6	71.3	5.1	365	66.3	100.0	0.0
Murchison city	594	593	-0.2	472	100.0	0.0	0.0	0.0	0.0	16.7	63.8	19.5	192	69.3	41.7	21.9
Murillo CDP	7,344	NA	NA	7,454	4.3	0.0	1.9	0.0	93.9	35.1	60.1	5.0	1,960	79.4	59.7	20.8
Murphy city	17,862	20,230	13.3	19,154	52.3	13.3	26.9	1.7	5.8	33.4	60.0	6.6	5,087	94.2	13.4	58.1
Mustang town	21	21	0.0	34	100.0	0.0	0.0	0.0	0.0	20.6	79.4	0.0	11	9.1	27.3	0.0
Mustang Ridge city	865	960	11.0	1,052	39.2	0.3	0.0	0.5	60.1	34.8	58.3	7.0	297	71.0	61.6	6.7
Myrtle Springs CDP	828	NA	NA	495	100.0	0.0	0.0	0.0	0.0	13.4	51.3	35.4	192	94.3	42.7	17.2
Nacogdoches city	32,899	33,687	2.4	33,589	47.6	29.8	2.3	1.7	18.7	21.6	68.2	10.3	11,941	38.9	30.2	28.9
Naples city	1,375	1,363	-0.9	1,368	68.1	24.8	0.0	4.6	2.6	19.4	61.6	18.9	626	68.5	48.9	10.9
Narciso Pena CDP	30	NA	NA	0	0.0	0.0	0.0	0.0	0.0	0.0	0.0	0.0	0	0.0	0.0	0.0
Nash city	2,960	3,142	6.1	3,060	49.1	31.3	0.0	2.2	17.4	29.9	59.4	10.7	1,190	48.4	40.9	10.2
Nassau Bay city	4,002	4,108	2.6	4,077	82.0	1.9	1.3	1.5	13.4	18.6	64.6	16.9	1,833	54.9	14.9	42.7
Natalia city	1,423	1,481	4.1	1,383	12.6	0.0	0.0	0.0	87.4	28.9	57.4	13.5	511	77.1	67.5	0.8
Navarro town	209	208	-0.5	368	82.3	3.0	0.3	1.9	12.5	34.5	60.1	5.4	120	93.3	61.7	3.3
Navasota city	7,127	7,351	3.1	7,215	28.7	26.8	0.0	1.7	42.8	24.3	61.7	13.9	2,394	54.9	64.6	12.7
Nazareth city	311	299	-3.9	278	96.0	0.0	0.0	0.7	3.2	24.5	56.7	19.1	106	86.8	38.7	17.0
Nederland city	16,993	17,108	0.7	17,018	81.8	1.9	0.6	3.0	12.7	23.0	63.0	13.9	6,991	76.9	37.0	20.1
Needville city	2,929	3,058	4.4	2,995	64.7	14.2	0.0	2.3	18.8	30.8	56.8	12.2	1,057	70.2	44.9	18.4
Nesbitt town	281	NA	NA	260	46.9	51.9	0.0	0.4	0.8	3.5	75.4	21.2	103	100.0	62.1	25.2
Netos CDP	31	NA	NA	15	0.0	0.0	0.0	0.0	100.0	0.0	0.0	100.0	15	100.0	100.0	0.0
Nevada city	822	942	14.6	1,072	79.2	3.5	3.0	2.6	11.8	24.0	68.5	7.5	346	85.0	43.4	17.9
Newark city	1,007	1,043	3.6	1,309	81.8	0.2	0.2	2.1	15.7	26.4	64.3	9.2	398	78.6	39.4	15.6
New Berlin city	511	529	3.5	589	84.4	0.0	0.0	0.5	15.1	19.2	54.9	26.0	196	89.8	42.3	28.6
New Boston city	4,794	4,749	-0.9	4,773	71.1	22.0	1.2	3.8	2.0	23.9	61.1	14.9	1,879	53.9	49.4	16.0
New Braunfels city	57,727	66,394	15.0	61,712	60.7	2.2	0.5	0.9	35.7	27.7	59.3	13.0	21,827	65.1	34.0	30.9

1 May be of any race.

Table A. All Places — Population and Housing

STATE City, town, township, borough, or CDP (county if applicable)	2010 census total population	2014 estimated population	Percent change 2010-2014	ACS total population estimate 2010-2014	White alone, not Hispanic or Latino	Black alone, not Hispanic or Latino	Asian alone, not Hispanic or Latino	All other races or 2 or more races, not Hispanic or Latino	Hispanic or Latino[1]	Under 18 years old	Age 18 to 64 years old	Age 65 years and older	Total occupied housing units	Percent owner occupied	High school diploma or less	Bachelor's degree or more
	1	2	3	4	5	6	7	8	9	10	11	12	13	14	15	16
TEXAS—Con.																
Newcastle city	585	570	-2.6	443	96.8	0.0	0.0	0.5	2.7	17.6	52.6	29.8	214	83.6	63.1	9.3
New Chapel Hill city	592	610	3.0	637	83.8	4.4	0.0	6.3	5.5	21.6	60.3	18.2	233	77.3	39.9	16.7
New Deal town	704	799	0.6	779	54.4	5.0	0.0	1.3	39.3	31.0	55.0	14.0	263	71.9	54.0	8.7
New Fairview city	1,258	1,309	4.1	1,090	63.3	1.5	0.9	10.7	23.6	27.2	63.8	9.1	367	80.4	62.1	3.5
New Falcon CDP	191	NA	NA	76	0.0	0.0	0.0	0.0	100.0	0.0	64.5	35.5	47	42.6	57.4	17.0
New Home city	334	336	0.6	314	34.7	0.0	0.0	1.3	64.0	30.0	53.7	16.2	96	72.9	58.3	19.8
New Hope town	614	639	4.1	759	82.7	0.4	0.4	3.8	12.6	16.9	70.3	12.8	258	86.8	47.7	27.1
New London city	999	999	0.0	1,316	69.8	5.3	0.2	1.2	23.4	26.1	58.8	15.2	382	86.9	49.2	8.4
New Summerfield city	1,111	1,098	-1.2	1,686	21.6	2.0	0.0	0.2	76.3	35.6	59.3	5.2	421	69.8	90.0	1.0
New Territory CDP	15,186	NA	NA	15,640	37.1	9.1	43.1	1.6	9.0	29.5	64.3	6.2	4,569	84.6	16.4	63.5
Newton city	2,473	2,420	-2.1	2,332	64.3	25.0	2.1	0.5	8.1	20.0	63.0	17.0	709	69.3	60.9	10.0
New Waverly city	1,032	1,030	-0.2	1,145	58.3	36.4	0.4	2.2	2.7	26.0	62.7	11.3	533	45.6	51.4	10.5
Neylandville town	97	99	2.1	139	4.3	38.8	0.0	0.0	56.8	20.9	56.2	23.0	67	92.5	34.3	11.9
Niederwald city	552	556	0.7	637	57.6	7.4	0.0	1.1	33.9	27.3	58.1	14.6	213	84.5	52.6	16.0
Nina CDP	141	NA	NA	299	0.0	0.0	0.0	0.0	100.0	30.1	70.0	0.0	44	63.6	100.0	0.0
Nixon city	2,385	2,459	3.1	2,591	13.8	1.9	0.0	0.4	83.9	34.2	54.8	10.9	775	64.0	75.6	3.0
Nocona city	3,031	2,971	-2.0	3,004	78.1	0.0	0.0	4.3	17.6	23.5	53.8	22.8	1,272	58.6	57.8	9.4
Nocona Hills CDP	675	NA	NA	779	91.5	0.0	0.0	1.2	7.3	11.1	54.5	34.4	368	89.1	32.3	18.5
Nolanville city	4,263	4,593	7.7	4,429	56.9	12.8	1.6	5.9	22.7	37.7	58.5	3.8	1,505	54.6	34.5	15.0
Nome city	577	561	-2.8	458	63.3	14.0	0.0	2.0	20.7	19.4	68.3	12.2	182	77.5	46.2	15.0
Noonday city	776	802	3.4	921	83.6	9.2	0.5	0.0	6.6	21.2	64.3	14.3	357	80.7	31.1	21.8
Nordheim city	307	316	2.9	335	58.5	0.0	0.0	0.3	41.2	20.9	49.7	29.6	126	90.5	57.9	27.8
Normangee town	685	685	0.0	676	70.1	21.2	0.0	0.1	8.6	26.5	57.4	16.3	228	70.6	60.1	15.4
Normanna CDP	113	NA	NA	65	80.0	3.1	0.0	0.0	16.9	7.7	61.6	30.8	21	90.5	85.7	0.0
North Alamo CDP	3,235	NA	NA	3,756	9.8	0.0	0.0	0.3	89.9	38.5	49.9	11.6	963	78.5	68.6	10.3
North Cleveland city	247	258	4.5	177	76.3	2.3	1.7	4.0	15.8	23.2	49.7	27.1	74	90.5	55.4	4.1
North Escobares CDP	118	NA	NA	217	0.0	0.0	0.0	0.0	100.0	46.5	35.0	18.4	38	0.0	100.0	0.0
Northlake town	1,725	1,916	11.1	2,410	86.1	1.8	0.6	1.2	10.3	25.7	67.9	6.4	1,052	29.6	17.0	40.2
North Pearsall CDP	614	NA	NA	730	22.6	0.0	0.0	3.2	74.2	30.6	51.4	17.9	246	60.2	63.0	6.9
North Richland Hills city	63,343	68,529	8.2	65,835	71.7	4.0	3.7	2.7	17.9	24.2	63.4	12.5	24,853	63.2	28.2	32.5
Northridge CDP	78	NA	NA	0	0.0	0.0	0.0	0.0	0.0	0.0	0.0	0.0	0	0.0	0.0	0.0
North San Pedro CDP	895	NA	NA	634	10.9	0.0	0.0	0.0	89.1	20.5	65.7	13.7	195	56.9	75.4	6.2
Novice city	139	132	-5.0	156	96.8	0.0	0.0	0.6	2.6	34.0	58.8	7.1	61	70.5	65.6	16.4
Oak Grove town	603	649	7.6	874	74.1	0.0	0.1	0.0	25.7	27.4	53.8	18.9	280	97.1	45.4	26.8
Oakhurst CDP	233	NA	NA	471	96.0	4.0	0.0	0.0	0.0	31.0	38.8	30.1	173	89.0	36.4	63.6
Oak Island CDP	363	NA	NA	246	49.6	13.0	37.4	0.0	0.0	21.9	44.4	33.7	104	93.3	64.4	26.9
Oak Leaf city	1,302	1,349	3.6	1,279	81.2	8.7	0.0	0.7	9.4	19.6	63.5	16.7	404	100.0	23.3	40.3
Oak Point city	2,786	3,178	14.1	3,011	82.6	0.7	2.9	3.4	10.4	23.4	68.4	8.2	1,058	88.9	29.0	34.7
Oak Ridge town (Cooke)	141	171	21.3	103	87.4	0.0	0.0	0.0	12.6	22.3	70.0	7.8	43	69.8	46.5	9.3
Oak Ridge town (Kaufman)	492	531	7.9	591	78.0	13.7	0.0	1.0	7.3	31.4	55.7	13.0	200	82.0	33.0	9.5
Oak Ridge North city	3,046	3,160	3.7	3,107	82.8	5.3	1.6	2.3	7.9	22.1	55.8	22.1	1,102	92.3	18.7	45.2
Oak Trail Shores CDP	2,755	NA	NA	3,064	71.8	0.0	0.0	4.6	23.6	27.3	62.8	10.0	1,028	66.1	65.0	9.0
Oak Valley town	368	375	1.9	373	80.4	7.5	0.0	1.6	10.5	23.0	65.2	11.8	140	92.1	50.0	14.3
Oakwood town	510	510	0.0	485	68.2	28.7	0.4	0.4	2.3	21.5	60.3	18.1	175	75.4	50.9	12.0
O'Brien city	106	104	-1.9	142	71.1	0.0	0.0	7.7	21.1	18.3	65.5	16.2	72	81.9	50.0	13.9
Odem city	2,440	2,487	1.9	2,563	19.6	0.3	0.0	0.0	80.0	27.2	61.0	11.9	854	69.0	54.7	14.1
Odessa city	99,880	114,597	14.7	107,325	39.1	5.2	1.2	1.6	52.8	28.6	61.2	10.0	38,130	61.0	48.1	19.1
O'Donnell city	831	815	-1.9	982	22.3	0.0	0.5	0.4	76.8	35.8	52.4	11.8	351	67.5	64.7	6.8
Oglesby city	484	469	-3.1	474	88.0	0.0	0.0	1.1	11.0	22.4	56.9	20.9	178	71.3	67.4	15.2
Oilton CDP	353	NA	NA	405	0.0	0.0	0.0	0.0	100.0	23.5	59.8	16.8	123	81.3	60.2	0.0
Old River-Winfree city	1,247	1,280	2.6	1,844	78.6	11.2	0.0	1.0	9.2	24.1	70.8	5.2	607	81.4	60.5	6.6
Olivarez CDP	3,827	NA	NA	4,317	0.0	0.0	1.5	0.0	98.4	44.0	54.3	1.6	875	78.3	69.6	5.8
Olivia Lopez de Gutierrez CDP	93	NA	NA	0	0.0	0.0	0.0	0.0	0.0	0.0	0.0	0.0	0	0.0	0.0	0.0
Olmito CDP	1,210	NA	NA	1,361	0.9	0.0	0.0	0.0	99.1	28.2	50.8	20.9	342	67.8	63.2	9.4
Olmito and Olmito CDP	271	NA	NA	277	0.0	0.0	0.0	0.0	100.0	45.1	33.2	21.7	68	100.0	100.0	0.0
Olmos Park city	2,237	2,361	5.5	2,023	79.2	4.4	0.0	0.6	15.8	25.6	57.2	17.3	867	72.9	5.9	85.1
Olney city	3,285	3,221	-1.9	3,242	69.0	1.2	0.3	6.6	22.9	28.4	54.6	17.2	1,207	59.9	62.4	10.5
Olton city	2,215	2,158	-2.6	1,904	25.6	0.0	0.7	0.0	73.7	27.0	55.5	17.5	700	69.6	62.9	4.9
Omaha city	1,031	1,008	-2.2	961	68.4	26.7	0.0	0.0	4.9	19.6	57.9	22.6	409	68.2	43.0	12.0
Onalaska city	1,740	1,713	-1.6	1,731	80.1	6.4	0.7	5.4	7.5	24.2	53.3	22.5	768	76.4	52.5	10.2
Opdyke West town	174	178	2.3	71	43.7	0.0	0.0	0.0	56.3	26.8	71.8	1.4	29	51.7	55.2	10.3
Orange city	18,612	18,913	1.6	18,810	59.4	31.4	1.5	2.6	5.2	23.8	60.1	16.2	7,585	60.5	51.5	16.2
Orange Grove city	1,319	1,335	1.2	1,476	55.9	3.6	0.0	0.0	40.5	28.3	55.7	16.1	517	72.3	52.0	29.4
Orason CDP	129	NA	NA	111	87.4	0.0	0.0	0.0	12.6	0.0	81.9	18.0	58	58.6	9.2	55.2
Orchard city	351	366	4.3	366	60.4	0.0	0.0	0.0	39.6	28.5	58.5	13.1	143	69.9	10.3	55.2
Ore City city	1,143	1,170	2.4	914	81.7	6.0	0.0	4.5	7.8	27.6	52.1	20.4	385	67.0	47.0	14.0
Overton city	2,554	2,537	-0.7	2,310	67.8	16.8	0.0	3.4	11.9	23.9	60.6	15.4	773	67.7	46.2	19.0
Ovilla city	3,482	3,619	3.9	3,460	83.7	8.3	0.1	1.1	6.8	25.1	63.4	11.6	1,279	93.9	27.6	34.4
Owl Ranch CDP	225	NA	NA	113	0.0	0.0	0.0	0.0	100.0	41.6	58.4	0.0	66	21.2	100.0	0.0
Oyster Creek city	1,111	1,133	2.0	1,037	68.8	2.9	0.7	2.6	25.1	27.8	60.8	11.4	348	73.9	62.6	8.6
Ozona CDP	3,225	NA	NA	3,295	28.8	0.0	0.0	0.8	70.5	25.9	58.1	16.1	1,195	70.8	69.6	11.0
Pablo Pena CDP	63	NA	NA	0	0.0	0.0	0.0	0.0	0.0	0.0	0.0	0.0	0	0.0	0.0	0.0
Paducah town	1,188	1,114	-6.2	1,287	58.4	14.3	0.0	0.2	27.1	19.3	49.4	31.3	589	74.4	61.1	11.9
Paint Rock town	273	264	-3.3	371	77.4	0.0	0.0	1.1	21.6	18.9	69.2	11.9	85	89.4	55.3	11.8
Paisano Park CDP	130	NA	NA	86	0.0	0.0	0.0	0.0	100.0	0.0	0.0	100.0	46	100.0	0.0	0.0
Palacios city	4,718	4,655	-1.3	4,691	27.9	0.7	10.4	0.3	60.7	29.8	59.7	10.3	1,661	71.5	65.3	8.9
Palestine city	18,774	18,393	-2.0	18,611	50.9	26.0	0.9	2.0	20.2	27.3	57.7	15.0	6,309	61.4	50.4	16.8
Palisades village	325	333	2.5	227	89.9	0.0	0.4	0.0	9.7	13.2	67.3	19.4	100	95.0	40.0	9.0
Palmer town	2,000	2,036	1.8	2,347	58.8	0.9	0.0	2.9	37.4	37.1	52.8	9.9	683	74.4	54.2	8.1
Palmhurst city	2,543	2,663	4.7	2,620	16.0	1.8	4.3	0.0	77.9	31.5	56.9	11.6	697	86.9	35.0	36.7
Palm Valley city	1,304	1,302	-0.2	1,628	63.9	6.0	0.0	1.2	28.9	18.0	43.3	38.6	742	80.6	16.7	51.3
Palmview city	5,469	5,661	3.5	5,577	1.8	0.0	0.0	0.0	98.2	35.8	58.2	6.2	1,358	76.8	63.5	15.5
Palmview South CDP	5,575	NA	NA	5,294	20.1	0.0	0.0	0.0	79.9	31.0	49.6	19.5	1,561	87.2	63.4	10.4
Palo Blanco CDP	204	NA	NA	173	0.0	0.0	0.0	0.0	100.0	20.2	68.2	11.6	36	100.0	55.6	0.0
Paloma Creek CDP	2,501	NA	NA	3,202	66.3	7.4	0.0	5.2	21.1	39.5	57.8	2.9	961	62.3	18.4	38.6
Paloma Creek South CDP	2,753	NA	NA	4,221	44.8	33.8	0.6	5.9	14.9	32.8	61.6	5.6	1,282	92.0	8.1	31.4
Palo Pinto CDP	333	NA	NA	286	57.3	5.2	0.0	2.8	34.6	4.2	81.4	14.3	98	94.9	41.8	15.3
Pampa city	17,994	18,399	2.3	18,180	65.8	2.4	0.4	3.0	28.4	27.0	56.9	16.4	7,222	72.7	48.0	16.9
Panhandle town	2,452	2,356	-3.9	2,250	89.8	2.6	1.0	2.2	4.4	26.3	57.3	16.4	845	89.3	19.3	31.6

1 May be of any race.

Table A. All Places — **Population and Housing**

STATE City, town, township, borough, or CDP (county if applicable)	Population: 2010 census total population	Population: 2014 estimated population	Population: Percent change 2010-2014	Population: ACS total population estimate 2010-2014	Race and Hispanic or Latino origin (percent), 2010–2014: White alone, not Hispanic or Latino	Black alone, not Hispanic or Latino	Asian alone, not Hispanic or Latino	All other races or 2 or more races, not Hispanic or Latino	Hispanic or Latino[1]	Age (percent), 2010–2014: Under 18 years old	Age 18 to 64 years old	Age 65 years and older	Households, 2010–2014: Total occupied housing units	Percent owner occupied	Householders by level of education (percent): High school diploma or less	Bachelor's degree or more
	1	2	3	4	5	6	7	8	9	10	11	12	13	14	15	16
TEXAS—Con.																
Panorama Village city	2,170	2,271	4.7	1,985	85.5	7.0	0.0	1.7	5.8	14.0	48.7	37.1	949	84.8	20.7	41.7
Pantego town	2,394	2,505	4.6	2,466	83.3	3.0	0.7	3.0	10.0	20.2	49.8	30.0	1,014	72.6	30.0	42.6
Paradise city	442	460	4.1	421	91.4	0.0	0.0	0.7	7.8	22.4	53.5	24.2	180	70.6	58.3	11.1
Paris city	25,163	24,895	-1.1	25,023	66.4	21.9	1.4	5.1	5.2	23.7	58.7	17.5	10,056	53.1	47.3	16.7
Parker city	3,700	4,247	14.8	3,974	67.8	5.0	10.8	0.8	15.5	29.1	55.3	15.6	1,183	95.9	6.5	76.5
Pasadena city	149,300	153,887	3.1	152,171	30.6	2.2	2.2	1.2	63.8	29.7	61.6	8.7	48,526	55.6	55.5	15.9
Pattison city	476	510	7.1	465	54.0	6.5	0.0	2.6	37.0	15.3	66.4	18.3	182	81.9	36.3	29.1
Patton Village city	1,557	1,618	3.9	1,541	62.8	0.0	0.0	2.3	34.9	30.5	63.4	6.2	477	74.6	80.7	2.5
Pawnee CDP	166	NA	NA	163	1.8	0.0	0.0	0.0	98.2	22.0	52.8	25.2	58	58.6	72.4	0.0
Payne Springs town	765	766	0.1	780	90.0	0.0	0.0	3.6	6.4	17.4	64.0	18.6	271	84.5	43.5	16.6
Pearland city	89,891	103,441	15.1	97,427	47.2	15.8	13.6	2.2	21.3	28.9	62.5	8.6	33,112	78.5	20.7	50.1
Pearsall city	9,150	9,852	7.7	9,482	11.8	2.8	0.4	0.5	84.5	25.6	61.7	12.6	2,474	69.7	61.1	10.5
Pecan Acres CDP	4,099	NA	NA	5,331	84.5	0.4	0.2	3.0	11.9	33.9	58.0	8.1	1,535	84.5	33.9	29.6
Pecan Gap city	201	201	0.0	211	87.7	8.1	0.0	4.3	0.0	14.3	65.4	20.4	82	74.4	57.3	4.9
Pecan Grove CDP	15,963	NA	NA	16,619	75.6	3.2	2.5	2.3	16.4	23.9	66.7	9.3	5,878	86.4	18.7	46.8
Pecan Hill city	626	635	1.4	699	80.3	4.9	0.0	2.1	12.7	19.1	69.4	11.4	271	86.3	45.4	18.1
Pecan Plantation CDP	5,294	NA	NA	5,607	91.9	0.0	0.0	1.1	7.0	12.2	41.6	46.3	2,428	92.3	19.8	47.5
Pecos city	8,780	9,213	4.9	8,919	19.4	4.2	0.2	0.8	75.3	28.4	57.4	14.2	2,835	70.1	63.2	12.3
Pelican Bay city	1,547	1,615	4.4	1,908	76.8	3.7	0.0	4.6	14.9	35.1	58.0	6.9	602	58.5	72.4	4.3
Pena CDP	118	NA	NA	125	0.0	0.0	0.0	0.0	100.0	54.4	45.6	0.0	27	100.0	100.0	0.0
Penelope town	198	196	-1.0	192	63.0	0.0	0.0	0.0	37.0	18.7	58.4	22.9	86	88.4	61.6	11.6
Penitas city	4,366	4,632	6.1	4,498	0.7	0.0	0.0	0.0	99.3	34.9	58.4	6.7	1,075	77.7	68.8	6.3
Perezville CDP	5,376	NA	NA	4,543	25.4	0.0	0.0	0.8	73.8	30.9	40.5	28.7	1,509	83.7	60.6	10.7
Perrin CDP	398	NA	NA	421	94.5	0.0	0.0	0.0	5.5	11.6	65.9	22.6	165	84.8	57.0	24.8
Perryton city	8,802	9,260	5.2	9,330	45.8	0.2	0.2	1.6	52.1	32.4	58.6	9.0	3,311	68.8	64.6	10.5
Petersburg city	1,202	1,142	-5.0	1,224	29.7	2.4	0.5	0.3	67.2	27.8	58.7	13.5	411	72.5	67.2	8.3
Petrolia city	686	662	-3.5	651	88.5	0.0	0.0	5.8	5.7	19.2	60.5	20.3	259	86.1	71.0	6.2
Petronila city	113	115	1.8	193	55.4	0.0	0.0	6.2	38.3	42.5	39.4	18.1	60	80.0	16.7	26.7
Pettus CDP	558	NA	NA	613	69.0	0.5	0.0	0.0	30.5	30.7	58.3	11.1	160	65.6	82.5	0.0
Pflugerville city	48,356	54,644	13.0	52,138	46.8	15.0	8.7	2.1	27.4	29.7	63.6	6.9	17,968	77.3	24.6	39.4
Pharr city	70,470	75,382	7.0	73,143	5.5	0.0	0.5	0.2	93.7	34.5	54.8	10.7	19,971	60.5	62.9	16.2
Pilot Point city	3,858	4,056	5.1	3,967	55.8	0.2	0.0	4.3	39.8	25.1	62.3	12.7	1,473	72.2	47.3	13.0
Pine Forest city	487	501	2.9	519	95.0	0.0	0.0	0.0	5.0	30.8	55.7	13.5	179	82.7	63.7	7.3
Pine Harbor CDP	810	NA	NA	597	89.4	0.0	0.0	1.2	9.4	14.2	64.2	21.6	298	77.2	76.5	0.0
Pinehurst CDP	4,624	NA	NA	4,835	53.1	0.3	0.0	1.1	45.5	31.4	60.6	8.1	1,504	86.5	57.0	15.0
Pinehurst city	2,094	2,083	-0.5	2,023	70.5	22.3	0.4	2.4	4.3	19.4	59.1	21.4	881	55.3	46.8	11.8
Pine Island town	977	1,038	6.2	1,182	47.7	6.1	0.0	0.4	45.8	22.9	61.9	15.1	366	74.6	52.5	19.4
Pineland city	855	815	-4.7	1,240	61.3	14.0	0.0	1.2	23.5	45.8	41.9	12.1	302	69.5	54.0	7.6
Pinewood Estates CDP	1,678	NA	NA	1,779	91.6	0.0	0.7	5.2	2.5	25.9	58.6	15.5	572	100.0	17.8	44.1
Piney Point Village city	3,125	3,342	6.9	3,228	79.2	0.0	12.4	1.6	6.8	22.4	56.4	21.1	1,135	95.3	2.4	93.3
Pittsburg city	4,500	4,580	1.8	4,517	25.5	29.4	0.9	2.1	42.1	28.7	58.0	13.4	1,594	50.8	62.0	14.6
Placedo CDP	692	NA	NA	816	13.0	11.5	0.0	1.3	74.1	39.2	52.7	8.1	249	66.3	68.7	0.0
Plains town	1,481	1,570	6.0	1,914	38.3	0.3	0.0	0.8	60.6	40.0	50.7	9.1	573	68.6	53.6	18.7
Plainview city	22,200	21,166	-4.7	21,952	34.6	3.9	0.4	2.1	59.0	30.2	57.4	12.4	7,485	59.1	59.1	16.0
Plano city	259,841	278,480	7.2	271,166	56.9	7.3	18.1	3.0	14.7	25.0	64.6	10.4	102,182	63.1	15.3	58.8
Pleak village	1,043	1,292	23.9	1,260	30.5	2.5	0.0	0.0	67.0	30.6	51.8	17.6	417	84.7	58.5	16.5
Pleasant Hill CDP	522	NA	NA	787	40.0	19.9	0.0	0.0	40.0	35.8	57.4	6.9	195	75.9	50.3	0.0
Pleasanton city	8,940	9,638	7.8	9,283	38.9	1.3	0.1	0.9	58.7	28.3	57.3	14.3	3,068	59.5	54.3	17.7
Pleasant Valley town	336	335	-0.3	358	97.2	0.0	1.4	0.0	1.4	16.4	67.3	16.2	149	87.2	48.3	27.5
Plum Grove city	599	622	3.8	519	93.3	0.0	0.0	0.0	6.7	23.5	59.4	17.1	219	67.6	69.4	0.9
Point city	820	826	0.7	727	83.1	5.2	0.6	0.0	11.1	25.8	61.1	13.1	268	47.0	67.9	8.2
Point Blank city	691	712	3.0	749	82.9	12.0	0.0	0.0	5.1	31.3	42.6	26.0	276	90.6	43.5	21.0
Point Comfort city	737	725	-1.6	620	55.2	3.5	4.8	3.5	32.9	27.3	58.1	14.5	215	59.1	40.5	8.8
Point Venture village	800	873	9.1	791	87.9	0.8	0.8	0.6	10.0	13.7	64.3	21.9	391	88.7	12.5	49.6
Ponder town	1,395	1,484	6.4	1,536	76.6	4.8	0.1	8.4	10.0	32.0	61.2	6.6	484	91.3	35.5	20.9
Port Aransas city	3,480	3,876	11.4	3,677	96.2	0.2	0.2	1.0	2.5	17.8	57.1	25.1	1,850	62.1	24.4	35.9
Port Arthur city	54,376	54,548	0.3	54,685	23.2	37.1	6.9	1.7	31.1	28.1	60.2	11.6	20,283	57.8	58.4	10.4
Porter Heights CDP	1,653	NA	NA	1,344	46.1	2.9	1.9	4.5	44.6	23.1	50.1	26.9	578	83.7	68.3	1.6
Port Isabel city	5,012	5,022	0.2	5,033	19.5	0.7	0.0	0.5	79.3	25.6	58.7	15.6	1,734	53.0	70.2	12.2
Portland city	15,102	15,915	5.4	15,420	56.3	2.2	1.5	1.8	38.1	30.9	58.6	10.6	5,239	62.3	29.9	29.1
Port Lavaca city	12,248	12,399	1.2	12,289	31.6	4.1	4.3	2.5	57.6	27.7	58.2	14.0	4,361	59.4	51.8	16.7
Port Mansfield CDP	226	NA	NA	104	93.3	0.0	0.0	0.0	6.7	9.6	39.5	51.0	61	82.0	45.9	47.5
Port Neches city	13,040	12,755	-2.2	12,877	82.3	3.6	3.9	1.7	8.6	23.6	61.4	15.1	4,818	76.8	34.5	29.5
Port O'Connor CDP	1,253	NA	NA	1,153	69.9	0.0	0.0	0.3	29.8	21.0	63.5	15.5	421	91.2	34.9	25.4
Post city	5,376	5,365	-0.2	4,841	31.2	6.5	0.1	0.5	61.7	18.0	72.5	9.5	1,111	70.0	63.8	9.3
Post Oak Bend City town	633	666	5.2	923	96.5	0.1	0.0	0.5	2.8	25.5	54.9	19.7	292	91.1	40.1	29.1
Poteet city	3,263	3,393	4.0	3,331	4.4	0.0	0.0	0.2	95.5	28.5	56.8	14.8	1,045	68.8	73.0	3.3
Poth town	1,908	2,103	10.2	2,070	37.0	0.0	0.0	1.3	61.6	29.6	58.0	12.3	668	72.8	56.0	18.9
Potosi CDP	2,991	NA	NA	3,335	85.2	0.0	0.2	2.9	11.6	37.5	50.2	12.4	1,011	92.9	31.7	32.1
Pottsboro town	2,160	2,218	2.7	2,360	93.0	0.3	0.0	3.8	3.0	27.3	58.0	14.7	835	67.8	19.3	27.8
Powderly CDP	1,178	NA	NA	1,050	92.9	3.1	0.0	3.3	0.7	18.7	58.9	22.3	439	89.1	44.0	21.4
Powell town	136	138	1.5	146	52.1	26.7	0.0	19.2	2.1	26.7	55.5	17.8	56	55.4	69.6	7.1
Poynor town	305	305	0.0	275	100.0	0.0	0.0	0.0	0.0	25.0	64.3	10.5	93	88.2	50.5	7.5
Prado Verde CDP	246	NA	NA	295	4.7	0.0	0.0	0.0	95.3	30.5	62.4	7.1	80	63.8	18.8	23.8
Prairie View city	5,571	6,197	11.2	5,890	10.7	71.3	2.2	4.1	11.7	5.2	91.7	3.1	738	39.4	27.0	20.6
Premont city	2,653	2,661	0.3	2,674	12.9	0.0	0.0	0.2	86.9	24.9	52.9	22.4	936	78.7	71.9	4.1
Presidio city	4,426	3,952	-10.7	4,237	2.1	0.0	2.9	0.4	94.5	33.6	49.5	16.8	1,359	66.0	84.8	8.6
Preston CDP	2,096	NA	NA	1,876	93.4	0.0	0.4	3.8	2.3	10.8	56.5	32.6	918	89.4	33.9	18.2
Primera town	4,059	4,208	3.7	4,138	5.4	0.3	0.0	0.0	94.3	30.1	60.5	9.4	1,203	78.8	51.3	15.8
Princeton city	6,774	8,140	20.2	7,520	63.3	9.8	0.4	1.3	25.2	31.0	59.3	9.6	2,703	68.5	45.6	17.9
Progreso city	5,506	5,861	6.4	5,709	0.9	0.0	0.0	0.0	99.1	30.7	60.9	8.4	1,348	77.4	78.3	1.0
Progreso Lakes city	239	251	5.0	336	28.0	0.0	0.0	0.0	72.0	16.7	60.4	22.9	115	100.0	55.7	19.1
Prosper town	9,523	14,416	51.4	12,503	79.8	7.4	3.1	0.5	9.2	37.3	57.3	5.5	3,783	77.3	14.0	48.6
Providence Village town	4,798	5,311	10.7	4,975	71.0	9.4	0.3	1.7	17.6	38.6	57.8	3.5	1,398	81.5	15.5	53.6
Pueblo East CDP	0	NA	NA	0	0.0	0.0	0.0	0.0	0.0	0.0	0.0	0.0	0	0.0	0.0	0.0
Pueblo Nuevo CDP	521	NA	NA	630	0.0	0.0	0.0	0.0	100.0	49.9	46.1	4.0	142	81.7	93.7	0.0
Putnam town	94	93	-1.1	49	100.0	0.0	0.0	0.0	0.0	20.4	63.3	16.3	17	70.6	64.7	0.0
Pyote town	114	123	7.9	121	86.8	0.0	0.0	0.0	13.2	38.0	48.9	13.2	48	70.8	43.8	14.6
Quail CDP	19	NA	NA	44	34.1	0.0	0.0	65.9	0.0	11.4	65.9	22.7	15	100.0	80.0	0.0
Quail Creek CDP	1,628	NA	NA	1,475	51.2	0.0	3.8	1.2	43.8	13.2	80.8	6.0	596	94.3	33.4	27.5
Quanah city	2,638	2,496	-5.4	2,744	62.4	13.1	1.0	0.6	23.0	29.3	55.2	15.5	1,111	64.7	55.2	17.5

1 May be of any race.

Table A. All Places — **Population and Housing**

STATE City, town, township, borough, or CDP (county if applicable)	2010 census total population	2014 estimated population	Percent change 2010-2014	ACS total population estimate 2010-2014	White alone, not Hispanic or Latino	Black alone, not Hispanic or Latino	Asian alone, not Hispanic or Latino	All other races or 2 or more races, not Hispanic or Latino	Hispanic or Latino[1]	Under 18 years old	Age 18 to 64 years old	Age 65 years and older	Total occupied housing units	Percent owner occupied	High school diploma or less	Bachelor's degree or more
	1	2	3	4	5	6	7	8	9	10	11	12	13	14	15	16
TEXAS—Con.																
Queen City city	1,482	1,471	-0.7	1,883	74.5	21.4	0.9	1.4	1.8	25.3	55.8	18.8	637	58.9	65.8	5.8
Quemado CDP	230	NA	NA	58	13.8	0.0	0.0	0.0	86.2	0.0	29.3	70.7	45	100.0	100.0	0.0
Quesada CDP	25	NA	NA	0	0.0	0.0	0.0	0.0	0.0	0.0	0.0	0.0	0	0.0	0.0	0.0
Quinlan city	1,394	1,416	1.6	1,618	83.8	0.0	0.0	0.6	15.6	26.9	58.9	14.2	543	54.1	65.6	5.9
Quintana town	56	63	12.5	45	95.6	0.0	0.0	4.4	13.3	80.1	6.7	17	47.1	64.7	0.0
Quitaque city	411	386	-6.1	401	51.4	4.5	0.0	2.5	41.6	22.9	57.8	19.2	158	64.6	51.9	22.2
Quitman city	1,809	1,815	0.3	2,082	83.7	4.6	0.1	2.3	9.4	18.9	53.8	27.2	819	61.7	49.7	17.7
Radar Base CDP	762	NA	NA	494	2.6	0.0	0.0	0.0	97.4	0.6	99.4	0.0	33	54.5	90.9	0.0
Rafael Pena CDP	17	NA	NA	0	0.0	0.0	0.0	0.0	0.0	0.0	0.0	0.0	0	0.0	0.0	0.0
Ralls city	1,944	1,878	-3.4	1,873	33.2	3.9	0.0	0.0	62.9	30.3	51.2	18.5	619	64.5	65.4	9.0
Ramireno CDP	35	NA	NA	0	0.0	0.0	0.0	0.0	0.0	0.0	0.0	0.0	0	0.0	0.0	0.0
Ramirez-Perez CDP	78	NA	NA	61	0.0	0.0	0.0	0.0	100.0	32.8	67.2	0.0	23	100.0	0.0	0.0
Ramos CDP	116	NA	NA	90	0.0	0.0	0.0	0.0	100.0	23.4	76.8	0.0	23	73.9	78.3	0.0
Ranchette Estates CDP	152	NA	NA	75	0.0	0.0	0.0	0.0	100.0	22.7	77.3	0.0	12	100.0	100.0	0.0
Ranchitos Del Norte CDP	112	NA	NA	16	0.0	0.0	0.0	0.0	100.0	0.0	56.3	43.8	7	100.0	100.0	0.0
Ranchitos East CDP	212	NA	NA	251	0.0	0.0	0.0	0.0	100.0	23.5	76.6	0.0	69	84.1	65.2	0.0
Ranchitos Las Lomas CDP	266	NA	NA	191	15.2	0.0	0.0	0.0	84.8	32.0	52.8	15.2	51	39.2	100.0	0.0
Rancho Alegre CDP	1,704	NA	NA	1,177	3.3	0.0	0.0	0.0	96.7	14.6	71.3	14.0	380	86.8	94.5	0.0
Rancho Banquete CDP	424	NA	NA	503	7.0	0.0	0.0	0.0	93.0	29.9	67.8	2.4	132	100.0	43.9	9.1
Rancho Chico CDP	396	NA	NA	330	34.5	0.0	0.0	0.0	65.5	12.7	63.0	24.2	142	59.9	77.5	0.0
Ranchos Penitas West CDP	573	NA	NA	910	0.0	0.0	0.0	0.0	100.0	36.7	50.4	12.9	184	82.6	95.7	4.3
Rancho Viejo town	2,432	2,495	2.6	2,440	38.9	0.0	1.6	0.9	58.6	23.5	49.6	26.8	950	80.7	19.9	65.4
Rancho Viejo CDP	228	NA	NA	331	0.0	0.0	0.0	0.0	100.0	27.2	65.8	6.9	61	100.0	59.0	0.0
Randolph AFB CDP	1,241	NA	NA	1,166	70.2	11.9	6.2	2.7	8.9	40.4	59.5	0.2	268	0.7	4.5	68.7
Ranger city	2,468	2,454	-0.6	2,921	63.5	5.3	0.2	0.7	30.2	29.2	57.0	13.9	923	62.1	59.7	5.6
Rangerville village	289	NA	NA	315	0.0	0.0	5.1	0.0	94.9	54.3	35.9	9.8	81	29.6	100.0	0.0
Rankin city	778	800	2.8	797	66.1	1.5	0.0	0.3	32.1	24.5	63.2	12.3	294	70.7	57.8	7.1
Ransom Canyon town	1,096	1,125	2.6	1,411	79.4	0.0	0.7	0.9	19.0	25.7	61.0	13.3	515	88.7	13.4	51.8
Ratamosa CDP	254	NA	NA	231	0.0	0.0	0.0	0.0	100.0	77.1	22.9	0.0	53	100.0	100.0	0.0
Ravenna city	209	207	-1.0	169	81.7	0.0	7.7	7.7	3.0	10.7	69.2	20.1	85	94.1	58.8	9.4
Raymondville city	11,277	11,117	-1.4	11,226	7.9	2.7	0.1	0.3	88.9	21.1	66.7	12.1	2,545	79.1	71.0	7.7
Realitos CDP	184	NA	NA	377	4.5	0.0	0.0	0.0	95.5	45.1	43.2	11.7	98	100.0	82.7	17.3
Redfield CDP	441	NA	NA	352	79.5	14.8	0.0	0.0	5.7	39.7	45.7	14.5	173	54.9	15.0	31.8
Redford CDP	90	NA	NA	25	0.0	0.0	0.0	72.0	28.0	0.0	72.0	28.0	16	56.3	43.8	0.0
Redland CDP	1,047	NA	NA	967	61.1	28.2	0.0	0.0	10.7	42.4	44.7	12.9	397	72.0	48.4	13.9
Red Lick city	1,011	1,006	-0.5	965	91.7	3.4	0.0	1.8	3.1	24.9	62.1	13.1	344	84.6	23.3	34.0
Red Oak city	10,769	11,560	7.3	11,149	55.9	14.2	2.9	0.9	26.1	28.7	62.2	9.2	3,617	69.6	40.5	19.9
Redwater city	1,058	1,060	0.2	1,190	91.6	4.1	0.3	2.9	1.1	32.2	57.5	10.4	404	55.4	53.2	14.1
Redwood CDP	4,338	NA	NA	4,034	5.6	4.1	0.0	0.0	90.4	28.8	64.3	6.8	927	77.7	77.2	6.4
Refugio town	2,893	2,838	-1.9	2,838	32.6	10.9	0.0	2.1	54.4	23.3	55.9	20.8	1,112	66.3	48.7	8.6
Regino Ramirez CDP	85	NA	NA	83	0.0	0.0	0.0	0.0	100.0	63.9	16.9	19.3	23	100.0	100.0	0.0
Reid Hope King CDP	786	NA	NA	548	0.0	0.0	0.0	0.0	100.0	31.9	63.0	5.1	177	43.5	83.1	6.2
Reklaw city	381	380	-0.3	376	76.3	0.0	3.7	3.7	16.2	22.9	54.6	22.6	127	96.1	58.3	18.9
Relampago CDP	132	NA	NA	22	0.0	0.0	0.0	0.0	100.0	0.0	0.0	100.0	22	0.0	100.0	0.0
Rendon CDP	12,552	NA	NA	13,743	74.0	4.2	1.1	2.1	18.5	26.8	62.0	11.2	4,433	82.5	35.7	24.5
Reno city (Lamar)	3,170	3,262	2.9	3,238	85.0	2.6	0.0	3.8	8.6	31.0	56.4	12.6	1,160	74.4	29.1	35.2
Reno city (Parker and Tarrant)	2,493	2,643	6.0	2,551	91.7	0.8	0.0	3.0	4.5	25.4	59.5	15.1	852	80.4	46.6	15.8
Retreat town	372	387	4.0	346	81.5	8.4	0.0	0.0	10.1	19.4	59.7	20.8	143	93.7	45.5	9.8
Rhome city	1,524	1,590	4.3	1,598	77.8	1.7	0.1	2.4	17.9	25.7	66.4	7.8	566	74.4	46.6	15.5
Ricardo CDP	1,048	NA	NA	884	30.0	0.0	0.0	0.0	70.0	9.9	75.3	14.7	254	85.4	49.2	15.4
Rice city	918	928	1.1	1,072	69.5	2.8	0.0	0.5	27.2	35.7	58.6	5.7	317	62.5	53.9	6.0
Richardson city	99,223	108,617	9.5	103,752	56.1	8.3	15.3	3.7	16.6	21.8	65.0	13.2	39,576	60.4	18.2	55.2
Richland town	266	265	-0.4	225	80.0	6.2	4.0	4.0	5.8	18.3	58.7	23.1	118	66.9	62.7	10.2
Richland Hills city	7,787	8,041	3.3	7,933	76.9	2.3	0.7	2.9	17.2	17.4	64.8	17.7	3,109	66.8	38.9	19.8
Richland Springs town	338	325	-3.8	332	73.2	0.0	0.0	3.3	23.5	33.7	49.0	17.2	120	75.0	38.3	5.0
Richmond city	11,588	12,018	3.7	11,769	26.1	12.3	0.4	0.2	61.0	25.4	62.6	12.1	3,520	55.0	61.8	14.0
Richwood city	3,512	3,755	6.9	3,618	49.7	13.1	0.0	2.4	34.7	28.0	61.4	10.4	1,472	64.5	40.4	20.2
Riesel city	1,007	1,020	1.3	947	88.3	0.0	0.0	2.7	9.0	29.6	55.4	14.9	342	77.2	44.7	17.3
Rio Bravo city	4,802	4,855	1.1	4,880	2.6	0.0	0.0	0.0	97.4	37.1	56.1	6.9	1,195	83.6	74.1	5.3
Rio Grande City city	13,803	14,227	3.1	14,033	5.6	0.0	0.1	0.8	93.5	34.8	56.2	9.1	3,837	66.7	65.2	15.2
Rio Hondo city	2,397	2,430	1.4	2,146	17.4	0.6	0.5	0.0	81.6	22.1	56.5	21.5	779	73.7	53.1	8.5
Rio Vista city	873	920	5.4	1,006	87.2	0.0	0.0	2.1	10.7	32.8	57.0	10.4	345	71.9	40.6	6.4
Rising Star town	835	822	-1.6	1,077	84.8	0.0	0.0	0.0	15.2	30.0	50.3	19.8	347	77.8	66.6	12.1
Rivereno CDP	61	NA	NA	0	0.0	0.0	0.0	0.0	0.0	0.0	0.0	0.0	0	0.0	0.0	0.0
River Oaks city	7,427	7,671	3.3	7,575	43.7	1.7	2.7	1.8	50.2	30.2	59.7	10.1	2,630	70.6	55.7	12.9
Riverside city	510	504	-1.2	549	77.6	13.3	0.0	0.0	9.1	22.0	59.7	18.2	240	78.3	65.4	9.6
Riviera CDP	689	NA	NA	751	30.6	0.0	0.0	0.0	69.4	29.7	57.2	13.2	241	79.3	59.8	5.0
Roanoke city	5,962	6,974	17.0	6,488	73.5	2.8	4.7	5.4	13.6	23.7	65.9	10.4	3,009	57.9	24.7	28.3
Roaring Springs town	234	223	-4.7	289	88.9	0.0	0.3	0.0	10.7	15.6	62.2	22.1	118	79.7	42.4	18.6
Robert Lee city	1,049	1,032	-1.6	1,106	66.2	0.0	0.0	1.2	32.6	21.0	53.4	25.7	500	70.0	63.8	9.4
Robinson city	10,508	11,416	8.6	11,051	80.7	2.6	0.0	0.7	16.0	24.7	60.6	14.6	3,826	78.7	39.2	25.5
Robstown city	11,487	11,657	1.5	11,599	6.7	0.5	0.1	0.3	92.4	28.5	57.7	13.9	3,446	59.0	66.8	6.9
Roby city	643	622	-3.3	602	55.8	6.1	0.7	0.7	36.7	26.4	51.0	22.6	221	75.1	59.7	10.9
Rochester town	324	317	-2.2	261	64.4	8.4	0.0	11.9	15.3	19.5	57.4	23.0	128	74.2	60.2	12.5
Rockdale city	5,579	5,556	-0.4	5,506	60.3	9.4	1.2	0.8	28.2	26.0	60.3	13.8	2,135	53.5	49.1	20.1
Rockport city	9,366	10,323	10.2	9,776	71.6	2.3	2.3	3.1	20.8	20.6	52.1	27.0	3,914	71.4	31.8	33.0
Rocksprings town	1,181	1,108	-6.2	1,414	34.5	1.1	0.0	0.0	64.4	20.8	54.1	25.2	498	87.6	67.3	15.9
Rockwall city	37,572	41,785	11.2	39,948	72.0	5.6	1.9	3.5	17.0	28.5	60.5	10.9	13,722	74.0	23.3	42.4
Rocky Mound town	68	69	1.5	68	70.6	26.5	0.0	0.0	2.9	33.9	51.6	14.7	25	64.0	68.0	12.0
Rogers town	1,218	1,209	-0.7	949	53.3	3.5	0.2	1.7	41.3	22.8	64.6	12.8	328	79.0	63.4	6.1
Rollingwood city	1,412	1,523	7.9	1,453	88.6	0.0	2.3	2.8	6.3	27.4	59.0	13.7	498	96.6	3.6	85.7
Roma city	9,765	10,088	3.3	9,938	2.1	0.0	0.0	0.4	97.4	30.3	53.2	16.6	2,812	67.4	73.2	11.9
Roma Creek CDP	350	NA	NA	371	0.0	0.0	0.0	0.0	100.0	46.4	50.0	3.5	83	73.5	36.1	54.2
Roman Forest town	1,541	1,814	17.7	2,008	66.0	5.6	2.2	1.4	24.8	27.6	57.0	15.2	642	91.1	43.0	15.1
Ropesville city	434	445	2.5	403	31.5	3.7	0.0	1.5	63.3	27.5	49.6	23.1	145	83.4	60.7	13.1
Roscoe city	1,334	1,324	-0.7	1,431	48.8	0.0	1.3	0.7	49.2	29.0	55.6	15.7	500	80.8	57.6	12.8
Rosebud city	1,431	1,381	-3.5	1,377	46.0	26.7	0.7	1.2	25.6	22.1	56.0	21.9	476	70.0	55.3	14.1
Rose City city	502	514	2.4	432	87.7	0.0	0.0	0.0	12.3	10.2	75.9	13.9	183	88.5	72.7	11.5

1 May be of any race.

Table A. All Places — **Population and Housing**

STATE City, town, township, borough, or CDP (county if applicable)	Population				Race and Hispanic or Latino origin (percent), 2010–2014					Age (percent), 2010–2014			Households, 2010–2014		Householders by level of education (percent)	
	2010 census total population	2014 estimated population	Percent change 2010-2014	ACS total population estimate 2010-2014	White alone, not Hispanic or Latino	Black alone, not Hispanic or Latino	Asian alone, not Hispanic or Latino	All other races or 2 or more races, not Hispanic or Latino	Hispanic or Latino[1]	Under 18 years old	Age 18 to 64 years old	Age 65 years and older	Total occupied housing units	Percent owner occupied	High school diploma or less	Bachelor's degree or more
	1	2	3	4	5	6	7	8	9	10	11	12	13	14	15	16
TEXAS—Con.																
Rose Hill Acres city	441	444	0.7	460	94.3	0.0	0.0	2.2	3.5	16.1	61.6	22.4	177	87.0	37.3	18.6
Rosenberg city	31,383	34,468	9.8	32,789	26.3	11.2	2.5	0.9	59.0	28.4	61.4	10.2	10,855	51.2	57.2	14.2
Rosharon CDP	1,152	NA	NA	1,940	23.8	41.9	0.0	0.0	34.3	27.2	66.2	6.6	561	71.8	70.8	5.3
Rosita CDP	2,704	NA	NA	2,286	0.1	0.0	0.0	20.8	79.1	40.6	54.8	4.4	575	79.0	67.7	6.3
Ross city	283	287	1.4	279	76.0	0.0	0.0	0.4	23.7	19.4	62.8	17.9	107	81.3	43.0	16.8
Rosser village	332	349	5.1	317	62.1	18.6	1.6	13.9	3.8	14.8	64.3	20.8	124	76.6	86.3	5.6
Rotan city	1,508	1,444	-4.2	1,588	49.4	4.9	0.7	2.0	42.9	20.3	58.5	21.3	649	66.3	59.8	11.9
Round Mountain town	181	181	0.0	331	85.5	0.0	0.0	0.3	14.2	12.9	60.0	26.9	113	79.6	71.7	15.9
Round Rock city	99,990	112,744	12.8	106,972	52.9	9.1	5.3	2.7	29.9	30.3	63.1	6.6	35,338	60.0	22.8	41.2
Round Top town	90	92	2.2	80	97.5	0.0	0.0	2.5	0.0	11.4	40.2	48.8	44	84.1	18.2	50.0
Rowlett city	56,242	58,407	3.8	57,532	56.3	14.0	7.0	2.2	20.5	25.8	65.0	9.1	18,251	86.0	27.8	35.0
Roxton city	650	643	-1.1	615	78.0	12.7	0.0	6.2	3.1	16.7	65.8	17.6	289	50.5	48.4	9.3
Royse City city	9,375	10,757	14.7	9,755	78.1	5.2	0.5	1.9	14.4	36.3	57.0	6.6	3,043	74.3	40.6	24.7
Rule town	636	623	-2.0	617	77.5	1.9	0.0	0.6	19.9	21.5	53.4	25.1	274	86.5	61.3	10.9
Runaway Bay city	1,286	1,381	7.4	1,653	82.0	0.0	0.3	3.2	14.5	18.9	60.2	20.9	685	81.8	36.8	27.2
Runge town	1,031	1,069	3.7	1,138	20.9	0.8	0.0	0.0	78.3	20.2	63.4	16.3	413	58.6	73.4	3.6
Rusk city	5,553	5,579	0.5	5,573	59.1	25.4	0.7	0.9	14.0	23.2	66.1	10.8	1,166	57.5	52.6	14.7
Sabinal city	1,695	1,710	0.9	1,703	26.8	0.8	0.0	0.0	72.4	36.0	46.3	17.5	539	78.3	52.7	9.1
Sachse city	20,329	23,681	16.5	21,790	57.8	12.6	11.3	1.9	16.4	26.8	66.1	7.2	7,147	86.5	23.6	37.5
Sadler city	349	352	0.9	379	100.0	0.0	0.0	0.0	0.0	25.3	62.7	11.9	160	60.6	45.6	13.8
Saginaw city	19,806	21,703	9.6	20,840	68.1	3.8	1.9	3.1	23.3	30.1	62.8	7.2	6,566	77.7	38.7	21.9
St. Hedwig town	2,089	2,289	9.6	1,872	86.0	0.1	0.1	0.5	13.4	16.7	67.3	16.0	651	86.3	50.7	18.9
St. Jo city	1,043	1,022	-2.0	1,072	96.1	0.0	1.1	0.6	2.2	25.6	57.9	16.5	392	74.0	53.3	16.1
St. Paul town	1,066	1,125	5.5	1,270	68.3	5.9	10.2	2.2	13.4	30.2	59.3	10.5	378	88.9	29.4	38.6
St. Paul CDP	584	NA	NA	991	27.7	0.0	0.0	0.0	72.3	22.0	70.5	7.7	243	68.7	59.7	0.0
Salado village	2,126	2,134	0.4	1,681	82.2	4.5	1.9	0.8	10.6	14.9	53.7	31.5	763	88.3	20.3	56.9
Salineño CDP	201	NA	NA	89	0.0	0.0	0.0	0.0	100.0	0.0	78.6	21.3	42	54.8	100.0	0.0
Salineño North CDP	115	NA	NA	26	0.0	0.0	0.0	0.0	100.0	0.0	84.6	15.4	20	100.0	100.0	0.0
Sammy Martinez CDP	110	NA	NA	107	0.0	0.0	0.0	0.0	100.0	65.4	34.5	0.0	23	100.0	73.9	0.0
Samnorwood CDP	51	NA	NA	22	100.0	0.0	0.0	0.0	0.0	27.3	40.9	31.8	9	100.0	0.0	66.7
Sam Rayburn CDP	1,181	NA	NA	1,162	99.5	0.0	0.0	0.5	0.0	5.9	66.7	27.6	453	100.0	47.5	28.0
San Angelo city	93,227	98,975	6.2	96,177	52.8	4.6	1.3	1.5	39.9	23.1	62.9	14.0	36,157	59.0	43.7	22.6
San Antonio city	1,327,556	1,436,697	8.2	1,385,438	26.3	6.4	2.3	1.6	63.3	26.1	62.7	11.0	484,219	55.0	39.3	27.8
San Augustine city	2,114	2,050	-3.0	2,409	41.5	43.9	0.0	0.5	14.2	24.9	49.5	25.6	692	62.7	60.4	15.0
San Benito city	24,253	24,506	1.0	24,447	6.4	0.1	0.3	0.4	92.9	32.7	54.5	12.9	7,329	66.3	66.0	11.2
San Carlos CDP	3,130	NA	NA	3,318	1.7	0.0	0.0	0.0	98.3	34.9	58.8	6.4	857	85.4	75.5	4.9
San Carlos I CDP	316	NA	NA	258	0.0	0.0	0.0	0.0	100.0	58.9	41.1	0.0	47	100.0	100.0	0.0
San Carlos II CDP	261	NA	NA	189	0.0	0.0	0.0	0.0	100.0	48.6	51.3	0.0	23	100.0	100.0	0.0
Sanctuary town	327	341	4.3	339	85.8	2.7	6.8	1.2	3.5	21.8	57.7	20.4	135	68.9	40.0	11.9
Sanderson CDP	837	NA	NA	746	33.0	1.7	1.6	0.0	63.7	16.4	56.9	26.8	375	66.1	60.0	18.1
Sandia CDP	379	NA	NA	642	6.2	0.0	0.0	0.0	93.8	59.0	30.4	10.6	154	94.2	87.7	0.0
San Diego city	4,477	4,400	-1.7	4,813	8.7	0.4	0.0	0.0	90.9	22.7	61.8	15.4	1,733	66.9	64.2	6.0
Sandoval CDP	32	NA	NA	9	0.0	0.0	0.0	0.0	100.0	33.3	66.6	0.0	3	100.0	0.0	100.0
Sand Springs CDP	835	NA	NA	921	84.1	0.0	0.0	0.0	15.9	20.2	63.0	16.7	368	81.0	58.4	8.2
Sandy Hollow-Escondidas CDP	296	NA	NA	633	66.8	0.0	0.0	0.0	33.2	21.8	54.1	24.0	185	88.6	84.3	6.5
Sandy Point city	207	212	2.4	1,284	30.5	29.7	0.0	0.0	39.8	0.5	97.3	2.3	78	55.1	56.4	12.8
San Elizario CDP	13,603	NA	NA	14,360	0.3	0.0	0.0	0.0	99.6	41.5	53.0	5.5	3,401	73.9	78.0	2.9
San Felipe town	746	770	3.2	739	53.0	28.8	0.0	5.0	13.1	12.5	74.6	12.7	345	66.1	62.9	14.5
San Fernando CDP	68	NA	NA	27	0.0	0.0	0.0	0.0	100.0	0.0	100.0	0.0	27	48.1	100.0	0.0
Sanford town	164	162	-1.2	128	84.4	0.0	3.1	3.1	9.4	20.3	48.5	31.3	49	87.8	51.0	2.0
Sanger city	6,922	7,601	9.8	7,237	72.1	6.2	0.3	1.4	20.0	32.4	59.7	8.0	2,399	64.4	39.6	20.3
San Isidro CDP	240	NA	NA	285	0.0	0.0	0.0	0.0	100.0	22.2	69.6	8.4	77	72.7	66.2	16.9
San Juan city	33,856	36,174	6.8	35,183	1.9	0.1	0.1	0.1	97.9	36.1	55.3	8.5	8,908	75.6	68.4	10.2
San Juan CDP	129	NA	NA	223	0.0	0.0	0.0	32.7	67.3	27.8	68.6	3.6	53	49.1	100.0	0.0
San Leanna village	497	533	7.2	537	76.9	2.0	0.4	0.0	20.7	12.5	66.8	20.7	226	86.7	16.4	35.8
San Leon CDP	4,970	NA	NA	5,255	64.3	1.4	9.8	1.8	22.7	16.7	70.8	12.5	2,129	72.9	49.5	19.5
San Marcos city	45,068	58,892	30.7	51,289	51.2	4.0	1.6	3.0	40.3	15.2	78.1	6.7	18,782	27.2	25.4	29.5
San Patricio city	390	395	1.3	517	58.4	0.0	0.0	0.0	41.6	13.9	73.0	13.2	186	87.6	55.9	4.3
San Pedro CDP	530	NA	NA	355	0.0	0.0	0.0	0.0	100.0	29.3	49.3	21.4	98	75.5	78.6	4.1
San Perlita city	573	567	-1.0	640	5.0	0.0	0.0	3.9	91.1	33.7	54.8	11.6	140	85.7	77.1	5.0
San Saba city	3,183	2,783	-12.6	3,006	53.1	4.2	0.5	1.6	40.7	24.9	58.4	16.9	884	70.8	57.1	13.6
Sansom Park city	4,686	4,825	3.0	4,769	41.3	0.2	2.4	1.3	54.8	30.6	61.2	8.4	1,319	68.6	67.3	6.7
Santa Anna town	1,099	1,045	-4.9	1,296	75.2	6.8	0.0	0.6	17.4	24.6	58.2	17.1	514	56.4	69.1	8.4
Santa Anna CDP	13	NA	NA	0	0.0	0.0	0.0	0.0	0.0	0.0	0.0	0.0	0	0.0	0.0	0.0
Santa Clara city	697	722	3.6	738	76.4	0.0	1.8	1.5	20.3	24.3	54.5	21.3	240	88.8	39.6	26.7
Santa Cruz CDP	54	NA	NA	155	0.0	0.0	0.0	0.0	100.0	0.0	59.4	40.6	45	100.0	100.0	0.0
Santa Fe city	12,347	12,860	4.2	12,572	85.4	0.2	0.3	1.4	12.7	23.5	61.2	15.3	4,798	81.2	45.3	12.2
Santa Maria CDP	733	NA	NA	930	1.1	0.0	0.0	0.0	98.9	34.4	50.1	15.8	253	79.8	81.4	2.0
Santa Monica CDP	83	NA	NA	100	38.0	0.0	0.0	0.0	62.0	7.0	76.0	17.0	34	100.0	67.6	0.0
Santa Rosa town	2,873	2,894	0.7	2,881	0.5	0.0	0.0	0.0	99.5	36.8	55.5	7.7	752	72.9	73.3	6.6
Santa Rosa CDP	241	NA	NA	130	0.0	0.0	0.0	0.0	100.0	17.7	75.3	6.9	35	82.9	85.7	0.0
Santel CDP	44	NA	NA	347	0.0	0.0	0.0	0.0	100.0	0.0	100.0	0.0	62	100.0	100.0	0.0
San Ygnacio CDP	667	NA	NA	335	0.0	0.0	0.0	0.0	100.0	26.3	57.4	16.4	109	79.8	33.0	20.2
Sarita CDP	238	NA	NA	442	19.0	0.0	0.0	0.0	81.0	29.7	56.6	13.8	101	33.7	64.4	0.0
Savannah CDP	3,318	NA	NA	4,115	76.3	3.8	1.7	3.5	14.6	38.6	57.3	4.0	1,099	79.3	15.4	43.9
Savoy city	828	835	0.8	542	85.8	3.0	0.0	5.2	6.1	13.1	49.9	37.1	205	70.7	45.9	10.2
Scenic Oaks CDP	4,957	NA	NA	5,456	64.2	4.0	4.9	1.8	25.1	29.0	59.9	11.1	1,734	94.9	10.3	59.9
Schertz city	31,793	36,896	16.1	35,093	57.7	8.8	3.0	3.9	26.6	26.8	61.4	11.9	12,273	77.4	24.4	37.1
Schulenburg city	2,853	2,893	1.4	2,885	64.5	11.9	0.0	1.2	22.3	28.2	43.8	28.0	1,012	61.8	65.8	12.4
Scissors CDP	3,186	NA	NA	3,014	0.5	0.0	0.0	0.0	99.5	40.3	53.1	6.5	693	72.3	97.0	0.0
Scotland city	501	485	-3.2	612	78.9	0.0	0.2	1.1	19.8	25.3	64.5	10.3	200	89.0	57.0	16.0
Scottsville city	362	362	0.0	410	50.5	29.3	1.2	13.2	5.9	29.5	58.6	11.7	134	86.6	68.7	17.2
Scurry town	681	716	5.1	685	89.2	1.9	0.0	4.4	4.5	21.1	67.2	11.7	246	81.3	31.7	17.1
Seabrook city	11,952	12,792	7.0	12,437	72.9	3.0	7.2	2.4	14.4	25.6	68.0	6.3	4,856	63.4	16.7	45.8
Seadrift city	1,364	1,446	6.0	1,677	50.9	0.8	1.4	11.7	35.2	31.5	57.2	11.2	513	70.0	56.1	9.6
Seagoville city	14,915	15,723	5.4	15,379	49.0	14.5	1.3	0.6	34.6	25.5	66.1	8.3	4,457	70.4	62.8	10.7
Seagraves city	2,417	2,683	11.0	2,544	19.8	3.2	0.0	0.0	77.0	36.4	53.1	10.5	871	57.4	69.2	5.1
Sealy city	6,088	6,286	3.3	6,181	50.0	13.6	0.0	1.1	35.3	29.8	53.7	16.4	2,159	62.3	52.8	13.2
Sebastian CDP	1,917	NA	NA	1,676	0.0	2.3	0.0	0.0	97.7	25.3	60.7	14.0	515	84.1	90.9	3.9
Seco Mines CDP	560	NA	NA	503	9.7	0.0	0.0	0.0	90.3	23.6	57.9	18.5	189	56.1	47.6	18.0

1 May be of any race.

Table A. All Places — **Population and Housing**

STATE City, town, township, borough, or CDP (county if applicable)	Population: 2010 census total population	Population: 2014 estimated population	Population: Percent change 2010-2014	Population: ACS total population estimate 2010-2014	Race and Hispanic or Latino origin (percent), 2010–2014: White alone, not Hispanic or Latino	Black alone, not Hispanic or Latino	Asian alone, not Hispanic or Latino	All other races or 2 or more races, not Hispanic or Latino	Hispanic or Latino[1]	Age (percent), 2010–2014: Under 18 years old	Age 18 to 64 years old	Age 65 years and older	Households, 2010–2014: Total occupied housing units	Percent owner occupied	Householders by level of education (percent): High school diploma or less	Bachelor's degree or more
	1	2	3	4	5	6	7	8	9	10	11	12	13	14	15	16
TEXAS—Con.																
Seguin city	25,173	27,041	7.4	26,237	37.7	8.4	1.2	1.1	51.6	23.9	59.2	16.9	9,382	63.8	57.8	16.7
Selma city	5,539	8,483	53.2	7,046	45.0	7.5	3.1	3.6	40.8	29.3	65.3	5.4	2,313	72.4	17.7	38.3
Seminole city	6,475	7,206	11.3	6,848	52.8	1.3	1.2	2.6	42.2	27.2	59.5	13.2	2,242	79.8	60.1	12.1
Serenada CDP	1,641	NA	NA	1,216	92.0	0.0	1.2	0.0	6.8	14.5	57.1	28.4	496	98.6	11.3	61.5
Seth Ward CDP	2,025	NA	NA	1,747	10.1	1.9	2.3	0.3	85.3	33.2	59.9	6.9	530	61.1	60.4	10.8
Seven Oaks city	112	111	-0.9	182	7.7	69.8	0.0	16.5	6.0	29.6	58.1	12.1	55	65.5	60.0	12.7
Seven Points city	1,452	1,450	-0.1	1,337	81.9	0.0	0.0	2.5	15.6	23.4	57.8	18.8	522	68.4	76.8	2.9
Seymour city	2,740	2,634	-3.9	2,521	80.4	2.1	0.0	2.3	15.3	25.5	49.7	24.7	1,211	66.3	50.4	14.2
Shadybrook CDP	1,967	NA	NA	1,969	99.0	0.4	0.0	0.6	0.0	19.2	70.5	10.4	776	61.0	36.1	22.2
Shady Hollow CDP	5,004	NA	NA	4,940	78.6	0.9	2.8	0.9	16.8	21.4	65.3	13.2	1,727	96.8	7.8	67.1
Shady Shores town	2,612	2,790	6.8	2,729	80.4	5.1	2.6	2.5	9.4	24.4	63.5	12.2	998	90.1	16.9	47.9
Shallowater city	2,478	2,536	2.3	2,514	71.3	0.0	1.1	0.7	26.9	28.9	61.8	9.2	863	71.6	37.5	31.9
Shamrock city	1,910	2,013	5.4	1,906	69.3	3.0	1.5	4.4	21.8	19.5	62.0	18.3	886	74.7	49.8	16.5
Shavano Park city	3,035	3,416	12.6	3,234	66.3	0.0	7.9	1.3	24.5	21.6	59.3	19.1	1,191	97.7	8.1	76.2
Sheldon CDP	1,990	NA	NA	1,585	17.0	5.1	1.0	1.1	75.7	20.0	62.3	17.6	521	82.3	58.5	15.0
Shenandoah city	2,135	2,664	24.8	2,397	83.1	3.3	3.5	1.2	8.9	17.8	60.6	21.6	1,059	52.2	21.2	40.7
Shepherd city	2,321	2,389	2.9	3,006	71.1	14.9	5.8	1.1	7.0	29.0	58.5	12.7	856	47.9	65.5	3.7
Sherman city	38,340	39,943	4.2	39,119	62.0	11.1	1.6	3.6	21.7	25.2	61.6	13.2	14,640	54.8	41.7	20.4
Sherwood Shores CDP	1,190	NA	NA	1,069	92.0	0.0	1.3	1.1	5.6	17.3	55.2	27.4	499	88.2	63.7	8.4
Shiner city	2,075	2,128	2.6	2,083	74.2	11.2	0.2	1.6	12.8	25.6	52.4	21.8	818	77.4	62.2	14.3
Shoreacres city	1,493	1,590	6.5	1,768	74.3	0.2	0.2	0.6	24.8	29.1	61.9	9.2	573	78.4	17.3	32.8
Sienna Plantation CDP	13,721	NA	NA	15,824	54.6	25.9	11.1	2.0	6.5	34.4	58.7	7.0	4,574	97.6	6.8	61.8
Sierra Blanca CDP	553	NA	NA	547	33.8	4.2	0.7	0.0	61.2	21.4	69.2	9.3	129	76.7	49.6	10.1
Siesta Acres CDP	1,885	NA	NA	1,894	0.0	0.0	0.0	0.0	100.0	23.7	65.3	10.9	528	75.0	76.7	9.7
Siesta Shores CDP	1,382	NA	NA	1,534	12.1	0.0	0.0	0.0	87.9	44.5	47.4	8.3	411	76.9	87.1	0.0
Silsbee city	6,599	6,692	1.4	6,676	56.3	29.6	1.7	2.1	10.3	25.0	57.9	17.0	2,684	65.5	49.7	14.3
Silverton city	731	686	-6.2	780	56.5	4.2	0.0	3.2	36.0	29.7	53.9	16.5	270	80.0	52.6	11.9
Simonton city	821	850	3.5	863	81.5	4.2	2.8	0.0	11.6	25.0	59.5	15.4	334	74.0	35.6	22.5
Sinton city	5,668	5,747	1.4	5,678	18.4	6.9	0.0	0.0	74.7	25.2	61.4	13.2	1,890	65.5	67.1	11.4
Skellytown town	473	460	-2.7	572	92.0	0.0	0.0	4.5	3.5	32.9	52.0	15.0	218	83.0	61.9	17.0
Skidmore CDP	925	NA	NA	1,055	24.5	6.9	0.0	0.0	68.5	10.2	67.2	22.5	391	65.5	59.1	3.6
Slaton city	6,104	6,068	-0.6	6,100	40.9	12.3	0.3	1.1	45.4	24.2	57.0	18.8	2,513	76.7	61.9	13.1
Smiley city	549	567	3.3	577	39.5	3.8	0.0	0.3	56.3	26.2	55.8	18.0	179	53.1	74.3	7.3
Smithville city	3,817	4,004	4.9	3,890	59.9	19.4	0.8	1.0	18.9	26.9	53.7	19.1	1,540	68.4	53.2	18.6
Smyer town	474	486	2.5	490	68.2	0.0	0.0	0.2	31.6	31.3	59.1	9.6	172	77.9	39.0	15.7
Snook city	511	508	-0.6	474	74.1	21.9	0.0	0.0	4.0	21.7	62.6	15.6	197	71.6	48.7	12.7
Snyder city	11,202	11,571	3.3	11,368	52.2	3.8	0.1	2.0	42.0	28.1	55.9	16.0	4,182	70.0	52.3	18.8
Socorro city	32,031	32,909	2.7	32,623	1.9	0.1	0.3	1.0	96.7	31.3	59.5	9.1	9,037	75.8	68.7	6.6
Solis CDP	512	NA	NA	561	11.4	0.0	0.0	0.0	88.6	41.5	40.3	18.2	157	82.2	66.9	19.7
Somerset city	1,631	1,750	7.3	1,488	21.3	0.3	0.1	2.7	75.7	26.7	59.9	13.6	483	66.3	54.9	8.7
Somerville city	1,376	1,367	-0.7	1,430	39.5	26.4	0.0	2.4	31.6	19.9	59.6	20.6	586	75.1	60.2	14.0
Sonora city	3,029	2,908	-4.0	2,877	43.4	0.2	0.0	0.8	55.6	29.4	56.7	13.9	1,072	64.5	50.0	17.4
Sour Lake city	1,813	1,783	-1.7	1,598	90.9	0.8	0.2	1.4	6.8	22.8	62.1	15.1	683	68.5	49.6	5.7
South Alamo CDP	3,361	NA	NA	3,907	0.0	0.0	0.0	0.0	100.0	41.9	52.3	5.9	729	83.3	95.5	0.0
South Fork Estates CDP	70	NA	NA	44	0.0	0.0	0.0	0.0	100.0	0.0	54.5	45.5	20	100.0	55.0	45.0
South Houston city	16,988	17,536	3.2	17,323	6.1	1.4	1.1	0.6	90.8	33.0	59.3	7.7	4,669	61.0	76.2	8.7
Southlake city	26,576	29,086	9.4	27,755	82.2	3.1	6.8	1.9	6.0	33.1	59.6	7.3	8,808	92.4	8.0	72.5
South La Paloma CDP	345	NA	NA	394	14.7	0.0	0.0	0.0	85.3	38.3	46.9	14.7	137	32.1	27.7	0.0
Southmayd city	992	1,001	0.9	895	79.7	0.0	0.4	3.9	16.0	25.6	61.5	12.8	315	85.7	53.3	7.0
South Mountain town	384	372	-3.1	422	74.2	0.0	0.7	0.0	25.1	16.3	67.8	15.9	126	89.7	59.5	15.9
South Padre Island town	2,820	2,889	2.4	2,886	68.7	4.3	0.0	0.0	27.0	9.3	59.0	31.6	1,708	68.1	25.5	37.4
South Point CDP	1,376	NA	NA	1,057	0.0	0.0	0.0	0.0	100.0	26.0	60.5	13.4	236	92.8	78.0	0.0
Southside Place city	1,715	1,819	6.1	1,816	73.9	1.3	14.4	1.6	8.8	29.6	60.2	10.2	622	67.2	7.4	82.2
South Toledo Bend CDP	524	NA	NA	559	87.7	3.2	0.0	9.1	0.0	19.3	44.7	36.0	230	78.7	47.8	20.0
Spade CDP	73	NA	NA	111	31.5	38.7	0.0	0.0	29.7	18.0	81.9	0.0	37	51.4	48.6	27.0
Sparks CDP	4,529	NA	NA	3,850	0.7	0.0	0.0	0.2	99.1	33.6	61.3	5.2	1,035	67.4	84.6	0.0
Spearman city	3,368	3,309	-1.8	3,409	50.8	0.2	0.4	0.9	47.8	28.1	56.3	15.5	1,247	80.8	53.3	20.4
Splendora city	1,616	1,679	3.9	1,569	88.0	0.9	0.3	0.7	10.2	26.9	58.5	14.6	518	76.8	64.9	5.4
Spofford city	95	93	-2.1	86	14.0	0.0	0.0	0.0	86.0	29.0	64.1	7.0	14	85.7	42.9	28.6
Spring CDP	54,298	NA	NA	54,992	43.4	21.1	3.3	2.5	29.6	30.3	61.9	7.9	18,084	76.2	33.7	24.3
Spring Gardens CDP	563	NA	NA	488	3.3	0.0	0.0	0.0	96.7	36.1	58.6	5.3	131	82.4	86.3	0.0
Springlake town	108	105	-2.8	134	52.2	4.5	0.0	0.0	43.3	32.9	47.8	19.4	46	65.2	58.7	4.3
Springtown city	2,661	2,756	3.6	2,710	87.6	0.5	0.0	1.1	10.8	24.0	61.8	13.9	1,030	58.0	47.7	12.3
Spring Valley Village city	3,715	4,142	11.5	3,938	84.9	0.0	8.4	1.2	5.5	28.1	60.2	11.8	1,378	93.6	7.8	81.8
Spur city	1,318	1,211	-8.1	1,204	54.4	8.1	0.2	1.2	36.0	21.1	61.3	17.6	427	71.4	61.4	8.7
Stafford city	17,698	18,344	3.7	17,990	26.9	25.1	22.7	1.4	23.9	21.5	70.0	8.3	6,779	42.0	28.4	36.2
Stagecoach town	552	580	5.1	554	92.2	0.0	0.7	1.3	5.8	24.2	63.2	12.6	197	93.4	40.1	21.3
Stamford city	3,124	3,003	-3.9	3,033	60.4	11.7	0.0	0.0	27.9	27.2	46.8	25.9	1,330	67.7	65.1	12.0
Stanton city	2,492	2,841	14.0	2,653	30.0	4.4	0.0	0.9	64.6	33.0	55.9	11.0	786	68.7	59.3	12.6
Staples city	267	276	3.4	460	39.6	0.9	0.0	1.3	58.3	16.3	72.8	10.9	168	54.2	33.3	16.7
Star Harbor city	444	452	1.8	555	96.8	0.0	0.0	2.3	0.9	9.2	54.1	36.8	232	96.1	22.0	38.4
Stephenville city	17,093	19,374	13.3	18,387	78.7	2.9	1.2	2.3	14.9	18.8	68.7	12.4	6,678	42.7	28.0	30.4
Sterling City city	888	1,039	17.0	942	58.9	0.3	0.0	0.0	40.8	31.2	53.4	15.4	306	81.7	57.5	5.2
Stinnett city	1,881	1,861	-1.1	1,618	84.4	0.9	0.0	1.5	13.1	24.7	62.3	13.1	572	81.8	41.3	10.5
Stockdale city	1,445	1,531	6.0	1,681	45.4	3.5	0.2	0.2	50.7	31.3	52.3	16.4	582	59.6	54.0	9.6
Stonewall CDP	505	NA	NA	501	69.7	0.0	0.0	0.0	30.3	23.6	62.4	14.2	198	77.3	34.3	40.4
Stowell CDP	1,756	NA	NA	1,417	75.4	18.6	1.5	0.8	3.7	33.5	54.1	12.4	459	74.3	69.9	11.5
Stratford city	2,017	2,075	2.9	2,223	48.8	0.2	0.0	2.6	48.4	31.1	56.4	12.5	708	75.8	45.8	22.3
Strawn city	653	648	-0.8	535	51.2	7.5	0.0	0.4	40.9	15.9	70.4	13.8	272	76.1	61.4	13.2
Streetman town	249	247	-0.8	283	78.4	1.1	0.0	0.0	20.5	26.8	55.4	17.7	103	86.4	70.9	2.9
Study Butte CDP	233	NA	NA	300	48.0	0.0	0.0	1.7	50.3	29.3	59.3	11.3	110	48.2	65.5	20.0
Sudan city	958	934	-2.5	1,051	45.2	2.8	0.0	2.4	49.7	34.2	52.1	13.9	368	76.1	54.1	13.3
Sugar Land city	78,592	86,777	10.4	82,420	43.0	6.9	36.5	2.4	11.1	23.4	64.8	11.7	26,635	82.1	13.3	60.3
Sullivan City city	3,998	4,152	3.9	4,087	1.1	0.0	0.0	0.0	98.9	31.6	57.1	11.2	1,096	75.5	80.3	4.7
Sulphur Springs city	15,450	15,975	3.4	15,673	65.5	13.7	0.5	3.4	16.9	27.1	57.8	15.1	5,769	56.6	52.1	15.2
Sundown city	1,397	1,435	2.7	1,314	51.5	0.0	0.0	2.0	46.5	35.0	60.6	4.4	429	73.0	42.2	21.0
Sunnyvale town	5,113	5,766	12.8	5,480	67.3	0.7	24.7	1.2	6.1	24.3	64.0	11.8	1,792	95.4	19.0	51.9
Sunray city	1,926	1,919	-0.4	2,178	58.2	0.1	0.5	2.2	39.0	25.8	59.3	15.0	874	79.6	56.8	9.6
Sunrise Beach Village city	713	719	0.8	808	95.8	0.9	0.0	0.4	3.0	12.4	52.8	34.9	376	96.0	28.2	34.8
Sunset CDP (Montague)	497	NA	NA	293	88.4	0.0	0.0	0.0	11.6	13.3	57.3	29.4	166	91.6	88.0	0.0
Sunset CDP (Starr)	47	NA	NA	19	0.0	0.0	0.0	0.0	100.0	0.0	100.0	0.0	19	0.0	100.0	0.0

1 May be of any race.

Table A. All Places — Population and Housing

STATE City, town, township, borough, or CDP (county if applicable)	Population				Race and Hispanic or Latino origin (percent), 2010–2014					Age (percent), 2010–2014			Households, 2010–2014			
	2010 census total population	2014 estimated population	Percent change 2010-2014	ACS total population estimate 2010-2014	White alone, not Hispanic or Latino	Black alone, not Hispanic or Latino	Asian alone, not Hispanic or Latino	All other races or 2 or more races, not Hispanic or Latino	Hispanic or Latino[1]	Under 18 years old	Age 18 to 64	Age 65 years and older	Total occupied housing units	Percent owner occupied	High school diploma or less	Bachelor's degree or more
	1	2	3	4	5	6	7	8	9	10	11	12	13	14	15	16
TEXAS—Con.																
Sunset Acres CDP	23	NA	NA	0	0.0	0.0	0.0	0.0	0.0	0.0	0.0	0.0	0	0.0	0.0	0.0
Sunset Valley city	648	697	7.6	697	58.7	0.0	6.3	2.7	32.3	23.2	63.4	13.6	269	90.0	7.4	71.4
Sun Valley city	69	68	-1.4	157	27.4	0.0	0.0	0.0	72.6	29.9	70.1	0.0	57	82.5	42.1	38.6
Surfside Beach city	482	531	10.2	611	83.1	2.5	1.5	0.8	12.1	20.1	62.3	17.7	271	75.3	19.6	28.4
Sweeny city	3,727	3,769	1.1	3,743	64.1	19.0	0.4	1.7	14.8	28.5	58.9	12.6	1,384	61.1	52.5	9.0
Sweetwater city	10,906	10,805	-0.9	10,809	53.2	5.5	0.0	2.3	39.0	25.3	58.7	16.1	3,918	64.4	54.6	10.3
Taft city	3,048	3,079	1.0	3,046	23.0	1.5	0.3	1.8	73.4	25.4	56.8	17.8	1,192	70.4	57.9	10.7
Taft Southwest CDP	1,460	NA	NA	1,373	7.7	0.0	0.0	0.0	92.3	35.4	47.5	17.1	434	75.8	75.3	0.0
Tahoka city	2,673	2,596	-2.9	2,623	47.3	2.6	0.0	2.9	47.2	24.7	57.3	18.0	1,022	70.3	50.2	22.1
Talco city	516	512	-0.8	528	54.7	16.1	1.3	1.7	26.1	30.3	59.2	10.4	186	65.1	67.2	6.5
Talty town	1,698	1,823	7.4	1,738	78.4	9.1	0.0	3.1	9.4	29.9	62.6	7.5	537	91.8	26.1	25.9
Tanquecitos South Acres CDP	233	NA	NA	466	4.1	0.0	0.0	0.0	95.9	52.8	43.1	4.1	53	79.2	56.6	43.4
Tanquecitos South Acres II CDP	50	NA	NA	91	0.0	0.0	0.0	0.0	100.0	13.2	70.4	16.5	11	100.0	100.0	0.0
Tatum city	1,385	1,383	-0.1	1,022	50.9	13.4	0.0	0.0	35.7	30.8	57.6	11.6	416	76.4	59.9	14.4
Taylor city	15,281	16,483	7.9	16,001	47.3	11.0	0.5	2.8	38.3	24.7	62.7	12.6	5,556	63.0	53.5	18.3
Taylor Lake Village city	3,546	3,653	3.0	3,613	86.4	1.1	1.1	1.2	10.2	23.4	58.5	18.1	1,283	94.5	10.0	74.4
Taylor Landing city	228	229	0.4	275	94.2	0.0	0.0	0.0	5.8	12.4	62.9	24.7	93	100.0	20.4	45.2
Teague city	3,562	3,590	0.8	3,551	72.7	13.1	0.0	1.1	13.1	27.7	54.1	18.2	1,419	75.8	50.0	14.0
Tehuacana town	283	284	0.4	244	71.3	24.2	0.0	0.0	4.5	18.5	60.2	21.3	115	77.4	20.9	33.9
Temple city	66,315	70,765	6.7	68,877	55.4	16.1	3.1	2.2	23.3	25.7	59.4	14.8	24,696	57.5	37.7	29.6
Tenaha town	1,157	1,157	0.0	1,515	28.8	47.5	0.0	1.5	22.3	29.6	58.9	11.4	500	51.2	77.8	3.6
Terlingua CDP	58	NA	NA	86	100.0	0.0	0.0	0.0	0.0	10.5	64.0	25.6	41	100.0	7.3	48.8
Terrell city	15,816	16,561	4.7	16,146	43.0	24.0	0.9	3.9	28.3	27.2	59.1	13.7	5,446	52.4	54.0	14.5
Terrell Hills city	4,878	5,214	6.9	5,037	74.8	1.5	0.4	2.4	21.0	28.0	58.5	13.5	1,877	88.6	10.7	68.2
Texarkana city	36,409	37,225	2.2	36,999	51.4	37.1	1.5	2.6	7.3	24.7	61.2	14.0	13,931	55.8	38.0	27.6
Texas City city	45,091	46,639	3.4	45,802	43.4	25.8	0.3	2.2	28.3	25.8	60.9	13.1	16,570	60.0	42.0	14.1
Texhoma city	346	343	-0.9	218	71.1	0.0	0.0	0.0	28.9	12.0	60.1	28.0	117	86.3	52.1	19.7
Texline town	508	528	3.9	485	69.9	0.0	1.4	1.4	27.2	21.0	55.6	23.3	173	75.1	43.9	20.8
The Colony city	36,328	41,352	13.8	38,690	64.3	7.2	7.2	3.3	18.0	25.7	68.2	6.1	13,978	63.5	23.7	39.1
The Hills village	2,449	2,573	5.1	2,533	88.8	0.0	4.2	2.8	4.2	26.3	54.7	18.9	907	91.3	7.2	71.7
The Woodlands CDP	93,847	NA	NA	102,911	76.3	2.3	5.1	2.4	13.9	29.0	60.3	10.8	37,339	73.1	12.2	64.0
Thompsons town	221	277	25.3	178	60.1	21.3	0.0	6.2	12.4	25.9	56.3	18.0	66	39.4	48.5	22.7
Thompsonville CDP	46	NA	NA	0	0.0	0.0	0.0	0.0	0.0	0.0	0.0	0.0	0	0.0	0.0	0.0
Thorndale city	1,336	1,305	-2.3	1,495	70.2	4.5	0.0	2.7	22.7	25.5	57.7	16.9	600	70.0	63.3	13.7
Thornton town	526	528	0.4	328	82.0	4.3	0.6	1.8	11.3	12.2	58.3	29.6	161	72.0	61.5	5.6
Thorntonville town	476	515	8.2	538	44.4	12.6	0.0	1.1	41.8	24.9	58.9	16.2	187	80.2	58.3	13.4
Thrall city	838	906	8.1	677	54.4	10.3	0.0	2.4	32.9	24.7	57.8	17.4	265	83.4	66.4	14.7
Three Rivers city	1,848	1,947	5.4	1,590	40.9	1.8	0.0	0.0	57.2	24.2	54.2	21.6	595	68.7	54.3	12.8
Throckmorton town	828	812	-1.9	796	82.2	0.5	0.9	2.9	13.6	15.9	51.5	32.7	383	70.5	55.1	18.0
Thunderbird Bay CDP	663	NA	NA	593	90.6	0.0	0.7	2.2	6.6	12.3	43.5	44.0	256	95.3	57.0	10.9
Tierra Bonita CDP	141	NA	NA	125	36.0	0.0	0.0	0.0	64.0	57.6	42.4	0.0	53	52.8	47.2	0.0
Tierra Dorada CDP	28	NA	NA	8	0.0	0.0	0.0	0.0	100.0	0.0	0.0	100.0	8	0.0	100.0	0.0
Tierra Grande CDP	403	NA	NA	139	51.8	28.1	0.0	0.0	20.1	20.9	71.2	7.9	48	22.9	18.8	22.9
Tierra Verde CDP	277	NA	NA	241	0.0	0.0	0.0	0.0	100.0	46.0	51.8	2.1	61	100.0	19.7	9.8
Tiki Island village	968	1,007	4.0	896	91.0	1.7	2.8	1.5	3.1	4.8	66.9	28.3	461	91.5	20.4	52.1
Tilden CDP	261	NA	NA	288	19.1	0.0	0.0	0.0	80.9	21.5	60.7	17.7	111	84.7	57.7	18.0
Timbercreek Canyon village	418	438	4.8	384	94.5	0.0	1.0	0.8	3.6	17.7	63.6	18.8	157	97.5	20.4	46.5
Timberwood Park CDP	13,447	NA	NA	25,086	61.2	3.1	4.8	2.2	28.7	30.4	62.0	7.6	8,189	80.0	14.3	54.5
Timpson city	1,155	1,155	0.0	1,462	49.0	39.7	0.0	0.6	10.7	28.1	59.5	12.3	539	56.0	67.2	6.3
Tioga town	799	825	3.3	1,006	80.3	0.3	0.8	1.4	17.2	27.8	58.5	14.0	398	68.8	51.0	13.8
Tira town	297	300	1.0	255	92.5	0.8	0.0	0.0	6.7	20.8	55.9	23.5	115	87.0	57.4	16.5
Tivoli CDP	479	NA	NA	588	21.4	0.7	0.0	0.0	77.9	27.2	61.5	11.4	201	69.2	54.7	10.0
Toco city	75	74	-1.3	133	3.0	63.9	0.0	0.0	33.1	36.9	50.4	12.8	41	73.2	73.2	0.0
Todd Mission city	107	109	1.9	103	98.1	0.0	0.0	0.0	1.9	25.3	72.8	1.9	36	83.3	41.7	5.6
Tolar city	681	776	14.0	1,109	87.7	0.2	1.7	0.8	9.6	32.2	57.2	10.6	358	72.9	37.4	27.7
Tomball city	10,753	11,299	5.1	11,030	65.6	7.4	1.5	1.9	23.6	28.6	53.0	18.4	4,145	42.2	46.6	28.2
Tom Bean city	1,041	1,043	0.2	1,064	93.8	0.6	0.0	2.7	2.9	28.4	54.7	16.9	383	66.1	33.9	9.7
Tool city	2,235	2,260	1.1	2,581	86.9	0.8	0.6	4.6	7.1	17.8	58.1	24.3	1,062	78.4	55.2	14.9
Tornillo CDP	1,568	NA	NA	1,388	0.0	0.0	0.4	0.0	99.6	32.7	54.6	12.7	359	81.6	66.6	3.6
Toyah town	90	95	5.6	127	22.8	0.0	0.0	0.0	77.2	41.7	39.3	18.9	39	76.9	82.1	0.0
Tradewinds CDP	180	NA	NA	120	0.0	0.0	0.0	0.0	100.0	0.0	99.9	0.0	42	100.0	50.0	0.0
Travis Ranch CDP	2,556	NA	NA	2,787	47.5	12.4	3.6	1.1	35.3	36.5	57.2	6.4	902	91.0	22.7	47.2
Trent town	337	341	1.2	311	89.1	1.6	0.0	1.6	7.7	24.5	52.9	22.8	134	76.9	42.5	11.9
Trenton city	642	631	-1.7	845	67.5	6.0	0.6	0.9	25.0	23.9	63.4	12.7	310	63.5	62.9	7.7
Trinidad city	886	877	-1.0	779	78.9	12.2	0.0	1.9	6.9	25.2	57.6	17.3	302	63.2	67.2	4.6
Trinity city	2,787	2,717	-2.5	2,755	55.6	22.8	0.0	0.2	21.3	22.0	57.4	20.3	933	63.3	66.7	9.5
Trophy Club town	8,024	11,227	39.9	9,451	84.5	1.1	3.0	2.8	8.6	29.3	59.5	11.3	3,301	92.7	5.8	70.1
Troup city	1,869	1,933	3.4	1,812	70.3	17.3	0.0	0.4	11.9	28.7	56.8	14.4	692	57.4	49.7	16.8
Troy city	1,645	1,750	6.4	1,771	76.1	1.7	0.5	3.6	18.2	26.6	62.3	10.9	596	71.3	49.3	12.2
Tuleta CDP	288	NA	NA	310	77.7	0.0	0.0	1.6	20.6	21.3	70.4	8.4	109	96.3	57.8	2.8
Tulia city	4,967	4,791	-3.5	4,923	41.0	8.5	0.2	2.3	48.0	25.2	58.2	16.6	1,639	67.4	64.2	14.0
Tulsita CDP	14	NA	NA	46	100.0	0.0	0.0	0.0	0.0	0.0	65.2	34.8	16	100.0	100.0	0.0
Turkey city	421	396	-5.9	426	64.3	3.1	0.0	0.5	32.2	31.4	44.8	23.7	157	65.0	42.7	25.5
Tuscola city	740	740	0.0	793	88.0	0.0	0.0	2.3	9.7	26.6	58.4	15.0	289	86.9	48.4	17.3
Tye city	1,240	1,251	0.9	1,167	78.9	0.9	0.0	0.4	19.7	32.6	59.3	7.9	413	69.5	59.8	9.2
Tyler city	96,945	101,421	4.6	99,344	49.8	23.8	2.1	1.6	22.7	23.7	61.6	14.7	37,996	53.5	31.2	33.1
Tynan CDP	278	NA	NA	318	8.2	0.0	0.0	0.0	91.8	26.1	56.8	17.0	115	87.0	69.6	4.3
Uhland city	1,014	1,035	2.1	1,263	26.0	2.1	0.8	2.4	68.8	40.6	54.3	5.0	389	62.5	57.8	13.9
Uncertain city	94	94	0.0	99	84.8	15.2	0.0	0.0	0.0	0.0	52.5	47.5	53	88.7	62.3	15.1
Union Grove city	359	366	1.9	332	91.0	0.6	3.3	0.0	5.1	22.0	62.5	15.4	137	83.9	47.4	11.7
Union Valley city	307	323	5.2	295	87.8	4.7	0.7	0.0	6.8	16.6	64.5	19.0	122	95.1	42.6	20.5
Universal City city	18,530	19,721	6.4	19,164	52.3	8.5	2.4	3.3	33.5	24.1	63.3	12.6	7,337	57.3	26.9	30.5
University Park city	23,068	24,396	5.8	23,761	90.4	0.7	3.0	1.5	4.4	29.5	63.4	7.0	7,186	75.9	4.2	80.3
Utopia CDP	227	NA	NA	167	88.0	0.0	0.0	0.0	12.0	36.6	39.6	24.0	55	65.5	18.2	12.7
Uvalde city	15,753	16,412	4.2	16,094	19.2	0.2	1.7	0.5	78.3	30.2	55.2	14.9	5,016	63.8	49.3	16.3
Uvalde Estates CDP	2,171	NA	NA	2,408	17.9	0.0	0.0	0.0	82.1	21.2	67.5	11.1	738	67.1	64.5	1.8
Valentine town	134	126	-6.0	121	38.8	0.0	0.0	0.0	61.2	19.8	57.8	22.3	46	67.4	52.2	39.1
Valle Hermoso CDP	0	NA	NA	0	0.0	0.0	0.0	0.0	0.0	0.0	0.0	0.0	0	0.0	0.0	0.0

1 May be of any race.

Table A. All Places — **Population and Housing**

STATE City, town, township, borough, or CDP (county if applicable)	Population: 2010 census total population	Population: 2014 estimated population	Population: Percent change 2010-2014	Population: ACS total population estimate 2010-2014	Race and Hispanic or Latino origin (percent), 2010–2014: White alone, not Hispanic or Latino	Black alone, not Hispanic or Latino	Asian alone, not Hispanic or Latino	All other races or 2 or more races, not Hispanic or Latino	Hispanic or Latino[1]	Age (percent), 2010–2014: Under 18 years old	Age 18 to 64 years old	Age 65 years and older	Households, 2010–2014: Total occupied housing units	Percent owner occupied	Householders by level of education (percent): High school diploma or less	Bachelor's degree or more
	1	2	3	4	5	6	7	8	9	10	11	12	13	14	15	16
TEXAS—Con.																
Valle Verde CDP	0	NA	NA	0	0.0	0.0	0.0	0.0	0.0	0.0	0.0	0.0	0	0.0	0.0	0.0
Valle Vista CDP	469	NA	NA	263	0.0	0.0	0.0	0.0	100.0	62.0	38.0	0.0	58	72.4	41.4	0.0
Valley Mills city	1,203	1,171	-2.7	1,449	78.9	3.5	0.0	0.7	17.0	27.7	60.9	11.2	505	71.9	43.6	13.1
Valley View city	757	760	0.4	1,027	90.7	0.1	1.7	1.0	6.5	27.7	65.3	7.0	331	58.9	44.7	15.7
Val Verde Park CDP	2,384	NA	NA	2,474	14.1	0.0	0.0	0.0	85.9	28.4	62.6	9.0	737	89.7	81.1	1.5
Van city	2,631	2,665	1.3	2,642	85.1	0.0	0.6	4.8	9.6	25.9	61.4	12.8	929	67.3	44.7	25.5
Van Alstyne city	3,046	3,221	5.7	3,101	89.6	0.6	0.4	1.5	7.9	28.2	56.2	15.7	1,277	65.6	48.2	18.0
Vanderbilt CDP	395	NA	NA	366	56.3	0.0	0.0	0.0	43.7	20.5	77.3	2.2	146	82.2	34.2	28.1
Van Horn town	2,063	1,954	-5.3	2,264	17.1	0.7	0.0	1.5	80.6	23.7	61.5	14.8	822	72.3	63.1	17.2
Van Vleck CDP	1,844	NA	NA	2,168	46.7	13.9	0.0	0.0	39.3	21.6	65.5	12.7	678	87.2	51.8	14.7
Vega city	884	900	1.8	813	89.4	0.1	0.5	3.0	7.0	24.9	57.3	17.8	352	88.1	39.8	31.3
Venus town	2,960	3,224	8.9	3,110	59.9	15.0	3.3	3.2	18.6	18.7	72.0	9.2	796	79.9	42.2	15.2
Vernon city	11,002	10,531	-4.3	11,005	55.8	9.5	0.9	2.7	31.1	24.3	60.0	15.6	4,343	61.5	51.5	15.7
Victoria city	62,601	66,094	5.6	64,275	41.6	6.6	1.4	1.4	48.9	26.9	59.7	13.5	23,649	58.3	45.9	18.3
Victoria Vera CDP	110	NA	NA	110	0.0	0.0	0.0	0.0	100.0	23.6	68.2	8.2	33	100.0	100.0	0.0
Vidor city	10,710	10,920	2.0	10,844	90.5	0.6	0.3	2.4	6.2	24.3	63.1	12.7	4,121	73.3	57.3	9.1
Villa del Sol CDP	175	NA	NA	46	0.0	0.0	0.0	0.0	100.0	0.0	100.0	0.0	23	0.0	100.0	0.0
Villa Pancho CDP	788	NA	NA	582	0.0	0.0	0.0	0.0	100.0	30.0	54.1	16.0	167	83.8	82.0	7.8
Villarreal CDP	131	NA	NA	234	0.0	0.0	0.0	0.0	100.0	59.0	38.5	2.6	45	4.4	100.0	0.0
Villa Verde CDP	874	NA	NA	711	1.8	0.0	0.0	0.0	98.2	22.0	54.9	23.1	301	57.8	95.7	0.0
Vinton village	1,971	1,969	-0.1	1,529	3.0	0.3	0.0	0.5	96.1	35.3	58.6	6.1	408	76.7	53.9	7.6
Volente village	520	559	7.5	716	81.0	0.0	3.4	3.8	11.9	27.6	63.4	8.9	278	85.6	11.5	71.2
Von Ormy city	1,085	1,153	6.3	1,031	15.0	0.0	1.8	0.0	83.1	32.0	54.2	13.8	290	72.8	77.6	5.9
Waco city	124,810	130,194	4.3	127,796	44.1	20.6	1.7	1.8	31.7	24.7	63.9	11.3	45,874	46.1	41.3	23.0
Waelder city	1,065	1,103	3.6	1,351	3.6	18.7	0.0	0.0	77.7	22.6	64.5	12.9	338	67.2	78.4	2.4
Wake Village city	5,492	5,471	-0.4	5,477	67.5	26.8	0.7	1.8	3.1	30.8	54.6	14.7	2,087	69.8	33.5	20.9
Waller city	2,334	2,454	5.1	1,956	48.8	24.5	0.9	1.0	24.7	27.3	59.1	13.8	690	58.7	45.7	21.4
Wallis city	1,252	1,278	2.1	1,137	65.5	12.1	0.0	7.0	15.3	20.4	64.3	15.3	458	68.1	51.5	9.8
Walnut Springs city	827	805	-2.7	798	69.9	0.0	0.0	2.0	28.1	33.4	52.3	14.3	270	78.9	60.4	12.6
Warren CDP	757	NA	NA	706	100.0	0.0	0.0	0.0	0.0	21.7	61.2	17.0	298	97.3	42.3	13.1
Warren City city	298	295	-1.0	278	90.6	7.6	0.0	0.4	1.4	24.1	64.7	11.2	111	83.8	39.6	12.6
Waskom city	2,164	2,170	0.3	2,156	68.3	13.3	0.0	2.6	15.9	19.4	65.1	15.4	743	70.4	54.1	10.2
Watauga city	23,497	24,345	3.6	23,999	65.2	5.4	5.0	2.0	22.4	29.2	61.9	8.7	8,161	78.0	38.8	20.5
Waxahachie city	29,603	32,344	9.3	31,045	58.0	14.9	0.5	2.4	24.2	27.6	60.9	11.4	10,684	56.1	39.2	26.0
Weatherford city	25,250	27,769	10.0	26,490	76.4	3.3	1.1	2.4	16.8	27.1	58.2	14.4	9,934	61.5	29.6	27.4
Webberville village	394	412	4.6	480	24.6	2.9	0.0	0.2	72.3	30.6	61.0	8.3	126	83.3	73.0	1.6
Webster city	10,622	11,115	4.6	10,898	50.0	11.8	2.4	1.1	34.7	20.4	69.9	9.7	4,730	12.7	26.2	29.4
Weimar city	2,151	2,133	-0.8	2,276	49.2	19.9	1.1	0.0	29.7	30.5	53.5	16.0	806	75.3	54.3	23.2
Weinert city	172	168	-2.3	192	75.5	8.3	0.0	4.7	11.5	12.5	48.3	39.1	103	93.2	56.3	20.4
Weir city	453	487	7.5	610	51.5	0.0	0.0	0.0	48.5	30.3	62.2	7.7	184	62.5	51.6	22.3
Welch CDP	222	NA	NA	178	56.7	0.0	0.0	0.0	43.3	22.5	59.5	18.0	59	69.5	44.1	32.2
Wellington city	2,189	2,155	-1.6	2,197	60.6	4.6	0.3	1.7	32.8	27.0	51.8	21.0	814	78.1	55.8	18.2
Wellman city	203	205	1.0	269	70.6	0.0	0.0	0.0	29.4	20.8	72.9	6.3	107	41.1	19.6	59.8
Wells town	790	788	-0.3	1,057	72.7	17.9	0.0	1.9	7.6	37.0	50.7	12.4	316	50.3	59.8	14.2
Wells Branch CDP	12,120	NA	NA	11,852	43.2	16.3	8.4	3.2	28.9	19.3	73.9	6.9	5,545	29.2	23.4	38.9
Weslaco city	35,437	37,601	6.1	36,752	14.6	0.3	0.7	0.1	84.2	31.2	52.3	16.5	11,570	63.7	54.3	19.0
West city	2,807	2,927	4.3	2,848	82.0	7.9	0.0	1.4	8.7	23.8	51.6	24.7	1,148	59.7	43.6	11.8
West Alto Bonito CDP	696	NA	NA	845	0.0	0.0	0.0	0.0	100.0	43.0	57.1	0.0	163	74.8	100.0	0.0
Westbrook city	253	255	0.8	223	63.2	0.0	0.0	5.8	30.9	30.0	61.4	8.5	81	79.0	60.5	14.8
West Columbia city	3,905	3,943	1.0	3,917	56.8	23.5	0.0	0.2	19.5	30.0	54.7	15.3	1,384	68.9	46.8	12.7
Westdale CDP	372	NA	NA	369	42.3	0.0	0.0	0.0	57.7	21.6	64.8	13.6	157	80.3	58.6	19.7
Western Lake CDP	1,525	NA	NA	1,260	64.4	0.0	0.0	2.2	33.3	24.7	63.8	11.7	431	84.2	67.7	0.0
Westlake town	986	1,194	21.1	1,171	85.5	0.3	8.3	1.5	4.4	34.3	57.1	8.5	355	94.6	7.3	66.5
West Lake Hills city	3,079	3,291	6.9	3,225	79.3	1.1	2.4	3.4	13.8	29.1	56.9	13.9	1,199	82.8	6.7	88.2
West Livingston CDP	8,071	NA	NA	7,849	57.5	17.8	0.3	0.4	24.0	12.4	77.6	9.9	1,624	74.8	58.6	13.3
Westminster CDP	861	NA	NA	703	94.6	0.0	0.0	0.0	5.4	18.9	69.0	12.1	216	93.5	58.3	6.9
West Odessa CDP	22,707	NA	NA	22,818	37.5	0.3	0.0	1.1	61.2	31.5	59.7	8.9	7,342	79.4	67.4	6.0
Weston city	313	329	5.1	429	83.2	0.0	0.0	0.0	16.8	23.3	73.3	3.5	149	91.9	61.1	14.1
Weston Lakes city	2,482	2,577	3.8	2,544	83.0	6.4	1.9	1.0	7.7	17.5	58.4	23.9	998	97.1	5.8	67.9
West Orange city	3,443	3,455	0.3	3,460	76.0	5.8	0.0	1.6	16.6	18.8	63.3	18.1	1,496	66.2	56.1	10.7
Westover Hills town	682	718	5.3	635	98.9	0.0	0.3	0.2	0.6	21.4	54.7	23.9	254	92.1	6.7	85.4
West Sharyland CDP	2,309	NA	NA	2,308	2.4	0.0	0.0	0.0	97.6	37.8	50.8	11.4	571	78.8	74.4	4.9
West Tawakoni city	1,576	1,623	3.0	1,683	88.0	0.0	0.0	3.1	8.9	23.6	59.8	16.5	681	71.5	64.5	7.0
West University Place city	14,787	15,604	5.5	15,223	83.7	0.4	8.1	2.0	5.9	29.7	59.3	11.0	5,428	87.5	1.9	89.8
Westway CDP	4,188	NA	NA	3,938	1.1	0.0	0.0	0.0	98.9	36.2	54.1	9.8	992	65.6	76.8	2.3
Westwood Shores CDP	1,162	NA	NA	1,075	98.8	0.0	0.0	1.2	0.0	12.4	53.0	34.6	488	93.0	44.7	17.6
Westworth Village city	2,472	2,632	6.5	2,541	66.2	0.9	2.2	3.0	27.7	25.3	63.9	10.8	974	56.7	30.9	30.2
Wharton city	8,826	8,659	-1.9	8,768	25.0	29.4	0.2	1.7	43.7	24.8	60.3	14.8	3,265	41.1	60.1	13.4
Wheeler city	1,592	1,671	5.0	1,619	51.5	0.0	0.6	0.2	47.7	32.1	53.0	15.1	539	78.5	54.4	8.3
White Deer town	1,000	976	-2.4	977	91.3	0.2	0.0	2.8	5.7	24.7	60.3	14.9	389	92.0	29.6	26.2
Whiteface town	449	420	-6.5	400	44.8	1.0	0.3	3.5	50.5	32.3	55.1	13.0	147	72.1	42.9	27.2
Whitehouse city	7,679	8,044	4.8	7,882	92.6	2.1	1.0	0.2	4.1	36.0	55.4	8.5	2,510	74.1	30.0	24.5
White Oak city	6,469	6,318	-2.3	6,431	84.3	5.5	0.2	1.6	8.4	29.8	59.7	10.5	2,263	72.5	34.9	20.5
Whitesboro city	3,793	3,862	1.8	3,829	84.6	1.3	0.4	1.3	12.4	22.7	61.0	16.4	1,562	51.2	43.2	11.8
White Settlement city	16,116	16,896	4.8	16,571	58.0	7.1	2.6	3.7	28.7	24.9	62.5	12.5	5,994	50.1	54.6	9.6
Whitewright town	1,604	1,617	0.8	1,944	83.7	12.4	0.3	1.9	1.7	25.9	59.5	14.5	753	55.0	44.8	25.9
Whitney town	2,085	2,086	0.0	2,277	84.8	3.8	0.0	0.4	10.9	30.0	49.7	20.3	791	50.8	45.3	6.3
Wichita Falls city	104,724	105,114	0.4	104,771	62.1	12.4	2.5	2.6	20.4	22.7	65.2	12.3	37,108	57.5	39.8	24.3
Wickett town	498	537	7.8	397	76.6	0.8	0.0	1.8	20.9	28.5	49.0	22.4	156	85.3	40.4	7.1
Wild Peach Village CDP	2,452	NA	NA	2,608	71.3	5.7	1.3	2.5	19.3	27.2	59.0	13.8	834	86.3	40.2	7.0
Wildwood CDP	1,235	NA	NA	805	97.0	0.0	0.0	2.1	0.9	17.2	55.9	27.0	347	96.0	17.9	29.1
Willis city	5,874	6,275	6.8	6,052	43.5	13.6	0.0	0.4	42.6	31.2	55.7	13.0	1,871	55.6	74.2	9.6
Willow Park city	3,982	4,738	19.0	4,305	93.4	2.9	0.0	2.1	1.6	27.2	61.2	11.5	1,612	87.0	21.0	46.5
Wills Point city	3,522	3,521	0.0	3,527	77.5	11.1	0.0	1.7	9.6	28.8	53.1	18.1	1,145	61.2	54.9	17.7
Wilmer city	3,681	3,848	4.5	3,779	19.3	21.9	0.0	0.6	58.2	29.7	64.3	6.0	1,076	62.6	60.6	14.5
Wilson city	489	479	-2.0	525	31.4	0.0	0.0	1.0	67.6	28.9	59.5	11.6	172	74.4	57.0	11.6
Wimberley city	2,626	2,615	-0.4	2,600	88.3	0.3	0.0	1.4	10.0	23.0	59.0	18.1	1,083	70.0	31.0	28.9
Windcrest city	5,364	5,717	6.6	5,562	61.3	9.5	1.4	2.3	25.5	13.1	54.0	32.9	2,202	86.2	31.2	36.8
Windemere CDP	1,037	NA	NA	787	37.2	32.0	0.0	0.0	30.7	28.1	68.3	3.6	325	3.7	33.2	41.2
Windom town	199	198	-0.5	164	89.6	0.0	0.0	7.3	3.0	21.9	56.9	21.3	65	81.5	56.9	18.5
Windthorst town	409	395	-3.4	364	83.8	0.0	0.0	0.0	16.2	20.0	57.2	22.8	152	75.7	67.8	17.1

1 May be of any race.

Table A. All Places — **Population and Housing**

STATE City, town, township, borough, or CDP (county if applicable)	Population				Race and Hispanic or Latino origin (percent), 2010–2014					Age (percent), 2010–2014			Households, 2010–2014		Householders by level of education (percent)	
	2010 census total population	2014 estimated population	Percent change 2010-2014	ACS total population estimate 2010-2014	White alone, not Hispanic or Latino	Black alone, not Hispanic or Latino	Asian alone, not Hispanic or Latino	All other races or 2 or more races, not Hispanic or Latino	Hispanic or Latino[1]	Under 18 years old	Age 18 to 64 years old	Age 65 years and older	Total occupied housing units	Percent owner occupied	High school diploma or less	Bachelor's degree or more
	1	2	3	4	5	6	7	8	9	10	11	12	13	14	15	16
TEXAS—Con.																
Winfield city	524	523	-0.2	533	33.0	0.8	0.0	3.2	63.0	39.0	54.8	6.2	156	80.1	73.1	9.0
Wink city	940	1,034	10.0	1,073	50.0	3.4	3.4	2.5	40.6	29.9	61.1	8.9	384	69.8	44.0	16.9
Winnie CDP	3,254	NA	NA	3,325	69.4	4.4	0.1	0.0	26.1	20.2	65.8	13.9	1,344	68.7	65.6	16.6
Winnsboro city	3,252	3,314	1.9	3,124	79.8	6.1	0.0	0.6	13.5	30.5	50.8	18.8	1,074	60.8	43.4	20.2
Winona town	576	593	3.0	810	66.2	22.1	0.0	0.4	11.4	26.5	64.4	9.0	255	60.0	54.1	13.3
Winters city	2,564	2,531	-1.3	2,532	48.1	0.6	0.3	0.3	50.6	31.6	49.8	18.6	929	69.4	68.4	11.2
Wixon Valley city	258	259	0.4	244	69.3	22.1	0.0	0.4	8.2	22.9	64.0	13.1	91	81.3	51.6	27.5
Wolfe City city	1,412	1,415	0.2	1,795	64.8	16.5	0.0	1.2	17.4	35.8	48.1	16.1	603	68.8	52.4	18.4
Wolfforth city	3,656	4,104	12.3	3,891	60.4	3.5	0.2	2.5	33.4	35.0	55.6	9.4	1,131	74.4	32.2	28.3
Woodbranch city	1,279	1,364	6.6	1,345	87.4	0.5	0.4	5.1	6.5	21.6	61.5	17.0	472	89.4	49.8	15.9
Woodcreek city	1,457	1,483	1.8	1,244	95.3	0.3	0.0	1.3	3.1	9.7	43.0	47.3	660	89.5	12.4	53.9
Woodloch town	207	214	3.4	202	94.1	0.0	0.0	0.0	5.9	22.8	62.9	14.4	69	84.1	26.1	11.6
Woodsboro town	1,512	1,493	-1.3	1,508	43.6	3.8	0.5	0.8	51.3	26.3	55.3	18.4	505	80.0	63.4	10.3
Woodson town	264	258	-2.3	276	81.2	0.0	0.0	0.0	18.8	31.2	56.2	12.7	120	62.5	65.0	13.3
Woodville town	2,586	2,490	-3.7	2,680	69.6	19.7	0.0	3.2	7.5	25.8	53.4	20.8	1,073	53.6	41.8	17.2
Woodway city	8,458	8,760	3.6	8,614	87.2	4.2	1.0	0.3	7.2	16.7	58.8	24.3	3,233	90.4	15.1	51.6
Wortham town	1,076	1,061	-1.4	1,113	77.7	15.8	0.0	3.0	3.5	28.9	53.0	18.1	422	60.7	39.3	17.1
Wyldwood CDP	2,505	NA	NA	3,587	49.5	30.1	0.0	0.5	19.8	26.4	68.2	5.5	993	78.7	36.1	18.1
Wylie city	41,393	45,913	10.9	43,531	62.5	12.6	5.1	3.1	16.7	31.5	62.2	6.4	13,675	84.5	28.0	37.8
Yantis town	388	392	1.0	459	78.9	0.4	0.0	0.4	20.3	21.2	65.5	13.5	153	48.4	71.2	8.5
Yoakum city	5,813	5,988	3.0	5,540	36.6	12.5	0.3	0.3	50.2	25.6	57.4	17.0	2,114	67.3	69.1	10.5
Yorktown city	2,092	2,132	1.9	2,386	54.6	6.3	0.0	1.9	37.3	25.4	53.9	20.7	834	81.5	60.4	14.5
Yznaga CDP	91	NA	NA	0	0.0	0.0	0.0	0.0	0.0	0.0	0.0	0.0	0	0.0	0.0	0.0
Zapata CDP	5,089	NA	NA	4,873	4.2	0.0	0.0	0.0	95.8	26.2	57.5	16.5	1,793	76.7	67.7	13.8
Zapata Ranch CDP	108	NA	NA	98	69.4	0.0	0.0	0.0	30.6	51.0	40.8	8.2	23	100.0	60.9	0.0
Zarate CDP	59	NA	NA	27	0.0	0.0	0.0	0.0	100.0	0.0	100.0	0.0	27	100.0	100.0	0.0
Zavalla city	713	711	-0.3	712	84.1	1.1	3.1	8.7	2.9	21.6	63.8	14.6	260	61.5	57.7	5.0
Zuehl CDP	376	NA	NA	463	63.7	0.0	0.0	7.3	28.9	4.8	66.1	29.2	195	85.1	47.7	38.5
UTAH	2,763,885	2,942,902	6.5	2,858,111	79.8	1.0	2.1	3.9	13.3	31.1	59.5	9.5	896,194	69.7	28.1	33.0
Alpine city	9,557	10,131	6.0	9,856	95.1	0.1	0.4	2.4	2.0	37.7	52.7	9.6	2,568	78.3	11.8	49.6
Alta town	383	390	1.8	342	100.0	0.0	0.0	0.0	0.0	5.0	90.1	5.0	54	64.8	25.9	59.3
Altamont town	232	251	8.2	284	97.2	0.0	0.0	2.8	0.0	33.8	54.6	11.6	100	78.0	53.0	14.0
Alton town	119	118	-0.8	115	79.1	0.0	0.0	3.5	17.4	47.8	32.2	20.0	37	94.6	13.5	21.6
Amalga town	488	501	2.7	527	82.4	0.8	0.0	2.5	14.4	36.6	52.4	11.0	148	84.5	39.9	28.4
American Fork city	26,439	28,152	6.5	27,366	87.9	0.4	1.2	3.9	6.6	37.7	53.0	9.3	7,471	72.6	22.4	36.6
Aneth CDP	501	NA	NA	426	0.0	0.0	0.0	100.0	0.0	35.2	55.2	9.6	103	93.2	64.1	18.4
Annabella town	788	794	0.8	894	96.2	0.2	0.9	0.0	2.7	41.1	51.8	7.0	251	84.1	29.1	23.9
Antimony town	125	120	-4.0	141	97.9	0.0	0.0	0.0	2.1	12.1	41.1	46.8	69	84.1	39.1	24.6
Apple Valley town	701	718	2.4	977	98.1	0.0	0.2	1.1	0.6	26.5	63.5	9.9	262	90.1	37.4	24.0
Aurora city	1,016	1,018	0.2	990	96.2	0.0	0.0	3.3	0.5	34.2	48.0	17.9	334	93.7	33.8	10.2
Avon CDP	367	NA	NA	318	100.0	0.0	0.0	0.0	0.0	15.4	69.5	15.1	122	100.0	45.1	41.0
Ballard town	801	1,010	26.1	748	78.5	0.0	0.0	10.2	11.4	27.8	66.1	6.0	253	82.6	69.2	7.9
Bear River City city	853	842	-1.3	857	88.3	0.0	0.0	1.8	9.9	30.2	56.4	13.3	294	85.4	40.8	19.7
Beaver city	3,122	3,061	-2.0	3,073	85.0	0.5	0.0	6.2	8.3	33.8	52.2	14.0	1,001	71.3	37.2	13.2
Benjamin CDP	1,145	NA	NA	1,171	94.0	0.0	0.0	0.7	5.3	26.3	57.3	16.2	349	89.1	47.3	25.2
Benson CDP	1,485	NA	NA	1,120	100.0	0.0	0.0	0.0	0.0	16.4	67.0	16.8	468	83.5	50.4	24.1
Beryl Junction CDP	197	NA	NA	86	15.1	0.0	0.0	0.0	84.9	0.0	100.0	0.0	42	0.0	100.0	0.0
Bicknell town	331	326	-1.5	375	95.5	0.0	0.0	0.5	4.0	23.5	46.7	29.9	135	90.4	32.6	33.3
Big Water town	479	474	-1.0	621	74.7	0.0	1.1	14.7	9.5	16.3	72.5	11.1	275	69.5	42.5	10.2
Blanding city	3,345	3,668	9.7	3,478	73.3	0.3	0.0	19.8	6.5	39.9	49.1	11.2	906	70.8	26.0	37.6
Bluebell CDP	293	NA	NA	233	100.0	0.0	0.0	0.0	0.0	25.8	66.5	7.7	89	76.4	58.4	23.6
Bluff CDP	258	NA	NA	401	89.3	0.0	2.7	4.2	3.7	0.0	85.9	14.0	222	77.5	21.2	74.8
Bluffdale city	7,597	9,887	30.1	8,319	90.6	0.6	0.3	2.1	6.4	35.0	59.3	5.6	2,220	82.7	28.2	29.7
Bonanza CDP	1	NA	NA	0	0.0	0.0	0.0	0.0	0.0	0.0	0.0	0.0	0	0.0	0.0	0.0
Boulder town	226	223	-1.3	141	97.9	0.0	2.1	0.0	0.0	4.2	82.4	13.5	68	60.3	25.0	42.6
Bountiful city	42,561	43,385	1.9	42,947	89.4	0.6	1.5	2.5	6.0	28.9	55.1	15.9	14,018	73.4	18.6	45.1
Brian Head town	85	86	1.2	50	76.0	0.0	0.0	0.0	24.0	20.0	54.0	26.0	28	46.4	17.9	57.1
Brigham City city	17,908	18,631	4.0	18,264	87.9	0.6	0.2	2.8	8.5	29.4	57.1	13.6	6,154	71.8	38.8	21.8
Bryce Canyon City town	230	223	-3.0	118	66.1	0.0	0.0	14.4	19.5	18.6	75.3	5.9	47	48.9	55.3	38.3
Cache CDP	38	NA	NA	0	0.0	0.0	0.0	0.0	0.0	0.0	0.0	0.0	0	0.0	0.0	0.0
Cannonville town	178	168	-5.6	243	97.9	0.0	0.0	2.1	0.0	35.0	51.1	14.0	73	91.8	42.5	23.3
Carbonville CDP	1,567	NA	NA	1,636	87.3	0.0	0.0	0.0	12.7	33.1	54.3	12.7	600	62.3	40.3	10.7
Castle Dale city	1,638	1,590	-2.9	1,899	90.6	0.0	0.3	4.9	4.2	35.0	56.1	9.0	584	82.7	43.8	13.7
Castle Valley town	322	334	3.7	380	95.5	0.8	2.1	0.5	1.1	5.8	64.3	30.0	165	96.4	13.9	43.6
Cedar City city	28,862	29,483	2.2	29,175	86.3	0.4	0.5	4.7	8.0	28.3	62.5	9.2	9,478	52.4	26.5	31.8
Cedar Fort town	368	383	4.1	355	88.5	0.0	1.1	7.3	3.1	23.9	58.2	17.7	121	92.6	38.0	13.2
Cedar Hills city	9,756	10,261	5.2	10,025	88.4	0.5	2.4	5.0	3.7	43.8	49.7	6.6	2,491	85.6	7.1	56.3
Centerfield town	1,367	1,384	1.2	1,257	69.6	0.0	0.0	4.9	25.5	34.6	52.8	12.6	371	84.6	42.3	7.5
Centerville city	15,326	16,819	9.7	16,104	92.9	0.2	1.5	2.3	3.1	29.2	57.9	12.8	5,347	87.0	17.4	47.8
Central CDP	613	NA	NA	650	97.1	0.0	2.5	0.0	0.5	16.6	57.2	26.5	265	80.4	31.7	21.1
Central Valley town	547	548	0.2	632	96.8	0.9	0.0	1.1	1.1	31.5	53.2	15.3	204	90.2	37.7	19.1
Charleston town	417	451	8.2	635	98.9	0.0	0.0	0.0	1.1	22.3	68.0	9.9	212	91.5	19.8	31.6
Circleville town	547	517	-5.5	775	80.6	0.0	0.0	2.7	16.6	21.4	63.9	14.8	202	81.2	55.0	18.8
Clarkston town	675	680	0.7	728	92.0	0.0	0.0	3.0	4.9	34.3	52.0	13.7	205	93.7	50.7	23.9
Clawson town	199	198	-0.5	175	77.7	0.0	0.0	17.1	5.1	36.6	48.5	14.9	45	82.2	42.2	0.0
Clear Creek CDP	4	NA	NA	0	0.0	0.0	0.0	0.0	0.0	0.0	0.0	0.0	0	0.0	0.0	0.0
Clearfield city	30,117	30,484	1.2	30,361	75.0	2.9	2.2	3.7	16.1	35.2	58.2	6.6	9,767	53.2	37.4	20.7
Cleveland town	464	453	-2.4	532	98.1	0.0	0.0	1.9	0.0	33.0	55.8	11.1	174	80.5	37.4	2.3
Clinton city	20,426	21,104	3.3	20,796	80.7	1.8	3.3	3.1	11.2	35.3	58.8	5.8	6,114	85.2	27.1	25.2
Coalville city	1,367	1,425	4.2	1,678	69.7	0.0	0.4	0.8	29.1	32.0	58.2	9.7	501	72.1	52.1	13.8
Copperton CDP	826	NA	NA	551	76.8	0.0	5.6	13.4	4.2	35.0	46.5	18.5	201	91.0	47.3	9.5
Corinne city	685	690	0.7	803	86.2	0.0	1.7	2.4	9.7	31.2	63.5	5.4	260	75.8	36.5	19.6
Cornish town	297	306	3.0	344	76.2	0.3	0.0	2.3	21.2	25.3	69.2	5.5	114	80.7	58.8	14.9
Cottonwood Heights city	33,435	34,166	2.2	33,932	86.3	0.6	5.5	3.0	4.6	23.6	63.1	13.4	12,042	71.7	16.1	50.8
Cove CDP	460	NA	NA	416	97.8	2.2	0.0	0.0	0.0	32.8	42.5	24.8	159	78.6	25.2	34.6
Dammeron Valley CDP	803	NA	NA	491	93.9	0.0	0.0	0.0	6.1	12.8	54.9	32.4	193	93.8	22.3	48.2
Daniel town	923	1,035	12.1	1,236	92.7	0.0	2.1	4.3	0.9	21.0	68.0	11.0	413	77.0	39.2	18.4
Delta city	3,436	3,474	1.1	3,461	86.8	0.1	0.0	0.6	12.5	34.3	53.2	12.4	1,137	71.6	40.0	24.0
Deseret CDP	353	NA	NA	326	100.0	0.0	0.0	0.0	0.0	33.4	44.1	22.4	115	70.4	54.8	23.5

1 May be of any race.

Table A. All Places — **Population and Housing**

STATE City, town, township, borough, or CDP (county if applicable)	Population				Race and Hispanic or Latino origin (percent), 2010–2014					Age (percent), 2010–2014			Households, 2010–2014			
	2010 census total population	2014 estimated population	Percent change 2010-2014	ACS total population estimate 2010-2014	White alone, not Hispanic or Latino	Black alone, not Hispanic or Latino	Asian alone, not Hispanic or Latino	All other races or 2 or more races, not Hispanic or Latino	Hispanic or Latino[1]	Under 18 years old	Age 18 to 64 years old	Age 65 years and older	Total occupied housing units	Percent owner occupied	Householders by level of education (percent): High school diploma or less	Householders by level of education (percent): Bachelor's degree or more
	1	2	3	4	5	6	7	8	9	10	11	12	13	14	15	16
UTAH—Con.																
Deweyville town	332	328	-1.2	365	93.4	0.0	0.8	1.6	4.1	24.4	63.1	12.6	131	77.9	42.7	19.8
Draper city	42,272	46,202	9.3	44,656	86.4	0.8	2.5	2.8	7.6	33.4	60.9	5.9	12,287	79.0	14.2	47.9
Duchesne city	1,688	1,801	6.7	2,007	92.5	0.0	0.0	1.5	6.0	30.8	56.0	13.1	690	63.5	57.0	10.0
Dugway CDP	795	NA	NA	820	64.6	6.5	1.8	9.5	17.6	18.5	81.4	0.0	255	0.0	42.0	17.6
Dutch John CDP	145	NA	NA	103	100.0	0.0	0.0	0.0	0.0	21.3	64.2	14.6	52	63.5	9.6	25.0
Eagle Mountain city	21,415	25,593	19.5	23,468	89.9	0.6	0.5	2.5	6.4	47.8	49.6	2.7	5,593	86.0	18.4	32.2
East Carbon-Sunnyside city	1,678	1,602	-4.5	1,600	76.0	0.0	0.0	3.4	20.6	24.3	55.5	20.2	705	75.2	54.5	2.3
Echo CDP	56	NA	NA	108	100.0	0.0	0.0	0.0	0.0	26.9	59.3	13.9	35	82.9	40.0	0.0
Eden CDP	600	NA	NA	708	97.6	0.0	0.0	2.4	0.0	26.7	54.2	19.1	214	80.8	15.0	65.9
Elberta CDP	256	NA	NA	366	63.1	0.0	0.0	0.0	36.9	32.8	29.5	37.7	105	71.4	36.2	56.2
Elk Ridge city	2,436	3,005	23.4	2,699	94.3	0.3	0.0	2.5	2.9	43.0	48.5	8.4	628	95.4	10.0	49.8
Elmo town	423	417	-1.4	398	93.7	0.0	2.5	0.0	3.8	29.4	54.7	15.8	136	67.6	47.1	5.9
Elsinore town	847	845	-0.2	864	93.2	0.0	0.2	4.1	2.5	28.6	52.0	19.4	298	80.5	36.9	12.1
Elwood town	1,034	1,034	0.0	1,334	94.7	0.0	0.6	0.4	4.3	33.4	53.7	13.0	370	96.8	38.9	24.3
Emery town	286	276	-3.5	303	93.1	1.3	0.7	2.0	3.0	23.4	59.9	16.8	106	97.2	54.7	14.2
Emigration Canyon CDP	1,567	NA	NA	1,649	85.4	0.0	3.9	0.0	10.6	24.8	66.1	9.2	553	85.0	4.2	77.0
Enoch city	5,849	6,115	4.5	6,006	92.4	0.0	0.4	2.5	4.7	40.8	51.6	7.6	1,595	88.5	29.3	20.6
Enterprise CDP	605	NA	NA	839	90.3	0.0	9.7	0.0	0.0	47.9	46.9	5.1	180	100.0	18.3	56.1
Enterprise city	1,708	1,780	4.2	1,763	89.9	0.0	0.0	3.1	7.0	46.2	45.5	8.3	440	78.0	33.6	24.8
Ephraim city	6,131	6,463	5.4	6,303	86.8	1.9	0.8	3.2	7.4	27.5	65.0	7.5	1,686	44.7	23.0	21.1
Erda CDP	4,642	NA	NA	5,409	88.9	0.3	2.1	0.0	8.7	39.5	56.3	4.2	1,437	78.7	33.1	24.4
Escalante city	820	793	-3.3	834	86.1	3.4	0.0	0.0	10.6	21.5	57.0	21.5	334	82.6	43.7	22.8
Eureka city	669	667	-0.3	615	95.1	0.0	0.0	4.1	0.8	20.5	61.6	18.0	257	83.7	37.4	13.6
Fairfield town	119	125	5.0	126	92.9	0.0	0.0	0.0	7.1	18.2	68.2	13.5	42	90.5	28.6	23.8
Fairview city	1,247	1,271	1.9	1,739	94.2	0.0	0.0	2.3	3.5	35.5	54.0	10.6	545	82.4	36.9	11.6
Farmington city	18,275	22,159	21.3	20,440	92.9	1.3	1.0	1.8	3.0	36.8	55.3	8.1	5,904	83.1	11.3	50.4
Farr West city	5,928	6,329	6.8	6,113	86.1	1.1	0.2	3.6	8.9	29.5	58.4	12.1	1,891	92.3	30.8	28.7
Fayette town	242	245	1.2	222	88.7	0.0	0.0	0.0	11.3	32.9	54.7	12.6	72	84.7	29.2	30.6
Ferron city	1,666	1,603	-3.8	1,541	99.9	0.0	0.0	0.0	0.1	31.2	52.9	16.0	506	87.4	40.5	8.3
Fielding town	453	447	-1.3	494	92.1	0.0	0.0	0.0	7.9	29.9	56.7	13.4	147	76.9	37.4	14.3
Fillmore city	2,461	2,492	1.3	2,835	71.1	0.8	0.6	4.1	23.4	34.4	49.9	15.7	841	80.6	52.7	14.7
Flaming Gorge CDP	83	NA	NA	60	100.0	0.0	0.0	0.0	0.0	38.3	41.6	20.0	22	81.8	40.9	27.3
Fort Duchesne CDP	714	NA	NA	852	1.4	0.0	3.5	94.0	1.1	39.5	54.1	6.3	237	67.5	69.2	21.9
Fountain Green city	1,071	1,088	1.6	1,118	90.4	0.0	0.0	3.0	6.5	29.6	58.1	12.3	359	85.8	45.4	12.5
Francis town	1,077	1,168	8.4	1,212	97.0	0.1	0.0	0.0	2.9	29.5	59.7	10.8	412	89.8	36.4	24.3
Fremont CDP	145	NA	NA	97	94.8	0.0	5.2	0.0	0.0	43.3	49.5	7.2	21	100.0	33.3	0.0
Fruit Heights city	4,987	5,859	17.5	5,353	89.5	1.8	0.8	4.1	3.7	31.3	57.5	11.1	1,447	93.6	14.5	54.2
Garden CDP	181	NA	NA	148	100.0	0.0	0.0	0.0	0.0	20.9	55.4	23.6	58	100.0	70.7	0.0
Garden City town	560	575	2.7	586	90.4	0.0	0.0	8.4	1.2	42.0	42.4	15.5	166	65.1	22.9	26.5
Garland city	2,428	2,422	-0.2	2,392	80.8	0.0	2.4	2.9	13.9	39.8	50.1	10.2	737	71.1	43.0	19.9
Genola town	1,370	1,408	2.8	1,261	87.1	0.0	0.0	1.7	11.3	32.9	55.0	12.3	329	83.3	37.4	14.3
Glendale town	381	374	-1.8	335	90.1	0.0	0.0	1.8	8.1	25.1	48.6	26.6	121	89.3	20.7	15.7
Glenwood town	460	463	0.7	415	94.5	0.0	2.7	0.5	2.4	28.2	51.5	20.2	134	93.3	38.8	35.1
Goshen town	921	950	3.1	986	88.8	0.3	0.0	0.3	10.5	36.1	54.7	9.2	299	84.6	53.5	8.7
Granite CDP	1,932	NA	NA	1,788	96.3	2.1	0.6	0.8	0.2	13.8	73.7	12.4	607	87.5	10.9	62.8
Grantsville city	8,916	9,838	10.3	9,391	94.8	0.0	0.9	0.4	3.9	38.2	55.4	6.6	2,799	84.0	37.1	27.4
Green River city	1,026	989	-3.6	1,191	63.5	3.8	0.0	0.0	32.7	36.4	50.2	13.4	367	60.5	56.1	14.2
Gunnison city	3,285	3,291	0.2	3,267	69.6	3.7	0.3	5.9	20.5	12.7	81.7	5.6	424	74.3	27.1	22.2
Halchita CDP	266	NA	NA	402	0.0	0.0	0.0	100.0	0.0	34.4	54.6	10.9	70	81.4	52.9	8.6
Halls Crossing CDP	6	NA	NA	0	0.0	0.0	0.0	0.0	0.0	0.0	0.0	0.0	0	0.0	0.0	0.0
Hanksville town	219	213	-2.7	115	96.5	0.0	0.0	0.0	3.5	24.3	55.6	20.0	54	61.1	50.0	0.0
Harrisville city	5,585	6,069	8.7	5,828	84.7	0.3	0.0	7.6	7.4	30.2	63.1	6.6	1,906	83.7	29.0	25.0
Hatch town	146	141	-3.4	239	100.0	0.0	0.0	0.0	0.0	30.5	45.1	24.3	80	92.5	30.0	25.0
Heber city	11,378	13,599	19.5	12,434	79.4	0.4	1.4	1.4	17.5	38.0	56.4	5.5	3,406	65.8	28.2	34.1
Helper city	2,203	2,144	-2.7	2,218	87.5	0.4	0.2	0.9	10.9	30.0	56.1	14.0	889	72.4	38.7	13.6
Henefer town	761	834	9.6	699	85.0	0.0	0.0	5.4	9.6	28.0	55.7	16.3	242	83.5	35.1	25.2
Henrieville town	230	220	-4.3	196	100.0	0.0	0.0	0.0	0.0	29.1	56.2	14.8	73	84.9	61.6	8.2
Herriman city	21,738	28,556	31.4	25,022	86.8	1.6	1.2	2.1	8.2	45.5	51.7	2.8	6,257	76.3	21.9	31.5
Hideout town	656	705	7.5	536	21.5	0.0	0.6	7.6	70.3	34.1	64.0	2.1	163	1.2	46.6	25.8
Highland city	15,507	17,456	12.6	16,491	93.4	0.4	0.9	2.3	2.9	42.9	51.1	6.0	3,759	92.6	8.5	66.0
Hildale city	2,745	2,926	6.6	2,894	100.0	0.0	0.0	0.0	0.0	55.2	43.0	1.8	319	16.0	49.8	2.5
Hinckley town	696	698	0.3	597	89.9	0.0	0.0	1.5	8.5	18.6	61.6	19.8	250	75.6	50.8	8.8
Holden town	378	373	-1.3	378	91.3	0.0	0.5	0.8	7.4	32.1	50.5	17.5	129	83.7	29.5	23.3
Holladay city	26,472	27,129	2.5	26,896	89.6	1.0	1.9	2.2	5.3	25.3	57.0	17.6	10,054	74.9	14.8	52.4
Honeyville city	1,441	1,441	0.0	1,299	92.3	0.0	1.0	0.6	6.1	29.6	55.9	14.5	451	90.2	37.5	18.0
Hooper city	7,218	8,107	12.3	7,720	88.5	1.4	0.6	3.1	6.4	34.7	58.2	7.1	2,271	95.3	24.7	28.9
Howell town	245	247	0.8	227	98.2	0.0	0.0	0.0	1.8	27.3	49.0	23.8	84	91.7	66.7	7.1
Hoytsville CDP	607	NA	NA	770	74.8	0.0	0.0	0.0	25.2	28.5	63.2	8.3	248	62.1	49.2	7.3
Huntington city	2,138	2,056	-3.8	2,040	93.8	0.0	0.0	0.0	6.2	29.2	59.4	11.4	739	81.3	40.2	6.5
Huntsville town	608	617	1.5	819	97.8	0.0	0.1	0.0	2.1	23.0	58.7	18.3	268	86.6	20.5	39.2
Hurricane city	13,749	15,032	9.3	14,338	90.4	0.1	0.3	2.6	6.6	29.6	49.9	20.4	4,756	71.7	32.2	25.4
Hyde Park city	3,840	4,274	11.3	4,085	94.1	0.2	0.3	3.6	1.7	37.1	52.9	9.9	1,130	92.1	15.5	51.9
Hyrum city	7,613	7,818	2.7	7,751	79.7	0.1	0.0	0.8	19.4	41.3	52.3	6.4	1,981	85.3	38.5	23.1
Independence town	156	167	7.1	213	92.0	0.0	0.0	0.0	8.0	20.2	55.0	24.9	83	94.0	28.9	21.7
Ivins city	6,755	7,665	13.5	7,184	92.1	0.3	0.0	2.3	5.3	24.8	51.1	24.3	2,772	78.7	26.5	37.0
Jensen CDP	412	NA	NA	259	76.1	0.0	0.0	23.9	0.0	42.8	57.2	0.0	55	67.3	56.4	0.0
Joseph town	344	341	-0.9	357	96.9	0.0	0.8	0.6	1.7	23.5	63.1	13.4	135	84.4	66.7	5.9
Junction town	191	180	-5.8	253	95.7	0.0	0.0	0.0	4.3	32.0	31.4	36.8	68	76.5	64.7	5.9
Kamas city	1,811	1,989	9.8	2,019	71.6	0.2	0.0	0.4	27.7	27.9	61.2	10.8	636	74.8	47.5	17.3
Kanab city	4,324	4,463	3.2	4,407	94.4	0.4	0.0	2.0	3.2	26.2	53.6	20.1	1,761	73.9	32.3	29.9
Kanarraville town	358	364	1.7	334	92.2	0.0	0.6	2.1	5.1	22.2	57.9	20.1	134	91.8	29.9	25.4
Kanosh town	474	470	-0.8	411	92.0	0.0	0.0	0.2	7.8	21.9	44.7	33.3	162	86.4	43.2	25.9
Kaysville city	27,410	29,494	7.6	28,480	93.8	0.5	0.7	1.1	3.8	37.6	55.7	6.7	7,868	86.3	15.5	50.6
Kearns CDP	35,731	NA	NA	34,865	59.8	0.8	1.6	5.7	32.1	33.1	60.7	6.1	9,646	82.7	51.8	12.0
Kenilworth CDP	180	NA	NA	90	67.8	0.0	0.0	0.0	32.2	0.0	52.2	47.8	53	100.0	30.2	0.0
Kingston town	173	163	-5.8	277	96.4	0.0	0.0	0.0	3.6	24.6	54.9	20.6	70	100.0	45.7	15.7
Koosharem town	327	326	-0.3	274	88.0	1.8	0.0	1.5	8.8	38.3	39.0	22.6	89	78.7	40.4	19.1
Lake Shore CDP	817	NA	NA	785	95.0	0.8	0.0	3.4	0.8	20.7	63.7	15.5	239	95.4	33.1	21.8
Laketown town	252	256	1.6	243	92.2	0.0	0.0	0.4	7.4	34.2	46.3	19.3	79	97.5	25.3	30.4
La Sal CDP	395	NA	NA	317	97.2	0.0	0.0	0.0	2.8	9.8	71.9	18.3	186	62.4	36.0	3.8

1 May be of any race.

Table A. All Places — **Population and Housing**

STATE City, town, township, borough, or CDP (county if applicable)	Population				Race and Hispanic or Latino origin (percent), 2010–2014					Age (percent), 2010–2014			Households, 2010–2014			
	2010 census total population	2014 estimated population	Percent change 2010-2014	ACS total population estimate 2010-2014	White alone, not Hispanic or Latino	Black alone, not Hispanic or Latino	Asian alone, not Hispanic or Latino	All other races or 2 or more races, not Hispanic or Latino	Hispanic or Latino[1]	Under 18 years old	Age 18 to 64 years old	Age 65 years and older	Total occupied housing units	Percent owner occupied	Householders by level of education (percent): High school diploma or less	Householders by level of education (percent): Bachelor's degree or more
	1	2	3	4	5	6	7	8	9	10	11	12	13	14	15	16
UTAH—Con.																
La Verkin city	4,060	4,163	2.5	4,144	87.7	0.7	0.0	0.7	10.9	30.4	56.7	13.0	1,299	74.7	36.4	21.2
Layton city	67,297	72,231	7.3	69,508	80.8	1.2	2.5	4.3	11.1	31.8	60.3	7.9	21,838	74.9	25.3	33.2
Leamington town	226	229	1.3	195	97.9	0.0	0.0	0.0	2.1	32.8	55.9	11.3	68	85.3	23.5	36.8
Leeds town	814	837	2.8	939	98.1	0.0	1.7	0.0	0.2	23.6	52.0	24.2	322	85.1	27.3	32.0
Lehi city	47,735	56,275	17.9	51,982	87.9	0.2	1.3	2.8	7.8	43.7	51.3	5.0	13,355	80.9	18.7	43.0
Levan town	843	862	2.3	779	95.4	0.0	0.0	0.0	4.6	26.8	62.8	10.5	280	72.9	61.1	16.8
Lewiston city	1,764	1,752	-0.7	1,978	89.7	0.0	0.2	1.0	9.1	34.3	54.9	10.9	615	83.3	37.1	27.0
Liberty CDP	1,257	NA	NA	1,974	98.8	0.0	0.0	0.0	1.2	39.5	55.1	5.4	536	88.1	29.3	31.9
Lindon city	10,082	10,723	6.4	10,434	83.2	0.0	1.8	4.6	10.4	37.8	55.4	6.8	2,546	80.4	13.4	44.9
Loa town	613	596	-2.8	606	95.4	0.0	0.0	0.2	4.5	35.1	49.0	15.7	210	88.6	33.3	21.9
Logan city	48,203	48,997	1.6	48,933	76.8	1.2	3.7	3.5	14.9	24.6	69.1	6.6	15,839	42.3	24.2	32.8
Lyman town	258	251	-2.7	330	90.6	0.0	0.0	0.0	9.4	41.7	48.1	10.0	91	87.9	8.8	13.2
Lynndyl town	106	109	2.8	133	95.5	0.0	0.0	0.0	4.5	22.6	54.1	23.3	51	94.1	54.9	21.6
Maeser CDP	3,601	NA	NA	3,963	86.2	0.0	0.0	4.6	9.2	35.1	56.2	8.8	1,255	79.3	38.6	29.3
Magna CDP	26,505	NA	NA	28,182	67.3	0.2	1.1	4.6	26.8	33.5	61.0	5.3	7,906	77.6	51.3	10.1
Manila town	327	334	2.1	193	84.5	0.0	0.0	15.5	0.0	13.0	55.5	31.6	70	78.6	45.7	22.9
Manti city	3,280	3,362	2.5	3,313	96.4	0.1	0.5	1.3	1.7	32.7	52.6	14.7	1,053	80.2	29.2	28.7
Mantua town	687	694	1.0	719	91.0	1.7	3.2	2.1	2.1	29.6	54.3	16.1	229	93.0	30.6	38.0
Mapleton city	8,029	9,071	13.0	8,545	88.1	0.5	0.0	7.4	4.1	39.3	49.5	11.2	2,081	88.6	16.6	43.7
Marion CDP	685	NA	NA	779	100.0	0.0	0.0	0.0	0.0	37.9	53.4	8.7	199	89.9	39.7	9.0
Marriott-Slaterville city	1,701	1,740	2.3	1,598	89.4	0.0	0.0	0.5	10.1	29.9	57.0	13.1	540	78.9	32.8	17.4
Marysvale town	399	388	-2.8	441	98.4	0.0	0.0	0.0	1.6	16.1	52.1	31.7	181	90.1	45.9	18.2
Mayfield town	496	503	1.4	391	97.2	1.3	0.0	1.3	0.3	20.2	55.3	24.6	155	81.3	20.6	27.1
Meadow town	310	313	1.0	289	96.2	0.0	0.0	0.3	3.5	33.6	47.8	18.7	107	71.0	43.0	25.2
Mendon city	1,333	1,315	-1.4	1,177	95.4	0.3	0.4	2.5	1.4	40.8	50.4	8.8	350	90.0	22.9	42.6
Mexican Hat CDP	31	NA	NA	64	100.0	0.0	0.0	0.0	0.0	0.0	71.9	28.1	18	100.0	100.0	0.0
Midvale city	27,983	31,725	13.4	29,957	67.9	1.9	3.3	3.0	23.9	23.5	67.4	9.2	11,434	45.2	34.0	24.9
Midway city	3,843	4,436	15.4	4,096	89.4	0.0	0.0	0.0	10.6	32.9	54.7	12.5	1,289	75.2	23.7	35.6
Milford city	1,408	1,353	-3.9	1,610	82.2	0.1	0.0	0.9	16.8	34.5	55.8	9.6	558	74.2	50.4	23.1
Millcreek CDP	62,139	NA	NA	63,311	84.2	1.9	3.5	3.7	6.7	22.1	62.1	15.9	24,921	62.1	21.7	44.5
Millville city	1,866	1,918	2.8	1,888	89.3	0.0	0.0	6.5	4.2	30.0	59.4	10.6	553	89.5	29.5	32.7
Minersville town	907	882	-2.8	960	87.1	0.0	0.0	0.6	12.3	33.0	59.0	8.1	307	85.7	53.7	14.3
Moab city	5,062	5,140	1.5	5,105	86.7	0.2	1.0	2.0	10.1	19.4	67.3	13.3	2,263	60.5	28.0	31.3
Mona city	1,540	1,578	2.5	1,414	95.2	0.7	1.6	1.3	1.3	36.4	55.7	7.8	418	84.9	39.2	18.9
Monroe city	2,257	2,262	0.2	2,756	96.8	0.0	0.0	1.3	1.9	30.9	51.4	17.7	864	83.9	39.8	23.7
Montezuma Creek CDP	335	NA	NA	385	3.4	0.0	7.8	88.8	0.0	37.2	55.6	7.3	67	95.5	58.2	0.0
Monticello city	1,974	1,999	1.3	2,325	76.6	0.6	0.0	8.5	14.3	33.2	51.9	14.9	662	68.4	27.8	24.6
Morgan city	3,663	3,957	8.0	3,787	92.5	0.0	0.7	1.3	5.5	36.4	48.8	14.8	1,188	83.1	34.8	34.8
Moroni city	1,423	1,451	2.0	1,407	69.4	0.0	0.0	0.4	30.2	34.2	49.9	15.8	449	83.5	43.7	20.9
Mountain Green CDP	2,309	NA	NA	2,621	96.9	0.0	0.8	0.8	1.5	37.4	54.3	8.4	684	87.3	23.7	46.8
Mount Pleasant city	3,259	3,305	1.4	3,290	88.0	0.6	0.6	0.9	9.9	32.1	51.9	16.0	985	79.8	40.3	18.2
Murray city	46,695	48,822	4.6	47,909	82.1	1.9	1.5	3.7	10.8	23.1	63.1	13.8	18,646	63.9	26.0	32.0
Myton city	569	619	8.8	580	69.0	0.0	0.3	14.8	15.9	26.0	69.0	5.0	248	52.8	71.4	5.2
Naples city	1,745	2,148	23.1	2,147	90.5	0.0	2.0	2.8	4.7	33.7	57.3	9.1	645	85.6	42.5	16.6
Navajo Mountain CDP	354	NA	NA	557	0.7	0.0	0.0	98.4	0.9	49.2	44.4	6.3	91	76.9	52.7	22.0
Neola CDP	461	NA	NA	455	61.8	0.0	0.0	29.0	9.2	42.9	50.0	7.3	138	88.4	43.5	15.2
Nephi city	5,387	5,508	2.2	5,442	92.0	0.0	0.1	1.3	6.5	34.5	53.5	12.1	1,676	84.7	38.2	17.4
Newcastle CDP	247	NA	NA	334	77.5	0.0	0.0	22.5	0.0	19.2	67.2	13.8	150	78.0	28.7	28.7
New Harmony town	207	210	1.4	212	97.6	0.0	0.9	1.4	0.0	21.2	44.8	34.0	83	84.3	32.5	31.3
Newton town	789	778	-1.4	810	95.9	0.0	0.0	0.2	3.8	35.2	52.1	12.8	240	93.3	38.3	23.3
Nibley city	5,465	6,172	12.9	5,866	86.6	1.0	0.0	1.1	11.3	44.4	51.9	3.6	1,508	89.2	19.6	43.7
North Logan city	8,269	9,874	19.4	9,007	89.3	0.2	5.6	1.1	3.8	32.6	58.6	8.8	2,799	67.3	17.1	52.2
North Ogden city	17,324	18,172	4.9	17,743	89.7	0.9	0.5	1.8	7.1	32.6	55.7	11.5	5,504	85.9	25.3	35.4
North Salt Lake city	16,322	19,193	17.6	17,465	75.1	0.3	2.7	7.4	14.5	31.0	62.0	7.1	5,594	72.8	22.2	45.1
Oak City town	578	598	3.5	651	96.2	0.0	0.0	3.8	0.0	33.8	52.1	14.1	206	84.0	21.4	29.6
Oakley city	1,470	1,576	7.2	1,495	88.3	0.0	0.7	0.0	11.0	29.9	65.6	4.5	464	81.9	36.4	23.1
Oasis CDP	75	NA	NA	0	0.0	0.0	0.0	0.0	0.0	0.0	0.0	0.0	0	0.0	0.0	0.0
Ogden city	82,827	84,316	1.8	83,767	63.5	1.6	1.3	3.7	29.8	27.6	62.5	9.8	29,454	54.9	42.4	20.6
Oljato-Monument Valley CDP	674	NA	NA	1,106	9.2	0.0	0.0	90.0	0.8	36.2	61.6	2.3	178	88.8	64.6	13.5
Ophir town	44	48	9.1	111	100.0	0.0	0.0	0.0	0.0	3.6	93.7	2.7	54	7.4	96.3	0.0
Orangeville city	1,470	1,423	-3.2	1,483	97.6	1.8	0.0	0.0	0.5	36.8	54.8	8.3	460	79.6	32.8	13.7
Orderville town	578	572	-1.0	715	90.9	0.0	2.2	1.0	5.9	25.0	56.7	18.3	237	82.3	36.3	13.1
Orem city	88,323	91,781	3.9	90,485	77.8	1.0	1.8	3.8	15.6	30.4	61.3	8.4	25,884	60.9	19.1	37.9
Palmyra CDP	491	NA	NA	571	100.0	0.0	0.0	0.0	0.0	22.9	66.3	10.9	199	63.3	31.7	15.6
Panguitch city	1,523	1,490	-2.2	1,891	87.7	0.2	2.0	4.6	5.4	27.1	59.3	13.6	605	73.7	39.3	15.9
Paradise town	900	923	2.6	1,154	94.6	0.0	0.0	0.8	4.6	35.5	55.4	9.0	319	91.5	30.7	35.7
Paragonah town	498	501	0.6	529	97.4	0.0	0.0	1.5	1.1	22.8	53.8	23.6	195	80.5	33.8	18.5
Park City city	7,558	8,058	6.6	7,845	77.9	0.3	2.8	0.2	18.8	20.7	68.6	10.7	3,192	64.3	15.4	64.8
Parowan city	2,801	2,862	2.2	2,827	88.5	0.7	0.0	5.9	4.8	28.7	56.6	14.8	951	74.1	39.5	20.6
Payson city	18,330	19,331	5.5	18,928	81.5	0.4	0.1	1.8	16.3	39.0	53.6	7.3	5,174	76.2	30.1	24.3
Peoa CDP	253	NA	NA	100	100.0	0.0	0.0	0.0	0.0	0.0	34.0	66.0	37	100.0	78.4	21.6
Perry city	4,512	4,621	2.4	4,529	88.3	0.2	1.7	6.0	3.8	39.4	49.1	11.5	1,348	91.5	19.7	39.9
Peter CDP	324	NA	NA	432	100.0	0.0	0.0	0.0	0.0	38.1	52.8	8.8	119	100.0	11.8	63.0
Pine Valley CDP	186	NA	NA	139	100.0	0.0	0.0	0.0	0.0	8.6	73.3	18.0	61	80.3	32.8	34.4
Plain City city	5,476	6,214	13.5	5,859	96.1	0.0	0.2	1.4	2.4	34.7	55.5	9.8	1,671	99.2	37.8	20.9
Pleasant Grove city	33,540	37,064	10.5	34,858	88.3	0.3	0.7	2.1	8.5	37.9	55.3	6.8	9,539	67.3	19.4	41.3
Pleasant View city	8,008	8,948	11.7	8,426	92.1	0.0	0.1	1.3	6.5	34.3	54.1	11.6	2,574	93.0	24.1	44.1
Plymouth town	404	405	0.2	368	95.1	0.8	0.0	0.0	4.1	29.7	57.6	12.8	128	92.2	57.0	10.9
Portage town	245	252	2.9	243	100.0	0.0	0.0	0.0	0.0	25.1	56.8	18.1	87	95.4	42.5	12.6
Price city	8,727	8,358	-4.2	8,585	82.4	1.3	1.3	1.5	13.4	25.1	61.8	13.2	3,047	60.9	40.2	15.2
Providence city	6,959	7,066	1.5	7,026	95.0	1.3	0.1	1.4	3.5	36.5	51.4	12.3	2,171	80.4	15.4	49.3
Provo city	112,494	114,801	2.1	114,804	75.7	0.6	2.4	4.4	16.8	22.8	71.2	6.1	32,332	42.1	17.3	35.6
Randlett CDP	220	NA	NA	232	8.2	0.0	0.0	91.8	0.0	44.4	42.3	13.4	73	100.0	91.8	0.0
Randolph town	462	462	0.0	578	91.7	0.3	0.0	0.5	7.4	31.1	52.8	16.1	147	83.0	53.1	9.5
Redmond town	730	732	0.3	638	89.2	0.3	0.0	0.0	10.5	19.6	57.3	23.0	236	89.0	59.3	10.6
Richfield city	7,569	7,518	-0.7	7,550	91.9	1.3	0.0	2.5	4.3	32.7	54.9	12.4	2,453	65.2	37.4	19.7
Richmond city	2,476	2,535	2.4	2,509	93.0	0.4	0.0	0.0	6.7	33.2	56.1	10.7	778	83.9	36.2	28.5
Riverdale city	8,428	8,592	1.9	8,532	80.9	0.4	0.8	1.3	16.6	24.8	62.5	12.8	3,052	70.5	34.9	21.4
River Heights city	1,843	1,894	2.8	1,944	91.0	0.0	2.8	4.0	2.2	32.1	57.2	10.7	608	85.5	25.8	53.9
Riverside CDP	760	NA	NA	755	100.0	0.0	0.0	0.0	0.0	45.2	54.5	0.3	201	58.7	15.9	12.9

1 May be of any race.

Table A. All Places — **Population and Housing**

STATE City, town, township, borough, or CDP (county if applicable)	Population: 2010 census total population	Population: 2014 estimated population	Population: Percent change 2010-2014	Population: ACS total population estimate 2010-2014	Race and Hispanic or Latino origin (percent), 2010–2014: White alone, not Hispanic or Latino	Black alone, not Hispanic or Latino	Asian alone, not Hispanic or Latino	All other races or 2 or more races, not Hispanic or Latino	Hispanic or Latino[1]	Age (percent), 2010–2014: Under 18 years old	Age 18 to 64 years old	Age 65 years and older	Households, 2010–2014: Total occupied housing units	Percent owner occupied	Householders by level of education (percent): High school diploma or less	Bachelor's degree or more
	1	2	3	4	5	6	7	8	9	10	11	12	13	14	15	16
UTAH—Con.																
Riverton city	38,801	41,457	6.8	40,274	90.6	0.3	1.6	1.9	5.6	35.5	58.1	6.4	11,044	89.0	20.9	36.0
Rockville town	245	255	4.1	398	97.7	0.0	1.0	0.0	1.3	17.8	61.8	20.4	136	84.6	21.3	44.1
Rocky Ridge town	733	761	3.8	1,274	98.1	0.0	0.0	1.9	0.0	58.3	40.6	1.0	199	56.3	57.8	10.6
Roosevelt city	6,049	6,777	12.0	6,390	78.5	0.2	1.1	10.5	9.7	38.8	55.1	6.1	2,131	65.4	43.2	18.3
Roy city	36,884	37,877	2.7	37,472	79.4	1.0	1.6	2.7	15.2	31.9	57.8	10.3	12,345	84.4	35.3	21.8
Rush Valley town	440	468	6.4	568	95.4	0.0	0.0	0.0	4.6	20.6	57.8	21.5	221	89.6	53.8	14.9
St. George city	72,763	78,505	7.9	75,469	81.5	0.6	0.8	4.2	13.0	27.9	52.7	19.3	25,736	64.7	26.8	30.5
Salem city	6,429	7,237	12.6	6,789	91.9	1.0	0.8	1.9	4.4	38.4	52.1	9.3	1,831	83.7	28.8	40.7
Salina city	2,489	2,494	0.2	2,283	89.1	0.0	0.3	1.4	9.2	28.5	56.7	14.7	949	72.4	55.4	6.4
Salt Lake City city	186,452	190,884	2.4	189,267	65.7	2.7	5.0	5.6	20.9	22.0	68.0	9.9	74,652	48.4	25.4	44.1
Samak CDP	287	NA	NA	164	100.0	0.0	0.0	0.0	0.0	20.7	79.2	0.0	68	79.4	22.1	58.8
Sandy city	87,720	91,148	3.9	89,521	85.5	0.5	3.0	2.7	8.2	28.9	60.7	10.5	28,478	77.0	20.3	42.0
Santa Clara city	6,145	6,671	8.6	6,404	90.7	0.4	2.4	2.1	4.4	35.1	52.7	12.0	1,709	75.1	13.9	41.9
Santaquin city	9,137	10,106	10.6	9,694	85.6	0.3	0.7	1.8	11.6	44.7	49.4	5.9	2,389	81.3	35.5	21.0
Saratoga Springs city	17,802	24,356	36.8	21,061	88.9	1.4	2.2	2.6	4.9	47.7	48.8	3.7	4,968	81.4	12.7	43.0
Scipio town	327	324	-0.9	433	96.1	0.0	0.0	3.9	0.0	27.2	51.4	21.5	160	82.5	48.1	18.1
Scofield town	24	23	-4.2	32	78.1	0.0	0.0	15.6	6.3	0.0	81.3	18.8	18	72.2	16.7	33.3
Sigurd town	427	426	-0.2	548	96.0	0.0	0.0	0.0	4.0	38.7	45.5	15.7	171	74.9	41.5	7.6
Silver Summit CDP	3,632	NA	NA	3,591	92.0	1.2	2.0	1.1	3.7	28.3	68.9	3.0	1,101	83.3	5.3	70.1
Smithfield city	9,628	11,014	14.4	10,233	89.6	0.0	1.6	3.7	5.1	37.7	53.2	9.0	2,945	87.9	29.0	29.9
Snowville town	167	170	1.8	138	84.1	0.0	2.2	0.0	13.8	18.7	60.1	21.0	51	70.6	52.9	3.9
Snyderville CDP	5,612	NA	NA	5,814	88.1	1.3	1.0	1.9	7.6	21.9	68.1	9.9	2,425	75.2	11.5	65.8
South Jordan city	50,420	62,781	24.5	56,528	88.6	0.4	2.1	3.8	5.1	33.4	58.6	7.8	15,713	81.3	15.7	45.0
South Ogden city	16,532	16,852	1.9	16,702	82.2	1.5	1.7	2.7	11.9	28.4	56.8	14.8	6,224	65.9	25.3	32.7
South Salt Lake city	23,615	24,748	4.8	24,315	54.2	3.7	9.7	3.9	28.5	26.3	67.2	6.5	8,540	40.8	39.3	25.9
South Weber city	6,051	6,731	11.2	6,386	91.4	0.7	0.1	2.0	5.8	36.1	55.7	8.1	1,782	88.9	21.2	37.6
South Willard CDP	1,571	NA	NA	1,825	73.2	0.0	0.3	6.7	19.8	44.8	50.0	5.3	473	81.6	37.4	23.0
Spanish Fork city	34,740	37,527	8.0	36,337	87.1	0.4	0.3	2.2	10.1	39.4	54.9	5.9	9,411	77.3	25.6	30.3
Spanish Valley CDP	491	NA	NA	308	100.0	0.0	0.0	0.0	0.0	29.6	55.2	15.3	94	100.0	38.3	31.9
Spring City city	988	1,001	1.3	812	96.1	0.0	0.0	0.1	3.8	26.4	57.8	16.0	314	74.8	34.7	25.2
Springdale town	529	548	3.6	409	91.0	0.0	0.0	0.2	8.8	3.4	67.2	29.3	215	57.7	13.0	48.8
Spring Glen CDP	1,126	NA	NA	1,055	95.9	0.0	0.0	1.2	2.8	23.3	57.8	18.9	436	70.6	36.5	7.6
Spring Lake CDP	458	NA	NA	477	81.3	0.0	0.0	15.9	2.7	42.1	51.1	6.7	128	65.6	24.2	5.5
Springville city	29,500	31,464	6.7	30,649	84.5	0.3	0.6	5.1	9.5	37.0	55.5	7.5	8,773	70.5	23.9	37.4
Stansbury Park CDP	5,145	NA	NA	5,079	89.6	0.4	2.1	0.0	7.9	41.4	51.5	7.2	1,381	97.9	24.5	38.0
Sterling town	272	276	1.5	248	94.8	0.0	1.2	4.0	0.0	28.6	48.4	23.0	91	96.7	31.9	28.6
Stockton town	632	638	0.9	674	85.8	0.0	0.0	0.6	13.6	25.2	65.9	8.8	248	66.9	48.8	2.8
Summit CDP	160	NA	NA	218	100.0	0.0	0.0	0.0	0.0	4.1	50.0	45.9	98	100.0	21.4	38.8
Summit Park CDP	7,775	NA	NA	7,843	84.9	0.3	5.0	0.9	8.9	30.7	62.1	7.1	2,582	84.2	6.9	69.3
Sunset city	5,122	5,149	0.5	5,145	69.2	3.3	1.7	1.8	24.1	34.5	55.4	10.2	1,739	72.1	43.5	15.2
Sutherland CDP	165	NA	NA	279	93.5	6.5	0.0	0.0	0.0	29.1	37.6	33.3	136	89.7	46.3	17.6
Syracuse city	24,369	26,639	9.3	25,374	89.9	1.3	1.3	1.1	6.4	41.4	52.7	6.0	6,778	92.0	18.7	41.1
Tabiona town	171	186	8.8	176	100.0	0.0	0.0	0.0	0.0	36.9	42.0	21.0	63	84.1	68.3	0.0
Taylorsville city	58,644	60,433	3.1	59,920	68.7	1.8	4.1	4.9	20.5	27.2	63.0	9.7	19,570	69.0	33.7	23.4
Teasdale CDP	191	NA	NA	88	85.2	0.0	14.8	0.0	0.0	19.3	14.7	65.9	45	100.0	8.9	57.8
Thatcher CDP	789	NA	NA	704	99.1	0.0	0.0	0.9	0.0	31.7	55.6	12.8	233	84.5	24.9	53.2
Thompson Springs CDP	39	NA	NA	90	100.0	0.0	0.0	0.0	0.0	44.4	43.3	12.2	29	100.0	37.9	0.0
Timber Lakes CDP	607	NA	NA	512	80.5	0.0	0.0	19.5	0.0	11.7	56.7	31.6	249	100.0	18.1	34.9
Tooele city	31,605	32,573	3.1	32,164	80.2	1.0	0.6	4.5	13.7	33.5	58.1	8.3	10,294	74.9	38.4	18.9
Toquerville city	1,372	1,448	5.5	1,884	97.7	0.0	0.0	0.2	2.1	35.0	51.4	13.5	548	82.8	20.4	33.6
Torrey town	184	181	-1.6	286	90.9	0.0	0.0	0.7	8.4	23.4	46.6	29.7	111	82.9	31.5	38.7
Tremonton city	7,614	8,066	5.9	7,833	82.8	0.0	1.6	0.9	14.7	36.2	54.8	9.1	2,442	75.3	39.3	15.1
Trenton town	489	497	1.6	519	86.9	1.3	0.4	2.5	8.9	38.2	49.7	12.1	162	90.7	42.6	13.0
Tropic town	530	513	-3.2	605	92.4	0.0	1.7	0.8	5.1	33.7	49.9	16.4	205	80.5	37.6	32.2
Tselakai Dezza CDP	109	NA	NA	175	0.0	0.0	1.7	98.3	0.0	17.7	81.1	1.1	31	100.0	67.7	0.0
Uintah town	1,322	1,333	0.8	1,254	94.7	0.0	0.2	4.0	1.1	31.2	58.6	10.2	391	84.7	40.4	24.8
Vernal city	9,111	10,844	19.0	9,882	85.9	0.2	0.0	3.2	10.8	29.5	59.8	10.5	3,400	61.8	47.8	15.2
Vernon town	248	264	6.5	250	90.8	0.0	0.0	0.0	9.2	38.0	51.2	10.8	72	81.9	44.4	9.7
Veyo CDP	483	NA	NA	340	100.0	0.0	0.0	0.0	0.0	24.4	54.7	20.9	116	79.3	69.0	8.6
Vineyard town	140	691	393.6	421	88.8	0.0	1.9	0.0	9.3	19.2	64.9	15.9	125	88.8	18.4	34.4
Virgin town	596	605	1.5	483	93.2	0.0	0.4	0.8	5.6	31.2	54.9	14.1	173	83.8	38.7	16.2
Wales town	298	302	1.3	289	97.6	2.1	0.0	0.0	0.3	41.5	42.6	15.9	82	87.8	41.5	2.4
Wallsburg town	256	303	18.4	331	94.3	0.0	3.0	2.1	0.6	10.5	79.4	10.0	116	97.4	29.3	6.9
Wanship CDP	400	NA	NA	439	96.1	0.0	0.0	3.9	0.0	24.4	65.5	10.0	147	70.7	38.1	34.7
Washington city	18,761	23,360	24.5	20,999	84.5	0.5	0.8	5.6	8.7	31.1	52.2	16.7	7,019	71.4	27.9	29.5
Washington Terrace city	9,065	9,177	1.2	9,140	84.1	0.2	0.5	3.6	11.6	23.5	60.4	15.9	3,521	61.2	34.6	22.4
Wellington city	1,682	1,641	-2.4	1,674	83.2	0.0	0.0	3.2	13.6	25.2	60.0	14.9	661	64.3	52.6	9.7
Wellsville city	3,486	3,578	2.6	3,557	95.0	0.0	0.0	1.5	3.6	36.2	55.3	8.6	1,029	87.4	34.1	34.8
Wendover city	1,400	1,397	-0.2	1,259	21.4	0.0	0.0	0.0	78.6	32.2	63.5	4.3	425	20.2	75.1	9.4
West Bountiful city	5,265	5,446	3.4	5,353	92.2	1.3	0.7	2.2	3.6	28.1	63.3	8.5	1,567	88.0	23.7	36.6
West Haven city	10,275	11,582	12.7	10,996	81.2	0.6	3.2	2.1	12.8	34.5	58.9	6.6	3,353	71.3	31.1	25.0
West Jordan city	103,708	110,920	7.0	108,062	73.5	1.0	2.5	4.1	18.8	33.7	61.0	5.4	31,116	76.4	32.0	26.7
West Mountain CDP	1,186	NA	NA	784	93.9	0.0	0.0	0.0	6.1	33.0	52.6	14.4	250	82.8	21.6	37.6
West Point city	9,511	10,204	7.3	9,863	88.2	0.0	2.6	3.3	5.8	39.0	54.5	6.6	2,694	90.6	29.4	27.2
West Valley City city	129,475	134,495	3.9	132,329	50.2	2.0	5.1	6.8	36.0	32.6	60.0	7.4	36,946	68.8	49.6	13.7
West Wood CDP	844	NA	NA	739	82.3	0.0	1.2	0.0	16.5	26.6	64.2	9.3	240	98.3	15.8	34.2
White City CDP	5,407	NA	NA	5,488	89.8	0.3	0.6	2.5	6.8	29.3	57.2	13.4	1,702	82.7	29.7	24.4
White Mesa CDP	242	NA	NA	337	0.0	0.0	1.2	89.3	9.5	45.7	46.3	8.0	87	64.4	88.5	0.0
Whiterocks CDP	289	NA	NA	177	12.4	0.0	0.0	87.6	0.0	22.0	74.0	4.0	93	50.5	87.1	12.9
Willard city	1,772	1,775	0.2	1,752	84.8	0.2	0.0	2.2	12.8	33.4	54.1	12.4	586	83.1	41.5	20.5
Wolf Creek CDP	1,336	NA	NA	845	100.0	0.0	0.0	0.0	0.0	14.8	71.9	13.1	456	69.5	13.4	54.6
Woodland CDP	343	NA	NA	379	100.0	0.0	0.0	0.0	0.0	33.5	58.1	8.4	138	56.5	29.0	20.3
Woodland Hills city	1,344	1,455	8.3	1,297	91.4	0.0	0.8	2.3	5.6	33.8	51.8	14.3	339	98.8	6.2	63.4
Woodruff town	184	186	1.1	332	100.0	0.0	0.0	0.0	0.0	31.6	60.2	8.1	51	90.2	19.6	7.8
Woods Cross city	9,761	11,097	13.7	10,389	87.3	0.6	1.0	3.5	7.6	35.2	58.9	5.9	3,219	81.3	17.3	34.3
VERMONT	625,745	626,562	0.1	626,358	93.9	1.0	1.3	2.2	1.6	20.0	64.3	15.7	257,252	70.9	35.8	36.4
Addison town (Addison)	1,375	1,365	-0.7	1,415	93.9	0.8	0.4	0.0	5.0	22.6	59.5	18.0	551	86.0	40.3	31.8
Albany village	193	187	-3.1	204	99.0	0.0	0.0	1.0	0.0	34.8	48.5	16.7	70	90.0	42.9	17.1
Albany town (Orleans)	941	920	-2.2	893	98.4	0.0	0.3	1.2	0.0	19.7	64.4	15.8	396	85.4	42.9	24.2

1 May be of any race.

Table A. All Places — **Population and Housing**

STATE City, town, township, borough, or CDP (county if applicable)	Population: 2010 census total population	Population: 2014 estimated population	Population: Percent change 2010-2014	Population: ACS total population estimate 2010-2014	Race and Hispanic or Latino origin (percent), 2010–2014: White alone, not Hispanic or Latino	Black alone, not Hispanic or Latino	Asian alone, not Hispanic or Latino	All other races or 2 or more races, not Hispanic or Latino	Hispanic or Latino[1]	Age (percent), 2010–2014: Under 18 years old	Age 18 to 64 years old	Age 65 years and older	Households, 2010–2014: Total occupied housing units	Percent owner occupied	Householders by level of education (percent): High school diploma or less	Bachelor's degree or more
	1	2	3	4	5	6	7	8	9	10	11	12	13	14	15	16
VERMONT—Con.																
Alburgh village	497	499	0.4	475	92.4	0.0	0.0	5.9	1.7	25.9	62.2	12.0	190	68.9	56.3	21.1
Alburgh town (Grand Isle)	1,998	2,008	0.5	1,623	97.4	0.0	0.2	1.8	0.5	18.9	66.2	14.9	705	75.2	48.7	24.4
Andover town (Windsor)	467	477	2.1	425	98.4	0.0	0.7	0.0	0.9	15.1	62.2	22.8	184	82.1	41.3	26.1
Arlington CDP	1,213	NA	NA	1,311	96.5	1.4	0.0	2.1	0.0	16.2	58.8	24.9	611	60.6	39.6	39.6
Arlington town (Bennington)	2,316	2,277	-1.7	2,354	96.3	0.8	0.0	2.1	0.7	14.9	60.0	25.1	1,070	70.7	36.9	41.2
Ascutney CDP	540	NA	NA	449	97.3	0.2	0.0	2.4	0.0	4.4	76.5	19.2	256	86.7	74.2	9.8
Athens town (Windham)	442	437	-1.1	402	95.8	0.0	0.2	1.7	2.2	25.6	56.2	18.2	173	75.1	54.3	23.7
Averill town (Essex)	24	23	-4.2	19	100.0	0.0	0.0	0.0	0.0	0.0	21.1	78.9	8	100.0	25.0	50.0
Avery's gore (Essex)	0	0	0.0	0	0.0	0.0	0.0	0.0	0.0	0.0	0.0	0.0	0	0.0	0.0	0.0
Bakersfield town (Franklin)	1,322	1,351	2.2	1,551	97.2	0.0	0.0	0.9	1.9	29.3	60.4	10.3	547	89.2	47.0	20.8
Baltimore town (Windsor)	248	255	2.8	234	98.7	0.0	0.0	0.4	0.9	19.7	68.8	11.5	80	93.8	41.3	20.0
Barnard town (Windsor)	947	931	-1.7	899	97.9	0.0	0.6	1.1	0.4	23.5	54.3	22.1	375	81.1	27.7	48.8
Barnet CDP	129	NA	NA	172	100.0	0.0	0.0	0.0	0.0	26.2	50.0	23.8	48	77.1	22.9	52.1
Barnet town (Caledonia)	1,704	1,683	-1.2	1,648	95.0	1.0	0.3	2.9	0.9	19.8	59.5	20.7	619	75.4	34.1	39.4
Barre city & MCD (Washington)	9,049	8,837	-2.3	8,955	93.5	2.9	0.4	2.0	1.3	21.0	61.5	17.5	4,066	52.7	46.5	22.2
Barre town (Washington)	7,926	7,857	-0.9	7,908	96.0	0.1	0.2	1.4	2.2	21.6	63.2	15.2	3,132	88.3	46.8	26.1
Barton village	737	708	-3.9	621	89.7	0.0	3.1	6.1	1.1	16.4	48.1	35.6	326	50.9	66.3	7.1
Barton town (Orleans)	2,810	2,702	-3.8	2,766	91.6	2.5	1.2	4.1	0.6	21.4	58.6	19.9	1,097	71.4	55.8	15.7
Beecher Falls CDP	177	NA	NA	143	97.9	0.0	0.0	0.0	2.1	23.8	66.5	9.8	70	70.0	62.9	8.6
Bellows Falls village	3,141	3,061	-2.5	2,766	92.3	2.1	0.0	3.0	2.6	19.3	67.5	13.2	1,303	47.0	56.0	14.7
Belvidere town (Lamoille)	348	355	2.0	364	95.1	0.0	0.8	2.2	1.9	31.4	60.7	8.0	133	87.2	48.9	19.5
Bennington CDP	9,074	NA	NA	8,933	92.7	1.2	1.3	3.2	1.7	23.1	58.0	18.8	3,641	50.6	43.5	28.5
Bennington town (Bennington)	15,764	15,431	-2.1	15,575	92.9	1.0	1.0	3.0	2.1	21.6	60.8	17.6	6,096	58.3	42.7	28.8
Benson CDP	308	NA	NA	319	100.0	0.0	0.0	0.0	0.0	19.5	63.5	16.9	137	88.3	59.9	19.7
Benson town (Rutland)	1,056	1,037	-1.8	1,065	97.8	0.2	0.0	1.6	0.4	24.4	61.9	13.6	390	83.3	59.0	21.8
Berkshire town (Franklin)	1,696	1,716	1.2	1,760	90.9	0.2	0.0	2.8	6.1	29.6	61.6	8.9	582	86.1	53.3	18.2
Berlin town (Washington)	2,882	2,840	-1.5	2,869	93.6	2.0	1.8	1.9	0.6	19.7	56.5	23.8	1,057	82.0	39.5	28.2
Bethel CDP	569	NA	NA	572	100.0	0.0	0.0	0.0	0.0	24.7	62.0	13.3	235	56.2	46.8	25.5
Bethel town (Windsor)	2,022	2,016	-0.3	1,919	99.1	0.0	0.0	0.9	0.0	22.0	62.8	15.3	821	74.2	42.8	27.5
Bloomfield town (Essex)	219	215	-1.8	207	99.5	0.0	0.0	0.5	0.0	14.5	57.1	28.5	101	86.1	53.5	22.8
Bolton town (Chittenden)	1,182	1,191	0.8	1,247	98.0	1.4	0.2	0.3	0.0	20.5	72.5	7.0	525	82.1	28.2	41.1
Bradford CDP	788	NA	NA	1,005	97.4	0.0	0.6	1.8	0.2	32.4	55.9	11.8	342	40.6	41.8	22.8
Bradford town (Orange)	2,795	2,765	-1.1	2,776	96.8	0.0	0.9	2.2	0.1	24.9	59.9	15.1	1,106	68.6	33.2	29.6
Braintree town (Orange)	1,244	1,231	-1.0	1,238	95.2	0.0	0.0	3.6	1.2	16.9	66.6	16.5	575	83.1	44.9	23.5
Brandon CDP	1,648	NA	NA	1,425	99.0	0.0	0.0	1.0	0.0	25.6	54.8	19.4	599	79.6	38.9	41.4
Brandon town (Rutland)	3,969	3,860	-2.7	3,906	97.8	0.5	0.0	1.7	0.0	23.0	60.1	16.8	1,615	78.5	46.1	29.4
Brattleboro town (Windham)	12,046	11,765	-2.3	11,876	90.8	1.8	2.5	1.9	2.9	18.4	63.9	17.9	5,461	53.4	37.1	37.9
Brattleboro CDP	7,414	NA	NA	7,132	91.9	1.5	2.7	1.2	2.7	17.4	65.1	17.5	3,397	42.6	35.4	37.2
Bridgewater town (Windsor)	934	930	-0.4	710	98.2	0.0	0.0	1.8	0.0	8.6	68.5	23.0	358	73.2	34.9	24.0
Bridport town (Addison)	1,218	1,221	0.2	1,180	93.6	1.2	0.0	0.5	4.7	19.2	59.7	21.2	491	74.1	54.4	24.6
Brighton town (Essex)	1,222	1,182	-3.3	939	96.4	1.1	0.5	2.0	0.0	19.0	57.6	23.2	447	69.4	61.7	15.7
Bristol CDP	2,030	NA	NA	1,871	96.7	0.0	1.7	0.0	1.6	26.4	52.2	21.4	771	56.7	34.0	35.3
Bristol town (Addison)	3,901	3,918	0.4	3,896	96.9	0.0	1.4	0.3	1.4	22.8	59.9	17.2	1,541	65.9	42.7	29.2
Brookfield town (Orange)	1,287	1,289	0.2	1,297	98.7	0.0	0.0	1.3	0.0	16.5	66.2	17.3	539	82.6	32.3	35.3
Brookline town (Windham)	530	524	-1.1	567	98.8	0.0	0.0	0.4	0.9	23.5	62.3	14.3	233	85.4	36.1	33.5
Brownington town (Orleans)	988	969	-1.9	973	98.6	0.0	0.0	0.8	0.6	22.6	63.2	14.2	380	86.6	62.6	17.4
Brunswick town (Essex)	114	115	0.9	84	100.0	0.0	0.0	0.0	0.0	15.5	54.9	29.8	44	86.4	59.1	9.1
Buels gore (Chittenden)	30	30	0.0	43	83.7	7.0	0.0	0.0	9.3	18.7	67.5	14.0	14	64.3	21.4	50.0
Burke town (Caledonia)	1,753	1,735	-1.0	1,711	96.5	2.0	0.2	0.8	0.5	25.9	56.7	17.4	676	75.6	40.2	28.6
Burlington city & MCD (Chittenden)	42,417	42,211	-0.5	42,342	85.3	3.6	5.4	3.0	2.7	12.9	77.1	9.9	16,337	40.6	25.1	45.4
Cabot CDP	233	NA	NA	246	97.2	0.0	1.2	1.6	0.0	23.6	60.1	16.3	105	75.2	38.1	36.2
Cabot town (Washington)	1,434	1,449	1.0	1,393	97.0	0.0	0.2	2.8	0.0	23.8	56.3	19.8	584	84.2	42.6	32.5
Calais town (Washington)	1,607	1,600	-0.4	1,556	90.9	0.0	1.2	5.3	2.6	20.6	65.1	14.3	632	92.4	24.5	50.5
Cambridge village	233	236	1.3	200	100.0	0.0	0.0	0.0	0.0	12.5	81.5	6.0	89	55.1	37.1	34.8
Cambridge town (Lamoille)	3,659	3,748	2.4	3,713	97.0	0.0	0.0	1.9	1.1	21.0	67.4	11.5	1,548	69.3	27.7	39.3
Canaan CDP	392	NA	NA	414	92.3	5.3	0.0	1.9	0.5	17.9	69.1	13.0	196	71.4	65.8	10.7
Canaan town (Essex)	972	934	-3.9	1,164	97.0	1.9	0.0	0.7	0.4	21.5	64.3	14.1	482	79.3	55.6	16.2
Castleton CDP	1,485	NA	NA	1,238	87.0	9.9	0.8	1.0	1.3	1.8	92.9	5.2	202	52.5	26.2	45.5
Castleton town (Rutland)	4,717	4,612	-2.2	4,669	93.8	3.0	0.2	2.2	0.7	14.7	74.9	10.6	1,531	66.9	38.9	26.9
Cavendish CDP	179	NA	NA	268	93.7	0.0	0.0	0.0	6.3	13.8	58.7	27.6	115	69.6	46.1	33.9
Cavendish town (Windsor)	1,367	1,361	-0.4	1,587	94.5	0.4	0.0	0.0	5.1	20.2	58.1	21.7	642	78.7	46.6	25.1
Charleston town (Orleans)	1,023	1,001	-2.2	939	98.1	0.0	0.6	0.9	0.4	13.2	67.7	19.2	425	76.5	62.4	11.8
Charlotte town (Chittenden)	3,754	3,856	2.7	3,810	94.0	0.0	1.0	1.4	3.5	21.7	66.9	11.6	1,442	86.5	19.2	65.3
Chelsea CDP	0	NA	NA	325	92.3	4.6	0.0	0.0	3.1	9.8	53.8	36.3	171	66.7	38.0	36.8
Chelsea town (Orange)	1,243	1,245	0.2	1,430	92.4	2.4	0.6	3.8	0.7	19.8	60.7	19.6	594	77.1	37.5	32.2
Chester CDP	1,005	NA	NA	991	97.9	0.0	0.0	0.7	1.4	14.3	57.7	27.9	540	50.2	51.9	25.2
Chester town (Windsor)	3,150	3,092	-1.8	3,128	92.0	0.0	0.8	1.6	5.6	17.3	63.8	18.8	1,442	70.2	41.6	29.4
Chittenden town (Rutland)	1,258	1,237	-1.7	1,198	96.3	0.0	1.8	0.5	1.4	18.5	63.2	18.0	508	80.5	28.3	45.7
Clarendon town (Rutland)	2,571	2,504	-2.6	2,535	94.2	0.9	1.1	2.2	1.6	15.4	66.2	18.3	1,119	78.6	51.3	20.6
Colchester town (Chittenden)	17,067	17,384	1.9	17,249	92.8	0.8	1.7	2.8	1.8	19.1	70.3	10.5	6,219	70.7	24.4	40.7
Concord CDP	271	NA	NA	281	97.5	0.0	1.1	0.0	1.4	12.8	63.8	23.5	138	73.9	69.6	5.8
Concord town (Essex)	1,235	1,203	-2.6	1,203	92.8	0.0	0.7	3.4	3.2	22.0	61.7	16.4	520	84.6	57.9	15.0
Corinth town (Orange)	1,366	1,366	0.0	1,302	95.2	0.6	0.0	3.9	0.3	21.8	62.3	16.0	557	90.5	42.7	30.3
Cornwall town (Addison)	1,187	1,189	0.2	1,089	95.5	0.0	0.8	1.6	2.1	19.8	62.9	17.3	460	80.4	23.5	60.0
Coventry CDP	97	NA	NA	111	100.0	0.0	0.0	0.0	0.0	16.2	69.3	14.4	55	78.2	74.5	12.7
Coventry town (Orleans)	1,086	1,059	-2.5	1,123	98.3	0.0	0.0	1.2	0.4	27.2	58.4	14.2	423	84.6	58.9	12.1
Craftsbury town (Orleans)	1,206	1,179	-2.2	1,238	89.7	0.9	0.8	4.9	3.6	22.1	55.3	22.5	467	85.4	35.8	37.7
Danby town (Rutland)	1,305	1,287	-1.4	1,366	95.9	0.0	0.3	1.4	2.4	22.8	61.4	15.9	551	79.5	49.7	22.9
Danville CDP	383	NA	NA	346	96.0	0.0	0.0	4.0	0.0	7.2	59.1	33.5	164	62.2	36.0	37.8
Danville town (Caledonia)	2,208	2,208	0.0	2,247	97.5	0.0	0.7	0.6	1.2	18.2	60.5	21.3	934	88.2	40.5	36.2
Derby town (Orleans)	4,623	4,502	-2.6	4,561	94.8	0.7	1.2	2.8	0.6	18.0	61.3	20.9	2,039	77.9	48.5	23.8

1 May be of any race.

Table A. All Places — Population and Housing

STATE City, town, township, borough, or CDP (county if applicable)	2010 census total population	2014 estimated population	Percent change 2010-2014	ACS total population estimate 2010-2014	White alone, not Hispanic or Latino	Black alone, not Hispanic or Latino	Asian alone, not Hispanic or Latino	All other races or 2 or more races, not Hispanic or Latino	Hispanic or Latino[1]	Under 18 years old	Age 18 to 64 years old	Age 65 years and older	Total occupied housing units	Percent owner occupied	High school diploma or less	Bachelor's degree or more
	1	2	3	4	5	6	7	8	9	10	11	12	13	14	15	16
VERMONT—Con.																
Derby Center village	597	580	-2.8	705	98.0	0.6	0.7	0.3	0.4	29.4	55.3	15.5	315	45.4	63.8	12.4
Derby Line village	675	656	-2.8	760	95.8	0.8	1.1	0.3	2.1	15.8	67.3	16.8	340	70.9	39.1	30.6
Dorset CDP	249	NA	NA	269	100.0	0.0	0.0	0.0	0.0	1.5	59.6	39.0	173	48.6	12.7	53.8
Dorset town (Bennington)	2,031	1,996	-1.7	2,118	98.2	0.0	0.5	0.2	1.0	21.4	56.1	22.4	937	79.9	19.1	46.2
Dover town (Windham)	1,124	1,108	-1.4	1,335	94.6	0.4	0.4	1.9	2.7	18.0	64.7	17.2	670	70.1	30.3	36.7
Dummerston town (Windham)	1,864	1,829	-1.9	1,933	99.1	0.4	0.2	0.0	0.4	18.0	61.4	20.5	896	84.9	28.8	49.9
Duxbury town (Washington)	1,337	1,337	0.0	1,409	93.8	0.0	0.6	0.0	5.5	19.4	69.1	11.4	553	88.8	29.7	48.1
East Barre CDP	826	NA	NA	942	94.2	0.0	0.0	0.0	5.8	23.4	68.7	7.9	341	85.6	40.8	36.4
East Burke CDP	132	NA	NA	143	100.0	0.0	0.0	0.0	0.0	36.4	49.7	14.0	45	100.0	15.6	73.3
East Haven town (Essex)	290	285	-1.7	338	94.1	0.0	0.0	5.0	0.9	16.3	64.0	19.8	135	91.1	64.4	15.6
East Middlebury CDP	425	NA	NA	295	100.0	0.0	0.0	0.0	0.0	20.4	72.2	7.5	156	76.3	28.8	34.6
East Montpelier CDP	80	NA	NA	62	100.0	0.0	0.0	0.0	0.0	0.0	100.0	0.0	54	70.4	14.8	25.9
East Montpelier town (Washington)	2,582	2,626	1.7	2,601	93.3	0.8	0.2	0.7	5.0	18.3	64.3	17.5	1,141	82.3	21.4	45.1
Eden town (Lamoille)	1,320	1,348	2.1	1,353	93.2	0.7	0.0	5.5	0.6	28.5	58.2	13.3	500	85.4	50.2	22.4
Elmore town (Lamoille)	855	872	2.0	946	97.0	0.6	0.0	1.8	0.5	21.6	64.9	13.4	380	86.3	37.1	42.9
Enosburg Falls village	1,329	1,314	-1.1	1,322	94.0	0.0	0.0	5.3	0.5	18.5	57.3	24.1	613	51.4	49.8	18.8
Enosburgh town (Franklin)	2,779	2,754	-0.9	2,771	95.3	0.0	0.1	4.0	0.5	21.1	62.1	17.0	1,151	62.5	49.7	21.1
Essex town (Chittenden)	19,593	20,724	5.8	20,172	92.2	2.2	2.3	1.7	1.7	23.6	64.5	12.0	8,298	72.5	21.2	49.9
Essex Junction village	9,273	9,881	6.6	9,552	91.2	2.0	3.8	2.7	0.3	23.0	64.4	12.7	4,131	61.8	23.5	46.4
Fairfax town (Franklin)	4,289	4,524	5.5	4,397	97.7	0.0	0.1	0.8	1.3	21.3	65.4	13.1	1,718	81.7	30.5	37.3
Fairfield town (Franklin)	1,896	1,911	0.8	1,856	98.2	0.0	0.0	0.6	1.2	22.9	67.0	10.0	668	82.8	44.8	29.3
Fair Haven town (Rutland)	2,734	2,650	-3.1	2,694	96.3	0.0	1.6	0.1	2.1	19.8	62.1	18.2	1,102	62.1	45.4	25.1
Fair Haven CDP	2,269	NA	NA	2,347	95.7	0.0	1.8	0.1	2.4	20.1	61.9	18.2	958	56.4	47.0	22.8
Fairlee CDP	189	NA	NA	264	95.8	0.0	0.0	4.2	0.0	35.9	57.1	6.8	98	28.6	36.7	34.7
Fairlee town (Orange)	980	987	0.7	1,029	95.7	0.5	1.5	2.0	0.3	19.4	64.5	16.1	444	61.9	42.6	36.0
Fayston town (Washington)	1,353	1,347	-0.4	1,314	98.0	0.0	1.1	0.9	0.0	22.9	61.9	15.2	557	86.0	13.1	71.6
Ferdinand town (Essex)	32	31	-3.1	28	100.0	0.0	0.0	0.0	0.0	25.0	60.8	14.3	11	100.0	63.6	0.0
Ferrisburgh town (Addison)	2,780	2,779	0.0	2,779	96.0	1.4	0.0	1.2	1.4	20.0	65.0	15.1	1,156	77.2	43.0	30.2
Fletcher town (Franklin)	1,279	1,314	2.7	1,244	97.1	0.0	0.2	2.7	0.0	22.0	69.3	8.7	503	93.0	25.4	28.2
Franklin town (Franklin)	1,405	1,424	1.4	1,240	96.9	0.0	0.1	1.5	1.5	20.9	62.3	16.8	516	88.2	52.5	20.5
Georgia town (Franklin)	4,515	4,684	3.7	4,610	95.3	0.0	0.2	3.4	1.1	29.0	61.0	10.0	1,653	84.7	36.8	31.9
Glastenbury town (Bennington)	8	8	0.0	9	100.0	0.0	0.0	0.0	0.0	0.0	77.7	22.2	5	60.0	0.0	60.0
Glover CDP	303	NA	NA	346	98.8	0.0	0.0	0.6	0.6	22.3	51.4	26.3	126	77.8	54.8	19.0
Glover town (Orleans)	1,122	1,099	-2.0	1,072	97.8	0.0	0.0	1.6	0.7	21.1	52.6	26.6	462	83.8	42.9	29.4
Goshen town (Addison)	164	163	-0.6	135	89.6	0.0	8.9	0.7	0.7	5.9	65.8	28.1	70	91.4	18.6	44.3
Grafton town (Windham)	679	670	-1.3	609	97.2	0.0	1.8	0.7	0.3	22.2	51.2	26.6	265	85.3	35.1	43.4
Granby town (Essex)	88	85	-3.4	85	100.0	0.0	0.0	0.0	0.0	12.9	54.1	32.9	41	92.7	73.2	7.3
Grand Isle town (Grand Isle)	2,067	2,081	0.7	2,264	96.1	0.0	0.3	1.8	1.9	20.2	65.0	14.8	957	79.9	34.8	30.3
Graniteville CDP	784	NA	NA	554	94.0	0.0	1.8	1.4	2.7	13.6	63.6	22.9	302	79.5	64.6	13.2
Granville town (Addison)	298	301	1.0	308	94.5	0.0	1.6	3.9	0.0	17.1	72.3	10.4	139	71.2	36.0	24.5
Greensboro CDP	109	NA	NA	79	100.0	0.0	0.0	0.0	0.0	2.5	35.5	62.0	49	77.6	14.3	77.6
Greensboro town (Orleans)	762	746	-2.1	723	96.7	0.3	0.0	2.2	0.8	15.6	60.7	23.5	316	87.0	33.5	49.4
Greensboro Bend CDP	232	NA	NA	218	91.7	0.9	0.0	7.3	0.0	23.8	62.9	13.3	87	88.5	51.7	28.7
Groton CDP	437	NA	NA	401	93.5	0.0	0.0	5.7	0.7	23.2	60.0	16.7	168	70.2	51.2	14.3
Groton town (Caledonia)	1,022	1,013	-0.9	1,013	96.8	0.0	0.0	2.9	0.3	20.8	60.8	18.4	387	82.2	43.4	15.2
Guildhall town (Essex)	261	255	-2.3	209	98.6	0.0	0.0	1.4	0.0	15.2	61.7	23.0	94	90.4	38.3	29.8
Guilford town (Windham)	2,121	2,093	-1.3	2,151	96.0	0.5	0.7	1.4	1.3	23.0	65.9	11.0	899	77.5	40.8	38.2
Halifax town (Windham)	728	723	-0.7	692	97.4	0.6	0.0	1.7	0.3	23.8	62.4	13.6	304	89.8	43.1	29.6
Hancock town (Addison)	323	326	0.9	395	96.2	0.0	0.8	2.3	0.8	23.7	59.3	17.0	161	80.1	50.9	22.4
Hardwick CDP	1,345	NA	NA	1,560	99.1	0.0	0.0	0.9	0.0	32.7	54.3	12.9	571	65.7	59.9	21.4
Hardwick town (Caledonia)	3,010	2,956	-1.8	2,976	95.9	0.0	0.7	3.4	0.0	25.6	57.9	16.4	1,144	79.5	54.3	22.9
Hartford town (Windsor)	9,952	9,829	-1.2	9,869	93.9	0.9	2.0	2.8	0.4	18.7	63.2	18.1	4,430	64.0	35.9	38.2
Hartland CDP	380	NA	NA	459	94.1	0.0	3.1	2.8	0.0	24.6	71.7	3.7	216	61.1	17.6	42.1
Hartland town (Windsor)	3,396	3,379	-0.5	3,397	97.6	0.0	1.1	1.3	0.0	21.8	65.5	12.6	1,460	75.4	40.0	30.9
Highgate town (Franklin)	3,537	3,608	2.0	3,576	92.6	0.0	0.2	7.2	0.0	22.3	60.1	17.6	1,409	80.8	63.8	12.8
Hinesburg CDP	0	NA	NA	853	99.9	0.0	0.0	0.0	0.1	25.2	65.5	9.4	384	61.7	3.6	81.0
Hinesburg town (Chittenden)	4,388	4,497	2.5	4,451	94.6	0.2	1.3	3.9	0.0	23.2	64.9	12.1	1,806	83.6	24.1	51.6
Holland town (Orleans)	629	617	-1.9	689	97.0	0.0	0.0	2.3	0.7	27.0	59.9	13.2	284	92.6	42.6	27.5
Hubbardton town (Rutland)	706	693	-1.8	624	98.4	0.0	0.3	0.0	1.3	10.0	68.0	21.8	293	96.2	39.6	31.7
Huntington town (Chittenden)	1,936	1,986	2.6	1,924	95.4	0.3	0.2	0.8	3.3	21.6	69.7	8.7	768	84.0	28.1	52.1
Hyde Park village	462	491	6.3	511	89.2	0.0	8.2	2.5	0.0	26.1	60.9	13.1	194	88.1	35.1	35.1
Hyde Park town (Lamoille)	2,953	3,040	2.9	3,011	94.4	0.0	1.4	1.2	3.1	19.9	62.4	17.6	1,287	80.7	51.6	24.6
Ira town (Rutland)	432	428	-0.9	441	99.1	0.0	0.0	0.9	0.0	22.5	65.0	12.5	186	90.9	33.9	29.0
Irasburg CDP	163	NA	NA	173	100.0	0.0	0.0	0.0	0.0	8.7	51.4	39.9	96	72.9	53.1	27.1
Irasburg town (Orleans)	1,163	1,138	-2.1	1,195	97.8	0.0	0.2	0.4	1.6	19.2	62.8	18.1	478	82.6	63.8	17.4
Island Pond CDP	821	NA	NA	644	94.7	1.6	0.8	3.0	0.0	22.5	56.6	20.8	313	56.2	65.8	12.8
Isle La Motte town (Grand Isle)	471	473	0.4	577	80.9	0.0	1.2	16.8	1.0	21.5	61.0	17.5	217	86.2	39.2	23.0
Jacksonville village	223	220	-1.3	226	96.9	0.0	0.0	0.0	3.1	23.4	64.3	12.4	95	74.7	52.6	22.1
Jamaica town (Windham)	1,035	1,022	-1.3	899	96.9	0.0	0.0	3.1	0.0	22.3	61.3	16.2	377	78.2	48.0	29.2
Jay town (Orleans)	515	552	7.2	818	97.7	0.4	0.1	0.2	1.6	30.5	63.2	6.2	276	74.3	41.7	23.9
Jeffersonville village	729	747	2.5	816	90.9	0.0	0.0	8.7	0.4	24.9	69.2	6.0	301	34.2	33.9	31.2
Jericho village	1,329	NA	NA	1,312	99.2	0.0	0.0	0.8	0.0	24.9	67.0	8.1	469	97.0	9.4	61.6
Jericho town (Chittenden)	5,009	5,074	1.3	5,040	96.2	0.6	0.5	2.5	0.3	27.7	61.2	11.2	1,863	89.4	17.7	60.3
Johnson village	1,423	1,444	1.5	1,316	94.2	2.1	0.5	1.7	1.5	14.2	75.8	10.0	389	50.9	49.6	19.3
Johnson town (Lamoille)	3,450	3,511	1.8	3,491	91.7	1.7	0.2	3.4	3.0	24.5	64.2	11.1	1,177	60.1	44.7	18.2
Killington town (Rutland)	813	795	-2.2	896	90.7	0.0	0.6	3.5	5.2	11.6	65.6	22.7	419	74.0	24.8	55.1
Kirby town (Caledonia)	490	499	1.8	435	96.1	0.0	0.5	0.0	3.4	19.1	70.3	10.6	167	91.0	41.3	31.7

1 May be of any race.

Table A. All Places — **Population and Housing**

	Population				Race and Hispanic or Latino origin (percent), 2010–2014					Age (percent), 2010–2014			Households, 2010–2014			
								All other races or 2 or more races, not Hispanic or Latino							Householders by level of education (percent)	
STATE City, town, township, borough, or CDP (county if applicable)	2010 census total population	2014 estimated population	Percent change 2010-2014	ACS total population estimate 2010-2014	White alone, not Hispanic or Latino	Black alone, not Hispanic or Latino	Asian alone, not Hispanic or Latino		Hispanic or Latino[1]	Under 18 years old	Age 18 to 64 years old	Age 65 years and older	Total occupied housing units	Percent owner occupied	High school diploma or less	Bachelor's degree or more
	1	2	3	4	5	6	7	8	9	10	11	12	13	14	15	16
VERMONT—Con.																
Landgrove town (Bennington)	158	160	1.3	132	98.5	0.0	0.0	1.5	0.0	8.3	43.2	48.5	71	94.4	18.3	57.7
Leicester town (Addison) ..	1,100	1,119	1.7	1,226	96.4	0.4	0.0	1.5	1.7	18.6	62.5	18.8	478	79.7	46.2	24.9
Lemington town (Essex) ...	104	101	-2.9	134	87.3	0.0	0.7	1.5	10.4	26.8	43.3	29.9	54	88.9	35.2	22.2
Lewis town (Essex)	0	0	0.0	0	0.0	0.0	0.0	0.0	0.0	0.0	0.0	0.0	0	0.0	0.0	0.0
Lincoln town (Addison)	1,271	1,272	0.1	1,221	95.7	0.0	0.7	0.7	2.9	20.4	64.0	15.5	498	89.0	28.5	46.4
Londonderry town (Windham)	1,769	1,756	-0.7	1,596	94.7	1.7	0.2	3.4	0.0	17.3	58.8	23.9	741	75.0	37.1	36.8
Lowell CDP	228	NA	NA	129	97.7	0.0	0.0	2.3	0.0	16.3	69.8	14.0	64	92.2	64.1	4.7
Lowell town (Orleans)	879	861	-2.0	810	86.9	0.2	0.4	1.9	10.6	22.7	65.2	12.1	322	84.8	54.3	16.8
Ludlow village	808	795	-1.6	940	91.4	0.5	2.7	0.4	5.0	11.9	63.5	24.7	456	42.1	42.8	27.6
Ludlow town (Windsor)	1,963	1,935	-1.4	2,131	92.7	0.2	1.2	3.4	2.4	13.7	64.8	21.5	955	60.5	41.7	33.7
Lunenburg town (Essex) ...	1,302	1,270	-2.5	1,331	97.7	0.7	0.2	1.5	0.0	16.0	61.9	22.2	571	77.1	58.1	11.6
Lyndon town (Caledonia)..	5,980	5,941	-0.7	5,966	95.6	1.0	1.2	1.3	1.0	19.1	66.7	14.1	2,262	59.9	52.5	16.6
Lyndonville village...........	1,207	1,199	-0.7	1,260	96.7	0.0	0.7	0.3	2.2	15.5	70.3	14.3	559	35.4	55.5	12.5
Maidstone town (Essex) ...	208	202	-2.9	217	93.1	0.5	0.9	0.9	4.6	12.5	52.2	35.5	113	83.2	46.9	15.0
Manchester village...........	746	728	-2.4	648	90.6	0.6	1.1	2.3	5.4	20.3	39.2	40.4	331	52.3	21.8	52.9
Manchester town (Bennington)	4,393	4,313	-1.8	4,352	97.5	0.5	0.2	0.7	1.2	20.0	57.5	22.5	2,044	70.2	32.9	42.0
Manchester Center CDP ..	2,120	NA	NA	2,211	97.8	0.8	0.0	0.7	0.7	26.1	54.5	19.4	1,012	61.0	42.7	30.1
Marlboro town (Windham) .	1,078	1,067	-1.0	1,196	94.1	0.7	0.5	2.7	2.1	13.8	73.6	12.4	375	81.6	16.3	61.3
Marshfield village.............	269	265	-1.5	298	90.6	0.0	0.0	6.0	3.4	36.3	43.9	19.8	98	88.8	36.7	40.8
Marshfield town (Washington)	1,582	1,550	-2.0	1,724	94.1	0.6	0.1	2.3	2.8	25.8	60.1	14.0	634	77.4	37.7	37.9
Mendon town (Rutland)	1,059	1,038	-2.0	862	97.0	0.5	1.7	0.8	0.0	16.9	64.8	18.2	429	74.1	25.4	51.0
Middlebury CDP	6,588	NA	NA	6,713	87.9	0.9	5.1	3.1	3.1	10.0	74.0	16.0	2,089	50.4	27.6	47.3
Middlebury town (Addison)	8,494	8,545	0.6	8,505	88.7	0.7	5.7	2.4	2.4	13.9	71.0	15.1	2,860	57.6	27.6	43.5
Middlesex town (Washington)	1,731	1,756	1.4	1,899	95.8	0.4	0.4	2.6	0.7	24.0	63.6	12.3	773	90.8	17.7	53.4
Middletown Springs town (Rutland)	744	732	-1.6	731	95.5	0.0	0.4	3.3	0.8	17.1	59.1	23.7	332	82.2	36.4	38.0
Milton CDP	1,861	NA	NA	1,363	95.7	0.0	0.0	3.2	1.1	11.8	69.7	18.6	680	69.7	42.1	20.3
Milton town (Chittenden)...	10,352	10,667	3.0	10,533	94.7	0.3	1.0	3.1	0.9	24.1	67.6	8.4	3,958	85.2	38.6	27.6
Monkton town (Addison)...	1,975	2,047	3.6	2,043	96.5	0.6	1.7	0.6	0.5	21.6	67.3	11.1	778	88.3	33.3	47.8
Montgomery town (Franklin)	1,201	1,195	-0.5	1,084	95.0	0.5	0.0	0.0	4.5	27.4	61.5	11.1	431	76.6	34.8	29.9
Montpelier city & MCD (Washington)................	7,849	7,671	-2.3	7,760	94.3	0.8	1.6	2.2	1.1	19.6	63.5	16.8	3,614	54.1	25.9	53.5
Moretown town (Washington)	1,658	1,664	0.4	1,653	90.6	0.0	0.5	5.7	3.1	20.5	65.1	14.6	728	78.8	21.8	53.4
Morgan town (Orleans)	749	742	-0.9	721	96.7	0.0	0.0	0.4	2.9	23.2	53.9	23.0	284	87.0	38.4	37.3
Morristown town (Lamoille)	5,227	5,389	3.1	5,314	94.6	0.6	0.6	3.7	0.6	21.5	60.5	18.0	2,252	71.0	36.7	34.0
Morrisville village	1,977	2,031	2.7	2,194	94.9	0.9	0.6	2.6	1.0	13.9	61.9	24.2	1,011	53.6	40.4	27.7
Mount Holly town (Rutland)	1,237	1,222	-1.2	1,258	95.2	0.0	0.2	4.6	0.0	13.7	66.1	20.1	567	86.9	42.3	27.3
Mount Tabor town (Rutland)	258	256	-0.8	271	96.3	0.0	0.0	1.1	2.6	14.8	67.1	18.1	107	68.2	45.8	31.8
Newark town (Caledonia) .	581	581	0.0	534	96.6	0.0	0.4	2.1	0.9	16.0	61.2	22.8	237	83.5	46.8	27.8
Newbury village	365	362	-0.8	306	97.4	0.7	1.6	0.3	0.0	16.4	56.2	27.5	153	75.8	37.9	38.6
Newbury town (Orange)....	2,216	2,202	-0.6	2,155	96.6	0.1	0.8	1.8	0.7	19.5	62.0	18.7	1,041	82.5	38.5	28.6
Newfane village	118	116	-1.7	58	100.0	0.0	0.0	0.0	0.0	25.8	44.8	29.3	29	41.4	27.6	48.3
Newfane town (Windham)	1,726	1,684	-2.4	1,819	98.8	0.0	0.0	0.4	0.8	17.1	64.0	19.0	805	84.8	23.5	43.1
New Haven town (Addison)	1,720	1,741	1.2	1,648	95.0	0.1	0.0	0.5	4.4	18.1	65.8	16.3	680	81.2	36.6	34.9
Newport city & MCD (Orleans)	4,587	4,473	-2.5	4,535	97.7	1.1	0.1	0.8	0.4	22.1	61.0	16.7	1,820	54.6	56.2	19.8
Newport town (Orleans)....	1,594	2,034	27.6	1,764	96.3	0.0	0.0	0.6	3.2	20.0	53.5	26.4	703	85.6	53.1	18.6
Newport Center CDP........	274	NA	NA	299	97.3	0.0	0.0	1.0	1.7	21.1	46.4	32.4	111	94.6	42.3	6.3
North Bennington village ..	1,643	1,622	-1.3	1,686	90.2	1.5	1.0	5.1	2.1	13.8	71.7	14.7	481	56.3	34.1	26.6
Northfield village	2,100	2,057	-2.0	2,677	95.5	0.5	0.1	1.0	2.9	18.1	70.0	11.8	836	59.1	42.1	22.7
Northfield town (Washington)	6,213	6,114	-1.6	6,175	94.3	0.6	1.4	1.0	2.7	15.2	72.4	12.4	1,867	75.5	32.6	36.1
North Hartland CDP	302	NA	NA	151	100.0	0.0	0.0	0.0	0.0	0.0	100.0	0.0	76	42.1	52.6	10.5
North Hero town (Grand Isle)	803	805	0.2	939	96.2	0.0	0.0	0.5	3.3	19.8	61.4	18.8	409	92.4	24.9	38.6
North Springfield CDP	573	NA	NA	486	100.0	0.0	0.0	0.0	0.0	8.2	62.1	29.6	325	78.8	52.9	6.5
North Troy village	620	600	-3.2	572	93.2	0.3	0.0	6.5	0.0	22.5	62.1	15.2	233	70.8	73.4	10.7
North Westminster CDP ...	247	NA	NA	294	91.5	0.0	0.0	2.4	6.1	13.2	75.9	10.9	135	55.6	42.2	11.1
Norton town (Essex)	169	160	-5.3	161	98.8	0.0	0.0	0.0	1.2	11.2	55.2	33.5	86	83.7	59.3	14.0
Norwich CDP	878	NA	NA	1,089	86.9	1.2	4.0	6.7	1.2	21.6	65.1	13.2	463	67.4	3.7	83.8
Norwich town (Windsor) ...	3,416	3,386	-0.9	3,400	91.9	0.8	1.8	3.1	2.3	22.3	63.2	14.6	1,480	75.7	6.3	77.4
Old Bennington village......	139	138	-0.7	150	98.7	0.0	0.7	0.7	0.0	23.4	58.7	18.0	58	91.4	10.3	79.3
Orange town (Orange)......	1,072	1,073	0.1	1,048	99.7	0.0	0.0	0.0	0.3	22.5	64.8	12.7	391	91.3	61.4	13.0
Orleans village	818	787	-3.8	898	87.2	7.8	0.0	4.0	1.0	29.1	56.0	15.1	300	62.0	51.0	11.3
Orwell town (Addison)	1,250	1,250	0.0	1,242	98.2	1.1	0.0	0.6	0.0	18.9	63.9	17.1	472	83.7	44.9	36.2
Panton town (Addison)	677	675	-0.3	740	94.3	0.0	0.3	5.1	0.3	22.6	64.5	13.0	297	78.1	49.2	23.6
Pawlet town (Rutland).......	1,477	1,438	-2.6	1,440	96.3	0.1	0.0	2.5	1.0	24.4	55.2	20.4	569	75.6	38.7	35.3
Peacham town (Caledonia)	734	735	0.1	695	97.0	1.4	0.0	0.0	1.6	16.4	63.8	19.7	285	85.3	18.2	52.6
Perkinsville village	130	128	-1.5	208	97.6	0.0	0.0	2.4	0.0	33.2	54.9	12.0	73	87.7	34.2	37.0
Peru town (Bennington)	373	365	-2.1	348	97.7	0.0	0.3	0.9	1.1	19.2	53.9	26.7	158	82.3	24.7	46.2
Pittsfield town (Rutland)....	548	543	-0.9	617	94.3	0.0	1.8	2.3	1.6	24.5	63.1	12.5	231	76.2	22.9	40.7
Pittsford CDP	740	NA	NA	570	99.1	0.0	0.0	0.9	0.0	16.1	52.6	31.2	290	59.3	34.1	42.8
Pittsford town (Rutland)	2,991	2,898	-3.1	2,940	99.5	0.0	0.0	0.2	0.3	21.0	62.8	16.3	1,249	77.2	35.5	30.3
Plainfield CDP	401	NA	NA	346	94.5	0.0	1.7	2.3	1.4	23.1	66.5	10.1	139	48.9	20.1	46.8
Plainfield town (Washington)	1,249	1,252	0.2	1,304	90.8	2.5	1.2	4.4	1.2	22.3	63.3	14.5	508	75.8	25.4	45.9
Plymouth town (Windsor) .	619	616	-0.5	471	98.5	0.0	0.0	1.5	0.0	13.5	58.3	28.2	233	90.6	19.7	48.1
Pomfret town (Windsor)	904	894	-1.1	963	95.4	0.0	1.1	0.0	3.4	14.2	58.9	27.0	447	92.2	23.5	54.4
Poultney village...............	1,613	1,579	-2.1	1,673	92.2	1.4	0.4	2.3	3.7	15.9	75.0	9.0	509	56.0	44.2	24.4

1 May be of any race.

Table A. All Places — **Population and Housing**

STATE City, town, township, borough, or CDP (county if applicable)	2010 census total population	2014 estimated population	Percent change 2010-2014	ACS total population estimate 2010-2014	White alone, not Hispanic or Latino	Black alone, not Hispanic or Latino	Asian alone, not Hispanic or Latino	All other races or 2 or more races, not Hispanic or Latino	Hispanic or Latino[1]	Under 18 years old	Age 18 to 64 years old	Age 65 years and older	Total occupied housing units	Percent owner occupied	High school diploma or less	Bachelor's degree or more
	1	2	3	4	5	6	7	8	9	10	11	12	13	14	15	16
VERMONT—Con.																
Poultney town (Rutland)	3,433	3,340	-2.7	3,382	94.5	0.9	0.2	2.3	2.0	15.1	68.5	16.4	1,266	70.8	43.8	26.4
Pownal town (Bennington)	3,527	3,476	-1.4	3,495	96.2	0.0	0.1	3.7	0.0	20.8	62.4	17.0	1,408	76.3	45.2	17.4
Proctor town (Rutland)	1,741	1,677	-3.7	1,650	97.4	0.4	0.2	0.1	1.9	22.2	62.3	15.6	736	71.5	36.0	25.4
Proctorsville CDP	454	NA	NA	515	89.1	1.0	0.0	0.0	9.9	16.3	51.5	32.2	217	76.0	54.8	13.8
Putney CDP	523	NA	NA	477	99.8	0.0	0.0	0.0	0.2	15.3	59.0	25.6	252	44.0	30.6	50.4
Putney town (Windham)	2,702	2,681	-0.8	2,696	95.0	0.9	0.4	1.1	2.7	14.7	70.2	15.0	917	67.6	26.5	52.0
Quechee CDP	656	NA	NA	665	96.7	1.2	0.0	2.1	0.0	19.3	73.0	7.7	309	52.4	13.3	68.9
Randolph CDP	1,974	NA	NA	2,361	97.2	0.0	0.0	0.0	2.8	19.3	52.8	27.8	1,085	61.1	47.6	32.8
Randolph town (Orange)	4,780	4,755	-0.5	4,768	97.1	0.3	0.9	0.3	1.4	18.8	62.4	18.7	1,910	75.9	40.1	40.6
Reading town (Windsor)	666	656	-1.5	739	99.6	0.0	0.4	0.0	0.0	25.2	56.4	18.5	284	81.7	32.0	40.8
Readsboro CDP	321	NA	NA	268	99.6	0.0	0.0	0.4	0.0	9.7	52.9	37.3	146	67.8	56.8	17.1
Readsboro town (Bennington)	763	742	-2.8	777	98.2	0.1	0.0	0.9	0.8	12.8	64.5	22.5	388	87.4	50.5	26.3
Richford CDP	1,361	NA	NA	1,418	94.6	1.0	0.0	4.4	0.0	22.2	64.7	13.0	565	74.0	65.0	7.8
Richford town (Franklin)	2,306	2,316	0.4	2,329	95.7	0.6	0.0	3.5	0.3	23.2	62.5	14.3	920	79.1	65.5	10.1
Richmond CDP	723	NA	NA	702	89.7	7.8	1.1	1.3	0.0	30.0	63.9	6.0	305	44.6	49.5	44.6
Richmond town (Chittenden)	4,081	4,129	1.2	4,114	94.2	1.3	1.9	2.2	0.4	25.7	64.9	9.4	1,555	80.2	25.6	53.5
Ripton town (Addison)	588	595	1.2	650	97.4	0.0	0.0	2.6	0.0	22.5	64.5	12.9	261	73.2	25.7	51.3
Rochester CDP	299	NA	NA	285	94.7	1.1	0.0	4.2	0.0	21.5	47.8	30.9	158	42.4	34.8	39.2
Rochester town (Windsor)	1,139	1,121	-1.6	1,095	96.1	0.5	0.0	2.5	0.9	17.5	59.2	23.3	513	70.2	32.7	34.5
Rockingham town (Windham)	5,275	5,140	-2.6	5,190	92.6	1.1	0.5	3.7	2.1	20.4	63.4	16.3	2,252	61.2	51.6	23.6
Roxbury town (Washington)	691	687	-0.6	684	95.3	0.0	0.1	0.0	4.5	17.6	70.6	11.8	289	76.5	46.0	29.1
Royalton town (Windsor)	2,781	2,765	-0.6	2,778	94.5	1.9	0.2	2.1	1.4	17.7	68.8	13.6	1,271	52.0	38.9	40.0
Rupert town (Bennington)	714	700	-2.0	620	95.8	0.6	0.0	3.5	0.0	13.1	55.2	31.6	281	84.3	46.6	24.2
Rutland city & MCD (Rutland)	16,495	15,942	-3.4	16,217	96.1	0.4	1.3	1.1	1.1	19.2	62.6	18.0	7,167	51.9	42.8	30.7
Rutland town (Rutland)	4,054	4,019	-0.9	4,048	97.1	1.2	0.3	1.0	0.3	16.2	59.7	24.1	1,809	75.5	35.1	39.1
Ryegate town (Caledonia)	1,171	1,148	-2.0	1,118	100.0	0.0	0.0	0.0	0.0	20.7	61.1	18.3	462	87.0	54.8	24.2
St. Albans city & MCD (Franklin)	6,922	6,860	-0.9	6,889	92.2	0.6	1.5	5.2	0.5	24.4	64.7	10.8	2,926	54.0	41.1	24.4
St. Albans town (Franklin)	5,995	6,313	5.3	6,157	93.8	1.8	0.3	3.5	0.6	22.8	61.7	15.6	2,252	79.5	42.2	25.2
St. George town (Chittenden)	697	708	1.6	772	96.4	0.8	0.0	2.3	0.5	22.9	68.1	9.1	306	71.6	43.8	31.0
St. Johnsbury CDP	6,193	NA	NA	5,922	92.1	0.4	2.3	1.5	3.7	18.2	61.1	20.8	2,660	56.1	37.6	28.6
St. Johnsbury town (Caledonia)	7,604	7,523	-1.1	7,573	92.3	0.3	1.8	2.8	2.9	19.4	62.7	17.9	3,236	60.8	37.7	28.0
Salisbury town (Addison)	1,136	1,131	-0.4	1,142	95.7	0.4	1.1	1.1	1.8	21.6	62.7	15.8	445	80.2	45.2	31.9
Sandgate town (Bennington)	405	398	-1.7	516	88.6	0.8	1.0	2.1	7.6	30.4	54.8	14.7	182	79.1	24.2	40.7
Saxtons River village	568	555	-2.3	627	78.6	0.0	1.3	15.5	4.6	25.3	62.1	12.4	220	59.1	29.1	54.5
Searsburg town (Bennington)	109	107	-1.8	97	91.8	0.0	0.0	8.2	0.0	20.6	67.1	12.4	35	80.0	48.6	5.7
Shaftsbury town (Bennington)	3,592	3,531	-1.7	3,558	95.6	0.0	0.4	1.1	2.8	18.1	61.2	20.4	1,548	82.2	38.2	32.0
Sharon town (Windsor)	1,502	1,495	-0.5	1,521	96.4	0.5	0.3	2.4	0.3	26.2	61.5	12.3	597	77.6	38.2	31.7
Sheffield town (Caledonia)	703	699	-0.6	568	98.8	0.0	0.0	0.5	0.7	21.1	65.4	13.4	233	87.1	36.9	26.6
Shelburne CDP	592	NA	NA	745	100.0	0.0	0.0	0.0	0.0	18.4	63.0	18.5	293	63.5	19.1	32.8
Shelburne town (Chittenden)	7,144	7,736	8.3	7,452	95.8	0.0	1.3	1.1	1.9	23.6	56.2	20.3	2,932	74.7	13.0	67.3
Sheldon town (Franklin)	2,185	2,230	2.1	2,329	92.9	0.8	0.3	1.8	4.2	22.0	66.9	11.0	834	80.6	57.7	15.6
Shoreham town (Addison)	1,265	1,272	0.6	1,179	94.7	1.3	0.5	2.2	1.3	16.8	66.5	16.8	483	85.3	48.2	31.9
Shrewsbury town (Rutland)	1,055	1,033	-2.1	1,158	96.4	0.0	0.0	0.4	3.2	17.1	65.4	17.6	436	88.8	28.2	40.6
Somerset town (Windham)	3	3	0.0	7	100.0	0.0	0.0	0.0	0.0	0.0	0.0	100.0	7	100.0	100.0	0.0
South Barre CDP	1,219	NA	NA	1,411	98.4	0.0	0.6	1.0	0.0	20.9	65.2	14.0	550	77.3	46.2	26.2
South Burlington city & MCD (Chittenden)	17,902	18,743	4.7	18,378	88.0	2.5	3.9	2.5	3.1	17.3	64.1	18.8	8,204	66.3	17.4	56.1
South Hero town (Grand Isle)	1,631	1,627	-0.2	1,576	90.7	0.4	0.4	7.5	1.0	18.1	66.0	15.9	693	76.5	30.4	49.1
South Royalton CDP	694	NA	NA	755	89.0	4.4	0.7	2.3	3.7	7.4	88.2	4.5	407	22.9	15.0	64.9
South Shaftsbury CDP	683	NA	NA	612	99.5	0.0	0.0	0.5	0.0	24.9	53.9	21.2	298	73.8	69.5	13.8
Springfield CDP	3,979	NA	NA	3,913	94.6	0.5	0.0	1.2	3.7	27.9	57.9	14.4	1,643	53.0	58.1	14.9
Springfield town (Windsor)	9,373	9,232	-1.5	9,301	94.2	0.5	0.2	3.5	1.6	21.2	59.0	19.8	3,835	66.4	54.1	19.5
Stamford town (Bennington)	824	818	-0.7	878	98.6	0.0	0.0	0.0	1.4	18.9	64.4	16.6	364	86.0	43.7	31.3
Stannard town (Caledonia)	218	222	1.8	278	91.4	0.0	0.0	7.9	0.7	31.3	60.8	7.9	94	84.0	50.0	29.8
Starksboro town (Addison)	1,776	1,774	-0.1	1,762	96.3	0.4	1.0	1.8	0.6	25.9	67.4	6.6	664	86.0	35.8	40.4
Stockbridge town (Windsor)	734	731	-0.4	735	97.7	0.0	0.4	1.5	0.4	22.0	59.1	18.9	325	83.1	44.9	28.6
Stowe CDP	495	NA	NA	587	96.9	0.3	0.0	2.7	0.0	3.1	75.4	21.5	415	29.2	14.9	62.7
Stowe town (Lamoille)	4,314	4,411	2.2	4,371	96.2	0.3	0.9	1.3	1.3	20.3	65.7	14.0	1,947	60.3	12.7	64.4
Strafford town (Orange)	1,098	1,107	0.8	1,037	95.0	0.0	0.0	4.3	0.7	21.1	63.5	15.5	430	84.4	20.5	57.4
Stratton town (Windham)	216	212	-1.9	171	98.8	0.0	0.0	1.2	0.0	21.1	59.6	19.3	76	90.8	22.4	53.9
Sudbury town (Rutland)	557	548	-1.6	499	97.8	0.0	0.2	1.0	1.0	14.2	57.8	27.9	228	92.1	31.1	33.8
Sunderland town (Bennington)	955	951	-0.4	934	99.1	0.0	0.0	0.6	0.2	14.9	64.0	21.2	405	88.1	29.6	41.0
Sutton town (Caledonia)	1,029	1,019	-1.0	948	97.6	1.1	0.0	0.5	0.8	24.1	62.7	13.2	390	92.3	56.2	20.0
Swanton village	2,373	2,374	0.0	2,389	93.1	0.4	0.0	5.4	1.2	15.9	62.0	22.0	1,077	64.0	59.4	9.7
Swanton town (Franklin)	6,425	6,442	0.3	6,433	93.9	0.1	0.0	4.3	1.6	22.4	63.3	14.2	2,641	72.4	47.2	17.6
Thetford town (Orange)	2,590	2,591	0.0	2,589	95.8	0.0	0.8	2.6	0.9	21.0	62.7	16.3	1,099	85.4	22.7	53.7
Tinmouth town (Rutland)	616	614	-0.3	558	96.6	0.7	0.7	2.0	0.0	15.8	63.3	21.0	264	89.4	44.7	26.5
Topsham town (Orange)	1,173	1,171	-0.2	1,228	96.5	0.0	0.0	1.9	1.6	23.1	65.5	11.5	476	89.9	54.6	19.3
Townshend town (Windham)	1,232	1,217	-1.2	1,126	92.2	0.5	0.5	4.0	2.8	16.4	58.1	25.4	539	78.7	38.8	35.1
Troy CDP	243	NA	NA	153	100.0	0.0	0.0	0.0	0.0	1.3	49.8	49.0	89	74.2	66.3	22.5
Troy town (Orleans)	1,668	1,622	-2.8	1,413	97.2	0.1	0.0	2.6	0.0	16.2	62.7	21.1	652	80.7	67.0	13.3
Tunbridge town (Orange)	1,284	1,286	0.2	1,237	95.1	0.0	0.0	4.5	0.3	16.7	69.2	14.2	547	87.0	33.3	40.8

1 May be of any race.

Table A. All Places — **Population and Housing**

STATE City, town, township, borough, or CDP (county if applicable)	2010 census total population	2014 estimated population	Percent change 2010-2014	ACS total population estimate 2010-2014	White alone, not Hispanic or Latino	Black alone, not Hispanic or Latino	Asian alone, not Hispanic or Latino	All other races or 2 or more races, not Hispanic or Latino	Hispanic or Latino[1]	Under 18 years old	Age 18 to 64 years old	Age 65 years and older	Total occupied housing units	Percent owner occupied	High school diploma or less	Bachelor's degree or more
	1	2	3	4	5	6	7	8	9	10	11	12	13	14	15	16
VERMONT—Con.																
Underhill town (Chittenden)	3,016	3,067	1.7	3,040	95.7	0.2	0.6	3.0	0.5	21.9	63.7	14.4	1,146	90.6	14.0	57.9
Vergennes city & MCD (Addison)	2,588	2,597	0.3	2,579	89.7	3.5	1.0	3.5	2.3	18.6	65.9	15.4	1,018	69.9	37.9	36.1
Vernon town (Windham) ...	2,206	2,184	-1.0	2,027	95.5	1.0	0.5	1.4	1.5	20.3	56.9	22.7	812	78.2	42.4	23.0
Vershire town (Orange).....	721	722	0.1	679	83.7	6.0	0.7	8.0	1.6	22.7	66.2	11.0	270	85.2	30.0	45.6
Victory town (Essex).........	62	60	-3.2	108	100.0	0.0	0.0	0.0	0.0	28.7	50.9	20.4	43	97.7	39.5	16.3
Waitsfield CDP...............	164	NA	NA	197	100.0	0.0	0.0	0.0	0.0	10.7	75.6	13.7	113	64.6	24.8	48.7
Waitsfield town (Washington)...............	1,719	1,723	0.2	1,607	96.7	0.2	0.2	2.0	0.8	18.1	66.1	15.7	754	76.4	19.0	59.2
Walden town (Caledonia) .	933	933	0.0	1,044	97.4	0.0	0.2	2.4	0.0	26.5	60.7	12.8	401	86.0	48.1	28.7
Wallingford CDP...............	830	NA	NA	813	95.4	0.0	2.0	0.0	2.6	11.8	58.6	29.5	381	74.3	48.0	29.1
Wallingford town (Rutland)	2,080	2,041	-1.9	2,098	96.5	0.0	1.0	0.7	1.8	16.8	61.3	21.9	898	80.2	38.6	29.7
Waltham town (Addison)...	486	477	-1.9	486	93.2	2.5	0.4	2.5	1.4	13.8	65.6	20.6	208	89.9	23.1	51.4
Wardsboro town (Windham)	900	886	-1.6	694	90.2	1.7	0.1	7.1	0.9	19.2	61.7	19.2	343	88.6	48.1	21.3
Warner's grant (Essex)	0	0	0.0	0	0.0	0.0	0.0	0.0	0.0	0.0	0.0	0.0	0	0.0	0.0	0.0
Warren town (Washington)	1,705	1,703	-0.1	1,651	97.9	0.0	0.5	1.0	0.5	20.0	66.2	13.9	743	79.8	18.2	61.4
Warren's gore (Essex)	4	4	0.0	4	100.0	0.0	0.0	0.0	0.0	0.0	50.0	50.0	2	100.0	0.0	0.0
Washington town (Orange)	1,040	1,029	-1.1	1,067	93.3	0.7	0.4	0.7	4.9	14.4	71.8	13.5	437	87.6	51.7	23.3
Waterbury village	1,759	1,801	2.4	1,914	95.4	0.0	1.1	1.1	2.4	19.7	68.1	12.1	873	58.6	28.2	45.2
Waterbury town (Washington)...............	5,064	5,098	0.7	5,083	96.2	0.0	1.1	1.8	0.9	18.5	68.8	12.8	2,274	73.1	29.7	48.2
Waterford town (Caledonia)	1,278	1,280	0.2	1,489	96.1	0.0	0.5	2.6	0.8	25.0	63.4	11.6	540	92.6	39.8	21.5
Waterville town (Lamoille)	673	687	2.1	724	99.2	0.4	0.0	0.4	0.0	22.5	64.7	12.8	297	80.5	43.4	30.6
Weathersfield town (Windsor)	2,825	2,791	-1.2	2,813	97.9	0.7	0.0	1.1	0.2	17.6	60.7	21.6	1,220	87.8	45.3	24.8
Websterville CDP	550	NA	NA	514	100.0	0.0	0.0	0.0	0.0	25.0	66.5	8.6	211	84.8	63.5	7.6
Wells CDP	397	NA	NA	322	100.0	0.0	0.0	0.0	0.0	20.8	52.4	26.7	142	85.2	50.0	25.4
Wells town (Rutland).........	1,150	1,137	-1.1	1,116	99.7	0.0	0.0	0.3	0.0	24.6	54.8	20.7	487	84.2	52.0	23.0
Wells River village	397	394	-0.8	364	94.5	0.0	3.0	1.9	0.5	17.9	60.4	21.7	182	47.3	50.5	20.3
West Brattleboro CDP	2,740	NA	NA	2,758	88.3	0.0	3.9	2.2	5.5	21.6	58.2	20.4	1,251	59.5	48.0	30.9
West Burke village	343	338	-1.5	340	96.5	2.4	0.0	1.2	0.0	27.3	60.3	12.4	130	53.8	57.7	18.5
West Fairlee town (Orange).....................	658	657	-0.2	650	97.4	0.0	0.0	2.6	0.0	23.0	63.8	13.1	289	79.2	50.2	28.4
Westfield town (Orleans) ..	536	524	-2.2	534	98.3	0.7	0.4	0.0	0.6	19.1	63.3	17.8	198	88.4	31.8	33.3
Westford town (Chittenden)	2,023	2,085	3.1	1,937	95.0	0.0	2.3	1.8	0.8	21.8	65.5	12.7	740	91.5	24.7	47.7
West Haven town (Rutland)	264	259	-1.9	290	99.0	0.0	0.0	1.0	0.0	14.8	63.2	22.1	133	82.7	45.1	36.1
Westminster village	291	285	-2.1	288	100.0	0.0	0.0	0.0	0.0	13.8	70.0	16.0	130	78.5	42.3	29.2
Westminster town (Windham)	3,185	3,111	-2.3	3,148	90.1	1.0	0.0	4.0	4.9	19.6	64.8	15.4	1,391	75.7	31.1	34.1
Westmore town (Orleans).	350	342	-2.3	393	96.2	0.0	0.0	3.8	0.0	13.0	53.7	33.3	192	90.1	27.6	41.1
Weston town (Windsor)	566	561	-0.9	598	98.2	0.0	0.7	0.5	0.7	11.9	53.8	34.3	279	73.1	29.7	54.1
West Rutland town (Rutland)	2,326	2,246	-3.4	2,335	94.2	0.0	0.5	1.2	4.2	20.4	60.1	19.5	1,013	79.2	55.4	18.1
West Rutland CDP	2,024	NA	NA	1,998	93.2	0.0	0.6	1.4	4.9	20.8	60.9	18.5	870	75.7	57.8	18.5
West Windsor town (Windsor)	1,099	1,089	-0.9	1,094	99.4	0.0	0.6	0.0	0.0	21.4	56.6	22.0	473	88.8	24.9	46.7
Weybridge town (Addison)	833	828	-0.6	854	92.5	1.4	0.0	4.3	1.8	24.6	60.7	14.9	343	82.8	19.8	54.5
Wheelock town (Caledonia)	808	806	-0.2	866	97.3	0.0	0.0	1.2	1.5	23.1	60.8	16.2	331	81.6	53.5	24.8
White River Junction CDP	2,286	NA	NA	2,327	94.9	0.3	3.1	1.0	0.7	18.1	65.1	16.8	1,097	53.9	42.5	21.0
Whiting town (Addison).....	419	424	1.2	409	94.9	1.5	0.0	1.2	2.4	24.4	63.1	12.5	161	75.2	52.2	27.3
Whitingham town (Windham)	1,357	1,344	-1.0	1,237	99.1	0.0	0.0	0.0	0.9	23.7	59.9	16.5	537	84.2	47.7	28.7
Wilder CDP	1,690	NA	NA	1,506	95.1	1.2	1.3	0.7	1.7	27.4	63.7	9.0	623	75.6	24.4	49.9
Williamstown CDP	1,162	NA	NA	1,149	100.0	0.0	0.0	0.0	0.0	15.9	67.8	16.4	530	60.4	54.2	17.4
Williamstown town (Orange).....................	3,389	3,383	-0.2	3,397	97.0	0.0	0.0	0.2	2.8	20.9	62.9	16.3	1,430	80.1	50.1	19.6
Williston town (Chittenden)	8,682	9,215	6.1	8,932	91.7	0.9	2.9	2.3	2.2	24.9	58.9	16.3	3,736	77.4	20.0	55.4
Wilmington CDP	463	NA	NA	512	98.4	0.0	0.0	1.6	0.0	28.7	53.2	18.2	223	70.0	11.2	35.0
Wilmington town (Windham)	1,876	1,842	-1.8	2,257	95.5	0.0	0.9	3.6	0.0	22.3	60.5	17.3	956	78.0	21.2	37.6
Windham town (Windham)	419	416	-0.7	422	96.2	1.7	0.9	1.2	0.0	20.2	53.7	26.1	194	92.3	35.6	44.8
Windsor town (Windsor) ...	3,553	3,476	-2.2	3,504	96.3	2.2	0.9	0.5	0.1	19.8	59.6	20.5	1,448	55.3	49.6	25.1
Windsor CDP	2,066	NA	NA	2,138	94.5	3.6	1.2	0.7	0.0	25.4	59.2	15.4	926	38.3	54.9	25.8
Winhall town (Bennington)	769	759	-1.3	654	97.1	0.5	0.0	0.0	2.4	16.9	50.8	32.6	332	82.8	22.0	51.8
Winooski city & MCD (Chittenden)	7,267	7,228	-0.5	7,250	86.4	6.9	3.1	1.8	1.8	16.0	74.6	9.4	3,237	38.7	35.3	35.9
Wolcott town (Lamoille)	1,676	1,721	2.7	1,556	97.8	0.0	0.0	1.9	0.3	24.0	63.7	12.3	600	83.8	43.0	22.3
Woodbury town (Washington)...............	906	895	-1.2	897	93.2	0.0	0.0	3.8	3.0	18.4	62.3	19.2	411	93.4	34.3	36.0
Woodford town (Bennington)	424	413	-2.6	322	97.5	0.0	1.2	1.2	0.0	12.7	67.5	19.9	153	82.4	44.4	19.0
Woodstock village............	895	879	-1.8	948	95.3	0.2	0.0	2.6	1.9	18.7	51.6	29.6	461	59.9	17.6	54.4
Woodstock town (Windsor)	3,043	2,996	-1.5	3,017	96.6	0.1	0.0	1.3	2.0	14.5	58.7	26.7	1,408	78.3	23.9	51.1
Worcester CDP	112	NA	NA	136	97.1	0.0	1.5	1.5	0.0	29.4	53.6	16.9	61	73.8	26.2	39.3
Worcester town (Washington)...............	998	992	-0.6	891	95.2	0.3	0.6	3.9	0.0	21.4	63.1	15.5	387	81.4	25.1	47.5
VIRGINIA	8,001,023	8,326,289	4.1	8,185,131	63.9	18.9	5.8	3.0	8.4	22.7	64.3	13.0	3,041,710	66.7	33.0	38.4
Abingdon town..................	8,181	8,146	-0.4	8,176	88.2	5.2	1.6	1.0	4.0	19.2	60.6	20.1	3,850	51.2	37.7	33.8
Accomac town..................	506	496	-2.0	485	72.8	11.8	0.0	1.9	13.6	21.4	59.4	19.2	179	63.7	41.9	34.6
Adwolf CDP	1,530	NA	NA	1,630	97.6	0.0	0.0	1.0	1.3	10.9	70.5	18.6	645	80.9	66.4	10.4

1 May be of any race.

Table A. All Places — **Population and Housing**

STATE City, town, township, borough, or CDP (county if applicable)	Population				Race and Hispanic or Latino origin (percent), 2010–2014					Age (percent), 2010–2014			Households, 2010–2014			
	2010 census total population	2014 estimated population	Percent change 2010-2014	ACS total population estimate 2010-2014	White alone, not Hispanic or Latino	Black alone, not Hispanic or Latino	Asian alone, not Hispanic or Latino	All other races or 2 or more races, not Hispanic or Latino	Hispanic or Latino[1]	Under 18 years old	Age 18 to 64 years old	Age 65 years and older	Total occupied housing units	Percent owner occupied	Householders by level of education (percent): High school diploma or less	Householders by level of education (percent): Bachelor's degree or more
	1	2	3	4	5	6	7	8	9	10	11	12	13	14	15	16
VIRGINIA—Con.																
Alberta town	298	286	-4.0	279	61.6	32.6	0.0	5.7	0.0	16.9	63.1	20.1	126	70.6	55.6	21.4
Alexandria city	140,006	150,575	7.5	146,422	52.7	21.2	6.3	3.4	16.5	17.6	73.1	9.6	65,916	42.7	14.9	67.1
Allisonia CDP	117	NA	NA	156	39.7	60.3	0.0	0.0	0.0	39.1	45.5	15.4	43	72.1	100.0	0.0
Altavista town	3,450	3,460	0.3	3,456	66.4	25.4	1.6	2.8	3.7	17.3	60.7	22.0	1,475	60.5	53.2	17.7
Amelia Court House CDP	1,099	NA	NA	825	77.8	21.5	0.0	0.7	0.0	32.4	50.0	17.6	278	42.8	54.0	37.4
Amherst town	2,231	2,206	-1.1	2,643	71.0	20.6	0.3	4.7	3.4	17.9	58.4	23.7	950	62.0	44.8	24.4
Annandale CDP	41,008	NA	NA	43,479	34.7	7.2	24.5	3.6	30.0	22.5	64.8	12.7	14,024	58.7	29.3	46.1
Appalachia town	1,751	1,684	-3.8	1,732	95.1	2.2	1.0	1.4	0.3	22.0	62.2	15.9	731	56.9	43.4	19.6
Apple Mountain Lake CDP	1,396	NA	NA	1,509	85.6	0.0	2.9	0.8	10.7	34.9	60.3	4.7	543	88.6	24.9	27.4
Appomattox town	1,707	1,744	2.2	2,132	62.6	34.6	0.1	1.1	1.6	17.4	58.3	24.3	867	64.0	59.7	14.0
Aquia Harbour CDP	6,727	NA	NA	6,544	76.8	11.0	1.7	3.5	7.0	23.5	64.8	11.7	2,254	86.5	10.6	56.0
Arcola CDP	233	NA	NA	182	95.1	0.0	4.9	0.0	0.0	9.3	90.5	0.0	43	65.1	34.9	39.5
Arlington CDP	207,627	NA	NA	220,173	63.2	8.2	9.7	3.4	15.4	16.4	74.8	8.9	96,264	44.8	11.0	77.0
Arrington CDP	708	NA	NA	850	62.9	37.1	0.0	0.0	0.0	27.7	66.5	5.9	361	71.7	57.6	20.5
Ashburn CDP	43,511	NA	NA	47,484	60.7	8.9	15.0	4.8	10.6	30.2	61.7	8.0	15,797	73.0	10.2	66.9
Ashland town	7,225	7,328	1.4	7,264	69.0	19.6	2.4	4.7	4.3	17.6	66.9	15.4	2,609	55.0	40.8	24.7
Atkins CDP	1,143	NA	NA	1,167	96.7	0.0	0.0	2.1	1.2	17.1	70.9	12.1	449	66.1	73.1	5.1
Atlantic CDP	862	NA	NA	1,240	75.9	21.9	0.0	0.0	2.2	9.9	67.0	23.1	501	91.2	43.9	38.7
Augusta Springs CDP	257	NA	NA	282	100.0	0.0	0.0	0.0	0.0	21.3	34.1	44.7	130	93.1	94.6	0.0
Bailey's Crossroads CDP	23,643	NA	NA	24,947	31.4	18.1	10.3	2.1	38.0	23.6	64.8	11.7	9,170	37.4	33.7	47.9
Baskerville CDP	128	NA	NA	91	100.0	0.0	0.0	0.0	0.0	23.1	58.3	18.7	32	100.0	46.9	53.1
Bassett CDP	1,100	NA	NA	1,139	60.4	33.3	0.0	0.0	6.3	24.3	55.5	20.2	454	57.0	49.6	13.4
Basye CDP	1,253	NA	NA	741	95.7	4.3	0.0	0.0	0.0	17.6	45.7	36.7	354	72.0	26.0	21.2
Bayside CDP	120	NA	NA	120	0.0	100.0	0.0	0.0	0.0	0.0	47.5	52.5	100	87.0	100.0	0.0
Bealeton CDP	4,435	NA	NA	4,521	82.3	6.1	0.2	2.2	9.2	26.2	67.3	6.4	1,342	78.9	33.2	33.7
Bedford town	6,570	6,466	-1.6	6,508	69.1	27.6	0.0	2.0	1.3	20.9	56.6	22.4	2,845	54.0	50.5	17.7
Belle Haven town	524	525	0.2	376	73.4	26.6	0.0	0.0	0.0	25.7	57.7	16.5	179	69.3	47.5	24.0
Belle Haven CDP	6,518	NA	NA	6,807	81.3	4.1	2.2	0.9	11.6	23.6	64.6	11.9	2,989	76.9	11.8	73.0
Bellwood CDP	6,352	NA	NA	5,889	46.2	25.8	2.0	2.8	23.2	25.2	62.0	12.9	2,172	60.6	65.7	10.7
Belmont CDP	5,966	NA	NA	5,910	64.3	5.0	25.0	3.8	1.9	33.6	58.8	7.7	1,843	93.1	6.0	80.4
Belmont Estates CDP	1,263	NA	NA	1,299	98.9	0.0	1.1	0.0	0.0	24.6	44.0	31.4	517	97.5	28.4	46.2
Belspring CDP	256	NA	NA	337	100.0	0.0	0.0	0.0	0.0	6.2	39.2	54.6	174	92.5	29.9	9.8
Belview CDP	891	NA	NA	1,189	100.0	0.0	0.0	0.0	0.0	37.1	45.3	17.7	377	45.6	80.9	11.7
Benns Church CDP	872	NA	NA	617	62.6	30.1	0.0	7.1	0.2	22.0	59.9	18.0	231	92.2	46.8	0.0
Bensley CDP	5,819	NA	NA	5,865	34.5	20.7	0.9	3.2	40.6	26.3	64.9	8.9	2,147	42.0	61.2	9.0
Berryville town	4,182	4,297	2.7	4,254	84.8	11.4	0.5	1.7	1.6	24.6	57.1	18.4	1,668	62.3	38.1	37.6
Bethel Manor CDP	3,792	NA	NA	3,761	63.1	19.4	0.9	5.6	11.1	46.0	54.0	0.0	1,059	0.0	13.5	28.4
Big Island CDP	303	NA	NA	289	100.0	0.0	0.0	0.0	0.0	16.2	64.3	19.4	117	94.0	48.7	28.2
Big Stone Gap town	5,610	5,457	-2.7	5,559	74.8	19.2	0.5	2.8	2.7	18.3	68.9	12.9	1,680	54.1	49.5	21.4
Blacksburg town	42,607	43,985	3.2	43,204	75.8	4.7	12.0	3.3	4.1	9.9	85.7	4.5	13,581	28.3	11.7	53.0
Blackstone town	3,620	3,553	-1.9	3,581	52.6	37.8	0.1	0.4	9.2	19.4	55.9	24.7	1,502	40.1	63.1	15.9
Blairs CDP	916	NA	NA	857	67.9	19.3	0.0	0.6	12.3	15.1	59.2	25.7	364	75.5	46.2	16.5
Bland CDP	409	NA	NA	587	99.5	0.0	0.0	0.0	0.5	23.6	49.1	27.1	266	59.0	53.0	12.8
Bloxom town	389	386	-0.8	422	74.6	13.7	0.0	1.4	10.2	30.1	57.9	11.8	170	69.4	63.5	10.0
Bluefield town	5,441	5,302	-2.6	5,375	86.6	7.6	0.7	2.6	2.5	20.4	60.6	19.2	2,211	72.2	42.2	18.9
Blue Ridge CDP	3,084	NA	NA	2,823	98.6	0.4	0.0	1.1	0.0	15.0	60.7	24.3	1,134	87.4	40.3	29.5
Blue Ridge Shores CDP	813	NA	NA	822	87.1	9.9	0.0	3.0	0.0	30.3	51.0	18.6	327	79.5	48.0	18.7
Bobtown CDP	211	NA	NA	394	55.1	0.0	0.0	0.0	44.9	21.3	53.6	25.1	165	87.3	6.1	57.0
Bon Air CDP	16,366	NA	NA	16,857	75.5	10.8	4.0	1.5	8.2	22.8	62.1	15.2	6,509	75.6	22.2	48.5
Boones Mill town	234	234	0.0	166	99.4	0.0	0.0	0.6	0.0	12.0	72.8	15.1	82	86.6	31.7	42.7
Boston CDP	504	NA	NA	625	1.8	98.2	0.0	0.0	0.0	13.9	76.9	9.1	319	74.0	83.1	9.1
Boswell's Corner CDP	1,375	NA	NA	1,416	31.4	7.7	7.1	8.5	45.3	34.3	57.1	8.5	429	50.6	44.1	37.5
Bowling Green town	1,111	1,152	3.7	1,154	80.0	18.9	0.0	0.8	0.3	22.8	49.2	28.0	463	58.3	47.1	22.2
Boyce town	599	614	2.5	732	68.9	7.1	1.2	4.9	17.9	30.9	57.3	11.9	228	85.1	32.9	39.9
Boydton town	431	419	-2.8	428	67.3	30.6	0.0	0.7	1.4	28.0	55.0	16.8	130	73.1	46.9	38.5
Boykins town	564	544	-3.5	680	62.6	28.7	1.3	7.4	0.0	23.7	59.3	17.1	218	72.5	46.3	20.2
Bracey CDP	1,554	NA	NA	1,207	90.2	8.8	0.0	0.0	1.0	7.3	61.1	31.6	678	93.5	23.9	16.8
Brambleton CDP	9,845	NA	NA	13,357	57.3	5.6	26.4	5.2	5.5	34.8	62.5	2.8	4,131	85.7	5.4	80.2
Branchville town	122	117	-4.1	133	59.4	39.1	0.0	1.5	0.0	30.8	60.9	8.3	43	83.7	58.1	7.0
Brandermill CDP	13,173	NA	NA	13,570	75.3	14.2	2.9	3.9	3.6	23.2	60.4	16.2	5,242	65.8	13.7	55.4
Bridgewater town	5,644	5,951	5.4	5,812	86.9	4.9	0.1	3.2	4.9	17.4	63.3	19.4	1,838	60.8	42.3	37.5
Brightwood CDP	1,001	NA	NA	1,428	89.2	2.0	0.0	8.8	0.0	18.1	60.8	21.3	501	86.8	66.5	11.0
Bristol city	17,841	17,184	-3.7	17,595	89.1	6.6	0.8	2.7	0.7	20.4	60.4	19.1	7,764	55.3	49.2	20.5
Broadlands CDP	12,313	NA	NA	13,138	63.2	7.1	20.4	3.9	5.3	38.6	59.6	1.8	3,996	86.0	3.6	83.2
Broadway town	3,686	3,780	2.6	3,748	87.5	5.2	1.2	0.9	5.2	28.1	58.2	13.8	1,502	71.8	42.1	21.0
Brodnax town	298	287	-3.7	263	49.0	49.4	0.0	0.4	1.1	21.6	58.4	19.8	105	74.3	56.2	14.3
Brookneal town	1,112	1,115	0.3	1,157	54.1	42.7	0.7	2.5	0.0	17.0	62.0	21.2	470	63.8	59.4	11.9
Buchanan town	1,178	1,171	-0.6	1,075	94.1	4.7	0.0	0.9	0.3	23.6	56.1	20.4	445	78.4	50.8	22.2
Buckhall CDP	16,293	NA	NA	17,265	66.8	6.5	6.5	3.0	17.2	28.7	62.9	8.4	5,105	91.4	21.9	45.6
Buckingham Courthouse CDP	133	NA	NA	165	78.2	0.0	4.8	17.0	0.0	7.9	48.0	44.2	62	82.3	9.7	41.9
Buena Vista city	6,651	6,603	-0.7	6,683	89.1	3.2	5.7	1.2	0.8	20.7	62.3	16.9	2,741	64.1	58.4	15.2
Bull Run CDP	14,983	NA	NA	14,570	30.9	15.6	6.6	4.8	42.0	24.4	71.1	4.8	5,356	34.0	32.4	36.6
Bull Run Mountain Estates CDP	1,251	NA	NA	1,051	87.5	0.9	3.0	2.3	6.3	13.3	79.1	7.6	465	100.0	26.2	54.6
Burke CDP	41,055	NA	NA	42,528	62.0	5.2	17.3	3.5	12.0	25.2	63.1	11.6	13,684	85.0	10.7	69.5
Burke Centre CDP	17,326	NA	NA	17,842	59.1	4.9	15.2	3.6	17.3	24.4	64.8	10.9	6,212	73.6	14.8	65.9
Burkeville town	432	420	-2.8	341	59.8	39.6	0.0	0.6	0.0	20.5	59.8	19.6	132	78.0	56.8	12.1
Callaghan CDP	348	NA	NA	197	93.4	2.5	0.0	0.0	4.1	0.0	57.9	42.1	105	68.6	38.1	6.7
Calverton CDP	239	NA	NA	175	100.0	0.0	0.0	0.0	0.0	0.0	64.0	36.0	96	18.8	77.1	22.9
Camptown CDP	766	NA	NA	556	29.0	71.0	0.0	0.0	0.0	14.2	67.4	18.7	300	48.7	86.0	6.7
Cana CDP	1,254	NA	NA	1,352	88.5	2.2	0.0	5.3	4.0	19.5	60.0	20.6	597	78.9	56.1	9.4
Cape Charles town	1,009	990	-1.9	926	70.3	26.5	0.9	0.0	2.4	15.2	55.5	29.4	498	55.8	44.2	36.9
Capron town	164	157	-4.3	96	76.0	19.8	0.0	4.2	0.0	10.5	67.7	21.9	45	82.2	48.9	17.8
Captains Cove CDP	1,042	NA	NA	863	100.0	0.0	0.0	0.0	0.0	15.0	55.5	29.7	362	71.8	39.2	41.4
Carrollton CDP	4,574	NA	NA	4,693	63.1	19.3	2.8	3.8	10.9	22.0	65.5	12.5	1,675	74.6	23.0	45.9
Carrsville CDP	359	NA	NA	277	88.4	9.4	0.0	2.2	0.0	4.3	73.9	21.7	157	73.9	51.6	24.2
Cascades CDP	11,912	NA	NA	12,231	66.5	7.1	16.8	3.0	6.6	25.8	64.4	9.8	4,466	77.5	8.9	68.5
Castlewood CDP	2,045	NA	NA	1,631	92.5	1.4	2.3	3.9	0.0	29.8	51.8	18.5	627	70.3	62.2	5.4
Catlett CDP	296	NA	NA	229	81.7	18.3	0.0	0.0	0.0	5.7	67.7	26.6	109	66.1	50.5	27.5
Cats Bridge CDP	229	NA	NA	323	0.0	100.0	0.0	0.0	0.0	37.7	50.4	11.8	148	66.2	48.0	0.0

1 May be of any race.

Table A. All Places — **Population and Housing**

STATE City, town, township, borough, or CDP (county if applicable)	Population: 2010 census total population	Population: 2014 estimated population	Population: Percent change 2010-2014	Population: ACS total population estimate 2010-2014	Race and Hispanic or Latino origin (percent), 2010–2014: White alone, not Hispanic or Latino	Black alone, not Hispanic or Latino	Asian alone, not Hispanic or Latino	All other races or 2 or more races, not Hispanic or Latino	Hispanic or Latino[1]	Age (percent), 2010–2014: Under 18 years old	Age 18 to 64 years old	Age 65 years and older	Households, 2010–2014: Total occupied housing units	Percent owner occupied	Householders by level of education (percent): High school diploma or less	Bachelor's degree or more
	1	2	3	4	5	6	7	8	9	10	11	12	13	14	15	16
VIRGINIA—Con.																
Cave Spring CDP	24,922	NA	NA	25,547	86.7	5.0	5.3	1.6	1.3	19.8	62.0	18.1	11,482	66.3	18.6	49.3
Cedar Bluff town	1,137	1,090	-4.1	1,172	97.2	0.0	0.0	2.8	0.0	23.8	54.4	21.8	506	62.8	51.0	8.3
Central Garage CDP	1,318	NA	NA	1,002	78.7	15.2	0.0	6.1	0.0	17.0	69.9	13.3	473	85.6	39.1	25.2
Centreville CDP	71,135	NA	NA	73,677	47.5	6.5	26.8	4.6	14.6	26.1	68.0	5.7	24,575	71.7	15.8	60.8
Chamberlayne CDP	5,456	NA	NA	5,867	30.7	57.8	4.7	3.3	3.6	18.2	61.9	19.8	2,198	94.5	21.8	47.2
Chantilly CDP	23,039	NA	NA	23,431	45.7	6.4	26.0	2.7	19.1	28.0	65.6	6.5	7,223	80.8	15.3	60.5
Charles City CDP	133	NA	NA	150	25.3	74.7	0.0	0.0	0.0	20.0	45.4	34.7	61	80.3	59.0	24.6
Charlotte Court House town	543	531	-2.2	794	52.8	34.6	1.8	0.1	10.7	36.6	45.9	17.4	227	69.2	45.4	21.1
Charlottesville city	43,435	45,593	5.0	44,505	66.4	19.5	6.8	2.4	4.9	15.2	75.4	9.2	17,604	41.6	29.1	49.7
Chase City town	2,351	2,304	-2.0	2,228	45.2	48.6	4.5	1.8	0.0	25.6	58.1	16.1	908	56.6	59.7	13.4
Chase Crossing CDP	377	NA	NA	439	14.8	15.0	0.0	0.0	70.2	44.9	55.2	0.0	137	52.6	71.5	22.6
Chatham town	1,269	1,476	16.3	987	76.3	18.8	0.0	2.1	2.7	11.4	63.8	24.7	406	69.7	22.4	43.3
Chatmoss CDP	1,698	NA	NA	1,535	71.7	23.4	0.8	0.0	4.0	14.9	62.8	22.3	666	93.8	40.1	25.8
Cheriton town	487	477	-2.1	471	48.6	45.6	0.0	0.0	5.7	11.4	70.1	18.5	219	74.4	59.8	2.7
Cherry Hill CDP	16,000	NA	NA	17,079	23.6	39.9	9.3	6.0	21.1	31.1	65.1	3.9	5,480	55.0	24.6	36.7
Chesapeake city	222,209	233,371	5.0	228,168	59.5	29.3	3.2	3.2	4.9	25.1	63.9	11.2	80,388	71.7	31.0	32.4
Chester CDP	20,987	NA	NA	21,355	64.8	23.0	1.3	2.0	8.9	25.7	61.2	13.2	8,119	65.3	38.9	28.8
Chester Gap CDP	839	NA	NA	745	97.2	0.0	0.0	2.8	0.0	18.3	69.5	11.9	306	82.4	46.7	31.7
Chilhowie town	1,781	1,749	-1.8	1,865	88.8	0.4	0.4	2.6	7.8	22.5	53.7	23.7	685	59.0	61.0	12.1
Chincoteague town	2,941	2,913	-1.0	2,933	92.3	3.4	0.0	3.2	1.1	15.3	56.7	28.1	1,427	81.3	43.4	26.4
Christiansburg town	20,961	21,805	4.0	21,427	87.8	7.0	1.2	1.0	3.0	23.5	63.1	13.2	8,963	62.7	28.2	41.2
Churchville CDP	194	NA	NA	60	100.0	0.0	0.0	0.0	0.0	0.0	100.0	0.0	46	28.3	60.9	39.1
Claremont town	372	358	-3.8	291	62.5	32.3	2.7	2.4	0.0	12.1	62.2	25.8	119	78.2	52.1	16.8
Clarksville town	1,139	1,117	-1.9	1,226	64.4	25.9	5.2	0.3	4.2	17.7	57.8	24.4	617	64.8	41.0	30.8
Claypool Hill CDP	1,776	NA	NA	1,706	99.1	0.9	0.0	0.0	0.0	18.4	58.8	22.9	718	82.9	48.7	14.5
Cleveland town	193	188	-2.6	296	100.0	0.0	0.0	0.0	0.0	30.7	58.5	10.8	112	54.5	50.9	7.1
Clifton town	282	295	4.6	254	95.7	0.8	2.8	0.4	0.4	29.9	54.7	15.4	83	97.6	0.0	74.7
Clifton Forge town	3,886	3,775	-2.9	3,850	84.2	10.8	0.3	2.0	2.8	21.8	55.2	23.0	1,610	60.3	49.4	16.1
Clinchco town	336	322	-4.2	365	95.1	4.4	0.0	0.5	0.0	21.2	68.7	10.1	146	54.8	72.6	2.1
Clinchport town	70	68	-2.9	83	100.0	0.0	0.0	0.0	0.0	26.5	64.9	8.4	35	80.0	91.4	0.0
Clintwood town	1,410	1,343	-4.8	1,448	91.0	2.7	0.1	0.3	5.9	13.8	60.3	26.0	603	71.1	49.4	22.7
Clover CDP	438	NA	NA	483	52.8	45.5	0.0	0.0	1.7	24.6	50.5	24.8	247	60.7	56.3	4.9
Cloverdale CDP	3,119	NA	NA	3,179	89.0	4.3	0.0	0.3	6.4	23.6	62.4	13.7	1,195	85.7	32.6	23.3
Cluster Springs CDP	811	NA	NA	745	85.6	14.4	0.0	0.0	0.0	28.4	54.2	17.4	312	87.8	55.1	6.4
Coeburn town	2,081	2,015	-3.2	2,309	94.3	1.4	0.6	0.3	3.4	27.1	63.5	9.5	889	59.7	51.4	9.2
Collinsville CDP	7,335	NA	NA	7,632	75.8	15.4	1.0	2.1	5.7	19.6	59.1	21.3	3,438	60.9	48.4	18.0
Colonial Beach town	3,540	3,541	0.0	3,551	88.3	9.3	1.4	1.0	0.0	15.1	61.6	23.4	1,592	64.6	57.7	21.0
Colonial Heights city	17,413	17,731	1.8	17,542	78.1	13.0	3.2	1.0	4.7	22.8	57.9	19.3	7,025	64.7	47.4	21.0
Columbia town	81	80	-1.2	87	28.7	34.5	0.0	27.6	9.2	43.7	50.4	5.7	20	80.0	45.0	15.0
Concord CDP	1,458	NA	NA	1,552	83.1	9.1	0.0	2.5	5.3	16.9	67.4	15.5	666	83.5	56.9	17.6
Countryside CDP	10,072	NA	NA	10,279	66.2	6.7	8.0	3.8	15.3	24.5	68.3	7.1	3,538	74.6	11.7	57.6
County Center CDP	3,270	NA	NA	2,547	40.2	31.6	8.0	5.5	14.6	28.6	68.9	2.5	944	60.8	17.9	47.7
Courtland town	1,281	1,247	-2.7	1,819	45.8	46.8	0.0	4.8	2.5	29.8	54.0	16.2	618	45.0	54.2	15.5
Covington city	5,954	5,802	-2.6	5,853	82.1	13.7	0.4	2.6	1.2	22.1	59.9	17.9	2,468	75.1	57.1	12.1
Craigsville town	923	925	0.2	1,362	97.7	0.0	0.0	0.4	1.9	21.9	60.4	17.8	545	59.8	75.2	5.3
Crewe town	2,326	2,282	-1.9	2,875	61.0	30.5	0.0	2.2	6.3	27.7	60.2	12.2	1,002	54.4	57.8	15.7
Crimora CDP	2,209	NA	NA	1,997	97.1	1.5	0.0	1.4	0.0	14.9	67.0	18.3	840	85.8	77.9	1.4
Crosspointe CDP	5,802	NA	NA	6,193	71.9	4.4	12.8	4.3	6.6	25.8	64.9	9.4	1,814	95.4	4.2	80.3
Crozet CDP	5,565	NA	NA	6,511	84.0	1.8	5.6	3.2	5.5	31.2	56.8	11.9	2,398	80.9	30.0	50.5
Culpeper town	16,651	17,411	4.6	16,968	57.8	18.7	1.8	5.1	16.7	30.5	59.3	10.3	6,041	55.1	43.3	27.6
Cumberland CDP	393	NA	NA	144	83.3	16.7	0.0	0.0	0.0	7.0	38.9	54.2	64	65.6	65.6	26.6
Dahlgren CDP	2,653	NA	NA	3,059	51.6	31.8	4.1	2.2	10.3	26.8	63.7	9.4	990	58.2	39.1	28.1
Dahlgren Center CDP	599	NA	NA	674	59.6	24.3	4.2	4.9	7.0	32.3	67.6	0.0	155	0.0	15.5	27.1
Dale City CDP	65,969	NA	NA	70,381	31.5	28.0	8.5	4.9	27.1	28.3	64.7	7.0	20,605	72.1	34.9	29.4
Daleville CDP	2,557	NA	NA	2,565	94.3	5.2	0.0	0.0	0.5	24.5	58.8	16.7	921	87.0	24.0	40.2
Damascus town	805	802	-0.4	796	99.2	0.0	0.0	0.3	0.5	24.1	51.3	24.5	427	52.7	55.5	13.3
Dante CDP	649	NA	NA	465	94.6	5.4	0.0	0.0	0.0	26.2	56.0	17.8	141	82.3	87.9	5.0
Danville city	43,066	42,444	-1.4	42,704	45.5	48.2	1.2	2.0	3.1	21.9	59.0	19.1	18,520	54.1	45.9	17.5
Dayton town	1,540	1,578	2.5	1,844	77.1	1.6	1.0	1.2	19.1	23.3	65.0	11.7	729	65.2	45.5	29.8
Deep Creek CDP	115	NA	NA	64	100.0	0.0	0.0	0.0	0.0	0.0	0.0	100.0	33	87.9	51.5	48.5
Deerfield CDP	132	NA	NA	122	100.0	0.0	0.0	0.0	0.0	0.0	76.1	23.8	59	100.0	59.3	0.0
Deltaville CDP	1,119	NA	NA	988	92.4	2.9	0.0	1.3	3.3	14.6	55.5	30.0	527	75.1	49.7	37.4
Dendron town	273	260	-4.8	395	36.2	62.0	0.0	0.8	1.0	26.3	60.5	13.2	136	68.4	64.0	16.9
Dillwyn town	444	443	-0.2	517	47.4	44.9	0.0	7.2	0.6	24.5	48.9	26.5	186	48.9	72.0	15.6
Dooms CDP	1,327	NA	NA	1,273	97.5	1.5	0.0	1.0	0.0	28.4	54.3	17.2	443	83.5	67.9	11.7
Drakes Branch town	530	515	-2.8	710	38.2	57.2	0.0	1.0	3.7	25.0	54.5	20.6	253	63.6	54.9	21.7
Dranesville CDP	11,921	NA	NA	12,128	66.5	3.7	11.5	5.6	12.7	27.0	64.6	8.5	3,881	90.9	7.1	75.8
Draper CDP	320	NA	NA	502	100.0	0.0	0.0	0.0	0.0	24.3	55.1	20.7	198	93.4	56.1	13.1
Dryden CDP	1,208	NA	NA	1,252	99.0	0.5	0.0	0.0	0.5	17.6	66.5	15.8	492	62.6	39.2	10.6
Dublin town	2,534	2,686	6.0	2,625	89.2	4.4	0.4	1.4	4.6	18.7	71.4	9.8	909	45.1	43.8	16.2
Duffield town	90	87	-3.3	139	97.1	2.9	0.0	0.0	0.0	30.2	42.4	27.3	53	75.5	60.4	17.0
Dulles Town Center CDP	4,601	NA	NA	4,847	37.6	14.6	18.9	9.4	19.5	24.5	71.1	4.3	1,813	31.9	17.6	66.0
Dumbarton CDP	7,879	NA	NA	8,346	41.9	28.3	2.4	3.2	24.2	16.6	72.1	11.3	3,417	26.1	41.3	22.9
Dumfries town	4,961	5,192	4.7	5,122	31.2	34.4	3.7	3.6	27.2	28.4	65.7	5.8	1,617	57.7	51.9	16.7
Dungannon town	328	317	-3.4	468	92.7	0.0	0.0	0.0	7.3	25.4	64.4	10.0	149	40.9	73.2	12.8
Dunn Loring CDP	8,803	NA	NA	9,360	63.8	3.7	23.2	3.5	5.9	25.8	58.9	15.3	2,979	88.4	8.0	76.0
East Highland Park CDP	14,796	NA	NA	14,235	8.8	84.5	1.1	3.6	2.0	21.6	64.0	14.4	5,880	73.6	43.5	20.7
East Lexington CDP	1,463	NA	NA	1,205	83.6	12.1	1.2	2.7	0.5	16.3	58.7	25.0	477	44.2	41.3	27.9
Eastville town	170	167	-1.8	236	74.6	25.4	0.0	0.0	0.0	27.6	52.1	20.3	92	70.7	33.7	34.8
Ebony CDP	161	NA	NA	89	88.8	11.2	0.0	0.0	0.0	12.4	73.0	14.6	63	84.1	52.4	31.7
Edinburg town	1,041	1,065	2.3	1,282	83.3	0.1	0.3	1.2	15.1	28.2	56.2	15.7	495	56.4	52.7	20.4
Elkton town	2,724	2,790	2.4	2,770	96.6	1.8	0.0	0.0	1.6	22.1	56.9	21.1	1,242	74.0	54.2	16.7
Elliston CDP	902	NA	NA	1,219	97.6	2.4	0.0	0.0	0.0	21.7	61.2	17.1	295	86.4	68.5	0.0
Emory CDP	1,251	NA	NA	1,326	84.9	7.3	4.4	0.8	2.6	8.7	88.4	3.0	215	74.4	32.6	50.7
Emporia city	5,927	5,462	-7.8	5,682	31.0	65.4	1.1	1.5	1.0	22.1	60.9	17.0	2,420	39.3	62.5	16.4
Enon CDP	3,466	NA	NA	3,752	72.1	20.1	1.5	2.2	4.0	21.5	67.3	11.3	1,524	71.8	39.6	24.8
Esmont CDP	528	NA	NA	595	59.5	40.5	0.0	0.0	0.0	26.3	67.4	6.4	186	78.5	53.8	14.5
Ettrick CDP	6,682	NA	NA	5,660	21.3	73.9	0.2	0.4	4.2	13.2	77.6	9.2	1,195	62.5	43.3	15.6
Ewing CDP	439	NA	NA	260	95.8	0.0	0.0	0.0	4.2	28.4	52.2	19.2	106	73.6	59.4	9.4
Exmore town	1,466	1,445	-1.4	1,595	60.6	33.6	0.3	0.8	4.8	24.6	50.8	24.8	742	52.8	69.9	5.7

1 May be of any race.

Table A. All Places — **Population and Housing**

STATE City, town, township, borough, or CDP (county if applicable)	Population: 2010 census total population	Population: 2014 estimated population	Population: Percent change 2010-2014	Population: ACS total population estimate 2010-2014	Race and Hispanic or Latino origin (percent), 2010–2014: White alone, not Hispanic or Latino	Black alone, not Hispanic or Latino	Asian alone, not Hispanic or Latino	All other races or 2 or more races, not Hispanic or Latino	Hispanic or Latino[1]	Age (percent), 2010–2014: Under 18 years old	Age 18 to 64 years old	Age 65 years and older	Households, 2010–2014: Total occupied housing units	Percent owner occupied	Householders by level of education (percent): High school diploma or less	Bachelor's degree or more
	1	2	3	4	5	6	7	8	9	10	11	12	13	14	15	16
VIRGINIA—Con.																
Fairfax city	22,542	24,483	8.6	23,507	60.2	4.6	14.7	4.3	16.3	21.6	64.1	14.2	8,480	70.1	19.3	59.3
Fairfax Station CDP	12,030	NA	NA	11,081	72.1	5.8	13.1	2.6	6.4	22.3	65.4	12.5	3,810	90.7	9.4	74.2
Fair Lakes CDP	7,942	NA	NA	7,368	44.1	5.8	37.4	4.6	8.1	21.0	72.2	6.8	3,017	59.6	7.1	71.0
Fairlawn CDP	2,367	NA	NA	2,476	92.6	1.8	0.0	4.1	1.4	18.7	58.9	22.5	1,160	78.4	33.8	30.2
Fair Oaks CDP	30,223	NA	NA	32,392	51.1	9.8	24.6	4.0	10.5	19.2	74.9	5.9	14,081	46.3	9.1	69.7
Fairview CDP	240	NA	NA	112	48.2	48.2	0.0	3.6	0.0	0.0	12.6	87.5	11	100.0	100.0	0.0
Fairview Beach CDP	391	NA	NA	504	93.8	6.2	0.0	0.0	0.0	4.2	85.5	10.5	175	40.6	18.3	57.1
Falls Church city	12,289	13,601	10.7	13,074	72.7	5.5	9.0	3.2	9.5	25.3	64.0	10.6	4,966	59.1	8.0	79.6
Falmouth CDP	4,274	NA	NA	4,518	76.6	9.9	0.7	2.2	10.5	30.8	58.6	10.8	1,575	65.1	34.7	36.2
Fancy Gap CDP	237	NA	NA	201	100.0	0.0	0.0	0.0	0.0	20.4	54.4	25.4	78	80.8	16.7	24.4
Farmville town	8,216	8,229	0.2	8,350	64.7	30.5	0.9	2.7	1.3	14.9	72.0	12.9	2,590	40.3	41.5	30.8
Ferrum CDP	2,043	NA	NA	1,888	54.2	33.7	1.2	2.7	8.3	10.3	86.9	2.9	326	66.9	28.5	28.8
Fieldale CDP	879	NA	NA	771	86.8	1.7	0.0	4.4	7.1	16.4	69.8	13.7	333	78.4	49.2	20.1
Fincastle town	353	340	-3.7	308	88.0	10.1	0.0	0.6	1.3	11.9	68.5	19.5	107	82.2	39.3	34.6
Fishersville CDP	7,462	NA	NA	7,567	88.0	4.5	2.0	3.2	2.3	22.9	56.6	20.5	2,860	76.3	35.0	31.5
Flint Hill CDP	209	NA	NA	150	100.0	0.0	0.0	0.0	0.0	10.0	63.3	26.7	62	85.5	41.9	35.5
Floris CDP	8,375	NA	NA	8,413	49.8	3.6	32.8	5.5	8.3	29.9	64.9	5.3	2,525	95.3	3.6	80.8
Floyd town	425	434	2.1	631	90.2	4.0	0.0	0.0	5.9	23.8	51.4	24.7	280	45.7	45.4	29.3
Forest CDP	9,106	NA	NA	9,999	90.1	4.1	4.1	0.4	1.2	22.9	59.0	18.1	3,954	82.7	23.8	44.4
Fort Belvoir CDP	7,100	NA	NA	7,942	51.8	21.8	1.8	6.7	17.9	44.1	55.7	0.1	1,950	0.5	11.2	37.7
Fort Chiswell CDP	939	NA	NA	860	99.8	0.0	0.2	0.0	0.0	14.2	66.1	19.9	363	79.6	40.2	7.2
Fort Hunt CDP	16,045	NA	NA	17,038	85.7	2.2	3.7	2.2	6.1	27.7	55.2	17.1	5,883	92.3	3.1	83.9
Fort Lee CDP	3,393	NA	NA	4,700	33.1	44.8	1.4	5.6	15.1	42.4	57.3	0.2	1,028	1.9	16.7	23.0
Franconia CDP	18,245	NA	NA	19,439	47.5	19.7	14.7	4.0	14.1	20.0	73.2	6.8	7,491	74.8	13.6	68.2
Franklin city	8,561	8,526	-0.4	8,534	38.2	58.0	0.9	2.4	0.6	25.2	57.6	17.2	3,580	43.5	46.1	19.4
Franklin Farm CDP	19,288	NA	NA	19,956	66.4	3.6	19.3	4.9	5.8	30.5	63.3	6.3	6,052	94.2	4.4	83.5
Fredericksburg city	24,023	28,350	18.0	26,632	60.2	22.2	2.8	4.1	10.8	20.2	69.9	10.0	9,849	36.2	31.1	39.9
Free Union CDP	193	NA	NA	265	84.2	0.0	4.9	10.9	0.0	9.8	66.8	23.4	125	55.2	6.4	37.6
Fries town	484	470	-2.9	534	94.0	0.7	0.0	1.9	3.4	18.9	51.2	30.1	259	54.4	57.1	13.9
Front Royal town	14,440	15,038	4.1	14,709	81.0	7.7	1.5	4.6	5.2	21.6	62.9	15.6	5,855	56.8	52.1	17.4
Gainesville CDP	11,481	NA	NA	12,145	62.9	10.7	13.0	4.4	9.0	31.2	61.9	6.8	3,913	82.3	14.0	60.8
Galax city	7,042	7,014	-0.4	6,981	75.6	4.5	0.2	1.2	18.5	22.3	56.9	20.9	2,968	59.2	54.4	15.4
Gargatha CDP	381	NA	NA	657	20.5	20.5	0.0	0.0	58.9	30.5	58.5	11.1	228	47.4	73.2	12.3
Gasburg CDP	481	NA	NA	450	100.0	0.0	0.0	0.0	0.0	13.1	49.2	37.8	242	93.4	45.5	14.0
Gate City town	2,047	1,976	-3.5	2,348	96.0	3.6	0.0	0.4	0.0	22.4	59.7	17.8	942	68.6	53.9	14.5
George Mason CDP	9,496	NA	NA	9,928	58.1	11.3	13.1	4.4	13.1	15.1	79.2	5.6	1,711	81.0	17.4	63.4
Glade Spring town	1,458	1,458	0.0	1,792	98.8	0.7	0.3	0.2	0.0	24.7	60.7	14.5	616	70.0	40.6	19.5
Glasgow town	1,113	1,113	0.0	1,258	78.3	9.9	0.5	1.0	10.3	26.5	59.7	13.8	484	61.8	73.6	7.2
Glen Allen CDP	14,774	NA	NA	15,464	62.7	23.5	4.0	5.1	4.7	24.5	64.1	11.5	5,881	72.8	26.3	38.0
Glen Lyn town	121	117	-3.3	158	100.0	0.0	0.0	0.0	0.0	39.3	43.7	17.1	54	44.4	51.9	0.0
Glenvar CDP	976	NA	NA	818	92.2	6.6	0.4	0.9	0.0	6.4	21.0	72.7	376	50.5	85.4	3.7
Gloucester Courthouse CDP	2,951	NA	NA	2,712	75.0	20.8	0.0	1.2	3.0	22.4	54.5	23.0	1,000	68.4	38.6	23.7
Gloucester Point CDP	9,402	NA	NA	9,784	87.9	6.8	0.0	1.8	3.5	22.6	59.9	17.3	3,869	70.4	36.1	25.4
Goochland CDP	861	NA	NA	794	99.2	0.0	0.8	0.0	0.0	22.3	67.9	9.8	359	83.3	30.1	43.2
Gordonsville town	1,488	1,560	4.8	1,535	72.9	25.3	0.0	1.8	0.0	18.9	61.4	19.7	687	43.4	53.7	17.5
Goshen town	358	355	-0.8	421	95.7	2.6	0.0	0.5	1.2	20.4	58.4	21.4	179	74.9	68.2	6.7
Gratton CDP	937	NA	NA	898	97.7	0.0	2.3	0.0	0.0	24.9	61.6	13.5	341	90.0	46.0	20.2
Great Falls CDP	15,427	NA	NA	16,207	71.1	1.7	16.1	4.5	6.6	28.5	56.0	15.4	5,024	93.8	4.4	86.2
Greenbackville CDP	192	NA	NA	190	100.0	0.0	0.0	0.0	0.0	16.3	76.8	6.8	75	29.3	12.0	88.0
Greenbriar CDP	8,166	NA	NA	7,994	64.5	4.1	14.2	5.4	11.8	23.2	64.8	12.1	3,046	70.4	16.0	59.4
Greenbush CDP	220	NA	NA	47	100.0	0.0	0.0	0.0	0.0	0.0	17.0	83.0	37	78.4	100.0	0.0
Greenville CDP	832	NA	NA	1,060	91.1	8.2	0.0	0.3	0.4	24.3	62.0	13.6	302	82.5	72.2	0.0
Gretna town	1,267	1,245	-1.7	1,315	59.4	34.4	2.7	3.3	0.3	15.6	50.0	34.6	641	54.8	61.2	10.3
Grottoes town	2,668	2,738	2.6	2,705	90.8	1.8	0.0	2.1	5.3	27.3	60.8	12.1	1,096	67.8	61.9	12.2
Groveton CDP	14,598	NA	NA	15,478	39.3	16.5	13.6	5.4	25.3	25.7	66.1	8.3	5,478	53.0	39.4	40.3
Grundy town	1,019	988	-3.0	1,063	76.0	15.8	5.8	0.0	2.4	24.8	61.1	14.1	349	61.6	26.9	51.6
Gwynn CDP	602	NA	NA	695	100.0	0.0	0.0	0.0	0.0	15.1	71.3	13.5	317	80.8	33.8	29.0
Halifax town	1,309	1,252	-4.4	1,402	62.6	32.0	2.8	2.3	0.4	19.1	59.4	21.5	567	63.5	44.3	25.7
Hallwood town	206	204	-1.0	371	94.3	2.2	0.0	0.0	3.5	36.9	53.2	9.7	130	66.9	58.5	10.8
Hamilton town	508	588	15.7	473	90.9	2.1	1.1	2.3	3.6	22.0	69.0	9.1	192	78.6	40.1	40.1
Hampden-Sydney CDP	1,450	NA	NA	1,674	81.4	15.2	0.1	1.0	2.2	2.3	94.8	2.9	138	74.6	26.1	66.7
Hampton city	137,508	136,879	-0.5	136,904	40.5	49.3	2.3	2.9	5.0	22.3	64.8	12.9	52,700	58.8	33.0	24.8
Hanover CDP	252	NA	NA	166	100.0	0.0	0.0	0.0	0.0	0.0	76.4	23.5	64	51.6	48.4	32.8
Harborton CDP	131	NA	NA	123	88.6	11.4	0.0	0.0	0.0	0.0	11.4	88.6	76	100.0	0.0	100.0
Harrisonburg city	48,907	52,478	7.3	50,821	69.8	6.5	3.6	2.9	17.3	15.7	76.4	7.8	15,881	35.7	35.1	32.9
Harriston CDP	909	NA	NA	1,012	81.2	4.4	1.4	4.2	8.8	31.3	62.8	6.1	303	62.0	73.9	4.0
Hayfield CDP	3,909	NA	NA	4,501	70.7	15.9	6.7	2.6	4.2	29.7	59.5	10.8	1,500	84.2	8.7	74.1
Haymarket town	1,782	1,973	10.7	1,736	66.9	7.4	10.6	6.5	8.5	32.0	65.4	2.6	552	81.5	14.7	51.3
Haysi town	494	476	-3.6	408	85.3	8.6	1.5	3.2	1.5	12.2	80.0	7.8	87	73.6	62.1	8.0
Heathsville CDP	142	NA	NA	129	100.0	0.0	0.0	0.0	0.0	12.4	54.3	33.3	57	100.0	33.3	66.7
Henry Fork CDP	1,234	NA	NA	1,142	56.9	32.0	0.0	0.0	11.0	29.8	61.5	8.7	373	71.3	33.0	9.4
Herndon town	23,292	24,554	5.4	24,141	35.7	9.5	17.4	2.9	34.5	24.3	68.5	7.2	7,680	59.8	25.1	57.6
Highland Springs CDP	15,711	NA	NA	16,673	24.6	69.4	0.5	1.1	4.3	25.5	64.6	10.0	6,260	58.1	52.9	17.1
Hillsboro town	80	93	16.3	73	98.6	1.4	0.0	0.0	0.0	17.8	67.0	15.1	25	96.0	4.0	72.0
Hillsville town	2,737	2,680	-2.1	2,717	98.9	0.0	0.0	0.0	1.1	17.2	63.8	18.8	1,232	49.1	50.5	10.3
Hiwassee CDP	264	NA	NA	169	100.0	0.0	0.0	0.0	0.0	24.3	66.3	9.5	77	77.9	77.9	22.1
Hollins CDP	14,673	NA	NA	14,844	82.5	9.2	1.9	2.9	3.6	20.0	57.2	22.7	6,006	71.5	37.2	28.7
Hollymead CDP	7,690	NA	NA	8,828	76.1	3.9	8.7	6.7	4.7	29.3	59.2	11.7	3,274	68.6	17.3	60.1
Honaker town	1,447	1,399	-3.3	1,626	99.4	0.2	0.1	0.2	0.0	22.0	61.2	16.9	560	75.0	57.3	10.5
Hopewell city	22,591	22,196	-1.7	22,375	51.8	37.6	1.3	2.5	6.7	25.2	59.4	15.4	8,774	52.8	56.4	12.3
Horntown CDP	574	NA	NA	315	14.6	85.4	0.0	0.0	0.0	0.0	31.2	68.9	226	100.0	89.4	0.0
Horse Pasture CDP	2,227	NA	NA	1,925	69.7	28.7	0.0	0.6	0.9	14.9	57.4	27.7	921	82.1	65.6	11.5
Hot Springs CDP	738	NA	NA	591	45.2	33.3	0.0	16.1	5.4	28.9	45.0	26.1	296	54.4	76.7	0.0
Huntington CDP	11,267	NA	NA	12,144	50.8	18.5	7.0	4.0	19.7	13.4	74.6	11.9	6,307	44.1	16.0	67.1
Hurt town	1,304	1,281	-1.8	1,388	83.4	10.6	3.0	1.8	1.2	25.8	58.2	15.7	553	78.3	45.2	19.5
Hybla Valley CDP	15,801	NA	NA	16,076	29.3	28.9	7.6	4.0	30.2	26.7	64.4	8.9	5,849	40.3	44.0	32.8
Idylwood CDP	17,288	NA	NA	17,643	48.1	5.0	24.0	3.5	19.4	21.9	69.5	8.7	6,687	52.0	17.1	64.9
Independence town	947	926	-2.2	1,259	78.4	15.6	0.0	0.0	6.0	23.4	52.8	23.8	516	42.1	60.7	2.7
Independent Hill CDP	7,419	NA	NA	7,973	63.6	14.9	5.1	8.3	8.1	30.5	62.9	6.6	2,449	88.1	16.3	59.6
Innsbrook CDP	7,753	NA	NA	7,749	57.3	10.4	23.3	4.4	4.6	25.3	66.8	7.9	3,089	68.7	14.2	57.4

1 May be of any race.

Table A. All Places — **Population and Housing**

STATE City, town, township, borough, or CDP (county if applicable)	Population: 2010 census total population	Population: 2014 estimated population	Population: Percent change 2010-2014	Population: ACS total population estimate 2010-2014	Race and Hispanic or Latino origin (percent), 2010–2014: White alone, not Hispanic or Latino	Black alone, not Hispanic or Latino	Asian alone, not Hispanic or Latino	All other races or 2 or more races, not Hispanic or Latino	Hispanic or Latino[1]	Age (percent), 2010–2014: Under 18 years old	Age 18 to 64 years old	Age 65 years and older	Households, 2010–2014: Total occupied housing units	Percent owner occupied	Householders by level of education (percent): High school diploma or less	Bachelor's degree or more
	1	2	3	4	5	6	7	8	9	10	11	12	13	14	15	16
VIRGINIA—Con.																
Iron Gate town	392	383	-2.3	369	84.8	2.7	0.0	12.5	0.0	23.1	50.6	26.3	141	91.5	49.6	14.2
Irvington town	432	418	-3.2	521	97.5	1.9	0.0	0.0	0.6	9.5	44.8	45.9	247	83.4	9.3	61.1
Ivanhoe CDP	551	NA	NA	450	98.9	0.0	0.0	1.1	0.0	16.5	53.5	30.0	244	88.5	87.3	6.1
Ivor town	339	329	-2.9	425	81.4	12.5	0.0	6.1	0.0	24.5	55.3	20.2	174	73.6	56.3	7.5
Ivy CDP	905	NA	NA	898	97.9	0.0	0.0	0.0	2.1	31.5	54.6	13.8	339	88.5	13.3	71.7
Jarratt town	638	630	-1.3	664	57.7	40.4	0.2	1.5	0.3	25.2	53.7	21.1	279	78.5	54.1	18.3
Jolivue CDP	1,129	NA	NA	1,282	85.1	11.2	0.0	1.2	2.6	28.4	60.6	10.8	593	51.8	58.7	5.2
Jonesville town	1,006	982	-2.4	1,303	82.1	15.0	1.6	0.0	1.2	17.7	64.8	17.3	563	51.9	57.7	11.0
Keller town	178	177	-0.6	170	95.9	4.1	0.0	0.0	0.0	38.8	38.8	22.4	54	77.8	74.1	3.7
Kenbridge town	1,264	1,241	-1.8	1,310	54.1	37.1	0.3	0.5	7.9	25.8	59.5	14.7	493	69.6	46.5	23.9
Keokee CDP	416	NA	NA	313	100.0	0.0	0.0	0.0	0.0	3.2	72.3	24.6	167	79.0	73.1	6.0
Keysville town	832	813	-2.3	1,154	56.1	38.1	0.0	2.9	2.9	31.8	51.6	16.6	396	40.2	48.2	15.4
Kilmarnock town	1,486	1,446	-2.7	1,513	55.7	42.0	0.6	0.7	1.0	12.4	53.8	33.6	760	58.4	44.1	16.6
King and Queen Court House CDP	85	NA	NA	168	79.2	20.8	0.0	0.0	0.0	32.1	68.0	0.0	64	82.8	60.9	10.9
King George CDP	4,457	NA	NA	4,971	76.6	18.6	0.5	4.3	0.0	28.9	61.7	9.5	1,654	63.7	31.8	35.5
Kings Park CDP	4,333	NA	NA	4,464	52.6	3.2	20.3	2.4	21.5	30.5	57.0	12.7	1,400	89.9	21.8	61.7
Kings Park West CDP	13,390	NA	NA	13,864	64.0	2.1	17.7	6.1	10.1	24.5	63.5	12.0	4,368	88.1	9.4	68.9
Kingstowne CDP	15,556	NA	NA	15,455	61.1	12.6	11.2	4.7	10.3	22.1	70.9	7.1	6,516	65.1	7.7	74.2
King William CDP	252	NA	NA	89	100.0	0.0	0.0	0.0	0.0	4.5	64.0	31.5	67	100.0	85.1	0.0
La Crosse town	604	591	-2.2	733	52.4	20.9	2.2	1.9	22.6	28.0	54.9	17.2	267	67.8	58.1	12.0
Lafayette CDP	449	NA	NA	606	98.2	0.0	0.0	1.8	0.0	42.2	45.2	12.5	245	71.8	44.5	4.9
Lake Barcroft CDP	9,558	NA	NA	9,592	61.1	6.5	10.5	3.9	18.1	21.8	62.8	15.5	3,456	75.0	15.0	69.2
Lake Caroline CDP	2,260	NA	NA	1,904	76.3	17.0	0.9	1.2	4.7	22.7	65.5	11.9	829	100.0	29.1	36.7
Lake Holiday CDP	1,905	NA	NA	2,512	90.3	7.8	0.0	0.0	1.9	31.3	58.9	9.8	853	83.5	5.3	53.1
Lake Land'Or CDP	4,223	NA	NA	3,676	67.8	25.8	0.0	3.3	3.1	30.6	61.2	8.1	1,319	81.8	29.2	36.2
Lake Monticello CDP	9,920	NA	NA	9,547	89.4	2.5	1.3	4.6	2.2	24.0	55.6	20.4	3,891	85.0	19.1	51.1
Lake of the Woods CDP	7,177	NA	NA	7,454	90.2	3.6	0.3	2.6	3.4	16.7	52.8	30.6	2,943	88.9	22.2	45.3
Lake Ridge CDP	41,058	NA	NA	44,593	48.9	21.5	7.5	5.4	16.6	26.5	65.4	8.1	15,049	73.6	15.2	55.4
Lakeside CDP	11,849	NA	NA	12,854	65.8	18.0	2.4	2.5	11.4	21.7	64.8	13.5	5,403	60.1	34.8	25.8
Lake Wilderness CDP	2,669	NA	NA	2,211	85.3	3.9	0.0	2.1	8.7	21.3	70.0	8.5	813	88.9	29.2	27.8
Lancaster CDP	0	NA	NA	176	91.5	5.1	0.0	0.0	3.4	16.5	69.8	13.6	36	80.6	47.2	52.8
Lansdowne CDP	11,253	NA	NA	11,678	61.4	9.7	16.9	2.4	9.5	28.4	59.1	12.3	4,313	72.8	9.3	69.3
Laurel CDP	16,713	NA	NA	16,123	55.1	29.5	4.4	3.9	7.0	19.5	68.9	11.5	6,595	53.5	31.9	29.4
Laurel Hill CDP	6,855	NA	NA	8,015	37.0	22.3	27.0	4.9	8.8	26.5	65.9	7.6	2,533	79.0	10.1	61.5
Laurel Park CDP	675	NA	NA	666	13.1	85.3	1.7	0.0	0.0	25.1	66.9	8.1	358	62.8	29.3	10.6
Lawrenceville town	1,439	1,081	-24.9	1,404	26.3	69.6	0.4	2.2	1.6	20.0	64.6	15.3	428	41.8	50.0	25.7
Laymantown CDP	1,979	NA	NA	2,720	92.3	0.7	0.0	6.7	0.4	27.0	55.0	17.9	977	95.3	30.6	37.2
Lebanon town	3,444	3,356	-2.6	3,399	95.0	3.8	0.5	0.1	0.6	17.5	58.9	23.7	1,412	52.9	41.1	25.3
Lee Mont CDP	125	NA	NA	236	100.0	0.0	0.0	0.0	0.0	15.3	69.0	15.7	105	83.8	72.4	11.4
Leesburg town	42,616	49,496	16.1	46,211	61.6	7.4	8.8	3.1	19.1	29.4	63.8	6.8	15,098	68.2	20.9	54.1
Lexington city	7,038	7,311	3.9	7,114	82.2	6.3	4.4	2.9	4.2	9.9	77.9	12.1	1,727	54.2	37.6	46.3
Lincolnia CDP	22,855	NA	NA	22,917	33.2	17.2	17.0	2.1	30.6	23.2	68.2	8.6	7,795	56.0	24.6	55.6
Linton Hall CDP	35,725	NA	NA	39,944	61.5	12.0	8.6	5.3	12.6	36.1	60.4	3.7	11,333	86.9	12.3	56.8
Loch Lomond CDP	3,701	NA	NA	4,292	44.6	2.0	4.4	1.3	47.7	22.4	69.3	8.1	1,112	79.6	56.0	18.3
Long Branch CDP	7,593	NA	NA	7,388	66.6	0.4	22.9	3.7	6.4	23.4	56.9	19.8	2,570	84.3	15.2	69.2
Lorton CDP	18,610	NA	NA	19,497	29.6	30.1	20.1	4.5	15.6	24.9	68.0	7.1	6,459	53.0	19.6	53.4
Loudoun Valley Estates CDP	3,656	NA	NA	4,860	22.8	8.4	60.2	4.4	4.1	37.6	57.6	4.9	1,332	88.7	5.4	88.8
Louisa town	1,555	1,610	3.5	2,254	59.1	22.2	1.6	1.6	15.5	27.2	58.5	14.2	791	43.6	47.8	22.0
Lovettsville town	1,613	1,869	15.9	1,785	88.3	4.9	2.8	1.2	2.7	34.1	58.8	7.1	574	80.0	24.4	47.2
Lovingston CDP	520	NA	NA	384	66.4	31.5	0.0	2.1	0.0	5.7	70.8	23.4	174	43.1	72.4	9.8
Lowes Island CDP	10,756	NA	NA	11,259	66.6	4.4	16.9	4.1	8.0	28.1	61.5	10.4	3,603	89.6	7.8	79.6
Low Moor CDP	258	NA	NA	301	58.8	35.9	0.0	5.3	0.0	19.9	67.1	13.0	141	100.0	69.5	5.7
Lunenburg CDP	165	NA	NA	128	96.9	3.1	0.0	0.0	0.0	24.2	52.5	23.4	53	100.0	66.0	0.0
Luray town	4,885	4,850	-0.7	4,864	87.8	6.1	1.7	1.8	2.6	17.0	55.8	27.2	1,999	61.2	55.3	19.6
Lynchburg city	75,613	79,047	4.5	77,626	62.9	28.0	2.8	3.1	3.2	19.8	66.4	13.7	28,424	52.1	33.7	33.5
Lyndhurst CDP	1,490	NA	NA	1,563	95.7	4.3	0.0	0.0	0.0	19.8	61.7	18.6	581	89.8	67.1	23.9
McKenney town	481	476	-1.0	359	62.1	34.8	0.3	2.2	0.6	18.7	64.9	16.4	153	62.7	60.8	12.4
McLean CDP	48,115	NA	NA	48,078	72.5	1.4	16.3	3.9	6.0	25.2	56.1	18.6	16,845	86.9	5.4	86.3
McMullin CDP	464	NA	NA	296	100.0	0.0	0.0	0.0	0.0	18.9	44.0	37.2	145	96.6	64.8	12.4
McNair CDP	17,513	NA	NA	19,321	27.4	16.4	40.9	3.4	11.9	23.0	73.6	3.4	7,545	25.2	11.8	69.7
Madison town	226	221	-2.2	168	83.9	8.9	0.0	3.6	3.6	16.1	62.4	21.4	79	36.7	50.6	22.8
Madison Heights CDP	11,285	NA	NA	10,359	69.8	22.9	1.3	4.0	2.0	20.9	59.9	19.3	4,435	67.4	52.7	18.6
Makemie Park CDP	155	NA	NA	126	8.7	91.3	0.0	0.0	0.0	0.0	86.5	13.5	113	76.1	95.6	0.0
Manassas city	37,839	42,081	11.2	40,436	45.5	13.6	5.1	3.3	32.5	27.7	64.9	7.5	12,274	64.7	37.8	33.8
Manassas Park city	14,241	15,174	6.6	14,992	40.0	12.4	7.9	5.6	34.0	26.2	67.3	6.5	4,526	63.9	36.3	32.6
Manchester CDP	10,804	NA	NA	10,402	54.4	33.6	2.8	1.5	7.6	20.5	65.4	14.1	4,231	66.6	30.2	35.2
Mantua CDP	7,135	NA	NA	7,487	64.3	3.6	18.4	4.8	8.9	25.8	56.7	17.6	2,447	72.6	22.5	66.9
Mappsburg CDP	60	NA	NA	33	72.7	27.3	0.0	0.0	0.0	0.0	100.0	0.0	21	76.2	0.0	42.9
Mappsville CDP	440	NA	NA	333	5.4	29.4	0.0	6.9	58.3	41.4	53.4	5.1	87	79.3	100.0	0.0
Marion town	5,968	5,875	-1.6	5,931	86.2	9.5	0.1	2.0	2.3	14.6	62.4	23.2	2,633	53.4	49.6	19.8
Marshall CDP	1,480	NA	NA	1,313	82.0	1.5	4.6	9.0	2.9	24.7	60.1	15.2	490	68.4	35.9	32.4
Martinsville city	13,821	13,711	-0.8	13,745	47.5	45.6	0.1	2.4	4.4	22.7	57.5	19.9	5,974	55.0	51.7	17.7
Marumsco CDP	35,036	NA	NA	38,894	25.8	20.7	6.8	3.9	42.8	28.8	64.6	6.5	11,745	52.1	46.1	25.5
Mason Neck CDP	2,005	NA	NA	2,016	88.3	7.1	1.7	0.7	2.1	21.5	60.9	17.8	696	89.7	19.7	64.1
Massanetta Springs CDP	4,833	NA	NA	4,668	86.5	0.9	4.5	3.4	4.8	25.2	52.6	22.1	1,870	68.2	12.9	66.2
Massanutten CDP	2,291	NA	NA	2,393	99.1	0.0	0.0	0.0	0.9	19.1	64.6	16.3	922	85.7	24.1	48.4
Mathews CDP	555	NA	NA	724	54.0	28.5	0.0	2.3	15.2	19.2	50.2	30.7	344	34.3	70.3	0.0
Matoaca CDP	2,403	NA	NA	2,199	57.3	33.8	0.0	3.0	6.0	23.1	63.2	13.6	869	70.5	51.6	8.1
Maurertown CDP	770	NA	NA	1,052	95.2	1.2	0.0	0.0	3.6	27.6	56.3	16.2	387	70.0	49.9	23.8
Max Meadows CDP	562	NA	NA	322	100.0	0.0	0.0	0.0	0.0	0.0	62.7	37.3	200	48.5	42.0	5.5
Meadowbrook CDP	18,312	NA	NA	19,263	35.8	43.0	4.8	2.7	13.7	23.3	64.0	12.8	6,558	75.4	34.9	21.9
Meadow View CDP	967	NA	NA	955	89.5	0.6	0.1	9.7	0.0	20.8	55.8	23.4	384	82.8	51.8	25.0
Mechanicsville CDP	36,348	NA	NA	36,991	83.8	8.9	1.6	2.8	2.9	24.9	60.1	15.0	14,003	79.7	32.3	35.6
Melfa town	400	401	0.3	411	90.8	6.6	0.0	1.0	1.7	18.5	64.9	16.5	176	82.4	54.0	22.2
Merrifield CDP	15,212	NA	NA	15,873	42.7	4.4	35.4	4.5	12.9	18.2	74.5	7.4	6,330	50.0	9.2	73.1
Merrimac CDP	2,133	NA	NA	1,989	94.3	2.4	2.2	0.4	0.7	13.9	52.8	33.3	1,052	39.1	41.4	26.5
Metompkin CDP	551	NA	NA	435	24.4	39.8	0.0	0.0	35.9	14.0	64.4	21.6	236	41.9	57.6	12.7
Middlebrook CDP	213	NA	NA	294	100.0	0.0	0.0	0.0	0.0	33.3	59.5	7.1	149	100.0	70.5	16.1
Middleburg town	673	781	16.0	774	74.9	20.9	1.4	1.7	1.0	23.0	54.7	22.2	388	39.2	23.2	50.8

1 May be of any race.

Table A. All Places — **Population and Housing**

STATE City, town, township, borough, or CDP (county if applicable)	Population: 2010 census total population	Population: 2014 estimated population	Population: Percent change 2010-2014	Population: ACS total population estimate 2010-2014	Race and Hispanic or Latino origin (percent), 2010–2014: White alone, not Hispanic or Latino	Race: Black alone, not Hispanic or Latino	Race: Asian alone, not Hispanic or Latino	Race: All other races or 2 or more races, not Hispanic or Latino	Race: Hispanic or Latino[1]	Age (percent), 2010–2014: Under 18 years old	Age: Age 18 to 64 years old	Age: Age 65 years and older	Households, 2010–2014: Total occupied housing units	Households: Percent owner occupied	Householders by level of education (percent): High school diploma or less	Householders by level of education (percent): Bachelor's degree or more
	1	2	3	4	5	6	7	8	9	10	11	12	13	14	15	16
VIRGINIA—Con.																
Middletown town	1,267	1,319	4.1	1,362	80.8	10.7	0.0	2.5	6.0	22.8	64.5	12.6	493	69.6	42.4	25.2
Midland CDP	218	NA	NA	229	86.0	8.3	2.6	3.1	0.0	31.4	56.4	12.2	80	83.8	55.0	0.0
Mineral town	467	479	2.6	679	78.8	4.7	0.0	8.7	7.8	36.8	56.8	6.3	181	60.8	48.1	16.6
Modest Town CDP	149	NA	NA	110	100.0	0.0	0.0	0.0	0.0	0.0	87.3	12.7	81	100.0	61.7	0.0
Montclair CDP	19,570	NA	NA	19,990	59.6	20.1	5.9	5.3	9.0	27.1	61.5	11.3	6,689	86.4	13.1	61.0
Monterey town	145	139	-4.1	174	100.0	0.0	0.0	0.0	0.0	18.4	63.7	17.8	87	80.5	40.2	32.2
Montrose CDP	7,993	NA	NA	7,686	25.0	66.6	1.3	3.4	3.6	25.6	62.9	11.6	3,244	40.4	58.2	15.8
Montross town	384	386	0.5	522	61.9	24.9	0.0	0.6	12.6	15.7	53.0	31.4	241	72.6	51.9	18.7
Montvale CDP	698	NA	NA	705	92.5	7.5	0.0	0.0	0.0	4.9	66.5	28.5	354	97.7	70.9	1.7
Moorefield Station CDP	77	NA	NA	833	33.4	16.9	33.0	16.7	0.0	33.7	62.6	3.6	296	15.9	8.1	61.8
Motley CDP	1,015	NA	NA	935	75.6	24.4	0.0	0.0	0.0	13.1	56.4	30.5	450	90.0	62.2	8.0
Mountain Road CDP	1,100	NA	NA	1,255	14.2	85.8	0.0	0.0	0.0	32.1	49.7	18.2	433	74.4	46.0	12.2
Mount Crawford town	433	442	2.1	454	93.4	0.7	0.7	4.4	0.9	16.3	71.3	12.6	197	73.1	48.7	32.5
Mount Hermon CDP	3,966	NA	NA	4,164	91.4	7.0	0.5	0.3	0.8	19.8	63.5	16.5	1,716	81.5	37.5	25.9
Mount Jackson town	1,994	2,036	2.1	2,051	67.5	0.8	2.0	1.2	28.5	24.9	62.9	12.1	765	56.6	59.1	18.0
Mount Sidney CDP	663	NA	NA	501	97.0	3.0	0.0	0.0	0.0	25.2	39.0	35.9	198	96.5	39.4	30.8
Mount Vernon CDP	12,416	NA	NA	12,917	62.6	11.6	7.9	3.3	14.6	26.4	57.4	16.0	4,540	79.2	21.1	61.9
Narrows town	2,014	1,964	-2.5	2,058	98.7	0.6	0.6	0.0	0.0	22.3	58.7	18.9	902	66.4	46.7	13.4
Nassawadox town	501	495	-1.2	771	44.7	53.4	0.0	1.3	0.5	15.4	56.8	27.8	264	56.1	59.1	16.3
Nathalie CDP	183	NA	NA	318	14.2	85.8	0.0	0.0	0.0	52.5	43.1	4.4	81	70.4	29.6	17.3
Neabsco CDP	12,068	NA	NA	14,775	31.9	31.7	11.8	7.3	17.3	28.2	67.0	4.9	4,567	77.7	17.4	53.5
Nellysford CDP	1,076	NA	NA	1,032	97.5	0.0	0.0	2.5	0.0	16.0	45.5	38.6	505	81.6	24.0	61.8
Nelsonia CDP	523	NA	NA	515	4.5	95.5	0.0	0.0	0.0	3.9	93.5	2.5	300	72.7	88.3	0.0
New Baltimore CDP	8,119	NA	NA	8,955	92.8	2.1	1.0	1.9	2.3	27.2	59.6	13.2	2,868	90.5	16.0	54.8
New Castle town	153	153	0.0	250	99.6	0.0	0.4	0.0	0.0	37.6	54.0	8.4	119	68.1	28.6	8.4
New Church CDP	205	NA	NA	175	79.4	5.1	0.0	0.0	15.4	16.6	74.3	9.1	46	34.8	39.1	0.0
New Hope CDP	797	NA	NA	1,043	97.9	2.1	0.0	0.0	0.0	36.2	48.9	15.0	366	88.3	46.7	32.0
Newington CDP	12,943	NA	NA	13,804	48.0	20.7	14.6	5.2	11.6	27.3	64.5	8.2	4,417	78.6	13.0	64.0
Newington Forest CDP	12,442	NA	NA	12,283	55.7	8.9	15.1	4.8	15.5	24.2	68.9	6.6	4,312	84.4	16.4	63.5
New Kent CDP	239	NA	NA	226	100.0	0.0	0.0	0.0	0.0	4.9	78.8	16.4	80	100.0	32.5	0.0
New Market town	2,146	2,199	2.5	2,294	84.5	0.8	0.9	2.2	11.6	22.8	52.8	24.2	977	48.2	47.9	28.2
Newport News city	180,918	182,965	1.1	181,362	45.5	39.3	2.8	4.4	8.0	23.9	65.0	11.1	68,987	50.6	34.3	25.6
New River CDP	244	NA	NA	251	52.2	47.8	0.0	0.0	0.0	8.8	51.5	39.8	127	100.0	44.1	33.1
Newsoms town	321	311	-3.1	486	36.6	61.7	0.0	1.0	0.6	13.8	71.7	14.6	189	36.5	58.2	15.9
Nickelsville town	390	377	-3.3	423	87.5	0.0	0.0	0.0	12.5	28.1	60.8	11.1	161	63.4	65.2	5.6
Nokesville CDP	1,354	NA	NA	1,989	68.0	0.2	2.8	0.6	28.4	29.1	54.7	16.0	538	88.3	18.8	30.9
Norfolk city	242,831	245,428	1.1	244,745	44.1	41.5	3.3	4.0	7.1	20.5	69.7	9.6	86,397	43.7	36.0	26.9
North Shore CDP	3,094	NA	NA	2,881	94.3	3.7	0.0	0.2	1.8	7.3	52.6	40.0	1,432	91.2	27.8	40.6
North Springfield CDP	7,274	NA	NA	7,487	46.6	5.4	20.1	2.5	25.5	23.7	67.3	9.2	2,417	78.9	31.2	38.9
Norton city	3,946	4,031	2.2	4,015	90.2	7.0	0.0	0.8	2.0	20.5	66.9	12.7	1,655	53.1	39.0	18.4
Nottoway Court House CDP	84	NA	NA	78	100.0	0.0	0.0	0.0	0.0	15.4	84.6	0.0	38	68.4	13.2	0.0
Oak Grove CDP	1,777	NA	NA	1,625	16.6	13.7	53.4	0.0	16.2	25.0	74.1	0.9	589	89.0	17.8	59.8
Oak Hall CDP	255	NA	NA	360	100.0	0.0	0.0	0.0	0.0	53.1	39.2	7.8	110	20.9	86.4	0.0
Oak Level CDP	857	NA	NA	537	94.2	5.8	0.0	0.0	0.0	7.1	56.6	36.3	318	65.7	63.2	1.9
Oakton CDP	34,166	NA	NA	36,860	55.3	6.5	20.0	4.0	14.2	23.4	65.1	11.6	13,270	61.3	11.3	74.0
Occoquan town	934	1,013	8.5	861	79.0	10.0	3.4	3.5	4.2	15.7	71.2	13.1	471	59.7	15.3	56.9
Onancock town	1,268	1,262	-0.5	1,226	60.3	33.8	0.2	5.0	0.7	15.9	58.4	25.8	649	60.7	45.6	33.9
Onley town	516	517	0.2	502	78.3	9.8	0.0	4.2	7.8	18.0	64.2	18.1	234	70.9	49.6	25.6
Opal CDP	691	NA	NA	722	62.0	14.8	10.9	10.0	2.2	19.3	70.1	10.8	242	78.9	19.4	41.3
Orange town	4,721	4,902	3.8	4,808	67.7	23.3	2.1	2.2	4.6	20.4	61.6	17.9	1,643	47.2	50.2	22.6
Painter town	229	227	-0.9	308	63.0	21.1	0.0	3.9	12.0	28.5	65.6	5.8	110	69.1	57.3	15.5
Palmyra CDP	104	NA	NA	137	84.7	0.0	0.0	15.3	0.0	29.2	55.4	15.3	49	63.3	36.7	0.0
Pamplin City town	219	220	0.5	205	77.6	17.6	0.0	1.5	3.4	30.7	52.7	16.6	78	87.2	59.0	10.3
Pantops CDP	0	NA	NA	3,400	73.7	18.2	4.0	4.0	0.1	17.3	53.2	29.5	1,683	30.3	16.6	69.2
Parksley town	842	841	-0.1	941	74.4	15.0	0.0	1.4	9.2	21.5	64.4	14.1	380	67.1	49.2	25.3
Parrott CDP	435	NA	NA	508	100.0	0.0	0.0	0.0	0.0	29.2	34.5	36.4	229	49.8	73.4	11.8
Passapatanzy CDP	1,283	NA	NA	1,131	85.1	13.1	1.8	0.0	0.0	38.3	49.7	12.0	390	96.4	20.0	36.4
Pastoria CDP	649	NA	NA	895	18.3	44.8	0.0	2.7	34.2	22.2	65.0	12.8	326	50.6	81.9	10.4
Patrick Springs CDP	1,845	NA	NA	1,532	94.1	5.9	0.0	0.0	0.0	11.7	52.4	35.8	746	85.3	45.6	19.7
Pearisburg town	2,790	2,699	-3.3	2,750	95.3	2.6	0.0	2.1	0.0	23.0	50.4	26.5	1,236	73.0	56.7	22.7
Pembroke town	1,118	1,087	-2.8	1,298	89.2	9.6	0.0	1.2	0.0	25.1	58.3	16.6	547	72.6	50.1	10.4
Penhook CDP	801	NA	NA	711	81.9	16.7	0.0	1.4	0.0	12.3	51.0	36.8	304	91.8	30.3	50.7
Pennington Gap town	1,873	1,823	-2.7	1,783	95.6	4.0	0.0	0.0	0.4	22.1	47.1	30.7	792	46.0	54.3	10.2
Petersburg city	32,420	32,701	0.9	32,439	15.5	77.0	1.0	2.3	4.1	21.2	63.6	15.2	12,515	44.6	51.9	18.1
Phenix town	226	219	-3.1	275	84.0	12.0	0.0	4.0	0.0	27.3	55.3	17.5	115	68.7	56.5	10.4
Pimmit Hills CDP	6,094	NA	NA	7,364	53.7	1.9	22.0	7.7	14.7	21.9	64.8	13.3	2,280	62.6	26.0	55.9
Piney Mountain CDP	1,130	NA	NA	1,446	38.4	19.2	5.4	5.5	31.5	31.0	61.5	7.4	480	84.8	38.8	42.5
Plum Creek CDP	1,524	NA	NA	1,380	99.0	1.0	0.0	0.0	0.0	25.9	63.5	10.7	596	60.2	55.4	9.4
Pocahontas town	402	387	-3.7	626	80.2	15.2	0.0	0.5	4.2	11.8	76.0	12.3	165	42.4	50.3	8.5
Poquoson city	12,157	12,048	-0.9	12,103	93.0	0.7	2.8	1.4	2.1	22.9	60.5	16.7	4,627	81.3	31.4	39.2
Port Royal town	126	129	2.4	142	27.5	56.3	0.0	16.2	0.0	20.4	71.0	8.5	67	68.7	68.7	6.0
Portsmouth city	95,535	96,004	0.5	96,007	39.8	52.3	1.1	3.3	3.5	23.5	63.0	13.5	36,764	55.8	43.0	20.5
Potomac Mills CDP	5,614	NA	NA	4,967	42.6	30.3	7.8	3.3	16.0	29.1	61.6	9.3	1,634	75.3	30.3	40.0
Pound town	1,011	976	-3.5	981	97.0	0.0	0.0	3.0	0.0	22.8	59.6	17.5	401	75.6	58.9	17.2
Powhatan CDP	0	NA	NA	213	93.4	6.6	0.0	0.0	0.0	0.0	21.2	78.9	143	93.0	46.2	46.9
Prices Fork CDP	1,066	NA	NA	1,663	100.0	0.0	0.0	0.0	0.0	21.7	75.0	3.1	551	49.9	32.8	56.4
Prince George CDP	2,066	NA	NA	2,016	55.3	27.6	4.2	1.0	12.0	24.6	62.5	12.9	633	72.8	56.1	9.8
Pulaski town	9,086	8,909	-1.9	8,993	87.5	10.2	0.3	0.9	1.0	19.2	63.2	17.8	4,028	58.9	55.3	11.9
Pungoteague CDP	347	NA	NA	244	48.4	51.6	0.0	0.0	0.0	23.8	66.8	9.4	162	44.4	45.7	29.0
Purcellville town	7,727	8,929	15.6	8,350	88.3	3.3	2.5	0.9	5.0	33.5	59.8	6.6	2,495	75.3	16.8	56.4
Quantico town	480	531	10.6	446	62.3	8.5	4.9	8.7	15.5	18.2	72.8	9.0	240	10.8	38.8	29.6
Quantico Base CDP	4,452	NA	NA	6,656	58.1	8.7	2.8	9.9	20.5	27.0	72.8	0.1	1,205	2.4	17.6	30.9
Quinby CDP	282	NA	NA	140	70.7	7.9	0.0	0.0	21.4	10.0	44.2	45.7	76	84.2	92.1	7.9
Radford city	16,408	17,646	7.5	16,993	84.0	8.8	1.7	2.7	2.8	13.3	78.7	7.9	5,333	47.2	25.2	30.0
Raven CDP	2,270	NA	NA	2,451	99.4	0.0	0.0	0.6	0.0	20.7	63.2	16.3	1,084	69.7	61.7	4.2
Ravensworth CDP	2,466	NA	NA	2,709	51.1	0.0	31.2	1.1	16.6	22.7	56.9	20.4	881	90.0	25.8	50.3
Remington town	594	621	4.5	499	70.5	16.4	0.6	7.6	4.8	22.0	69.0	8.8	198	46.5	54.0	15.7
Reston CDP	58,404	NA	NA	59,217	62.5	8.8	10.3	3.8	14.5	20.4	66.9	12.5	25,351	60.8	9.9	72.0
Rich Creek town	767	752	-2.0	716	86.2	0.3	0.3	2.7	10.6	16.9	49.6	33.5	283	69.3	53.4	13.4
Richlands town	5,823	5,583	-4.1	5,698	96.8	0.0	1.3	1.6	0.3	24.2	59.5	16.4	2,414	65.1	61.1	8.9

1 May be of any race.

Table A. All Places — **Population and Housing**

STATE City, town, township, borough, or CDP (county if applicable)	2010 census total population	2014 estimated population	Percent change 2010-2014	ACS total population estimate 2010-2014	White alone, not Hispanic or Latino	Black alone, not Hispanic or Latino	Asian alone, not Hispanic or Latino	All other races or 2 or more races, not Hispanic or Latino	Hispanic or Latino[1]	Under 18 years old	Age 18 to 64 years old	Age 65 years and older	Total occupied housing units	Percent owner occupied	High school diploma or less	Bachelor's degree or more
	1	2	3	4	5	6	7	8	9	10	11	12	13	14	15	16
VIRGINIA—Con.																
Richmond city	204,246	217,853	6.7	211,063	39.7	48.6	2.2	3.1	6.4	18.6	70.2	11.3	85,913	42.7	35.6	36.9
Ridgeway town	742	712	-4.0	829	67.7	15.4	0.8	0.5	15.6	25.0	55.7	19.4	343	65.6	38.5	23.9
Riner CDP	859	NA	NA	766	95.3	0.0	0.0	0.0	4.7	17.6	65.4	17.1	306	80.1	47.7	28.4
Rivanna CDP	1,860	NA	NA	1,772	94.4	1.5	0.0	0.6	3.5	19.7	47.2	33.0	719	94.9	6.0	86.8
Riverdale CDP	956	NA	NA	1,361	59.7	26.3	0.0	3.4	10.7	24.5	52.7	22.6	484	82.9	52.7	8.5
Riverview CDP	782	NA	NA	582	99.5	0.0	0.0	0.0	0.5	10.1	69.6	20.3	296	53.4	63.9	6.8
Roanoke city	96,919	99,428	2.6	97,949	61.3	27.7	2.1	3.2	5.7	21.8	63.6	14.5	42,549	54.5	42.1	26.7
Rockwood CDP	8,431	NA	NA	8,281	67.6	15.0	5.5	1.9	10.1	26.1	59.6	14.1	3,243	90.3	24.9	39.9
Rocky Mount town	4,777	4,798	0.4	4,795	76.2	18.6	0.0	2.8	2.3	18.8	55.2	26.1	2,376	53.4	53.2	17.0
Rose Hill CDP (Fairfax)	20,226	NA	NA	19,259	55.4	13.5	11.3	3.4	16.4	23.0	64.1	12.8	6,951	77.1	23.5	51.0
Rose Hill CDP (Lee)	799	NA	NA	796	100.0	0.0	0.0	0.0	0.0	25.0	54.7	20.4	307	86.6	73.6	3.3
Round Hill town	539	621	15.2	576	95.5	0.3	0.5	0.3	3.3	28.3	61.5	10.2	209	84.2	21.1	59.3
Ruckersville CDP	1,141	NA	NA	890	69.8	7.2	0.0	0.0	23.0	25.5	48.7	25.7	371	73.6	36.7	35.3
Rural Retreat town	1,479	1,485	0.4	1,631	98.6	0.0	0.0	1.1	0.3	22.6	57.1	20.4	654	81.2	43.4	20.9
Rushmere CDP	1,018	NA	NA	910	45.7	54.3	0.0	0.0	0.0	17.2	65.2	17.8	400	66.8	61.3	12.3
Rustburg CDP	1,431	NA	NA	916	81.6	12.8	0.8	4.9	0.0	18.8	68.6	12.7	368	67.9	47.8	15.8
St. Charles town	123	120	-2.4	119	100.0	0.0	0.0	0.0	0.0	19.3	67.2	13.4	40	60.0	65.0	0.0
St. Paul town	956	925	-3.2	1,062	96.1	2.7	0.3	0.0	0.8	14.6	66.1	19.3	446	64.6	38.1	20.6
Salem city	24,848	25,483	2.6	25,120	86.3	7.8	2.0	1.0	2.8	19.9	63.1	16.9	9,953	67.4	32.7	31.9
Saltville town	2,077	2,042	-1.7	2,374	93.6	0.0	0.0	3.7	2.6	27.6	57.1	15.3	900	70.3	54.1	11.3
Saluda CDP	769	NA	NA	522	61.9	34.1	0.0	2.3	1.7	2.1	70.9	27.0	110	93.6	77.3	6.4
Sandston CDP	7,571	NA	NA	7,631	52.1	32.9	0.2	4.0	10.9	29.0	60.8	10.3	3,090	57.8	50.5	16.0
Sandy Level CDP	484	NA	NA	395	33.2	66.8	0.0	0.0	0.0	3.0	66.0	30.9	190	86.8	83.7	0.0
Sanford CDP	212	NA	NA	196	57.1	35.2	0.0	7.7	0.0	29.6	66.9	3.6	69	58.0	71.0	0.0
Savage Town CDP	78	NA	NA	179	0.0	100.0	0.0	0.0	0.0	50.3	49.8	0.0	71	0.0	42.3	0.0
Savageville CDP	175	NA	NA	76	0.0	100.0	0.0	0.0	0.0	0.0	31.6	68.4	51	80.4	27.5	19.6
Saxis town	241	239	-0.8	216	98.6	0.0	0.0	1.4	0.0	11.1	52.8	36.1	118	83.1	80.5	3.4
Schuyler CDP	298	NA	NA	263	100.0	0.0	0.0	0.0	0.0	35.3	55.3	9.5	115	73.0	94.8	0.0
Scotland CDP	203	NA	NA	188	56.4	43.6	0.0	0.0	0.0	30.9	44.2	25.0	82	62.2	47.6	26.8
Scottsburg town	137	132	-3.6	112	71.4	9.8	0.0	5.4	13.4	20.5	69.7	9.8	41	73.2	48.8	12.2
Scottsville town	566	597	5.5	513	96.3	2.1	0.6	0.2	0.8	20.8	53.4	25.5	240	56.3	56.3	19.6
Sedley CDP	470	NA	NA	534	86.7	5.2	0.0	5.2	2.8	33.3	51.4	15.4	162	71.0	39.5	17.3
Selma CDP	529	NA	NA	439	100.0	0.0	0.0	0.0	0.0	13.9	56.0	30.1	163	55.2	52.1	5.5
Seven Corners CDP	9,255	NA	NA	8,343	33.0	12.3	16.4	0.9	37.5	21.8	68.3	9.9	3,642	31.7	40.0	38.3
Seven Mile Ford CDP	783	NA	NA	641	94.1	5.9	0.0	0.0	0.0	18.8	60.5	20.7	278	55.4	52.2	11.5
Shawneeland CDP	1,873	NA	NA	1,706	95.9	0.0	0.8	1.3	2.0	23.9	66.4	9.8	647	82.7	51.9	14.2
Shawsville CDP	1,310	NA	NA	1,205	100.0	0.0	0.0	0.0	0.0	23.5	58.4	17.9	497	69.4	57.7	12.9
Shenandoah town	2,370	2,352	-0.8	2,134	93.6	1.4	0.0	2.5	2.5	14.0	66.6	19.3	944	77.2	66.9	7.1
Shenandoah Farms CDP	3,033	NA	NA	2,864	90.2	3.6	0.3	3.3	2.6	22.3	68.9	8.8	1,167	85.9	49.4	26.7
Shenandoah Retreat CDP	518	NA	NA	494	100.0	0.0	0.0	0.0	0.0	13.9	77.1	9.1	230	96.5	25.7	42.6
Shenandoah Shores CDP	934	NA	NA	996	89.6	0.0	2.0	8.4	0.0	42.3	49.8	7.8	303	96.4	45.9	27.1
Sherando CDP	688	NA	NA	584	100.0	0.0	0.0	0.0	0.0	19.0	57.5	23.6	259	57.9	42.9	27.4
Shipman CDP	507	NA	NA	349	85.4	4.3	0.0	2.9	7.4	9.5	76.8	13.8	184	50.0	46.2	32.6
Short Pump CDP	24,729	NA	NA	27,034	72.2	4.9	18.5	1.8	2.6	30.3	62.6	7.3	9,528	63.9	10.3	75.4
Skyland Estates CDP	830	NA	NA	633	97.8	1.3	0.0	0.9	0.0	23.5	66.5	10.0	237	88.2	42.6	24.5
Smithfield town	8,089	8,287	2.4	8,159	64.8	32.6	0.2	1.4	1.0	22.8	62.7	14.5	3,200	70.8	25.8	34.4
Snowville CDP	149	NA	NA	157	100.0	0.0	0.0	0.0	0.0	10.2	61.9	28.0	70	72.9	31.4	27.1
Southampton Meadows CDP	0	NA	NA	311	13.8	86.2	0.0	0.0	0.0	12.9	66.3	20.9	146	93.2	54.8	0.0
South Boston town	8,142	7,986	-1.9	8,069	53.5	45.3	0.6	0.6	0.1	20.6	58.6	20.8	3,323	60.4	57.6	18.0
Southern Gateway CDP	2,805	NA	NA	2,987	57.2	30.4	5.1	2.8	4.5	21.4	74.4	4.1	1,243	24.9	38.4	32.7
South Hill town	4,650	4,541	-2.3	4,603	56.3	37.4	0.0	4.4	1.9	26.8	54.6	18.6	1,926	55.6	48.6	19.8
South Riding CDP	24,256	NA	NA	26,762	51.9	6.3	29.3	5.3	7.2	35.6	60.0	4.3	8,008	84.7	10.5	72.1
South Run CDP	6,389	NA	NA	6,607	77.9	4.4	10.7	4.0	3.0	27.5	59.1	13.3	2,156	93.6	3.9	85.9
Southside Chesconessex CDP	131	NA	NA	157	100.0	0.0	0.0	0.0	0.0	41.4	36.3	22.3	47	48.9	100.0	0.0
Sperryville CDP	342	NA	NA	207	100.0	0.0	0.0	0.0	0.0	16.9	49.8	33.3	81	84.0	19.8	50.6
Spotsylvania Courthouse CDP	4,239	NA	NA	4,289	67.6	22.2	1.0	5.8	3.3	30.7	61.2	7.9	1,393	74.3	32.4	24.3
Springfield CDP	30,484	NA	NA	30,154	37.8	10.4	24.7	2.9	24.2	21.4	63.3	15.3	9,853	63.8	31.2	45.2
Springville CDP	1,371	NA	NA	1,589	85.7	4.7	0.0	9.6	0.0	15.3	74.0	10.8	664	50.5	52.4	15.5
Stafford Courthouse CDP	4,320	NA	NA	4,405	46.3	25.9	8.1	1.2	18.4	21.1	74.8	4.1	1,065	41.3	41.8	29.7
Stanardsville town	365	378	3.6	334	78.1	20.4	0.6	0.3	0.6	27.3	53.7	19.2	148	41.2	52.0	25.7
Stanley town	1,682	1,663	-1.1	1,876	95.0	0.0	0.7	4.0	0.3	23.6	61.2	15.2	735	50.9	72.4	8.2
Stanleytown CDP	1,422	NA	NA	1,207	89.5	3.7	0.0	0.0	6.8	16.1	58.0	26.2	550	84.0	44.2	13.1
Staunton city	23,746	24,538	3.3	24,132	82.0	11.6	1.0	2.9	2.5	18.9	61.2	19.9	10,503	57.9	40.1	33.7
Stephens City town	1,829	1,921	5.0	1,856	85.2	6.1	1.0	1.3	6.4	20.0	68.0	12.1	731	52.3	43.4	27.2
Sterling CDP	27,822	NA	NA	29,016	40.6	7.0	10.7	4.4	37.3	26.1	65.6	8.4	9,286	72.0	35.2	39.2
Stone Ridge CDP	7,214	NA	NA	8,667	48.3	8.6	26.6	6.3	10.2	33.1	63.4	3.6	2,828	87.1	8.9	66.3
Stony Creek town	200	191	-4.5	162	79.0	16.7	0.0	0.0	4.3	18.5	67.4	14.2	88	52.3	53.4	23.9
Strasburg town	6,398	6,559	2.5	6,486	87.4	3.2	0.9	2.1	6.3	22.5	59.8	17.6	2,831	57.7	56.3	18.7
Stuart town	1,406	1,455	3.5	1,476	90.5	8.3	0.0	0.9	0.3	17.2	53.1	29.7	604	51.2	43.5	13.7
Stuarts Draft CDP	9,235	NA	NA	8,415	93.5	3.1	0.0	1.3	2.1	19.6	65.9	14.4	3,392	73.4	54.1	16.0
Sudley CDP	16,203	NA	NA	16,221	36.3	14.9	10.3	4.2	34.3	29.0	64.7	6.5	5,147	57.3	33.3	26.7
Suffolk city	84,596	86,806	2.6	85,477	50.4	41.4	1.3	3.5	3.3	25.5	62.4	12.2	30,798	71.6	36.9	27.6
Sugar Grove CDP	758	NA	NA	713	99.0	0.0	1.0	0.0	0.0	19.2	54.1	26.6	327	61.2	67.0	13.1
Sugarland Run CDP	11,799	NA	NA	12,473	41.7	10.8	17.4	4.2	25.9	25.4	67.0	7.5	3,616	75.2	29.8	40.2
Surry town	243	234	-3.7	274	74.1	23.7	0.0	1.5	0.7	21.8	60.5	17.5	104	59.6	48.1	29.8
Sussex CDP	256	NA	NA	127	63.8	36.2	0.0	0.0	0.0	15.0	47.1	37.8	50	100.0	50.0	50.0
Tangier town	727	727	0.0	485	98.8	0.0	0.0	1.2	0.0	14.9	60.9	24.3	220	95.5	71.8	12.7
Tappahannock town	2,385	2,380	-0.2	2,161	48.9	48.8	0.0	1.7	0.6	20.8	62.3	16.9	894	46.4	59.5	13.2
Tasley CDP	300	NA	NA	184	13.0	87.0	0.0	0.0	0.0	20.6	44.1	35.3	86	60.5	70.9	0.0
Tazewell town	4,644	4,479	-3.6	4,568	87.8	8.0	0.7	3.3	0.3	23.1	54.9	21.9	1,995	55.0	60.6	19.0
Temperanceville CDP	358	NA	NA	477	44.0	43.6	0.0	0.6	11.7	0.6	76.5	22.9	317	56.2	71.6	12.0
Templeton CDP	431	NA	NA	550	91.3	8.7	0.0	0.0	0.0	14.9	67.5	17.6	232	62.9	71.1	10.3
The Plains town	217	224	3.2	162	96.9	0.0	0.0	0.0	3.1	22.8	58.2	19.1	61	68.9	19.7	55.7
Thynedale CDP	197	NA	NA	64	0.0	100.0	0.0	0.0	0.0	0.0	45.3	54.7	45	77.8	77.8	0.0
Timberlake CDP	12,183	NA	NA	12,478	83.7	7.8	1.6	5.2	1.8	21.5	59.4	19.0	4,868	66.8	38.5	25.8
Timberville town	2,526	2,586	2.4	2,557	91.9	2.0	0.0	1.5	4.6	21.4	61.1	17.5	1,120	60.2	56.4	17.4
Toms Brook town	258	262	1.6	289	75.4	4.2	0.0	2.1	18.3	28.3	58.1	13.5	104	84.6	60.6	5.8
Triangle CDP	8,188	NA	NA	9,048	35.3	40.9	7.2	5.9	10.6	28.8	66.4	4.7	3,161	49.5	38.5	34.5

1 May be of any race.

Table A. All Places — **Population and Housing**

STATE City, town, township, borough, or CDP (county if applicable)	Population: 2010 census total population	Population: 2014 estimated population	Population: Percent change 2010-2014	Population: ACS total population estimate 2010-2014	Race and Hispanic or Latino origin (percent), 2010–2014: White alone, not Hispanic or Latino	Black alone, not Hispanic or Latino	Asian alone, not Hispanic or Latino	All other races or 2 or more races, not Hispanic or Latino	Hispanic or Latino[1]	Age (percent), 2010–2014: Under 18 years old	Age 18 to 64 years old	Age 65 years and older	Households, 2010–2014: Total occupied housing units	Percent owner occupied	Householders by level of education (percent): High school diploma or less	Bachelor's degree or more
	1	2	3	4	5	6	7	8	9	10	11	12	13	14	15	16
VIRGINIA—Con.																
Troutdale town	178	173	-2.8	160	95.6	0.0	0.0	1.9	2.5	15.0	55.1	30.0	72	84.7	69.4	6.9
Troutville town	431	428	-0.7	543	97.1	1.7	0.0	0.0	1.3	11.3	53.3	35.5	266	72.6	53.0	14.3
Tuckahoe CDP	44,990	NA	NA	46,235	77.5	9.9	5.2	1.7	5.8	22.2	60.5	17.3	18,446	64.4	21.8	54.6
Twin Lakes CDP	1,647	NA	NA	1,986	80.2	10.6	0.0	8.8	0.4	33.6	53.6	12.6	648	86.7	29.5	34.0
Tysons Corner CDP	19,627	NA	NA	21,828	53.9	4.9	25.0	4.4	11.7	20.3	69.4	10.3	9,741	43.0	9.4	76.2
Union Hall CDP	1,138	NA	NA	1,329	97.4	2.6	0.0	0.0	0.0	16.6	51.2	32.1	605	90.2	30.4	38.0
Union Level CDP	188	NA	NA	184	76.6	17.9	0.0	0.0	5.4	27.2	56.6	16.3	97	66.0	60.8	17.5
University Center CDP	3,586	NA	NA	3,967	42.5	11.0	18.7	2.4	25.4	23.3	74.8	2.0	1,649	26.7	19.7	53.1
University of Virginia CDP	7,704	NA	NA	8,515	65.4	7.2	15.9	5.6	5.9	3.9	94.1	1.9	1,198	10.1	11.6	73.5
Urbanna town	478	467	-2.3	505	90.9	8.7	0.0	0.4	0.0	8.3	54.9	36.8	244	73.4	49.6	27.5
Vansant CDP	470	NA	NA	433	95.8	0.0	0.0	0.0	4.2	16.6	52.9	30.5	241	46.1	63.5	9.5
Verona CDP	4,239	NA	NA	3,405	86.5	4.6	3.3	2.6	3.0	19.2	64.9	15.8	1,427	80.2	62.8	17.4
Victoria town	1,725	1,696	-1.7	1,832	71.7	25.0	0.0	2.7	0.5	17.1	58.7	24.1	841	60.9	57.1	13.7
Vienna town	15,685	16,459	4.9	16,173	72.0	2.8	11.3	2.8	11.1	27.2	58.5	14.2	5,542	79.9	14.4	69.8
Villa Heights CDP	717	NA	NA	605	72.1	20.3	0.0	7.6	0.0	16.3	51.4	32.2	285	61.1	62.8	4.6
Vinton town	8,057	8,180	1.5	8,129	84.5	7.9	1.6	1.5	4.4	22.8	59.8	17.4	3,438	54.8	52.8	19.7
Virgilina town	148	143	-3.4	157	89.8	6.4	0.0	1.3	2.5	17.7	50.4	31.8	74	74.3	35.1	23.0
Virginia Beach city	437,966	450,980	3.0	445,623	63.6	18.6	6.4	4.2	7.2	23.3	65.3	11.4	165,296	64.1	25.1	35.6
Wachapreague town	232	230	-0.9	203	92.6	0.0	0.0	0.0	7.4	8.9	48.3	42.9	112	75.0	53.6	18.8
Wakefield CDP	11,275	NA	NA	12,684	65.6	2.9	17.5	1.7	12.3	25.2	57.3	17.4	3,920	92.1	8.6	75.9
Wakefield town	923	886	-4.0	769	63.2	34.6	0.1	1.2	0.9	24.4	51.5	24.3	381	58.0	61.2	11.0
Warfield CDP	115	NA	NA	110	36.4	63.6	0.0	0.0	0.0	4.5	59.2	36.4	80	68.8	91.3	8.8
Warm Springs CDP	123	NA	NA	96	100.0	0.0	0.0	0.0	0.0	10.4	66.7	22.9	67	40.3	0.0	40.3
Warrenton town	9,600	9,907	3.2	9,774	73.2	11.3	1.5	4.3	9.7	25.6	56.3	18.0	3,839	60.0	32.3	38.0
Warsaw town	1,512	1,501	-0.7	1,229	75.3	21.9	0.3	0.4	2.0	19.2	50.2	30.5	461	53.6	40.3	30.6
Washington town	130	128	-1.5	156	89.7	7.7	0.0	2.6	0.0	4.5	69.9	25.6	84	53.6	21.4	46.4
Wattsville CDP	1,128	NA	NA	1,213	69.9	30.1	0.0	0.0	0.0	18.1	61.1	20.8	586	78.8	65.0	7.2
Waverly town	2,155	2,081	-3.4	1,534	35.4	58.1	0.1	0.0	6.4	30.4	45.7	23.8	637	58.9	70.6	6.6
Waynesboro city	21,020	21,366	1.6	21,177	78.6	11.0	0.9	3.0	6.6	23.9	58.7	17.4	8,878	57.5	52.1	19.1
Weber City town	1,318	1,275	-3.3	1,473	95.7	0.8	2.5	0.6	0.4	17.7	55.2	27.1	679	58.0	62.4	10.5
West Falls Church CDP	0	NA	NA	28,277	41.3	5.2	19.0	3.6	30.9	23.1	67.1	9.8	9,935	65.8	28.6	52.0
Westlake Corner CDP	976	NA	NA	940	96.4	0.0	0.0	3.6	0.0	15.3	56.0	28.8	411	83.0	25.8	43.3
West Point town	3,306	3,333	0.8	3,319	83.7	9.5	0.0	4.7	2.1	22.0	59.1	18.9	1,408	68.7	35.2	27.6
West Springfield CDP	22,460	NA	NA	22,956	61.0	8.7	16.4	2.7	11.2	23.9	63.2	12.8	8,316	80.5	13.0	65.9
Weyers Cave CDP	2,473	NA	NA	3,024	90.8	0.8	0.0	1.0	7.4	34.3	54.4	11.3	1,081	75.1	40.3	31.8
White Stone town	356	345	-3.1	395	85.1	8.9	0.3	3.8	2.0	22.0	61.8	16.2	195	57.9	42.1	30.8
Whitesville CDP	219	NA	NA	289	53.3	45.0	0.0	0.0	1.7	25.6	69.6	4.8	134	81.3	72.4	0.0
Williamsburg city	13,673	14,691	7.4	14,401	69.6	14.5	5.4	3.5	7.0	10.7	74.6	14.6	4,365	46.3	21.0	50.2
Winchester city	26,203	27,543	5.1	27,031	68.2	10.5	2.4	2.8	16.0	22.7	63.1	14.1	10,692	47.7	42.9	30.1
Windsor town	2,620	2,654	1.3	2,624	78.3	18.6	0.6	2.6	0.0	24.4	61.4	14.3	988	74.1	55.6	10.0
Wintergreen CDP	165	NA	NA	286	100.0	0.0	0.0	0.0	0.0	0.0	32.5	67.5	168	71.4	45.8	20.8
Wise town	3,246	3,144	-3.1	3,204	96.1	2.4	0.8	0.0	0.7	17.8	68.9	13.4	1,415	63.8	38.5	27.5
Wolf Trap CDP	16,131	NA	NA	16,577	78.2	1.2	12.6	4.2	3.9	27.3	57.9	14.9	5,296	94.6	4.5	86.1
Woodbridge CDP	4,055	NA	NA	4,527	52.1	15.4	10.7	4.3	17.5	23.4	68.6	8.1	1,788	68.0	23.5	53.2
Woodburn CDP	8,480	NA	NA	8,742	57.3	8.5	22.3	3.1	8.8	20.6	68.1	11.4	3,114	63.9	16.2	65.2
Woodlake CDP	7,319	NA	NA	7,266	84.9	8.7	1.9	2.1	2.3	26.5	63.6	9.9	2,525	88.1	17.3	64.5
Woodlawn CDP (Carroll)	2,343	NA	NA	2,082	98.2	0.4	1.0	0.4	0.0	15.6	69.2	15.0	891	82.0	44.6	20.2
Woodlawn CDP (Fairfax)	20,804	NA	NA	20,811	20.4	30.5	9.3	3.3	36.5	24.5	69.0	6.3	6,775	55.9	47.9	29.0
Woodstock town	5,097	5,226	2.5	5,164	83.2	5.2	0.2	1.9	9.7	26.9	53.7	19.5	2,026	53.0	47.9	21.1
Wyndham CDP	9,785	NA	NA	10,101	78.0	2.1	16.1	0.7	3.1	34.3	58.1	7.4	3,242	86.9	5.3	77.2
Wytheville town	8,211	8,133	-0.9	8,193	87.3	8.1	1.3	0.2	3.1	16.9	56.7	26.4	3,946	56.7	53.8	20.2
Yogaville CDP	226	NA	NA	140	99.3	0.7	0.0	0.0	0.0	0.0	66.4	33.6	128	33.6	0.0	70.3
Yorkshire CDP	7,541	NA	NA	8,091	39.7	10.6	5.6	3.0	41.1	29.8	64.3	6.0	2,390	59.9	50.6	25.7
Yorktown CDP	195	NA	NA	122	100.0	0.0	0.0	0.0	0.0	0.0	63.1	36.9	80	48.8	0.0	63.8
WASHINGTON	6,724,543	7,061,530	5.0	6,899,123	71.3	3.5	7.4	6.0	11.7	23.0	63.8	13.2	2,645,396	62.7	28.9	34.5
Aberdeen city	16,894	16,255	-3.8	16,544	72.9	0.8	1.6	6.9	17.9	24.8	62.3	13.0	6,074	54.0	42.9	17.7
Aberdeen Gardens CDP	279	NA	NA	236	86.9	0.0	0.0	0.8	12.3	11.5	61.0	27.5	105	79.0	49.5	10.5
Acme CDP	246	NA	NA	310	100.0	0.0	0.0	0.0	0.0	16.5	83.6	0.0	97	44.3	55.7	0.0
Addy CDP	268	NA	NA	86	100.0	0.0	0.0	0.0	0.0	22.1	60.5	17.4	39	17.9	46.2	0.0
Ahtanum CDP	3,601	NA	NA	3,785	74.3	1.4	0.6	0.0	23.7	34.0	54.0	12.0	1,248	73.7	52.6	11.7
Airway Heights city	6,114	6,545	7.0	6,356	67.1	5.6	3.8	9.4	14.2	14.9	78.8	6.3	1,409	50.2	36.9	13.0
Albion town	579	574	-0.9	546	93.4	0.0	0.0	6.6	0.0	15.3	67.2	17.8	263	74.5	27.8	28.1
Alder CDP	227	NA	NA	133	100.0	0.0	0.0	0.0	0.0	26.3	73.8	0.0	43	41.9	0.0	41.9
Alderton CDP	2,893	NA	NA	2,937	86.0	0.2	2.5	1.0	10.4	26.0	62.1	12.0	1,074	82.0	38.3	22.9
Alderwood Manor CDP	8,442	NA	NA	8,628	63.1	4.0	17.0	9.4	6.5	19.3	68.5	12.3	3,252	69.6	27.1	37.6
Alger CDP	403	NA	NA	164	79.3	0.0	0.0	20.7	0.0	0.0	72.0	28.0	93	100.0	33.3	6.5
Algona city	3,014	3,133	3.9	3,090	57.4	1.3	7.9	10.8	22.6	30.5	64.1	5.3	941	78.3	48.7	7.0
Allyn CDP	1,963	NA	NA	2,098	85.3	0.0	0.0	3.5	11.2	17.6	54.9	27.7	778	94.5	12.2	45.4
Almira town	284	269	-5.3	254	93.7	0.0	2.0	4.3	0.0	21.2	47.5	31.1	116	75.0	34.5	13.8
Altoona CDP	39	NA	NA	40	80.0	0.0	0.0	20.0	0.0	0.0	42.5	57.5	22	100.0	0.0	0.0
Amanda Park CDP	252	NA	NA	175	61.7	0.0	0.0	21.7	16.6	17.1	72.4	10.3	74	40.5	50.0	20.3
Amboy CDP	1,608	NA	NA	1,558	96.8	0.0	0.0	2.4	0.8	35.2	52.3	12.5	489	77.5	54.6	9.4
Ames Lake CDP	1,486	NA	NA	1,231	85.4	1.4	7.6	4.0	1.6	24.5	65.6	9.8	503	77.3	25.0	57.9
Anacortes city	15,766	16,232	3.0	15,965	88.3	0.5	2.2	3.5	5.4	18.0	57.9	23.9	6,958	65.5	25.6	38.5
Anderson Island CDP	1,037	NA	NA	877	92.2	1.9	4.7	0.0	1.1	0.0	48.8	51.3	483	88.0	30.2	30.2
Arlington city	17,951	18,808	4.8	18,370	80.9	0.9	2.5	5.0	10.7	26.2	62.1	11.5	6,687	65.6	41.1	15.1
Arlington Heights CDP	2,284	NA	NA	2,827	96.0	0.1	0.0	3.6	0.3	25.0	65.0	10.3	899	87.7	37.7	24.1
Artondale CDP	12,653	NA	NA	13,089	89.3	0.5	1.7	3.5	4.9	25.8	61.9	12.4	4,439	82.8	18.7	48.3
Ashford CDP	217	NA	NA	280	100.0	0.0	0.0	0.0	0.0	0.0	75.7	24.3	177	58.8	42.9	13.0
Asotin city	1,251	1,290	3.1	1,420	84.9	0.0	0.6	12.3	2.2	30.1	56.4	13.5	472	67.8	37.3	25.0
Auburn city	70,172	76,347	8.8	73,403	61.7	4.9	9.4	9.4	14.6	25.9	63.1	11.2	27,371	59.7	36.7	23.5
Bainbridge Island city	23,025	23,293	1.2	23,206	86.4	1.3	3.7	4.1	4.5	24.1	57.4	18.6	9,404	75.2	7.6	71.0
Bangor Base CDP	6,054	NA	NA	6,355	66.4	4.0	4.7	5.3	19.7	28.9	71.0	0.0	1,321	0.0	27.4	10.1
Banks Lake South CDP	174	NA	NA	218	89.0	6.9	0.0	4.1	0.0	36.7	44.1	19.3	69	73.9	43.5	13.0
Barberton CDP	5,661	NA	NA	5,895	83.3	0.9	3.3	1.5	11.0	27.1	59.5	13.4	2,130	83.1	28.6	33.0
Baring CDP	220	NA	NA	159	95.0	0.0	0.0	5.0	0.0	10.1	88.1	1.9	100	53.0	52.0	0.0
Barney's Junction CDP	146	NA	NA	201	100.0	0.0	0.0	0.0	0.0	8.0	70.7	21.4	125	79.2	39.2	0.0
Barstow CDP	59	NA	NA	81	100.0	0.0	0.0	0.0	0.0	29.6	53.0	17.3	28	57.1	0.0	35.7
Basin City CDP	1,092	NA	NA	1,526	13.4	0.0	0.0	0.0	86.6	42.3	56.8	1.0	341	62.8	67.2	0.0

1 May be of any race.

Table A. All Places — **Population and Housing**

STATE City, town, township, borough, or CDP (county if applicable)	Population				Race and Hispanic or Latino origin (percent), 2010–2014					Age (percent), 2010–2014			Households, 2010–2014			
	2010 census total population	2014 estimated population	Percent change 2010-2014	ACS total population estimate 2010-2014	White alone, not Hispanic or Latino	Black alone, not Hispanic or Latino	Asian alone, not Hispanic or Latino	All other races or 2 or more races, not Hispanic or Latino	Hispanic or Latino[1]	Under 18 years old	Age 18 to 64 years old	Age 65 years and older	Total occupied housing units	Percent owner occupied	Householders by level of education (percent): High school diploma or less	Householders by level of education (percent): Bachelor's degree or more
	1	2	3	4	5	6	7	8	9	10	11	12	13	14	15	16
WASHINGTON—Con.																
Battle Ground city	17,682	18,930	7.1	18,168	87.4	1.0	2.3	2.9	6.5	33.1	58.2	8.7	5,901	65.7	33.5	22.6
Bay Center CDP	276	NA	NA	191	66.5	0.0	0.0	17.8	15.7	6.8	56.4	36.6	116	92.2	24.1	27.6
Bay View CDP	696	NA	NA	798	90.9	0.0	8.5	0.6	0.0	21.5	64.4	14.2	331	97.3	16.3	65.0
Beaux Arts Village town	299	323	8.0	425	87.1	0.0	3.8	4.0	5.2	27.3	58.4	14.1	137	95.6	1.5	83.9
Belfair CDP	3,931	NA	NA	3,508	78.7	0.0	1.2	2.8	17.3	27.1	61.3	11.7	1,234	70.4	36.5	13.9
Bellevue city	127,887	136,426	6.7	132,268	56.8	2.4	29.6	4.6	6.6	20.7	65.4	14.0	53,231	56.4	11.6	66.2
Bell Hill CDP	837	NA	NA	1,062	96.1	0.0	2.2	1.7	0.0	2.8	59.0	38.1	450	91.3	12.2	54.9
Bellingham city	80,867	83,365	3.1	82,080	79.8	1.1	5.2	5.5	8.3	16.1	70.7	13.2	33,847	45.7	22.4	37.8
Benton City city	3,032	3,191	5.2	3,130	62.4	0.9	0.0	5.7	31.1	26.2	61.2	12.6	1,122	71.6	47.1	11.3
Bethel CDP	3,713	NA	NA	3,523	76.5	4.3	3.5	8.0	7.6	17.4	69.2	13.5	1,327	86.3	27.9	19.1
Bickleton CDP	88	NA	NA	55	92.7	0.0	0.0	0.0	7.3	20.0	63.6	16.4	25	68.0	28.0	32.0
Big Lake CDP	1,835	NA	NA	1,773	89.6	0.0	0.0	4.4	6.0	19.2	63.1	17.7	752	82.7	16.0	47.5
Bingen city	712	719	1.0	888	60.4	0.0	0.0	1.9	37.7	29.7	62.6	7.7	274	46.0	44.5	15.0
Birch Bay CDP	8,413	NA	NA	8,475	81.3	1.7	11.0	3.3	2.7	19.6	60.0	20.4	3,641	81.7	29.3	37.6
Black Diamond city	4,151	4,338	4.5	4,257	86.2	0.0	2.2	5.0	6.6	26.8	60.1	13.0	1,658	88.8	42.8	21.5
Blaine city	4,684	4,976	6.2	4,829	83.4	0.3	8.2	5.1	3.1	25.7	52.5	21.9	2,103	63.5	31.1	32.3
Blyn CDP	101	NA	NA	35	94.3	0.0	0.0	5.7	0.0	2.9	34.3	62.9	29	75.9	89.7	6.9
Bonney Lake city	17,374	18,809	8.3	18,040	86.2	0.9	2.1	6.5	4.2	27.7	65.6	6.7	6,039	81.1	30.5	23.7
Bothell city	33,522	36,567	9.1	34,920	74.2	0.9	12.9	4.5	7.5	21.7	65.8	12.4	13,922	66.1	20.7	48.0
Bothell East CDP	8,018	NA	NA	8,959	60.7	2.2	23.2	5.1	8.8	29.4	62.9	7.6	3,088	67.0	13.7	55.3
Bothell West CDP	16,607	NA	NA	18,243	70.1	3.3	12.4	6.3	7.9	26.2	63.4	10.3	6,535	81.4	23.3	43.0
Boulevard Park CDP	5,287	NA	NA	4,027	43.7	13.9	4.7	11.0	26.7	23.2	66.6	10.2	1,661	43.5	50.3	12.1
Boyds CDP	34	NA	NA	89	65.2	0.0	0.0	0.0	34.8	34.9	65.2	0.0	28	42.9	100.0	0.0
Brady CDP	676	NA	NA	922	92.3	0.0	3.5	2.0	2.3	29.9	65.0	5.1	337	86.1	41.2	9.2
Bremerton city	37,830	38,572	2.0	38,664	70.9	4.9	4.4	8.1	11.7	18.5	69.7	11.8	15,347	41.9	31.1	19.4
Brewster city	2,370	2,354	-0.7	2,332	27.2	0.2	0.3	2.5	69.7	34.6	54.0	11.4	662	57.6	70.7	11.0
Bridgeport city	2,409	2,434	1.0	2,372	23.4	0.0	2.5	0.5	73.6	33.3	52.3	14.3	739	60.1	71.0	9.5
Brier city	6,087	6,434	5.7	6,255	80.8	0.6	9.1	3.6	5.8	20.3	68.2	11.7	2,220	86.9	21.3	39.7
Brinnon CDP	797	NA	NA	767	94.5	0.0	1.0	4.4	0.0	10.4	53.4	36.2	397	87.2	30.0	23.7
Browns Point CDP	0	NA	NA	1,310	85.6	1.8	1.0	5.9	5.8	19.3	60.3	20.5	563	67.1	18.5	45.1
Brush Prairie CDP	2,652	NA	NA	2,692	87.3	0.8	0.4	2.3	9.2	23.7	57.9	18.3	930	94.2	26.7	20.3
Bryant CDP	1,870	NA	NA	1,867	94.4	1.4	0.0	0.5	3.7	22.0	66.7	11.4	654	81.3	36.4	25.1
Bryn Mawr-Skyway CDP	15,645	NA	NA	15,339	29.0	28.7	30.0	6.9	5.4	22.1	64.1	14.0	5,755	58.9	32.1	29.6
Buckley city	4,354	4,520	3.8	4,430	86.7	0.2	0.7	11.5	0.9	24.9	61.1	14.0	1,522	66.6	40.9	21.0
Bucoda town	562	565	0.5	522	92.9	0.0	0.0	0.0	7.1	21.2	63.8	14.9	216	62.0	32.9	5.6
Buena CDP	990	NA	NA	1,602	1.6	0.0	0.4	0.0	98.1	53.2	44.6	2.1	338	33.7	84.9	0.0
Bunk Foss CDP	3,570	NA	NA	3,336	85.2	3.3	1.4	4.3	5.8	28.8	60.0	11.1	1,154	84.9	29.7	24.4
Burbank CDP	3,291	NA	NA	3,125	81.2	0.3	0.4	0.3	17.8	27.9	58.9	13.2	1,072	89.8	29.8	17.4
Burien city	48,072	50,188	4.4	49,291	51.1	7.2	10.9	7.1	23.6	24.2	63.0	12.8	18,266	52.3	40.5	23.7
Burley CDP	2,057	NA	NA	1,629	83.6	0.5	2.0	12.0	1.9	20.1	71.3	8.6	629	85.1	35.5	17.6
Burlington city	8,374	8,568	2.3	8,466	63.6	1.3	1.7	8.4	25.0	25.6	61.1	13.4	3,245	53.5	43.0	16.3
Camano CDP	0	NA	NA	15,201	90.8	0.3	0.8	3.6	4.4	19.0	54.4	26.6	6,285	84.6	28.5	26.0
Camas city	19,395	21,220	9.4	20,458	85.5	1.6	6.2	3.3	3.5	30.0	60.6	9.4	6,836	76.1	19.8	45.1
Canterwood CDP	3,079	NA	NA	3,777	74.2	0.0	16.2	2.2	7.4	22.5	66.9	10.6	1,334	85.0	16.1	48.1
Canyon Creek CDP	3,200	NA	NA	3,230	91.9	0.0	0.3	4.3	3.5	25.2	67.6	7.2	1,135	82.7	41.4	12.7
Carbonado town	610	623	2.1	530	90.6	1.3	0.0	5.3	2.8	27.3	56.7	16.0	207	70.0	46.4	4.8
Carlsborg CDP	995	NA	NA	627	92.3	0.0	0.0	3.5	4.1	0.0	33.0	67.0	452	90.9	44.7	15.9
Carnation city	1,786	1,853	3.8	1,830	80.0	1.1	3.3	4.3	11.3	29.1	63.3	7.7	654	71.1	40.4	25.1
Carson CDP	2,279	NA	NA	2,262	80.0	0.0	1.9	7.3	10.7	23.1	62.9	13.8	862	75.2	47.7	8.1
Cascade Valley CDP	2,246	NA	NA	2,700	82.4	3.4	0.5	1.9	11.9	28.2	55.1	16.6	988	56.1	47.9	16.2
Cashmere city	3,118	3,137	0.6	3,141	69.3	0.5	0.8	3.1	26.4	22.0	58.6	19.4	1,121	57.4	45.5	25.2
Castle Rock city	2,120	2,140	0.9	2,030	81.7	0.0	1.3	12.6	4.4	19.5	64.7	15.9	908	62.8	43.1	18.0
Cathcart CDP	2,458	NA	NA	2,593	94.4	0.0	2.6	0.5	2.5	21.0	66.6	12.2	913	82.5	23.9	41.7
Cathlamet town	532	537	0.9	657	91.2	0.0	1.5	3.5	3.8	22.8	42.4	34.9	263	55.9	28.1	23.6
Cavalero CDP	4,660	NA	NA	5,251	82.3	0.2	2.1	5.6	9.8	29.9	64.3	5.8	1,690	84.1	28.4	28.9
Centerville CDP	112	NA	NA	188	94.7	0.0	2.1	3.2	0.0	22.3	69.1	8.5	67	76.1	29.9	6.0
Centralia city	16,553	16,623	0.4	16,664	74.3	0.4	0.9	4.3	20.1	24.1	57.9	17.9	6,557	48.7	41.1	14.9
Central Park CDP	2,685	NA	NA	2,492	88.0	0.0	3.7	3.2	5.1	18.2	59.0	22.7	1,048	81.8	35.7	20.8
Chain Lake CDP	3,741	NA	NA	4,566	90.3	0.0	3.5	4.0	2.1	31.1	59.1	9.8	1,357	91.3	21.0	34.3
Chehalis city	7,261	7,261	0.0	7,265	81.7	2.9	0.9	3.1	11.3	26.0	60.8	13.2	2,720	44.5	37.6	20.6
Chelan city	3,890	3,981	2.3	3,945	71.8	0.0	0.0	0.4	27.8	22.1	58.0	19.9	1,650	72.7	41.7	21.1
Chelan Falls CDP	329	NA	NA	201	85.6	0.0	0.0	0.0	14.4	0.0	71.7	28.4	118	89.0	59.3	0.0
Cheney city	10,590	11,420	7.8	11,014	79.9	3.2	3.1	6.1	7.6	14.0	81.1	4.9	3,803	30.5	14.8	34.7
Cherry Grove CDP	546	NA	NA	523	97.3	0.0	0.2	2.5	0.0	8.6	65.6	25.8	227	100.0	13.2	42.3
Chewelah city	2,607	2,602	-0.2	2,608	89.2	2.4	0.5	5.6	2.3	23.3	50.7	25.9	1,171	53.2	46.6	15.3
Chico CDP	2,259	NA	NA	2,113	80.6	1.3	12.9	2.6	2.6	21.1	64.2	14.6	832	89.1	22.8	37.5
Chinook CDP	466	NA	NA	336	90.2	0.0	0.0	1.8	8.0	21.2	67.0	11.9	137	95.6	25.5	8.0
Clallam Bay CDP	363	NA	NA	341	66.0	4.4	0.0	0.0	29.6	32.5	53.3	14.1	153	35.3	35.3	20.9
Clarkston city	7,229	7,359	1.8	7,318	91.2	1.0	0.2	2.6	5.1	22.4	60.1	17.5	3,263	47.9	42.7	11.5
Clarkston Heights-Vineland CDP	6,326	NA	NA	6,754	92.7	0.3	2.0	3.3	1.7	20.0	55.2	24.6	2,793	86.3	35.3	27.6
Clayton CDP	443	NA	NA	376	79.0	0.0	0.0	0.0	21.0	37.0	56.1	6.9	122	47.5	27.9	0.0
Clear Lake CDP (Pierce)	1,419	NA	NA	1,099	94.2	0.0	4.8	0.6	0.4	13.3	69.2	17.6	391	66.0	62.7	13.6
Clear Lake CDP (Skagit)	1,002	NA	NA	994	94.9	0.0	0.0	2.1	3.0	20.6	62.7	16.5	430	68.1	38.4	14.0
Clearview CDP	3,324	NA	NA	3,656	90.4	0.9	2.3	1.6	4.8	22.1	69.0	8.8	1,321	86.8	29.2	31.0
Cle Elum city	1,872	1,883	0.6	2,551	87.3	0.0	0.5	4.5	7.6	22.7	60.6	16.7	1,085	60.8	40.6	26.3
Cliffdell CDP	104	NA	NA	80	97.5	2.5	0.0	0.0	0.0	32.6	56.4	11.3	20	60.0	0.0	40.0
Clinton CDP	928	NA	NA	759	96.0	0.1	1.3	1.3	1.2	17.5	51.8	30.7	373	83.6	16.1	52.5
Clover Creek CDP	6,522	NA	NA	7,052	73.2	5.5	4.6	9.7	7.0	22.7	63.5	13.8	2,627	68.1	37.8	15.2
Clyde Hill city	2,988	3,198	7.0	3,097	83.7	0.0	12.5	1.4	2.4	31.2	52.1	16.7	1,016	90.4	6.2	81.4
Cohassett Beach CDP	722	NA	NA	605	84.1	0.0	0.0	0.5	15.4	26.6	65.9	7.4	267	59.9	65.2	13.9
Colfax city	2,805	2,828	0.8	2,826	93.4	1.2	3.1	0.1	2.2	24.2	55.6	20.4	1,252	61.7	25.2	32.7
College Place city	8,776	8,997	2.5	8,905	79.6	0.9	0.8	2.4	16.3	17.7	65.6	16.7	3,433	50.7	29.4	30.0
Colton town	418	431	3.1	374	97.9	0.0	0.0	1.6	0.5	19.5	59.9	20.6	165	96.4	29.7	29.1
Colville city	4,682	4,706	0.5	4,681	88.6	0.5	0.9	4.9	5.1	25.2	54.8	20.0	2,183	57.0	43.7	19.4
Conconully town	210	212	1.0	153	94.1	0.0	2.0	2.0	2.0	4.6	52.9	42.5	89	62.9	43.8	7.9
Concrete town	705	714	1.3	751	87.1	0.9	1.1	9.6	1.3	19.9	67.7	12.6	290	53.1	44.8	16.2
Connell city	4,203	5,388	28.2	5,130	42.6	4.6	1.3	4.8	46.7	27.0	67.6	5.4	1,123	52.6	56.8	5.8
Conway CDP	91	NA	NA	12	100.0	0.0	0.0	0.0	0.0	0.0	0.0	100.0	6	100.0	0.0	100.0
Copalis Beach CDP	415	NA	NA	338	71.3	8.0	3.3	13.3	4.1	0.0	72.2	27.8	165	49.7	27.3	0.0
Cosmopolis city	1,649	1,589	-3.6	1,479	87.8	0.0	1.5	5.6	5.1	19.9	64.1	16.0	588	74.8	38.6	12.1

1 May be of any race.

Table A. All Places — **Population and Housing**

STATE City, town, township, borough, or CDP (county if applicable)	Population: 2010 census total population	Population: 2014 estimated population	Population: Percent change 2010-2014	Population: ACS total population estimate 2010-2014	Race and Hispanic or Latino origin (percent), 2010–2014: White alone, not Hispanic or Latino	Black alone, not Hispanic or Latino	Asian alone, not Hispanic or Latino	All other races or 2 or more races, not Hispanic or Latino	Hispanic or Latino[1]	Age (percent), 2010–2014: Under 18 years old	Age 18 to 64 years old	Age 65 years and older	Households, 2010–2014: Total occupied housing units	Percent owner occupied	Householders by level of education (percent): High school diploma or less	Bachelor's degree or more
	1	2	3	4	5	6	7	8	9	10	11	12	13	14	15	16
WASHINGTON—Con.																
Cottage Lake CDP	22,494	NA	NA	23,318	86.2	0.9	5.4	3.5	4.0	26.2	64.2	9.6	7,941	92.2	11.1	63.4
Coulee City town	562	575	2.3	644	94.4	0.0	0.0	2.8	2.8	22.3	56.2	21.4	240	70.4	60.0	11.7
Coulee Dam town	1,098	1,091	-0.6	1,277	50.0	0.6	1.6	42.5	5.3	23.4	61.1	15.4	515	66.6	30.9	26.0
Country Homes CDP	5,841	NA	NA	5,566	86.8	0.8	4.4	4.2	3.8	14.7	71.4	14.0	1,827	54.1	22.9	31.0
Coupeville town	1,831	1,860	1.6	2,128	78.5	0.1	3.1	1.8	16.5	19.5	53.4	27.1	896	50.6	25.2	34.2
Covington city	17,565	19,134	8.9	18,361	71.6	6.5	8.4	5.3	8.2	27.9	65.3	6.7	6,199	80.4	26.8	33.0
Cowiche CDP	428	NA	NA	712	8.4	0.0	0.0	0.0	91.6	43.8	50.9	5.3	135	28.1	88.9	11.1
Creston town	233	217	-6.9	228	96.9	0.0	0.0	3.1	0.0	15.3	52.6	32.0	108	84.3	46.3	23.1
Crocker CDP	1,268	NA	NA	1,240	96.9	0.0	0.0	2.3	0.8	21.7	68.7	9.6	431	88.6	32.9	13.0
Curlew CDP	118	NA	NA	80	68.8	0.0	0.0	25.0	6.3	18.8	58.8	22.5	29	86.2	65.5	13.8
Curlew Lake CDP	462	NA	NA	622	93.7	0.0	0.0	6.3	0.0	23.8	51.4	24.9	227	66.1	52.9	19.4
Cusick town	206	204	-1.0	99	86.9	0.0	0.0	11.1	2.0	13.2	66.8	20.2	49	93.9	34.7	8.2
Custer CDP	366	NA	NA	808	93.1	0.0	0.0	0.0	6.9	20.2	71.6	8.4	211	64.5	84.4	0.0
Dallesport CDP	1,202	NA	NA	1,254	93.7	0.0	0.0	0.3	6.0	15.5	51.8	32.8	528	76.5	65.0	9.1
Danville CDP	34	NA	NA	41	70.7	0.0	0.0	29.3	0.0	9.8	90.3	0.0	17	88.2	0.0	35.3
Darrington town	1,347	1,370	1.7	1,553	92.5	0.7	0.0	6.8	0.0	26.6	56.4	17.1	593	57.0	43.2	10.8
Dash Point CDP	931	NA	NA	824	80.6	0.4	6.7	7.2	5.2	12.3	64.4	23.3	373	88.7	19.6	45.0
Davenport city	1,734	1,665	-4.0	1,635	96.2	0.1	0.0	1.8	2.0	21.8	56.5	21.7	680	79.3	38.1	16.5
Dayton city	2,526	2,460	-2.6	2,905	87.7	0.1	0.6	3.9	7.7	22.4	56.4	21.4	1,192	72.4	29.1	23.4
Deep River CDP	204	NA	NA	146	96.6	0.0	0.0	3.4	0.0	7.5	45.3	47.3	70	72.9	32.9	20.0
Deer Park city	3,652	3,864	5.8	3,739	90.3	0.0	0.2	5.0	4.6	24.9	57.8	17.2	1,398	64.8	34.1	19.7
Deming CDP	353	NA	NA	422	84.8	0.0	8.1	7.1	0.0	26.1	74.0	0.0	127	81.1	30.7	35.4
Desert Aire CDP	1,626	NA	NA	1,791	28.3	0.0	0.6	0.0	71.2	47.6	40.4	12.1	444	78.4	55.6	18.5
Des Moines city	29,673	31,011	4.5	30,403	54.1	8.4	13.2	7.7	16.6	21.3	63.9	14.7	11,347	58.3	35.4	26.2
Disautel CDP	78	NA	NA	15	33.3	0.0	0.0	66.7	0.0	0.0	100.0	0.0	10	0.0	100.0	0.0
Dixie CDP	197	NA	NA	252	97.2	0.0	0.0	2.8	0.0	21.4	62.0	16.7	95	78.9	33.7	13.7
Dollars Corner CDP	0	NA	NA	1,183	97.7	0.0	1.0	0.3	0.9	10.5	59.6	29.9	528	91.1	33.0	32.8
Donald CDP	91	NA	NA	73	0.0	0.0	0.0	0.0	100.0	0.0	100.0	0.0	14	0.0	100.0	0.0
Duluth CDP	1,544	NA	NA	1,184	90.6	0.0	0.0	4.7	4.6	22.7	60.9	16.4	436	76.6	20.6	18.3
DuPont city	8,199	9,313	13.6	8,851	63.7	9.6	9.8	7.4	9.4	34.6	59.3	6.1	3,090	57.4	6.0	54.3
Duvall city	6,713	7,639	13.8	7,185	87.4	3.1	2.3	3.4	3.8	33.4	63.1	3.5	2,292	83.8	17.4	44.4
East Cathlamet CDP	491	NA	NA	485	87.0	0.0	0.0	9.7	3.3	4.1	69.7	26.2	216	85.6	25.0	7.9
Eastmont CDP	20,101	NA	NA	20,443	73.0	2.6	11.4	6.9	6.1	24.9	64.4	10.7	6,958	84.1	21.4	42.0
Easton CDP	478	NA	NA	427	98.4	0.0	0.0	0.7	0.9	21.5	64.0	14.5	157	51.6	55.4	7.0
East Port Orchard CDP	5,919	NA	NA	5,098	74.7	2.2	2.4	8.3	12.5	23.2	63.0	13.7	1,982	58.1	31.7	19.3
East Renton Highlands CDP	11,140	NA	NA	11,674	75.0	2.3	6.2	7.0	9.5	25.5	59.6	15.0	4,115	87.6	25.3	40.7
East Wenatchee city	13,190	13,505	2.4	13,403	70.7	0.1	1.0	3.4	24.8	26.3	58.3	15.2	4,939	62.5	42.1	18.1
Eatonville town	2,758	2,865	3.9	2,805	89.8	0.2	0.7	3.8	5.6	33.5	50.7	15.8	1,089	69.0	42.5	19.7
Edgewood city	9,387	9,749	3.9	9,538	85.2	0.3	1.3	6.9	6.3	19.1	64.4	16.5	3,663	79.9	38.4	26.4
Edison CDP	133	NA	NA	236	100.0	0.0	0.0	0.0	0.0	32.2	46.6	21.2	73	79.5	64.4	35.6
Edmonds city	39,698	40,896	3.0	40,343	79.2	2.4	9.3	4.6	4.5	17.5	63.1	19.4	17,440	68.7	16.4	50.2
Elbe CDP	29	NA	NA	0	0.0	0.0	0.0	0.0	0.0	0.0	0.0	0.0	0	0.0	0.0	0.0
Electric City city	982	1,018	3.7	1,084	80.7	0.0	0.5	9.4	9.4	22.9	55.0	22.0	470	70.2	42.3	18.5
Elk Plain CDP	14,205	NA	NA	13,947	71.7	6.4	2.6	6.4	12.9	25.4	65.7	8.8	4,662	75.3	37.8	17.9
Ellensburg city	18,251	18,774	2.9	18,455	79.6	1.8	3.5	4.8	10.3	14.9	76.6	8.4	7,103	30.1	24.2	34.3
Elma city	3,103	3,018	-2.7	3,048	86.7	0.5	6.5	4.1	2.1	30.6	58.5	10.9	1,106	45.2	39.9	10.7
Elmer City town	238	239	0.4	317	42.9	1.3	1.6	54.3	0.0	21.4	57.4	21.1	121	68.6	43.0	18.2
Endicott town	289	286	-1.0	236	99.6	0.0	0.0	0.4	0.0	22.0	58.6	19.5	114	86.8	43.9	20.2
Enetai CDP	2,286	NA	NA	2,104	81.3	0.9	4.0	10.0	3.8	22.0	61.0	17.2	881	85.5	26.2	25.2
Entiat city	1,112	1,154	3.8	1,225	76.6	0.0	0.0	4.0	19.4	20.2	57.3	22.5	483	66.7	49.9	12.2
Enumclaw city	11,092	11,548	4.1	11,388	83.6	1.6	1.9	4.9	8.0	24.4	62.4	13.2	4,426	60.9	41.4	18.2
Ephrata city	7,664	8,031	4.8	7,888	73.5	0.1	2.7	3.4	20.3	30.0	58.9	11.1	2,735	58.9	45.1	20.4
Erlands Point-Kitsap Lake CDP	2,935	NA	NA	2,896	78.9	0.0	2.6	11.8	6.7	23.8	61.1	15.1	1,151	64.7	29.8	17.9
Eschbach CDP	415	NA	NA	313	95.5	0.0	0.0	4.5	0.0	27.1	38.3	34.5	114	90.4	51.8	9.6
Esperance CDP	3,601	NA	NA	4,039	75.2	2.5	7.5	7.6	7.3	22.9	61.1	16.0	1,594	73.7	19.6	42.6
Everett city	103,022	106,736	3.6	104,708	64.9	3.7	8.2	7.0	16.1	22.5	67.1	10.5	41,500	45.1	35.1	22.9
Everson city	2,483	2,565	3.3	2,528	77.0	0.0	0.2	1.0	21.8	27.0	63.4	9.5	818	76.0	44.9	15.4
Fairchild AFB CDP	2,776	NA	NA	3,097	77.2	11.8	2.8	2.6	5.6	33.1	66.8	0.0	749	1.3	13.5	16.7
Fairfield town	611	606	-0.8	457	89.9	1.1	0.0	7.2	1.8	17.5	59.0	23.6	188	73.9	44.1	8.5
Fairwood CDP (King)	19,102	NA	NA	19,088	58.9	7.8	19.6	7.3	6.4	23.0	65.3	11.7	7,020	72.2	19.1	45.0
Fairwood CDP (Spokane)	7,905	NA	NA	8,312	90.3	1.6	0.8	2.6	4.7	30.4	56.0	13.5	3,066	69.2	20.5	38.3
Fall City CDP	1,993	NA	NA	1,958	88.5	0.0	0.0	1.2	10.3	15.6	74.3	10.1	799	58.7	42.7	33.2
Farmington town	146	148	1.4	126	88.1	0.0	0.0	4.8	7.1	34.1	55.5	10.3	39	89.7	43.6	25.6
Federal Way city	89,306	93,425	4.6	91,676	50.3	9.5	14.6	8.3	17.3	24.0	64.3	11.6	34,064	55.0	32.9	27.6
Felida CDP	7,385	NA	NA	7,416	86.5	1.1	4.9	4.5	3.0	26.0	59.8	14.1	2,502	88.9	10.1	53.8
Ferndale city	11,431	12,704	11.1	12,040	75.6	1.8	5.6	5.4	11.6	26.2	61.1	12.8	4,428	62.3	32.3	29.0
Fern Prairie CDP	1,884	NA	NA	2,238	87.0	0.8	0.0	5.6	6.5	24.2	59.2	16.6	736	87.2	32.6	22.7
Fife city	9,173	9,550	4.1	9,346	45.3	10.8	16.1	10.9	16.9	26.1	67.8	6.1	3,472	40.9	38.9	20.7
Fife Heights CDP	2,137	NA	NA	1,977	77.7	1.5	6.8	7.3	6.8	27.5	63.3	9.2	643	66.4	33.1	23.8
Finley CDP	6,012	NA	NA	6,204	70.7	0.7	0.0	2.5	26.1	27.4	62.6	9.9	2,019	85.1	43.3	10.2
Fircrest city	6,495	6,658	2.5	6,592	73.0	6.6	6.2	11.0	3.3	23.0	60.4	16.6	2,819	63.3	19.4	41.6
Five Corners CDP	18,159	NA	NA	19,787	81.5	3.1	4.1	4.9	6.3	29.8	62.0	8.2	6,163	69.5	35.8	18.8
Fobes Hill CDP	2,418	NA	NA	2,427	96.0	0.0	2.1	1.8	0.1	17.1	67.6	15.2	956	82.2	29.4	34.1
Fords Prairie CDP	1,959	NA	NA	1,680	87.3	6.2	0.2	1.3	4.9	23.8	56.7	19.4	835	68.3	51.3	4.0
Forks city	3,552	3,717	4.6	3,656	70.5	0.5	1.3	9.8	17.8	22.7	63.6	13.8	1,525	62.4	49.6	11.0
Fort Lewis CDP	11,046	NA	NA	13,776	61.2	13.2	1.6	5.2	18.7	39.1	61.0	0.1	3,049	0.7	32.4	10.6
Four Lakes CDP	512	NA	NA	143	79.0	0.0	0.0	20.3	0.7	0.0	48.3	51.7	115	100.0	47.8	15.7
Fox Island CDP	3,633	NA	NA	3,556	89.8	0.6	4.3	4.5	0.9	21.0	63.5	15.5	1,355	86.6	8.0	52.3
Fredrickson CDP	18,719	NA	NA	19,754	61.1	10.1	5.8	11.9	11.1	28.4	63.0	8.5	6,500	72.5	30.2	19.6
Freeland CDP	2,045	NA	NA	1,486	94.8	0.0	0.5	3.2	1.5	14.8	52.4	32.7	699	63.7	30.5	31.2
Friday Harbor town	2,168	2,306	6.4	2,223	81.1	0.4	1.8	3.0	13.7	19.9	60.8	19.4	1,018	49.4	34.2	33.5
Garfield town	597	598	0.2	479	92.9	0.2	0.0	0.4	6.5	18.1	57.7	24.0	229	69.4	37.6	16.2
Garrett CDP	1,419	NA	NA	1,446	69.2	0.4	0.7	1.9	27.8	24.2	56.5	19.4	547	66.5	34.9	33.5
Geneva CDP	2,321	NA	NA	2,429	86.0	0.1	1.6	6.8	5.6	20.2	61.3	18.5	878	87.0	12.5	53.9
George city	501	505	0.8	735	10.3	0.0	0.1	0.0	89.5	36.5	59.7	3.8	181	35.9	84.5	0.6
Gig Harbor city	7,126	8,375	17.5	7,620	82.3	0.8	3.2	5.5	8.1	16.3	60.2	23.6	3,420	55.0	19.5	49.7
Glacier CDP	211	NA	NA	76	80.3	0.0	0.0	19.7	0.0	0.0	100.0	0.0	44	65.9	0.0	65.9
Gleed CDP	2,906	NA	NA	3,034	77.3	1.2	0.0	5.3	16.2	22.6	61.0	16.4	1,072	84.7	50.8	16.4
Glenwood CDP	0	NA	NA	176	89.8	1.1	0.0	4.5	4.5	22.2	59.1	18.8	76	65.8	43.4	17.1

1 May be of any race.

Table A. All Places — Population and Housing

STATE City, town, township, borough, or CDP (county if applicable)	2010 census total population	2014 estimated population	Percent change 2010-2014	ACS total population estimate 2010-2014	White alone, not Hispanic or Latino	Black alone, not Hispanic or Latino	Asian alone, not Hispanic or Latino	All other races or 2 or more races, not Hispanic or Latino	Hispanic or Latino[1]	Under 18 years old	Age 18 to 64 years old	Age 65 years and older	Total occupied housing units	Percent owner occupied	High school diploma or less	Bachelor's degree or more
	1	2	3	4	5	6	7	8	9	10	11	12	13	14	15	16
Gold Bar city	2,075	2,101	1.3	2,300	89.7	0.0	0.4	4.2	5.7	26.9	67.3	5.9	803	74.2	46.9	10.0
Goldendale city	3,407	3,428	0.6	3,423	85.6	2.7	0.3	8.7	2.6	19.7	61.1	19.0	1,439	46.9	39.4	21.3
Gorst CDP	592	NA	NA	385	72.7	0.0	0.0	14.8	12.5	13.8	48.6	37.7	176	73.3	38.1	45.5
Graham CDP	23,491	NA	NA	24,330	82.8	3.3	1.6	6.1	6.3	28.8	63.3	8.0	8,070	84.2	35.1	20.6
Grand Coulee city	1,020	1,050	2.9	999	68.4	0.2	1.0	26.9	3.5	20.2	53.1	26.6	450	45.8	44.9	16.7
Grand Mound CDP	2,981	NA	NA	2,921	67.8	0.0	0.3	4.8	27.1	29.0	58.6	12.4	1,013	62.1	57.7	10.5
Grandview city	10,862	11,140	2.6	11,023	20.2	0.3	0.1	1.8	77.5	38.5	52.1	9.6	2,956	62.2	58.3	11.8
Granger city	3,241	3,394	4.7	3,330	7.4	0.2	0.0	3.1	89.3	44.4	52.1	3.7	739	57.2	64.3	10.0
Granite Falls city	3,372	3,468	2.8	3,416	82.6	2.8	1.5	5.8	7.3	22.5	64.5	13.0	1,440	63.4	45.1	15.1
Grapeview CDP	954	NA	NA	999	89.9	0.0	0.0	8.3	1.8	13.8	63.7	22.4	401	78.8	23.9	27.9
Grayland CDP	953	NA	NA	589	92.2	0.0	0.0	5.9	1.9	1.8	47.3	50.8	302	78.8	58.6	14.9
Grays River CDP	263	NA	NA	540	91.9	0.0	0.0	3.0	5.2	28.2	49.4	22.4	198	76.3	50.5	13.1
Green Bluff CDP	761	NA	NA	916	100.0	0.0	0.0	0.0	0.0	26.0	65.2	8.7	275	83.3	27.6	31.6
Greenwater CDP	67	NA	NA	108	100.0	0.0	0.0	0.0	0.0	0.0	73.2	26.9	62	62.9	16.1	22.6
Hamilton town	301	299	-0.7	252	90.5	0.0	0.0	9.5	0.0	6.0	78.2	15.9	99	79.8	50.5	6.1
Hansville CDP	3,091	NA	NA	3,573	86.8	0.5	3.9	6.3	2.5	19.0	58.2	22.8	1,564	88.6	15.9	43.5
Harrah town	625	627	0.3	677	24.7	0.4	0.3	19.9	54.7	32.5	57.6	9.9	196	57.1	65.3	10.7
Harrington city	424	400	-5.7	339	92.9	0.0	0.0	7.1	0.0	13.0	58.9	28.0	167	70.7	53.9	18.0
Hartline town	151	156	3.3	106	100.0	0.0	0.0	0.0	0.0	21.7	67.0	11.3	52	76.9	26.9	19.2
Hat Island CDP	41	NA	NA	18	50.0	0.0	50.0	0.0	0.0	0.0	100.0	0.0	9	100.0	100.0	0.0
Hatton town	101	102	1.0	93	64.5	0.0	3.2	1.1	31.2	21.5	69.0	9.7	49	40.8	22.4	59.2
Hazel Dell CDP	19,435	NA	NA	19,590	77.1	2.4	3.3	3.7	13.5	22.5	64.2	13.3	7,693	54.8	29.9	22.1
Herron Island CDP	151	NA	NA	74	100.0	0.0	0.0	0.0	0.0	0.0	20.3	79.7	40	100.0	65.0	35.0
High Bridge CDP	2,994	NA	NA	3,067	91.0	1.2	1.3	3.1	3.5	22.3	67.4	10.4	1,020	97.9	19.8	40.3
Hobart CDP	6,221	NA	NA	6,548	90.6	1.2	1.4	2.6	4.2	22.2	61.4	16.5	2,382	92.1	26.6	33.7
Hockinson CDP	4,771	NA	NA	5,129	92.0	0.1	1.7	2.7	3.5	31.1	57.5	11.4	1,594	89.3	29.0	32.3
Hogans Corner CDP	85	NA	NA	123	100.0	0.0	0.0	0.0	0.0	32.5	67.5	0.0	43	100.0	100.0	0.0
Home CDP	1,377	NA	NA	1,647	94.2	0.0	0.8	4.9	0.1	30.2	58.2	11.6	647	74.3	38.3	32.9
Hoodsport CDP	376	NA	NA	952	82.8	0.0	0.0	9.3	7.9	23.3	60.9	15.9	343	72.0	44.6	14.0
Hoquiam city	8,726	8,389	-3.9	8,560	76.5	0.8	0.4	9.2	13.0	24.5	59.1	16.4	3,349	59.8	42.7	14.1
Humptulips CDP	255	NA	NA	249	95.6	0.0	0.0	1.6	2.8	31.7	59.0	9.2	99	92.9	47.5	0.0
Hunts Point town	396	434	9.6	487	78.4	0.0	15.8	4.1	1.6	23.4	58.4	18.3	174	87.9	4.6	72.4
Ilwaco city	936	905	-3.3	1,086	78.6	1.5	0.0	9.1	10.8	24.5	57.3	18.1	439	51.9	39.6	16.9
Inchelium CDP	409	NA	NA	515	12.4	0.0	0.0	87.6	0.0	34.1	55.1	10.7	163	61.3	39.9	7.4
Index town	176	190	8.0	217	99.1	0.0	0.9	0.0	0.0	20.7	75.6	3.7	87	62.1	16.1	28.7
Indianola CDP	3,500	NA	NA	3,455	87.1	0.2	2.6	6.8	3.3	22.1	64.6	13.4	1,399	78.0	23.7	38.2
Ione town	449	448	-0.2	377	95.2	0.0	0.0	3.4	1.3	19.1	62.6	18.3	158	79.1	43.7	12.7
Issaquah city	30,434	34,056	11.9	32,551	72.4	2.3	15.4	4.1	5.8	24.4	63.4	12.3	13,869	59.7	9.2	62.6
Jamestown CDP	361	NA	NA	366	97.3	0.0	0.0	2.7	0.0	33.4	47.6	19.1	164	78.0	19.5	32.9
Junction City CDP	18	NA	NA	9	100.0	0.0	0.0	0.0	0.0	0.0	0.0	100.0	9	100.0	100.0	0.0
Kahlotus city	193	191	-1.0	143	95.1	3.5	0.0	1.4	0.0	30.8	58.1	11.2	58	62.1	50.0	29.3
Kalama city	2,344	2,347	0.1	2,616	91.7	0.0	0.5	2.7	5.2	26.0	55.6	18.5	1,027	65.5	37.4	17.7
Kapowsin CDP	333	NA	NA	210	100.0	0.0	0.0	0.0	0.0	13.8	77.1	9.0	79	100.0	26.6	5.1
Kayak Point CDP	0	NA	NA	1,587	96.2	0.4	0.0	1.6	1.8	21.9	62.7	15.4	530	94.7	27.4	39.8
Keller CDP	234	NA	NA	187	15.5	0.0	0.0	81.3	3.2	31.0	53.6	15.5	63	49.2	55.6	4.8
Kelso city	11,925	11,788	-1.1	11,837	76.7	1.7	0.6	4.2	16.8	24.5	63.5	12.1	4,466	47.9	40.7	11.8
Kendall CDP	191	NA	NA	197	100.0	0.0	0.0	0.0	0.0	32.5	58.9	8.6	72	77.8	18.1	0.0
Kenmore city	20,460	21,839	6.7	21,263	74.4	1.3	9.6	4.7	10.0	24.5	62.5	13.0	8,001	73.2	14.6	56.4
Kennewick city	73,874	77,421	4.8	75,971	67.8	2.3	2.5	2.8	24.6	27.9	60.5	11.5	27,250	61.5	39.2	23.3
Kent city	118,593	125,560	5.9	122,620	48.3	9.7	17.7	8.5	15.9	26.2	64.2	9.4	42,457	53.8	34.7	27.4
Ketron Island CDP	17	NA	NA	0	0.0	0.0	0.0	0.0	0.0	0.0	0.0	0.0	0	0.0	0.0	0.0
Kettle Falls city	1,602	1,592	-0.6	1,507	90.4	0.0	0.5	9.0	0.0	21.1	60.7	18.2	735	66.3	50.5	18.0
Key Center CDP	3,692	NA	NA	4,172	88.1	0.1	0.3	2.6	8.9	26.7	61.0	12.5	1,434	85.2	25.2	27.0
Keyport CDP	554	NA	NA	543	98.7	0.0	0.0	1.3	0.0	14.4	76.2	9.4	227	78.9	26.4	35.2
Kingston CDP	2,099	NA	NA	2,079	82.5	0.0	3.9	12.1	1.5	21.5	59.3	19.2	908	70.5	18.7	44.9
Kirkland city	80,585	85,763	6.4	83,320	74.3	1.4	12.9	5.0	6.4	20.7	67.9	11.4	34,762	63.6	12.8	58.4
Kittitas city	1,380	1,417	2.7	1,241	86.7	0.1	1.3	3.4	8.5	22.0	67.5	10.6	486	55.6	50.8	13.6
Klahanie CDP	0	NA	NA	11,538	63.4	3.0	22.9	5.6	5.1	28.7	65.2	5.8	4,057	78.1	7.6	70.4
Klickitat CDP	362	NA	NA	380	84.7	1.3	0.0	13.9	0.0	17.4	67.0	15.8	142	51.4	28.2	4.9
Krupp town	48	50	4.2	28	100.0	0.0	0.0	0.0	0.0	10.7	42.6	46.4	20	100.0	50.0	20.0
La Center city	2,951	3,099	5.0	3,036	86.6	1.2	0.2	3.6	8.4	29.8	60.8	9.3	1,065	81.9	26.1	33.7
Lacey city	42,395	45,446	7.2	44,031	67.8	6.0	10.8	7.1	8.2	23.2	61.8	15.1	17,346	53.8	26.0	33.5
La Conner town	891	917	2.9	783	89.8	0.0	0.0	1.9	8.3	15.4	52.0	32.3	399	47.6	21.8	27.1
LaCrosse town	313	312	-0.3	261	93.5	0.0	0.0	5.7	0.8	8.3	61.7	29.9	140	80.7	48.6	27.9
La Grande CDP	109	NA	NA	129	100.0	0.0	0.0	0.0	0.0	6.2	93.8	0.0	64	100.0	0.0	100.0
Lake Bosworth CDP	667	NA	NA	475	98.1	0.0	0.0	0.0	1.9	17.7	60.6	21.7	217	65.4	58.1	10.6
Lake Cassidy CDP	3,415	NA	NA	3,297	96.9	0.0	0.7	1.7	0.8	27.4	58.9	13.8	1,109	93.7	42.0	17.0
Lake Cavanaugh CDP	167	NA	NA	150	100.0	0.0	0.0	0.0	0.0	8.7	40.7	50.7	104	70.2	22.1	14.4
Lake Forest Park city	12,599	13,184	4.6	12,938	81.7	2.3	6.4	5.7	3.9	18.6	63.6	17.8	5,183	80.7	10.3	58.9
Lake Goodwin CDP	0	NA	NA	3,621	92.6	0.0	1.5	1.9	3.9	21.5	67.4	11.2	1,336	71.5	32.9	26.2
Lake Holm CDP	3,221	NA	NA	3,421	91.7	0.0	4.0	1.6	2.7	16.3	68.3	15.3	1,300	92.4	19.8	40.4
Lake Ketchum CDP	930	NA	NA	816	88.5	0.0	0.0	4.5	7.0	15.1	62.4	22.5	388	90.7	30.2	23.2
Lakeland North CDP	12,942	NA	NA	12,860	63.2	6.5	12.0	4.2	14.1	23.7	65.3	10.9	4,553	75.3	33.7	23.6
Lakeland South CDP	11,574	NA	NA	13,047	73.2	2.7	9.7	5.9	8.4	25.5	63.1	11.3	4,539	84.0	29.2	26.5
Lake McMurray CDP	192	NA	NA	169	84.0	0.0	6.5	4.1	5.3	5.3	65.0	29.6	76	100.0	51.3	7.9
Lake Marcel-Stillwater CDP	1,277	NA	NA	1,305	77.2	0.0	0.0	7.2	15.6	28.7	67.0	4.3	474	96.6	15.6	47.9
Lake Morton-Berrydale CDP	10,160	NA	NA	9,654	85.7	1.1	3.7	5.1	4.5	21.7	64.5	13.9	3,638	89.4	28.4	30.1
Lake Roesiger CDP	503	NA	NA	815	98.0	0.0	0.0	0.0	2.0	28.1	58.6	13.4	291	62.9	17.9	43.0
Lake Shore CDP	6,571	NA	NA	6,560	84.8	1.1	2.8	5.1	6.2	22.1	59.4	18.5	2,502	87.8	17.5	38.1
Lake Stevens city	28,060	30,284	7.9	29,258	82.9	0.1	3.0	5.3	8.7	30.0	62.3	7.8	10,026	71.7	32.8	24.5
Lake Stickney CDP	7,777	NA	NA	8,324	42.0	4.5	27.6	6.0	20.0	24.2	65.7	10.1	2,785	57.8	34.1	21.5
Lake Tapps CDP	11,859	NA	NA	12,306	90.4	0.0	1.0	6.2	2.4	26.4	63.5	9.9	4,224	86.9	24.5	35.8
Lakeview CDP	915	NA	NA	913	82.3	0.0	0.0	3.6	14.1	13.2	54.1	32.6	466	68.0	45.1	15.9
Lakewood city	58,163	59,610	2.5	58,890	53.7	9.9	8.2	11.3	16.8	21.5	64.1	14.4	24,107	46.0	33.2	22.2
Lamont town	70	71	1.4	88	94.3	0.0	0.0	3.4	2.3	34.1	45.5	20.5	35	74.3	48.6	2.9
Langley city	1,035	1,052	1.6	1,281	86.3	1.6	2.3	5.9	3.8	24.0	46.0	30.0	577	50.4	23.7	42.1
Larch Way CDP	3,318	NA	NA	3,760	61.1	0.7	31.5	3.1	3.7	29.6	60.9	9.5	1,191	83.7	22.0	41.1
Latah town	183	184	0.5	162	87.0	0.0	0.0	4.3	8.6	38.9	53.8	7.4	56	80.4	46.4	19.6
Laurier CDP	1	NA	NA	0	0.0	0.0	0.0	0.0	0.0	0.0	0.0	0.0	0	0.0	0.0	0.0

1 May be of any race.

Table A. All Places — **Population and Housing**

STATE City, town, township, borough, or CDP (county if applicable)	2010 census total population	2014 estimated population	Percent change 2010-2014	ACS total population estimate 2010-2014	White alone, not Hispanic or Latino	Black alone, not Hispanic or Latino	Asian alone, not Hispanic or Latino	All other races or 2 or more races, not Hispanic or Latino	Hispanic or Latino[1]	Under 18 years old	Age 18 to 64 years old	Age 65 years and older	Total occupied housing units	Percent owner occupied	High school diploma or less	Bachelor's degree or more
	1	2	3	4	5	6	7	8	9	10	11	12	13	14	15	16
WASHINGTON—Con.																
Leavenworth city	1,962	1,979	0.9	2,313	79.3	0.0	0.8	3.7	16.2	19.3	55.4	25.3	1,107	57.7	41.6	34.6
Lebam CDP	160	NA	NA	204	71.1	0.0	0.0	12.3	16.7	13.2	81.9	4.9	90	55.6	38.9	16.7
Lewisville CDP	1,722	NA	NA	1,945	97.9	0.0	0.4	0.2	1.5	30.1	56.3	13.8	683	84.6	31.5	26.6
Liberty Lake city	7,601	8,637	13.6	8,027	88.8	0.0	2.3	4.0	4.9	31.1	58.1	10.8	2,968	64.5	16.4	43.7
Lind town	564	569	0.9	557	89.2	0.0	0.0	2.9	7.9	33.8	55.2	11.0	194	71.1	26.3	23.7
Lochsloy CDP	2,533	NA	NA	2,584	94.1	0.0	1.1	2.6	2.2	18.6	65.9	15.5	929	84.0	42.0	18.2
Lofall CDP	2,289	NA	NA	2,040	90.2	3.0	2.1	1.0	3.7	20.8	61.6	17.5	836	88.2	18.7	23.7
Long Beach city	1,392	1,346	-3.3	1,469	85.1	0.1	0.2	1.1	13.5	14.4	56.5	29.2	772	50.9	34.2	21.5
Longbranch CDP	3,784	NA	NA	3,147	91.8	1.8	0.0	5.0	1.5	19.9	62.9	17.1	1,340	88.2	35.1	23.1
Longview city	36,834	36,483	-1.0	36,589	82.2	0.4	2.0	6.4	9.0	22.1	59.5	18.4	15,266	55.0	35.8	16.3
Longview Heights CDP	3,851	NA	NA	3,588	93.5	0.0	0.4	2.2	3.9	22.7	60.4	16.8	1,410	79.9	26.6	23.6
Loomis CDP	159	NA	NA	82	100.0	0.0	0.0	0.0	0.0	0.0	20.7	79.3	64	100.0	42.2	0.0
Loon Lake CDP	783	NA	NA	746	96.2	2.0	0.0	0.7	1.1	20.7	56.6	22.8	320	86.9	25.9	20.6
Lower Elochoman CDP	185	NA	NA	131	100.0	0.0	0.0	0.0	0.0	0.0	16.1	84.0	72	100.0	13.9	22.2
Lyle CDP	499	NA	NA	344	99.1	0.0	0.3	0.6	0.0	10.7	67.2	22.1	150	85.3	30.0	16.7
Lyman town	438	447	2.1	549	86.7	0.9	0.0	7.5	4.9	24.6	65.2	10.2	202	87.6	38.1	8.4
Lynden city	12,002	13,165	9.7	12,579	83.1	0.5	2.4	4.6	9.5	25.2	54.3	20.5	4,809	69.3	32.0	29.5
Lynnwood city	35,845	36,687	2.3	36,267	56.3	5.8	18.8	5.8	13.3	20.3	64.8	14.9	13,919	51.5	31.9	28.0
Mabton city	2,297	2,303	0.3	2,300	4.7	0.0	0.0	0.1	95.2	35.2	56.5	8.3	507	64.3	83.8	0.0
McChord AFB CDP	2,507	NA	NA	3,167	52.0	15.7	2.7	6.1	23.5	39.4	60.6	0.0	772	0.0	17.4	21.5
McCleary city	1,649	1,609	-2.4	1,805	89.4	0.6	0.7	6.5	2.8	25.8	58.3	15.9	677	60.7	31.9	15.1
Machias CDP	1,178	NA	NA	1,135	90.4	0.0	0.0	3.7	5.9	28.9	63.8	7.2	361	90.9	41.6	27.7
McKenna CDP	716	NA	NA	701	96.1	0.0	0.0	0.0	3.9	21.7	55.8	22.5	273	89.0	59.7	17.2
McMillin CDP	1,547	NA	NA	1,324	89.9	0.0	3.9	0.6	5.6	17.4	63.7	19.0	509	99.0	29.5	30.1
Malden town	203	199	-2.0	173	95.4	0.0	2.9	1.7	0.0	16.8	56.6	26.6	90	82.2	45.6	10.0
Malo CDP	28	NA	NA	0	0.0	0.0	0.0	0.0	0.0	0.0	0.0	0.0	0	0.0	0.0	0.0
Malone CDP	475	NA	NA	474	86.1	0.0	0.0	11.4	2.5	23.8	66.8	9.3	186	59.7	65.6	10.2
Malott CDP	487	NA	NA	494	32.6	0.0	0.0	3.4	64.0	38.3	50.5	11.3	186	37.6	74.7	0.0
Maltby CDP	10,830	NA	NA	11,447	91.5	0.0	3.3	3.0	2.2	24.5	65.5	10.2	3,783	92.8	24.5	42.6
Manchester CDP	5,413	NA	NA	5,081	84.1	0.9	5.6	7.2	2.2	20.8	62.6	16.8	1,997	77.6	22.6	30.8
Mansfield town	320	327	2.2	319	96.2	0.0	0.0	0.6	3.1	19.8	53.3	27.0	151	67.5	43.0	22.5
Manson CDP	1,468	NA	NA	1,418	73.8	0.0	0.0	2.2	24.0	22.1	54.5	23.6	636	61.6	45.1	19.3
Maple Falls CDP	324	NA	NA	177	73.4	0.0	0.0	26.6	0.0	0.0	78.5	21.5	82	100.0	20.7	0.0
Maple Heights-Lake Desire CDP	3,152	NA	NA	3,282	66.9	4.2	14.4	8.3	6.2	19.4	69.9	10.7	1,232	91.7	26.3	40.3
Maple Valley city	22,684	25,125	10.8	24,040	80.6	2.6	5.0	6.2	5.7	31.2	60.6	8.3	8,226	82.7	21.8	36.9
Maplewood CDP	5,138	NA	NA	4,972	88.2	1.0	3.8	3.4	3.5	23.2	58.1	18.5	1,910	83.7	25.2	48.5
Marblemount CDP	203	NA	NA	66	63.6	0.0	0.0	0.0	36.4	12.1	87.9	0.0	42	45.2	0.0	0.0
Marcus town	183	184	0.5	169	87.6	0.0	1.8	10.7	0.0	15.4	59.3	25.4	82	100.0	54.9	19.5
Marietta-Alderwood CDP	3,906	NA	NA	4,435	80.2	0.3	5.3	0.9	13.3	24.9	66.5	8.5	1,682	47.3	27.1	25.6
Markham CDP	111	NA	NA	153	100.0	0.0	0.0	0.0	0.0	0.0	65.3	34.6	73	100.0	23.3	27.4
Marrowstone CDP	844	NA	NA	1,218	96.7	0.0	0.6	2.7	0.0	25.4	53.6	21.1	463	85.5	16.2	47.7
Martha Lake CDP	15,473	NA	NA	16,441	63.7	5.5	12.2	6.7	12.0	25.7	65.3	9.0	5,731	62.1	23.8	36.2
Maryhill CDP	58	NA	NA	0	0.0	0.0	0.0	0.0	0.0	0.0	0.0	0.0	0	0.0	0.0	0.0
Marysville city	60,024	65,087	8.4	62,472	75.9	1.5	6.4	6.5	9.7	26.0	63.2	10.9	22,456	68.9	36.3	19.4
Mattawa city	4,433	4,579	3.3	4,502	1.0	0.0	0.3	0.2	98.5	42.8	55.6	1.8	857	28.5	89.1	4.8
May Creek CDP	818	NA	NA	773	79.8	0.0	0.0	20.2	0.0	28.0	65.5	6.6	280	96.1	20.7	36.1
Mead CDP	7,275	NA	NA	7,314	93.6	0.0	0.0	3.1	3.3	23.1	62.4	14.5	2,820	84.2	27.4	28.8
Meadowdale CDP	2,826	NA	NA	2,720	82.6	4.7	6.8	3.9	2.0	22.5	64.3	13.2	1,017	81.9	19.7	42.3
Meadow Glade CDP	2,541	NA	NA	2,485	89.9	0.5	1.4	3.3	4.9	28.1	56.9	15.1	747	90.4	17.4	44.4
Medical Lake city	5,060	4,952	-2.1	4,950	83.9	2.7	1.6	6.8	5.1	23.6	66.8	9.6	1,642	67.6	33.9	21.7
Medina city	2,967	3,188	7.4	3,080	78.7	0.3	14.5	6.6	0.0	32.0	50.6	17.5	1,054	90.1	4.1	85.2
Mercer Island city	22,691	24,326	7.2	23,636	75.2	1.8	16.1	3.7	3.3	24.6	55.1	20.3	9,431	74.1	7.2	77.0
Mesa city	489	491	0.4	398	23.9	0.0	0.5	0.0	75.6	35.0	60.1	5.0	104	59.6	80.8	6.7
Metaline town	173	171	-1.2	195	84.6	0.0	0.0	3.6	11.8	18.5	53.3	28.2	94	63.8	36.2	13.8
Metaline Falls town	238	238	0.0	176	85.2	0.0	0.0	11.9	2.8	10.2	62.4	27.3	117	30.8	48.7	19.7
Methow CDP	68	NA	NA	20	70.0	0.0	0.0	0.0	30.0	0.0	100.0	0.0	16	100.0	0.0	0.0
Midland CDP	8,962	NA	NA	8,526	46.9	12.7	17.3	6.0	17.1	26.6	62.8	10.7	3,216	54.9	51.4	12.0
Mill Creek city	18,229	19,200	5.3	18,667	66.4	1.8	21.4	6.1	4.2	22.8	64.1	13.2	7,614	61.6	15.3	50.6
Mill Creek East CDP	15,709	NA	NA	16,754	62.1	1.3	23.8	4.7	7.3	27.1	65.4	7.5	5,865	87.7	13.5	56.2
Millwood city	1,786	1,776	-0.6	1,760	89.1	4.3	1.3	3.4	1.9	22.3	64.3	13.3	747	66.9	33.9	22.5
Milton city	7,129	7,360	3.2	7,260	80.8	1.7	6.2	6.7	4.5	24.7	63.7	11.5	2,875	58.9	31.7	21.0
Mineral CDP	202	NA	NA	152	84.9	0.0	0.0	15.1	0.0	0.0	65.1	34.9	136	57.4	68.4	0.0
Minnehaha CDP	9,771	NA	NA	8,864	79.0	1.0	6.2	4.8	9.0	23.8	64.5	11.7	3,528	76.1	33.6	26.3
Mirrormont CDP	3,659	NA	NA	4,001	94.0	0.5	2.9	1.1	1.4	21.2	63.9	14.8	1,475	93.0	5.9	66.8
Moclips CDP	207	NA	NA	73	100.0	0.0	0.0	0.0	0.0	0.0	0.0	100.0	36	100.0	100.0	0.0
Monroe city	17,304	17,899	3.4	17,564	69.5	4.1	3.5	3.8	19.1	26.6	65.0	8.4	4,940	65.0	33.6	24.9
Monroe North CDP	1,666	NA	NA	1,637	91.1	0.0	0.0	5.3	3.6	31.7	57.0	11.2	501	88.4	24.0	28.5
Montesano city	3,971	3,861	-2.8	3,915	84.9	1.3	0.1	7.3	6.4	20.3	65.4	14.2	1,470	68.6	27.3	20.5
Morton city	1,122	1,116	-0.5	1,111	86.7	0.5	0.1	4.0	8.8	17.5	58.5	24.1	502	56.2	49.6	14.1
Moses Lake city	20,366	21,713	6.6	21,141	63.9	1.8	1.5	2.2	30.5	32.6	55.6	11.6	7,823	53.1	40.1	18.5
Moses Lake North CDP	4,418	NA	NA	4,583	57.7	2.7	0.5	5.9	33.3	32.2	61.1	6.7	1,372	27.3	49.1	9.9
Mossyrock city	759	745	-1.8	825	64.2	0.0	0.0	5.3	30.4	23.4	59.4	17.3	312	65.1	62.5	6.1
Mountlake Terrace city	19,884	20,817	4.7	20,318	69.1	3.4	10.7	6.2	10.6	20.1	68.0	12.1	8,209	61.0	29.0	30.2
Mount Vernon city	31,762	33,132	4.3	32,356	59.3	0.7	2.5	3.1	34.3	28.2	58.2	13.7	11,308	55.0	42.6	21.0
Mount Vista CDP	7,850	NA	NA	7,745	86.8	1.4	3.0	3.6	5.2	21.3	61.5	17.2	3,155	70.0	19.3	42.0
Moxee city	3,408	3,784	11.0	3,631	48.4	0.4	0.4	4.2	46.6	34.7	59.9	5.3	1,064	81.5	46.0	11.7
Mukilteo city	20,254	20,993	3.6	20,635	73.3	1.1	17.5	5.2	2.9	22.5	67.3	10.3	7,975	64.7	15.8	50.4
Naches town	795	801	0.8	936	91.7	0.0	0.0	7.3	0.3	24.1	65.6	10.4	346	54.6	49.4	13.6
Napavine city	1,765	1,778	0.7	1,660	93.6	0.0	0.0	3.6	2.8	26.6	56.1	17.3	612	83.0	50.5	5.2
Naselle CDP	419	NA	NA	387	91.0	0.0	0.0	1.0	8.0	24.6	50.9	24.5	163	82.8	55.2	9.2
Navy Yard City CDP	2,477	NA	NA	2,590	67.0	3.8	2.0	9.9	17.2	25.6	65.8	8.6	1,087	51.4	31.0	15.7
Neah Bay CDP	865	NA	NA	1,002	12.9	1.5	0.0	77.9	7.7	27.2	62.1	10.9	301	72.4	44.5	14.0
Neilton CDP	315	NA	NA	400	58.3	0.0	0.0	8.8	33.0	30.3	61.8	8.3	141	68.8	46.1	20.6
Nespelem town	232	243	4.7	173	5.8	0.0	0.0	85.0	9.2	39.3	53.7	6.9	62	72.6	46.8	6.5
Nespelem Community CDP	253	NA	NA	294	1.4	0.0	0.0	97.6	1.0	33.0	61.2	5.8	75	78.7	48.0	12.0
Newcastle city	10,368	11,201	8.0	10,792	61.8	1.8	27.8	5.8	2.8	21.7	66.7	11.6	4,173	71.1	10.8	65.5
Newport city	2,146	2,123	-1.1	2,230	90.1	0.0	0.0	5.0	4.8	26.1	57.6	16.3	859	56.0	48.1	14.0
Nile CDP	140	NA	NA	112	100.0	0.0	0.0	0.0	0.0	0.0	18.8	81.3	59	100.0	89.8	0.0

1 May be of any race.

Table A. All Places — **Population and Housing**

STATE City, town, township, borough, or CDP (county if applicable)	2010 census total population	2014 estimated population	Percent change 2010-2014	ACS total population estimate 2010-2014	White alone, not Hispanic or Latino	Black alone, not Hispanic or Latino	Asian alone, not Hispanic or Latino	All other races or 2 or more races, not Hispanic or Latino	Hispanic or Latino[1]	Under 18 years old	Age 18 to 64 years old	Age 65 years and older	Total occupied housing units	Percent owner occupied	High school diploma or less	Bachelor's degree or more
	1	2	3	4	5	6	7	8	9	10	11	12	13	14	15	16
WASHINGTON—Con.																
Nisqually Indian Community CDP	575	NA	NA	655	22.1	2.6	2.1	67.6	5.5	29.3	60.0	10.7	183	71.6	47.0	14.2
Nooksack city	1,338	1,443	7.8	1,565	83.0	0.8	0.0	1.1	15.1	37.2	53.6	9.2	483	82.8	38.7	15.3
Normandy Park city	6,335	6,615	4.4	6,491	81.5	0.4	4.9	5.3	7.9	20.7	58.0	21.5	2,595	74.9	15.5	57.1
North Bend city	5,821	6,578	13.0	6,127	87.2	0.5	0.5	3.4	8.5	30.2	59.4	10.4	2,276	62.5	24.9	38.0
North Bonneville city	956	971	1.6	1,141	96.6	1.0	0.0	2.3	0.2	21.6	61.1	17.2	468	54.1	34.4	21.4
North Fort Lewis CDP	2,699	NA	NA	3,434	57.7	19.6	2.6	7.9	12.2	26.9	73.2	0.0	501	0.0	20.2	14.8
North Lynnwood CDP	16,574	NA	NA	17,602	54.0	5.9	18.2	12.5	9.3	22.8	70.7	6.7	6,588	47.9	20.8	37.0
North Marysville CDP	108	NA	NA	115	100.0	0.0	0.0	0.0	0.0	11.3	46.1	42.6	33	100.0	42.4	0.0
North Omak CDP	688	NA	NA	751	32.1	0.0	0.0	37.8	30.1	37.4	57.8	4.9	242	33.5	26.9	27.3
Northport town	295	289	-2.0	368	96.7	1.4	1.1	0.8	0.0	19.0	56.9	24.2	182	57.7	53.3	17.6
North Puyallup CDP	1,743	NA	NA	1,746	92.2	1.7	2.7	0.9	2.6	13.0	51.8	35.2	891	77.7	58.1	9.9
North Sultan CDP	264	NA	NA	305	100.0	0.0	0.0	0.0	0.0	18.4	73.1	8.5	109	84.4	42.2	24.8
Northwest Stanwood CDP	149	NA	NA	21	100.0	0.0	0.0	0.0	0.0	0.0	0.0	100.0	10	100.0	100.0	0.0
North Yelm CDP	2,906	NA	NA	2,808	87.6	0.5	1.3	4.8	5.7	32.1	53.0	15.0	1,005	76.0	38.1	12.5
Oakesdale town	422	424	0.5	498	91.8	2.0	0.4	2.8	3.0	20.2	60.0	19.5	192	74.5	25.0	35.4
Oak Harbor city	22,130	22,306	0.8	22,220	64.0	5.0	10.8	8.1	12.2	26.6	61.9	11.4	9,080	43.2	29.8	21.7
Oakville city	684	663	-3.1	706	83.3	0.1	0.8	4.8	10.9	29.8	49.1	21.1	233	76.8	42.9	6.0
Ocean City CDP	200	NA	NA	144	67.4	0.0	0.0	26.4	6.3	0.0	75.0	25.0	110	56.4	53.6	34.5
Ocean Park CDP	1,573	NA	NA	1,150	97.1	0.0	0.0	0.0	2.9	7.9	52.1	39.9	596	73.3	22.1	31.4
Ocean Shores city	5,569	5,628	1.1	5,609	90.1	0.0	2.7	4.5	2.7	13.2	52.1	34.6	2,675	84.9	27.4	22.3
Odessa town	910	868	-4.6	768	87.1	0.4	1.7	8.7	2.1	14.7	58.3	27.1	377	73.2	30.5	26.5
Okanogan city	2,603	2,571	-1.2	2,579	78.6	3.9	0.5	8.6	8.4	22.3	59.5	18.2	1,043	53.3	54.4	12.1
Olympia city	46,476	49,218	5.9	47,847	80.2	1.3	6.0	4.6	7.8	19.9	66.8	13.5	20,657	49.0	19.6	43.9
Omak city	4,845	4,848	0.1	4,835	65.4	0.1	2.2	17.1	15.2	22.6	58.0	19.3	1,910	49.6	40.7	16.1
Onalaska CDP	621	NA	NA	994	85.0	0.0	0.0	11.2	3.8	26.3	60.3	13.3	332	69.3	27.1	5.1
Orchards CDP	19,556	NA	NA	21,259	79.7	1.7	3.8	6.0	8.7	32.7	59.8	7.7	6,667	66.4	35.6	18.5
Orient CDP	115	NA	NA	74	100.0	0.0	0.0	0.0	0.0	6.8	69.0	24.3	56	80.4	69.6	0.0
Oroville city	1,686	1,679	-0.4	1,786	70.4	0.0	0.0	10.6	19.0	22.4	60.3	17.5	822	57.4	46.4	12.2
Orting city	6,746	7,266	7.7	6,941	83.5	0.7	1.0	8.7	6.1	31.2	58.3	10.7	2,298	79.5	39.9	15.1
Oso CDP	180	NA	NA	122	86.9	0.0	13.1	0.0	0.0	13.1	55.7	31.1	75	58.7	77.3	10.7
Othello city	7,364	7,703	4.6	7,524	22.4	0.2	1.0	0.6	75.7	36.7	54.4	8.9	2,261	62.3	59.6	10.9
Otis Orchards-East Farms CDP	6,220	NA	NA	6,538	94.4	0.0	1.1	3.1	1.4	22.2	64.7	13.1	2,312	88.8	36.4	18.2
Outlook CDP	292	NA	NA	473	3.8	0.0	0.0	0.0	96.2	40.8	58.1	1.1	79	50.6	93.7	6.3
Oyehut CDP	85	NA	NA	13	100.0	0.0	0.0	0.0	0.0	0.0	0.0	100.0	13	100.0	100.0	0.0
Pacific city	6,604	7,079	7.2	6,845	62.4	1.5	6.0	12.6	17.4	26.5	66.3	7.1	2,419	53.9	46.1	13.1
Pacific Beach CDP	291	NA	NA	138	100.0	0.0	0.0	0.0	0.0	0.0	81.2	18.8	57	100.0	0.0	0.0
Packwood CDP	342	NA	NA	307	95.4	0.0	0.0	4.6	0.0	5.2	38.1	56.7	172	84.3	43.0	6.4
Palouse city	998	1,012	1.4	1,092	96.5	0.0	0.5	1.4	1.6	29.1	60.2	10.7	415	76.4	20.2	39.8
Parker CDP	154	NA	NA	93	58.1	0.0	0.0	41.9	0.0	45.3	54.9	0.0	22	40.9	59.1	0.0
Parkland CDP	35,803	NA	NA	36,263	54.0	11.1	7.0	13.7	14.3	24.2	65.0	10.6	12,846	46.1	43.5	14.4
Parkwood CDP	7,126	NA	NA	7,312	76.3	6.9	4.3	6.9	5.7	24.1	62.8	13.2	2,767	63.1	24.4	24.9
Pasco city	61,083	68,648	12.4	65,858	38.6	1.7	1.9	2.3	55.5	34.3	58.7	7.0	19,055	66.3	50.5	17.5
Pateros city	667	656	-1.6	560	42.1	0.7	0.0	10.7	46.4	35.4	53.8	10.9	209	56.0	59.3	8.6
Peaceful Valley CDP	3,324	NA	NA	3,893	90.5	0.0	0.3	0.3	8.9	24.1	69.6	6.2	1,338	62.4	51.6	6.7
Pe Ell town	632	628	-0.6	605	91.6	0.0	0.0	4.8	3.6	22.6	62.4	15.0	250	81.2	42.0	11.2
Picnic Point CDP	8,809	NA	NA	8,969	74.5	1.4	12.5	7.6	4.0	23.8	64.8	11.1	3,226	74.1	18.8	36.4
Pine Grove CDP	145	NA	NA	114	93.9	0.0	0.0	6.1	0.0	11.4	32.4	56.1	44	100.0	34.1	45.5
Point Roberts CDP	1,314	NA	NA	1,323	91.2	1.2	4.5	2.1	1.0	19.9	58.3	21.8	663	71.0	25.9	35.1
Pomeroy city	1,425	1,386	-2.7	1,380	87.2	0.0	0.7	4.6	7.5	18.3	54.0	27.7	544	77.6	36.0	19.1
Port Angeles city	19,038	19,256	1.1	19,125	85.9	1.7	2.0	5.5	4.9	20.4	59.6	20.2	8,308	55.9	34.6	22.8
Port Angeles East CDP	3,036	NA	NA	3,338	93.7	0.2	0.0	3.2	2.8	18.3	63.1	18.7	1,332	77.4	31.6	22.4
Porter CDP	207	NA	NA	210	91.9	0.0	0.0	8.1	0.0	21.5	78.7	0.0	74	86.5	24.3	0.0
Port Gamble Tribal Community CDP	916	NA	NA	899	30.9	0.0	1.3	63.4	4.3	25.3	65.3	9.6	255	76.5	43.9	11.4
Port Hadlock-Irondale CDP	3,580	NA	NA	3,512	91.4	0.0	1.7	2.5	4.4	12.6	68.4	18.8	1,564	70.8	41.9	13.2
Port Ludlow CDP	2,603	NA	NA	2,461	90.9	0.8	3.3	4.5	0.5	11.2	39.4	49.4	1,121	94.0	15.3	51.3
Port Orchard city	12,200	13,266	8.7	12,715	72.2	2.4	8.0	9.4	8.0	25.4	60.1	14.5	4,442	56.0	27.6	25.6
Port Townsend city	9,113	9,255	1.6	9,168	90.0	0.9	2.8	4.4	1.9	13.9	57.6	28.5	4,488	63.1	21.8	45.6
Poulsbo city	9,247	9,702	4.9	9,436	75.9	1.0	3.5	7.6	12.0	24.3	55.0	20.8	3,759	64.9	23.9	37.7
Prairie Heights CDP	4,405	NA	NA	4,363	88.8	1.1	0.9	3.1	6.1	28.7	63.0	8.3	1,471	89.0	42.8	19.9
Prairie Ridge CDP	11,464	NA	NA	11,935	81.6	2.2	1.1	4.0	11.0	27.7	64.8	7.5	3,992	83.5	46.4	13.9
Prescott city	318	309	-2.8	272	87.9	1.5	0.0	1.8	8.8	23.1	56.2	20.6	121	76.0	45.5	21.5
Prosser city	5,709	5,802	1.6	5,793	68.1	0.0	0.2	2.1	29.6	28.5	56.6	15.1	2,221	56.6	36.2	20.9
Puget Island CDP	831	NA	NA	804	96.0	0.0	2.6	1.0	0.4	18.9	62.9	18.2	299	83.3	29.8	12.4
Pullman city	29,799	31,682	6.3	30,851	74.4	2.7	11.0	5.5	6.4	11.4	84.1	4.5	10,536	28.4	9.8	49.4
Purdy CDP	1,544	NA	NA	1,229	83.4	0.0	6.8	5.1	4.7	18.6	60.2	21.3	583	85.1	20.4	36.4
Puyallup city	37,028	39,105	5.6	38,092	78.3	3.5	4.1	5.7	8.4	21.6	65.9	12.5	14,966	50.7	35.0	25.6
Queets CDP	174	NA	NA	167	1.2	0.0	0.0	98.8	0.0	27.0	58.8	14.4	51	51.0	54.9	0.0
Quilcene CDP	596	NA	NA	498	90.8	0.0	0.0	3.4	5.8	16.0	70.5	13.3	225	90.7	46.2	21.8
Qui-nai-elt Village CDP	54	NA	NA	53	5.7	0.0	0.0	94.3	0.0	47.2	34.0	18.9	10	100.0	20.0	30.0
Quincy city	6,756	7,355	8.9	7,075	20.6	0.0	0.1	1.7	77.7	35.1	57.7	7.2	2,016	60.7	56.3	14.2
Raft Island CDP	459	NA	NA	333	100.0	0.0	0.0	0.0	0.0	5.1	54.6	40.2	181	92.3	8.3	76.8
Rainier city	1,794	1,948	8.6	1,901	86.7	2.1	0.5	3.3	7.5	25.5	62.9	11.5	677	79.9	39.3	20.8
Ravensdale CDP	1,101	NA	NA	980	92.1	0.0	0.0	5.9	1.9	24.3	65.6	10.0	357	68.6	29.1	28.3
Raymond city	2,882	2,787	-3.3	2,827	68.2	1.0	9.1	4.5	17.2	21.2	53.5	25.3	1,168	60.7	51.3	14.3
Reardan town	571	548	-4.0	756	95.8	0.0	0.0	0.0	4.2	27.0	57.6	15.5	313	70.6	32.9	9.3
Redmond city	54,313	59,285	9.2	56,704	56.2	1.5	29.2	3.9	9.3	22.2	68.3	9.6	23,520	50.9	11.8	66.5
Renton city	91,819	98,404	7.2	95,479	46.7	10.2	21.9	7.6	13.6	22.6	67.3	10.1	37,207	53.2	31.5	32.8
Republic city	1,073	1,083	0.9	1,252	85.2	0.7	0.0	9.2	4.9	18.9	58.0	23.0	570	44.7	32.1	20.2
Richland city	48,104	53,019	10.2	51,116	80.2	1.6	5.3	3.9	9.0	25.3	60.1	14.8	20,401	66.1	20.8	44.6
Ridgefield city	4,763	6,123	28.6	5,373	86.4	0.8	3.5	2.9	6.4	30.3	62.3	7.5	1,810	78.9	18.5	34.9
Ritzville city	1,673	1,671	-0.1	1,803	89.6	0.1	1.2	2.8	6.4	21.4	59.9	18.7	774	66.9	35.1	26.5
Riverbend CDP	2,132	NA	NA	2,172	86.0	0.0	1.0	0.0	13.0	28.6	64.0	7.3	856	80.4	29.6	33.8
River Road CDP	454	NA	NA	471	78.3	0.0	0.0	21.7	0.0	14.2	60.9	24.8	196	72.4	26.5	16.3
Riverside town	280	272	-2.9	451	79.6	0.0	0.4	11.5	8.4	23.3	62.5	14.0	185	68.6	50.8	7.0
Rochester CDP	2,388	NA	NA	2,062	85.1	0.0	0.0	13.0	1.9	26.3	66.4	7.3	761	78.1	23.9	34.4
Rockford town	471	469	-0.4	456	84.2	0.0	0.0	5.9	9.9	24.4	64.4	11.4	169	66.9	43.2	10.1
Rock Island city	788	792	0.5	874	42.4	0.0	0.0	4.3	53.2	25.2	63.1	11.7	306	82.0	64.1	3.3

1 May be of any race.

Table A. All Places — **Population and Housing**

STATE City, town, township, borough, or CDP (county if applicable)	Population: 2010 census total population	Population: 2014 estimated population	Population: Percent change 2010-2014	Population: ACS total population estimate 2010-2014	Race and Hispanic or Latino origin (percent), 2010–2014: White alone, not Hispanic or Latino	Black alone, not Hispanic or Latino	Asian alone, not Hispanic or Latino	All other races or 2 or more races, not Hispanic or Latino	Hispanic or Latino[1]	Age (percent), 2010–2014: Under 18 years old	Age 18 to 64 years old	Age 65 years and older	Households, 2010–2014: Total occupied housing units	Percent owner occupied	Householders by level of education (percent): High school diploma or less	Bachelor's degree or more
	1	2	3	4	5	6	7	8	9	10	11	12	13	14	15	16
WASHINGTON—Con.																
Rockport CDP	109	NA	NA	83	100.0	0.0	0.0	0.0	0.0	0.0	74.7	25.3	51	82.4	82.4	0.0
Rocky Point CDP	1,564	NA	NA	1,582	91.0	0.0	1.9	5.8	1.3	18.7	64.7	16.6	731	69.4	19.0	24.8
Ronald CDP	308	NA	NA	220	100.0	0.0	0.0	0.0	0.0	0.0	46.4	53.6	120	85.8	72.5	0.0
Roosevelt CDP	156	NA	NA	193	32.6	0.0	0.0	0.0	67.4	41.9	50.7	7.3	57	29.8	93.0	0.0
Rosalia town	550	549	-0.2	607	81.5	2.1	0.0	7.9	8.4	25.3	53.1	21.4	255	68.2	47.1	27.8
Rosburg CDP	317	NA	NA	396	96.5	0.0	0.5	3.0	0.0	23.7	58.2	17.9	171	85.4	39.8	28.7
Rosedale CDP	4,044	NA	NA	4,542	82.0	3.4	1.9	10.5	2.2	22.2	65.2	12.6	1,242	81.2	15.7	53.4
Roslyn city	893	896	0.3	947	96.5	0.0	0.0	0.2	3.3	27.7	57.8	14.6	375	64.8	38.4	27.5
Roy city	793	805	1.5	654	82.0	0.5	2.9	6.3	8.4	20.1	63.6	16.2	245	66.5	39.6	18.8
Royal City city	2,140	2,217	3.6	1,848	8.4	0.0	0.0	0.0	91.6	37.4	59.8	2.9	509	38.5	86.1	5.5
Ruston town	749	791	5.6	953	81.0	5.8	1.5	8.3	3.5	19.2	69.9	11.0	428	61.9	19.2	43.0
Ryderwood CDP	395	NA	NA	192	100.0	0.0	0.0	0.0	0.0	0.0	30.7	69.3	116	100.0	23.3	8.6
St. John town	537	545	1.5	524	92.6	3.4	0.0	1.5	2.5	17.4	47.5	35.1	314	58.9	46.8	18.5
Salmon Creek CDP	19,686	NA	NA	20,985	81.5	0.4	2.7	5.5	9.9	25.5	61.5	13.0	7,676	71.0	25.9	34.4
Sammamish city	46,763	51,229	9.6	49,077	70.4	0.8	20.7	4.1	4.1	33.1	60.1	6.7	15,820	87.6	5.4	76.0
Santiago CDP	42	NA	NA	14	0.0	0.0	0.0	100.0	0.0	35.7	35.7	28.6	9	66.7	77.8	22.2
Satsop CDP	675	NA	NA	652	97.4	0.0	0.0	2.6	0.0	14.6	67.8	17.6	254	83.5	56.3	16.1
Seabeck CDP	1,105	NA	NA	1,245	88.6	0.0	9.1	0.0	2.3	14.8	56.5	28.8	585	86.2	17.6	44.4
SeaTac city	26,909	28,126	4.5	27,606	34.6	21.7	14.6	9.5	19.6	21.1	68.2	10.6	9,945	51.6	45.7	20.2
Seattle city	608,658	668,342	9.8	637,850	66.2	7.2	14.2	6.1	6.4	15.5	73.2	11.3	290,822	46.2	15.0	59.8
Sedro-Woolley city	10,596	10,764	1.6	10,645	79.3	1.0	1.1	4.3	14.3	26.7	58.0	15.4	4,092	53.3	39.5	15.1
Sekiu CDP	27	NA	NA	0	0.0	0.0	0.0	0.0	0.0	0.0	0.0	0.0	0	0.0	0.0	0.0
Selah city	7,176	7,444	3.7	7,328	79.0	1.7	0.8	0.6	17.9	28.6	58.8	12.5	2,937	57.4	33.0	36.4
Sequim city	6,606	6,737	2.0	6,651	80.1	1.2	2.5	5.4	10.7	15.0	44.9	40.0	3,166	54.3	35.4	24.4
Shadow Lake CDP	2,262	NA	NA	2,695	75.5	10.9	1.7	2.8	9.1	16.6	71.0	12.7	1,018	85.7	31.9	32.8
Shelton city	9,849	9,777	-0.7	9,798	72.3	0.6	1.0	5.8	20.3	26.5	60.2	13.4	3,222	56.9	42.4	15.7
Shoreline city	53,031	55,174	4.0	54,254	66.3	5.7	14.5	5.4	8.1	18.8	65.4	15.8	21,360	64.2	20.8	45.6
Silvana CDP	90	NA	NA	152	100.0	0.0	0.0	0.0	0.0	0.0	89.6	10.5	64	100.0	0.0	0.0
Silverdale CDP	19,204	NA	NA	20,364	69.0	4.7	10.3	8.5	7.6	20.3	65.6	14.1	8,291	52.5	24.2	31.9
Silver Firs CDP	20,891	NA	NA	22,398	78.4	1.0	9.7	4.2	6.7	28.8	65.6	5.5	7,064	88.8	12.1	53.6
Sisco Heights CDP	2,696	NA	NA	2,605	92.8	0.0	1.6	2.0	3.6	21.0	66.3	12.6	942	84.1	28.0	26.1
Skamokawa Valley CDP	401	NA	NA	260	73.8	0.0	0.0	26.2	0.0	6.2	55.5	38.5	127	84.3	37.0	18.9
Skokomish CDP	617	NA	NA	687	18.6	4.4	1.2	69.7	6.1	26.8	61.9	11.2	198	72.2	51.0	12.6
Skykomish town	197	204	3.6	118	89.0	7.6	3.4	0.0	0.0	6.8	71.2	22.0	51	100.0	31.4	15.7
Snohomish city	9,139	9,544	4.4	9,326	87.2	0.4	2.4	4.8	5.2	22.9	63.1	14.0	3,606	54.8	29.5	23.6
Snoqualmie city	10,670	12,630	18.4	11,625	82.3	0.0	10.7	5.0	2.0	36.1	60.4	3.6	3,882	78.1	9.0	61.7
Snoqualmie Pass CDP	311	NA	NA	230	92.2	0.9	0.0	4.3	2.6	3.1	87.0	10.0	128	77.3	22.7	43.0
Soap Lake city	1,544	1,585	2.7	1,629	78.8	0.1	0.9	8.3	11.9	22.3	53.1	24.5	755	55.1	54.4	8.6
South Bend city	1,630	1,594	-2.2	1,815	58.8	0.0	8.6	6.7	25.9	24.1	57.2	18.7	771	58.8	46.4	11.8
South Cle Elum town	532	532	0.0	530	88.3	1.1	0.0	0.0	10.6	19.3	65.7	15.1	251	63.3	70.9	10.0
South Creek CDP	2,507	NA	NA	2,045	97.1	0.0	0.0	2.9	0.0	9.8	69.6	20.4	843	84.1	58.1	6.2
South Hill CDP	52,431	NA	NA	54,878	70.5	4.1	5.7	10.1	9.6	29.8	60.6	9.6	18,394	73.1	31.6	26.9
South Prairie town	434	435	0.2	369	94.0	0.0	1.6	4.3	0.0	27.3	70.9	1.9	121	95.9	45.5	11.6
South Wenatchee CDP	1,553	NA	NA	1,549	53.5	0.0	1.7	0.0	44.8	19.3	79.2	1.6	514	48.2	62.5	6.8
Southworth CDP	2,185	NA	NA	2,142	94.0	0.0	2.2	2.2	1.5	19.0	60.4	20.6	803	79.5	30.8	36.7
Spanaway CDP	27,227	NA	NA	29,113	61.7	9.8	4.9	10.9	12.7	28.2	62.7	9.2	9,904	67.6	40.8	13.8
Spangle city	278	288	3.6	210	84.8	0.0	7.1	3.8	4.3	14.3	62.4	23.3	96	72.9	39.6	25.0
Spokane city	209,440	212,052	1.2	210,142	83.1	2.6	2.9	5.8	5.7	22.0	64.0	14.0	87,235	56.2	30.5	29.9
Spokane Valley city	89,745	91,729	2.2	90,829	87.9	1.0	2.0	4.3	4.7	23.4	61.7	14.9	36,802	62.2	34.7	22.2
Sprague city	446	423	-5.2	531	84.2	0.0	1.5	7.5	6.8	22.2	50.1	27.7	251	82.9	35.5	6.8
Springdale town	285	276	-3.2	230	84.8	5.2	0.0	7.0	3.0	38.3	42.8	18.7	85	65.9	56.5	7.1
Stansberry Lake CDP	2,101	NA	NA	2,389	83.5	2.3	3.3	7.8	3.1	25.1	67.6	7.2	781	87.5	29.8	16.9
Stanwood city	6,231	6,739	8.2	6,468	86.1	0.0	0.0	6.3	7.7	30.7	55.7	13.8	2,362	56.8	31.1	24.0
Starbuck town	129	127	-1.6	87	79.3	0.0	0.0	20.7	0.0	1.1	68.7	29.9	48	60.4	37.5	27.1
Startup CDP	676	NA	NA	738	82.9	0.0	0.0	0.0	17.1	16.4	66.2	17.2	343	80.5	74.9	21.0
Steilacoom town	5,989	6,179	3.2	6,083	73.8	4.0	8.3	7.0	6.9	20.0	61.8	18.1	2,655	58.0	21.0	36.1
Steptoe CDP	180	NA	NA	190	95.3	0.0	0.0	4.7	0.0	15.7	66.4	17.9	89	65.2	36.0	21.3
Stevenson city	1,465	1,499	2.3	1,427	87.5	1.6	0.8	5.1	4.9	22.3	63.9	13.8	635	54.3	35.3	29.9
Sudden Valley CDP	6,441	NA	NA	6,749	84.7	0.5	0.6	5.3	8.9	18.3	62.7	19.1	2,681	77.6	10.6	55.7
Sultan city	4,651	4,769	2.5	4,715	82.3	0.0	1.1	4.1	12.5	25.5	66.6	7.8	1,706	67.2	37.1	12.7
Sumas city	1,307	1,348	3.1	1,256	81.4	0.0	1.4	1.6	15.7	24.2	64.9	10.8	436	63.5	43.1	19.3
Summit CDP	7,985	NA	NA	8,025	81.7	2.4	6.0	6.4	3.6	19.2	61.6	19.2	3,212	82.0	34.9	26.1
Summit View CDP	7,236	NA	NA	7,033	71.1	7.3	6.3	9.0	6.3	25.6	68.1	6.3	2,599	54.7	32.6	19.4
Summitview CDP	967	NA	NA	1,230	81.5	0.0	0.0	4.0	14.6	36.6	58.3	5.2	374	77.8	22.5	20.9
Sumner city	9,451	9,677	2.4	9,548	75.7	0.9	2.4	10.2	10.8	28.1	59.3	12.6	3,859	48.9	44.8	18.6
Sunday Lake CDP	640	NA	NA	802	91.3	0.0	2.0	2.1	4.6	28.2	68.3	3.5	252	80.6	19.0	48.4
Sunnyside city	15,855	16,140	1.8	16,038	15.6	0.0	0.4	1.6	82.4	36.5	55.3	8.2	4,257	54.9	72.6	10.8
Sunnyslope CDP	3,252	NA	NA	3,327	91.7	0.7	2.3	0.6	4.7	21.6	61.8	16.4	1,246	85.6	26.8	37.9
Suquamish CDP	4,140	NA	NA	4,158	74.1	0.8	3.3	17.4	4.5	20.0	63.4	16.8	1,751	73.9	26.4	31.0
Swede Heaven CDP	768	NA	NA	843	95.4	0.0	1.1	2.6	0.9	28.4	49.4	22.3	316	80.7	43.7	9.2
Tacoma city	198,397	205,159	3.4	201,794	60.5	10.1	8.6	9.7	11.0	22.2	65.6	12.3	78,761	51.1	34.9	27.8
Taholah CDP	840	NA	NA	829	6.2	1.0	0.0	87.1	5.8	28.3	59.6	12.2	239	68.6	41.0	20.5
Tampico CDP	312	NA	NA	388	95.6	0.0	0.0	4.4	0.0	22.7	70.3	7.0	136	61.8	75.7	0.0
Tanglewilde CDP	5,892	NA	NA	5,865	67.2	1.6	5.7	11.0	14.7	23.7	67.4	8.8	2,147	57.0	31.0	20.0
Tanner CDP	1,018	NA	NA	1,031	95.2	0.0	0.0	0.0	4.8	29.1	61.7	9.0	338	100.0	10.9	61.5
Tekoa city	778	784	0.8	789	83.3	0.5	0.4	5.6	10.3	24.6	50.6	24.7	331	66.5	44.7	23.3
Tenino city	1,695	1,729	2.0	1,887	89.1	0.3	1.5	3.5	5.6	26.1	64.0	9.9	701	70.8	41.7	16.8
Terrace Heights CDP	6,937	NA	NA	6,701	75.4	0.1	1.1	5.7	17.6	22.5	60.4	17.2	2,686	80.3	34.5	26.8
Thorp CDP	240	NA	NA	304	99.0	0.0	0.0	1.0	0.0	18.4	59.2	22.4	110	51.8	48.2	26.4
Three Lakes CDP	3,184	NA	NA	2,691	92.2	0.7	0.3	4.2	2.7	15.0	70.4	14.4	1,097	92.4	25.5	32.5
Tieton city	1,191	1,247	4.7	1,319	32.7	0.0	0.2	2.5	64.6	36.4	55.7	7.7	356	60.7	64.9	7.9
Tokeland CDP	151	NA	NA	181	92.8	0.0	0.0	7.2	0.0	7.2	66.3	26.5	95	70.5	65.3	0.0
Toledo city	725	721	-0.6	668	80.7	0.7	0.0	5.5	13.0	20.3	61.6	18.0	259	62.2	42.9	13.1
Tonasket city	1,032	1,018	-1.4	1,190	75.6	0.8	0.4	9.7	13.5	20.6	56.8	22.6	594	42.1	52.7	11.8
Toppenish city	8,951	8,996	0.5	9,007	9.7	0.7	0.8	7.2	81.6	37.6	55.3	7.1	2,364	52.1	70.3	8.0
Torboy CDP	49	NA	NA	128	80.5	0.0	0.0	19.5	0.0	28.1	52.3	19.5	56	87.5	0.0	0.0
Touchet CDP	421	NA	NA	491	60.9	0.0	0.8	3.7	34.6	36.3	48.9	14.9	154	56.5	41.6	13.6
Town and Country CDP	4,857	NA	NA	5,450	86.1	1.3	2.8	7.7	2.1	27.3	58.1	14.5	1,984	73.1	26.4	33.4
Tracyton CDP	5,233	NA	NA	5,909	68.3	4.5	12.3	12.6	2.3	21.8	64.3	14.0	2,246	74.5	26.3	26.5
Trout Lake CDP	557	NA	NA	464	92.5	0.0	1.1	1.5	5.0	31.3	48.8	20.0	165	78.8	17.6	44.8
Tukwila city	19,107	19,920	4.3	19,573	34.7	20.3	21.4	10.5	13.1	24.9	65.6	9.5	7,280	38.9	42.0	24.7

1 May be of any race.

Table A. All Places — **Population and Housing**

STATE City, town, township, borough, or CDP (county if applicable)	Population: 2010 census total population	Population: 2014 estimated population	Population: Percent change 2010-2014	Population: ACS total population estimate 2010-2014	Race and Hispanic or Latino origin (percent), 2010–2014: White alone, not Hispanic or Latino	Black alone, not Hispanic or Latino	Asian alone, not Hispanic or Latino	All other races or 2 or more races, not Hispanic or Latino	Hispanic or Latino[1]	Age (percent), 2010–2014: Under 18 years old	Age 18 to 64 years old	Age 65 years and older	Households, 2010–2014: Total occupied housing units	Percent owner occupied	Householders by level of education (percent): High school diploma or less	Bachelor's degree or more
	1	2	3	4	5	6	7	8	9	10	11	12	13	14	15	16
WASHINGTON—Con.																
Tumwater city	17,371	18,820	8.3	18,128	80.4	2.8	4.3	7.1	5.3	20.0	65.8	14.2	7,773	54.4	22.5	36.0
Twin Lakes CDP	59	NA	NA	117	51.3	0.0	0.0	48.7	0.0	10.3	62.4	27.4	54	92.6	50.0	11.1
Twisp town	919	937	2.0	1,027	84.6	0.2	0.0	1.4	13.8	18.7	64.5	16.7	554	56.7	44.0	22.6
Union CDP	631	NA	NA	459	100.0	0.0	0.0	0.0	0.0	0.0	44.0	56.0	265	100.0	23.4	39.6
Union Gap city	6,048	6,030	-0.3	6,061	44.2	1.1	0.6	4.6	49.5	30.4	58.4	11.1	1,981	58.6	61.3	5.5
Union Hill-Novelty Hill CDP	18,805	NA	NA	21,313	75.3	0.7	17.9	2.8	3.3	24.8	61.1	14.2	7,823	83.7	6.7	71.7
Uniontown town	294	322	9.5	455	93.2	0.0	0.0	3.1	3.7	22.4	56.3	21.3	175	82.9	36.0	18.3
University Place city	31,146	32,282	3.6	31,670	67.5	6.9	8.2	9.6	7.8	23.6	61.9	14.6	12,806	55.3	25.2	37.9
Upper Elochoman CDP	193	NA	NA	163	100.0	0.0	0.0	0.0	0.0	25.2	62.0	12.9	76	46.1	88.2	11.8
Vader city	620	614	-1.0	645	80.2	0.0	0.0	10.4	9.5	28.1	57.4	14.6	240	75.8	42.9	2.5
Valley CDP	146	NA	NA	203	96.1	0.0	0.0	0.0	3.9	28.5	69.9	1.5	80	33.8	38.8	22.5
Vancouver city	161,849	169,294	4.6	165,554	73.5	2.9	5.4	7.0	11.2	23.4	63.3	13.3	65,666	50.3	31.2	27.4
Vantage CDP	74	NA	NA	9	100.0	0.0	0.0	0.0	0.0	0.0	100.0	0.0	9	100.0	0.0	0.0
Vashon CDP	10,624	NA	NA	10,447	92.5	0.2	2.3	1.4	3.6	18.0	63.2	18.9	4,704	80.7	19.7	56.6
Vaughn CDP	544	NA	NA	498	85.3	0.6	2.0	3.0	9.0	11.4	45.3	43.2	218	100.0	41.3	16.5
Venersborg CDP	3,745	NA	NA	3,600	95.5	0.4	1.4	2.6	0.0	26.3	58.2	15.4	1,175	93.1	35.7	33.4
Verlot CDP	285	NA	NA	93	100.0	0.0	0.0	0.0	0.0	30.1	69.9	0.0	45	100.0	37.8	26.7
Waitsburg city	1,217	1,196	-1.7	1,065	96.0	0.8	0.3	2.2	0.8	24.0	58.6	17.3	445	67.6	32.4	20.0
Walla Walla city	31,731	31,910	0.6	31,895	68.7	2.4	2.3	4.2	22.3	20.7	64.5	14.8	11,614	56.8	34.1	26.4
Walla Walla East CDP	1,672	NA	NA	1,556	89.1	0.0	3.1	1.0	6.7	28.0	55.7	16.2	583	88.3	19.6	36.0
Waller CDP	7,922	NA	NA	7,681	82.9	4.2	2.6	5.7	4.6	17.1	62.8	20.2	3,145	77.5	39.5	21.2
Wallula CDP	179	NA	NA	21	100.0	0.0	0.0	0.0	0.0	0.0	0.0	100.0	11	0.0	100.0	0.0
Walnut Grove CDP	9,790	NA	NA	10,705	84.5	2.0	3.4	4.5	5.6	23.5	58.4	18.1	4,239	61.5	28.8	29.4
Wapato city	4,997	5,051	1.1	5,043	7.3	0.4	0.0	6.0	86.3	35.8	56.6	7.5	1,287	53.3	77.4	3.8
Warden city	2,692	2,749	2.1	2,734	21.4	0.0	0.0	0.8	77.8	36.7	55.0	8.3	806	60.9	63.4	5.7
Warm Beach CDP	2,437	NA	NA	2,458	88.5	0.3	0.8	5.5	4.9	16.9	67.5	15.5	971	83.0	37.3	25.3
Washougal city	14,102	14,999	6.4	14,563	88.5	0.8	2.0	4.2	4.5	25.6	62.8	11.5	5,322	69.2	28.7	26.9
Washtucna town	208	204	-1.9	238	96.6	0.0	1.3	2.1	0.0	21.4	55.8	22.7	116	83.6	49.1	12.1
Waterville town	1,138	1,161	2.0	1,822	87.3	0.0	0.2	11.6	0.9	36.5	51.9	11.7	619	53.0	53.2	7.6
Wauna CDP	4,186	NA	NA	4,392	88.3	0.3	2.7	6.8	1.9	20.8	64.7	14.5	1,635	85.7	23.2	36.9
Waverly town	106	107	0.9	101	87.1	0.0	0.0	12.9	0.0	17.9	60.3	21.8	48	93.8	35.4	20.8
Wenatchee city	32,105	33,261	3.6	32,627	64.2	0.4	0.9	3.4	31.1	27.6	57.4	15.1	11,586	56.2	41.2	24.9
West Clarkston-Highland CDP	5,261	NA	NA	5,224	92.1	0.5	0.2	2.9	4.2	20.3	60.8	19.0	2,294	65.4	43.6	20.4
West Pasco CDP	3,739	NA	NA	2,437	88.9	0.3	1.5	3.6	5.7	23.0	55.0	22.1	840	93.3	34.2	34.2
Westport city	2,079	2,018	-2.9	1,869	82.9	0.1	0.0	7.5	9.5	20.9	61.8	17.3	927	50.8	32.3	17.2
West Richland city	11,832	13,351	12.8	12,680	84.8	0.5	1.3	3.2	10.2	27.6	62.2	10.1	4,455	83.4	18.1	36.2
West Side Highway CDP	5,517	NA	NA	5,659	80.7	1.1	5.1	6.0	7.0	27.1	60.5	12.3	1,974	81.0	35.2	15.8
Whidbey Island Station CDP	1,541	NA	NA	1,882	68.6	10.5	1.5	6.8	12.6	5.7	94.2	0.0	192	0.0	39.1	6.3
White Center CDP	13,495	NA	NA	14,228	32.3	11.6	16.4	12.9	26.8	23.7	65.7	10.6	5,147	44.4	48.0	18.9
White Salmon city	2,238	2,314	3.4	2,221	69.0	0.0	1.1	0.7	29.2	22.8	60.6	16.6	899	50.9	28.4	32.0
White Swan CDP	793	NA	NA	671	3.0	0.0	0.0	86.4	10.6	43.7	51.1	5.4	157	60.5	70.7	0.0
Wilbur town	882	846	-4.1	724	85.5	0.6	0.0	11.9	2.1	19.5	49.0	31.4	367	83.7	56.9	10.6
Wilderness Rim CDP	1,523	NA	NA	1,443	92.0	0.0	1.4	4.0	2.6	17.6	75.4	6.9	607	92.9	20.4	38.4
Wilkeson town	477	486	1.9	461	95.4	0.2	0.0	1.7	2.6	26.0	64.2	9.8	183	80.3	51.4	12.0
Willapa CDP	210	NA	NA	211	100.0	0.0	0.0	0.0	0.0	18.0	58.7	23.2	90	87.8	40.0	21.1
Wilson Creek town	205	212	3.4	233	91.8	1.7	0.4	3.9	2.1	28.4	54.1	17.6	99	64.6	29.3	31.3
Winlock city	1,336	1,308	-2.1	1,728	72.3	0.0	1.3	6.3	20.0	27.6	65.9	6.5	537	55.1	48.2	8.6
Winthrop town	394	412	4.6	384	91.4	0.0	0.0	0.0	8.6	20.4	67.0	12.8	190	63.7	32.6	22.6
Wishram CDP	342	NA	NA	325	96.6	0.0	0.0	3.4	0.0	22.5	57.5	20.0	153	62.7	53.6	12.4
Wollochet CDP	6,651	NA	NA	6,332	87.0	3.3	4.0	3.4	2.3	20.6	56.6	22.8	2,485	74.7	12.7	55.7
Woodinville city	10,938	11,372	4.0	11,201	80.3	0.9	9.2	5.2	4.5	24.2	65.1	10.7	4,586	60.4	17.2	54.1
Woodland city	5,552	5,708	2.8	5,535	76.7	0.2	2.6	2.6	17.9	36.5	53.9	9.6	1,641	65.4	35.6	18.6
Woods Creek CDP	5,589	NA	NA	5,881	84.2	0.1	2.0	3.0	10.6	23.2	66.5	10.4	1,933	85.2	31.6	27.8
Woodway city	1,307	1,351	3.4	1,330	80.6	4.4	8.0	3.6	3.5	26.3	57.7	16.1	451	93.8	11.1	64.7
Yacolt town	1,566	1,657	5.8	1,876	96.7	0.0	0.0	1.7	1.6	33.4	61.3	5.3	544	77.9	54.2	5.7
Yakima city	91,276	93,357	2.3	92,806	49.6	1.0	1.1	4.2	44.0	27.5	58.9	13.7	33,023	53.8	47.5	18.6
Yarrow Point town	1,001	1,063	6.2	1,081	79.3	0.2	15.4	4.8	0.3	26.6	51.1	22.3	396	90.9	5.6	84.3
Yelm city	6,848	8,223	20.1	7,398	72.3	2.7	4.6	5.7	14.7	36.3	57.2	6.4	2,500	53.6	32.2	24.2
Zillah city	3,026	3,118	3.0	3,078	58.6	0.0	1.0	3.8	36.6	31.9	60.1	8.1	1,002	70.0	48.7	19.0
WEST VIRGINIA	1,853,033	1,850,326	-0.1	1,853,881	92.7	3.2	0.7	2.1	1.3	20.8	62.6	16.8	742,359	73.0	53.5	20.1
Accoville CDP	574	NA	NA	460	98.0	0.0	0.0	0.0	2.0	34.8	56.9	8.0	159	88.1	76.7	7.5
Addison (Webster Springs) town	772	741	-4.0	1,133	97.4	0.0	0.0	1.2	1.3	18.7	60.8	20.5	479	64.3	63.5	17.1
Albright town	299	303	1.3	295	98.0	0.7	0.0	1.4	0.0	21.3	62.0	16.6	113	70.8	73.5	1.8
Alderson town	1,184	1,184	0.0	990	93.8	4.0	0.0	1.5	0.6	22.0	53.7	24.4	469	58.8	51.8	18.8
Alum Creek CDP	1,749	NA	NA	1,832	97.4	0.0	1.7	0.5	0.4	21.1	65.1	13.7	735	76.3	45.0	19.0
Amherstdale CDP	350	NA	NA	201	64.7	27.9	0.0	7.5	0.0	29.3	61.2	9.5	80	65.0	80.0	0.0
Anawalt town	226	212	-6.2	212	92.5	7.5	0.0	0.0	0.0	28.3	60.2	11.3	77	77.9	59.7	16.9
Anmoore town	774	761	-1.7	866	86.8	11.3	0.0	0.0	1.8	31.6	60.0	8.4	317	55.8	53.3	3.8
Ansted town	1,412	1,398	-1.0	1,593	97.2	1.1	0.0	0.0	1.7	21.6	56.5	21.9	590	81.2	63.7	10.8
Apple Grove CDP	204	NA	NA	183	100.0	0.0	0.0	0.0	0.0	27.9	50.2	21.9	84	100.0	66.7	9.5
Arbovale CDP	0	NA	NA	210	100.0	0.0	0.0	0.0	0.0	27.2	62.0	11.0	93	83.9	83.9	9.7
Athens town	1,047	960	-8.3	1,062	91.1	4.4	1.1	1.7	1.6	9.2	83.8	7.0	250	51.2	17.2	32.4
Auburn town	97	93	-4.1	126	100.0	0.0	0.0	0.0	0.0	23.9	67.4	8.7	47	91.5	89.4	2.1
Aurora CDP	201	NA	NA	221	100.0	0.0	0.0	0.0	0.0	31.6	60.7	7.7	88	85.2	60.2	0.0
Bancroft town	587	595	1.4	534	100.0	0.0	0.0	0.0	0.0	16.1	67.6	16.3	227	75.3	65.6	13.2
Barboursville village	3,963	4,175	5.3	4,075	92.8	4.3	1.9	0.2	0.8	13.2	64.9	21.8	1,619	63.2	32.6	24.7
Barrackville town	1,302	1,317	1.2	1,250	93.3	4.5	0.0	2.0	0.2	23.8	56.7	19.4	515	81.6	57.1	19.4
Bartley CDP	224	NA	NA	279	100.0	0.0	0.0	0.0	0.0	12.9	64.5	22.6	110	75.5	100.0	0.0
Bartow CDP	111	NA	NA	68	100.0	0.0	0.0	0.0	0.0	0.0	75.0	25.0	40	10.0	100.0	0.0
Bath (Berkeley Springs) town	624	610	-2.2	673	94.7	1.6	1.8	0.1	1.8	23.2	57.7	19.2	327	33.9	52.3	24.8
Bayard town	290	276	-4.8	448	100.0	0.0	0.0	0.0	0.0	26.0	56.4	17.9	160	88.1	88.8	3.8
Beards Fork CDP	199	NA	NA	108	74.1	25.9	0.0	0.0	0.0	0.0	45.4	54.6	41	100.0	100.0	0.0
Beaver CDP	1,308	NA	NA	1,299	100.0	0.0	0.0	0.0	0.0	13.2	65.2	21.5	557	74.9	63.2	12.4
Beckley city	17,614	17,238	-2.1	17,529	65.8	25.6	3.9	3.9	0.8	22.2	61.8	16.0	7,439	56.0	39.9	25.8

1 May be of any race.

Table A. All Places — **Population and Housing**

STATE City, town, township, borough, or CDP (county if applicable)	2010 census total population	2014 estimated population	Percent change 2010-2014	ACS total population estimate 2010-2014	White alone, not Hispanic or Latino	Black alone, not Hispanic or Latino	Asian alone, not Hispanic or Latino	All other races or 2 or more races, not Hispanic or Latino	Hispanic or Latino[1]	Under 18 years old	Age 18 to 64 years old	Age 65 years and older	Total occupied housing units	Percent owner occupied	High school diploma or less	Bachelor's degree or more
	1	2	3	4	5	6	7	8	9	10	11	12	13	14	15	16
WEST VIRGINIA—Con.																
Beech Bottom village	523	506	-3.3	770	100.0	0.0	0.0	0.0	0.0	23.7	62.5	13.9	285	83.2	73.3	8.1
Belington town	1,921	1,944	1.2	2,145	93.7	0.0	0.0	5.7	0.6	26.2	57.5	16.4	717	78.7	67.2	8.6
Belle town	1,260	1,228	-2.5	1,256	88.3	0.4	0.2	9.7	1.4	17.0	60.5	22.6	567	65.6	47.1	14.8
Belmont city	903	903	0.0	1,118	93.5	0.0	0.0	3.5	3.0	26.2	54.9	19.0	429	65.5	50.8	17.0
Belva CDP	95	NA	NA	116	100.0	0.0	0.0	0.0	0.0	10.3	52.5	37.1	62	61.3	87.1	0.0
Benwood city	1,420	1,378	-3.0	1,286	93.5	4.7	0.0	1.1	0.7	21.7	58.7	19.8	627	56.0	51.5	9.1
Bergoo CDP	94	NA	NA	59	100.0	0.0	0.0	0.0	0.0	0.0	55.8	44.1	28	100.0	53.6	21.4
Berwind CDP	278	NA	NA	544	100.0	0.0	0.0	0.0	0.0	36.0	56.5	7.5	145	77.2	71.7	11.7
Bethany town	1,036	1,030	-0.6	1,147	84.7	8.4	2.4	0.9	3.6	6.7	86.9	6.4	188	68.1	27.1	47.3
Bethlehem village	2,499	2,444	-2.2	2,616	97.5	0.0	1.8	0.5	0.2	21.3	62.0	16.7	1,030	84.5	38.9	30.4
Beverly town	701	693	-1.1	648	94.9	2.0	0.0	3.1	0.0	26.2	66.1	7.7	276	39.5	55.4	23.9
Big Chimney CDP	627	NA	NA	372	100.0	0.0	0.0	0.0	0.0	0.0	33.3	66.7	247	88.3	57.1	19.4
Big Creek CDP	237	NA	NA	440	100.0	0.0	0.0	0.0	0.0	18.0	80.5	1.6	114	81.6	62.3	12.3
Big Sandy CDP	168	NA	NA	109	100.0	0.0	0.0	0.0	0.0	0.0	58.7	41.3	74	83.8	60.8	0.0
Birch River CDP	107	NA	NA	70	100.0	0.0	0.0	0.0	0.0	48.6	51.4	0.0	26	34.6	100.0	0.0
Blacksville town	171	180	5.3	152	100.0	0.0	0.0	0.0	0.0	32.2	56.0	11.8	55	87.3	61.8	21.8
Blennerhassett CDP	3,089	NA	NA	2,893	99.8	0.0	0.0	0.2	0.0	18.9	60.7	20.5	1,183	90.2	45.3	24.3
Bluefield city	10,443	10,448	0.0	10,465	73.5	22.7	1.3	1.0	1.5	21.6	57.9	20.6	4,495	68.1	44.5	25.2
Bluewell CDP	2,184	NA	NA	2,245	95.9	4.0	0.0	0.1	0.0	19.9	68.8	11.1	908	78.4	62.0	8.1
Boaz CDP	1,297	NA	NA	1,400	99.5	0.0	0.0	0.0	0.5	19.3	60.3	20.4	540	90.9	29.4	35.2
Bolivar town	1,039	1,054	1.4	1,162	92.9	3.8	0.0	3.4	0.0	17.5	63.0	19.5	539	65.9	40.6	38.0
Bolt CDP	548	NA	NA	628	100.0	0.0	0.0	0.0	0.0	23.0	65.8	11.3	209	100.0	48.3	27.3
Boomer CDP	615	NA	NA	926	95.1	3.1	0.4	1.3	0.0	24.2	59.4	16.4	352	72.4	61.6	6.0
Bowden CDP	9	NA	NA	0	0.0	0.0	0.0	0.0	0.0	0.0	0.0	0.0	0	0.0	0.0	0.0
Bradley CDP	2,040	NA	NA	1,905	88.1	1.6	1.5	2.9	5.9	18.9	68.5	12.6	682	60.1	45.7	25.8
Bradshaw town	336	313	-6.8	281	100.0	0.0	0.0	0.0	0.0	27.8	60.4	11.7	104	86.5	83.7	1.9
Bramwell town	364	365	0.3	413	97.3	2.7	0.0	0.0	0.0	13.5	66.3	20.3	160	81.3	61.9	10.0
Brandonville town	101	103	2.0	195	100.0	0.0	0.0	0.0	0.0	23.0	37.3	39.5	82	76.8	39.0	19.5
Brandywine CDP	218	NA	NA	158	100.0	0.0	0.0	0.0	0.0	5.7	74.6	19.6	91	49.5	86.8	0.0
Brenton CDP	249	NA	NA	159	100.0	0.0	0.0	0.0	0.0	14.5	57.2	28.3	93	100.0	72.0	28.0
Bridgeport city	8,127	8,358	2.8	8,316	91.8	2.3	1.2	3.3	1.4	20.8	61.0	18.3	3,272	78.1	22.6	48.6
Brookhaven CDP	5,171	NA	NA	5,412	93.8	2.0	0.1	0.2	3.9	21.6	67.6	10.8	2,092	78.8	43.1	28.4
Bruceton Mills town	85	86	1.2	55	100.0	0.0	0.0	0.0	0.0	12.8	78.1	9.1	23	73.9	78.3	0.0
Bruno CDP	544	NA	NA	804	92.9	0.0	0.0	0.0	7.1	22.6	63.2	14.2	231	57.6	46.3	6.5
Brush Fork CDP	1,197	NA	NA	1,309	95.6	0.0	1.9	1.8	0.7	14.4	74.7	10.8	583	72.0	49.1	27.4
Buckhannon city	5,635	5,679	0.8	5,646	92.8	2.0	0.1	1.5	3.5	18.8	67.4	13.8	1,812	57.9	53.0	28.9
Bud CDP	487	NA	NA	334	73.4	26.6	0.0	0.0	0.0	15.6	60.8	23.7	181	94.5	73.5	0.0
Buffalo town	1,236	1,255	1.5	1,295	98.9	0.0	0.0	0.5	0.6	20.4	63.8	15.7	496	85.3	68.1	9.9
Burlington CDP	182	NA	NA	205	98.0	1.0	0.0	1.0	0.0	43.0	29.7	27.3	47	36.2	57.4	12.8
Burnsville town	508	501	-1.4	523	99.4	0.0	0.0	0.6	0.0	18.2	65.1	16.8	209	62.7	64.6	3.8
Cairo town	281	271	-3.6	390	88.7	0.0	0.0	0.0	11.3	30.0	53.7	16.4	132	87.1	70.5	9.8
Camden-on-Gauley town	165	160	-3.0	140	100.0	0.0	0.0	0.0	0.0	30.7	58.6	10.7	55	81.8	74.5	9.1
Cameron city	946	915	-3.3	1,043	96.6	0.0	1.2	1.2	1.0	27.9	56.4	15.8	399	74.4	69.9	9.0
Capon Bridge town	355	359	1.1	393	98.5	0.8	0.0	0.0	0.8	34.8	50.0	15.3	181	37.0	76.2	7.7
Carolina CDP	411	NA	NA	318	100.0	0.0	0.0	0.0	0.0	6.3	69.5	24.2	124	71.0	63.7	8.9
Carpendale town	977	944	-3.4	900	99.3	0.0	0.0	0.6	0.1	13.7	64.3	22.0	367	71.4	70.0	7.9
Cass CDP	52	NA	NA	9	100.0	0.0	0.0	0.0	0.0	0.0	0.0	100.0	4	0.0	100.0	0.0
Cassville CDP	701	NA	NA	708	100.0	0.0	0.0	0.0	0.0	22.5	70.8	6.9	325	83.1	46.5	29.5
Cedar Grove town	997	966	-3.1	1,082	71.6	0.6	0.0	27.7	0.0	31.3	57.8	10.9	337	72.1	74.5	9.5
Century CDP	115	NA	NA	187	87.2	0.0	0.0	0.0	12.8	23.6	46.0	30.5	33	100.0	100.0	0.0
Ceredo city	1,446	1,395	-3.5	1,493	98.2	0.3	0.0	0.2	1.3	14.3	65.1	20.7	635	63.6	52.6	16.5
Chapmanville town	1,232	1,227	-0.4	1,242	99.0	0.0	0.0	0.0	1.0	23.6	58.1	18.3	520	41.0	62.1	7.9
Charleston city	51,347	50,404	-1.8	50,911	81.5	8.3	2.3	6.4	1.5	20.1	63.1	16.9	22,919	60.1	33.9	40.4
Charles Town city	5,262	5,706	8.4	5,464	73.8	13.4	2.3	0.9	9.6	27.0	60.7	12.2	2,033	58.5	40.5	34.7
Charlton Heights CDP	406	NA	NA	487	97.5	0.0	0.0	2.5	0.0	30.6	44.7	24.6	137	81.8	65.0	5.1
Chattaroy CDP	756	NA	NA	584	94.0	0.0	0.0	0.0	6.0	17.4	69.4	13.0	236	88.6	47.9	23.3
Chauncey CDP	283	NA	NA	255	100.0	0.0	0.0	0.0	0.0	10.6	89.4	0.0	84	100.0	52.4	47.6
Cheat Lake CDP	7,988	NA	NA	9,220	92.3	3.7	2.8	0.6	0.7	24.2	65.9	9.9	3,259	82.0	22.0	57.6
Chelyan CDP	776	NA	NA	833	88.1	2.8	0.0	9.1	0.0	20.0	52.0	28.1	379	89.7	81.3	9.0
Chesapeake town	1,554	1,522	-2.1	1,469	87.3	4.3	0.0	8.2	0.2	15.9	62.7	21.4	671	70.2	65.1	10.1
Chester city	2,588	2,527	-2.4	2,564	99.4	0.0	0.0	0.6	0.0	19.6	59.6	20.8	1,181	60.9	55.5	8.6
Clarksburg city	16,570	16,242	-2.0	16,437	92.1	3.5	0.4	2.7	1.3	21.5	63.2	15.3	6,725	64.8	45.9	22.8
Clay town	491	468	-4.7	515	97.9	0.0	0.0	1.6	0.6	17.5	59.5	23.1	225	58.7	71.6	6.7
Clearview village	565	556	-1.6	581	98.3	0.0	0.0	0.9	0.9	19.3	62.7	18.1	228	88.2	36.4	31.1
Clendenin town	1,227	1,202	-2.0	984	84.0	0.0	0.0	15.1	0.8	18.7	60.2	21.0	416	68.8	57.9	15.9
Coal City CDP	1,815	NA	NA	1,632	89.7	0.0	0.0	4.1	6.2	20.5	53.8	25.7	646	79.9	67.6	11.6
Coal Fork CDP	1,233	NA	NA	1,037	95.9	0.0	0.0	3.8	0.4	17.9	52.1	30.1	477	81.1	67.7	11.5
Comfort CDP	306	NA	NA	501	95.2	0.0	1.2	3.6	0.0	37.6	51.6	11.0	138	63.0	47.8	9.4
Corinne CDP	362	NA	NA	187	100.0	0.0	0.0	0.0	0.0	18.2	81.9	0.0	87	100.0	100.0	0.0
Covel CDP	142	NA	NA	233	100.0	0.0	0.0	0.0	0.0	30.0	32.8	37.3	85	100.0	77.6	22.4
Cowen town	533	509	-4.5	487	100.0	0.0	0.0	0.0	0.0	27.2	55.7	16.8	189	67.2	66.7	7.4
Crab Orchard CDP	2,678	NA	NA	2,644	99.4	0.0	0.0	0.0	0.6	25.1	59.7	15.3	1,100	83.6	42.1	25.9
Craigsville CDP	2,213	NA	NA	1,599	100.0	0.0	0.0	0.0	0.0	23.3	49.4	27.3	760	75.4	68.9	5.4
Cross Lanes CDP	9,995	NA	NA	11,061	91.6	3.3	1.6	1.4	2.0	25.3	63.5	11.3	4,312	69.2	41.6	30.6
Crum CDP	182	NA	NA	157	41.4	0.0	0.0	58.6	0.0	0.0	77.6	22.3	53	86.8	32.1	26.4
Crumpler CDP	204	NA	NA	280	86.8	13.2	0.0	0.0	0.0	23.9	69.0	7.1	117	88.9	63.2	29.9
Cucumber CDP	94	NA	NA	30	100.0	0.0	0.0	0.0	0.0	0.0	100.0	0.0	15	100.0	100.0	0.0
Culloden CDP	3,061	NA	NA	3,274	99.6	0.0	0.0	0.4	0.0	25.7	60.5	13.8	1,160	87.6	45.1	24.9
Dailey CDP	114	NA	NA	92	100.0	0.0	0.0	0.0	0.0	0.0	61.9	38.0	50	76.0	76.0	24.0
Daniels CDP	1,881	NA	NA	2,023	99.9	0.0	0.0	0.1	0.0	21.8	51.1	27.1	797	91.1	46.9	16.3
Danville town	691	664	-3.9	739	98.1	1.4	0.0	0.4	0.1	18.7	51.6	29.8	339	38.6	68.7	3.2
Davis town	660	651	-1.4	758	97.2	0.0	0.0	0.0	2.8	16.9	68.4	14.6	314	69.7	61.5	19.4
Davy town	420	392	-6.7	257	100.0	0.0	0.0	0.0	0.0	16.7	60.3	23.0	110	78.2	75.5	10.0
Deep Water CDP	280	NA	NA	214	100.0	0.0	0.0	0.0	0.0	35.6	37.8	26.6	91	72.5	86.8	0.0
Delbarton town	577	549	-4.9	704	99.1	0.0	0.0	0.0	0.9	30.5	58.9	10.8	263	73.8	69.2	1.9
Despard CDP	1,004	NA	NA	1,443	100.0	0.0	0.0	0.0	0.0	31.5	48.3	20.3	465	70.5	69.2	2.4
Dixie CDP	291	NA	NA	185	100.0	0.0	0.0	0.0	0.0	24.9	61.1	14.1	73	100.0	53.4	26.0
Dunbar city	7,907	7,749	-2.0	7,844	88.3	6.5	1.7	1.8	1.7	17.8	62.3	20.0	3,636	63.0	44.8	23.7
Durbin town	294	286	-2.7	252	90.5	3.6	0.0	6.0	0.0	17.1	62.4	20.6	108	79.6	77.8	5.6
East Bank town	961	944	-1.8	928	84.6	0.0	0.3	10.9	4.2	19.6	62.6	17.8	349	81.7	72.5	9.5
East Dailey CDP	557	NA	NA	452	100.0	0.0	0.0	0.0	0.0	23.9	74.5	1.5	178	89.9	54.5	0.0

1 May be of any race.

Table A. All Places — **Population and Housing**

STATE City, town, township, borough, or CDP (county if applicable)	Population: 2010 census total population	Population: 2014 estimated population	Population: Percent change 2010-2014	Population: ACS total population estimate 2010-2014	Race and Hispanic or Latino origin (percent), 2010–2014: White alone, not Hispanic or Latino	Black alone, not Hispanic or Latino	Asian alone, not Hispanic or Latino	All other races or 2 or more races, not Hispanic or Latino	Hispanic or Latino[1]	Age (percent), 2010–2014: Under 18 years old	Age 18 to 64 years old	Age 65 years and older	Households, 2010–2014: Total occupied housing units	Percent owner occupied	Householders by level of education (percent): High school diploma or less	Bachelor's degree or more
	1	2	3	4	5	6	7	8	9	10	11	12	13	14	15	16
WEST VIRGINIA—Con.																
Eccles CDP	362	NA	NA	141	100.0	0.0	0.0	0.0	0.0	0.0	56.7	43.3	118	100.0	0.0	27.1
Eleanor town	1,518	1,575	3.8	1,976	92.7	0.0	0.0	2.1	5.2	19.3	64.4	16.3	779	78.7	37.7	22.3
Elizabeth town	823	835	1.5	876	96.8	0.0	0.0	3.2	0.0	28.8	57.2	14.2	353	58.1	65.2	15.0
Elk Garden town	232	225	-3.0	204	99.5	0.5	0.0	0.0	0.0	21.5	64.7	13.7	84	45.2	86.9	2.4
Elkins city	7,197	7,286	1.2	7,241	91.1	2.7	1.3	2.7	2.2	19.8	63.1	17.1	3,034	60.3	51.6	28.0
Elkview CDP	1,222	NA	NA	1,203	88.0	0.0	0.0	11.0	1.0	24.7	55.8	19.5	428	78.0	66.6	19.9
Ellenboro town	363	348	-4.1	482	99.8	0.0	0.0	0.2	0.0	23.4	66.4	10.2	176	85.2	52.8	10.8
Enterprise CDP	961	NA	NA	786	93.1	0.0	4.1	2.8	0.0	15.0	60.6	24.3	325	80.9	58.2	9.8
Fairlea CDP	1,747	NA	NA	2,047	93.2	1.2	0.0	4.0	1.7	23.0	56.0	21.0	942	70.5	76.0	6.7
Fairmont city	18,709	18,740	0.2	18,746	88.3	8.2	0.4	1.8	1.2	19.5	64.1	16.4	7,598	67.8	42.5	25.3
Fairview town	408	413	1.2	435	99.5	0.0	0.0	0.5	0.0	24.8	51.5	23.7	168	85.1	73.8	4.2
Falling Spring town	211	209	-0.9	217	97.2	1.8	0.0	0.9	0.0	13.8	73.8	12.4	111	61.3	59.5	9.9
Falling Waters CDP	876	NA	NA	887	81.2	14.8	0.0	4.1	0.0	7.0	66.4	26.7	363	72.7	46.8	24.2
Falls View CDP	238	NA	NA	131	100.0	0.0	0.0	0.0	0.0	37.4	34.4	28.2	71	87.3	46.5	0.0
Farmington town	375	377	0.5	418	90.7	1.0	0.2	7.2	1.0	19.6	57.8	22.5	157	87.3	72.6	8.3
Fayetteville town	2,930	2,892	-1.3	2,916	93.8	0.8	0.0	5.5	0.0	19.2	62.7	18.2	1,319	78.5	33.8	31.3
Fenwick CDP	116	NA	NA	72	100.0	0.0	0.0	0.0	0.0	27.8	44.4	27.8	25	64.0	56.0	24.0
Flatwoods town	277	277	0.0	340	85.6	0.0	0.0	14.1	0.3	33.9	54.9	11.2	106	77.4	70.8	3.8
Flemington town	311	316	1.6	356	98.0	0.0	0.0	0.0	2.0	31.5	57.3	11.2	126	77.0	77.0	4.8
Follansbee city	2,986	2,911	-2.5	2,949	96.6	2.7	0.0	0.4	0.3	15.4	63.5	21.1	1,384	66.8	61.7	17.3
Fort Ashby CDP	1,380	NA	NA	1,511	100.0	0.0	0.0	0.0	0.0	21.6	60.5	18.0	721	65.0	59.9	10.7
Fort Gay town	707	684	-3.3	808	97.8	0.2	0.0	2.0	0.0	24.8	63.3	12.0	335	28.7	76.1	4.8
Frank CDP	90	NA	NA	49	100.0	0.0	0.0	0.0	0.0	32.6	49.0	18.4	28	64.3	100.0	0.0
Franklin town	723	685	-5.3	782	96.7	2.6	0.8	0.0	0.0	15.1	60.1	24.8	316	65.5	53.2	30.4
Friendly town	132	131	-0.8	71	98.6	0.0	0.0	1.4	0.0	7.0	69.0	23.9	48	62.5	41.7	0.0
Gallipolis Ferry CDP	817	NA	NA	1,077	97.7	0.0	0.0	0.0	2.3	18.1	62.9	18.9	397	56.7	73.6	0.0
Galloway CDP	143	NA	NA	191	100.0	0.0	0.0	0.0	0.0	0.0	80.6	19.4	62	66.1	61.3	19.4
Gary city	970	908	-6.4	852	78.5	17.6	0.0	3.9	0.0	15.3	53.1	31.6	304	90.8	68.8	9.5
Gassaway town	908	906	-0.2	897	96.8	0.0	2.5	0.6	0.2	19.4	59.2	21.5	406	57.1	59.9	15.5
Gauley Bridge town	614	598	-2.6	603	96.5	1.2	0.0	2.3	0.0	21.6	65.6	12.8	240	52.5	63.8	9.6
Ghent CDP	457	NA	NA	486	100.0	0.0	0.0	0.0	0.0	15.2	76.9	8.0	218	90.4	38.5	45.9
Gilbert town	446	429	-3.8	411	100.0	0.0	0.0	0.0	0.0	22.3	61.7	16.1	173	70.5	49.7	17.3
Gilbert Creek CDP	1,090	NA	NA	1,111	99.4	0.0	0.0	0.6	0.0	22.2	63.8	14.0	523	88.5	76.9	3.4
Glasgow town	903	888	-1.7	748	84.6	0.5	0.0	14.8	0.0	16.1	54.0	29.7	253	77.5	62.1	10.3
Glen Dale city	1,526	1,483	-2.8	1,627	97.2	1.8	0.3	0.4	0.3	19.3	54.9	25.9	704	75.1	39.5	34.5
Glen Ferris CDP	203	NA	NA	129	100.0	0.0	0.0	0.0	0.0	0.0	47.4	52.7	75	38.7	100.0	0.0
Glen Fork CDP	487	NA	NA	516	100.0	0.0	0.0	0.0	0.0	16.7	55.8	27.3	206	81.1	46.1	25.7
Glen Jean CDP	210	NA	NA	433	50.6	49.4	0.0	0.0	0.0	22.6	53.2	24.0	119	63.9	68.9	0.0
Glenville town	1,543	1,541	-0.1	1,906	79.4	9.7	0.0	9.3	1.6	13.7	75.8	10.4	575	39.5	27.5	25.0
Glen White CDP	266	NA	NA	495	97.6	0.0	0.0	2.4	0.0	10.7	71.5	17.8	195	56.9	61.0	39.0
Grafton city	5,164	5,199	0.7	5,179	94.6	1.1	2.1	1.1	1.1	17.1	61.5	21.3	2,198	68.9	68.5	10.3
Grantsville town	557	550	-1.3	634	95.6	0.0	0.2	0.6	3.6	21.6	55.6	22.9	249	62.7	68.3	14.1
Grant Town town	613	616	0.5	482	92.1	6.6	0.0	0.0	1.2	18.1	65.1	16.8	208	89.4	58.2	16.3
Granville town	781	2,529	223.8	1,628	98.3	0.5	0.0	1.2	0.0	17.7	67.1	15.2	653	52.7	60.9	4.9
Great Cacapon CDP	386	NA	NA	318	73.6	0.0	0.0	18.6	7.9	13.5	86.6	0.0	119	61.3	31.9	16.0
Green Bank CDP	143	NA	NA	93	100.0	0.0	0.0	0.0	0.0	30.2	48.4	21.5	31	100.0	25.8	74.2
Green Spring CDP	218	NA	NA	178	92.7	0.0	0.0	0.0	7.3	0.0	71.4	28.7	144	6.9	88.9	0.0
Greenview CDP	378	NA	NA	240	97.1	0.0	0.0	2.9	0.0	35.8	58.0	6.3	89	30.3	96.6	3.4
Gypsy CDP	328	NA	NA	386	99.2	0.8	0.0	0.0	0.0	11.7	69.4	18.9	162	87.7	57.4	33.3
Hambleton town	232	224	-3.4	271	100.0	0.0	0.0	0.0	0.0	15.5	65.6	18.8	118	76.3	76.3	9.3
Hamlin town	1,140	1,131	-0.8	1,426	99.6	0.0	0.4	0.0	0.0	20.6	59.5	19.9	544	69.5	54.0	18.0
Handley town	349	344	-1.4	284	75.4	1.4	0.0	19.7	3.5	27.1	56.0	16.9	109	73.4	59.6	5.5
Harman town	142	143	0.7	139	100.0	0.0	0.0	0.0	0.0	25.1	63.4	11.5	51	60.8	62.7	13.7
Harpers Ferry town	287	293	2.1	231	92.2	2.6	0.0	5.2	0.0	8.6	68.0	23.4	133	83.5	11.3	67.7
Harrisville town	1,875	1,786	-4.7	2,194	98.1	0.4	0.0	1.0	0.4	22.4	61.1	16.5	791	71.9	58.4	16.3
Hartford City town	612	601	-1.8	651	98.5	0.9	0.0	0.6	0.0	23.0	62.6	14.6	263	76.4	67.7	0.0
Harts CDP	656	NA	NA	656	87.0	4.0	2.0	7.0	0.0	15.9	66.6	17.5	261	75.1	69.0	9.6
Hedgesville town	311	320	2.9	270	89.6	2.6	0.7	1.9	5.2	18.9	74.5	6.7	98	61.2	36.7	12.2
Helen CDP	219	NA	NA	112	100.0	0.0	0.0	0.0	0.0	0.0	100.0	0.0	50	0.0	100.0	0.0
Helvetia CDP	59	NA	NA	33	100.0	0.0	0.0	0.0	0.0	0.0	24.2	75.8	15	100.0	0.0	100.0
Henderson town	270	268	-0.7	175	100.0	0.0	0.0	0.0	0.0	21.7	51.4	26.9	70	65.7	62.9	5.7
Hendricks town	272	265	-2.6	270	97.0	0.0	0.0	0.0	3.0	7.4	64.3	28.1	116	85.3	73.3	4.3
Henlawson CDP	442	NA	NA	239	100.0	0.0	0.0	0.0	0.0	20.1	53.2	26.8	74	100.0	100.0	0.0
Hepzibah CDP	566	NA	NA	596	100.0	0.0	0.0	0.0	0.0	13.9	64.7	21.3	223	69.1	79.8	13.5
Hico CDP	272	NA	NA	117	100.0	0.0	0.0	0.0	0.0	0.0	91.4	8.5	30	100.0	33.3	66.7
Hillsboro town	257	256	-0.4	403	89.6	4.2	0.0	4.0	2.2	15.4	73.2	11.4	119	62.2	63.9	11.8
Hilltop CDP	624	NA	NA	609	98.7	0.0	0.0	1.3	0.0	21.2	52.7	26.1	190	77.4	65.3	11.1
Hinton city	2,676	2,556	-4.5	2,615	87.2	8.9	0.0	1.2	2.7	13.9	53.5	32.6	1,328	70.0	62.1	16.7
Holden CDP	876	NA	NA	701	88.4	11.6	0.0	0.0	0.0	29.6	59.6	10.8	239	72.0	57.7	12.1
Hometown CDP	668	NA	NA	477	100.0	0.0	0.0	0.0	0.0	11.8	59.2	28.9	197	84.3	68.5	5.6
Hooverson Heights CDP	2,590	NA	NA	2,601	98.5	0.2	0.2	1.0	0.1	20.1	54.3	25.5	989	82.4	59.7	13.7
Hundred town	299	289	-3.3	284	95.4	0.0	0.0	1.8	2.8	12.7	71.9	15.5	116	78.4	59.5	9.5
Huntersville CDP	73	NA	NA	160	100.0	0.0	0.0	0.0	0.0	21.9	70.7	7.5	65	100.0	63.1	0.0
Huntington city	49,135	48,807	-0.7	49,053	85.9	8.0	1.1	3.9	1.2	18.1	67.2	14.8	21,148	51.6	37.9	29.5
Hurricane city	6,279	6,396	1.9	6,352	96.6	0.0	0.3	1.8	1.3	24.4	61.9	13.5	2,407	75.9	40.8	27.2
Huttonsville town	221	221	0.0	767	93.7	6.3	0.0	0.0	0.0	10.3	84.7	5.0	91	64.8	74.7	12.1
Iaeger town	305	283	-7.2	281	98.9	0.0	0.0	1.1	0.0	18.1	55.9	26.0	114	86.0	75.4	0.0
Idamay CDP	611	NA	NA	276	100.0	0.0	0.0	0.0	0.0	18.9	51.8	29.3	116	84.5	35.3	10.3
Inwood CDP	2,954	NA	NA	2,222	77.0	15.1	2.9	3.7	1.3	21.2	68.2	10.7	856	86.3	65.8	16.2
Itmann CDP	293	NA	NA	349	100.0	0.0	0.0	0.0	0.0	26.3	70.2	3.4	109	67.9	48.6	0.0
Jacksonburg CDP	182	NA	NA	93	100.0	0.0	0.0	0.0	0.0	0.0	64.5	35.5	51	100.0	82.4	0.0
Jane Lew town	405	408	0.7	470	100.0	0.0	0.0	0.0	0.0	23.3	64.1	12.6	211	53.6	62.6	22.3
Jefferson CDP	676	NA	NA	792	76.3	10.6	0.0	11.7	1.4	26.2	54.8	19.1	253	31.2	54.9	6.7
Junior town	520	508	-2.3	503	98.2	0.0	0.0	1.8	0.0	21.5	65.6	13.1	187	71.1	79.7	6.4
Justice CDP	412	NA	NA	369	100.0	0.0	0.0	0.0	0.0	23.9	59.4	16.8	139	100.0	82.7	0.0
Kenova city	3,216	3,096	-3.7	3,151	98.5	0.0	0.0	1.5	0.0	20.1	57.9	22.1	1,424	70.8	62.7	6.7
Kermit town	402	387	-3.7	281	95.4	0.0	0.0	0.0	4.6	14.6	70.6	14.6	126	78.6	55.6	15.1
Keyser city	5,434	5,264	-3.1	5,350	82.1	9.2	0.3	7.7	0.7	21.5	59.2	19.3	2,201	46.4	54.8	19.1
Keystone city	282	259	-8.2	246	37.8	58.9	0.0	3.3	0.0	30.8	48.3	20.7	80	76.3	72.5	0.0
Kimball town	194	182	-6.2	201	42.8	48.8	0.0	5.0	3.5	23.9	62.8	13.4	72	79.2	68.1	13.9
Kimberly CDP	287	NA	NA	296	94.9	5.1	0.0	0.0	0.0	10.1	67.2	22.6	158	100.0	69.6	7.6

1 May be of any race.

Table A. All Places — **Population and Housing**

STATE City, town, township, borough, or CDP (county if applicable)	2010 census total population	2014 estimated population	Percent change 2010-2014	ACS total population estimate 2010-2014	White alone, not Hispanic or Latino	Black alone, not Hispanic or Latino	Asian alone, not Hispanic or Latino	All other races or 2 or more races, not Hispanic or Latino	Hispanic or Latino[1]	Under 18 years old	Age 18 to 64 years old	Age 65 years and older	Total occupied housing units	Percent owner occupied	High school diploma or less	Bachelor's degree or more
	1	2	3	4	5	6	7	8	9	10	11	12	13	14	15	16
WEST VIRGINIA—Con.																
Kincaid CDP	260	NA	NA	404	93.3	0.0	0.0	0.0	6.7	50.0	33.2	16.8	110	74.5	82.7	1.8
Kingwood city	2,939	2,956	0.6	2,953	93.4	2.9	0.0	3.1	0.5	22.0	61.2	16.7	1,252	67.7	49.3	20.5
Kistler CDP	528	NA	NA	515	100.0	0.0	0.0	0.0	0.0	19.2	71.3	9.5	252	64.7	61.9	9.5
Kopperston CDP	616	NA	NA	546	95.6	0.0	0.0	4.4	0.0	20.8	77.1	2.0	210	69.5	42.9	9.5
Lashmeet CDP	479	NA	NA	390	100.0	0.0	0.0	0.0	0.0	19.0	58.3	22.8	159	83.0	91.8	0.0
Lavalette CDP	1,073	NA	NA	1,171	97.2	0.0	0.0	2.8	0.0	32.2	54.4	13.2	436	77.3	54.8	21.1
Leon town	158	157	-0.6	114	100.0	0.0	0.0	0.0	0.0	27.2	56.9	15.8	50	86.0	84.0	4.0
Lesage CDP	1,358	NA	NA	1,587	91.9	2.5	1.4	4.2	0.0	16.5	55.4	28.3	738	69.5	56.9	18.8
Lester town	344	333	-3.2	350	82.0	12.6	0.0	3.1	2.3	24.9	63.0	12.0	138	76.1	68.1	9.4
Lewisburg city	3,830	3,939	2.8	3,917	87.0	5.7	2.9	3.1	1.2	15.9	62.7	21.4	1,929	62.4	23.6	55.8
Littleton CDP	198	NA	NA	172	100.0	0.0	0.0	0.0	0.0	63.4	29.7	7.0	45	64.4	73.3	26.7
Logan city	1,779	1,682	-5.5	1,896	92.7	4.9	0.6	0.9	0.9	18.9	66.4	14.6	830	49.4	49.8	10.6
Lost Creek town	493	482	-2.2	475	95.4	0.8	0.0	1.3	2.5	24.2	58.2	17.5	165	75.2	41.8	21.2
Lubeck CDP	1,311	NA	NA	1,304	96.9	0.0	0.0	3.1	0.0	18.2	66.1	15.7	565	84.2	40.0	25.3
Lumberport town	879	871	-0.9	1,052	90.8	0.0	0.0	2.2	7.0	25.8	58.9	15.4	438	72.6	51.6	9.8
Mabscott town	1,408	1,388	-1.4	1,395	87.1	8.8	0.0	2.5	1.6	21.6	60.9	17.5	574	82.1	53.7	21.8
MacArthur CDP	1,500	NA	NA	1,610	98.8	0.6	0.0	0.6	0.0	20.0	63.0	17.1	736	76.2	60.3	19.2
McConnell CDP	514	NA	NA	610	100.0	0.0	0.0	0.0	0.0	28.5	39.1	32.5	237	96.2	31.2	32.5
McMechen city	1,926	1,866	-3.1	1,686	98.5	0.0	0.0	1.3	0.2	20.6	62.2	17.1	774	73.4	54.4	14.1
Madison city	3,076	2,968	-3.5	3,021	93.4	5.4	0.0	0.8	0.4	23.7	61.8	14.5	1,224	68.7	49.4	19.6
Mallory CDP	1,654	NA	NA	1,183	99.3	0.0	0.0	0.0	0.7	13.7	69.1	17.1	520	90.6	68.7	7.7
Man town	758	718	-5.3	1,050	96.5	0.5	2.2	0.9	0.0	19.8	64.8	15.2	457	77.2	37.9	14.7
Mannington city	2,063	2,072	0.4	1,961	94.4	0.0	0.0	5.4	0.2	29.4	51.8	18.7	714	77.5	60.1	13.0
Marlinton town	1,059	1,043	-1.5	1,039	92.7	3.7	0.0	3.2	0.5	15.6	60.4	24.1	457	58.6	61.7	17.1
Marmet city	1,503	1,469	-2.3	1,641	92.3	0.5	0.0	6.9	0.2	15.5	60.4	24.1	666	65.6	63.8	12.3
Martinsburg city	17,227	17,743	3.0	17,508	74.1	13.4	0.9	5.6	6.0	24.9	62.0	13.0	7,048	51.5	51.1	18.1
Mason city	966	946	-2.1	1,059	91.5	3.3	0.0	5.2	0.0	12.5	58.6	29.0	504	81.2	67.9	10.3
Masontown town	546	547	0.2	777	100.0	0.0	0.0	0.0	0.0	29.0	60.2	10.8	297	74.7	63.3	10.4
Matewan town	501	476	-5.0	680	88.7	3.8	0.0	0.3	7.2	20.7	66.6	12.5	331	45.9	74.6	15.1
Matheny CDP	531	NA	NA	422	97.9	0.0	0.0	2.1	0.0	4.5	77.6	18.0	192	96.4	86.5	0.0
Matoaka town	223	222	-0.4	252	96.8	0.0	0.0	3.2	0.0	21.1	61.0	17.9	95	52.6	88.4	4.2
Maybeury CDP	234	NA	NA	238	79.8	20.2	0.0	0.0	0.0	8.4	85.3	6.3	103	78.6	39.8	42.7
Meadow Bridge town	379	365	-3.7	383	96.3	0.0	0.0	0.8	2.9	30.3	53.7	15.9	140	84.3	81.4	6.4
Middlebourne town	812	803	-1.1	890	97.6	1.2	0.0	0.3	0.8	21.5	55.7	22.8	373	65.4	59.0	11.0
Middleway CDP	441	NA	NA	422	92.4	7.6	0.0	0.0	0.0	16.4	63.1	20.6	206	84.0	63.1	36.9
Mill Creek town	724	715	-1.2	796	100.0	0.0	0.0	0.0	0.0	20.4	64.7	14.8	315	73.7	75.6	7.0
Milton town	2,413	2,631	9.0	2,507	97.5	0.8	0.4	1.2	0.0	13.9	66.5	19.6	1,206	62.5	58.6	19.2
Minden CDP	250	NA	NA	441	98.6	0.0	0.0	1.4	0.0	10.4	68.9	20.6	160	61.9	96.3	0.0
Mineralwells CDP	1,950	NA	NA	1,441	95.4	0.4	0.0	4.2	0.0	20.3	63.5	16.3	601	76.9	41.6	25.0
Mitchell Heights town	323	312	-3.4	447	91.3	0.0	4.0	3.8	0.9	11.6	57.5	30.9	208	95.7	22.1	37.5
Monaville CDP	309	NA	NA	182	96.2	0.0	0.0	0.0	3.8	26.3	39.5	34.1	86	64.0	100.0	0.0
Monongah town	1,047	1,070	2.2	1,029	94.8	2.5	0.0	2.4	0.3	20.1	64.8	15.1	459	82.8	54.7	8.1
Montcalm CDP	726	NA	NA	494	100.0	0.0	0.0	0.0	0.0	4.3	82.6	13.0	240	81.7	62.9	6.3
Montgomery city	1,638	1,607	-1.9	1,833	71.7	16.0	0.9	9.9	1.6	14.8	71.0	14.2	656	46.2	47.4	18.6
Montrose town	158	158	0.0	169	100.0	0.0	0.0	0.0	0.0	17.2	73.3	9.5	71	95.8	69.0	16.9
Moorefield town	2,555	2,505	-2.0	2,532	71.2	16.2	0.4	3.0	9.2	14.2	68.3	17.6	1,078	52.2	67.5	8.3
Morgantown city	28,827	31,073	7.8	30,133	85.0	5.6	4.2	2.6	2.6	8.4	82.8	8.7	10,055	41.6	19.5	45.0
Moundsville city	9,066	8,891	-1.9	8,960	95.7	1.2	0.8	0.8	1.4	17.6	62.7	19.7	4,105	69.5	58.9	13.9
Mount Carbon CDP	428	NA	NA	369	93.2	0.0	0.0	6.8	0.0	20.6	57.8	21.7	180	93.3	37.8	11.1
Mount Gay-Shamrock CDP	1,779	NA	NA	1,522	97.2	1.6	0.0	0.0	1.2	17.2	66.9	15.9	657	68.2	65.1	8.8
Mount Hope city	1,408	1,370	-2.7	1,384	79.3	17.4	0.0	2.5	0.9	27.1	63.9	9.0	561	49.2	54.5	6.1
Mullens city	1,570	1,494	-4.8	2,020	91.3	1.8	0.2	6.1	0.5	23.4	63.7	12.9	818	80.2	43.9	27.6
Neibert CDP	183	NA	NA	160	100.0	0.0	0.0	0.0	0.0	10.6	84.4	5.0	61	77.0	100.0	0.0
Nettie CDP	568	NA	NA	874	100.0	0.0	0.0	0.0	0.0	9.0	67.7	23.3	372	96.0	53.8	9.1
Newburg town	326	322	-1.2	325	97.5	0.0	0.9	0.6	0.9	19.7	66.7	13.5	118	83.1	73.7	11.0
New Cumberland city	1,103	1,076	-2.4	1,154	99.9	0.0	0.0	0.1	0.0	18.9	66.1	14.8	528	56.6	77.1	7.6
Newell CDP	1,376	NA	NA	1,156	90.9	9.1	0.0	0.0	0.0	22.9	48.9	28.2	486	73.5	77.2	7.4
New Haven town	1,555	1,536	-1.2	1,414	98.2	0.0	0.0	1.8	0.0	18.2	57.9	23.9	616	87.8	58.1	10.4
New Martinsville city	5,366	5,254	-2.1	5,322	96.8	0.2	1.1	0.6	1.3	24.2	54.2	21.5	2,166	75.2	57.0	15.3
New Richmond CDP	238	NA	NA	315	100.0	0.0	0.0	0.0	0.0	18.4	61.3	20.3	105	68.6	83.8	0.0
Nitro city	6,936	6,837	-1.4	6,860	97.5	0.6	0.1	1.5	0.3	18.9	63.9	17.3	3,110	69.3	50.7	18.2
Northfork town	427	394	-7.7	358	46.4	53.6	0.0	0.0	0.0	27.4	54.9	17.9	147	76.9	70.1	11.6
North Hills town	832	827	-0.6	826	97.2	1.6	1.2	0.0	0.0	26.2	57.4	16.3	307	90.6	12.7	59.3
Nutter Fort town	1,593	1,572	-1.3	1,388	89.3	4.1	0.8	4.4	1.4	20.8	57.8	21.5	663	64.3	40.1	22.2
Oak Hill city	8,330	8,175	-1.9	8,270	90.0	7.7	0.0	1.1	1.2	24.4	59.9	15.6	3,165	70.4	59.0	18.2
Oakvale town	117	118	0.9	151	100.0	0.0	0.0	0.0	0.0	15.9	64.9	19.2	54	70.4	90.7	5.6
Oceana town	1,394	1,326	-4.9	1,452	96.3	0.0	0.0	2.0	1.7	20.4	61.8	17.8	595	84.4	75.6	6.1
Omar CDP	552	NA	NA	571	100.0	0.0	0.0	0.0	0.0	11.9	73.2	15.1	264	85.6	59.8	0.0
Paden City city	2,633	2,540	-3.5	2,528	97.9	0.4	0.0	1.2	0.4	21.5	57.0	21.5	1,172	75.6	65.6	11.2
Page CDP	224	NA	NA	254	98.4	1.6	0.0	0.0	0.0	34.6	55.9	9.4	91	69.2	48.4	0.0
Pageton CDP	187	NA	NA	48	100.0	0.0	0.0	0.0	0.0	10.4	12.5	77.1	37	100.0	100.0	0.0
Parcoal CDP	0	NA	NA	55	100.0	0.0	0.0	0.0	0.0	0.0	80.0	20.0	31	100.0	100.0	0.0
Parkersburg city	31,381	30,981	-1.3	31,195	94.4	1.6	0.4	2.8	0.9	20.6	61.1	18.1	13,314	60.8	50.8	16.9
Parsons city	1,473	1,427	-3.1	1,390	98.8	0.0	0.4	0.8	0.0	23.5	54.9	21.7	612	73.5	60.5	17.8
Paw Paw town	508	494	-2.8	506	93.9	0.8	0.6	0.8	4.0	30.1	50.7	19.2	185	60.5	71.4	0.0
Pax town	167	164	-1.8	201	92.0	0.0	0.0	0.0	8.0	26.9	55.2	17.9	80	81.3	57.5	0.0
Pea Ridge CDP	6,650	NA	NA	6,321	90.5	2.0	3.9	1.7	1.9	18.5	61.2	20.3	2,817	60.7	29.1	41.7
Pennsboro city	1,142	1,085	-5.0	1,244	97.3	0.0	0.0	0.2	2.6	19.8	63.5	16.8	481	69.6	63.8	14.1
Pentress CDP	175	NA	NA	274	100.0	0.0	0.0	0.0	0.0	29.2	60.1	10.6	89	53.9	43.8	0.0
Petersburg city	2,404	2,451	2.0	2,032	95.0	3.6	0.0	0.0	1.3	21.8	56.4	21.8	970	56.6	64.1	18.9
Peterstown town	651	650	-0.2	442	100.0	0.0	0.0	0.0	0.0	19.7	59.4	20.8	222	66.7	59.9	18.0
Philippi city	2,963	3,233	9.1	3,131	94.7	1.6	1.9	1.2	0.6	16.3	65.9	17.9	1,273	52.7	49.1	26.3
Pickens CDP	66	NA	NA	32	100.0	0.0	0.0	0.0	0.0	0.0	0.0	100.0	24	33.3	100.0	0.0
Piedmont town	876	844	-3.7	867	75.3	19.0	0.0	5.0	0.7	20.2	66.1	13.7	306	48.0	83.0	2.3
Pinch CDP	3,262	NA	NA	2,783	91.2	0.0	0.0	8.8	0.0	19.4	65.3	15.2	1,159	68.8	45.0	37.4
Pine Grove town	552	525	-4.9	708	99.2	0.0	0.0	0.8	0.0	30.4	58.0	11.6	271	62.0	67.5	8.9
Pineville town	668	639	-4.3	692	97.3	2.2	0.0	0.1	0.0	15.4	59.7	24.9	292	62.3	39.7	14.4
Piney View CDP	989	NA	NA	1,003	100.0	0.0	0.0	0.0	0.0	14.2	63.0	23.0	460	84.6	65.9	13.9
Pleasant Valley city	3,149	3,185	1.1	3,175	96.9	0.5	0.0	1.6	1.0	18.7	61.7	19.7	1,374	76.3	41.8	36.2
Poca town	972	990	1.9	1,048	98.0	0.7	0.5	0.0	0.9	17.8	62.2	20.0	433	84.3	55.4	18.9

1 May be of any race.

Table A. All Places — Population and Housing

STATE City, town, township, borough, or CDP (county if applicable)	Population 2010 census total population	2014 estimated population	Percent change 2010-2014	ACS total population estimate 2010-2014	White alone, not Hispanic or Latino	Black alone, not Hispanic or Latino	Asian alone, not Hispanic or Latino	All other races or 2 or more races, not Hispanic or Latino	Hispanic or Latino[1]	Under 18 years old	Age 18 to 64 years old	Age 65 years and older	Total occupied housing units	Percent owner occupied	High school diploma or less	Bachelor's degree or more
	1	2	3	4	5	6	7	8	9	10	11	12	13	14	15	16
WEST VIRGINIA—Con.																
Point Pleasant city	4,347	4,284	-1.4	4,326	95.4	1.7	0.0	1.3	1.6	22.9	53.6	23.3	1,998	68.0	55.7	15.0
Powellton CDP	619	NA	NA	533	97.4	2.6	0.0	0.0	0.0	29.6	54.2	16.3	175	62.3	67.4	0.0
Pratt town	602	590	-2.0	532	93.6	0.8	0.0	5.6	0.0	20.6	56.9	22.4	209	72.2	39.2	21.1
Prichard CDP	527	NA	NA	408	100.0	0.0	0.0	0.0	0.0	10.8	63.8	25.2	177	79.1	67.2	8.5
Prince CDP	116	NA	NA	119	100.0	0.0	0.0	0.0	0.0	22.7	77.3	0.0	53	26.4	26.4	22.6
Princeton city	6,379	6,359	-0.3	6,387	86.8	6.7	0.7	3.3	2.6	20.7	55.0	24.2	2,868	62.4	57.8	19.7
Prosperity CDP	1,498	NA	NA	1,745	99.9	0.1	0.0	0.0	0.0	20.1	67.1	12.8	723	74.0	62.7	10.9
Pullman town	154	148	-3.9	195	95.4	0.0	0.0	4.6	0.0	17.9	62.5	19.5	80	53.8	61.3	2.5
Quinwood town	290	288	-0.7	243	98.8	0.0	0.0	1.2	0.0	18.9	65.8	15.2	106	75.5	66.0	4.7
Rachel CDP	248	NA	NA	283	95.4	0.0	4.6	0.0	0.0	27.1	64.2	8.5	115	100.0	87.0	13.0
Racine CDP	256	NA	NA	219	100.0	0.0	0.0	0.0	0.0	18.3	72.1	9.6	134	91.0	59.7	13.4
Rainelle town	1,486	1,477	-0.6	1,517	94.6	1.3	0.0	2.5	1.6	18.6	59.9	21.4	624	64.6	74.4	8.5
Rand CDP	1,631	NA	NA	1,164	71.3	21.6	0.0	7.0	0.0	22.5	65.6	11.9	532	54.1	56.8	8.1
Ranson corporation	4,399	4,830	9.8	4,602	59.5	14.5	4.5	3.1	18.4	28.0	64.7	7.4	1,712	62.1	45.9	21.3
Ravenswood city	3,868	3,834	-0.9	3,853	96.0	0.0	0.0	4.0	0.0	24.2	55.2	20.7	1,589	55.6	45.3	26.7
Raysal CDP	465	NA	NA	558	94.4	0.0	0.0	5.6	0.0	26.9	61.9	11.3	178	70.2	95.5	0.0
Reader CDP	397	NA	NA	436	100.0	0.0	0.0	0.0	0.0	22.7	57.1	20.2	175	97.7	69.1	2.3
Red Jacket CDP	581	NA	NA	631	84.8	8.2	0.0	7.0	0.0	22.2	56.1	21.7	293	76.1	69.3	14.0
Reedsville town	591	600	1.5	518	100.0	0.0	0.0	0.0	0.0	22.2	59.4	18.5	218	73.4	59.6	16.5
Reedy town	182	177	-2.7	165	97.0	0.0	0.0	3.0	0.0	19.4	66.0	14.5	60	88.3	56.7	11.7
Rhodell town	173	172	-0.6	188	98.4	1.6	0.0	0.0	0.0	21.9	64.9	13.3	71	71.8	69.0	7.0
Richwood city	2,051	2,001	-2.4	2,267	93.4	0.0	1.6	4.2	0.7	24.8	51.2	23.9	891	73.3	60.0	17.6
Ridgeley town	675	649	-3.9	694	98.4	0.0	1.0	0.6	0.0	24.0	56.1	20.0	279	49.8	76.0	7.9
Ripley city	3,249	3,242	-0.2	3,259	98.6	0.0	0.0	1.4	0.0	21.4	52.8	25.8	1,447	60.9	39.5	18.2
Rivesville town	934	943	1.0	1,095	90.8	8.9	0.0	0.0	0.3	30.6	55.9	13.6	396	70.2	47.2	28.5
Robinette CDP	663	NA	NA	624	94.1	0.0	0.0	5.9	0.0	25.0	71.3	3.7	215	79.1	73.5	3.7
Roderfield CDP	188	NA	NA	66	100.0	0.0	0.0	0.0	0.0	15.2	37.9	47.0	43	100.0	58.1	41.9
Romney city	1,848	1,788	-3.2	2,137	93.7	3.9	0.0	0.5	1.9	19.4	56.3	24.3	920	40.4	62.6	14.7
Ronceverte city	1,764	1,753	-0.6	1,644	93.8	4.1	0.0	1.3	0.8	17.4	62.1	20.5	762	67.8	60.4	13.3
Rossmore CDP	301	NA	NA	434	97.5	0.0	0.0	0.0	2.5	18.9	62.3	18.7	143	83.9	58.0	0.0
Rowlesburg town	580	581	0.2	814	99.0	0.2	0.0	0.7	0.0	25.6	58.3	16.2	287	72.1	78.7	9.1
Rupert town	942	932	-1.1	993	92.2	0.7	0.0	2.4	4.6	21.7	60.1	18.2	434	56.9	69.4	7.6
St. Albans city	11,039	10,835	-1.8	10,939	92.8	3.2	0.7	2.6	0.7	19.1	60.6	20.3	4,940	69.9	46.8	23.3
St. George CDP	0	NA	NA	108	100.0	0.0	0.0	0.0	0.0	13.0	76.8	10.2	54	88.9	61.1	7.4
St. Marys city	1,860	1,860	0.0	1,910	99.0	0.1	0.0	0.4	0.5	15.5	64.9	19.6	793	81.6	51.6	17.0
Salem city	1,586	1,557	-1.8	1,861	93.3	3.3	0.2	1.6	1.6	23.4	62.7	13.9	628	67.0	52.1	18.5
Salt Rock CDP	388	NA	NA	702	100.0	0.0	0.0	0.0	0.0	15.2	64.4	20.2	262	85.9	77.1	5.7
Sand Fork town	158	156	-1.3	191	92.1	0.0	0.0	7.9	0.0	35.1	52.9	12.0	59	79.7	59.3	16.9
Sarah Ann CDP	345	NA	NA	288	100.0	0.0	0.0	0.0	0.0	33.7	56.7	9.7	135	91.9	74.1	0.0
Scarbro CDP	486	NA	NA	380	87.1	6.6	0.0	6.3	0.0	11.8	72.0	16.3	172	95.3	75.0	11.0
Shady Spring CDP	2,998	NA	NA	3,078	95.0	0.0	0.1	1.9	3.0	24.7	57.9	17.4	1,308	75.1	50.8	24.9
Shannondale CDP	3,358	NA	NA	3,295	87.9	1.8	0.9	4.0	5.4	29.5	64.3	6.2	1,244	85.0	31.6	24.4
Shenandoah Junction CDP	703	NA	NA	632	89.1	5.4	0.0	5.5	0.0	27.5	67.7	4.7	189	73.0	48.1	18.0
Shepherdstown town	2,149	2,095	-2.5	1,632	76.2	11.7	2.3	4.9	4.9	3.8	87.7	8.5	357	30.3	23.8	51.0
Shinnston city	2,203	2,178	-1.1	2,476	96.8	0.0	3.0	0.0	0.2	19.9	60.1	20.0	1,032	73.4	57.8	14.6
Shrewsbury CDP	652	NA	NA	745	82.8	0.0	0.0	17.2	0.0	17.0	58.4	24.4	271	74.9	62.7	0.0
Sissonville CDP	4,028	NA	NA	5,017	92.9	0.0	0.0	7.0	0.1	23.5	61.1	15.4	2,106	85.9	40.2	28.1
Sistersville city	1,396	1,375	-1.5	1,583	98.9	0.4	0.1	0.6	0.0	24.7	59.9	15.3	620	71.0	60.3	12.4
Smithers city	813	793	-2.5	987	83.9	11.0	0.0	4.2	0.9	22.7	59.8	17.4	415	53.0	58.6	4.1
Smithfield town	166	161	-3.0	166	100.0	0.0	0.0	0.0	0.0	30.7	66.1	3.0	63	65.1	88.9	0.0
Sophia town	1,344	1,331	-1.0	1,337	94.8	1.6	0.0	3.7	0.0	20.5	66.9	12.6	533	62.1	63.8	9.9
South Charleston city	13,508	13,214	-2.2	13,380	89.7	4.0	0.3	5.4	0.5	18.7	60.4	20.9	6,293	69.0	36.3	32.0
Spelter CDP	346	NA	NA	519	96.0	0.0	0.0	0.0	4.0	34.9	49.1	16.0	223	69.5	71.7	10.8
Spencer city	2,306	2,234	-3.1	2,303	95.2	0.2	0.1	0.8	3.8	22.4	56.2	21.3	997	56.2	67.8	12.7
Springfield CDP	477	NA	NA	547	100.0	0.0	0.0	0.0	0.0	19.0	74.6	6.4	235	67.7	84.3	0.0
Stanaford CDP	1,350	NA	NA	1,629	88.5	4.9	0.6	6.1	0.0	21.6	57.8	20.6	622	89.4	48.1	17.2
Star City town	1,814	1,917	5.7	1,888	84.9	7.0	5.7	2.2	0.2	13.4	72.1	14.5	817	44.1	26.4	45.4
Stollings CDP	316	NA	NA	452	80.3	0.0	0.0	19.7	0.0	26.9	52.7	20.4	190	79.5	38.9	0.0
Stonewood city	1,806	1,772	-1.9	1,962	91.9	1.8	0.0	3.7	2.5	20.2	57.0	22.9	834	77.7	61.0	12.2
Summersville city	3,575	3,513	-1.7	3,549	99.9	0.1	0.0	0.0	0.0	16.3	66.1	17.6	1,587	67.2	56.8	18.8
Sutton town	994	988	-0.6	1,191	96.6	1.3	0.0	0.9	1.2	20.8	58.6	20.6	490	63.1	55.7	19.2
Switzer CDP	595	NA	NA	601	95.5	0.0	0.0	0.0	4.5	9.6	81.3	9.2	287	65.5	60.3	4.2
Sylvester town	160	154	-3.8	122	99.2	0.0	0.0	0.8	0.0	19.6	59.8	20.5	49	81.6	69.4	14.3
Teays Valley CDP	13,175	NA	NA	13,461	92.1	4.3	1.4	1.6	0.6	24.2	58.4	17.4	5,286	80.5	26.9	41.5
Terra Alta town	1,477	1,490	0.9	1,676	98.2	0.4	0.0	0.5	0.9	23.0	67.6	9.3	637	63.9	60.1	9.4
Thomas city	586	564	-3.8	573	93.5	1.0	0.0	3.7	1.7	15.0	47.1	37.9	263	71.1	63.9	9.1
Thurmond town	5	5	0.0	7	100.0	0.0	0.0	0.0	0.0	0.0	100.0	0.0	4	100.0	0.0	50.0
Tioga CDP	98	NA	NA	66	100.0	0.0	0.0	0.0	0.0	0.0	62.2	37.9	25	100.0	100.0	0.0
Tornado CDP	0	NA	NA	1,287	94.3	0.0	0.0	5.7	0.0	26.0	61.0	13.0	480	88.3	30.6	34.4
Triadelphia town	804	780	-3.0	779	98.7	1.3	0.0	0.0	0.0	17.5	63.7	18.9	348	67.0	65.2	7.8
Tunnelton town	294	298	1.4	333	96.7	0.6	0.0	0.0	2.7	21.9	65.4	12.6	112	80.4	67.9	6.3
Twilight CDP	90	NA	NA	151	100.0	0.0	0.0	0.0	0.0	38.5	61.6	0.0	54	66.7	92.6	0.0
Union town	565	563	-0.4	647	70.9	11.7	0.0	14.4	2.9	28.2	47.4	24.3	285	61.1	52.3	22.8
Valley Bend CDP	485	NA	NA	472	100.0	0.0	0.0	0.0	0.0	38.6	47.4	14.0	146	85.6	79.5	5.5
Valley Grove village	379	371	-2.1	320	99.4	0.0	0.0	0.6	0.0	5.5	83.9	10.6	119	100.0	49.6	9.2
Valley Head CDP	267	NA	NA	273	100.0	0.0	0.0	0.0	0.0	27.5	64.3	8.3	43	60.5	48.8	11.6
Van CDP	211	NA	NA	109	98.5	0.0	0.0	0.0	1.5	8.1	67.6	24.3	357	84.3	66.7	14.8
Verdunville CDP	687	NA	NA	839	98.5	0.0	0.0	0.0	1.5	8.1	67.6	24.3	357	84.3	66.7	14.8
Vienna city	10,751	10,562	-1.8	10,654	94.3	0.7	1.5	2.1	1.5	21.1	58.6	20.4	4,723	75.5	36.6	28.3
Vivian CDP	82	NA	NA	28	100.0	0.0	0.0	0.0	0.0	0.0	100.0	0.0	15	100.0	0.0	0.0
Wallace CDP	0	NA	NA	488	100.0	0.0	0.0	0.0	0.0	42.8	53.0	4.1	135	88.1	63.0	33.3
War city	853	793	-7.0	779	98.1	1.9	0.0	0.0	0.0	22.0	56.9	21.2	328	61.9	77.1	7.6
Wardensville town	271	276	1.8	253	95.7	2.4	0.0	1.2	0.8	21.0	60.9	18.2	104	51.9	61.5	15.4
Washington CDP	1,175	NA	NA	1,380	93.4	0.0	4.3	2.3	0.0	22.3	58.7	18.9	483	83.9	26.5	30.4
Waverly CDP	395	NA	NA	234	83.8	11.1	0.0	5.1	0.0	11.1	65.8	23.1	117	50.4	75.2	6.8
Wayne town	1,431	1,385	-3.2	2,032	97.7	0.0	0.0	0.2	2.1	25.9	61.5	12.6	804	53.0	72.4	6.0
Weirton city	19,745	19,362	-1.9	19,523	92.8	3.2	0.2	2.2	1.6	19.1	59.7	21.3	8,764	68.9	47.7	21.1
Welch city	2,398	2,154	-10.2	3,015	69.0	23.8	0.3	2.2	4.6	13.4	69.6	16.9	978	71.5	59.9	13.7
Wellsburg city	2,807	2,725	-2.9	2,763	98.4	1.5	0.0	0.1	0.0	16.5	60.9	22.4	1,318	64.9	52.8	16.3
West Hamlin town	774	768	-0.8	814	93.9	0.0	0.0	5.8	0.4	24.1	61.9	14.0	345	49.6	79.1	0.6

1 May be of any race.

Table A. All Places — **Population and Housing**

STATE City, town, township, borough, or CDP (county if applicable)	Population				Race and Hispanic or Latino origin (percent), 2010–2014					Age (percent), 2010–2014			Households, 2010–2014			
	2010 census total population	2014 estimated population	Percent change 2010-2014	ACS total population estimate 2010-2014	White alone, not Hispanic or Latino	Black alone, not Hispanic or Latino	Asian alone, not Hispanic or Latino	All other races or 2 or more races, not Hispanic or Latino	Hispanic or Latino[1]	Under 18 years old	Age 18 to 64 years old	Age 65 years and older	Total occupied housing units	Percent owner occupied	High school diploma or less	Bachelor's degree or more
	1	2	3	4	5	6	7	8	9	10	11	12	13	14	15	16
WEST VIRGINIA—Con.																
West Liberty town............	1,746	1,634	-6.4	1,517	86.0	7.2	2.1	2.4	2.4	5.8	90.7	3.6	269	37.2	21.9	33.8
West Logan town............	424	406	-4.2	508	80.1	0.0	15.4	4.5	0.0	20.9	62.8	16.3	217	61.8	54.4	18.0
West Milford town............	630	618	-1.9	710	91.1	0.0	2.1	5.5	1.3	17.9	64.7	17.3	297	89.9	45.1	18.9
Weston city....................	4,095	4,079	-0.4	4,088	95.3	2.6	0.2	1.2	0.7	26.0	58.4	15.8	1,529	59.6	58.9	20.0
Westover city..................	3,983	4,173	4.8	4,099	91.9	3.5	0.1	4.3	0.2	17.9	68.4	13.7	1,696	59.1	37.6	29.7
West Union town.............	824	832	1.0	1,177	90.2	0.9	0.0	3.9	4.9	31.6	56.6	11.8	366	65.6	67.2	8.7
Wheeling city..................	28,479	27,790	-2.4	28,129	90.0	5.6	1.1	2.2	1.2	19.1	60.2	20.6	12,738	62.0	42.6	27.9
White Hall town...............	653	660	1.1	624	93.9	1.1	1.6	1.4	1.9	16.0	71.4	12.5	285	47.7	22.1	34.0
White Sulphur Springs city	2,437	2,441	0.2	2,504	82.1	12.6	0.7	3.6	1.0	20.8	56.1	23.0	1,122	61.7	53.7	9.8
Whitesville town..............	507	483	-4.7	545	100.0	0.0	0.0	0.0	0.0	19.7	60.3	20.0	265	41.9	75.8	2.6
Whitmer CDP...................	106	NA	NA	81	100.0	0.0	0.0	0.0	0.0	16.0	39.5	44.4	35	68.6	100.0	0.0
Wiley Ford CDP...............	1,026	NA	NA	688	100.0	0.0	0.0	0.0	0.0	9.5	65.8	24.6	326	57.7	71.5	9.8
Williamson city................	3,195	3,051	-4.5	3,118	79.3	9.8	3.9	7.0	0.0	20.4	58.5	21.2	1,405	54.6	46.4	26.0
Williamstown city............	2,906	2,936	1.0	2,919	97.9	0.5	0.0	0.5	1.1	18.3	59.7	22.2	1,268	77.8	29.0	31.0
Windsor Heights village....	423	407	-3.8	491	91.4	0.8	0.6	5.1	2.0	20.6	67.2	12.2	202	93.6	50.0	13.9
Winfield town..................	2,299	2,333	1.5	2,538	90.3	0.2	0.5	8.6	0.4	24.1	60.7	15.2	984	83.8	35.7	26.3
Wolf Summit CDP............	272	NA	NA	106	100.0	0.0	0.0	0.0	0.0	0.0	52.0	48.1	48	100.0	83.3	0.0
Womelsdorf (Coalton) town	246	246	0.0	264	100.0	0.0	0.0	0.0	0.0	12.1	59.1	28.8	107	88.8	68.2	18.7
Worthington town............	158	160	1.3	176	100.0	0.0	0.0	0.0	0.0	10.2	64.7	25.0	84	96.4	72.6	0.0
WISCONSIN	5,687,289	5,757,564	1.2	5,724,692	82.7	6.1	2.4	2.6	6.2	23.0	62.6	14.4	2,293,250	67.7	38.6	28.5
Abbotsford city...............	2,310	2,278	-1.4	2,134	75.4	0.0	0.0	1.2	23.4	28.0	53.1	18.7	835	68.5	61.3	10.2
Abbotsford city (Clark).....	1,616	1,600		1,625	76.4	0.0	0.0	1.3	22.3	30.9	52.5	16.7	669	62.6	58.7	12.7
Abbotsford city (Marathon)	694	678	-2.3	509	72.3	0.0	0.0	0.8	26.9	18.8	56.1	25.1	166	92.2	71.7	0.0
Abrams CDP....................	340	NA	NA	384	93.0	0.0	0.0	2.6	4.4	17.4	69.5	13.0	154	86.4	62.3	13.6
Abrams town (Oconto)......	1,856	1,851	-0.3	1,984	96.8	0.0	0.0	1.1	2.1	24.8	67.0	8.2	739	90.9	49.7	18.5
Ackley town (Langlade)....	524	512	-2.3	518	98.5	0.0	0.0	1.5	0.0	27.2	61.9	11.0	194	79.9	58.8	10.8
Adams city & MCD (Adams)	1,967	1,899	-3.5	1,570	84.4	0.1	0.3	10.3	4.8	20.5	50.7	28.9	679	53.0	60.8	14.3
Adams town (Adams)........	1,343	1,302	-3.1	1,516	89.8	0.3	0.9	4.1	4.9	22.2	51.8	26.0	557	80.6	51.5	14.4
Adams town (Green)........	525	533	1.5	534	99.1	0.0	0.0	0.0	0.9	23.4	63.4	13.3	199	84.4	48.7	18.6
Adams town (Jackson)	1,362	1,400	2.8	1,440	93.8	0.0	0.4	4.9	0.9	20.8	54.2	25.0	611	89.0	50.2	15.4
Addison town (Washington)	3,493	3,449	-1.3	3,470	100.0	0.0	0.0	0.0	0.0	21.9	68.3	9.8	1,272	80.6	45.0	20.8
Adell village & MCD (Sheboygan)	516	520	0.8	465	92.7	0.0	0.0	6.5	0.9	20.9	68.2	11.0	217	68.2	60.8	12.4
Adrian town (Monroe)......	759	774	2.0	689	98.5	0.0	0.3	0.3	0.9	23.9	66.0	10.2	268	92.2	40.7	25.0
Agenda town (Ashland)	423	422	-0.2	480	96.0	0.0	0.2	3.8	0.0	23.6	64.8	11.9	202	78.2	59.9	12.9
Ahnapee town (Kewaunee)	930	924	-0.6	979	98.0	0.0	0.3	0.0	1.7	20.7	60.2	19.0	376	94.1	50.3	21.8
Ainsworth town (Langlade)	469	457	-2.6	394	99.5	0.0	0.0	0.0	0.5	10.6	56.4	33.0	193	91.7	77.2	5.7
Akan town (Richland)	403	396	-1.7	369	99.7	0.0	0.0	0.3	0.0	20.2	56.9	22.8	164	86.0	45.7	18.9
Alban town (Portage)........	885	895	1.1	815	99.3	0.0	0.4	0.0	0.4	18.0	59.7	22.3	356	95.2	65.2	10.7
Albany village & MCD (Green)	1,018	1,016	-0.2	1,167	93.3	0.2	0.2	5.1	1.2	25.8	63.2	11.2	470	57.2	56.2	9.8
Albany town (Green)........	1,106	1,125	1.7	873	97.1	0.0	0.0	2.3	0.6	18.4	65.5	16.2	360	88.9	42.8	22.5
Albany town (Pepin)........	676	708	4.7	915	100.0	0.0	0.0	0.0	0.0	35.4	54.1	10.5	274	88.7	62.8	17.5
Albion town (Dane)..........	1,987	2,072	4.3	1,885	96.8	0.1	0.7	0.9	1.5	18.7	68.3	13.2	806	81.3	36.0	23.7
Albion town (Jackson)......	1,210	1,243	2.7	1,189	95.3	0.0	0.0	2.7	1.9	20.3	60.5	19.3	474	87.8	50.0	15.6
Albion town (Trempealeau)	653	673	3.1	558	98.9	0.0	1.1	0.0	0.0	21.0	62.7	16.3	228	83.3	44.7	21.5
Alden town (Polk)............	2,786	2,758	-1.0	2,771	99.5	0.0	0.0	0.4	0.2	26.1	60.5	13.4	1,052	86.1	41.3	18.7
Algoma city & MCD (Kewaunee)	3,177	3,117	-1.9	3,152	96.0	1.2	0.0	0.2	2.6	23.9	54.4	21.8	1,342	66.5	58.0	11.6
Algoma town (Winnebago)	6,822	7,110	4.2	6,952	90.3	0.0	3.8	2.5	3.3	21.4	62.6	16.0	2,748	95.0	26.0	47.3
Allenton CDP...................	823	NA	NA	928	100.0	0.0	0.0	0.0	0.0	29.1	62.2	8.8	356	66.0	58.1	25.3
Allouez village & MCD (Brown)	13,975	13,943	-0.2	13,948	81.1	5.4	2.4	4.5	6.6	21.0	63.0	16.0	5,202	83.9	25.7	43.6
Alma city & MCD (Buffalo)	781	752	-3.7	766	95.6	1.8	0.0	0.0	2.6	11.6	59.8	28.6	379	67.5	55.4	18.5
Alma town (Buffalo)	297	287	-3.4	281	95.0	0.0	0.0	1.4	3.6	14.6	69.1	16.4	124	96.0	42.7	20.2
Alma town (Jackson)........	1,050	1,069	1.8	893	91.4	0.0	0.7	1.1	6.8	23.8	59.1	17.0	349	77.1	63.6	12.3
Alma Center village & MCD (Jackson)	503	500	-0.6	518	92.3	0.0	0.0	1.9	5.8	26.8	59.0	14.1	217	64.5	55.3	16.6
Almena village & MCD (Barron)	677	664	-1.9	688	90.0	1.2	0.0	2.9	6.0	21.0	62.9	16.3	303	59.1	58.4	12.2
Almena town (Barron)......	858	860	0.2	727	97.7	0.0	0.8	0.7	0.8	15.9	59.7	24.6	302	90.4	48.3	13.9
Almon town (Shawano).....	584	582	-0.3	573	93.2	0.0	0.0	6.1	0.7	24.2	59.6	16.2	221	89.6	69.7	5.0
Almond village & MCD (Portage)	448	437	-2.5	452	84.1	0.0	0.0	0.0	15.9	25.9	59.0	15.0	183	78.1	54.1	14.2
Almond town (Portage).....	680	688	1.2	751	96.8	0.0	0.0	1.3	1.9	28.7	58.7	12.8	266	92.1	54.0	12.8
Alto town (Fond du Lac)....	1,049	1,045	-0.4	1,054	91.4	0.3	0.8	0.2	7.4	28.8	64.1	6.9	347	90.8	56.8	9.2
Altoona city & MCD (Eau Claire)	6,715	7,155	6.6	6,940	93.0	0.0	3.2	3.5	0.3	23.2	59.1	17.8	2,905	66.6	35.0	27.9
Alvin town (Forest)...........	157	153	-2.5	126	100.0	0.0	0.0	0.0	0.0	5.6	47.7	46.8	69	95.7	73.9	7.2
Amberg CDP....................	180	NA	NA	172	100.0	0.0	0.0	0.0	0.0	22.7	46.0	31.4	91	67.0	71.4	4.4
Amberg town (Marinette) ..	726	718	-1.1	725	96.0	0.0	0.6	3.2	0.3	16.9	59.1	24.1	360	88.3	63.3	8.9
Amery city & MCD (Polk)..	2,926	2,856	-2.4	2,890	95.6	1.8	0.0	1.5	1.2	19.2	50.4	30.4	1,284	63.6	38.8	20.9
Amherst village & MCD (Portage)	1,035	1,043	0.8	1,180	94.2	1.2	0.3	1.9	2.4	33.8	52.6	13.6	459	66.2	50.8	13.1
Amherst town (Portage)....	1,325	1,340	1.1	1,328	97.6	0.7	0.5	1.2	0.0	19.9	61.1	18.9	546	93.8	39.0	28.4
Amherst Junction village & MCD (Portage)	377	375	-0.5	391	99.7	0.0	0.0	0.3	0.0	31.7	59.9	8.4	134	88.1	43.3	32.1
Amnicon town (Douglas) ..	1,155	1,164	0.8	1,354	94.0	0.0	0.2	3.5	2.3	29.2	64.1	6.8	508	91.3	31.1	30.1
Anderson town (Burnett)...	398	396	-0.5	428	99.1	0.0	0.0	0.9	0.0	20.5	67.7	11.9	188	86.2	47.9	18.1
Anderson town (Iron)	58	58	0.0	106	100.0	0.0	0.0	0.0	0.0	12.2	68.0	19.8	54	98.1	37.0	22.2
Angelica CDP...................	92	NA	NA	87	100.0	0.0	0.0	0.0	0.0	19.5	51.6	28.7	40	85.0	52.5	5.0
Angelica town (Shawano).	1,791	1,792	0.1	1,665	96.1	0.0	0.0	3.9	0.0	26.3	57.1	16.6	665	93.1	51.6	13.2
Angelo town (Monroe)	1,306	1,322	1.2	1,115	95.1	0.0	0.5	0.3	4.1	20.7	66.2	13.3	470	79.1	53.2	13.8

1 May be of any race.

Table A. All Places — Population and Housing

STATE City, town, township, borough, or CDP (county if applicable)	Population				Race and Hispanic or Latino origin (percent), 2010–2014					Age (percent), 2010–2014			Households, 2010–2014			
	2010 census total population	2014 estimated population	Percent change 2010-2014	ACS total population estimate 2010-2014	White alone, not Hispanic or Latino	Black alone, not Hispanic or Latino	Asian alone, not Hispanic or Latino	All other races or 2 or more races, not Hispanic or Latino	Hispanic or Latino[1]	Under 18 years old	Age 18 to 64 years old	Age 65 years and older	Total occupied housing units	Percent owner occupied	High school diploma or less	Bachelor's degree or more
	1	2	3	4	5	6	7	8	9	10	11	12	13	14	15	16
WISCONSIN—Con.																
Aniwa village & MCD (Shawano)	260	250	-3.8	242	97.9	0.4	0.8	0.4	0.4	26.0	52.4	21.5	96	87.5	58.3	6.3
Aniwa town (Shawano)	541	537	-0.7	533	95.7	0.4	0.0	2.1	1.9	18.6	65.5	15.9	199	95.0	59.3	12.6
Anson town (Chippewa)	2,076	2,125	2.4	2,234	98.6	0.0	0.4	0.9	0.2	20.0	65.1	14.9	879	89.8	38.5	26.2
Antigo city & MCD (Langlade)	8,234	7,921	-3.8	8,075	93.1	1.3	0.0	2.6	3.1	21.5	59.4	19.2	3,828	56.5	52.5	12.7
Antigo town (Langlade)	1,412	1,385	-1.9	1,365	96.8	0.0	2.3	0.8	0.1	19.5	57.9	22.6	572	91.4	59.1	23.6
Apple River town (Polk)	1,146	1,132	-1.2	1,099	92.2	0.7	0.3	5.3	1.5	24.9	58.8	16.3	425	86.6	44.2	21.6
Appleton city	72,628	73,971	1.8	72,861	84.4	1.5	5.7	2.9	5.5	24.9	63.7	11.6	28,741	67.9	33.6	32.8
Appleton city (Calumet)	11,082	11,256	1.6	11,218	83.3	1.1	5.4	2.5	7.7	26.5	65.0	8.6	4,222	72.9	29.9	33.6
Appleton city (Outagamie)	60,056	61,190	1.9	60,492	84.5	1.6	5.9	3.0	5.0	24.9	63.4	11.8	23,813	68.8	34.0	32.7
Appleton city (Winnebago)	1,490	1,525	2.3	1,151	90.9	0.0	0.0	0.0	9.1	12.5	60.8	26.8	706	7.1	41.5	31.6
Arbor Vitae town (Vilas)	3,316	3,307	-0.3	3,310	94.7	0.1	0.0	3.9	1.3	16.0	61.0	23.0	1,690	81.2	34.4	19.9
Arcadia city & MCD (Trempealeau)	2,925	2,946	0.7	2,953	64.0	1.3	0.0	0.2	34.6	27.8	58.2	14.1	1,127	55.6	66.8	11.1
Arcadia town (Trempealeau)	1,779	1,837	3.3	1,821	93.8	0.0	0.2	1.2	4.8	28.1	59.3	12.5	669	86.7	52.0	22.1
Arena village & MCD (Iowa)	834	831	-0.4	807	97.8	0.6	0.6	0.5	0.5	26.4	60.7	13.0	336	70.8	46.7	15.8
Arena town (Iowa)	1,456	1,480	1.6	1,519	97.3	0.1	0.0	2.0	0.6	20.5	67.4	12.0	623	80.1	46.9	23.4
Argonne CDP	160	NA	NA	188	90.4	0.0	0.0	9.6	0.0	25.6	55.5	19.1	70	81.4	54.3	10.0
Argonne town (Forest)	512	507	-1.0	524	94.7	0.0	0.8	4.6	0.0	21.1	64.0	14.9	216	83.3	46.8	13.9
Argyle village & MCD (Lafayette)	857	851	-0.7	813	95.6	0.0	0.0	1.0	3.4	28.9	51.7	19.4	349	72.2	59.9	11.7
Argyle town (Lafayette)	436	441	1.1	404	99.5	0.0	0.0	0.0	0.5	26.0	55.0	19.1	153	88.2	44.4	23.5
Arkansaw CDP	177	NA	NA	169	92.9	0.0	0.0	7.1	0.0	14.9	61.6	23.7	81	88.9	55.6	11.1
Arkdale CDP	158	NA	NA	166	95.2	0.0	0.0	4.8	0.0	15.0	51.1	33.7	83	97.6	47.0	20.5
Arland town (Barron)	789	781	-1.0	738	98.9	0.0	0.0	0.3	0.8	24.9	60.7	14.2	257	94.6	51.0	16.7
Arlington village & MCD (Columbia)	817	815	-0.2	829	92.6	0.0	0.7	2.3	4.3	29.1	60.0	11.1	294	82.7	39.5	21.1
Arlington town (Columbia)	808	808	0.0	921	99.6	0.0	0.0	0.4	0.0	22.6	65.8	11.6	348	79.3	43.1	21.8
Armenia town (Juneau)	699	704	0.7	623	88.4	0.0	0.0	2.4	9.1	21.7	58.1	20.2	278	86.7	62.2	11.2
Armstrong Creek town (Forest)	409	400	-2.2	416	99.8	0.0	0.0	0.2	0.0	21.6	61.8	16.6	185	93.0	54.6	11.9
Arpin village & MCD (Wood)	333	325	-2.4	353	95.2	0.8	0.8	2.8	0.3	23.8	63.1	13.0	146	78.8	71.9	6.2
Arpin town (Wood)	929	922	-0.8	1,026	99.2	0.0	0.0	0.0	0.8	31.5	60.7	7.9	343	94.5	54.5	10.8
Arthur town (Chippewa)	759	770	1.4	718	92.5	0.0	0.0	2.4	5.2	29.8	61.3	8.9	251	79.7	57.8	10.0
Ashford town (Fond du Lac)	1,743	1,723	-1.1	1,706	95.7	0.0	0.0	1.7	2.6	18.4	67.9	13.6	703	89.0	56.0	11.9
Ashippun CDP	333	NA	NA	284	100.0	0.0	0.0	0.0	0.0	15.4	79.5	4.9	98	70.4	20.4	38.8
Ashippun town (Dodge)	2,559	2,559	0.0	2,559	97.9	0.8	0.0	0.2	1.2	25.9	57.5	16.6	919	77.8	43.5	18.3
Ashland city	8,216	8,179	-0.5	8,167	83.9	0.4	0.7	12.4	2.5	20.2	62.6	17.3	3,513	60.4	34.1	31.1
Ashland city (Ashland)	8,216	8,179	-0.5	8,159	83.9	0.4	0.7	12.4	2.5	20.2	62.5	17.3	3,509	60.4	34.1	31.1
Ashland city (Bayfield)	0	0	0.0	8	100.0	0.0	0.0	0.0	0.0	0.0	50.0	50.0	4	100.0	100.0	0.0
Ashland town (Ashland)	594	593	-0.2	602	96.2	0.0	0.3	3.5	0.0	24.5	56.4	19.1	246	93.5	44.7	15.9
Ashwaubenon village & MCD (Brown)	16,943	17,111	1.0	17,065	87.9	1.7	3.6	4.4	2.4	21.9	61.8	16.2	7,271	62.2	33.8	26.5
Athelstane town (Marinette)	504	506	0.4	610	98.0	0.0	0.0	2.0	0.0	11.1	57.3	31.5	310	92.3	61.3	5.8
Athens village & MCD (Marathon)	1,105	1,100	-0.5	1,008	91.2	0.0	0.0	0.4	8.4	21.6	59.8	18.8	444	74.5	59.9	14.2
Atlanta town (Rusk)	592	584	-1.4	598	99.7	0.0	0.0	0.3	0.0	18.1	62.6	19.2	261	90.4	57.5	12.6
Auburn town (Chippewa)	697	709	1.7	638	98.7	0.9	0.3	0.0	0.0	21.8	66.1	12.2	236	84.7	48.3	19.1
Auburn town (Fond du Lac)	2,352	2,335	-0.7	2,552	96.5	0.0	0.0	2.6	0.9	21.9	63.1	14.9	960	92.0	52.0	16.6
Auburndale village & MCD (Wood)	703	679	-3.4	604	97.4	0.0	0.0	1.8	0.8	20.9	64.4	14.7	253	78.7	47.8	20.2
Auburndale town (Wood)	860	836	-2.8	754	97.6	0.0	0.0	2.0	0.4	24.5	60.3	15.3	296	90.5	63.9	11.5
Augusta city & MCD (Eau Claire)	1,546	1,532	-0.9	1,556	91.3	1.3	0.3	1.8	5.4	25.4	54.8	19.6	644	56.1	50.0	17.7
Aurora town (Florence)	1,036	1,050	1.4	897	98.7	0.0	0.0	0.3	1.0	14.8	68.3	17.1	371	91.6	48.8	6.5
Aurora town (Taylor)	422	419	-0.7	347	92.5	0.0	0.0	0.0	7.5	31.7	53.5	14.7	126	87.3	70.6	4.8
Aurora town (Waushara)	985	974	-1.1	1,013	97.6	0.1	0.3	0.3	1.7	23.2	61.3	15.3	419	90.9	58.0	9.5
Avoca village & MCD (Iowa)	637	627	-1.6	625	99.4	0.0	0.0	0.2	0.5	17.6	57.5	24.8	286	67.5	58.0	7.3
Avon town (Rock)	606	604	-0.3	582	97.6	0.0	0.0	0.9	1.5	23.0	60.9	16.2	217	90.8	51.2	15.7
Aztalan town (Jefferson)	1,454	1,484	2.1	1,426	95.9	0.4	0.0	1.0	2.7	20.1	65.1	14.9	525	89.1	42.5	19.4
Babcock CDP	126	NA	NA	66	98.5	0.0	0.0	0.0	1.5	10.6	62.1	27.3	43	83.7	69.8	2.3
Bagley village & MCD (Grant)	379	366	-3.4	493	95.9	0.0	2.0	1.8	0.2	14.9	52.7	32.5	210	95.7	68.1	2.4
Bagley town (Oconto)	291	288	-1.0	381	97.1	0.0	1.0	1.8	0.0	27.0	55.1	17.8	155	85.8	68.4	7.7
Baileys Harbor CDP	257	NA	NA	268	100.0	0.0	0.0	0.0	0.0	6.3	66.7	26.9	151	76.2	25.8	37.1
Baileys Harbor town (Door)	1,022	1,035	1.3	1,312	90.2	1.1	0.3	0.9	7.5	16.5	57.7	25.7	661	77.6	24.1	38.1
Baldwin village & MCD (St. Croix)	3,960	3,960	0.0	3,959	95.9	0.2	0.2	3.7	0.0	31.0	55.7	13.4	1,585	56.5	37.9	20.0
Baldwin town (St. Croix)	928	928	0.0	955	98.5	0.0	0.3	0.2	0.9	19.1	69.2	11.7	347	91.4	46.4	20.5
Balsam Lake village & MCD (Polk)	1,009	986	-2.3	829	95.1	3.7	0.7	0.0	0.5	21.7	55.2	23.2	346	71.7	46.0	20.2
Balsam Lake town (Polk)	1,411	1,394	-1.2	1,365	96.2	0.0	0.2	3.0	0.6	19.0	60.5	20.6	529	91.9	46.3	22.1
Bancroft CDP	535	NA	NA	607	64.7	0.0	0.0	0.0	35.3	26.3	66.2	7.4	217	91.2	70.5	10.1
Bangor village & MCD (La Crosse)	1,459	1,491	2.2	1,523	96.1	0.5	0.0	0.6	2.8	28.9	54.6	16.6	598	73.2	47.7	20.1
Bangor town (La Crosse)	615	631	2.6	671	90.5	0.4	1.8	0.4	6.9	27.8	63.5	8.6	272	59.2	53.7	15.8
Baraboo city & MCD (Sauk)	12,050	12,085	0.3	12,046	93.5	1.6	0.8	0.9	3.1	22.0	62.3	15.8	5,079	57.5	44.8	22.6
Baraboo town (Sauk)	1,673	1,724	3.0	1,679	95.1	0.1	0.2	3.2	1.3	21.5	63.9	14.7	655	90.1	37.3	34.4
Barksdale town (Bayfield)	723	725	0.3	727	97.2	0.0	0.3	1.7	0.8	22.2	62.1	15.8	322	93.5	33.9	28.3
Barnes town (Bayfield)	769	773	0.5	798	97.2	0.9	0.0	0.9	1.0	10.3	51.0	39.0	387	89.7	38.2	33.3

1 May be of any race.

Table A. All Places — Population and Housing

STATE City, town, township, borough, or CDP (county if applicable)	2010 census total population	2014 estimated population	Percent change 2010-2014	ACS total population estimate 2010-2014	White alone, not Hispanic or Latino	Black alone, not Hispanic or Latino	Asian alone, not Hispanic or Latino	All other races or 2 or more races, not Hispanic or Latino	Hispanic or Latino[1]	Under 18 years old	Age 18 to 64 years old	Age 65 years and older	Total occupied housing units	Percent owner occupied	High school diploma or less	Bachelor's degree or more
	1	2	3	4	5	6	7	8	9	10	11	12	13	14	15	16
WISCONSIN—Con.																
Barneveld village & MCD (Iowa)	1,231	1,233	0.2	1,223	96.7	1.6	0.7	0.7	0.3	33.2	57.8	8.9	443	77.4	28.9	29.8
Barre town (La Crosse)	1,234	1,261	2.2	1,252	98.0	0.5	0.6	0.0	1.0	27.2	60.1	12.7	465	89.2	35.5	30.1
Barron city & MCD (Barron)	3,423	3,344	-2.3	3,392	86.4	11.8	0.0	0.2	1.6	19.4	63.8	16.7	1,381	53.9	53.1	9.2
Barron town (Barron)	873	874	0.1	773	92.9	4.9	0.0	0.4	1.8	25.0	56.3	18.9	300	73.0	57.3	16.0
Barronett CDP	111	NA	NA	124	95.2	0.0	0.0	4.8	0.0	12.9	82.2	4.8	81	81.5	77.8	3.7
Barronett town (Washburn)	442	434	-1.8	437	98.6	0.0	0.0	0.7	0.7	28.6	60.2	11.2	164	86.0	53.0	17.7
Bartelme town (Shawano)	825	819	-0.7	990	14.4	1.0	0.0	83.1	1.4	27.0	57.3	16.0	366	77.0	53.3	16.4
Barton town (Washington)	2,611	2,614	0.1	2,602	98.6	0.0	0.0	0.2	1.2	16.3	65.0	18.9	1,089	82.9	34.9	27.0
Bashaw town (Washburn)	946	934	-1.3	944	98.4	0.4	0.0	0.7	0.4	22.4	59.1	18.5	408	89.0	42.2	25.5
Bass Lake town (Sawyer)	2,375	2,374	0.0	2,465	59.8	0.0	0.9	35.9	3.4	26.1	57.1	16.7	1,062	71.8	37.3	22.3
Bass Lake town (Washburn)	505	499	-1.2	461	75.5	0.0	0.7	22.8	1.1	26.9	54.5	18.9	179	82.1	45.8	20.7
Bay City village & MCD (Pierce)	500	489	-2.2	512	94.5	0.2	0.0	3.9	1.4	19.9	67.0	13.1	226	74.3	66.4	7.5
Bayfield city & MCD (Bayfield)	487	481	-1.2	550	69.3	5.5	0.9	22.4	2.0	15.9	64.6	19.6	287	62.7	14.3	44.3
Bayfield town (Bayfield)	680	683	0.4	753	74.8	0.0	0.0	25.2	0.0	14.6	54.6	30.8	347	89.0	30.8	35.7
Bayside village (Bayfield)	4,389	4,420	0.7	4,479	90.1	3.0	2.8	2.2	1.8	25.6	53.2	21.3	1,831	81.6	9.5	74.3
Bayside village (Milwaukee)	4,300	4,331	0.7	4,434	90.0	3.0	2.9	2.3	1.8	25.9	52.5	21.5	1,805	81.3	9.6	74.0
Bayside village (Ozaukee)	89	89	0.0	45	100.0	0.0	0.0	0.0	0.0	0.0	100.0	0.0	26	100.0	0.0	100.0
Bayview town (Bayfield)	487	488	0.2	417	87.3	0.0	1.2	9.4	2.2	13.9	61.3	24.9	205	86.8	24.4	47.8
Bear Bluff town (Jackson)	138	139	0.7	91	96.7	0.0	0.0	0.0	3.3	15.4	75.9	8.8	47	63.8	68.1	6.4
Bear Creek village & MCD (Outagamie)	448	439	-2.0	437	58.8	0.0	0.0	1.6	39.6	21.7	64.7	13.5	157	63.7	72.0	5.7
Bear Creek town (Sauk)	595	613	3.0	495	98.6	0.2	0.2	0.0	1.0	21.6	62.5	16.0	206	81.1	50.5	19.9
Bear Creek town (Waupaca)	823	816	-0.9	862	89.3	0.0	6.4	0.5	3.8	20.4	62.6	17.1	326	87.7	49.1	11.0
Bear Lake town (Barron)	659	659	0.0	648	99.1	0.0	0.0	0.3	0.6	19.8	61.5	18.7	260	88.5	49.6	18.8
Beaver town (Clark)	885	882	-0.3	944	99.4	0.0	0.0	0.5	0.1	41.5	52.0	6.4	269	80.7	66.9	11.9
Beaver town (Marinette)	1,146	1,149	0.3	1,212	96.8	0.0	0.0	1.9	1.3	18.1	60.0	21.9	541	82.8	63.6	10.5
Beaver town (Polk)	835	825	-1.2	731	96.9	0.0	0.0	1.8	1.4	16.7	60.4	23.0	334	85.6	50.9	11.7
Beaver Brook town (Washburn)	713	707	-0.8	754	96.9	0.5	2.3	0.3	0.0	24.4	63.1	12.6	307	72.0	42.3	19.2
Beaver Dam city & MCD (Dodge)	16,214	16,536	2.0	16,331	88.0	1.6	0.5	2.0	7.9	24.4	59.8	15.9	6,576	60.3	45.2	20.3
Beaver Dam town (Dodge)	3,948	3,898	-1.3	3,935	92.8	0.0	0.0	1.4	5.8	22.1	63.2	14.9	1,529	97.4	44.7	23.5
Beecher town (Marinette)	724	715	-1.2	668	96.1	0.0	0.0	3.6	0.3	14.7	57.7	27.2	314	83.1	61.1	11.8
Beetown town (Grant)	777	770	-0.9	645	98.8	0.0	1.2	0.0	0.0	25.1	58.0	16.7	228	84.6	56.6	8.8
Belgium village & MCD (Ozaukee)	2,231	2,255	1.1	2,088	87.7	0.1	0.2	0.9	11.0	29.4	63.3	7.3	759	72.6	34.4	32.8
Belgium town (Ozaukee)	1,429	1,430	0.1	1,428	89.2	0.0	3.1	4.9	2.8	22.6	57.5	19.8	562	84.5	42.0	33.5
Bell town (Bayfield)	263	264	0.4	222	97.7	0.0	0.0	0.0	2.3	1.8	52.0	46.4	139	93.5	28.8	29.5
Bell Center village & MCD (Crawford)	117	115	-1.7	118	96.6	2.5	0.0	0.0	0.8	15.3	66.1	18.6	50	88.0	70.0	16.0
Belle Plaine town (Shawano)	1,856	1,848	-0.4	1,832	95.1	0.0	0.2	1.9	2.7	12.6	64.4	22.8	779	89.6	53.3	15.8
Belleville village	2,382	2,424	1.8	2,759	95.0	0.6	0.7	1.6	2.1	30.8	61.8	7.4	1,037	75.7	33.9	27.8
Belleville village (Dane)	1,847	1,890	2.3	2,193	96.5	0.7	0.9	1.7	0.2	30.2	60.7	9.1	820	72.4	33.5	27.8
Belleville village (Green)	535	534	-0.2	566	89.2	0.2	0.0	1.2	9.4	33.4	65.6	0.9	217	88.0	35.5	27.6
Bellevue village & MCD (Brown)	14,710	15,215	3.4	14,936	82.9	0.3	5.1	1.4	10.3	24.0	62.9	13.0	6,259	59.6	38.6	28.1
Belmont village & MCD (Lafayette)	986	985	-0.1	959	87.6	1.7	0.4	5.2	5.1	21.8	61.1	17.0	417	65.2	51.3	16.5
Belmont town (Lafayette)	767	775	1.0	612	95.9	0.0	0.7	0.0	3.4	21.4	61.2	17.5	254	92.1	44.5	27.2
Belmont town (Portage)	616	608	-1.3	668	93.0	0.0	0.0	3.3	3.7	18.7	62.0	19.2	290	91.4	55.5	15.2
Beloit city & MCD (Rock)	37,004	36,881	-0.3	36,876	64.0	10.5	1.0	5.6	18.9	25.9	61.0	12.9	14,140	59.1	53.4	16.2
Beloit town (Rock)	7,623	7,666	0.6	7,641	89.3	3.5	0.7	3.5	3.0	19.1	60.2	20.7	3,192	82.1	48.9	22.1
Belvidere town (Buffalo)	396	390	-1.5	412	94.2	2.9	0.0	0.2	2.7	16.7	51.0	32.3	178	90.4	55.6	19.1
Bennett town (Douglas)	597	604	1.2	551	92.4	0.5	0.0	3.4	3.6	21.1	62.3	16.7	212	93.4	39.2	24.5
Benton village & MCD (Lafayette)	973	967	-0.6	927	98.2	1.8	0.0	0.0	0.0	27.6	52.1	20.3	366	80.6	47.5	15.8
Benton town (Lafayette)	504	519	3.0	521	99.8	0.0	0.0	0.2	0.0	23.1	64.2	12.9	184	84.8	45.1	19.6
Bergen town (Marathon)	641	644	0.5	630	99.7	0.0	0.0	0.0	0.3	15.8	61.1	23.0	256	98.0	33.2	28.5
Bergen town (Vernon)	1,357	1,385	2.1	1,289	96.2	0.0	0.5	1.3	2.0	21.4	60.6	18.0	539	89.2	33.2	26.0
Berlin city	5,524	5,431	-1.7	5,451	89.0	0.3	0.0	1.9	8.9	23.1	56.6	20.5	2,344	63.1	59.0	11.2
Berlin city (Green Lake)	5,435	5,343	-1.7	5,401	88.9	0.3	0.0	1.9	9.0	22.9	56.6	20.4	2,318	62.6	59.7	11.0
Berlin city (Waushara)	89	88	-1.1	50	100.0	0.0	0.0	0.0	0.0	32.0	34.0	34.0	26	100.0	0.0	34.6
Berlin town (Green Lake)	1,140	1,133	-0.6	1,150	98.4	0.3	0.0	0.3	1.0	22.9	57.2	19.9	443	83.3	40.4	16.5
Berlin town (Marathon)	945	944	-0.1	964	94.7	0.0	0.2	1.5	3.6	29.5	57.7	12.8	361	90.0	55.1	17.5
Bern town (Marathon)	591	592	0.2	648	99.8	0.0	0.0	0.2	0.0	30.7	58.3	11.0	197	89.3	66.0	12.7
Berry town (Dane)	1,115	1,170	4.9	1,188	97.8	0.0	0.0	0.6	1.6	18.3	63.0	18.7	494	90.9	37.4	39.1
Bevent town (Marathon)	1,118	1,120	0.2	1,145	96.5	0.0	1.0	2.1	0.3	21.9	62.1	16.0	477	84.3	65.6	11.3
Big Bend town (Rusk)	358	352	-1.7	470	97.0	0.0	0.0	0.6	2.3	13.2	62.0	24.9	216	76.9	56.9	18.1
Big Bend village & MCD (Waukesha)	1,285	1,310	1.9	1,327	93.7	0.0	1.2	3.6	1.4	23.9	64.8	11.4	470	85.1	34.7	25.3
Big Falls town (Rusk)	140	134	-4.3	131	85.5	0.0	5.3	9.2	0.0	18.3	68.7	13.0	56	100.0	44.6	16.1
Big Falls village & MCD (Waupaca)	61	61	0.0	126	100.0	0.0	0.0	0.0	0.0	23.0	51.6	25.4	58	79.3	69.0	3.4
Big Flats town (Adams)	1,018	985	-3.2	905	93.5	0.3	0.0	0.7	5.5	11.4	59.5	29.0	364	86.5	60.2	6.3
Birch town (Lincoln)	594	955	60.8	666	74.0	15.0	0.8	7.8	2.4	40.9	48.4	11.0	226	90.7	50.9	11.9
Birch Creek town (Chippewa)	517	528	2.1	454	99.3	0.0	0.0	0.4	0.2	9.9	55.5	34.6	217	87.6	50.7	18.9
Birch Hill CDP	293	NA	NA	302	2.3	0.0	3.3	89.1	5.3	42.8	53.9	3.3	96	7.3	46.9	5.2
Birchwood village & MCD (Washburn)	442	431	-2.5	497	94.6	0.0	0.0	3.0	2.4	18.7	58.6	22.5	264	64.0	51.5	21.2
Birchwood town (Washburn)	478	473	-1.0	451	98.2	0.0	0.0	1.1	0.7	9.5	55.9	34.6	229	90.0	28.4	35.4

1 May be of any race.

Table A. All Places — **Population and Housing**

STATE City, town, township, borough, or CDP (county if applicable)	2010 census total population	2014 estimated population	Percent change 2010-2014	ACS total population estimate 2010-2014	White alone, not Hispanic or Latino	Black alone, not Hispanic or Latino	Asian alone, not Hispanic or Latino	All other races or 2 or more races, not Hispanic or Latino	Hispanic or Latino[1]	Under 18 years old	Age 18 to 64 years old	Age 65 years and older	Total occupied housing units	Percent owner occupied	High school diploma or less	Bachelor's degree or more
	1	2	3	4	5	6	7	8	9	10	11	12	13	14	15	16
WISCONSIN—Con.																
Birnamwood village	818	806	-1.5	903	95.8	0.0	0.0	4.2	0.0	22.0	50.2	27.9	343	59.5	56.0	11.1
Birnamwood village (Marathon)	16	16	0.0	5	100.0	0.0	0.0	0.0	0.0	0.0	100.0	0.0	5	60.0	100.0	0.0
Birnamwood village (Shawano)	802	790	-1.5	898	95.8	0.0	0.0	4.2	0.0	22.0	49.8	28.1	338	59.5	55.3	11.2
Birnamwood town (Shawano)	763	758	-0.7	692	88.3	0.6	0.0	11.1	0.0	23.7	58.9	17.3	265	83.4	57.0	11.7
Biron village & MCD (Wood)	839	811	-3.3	913	94.3	0.0	0.3	0.0	5.4	19.7	58.8	21.6	363	84.8	54.8	18.7
Black Brook town (Polk)	1,329	1,313	-1.2	1,440	96.8	0.0	0.7	2.0	0.5	20.7	68.6	11.0	606	76.7	43.1	27.6
Black Creek village & MCD (Outagamie)	1,316	1,320	0.3	1,305	97.6	0.0	0.0	1.8	0.6	32.3	55.2	12.6	491	72.9	52.5	11.0
Black Creek town (Outagamie)	1,259	1,260	0.1	1,209	96.4	0.0	0.6	3.1	0.0	23.8	61.4	14.9	457	92.6	62.8	12.5
Black Earth village & MCD (Dane)	1,340	1,391	3.8	1,410	94.8	0.9	1.3	0.5	2.6	21.9	60.1	18.1	591	79.7	40.1	26.2
Black Earth town (Dane)	484	508	5.0	538	97.8	0.0	0.4	0.9	0.9	24.7	61.0	14.1	191	93.2	31.9	33.5
Black River Falls city & MCD (Jackson)	3,602	3,582	-0.6	3,591	92.4	1.2	1.0	3.5	1.9	18.5	61.4	20.1	1,723	58.7	41.3	18.5
Blackwell town (Forest)	332	311	-6.3	229	73.8	23.1	0.0	0.0	3.1	8.7	44.9	46.3	32	71.9	78.1	6.3
Black Wolf town (Winnebago)	2,410	2,442	1.3	2,385	93.5	0.2	2.2	3.1	1.0	20.7	57.5	21.6	1,010	96.5	32.2	32.0
Blaine town (Burnett)	197	192	-2.5	177	94.4	0.0	0.0	5.6	0.0	20.3	47.5	32.2	86	89.5	50.0	10.5
Blair city & MCD (Trempealeau)	1,366	1,366	0.0	1,299	97.2	0.0	0.7	0.0	2.2	25.5	54.1	20.6	546	69.8	59.3	11.4
Blanchard town (Lafayette)	264	265	0.4	259	98.1	0.0	0.0	0.0	1.9	27.4	59.4	13.1	99	82.8	41.4	26.3
Blanchardville village	825	821	-0.5	805	97.0	0.4	0.0	0.4	2.2	22.1	59.5	18.4	344	74.1	57.6	15.7
Blanchardville village (Iowa)	177	177	0.0	144	100.0	0.0	0.0	0.0	0.0	24.3	55.7	20.1	63	68.3	55.6	15.9
Blanchardville village (Lafayette)	648	644	-0.6	661	96.4	0.5	0.0	0.5	2.7	21.6	60.5	18.0	281	75.4	58.0	15.7
Bloom town (Richland)	512	504	-1.6	507	91.7	0.0	0.0	8.3	0.0	23.0	56.6	20.3	210	76.7	50.0	13.8
Bloomer city & MCD (Chippewa)	3,541	3,535	-0.2	3,558	92.1	0.0	0.0	2.2	5.6	28.2	52.5	19.3	1,463	69.2	45.1	17.4
Bloomer town (Chippewa)	1,050	1,067	1.6	1,043	98.1	0.0	0.0	0.6	1.3	24.0	64.3	11.7	351	90.0	51.0	8.5
Bloomfield village & MCD (Walworth)	4,644	4,642	0.0	4,629	90.7	0.5	2.4	0.7	5.7	19.8	70.7	9.6	1,745	77.5	45.4	21.8
Bloomfield town (Walworth)	1,631	1,643	0.7	1,503	69.7	3.5	0.0	12.1	14.7	26.6	62.1	11.5	519	75.1	53.2	15.8
Bloomfield town (Waushara)	1,052	1,044	-0.8	986	96.3	0.8	0.0	1.7	1.1	17.3	65.3	17.2	390	89.0	52.3	12.3
Blooming Grove town (Dane)	1,792	1,880	4.9	1,823	89.9	3.9	0.9	3.2	2.0	20.3	66.2	13.5	767	77.6	23.5	36.4
Bloomington village & MCD (Grant)	735	719	-2.2	836	98.8	0.0	0.0	0.0	1.2	26.9	54.9	18.2	342	83.0	49.7	9.9
Bloomington town (Grant)	350	352	0.6	371	98.1	0.0	0.0	1.9	0.0	24.3	59.0	16.7	141	75.2	49.6	18.4
Blue Mounds village & MCD (Dane)	857	930	8.5	870	97.6	0.0	0.2	1.4	0.8	27.3	62.4	10.2	345	86.1	34.8	25.8
Blue Mounds town (Dane)	864	905	4.7	944	93.3	0.0	1.4	3.9	1.4	25.4	62.4	12.4	334	79.6	31.1	35.6
Blue River village & MCD (Grant)	434	421	-3.0	461	93.7	0.7	2.2	1.3	2.2	19.3	62.1	18.7	229	73.8	58.5	9.2
Bluffview CDP	742	NA	NA	793	43.1	1.8	0.0	0.9	54.2	39.4	54.5	6.1	261	66.3	66.7	3.1
Boaz village & MCD (Richland)	156	153	-1.9	116	100.0	0.0	0.0	0.0	0.0	16.4	65.3	18.1	54	70.4	70.4	5.6
Bohners Lake CDP	2,444	NA	NA	2,389	98.0	0.0	0.3	0.0	1.6	22.2	61.9	16.0	922	82.6	55.3	13.6
Bonduel village & MCD (Shawano)	1,478	1,468	-0.7	1,426	95.4	0.0	0.4	0.1	4.2	29.4	55.2	15.5	563	66.6	51.7	13.9
Bone Lake town (Polk)	717	710	-1.0	605	96.2	0.0	0.0	3.8	0.0	21.5	60.9	17.7	259	95.0	42.1	18.5
Boscobel city & MCD (Grant)	3,231	3,188	-1.3	3,201	87.8	8.4	0.0	2.5	1.3	17.8	69.1	13.2	1,229	62.1	45.8	22.4
Boscobel town (Grant)	376	379	0.8	397	97.5	0.0	0.0	1.8	0.8	20.4	58.4	21.2	168	74.4	53.0	13.7
Boulder Junction CDP	183	NA	NA	132	93.2	0.0	0.0	6.8	0.0	2.3	48.5	49.2	73	78.1	31.5	24.7
Boulder Junction town (Vilas)	933	933	0.0	938	96.6	0.0	0.0	3.4	0.0	11.0	47.3	41.8	482	82.8	28.0	42.1
Bovina town (Outagamie)	1,143	1,139	-0.3	1,071	92.6	0.0	0.0	0.7	6.7	19.0	68.1	12.9	434	91.5	65.0	13.1
Bowler village & MCD (Shawano)	302	300	-0.7	384	66.1	0.0	0.0	23.2	10.7	31.6	57.7	10.7	130	67.7	66.9	10.8
Boyceville village & MCD (Dunn)	1,086	1,104	1.7	1,020	97.8	0.0	0.7	1.3	0.2	20.6	65.1	14.4	446	63.2	63.9	9.2
Boyd village & MCD (Chippewa)	552	545	-1.3	610	93.9	1.3	0.0	4.8	0.0	19.7	62.5	17.7	259	83.8	54.8	10.8
Bradford town (Rock)	1,120	1,114	-0.5	1,156	75.8	0.0	0.0	4.2	20.0	27.5	61.2	11.5	408	82.8	47.3	14.0
Bradley town (Lincoln)	2,408	2,381	-1.1	2,173	98.5	0.1	0.0	0.5	0.9	9.0	56.8	34.1	1,089	89.6	43.3	18.3
Brandon village & MCD (Fond du Lac)	879	862	-1.9	920	87.7	2.0	0.0	0.2	10.1	26.6	58.8	14.5	338	75.7	55.6	13.0
Brazeau town (Oconto)	1,284	1,276	-0.6	1,238	98.1	1.1	0.0	0.8	0.0	15.5	54.3	30.2	583	88.9	60.0	8.2
Breed town (Oconto)	712	707	-0.7	593	98.0	0.0	0.0	2.0	0.0	10.8	61.3	27.8	282	90.1	67.0	5.7
Brice Prairie CDP	1,887	NA	NA	1,762	97.7	1.1	0.0	0.9	0.3	20.8	67.5	11.5	727	94.8	34.0	28.5
Bridge Creek town (Eau Claire)	1,904	1,966	3.3	2,073	93.9	0.4	0.4	1.4	4.0	32.0	58.3	9.6	615	73.7	62.9	12.0
Bridgeport town (Crawford)	1,005	1,005	0.0	1,010	99.4	0.0	0.0	0.0	0.6	23.3	60.7	15.8	354	95.2	41.5	29.4
Brigham town (Iowa)	1,034	1,053	1.8	1,056	94.6	0.5	0.0	0.2	4.7	23.6	63.6	12.8	399	86.7	35.3	30.3
Brighton town (Kenosha)	1,456	1,485	2.0	1,291	91.1	0.0	4.1	0.7	4.1	16.5	65.5	18.0	569	84.9	45.5	22.7
Brighton town (Marathon)	612	636	3.9	554	98.4	0.0	0.0	0.0	1.6	28.3	59.3	12.5	205	84.4	58.0	14.1
Brillion city & MCD (Calumet)	3,146	3,159	0.4	3,183	92.6	1.2	0.4	0.3	5.5	29.2	55.8	14.8	1,203	74.0	52.0	17.9
Brillion town (Calumet)	1,488	1,497	0.6	1,452	97.9	0.0	0.0	1.4	0.7	22.0	66.9	11.1	592	83.1	53.9	17.1
Bristol town (Dane)	3,695	3,883	5.1	3,795	90.6	0.5	0.8	2.2	5.9	30.4	60.0	9.6	1,265	89.5	27.7	42.8

1 May be of any race.

Table A. All Places — **Population and Housing**

	Population				Race and Hispanic or Latino origin (percent), 2010–2014					Age (percent), 2010–2014			Households, 2010–2014			
STATE City, town, township, borough, or CDP (county if applicable)	2010 census total population	2014 estimated population	Percent change 2010–2014	ACS total population estimate 2010–2014	White alone, not Hispanic or Latino	Black alone, not Hispanic or Latino	Asian alone, not Hispanic or Latino	All other races or 2 or more races, not Hispanic or Latino	Hispanic or Latino[1]	Under 18 years old	Age 18 to 64 years old	Age 65 years and older	Total occupied housing units	Percent owner occupied	Householders by level of education (percent): High school diploma or less	Householders by level of education (percent): Bachelor's degree or more
	1	2	3	4	5	6	7	8	9	10	11	12	13	14	15	16
WISCONSIN—Con.																
Bristol village & MCD (Kenosha)	4,912	4,931	0.4	4,909	91.7	1.2	0.3	1.3	5.5	21.0	62.8	16.2	1,879	81.7	45.4	22.2
Brockway town (Jackson)	2,828	2,857	1.0	2,831	65.8	13.2	0.8	16.3	3.8	16.4	71.8	11.9	718	58.6	60.6	10.9
Brodhead city	3,293	3,284	-0.3	3,285	97.2	0.0	0.0	1.1	1.7	22.7	59.0	18.3	1,391	71.6	49.2	15.0
Brodhead city (Green)	3,204	3,196	-0.2	3,201	97.1	0.0	0.0	1.1	1.8	23.3	60.2	16.6	1,336	72.4	51.3	12.5
Brodhead city (Rock)	89	88	-1.1	84	100.0	0.0	0.0	0.0	0.0	0.0	16.7	83.3	55	52.7	0.0	76.4
Brokaw village & MCD (Marathon)	251	253	0.8	178	100.0	0.0	0.0	0.0	0.0	6.2	73.0	20.8	108	21.3	39.8	22.2
Brookfield city & MCD (Waukesha)	37,931	37,982	0.1	37,971	89.9	1.2	4.9	1.4	2.6	22.8	57.3	20.0	14,557	88.4	16.4	59.6
Brookfield town (Waukesha)	6,105	6,104	0.0	6,111	88.2	0.9	6.2	1.2	3.5	18.2	55.1	26.7	2,716	61.5	30.4	41.1
Brooklyn village	1,403	1,446	3.1	1,439	95.2	0.0	0.4	1.1	3.3	29.6	65.2	5.1	478	83.9	26.8	28.0
Brooklyn village (Dane)	938	976	4.1	837	98.1	0.0	0.0	0.6	1.3	29.9	65.8	4.3	281	86.1	26.0	30.2
Brooklyn village (Green)	465	470	1.1	602	91.2	0.0	1.0	1.8	6.0	29.0	64.7	6.3	197	80.7	27.9	24.9
Brooklyn town (Green)	1,083	1,100	1.6	1,109	97.2	0.0	0.0	1.4	1.4	22.5	60.3	17.2	422	94.5	30.8	32.5
Brooklyn town (Green Lake)	1,826	1,821	-0.3	1,504	96.3	2.1	0.0	0.3	1.3	15.2	59.5	25.4	689	88.8	37.2	35.8
Brooklyn town (Washburn)	254	252	-0.8	261	97.3	0.0	0.0	0.8	1.9	13.0	59.1	28.0	125	94.4	54.4	14.4
Brothertown town (Calumet)	1,329	1,328	-0.1	1,419	94.5	0.0	0.0	2.0	3.5	24.4	63.6	12.1	562	89.1	58.2	14.8
Brown Deer village & MCD (Milwaukee)	12,000	12,102	0.9	12,067	56.3	32.8	3.1	3.9	3.9	18.4	63.6	18.1	5,449	66.5	22.2	41.4
Browning town (Taylor)	905	914	1.0	934	89.8	0.0	0.0	0.5	9.6	24.1	66.3	9.6	353	77.9	73.7	4.5
Browns Lake CDP	2,039	NA	NA	2,084	95.1	0.0	0.0	0.0	4.9	20.0	64.6	15.5	809	85.9	50.8	14.1
Brownsville village & MCD (Dodge)	581	583	0.3	648	94.6	0.0	0.3	1.4	0.0	23.4	66.8	9.9	227	74.9	48.9	29.5
Browntown village & MCD (Green)	280	282	0.7	280	96.1	0.0	0.0	3.9	0.0	26.4	59.3	14.3	106	86.8	69.8	17.0
Bruce village & MCD (Rusk)	782	744	-4.9	754	94.8	0.0	0.0	2.1	3.1	26.5	54.5	19.0	358	61.5	65.1	10.9
Brule CDP	254	NA	NA	209	96.7	1.9	0.0	1.4	0.0	21.6	59.0	19.6	86	86.0	39.5	19.8
Brule town (Douglas)	656	661	0.8	500	96.6	0.8	0.0	2.6	0.0	16.0	59.4	24.6	219	94.5	45.7	16.9
Brunswick town (Eau Claire)	1,626	1,669	2.6	1,628	95.8	0.0	0.1	1.2	2.9	19.4	66.1	14.6	642	91.9	38.6	28.2
Brussels town (Door)	1,136	1,125	-1.0	998	96.0	1.2	0.0	2.1	0.7	24.8	60.7	14.3	409	87.3	59.9	11.0
Buchanan town (Outagamie)	6,753	7,072	4.7	6,961	94.1	0.6	1.2	2.5	1.6	28.4	62.6	9.0	2,494	75.8	31.0	35.3
Buena Vista town (Portage)	1,198	1,211	1.1	1,286	97.3	0.0	0.0	0.7	2.0	26.6	60.5	13.1	476	87.4	51.9	20.6
Buena Vista town (Richland)	1,865	1,837	-1.5	1,854	89.6	0.1	0.6	1.7	8.0	28.6	61.3	10.1	714	84.9	49.2	11.3
Buffalo town (Buffalo)	705	691	-2.0	749	99.7	0.0	0.0	0.3	0.0	22.2	60.1	17.6	316	88.6	49.1	23.7
Buffalo town (Marquette)	1,221	1,188	-2.7	1,180	98.2	0.0	0.0	0.9	0.8	23.4	60.5	16.1	441	85.3	56.2	12.0
Buffalo City city & MCD (Buffalo)	1,023	976	-4.6	1,057	97.4	0.0	0.2	0.6	1.8	19.5	58.3	22.1	484	92.4	49.2	17.1
Burke town (Dane)	3,219	3,384	5.1	3,310	95.9	3.3	0.0	0.6	0.2	22.6	60.2	17.1	1,216	85.0	21.4	35.9
Burlington city	10,529	10,541	0.1	10,528	87.3	4.2	0.9	1.7	5.9	25.2	59.7	15.1	4,329	54.7	41.7	19.4
Burlington city (Racine)	10,529	10,541	0.1	10,528	87.3	4.2	0.9	1.7	5.9	25.2	59.7	15.1	4,329	54.7	41.7	19.4
Burlington city (Walworth)	0	0	0.0	0	0.0	0.0	0.0	0.0	0.0	0.0	0.0	0.0	0	0.0	0.0	0.0
Burlington town (Racine)	6,437	6,518	1.3	6,468	96.6	0.6	0.3	0.1	2.4	21.7	60.5	17.9	2,454	87.1	48.9	19.3
Burnett CDP	256	NA	NA	246	96.7	0.0	0.0	3.3	0.0	24.5	61.4	14.2	102	77.5	48.0	5.9
Burnett town (Dodge)	904	885	-2.1	853	97.8	0.6	0.2	0.9	0.5	19.4	62.8	17.8	336	84.2	57.4	13.7
Burns town (La Crosse)	947	959	1.3	940	98.6	0.0	0.0	0.7	0.6	22.7	64.1	13.2	355	87.6	51.3	12.4
Burnside town (Trempealeau)	511	529	3.5	408	94.6	0.0	0.0	0.0	5.4	21.1	63.5	15.4	171	85.4	46.8	21.1
Butler town (Clark)	96	96	0.0	95	95.8	4.2	0.0	0.0	0.0	42.1	45.4	12.6	33	75.8	48.5	18.2
Butler village & MCD (Waukesha)	1,841	1,831	-0.5	1,746	85.9	1.9	1.9	3.0	7.4	14.5	67.3	18.3	863	50.8	46.2	21.4
Butte des Morts CDP	962	NA	NA	773	100.0	0.0	0.0	0.0	0.0	26.5	56.7	16.8	319	89.3	28.2	25.4
Butternut village & MCD (Ashland)	375	371	-1.1	432	94.2	0.0	0.0	1.9	3.9	22.2	57.1	20.8	208	59.6	56.3	6.7
Byron town (Fond du Lac)	1,638	1,615	-1.4	1,686	95.9	0.6	0.0	0.0	3.5	21.2	65.5	13.4	646	86.5	48.1	17.6
Byron town (Monroe)	1,343	1,341	-0.1	1,355	79.6	0.0	1.0	14.7	4.6	28.2	57.2	14.6	517	71.0	52.6	7.0
Cable CDP	206	NA	NA	206	74.3	5.3	0.0	20.4	0.0	30.1	37.9	32.0	108	75.0	41.7	25.0
Cable town (Bayfield)	825	827	0.2	806	87.0	3.2	0.0	6.8	3.0	18.9	58.9	22.2	407	87.5	37.3	21.1
Cadiz town (Green)	815	824	1.1	909	100.0	0.0	0.0	0.0	0.0	14.5	71.2	14.4	336	81.0	45.5	10.4
Cadott village & MCD (Chippewa)	1,436	1,431	-0.3	1,384	97.9	0.0	0.7	0.1	0.1	24.1	58.7	17.1	593	60.2	52.1	18.0
Cady town (St. Croix)	821	840	2.3	782	96.5	0.3	0.0	0.5	2.7	21.5	66.0	12.5	301	91.7	53.8	15.6
Calamus town (Dodge)	1,048	1,036	-1.1	947	98.4	0.0	0.0	0.3	1.3	20.2	65.6	14.3	393	81.4	51.9	22.9
Caledonia town (Columbia)	1,378	1,380	0.1	1,442	95.7	0.2	0.0	1.7	2.4	15.7	67.9	16.4	606	89.6	36.0	30.2
Caledonia village & MCD (Racine)	24,705	24,708	0.0	24,689	86.3	4.0	2.5	2.5	4.8	20.6	63.1	16.3	9,729	82.7	32.0	33.0
Caledonia town (Trempealeau)	920	948	3.0	871	96.7	0.0	1.1	1.6	0.6	21.0	64.4	14.5	335	93.1	43.0	20.3
Caledonia town (Waupaca)	1,627	1,657	1.8	1,471	96.3	1.8	0.0	1.4	0.5	19.1	67.4	13.5	598	97.0	51.8	21.2
Calumet town (Fond du Lac)	1,470	1,457	-0.9	1,423	97.2	0.0	0.4	1.9	0.5	17.6	58.7	23.5	614	91.2	52.9	18.2
Cambria village & MCD (Columbia)	767	758	-1.2	771	77.6	1.8	1.2	1.0	18.4	25.5	65.0	9.3	281	74.4	47.0	15.7
Cambridge village	1,451	1,488	2.5	1,362	96.0	1.1	0.0	1.9	1.0	23.9	56.4	19.8	607	73.8	28.3	36.9
Cambridge village (Dane)	1,342	1,378	2.7	1,254	96.7	1.2	0.0	1.6	0.6	21.9	57.0	21.1	576	74.5	29.0	36.8
Cambridge village (Jefferson)	109	110	0.9	108	88.0	0.0	0.0	5.6	6.5	48.2	47.3	4.6	31	61.3	16.1	38.7
Cameron village & MCD (Barron)	1,783	1,783	0.0	1,912	94.1	0.0	1.6	3.6	0.7	27.9	57.6	14.5	771	61.7	51.0	13.5
Cameron town (Wood)	518	508	-1.9	551	98.2	0.0	0.4	1.1	0.4	20.0	57.3	22.7	222	88.7	43.7	16.7

1 May be of any race.

Table A. All Places — **Population and Housing**

STATE City, town, township, borough, or CDP (county if applicable)	2010 census total population	2014 estimated population	Percent change 2010-2014	ACS total population estimate 2010-2014	White alone, not Hispanic or Latino	Black alone, not Hispanic or Latino	Asian alone, not Hispanic or Latino	All other races or 2 or more races, not Hispanic or Latino	Hispanic or Latino[1]	Under 18 years old	Age 18 to 64 years old	Age 65 years and older	Total occupied housing units	Percent owner occupied	High school diploma or less	Bachelor's degree or more
	1	2	3	4	5	6	7	8	9	10	11	12	13	14	15	16
WISCONSIN—Con.																
Campbell town (La Crosse)	4,311	4,407	2.2	4,384	98.3	0.1	0.7	0.9	0.0	16.8	68.9	14.1	2,000	68.6	35.1	29.6
Campbellsport village & MCD (Fond du Lac)	2,020	1,983	-1.8	1,906	96.9	0.1	0.3	2.6	0.1	23.4	55.3	21.4	734	72.6	54.1	15.5
Camp Douglas village & MCD (Juneau)	601	614	2.2	539	96.1	1.5	0.7	0.7	0.9	22.3	57.6	20.0	239	66.5	50.6	15.9
Camp Lake CDP	3,665	NA	NA	3,898	90.3	0.0	0.0	0.4	9.3	28.7	65.9	5.4	1,381	81.4	43.0	23.3
Canton town (Buffalo)	305	295	-3.3	305	97.7	0.0	0.0	0.0	2.3	19.7	63.4	17.0	134	78.4	50.0	14.9
Carey town (Iron)	163	163	0.0	140	94.3	1.4	0.0	2.9	1.4	11.4	53.6	35.0	74	82.4	36.5	17.6
Carlton town (Kewaunee)	1,014	1,012	-0.2	1,005	98.8	0.0	0.0	0.4	0.8	20.3	62.0	18.0	401	88.0	51.6	8.7
Caroline CDP	270	NA	NA	254	99.2	0.0	0.8	0.0	0.0	18.0	66.5	15.4	95	97.9	53.7	16.8
Carson town (Portage)	1,305	1,321	1.2	1,274	97.3	0.0	0.0	1.0	1.7	22.3	61.7	16.2	492	92.1	44.1	21.1
Cary town (Wood)	424	414	-2.4	487	92.8	0.0	0.0	0.0	7.2	21.9	60.8	17.2	208	89.4	52.9	20.7
Cascade village & MCD (Sheboygan)	709	701	-1.1	676	92.3	0.0	0.0	5.0	2.7	25.3	61.7	13.2	276	77.2	51.8	8.0
Casco village & MCD (Kewaunee)	592	581	-1.9	520	84.4	0.4	0.0	11.0	4.2	29.4	52.2	18.5	220	70.5	53.2	20.0
Casco town (Kewaunee)	1,156	1,165	0.8	1,145	99.3	0.0	0.0	0.3	0.4	18.8	61.4	19.8	456	88.6	52.0	12.1
Casey town (Washburn)	353	350	-0.8	386	98.7	0.0	0.0	0.5	0.8	10.3	56.5	33.2	198	94.4	36.4	32.8
Cashton village & MCD (Monroe)	1,104	1,093	-1.0	1,034	91.9	2.6	0.0	0.3	5.2	24.6	58.9	16.6	424	70.3	49.3	15.8
Cassel town (Marathon)	911	915	0.4	967	96.7	0.0	0.2	2.6	0.5	23.0	63.6	13.2	341	91.5	51.0	15.2
Cassian town (Oneida)	983	978	-0.5	922	96.1	0.0	0.0	0.4	3.5	17.3	58.9	23.8	391	94.9	39.4	27.6
Cassville village & MCD (Grant)	947	922	-2.6	804	98.9	0.0	0.0	0.1	1.0	18.0	52.4	29.6	366	74.0	53.6	19.1
Cassville town (Grant)	416	411	-1.2	435	98.9	0.0	0.0	0.5	0.7	20.7	59.4	19.8	177	94.4	52.0	11.9
Castle Rock town (Grant)	248	251	1.2	256	97.3	0.0	0.0	0.0	2.7	10.9	71.4	17.6	110	73.6	49.1	19.1
Caswell town (Forest)	91	86	-5.5	43	76.7	0.0	0.0	23.3	0.0	28.0	65.0	7.0	19	84.2	57.9	10.5
Cataract CDP	186	NA	NA	136	100.0	0.0	0.0	0.0	0.0	14.0	58.0	27.9	65	72.3	61.5	7.7
Catawba village & MCD (Price)	110	106	-3.6	100	93.0	0.0	0.0	0.0	7.0	23.0	54.0	23.0	56	91.1	69.6	3.6
Catawba town (Price)	277	268	-3.2	235	99.1	0.0	0.0	0.0	0.9	20.1	62.9	17.0	109	83.5	41.3	14.7
Cato town (Manitowoc)	1,563	1,549	-0.9	1,528	98.6	0.0	0.2	1.2	0.0	20.8	64.2	15.0	593	92.7	47.9	20.9
Cazenovia village	324	325	0.3	367	95.4	0.0	2.2	2.5	0.0	16.1	61.7	22.3	174	67.8	64.4	2.9
Cazenovia village (Richland)	314	315	0.3	353	95.2	0.0	2.3	2.5	0.0	16.6	60.5	22.7	170	67.1	64.7	2.9
Cazenovia village (Sauk)	10	10	0.0	14	100.0	0.0	0.0	0.0	0.0	0.0	85.7	14.3	4	100.0	50.0	0.0
Cecil village & MCD (Shawano)	570	559	-1.9	608	97.2	0.0	0.0	1.8	1.0	15.2	64.9	20.1	286	58.7	41.6	15.7
Cedarburg city & MCD (Ozaukee)	11,461	11,506	0.4	11,485	91.7	0.8	2.6	0.7	4.1	26.3	58.0	15.7	4,657	71.0	19.6	52.4
Cedarburg town (Ozaukee)	5,729	5,845	2.0	5,788	96.4	0.2	0.8	0.4	2.2	23.6	59.4	16.9	1,946	94.2	17.9	57.3
Cedar Grove village & MCD (Sheboygan)	2,113	2,109	-0.2	2,139	97.0	0.0	0.0	1.2	1.7	27.6	59.0	13.4	835	75.9	45.5	24.6
Cedar Lake town (Barron)	948	948	0.0	1,091	96.2	0.1	1.1	1.6	1.0	13.7	61.2	25.0	511	92.2	47.0	17.2
Cedar Rapids town (Rusk)	41	40	-2.4	21	100.0	0.0	0.0	0.0	0.0	14.3	66.7	19.0	11	100.0	63.6	9.1
Center town (Outagamie)	3,402	3,486	2.5	3,440	100.0	0.0	0.0	0.0	0.0	19.4	68.1	12.4	1,342	94.9	50.8	20.4
Center town (Rock)	1,064	1,068	0.4	1,053	91.5	0.3	0.0	1.8	6.5	19.7	61.3	19.0	411	88.3	44.5	20.9
Centerville town (Manitowoc)	641	631	-1.6	664	94.0	0.9	0.0	0.8	4.4	22.5	59.3	18.2	258	77.9	41.9	24.4
Centuria village & MCD (Polk)	947	922	-2.6	1,001	88.8	1.3	1.8	4.4	3.7	36.3	51.5	12.3	387	50.1	60.5	10.1
Chain O' Lakes CDP	981	NA	NA	1,011	100.0	0.0	0.0	0.0	0.0	7.9	56.8	35.4	556	84.2	23.0	46.0
Charlestown town (Calumet)	775	782	0.9	805	93.8	2.6	0.0	3.6	0.0	25.2	56.0	18.8	293	89.8	55.3	15.7
Chase town (Oconto)	3,005	3,002	-0.1	3,020	96.8	0.2	0.2	0.6	2.2	32.6	61.1	6.3	939	94.7	44.4	22.5
Chaseburg village & MCD (Vernon)	288	299	3.8	234	96.6	0.0	0.4	1.7	1.3	17.9	65.6	16.2	112	65.2	49.1	8.9
Chelsea CDP	113	NA	NA	109	96.3	0.0	0.0	0.0	3.7	21.1	51.4	27.5	42	100.0	76.2	0.0
Chelsea town (Taylor)	804	799	-0.6	775	97.9	0.0	0.0	0.4	1.7	22.9	63.9	13.2	336	90.8	64.9	7.4
Chenequa village & MCD (Waukesha)	587	600	2.2	536	97.8	0.0	0.7	0.9	0.6	14.9	48.9	36.2	238	89.9	15.5	71.4
Chester town (Dodge)	687	678	-1.3	756	97.1	0.0	0.0	0.0	2.9	22.9	61.8	15.3	265	90.2	52.1	16.2
Chetek city & MCD (Barron)	2,221	2,191	-1.4	2,413	94.3	0.0	0.0	0.8	4.8	21.7	56.9	21.3	995	60.4	48.2	16.6
Chetek town (Barron)	1,644	1,628	-1.0	1,712	97.4	1.1	0.0	0.9	0.7	14.4	56.8	29.0	750	91.9	42.3	16.5
Chicog town (Washburn)	234	232	-0.9	276	96.7	0.0	0.0	3.3	0.0	2.9	65.7	31.5	172	92.4	54.7	16.9
Chief Lake CDP	583	NA	NA	555	29.2	0.0	0.0	62.3	8.5	23.8	49.9	26.3	219	71.2	54.3	7.8
Chili CDP	226	NA	NA	298	97.7	0.0	0.0	2.3	0.0	36.2	56.9	6.7	107	76.6	50.5	37.4
Chilton city & MCD (Calumet)	3,947	3,922	-0.6	3,953	96.6	0.1	0.0	0.1	3.2	22.4	60.5	16.9	1,658	65.2	57.2	15.7
Chilton town (Calumet)	1,127	1,125	-0.2	1,228	98.8	0.0	0.0	0.0	1.2	23.1	61.9	15.1	441	91.2	48.8	26.8
Chimney Rock town (Trempealeau)	241	248	2.9	167	98.2	0.0	0.0	0.6	1.2	22.2	63.6	14.4	64	89.1	54.7	17.2
Chippewa town (Ashland)	374	374	0.0	316	98.4	0.0	0.0	1.3	0.3	13.9	66.3	19.6	150	93.3	70.7	12.7
Chippewa Falls city & MCD (Chippewa)	13,727	13,965	1.7	13,803	94.9	1.8	0.6	1.8	1.0	22.3	59.4	18.3	6,240	53.9	46.3	21.5
Christiana town (Dane)	1,243	1,297	4.3	1,240	92.9	2.7	0.2	4.0	0.2	22.9	62.8	14.4	495	72.3	47.7	26.7
Christiana town (Vernon)	931	961	3.2	915	97.9	0.4	0.0	0.5	1.1	17.6	70.1	12.0	360	91.4	45.6	22.5
Cicero town (Outagamie)	1,103	1,096	-0.6	1,154	97.1	0.0	0.0	1.6	1.4	24.8	60.9	14.2	406	93.8	60.6	12.8
City Point town (Jackson)	182	181	-0.5	225	99.6	0.4	0.0	0.0	0.0	16.8	55.2	28.0	110	62.7	55.5	26.4
Clam Falls town (Polk)	596	587	-1.5	529	97.0	0.0	0.0	2.1	0.9	20.6	59.5	19.8	224	92.0	47.3	13.8
Clam Lake CDP	37	NA	NA	61	98.4	0.0	0.0	1.6	0.0	0.0	45.8	54.1	33	87.9	63.6	9.1
Clarno town (Green)	1,177	1,194	1.4	1,061	91.0	0.0	0.0	0.0	9.0	20.7	66.0	13.2	434	75.1	50.7	15.7
Clay Banks town (Door)	382	388	1.6	350	94.3	0.0	0.0	0.0	5.7	20.8	56.1	22.9	146	91.1	44.5	32.2
Clayton town (Crawford)	958	927	-3.2	962	97.4	0.1	0.0	0.2	2.3	21.1	62.6	16.4	351	84.6	53.0	19.1
Clayton village & MCD (Polk)	571	551	-3.5	742	89.1	2.4	0.0	2.6	5.9	37.6	57.9	4.4	246	61.8	60.2	11.8
Clayton town (Polk)	975	964	-1.1	1,044	99.4	0.0	0.0	0.6	0.0	19.5	61.8	18.6	427	81.0	44.5	19.0
Clayton town (Winnebago)	3,951	4,070	3.0	4,010	90.6	0.3	4.2	3.4	1.5	23.5	62.2	14.5	1,548	95.5	32.4	36.4

1 May be of any race.

Table A. All Places — Population and Housing

STATE City, town, township, borough, or CDP (county if applicable)	2010 census total population	2014 estimated population	Percent change 2010-2014	ACS total population estimate 2010-2014	White alone, not Hispanic or Latino	Black alone, not Hispanic or Latino	Asian alone, not Hispanic or Latino	All other races or 2 or more races, not Hispanic or Latino	Hispanic or Latino[1]	Under 18 years old	Age 18 to 64 years old	Age 65 years and older	Total occupied housing units	Percent owner occupied	High school diploma or less	Bachelor's degree or more
	1	2	3	4	5	6	7	8	9	10	11	12	13	14	15	16
WISCONSIN—Con.																
Clear Creek town (Eau Claire)	821	844	2.8	814	97.9	0.0	0.0	1.6	0.5	23.9	57.9	18.3	297	87.9	41.1	19.5
Clearfield town (Juneau)	728	712	-2.2	630	95.2	0.0	0.0	1.3	3.5	16.5	60.0	23.5	258	92.2	51.9	17.8
Clear Lake village & MCD (Polk)	1,070	1,039	-2.9	919	96.6	0.0	0.2	0.0	3.2	20.3	56.0	23.7	440	69.8	55.5	13.4
Clear Lake town (Polk)	899	883	-1.8	783	98.9	0.0	0.0	1.0	0.1	26.3	62.6	11.0	292	91.1	44.5	15.4
Cleveland town (Chippewa)	864	881	2.0	1,007	94.1	1.3	0.0	1.8	2.8	20.1	69.9	10.0	354	85.6	62.4	12.4
Cleveland town (Jackson)	473	484	2.3	524	98.1	0.0	0.0	0.6	1.3	27.4	60.1	12.4	183	86.3	48.6	16.9
Cleveland village & MCD (Manitowoc)	1,489	1,480	-0.6	1,599	88.4	0.4	1.4	1.3	8.6	32.4	56.6	10.9	573	87.1	42.8	29.1
Cleveland town (Marathon)	1,488	1,496	0.5	1,542	95.3	1.0	0.5	2.7	0.5	27.8	60.7	11.5	544	91.0	47.8	19.5
Cleveland town (Taylor)	268	261	-2.6	251	100.0	0.0	0.0	0.0	0.0	16.4	68.3	15.5	117	89.7	58.1	21.4
Clifton town (Grant)	385	385	0.0	409	99.5	0.0	0.0	0.0	0.5	31.8	55.3	13.0	127	89.8	55.1	23.6
Clifton town (Monroe)	690	690	0.0	717	99.0	0.0	0.4	0.6	0.0	40.5	49.8	9.6	194	85.1	51.5	18.0
Clifton town (Pierce)	2,012	2,014	0.1	1,973	97.4	0.8	0.2	0.7	1.0	29.2	61.2	9.6	692	94.7	24.9	49.7
Clinton town (Barron)	879	873	-0.7	806	94.9	0.0	1.1	4.0	0.0	27.5	55.7	16.9	291	89.3	66.0	11.7
Clinton village & MCD (Rock)	2,152	2,133	-0.9	1,997	91.6	1.8	0.4	2.5	3.8	22.0	63.6	14.5	775	61.8	49.2	16.3
Clinton town (Rock)	932	951	2.0	912	94.1	0.2	0.1	2.4	3.2	26.0	63.6	10.2	325	88.0	51.4	18.8
Clinton town (Vernon)	1,356	1,363	0.5	1,614	99.5	0.0	0.0	0.0	0.5	48.6	44.7	6.8	370	76.2	72.4	6.5
Clintonville city & MCD (Waupaca)	4,567	4,481	-1.9	4,516	94.7	0.0	0.0	0.3	5.0	24.0	58.5	17.6	1,960	70.2	56.7	11.1
Clover town (Bayfield)	223	224	0.4	187	92.0	0.0	0.0	3.2	4.8	8.0	59.4	32.6	96	96.9	29.2	32.3
Cloverland town (Douglas)	210	208	-1.0	212	94.3	0.9	0.5	4.2	0.0	21.2	60.8	17.9	87	90.8	49.4	17.2
Cloverland town (Vilas)	1,029	1,030	0.1	996	95.5	0.6	0.2	0.9	2.8	17.8	51.3	30.6	485	80.0	31.3	40.6
Clyde town (Iowa)	306	312	2.0	283	97.2	0.4	0.0	1.8	0.7	16.2	65.4	18.4	125	87.2	36.8	32.0
Clyman village & MCD (Dodge)	422	407	-3.6	376	86.2	2.1	1.1	7.2	3.5	18.9	68.4	12.8	150	64.7	64.0	6.7
Clyman town (Dodge)	774	764	-1.3	742	96.2	0.8	0.0	1.6	1.3	16.8	63.6	19.5	288	84.4	57.6	10.8
Cobb village & MCD (Iowa)	458	461	0.7	506	87.2	0.0	11.7	0.0	1.2	26.6	59.8	13.6	206	79.6	37.4	14.1
Cochrane village & MCD (Buffalo)	450	428	-4.9	470	98.9	0.0	0.0	0.0	1.1	26.6	50.6	22.8	211	61.6	63.5	12.3
Colburn town (Adams)	221	216	-2.3	232	97.8	0.4	0.0	0.0	1.7	13.3	56.8	29.7	102	78.4	72.5	2.9
Colburn town (Chippewa)	856	874	2.1	919	93.5	0.0	0.5	3.3	2.7	20.4	64.2	15.5	350	85.7	58.6	8.9
Colby city	1,852	1,832	-1.1	1,788	84.1	0.1	0.8	2.3	12.6	24.8	53.2	22.0	723	58.8	64.2	10.1
Colby city (Clark)	1,354	1,342	-0.9	1,186	90.1	0.0	0.0	1.8	8.2	23.2	54.6	22.3	468	66.2	57.3	13.9
Colby city (Marathon)	498	490	-1.6	602	72.4	0.3	2.5	3.5	21.3	27.8	50.9	21.3	255	45.1	76.9	3.1
Colby town (Clark)	872	872	0.0	758	95.0	0.0	0.0	1.6	3.4	36.9	52.4	10.7	241	90.5	64.3	10.8
Cold Spring town (Jefferson)	727	740	1.8	843	92.8	0.0	0.0	2.5	4.7	26.7	57.7	15.7	276	85.9	33.7	33.7
Coleman village & MCD (Marinette)	724	711	-1.8	697	97.1	0.1	0.0	0.3	2.4	22.9	58.5	18.5	324	63.3	47.8	11.7
Colfax village & MCD (Dunn)	1,158	1,161	0.3	1,135	96.8	0.8	0.0	1.8	0.6	26.8	51.2	22.0	453	61.4	57.6	12.6
Colfax town (Dunn)	1,186	1,212	2.2	1,077	91.4	0.0	0.4	1.9	6.4	26.4	61.9	11.5	407	84.0	43.7	20.9
Collins CDP	164	NA	NA	178	100.0	0.0	0.0	0.0	0.0	16.3	75.4	8.4	68	88.2	61.8	10.3
Coloma village & MCD (Waushara)	450	441	-2.0	415	98.1	0.5	0.0	1.2	0.2	23.1	59.8	17.1	170	81.2	50.6	10.0
Coloma town (Waushara)	753	747	-0.8	676	95.4	0.0	0.7	0.7	3.1	13.8	59.8	26.3	306	92.5	54.6	18.3
Columbus city	4,992	4,998	0.1	5,014	93.8	0.9	1.4	1.4	2.5	25.3	59.7	15.1	2,006	70.2	36.3	33.8
Columbus city (Columbia)	4,992	4,998	0.1	5,014	93.8	0.9	1.4	1.4	2.5	25.3	59.7	15.1	2,006	70.2	36.3	33.8
Columbus city (Dodge)	0	0	0.0	0	0.0	0.0	0.0	0.0	0.0	0.0	0.0	0.0	0	0.0	0.0	0.0
Columbus town (Columbia)	645	643	-0.3	596	95.8	1.3	0.7	0.2	2.0	17.6	59.0	23.3	247	74.9	48.6	21.9
Combined Locks village & MCD (Outagamie)	3,323	3,503	5.4	3,407	95.1	2.1	0.0	0.6	2.1	25.6	56.4	17.8	1,281	92.4	38.8	23.8
Commonwealth town (Florence)	399	404	1.3	433	96.5	0.0	0.5	0.5	2.5	18.4	60.2	21.2	169	93.5	50.9	19.5
Como CDP	2,631	NA	NA	2,582	81.5	0.0	1.5	0.8	16.2	27.8	62.1	10.1	1,011	73.9	47.3	22.7
Concord town (Jefferson)	2,049	2,068	0.9	2,158	96.8	0.3	0.2	0.7	2.0	23.6	61.5	14.9	795	91.4	46.3	18.5
Conover town (Vilas)	1,235	1,237	0.2	1,223	97.0	0.0	0.5	2.0	0.6	12.9	53.4	33.6	606	86.8	45.7	20.1
Conrath village & MCD (Rusk)	98	94	-4.1	109	100.0	0.0	0.0	0.0	0.0	18.4	63.4	18.3	51	60.8	76.5	9.8
Cooks Valley town (Chippewa)	805	818	1.6	882	99.7	0.0	0.0	0.0	0.3	27.5	67.3	5.3	286	87.8	51.0	12.6
Coon town (Vernon)	728	749	2.9	702	98.4	0.0	0.1	1.0	0.4	16.7	60.6	22.6	314	92.4	43.0	20.7
Coon Valley village & MCD (Vernon)	765	779	1.8	766	99.5	0.1	0.4	0.0	0.0	23.5	60.7	15.7	325	84.0	47.1	21.8
Cooperstown town (Manitowoc)	1,292	1,282	-0.8	1,344	99.5	0.0	0.5	0.0	0.0	20.1	67.7	12.2	504	92.7	53.4	16.5
Cornell city & MCD (Chippewa)	1,465	1,448	-1.2	1,401	96.8	1.4	0.0	1.6	0.2	20.9	60.6	18.4	582	70.1	44.2	20.1
Corning town (Lincoln)	883	872	-1.2	729	98.9	0.0	0.0	0.7	0.4	21.8	65.1	13.0	314	91.4	50.3	7.0
Cornucopia CDP	98	NA	NA	76	100.0	0.0	0.0	0.0	0.0	1.3	48.6	50.0	48	95.8	29.2	8.3
Cottage Grove village & MCD (Dane)	6,357	6,664	4.8	6,533	78.2	0.7	7.0	0.8	13.3	30.7	61.9	7.5	2,268	76.9	22.9	49.0
Cottage Grove town (Dane)	3,732	3,924	5.1	3,846	97.3	0.5	0.9	1.4	0.0	22.5	65.7	11.6	1,544	92.9	28.1	22.5
Couderay village & MCD (Sawyer)	88	88	0.0	102	60.8	0.0	0.0	34.3	4.9	18.6	59.6	21.6	40	97.5	35.0	30.0
Couderay town (Sawyer)	401	399	-0.5	550	25.8	0.0	0.5	57.5	16.2	34.5	54.5	10.9	201	39.3	60.2	6.5
Courtland town (Columbia)	525	521	-0.8	547	95.2	0.0	0.7	1.3	2.7	29.9	59.6	10.6	198	85.9	59.6	15.2
Crandon city & MCD (Forest)	1,922	1,886	-1.9	1,843	85.3	1.1	0.2	13.0	0.4	22.7	59.3	18.0	718	65.7	54.3	16.4
Crandon town (Forest)	650	646	-0.6	703	88.6	0.0	0.0	6.3	5.1	24.0	61.3	14.8	252	80.6	56.3	15.1
Cranmoor town (Wood)	168	164	-2.4	167	88.0	0.0	0.0	10.8	1.2	32.4	58.2	9.6	53	45.3	52.8	18.9
Crescent town (Oneida)	2,013	2,004	-0.4	2,138	98.1	0.1	0.5	0.8	0.5	16.5	63.9	19.5	831	88.4	29.6	35.1

1 May be of any race.

Table A. All Places — Population and Housing

STATE City, town, township, borough, or CDP (county if applicable)	2010 census total population	2014 estimated population	Percent change 2010-2014	ACS total population estimate 2010-2014	White alone, not Hispanic or Latino	Black alone, not Hispanic or Latino	Asian alone, not Hispanic or Latino	All other races or 2 or more races, not Hispanic or Latino	Hispanic or Latino[1]	Under 18 years old	Age 18 to 64 years old	Age 65 years and older	Total occupied housing units	Percent owner occupied	High school diploma or less	Bachelor's degree or more
	1	2	3	4	5	6	7	8	9	10	11	12	13	14	15	16
WISCONSIN—Con.																
Crivitz village & MCD (Marinette)	984	972	-1.2	1,071	97.4	0.0	0.0	1.2	1.4	22.5	48.7	28.9	465	57.8	49.2	6.9
Cross town (Buffalo)	377	371	-1.6	320	99.7	0.0	0.0	0.0	0.3	22.2	63.9	14.1	135	88.1	51.1	22.2
Cross Plains village & MCD (Dane)	3,652	3,885	6.4	3,755	97.6	0.3	0.2	0.9	1.1	26.6	63.2	10.1	1,486	71.1	34.5	36.3
Cross Plains town (Dane)	1,407	1,475	4.8	1,561	95.5	0.4	0.3	1.1	2.7	22.5	64.0	13.7	571	89.5	27.0	41.0
Crystal town (Washburn)	267	265	-0.7	283	100.0	0.0	0.0	0.0	0.0	24.0	55.1	20.8	107	91.6	47.7	34.6
Crystal Lake town (Barron)	759	758	-0.1	748	95.1	0.7	0.0	2.4	1.9	19.4	62.4	18.2	319	88.7	50.8	14.1
Crystal Lake town (Marquette)	484	475	-1.9	507	90.9	0.0	1.8	7.3	0.0	11.7	59.9	28.6	238	94.1	49.6	23.5
Cuba City city (Grant)	2,086	2,046	-1.9	1,899	92.5	2.8	1.0	2.2	1.5	19.7	57.8	22.5	832	76.3	46.8	29.8
Cuba City city (Grant)	1,877	1,836	-2.2	1,677	92.7	3.2	1.1	1.3	1.7	20.5	55.9	23.6	735	73.2	47.8	29.4
Cuba City city (Lafayette)	209	210	0.5	222	91.0	0.0	0.0	9.0	0.0	13.1	72.6	14.4	97	100.0	39.2	33.0
Cudahy city & MCD (Milwaukee)	18,271	18,341	0.4	18,321	80.7	2.7	1.2	3.4	12.0	23.4	60.6	16.0	7,566	58.3	44.4	21.7
Cumberland city & MCD (Barron)	2,168	2,139	-1.3	2,414	91.5	0.0	0.0	2.0	6.5	23.6	53.5	23.0	1,004	61.0	47.1	24.6
Cumberland town (Barron)	876	875	-0.1	824	98.5	0.0	0.0	0.4	1.1	17.2	62.9	19.8	329	87.5	45.0	22.5
Curran town (Jackson)	343	345	0.6	361	96.7	0.0	0.0	0.6	2.8	26.9	60.8	12.2	147	88.4	57.1	8.8
Curtiss village & MCD (Clark)	216	215	-0.5	298	31.9	0.0	0.0	0.0	68.1	39.9	50.7	9.4	83	54.2	85.5	3.6
Cutler town (Juneau)	326	322	-1.2	300	88.7	0.0	5.0	6.3	0.0	15.3	62.4	22.3	125	79.2	53.6	7.2
Cylon town (St. Croix)	683	684	0.1	803	96.6	0.0	0.2	1.0	2.1	20.1	67.4	12.7	276	83.7	49.6	16.7
Dairyland town (Douglas)	184	186	1.1	181	99.4	0.0	0.0	0.0	0.6	13.3	61.2	25.4	100	86.0	62.0	5.0
Dakota town (Waushara)	1,230	1,213	-1.4	1,271	80.8	0.0	0.0	1.1	18.1	21.7	58.1	20.2	495	79.6	57.4	20.4
Dale CDP	528	NA	NA	538	95.9	0.0	0.0	4.1	0.0	25.8	58.9	15.4	199	100.0	39.7	14.6
Dale town (Outagamie)	2,738	2,800	2.3	2,766	98.3	0.0	0.0	0.4	1.1	23.7	65.4	10.7	981	97.0	40.1	22.9
Dallas village & MCD (Barron)	409	396	-3.2	388	99.7	0.0	0.0	0.0	0.3	18.1	61.0	20.9	150	68.0	46.0	8.0
Dallas town (Barron)	565	559	-1.1	551	91.1	0.0	0.9	1.3	6.7	25.3	59.9	14.9	208	86.1	54.3	15.4
Dalton CDP	206	NA	NA	225	94.2	0.0	0.0	1.8	4.0	30.2	56.5	13.3	82	86.6	35.4	29.3
Danbury CDP	172	NA	NA	238	81.9	0.0	0.0	18.1	0.0	37.5	49.6	13.0	92	78.3	59.8	3.3
Dane village & MCD (Dane)	997	1,100	10.3	1,154	86.8	1.0	0.0	1.0	11.1	28.6	66.0	5.4	414	59.4	40.6	21.5
Dane town (Dane)	986	1,031	4.6	943	93.7	0.0	1.6	0.2	4.5	13.4	70.4	16.2	374	81.3	51.6	22.5
Daniels town (Burnett)	649	646	-0.5	635	97.5	1.3	0.3	0.6	0.3	19.9	56.3	23.8	316	88.0	46.2	19.3
Darien village & MCD (Walworth)	1,580	1,605	1.6	1,598	77.1	1.8	0.4	1.8	19.0	23.9	69.7	6.4	568	62.5	49.6	18.3
Darien town (Walworth)	1,693	1,698	0.3	2,015	78.8	1.8	0.0	1.5	18.0	22.4	60.7	16.9	688	87.1	50.7	15.1
Darlington city & MCD (Lafayette)	2,454	2,411	-1.8	2,284	89.0	0.5	0.4	1.0	9.2	23.0	57.5	19.4	996	66.8	49.9	17.4
Darlington town (Lafayette)	872	877	0.6	890	99.0	0.0	0.2	0.8	0.0	27.0	56.9	16.1	328	86.9	43.9	25.6
Day town (Marathon)	1,085	1,133	4.4	919	99.7	0.0	0.0	0.1	0.2	20.5	66.9	12.6	368	87.2	51.9	15.5
Dayton town (Richland)	693	682	-1.6	565	98.6	0.0	0.0	0.9	0.5	21.9	61.9	16.3	236	76.7	52.5	18.2
Dayton town (Waupaca)	2,744	2,697	-1.7	2,722	93.3	0.0	0.3	0.0	6.5	21.9	61.5	16.6	1,014	87.8	34.4	32.8
Decatur town (Green)	1,766	1,794	1.6	1,704	95.7	0.1	0.8	2.4	1.0	19.3	66.0	14.7	637	84.3	44.9	27.5
Deer Creek town (Outagamie)	637	648	1.7	571	98.8	0.0	0.0	0.4	0.9	19.0	69.0	12.1	212	93.9	59.0	6.1
Deer Creek town (Taylor)	768	759	-1.2	654	99.4	0.0	0.0	0.6	0.0	32.0	57.9	10.1	241	83.4	69.3	6.6
Deerfield village & MCD (Dane)	2,311	2,492	7.8	2,468	93.3	1.6	0.3	1.6	3.2	28.1	64.2	7.6	897	77.6	26.5	35.8
Deerfield town (Dane)	1,597	1,665	4.3	1,702	91.8	7.1	0.2	0.4	0.6	20.7	69.8	9.7	556	86.9	31.7	33.6
Deerfield town (Waushara)	737	731	-0.8	583	97.4	0.9	0.0	1.0	0.7	13.5	54.2	32.2	266	93.2	43.6	31.6
Deer Park village & MCD (St. Croix)	216	218	0.9	216	96.8	0.0	0.5	1.9	0.9	23.2	51.9	25.0	101	68.3	62.4	5.0
DeForest village & MCD (Dane)	8,942	9,466	5.9	9,232	92.4	0.2	2.6	2.2	2.6	28.5	62.8	8.7	3,505	72.0	29.5	34.2
Dekorra town (Columbia)	2,304	2,309	0.2	1,917	94.9	0.0	0.2	1.6	3.3	13.5	66.4	20.1	851	90.6	32.9	23.1
Delafield city & MCD (Waukesha)	7,090	7,166	1.1	7,136	94.8	0.2	1.1	3.6	0.3	25.2	59.5	15.2	2,892	64.4	20.7	51.7
Delafield town (Waukesha)	8,385	8,296	-1.1	8,297	88.3	1.4	1.3	3.1	5.8	23.4	62.5	14.0	2,873	94.1	14.3	56.1
Delavan city & MCD (Walworth)	8,463	8,443	-0.2	8,467	68.7	0.0	0.4	1.6	29.3	25.4	59.8	14.8	3,134	57.5	48.1	18.6
Delavan town (Walworth)	5,285	5,338	1.0	5,307	83.3	0.7	0.9	1.6	13.5	21.7	60.5	17.8	2,174	76.0	34.5	29.6
Delavan Lake CDP	2,649	NA	NA	2,665	90.9	1.4	0.6	2.0	5.1	19.8	65.0	15.3	1,132	78.9	27.6	37.0
Dellona town (Sauk)	1,552	1,605	3.4	1,314	91.9	0.2	1.1	3.8	3.0	17.7	60.4	21.9	554	86.8	45.5	20.6
Dell Prairie town (Adams)	1,590	1,545	-2.8	1,542	94.9	0.5	0.0	1.8	2.8	21.6	61.3	17.1	576	89.2	46.4	14.6
Dellwood CDP	563	NA	NA	603	97.8	0.0	0.0	0.0	2.2	9.7	59.2	31.2	296	87.2	50.3	7.8
Delmar town (Chippewa)	935	954	2.0	1,070	98.4	0.0	0.0	1.3	0.3	24.0	65.5	10.6	378	87.8	49.7	18.3
Delta town (Bayfield)	273	275	0.7	294	96.9	0.0	0.0	3.1	0.0	10.5	57.6	32.0	150	97.3	36.0	36.7
Delton town (Sauk)	2,350	2,400	2.1	2,686	75.7	0.2	2.5	15.6	6.0	23.5	63.5	13.1	999	74.8	46.2	22.7
Denmark village & MCD (Brown)	2,122	2,182	2.8	2,172	96.4	0.2	0.0	2.1	1.2	27.5	58.6	14.0	903	67.9	59.7	16.6
De Pere city & MCD (Brown)	23,806	24,555	3.1	24,216	89.9	0.8	1.8	3.2	4.3	24.5	63.5	11.9	9,122	61.9	30.9	34.9
De Soto village	287	288	0.3	291	96.6	0.0	0.0	0.0	3.4	21.3	54.2	24.4	134	88.1	47.8	14.2
De Soto village (Crawford)	108	106	-1.9	96	89.6	0.0	0.0	0.0	10.4	29.2	63.6	7.3	39	89.7	33.3	7.7
De Soto village (Vernon)	179	182	1.7	195	100.0	0.0	0.0	0.0	0.0	17.4	49.8	32.8	95	87.4	53.7	16.8
Dewey town (Burnett)	516	516	0.0	550	82.9	0.0	0.9	14.2	2.0	25.4	52.0	22.5	207	76.3	47.3	15.9
Dewey town (Portage)	932	943	1.2	919	96.8	0.3	1.3	1.5	0.0	19.9	61.6	18.5	365	92.1	45.5	19.7
Dewey town (Rusk)	545	529	-2.9	633	99.2	0.0	0.0	0.8	0.0	25.0	54.8	20.1	268	84.3	41.0	17.2
Dewhurst town (Clark)	323	327	1.2	314	97.5	0.0	0.6	1.3	0.6	18.1	49.5	32.5	163	82.8	40.5	15.3
Dexter town (Wood)	359	352	-1.9	380	98.7	0.0	0.0	0.5	0.8	19.7	62.9	17.4	164	87.8	64.6	12.8
Diamond Bluff CDP	194	NA	NA	202	100.0	0.0	0.0	0.0	0.0	18.9	57.5	23.8	87	95.4	43.7	8.0
Diamond Bluff town (Pierce)	469	467	-0.4	464	98.1	0.0	0.0	1.5	0.4	21.6	61.3	17.2	188	82.4	45.2	13.3
Diaperville CDP	70	NA	NA	55	0.0	0.0	5.5	94.5	0.0	34.6	63.7	1.8	17	100.0	70.6	17.6

1 May be of any race.

Table A. All Places — **Population and Housing**

STATE City, town, township, borough, or CDP (county if applicable)	2010 census total population	2014 estimated population	Percent change 2010-2014	ACS total population estimate 2010-2014	White alone, not Hispanic or Latino	Black alone, not Hispanic or Latino	Asian alone, not Hispanic or Latino	All other races or 2 or more races, not Hispanic or Latino	Hispanic or Latino[1]	Under 18 years old	Age 18 to 64 years old	Age 65 years and older	Total occupied housing units	Percent owner occupied	High school diploma or less	Bachelor's degree or more
	1	2	3	4	5	6	7	8	9	10	11	12	13	14	15	16
Dickeyville village & MCD (Grant)......................	1,061	1,040	-2.0	1,024	99.3	0.0	0.0	0.7	0.0	18.8	61.7	19.5	458	70.5	58.7	17.5
Dodge CDP	121	NA	NA	133	100.0	0.0	0.0	0.0	0.0	16.6	64.7	18.8	66	40.9	40.9	24.2
Dodge town (Trempealeau)..........	389	401	3.1	413	98.5	0.0	0.5	0.0	1.0	18.9	65.6	15.5	187	72.7	47.1	21.4
Dodgeville city & MCD (Iowa)...............	4,693	4,686	-0.1	4,693	96.2	0.6	0.7	1.6	0.9	24.9	58.7	16.5	1,977	65.0	35.0	27.6
Dodgeville town (Iowa)	1,708	1,739	1.8	1,734	97.5	0.0	0.9	1.6	0.0	22.4	61.7	15.9	658	85.9	32.8	33.7
Dorchester village	876	863	-1.5	929	86.3	0.0	0.0	0.0	13.7	28.9	59.9	11.1	370	65.9	71.6	5.9
Dorchester village (Clark).	871	858	-1.5	929	86.3	0.0	0.0	0.0	13.7	28.9	59.9	11.1	370	65.9	71.6	5.9
Dorchester village (Marathon)..............	5	5	0.0	0	0.0	0.0	0.0	0.0	0.0	0.0	0.0	0.0	0	0.0	0.0	0.0
Doty town (Oconto)..........	260	258	-0.8	247	99.6	0.0	0.0	0.4	0.0	6.0	51.5	42.5	144	94.4	56.3	11.8
Douglas town (Marquette)	725	711	-1.9	686	97.4	0.0	0.0	0.7	1.9	21.0	55.9	23.2	291	89.3	51.2	24.7
Dousman village & MCD (Waukesha)..............	2,282	2,331	2.1	2,274	95.3	0.2	1.0	1.1	2.4	23.4	55.0	21.7	926	57.7	35.1	25.5
Dover town (Buffalo)........	486	477	-1.9	553	96.6	0.0	0.0	2.2	1.3	32.0	62.0	6.1	183	91.8	54.6	11.5
Dover town (Racine)........	4,071	4,089	0.4	4,043	89.5	5.8	0.0	1.9	2.8	19.3	68.2	12.5	1,244	89.8	39.1	24.3
Dovre town (Barron)........	849	841	-0.9	797	99.7	0.0	0.0	0.0	0.3	27.3	62.9	9.9	292	88.4	56.5	10.6
Downing village & MCD (Dunn)......................	265	267	0.8	279	96.8	0.0	0.0	0.7	2.5	29.3	60.7	10.0	90	78.9	63.3	20.0
Downsville CDP	146	NA	NA	129	100.0	0.0	0.0	0.0	0.0	33.4	55.8	10.9	53	62.3	45.3	32.1
Doyle town (Barron).........	453	449	-0.9	492	97.8	0.0	0.0	2.0	0.2	25.8	63.9	10.4	193	93.8	60.1	15.5
Doylestown village & MCD (Columbia)...................	297	296	-0.3	303	98.0	0.0	0.0	1.0	1.0	23.5	68.0	8.6	119	85.7	56.3	5.0
Drammen town (Eau Claire).....................	783	806	2.9	791	91.3	0.0	0.0	5.9	2.8	25.0	55.2	20.1	313	93.3	28.8	20.4
Draper town (Sawyer).......	204	204	0.0	196	98.5	0.0	0.5	0.0	1.0	3.0	57.1	39.8	102	83.3	63.7	11.8
Dresser village & MCD (Polk).....................	888	863	-2.8	871	96.7	0.9	1.0	0.6	0.8	28.6	60.9	10.7	375	68.3	46.7	9.9
Drummond CDP	154	NA	NA	159	95.6	0.0	1.3	3.1	0.0	18.9	58.4	22.6	82	57.3	42.7	28.0
Drummond town (Bayfield)	463	458	-1.1	486	97.1	0.0	0.6	2.3	0.0	9.9	60.2	30.0	241	80.1	34.0	29.0
Dunbar CDP	50	NA	NA	116	81.0	0.0	0.0	19.0	0.0	44.9	41.4	13.8	39	64.1	56.4	15.4
Dunbar town (Marinette)...	1,094	852	-22.1	1,103	94.7	0.0	0.4	4.4	0.5	14.2	71.7	14.1	267	73.0	38.6	35.6
Dunkirk town (Dane)........	1,902	1,999	5.1	1,835	96.6	0.3	0.0	2.0	1.0	17.1	67.0	15.9	780	91.8	31.7	29.1
Dunn town (Dane)...........	4,930	5,159	4.6	5,049	96.0	0.8	0.0	2.0	1.2	17.3	63.5	19.2	2,257	89.2	30.4	35.6
Dunn town (Dunn)	1,524	1,551	1.8	1,341	99.7	0.0	0.3	0.0	0.0	20.8	61.5	17.7	568	78.5	48.4	19.2
Dupont town (Waupaca) ...	738	737	-0.1	786	96.6	0.0	0.0	1.5	1.9	31.5	53.7	15.0	275	88.4	67.6	12.4
Durand city & MCD (Pepin).....................	1,931	1,869	-3.2	1,755	97.4	0.7	0.1	0.5	1.2	19.6	57.2	23.2	793	67.6	55.4	17.4
Durand town (Pepin)........	742	723	-2.6	651	95.9	0.6	0.0	2.9	0.6	22.2	66.7	11.2	250	93.6	46.0	20.0
Dyckesville CDP	538	NA	NA	502	95.4	0.0	1.4	0.0	3.2	22.3	51.4	26.5	214	86.0	31.3	50.0
Eagle town (Richland)	531	523	-1.5	526	98.7	0.4	0.0	0.4	0.6	27.0	53.8	19.4	198	82.8	52.5	13.6
Eagle village & MCD (Waukesha)..............	1,953	1,953	0.0	1,864	95.8	0.3	0.0	0.9	3.0	28.1	64.4	7.5	676	88.9	33.7	29.3
Eagle town (Waukesha).....	3,504	3,533	0.8	3,531	95.4	1.7	1.2	1.7	0.0	25.4	62.9	11.7	1,212	94.4	30.0	29.9
Eagle Lake CDP	1,192	NA	NA	1,229	97.2	0.0	0.0	0.0	2.8	14.7	74.3	10.8	467	91.2	42.2	27.2
Eagle Point town (Chippewa)..................	3,049	3,124	2.5	3,095	98.5	0.0	0.0	1.5	0.0	19.8	61.9	18.2	1,155	87.8	42.6	17.8
Eagle River city & MCD (Vilas).....................	1,398	1,358	-2.9	1,647	88.1	1.8	0.4	6.9	2.8	20.9	59.5	19.7	759	43.1	46.1	21.1
Eastman village & MCD (Crawford)	428	411	-4.0	395	99.7	0.0	0.0	0.3	0.0	24.3	60.1	15.7	160	73.8	63.1	12.5
Eastman town (Crawford) .	739	717	-3.0	790	98.7	0.0	0.0	0.4	0.9	25.6	59.1	15.3	273	83.5	52.0	18.7
Easton town (Adams)	1,130	1,087	-3.8	1,008	98.1	0.0	0.0	1.9	0.0	19.9	59.3	20.8	384	88.3	61.5	8.9
Easton town (Marathon) ...	1,111	1,140	2.6	1,071	99.3	0.0	0.0	0.2	0.5	24.5	60.9	14.7	404	98.5	47.3	22.0
East Troy village & MCD (Walworth)................	4,281	4,306	0.6	4,300	95.8	0.5	0.0	0.7	2.9	30.9	57.0	12.2	1,682	57.8	35.3	23.5
East Troy town (Walworth)	4,021	4,089	1.7	4,062	94.2	2.3	0.0	3.2	0.3	14.2	68.0	17.7	1,802	86.8	34.5	30.1
Eaton town (Brown)..........	1,508	1,560	3.4	1,422	98.2	0.0	0.0	0.0	1.8	24.0	66.5	9.7	501	89.2	55.3	15.0
Eaton town (Clark)...........	712	701	-1.5	654	99.5	0.0	0.0	0.5	0.0	28.9	62.2	8.9	232	87.1	48.3	14.7
Eaton town (Manitowoc) ...	836	823	-1.6	762	96.6	0.0	3.4	0.0	0.0	22.5	65.5	11.9	297	92.3	53.2	12.1
Eau Claire city	66,190	67,684	2.3	67,036	89.8	0.8	4.0	3.1	2.4	19.3	69.0	11.9	27,255	53.4	28.8	31.0
Eau Claire city (Chippewa)	1,974	2,002	1.4	1,826	79.7	0.1	15.2	4.3	0.7	28.1	58.4	13.6	761	67.9	45.1	15.2
Eau Claire city (Eau Claire).....................	64,216	65,682	2.3	65,210	90.1	0.9	3.7	3.0	2.4	19.0	69.4	11.8	26,494	53.0	28.3	31.4
Eau Galle town (Dunn)	757	772	2.0	754	99.2	0.0	0.0	0.4	0.4	19.1	61.0	19.8	323	84.5	50.5	20.1
Eau Galle town (St. Croix)	1,139	1,176	3.2	1,029	93.8	0.0	3.8	1.5	1.0	21.8	66.1	12.2	389	87.9	37.5	29.0
Eau Pleine town (Marathon)	773	809	4.7	824	99.5	0.0	0.0	0.0	0.5	21.2	64.9	13.7	311	88.1	64.3	12.9
Eau Pleine town (Portage)	906	917	1.2	1,079	96.5	0.4	0.6	1.8	0.7	25.2	62.0	12.9	394	86.5	44.7	20.1
Eden village & MCD (Fond du Lac)....................	875	868	-0.8	749	97.5	0.0	0.0	0.7	1.9	29.7	57.1	13.1	304	79.6	54.9	11.8
Eden town (Fond du Lac) .	1,024	1,035	1.1	998	93.9	0.8	0.0	1.1	3.3	21.8	61.8	16.2	369	86.4	54.7	19.5
Eden town (Iowa).............	355	360	1.4	336	99.1	0.0	0.0	0.0	0.9	24.2	58.4	17.6	136	83.1	33.1	31.6
Edgar village & MCD (Marathon)	1,479	1,470	-0.6	1,561	96.6	0.0	0.0	1.7	1.7	28.1	57.7	14.2	593	78.4	55.8	13.8
Edgerton city	5,418	5,513	1.8	5,478	93.6	0.0	0.0	1.2	5.3	24.0	60.8	15.4	2,430	65.2	40.0	20.5
Edgerton city (Dane)	59	61	3.4	89	100.0	0.0	0.0	0.0	0.0	13.5	75.3	11.2	57	86.0	78.9	14.0
Edgerton city (Rock).........	5,359	5,452	1.7	5,389	93.5	0.0	0.0	1.2	5.4	24.2	60.4	15.4	2,373	64.7	39.1	20.7
Edgewater town (Sawyer).	519	518	-0.2	526	95.6	0.0	1.0	2.9	0.6	6.3	62.1	31.6	285	89.5	41.1	19.3
Edmund CDP	173	NA	NA	163	96.3	0.0	0.0	3.7	0.0	30.1	61.3	8.6	75	60.0	46.7	4.0
Edson town (Chippewa)....	1,089	1,111	2.0	1,170	98.0	0.0	0.0	0.2	1.0	29.6	58.9	11.5	388	84.5	65.5	3.9
Egg Harbor village & MCD (Door).....................	201	203	1.0	278	98.6	0.4	0.0	0.0	1.1	9.7	49.6	40.6	152	69.7	19.7	57.9
Egg Harbor town (Door) ...	1,342	1,339	-0.2	1,385	81.7	0.0	0.7	1.9	15.7	16.3	55.3	28.3	632	84.8	43.4	29.0
Eileen town (Bayfield).......	681	683	0.3	664	95.0	0.0	0.2	4.4	0.5	17.9	60.8	21.2	303	86.5	38.3	22.8
Eisenstein town (Price).....	630	615	-2.4	553	95.7	0.0	0.0	4.3	0.0	18.4	59.5	22.1	269	93.3	54.6	16.7
Eland village & MCD (Shawano)..................	202	203	0.5	266	72.9	0.4	0.0	5.6	21.1	24.9	65.6	9.4	91	83.5	65.9	11.0
Elba town (Dodge)............	996	985	-1.1	1,078	99.0	0.0	0.0	0.6	0.4	18.4	66.8	14.8	433	84.1	45.0	30.0

1 May be of any race.

Table A. All Places — **Population and Housing**

STATE City, town, township, borough, or CDP (county if applicable)	2010 census total population	2014 estimated population	Percent change 2010-2014	ACS total population estimate 2010-2014	White alone, not Hispanic or Latino	Black alone, not Hispanic or Latino	Asian alone, not Hispanic or Latino	All other races or 2 or more races, not Hispanic or Latino	Hispanic or Latino[1]	Under 18 years old	Age 18 to 64 years old	Age 65 years and older	Total occupied housing units	Percent owner occupied	High school diploma or less	Bachelor's degree or more
	1	2	3	4	5	6	7	8	9	10	11	12	13	14	15	16
WISCONSIN—Con.																
Elcho CDP	339	NA	NA	275	92.4	0.0	0.0	5.8	1.8	7.0	70.2	22.9	167	68.9	46.1	8.4
Elcho town (Langlade)	1,233	1,209	-1.9	1,208	97.4	0.0	0.0	2.2	0.4	12.4	53.9	33.6	593	83.5	53.1	10.8
Elderon village & MCD (Marathon)	179	181	1.1	161	92.5	0.0	0.0	5.6	1.9	28.6	56.5	14.9	69	69.6	65.2	14.5
Elderon town (Marathon)	606	635	4.8	597	97.7	0.0	0.0	1.8	0.5	17.0	58.2	24.8	253	88.1	67.2	10.7
Eldorado town (Fond du Lac)	1,462	1,446	-1.1	1,428	98.3	0.0	0.4	0.6	0.8	23.0	61.2	15.8	556	90.1	48.2	18.5
Eleva village & MCD (Trempealeau)	670	678	1.2	735	95.8	3.1	0.0	0.3	0.8	22.9	59.0	18.2	335	63.9	51.6	12.5
Elk town (Price)	978	958	-2.0	969	97.3	0.0	1.0	1.3	0.3	13.6	58.8	27.8	489	87.3	40.1	21.3
Elk Grove town (Lafayette)	551	553	0.4	518	99.4	0.2	0.0	0.4	0.0	32.8	57.0	10.2	157	80.9	37.6	28.0
Elkhart Lake village & MCD (Sheboygan)	967	961	-0.6	961	99.9	0.0	0.0	0.1	0.0	16.1	56.8	27.2	455	74.5	32.3	34.7
Elkhorn city & MCD (Walworth)	10,084	9,975	-1.1	10,020	86.9	1.9	0.0	1.6	9.5	25.9	62.2	11.9	4,009	60.2	37.0	21.5
Elk Mound village & MCD (Dunn)	878	875	-0.3	981	88.4	0.0	5.1	1.0	5.5	29.8	60.7	9.5	366	58.2	47.8	17.8
Elk Mound town (Dunn)	1,792	1,838	2.6	1,793	95.0	0.3	3.5	0.8	0.4	32.5	57.8	9.7	617	77.3	33.5	29.5
Ellenboro town (Grant)	525	527	0.4	659	91.8	0.0	1.7	6.2	0.3	28.4	64.2	7.4	219	88.6	50.7	24.7
Ellington town (Outagamie)	2,758	2,888	4.7	2,819	96.3	1.3	0.0	1.8	0.6	25.0	65.0	10.2	998	94.1	42.4	24.2
Ellison Bay CDP	165	NA	NA	242	69.0	0.4	1.7	28.9	0.0	10.0	60.0	30.2	105	91.4	26.7	59.0
Ellsworth village & MCD (Pierce)	3,284	3,236	-1.5	3,248	95.9	0.5	0.7	1.4	1.5	28.2	57.7	14.1	1,251	61.7	49.6	17.5
Ellsworth town (Pierce)	1,146	1,144	-0.2	1,111	99.8	0.0	0.0	0.2	0.0	19.6	69.1	11.4	438	97.5	43.6	19.4
Elm Grove village & MCD (Waukesha)	5,934	6,176	4.1	5,985	94.6	0.2	4.3	0.3	0.6	24.6	53.9	21.5	2,263	92.7	9.8	76.0
Elmwood village & MCD (Pierce)	817	811	-0.7	957	99.4	0.0	0.0	0.4	0.2	24.9	52.6	22.5	371	69.3	63.6	7.8
Elmwood Park village & MCD (Racine)	497	496	-0.2	552	86.6	6.2	1.3	3.4	2.5	30.3	48.6	21.0	191	96.3	30.4	32.5
El Paso town (Pierce)	681	681	0.0	692	95.2	0.0	0.0	0.0	4.8	22.5	67.2	10.3	251	91.2	43.0	16.3
Elroy city & MCD (Juneau)	1,441	1,389	-3.6	1,385	95.2	2.5	0.0	1.9	0.4	22.0	58.5	19.5	520	63.7	56.3	10.0
Embarrass village & MCD (Waupaca)	404	398	-1.5	603	98.7	0.0	0.0	1.3	0.0	21.7	48.8	29.7	206	66.5	42.7	10.2
Emerald CDP	161	NA	NA	177	67.2	0.0	14.7	0.0	18.1	35.5	58.7	5.6	60	70.0	63.3	10.0
Emerald town (St. Croix)	853	866	1.5	867	88.7	0.0	0.7	0.8	9.8	29.5	60.5	10.0	281	92.9	40.6	20.6
Emery town (Price)	297	290	-2.4	301	94.7	0.0	5.0	0.0	0.3	23.3	67.0	10.0	124	87.9	53.2	12.1
Emmet town (Dodge)	1,300	1,300	0.0	1,196	98.9	0.1	0.3	0.4	0.3	17.5	65.6	17.0	452	85.0	49.8	18.6
Emmet town (Marathon)	931	938	0.8	1,013	98.8	0.0	0.0	0.7	0.5	25.8	61.9	12.1	334	91.0	63.5	14.4
Empire town (Fond du Lac)	2,797	2,808	0.4	2,798	94.9	0.9	1.5	1.7	1.1	24.0	65.5	10.5	980	96.1	34.8	34.4
Endeavor village & MCD (Marquette)	468	459	-1.9	464	87.5	0.2	1.9	1.5	8.8	25.0	65.7	9.3	180	77.2	53.9	11.1
Enterprise town (Oneida)	312	308	-1.3	302	91.1	0.0	0.0	4.6	4.3	13.9	55.5	30.5	129	86.8	55.8	10.1
Ephraim village & MCD (Door)	288	287	-0.3	218	100.0	0.0	0.0	0.0	0.0	10.0	40.5	49.5	124	85.5	16.1	63.7
Erin town (Washington)	3,747	3,786	1.0	3,763	95.8	0.1	0.3	1.0	2.9	22.6	62.1	15.2	1,470	90.3	33.3	37.8
Erin Prairie town (St. Croix)	688	691	0.4	676	95.0	0.0	2.2	0.3	2.5	20.5	67.0	12.4	244	84.8	28.7	29.5
Estella town (Chippewa)	435	443	1.8	442	99.3	0.0	0.0	0.7	0.0	18.6	62.6	18.8	162	88.9	61.7	11.7
Ettrick village & MCD (Trempealeau)	524	522	-0.4	617	98.5	0.0	0.0	0.6	0.8	20.9	62.1	17.0	266	65.8	58.6	11.7
Ettrick town (Trempealeau)	1,237	1,278	3.3	1,334	99.1	0.0	0.0	0.3	0.6	22.9	60.9	16.1	522	86.8	43.3	21.8
Eureka town (Polk)	1,649	1,626	-1.4	1,676	97.6	0.0	0.8	1.6	0.1	23.6	62.2	14.3	679	89.2	47.9	19.0
Eureka CDP	220	NA	NA	268	98.9	0.0	0.0	1.1	0.0	28.3	57.6	14.2	98	84.7	59.2	9.2
Evansville city & MCD (Rock)	5,025	5,178	3.0	5,089	92.7	0.3	1.3	1.9	3.8	28.6	58.6	12.8	1,940	67.2	31.1	30.4
Evergreen town (Langlade)	495	483	-2.4	390	98.2	0.0	0.0	1.8	0.0	21.3	53.2	25.4	164	82.9	62.8	5.5
Evergreen town (Washburn)	1,135	1,127	-0.7	1,091	98.3	0.0	0.0	1.7	0.0	24.2	61.6	14.0	455	89.0	33.2	21.5
Excelsior town (Sauk)	1,575	1,627	3.3	1,537	98.3	0.1	0.0	1.4	0.2	17.5	61.4	21.1	624	92.0	46.3	19.9
Exeland village & MCD (Sawyer)	201	197	-2.0	208	91.3	4.3	0.0	3.8	0.5	31.7	54.7	13.5	81	69.1	66.7	12.3
Exeter town (Green)	2,025	2,059	1.7	1,986	95.9	0.7	0.6	1.4	1.6	33.0	61.6	5.5	658	83.0	33.4	31.8
Fairbanks town (Shawano)	616	612	-0.6	608	95.2	0.0	0.0	4.4	0.3	17.6	66.2	16.3	244	84.8	62.7	13.1
Fairchild village & MCD (Eau Claire)	555	564	1.6	493	97.2	0.0	0.0	1.0	1.8	20.9	58.1	21.1	207	60.9	76.3	5.8
Fairchild town (Eau Claire)	345	355	2.9	403	95.0	0.0	0.0	1.7	3.2	25.8	53.4	20.8	139	93.5	68.3	10.8
Fairfield town (Sauk)	1,077	1,098	1.9	833	96.5	0.0	1.0	2.0	0.5	17.7	65.2	17.0	367	91.0	45.0	28.3
Fairwater village & MCD (Fond du Lac)	371	367	-1.1	370	93.2	0.5	0.0	0.0	6.2	21.3	65.6	13.0	146	59.6	47.3	8.2
Fall Creek village & MCD (Eau Claire)	1,315	1,305	-0.8	1,316	95.3	0.6	0.3	3.3	0.5	24.9	55.8	19.3	537	66.7	36.5	23.6
Fall River village & MCD (Columbia)	1,713	1,690	-1.3	1,563	92.3	3.5	1.0	0.5	2.8	29.6	63.9	6.4	603	68.3	33.3	28.0
Farmington town (Jefferson)	1,414	1,438	1.7	1,471	98.8	0.3	0.0	0.1	0.8	19.4	65.3	15.2	581	89.2	46.5	17.9
Farmington town (La Crosse)	2,061	2,114	2.6	2,120	95.7	0.0	3.9	0.2	0.2	23.9	61.1	15.0	832	83.7	43.0	21.8
Farmington town (Polk)	1,841	1,822	-1.0	1,801	93.8	0.2	0.3	0.4	5.4	23.7	64.1	12.2	686	86.6	37.9	24.9
Farmington town (Washington)	4,014	4,020	0.1	4,011	96.7	0.0	0.5	2.3	0.4	24.5	63.2	12.4	1,457	91.4	46.1	20.7
Farmington town (Waupaca)	3,978	3,967	-0.3	3,976	96.1	0.6	0.3	0.9	2.1	11.0	53.9	35.1	1,580	79.7	41.1	32.4
Fayette town (Lafayette)	376	382	1.6	406	99.8	0.2	0.0	0.0	0.0	23.8	60.6	15.5	161	77.0	50.9	14.3
Fence town (Florence)	192	195	1.6	146	95.2	0.0	0.0	0.7	4.1	19.1	52.7	28.1	58	82.8	63.8	13.8
Fennimore city & MCD (Grant)	2,497	2,477	-0.8	2,416	99.3	0.0	0.0	0.0	0.7	22.1	58.8	19.0	1,059	75.7	35.7	17.8

1 May be of any race.

Table A. All Places — Population and Housing

STATE City, town, township, borough, or CDP (county if applicable)	Population				Race and Hispanic or Latino origin (percent), 2010–2014					Age (percent), 2010–2014			Households, 2010–2014			
	2010 census total population	2014 estimated population	Percent change 2010–2014	ACS total population estimate 2010–2014	White alone, not Hispanic or Latino	Black alone, not Hispanic or Latino	Asian alone, not Hispanic or Latino	All other races or 2 or more races, not Hispanic or Latino	Hispanic or Latino[1]	Under 18 years old	Age 18 to 64 years old	Age 65 years and older	Total occupied housing units	Percent owner occupied	High school diploma or less	Bachelor's degree or more
	1	2	3	4	5	6	7	8	9	10	11	12	13	14	15	16
WISCONSIN—Con.																
Fennimore town (Grant)....	612	613	0.2	595	99.7	0.0	0.0	0.0	0.3	25.7	61.0	13.3	237	68.4	52.7	14.8
Fenwood village & MCD (Marathon)	152	152	0.0	127	100.0	0.0	0.0	0.0	0.0	25.2	66.1	8.7	53	88.7	56.6	7.5
Fern town (Florence)........	150	102	1.9	102	100.0	0.0	0.0	0.0	0.0	10.8	60.8	28.4	52	94.2	42.3	23.1
Ferryville village & MCD (Crawford)	176	179	1.7	163	100.0	0.0	0.0	0.0	0.0	9.2	49.7	41.1	86	72.1	45.3	14.0
Fifield town (Price)...........	901	880	-2.3	1,026	92.7	0.3	0.0	5.5	1.6	11.6	64.4	23.9	544	71.3	53.7	10.8
Finley town (Juneau)	97	96	-1.0	82	97.6	0.0	0.0	2.4	0.0	4.9	58.5	36.6	38	89.5	65.8	2.6
Fitchburg city & MCD (Dane)	25,163	27,154	7.9	26,050	61.5	9.9	6.1	2.9	19.6	23.7	67.6	8.8	10,407	50.3	24.0	50.9
Flambeau town (Price)	489	477	-2.5	466	97.0	0.0	1.3	1.1	0.6	15.5	63.6	21.0	219	88.6	61.6	11.4
Flambeau town (Rusk)	1,060	1,014	-4.3	1,024	96.3	0.7	0.2	0.4	2.4	18.9	64.4	16.8	461	89.2	48.2	15.8
Florence CDP	592	NA	NA	573	96.5	0.0	0.0	3.5	0.0	20.9	51.3	27.7	224	58.0	45.1	7.1
Florence town (Florence)..	2,002	2,028	1.3	2,273	94.3	0.0	0.0	5.2	0.5	21.2	58.9	20.0	925	78.9	45.1	20.1
Fond du Lac city & MCD (Fond du Lac)...............	43,023	42,917	-0.2	43,007	87.1	2.2	1.7	2.4	6.6	22.1	62.7	15.2	18,271	56.9	43.0	22.3
Fond du Lac town (Fond du Lac)	3,017	3,399	12.7	3,283	94.4	0.4	3.4	0.6	1.2	24.5	58.5	16.9	1,283	90.5	34.1	32.6
Fontana-on-Geneva Lake village & MCD (Walworth)	1,672	1,701	1.7	1,411	96.5	0.0	0.2	1.7	1.6	14.0	56.3	29.9	666	91.0	13.2	63.2
Footville village & MCD (Rock)	808	806	-0.2	752	97.9	0.0	0.0	2.1	0.0	16.9	62.8	20.5	312	73.1	64.4	16.3
Ford town (Taylor)	268	268	0.0	274	97.4	1.1	0.0	0.7	0.7	21.5	53.6	24.8	115	93.9	65.2	7.8
Forest town (Fond du Lac)	1,080	1,083	0.3	1,192	97.1	0.0	0.4	1.1	1.4	20.7	66.0	13.2	458	88.6	56.1	13.5
Forest town (Richland)......	352	346	-1.7	351	94.6	0.0	0.0	3.1	2.3	16.8	59.3	23.9	135	88.9	35.6	32.6
Forest town (St. Croix)......	629	629	0.0	609	97.2	0.2	0.0	1.1	1.5	30.1	56.7	13.3	231	87.4	50.6	14.7
Forest town (Vernon)	634	635	0.2	638	99.4	0.0	0.0	0.0	0.6	29.1	58.3	12.4	244	87.3	53.7	14.3
Forest Junction CDP	616	NA	NA	635	100.0	0.0	0.0	0.0	0.0	25.2	66.3	8.5	263	84.4	47.5	19.8
Forestville village & MCD (Door)	430	417	-3.0	447	95.7	0.0	0.0	2.9	1.3	23.5	61.0	15.4	194	79.4	52.6	13.4
Forestville town (Door)......	1,096	1,079	-1.6	1,000	93.6	1.2	0.0	2.8	2.4	24.2	62.9	12.9	398	88.7	54.3	14.1
Fort Atkinson city & MCD (Jefferson)	12,393	12,430	0.3	12,436	85.1	0.6	0.7	2.2	11.4	24.9	61.2	14.1	5,077	67.2	40.8	28.2
Fort Winnebago town (Columbia)	825	829	0.5	1,133	79.8	14.5	0.0	1.1	4.6	7.6	79.8	12.7	357	91.3	55.8	21.6
Foster town (Clark)	95	96	1.1	75	96.0	0.0	0.0	0.0	4.0	4.0	42.7	53.3	42	97.6	71.4	19.0
Fountain town (Juneau)	555	555	0.0	614	96.9	1.8	0.0	0.0	1.3	16.5	62.9	20.7	244	95.5	37.3	16.8
Fountain City city & MCD (Buffalo)	859	830	-3.4	910	98.1	0.0	0.0	1.9	0.0	18.9	62.7	18.5	413	65.6	42.4	22.8
Fountain Prairie town (Columbia)	886	886	0.0	902	97.7	0.8	0.0	1.3	0.2	21.0	58.4	20.5	366	77.6	51.9	14.8
Fox Lake city & MCD (Dodge)	1,519	1,484	-2.3	1,544	91.1	3.1	0.8	0.6	4.3	18.3	67.7	14.1	618	73.5	57.4	14.4
Fox Lake town (Dodge).....	2,469	2,734	10.7	2,579	67.0	23.4	0.9	3.0	5.7	8.0	79.4	12.9	505	81.4	45.5	22.4
Fox Point village & MCD (Milwaukee)	6,701	6,740	0.6	6,695	89.9	2.9	2.8	2.4	2.0	24.3	56.2	19.4	2,725	84.8	8.1	79.2
Francis Creek village & MCD (Manitowoc)	673	658	-2.2	529	100.0	0.0	0.0	0.0	0.0	14.7	72.1	13.0	249	75.1	52.2	14.9
Frankfort town (Marathon)	670	701	4.6	660	96.8	0.0	0.0	1.1	2.1	26.7	58.3	14.8	232	98.3	56.0	5.6
Frankfort town (Pepin)	343	333	-2.9	477	98.7	0.0	0.0	0.8	0.4	23.5	62.1	14.5	176	79.0	36.4	16.5
Franklin town (Jackson)	448	453	1.1	444	97.1	0.0	0.0	0.5	2.5	25.0	55.1	19.8	180	89.4	41.1	22.8
Franklin town (Kewaunee)	993	975	-1.8	1,046	94.7	0.0	0.4	1.9	3.0	22.2	62.9	14.8	379	92.9	59.6	13.2
Franklin town (Manitowoc)	1,264	1,245	-1.5	1,143	99.7	0.0	0.0	0.3	0.0	24.8	61.6	13.5	437	91.1	54.0	10.8
Franklin city & MCD (Milwaukee)	35,451	36,278	2.3	35,920	81.4	4.7	6.4	3.3	4.2	21.7	64.1	14.4	13,126	77.6	27.9	39.9
Franklin town (Sauk)........	652	672	3.1	740	97.6	0.0	0.0	0.0	2.4	22.4	62.8	14.7	290	80.0	54.5	15.5
Franklin town (Vernon)......	1,140	1,173	2.9	1,118	96.8	0.0	0.6	2.6	0.0	30.1	56.2	13.6	427	77.8	48.9	23.4
Franks Field CDP	154	NA	NA	129	13.2	0.0	0.0	72.1	14.7	22.5	73.8	3.9	67	55.2	35.8	1.5
Franzen town (Marathon)..	578	574	-0.7	519	93.4	0.0	0.4	0.0	6.2	22.6	60.5	17.0	215	86.5	62.3	15.3
Frederic village & MCD (Polk)	1,133	1,106	-2.4	1,032	96.4	0.0	0.0	3.2	0.4	22.9	49.2	27.9	488	62.1	58.8	14.3
Fredonia village & MCD (Ozaukee)	2,162	2,224	2.9	2,089	93.4	0.2	0.0	1.6	4.7	25.6	62.5	12.0	850	74.1	45.9	17.9
Fredonia town (Ozaukee) .	2,169	2,157	-0.6	2,124	96.8	0.5	0.2	2.2	0.2	21.5	66.0	12.4	761	87.6	41.0	20.2
Freedom town (Forest)	345	336	-2.6	295	97.3	0.0	0.0	1.0	1.7	14.5	54.9	30.5	132	89.4	49.2	14.4
Freedom town (Outagamie)	5,842	6,019	3.0	5,932	98.9	0.0	0.0	0.4	0.8	27.0	62.9	10.4	2,220	83.3	43.2	18.5
Freedom town (Sauk)	447	462	3.4	414	93.5	0.0	0.0	0.0	6.5	19.6	63.1	17.4	161	86.3	50.1	17.4
Freeman town (Crawford).	686	686	0.0	718	99.3	0.0	0.0	0.3	0.4	13.1	59.0	27.9	331	80.4	57.7	20.5
Fremont town (Clark)	1,265	1,260	-0.4	1,444	96.6	0.3	0.8	1.1	1.1	34.8	56.7	8.4	473	76.7	57.7	18.8
Fremont village & MCD (Waupaca)	679	668	-1.6	744	99.2	0.0	0.0	0.0	0.8	27.2	57.1	15.9	315	82.9	45.4	15.9
Fremont town (Waupaca) .	597	592	-0.8	607	99.2	0.0	0.0	0.0	0.8	15.3	65.0	19.8	255	91.4	51.0	18.8
French Island CDP	4,207	NA	NA	4,384	98.3	0.1	0.7	0.9	0.0	16.8	68.9	14.1	2,000	68.6	35.1	29.6
Friendship village & MCD (Adams)	727	663	-8.8	631	94.9	1.9	0.8	0.0	2.4	16.0	60.1	23.9	205	60.0	49.3	15.1
Friendship town (Fond du Lac)	2,671	2,600	-2.7	2,644	94.3	0.3	0.0	0.0	5.4	23.8	58.3	18.0	1,094	90.1	50.2	15.7
Friesland village & MCD (Columbia)	356	355	-0.3	405	89.6	0.0	0.0	0.5	9.9	29.9	54.0	16.0	145	75.2	62.8	18.6
Frog Creek town (Washburn)	130	128	-1.5	134	99.3	0.0	0.0	0.7	0.0	20.9	67.9	11.2	59	81.4	47.5	11.9
Fulton town (Rock)...........	3,257	3,270	0.4	3,256	93.9	0.0	0.0	3.4	2.7	19.0	61.4	19.7	1,302	86.3	45.8	21.9
Gale town (Trempealeau) .	1,692	1,748	3.3	1,736	97.7	0.2	0.0	0.6	1.3	21.7	64.9	13.4	671	86.3	42.9	22.4
Galesville city & MCD (Trempealeau)	1,484	1,537	3.6	1,539	96.6	0.0	0.0	1.2	2.1	21.4	60.3	18.4	682	60.9	35.6	22.0
Garden Valley town (Jackson)	418	428	2.4	439	94.3	0.2	0.0	1.6	3.9	25.6	56.6	17.8	158	89.9	48.1	17.1
Gardner town (Door)........	1,194	1,175	-1.6	1,112	93.1	0.2	0.2	2.2	4.3	17.0	63.9	19.0	490	86.7	46.9	23.7
Garfield town (Jackson)	638	661	3.6	624	94.6	1.0	0.2	1.3	3.0	18.6	65.1	16.3	246	91.9	60.6	10.2

1 May be of any race.

Table A. All Places — **Population and Housing**

STATE City, town, township, borough, or CDP (county if applicable)	2010 census total population	2014 estimated population	Percent change 2010-2014	ACS total population estimate 2010-2014	White alone, not Hispanic or Latino	Black alone, not Hispanic or Latino	Asian alone, not Hispanic or Latino	All other races or 2 or more races, not Hispanic or Latino	Hispanic or Latino[1]	Under 18 years old	Age 18 to 64 years old	Age 65 years and older	Total occupied housing units	Percent owner occupied	High school diploma or less	Bachelor's degree or more
	1	2	3	4	5	6	7	8	9	10	11	12	13	14	15	16
WISCONSIN—Con.																
Garfield town (Polk)	1,692	1,651	-2.4	1,646	95.6	0.0	0.0	0.4	4.0	21.2	63.5	15.2	644	85.4	46.4	21.7
Gays Mills village & MCD (Crawford)	491	532	8.4	483	99.6	0.0	0.0	0.4	0.0	32.7	52.2	15.1	189	73.0	59.3	12.7
Genesee town (Waukesha)	7,338	7,344	0.1	7,346	94.1	0.0	0.2	3.6	2.1	25.1	60.3	14.6	2,613	94.8	26.8	44.4
Geneva town (Walworth) ..	4,993	5,048	1.1	5,010	85.9	0.6	1.4	0.4	11.7	24.6	57.3	18.1	1,960	76.9	42.7	28.3
Genoa village & MCD (Vernon)	264	268	1.5	259	89.6	1.9	0.0	8.5	0.0	27.8	44.8	27.4	103	80.6	53.4	6.8
Genoa town (Vernon)	782	784	0.3	670	96.9	0.0	0.0	1.9	1.2	25.8	58.3	15.8	271	90.4	57.9	15.5
Genoa City village	3,045	3,045	0.0	3,032	87.2	0.3	0.0	2.8	9.7	30.4	60.2	9.5	1,024	78.2	36.7	16.5
Genoa City village (Kenosha).....................	6	6	0.0	0	0.0	0.0	0.0	0.0	0.0	0.0	0.0	0.0	0	0.0	0.0	0.0
Genoa City village (Walworth)....................	3,039	3,039	0.0	3,032	87.2	0.3	0.0	2.8	9.7	30.4	60.2	9.5	1,024	78.2	36.7	16.5
Georgetown town (Polk) ...	977	968	-0.9	1,092	88.5	0.0	0.0	11.5	0.0	15.3	57.5	27.2	526	83.5	48.7	15.8
Georgetown town (Price)..	171	165	-3.5	206	100.0	0.0	0.0	0.0	0.0	20.4	59.3	20.4	86	94.2	57.0	18.6
Germania town (Shawano)	332	330	-0.6	279	91.8	1.1	0.0	7.2	0.0	16.9	58.9	24.4	126	88.9	59.5	10.3
Germantown town (Juneau)	1,471	1,548	5.2	1,492	95.6	1.3	0.0	1.3	1.7	17.5	50.8	31.6	657	82.3	55.1	17.2
Germantown village & MCD (Washington)........	19,753	19,901	0.7	19,791	91.2	2.2	1.7	1.6	3.4	25.4	61.3	13.2	7,833	78.7	27.0	39.6
Germantown town (Washington)...............	250	249	-0.4	217	98.6	0.0	0.0	1.4	0.0	20.2	73.7	6.0	77	90.9	46.8	20.8
Gibbsville CDP	512	NA	NA	573	90.6	0.0	0.0	4.4	5.1	28.2	60.1	11.7	191	97.4	50.8	22.0
Gibraltar town (Door)	1,021	1,035	1.4	1,080	90.7	0.0	0.0	1.1	8.1	16.9	44.4	38.7	500	91.6	31.4	45.8
Gibson town (Manitowoc) .	1,344	1,326	-1.3	1,333	98.1	0.5	0.0	1.4	0.0	21.2	63.5	15.4	528	86.9	54.7	17.2
Gillett city & MCD (Oconto)	1,386	1,351	-2.5	1,417	86.9	0.0	0.0	3.2	10.0	22.4	58.9	18.6	605	63.1	65.1	11.2
Gillett town (Oconto).........	1,043	1,037	-0.6	959	96.1	0.0	0.0	3.9	0.0	19.1	62.6	18.4	378	89.9	64.8	7.4
Gilman town (Pierce)........	959	957	-0.2	1,082	95.6	0.3	2.7	0.3	1.2	31.1	59.1	10.0	378	86.8	45.2	22.5
Gilman village & MCD (Taylor)	410	400	-2.4	414	94.9	2.2	0.0	1.4	1.4	15.7	53.3	31.2	216	62.5	52.8	18.5
Gilmanton town (Buffalo) ..	426	419	-1.6	354	100.0	0.0	0.0	0.0	0.0	20.6	59.0	20.3	147	79.6	63.3	9.5
Gingles town (Ashland)	778	786	1.0	738	91.6	0.0	0.5	7.3	0.5	23.0	68.5	8.4	293	94.9	32.8	19.5
Glenbeulah village & MCD (Sheboygan)	463	460	-0.6	442	99.0	0.0	0.0	0.2	0.0	20.1	65.0	14.9	191	85.3	48.7	19.9
Glencoe town (Buffalo)	485	476	-1.9	502	92.8	1.2	0.0	0.0	6.0	25.3	59.8	15.1	193	77.2	50.3	18.1
Glendale city & MCD (Milwaukee)................	12,879	12,887	0.1	12,893	76.7	13.0	1.8	2.2	6.3	18.3	59.8	21.7	5,698	68.5	21.4	52.5
Glendale town (Monroe) ...	662	664	0.3	661	97.6	0.0	0.0	2.4	0.0	26.5	57.3	16.3	241	78.4	53.1	10.4
Glen Flora village & MCD (Rusk)	92	88	-4.3	74	100.0	0.0	0.0	0.0	0.0	29.7	59.5	10.8	35	45.7	51.4	14.3
Glen Haven CDP	73	NA	NA	80	100.0	0.0	0.0	0.0	0.0	17.5	45.1	37.5	40	82.5	75.0	7.5
Glen Haven town (Grant)..	417	414	-0.7	408	98.8	0.0	1.2	0.0	0.0	19.4	62.0	18.6	165	74.5	69.1	5.5
Glenmore town (Brown)....	1,134	1,143	0.8	1,145	99.3	0.0	0.3	0.0	0.3	23.2	64.3	12.5	431	91.4	50.6	15.5
Glenwood town (St. Croix)	785	784	-0.1	769	90.1	0.1	2.9	3.6	3.3	27.9	63.8	8.3	254	87.8	45.3	10.2
Glenwood City city & MCD (St. Croix)	1,242	1,225	-1.4	1,250	97.8	0.0	0.2	0.9	1.1	22.8	55.0	22.2	555	63.2	51.9	22.5
Glidden CDP	507	NA	NA	399	97.5	0.0	0.0	2.5	0.0	19.1	60.9	20.1	205	67.3	61.5	12.2
Goetz town (Chippewa)	762	774	1.6	832	96.3	0.7	0.5	1.6	1.0	22.9	64.3	12.9	281	87.2	47.0	20.3
Goodman CDP	271	NA	NA	267	98.9	0.0	0.0	0.4	0.7	21.0	51.6	27.3	129	70.5	57.4	10.1
Goodman town (Marinette)..................	619	615	-0.6	716	98.5	0.0	0.0	0.6	1.0	11.3	62.0	26.7	351	84.9	60.4	11.7
Goodrich town (Taylor).....	510	506	-0.8	530	96.0	0.6	0.0	1.1	2.3	26.8	59.0	14.2	194	93.3	63.4	10.8
Gordon town (Ashland).....	283	287	1.4	283	98.6	0.0	0.0	1.4	0.0	6.7	67.1	26.1	138	94.2	63.0	15.9
Gordon CDP	176	NA	NA	203	98.0	0.0	0.0	2.0	0.0	26.1	41.4	32.5	83	77.1	39.8	10.8
Gordon town (Douglas)	636	642	0.9	698	97.0	0.3	0.3	2.3	0.1	11.6	57.9	30.5	347	86.7	38.9	15.9
Gotham CDP	191	NA	NA	234	97.0	0.0	0.0	3.0	0.0	23.9	62.4	13.7	100	91.0	29.0	7.0
Grafton village & MCD (Ozaukee)	11,477	11,531	0.5	11,539	92.1	0.7	4.5	1.8	0.9	21.3	62.3	16.5	4,738	67.7	28.5	40.7
Grafton town (Ozaukee) ...	4,020	4,111	2.3	4,065	94.3	3.1	0.4	0.8	1.4	20.4	63.8	15.9	1,509	87.3	32.3	33.6
Grand Chute town (Outagamie)	20,908	22,097	5.7	21,473	84.5	0.8	6.3	1.7	6.7	19.3	66.1	14.8	9,704	50.3	31.9	33.8
Grand Marsh CDP	127	NA	NA	70	64.3	4.3	0.0	31.4	0.0	22.9	52.9	24.3	26	76.9	42.3	11.5
Grand Rapids town (Wood)	7,642	7,533	-1.4	7,618	92.3	0.0	3.7	1.2	2.8	21.0	62.6	16.3	3,097	92.0	34.6	29.0
Grand View CDP	163	NA	NA	177	92.1	0.0	0.0	4.0	4.0	31.6	52.6	15.8	73	78.1	35.6	15.1
Grandview town (Bayfield)	468	470	0.4	493	94.7	0.0	0.0	3.0	2.2	16.1	56.2	27.8	230	92.2	40.9	15.7
Grant town (Clark)	916	908	-0.9	721	92.6	0.6	1.9	1.8	3.1	19.2	62.5	18.2	324	86.4	58.0	9.6
Grant town (Dunn)	385	393	2.1	352	99.7	0.0	0.0	0.0	0.3	17.3	68.2	14.5	142	94.4	42.3	21.1
Grant town (Monroe)	493	489	-0.8	436	95.9	0.0	0.0	0.9	3.2	21.6	59.4	19.0	178	87.6	49.4	12.9
Grant town (Portage)	1,906	1,953	2.5	1,859	98.5	0.0	0.1	0.8	0.6	20.8	66.9	12.3	770	92.9	45.6	14.7
Grant town (Rusk)	813	806	-0.9	772	98.6	0.4	0.0	0.1	0.9	21.8	59.5	18.8	315	86.3	57.1	16.8
Grant town (Shawano)......	991	986	-0.5	993	94.6	0.0	0.2	4.4	0.8	21.1	62.0	16.8	353	90.1	63.7	11.6
Granton village & MCD (Clark)	355	347	-2.3	397	89.7	8.6	0.0	0.3	1.5	27.2	61.9	10.8	150	84.7	54.7	7.3
Grantsburg village & MCD (Burnett)....................	1,341	1,308	-2.5	1,227	93.0	0.2	0.0	6.8	0.1	21.4	52.1	26.6	581	62.3	47.2	15.5
Grantsburg town (Burnett)	1,136	1,129	-0.6	1,185	86.8	0.0	0.0	8.4	4.8	24.1	59.3	16.6	536	78.5	56.0	14.2
Gratiot village & MCD (Lafayette)	236	237	0.4	176	98.9	0.0	0.0	1.1	0.0	19.9	59.2	21.0	75	84.0	58.7	16.0
Gratiot town (Lafayette)	550	556	1.1	529	96.4	0.4	0.6	0.6	2.1	22.2	60.3	17.6	216	81.0	54.6	13.9
Green Bay city & MCD (Brown)	103,913	104,891	0.9	104,574	74.0	3.5	3.9	5.8	12.8	24.2	63.8	11.9	42,358	57.5	43.1	24.0
Green Bay town (Brown) ..	2,035	2,080	2.2	2,088	95.9	0.0	2.6	0.4	1.1	24.7	59.6	15.7	818	88.5	40.0	26.3
Greenbush CDP	162	NA	NA	144	97.2	0.0	2.8	0.0	0.0	37.5	59.0	3.5	41	70.7	41.5	29.3
Greenbush town (Sheboygan)	2,565	2,571	0.2	2,581	69.0	16.9	0.2	5.1	8.8	12.7	80.5	6.9	502	91.8	49.6	24.1
Greendale village & MCD (Milwaukee)................	14,046	14,332	2.0	14,208	90.1	1.1	2.9	2.0	3.9	22.2	55.3	22.4	5,856	65.5	28.5	41.0

1 May be of any race.

Table A. All Places — **Population and Housing**

STATE City, town, township, borough, or CDP (county if applicable)	2010 census total population	2014 estimated population	Percent change 2010-2014	ACS total population estimate 2010-2014	White alone, not Hispanic or Latino	Black alone, not Hispanic or Latino	Asian alone, not Hispanic or Latino	All other races or 2 or more races, not Hispanic or Latino	Hispanic or Latino[1]	Under 18 years old	Age 18 to 64 years old	Age 65 years and older	Total occupied housing units	Percent owner occupied	High school diploma or less	Bachelor's degree or more
	1	2	3	4	5	6	7	8	9	10	11	12	13	14	15	16
WISCONSIN—Con.																
Greenfield town (La Crosse)	2,060	2,111	2.5	2,120	96.6	0.0	0.9	0.2	2.4	26.2	60.6	13.1	737	91.0	35.1	31.5
Greenfield city & MCD (Milwaukee)	36,746	37,157	1.1	36,990	80.9	2.6	5.2	1.7	9.6	17.1	62.0	20.8	16,661	57.9	38.0	30.0
Greenfield town (Monroe)	707	709	0.3	1,016	92.2	1.7	1.9	3.1	1.1	25.8	59.4	14.9	356	82.0	50.0	15.2
Greenfield town (Sauk)	932	960	3.0	868	97.8	0.3	0.0	1.5	0.3	13.8	69.2	17.2	353	90.1	39.9	30.3
Green Grove town (Clark)	756	753	-0.4	715	99.2	0.0	0.0	0.6	0.3	35.9	52.9	11.2	236	79.7	75.0	5.9
Green Lake city & MCD (Green Lake)	960	952	-0.8	1,022	84.5	1.9	2.2	5.1	6.4	18.3	57.8	23.9	488	70.5	37.5	38.7
Green Lake town (Green Lake)	1,154	1,153	-0.1	1,232	98.5	0.0	0.0	0.2	1.4	19.3	52.0	28.7	543	85.6	53.2	25.8
Greenleaf CDP	607	NA	NA	694	74.1	0.0	0.0	24.6	1.3	34.7	56.3	8.9	230	63.0	60.4	2.6
Green Valley town (Marathon)	541	566	4.6	504	98.8	0.0	0.0	1.2	0.0	18.1	61.9	20.0	210	95.2	42.4	21.0
Green Valley CDP	133	NA	NA	90	38.9	0.0	0.0	13.3	47.8	40.0	45.7	14.4	34	58.8	79.4	0.0
Green Valley town (Shawano)	1,089	1,084	-0.5	1,145	93.3	0.0	0.0	2.1	4.6	25.9	59.2	14.8	414	88.4	51.9	14.5
Greenville town (Outagamie)	10,309	11,235	9.0	10,787	93.1	3.0	0.6	1.5	1.7	28.4	61.9	9.6	3,716	90.0	28.4	37.9
Greenwood city & MCD (Clark)	1,026	1,014	-1.2	1,059	97.6	0.0	0.0	0.3	2.1	20.3	55.9	23.8	494	62.6	52.0	14.8
Greenwood town (Taylor)	638	639	0.2	616	97.2	0.6	0.0	0.5	1.6	23.0	57.5	19.5	271	89.3	64.9	5.9
Greenwood town (Vernon)	847	851	0.5	851	99.2	0.8	0.0	0.0	0.0	44.3	48.2	7.5	218	91.7	61.9	20.2
Gresham village & MCD (Shawano)	586	578	-1.4	445	70.6	0.0	0.0	29.4	0.0	25.6	63.0	11.5	214	56.5	51.4	7.0
Grover town (Marinette)	1,768	1,774	0.3	1,564	98.1	0.0	0.3	1.4	0.1	19.1	68.4	12.5	639	88.6	47.3	12.1
Grover town (Taylor)	256	266	3.9	281	98.9	0.0	0.0	0.0	1.1	24.1	61.2	14.6	123	98.4	60.2	13.8
Grow town (Rusk)	424	420	-0.9	394	96.4	1.8	0.8	0.8	0.3	21.6	60.3	18.3	145	93.1	69.0	13.1
Guenther town (Marathon)	341	357	4.7	286	98.3	0.3	0.0	1.4	0.0	18.1	68.7	12.9	129	87.6	51.9	9.3
Gull Lake town (Washburn)	186	184	-1.1	204	97.1	0.0	0.0	2.9	0.0	18.2	51.1	30.9	91	81.3	58.2	22.0
Gurney town (Iron)	159	159	0.0	173	94.8	0.0	0.0	5.2	0.0	26.0	60.7	13.3	71	91.5	43.7	25.4
Hackett town (Price)	169	163	-3.6	156	97.4	0.0	1.9	0.0	0.6	20.5	68.7	10.9	63	93.7	38.1	6.3
Hager City CDP	338	NA	NA	283	96.5	0.0	1.4	2.1	0.0	26.2	64.0	9.9	111	82.0	44.1	15.3
Hale town (Trempealeau)	1,037	1,069	3.1	1,152	94.1	0.0	1.5	1.7	2.7	24.6	59.1	16.2	415	82.7	50.8	23.6
Hales Corners village & MCD (Milwaukee)	7,695	7,757	0.8	7,749	91.3	0.4	0.4	2.2	5.7	20.2	61.4	18.3	3,245	64.2	35.5	36.4
Hallie town (Chippewa)	161	161	0.0	165	98.2	0.0	1.8	0.0	0.0	15.7	52.1	32.1	79	69.6	60.8	17.7
Halsey town (Marathon)	651	681	4.6	649	93.8	0.0	0.0	6.2	0.0	31.6	55.6	12.9	209	94.7	74.2	5.7
Hamburg town (Marathon)	918	944	2.8	845	95.5	0.0	0.0	1.9	2.6	26.3	64.0	9.8	279	93.5	64.2	11.1
Hamburg town (Vernon)	969	992	2.4	930	94.9	0.0	0.0	0.4	4.6	26.1	56.6	17.3	351	89.2	42.5	22.2
Hamilton town (La Crosse)	2,436	2,515	3.2	2,477	98.8	0.0	0.0	0.5	0.7	25.8	63.0	11.1	935	95.1	30.5	34.4
Hammel town (Taylor)	713	704	-1.3	746	96.2	0.0	0.0	3.5	0.3	21.3	66.0	12.7	314	95.2	47.1	11.5
Hammond village & MCD (St. Croix)	1,922	1,910	-0.6	1,928	99.1	0.2	0.2	0.4	0.3	29.1	60.4	10.4	710	68.7	37.3	22.1
Hammond town (St. Croix)	2,099	2,172	3.5	1,865	96.4	0.1	0.9	1.0	1.6	27.0	64.9	8.2	642	94.5	27.9	34.9
Hampden town (Columbia)	574	572	-0.3	490	99.6	0.0	0.0	0.4	0.0	22.5	54.1	23.5	198	86.9	51.0	21.7
Hancock village & MCD (Waushara)	417	404	-3.1	286	86.4	0.0	1.0	1.4	11.2	17.8	59.9	22.0	130	76.9	63.1	9.2
Hancock town (Waushara)	528	525	-0.6	604	85.3	0.0	2.5	0.0	12.3	23.9	57.2	18.9	230	91.3	57.8	14.8
Haney town (Crawford)	309	300	-2.9	287	100.0	0.0	0.0	0.0	0.0	18.2	62.0	19.9	109	78.9	51.4	11.9
Hanover CDP	181	NA	NA	178	100.0	0.0	0.0	0.0	0.0	29.3	70.7	0.0	67	68.7	53.7	28.4
Hansen town (Wood)	690	664	-3.8	594	99.3	0.5	0.0	0.2	0.0	22.2	61.7	16.0	243	96.7	52.3	14.4
Harding town (Lincoln)	372	369	-0.8	420	97.9	0.7	0.0	0.5	1.0	25.7	63.5	10.7	160	92.5	48.1	14.4
Harmony town (Price)	222	218	-1.8	263	98.1	0.0	0.0	0.8	1.1	12.9	54.3	32.7	126	92.9	46.8	19.0
Harmony town (Rock)	2,533	2,580	1.9	2,556	95.7	0.5	1.6	0.2	2.0	21.9	65.3	13.0	960	90.2	30.5	27.6
Harmony town (Vernon)	755	864	14.4	778	96.0	0.0	0.0	2.2	1.8	27.7	61.0	11.4	264	93.2	53.8	24.2
Harris town (Marquette)	790	775	-1.9	893	97.8	0.2	0.8	0.0	1.2	16.7	55.0	28.3	358	84.6	52.8	10.9
Harrison village	7,379	7,331	-0.7	7,408	91.4	0.0	4.7	2.6	1.3	34.1	61.6	4.2	2,359	93.6	17.8	52.3
Harrison village (Calumet)	7,379	7,331	-0.7	7,401	91.4	0.0	4.7	2.6	1.3	34.3	61.6	4.2	2,359	93.6	17.8	52.3
Harrison village (Outagamie)	0	0	0.0	7	100.0	0.0	0.0	0.0	0.0	0.0	100.0	0.0	0	0.0	0.0	0.0
Harrison town (Calumet)	3,468	3,783	9.1	3,635	97.2	0.8	0.4	0.7	0.9	23.8	59.7	16.5	1,305	96.6	36.5	31.0
Harrison town (Grant)	495	497	0.4	460	98.5	0.0	0.7	0.9	0.0	23.3	60.1	16.5	176	91.5	44.9	25.6
Harrison town (Lincoln)	833	818	-1.8	798	96.1	0.0	1.4	1.0	1.5	13.9	59.3	27.1	366	92.3	39.9	18.6
Harrison town (Marathon)	374	370	-1.1	371	99.7	0.0	0.0	0.3	0.0	21.0	69.0	10.0	148	87.2	60.1	6.8
Harrison town (Waupaca)	467	464	-0.6	465	97.6	0.6	1.1	0.6	0.0	19.2	55.6	25.2	205	84.9	58.0	18.0
Hartford city	14,221	14,280	0.4	14,251	90.1	0.8	1.7	1.9	5.6	25.0	61.3	13.6	5,849	68.1	38.9	21.6
Hartford city (Dodge)	0	0	0.0	0	0.0	0.0	0.0	0.0	0.0	0.0	0.0	0.0	0	0.0	0.0	0.0
Hartford city (Washington)	14,221	14,280	0.4	14,251	90.1	0.8	1.7	1.9	5.6	25.0	61.3	13.6	5,849	68.1	38.9	21.6
Hartford town (Washington)	3,606	3,597	-0.2	3,593	98.6	0.7	0.0	0.4	0.3	20.0	66.4	13.7	1,338	91.9	41.0	25.8
Hartland town (Pierce)	827	826	-0.1	795	96.6	0.0	0.0	2.3	1.1	20.9	66.1	13.1	356	81.7	49.2	15.2
Hartland town (Shawano)	904	898	-0.7	920	97.6	0.0	1.4	0.5	0.4	31.2	57.5	11.4	308	90.6	54.2	13.3
Hartland village & MCD (Waukesha)	9,118	9,205	1.0	9,161	93.0	0.6	2.4	1.0	2.9	26.3	62.2	11.5	3,602	60.8	25.9	37.2
Hatfield CDP	141	NA	NA	201	94.0	0.0	0.0	6.0	0.0	26.8	45.5	27.9	78	75.6	62.8	17.9
Hatley village & MCD (Marathon)	574	602	4.9	481	95.6	0.6	1.0	1.5	1.2	16.4	71.0	12.5	206	86.9	51.5	16.5
Haugen village & MCD (Barron)	287	284	-1.0	333	98.8	0.0	0.0	0.6	0.6	24.6	61.5	13.8	134	90.3	41.0	14.2
Hawkins village & MCD (Rusk)	305	288	-5.6	342	98.8	0.0	0.6	0.6	0.0	21.1	52.9	26.0	169	87.6	60.4	6.5
Hawkins town (Rusk)	153	152	-0.7	143	97.2	0.0	0.0	2.8	0.0	11.9	64.4	23.8	65	100.0	78.5	3.1
Hawthorne town (Douglas)	1,136	1,129	-0.6	1,042	96.0	0.0	0.0	2.6	1.4	21.7	61.4	16.9	380	88.2	42.4	17.1
Hay River town (Dunn)	563	572	1.6	562	96.6	0.0	0.0	2.0	1.4	24.2	62.2	13.7	206	88.3	43.7	17.0
Hayward city & MCD (Sawyer)	2,344	2,317	-1.2	1,951	86.0	3.0	0.1	10.3	0.6	20.3	56.1	23.6	966	48.2	47.8	18.8
Hayward town (Sawyer)	3,535	3,516	-0.5	3,518	69.8	0.2	0.3	29.2	0.5	27.4	58.9	13.8	1,300	70.2	30.8	26.8
Hazel Green village	1,256	1,241	-1.2	1,173	97.7	0.0	0.0	2.3	0.0	23.7	62.6	13.7	487	74.9	37.8	23.2

1 May be of any race.

Table A. All Places — **Population and Housing**

STATE City, town, township, borough, or CDP (county if applicable)	2010 census total population	2014 estimated population	Percent change 2010-2014	ACS total population estimate 2010-2014	White alone, not Hispanic or Latino	Black alone, not Hispanic or Latino	Asian alone, not Hispanic or Latino	All other races or 2 or more races, not Hispanic or Latino	Hispanic or Latino[1]	Under 18 years old	Age 18 to 64 years old	Age 65 years and older	Total occupied housing units	Percent owner occupied	High school diploma or less	Bachelor's degree or more
	1	2	3	4	5	6	7	8	9	10	11	12	13	14	15	16
WISCONSIN—Con.																
Hazel Green village (Grant)	1,243	1,228	-1.2	1,161	97.7	0.0	0.0	2.3	0.0	24.0	62.3	13.9	483	74.7	38.1	22.6
Hazel Green village (Lafayette)	13	13	0.0	12	100.0	0.0	0.0	0.0	0.0	0.0	99.9	0.0	4	100.0	0.0	100.0
Hazel Green town (Grant)	1,132	1,119	-1.1	1,034	96.0	0.8	1.0	1.2	1.1	18.7	44.1	37.2	325	82.5	56.3	21.8
Hazelhurst town (Oneida)	1,272	1,269	-0.2	1,208	97.0	0.0	0.6	0.0	2.4	22.9	56.8	20.2	507	90.9	29.4	30.0
Hebron CDP	224	NA	NA	172	100.0	0.0	0.0	0.0	0.0	9.3	73.9	16.9	83	91.6	59.0	7.2
Hebron town (Jefferson)	1,094	1,110	1.5	1,096	93.2	0.0	0.0	0.5	6.4	17.7	64.3	17.8	428	87.1	48.8	16.1
Helenville CDP	249	NA	NA	239	97.1	0.0	0.0	2.9	0.0	20.0	72.4	7.5	103	100.0	54.4	13.6
Helvetia town (Waupaca)	636	627	-1.4	696	96.3	0.0	0.4	2.4	0.9	20.0	57.5	22.3	293	88.1	56.7	14.7
Hendren town (Clark)	499	497	-0.4	400	99.8	0.0	0.0	0.0	0.3	14.3	67.8	18.3	165	93.9	61.2	8.5
Henrietta town (Richland)	493	485	-1.6	440	99.5	0.5	0.0	0.0	0.0	17.1	57.3	25.7	205	86.3	64.4	13.2
Herbster CDP	104	NA	NA	62	100.0	0.0	0.0	0.0	0.0	4.8	38.8	56.5	33	90.9	21.2	48.5
Herman town (Dodge)	1,110	1,124	1.3	1,061	97.9	0.0	0.0	0.7	1.4	21.3	62.8	15.9	383	85.6	52.0	14.6
Herman town (Shawano)	776	771	-0.6	793	83.6	0.0	0.5	12.1	3.8	27.7	52.5	19.7	296	78.7	61.5	15.9
Herman town (Sheboygan)	2,151	2,191	1.9	2,125	88.2	5.3	2.3	0.7	3.6	12.2	74.7	12.9	610	80.8	50.3	14.9
Hewett town (Clark)	293	289	-1.4	253	100.0	0.0	0.0	0.0	0.0	15.0	67.1	17.8	115	87.8	48.7	20.0
Hewitt town (Marathon)	606	635	4.8	693	98.3	0.0	1.0	0.6	0.1	19.5	67.5	13.0	276	98.9	52.5	13.8
Hewitt village & MCD (Wood)	828	821	-0.8	805	98.3	0.0	1.4	0.0	0.4	26.1	62.9	11.1	320	92.8	37.2	31.9
Hickory Grove town (Grant)	455	458	0.7	405	100.0	0.0	0.0	0.0	0.0	27.9	59.4	12.6	164	75.6	62.2	11.0
Highland town (Douglas)	311	314	1.0	265	98.5	0.0	1.5	0.0	0.0	12.1	57.5	30.6	142	94.4	40.8	29.6
Highland village & MCD (Iowa)	842	844	0.2	914	92.5	1.2	0.4	2.8	3.1	23.6	61.6	15.1	379	74.1	54.6	10.0
Highland town (Iowa)	750	762	1.6	655	98.0	0.0	0.0	2.0	0.0	21.2	62.9	15.9	270	90.0	47.4	24.4
Hilbert village & MCD (Calumet)	1,132	1,114	-1.6	1,048	89.6	0.0	0.0	0.0	10.4	23.3	60.6	16.0	468	78.2	68.6	16.9
Hiles town (Forest)	311	309	-0.6	357	96.4	0.0	0.0	0.8	2.8	12.8	47.2	39.8	179	94.4	48.6	23.5
Hiles town (Wood)	167	166	-0.6	152	100.0	0.0	0.0	0.0	0.0	17.8	75.2	7.2	57	84.2	47.4	5.3
Hill town (Price)	333	321	-3.6	429	98.8	0.0	0.0	0.2	0.9	26.8	59.0	14.2	174	94.8	56.3	13.2
Hillsboro city & MCD (Vernon)	1,413	1,420	0.5	1,412	94.1	0.4	0.0	0.8	4.7	20.5	57.5	21.9	623	57.5	46.5	18.5
Hillsboro town (Vernon)	811	826	1.8	677	97.6	0.0	0.0	2.4	0.0	20.8	58.5	20.7	294	86.1	59.9	11.2
Hingham CDP	886	NA	NA	999	97.0	0.0	0.0	3.0	0.0	26.9	62.9	10.1	339	92.0	48.1	18.6
Hixon town (Clark)	808	802	-0.7	815	96.4	0.0	0.0	3.6	0.0	38.2	54.9	6.9	241	90.9	66.0	7.1
Hixton village & MCD (Jackson)	435	430	-1.1	525	97.3	0.0	0.0	2.7	0.0	28.7	58.7	12.4	203	75.4	61.6	5.4
Hixton town (Jackson)	652	663	1.7	535	93.5	0.2	0.0	3.2	3.2	19.9	63.4	16.6	239	80.3	60.3	13.8
Hoard town (Clark)	841	816	-3.0	674	95.3	0.0	0.6	2.5	1.6	27.4	51.5	21.1	208	87.0	70.2	12.5
Hobart village & MCD (Brown)	6,187	7,861	27.1	6,951	79.0	0.0	0.6	19.6	0.8	27.5	60.5	11.9	2,520	88.0	27.8	40.6
Holcombe CDP	267	NA	NA	190	97.9	0.0	0.0	2.1	0.0	25.3	58.0	16.8	80	81.3	60.0	16.3
Holland town (Brown)	1,514	1,540	1.7	1,518	96.9	0.3	0.0	0.1	2.7	27.8	61.6	10.7	531	90.2	50.5	15.6
Holland town (La Crosse)	3,701	3,823	3.3	3,757	90.2	0.0	7.7	1.0	1.1	21.7	67.9	10.4	1,345	98.7	39.7	29.4
Holland town (Sheboygan)	2,239	2,253	0.6	2,360	97.4	0.0	0.2	0.8	1.7	22.7	60.4	16.8	922	89.7	49.2	23.3
Hollandale village & MCD (Iowa)	288	291	1.0	330	99.4	0.0	0.0	0.3	0.3	29.6	60.4	10.0	124	84.7	35.5	17.7
Holmen village & MCD (La Crosse)	9,015	9,564	6.1	9,335	92.5	0.1	4.8	1.9	0.7	29.2	57.3	13.5	3,766	70.9	34.1	24.5
Holton town (Marathon)	873	912	4.5	938	95.1	0.0	0.0	0.2	4.7	28.0	58.4	13.8	333	83.2	67.9	10.2
Holway town (Taylor)	973	962	-1.1	975	99.0	0.0	0.6	0.4	0.0	32.9	56.0	10.9	336	86.0	65.5	7.7
Homestead town (Florence)	336	341	1.5	331	99.1	0.0	0.0	0.9	0.0	18.5	59.4	22.1	140	95.7	49.3	12.1
Honey Creek town (Sauk)	733	754	2.9	792	95.6	0.0	0.6	0.4	3.4	23.7	62.4	13.9	285	75.8	47.4	20.7
Horicon city & MCD (Dodge)	3,655	3,695	1.1	3,658	92.1	1.3	1.6	0.7	4.3	25.6	62.3	12.1	1,393	73.7	47.7	15.1
Hortonia town (Outagamie)	1,093	1,086	-0.6	1,170	96.0	0.0	0.3	0.8	2.9	21.4	66.3	12.3	418	83.0	41.9	25.6
Hortonville village & MCD (Outagamie)	2,705	2,714	0.3	2,701	94.2	0.0	2.9	1.2	1.6	29.9	58.6	11.5	967	77.7	38.8	23.5
Houlton CDP	386	NA	NA	305	100.0	0.0	0.0	0.0	0.0	5.2	36.4	58.4	142	100.0	38.0	11.3
How town (Oconto)	516	515	-0.2	649	85.4	0.0	0.0	14.6	0.0	21.1	57.1	21.9	240	85.4	50.8	23.8
Howard village (Outagamie)	17,399	18,987	9.1	18,313	87.7	0.6	2.1	3.6	6.0	26.4	62.9	10.8	7,130	64.9	36.4	30.4
Howard village (Brown)	17,399	18,987	9.1	18,313	87.7	0.6	2.1	3.6	6.0	26.4	62.9	10.8	7,130	64.9	36.4	30.4
Howard town (Outagamie)	0	0	0.0	0	0.0	0.0	0.0	0.0	0.0	0.0	0.0	0.0	0	0.0	0.0	0.0
Howard town (Chippewa)	798	810	1.5	659	99.5	0.0	0.3	0.2	0.0	22.9	70.1	7.0	262	93.1	35.5	20.6
Howards Grove village & MCD (Sheboygan)	3,188	3,257	2.2	3,212	96.9	0.0	0.7	1.0	1.4	22.3	66.2	11.4	1,250	84.2	39.5	26.2
Hubbard town (Dodge)	1,774	1,752	-1.2	1,662	97.7	0.0	0.0	0.0	2.3	18.9	64.7	16.5	651	93.7	48.4	20.4
Hubbard town (Rusk)	204	198	-2.9	195	94.4	1.5	0.0	2.6	1.5	20.0	52.4	27.7	95	80.0	65.3	12.6
Hudson city & MCD (St. Croix)	12,715	13,415	5.5	13,023	92.3	2.2	1.3	1.8	2.4	23.1	62.4	14.5	5,754	63.4	25.7	44.4
Hudson town (St. Croix)	8,453	8,736	3.3	8,589	95.7	0.2	1.3	1.0	1.9	25.9	66.6	7.4	2,860	93.6	17.1	48.4
Hughes town (Bayfield)	383	385	0.5	474	89.2	0.4	0.2	6.5	3.6	26.2	53.6	20.3	181	94.5	45.3	25.4
Hull town (Marathon)	750	782	4.3	708	99.2	0.4	0.0	0.0	0.4	35.3	50.8	14.0	222	89.2	61.3	10.8
Hull town (Portage)	5,360	5,423	1.2	5,390	96.5	0.0	2.0	0.8	0.7	22.8	62.2	15.0	2,170	91.5	40.2	37.2
Humbird CDP	266	NA	NA	198	98.5	0.0	0.0	1.5	0.0	18.1	50.2	31.8	82	89.0	74.4	4.9
Humboldt town (Brown)	1,311	1,332	1.6	1,242	98.6	0.0	0.0	0.2	1.2	22.5	61.5	15.9	492	88.8	52.6	14.4
Hunter town (Sawyer)	678	673	-0.7	770	64.5	0.8	0.0	34.3	0.4	15.2	53.3	31.4	412	78.9	43.4	21.8
Hurley city & MCD (Iron)	1,547	1,524	-1.5	1,570	94.1	2.5	0.0	1.5	1.8	20.5	52.0	27.3	776	61.9	39.9	16.8
Hustisford village & MCD (Dodge)	1,123	1,100	-2.0	1,149	93.7	0.0	1.0	1.2	4.1	25.4	60.4	14.1	467	52.7	52.0	16.5
Hustisford town (Dodge)	1,373	1,362	-0.8	1,403	95.1	0.0	0.0	0.3	4.1	19.8	66.3	14.0	531	85.9	50.1	14.1
Hustler village & MCD (Juneau)	194	193	-0.5	184	85.9	0.0	1.6	12.5	0.0	25.0	43.4	31.5	72	66.7	58.3	18.1
Hutchins town (Shawano)	600	596	-0.7	614	87.1	0.0	0.0	3.9	9.0	23.0	58.1	18.9	252	86.5	55.6	8.3
Independence city & MCD (Trempealeau)	1,336	1,350	1.0	1,557	74.2	2.2	1.7	1.0	21.0	25.9	58.4	15.7	700	52.3	62.7	9.4

1 May be of any race.

Table A. All Places — **Population and Housing**

STATE City, town, township, borough, or CDP (county if applicable)	2010 census total population	2014 estimated population	Percent change 2010-2014	ACS total population estimate 2010-2014	White alone, not Hispanic or Latino	Black alone, not Hispanic or Latino	Asian alone, not Hispanic or Latino	All other races or 2 or more races, not Hispanic or Latino	Hispanic or Latino[1]	Under 18 years old	Age 18 to 64 years old	Age 65 years and older	Total occupied housing units	Percent owner occupied	High school diploma or less	Bachelor's degree or more
	1	2	3	4	5	6	7	8	9	10	11	12	13	14	15	16
WISCONSIN—Con.																
Ingram village & MCD (Rusk)	78	75	-3.8	87	100.0	0.0	0.0	0.0	0.0	28.7	43.6	27.6	37	89.2	35.1	24.3
Iola village & MCD (Waupaca)	1,301	1,278	-1.8	1,336	96.6	0.0	0.0	2.5	0.8	22.3	53.2	24.6	599	63.1	44.7	23.0
Iola town (Waupaca)	970	965	-0.5	886	98.3	0.0	1.4	0.1	0.2	20.3	55.0	24.7	378	89.4	41.3	23.3
Iron Belt CDP	173	NA	NA	209	97.1	0.0	0.0	2.9	0.0	16.3	65.5	18.2	111	79.3	36.0	13.5
Iron Ridge village & MCD (Dodge)	929	905	-2.6	927	95.0	0.0	0.0	3.8	1.2	24.1	64.8	11.1	355	75.5	52.1	6.5
Iron River CDP	761	NA	NA	799	95.4	0.0	0.4	4.3	0.0	19.5	56.3	24.2	389	71.5	39.8	27.2
Iron River town (Bayfield)	1,123	1,126	0.3	1,153	96.0	0.0	0.3	3.7	0.0	17.9	59.1	23.0	555	79.5	36.9	29.5
Ironton village & MCD (Sauk)	253	255	0.8	280	100.0	0.0	0.0	0.0	0.0	33.5	60.9	5.7	100	82.0	62.0	1.0
Ironton town (Sauk)	654	675	3.2	536	88.6	0.7	0.0	0.0	10.6	16.4	68.5	15.3	175	92.6	51.4	19.4
Irving town (Jackson)	751	766	2.0	742	95.0	0.0	0.5	4.4	0.0	29.0	60.2	10.8	266	80.1	50.8	12.0
Isabelle town (Pierce)	281	280	-0.4	259	98.1	0.0	0.0	0.0	1.9	11.2	76.8	12.0	123	85.4	43.1	26.0
Ithaca town (Richland)	619	609	-1.6	671	100.0	0.0	0.0	0.0	0.0	23.2	56.3	20.7	264	80.3	58.0	13.3
Ixonia CDP	1,624	NA	NA	1,690	93.8	2.5	0.0	1.3	2.4	26.2	64.3	9.4	611	72.7	38.1	23.1
Ixonia town (Jefferson)	4,385	4,469	1.9	4,437	94.2	1.4	0.0	0.8	3.6	23.4	65.9	10.7	1,655	77.4	38.4	21.0
Jackson town (Adams)	1,003	975	-2.8	1,197	91.4	0.0	1.4	2.3	4.8	15.0	58.6	26.5	462	89.0	47.6	19.5
Jackson town (Burnett)	773	774	0.1	868	94.0	0.3	0.2	5.0	0.5	6.9	49.0	43.9	463	90.3	45.1	22.9
Jackson village & MCD (Washington)	6,773	6,802	0.4	6,773	96.3	0.0	0.4	0.7	2.6	26.1	60.6	13.3	2,840	74.6	39.4	21.9
Jackson town (Washington)	4,114	4,356	5.9	4,243	90.9	1.7	0.5	4.1	2.7	16.9	70.6	12.5	1,573	95.9	26.9	31.3
Jacksonport town (Door)	705	714	1.3	768	97.9	0.4	0.0	0.0	1.7	14.8	53.3	31.9	336	93.5	39.6	31.5
Jacobs town (Ashland)	722	715	-1.0	672	96.3	0.0	0.0	1.8	1.9	22.5	56.9	20.5	308	78.2	59.7	14.3
Jamestown town (Grant)	2,076	2,084	0.4	1,932	97.3	0.0	0.0	1.6	1.1	22.2	58.8	18.9	840	79.3	48.9	12.0
Janesville city & MCD (Rock)	63,606	64,009	0.6	63,674	88.5	1.7	1.6	3.1	5.1	25.0	61.1	13.8	25,581	66.9	43.0	21.2
Janesville town (Rock)	3,427	3,454	0.8	3,438	86.7	2.7	1.0	3.5	6.1	19.8	68.2	12.0	1,097	96.4	28.6	31.4
Jefferson town (Green)	1,217	1,235	1.5	1,225	98.2	0.3	0.0	1.0	0.5	24.2	62.6	13.1	469	86.4	61.0	9.6
Jefferson city & MCD (Jefferson)	7,973	7,955	-0.2	7,968	80.8	1.2	0.5	1.6	15.9	24.5	57.6	18.0	3,030	59.7	52.4	16.7
Jefferson town (Jefferson)	2,185	2,222	1.7	2,030	98.0	0.0	0.0	0.3	1.6	22.5	57.7	19.9	813	84.1	45.4	17.8
Jefferson town (Monroe)	823	842	2.3	637	91.8	0.6	0.5	3.8	3.3	26.7	56.7	16.8	207	78.3	68.1	9.7
Jefferson town (Vernon)	1,143	1,168	2.2	1,161	96.1	2.8	0.0	0.2	0.9	28.4	54.5	17.1	459	88.7	43.8	18.1
Jim Falls CDP	237	NA	NA	157	100.0	0.0	0.0	0.0	0.0	18.4	63.1	18.5	70	75.7	80.0	10.0
Johnson town (Marathon)	985	981	-0.4	1,172	93.3	0.0	4.4	0.3	2.0	35.2	51.1	13.7	341	83.9	78.6	5.3
Johnson Creek village & MCD (Jefferson)	2,729	2,871	5.2	2,813	90.5	0.7	1.5	1.7	5.6	27.9	63.3	8.6	1,085	71.6	36.9	27.9
Johnstown town (Polk)	534	528	-1.1	523	76.5	0.0	2.9	18.4	2.3	21.2	58.4	20.3	216	76.9	50.0	13.0
Johnstown town (Rock)	776	783	0.9	779	97.8	0.0	0.0	1.0	1.2	15.8	65.9	18.4	290	87.6	50.7	17.6
Jordan town (Green)	641	650	1.4	559	99.6	0.0	0.0	0.4	0.0	19.0	68.7	12.3	219	78.1	38.8	36.1
Juda CDP	357	NA	NA	335	95.2	1.2	0.0	3.6	0.0	26.3	64.1	9.6	116	92.2	57.8	2.6
Jump River CDP	52	NA	NA	47	100.0	0.0	0.0	0.0	0.0	19.2	44.6	36.2	22	72.7	86.4	0.0
Jump River town (Taylor)	375	365	-2.7	320	98.1	1.9	0.0	0.0	0.0	21.9	57.2	20.9	136	90.4	64.7	16.9
Junction City village & MCD (Portage)	441	435	-1.4	457	87.1	0.0	2.0	1.3	9.6	31.3	55.7	12.9	181	65.7	53.6	13.8
Juneau city & MCD (Dodge)	2,814	2,700	-4.1	2,750	89.8	1.1	0.0	2.1	7.1	24.1	58.6	17.3	909	62.4	43.9	9.8
Kaukauna city	15,460	15,799	2.2	15,649	92.9	0.4	0.2	2.8	3.6	24.7	63.7	11.6	6,191	70.1	45.1	21.7
Kaukauna city (Calumet)	0	0	0.0	0	0.0	0.0	0.0	0.0	0.0	0.0	0.0	0.0	0	0.0	0.0	0.0
Kaukauna city (Outagamie)	15,460	15,799	2.2	15,649	92.9	0.4	0.2	2.8	3.6	24.7	63.7	11.6	6,191	70.1	45.1	21.7
Kaukauna town (Outagamie)	1,242	1,271	2.3	1,269	94.0	1.2	1.1	1.3	2.4	29.3	60.5	10.2	451	84.7	48.8	19.5
Kekoskee village & MCD (Dodge)	161	159	-1.2	168	98.2	0.0	0.0	0.0	1.8	17.3	64.3	18.5	77	85.7	59.7	7.8
Kellnersville village & MCD (Manitowoc)	332	325	-2.1	455	96.3	0.0	0.0	2.2	1.5	20.6	65.8	13.6	196	78.1	57.7	6.1
Kelly town (Bayfield)	463	464	0.2	434	93.3	0.0	0.2	6.5	0.0	29.5	59.9	10.6	181	85.6	42.5	15.5
Kendall town (Lafayette)	454	462	1.8	522	99.6	0.4	0.0	0.0	0.0	38.6	52.7	8.8	134	86.6	40.3	26.9
Kendall village & MCD (Monroe)	477	477	0.0	476	97.9	0.0	0.4	0.6	1.1	18.9	57.5	23.5	222	74.3	60.4	10.4
Kennan village & MCD (Price)	135	130	-3.7	134	100.0	0.0	0.0	0.0	0.0	23.1	58.8	17.9	63	87.3	69.8	11.1
Kennan town (Price)	356	339	-4.8	326	96.0	0.3	0.0	3.4	0.3	22.1	63.8	14.1	137	94.9	51.1	8.0
Kenosha city & MCD (Kenosha)	99,228	99,894	0.7	99,709	69.1	10.3	1.5	2.5	16.6	26.4	62.4	11.2	37,305	57.8	41.3	24.3
Keshena CDP	1,262	NA	NA	1,284	3.3	0.6	5.8	84.7	5.6	42.2	52.2	5.5	304	36.8	46.1	3.3
Kewaskum village	3,988	4,069	2.0	4,030	94.3	4.2	0.0	0.4	1.0	26.4	59.9	13.7	1,564	70.1	39.4	21.5
Kewaskum village (Fond du Lac)	0	0	0.0	0	0.0	0.0	0.0	0.0	0.0	0.0	0.0	0.0	0	0.0	0.0	0.0
Kewaskum village (Washington)	3,988	4,069	2.0	4,030	94.3	4.2	0.0	0.4	1.0	26.4	59.9	13.7	1,564	70.1	39.4	21.5
Kewaskum town (Washington)	1,069	1,072	0.3	952	98.2	0.0	0.0	0.8	0.9	18.3	61.8	20.0	392	86.5	34.9	24.2
Kewaunee city & MCD (Kewaunee)	2,950	2,896	-1.8	2,925	95.9	0.0	1.5	2.6	0.0	17.7	64.6	17.8	1,358	74.9	46.7	18.1
Keystone town (Bayfield)	378	380	0.5	365	91.8	0.0	0.0	8.2	0.0	15.6	64.7	19.7	155	78.7	57.4	12.3
Kickapoo town (Vernon)	628	636	1.3	718	94.2	0.1	0.0	1.4	4.3	30.1	53.5	16.4	254	90.2	50.8	22.0
Kiel city	3,722	3,747	0.7	3,757	97.4	0.4	1.0	0.0	1.2	25.9	58.9	15.3	1,654	75.2	50.1	14.3
Kiel city (Calumet)	309	308	-0.3	341	95.0	0.0	5.0	0.0	0.0	34.3	65.7	0.0	127	100.0	62.2	0.0
Kiel city (Manitowoc)	3,413	3,439	0.8	3,416	97.6	0.4	0.6	0.0	1.3	25.1	58.2	16.8	1,527	73.1	49.1	15.5
Kieler CDP	497	NA	NA	428	96.7	0.0	0.0	3.3	0.0	18.0	53.7	28.3	218	67.4	65.6	8.3
Kildare town (Juneau)	681	687	0.9	578	97.1	0.0	0.0	0.0	2.9	10.3	71.5	18.2	215	95.3	62.8	14.4
Kimball town (Iron)	498	501	0.6	465	96.3	0.0	0.0	2.4	1.3	18.4	58.5	23.0	210	99.0	25.2	27.1
Kimberly village & MCD (Outagamie)	6,473	6,691	3.4	6,590	96.2	1.8	0.0	1.0	1.0	22.8	58.8	18.4	2,852	71.3	44.8	24.1
King town (Lincoln)	855	846	-1.1	949	97.5	0.0	0.0	1.1	1.5	16.0	62.3	21.7	440	83.4	52.5	17.3
King CDP	1,750	NA	NA	1,626	97.7	0.9	0.0	0.7	0.7	4.0	46.3	49.6	492	73.0	49.8	25.4

1 May be of any race.

Table A. All Places — **Population and Housing**

	Population				Race and Hispanic or Latino origin (percent), 2010–2014					Age (percent), 2010–2014			Households, 2010–2014			
STATE City, town, township, borough, or CDP (county if applicable)	2010 census total population	2014 estimated population	Percent change 2010–2014	ACS total population estimate 2010–2014	White alone, not Hispanic or Latino	Black alone, not Hispanic or Latino	Asian alone, not Hispanic or Latino	All other races or 2 or more races, not Hispanic or Latino	Hispanic or Latino[1]	Under 18 years old	Age 18 to 64 years old	Age 65 years and older	Total occupied housing units	Percent owner occupied	High school diploma or less	Bachelor's degree or more
	1	2	3	4	5	6	7	8	9	10	11	12	13	14	15	16

WISCONSIN—Con.

STATE	1	2	3	4	5	6	7	8	9	10	11	12	13	14	15	16
Kingston village & MCD (Green Lake)	326	327	0.3	318	99.4	0.0	0.0	0.0	0.6	26.1	55.6	18.2	133	86.5	52.6	11.3
Kingston town (Green Lake)	1,064	1,071	0.7	979	97.2	0.0	0.4	0.6	1.7	43.7	47.8	8.7	276	87.7	62.3	17.0
Kingston town (Juneau)	91	90	-1.1	79	100.0	0.0	0.0	0.0	0.0	30.4	50.7	19.0	32	65.6	65.6	0.0
Kinnickinnic town (St. Croix)	1,722	1,769	2.7	1,735	98.2	0.2	0.3	0.2	1.2	21.7	64.0	14.3	639	87.6	30.8	38.0
Knapp village & MCD (Dunn)	463	459	-0.9	458	98.3	0.0	0.0	1.7	0.0	18.1	56.2	25.5	208	63.9	70.7	4.3
Knapp town (Jackson)	299	303	1.3	250	100.0	0.0	0.0	0.0	0.0	19.6	64.4	16.0	109	74.3	66.1	5.5
Knight town (Iron)	211	212	0.5	233	96.6	0.0	0.0	3.4	0.0	14.6	66.5	18.9	124	81.5	35.5	12.9
Knowlton CDP	120	NA	NA	130	100.0	0.0	0.0	0.0	0.0	31.5	43.8	24.6	50	94.0	62.0	28.0
Knowlton town (Marathon)	1,910	1,995	4.5	1,987	92.1	0.2	1.4	1.0	5.4	25.2	61.1	13.5	739	91.7	44.2	34.4
Knox town (Price)	341	333	-2.3	295	99.7	0.0	0.0	0.3	0.0	19.4	57.6	23.1	142	89.4	57.0	12.0
Kohler village & MCD (Sheboygan)	2,120	2,109	-0.5	2,315	93.9	0.2	1.6	2.9	1.4	29.7	52.2	18.0	869	86.4	15.1	61.2
Komensky town (Jackson)	509	515	1.2	663	15.4	1.8	0.0	67.0	15.8	35.9	56.8	7.2	166	61.4	68.7	6.0
Koshkonong town (Jefferson)	3,657	3,729	2.0	3,696	96.3	0.6	0.4	0.9	1.8	19.8	64.1	16.0	1,418	91.5	42.2	30.9
Kossuth town (Manitowoc)	2,086	2,065		1,926	95.4	0.0	0.5	0.5	3.6	19.9	63.0	17.1	775	94.8	49.7	19.1
Krakow CDP	354	NA	NA	363	88.2	0.0	0.0	11.8	0.0	25.4	54.9	19.8	173	100.0	51.4	13.3
Kronenwetter village & MCD (Marathon)	7,210	7,427	3.0	7,330	96.1	0.0	3.5	0.2	0.2	26.1	64.2	10.0	2,625	80.2	33.1	38.1
Lac du Flambeau CDP	1,969	NA	NA	1,835	10.0	0.1	2.8	85.4	1.7	30.7	59.7	9.6	835	48.3	52.6	11.6
Lac du Flambeau town (Vilas)	3,441	3,443	0.1	3,439	35.7	0.0	1.5	59.8	2.9	26.2	53.0	20.7	1,560	66.7	46.4	22.3
Lac La Belle village	286	293	2.4	277	99.6	0.0	0.4	0.0	0.0	20.2	62.8	17.0	106	90.6	10.4	58.5
Lac La Belle village (Jefferson)	1	1	0.0	0	0.0	0.0	0.0	0.0	0.0	0.0	0.0	0.0	0	0.0	0.0	0.0
Lac La Belle village (Waukesha)	285	292	2.5	277	99.6	0.0	0.4	0.0	0.0	20.2	62.8	17.0	106	90.6	10.4	58.5
La Crosse city & MCD (La Crosse)	51,323	52,440	2.2	51,864	89.3	2.1	4.2	2.4	2.0	16.1	70.8	13.1	20,749	50.2	28.6	29.9
Ladysmith city & MCD (Rusk)	3,413	3,266	-4.3	3,327	92.2	1.7	1.0	2.5	2.7	22.6	54.0	23.3	1,400	54.1	45.9	20.8
La Farge village & MCD (Vernon)	746	769	3.1	668	98.7	0.3	0.0	0.1	0.9	13.1	63.8	23.1	327	73.4	63.3	11.6
Lafayette town (Chippewa)	5,770	5,902	2.3	5,850	98.8	0.0	0.6	0.0	0.6	21.3	63.3	15.4	2,432	78.9	32.1	31.8
Lafayette town (Monroe)	396	400	1.0	373	91.2	3.2	1.6	2.7	1.3	18.4	65.2	16.4	112	92.0	50.0	25.0
Lafayette town (Walworth)	1,979	1,998	1.0	2,166	91.6	1.3	0.2	0.5	6.4	22.9	62.2	14.8	745	83.6	39.5	33.0
La Follette town (Burnett)	536	535	-0.2	556	76.1	0.0	0.7	19.2	4.0	24.5	55.9	19.6	248	81.9	50.0	10.9
La Grange town (Monroe)	1,988	2,042	2.7	2,042	91.5	0.7	0.5	5.1	2.2	25.0	62.2	12.8	788	82.0	43.9	23.4
La Grange town (Walworth)	2,454	2,482	1.1	2,790	96.1	0.1	0.6	1.0	2.3	24.6	57.1	18.4	1,040	89.4	32.3	35.3
Lake town (Marinette)	1,135	1,145	0.9	1,084	99.0	0.0	0.0	0.6	0.5	19.4	60.0	20.5	463	93.3	45.6	17.1
Lake town (Price)	1,128	1,102	-2.3	1,179	98.8	0.0	0.0	1.2	0.0	13.6	63.4	23.0	555	87.9	56.4	13.9
Lake Arrowhead CDP	838	NA	NA	691	97.5	0.0	2.5	0.0	0.0	4.1	42.6	53.4	376	100.0	24.2	51.9
Lake Camelot CDP	826	NA	NA	1,002	99.1	0.0	0.0	0.0	0.9	14.6	48.3	37.2	405	96.0	44.9	24.4
Lake Delton village & MCD (Sauk)	2,917	2,953	1.2	2,936	80.7	0.9	2.1	1.7	14.6	16.6	60.2	23.2	1,406	44.5	37.8	25.7
Lake Geneva city & MCD (Walworth)	7,651	7,746	1.2	7,693	78.4	0.1	1.7	0.7	19.0	23.0	61.5	15.4	3,224	48.9	41.7	32.5
Lake Hallie village & MCD (Chippewa)	6,468	6,565	1.5	6,550	91.8	2.6	2.0	3.3	0.4	25.6	63.4	11.0	2,361	68.6	31.4	28.8
Lake Holcombe town (Chippewa)	1,034	1,055	2.0	912	96.3	0.0	0.0	0.0	3.7	18.3	54.1	27.6	397	90.4	47.4	18.6
Lake Ivanhoe CDP	435	NA	NA	512	47.3	10.2	0.0	30.9	11.7	31.4	65.1	3.5	139	87.8	35.3	17.3
Lake Koshkonong CDP	1,204	NA	NA	1,235	98.6	0.8	0.0	0.1	0.5	18.6	62.7	18.9	490	84.9	40.2	29.2
Lakeland town (Barron)	975	968	-0.7	868	97.6	0.0	0.0	1.0	1.4	17.8	63.4	18.7	401	86.3	58.6	16.2
Lake Lorraine CDP	324	NA	NA	286	100.0	0.0	0.0	0.0	0.0	11.9	66.3	21.7	137	94.9	64.2	21.2
Lake Mills city & MCD (Jefferson)	5,707	5,785	1.4	5,768	94.3	0.7	0.7	1.0	3.3	24.7	60.2	15.1	2,362	59.3	22.4	37.9
Lake Mills town (Jefferson)	2,074	2,111	1.8	2,052	96.4	0.4	0.9	2.0	0.2	21.0	61.7	17.3	848	85.5	28.2	34.7
Lake Nebagamon village & MCD (Douglas)	1,069	1,061	-0.7	1,268	93.5	0.0	0.9	5.5	0.0	22.8	57.1	20.2	550	85.3	25.1	40.5
Lake Ripley CDP	1,779	NA	NA	1,727	97.4	0.0	0.0	2.3	0.3	13.9	69.7	16.4	782	85.3	36.3	27.4
Lake Sherwood CDP	372	NA	NA	343	100.0	0.0	0.0	0.0	0.0	0.0	51.9	48.1	166	83.7	38.0	45.2
Lakeside town (Douglas)	693	694	0.1	596	91.6	0.3	0.0	7.4	0.7	25.6	63.7	11.1	247	89.9	36.0	24.3
Lake Tomahawk CDP	228	NA	NA	187	95.2	0.0	0.0	3.7	1.1	4.3	57.4	38.5	96	70.8	37.5	31.3
Lake Tomahawk town (Oneida)	1,045	1,028	-1.6	1,030	91.7	4.1	0.0	1.7	2.6	9.6	64.6	25.8	440	92.5	32.5	30.0
Laketown town (Polk)	961	944	-1.8	1,015	96.3	0.0	1.9	0.5	1.4	23.1	61.6	15.2	393	86.8	49.6	21.1
Lake Wazeecha CDP	2,651	NA	NA	2,611	98.5	0.0	0.6	0.3	0.5	21.1	60.5	18.4	1,110	93.2	37.0	22.3
Lake Wisconsin CDP	4,189	NA	NA	4,369	96.9	0.0	1.3	1.0	0.8	22.2	60.5	17.4	1,763	93.8	20.0	39.6
Lake Wissota CDP	2,738	NA	NA	3,017	99.5	0.0	0.5	0.0	0.0	25.3	60.2	14.4	1,250	71.2	36.6	23.4
Lakewood CDP	323	NA	NA	285	99.3	0.0	0.0	0.0	0.7	20.0	48.5	31.6	143	76.9	60.1	20.3
Lakewood town (Oconto)	816	813	-0.4	760	96.2	0.0	0.0	3.0	0.3	9.3	51.2	39.5	399	86.7	54.6	15.8
Lamartine town (Fond du Lac)	1,735	1,721	-0.8	1,894	91.7	0.6	1.6	1.5	4.5	23.3	63.2	13.5	725	89.5	39.9	20.7
Lamont town (Lafayette)	314	315	0.3	398	100.0	0.0	0.0	0.0	0.0	31.6	55.0	13.3	126	81.0	55.6	17.5
Lanark town (Portage)	1,527	1,540	0.9	1,423	99.1	0.0	0.0	0.4	0.6	23.7	62.3	13.9	582	91.1	41.8	26.1
Lancaster city & MCD (Grant)	3,868	3,785	-2.1	3,830	97.6	0.8	0.0	0.0	1.6	23.3	54.8	21.8	1,655	70.0	43.7	21.8
Land O'Lakes town (Vilas)	861	861	0.0	842	97.3	0.0	0.0	2.4	0.4	13.9	53.9	32.3	460	76.3	33.9	29.3
Langlade town (Langlade)	473	459	-3.0	546	98.4	0.0	0.0	0.9	0.7	17.8	57.4	24.9	221	97.3	48.4	13.1
Lannon village & MCD (Waukesha)	1,107	1,089	-1.6	1,139	87.4	0.3	0.0	1.0	11.3	19.6	64.3	16.0	497	82.5	38.0	16.9
Laona CDP	583	NA	NA	466	96.6	0.0	0.0	3.4	0.0	25.7	55.8	18.5	193	61.7	77.2	13.5
Laona town (Forest)	1,208	1,200	-0.7	1,058	95.6	0.4	0.0	4.1	0.0	25.5	57.1	17.4	427	78.9	56.4	17.1
La Pointe town (Ashland)	261	268	2.7	227	87.2	0.0	0.0	0.0	12.8	9.7	64.0	26.4	124	96.8	22.6	65.3
La Prairie town (Rock)	842	840	-0.2	799	95.5	0.0	0.0	0.9	3.6	15.2	67.3	17.5	354	64.7	55.4	18.4

1 May be of any race.

Table A. All Places — **Population and Housing**

STATE City, town, township, borough, or CDP (county if applicable)	2010 census total population	2014 estimated population	Percent change 2010–2014	ACS total population estimate 2010–2014	White alone, not Hispanic or Latino	Black alone, not Hispanic or Latino	Asian alone, not Hispanic or Latino	All other races or 2 or more races, not Hispanic or Latino	Hispanic or Latino[1]	Under 18 years old	Age 18 to 64 years old	Age 65 years and older	Total occupied housing units	Percent owner occupied	High school diploma or less	Bachelor's degree or more
	1	2	3	4	5	6	7	8	9	10	11	12	13	14	15	16
WISCONSIN—Con.																
Larrabee town (Waupaca)	1,373	1,359	-1.0	1,321	93.7	0.0	0.2	3.1	3.0	24.7	61.5	14.0	480	92.5	52.7	14.2
Lauderdale Lakes CDP	1,172	NA	NA	1,100	92.2	1.6	1.1	1.0	4.1	20.9	49.4	29.7	488	92.6	32.0	37.5
La Valle village & MCD (Sauk)	367	366	-0.3	391	90.5	4.9	0.0	4.6	0.0	21.0	58.8	20.2	153	81.0	69.9	7.8
La Valle town (Sauk)	1,302	1,349	3.6	1,234	97.4	0.0	0.0	1.6	1.0	19.5	58.8	21.7	525	92.0	41.0	20.2
Lawrence town (Brown)....	4,282	4,790	11.9	4,557	92.3	0.0	3.8	2.8	1.2	24.8	66.1	9.0	1,887	65.9	20.1	49.0
Lawrence town (Rusk)......	311	302	-2.9	248	98.0	0.0	0.0	2.0	0.0	23.7	58.9	17.3	108	79.6	46.3	4.6
Lebanon CDP	204	NA	NA	340	97.6	0.0	2.4	0.0	0.0	21.1	72.4	6.5	110	72.7	44.5	4.5
Lebanon town (Dodge).....	1,659	1,642	-1.0	1,730	98.3	0.0	0.5	0.1	1.1	19.7	64.6	15.6	647	86.2	55.2	9.0
Lebanon town (Waupaca).	1,665	1,641	-1.4	1,610	95.1	0.7	0.0	1.7	2.5	24.4	64.2	11.4	632	87.0	52.4	13.1
Ledgeview town (Brown) ..	6,603	7,566	14.6	7,134	90.5	1.6	3.5	3.6	0.9	30.1	61.4	8.6	2,609	63.4	21.5	44.6
Leeds town (Columbia)	774	774	0.0	837	97.7	0.0	0.6	1.7	0.0	21.3	68.8	9.8	322	72.0	46.0	17.1
Legend Lake CDP	1,525	NA	NA	1,492	26.9	0.0	0.0	67.8	5.3	22.4	55.8	21.9	498	95.0	38.6	24.7
Lemonweir town (Juneau)	1,743	1,700	-2.5	1,800	93.0	0.0	0.0	2.9	4.1	24.9	62.4	12.6	686	84.4	52.2	13.8
Lena village & MCD (Oconto)	564	550	-2.5	488	90.0	0.0	0.0	4.1	5.9	23.6	57.6	19.1	207	52.7	64.3	7.2
Lena town (Oconto)	727	724	-0.4	690	95.2	0.0	1.4	0.3	3.0	18.7	62.9	18.4	281	93.2	68.3	10.7
Lenroot town (Sawyer)......	1,279	1,273	-0.5	1,203	93.8	0.0	0.2	4.3	1.7	19.5	57.0	23.5	543	89.9	32.8	30.6
Leola town (Adams).........	310	300	-3.2	306	100.0	0.0	0.0	0.0	0.0	21.9	64.8	13.4	114	68.4	71.9	11.4
Leon town (Monroe)	1,088	1,116	2.6	1,107	95.8	0.2	0.4	1.2	2.5	20.1	67.4	12.5	441	80.7	42.2	15.0
Leon town (Waushara)	1,439	1,428	-0.8	1,276	98.7	0.5	0.1	0.5	0.2	18.1	62.1	19.7	561	85.4	61.0	10.2
Leopolis CDP	87	NA	NA	67	100.0	0.0	0.0	0.0	0.0	52.2	26.9	20.9	25	48.0	60.0	28.0
Leroy town (Dodge)	1,002	1,001	-0.1	927	98.0	0.0	0.0	0.3	1.7	24.9	60.4	14.7	363	89.0	54.0	14.9
Lessor town (Shawano)....	1,263	1,257	-0.5	1,125	98.0	0.0	0.0	1.9	0.1	25.7	62.4	11.7	415	93.7	57.6	14.7
Levis town (Clark)	492	492	0.0	450	95.8	0.0	0.0	3.8	0.4	18.9	55.0	26.2	211	77.3	70.1	3.8
Lewis CDP	164	NA	NA	99	100.0	0.0	0.0	0.0	0.0	19.1	54.5	26.3	49	91.8	65.3	10.2
Lewiston town (Columbia)	1,225	1,221	-0.3	1,246	93.1	0.2	0.0	1.5	5.2	13.5	68.1	18.2	544	83.1	45.8	10.1
Liberty town (Grant).........	553	554	0.2	663	99.8	0.0	0.0	0.0	0.2	35.6	53.1	11.2	220	74.1	67.3	7.7
Liberty town (Manitowoc)..	1,281	1,270	-0.9	1,368	98.6	0.0	0.1	0.2	1.0	26.0	60.9	13.0	517	92.1	46.0	21.7
Liberty town (Outagamie) .	874	909	4.0	825	96.0	0.0	0.0	0.7	3.3	22.7	63.0	14.3	308	92.5	46.1	15.3
Liberty town (Vernon)	252	265	5.2	254	98.8	0.0	0.4	0.8	0.0	25.2	59.0	15.7	93	88.2	31.2	23.7
Liberty Grove town (Door)	1,734	1,761	1.6	1,789	95.4	0.2	0.5	3.9	0.0	10.0	54.7	35.2	896	82.0	36.0	42.4
Lily Lake CDP.................	0	NA	NA	525	86.5	0.0	0.0	0.0	13.5	15.0	68.7	16.2	195	100.0	51.8	0.0
Lima town (Grant)	805	790	-1.9	752	97.5	1.2	0.0	0.8	0.5	28.6	58.4	12.9	266	78.2	39.5	27.1
Lima town (Pepin)	702	690	-1.7	686	94.2	0.3	0.0	0.7	4.8	26.4	52.5	21.3	273	82.4	71.8	11.0
Lima town (Rock)....	1,282	1,283	0.1	1,201	77.4	0.2	0.0	0.7	21.7	22.9	63.1	13.9	476	88.2	47.7	23.7
Lima town (Sheboygan)....	2,982	2,993	0.4	2,983	93.9	0.1	0.0	4.6	1.4	26.8	59.4	14.0	1,051	92.0	48.5	19.7
Lime Ridge village & MCD (Sauk)	162	165	1.9	204	94.6	0.0	0.0	2.5	2.9	24.5	54.9	20.6	78	61.5	76.9	9.0
Lincoln town (Adams).......	296	289	-2.4	344	97.7	1.2	0.3	0.0	0.9	20.9	52.0	27.0	119	93.3	58.0	11.8
Lincoln town (Bayfield)......	287	285	-0.7	225	92.0	0.0	2.2	2.2	3.6	13.7	60.3	25.8	118	86.4	44.1	26.3
Lincoln town (Buffalo)......	162	157	-3.1	128	98.4	0.0	0.0	1.6	0.0	7.0	71.9	21.1	56	91.1	48.2	14.3
Lincoln town (Burnett).......	309	306	-1.0	241	94.6	0.0	0.0	2.9	2.5	11.1	60.6	28.2	132	93.2	61.4	6.8
Lincoln town (Eau Claire) .	1,096	1,129	3.0	966	100.0	0.0	0.0	0.0	0.0	22.8	64.2	12.8	370	91.9	43.5	23.8
Lincoln town (Forest)	953	933	-2.1	989	66.5	0.8	0.0	26.5	6.2	17.9	60.6	21.7	433	80.1	45.3	17.1
Lincoln town (Kewaunee) .	948	950	0.2	902	94.5	0.7	0.3	1.0	3.5	22.7	62.6	14.7	320	86.3	64.1	7.8
Lincoln town (Monroe)	844	842	-0.2	1,007	93.2	0.6	0.3	5.9	0.0	20.1	61.3	18.8	425	75.1	54.1	14.1
Lincoln town (Polk)	2,180	2,158	-1.0	2,230	97.0	0.0	0.0	0.0	3.0	20.2	59.8	20.0	947	83.9	47.1	21.0
Lincoln town (Trempealeau)..............	823	857	4.1	839	94.8	1.9	0.0	0.6	2.7	25.5	55.7	19.0	260	82.7	59.6	20.0
Lincoln town (Vilas).........	2,423	2,423	0.0	2,234	98.5	0.0	0.0	0.9	0.6	13.1	63.3	23.5	1,175	76.3	47.5	16.4
Lincoln town (Wood)........	1,573	1,570	-0.2	1,682	96.8	0.0	0.5	0.8	1.8	22.8	63.4	13.8	664	88.4	50.2	29.1
Lind town (Waupaca).......	1,579	1,669	5.7	1,656	95.8	0.6	0.4	1.8	1.4	25.2	59.5	15.5	602	80.4	50.0	16.1
Linden village & MCD (Iowa)	549	541	-1.5	541	100.0	0.0	0.0	0.0	0.0	24.8	62.3	12.8	212	83.5	41.5	3.3
Linden town (Iowa)	847	848	0.1	739	98.8	0.3	0.0	0.9	0.0	22.5	56.3	21.1	282	74.8	43.6	16.7
Lindina town (Juneau)	718	703	-2.1	580	97.8	1.2	0.0	0.3	0.7	17.8	59.5	22.6	239	89.1	49.4	19.7
Linn town (Walworth)	2,383	2,405	0.9	2,288	91.8	0.0	0.6	0.1	7.5	19.5	57.0	23.5	1,008	81.6	32.9	41.1
Linwood town (Portage)....	1,121	1,137	1.4	1,058	97.9	0.0	0.4	1.5	0.2	18.4	63.3	18.2	445	93.9	44.3	27.2
Lisbon town (Juneau)	912	898	-1.5	918	97.3	0.0	0.7	1.6	0.4	15.9	66.8	17.3	374	85.8	58.0	16.3
Lisbon town (Waukesha) ..	10,182	10,333	1.5	10,259	95.9	0.2	1.0	1.5	1.4	22.9	60.4	16.6	3,797	98.0	28.8	36.3
Little Black town (Taylor)..	1,140	1,126	-1.2	1,173	91.8	0.0	0.9	1.9	5.5	23.1	62.4	14.6	466	85.4	63.1	17.4
Little Chute village & MCD (Outagamie)	10,450	10,813	3.5	10,520	95.3	0.1	0.1	3.0	1.5	22.5	64.3	13.2	4,160	70.1	43.2	21.5
Little Falls town (Monroe) .	1,523	1,556	2.2	1,612	94.5	0.0	3.8	0.0	1.7	28.8	57.7	13.3	570	81.6	49.5	20.4
Little Grant town (Grant) ...	283	283	0.0	287	99.0	0.0	1.0	0.0	0.0	28.9	59.9	11.1	110	83.6	48.2	14.5
Little Rice town (Oneida)...	306	301	-1.6	396	98.0	0.0	1.3	0.3	0.5	6.6	61.7	31.8	164	97.0	50.6	19.5
Little River town (Oconto) .	1,094	1,089	-0.5	1,142	95.1	1.1	0.0	3.1	0.8	24.4	59.4	16.3	427	84.5	55.0	15.2
Little Round Lake CDP	1,081	NA	NA	1,301	7.4	0.5	2.0	88.7	1.5	38.9	58.2	2.9	455	22.0	47.5	1.3
Little Sturgeon CDP	136	NA	NA	169	96.4	0.0	0.0	0.0	3.6	6.5	61.7	32.0	92	75.0	41.3	35.9
Little Suamico town (Oconto)	4,799	4,797	0.0	4,776	97.3	0.0	0.5	2.2	0.0	23.4	70.4	6.1	1,755	96.2	37.6	19.8
Little Wolf town (Waupaca)	1,424	1,410	-1.0	1,400	97.1	0.0	0.0	0.0	2.9	20.7	64.0	15.2	546	89.2	53.3	10.1
Livingston village	664	651	-2.0	645	98.1	1.1	0.0	0.5	0.3	28.9	52.6	18.3	250	85.2	52.8	16.8
Livingston village (Grant)..	657	644	-2.0	642	98.1	1.1	0.0	0.5	0.3	29.1	53.0	17.9	247	85.0	52.2	17.0
Livingston village (Iowa) ...	7	7	0.0	3	100.0	0.0	0.0	0.0	0.0	0.0	0.0	100.0	3	100.0	100.0	0.0
Lodi city & MCD (Columbia)	3,050	3,049	0.0	3,050	97.4	0.7	0.4	1.0	0.5	22.9	62.0	14.9	1,344	66.6	37.3	32.4
Lodi town (Columbia)........	3,273	3,290	0.5	3,268	97.9	0.0	1.3	0.8	0.0	21.9	64.0	14.2	1,246	96.4	24.3	37.9
Loganville village & MCD (Sauk)	302	308	2.0	262	96.9	0.0	0.0	1.1	1.9	20.3	64.4	15.3	115	68.7	53.0	6.1
Lohrville village & MCD (Waushara)	402	388	-3.5	398	81.2	0.5	0.3	12.1	6.0	22.1	56.6	21.4	179	86.0	69.3	5.0
Lomira village & MCD (Dodge)	2,430	2,375	-2.3	2,340	86.9	0.0	0.0	2.1	11.0	23.9	63.8	12.1	967	47.7	47.6	13.4
Lomira town (Dodge)	1,137	1,134	-0.3	1,257	96.7	0.0	0.0	0.6	2.7	21.1	65.8	13.0	478	79.5	58.6	9.2
Lone Rock village & MCD (Richland)	892	860	-3.6	868	95.2	0.9	1.6	1.6	0.7	22.6	62.6	14.9	398	75.6	67.3	10.3
Long Lake CDP	50	NA	NA	23	100.0	0.0	0.0	0.0	0.0	8.7	86.9	4.3	11	100.0	81.8	0.0
Long Lake town (Florence)...................	157	158	0.6	128	93.8	6.3	0.0	0.0	0.0	9.4	61.0	29.7	73	95.9	46.6	2.7

1 May be of any race.

Table A. All Places — **Population and Housing**

STATE City, town, township, borough, or CDP (county if applicable)	2010 census total population	2014 estimated population	Percent change 2010-2014	ACS total population estimate 2010-2014	White alone, not Hispanic or Latino	Black alone, not Hispanic or Latino	Asian alone, not Hispanic or Latino	All other races or 2 or more races, not Hispanic or Latino	Hispanic or Latino[1]	Under 18 years old	Age 18 to 64 years old	Age 65 years and older	Total occupied housing units	Percent owner occupied	High school diploma or less	Bachelor's degree or more
	1	2	3	4	5	6	7	8	9	10	11	12	13	14	15	16
WISCONSIN—Con.																
Long Lake town (Washburn)	627	623	-0.6	549	95.6	0.0	2.4	2.0	0.0	6.2	64.9	28.8	263	94.3	41.8	30.0
Longwood town (Clark)	861	858	-0.3	796	99.6	0.0	0.4	0.0	0.0	34.0	50.8	15.1	261	77.8	65.5	9.2
Lorain town (Polk)	284	279	-1.8	289	92.0	0.0	2.1	5.9	0.0	17.7	56.1	26.3	124	78.2	60.5	5.6
Lowell village & MCD (Dodge)	340	327	-3.8	322	98.8	1.2	0.0	0.0	0.0	21.2	60.5	18.3	122	71.3	63.1	10.7
Lowell town (Dodge)	1,190	1,165	-2.1	1,045	99.5	0.0	0.0	0.2	0.3	19.4	65.3	15.3	449	93.1	58.4	12.2
Lowville town (Columbia)	1,008	1,012	0.4	970	96.7	0.0	0.2	1.0	2.1	21.0	62.8	16.1	384	85.2	40.1	20.1
Loyal city & MCD (Clark)	1,261	1,239	-1.7	1,239	97.0	0.0	0.0	0.3	2.7	22.3	55.0	22.7	544	71.7	63.8	4.6
Loyal town (Clark)	826	823	-0.4	822	99.6	0.0	0.0	0.0	0.4	44.2	46.9	9.0	232	74.6	61.2	11.2
Lublin village & MCD (Taylor)	118	117	-0.8	91	100.0	0.0	0.0	0.0	0.0	11.0	72.6	16.5	55	60.0	56.4	7.3
Lucas town (Dunn)	764	780	2.1	801	95.6	0.0	0.7	0.9	2.7	21.1	65.5	13.4	317	84.5	50.5	32.2
Luck village & MCD (Polk)	1,119	1,071	-4.3	1,031	97.5	0.6	0.0	1.5	0.5	19.1	53.2	27.5	449	65.0	45.0	16.3
Luck town (Polk)	930	919	-1.2	919	94.1	0.3	0.8	0.3	4.5	20.2	63.8	16.1	398	90.5	49.2	11.1
Ludington town (Eau Claire)	1,063	1,085	2.1	1,089	97.2	0.3	0.3	1.3	1.0	24.7	63.3	12.0	404	88.4	42.6	22.0
Luxemburg village & MCD (Kewaunee)	2,524	2,562	1.5	2,557	95.9	0.5	0.0	1.6	2.0	33.9	54.4	11.8	878	69.4	44.2	13.7
Luxemburg town (Kewaunee)	1,460	1,463	0.2	1,402	99.3	0.1	0.2	0.0	0.4	20.8	62.5	16.7	537	96.5	63.5	11.2
Lyndon town (Juneau)	1,384	1,361	-1.7	1,463	79.2	0.1	0.0	17.3	3.3	21.1	67.5	11.5	533	78.0	56.3	10.9
Lyndon town (Sheboygan)	1,542	1,542	0.0	1,273	92.5	0.0	4.3	3.1	0.0	17.2	67.1	15.6	504	87.5	48.6	18.3
Lyndon Station village & MCD (Juneau)	500	486	-2.8	659	98.9	0.0	0.0	0.5	0.6	24.1	61.5	14.4	228	58.3	54.8	11.8
Lynn town (Clark)	861	860	-0.1	949	97.9	0.4	0.0	1.3	0.4	43.2	46.1	10.9	258	84.9	65.5	13.2
Lynne town (Oneida)	141	141	0.0	201	96.5	0.0	0.0	3.5	0.0	13.5	64.4	22.4	83	98.8	59.0	10.8
Lynxville village & MCD (Crawford)	132	128	-3.0	161	94.4	0.0	0.0	1.9	3.7	20.5	54.7	24.8	68	82.4	41.2	8.8
Lyons town (Walworth)	3,698	3,720	0.6	3,706	93.8	0.5	0.9	4.2	0.5	23.2	61.4	15.4	1,338	82.2	39.2	33.6
McFarland village & MCD (Dane)	7,805	8,182	4.8	8,009	96.0	0.2	0.8	1.6	1.3	24.7	61.8	13.5	3,260	73.9	15.1	50.7
Mackford town (Green Lake)	560	554	-1.1	518	96.3	0.0	2.7	1.0	0.0	25.7	66.2	8.1	199	85.9	55.3	10.1
McKinley town (Polk)	347	343	-1.2	349	91.1	0.0	0.9	6.3	1.7	21.2	58.3	20.6	157	87.3	47.1	29.3
McKinley town (Taylor)	458	446	-2.6	398	100.0	0.0	0.0	0.0	0.0	29.6	53.0	17.3	142	90.1	62.7	6.3
McMillan town (Marathon)	1,981	2,078	4.9	2,168	94.6	0.7	3.9	0.7	0.1	31.2	55.9	12.9	745	96.9	30.1	45.1
Madge town (Washburn)	505	500	-1.0	496	99.2	0.0	0.0	0.4	0.4	12.9	56.5	30.4	238	97.5	42.4	28.2
Madison city & MCD (Dane)	233,059	245,691	5.4	239,848	75.0	7.0	8.1	3.3	6.6	17.8	72.2	10.0	103,169	48.7	17.0	54.8
Madison town (Dane)	6,449	6,760	4.8	6,630	45.1	15.5	4.1	3.9	31.5	21.7	72.6	5.6	3,108	26.4	33.9	30.1
Magnolia town (Rock)	767	771	0.5	740	96.4	0.0	0.0	0.7	3.0	16.1	67.5	16.4	308	85.4	57.8	16.6
Maiden Rock village & MCD (Pierce)	119	120	0.8	94	100.0	0.0	0.0	0.0	0.0	29.8	67.0	3.2	33	97.0	63.6	21.2
Maiden Rock town (Pierce)	589	588	-0.2	584	98.8	0.2	0.5	0.0	0.5	17.5	59.7	22.9	258	92.2	45.3	24.4
Maine town (Marathon)	2,336	2,372	1.5	2,298	98.8	0.0	0.0	1.2	0.0	22.1	64.0	14.1	874	93.9	38.4	29.2
Maine town (Outagamie)	866	878	1.4	885	95.1	0.0	0.0	0.0	4.9	24.2	60.6	15.4	332	87.3	68.1	6.3
Manawa city & MCD (Waupaca)	1,371	1,325	-3.4	1,273	98.3	0.5	0.2	0.0	1.1	22.2	62.3	15.6	577	64.3	52.5	15.1
Manchester town (Green Lake)	1,022	1,017	-0.5	1,190	100.0	0.0	0.0	0.0	0.0	34.0	54.1	11.8	368	85.3	62.8	9.2
Manchester town (Jackson)	704	719	2.1	680	95.0	0.3	0.0	3.7	1.0	16.5	61.1	22.4	295	91.2	57.3	13.6
Manitowish Waters town (Vilas)	566	567	0.2	618	99.5	0.0	0.0	0.0	0.5	4.5	56.9	38.7	354	82.8	20.9	45.2
Manitowoc city & MCD (Manitowoc)	33,740	33,102	-1.9	33,443	87.4	0.4	4.9	2.3	5.0	21.5	60.0	18.4	14,839	66.8	48.1	21.4
Manitowoc town (Manitowoc)	1,084	1,077	-0.6	931	97.0	0.0	1.5	1.5	0.0	16.8	59.2	24.0	394	90.6	43.9	26.9
Manitowoc Rapids town (Manitowoc)	2,143	2,127	-0.7	2,097	97.3	0.0	1.8	0.6	0.3	17.8	60.9	21.3	762	97.2	33.2	32.7
Maple town (Douglas)	744	745	0.1	770	87.5	0.4	0.3	11.4	0.4	28.3	60.7	11.0	287	81.2	35.2	23.3
Maple Bluff village & MCD (Dane)	1,317	1,343	2.0	1,445	97.3	0.3	0.0	0.7	1.7	21.0	61.0	18.1	581	87.4	4.5	83.8
Maple Creek town (Outagamie)	616	616	0.0	638	98.3	0.0	0.3	0.6	0.8	24.4	63.4	12.1	226	88.9	67.7	11.9
Maple Grove town (Barron)	979	980	0.1	950	95.2	0.9	0.2	2.4	1.3	20.2	63.7	16.1	353	92.1	50.7	12.7
Maple Grove town (Manitowoc)	832	819	-1.6	782	98.3	0.0	0.0	1.7	0.0	21.6	63.4	15.0	287	97.2	59.6	10.8
Maple Grove town (Shawano)	972	968	-0.4	926	97.9	0.0	1.6	0.4	0.0	18.0	65.7	16.3	376	89.4	56.6	13.0
Maplehurst town (Taylor)	335	330	-1.5	350	98.6	0.0	0.0	0.0	1.4	20.3	57.2	22.6	158	84.8	79.1	6.3
Maple Plain town (Barron)	803	805	0.2	652	86.0	0.0	0.6	11.2	2.1	19.5	59.1	21.5	280	84.3	48.6	24.6
Maple Valley town (Oconto)	662	660	-0.3	687	98.3	0.0	0.0	1.7	0.0	22.1	55.6	22.3	302	84.1	54.6	14.6
Marathon town (Marathon)	1,048	1,098	4.8	1,059	96.1	0.0	1.3	2.0	0.6	22.4	65.4	12.1	397	88.9	46.3	15.9
Marathon City village & MCD (Marathon)	1,524	1,527	0.2	1,472	96.5	0.0	1.3	1.2	1.0	18.6	59.6	21.7	635	78.4	56.4	17.6
Marcellon town (Columbia)	1,102	1,106	0.4	1,125	98.8	0.0	0.3	1.0	0.0	26.9	58.0	15.1	408	90.0	50.0	19.1
Marengo CDP	111	NA	NA	139	94.2	0.0	0.0	5.8	0.0	28.8	48.2	23.0	50	94.0	70.0	0.0
Marengo town (Ashland)	390	390	0.0	445	95.1	0.0	0.2	1.6	3.1	38.7	49.2	12.1	132	94.7	50.0	15.2
Maribel village & MCD (Manitowoc)	351	346	-1.4	346	95.1	0.0	0.0	4.3	0.6	22.3	63.7	13.9	140	80.7	66.4	8.6
Marietta town (Crawford)	470	454	-3.4	469	97.9	0.9	0.2	0.6	0.4	14.9	64.9	20.0	203	84.7	62.1	11.8
Marinette city & MCD (Marinette)	10,968	10,897	-0.6	10,890	93.2	0.9	0.5	2.8	2.7	21.4	59.9	18.6	5,105	61.8	49.6	12.3
Marion town (Grant)	572	567	-0.9	802	98.8	0.0	0.0	1.2	0.0	28.5	61.7	10.0	261	90.8	46.0	16.9
Marion town (Juneau)	426	417	-2.1	413	96.1	0.0	0.0	2.2	1.7	14.3	60.6	24.9	189	91.0	51.3	11.1

1 May be of any race.

Table A. All Places — **Population and Housing**

STATE City, town, township, borough, or CDP (county if applicable)	Population				Race and Hispanic or Latino origin (percent), 2010–2014					Age (percent), 2010–2014			Households, 2010–2014			
	2010 census total population	2014 estimated population	Percent change 2010-2014	ACS total population estimate 2010-2014	White alone, not Hispanic or Latino	Black alone, not Hispanic or Latino	Asian alone, not Hispanic or Latino	All other races or 2 or more races, not Hispanic or Latino	Hispanic or Latino[1]	Under 18 years old	Age 18 to 64 years old	Age 65 years and older	Total occupied housing units	Percent owner occupied	Householders by level of education (percent): High school diploma or less	Bachelor's degree or more
	1	2	3	4	5	6	7	8	9	10	11	12	13	14	15	16
WISCONSIN—Con.																
Marion city	1,260	1,233	-2.1	1,171	96.1	0.0	0.0	0.2	3.8	22.2	59.9	17.6	509	62.7	57.8	10.4
Marion city (Shawano)......	25	25	0.0	0	0.0	0.0	0.0	0.0	0.0	0.0	0.0	0.0	0	0.0	0.0	0.0
Marion city (Waupaca)......	1,235	1,208	-2.2	1,171	96.1	0.0	0.0	0.2	3.8	22.2	59.9	17.6	509	62.7	57.8	10.4
Marion town (Waushara) ..	2,038	2,025	-0.6	1,980	99.3	0.0	0.0	0.4	0.3	14.9	55.6	29.5	905	93.9	44.0	24.4
Markesan city & MCD (Green Lake)..............	1,476	1,427	-3.3	1,510	86.8	0.3	1.1	0.0	11.7	22.9	54.3	22.7	624	58.7	58.5	15.2
Marquette village & MCD (Green Lake)..............	150	148	-1.3	114	100.0	0.0	0.0	0.0	0.0	10.6	48.2	41.2	60	80.0	55.0	10.0
Marquette town (Green Lake).........................	531	527	-0.8	514	98.8	0.0	0.0	1.2	0.0	13.0	61.5	25.5	235	75.3	50.6	11.1
Marshall village & MCD (Dane).........................	3,857	3,928	1.8	3,912	82.9	5.4	0.0	0.0	11.7	32.0	58.3	9.9	1,416	73.2	46.3	13.7
Marshall town (Richland)..	567	558	-1.6	665	99.2	0.0	0.0	0.8	0.0	26.6	56.8	16.7	261	84.7	49.0	19.5
Marshall town (Rusk).......	688	677	-1.6	667	99.3	0.0	0.0	0.7	0.0	33.6	54.3	11.8	235	84.3	66.4	7.2
Marshfield town (Fond du Lac)...........................	1,136	1,125	-1.0	989	99.1	0.0	0.0	0.0	0.9	19.4	58.3	22.3	387	84.0	61.5	18.1
Marshfield city.................	19,079	18,691	-2.0	18,514	93.5	0.3	2.2	1.0	3.0	21.6	59.6	19.0	8,439	61.2	40.2	27.7
Marshfield city (Marathon)	901	901	0.0	524	99.4	0.0	0.0	0.6	0.0	1.3	59.7	39.1	302	26.5	28.5	31.5
Marshfield city (Wood)....	18,178	17,790	-2.1	17,990	93.3	0.3	2.2	1.0	3.1	22.2	59.5	18.4	8,137	62.5	40.7	27.6
Marshfield town (Wood)....	788	796	1.0	862	98.3	0.0	0.0	0.0	1.7	19.4	51.6	29.1	354	93.8	56.5	16.7
Martell town (Pierce).......	1,185	1,183	-0.2	1,083	97.5	0.5	0.5	1.1	0.5	20.6	67.4	11.8	443	89.6	38.1	25.7
Mason village & MCD (Bayfield).....................	93	92	-1.1	84	88.1	0.0	0.0	11.9	0.0	32.1	60.7	7.1	32	93.8	50.0	0.0
Mason town (Bayfield)......	315	317	0.6	319	83.7	0.0	0.0	2.8	13.5	28.9	56.5	14.7	122	78.7	51.6	15.6
Matteson town (Waupaca)	936	924	-1.3	1,033	98.5	0.0	0.0	0.8	0.8	24.8	61.5	13.7	413	91.0	56.9	12.3
Mattoon village & MCD (Shawano)...................	438	426	-2.7	467	64.5	0.0	0.0	0.9	34.7	22.9	63.9	13.3	170	60.6	72.4	5.9
Mauston city & MCD (Juneau)......................	4,423	4,392	-0.7	4,446	91.7	2.7	0.4	1.6	3.5	20.8	58.6	20.6	1,626	60.6	47.5	20.0
Maxville town (Buffalo)......	309	305	-1.3	365	90.7	0.0	0.0	0.3	9.0	24.1	62.5	13.4	142	76.1	54.9	16.9
Mayville town (Clark)	963	951	-1.2	939	92.7	0.0	1.4	3.7	2.2	31.2	54.8	14.0	319	81.2	70.8	9.1
Mayville city & MCD (Dodge)........................	5,154	5,009	-2.8	5,086	92.4	0.6	2.2	1.1	3.7	22.8	59.9	17.3	2,026	68.0	55.0	13.9
Mazomanie village & MCD (Dane).........................	1,642	1,701	3.6	1,585	93.6	0.4	0.4	1.1	4.5	23.8	63.7	12.2	660	74.7	43.0	25.2
Mazomanie town (Dane) ..	1,095	1,143	4.4	1,045	97.0	0.0	0.7	0.2	2.1	19.6	68.0	12.3	418	92.6	30.4	32.3
Mead town (Clark)	321	320	-0.3	300	91.0	0.0	1.0	2.7	5.3	28.7	51.6	19.7	120	85.8	67.5	9.2
Meadowbrook town (Sawyer)........................	131	129	-1.5	104	90.4	0.0	1.9	0.0	7.7	18.2	58.6	23.1	50	80.0	66.0	10.0
Mecan town (Marquette)...	686	663	-3.4	623	98.7	0.0	0.3	1.0	0.0	11.9	54.2	33.9	307	86.3	62.5	14.7
Medary town (La Crosse) .	1,446	1,493	3.3	1,414	93.4	0.0	2.2	2.8	1.6	22.7	61.6	15.6	558	91.8	21.5	45.0
Medford city & MCD (Taylor).........................	4,368	4,344	-0.5	4,349	97.0	0.2	0.0	1.1	1.7	21.0	56.2	22.8	2,110	58.6	52.7	18.0
Medford town (Taylor)	2,564	2,582	0.7	2,581	99.7	0.0	0.0	0.3	0.0	24.9	61.6	13.6	1,035	86.1	50.3	19.2
Medina town (Dane)	1,383	1,450	4.8	1,328	92.8	0.0	0.5	2.0	4.7	23.2	66.5	10.2	524	82.1	38.4	24.0
Meeme town (Manitowoc) .	1,446	1,428	-1.2	1,273	95.9	0.5	1.4	2.2	0.0	17.2	65.7	17.1	512	94.3	54.5	15.2
Meenon town (Burnett).....	1,163	1,152	-0.9	1,210	90.0	1.1	0.9	5.4	2.6	24.6	61.0	14.2	479	86.8	40.1	16.7
Mellen city & MCD (Ashland)......................	731	717	-1.9	774	95.3	1.7	0.0	2.5	0.5	21.2	58.7	20.0	342	69.0	63.5	7.3
Melrose village & MCD (Jackson)......................	503	499	-0.8	549	93.3	0.0	0.0	2.4	4.4	25.2	58.3	16.6	230	58.7	58.7	14.3
Melrose town (Jackson)....	470	471	0.2	389	95.1	0.0	1.3	0.8	2.8	27.8	59.4	12.9	144	83.3	53.5	20.8
Melvina village & MCD (Monroe)	104	104	0.0	80	87.5	0.0	0.0	12.5	0.0	35.0	55.2	10.0	31	83.9	67.7	12.9
Menasha city	17,351	17,604	1.5	17,535	86.0	2.3	5.1	2.0	4.6	24.1	63.0	12.7	7,299	63.1	42.3	19.5
Menasha city (Calumet)....	2,207	2,235	1.3	2,262	91.7	1.8	0.0	0.0	6.5	27.6	65.3	7.2	808	85.4	27.2	47.9
Menasha city (Winnebago)	15,144	15,369	1.5	15,273	85.1	2.4	5.9	2.3	4.3	23.7	62.8	13.5	6,491	60.3	44.1	15.9
Menasha town (Winnebago)	18,498	18,867	2.0	18,729	90.5	1.1	2.1	1.9	4.4	22.4	63.6	14.0	8,002	64.0	38.1	27.9
Menominee town (Menominee)	4,232	4,522	6.9	4,382	12.2	0.3	2.0	80.3	5.2	30.2	55.2	14.5	1,238	73.8	47.3	15.5
Menomonee Falls village & MCD (Waukesha).......	35,625	35,974	1.0	35,828	88.8	2.5	4.7	1.7	2.4	22.3	58.7	19.1	14,539	75.2	30.5	40.5
Menomonie city & MCD (Dunn)..........................	16,284	16,237	-0.3	16,219	88.1	1.2	5.6	2.8	2.3	13.3	75.0	11.7	5,679	40.7	33.5	27.8
Menomonie town (Dunn) ..	3,346	3,412	2.0	3,379	96.2	0.0	0.0	3.1	0.7	28.9	57.2	13.8	1,208	89.4	36.8	32.9
Mentor town (Clark)	585	576	-1.5	572	94.2	0.0	0.0	0.5	5.2	17.2	61.5	21.3	254	81.5	60.2	11.4
Mequon city & MCD (Ozaukee).....................	23,139	23,509	1.6	23,300	91.3	2.6	2.7	1.4	2.0	21.8	58.1	20.1	9,105	87.0	14.5	65.5
Mercer CDP	516	NA	NA	585	99.1	0.0	0.0	0.9	0.0	13.0	55.7	31.3	317	61.2	57.4	13.2
Mercer town (Iron)	1,407	1,421	1.0	1,354	98.7	0.0	0.0	1.3	0.0	12.4	54.9	32.6	717	78.2	47.6	18.5
Merrill city & MCD (Lincoln)......................	9,661	9,364	-3.1	9,491	94.7	0.8	0.8	1.4	2.3	22.3	60.1	17.6	4,173	59.6	55.0	14.4
Merrill town (Lincoln)	2,980	2,944	-1.2	2,956	99.6	0.4	0.0	0.0	0.0	20.5	61.6	17.7	1,199	93.0	51.5	18.9
Merrillan village & MCD (Jackson)......................	538	538	0.0	650	90.9	0.3	0.0	5.1	3.7	19.6	62.6	17.8	309	66.7	59.2	9.1
Merrimac village & MCD (Sauk).........................	419	439	4.8	448	92.6	1.8	0.2	2.0	3.3	19.6	60.7	19.6	181	72.9	43.1	23.8
Merrimac town (Sauk)	945	985	4.2	784	96.9	0.0	0.4	0.5	2.2	9.6	64.1	26.4	356	93.8	38.2	32.0
Merton village & MCD (Waukesha).................	3,388	3,529	4.2	3,463	96.2	1.2	1.0	0.0	1.6	36.9	57.3	5.6	1,036	95.8	16.6	52.9
Merton town (Waukesha)..	8,258	8,406	1.8	8,338	96.8	0.3	0.8	0.9	1.2	26.0	61.3	12.7	2,922	94.1	24.6	46.5
Meteor town (Sawyer).......	158	157	-0.6	163	96.3	0.0	0.0	3.7	0.0	12.2	69.9	17.8	78	89.7	41.0	7.7
Metomen town (Fond du Lac)...........................	741	722	-2.6	828	99.5	0.0	0.0	0.5	0.0	21.1	67.0	12.0	302	87.4	55.6	16.2
Middle Inlet town (Marinette)...................	840	832	-1.0	880	98.0	0.0	0.0	2.0	0.0	15.6	57.4	26.9	403	93.1	54.8	11.4
Middleton city & MCD (Dane).........................	17,547	18,671	6.4	18,185	80.7	5.6	6.5	1.9	5.3	18.9	66.8	14.3	8,549	54.6	17.7	58.2
Middleton town (Dane)	5,862	6,171	5.3	6,041	87.8	0.4	5.4	0.7	5.7	30.3	59.2	10.4	2,038	97.5	8.3	74.5

1 May be of any race.

Table A. All Places — **Population and Housing**

STATE City, town, township, borough, or CDP (county if applicable)	2010 census total population	2014 estimated population	Percent change 2010-2014	ACS total population estimate 2010-2014	White alone, not Hispanic or Latino	Black alone, not Hispanic or Latino	Asian alone, not Hispanic or Latino	All other races or 2 or more races, not Hispanic or Latino	Hispanic or Latino[1]	Under 18 years old	Age 18 to 64 years old	Age 65 years and older	Total occupied housing units	Percent owner occupied	High school diploma or less	Bachelor's degree or more
	1	2	3	4	5	6	7	8	9	10	11	12	13	14	15	16
WISCONSIN—Con.																
Middle Village CDP..........	281	NA	NA	262	0.0	0.0	0.0	100.0	0.0	33.2	58.8	8.0	88	21.6	60.2	5.7
Mifflin town (Iowa)............	580	591	1.9	647	86.4	0.0	0.0	0.2	13.4	29.1	57.5	13.4	225	76.0	55.1	23.1
Milford town (Jefferson)	1,099	1,115	1.5	1,144	98.9	1.0	0.2	0.0	0.0	21.6	64.7	13.6	452	84.5	40.5	26.1
Milladore village..............	276	276	0.0	245	98.8	0.0	0.0	1.2	0.0	22.4	67.7	9.8	109	78.0	59.6	18.3
Milladore village (Portage)	0	0	0.0	0	0.0	0.0	0.0	0.0	0.0	0.0	0.0	0.0	0	0.0	0.0	0.0
Milladore village (Wood) ...	276	276	0.0	245	98.8	0.0	0.0	1.2	0.0	22.4	67.7	9.8	109	78.0	59.6	18.3
Milladore town (Wood)......	690	669	-3.0	845	96.7	0.0	0.0	0.7	2.6	28.5	59.9	11.6	287	79.1	63.4	7.3
Millston CDP....................	125	NA	NA	143	98.6	0.0	1.4	0.0	0.0	15.4	57.4	27.3	67	68.7	58.2	19.4
Millston town (Jackson)	159	160	0.6	167	98.8	0.0	1.2	0.0	0.0	13.8	59.4	26.9	80	68.8	56.3	18.8
Milltown village & MCD (Polk).......................	917	886	-3.4	1,062	95.8	0.0	0.5	2.4	1.3	22.7	67.5	9.8	460	63.9	59.3	6.3
Milltown town (Polk)..........	1,226	1,214	-1.0	1,224	97.5	0.0	0.0	0.8	1.7	22.1	61.2	16.7	518	89.4	46.7	14.5
Millville town (Grant).........	166	165	-0.6	151	100.0	0.0	0.0	0.0	0.0	15.2	72.2	12.6	58	93.1	44.8	25.9
Milton town (Buffalo).........	534	523	-2.1	526	100.0	0.0	0.0	0.0	0.0	29.0	53.5	17.5	198	99.0	33.3	38.9
Milton city & MCD (Rock) .	5,549	5,585	0.6	5,562	95.8	1.1	0.2	0.8	2.2	25.6	59.2	15.3	2,212	69.8	40.5	30.2
Milton town (Rock)............	2,920	3,014	3.2	2,965	93.6	0.4	3.1	2.9	0.0	18.7	65.7	15.6	1,242	82.7	46.8	23.6
Milwaukee city	594,738	599,642	0.8	598,078	36.6	38.8	3.7	3.2	17.7	26.8	64.1	9.2	230,181	43.0	42.9	24.4
Milwaukee city (Milwaukee).................	594,738	599,642	0.8	598,078	36.6	38.8	3.7	3.2	17.7	26.8	64.1	9.2	230,181	43.0	42.9	24.4
Milwaukee city (Washington)................	0	0	0.0	0	0.0	0.0	0.0	0.0	0.0	0.0	0.0	0.0	0	0.0	0.0	0.0
Mineral Point city & MCD (Iowa)........................	2,487	2,489	0.1	2,659	95.6	0.0	0.0	1.4	3.0	22.4	61.1	16.6	1,165	66.8	38.5	30.7
Mineral Point town (Iowa) .	1,033	1,048	1.5	1,073	99.6	0.0	0.0	0.4	0.0	28.1	58.9	12.9	365	90.1	46.6	24.7
Minocqua CDP..................	451	NA	NA	350	78.0	0.0	15.7	5.4	0.9	10.0	48.9	41.1	210	47.1	33.8	23.3
Minocqua town (Oneida) ..	4,454	4,453	0.0	4,446	94.9	0.5	2.8	1.2	0.7	12.6	54.4	32.9	2,101	85.6	32.7	33.0
Minong village & MCD (Washburn)	527	512	-2.8	394	97.0	0.0	0.0	0.0	3.0	22.8	48.5	28.7	190	72.1	54.7	12.1
Minong town (Washburn)..	917	910	-0.8	734	97.5	0.3	0.0	1.8	0.4	14.3	50.5	35.3	365	82.5	44.1	20.0
Mishicot village & MCD (Manitowoc)	1,438	1,412	-1.8	1,349	97.7	0.0	0.0	1.9	0.4	22.9	55.2	21.9	550	85.6	49.3	16.9
Mishicot town (Manitowoc)	1,285	1,270	-1.2	1,395	98.2	1.1	0.0	0.6	0.0	21.4	67.6	11.0	494	88.7	49.8	9.3
Mitchell town (Sheboygan)	1,304	1,313	0.7	1,347	96.0	1.0	0.0	1.0	1.9	22.3	62.6	15.1	473	93.2	38.5	19.9
Modena town (Buffalo)......	354	347	-2.0	330	91.2	0.0	0.0	1.2	7.6	25.1	51.6	23.3	136	77.9	48.5	22.8
Mole Lake CDP.................	435	NA	NA	598	12.4	0.0	0.0	85.1	2.5	25.8	67.5	6.9	206	21.4	55.8	1.5
Molitor town (Taylor)	326	323	-0.9	386	94.6	1.0	2.1	1.6	0.8	22.0	58.0	19.9	159	98.1	56.6	13.8
Mondovi city & MCD (Buffalo)	2,777	2,672	-3.8	2,723	96.0	0.0	0.0	3.8	0.2	23.3	56.7	20.0	1,265	53.7	54.4	17.1
Mondovi town (Buffalo).....	469	461	-1.7	454	95.2	4.0	0.0	0.7	0.2	25.8	60.8	13.4	173	86.7	46.2	17.3
Monico town (Oneida)	309	306	-1.0	253	98.8	0.0	0.0	0.8	0.4	15.8	64.5	19.8	111	84.7	64.0	9.9
Monona town (Dane)........	7,567	7,859	3.9	7,711	89.8	2.3	1.5	1.3	5.1	17.1	63.2	19.8	3,972	54.0	20.7	44.0
Monroe town (Adams)	398	386	-3.0	469	98.9	0.0	0.0	1.1	0.0	16.0	53.1	30.9	215	90.7	68.4	7.0
Monroe city & MCD (Green)......................	10,817	10,781	-0.3	10,807	92.4	0.4	0.8	2.0	4.4	21.5	58.6	19.8	4,767	60.5	48.0	20.7
Monroe town (Green)	1,244	1,248	0.3	1,142	98.0	0.0	1.0	0.2	0.9	19.2	52.4	28.5	390	91.5	45.6	25.9
Montana town (Buffalo).....	284	279	-1.8	266	95.1	0.0	0.0	2.3	2.6	27.4	63.1	9.4	94	92.6	50.0	19.1
Montello city & MCD (Marquette)	1,495	1,460	-2.3	1,494	93.9	1.6	1.4	1.5	1.6	15.6	60.6	23.8	641	63.0	53.7	17.6
Montello town (Marquette)	1,033	1,010	-2.2	1,155	97.3	0.0	0.0	2.4	0.3	16.9	59.6	23.5	492	86.0	57.5	8.9
Montfort village	718	701	-2.4	710	95.5	1.3	0.0	0.8	2.4	20.4	65.3	14.2	281	90.4	44.5	16.0
Montfort village (Grant).....	622	605	-2.7	610	94.8	1.5	0.0	1.0	2.8	18.9	67.9	13.3	250	89.2	46.0	18.0
Montfort village (Iowa)......	96	96	0.0	100	100.0	0.0	0.0	0.0	0.0	30.0	50.0	20.0	31	100.0	32.3	0.0
Monticello village & MCD (Green).....................	1,212	1,220	0.7	1,270	95.7	1.0	0.6	0.5	2.3	23.4	62.9	13.9	567	61.6	40.9	16.9
Monticello town (Lafayette)	133	133	0.0	167	100.0	0.0	0.0	0.0	0.0	30.0	49.2	21.0	63	93.7	60.3	19.0
Montpelier town (Kewaunee)...................	1,306	1,287	-1.5	1,206	90.7	0.0	0.0	0.2	9.1	25.1	61.0	14.0	440	91.6	45.2	14.1
Montreal city & MCD (Iron).........................	807	804	-0.4	760	96.7	0.0	0.0	2.1	1.2	22.7	66.1	11.1	347	82.7	38.9	25.4
Montrose town (Dane)......	1,075	1,123	4.5	1,009	99.6	0.0	0.0	0.4	0.0	18.0	61.4	20.7	418	84.2	30.4	31.6
Morgan town (Oconto)......	984	979	-0.5	935	97.2	0.0	0.0	2.4	0.4	17.7	66.6	15.7	401	95.8	44.9	19.7
Morris town (Shawano).....	453	450	-0.7	356	99.2	0.0	0.0	0.8	0.0	18.6	60.7	20.8	157	88.5	51.6	13.4
Morrison town (Brown).....	1,599	1,608	0.6	1,561	94.0	0.4	0.0	1.9	3.7	23.8	62.1	14.0	583	89.2	54.4	10.5
Morse town (Ashland).......	493	494	0.2	524	97.5	0.0	0.0	2.5	0.0	29.4	54.0	16.6	194	97.4	46.4	13.9
Moscow town (Iowa).........	576	587	1.9	527	99.4	0.0	0.0	0.0	0.6	20.7	60.4	19.0	221	92.3	36.2	31.7
Mosel town (Sheboygan) ..	790	792	0.3	827	96.1	0.6	2.5	0.0	0.7	22.3	61.7	16.1	316	88.0	48.4	20.9
Mosinee city & MCD (Marathon)..................	3,988	4,046	1.5	4,008	96.7	0.7	0.0	2.4	0.2	20.8	64.2	15.0	1,636	74.5	54.2	20.2
Mosinee town (Marathon).	2,174	2,188	0.6	2,099	95.3	0.0	1.2	2.1	1.3	24.5	59.8	15.8	753	91.8	38.5	22.4
Moundville town (Marquette)	552	541	-2.0	469	91.3	0.4	1.5	0.0	6.8	20.1	64.8	15.4	184	79.9	54.3	12.5
Mountain CDP..................	363	NA	NA	310	79.0	0.0	0.0	20.3	0.6	23.6	54.3	22.3	135	83.0	64.4	3.0
Mountain town (Oconto) ...	822	816	-0.7	797	87.5	0.4	0.0	10.9	1.3	14.8	57.2	27.9	361	85.6	56.5	8.6
Mount Calvary village & MCD (Fond du Lac)	764	749	-2.0	637	95.1	0.2	0.6	4.1	0.0	22.2	54.2	23.4	218	92.7	55.5	13.8
Mount Hope village & MCD (Grant)	225	221	-1.8	166	91.0	0.0	0.0	0.6	8.4	23.5	57.6	18.7	82	76.8	63.4	6.1
Mount Hope town (Grant) .	300	300	0.0	419	84.7	0.0	0.0	0.0	15.3	34.6	58.8	6.7	115	75.7	52.2	5.2
Mount Horeb village & MCD (Dane)...............	7,128	7,388	3.6	7,286	97.7	0.2	0.0	1.2	0.9	27.7	61.8	10.6	2,981	62.1	30.3	38.4
Mount Ida town (Grant).....	561	562	0.2	536	97.8	0.0	0.0	0.4	1.9	25.2	58.4	16.4	199	86.4	46.2	13.1
Mount Morris town (Waushara)	1,097	1,091	-0.5	1,033	97.1	1.2	0.5	0.0	1.3	13.9	53.2	32.7	481	91.9	44.5	19.8
Mount Pleasant town (Green).......................	603	612	1.5	567	98.4	0.4	0.0	0.0	1.2	26.0	60.0	14.1	229	84.3	48.9	12.7
Mount Pleasant village & MCD (Racine)	26,197	26,293	0.4	26,220	80.6	6.2	2.4	2.0	8.9	20.2	60.9	18.9	11,053	77.9	31.8	33.3
Mount Sterling village & MCD (Crawford)............	211	207	-1.9	244	99.6	0.0	0.4	0.0	0.0	27.9	48.7	23.4	100	89.0	35.0	12.0

1 May be of any race.

Table A. All Places — **Population and Housing**

STATE City, town, township, borough, or CDP (county if applicable)	Population				Race and Hispanic or Latino origin (percent), 2010–2014					Age (percent), 2010–2014			Households, 2010–2014			
	2010 census total population	2014 estimated population	Percent change 2010-2014	ACS total population estimate 2010-2014	White alone, not Hispanic or Latino	Black alone, not Hispanic or Latino	Asian alone, not Hispanic or Latino	All other races or 2 or more races, not Hispanic or Latino	Hispanic or Latino[1]	Under 18 years old	Age 18 to 64 years old	Age 65 years and older	Total occupied housing units	Percent owner occupied	High school diploma or less	Bachelor's degree or more
	1	2	3	4	5	6	7	8	9	10	11	12	13	14	15	16
WISCONSIN—Con.																
Mukwa town (Waupaca) ...	2,930	2,895	-1.2	2,928	98.2	1.1	0.0	0.4	0.3	22.0	63.0	15.0	1,146	94.4	47.7	18.5
Mukwonago village	7,355	7,595	3.3	7,426	94.6	0.4	0.6	1.5	2.9	25.1	60.4	14.5	3,020	69.0	37.1	30.8
Mukwonago village (Walworth)...................	101	102	1.0	70	100.0	0.0	0.0	0.0	0.0	0.0	81.5	18.6	29	100.0	55.2	0.0
Mukwonago village (Waukesha)..................	7,254	7,493	3.3	7,356	94.6	0.4	0.6	1.5	3.0	25.3	60.3	14.4	2,991	68.7	36.9	31.1
Mukwonago town (Waukesha)..................	7,966	8,086	1.5	8,022	95.2	0.3	0.4	3.2	0.8	25.0	63.2	11.8	2,885	97.4	26.7	37.9
Murry town (Rusk)	277	269	-2.9	266	98.1	0.0	0.0	0.4	1.5	18.0	50.8	31.2	130	91.5	73.1	9.2
Muscoda village	1,299	1,270	-2.2	1,387	99.6	0.0	0.0	0.0	0.4	24.2	54.2	21.6	607	60.3	53.2	9.6
Muscoda village (Grant) ...	1,249	1,220	-2.3	1,306	99.6	0.0	0.0	0.0	0.4	23.7	54.1	22.2	577	61.9	52.0	10.1
Muscoda village (Iowa).....	50	50	0.0	81	100.0	0.0	0.0	0.0	0.0	33.3	55.5	11.1	30	30.0	76.7	0.0
Muscoda town (Grant)	769	767	-0.3	821	93.9	0.2	4.5	1.3	0.0	19.7	69.0	11.3	293	78.5	50.5	16.4
Muskego city & MCD (Waukesha)...............	24,135	24,621	2.0	24,387	95.6	0.0	1.5	0.4	2.4	23.7	61.8	14.5	9,220	86.2	34.9	35.9
Namakagon town (Bayfield)...................	246	247	0.4	261	98.9	0.0	0.0	0.0	1.1	1.5	39.1	59.4	156	92.3	38.5	35.9
Naples town (Buffalo)	691	676	-2.2	647	99.8	0.0	0.2	0.0	0.0	23.2	59.8	17.0	251	74.5	37.5	21.1
Nasewaupee town (Door) .	2,061	2,044	-0.8	1,830	96.4	0.0	0.2	2.1	1.3	15.1	64.4	20.7	910	88.0	47.9	24.4
Nashotah village & MCD (Waukesha)...............	1,395	1,397	0.1	1,524	95.5	0.0	2.6	1.5	0.4	25.8	59.9	14.2	577	89.8	16.5	52.7
Nashville town (Forest).....	1,064	1,046	-1.7	1,301	58.9	0.0	0.0	40.0	1.2	20.7	56.8	22.4	533	63.6	55.0	10.7
Navarino CDP..................	177	NA	NA	147	100.0	0.0	0.0	0.0	0.0	18.4	68.6	12.9	64	76.6	56.3	10.9
Navarino town (Shawano) .	446	443	-0.7	417	98.6	0.0	0.0	1.2	0.2	20.8	67.4	11.8	180	89.4	56.7	16.1
Necedah village & MCD (Juneau)....................	916	915	-0.1	1,011	94.8	3.0	0.0	0.8	1.5	29.4	59.6	10.9	338	55.6	50.9	17.2
Necedah town (Juneau) ...	2,327	2,296	-1.3	2,323	93.6	0.0	1.5	1.0	3.8	26.6	53.3	20.0	887	87.7	52.1	10.1
Neenah city & MCD (Winnebago)	25,504	25,855	1.4	25,697	88.7	0.8	2.5	3.0	4.9	24.5	62.4	13.2	10,798	66.9	38.3	29.7
Neenah town (Winnebago)	3,234	3,362	4.0	3,284	98.0	0.0	0.0	0.6	1.5	21.6	65.1	13.2	1,370	94.1	24.2	31.4
Neillsville city & MCD (Clark)......................	2,463	2,418	-1.8	2,287	95.9	1.0	0.5	1.0	1.6	20.3	54.5	25.2	1,053	67.1	53.8	16.8
Nekimi town (Winnebago)	1,429	1,480	3.6	1,570	98.6	0.0	0.0	0.3	1.1	17.9	68.8	13.2	639	89.7	43.3	26.8
Nekoosa city & MCD (Wood)...................	2,580	2,498	-3.2	2,361	95.0	0.3	0.0	3.3	1.5	25.3	57.4	17.4	1,021	66.3	61.9	8.4
Nelson village & MCD (Buffalo)	374	355	-5.1	308	93.5	0.0	0.0	1.6	4.9	16.2	62.9	20.8	158	69.6	62.0	15.2
Nelson town (Buffalo)	571	558	-2.3	538	91.8	0.2	0.0	0.0	8.0	16.2	68.9	14.9	226	82.7	58.4	9.7
Nelsonville village & MCD (Portage)	155	154	-0.6	117	93.2	0.0	0.0	0.9	6.0	24.7	56.4	18.8	45	82.2	33.3	26.7
Neopit CDP.....................	690	NA	NA	603	1.3	1.2	0.0	92.2	5.3	37.1	56.0	6.8	160	53.8	63.1	13.1
Neosho village & MCD (Dodge)	574	557	-3.0	600	95.8	0.0	0.0	1.0	3.2	26.1	64.1	9.8	241	75.9	55.2	10.8
Nepeuskun town (Winnebago)	710	725	2.1	726	96.8	0.0	0.4	0.3	2.5	22.2	61.9	15.8	309	84.5	56.3	14.2
Neshkoro village & MCD (Marquette)	434	424	-2.3	406	93.3	6.7	0.0	0.0	0.0	21.6	57.8	20.4	165	75.8	63.0	8.5
Neshkoro town (Marquette)	561	550	-2.0	522	94.3	1.3	0.8	3.6	0.0	10.7	57.4	31.8	256	100.0	60.2	18.8
Neva town (Langlade).......	902	885	-1.9	878	91.1	0.0	0.0	3.6	5.2	23.5	57.8	18.7	351	92.0	53.8	13.7
Newald CDP	95	NA	NA	148	95.3	3.4	0.0	1.4	0.0	14.9	68.4	16.9	59	100.0	61.0	0.0
Newark town (Rock)	1,543	1,551	0.5	1,709	94.5	0.0	0.7	3.3	1.5	22.0	62.8	15.3	644	97.8	54.0	16.3
New Auburn village	548	559	2.0	540	98.7	0.0	0.0	1.3	0.0	27.0	60.8	12.2	193	80.8	54.9	12.4
New Auburn village (Barron)....................	20	20	0.0	10	100.0	0.0	0.0	0.0	0.0	0.0	60.0	40.0	5	100.0	100.0	0.0
New Auburn village (Chippewa).................	528	539	2.1	530	98.7	0.0	0.0	1.3	0.0	27.5	60.7	11.7	188	80.3	53.7	12.8
New Berlin city & MCD (Waukesha)..................	39,584	39,842	0.7	39,712	90.5	0.8	4.1	1.8	2.8	19.4	62.5	18.1	16,612	76.0	26.5	41.3
Newbold town (Oneida)	2,734	2,723	-0.4	2,722	95.7	0.5	0.0	2.1	1.7	21.6	62.2	16.3	1,061	95.4	30.4	26.7
Newburg village	1,252	1,237	-1.2	1,130	96.7	0.0	0.0	1.0	2.3	17.5	65.1	17.4	516	75.6	50.0	15.9
Newburg village (Ozaukee)..................	97	97	0.0	70	95.7	0.0	0.0	0.0	4.3	21.5	74.3	4.3	45	37.8	26.7	46.7
Newburg village (Washington)..............	1,155	1,140	-1.3	1,060	96.8	0.0	0.0	1.0	2.2	17.1	64.6	18.3	471	79.2	52.2	13.0
New Chester town (Adams)	2,254	2,148	-4.7	2,083	53.6	27.2	0.7	3.8	14.7	7.5	82.2	10.3	391	93.1	53.2	5.4
New Denmark town (Brown)	1,542	1,570	1.8	1,622	93.2	0.3	0.0	5.0	1.5	25.5	63.1	11.3	576	90.8	49.3	16.3
New Diggings town (Lafayette)	502	506	0.8	577	97.9	0.0	0.0	2.1	0.0	22.0	68.8	9.2	228	80.7	47.8	9.2
New Glarus village & MCD (Green)	2,168	2,166	-0.1	2,177	94.2	0.3	0.4	0.1	5.0	24.2	52.6	23.1	883	76.6	37.1	25.4
New Glarus town (Green).	1,331	1,355	1.8	1,411	95.5	0.0	0.8	1.8	1.8	30.3	60.7	9.0	494	93.5	32.8	36.8
New Haven town (Adams)	655	636	-2.9	690	98.1	0.0	0.0	0.7	1.2	19.7	56.9	23.3	282	89.4	55.0	12.1
New Haven town (Dunn)...	677	673	-0.6	608	97.5	0.0	0.0	0.2	2.3	20.0	62.9	16.9	246	89.4	46.3	24.4
New Holstein city & MCD (Calumet).................	3,237	3,181	-1.7	3,223	98.7	0.0	0.0	0.7	0.6	17.7	53.5	28.7	1,417	70.2	53.8	13.3
New Holstein town (Calumet).................	1,507	1,523	1.1	1,728	97.1	0.6	0.3	0.2	1.8	28.9	59.7	11.4	597	92.1	50.4	18.4
New Hope town (Portage)	718	726	1.1	741	98.5	0.0	0.4	0.0	1.1	19.2	64.5	16.3	297	89.2	40.1	38.4
New Lisbon city & MCD (Juneau)..................	2,554	2,500	-2.1	2,545	79.8	11.7	0.0	2.4	6.0	16.9	73.0	10.1	741	65.5	49.9	9.0
New London city	7,294	7,216	-1.1	7,091	89.8	1.2	0.3	0.8	7.8	23.6	62.2	14.3	2,949	62.4	54.3	16.1
New London city (Outagamie)...............	1,609	1,607	-0.1	1,447	78.9	0.4	0.0	0.0	20.7	23.0	66.7	10.4	549	49.4	56.1	23.9
New London city (Waupaca).................	5,685	5,609	-1.3	5,644	92.6	1.4	0.4	1.1	4.5	23.8	61.0	15.3	2,400	65.3	53.9	14.4
New Lyme town (Monroe).	168	171	1.8	180	100.0	0.0	0.0	0.0	0.0	18.9	59.4	21.7	71	90.1	35.2	45.1
New Odanah CDP	472	NA	NA	445	4.9	2.0	2.7	89.7	0.7	23.6	60.9	15.5	162	59.3	43.8	5.6

1 May be of any race.

Table A. All Places — **Population and Housing**

STATE City, town, township, borough, or CDP (county if applicable)	Population				Race and Hispanic or Latino origin (percent), 2010–2014					Age (percent), 2010–2014			Households, 2010–2014			
	2010 census total population	2014 estimated population	Percent change 2010-2014	ACS total population estimate 2010-2014	White alone, not Hispanic or Latino	Black alone, not Hispanic or Latino	Asian alone, not Hispanic or Latino	All other races or 2 or more races, not Hispanic or Latino	Hispanic or Latino[1]	Under 18 years old	Age 18 to 64 years old	Age 65 years and older	Total occupied housing units	Percent owner occupied	High school diploma or less	Bachelor's degree or more
	1	2	3	4	5	6	7	8	9	10	11	12	13	14	15	16
WISCONSIN—Con.																
Newport town (Columbia).	586	588	0.3	587	94.7	0.7	0.9	0.3	3.4	23.3	55.7	21.1	242	91.7	42.1	28.1
New Post CDP	305	NA	NA	278	37.4	1.1	0.0	60.4	1.1	13.7	51.1	35.3	162	63.0	57.4	17.3
New Richmond city & MCD (St. Croix)	8,367	8,679	3.7	8,501	94.9	1.0	0.3	3.3	0.5	30.6	58.2	11.3	3,206	61.1	32.9	25.8
Newton town (Manitowoc)	2,266	2,259	-0.3	2,181	96.9	0.0	0.6	2.4	0.1	20.8	63.2	16.0	853	92.6	42.1	21.6
Newton town (Marquette) .	547	532	-2.7	457	97.6	0.4	0.0	0.0	2.0	19.7	57.2	23.2	185	90.8	60.0	9.2
Niagara city & MCD (Marinette)	1,624	1,601	-1.4	1,633	96.1	0.0	0.2	1.5	2.2	27.4	57.9	14.6	678	83.5	54.0	13.6
Niagara town (Marinette)..	853	864	1.3	842	98.8	0.0	0.1	1.1	0.0	18.2	63.1	18.6	356	91.0	46.9	18.0
Nichols village & MCD (Outagamie)	273	269	-1.5	189	98.9	0.0	0.0	1.1	0.0	17.4	67.0	15.3	97	79.4	83.5	2.1
Nokomis town (Oneida)	1,373	1,367	-0.4	1,379	95.0	0.0	0.3	2.8	1.9	19.2	58.0	22.8	578	95.7	48.8	19.9
Norrie town (Marathon).....	976	984	0.8	958	93.8	0.0	0.3	1.7	4.2	20.6	66.2	13.2	370	90.5	49.7	23.2
North Bay village & MCD (Racine)	241	241	0.0	253	92.9	2.0	1.2	2.0	2.0	21.8	62.8	15.4	89	94.4	16.9	69.7
North Bend town (Jackson)	488	496	1.6	421	98.3	0.0	1.0	0.0	0.7	21.2	61.0	18.1	172	87.8	64.5	14.0
Northfield town (Jackson) .	639	648	1.4	698	77.9	0.0	0.0	21.3	0.7	30.5	51.3	18.3	258	86.4	53.1	21.7
North Fond du Lac village & MCD (Fond du Lac).	5,014	5,027	0.3	5,000	90.6	0.6	2.6	2.4	3.8	25.2	62.2	12.5	2,038	73.1	55.2	12.1
North Freedom village & MCD (Sauk)	701	707	0.9	670	94.3	0.0	0.3	0.6	4.8	22.1	66.9	11.0	271	79.0	55.7	11.8
North Hudson village & MCD (St. Croix)	3,768	3,815	1.2	3,776	92.2	0.4	0.3	3.2	3.8	27.2	62.0	10.8	1,457	79.9	32.2	37.2
North Lancaster town (Grant)	509	511	0.4	471	99.4	0.0	0.0	0.0	0.6	26.4	64.0	9.6	165	88.5	42.4	20.0
Northport CDP	491	NA	NA	466	97.6	1.5	0.0	0.9	0.0	18.3	67.6	14.2	191	83.2	59.7	14.7
North Prairie village & MCD (Waukesha)	2,136	2,145	0.4	2,284	94.9	2.1	0.0	0.0	2.9	25.4	62.3	12.3	807	85.0	28.6	33.1
Norwalk village & MCD (Monroe)	651	640	-1.7	632	56.6	0.0	0.6	0.9	41.8	40.8	48.4	10.6	216	70.8	78.7	7.9
Norway town (Racine)	7,948	8,078	1.6	8,017	96.7	0.2	0.1	1.4	1.6	24.4	61.9	13.9	2,937	88.4	34.1	26.3
Norwood town (Langlade)	913	896	-1.9	1,000	95.2	0.0	2.2	1.5	1.1	23.2	57.2	19.6	382	86.6	63.4	9.2
Oak Creek city & MCD (Milwaukee)	34,452	35,053	1.7	34,823	82.9	2.2	4.4	2.1	8.5	23.8	65.2	11.0	14,140	60.6	33.9	31.2
Oakdale village & MCD (Monroe)	294	290	-1.4	257	98.8	0.0	0.0	0.4	0.8	18.7	57.0	24.1	114	69.3	64.0	9.6
Oakdale town (Monroe)	775	791	2.1	1,046	98.1	0.6	0.0	0.9	0.5	33.3	52.7	14.1	333	83.2	55.3	15.3
Oakfield village & MCD (Fond du Lac)	1,075	1,073	-0.2	1,080	93.1	0.0	0.5	0.8	5.6	23.1	61.4	15.6	425	77.9	45.9	22.6
Oakfield town (Fond du Lac)	705	710	0.7	714	97.5	0.0	0.6	0.6	1.4	21.2	63.1	15.8	272	87.1	55.5	12.9
Oak Grove town (Barron)..	948	948	0.0	922	96.9	0.0	1.4	1.7	0.0	23.4	61.6	15.1	343	94.2	38.2	22.2
Oak Grove town (Dodge)..	1,080	1,077	-0.3	1,166	91.4	0.0	0.9	0.0	7.7	21.9	60.3	17.7	458	79.5	56.3	15.3
Oak Grove town (Pierce) ..	2,150	2,155	0.2	2,251	94.5	1.3	1.0	0.8	2.4	29.9	61.2	8.8	783	91.3	26.7	35.5
Oakland town (Burnett).....	827	826	-0.1	908	96.7	0.8	0.0	2.4	0.1	8.7	52.4	39.0	486	95.7	42.2	22.8
Oakland town (Douglas)...	1,136	1,144	0.7	1,178	92.7	0.0	0.1	4.4	2.8	20.9	64.6	14.4	464	95.7	42.5	20.3
Oakland town (Jefferson)..	3,100	3,140	1.3	3,117	97.4	0.0	0.0	1.9	0.6	14.9	68.4	16.8	1,293	89.0	36.4	26.0
Oasis town (Waushara)	389	388	-0.3	337	98.2	1.2	0.6	0.0	0.0	16.6	68.9	14.5	122	91.0	66.4	15.6
Oconomowoc city & MCD (Waukesha)	15,759	16,319	3.6	15,990	89.6	1.0	0.9	1.5	7.0	27.2	58.9	13.9	6,278	71.4	28.3	40.7
Oconomowoc town (Waukesha)	8,422	8,609	2.2	8,546	97.5	0.2	0.0	1.2	1.1	22.4	63.9	13.6	3,335	86.8	22.2	46.5
Oconomowoc Lake village & MCD (Waukesha)	595	607	2.0	547	93.4	1.1	0.0	0.0	5.5	18.9	54.3	26.7	216	94.4	13.0	65.7
Oconto city & MCD (Oconto)	4,513	4,483	-0.7	4,510	95.0	1.2	0.7	1.7	1.4	18.8	64.4	16.8	1,948	66.9	56.6	11.5
Oconto town (Oconto)	1,335	1,332	-0.2	1,394	95.6	0.0	0.5	1.4	2.6	25.6	56.3	18.1	561	92.5	51.5	10.9
Oconto Falls city & MCD (Oconto)	2,891	2,846	-1.6	2,859	95.0	0.0	1.7	1.9	1.4	23.4	58.9	17.7	1,241	60.0	51.0	16.3
Oconto Falls town (Oconto)	1,265	1,258	-0.6	1,118	95.0	0.0	0.0	0.7	4.3	18.9	66.5	14.6	457	87.5	54.5	16.6
Odanah CDP	13	NA	NA	9	0.0	0.0	0.0	100.0	0.0	11.1	88.9	0.0	8	100.0	25.0	0.0
Ogdensburg village & MCD (Waupaca)	185	184	-0.5	226	95.6	0.0	0.4	4.0	0.0	24.0	66.2	9.7	90	66.7	66.7	10.0
Ogema CDP	186	NA	NA	211	66.4	0.9	0.0	0.9	31.8	36.0	50.4	13.7	85	74.1	65.9	12.9
Ogema town (Price)	705	684	-3.0	750	87.5	0.3	0.5	0.9	10.8	23.0	57.5	19.5	351	81.2	60.1	12.0
Ojibwa town (Sawyer).......	249	248	-0.4	285	88.8	0.0	2.1	1.8	7.4	14.1	63.2	22.8	160	91.9	68.1	10.6
Okauchee Lake CDP.........	4,422	NA	NA	4,581	98.6	0.3	0.0	0.0	1.1	23.4	64.7	12.0	1,788	81.9	17.3	52.3
Oliver village & MCD (Douglas)	399	399	0.0	295	92.2	0.0	1.0	5.4	1.4	22.0	65.4	12.5	120	85.8	42.5	15.8
Oma town (Iron)	289	293	1.4	262	99.6	0.0	0.0	0.4	0.0	6.2	49.3	44.7	138	100.0	23.9	40.6
Omro city & MCD (Winnebago)	3,517	3,542	0.7	3,541	81.8	0.0	0.0	0.7	17.5	31.1	57.9	11.0	1,330	66.3	47.1	21.2
Omro town (Winnebago) ..	2,116	2,152	1.7	2,507	93.5	0.0	0.0	0.3	6.2	21.4	61.7	16.9	1,047	83.4	49.5	27.6
Onalaska city & MCD (La Crosse)	17,790	18,385	3.3	18,148	84.4	2.0	9.5	2.6	1.6	24.4	59.7	16.1	7,372	64.9	28.8	37.0
Onalaska town (La Crosse)	5,574	5,761	3.4	5,678	92.1	1.3	4.3	1.9	0.3	25.1	65.1	9.9	2,029	94.9	23.6	40.0
Oneida town (Outagamie)	4,678	4,686	0.2	4,678	51.9	0.6	2.4	41.0	4.1	31.1	56.8	12.1	1,551	89.5	45.0	17.6
Ontario village & MCD (Vernon)	554	554	0.0	517	76.2	0.0	0.8	1.5	21.5	31.9	53.0	15.1	197	75.1	62.9	8.1
Oostburg village & MCD (Sheboygan)	2,887	2,942	1.9	2,905	96.2	0.9	0.2	0.7	2.0	25.5	56.5	18.1	1,121	79.9	38.6	26.2
Orange town (Juneau)......	570	559	-1.9	608	91.4	0.7	0.0	5.9	2.0	25.0	51.9	23.0	206	93.7	58.7	7.8
Oregon village & MCD (Dane)	9,318	9,871	5.9	9,629	94.5	0.6	0.6	2.8	1.6	28.0	62.3	9.9	3,779	68.2	22.4	37.5
Oregon town (Dane)	3,110	3,271	5.2	3,206	98.7	0.3	0.2	0.6	0.2	23.5	65.2	11.3	1,164	94.6	18.2	50.6
Orfordville village & MCD (Rock)	1,442	1,487	3.1	1,437	95.3	0.0	0.3	0.3	4.0	29.4	57.4	13.2	525	69.5	42.9	14.5
Orienta town (Bayfield)	122	122	0.0	107	92.5	0.0	0.0	7.5	0.0	14.0	64.5	21.5	55	89.1	38.2	34.5

1 May be of any race.

STATE City, town, township, borough, or CDP (county if applicable)	Population				Race and Hispanic or Latino origin (percent), 2010–2014					Age (percent), 2010–2014			Households, 2010–2014			
	2010 census total population	2014 estimated population	Percent change 2010–2014	ACS total population estimate 2010–2014	White alone, not Hispanic or Latino	Black alone, not Hispanic or Latino	Asian alone, not Hispanic or Latino	All other races or 2 or more races, not Hispanic or Latino	Hispanic or Latino[1]	Under 18 years old	Age 18 to 64 years old	Age 65 years and older	Total occupied housing units	Percent owner occupied	High school diploma or less	Bachelor's degree or more
	1	2	3	4	5	6	7	8	9	10	11	12	13	14	15	16
WISCONSIN—Con.																
Orion town (Richland).......	579	570	-1.6	621	97.7	0.0	0.0	0.6	1.6	23.5	55.5	21.1	246	87.4	44.3	24.0
Osborn town (Outagamie)	1,170	1,213	3.7	1,145	98.1	0.0	0.0	1.9	0.0	25.8	65.4	9.0	410	93.2	45.6	20.5
Osceola town (Fond du Lac)....................	1,865	1,846	-1.0	1,850	98.2	0.0	0.5	0.6	0.6	19.6	60.8	19.5	753	83.4	49.0	10.2
Osceola village & MCD (Polk)...................	2,559	2,511	-1.9	2,522	95.0	0.4	2.9	0.2	1.4	26.2	60.3	13.6	1,042	60.7	44.2	25.3
Osceola town (Polk).........	2,866	2,841	-0.9	2,843	98.7	0.0	0.4	0.6	0.3	25.0	64.7	10.2	1,126	88.8	37.8	31.0
Oshkosh city & MCD (Winnebago)	66,083	66,621	0.8	66,430	89.7	2.9	2.1	2.3	3.0	18.7	68.4	12.9	25,987	54.6	38.2	25.0
Oshkosh town (Winnebago)	2,475	2,525	2.0	2,510	85.8	5.3	0.4	2.9	5.7	16.7	66.2	17.0	850	80.0	39.9	27.5
Osseo city & MCD (Trempealeau).............	1,701	1,705	0.2	1,690	96.0	0.0	1.5	1.5	0.9	23.9	59.3	16.9	740	72.6	47.0	20.1
Otsego town (Columbia)...	693	693	0.0	636	98.0	0.0	0.0	0.9	1.1	15.9	66.0	18.1	277	80.5	58.1	11.6
Ottawa town (Waukesha)..	3,880	3,888	0.2	3,884	92.9	0.6	5.0	0.1	1.5	18.7	66.3	14.9	1,422	97.3	27.0	38.5
Otter Creek town (Dunn) ..	501	512	2.2	550	98.9	0.0	0.0	1.1	0.0	19.5	69.9	10.7	207	87.0	55.6	14.5
Otter Creek town (Eau Claire)	500	515	3.0	549	96.4	0.0	0.0	0.7	2.9	30.6	59.1	10.2	175	84.0	52.6	14.9
Oulu town (Bayfield)	527	528	0.2	493	97.2	0.0	0.0	2.8	0.0	23.2	63.5	13.4	212	88.2	37.3	16.5
Owen city & MCD (Clark) .	937	930	-0.7	1,044	94.5	0.0	1.3	0.5	3.6	21.9	49.3	28.8	463	69.8	57.2	14.3
Oxford village & MCD (Marquette)..............	607	591	-2.6	634	97.3	0.0	0.0	0.0	2.7	23.0	64.8	12.1	253	56.9	63.2	5.1
Oxford town (Marquette)...	885	864	-2.4	770	96.6	0.0	0.9	2.1	0.4	15.9	57.8	26.5	324	89.2	54.6	6.8
Pacific town (Columbia)....	2,707	2,724	0.6	2,712	97.0	0.0	0.4	1.1	1.4	21.2	55.9	22.9	1,180	90.2	37.5	28.0
Packwaukee CDP.............	262	NA	NA	281	94.3	0.0	0.0	0.0	5.7	22.1	66.6	11.4	106	67.9	51.9	2.8
Packwaukee town (Marquette)..............	1,416	1,384	-2.3	1,386	94.8	0.0	0.0	1.4	3.8	21.4	54.8	23.9	580	86.7	54.1	10.3
Paddock Lake village & MCD (Kenosha)	2,992	3,013	0.7	2,999	93.8	0.0	0.7	1.0	4.5	25.9	65.3	8.6	1,089	82.2	46.5	20.7
Palmyra village & MCD (Jefferson)................	1,784	1,780	-0.2	1,668	85.0	0.0	0.0	2.7	12.3	21.6	58.9	19.5	644	74.4	55.4	10.6
Palmyra town (Jefferson)..	1,183	1,206	1.9	1,413	87.0	0.1	0.1	1.0	11.7	25.7	60.1	14.1	504	81.3	34.3	31.5
Pardeeville village & MCD (Columbia)	2,115	2,096	-0.9	2,156	94.8	0.6	1.5	2.0	1.1	25.6	58.7	15.7	907	71.6	43.6	16.2
Paris town (Grant)............	702	706	0.6	810	96.7	0.0	0.5	0.7	2.1	26.0	62.3	11.5	296	85.8	49.3	22.6
Paris town (Kenosha)	1,504	1,521	1.1	1,867	94.9	0.0	0.6	0.3	4.2	27.9	58.0	14.3	645	83.7	41.9	22.8
Park Falls city & MCD (Price)...................	2,462	2,359	-4.2	2,256	98.4	0.3	0.4	0.0	0.9	20.3	54.9	24.7	1,098	67.2	44.3	20.2
Parkland town (Douglas)..	1,220	1,227	0.6	1,297	93.5	1.9	0.4	4.2	0.0	25.4	63.3	11.4	519	88.4	41.0	15.4
Park Ridge village & MCD (Portage).............	491	506	3.1	563	95.0	0.0	2.0	0.5	2.5	26.7	50.0	23.4	227	91.2	16.7	54.6
Parrish town (Langlade)....	91	89	-2.2	99	97.0	3.0	0.0	0.0	0.0	19.2	67.7	13.1	37	94.6	48.6	5.4
Patch Grove village & MCD (Grant)	198	195	-1.5	137	100.0	0.0	0.0	0.0	0.0	24.1	56.8	19.0	57	87.7	54.4	5.3
Patch Grove town (Grant) .	339	343	1.2	400	94.0	0.0	0.0	0.0	6.0	28.1	63.2	9.0	144	65.3	66.0	6.9
Peck town (Langlade)	349	339	-2.9	402	93.3	0.0	4.2	2.2	0.2	24.9	57.0	18.2	154	89.6	57.8	8.4
Peeksville town (Ashland).	140	140	0.0	136	97.8	0.0	0.7	0.0	1.5	13.2	67.6	19.1	63	92.1	22.2	23.8
Pelican town (Oneida)	2,771	2,756	-0.5	2,761	97.5	0.0	1.4	0.8	0.3	19.8	62.7	17.4	1,100	92.6	35.5	28.4
Pella CDP......................	185	NA	NA	189	88.9	0.0	6.9	4.2	0.0	19.5	47.1	33.3	89	88.8	56.2	25.8
Pella town (Shawano)	865	865	0.0	807	93.9	0.0	1.6	4.2	0.2	17.4	58.5	24.3	365	91.8	62.2	13.7
Pembine CDP..................	193	NA	NA	202	98.5	0.0	0.0	1.5	0.0	40.1	45.6	14.4	63	95.2	60.3	3.2
Pembine town (Marinette).	889	886	-0.3	784	98.7	0.0	0.0	1.3	0.0	20.3	55.1	24.5	340	93.5	46.8	15.6
Pence CDP......................	131	NA	NA	120	100.0	0.0	0.0	0.0	0.0	10.8	66.7	22.5	60	96.7	48.3	11.7
Pence town (Iron)	163	163	0.0	143	100.0	0.0	0.0	0.0	0.0	10.5	70.0	19.6	71	97.2	50.7	14.1
Pensaukee town (Oconto)	1,381	1,375	-0.4	1,457	98.0	0.2	0.0	0.9	0.9	21.4	62.7	15.9	598	87.0	59.7	15.2
Pepin village & MCD (Pepin)....................	837	805	-3.8	796	97.7	0.4	1.0	0.0	0.9	15.1	53.6	31.3	376	76.9	52.4	16.5
Pepin town (Pepin)...........	721	710	-1.5	671	98.5	0.0	0.0	0.9	0.6	19.9	60.5	19.5	275	92.4	50.5	29.1
Perry town (Dane)..	731	764	4.5	715	96.8	0.3	0.0	0.8	2.1	18.2	64.7	17.1	285	84.6	36.1	38.2
Pershing town (Taylor)	180	179	-0.6	202	100.0	0.0	0.0	0.0	0.0	34.6	53.6	11.9	80	66.3	66.3	7.5
Peru town (Dunn)	242	244	0.8	242	99.6	0.0	0.4	0.0	0.0	12.0	66.3	21.9	100	87.0	41.0	19.0
Peshtigo city & MCD (Marinette).................	3,502	3,449	-1.5	3,481	94.6	0.0	2.2	0.9	2.3	20.6	53.1	26.3	1,580	61.8	48.4	18.6
Peshtigo town (Marinette).	4,057	4,047	-0.2	4,049	96.9	0.0	1.1	1.4	0.6	23.9	60.7	15.4	1,532	93.9	45.9	15.7
Pewaukee city & MCD (Waukesha).................	13,204	13,942	5.6	13,599	94.1	0.7	2.9	0.2	2.2	22.0	60.8	17.2	5,451	83.4	19.8	49.6
Pewaukee village & MCD (Waukesha).................	8,213	8,236	0.3	8,233	91.0	0.9	4.9	1.3	1.8	20.2	61.5	18.2	3,910	59.5	29.3	38.4
Phelps town (Vilas)	1,200	1,205	0.4	1,267	93.4	0.1	1.8	3.1	1.7	16.2	52.5	31.2	584	79.6	42.6	24.1
Phillips city & MCD (Price)	1,481	1,401	-5.4	1,505	91.1	0.0	1.7	5.4	1.9	18.4	62.2	19.1	721	51.5	49.0	19.7
Piehl town (Oneida)	85	84	-1.2	100	91.0	0.0	0.0	9.0	0.0	24.0	52.0	24.0	46	80.4	43.5	10.9
Pierce town (Kewaunee)...	833	816	-2.0	836	97.0	0.0	1.0	1.2	0.8	13.0	61.3	25.6	344	86.3	49.7	25.0
Pigeon town (Trempealeau)	891	920	3.3	875	96.8	0.0	0.0	2.6	0.6	31.0	56.9	12.0	306	88.9	56.2	10.5
Pigeon Falls village & MCD (Trempealeau)......	411	418	1.7	381	100.0	0.0	0.0	0.0	0.0	17.6	55.3	27.0	153	70.6	52.3	22.2
Pilsen town (Bayfield)	210	209	-0.5	198	100.0	0.0	0.0	0.0	0.0	20.2	60.7	19.2	90	96.7	44.4	26.7
Pine Grove town (Portage)	937	932	-0.5	928	72.7	0.0	0.0	0.0	27.3	25.0	63.9	11.0	360	86.9	72.2	9.4
Pine Lake town (Oneida)..	2,738	2,726	-0.4	2,746	97.6	0.0	0.0	2.4	0.0	16.7	65.7	17.6	1,207	89.2	33.0	27.5
Pine River town (Lincoln)..	1,869	1,838	-1.7	1,860	98.3	0.0	0.0	1.5	0.2	18.8	65.3	15.9	793	89.9	49.4	17.9
Pine River CDP...............	147	NA	NA	97	100.0	0.0	0.0	0.0	0.0	19.6	66.0	14.4	44	84.1	65.9	0.0
Pine Valley town (Clark)....	1,157	1,152	-0.4	1,370	89.1	1.5	1.6	3.9	3.9	25.6	59.5	14.8	544	84.6	53.3	19.1
Pittsfield town (Brown)	2,608	2,682	2.8	2,648	96.7	0.5	0.0	0.9	1.9	22.9	63.9	13.3	999	97.8	37.6	29.7
Pittsville city & MCD (Wood)	874	855	-2.2	872	98.9	0.0	0.0	0.5	0.7	26.7	55.4	17.9	339	62.5	58.1	11.8
Plain village & MCD (Sauk)	773	779	0.8	804	95.6	0.0	0.0	3.1	1.2	24.9	56.4	18.8	324	79.6	48.1	21.9
Plainfield village & MCD (Waushara)	862	840	-2.6	981	71.0	0.3	0.2	3.5	25.0	32.3	55.4	12.3	317	76.0	53.0	10.4
Plainfield town (Waushara)	550	542	-1.5	477	92.2	0.0	0.2	0.0	7.5	19.4	65.4	15.1	195	85.6	58.5	6.7

1 May be of any race.

Table A. All Places — **Population and Housing**

STATE City, town, township, borough, or CDP (county if applicable)	Population				Race and Hispanic or Latino origin (percent), 2010–2014					Age (percent), 2010–2014			Households, 2010–2014			
	2010 census total population	2014 estimated population	Percent change 2010-2014	ACS total population estimate 2010-2014	White alone, not Hispanic or Latino	Black alone, not Hispanic or Latino	Asian alone, not Hispanic or Latino	All other races or 2 or more races, not Hispanic or Latino	Hispanic or Latino[1]	Under 18 years old	Age 18 to 64 years old	Age 65 years and older	Total occupied housing units	Percent owner occupied	High school diploma or less	Bachelor's degree or more
	1	2	3	4	5	6	7	8	9	10	11	12	13	14	15	16

WISCONSIN—Con.

STATE City, town, township, borough, or CDP (county if applicable)	1	2	3	4	5	6	7	8	9	10	11	12	13	14	15	16
Platteville city & MCD (Grant)	11,255	12,281	9.1	11,480	93.7	2.1	1.2	1.1	1.8	12.9	78.1	9.2	3,553	45.9	24.9	29.6
Platteville town (Grant)	1,478	1,477	-0.1	1,423	95.2	0.0	1.1	3.7	0.0	24.0	58.9	16.9	582	72.0	36.8	41.4
Pleasant Prairie village & MCD (Kenosha)	19,719	20,400	3.5	20,015	84.7	4.8	2.1	2.1	6.2	22.9	63.8	13.0	7,413	79.7	35.1	36.1
Pleasant Springs town (Dane)	3,165	3,321	4.9	3,252	94.3	0.7	3.5	0.8	0.8	20.4	61.7	17.8	1,269	97.3	28.1	37.7
Pleasant Valley town (Eau Claire)	3,044	3,151	3.5	3,108	93.1	0.2	3.4	2.6	0.7	28.6	58.4	12.9	1,033	94.0	22.6	39.6
Pleasant Valley town (St. Croix)	515	533	3.5	524	99.6	0.0	0.0	0.0	0.4	27.5	66.6	5.9	197	75.6	32.5	39.1
Plover town (Marathon)	689	685	-0.6	682	99.3	0.0	0.0	0.0	0.7	24.9	65.5	9.5	280	90.0	55.7	11.4
Plover village & MCD (Portage)	12,123	12,326	1.7	12,195	91.7	0.1	4.0	1.6	2.5	23.9	63.4	12.7	4,898	60.9	34.6	30.7
Plover town (Portage)	1,701	1,725	1.4	1,742	89.0	2.5	1.0	1.1	6.3	18.2	69.7	12.1	654	78.3	48.5	17.6
Plum City village & MCD (Pierce)	599	585	-2.3	618	84.5	0.0	0.0	2.9	12.6	28.4	49.1	22.5	218	69.7	52.3	11.5
Plum Lake town (Vilas)	491	493	0.4	389	100.0	0.0	0.0	0.0	0.0	10.6	56.1	33.4	204	90.7	24.5	30.4
Plymouth town (Juneau)	598	604	1.0	658	100.0	0.0	0.0	0.0	0.0	20.3	57.6	22.2	274	88.7	49.6	19.7
Plymouth town (Rock)	1,235	1,243	0.6	1,251	96.3	1.0	0.4	1.6	0.7	24.4	62.7	12.9	449	84.2	45.2	18.7
Plymouth city & MCD (Sheboygan)	8,445	8,433	-0.1	8,408	93.9	1.8	2.0	1.1	1.3	22.7	57.6	19.6	3,929	59.5	41.4	27.0
Plymouth town (Sheboygan)	3,195	3,195	0.0	3,192	99.0	0.3	0.1	0.4	0.2	24.5	58.7	16.9	1,059	90.5	37.3	30.6
Polar town (Langlade)	984	966	-1.8	924	97.2	1.0	0.0	0.4	1.4	21.9	60.8	17.3	366	87.2	49.5	24.0
Polk town (Washington)	3,931	3,949	0.5	3,934	99.4	0.2	0.0	0.4	0.0	24.9	59.3	15.9	1,409	94.4	32.4	40.4
Polonia CDP	526	NA	NA	562	97.7	0.0	0.0	0.9	1.4	29.2	63.6	7.1	201	81.6	52.2	18.4
Poplar village & MCD (Douglas)	603	601	-0.3	602	94.0	0.0	1.5	4.5	0.0	27.6	56.6	15.8	233	85.4	35.2	24.0
Popple River town (Forest)	44	44	0.0	28	100.0	0.0	0.0	0.0	0.0	0.0	53.6	46.4	20	100.0	95.0	0.0
Portage city & MCD (Columbia)	10,324	10,178	-1.4	10,227	89.1	4.4	0.3	1.7	4.5	23.3	62.6	14.1	4,070	51.9	40.8	19.4
Port Edwards village & MCD (Wood)	1,818	1,751	-3.7	1,804	91.0	4.7	0.2	2.2	1.9	23.2	53.3	23.6	718	82.9	34.1	24.0
Port Edwards town (Wood)	1,427	1,381	-3.2	1,314	77.1	0.0	1.8	11.4	9.7	18.4	63.7	18.0	586	90.6	58.2	9.0
Porter town (Rock)	947	962	1.6	914	95.3	0.0	0.5	3.2	1.0	17.1	61.4	21.7	384	81.3	41.9	20.8
Porterfield town (Marinette)	1,971	1,962	-0.5	1,853	99.2	0.0	0.0	0.4	0.4	21.6	60.1	18.4	781	96.8	54.4	15.1
Portland town (Dodge)	1,079	1,067	-1.1	1,090	91.9	0.0	0.0	1.4	6.7	24.9	61.9	13.1	436	78.7	50.0	15.6
Portland town (Monroe)	804	816	1.5	641	97.8	0.3	0.0	1.1	0.8	22.6	62.8	14.7	254	83.9	52.0	13.8
Port Washington city & MCD (Ozaukee)	11,290	11,586	2.6	11,401	94.2	0.3	1.1	0.9	3.5	22.3	64.6	13.4	4,709	63.9	30.5	37.8
Port Washington town (Ozaukee)	1,606	1,607	0.1	1,868	91.2	3.6	0.0	2.6	2.6	21.6	65.7	12.7	632	86.7	33.7	29.1
Port Wing CDP	164	NA	NA	136	100.0	0.0	0.0	0.0	0.0	8.8	50.7	40.4	85	96.5	27.1	30.6
Port Wing town (Bayfield)	368	369	0.3	359	95.5	0.0	0.0	0.0	4.5	11.6	55.7	32.6	196	96.4	30.1	31.1
Post Lake CDP	374	NA	NA	405	100.0	0.0	0.0	0.0	0.0	9.9	52.0	38.0	189	92.1	55.0	8.5
Potosi village & MCD (Grant)	688	677	-1.6	687	99.1	0.0	0.7	0.0	0.1	19.8	56.3	23.9	313	76.7	57.8	22.0
Potosi town (Grant)	849	848	-0.1	878	99.1	0.0	0.0	0.0	0.9	27.8	58.2	13.9	322	85.1	58.7	15.8
Potter village & MCD (Calumet)	253	252	-0.4	251	96.0	0.0	0.0	2.8	1.2	20.8	65.5	13.9	92	79.3	54.3	13.0
Potter Lake CDP	1,107	NA	NA	1,109	98.4	1.6	0.0	0.0	0.0	17.3	63.6	19.0	484	100.0	26.9	19.2
Pound village & MCD (Marinette)	377	375	-0.5	484	93.0	0.0	0.0	2.3	4.8	24.4	64.9	10.7	180	67.8	60.6	11.7
Pound town (Marinette)	1,425	1,419	-0.4	1,432	94.4	0.0	0.0	1.3	4.3	22.3	64.2	13.3	616	83.3	56.0	13.1
Powers Lake CDP	1,615	NA	NA	1,092	96.2	0.1	0.0	1.5	2.3	13.8	70.8	15.4	432	85.2	31.5	28.7
Poygan town (Winnebago)	1,301	1,315	1.1	1,313	99.2	0.0	0.0	0.4	0.5	18.2	59.8	21.9	543	93.7	52.9	18.4
Poynette village & MCD (Columbia)	2,535	2,505	-1.2	2,516	94.0	1.6	0.2	2.7	1.5	27.9	63.1	9.1	964	68.3	38.8	16.0
Poy Sippi CDP	371	NA	NA	377	94.4	0.0	0.0	0.0	5.6	33.9	56.7	9.3	139	59.0	53.2	5.0
Poy Sippi town (Waushara)	931	925	-0.6	898	96.1	0.3	0.0	0.0	3.6	24.0	54.6	21.5	384	75.3	53.9	12.5
Prairie du Chien city & MCD (Crawford)	5,896	5,757	-2.4	5,829	94.1	3.8	0.3	0.4	1.3	21.2	58.7	20.1	2,342	61.0	48.8	17.0
Prairie du Chien town (Crawford)	1,073	1,030	-4.0	987	97.4	0.0	0.3	0.0	2.3	22.6	61.3	16.1	394	76.6	53.0	15.7
Prairie du Sac village & MCD (Sauk)	4,052	4,225	4.3	4,137	91.2	0.5	0.0	2.3	6.1	26.4	57.0	16.7	1,715	69.7	33.4	38.2
Prairie du Sac town (Sauk)	1,078	1,119	3.8	1,190	95.8	0.3	0.3	2.3	1.4	25.2	59.7	15.2	424	80.9	42.7	25.5
Prairie Farm village & MCD (Barron)	473	455	-3.8	476	90.8	0.2	0.0	0.6	8.4	22.5	54.1	23.3	214	61.7	58.4	17.8
Prairie Farm town (Barron)	573	570	-0.5	618	94.5	0.0	0.3	5.2	0.0	32.0	54.4	13.6	204	85.3	51.5	21.6
Prairie Lake town (Barron)	1,532	1,532	0.0	1,355	93.1	0.0	0.2	4.4	2.3	18.6	59.6	22.0	567	92.1	50.8	23.6
Prentice village & MCD (Price)	660	630	-4.5	566	94.7	0.0	1.4	1.6	2.3	21.6	60.2	18.0	299	60.5	57.5	9.7
Prentice town (Price)	475	462	-2.7	492	87.8	0.0	0.6	11.6	0.0	21.1	56.7	22.2	219	84.5	56.2	6.8
Prescott city & MCD (Pierce)	4,258	4,227	-0.7	4,222	95.2	0.0	0.3	1.8	2.7	25.5	62.4	12.3	1,617	76.2	37.4	20.2
Presque Isle town (Vilas)	618	616	-0.3	666	99.4	0.0	0.0	0.6	0.0	19.0	40.1	41.1	322	92.2	27.3	40.1
Preston town (Adams)	1,395	1,356	-2.8	1,510	97.5	0.1	0.0	0.9	1.4	13.0	63.2	23.8	544	92.3	57.7	16.0
Preston town (Trempealeau)	953	983	3.1	881	98.8	0.0	0.3	0.3	0.6	24.6	56.9	18.4	317	86.8	59.0	12.3
Price town (Langlade)	228	224	-1.8	233	100.0	0.0	0.0	0.0	0.0	24.4	64.8	10.7	99	73.7	56.6	18.2
Primrose town (Dane)	728	762	4.7	758	94.5	0.3	1.1	4.2	0.0	23.2	60.4	16.4	276	86.6	37.3	32.2
Princeton city & MCD (Green Lake)	1,214	1,187	-2.2	1,187	97.8	0.0	0.8	0.8	0.7	24.5	59.3	16.3	506	74.1	54.7	15.0
Princeton town (Green Lake)	1,434	1,424	-0.7	1,605	96.4	1.0	0.2	0.9	1.4	19.2	60.9	19.9	686	86.7	52.5	15.9

1 May be of any race.

Table A. All Places — **Population and Housing**

STATE City, town, township, borough, or CDP (county if applicable)	Population				Race and Hispanic or Latino origin (percent), 2010–2014					Age (percent), 2010–2014			Households, 2010–2014			
	2010 census total population	2014 estimated population	Percent change 2010-2014	ACS total population estimate 2010-2014	White alone, not Hispanic or Latino	Black alone, not Hispanic or Latino	Asian alone, not Hispanic or Latino	All other races or 2 or more races, not Hispanic or Latino	Hispanic or Latino[1]	Under 18 years old	Age 18 to 64 years old	Age 65 years and older	Total occupied housing units	Percent owner occupied	High school diploma or less	Bachelor's degree or more
	1	2	3	4	5	6	7	8	9	10	11	12	13	14	15	16
WISCONSIN—Con.																
Pulaski village..............	3,539	3,548	0.3	3,507	99.3	0.1	0.0	0.6	0.0	26.2	56.8	16.9	1,476	63.9	37.5	22.1
Pulaski village (Brown)	3,321	3,331	0.3	3,334	99.3	0.1	0.0	0.7	0.0	25.5	56.5	17.8	1,431	63.9	38.3	21.9
Pulaski village (Oconto)....	0	0	0.0	0	0.0	0.0	0.0	0.0	0.0	0.0	0.0	0.0	0	0.0	0.0	0.0
Pulaski village (Shawano)	218	217	-0.5	173	100.0	0.0	0.0	0.0	0.0	38.1	61.7	0.0	45	62.2	11.1	26.7
Pulaski town (Iowa)..........	400	403	0.8	325	92.6	0.0	0.9	4.3	2.2	21.9	63.0	15.1	140	80.7	56.4	15.0
Pulcifer CDP..................	134	NA	NA	123	100.0	0.0	0.0	0.0	0.0	22.0	57.7	20.3	50	88.0	38.0	22.0
Quincy town (Adams)	1,163	1,125	-3.3	1,229	94.3	0.4	0.0	1.2	4.1	12.1	57.2	30.8	541	87.4	55.3	6.1
Racine city & MCD (Racine)	78,860	78,065	-1.0	78,347	53.2	21.1	0.9	3.1	21.7	28.1	60.7	11.2	29,979	56.0	47.3	18.7
Radisson village & MCD (Sawyer)......................	249	244	-2.0	144	93.1	0.0	0.0	6.9	0.0	16.6	50.1	33.3	69	76.8	68.1	8.7
Radisson town (Sawyer)...	397	395	-0.5	285	94.4	0.0	0.0	5.3	0.4	16.9	58.3	24.9	129	91.5	47.3	17.1
Randall town (Kenosha) ...	3,186	3,214	0.9	3,198	96.9	0.0	0.7	1.1	1.3	20.6	62.1	17.5	1,213	83.8	40.2	23.4
Randolph village	1,807	1,777	-1.7	1,695	94.0	0.6	1.1	1.1	3.2	26.9	52.5	20.8	607	75.3	55.8	10.4
Randolph village (Columbia)	472	466	-1.3	425	92.0	2.1	0.0	0.9	4.9	28.1	57.1	14.8	165	77.6	54.5	8.5
Randolph village (Dodge).	1,335	1,311	-1.8	1,270	94.7	0.1	1.4	1.2	2.6	26.5	50.7	22.8	442	74.4	56.3	11.1
Randolph town (Columbia)	769	772	0.4	655	99.2	0.0	0.3	0.5	0.0	28.5	56.2	15.3	230	85.7	60.9	13.0
Random Lake village & MCD (Sheboygan)	1,594	1,589	-0.3	1,451	97.5	0.0	0.6	0.7	1.2	23.9	61.6	14.6	662	68.3	42.6	20.7
Rantoul town (Calumet)....	798	803	0.6	716	96.4	1.0	0.7	2.0	0.0	20.4	68.7	10.9	260	91.9	57.3	11.9
Raymond town (Racine)....	3,870	3,925	1.4	3,885	95.0	0.3	0.0	0.4	4.4	24.0	60.9	15.0	1,398	86.9	47.9	14.9
Readstown village & MCD (Vernon)....	413	417	1.0	409	97.8	0.0	0.5	1.5	0.2	21.8	55.9	22.2	193	71.5	57.5	11.9
Red Cedar town (Dunn)...	2,086	2,140	2.6	2,068	96.5	0.4	0.5	0.9	1.8	23.1	65.5	11.5	812	89.5	30.5	27.6
Redgranite village & MCD (Waushara)	2,149	2,130	-0.9	2,143	74.4	14.8	0.7	4.9	5.2	9.4	76.1	14.6	553	59.3	58.0	23.0
Red River town (Kewaunee).................	1,393	1,385	-0.6	1,476	94.4	1.0	0.5	1.5	2.6	23.3	58.1	18.8	576	88.0	48.3	20.0
Red Springs town (Shawano).................	925	922	-0.3	961	36.3	0.3	0.0	63.1	0.3	22.8	58.5	18.7	370	71.1	50.8	12.7
Reedsburg city & MCD (Sauk)	9,263	9,533	2.9	9,411	91.9	0.1	1.5	1.0	5.5	27.8	58.6	13.5	3,944	60.1	48.1	19.4
Reedsburg town (Sauk)....	1,226	1,264	3.1	1,267	94.6	0.2	0.2	0.2	4.7	16.3	62.4	21.2	474	86.3	49.4	17.3
Reedsville village & MCD (Manitowoc)	1,209	1,183	-2.2	1,070	91.0	0.0	0.3	1.4	7.3	28.4	54.0	17.6	434	79.7	58.5	11.8
Reeseville village & MCD (Dodge)..	708	690	-2.5	668	93.1	0.0	0.0	1.6	5.2	23.3	62.2	14.4	290	74.1	59.7	6.6
Reid town (Marathon)	1,215	1,266	4.2	1,211	98.6	0.0	0.0	0.8	0.6	18.3	69.8	12.0	514	89.1	58.8	17.1
Remington town (Wood)...	268	256	-4.5	185	98.9	0.0	0.0	0.5	0.5	20.0	60.0	20.0	86	82.6	55.8	4.7
Reseburg town (Clark)......	776	764	-1.5	757	97.8	0.0	0.0	0.0	2.2	40.6	50.0	9.5	207	91.3	57.0	7.2
Reserve CDP..................	429	NA	NA	524	6.1	1.1	0.4	75.4	17.0	27.5	59.3	13.2	198	41.4	59.6	6.6
Rewey village & MCD (Iowa).....................	297	297	0.0	300	95.7	0.0	0.0	4.3	0.0	26.0	61.8	12.0	119	66.4	49.6	12.6
Rhine town (Sheboygan) ..	2,134	2,148	0.7	2,057	97.4	0.1	0.0	0.6	1.8	16.7	67.5	15.7	914	81.9	39.7	25.3
Rhinelander city & MCD (Oneida).....................	7,799	7,497	-3.9	7,642	93.4	1.8	0.1	2.8	1.9	21.9	59.4	18.7	3,337	61.9	42.3	20.6
Rib Falls town (Marathon).	993	1,036	4.3	1,125	98.8	0.0	0.5	0.0	0.7	26.0	62.5	11.6	375	89.1	53.1	16.5
Rib Lake village & MCD (Taylor).....................	910	900	-1.1	1,025	91.1	4.0	0.0	3.3	1.6	26.3	50.9	22.8	443	58.0	59.8	14.0
Rib Lake town (Taylor)	852	848	-0.5	738	98.5	0.0	0.0	0.0	1.5	17.5	66.0	16.5	327	83.5	56.3	14.4
Rib Mountain CDP............	5,651	NA	NA	5,512	95.1	0.5	1.3	2.0	1.1	23.1	57.3	19.6	2,088	83.8	26.5	38.3
Rib Mountain town (Marathon)	6,825	6,925	1.5	6,863	95.7	0.4	1.4	1.6	0.9	23.7	59.2	17.1	2,530	84.1	25.8	37.1
Rice Lake city & MCD (Barron)....................	8,401	8,286	-1.4	8,353	96.5	0.1	0.4	1.8	1.1	19.5	57.5	22.8	3,874	55.3	43.4	19.5
Rice Lake town (Barron)...	3,078	3,070	-0.3	3,081	95.1	0.0	0.0	0.6	4.3	18.0	59.7	22.4	1,322	94.8	39.6	20.3
Richfield town (Adams).....	158	154	-2.5	149	94.0	0.7	0.0	0.0	5.4	14.7	61.0	24.2	67	98.5	64.2	7.5
Richfield village & MCD (Washington)................	11,300	11,460	1.4	11,365	95.2	1.1	1.0	0.9	1.9	23.4	62.4	14.1	4,224	97.6	23.4	37.5
Richfield town (Wood).......	1,628	1,602	-1.6	1,655	98.9	0.3	0.0	0.3	0.5	27.9	59.4	12.8	541	93.2	50.5	20.7
Richford town (Waushara).	612	607	-0.8	847	93.5	0.4	0.0	0.6	5.5	30.1	59.0	11.0	251	92.0	68.1	13.1
Richland town (Richland)..	1,370	1,342	-2.0	1,526	98.2	0.5	0.0	1.1	0.3	22.6	53.3	24.0	589	75.2	47.4	20.0
Richland town (Rusk)	232	225	-3.0	227	95.2	0.0	1.3	3.1	0.4	24.2	52.3	23.3	98	92.9	66.3	13.3
Richland Center city & MCD (Richland)	5,193	5,066	-2.4	5,128	93.8	0.8	0.6	1.4	3.4	20.8	58.8	20.3	2,286	57.1	40.5	18.2
Richmond town (St. Croix)	3,272	3,402	4.0	3,331	96.1	1.9	0.0	0.7	1.3	29.6	63.6	6.8	1,178	92.2	32.5	30.9
Richmond town (Shawano)..................	1,864	1,858	-0.3	1,956	86.9	0.0	0.1	6.5	6.4	20.6	60.6	18.6	807	84.6	43.5	18.7
Richmond town (Walworth).................	1,884	1,902	1.0	1,711	93.7	0.2	0.6	1.1	4.5	16.1	64.6	19.2	762	92.0	43.4	22.2
Richwood town (Richland)	533	524	-1.7	474	90.5	3.8	0.0	0.0	5.7	15.5	57.1	27.4	224	87.1	49.1	19.2
Ridgeland village & MCD (Dunn).....................	273	277	1.5	233	100.0	0.0	0.0	0.0	0.0	24.0	55.0	21.0	107	75.7	55.1	6.5
Ridgeville town (Monroe)..	488	497	1.8	520	88.7	0.4	0.0	7.5	3.5	27.5	59.6	12.9	186	88.2	64.0	11.8
Ridgeway village & MCD (Iowa).....................	653	645	-1.2	584	90.4	0.5	0.0	0.7	8.4	22.0	64.7	13.4	237	78.1	61.6	11.4
Ridgeway town (Iowa).......	568	578	1.8	541	97.2	0.6	2.2	0.0	0.0	16.9	62.7	20.3	248	87.5	41.9	23.4
Rietbrock town (Marathon)	981	977	-0.4	1,009	91.9	0.0	0.0	1.3	6.8	26.1	64.3	9.6	359	82.7	61.3	14.5
Ringle town (Marathon)	1,711	1,767	3.3	1,905	91.1	0.0	6.5	1.2	1.2	25.9	63.6	10.4	647	91.7	49.3	22.9
Rio village & MCD (Columbia)	1,059	1,049	-0.9	1,059	96.1	0.8	0.0	1.8	1.2	25.4	60.9	13.8	434	65.9	41.5	12.7
Ripon city & MCD (Fond du Lac).....................	7,733	7,778	0.6	7,699	92.1	0.8	1.1	0.8	5.2	21.7	60.9	17.5	2,986	59.6	45.1	23.3
Ripon town (Fond du Lac).	1,400	1,391	-0.6	1,494	96.5	0.2	0.3	0.6	2.3	20.7	62.2	17.2	615	89.1	50.2	20.8
River Falls city	15,003	15,175	1.1	15,050	93.1	1.0	2.1	1.9	1.9	16.0	74.7	9.4	5,330	49.9	22.8	32.6
River Falls city (Pierce)...	11,854	11,897	0.4	11,827	93.1	1.2	2.7	2.0	1.0	13.8	78.4	7.8	3,984	47.0	21.6	30.9
River Falls city (St. Croix) .	3,149	3,278	4.1	3,223	93.0	0.0	0.0	1.8	5.2	23.4	61.3	15.5	1,346	58.5	26.2	37.7
River Falls town (Pierce)...	2,268	2,289	0.9	2,219	92.7	0.6	0.5	3.0	3.2	21.9	67.1	11.0	893	77.7	27.9	39.0
River Hills village & MCD (Milwaukee).................	1,597	1,607	0.6	1,501	81.3	1.5	8.5	4.3	4.5	22.9	55.1	22.1	542	98.2	7.2	85.1

1 May be of any race.

Table A. All Places — **Population and Housing**

STATE City, town, township, borough, or CDP (county if applicable)	Population				Race and Hispanic or Latino origin (percent), 2010–2014					Age (percent), 2010–2014			Households, 2010–2014			
								All other races or 2 or more races, not Hispanic or Latino							Householders by level of education (percent)	
	2010 census total population	2014 estimated population	Percent change 2010-2014	ACS total population estimate 2010-2014	White alone, not Hispanic or Latino	Black alone, not Hispanic or Latino	Asian alone, not Hispanic or Latino		Hispanic or Latino[1]	Under 18 years old	Age 18 to 64 years old	Age 65 years and older	Total occupied housing units	Percent owner occupied	High school diploma or less	Bachelor's degree or more
	1	2	3	4	5	6	7	8	9	10	11	12	13	14	15	16

WISCONSIN—Con.

STATE City, town, township, borough, or CDP (county if applicable)	1	2	3	4	5	6	7	8	9	10	11	12	13	14	15	16
Riverview town (Oconto) ..	725	722	-0.4	896	98.7	0.0	0.0	1.3	0.0	8.4	45.9	45.8	460	94.8	60.4	11.3
Roberts village & MCD (St. Croix)	1,651	1,637	-0.8	1,701	92.9	0.6	0.4	3.4	2.7	28.5	65.6	5.9	642	75.9	32.1	26.5
Rochester village & MCD (Racine)	3,682	3,732	1.4	3,687	88.7	0.0	0.0	0.5	10.8	21.1	63.6	15.3	1,457	89.4	54.1	28.9
Rock town (Rock)	3,201	3,175	-0.8	3,177	80.5	0.8	0.4	8.9	9.4	24.0	61.6	14.2	1,246	86.0	54.3	9.0
Rock town (Wood)	855	1,264	47.8	823	97.7	0.0	0.2	0.0	2.1	20.0	67.9	12.0	318	95.0	50.0	25.8
Rockbridge town (Richland)	734	718	-2.2	789	97.3	0.0	0.0	2.7	0.0	20.7	58.3	21.0	346	90.5	57.8	18.2
Rock Creek town (Dunn) ..	1,000	1,021	2.1	877	96.8	0.1	0.0	1.6	1.5	25.2	63.3	11.5	331	90.9	36.9	23.0
Rockdale village & MCD (Dane)	214	220	2.8	195	85.6	3.1	0.5	0.0	10.8	24.1	64.7	11.3	87	69.0	33.3	31.0
Rock Elm town (Pierce)	485	483	-0.4	462	96.8	0.0	0.0	2.8	0.4	20.5	60.9	18.6	188	86.7	58.0	9.0
Rock Falls town (Lincoln)..	618	610	-1.3	608	95.1	0.0	3.0	0.0	2.0	14.8	68.1	17.1	271	92.3	47.2	21.0
Rockland town (Brown).....	1,702	1,768	3.9	1,715	93.5	0.0	0.1	2.0	4.4	26.4	62.7	10.9	563	89.5	32.3	35.5
Rockland village & MCD (La Crosse)	594	624	5.1	638	97.6	0.0	0.0	0.8	1.6	22.8	68.3	8.9	223	74.9	36.8	6.7
Rockland town (Manitowoc)	998	985	-1.3	1,108	97.8	0.0	0.0	0.3	1.9	23.0	66.0	10.8	371	91.6	55.3	15.9
Rock Springs village & MCD (Sauk)	362	369	1.9	352	88.6	0.0	0.0	4.8	6.5	27.6	62.5	9.9	133	79.7	63.2	7.5
Rolling town (Langlade)....	1,504	1,470	-2.3	1,426	94.5	0.0	0.0	3.6	1.8	26.5	60.6	12.9	548	89.1	52.4	17.0
Rome town (Adams).........	2,720	2,689	-1.1	2,717	99.0	0.0	0.6	0.0	0.3	11.8	50.1	37.9	1,217	94.4	36.7	35.7
Rome CDP	689	NA	NA	680	98.2	0.0	0.0	1.0	0.7	21.9	61.9	16.0	255	84.7	43.1	17.6
Roosevelt town (Burnett)..	199	197	-1.0	131	99.2	0.0	0.0	0.8	0.0	16.0	56.4	27.5	61	93.4	49.2	18.0
Roosevelt town (Taylor)	473	461	-2.5	482	99.4	0.0	0.0	0.6	0.0	27.5	57.4	14.9	183	84.7	74.3	10.9
Rose town (Waushara)	640	632	-1.3	644	95.5	0.0	0.0	1.7	2.8	11.6	64.8	23.6	291	91.8	57.0	18.6
Rosendale village & MCD (Fond du Lac)...............	1,063	1,046	-1.6	860	96.9	0.7	0.0	0.9	1.5	22.9	58.5	18.7	355	85.1	48.5	25.1
Rosendale town (Fond du Lac)............................	695	687	-1.2	770	98.2	0.1	0.0	1.7	0.0	20.6	68.2	11.0	292	91.4	36.3	30.1
Rosholt village & MCD (Portage)	506	497	-1.8	453	97.8	0.0	0.0	0.0	2.2	25.9	58.2	15.9	200	71.0	71.0	9.5
Ross town (Forest)	136	130	-4.4	188	96.3	2.7	0.0	1.1	0.0	11.7	67.6	20.7	80	100.0	65.0	0.0
Rothschild village & MCD (Marathon)	5,269	5,305	0.7	5,279	97.8	0.0	1.3	0.8	0.2	21.0	64.5	14.5	2,323	72.6	42.5	27.7
Round Lake town (Sawyer).....................	983	983	0.0	1,116	98.7	0.0	0.0	1.3	0.0	11.2	53.9	35.0	555	91.4	34.4	33.7
Roxbury town (Dane)	1,794	1,882	4.9	1,806	97.6	0.2	0.8	0.7	0.8	23.5	62.3	14.1	708	88.0	39.1	28.2
Royalton town (Waupaca)	1,434	1,416	-1.3	1,487	96.2	0.1	0.0	3.5	0.2	18.2	58.9	22.9	586	88.1	52.9	13.5
Rubicon town (Dodge)	2,207	2,207	0.0	2,264	97.1	1.1	0.0	0.4	1.3	19.3	70.6	10.2	788	86.4	50.0	11.5
Ruby town (Chippewa)	491	499	1.6	506	97.8	2.2	0.0	0.0	0.0	41.1	46.3	12.5	148	91.2	68.2	5.4
Rudolph village & MCD (Wood)	439	433	-1.4	539	94.1	0.0	0.2	0.2	5.6	22.2	65.8	11.9	205	77.1	62.0	15.1
Rudolph town (Wood).......	1,028	998	-2.9	1,062	94.7	0.0	0.0	0.7	3.8	24.2	60.7	15.2	398	93.2	50.5	14.1
Rushford town (Winnebago)	1,561	1,578	1.1	1,532	98.8	0.0	0.2	0.4	0.7	25.7	59.6	14.6	616	94.2	46.8	17.4
Rush River town (St. Croix)	508	507	-0.2	515	96.3	0.0	1.4	0.6	1.7	20.2	68.4	11.5	203	92.1	30.5	28.1
Rusk town (Burnett).........	409	409	0.0	462	87.2	4.1	0.0	7.6	1.1	22.1	55.2	22.7	198	83.3	52.0	15.2
Rusk town (Rusk)	525	517	-1.5	533	99.6	0.0	0.0	0.2	0.2	16.3	59.9	23.8	232	89.2	59.5	15.1
Russell town (Bayfield)	1,279	1,279	0.0	1,233	21.2	0.2	2.1	76.4	0.1	28.8	60.5	10.8	474	65.6	36.3	14.6
Russell town (Lincoln)	677	668	-1.3	682	94.1	2.8	0.7	0.7	1.6	26.7	51.0	22.4	273	77.7	56.4	12.1
Russell town (Sheboygan)	377	371	-1.6	362	97.5	0.6	0.0	1.7	0.3	24.9	61.3	13.8	145	80.7	55.9	11.7
Rutland town (Dane)........	1,956	2,054	5.0	2,095	95.7	0.4	0.5	0.7	2.7	23.6	63.4	13.1	793	92.8	31.5	34.9
St. Cloud village & MCD (Fond du Lac)...............	477	463	-2.9	490	100.0	0.0	0.0	0.0	0.0	19.4	64.3	16.3	214	81.8	61.7	10.3
St. Croix Falls city & MCD (Polk).........................	2,129	2,076	-2.5	2,059	97.1	0.4	0.0	1.3	1.2	17.6	60.7	21.5	1,030	57.3	34.4	26.5
St. Croix Falls town (Polk).	1,170	1,151	-1.6	1,211	95.0	0.2	0.0	3.1	1.7	24.0	62.2	13.8	456	89.0	41.2	18.9
St. Francis city & MCD (Milwaukee).................	9,359	9,547	2.0	9,488	78.0	2.7	3.3	4.9	11.0	14.1	67.7	18.2	4,590	49.6	41.0	29.0
St. Germain town (Vilas)...	2,085	2,091	0.3	1,975	94.0	2.5	0.3	0.3	3.0	17.1	52.6	30.1	959	76.1	46.9	21.8
St. Joseph CDP	0	NA	NA	447	100.0	0.0	0.0	0.0	0.0	19.9	54.7	25.3	137	80.3	40.9	35.8
St. Joseph town (St. Croix)	3,842	3,951	2.8	3,898	96.7	0.0	0.7	0.0	2.6	23.7	63.0	13.1	1,384	98.8	21.1	39.5
St. Lawrence town (Waupaca)	710	706	-0.6	788	99.5	0.0	0.0	0.0	0.5	19.7	61.8	18.4	338	89.1	63.9	11.8
St. Marie town (Green Lake)	351	346	-1.4	348	93.4	0.0	0.0	6.6	0.0	11.7	71.9	16.4	161	84.5	53.4	9.3
St. Nazianz village & MCD (Manitowoc)	783	764	-2.4	732	84.4	0.0	4.8	0.3	10.5	26.5	62.8	10.7	297	69.4	60.3	11.4
St. Peter CDP	1,489	NA	NA	1,384	99.1	0.0	0.0	0.0	0.9	15.9	67.5	16.7	571	87.2	40.8	20.7
Salem town (Kenosha)	12,061	12,184	1.0	12,116	92.7	0.4	0.5	0.9	5.5	25.3	65.3	9.3	4,507	83.2	43.2	25.3
Salem town (Pierce)	510	508	-0.4	501	99.4	0.0	0.0	0.6	0.0	24.4	58.6	17.2	194	85.1	54.1	14.9
Sampson town (Chippewa)	892	910	2.0	973	98.8	0.0	0.3	0.9	0.0	22.6	58.7	18.5	391	84.1	40.2	20.7
Sanborn town (Ashland)...	1,331	1,318	-1.0	1,260	13.8	0.7	2.0	78.7	4.8	29.2	59.5	11.3	488	58.8	44.1	9.4
Sand Creek town (Dunn)..	570	573	0.5	636	95.0	0.0	0.0	5.0	0.0	25.6	60.1	14.3	259	75.7	37.5	22.4
Sand Lake town (Burnett).	531	531	0.0	441	71.2	0.0	0.5	27.4	0.9	20.8	58.7	20.4	193	71.5	38.9	13.5
Sand Lake town (Sawyer).	815	814	-0.1	957	83.5	0.9	0.0	14.9	0.6	15.2	54.7	30.4	444	81.3	45.7	23.0
Sandy Hook CDP	309	NA	NA	442	99.1	0.0	0.0	0.0	0.9	30.8	49.5	19.7	171	80.1	34.5	21.1
Saratoga town (Wood)......	5,142	5,048	-1.8	5,102	98.6	0.0	0.2	0.5	0.7	17.7	63.6	18.6	2,267	94.2	52.3	10.1
Sarona town (Washburn)..	384	382	-0.5	463	96.5	0.0	0.0	3.0	0.4	18.1	68.9	13.0	211	72.5	51.7	18.5
Sauk City village & MCD (Sauk)	3,396	3,479	2.4	3,445	97.5	0.0	0.3	1.9	0.3	23.6	59.0	17.4	1,417	58.0	42.8	24.8
Saukville village & MCD (Ozaukee)	4,453	4,482	0.7	4,479	95.7	0.7	0.0	2.5	1.1	24.1	68.4	7.4	1,754	71.0	44.1	25.8
Saukville town (Ozaukee)	1,832	1,855	1.3	1,963	94.7	0.5	0.0	1.5	3.3	21.4	57.5	21.0	723	85.2	39.0	28.8
Saxeville town (Waushara)	986	978	-0.8	1,030	95.0	0.0	0.4	2.1	2.4	18.3	59.2	22.4	441	93.2	49.9	21.8
Saxon CDP	90	NA	NA	73	98.6	0.0	0.0	1.4	0.0	2.8	49.2	47.9	48	70.8	64.6	16.7
Saxon town (Iron)	324	325	0.3	338	98.2	0.0	0.6	1.2	0.0	13.9	60.4	25.7	160	86.3	54.4	10.6

1 May be of any race.

Table A. All Places — **Population and Housing**

STATE City, town, township, borough, or CDP (county if applicable)	2010 census total population	2014 estimated population	Percent change 2010-2014	ACS total population estimate 2010-2014	White alone, not Hispanic or Latino	Black alone, not Hispanic or Latino	Asian alone, not Hispanic or Latino	All other races or 2 or more races, not Hispanic or Latino	Hispanic or Latino[1]	Under 18 years old	Age 18 to 64 years old	Age 65 years and older	Total occupied housing units	Percent owner occupied	High school diploma or less	Bachelor's degree or more
	1	2	3	4	5	6	7	8	9	10	11	12	13	14	15	16
WISCONSIN—Con.																
Sayner CDP....................	207	NA	NA	139	100.0	0.0	0.0	0.0	0.0	10.0	69.0	20.9	72	79.2	27.8	5.6
Scandinavia village & MCD (Waupaca)	363	362	-0.3	357	99.2	0.0	0.0	0.6	0.3	27.2	58.2	14.6	138	73.9	52.2	12.3
Scandinavia town (Waupaca)....................	1,068	1,063	-0.5	1,033	95.8	0.1	2.3	1.3	0.5	19.8	61.4	18.8	424	90.8	46.0	27.1
Schleswig town (Manitowoc)	1,979	1,957	-1.1	2,343	93.0	0.6	0.8	1.7	3.9	19.8	64.7	15.5	911	90.9	44.2	20.1
Schley town (Lincoln)........	934	920	-1.5	1,025	96.6	0.3	0.0	2.2	0.9	20.9	67.2	11.9	433	85.7	45.3	16.2
Schoepke town (Oneida) ..	390	388	-0.5	440	95.9	0.0	0.5	3.6	0.0	12.3	62.1	25.7	201	86.6	39.8	23.4
Schofield city & MCD (Marathon)	2,169	2,149	-0.9	2,204	88.3	0.0	7.5	1.4	2.8	22.4	60.8	16.8	1,026	57.8	52.3	16.6
Scott town (Brown)	3,545	3,676	3.7	3,613	97.0	0.2	1.9	0.0	0.8	21.1	61.3	17.6	1,472	94.4	23.6	36.3
Scott town (Burnett).........	494	495	0.2	634	92.9	1.6	0.0	4.3	1.3	7.9	46.2	45.9	331	97.0	39.6	21.8
Scott town (Columbia)	905	911	0.7	1,063	91.6	0.0	0.0	1.4	7.0	31.4	58.7	10.0	301	87.4	56.5	9.6
Scott town (Crawford)	462	453	-1.9	411	97.8	0.0	0.0	0.0	2.2	10.9	59.9	29.2	194	92.8	52.1	12.9
Scott town (Lincoln)	1,432	1,417	-1.0	1,552	95.8	0.0	0.0	4.2	0.0	26.0	63.3	10.6	605	89.3	50.2	9.8
Scott town (Monroe)	136	140	2.9	91	100.0	0.0	0.0	0.0	0.0	0.0	81.4	18.7	48	75.0	58.3	16.7
Scott town (Sheboygan) ...	1,836	1,842	0.3	1,717	93.4	0.0	0.2	4.5	1.9	21.8	62.2	16.0	672	91.5	45.5	17.3
Seif town (Clark)	172	171	-0.6	196	100.0	0.0	0.0	0.0	0.0	14.8	64.9	20.4	84	96.4	69.0	4.8
Seneca town (Crawford) ...	866	892	3.0	870	99.4	0.0	0.2	0.0	0.3	19.5	62.6	17.9	351	88.6	55.0	13.1
Seneca town (Green Lake)	408	406	-0.5	409	100.0	0.0	0.0	0.0	0.0	19.5	64.1	16.4	169	92.3	64.5	11.2
Seneca town (Shawano)...	558	554	-0.7	548	98.4	0.0	0.0	1.6	0.0	19.1	58.1	22.6	210	93.3	64.3	8.6
Seneca town (Wood).......	1,120	1,095	-2.2	1,036	94.2	0.0	2.3	3.5	0.0	19.0	62.6	18.4	410	90.0	52.2	13.2
Sevastopol town (Door)	2,628	2,662	1.3	2,646	98.9	0.2	0.2	0.0	0.7	15.2	60.7	23.9	1,218	90.1	34.7	28.8
Seven Mile Creek town (Juneau).....................	358	353	-1.4	307	97.1	2.6	0.0	0.3	0.0	18.2	54.3	27.4	134	72.4	60.4	13.4
Sextonville CDP..............	551	NA	NA	390	93.1	0.0	0.0	3.6	3.3	27.9	64.9	7.2	170	95.9	46.5	4.1
Seymour CDP.................	1,418	NA	NA	1,582	98.0	0.0	2.0	0.0	0.0	27.3	57.9	14.7	592	90.9	47.3	19.3
Seymour town (Eau Claire)	3,178	3,254	2.4	3,221	97.7	1.1	1.0	0.2	0.0	25.7	60.1	14.5	1,207	93.4	39.4	22.5
Seymour town (Lafayette).	446	450	0.9	568	77.1	0.0	0.0	0.0	22.9	30.8	60.7	8.5	171	63.7	73.7	9.9
Seymour city & MCD (Outagamie).................	3,451	3,442	-0.3	3,449	96.1	0.0	0.0	2.2	1.7	29.4	54.3	16.4	1,494	54.0	46.1	16.7
Seymour town (Outagamie).................	1,193	1,202	0.8	1,273	88.1	0.0	0.0	3.9	8.0	20.1	64.3	15.5	446	87.9	66.8	13.2
Shanagolden town (Ashland)....................	125	125	0.0	113	98.2	0.0	0.0	1.8	0.0	8.0	50.5	41.6	63	82.5	52.4	22.2
Sharon town (Portage)	1,982	2,008	1.3	1,903	94.7	0.0	3.0	0.4	1.9	21.3	63.3	15.4	773	87.8	54.2	17.7
Sharon village & MCD (Walworth).................	1,605	1,596	-0.6	1,607	85.6	1.1	0.0	1.4	11.8	27.6	62.2	10.1	636	58.5	48.9	13.4
Sharon town (Walworth) ...	907	915	0.9	728	93.0	0.4	0.1	1.9	4.5	18.1	64.1	17.9	302	89.1	49.7	9.9
Shawano city & MCD (Shawano).................	9,304	9,169	-1.5	9,202	84.3	1.0	0.1	12.1	2.6	24.3	55.5	20.3	3,874	56.2	48.1	19.3
Sheboygan city & MCD (Sheboygan)	49,290	48,775	-1.0	48,918	75.8	1.8	9.9	1.9	10.6	24.6	60.6	14.8	20,151	61.7	47.1	20.1
Sheboygan town (Sheboygan)	7,271	7,307	0.5	7,272	93.3	0.0	2.5	0.6	3.6	21.3	61.4	17.4	3,035	79.1	40.9	32.6
Sheboygan Falls city & MCD (Sheboygan)	7,775	7,816	0.5	7,796	94.2	0.0	1.1	1.6	3.1	23.4	61.1	15.5	3,439	67.2	41.5	23.0
Sheboygan Falls town (Sheboygan)	1,718	1,741	1.3	1,975	94.0	0.0	2.7	1.1	2.2	18.2	63.8	17.9	815	90.3	47.5	17.4
Shelby town (La Crosse) ..	4,715	4,851	2.9	4,776	94.2	1.0	0.8	0.3	3.7	20.0	58.3	21.8	2,008	88.5	25.9	45.1
Sheldon town (Monroe)	727	747	2.8	559	99.1	0.0	0.0	0.0	0.9	30.9	55.5	13.4	189	79.9	57.7	14.8
Sheldon village & MCD (Rusk)	237	228	-3.8	209	99.5	0.0	0.0	0.5	0.0	23.5	54.5	22.0	92	77.2	60.9	15.2
Shell Lake city & MCD (Washburn)	1,347	1,327	-1.5	1,402	91.4	1.0	1.2	3.0	3.4	21.0	51.2	27.8	647	67.1	42.8	26.3
Sheridan town (Dunn).......	454	467	2.9	433	100.0	0.0	0.0	0.0	0.0	23.4	63.0	13.6	171	83.0	40.9	25.1
Sherman town (Clark)	882	893	1.2	926	94.4	0.0	0.0	0.0	5.6	36.7	53.7	9.5	283	85.5	65.7	13.8
Sherman town (Dunn)	849	868	2.2	884	99.2	0.0	0.1	0.7	0.0	19.6	67.2	13.2	360	87.5	41.4	24.7
Sherman town (Iron)........	290	294	1.4	383	98.4	0.0	0.0	1.6	0.0	3.6	49.3	47.0	216	98.1	51.4	23.1
Sherman town (Sheboygan)	1,505	1,527	1.5	1,459	98.6	0.0	0.0	0.8	0.6	20.5	66.4	13.0	537	88.6	44.3	20.7
Sherry town (Wood)..........	803	801	-0.2	825	98.1	0.0	0.0	0.5	1.5	22.6	67.2	10.3	322	86.3	64.6	8.4
Sherwood village & MCD (Calumet)..................	2,713	2,821	4.0	2,770	92.9	0.0	1.0	2.1	4.0	29.4	61.3	9.2	1,010	92.5	22.5	49.4
Sherwood town (Clark)	220	218	-0.9	215	94.9	0.0	0.9	1.9	2.3	13.5	66.6	20.0	95	91.6	63.2	9.5
Shields town (Dodge)	554	549	-0.9	567	96.6	0.0	0.0	2.3	1.1	17.9	58.9	23.3	218	90.8	60.6	15.1
Shields town (Marquette)..	550	535	-2.7	523	99.6	0.0	0.0	0.0	0.4	13.1	61.6	25.0	254	87.0	53.9	18.5
Shiocton village & MCD (Outagamie).................	923	924	0.1	916	95.3	0.2	0.0	0.3	4.1	26.3	60.9	12.9	372	56.2	64.5	9.7
Shorewood village & MCD (Milwaukee).................	13,162	13,331	1.3	13,245	87.0	2.7	4.8	2.7	2.8	19.1	66.9	14.0	6,221	48.6	12.0	67.3
Shorewood Hills village & MCD (Dane)...............	1,570	2,039	29.9	1,783	87.2	3.2	3.3	3.5	2.9	25.5	52.8	21.6	657	90.3	4.3	88.6
Shullsburg city & MCD (Lafayette).................	1,226	1,215	-0.9	1,151	95.7	0.0	0.5	2.2	1.7	18.9	61.6	19.5	530	75.8	53.8	17.2
Shullsburg town (Lafayette).................	354	360	1.7	322	99.1	0.3	0.0	0.6	0.0	20.3	66.6	13.4	126	83.3	58.7	14.3
Sigel town (Chippewa)......	1,045	1,063	1.7	1,037	99.3	0.0	0.6	0.1	0.0	24.1	64.7	11.1	389	85.3	47.0	17.0
Sigel town (Wood)	1,051	1,032	-1.8	1,075	99.0	0.0	0.0	1.0	0.0	18.6	63.8	17.6	450	91.8	50.0	14.9
Silver Cliff town (Marinette).................	491	490	-0.2	502	97.2	0.0	0.0	2.8	0.0	15.4	49.6	35.1	249	93.2	61.4	5.2
Silver Lake village & MCD (Kenosha).................	2,411	2,419	0.3	2,257	93.3	0.9	1.2	3.2	1.3	32.1	59.1	8.6	852	67.6	39.3	19.2
Sioux Creek town (Barron)	655	639	-2.4	810	99.3	0.0	0.0	0.7	0.0	36.2	54.3	9.5	240	92.1	54.6	17.1
Siren village & MCD (Burnett)...................	806	789	-2.1	811	91.5	0.2	0.7	5.7	1.8	16.9	58.7	24.5	448	51.8	52.9	11.6
Siren town (Burnett)..........	936	935	-0.1	858	93.0	0.0	0.0	6.5	0.5	19.8	57.5	22.5	406	82.5	49.0	19.5

1 May be of any race.

Table A. All Places — **Population and Housing**

STATE City, town, township, borough, or CDP (county if applicable)	Population				Race and Hispanic or Latino origin (percent), 2010–2014					Age (percent), 2010–2014			Households, 2010–2014			
	2010 census total population	2014 estimated population	Percent change 2010-2014	ACS total population estimate 2010-2014	White alone, not Hispanic or Latino	Black alone, not Hispanic or Latino	Asian alone, not Hispanic or Latino	All other races or 2 or more races, not Hispanic or Latino	Hispanic or Latino[1]	Under 18 years old	Age 18 to 64 years old	Age 65 years and older	Total occupied housing units	Percent owner occupied	High school diploma or less	Bachelor's degree or more
	1	2	3	4	5	6	7	8	9	10	11	12	13	14	15	16
WISCONSIN—Con.																
Sister Bay village & MCD (Door)	876	919	4.9	694	95.1	0.3	0.7	2.9	1.0	5.1	39.3	55.5	381	63.8	30.7	41.5
Skanawan town (Lincoln)	391	388	-0.8	460	97.0	0.0	0.0	2.6	0.4	22.8	61.4	15.9	188	87.2	44.1	11.7
Slinger village & MCD (Washington)	5,079	5,172	1.8	5,131	95.7	0.0	0.3	0.0	4.0	24.3	61.1	14.6	2,094	74.4	51.3	24.9
Smelser town (Grant)	794	794	0.0	766	99.1	0.0	0.0	0.7	0.3	20.8	64.7	14.6	308	84.4	59.1	18.5
Sobieski CDP	259	NA	NA	589	100.0	0.0	0.0	0.0	0.0	24.9	71.5	3.4	183	89.6	22.4	0.0
Soldiers Grove village & MCD (Crawford)	592	561	-5.2	572	99.0	0.0	0.0	1.0	0.0	18.1	44.6	37.2	261	63.6	69.3	11.1
Solon Springs village & MCD (Douglas)	600	604	0.7	559	96.6	0.0	0.4	3.0	0.0	14.9	68.9	16.3	275	70.9	37.5	15.6
Solon Springs town (Douglas)	910	917	0.8	917	86.6	0.4	0.2	12.5	0.2	23.6	53.3	23.1	396	86.9	33.8	29.3
Somers town (Kenosha)	9,589	9,523	-0.7	9,500	83.2	2.0	2.1	1.8	10.9	14.5	72.0	13.5	3,536	73.7	36.3	27.4
Somerset village & MCD (St. Croix)	2,635	2,674	1.5	2,655	91.6	2.2	0.4	2.9	2.9	35.8	59.1	5.1	966	61.2	41.6	26.0
Somerset town (St. Croix)	4,036	4,142	2.6	4,090	88.8	0.5	1.6	1.1	8.1	27.8	63.7	8.3	1,416	91.9	39.3	20.7
Somo town (Lincoln)	114	111	-2.6	141	100.0	0.0	0.0	0.0	0.0	14.2	63.7	22.0	73	97.3	65.8	0.0
South Fork town (Rusk)	120	115	-4.2	109	94.5	0.0	0.0	4.6	0.9	12.9	61.6	25.7	57	93.0	49.1	7.0
South Lancaster town (Grant)	843	847	0.5	846	95.2	0.8	0.0	0.7	3.3	23.2	50.9	25.9	280	71.1	47.9	24.3
South Milwaukee city & MCD (Milwaukee)	21,155	21,236	0.4	21,210	85.7	1.6	0.9	3.4	8.5	22.3	62.8	15.1	8,451	63.3	42.8	20.9
South Wayne village & MCD (Lafayette)	489	482	-1.4	457	93.4	0.0	0.0	6.6	0.0	26.6	60.4	13.1	196	68.4	61.7	13.3
Sparta city & MCD (Monroe)	9,523	9,667	1.5	9,610	86.3	2.0	0.4	2.1	9.2	24.3	61.2	14.5	4,092	51.8	45.7	19.4
Sparta town (Monroe)	3,120	3,189	2.2	3,156	98.6	0.2	0.3	0.6	0.2	25.8	59.6	14.6	1,130	88.6	34.9	28.1
Spencer village & MCD (Marathon)	1,925	1,935	0.5	1,914	97.4	0.3	0.0	1.0	1.3	22.5	63.3	14.1	803	84.7	56.3	14.4
Spencer town (Marathon)	1,567	1,638	4.5	1,645	97.8	0.5	0.5	0.6	0.6	26.3	63.1	10.8	603	91.7	45.9	20.6
Spider Lake town (Sawyer)	351	347	-1.1	373	98.1	0.0	0.5	1.3	0.0	7.7	55.6	36.7	195	92.8	31.3	44.6
Spirit town (Price)	277	270	-2.5	234	98.3	0.0	0.0	0.4	1.3	17.2	50.8	32.1	102	95.1	48.0	20.6
Spooner city & MCD (Washburn)	2,682	2,616	-2.5	2,634	94.0	1.3	1.0	2.0	1.7	22.7	52.0	25.1	1,324	57.3	52.0	18.4
Spooner town (Washburn)	706	700	-0.8	768	87.9	1.3	0.8	0.0	10.0	21.3	62.0	16.7	292	83.9	40.4	28.4
Spring Brook town (Dunn)	1,558	1,599	2.6	1,542	95.0	0.5	0.3	2.8	1.4	22.1	66.4	11.3	593	82.6	35.9	24.1
Springbrook town (Washburn)	445	443	-0.4	468	97.9	0.0	0.0	2.1	0.0	19.5	62.7	17.9	217	84.8	63.1	12.9
Springdale town (Dane)	1,888	1,984	5.1	2,003	97.9	0.4	0.8	0.1	0.7	23.9	63.0	12.8	720	87.1	27.2	39.3
Springfield town (Dane)	2,740	2,870	4.7	2,814	94.4	0.4	0.6	2.3	2.4	27.3	61.0	11.9	998	90.5	34.8	42.4
Springfield town (Jackson)	623	625	0.3	642	90.2	0.0	0.0	9.8	0.0	34.8	53.9	11.4	189	78.8	55.0	8.5
Springfield town (Marquette)	830	815	-1.8	744	98.1	0.0	0.7	1.2	0.0	17.7	59.6	22.7	316	91.5	45.9	18.0
Springfield town (St. Croix)	932	960	3.0	857	98.6	0.0	0.7	0.7	0.0	27.9	58.6	13.3	313	91.1	42.8	19.2
Springfield CDP	158	NA	NA	235	100.0	0.0	0.0	0.0	0.0	25.1	75.0	0.0	69	59.4	11.6	0.0
Spring Green village & MCD (Sauk)	1,613	1,648	2.2	1,701	95.5	0.2	0.0	3.6	0.8	24.4	56.1	19.5	701	63.3	32.1	33.0
Spring Green town (Sauk)	1,712	1,762	2.9	1,580	95.1	0.0	0.3	3.0	1.6	22.5	58.9	18.5	673	90.3	51.7	22.6
Spring Grove town (Green)	874	887	1.5	922	93.0	0.0	0.2	1.5	5.3	25.6	58.6	15.8	314	87.6	52.9	13.4
Spring Lake town (Pierce)	563	561	-0.4	599	98.8	0.3	0.2	0.7	0.0	23.4	65.3	11.4	219	90.0	48.4	23.7
Spring Prairie town (Walworth)	2,181	2,202	1.0	2,190	86.1	0.0	2.6	1.8	9.4	20.7	65.5	13.7	755	92.2	39.3	17.9
Springvale town (Columbia)	520	518	-0.4	639	97.8	0.5	0.0	0.9	0.8	24.9	60.6	14.4	247	91.5	58.3	15.0
Springvale town (Fond du Lac)	707	699	-1.1	643	97.2	0.3	0.0	1.7	0.8	19.1	60.9	20.1	276	94.2	48.2	16.3
Spring Valley village	1,352	1,356	0.3	1,410	93.7	0.4	0.7	0.3	5.0	28.4	55.7	15.9	557	78.8	36.6	21.0
Spring Valley village (Pierce)	1,346	1,350	0.3	1,397	93.6	0.4	0.7	0.3	5.0	28.6	56.1	15.3	550	78.5	37.1	21.3
Spring Valley village (St. Croix)	6	6	0.0	13	100.0	0.0	0.0	0.0	0.0	0.0	23.1	76.9	7	100.0	0.0	0.0
Spring Valley town (Rock)	747	751	0.5	858	95.2	0.8	0.5	3.4	0.1	20.9	63.8	15.3	336	83.3	50.3	21.1
Springville town (Adams)	1,318	1,277	-3.1	1,299	97.1	0.0	0.0	0.5	2.5	21.4	55.4	23.3	500	82.2	57.4	5.4
Springwater town (Waushara)	1,274	1,256	-1.4	1,481	97.7	0.2	1.1	0.2	0.8	14.4	57.0	28.8	652	88.7	36.5	24.7
Spruce town (Oconto)	835	829	-0.7	858	97.8	0.0	0.0	0.7	1.5	24.4	59.2	16.6	352	82.7	54.0	17.9
Stanfold town (Barron)	719	714	-0.7	657	97.0	0.5	0.0	2.6	0.0	25.5	61.3	13.2	253	88.5	42.7	14.2
Stanley town (Barron)	2,546	2,543	-0.1	2,538	95.5	0.0	2.5	0.9	1.1	25.7	59.2	15.0	1,015	86.7	43.5	16.7
Stanley city	3,609	3,617	0.2	3,606	76.2	10.8	0.7	5.9	6.4	18.6	68.2	13.1	1,004	49.5	59.2	9.2
Stanley city (Chippewa)	3,603	3,611	0.2	3,606	76.2	10.8	0.7	5.9	6.4	18.6	68.2	13.1	1,004	49.5	59.2	9.2
Stanley city (Clark)	6	6	0.0	0	0.0	0.0	0.0	0.0	0.0	0.0	0.0	0.0	0	0.0	0.0	0.0
Stanton town (Dunn)	791	802	1.4	723	99.3	0.0	0.0	0.0	0.7	21.2	65.7	13.0	292	93.2	52.4	14.4
Stanton town (St. Croix)	900	908	0.9	1,006	97.8	0.1	0.0	0.9	1.2	23.3	64.1	12.8	370	90.5	54.1	14.6
Stark town (Vernon)	362	368	1.7	322	94.7	4.3	0.0	0.6	0.3	12.5	59.6	28.0	138	89.1	55.8	29.0
Star Prairie village & MCD (St. Croix)	561	568	1.2	632	98.9	0.0	0.2	0.6	0.3	28.0	61.9	10.1	242	74.0	38.0	19.4
Star Prairie town (St. Croix)	3,512	3,547	1.0	3,535	97.9	0.1	1.0	1.0	0.0	28.4	62.8	8.9	1,210	93.2	39.3	24.8
Stella town (Oneida)	650	647	-0.5	680	96.9	0.3	0.0	1.3	1.5	23.5	59.5	17.1	261	95.4	38.3	14.2
Stephenson town (Marinette)	3,006	2,990	-0.5	2,980	98.6	0.4	0.7	0.3	0.0	12.5	56.8	30.8	1,528	90.5	54.1	14.8
Sterling town (Polk)	790	777	-1.6	680	96.2	0.1	0.0	1.9	1.8	20.8	65.6	13.5	310	78.7	43.9	14.5
Sterling town (Vernon)	633	636	0.5	672	92.9	0.0	3.1	1.9	2.1	25.4	61.1	13.5	258	71.3	60.9	10.9
Stetsonville village & MCD (Taylor)	541	530	-2.0	586	97.4	0.0	1.0	0.9	0.7	25.8	57.3	16.9	281	59.4	62.3	16.0
Stettin town (Marathon)	2,544	2,565	0.8	2,551	96.0	0.2	2.0	1.2	0.6	23.8	62.8	13.5	1,002	86.2	29.8	35.4

1 May be of any race.

Table A. All Places — **Population and Housing**

STATE City, town, township, borough, or CDP (county if applicable)	Population				Race and Hispanic or Latino origin (percent), 2010–2014					Age (percent), 2010–2014			Households, 2010–2014			
	2010 census total population	2014 estimated population	Percent change 2010–2014	ACS total population estimate 2010–2014	White alone, not Hispanic or Latino	Black alone, not Hispanic or Latino	Asian alone, not Hispanic or Latino	All other races or 2 or more races, not Hispanic or Latino	Hispanic or Latino[1]	Under 18 years old	Age 18 to 64 years old	Age 65 years and older	Total occupied housing units	Percent owner occupied	High school diploma or less	Bachelor's degree or more
	1	2	3	4	5	6	7	8	9	10	11	12	13	14	15	16

WISCONSIN—Con.

STATE City, town, township, borough, or CDP (county if applicable)	1	2	3	4	5	6	7	8	9	10	11	12	13	14	15	16
Steuben village & MCD (Crawford)	131	129	-1.5	106	99.1	0.0	0.0	0.9	0.0	34.9	55.7	9.4	38	76.3	63.2	2.6
Stevens Point city & MCD (Portage)	26,703	26,658	-0.2	26,778	89.3	1.3	4.2	2.3	3.0	15.5	73.2	11.3	10,529	49.0	29.1	32.1
Stiles town (Oconto)	1,489	1,479	-0.7	1,580	98.3	0.0	0.0	0.3	1.4	18.5	65.1	16.3	677	92.2	55.5	14.2
Stinnett town (Washburn)	246	242	-1.6	280	93.9	0.0	0.0	3.2	2.9	13.3	68.2	18.6	126	79.4	43.7	21.4
Stockbridge village & MCD (Calumet)	636	630	-0.9	745	97.0	0.0	0.9	0.9	1.1	13.9	63.4	23.0	322	85.4	49.7	20.2
Stockbridge town (Calumet)	1,458	1,454	-0.3	1,242	96.9	0.0	0.0	2.3	0.8	14.4	65.6	20.0	554	94.9	48.9	16.6
Stockholm village & MCD (Pepin)	66	66	0.0	85	95.3	4.7	0.0	0.0	0.0	5.9	53.0	41.2	39	84.6	30.8	30.8
Stockholm town (Pepin)	197	196	-0.5	185	98.4	1.1	0.0	0.0	0.5	17.3	57.3	25.4	78	88.5	32.1	47.4
Stockton town (Portage)	2,917	2,951	1.2	2,934	96.6	0.4	0.0	1.6	1.5	23.0	62.9	14.3	1,101	94.6	43.0	26.2
Stoddard village & MCD (Vernon)	777	805	3.6	790	98.9	0.0	0.0	0.1	1.0	22.7	59.7	17.5	346	78.9	44.8	17.9
Stone Lake CDP	178	NA	NA	184	100.0	0.0	0.0	0.0	0.0	9.8	74.4	15.8	89	78.7	59.6	16.9
Stone Lake town (Washburn)	508	504	-0.8	555	94.1	0.2	0.0	5.8	0.0	21.7	57.4	21.1	246	85.4	58.1	14.6
Stoughton city & MCD (Dane)	12,649	13,039	3.1	12,886	92.8	2.3	0.6	2.4	1.9	23.5	61.5	15.0	5,269	65.9	32.5	40.9
Stratford village & MCD (Marathon)	1,578	1,576	-0.1	1,674	96.7	0.8	0.2	0.5	1.8	28.9	56.0	15.1	664	77.3	48.5	16.1
Strickland town (Rusk)	280	279	-0.4	301	98.0	0.0	0.0	0.0	2.0	19.0	61.2	19.9	129	81.4	56.6	1.6
Strongs Prairie town (Adams)	1,148	1,123	-2.2	1,192	96.7	0.0	0.0	1.3	2.0	13.7	57.7	28.5	506	90.7	50.0	13.0
Strum village & MCD (Trempealeau)	1,114	1,130	1.4	972	94.7	0.0	0.0	0.0	5.3	24.2	58.4	17.4	397	71.8	47.6	16.9
Stubbs town (Rusk)	576	572	-0.7	547	97.8	0.0	0.0	0.0	2.2	14.0	60.8	25.2	238	85.3	45.4	17.6
Sturgeon Bay city & MCD (Door)	9,144	9,044	-1.1	9,093	95.9	0.6	1.0	1.1	1.4	19.4	60.1	20.7	4,476	62.2	39.1	28.0
Sturgeon Bay town (Door)	818	826	1.0	923	96.1	0.4	0.0	2.8	0.7	18.5	59.9	21.6	411	96.1	44.8	22.6
Sturtevant village & MCD (Racine)	6,970	6,981	0.2	6,981	74.1	12.4	0.9	2.5	10.0	20.2	70.5	9.3	2,043	73.7	42.6	17.8
Suamico village & MCD (Brown)	11,346	11,878	4.7	11,621	97.6	0.2	0.0	1.8	0.3	26.1	64.2	9.6	4,230	93.1	32.0	36.9
Sugar Camp town (Oneida)	1,694	1,675	-1.1	1,745	97.4	0.0	0.9	0.9	0.9	18.7	57.8	23.5	753	91.6	32.4	28.6
Sugar Creek town (Walworth)	3,943	3,978	0.9	3,957	89.8	0.5	0.0	0.5	9.3	26.5	68.2	5.2	1,404	85.3	39.0	26.1
Sullivan village & MCD (Jefferson)	667	668	0.1	731	97.8	0.0	0.0	1.9	0.3	17.6	74.8	7.7	335	39.7	41.5	14.0
Sullivan town (Jefferson)	2,212	2,237	1.1	2,235	97.7	0.1	0.0	1.5	0.7	18.9	69.9	11.2	885	86.2	44.3	19.2
Summit town (Douglas)	1,063	1,068	0.5	1,060	96.1	0.0	1.0	1.1	1.7	22.4	66.7	10.9	423	93.6	47.8	14.4
Summit town (Juneau)	646	638	-1.2	575	99.7	0.0	0.0	0.3	0.0	15.3	66.8	18.1	254	84.6	59.4	8.3
Summit town (Langlade)	163	158	-3.1	241	95.9	0.0	0.0	4.1	0.0	20.4	67.1	12.4	99	85.9	54.5	9.1
Summit village & MCD (Waukesha)	4,673	4,814	3.0	4,744	95.7	0.6	1.0	0.3	2.4	26.6	60.5	12.8	1,685	91.1	18.3	53.0
Summit Lake CDP	144	NA	NA	121	99.2	0.0	0.0	0.8	0.0	30.5	56.2	13.2	37	81.1	67.6	13.5
Sumner town (Barron)	798	801	0.4	695	97.4	0.0	0.0	0.4	2.2	17.6	70.1	12.2	290	89.3	44.1	21.7
Sumner town (Jefferson)	832	846	1.7	771	99.1	0.0	0.0	0.1	0.8	17.0	64.6	18.4	311	86.5	41.2	23.2
Sumner town (Trempealeau)	810	838	3.5	823	92.3	0.0	1.6	4.5	1.6	24.6	62.5	13.2	311	79.4	49.2	18.0
Sumpter town (Sauk)	1,189	1,209	1.7	1,437	63.7	1.0	0.0	3.3	31.9	37.4	56.9	5.8	449	70.8	49.0	14.7
Sun Prairie city & MCD (Dane)	29,541	31,752	7.5	30,601	84.8	5.3	3.7	2.7	3.6	27.6	62.9	9.5	12,029	58.7	23.1	45.7
Sun Prairie town (Dane)	2,305	2,420	5.0	2,662	83.7	1.6	2.8	1.5	10.4	28.1	61.7	10.1	872	86.7	37.7	28.6
Superior city & MCD (Douglas)	27,244	26,705	-2.0	26,932	91.6	1.5	1.6	4.3	1.0	20.6	65.6	13.8	11,669	55.7	36.1	21.3
Superior village & MCD (Douglas)	664	665	0.2	653	97.2	0.3	0.3	1.7	0.5	17.3	59.1	23.6	246	75.6	54.1	10.2
Superior town (Douglas)	2,166	2,188	1.0	2,089	92.0	0.0	0.0	3.2	4.9	23.9	58.3	17.8	787	91.6	42.6	16.1
Suring village & MCD (Oconto)	544	530	-2.6	379	97.1	0.0	0.0	2.9	0.0	17.1	45.2	37.5	183	66.1	60.1	6.6
Sussex village & MCD (Waukesha)	10,518	10,740	2.1	10,632	93.3	1.5	2.6	0.6	2.0	28.5	61.8	9.8	3,880	66.1	28.4	37.0
Swiss town (Burnett)	790	791	0.1	816	76.1	1.1	0.7	20.8	1.2	20.3	55.3	24.4	394	79.4	49.5	14.2
Sylvan town (Richland)	555	547	-1.4	527	95.4	0.0	0.0	3.0	1.5	30.3	57.6	12.0	177	80.8	53.7	16.4
Sylvester town (Green)	1,004	1,021	1.7	1,039	97.8	0.5	0.8	0.5	0.5	28.8	57.5	13.6	355	91.5	40.3	30.7
Taft town (Taylor)	430	418	-2.8	391	100.0	0.0	0.0	0.0	0.0	24.5	61.1	14.3	165	81.8	61.8	13.3
Tainter town (Dunn)	2,319	2,378	2.5	3,014	98.0	0.0	0.4	1.2	0.4	23.7	60.0	16.3	1,145	78.0	32.4	32.0
Tainter Lake CDP	2,242	NA	NA	2,927	98.0	0.0	0.4	1.2	0.4	22.7	60.4	16.8	1,125	79.6	28.8	33.9
Taycheedah CDP	704	NA	NA	901	98.3	0.0	0.0	1.7	0.0	14.0	74.4	11.7	340	85.3	51.8	18.8
Taycheedah town (Fond du Lac)	4,205	4,338	3.2	4,270	95.7	0.0	0.0	0.8	3.5	16.8	64.2	19.1	1,750	90.3	40.1	27.7
Taylor village & MCD (Jackson)	476	477	0.2	462	91.1	0.0	0.0	0.0	8.9	24.7	64.8	10.4	215	48.4	66.0	1.9
Tennyson village & MCD (Grant)	355	349	-1.7	345	99.4	0.0	0.0	0.6	0.0	22.4	58.4	19.1	153	79.7	63.4	15.0
Texas town (Marathon)	1,615	1,620	0.3	1,714	98.9	0.0	0.0	1.1	0.0	19.0	63.4	17.6	681	94.7	56.1	17.8
Theresa village & MCD (Dodge)	1,262	1,220	-3.3	1,236	86.8	10.0	0.0	0.2	3.0	27.3	60.5	12.2	482	83.4	51.5	9.8
Theresa town (Dodge)	1,075	1,061	-1.3	1,087	100.0	0.0	0.0	0.0	0.0	21.2	65.0	13.8	394	89.1	53.8	12.7
Thiensville village & MCD (Ozaukee)	3,211	3,186	-0.8	3,198	94.9	1.3	1.2	2.2	0.4	18.5	61.1	20.4	1,543	66.6	22.8	46.1
Thornapple town (Rusk)	774	765	-1.2	766	96.1	3.0	0.7	0.0	0.3	22.2	58.1	19.7	340	85.6	53.5	16.5
Thornton CDP	65	NA	NA	91	86.8	0.0	0.0	13.2	0.0	23.1	50.6	26.4	50	70.0	32.0	4.0
Thorp city & MCD (Clark)	1,621	1,620	-0.1	1,678	96.5	0.0	0.0	1.4	2.1	24.4	54.6	21.0	734	61.4	63.9	12.1
Thorp town (Clark)	808	833	3.1	820	96.1	0.6	0.5	2.8	0.0	33.2	56.6	10.0	280	81.4	62.9	12.5
Three Lakes CDP	605	NA	NA	519	100.0	0.0	0.0	0.0	0.0	6.7	60.8	32.4	303	77.6	41.6	25.4

1 May be of any race.

Table A. All Places — **Population and Housing**

STATE City, town, township, borough, or CDP (county if applicable)	2010 census total population	2014 estimated population	Percent change 2010-2014	ACS total population estimate 2010-2014	White alone, not Hispanic or Latino	Black alone, not Hispanic or Latino	Asian alone, not Hispanic or Latino	All other races or 2 or more races, not Hispanic or Latino	Hispanic or Latino[1]	Under 18 years old	Age 18 to 64 years old	Age 65 years and older	Total occupied housing units	Percent owner occupied	High school diploma or less	Bachelor's degree or more
	1	2	3	4	5	6	7	8	9	10	11	12	13	14	15	16
WISCONSIN—Con.																
Three Lakes town (Oneida)	2,131	2,124	-0.3	1,858	98.7	0.0	1.1	0.0	0.2	9.4	55.3	35.3	918	89.5	37.6	30.5
Tichigan CDP	5,133	NA	NA	5,332	93.2	0.8	0.3	1.5	4.2	24.9	63.7	11.4	2,020	92.2	37.6	32.2
Tiffany town (Dunn)	618	628	1.6	607	99.2	0.0	0.0	0.5	0.3	22.8	60.1	16.8	236	87.3	51.3	18.2
Tigerton village & MCD (Shawano)	741	728	-1.8	865	92.4	0.0	0.0	3.7	3.9	27.9	56.4	15.7	371	64.7	56.9	14.6
Tilden town (Chippewa)	1,485	1,509	1.6	1,481	96.8	0.0	0.0	0.0	3.2	23.8	63.8	12.2	540	91.9	40.2	25.0
Tilleda CDP	91	NA	NA	90	100.0	0.0	0.0	0.0	0.0	27.8	57.8	14.4	36	91.7	55.6	11.1
Tipler town (Florence)	142	143	0.7	163	89.6	0.0	0.0	8.6	1.8	7.4	55.1	37.4	56	92.9	76.8	3.6
Tomah city & MCD (Monroe)	9,118	9,328	2.3	9,281	92.0	2.7	1.0	2.3	1.9	24.6	59.2	16.2	3,968	48.4	46.1	18.8
Tomah town (Monroe)	1,392	1,431	2.8	1,439	95.1	0.6	0.2	2.9	1.2	26.7	58.4	14.8	553	86.3	41.2	24.8
Tomahawk city & MCD (Lincoln)	3,397	3,277	-3.5	3,335	95.5	0.1	1.3	1.4	1.6	23.4	53.9	22.7	1,526	61.7	50.9	14.5
Tomahawk town (Lincoln)	416	410	-1.4	417	100.0	0.0	0.0	0.0	0.0	10.8	67.8	21.3	215	92.1	55.8	13.0
Tony village & MCD (Rusk)	113	109	-3.5	82	98.8	0.0	1.2	0.0	0.0	3.6	52.5	43.9	49	77.6	61.2	4.1
Townsend CDP	146	NA	NA	132	100.0	0.0	0.0	0.0	0.0	11.4	67.5	21.2	69	56.5	50.7	4.3
Townsend town (Oconto)	979	975	-0.4	942	100.0	0.0	0.0	0.0	0.0	13.1	51.6	35.1	454	83.7	54.2	14.5
Trade Lake town (Burnett)	823	820	-0.4	790	96.2	0.6	0.0	0.8	2.4	23.5	58.4	18.4	338	89.6	44.1	24.9
Trego CDP	227	NA	NA	107	98.1	0.0	0.0	1.9	0.0	4.7	52.4	43.0	62	85.5	58.1	22.6
Trego town (Washburn)	932	919	-1.4	863	94.4	0.5	0.0	4.1	1.0	23.3	58.1	18.5	382	86.4	39.8	22.3
Trempealeau village & MCD (Trempealeau)	1,529	1,613	5.5	1,698	97.9	0.1	0.0	0.2	1.8	24.5	57.8	17.7	761	57.3	37.2	25.9
Trempealeau town (Trempealeau)	1,756	1,818	3.5	1,676	98.6	0.4	0.0	0.8	0.2	23.0	59.1	18.0	673	85.0	38.3	22.1
Trenton town (Dodge)	1,293	1,289	-0.3	1,351	97.0	0.0	1.1	1.1	0.7	20.7	64.6	14.7	445	88.3	44.9	18.9
Trenton town (Pierce)	1,829	1,829	0.0	1,768	98.4	0.0	0.2	0.5	1.0	26.8	60.7	12.3	664	92.9	38.7	22.3
Trenton town (Washington)	4,710	4,700	-0.2	4,709	96.2	0.0	1.0	1.7	1.1	24.2	61.9	13.9	1,744	92.1	44.4	17.4
Trimbelle town (Pierce)	1,679	1,672	-0.4	1,524	97.8	0.2	0.5	0.3	1.2	18.5	67.7	13.7	651	89.9	45.0	21.8
Tripp town (Bayfield)	231	230	-0.4	262	93.1	0.0	1.9	5.0	0.0	17.6	67.6	14.9	113	86.7	57.5	18.6
Troy town (St. Croix)	4,717	4,968	5.3	4,816	93.2	0.2	4.4	0.3	1.9	24.8	65.6	9.6	1,696	95.0	10.8	55.6
Troy town (Sauk)	794	817	2.9	821	97.7	0.0	0.0	1.7	0.6	24.1	63.2	12.8	300	77.7	50.7	20.0
Troy town (Walworth)	2,353	2,369	0.7	2,433	97.0	0.0	0.2	1.3	1.5	18.2	64.3	17.4	917	93.2	37.3	28.5
True town (Rusk)	296	290	-2.0	341	100.0	0.0	0.0	0.0	0.0	22.0	62.6	15.5	134	94.8	66.4	14.9
Tunnel City CDP	106	NA	NA	179	93.3	0.0	3.4	3.4	0.0	26.8	62.0	11.2	55	76.4	34.5	12.7
Turtle town (Rock)	2,389	2,400	0.5	2,235	91.3	1.2	0.4	2.5	4.5	22.1	59.4	18.6	934	84.6	45.6	22.5
Turtle Lake village	1,050	1,035	-1.4	1,168	78.1	4.3	0.9	7.7	9.0	24.4	62.1	13.5	480	52.5	55.6	10.8
Turtle Lake village (Barron)	957	944	-1.4	1,086	76.4	4.6	1.0	8.3	9.7	24.0	62.1	14.0	440	53.0	57.3	11.1
Turtle Lake village (Polk)	93	91	-2.2	82	100.0	0.0	0.0	0.0	0.0	31.7	61.1	7.3	40	47.5	37.5	7.5
Turtle Lake CDP	343	NA	NA	343	82.8	0.0	0.0	2.6	14.6	22.8	66.7	10.5	166	92.8	20.5	16.3
Turtle Lake town (Barron)	624	620	-0.6	553	100.0	0.0	0.0	0.0	0.0	23.7	62.5	13.9	230	88.3	66.1	12.6
Tustin CDP	117	NA	NA	88	100.0	0.0	0.0	0.0	0.0	0.0	85.1	14.8	47	95.7	38.3	19.1
Twin Lakes village & MCD (Kenosha)	5,989	6,102	1.9	6,033	96.9	0.1	0.2	0.5	2.3	27.3	61.8	11.0	2,225	75.9	36.5	25.2
Two Creeks town (Manitowoc)	442	435	-1.6	469	99.1	0.0	0.0	0.0	0.9	17.4	66.2	16.4	173	87.9	64.7	9.2
Two Rivers city & MCD (Manitowoc)	11,723	11,437	-2.4	11,577	92.6	2.0	0.7	2.4	2.4	22.2	55.9	21.9	4,945	70.2	51.0	16.3
Two Rivers town (Manitowoc)	1,787	1,770	-1.0	1,886	97.5	0.0	0.4	1.7	0.3	13.2	67.2	19.7	768	91.8	48.0	18.5
Underhill town (Oconto)	882	875	-0.8	727	89.5	0.0	0.4	6.5	3.6	18.6	62.5	19.0	312	94.2	61.9	7.7
Union town (Burnett)	340	340	0.0	339	97.6	0.0	0.6	1.8	0.0	11.2	57.2	31.6	168	75.0	52.4	19.6
Union town (Door)	999	996	-0.3	1,060	98.0	0.3	0.0	0.6	1.1	21.0	61.6	17.5	427	91.3	48.0	19.2
Union town (Eau Claire)	2,620	2,730	4.2	2,684	92.2	1.6	4.3	0.0	1.8	23.1	60.8	16.2	941	89.5	35.0	27.7
Union town (Pierce)	609	606	-0.5	617	96.8	0.0	0.0	2.9	0.3	24.2	64.3	11.7	229	86.9	47.6	23.1
Union town (Rock)	2,086	2,089	0.1	2,383	93.7	0.5	0.6	2.7	2.4	28.0	64.0	8.0	897	83.9	46.5	26.6
Union town (Vernon)	700	701	0.1	770	97.3	0.0	1.6	0.1	1.0	35.8	53.6	10.6	219	92.2	45.2	24.2
Union town (Waupaca)	806	852	5.7	830	93.6	0.0	0.4	5.3	0.7	24.4	59.0	16.6	335	88.4	63.3	16.1
Union Center village & MCD (Juneau)	200	197	-1.5	226	100.0	0.0	0.0	0.0	0.0	22.6	61.6	15.9	86	79.1	81.4	3.5
Union Grove village & MCD (Racine)	4,915	4,898	-0.3	4,883	92.7	0.1	0.6	1.9	4.6	24.8	63.7	11.6	1,823	62.0	45.9	20.6
Unity town (Clark)	878	881	0.3	840	98.9	0.7	0.0	0.4	0.0	37.3	52.6	10.0	253	85.4	68.0	7.9
Unity village	343	342	-0.3	363	91.2	0.0	0.0	6.1	2.8	22.8	63.8	13.2	157	84.7	70.7	7.6
Unity village (Clark)	139	138	-0.7	100	88.0	0.0	0.0	2.0	10.0	19.0	74.0	7.0	46	97.8	69.6	6.5
Unity village (Marathon)	204	204	0.0	263	92.4	0.0	0.0	7.6	0.0	24.3	59.9	15.6	111	79.3	71.2	8.1
Unity town (Trempealeau)	506	524	3.6	618	96.8	0.0	1.6	0.3	1.3	25.9	56.3	17.8	232	92.2	65.5	8.6
Upham town (Langlade)	676	661	-2.2	743	98.9	0.0	0.9	0.1	0.0	13.5	52.7	33.9	351	95.7	49.9	20.2
Utica town (Crawford)	661	668	1.1	699	97.4	0.0	0.9	1.7	0.0	22.7	58.1	19.0	283	90.8	51.2	21.6
Utica town (Winnebago)	1,299	1,329	2.3	1,464	97.4	0.0	0.0	2.6	0.0	25.1	60.8	14.1	531	86.1	46.5	29.2
Valders village & MCD (Manitowoc)	962	945	-1.8	1,042	89.2	0.0	0.0	0.4	10.5	25.3	58.9	15.8	429	71.1	54.8	12.1
Vance Creek town (Barron)	669	654	-2.2	647	97.7	0.8	0.0	1.5	0.0	30.0	56.2	13.8	248	84.3	54.4	20.6
Vandenbroek town (Outagamie)	1,473	1,522	3.3	1,726	97.5	0.0	0.6	0.1	1.7	29.3	60.8	9.9	536	91.6	37.1	24.6
Van Dyne CDP	279	NA	NA	331	100.0	0.0	0.0	0.0	0.0	29.9	61.6	8.5	118	100.0	47.5	31.4
Vermont town (Dane)	821	859	4.6	759	97.0	0.5	0.3	2.0	0.3	20.1	66.1	13.8	314	85.7	29.9	48.7
Vernon town (Waukesha)	7,606	7,636	0.4	7,637	94.9	0.7	0.5	2.7	1.1	22.9	61.2	15.8	2,843	94.3	31.4	29.5
Verona city & MCD (Dane)	10,678	12,003	12.4	11,353	95.2	1.7	1.3	1.8	0.0	26.8	61.4	11.7	4,800	65.1	18.8	53.9
Verona town (Dane)	1,821	1,924	5.7	1,780	93.9	1.3	0.8	2.1	1.8	21.4	63.9	14.7	676	86.4	21.7	50.3
Vesper village & MCD (Wood)	584	565	-3.3	640	96.3	0.0	0.0	3.4	0.3	28.6	57.7	13.9	263	75.7	50.2	10.3
Vienna town (Dane)	1,476	1,548	4.9	1,315	97.3	0.4	0.0	0.1	2.3	21.0	67.8	11.1	505	90.3	28.3	33.3
Vilas town (Langlade)	233	227	-2.6	243	98.8	0.0	1.2	0.0	0.0	17.7	70.4	11.9	94	86.2	57.4	6.4
Vinland town (Winnebago)	1,765	1,783	1.0	1,990	98.9	0.0	0.2	0.7	0.3	17.9	65.6	16.4	791	91.2	39.9	24.1
Viola town (Richland)	699	684	-2.1	713	97.2	0.0	0.0	0.1	2.7	28.2	56.4	15.4	285	69.5	54.0	13.0
Viola village (Richland)	477	462	-3.1	398	99.7	0.0	0.0	0.3	0.0	26.4	59.3	14.3	174	74.7	47.1	12.6

1 May be of any race.

Table A. All Places — **Population and Housing**

STATE City, town, township, borough, or CDP (county if applicable)	2010 census total population	2014 estimated population	Percent change 2010–2014	ACS total population estimate 2010-2014	White alone, not Hispanic or Latino	Black alone, not Hispanic or Latino	Asian alone, not Hispanic or Latino	All other races or 2 or more races, not Hispanic or Latino	Hispanic or Latino[1]	Under 18 years old	Age 18 to 64 years old	Age 65 years and older	Total occupied housing units	Percent owner occupied	High school diploma or less	Bachelor's degree or more
	1	2	3	4	5	6	7	8	9	10	11	12	13	14	15	16
WISCONSIN—Con.																
Viola village (Vernon)........	222	222	0.0	315	94.0	0.0	0.0	0.0	6.0	30.5	52.7	16.8	111	61.3	64.9	13.5
Viroqua city & MCD (Vernon)	4,360	4,369	0.2	4,378	96.0	0.7	0.8	2.4	0.2	23.3	52.6	24.1	1,963	62.6	37.4	28.8
Viroqua town (Vernon)......	1,721	1,789	4.0	1,686	98.5	0.0	0.1	1.0	0.5	20.4	60.6	19.1	624	92.0	39.4	27.6
Wabeno CDP...................	575	NA	NA	530	84.9	0.0	0.0	15.1	0.0	23.1	54.0	22.8	208	74.0	57.2	0.0
Wabeno town (Forest)	1,170	1,140	-2.6	1,098	69.9	0.5	0.0	27.3	2.4	24.2	55.3	20.5	422	76.3	55.9	4.0
Wagner town (Marinette) ..	681	686	0.7	635	99.7	0.0	0.0	0.3	0.0	14.0	64.3	21.7	302	86.8	48.3	11.3
Waldo village & MCD (Sheboygan)	503	495	-1.6	627	93.3	0.0	1.0	4.8	1.0	25.5	66.4	8.1	219	72.6	54.8	12.8
Waldwick town (Iowa)	473	481	1.7	545	100.0	0.0	0.0	0.0	0.0	23.5	61.9	14.7	206	81.6	56.3	24.3
Wales village & MCD (Waukesha).................	2,549	2,570	0.8	2,561	90.9	1.3	0.3	2.1	5.3	20.8	66.5	12.8	1,013	82.9	18.7	53.7
Walworth village & MCD (Walworth)	2,816	2,830	0.5	2,825	83.5	0.8	0.2	0.2	15.3	27.3	58.1	14.5	1,094	56.5	42.5	28.2
Walworth town (Walworth)	1,702	1,717	0.9	1,829	94.8	0.0	0.1	0.7	4.4	21.3	64.2	14.5	708	74.7	43.5	26.1
Warner town (Clark)	669	656	-1.9	729	99.0	0.0	0.0	0.5	0.4	38.4	52.8	8.8	208	88.0	61.5	13.5
Warren town (St. Croix)	1,591	1,638	3.0	1,776	95.9	1.2	0.2	2.0	0.7	31.1	60.6	8.3	572	87.1	25.2	39.2
Warren town (Waushara)..	668	652	-2.4	728	93.8	1.5	1.4	1.5	1.8	21.4	65.7	12.9	288	83.0	53.5	14.2
Warrens village & MCD (Monroe)	356	352	-1.1	354	85.3	2.8	0.0	11.6	0.3	22.0	64.4	13.6	151	51.0	60.9	15.2
Wascott town (Douglas)....	763	772	1.2	882	87.6	6.5	0.0	0.1	5.8	9.5	60.6	29.9	387	95.1	32.6	29.7
Washburn city & MCD (Bayfield)	2,117	2,068	-2.3	2,190	91.3	0.9	0.3	6.5	1.0	21.1	61.5	17.5	973	68.9	31.0	38.4
Washburn town (Bayfield).	530	533	0.6	502	92.4	0.0	0.0	7.0	0.6	16.0	68.4	15.7	218	91.7	19.7	50.9
Washburn town (Clark).....	290	283	-2.4	334	93.1	0.0	0.0	0.6	6.3	25.2	61.2	13.8	134	87.3	66.4	7.5
Washington town (Door)...	708	717	1.3	806	94.7	1.5	0.0	2.9	1.0	13.9	47.0	39.2	393	86.3	24.4	43.8
Washington town (Eau Claire)	7,073	7,324	3.5	7,233	91.7	0.0	3.1	3.3	1.9	19.1	63.9	17.0	2,961	81.5	30.7	40.2
Washington town (Green).	817	830	1.6	863	97.7	0.0	0.3	2.0	0.0	26.5	61.8	11.7	323	84.5	57.3	22.6
Washington town (La Crosse)	558	573	2.7	478	92.1	0.0	3.3	0.0	4.6	19.9	64.4	15.5	199	78.9	42.7	22.1
Washington town (Rusk)...	339	335	-1.2	306	98.0	0.0	0.3	1.3	0.3	18.0	54.2	27.8	151	93.4	53.6	12.6
Washington town (Sauk)...	1,007	1,026	1.9	940	99.6	0.0	0.1	0.2	0.1	28.8	56.9	14.5	306	76.8	57.8	15.4
Washington town (Shawano)	1,895	1,878	-0.9	1,920	99.0	0.0	0.0	1.0	0.0	13.1	60.0	27.0	894	92.4	59.5	13.1
Washington town (Vilas)...	1,451	1,450	-0.1	1,435	96.3	0.0	0.6	2.4	0.8	15.0	59.7	25.4	707	88.5	35.1	26.9
Waterford village & MCD (Racine)	5,368	5,349	-0.4	5,346	90.8	2.8	0.7	3.2	2.5	25.6	58.1	16.1	2,031	70.7	36.8	28.1
Waterford town (Racine)...	6,344	6,441	1.5	6,396	94.0	0.6	0.3	1.3	3.8	22.5	65.9	11.5	2,472	89.0	35.8	32.4
Waterloo town (Grant)	550	545	-0.9	704	94.3	0.0	0.4	5.3	0.0	34.7	55.2	10.2	238	87.8	54.6	8.0
Waterloo city & MCD (Jefferson)	3,333	3,345	0.4	3,346	86.8	0.0	0.4	1.2	11.6	22.4	63.8	13.6	1,304	72.2	51.5	9.7
Waterloo town (Jefferson).	907	924	1.9	899	99.4	0.1	0.2	0.2	0.0	21.9	64.8	13.2	363	85.4	42.7	28.7
Watertown city	23,855	23,891	0.2	23,899	91.5	0.7	1.0	2.4	4.4	25.7	59.2	15.1	9,115	64.4	45.2	21.4
Watertown city (Dodge)....	8,461	8,387	-0.9	8,435	93.3	0.9	0.6	2.8	2.4	22.7	56.6	20.7	3,139	70.5	41.9	24.3
Watertown city (Jefferson)	15,394	15,504	0.7	15,464	90.6	0.6	1.2	2.1	5.4	27.2	60.9	12.0	5,976	61.1	47.0	19.8
Watertown town (Jefferson)	1,979	2,012	1.7	1,906	98.8	0.0	0.2	0.0	1.0	21.8	60.1	18.2	728	87.6	48.4	18.7
Waterville town (Pepin).....	831	816	-1.8	722	95.7	0.0	0.0	2.5	1.8	16.2	64.8	18.8	346	78.6	56.1	13.0
Watterstown town (Grant).	330	326	-1.2	331	97.0	0.0	0.9	2.1	0.0	21.7	60.3	17.8	142	89.4	51.4	18.3
Waubeek town (Pepin)......	423	419	-0.9	447	96.4	0.0	0.4	1.8	1.3	31.1	57.3	11.6	147	93.2	46.9	23.1
Waubeka CDP.................	657	NA	NA	801	95.8	0.6	0.6	3.0	0.0	29.5	63.3	7.2	269	77.3	30.9	21.2
Waukau CDP..................	255	NA	NA	293	99.0	0.0	0.0	0.0	1.0	21.9	64.4	13.7	132	86.4	45.5	12.1
Waukechon town (Shawano)	1,023	1,021	-0.2	1,019	98.2	0.0	0.4	1.2	0.2	22.9	63.5	13.5	390	93.8	54.4	18.7
Waukesha city & MCD (Waukesha)	70,706	71,489	1.1	71,083	78.8	3.0	3.3	2.5	12.4	23.1	66.1	10.9	28,466	58.9	28.9	36.2
Waukesha town (Waukesha)	9,145	9,230	0.9	9,181	93.9	0.3	0.2	1.7	4.0	18.9	63.3	18.1	3,493	91.7	24.2	39.1
Waumandee CDP............	68	NA	NA	68	100.0	0.0	0.0	0.0	0.0	10.3	54.5	35.3	37	86.5	64.9	8.1
Waumandee town (Buffalo)	472	463	-1.9	410	95.9	0.0	0.0	0.0	4.1	15.4	62.7	22.0	187	82.9	65.2	8.0
Waunakee village & MCD (Dane)	12,099	13,067	8.0	12,613	90.6	0.6	1.3	2.3	5.2	30.8	58.8	10.4	4,530	77.2	19.2	50.4
Waupaca city & MCD (Waupaca)	6,069	6,018	-0.8	6,016	94.7	0.3	1.0	2.3	1.7	22.2	58.6	19.3	2,540	48.4	50.8	14.8
Waupaca town (Waupaca)	1,173	1,239	5.6	1,116	98.8	0.0	0.0	0.3	0.9	23.8	58.6	17.7	448	83.7	46.2	15.0
Waupun city	11,352	11,377	0.2	11,336	82.9	9.5	0.4	1.9	5.4	18.8	67.4	13.8	3,745	69.6	53.4	13.2
Waupun city (Dodge)........	7,864	7,887	0.3	7,858	79.2	13.8	0.5	1.7	4.9	15.5	72.0	12.4	2,367	65.5	55.3	13.2
Waupun city (Fond du Lac)	3,488	3,490	0.1	3,478	91.1	0.0	0.3	2.3	6.4	26.0	56.8	17.0	1,378	76.6	49.9	13.3
Waupun town (Fond du Lac)	1,359	1,351	-0.6	1,297	99.6	0.0	0.0	0.0	0.4	18.4	65.4	16.1	501	90.6	50.1	19.6
Wausau city & MCD (Marathon)	39,114	39,302	0.5	39,209	77.2	1.8	13.3	3.8	4.0	23.7	59.7	16.7	16,562	58.9	41.0	25.9
Wausau town (Marathon) .	2,232	2,243	0.5	2,519	88.3	1.1	0.4	0.0	10.2	16.1	64.9	19.0	924	81.6	51.6	14.1
Wausaukee village & MCD (Marinette)	575	574	-0.2	520	91.2	0.0	2.1	6.7	0.0	20.2	56.6	23.3	270	47.8	68.5	7.4
Wausaukee town (Marinette)	1,066	1,069	0.3	1,073	98.8	0.3	0.2	0.7	0.0	18.7	55.9	25.3	465	89.5	46.5	15.3
Wautoma city & MCD (Waushara)	2,215	2,153	-2.8	2,010	73.6	3.7	0.0	1.6	21.0	27.4	57.7	15.1	820	42.2	52.6	10.9
Wautoma town (Waushara)	1,278	1,272	-0.5	1,507	95.8	0.0	0.1	1.1	3.0	20.8	56.4	22.6	596	93.1	36.6	22.8
Wauwatosa city & MCD (Milwaukee)	46,449	47,102	1.4	46,838	88.0	4.2	2.6	2.3	2.9	22.1	62.6	15.3	20,515	64.3	16.8	57.8
Wauzeka village & MCD (Crawford)	711	721	1.4	669	96.9	0.3	0.0	2.8	0.0	31.3	59.0	9.6	246	76.4	42.7	16.7
Wauzeka town (Crawford)	422	414	-1.9	486	99.6	0.0	0.0	0.4	0.0	22.0	63.2	14.6	185	75.7	50.8	16.2
Wayne town (Lafayette).....	490	497	1.4	484	99.4	0.0	0.0	0.0	0.6	22.9	60.3	16.7	172	88.4	55.8	5.8
Wayne town (Washington)	2,169	2,192	1.1	2,404	96.2	0.6	0.3	0.4	2.5	23.6	65.8	10.4	867	89.5	40.9	23.2

1 May be of any race.

Table A. All Places — Population and Housing

STATE City, town, township, borough, or CDP (county if applicable)	2010 census total population	2014 estimated population	Percent change 2010-2014	ACS total population estimate 2010-2014	White alone, not Hispanic or Latino	Black alone, not Hispanic or Latino	Asian alone, not Hispanic or Latino	All other races or 2 or more races, not Hispanic or Latino	Hispanic or Latino[1]	Under 18 years old	Age 18 to 64 years old	Age 65 years and older	Total occupied housing units	Percent owner occupied	High school diploma or less	Bachelor's degree or more
	1	2	3	4	5	6	7	8	9	10	11	12	13	14	15	16
WISCONSIN—Con.																
Webb Lake town (Burnett)	311	311	0.0	366	96.4	0.0	0.8	0.0	2.7	12.1	45.9	42.1	199	93.0	42.7	23.1
Webster village & MCD (Burnett)	653	636	-2.6	644	89.6	0.9	1.1	6.7	1.7	22.7	58.8	18.6	329	57.4	56.5	8.5
Webster town (Vernon)	778	792	1.8	1,012	98.9	0.0	0.0	0.0	1.1	35.6	54.8	9.6	312	83.3	44.6	23.4
Weirgor town (Sawyer)	327	325	-0.6	336	90.5	1.5	0.0	7.7	0.3	12.3	67.9	19.9	196	92.3	41.8	9.2
Wellington town (Monroe)	621	635	2.3	603	93.9	0.0	0.5	0.3	5.3	36.8	47.9	15.3	192	78.1	60.4	11.5
Wells town (Monroe)	517	530	2.5	493	100.0	0.0	0.0	0.0	0.0	19.7	60.8	19.5	214	81.8	52.8	13.6
Wescott town (Shawano)	3,183	3,171	-0.4	3,178	90.9	0.2	3.6	5.1	0.1	15.7	58.7	25.6	1,424	82.4	48.5	20.9
West Allis city & MCD (Milwaukee)	60,419	60,624	0.3	60,595	80.1	4.0	2.6	2.7	10.5	20.6	64.6	14.5	27,294	55.1	41.7	23.7
West Baraboo village & MCD (Sauk)	1,411	1,436	1.8	1,584	87.1	0.0	2.0	2.5	8.5	25.9	64.3	9.7	621	49.8	41.9	22.5
West Bend city & MCD (Washington)	31,199	31,692	1.6	31,496	91.9	1.3	1.8	1.2	3.7	24.5	60.8	14.8	13,009	65.7	35.9	26.3
West Bend town (Washington)	4,703	4,751	1.0	4,731	97.3	0.0	1.4	0.7	0.7	16.9	54.4	28.9	1,982	80.6	36.9	34.4
Westboro CDP	190	NA	NA	208	100.0	0.0	0.0	0.0	0.0	26.9	60.5	12.5	90	78.9	61.1	11.1
Westboro town (Taylor)	684	674	-1.5	727	99.6	0.0	0.0	0.4	0.0	25.8	58.1	16.2	302	86.4	59.6	12.9
Westby city & MCD (Vernon)	2,200	2,259	2.7	2,246	96.4	0.7	1.1	0.9	0.9	26.1	52.9	21.1	907	66.6	43.4	23.9
Westfield village & MCD (Marquette)	1,254	1,225	-2.3	1,276	87.9	0.0	0.0	0.5	11.5	32.6	56.2	11.2	476	57.4	52.9	19.5
Westfield town (Marquette)	866	848	-2.1	1,035	88.5	0.4	0.0	4.7	6.4	26.0	57.6	16.4	381	75.3	50.7	19.9
Westfield town (Sauk)	569	587	3.2	635	100.0	0.0	0.0	0.0	0.0	25.7	58.3	16.1	219	84.9	46.6	21.0
Westford town (Dodge)	1,242	1,225	-1.4	1,246	99.8	0.0	0.0	0.2	0.0	16.4	63.9	19.7	489	90.4	47.2	19.4
Westford town (Richland)	530	522	-1.5	534	98.9	0.4	0.7	0.0	0.0	23.4	58.6	18.0	204	82.4	68.1	8.3
West Kewaunee town (Kewaunee)	1,298	1,311	1.0	1,394	93.6	0.2	0.5	0.6	5.1	21.9	61.2	16.9	498	85.3	52.6	19.3
West Marshland town (Burnett)	367	364	-0.8	358	93.3	0.8	2.2	3.6	0.0	19.6	71.4	8.9	163	88.3	58.3	8.0
West Milwaukee village & MCD (Milwaukee)	4,206	4,217	0.3	4,214	50.1	11.1	5.1	4.4	29.3	22.4	67.7	9.8	2,014	30.6	46.3	17.8
Weston town (Clark)	699	688	-1.6	711	94.9	0.0	0.0	2.8	2.3	29.0	54.3	16.7	271	87.5	57.2	11.8
Weston town (Dunn)	594	609	2.5	640	99.4	0.0	0.6	0.0	0.0	26.9	58.7	14.4	240	87.1	53.8	17.9
Weston village & MCD (Marathon)	14,868	14,988	0.8	14,937	90.9	0.2	5.9	1.1	1.9	25.5	60.4	14.1	5,880	63.1	42.7	24.7
Weston town (Marathon)	639	666	4.2	590	96.4	0.0	1.0	1.2	1.4	23.7	63.0	13.2	219	94.1	32.4	34.2
West Point town (Columbia)	1,955	1,952	-0.2	1,948	96.5	0.0	0.4	0.3	2.8	22.8	56.1	21.0	830	93.0	27.5	40.0
Westport town (Dane)	3,935	4,139	5.2	4,061	95.7	0.0	1.4	2.0	0.9	14.3	56.7	29.0	1,821	77.9	23.9	40.5
West Salem village & MCD (La Crosse)	4,799	5,008	4.4	4,895	98.6	0.2	0.3	0.4	0.5	28.1	54.5	17.4	1,860	71.1	37.2	31.9
West Sweden town (Polk)	703	692	-1.6	793	93.4	0.0	0.0	0.6	5.9	23.8	63.0	13.2	310	83.2	53.2	17.7
Weyauwega city & MCD (Waupaca)	1,900	1,875	-1.3	1,709	86.5	0.0	0.0	0.7	12.8	28.2	54.1	17.7	662	63.1	55.7	13.9
Weyauwega town (Waupaca)	583	578	-0.9	500	88.0	0.0	0.0	2.4	9.6	17.2	70.4	12.4	198	83.8	63.1	17.2
Weyerhaeuser village & MCD (Rusk)	238	229	-3.8	227	91.6	2.2	0.0	3.1	3.1	16.7	58.1	25.1	118	75.4	57.6	8.5
Wheatland town (Kenosha)	3,373	3,376	0.1	3,374	88.2	1.9	0.7	4.5	4.7	19.2	62.7	18.0	1,340	95.1	54.2	17.5
Wheatland town (Vernon)	561	575	2.5	566	99.3	0.4	0.0	0.0	0.4	9.5	67.4	23.1	293	89.8	48.8	17.7
Wheaton town (Chippewa)	2,711	2,778	2.5	2,746	92.6	0.0	6.6	0.3	0.5	23.9	64.0	12.0	927	87.4	38.1	20.7
Wheeler village & MCD (Dunn)	343	336	-2.0	340	93.8	0.0	1.2	1.5	3.5	27.6	61.0	11.2	131	52.7	69.5	3.1
Whitefish Bay village & MCD (Milwaukee)	14,110	14,122	0.1	14,132	88.0	2.0	3.7	3.2	3.0	28.1	59.7	12.2	5,367	81.3	10.0	76.1
Whitehall city & MCD (Trempealeau)	1,558	1,573	1.0	1,661	94.5	0.1	0.2	1.1	4.0	23.3	57.7	19.1	708	62.4	53.7	19.1
White Lake village & MCD (Langlade)	352	342	-2.8	303	94.4	0.0	0.0	4.0	1.7	20.4	44.9	34.7	149	66.4	63.8	7.4
Whitelaw village & MCD (Manitowoc)	760	751	-1.2	714	96.4	0.0	0.0	1.1	2.5	18.5	66.8	14.7	304	85.5	57.9	14.1
White Oak Springs town (Lafayette)	118	118	0.0	101	100.0	0.0	0.0	0.0	0.0	17.8	65.3	16.8	44	68.2	47.7	27.3
White River town (Ashland)	921	924	0.3	904	98.0	0.0	0.0	2.0	0.0	40.7	48.8	10.6	281	83.6	52.7	11.0
Whitestown town (Vernon)	502	506	0.8	592	98.8	0.0	0.5	0.0	0.7	29.4	54.4	16.4	211	62.1	62.1	15.2
Whitewater city	14,390	15,040	4.5	14,801	82.9	2.6	2.4	1.6	10.4	13.3	78.3	8.2	4,833	34.7	25.3	24.9
Whitewater city (Jefferson)	3,240	3,095	-4.5	3,205	74.8	4.1	2.3	1.5	17.4	6.7	90.7	2.5	548	32.1	17.5	29.4
Whitewater city (Walworth)	11,150	11,945	7.1	11,596	85.2	2.2	2.4	1.7	8.5	15.2	74.9	9.7	4,285	35.0	26.3	24.3
Whitewater town (Walworth)	1,471	1,488	1.2	1,373	89.3	2.7	1.2	1.4	5.4	19.2	60.2	20.6	547	89.0	23.8	45.2
Whiting village & MCD (Portage)	1,724	1,733	0.5	1,653	89.5	0.0	3.7	0.0	6.8	15.8	48.7	35.4	761	65.4	49.8	22.7
Whittlesey CDP	105	NA	NA	129	100.0	0.0	0.0	0.0	0.0	24.9	67.5	7.8	64	100.0	64.1	9.4
Wien town (Marathon)	825	865	4.8	838	98.1	0.0	0.0	0.5	1.4	34.3	50.6	15.2	269	96.7	57.6	9.3
Wild Rose village & MCD (Waushara)	725	704	-2.9	755	94.8	0.0	0.0	0.4	4.4	15.6	46.2	38.3	318	52.8	58.2	14.2
Wilkinson town (Rusk)	40	40	0.0	30	100.0	0.0	0.0	0.0	0.0	6.6	63.3	30.0	17	100.0	76.5	0.0
Willard town (Rusk)	505	493	-2.4	410	98.8	0.0	0.0	0.7	0.5	20.3	57.9	22.0	190	91.1	64.7	9.5
Williams Bay village & MCD (Walworth)	2,564	2,605	1.6	2,604	84.4	0.4	0.4	2.2	12.7	27.8	49.8	22.4	1,081	71.7	22.6	48.5
Williamstown town (Dodge)	755	748	-0.9	722	100.0	0.0	0.0	0.0	0.0	19.7	63.2	17.2	281	95.0	48.0	16.7
Willow town (Richland)	579	571	-1.4	474	97.3	0.0	0.0	0.8	1.9	24.4	59.1	16.5	181	82.3	45.3	18.8
Willow Springs town (Lafayette)	758	766	1.1	1,023	92.0	0.0	0.0	0.0	8.0	33.1	55.8	11.0	335	80.0	55.8	16.4
Wilmot CDP	442	NA	NA	282	100.0	0.0	0.0	0.0	0.0	15.6	32.9	51.4	183	80.3	86.3	13.7
Wilson town (Dunn)	531	545	2.6	497	97.0	0.0	0.0	0.0	3.0	15.0	66.1	18.7	200	93.5	54.5	11.0

1 May be of any race.

Table A. All Places — **Population and Housing**

STATE City, town, township, borough, or CDP (county if applicable)	2010 census total population	2014 estimated population	Percent change 2010-2014	ACS total population estimate 2010-2014	White alone, not Hispanic or Latino	Black alone, not Hispanic or Latino	Asian alone, not Hispanic or Latino	All other races or 2 or more races, not Hispanic or Latino	Hispanic or Latino[1]	Under 18 years old	Age 18 to 64 years old	Age 65 years and older	Total occupied housing units	Percent owner occupied	High school diploma or less	Bachelor's degree or more
	1	2	3	4	5	6	7	8	9	10	11	12	13	14	15	16
WISCONSIN—Con.																
Wilson town (Eau Claire)..	485	498	2.7	533	98.1	0.0	0.6	1.3	0.0	30.8	58.6	10.5	188	75.0	60.6	10.6
Wilson town (Lincoln)	309	305	-1.3	304	99.0	0.0	0.0	1.0	0.0	15.1	57.5	27.3	139	96.4	50.4	10.8
Wilson town (Rusk)...........	106	104	-1.9	125	92.0	0.0	0.0	0.0	8.0	38.4	46.4	15.2	45	57.8	53.3	22.2
Wilson village & MCD (St. Croix)	184	185	0.5	256	97.3	0.0	0.0	2.7	0.0	26.2	59.4	14.5	90	96.7	28.9	10.0
Wilson town (Sheboygan).	3,328	3,337	0.3	3,323	99.0	0.0	0.2	0.0	0.8	24.0	60.9	15.2	1,264	95.4	25.3	37.9
Wilton village & MCD (Monroe)	514	507	-1.4	534	98.7	0.0	0.0	0.6	0.7	24.9	59.2	15.9	223	76.7	56.1	14.8
Wilton town (Monroe)	1,017	1,040	2.3	1,208	99.3	0.0	0.0	0.7	0.0	37.4	55.3	7.3	283	90.1	64.0	5.3
Winchester town (Vilas)....	383	384	0.3	389	98.7	0.0	0.0	0.0	1.3	12.8	43.8	43.4	205	90.7	36.6	34.1
Winchester CDP	671	NA	NA	620	99.4	0.0	0.0	0.0	0.6	15.2	64.6	20.2	278	93.5	41.4	19.4
Winchester town (Winnebago)	1,763	1,788	1.4	1,672	96.8	0.0	0.0	1.4	1.7	19.2	66.3	14.4	672	93.6	43.6	21.1
Wind Lake CDP	5,342	NA	NA	5,347	97.0	0.0	0.1	1.7	1.3	22.5	63.2	14.3	2,005	86.5	32.3	25.7
Wind Point village & MCD (Racine)	1,723	1,713	-0.6	1,634	94.4	0.2	3.1	0.6	1.8	17.8	58.0	24.3	689	94.8	11.0	64.7
Windsor CDP.................	3,573	NA	NA	3,902	83.8	0.8	4.4	1.6	9.4	22.5	63.7	13.6	1,604	65.6	31.2	33.3
Windsor town (Dane)........	6,340	6,663	5.1	6,517	88.5	0.5	4.1	1.2	5.8	23.8	63.3	12.9	2,546	76.1	26.9	36.2
Winfield town (Sauk)........	859	883	2.8	925	99.5	0.0	0.0	0.5	0.0	24.1	64.2	11.9	355	81.4	41.7	15.5
Wingville town (Grant)	357	356	-0.3	326	92.0	0.6	0.9	0.0	6.4	28.5	58.0	13.5	125	80.0	43.2	32.8
Winneconne village & MCD (Winnebago)	2,383	2,441	2.4	2,506	97.3	0.0	0.0	2.2	0.4	24.8	58.6	16.6	1,066	74.7	38.0	24.6
Winneconne town (Winnebago)	2,350	2,430	3.4	1,993	98.9	0.0	0.0	1.1	0.0	18.9	60.7	20.4	902	94.2	36.5	24.6
Winter village & MCD (Sawyer)	313	302	-3.5	343	91.8	0.0	0.3	7.9	0.0	27.7	48.1	24.2	168	47.6	66.1	10.7
Winter town (Sawyer)	960	934	-2.7	921	82.8	2.8	0.2	9.4	4.7	10.2	70.1	19.5	403	92.8	45.9	19.4
Wiota town (Lafayette)	856	863	0.8	884	100.0	0.0	0.0	0.0	0.0	19.3	65.5	15.4	350	83.1	56.0	14.3
Wisconsin Dells city	2,717	2,712	-0.2	2,369	90.7	0.0	0.0	4.2	5.1	21.2	58.8	19.9	955	60.7	44.7	24.9
Wisconsin Dells city (Adams)	61	60	-1.6	15	100.0	0.0	0.0	0.0	0.0	46.7	53.4	0.0	4	100.0	0.0	100.0
Wisconsin Dells city (Columbia)	2,440	2,432	-0.3	2,182	91.6	0.0	0.0	3.5	4.9	22.6	57.4	19.9	878	60.8	44.1	26.1
Wisconsin Dells city (Juneau)	2	2	0.0	23	100.0	0.0	0.0	0.0	0.0	0.0	69.6	30.4	7	100.0	0.0	0.0
Wisconsin Dells city (Sauk)	214	218	1.9	149	75.8	0.0	0.0	16.1	8.1	2.7	77.9	19.5	66	53.0	60.6	7.6
Wisconsin Rapids city & MCD (Wood)	18,371	17,966	-2.2	18,162	89.8	1.2	3.9	2.2	3.0	22.8	57.5	19.5	8,558	62.8	42.5	17.1
Withee village & MCD (Clark)	487	477	-2.1	528	92.6	0.0	0.0	3.6	3.2	24.5	57.2	18.4	233	68.7	55.4	4.7
Withee town (Clark)	966	953	-1.3	990	96.1	0.0	0.7	2.2	1.0	34.9	52.8	12.3	280	86.4	72.1	3.9
Wittenberg village & MCD (Shawano)	1,081	1,036	-4.2	1,037	87.9	0.8	0.3	8.2	2.8	24.9	52.4	22.8	428	54.9	63.3	7.5
Wittenberg town (Shawano)	833	830	-0.4	834	95.0	1.7	0.0	3.2	0.1	20.9	61.5	17.7	337	84.3	60.2	13.1
Wolf River town (Langlade)	742	727	-2.0	718	98.3	0.7	0.0	0.8	0.1	11.8	59.6	28.6	347	85.3	52.7	19.0
Wolf River town (Winnebago)	1,189	1,202	1.1	1,178	98.1	0.0	0.2	1.2	0.5	17.1	53.8	29.2	528	92.2	54.0	15.7
Wonewoc village & MCD (Juneau)	816	796	-2.5	877	94.1	1.1	0.5	1.0	3.3	23.5	62.4	14.1	347	71.2	65.1	9.8
Wonewoc town (Juneau) ..	687	668	-2.8	669	97.8	0.4	0.0	0.4	1.3	23.1	60.9	16.0	247	88.3	59.1	7.3
Wood town (Wood)	796	767	-3.6	778	98.3	0.0	0.0	1.7	0.0	19.0	63.2	17.9	317	94.3	60.3	13.9
Woodboro town (Oneida)..	811	808	-0.4	843	98.1	0.1	0.0	1.5	0.2	14.3	66.3	19.5	371	87.6	37.7	26.4
Woodford CDP	69	NA	NA	88	100.0	0.0	0.0	0.0	0.0	25.0	64.9	10.2	41	53.7	70.7	0.0
Woodland town (Sauk)	790	813	2.9	1,140	93.0	0.0	0.0	0.0	7.0	37.6	48.6	13.9	342	91.5	50.0	21.3
Woodman village & MCD (Grant)...................	132	130	-1.5	114	92.1	0.0	0.0	0.0	7.9	18.4	62.2	19.3	45	73.3	48.9	4.4
Woodman town (Grant)	185	184	-0.5	157	100.0	0.0	0.0	0.0	0.0	17.2	62.4	20.4	70	85.7	47.1	22.9
Woodmohr town (Chippewa)	930	954	2.6	950	98.4	0.0	0.3	0.2	1.1	24.8	65.6	9.6	339	93.5	56.0	9.1
Wood River town (Burnett)	953	930	-2.4	752	98.3	0.0	0.3	1.5	0.0	19.0	60.9	20.1	338	85.5	39.9	19.5
Woodruff CDP	966	NA	NA	896	92.7	0.0	0.0	3.3	3.9	19.9	48.0	32.1	466	60.3	45.7	8.8
Woodruff town (Oneida) ...	1,987	1,980	-0.4	1,942	92.8	0.0	0.0	4.6	2.5	19.3	50.2	30.5	929	70.9	41.2	19.2
Woodville town (Calumet).	980	987	0.7	882	93.8	0.0	0.8	2.3	3.2	23.2	62.1	14.6	316	91.8	64.2	12.7
Woodville village & MCD (St. Croix)	1,344	1,358	1.0	1,282	97.9	0.3	0.0	1.6	0.2	26.0	59.0	15.1	535	66.9	44.5	15.1
Worcester town (Price)	1,562	1,504	-3.7	1,447	98.5	0.0	0.4	0.6	0.5	15.6	56.6	27.8	708	91.0	45.9	16.5
Worden town (Clark)	666	677	1.7	648	97.1	0.0	0.0	1.1	1.9	29.8	60.2	9.9	228	86.8	64.5	6.1
Wrightstown village..........	2,841	3,308	16.4	3,132	88.8	0.9	0.8	1.0	8.5	32.5	61.3	6.1	1,077	74.0	34.5	27.2
Wrightstown village (Brown)	2,690	3,136	16.6	2,894	87.9	1.0	0.9	1.0	9.2	32.7	60.9	6.5	999	72.0	33.8	26.4
Wrightstown village (Outagamie)................	151	172	13.9	238	100.0	0.0	0.0	0.0	0.0	30.2	67.6	2.1	78	100.0	43.6	37.2
Wrightstown town (Brown)	2,212	2,265	2.4	2,409	85.8	0.0	0.0	8.3	5.9	27.2	65.4	7.4	818	80.4	48.3	19.2
Wyalusing town (Grant)	346	340	-1.7	333	95.2	0.0	0.0	2.4	2.4	14.1	59.1	26.7	158	76.6	49.4	20.9
Wyeville village & MCD (Monroe)	147	147	0.0	155	98.1	0.0	0.0	1.9	0.0	25.8	58.0	16.1	66	81.8	60.6	16.7
Wyocena village & MCD (Columbia)	768	750	-2.3	682	98.1	0.0	0.0	1.3	0.6	17.7	56.7	25.8	252	71.4	49.2	13.9
Wyocena town (Columbia)	1,666	1,669	0.2	1,843	98.5	0.0	0.0	0.8	0.7	21.1	62.4	16.5	727	90.4	48.4	22.6
Wyoming town (Iowa)	302	308	2.0	264	98.5	0.0	0.0	1.1	0.4	11.0	60.5	28.4	147	68.0	34.7	42.9
Wyoming town (Waupaca)	329	325	-1.2	318	98.7	0.0	0.0	0.6	0.6	21.7	56.0	22.3	136	93.4	64.0	12.5
York town (Clark)	886	871	-1.7	979	95.5	0.8	0.0	0.9	2.8	34.5	53.5	11.8	311	93.9	70.7	8.4
York town (Dane).............	652	683	4.8	643	98.1	0.6	0.0	1.2	0.0	17.5	67.1	15.4	260	91.5	40.0	22.3
York town (Green)............	915	931	1.7	997	98.6	0.0	0.7	0.0	0.7	27.0	62.3	10.5	366	91.3	32.8	40.4
Yorkville town (Racine)	3,071	3,095	0.8	3,110	96.7	0.1	0.4	0.5	2.3	20.4	65.2	14.5	1,160	93.0	42.8	24.7
Yuba village & MCD (Richland).................	74	72	-2.7	86	100.0	0.0	0.0	0.0	0.0	5.8	62.9	31.4	53	79.2	66.0	1.9
Zoar CDP.....................	98	NA	NA	183	1.6	0.0	0.0	73.8	24.6	32.3	57.5	10.4	44	61.4	31.8	0.0

1 May be of any race.

Table A. All Places — Population and Housing

STATE City, town, township, borough, or CDP (county if applicable)	2010 census total population	2014 estimated population	Percent change 2010-2014	ACS total population estimate 2010-2014	White alone, not Hispanic or Latino	Black alone, not Hispanic or Latino	Asian alone, not Hispanic or Latino	All other races or 2 or more races, not Hispanic or Latino	Hispanic or Latino[1]	Under 18 years old	Age 18 to 64 years old	Age 65 years and older	Total occupied housing units	Percent owner occupied	High school diploma or less	Bachelor's degree or more
	1	2	3	4	5	6	7	8	9	10	11	12	13	14	15	16
WYOMING	563,767	584,153	3.6	575,251	84.8	1.0	0.9	3.8	9.4	23.8	63.2	13.1	225,514	69.3	34.1	26.0
Afton town	1,916	1,968	2.7	2,065	87.6	0.3	0.0	4.2	7.9	33.8	54.0	12.3	675	76.0	34.4	20.9
Albany CDP	55	NA	NA	40	100.0	0.0	0.0	0.0	0.0	0.0	52.5	47.5	27	100.0	22.2	44.4
Albin town	181	185	2.2	180	78.9	0.0	0.0	0.0	21.1	26.1	62.1	11.7	73	64.4	39.7	11.0
Alcova CDP	76	NA	NA	0	0.0	0.0	0.0	0.0	0.0	0.0	0.0	0.0	0	0.0	0.0	0.0
Alpine town	828	845	2.1	744	82.5	0.8	0.0	1.3	15.3	25.7	71.1	3.2	290	72.8	40.3	28.6
Alpine Northeast CDP	196	NA	NA	10	100.0	0.0	0.0	0.0	0.0	0.0	100.0	0.0	10	0.0	0.0	100.0
Alpine Northwest CDP	244	NA	NA	295	100.0	0.0	0.0	0.0	0.0	5.8	79.1	15.3	162	87.7	76.5	7.4
Alta CDP	394	NA	NA	390	100.0	0.0	0.0	0.0	0.0	27.4	72.6	0.0	204	72.5	21.1	29.4
Antelope Hills CDP	97	NA	NA	0	0.0	0.0	0.0	0.0	0.0	0.0	0.0	0.0	0	0.0	0.0	0.0
Antelope Valley-Crestview CDP	1,658	NA	NA	1,762	94.2	0.0	0.0	5.5	0.3	27.3	66.9	5.9	612	72.2	34.5	28.4
Arapahoe CDP	1,656	NA	NA	1,398	16.1	0.4	0.0	73.6	9.9	33.5	59.5	6.9	330	75.2	43.9	9.1
Arlington CDP	25	NA	NA	33	100.0	0.0	0.0	0.0	0.0	51.5	33.4	15.2	11	45.5	0.0	0.0
Arrowhead Springs CDP	63	NA	NA	22	100.0	0.0	0.0	0.0	0.0	0.0	72.8	27.3	11	100.0	0.0	100.0
Arvada CDP	43	NA	NA	46	100.0	0.0	0.0	0.0	0.0	10.9	73.9	15.2	26	7.7	19.2	26.9
Atlantic City CDP	37	NA	NA	25	100.0	0.0	0.0	0.0	0.0	0.0	72.0	28.0	18	100.0	0.0	100.0
Auburn CDP	328	NA	NA	199	100.0	0.0	0.0	0.0	0.0	11.5	80.4	8.0	101	73.3	50.5	18.8
Baggs town	440	439	-0.2	369	82.1	0.0	0.0	3.0	14.9	29.3	55.2	15.4	146	64.4	47.3	22.6
Bairoil town	106	107	0.9	142	95.8	0.0	0.0	0.0	4.2	13.3	75.2	11.3	64	89.1	39.1	21.9
Bar Nunn town	2,213	2,735	23.6	2,447	88.2	0.4	1.5	2.5	7.4	27.4	63.6	8.8	903	93.4	36.4	17.8
Basin town	1,285	1,300	1.2	1,243	91.9	0.2	1.0	4.5	2.4	20.5	55.3	24.2	449	69.5	39.4	20.5
Bear River town	519	521	0.4	730	91.8	0.0	0.0	1.6	6.6	24.4	68.4	7.1	255	97.6	45.1	14.1
Bedford CDP	201	NA	NA	41	100.0	0.0	0.0	0.0	0.0	19.5	80.5	0.0	18	100.0	0.0	0.0
Bessemer Bend CDP	199	NA	NA	136	89.7	0.0	0.0	0.0	10.3	30.9	52.9	16.2	68	91.2	10.3	29.4
Beulah CDP	73	NA	NA	108	48.1	0.0	0.0	0.0	51.9	0.0	75.0	25.0	52	51.9	0.0	0.0
Big Horn CDP	490	NA	NA	410	100.0	0.0	0.0	0.0	0.0	11.7	81.8	6.6	189	100.0	5.8	24.3
Big Piney town	562	538	-4.3	529	97.4	0.0	0.0	1.5	1.1	23.6	58.0	18.3	196	70.9	48.5	15.3
Bondurant CDP	93	NA	NA	51	100.0	0.0	0.0	0.0	0.0	0.0	52.9	47.1	24	100.0	0.0	0.0
Boulder CDP	170	NA	NA	253	100.0	0.0	0.0	0.0	0.0	53.8	46.2	0.0	67	100.0	0.0	0.0
Boulder Flats CDP	408	NA	NA	413	26.4	1.0	0.0	68.0	4.6	30.0	58.4	11.4	137	86.1	36.5	13.1
Brookhurst CDP	185	NA	NA	201	100.0	0.0	0.0	0.0	0.0	6.0	94.0	0.0	87	37.9	20.7	0.0
Buffalo city	4,585	4,615	0.7	4,620	88.0	0.0	2.1	4.0	6.0	22.9	58.8	18.3	2,110	69.1	40.5	20.0
Burlington town	288	332	15.3	244	89.3	0.0	0.0	5.7	4.9	36.4	48.3	15.2	86	72.1	33.7	18.6
Burns town	301	305	1.3	286	100.0	0.0	0.0	0.0	0.0	25.5	51.9	22.4	124	58.9	33.9	12.9
Byron town	593	609	2.7	691	87.0	0.0	0.0	1.7	11.3	33.7	54.6	11.7	208	81.3	57.2	14.9
Carpenter CDP	94	NA	NA	133	12.8	0.0	0.0	0.0	87.2	76.0	24.1	0.0	17	0.0	100.0	0.0
Carter CDP	10	NA	NA	0	0.0	0.0	0.0	0.0	0.0	0.0	0.0	0.0	0	0.0	0.0	0.0
Casper city	55,323	60,086	8.6	57,815	86.9	1.2	0.9	3.2	7.8	23.8	63.6	12.6	23,535	65.2	30.8	23.8
Casper Mountain CDP	401	NA	NA	316	94.3	0.0	0.0	5.7	0.0	12.0	64.1	24.1	150	100.0	12.7	40.7
Centennial CDP	270	NA	NA	228	77.6	0.0	0.0	18.9	3.5	10.5	76.8	12.7	134	88.1	6.0	53.0
Cheyenne city	59,631	62,845	5.4	61,470	76.7	3.4	1.5	3.4	15.0	24.4	61.8	13.8	25,007	62.4	26.7	28.8
Chugcreek CDP	156	NA	NA	325	100.0	0.0	0.0	0.0	0.0	54.8	45.2	0.0	102	100.0	0.0	0.0
Chugwater town	212	216	1.9	210	91.4	0.0	0.0	1.0	7.6	4.3	74.3	21.4	79	72.2	55.7	13.9
Clearmont town	142	142	0.0	128	76.6	0.0	0.0	0.0	23.4	21.8	64.8	13.3	58	81.0	70.7	10.3
Clearview Acres CDP	795	NA	NA	1,055	77.8	0.0	0.0	1.4	20.8	17.3	69.8	12.9	369	100.0	76.2	0.0
Cody city	9,520	9,740	2.3	9,687	88.6	1.5	1.1	2.7	6.1	22.8	59.6	17.6	3,905	62.5	42.4	29.2
Cokeville town	535	542	1.3	622	96.5	0.0	0.0	0.0	3.5	43.7	44.3	11.9	173	83.2	32.9	22.0
Cora CDP	142	NA	NA	90	100.0	0.0	0.0	0.0	0.0	36.7	34.4	28.9	31	0.0	0.0	0.0
Cowley town	655	718	9.6	789	96.7	0.0	0.0	1.1	2.2	30.5	59.3	10.1	226	85.0	35.0	18.6
Crowheart CDP	141	NA	NA	85	32.9	0.0	0.0	61.2	5.9	0.0	58.8	41.2	49	100.0	22.4	14.3
Daniel CDP	150	NA	NA	274	89.8	0.0	0.0	10.2	0.0	34.3	54.4	11.3	88	79.5	88.6	11.4
Dayton town	759	794	4.6	807	84.8	0.0	0.0	10.9	4.3	22.7	62.1	15.1	359	81.3	30.9	29.0
Deaver town	178	184	3.4	174	93.1	0.0	1.1	0.0	5.7	17.9	72.4	9.8	59	67.8	50.8	15.3
Diamondville town	737	740	0.4	675	83.1	0.9	0.1	6.1	9.8	19.0	64.4	16.7	299	83.9	54.2	14.4
Dixon town	97	97	0.0	78	91.0	0.0	0.0	0.0	9.0	14.1	67.8	17.9	37	97.3	59.5	5.4
Douglas city	6,114	6,423	5.1	6,272	87.5	0.0	1.1	2.5	8.9	26.9	61.8	11.4	2,735	68.0	39.7	16.4
Dubois town	982	998	1.6	740	93.9	3.5	0.0	1.2	1.4	13.2	60.1	26.8	418	62.4	27.5	38.5
East Thermopolis town	254	252	-0.8	299	97.0	0.3	0.0	1.7	1.0	14.7	47.0	38.1	177	41.8	49.2	6.2
Eden CDP	281	NA	NA	254	100.0	0.0	0.0	0.0	0.0	24.0	54.8	21.3	89	70.8	24.7	9.0
Edgerton town	195	199	2.1	401	65.1	0.0	0.0	0.0	34.9	34.4	50.5	15.0	140	62.1	44.3	17.9
Elk Mountain town	191	196	2.6	133	96.2	0.0	0.0	0.0	3.8	18.8	64.0	17.3	63	73.0	38.1	33.3
Encampment town	450	447	-0.7	411	97.1	0.0	0.0	2.9	0.0	16.2	58.0	25.5	204	76.0	30.4	18.1
Esterbrook CDP	52	NA	NA	63	100.0	0.0	0.0	0.0	0.0	0.0	68.3	31.7	45	100.0	75.6	24.4
Ethete CDP	1,553	NA	NA	1,850	4.2	0.3	0.0	88.9	6.6	35.8	59.3	5.0	371	63.3	36.1	8.4
Etna CDP	164	NA	NA	278	100.0	0.0	0.0	0.0	0.0	0.0	72.4	27.7	81	100.0	19.8	0.0
Evanston city	12,387	12,190	-1.6	12,253	84.9	0.1	0.1	3.3	11.6	31.4	60.5	8.0	4,368	63.3	44.5	21.6
Evansville town	2,535	2,831	11.7	2,776	83.6	1.6	0.0	1.2	13.6	29.1	61.9	9.0	1,111	69.2	52.3	5.9
Fairview CDP	275	NA	NA	357	100.0	0.0	0.0	0.0	0.0	29.4	63.5	7.3	92	95.7	14.1	21.7
Farson CDP	313	NA	NA	458	100.0	0.0	0.0	0.0	0.0	32.5	60.3	7.0	170	63.5	18.2	48.2
Fontenelle CDP	13	NA	NA	0	0.0	0.0	0.0	0.0	0.0	0.0	0.0	0.0	0	0.0	0.0	0.0
Fort Bridger CDP	345	NA	NA	214	94.9	0.0	0.0	0.0	5.1	0.0	66.0	34.1	131	71.8	51.9	9.2
Fort Laramie town	230	227	-1.3	188	100.0	0.0	0.0	0.0	0.0	3.7	54.4	42.0	102	87.3	53.9	11.8
Fort Washakie CDP	1,759	NA	NA	1,899	7.2	1.2	0.0	85.9	5.7	37.5	50.3	12.2	472	53.0	40.7	17.6
Fox Farm-College CDP	3,647	NA	NA	3,959	78.8	0.1	0.0	2.2	18.9	21.6	68.0	10.3	1,532	70.5	50.7	10.8
Fox Park CDP	0	NA	NA	0	0.0	0.0	0.0	0.0	0.0	0.0	0.0	0.0	0	0.0	0.0	0.0
Frannie town	157	162	3.2	153	61.4	2.6	19.6	7.8	8.5	36.6	45.2	18.3	63	74.6	42.9	14.3
Freedom CDP	214	NA	NA	319	86.8	0.0	0.0	0.0	13.2	50.5	49.5	0.0	86	39.5	11.6	10.5
Garland CDP	115	NA	NA	141	91.5	0.0	0.0	0.0	8.5	0.0	100.0	0.0	73	47.9	47.9	19.2
Gillette city	29,812	31,971	7.2	31,110	86.2	1.2	0.8	1.9	10.0	29.6	64.5	5.9	11,342	68.9	41.6	20.8
Glendo town	205	201	-2.0	334	96.7	0.0	0.0	1.2	2.1	20.4	63.6	16.2	127	63.0	33.9	4.7
Glenrock town	2,575	2,583	0.3	2,576	85.5	1.2	0.0	5.6	7.7	22.7	61.5	15.6	1,039	68.0	41.7	15.1
Granger town	139	140	0.7	206	84.0	0.0	0.0	0.0	16.0	29.1	64.2	6.8	71	77.5	67.6	0.0
Green River city	12,515	12,630	0.9	12,600	83.5	0.4	0.1	2.1	14.0	27.8	63.7	8.6	4,434	71.3	39.0	22.0
Greybull town	1,847	1,868	1.1	2,116	80.5	0.0	0.3	1.9	17.2	24.1	58.8	17.1	803	73.3	51.1	13.7
Grover CDP	147	NA	NA	248	100.0	0.0	0.0	0.0	0.0	36.3	54.7	8.9	77	85.7	31.2	40.3
Guernsey town	1,147	1,193	4.0	1,271	83.0	0.1	1.7	0.4	14.9	19.4	58.3	22.3	545	67.0	36.5	14.5
Hanna town	841	831	-1.2	798	87.2	1.8	0.0	2.4	8.6	18.5	59.2	22.3	354	75.1	54.0	9.0
Hartrandt CDP	693	NA	NA	850	89.8	0.0	0.0	0.0	10.2	28.7	65.6	5.8	349	42.1	30.9	2.9

1 May be of any race.

Table A. All Places — **Population and Housing**

STATE City, town, township, borough, or CDP (county if applicable)	2010 census total population	2014 estimated population	Percent change 2010-2014	ACS total population estimate 2010-2014	White alone, not Hispanic or Latino	Black alone, not Hispanic or Latino	Asian alone, not Hispanic or Latino	All other races or 2 or more races, not Hispanic or Latino	Hispanic or Latino[1]	Under 18 years old	Age 18 to 64 years old	Age 65 years and older	Total occupied housing units	Percent owner occupied	High school diploma or less	Bachelor's degree or more
	1	2	3	4	5	6	7	8	9	10	11	12	13	14	15	16
WYOMING—Con.																
Hartville town	62	62	0.0	73	86.3	0.0	0.0	0.0	13.7	1.4	69.8	28.8	34	94.1	52.9	29.4
Hawk Springs CDP	45	NA	NA	44	95.5	0.0	0.0	0.0	4.5	0.0	79.6	20.5	16	56.3	25.0	0.0
Hillsdale CDP	47	NA	NA	122	100.0	0.0	0.0	0.0	0.0	50.0	50.0	0.0	61	100.0	0.0	0.0
Hill View Heights CDP	170	NA	NA	50	100.0	0.0	0.0	0.0	0.0	0.0	56.0	44.0	24	100.0	33.3	25.0
Hoback CDP	1,176	NA	NA	1,344	90.7	0.0	0.0	0.0	9.3	16.1	76.6	7.3	568	79.6	25.0	43.1
Homa Hills CDP	278	NA	NA	262	100.0	0.0	0.0	0.0	0.0	24.8	61.4	13.7	112	70.5	45.5	0.0
Hudson town	461	462	0.2	521	83.1	0.0	0.0	16.1	0.8	31.9	56.6	11.5	193	62.7	50.3	13.0
Hulett town	383	400	4.4	399	98.7	1.0	0.0	0.3	0.0	28.4	61.9	9.8	153	71.2	47.1	13.1
Huntley CDP	30	NA	NA	0	0.0	0.0	0.0	0.0	0.0	0.0	0.0	0.0	0	0.0	0.0	0.0
Hyattville CDP	75	NA	NA	37	100.0	0.0	0.0	0.0	0.0	0.0	51.3	48.6	19	100.0	0.0	73.7
Jackson town	9,621	10,449	8.6	9,967	67.5	0.1	3.2	2.6	26.6	20.5	74.2	5.2	3,328	39.7	34.5	43.5
James Town CDP	536	NA	NA	529	87.0	9.6	0.0	3.4	0.0	11.7	55.9	32.3	283	82.0	45.2	14.1
Jeffrey City CDP	58	NA	NA	0	0.0	0.0	0.0	0.0	0.0	0.0	0.0	0.0	0	0.0	0.0	0.0
Johnstown CDP	242	NA	NA	306	45.1	0.0	0.0	51.3	3.6	28.1	51.0	20.9	97	87.6	35.1	9.3
Kaycee town	263	260	-1.1	228	94.3	0.0	0.0	0.0	5.7	32.0	53.9	14.0	98	70.4	44.9	25.5
Kelly CDP	138	NA	NA	45	100.0	0.0	0.0	0.0	0.0	0.0	100.0	0.0	13	0.0	0.0	0.0
Kemmerer city	2,656	2,732	2.9	2,672	91.8	0.0	0.0	1.0	7.1	25.8	63.5	10.7	1,001	77.3	38.5	21.7
Kirby town	92	93	1.1	128	99.2	0.0	0.0	0.0	0.8	24.2	65.5	10.2	47	85.1	66.0	10.6
La Barge town	551	553	0.4	581	86.2	0.0	0.3	13.4	0.0	28.8	65.2	6.0	202	80.7	40.1	5.0
La Grange town	448	455	1.6	403	88.1	0.0	0.0	1.7	10.2	24.3	68.9	6.7	98	55.1	13.3	18.4
Lakeview North CDP	84	NA	NA	40	100.0	0.0	0.0	0.0	0.0	0.0	100.0	0.0	21	100.0	100.0	0.0
Lance Creek CDP	43	NA	NA	25	100.0	0.0	0.0	0.0	0.0	32.0	68.0	0.0	8	100.0	37.5	0.0
Lander city	7,480	7,642	2.2	7,627	79.6	0.1	0.8	13.3	6.1	24.4	59.0	16.7	3,076	61.8	36.8	33.4
Laramie city	30,815	32,081	4.1	31,601	82.9	1.6	3.4	2.5	9.6	16.4	76.6	7.1	12,992	43.9	15.1	44.6
Lingle town	468	467	-0.2	653	98.8	0.0	0.0	0.8	0.5	32.8	54.4	13.0	188	84.0	29.8	21.8
Little America CDP	68	NA	NA	34	100.0	0.0	0.0	0.0	0.0	0.0	100.0	0.0	34	0.0	100.0	0.0
Lonetree CDP	49	NA	NA	0	0.0	0.0	0.0	0.0	0.0	0.0	0.0	0.0	0	0.0	0.0	0.0
Lost Springs town	4	4	0.0	6	100.0	0.0	0.0	0.0	0.0	0.0	0.0	100.0	6	100.0	0.0	0.0
Lovell town	2,360	2,404	1.9	2,409	86.8	0.0	0.2	2.9	10.1	28.5	54.1	17.4	891	64.0	40.1	14.7
Lucerne CDP	535	NA	NA	688	96.7	0.0	2.0	1.3	0.0	22.3	56.7	21.2	282	89.0	37.2	31.2
Lusk town	1,567	1,578	0.7	1,780	89.7	0.0	1.0	5.8	3.5	16.2	67.3	16.6	688	57.3	33.3	20.3
Lyman town	2,104	2,077	-1.3	2,186	91.9	0.0	0.0	1.4	6.7	33.0	61.0	6.0	714	81.8	46.4	14.3
McKinnon CDP	60	NA	NA	0	0.0	0.0	0.0	0.0	0.0	0.0	0.0	0.0	0	0.0	0.0	0.0
Mammoth CDP	263	NA	NA	302	99.3	0.7	0.0	0.0	0.0	0.0	95.7	4.3	131	0.0	0.0	58.8
Manderson town	114	117	2.6	98	86.7	0.0	0.0	6.1	7.1	24.5	50.9	24.5	45	82.2	51.1	13.3
Manville town	95	93	-2.1	50	88.0	12.0	0.0	0.0	0.0	10.0	16.0	74.0	27	77.8	88.9	0.0
Marbleton town	1,082	1,114	3.0	1,188	87.5	0.0	0.0	2.9	9.7	32.2	60.2	7.6	374	77.5	45.2	13.9
Meadow Acres CDP	198	NA	NA	108	89.8	0.0	0.0	10.2	0.0	0.0	77.7	22.2	44	100.0	38.6	20.5
Medicine Bow town	284	277	-2.5	237	90.7	0.0	0.0	2.1	7.2	23.3	44.4	32.5	103	78.6	57.3	9.7
Meeteetse town	327	327	0.0	286	94.8	0.0	0.0	4.9	0.3	16.3	58.9	24.5	151	70.2	41.1	31.8
Midwest town	404	412	2.0	426	93.4	1.2	0.0	0.7	4.7	29.1	63.3	7.5	155	76.8	44.5	12.9
Mills town	3,463	3,690	6.6	3,545	88.9	0.6	0.0	3.2	7.3	24.4	63.2	12.3	1,600	53.0	50.7	5.1
Moorcroft town	1,009	1,036	2.7	1,169	95.5	0.0	0.0	0.5	4.0	28.8	62.5	8.6	452	59.3	39.6	16.6
Moose Wilson Road CDP	1,821	NA	NA	2,009	92.7	0.0	0.0	0.2	7.0	22.6	71.1	6.4	696	68.4	3.0	75.1
Mountain View CDP	96	NA	NA	67	100.0	0.0	0.0	0.0	0.0	0.0	77.6	22.4	67	89.6	64.2	10.4
Mountain View town	1,290	1,304	1.1	1,343	84.4	0.7	0.0	7.1	7.7	35.2	55.7	9.2	462	72.3	45.9	19.0
Newcastle city	3,533	3,513	-0.6	3,495	87.2	0.3	2.8	2.6	7.0	24.0	57.4	18.6	1,367	70.0	41.0	14.4
Nordic CDP	602	NA	NA	657	90.0	0.0	10.0	0.0	0.0	19.9	80.2	0.0	317	70.0	16.4	35.6
North Rock Springs CDP	2,207	NA	NA	2,239	82.1	0.0	0.0	0.7	17.2	29.2	62.3	8.4	859	85.7	53.6	16.2
Oakley CDP	49	NA	NA	0	0.0	0.0	0.0	0.0	0.0	0.0	0.0	0.0	0	0.0	0.0	0.0
Opal town	96	99	3.1	65	95.4	0.0	1.5	0.0	3.1	10.7	87.7	1.5	28	92.9	46.4	0.0
Orin CDP	46	NA	NA	55	100.0	0.0	0.0	0.0	0.0	27.2	72.7	0.0	21	100.0	52.4	0.0
Osage CDP	208	NA	NA	282	100.0	0.0	0.0	0.0	0.0	12.8	58.6	28.7	152	67.1	82.2	7.2
Osmond CDP	397	NA	NA	362	100.0	0.0	0.0	0.0	0.0	41.6	49.5	8.8	89	100.0	15.7	27.0
Owl Creek CDP	5	NA	NA	0	0.0	0.0	0.0	0.0	0.0	0.0	0.0	0.0	0	0.0	0.0	0.0
Parkman CDP	151	NA	NA	156	100.0	0.0	0.0	0.0	0.0	9.6	79.5	10.9	75	84.0	64.0	16.0
Pavillion town	233	240	3.0	220	85.5	0.0	0.0	11.4	3.2	18.2	68.6	13.2	90	80.0	35.6	27.8
Pine Bluffs town	1,129	1,146	1.5	1,035	83.8	0.6	0.0	5.4	10.2	21.0	53.1	26.1	471	81.3	33.1	27.2
Pinedale town	2,026	1,958	-3.4	1,913	85.3	0.0	5.5	0.7	8.5	31.6	58.6	9.7	644	52.6	27.8	33.1
Pine Haven town	490	498	1.6	429	89.5	0.0	0.0	1.2	9.3	18.9	61.7	19.6	203	96.1	39.4	22.2
Point of Rocks CDP	0	NA	NA	83	88.0	0.0	0.0	0.0	12.0	41.0	59.0	0.0	40	100.0	15.0	57.5
Powder River CDP	44	NA	NA	13	100.0	0.0	0.0	0.0	0.0	0.0	100.0	0.0	8	100.0	0.0	0.0
Powell city	6,314	6,407	1.5	6,365	88.7	0.4	0.3	2.3	8.3	22.3	61.2	16.5	2,499	76.5	37.3	21.2
Purple Sage CDP	535	NA	NA	755	77.6	0.0	0.0	0.0	22.4	41.0	59.0	0.0	231	35.1	64.1	10.8
Rafter J Ranch CDP	1,075	NA	NA	1,431	92.2	0.0	0.0	0.0	7.8	13.4	75.1	11.4	555	77.7	11.5	68.5
Ralston CDP	280	NA	NA	173	93.6	0.0	0.0	6.4	0.0	35.3	36.5	28.3	67	100.0	38.8	31.3
Ranchester town	857	943	10.0	889	95.4	0.4	0.0	3.1	1.0	26.3	59.1	14.6	371	71.7	34.2	20.2
Ranchettes CDP	5,798	NA	NA	6,028	88.0	0.3	0.6	0.6	10.5	19.3	61.4	19.3	2,319	94.0	21.9	43.5
Rawlins city	9,259	9,227	-0.3	9,198	70.4	1.5	1.3	1.9	24.9	23.1	66.2	10.7	3,419	66.0	46.2	18.5
Red Butte CDP	449	NA	NA	451	73.8	0.0	8.4	2.0	15.7	13.1	73.4	13.5	190	100.0	23.2	35.3
Reliance CDP	714	NA	NA	650	94.9	0.0	0.0	0.0	5.1	30.5	66.9	2.6	249	86.3	51.4	32.1
Riverside town	52	53	1.9	66	98.5	0.0	0.0	1.5	0.0	6.1	50.1	43.9	35	100.0	42.9	22.9
Riverton city	10,695	10,953	2.4	10,902	77.9	0.9	0.4	11.6	9.2	22.4	63.4	14.1	4,459	62.8	39.9	19.2
Robertson CDP	97	NA	NA	172	100.0	0.0	0.0	0.0	0.0	27.9	72.1	0.0	74	100.0	0.0	0.0
Rock River town	245	245	0.0	250	81.2	2.4	0.0	0.0	16.4	16.8	63.2	20.0	108	72.2	16.7	23.1
Rock Springs city	23,036	24,045	4.4	23,684	76.6	1.2	1.2	3.5	17.5	26.6	64.7	8.7	9,128	67.5	42.6	18.9
Rolling Hills town	438	439	0.2	522	89.1	0.0	0.0	5.4	5.6	34.8	57.5	7.5	147	98.6	47.6	19.0
Ryan Park CDP	38	NA	NA	0	0.0	0.0	0.0	0.0	0.0	0.0	0.0	0.0	0	0.0	0.0	0.0
Saratoga town	1,690	1,692	0.1	1,929	90.6	0.0	0.5	2.4	6.5	24.1	58.6	17.4	811	85.5	41.7	23.8
Shell CDP	83	NA	NA	58	58.6	0.0	0.0	13.8	27.6	0.0	89.7	10.3	30	46.7	0.0	0.0
Sheridan city	17,450	17,916	2.7	17,699	90.0	1.1	1.0	2.8	5.2	22.3	60.7	17.0	7,703	62.3	32.5	29.2
Shoshoni town	649	655	0.9	550	77.6	2.2	0.0	6.4	13.8	16.6	59.9	23.6	263	72.2	58.6	12.9
Sinclair town	433	424	-2.1	407	94.6	0.0	0.0	0.2	5.2	23.2	67.9	9.1	172	77.3	27.9	22.1
Slater CDP	80	NA	NA	95	100.0	0.0	0.0	0.0	0.0	0.0	49.4	50.5	69	100.0	30.4	69.6
Sleepy Hollow CDP	1,308	NA	NA	1,050	96.5	0.0	0.0	1.5	2.0	22.2	76.0	1.8	393	97.2	48.1	24.2
Smoot CDP	195	NA	NA	274	95.3	0.0	0.0	0.0	4.7	64.6	35.4	0.0	42	100.0	0.0	28.6
South Greeley CDP	4,217	NA	NA	4,702	73.4	2.6	0.3	2.0	21.7	27.0	64.7	8.2	1,751	76.6	39.9	11.4
South Park CDP	1,731	NA	NA	1,502	96.7	0.0	0.0	0.0	3.3	28.0	60.7	11.3	571	79.3	4.2	64.6
Star Valley Ranch town	1,503	1,541	2.5	1,334	88.2	0.0	0.0	6.4	5.4	18.3	57.3	24.4	569	92.8	27.6	41.1
Story CDP	828	NA	NA	957	100.0	0.0	0.0	0.0	0.0	19.4	55.3	25.2	451	65.4	31.9	43.0
Sundance town	1,182	1,239	4.8	1,266	99.1	0.0	0.4	0.5	0.1	16.8	57.2	26.1	584	79.8	28.4	27.1

1 May be of any race.

STATE City, town, township, borough, or CDP (county if applicable)	Population				Race and Hispanic or Latino origin (percent), 2010–2014					Age (percent), 2010–2014			Households, 2010–2014			
								All other races or 2 or more races, not Hispanic or Latino							Householders by level of education (percent)	
	2010 census total population	2014 estimated population	Percent change 2010-2014	ACS total population estimate 2010-2014	White alone, not Hispanic or Latino	Black alone, not Hispanic or Latino	Asian alone, not Hispanic or Latino		Hispanic or Latino[1]	Under 18 years old	Age 18 to 64 years old	Age 65 years and older	Total occupied housing units	Percent owner occupied	High school diploma or less	Bachelor's degree or more
	1	2	3	4	5	6	7	8	9	10	11	12	13	14	15	16
WYOMING—Con.																
Superior town	336	332	-1.2	209	80.9	0.0	0.0	1.0	18.2	36.8	55.9	7.2	70	72.9	21.4	17.1
Table Rock CDP	0	NA	NA	0	0.0	0.0	0.0	0.0	0.0	0.0	0.0	0.0	0	0.0	0.0	0.0
Taylor CDP.....................	90	NA	NA	66	100.0	0.0	0.0	0.0	0.0	31.8	41.0	27.3	25	100.0	40.0	0.0
Ten Sleep town	260	253	-2.7	300	95.3	0.0	0.0	2.3	2.3	14.7	56.2	29.0	132	68.2	43.9	15.9
Teton Village CDP............	330	NA	NA	121	100.0	0.0	0.0	0.0	0.0	23.1	76.8	0.0	69	15.9	18.8	81.2
Thayne town	366	364	-0.5	432	87.5	0.7	0.0	0.5	11.3	33.7	57.4	9.0	141	61.0	55.3	14.2
Thermopolis town	3,009	3,020	0.4	2,899	94.8	0.0	0.0	2.1	3.1	22.1	53.3	24.6	1,375	72.4	35.3	22.2
Torrington city	6,501	6,736	3.6	6,732	85.2	0.4	0.1	2.7	11.6	17.8	62.4	19.8	2,642	70.6	32.5	24.6
Turnerville CDP	192	NA	NA	236	100.0	0.0	0.0	0.0	0.0	0.0	35.1	64.8	114	100.0	18.4	0.0
Upton town	1,100	1,104	0.4	871	97.7	0.0	0.0	1.3	1.0	22.2	59.8	17.9	435	64.1	43.4	15.4
Urie CDP	262	NA	NA	423	96.2	0.0	0.0	0.0	3.8	14.2	65.0	20.8	154	75.3	34.4	22.7
Van Tassell town	15	15	0.0	7	100.0	0.0	0.0	0.0	0.0	28.6	71.5	0.0	3	100.0	33.3	0.0
Veteran CDP....................	23	NA	NA	10	100.0	0.0	0.0	0.0	0.0	0.0	0.0	100.0	10	100.0	0.0	0.0
Vista West CDP	951	NA	NA	904	100.0	0.0	0.0	0.0	0.0	17.3	72.0	10.8	345	92.5	34.2	21.4
Wamsutter town	451	503	11.5	371	73.9	4.0	2.4	4.3	15.4	30.0	66.1	4.0	125	54.4	44.0	15.2
Warren AFB CDP	3,072	NA	NA	2,746	65.8	11.4	1.2	7.0	14.6	30.3	68.5	1.3	686	1.9	17.2	35.9
Washam CDP...................	51	NA	NA	41	100.0	0.0	0.0	0.0	0.0	0.0	100.0	0.0	12	100.0	0.0	100.0
Westview Circle CDP........	52	NA	NA	31	100.0	0.0	0.0	0.0	0.0	0.0	100.0	0.0	31	100.0	100.0	0.0
Wheatland town	3,627	3,659	0.9	3,633	87.3	0.0	0.0	1.4	11.2	20.9	53.1	26.0	1,585	68.3	36.5	23.7
Whiting CDP	83	NA	NA	149	100.0	0.0	0.0	0.0	0.0	0.0	41.6	58.4	90	100.0	0.0	50.0
Wilson CDP	1,482	NA	NA	1,647	95.3	0.0	1.8	2.9	0.0	17.2	55.4	27.5	625	80.2	17.4	41.3
Woods Landing-Jelm CDP	97	NA	NA	33	100.0	0.0	0.0	0.0	0.0	0.0	63.6	36.4	23	100.0	0.0	0.0
Worland city....................	5,487	5,366	-2.2	5,445	80.7	0.0	0.2	2.2	16.9	27.0	55.5	17.6	2,265	62.6	41.8	19.2
Wright town.....................	1,807	1,847	2.2	2,373	85.5	0.2	0.2	2.5	11.7	34.4	62.6	3.1	807	64.6	49.7	12.3
Yoder town	151	161	6.6	124	96.8	0.0	0.0	1.6	1.6	37.9	46.7	15.3	42	83.3	42.9	26.2
Y-O Ranch CDP...............	195	NA	NA	188	92.0	0.0	0.0	0.0	8.0	14.9	85.1	0.0	66	100.0	19.7	0.0

1 May be of any race.

TABLE B.

Incorporated Places, Census Designated Places (CDPs), and Minor Civil Divisions (MCDs) of 10,000 or More Population

(For explanation of symbols see page xvi)

Table B—Incorporated Places, Census Designated Places (CDPs), and Minor Civil Divisions (MCDs) of 10,000 or More Population

513

Table B. Incorporated Places, Census Designated Places (CDPs), and Minor Civil Divisions (MCDs) of 10,000 or More Population — **Land Area, Population, and Households, and Employment**

STATE City, town, township, borough, or CDP (county if applicable)	Land area,[1] 2010 (sq mi)	Population: Total persons 2010	Population: Total persons 2014	Population: Percent change 2010–2014	Population: Persons per square mile, 2014	Population characteristics 2010–2014: Foreign born	Population characteristics 2010–2014: Lives in same house as previous year	Household income and poverty, 2010–2014: Median household income (dollars	Household income and poverty, 2010–2014: Percent of households: Income of $100,000 or more	Household income and poverty, 2010–2014: Percent of households: Income below poverty level	Employment,[2] 2010–2014: Percent in labor force	Employment,[2] 2010–2014: Unemployment rate	Households, 2010–2014 (percent of households): Family households	Households, 2010–2014 (percent of households): One person households
	1	2	3	4	5	6	7	8	9	10	11	12	13	14
United States	3,531,905.283	308,758,105	318,907,401	3.3	90.3	13.1	85.0	$53,482	23.1	14.4	63.9	9.2	66.2	27.6
ALABAMA	50,645.324	4,780,127	4,849,377	1.4	95.8	3.5	85.0	$43,511	16.3	18.2	58.8	10.2	67.3	28.5
Alabaster city	24.458	30,360	31,545	3.9	1,289.7	8.4	88.7	$70,173	27.2	8.2	70.7	5.6	76.9	20.5
Albertville city	26.538	21,127	21,458	1.6	808.6	17.8	82.2	$36,210	13.5	19.4	61.5	6.0	71.2	26.0
Alexander City city	40.848	14,875	14,849	-0.2	363.5	4.0	84.4	$30,500	7.6	25.5	51.7	11.1	71.6	25.4
Anniston city	45.641	23,120	22,457	-2.9	492.0	2.0	80.1	$31,399	10.9	27.8	54.2	16.3	57.7	37.8
Athens city	39.518	21,891	24,522	12.0	620.5	5.1	87.3	$47,354	20.1	15.1	60.2	9.9	64.2	32.4
Atmore city	21.852	10,194	10,006	-1.8	457.9	1.1	88.2	$24,165	8.7	30.2	41.5	18.1	66.2	33.2
Auburn city	58.832	53,393	60,258	12.9	1,024.2	10.0	64.1	$37,406	19.2	32.8	59.1	8.2	48.0	31.4
Bessemer city	40.464	27,463	26,949	-1.9	666.0	2.5	83.8	$30,369	7.9	28.9	51.2	14.2	62.2	33.8
Birmingham city	146.025	212,193	212,247	0.0	1,453.5	3.4	78.8	$31,217	8.4	28.3	59.0	14.5	54.0	39.3
Calera city	24.091	11,606	12,972	11.8	538.5	2.6	85.0	$61,481	12.7	6.6	72.9	7.6	70.6	24.1
Center Point city	6.204	16,924	16,777	-0.9	2,704.2	1.8	80.2	$38,828	8.6	20.6	64.9	10.0	71.2	23.8
Chelsea city	21.788	10,488	11,758	12.1	539.7	4.3	85.8	$85,106	37.0	3.6	70.7	2.6	79.6	15.1
Cullman city	19.362	14,802	15,145	2.3	782.2	5.0	81.5	$37,995	12.4	22.2	52.7	6.7	60.9	36.6
Daphne city	16.441	21,581	24,395	13.0	1,483.8	2.9	77.1	$61,986	26.5	9.0	68.0	7.8	64.8	29.7
Decatur city	54.107	55,704	55,532	-0.3	1,026.3	7.6	85.5	$42,867	16.4	17.4	62.7	10.4	62.8	33.4
Dothan city	89.415	65,916	68,409	3.8	765.1	2.6	84.4	$42,026	16.0	18.1	60.1	8.6	65.8	30.1
Enterprise city	30.620	26,615	27,772	4.3	907.0	5.9	81.6	$51,692	22.2	16.6	60.5	7.2	67.8	27.8
Eufaula city	59.389	13,134	12,781	-2.7	215.2	3.1	87.4	$37,393	13.0	21.2	59.2	15.7	67.7	29.8
Fairfield city	3.469	11,117	10,988	-1.2	3,167.4	0.5	80.7	$34,556	11.5	23.6	56.0	14.4	58.4	40.0
Fairhope city	12.051	15,338	18,089	17.9	1,501.1	6.2	88.0	$58,767	27.4	9.6	54.6	5.9	66.5	30.6
Florence city	26.104	39,339	40,215	2.2	1,540.5	2.8	79.0	$35,632	11.2	25.3	55.9	8.2	55.3	38.0
Foley city	29.269	14,658	16,243	10.8	554.9	4.4	83.7	$43,202	8.5	14.1	51.0	12.7	61.0	33.4
Forestdale CDP	6.869	10,162	NA	NA	NA	1.5	88.0	$49,000	14.8	12.5	60.5	11.0	75.5	21.0
Fort Payne city	56.773	14,113	14,125	0.1	248.8	15.3	86.8	$34,689	8.2	23.4	59.4	12.1	61.1	36.7
Gadsden city	37.263	36,879	36,295	-1.6	974.0	3.2	81.7	$27,922	7.8	26.8	50.7	13.2	60.5	35.6
Gardendale city	22.691	13,881	13,729	-1.1	605.0	1.5	89.2	$56,852	21.8	8.7	60.7	4.0	70.6	26.8
Gulf Shores city	26.480	10,113	10,963	8.4	414.0	5.7	75.2	$45,777	14.1	16.5	61.1	16.4	69.1	27.4
Hartselle city	16.344	14,247	14,459	1.5	884.7	0.8	83.8	$53,221	17.1	10.6	65.5	13.5	74.3	23.9
Helena city	20.836	16,951	17,883	5.5	858.3	2.7	92.8	$86,018	35.9	3.7	77.1	5.7	75.5	21.4
Homewood city	8.362	25,165	25,802	2.5	3,085.7	7.1	75.7	$62,431	29.8	12.5	70.1	4.4	58.8	31.4
Hoover city	46.976	81,024	84,353	4.1	1,795.7	8.9	83.1	$76,469	37.5	5.4	68.7	5.7	68.3	27.8
Hueytown city	19.429	16,104	15,815	-1.8	814.0	1.4	86.9	$41,768	13.2	13.7	58.2	8.8	68.7	28.6
Huntsville city	212.401	180,241	188,226	4.4	886.2	6.6	81.2	$49,060	23.1	16.4	64.8	10.9	58.2	36.8
Irondale city	17.317	12,354	12,444	0.7	718.6	7.3	87.6	$48,361	14.0	18.7	63.9	9.9	61.8	33.5
Jacksonville city	9.924	12,556	12,250	-2.4	1,234.4	2.6	65.4	$38,192	11.3	30.5	56.5	16.6	58.6	25.3
Jasper city	28.527	14,386	14,109	-1.9	494.6	2.2	79.8	$40,786	17.8	21.6	55.0	11.7	69.8	26.6
Leeds city	22.482	11,772	11,939	1.4	531.0	5.2	88.0	$50,805	15.8	14.1	60.5	8.5	71.2	26.9
Madison city	29.606	42,939	46,450	8.2	1,568.9	7.8	84.8	$92,965	46.5	6.4	70.5	7.3	71.8	23.5
Millbrook city	12.819	14,637	15,169	3.6	1,183.3	1.1	85.3	$60,489	18.7	7.9	69.7	5.6	70.5	26.1
Mobile city	139.161	195,243	194,675	-0.3	1,398.9	3.2	83.4	$39,241	14.4	21.6	58.4	12.0	59.9	34.8
Montgomery city	159.800	205,595	200,481	-2.5	1,254.6	4.5	77.3	$43,535	16.8	20.8	61.9	9.3	62.6	32.0
Moody city	24.494	11,727	12,457	6.2	508.6	1.0	87.0	$60,829	16.7	10.7	64.2	5.1	71.7	24.4
Mountain Brook city	12.830	20,484	20,734	1.2	1,616.1	2.3	90.1	$130,259	61.7	3.6	63.0	2.2	77.7	21.2
Muscle Shoals city	15.550	13,156	13,614	3.5	875.5	0.4	90.8	$50,502	14.5	11.6	58.8	6.9	69.5	27.4
Northport city	16.737	23,360	24,709	5.8	1,476.3	2.6	82.5	$54,354	17.7	11.3	63.2	6.8	66.5	29.4
Opelika city	59.650	26,425	29,171	10.4	489.0	6.2	83.5	$39,506	15.2	21.0	60.3	6.8	65.9	30.1
Oxford city	30.822	21,329	21,155	-0.8	686.4	3.8	84.4	$50,934	18.7	12.6	62.7	13.1	76.1	21.9
Ozark city	34.091	14,899	14,700	-1.3	431.2	2.2	86.3	$38,392	11.4	21.0	55.4	9.8	59.5	35.4
Pelham city	38.839	21,448	22,699	5.8	584.4	8.2	88.1	$68,197	29.1	4.9	74.5	6.5	68.6	26.7
Pell City city	24.878	12,684	13,573	7.0	545.6	1.8	77.0	$40,961	16.9	17.4	56.9	12.2	69.1	27.6
Phenix City city	27.980	32,871	37,540	14.2	1,341.7	2.5	75.7	$36,225	11.8	22.5	63.5	11.5	62.9	32.5
Pleasant Grove city	9.897	10,110	10,325	2.1	1,043.3	0.8	88.4	$64,278	23.4	7.5	60.2	6.8	80.5	17.5
Prattville city	33.038	33,974	35,317	4.0	1,069.0	1.9	80.3	$57,478	24.2	10.6	65.1	7.3	67.9	27.1
Prichard city	25.316	22,671	22,312	-1.6	881.3	1.2	84.5	$21,860	4.0	37.0	49.1	20.9	62.8	33.5
Saks CDP	12.152	10,744	NA	NA	NA	3.6	87.2	$42,414	15.3	18.2	60.6	13.6	68.4	27.1
Saraland city	24.679	13,631	13,744	0.8	556.9	4.7	85.9	$53,646	17.2	11.9	60.2	9.4	71.7	22.9
Scottsboro city	50.655	14,778	14,748	-0.2	291.1	4.0	89.1	$36,470	11.7	16.1	54.0	10.4	64.8	32.5
Selma city	13.809	20,756	19,814	-4.5	1,434.8	0.9	86.5	$21,635	7.7	38.9	48.8	23.6	55.8	41.5
Sylacauga city	20.251	12,864	12,703	-1.3	627.3	1.6	83.0	$31,587	11.4	30.7	54.2	13.6	68.4	28.6
Talladega city	25.504	16,082	16,012	-0.4	627.8	4.0	82.5	$30,307	8.8	28.6	50.3	22.0	65.5	30.2
Tillmans Corner CDP	12.972	17,398	NA	NA	NA	3.5	81.0	$46,773	11.8	17.0	61.1	10.3	73.1	22.4
Troy city	28.218	18,180	19,138	5.3	678.2	5.1	75.1	$32,015	15.5	33.4	61.3	10.3	59.2	26.4
Trussville city	33.241	19,997	20,702	3.5	622.8	1.7	89.6	$86,518	42.2	4.9	67.4	5.5	80.5	18.1
Tuscaloosa city	61.465	90,524	96,122	6.2	1,563.8	4.8	73.2	$38,762	15.3	23.4	54.9	8.8	57.8	33.0
Vestavia Hills city	19.570	34,055	34,124	0.2	1,743.7	6.4	88.1	$81,352	43.1	5.2	63.5	3.6	67.3	29.8
ALASKA	570,640.925	710,249	736,732	3.7	1.3	7.1	80.9	$71,829	33.0	8.5	70.8	8.4	67.0	25.5
Anchorage municipality	1,704.880	291,826	301,010	3.1	176.6	9.7	80.3	$78,121	37.5	6.5	74.1	6.9	66.6	25.0
Badger CDP	65.636	19,482	NA	NA	NA	3.0	80.3	$78,157	34.1	5.3	75.4	8.8	69.7	21.3
College CDP	18.781	12,964	NA	NA	NA	7.0	69.4	$75,871	36.9	6.3	71.4	8.2	60.1	29.4
Fairbanks city	31.693	31,535	32,469	3.0	1,024.5	7.3	64.8	$55,778	20.5	12.1	71.9	11.5	62.2	29.8
Juneau city and borough	2,702.013	31,275	32,406	3.6	12.0	6.9	82.2	$84,750	38.4	5.5	71.7	5.6	65.3	25.7
Knik-Fairview CDP	83.101	14,923	NA	NA	NA	3.7	84.6	$81,534	36.6	7.9	65.4	11.0	73.3	20.3
ARIZONA	113,594.079	6,392,310	6,731,484	5.3	59.3	13.5	80.9	$49,928	19.6	15.6	60.1	9.9	65.7	27.2
Anthem CDP	7.986	21,700	NA	NA	NA	5.7	80.0	$79,351	37.4	4.3	65.0	7.1	81.5	16.3
Apache Junction city	34.995	35,838	38,131	6.4	1,089.6	7.4	82.0	$36,771	8.5	21.6	45.5	16.3	64.3	29.3
Avondale city	45.183	76,130	79,646	4.6	1,762.8	15.6	81.9	$57,170	18.5	14.9	69.9	9.5	77.6	15.4
Buckeye town	392.151	50,891	59,470	16.9	151.7	11.0	79.3	$58,703	17.1	13.7	53.8	9.0	80.0	15.3
Bullhead City city	59.382	39,540	39,364	-0.4	662.9	10.8	75.6	$37,121	8.5	16.1	50.0	14.5	62.4	30.4
Camp Verde town	43.119	10,873	11,097	2.1	257.4	2.3	77.4	$35,809	8.0	23.5	49.8	12.7	65.6	30.9
Casa Grande city	110.256	48,583	51,478	6.0	466.9	11.0	81.8	$44,719	12.7	14.8	55.1	11.7	71.2	24.4

1 Dry land or land partially or temporarily covered by water.
2 16 years old and over.

Table B. Incorporated Places, Census Designated Places (CDPs), and Minor Civil Divisions (MCDs) of 10,000 or More Population — **Crime, Construction, and Local Government Finance**

STATE City, town, township, borough, or CDP (county if applicable)	Serious crimes known to police, 2014[1] Total number	Rate[2] Total	Rate[2] Violent	Rate[2] Property	New residential construction authorized by building permits, 2014 Value ($1,000)	Number of housing units	Percent single family	Local government finance, 2012 — General revenue Total (mil dol)	Intergovernmental Total (mil dol)	Intergovernmental Percent from state gov.	Taxes per capita[3]	General expenditure Total (mil dol)	Per capita[3] Total	Per capita[3] Capital outlays	Debt outstanding (mil dol)
	15	16	17	18	19	20	21	22	23	24	25	26	27	28	29
United States	9,443,212	2962	366	2596	193,243,022	1,046,363	60.6	X	X	X	X	X	X	X	X
ALABAMA	174,821	3605	427	3178	2,204,675	13,369	71.1	X	X	X	X	X	X	X	X
Alabaster city	670	2122	184	1939	18,578	214	100.0	27.6	0.0	0.0	619	23.9	773	0	101.5
Albertville city	779	3597	106	3491	686	5	100.0	31.7	5.3	100.0	756	28.5	1,329	238	71.2
Alexander City city	797	5354	544	4810	3,582	16	100.0	21.9	1.7	82.0	813	25.8	1,750	179	36.1
Anniston city	2,247	9957	2375	7582	193	2	100.0	37.9	3.9	94.7	1266	46.5	2,041	345	39.6
Athens city	757	3087	24	3063	20,531	136	58.8	30.3	0.6	63.8	745	74.7	3,185	797	118.6
Atmore city	354	3507	733	2774	129	2	0.0	7.0	0.0	0.0	619	7.8	770	335	0.0
Auburn city	1,780	2974	211	2763	155,035	615	69.4	94.7	3.9	77.7	1135	67.3	1,180	135	229.8
Bessemer city	2,226	8258	1339	6918	311	1	100.0	51.9	5.8	81.8	1279	52.4	1,924	4	103.0
Birmingham city	17,298	8155	1588	6567	105,012	1,005	7.6	436.4	42.3	52.9	1583	466.4	2,207	235	573.7
Calera city	NA	NA	NA	NA	17,460	120	100.0	14.9	0.0	0.0	823	14.1	1,136	80	52.2
Center Point city	NA	NA	NA	NA	0	0	0.0	3.9	1.1	100.0	161	3.6	213	43	0.0
Chelsea city	NA	NA	NA	NA	24,346	110	100.0	4.4	0.0	54.1	370	3.9	357	56	6.3
Cullman city	702	4653	172	4481	8,886	57	89.5	32.5	1.4	100.0	1327	35.4	2,382	84	115.8
Daphne city	518	2148	170	1978	28,040	167	100.0	29.2	1.9	18.6	1012	29.1	1,272	300	40.7
Decatur city	2,563	4590	201	4390	7,793	37	100.0	174.2	68.7	100.0	1103	202.0	3,616	209	508.8
Dothan city	1,998	2918	304	2614	57,161	289	60.9	93.4	4.5	88.0	1046	98.8	1,467	83	84.7
Enterprise city	1,059	3778	375	3403	9,539	54	100.0	30.6	1.8	95.9	826	32.1	1,155	209	79.9
Eufaula city	551	4280	567	3713	1,608	8	75.0	16.9	1.3	99.9	720	14.0	1,082	28	19.7
Fairfield city	909	8330	1090	7239	0	0	0.0	10.4	0.0	0.0	709	8.5	770	0	61.4
Fairhope city	618	3450	301	3148	65,214	266	100.0	23.9	0.6	63.0	758	23.5	1,425	91	38.8
Florence city	1,678	4170	502	3668	5,905	45	100.0	64.7	4.1	76.8	1107	58.6	1,477	59	116.3
Foley city	834	5180	317	4863	27,345	172	100.0	35.7	3.0	33.4	1475	31.7	2,068	177	33.5
Forestdale CDP	NA	NA	NA	NA	NA	NA	NA	NA	NA	NA	NA	NA	NA	NA	NA
Fort Payne city	NA	NA	NA	NA	2,018	16	100.0	19.6	0.6	90.7	975	20.0	1,423	102	20.9
Gadsden city	3,164	8679	982	7697	651	11	100.0	64.3	6.9	28.4	1206	60.4	1,647	45	75.3
Gardendale city	591	4315	212	4103	6,112	34	100.0	17.8	1.2	100.0	849	14.3	1,037	0	5.6
Gulf Shores city	NA	NA	NA	NA	34,878	132	97.0	31.4	1.2	57.4	2161	29.3	2,789	96	45.9
Hartselle city	349	2404	124	2280	4,852	37	100.0	17.1	0.7	100.0	690	16.6	1,152	86	26.1
Helena city	162	915	96	819	32,228	153	100.0	7.2	0.4	100.0	284	6.9	398	12	3.3
Homewood city	1,101	4251	259	3992	7,867	19	100.0	54.6	1.8	36.5	1996	51.4	2,034	100	49.2
Hoover city	2,357	2778	116	2663	109,394	413	100.0	104.2	6.8	51.4	998	95.0	1,143	78	108.5
Hueytown city	636	4023	272	3751	115	1	100.0	11.1	0.5	0.0	542	9.8	612	10	2.6
Huntsville city	10,628	5665	782	4883	116,562	1,874	47.9	329.0	28.2	93.3	1186	337.4	1,836	440	774.8
Irondale city	461	3722	468	3253	4,531	34	100.0	25.3	1.3	11.8	927	13.3	1,073	40	67.3
Jacksonville city	527	4229	538	3691	956	4	100.0	11.4	0.6	79.6	668	11.3	907	141	4.3
Jasper city	1,231	8680	811	7869	1,431	7	100.0	27.5	4.9	97.6	1162	28.3	1,991	262	23.2
Leeds city	583	4885	511	4374	4,011	31	100.0	17.4	0.2	100.0	1332	13.1	1,108	273	20.9
Madison city	1,093	2354	323	2031	130,024	338	100.0	51.4	5.9	79.3	777	50.2	1,117	123	75.1
Millbrook city	753	4947	486	4461	9,783	71	100.0	12.1	0.5	100.0	559	12.4	829	33	23.8
Mobile city	13,091	5223	594	4629	22,235	109	100.0	353.3	20.4	65.4	1275	344.5	1,767	296	547.6
Montgomery city	10,071	5031	522	4508	73,538	571	52.0	280.1	36.3	46.1	830	218.0	1,065	80	275.9
Moody city	236	1881	120	1761	6,439	53	100.0	3.2	0.0	0.0	247	1.5	121	0	0.9
Mountain Brook city	221	1087	49	1038	32,567	48	100.0	36.6	4.5	22.7	1414	38.1	1,869	514	4.5
Muscle Shoals city	831	6117	331	5786	11,702	99	100.0	25.6	2.1	56.8	1345	19.4	1,450	81	22.7
Northport city	1,082	4369	363	4006	29,324	118	100.0	25.4	3.5	100.0	660	22.1	919	0	38.2
Opelika city	1,810	6198	644	5555	29,672	135	100.0	54.6	2.4	35.3	1425	51.4	1,834	224	162.2
Oxford city	1,113	5248	344	4904	10,762	87	86.2	40.1	0.8	100.0	1517	30.4	1,430	272	103.4
Ozark city	967	6514	451	6063	554	8	100.0	16.8	1.7	60.6	788	15.9	1,066	102	6.4
Pelham city	433	1924	89	1835	20,583	91	100.0	33.9	0.0	0.0	1133	30.2	1,367	21	68.0
Pell City city	305	2254	140	2114	5,119	26	100.0	17.6	2.3	100.0	1053	19.4	1,479	133	58.7
Phenix City city	2,499	6462	644	5818	21,553	113	100.0	33.7	1.9	100.0	717	36.4	1,007	213	139.4
Pleasant Grove city	132	1266	115	1151	615	3	100.0	4.1	0.2	23.6	296	6.2	600	0	0.0
Prattville city	1,355	3814	228	3586	34,660	131	100.0	35.5	1.0	99.2	765	28.2	814	6	61.2
Prichard city	1,642	7349	1410	5939	296	3	100.0	9.3	0.1	0.0	328	9.7	432	4	1.1
Saks CDP	NA	NA	NA	NA	NA	NA	NA	NA	NA	NA	NA	NA	NA	NA	NA
Saraland city	571	4157	299	3859	20,172	95	100.0	18.8	0.5	23.4	968	16.6	1,219	21	45.3
Scottsboro city	661	4452	431	4021	6,657	38	100.0	53.4	23.6	92.3	1409	55.4	3,742	94	66.5
Selma city	2,340	11875	1370	10505	0	0	0.0	21.4	2.2	100.0	876	35.1	1,728	29	27.3
Sylacauga city	805	6328	558	5770	528	2	100.0	16.2	0.5	100.0	865	14.3	1,116	56	35.7
Talladega city	1,157	7323	785	6538	268	2	100.0	26.7	9.9	17.9	716	17.4	1,077	179	28.5
Tillmans Corner CDP	NA	NA	NA	NA	NA	NA	NA	NA	NA	NA	NA	NA	NA	NA	NA
Troy city	1,068	5593	660	4933	5,501	44	95.5	45.6	3.8	100.0	638	47.8	2,600	209	49.0
Trussville city	NA	NA	NA	NA	42,053	185	100.0	26.5	0.2	100.0	1197	23.4	1,164	16	83.2
Tuscaloosa city	4,604	4775	483	4292	166,832	1,232	23.2	163.4	34.6	20.3	834	163.0	1,750	124	198.6
Vestavia Hills city	478	1406	65	1341	43,841	109	100.0	34.2	1.8	33.1	857	34.6	1,017	160	41.6
ALASKA	25,018	3396	636	2760	353,712	1,518	74.1	X	X	X	X	X	X	X	X
Anchorage municipality	14,136	4692	865	3827	211,518	770	74.3	1296.8	572.1	91.3	1830	1251.1	4,190	417	1789.0
Badger CDP	NA	NA	NA	NA	NA	NA	NA	NA	NA	NA	NA	NA	NA	NA	NA
College CDP	NA	NA	NA	NA	NA	NA	NA	NA	NA	NA	NA	NA	NA	NA	NA
Fairbanks city	1,461	4499	659	3840	0	0	0.0	42.7	11.6	100.0	659	39.7	1,220	110	2.3
Juneau city and borough	1,061	3216	573	2643	29,697	204	33.3	316.5	94.8	75.9	2561	302.2	9,325	1,605	193.0
Knik-Fairview CDP	NA	NA	NA	NA	NA	NA	NA	NA	NA	NA	NA	NA	NA	NA	NA
ARIZONA	242,156	3597	400	3198	5,666,004	26,997	62.4	X	X	X	X	X	X	X	X
Anthem CDP	NA	NA	NA	NA	NA	NA	NA	NA	NA	NA	NA	NA	NA	NA	NA
Apache Junction city	1,323	3549	247	3303	5,259	41	92.7	26.7	11.0	100.0	316	29.2	793	0	10.8
Avondale city	3,797	4778	287	4491	12,222	42	100.0	84.4	25.7	100.0	523	73.8	945	93	93.9
Buckeye town	1,170	2013	50	1963	194,595	749	100.0	61.1	12.9	69.2	512	48.2	882	7	160.3
Bullhead City city	1,684	4281	206	4075	14,497	61	100.0	48.4	17.4	91.6	286	42.5	1,075	35	73.4
Camp Verde town	309	2795	326	2469	1,760	9	100.0	4.4	1.6	94.8	217	4.3	390	4	2.7
Casa Grande city	2,035	4053	478	3575	23,901	106	100.0	70.3	17.3	83.1	586	77.3	1,541	234	119.9

1 Data for serious crimes have not been adjusted for underreporting. This may affect comparability between geographic areas over time.
2 Per 100,000 population estimated by the FBI. 3 Based on population estimated as of July 1 of the year shown.

Table B. Incorporated Places, Census Designated Places (CDPs), and Minor Civil Divisions (MCDs) of 10,000 or More Population — **Land Area, Population, and Households, and Employment**

STATE City, town, township, borough, or CDP (county if applicable)	Land area,[1] 2010 (sq mi)	Total persons 2010	Total persons 2014	Percent change 2010–2014	Persons per square mile, 2014	Foreign born	Lives in same house as previous year	Median household income (dollars)	Income of $100,000 or more	Income below poverty level	Percent in labor force	Unemploy-ment rate	Family households	One person households
	1	2	3	4	5	6	7	8	9	10	11	12	13	14
ARIZONA—Con.														
Casas Adobes CDP	26.813	66,795	NA	NA	NA	9.5	81.0	$56,164	21.3	9.5	64.7	9.0	63.4	30.2
Catalina Foothills CDP	41.871	50,796	NA	NA	NA	13.0	84.4	$79,568	39.0	6.4	55.6	6.1	60.7	33.7
Chandler city	64.587	236,167	254,276	7.7	3,937.0	14.5	79.9	$72,072	33.0	8.3	73.0	6.7	69.9	23.1
Chino Valley town	63.371	10,817	11,019	1.9	173.9	5.4	86.0	$43,238	8.7	16.0	48.9	7.9	69.1	23.2
Coolidge city	56.488	11,825	12,209	3.2	216.1	5.9	74.0	$40,875	9.3	20.8	55.6	13.4	73.0	21.8
Cottonwood city	16.588	11,271	11,595	2.9	699.0	17.3	75.6	$32,712	6.8	17.6	51.1	12.2	59.5	35.8
Douglas city	9.991	17,504	16,744	-4.3	1,675.9	25.5	78.2	$26,222	5.9	30.7	33.5	12.2	73.9	24.4
Drexel Heights CDP	20.201	27,749	NA	NA	NA	17.2	86.4	$45,981	12.7	16.4	63.4	12.0	75.8	18.3
El Mirage city	9.888	31,797	33,532	5.5	3,391.3	15.7	86.6	$47,564	10.0	15.6	63.8	9.1	76.3	18.7
Eloy city	112.522	16,676	16,738	0.4	148.8	22.5	74.7	$27,701	4.9	33.4	26.3	19.7	70.8	25.4
Flagstaff city	64.409	66,067	68,785	4.1	1,067.9	7.6	70.2	$48,120	20.3	22.6	69.7	8.5	57.6	25.1
Florence town	62.015	25,526	26,912	5.4	434.0	21.9	63.1	$48,503	8.4	13.7	15.2	7.2	62.6	32.2
Flowing Wells CDP	4.026	16,419	NA	NA	NA	12.6	85.4	$34,397	5.9	19.7	55.4	11.2	58.0	34.3
Fort Mohave CDP	16.697	14,364	NA	NA	NA	11.6	79.7	$41,466	9.5	9.7	53.2	17.0	67.2	27.7
Fortuna Foothills CDP	40.171	26,265	NA	NA	NA	10.7	86.3	$51,886	15.0	9.5	37.9	9.7	71.3	22.6
Fountain Hills town	20.326	22,489	23,573	4.8	1,159.7	6.8	84.9	$72,462	31.5	2.9	54.6	7.7	65.9	29.3
Gilbert town	67.871	208,399	239,277	14.8	3,525.5	9.3	80.9	$81,485	38.5	6.4	73.6	6.3	77.8	16.1
Glendale city	58.754	226,437	237,517	4.9	4,042.6	16.8	81.8	$46,855	17.8	18.8	64.2	11.1	68.1	25.7
Goodyear city	191.196	65,225	75,664	16.0	395.7	10.8	82.9	$70,293	28.0	8.6	59.6	6.6	78.6	17.7
Green Valley CDP	32.243	21,391	NA	NA	NA	6.7	87.4	$46,732	15.0	5.0	17.4	6.9	57.3	38.3
Kingman city	34.820	28,068	28,549	1.7	819.9	4.8	71.5	$42,859	10.0	16.9	49.4	11.0	60.0	29.6
Lake Havasu City city	46.177	52,532	53,103	1.1	1,150.0	6.2	82.2	$42,718	11.9	12.1	48.5	10.8	66.9	26.4
Marana town	120.732	34,575	39,888	15.4	330.4	8.0	80.0	$74,817	30.2	3.5	64.8	7.3	77.6	17.8
Maricopa city	47.474	43,482	47,442	9.1	999.3	9.2	83.7	$65,214	22.9	4.8	66.3	7.4	76.2	17.5
Mesa city	137.602	439,865	464,704	5.6	3,377.2	12.4	79.8	$48,259	17.9	14.0	61.9	9.1	65.1	27.8
New Kingman-Butler CDP	4.969	12,134	NA	NA	NA	4.8	83.5	$25,701	4.4	27.4	51.7	24.7	60.8	30.8
New River CDP	56.086	14,952	NA	NA	NA	4.3	87.2	$76,022	39.3	5.8	70.6	6.3	77.3	17.5
Nogales city	20.817	20,837	20,407	-2.1	980.3	39.5	83.9	$27,567	9.5	33.3	55.9	14.9	73.8	24.1
Oro Valley town	35.469	41,007	42,018	2.5	1,184.6	7.6	84.3	$74,480	35.1	5.7	52.8	7.4	71.2	24.3
Paradise Valley town	15.408	12,780	13,663	6.9	886.7	11.0	91.0	$134,097	59.5	8.9	52.8	3.3	75.7	21.7
Payson town	19.466	15,299	15,245	-0.4	783.2	4.9	86.6	$42,987	9.3	12.4	43.4	8.9	65.4	30.4
Peoria city	175.346	154,083	166,934	8.3	952.0	9.1	85.8	$63,025	26.5	8.6	64.5	7.6	70.4	24.2
Phoenix city	517.506	1,447,617	1,537,058	6.2	2,970.1	20.2	79.8	$46,881	19.0	19.2	65.8	9.9	63.3	28.7
Prescott city	41.360	39,827	40,958	2.8	990.3	6.2	76.1	$45,190	16.8	15.0	44.3	11.2	54.8	37.1
Prescott Valley town	38.663	38,822	41,075	5.8	1,062.4	6.5	80.4	$42,973	8.9	14.0	57.7	10.0	67.7	26.0
Queen Creek town	28.220	26,348	32,236	22.3	1,142.3	4.0	78.6	$83,809	41.6	7.0	69.5	4.2	84.1	13.6
Rio Rico CDP	62.257	18,962	NA	NA	NA	32.0	88.3	$50,754	14.4	13.5	59.9	10.3	82.2	12.6
Sahuarita town	31.123	25,259	27,547	9.1	885.1	10.0	84.2	$65,183	22.0	4.4	59.5	3.8	78.1	17.0
San Luis city	32.087	27,909	31,091	11.4	969.0	45.2	89.4	$31,064	3.3	32.3	53.1	17.2	90.6	7.6
San Tan Valley CDP	36.681	81,321	NA	NA	NA	7.5	76.7	$59,874	17.4	9.4	65.6	9.2	80.2	15.8
Scottsdale city	183.941	217,434	230,512	6.0	1,253.2	10.7	81.1	$72,455	36.7	8.2	63.9	6.3	57.9	33.5
Sedona city	19.032	10,036	10,281	2.4	540.2	15.3	82.3	$50,133	23.3	8.0	56.9	8.9	53.9	38.9
Show Low city	65.145	10,667	10,841	1.6	166.4	3.6	78.8	$39,795	10.8	16.8	53.0	16.1	68.0	28.2
Sierra Vista city	152.404	45,140	43,806	-3.0	287.4	8.7	74.0	$58,818	23.8	11.9	63.9	8.2	69.3	26.1
Sierra Vista Southeast CDP	110.865	14,797	NA	NA	NA	7.7	89.5	$53,593	27.2	12.3	51.2	9.4	71.8	24.2
Somerton city	7.417	14,297	14,912	4.3	2,010.5	39.3	87.2	$31,178	5.8	32.7	63.7	17.0	89.6	8.0
Sun City CDP	14.418	37,499	NA	NA	NA	4.6	86.6	$36,464	5.4	7.6	18.7	13.6	49.4	46.4
Sun City West CDP	10.869	24,535	NA	NA	NA	6.1	90.0	$45,157	12.9	5.1	10.9	8.5	55.6	41.4
Sun Lakes CDP	5.344	13,975	NA	NA	NA	5.8	90.1	$52,937	14.8	6.5	19.8	8.1	60.8	34.4
Surprise city	107.853	117,517	126,275	7.5	1,170.8	8.8	86.1	$59,094	20.5	9.0	55.8	9.4	74.4	21.5
Tanque Verde CDP	32.926	16,901	NA	NA	NA	6.2	89.1	$95,019	47.4	5.5	58.7	7.3	78.6	17.4
Tempe city	39.988	161,781	172,816	6.8	4,321.7	13.3	67.0	$48,183	19.4	20.4	69.3	9.0	48.5	33.2
Tucson city	230.805	520,561	527,972	1.4	2,287.5	14.9	74.9	$37,149	11.4	22.7	61.7	12.1	55.3	35.5
Tucson Estates CDP	12.994	12,192	NA	NA	NA	6.1	80.7	$44,556	9.0	14.9	45.9	18.9	63.6	30.0
Vail CDP	22.674	10,208	NA	NA	NA	6.1	86.8	$82,935	37.9	5.2	61.4	2.8	81.5	15.7
Valencia West CDP	10.448	9,355	NA	NA	NA	14.5	90.6	$55,561	15.5	11.7	70.0	8.4	76.2	17.5
Verde Village CDP	6.962	11,605	NA	NA	NA	7.6	81.8	$44,375	12.8	17.2	60.2	12.8	69.5	27.2
Yuma city	120.636	90,702	93,400	3.0	774.2	20.9	76.5	$44,166	13.4	16.4	61.9	12.4	73.8	20.5
ARKANSAS	52,035.475	2,915,958	2,966,369	1.7	57.0	4.6	83.8	$41,264	14.1	18.2	59.2	8.4	67.2	27.9
Arkadelphia city	7.260	10,714	10,649	-0.6	1,466.7	3.5	72.5	$29,848	12.2	31.1	53.0	6.5	54.5	40.2
Batesville city	11.424	10,243	10,497	2.5	918.9	10.3	81.0	$37,150	16.4	17.9	57.9	6.4	64.7	30.1
Bella Vista town	44.262	26,461	27,688	4.6	625.5	3.6	87.6	$62,500	24.3	4.9	49.9	5.1	75.9	19.6
Benton city	22.225	30,683	33,625	9.6	1,512.9	2.6	86.9	$52,341	22.0	12.0	64.2	5.5	68.4	25.6
Bentonville city	31.471	35,300	41,613	17.9	1,322.3	12.8	73.7	$71,461	33.1	9.1	69.1	5.0	69.4	22.5
Blytheville city	20.772	15,620	14,884	-4.7	716.5	2.6	83.2	$32,832	11.6	25.2	59.8	10.8	63.3	31.5
Bryant city	20.792	16,691	19,625	17.6	943.9	1.8	88.8	$63,448	22.0	5.1	71.6	3.1	66.8	27.8
Cabot city	20.209	23,792	25,627	7.7	1,268.1	3.0	83.4	$57,635	21.1	12.0	69.9	6.2	73.2	22.0
Camden city	16.446	12,183	11,569	-5.0	703.4	1.4	87.1	$26,229	8.3	28.2	53.4	10.8	60.3	37.8
Centerton city	11.757	9,526	11,193	17.5	952.0	7.6	80.5	$58,007	26.5	5.0	76.1	3.7	76.8	17.2
Conway city	45.544	58,906	64,490	9.5	1,416.0	4.5	76.9	$47,126	19.0	18.1	67.0	7.0	58.9	30.0
El Dorado city	16.266	18,884	18,352	-2.8	1,128.2	2.2	81.2	$33,725	10.3	24.6	58.9	13.5	64.5	31.5
Fayetteville city	54.007	73,581	80,621	9.6	1,492.8	7.1	65.9	$37,350	20.2	26.4	65.6	7.0	46.6	37.2
Forrest City city	16.291	15,371	14,823	-3.6	909.9	4.0	79.6	$28,656	7.1	31.5	41.9	13.9	64.3	31.8
Fort Smith city	63.156	86,261	87,351	1.3	1,383.1	12.4	82.6	$36,777	12.7	21.8	60.3	6.6	61.5	33.1
Harrison city	11.088	12,941	13,130	1.5	1,184.1	2.7	78.9	$32,495	8.8	21.4	54.9	7.8	59.0	36.2
Helena-West Helena city	13.332	12,282	11,320	-7.8	849.1	0.7	79.3	$22,451	8.6	38.9	58.7	21.9	62.8	33.2
Hope city	10.014	10,095	10,004	-0.9	999.0	11.1	85.1	$24,423	4.7	29.8	55.5	10.1	63.1	33.8
Hot Springs city	35.020	35,193	35,673	1.4	1,018.6	6.0	77.5	$31,302	9.3	27.0	53.1	11.7	55.1	38.4
Hot Springs Village CDP	57.168	12,807	NA	NA	NA	3.1	91.8	$54,326	19.3	5.0	24.9	7.9	71.6	25.5
Jacksonville city	28.969	28,388	28,808	1.5	994.4	5.9	75.9	$40,720	10.3	14.8	62.3	7.5	64.2	28.6
Jonesboro city	80.341	67,388	72,210	7.2	898.8	5.1	71.7	$40,583	16.3	23.2	62.5	8.9	64.2	27.4
Little Rock city	119.343	193,524	197,706	2.2	1,656.6	6.8	83.7	$46,409	20.2	16.7	65.9	6.8	57.6	36.7
Magnolia city	13.242	11,577	11,489	-0.8	867.6	3.6	73.3	$34,461	13.1	32.4	54.9	9.4	62.3	29.0
Malvern city	8.671	10,320	10,826	4.9	1,248.5	1.4	76.5	$30,983	8.7	24.3	50.0	8.5	61.3	33.7

1 Dry land or land partially or temporarily covered by water.
2 16 years old and over.

Table B. Incorporated Places, Census Designated Places (CDPs), and Minor Civil Divisions (MCDs) of 10,000 or More Population — **Crime, Construction, and Local Government Finance**

STATE City, town, township, borough, or CDP (county if applicable)	Serious crimes known to police, 2014[1]				New residential construction authorized by building permits, 2014			Local government finance, 2012							
		Rate[2]						General revenue				General expenditure			
									Intergovernmental				Per capita[3]		
	Total number	Total	Violent	Property	Value ($1,000)	Number of housing units	Percent single family	Total (mil dol)	Total (mil dol)	Percent from state gov.	Taxes per capita[3]	Total (mil dol)	Total	Capital outlays	Debt outstanding (mil dol)
	15	16	17	18	19	20	21	22	23	24	25	26	27	28	29
ARIZONA—Con.															
Casas Adobes CDP	NA	NA	NA	NA	NA	NA	NA	NA	NA	NA	NA	NA	NA	NA	NA
Catalina Foothills CDP	NA	NA	NA	NA	NA	NA	NA	NA	NA	NA	NA	NA	NA	NA	NA
Chandler city	6,109	2421	185	2236	339,919	1,683	38.8	333.6	72.6	90.2	617	266.6	1,089	179	579.4
Chino Valley town	370	3370	692	2678	2,012	29	100.0	9.3	3.7	100.0	364	9.8	907	53	21.7
Coolidge city	550	4645	414	4231	660	5	100.0	14.0	5.3	90.8	502	13.3	1,109	113	5.0
Cottonwood city	534	4648	348	4299	4,186	29	100.0	17.7	4.0	100.0	828	18.3	1,620	116	102.4
Douglas city	NA	NA	NA	NA	7,948	76	5.3	20.1	5.7	82.8	407	17.3	1,022	61	24.3
Drexel Heights CDP	NA	NA	NA	NA	NA	NA	NA	NA	NA	NA	NA	NA	NA	NA	NA
El Mirage city	1,071	3216	168	3047	13,185	69	100.0	30.1	8.5	100.0	290	33.0	1,011	114	27.3
Eloy city	583	3429	500	2929	14,497	87	95.4	57.2	47.6	16.7	375	54.1	3,108	110	10.9
Flagstaff city	3,295	4742	396	4346	67,761	383	40.5	130.0	35.8	90.1	801	120.0	1,768	130	118.5
Florence town	182	726	128	598	47,676	146	100.0	23.1	8.7	80.8	254	20.6	772	122	18.6
Flowing Wells CDP	NA	NA	NA	NA	NA	NA	NA	NA	NA	NA	NA	NA	NA	NA	NA
Fort Mohave CDP	NA	NA	NA	NA	NA	NA	NA	NA	NA	NA	NA	NA	NA	NA	NA
Fortuna Foothills CDP	NA	NA	NA	NA	NA	NA	NA	NA	NA	NA	NA	NA	NA	NA	NA
Fountain Hills town	NA	NA	NA	NA	24,440	48	91.7	17.1	6.0	100.0	433	15.7	679	0	13.9
Gilbert town	3,730	1584	90	1494	277,937	1,484	96.7	261.7	63.3	83.0	614	189.6	854	154	479.5
Glendale city	13,499	5701	389	5312	8,641	21	100.0	324.3	103.3	81.2	625	226.0	974	13	1053.0
Goodyear city	1,684	2251	148	2102	227,127	842	94.1	108.3	19.5	99.3	864	78.8	1,135	56	426.4
Green Valley CDP	NA	NA	NA	NA	NA	NA	NA	NA	NA	NA	NA	NA	NA	NA	NA
Kingman city	1,544	5413	256	5157	26,920	149	100.0	39.6	14.2	100.0	439	31.4	1,108	1	55.1
Lake Havasu City city	1,197	2263	166	2097	44,837	246	94.3	80.6	21.3	85.8	509	98.9	1,874	405	321.9
Marana town	1,090	2777	51	2726	172,027	639	100.0	50.4	18.1	58.5	760	43.7	1,189	179	94.8
Maricopa city	738	1613	175	1439	61,825	284	100.0	36.8	14.6	100.0	428	33.5	747	45	19.3
Mesa city	15,059	3259	459	2800	333,102	1,010	99.6	511.1	172.3	70.6	346	601.2	1,330	186	1494.6
New Kingman-Butler CDP	NA	NA	NA	NA	NA	NA	NA	NA	NA	NA	NA	NA	NA	NA	NA
New River CDP	NA	NA	NA	NA	NA	NA	NA	NA	NA	NA	NA	NA	NA	NA	NA
Nogales city	587	2880	236	2644	626	2	100.0	29.6	8.4	92.1	550	24.9	1,198	0	78.8
Oro Valley town	665	1592	36	1556	60,908	134	100.0	29.7	10.8	100.0	373	29.9	723	49	64.1
Paradise Valley town	189	1396	44	1352	53,074	50	100.0	20.6	3.3	100.0	959	21.7	1,635	162	10.4
Payson town	431	2828	361	2468	19,604	63	100.0	18.8	6.6	76.5	490	18.9	1,248	82	4.1
Peoria city	3,543	2151	148	2003	260,674	1,039	99.4	190.2	41.3	95.5	566	239.6	1,498	187	511.6
Phoenix city	65,726	4296	572	3724	935,003	5,138	31.3	2902.9	848.4	63.4	663	2651.7	1,780	445	8278.0
Prescott city	1,370	3342	344	2998	58,066	204	100.0	74.7	16.1	77.8	761	77.2	1,928	429	73.2
Prescott Valley town	1,016	2538	220	2318	74,912	337	97.6	38.2	14.1	87.4	357	41.2	1,051	74	104.9
Queen Creek town	NA	NA	NA	NA	269,930	693	100.0	50.6	8.0	99.8	739	52.0	1,861	347	165.6
Rio Rico CDP	NA	NA	NA	NA	NA	NA	NA	NA	NA	NA	NA	NA	NA	NA	NA
Sahuarita town	402	1478	33	1444	43,126	183	100.0	26.6	12.6	63.4	379	22.4	852	221	56.9
San Luis city	507	1581	156	1425	20,336	136	100.0	21.1	8.0	87.4	228	26.1	861	37	169.5
San Tan Valley CDP	NA	NA	NA	NA	NA	NA	NA	NA	NA	NA	NA	NA	NA	NA	NA
Scottsdale city	5,663	2469	158	2312	488,017	2,517	19.8	477.7	126.1	80.7	1068	562.4	2,518	823	1200.6
Sedona city	203	2005	158	1847	17,689	46	100.0	24.3	4.1	100.0	1428	21.8	2,175	455	55.1
Show Low city	540	5027	763	4264	12,043	55	100.0	19.4	4.2	100.0	868	16.6	1,545	158	19.0
Sierra Vista city	1,396	3092	171	2922	14,678	87	88.5	48.4	13.6	97.0	407	48.8	1,052	142	37.2
Sierra Vista Southeast CDP	NA	NA	NA	NA	NA	NA	NA	NA	NA	NA	NA	NA	NA	NA	NA
Somerton city	240	1585	165	1420	4,882	65	100.0	12.1	5.7	100.0	142	10.9	742	146	20.4
Sun City CDP	NA	NA	NA	NA	NA	NA	NA	NA	NA	NA	NA	NA	NA	NA	NA
Sun City West CDP	NA	NA	NA	NA	NA	NA	NA	NA	NA	NA	NA	NA	NA	NA	NA
Sun Lakes CDP	NA	NA	NA	NA	NA	NA	NA	NA	NA	NA	NA	NA	NA	NA	NA
Surprise city	2,236	1788	110	1679	100,955	320	100.0	112.2	31.8	91.0	332	106.8	880	55	37.0
Tanque Verde CDP	NA	NA	NA	NA	NA	NA	NA	NA	NA	NA	NA	NA	NA	NA	NA
Tempe city	8,843	5208	471	4737	252,172	2,120	2.6	344.4	69.4	71.3	1097	286.8	1,715	177	740.2
Tucson city	35,048	6646	653	5993	208,900	1,471	35.1	736.3	277.8	53.0	534	608.5	1,159	174	1174.4
Tucson Estates CDP	NA	NA	NA	NA	NA	NA	NA	NA	NA	NA	NA	NA	NA	NA	NA
Vail CDP	NA	NA	NA	NA	NA	NA	NA	NA	NA	NA	NA	NA	NA	NA	NA
Valencia West CDP	NA	NA	NA	NA	NA	NA	NA	NA	NA	NA	NA	NA	NA	NA	NA
Verde Village CDP	NA	NA	NA	NA	NA	NA	NA	NA	NA	NA	NA	NA	NA	NA	NA
Yuma city	5,223	3397	442	2956	54,410	300	100.0	125.5	30.9	90.5	545	125.6	1,341	167	302.8
ARKANSAS	113,261	3818	480	3338	1,250,185	7,666	68.6	X	X	X	X	X	X	X	X
Arkadelphia city	354	3302	382	2920	116	1	100.0	9.8	0.9	91.3	299	9.4	876	18	75.8
Batesville city	NA	NA	NA	NA	5,143	48	50.0	15.6	2.8	53.6	554	15.2	1,461	674	17.5
Bella Vista town	213	763	158	605	14,564	51	100.0	12.2	6.0	28.9	122	12.1	440	15	0.0
Benton city	1,576	4669	376	4292	33,913	204	99.0	23.3	4.6	40.9	398	22.8	712	138	44.1
Bentonville city	751	1817	150	1667	185,952	1,089	41.2	57.6	8.2	48.3	790	57.0	1,486	389	97.5
Blytheville city	1,520	10127	1732	8395	775	4	100.0	44.2	4.1	36.0	385	42.5	2,772	34	718.1
Bryant city	NA	NA	NA	NA	14,233	78	100.0	20.5	1.7	73.9	712	17.5	936	114	30.8
Cabot city	801	3102	201	2901	11,022	67	83.6	20.5	4.7	45.3	430	17.1	696	29	31.7
Camden city	579	5012	623	4389	263	3	100.0	10.8	3.1	32.7	436	9.2	775	34	13.7
Centerton city	NA	NA	NA	NA	77,999	296	100.0	6.1	2.0	31.8	213	4.4	427	52	14.2
Conway city	3,265	5031	391	4640	31,097	213	55.9	95.8	7.8	55.2	532	88.6	1,408	244	383.2
El Dorado city	1,050	5688	959	4729	5,235	83	6.0	26.7	10.0	16.1	458	26.9	1,451	354	9.0
Fayetteville city	3,799	4733	496	4237	137,137	649	84.6	107.6	24.4	45.2	626	96.7	1,256	246	139.6
Forrest City city	NA	NA	NA	NA	0	0	0.0	10.5	4.4	32.2	262	9.6	629	11	0.1
Fort Smith city	5,339	6068	752	5315	47,650	372	44.6	133.9	29.8	38.6	700	126.0	1,439	456	454.0
Harrison city	767	5769	790	4979	1,655	10	100.0	11.9	2.8	36.0	454	10.2	772	0	0.0
Helena-West Helena city	867	7598	1376	6222	2,778	34	100.0	12.2	4.7	28.7	386	12.0	1,018	46	10.2
Hope city	596	5901	693	5208	631	3	100.0	9.4	2.5	42.3	259	9.7	972	234	7.6
Hot Springs city	NA	NA	NA	NA	12,298	43	100.0	69.7	12.2	60.6	752	69.2	1,951	328	68.3
Hot Springs Village CDP	NA	NA	NA	NA	NA	NA	NA	NA	NA	NA	NA	NA	NA	NA	NA
Jacksonville city	1,505	5219	728	4491	7,337	46	69.6	66.7	10.5	44.6	344	75.1	2,619	339	28.9
Jonesboro city	3,578	4930	539	4392	61,384	598	54.7	78.3	23.6	30.3	435	71.4	1,014	147	298.0
Little Rock city	17,457	8807	1405	7402	130,768	779	43.4	376.0	98.2	37.1	617	369.8	1,881	297	511.4
Magnolia city	371	3221	356	2865	6,677	49	18.4	35.5	1.5	61.2	530	33.2	2,849	111	62.6
Malvern city	NA	NA	NA	NA	0	0	0.0	7.7	2.1	44.2	297	6.2	572	45	19.3

1 Data for serious crimes have not been adjusted for underreporting. This may affect comparability between geographic areas over time.
2 Per 100,000 population estimated by the FBI. 3 Based on population estimated as of July 1 of the year shown.

Table B. Incorporated Places, Census Designated Places (CDPs), and Minor Civil Divisions (MCDs) of 10,000 or More Population — Land Area, Population, and Households, and Employment

STATE City, town, township, borough, or CDP (county if applicable)	Land area,[1] 2010 (sq mi)	Total persons 2010	Total persons 2014	Percent change 2010–2014	Persons per square mile, 2014	Foreign born	Lives in same house as previous year	Median household income (dollars)	Income of $100,000 or more	Income below poverty level	Percent in labor force	Unemploy-ment rate	Family households	One person households
	1	2	3	4	5	6	7	8	9	10	11	12	13	14
ARKANSAS—Con.														
Marion city	20.366	12,369	12,321	-0.4	605.0	3.4	87.3	$62,740	24.8	6.0	73.3	7.9	76.3	19.8
Maumelle city	12.007	17,168	17,804	3.7	1,482.8	2.1	85.4	$79,182	37.8	6.6	72.9	4.1	70.6	26.6
Mountain Home city	11.736	12,448	12,278	-1.4	1,046.2	2.6	82.0	$32,884	6.4	14.9	46.4	6.2	55.9	39.8
North Little Rock city	51.840	62,368	66,810	7.1	1,288.8	4.6	79.7	$40,305	11.9	17.5	63.6	9.3	57.8	35.6
Paragould city	31.203	26,111	27,465	5.2	880.2	1.4	78.0	$38,481	10.4	17.4	57.6	8.8	64.7	30.1
Pine Bluff city	44.575	49,080	45,332	-7.6	1,017.0	1.5	83.3	$30,415	8.4	28.3	55.4	16.5	59.7	37.0
Rogers city	37.923	55,983	61,464	9.8	1,620.7	18.6	81.1	$52,386	22.2	12.5	68.4	5.4	72.3	23.4
Russellville city	28.267	27,917	28,993	3.9	1,025.7	6.6	76.1	$36,360	10.5	22.8	62.3	8.6	62.6	31.7
Searcy city	18.342	22,858	23,983	4.9	1,307.5	3.4	72.1	$42,181	13.4	19.8	54.9	6.1	63.8	29.8
Sherwood city	20.943	29,680	30,407	2.4	1,451.9	4.3	84.5	$58,300	20.8	10.8	69.4	4.8	65.2	30.0
Siloam Springs city	11.068	15,038	15,944	6.0	1,440.6	11.3	80.9	$44,390	10.6	15.0	59.4	4.3	73.7	22.5
Springdale city	46.468	70,747	76,565	8.2	1,647.7	24.2	77.4	$41,385	14.1	19.6	69.2	8.1	72.7	22.3
Texarkana city	41.635	29,911	30,014	0.3	720.9	0.7	75.7	$40,422	11.6	18.8	59.8	8.9	63.7	32.6
Van Buren city	15.297	22,791	23,070	1.2	1,508.1	8.8	79.5	$39,634	10.2	20.9	61.4	8.0	71.5	24.7
West Memphis city	28.399	26,247	25,423	-3.1	895.2	0.7	80.2	$29,764	8.2	29.5	58.0	14.9	65.6	29.7
CALIFORNIA	155,779.213	37,254,503	38,802,500	4.2	249.1	27.0	84.6	$61,489	29.4	14.5	63.8	11.0	68.7	24.1
Adelanto city	56.009	31,765	32,728	3.0	584.3	20.5	72.5	$35,262	5.3	35.9	46.6	25.5	85.1	10.7
Agoura Hills city	7.793	20,330	20,843	2.5	2,674.5	18.6	89.7	$107,268	54.9	6.0	67.6	8.3	77.0	16.8
Alameda city	10.442	73,812	77,660	5.2	7,437.1	26.7	84.0	$76,439	37.3	10.0	67.9	8.7	62.8	29.3
Alamo CDP	9.669	14,570	NA	NA	NA	10.5	91.6	$163,151	71.4	3.3	58.3	5.7	86.8	10.2
Albany city	1.788	18,543	19,488	5.1	10,898.2	32.2	81.0	$78,769	39.8	10.7	67.4	7.6	72.4	22.6
Alhambra city	7.631	83,089	85,569	3.0	11,214.0	50.7	86.1	$53,195	22.5	15.0	62.6	7.4	69.2	25.0
Aliso Viejo city	6.919	48,053	50,231	4.5	7,259.4	22.5	83.4	$102,325	51.3	5.2	77.5	7.4	68.7	24.8
Alpine CDP	26.781	14,236	NA	NA	NA	9.4	84.1	$78,433	40.3	7.3	62.9	7.1	72.7	21.3
Altadena CDP	8.714	42,777	NA	NA	NA	20.8	90.2	$83,917	41.6	9.8	65.8	9.5	70.7	23.4
Alum Rock CDP	0.849	15,536	NA	NA	NA	33.9	86.9	$70,202	31.9	7.3	65.4	13.1	85.0	12.1
American Canyon city	6.081	19,540	20,470	4.8	3,366.3	36.0	89.1	$81,955	39.0	6.9	67.8	9.1	82.1	13.3
Anaheim city	49.977	336,440	346,997	3.1	6,943.1	37.0	84.4	$59,707	26.9	14.9	67.5	10.9	76.0	17.9
Anderson city	6.372	9,932	10,209	2.8	1,602.1	2.9	84.9	$35,225	5.8	22.8	55.8	12.8	58.3	33.5
Antelope CDP	6.835	45,770	NA	NA	NA	27.0	85.5	$64,122	25.0	11.0	65.1	9.9	79.4	16.8
Antioch city	28.330	102,365	108,930	6.4	3,845.1	21.0	81.8	$65,770	29.6	13.5	64.7	13.4	76.7	18.6
Apple Valley town	74.441	69,139	71,595	3.6	961.8	8.1	82.5	$48,337	20.4	16.3	51.7	14.3	76.9	20.1
Arcadia city	10.925	56,364	58,232	3.3	5,330.1	48.7	88.6	$80,147	41.0	10.3	60.8	6.3	77.2	19.5
Arcata city	9.092	17,231	17,730	2.9	1,950.0	5.5	60.4	$30,244	9.8	34.7	60.5	16.9	40.5	37.7
Arden-Arcade CDP	17.829	92,186	NA	NA	NA	14.1	76.4	$45,750	21.1	19.4	61.5	14.9	54.7	37.4
Arroyo Grande city	5.833	17,249	17,908	3.8	3,070.2	8.8	85.8	$63,558	30.4	8.6	60.2	8.2	68.3	27.4
Artesia city	1.621	16,522	16,895	2.3	10,424.9	49.2	85.6	$60,544	27.7	12.7	61.7	7.0	84.8	13.8
Arvin city	4.819	19,304	20,583	6.6	4,270.9	47.6	87.7	$35,359	6.5	27.9	66.8	15.9	88.7	9.0
Ashland CDP	1.838	21,925	NA	NA	NA	33.1	87.1	$45,074	13.7	17.1	63.0	13.6	67.0	27.9
Atascadero city	25.713	28,306	29,134	2.9	1,133.0	6.3	86.7	$66,342	27.9	10.8	60.7	5.4	71.2	21.3
Atwater city	6.114	28,172	29,022	3.0	4,746.6	21.6	82.7	$41,619	13.5	23.0	60.2	16.2	76.7	18.6
Auburn city	7.154	13,305	13,960	4.9	1,951.3	5.9	84.7	$54,085	25.7	11.2	58.9	11.4	58.5	36.2
Avenal city	19.422	15,505	13,308	-14.2	685.2	36.9	78.0	$29,302	4.4	37.0	39.3	19.7	84.1	12.9
Avocado Heights CDP	2.706	15,411	NA	NA	NA	35.4	95.5	$72,174	30.3	11.5	62.4	12.9	82.8	13.0
Azusa city	9.656	46,361	48,799	5.3	5,053.6	31.8	83.3	$52,087	19.9	16.8	64.1	8.5	76.7	17.3
Bakersfield city	148.548	347,587	368,759	6.1	2,482.4	18.5	80.9	$56,842	24.2	17.5	64.3	11.6	74.6	19.5
Baldwin Park city	6.631	75,390	77,119	2.3	11,629.6	44.7	89.9	$51,189	15.5	16.3	62.6	13.7	89.0	8.6
Banning city	23.099	29,603	30,769	3.9	1,332.1	16.4	85.3	$39,556	9.8	15.5	44.4	13.5	63.6	30.8
Barstow city	41.343	22,639	23,498	3.8	568.4	11.4	77.8	$40,648	12.7	26.9	55.9	14.6	69.7	24.3
Bay Point CDP	6.580	21,349	NA	NA	NA	33.2	83.4	$41,749	14.6	24.4	69.9	18.2	73.4	22.4
Beaumont city	30.968	36,878	42,277	14.6	1,365.2	18.0	87.0	$66,775	30.4	11.8	63.6	8.2	75.6	19.4
Bell city	2.501	35,477	36,217	2.1	14,483.9	43.6	90.1	$36,496	7.0	27.5	62.1	14.8	85.0	12.9
Bellflower city	6.118	76,610	78,236	2.1	12,788.7	29.2	88.1	$49,360	17.3	17.2	63.9	11.0	74.3	21.0
Bell Gardens city	2.459	42,072	43,146	2.6	17,549.3	45.1	89.6	$37,103	6.3	27.4	64.1	13.0	87.4	9.1
Belmont city	4.625	25,844	27,073	4.8	5,853.1	28.7	86.5	$106,287	53.0	6.4	69.5	7.2	64.2	29.7
Benicia city	12.929	26,997	27,930	3.5	2,160.3	10.4	85.9	$89,094	44.8	7.0	67.3	8.1	68.4	25.2
Berkeley city	10.466	112,489	118,853	5.7	11,356.4	20.8	69.9	$65,283	35.4	19.2	59.5	8.3	44.0	35.3
Beverly Hills city	5.708	34,109	34,871	2.2	6,109.0	36.5	84.5	$87,366	46.3	12.5	64.1	10.1	55.1	37.9
Big Bear City CDP	31.953	12,304	NA	NA	NA	6.8	86.7	$43,404	13.2	20.9	59.9	16.9	59.4	31.0
Bloomington CDP	5.987	23,851	NA	NA	NA	36.0	88.0	$48,985	12.7	20.8	62.3	19.4	85.1	12.0
Blythe city	26.190	20,817	19,258	-7.5	735.3	16.8	77.6	$46,393	18.8	23.7	39.3	15.2	72.8	22.1
Bonita CDP	5.017	12,538	NA	NA	NA	22.4	86.2	$87,666	41.8	11.1	58.2	10.5	78.6	14.9
Bostonia CDP	1.932	15,379	NA	NA	NA	16.4	87.0	$42,333	12.2	18.6	65.2	13.9	69.8	25.2
Brawley city	7.682	24,953	25,820	3.5	3,361.3	23.4	83.9	$41,718	14.9	23.8	58.0	20.1	76.4	19.8
Brea city	12.193	39,189	41,508	5.9	3,404.3	21.4	85.7	$81,857	40.0	6.4	68.7	8.6	71.9	22.1
Brentwood city	14.851	51,624	57,019	10.5	3,839.4	14.8	86.1	$88,697	45.8	5.2	63.9	8.8	81.4	15.5
Buena Park city	10.524	80,613	83,105	3.1	7,896.9	37.7	86.2	$68,884	30.4	11.6	63.1	6.6	82.7	12.6
Burbank city	17.341	103,340	105,368	2.0	6,076.2	35.0	87.5	$66,111	30.5	10.5	68.2	8.9	61.5	31.6
Burlingame city	4.405	28,806	30,298	5.2	6,877.6	26.0	84.2	$90,890	47.1	6.0	69.2	5.0	57.0	35.7
Calabasas city	13.706	23,462	24,296	3.6	1,772.7	26.6	85.1	$117,176	57.4	8.8	62.7	6.9	76.1	18.1
Calexico city	8.632	38,573	39,799	3.2	4,610.5	46.9	86.9	$35,233	10.6	29.9	56.0	20.5	85.9	12.6
California City city	203.546	14,120	13,263	-6.1	65.2	12.9	74.1	$57,660	24.8	18.0	54.2	24.1	73.9	22.7
Camarillo city	19.532	65,221	66,923	2.6	3,426.3	14.6	85.1	$87,120	43.0	5.5	64.9	7.7	69.2	24.9
Cameron Park CDP	11.107	18,228	NA	NA	NA	5.9	84.6	$74,690	34.6	6.4	62.9	10.4	71.1	21.6
Campbell city	5.804	39,348	41,119	4.5	7,084.3	22.9	86.0	$91,269	44.9	7.8	71.7	6.1	63.1	26.7
Camp Pendleton South CDP	3.913	10,616	NA	NA	NA	6.5	65.7	$43,742	3.4	9.8	72.9	17.6	99.3	0.7
Canyon Lake city	3.911	10,561	11,010	4.3	2,814.9	4.5	89.0	$74,682	31.9	3.1	62.1	11.4	77.3	19.6
Capitola city	1.593	9,918	10,146	2.3	6,368.6	14.2	85.9	$56,607	23.0	7.3	69.6	7.1	53.2	36.0
Carlsbad city	37.727	105,459	112,299	6.5	2,976.6	14.0	86.1	$87,415	45.2	9.7	63.5	8.8	67.7	25.6
Carmichael CDP	13.528	61,762	NA	NA	NA	11.2	81.3	$54,598	23.3	12.9	60.4	15.2	63.4	30.2
Carpinteria city	2.586	13,044	13,671	4.8	5,286.7	25.5	83.7	$65,467	32.7	8.2	68.2	7.2	69.0	24.9
Carson city	18.723	91,714	93,271	1.7	4,981.7	34.4	88.3	$71,420	31.8	10.0	64.1	14.6	80.3	15.9
Casa de Oro-Mount Helix CDP	6.850	18,762	NA	NA	NA	13.4	90.8	$75,637	40.1	8.6	60.7	11.5	73.6	21.5
Castaic CDP	7.262	19,015	NA	NA	NA	17.9	92.0	$105,523	54.3	6.2	74.5	8.6	81.8	13.7

1 Dry land or land partially or temporarily covered by water.
2 16 years old and over.

Table B. Incorporated Places, Census Designated Places (CDPs), and Minor Civil Divisions (MCDs) of 10,000 or More Population — **Crime, Construction, and Local Government Finance**

STATE City, town, township, borough, or CDP (county if applicable)	Serious crimes known to police, 2014[1] Total number	Rate[2] Total	Rate[2] Violent	Rate[2] Property	New residential construction authorized by building permits, 2014 Value ($1,000)	New residential construction authorized by building permits, 2014 Number of housing units	New residential construction authorized by building permits, 2014 Percent single family	Local government finance, 2012 General revenue Total (mil dol)	Local government finance, 2012 General revenue Intergovernmental Total (mil dol)	Local government finance, 2012 General revenue Intergovernmental Percent from state gov.	Local government finance, 2012 General revenue Taxes per capita[3]	Local government finance, 2012 General expenditure Total (mil dol)	Local government finance, 2012 General expenditure Per capita[3] Total	Local government finance, 2012 General expenditure Per capita[3] Capital outlays	Local government finance, 2012 Debt outstanding (mil dol)
	15	16	17	18	19	20	21	22	23	24	25	26	27	28	29
ARKANSAS—Con.															
Marion city	595	4834	471	4363	11,448	70	77.1	15.9	1.9	60.4	288	14.1	1,148	30	203.3
Maumelle city	418	2341	106	2234	23,671	99	100.0	15.6	4.5	24.4	475	13.3	758	74	10.2
Mountain Home city	497	4060	106	3954	830	4	100.0	12.3	2.7	30.2	474	12.0	972	27	12.1
North Little Rock city	3,277	4889	639	4250	12,482	71	97.2	90.5	26.5	30.0	606	97.5	1,506	165	204.0
Paragould city	2,112	7736	432	7304	16,670	178	57.9	29.1	6.0	40.6	270	27.7	1,027	152	25.8
Pine Bluff city	3,232	7119	1269	5850	2,041	27	40.7	45.8	15.6	31.1	370	42.9	915	56	29.1
Rogers city	1,998	3270	347	2923	77,071	543	60.4	66.9	18.0	35.4	565	49.1	832	178	160.5
Russellville city	1,409	4923	321	4602	3,917	40	57.5	28.8	7.4	31.7	492	23.4	820	49	0.0
Searcy city	NA	NA	NA	NA	7,888	61	88.5	21.3	6.6	41.9	242	21.5	907	43	57.0
Sherwood city	1,316	4364	497	3866	23,251	147	100.0	26.4	11.3	17.7	261	26.0	868	128	8.3
Siloam Springs city	553	3446	287	3159	2,913	23	91.3	19.4	3.8	36.9	469	22.7	1,447	343	39.1
Springdale city	NA	NA	NA	NA	63,025	224	100.0	72.7	20.3	30.2	406	53.9	732	67	110.5
Texarkana city	2,041	6797	749	6048	5,654	37	94.6	31.4	6.9	34.8	449	26.4	879	33	34.1
Van Buren city	894	3867	290	3577	4,037	25	100.0	17.4	5.3	34.4	265	19.9	866	49	13.4
West Memphis city	1,841	7257	1435	5822	2,590	18	77.8	33.0	8.5	26.7	507	32.5	1,262	139	31.2
CALIFORNIA	1,100,901	2837	396	2441	18,742,105	83,645	46.9	X	X	X	X	X	X	X	X
Adelanto city	979	3137	606	2531	9,503	34	100.0	12.0	0.9	64.5	197	18.3	586	65	0.0
Agoura Hills city	251	1209	82	1127	9,022	33	100.0	18.5	1.5	46.7	673	21.0	1,018	324	11.1
Alameda city	1,868	2424	188	2236	7,795	57	8.8	117.1	11.9	69.1	961	118.5	1,564	250	152.6
Alamo CDP	NA	NA	NA	NA	NA	NA	NA	NA	NA	NA	NA	NA	NA	NA	NA
Albany city	509	2630	160	2470	882	3	100.0	25.4	1.3	91.1	923	27.1	1,428	288	27.2
Alhambra city	1,911	2250	198	2052	3,400	17	64.7	94.9	11.0	57.2	570	85.5	1,012	77	70.5
Aliso Viejo city	308	608	69	539	0	0	0.0	19.0	1.4	100.0	283	22.2	448	112	34.0
Alpine CDP	NA	NA	NA	NA	NA	NA	NA	NA	NA	NA	NA	NA	NA	NA	NA
Altadena CDP	NA	NA	NA	NA	NA	NA	NA	NA	NA	NA	NA	NA	NA	NA	NA
Alum Rock CDP	NA	NA	NA	NA	NA	NA	NA	NA	NA	NA	NA	NA	NA	NA	NA
American Canyon city	623	3057	270	2787	0	0	0.0	25.3	2.1	100.0	781	28.7	1,429	74	19.5
Anaheim city	9,297	2680	317	2362	206,092	1,241	4.1	697.7	119.6	21.0	779	658.5	1,917	451	1822.5
Anderson city	NA	NA	NA	NA	4,497	23	91.3	9.9	3.1	81.9	452	10.6	1,054	177	13.1
Antelope CDP	NA	NA	NA	NA	NA	NA	NA	NA	NA	NA	NA	NA	NA	NA	NA
Antioch city	5,039	4656	784	3872	25,338	83	100.0	69.2	16.1	79.1	336	57.9	550	87	41.8
Apple Valley town	1,866	2616	297	2319	17,099	129	96.9	55.7	5.3	91.3	389	55.8	790	105	63.0
Arcadia city	1,219	2104	104	2000	39,146	215	27.4	68.8	2.9	73.3	848	64.5	1,130	99	40.4
Arcata city	780	4395	439	3955	2,145	25	28.0	26.9	8.8	67.6	651	28.9	1,633	480	13.6
Arden-Arcade CDP	NA	NA	NA	NA	NA	NA	NA	NA	NA	NA	NA	NA	NA	NA	NA
Arroyo Grande city	408	2288	292	1997	6,369	54	83.3	17.5	1.3	95.7	740	19.2	1,095	179	8.7
Artesia city	343	2043	292	1751	2,970	24	29.2	11.6	1.8	100.0	442	11.1	662	118	15.7
Arvin city	660	3213	862	2351	9,174	59	1.8	9.6	2.3	100.0	216	9.6	476	54	14.5
Ashland CDP	NA	NA	NA	NA	NA	NA	NA	NA	NA	NA	NA	NA	NA	NA	NA
Atascadero city	520	1777	246	1531	33,060	185	76.2	31.8	7.6	92.3	555	28.1	978	301	27.6
Atwater city	1,206	4164	628	3536	673	4	100.0	26.6	3.9	48.1	291	49.2	1,714	675	93.3
Auburn city	339	2414	313	2101	5,443	15	86.7	15.9	0.8	89.2	644	15.9	1,165	181	11.7
Avenal city	172	1236	129	1107	278	4	100.0	11.9	3.5	68.0	264	10.6	714	129	12.4
Avocado Heights CDP	NA	NA	NA	NA	NA	NA	NA	NA	NA	NA	NA	NA	NA	NA	NA
Azusa city	1,230	2551	342	2208	101,432	297	100.0	58.3	7.2	30.8	767	55.0	1,161	37	235.4
Bakersfield city	16,273	4429	457	3972	316,961	1,659	77.0	360.1	84.2	69.9	417	382.6	1,069	301	345.9
Baldwin Park city	1,561	2029	285	1744	4,159	17	100.0	50.2	15.9	46.5	328	43.8	572	46	66.8
Banning city	747	2433	417	2016	0	0	0.0	33.1	4.9	90.4	427	30.4	1,003	237	48.2
Barstow city	998	4274	929	3345	5,095	50	100.0	34.6	1.4	72.5	1008	34.6	1,501	225	9.8
Bay Point CDP	NA	NA	NA	NA	NA	NA	NA	NA	NA	NA	NA	NA	NA	NA	NA
Beaumont city	1,045	2529	172	2357	74,958	454	100.0	83.3	0.7	100.0	366	79.5	2,017	1,172	9.6
Bell city	935	2593	602	1991	0	0	0.0	29.7	1.8	72.8	471	30.0	835	223	55.7
Bellflower city	1,916	2462	376	2085	16,090	73	100.0	32.9	3.7	60.2	328	34.3	442	71	31.8
Bell Gardens city	818	1898	251	1648	3,087	12	83.3	36.8	3.6	71.1	531	31.1	726	78	36.7
Belmont city	408	1514	134	1380	6,945	17	41.2	43.6	2.2	83.1	965	44.8	1,687	160	38.8
Benicia city	510	1837	94	1743	1,380	5	100.0	43.3	1.4	100.0	1061	46.0	1,679	414	55.1
Berkeley city	5,533	4699	366	4333	39,795	364	5.5	293.3	31.1	90.2	1281	300.7	2,605	242	188.8
Beverly Hills city	1,182	3398	319	3079	63,406	30	100.0	261.2	5.5	72.9	4124	226.1	6,532	1,003	142.3
Big Bear City CDP	NA	NA	NA	NA	NA	NA	NA	NA	NA	NA	NA	NA	NA	NA	NA
Bloomington CDP	NA	NA	NA	NA	NA	NA	NA	NA	NA	NA	NA	NA	NA	NA	NA
Blythe city	836	4250	447	3803	925	6	100.0	20.5	2.5	97.0	474	19.9	963	119	53.2
Bonita CDP	NA	NA	NA	NA	NA	NA	NA	NA	NA	NA	NA	NA	NA	NA	NA
Bostonia CDP	NA	NA	NA	NA	NA	NA	NA	NA	NA	NA	NA	NA	NA	NA	NA
Brawley city	1,089	4238	269	3970	4,040	29	79.3	29.2	9.3	38.4	420	34.0	1,327	347	18.8
Brea city	1,177	2846	128	2718	42,827	172	74.4	90.0	3.5	86.5	1395	87.6	2,176	593	39.1
Brentwood city	1,352	2422	183	2239	83,020	476	100.0	78.8	1.8	100.0	628	88.6	1,654	238	194.1
Buena Park city	2,247	2694	260	2434	9,231	71	1.4	87.0	7.0	64.8	788	105.8	1,285	278	115.5
Burbank city	2,576	2452	143	2310	8,945	27	81.5	265.6	36.3	55.0	1412	282.4	2,701	443	463.3
Burlingame city	797	2642	156	2487	14,269	25	76.0	72.1	2.7	100.0	1436	70.0	2,356	686	33.1
Calabasas city	271	1114	78	1036	8,398	15	20.0	36.6	3.9	79.6	947	40.5	1,690	503	36.5
Calexico city	1,726	4362	243	4119	9,210	56	1.8	34.0	6.5	59.4	405	33.5	852	103	2.8
California City city	560	4253	600	3653	275	1	100.0	15.6	1.3	88.6	845	16.3	1,217	350	21.4
Camarillo city	1,037	1565	109	1456	54,987	295	30.8	73.4	5.0	40.6	617	73.6	1,117	261	90.1
Cameron Park CDP	NA	NA	NA	NA	NA	NA	NA	NA	NA	NA	NA	NA	NA	NA	NA
Campbell city	1,469	3594	198	3396	11,472	38	100.0	46.2	3.4	53.9	823	49.3	1,222	160	28.0
Camp Pendleton South CDP	NA	NA	NA	NA	NA	NA	NA	NA	NA	NA	NA	NA	NA	NA	NA
Canyon Lake city	141	1283	118	1165	1,396	4	100.0	5.8	2.9	16.3	255	5.5	511	253	0.8
Capitola city	657	6483	296	6187	2,251	6	100.0	17.1	0.5	71.1	1170	16.9	1,687	77	1.0
Carlsbad city	1,935	1723	182	1541	97,105	283	100.0	179.5	13.2	50.3	1033	160.2	1,465	200	65.0
Carmichael CDP	NA	NA	NA	NA	NA	NA	NA	NA	NA	NA	NA	NA	NA	NA	NA
Carpinteria city	216	1582	139	1443	1,200	4	100.0	10.9	1.6	100.0	564	9.9	750	20	0.9
Carson city	2,455	2644	365	2279	11,858	28	100.0	105.5	19.8	56.9	799	135.1	1,459	403	217.3
Casa de Oro-Mount Helix CDP	NA	NA	NA	NA	NA	NA	NA	NA	NA	NA	NA	NA	NA	NA	NA
Castaic CDP	NA	NA	NA	NA	NA	NA	NA	NA	NA	NA	NA	NA	NA	NA	NA

1 Data for serious crimes have not been adjusted for underreporting. This may affect comparability between geographic areas over time.
2 Per 100,000 population estimated by the FBI.   3 Based on population estimated as of July 1 of the year shown.

Table B. Incorporated Places, Census Designated Places (CDPs), and Minor Civil Divisions (MCDs) of 10,000 or More Population — **Land Area, Population, and Households, and Employment**

STATE City, town, township, borough, or CDP (county if applicable)	Land area,[1] 2010 (sq mi)	Total persons 2010	Total persons 2014	Percent change 2010–2014	Persons per square mile, 2014	Foreign born	Lives in same house as previous year	Median household income (dollars)	Income of $100,000 or more	Income below poverty level	Percent in labor force	Unemployment rate	Family households	One person households
	1	2	3	4	5	6	7	8	9	10	11	12	13	14
CALIFORNIA—Con.														
Castro Valley CDP	16.740	61,388	NA	NA	NA	23.3	87.6	$83,442	41.3	6.3	65.0	8.3	73.3	21.7
Cathedral City city	21.500	51,200	53,437	4.4	2,485.5	34.0	82.4	$43,128	15.3	19.4	63.3	11.5	65.7	24.9
Ceres city	9.328	45,897	47,343	3.2	5,075.1	26.9	82.2	$46,132	15.8	20.7	63.8	17.5	80.5	14.9
Cerritos city	8.722	49,047	50,004	2.0	5,733.1	45.4	94.2	$91,487	45.8	4.4	59.4	7.5	84.7	12.7
Cherryland CDP	1.197	14,728	NA	NA	NA	32.5	85.7	$50,374	16.4	19.4	63.7	16.6	69.5	23.9
Chico city	32.922	86,198	89,180	3.5	2,708.8	7.8	69.2	$42,334	17.5	23.7	63.9	10.7	50.8	32.4
Chino city	29.664	77,972	84,723	8.7	2,856.1	23.0	79.5	$72,554	31.9	10.9	58.4	10.8	79.7	16.2
Chino Hills city	44.685	74,799	77,005	2.9	1,723.3	29.4	89.4	$97,609	48.2	5.8	69.9	10.0	82.3	14.4
Chowchilla city	11.137	18,782	18,909	0.7	1,697.9	14.2	71.9	$36,852	12.3	22.6	28.6	9.9	76.9	19.4
Chula Vista city	49.631	243,916	260,988	7.0	5,258.5	30.5	88.9	$66,110	29.1	12.2	65.1	12.0	77.4	18.8
Citrus CDP	0.887	10,866	NA	NA	NA	35.1	91.0	$58,626	21.6	12.5	61.7	14.2	88.1	8.8
Citrus Heights city	14.229	83,255	86,145	3.5	6,054.4	13.4	79.5	$51,150	16.6	11.9	65.1	13.8	63.4	27.8
Claremont city	13.350	34,926	36,054	3.2	2,700.6	18.3	83.9	$89,648	46.0	8.2	58.6	9.5	67.4	27.9
Clayton city	3.840	10,918	11,690	7.1	3,043.9	11.8	92.4	$131,136	66.3	3.7	62.5	9.3	79.5	17.9
Clearlake city	10.129	15,250	15,089	-1.1	1,489.7	10.6	78.4	$25,532	3.9	31.3	50.3	23.2	52.4	38.6
Clovis city	23.467	95,633	102,189	6.9	4,354.6	11.8	85.2	$63,662	28.0	12.5	64.1	11.7	72.9	22.0
Coachella city	28.950	40,704	44,132	8.4	1,524.4	41.2	85.8	$40,423	9.1	27.7	70.6	20.1	90.0	8.5
Coalinga city	6.676	18,089	16,452	-9.0	2,464.3	19.1	77.4	$50,373	22.5	20.1	51.7	10.5	69.6	25.1
Colton city	15.324	52,155	54,053	3.6	3,527.3	25.5	81.9	$39,915	12.0	22.4	64.9	14.7	76.4	19.6
Commerce city	6.538	12,827	13,076	1.9	2,000.0	35.1	90.5	$45,846	14.8	20.2	59.3	15.2	77.6	19.3
Compton city	10.012	96,412	98,597	2.3	9,847.8	29.9	87.9	$43,230	12.3	25.0	61.0	16.7	82.6	14.4
Concord city	30.544	122,282	127,522	4.3	4,175.0	25.8	85.2	$67,122	32.1	11.7	67.5	10.8	68.9	23.3
Corcoran city	7.504	24,813	22,815	-8.1	3,040.2	21.7	77.9	$34,082	6.2	30.4	24.1	16.0	77.3	17.9
Corona city	38.836	152,374	161,486	6.0	4,158.2	25.8	89.1	$77,021	35.4	10.2	67.1	10.5	79.3	16.0
Coronado city	7.931	24,697	24,910	0.9	3,140.8	10.1	81.0	$90,876	45.7	6.9	65.1	5.7	64.9	29.9
Costa Mesa city	15.700	109,929	112,784	2.6	7,183.7	24.2	83.3	$66,491	32.1	12.0	74.0	8.9	60.3	27.3
Coto de Caza CDP	7.721	14,866	NA	NA	NA	11.5	89.8	$166,328	72.5	3.6	64.7	8.2	89.8	7.5
Country Club CDP	1.917	9,379	NA	NA	NA	9.7	83.0	$43,323	9.8	17.0	59.9	20.1	67.3	25.5
Covina city	7.028	47,796	49,002	2.5	6,972.2	22.2	85.2	$64,496	28.4	11.2	66.0	12.6	72.7	21.8
Cudahy city	1.175	23,805	24,291	2.0	20,672.9	47.6	90.4	$37,759	6.5	33.1	65.4	14.6	88.7	8.0
Culver City city	5.111	38,885	39,691	2.1	7,766.0	23.4	84.6	$79,292	40.6	9.7	70.2	7.8	56.5	35.2
Cupertino city	11.311	58,572	60,668	3.6	5,363.5	50.3	83.7	$134,872	64.5	5.8	61.7	7.9	77.1	19.7
Cypress city	6.611	47,863	49,240	2.9	7,448.2	28.3	88.5	$83,819	40.5	6.1	63.6	5.7	80.4	16.5
Daly City city	7.640	101,146	106,094	4.9	13,886.0	52.3	87.7	$74,489	34.8	9.1	69.5	8.7	72.3	20.4
Dana Point city	6.499	33,278	34,116	2.5	5,249.4	13.9	81.1	$84,404	43.1	6.8	67.3	8.2	60.6	30.4
Danville town	18.077	41,859	43,909	4.9	2,429.0	12.6	89.5	$140,616	65.5	3.8	63.5	6.4	75.8	20.7
Davis city	9.883	65,611	66,742	1.7	6,753.2	18.8	67.8	$57,454	32.9	22.7	60.6	7.6	49.2	25.8
Del Aire CDP	1.014	10,001	NA	NA	NA	28.2	87.8	$79,943	37.3	10.7	70.2	10.1	73.4	23.5
Delano city	14.303	53,041	52,651	-0.7	3,681.1	37.9	79.1	$36,244	7.8	28.6	48.5	15.8	88.4	10.3
Desert Hot Springs city	30.200	27,049	28,164	4.1	932.6	24.0	78.2	$33,575	6.1	29.5	59.2	18.0	66.5	25.8
Diamond Bar city	14.879	55,544	56,784	2.2	3,816.4	42.1	88.7	$90,901	44.6	6.0	63.9	8.0	83.7	11.5
Diamond Springs CDP	16.642	11,037	NA	NA	NA	7.2	88.8	$52,483	21.3	13.3	53.9	15.0	63.2	31.4
Dinuba city	6.470	21,453	23,667	10.3	3,657.9	33.9	84.3	$38,509	6.3	22.8	65.2	16.9	82.7	12.7
Discovery Bay CDP	6.300	13,352	NA	NA	NA	7.1	86.6	$112,063	56.6	4.9	69.3	8.7	80.4	14.9
Dixon city	7.128	18,392	19,164	4.2	2,688.7	16.9	82.1	$66,818	28.8	11.5	70.0	10.7	81.0	13.5
Downey city	12.408	111,791	114,172	2.1	9,201.4	34.9	89.5	$60,374	23.7	10.5	66.2	10.1	78.6	17.0
Duarte city	6.690	21,321	22,006	3.2	3,289.2	34.3	90.3	$62,186	29.2	12.9	61.8	11.0	70.0	26.3
Dublin city	15.233	46,036	54,695	18.8	3,590.5	28.7	78.5	$114,699	59.2	3.9	65.8	5.3	73.6	21.0
East Hemet CDP	5.213	17,418	NA	NA	NA	13.1	82.7	$45,374	16.6	17.2	57.7	18.6	79.8	15.1
East Los Angeles CDP	7.450	126,496	NA	NA	NA	43.0	92.0	$39,103	8.6	27.6	62.1	13.9	80.5	15.9
East Palo Alto city	2.506	28,155	29,530	4.9	11,782.6	41.1	84.9	$52,716	24.0	17.1	69.9	11.8	73.8	17.9
East Rancho Dominguez CDP	0.822	15,135	NA	NA	NA	38.0	90.1	$44,964	13.4	20.7	63.8	15.2	84.6	11.9
East San Gabriel CDP	1.560	14,874	NA	NA	NA	47.4	87.4	$72,500	35.7	10.0	62.8	3.8	73.3	21.3
Eastvale city	12.663	53,683	57,016	6.2	4,502.5	31.0	87.5	$109,783	55.4	5.4	69.3	11.5	89.9	6.6
East Whittier CDP	1.090	NA	NA	NA	NA	15.1	90.3	$66,377	30.9	8.4	64.3	8.1	74.7	18.8
El Cajon city	14.478	99,476	103,091	3.6	7,120.5	29.6	80.5	$45,957	17.2	21.4	62.4	14.9	72.3	21.7
El Centro city	11.084	42,596	43,763	2.7	3,948.5	34.0	80.7	$41,677	17.9	23.9	59.6	17.3	75.6	20.4
El Cerrito city	3.657	23,586	24,599	4.3	6,726.8	27.7	86.2	$88,380	43.3	7.8	66.6	9.1	63.7	26.9
El Dorado Hills CDP	48.451	42,108	NA	NA	NA	14.3	88.0	$118,306	58.4	5.5	63.2	7.4	83.3	13.5
Elk Grove city	42.193	153,015	163,553	6.9	3,876.3	22.9	84.0	$79,051	37.6	8.9	67.0	10.6	80.0	15.9
El Monte city	9.562	113,475	116,631	2.8	12,196.9	50.6	92.0	$38,906	12.2	22.1	60.0	12.6	82.8	13.5
El Paso de Robles (Paso Robles) city	19.147	29,793	31,287	5.0	1,634.1	18.1	80.9	$59,978	25.2	11.2	67.9	8.1	70.4	22.2
El Segundo city	5.463	16,654	17,063	2.5	3,123.4	12.1	88.5	$84,004	42.1	7.3	71.3	6.3	62.5	29.8
El Sobrante CDP (Contra Costa County)	2.765	12,669	NA	NA	NA	24.0	87.7	$60,732	24.8	12.4	65.7	10.3	68.7	22.3
El Sobrante CDP (Riverside County)	7.213	12,723	NA	NA	NA	20.1	87.1	$99,080	48.0	6.2	70.2	20.4	91.1	7.6
Emeryville city	1.281	10,015	11,227	12.1	8,765.2	26.6	70.1	$69,329	34.2	10.0	76.8	7.5	32.7	52.8
Encinitas city	18.812	59,518	62,254	4.6	3,309.3	13.2	87.1	$92,564	47.1	8.4	66.1	7.7	65.1	24.9
Escondido city	37.059	143,913	150,243	4.4	4,054.2	28.3	85.6	$49,409	20.3	17.6	62.4	8.9	72.8	19.9
Eureka city	9.384	27,191	26,925	-1.0	2,869.2	7.5	76.2	$38,007	10.0	21.0	61.5	11.6	50.5	36.8
Exeter city	2.463	10,332	10,558	2.2	4,286.6	11.6	82.2	$41,341	16.2	22.1	64.0	11.4	76.6	18.1
Fairfield city	37.388	105,318	111,125	5.5	2,972.2	21.5	80.8	$66,190	30.2	11.8	66.1	11.5	75.0	19.4
Fair Oaks CDP	10.796	30,912	NA	NA	NA	11.4	84.2	$73,295	35.9	9.6	63.1	11.8	66.2	27.4
Fallbrook CDP	17.525	30,534	NA	NA	NA	23.5	85.1	$51,765	21.1	15.7	57.5	9.6	76.1	18.2
Farmersville city	2.258	10,588	10,786	1.9	4,775.9	27.6	85.7	$32,455	8.0	31.8	62.3	17.0	86.2	11.2
Fillmore city	3.364	15,002	15,420	2.8	4,584.3	28.0	90.7	$54,519	21.4	18.8	64.6	10.9	82.6	15.6
Florence-Graham CDP	3.580	63,387	NA	NA	NA	43.2	90.1	$33,902	6.8	34.1	60.9	13.1	87.2	10.1
Florin CDP	8.705	47,513	NA	NA	NA	30.6	81.5	$40,183	10.9	22.6	56.5	18.5	73.1	22.0
Folsom city	21.947	72,199	75,361	4.4	3,433.8	15.3	84.1	$100,163	50.1	5.3	61.9	8.1	69.7	24.6
Fontana city	42.430	196,074	204,950	4.5	4,830.3	29.3	86.0	$64,995	26.0	15.4	66.3	14.6	84.8	10.8
Foothill Farms CDP	4.200	33,121	NA	NA	NA	19.6	80.5	$44,590	12.1	21.1	65.9	13.1	68.3	22.7
Fortuna city	4.845	11,926	11,888	-0.3	2,453.6	9.0	82.7	$42,450	12.4	16.7	53.0	10.4	66.3	26.1
Foster City city	3.796	30,567	32,754	7.2	8,629.1	43.1	81.8	$114,651	58.8	3.8	66.5	6.6	70.9	23.9
Fountain Valley city	9.072	55,371	57,010	3.0	6,283.9	30.5	89.5	$82,532	40.3	7.0	62.3	8.3	76.7	18.4

1 Dry land or land partially or temporarily covered by water.
2 16 years old and over.

Table B. Incorporated Places, Census Designated Places (CDPs), and Minor Civil Divisions (MCDs) of 10,000 or More Population — **Crime, Construction, and Local Government Finance**

STATE City, town, township, borough, or CDP (county if applicable)	Serious crimes known to police, 2014[1]: Total number	Rate[2]: Total	Rate[2]: Violent	Rate[2]: Property	New residential construction authorized by building permits, 2014: Value ($1,000)	Number of housing units	Percent single family	Local government finance, 2012: General revenue: Total (mil dol)	Intergovernmental: Total (mil dol)	Intergovernmental: Percent from state gov.	Taxes per capita[3]	General expenditure: Total (mil dol)	Per capita[3]: Total	Per capita[3]: Capital outlays	Debt outstanding (mil dol)
	15	16	17	18	19	20	21	22	23	24	25	26	27	28	29
CALIFORNIA—Con.															
Castro Valley CDP	NA	NA	NA	NA	NA	NA	NA	NA	NA	NA	NA	NA	NA	NA	NA
Cathedral City city	1,322	2477	240	2237	6,566	32	100.0	70.1	6.3	64.9	1002	69.7	1,324	144	271.4
Ceres city	1,729	3686	309	3377	11,021	52	100.0	34.3	3.7	83.6	406	38.7	834	89	50.3
Cerritos city	1,611	3231	172	3058	0	0	0.0	96.9	2.0	89.7	1320	96.8	1,950	141	153.8
Cherryland CDP	NA	NA	NA	NA	NA	NA	NA	NA	NA	NA	NA	NA	NA	NA	NA
Chico city	3,553	4012	384	3628	58,752	396	50.8	99.3	7.9	55.7	799	91.9	1,050	275	163.2
Chino city	2,002	2453	228	2225	120,592	431	68.9	102.9	7.3	90.6	677	109.3	1,365	144	211.8
Chino Hills city	1,091	1417	79	1338	43,650	326	12.3	60.2	3.8	89.2	283	65.7	861	137	127.2
Chowchilla city	421	2465	521	1944	248	1	100.0	20.3	9.0	2.8	328	31.9	1,762	797	35.2
Chula Vista city	5,136	1976	235	1741	191,131	1,086	19.8	240.2	25.5	80.3	501	247.0	976	73	512.8
Citrus CDP	NA	NA	NA	NA	NA	NA	NA	NA	NA	NA	NA	NA	NA	NA	NA
Citrus Heights city	3,080	3592	454	3138	4,236	18	100.0	52.7	10.0	85.5	382	48.9	578	136	28.5
Claremont city	892	2475	108	2367	25,710	104	100.0	35.2	1.7	82.5	653	34.7	978	122	26.2
Clayton city	115	987	34	953	NA	NA	NA	10.0	1.0	100.0	640	7.2	634	151	5.1
Clearlake city	778	5217	650	4566	851	5	100.0	6.3	0.7	66.1	331	6.4	423	28	0.0
Clovis city	3,280	3257	214	3043	158,671	604	100.0	110.7	10.2	67.2	470	105.9	1,074	201	232.4
Coachella city	1,318	3021	380	2640	10,914	62	80.6	37.8	11.0	71.9	421	49.1	1,150	551	94.7
Coalinga city	436	2651	736	1915	1,286	6	100.0	20.8	1.3	67.4	451	16.6	985	87	24.6
Colton city	1,712	3201	256	2945	10,929	119	15.1	50.0	6.2	92.7	524	44.1	829	84	96.4
Commerce city	1,042	7995	591	7404	NA	NA	NA	57.6	2.7	89.3	3502	64.3	4,952	453	118.2
Compton city	3,748	3816	1149	2666	186	1	100.0	98.6	17.9	28.9	558	114.4	1,170	108	73.6
Concord city	5,661	4466	367	4100	2,278	7	100.0	120.0	9.6	80.8	566	128.3	1,026	86	63.7
Corcoran city	378	1639	373	1266	3,914	30	100.0	13.3	3.3	75.8	251	12.5	530	73	27.5
Corona city	3,611	2241	106	2135	72,458	654	4.6	225.6	16.4	78.9	672	219.2	1,388	272	346.1
Coronado city	562	2403	73	2331	25,667	37	100.0	75.0	5.1	70.4	2107	78.7	3,223	989	132.5
Costa Mesa city	3,780	3354	282	3072	40,563	196	90.8	117.6	9.7	76.3	823	111.9	1,001	113	38.8
Coto de Caza CDP	NA	NA	NA	NA	NA	NA	NA	NA	NA	NA	NA	NA	NA	NA	NA
Country Club CDP	NA	NA	NA	NA	NA	NA	NA	NA	NA	NA	NA	NA	NA	NA	NA
Covina city	1,218	2502	226	2276	640	2	100.0	49.3	4.1	69.9	672	49.1	1,013	132	86.2
Cudahy city	413	1708	335	1373	665	6	100.0	11.8	2.6	82.6	333	11.1	459	8	23.8
Culver City city	1,862	4707	427	4279	5,913	16	100.0	173.5	27.4	43.4	2528	143.8	3,651	482	206.5
Cupertino city	1,066	1760	66	1694	16,345	43	95.3	60.4	2.0	89.4	716	59.2	989	78	43.9
Cypress city	803	1626	103	1523	7,194	41	100.0	43.8	2.7	66.2	683	44.8	917	226	8.8
Daly City city	1,879	1779	184	1595	3,111	9	100.0	103.9	12.0	48.5	551	112.7	1,082	108	45.3
Dana Point city	534	1559	207	1352	51,252	39	100.0	29.3	1.6	100.0	740	31.5	929	121	8.2
Danville town	456	1044	39	1005	23,277	45	64.4	35.0	6.4	100.0	508	34.7	809	181	12.9
Davis city	1,539	2319	127	2193	2,508	11	81.8	96.8	18.9	87.5	714	90.4	1,372	150	55.0
Del Aire CDP	NA	NA	NA	NA	NA	NA	NA	NA	NA	NA	NA	NA	NA	NA	NA
Delano city	1,701	3257	412	2845	383	4	100.0	32.5	6.6	92.1	313	31.3	597	53	62.8
Desert Hot Springs city	1,328	4728	598	4130	0	0	0.0	20.2	3.1	33.2	446	27.4	988	219	12.2
Diamond Bar city	771	1361	86	1274	13,270	44	100.0	24.3	2.3	77.9	300	31.6	561	189	0.0
Diamond Springs CDP	NA	NA	NA	NA	NA	NA	NA	NA	NA	NA	NA	NA	NA	NA	NA
Dinuba city	1,120	4703	785	3918	2,923	24	100.0	39.7	6.1	55.9	855	35.6	1,555	336	85.4
Discovery Bay CDP	NA	NA	NA	NA	NA	NA	NA	NA	NA	NA	NA	NA	NA	NA	NA
Dixon city	481	2518	277	2240	3,017	23	100.0	20.1	1.3	92.7	781	19.2	1,028	178	3.8
Downey city	3,178	2798	247	2550	10,440	42	100.0	89.0	11.9	58.4	468	98.0	866	54	63.1
Duarte city	406	1861	248	1613	0	0	0.0	24.4	4.0	88.0	758	18.8	867	58	22.7
Dublin city	868	1614	130	1483	383,156	1,095	74.5	67.1	3.0	97.7	1032	63.3	1,298	122	6.2
East Hemet CDP	NA	NA	NA	NA	NA	NA	NA	NA	NA	NA	NA	NA	NA	NA	NA
East Los Angeles CDP	NA	NA	NA	NA	NA	NA	NA	NA	NA	NA	NA	NA	NA	NA	NA
East Palo Alto city	698	2376	422	1954	188	2	100.0	36.0	3.8	90.2	858	31.6	1,090	142	47.6
East Rancho Dominguez CDP	NA	NA	NA	NA	NA	NA	NA	NA	NA	NA	NA	NA	NA	NA	NA
East San Gabriel CDP	NA	NA	NA	NA	NA	NA	NA	NA	NA	NA	NA	NA	NA	NA	NA
Eastvale city	NA	NA	NA	NA	133,120	428	100.0	15.0	2.3	100.0	226	10.8	196	3	0.0
East Whittier CDP	NA	NA	NA	NA	NA	NA	NA	NA	NA	NA	NA	NA	NA	NA	NA
El Cajon city	2,579	2508	318	2190	6,603	28	100.0	103.0	8.1	84.7	695	103.4	1,017	157	68.2
El Centro city	2,262	5196	384	4813	7,998	43	100.0	182.9	11.7	52.8	582	173.8	4,019	507	100.3
El Cerrito city	1,003	4096	314	3782	9,545	57	1.8	41.0	4.4	100.0	961	43.0	1,784	249	24.7
El Dorado Hills CDP	NA	NA	NA	NA	NA	NA	NA	NA	NA	NA	NA	NA	NA	NA	NA
Elk Grove city	3,694	2267	382	1885	126,048	571	100.0	117.6	21.2	77.7	352	116.8	737	118	95.6
El Monte city	2,546	2191	287	1904	9,395	43	100.0	92.1	16.0	67.9	561	92.7	803	118	168.9
El Paso de Robles (Paso Robles) city	913	2934	402	2532	18,277	61	100.0	46.5	6.6	62.1	983	43.1	1,414	272	54.4
El Segundo city	586	3449	283	3167	0	0	0.0	63.4	7.3	7.6	2549	65.3	3,872	520	0.0
El Sobrante CDP (Contra Costa County)	NA	NA	NA	NA	NA	NA	NA	NA	NA	NA	NA	NA	NA	NA	NA
El Sobrante CDP (Riverside County)	NA	NA	NA	NA	NA	NA	NA	NA	NA	NA	NA	NA	NA	NA	NA
Emeryville city	1,720	15676	1066	14610	42,826	209	0.0	80.2	2.5	51.5	5980	70.8	6,900	1,969	162.2
Encinitas city	1,012	1630	168	1463	46,676	157	100.0	74.3	4.1	60.5	809	77.2	1,265	265	40.7
Escondido city	3,538	2361	342	2020	13,260	139	12.2	143.3	14.3	60.1	531	135.9	919	78	191.9
Eureka city	2,321	8647	540	8106	1,583	11	36.4	46.5	7.0	68.0	1036	49.7	1,845	324	109.2
Exeter city	352	3345	447	2898	NA	NA	NA	7.0	1.0	68.3	350	6.6	632	45	9.5
Fairfield city	4,392	3982	471	3511	85,588	316	100.0	135.2	23.7	86.3	811	120.8	1,122	219	271.5
Fair Oaks CDP	NA	NA	NA	NA	NA	NA	NA	NA	NA	NA	NA	NA	NA	NA	NA
Fallbrook CDP	NA	NA	NA	NA	NA	NA	NA	NA	NA	NA	NA	NA	NA	NA	NA
Farmersville city	217	2018	484	1535	NA	NA	NA	6.5	2.2	85.7	220	7.4	692	114	2.8
Fillmore city	168	1097	300	797	15,665	41	100.0	18.3	0.6	87.1	797	16.6	1,092	252	51.3
Florence-Graham CDP	NA	NA	NA	NA	NA	NA	NA	NA	NA	NA	NA	NA	NA	NA	NA
Florin CDP	NA	NA	NA	NA	NA	NA	NA	NA	NA	NA	NA	NA	NA	NA	NA
Folsom city	1,384	1887	108	1780	80,474	300	100.0	106.2	4.7	81.7	840	106.9	1,459	214	237.5
Fontana city	4,420	2161	347	1814	97,280	396	84.8	243.1	25.3	66.9	748	241.4	1,198	265	677.9
Foothill Farms CDP	NA	NA	NA	NA	NA	NA	NA	NA	NA	NA	NA	NA	NA	NA	NA
Fortuna city	529	4501	281	4221	4,391	32	31.3	13.6	1.0	76.5	484	13.7	1,155	149	37.0
Foster City city	380	1157	43	1115	48,667	232	0.0	51.6	1.9	100.0	1203	53.2	1,654	65	0.0
Fountain Valley city	1,109	1945	151	1794	1,828	7	100.0	51.8	4.2	91.1	630	53.9	954	197	9.7

1 Data for serious crimes have not been adjusted for underreporting. This may affect comparability between geographic areas over time.
2 Per 100,000 population estimated by the FBI. 3 Based on population estimated as of July 1 of the year shown.

Table B. Incorporated Places, Census Designated Places (CDPs), and Minor Civil Divisions (MCDs) of 10,000 or More Population — **Land Area, Population, and Households, and Employment**

STATE City, town, township, borough, or CDP (county if applicable)	Land area,[1] 2010 (sq mi)	Population: Total persons 2010	Population: Total persons 2014	Population: Percent change 2010–2014	Population: Persons per square mile, 2014	Population characteristics 2010–2014: Foreign born	Population characteristics 2010–2014: Lives in same house as previous year	Household income and poverty, 2010–2014: Median household income (dollars)	Household income and poverty, 2010–2014: Percent of households: Income of $100,000 or more	Household income and poverty, 2010–2014: Percent of households: Income below poverty level	Employment,[2] 2010–2014: Percent in labor force	Employment,[2] 2010–2014: Unemploy-ment rate	Households, 2010–2014 (percent of households): Family households	Households, 2010–2014 (percent of households): One person households
	1	2	3	4	5	6	7	8	9	10	11	12	13	14
CALIFORNIA—Con.														
Fremont city	77.465	214,079	228,758	6.9	2,953.1	44.0	87.2	$103,591	52.2	5.7	66.5	7.6	79.0	16.3
French Valley CDP	10.891	23,067	NA	NA	NA	15.6	79.6	$88,699	41.4	4.1	66.3	9.0	87.7	9.4
Fresno city	113.224	496,080	515,986	4.0	4,557.2	21.1	80.8	$41,455	15.6	25.6	61.9	15.4	70.2	22.9
Fullerton city	22.433	135,235	139,677	3.3	6,226.4	31.2	79.9	$65,909	31.4	14.6	65.0	10.1	71.3	20.2
Galt city	5.995	23,647	24,817	4.9	4,139.6	18.5	82.2	$59,375	18.8	17.3	65.2	16.1	78.2	18.5
Gardena city	5.829	58,829	60,395	2.7	10,360.8	33.0	87.7	$47,856	18.5	14.8	63.4	10.5	67.4	27.8
Garden Acres CDP	2.589	10,648	NA	NA	NA	33.8	85.1	$38,940	8.0	25.1	67.2	25.2	82.2	9.7
Garden Grove city	17.957	170,964	175,078	2.4	9,750.1	43.9	89.1	$59,360	25.3	16.0	63.9	10.7	79.8	15.1
Gilroy city	16.142	48,810	52,533	7.6	3,254.4	25.3	84.6	$81,056	37.8	12.3	70.4	11.2	81.8	14.8
Glendale city	30.444	191,713	200,167	4.4	6,575.0	54.9	87.2	$52,451	25.4	15.0	62.1	10.7	69.2	25.8
Glendora city	19.399	50,073	51,442	2.7	2,651.8	15.8	88.9	$74,169	34.1	9.2	62.9	10.2	75.6	19.6
Goleta city	7.851	29,902	30,797	3.0	3,922.6	22.9	79.2	$75,766	35.8	8.6	67.4	6.0	63.2	26.5
Grand Terrace city	3.502	12,040	12,414	3.1	3,544.5	17.0	89.2	$64,140	27.7	7.8	65.4	11.3	63.8	30.7
Granite Bay CDP	21.528	20,402	NA	NA	NA	7.0	91.3	$118,063	57.7	3.4	61.2	9.0	84.0	13.2
Grass Valley city	4.743	12,861	12,878	0.1	2,715.1	7.3	74.4	$33,325	8.0	22.7	48.2	11.8	44.6	45.1
Greenfield city	2.135	16,330	16,929	3.7	7,928.7	46.6	83.5	$52,374	11.0	20.3	68.2	14.3	86.6	9.6
Grover Beach city	2.310	13,156	13,505	2.7	5,846.1	10.9	79.1	$49,418	20.7	13.9	64.0	9.9	64.3	25.9
Hacienda Heights CDP	11.175	54,038	NA	NA	NA	42.3	93.0	$76,435	35.8	7.7	58.5	8.2	81.5	13.9
Half Moon Bay city	6.423	11,324	12,371	9.2	1,926.1	24.4	89.4	$103,239	53.1	4.5	69.6	7.7	69.1	25.4
Hanford city	16.804	54,076	55,065	1.8	3,277.0	15.4	82.1	$53,543	21.0	19.2	62.5	12.8	76.8	19.0
Hawaiian Gardens city	0.948	14,259	14,557	2.1	15,354.3	40.6	87.5	$39,073	9.5	27.8	57.4	10.0	85.8	10.7
Hawthorne city	6.081	84,293	87,583	3.9	14,402.2	33.8	83.9	$44,384	13.7	17.1	68.5	10.3	67.7	27.2
Hayward city	45.420	144,369	154,612	7.1	3,404.0	38.1	85.3	$62,691	28.2	13.8	68.0	12.8	72.7	20.5
Healdsburg city	4.457	11,254	11,656	3.6	2,615.3	21.4	82.1	$58,176	29.4	10.2	59.6	8.8	67.1	25.2
Hemet city	27.847	78,658	83,032	5.6	2,981.7	15.1	77.7	$33,932	8.7	21.1	48.5	20.7	62.5	31.8
Hercules city	6.412	24,084	25,086	4.2	3,912.2	32.0	86.1	$100,267	50.2	6.5	68.3	5.7	75.5	20.0
Hermosa Beach city	1.427	19,506	19,891	2.0	13,943.4	10.3	81.3	$105,029	52.4	4.0	75.7	4.8	43.7	41.0
Hesperia city	73.096	90,173	92,749	2.9	1,268.9	14.2	84.9	$44,472	13.9	21.2	55.2	17.5	79.6	16.6
Highland city	18.755	53,104	54,651	2.9	2,914.0	21.1	85.2	$53,385	26.0	17.8	62.2	13.2	81.0	15.3
Hillsborough town	6.190	10,825	11,413	5.4	1,843.7	23.0	88.5	$250,000	82.2	2.5	57.5	5.8	89.1	8.8
Hollister city	7.324	34,898	37,086	6.3	5,063.4	24.3	81.5	$66,045	26.0	11.4	70.8	14.0	82.1	14.4
Home Gardens CDP	1.556	11,570	NA	NA	NA	38.8	93.2	$52,704	14.4	25.1	62.8	11.2	81.6	13.7
Huntington Beach city	26.934	191,037	200,809	5.1	7,455.6	16.9	87.2	$82,554	41.0	8.1	67.5	8.4	66.4	24.9
Huntington Park city	3.013	58,114	59,362	2.1	19,704.9	50.4	88.9	$34,777	6.6	29.5	65.8	14.7	83.6	12.3
Imperial city	5.856	14,752	16,811	14.0	2,870.5	25.7	80.0	$73,683	27.8	10.4	66.4	14.2	76.9	19.0
Imperial Beach city	4.161	26,324	27,149	3.1	6,524.1	20.5	79.0	$48,117	13.7	16.6	64.0	14.5	67.4	25.0
Indio city	30.657	79,116	85,633	8.2	2,793.3	27.9	81.5	$47,922	20.4	18.6	62.6	15.5	75.2	20.6
Inglewood city	9.068	109,673	111,905	2.0	12,340.7	28.3	88.0	$42,249	14.4	19.7	67.1	14.6	67.4	27.6
Irvine city	65.571	211,906	248,531	17.3	3,790.3	36.6	78.1	$91,999	46.4	11.1	65.6	7.1	66.7	23.8
Isla Vista CDP	1.850	23,096	NA	NA	NA	15.8	25.4	$19,237	5.9	61.5	52.0	15.6	17.3	21.3
Jurupa Valley city	42.930	95,004	98,842	4.0	2,302.4	27.7	85.9	$55,898	19.9	14.6	64.9	17.4	80.8	14.8
Kerman city	3.233	13,544	14,394	6.3	4,452.9	32.4	95.5	$45,539	14.8	24.0	66.7	10.9	81.8	16.2
King City city	3.845	12,872	13,580	5.5	3,532.2	46.9	84.5	$40,500	12.5	22.2	62.2	17.3	84.8	11.8
Kingsburg city	2.824	11,397	11,732	2.9	4,154.7	13.1	93.6	$60,361	21.3	15.0	65.9	12.3	72.2	25.6
La Cañada Flintridge city	8.628	20,246	20,662	2.1	2,394.7	25.0	91.6	$151,786	70.1	2.9	58.6	5.7	85.8	13.1
La Crescenta-Montrose CDP	3.426	19,653	NA	NA	NA	36.3	90.7	$89,737	44.5	7.3	66.2	5.5	75.4	21.0
Ladera Ranch CDP	4.841	22,980	NA	NA	NA	14.5	86.7	$131,952	67.7	5.2	74.4	4.8	81.7	14.2
Lafayette city	15.047	23,794	25,473	7.1	1,692.9	13.6	92.1	$138,073	61.7	4.6	61.6	5.9	74.6	18.3
Laguna Beach city	8.894	22,730	23,341	2.7	2,624.4	11.8	85.8	$97,881	48.6	7.6	65.7	7.1	51.6	38.2
Laguna Hills city	6.601	30,257	30,972	2.4	4,691.8	26.4	85.2	$91,460	46.9	5.8	68.6	8.5	74.9	20.1
Laguna Niguel city	14.741	62,985	65,448	3.9	4,439.9	21.0	86.8	$98,957	49.6	6.1	68.7	8.1	69.3	23.5
Laguna Woods city	3.345	16,046	16,415	2.3	4,908.0	25.9	87.0	$36,708	10.5	12.0	26.5	8.8	33.3	61.8
La Habra city	7.354	60,281	62,066	3.0	8,439.9	27.0	86.2	$61,364	26.8	12.8	66.9	10.2	75.7	20.0
Lake Arrowhead CDP	17.727	12,424	NA	NA	NA	10.3	92.6	$64,461	30.2	11.1	57.3	9.3	76.1	19.6
Lake Elsinore city	38.349	52,861	60,029	13.6	1,565.3	21.9	82.3	$63,303	27.7	13.3	67.0	14.2	81.7	12.8
Lake Forest city	16.636	77,448	80,148	3.5	4,817.8	23.3	88.5	$92,781	47.1	6.3	72.9	6.4	75.0	21.0
Lakeland Village CDP	8.676	11,541	NA	NA	NA	19.4	78.4	$41,289	14.1	23.5	65.0	19.3	72.4	20.0
Lake Los Angeles CDP	9.741	12,328	NA	NA	NA	14.4	90.3	$40,227	14.0	26.2	50.6	16.1	80.2	14.9
Lakeside CDP	6.900	20,648	NA	NA	NA	9.2	88.3	$62,037	26.7	12.2	62.5	11.0	76.6	20.1
Lakewood city	9.419	80,048	81,653	2.0	8,669.2	21.5	88.7	$79,113	36.2	7.4	67.3	8.7	75.0	20.3
La Mesa city	9.079	57,065	59,177	3.7	6,518.3	14.6	77.7	$54,630	22.9	12.8	65.9	9.7	58.2	32.5
La Mirada city	7.822	48,527	49,459	1.9	6,323.0	24.2	90.3	$81,178	39.1	7.7	59.4	8.4	79.0	18.1
Lamont CDP	4.590	15,120	NA	NA	NA	44.4	90.2	$33,433	7.3	34.5	64.7	9.6	90.4	6.6
Lancaster city	94.297	156,633	161,043	2.8	1,707.8	13.6	87.8	$49,057	18.2	20.9	54.4	12.8	72.9	22.1
La Palma city	1.783	15,526	15,911	2.5	8,921.6	33.4	90.1	$84,026	40.1	8.1	58.9	7.2	80.3	17.1
La Presa CDP	5.497	34,169	NA	NA	NA	26.1	90.5	$60,817	20.5	11.4	65.5	12.7	75.3	18.3
La Puente city	3.479	39,816	40,735	2.3	11,709.5	40.7	89.1	$54,660	17.2	15.1	63.9	10.2	86.5	10.5
La Quinta city	35.134	37,467	39,964	6.7	1,137.5	13.6	87.8	$71,074	34.6	10.3	54.6	9.8	72.5	22.0
La Riviera CDP	1.850	10,802	NA	NA	NA	11.7	78.4	$58,694	20.6	15.1	67.1	12.6	57.1	27.5
Larkspur city	3.027	11,926	12,325	3.3	4,071.8	21.1	82.7	$82,568	41.5	5.6	66.3	9.1	52.1	42.7
Lathrop city	21.931	18,023	20,075	11.4	915.4	26.6	80.7	$63,087	20.4	10.5	56.8	13.1	86.5	8.8
La Verne city	8.430	31,063	32,288	3.9	3,830.1	14.8	87.2	$75,662	37.8	9.0	60.3	7.8	71.2	22.2
Lawndale city	1.974	32,769	33,442	2.1	16,939.9	40.1	88.1	$48,376	14.1	17.9	69.8	10.1	73.7	19.3
Lemon Grove city	3.879	25,320	26,511	4.7	6,835.3	19.5	90.6	$52,339	17.1	13.7	64.0	13.5	66.4	25.7
Lemon Hill CDP	1.627	13,729	NA	NA	NA	34.6	78.6	$27,101	6.6	35.2	55.2	20.7	76.3	18.4
Lemoore city	8.517	24,531	25,186	2.7	2,957.3	15.3	79.8	$52,701	22.8	11.4	72.1	12.3	72.5	21.2
Lennox CDP	1.093	22,753	NA	NA	NA	49.3	92.1	$36,573	6.9	31.3	63.6	10.7	86.6	9.1
Lincoln city	20.093	42,781	45,902	7.3	2,284.5	12.6	88.7	$70,870	30.3	8.2	53.3	9.9	71.4	21.9
Linda CDP	8.589	17,773	NA	NA	NA	17.0	75.7	$36,063	8.7	29.2	54.1	18.6	76.4	17.5
Lindsay city	2.610	11,744	13,192	12.3	5,055.3	33.5	88.3	$30,198	5.0	39.9	63.2	16.7	81.1	14.3
Live Oak CDP	3.243	17,158	NA	NA	NA	18.8	86.4	$64,957	31.4	13.1	67.9	7.2	59.3	28.2
Livermore city	26.866	81,108	86,870	7.1	3,233.4	17.3	88.5	$99,683	49.9	5.4	71.0	6.7	74.4	20.2
Livingston city	3.677	13,027	13,815	6.0	3,756.8	45.9	89.8	$50,674	9.3	19.9	63.8	21.9	84.8	12.0
Lodi city	13.671	62,134	63,950	2.9	4,677.6	20.3	81.9	$48,662	19.6	16.4	62.5	14.3	68.6	25.5
Loma Linda city	7.516	23,261	23,853	2.5	3,173.4	32.8	83.1	$58,259	26.3	16.4	60.7	8.5	63.5	30.0
Lomita city	1.911	20,256	20,768	2.5	10,867.7	28.6	82.8	$57,245	24.8	16.1	70.6	9.1	63.5	30.7

1 Dry land or land partially or temporarily covered by water.
2 16 years old and over.

Table B. Incorporated Places, Census Designated Places (CDPs), and Minor Civil Divisions (MCDs) of 10,000 or More Population — **Crime, Construction, and Local Government Finance**

STATE City, town, township, borough, or CDP (county if applicable)	Serious crimes known to police, 2014[1] Total number	Rate[2] Total	Rate[2] Violent	Rate[2] Property	New residential construction authorized by building permits, 2014 Value ($1,000)	New residential construction authorized by building permits, 2014 Number of housing units	New residential construction authorized by building permits, 2014 Percent single family	Local government finance, 2012 General revenue Total (mil dol)	Intergovernmental Total (mil dol)	Intergovernmental Percent from state gov.	Taxes per capita[3]	General expenditure Total (mil dol)	Per capita[3] Total	Per capita[3] Capital outlays	Debt outstanding (mil dol)
	15	16	17	18	19	20	21	22	23	24	25	26	27	28	29
CALIFORNIA—Con.															
Fremont city	4,194	1843	125	1718	89,403	274	94.2	214.4	29.7	64.9	637	244.1	1,100	468	313.6
French Valley CDP	NA	NA	NA	NA	NA	NA	NA	NA	NA	NA	NA	NA	NA	NA	NA
Fresno city	23,483	4576	464	4112	195,072	918	69.8	632.4	127.3	42.9	529	528.7	1,045	197	1062.2
Fullerton city	3,545	2534	242	2292	60,487	446	33.0	151.4	23.8	80.4	576	188.8	1,362	506	195.2
Galt city	644	2610	284	2327	12,814	72	100.0	41.3	10.3	19.8	716	52.7	2,169	1,195	37.8
Gardena city	1,665	2764	458	2306	4,311	28	78.6	78.5	10.8	48.9	938	63.5	1,065	158	24.8
Garden Acres CDP	NA	NA	NA	NA	NA	NA	NA	NA	NA	NA	NA	NA	NA	NA	NA
Garden Grove city	3,504	1990	231	1759	4,320	22	100.0	143.3	12.1	44.0	448	176.5	1,012	138	179.2
Gilroy city	1,683	3211	376	2835	75,501	243	100.0	73.7	6.7	42.5	762	72.6	1,432	389	54.9
Glendale city	3,259	1654	94	1559	43,555	373	4.6	315.9	29.1	55.9	748	334.4	1,717	239	322.6
Glendora city	1,307	2548	129	2419	33,705	284	1.4	41.0	5.3	97.4	553	34.8	685	69	46.8
Goleta city	457	1490	114	1376	583	4	100.0	31.1	4.4	87.8	727	33.8	1,118	384	15.7
Grand Terrace city	266	2144	145	1999	771	2	100.0	13.8	0.7	97.7	786	12.3	1,005	176	22.8
Granite Bay CDP	NA	NA	NA	NA	NA	NA	NA	NA	NA	NA	NA	NA	NA	NA	NA
Grass Valley city	785	6144	853	5291	5,397	83	3.6	17.2	2.1	69.3	702	17.7	1,378	64	23.2
Greenfield city	410	2414	536	1878	4,708	40	20.0	10.8	1.2	93.3	322	12.8	764	240	31.5
Grover Beach city	376	2786	385	2401	2,790	13	100.0	10.7	0.8	91.1	530	11.1	831	60	4.0
Hacienda Heights CDP	NA	NA	NA	NA	NA	NA	NA	NA	NA	NA	NA	NA	NA	NA	NA
Half Moon Bay city	NA	NA	NA	NA	13,837	84	15.5	17.6	0.5	100.0	863	19.7	1,680	282	16.3
Hanford city	2,162	3944	556	3387	26,241	194	62.9	41.5	3.7	86.5	355	40.0	736	127	43.0
Hawaiian Gardens city	238	1643	380	1263	1,094	6	50.0	26.6	4.8	28.9	1416	24.8	1,717	311	82.7
Hawthorne city	3,246	3745	759	2986	52,693	331	39.0	103.1	37.8	12.8	564	99.8	1,163	96	104.9
Hayward city	5,478	3573	395	3178	128,125	586	37.9	216.5	39.7	29.1	724	190.5	1,273	255	196.8
Healdsburg city	257	2221	164	2057	5,358	28	100.0	35.8	2.5	92.7	1683	37.8	3,312	921	56.6
Hemet city	3,787	4595	522	4073	31,856	138	100.0	71.2	3.5	72.5	552	68.8	846	126	13.7
Hercules city	313	1251	108	1143	351	1	100.0	27.4	1.4	100.0	597	29.1	1,184	149	131.8
Hermosa Beach city	580	2919	186	2732	31,236	57	100.0	32.2	1.5	47.4	1063	31.8	1,610	100	0.0
Hesperia city	2,599	2807	320	2487	15,478	75	100.0	73.7	15.0	93.8	483	101.5	1,103	350	168.7
Highland city	1,565	2868	469	2399	1,609	7	100.0	29.3	5.5	73.6	315	34.1	631	199	73.8
Hillsborough town	104	914	9	905	20,205	14	100.0	27.1	0.5	100.0	1301	27.5	2,462	227	35.8
Hollister city	634	1715	368	1347	19,757	76	100.0	49.1	1.4	100.0	753	40.2	1,115	356	43.7
Home Gardens CDP	NA	NA	NA	NA	NA	NA	NA	NA	NA	NA	NA	NA	NA	NA	NA
Huntington Beach city	4,629	2324	196	2128	59,297	503	10.3	237.1	14.8	87.5	732	245.0	1,257	137	257.9
Huntington Park city	2,215	3750	692	3058	366	2	100.0	53.9	9.0	53.2	605	47.0	799	63	42.4
Imperial city	51	308	30	278	22,131	116	100.0	15.1	1.6	98.6	449	17.7	1,130	265	23.8
Imperial Beach city	528	1939	411	1528	5,265	29	65.5	31.4	1.9	89.6	640	27.2	1,012	70	40.1
Indio city	2,676	3165	551	2614	100,696	517	100.0	79.4	8.3	78.1	577	80.9	980	123	184.2
Inglewood city	3,523	3146	699	2446	551	3	33.3	168.9	42.5	51.9	874	161.6	1,451	100	277.3
Irvine city	3,165	1303	49	1253	646,474	3,248	48.2	221.8	16.6	67.8	656	296.0	1,289	255	1400.1
Isla Vista CDP	NA	NA	NA	NA	NA	NA	NA	NA	NA	NA	NA	NA	NA	NA	NA
Jurupa Valley city	NA	NA	NA	NA	60,559	250	100.0	12.9	4.1	100.0	89	4.3	44	0	0.0
Kerman city	496	3412	261	3150	1,642	12	100.0	9.4	0.7	95.3	347	9.6	670	117	11.9
King City city	298	2235	412	1822	5,679	61	9.8	9.4	0.8	50.4	415	8.0	609	58	15.4
Kingsburg city	352	2993	289	2704	2,872	12	83.3	9.3	1.2	83.7	359	11.1	952	189	8.3
La Cañada Flintridge city	324	1571	87	1483	8,408	7	100.0	23.6	2.5	26.5	480	25.1	1,225	157	35.7
La Crescenta-Montrose CDP	NA	NA	NA	NA	NA	NA	NA	NA	NA	NA	NA	NA	NA	NA	NA
Ladera Ranch CDP	NA	NA	NA	NA	NA	NA	NA	NA	NA	NA	NA	NA	NA	NA	NA
Lafayette city	456	1798	67	1731	NA	NA	NA	22.5	1.2	100.0	628	22.9	929	219	33.2
Laguna Beach city	526	2251	274	1977	13,053	22	100.0	70.1	4.2	69.5	1938	61.4	2,650	401	13.5
Laguna Hills city	486	1566	145	1421	39,273	289	0.0	26.8	8.5	93.2	524	23.6	764	235	15.6
Laguna Niguel city	627	964	112	852	39,699	157	9.6	38.2	3.2	97.6	495	40.3	626	203	0.0
Laguna Woods city	124	752	36	716	0	0	0.0	6.0	1.4	90.5	257	6.1	372	106	0.0
La Habra city	1,154	1862	169	1693	5,157	31	61.3	54.3	8.3	81.6	521	52.1	847	84	55.8
Lake Arrowhead CDP	NA	NA	NA	NA	NA	NA	NA	NA	NA	NA	NA	NA	NA	NA	NA
Lake Elsinore city	1,790	3051	218	2833	90,540	491	100.0	62.9	4.4	97.8	682	70.3	1,261	194	410.2
Lake Forest city	786	986	130	855	138,429	833	31.0	48.6	4.3	66.7	491	69.4	879	338	18.8
Lake Los Angeles CDP	NA	NA	NA	NA	NA	NA	NA	NA	NA	NA	NA	NA	NA	NA	NA
Lakeland Village CDP	NA	NA	NA	NA	NA	NA	NA	NA	NA	NA	NA	NA	NA	NA	NA
Lakeside CDP	NA	NA	NA	NA	NA	NA	NA	NA	NA	NA	NA	NA	NA	NA	NA
Lakewood city	1,939	2383	248	2134	NA	NA	NA	58.5	5.6	92.9	474	55.1	680	68	42.5
La Mesa city	1,792	3037	353	2685	38,938	309	13.6	60.0	3.3	82.3	729	58.2	999	181	46.3
La Mirada city	724	1469	181	1289	8,793	35	100.0	53.4	5.0	48.8	744	62.4	1,271	395	92.9
Lamont CDP	NA	NA	NA	NA	NA	NA	NA	NA	NA	NA	NA	NA	NA	NA	NA
Lancaster city	4,552	2842	556	2285	25,862	93	100.0	155.7	14.4	70.0	621	158.8	999	170	431.7
La Palma city	259	1621	75	1546	0	0	0.0	16.2	0.9	100.0	818	13.7	865	109	6.6
La Presa CDP	NA	NA	NA	NA	NA	NA	NA	NA	NA	NA	NA	NA	NA	NA	NA
La Puente city	576	1419	335	1084	1,516	8	100.0	17.0	3.2	83.5	251	16.8	417	64	9.5
La Quinta city	1,411	3549	219	3331	59,233	182	95.6	92.3	4.4	99.5	1801	79.1	2,049	214	324.4
La Riviera CDP	NA	NA	NA	NA	NA	NA	NA	NA	NA	NA	NA	NA	NA	NA	NA
Larkspur city	NA	NA	NA	NA	27,945	62	54.8	15.7	1.6	96.2	950	16.3	1,344	139	1.4
Lathrop city	NA	NA	NA	NA	54,144	173	100.0	28.7	8.3	13.4	552	25.4	1,326	210	9.5
La Verne city	866	2701	143	2557	17,742	78	53.8	36.0	1.3	97.5	756	35.3	1,123	55	19.4
Lawndale city	555	1665	471	1194	674	4	100.0	21.9	4.6	43.6	470	22.6	682	195	21.1
Lemon Grove city	641	2434	475	1960	6,106	22	100.0	23.6	3.5	40.3	495	23.1	888	142	26.5
Lemon Hill CDP	NA	NA	NA	NA	NA	NA	NA	NA	NA	NA	NA	NA	NA	NA	NA
Lemoore city	779	3106	474	2632	24,375	193	54.4	32.9	7.9	11.0	478	23.7	959	196	45.2
Lennox CDP	NA	NA	NA	NA	NA	NA	NA	NA	NA	NA	NA	NA	NA	NA	NA
Lincoln city	480	1048	37	1011	81,253	286	100.0	39.4	1.9	82.7	363	39.2	887	142	35.5
Linda CDP	NA	NA	NA	NA	NA	NA	NA	NA	NA	NA	NA	NA	NA	NA	NA
Lindsay city	284	2135	308	1827	4,032	20	100.0	15.1	1.7	22.7	502	15.1	1,181	415	14.0
Live Oak CDP	NA	NA	NA	NA	NA	NA	NA	NA	NA	NA	NA	NA	NA	NA	NA
Livermore city	1,737	2016	274	1742	21,299	86	82.6	144.6	12.8	81.4	848	146.1	1,746	314	175.1
Livingston city	295	2155	365	1790	227	2	0.0	17.3	0.7	67.3	341	10.7	797	67	9.5
Lodi city	2,385	3750	456	3294	4,361	16	100.0	74.4	14.8	61.1	591	65.7	1,040	203	0.2
Loma Linda city	730	3067	172	2895	3,982	48	4.2	28.0	2.5	95.9	727	24.5	1,035	108	50.1
Lomita city	432	2089	372	1717	3,239	16	100.0	11.1	2.0	89.5	340	11.1	539	75	7.1

1 Data for serious crimes have not been adjusted for underreporting. This may affect comparability between geographic areas over time.
2 Per 100,000 population estimated by the FBI.   3 Based on population estimated as of July 1 of the year shown.

Table B. Incorporated Places, Census Designated Places (CDPs), and Minor Civil Divisions (MCDs) of 10,000 or More Population — **Land Area, Population, and Households, and Employment**

STATE City, town, township, borough, or CDP (county if applicable)	Land area,[1] 2010 (sq mi)	Total persons 2010	Total persons 2014	Percent change 2010–2014	Persons per square mile, 2014	Foreign born	Lives in same house as previous year	Median household income (dollars)	Income of $100,000 or more	Income below poverty level	Percent in labor force	Unemploy-ment rate	Family households	One person households
	1	2	3	4	5	6	7	8	9	10	11	12	13	14
CALIFORNIA—Con.														
Lompoc city	11.594	42,438	44,013	3.7	3,796.2	21.8	79.4	$47,908	16.3	18.1	58.9	12.7	68.4	25.5
Long Beach city	50.301	462,257	473,577	2.4	9,414.8	26.1	82.6	$52,944	23.7	18.1	66.5	12.1	60.6	30.4
Los Alamitos city	4.022	11,409	11,716	2.7	2,913.2	15.0	86.5	$82,258	40.1	10.1	64.8	8.2	75.1	21.2
Los Altos city	6.474	28,999	30,288	4.4	4,678.2	23.3	90.9	$157,500	66.9	3.3	58.5	5.5	77.3	20.3
Los Angeles city	468.669	3,792,657	3,928,864	3.6	8,383.0	38.6	85.4	$49,682	23.3	20.4	66.3	11.5	60.2	30.1
Los Banos city	9.993	35,967	37,126	3.2	3,715.1	24.8	81.2	$45,665	14.4	21.4	60.5	17.5	81.6	14.8
Los Gatos town	11.166	29,436	30,735	4.4	2,752.6	18.1	86.0	$122,860	55.5	5.4	62.6	5.6	65.2	28.8
Los Osos CDP	12.763	14,276	NA	NA	NA	8.0	86.8	$56,860	21.4	9.5	59.1	8.2	63.2	30.2
Lynwood city	4.840	69,772	71,839	3.0	14,842.6	40.3	90.2	$41,930	11.1	24.9	59.8	13.0	86.6	10.9
McFarland city	2.668	12,707	13,605	7.1	5,099.2	38.7	89.0	$34,750	4.8	30.5	60.1	19.2	91.3	6.1
McKinleyville CDP	20.797	15,177	NA	NA	NA	4.1	81.0	$50,298	17.4	13.8	66.7	8.8	64.4	28.0
Madera city	15.789	61,416	63,605	3.6	4,028.4	32.0	89.1	$42,027	12.3	25.9	59.3	8.3	80.0	17.1
Magalia CDP	14.015	11,310	NA	NA	NA	3.2	88.0	$39,514	8.3	15.6	43.5	21.6	65.4	28.0
Malibu city	19.789	12,645	12,958	2.5	654.8	16.9	83.9	$130,432	61.8	9.7	57.1	7.6	61.9	31.6
Manhattan Beach city	3.937	35,135	35,881	2.1	9,113.3	11.4	88.9	$142,071	65.2	3.1	67.4	5.1	64.4	27.1
Manteca city	20.547	67,276	73,494	9.2	3,576.9	15.4	83.5	$62,032	23.5	10.1	67.0	14.8	76.9	17.0
Marina city	8.883	19,718	20,817	5.6	2,343.5	21.8	82.8	$53,828	20.6	16.7	64.4	8.8	64.4	25.3
Martinez city	12.631	36,040	37,567	4.2	2,974.2	11.7	86.5	$85,736	42.2	6.3	68.4	8.5	64.8	26.8
Marysville city	3.464	12,072	12,231	1.3	3,531.2	10.7	62.7	$34,942	6.2	23.9	56.0	17.6	61.0	30.7
Maywood city	1.178	27,395	27,937	2.0	23,707.5	46.1	90.7	$36,492	8.2	28.7	66.1	11.0	86.4	10.9
Mead Valley CDP	19.196	18,510	NA	NA	NA	29.9	86.3	$41,962	20.0	29.3	59.6	21.3	83.9	12.5
Mendota city	3.296	11,148	11,412	2.4	3,462.7	51.3	88.7	$25,229	2.3	48.6	68.3	29.7	79.0	11.5
Menifee city	46.472	77,519	85,182	9.9	1,833.0	13.9	83.0	$56,671	18.9	9.9	57.6	16.0	71.7	23.1
Menlo Park city	9.775	32,026	33,309	4.0	3,407.4	23.6	84.8	$115,650	58.3	5.6	67.6	5.9	61.5	28.3
Merced city	23.226	78,957	81,743	3.5	3,519.4	21.4	78.3	$38,917	14.1	25.9	60.6	16.9	71.2	22.2
Millbrae city	3.250	21,532	22,703	5.4	6,986.4	36.8	90.9	$91,846	45.8	6.3	61.7	6.8	72.3	23.7
Mill Valley city	4.763	13,903	14,403	3.6	3,023.9	14.2	88.2	$132,192	61.1	3.6	63.7	4.1	63.6	31.1
Milpitas city	13.581	66,815	73,672	10.3	5,424.6	50.7	84.8	$99,072	49.5	7.3	65.3	8.7	79.9	15.9
Mission Viejo city	17.627	93,105	97,209	4.4	5,514.9	19.3	88.4	$98,157	49.1	5.3	66.4	7.7	75.8	19.5
Modesto city	44.587	203,116	209,286	3.0	4,693.9	17.5	80.6	$47,607	19.0	18.5	61.2	15.8	70.3	24.1
Monrovia city	13.605	36,590	37,415	2.3	2,750.1	25.1	85.9	$72,034	35.9	11.5	72.8	9.5	67.8	24.9
Montclair city	5.517	36,664	38,465	4.9	6,971.9	34.5	90.2	$48,767	15.2	18.1	62.2	12.0	78.4	18.1
Montebello city	8.333	62,500	63,929	2.3	7,672.2	36.8	91.1	$47,562	18.4	14.0	57.1	8.6	72.5	22.6
Monterey city	8.692	27,241	28,276	3.8	3,253.1	18.8	75.1	$64,772	26.3	11.5	64.5	6.6	52.0	38.0
Monterey Park city	7.668	60,269	61,458	2.0	8,014.5	53.8	90.2	$54,821	24.6	17.7	58.1	10.1	78.9	16.5
Moorpark city	12.579	34,421	35,550	3.3	2,826.1	17.4	89.8	$99,353	49.7	5.7	72.0	7.6	83.6	12.3
Moraga town	9.465	16,006	17,032	6.4	1,799.5	12.9	84.2	$132,651	61.8	5.0	53.7	8.1	75.6	20.6
Moreno Valley city	51.275	193,365	202,976	5.0	3,958.6	24.5	81.4	$54,229	18.9	17.6	63.7	15.7	84.2	12.2
Morgan Hill city	12.749	37,879	42,068	11.1	3,299.8	19.5	88.4	$96,232	47.1	9.1	68.8	10.0	81.1	15.1
Morro Bay city	5.303	10,234	10,544	3.0	1,988.4	12.6	80.8	$50,914	20.7	12.0	58.7	8.0	51.1	40.9
Mountain House CDP	3.193	9,675	NA	NA	NA	31.2	87.8	$106,119	53.7	7.2	69.5	16.3	83.3	12.8
Mountain View city	11.993	74,020	79,378	7.2	6,618.5	37.2	81.1	$100,028	50.0	8.0	74.0	7.2	56.1	33.5
Murrieta city	33.581	103,429	108,368	4.8	3,227.0	13.4	79.3	$74,401	33.5	7.2	66.0	11.5	77.9	17.6
Muscoy CDP	3.143	10,644	NA	NA	NA	31.6	82.5	$35,660	6.6	33.9	58.0	21.7	83.7	10.9
Napa city	17.855	76,989	80,011	3.9	4,481.2	23.4	85.2	$64,058	29.6	9.1	68.1	9.1	67.9	25.3
National City city	7.279	58,578	60,343	3.0	8,289.8	40.7	88.6	$39,517	11.8	23.9	62.6	12.3	76.4	19.1
Newark city	13.875	42,573	44,723	5.1	3,223.3	34.6	90.8	$86,521	41.7	7.4	66.8	7.4	77.6	16.5
Newman city	2.014	10,219	10,748	5.2	5,335.5	24.6	84.9	$43,722	12.7	24.7	64.7	18.8	81.7	15.2
Newport Beach city	23.778	85,199	87,266	2.4	3,670.0	13.6	81.9	$107,991	53.8	8.0	63.2	7.2	55.6	33.9
Nipomo CDP	14.853	16,714	NA	NA	NA	13.1	85.8	$57,185	27.1	13.0	64.0	8.7	75.6	20.6
Norco city	13.777	27,063	26,959	-0.4	1,956.9	13.1	87.2	$85,142	40.4	6.5	53.4	9.3	77.8	17.7
North Auburn CDP	7.811	13,022	NA	NA	NA	14.4	81.1	$48,052	20.9	10.2	50.2	9.8	66.5	28.6
North Fair Oaks CDP	1.200	14,687	NA	NA	NA	54.4	86.9	$63,343	32.8	17.7	73.7	7.7	73.3	17.8
North Highlands CDP	8.825	42,694	NA	NA	NA	24.0	77.4	$40,986	9.9	22.8	54.5	12.5	70.1	23.2
North Tustin CDP	6.611	24,917	NA	NA	NA	13.4	91.0	$123,270	61.9	3.0	61.1	5.0	81.0	16.2
Norwalk city	9.709	105,549	107,096	1.5	11,031.1	35.2	91.5	$60,523	22.1	13.5	62.6	10.3	82.7	13.5
Novato city	27.443	51,904	55,005	6.0	2,004.3	19.3	86.3	$76,609	39.5	7.4	66.2	7.4	65.6	28.4
Oakdale city	6.045	20,675	21,854	5.7	3,615.5	10.7	77.9	$53,785	22.5	15.3	60.6	13.5	74.3	21.5
Oak Hills CDP	24.390	8,879	NA	NA	NA	10.1	94.1	$74,257	34.8	8.5	57.3	16.5	86.3	10.5
Oakland city	55.893	390,905	413,775	5.9	7,403.0	27.1	83.0	$52,962	26.2	18.7	66.3	11.8	54.4	35.1
Oakley city	15.873	35,428	39,224	10.7	2,471.1	17.3	90.7	$78,597	36.7	9.2	67.7	10.7	79.9	15.6
Oak Park CDP	5.291	13,811	NA	NA	NA	18.5	82.1	$117,326	58.4	5.7	67.4	9.7	75.2	19.1
Oceanside city	41.252	167,086	174,558	4.5	4,231.5	20.0	83.2	$58,385	24.4	13.1	62.4	9.3	68.0	24.1
Oildale CDP	6.533	32,684	NA	NA	NA	4.3	71.8	$33,818	9.6	29.3	55.5	16.1	69.7	23.9
Olivehurst CDP	7.460	13,656	NA	NA	NA	19.7	81.6	$43,044	6.5	14.0	62.3	24.1	74.2	17.7
Ontario city	49.934	163,924	169,089	3.2	3,386.2	30.2	86.0	$54,156	18.1	16.6	66.8	13.0	75.8	19.7
Orange city	25.358	136,419	139,812	2.5	5,513.4	25.7	84.4	$77,086	36.9	10.7	66.1	9.0	72.4	19.7
Orangevale CDP	11.516	33,960	NA	NA	NA	8.3	86.0	$65,288	29.0	7.8	64.9	12.3	69.3	23.3
Orcutt CDP	11.125	28,905	NA	NA	NA	9.3	88.5	$71,830	33.6	6.9	60.2	7.6	72.8	23.7
Orinda city	12.853	17,751	19,003	7.1	1,478.4	14.6	91.5	$166,866	71.7	2.1	59.8	4.9	79.0	18.2
Oroville city	13.237	15,971	16,220	1.6	1,225.3	6.9	77.1	$36,581	10.0	22.9	51.7	12.9	64.3	30.1
Oxnard city	26.901	197,899	205,437	3.8	7,636.9	36.9	88.3	$62,349	25.7	13.9	69.0	10.5	81.2	14.0
Pacifica city	12.662	37,295	39,088	4.8	3,087.1	20.0	90.9	$96,875	48.1	6.0	70.5	6.6	68.0	25.5
Pacific Grove city	2.858	15,039	15,601	3.7	5,459.0	10.7	81.1	$70,230	33.6	7.8	61.5	7.6	55.9	35.2
Palmdale city	105.967	152,750	158,279	3.6	1,493.7	25.8	84.2	$54,921	22.1	18.9	59.6	14.3	80.9	14.5
Palm Desert city	26.809	48,443	51,202	5.7	1,909.9	18.8	81.0	$52,053	23.8	10.1	53.8	10.4	54.8	39.2
Palm Springs city	94.039	44,531	46,854	5.2	498.2	21.5	81.1	$45,497	19.9	14.7	53.7	12.4	39.4	44.3
Palo Alto city	23.873	64,409	66,955	4.0	2,804.7	32.2	81.6	$126,771	59.4	6.4	64.2	5.7	65.0	28.6
Palos Verdes Estates city	4.774	13,438	13,680	1.8	2,865.7	16.4	89.6	$171,328	70.3	3.9	55.3	2.1	82.8	13.9
Paradise town	18.318	26,217	26,449	0.9	1,443.9	3.9	84.0	$41,482	16.0	13.1	49.6	12.6	58.7	34.8
Paramount city	4.730	54,098	55,406	2.4	11,715.0	37.6	88.0	$43,784	11.7	22.8	62.8	13.3	81.2	15.0
Parkway CDP	2.418	14,670	NA	NA	NA	26.4	78.0	$33,959	10.9	28.8	59.6	16.8	70.9	23.6
Parlier city	2.286	14,508	14,990	3.3	6,556.6	42.7	84.5	$31,832	9.1	39.2	67.1	15.9	90.3	7.2
Pasadena city	22.983	137,122	140,881	2.7	6,129.9	30.5	82.7	$70,845	35.7	13.8	66.9	8.9	55.9	34.0
Patterson city	5.954	20,413	21,212	3.9	3,562.7	24.1	86.0	$54,422	21.1	15.3	65.8	15.4	83.1	14.7
Perris city	31.394	68,383	73,756	7.9	2,349.4	27.9	85.1	$48,591	10.5	22.9	64.2	19.9	88.9	7.8

1 Dry land or land partially or temporarily covered by water.
2 16 years old and over.

Table B. Incorporated Places, Census Designated Places (CDPs), and Minor Civil Divisions (MCDs) of 10,000 or More Population — Crime, Construction, and Local Government Finance

STATE City, town, township, borough, or CDP (county if applicable)	Serious crimes known to police, 2014[1] Total number	Rate[2] Total	Rate[2] Violent	Rate[2] Property	New residential construction authorized by building permits, 2014 Value ($1,000)	Number of housing units	Percent single family	Local government finance, 2012 General revenue Total (mil dol)	Intergovernmental Total (mil dol)	Intergovernmental Percent from state gov.	Taxes per capita[3]	General expenditure Total (mil dol)	Per capita[3] Total	Per capita[3] Capital outlays	Debt outstanding (mil dol)
	15	16	17	18	19	20	21	22	23	24	25	26	27	28	29
CALIFORNIA—Con.															
Lompoc city	1,007	2299	349	1949	4,036	22	100.0	49.0	7.6	70.8	479	57.4	1,329	168	54.1
Long Beach city	14,742	3129	489	2640	59,121	323	7.7	1850.9	195.5	44.1	877	1760.6	3,753	846	2390.0
Los Alamitos city	220	1879	137	1742	0	0	0.0	11.0	0.6	76.6	716	11.5	985	184	0.0
Los Altos city	329	1087	23	1064	73,195	217	16.1	38.7	1.3	98.4	820	41.7	1,397	179	1.9
Los Angeles city	102,310	2619	491	2128	2,325,891	11,264	14.8	9274.5	847.5	41.5	997	8678.1	2,247	524	23104.2
Los Banos city	1,033	2791	359	2432	7,025	36	88.9	30.8	1.2	94.3	437	30.9	844	146	28.4
Los Gatos town	639	2087	75	2012	42,013	39	100.0	39.5	1.7	100.0	1010	44.6	1,477	382	23.8
Los Osos CDP	NA	NA	NA	NA	NA	NA	NA	NA	NA	NA	NA	NA	NA	NA	NA
Lynwood city	1,825	2541	558	1983	3,890	23	100.0	48.4	7.5	65.9	465	48.6	685	116	30.0
McFarland city	295	2389	526	1863	6,571	74	86.5	8.1	0.8	54.1	298	7.3	587	138	1.6
McKinleyville CDP	NA	NA	NA	NA	NA	NA	NA	NA	NA	NA	NA	NA	NA	NA	NA
Madera city	2,101	3309	654	2655	40,536	156	100.0	61.9	6.4	52.4	571	58.8	939	220	114.1
Magalia CDP	NA	NA	NA	NA	NA	NA	NA	NA	NA	NA	NA	NA	NA	NA	NA
Malibu city	337	2610	194	2416	13,109	11	100.0	28.4	5.1	13.7	1566	30.4	2,368	525	6.2
Manhattan Beach city	915	2551	103	2448	62,231	98	98.0	64.9	2.0	100.0	1132	68.9	1,939	189	37.6
Manteca city	2,276	3115	241	2875	80,748	427	100.0	96.8	11.6	80.0	571	94.8	1,335	419	214.3
Marina city	521	2538	283	2255	2,470	11	100.0	25.2	2.6	26.5	643	25.9	1,281	243	9.1
Martinez city	1,047	2798	195	2603	12,018	83	45.8	24.4	2.4	100.0	493	24.1	653	42	29.2
Marysville city	593	4844	702	4141	0	0	0.0	11.7	1.3	58.9	394	13.0	1,072	82	9.2
Maywood city	338	1214	316	898	0	0	0.0	11.1	1.5	55.8	321	10.0	361	22	0.0
Mead Valley CDP	NA	NA	NA	NA	NA	NA	NA	NA	NA	NA	NA	NA	NA	NA	NA
Mendota city	359	3127	627	2500	0	0	0.0	6.8	1.8	17.3	216	6.2	547	134	7.6
Menifee city	1,608	1895	126	1769	167,929	570	86.0	33.2	8.6	100.0	243	27.8	341	43	20.0
Menlo Park city	617	1852	156	1696	32,340	49	100.0	57.5	3.5	90.3	1149	61.2	1,859	334	89.8
Merced city	3,202	3924	699	3225	11,678	46	100.0	96.3	17.9	51.3	401	102.4	1,271	255	93.3
Millbrae city	NA	NA	NA	NA	0	0	0.0	33.8	1.3	99.2	819	35.7	1,609	229	75.3
Mill Valley city	199	1381	76	1305	14,185	16	100.0	30.3	1.3	100.0	1313	29.0	2,048	215	9.2
Milpitas city	2,243	3178	159	3020	270,416	1,200	10.6	117.5	7.2	69.9	1162	122.5	1,776	418	171.2
Mission Viejo city	935	963	73	890	850	2	100.0	74.4	7.3	60.1	588	78.4	825	168	47.5
Modesto city	10,891	5292	864	4428	9,726	62	19.4	229.0	48.3	51.3	440	226.5	1,101	147	441.0
Monrovia city	765	2055	126	1929	7,190	34	100.0	51.2	2.2	84.3	1042	56.5	1,525	198	103.5
Montclair city	1,716	4475	548	3927	5,196	28	35.7	47.1	5.3	94.7	892	50.6	1,346	152	77.9
Montebello city	1,583	2484	210	2273	1,618	11	100.0	97.7	20.3	71.7	904	66.8	1,053	70	88.0
Monterey city	1,137	3988	403	3584	799	2	100.0	96.6	3.5	87.7	1575	99.9	3,520	328	14.8
Monterey Park city	1,130	1844	148	1695	9,170	31	87.1	60.2	3.6	69.4	674	56.7	929	44	83.1
Moorpark city	316	895	110	785	67,704	178	100.0	30.0	1.5	80.3	500	35.7	1,021	81	27.6
Moraga town	158	932	47	885	NA	NA	NA	7.5	1.0	100.0	327	7.7	469	71	1.5
Moreno Valley city	6,994	3447	288	3159	12,681	46	100.0	147.5	17.1	68.1	446	166.7	838	157	91.6
Morgan Hill city	677	1628	156	1472	88,145	342	90.9	67.3	2.7	96.6	960	61.1	1,548	436	124.6
Morro Bay city	284	2701	475	2225	4,525	31	32.3	18.9	2.5	81.1	872	20.8	2,001	373	1.1
Mountain House CDP	NA	NA	NA	NA	NA	NA	NA	NA	NA	NA	NA	NA	NA	NA	NA
Mountain View city	1,764	2240	198	2042	128,665	669	15.8	174.0	5.3	63.1	1337	183.3	2,392	549	83.5
Murrieta city	1,526	1408	63	1345	35,975	280	5.7	80.7	26.1	46.3	366	83.1	780	255	90.8
Muscoy CDP	NA	NA	NA	NA	NA	NA	NA	NA	NA	NA	NA	NA	NA	NA	NA
Napa city	1,564	1966	313	1653	13,167	80	31.3	110.6	18.2	18.2	732	117.8	1,502	144	95.7
National City city	1,856	3087	444	2643	26,312	128	11.7	79.9	19.2	23.1	801	70.4	1,183	258	84.5
Newark city	1,080	2429	245	2184	9,292	26	100.0	41.0	2.5	91.0	766	40.3	924	81	11.4
Newman city	182	1694	233	1462	3,947	17	100.0	8.0	0.4	87.4	257	7.4	700	135	2.7
Newport Beach city	1,989	2266	124	2142	84,339	127	66.1	200.4	9.9	61.5	1472	233.0	2,684	829	270.0
Nipomo CDP	NA	NA	NA	NA	NA	NA	NA	NA	NA	NA	NA	NA	NA	NA	NA
Norco city	688	2554	171	2384	394	1	100.0	33.0	2.3	44.5	787	36.0	1,314	451	136.8
North Auburn CDP	NA	NA	NA	NA	NA	NA	NA	NA	NA	NA	NA	NA	NA	NA	NA
North Fair Oaks CDP	NA	NA	NA	NA	NA	NA	NA	NA	NA	NA	NA	NA	NA	NA	NA
North Highlands CDP	NA	NA	NA	NA	NA	NA	NA	NA	NA	NA	NA	NA	NA	NA	NA
North Tustin CDP	NA	NA	NA	NA	NA	NA	NA	NA	NA	NA	NA	NA	NA	NA	NA
Norwalk city	2,317	2169	296	1873	264	1	100.0	85.6	27.5	48.8	464	67.8	637	38	142.9
Novato city	850	1552	146	1406	44,221	258	34.9	49.0	2.3	100.0	669	48.6	913	211	141.1
Oakdale city	865	3995	199	3797	18,110	76	100.0	17.7	1.2	68.4	436	18.9	889	146	41.3
Oak Hills CDP	NA	NA	NA	NA	NA	NA	NA	NA	NA	NA	NA	NA	NA	NA	NA
Oakland city	31,277	7629	1685	5943	49,131	257	31.5	1343.3	204.3	54.6	1420	1312.4	3,266	765	2294.4
Oakley city	514	1323	116	1207	23,863	73	100.0	29.3	2.8	84.6	447	25.9	696	242	39.5
Oak Park CDP	NA	NA	NA	NA	NA	NA	NA	NA	NA	NA	NA	NA	NA	NA	NA
Oceanside city	4,636	2663	374	2288	28,163	86	100.0	233.9	38.0	49.7	620	212.9	1,241	113	200.5
Oildale CDP	NA	NA	NA	NA	NA	NA	NA	NA	NA	NA	NA	NA	NA	NA	NA
Olivehurst CDP	NA	NA	NA	NA	NA	NA	NA	NA	NA	NA	NA	NA	NA	NA	NA
Ontario city	5,085	3022	256	2766	45,594	438	30.1	317.2	21.8	84.9	1031	290.2	1,736	274	212.5
Orange city	2,383	1693	101	1592	29,261	349	2.0	142.3	16.7	75.8	726	160.6	1,151	284	107.1
Orangevale CDP	NA	NA	NA	NA	NA	NA	NA	NA	NA	NA	NA	NA	NA	NA	NA
Orcutt CDP	NA	NA	NA	NA	NA	NA	NA	NA	NA	NA	NA	NA	NA	NA	NA
Orinda city	191	1010	21	989	NA	NA	NA	12.5	0.7	100.0	428	11.8	640	72	0.0
Oroville city	1,085	6743	566	6178	2,850	16	100.0	30.8	8.4	32.8	900	28.8	1,811	287	32.6
Oxnard city	7,266	3559	433	3126	70,849	502	14.1	312.9	40.3	93.9	575	320.7	1,592	328	484.3
Pacifica city	729	1873	234	1639	1,155	4	100.0	41.0	2.7	100.0	544	44.4	1,157	119	52.3
Pacific Grove city	331	2120	192	1928	2,669	9	100.0	23.4	1.4	84.1	928	20.5	1,333	223	20.7
Palmdale city	4,059	2566	531	2035	7,899	42	100.0	135.7	21.8	54.2	550	117.3	753	85	251.2
Palm Desert city	2,318	4548	275	4273	89,997	304	68.4	168.1	3.9	64.2	2515	156.3	3,132	538	450.5
Palm Springs city	3,017	6465	632	5833	58,046	203	95.6	141.9	13.2	18.3	1662	157.5	3,436	660	165.5
Palo Alto city	1,358	2022	88	1934	53,294	91	95.6	217.5	3.5	57.6	1269	250.9	3,789	623	142.0
Palos Verdes Estates city	126	922	37	885	8,057	11	100.0	17.0	0.7	100.0	668	17.8	1,308	204	0.0
Paradise town	568	2159	198	1962	5,065	22	100.0	16.8	4.1	95.7	420	14.4	551	19	14.9
Paramount city	1,647	2984	433	2551	1,147	5	100.0	37.4	3.7	65.3	546	36.2	660	87	69.2
Parkway CDP	NA	NA	NA	NA	NA	NA	NA	NA	NA	NA	NA	NA	NA	NA	NA
Parlier city	350	2341	776	1565	2,959	25	100.0	11.9	3.8	17.3	344	9.7	658	94	2.3
Pasadena city	3,863	2752	281	2471	125,479	684	2.2	411.2	38.8	79.2	1402	403.1	2,905	429	766.2
Patterson city	666	3175	191	2984	3,386	29	100.0	16.3	1.4	69.7	266	19.9	963	75	64.5
Perris city	2,085	2847	246	2602	19,398	200	59.5	49.1	3.7	86.4	376	54.9	770	150	262.8

1 Data for serious crimes have not been adjusted for underreporting. This may affect comparability between geographic areas over time.
2 Per 100,000 population estimated by the FBI. 3 Based on population estimated as of July 1 of the year shown.

Table B. Incorporated Places, Census Designated Places (CDPs), and Minor Civil Divisions (MCDs) of 10,000 or More Population — Land Area, Population, and Households, and Employment

STATE City, town, township, borough, or CDP (county if applicable)	Land area,[1] 2010 (sq mi)	Population Total persons 2010	Population Total persons 2014	Population Percent change 2010–2014	Population Persons per square mile, 2014	Population characteristics 2010–2014 Foreign born	Population characteristics 2010–2014 Lives in same house as previous year	Household income and poverty, 2010–2014 Median household income (dollars)	Household income and poverty, 2010–2014 Percent of households Income of $100,000 or more	Household income and poverty, 2010–2014 Percent of households Income below poverty level	Employment,[2] 2010–2014 Percent in labor force	Employment,[2] 2010–2014 Unemployment rate	Households, 2010–2014 (percent of households) Family households	Households, 2010–2014 (percent of households) One person households
	1	2	3	4	5	6	7	8	9	10	11	12	13	14
CALIFORNIA—Con.														
Petaluma city	14.382	57,941	59,953	3.5	4,168.5	18.2	86.7	$80,590	37.1	9.0	69.3	7.6	67.1	25.5
Phelan CDP	60.097	14,304	NA	NA	NA	9.0	90.5	$53,093	20.0	13.4	50.1	15.1	71.8	25.6
Pico Rivera city	8.296	62,942	64,235	2.1	7,743.3	32.9	90.0	$56,576	20.2	13.5	62.0	11.6	80.8	15.7
Piedmont city	1.700	10,686	11,236	5.1	6,610.6	15.2	89.1	$212,222	77.7	3.4	66.1	4.6	84.1	12.2
Pinole city	5.150	18,330	19,100	4.2	3,708.8	24.6	88.0	$74,379	34.5	7.9	62.2	8.3	72.5	22.1
Pittsburg city	17.188	63,260	68,140	7.7	3,964.5	31.6	82.4	$60,376	25.8	16.5	66.0	13.1	75.6	18.0
Placentia city	6.614	50,893	52,397	3.0	7,922.5	25.8	86.2	$79,275	38.5	9.1	66.1	9.6	78.0	16.5
Placerville city	5.812	10,389	10,556	1.6	1,816.3	8.8	74.7	$46,199	15.3	16.7	56.7	14.0	58.1	35.5
Pleasant Hill city	7.076	33,110	34,497	4.2	4,875.5	19.0	83.4	$81,556	42.0	8.3	64.3	6.9	58.6	32.3
Pleasanton city	24.427	70,317	77,682	10.5	3,180.1	25.1	87.1	$123,608	61.0	4.4	66.7	7.1	79.2	16.7
Pomona city	22.952	149,058	153,350	2.9	6,681.2	34.2	83.5	$48,993	15.9	20.3	60.8	12.9	78.0	16.1
Porterville city	17.608	54,165	55,466	2.4	3,150.1	20.9	86.9	$41,267	13.6	24.3	60.1	13.6	77.0	18.0
Port Hueneme city	4.451	21,723	22,139	1.9	4,974.1	22.1	79.5	$52,826	17.8	18.2	67.2	12.3	69.4	25.5
Poway city	39.079	47,811	49,848	4.3	1,275.6	16.0	90.2	$96,315	48.3	6.0	65.9	6.8	80.6	15.3
Prunedale CDP	46.058	17,560	NA	NA	NA	25.8	88.8	$72,933	33.1	7.9	64.2	9.7	80.3	15.1
Quartz Hill CDP	3.763	10,912	NA	NA	NA	7.9	91.2	$53,929	22.9	19.8	55.4	14.1	74.9	21.3
Ramona CDP	38.412	20,292	NA	NA	NA	18.6	85.7	$62,919	26.8	10.4	64.8	10.2	76.3	17.9
Rancho Cordova city	34.853	64,805	69,740	7.6	2,001.0	24.3	78.4	$53,563	20.4	15.0	67.2	14.1	68.0	23.9
Rancho Cucamonga city	39.864	165,350	174,305	5.4	4,372.5	20.5	83.1	$77,061	37.5	7.7	68.6	10.6	74.1	20.7
Rancho Mirage city	24.463	17,218	17,982	4.4	735.1	14.1	83.3	$71,688	39.1	8.6	41.7	12.7	55.3	33.1
Rancho Palos Verdes city	13.465	41,643	42,726	2.6	3,173.0	26.5	91.2	$120,697	58.2	4.4	55.4	4.7	75.9	20.9
Rancho San Diego CDP	8.701	21,208	NA	NA	NA	19.1	85.4	$80,591	36.1	6.6	62.2	10.3	73.9	23.0
Rancho Santa Margarita city	12.897	47,855	49,359	3.1	3,827.0	17.4	86.8	$104,952	54.1	4.0	75.3	5.0	77.9	18.8
Red Bluff city	7.563	14,076	14,057	-0.1	1,858.8	7.3	76.4	$32,393	7.4	22.3	54.2	17.5	64.1	29.2
Redding city	59.647	89,861	91,593	1.9	1,535.6	5.2	77.7	$43,773	16.0	16.6	56.5	11.4	61.6	30.2
Redlands city	36.031	68,667	70,622	2.8	1,960.0	13.9	85.4	$67,112	32.7	12.8	60.1	7.8	68.1	26.6
Redondo Beach city	6.198	66,748	68,149	2.1	10,994.6	18.4	84.8	$103,064	51.5	5.1	74.0	6.9	60.1	30.9
Redwood City city	19.452	76,802	82,881	7.9	4,260.7	31.9	87.8	$81,955	42.3	7.8	71.4	6.6	65.1	27.5
Reedley city	5.137	24,194	25,426	5.1	4,949.6	31.2	88.7	$46,002	15.4	21.2	66.0	13.9	82.9	15.4
Rialto city	22.343	99,150	102,741	3.6	4,598.4	27.2	83.7	$50,277	14.7	17.7	63.2	16.8	82.1	14.0
Richmond city	30.052	103,671	108,565	4.7	3,612.6	32.4	82.4	$54,857	22.3	16.4	65.8	11.8	66.6	27.7
Ridgecrest city	20.766	27,616	28,726	4.0	1,383.3	10.2	81.4	$61,480	24.1	10.5	64.6	10.0	61.6	31.9
Rio Linda CDP	9.919	15,106	NA	NA	NA	11.1	83.2	$50,873	16.9	14.4	56.9	12.8	70.3	20.9
Ripon city	5.305	14,297	14,966	4.7	2,821.3	6.4	86.0	$75,420	37.2	8.1	64.3	6.9	79.7	15.8
Riverbank city	4.092	22,682	23,798	4.9	5,815.5	22.2	88.8	$59,183	21.6	12.2	68.5	16.5	82.4	12.4
Riverside city	81.178	303,987	319,504	5.1	3,935.8	22.9	82.4	$56,089	22.7	16.8	62.5	13.9	71.4	21.1
Rocklin city	19.545	57,019	60,344	5.8	3,087.5	10.1	83.8	$79,274	38.3	8.5	67.7	9.5	73.2	21.3
Rohnert Park city	7.003	40,818	42,262	3.5	6,034.6	15.3	81.4	$57,557	22.5	14.0	68.1	10.7	57.1	30.5
Rosamond CDP	52.122	18,150	NA	NA	NA	13.3	86.7	$59,099	20.9	15.1	57.8	13.2	74.6	20.0
Rosedale CDP	29.521	14,058	NA	NA	NA	6.6	91.7	$111,273	53.8	5.2	65.6	8.9	82.6	13.0
Rosemead city	5.162	53,764	54,947	2.2	10,644.0	57.0	92.3	$44,524	15.5	19.3	58.8	13.1	83.3	13.1
Rosemont CDP	4.348	22,681	NA	NA	NA	18.8	82.3	$54,384	17.8	15.4	67.2	14.3	63.0	27.1
Roseville city	42.212	118,660	128,615	8.4	3,046.9	12.5	83.4	$76,712	37.8	8.4	65.6	8.3	68.0	25.1
Rossmoor CDP	1.543	10,244	NA	NA	NA	10.6	90.9	$114,239	55.7	3.0	63.3	5.1	80.8	15.7
Rowland Heights CDP	13.075	48,993	NA	NA	NA	56.3	89.3	$61,375	29.2	12.6	58.0	6.1	83.9	12.6
Sacramento city	97.924	466,488	485,199	4.0	4,954.9	22.1	78.8	$50,013	20.4	19.5	63.7	13.7	58.6	32.3
Salida CDP	5.385	13,722	NA	NA	NA	20.7	87.7	$72,872	23.6	8.7	68.9	11.0	84.4	9.3
Salinas city	23.610	150,498	156,677	4.1	6,636.0	37.2	87.3	$49,728	17.8	18.6	63.9	9.9	79.0	16.9
San Anselmo town	2.677	12,336	12,676	2.8	4,734.9	9.3	91.5	$100,681	50.5	5.7	66.5	8.0	63.5	31.2
San Bernardino city	61.507	209,961	215,213	2.5	3,499.0	23.0	79.5	$38,774	11.6	29.1	56.9	17.8	75.0	19.6
San Bruno city	5.461	41,053	43,009	4.8	7,875.4	36.0	90.0	$81,420	38.9	6.2	71.4	7.8	65.8	26.5
San Buenaventura (Ventura) city	21.816	107,231	109,484	2.1	5,018.6	14.5	85.1	$66,485	29.7	9.7	65.6	9.2	62.7	29.2
San Carlos city	5.526	28,406	29,803	4.9	5,392.9	18.8	89.6	$125,747	57.6	3.9	71.3	7.5	66.1	27.5
San Clemente city	18.356	63,497	65,326	2.9	3,558.8	11.2	84.7	$91,749	46.5	7.6	65.0	7.5	70.0	23.7
San Diego city	325.190	1,301,621	1,381,069	6.1	4,247.0	26.3	81.8	$65,753	31.6	13.8	67.6	9.2	59.8	28.6
San Diego Country Estates CDP	16.850	10,109	NA	NA	NA	6.0	86.6	$100,849	51.1	4.2	66.8	8.0	79.8	13.6
San Dimas city	15.037	33,371	34,637	3.8	2,303.4	19.9	84.7	$78,911	38.1	7.6	61.7	8.8	70.5	24.0
San Fernando city	2.374	23,646	24,587	4.0	10,356.7	36.2	92.8	$55,044	19.2	17.7	66.2	9.7	81.5	13.8
San Francisco city	46.893	805,195	852,469	5.9	18,179.1	35.5	84.4	$78,378	41.0	13.4	69.3	7.6	45.8	38.2
San Gabriel city	4.145	39,718	40,519	2.0	9,776.4	54.6	88.2	$56,238	26.3	12.7	62.4	7.5	76.1	19.1
Sanger city	5.720	24,270	24,810	2.2	4,337.7	22.7	85.0	$42,094	15.0	22.8	64.7	16.6	76.0	19.1
San Jacinto city	25.717	44,199	46,490	5.2	1,807.8	22.0	82.1	$46,714	12.9	17.9	58.3	19.9	75.1	19.5
San Jose city	176.571	952,560	1,015,785	6.6	5,752.9	38.7	86.0	$83,787	42.2	10.6	67.8	9.8	73.5	19.7
San Juan Capistrano city	14.235	34,709	36,282	4.5	2,548.8	25.9	87.1	$72,568	37.2	11.3	64.6	11.1	75.1	21.1
San Leandro city	13.347	84,950	89,351	5.2	6,694.5	35.4	88.1	$64,279	29.3	10.1	67.3	9.4	67.8	26.5
San Lorenzo CDP	2.768	23,452	NA	NA	NA	32.6	88.7	$74,283	32.7	8.7	65.4	13.2	77.2	18.4
San Luis Obispo city	13.130	45,170	46,730	3.5	3,559.1	10.0	63.2	$44,894	21.4	26.3	60.5	8.0	41.4	31.5
San Marcos city	24.365	83,650	92,929	11.1	3,814.0	23.4	88.6	$56,139	25.2	15.4	59.3	7.6	71.6	20.1
San Marino city	3.767	13,147	13,423	2.1	3,563.1	37.3	91.1	$119,300	58.2	9.2	52.2	5.6	83.7	14.0
San Mateo city	12.130	97,207	102,893	5.8	8,482.7	32.7	84.6	$90,087	44.7	6.3	70.9	7.4	63.0	29.4
San Pablo city	2.630	29,134	30,050	3.1	11,427.4	41.1	84.1	$42,746	12.1	20.8	64.8	14.1	74.6	19.6
San Rafael city	16.567	57,717	59,237	2.6	3,575.6	28.2	84.2	$75,668	38.2	10.9	67.1	7.4	59.2	31.7
San Ramon city	18.591	72,211	75,332	4.3	4,052.1	32.1	86.1	$129,062	64.8	2.9	72.0	6.0	76.4	18.6
Santa Ana city	27.146	324,782	334,909	3.1	12,337.5	47.3	87.0	$52,519	18.6	19.9	67.4	9.9	81.6	13.3
Santa Barbara city	19.490	88,411	91,196	3.2	4,679.2	25.9	79.5	$65,916	32.4	12.3	68.1	6.8	55.2	32.5
Santa Clara city	18.409	116,491	122,192	4.9	6,637.7	41.0	82.0	$93,840	47.5	8.0	67.6	7.6	66.2	25.7
Santa Clarita city	52.730	176,313	181,557	3.0	3,443.1	20.2	84.2	$83,178	38.8	8.2	68.7	10.0	75.2	19.9
Santa Cruz city	12.740	59,948	63,364	5.7	4,973.5	13.3	72.6	$61,533	29.4	20.7	61.1	7.6	47.5	31.8
Santa Fe Springs city	8.872	16,229	17,537	8.1	1,976.6	23.5	89.8	$51,786	22.6	12.1	58.5	10.8	74.3	22.3
Santa Maria city	22.780	99,597	103,410	3.8	4,539.5	34.3	83.2	$50,753	18.9	18.4	66.3	10.6	76.2	18.6
Santa Monica city	8.415	89,736	92,987	3.6	11,049.9	22.8	80.5	$74,534	39.1	12.3	70.8	9.6	38.4	48.4
Santa Paula city	4.593	29,321	30,441	3.8	6,628.2	29.4	86.6	$53,692	20.3	17.1	65.6	10.1	77.3	18.8
Santa Rosa city	41.292	167,834	174,170	3.8	4,218.0	18.8	82.1	$60,758	25.4	11.5	66.1	10.2	62.0	29.2
Santee city	16.230	53,415	57,052	6.8	3,515.2	8.2	86.2	$74,213	33.0	7.4	67.6	9.5	72.4	21.6

1 Dry land or land partially or temporarily covered by water.
2 16 years old and over.

Table B. Incorporated Places, Census Designated Places (CDPs), and Minor Civil Divisions (MCDs) of 10,000 or More Population — Crime, Construction, and Local Government Finance

STATE City, town, township, borough, or CDP (county if applicable)	Serious crimes known to police, 2014[1] Total number	Rate[2] Total	Rate[2] Violent	Rate[2] Property	New residential construction authorized by building permits, 2014 Value ($1,000)	Number of housing units	Percent single family	Local government finance, 2012 General revenue Total (mil dol)	Intergovernmental Total (mil dol)	Percent from state gov.	Taxes per capita[3]	General expenditure Total (mil dol)	Per capita[3] Total	Capital outlays	Debt outstanding (mil dol)
	15	16	17	18	19	20	21	22	23	24	25	26	27	28	29
CALIFORNIA—Con.															
Petaluma city	1,274	2130	334	1796	19,005	159	9.4	90.6	5.2	59.0	792	83.8	1,424	233	244.3
Phelan CDP	NA	NA	NA	NA	NA	NA	NA	NA	NA	NA	NA	NA	NA	NA	NA
Pico Rivera city	1,635	2556	430	2126	941	4	100.0	61.1	23.1	28.9	422	71.3	1,118	307	49.9
Piedmont city	240	2149	72	2077	300	1	100.0	24.3	1.2	100.0	1405	25.4	2,315	229	11.6
Pinole city	701	3683	363	3320	0	0	0.0	24.9	3.0	100.0	609	28.4	1,517	153	67.0
Pittsburg city	2,537	3758	259	3499	48,231	217	100.0	89.1	17.2	34.3	708	101.3	1,544	207	474.6
Placentia city	814	1550	156	1394	10,203	47	78.7	41.3	4.4	89.2	512	39.0	750	113	28.8
Placerville city	330	3147	544	2603	2,308	10	100.0	14.9	2.5	36.1	633	15.2	1,467	328	17.2
Pleasant Hill city	1,798	5232	175	5058	741	2	100.0	28.8	3.6	100.0	664	29.7	877	199	21.7
Pleasanton city	1,305	1739	81	1657	80,572	333	23.4	134.8	6.1	84.2	1125	130.6	1,807	174	82.6
Pomona city	5,180	3410	512	2899	7,658	39	89.7	196.5	41.6	62.7	692	201.6	1,334	134	411.1
Porterville city	1,362	2459	285	2174	26,052	280	11.4	49.1	8.8	73.5	387	51.3	933	177	72.6
Port Hueneme city	436	1960	400	1560	8,405	68	32.4	32.4	2.7	47.9	667	38.2	1,750	147	22.5
Poway city	506	1016	141	876	9,623	19	100.0	88.7	1.8	88.7	1375	85.0	1,731	191	246.1
Prunedale CDP	NA	NA	NA	NA	NA	NA	NA	NA	NA	NA	NA	NA	NA	NA	NA
Quartz Hill CDP	NA	NA	NA	NA	NA	NA	NA	NA	NA	NA	NA	NA	NA	NA	NA
Ramona CDP	NA	NA	NA	NA	NA	NA	NA	NA	NA	NA	NA	NA	NA	NA	NA
Rancho Cordova city	1,949	2840	444	2395	55,807	222	74.8	68.7	14.0	40.7	660	65.9	985	308	23.3
Rancho Cucamonga city	3,951	2288	164	2124	67,384	261	97.7	230.6	19.5	59.9	950	207.7	1,218	193	503.8
Rancho Mirage city	NA	NA	NA	NA	22,137	38	100.0	70.4	1.0	88.1	2819	66.2	3,750	364	164.3
Rancho Palos Verdes city	496	1163	56	1107	3,210	8	100.0	29.2	1.6	88.9	577	28.5	673	66	24.4
Rancho San Diego CDP	NA	NA	NA	NA	NA	NA	NA	NA	NA	NA	NA	NA	NA	NA	NA
Rancho Santa Margarita city	230	464	54	410	0	0	0.0	16.9	2.4	90.6	285	17.3	354	60	11.4
Red Bluff city	1,040	7374	915	6460	3,754	21	100.0	10.6	1.4	94.6	391	11.1	787	18	6.3
Redding city	4,534	4959	667	4292	24,102	112	100.0	182.1	39.5	29.9	638	162.8	1,795	572	140.7
Redlands city	2,984	4245	209	4036	15,598	67	86.6	93.8	3.7	75.1	805	85.8	1,228	162	63.1
Redondo Beach city	1,605	2358	232	2126	34,381	102	100.0	117.9	8.1	72.6	867	113.6	1,680	108	53.3
Redwood City city	1,922	2348	237	2111	168,414	781	1.3	145.3	7.3	85.5	1028	149.2	1,881	250	164.1
Reedley city	659	2617	790	1826	391	1	100.0	22.3	3.4	26.5	358	18.6	751	85	26.3
Rialto city	2,482	2421	320	2101	5,903	28	85.7	107.1	8.8	38.5	639	111.4	1,095	208	226.0
Richmond city	5,124	4724	777	3947	1,749	8	100.0	254.5	35.4	49.7	1416	274.3	2,573	398	657.3
Ridgecrest city	588	2040	409	1630	954	8	100.0	21.9	1.1	90.4	556	20.8	736	131	40.5
Rio Linda CDP	NA	NA	NA	NA	NA	NA	NA	NA	NA	NA	NA	NA	NA	NA	NA
Ripon city	276	1857	121	1736	5,029	17	100.0	19.1	0.7	98.9	894	16.4	1,116	188	40.9
Riverbank city	716	3022	118	2904	4,682	32	100.0	13.0	1.1	59.7	285	13.7	587	131	4.0
Riverside city	11,248	3521	433	3088	70,655	315	73.0	410.7	63.1	60.7	631	486.0	1,551	356	1908.6
Rocklin city	1,089	1804	83	1721	110,269	408	72.8	52.5	5.7	74.5	549	53.8	911	89	85.0
Rohnert Park city	895	2155	385	1770	2,464	32	0.0	59.0	3.3	100.0	780	57.7	1,402	280	71.7
Rosamond CDP	NA	NA	NA	NA	NA	NA	NA	NA	NA	NA	NA	NA	NA	NA	NA
Rosedale CDP	NA	NA	NA	NA	NA	NA	NA	NA	NA	NA	NA	NA	NA	NA	NA
Rosemead city	1,333	2435	269	2166	1,120	4	100.0	34.4	2.8	59.2	469	32.2	592	173	43.5
Rosemont CDP	NA	NA	NA	NA	NA	NA	NA	NA	NA	NA	NA	NA	NA	NA	NA
Roseville city	3,263	2530	150	2380	171,031	809	79.7	251.3	19.4	55.2	738	243.4	1,960	236	1069.1
Rossmoor CDP	NA	NA	NA	NA	NA	NA	NA	NA	NA	NA	NA	NA	NA	NA	NA
Rowland Heights CDP	NA	NA	NA	NA	NA	NA	NA	NA	NA	NA	NA	NA	NA	NA	NA
Sacramento city	18,046	3738	615	3123	60,400	281	91.1	884.8	128.8	66.1	771	806.3	1,695	296	1087.3
Salida CDP	NA	NA	NA	NA	NA	NA	NA	NA	NA	NA	NA	NA	NA	NA	NA
Salinas city	6,224	3967	635	3331	10,784	66	45.5	117.7	16.6	57.5	532	122.6	794	103	42.6
San Anselmo town	NA	NA	NA	NA	1,965	3	100.0	14.8	0.5	100.0	1005	20.0	1,596	143	11.8
San Bernardino city	11,367	5297	992	4305	31,845	115	82.6	250.9	21.3	61.3	621	230.8	1,081	128	121.7
San Bruno city	1,164	2720	257	2463	0	0	0.0	58.6	3.4	100.0	704	51.8	1,228	135	11.6
San Buenaventura (Ventura) city	4,143	3792	253	3540	11,532	96	32.3	132.2	9.8	64.9	662	135.5	1,247	155	122.9
San Carlos city	NA	NA	NA	NA	1,420	2	100.0	46.8	1.0	100.0	933	38.4	1,315	156	24.3
San Clemente city	756	1156	106	1051	43,713	103	62.1	74.5	6.4	93.0	685	82.7	1,276	289	18.2
San Diego city	32,026	2340	381	1959	524,088	2,743	26.0	2616.7	370.0	40.2	838	2361.5	1,763	396	3433.7
San Diego Country Estates CDP	NA	NA	NA	NA	NA	NA	NA	NA	NA	NA	NA	NA	NA	NA	NA
San Dimas city	700	2062	203	1858	642	2	100.0	30.5	1.5	86.2	690	33.2	982	105	19.7
San Fernando city	481	1974	308	1667	10,100	82	0.0	31.5	1.9	69.0	786	30.5	1,275	44	12.9
San Francisco city	51,854	6098	795	5303	768,892	2,711	1.3	7274.1	2355.9	68.6	3430	5704.0	6,875	846	13075.2
San Gabriel city	638	1579	205	1373	7,554	24	100.0	37.1	3.0	81.2	626	40.2	999	177	3.0
Sanger city	646	2608	392	2216	2,192	16	100.0	23.9	2.0	95.3	389	21.6	877	111	20.1
San Jacinto city	1,976	4276	219	4057	9,141	56	100.0	28.1	1.5	100.0	318	31.0	681	34	24.5
San Jose city	27,819	2755	321	2434	595,056	4,445	8.6	1721.1	116.7	56.0	876	1428.0	1,449	178	5924.6
San Juan Capistrano city	445	1232	172	1060	26,097	59	100.0	47.2	4.4	76.8	856	40.6	1,144	265	68.5
San Leandro city	4,126	4652	416	4236	22,960	116	0.9	123.0	8.3	72.0	1016	121.7	1,398	127	78.3
San Lorenzo CDP	NA	NA	NA	NA	NA	NA	NA	NA	NA	NA	NA	NA	NA	NA	NA
San Luis Obispo city	1,679	3597	514	3083	44,060	200	69.5	81.4	6.3	56.0	1049	76.5	1,668	350	65.5
San Marcos city	1,482	1632	216	1416	41,025	101	94.1	121.3	7.6	84.2	879	132.6	1,523	283	501.2
San Marino city	226	1690	37	1653	10,026	15	100.0	23.1	1.3	99.2	1177	23.8	1,789	282	6.0
San Mateo city	2,174	2130	225	1904	23,644	96	100.0	145.7	11.0	62.3	867	148.4	1,483	264	159.9
San Pablo city	1,403	4703	808	3895	7,751	31	100.0	44.1	1.8	97.0	1326	38.0	1,291	386	81.2
San Rafael city	1,857	3132	326	2806	113	1	100.0	85.9	4.1	86.9	903	87.5	1,496	47	46.5
San Ramon city	771	1027	31	997	6,076	48	0.0	74.2	3.7	100.0	557	75.1	1,017	190	108.0
Santa Ana city	7,044	2094	374	1719	19,782	95	100.0	440.5	127.5	23.8	621	391.8	1,181	145	358.1
Santa Barbara city	2,691	2961	332	2628	25,749	119	5.9	246.8	36.0	63.6	1149	228.4	2,550	530	112.5
Santa Clara city	3,430	2832	134	2698	305,287	1,687	3.3	280.5	11.7	71.5	1039	212.3	1,776	110	388.8
Santa Clarita city	2,744	1326	148	1178	90,637	322	94.1	152.4	24.6	54.9	448	145.6	814	191	94.2
Santa Cruz city	3,794	5980	826	5154	16,675	50	100.0	132.1	4.8	59.8	977	145.4	2,345	279	79.2
Santa Fe Springs city	1,198	6943	429	6514	21,780	156	3.8	73.4	1.5	98.2	3786	79.3	4,718	1,088	133.9
Santa Maria city	3,484	3386	427	2960	52,179	344	37.8	117.0	16.8	78.0	574	112.6	1,111	201	66.7
Santa Monica city	3,364	3611	363	3248	65,012	228	18.0	560.2	57.7	51.4	3618	538.6	5,867	1,727	353.1
Santa Paula city	532	1758	281	1477	604	2	100.0	29.3	4.2	87.4	428	23.2	771	142	69.0
Santa Rosa city	4,486	2593	368	2226	44,969	248	74.2	262.1	24.5	59.6	702	250.3	1,470	305	483.1
Santee city	924	1629	229	1399	19,963	176	2.3	44.7	2.6	60.7	616	49.1	885	180	52.7

1 Data for serious crimes have not been adjusted for underreporting. This may affect comparability between geographic areas over time.
2 Per 100,000 population estimated by the FBI.   3 Based on population estimated as of July 1 of the year shown.

Table B. Incorporated Places, Census Designated Places (CDPs), and Minor Civil Divisions (MCDs) of 10,000 or More Population — **Land Area, Population, and Households, and Employment**

STATE City, town, township, borough, or CDP (county if applicable)	Land area,[1] 2010 (sq mi)	Total persons 2010	Total persons 2014	Percent change 2010–2014	Persons per square mile, 2014	Foreign born	Lives in same house as previous year	Median household income (dollars)	Income of $100,000 or more	Income below poverty level	Percent in labor force	Unemploy-ment rate	Family households	One person households
	1	2	3	4	5	6	7	8	9	10	11	12	13	14
CALIFORNIA—Con.														
Saratoga city	12.479	29,971	31,001	3.4	2,484.3	37.9	90.3	$167,917	70.5	3.9	57.9	6.3	83.9	14.2
Scotts Valley city	4.618	11,581	11,858	2.4	2,567.8	11.2	89.5	$102,927	52.1	5.4	63.8	7.3	69.9	24.3
Seal Beach city	11.297	24,072	24,662	2.5	2,183.0	13.7	83.8	$54,026	30.0	11.3	49.5	6.8	48.4	44.7
Seaside city	9.240	33,025	34,182	3.5	3,699.3	31.6	81.0	$52,538	22.0	15.3	68.6	10.4	72.2	20.9
Selma city	5.138	23,219	24,283	4.6	4,726.2	28.1	86.7	$43,143	11.4	25.3	61.6	14.8	82.8	14.7
Shafter city	27.945	16,988	17,559	3.4	628.4	29.3	82.6	$41,107	12.0	20.2	57.6	15.5	87.4	9.1
Shasta Lake city	10.921	10,164	10,166	0.0	930.9	5.8	85.9	$40,295	12.8	19.7	54.9	12.7	66.4	28.3
Sierra Madre city	2.953	10,917	11,165	2.3	3,781.5	15.6	89.1	$90,780	42.8	6.1	65.3	5.1	66.2	27.8
Signal Hill city	2.176	11,016	11,526	4.6	5,295.9	30.1	92.1	$67,320	27.3	13.9	71.1	10.5	66.5	25.6
Simi Valley city	41.476	124,239	126,871	2.1	3,058.9	19.1	88.3	$89,595	43.9	6.0	70.0	8.2	76.3	17.8
Solana Beach city	3.520	12,867	13,337	3.7	3,789.5	18.6	83.9	$90,579	46.6	6.4	63.3	9.1	60.3	29.7
Soledad city	4.414	25,740	25,336	-1.6	5,740.1	31.6	78.2	$46,010	17.5	18.9	33.1	12.5	89.6	7.8
Sonoma city	2.744	10,652	11,017	3.4	4,015.5	7.8	87.4	$66,951	34.4	6.7	58.9	7.7	55.9	37.6
Soquel CDP	4.598	9,644	NA	NA	NA	12.1	87.3	$78,703	35.7	11.3	66.8	8.5	63.8	27.8
South El Monte city	2.843	20,116	20,569	2.3	7,234.3	44.8	92.8	$44,498	13.6	16.0	58.7	5.8	84.2	11.2
South Gate city	7.236	94,396	96,312	2.0	13,309.7	43.8	88.3	$43,526	12.0	21.8	63.7	14.3	85.2	11.7
South Lake Tahoe city	10.158	21,400	21,529	0.6	2,119.4	19.8	80.8	$41,380	15.5	19.1	68.0	12.4	55.0	34.7
South Pasadena city	3.405	25,619	26,156	2.1	7,680.7	28.3	85.1	$80,479	40.7	7.7	70.8	7.3	61.7	31.8
South San Francisco city	9.178	63,664	67,009	5.3	7,301.4	41.6	90.0	$78,101	37.5	8.0	67.8	7.9	72.0	21.8
South San Jose Hills CDP	1.508	20,551	NA	NA	NA	40.7	94.6	$58,154	19.7	17.1	60.6	11.5	88.1	7.7
South Whittier CDP	5.337	57,156	NA	NA	NA	25.3	91.0	$64,112	26.5	12.4	61.6	8.6	84.3	12.3
Spring Valley CDP (San Diego County)	7.164	28,205	NA	NA	NA	16.5	93.8	$64,517	29.6	11.6	66.0	10.4	75.6	17.7
Stanford CDP	2.731	13,809	NA	NA	NA	25.6	50.3	$51,622	35.1	20.1	46.5	5.1	38.6	33.2
Stanton city	3.097	37,827	38,719	2.4	12,503.2	43.6	88.1	$45,842	16.2	18.1	65.3	11.9	73.6	20.5
Stevenson Ranch CDP	6.357	17,557	NA	NA	NA	19.8	85.9	$114,555	57.2	4.4	70.7	8.0	76.9	16.1
Stockton city	61.667	291,731	302,389	3.7	4,903.6	26.2	79.4	$45,347	18.2	23.0	60.4	16.3	73.1	21.3
Suisun City city	4.105	28,104	29,256	4.1	7,126.5	21.7	81.3	$71,306	32.0	11.4	68.8	9.9	79.5	15.7
Sunnyvale city	21.983	140,058	149,980	7.1	6,822.4	44.6	82.2	$103,257	52.3	6.9	69.9	7.8	67.6	24.4
Sun Village CDP	10.679	11,565	NA	NA	NA	22.6	90.6	$57,840	16.8	14.0	55.3	14.5	78.9	17.8
Susanville city	7.945	17,943	15,543	-13.4	1,956.4	7.2	63.6	$49,430	16.1	21.6	30.0	16.4	57.0	34.8
Tamalpais-Homestead Valley CDP	4.685	10,735	NA	NA	NA	12.3	84.8	$138,598	64.8	5.6	71.6	7.6	68.7	22.7
Tehachapi city	9.875	14,414	13,236	-8.2	1,340.4	11.3	69.5	$42,654	18.4	16.3	36.2	9.0	70.2	29.0
Temecula city	37.211	100,156	109,428	9.3	2,940.7	15.3	82.2	$78,535	36.5	7.8	66.2	10.6	79.6	15.1
Temescal Valley CDP	19.276	22,535	NA	NA	NA	16.9	89.5	$89,259	43.6	7.7	64.6	12.2	81.6	12.4
Temple City city	4.006	35,558	36,334	2.2	9,070.7	47.2	89.3	$63,803	30.2	12.1	60.0	7.6	78.3	18.0
Thousand Oaks city	55.183	126,555	129,342	2.2	2,343.9	18.8	86.7	$99,115	49.6	6.8	66.5	9.7	72.6	22.3
Torrance city	20.478	145,438	148,495	2.1	7,251.4	28.9	87.6	$78,286	38.0	7.8	64.8	8.1	69.2	25.9
Tracy city	22.562	83,101	85,841	3.3	3,804.7	24.8	84.6	$74,748	35.0	8.7	69.5	12.9	81.4	13.5
Truckee town	32.322	16,164	16,297	0.8	504.2	13.0	85.2	$72,159	33.9	9.6	76.6	9.9	65.9	24.1
Tulare city	20.375	59,312	61,867	4.3	3,036.4	20.1	85.5	$46,387	15.2	19.7	61.6	11.8	78.4	16.5
Turlock city	16.928	68,549	71,245	3.9	4,208.6	24.1	80.0	$51,594	20.0	16.8	63.7	14.5	72.1	21.2
Tustin city	11.128	75,314	80,621	7.0	7,245.1	36.5	81.7	$71,105	33.5	11.5	72.1	8.9	71.6	21.9
Twentynine Palms city	59.143	25,048	25,902	3.4	438.0	5.5	57.7	$40,890	10.7	16.8	69.0	18.5	71.4	24.5
Ukiah city	4.670	16,075	15,977	-0.6	3,420.9	12.3	80.4	$42,237	13.9	18.5	60.6	17.9	55.6	36.2
Union City city	19.400	69,524	73,621	5.9	3,795.0	46.0	90.8	$82,564	41.5	8.2	65.1	8.9	81.2	15.0
Upland city	15.617	73,732	76,043	3.1	4,869.4	18.6	84.2	$61,551	27.4	13.9	63.9	9.2	68.4	25.3
Vacaville city	28.383	92,422	95,856	3.7	3,377.3	12.9	83.0	$74,207	32.4	9.2	62.3	10.1	69.4	25.1
Valinda CDP	2.014	22,822	NA	NA	NA	37.8	92.6	$66,697	26.6	12.5	63.7	11.6	89.4	7.3
Vallejo city	30.671	115,940	120,228	3.7	3,919.9	28.3	82.7	$58,472	24.5	16.3	63.4	15.3	67.9	25.2
Valle Vista CDP	6.868	14,578	NA	NA	NA	11.5	86.5	$40,010	14.5	20.8	51.7	15.6	67.6	25.7
Victorville city	73.330	115,921	121,901	5.2	1,662.4	18.1	82.2	$47,142	15.1	21.8	53.3	15.2	79.7	15.5
View Park-Windsor Hills CDP	1.841	11,075	NA	NA	NA	7.3	90.0	$76,461	39.4	6.6	63.0	12.1	59.0	35.2
Vincent CDP	1.472	15,922	NA	NA	NA	32.1	93.8	$76,682	29.0	8.1	66.2	9.7	87.5	9.6
Vineyard CDP	17.203	24,836	NA	NA	NA	24.9	84.0	$76,084	35.8	10.3	67.0	10.6	81.0	12.2
Visalia city	37.258	124,457	129,281	3.9	3,469.9	13.8	82.7	$52,262	21.6	17.6	63.5	11.0	74.0	21.5
Vista city	18.680	93,854	98,079	4.5	5,250.6	25.9	88.2	$47,782	16.9	16.1	60.0	7.4	68.9	20.8
Walnut city	8.992	29,172	30,214	3.6	3,360.0	48.4	91.7	$100,934	50.4	6.9	62.2	7.5	88.9	8.5
Walnut Creek city	19.759	64,174	67,673	5.5	3,425.0	22.4	83.2	$80,399	40.5	6.1	58.7	7.1	55.6	37.6
Walnut Park CDP	0.748	15,966	NA	NA	NA	49.1	91.6	$41,202	12.8	22.6	61.8	13.8	87.6	10.1
Wasco city	9.426	25,552	26,303	2.9	2,790.5	29.1	72.3	$39,273	9.1	30.0	43.8	16.4	84.4	12.7
Watsonville city	6.688	51,199	53,111	3.7	7,941.7	39.3	90.5	$46,691	16.1	19.3	66.6	10.2	78.9	18.2
West Carson CDP	2.266	21,699	NA	NA	NA	35.4	89.3	$62,414	28.6	9.1	61.6	10.2	68.7	27.3
West Covina city	16.041	106,098	108,455	2.2	6,761.0	34.5	85.9	$67,069	28.1	9.6	65.2	13.7	79.6	15.8
West Hollywood city	1.887	34,399	35,883	4.3	19,011.8	26.5	79.7	$56,025	26.6	15.8	77.0	9.1	20.5	60.2
Westminster city	10.043	89,614	92,068	2.7	9,167.4	45.8	86.3	$53,660	24.1	16.3	61.1	11.1	77.4	17.4
Westmont CDP	1.848	31,853	NA	NA	NA	22.7	88.4	$27,072	7.4	34.3	56.1	17.5	67.8	28.6
West Puente Valley CDP	1.869	22,636	NA	NA	NA	37.3	92.8	$62,669	22.3	11.2	61.2	13.3	88.3	9.9
West Rancho Dominguez CDP	3.974	5,669	NA	NA	NA	21.8	90.3	$44,909	12.6	18.8	58.4	14.8	75.5	21.7
West Sacramento city	21.496	48,744	51,847	6.4	2,412.0	22.9	81.7	$53,307	24.4	18.6	65.3	11.1	66.2	24.8
West Whittier-Los Nietos CDP	2.519	25,540	NA	NA	NA	26.8	93.3	$62,486	23.6	13.6	61.9	11.0	82.8	13.3
Whittier city	14.649	85,328	87,318	2.3	5,960.8	18.1	89.2	$65,583	31.3	11.8	63.9	8.7	73.4	22.0
Wildomar city	23.688	32,220	35,377	9.8	1,493.5	19.0	84.5	$60,816	23.9	11.5	65.7	14.0	79.9	14.7
Willowbrook CDP	1.547	35,983	NA	NA	NA	32.3	86.8	$37,760	8.5	29.9	63.4	17.9	81.8	14.9
Windsor town	7.268	26,795	27,414	2.3	3,771.8	14.9	88.9	$81,442	39.7	4.3	67.7	8.7	75.7	21.1
Winter Gardens CDP	4.429	20,631	NA	NA	NA	12.3	86.9	$61,759	23.9	7.6	65.5	10.3	71.1	21.9
Winton CDP	3.041	10,613	NA	NA	NA	33.3	77.3	$41,091	8.7	22.4	68.3	21.5	85.3	11.4
Woodcrest CDP	11.411	14,347	NA	NA	NA	15.8	89.8	$86,095	43.8	7.6	63.2	14.5	89.1	8.3
Woodland city	15.306	55,468	57,432	3.5	3,752.2	21.9	83.9	$54,532	24.0	13.5	64.6	9.8	70.8	23.3
Yorba Linda city	19.314	64,193	67,826	5.7	3,511.8	18.0	89.2	$115,994	58.3	3.3	67.9	8.0	83.8	13.6
Yuba City city	14.649	64,925	65,773	1.3	4,489.9	25.0	83.8	$50,494	19.7	16.5	61.4	14.7	71.7	22.6
Yucaipa city	28.401	51,371	53,096	3.4	1,869.5	9.6	86.4	$58,506	26.6	14.0	60.7	13.7	74.5	21.1
Yucca Valley town	40.015	20,700	21,485	3.8	536.9	6.6	76.4	$43,086	11.3	16.8	52.4	16.8	60.3	33.4
COLORADO	103,641.884	5,029,324	5,355,866	6.5	51.7	9.8	80.6	$59,448	26.2	12.1	68.7	7.9	64.2	28.0
Arvada city	38.332	106,474	113,574	6.7	2,962.9	5.0	84.9	$69,550	29.9	8.6	70.9	7.1	67.0	27.0

1 Dry land or land partially or temporarily covered by water.
2 16 years old and over.

Table B. Incorporated Places, Census Designated Places (CDPs), and Minor Civil Divisions (MCDs) of 10,000 or More Population — Crime, Construction, and Local Government Finance

STATE City, town, township, borough, or CDP (county if applicable)	Serious crimes known to police, 2014[1] Total number	Rate[2] Total	Rate[2] Violent	Rate[2] Property	New residential construction authorized by building permits, 2014 Value ($1,000)	Number of housing units	Percent single family	Local government finance, 2012 General revenue Total (mil dol)	Intergovernmental Total (mil dol)	Percent from state gov.	Taxes per capita[3]	General expenditure Total (mil dol)	Per capita[3] Total	Per capita[3] Capital outlays	Debt outstanding (mil dol)
	15	16	17	18	19	20	21	22	23	24	25	26	27	28	29
CALIFORNIA—Con.															
Saratoga city	307	986	61	925	14,667	19	100.0	20.9	1.1	97.2	490	22.6	736	169	12.0
Scotts Valley city	281	2382	144	2238	1,910	5	100.0	15.5	1.0	100.0	935	16.1	1,375	117	21.1
Seal Beach city	520	2103	105	1998	2,290	4	100.0	37.3	4.5	86.7	973	39.1	1,593	460	18.8
Seaside city	623	1814	338	1476	0	0	0.0	27.0	2.8	39.4	662	30.5	899	206	39.4
Selma city	1,140	4671	631	4040	2,579	12	100.0	15.6	1.6	71.0	409	16.9	712	115	16.4
Shafter city	508	2947	267	2681	14,804	105	100.0	30.5	1.0	76.2	900	28.5	1,666	536	18.0
Shasta Lake city	NA	NA	NA	NA	2,496	20	100.0	11.7	1.2	25.8	494	11.7	1,156	290	22.9
Sierra Madre city	105	947	117	830	2,178	10	70.0	13.9	1.0	92.1	816	13.7	1,241	129	12.3
Signal Hill city	540	4732	351	4382	4,905	18	100.0	31.0	1.0	69.6	2327	35.1	3,133	934	116.1
Simi Valley city	1,758	1389	111	1278	2,286	3	100.0	96.1	10.2	52.4	497	92.5	736	103	147.8
Solana Beach city	210	1576	165	1411	19,365	24	100.0	20.2	0.6	88.8	918	22.9	1,744	353	13.8
Soledad city	285	1104	205	899	0	0	0.0	15.7	1.0	97.1	229	14.9	563	43	45.3
Sonoma city	200	1826	311	1516	1,764	9	77.8	19.8	0.6	92.2	1338	20.1	1,859	487	46.6
Soquel CDP	NA	NA	NA	NA	NA	NA	NA	NA	NA	NA	NA	NA	NA	NA	NA
South El Monte city	767	3748	586	3161	16,432	80	100.0	16.7	1.2	67.4	726	19.3	946	256	34.7
South Gate city	3,193	3327	527	2800	35,943	224	1.3	80.6	17.7	38.8	383	67.6	707	121	167.3
South Lake Tahoe city	628	2937	524	2414	17,219	56	50.0	55.8	3.8	66.5	1454	64.9	3,048	601	197.1
South Pasadena city	505	1939	115	1824	1,921	5	100.0	28.7	3.5	84.1	731	28.2	1,089	148	7.3
South San Francisco city	1,430	2141	234	1907	731	5	100.0	128.4	5.4	89.0	1179	122.6	1,863	259	146.4
South San Jose Hills CDP	NA	NA	NA	NA	NA	NA	NA	NA	NA	NA	NA	NA	NA	NA	NA
South Whittier CDP	NA	NA	NA	NA	NA	NA	NA	NA	NA	NA	NA	NA	NA	NA	NA
Spring Valley CDP (San Diego County)	NA	NA	NA	NA	NA	NA	NA	NA	NA	NA	NA	NA	NA	NA	NA
Stanford CDP	NA	NA	NA	NA	NA	NA	NA	NA	NA	NA	NA	NA	NA	NA	NA
Stanton city	808	2083	320	1763	9,574	52	100.0	32.9	2.6	78.3	682	38.1	989	253	76.1
Stevenson Ranch CDP	NA	NA	NA	NA	NA	NA	NA	NA	NA	NA	NA	NA	NA	NA	NA
Stockton city	17,136	5721	1331	4390	21,907	96	79.2	381.7	98.9	79.6	544	384.7	1,293	244	572.9
Suisun City city	674	2325	235	2091	0	0	0.0	27.1	4.4	39.6	458	30.3	1,061	113	69.5
Sunnyvale city	2,523	1689	112	1577	133,544	821	23.9	274.8	32.4	34.0	770	274.4	1,871	145	125.4
Sun Village CDP	NA	NA	NA	NA	NA	NA	NA	NA	NA	NA	NA	NA	NA	NA	NA
Susanville city	422	2804	711	2093	0	0	0.0	7.0	1.1	82.5	265	6.6	397	18	37.4
Tamalpais-Homestead Valley CDP	NA	NA	NA	NA	NA	NA	NA	NA	NA	NA	NA	NA	NA	NA	NA
Tehachapi city	360	2770	392	2377	2,065	6	100.0	14.4	3.1	95.6	485	15.3	1,107	323	20.2
Temecula city	2,635	2433	92	2341	79,397	662	35.3	113.3	14.0	33.6	665	129.7	1,238	371	96.6
Temescal Valley CDP	NA	NA	NA	NA	NA	NA	NA	NA	NA	NA	NA	NA	NA	NA	NA
Temple City city	473	1304	124	1180	37,086	104	100.0	15.4	1.3	81.7	305	14.2	393	12	6.3
Thousand Oaks city	1,727	1337	99	1238	13,270	48	33.3	143.2	11.9	64.9	660	145.4	1,135	190	133.2
Torrance city	2,778	1877	105	1773	7,377	27	100.0	261.0	41.4	39.9	1056	234.0	1,589	118	148.8
Tracy city	2,391	2810	152	2659	44,538	135	100.0	114.6	11.3	53.2	556	128.6	1,519	332	222.9
Truckee town	182	1126	111	1015	25,762	87	100.0	29.5	4.5	97.0	1155	30.0	1,863	578	22.8
Tulare city	2,511	4077	742	3335	32,642	203	100.0	97.1	4.2	71.5	632	90.8	1,492	464	200.3
Turlock city	2,882	4071	526	3546	19,356	95	100.0	69.6	5.8	56.0	496	83.2	1,193	431	69.6
Tustin city	1,488	1882	167	1715	920	3	100.0	77.0	3.6	66.8	661	77.9	1,001	98	193.5
Twentynine Palms city	363	1400	239	1161	909	8	100.0	11.2	1.2	85.8	370	12.3	477	86	11.0
Ukiah city	685	4326	846	3479	0	0	0.0	30.2	2.2	38.4	904	30.8	1,934	342	108.9
Union City city	1,809	2469	283	2186	66	1	100.0	85.1	5.7	83.5	850	92.0	1,283	294	178.1
Upland city	2,335	3081	224	2857	14,193	54	100.0	71.1	4.5	65.1	502	74.2	987	59	41.7
Vacaville city	2,855	3015	283	2732	41,786	138	100.0	153.8	33.0	26.6	848	156.0	1,662	571	190.4
Valinda CDP	NA	NA	NA	NA	NA	NA	NA	NA	NA	NA	NA	NA	NA	NA	NA
Vallejo city	5,911	4946	865	4081	4,366	17	100.0	195.2	49.6	22.5	549	152.7	1,295	112	192.2
Valle Vista CDP	NA	NA	NA	NA	NA	NA	NA	NA	NA	NA	NA	NA	NA	NA	NA
Victorville city	5,016	4101	525	3576	13,341	46	100.0	115.4	9.5	68.3	448	130.1	1,082	123	370.9
View Park-Windsor Hills CDP	NA	NA	NA	NA	NA	NA	NA	NA	NA	NA	NA	NA	NA	NA	NA
Vincent CDP	NA	NA	NA	NA	NA	NA	NA	NA	NA	NA	NA	NA	NA	NA	NA
Vineyard CDP	NA	NA	NA	NA	NA	NA	NA	NA	NA	NA	NA	NA	NA	NA	NA
Visalia city	4,280	3331	377	2954	108,591	435	98.2	157.6	23.1	61.9	540	143.8	1,134	282	31.2
Vista city	2,026	2075	348	1727	108,020	753	7.2	132.0	9.1	80.1	601	117.1	1,217	321	245.6
Walnut city	323	1067	96	971	6,129	14	100.0	21.5	1.3	82.0	436	20.0	668	25	28.7
Walnut Creek city	2,513	3720	110	3610	73,610	325	4.3	70.1	2.6	97.1	699	80.4	1,224	103	4.9
Walnut Park CDP	NA	NA	NA	NA	NA	NA	NA	NA	NA	NA	NA	NA	NA	NA	NA
Wasco city	NA	NA	NA	NA	2,400	24	100.0	13.5	2.6	29.2	217	13.2	517	75	4.4
Watsonville city	1,754	3323	502	2821	6,357	71	43.7	67.3	6.4	30.2	599	72.0	1,387	113	36.2
West Carson CDP	NA	NA	NA	NA	NA	NA	NA	NA	NA	NA	NA	NA	NA	NA	NA
West Covina city	3,057	2827	208	2619	8,078	18	100.0	102.2	8.7	74.3	594	91.9	854	133	181.9
West Hollywood city	1,592	4484	752	3732	67,415	292	3.8	88.9	5.0	44.0	1601	93.6	2,685	485	100.2
Westminster city	2,404	2607	210	2397	5,784	21	85.7	91.7	10.4	70.7	750	114.0	1,245	487	142.2
Westmont CDP	NA	NA	NA	NA	NA	NA	NA	NA	NA	NA	NA	NA	NA	NA	NA
West Puente Valley CDP	NA	NA	NA	NA	NA	NA	NA	NA	NA	NA	NA	NA	NA	NA	NA
West Rancho Dominguez CDP	NA	NA	NA	NA	NA	NA	NA	NA	NA	NA	NA	NA	NA	NA	NA
West Sacramento city	1,557	3105	522	2582	17,338	61	100.0	140.9	23.6	64.6	1344	129.2	2,601	822	368.8
West Whittier-Los Nietos CDP	NA	NA	NA	NA	NA	NA	NA	NA	NA	NA	NA	NA	NA	NA	NA
Whittier city	2,486	2859	275	2584	15,342	71	1.4	79.8	8.9	72.4	483	82.4	954	94	98.6
Wildomar city	589	1736	115	1621	470	3	100.0	9.4	3.2	100.0	177	9.3	280	7	0.0
Willowbrook CDP	NA	NA	NA	NA	NA	NA	NA	NA	NA	NA	NA	NA	NA	NA	NA
Windsor town	340	1243	314	929	3,585	8	100.0	23.5	2.8	29.7	603	23.2	859	257	27.1
Winter Gardens CDP	NA	NA	NA	NA	NA	NA	NA	NA	NA	NA	NA	NA	NA	NA	NA
Winton CDP	NA	NA	NA	NA	NA	NA	NA	NA	NA	NA	NA	NA	NA	NA	NA
Woodcrest CDP	NA	NA	NA	NA	NA	NA	NA	NA	NA	NA	NA	NA	NA	NA	NA
Woodland city	2,054	3613	524	3089	39,854	128	100.0	72.5	12.3	93.9	793	78.0	1,385	376	111.4
Yorba Linda city	747	1103	66	1037	32,609	94	100.0	62.1	4.6	47.2	526	79.9	1,201	263	117.7
Yuba City city	1,922	2933	340	2593	16,724	57	82.5	54.9	5.2	89.4	508	59.0	910	163	63.6
Yucaipa city	1,049	1987	134	1852	902	4	100.0	28.1	0.9	94.5	398	29.1	554	111	35.9
Yucca Valley town	608	2864	353	2511	2,204	18	100.0	14.5	2.7	93.7	499	14.3	677	167	10.2
COLORADO	152,064	2839	309	2530	6,479,529	28,686	59.6	X	X	X	X	X	X	X	X
Arvada city	2,835	2509	150	2359	157,518	597	100.0	132.6	21.2	32.5	619	119.2	1,086	160	120.5

1 Data for serious crimes have not been adjusted for underreporting. This may affect comparability between geographic areas over time.
2 Per 100,000 population estimated by the FBI. 3 Based on population estimated as of July 1 of the year shown.

Table B. Incorporated Places, Census Designated Places (CDPs), and Minor Civil Divisions (MCDs) of 10,000 or More Population — Land Area, Population, and Households, and Employment

STATE City, town, township, borough, or CDP (county if applicable)	Land area,[1] 2010 (sq mi)	Population				Population characteristics 2010–2014		Household income and poverty, 2010–2014	Percent of households		Employment,[2] 2010–2014		Households, 2010–2014 (percent of households)	
		Total persons 2010	Total persons 2014	Percent change 2010–2014	Persons per square mile, 2014	Foreign born	Lives in same house as previous year	Median household income (dollars)	Income of $100,000 or more	Income below poverty level	Percent in labor force	Unemploy-ment rate	Family households	One person households
	1	2	3	4	5	6	7	8	9	10	11	12	13	14
COLORADO—Con.														
Aurora city	153.829	324,688	353,108	8.8	2,295.5	20.2	76.9	$52,275	19.1	13.4	71.3	10.1	65.6	27.7
Berkley CDP	3.645	11,207	NA	NA	NA	20.7	80.6	$49,398	13.6	17.3	70.9	9.6	65.3	24.3
Black Forest CDP	100.631	13,116	NA	NA	NA	4.0	88.5	$105,760	53.0	6.3	65.3	7.0	86.5	10.8
Boulder city	24.848	97,468	105,112	7.8	4,230.2	10.4	62.7	$58,062	30.0	20.6	67.4	7.4	42.5	33.5
Brighton city	20.761	33,780	36,765	8.8	1,770.8	13.3	85.8	$60,319	22.8	9.9	65.9	7.6	75.5	21.3
Broomfield city	33.003	55,860	62,138	11.2	1,882.8	9.2	82.1	$80,430	38.7	7.1	71.5	6.0	68.5	25.8
Cañon City city	12.512	16,415	16,337	-0.5	1,305.7	3.1	82.1	$38,540	10.7	21.6	48.8	8.0	61.6	31.5
Castle Pines city	9.567	10,360	10,796	4.2	1,128.4	5.6	89.2	$137,426	63.7	0.9	64.7	4.9	82.0	15.8
Castle Rock town	33.864	48,262	55,747	15.5	1,646.2	5.9	80.7	$86,563	41.8	5.9	74.8	5.8	78.2	17.1
Centennial city	28.901	100,547	107,201	6.6	3,709.2	8.7	87.0	$90,090	44.4	5.2	70.4	6.0	75.6	20.1
Cherry Creek CDP	1.678	11,120	NA	NA	NA	13.3	82.7	$93,976	47.3	6.6	73.3	4.3	72.0	22.3
Cimarron Hills CDP	6.055	16,161	NA	NA	NA	7.4	84.4	$51,421	17.7	6.7	69.9	8.1	72.0	22.4
Clifton CDP	6.081	19,889	NA	NA	NA	5.0	82.6	$39,418	9.6	18.2	68.2	14.0	67.8	23.5
Colorado Springs city	194.870	417,341	445,830	6.8	2,287.8	8.2	75.9	$54,228	23.0	12.7	68.2	9.7	63.9	29.4
Columbine CDP	6.631	24,280	NA	NA	NA	4.7	91.5	$82,000	40.2	4.5	68.1	6.4	72.8	23.3
Commerce City city	34.911	45,917	51,762	12.7	1,482.7	15.7	85.4	$64,672	24.3	12.2	71.1	7.3	77.5	17.7
Dakota Ridge CDP	9.318	32,005	NA	NA	NA	6.1	88.1	$84,710	38.9	4.1	75.5	4.9	76.3	18.6
Denver city	153.037	600,025	663,862	10.6	4,337.9	16.0	77.0	$51,800	23.6	16.1	71.0	7.8	48.1	40.1
Durango city	11.071	16,891	17,834	5.6	1,610.8	3.3	67.7	$53,621	20.1	12.5	68.5	5.3	48.7	32.9
Englewood city	6.552	30,255	32,480	7.4	4,957.6	9.3	77.4	$46,776	14.2	14.9	72.4	8.9	50.6	40.9
Erie town	17.266	18,133	20,493	13.0	1,186.9	8.1	84.0	$108,857	58.1	2.6	79.1	3.8	81.4	12.9
Evans city	10.152	18,545	20,473	10.4	2,016.6	13.3	78.3	$47,798	13.0	16.6	70.9	7.2	69.9	22.1
Federal Heights city	1.776	11,472	12,178	6.2	6,857.5	23.1	77.0	$36,823	4.4	17.2	72.8	9.0	66.4	28.8
Firestone town	11.409	10,161	11,537	13.5	1,011.2	5.7	88.7	$81,559	38.4	2.0	76.3	5.9	81.8	12.5
Fort Carson CDP	8.702	13,813	NA	NA	NA	3.5	45.9	$43,632	4.1	17.1	79.4	10.0	96.1	3.4
Fort Collins city	54.618	144,073	156,480	8.6	2,865.0	6.4	70.6	$53,775	22.6	17.4	69.8	7.9	55.4	26.1
Fort Morgan city	4.403	11,348	11,329	-0.2	2,573.2	17.8	79.3	$42,633	10.6	14.2	64.5	6.5	72.4	23.8
Fountain city	24.502	25,885	27,631	6.7	1,127.7	5.2	76.8	$56,687	18.9	10.9	68.4	9.2	77.9	18.3
Fruita city	7.624	12,685	12,761	0.6	1,673.9	4.3	83.3	$54,875	20.8	16.1	67.0	7.1	71.3	23.9
Golden city	9.956	18,905	20,201	6.9	2,029.1	8.1	71.9	$58,630	28.8	15.3	63.1	6.0	51.7	33.3
Grand Junction city	38.938	59,005	60,210	2.0	1,546.3	3.9	72.0	$44,887	16.6	17.7	62.9	9.4	57.9	32.7
Greeley city	47.122	92,881	98,596	6.2	2,092.4	10.6	73.7	$47,342	17.1	19.8	64.2	9.9	65.4	26.3
Greenwood Village city	8.254	13,925	15,385	10.5	1,864.0	13.8	85.9	$109,180	55.2	5.2	66.9	3.6	68.7	28.8
Highlands Ranch CDP	24.269	96,713	NA	NA	NA	7.4	86.3	$110,221	56.4	3.2	74.5	4.3	79.2	16.9
Johnstown town	13.803	9,879	13,306	34.7	964.0	4.1	85.6	$78,298	33.1	2.6	74.1	5.3	86.4	12.3
Ken Caryl CDP	9.698	32,438	NA	NA	NA	4.7	87.4	$85,655	39.5	3.8	76.8	6.8	69.4	26.1
Lafayette city	9.320	24,452	27,081	10.8	2,905.7	10.8	82.4	$71,038	33.7	7.7	75.6	7.6	64.5	29.1
Lakewood city	42.872	142,995	149,643	4.6	3,490.4	8.5	80.2	$56,134	22.5	11.5	68.1	8.1	57.5	34.2
Littleton city	12.736	41,733	44,669	7.0	3,507.4	7.6	80.2	$62,683	28.3	10.7	67.5	6.8	58.3	35.8
Lone Tree city	9.676	11,104	13,545	22.0	1,399.9	15.1	78.3	$110,694	53.7	6.4	73.4	4.8	66.8	22.8
Longmont city	27.255	86,303	90,237	4.6	3,310.8	13.4	79.7	$60,218	26.6	13.0	70.5	8.2	67.2	25.6
Louisville city	7.960	18,405	20,112	9.3	2,526.7	6.8	86.4	$92,121	46.4	8.2	71.4	4.7	67.9	27.1
Loveland city	33.934	66,824	72,651	8.7	2,140.9	4.1	83.4	$55,580	20.0	9.0	67.4	7.5	65.6	28.2
Montrose city	17.609	19,143	19,045	-0.5	1,081.6	7.5	77.6	$43,281	11.0	17.2	57.8	12.0	62.7	32.0
Northglenn city	7.356	35,769	38,596	7.9	5,247.0	9.3	82.9	$53,616	17.0	11.5	70.7	9.7	62.8	30.5
Parker town	21.182	45,297	49,857	10.1	2,353.7	5.0	84.1	$98,170	48.8	5.0	78.6	5.0	76.9	19.2
Pueblo city	53.592	106,544	108,423	1.8	2,023.1	4.7	79.2	$34,889	9.6	22.2	56.5	12.5	58.8	35.4
Pueblo West CDP	70.426	29,637	NA	NA	NA	3.5	86.8	$64,560	20.4	7.5	64.2	8.7	76.2	18.7
Security-Widefield CDP	13.244	32,882	NA	NA	NA	6.0	85.3	$57,428	18.3	9.0	66.8	9.6	78.4	16.7
Sherrelwood CDP	2.429	18,287	NA	NA	NA	19.4	86.6	$47,176	11.0	18.5	67.7	12.7	74.9	18.3
Steamboat Springs city	10.147	12,088	12,260	1.4	1,208.3	7.5	79.9	$54,218	22.3	11.2	76.5	6.8	55.3	32.6
Sterling city	7.610	14,777	14,629	-1.0	1,922.4	9.6	74.8	$36,204	8.1	18.8	62.7	15.9	56.1	38.1
Superior town	3.970	12,483	12,855	3.0	3,237.7	17.2	80.5	$116,250	60.7	3.1	80.6	4.1	77.2	13.2
The Pinery CDP	10.387	10,517	NA	NA	NA	3.3	85.2	$122,581	60.8	2.3	73.7	4.6	87.5	8.3
Thornton city	35.106	118,792	130,307	9.7	3,711.9	11.6	85.2	$66,160	27.2	7.6	74.0	7.5	73.9	20.2
Welby CDP	3.696	14,846	NA	NA	NA	17.8	85.6	$46,309	8.7	15.2	66.7	11.8	71.4	19.7
Westminster city	31.676	106,129	112,090	5.6	3,538.6	10.5	83.4	$66,300	27.3	9.5	73.4	8.5	66.1	26.3
Wheat Ridge city	9.367	30,192	31,034	2.8	3,313.1	6.4	81.0	$49,003	20.2	12.7	65.4	8.5	54.1	37.6
Windsor town	24.432	18,637	21,106	13.2	863.9	4.1	83.5	$82,724	39.0	4.3	72.4	4.4	76.4	19.7
CONNECTICUT	4,842.355	3,574,096	3,596,677	0.6	742.8	13.7	87.8	$69,899	33.9	10.3	67.8	9.6	66.3	27.9
Ansonia city & town (New Haven)	6.019	19,251	18,959	-1.5	3,150.0	13.2	89.8	$43,144	20.4	19.9	64.0	13.1	64.1	28.7
Avon town (Hartford)	23.153	18,098	18,421	1.8	795.6	12.2	90.8	$116,565	56.6	4.7	64.4	6.5	70.2	25.0
Berlin town (Hartford)	26.336	19,870	20,610	3.7	782.6	12.6	93.9	$87,518	43.7	4.2	70.4	6.9	71.3	24.2
Bethel town (Fairfield)	16.889	18,584	19,372	4.2	1,147.0	11.3	92.6	$85,377	43.4	4.6	75.0	9.5	72.9	23.3
Bloomfield town (Hartford)	26.086	20,486	20,819	1.6	798.1	21.0	91.0	$73,519	32.8	6.9	64.5	12.1	58.9	33.2
Branford town (New Haven)	21.840	28,026	28,225	0.7	1,292.4	8.4	90.7	$71,058	31.8	7.9	68.8	10.5	59.0	36.2
Bridgeport city & town (Fairfield)	16.058	144,236	147,612	2.3	9,192.2	27.7	81.4	$41,204	14.5	22.5	68.6	16.6	64.1	28.8
Bristol city & town (Hartford)	26.407	60,477	60,570	0.2	2,293.7	10.0	89.2	$60,208	24.4	9.7	68.7	10.6	61.7	32.2
Brookfield town (Fairfield)	19.773	16,452	17,055	3.7	862.5	10.0	91.4	$106,920	52.7	3.0	70.4	5.3	78.7	18.2
Canton town (Hartford)	24.586	10,292	10,345	0.5	420.8	5.0	93.6	$89,452	42.8	4.3	68.3	6.1	71.3	24.1
Cheshire town (New Haven)	33.039	29,258	29,250	0.0	884.2	10.2	90.4	$107,716	54.4	2.6	63.4	4.4	75.1	23.1
Clinton town (Middlesex)	16.207	13,260	13,129	-1.0	810.1	6.4	91.0	$71,028	32.2	8.2	69.4	7.3	68.9	25.6
Colchester town (New London)	48.983	16,059	16,192	0.8	330.6	4.9	89.4	$98,899	49.5	4.5	75.2	5.4	75.2	20.0
Conning Towers Nautilus Park CDP	4.985	8,834	NA	NA	NA	5.0	54.9	$56,891	21.0	9.3	82.9	10.8	79.1	15.6
Coventry town (Tolland)	37.569	12,435	12,419	-0.1	330.6	6.2	90.5	$92,663	44.4	2.2	74.4	4.8	78.7	15.8
Cromwell town (Middlesex)	12.452	14,005	14,113	0.8	1,133.4	10.0	92.5	$80,028	39.6	2.6	69.0	7.8	67.4	27.4
Danbury city & town (Fairfield)	41.941	80,897	83,784	3.6	1,997.7	32.0	85.8	$65,981	30.9	10.9	72.6	8.5	65.4	27.0
Darien CDP & town (Fairfield)	12.654	20,732	21,689	4.6	1,714.0	10.3	89.9	$199,444	70.1	5.7	60.3	7.5	83.6	13.7
Derby city & town (New Haven)	5.056	12,900	12,768	-1.0	2,525.5	19.2	85.6	$52,136	21.9	12.5	69.9	11.6	61.2	34.3
East Hampton town (Middlesex)	35.650	12,959	12,874	-0.7	361.1	6.3	94.7	$96,066	47.8	5.2	75.2	5.4	70.8	23.2

1 Dry land or land partially or temporarily covered by water.
2 16 years old and over.

Table B. Incorporated Places, Census Designated Places (CDPs), and Minor Civil Divisions (MCDs) of 10,000 or More Population — Crime, Construction, and Local Government Finance

STATE City, town, township, borough, or CDP (county if applicable)	Serious crimes known to police, 2014[1] Total number	Rate[2] Total	Rate[2] Violent	Rate[2] Property	New residential construction authorized by building permits, 2014 Value ($1,000)	Number of housing units	Percent single family	Local government finance, 2012 General revenue Total (mil dol)	Intergovernmental Total (mil dol)	Percent from state gov.	Taxes per capita[3]	General expenditure Total (mil dol)	Per capita[3] Total	Capital outlays	Debt outstanding (mil dol)
	15	16	17	18	19	20	21	22	23	24	25	26	27	28	29
COLORADO—Con.															
Aurora city	11,393	3246	407	2839	220,809	1,024	81.3	380.8	48.7	50.2	638	400.3	1,180	162	1215.3
Berkley CDP	NA	NA	NA	NA	NA	NA	NA	NA	NA	NA	NA	NA	NA	NA	NA
Black Forest CDP	NA	NA	NA	NA	NA	NA	NA	NA	NA	NA	NA	NA	NA	NA	NA
Boulder city	3,025	2901	235	2666	114,852	608	17.1	219.5	16.4	84.1	1471	210.4	2,063	39	155.7
Brighton city	1,280	3537	370	3167	18,993	98	100.0	32.9	3.4	84.3	624	24.3	691	69	76.1
Broomfield city	1,071	1765	51	1714	190,713	820	53.5	149.9	15.4	40.7	1924	109.7	1,860	53	293.0
Cañon City city	620	3806	381	3425	2,319	11	100.0	12.2	1.7	90.0	404	11.4	691	94	14.1
Castle Pines city	NA	NA	NA	NA	645	1	100.0	4.2	1.0	100.0	290	5.3	501	249	0.0
Castle Rock town	452	833	76	758	211,220	821	100.0	72.3	4.3	100.0	764	61.6	1,198	135	110.8
Centennial city	1,440	1340	132	1208	13,891	92	81.5	67.4	9.9	66.5	505	66.6	640	152	2.8
Cherry Creek CDP	NA	NA	NA	NA	NA	NA	NA	NA	NA	NA	NA	NA	NA	NA	NA
Cimarron Hills CDP	NA	NA	NA	NA	NA	NA	NA	NA	NA	NA	NA	NA	NA	NA	NA
Clifton CDP	NA	NA	NA	NA	NA	NA	NA	NA	NA	NA	NA	NA	NA	NA	NA
Colorado Springs city	18,348	4124	456	3668	NA	NA	NA	1020.1	65.7	31.6	494	968.4	2,233	239	2643.8
Columbine CDP	NA	NA	NA	NA	NA	NA	NA	NA	NA	NA	NA	NA	NA	NA	NA
Commerce City city	1,832	3610	398	3212	60,022	354	97.7	59.2	2.8	60.8	984	61.0	1,256	0	182.6
Dakota Ridge CDP	NA	NA	NA	NA	NA	NA	NA	NA	NA	NA	NA	NA	NA	NA	NA
Denver city	26,407	3969	601	3367	811,547	5,958	28.7	2940.6	477.1	60.5	1748	2623.4	4,139	261	7039.4
Durango city	553	3123	271	2851	20,508	138	63.8	43.8	5.9	96.9	1564	41.7	2,430	463	36.8
Englewood city	1,833	5762	201	5561	4,112	19	89.5	60.4	3.3	42.3	1002	53.0	1,698	1	89.9
Erie town	NA	NA	NA	NA	84,968	287	100.0	22.4	2.2	82.3	477	20.5	1,061	252	104.5
Evans city	468	2307	296	2011	6,320	48	66.7	14.8	2.1	97.1	453	13.4	683	111	2.9
Federal Heights city	688	5688	438	5250	2,317	12	0.0	13.0	2.2	12.7	629	10.9	927	105	4.5
Firestone town	115	1007	53	955	37,315	130	100.0	6.2	0.6	66.5	456	5.2	478	73	1.8
Fort Carson CDP	NA	NA	NA	NA	NA	NA	NA	NA	NA	NA	NA	NA	NA	NA	NA
Fort Collins city	4,104	2665	209	2456	230,800	1,152	64.4	238.1	30.8	16.5	843	233.7	1,569	354	216.4
Fort Morgan city	329	2880	368	2513	200	2	0.0	16.8	4.4	91.6	662	17.8	1,556	261	25.6
Fountain city	773	2804	301	2503	NA	NA	NA	12.7	1.1	60.7	374	26.4	981	22	29.0
Fruita city	236	1852	165	1687	NA	NA	NA	17.9	4.3	35.6	532	27.1	2,135	1,375	34.0
Golden city	419	2143	225	1918	17,256	126	9.5	37.0	2.4	47.8	1147	35.1	1,773	250	39.0
Grand Junction city	2,820	4702	477	4225	NA	NA	NA	114.1	18.2	45.4	1009	130.2	2,176	564	74.2
Greeley city	3,780	3881	496	3385	98,826	789	45.8	114.2	13.2	62.0	630	99.4	1,042	109	155.4
Greenwood Village city	518	3494	209	3285	10,776	13	100.0	41.2	2.1	43.0	2400	36.5	2,525	310	0.0
Highlands Ranch CDP	NA	NA	NA	NA	NA	NA	NA	NA	NA	NA	NA	NA	NA	NA	NA
Johnstown town	NA	NA	NA	NA	95,460	527	51.8	5.9	3.4	97.4	75	3.2	291	0	7.8
Ken Caryl CDP	NA	NA	NA	NA	NA	NA	NA	NA	NA	NA	NA	NA	NA	NA	NA
Lafayette city	504	1841	95	1746	33,988	209	49.8	34.4	1.6	88.9	748	32.2	1,252	149	52.4
Lakewood city	7,558	5099	481	4618	181,727	1,195	14.9	155.5	22.9	36.1	663	144.6	994	114	74.1
Littleton city	1,023	2280	89	2191	51,415	447	4.3	70.6	17.6	14.5	749	75.6	1,725	102	52.5
Lone Tree city	890	6438	43	6395	27,210	84	100.0	31.0	5.7	11.2	1906	36.4	3,058	1,142	24.3
Longmont city	2,376	2616	344	2273	82,850	411	50.9	98.1	6.6	75.4	650	98.8	1,114	42	86.1
Louisville city	191	960	75	885	17,451	63	100.0	25.3	1.4	76.7	880	21.7	1,138	214	16.2
Loveland city	2,121	2927	233	2694	145,897	772	40.3	115.2	11.2	96.5	847	109.1	1,554	315	5.0
Montrose city	771	4061	158	3903	7,950	42	100.0	24.8	4.1	99.8	800	27.3	1,441	506	7.7
Northglenn city	1,130	2981	314	2667	0	0	0.0	32.1	4.4	67.4	539	33.8	914	210	9.0
Parker town	677	1370	134	1236	154,622	654	53.2	53.8	8.3	22.1	699	55.5	1,175	321	55.9
Pueblo city	7,980	7349	819	6530	NA	NA	NA	152.7	29.0	69.9	734	141.8	1,315	332	144.1
Pueblo West CDP	NA	NA	NA	NA	NA	NA	NA	NA	NA	NA	NA	NA	NA	NA	NA
Security-Widefield CDP	NA	NA	NA	NA	NA	NA	NA	NA	NA	NA	NA	NA	NA	NA	NA
Sherrelwood CDP	NA	NA	NA	NA	NA	NA	NA	NA	NA	NA	NA	NA	NA	NA	NA
Steamboat Springs city	344	2840	198	2642	NA	NA	NA	40.7	7.8	51.8	1843	39.1	3,279	1,081	47.8
Sterling city	507	3476	418	3058	771	6	100.0	43.3	1.3	30.8	609	17.6	1,194	252	32.1
Superior town	NA	NA	NA	NA	6,444	17	100.0	17.0	0.3	95.1	1053	10.7	841	55	60.3
The Pinery CDP	NA	NA	NA	NA	NA	NA	NA	NA	NA	NA	NA	NA	NA	NA	NA
Thornton city	4,090	3160	255	2905	92,742	376	98.4	147.1	14.0	41.5	717	134.0	1,078	204	191.4
Welby CDP	NA	NA	NA	NA	NA	NA	NA	NA	NA	NA	NA	NA	NA	NA	NA
Westminster city	3,528	3147	234	2913	10,370	34	88.2	153.4	13.5	40.6	914	145.3	1,330	246	297.6
Wheat Ridge city	1,182	3801	312	3489	15,063	49	91.8	30.8	2.8	58.9	752	32.0	1,043	219	2.7
Windsor town	233	1117	24	1093	52,494	194	92.3	23.9	1.4	67.0	587	22.5	1,135	468	12.0
CONNECTICUT	77,592	2157	237	1920	1,148,276	5,329	51.8	X	X	X	X	X	X	X	X
Ansonia city & town (New Haven)	411	2167	200	1967	0	0	0.0	62.1	25.1	100.0	1578	59.3	3,091	308	55.5
Avon (Hartford)	173	938	11	927	7,669	22	100.0	80.8	8.1	69.0	3660	82.1	4,482	386	36.6
Berlin town (Hartford)	317	1526	53	1473	1,252	10	100.0	76.3	12.4	90.0	2813	80.9	3,951	373	37.1
Bethel town (Fairfield)	164	844	NA	844	15,386	86	100.0	81.1	12.8	99.9	2852	73.4	3,833	296	57.7
Bloomfield town (Hartford)	554	2674	193	2481	857	6	33.3	99.4	28.4	98.8	3248	109.7	5,313	1,332	51.5
Branford town (New Haven)	689	2463	89	2373	7,310	29	100.0	104.2	10.5	86.8	3017	107.4	3,831	504	57.9
Bridgeport city & town (Fairfield)	5,623	3804	905	2899	10,037	134	11.2	693.1	370.2	98.3	1888	743.6	5,058	849	742.4
Bristol city & town (Hartford)	1,580	2608	120	2487	5,055	61	24.6	263.8	119.3	99.5	1987	318.7	5,258	1,671	95.9
Brookfield town (Fairfield)	165	973	18	955	7,438	50	52.0	63.4	6.4	100.0	3108	63.4	3,778	437	57.0
Canton town (Hartford)	77	742	19	723	2,918	10	100.0	39.4	7.1	93.7	2908	37.0	3,574	198	10.5
Cheshire town (New Haven)	248	852	27	824	8,226	41	100.0	106.3	21.9	97.9	2621	105.8	3,608	306	57.2
Clinton town (Middlesex)	279	2119	137	1983	2,804	10	100.0	49.2	10.3	99.6	2837	54.2	4,107	667	20.8
Colchester town (New London)	NA	NA	NA	NA	5,098	31	100.0	55.4	17.9	100.0	2121	54.9	3,393	207	18.5
Conning Towers Nautilus Park CDP	NA	NA	NA	NA	NA	NA	NA	NA	NA	NA	NA	NA	NA	NA	NA
Coventry town (Tolland)	144	1161	73	1088	5,930	33	93.9	44.8	14.7	97.3	2149	48.8	3,922	552	23.7
Cromwell town (Middlesex)	315	2215	49	2166	5,966	23	100.0	48.2	7.3	95.7	2684	43.5	3,084	205	27.6
Danbury city & town (Fairfield)	1,505	1786	178	1608	68,156	317	63.4	280.7	82.5	95.8	2074	248.5	3,001	199	169.5
Darien CDP & town (Fairfield)	195	908	23	885	61,322	56	100.0	123.5	6.6	100.0	5174	130.9	6,191	766	99.0
Derby city & town (New Haven)	356	2786	188	2599	510	5	100.0	42.3	11.3	99.4	2004	44.1	3,434	151	20.7
East Hampton town (Middlesex)	77	597	23	574	4,168	35	54.3	43.5	10.9	100.0	2228	43.3	3,348	302	6.4

1 Data for serious crimes have not been adjusted for underreporting. This may affect comparability between geographic areas over time.
2 Per 100,000 population estimated by the FBI.   3 Based on population estimated as of July 1 of the year shown.

Table B. Incorporated Places, Census Designated Places (CDPs), and Minor Civil Divisions (MCDs) of 10,000 or More Population — **Land Area, Population, and Households, and Employment**

STATE City, town, township, borough, or CDP (county if applicable)	Land area,[1] 2010 (sq mi)	Total persons 2010	Total persons 2014	Percent change 2010–2014	Persons per square mile, 2014	Foreign born	Lives in same house as previous year	Median household income (dollars)	Income of $100,000 or more	Income below poverty level	Percent in labor force	Unemployment rate	Family households	One person households
	1	2	3	4	5	6	7	8	9	10	11	12	13	14
CONNECTICUT—Con.														
East Hartford CDP & town (Hartford)	17.997	51,249	51,033	-0.4	2,835.7	21.5	86.6	$50,355	17.0	14.5	69.5	13.6	64.5	29.6
East Haven CDP & town (New Haven)	12.296	29,209	29,044	-0.6	2,362.1	9.2	89.6	$61,435	24.3	9.2	65.8	8.6	63.2	29.0
East Lyme town (New London)	34.022	19,159	19,140	-0.1	562.6	8.5	85.6	$81,711	39.8	4.1	58.4	6.3	69.0	26.4
East Windsor town (Hartford)	26.251	11,162	11,423	2.3	435.2	10.6	86.5	$72,866	33.5	5.1	72.5	10.4	65.3	26.6
Ellington town (Tolland)	34.060	15,602	15,795	1.2	463.7	4.9	89.2	$84,339	40.8	3.2	74.3	5.9	67.3	27.5
Enfield town (Hartford)	33.272	44,654	44,626	-0.1	1,341.2	6.7	87.4	$68,162	28.8	7.6	63.7	8.7	68.5	25.4
Fairfield town (Fairfield)	29.903	59,404	61,347	3.3	2,051.6	10.6	89.2	$120,082	58.5	4.9	64.1	7.5	72.9	23.1
Farmington town (Hartford)	28.056	25,340	25,627	1.1	913.4	15.6	89.5	$92,933	47.5	5.5	67.4	4.8	63.7	30.7
Glastonbury town (Hartford)	51.270	34,427	34,754	0.9	677.9	12.4	91.7	$108,157	53.9	4.5	68.5	6.2	72.0	23.1
Granby town (Hartford)	40.678	11,282	11,310	0.2	278.0	2.8	94.2	$100,262	50.1	2.0	72.0	5.5	74.3	20.8
Greenwich town (Fairfield)	47.705	61,172	62,610	2.4	1,312.4	21.9	87.1	$135,258	60.9	5.4	62.5	7.7	72.6	23.8
Greenwich CDP	4.112	12,942	NA	NA	NA	26.0	83.7	$90,359	45.8	8.3	68.3	9.1	59.7	35.8
Griswold town (New London)*	34.709	11,951	11,916	-0.3	343.3	5.7	89.6	$59,545	26.6	10.5	69.5	9.6	68.9	23.9
Groton town (New London)*	31.099	40,115	40,167	0.1	1,291.6	7.4	74.8	$60,157	26.5	9.9	73.1	6.7	59.4	32.8
Guilford town (New Haven)	47.084	22,375	22,413	0.2	476.0	5.2	91.0	$99,441	49.6	5.9	69.6	5.6	71.2	23.8
Hamden town (New Haven)	32.643	60,887	61,422	0.9	1,881.6	13.1	85.1	$67,771	32.5	8.9	67.6	8.5	61.1	32.5
Hartford city (Hartford)	17.381	124,775	124,705	-0.1	7,174.8	22.2	77.7	$29,313	8.2	32.4	62.0	20.2	58.6	34.9
Killingly town (Windham)*	48.352	17,370	17,172	-1.1	355.1	5.1	85.2	$57,016	22.4	10.6	69.0	9.1	62.3	31.2
Ledyard town (New London)	38.219	15,051	15,121	0.5	395.6	7.5	87.6	$87,101	41.2	5.4	71.9	6.3	77.8	17.1
Madison town (New Haven)	36.148	18,269	18,259	-0.1	505.1	6.6	92.9	$108,231	54.1	3.7	61.2	4.6	75.7	21.5
Manchester CDP	6.463	30,577	NA	NA	NA	10.3	83.7	$54,364	18.8	12.9	70.6	12.3	60.2	32.8
Manchester town (Hartford)	27.403	58,253	58,106	-0.3	2,120.4	14.7	84.8	$63,198	26.0	10.3	70.9	10.2	61.9	30.1
Mansfield town (Tolland)	44.599	26,543	25,977	-2.1	582.5	11.2	68.4	$66,404	30.8	15.2	55.4	7.5	57.3	26.7
Meriden city & town (New Haven)	23.793	60,868	60,293	-0.9	2,534.1	9.5	87.1	$53,401	20.1	11.9	66.0	11.9	64.2	29.4
Middletown city & town (Middlesex)	41.018	47,648	47,043	-1.3	1,146.9	11.0	82.2	$61,373	29.1	11.1	67.6	7.4	55.7	35.3
Milford city & town (New Haven)	22.175	52,759	53,358	1.1	2,406.2	9.6	89.6	$80,743	38.5	6.4	69.0	8.0	64.0	29.7
Milford city (balance)	21.903	51,271	51,857	1.1	2,367.6	9.6	89.6	$80,793	38.8	6.5	69.1	8.1	64.1	29.6
Monroe town (Fairfield)	26.071	19,480	19,867	2.0	762.0	6.6	95.4	$108,688	53.9	4.4	69.3	5.7	81.0	16.0
Montville town (New London)	41.954	19,571	19,635	0.3	468.0	7.3	88.4	$67,044	29.0	5.4	62.2	7.4	69.3	25.7
Naugatuck borough & town (New Haven)	16.301	31,884	31,659	-0.7	1,942.1	12.1	91.1	$58,641	27.7	10.3	70.2	11.5	66.9	27.3
New Britain city & town (Hartford)	13.355	73,202	72,878	-0.4	5,457.2	19.5	83.6	$40,515	12.9	22.2	66.9	14.1	60.7	32.1
New Canaan town (Fairfield)	22.195	19,749	20,314	2.9	915.3	11.6	88.5	$179,810	69.7	3.7	55.6	6.4	78.4	19.8
New Fairfield town (Fairfield)	20.443	13,881	14,149	1.9	692.1	9.7	95.2	$101,750	51.7	2.0	71.3	8.2	79.0	16.3
New Haven city & town (New Haven)	18.690	129,890	130,282	0.3	6,970.6	15.8	80.7	$37,508	16.0	24.9	64.8	13.7	51.6	39.7
Newington CDP & town (Hartford)	13.141	30,562	30,685	0.4	2,335.1	17.9	89.0	$79,008	34.9	5.3	67.5	7.3	64.5	30.2
New London city & town (New London)	5.621	27,620	27,374	-0.9	4,870.0	15.4	73.8	$41,230	13.4	23.0	67.1	15.5	50.2	38.7
New Milford town (Litchfield)	61.574	28,142	27,474	-2.4	446.2	9.2	89.7	$79,028	37.5	6.3	74.6	9.3	70.9	23.3
Newtown town (Fairfield)*	57.663	27,559	28,152	2.2	488.2	8.2	93.1	$108,667	53.6	4.0	66.9	6.8	76.2	20.0
North Branford town (New Haven)	24.758	14,407	14,322	-0.6	578.5	4.1	94.7	$87,408	43.6	5.3	67.4	5.7	72.6	24.6
North Haven CDP & town (New Haven)	20.840	24,088	23,909	-0.7	1,147.3	9.7	92.2	$84,078	41.4	4.5	68.5	8.6	73.1	23.2
Norwalk city & town (Fairfield)	22.886	85,621	88,145	2.9	3,851.4	24.4	89.5	$76,051	37.1	8.6	73.1	9.3	60.6	33.8
Norwich city & town (New London)	28.062	40,493	40,178	-0.8	1,431.8	15.5	84.5	$49,695	19.2	13.2	69.8	11.4	57.3	34.0
Old Saybrook town (Middlesex)	15.059	10,242	10,217	-0.2	678.5	5.8	90.1	$74,896	40.0	6.0	60.1	4.9	69.8	26.6
Orange CDP & town (New Haven)	17.181	13,956	13,955	0.0	812.2	11.4	93.2	$105,190	53.4	4.5	66.3	8.5	78.9	17.3
Oxford town (New Haven)	32.743	12,690	12,914	1.8	394.4	4.4	96.3	$98,504	49.2	1.9	72.5	10.8	83.8	14.0
Plainfield town (Windham)	42.389	15,399	15,135	-1.7	357.0	3.1	88.1	$62,630	20.4	8.5	69.6	11.5	70.3	22.3
Plainville town (Hartford)	9.711	17,716	17,801	0.5	1,833.2	7.3	89.3	$55,506	20.7	8.8	71.6	9.0	59.6	34.9
Plymouth town (Litchfield)	21.868	12,243	11,914	-2.7	544.8	5.1	91.2	$71,441	30.8	8.7	71.1	8.1	68.5	23.3
Ridgefield town (Fairfield)	34.474	24,634	25,205	2.3	731.1	9.4	91.9	$147,936	64.1	4.0	65.1	5.3	80.1	18.2
Rocky Hill town (Hartford)	13.463	19,709	20,094	2.0	1,492.6	21.2	82.4	$75,442	37.1	6.8	69.4	8.3	60.6	32.1
Seymour town (New Haven)	14.518	16,533	16,537	0.0	1,139.1	10.1	89.8	$77,465	34.4	5.1	71.0	10.8	67.8	27.7
Shelton city & town (Fairfield)	30.626	39,559	41,295	4.4	1,348.4	10.7	90.8	$88,369	44.1	5.2	67.7	8.6	71.1	25.6
Simsbury town (Hartford)	33.925	23,511	23,975	2.0	706.7	8.5	89.9	$109,823	53.8	3.2	68.8	5.8	75.9	20.7
Somers town (Tolland)	28.368	11,444	11,303	-1.2	398.4	5.5	87.6	$95,139	46.5	4.8	56.1	8.1	77.7	17.9
Southbury town (New Haven)	38.992	19,904	19,881	-0.1	509.9	7.8	92.1	$76,896	38.3	5.5	56.0	8.2	64.2	33.8
Southington town (Hartford)	35.903	43,072	43,815	1.7	1,220.4	7.3	93.7	$81,285	41.1	5.0	69.7	6.3	71.2	24.9
South Windsor town (Hartford)	28.063	25,703	25,823	0.5	920.2	13.9	91.5	$94,217	47.8	4.0	71.3	6.9	73.8	22.8
Stafford town (Tolland)	58.038	12,087	11,881	-1.7	204.7	3.7	90.7	$62,859	24.5	11.3	72.1	9.8	68.7	25.8
Stamford city & town (Fairfield)	37.618	122,630	128,278	4.6	3,410.0	34.4	87.1	$77,221	39.3	9.8	73.4	10.2	64.1	28.6
Stonington town (New London)	38.656	18,545	18,512	-0.2	478.9	4.8	89.8	$81,673	39.2	5.8	66.2	5.8	63.7	31.8
Storrs CDP	5.589	15,344	NA	NA	NA	10.6	58.2	$31,925	22.6	28.9	52.4	8.7	32.2	37.1
Stratford CDP & town (Fairfield)	17.487	51,384	52,734	2.6	3,015.6	13.3	94.3	$66,451	31.6	8.5	67.2	10.5	66.5	29.0
Suffield town (Hartford)	42.263	15,735	15,814	0.5	374.2	6.7	87.5	$94,610	47.0	5.2	57.8	5.9	74.2	22.0
Tolland town (Tolland)	39.627	15,052	14,872	-1.2	375.3	4.5	94.6	$107,290	54.2	2.3	74.9	5.7	82.4	14.2
Torrington city & town (Litchfield)	39.759	36,383	35,190	-3.3	885.1	9.4	89.0	$55,460	20.7	11.5	66.5	9.5	61.0	33.1
Trumbull CDP & town (Fairfield)	23.239	36,011	36,578	1.6	1,574.0	10.7	92.9	$108,554	53.7	4.5	65.4	7.0	78.0	20.2
Vernon town (Tolland)	17.699	29,179	29,098	-0.3	1,644.0	8.2	84.5	$60,556	26.5	8.7	70.3	10.5	56.3	35.7
Wallingford town (New Haven)	39.040	45,135	45,074	-0.1	1,154.6	9.7	91.9	$75,533	36.3	5.0	69.5	7.3	67.7	26.8
Wallingford Center CDP	7.258	18,209	NA	NA	NA	11.2	89.9	$60,227	24.6	8.3	69.3	9.6	61.5	31.9
Waterbury city & town (New Haven)	28.525	110,331	109,307	-0.9	3,831.9	14.5	85.8	$41,136	13.6	23.6	62.4	13.7	63.0	31.8

1 Dry land or land partially or temporarily covered by water.
2 16 years old and over.

Table B. Incorporated Places, Census Designated Places (CDPs), and Minor Civil Divisions (MCDs) of 10,000 or More Population — Crime, Construction, and Local Government Finance

STATE City, town, township, borough, or CDP (county if applicable)	Serious crimes known to police, 2014[1] — Total number	Rate[2] Total	Rate[2] Violent	Rate[2] Property	New residential construction — Value ($1,000)	Number of housing units	Percent single family	Local gov finance 2012 General revenue Total (mil dol)	Intergovernmental Total (mil dol)	Percent from state gov.	Taxes per capita[3]	General expenditure Total (mil dol)	Per capita[3] Total	Per capita[3] Capital outlays	Debt outstanding (mil dol)
	15	16	17	18	19	20	21	22	23	24	25	26	27	28	29
CONNECTICUT—Con.															
East Hartford CDP & town (Hartford)	1,358	2653	266	2387	337	3	100.0	195.1	72.6	90.3	2264	161.7	3,152	197	45.9
East Haven CDP & town (New Haven)	752	2585	113	2471	2,032	18	88.9	92.3	27.9	99.9	2077	95.8	3,286	337	47.2
East Lyme town (New London)	NA	NA	NA	NA	39,727	363	10.5	65.1	14.5	80.6	2471	70.3	3,712	549	48.1
East Windsor town (Hartford)	424	3699	209	3490	1,534	10	100.0	41.4	8.9	98.2	2379	39.6	3,474	480	8.7
Ellington town (Tolland)	NA	NA	NA	NA	14,160	84	52.4	56.5	17.1	95.3	2217	50.0	3,166	111	14.3
Enfield town (Hartford)	813	1816	118	1698	5,260	63	4.8	141.5	47.1	96.4	1718	149.7	3,348	349	23.9
Fairfield town (Fairfield)	1,203	1967	54	1913	40,101	111	92.8	293.2	26.2	97.6	3985	308.7	5,079	675	230.7
Farmington town (Hartford)	674	2625	78	2547	9,311	34	100.0	101.6	11.2	97.0	3164	105.0	4,111	416	52.6
Glastonbury town (Hartford)	308	884	29	855	6,601	25	100.0	169.6	34.6	96.9	3666	143.7	4,142	261	94.4
Granby town (Hartford)	93	821	26	794	2,541	11	100.0	45.1	10.5	74.5	2811	42.6	3,761	267	22.3
Greenwich town (Fairfield)	491	783	29	755	135,713	115	100.0	396.6	25.9	98.8	5239	434.0	6,964	631	133.2
Greenwich CDP	NA	NA	NA	NA	NA	NA	NA	NA	NA	NA	NA	NA	NA	NA	NA
Griswold town (New London)*	NA	NA	NA	NA	1,841	11	100.0	35.7	18.8	91.7	1316	46.8	3,900	1,265	24.2
Groton town (New London)*	608	2004	138	1866	8,804	34	64.7	132.9	41.5	96.6	1943	129.1	3,204	237	48.0
Guilford town (New Haven)	356	1588	76	1512	7,545	17	100.0	89.4	10.0	100.0	3303	84.7	3,778	251	42.7
Hamden town (New Haven)	1,586	2575	377	2198	2,909	37	10.8	190.7	44.1	97.6	2275	214.1	3,465	241	215.1
Hartford city & town (Hartford)	6,660	5330	1105	4226	1,068	10	70.0	809.1	477.2	84.9	2262	793.7	6,336	712	413.5
Killingly town (Windham)*	NA	NA	NA	NA	2,963	20	100.0	59.7	25.1	93.3	1639	61.0	3,530	400	35.9
Ledyard town (New London)	NA	NA	NA	NA	2,657	16	100.0	53.7	19.8	90.2	2018	54.9	3,638	266	26.0
Madison town (New Haven)	122	667	11	656	8,573	20	100.0	76.3	5.1	100.0	3652	83.7	4,575	402	39.4
Manchester CDP	NA	NA	NA	NA	NA	NA	NA	NA	NA	NA	NA	NA	NA	NA	NA
Manchester town (Hartford)	1,692	2907	191	2716	8,410	65	3.1	251.4	96.9	97.1	2294	237.4	4,072	751	97.9
Mansfield town (Tolland)	NA	NA	NA	NA	4,755	14	100.0	66.5	34.8	98.3	1023	64.3	2,486	576	3.5
Meriden city & town (New Haven)	1,595	2643	300	2343	770	5	100.0	212.7	85.0	99.7	1819	226.8	3,739	412	121.0
Middletown city & town (Middlesex)	940	1989	169	1820	7,883	61	60.7	189.7	68.5	99.3	2142	158.3	3,339	308	145.6
Milford city & town (New Haven)	NA	NA	NA	NA	16,345	217	13.4	NA	NA	NA	NA	NA	NA	NA	NA
Milford city (balance)	1,422	2672	66	2606	NA	NA	NA	203.4	27.7	97.5	3160	206.1	4,000	448	167.9
Monroe town (Fairfield)	163	818	15	803	541	3	100.0	83.9	10.8	98.1	3369	75.4	3,803	115	45.9
Montville town (New London)	NA	NA	NA	NA	2,777	11	100.0	64.7	21.8	98.8	1738	64.6	3,275	346	49.1
Naugatuck borough & town (New Haven)	645	2037	85	1951	2,442	19	100.0	113.1	38.6	96.7	2115	123.1	3,870	120	75.9
New Britain city & town (Hartford)	2,439	3347	441	2907	9,704	102	20.6	264.0	124.4	97.4	1521	274.7	3,758	394	280.1
New Canaan town (Fairfield)	132	650	5	645	39,589	49	100.0	129.6	6.3	100.0	5865	121.0	6,007	617	127.4
New Fairfield town (Fairfield)	NA	NA	NA	NA	919	5	100.0	59.2	16.7	96.8	2861	71.5	5,062	1,141	31.2
New Haven city & town (New Haven)	6,653	5083	1089	3994	36,053	412	5.8	723.5	431.0	93.9	1776	1130.4	8,633	3,741	585.6
Newington CDP & town (Hartford)	770	2500	75	2425	1,922	8	100.0	111.4	25.8	94.3	2651	112.8	3,682	377	14.3
New London city & town (New London)	1,012	3677	596	3081	6,786	41	100.0	123.5	69.0	97.3	1438	112.6	4,081	298	63.6
New Milford town (Litchfield)	344	1243	61	1181	4,986	20	100.0	102.8	22.9	90.2	2551	104.9	3,772	396	61.1
Newtown town (Fairfield)*	187	662	42	620	5,057	19	100.0	118.2	14.6	89.3	3410	117.0	4,170	363	90.3
North Branford town (New Haven)	194	1353	21	1332	788	3	100.0	57.4	14.9	99.0	2581	50.6	3,515	225	47.7
North Haven CDP & town (New Haven)	580	2427	92	2335	6,218	18	100.0	95.6	13.4	96.8	3167	83.9	3,500	99	47.7
Norwalk city & town (Fairfield)	1,864	2113	298	1815	34,031	236	14.8	353.8	52.6	97.8	3023	360.1	4,125	476	269.9
Norwich city & town (New London)	1,001	2484	380	2104	4,298	42	50.0	159.1	79.8	97.7	1584	163.0	4,029	489	48.2
Old Saybrook town (Middlesex)	168	1639	117	1522	4,353	12	83.3	39.3	2.6	83.7	3425	37.3	3,645	163	20.1
Orange CDP & town (New Haven)	365	2616	65	2552	7,693	26	100.0	62.1	4.3	99.9	3832	66.6	4,774	521	23.5
Oxford town (New Haven)	NA	NA	NA	NA	10,234	61	100.0	43.1	7.9	100.0	2552	40.9	3,186	162	32.2
Plainfield town (Windham)	115	757	86	672	1,236	10	100.0	46.9	21.5	92.1	1512	43.4	2,839	71	15.1
Plainville town (Hartford)	516	2892	219	2673	3,748	21	100.0	63.8	18.7	98.3	2285	60.6	3,399	168	60.4
Plymouth town (Litchfield)	179	1491	42	1450	720	6	100.0	44.0	13.5	99.2	2151	43.3	3,579	417	21.6
Ridgefield town (Fairfield)	66	261	4	257	17,629	42	52.4	144.0	13.9	100.0	4578	136.0	5,423	441	102.3
Rocky Hill town (Hartford)	379	1898	10	1888	5,597	49	26.5	62.6	7.2	99.0	2714	62.0	3,135	81	14.8
Seymour town (New Haven)	172	1037	78	959	914	6	100.0	71.9	29.8	96.8	2336	68.5	4,130	1,003	46.1
Shelton city & town (Fairfield)	414	1001	56	946	4,998	47	70.2	121.4	15.0	88.2	2457	115.7	2,872	166	84.7
Simsbury town (Hartford)	176	736	29	707	15,095	176	4.5	105.3	17.4	81.9	3451	98.4	4,172	395	45.4
Somers town (Tolland)	NA	NA	NA	NA	2,533	13	100.0	32.3	12.7	100.0	1587	30.8	2,681	152	13.6
Southbury town (New Haven)	NA	NA	NA	NA	2,918	20	100.0	63.9	4.8	91.0	2802	59.0	2,969	89	10.7
Southington town (Hartford)	853	1948	80	1868	7,089	78	83.3	149.8	37.5	97.1	2304	139.3	3,201	190	70.5
South Windsor town (Hartford)	360	1391	35	1356	4,128	25	100.0	116.3	27.7	99.2	3110	114.2	4,421	727	34.5
Stafford town (Tolland)	NA	NA	NA	NA	880	7	100.0	44.0	17.9	98.1	1949	38.6	3,218	211	23.2
Stamford city & town (Fairfield)	2,373	1863	243	1619	44,578	391	11.5	535.4	50.2	94.1	3408	551.6	4,408	402	448.3
Stonington town (New London)	333	1796	92	1704	6,956	19	100.0	61.6	5.4	99.8	2707	57.9	3,117	118	57.2
Storrs CDP	NA	NA	NA	NA	NA	NA	NA	NA	NA	NA	NA	NA	NA	NA	NA
Stratford CDP & town (Fairfield)	1,379	2638	126	2512	2,792	13	100.0	213.5	38.7	97.2	2942	210.5	4,036	398	174.3
Suffield town (Hartford)	83	526	51	475	8,854	27	100.0	64.4	24.4	82.8	2209	63.3	4,052	859	12.9
Tolland town (Tolland)	NA	NA	NA	NA	4,737	17	76.5	57.6	16.4	95.5	2577	57.0	3,807	327	38.3
Torrington city & town (Litchfield)	681	1922	124	1798	1,177	7	100.0	128.3	39.4	97.2	2158	121.9	3,409	87	36.3
Trumbull CDP & town (Fairfield)	629	1714	79	1635	934	4	100.0	164.8	17.1	86.6	3589	180.4	4,935	863	177.3
Vernon town (Tolland)	366	1255	113	1142	1,000	10	80.0	102.6	33.2	92.3	1997	96.6	3,310	289	53.1
Wallingford town (New Haven)	637	1411	51	1360	3,985	22	100.0	158.5	36.4	96.1	2365	160.3	3,546	150	43.7
Wallingford Center CDP	NA	NA	NA	NA	NA	NA	NA	NA	NA	NA	NA	NA	NA	NA	NA
Waterbury city & town (New Haven)	4,999	4566	373	4193	3,890	44	29.5	498.5	253.0	94.0	2006	626.2	5,696	845	472.8

1 Data for serious crimes have not been adjusted for underreporting. This may affect comparability between geographic areas over time.
2 Per 100,000 population estimated by the FBI.   3 Based on population estimated as of July 1 of the year shown.

Table B. Incorporated Places, Census Designated Places (CDPs), and Minor Civil Divisions (MCDs) of 10,000 or More Population — Land Area, Population, and Households, and Employment

STATE City, town, township, borough, or CDP (county if applicable)	Land area,[1] 2010 (sq mi)	Total persons 2010	Total persons 2014	Percent change 2010–2014	Persons per square mile, 2014	Foreign born	Lives in same house as previous year	Median household income (dollars)	Income of $100,000 or more	Income below poverty level	Percent in labor force	Unemploy- ment rate	Family households	One person households
	1	2	3	4	5	6	7	8	9	10	11	12	13	14
CONNECTICUT—Con.														
Waterford town (New London)..	32.701	19,517	19,427	-0.5	594.1	7.9	92.7	$75,181	34.4	6.9	65.9	7.3	66.5	29.3
Watertown town (Litchfield)	29.004	22,528	22,046	-2.1	760.1	7.4	95.2	$78,767	35.9	4.6	71.0	7.1	70.2	25.4
West Hartford CDP & town (Hartford)	21.837	63,268	63,324	0.1	2,899.8	17.3	88.9	$84,092	43.0	9.6	67.5	6.8	65.9	27.8
West Haven city & town (New Haven)	10.747	55,564	54,905	-1.2	5,108.8	15.4	86.2	$49,993	21.5	13.3	69.7	13.1	61.4	32.4
Weston town (Fairfield)	19.773	10,179	10,388	2.1	525.4	11.4	92.3	$208,078	72.5	2.1	64.5	5.5	86.3	12.9
Westport CDP & town (Fairfield)	19.961	26,391	27,561	4.4	1,380.7	12.4	92.6	$151,771	63.8	5.2	63.2	7.5	76.9	19.0
Wethersfield CDP & town (Hartford)	12.302	26,668	26,446	-0.8	2,149.7	15.5	93.6	$78,008	38.6	6.4	64.4	7.4	66.3	29.7
Willimantic CDP	4.397	17,737	NA	NA	NA	12.9	77.7	$33,008	10.7	27.1	63.8	13.2	59.0	30.8
Wilton town (Fairfield)	26.787	18,044	18,692	3.6	697.8	11.4	88.0	$175,019	71.9	2.1	66.4	4.5	81.3	16.3
Winchester town (Litchfield)	32.512	11,242	10,929	-2.8	336.2	7.3	89.0	$60,163	23.5	10.0	66.4	8.1	64.9	30.9
Windham town (Windham)	26.760	25,268	25,005		934.4	10.7	79.8	$41,019	13.1	23.5	63.8	12.3	63.4	28.8
Windsor town (Hartford)	29.504	29,044	29,069	0.1	985.3	15.2	90.0	$79,244	36.7	5.4	71.1	9.5	73.0	22.9
Windsor Locks CDP & town (Hartford)	9.023	12,498	12,565	0.5	1,392.5	8.2	88.7	$67,222	26.6	6.1	70.5	8.2	61.8	32.7
Wolcott town (New Haven)	20.435	16,695	16,716	0.1	818.0	7.8	95.9	$83,317	38.3	3.2	70.0	8.5	75.0	21.1
DELAWARE.............	1,948.543	897,936	935,614	4.2	480.2	8.4	86.6	$60,231	26.0	10.9	63.8	8.5	67.2	26.6
Bear CDP	5.712	19,371	NA	NA	NA	14.4	81.7	$60,647	25.0	12.5	69.5	7.9	74.7	19.0
Brookside CDP	3.947	14,353	NA	NA	NA	9.1	86.5	$58,470	20.9	9.7	69.0	9.4	65.2	27.7
Dover city	23.182	35,934	37,355	4.0	1,611.4	6.3	75.8	$45,660	14.7	16.6	59.8	10.0	58.1	34.1
Glasgow CDP	9.925	14,303	NA	NA	NA	8.9	89.3	$86,879	41.4	4.4	72.0	9.2	78.8	13.3
Hockessin CDP	10.041	13,527	NA	NA	NA	10.8	94.5	$121,432	61.0	1.9	64.3	4.6	80.9	17.3
Middletown town	11.768	18,871	19,910	5.5	1,691.9	6.4	92.9	$83,701	40.1	4.4	73.3	5.7	78.2	16.8
Newark city	9.187	31,513	33,008	4.7	3,592.8	10.5	63.0	$53,125	27.1	23.3	51.0	6.1	49.9	29.2
Pike Creek Valley CDP	2.583	11,217	NA	NA	NA	8.6	86.3	$73,149	30.0	3.7	76.0	5.8	52.2	40.2
Smyrna town	5.936	10,001	11,170	11.7	1,881.8	5.7	86.2	$52,243	18.7	6.6	68.3	9.9	71.4	22.0
Wilmington city	10.904	70,852	71,817	1.4	6,586.2	7.0	79.5	$38,979	15.8	23.2	62.9	12.8	52.3	39.5
DISTRICT OF COLUMBIA	61.048	601,767	658,893	9.5	10,793.0	14.0	80.0	$69,235	36.0	15.7	68.5	10.6	42.5	45.1
Washington city	61.048	601,767	658,893	9.5	10,793.0	14.0	80.0	$69,235	36.0	15.7	68.5	10.6	42.5	45.1
FLORIDA.............	53,624.756	18,804,623	19,893,297	5.8	371.0	19.6	83.7	$47,212	18.3	15.2	59.5	10.9	64.4	29.0
Alafaya CDP	37.922	78,113	NA	NA	NA	21.0	82.4	$63,022	28.3	12.5	73.5	8.6	74.5	17.1
Altamonte Springs city............	9.033	41,499	42,225	1.7	4,674.5	14.9	82.2	$50,013	14.9	8.5	69.4	9.5	52.7	40.1
Apollo Beach CDP	19.812	14,055	NA	NA	NA	9.3	85.9	$70,138	32.5	7.0	64.5	8.5	72.2	21.6
Apopka city	31.823	41,671	47,084	13.0	1,479.5	19.8	89.2	$57,925	24.1	13.9	67.5	9.3	77.5	17.7
Atlantic Beach city	3.494	12,655	13,031	3.0	3,729.6	7.8	82.0	$70,095	32.8	8.0	65.6	5.4	60.3	29.2
Auburndale city	13.485	13,502	14,518	7.5	1,076.6	11.0	84.0	$40,851	13.1	17.0	60.9	11.8	73.0	22.4
Aventura city	2.652	35,762	37,451	4.7	14,124.3	46.4	82.3	$59,657	29.4	13.0	53.4	8.3	52.5	41.8
Azalea Park CDP	3.167	12,556	NA	NA	NA	21.3	83.5	$35,671	4.8	21.9	66.2	13.7	69.1	24.5
Bartow city	45.907	17,298	18,420	6.5	401.2	4.9	81.7	$42,551	11.7	20.1	56.3	11.3	67.9	26.1
Bayonet Point CDP	5.747	23,467	NA	NA	NA	6.3	86.0	$30,684	3.7	15.0	43.1	13.3	56.7	38.6
Bayshore Gardens CDP	3.518	16,323	NA	NA	NA	16.8	85.8	$36,977	8.8	17.7	55.9	10.4	56.4	37.0
Bellair-Meadowbrook Terrace CDP	4.192	13,343	NA	NA	NA	9.7	74.8	$45,860	10.2	6.9	63.6	11.1	64.1	28.1
Belle Glade city	5.596	17,461	18,061	3.4	3,227.6	29.6	90.5	$31,667	6.8	30.9	61.0	19.1	69.9	25.1
Bellview CDP	11.644	23,355	NA	NA	NA	6.6	89.6	$48,984	13.2	8.4	63.5	9.0	65.7	30.5
Bloomingdale CDP	8.134	22,711	NA	NA	NA	9.7	88.3	$80,274	35.9	6.7	68.3	8.4	81.2	13.4
Boca Raton city	29.322	84,401	91,332	8.2	3,114.8	19.5	81.6	$71,867	37.3	8.7	62.2	8.7	60.1	32.7
Bonita Springs city	38.393	43,832	49,299	12.5	1,284.1	23.6	83.8	$53,530	25.4	12.8	47.2	9.0	65.5	28.5
Boynton Beach city	16.185	68,215	73,124	7.2	4,518.1	24.7	83.7	$44,973	16.6	14.7	63.1	13.3	54.7	36.9
Bradenton city	14.284	49,283	52,769	7.1	3,694.3	13.6	78.4	$40,592	10.5	16.3	56.1	10.9	56.2	36.2
Brandon CDP	33.102	103,483	NA	NA	NA	12.3	80.0	$56,012	18.4	10.5	67.7	6.9	64.6	26.4
Brent CDP	10.380	21,804	NA	NA	NA	6.7	82.7	$35,122	6.0	23.7	63.8	12.8	63.7	29.3
Brownsville CDP	2.276	15,313	NA	NA	NA	19.2	91.9	$20,804	2.0	42.6	51.9	23.7	59.1	36.1
Buenaventura Lakes CDP	5.581	26,079	NA	NA	NA	24.4	90.7	$41,155	6.8	16.5	62.5	10.9	78.3	16.5
Callaway city	8.910	14,336	15,006	4.7	1,684.1	5.6	83.2	$49,986	16.3	12.8	65.7	11.4	72.3	22.6
Cape Coral city	105.652	154,301	169,854	10.1	1,607.7	14.2	81.4	$49,841	15.8	12.0	59.5	13.0	72.1	22.2
Carrollwood CDP	9.219	33,365	NA	NA	NA	18.7	87.9	$60,010	27.4	9.3	69.0	7.8	66.0	29.0
Casselberry city	7.039	26,264	26,707	1.7	3,794.1	10.9	86.4	$41,960	12.1	14.4	64.7	11.6	56.5	37.4
Cheval CDP	5.955	10,702	NA	NA	NA	13.4	79.1	$63,194	30.6	8.1	75.0	6.0	63.1	32.6
Citrus Park CDP	10.163	24,252	NA	NA	NA	19.3	87.2	$60,295	22.3	10.7	71.1	9.7	70.5	23.9
Clearwater city	25.677	108,334	110,703	2.2	4,311.4	14.4	83.5	$43,306	17.0	14.9	59.5	8.7	54.9	38.4
Clermont city	14.258	28,740	30,600	6.5	2,146.1	13.0	85.5	$55,336	22.8	12.5	57.7	9.5	76.9	19.3
Cocoa city	13.331	17,134	17,419	1.7	1,306.6	10.1	77.3	$30,804	9.4	26.7	61.4	16.1	58.3	34.7
Cocoa Beach city	4.657	11,231	11,400	1.5	2,448.1	6.6	83.4	$51,866	23.5	8.6	52.0	9.5	53.2	38.7
Coconut Creek city	11.858	52,934	58,536	10.6	4,936.4	26.8	82.5	$53,316	20.7	9.0	67.0	9.5	59.6	33.6
Conway CDP	3.416	13,467	NA	NA	NA	7.7	88.6	$66,096	29.9	7.7	69.2	6.6	72.2	20.0
Cooper City city	8.062	28,548	34,923	22.3	4,332.0	22.8	90.7	$91,285	45.0	4.3	73.4	8.4	82.8	14.5
Coral Gables city	12.929	46,776	51,227	9.5	3,962.2	37.3	79.5	$93,590	47.8	9.2	60.5	7.2	63.2	30.8
Coral Springs city	23.789	121,098	127,952	5.7	5,378.6	27.5	83.0	$66,271	30.6	9.8	73.6	11.1	78.8	17.2
Coral Terrace CDP	3.377	24,376	NA	NA	NA	62.1	91.0	$48,938	18.1	15.8	59.4	12.2	78.6	17.4
Country Club CDP	4.144	47,105	NA	NA	NA	54.6	93.3	$46,479	10.9	19.6	68.2	7.0	75.6	18.3
Country Walk CDP	2.579	15,997	NA	NA	NA	44.5	89.7	$77,451	38.0	10.3	70.3	8.0	80.6	14.4
Crestview city	16.033	20,980	22,955	9.4	1,431.7	4.1	77.7	$51,115	15.1	19.7	63.9	9.0	68.0	25.9
Cutler Bay town	9.826	40,286	44,321	10.0	4,510.7	36.1	88.4	$62,130	24.5	11.2	66.3	8.1	75.1	20.3
Cypress Lake CDP	3.858	11,846	NA	NA	NA	8.6	81.8	$44,793	12.5	9.8	46.3	9.5	48.4	42.5
Dania Beach city	8.107	29,639	31,117	5.0	3,838.2	26.9	79.8	$40,222	15.3	22.2	66.6	14.5	56.1	34.7
Davie town	34.884	91,992	98,895	7.5	2,835.0	27.1	83.1	$58,924	29.1	13.5	68.8	9.1	68.9	23.5

1 Dry land or land partially or temporarily covered by water.
2 16 years old and over.

Table B. Incorporated Places, Census Designated Places (CDPs), and Minor Civil Divisions (MCDs) of 10,000 or More Population — Crime, Construction, and Local Government Finance

STATE City, town, township, borough, or CDP (county if applicable)	Serious crimes known to police, 2014[1] Total number	Rate[2] Total	Rate[2] Violent	Rate[2] Property	New residential construction authorized by building permits, 2014 Value ($1,000)	Number of housing units	Percent single family	Local government finance, 2012 General revenue Total (mil dol)	Intergovernmental Total (mil dol)	Percent from state gov.	Taxes per capita[3]	General expenditure Total (mil dol)	Per capita[3] Total	Capital outlays	Debt outstanding (mil dol)
	15	16	17	18	19	20	21	22	23	24	25	26	27	28	29
CONNECTICUT—Con.															
Waterford town (New London)..	483	2476	220	2256	3,355	14	100.0	86.7	9.5	97.2	3560	112.2	5,738	1,722	83.6
Watertown town (Litchfield)	515	2324	144	2180	6,782	31	100.0	65.5	15.5	100.0	2038	56.6	2,542	42	75.0
West Hartford CDP & town (Hartford)	1,449	2287	79	2208	5,283	59	18.6	267.9	42.0	74.8	3180	224.2	3,534	172	145.6
West Haven city & town (New Haven)..	1,665	3032	264	2768	1,289	11	100.0	172.1	67.7	99.0	1617	169.2	3,062	287	122.2
Weston town (Fairfield)	35	336	19	317	18,000	9	100.0	69.8	2.6	97.5	6103	64.7	6,242	181	56.4
Westport CDP & town (Fairfield)	337	1224	29	1195	81,685	163	66.9	196.9	8.0	87.0	6212	167.9	6,194	193	142.6
Wethersfield CDP & town (Hartford)	399	1507	64	1443	2,261	10	100.0	93.0	15.8	97.6	2754	89.8	3,385	101	27.7
Willimantic CDP	NA	NA	NA	NA	NA	NA	NA	NA	NA	NA	NA	NA	NA	NA	NA
Wilton town (Fairfield)	63	335	5	330	16,381	25	100.0	119.4	6.3	99.3	5680	111.8	6,000	210	59.6
Winchester town (Litchfield)	168	1533	73	1460	477	3	100.0	35.7	12.6	99.5	1883	35.4	3,201	182	9.7
Windham town (Windham)	NA	NA	NA	NA	1,224	10	100.0	104.8	66.5	95.4	1262	98.2	3,878	714	34.3
Windsor town (Hartford)	483	1657	79	1578	5,928	28	100.0	124.4	36.5	97.1	2756	109.6	3,760	268	39.3
Windsor Locks CDP & town (Hartford)	257	2041	119	1922	1,811	11	100.0	50.6	16.2	98.9	2392	46.4	3,692	227	17.7
Wolcott town (New Haven)	314	1876	42	1835	1,680	20	60.0	54.2	19.5	99.6	1887	54.3	3,239	190	35.1
DELAWARE..........................	32,476	3471	489	2982	615,472	5,194	79.8	X	X	X	X	X	X	X	X
Bear CDP	NA	NA	NA	NA	NA	NA	NA	NA	NA	NA	NA	NA	NA	NA	NA
Brookside CDP	NA	NA	NA	NA	NA	NA	NA	NA	NA	NA	NA	NA	NA	NA	NA
Dover city...............................	2,112	5606	637	4969	16,365	116	37.9	42.7	9.6	91.3	426	55.8	1,506	400	41.3
Glasgow CDP	NA	NA	NA	NA	NA	NA	NA	NA	NA	NA	NA	NA	NA	NA	NA
Hockessin CDP.......................	NA	NA	NA	NA	NA	NA	NA	NA	NA	NA	NA	NA	NA	NA	NA
Middletown town	531	2687	309	2378	13,874	180	100.0	13.7	0.4	100.0	310	21.0	1,080	308	46.8
Newark city.............................	850	2590	317	2273	29,025	361	21.1	23.4	3.3	100.0	258	32.7	1,010	108	13.6
Pike Creek Valley CDP	NA	NA	NA	NA	NA	NA	NA	NA	NA	NA	NA	NA	NA	NA	NA
Smyrna town............................	386	3456	555	2901	10,644	85	97.6	9.2	1.4	61.3	262	10.5	980	119	13.7
Wilmington city........................	4,941	6890	1636	5254	3,315	133	21.1	193.4	38.2	53.3	1550	166.5	2,334	116	353.0
DISTRICT OF COLUMBIA	42,346	6427	1244	5182	374,396	4,189	6.9	X	X	X	X	X	X	X	X
Washington city	40,837	6198	1185	5012	374,397	4,189	6.9	10710.4	3077.7	0.0	9344	11199.3	17,636	2,228	11278.8
FLORIDA.............................	786,967	3956	540	3415	19,548,769	84,075	66.9	X	X	X	X	X	X	X	X
Alafaya CDP	NA	NA	NA	NA	NA	NA	NA	NA	NA	NA	NA	NA	NA	NA	NA
Altamonte Springs city.............	1,503	3553	364	3189	22,126	265	1.1	42.8	3.7	94.1	515	30.6	731	144	0.0
Apollo Beach CDP...................	NA	NA	NA	NA	NA	NA	NA	NA	NA	NA	NA	NA	NA	NA	NA
Apopka city.............................	1,676	3599	363	3236	95,306	292	100.0	48.2	9.5	80.2	437	45.1	1,012	64	33.4
Atlantic Beach city...................	362	2794	363	2431	9,424	22	100.0	19.5	3.1	86.4	588	18.9	1,470	95	21.1
Auburndale city.......................	822	5690	256	5434	22,645	112	100.0	21.5	4.2	31.3	618	18.5	1,329	215	56.0
Aventura city...........................	2,055	5475	202	5272	0	0	0.0	42.7	11.2	85.4	671	38.3	1,028	79	32.5
Azalea Park CDP.....................	NA	NA	NA	NA	NA	NA	NA	NA	NA	NA	NA	NA	NA	NA	NA
Bartow city..............................	1,068	5879	666	5213	22,055	113	100.0	24.3	2.1	86.3	364	32.9	1,862	219	39.3
Bayonet Point CDP..................	NA	NA	NA	NA	NA	NA	NA	NA	NA	NA	NA	NA	NA	NA	NA
Bayshore Gardens CDP	NA	NA	NA	NA	NA	NA	NA	NA	NA	NA	NA	NA	NA	NA	NA
Bellair-Meadowbrook Terrace CDP	NA	NA	NA	NA	NA	NA	NA	NA	NA	NA	NA	NA	NA	NA	NA
Belle Glade city.......................	1,231	6867	1383	5483	584	5	100.0	13.7	4.3	70.6	298	13.1	734	105	0.0
Bellview CDP...........................	NA	NA	NA	NA	NA	NA	NA	NA	NA	NA	NA	NA	NA	NA	NA
Bloomingdale CDP...................	NA	NA	NA	NA	NA	NA	NA	NA	NA	NA	NA	NA	NA	NA	NA
Boca Raton city.......................	2,233	2468	185	2283	123,609	469	14.1	195.4	30.0	30.6	1242	210.8	2,397	278	139.0
Bonita Springs city..................	NA	NA	NA	NA	255,257	902	67.1	18.8	4.9	87.3	243	17.6	382	76	24.3
Boynton Beach city..................	3,257	4536	526	4010	5,197	29	100.0	116.4	15.6	61.0	721	120.3	1,714	146	126.0
Bradenton city.........................	2,347	4483	646	3838	60,241	511	24.1	58.2	10.3	29.0	488	58.4	1,157	9	34.5
Brandon CDP	NA	NA	NA	NA	NA	NA	NA	NA	NA	NA	NA	NA	NA	NA	NA
Brent CDP	NA	NA	NA	NA	NA	NA	NA	NA	NA	NA	NA	NA	NA	NA	NA
Brownsville CDP......................	NA	NA	NA	NA	NA	NA	NA	NA	NA	NA	NA	NA	NA	NA	NA
Buenaventura Lakes CDP	NA	NA	NA	NA	NA	NA	NA	NA	NA	NA	NA	NA	NA	NA	NA
Callaway city...........................	NA	NA	NA	NA	260	3	100.0	11.0	2.0	96.2	263	9.8	671	31	37.4
Cape Coral city........................	3,513	2082	143	1939	160,093	663	100.0	245.7	47.7	80.3	572	240.6	1,492	184	907.6
Carrollwood CDP.....................	NA	NA	NA	NA	NA	NA	NA	NA	NA	NA	NA	NA	NA	NA	NA
Casselberry city.......................	1,235	4635	499	4136	9,395	48	100.0	34.0	7.5	31.2	484	41.1	1,552	195	20.3
Cheval CDP	NA	NA	NA	NA	NA	NA	NA	NA	NA	NA	NA	NA	NA	NA	NA
Citrus Park CDP......................	NA	NA	NA	NA	NA	NA	NA	NA	NA	NA	NA	NA	NA	NA	NA
Clearwater city........................	4,924	4473	582	3891	36,942	495	7.5	200.9	27.4	47.6	751	194.0	1,782	189	247.9
Clermont city...........................	950	3131	224	2907	64,619	551	47.7	32.1	6.1	87.7	423	30.7	1,043	125	19.7
Cocoa city...............................	1,402	8109	1810	6299	3,649	16	100.0	27.6	5.3	27.1	496	31.3	1,814	74	88.8
Cocoa Beach city.....................	725	6389	846	5543	3,120	12	100.0	18.8	1.6	41.1	919	22.1	1,962	184	3.9
Coconut Creek city..................	1,353	2342	147	2195	4,902	41	100.0	61.2	5.4	70.6	537	52.9	959	77	22.8
Conway CDP	NA	NA	NA	NA	NA	NA	NA	NA	NA	NA	NA	NA	NA	NA	NA
Cooper City city......................	482	1351	118	1233	2,315	10	100.0	35.4	2.6	92.2	547	32.2	994	12	6.1
Coral Gables city.....................	2,063	4100	151	3949	46,614	60	93.3	158.0	11.2	62.7	1954	127.4	2,504	171	79.3
Coral Springs city....................	2,684	2090	159	1939	949	2	100.0	123.2	15.5	67.5	521	133.1	1,060	84	71.6
Coral Terrace CDP...................	NA	NA	NA	NA	NA	NA	NA	NA	NA	NA	NA	NA	NA	NA	NA
Country Club CDP....................	NA	NA	NA	NA	NA	NA	NA	NA	NA	NA	NA	NA	NA	NA	NA
Country Walk CDP....................	NA	NA	NA	NA	NA	NA	NA	NA	NA	NA	NA	NA	NA	NA	NA
Crestview city..........................	868	3733	551	3183	15,956	62	100.0	21.6	0.9	77.8	472	21.2	949	51	24.4
Cutler Bay town.......................	1,973	4476	288	4188	4,210	115	2.6	23.2	9.8	41.7	260	26.0	611	269	18.6
Cypress Lake CDP...................	NA	NA	NA	NA	NA	NA	NA	NA	NA	NA	NA	NA	NA	NA	NA
Dania Beach city......................	1,344	4336	494	3842	1,615	7	71.4	52.7	10.5	66.3	793	52.7	1,718	156	30.3
Davie town..............................	3,464	3534	262	3272	23,578	378	12.2	104.7	13.7	53.9	738	98.2	1,027	73	144.9

1 Data for serious crimes have not been adjusted for underreporting. This may affect comparability between geographic areas over time.
2 Per 100,000 population estimated by the FBI.   3 Based on population estimated as of July 1 of the year shown.

Table B. Incorporated Places, Census Designated Places (CDPs), and Minor Civil Divisions (MCDs) of 10,000 or More Population — Land Area, Population, and Households, and Employment

STATE City, town, township, borough, or CDP (county if applicable)	Land area,[1] 2010 (sq mi)	Total persons 2010	Total persons 2014	Percent change 2010–2014	Persons per square mile, 2014	Foreign born	Lives in same house as previous year	Median household income (dollars)	Income of $100,000 or more	Income below poverty level	Percent in labor force	Unemployment rate	Family households	One person households
	1	2	3	4	5	6	7	8	9	10	11	12	13	14
FLORIDA—Con.														
Daytona Beach city	58.410	61,005	63,011	3.3	1,078.8	8.9	80.4	$28,164	7.3	27.5	49.9	12.1	46.9	42.7
DeBary city	18.969	19,315	19,648	1.7	1,035.8	6.6	89.5	$52,258	17.0	8.7	53.7	9.5	66.6	27.6
Deerfield Beach city	15.092	75,018	78,881	5.1	5,226.7	31.6	81.1	$38,209	12.5	17.2	60.4	11.0	54.4	37.3
DeLand city	18.501	26,957	29,194	8.3	1,578.0	8.7	81.2	$37,417	11.5	16.5	49.0	11.3	61.4	35.0
Delray Beach city	15.924	60,601	65,055	7.3	4,085.3	23.0	84.2	$50,833	22.0	14.5	62.0	12.2	51.2	38.4
Deltona city	37.531	85,182	86,890	2.0	2,315.2	9.6	89.8	$44,046	10.0	14.8	58.2	11.6	73.8	20.9
Destin city	7.690	12,305	13,355	8.5	1,736.6	8.5	83.1	$66,324	28.4	7.3	69.6	6.8	61.9	29.4
Doctor Phillips CDP	3.399	10,981	NA	NA	NA	28.6	86.2	$76,857	37.4	6.9	60.6	4.2	76.1	15.9
Doral city	13.854	45,709	54,116	18.4	3,906.3	62.4	80.5	$72,623	32.3	11.3	67.6	6.3	81.7	13.9
Dunedin city	10.393	35,356	35,819	1.3	3,446.6	10.0	84.0	$46,310	15.4	9.0	57.9	8.1	53.3	39.4
East Lake CDP	28.670	30,962	NA	NA	NA	10.9	85.9	$73,843	35.7	5.8	58.1	8.3	69.4	26.1
East Lake-Orient Park CDP	16.112	22,753	NA	NA	NA	13.8	80.7	$38,290	6.4	22.8	66.8	12.7	60.6	32.1
East Milton CDP	28.708	11,074	NA	NA	NA	3.5	71.4	$43,864	12.1	25.7	35.0	20.3	69.6	22.2
Edgewater city	22.167	20,759	21,121	1.7	952.8	3.7	85.2	$43,942	10.9	11.0	54.4	11.9	66.0	27.0
Egypt Lake-Leto CDP	5.907	35,282	NA	NA	NA	34.5	77.9	$36,976	9.6	21.8	66.0	9.4	63.3	28.9
Elfers CDP	3.543	13,986	NA	NA	NA	10.3	90.9	$33,340	4.1	19.2	48.1	12.2	63.6	31.1
Englewood CDP	9.815	14,863	NA	NA	NA	6.0	86.5	$41,949	12.9	10.2	35.5	15.3	58.6	35.2
Ensley CDP	12.175	20,602	NA	NA	NA	7.1	85.1	$41,782	9.4	16.1	63.9	11.9	53.1	36.3
Estero CDP	20.626	22,612	NA	NA	NA	13.7	87.5	$66,439	33.9	5.1	40.1	7.6	69.6	26.4
Eustis city	10.395	18,490	19,455	5.2	1,871.6	6.7	88.8	$37,203	10.8	20.8	54.8	11.9	62.5	32.4
Fairview Shores CDP	3.020	10,239	NA	NA	NA	12.1	67.2	$41,284	14.7	20.1	71.3	12.3	50.5	36.4
Fernandina Beach city	11.160	11,583	12,103	4.5	1,084.5	4.7	79.8	$52,165	22.9	12.8	53.3	9.4	62.2	33.6
Ferry Pass CDP	13.988	28,921	NA	NA	NA	6.0	73.8	$40,893	13.3	14.4	60.0	9.3	48.4	41.0
Fish Hawk CDP	16.216	14,087	NA	NA	NA	7.2	86.0	$107,153	54.8	4.4	71.2	7.3	84.0	13.5
Fleming Island CDP	15.838	27,126	NA	NA	NA	6.9	85.0	$88,672	42.3	5.5	63.7	9.1	80.3	15.9
Florida City city	5.958	11,245	12,062	7.3	2,024.6	32.8	80.6	$26,539	1.9	45.7	53.0	28.7	81.3	16.1
Florida Ridge CDP	10.770	18,164	NA	NA	NA	12.9	84.4	$40,923	12.7	11.2	55.2	13.5	63.7	32.5
Forest City CDP	4.267	13,854	NA	NA	NA	16.8	79.8	$55,091	20.9	14.1	69.2	10.3	69.2	24.9
Fort Lauderdale city	34.598	165,578	176,013	6.3	5,087.4	22.8	79.3	$48,898	23.4	17.0	65.5	12.2	46.5	42.0
Fort Myers city	39.637	62,202	70,918	14.0	1,789.2	16.3	74.5	$37,360	14.0	20.8	53.1	14.2	57.6	35.4
Fort Pierce city	22.663	41,853	43,601	4.2	1,923.9	19.0	84.9	$25,976	7.4	33.2	52.7	16.3	59.8	34.8
Fort Walton Beach city	7.491	19,516	21,558	10.5	2,878.0	6.7	82.0	$49,552	16.8	15.2	65.5	9.5	60.1	32.6
Fountainebleau CDP	3.863	59,764	NA	NA	NA	70.0	84.1	$42,273	9.8	15.9	64.5	10.7	72.2	20.4
Four Corners CDP	46.414	26,116	NA	NA	NA	12.6	75.5	$48,883	12.9	12.2	68.9	9.1	73.1	20.0
Fruit Cove CDP	16.080	29,362	NA	NA	NA	6.7	88.4	$97,555	48.2	4.0	69.7	6.9	87.0	11.1
Fruitville CDP	6.799	13,224	NA	NA	NA	10.3	86.7	$56,174	18.6	8.8	64.6	8.6	62.6	30.9
Gainesville city	61.597	124,486	128,460	3.2	2,085.5	11.7	65.9	$32,108	11.7	30.8	56.7	9.7	40.3	37.8
Gibsonton CDP	12.806	14,234	NA	NA	NA	14.5	83.1	$42,547	10.3	19.8	63.2	9.5	70.2	22.4
Gladeview CDP	2.559	11,535	NA	NA	NA	18.5	86.5	$23,321	3.4	41.7	58.7	25.4	67.9	23.3
Glenvar Heights CDP	4.118	16,898	NA	NA	NA	45.1	85.9	$57,103	27.6	12.1	68.8	6.1	58.4	33.6
Golden Gate CDP	3.902	23,961	NA	NA	NA	49.2	80.7	$38,644	7.9	24.2	74.2	11.3	78.4	16.6
Golden Glades CDP	4.887	33,145	NA	NA	NA	47.2	84.8	$37,778	7.4	25.2	63.0	16.2	72.2	22.2
Goldenrod CDP	2.516	12,039	NA	NA	NA	11.1	78.7	$39,034	10.1	24.5	66.0	11.8	51.9	33.6
Gonzalez CDP	15.109	13,273	NA	NA	NA	4.9	92.4	$62,857	19.9	6.8	64.2	8.9	81.1	16.1
Goulds CDP	2.907	10,103	NA	NA	NA	33.0	87.9	$28,738	3.8	35.3	55.5	21.6	80.6	15.8
Greenacres city	5.868	37,580	39,157	4.2	6,673.2	36.0	84.0	$43,235	10.3	16.4	68.2	11.4	66.7	27.5
Gulf Gate Estates CDP	2.712	10,911	NA	NA	NA	15.1	84.3	$42,469	8.2	14.2	56.1	9.8	50.9	44.4
Gulfport city	2.758	12,029	12,198	1.4	4,422.6	10.9	83.0	$38,315	12.3	19.9	53.4	10.5	46.6	42.1
Haines City city	18.549	20,577	22,072	7.3	1,190.0	22.1	87.7	$33,305	6.4	25.6	56.8	7.9	71.2	24.6
Hallandale Beach city	4.214	37,113	39,051	5.2	9,265.9	45.7	78.8	$33,838	11.4	20.5	57.2	14.7	51.1	42.3
Hialeah city	21.433	224,667	235,563	4.8	10,990.6	73.0	93.6	$29,959	6.1	29.2	58.3	13.1	75.1	20.5
Hialeah Gardens city	3.258	21,744	23,555	8.3	7,229.9	69.5	97.3	$41,967	11.3	20.8	63.4	12.2	79.4	18.7
Highland City CDP	7.862	10,834	NA	NA	NA	8.4	92.4	$63,258	23.1	5.6	66.7	6.0	78.1	19.0
Hobe Sound CDP	7.049	11,521	NA	NA	NA	8.2	83.9	$45,908	15.9	11.1	52.4	9.5	59.5	35.2
Holiday CDP	5.369	22,403	NA	NA	NA	10.6	89.3	$33,595	4.8	17.9	51.6	13.5	59.5	34.8
Holly Hill city	3.934	11,657	11,765	0.9	2,990.8	4.0	80.8	$26,699	3.8	24.1	56.2	15.8	49.5	40.1
Hollywood city	27.273	140,769	148,047	5.2	5,428.3	32.8	82.8	$46,419	18.6	15.8	66.2	11.9	59.6	33.0
Homestead city	15.137	60,509	65,524	8.3	4,328.7	36.0	77.0	$40,250	14.6	27.7	65.8	12.3	69.8	23.0
Homosassa Springs CDP	25.159	13,791	NA	NA	NA	6.1	85.7	$28,767	9.2	25.7	45.9	19.7	64.7	28.2
Horizon West CDP	33.020	14,000	NA	NA	NA	20.5	80.8	$84,215	38.0	5.7	78.9	5.0	72.5	19.4
Hudson CDP	6.359	12,158	NA	NA	NA	5.5	86.9	$36,692	10.6	15.2	39.5	13.8	56.1	36.0
Hunters Creek CDP	7.075	14,321	NA	NA	NA	25.9	86.1	$61,834	22.7	7.5	76.2	7.1	71.9	20.8
Immokalee CDP	22.713	24,154	NA	NA	NA	41.4	84.6	$25,725	6.0	45.1	66.1	15.5	79.4	15.3
Iona CDP	6.611	15,369	NA	NA	NA	8.4	88.9	$53,395	23.8	7.9	38.8	7.8	55.6	38.2
Ives Estates CDP	2.507	19,525	NA	NA	NA	40.0	89.2	$49,627	12.5	15.0	65.5	12.3	68.7	28.0
Jacksonville city	747.444	821,784	853,382	3.8	1,141.7	9.7	80.9	$46,768	17.3	16.2	65.8	11.4	62.8	30.8
Jacksonville Beach city	7.333	21,362	22,665	6.1	3,090.7	6.4	80.7	$58,792	26.3	10.3	68.5	5.3	49.9	39.5
Jasmine Estates CDP	3.550	18,989	NA	NA	NA	14.0	90.2	$30,851	3.2	22.8	52.8	16.0	61.8	28.9
Jensen Beach CDP	6.958	11,707	NA	NA	NA	3.8	85.9	$43,181	18.0	10.5	56.5	10.0	59.1	32.7
Jupiter town	21.858	55,266	60,681	9.8	2,776.2	13.5	87.3	$70,240	33.1	7.9	63.3	5.7	61.9	30.9
Jupiter Farms CDP	14.948	11,994	NA	NA	NA	8.0	90.3	$90,227	43.4	4.6	70.9	7.3	80.9	16.3
Kendale Lakes CDP	8.102	56,148	NA	NA	NA	61.9	90.5	$50,032	17.6	14.8	65.1	11.1	79.6	16.2
Kendall CDP	16.080	75,371	NA	NA	NA	44.7	87.0	$59,753	29.5	9.4	67.3	8.1	66.2	29.0
Kendall West CDP	2.750	36,154	NA	NA	NA	62.8	87.6	$44,237	15.5	17.3	63.3	9.5	80.6	15.9
Key Biscayne village	1.230	12,344	12,924	4.7	10,505.8	44.0	89.2	$121,023	56.8	6.3	56.7	4.7	78.4	18.3
Key Largo CDP	12.059	10,433	NA	NA	NA	21.3	82.1	$56,809	21.7	14.4	60.7	8.4	57.6	31.0
Keystone CDP	35.126	24,039	NA	NA	NA	9.8	91.3	$113,971	58.3	2.7	68.9	4.6	85.7	11.7
Key West city	5.600	24,649	25,704	4.3	4,590.0	19.1	76.2	$54,306	20.5	10.4	70.4	6.3	51.1	36.9
Kissimmee city	20.797	59,620	66,722	11.9	3,208.2	26.9	85.6	$35,452	9.3	21.0	66.4	11.3	71.0	21.8
Lady Lake town	8.181	13,927	14,455	3.8	1,766.8	7.0	80.8	$38,222	5.7	10.0	37.8	13.0	57.3	37.8
Lake Butler CDP	11.806	15,400	NA	NA	NA	15.5	84.7	$107,266	53.4	2.6	68.0	3.9	79.9	13.6
Lake City city	12.051	12,031	12,100	0.6	1,004.1	3.6	70.4	$33,571	8.2	24.6	59.2	20.0	53.8	43.1
Lakeland city	65.610	97,433	102,346	5.0	1,559.9	8.7	79.3	$39,238	12.1	16.6	54.7	13.0	58.7	35.1
Lakeland Highlands CDP	4.860	11,056	NA	NA	NA	6.8	90.1	$81,263	35.9	4.3	61.2	8.6	78.3	17.7
Lake Magdalene CDP	10.228	28,509	NA	NA	NA	13.5	85.4	$52,911	25.1	13.0	65.0	8.3	60.6	32.2
Lake Mary city	9.153	13,818	15,801	14.4	1,726.3	12.0	88.5	$84,741	40.6	5.7	64.7	9.3	71.7	23.4

1 Dry land or land partially or temporarily covered by water.
2 16 years old and over.

Table B. Incorporated Places, Census Designated Places (CDPs), and Minor Civil Divisions (MCDs) of 10,000 or More Population — Crime, Construction, and Local Government Finance

STATE City, town, township, borough, or CDP (county if applicable)	Serious crimes known to police, 2014[1] Total number	Rate[2] Total	Rate[2] Violent	Rate[2] Property	New residential construction authorized by building permits, 2014 Value ($1,000)	Number of housing units	Percent single family	Local government finance, 2012 General revenue Total (mil dol)	Intergovernmental Total (mil dol)	Intergovernmental Percent from state gov.	Taxes per capita[3]	General expenditure Total (mil dol)	Per capita[3] Total	Per capita[3] Capital outlays	Debt outstanding (mil dol)
	15	16	17	18	19	20	21	22	23	24	25	26	27	28	29
FLORIDA—Con.															
Daytona Beach city	4,778	7629	1284	6345	48,701	302	43.0	124.9	15.8	46.5	724	118.4	1,915	146	154.8
DeBary city	NA	NA	NA	NA	6,605	24	100.0	14.0	3.2	43.1	403	11.4	589	129	11.4
Deerfield Beach city	2,442	3100	468	2632	3,600	10	100.0	110.6	11.2	65.6	667	119.1	1,535	67	72.1
DeLand city	1,424	4988	501	4487	116,130	335	100.0	35.7	3.0	61.4	614	31.5	1,139	109	33.4
Delray Beach city	3,165	4875	665	4210	53,093	283	39.2	122.1	11.8	68.8	1240	117.6	1,882	71	86.4
Deltona city	NA	NA	NA	NA	21,644	61	100.0	54.5	13.8	48.2	348	53.3	623	113	97.2
Destin city	NA	NA	NA	NA	24,869	65	87.7	12.9	1.6	81.6	826	11.7	916	169	35.1
Doctor Phillips CDP	NA	NA	NA	NA	NA	NA	NA	NA	NA	NA	NA	NA	NA	NA	NA
Doral city	2,142	4171	140	4031	97,010	605	67.8	55.0	5.7	60.4	848	61.9	1,277	597	26.4
Dunedin city	794	2219	268	1951	518	2	100.0	36.4	4.4	84.4	493	42.1	1,185	73	35.3
East Lake CDP	NA	NA	NA	NA	NA	NA	NA	NA	NA	NA	NA	NA	NA	NA	NA
East Lake-Orient Park CDP	NA	NA	NA	NA	NA	NA	NA	NA	NA	NA	NA	NA	NA	NA	NA
East Milton CDP	NA	NA	NA	NA	NA	NA	NA	NA	NA	NA	NA	NA	NA	NA	NA
Edgewater city	436	2078	205	1873	7,107	45	100.0	22.0	3.0	55.6	434	20.3	973	128	19.7
Egypt Lake-Leto CDP	NA	NA	NA	NA	NA	NA	NA	NA	NA	NA	NA	NA	NA	NA	NA
Elfers CDP	NA	NA	NA	NA	NA	NA	NA	NA	NA	NA	NA	NA	NA	NA	NA
Englewood CDP	NA	NA	NA	NA	NA	NA	NA	NA	NA	NA	NA	NA	NA	NA	NA
Ensley CDP	NA	NA	NA	NA	NA	NA	NA	NA	NA	NA	NA	NA	NA	NA	NA
Estero CDP	NA	NA	NA	NA	NA	NA	NA	NA	NA	NA	NA	NA	NA	NA	NA
Eustis city	761	3929	320	3609	32,655	112	100.0	21.6	3.7	54.7	601	22.1	1,171	252	7.4
Fairview Shores CDP	NA	NA	NA	NA	NA	NA	NA	NA	NA	NA	NA	NA	NA	NA	NA
Fernandina Beach city	308	2553	282	2272	23,963	78	100.0	28.9	4.6	64.4	928	28.2	2,386	244	52.3
Ferry Pass CDP	NA	NA	NA	NA	NA	NA	NA	NA	NA	NA	NA	NA	NA	NA	NA
Fish Hawk CDP	NA	NA	NA	NA	NA	NA	NA	NA	NA	NA	NA	NA	NA	NA	NA
Fleming Island CDP	NA	NA	NA	NA	NA	NA	NA	NA	NA	NA	NA	NA	NA	NA	NA
Florida City city	1,436	11811	2772	9039	NA	NA	NA	15.4	4.5	21.2	415	15.4	1,287	279	1.4
Florida Ridge CDP	NA	NA	NA	NA	NA	NA	NA	NA	NA	NA	NA	NA	NA	NA	NA
Forest City CDP	NA	NA	NA	NA	NA	NA	NA	NA	NA	NA	NA	NA	NA	NA	NA
Fort Lauderdale city	10,278	5905	773	5132	50,627	362	21.8	351.8	52.9	32.9	1007	357.5	2,086	178	587.6
Fort Myers city	2,945	4224	1103	3121	178,249	849	84.3	148.2	15.3	59.3	943	154.4	2,352	195	377.2
Fort Pierce city	2,620	6044	1061	4983	6,280	21	76.2	68.9	10.3	85.1	609	79.2	1,855	305	216.8
Fort Walton Beach city	764	3659	340	3319	6,280	46	100.0	28.0	3.1	84.6	617	26.8	1,317	109	16.1
Fountainebleau CDP	NA	NA	NA	NA	NA	NA	NA	NA	NA	NA	NA	NA	NA	NA	NA
Four Corners CDP	NA	NA	NA	NA	NA	NA	NA	NA	NA	NA	NA	NA	NA	NA	NA
Fruit Cove CDP	NA	NA	NA	NA	NA	NA	NA	NA	NA	NA	NA	NA	NA	NA	NA
Fruitville CDP	NA	NA	NA	NA	NA	NA	NA	NA	NA	NA	NA	NA	NA	NA	NA
Gainesville city	5,397	4210	637	3573	23,681	330	20.3	206.3	24.2	47.3	510	208.2	1,648	273	1189.9
Gibsonton CDP	NA	NA	NA	NA	NA	NA	NA	NA	NA	NA	NA	NA	NA	NA	NA
Gladeview CDP	NA	NA	NA	NA	NA	NA	NA	NA	NA	NA	NA	NA	NA	NA	NA
Glenvar Heights CDP	NA	NA	NA	NA	NA	NA	NA	NA	NA	NA	NA	NA	NA	NA	NA
Golden Gate CDP	NA	NA	NA	NA	NA	NA	NA	NA	NA	NA	NA	NA	NA	NA	NA
Golden Glades CDP	NA	NA	NA	NA	NA	NA	NA	NA	NA	NA	NA	NA	NA	NA	NA
Goldenrod CDP	NA	NA	NA	NA	NA	NA	NA	NA	NA	NA	NA	NA	NA	NA	NA
Gonzalez CDP	NA	NA	NA	NA	NA	NA	NA	NA	NA	NA	NA	NA	NA	NA	NA
Goulds CDP	NA	NA	NA	NA	NA	NA	NA	NA	NA	NA	NA	NA	NA	NA	NA
Greenacres city	1,788	4590	680	3909	7,209	40	100.0	21.6	4.0	80.4	347	20.5	533	30	4.0
Gulf Gate Estates CDP	NA	NA	NA	NA	NA	NA	NA	NA	NA	NA	NA	NA	NA	NA	NA
Gulfport city	703	5763	287	5476	1,645	4	100.0	15.8	1.9	63.8	510	17.3	1,433	79	0.0
Haines City city	710	3269	239	3030	47,698	166	100.0	25.4	2.5	66.1	577	27.1	1,287	106	55.3
Hallandale Beach city	1,766	4528	615	3913	2,691	4	100.0	73.9	8.7	37.1	827	76.5	1,992	86	31.5
Hialeah city	7,318	3108	332	2776	27,120	127	84.3	219.5	58.6	43.0	442	207.3	887	63	169.3
Hialeah Gardens city	891	3898	249	3649	5,124	76	5.3	14.0	3.6	67.6	411	19.5	861	55	6.9
Highland City CDP	NA	NA	NA	NA	NA	NA	NA	NA	NA	NA	NA	NA	NA	NA	NA
Hobe Sound CDP	NA	NA	NA	NA	NA	NA	NA	NA	NA	NA	NA	NA	NA	NA	NA
Holiday CDP	NA	NA	NA	NA	NA	NA	NA	NA	NA	NA	NA	NA	NA	NA	NA
Holly Hill city	674	5768	650	5117	210	3	100.0	14.6	2.4	38.2	566	11.6	1,000	95	30.2
Hollywood city	7,116	4811	494	4317	5,804	22	36.4	276.4	29.3	52.2	843	276.3	1,896	231	379.0
Homestead city	3,825	5890	1327	4563	48,088	246	100.0	81.0	20.4	49.7	395	68.8	1,081	164	18.5
Homosassa Springs CDP	NA	NA	NA	NA	NA	NA	NA	NA	NA	NA	NA	NA	NA	NA	NA
Horizon West CDP	NA	NA	NA	NA	NA	NA	NA	NA	NA	NA	NA	NA	NA	NA	NA
Hudson CDP	NA	NA	NA	NA	NA	NA	NA	NA	NA	NA	NA	NA	NA	NA	NA
Hunters Creek CDP	NA	NA	NA	NA	NA	NA	NA	NA	NA	NA	NA	NA	NA	NA	NA
Immokalee CDP	NA	NA	NA	NA	NA	NA	NA	NA	NA	NA	NA	NA	NA	NA	NA
Iona CDP	NA	NA	NA	NA	NA	NA	NA	NA	NA	NA	NA	NA	NA	NA	NA
Ives Estates CDP	NA	NA	NA	NA	NA	NA	NA	NA	NA	NA	NA	NA	NA	NA	NA
Jacksonville city	39,585	4624	684	3941	543,925	3,302	63.8	1946.9	245.5	61.0	1104	1888.1	2,255	340	10439.0
Jacksonville Beach city	948	4322	615	3706	33,732	109	92.7	40.0	6.9	54.3	917	36.4	1,675	375	48.2
Jasmine Estates CDP	NA	NA	NA	NA	NA	NA	NA	NA	NA	NA	NA	NA	NA	NA	NA
Jensen Beach CDP	NA	NA	NA	NA	NA	NA	NA	NA	NA	NA	NA	NA	NA	NA	NA
Jupiter town	1,175	1990	213	1777	159,676	706	51.6	55.9	5.9	86.7	621	60.5	1,056	189	66.9
Jupiter Farms CDP	NA	NA	NA	NA	NA	NA	NA	NA	NA	NA	NA	NA	NA	NA	NA
Kendale Lakes CDP	NA	NA	NA	NA	NA	NA	NA	NA	NA	NA	NA	NA	NA	NA	NA
Kendall CDP	NA	NA	NA	NA	NA	NA	NA	NA	NA	NA	NA	NA	NA	NA	NA
Kendall West CDP	NA	NA	NA	NA	NA	NA	NA	NA	NA	NA	NA	NA	NA	NA	NA
Key Biscayne village	212	1638	15	1622	134	1	100.0	29.3	2.1	47.6	1793	26.1	2,027	153	36.4
Key Largo CDP	NA	NA	NA	NA	NA	NA	NA	NA	NA	NA	NA	NA	NA	NA	NA
Keystone CDP	NA	NA	NA	NA	NA	NA	NA	NA	NA	NA	NA	NA	NA	NA	NA
Key West city	1,518	5890	788	5102	420	1	100.0	94.5	20.7	30.3	1042	92.7	3,686	794	36.2
Kissimmee city	3,261	4895	668	4227	82,884	441	61.5	69.7	20.4	62.5	438	82.5	1,296	259	457.1
Lady Lake town	218	1522	182	1341	4,665	42	100.0	11.1	1.6	27.2	525	11.9	846	230	5.5
Lake Butler CDP	NA	NA	NA	NA	NA	NA	NA	NA	NA	NA	NA	NA	NA	NA	NA
Lake City city	1,113	9182	1378	7805	580	3	100.0	23.5	4.1	81.5	665	23.6	1,952	427	47.0
Lakeland city	5,738	5657	447	5211	26,867	104	98.1	186.5	38.4	30.2	502	203.7	2,048	303	951.3
Lakeland Highlands CDP	NA	NA	NA	NA	NA	NA	NA	NA	NA	NA	NA	NA	NA	NA	NA
Lake Magdalene CDP	NA	NA	NA	NA	NA	NA	NA	NA	NA	NA	NA	NA	NA	NA	NA
Lake Mary city	326	2164	206	1958	6,622	25	100.0	22.4	1.7	82.3	1122	18.3	1,253	78	5.8

1 Data for serious crimes have not been adjusted for underreporting. This may affect comparability between geographic areas over time.
2 Per 100,000 population estimated by the FBI.   3 Based on population estimated as of July 1 of the year shown.

Table B. Incorporated Places, Census Designated Places (CDPs), and Minor Civil Divisions (MCDs) of 10,000 or More Population — **Land Area, Population, and Households, and Employment**

STATE City, town, township, borough, or CDP (county if applicable)	Land area,[1] 2010 (sq mi)	Total persons 2010	Total persons 2014	Percent change 2010–2014	Persons per square mile, 2014	Foreign born	Lives in same house as previous year	Median household income (dollars	Income of $100,000 or more	Income below poverty level	Percent in labor force	Unemployment rate	Family households	One person households
	1	2	3	4	5	6	7	8	9	10	11	12	13	14
FLORIDA—Con.														
Lakeside CDP	13.525	30,943	NA	NA	NA	5.3	83.2	$56,127	21.5	10.3	66.5	11.7	76.5	20.1
Lake Wales city	18.934	14,205	15,140	6.6	799.6	8.9	74.8	$35,785	8.0	23.5	53.3	19.1	62.8	32.4
Lakewood Park CDP	6.647	11,323	NA	NA	NA	7.7	88.4	$48,361	10.2	13.3	56.7	8.8	66.5	26.1
Lake Worth city	5.876	34,910	37,097	6.3	6,313.5	36.0	77.9	$37,036	11.8	24.8	72.0	15.8	55.8	30.9
Land O' Lakes CDP	19.070	31,996	NA	NA	NA	10.3	87.6	$65,612	30.3	6.7	66.6	8.2	75.7	17.8
Lantana town	2.310	10,616	10,996	3.6	4,760.7	21.3	81.5	$43,458	13.5	20.6	66.3	14.1	57.6	32.9
Largo city	17.976	78,135	79,019	1.1	4,395.7	12.2	79.0	$39,722	9.7	14.3	58.0	11.9	51.0	39.4
Lauderdale Lakes city	3.687	32,653	34,410	5.4	9,333.0	47.5	85.9	$33,070	5.3	22.1	68.2	19.4	67.7	27.8
Lauderhill city	8.523	66,954	70,626	5.5	8,286.5	35.5	82.1	$37,691	10.5	20.7	66.9	16.4	66.0	27.6
Lealman CDP	3.998	19,879	NA	NA	NA	12.7	81.7	$30,263	6.5	26.6	53.7	14.4	50.1	40.7
Leesburg city	31.735	20,364	21,524	5.7	678.3	6.3	71.3	$33,846	8.0	19.1	52.7	17.1	57.6	35.8
Lehigh Acres CDP	92.630	86,784	NA	NA	NA	23.7	72.2	$39,686	7.8	19.2	63.1	14.7	75.3	19.5
Leisure City CDP	3.330	22,655	NA	NA	NA	42.7	83.3	$34,000	6.3	36.5	59.8	16.8	81.4	13.0
Lighthouse Point city	2.307	10,344	10,953	5.9	4,748.1	18.6	86.7	$74,732	38.3	7.9	63.3	8.4	60.7	34.4
Lockhart CDP	4.439	13,060	NA	NA	NA	11.4	78.5	$47,686	13.6	15.5	73.5	14.6	68.1	22.3
Longwood city	5.461	13,659	13,877	1.6	2,541.1	9.9	91.2	$56,163	20.6	8.9	66.3	12.2	66.6	27.9
Lutz CDP	24.654	19,344	NA	NA	NA	8.2	90.3	$69,971	35.5	7.2	66.4	7.7	70.7	24.6
Lynn Haven city	10.374	18,474	19,792	7.1	1,907.8	4.9	76.9	$57,529	18.6	11.3	64.5	7.6	66.5	30.6
Maitland city	5.278	15,739	16,823	6.9	3,187.4	10.2	79.4	$69,080	33.9	9.9	69.7	4.9	54.0	35.1
Mango CDP	4.668	11,313	NA	NA	NA	10.3	79.7	$34,137	7.0	23.1	62.7	14.0	67.5	27.7
Marco Island city	12.145	16,413	17,460	6.4	1,437.6	11.3	87.7	$73,031	37.3	8.2	37.4	5.4	69.1	26.8
Margate city	8.858	53,284	56,061	5.2	6,328.5	33.1	86.7	$42,599	13.4	14.0	65.2	11.4	62.7	32.5
Meadow Woods CDP	11.402	25,558	NA	NA	NA	28.2	84.5	$47,817	12.1	15.2	66.3	14.0	86.3	11.3
Melbourne city	33.977	76,196	78,490	3.0	2,310.1	10.1	83.3	$40,400	13.0	16.0	57.3	11.7	54.8	38.2
Merritt Island CDP	17.525	34,743	NA	NA	NA	7.6	83.5	$53,421	23.6	13.0	59.6	11.6	62.2	30.1
Miami city	35.892	399,508	430,332	7.7	11,989.7	57.6	83.7	$30,858	13.1	29.9	61.5	12.5	55.7	36.5
Miami Beach city	7.669	87,784	91,732	4.5	11,961.7	52.2	74.9	$42,547	22.3	18.1	68.1	5.7	42.3	47.5
Miami Gardens city	18.230	107,163	112,265	4.8	6,158.2	29.8	91.5	$39,545	10.9	21.9	62.8	16.6	73.6	22.7
Miami Lakes town	5.643	29,364	30,791	4.9	5,456.6	49.7	93.7	$65,269	25.3	11.6	63.0	7.0	72.1	22.4
Miami Shores village	2.489	10,329	10,861	5.2	4,363.1	24.7	87.3	$88,977	43.6	6.9	66.8	11.6	69.0	20.4
Miami Springs city	2.890	13,809	14,415	4.4	4,987.2	48.0	88.9	$52,021	22.8	13.0	68.9	11.4	66.6	29.0
Middleburg CDP	19.629	13,008	NA	NA	NA	3.5	86.7	$47,856	14.4	16.6	59.3	11.3	75.7	17.6
Midway CDP (Santa Rosa County)	12.006	16,115	NA	NA	NA	3.3	82.0	$65,929	23.4	8.4	64.9	7.1	72.3	22.7
Miramar city	29.382	122,041	134,989	10.6	4,594.3	43.9	88.1	$64,987	26.3	9.4	72.5	11.4	79.9	15.7
Mount Dora city	7.917	12,151	13,182	8.5	1,665.0	9.9	86.6	$48,434	13.9	15.2	52.7	8.1	63.3	30.9
Myrtle Grove CDP	6.644	15,870	NA	NA	NA	6.0	76.9	$38,283	7.8	20.7	67.5	10.6	58.6	32.8
Naples city	12.323	19,537	20,968	7.3	1,701.6	12.5	86.8	$80,571	43.0	8.6	37.7	5.9	58.7	37.1
Navarre CDP	23.066	31,378	NA	NA	NA	5.6	78.8	$66,906	28.3	8.4	67.1	8.0	72.2	19.2
New Port Richey city	4.531	14,903	15,527	4.2	3,426.7	7.5	85.2	$30,660	5.9	21.6	45.1	13.8	53.4	39.0
New Smyrna Beach city	34.984	22,556	23,658	4.9	676.2	5.3	80.7	$50,918	18.0	13.7	45.3	6.6	60.4	34.6
Niceville city	11.439	12,752	14,387	12.8	1,257.7	6.0	84.0	$62,538	29.8	11.7	68.8	4.6	69.6	25.6
Northdale CDP	8.088	22,079	NA	NA	NA	15.2	85.9	$65,839	29.7	9.6	70.9	9.2	68.8	23.3
North Fort Myers CDP	50.598	39,407	NA	NA	NA	7.3	88.6	$38,598	10.7	11.7	36.7	13.1	55.4	38.9
North Lauderdale city	4.602	41,055	43,214	5.3	9,390.3	43.6	80.9	$42,610	9.2	18.8	72.4	11.2	76.1	17.0
North Miami city	8.401	58,896	61,420	4.3	7,310.6	49.1	84.5	$36,776	11.8	24.2	64.0	14.1	65.7	27.8
North Miami Beach city	4.828	41,523	43,664	5.2	9,043.7	50.4	87.4	$38,130	9.8	22.0	66.1	14.6	64.1	29.2
North Palm Beach village	3.602	12,013	12,483	3.9	3,465.8	8.1	89.4	$56,460	29.7	8.2	57.1	5.2	50.7	41.2
North Port city	99.420	57,333	60,380	5.3	607.3	11.8	84.8	$50,855	13.4	10.9	55.7	10.7	68.3	24.9
Oakland Park city	7.514	41,394	43,800	5.8	5,828.9	32.3	79.0	$45,137	13.6	17.0	75.0	12.7	49.9	37.3
Oakleaf Plantation CDP	16.576	20,315	NA	NA	NA	14.4	81.8	$73,707	34.8	6.8	74.5	9.2	85.8	9.3
Oak Ridge CDP	3.563	22,685	NA	NA	NA	36.2	80.4	$30,679	4.7	25.5	71.1	9.8	68.1	25.1
Ocala city	44.964	56,324	57,586	2.2	1,280.7	6.4	75.4	$37,442	12.9	19.0	56.8	13.1	57.6	35.9
Ocoee city	14.990	35,736	41,073	14.9	2,740.1	18.4	86.5	$62,487	23.1	8.6	71.6	9.9	77.4	18.4
Ojus CDP	2.641	18,036	NA	NA	NA	45.2	91.9	$46,679	22.6	16.9	63.2	7.9	68.6	29.1
Oldsmar city	8.936	13,617	13,913	2.2	1,556.9	9.8	82.3	$54,186	18.8	12.1	69.2	9.6	70.1	21.5
Olympia Heights CDP	2.653	13,488	NA	NA	NA	55.6	95.0	$54,167	26.3	17.6	61.6	6.7	79.8	17.2
Opa-locka city	4.304	15,219	16,460	8.2	3,824.2	31.6	97.0	$19,243	2.9	44.6	52.1	13.6	68.3	28.3
Orange City city	7.271	10,962	11,056	0.9	1,520.6	6.0	86.3	$31,445	5.9	19.8	47.4	13.1	45.7	45.0
Orlando city	102.707	238,834	262,372	9.9	2,554.6	18.3	72.7	$41,901	14.6	16.9	72.6	10.2	52.5	36.8
Ormond Beach city	32.032	38,171	39,075	2.4	1,219.9	8.6	89.7	$49,000	19.2	10.8	48.7	8.8	64.9	30.0
Oviedo city	15.223	33,467	38,020	13.6	2,497.5	11.8	88.7	$82,259	39.1	6.6	71.0	8.4	81.6	14.1
Pace CDP	24.228	20,039	NA	NA	NA	5.2	84.3	$62,298	22.6	9.0	65.9	7.8	79.2	16.6
Palatka city	8.534	10,546	10,387	-1.5	1,217.2	2.8	80.5	$21,864	5.6	40.3	50.3	14.6	60.6	34.7
Palm Bay city	65.722	103,203	105,838	2.6	1,610.4	12.8	85.0	$43,064	10.9	15.6	58.7	13.0	70.6	24.1
Palm Beach Gardens city	56.013	48,567	51,919	6.9	926.9	15.1	84.2	$67,102	33.2	7.2	58.9	6.9	58.6	34.6
Palm City CDP	13.870	23,120	NA	NA	NA	5.5	88.2	$74,699	36.3	5.6	53.8	8.6	69.3	27.6
Palm Coast city	94.859	75,197	80,600	7.2	849.7	14.9	88.7	$47,634	12.6	12.6	48.4	10.0	72.5	22.3
Palmetto city	5.398	12,629	13,082	3.6	2,423.7	7.4	84.7	$37,976	12.7	14.6	52.4	8.8	59.9	33.7
Palmetto Bay village	8.290	23,408	24,513	4.7	2,956.9	28.3	91.5	$108,360	53.7	6.4	65.4	8.6	83.2	14.7
Palmetto Estates CDP	2.162	13,535	NA	NA	NA	42.3	94.3	$58,864	23.4	13.4	67.8	13.4	83.5	13.2
Palm Harbor CDP	17.350	57,439	NA	NA	NA	10.1	83.9	$53,232	22.0	10.0	57.5	8.0	58.6	35.2
Palm River-Clair Mel CDP	11.503	21,024	NA	NA	NA	22.8	81.8	$36,167	9.1	24.0	62.3	14.7	70.1	24.1
Palm Springs village	3.590	20,825	21,728	4.3	6,052.9	39.2	78.9	$34,081	5.3	23.5	71.6	14.2	61.6	29.2
Palm Valley CDP	12.180	20,019	NA	NA	NA	5.9	84.2	$81,652	43.8	6.5	62.6	7.3	64.2	28.3
Panama City city	29.324	35,520	37,681	6.1	1,285.0	5.8	75.8	$37,453	12.2	19.2	59.4	12.6	57.7	34.2
Panama City Beach city	19.276	11,554	12,408	7.4	643.7	9.8	79.3	$53,242	17.9	11.9	66.1	6.3	63.2	29.8
Parkland city	12.247	23,960	28,131	17.4	2,296.9	22.6	87.4	$126,905	60.4	4.1	70.6	6.9	87.5	9.1
Pembroke Pines city	32.901	154,019	164,626	6.9	5,003.6	35.3	86.1	$61,539	26.8	10.3	66.6	9.9	70.3	26.4
Pensacola city	22.576	51,956	53,068	2.1	2,350.7	6.2	80.9	$46,424	16.6	15.7	64.2	9.4	53.9	38.1
Pine Castle CDP	2.433	10,805	NA	NA	NA	34.5	82.9	$32,674	9.1	30.6	67.7	11.8	63.4	27.5
Pinecrest village	7.442	18,223	19,251	5.6	2,586.9	33.7	90.5	$122,235	57.2	5.3	65.2	6.4	79.4	19.2
Pine Hills CDP	12.229	60,076	NA	NA	NA	29.3	78.2	$36,423	6.9	22.8	70.5	15.7	71.8	23.0
Pinellas Park city	15.640	49,175	50,946	3.6	3,257.4	14.5	87.9	$41,877	10.8	13.5	59.2	10.1	57.5	36.2
Pinewood CDP	1.753	16,520	NA	NA	NA	44.5	84.1	$27,983	3.2	31.9	57.2	19.2	68.3	27.5
Plantation city	21.632	84,877	91,457	7.8	4,227.8	26.8	82.8	$66,886	29.8	8.7	69.2	8.1	65.2	27.0

1 Dry land or land partially or temporarily covered by water.
2 16 years old and over.

Table B. Incorporated Places, Census Designated Places (CDPs), and Minor Civil Divisions (MCDs) of 10,000 or More Population — **Crime, Construction, and Local Government Finance**

STATE City, town, township, borough, or CDP (county if applicable)	Serious crimes known to police, 2014[1] Total number	Rate[2] Total	Rate[2] Violent	Rate[2] Property	New residential construction authorized by building permits, 2014 Value ($1,000)	Number of housing units	Percent single family	Local government finance, 2012 General revenue Total (mil dol)	Intergovernmental Total (mil dol)	Percent from state gov.	Taxes per capita[3]	General expenditure Total (mil dol)	Per capita[3] Total	Capital outlays	Debt outstanding (mil dol)
	15	16	17	18	19	20	21	22	23	24	25	26	27	28	29
FLORIDA—Con.															
Lakeside CDP	NA	NA	NA	NA	NA	NA	NA	NA	NA	NA	NA	NA	NA	NA	NA
Lake Wales city	736	4877	444	4433	20,162	74	86.5	20.4	5.2	34.2	607	18.7	1,275	234	25.6
Lakewood Park CDP	NA	NA	NA	NA	NA	NA	NA	NA	NA	NA	NA	NA	NA	NA	NA
Lake Worth city	2,401	6622	1147	5475	4,499	17	100.0	47.4	10.9	39.7	389	55.1	1,538	116	74.3
Land O' Lakes CDP	NA	NA	NA	NA	NA	NA	NA	NA	NA	NA	NA	NA	NA	NA	NA
Lantana town	605	5537	613	4924	4,393	14	42.9	12.5	1.5	60.3	483	13.1	1,209	212	10.1
Largo city	3,214	4094	431	3664	28,420	197	22.3	106.7	10.7	72.0	505	110.7	1,416	238	31.5
Lauderdale Lakes city	1,771	5148	773	4375	0	0	0.0	26.2	4.3	77.6	352	26.8	792	44	28.4
Lauderhill city	2,932	4159	654	3505	6,647	62	100.0	67.1	12.7	52.9	394	71.1	1,026	65	118.7
Lealman CDP	NA	NA	NA	NA	NA	NA	NA	NA	NA	NA	NA	NA	NA	NA	NA
Leesburg city	1,198	5620	624	4996	10,327	77	100.0	37.9	3.3	59.0	616	48.3	2,319	270	132.2
Lehigh Acres CDP	NA	NA	NA	NA	NA	NA	NA	NA	NA	NA	NA	NA	NA	NA	NA
Leisure City CDP	NA	NA	NA	NA	NA	NA	NA	NA	NA	NA	NA	NA	NA	NA	NA
Lighthouse Point city	225	2056	91	1965	5,487	15	100.0	14.6	1.4	89.0	876	14.7	1,364	27	4.0
Lockhart CDP	NA	NA	NA	NA	NA	NA	NA	NA	NA	NA	NA	NA	NA	NA	NA
Longwood city	461	3325	454	2871	4,272	28	92.9	18.3	1.3	96.1	814	19.2	1,397	406	0.0
Lutz CDP	NA	NA	NA	NA	NA	NA	NA	NA	NA	NA	NA	NA	NA	NA	NA
Lynn Haven city	537	2745	256	2489	16,673	63	100.0	16.5	2.0	83.5	460	16.2	857	141	21.6
Maitland city	464	2788	186	2602	16,125	231	7.4	29.4	3.2	89.5	995	31.0	1,899	301	26.7
Mango CDP	NA	NA	NA	NA	NA	NA	NA	NA	NA	NA	NA	NA	NA	NA	NA
Marco Island city	123	709	29	680	78,391	105	100.0	48.2	4.7	64.7	1177	43.2	2,563	1,307	225.8
Margate city	1,027	1835	225	1609	6,584	240	0.0	70.3	9.0	65.1	598	69.8	1,266	200	53.5
Meadow Woods CDP	NA	NA	NA	NA	NA	NA	NA	NA	NA	NA	NA	NA	NA	NA	NA
Melbourne city	3,713	4773	785	3987	42,644	146	100.0	117.4	17.7	39.8	584	113.2	1,469	76	132.5
Merritt Island CDP	NA	NA	NA	NA	NA	NA	NA	NA	NA	NA	NA	NA	NA	NA	NA
Miami city	24,867	5893	1060	4833	950,530	3,786	1.9	722.3	172.2	31.3	976	740.7	1,777	262	873.2
Miami Beach city	10,316	11241	973	10268	109,144	140	45.0	529.5	21.7	43.5	3597	497.2	5,448	572	465.1
Miami Gardens city	5,260	4681	655	4026	6,790	125	10.4	83.2	27.7	43.3	368	85.3	765	86	111.4
Miami Lakes town	688	2230	68	2162	2,546	7	100.0	18.1	3.9	79.9	422	19.4	635	118	7.5
Miami Shores village	588	5480	522	4959	1,177	2	100.0	16.6	1.6	93.0	885	16.3	1,498	103	8.9
Miami Springs city	574	3976	263	3713	1,432	6	100.0	18.1	3.2	38.4	668	19.7	1,372	135	4.9
Middleburg CDP	NA	NA	NA	NA	NA	NA	NA	NA	NA	NA	NA	NA	NA	NA	NA
Midway CDP (Santa Rosa County)	NA	NA	NA	NA	NA	NA	NA	NA	NA	NA	NA	NA	NA	NA	NA
Miramar city	3,167	2393	315	2078	35,597	177	100.0	143.9	25.7	45.7	562	135.3	1,048	75	182.5
Mount Dora city	521	3987	467	3520	15,839	71	95.8	20.6	2.3	35.3	675	23.0	1,820	268	12.0
Myrtle Grove CDP	NA	NA	NA	NA	NA	NA	NA	NA	NA	NA	NA	NA	NA	NA	NA
Naples city	557	2681	77	2604	375,458	356	52.0	87.7	8.9	33.6	1591	80.4	3,988	140	46.2
Navarre CDP	NA	NA	NA	NA	NA	NA	NA	NA	NA	NA	NA	NA	NA	NA	NA
New Port Richey city	810	5353	800	4553	5,020	56	17.9	24.2	4.5	43.9	773	22.7	1,521	165	32.1
New Smyrna Beach city	824	3523	385	3138	59,968	199	100.0	51.3	5.1	45.8	928	46.0	2,006	320	81.3
Niceville city	190	1319	104	1215	21,640	93	100.0	15.4	2.2	93.5	418	15.3	1,123	224	17.1
Northdale CDP	NA	NA	NA	NA	NA	NA	NA	NA	NA	NA	NA	NA	NA	NA	NA
North Fort Myers CDP	NA	NA	NA	NA	NA	NA	NA	NA	NA	NA	NA	NA	NA	NA	NA
North Lauderdale city	1,291	2991	426	2564	0	0	0.0	36.7	5.7	71.1	327	33.0	775	30	8.6
North Miami city	3,383	5501	938	4563	2,400	6	100.0	74.3	14.3	45.8	493	78.4	1,282	99	21.9
North Miami Beach city	1,991	4561	843	3718	6,197	44	100.0	69.4	10.5	84.8	528	79.6	1,838	147	111.2
North Palm Beach village	307	2470	153	2317	1,600	146	0.0	21.8	1.3	89.6	1206	19.2	1,558	135	3.8
North Port city	995	1668	173	1495	136,629	557	100.0	74.1	8.3	65.2	389	78.1	1,339	244	54.0
Oakland Park city	2,019	4615	519	4096	1,879	13	61.5	60.8	8.4	54.6	546	60.3	1,403	122	38.9
Oakleaf Plantation CDP	NA	NA	NA	NA	NA	NA	NA	NA	NA	NA	NA	NA	NA	NA	NA
Oak Ridge CDP	NA	NA	NA	NA	NA	NA	NA	NA	NA	NA	NA	NA	NA	NA	NA
Ocala city	3,363	5824	623	5201	24,381	84	100.0	118.1	16.3	79.4	707	106.1	1,865	168	201.6
Ocoee city	1,549	3870	345	3525	97,664	723	33.1	39.5	8.6	94.4	428	40.9	1,066	54	54.8
Ojus CDP	NA	NA	NA	NA	NA	NA	NA	NA	NA	NA	NA	NA	NA	NA	NA
Oldsmar city	482	3482	108	3374	10,439	44	90.9	21.2	3.0	38.6	751	21.5	1,572	439	14.8
Olympia Heights CDP	NA	NA	NA	NA	NA	NA	NA	NA	NA	NA	NA	NA	NA	NA	NA
Opa-locka city	1,567	9705	2428	7277	2,000	12	0.0	20.4	3.4	100.0	662	25.3	1,599	312	10.7
Orange City city	900	8227	548	7678	694	2	100.0	9.1	0.7	95.9	606	8.9	817	41	3.7
Orlando city	18,855	7261	901	6360	525,686	2,849	32.1	675.7	172.2	30.5	895	644.8	2,578	124	1055.4
Ormond Beach city	1,721	4438	428	4010	37,277	104	100.0	49.2	7.5	40.8	554	51.7	1,346	298	54.1
Oviedo city	517	1380	149	1230	10,984	42	100.0	37.7	4.2	64.8	531	40.7	1,151	91	79.7
Pace CDP	NA	NA	NA	NA	NA	NA	NA	NA	NA	NA	NA	NA	NA	NA	NA
Palatka city	618	5903	640	5263	214	1	100.0	18.5	5.4	42.2	702	15.4	1,472	328	18.3
Palm Bay city	2,826	2684	570	2114	36,082	162	100.0	95.5	22.5	37.8	421	96.4	925	142	157.8
Palm Beach Gardens city	1,523	2974	148	2826	86,742	237	79.3	72.5	6.7	77.4	1116	73.8	1,475	130	25.8
Palm City CDP	NA	NA	NA	NA	NA	NA	NA	NA	NA	NA	NA	NA	NA	NA	NA
Palm Coast city	NA	NA	NA	NA	95,293	339	100.0	61.9	7.9	63.6	306	75.5	974	151	176.4
Palmetto city	561	4302	867	3436	2,591	9	100.0	19.7	2.8	91.9	710	20.9	1,625	146	16.9
Palmetto Bay village	880	3583	179	3404	575	3	100.0	17.5	3.3	69.4	525	17.9	736	188	17.7
Palmetto Estates CDP	NA	NA	NA	NA	NA	NA	NA	NA	NA	NA	NA	NA	NA	NA	NA
Palm Harbor CDP	NA	NA	NA	NA	NA	NA	NA	NA	NA	NA	NA	NA	NA	NA	NA
Palm River-Clair Mel CDP	NA	NA	NA	NA	NA	NA	NA	NA	NA	NA	NA	NA	NA	NA	NA
Palm Springs village	1,285	6116	662	5454	4,244	26	53.8	17.8	2.0	84.8	323	22.8	1,070	122	18.3
Palm Valley CDP	NA	NA	NA	NA	NA	NA	NA	NA	NA	NA	NA	NA	NA	NA	NA
Panama City city	2,924	7859	922	6937	NA	NA	NA	60.3	8.8	82.6	771	64.4	1,779	119	35.5
Panama City Beach city	1,225	10053	1009	9043	24,341	111	100.0	40.3	11.2	21.5	1118	52.6	4,457	2,089	122.7
Parkland city	180	663	26	637	183,768	556	98.4	22.7	2.1	77.2	638	20.8	809	56	10.0
Pembroke Pines city	4,052	2465	169	2297	398	2	100.0	252.5	67.1	81.6	581	310.7	1,942	78	388.8
Pensacola city	2,763	5226	705	4520	10,802	46	100.0	126.4	46.1	16.9	804	157.0	2,977	968	213.6
Pine Castle CDP	NA	NA	NA	NA	NA	NA	NA	NA	NA	NA	NA	NA	NA	NA	NA
Pinecrest village	NA	NA	NA	NA	40,312	39	100.0	19.8	3.4	65.2	718	18.8	990	89	13.1
Pine Hills CDP	NA	NA	NA	NA	NA	NA	NA	NA	NA	NA	NA	NA	NA	NA	NA
Pinellas Park city	3,156	6285	456	5829	13,628	66	100.0	65.8	7.8	64.1	631	68.5	1,377	108	31.8
Pinewood CDP	NA	NA	NA	NA	NA	NA	NA	NA	NA	NA	NA	NA	NA	NA	NA
Plantation city	3,067	3350	341	3009	9,884	19	100.0	103.5	13.9	50.3	628	108.1	1,225	75	39.9

1 Data for serious crimes have not been adjusted for underreporting. This may affect comparability between geographic areas over time.
2 Per 100,000 population estimated by the FBI. 3 Based on population estimated as of July 1 of the year shown.

Table B. Incorporated Places, Census Designated Places (CDPs), and Minor Civil Divisions (MCDs) of 10,000 or More Population — Land Area, Population, and Households, and Employment

STATE City, town, township, borough, or CDP (county if applicable)	Land area,[1] 2010 (sq mi)	Population Total persons 2010	Total persons 2014	Percent change 2010–2014	Persons per square mile, 2014	Population characteristics 2010–2014 Foreign born	Lives in same house as previous year	Household income and poverty, 2010–2014 Median household income (dollars)	Percent of households Income of $100,000 or more	Income below poverty level	Employment,[2] 2010–2014 Percent in labor force	Unemploy-ment rate	Households, 2010–2014 (percent of households) Family households	One person households
	1	2	3	4	5	6	7	8	9	10	11	12	13	14
FLORIDA—Con.														
Plant City city	27.165	34,688	36,627	5.6	1,348.3	15.2	82.5	$45,794	14.7	16.5	65.9	10.7	70.8	25.3
Poinciana CDP	71.878	53,193	NA	NA	NA	18.8	83.9	$39,745	8.4	18.8	55.3	16.7	80.3	17.0
Pompano Beach city	24.039	99,844	106,105	6.3	4,413.8	25.1	79.4	$40,534	14.0	19.2	58.1	13.5	52.4	38.9
Port Charlotte CDP	28.480	54,392	NA	NA	NA	12.9	83.9	$39,387	10.9	14.6	52.0	11.7	60.8	34.1
Port Orange city	26.823	56,595	58,742	3.8	2,190.0	6.7	85.8	$44,981	14.3	11.5	53.4	7.7	62.9	30.8
Port St. John CDP	3.875	12,267	NA	NA	NA	4.4	87.5	$52,733	14.2	15.0	67.4	11.6	66.0	27.0
Port St. Lucie city	113.870	164,716	174,110	5.7	1,529.0	16.9	83.2	$48,898	15.3	13.3	61.8	13.7	72.9	21.6
Port Salerno CDP	3.551	10,091	NA	NA	NA	8.5	83.8	$43,036	17.6	12.3	60.0	10.9	63.0	30.4
Princeton CDP	7.376	22,038	NA	NA	NA	35.9	79.8	$48,170	17.3	19.8	65.6	15.5	86.3	10.5
Punta Gorda city	15.017	16,641	17,596	5.7	1,171.7	6.9	86.6	$56,081	19.8	10.5	34.5	12.2	67.2	28.5
Richmond West CDP	4.168	31,973	NA	NA	NA	51.5	92.0	$70,273	28.7	8.4	68.7	8.9	89.5	7.3
Riverview CDP	46.183	71,050	NA	NA	NA	11.8	83.6	$65,874	24.7	8.8	69.1	9.1	74.1	19.5
Riviera Beach city	8.519	32,488	33,649	3.6	3,949.9	16.8	85.4	$38,300	15.2	21.6	65.0	17.2	62.2	31.8
Rockledge city	12.155	24,930	26,071	4.6	2,144.8	8.2	89.5	$59,905	20.8	8.2	62.8	13.2	68.2	25.3
Royal Palm Beach village	11.143	34,140	37,015	8.4	3,321.7	19.3	87.9	$66,620	28.6	8.2	68.4	8.6	78.8	17.5
Ruskin CDP	18.014	17,208	NA	NA	NA	17.1	88.4	$49,247	16.3	14.2	65.7	5.0	75.8	17.5
Safety Harbor city	4.917	16,885	17,234	2.1	3,505.3	11.4	90.8	$58,375	25.4	9.0	61.3	6.4	62.4	32.9
St. Augustine city	9.429	12,975	13,841	6.7	1,467.9	6.5	70.8	$43,204	18.0	19.3	59.5	8.6	51.4	35.8
St. Cloud city	18.054	36,332	43,005	18.4	2,382.1	10.9	84.2	$48,911	13.7	16.7	63.0	12.6	72.9	22.7
St. Petersburg city	61.752	245,193	253,693	3.5	4,108.3	10.5	82.9	$45,483	16.8	15.7	64.5	10.1	53.6	38.0
San Carlos Park CDP	4.747	16,824	NA	NA	NA	16.0	82.7	$46,133	13.0	14.0	72.8	10.2	67.4	21.6
Sanford city	23.028	53,711	57,525	7.1	2,498.1	10.2	83.5	$39,776	10.2	18.3	62.7	14.8	61.3	31.5
Sarasota city	14.681	52,056	54,214	4.1	3,692.7	17.4	77.5	$41,670	16.7	18.1	58.1	12.1	51.5	39.3
Sarasota Springs CDP	3.504	14,395	NA	NA	NA	10.3	86.1	$51,646	17.2	8.9	64.8	8.7	63.4	27.7
Satellite Beach city	2.918	10,109	10,418	3.1	3,569.8	8.3	80.8	$63,793	24.7	3.3	61.9	6.0	64.5	27.6
Sebastian city	13.677	21,929	23,344	6.5	1,706.8	6.8	86.9	$42,591	13.1	8.5	52.7	15.4	65.7	27.8
Sebring city	10.064	10,413	10,372	-0.4	1,030.6	11.7	77.7	$27,383	6.8	27.0	44.5	16.7	51.3	41.8
Seminole city	5.134	17,159	17,923	4.5	3,491.1	9.8	86.0	$47,588	19.0	11.3	48.4	7.3	53.2	43.2
Shady Hills CDP	28.591	11,523	NA	NA	NA	3.7	89.6	$38,802	11.4	16.7	49.5	15.4	68.1	20.4
South Bradenton CDP	4.493	22,178	NA	NA	NA	16.8	78.1	$31,738	4.7	19.3	53.9	12.2	52.4	40.1
Southchase CDP	6.843	15,921	NA	NA	NA	31.0	88.4	$52,661	19.0	10.7	71.5	10.6	84.0	12.8
South Daytona city	3.714	12,252	12,397	1.2	3,337.7	5.2	81.5	$33,328	8.9	21.2	56.2	13.6	58.3	33.5
South Miami city	2.266	11,655	12,183	4.5	5,376.0	34.5	86.0	$54,101	29.8	16.5	68.6	11.9	64.2	28.1
South Miami Heights CDP	4.885	35,696	NA	NA	NA	50.2	86.8	$39,195	10.7	21.1	61.4	9.6	76.0	21.0
South Venice CDP	6.015	13,949	NA	NA	NA	9.7	81.7	$43,930	11.8	9.0	53.6	10.6	64.3	27.7
Spring Hill CDP	59.840	98,621	NA	NA	NA	7.8	85.9	$40,969	8.6	14.1	49.6	16.5	69.9	25.4
Stuart city	6.649	15,589	16,197	3.9	2,436.1	11.1	80.2	$36,637	11.3	15.8	57.8	13.4	44.0	49.0
Sun City Center CDP	15.751	19,258	NA	NA	NA	7.0	87.7	$43,369	13.1	6.7	18.1	15.7	51.1	46.2
Sunny Isles Beach city	1.008	20,832	21,946	5.3	21,771.4	60.2	84.6	$45,972	23.3	17.1	53.6	6.2	48.8	45.7
Sunrise city	16.346	84,381	91,256	8.1	5,582.9	35.8	85.8	$49,370	19.8	13.1	68.6	9.9	66.8	27.3
Sunset CDP	3.485	16,389	NA	NA	NA	49.0	94.2	$65,727	36.3	9.3	63.3	6.8	80.0	17.0
Sweetwater city	2.270	19,958	20,751	4.0	9,143.1	73.6	83.0	$31,858	4.4	28.9	57.9	10.1	79.0	15.1
Tallahassee city	100.353	181,383	188,107	3.7	1,874.4	7.7	65.1	$39,407	16.2	28.2	65.6	13.1	47.1	33.1
Tamarac city	11.623	60,503	63,793	5.4	5,488.6	32.9	81.1	$43,250	12.2	11.5	61.0	10.0	58.6	37.1
Tamiami CDP	7.068	55,271	NA	NA	NA	67.0	92.8	$48,254	18.7	15.2	62.1	9.1	82.7	13.5
Tampa city	113.406	335,715	358,699	6.8	3,163.0	15.4	78.6	$43,740	20.2	19.5	65.0	11.5	54.6	36.5
Tarpon Springs city	9.102	23,515	24,239	3.1	2,663.0	12.4	84.4	$43,024	18.8	13.9	52.2	14.0	58.7	35.5
Tavares city	11.537	13,956	14,930	7.0	1,294.1	8.4	82.5	$38,872	9.4	13.1	39.8	12.7	62.4	34.3
Temple Terrace city	7.059	24,501	25,419	3.7	3,600.7	13.5	80.8	$50,978	18.2	14.7	67.9	8.9	56.9	36.6
The Acreage CDP	40.820	38,704	NA	NA	NA	17.7	92.7	$73,560	29.5	6.2	69.6	9.0	83.5	12.0
The Crossings CDP	3.461	22,758	NA	NA	NA	43.9	91.5	$62,031	27.8	13.5	66.3	9.2	72.6	22.6
The Hammocks CDP	7.883	51,003	NA	NA	NA	52.7	86.7	$58,071	21.7	10.6	66.0	9.6	80.2	16.5
The Villages CDP	30.838	51,442	NA	NA	NA	5.7	88.8	$55,708	17.2	4.7	15.5	10.5	73.1	23.1
Thonotosassa CDP	26.481	13,014	NA	NA	NA	8.5	87.3	$41,381	14.4	17.7	60.2	15.6	68.1	26.2
Three Lakes CDP	3.199	15,047	NA	NA	NA	47.9	87.9	$70,011	29.6	8.9	73.0	8.7	79.7	15.7
Titusville city	29.337	43,749	44,557	1.8	1,518.8	5.4	81.1	$40,420	12.2	17.6	54.7	13.5	62.1	31.8
Town 'n' Country CDP	22.093	78,442	NA	NA	NA	28.1	83.0	$49,714	17.3	12.8	69.7	11.3	63.9	26.5
Trinity CDP	4.608	10,907	NA	NA	NA	6.6	94.6	$72,593	30.7	5.6	54.3	3.6	81.9	16.6
Union Park CDP	2.855	9,765	NA	NA	NA	12.3	77.1	$40,677	10.3	22.1	68.6	12.6	68.4	19.9
University CDP (Hillsborough County)	6.423	41,163	NA	NA	NA	21.2	69.0	$22,523	2.7	42.1	64.6	17.6	43.5	43.1
University CDP (Orange County)	9.086	31,084	NA	NA	NA	14.8	60.4	$37,297	10.8	31.8	40.8	11.0	50.2	30.3
University Park CDP	3.972	26,995	NA	NA	NA	63.6	86.4	$43,863	17.3	18.8	56.4	8.4	75.1	17.9
Upper Grand Lagoon CDP	8.092	13,963	NA	NA	NA	3.5	77.8	$54,035	20.5	7.6	68.2	7.8	66.9	27.0
Valrico CDP	13.806	35,545	NA	NA	NA	8.6	87.3	$71,893	31.9	7.4	63.8	7.2	78.4	18.1
Venice city	15.429	20,746	21,730	4.7	1,408.4	6.9	85.5	$48,103	15.4	8.6	30.0	13.5	53.8	41.0
Vero Beach city	11.438	15,225	16,017	5.2	1,400.3	7.7	79.7	$37,937	19.2	20.3	52.3	13.1	48.4	41.9
Vero Beach South CDP	10.251	23,092	NA	NA	NA	7.6	86.2	$43,820	16.0	12.2	57.8	14.1	63.8	32.3
Viera East CDP	5.062	10,757	NA	NA	NA	8.4	86.2	$65,767	24.2	2.8	51.4	9.7	70.2	24.2
Villas CDP	4.649	11,569	NA	NA	NA	16.3	78.1	$44,464	9.7	8.5	62.9	6.2	42.6	46.7
Warrington CDP	6.930	14,531	NA	NA	NA	3.9	83.5	$36,485	7.4	21.3	59.2	14.7	48.6	42.4
Wekiwa Springs CDP	8.590	21,998	NA	NA	NA	10.4	91.0	$76,462	34.9	5.5	61.8	8.9	73.1	23.0
Wellington village	45.143	56,712	61,485	8.4	1,362.0	21.5	86.6	$81,481	38.9	6.9	67.0	8.3	80.0	15.9
Wesley Chapel CDP	43.930	44,092	NA	NA	NA	14.4	85.3	$71,722	25.3	7.0	71.3	7.1	76.9	18.5
Westchase CDP	9.942	21,747	NA	NA	NA	13.2	76.7	$91,250	46.7	5.8	74.5	7.2	68.5	22.7
Westchester CDP	3.941	29,862	NA	NA	NA	60.4	94.4	$45,083	16.4	13.4	59.1	10.3	77.2	19.7
West Lealman CDP	3.129	15,651	NA	NA	NA	12.7	84.6	$32,192	7.5	15.5	51.8	11.7	46.3	45.4
West Little River CDP	4.576	34,699	NA	NA	NA	40.6	91.2	$32,688	8.0	27.6	62.7	17.9	68.4	28.3
West Melbourne city	10.547	18,370	20,078	9.3	1,903.7	9.3	86.1	$52,563	20.1	9.3	58.7	11.4	64.0	30.3
Weston city	24.362	65,333	69,100	5.8	2,836.4	39.9	83.9	$91,613	46.6	7.2	67.5	8.5	84.5	12.9
West Palm Beach city	55.172	100,347	104,031	3.7	1,885.6	26.4	78.9	$45,027	17.5	17.2	64.0	10.3	51.9	37.9
West Park city	2.197	14,156	14,914	5.4	6,787.6	29.0	83.0	$40,140	11.6	18.1	67.3	18.1	74.6	20.3
West Pensacola CDP	7.172	21,339	NA	NA	NA	5.3	86.7	$29,293	3.7	23.3	59.9	19.0	55.3	37.5
West Perrine CDP	1.756	9,460	NA	NA	NA	28.3	85.7	$39,344	9.1	25.8	56.4	15.3	77.6	19.4
Westview CDP	3.023	9,650	NA	NA	NA	30.7	89.5	$35,588	9.9	28.8	56.2	12.6	66.9	25.6

1 Dry land or land partially or temporarily covered by water.
2 16 years old and over.

Table B. Incorporated Places, Census Designated Places (CDPs), and Minor Civil Divisions (MCDs) of 10,000 or More Population — Crime, Construction, and Local Government Finance

STATE City, town, township, borough, or CDP (county if applicable)	Serious crimes known to police, 2014[1] Total number	Rate[2] Total	Rate[2] Violent	Rate[2] Property	New residential construction authorized by building permits, 2014 Value ($1,000)	Number of housing units	Percent single family	Local government finance, 2012 General revenue Total (mil dol)	Intergovernmental Total (mil dol)	Percent from state gov.	Taxes per capita[3]	General expenditure Total (mil dol)	Per capita[3] Total	Capital outlays	Debt outstanding (mil dol)
	15	16	17	18	19	20	21	22	23	24	25	26	27	28	29
FLORIDA—Con.															
Plant City city	1,617	4439	464	3975	20,222	142	100.0	47.9	7.5	73.4	554	40.6	1,128	97	68.0
Poinciana CDP	NA	NA	NA	NA	NA	NA	NA	NA	NA	NA	NA	NA	NA	NA	NA
Pompano Beach city	5,437	5152	824	4329	27,939	281	29.5	157.1	12.7	50.4	819	202.4	1,959	236	88.3
Port Charlotte CDP	NA	NA	NA	NA	NA	NA	NA	NA	NA	NA	NA	NA	NA	NA	NA
Port Orange city	1,168	2036	56	1981	40,432	131	100.0	65.3	6.6	74.6	440	62.8	1,105	37	156.3
Port St. John CDP	NA	NA	NA	NA	NA	NA	NA	NA	NA	NA	NA	NA	NA	NA	NA
Port St. Lucie city	2,741	1589	141	1449	100,987	820	66.5	168.3	26.2	39.2	422	184.5	1,092	286	1015.1
Port Salerno CDP	NA	NA	NA	NA	NA	NA	NA	NA	NA	NA	NA	NA	NA	NA	NA
Princeton CDP	NA	NA	NA	NA	NA	NA	NA	NA	NA	NA	NA	NA	NA	NA	NA
Punta Gorda city	295	1705	46	1658	36,395	108	100.0	36.5	4.7	85.6	874	37.8	2,236	190	35.5
Richmond West CDP	NA	NA	NA	NA	NA	NA	NA	NA	NA	NA	NA	NA	NA	NA	NA
Riverview CDP	NA	NA	NA	NA	NA	NA	NA	NA	NA	NA	NA	NA	NA	NA	NA
Riviera Beach city	1,954	5842	1190	4652	1,121	3	100.0	85.9	14.2	26.9	1438	92.1	2,775	315	67.2
Rockledge city	561	2176	209	1966	17,754	69	100.0	23.1	1.9	98.9	501	26.5	1,041	164	10.6
Royal Palm Beach village	984	2671	269	2402	18,785	74	100.0	21.1	5.0	54.1	338	26.3	747	203	20.5
Ruskin CDP	NA	NA	NA	NA	NA	NA	NA	NA	NA	NA	NA	NA	NA	NA	NA
Safety Harbor city	341	1982	221	1761	6,818	25	100.0	23.4	2.1	87.5	546	23.5	1,385	180	14.6
St. Augustine city	814	5879	744	5135	11,904	59	100.0	37.5	2.6	88.2	1046	39.9	2,966	304	69.3
St. Cloud city	1,001	2377	325	2052	82,879	554	100.0	51.0	4.2	78.7	386	64.8	1,632	228	123.7
St. Petersburg city	16,319	6508	865	5643	98,686	538	32.9	377.4	80.5	33.2	565	403.2	1,630	142	562.7
San Carlos Park CDP	NA	NA	NA	NA	NA	NA	NA	NA	NA	NA	NA	NA	NA	NA	NA
Sanford city	3,437	6072	804	5268	4,194	20	100.0	92.0	18.1	67.1	597	78.2	1,427	372	79.7
Sarasota city	2,894	5397	666	4731	77,951	157	58.6	157.9	32.8	32.3	1023	163.4	3,091	774	156.6
Sarasota Springs CDP	NA	NA	NA	NA	NA	NA	NA	NA	NA	NA	NA	NA	NA	NA	NA
Satellite Beach city	148	1425	116	1310	5,240	25	100.0	11.0	2.4	74.6	724	12.3	1,199	154	6.7
Sebastian city	502	2193	170	2023	36,831	165	100.0	16.7	3.0	97.9	462	17.1	765	158	10.0
Sebring city	521	5052	417	4635	1,153	5	100.0	20.6	4.0	39.9	699	21.5	2,077	170	27.3
Seminole city	568	3154	355	2799	9,233	43	100.0	16.8	1.8	88.7	428	15.4	894	23	5.4
Shady Hills CDP	NA	NA	NA	NA	NA	NA	NA	NA	NA	NA	NA	NA	NA	NA	NA
South Bradenton CDP	NA	NA	NA	NA	NA	NA	NA	NA	NA	NA	NA	NA	NA	NA	NA
Southchase CDP	NA	NA	NA	NA	NA	NA	NA	NA	NA	NA	NA	NA	NA	NA	NA
South Daytona city	472	3841	244	3597	905	2	100.0	14.4	2.3	43.8	517	16.0	1,306	75	24.4
South Miami city	725	5948	353	5595	1,162	3	100.0	20.8	2.7	66.4	974	19.2	1,581	89	16.8
South Venice CDP	NA	NA	NA	NA	NA	NA	NA	NA	NA	NA	NA	NA	NA	NA	NA
Spring Hill CDP	NA	NA	NA	NA	NA	NA	NA	NA	NA	NA	NA	NA	NA	NA	NA
Stuart city	709	4377	395	3982	8,061	20	100.0	32.3	4.6	51.5	1038	35.9	2,271	362	35.9
Sun City Center CDP	NA	NA	NA	NA	NA	NA	NA	NA	NA	NA	NA	NA	NA	NA	NA
Sunny Isles Beach city	450	2052	137	1915	108,626	62	1.6	34.6	3.3	68.1	1128	35.5	1,638	552	58.3
Sunrise city	3,331	3639	303	3336	14,205	160	0.0	184.3	17.8	52.4	698	170.9	1,920	274	298.7
Sunset CDP	NA	NA	NA	NA	NA	NA	NA	NA	NA	NA	NA	NA	NA	NA	NA
Sweetwater city	690	3330	232	3099	120	2	100.0	11.9	5.6	61.9	223	14.4	698	253	4.9
Tallahassee city	10,838	5778	937	4841	112,530	903	30.0	339.4	52.0	38.9	565	370.9	1,983	425	1263.4
Tamarac city	1,432	2245	277	1967	5,990	75	49.3	73.4	11.5	50.2	507	68.8	1,097	20	60.4
Tamiami CDP	NA	NA	NA	NA	NA	NA	NA	NA	NA	NA	NA	NA	NA	NA	NA
Tampa city	10,750	3010	582	2428	406,253	2,555	27.9	643.2	135.9	37.9	774	634.2	1,817	201	1377.0
Tarpon Springs city	774	3230	442	2787	13,054	78	74.4	36.1	3.3	59.4	649	35.3	1,492	204	7.1
Tavares city	474	3265	510	2755	42,226	191	100.0	17.9	2.0	70.0	649	20.7	1,454	137	30.6
Temple Terrace city	879	3470	316	3154	1,619	6	100.0	35.7	5.8	60.9	609	39.0	1,549	237	44.1
The Acreage CDP	NA	NA	NA	NA	NA	NA	NA	NA	NA	NA	NA	NA	NA	NA	NA
The Crossings CDP	NA	NA	NA	NA	NA	NA	NA	NA	NA	NA	NA	NA	NA	NA	NA
The Hammocks CDP	NA	NA	NA	NA	NA	NA	NA	NA	NA	NA	NA	NA	NA	NA	NA
The Villages CDP	NA	NA	NA	NA	NA	NA	NA	NA	NA	NA	NA	NA	NA	NA	NA
Thonotosassa CDP	NA	NA	NA	NA	NA	NA	NA	NA	NA	NA	NA	NA	NA	NA	NA
Three Lakes CDP	NA	NA	NA	NA	NA	NA	NA	NA	NA	NA	NA	NA	NA	NA	NA
Titusville city	1,714	3868	603	3266	19,351	77	97.4	55.0	7.1	79.7	589	44.4	1,010	129	56.5
Town 'n' Country CDP	NA	NA	NA	NA	NA	NA	NA	NA	NA	NA	NA	NA	NA	NA	NA
Trinity CDP	NA	NA	NA	NA	NA	NA	NA	NA	NA	NA	NA	NA	NA	NA	NA
Union Park CDP	NA	NA	NA	NA	NA	NA	NA	NA	NA	NA	NA	NA	NA	NA	NA
University CDP (Hillsborough County)	NA	NA	NA	NA	NA	NA	NA	NA	NA	NA	NA	NA	NA	NA	NA
University CDP (Orange County)	NA	NA	NA	NA	NA	NA	NA	NA	NA	NA	NA	NA	NA	NA	NA
University Park CDP	NA	NA	NA	NA	NA	NA	NA	NA	NA	NA	NA	NA	NA	NA	NA
Upper Grand Lagoon CDP	NA	NA	NA	NA	NA	NA	NA	NA	NA	NA	NA	NA	NA	NA	NA
Valrico CDP	NA	NA	NA	NA	NA	NA	NA	NA	NA	NA	NA	NA	NA	NA	NA
Venice city	436	2039	187	1852	54,095	189	66.1	40.7	3.1	85.9	873	39.5	1,877	184	25.1
Vero Beach city	676	4258	441	3817	NA	NA	NA	35.4	3.9	80.6	690	39.1	2,516	324	160.9
Vero Beach South CDP	NA	NA	NA	NA	NA	NA	NA	NA	NA	NA	NA	NA	NA	NA	NA
Viera East CDP	NA	NA	NA	NA	NA	NA	NA	NA	NA	NA	NA	NA	NA	NA	NA
Villas CDP	NA	NA	NA	NA	NA	NA	NA	NA	NA	NA	NA	NA	NA	NA	NA
Warrington CDP	NA	NA	NA	NA	NA	NA	NA	NA	NA	NA	NA	NA	NA	NA	NA
Wekiwa Springs CDP	NA	NA	NA	NA	NA	NA	NA	NA	NA	NA	NA	NA	NA	NA	NA
Wellington village	1,312	2148	167	1981	52,618	144	98.6	61.9	10.3	59.9	481	61.6	1,048	256	22.8
Wesley Chapel CDP	NA	NA	NA	NA	NA	NA	NA	NA	NA	NA	NA	NA	NA	NA	NA
Westchase CDP	NA	NA	NA	NA	NA	NA	NA	NA	NA	NA	NA	NA	NA	NA	NA
Westchester CDP	NA	NA	NA	NA	NA	NA	NA	NA	NA	NA	NA	NA	NA	NA	NA
West Lealman CDP	NA	NA	NA	NA	NA	NA	NA	NA	NA	NA	NA	NA	NA	NA	NA
West Little River CDP	NA	NA	NA	NA	NA	NA	NA	NA	NA	NA	NA	NA	NA	NA	NA
West Melbourne city	653	3267	225	3042	35,806	138	100.0	15.4	2.1	55.5	391	13.9	726	89	19.9
Weston city	425	615	65	550	3,508	4	100.0	90.1	5.2	88.6	569	83.3	1,228	132	12.6
West Palm Beach city	5,637	5471	824	4647	110,682	904	11.8	226.7	39.5	30.6	1069	255.4	2,491	117	437.5
West Park city	634	4254	798	3455	481	6	100.0	11.2	1.4	80.1	382	11.1	759	19	0.0
West Pensacola CDP	NA	NA	NA	NA	NA	NA	NA	NA	NA	NA	NA	NA	NA	NA	NA
West Perrine CDP	NA	NA	NA	NA	NA	NA	NA	NA	NA	NA	NA	NA	NA	NA	NA
Westview CDP	NA	NA	NA	NA	NA	NA	NA	NA	NA	NA	NA	NA	NA	NA	NA

1 Data for serious crimes have not been adjusted for underreporting. This may affect comparability between geographic areas over time.
2 Per 100,000 population estimated by the FBI.   3 Based on population estimated as of July 1 of the year shown.

Table B. Incorporated Places, Census Designated Places (CDPs), and Minor Civil Divisions (MCDs) of 10,000 or More Population — **Land Area, Population, and Households, and Employment**

STATE City, town, township, borough, or CDP (county if applicable)	Land area,[1] 2010 (sq mi)	Population				Population characteristics 2010–2014		Household income and poverty, 2010–2014	Percent of households		Employment,[2] 2010–2014		Households, 2010–2014 (percent of households)	
		Total persons 2010	Total persons 2014	Percent change 2010–2014	Persons per square mile, 2014	Foreign born	Lives in same house as previous year	Median household income (dollars	Income of $100,000 or more	Income below poverty level	Percent in labor force	Unemploy-ment rate	Family households	One person households
	1	2	3	4	5	6	7	8	9	10	11	12	13	14
FLORIDA—Con.														
Westwood Lakes CDP	1.644	11,838	NA	NA	NA	65.7	92.1	$49,418	18.3	15.4	61.2	8.8	80.8	17.2
Wilton Manors city	1.964	11,632	12,243	5.3	6,232.4	22.8	78.8	$50,618	22.5	12.0	68.5	12.1	30.4	52.3
Winter Garden city	15.734	34,648	38,746	11.8	2,462.5	15.9	86.6	$58,355	27.9	9.2	69.5	8.6	75.0	20.6
Winter Haven city	31.304	33,874	36,371	7.4	1,161.9	10.8	81.6	$36,602	10.6	20.4	53.4	11.7	62.5	33.4
Winter Park city	8.686	27,856	29,442	5.7	3,389.7	9.0	81.6	$56,995	33.0	11.6	55.4	7.3	53.4	37.7
Winter Springs city	14.658	33,282	34,169	2.7	2,331.1	10.9	87.1	$64,038	30.7	8.8	67.7	11.7	70.4	24.5
World Golf Village CDP	26.857	12,310	NA	NA	NA	6.4	87.9	$75,224	33.4	6.6	67.1	5.2	74.5	19.9
Wright CDP	5.526	23,127	NA	NA	NA	10.5	78.2	$45,096	11.5	16.9	70.6	9.2	58.1	35.7
Yulee CDP	23.159	11,491	NA	NA	NA	5.3	83.4	$54,715	19.1	8.0	62.0	8.3	73.9	21.3
Zephyrhills city	9.294	13,538	14,381	6.2	1,547.4	8.0	85.2	$37,253	8.1	16.1	49.3	10.7	56.0	40.1
GEORGIA	57,513.483	9,688,681	10,097,343	4.2	175.6	9.7	83.8	$49,342	20.0	16.8	63.3	10.8	68.0	26.7
Acworth city	8.253	20,439	21,867	7.0	2,649.7	20.4	83.2	$50,668	16.1	11.0	71.1	9.7	65.3	28.4
Albany city	55.064	77,434	75,769	-2.2	1,376.0	2.5	81.4	$28,303	7.9	31.3	57.5	19.4	61.2	33.4
Alpharetta city	26.895	57,500	63,038	9.6	2,343.9	22.0	84.3	$87,837	43.0	5.8	70.0	5.8	70.8	25.6
Americus city	11.269	17,085	16,283	-4.7	1,445.0	2.1	79.3	$26,227	7.6	33.9	56.4	19.9	60.0	36.7
Athens-Clarke County unified government	119.200	116,707	120,938	3.6	1,014.6	10.1	74.3	$33,430	12.9	31.5	57.7	9.8	49.1	33.9
Athens-Clarke County unified government (balance)	116.359	115,453	119,648	3.6	1,028.3	10.1	74.1	$33,293	12.8	31.7	57.6	9.8	48.9	34.0
Atlanta city	133.098	420,256	456,002	8.5	3,426.1	7.6	76.4	$46,439	23.6	21.1	64.8	12.9	43.3	46.4
Augusta-Richmond County consolidated government	324.326	200,549	201,368	0.4	620.9	3.6	81.0	$37,704	11.7	22.6	59.7	13.0	60.7	34.0
Augusta-Richmond County consolidated government (balance)	302.465	195,844	196,741	0.5	650.5	3.6	80.9	$37,593	11.7	22.9	59.7	13.0	60.4	34.2
Bainbridge city	18.799	12,697	12,496	-1.6	664.7	2.2	86.9	$25,366	8.3	32.5	48.5	11.2	58.1	39.1
Belvedere Park CDP	4.922	15,152	NA	NA	NA	4.9	69.1	$38,779	12.6	20.7	67.9	21.5	60.5	31.9
Brookhaven city	11.246	49,219	51,079	3.8	4,542.0	25.6	83.5	$67,916	35.2	12.1	75.1	4.5	47.3	41.2
Brunswick city	17.076	15,383	15,903	3.4	931.3	8.8	78.5	$26,775	6.7	32.8	61.8	16.2	58.8	37.8
Buford city	17.033	12,235	13,392	9.5	786.2	23.0	83.5	$43,750	17.2	19.6	65.1	8.9	75.0	24.1
Calhoun city	14.932	15,667	16,052	2.5	1,075.0	21.5	80.7	$35,517	13.6	22.0	58.1	6.3	64.6	27.2
Candler-McAfee CDP	7.007	23,025	NA	NA	NA	2.3	85.2	$33,402	7.8	23.5	58.3	21.9	59.7	34.4
Canton city	18.644	22,959	24,801	8.0	1,330.2	15.5	79.9	$50,071	16.8	14.8	68.9	9.7	68.8	25.8
Carrollton city	22.311	24,392	26,690	9.4	1,196.3	10.9	71.6	$32,969	13.8	28.9	59.8	15.4	56.4	31.9
Cartersville city	29.170	19,786	20,015	1.2	686.2	6.2	72.4	$46,909	12.4	14.7	59.9	7.7	62.3	31.7
Chamblee city	4.793	15,514	16,112	3.9	3,361.5	38.1	84.5	$50,209	20.4	18.7	76.6	8.1	52.1	32.4
College Park city	10.071	13,942	14,598	4.7	1,449.5	5.9	69.2	$26,150	7.8	34.1	67.0	16.0	53.7	38.6
Columbus city	216.422	190,545	200,887	5.4	928.2	5.5	75.5	$41,362	13.9	19.6	62.9	11.3	64.7	30.4
Conyers city	11.665	15,195	15,718	3.4	1,347.5	14.7	72.3	$39,423	7.8	18.8	64.4	14.3	66.8	27.7
Cordele city	10.141	11,147	10,939	-1.9	1,078.7	2.3	81.6	$22,143	6.2	42.3	58.6	20.3	70.1	26.0
Covington city	15.805	13,116	13,667	4.2	864.7	6.1	72.9	$32,171	12.5	24.4	60.9	10.8	62.4	33.3
Cusseta-Chattahoochee County unified government	248.736	11,267	11,837	5.1	47.6	7.8	48.9	$48,488	8.6	6.2	78.3	18.1	77.1	16.3
Dallas city	7.384	11,564	12,629	9.2	1,710.4	11.0	77.3	$50,113	8.7	22.6	72.3	13.3	72.2	23.0
Dalton city	20.290	33,103	33,529	1.3	1,652.5	27.7	79.7	$35,530	11.5	23.7	65.3	11.9	65.0	28.0
Decatur city	4.318	19,334	20,380	5.4	4,719.9	7.9	83.8	$77,202	41.6	15.8	70.8	7.4	55.0	37.4
Doraville city	4.015	10,326	10,714	3.8	2,668.2	48.8	85.2	$42,407	8.9	22.9	75.3	8.4	65.6	26.1
Douglas city	13.390	11,590	11,665	0.6	871.1	4.9	86.2	$31,943	8.6	28.9	51.0	7.9	63.1	35.1
Douglasville city	22.467	30,956	32,523	5.1	1,447.6	8.0	77.5	$47,563	17.2	17.4	65.4	11.2	66.8	28.9
Druid Hills CDP	4.142	14,568	NA	NA	NA	13.4	67.6	$80,278	44.2	9.8	54.0	5.1	50.6	37.7
Dublin city	15.935	16,206	16,182	-0.1	1,015.5	2.7	83.5	$28,491	10.4	30.7	45.2	8.5	61.3	35.0
Duluth city	10.132	26,602	28,838	8.4	2,846.2	28.6	87.6	$56,849	22.5	12.3	69.9	8.5	68.0	26.9
Dunwoody city	12.969	46,268	48,000	3.7	3,701.2	21.3	84.4	$78,063	37.4	8.3	69.6	7.4	58.0	36.1
East Point city	14.677	33,712	35,488	5.3	2,417.9	8.9	79.2	$37,646	9.5	23.7	66.0	19.5	57.2	35.8
Evans CDP	25.266	29,011	NA	NA	NA	7.7	85.0	$90,259	41.1	4.3	64.6	6.0	83.8	14.3
Fairburn city	16.924	13,028	13,696	5.1	809.2	9.0	87.5	$43,830	9.3	15.7	69.7	14.0	72.4	25.4
Fayetteville city	10.825	16,097	16,725	3.9	1,545.0	9.1	87.0	$63,750	26.1	8.6	61.3	7.9	69.1	29.3
Forest Park city	9.277	18,468	18,949	2.6	2,042.5	28.0	72.0	$30,814	4.7	29.7	64.2	17.1	63.2	28.7
Gainesville city	31.977	33,809	36,306	7.4	1,135.4	25.5	77.3	$39,791	12.5	24.4	65.7	9.5	63.6	29.8
Georgetown CDP	8.145	11,823	NA	NA	NA	9.8	78.7	$47,877	21.7	16.4	71.1	5.3	62.2	27.8
Griffin city	13.938	23,637	23,329	-1.3	1,673.7	4.4	81.5	$29,119	9.8	29.2	53.4	14.8	64.1	30.2
Grovetown city	4.831	11,272	12,746	13.1	2,638.5	11.7	85.9	$53,223	12.1	14.3	69.6	11.5	78.3	21.5
Hinesville city	20.427	33,439	34,815	4.1	1,704.4	7.2	73.2	$44,896	11.8	16.0	70.4	13.0	74.0	20.2
Jesup city	16.411	10,214	10,285	0.7	626.7	5.9	76.0	$31,309	7.7	27.7	40.6	9.5	64.2	31.8
Johns Creek city	30.753	76,727	83,102	8.3	2,702.3	25.4	87.9	$108,114	53.5	5.3	70.0	7.3	80.8	16.9
Kennesaw city	9.476	30,294	32,400	7.0	3,419.2	15.9	80.5	$58,483	23.4	9.5	75.6	9.4	60.6	30.9
Kingsland city	42.732	15,944	16,416	3.0	384.2	2.9	83.0	$57,278	15.6	13.7	68.3	8.8	76.7	16.6
LaGrange city	40.743	29,430	30,557	3.8	750.0	7.2	73.8	$34,056	10.4	27.2	58.8	14.7	64.2	30.6
Lawrenceville city	13.394	28,391	30,212	6.4	2,255.6	26.7	83.3	$42,459	11.1	18.3	64.9	13.7	68.8	25.0
Lilburn city	6.393	11,660	12,543	7.6	1,962.1	31.5	87.7	$49,081	20.9	19.2	66.4	10.4	74.1	24.0
Lithia Springs CDP	13.686	15,491	NA	NA	NA	13.9	76.0	$38,221	10.1	24.4	67.3	17.2	64.8	28.2
Loganville city	7.339	10,458	11,022	5.4	1,501.8	16.6	88.4	$59,205	16.2	10.4	66.4	8.9	74.5	22.9
Mableton CDP	20.576	37,115	NA	NA	NA	17.6	83.2	$55,532	24.0	14.5	73.6	10.5	72.1	22.5
McDonough city	12.616	22,019	23,004	4.5	1,823.5	9.2	76.5	$45,263	11.8	18.4	62.0	12.6	59.7	35.4
Macon-Bibb County	249.269	155,292	153,691	-1.0	616.6	3.7	82.0	$36,671	13.9	24.1	56.8	12.7	63.3	31.7
Marietta city	23.123	56,605	60,014	6.0	2,595.5	20.5	70.5	$42,688	18.8	18.5	70.6	10.5	57.9	33.1
Martinez CDP	14.500	35,795	NA	NA	NA	7.0	90.5	$63,422	25.1	7.6	64.7	7.9	75.0	20.4
Milledgeville city	20.337	18,380	19,211	4.5	944.6	4.5	65.7	$22,500	5.5	41.2	43.9	10.7	45.4	37.3
Milton city	38.534	32,712	36,662	12.1	951.4	16.8	87.1	$110,891	53.5	4.7	67.1	4.4	81.5	15.8
Monroe city	15.202	13,219	13,664	3.4	898.8	3.4	80.4	$31,947	5.4	35.2	55.5	14.5	67.2	26.5
Moultrie city	16.481	14,268	14,507	1.7	880.2	8.9	72.9	$22,935	7.4	36.4	51.1	9.1	62.9	33.6
Mountain Park CDP	5.681	11,554	NA	NA	NA	15.0	88.7	$69,178	29.7	8.3	63.2	8.7	77.7	19.6
Newnan city	19.070	33,191	36,203	9.1	1,898.4	9.2	81.2	$50,175	21.4	19.1	63.9	8.5	66.6	28.6

1 Dry land or land partially or temporarily covered by water.
2 16 years old and over.

Table B. Incorporated Places, Census Designated Places (CDPs), and Minor Civil Divisions (MCDs) of 10,000 or More Population — Crime, Construction, and Local Government Finance

STATE City, town, township, borough, or CDP (county if applicable)	Serious crimes known to police, 2014[1] Total number	Rate[2] Total	Rate[2] Violent	Rate[2] Property	New residential construction authorized by building permits, 2014 Value ($1,000)	Number of housing units	Percent single family	Local government finance, 2012 General revenue Total (mil dol)	Intergovernmental Total (mil dol)	Intergovernmental Percent from state gov.	Taxes per capita[3]	General expenditure Total (mil dol)	Per capita[3] Total	Per capita[3] Capital outlays	Debt outstanding (mil dol)
	15	16	17	18	19	20	21	22	23	24	25	26	27	28	29
FLORIDA—Con.															
Westwood Lakes CDP	NA	NA	NA	NA	NA	NA	NA	NA	NA	NA	NA	NA	NA	NA	NA
Wilton Manors city	679	5555	597	4958	1,110	6	100.0	17.3	1.5	77.8	814	15.5	1,288	41	14.0
Winter Garden city	1,276	3318	424	2894	100,326	456	100.0	39.8	5.5	93.8	560	40.6	1,096	279	22.0
Winter Haven city	1,575	4383	623	3760	59,123	359	100.0	52.2	3.8	56.0	594	58.7	1,677	299	89.2
Winter Park city	1,185	4013	274	3739	60,278	117	96.6	63.4	8.3	60.7	1019	65.0	2,246	474	187.9
Winter Springs city	432	1270	185	1085	21,427	115	68.7	27.7	4.0	89.0	389	26.4	786	144	34.5
World Golf Village CDP	NA	NA	NA	NA	NA	NA	NA	NA	NA	NA	NA	NA	NA	NA	NA
Wright CDP	NA	NA	NA	NA	NA	NA	NA	NA	NA	NA	NA	NA	NA	NA	NA
Yulee CDP	NA	NA	NA	NA	NA	NA	NA	NA	NA	NA	NA	NA	NA	NA	NA
Zephyrhills city	958	6757	409	6348	2,056	19	100.0	20.0	2.4	85.9	624	16.4	1,162	189	19.3
GEORGIA	369,413	3659	377	3281	6,541,383	39,423	69.8	X	X	X	X	X	X	X	X
Acworth city	NA	NA	NA	NA	5,910	46	100.0	16.0	3.6	0.7	399	15.5	730	188	14.4
Albany city	4,971	6553	1022	5531	7,154	80	55.0	124.2	55.1	36.8	312	134.7	1,739	76	71.8
Alpharetta city	1,292	2035	60	1975	103,284	288	100.0	73.1	15.6	8.8	678	72.3	1,166	291	54.6
Americus city	1,485	9167	1173	7994	70	1	100.0	16.3	2.5	12.3	422	19.9	1,213	267	19.3
Athens-Clarke County unified government	NA	NA	NA	NA	NA	NA	NA	206.5	69.1	26.0	592	249.4	2,073	479	263.4
Athens-Clarke County unified government (balance)	4,164	3427	306	3121	50,528	538	21.6	NA	NA	NA	NA	NA	NA	NA	NA
Atlanta city	31,691	6975	1227	5747	618,660	4,505	12.1	1789.4	282.2	8.0	1173	1567.5	3,530	1,093	7446.5
Augusta-Richmond County consolidated government	NA	NA	NA	NA	78,026	720	47.8	NA	NA	NA	NA	NA	NA	NA	NA
Augusta-Richmond County consolidated government (balance)	3,224	1626	127	1499	NA	NA	NA	364.7	133.0	12.9	524	341.5	1,731	350	619.6
Bainbridge city	1,931	15357	1734	13623	784	12	100.0	13.9	2.9	0.2	282	15.7	1,245	257	5.6
Belvedere Park CDP	NA	NA	NA	NA	NA	NA	NA	NA	NA	NA	NA	NA	NA	NA	NA
Brookhaven city	NA	NA	NA	NA	NA	NA	NA	NA	NA	NA	NA	NA	NA	NA	NA
Brunswick city	1,427	8968	1414	7554	NA	NA	NA	19.0	9.6	4.0	468	20.7	1,321	276	2.0
Buford city	NA	NA	NA	NA	17,812	100	100.0	22.8	2.4	12.9	1079	41.3	3,252	855	13.2
Calhoun city	784	4914	226	4688	2,919	22	86.4	25.6	8.6	2.5	365	22.6	1,428	135	56.4
Candler-McAfee CDP	NA	NA	NA	NA	NA	NA	NA	NA	NA	NA	NA	NA	NA	NA	NA
Canton city	542	2217	143	2074	45,244	282	100.0	18.6	3.3	4.3	386	16.2	683	69	52.7
Carrollton city	1,314	5191	435	4756	1,699	14	100.0	34.9	9.5	4.2	363	28.4	1,136	174	22.2
Cartersville city	1,607	8012	304	7708	12,921	73	100.0	46.9	9.5	2.5	1199	57.2	2,887	660	50.7
Chamblee city	NA	NA	NA	NA	8,760	40	100.0	13.2	0.8	10.3	543	10.1	639	34	0.0
College Park city	1,962	13275	2152	11123	801	5	100.0	70.7	4.6	0.3	2197	106.3	7,254	3,048	415.1
Columbus city	14,479	7004	533	6472	53,634	585	56.9	354.1	116.0	29.3	675	364.1	1,820	349	514.9
Conyers city	980	6237	675	5562	1,181	5	100.0	19.6	2.6	0.0	647	19.0	1,233	57	6.1
Cordele city	755	6740	634	6106	340	2	100.0	11.8	2.9	0.0	496	11.5	1,014	114	6.6
Covington city	993	7337	473	6864	3,868	33	84.8	26.8	4.4	2.1	567	28.0	2,108	199	17.2
Cusseta-Chattahoochee County unified government	NA	NA	NA	NA	300	3	100.0	2.9	1.3	17.7	46	4.1	325	0	1.0
Dallas city	NA	NA	NA	NA	11,364	74	100.0	8.1	3.5	18.4	202	8.2	679	251	10.6
Dalton city	1,332	3980	269	3711	NA	NA	NA	69.4	16.5	0.3	427	82.6	2,478	515	51.3
Decatur city	653	3226	148	3078	79,722	494	23.5	31.3	3.7	1.5	980	35.1	1,767	375	51.1
Doraville city	NA	NA	NA	NA	2,172	9	100.0	10.7	0.8	51.0	604	9.8	934	41	0.0
Douglas city	1,214	10181	906	9275	236	4	50.0	15.3	4.8	31.0	333	20.1	1,696	284	1.9
Douglasville city	2,241	6979	579	6399	14,879	44	100.0	27.0	7.1	10.3	441	34.0	1,088	313	43.7
Druid Hills CDP	NA	NA	NA	NA	NA	NA	NA	NA	NA	NA	NA	NA	NA	NA	NA
Dublin city	1,000	6089	542	5547	653	7	100.0	23.2	8.5	22.5	400	29.7	1,836	251	12.9
Duluth city	624	2163	94	2069	10,071	38	100.0	24.7	9.0	7.9	419	21.2	761	234	10.1
Dunwoody city	2,244	4683	121	4562	18,011	40	100.0	20.5	0.6	15.1	372	26.5	560	185	7.3
East Point city	4,220	11745	1291	10454	5,071	40	100.0	49.3	11.3	1.5	582	55.0	1,547	287	99.0
Evans CDP	NA	NA	NA	NA	NA	NA	NA	NA	NA	NA	NA	NA	NA	NA	NA
Fairburn city	580	4187	375	3812	15,879	129	25.6	12.2	1.3	0.6	479	13.9	1,013	51	36.5
Fayetteville city	489	2977	164	2813	16,297	73	100.0	13.1	2.5	0.5	383	14.9	918	194	25.4
Forest Park city	1,158	6142	615	5526	350	12	0.0	29.9	11.5	5.6	607	31.6	1,669	337	0.0
Gainesville city	1,623	4512	364	4148	43,507	259	97.7	78.3	19.3	20.5	626	70.8	2,035	502	711.3
Georgetown CDP	NA	NA	NA	NA	NA	NA	NA	NA	NA	NA	NA	NA	NA	NA	NA
Griffin city	1,814	7792	1125	6667	431	2	100.0	33.5	5.3	7.0	339	37.7	1,613	65	65.7
Grovetown city	123	970	32	939	13,983	89	100.0	6.6	3.0	0.1	112	8.4	683	176	2.4
Hinesville city	1,599	4631	469	4162	37,183	171	74.3	30.4	10.9	1.3	287	30.3	873	89	24.5
Jesup city	859	8321	746	7575	631	4	100.0	9.6	4.3	0.4	307	8.4	813	195	0.0
Johns Creek city	622	738	33	705	46,501	125	100.0	48.5	16.3	1.2	352	41.5	504	64	3.2
Kennesaw city	545	1681	114	1566	33,658	289	12.8	26.5	5.0	1.3	449	24.9	796	112	25.6
Kingsland city	541	3317	331	2986	8,481	64	100.0	15.6	3.7	4.8	397	15.5	955	44	19.8
LaGrange city	1,903	6203	411	5792	8,995	38	100.0	35.7	9.6	8.9	155	44.0	1,454	186	38.1
Lawrenceville city	957	3166	175	2991	9,152	48	91.7	22.3	5.6	4.6	185	28.0	952	219	0.0
Lilburn city	736	5837	317	5519	392	1	100.0	8.4	2.7	2.8	337	8.0	658	125	1.3
Lithia Springs CDP	NA	NA	NA	NA	NA	NA	NA	NA	NA	NA	NA	NA	NA	NA	NA
Loganville city	250	2294	64	2230	6,719	71	100.0	12.6	2.1	13.4	528	13.4	1,259	150	7.8
Mableton CDP	NA	NA	NA	NA	NA	NA	NA	NA	NA	NA	NA	NA	NA	NA	NA
McDonough city	886	3852	235	3617	15,266	122	100.0	6.5	2.2	0.1	67	7.2	318	25	4.5
Macon-Bibb County	NA	NA	NA	NA	762	7	100.0	105.9	49.5	9.0	239	116.6	748	73	46.4
Marietta city	2,957	4956	508	4448	36,810	145	92.4	82.2	22.8	7.9	524	98.4	1,683	284	100.1
Martinez CDP	NA	NA	NA	NA	NA	NA	NA	NA	NA	NA	NA	NA	NA	NA	NA
Milledgeville city	794	4068	333	3735	408	12	58.3	18.4	5.3	7.4	341	14.5	746	22	9.2
Milton city	372	1014	19	994	72,956	344	100.0	21.7	4.6	14.9	433	20.2	577	192	1.1
Monroe city	2,460	18207	1599	16609	4,007	12	100.0	23.3	5.1	7.4	345	24.4	1,821	119	30.0
Moultrie city	1,070	7283	497	6786	2,168	14	100.0	27.1	10.0	58.3	387	24.0	1,654	265	17.9
Mountain Park CDP	NA	NA	NA	NA	NA	NA	NA	NA	NA	NA	NA	NA	NA	NA	NA
Newnan city	1,202	3412	483	2929	94,154	316	100.0	30.9	10.4	1.6	320	29.9	875	209	38.2

1 Data for serious crimes have not been adjusted for underreporting. This may affect comparability between geographic areas over time.
2 Per 100,000 population estimated by the FBI.   3 Based on population estimated as of July 1 of the year shown.

Table B. Incorporated Places, Census Designated Places (CDPs), and Minor Civil Divisions (MCDs) of 10,000 or More Population — Land Area, Population, and Households, and Employment

STATE City, town, township, borough, or CDP (county if applicable)	Land area,[1] 2010 (sq mi)	Population				Population characteristics 2010–2014		Household income and poverty, 2010–2014			Employment,[2] 2010–2014		Households, 2010–2014 (percent of households)	
		Total persons 2010	Total persons 2014	Percent change 2010–2014	Persons per square mile, 2014	Foreign born	Lives in same house as previous year	Median household income (dollars	Percent of households		Percent in labor force	Unemploy-ment rate	Family households	One person households
									Income of $100,000 or more	Income below poverty level				
	1	2	3	4	5	6	7	8	9	10	11	12	13	14
GEORGIA—Con.														
Norcross city	6.117	15,174	16,349	7.7	2,672.6	40.2	83.6	$39,436	18.9	23.9	72.9	9.9	71.5	24.1
North Decatur CDP	4.916	16,698	NA	NA	NA	17.0	79.8	$55,821	24.8	14.4	67.9	8.8	45.5	44.0
North Druid Hills CDP	5.050	18,947	NA	NA	NA	20.8	76.2	$51,365	27.2	15.3	72.7	6.5	34.0	51.2
Peachtree City city	24.544	34,364	35,063	2.0	1,428.6	11.7	86.1	$86,352	42.6	7.0	65.4	7.3	75.6	22.0
Peachtree Corners city	16.180	38,011	40,531	6.6	2,504.9	22.8	82.0	$63,431	31.9	9.3	72.7	8.3	65.3	28.3
Perry city	26.302	13,829	15,144	9.5	575.8	4.3	76.3	$49,140	17.5	20.4	58.6	14.5	68.5	24.7
Pooler city	29.647	19,104	22,251	16.5	750.5	9.8	84.7	$68,787	26.7	7.8	69.1	3.8	64.0	29.6
Powder Springs city	7.186	13,939	14,590	4.7	2,030.4	8.9	85.0	$56,768	18.7	13.3	64.0	13.3	73.5	21.0
Redan CDP	9.612	33,015	NA	NA	NA	9.3	83.3	$45,484	10.6	15.1	74.1	17.1	67.3	27.7
Richmond Hill city	14.443	9,281	11,229	21.0	777.5	7.3	74.8	$64,381	20.7	10.1	74.4	7.2	78.4	16.0
Riverdale city	4.560	15,235	15,669	2.8	3,436.5	14.3	77.0	$34,354	12.7	27.6	69.4	17.3	63.7	31.8
Rome city	30.917	36,306	35,997	-0.9	1,164.3	10.8	78.9	$33,787	11.3	25.9	56.7	13.9	57.8	34.5
Roswell city	40.713	88,347	94,089	6.5	2,311.0	18.8	87.2	$79,359	41.8	7.5	70.6	6.8	68.2	27.5
St. Marys city	22.630	17,126	17,949	4.8	793.2	1.9	75.8	$51,442	16.8	14.8	66.8	12.3	73.2	19.1
St. Simons CDP	16.114	12,743	NA	NA	NA	4.7	82.8	$62,205	30.8	7.4	58.8	7.7	57.7	37.1
Sandy Springs city	37.657	93,852	101,908	8.6	2,706.2	18.7	78.5	$63,401	33.7	11.5	73.5	7.3	54.6	37.6
Savannah city	103.280	136,340	144,352	5.9	1,397.7	6.0	79.2	$36,628	11.5	23.6	61.0	12.7	55.5	35.1
Smyrna city	15.359	51,265	54,958	7.2	3,578.3	16.8	75.3	$61,333	31.0	11.4	77.8	7.7	55.4	36.2
Snellville city	10.466	18,265	19,439	6.4	1,857.3	14.8	92.7	$56,654	23.2	9.4	62.5	13.2	79.4	19.1
Statesboro city	13.993	28,404	30,367	6.9	2,170.1	4.4	65.8	$22,196	6.0	47.0	52.0	11.3	42.1	26.9
Stockbridge city	13.179	26,319	27,619	4.9	2,095.6	14.6	84.3	$54,864	15.6	11.5	67.5	14.3	75.0	20.8
Sugar Hill city	10.607	18,524	20,821	12.4	1,963.0	17.6	87.5	$67,426	25.1	11.5	73.7	10.7	81.6	15.1
Suwanee city	10.883	15,355	18,164	18.3	1,669.1	17.4	90.7	$83,780	38.6	4.6	73.2	5.7	81.9	14.7
Thomasville city	15.012	18,554	18,700	0.8	1,245.7	2.1	82.5	$31,240	8.6	31.9	53.6	15.7	62.8	33.5
Tifton city	12.516	16,346	16,701	2.2	1,334.3	5.3	77.9	$30,615	10.0	33.2	48.4	9.7	60.8	33.3
Tucker CDP	11.980	27,581	NA	NA	NA	19.5	85.6	$60,536	29.1	13.0	67.5	10.0	63.3	30.9
Union City city	19.612	19,463	20,427	5.0	1,041.5	6.3	78.0	$32,324	2.9	23.6	59.7	14.6	55.2	40.8
Valdosta city	35.859	54,764	56,595	3.3	1,578.3	5.0	72.4	$29,828	9.4	29.3	62.7	14.9	55.3	31.5
Vidalia city	17.361	10,442	10,670	2.2	614.6	2.9	90.8	$30,294	9.3	29.0	60.2	13.3	61.3	34.9
Villa Rica city	14.239	13,956	14,700	5.3	1,032.3	7.7	80.2	$50,759	16.2	16.6	64.8	13.6	65.7	29.2
Vinings CDP	3.127	9,734	NA	NA	NA	12.3	67.4	$58,550	28.5	8.8	74.6	5.7	39.9	50.3
Warner Robins city	36.124	68,618	73,271	6.8	2,028.3	6.3	82.2	$44,661	12.3	19.0	65.4	11.1	64.3	32.0
Waycross city	11.717	14,651	14,166	-3.3	1,209.0	4.5	80.2	$25,942	6.3	31.3	45.6	10.8	59.0	37.2
Wilmington Island CDP	8.260	15,138	NA	NA	NA	6.1	92.2	$75,333	32.1	6.2	67.0	4.6	65.5	28.2
Winder city	12.544	14,139	14,930	5.6	1,190.2	5.5	82.9	$44,327	10.9	16.2	61.9	13.7	65.8	28.4
Woodstock city	11.719	23,904	27,823	16.4	2,374.1	11.9	83.1	$68,499	30.4	5.4	73.8	7.7	70.6	24.8
HAWAII	6,422.628	1,360,301	1,419,561	4.4	221.0	17.9	85.0	$68,201	31.2	11.0	65.4	6.7	69.2	23.9
East Honolulu CDP	23.012	49,914	NA	NA	NA	14.4	92.2	$111,582	56.0	3.8	64.0	3.2	78.7	16.4
Ewa Beach CDP	1.206	14,955	NA	NA	NA	26.9	89.6	$78,388	36.5	11.6	59.7	9.8	85.7	11.8
Ewa Gentry CDP	2.180	22,690	NA	NA	NA	21.5	80.7	$85,431	40.4	2.2	75.4	4.7	77.3	16.3
Halawa CDP	2.367	14,014	NA	NA	NA	21.6	88.9	$89,367	43.2	8.0	66.3	4.0	76.5	18.3
Hawaiian Paradise Park CDP	15.213	11,404	NA	NA	NA	13.6	86.2	$46,152	15.3	30.0	45.0	7.0	71.3	21.2
Hilo CDP	53.389	43,263	NA	NA	NA	7.2	89.6	$52,563	21.6	17.9	56.2	7.5	64.8	29.0
Kahului CDP	14.447	26,337	NA	NA	NA	32.8	81.7	$62,038	28.6	10.1	64.2	11.7	75.3	20.0
Kailua CDP (Hawaii County)	35.634	11,975	NA	NA	NA	15.6	77.3	$56,429	21.3	14.7	64.6	8.7	67.1	25.5
Kailua CDP (Honolulu County)	7.753	38,635	NA	NA	NA	8.4	87.5	$104,911	52.9	4.9	67.4	5.9	76.2	18.6
Kalaoa CDP	39.169	9,644	NA	NA	NA	9.5	79.4	$62,272	24.7	14.0	73.7	6.0	64.9	22.5
Kaneohe CDP	6.529	34,597	NA	NA	NA	7.9	88.0	$81,907	38.1	6.4	65.0	5.2	78.7	17.0
Kaneohe Station CDP	4.384	9,517	NA	NA	NA	3.9	62.3	$50,336	14.0	11.7	81.6	5.0	92.4	6.8
Kapaa CDP	10.007	10,699	NA	NA	NA	10.2	87.5	$62,923	21.0	10.1	61.5	8.5	64.4	25.7
Kapolei CDP	4.136	15,186	NA	NA	NA	16.4	84.6	$97,943	47.4	4.1	74.1	5.5	82.5	13.0
Kihei CDP	9.278	20,881	NA	NA	NA	17.9	74.0	$63,804	23.9	11.0	73.3	8.9	63.2	25.7
Lahaina CDP	7.785	11,704	NA	NA	NA	26.1	81.3	$62,542	25.7	9.7	78.4	7.8	65.2	19.5
Makakilo CDP	3.817	18,248	NA	NA	NA	15.4	82.8	$104,966	52.6	3.7	76.1	7.5	82.8	12.3
Mililani Mauka CDP	3.979	21,039	NA	NA	NA	9.3	85.9	$101,141	51.3	2.8	77.2	3.1	75.0	17.4
Mililani Town CDP	4.010	27,629	NA	NA	NA	10.5	90.0	$94,410	45.8	4.0	66.8	5.5	81.7	15.5
Nanakuli CDP	2.989	12,666	NA	NA	NA	4.4	91.5	$59,148	27.6	18.4	64.2	14.9	84.5	12.8
Ocean Pointe CDP	2.024	8,361	NA	NA	NA	15.4	79.2	$108,319	58.3	2.9	73.3	6.2	87.5	7.1
Pearl City CDP	9.112	47,698	NA	NA	NA	13.2	86.8	$82,895	40.3	5.9	63.1	5.6	77.8	18.8
Royal Kunia CDP	3.007	14,525	NA	NA	NA	28.3	84.0	$109,196	56.3	2.3	71.4	5.1	86.6	10.3
Schofield Barracks CDP	2.773	16,370	NA	NA	NA	5.6	63.4	$51,584	12.0	11.2	77.4	15.9	94.2	2.3
Urban Honolulu CDP	60.521	337,256	350,399	3.9	5,789.8	25.7	84.7	$60,548	26.4	11.9	64.0	5.3	58.3	33.3
Wahiawa CDP	2.066	17,821	NA	NA	NA	19.9	84.4	$57,049	26.2	13.1	64.6	6.7	65.7	26.1
Waianae CDP	5.358	13,177	NA	NA	NA	6.7	86.9	$68,348	28.4	25.6	60.6	12.3	84.6	10.7
Wailuku CDP	5.319	15,313	NA	NA	NA	13.1	86.3	$70,409	29.6	10.6	66.3	9.9	69.9	25.8
Waimalu CDP	1.831	13,730	NA	NA	NA	18.4	82.6	$69,826	28.4	7.1	69.4	3.3	56.2	36.7
Waipahu CDP	2.650	38,216	NA	NA	NA	38.1	90.2	$68,352	33.1	12.9	63.6	5.8	81.3	13.8
Waipio CDP	1.251	11,674	NA	NA	NA	17.1	85.2	$74,091	32.9	5.3	70.4	4.5	67.6	29.6
IDAHO	82,643.113	1,567,652	1,634,464	4.3	19.8	6.0	82.7	$47,334	15.4	14.7	63.2	8.1	69.5	24.4
Ammon city	7.305	13,814	14,685	6.3	2,010.1	1.8	86.4	$59,497	22.8	9.4	65.9	5.6	78.6	20.0
Blackfoot city	5.826	11,899	11,814	-0.7	2,028.0	7.6	78.3	$39,524	9.7	19.6	61.9	5.6	65.0	30.4
Boise City city	80.486	206,105	216,282	4.9	2,687.2	7.3	78.9	$49,209	20.4	14.5	68.4	7.7	59.1	30.9
Burley city	6.118	10,345	10,480	1.3	1,713.1	7.6	80.3	$32,202	7.0	21.0	56.2	7.2	66.4	31.1
Caldwell city	22.151	46,301	50,224	8.5	2,267.3	10.9	82.0	$41,368	6.8	21.5	64.9	11.0	69.5	25.7
Chubbuck city	4.173	13,954	14,229	2.0	3,409.4	2.2	84.7	$44,650	13.2	12.9	68.2	5.8	70.1	25.7
Coeur d'Alene city	15.590	44,137	47,912	8.6	3,073.3	3.0	77.4	$41,336	13.0	14.9	62.1	9.9	59.0	31.6
Eagle city	29.435	19,921	22,502	13.0	764.5	4.3	91.5	$82,264	40.2	5.9	60.6	5.8	81.0	14.5
Garden City city	4.041	10,977	11,420	4.0	2,825.9	4.3	78.1	$38,212	16.7	16.9	62.4	12.5	63.3	29.8
Hayden city	9.588	13,304	13,870	4.3	1,446.6	1.3	81.8	$54,481	10.7	7.9	64.8	9.3	67.9	25.0
Idaho Falls city	22.436	56,891	58,691	3.2	2,615.9	5.8	82.7	$45,680	17.5	14.9	64.4	6.7	69.9	25.2
Jerome city	5.518	10,890	11,189	2.7	2,027.6	19.5	82.8	$35,317	3.2	23.6	63.4	10.3	72.3	25.1
Kuna city	18.137	15,234	16,999	11.6	937.2	3.0	92.9	$56,533	11.0	14.2	69.1	9.3	83.2	12.8

1 Dry land or land partially or temporarily covered by water.
2 16 years old and over.

Table B. Incorporated Places, Census Designated Places (CDPs), and Minor Civil Divisions (MCDs) of 10,000 or More Population — Crime, Construction, and Local Government Finance

STATE City, town, township, borough, or CDP (county if applicable)	Serious crimes known to police, 2014[1] — Total number	Rate[2] — Total	Rate[2] — Violent	Rate[2] — Property	New residential construction authorized by building permits, 2014 — Value ($1,000)	Number of housing units	Percent single family	Local government finance, 2012 — General revenue — Total (mil dol)	Intergovernmental Total (mil dol)	Percent from state gov.	Taxes per capita[3]	General expenditure — Total (mil dol)	Per capita[3] — Total	Capital outlays	Debt outstanding (mil dol)
	15	16	17	18	19	20	21	22	23	24	25	26	27	28	29
GEORGIA—Con.															
Norcross city	NA	NA	NA	NA	12,877	49	100.0	13.5	2.5	23.3	402	13.0	821	121	0.7
North Decatur CDP	NA	NA	NA	NA	NA	NA	NA	NA	NA	NA	NA	NA	NA	NA	NA
North Druid Hills CDP	NA	NA	NA	NA	NA	NA	NA	NA	NA	NA	NA	NA	NA	NA	NA
Peachtree City city	453	1295	29	1266	12,022	39	100.0	37.7	9.3	2.0	559	41.6	1,200	340	15.8
Peachtree Corners city	NA	NA	NA	NA	NA	NA	NA	NA	NA	NA	NA	NA	NA	NA	NA
Perry city	207	1363	151	1211	28,589	190	100.0	18.9	2.7	26.7	610	17.5	1,187	141	15.7
Pooler city	660	3040	184	2856	59,302	341	93.0	17.9	3.6	1.3	428	14.6	709	118	21.5
Powder Springs city	861	5928	1095	4833	16,797	54	100.0	11.4	2.7	0.1	348	14.4	1,010	428	0.9
Redan CDP	NA	NA	NA	NA	NA	NA	NA	NA	NA	NA	NA	NA	NA	NA	NA
Richmond Hill city	NA	NA	NA	NA	27,779	233	65.7	11.6	4.0	1.3	447	9.0	862	62	5.9
Riverdale city	988	6330	442	5888	0	0	0.0	16.0	6.0	0.0	328	15.1	967	153	18.5
Rome city	2,442	6806	672	6135	0	NA	NA	65.6	22.8	6.9	526	61.5	1,706	503	63.5
Roswell city	1,899	1991	115	1876	71,098	172	100.0	94.1	26.7	5.7	478	94.3	1,006	196	12.2
St. Marys city	656	3672	515	3157	11,622	44	100.0	13.8	2.8	0.6	331	13.0	737	47	47.3
St. Simons CDP	NA	NA	NA	NA	NA	NA	NA	NA	NA	NA	NA	NA	NA	NA	NA
Sandy Springs city	2,904	2870	157	2713	103,725	1,743	14.7	95.9	28.3	2.8	604	75.2	757	151	2.8
Savannah city	9,434	3986	392	3594	83,848	364	93.7	345.6	126.6	7.8	739	307.5	2,161	358	184.3
Smyrna city	1,707	3163	287	2876	30,160	429	36.1	56.3	11.1	0.4	513	52.4	994	224	50.4
Snellville city	732	3758	175	3583	10,315	46	100.0	16.6	4.4	1.2	409	16.1	850	281	4.3
Statesboro city	1,166	3848	271	3578	25,487	348	10.1	31.5	5.9	3.1	316	31.3	1,045	125	18.7
Stockbridge city	NA	NA	NA	NA	NA	NA	NA	16.8	7.3	22.1	149	12.9	481	83	17.6
Sugar Hill city	NA	NA	NA	NA	51,097	247	100.0	9.0	2.7	0.3	225	11.4	582	332	0.0
Suwanee city	482	2632	93	2539	36,057	133	100.0	16.8	4.3	2.5	674	13.7	847	237	20.3
Thomasville city	1,316	7018	389	6629	4,409	26	100.0	61.9	6.9	11.7	202	54.5	2,957	494	22.9
Tifton city	1,190	7250	792	6458	3,078	34	35.3	25.3	9.1	3.4	380	23.3	1,399	158	11.1
Tucker CDP	NA	NA	NA	NA	NA	NA	NA	NA	NA	NA	NA	NA	NA	NA	NA
Union City city	1,526	7375	913	6462	19,378	190	21.1	22.1	3.1	0.1	443	29.4	1,433	210	22.6
Valdosta city	3,492	6141	329	5812	9,924	76	81.6	56.4	22.7	6.1	302	59.7	1,036	254	48.0
Vidalia city	813	7581	774	6807	1,370	20	10.0	11.8	4.3	9.0	329	11.7	1,105	137	0.0
Villa Rica city	769	5278	343	4935	2,014	19	100.0	18.4	2.7	3.7	382	12.6	885	39	35.9
Vinings CDP	NA	NA	NA	NA	NA	NA	NA	NA	NA	NA	NA	NA	NA	NA	NA
Warner Robins city	4,853	6610	448	6162	36,837	195	96.9	55.2	4.5	3.8	390	54.2	755	88	39.6
Waycross city	1,073	7584	466	7117	0	0	0.0	15.1	3.6	0.4	457	17.4	1,213	129	8.8
Wilmington Island CDP	NA	NA	NA	NA	NA	NA	NA	NA	NA	NA	NA	NA	NA	NA	NA
Winder city	650	4392	277	4115	5,122	50	100.0	16.2	2.4	2.3	227	19.1	1,337	135	23.2
Woodstock city	680	2458	116	2342	143,103	827	33.9	21.5	3.0	3.9	515	22.0	875	72	42.4
HAWAII	46,977	3309	259	3050	1,011,786	3,066	71.7	X	X	X	X	X	X	X	X
East Honolulu CDP	NA	NA	NA	NA	NA	NA	NA	NA	NA	NA	NA	NA	NA	NA	NA
Ewa Beach CDP	NA	NA	NA	NA	NA	NA	NA	NA	NA	NA	NA	NA	NA	NA	NA
Ewa Gentry CDP	NA	NA	NA	NA	NA	NA	NA	NA	NA	NA	NA	NA	NA	NA	NA
Halawa CDP	NA	NA	NA	NA	NA	NA	NA	NA	NA	NA	NA	NA	NA	NA	NA
Hawaiian Paradise Park CDP	NA	NA	NA	NA	NA	NA	NA	NA	NA	NA	NA	NA	NA	NA	NA
Hilo CDP	NA	NA	NA	NA	NA	NA	NA	NA	NA	NA	NA	NA	NA	NA	NA
Kahului CDP	NA	NA	NA	NA	NA	NA	NA	NA	NA	NA	NA	NA	NA	NA	NA
Kailua CDP (Hawaii County)	NA	NA	NA	NA	NA	NA	NA	NA	NA	NA	NA	NA	NA	NA	NA
Kailua CDP (Honolulu County)	NA	NA	NA	NA	NA	NA	NA	NA	NA	NA	NA	NA	NA	NA	NA
Kalaoa CDP	NA	NA	NA	NA	NA	NA	NA	NA	NA	NA	NA	NA	NA	NA	NA
Kaneohe CDP	NA	NA	NA	NA	NA	NA	NA	NA	NA	NA	NA	NA	NA	NA	NA
Kaneohe Station CDP	NA	NA	NA	NA	NA	NA	NA	NA	NA	NA	NA	NA	NA	NA	NA
Kapaa CDP	NA	NA	NA	NA	NA	NA	NA	NA	NA	NA	NA	NA	NA	NA	NA
Kapolei CDP	NA	NA	NA	NA	NA	NA	NA	NA	NA	NA	NA	NA	NA	NA	NA
Kihei CDP	NA	NA	NA	NA	NA	NA	NA	NA	NA	NA	NA	NA	NA	NA	NA
Lahaina CDP	NA	NA	NA	NA	NA	NA	NA	NA	NA	NA	NA	NA	NA	NA	NA
Makakilo CDP	NA	NA	NA	NA	NA	NA	NA	NA	NA	NA	NA	NA	NA	NA	NA
Mililani Mauka CDP	NA	NA	NA	NA	NA	NA	NA	NA	NA	NA	NA	NA	NA	NA	NA
Mililani Town CDP	NA	NA	NA	NA	NA	NA	NA	NA	NA	NA	NA	NA	NA	NA	NA
Nanakuli CDP	NA	NA	NA	NA	NA	NA	NA	NA	NA	NA	NA	NA	NA	NA	NA
Ocean Pointe CDP	NA	NA	NA	NA	NA	NA	NA	NA	NA	NA	NA	NA	NA	NA	NA
Pearl City CDP	NA	NA	NA	NA	NA	NA	NA	NA	NA	NA	NA	NA	NA	NA	NA
Royal Kunia CDP	NA	NA	NA	NA	NA	NA	NA	NA	NA	NA	NA	NA	NA	NA	NA
Schofield Barracks CDP	NA	NA	NA	NA	NA	NA	NA	NA	NA	NA	NA	NA	NA	NA	NA
Urban Honolulu CDP	NA	NA	NA	NA	NA	NA	NA	NA	NA	NA	NA	NA	NA	NA	NA
Wahiawa CDP	NA	NA	NA	NA	NA	NA	NA	NA	NA	NA	NA	NA	NA	NA	NA
Waianae CDP	NA	NA	NA	NA	NA	NA	NA	NA	NA	NA	NA	NA	NA	NA	NA
Wailuku CDP	NA	NA	NA	NA	NA	NA	NA	NA	NA	NA	NA	NA	NA	NA	NA
Waimalu CDP	NA	NA	NA	NA	NA	NA	NA	NA	NA	NA	NA	NA	NA	NA	NA
Waipahu CDP	NA	NA	NA	NA	NA	NA	NA	NA	NA	NA	NA	NA	NA	NA	NA
Waipio CDP	NA	NA	NA	NA	NA	NA	NA	NA	NA	NA	NA	NA	NA	NA	NA
IDAHO	33,784	2067	212	1855	1,654,793	8,797	71.5	X	X	X	X	X	X	X	X
Ammon city	NA	NA	NA	NA	12,986	74	100.0	6.4	0.8	89.7	139	16.5	1,160	702	33.3
Blackfoot city	340	2873	194	2679	1,694	22	45.5	9.5	1.2	94.6	283	11.0	931	42	1.8
Boise City city	5,137	2375	289	2087	195,635	1,260	37.1	272.0	25.8	66.8	555	267.8	1,262	173	79.7
Burley city	NA	NA	NA	NA	783	7	100.0	12.4	2.3	100.0	233	10.6	1,018	82	20.3
Caldwell city	1,541	3107	325	2782	55,613	415	99.0	38.9	8.0	82.7	300	36.7	769	225	12.5
Chubbuck city	706	4986	283	4704	6,429	71	71.8	11.4	0.9	100.0	451	8.4	590	10	5.3
Coeur d'Alene city	2,067	4402	513	3889	64,628	458	53.1	48.9	9.7	58.0	502	55.8	1,224	307	31.6
Eagle city	NA	NA	NA	NA	159,473	477	83.2	5.3	1.5	100.0	173	4.7	226	2	3.6
Garden City city	506	4465	627	3839	16,338	113	41.6	11.4	0.8	100.0	361	10.7	957	17	2.4
Hayden city	NA	NA	NA	NA	21,154	81	97.5	6.4	1.3	72.8	128	6.4	471	31	0.7
Idaho Falls city	1,627	2776	215	2561	9,971	106	100.0	69.3	13.2	98.9	500	71.2	1,228	104	21.5
Jerome city	265	2395	343	2052	4,348	28	100.0	9.6	1.2	73.1	343	14.0	1,264	450	12.2
Kuna city	NA	NA	NA	NA	25,940	116	100.0	5.9	0.6	100.0	105	2.1	128	0	0.7

1 Data for serious crimes have not been adjusted for underreporting. This may affect comparability between geographic areas over time.
2 Per 100,000 population estimated by the FBI.   3 Based on population estimated as of July 1 of the year shown.

Table B. Incorporated Places, Census Designated Places (CDPs), and Minor Civil Divisions (MCDs) of 10,000 or More Population — Land Area, Population, and Households, and Employment

STATE City, town, township, borough, or CDP (county if applicable)	Land area,[1] 2010 (sq mi)	Total persons 2010	Total persons 2014	Percent change 2010–2014	Persons per square mile, 2014	Foreign born	Lives in same house as previous year	Median household income (dollars)	Income of $100,000 or more	Income below poverty level	Percent in labor force	Unemployment rate	Family households	One person households
	1	2	3	4	5	6	7	8	9	10	11	12	13	14
IDAHO—Con.														
Lewiston city	17.231	31,894	32,482	1.8	1,885.1	1.9	84.7	$45,148	12.5	11.2	64.0	5.7	61.5	31.2
Meridian city	27.305	75,130	87,743	16.8	3,213.4	4.9	86.0	$63,225	22.3	8.1	68.8	7.3	77.5	19.3
Moscow city	6.875	23,809	24,767	4.0	3,602.2	6.2	63.1	$33,591	15.4	30.5	63.7	9.2	44.9	29.0
Mountain Home city	6.090	14,209	13,780	-3.0	2,262.5	5.8	77.9	$46,836	11.3	14.6	69.0	7.5	66.6	27.4
Nampa city	31.051	81,748	88,211	7.9	2,840.9	8.4	78.8	$40,083	7.1	20.3	63.3	10.4	71.5	23.6
Pocatello city	32.487	54,230	54,292	0.1	1,671.2	4.0	78.3	$40,792	13.7	18.2	66.6	7.7	62.1	30.1
Post Falls city	14.346	27,572	29,896	8.4	2,083.9	1.8	84.5	$49,736	10.7	14.9	69.5	7.8	72.8	22.3
Rexburg city	9.687	25,468	27,094	6.4	2,797.0	4.5	49.7	$25,606	7.7	40.5	60.6	12.1	75.8	11.2
Twin Falls city	18.318	44,308	46,528	5.0	2,540.0	9.4	77.3	$41,880	10.6	17.6	64.7	7.4	67.7	24.9
Addison village	9.779	36,964	37,297	0.9	3,814.1	33.1	84.4	$53,469	22.2	13.2	70.5	11.7	77.5	19.3
Algonquin village	12.251	30,049	30,410	1.2	2,482.2	12.4	91.8	$100,534	50.4	3.7	75.3	10.0	79.5	15.5
Alsip village	6.503	19,277	19,427	0.8	2,987.6	12.8	90.1	$53,584	20.6	10.9	68.9	12.6	65.0	31.2
Alton city	15.469	27,918	27,177	-2.7	1,756.8	1.1	87.1	$36,076	8.7	20.6	59.6	14.6	57.1	35.4
Antioch village	8.059	14,456	14,411	-0.3	1,788.3	9.4	91.9	$78,942	38.3	11.3	72.2	7.1	74.8	19.9
ILLINOIS	55,518.928	12,831,587	12,880,580	0.4	232.0	13.9	86.8	$57,166	25.2	13.4	66.1	10.0	65.5	28.7
Arlington Heights village	16.602	75,101	76,024	1.2	4,579.3	17.5	89.1	$78,865	38.8	6.6	67.4	6.6	66.4	29.4
Aurora city	44.880	197,952	200,456	1.3	4,466.5	25.7	85.8	$63,569	29.0	12.5	73.1	9.9	74.9	19.9
Barrington village	4.616	10,321	10,373	0.5	2,247.1	9.1	89.8	$110,469	55.8	8.1	63.8	7.8	75.5	19.6
Bartlett village	15.777	41,227	41,632	1.0	2,638.7	19.4	92.1	$94,919	46.6	4.2	73.9	7.0	81.0	16.1
Batavia city	9.591	26,158	26,424	1.0	2,755.0	5.2	92.9	$92,015	45.7	7.6	71.4	8.3	71.9	23.7
Beach Park village	7.108	13,795	13,988	1.4	1,968.0	15.1	89.1	$70,581	25.6	2.5	71.0	8.4	80.0	12.1
Belleville city	22.407	44,074	42,529	-3.5	1,898.0	2.3	88.9	$46,558	16.2	16.4	64.1	7.0	58.3	35.3
Bellwood village	2.398	19,071	19,152	0.4	7,986.2	6.2	91.2	$50,316	16.2	12.1	68.3	15.1	72.5	23.8
Belvidere city	12.085	25,585	25,282	-1.2	2,092.0	15.7	86.3	$49,423	13.2	14.8	66.4	14.0	72.4	23.7
Bensenville village	5.557	18,352	18,487	0.7	3,326.9	33.3	86.6	$60,578	19.9	13.8	73.2	7.8	69.0	26.1
Berwyn city	3.905	56,657	56,693	0.1	14,518.0	25.7	87.9	$54,392	19.2	13.9	68.9	12.7	70.6	24.0
Bloomingdale village	6.787	22,063	22,299	1.1	3,285.3	20.9	85.5	$71,032	30.3	4.9	67.3	6.9	63.4	31.7
Bloomington city	27.272	76,616	78,730	2.8	2,886.8	9.6	82.4	$62,046	28.7	12.1	70.8	6.6	60.2	31.7
Blue Island city	4.071	23,706	23,785	0.3	5,842.4	22.4	89.2	$39,023	11.2	20.2	66.9	15.6	63.4	31.4
Bolingbrook village	24.106	73,366	74,180	1.1	3,077.3	20.4	92.6	$78,230	35.8	7.8	72.1	8.4	81.1	15.8
Bourbonnais village	9.468	18,645	18,534	-0.6	1,957.4	2.5	86.1	$63,707	24.9	11.9	63.2	7.9	73.9	20.3
Bradley village	7.262	15,895	15,677	-1.4	2,158.8	4.6	88.5	$54,187	19.9	9.2	70.2	8.1	63.4	29.0
Bridgeview village	4.149	16,446	16,491	0.3	3,975.0	29.4	88.6	$51,270	13.9	17.4	62.2	11.2	69.0	26.6
Brookfield village	3.063	18,978	19,023	0.2	6,210.4	8.0	88.7	$76,735	33.7	10.7	68.9	6.7	69.9	25.6
Buffalo Grove village	9.470	41,431	41,701	0.7	4,403.4	28.5	89.4	$96,768	48.1	5.5	73.4	6.6	71.8	24.7
Burbank city	4.170	28,925	29,218	1.0	7,007.1	30.4	91.5	$56,869	19.1	10.1	63.6	10.8	77.5	19.6
Burr Ridge village	6.998	10,559	10,761	1.9	1,537.7	20.5	88.5	$113,576	54.9	6.4	59.2	5.2	74.8	21.8
Cahokia village	9.555	15,238	14,588	-4.3	1,526.8	0.7	92.8	$30,394	6.3	31.2	54.7	15.9	68.9	26.5
Calumet City city	7.181	37,042	37,213	0.5	5,182.3	8.3	88.0	$39,530	10.7	21.0	66.1	19.0	59.8	36.0
Campton Hills village	16.909	11,106	11,317	1.9	669.3	5.2	96.3	$117,556	60.5	5.3	66.3	5.8	86.1	10.8
Canton city	7.904	14,704	14,307	-2.7	1,810.0	2.8	80.2	$40,206	11.2	18.0	49.9	8.9	58.1	33.9
Carbondale city	17.240	26,229	26,324	0.4	1,526.9	9.8	62.2	$17,677	8.9	49.3	52.3	11.2	36.1	43.0
Carol Stream village	9.099	39,718	40,349	1.6	4,434.7	21.5	89.1	$74,026	33.4	8.8	77.5	8.5	69.2	27.0
Carpentersville village	7.894	37,691	38,407	1.9	4,865.2	30.4	87.6	$57,978	25.3	13.5	75.1	10.8	80.5	14.2
Cary village	6.244	18,269	17,991	-1.5	2,881.1	9.2	92.2	$104,343	53.0	6.3	75.8	8.0	85.9	10.4
Centralia city	8.194	13,034	12,742	-2.2	1,555.0	2.0	84.0	$32,253	8.2	21.0	56.6	17.5	55.1	39.3
Champaign city	22.584	81,072	84,513	4.2	3,742.1	13.9	67.5	$42,077	18.0	24.5	64.1	7.5	46.8	37.3
Channahon village	15.003	12,560	12,616	0.4	840.9	2.8	97.1	$90,859	45.2	2.6	76.4	6.5	84.8	11.1
Charleston city	8.991	21,836	21,838	0.0	2,428.9	3.4	60.9	$26,844	9.2	32.1	58.8	11.9	44.1	36.0
Chatham village	6.537	11,599	12,212	5.3	1,868.1	2.0	84.0	$78,455	34.3	5.4	76.1	6.1	80.4	16.7
Chicago city	227.766	2,695,598	2,722,389	1.0	11,952.6	20.9	83.6	$47,831	21.6	20.3	66.3	13.2	54.9	36.2
Chicago Heights city	10.194	30,321	30,436	0.4	2,985.8	11.8	90.3	$44,272	13.1	26.2	62.4	18.5	67.8	29.8
Chicago Ridge village	2.268	14,308	14,434	0.9	6,364.3	21.1	83.4	$46,819	14.3	17.1	69.9	11.3	59.1	31.2
Cicero town	5.865	84,241	84,354	0.1	14,383.7	41.0	89.2	$41,882	10.3	20.1	67.3	13.6	80.7	15.2
Collinsville city	14.640	25,558	24,883	-2.6	1,699.7	1.8	86.2	$52,821	17.6	14.8	66.9	10.2	61.6	32.1
Country Club Hills city	4.830	16,543	16,865	1.9	3,492.0	2.0	93.6	$60,100	22.1	13.3	64.0	17.5	68.5	29.0
Crest Hill city	9.041	20,840	20,771	-0.3	2,297.5	9.8	85.7	$48,842	14.1	12.2	54.5	8.5	60.7	34.2
Crestwood village	3.048	10,950	11,029	0.7	3,619.0	6.8	92.4	$54,330	16.4	9.4	60.4	10.4	48.8	44.9
Crystal Lake city	18.258	40,739	40,493	-0.6	2,217.8	10.8	89.7	$80,136	36.5	5.7	72.8	7.1	73.0	22.2
Danville city	17.980	33,019	32,243	-2.4	1,793.2	3.9	83.8	$35,581	9.5	25.1	54.2	14.3	59.2	36.0
Darien city	6.200	22,087	22,315	1.0	3,599.4	17.3	91.1	$77,188	36.2	6.7	64.4	8.4	68.5	27.3
Decatur city	42.245	76,126	74,010	-2.8	1,751.9	2.4	79.8	$39,588	12.0	20.7	61.5	13.9	56.3	37.4
Deerfield village	5.528	18,233	18,385	0.8	3,325.9	9.0	95.3	$135,754	62.4	2.3	68.4	5.8	75.0	22.6
DeKalb city	15.214	44,117	44,054	-0.1	2,895.7	8.8	65.8	$38,357	15.0	29.4	65.2	12.0	50.7	32.6
Des Plaines city	14.282	58,364	58,947	1.0	4,127.4	29.7	91.5	$65,953	27.1	6.8	66.6	6.7	65.0	30.3
Dixon city	7.389	15,735	15,285	-2.9	2,068.7	2.6	81.6	$45,250	12.8	15.0	53.5	8.7	59.7	32.9
Dolton village	4.568	23,153	23,307	0.7	5,102.4	2.6	88.3	$46,184	13.2	20.1	66.1	24.1	72.5	23.0
Downers Grove village	14.441	48,867	49,715	1.7	3,442.6	9.7	89.8	$85,020	42.8	6.7	68.3	6.9	69.3	27.1
East Moline city	14.701	21,302	21,175	-0.6	1,440.4	13.2	82.5	$40,647	10.6	19.8	56.2	10.0	58.8	36.6
East Peoria city	20.228	23,437	23,375	-0.3	1,155.6	1.7	88.9	$49,873	18.7	11.9	64.4	7.4	64.0	30.2
East St. Louis city	13.901	26,917	26,672	-0.9	1,918.7	0.4	87.7	$19,856	2.7	41.9	47.0	16.4	58.0	38.6
Edwardsville city	19.627	24,293	24,758	1.9	1,261.4	4.1	76.2	$70,791	32.5	15.0	65.2	5.0	62.7	24.4
Effingham city	9.926	12,329	12,577	2.0	1,267.0	1.6	82.9	$44,674	12.3	15.5	65.8	7.0	54.9	37.2
Elgin city	37.306	108,146	111,117	2.7	2,978.5	26.0	86.6	$59,832	24.4	12.7	71.0	9.6	71.7	23.4
Elk Grove Village village	11.445	33,127	33,379	0.8	2,916.5	18.6	90.9	$68,188	30.6	7.0	69.7	6.2	64.5	31.2
Elmhurst city	10.258	44,136	45,751	3.7	4,460.0	8.8	89.8	$95,240	48.3	4.2	65.7	7.3	72.0	24.3
Elmwood Park village	1.908	24,883	24,954	0.3	13,075.9	27.2	90.4	$55,905	22.4	8.9	66.2	10.4	65.9	29.6
Evanston city	7.779	74,486	75,658	1.6	9,725.7	19.0	78.1	$69,347	36.0	13.6	64.5	8.2	54.1	36.7
Evergreen Park village	3.163	19,852	19,935	0.4	6,303.5	5.4	91.4	$65,744	29.5	9.1	67.8	11.4	68.2	28.3
Fairview Heights city	11.368	17,078	16,901	-1.0	1,486.7	5.1	90.0	$60,427	20.4	7.9	68.0	5.7	63.0	31.7
Forest Park village	2.402	14,167	14,196	0.2	5,910.7	13.7	82.2	$50,749	18.2	9.1	74.9	11.6	46.1	49.4
Fox Lake village	7.992	10,623	10,578	-0.4	1,323.6	11.0	87.6	$54,013	17.4	11.8	67.8	14.1	62.2	34.0
Frankfort village	15.058	17,808	18,446	3.6	1,225.0	4.5	91.7	$110,829	54.5	4.5	66.8	7.0	83.6	14.0
Franklin Park village	4.768	18,330	18,404	0.4	3,860.0	35.5	92.9	$56,985	19.6	10.9	70.6	9.0	70.0	25.0

1 Dry land or land partially or temporarily covered by water.
2 16 years old and over.

Table B. Incorporated Places, Census Designated Places (CDPs), and Minor Civil Divisions (MCDs) of 10,000 or More Population — Crime, Construction, and Local Government Finance

STATE City, town, township, borough, or CDP (county if applicable)	Serious crimes known to police, 2014[1] Total number	Rate[2] Total	Rate[2] Violent	Rate[2] Property	New residential construction authorized by building permits, 2014 Value ($1,000)	Number of housing units	Percent single family	Local government finance, 2012 General revenue Total (mil dol)	Intergovernmental Total (mil dol)	Intergovernmental Percent from state gov.	Taxes per capita[3]	General expenditure Total (mil dol)	Per capita[3] Total	Per capita[3] Capital outlays	Debt outstanding (mil dol)
	15	16	17	18	19	20	21	22	23	24	25	26	27	28	29
IDAHO—Con.															
Lewiston city	1,193	3668	172	3496	9,573	55	47.3	41.1	7.7	98.7	511	40.2	1,252	159	6.6
Meridian city	1,308	1526	89	1437	236,665	1,260	60.6	53.9	9.9	100.0	290	42.4	528	89	1.3
Moscow city	715	2894	49	2846	12,119	88	25.0	21.7	4.5	71.6	260	21.8	891	90	16.8
Mountain Home city	299	2183	343	1840	7,334	45	73.3	9.9	1.5	82.0	383	10.5	761	95	14.4
Nampa city	2,806	3198	320	2878	52,956	389	78.7	96.5	19.8	60.9	476	87.0	1,036	141	58.7
Pocatello city	1,359	2500	258	2242	7,408	65	100.0	63.5	14.4	48.1	493	67.9	1,239	121	24.5
Post Falls city	903	3033	171	2861	32,476	161	96.3	27.0	5.7	100.0	307	21.0	732	124	11.1
Rexburg city	277	1035	34	1001	50,697	355	14.9	28.6	9.7	87.9	188	28.9	1,102	434	14.4
Twin Falls city	1,586	3421	255	3167	37,828	250	80.4	39.5	5.6	70.4	433	33.6	747	116	43.5
Addison village	677	1806	173	1633	2,260	6	100.0	44.5	12.7	100.0	594	39.8	1,067	5	59.7
Algonquin village	465	1521	59	1462	14,262	81	22.2	27.6	11.4	100.0	415	21.1	704	36	13.6
Alsip village	NA	NA	NA	NA	145	1	100.0	26.7	6.3	100.0	718	22.1	1,138	47	23.7
Alton city	1,383	5093	545	4548	70	1	100.0	40.8	15.1	100.0	535	34.8	1,267	124	20.7
Antioch village	241	1674	111	1563	0	0	0.0	14.3	5.7	85.2	381	13.8	957	147	20.9
ILLINOIS	315,048	2446	370	2076	4,211,740	20,578	51.3	X	X	X	X	X	X	X	X
Arlington Heights village	786	1031	56	975	32,625	100	96.0	98.7	20.5	94.8	897	81.7	1,078	28	53.7
Aurora city	3,540	1766	278	1488	26,275	101	100.0	238.0	71.0	89.2	671	225.1	1,127	121	553.2
Barrington village	106	1022	19	1003	7,271	16	100.0	24.8	6.0	83.6	683	24.0	2,322	415	27.3
Bartlett village	250	598	34	565	3,280	16	100.0	31.0	7.0	96.0	415	29.2	703	48	54.9
Batavia city	408	1543	136	1407	6,395	22	100.0	30.0	8.1	95.0	500	38.7	1,468	511	54.8
Beach Park village	NA	NA	NA	NA	6,223	32	100.0	4.0	2.4	100.0	58	4.3	313	51	4.1
Belleville city	1,731	4063	422	3640	4,147	28	100.0	58.9	17.0	97.2	641	95.3	2,198	622	71.6
Bellwood village	549	2862	600	2263	19,000	89	0.0	35.3	4.2	93.8	1270	31.6	1,649	101	94.0
Belvidere city	481	1902	182	1720	790	5	100.0	21.8	7.4	92.3	331	17.2	679	20	5.1
Bensenville village	300	1615	118	1496	1,435	5	100.0	33.7	10.2	98.9	541	35.0	1,895	494	66.0
Berwyn city	1,290	2272	224	2048	282	1	100.0	69.4	14.0	73.5	679	80.9	1,425	107	97.3
Bloomingdale village	582	2597	71	2525	300	1	100.0	30.2	10.8	97.3	584	29.6	1,330	263	37.6
Bloomington city	2,029	2554	419	2135	20,013	108	94.4	114.7	26.3	94.5	704	104.9	1,349	122	96.3
Blue Island city	773	3246	571	2675	0	0	0.0	25.0	5.8	94.7	497	24.5	1,028	65	10.0
Bolingbrook village	1,142	1542	211	1332	20,448	124	100.0	85.6	23.0	91.1	588	83.2	1,124	65	272.1
Bourbonnais village	410	2208	162	2047	6,556	44	100.0	15.6	6.1	94.7	94	14.4	771	64	40.0
Bradley village	673	4269	140	4129	4,697	24	66.7	14.8	8.3	100.0	198	16.1	1,014	82	11.3
Bridgeview village	503	3053	170	2883	0	0	0.0	32.4	11.3	99.5	802	39.7	2,401	234	222.0
Brookfield village	249	1307	152	1155	1,115	10	10.0	21.5	4.1	83.3	687	19.9	1,047	83	13.9
Buffalo Grove village	299	715	24	691	2,179	8	100.0	47.2	12.4	82.1	535	50.5	1,215	102	2.2
Burbank city	445	1520	150	1370	1,638	14	100.0	19.3	6.5	97.7	410	17.0	584	9	10.1
Burr Ridge village	105	973	28	945	16,116	28	100.0	10.7	4.2	88.2	373	8.7	816	38	8.2
Cahokia village	521	3565	315	3250	0	0	0.0	12.8	4.1	82.9	391	10.8	727	20	4.0
Calumet City city	1,752	4699	515	4184	0	0	0.0	50.9	11.6	90.1	919	45.9	1,232	103	52.6
Campton Hills village	36	317	18	300	3,580	6	100.0	2.4	1.7	100.0	57	2.2	192	29	0.1
Canton city	290	2018	132	1886	135	1	100.0	12.8	5.6	86.1	273	16.6	1,143	308	21.8
Carbondale city	1,078	4088	523	3565	16,260	130	6.9	32.4	10.9	88.9	533	31.8	1,202	47	33.7
Carol Stream village	427	1053	109	945	4,648	36	100.0	28.1	11.1	91.6	252	25.3	631	60	7.2
Carpentersville village	622	1621	86	1535	5,221	26	100.0	32.2	12.8	86.2	332	36.5	955	239	49.4
Cary village	137	763	100	663	3,920	12	100.0	11.8	3.4	99.5	257	10.5	581	125	11.6
Centralia city	716	5626	778	4848	0	0	0.0	15.4	5.5	93.6	233	16.6	1,289	81	7.5
Champaign city	3,064	3648	770	2878	142,414	914	10.1	100.8	38.9	81.8	597	101.7	1,229	343	74.8
Channahon village	65	516	32	484	2,343	11	81.8	34.9	12.3	99.5	1507	32.0	2,546	0	36.5
Charleston city	135	614	132	482	2,116	9	100.0	18.2	7.5	92.8	259	20.8	950	174	12.9
Chatham village	105	862	148	714	9,813	81	82.7	5.9	2.5	98.5	190	7.9	661	10	6.6
Chicago city	109,484	4019	886	3133	959,625	5,750	9.3	6690.6	1758.6	65.4	930	7439.1	2,740	425	21209.6
Chicago Heights city	1,114	3658	653	3004	0	0	0.0	44.6	13.6	76.8	750	45.7	1,500	202	67.7
Chicago Ridge village	612	4226	145	4081	0	0	0.0	16.9	5.7	87.2	614	14.7	1,020	62	8.2
Cicero town	2,128	2529	385	2144	0	0	0.0	111.4	23.7	88.5	863	108.6	1,285	185	108.3
Collinsville city	805	3228	208	3019	2,548	18	100.0	30.2	11.1	94.1	478	29.1	1,154	106	47.8
Country Club Hills city	663	3907	289	3618	0	0	0.0	20.1	4.8	96.4	742	36.8	2,184	224	24.4
Crest Hill city	264	1271	193	1079	920	7	100.0	14.5	6.7	83.9	179	15.3	733	188	28.8
Crestwood village	NA	NA	NA	NA	0	0	0.0	10.1	5.4	99.7	282	10.0	906	35	33.7
Crystal Lake city	894	2219	129	2090	2,949	18	100.0	53.2	19.4	99.7	576	54.2	1,341	305	42.4
Danville city	2,226	6870	1074	5796	760	5	100.0	42.4	15.6	82.1	590	42.8	1,309	210	12.0
Darien city	343	1530	58	1472	400	1	100.0	14.9	8.0	100.0	251	14.7	661	131	7.7
Decatur city	2,580	3469	477	2992	441	2	100.0	75.9	32.1	85.6	458	89.1	1,182	206	96.9
Deerfield village	136	743	38	705	48,076	287	13.6	32.2	8.0	93.1	915	48.5	2,655	1,133	102.0
DeKalb city	1,345	3071	409	2663	0	0	0.0	53.3	19.6	68.3	614	45.2	1,031	260	29.2
Des Plaines city	771	1306	90	1216	2,312	4	100.0	103.1	31.2	96.3	982	92.0	1,563	249	71.7
Dixon city	246	1614	92	1522	75	1	100.0	16.1	6.4	97.3	318	17.6	1,136	328	37.3
Dolton village	NA	NA	NA	NA	0	0	0.0	9.0	3.3	100.0	119	10.8	465	0	2.4
Downers Grove village	683	1370	62	1308	30,575	76	100.0	65.8	18.9	98.8	793	58.7	1,190	157	80.1
East Moline city	520	2433	370	2063	300	2	0.0	29.9	13.2	91.7	378	34.8	1,632	680	37.7
East Peoria city	727	3091	332	2759	9,085	47	100.0	58.2	29.9	97.8	691	80.5	3,426	2,029	102.0
East St. Louis city	2,062	7774	3646	4128	24,904	207	2.4	38.6	19.9	85.1	592	38.3	1,439	101	25.4
Edwardsville city	350	1414	77	1337	22,467	155	22.6	27.3	9.0	100.0	468	26.8	1,097	107	25.9
Effingham city	461	3653	412	3241	3,623	17	100.0	23.9	12.5	88.0	601	29.8	2,372	965	16.7
Elgin city	2,217	2005	199	1806	56,032	393	84.7	136.9	44.5	93.0	605	125.2	1,141	155	106.3
Elk Grove Village village	529	1580	63	1517	0	0	0.0	60.1	13.5	93.1	1113	64.9	1,946	411	52.6
Elmhurst city	526	1146	44	1102	67,001	145	100.0	70.4	17.9	99.2	806	65.4	1,450	192	61.9
Elmwood Park village	345	1380	68	1312	1,200	6	100.0	24.8	4.6	97.7	717	23.5	940	4	5.0
Evanston city	2,051	2705	199	2506	7,818	24	79.2	123.4	24.9	70.5	858	116.5	1,544	176	237.9
Evergreen Park village	596	2983	135	2848	575	3	100.0	28.9	10.7	89.6	574	28.8	1,444	308	20.4
Fairview Heights city	701	4152	142	4009	10,579	68	100.0	19.4	9.4	100.0	533	16.4	967	39	7.1
Forest Park village	575	4043	323	3719	150	1	100.0	22.8	6.7	94.7	802	23.8	1,671	106	14.7
Fox Lake village	156	1482	105	1378	80	1	100.0	18.0	4.3	98.7	432	15.3	1,451	49	7.9
Frankfort village	152	833	22	811	32,054	103	100.0	20.5	7.8	100.0	337	20.2	1,119	192	3.7
Franklin Park village	315	1708	168	1539	0	0	0.0	34.0	5.6	100.0	1173	34.0	1,849	293	56.0

1 Data for serious crimes have not been adjusted for underreporting. This may affect comparability between geographic areas over time.
2 Per 100,000 population estimated by the FBI.   3 Based on population estimated as of July 1 of the year shown.

Table B. Incorporated Places, Census Designated Places (CDPs), and Minor Civil Divisions (MCDs) of 10,000 or More Population — **Land Area, Population, and Households, and Employment**

STATE City, town, township, borough, or CDP (county if applicable)	Land area,[1] 2010 (sq mi)	Total persons 2010	Total persons 2014	Percent change 2010–2014	Persons per square mile, 2014	Foreign born	Lives in same house as previous year	Median household income (dollars)	Income of $100,000 or more	Income below poverty level	Percent in labor force	Unemployment rate	Family households	One person households
	1	2	3	4	5	6	7	8	9	10	11	12	13	14
ILLINOIS—Con.														
Freeport city	11.763	25,637	24,851	-3.1	2,112.6	1.9	82.1	$36,250	9.5	19.2	60.1	15.2	57.1	37.2
Gages Lake CDP	2.992	10,198	NA	NA	NA	11.6	89.0	$80,476	41.2	5.9	74.6	12.0	74.7	23.9
Galesburg city	17.687	32,189	31,659	-1.6	1,789.9	3.2	85.9	$33,369	9.9	21.0	50.9	10.3	51.4	40.6
Geneva city	9.756	21,495	21,742	1.1	2,228.6	4.2	91.5	$93,588	47.4	5.7	70.5	7.6	76.3	21.3
Glen Carbon village	10.062	12,936	12,947	0.1	1,286.7	4.9	83.7	$69,419	33.0	8.9	70.5	6.1	67.4	23.8
Glendale Heights village	5.370	34,212	34,530	0.9	6,430.6	36.8	84.9	$60,879	19.9	10.7	75.1	10.5	72.0	23.3
Glen Ellyn village	6.626	27,369	27,763	1.4	4,189.8	11.8	88.6	$91,051	46.6	8.4	67.6	9.1	69.0	27.9
Glenview village	13.981	44,695	46,767	4.6	3,345.0	21.8	90.8	$92,304	47.6	4.3	61.2	5.5	70.8	27.2
Godfrey village	34.680	18,007	17,782	-1.2	512.7	2.1	88.7	$60,909	24.2	6.4	60.1	7.3	67.5	29.3
Granite City city	19.355	29,849	29,183	-2.2	1,507.8	2.0	87.0	$43,759	13.7	17.9	59.2	10.6	61.1	33.8
Grayslake village	9.866	20,883	21,018	0.6	2,130.4	12.7	87.7	$87,967	42.3	5.3	75.0	5.0	73.8	22.0
Gurnee village	13.488	31,232	31,207	-0.1	2,313.7	15.1	88.0	$85,141	40.8	4.9	72.4	7.9	69.2	26.2
Hanover Park village	6.331	37,958	38,476	1.4	6,077.2	34.8	87.7	$66,359	23.0	11.6	73.2	9.6	83.4	13.2
Harvey city	6.308	25,282	25,347	0.3	4,018.2	7.6	90.3	$25,074	6.6	37.6	54.3	25.6	60.2	37.3
Hazel Crest village	3.390	14,100	14,182	0.6	4,183.4	2.3	90.0	$50,042	17.9	17.4	61.0	19.6	65.0	32.3
Herrin city	9.723	12,523	12,852	2.6	1,321.8	0.6	88.0	$40,549	11.6	15.3	61.9	9.0	63.5	33.4
Hickory Hills city	2.827	14,049	14,177	0.9	5,014.1	28.1	89.3	$57,880	22.4	12.5	65.6	11.6	75.9	21.6
Highland Park city	12.200	29,728	29,871	0.5	2,448.4	12.5	90.6	$115,382	56.5	5.0	62.7	6.3	73.7	24.6
Hinsdale village	4.615	16,816	17,446	3.7	3,780.4	10.8	89.8	$163,558	62.7	6.4	58.9	6.1	85.5	13.2
Hoffman Estates village	20.808	51,890	52,347	0.9	2,515.7	30.0	87.8	$83,518	40.4	4.9	74.8	6.6	78.5	17.3
Homer Glen village	22.231	24,224	24,364	0.6	1,096.0	11.2	95.4	$92,547	44.8	3.6	68.5	6.9	82.4	15.7
Homewood village	5.217	19,323	19,464	0.7	3,730.6	4.3	91.7	$68,998	31.3	7.2	68.1	10.4	68.7	28.4
Huntley village	14.074	24,292	25,603	5.4	1,819.2	9.0	91.0	$75,792	35.7	1.4	54.1	5.6	71.4	26.4
Jacksonville city	10.462	19,446	19,159	-1.5	1,831.3	2.5	76.5	$39,171	13.2	17.0	59.2	10.5	59.2	35.0
Joliet city	62.712	147,459	147,928	0.3	2,358.8	15.1	87.4	$62,008	24.5	11.8	70.3	11.0	72.5	22.3
Justice village	2.839	12,926	13,022	0.7	4,587.2	21.8	83.5	$52,203	16.0	14.3	74.5	12.6	72.7	19.1
Kankakee city	14.835	27,537	26,860	-2.5	1,810.5	9.9	84.0	$32,265	8.6	29.0	58.1	15.5	60.3	33.0
Kewanee city	6.713	12,916	12,596	-2.5	1,876.3	6.1	88.6	$37,881	8.2	16.9	58.4	8.6	60.1	34.7
La Grange village	2.524	15,550	15,759	1.3	6,244.7	8.8	89.2	$98,971	49.3	7.4	65.2	6.7	72.8	23.7
La Grange Park village	2.232	13,579	13,665	0.6	6,123.2	10.9	90.3	$70,399	34.8	6.8	64.2	7.4	64.5	32.6
Lake Forest city	17.194	19,377	19,379	0.0	1,127.1	8.7	88.5	$151,000	65.5	3.8	54.6	6.2	78.9	19.3
Lake in the Hills village	10.433	28,971	28,893	-0.3	2,769.3	10.6	92.3	$83,149	38.6	3.5	78.1	8.8	77.4	18.5
Lake Zurich village	6.882	19,676	20,054	1.9	2,914.1	16.4	93.2	$108,294	55.9	4.2	76.5	6.9	81.6	16.3
Lansing village	7.461	28,374	28,522	0.5	3,822.7	7.5	92.6	$49,684	19.8	12.9	67.1	13.2	63.4	32.7
Lemont village	8.162	16,091	16,661	3.5	2,041.3	14.5	91.0	$87,410	42.7	4.1	68.4	8.1	72.9	23.1
Libertyville village	8.802	20,327	20,512	0.9	2,330.3	9.4	89.6	$112,572	55.4	4.4	66.1	5.2	74.1	23.7
Lincoln city	6.396	14,502	14,162	-2.3	2,214.1	1.6	81.9	$42,818	11.7	18.2	58.7	8.2	61.4	33.1
Lincolnwood village	2.692	12,590	12,687	0.8	4,713.5	39.1	94.6	$95,680	47.4	4.5	60.1	5.8	80.0	18.2
Lindenhurst village	4.538	14,384	14,468	0.6	3,188.2	8.8	89.5	$88,633	42.7	4.4	74.3	9.1	77.7	18.7
Lisle village	6.876	22,451	22,827	1.7	3,319.6	13.8	82.6	$74,041	38.4	7.8	70.0	7.2	62.4	30.9
Lockport city	11.381	24,886	25,119	0.9	2,207.0	7.4	93.6	$79,845	37.0	4.6	75.4	9.2	73.5	23.5
Lombard village	10.236	43,395	43,893	1.1	4,288.0	11.6	88.6	$70,415	30.6	6.4	69.8	8.0	63.1	31.8
Loves Park city	16.416	24,001	23,551	-1.9	1,434.6	5.7	90.1	$50,593	14.5	10.7	69.3	10.9	62.2	32.2
Lyons village	2.186	10,729	10,773	0.4	4,928.6	22.5	90.0	$51,281	12.6	12.3	66.3	8.5	63.5	31.5
McHenry city	14.605	26,994	26,630	-1.3	1,823.3	8.9	89.3	$62,580	24.8	8.5	72.2	11.4	68.7	26.6
Machesney Park village	12.685	23,495	23,036	-2.0	1,815.9	4.5	89.0	$54,395	15.8	9.6	69.5	11.5	72.9	21.3
Macomb city	10.894	19,294	18,943	-1.8	1,738.9	4.9	61.6	$27,007	14.4	36.6	54.1	12.9	44.5	39.8
Marion city	16.240	17,192	17,438	1.4	1,073.8	3.4	81.9	$42,489	15.3	18.0	59.3	7.6	61.4	32.2
Markham city	5.303	12,508	12,688	1.4	2,392.6	3.1	95.0	$34,055	8.7	30.1	53.2	21.9	65.3	29.9
Matteson village	9.319	19,009	19,156	0.8	2,055.7	4.1	91.0	$67,170	30.5	9.8	70.4	15.0	71.0	27.2
Mattoon city	10.312	18,555	18,221	-1.9	1,765.9	0.8	81.4	$36,803	9.5	18.9	63.3	12.0	60.4	33.7
Maywood village	2.717	24,090	24,133	0.2	8,883.2	10.6	88.9	$43,884	14.4	19.1	61.5	18.5	73.4	23.4
Melrose Park village	4.239	25,414	25,511	0.4	6,018.7	38.7	86.8	$45,697	14.4	14.6	69.4	11.4	74.4	22.4
Midlothian village	2.819	14,819	14,911	0.6	5,289.0	8.6	90.3	$62,036	19.4	10.1	72.1	13.9	70.9	26.2
Minooka village	9.412	10,924	11,194	2.5	1,189.3	4.3	92.9	$84,453	37.4	6.0	75.5	8.1	84.6	13.4
Mokena village	8.817	18,738	19,447	3.8	2,205.5	5.2	95.5	$100,887	50.5	3.4	72.4	7.1	81.4	15.5
Moline city	16.547	43,471	42,685	-1.8	2,579.6	9.4	88.1	$50,209	16.0	10.7	65.5	8.0	61.7	34.4
Montgomery village	9.329	18,377	19,301	5.0	2,068.8	14.4	86.2	$76,207	30.0	5.0	75.3	7.6	76.0	21.0
Morris city	9.470	13,636	14,135	3.7	1,492.7	5.2	85.2	$57,796	24.1	12.2	64.3	8.1	63.5	30.6
Morton village	12.957	16,273	16,499	1.4	1,273.3	2.8	88.7	$70,878	30.6	5.4	63.4	3.9	67.4	28.5
Morton Grove village	5.088	23,270	23,497	1.0	4,618.0	39.9	90.8	$73,939	34.5	7.1	60.8	6.6	76.4	21.6
Mount Prospect village	10.346	54,243	54,951	1.3	5,311.3	32.3	89.5	$69,155	30.8	4.1	68.8	6.6	69.7	25.7
Mount Vernon city	14.421	15,283	15,177	-0.7	1,052.4	2.1	76.1	$33,943	10.7	23.7	60.0	13.4	53.4	40.8
Mundelein village	9.571	31,012	31,562	1.8	3,297.7	28.9	88.2	$78,635	37.9	6.3	74.3	9.4	76.2	20.3
Naperville city	38.636	142,087	146,128	2.8	3,782.2	18.1	87.6	$109,512	54.2	4.9	70.1	6.6	76.7	19.5
New Lenox village	15.976	24,381	25,426	4.3	1,591.5	2.8	91.4	$96,327	47.8	2.9	72.8	5.8	81.1	16.0
Niles village	5.846	29,803	30,000	0.7	5,132.0	43.5	90.7	$48,666	21.3	10.7	55.1	7.5	66.9	30.7
Normal town	18.646	52,535	54,594	3.9	2,928.0	5.1	68.7	$52,134	24.0	22.9	67.7	5.6	52.8	29.0
Norridge village	1.810	14,572	14,674	0.7	8,105.8	34.1	94.6	$55,707	20.1	9.9	57.6	7.1	67.5	30.4
North Aurora village	7.236	16,732	17,342	3.6	2,396.7	9.7	89.9	$81,350	37.1	6.5	74.3	7.8	74.5	21.2
Northbrook village	13.194	33,173	33,655	1.5	2,550.7	19.1	91.1	$115,085	56.5	4.3	58.8	5.4	76.3	21.7
North Chicago city	7.942	32,575	30,395	-6.7	3,827.4	16.4	58.4	$41,866	13.2	23.9	77.0	16.2	67.7	25.6
Northlake city	3.167	12,326	12,372	0.4	3,906.0	27.8	92.0	$58,262	19.6	11.5	67.3	8.0	70.2	26.5
Oak Forest city	5.950	27,962	28,174	0.8	4,734.9	9.0	92.4	$71,082	31.7	7.8	71.5	11.8	71.3	24.5
Oak Lawn village	8.571	56,687	57,034	0.6	6,654.4	15.3	92.6	$57,567	23.5	8.7	63.6	11.8	65.0	30.6
Oak Park village	4.700	51,878	52,008	0.3	11,065.9	10.8	86.0	$78,895	40.0	9.1	72.9	8.1	59.5	34.8
O'Fallon city	14.855	28,674	29,069	1.4	1,956.8	3.9	85.5	$79,795	41.3	7.1	68.6	9.0	71.3	25.1
Orland Park village	21.915	56,680	58,666	3.5	2,677.0	13.2	92.2	$79,334	39.1	5.3	64.1	7.4	71.6	25.1
Oswego village	15.556	30,345	33,099	9.1	2,127.7	4.9	91.7	$97,323	47.0	4.0	76.5	5.4	84.0	13.8
Ottawa city	11.951	18,758	18,428	-1.8	1,541.9	2.1	87.3	$46,422	17.7	16.1	64.5	12.4	64.3	30.2
Palatine village	13.617	68,555	69,387	1.2	5,095.5	25.2	86.6	$72,180	35.1	7.7	72.5	7.6	66.0	28.2
Palos Heights city	3.772	12,515	12,597	0.7	3,339.3	9.0	92.0	$77,575	41.3	3.8	55.4	9.9	70.7	25.7
Palos Hills city	4.248	17,484	17,627	0.8	4,149.1	29.3	92.1	$53,892	20.9	8.1	64.2	8.9	61.1	33.8
Park Forest village	4.963	21,971	22,034	0.3	4,440.1	3.1	91.5	$48,319	12.3	17.9	66.0	19.0	60.8	34.9
Park Ridge city	7.090	37,480	37,856	1.0	5,339.4	15.0	93.1	$87,626	44.0	4.2	63.8	5.5	73.0	25.0
Pekin city	14.868	34,096	33,824	-0.8	2,274.9	1.4	85.4	$48,544	13.8	13.2	61.3	8.3	62.4	31.6

1 Dry land or land partially or temporarily covered by water.
2 16 years old and over.

Table B. Incorporated Places, Census Designated Places (CDPs), and Minor Civil Divisions (MCDs) of 10,000 or More Population — **Crime, Construction, and Local Government Finance**

STATE City, town, township, borough, or CDP (county if applicable)	Serious crimes known to police, 2014[1]: Total number	Serious crimes: Rate[2]: Total	Rate[2]: Violent	Rate[2]: Property	New residential construction authorized by building permits, 2014: Value ($1,000)	Number of housing units	Percent single family	Local government finance, 2012: General revenue: Total (mil dol)	General revenue: Intergovernmental: Total (mil dol)	Intergovernmental: Percent from state gov.	Taxes per capita[3]	General expenditure: Total (mil dol)	General expenditure: Per capita[3]: Total	Per capita[3]: Capital outlays	Debt outstanding (mil dol)
	15	16	17	18	19	20	21	22	23	24	25	26	27	28	29
ILLINOIS—Con.															
Freeport city	686	2756	193	2563	272	1	100.0	29.6	13.3	99.7	317	28.8	1,144	64	32.6
Gages Lake CDP	NA	NA	NA	NA	NA	NA	NA	NA	NA	NA	NA	NA	NA	NA	NA
Galesburg city	1,161	3681	400	3282	396	3	100.0	39.9	19.3	93.4	455	38.4	1,207	64	27.4
Geneva city	184	846	32	814	7,985	20	100.0	27.4	9.8	99.8	450	25.4	1,171	125	61.3
Glen Carbon village	NA	NA	NA	NA	12,567	38	100.0	12.0	4.0	98.2	372	9.3	718	34	9.7
Glendale Heights village	537	1547	78	1469	0	0	0.0	35.6	10.2	99.2	460	43.0	1,246	422	49.6
Glen Ellyn village	366	1314	83	1231	22,236	52	100.0	37.6	7.6	88.9	602	32.5	1,176	174	13.3
Glenview village	404	886	39	847	85,084	359	23.7	101.0	27.2	76.5	1377	95.5	2,120	282	137.4
Godfrey village	NA	NA	NA	NA	4,396	32	15.6	8.2	4.1	100.0	88	8.3	465	114	0.8
Granite City city	NA	NA	NA	NA	4,324	26	23.1	40.9	13.0	100.0	629	45.0	1,521	211	30.0
Grayslake village	300	1420	114	1306	475	1	100.0	19.0	5.6	83.6	244	15.3	729	166	0.0
Gurnee village	1,420	4541	106	4435	1,353	4	100.0	38.2	22.9	85.8	307	34.9	1,121	11	16.1
Hanover Park village	378	978	106	872	0	0	0.0	38.2	10.2	89.4	563	53.4	1,392	426	24.0
Harvey city	1,539	6065	1296	4768	0	0	0.0	23.0	6.4	100.0	543	25.1	990	34	50.8
Hazel Crest village	545	3832	506	3326	0	0	0.0	15.4	2.6	97.8	660	12.0	845	3	2.4
Herrin city	397	3074	85	2989	6,613	35	82.9	9.5	4.4	92.4	217	10.3	810	71	5.3
Hickory Hills city	185	1302	106	1197	614	3	100.0	9.8	3.8	98.2	268	10.4	739	41	0.9
Highland Park city	354	1183	64	1120	20,218	28	100.0	56.2	12.1	93.3	978	47.5	1,591	94	44.8
Hinsdale village	177	1019	6	1013	51,239	90	74.4	25.7	7.2	99.4	781	22.5	1,312	201	12.5
Hoffman Estates village	608	1158	95	1063	400	1	100.0	82.1	13.5	91.6	982	64.6	1,237	110	193.6
Homer Glen village	172	707	21	686	12,525	40	100.0	11.2	9.9	87.2	48	7.6	314	16	0.0
Homewood village	607	3118	175	2943	0	0	0.0	20.2	6.7	100.0	432	26.7	1,372	186	1.9
Huntley village	215	843	27	816	24,426	193	100.0	18.4	6.4	75.7	344	15.7	635	202	46.7
Jacksonville city	526	2743	94	2649	468	2	100.0	19.7	7.1	95.7	377	19.5	1,010	53	31.7
Joliet city	3,483	2356	335	2021	26,480	122	100.0	202.1	70.4	93.0	488	177.8	1,199	22	61.9
Justice village	151	1157	138	1019	320	2	100.0	9.0	2.6	73.5	318	8.8	673	47	12.8
Kankakee city	1,453	5376	818	4559	562	6	100.0	60.8	25.8	88.2	735	66.7	2,438	258	78.1
Kewanee city	462	3661	293	3367	840	3	100.0	11.5	4.3	99.8	208	11.5	898	176	15.7
La Grange village	170	1078	51	1027	8,269	19	100.0	17.3	4.8	100.0	669	17.5	1,113	151	8.4
La Grange Park village	87	636	37	600	1,344	4	100.0	9.4	2.7	98.3	353	9.6	706	124	5.3
Lake Forest city	147	760	10	750	13,677	15	100.0	53.9	6.5	100.0	1900	55.0	2,844	536	61.4
Lake in the Hills village	157	543	59	484	8,698	62	9.7	20.2	7.5	78.9	314	18.0	620	82	7.6
Lake Zurich village	315	1571	30	1541	3,541	18	100.0	32.7	11.0	92.4	581	29.1	1,461	91	36.4
Lansing village	1,262	4421	319	4102	0	0	0.0	33.0	8.0	94.6	649	35.4	1,241	283	20.8
Lemont village	178	1071	42	1029	17,178	78	100.0	13.4	4.0	88.4	443	14.6	894	224	37.7
Libertyville village	276	1349	54	1295	11,653	20	100.0	35.9	8.7	95.2	634	32.1	1,577	211	26.2
Lincoln city	482	3386	492	2894	1,275	2	100.0	10.2	5.3	100.0	114	9.0	626	20	7.2
Lincolnwood village	443	3482	63	3420	4,088	7	100.0	22.8	6.2	95.9	1105	21.0	1,656	162	12.4
Lindenhurst village	60	413	48	365	1,505	7	100.0	9.1	2.5	99.6	184	8.0	557	72	5.1
Lisle village	260	1139	26	1113	19,593	93	100.0	24.0	6.5	97.1	611	19.8	874	148	39.3
Lockport city	310	1237	40	1197	15,119	55	89.1	23.5	6.3	92.0	357	16.1	640	36	26.1
Lombard village	908	2062	70	1992	3,340	16	100.0	90.1	27.3	90.2	464	97.6	2,231	83	219.0
Loves Park city	732	3098	309	2789	1,924	23	47.8	12.9	8.3	99.4	143	12.9	542	82	10.8
Lyons village	145	1343	102	1242	125	1	100.0	11.6	2.8	98.7	552	13.2	1,222	212	26.1
McHenry city	356	1339	90	1249	4,254	41	17.1	24.8	12.3	96.4	249	23.4	873	150	17.9
Machesney Park village	440	1902	233	1669	2,016	13	100.0	12.0	9.2	92.3	103	12.2	523	143	11.7
Macomb city	354	1838	280	1557	1,488	8	25.0	23.8	15.8	58.1	181	24.2	1,256	360	5.4
Marion city	187	1071	46	1025	5,215	42	52.4	29.6	11.4	83.0	788	28.9	1,665	284	33.9
Markham city	NA	NA	NA	NA	1,109	10	100.0	19.3	3.6	96.6	1035	21.5	1,698	267	44.0
Matteson village	960	5005	292	4713	6,611	41	2.4	26.7	7.9	95.3	721	26.2	1,370	27	58.2
Mattoon city	377	2058	371	1687	1,042	7	100.0	27.3	12.9	74.6	398	27.3	1,489	166	21.0
Maywood village	893	3694	881	2813	0	0	0.0	34.0	5.8	96.7	978	33.3	1,378	281	25.7
Melrose Park village	413	1617	106	1511	275	1	100.0	43.6	13.9	98.6	918	48.9	1,914	285	80.3
Midlothian village	346	2315	194	2121	560	2	100.0	12.7	3.4	100.0	438	14.5	972	76	20.7
Minooka village	125	1119	63	1056	7,585	34	100.0	8.0	2.9	100.0	283	8.5	770	135	16.1
Mokena village	210	1090	42	1048	36,341	187	29.4	15.3	7.2	100.0	171	16.1	845	211	11.5
Moline city	1,603	3726	363	3364	18,248	108	9.3	72.2	20.2	84.2	819	74.2	1,720	148	79.9
Montgomery village	281	1456	140	1316	5,346	31	100.0	11.9	4.9	97.1	222	10.8	572	16	27.3
Morris city	345	2466	150	2315	9,024	144	10.4	18.2	7.3	97.4	554	16.1	1,164	182	6.1
Morton village	172	1037	42	995	10,358	37	100.0	16.0	6.3	98.7	247	13.6	830	212	2.8
Morton Grove village	328	1391	106	1285	4,914	24	29.2	37.3	6.9	98.7	991	31.9	1,361	20	56.4
Mount Prospect village	608	1108	44	1064	4,975	17	29.4	70.6	19.0	93.5	805	70.0	1,283	142	40.7
Mount Vernon city	1,140	7484	1261	6224	896	7	100.0	21.5	9.1	84.7	525	24.3	1,598	350	10.6
Mundelein village	277	880	57	823	9,284	73	100.0	36.2	9.6	91.1	577	32.6	1,046	94	21.6
Naperville city	1,747	1201	78	1123	121,012	460	81.5	169.6	55.1	89.1	555	143.7	999	101	178.8
New Lenox village	329	1311	96	1215	59,440	162	100.0	25.2	7.3	97.2	354	19.7	800	30	38.4
Niles village	727	2418	90	2328	1,883	3	100.0	48.5	18.9	99.5	776	41.3	1,378	19	18.8
Normal town	1,160	2102	185	1917	8,273	87	93.1	80.5	31.2	99.5	581	77.3	1,435	387	87.9
Norridge village	476	3235	82	3154	2,340	6	100.0	16.4	8.4	100.0	514	15.8	1,078	0	0.8
North Aurora village	244	1417	134	1284	7,408	40	100.0	14.7	6.9	98.6	380	13.4	790	175	15.0
Northbrook village	363	1077	21	1056	26,682	46	100.0	51.6	18.4	98.1	715	52.8	1,578	131	72.5
North Chicago city	381	1293	343	951	0	0	0.0	26.1	8.5	79.5	441	26.6	885	25	31.9
Northlake city	262	2114	65	2050	0	0	0.0	22.2	5.2	100.0	1096	15.4	1,247	119	50.2
Oak Forest city	362	1281	92	1189	299	2	100.0	21.4	5.3	98.7	444	20.9	744	55	30.0
Oak Lawn village	1,101	1926	157	1769	1,079	5	100.0	62.1	19.1	99.2	496	68.1	1,194	211	87.5
Oak Park village	1,667	3199	198	3001	74,412	280	3.6	89.0	14.1	80.8	1115	90.4	1,737	226	104.7
O'Fallon city	512	1750	140	1610	32,543	126	100.0	33.2	13.4	98.6	370	31.4	1,072	258	47.3
Orland Park village	1,315	2227	37	2189	19,540	81	100.0	85.4	30.2	96.4	592	81.3	1,420	303	81.7
Oswego village	524	1607	80	1528	30,411	182	65.4	21.0	9.6	98.5	198	17.5	553	6	34.4
Ottawa city	502	2711	81	2630	5,064	27	100.0	26.7	9.5	84.0	653	28.3	1,523	562	23.7
Palatine village	659	948	52	896	21,170	89	38.2	81.2	22.0	76.2	660	87.2	1,262	293	119.0
Palos Heights city	152	1203	47	1156	0	0	0.0	14.5	2.7	100.0	665	13.8	1,098	75	3.3
Palos Hills city	133	753	158	594	1,420	6	100.0	10.7	3.3	100.0	291	9.6	545	34	6.2
Park Forest village	452	2048	308	1740	0	0	0.0	30.5	5.3	67.9	795	32.4	1,470	190	27.1
Park Ridge city	463	1221	32	1189	16,644	37	94.6	46.1	10.0	100.0	818	47.4	1,255	36	45.7
Pekin city	832	2441	282	2160	4,687	28	100.0	40.2	14.5	81.3	404	48.4	1,417	388	49.3

1 Data for serious crimes have not been adjusted for underreporting. This may affect comparability between geographic areas over time.
2 Per 100,000 population estimated by the FBI. 3 Based on population estimated as of July 1 of the year shown.

Table B. Incorporated Places, Census Designated Places (CDPs), and Minor Civil Divisions (MCDs) of 10,000 or More Population — Land Area, Population, and Households, and Employment

STATE City, town, township, borough, or CDP (county if applicable)	Land area,[1] 2010 (sq mi)	Total persons 2010	Total persons 2014	Percent change 2010–2014	Persons per square mile, 2014	Foreign born	Lives in same house as previous year	Median household income (dollars	Income of $100,000 or more	Income below poverty level	Percent in labor force	Unemploy- ment rate	Family households	One person households
	1	2	3	4	5	6	7	8	9	10	11	12	13	14
ILLINOIS—Con.														
Peoria city	48.002	115,021	115,828	0.7	2,413.0	7.8	80.2	$46,042	17.9	19.5	63.4	10.7	58.3	35.0
Peru city	9.012	10,297	10,016	-2.7	1,111.4	2.5	93.8	$48,689	16.5	11.3	63.0	12.1	59.2	35.4
Plainfield village	23.320	39,840	42,138	5.8	1,806.9	11.5	90.5	$111,536	56.2	3.7	76.5	5.7	85.1	12.3
Plano city	7.445	10,859	11,175	2.9	1,500.9	15.0	80.1	$54,514	21.4	9.8	75.1	11.1	70.7	20.3
Pontiac city	7.714	11,931	11,599	-2.8	1,503.7	1.9	80.8	$48,435	15.6	11.6	49.3	8.0	58.9	36.1
Prospect Heights city	4.256	16,256	16,418	1.0	3,857.8	38.9	87.3	$62,013	23.3	9.3	66.2	6.4	68.8	27.6
Quincy city	15.872	40,636	40,805	0.4	2,570.8	1.8	86.6	$40,886	10.0	17.2	64.3	7.9	59.2	35.5
Rantoul village	8.421	12,941	13,100	1.2	1,555.6	8.2	76.2	$38,052	8.4	21.8	66.8	13.2	62.2	33.5
Richton Park village	3.976	13,646	13,751	0.8	3,458.8	5.3	88.6	$54,887	19.0	13.0	68.6	16.1	64.3	33.9
Riverdale village	3.575	13,549	13,604	0.4	3,805.0	2.1	86.0	$39,623	8.3	27.7	63.9	18.2	59.5	38.0
River Forest village	2.480	11,172	11,208	0.3	4,519.8	10.3	84.1	$108,563	52.1	4.5	60.9	4.1	73.0	23.6
River Grove village	2.391	10,227	10,271	0.4	4,296.4	29.7	93.1	$45,008	13.5	15.7	67.2	8.5	61.1	34.2
Rockford city	63.348	153,054	149,123	-2.6	2,354.0	11.1	82.9	$38,231	12.2	22.6	62.8	15.5	62.0	32.6
Rock Island city	16.829	39,005	38,642	-0.9	2,296.1	6.4	83.7	$40,654	13.9	18.6	61.4	8.9	57.4	37.1
Rolling Meadows city	5.629	24,094	24,279	0.8	4,313.1	26.4	89.5	$62,609	25.0	9.7	69.6	9.2	67.6	28.0
Romeoville village	18.520	39,611	39,679	0.2	2,142.5	20.7	89.9	$66,705	25.2	7.3	70.2	8.8	80.3	16.4
Roscoe village	10.315	10,782	10,603	-1.7	1,027.9	5.1	89.8	$68,253	25.2	7.8	72.1	6.8	76.3	19.7
Roselle village	5.417	22,746	23,030	1.2	4,251.4	16.3	90.5	$77,071	35.0	4.6	75.0	7.5	71.5	24.0
Round Lake village	5.514	18,310	18,536	1.2	3,361.8	24.2	85.6	$79,109	33.8	5.2	75.9	5.7	77.5	18.9
Round Lake Beach village	5.061	28,108	28,012	-0.3	5,534.6	29.4	91.5	$61,113	21.4	14.2	73.0	9.0	79.8	16.1
St. Charles city	14.698	32,949	33,387	1.3	2,271.6	11.0	87.5	$83,997	42.4	4.5	69.0	4.1	68.5	26.4
Sauk Village village	3.835	10,506	10,545	0.4	2,749.4	2.2	91.4	$42,278	13.6	17.7	64.0	22.8	71.6	23.8
Schaumburg village	19.197	74,227	74,896	0.9	3,901.4	26.4	83.7	$72,745	30.7	7.2	71.7	6.6	61.8	32.1
Schiller Park village	2.769	11,793	11,857	0.5	4,282.3	46.2	94.2	$45,646	13.6	9.0	69.6	11.3	65.6	28.9
Shiloh village	10.766	12,411	12,907	4.0	1,198.9	5.1	87.7	$81,731	41.9	5.5	71.1	5.7	72.0	25.7
Shorewood village	7.781	15,615	16,569	6.1	2,129.3	8.2	95.4	$90,882	43.1	7.8	68.4	8.6	77.6	17.1
Skokie village	10.064	64,784	65,112	0.5	6,469.9	41.6	91.8	$66,586	30.6	11.7	63.3	9.2	73.3	23.6
South Elgin village	7.014	21,985	22,226	1.1	3,169.0	11.0	91.1	$86,600	40.8	3.0	74.6	5.6	78.4	18.3
South Holland village	7.239	22,030	22,144	0.5	3,059.1	4.7	90.7	$65,478	26.0	8.1	63.5	16.6	75.0	22.1
Springfield city	59.632	116,365	116,809	0.4	1,958.8	4.4	81.8	$48,848	19.9	16.5	65.4	9.1	55.5	37.3
Sterling city	5.840	15,438	15,011	-2.8	2,570.4	5.4	89.7	$41,413	9.6	12.8	64.5	9.1	62.7	32.2
Streamwood village	7.789	39,858	40,345	1.2	5,179.7	30.4	91.7	$72,720	31.9	4.6	76.1	9.7	76.9	19.7
Streator city	6.065	13,705	13,289	-3.0	2,191.0	6.7	86.4	$39,464	8.5	16.3	59.2	15.9	61.7	32.5
Summit village	2.119	11,054	11,447	3.6	5,402.7	33.0	87.3	$47,975	11.5	18.0	65.4	13.9	77.9	14.4
Swansea village	6.293	13,455	13,651	1.5	2,169.3	1.9	87.5	$66,491	30.7	9.6	68.3	6.2	70.7	26.9
Sycamore city	9.726	17,519	17,753	1.3	1,825.3	6.0	83.1	$62,944	26.1	11.0	73.1	7.7	63.4	28.4
Taylorville city	10.292	11,278	10,971	-2.7	1,066.0	1.4	87.1	$43,457	13.4	13.4	59.8	8.2	57.0	36.5
Tinley Park village	16.023	56,736	57,280	1.0	3,574.9	9.8	90.7	$75,991	35.0	6.9	69.4	6.7	71.3	25.0
Urbana city	11.867	41,452	42,044	1.4	3,542.9	19.1	58.8	$30,834	13.3	32.3	59.7	7.5	37.4	39.0
Vernon Hills village	7.705	25,024	25,911	3.5	3,363.0	29.9	86.8	$89,667	45.9	3.7	73.0	6.3	69.7	26.4
Villa Park village	4.718	21,907	22,038	0.6	4,671.4	15.6	88.5	$70,334	27.8	8.2	72.3	9.1	72.4	22.2
Warrenville city	5.424	13,176	13,336	1.2	2,458.6	13.2	83.7	$74,716	32.6	5.7	78.0	9.6	67.6	25.4
Washington city	8.021	15,201	15,816	4.0	1,971.7	3.3	89.2	$72,247	33.4	4.9	66.4	4.2	74.9	21.8
Waterloo city	8.130	9,982	10,178	2.0	1,251.9	0.8	87.3	$70,976	26.7	6.6	69.6	4.2	71.4	25.6
Wauconda village	5.103	13,635	13,896	1.9	2,723.3	15.5	83.4	$72,987	33.0	6.8	73.1	7.3	65.2	28.9
Waukegan city	23.681	89,099	88,915	-0.2	3,754.7	30.7	82.5	$45,983	16.1	19.4	69.3	11.6	71.2	23.7
Westchester village	3.686	16,718	16,807	0.5	4,559.8	13.3	92.3	$68,017	30.9	6.3	62.3	7.5	66.7	28.9
West Chicago city	15.153	27,200	27,507	1.1	1,815.3	33.0	90.4	$69,252	31.6	12.5	73.0	9.7	79.3	14.8
Western Springs village	2.789	12,975	13,284	2.4	4,763.3	2.7	93.3	$140,361	65.4	1.8	64.9	5.3	82.0	17.1
Westmont village	5.009	24,663	24,963	1.2	4,983.7	19.8	84.0	$57,547	24.5	9.6	66.8	10.4	58.8	34.7
Wheaton city	11.251	52,978	53,644	1.3	4,767.8	10.7	83.8	$84,833	42.3	6.5	67.7	6.9	69.6	25.4
Wheeling village	8.668	37,636	38,010	1.0	4,384.9	41.7	87.0	$57,543	22.6	12.1	74.3	6.7	64.6	28.8
Wilmette village	5.403	27,087	27,446	1.3	5,079.6	17.7	90.5	$126,471	59.5	3.7	60.7	4.3	77.5	20.5
Winnetka village	3.807	12,187	12,490	2.5	3,280.9	6.4	88.3	$207,540	75.0	2.3	58.9	4.8	83.2	15.7
Wood Dale city	4.727	13,770	13,945	1.3	2,950.0	23.2	89.5	$62,240	21.4	8.5	66.9	8.7	66.7	29.5
Woodridge village	9.468	32,967	33,378	1.2	3,525.5	21.1	87.7	$77,164	35.6	5.2	76.8	8.3	66.6	27.5
Wood River city	6.982	10,657	10,355	-2.8	1,483.1	2.0	90.6	$43,075	13.1	15.7	61.8	10.6	60.8	31.3
Woodstock city	13.534	24,771	25,178	1.6	1,860.3	13.6	84.6	$57,583	21.4	14.4	73.1	10.8	66.4	27.8
Worth village	2.369	10,789	10,838	0.5	4,575.5	17.3	85.2	$51,080	16.0	13.0	69.1	13.2	62.7	32.6
Yorkville city	19.888	16,919	18,096	7.0	909.9	5.2	84.3	$86,387	40.6	4.0	76.4	6.1	74.5	19.1
Zion city	9.818	24,346	24,264	-0.3	2,471.5	13.4	84.1	$50,485	14.9	17.8	67.7	15.3	65.8	29.0
INDIANA	35,826.108	6,484,192	6,596,855	1.7	184.1	4.8	85.0	$48,737	17.0	14.2	64.1	8.8	66.5	27.8
Anderson city	42.572	56,176	55,455	-1.3	1,302.6	2.9	77.7	$33,854	6.3	24.3	55.8	14.7	57.5	36.1
Auburn city	7.166	12,742	12,834	0.7	1,790.9	1.2	85.1	$45,317	15.1	13.9	62.6	6.2	61.6	32.6
Avon town	18.094	13,566	15,971	17.7	882.7	7.2	89.5	$89,034	42.1	3.6	75.1	3.6	77.9	16.6
Bedford city	12.160	13,407	13,355	-0.4	1,098.2	2.7	82.3	$35,126	8.0	19.3	54.0	10.3	61.2	35.0
Beech Grove city	4.396	14,194	14,514	2.3	3,301.8	2.4	84.1	$37,624	9.5	16.5	61.7	10.5	62.3	32.7
Bloomington city	23.252	80,307	83,322	3.8	3,583.5	12.2	54.4	$28,660	12.4	34.3	55.7	8.8	38.9	40.0
Brownsburg town	14.670	21,542	23,322	8.3	1,589.8	3.5	87.0	$65,492	26.0	5.6	70.3	5.6	68.0	29.1
Carmel city	47.469	79,191	86,682	9.5	1,826.1	11.9	86.2	$107,916	54.6	4.1	70.9	5.0	76.3	20.2
Cedar Lake town	8.423	11,560	11,854	2.5	1,407.4	2.3	89.6	$64,071	18.5	6.9	70.4	11.8	73.7	21.9
Chesterton town	9.334	13,092	13,403	2.4	1,435.9	5.1	88.9	$66,919	32.7	8.9	67.3	8.8	75.9	19.2
Clarksville town	10.048	21,724	21,879	0.7	2,177.5	5.9	87.6	$41,788	9.6	15.6	63.6	6.9	57.1	35.6
Columbus city	27.594	44,077	46,124	4.6	1,671.5	10.6	82.6	$55,288	22.3	10.9	65.4	6.3	63.6	31.3
Connersville city	7.745	13,506	13,032	-3.5	1,682.7	0.8	80.7	$31,299	5.9	22.4	53.6	16.1	61.5	34.2
Crawfordsville city	9.147	15,924	15,988	0.4	1,747.9	4.7	77.6	$33,085	5.4	19.6	58.5	11.6	59.1	36.3
Crown Point city	17.813	27,837	28,623	2.8	1,606.8	8.7	87.0	$64,250	27.1	6.2	61.8	8.6	67.4	29.0
Dyer town	6.140	16,390	16,169	-1.3	2,633.4	6.2	93.3	$79,859	36.6	3.1	65.5	7.6	75.7	19.7
East Chicago city	14.085	29,698	28,990	-2.4	2,058.2	14.9	83.7	$27,215	5.8	32.3	54.6	17.0	66.7	29.3
Elkhart city	23.457	50,904	51,421	1.0	2,192.2	14.1	77.8	$35,505	6.7	21.8	65.1	12.8	62.1	31.3
Evansville city	47.347	120,081	120,346	0.2	2,541.8	2.3	81.2	$35,996	8.4	18.6	62.4	8.2	56.1	37.0
Fishers town	34.414	76,880	86,325	12.3	2,508.5	7.9	88.5	$91,646	44.3	3.3	76.2	5.0	74.3	21.1
Fort Wayne city	110.614	253,700	258,522	1.9	2,337.2	7.5	84.0	$43,994	13.2	16.8	65.8	10.0	61.2	32.7
Frankfort city	7.429	16,442	16,153	-1.8	2,174.2	11.4	81.9	$40,803	8.8	13.5	66.0	10.9	65.0	28.8

1 Dry land or land partially or temporarily covered by water.
2 16 years old and over.

Table B. Incorporated Places, Census Designated Places (CDPs), and Minor Civil Divisions (MCDs) of 10,000 or More Population — Crime, Construction, and Local Government Finance

STATE City, town, township, borough, or CDP (county if applicable)	Serious crimes known to police, 2014[1] Total number	Rate[2] Total	Rate[2] Violent	Rate[2] Property	New residential construction authorized by building permits, 2014 Value ($1,000)	Number of housing units	Percent single family	Local government finance, 2012 General revenue Total (mil dol)	Intergovernmental Total (mil dol)	Percent from state gov.	Taxes per capita[3]	General expenditure Total (mil dol)	Per capita[3] Total	Capital outlays	Debt outstanding (mil dol)
	15	16	17	18	19	20	21	22	23	24	25	26	27	28	29
ILLINOIS—Con.															
Peoria city	5,617	4804	649	4155	14,768	51	100.0	185.6	76.4	95.2	702	173.5	1,500	288	222.0
Peru city	216	2147	60	2087	1,726	6	100.0	17.6	6.6	98.2	585	17.9	1,758	231	28.6
Plainfield village	357	846	76	770	49,525	163	100.0	34.8	10.0	90.4	348	27.5	680	54	63.7
Plano city	115	1032	18	1014	140	1	100.0	8.4	3.0	97.0	223	11.3	1,022	411	5.8
Pontiac city	371	3189	378	2810	355	6	0.0	12.4	4.2	100.0	318	13.4	1,133	150	6.9
Prospect Heights city	178	1083	128	955	3,515	16	100.0	11.2	3.7	90.7	295	12.6	773	283	23.0
Quincy city	1,553	3790	464	3327	11,695	83	83.1	46.5	24.3	86.8	330	36.7	898	111	20.2
Rantoul village	349	2672	398	2274	0	0	0.0	16.3	5.8	82.1	444	14.3	1,099	127	13.7
Richton Park village	375	2719	355	2364	0	0	0.0	12.0	2.2	97.1	501	12.2	886	138	3.9
Riverdale village	NA	NA	NA	NA	0	0	0.0	17.8	3.0	71.0	903	15.9	1,166	118	31.4
River Forest village	262	2336	169	2166	0	0	0.0	17.2	4.0	91.5	874	16.4	1,465	84	16.6
River Grove village	127	1234	87	1147	0	0	0.0	10.8	2.9	80.7	585	10.6	1,027	74	13.8
Rockford city	8,306	5553	1245	4307	4,384	37	89.2	205.7	107.8	79.0	497	178.2	1,180	127	164.6
Rock Island city	1,036	2667	409	2258	9,736	68	20.6	69.8	23.7	74.6	601	75.1	1,934	393	36.5
Rolling Meadows city	262	1077	66	1011	1,378	5	100.0	38.8	6.2	92.0	1011	38.6	1,591	156	19.6
Romeoville village	679	1713	119	1594	3,124	16	100.0	58.3	11.7	84.0	726	58.2	1,465	267	169.7
Roscoe village	108	1014	122	892	NA	NA	NA	5.6	3.9	82.6	121	6.0	561	116	3.9
Roselle village	254	1100	35	1065	4,295	13	100.0	20.5	5.0	96.2	440	17.7	770	66	16.3
Round Lake village	174	940	124	816	946	11	100.0	9.0	2.7	100.0	277	8.2	448	88	42.2
Round Lake Beach village	697	2483	125	2359	0	0	0.0	17.9	8.1	98.7	305	22.5	802	338	25.1
St. Charles city	510	1530	60	1470	7,326	23	100.0	51.7	14.2	98.9	807	54.5	1,637	225	142.6
Sauk Village village	338	3201	474	2728	0	0	0.0	12.3	2.4	80.9	743	9.0	850	89	42.9
Schaumburg village	1,943	2589	97	2491	7,869	46	65.2	155.0	40.4	92.8	937	138.1	1,847	106	302.1
Schiller Park village	270	2270	67	2203	298	2	100.0	20.1	5.4	100.0	1046	21.0	1,775	89	28.6
Shiloh village	208	1601	185	1416	10,762	62	100.0	7.4	3.5	98.2	238	11.6	900	44	18.0
Shorewood village	145	879	49	831	16,873	92	100.0	15.4	5.3	100.0	331	12.7	782	22	9.6
Skokie village	1,502	2301	265	2036	3,719	8	100.0	104.2	37.0	66.4	929	82.4	1,265	140	66.5
South Elgin village	263	1182	117	1065	11,888	40	100.0	17.2	7.6	93.7	261	16.8	757	131	7.1
South Holland village	443	1995	284	1712	0	0	0.0	32.0	5.5	95.5	860	25.6	1,157	62	28.1
Springfield city	6,783	5791	1065	4725	46,778	226	39.4	137.9	49.3	90.7	587	135.8	1,159	63	703.4
Sterling city	581	3852	219	3633	650	3	100.0	216.0	8.3	73.4	401	202.3	13,320	844	43.3
Streamwood village	705	1743	101	1641	3,516	128	0.0	29.9	8.7	93.2	390	26.2	650	57	10.0
Streator city	486	3639	202	3437	475	2	100.0	14.4	5.4	100.0	314	15.1	1,113	145	15.8
Summit village	317	2742	389	2353	0	0	0.0	10.5	3.1	85.3	491	11.6	1,011	56	0.6
Swansea village	231	1681	146	1536	8,483	29	100.0	9.7	3.5	97.5	181	10.5	763	143	24.0
Sycamore city	224	1277	91	1186	5,569	30	100.0	54.1	18.1	99.2	1747	54.5	3,119	147	16.6
Taylorville city	165	1493	217	1276	330	2	100.0	10.7	5.4	100.0	253	14.2	1,272	553	16.2
Tinley Park village	975	1698	80	1618	5,781	34	100.0	70.3	22.1	99.9	632	61.1	1,069	254	45.9
Urbana city	1,597	3820	311	3509	33,374	241	18.3	47.8	17.7	62.5	531	48.4	1,159	285	11.4
Vernon Hills village	518	2011	35	1976	26,202	220	27.3	21.2	13.2	99.1	222	18.9	740	29	24.7
Villa Park village	515	2327	86	2241	325	2	100.0	30.1	9.5	93.3	606	26.4	1,196	105	28.0
Warrenville city	111	828	82	746	1,488	7	100.0	14.7	3.4	97.0	633	13.9	1,044	174	0.0
Washington city	NA	NA	NA	NA	116,515	477	100.0	12.6	7.1	92.6	168	12.0	775	231	13.0
Waterloo city	NA	NA	NA	NA	8,833	40	90.0	8.3	3.5	100.0	177	10.1	1,000	219	13.7
Wauconda village	118	851	58	793	0	0	0.0	12.1	3.3	96.9	372	11.0	801	65	18.7
Waukegan city	2,966	3342	439	2903	6,299	41	65.9	87.3	16.1	90.5	525	72.7	819	47	133.5
Westchester village	163	967	30	938	0	0	0.0	18.2	3.5	97.8	636	19.7	1,173	74	5.8
West Chicago city	371	1342	90	1252	1,617	6	100.0	29.0	8.4	99.1	324	28.0	1,022	227	20.8
Western Springs village	46	348	15	333	27,967	54	100.0	15.7	3.4	67.1	665	16.4	1,251	199	60.0
Westmont village	298	1190	76	1114	8,304	25	80.0	26.4	9.6	100.0	577	23.2	932	40	2.9
Wheaton city	398	740	52	688	21,987	61	100.0	56.0	12.7	96.7	616	46.6	872	33	45.4
Wheeling village	546	1433	118	1315	9,450	96	0.0	45.9	10.7	93.0	765	45.1	1,188	197	84.5
Wilmette village	362	1320	36	1283	26,485	44	100.0	38.5	7.6	85.0	821	38.9	1,425	199	76.2
Winnetka village	103	826	16	809	20,997	19	100.0	25.8	3.0	94.1	1344	25.7	2,079	237	1.3
Wood Dale city	159	1134	64	1070	1,130	6	33.3	20.6	7.3	98.2	500	19.1	1,374	401	10.0
Woodridge village	410	1224	110	1113	8,010	29	100.0	30.1	9.8	82.4	434	26.2	789	18	24.8
Wood River city	483	4658	270	4388	403	2	100.0	15.6	7.5	97.9	228	21.2	2,022	882	7.9
Woodstock city	393	1558	135	1423	4,005	46	100.0	25.4	7.2	92.8	447	23.7	947	107	50.6
Worth village	141	1298	92	1206	0	0	0.0	10.6	3.5	100.0	331	9.8	903	37	7.6
Yorkville city	178	993	50	943	12,373	74	100.0	19.9	5.0	99.0	578	15.8	901	2	42.9
Zion city	NA	NA	NA	NA	0	0	0.0	21.9	5.6	99.7	494	24.2	999	63	33.8
INDIANA	198,875	3015	365	2649	3,222,176	17,816	68.1	X	X	X	X	X	X	X	X
Anderson city	2,680	4825	342	4483	3,519	24	83.3	84.2	19.0	48.2	652	65.2	1,172	281	127.1
Auburn city	278	2172	63	2110	7,420	40	100.0	16.1	5.2	36.8	397	12.6	986	150	6.5
Avon town	670	4783	378	4404	38,492	208	88.5	9.2	3.2	46.8	355	5.6	387	40	4.7
Bedford city	523	3911	112	3799	6,336	42	19.0	17.3	7.0	51.0	476	12.4	924	71	8.9
Beech Grove city	650	4472	172	4300	0	0	0.0	14.4	3.1	84.7	478	16.6	1,155	53	7.1
Bloomington city	2,760	3322	354	2968	NA	NA	NA	85.2	17.5	64.4	539	72.9	886	129	159.2
Brownsburg town	404	1716	187	1529	62,930	564	27.0	28.8	8.8	21.5	575	29.7	1,319	204	4.7
Carmel city	828	946	14	932	210,549	1,066	33.0	111.9	17.9	66.3	871	93.8	1,122	60	367.8
Cedar Lake town	242	2062	170	1892	15,668	110	100.0	12.7	1.0	88.1	439	8.8	752	6	16.2
Chesterton town	155	1159	82	1077	7,003	27	92.6	14.1	1.8	90.9	460	11.2	848	9	12.6
Clarksville town	1,873	8569	554	8015	691	3	100.0	29.2	6.6	25.4	721	25.5	1,169	239	18.1
Columbus city	2,046	4429	97	4332	NA	NA	NA	72.5	21.0	50.2	657	59.6	1,314	244	109.4
Connersville city	NA	NA	NA	NA	NA	NA	NA	19.0	5.8	59.0	580	15.6	1,170	10	10.9
Crawfordsville city	656	4096	1261	2834	3,339	22	100.0	18.6	3.8	83.0	604	15.4	960	71	23.8
Crown Point city	NA	NA	NA	NA	56,991	225	88.4	35.9	4.6	85.5	616	21.8	773	94	22.4
Dyer town	205	1262	98	1164	2,515	10	100.0	19.5	2.2	77.9	607	14.4	879	31	6.2
East Chicago city	1,471	5057	856	4201	235	1	100.0	103.6	44.0	82.6	1697	63.2	2,147	65	42.0
Elkhart city	2,929	5702	1258	4445	735	4	100.0	70.5	21.2	34.3	606	59.6	1,167	88	28.7
Evansville city	7,506	6236	518	5718	14,057	92	95.7	183.6	54.1	55.1	568	192.0	1,598	442	274.1
Fishers town	832	972	21	951	228,408	1,112	50.7	58.2	7.3	74.3	430	55.3	676	109	131.1
Fort Wayne city	9,168	3565	317	3248	NA	NA	NA	289.9	59.4	54.7	554	257.6	1,011	147	435.4
Frankfort city	841	5190	123	5066	600	4	100.0	17.4	4.8	37.4	334	19.0	1,167	90	15.5

1 Data for serious crimes have not been adjusted for underreporting. This may affect comparability between geographic areas over time.
2 Per 100,000 population estimated by the FBI. 3 Based on population estimated as of July 1 of the year shown.

Table B. Incorporated Places, Census Designated Places (CDPs), and Minor Civil Divisions (MCDs) of 10,000 or More Population — Land Area, Population, and Households, and Employment

STATE City, town, township, borough, or CDP (county if applicable)	Land area,[1] 2010 (sq mi)	Total persons 2010	Total persons 2014	Percent change 2010–2014	Persons per square mile, 2014	Foreign born	Lives in same house as previous year	Median household income (dollars)	Income of $100,000 or more	Income below poverty level	Percent in labor force	Unemployment rate	Family households	One person households
	1	2	3	4	5	6	7	8	9	10	11	12	13	14
INDIANA—Con.														
Franklin city	13.013	23,731	24,356	2.6	1,871.7	2.4	81.4	$51,397	20.2	12.4	65.0	7.3	65.7	28.6
Gary city	49.873	80,314	77,909	-3.0	1,562.1	1.8	85.0	$27,458	6.2	33.8	51.7	18.8	60.9	34.6
Goshen city	16.375	31,613	32,267	2.1	1,970.5	15.7	80.9	$40,259	8.0	19.1	62.7	8.7	69.1	26.8
Granger CDP	25.073	30,465	NA	NA	NA	6.2	92.8	$93,830	46.5	2.9	67.3	5.3	83.3	14.2
Greencastle city	5.242	10,315	10,362	0.5	1,976.7	4.3	70.4	$41,365	12.4	12.8	50.1	6.5	64.1	31.3
Greenfield city	12.854	20,624	21,398	3.8	1,664.7	1.6	84.1	$53,819	15.2	10.2	64.9	7.7	67.3	26.4
Greensburg city	9.268	11,492	11,817	2.8	1,275.0	2.3	78.1	$45,363	10.0	17.2	66.4	9.4	62.7	33.2
Greenwood city	24.939	50,979	54,491	6.9	2,184.9	7.1	82.0	$52,621	19.3	12.0	68.3	8.1	65.6	28.6
Griffith town	7.735	16,893	16,516	-2.2	2,135.1	5.3	84.7	$52,800	16.7	11.2	68.0	8.9	69.7	26.3
Hammond city	22.780	80,823	78,384	-3.0	3,441.0	11.6	86.9	$39,771	9.6	20.8	61.4	13.7	65.8	29.4
Highland town	6.952	23,727	23,127	-2.5	3,326.9	5.2	91.1	$62,738	22.1	6.3	66.5	5.9	63.5	30.8
Hobart city	26.346	29,349	28,635	-2.4	1,086.9	4.4	89.1	$55,840	17.0	9.0	68.4	10.1	66.3	29.7
Huntington city	8.506	17,367	17,166	-1.2	2,018.2	2.2	80.9	$39,542	7.0	14.2	63.2	11.4	60.6	30.7
Indianapolis city	366.456	829,668	858,325	3.5	2,342.2	8.6	82.7	$42,169	14.7	18.8	67.5	11.2	58.3	34.1
Indianapolis city (balance)	361.479	820,441	848,788	3.5	2,348.1	8.7	82.7	$42,076	14.6	18.9	67.6	11.2	58.3	34.1
Jasper city	13.149	15,048	15,325	1.8	1,165.5	4.7	86.2	$53,568	15.7	7.0	67.3	4.1	64.1	31.9
Jeffersonville city	34.101	45,031	46,440	3.1	1,361.8	3.8	89.7	$51,706	15.5	11.2	67.3	8.8	64.6	28.7
Kokomo city	30.343	56,842	57,085	0.4	1,881.3	2.7	79.6	$35,690	10.8	19.4	59.0	11.8	57.5	37.3
Lafayette city	29.471	68,867	70,654	2.6	2,397.4	7.8	76.5	$39,378	9.4	18.5	69.8	8.7	56.7	34.3
Lake Station city	8.296	12,572	12,175	-3.2	1,467.5	5.2	88.1	$35,625	6.4	21.8	56.2	16.5	72.4	22.0
La Porte city	11.666	22,043	22,007	-0.2	1,886.4	5.7	82.8	$37,225	6.8	16.6	63.1	12.3	59.9	32.2
Lawrence city	20.144	46,003	47,550	3.4	2,360.6	7.4	86.0	$49,849	17.8	13.4	74.9	11.2	67.9	27.0
Lebanon city	15.627	15,794	15,836	0.3	1,013.4	2.2	83.0	$44,709	10.8	12.2	68.6	5.8	64.1	29.8
Logansport city	8.748	18,266	18,019	-1.4	2,059.9	15.5	80.3	$33,164	5.9	20.6	61.8	12.8	60.4	33.2
Madison city	8.575	11,967	12,035	0.6	1,403.5	1.8	78.2	$45,569	13.9	13.0	54.3	11.0	64.0	32.8
Marion city	15.617	29,920	29,308	-2.0	1,876.6	2.4	80.2	$32,334	6.8	22.9	53.8	10.2	55.2	39.0
Martinsville city	4.490	11,771	11,744	-0.2	2,615.8	1.5	77.2	$36,379	7.2	17.7	58.4	11.8	65.4	27.8
Merrillville town	33.206	34,969	35,450	1.4	1,067.6	5.9	82.9	$49,711	14.4	12.9	64.4	11.2	62.1	33.1
Michigan City city	19.586	31,484	31,487	0.0	1,607.6	3.8	80.6	$35,710	7.7	24.8	57.1	15.5	57.6	35.0
Mishawaka city	17.623	48,260	48,174	-0.2	2,733.7	6.1	80.4	$37,542	8.4	16.5	67.8	10.6	54.3	37.6
Muncie city	27.406	70,201	70,211	0.0	2,561.9	2.8	63.3	$30,570	6.8	30.3	57.4	14.1	50.4	34.5
Munster town	7.553	23,560	23,103	-1.9	3,058.7	11.2	91.4	$72,532	36.2	7.6	61.5	6.5	72.8	24.7
New Albany city	14.939	36,345	36,589	0.7	2,449.3	2.2	82.3	$40,061	9.6	19.2	64.5	10.7	59.8	34.6
New Castle city	7.355	18,106	17,653	-2.5	2,400.1	1.1	80.5	$32,908	4.4	23.6	53.6	14.1	59.6	36.6
New Haven city	9.872	14,794	15,608	5.5	1,581.0	2.0	88.2	$46,952	10.9	9.7	69.1	7.7	65.1	29.0
Noblesville city	31.600	52,135	57,584	10.5	1,822.3	4.2	84.0	$67,939	28.8	6.5	74.1	4.7	70.7	24.7
Peru city	5.105	11,417	11,079	-3.0	2,170.2	0.4	82.9	$33,713	6.7	22.5	56.5	14.4	62.7	32.7
Plainfield town	22.153	27,634	30,409	10.0	1,372.7	6.9	82.5	$58,625	20.2	8.7	60.9	8.1	68.6	27.2
Plymouth city	7.534	10,033	10,095	0.6	1,340.0	12.3	80.4	$32,988	6.1	21.7	66.1	15.1	65.3	31.7
Portage city	25.516	36,828	36,760	-0.2	1,440.7	4.5	86.0	$51,180	18.7	13.0	62.5	11.0	69.2	26.0
Purdue University CDP	1.297	12,183	NA	NA	NA	24.8	33.3	$19,411	0.4	48.3	31.5	12.1	46.9	20.0
Richmond city	23.997	36,797	36,159	-1.7	1,506.8	3.4	78.0	$29,802	7.5	24.5	54.0	12.5	59.2	34.8
St. John town	11.653	14,853	16,117	8.5	1,383.0	4.9	95.3	$93,802	47.0	4.3	70.2	3.9	80.3	15.9
Schererville town	14.717	29,243	28,926	-1.1	1,965.5	9.7	90.1	$69,011	31.5	5.7	68.8	6.7	66.1	28.2
Seymour city	11.959	18,021	19,094	6.0	1,596.6	9.2	86.3	$43,890	9.2	13.9	64.3	9.5	67.4	27.5
Shelbyville city	11.564	19,152	19,163	0.1	1,657.1	4.5	81.7	$41,525	9.7	15.0	65.7	11.2	62.1	31.3
South Bend city	41.346	101,046	101,190	0.1	2,447.4	7.3	80.0	$34,656	9.0	23.6	65.2	13.7	57.9	35.1
Speedway town	4.753	11,812	12,101	2.4	2,545.9	11.1	81.6	$39,805	9.3	15.4	65.7	10.7	52.2	43.8
Terre Haute city	34.549	60,785	60,956	0.3	1,764.4	3.5	78.7	$33,317	8.4	24.1	54.6	9.8	55.9	35.8
Valparaiso city	15.567	31,734	32,369	2.0	2,079.4	6.0	80.1	$49,656	19.0	15.3	60.9	6.8	57.3	35.6
Vincennes city	7.412	18,422	18,032	-2.1	2,432.9	1.2	76.8	$34,036	6.2	22.5	53.2	8.3	57.6	36.7
Wabash city	9.330	10,670	10,433	-2.2	1,118.2	1.0	81.6	$39,078	6.2	16.8	64.3	11.2	65.2	31.4
Warsaw city	12.060	13,562	14,280	5.3	1,184.1	8.7	78.9	$46,530	14.2	14.1	64.3	8.5	60.7	32.8
Washington city	4.731	11,497	12,020	4.5	2,540.9	4.9	86.6	$40,302	10.8	17.9	61.0	8.5	63.2	32.7
Westfield city	28.261	30,090	35,297	17.3	1,248.9	4.9	88.8	$85,071	42.6	4.8	74.8	3.5	76.0	19.6
West Lafayette city	7.614	29,596	32,109	8.5	4,216.9	23.0	55.8	$28,507	15.3	36.7	50.0	7.0	32.7	38.8
Yorktown town	31.930	11,303	11,220	-0.7	351.4	1.4	89.4	$60,552	25.5	7.7	64.2	6.3	74.1	21.6
Zionsville town	53.366	23,520	25,734	9.4	482.2	6.0	91.3	$103,951	52.7	2.8	70.2	3.4	78.5	18.6
IOWA	55,857.128	3,046,869	3,107,126	2.0	55.6	4.7	84.9	$52,716	19.0	12.1	67.9	5.4	64.7	28.8
Altoona city	9.351	14,541	16,105	10.8	1,722.3	1.3	89.3	$66,730	30.4	5.8	75.8	5.1	73.4	21.7
Ames city	24.350	58,967	63,266	7.3	2,598.2	11.8	58.0	$42,373	18.4	27.9	66.4	6.2	43.9	30.4
Ankeny city	29.358	45,582	53,801	18.0	1,832.6	3.4	81.7	$75,069	32.4	7.0	77.8	3.6	69.6	23.6
Bettendorf city	21.297	33,213	35,122	5.7	1,649.2	5.4	85.9	$74,529	34.8	6.7	66.0	4.3	67.1	29.2
Boone city	9.091	12,661	12,633	-0.2	1,389.6	0.8	81.2	$45,012	14.7	10.8	67.0	6.1	59.3	32.1
Burlington city	14.485	25,625	25,539	-0.3	1,763.1	1.4	82.9	$37,223	9.8	19.6	68.6	8.6	62.5	32.1
Carroll city	5.694	10,103	10,007	-1.0	1,757.3	0.7	87.2	$44,972	12.9	14.2	68.6	0.8	58.2	39.1
Cedar Falls city	28.749	39,260	40,859	4.1	1,421.3	4.8	76.0	$52,678	22.6	16.9	68.9	7.1	56.5	27.5
Cedar Rapids city	70.798	126,326	129,195	2.3	1,824.8	3.4	82.8	$54,465	20.2	12.2	70.9	5.7	59.2	32.3
Clinton city	35.153	26,885	26,246	-2.4	746.6	2.8	85.1	$41,848	14.6	15.3	62.1	6.3	59.2	34.0
Clive city	7.592	15,407	17,052	10.7	2,246.1	13.3	89.3	$91,696	45.7	2.6	72.5	2.2	75.7	20.6
Coralville city	12.177	18,908	20,349	7.6	1,671.4	12.1	79.7	$59,822	26.8	11.5	72.6	3.5	57.3	30.0
Council Bluffs city	42.857	62,228	62,245	0.0	1,452.4	4.0	82.8	$45,204	12.6	15.7	67.5	7.0	62.5	31.0
Davenport city	62.894	99,687	102,448	2.8	1,628.9	3.9	84.3	$45,424	15.7	16.2	65.9	6.7	58.8	33.2
Des Moines city	88.974	204,186	209,220	2.5	2,351.5	11.3	78.1	$46,430	13.8	17.0	70.3	8.4	60.3	31.6
Dubuque city	30.154	57,532	58,436	1.6	1,937.9	2.8	82.2	$46,806	13.4	12.6	67.1	6.1	57.9	33.5
Fort Dodge city	16.052	25,206	24,594	-2.4	1,532.2	2.9	80.9	$38,380	12.7	18.3	60.3	10.7	53.9	39.3
Fort Madison city	9.492	11,051	10,764	-2.6	1,134.0	2.6	88.2	$41,875	8.9	16.2	65.6	10.2	61.3	34.1
Indianola city	11.248	14,777	15,305	3.6	1,360.7	1.4	79.9	$52,131	19.2	8.7	72.6	7.1	64.0	30.4
Iowa City city	25.717	67,894	73,415	8.1	2,854.7	13.4	63.3	$42,119	19.1	25.6	73.0	4.6	44.7	35.2
Johnston city	17.139	17,266	20,359	17.9	1,187.8	5.0	86.1	$94,821	46.2	7.2	73.0	3.6	72.5	21.9
Keokuk city	9.133	10,780	10,692	-0.8	1,170.7	1.9	84.9	$33,040	6.6	23.1	58.6	9.8	59.4	34.8
Marion city	16.050	34,768	36,774	5.8	2,291.2	3.9	85.9	$62,532	24.3	6.9	72.0	4.8	64.7	28.6
Marshalltown city	19.281	27,552	27,727	0.6	1,438.1	16.9	81.9	$48,750	12.3	12.4	63.0	7.6	66.1	29.5
Mason City city	27.789	28,079	27,458	-2.2	988.1	2.1	86.2	$42,009	11.9	15.6	67.3	5.9	53.4	40.3

1 Dry land or land partially or temporarily covered by water.
2 16 years old and over.

Table B. Incorporated Places, Census Designated Places (CDPs), and Minor Civil Divisions (MCDs) of 10,000 or More Population — Crime, Construction, and Local Government Finance

STATE City, town, township, borough, or CDP (county if applicable)	Serious crimes known to police, 2014[1] Total number	Rate[2] Total	Rate[2] Violent	Rate[2] Property	New residential construction authorized by building permits, 2014 Value ($1,000)	Number of housing units	Percent single family	Local government finance, 2012 General revenue Total (mil dol)	Intergovernmental Total (mil dol)	Intergovernmental Percent from state gov.	Taxes per capita[3]	General expenditure Total (mil dol)	Per capita[3] Total	Per capita[3] Capital outlays	Debt outstanding (mil dol)
	15	16	17	18	19	20	21	22	23	24	25	26	27	28	29
INDIANA—Con.															
Franklin city	1,027	4225	309	3916	9,985	75	100.0	26.5	9.0	26.4	491	22.8	951	136	7.4
Gary city	4,764	6107	913	5194	1,315	7	100.0	181.4	65.4	74.4	1028	145.6	1,839	385	85.2
Goshen city	1,276	3946	111	3835	6,678	40	100.0	35.1	9.7	53.7	454	47.8	1,498	416	101.3
Granger CDP	NA	NA	NA	NA	NA	NA	NA	NA	NA	NA	NA	NA	NA	NA	NA
Greencastle city	NA	NA	NA	NA	4,659	31	3.2	10.1	3.0	35.4	357	7.1	691	131	13.0
Greenfield city	392	1833	136	1698	14,685	96	89.6	21.3	6.1	39.1	400	15.1	719	41	13.2
Greensburg city	NA	NA	NA	NA	2,185	23	100.0	12.5	4.0	37.6	402	11.2	963	51	40.1
Greenwood city	2,112	3886	351	3535	54,630	308	100.0	47.0	10.2	33.2	376	34.0	645	24	30.0
Griffith town	506	3057	254	2803	670	6	100.0	18.0	3.1	92.5	583	9.1	542	4	1.8
Hammond city	3,478	4429	811	3618	862	4	100.0	192.8	73.8	83.1	797	155.5	1,953	159	112.1
Highland town	632	2727	65	2662	1,727	6	100.0	22.8	3.5	89.6	539	18.2	776	169	30.7
Hobart city	1,823	6422	292	6129	3,945	18	100.0	40.0	5.7	88.9	794	36.0	1,242	112	25.7
Huntington city	328	1910	116	1793	1,364	8	100.0	20.1	5.9	40.0	496	19.7	1,138	185	12.5
Indianapolis city	52,162	6078	1255	4823	167,626	1,126	50.8	2604.6	712.4	81.1	1064	3151.6	3,777	1,038	6001.3
Indianapolis city (balance)	NA	NA	NA	NA	NA	NA	NA	NA	NA	NA	NA	NA	NA	NA	NA
Jasper city	181	1178	234	943	15,931	69	100.0	15.8	1.3	89.0	593	9.3	613	67	9.9
Jeffersonville city	1,708	3704	579	3125	26,076	250	47.2	55.6	10.3	33.9	605	57.7	1,264	472	54.0
Kokomo city	2,236	3929	285	3645	14,766	108	70.4	76.1	16.8	67.8	777	63.7	1,118	63	32.5
Lafayette city	3,777	5339	496	4842	16,209	166	50.6	99.8	25.3	67.7	637	75.9	1,086	2	133.7
Lake Station city	638	5242	181	5062	240	2	100.0	14.9	1.1	85.2	372	13.8	1,117	261	3.0
La Porte city	781	3550	155	3395	1,491	10	100.0	24.3	6.0	39.5	531	18.7	846	88	22.2
Lawrence city	NA	NA	NA	NA	10,139	69	100.0	36.4	5.3	60.9	411	34.5	739	4	27.5
Lebanon city	NA	NA	NA	NA	2,445	14	57.1	16.6	1.1	89.6	491	12.1	770	64	12.4
Logansport city	845	4701	89	4612	NA	NA	NA	20.8	5.6	45.2	384	12.7	699	2	4.0
Madison city	NA	NA	NA	NA	1,988	11	81.8	18.7	5.0	87.3	580	13.1	1,089	243	14.3
Marion city	1,341	4550	299	4251	3,284	36	41.7	32.5	6.6	85.0	665	37.1	1,252	46	11.4
Martinsville city	179	1510	42	1468	120	1	100.0	14.1	5.6	28.0	329	13.2	1,127	40	7.5
Merrillville town	1,349	3777	333	3444	5,009	39	64.1	30.3	3.8	91.0	587	18.3	518	137	22.7
Michigan City city	1,482	4704	317	4386	1,600	40	40.0	59.4	25.0	70.4	553	50.5	1,621	213	54.0
Mishawaka city	2,458	5128	221	4907	8,232	59	72.9	83.6	10.9	75.5	1142	78.3	1,630	554	117.0
Muncie city	3,176	4515	394	4121	7,151	62	29.0	72.4	20.0	73.9	414	72.9	1,040	117	33.5
Munster town	407	1755	91	1665	12,233	23	100.0	38.1	4.5	60.6	1116	35.5	1,521	650	42.0
New Albany city	2,165	5866	244	5622	4,652	32	100.0	59.3	15.9	55.8	564	50.5	1,385	371	61.3
New Castle city	NA	NA	NA	NA	134	1	100.0	22.8	3.7	43.6	419	22.8	1,283	0	10.0
New Haven city	347	2219	102	2117	NA	NA	NA	15.5	2.6	94.6	422	13.0	843	96	20.5
Noblesville city	NA	NA	NA	NA	132,478	799	55.4	84.0	18.9	89.5	823	67.7	1,226	347	240.4
Peru city	391	3522	315	3207	799	3	100.0	15.4	2.2	88.6	607	16.7	1,481	203	20.3
Plainfield town	947	3082	179	2903	28,627	155	96.1	48.8	11.2	29.1	854	35.1	1,203	268	56.2
Plymouth city	228	2272	139	2132	2,058	16	100.0	14.8	5.5	47.7	460	11.3	1,130	76	5.4
Portage city	846	2299	163	2136	4,536	38	78.9	42.2	5.4	93.6	604	46.8	1,270	181	59.2
Purdue University CDP	NA	NA	NA	NA	NA	NA	NA	NA	NA	NA	NA	NA	NA	NA	NA
Richmond city	NA	NA	NA	NA	7,381	71	11.3	48.2	15.7	58.1	368	46.4	1,269	343	34.6
St. John town	106	668	32	636	47,302	178	100.0	15.9	2.3	87.9	580	9.8	641	63	13.1
Schererville town	150	518	14	504	14,172	50	76.0	33.2	3.7	90.7	734	19.4	667	73	18.2
Seymour city	1,015	5328	336	4992	19,468	178	34.3	NA	NA	NA	NA	NA	NA	NA	NA
Shelbyville city	752	3901	1001	2900	2,871	32	37.5	158.8	37.2	31.6	797	116.8	6,115	205	43.4
South Bend city	5,435	5389	685	4704	NA	NA	NA	201.3	37.3	61.0	1060	141.5	1,404	147	230.5
Speedway town	659	5437	322	5116	0	0	0.0	18.9	1.8	90.5	939	32.5	2,721	863	51.6
Terre Haute city	3,210	5255	324	4931	17,050	186	5.9	82.6	28.3	35.8	519	64.3	1,051	189	52.7
Valparaiso city	654	2020	108	1912	34,025	156	59.0	44.4	6.4	59.9	713	35.7	1,116	232	56.6
Vincennes city	NA	NA	NA	NA	560	6	100.0	15.1	1.6	91.1	407	13.6	752	53	26.7
Wabash city	NA	NA	NA	NA	210	1	100.0	14.2	4.0	80.6	379	10.8	1,026	12	4.4
Warsaw city	503	3552	381	3171	3,992	128	0.0	29.5	1.1	90.2	1161	21.7	1,573	123	10.3
Washington city	678	5658	451	5208	400	4	0.0	20.1	12.4	37.9	205	11.4	970	136	34.4
Westfield city	457	1336	105	1230	142,575	647	64.1	33.7	3.8	75.3	572	25.9	808	40	55.7
West Lafayette city	381	1221	103	1119	49,719	432	29.9	32.5	8.8	47.0	416	24.7	808	153	40.9
Yorktown town	NA	NA	NA	NA	5,125	20	100.0	5.1	1.1	82.0	209	5.3	468	14	8.8
Zionsville town	155	606	23	583	70,256	190	100.0	17.4	2.4	70.0	433	8.3	340	51	17.7
IOWA	73,553	2367	273	2094	1,907,579	10,256	68.1	X	X	X	X	X	X	X	X
Altoona city	NA	NA	NA	NA	40,975	323	29.4	25.3	3.1	45.4	1011	23.0	1,492	226	101.4
Ames city	1,192	1907	120	1787	66,548	441	20.6	250.4	24.1	59.9	475	219.0	3,578	476	127.9
Ankeny city	748	1409	115	1294	243,075	1,180	82.5	57.6	6.0	79.4	658	69.7	1,421	618	178.3
Bettendorf city	513	1464	148	1315	44,416	168	100.0	52.9	7.7	67.3	883	55.4	1,617	483	119.0
Boone city	303	2400	499	1901	1,551	10	80.0	15.3	3.0	41.5	613	12.1	961	201	32.4
Burlington city	1,038	4029	633	3396	4,387	29	100.0	34.5	5.6	56.2	700	35.7	1,395	364	62.6
Carroll city	107	1071	130	941	3,227	10	100.0	13.5	2.1	58.6	730	10.8	1,071	242	13.2
Cedar Falls city	840	2055	122	1932	44,807	181	83.4	77.7	19.4	43.0	783	81.6	2,049	977	86.6
Cedar Rapids city	5,431	4213	301	3912	45,054	449	72.4	405.0	168.3	22.7	905	457.5	3,573	2,065	538.7
Clinton city	1,386	5255	626	4629	8,294	61	27.9	48.5	10.4	28.4	761	67.1	2,521	1,417	83.3
Clive city	386	2287	113	2174	49,685	191	65.4	26.7	2.8	96.1	1080	25.9	1,596	291	63.1
Coralville city	584	2864	103	2761	21,254	164	54.3	73.7	16.3	48.8	1569	113.1	5,711	3,470	269.5
Council Bluffs city	4,459	7208	548	6660	14,891	73	100.0	118.7	29.8	38.3	983	111.9	1,801	467	125.8
Davenport city	4,831	4703	619	4084	20,744	120	75.0	165.6	37.9	52.7	837	177.4	1,749	508	324.8
Des Moines city	10,148	4873	613	4260	46,376	283	41.0	404.2	93.7	24.5	757	460.9	2,228	484	556.3
Dubuque city	1,665	2850	248	2602	11,662	82	100.0	135.5	48.8	22.7	780	160.4	2,763	1,348	185.8
Fort Dodge city	1,398	5701	689	5011	1,415	9	55.6	36.9	6.2	50.6	717	39.3	1,589	605	80.9
Fort Madison city	272	2464	516	1947	1,590	16	50.0	16.7	5.3	38.7	549	14.6	1,323	243	28.5
Indianola city	431	2839	527	2312	7,963	53	54.7	14.0	2.0	74.2	429	19.6	1,310	452	41.5
Iowa City city	1,969	2715	294	2421	81,693	445	50.8	138.3	36.0	53.0	906	128.1	1,819	366	187.9
Johnston city	191	935	88	847	42,805	174	72.4	25.6	5.6	95.3	837	24.7	1,317	482	48.9
Keokuk city	536	4978	873	4105	95	2	100.0	15.5	2.6	56.7	732	14.0	1,305	242	40.3
Marion city	585	1604	134	1469	25,765	221	66.1	36.5	5.5	81.7	630	37.9	1,056	306	67.4
Marshalltown city	958	3432	552	2880	411	4	0.0	34.2	10.2	31.7	595	35.1	1,262	431	31.2
Mason City city	969	3509	94	3414	10,743	67	28.4	52.9	17.0	23.3	748	45.1	1,625	357	60.3

1 Data for serious crimes have not been adjusted for underreporting. This may affect comparability between geographic areas over time.
2 Per 100,000 population estimated by the FBI.   3 Based on population estimated as of July 1 of the year shown.

Table B. Incorporated Places, Census Designated Places (CDPs), and Minor Civil Divisions (MCDs) of 10,000 or More Population — Land Area, Population, and Households, and Employment

STATE City, town, township, borough, or CDP (county if applicable)	Land area,[1] 2010 (sq mi)	Total persons 2010	Total persons 2014	Percent change 2010–2014	Persons per square mile, 2014	Foreign born	Lives in same house as previous year	Median household income (dollars)	Income of $100,000 or more	Income below poverty level	Percent in labor force	Unemploy-ment rate	Family households	One person households
	1	2	3	4	5	6	7	8	9	10	11	12	13	14
IOWA—Con.														
Muscatine city	18.170	23,772	23,888	0.5	1,314.7	6.2	86.0	$44,535	12.2	15.8	66.0	5.9	65.8	27.8
Newton city	11.187	15,254	15,150	-0.7	1,354.3	1.4	78.8	$45,421	12.4	15.3	60.3	6.1	59.5	32.6
North Liberty city	7.833	13,374	15,386	15.0	1,964.3	3.7	81.5	$72,470	29.7	5.3	84.8	0.7	57.0	29.9
Oskaloosa city	7.988	11,502	11,541	0.3	1,444.8	2.0	77.8	$39,385	8.5	20.2	66.0	9.9	55.5	38.6
Ottumwa city	15.860	25,023	24,682	-1.4	1,556.3	9.7	82.6	$38,095	9.2	21.4	63.1	10.1	62.5	31.5
Pella city	8.928	10,357	10,337	-0.2	1,157.8	4.5	76.0	$57,096	14.9	9.1	68.8	4.7	64.9	33.1
Sioux City city	58.071	82,684	82,517	-0.2	1,421.0	10.7	81.3	$43,629	12.1	15.9	69.3	6.1	64.1	29.9
Spencer city	10.831	11,241	11,206	-0.3	1,034.6	2.6	83.4	$44,467	14.3	13.4	66.5	4.4	59.5	32.1
Storm Lake city	5.273	10,641	10,895	2.4	2,066.1	31.6	78.5	$44,164	12.8	15.8	71.8	5.1	62.2	33.1
Urbandale city	22.126	39,457	43,150	9.4	1,950.2	7.8	90.3	$79,909	38.7	4.7	75.4	3.9	70.0	24.5
Waterloo city	61.389	68,406	68,364	-0.1	1,113.6	6.3	84.8	$41,461	10.3	16.8	66.4	9.6	57.0	36.3
Waukee city	13.492	13,800	17,705	28.3	1,312.3	5.8	84.9	$78,786	38.6	4.8	78.9	0.6	73.8	18.4
West Des Moines city	46.281	56,700	63,325	11.7	1,368.3	11.1	79.2	$70,882	31.6	7.5	76.6	4.3	60.4	30.6
KANSAS	81,758.714	2,853,132	2,904,021	1.8	35.5	6.8	83.4	$51,872	19.9	13.0	67.4	6.6	65.7	28.5
Andover city	10.000	11,791	12,509	6.1	1,250.9	3.0	84.2	$81,622	35.6	4.7	75.3	4.3	75.6	23.9
Arkansas City city	9.268	12,405	12,205	-1.6	1,316.9	4.8	76.3	$37,139	7.3	22.1	61.3	11.9	59.3	33.6
Atchison city	7.852	11,027	10,771	-2.3	1,371.7	1.0	80.5	$41,283	13.8	18.5	63.9	9.3	59.7	35.3
Coffeyville city	9.396	10,295	9,876	-4.1	1,051.1	4.9	77.9	$32,758	5.5	23.8	61.1	8.8	54.8	39.8
Derby city	9.913	22,227	23,234	4.5	2,343.8	2.7	85.8	$67,720	27.0	6.5	72.3	4.5	73.4	21.5
Dodge City city	14.577	27,340	28,117	2.8	1,928.8	30.8	86.8	$49,083	12.9	15.7	70.7	7.6	74.4	21.1
El Dorado city	8.968	13,026	12,879	-1.1	1,436.1	0.9	76.5	$44,233	12.4	15.5	63.4	6.6	62.1	33.2
Emporia city	11.963	24,923	24,560	-1.5	2,052.9	12.8	73.1	$36,697	8.4	25.5	69.3	8.9	56.4	32.5
Garden City city	8.826	26,666	27,004	1.3	3,059.5	22.1	84.1	$46,611	14.2	13.6	73.4	4.5	70.5	23.7
Gardner city	10.170	19,115	20,667	8.1	2,032.1	3.4	85.0	$65,938	23.4	3.0	77.9	6.4	76.6	18.3
Great Bend city	10.602	15,995	15,840	-1.0	1,494.0	9.2	82.7	$38,533	12.8	18.6	64.8	9.4	63.1	33.7
Hays city	8.020	20,533	21,044	2.5	2,623.8	3.4	70.6	$42,166	14.3	20.9	74.0	5.2	50.9	35.1
Haysville city	4.660	10,826	11,112	2.6	2,384.6	2.2	88.4	$52,951	13.0	8.5	64.2	5.8	74.6	23.0
Hutchinson city	24.643	42,192	41,642	-1.3	1,689.8	3.3	78.1	$41,677	9.9	13.9	60.8	6.9	62.4	32.5
Junction City city	11.075	23,349	24,665	5.6	2,227.0	9.2	73.6	$45,106	10.9	14.6	72.6	9.0	65.9	26.6
Kansas City city	124.812	145,786	149,636	2.6	1,198.9	15.8	82.7	$38,073	9.9	22.9	65.7	12.7	64.1	29.7
Lansing city	12.385	11,265	11,713	4.0	945.8	3.1	77.8	$82,288	34.8	9.7	52.8	6.5	78.9	17.6
Lawrence city	34.325	87,643	92,763	5.8	2,702.5	7.9	67.9	$46,929	18.5	19.7	69.9	6.8	49.6	31.8
Leavenworth city	24.043	35,251	36,000	2.1	1,497.3	4.7	69.2	$52,022	21.7	13.4	57.6	8.8	63.7	30.4
Leawood city	15.068	31,867	34,395	7.9	2,282.7	5.2	90.0	$133,702	63.6	4.1	65.4	3.3	77.7	19.5
Lenexa city	34.109	48,190	51,042	5.9	1,496.5	8.8	81.9	$75,400	35.6	6.7	74.1	5.6	66.7	25.7
Liberal city	11.532	20,525	21,012	2.4	1,822.1	32.3	82.3	$47,286	12.8	17.9	71.3	8.7	73.4	20.5
McPherson city	7.487	13,157	13,189	0.2	1,761.6	1.8	83.1	$53,970	19.4	7.4	67.1	2.8	65.8	29.2
Manhattan city	18.883	52,297	56,078	7.2	2,969.7	7.9	72.3	$43,275	16.1	22.4	65.7	5.2	46.9	33.0
Merriam city	4.325	11,032	11,290	2.3	2,610.2	8.4	85.2	$55,103	16.3	10.4	73.7	5.0	55.5	35.2
Newton city	13.298	19,139	19,120	-0.1	1,437.8	6.8	84.4	$44,210	12.6	14.5	64.5	5.7	63.4	31.4
Olathe city	60.096	125,875	133,062	5.7	2,214.2	10.9	84.7	$76,519	35.1	7.0	77.1	5.3	74.2	20.8
Ottawa city	9.752	12,651	12,403	-2.0	1,271.9	2.2	80.7	$43,828	10.1	15.3	69.1	8.0	62.9	30.7
Overland Park city	74.885	173,333	184,525	6.5	2,464.1	9.9	83.6	$72,231	34.0	6.4	71.8	5.1	63.7	31.0
Parsons city	10.606	10,500	10,174	-3.1	959.3	1.9	81.8	$37,948	7.9	17.1	61.5	8.0	61.3	34.2
Pittsburg city	12.798	20,233	20,394	0.8	1,593.6	5.0	74.1	$32,655	9.2	29.8	63.6	6.6	50.6	35.7
Prairie Village city	6.203	21,447	21,877	2.0	3,526.8	2.8	85.8	$81,422	39.1	4.2	69.6	3.4	60.1	34.4
Salina city	25.108	47,707	47,867	0.3	1,906.4	6.1	83.7	$44,398	12.7	15.2	68.7	6.0	62.1	31.2
Shawnee city	41.854	62,209	64,599	3.8	1,543.4	5.3	86.0	$74,992	34.3	7.6	72.3	4.9	71.4	23.3
Topeka city	60.858	127,474	127,215	-0.2	2,090.4	5.6	79.9	$41,412	13.2	18.8	64.0	8.2	57.0	36.0
Wichita city	160.437	382,386	388,413	1.6	2,421.0	10.2	82.7	$45,907	16.4	16.2	67.3	8.7	61.8	32.5
Winfield city	11.142	12,347	12,258	-0.7	1,100.1	3.7	73.8	$40,713	14.9	16.5	58.3	7.7	58.3	34.7
KENTUCKY	39,486.336	4,339,349	4,413,457	1.7	111.8	3.4	84.7	$43,342	15.5	18.5	59.8	9.3	66.6	28.1
Ashland city	10.743	21,684	21,335	-1.6	1,986.0	1.8	85.0	$37,789	13.1	25.0	55.3	12.5	61.0	34.2
Bardstown city	12.010	12,604	12,998	3.1	1,082.2	2.8	77.9	$32,000	11.8	26.1	61.0	18.0	66.2	28.8
Berea city	16.412	13,561	14,658	8.1	893.2	3.9	73.2	$38,513	8.3	28.2	59.2	7.3	62.5	27.9
Bowling Green city	38.214	58,888	62,479	6.1	1,635.0	12.7	65.3	$34,036	10.3	26.4	63.9	11.7	52.9	33.7
Burlington CDP	8.840	15,926	NA	NA	NA	2.0	83.4	$71,064	28.3	8.0	71.0	4.4	79.4	15.7
Campbellsville city	7.228	10,638	11,282	6.1	1,560.8	3.0	82.4	$31,026	8.0	26.0	53.6	11.0	61.0	36.4
Covington city	13.191	40,516	40,944	1.1	3,103.8	2.0	79.5	$35,460	8.6	23.5	62.1	12.1	51.8	39.3
Danville city	15.821	16,218	16,620	2.5	1,050.5	2.9	77.5	$38,198	12.6	20.6	56.2	10.1	61.3	33.1
Elizabethtown city	26.007	28,541	29,974	5.0	1,152.5	5.1	75.1	$42,735	19.0	14.7	62.3	8.5	61.1	34.1
Erlanger city	8.303	18,127	18,647	2.9	2,245.8	2.6	83.1	$56,625	20.4	10.5	71.1	8.6	68.7	27.0
Florence city	10.341	29,953	31,888	6.5	3,083.8	6.8	78.9	$52,878	18.4	10.2	68.7	6.6	61.1	32.5
Fort Campbell North CDP	5.070	13,685	NA	NA	NA	6.1	59.3	$36,642	2.9	19.0	76.4	23.1	95.4	4.4
Fort Knox CDP	20.610	10,124	NA	NA	NA	5.0	46.6	$50,988	12.2	10.6	77.8	19.0	94.1	5.6
Fort Thomas city	5.672	16,194	16,329	0.8	2,879.1	2.9	85.9	$62,454	31.1	8.8	71.7	6.3	63.0	31.1
Frankfort city	14.767	27,269	27,557	1.1	1,866.1	4.7	74.1	$40,622	13.6	19.0	62.4	11.4	55.2	38.4
Georgetown city	16.564	29,119	31,653	8.7	1,911.0	3.2	79.8	$56,854	18.6	13.1	71.8	8.2	70.2	25.0
Glasgow city	15.461	14,049	14,339	2.1	927.4	2.2	80.3	$28,155	9.7	27.3	52.7	10.5	58.6	39.5
Henderson city	15.376	28,757	28,900	0.5	1,879.6	1.4	81.7	$35,725	9.6	21.8	60.6	10.7	59.6	36.5
Hopkinsville city	31.120	32,035	32,634	1.9	1,048.7	2.9	79.2	$34,670	11.2	21.0	56.8	16.4	61.2	34.0
Independence city	17.428	24,753	26,378	6.6	1,513.5	2.2	87.5	$65,776	23.4	8.6	73.2	6.9	80.3	15.7
Jeffersontown city	9.926	26,595	26,949	1.3	2,714.9	7.4	80.6	$60,251	24.9	8.5	74.2	6.9	64.9	28.6
Lawrenceburg city	6.003	10,908	11,093	1.7	1,847.8	1.2	88.8	$50,696	8.7	11.4	68.1	6.8	65.5	27.9
Lexington-Fayette urban county	283.649	295,803	310,797	5.1	1,095.7	9.1	75.7	$48,667	20.8	17.9	68.4	8.0	57.3	32.6
Louisville/Jefferson County metro government	380.416	741,096	760,026	2.6	1,997.9	6.7	85.3	$47,692	19.2	15.9	65.8	9.3	60.6	33.0
Louisville/Jefferson County metro government (balance)	263.761	597,265	612,780	2.6	2,323.2	6.7	85.3	$44,806	17.2	17.6	65.4	10.2	60.4	33.2
Lyndon city	3.599	11,002	11,311	2.8	3,143.0	10.9	76.8	$50,516	17.1	9.3	73.6	5.1	51.1	39.7
Madisonville city	17.946	19,929	19,622	-1.5	1,093.4	1.6	82.3	$40,565	11.3	18.2	58.2	7.5	59.1	36.3
Mayfield city	6.890	10,024	10,122	1.0	1,469.1	6.4	84.8	$24,839	9.5	32.9	51.7	15.0	60.1	36.2

1 Dry land or land partially or temporarily covered by water.
2 16 years old and over.

Table B. Incorporated Places, Census Designated Places (CDPs), and Minor Civil Divisions (MCDs) of 10,000 or More Population — Crime, Construction, and Local Government Finance

STATE City, town, township, borough, or CDP (county if applicable)	Serious crimes known to police, 2014[1] Total number	Rate[2] Total	Rate[2] Violent	Rate[2] Property	New residential construction authorized by building permits, 2014 Value ($1,000)	Number of housing units	Percent single family	Local government finance, 2012 General revenue Total (mil dol)	General revenue Intergovernmental Total (mil dol)	Intergovernmental Percent from state gov.	Taxes per capita[3]	General expenditure Total (mil dol)	Per capita[3] Total	Per capita[3] Capital outlays	Debt outstanding (mil dol)
	15	16	17	18	19	20	21	22	23	24	25	26	27	28	29
IOWA—Con.															
Muscatine city	607	2633	603	2030	2,574	22	18.2	51.6	8.5	41.2	698	49.5	2,073	465	35.3
Newton city	657	4348	371	3977	673	3	100.0	56.3	2.4	73.6	754	55.0	3,639	215	34.8
North Liberty city	186	1211	345	866	42,286	255	63.5	17.0	2.3	92.9	665	18.7	1,284	548	44.0
Oskaloosa city	364	3143	397	2746	8,782	62	12.9	13.3	3.4	33.3	560	10.7	924	138	14.2
Ottumwa city	1,147	4626	290	4336	316	4	50.0	40.4	7.9	63.1	679	37.3	1,505	459	37.1
Pella city	183	1769	164	1604	10,759	38	78.9	22.5	2.6	40.1	653	11.2	1,081	345	8.9
Sioux City city	3,479	4224	353	3870	17,741	88	86.4	139.6	32.9	58.3	766	143.7	1,737	477	249.2
Spencer city	281	2523	162	2361	2,270	10	80.0	93.9	2.2	70.2	680	79.9	7,152	612	39.6
Storm Lake city	268	2477	471	2006	1,132	4	100.0	19.3	3.8	38.3	524	18.8	1,748	477	38.4
Urbandale city	781	1845	198	1646	63,123	246	63.4	41.8	4.8	80.6	721	40.8	995	315	55.3
Waterloo city	3,336	4880	958	3922	10,786	93	84.9	115.1	25.8	46.6	865	119.5	1,749	524	115.2
Waukee city	162	902	84	819	97,919	554	53.1	19.6	2.0	81.9	665	16.4	1,028	267	31.8
West Des Moines city	1,694	2717	186	2531	76,606	319	75.5	100.9	15.8	70.7	1076	85.4	1,439	353	136.6
KANSAS	89,554	3084	349	2735	1,417,358	7,459	65.3	X	X	X	X	X	X	X	X
Andover city	300	2424	145	2279	21,733	75	100.0	16.1	0.7	60.3	705	22.8	1,890	1,188	50.4
Arkansas City city	546	4446	529	3916	390	5	20.0	47.4	3.7	47.8	619	40.6	3,293	644	37.8
Atchison city	424	3887	348	3539	160	2	100.0	11.5	1.0	92.6	703	14.3	1,305	535	9.9
Coffeyville city	861	8721	1114	7607	50	1	100.0	18.3	1.9	32.9	1030	18.0	1,801	333	23.4
Derby city	591	2548	103	2444	13,513	75	78.7	27.8	4.4	23.1	629	24.0	1,046	286	77.8
Dodge City city	895	3160	420	2740	5,751	33	93.9	42.1	4.4	73.2	676	61.8	2,199	497	220.7
El Dorado city	494	3857	281	3576	2,120	10	100.0	16.3	0.6	100.0	617	14.3	1,110	18	25.2
Emporia city	386	1558	117	1441	1,555	10	100.0	34.5	3.8	32.2	657	25.8	1,039	28	44.1
Garden City city	976	3613	611	3003	2,253	14	71.4	32.6	5.3	13.6	508	32.2	1,196	137	42.2
Gardner city	NA	NA	NA	NA	15,790	91	93.4	18.8	2.6	31.7	413	15.7	772	50	118.5
Great Bend city	974	6135	510	5625	4,550	51	5.9	16.2	3.0	20.9	541	16.9	1,061	278	15.6
Hays city	530	2504	279	2225	13,483	66	63.6	27.0	1.1	87.1	964	19.9	944	66	20.2
Haysville city	324	2933	253	2680	4,069	38	73.7	7.6	2.0	29.2	255	7.6	695	24	19.5
Hutchinson city	1,916	4583	490	4093	3,459	19	68.4	47.8	10.1	16.6	572	36.3	867	15	54.3
Junction City city	717	2781	500	2280	NA	NA	NA	35.4	4.6	40.2	705	27.0	1,045	37	196.5
Kansas City city	8,376	5618	711	4907	55,076	481	35.1	345.7	20.8	59.0	1342	304.9	2,068	35	1786.2
Lansing city	159	1356	281	1074	5,996	22	90.9	9.1	1.0	32.9	416	8.3	716	121	24.1
Lawrence city	2,128	2325	231	2095	42,430	276	47.5	300.0	35.4	66.1	569	265.3	2,952	315	287.4
Leavenworth city	1,427	3962	694	3268	2,206	10	100.0	35.9	6.9	24.9	523	39.7	1,108	180	32.8
Leawood city	432	1299	69	1229	26,414	81	90.1	52.4	9.2	26.4	1121	38.2	1,173	233	60.6
Lenexa city	870	1710	110	1600	121,164	639	30.2	84.1	15.1	53.5	979	101.5	2,056	664	280.1
Liberal city	667	3168	385	2783	6,293	58	17.2	24.5	6.4	49.9	552	23.0	1,096	135	10.5
McPherson city	768	5745	209	5535	10,070	100	22.0	18.9	0.6	85.4	889	19.9	1,503	243	41.3
Manhattan city	NA	NA	NA	NA	51,847	270	71.5	75.3	14.5	19.2	675	70.4	1,243	66	344.8
Merriam city	558	4920	309	4612	938	6	100.0	19.5	3.0	11.5	1262	20.4	1,820	352	19.2
Newton city	602	3152	618	2534	3,845	23	100.0	28.8	5.8	21.1	429	22.3	1,165	21	69.8
Olathe city	1,847	1385	76	1309	145,127	502	98.4	165.1	23.5	34.3	697	149.2	1,147	163	1141.4
Ottawa city	415	3336	265	3071	669	6	33.3	12.2	1.5	29.6	546	12.4	985	59	27.8
Overland Park city	3,360	1835	179	1656	210,187	936	41.0	224.8	42.2	25.4	506	208.7	1,166	223	1428.3
Parsons city	445	4410	595	3816	210	2	100.0	10.3	1.4	41.4	528	9.7	943	108	17.0
Pittsburg city	1,226	6001	264	5736	12,001	92	15.2	25.0	4.7	21.3	592	22.3	1,096	101	39.5
Prairie Village city	239	1086	50	1036	6,935	16	100.0	23.6	4.3	44.4	653	21.7	995	355	27.4
Salina city	2,028	4238	403	3835	8,613	56	96.4	68.5	10.3	26.4	535	75.4	1,572	264	168.5
Shawnee city	1,173	1809	163	1646	51,330	201	76.6	54.4	10.0	26.2	607	48.9	769	62	215.7
Topeka city	6,911	5413	510	4903	21,242	114	75.4	206.4	27.9	31.8	835	153.6	1,201	139	364.4
Wichita city	21,240	5481	758	4723	105,584	732	75.1	562.5	102.8	20.6	435	543.6	1,410	223	3471.3
Winfield city	441	3577	195	3382	1,272	10	100.0	42.6	1.0	93.3	513	38.8	3,144	160	39.1
KENTUCKY	108,506	2459	212	2247	1,304,713	9,536	63.7	X	X	X	X	X	X	X	X
Ashland city	1,132	5309	239	5070	363	5	60.0	38.8	6.4	36.2	855	30.3	1,402	84	205.4
Bardstown city	389	2991	161	2830	NA	NA	NA	21.6	1.2	39.8	324	21.9	1,701	253	106.4
Berea city	331	2272	69	2203	3,399	54	37.0	17.9	1.0	84.8	684	14.2	997	86	99.3
Bowling Green city	3,160	5087	335	4752	38,793	302	39.1	98.4	10.3	24.6	916	76.0	1,251	71	283.6
Burlington CDP	NA	NA	NA	NA	0	0	0.0	NA	NA	NA	NA	NA	NA	NA	NA
Campbellsville city	NA	NA	NA	NA	2,200	25	100.0	15.5	4.3	18.9	475	14.1	1,267	218	25.4
Covington city	1,888	4597	497	4100	0	0	0.0	71.2	13.5	27.4	989	54.8	1,350	183	162.2
Danville city	466	2832	188	2644	NA	NA	NA	20.1	3.4	29.0	619	15.1	914	97	29.6
Elizabethtown city	1,113	3684	136	3549	12,812	186	32.3	45.8	8.2	36.9	863	37.6	1,280	347	55.2
Erlanger city	545	2410	97	2313	10,379	43	100.0	18.1	1.1	66.5	695	13.2	719	135	27.1
Florence city	1,548	4873	195	4678	NA	NA	NA	43.3	5.6	79.1	928	28.8	926	346	69.3
Fort Campbell North CDP	NA	NA	NA	NA	NA	NA	NA	NA	NA	NA	NA	NA	NA	NA	NA
Fort Knox CDP	NA	NA	NA	NA	NA	NA	NA	NA	NA	NA	NA	NA	NA	NA	NA
Fort Thomas city	125	770	37	733	6,812	23	87.0	12.7	1.2	100.0	587	11.7	720	210	2.5
Frankfort city	1,126	4096	338	3758	5,863	52	30.8	67.6	2.6	55.3	937	57.0	2,091	104	46.6
Georgetown city	1,005	3213	205	3008	NA	NA	NA	46.6	3.3	36.0	523	38.6	1,277	68	473.4
Glasgow city	497	3472	161	3311	2,041	25	100.0	23.5	4.2	15.9	804	17.6	1,245	166	82.6
Henderson city	1,052	3647	236	3412	2,915	23	52.2	46.8	13.7	10.5	597	40.9	1,415	213	50.4
Hopkinsville city	1,133	3465	315	3150	3,748	32	71.9	42.0	7.0	7.7	702	37.4	1,128	88	170.2
Independence city	218	825	49	776	14,853	131	81.7	8.3	0.8	74.2	227	6.6	259	52	8.2
Jeffersontown city	675	2489	129	2360	3,347	18	100.0	25.4	1.1	76.1	637	23.6	876	92	160.3
Lawrenceburg city	93	836	90	746	1,294	6	100.0	5.8	0.5	62.0	242	5.4	490	41	15.5
Lexington-Fayette urban county	13,251	4249	337	3912	134,483	1,225	56.1	544.8	60.2	29.6	1045	440.5	1,443	142	1000.4
Louisville/Jefferson County metro government	32,453	4789	592	4196	289,055	2,413	40.0	935.3	222.4	25.0	607	992.9	1,322	270	1594.3
Louisville/Jefferson County metro government (balance)	NA	NA	NA	NA	NA	NA	NA	NA	NA	NA	NA	NA	NA	NA	NA
Lyndon city	NA	NA	NA	NA	NA	NA	NA	2.3	0.2	100.0	187	2.3	206	0	11.1
Madisonville city	414	2095	96	1999	2,582	20	70.0	29.9	1.6	74.2	642	28.2	1,425	102	221.4
Mayfield city	301	2971	128	2843	0	0	0.0	10.9	1.1	54.4	616	12.2	1,207	57	109.9

1 Data for serious crimes have not been adjusted for underreporting. This may affect comparability between geographic areas over time.
2 Per 100,000 population estimated by the FBI.   3 Based on population estimated as of July 1 of the year shown.

Table B. Incorporated Places, Census Designated Places (CDPs), and Minor Civil Divisions (MCDs) of 10,000 or More Population — Land Area, Population, and Households, and Employment

STATE City, town, township, borough, or CDP (county if applicable)	Land area,[1] 2010 (sq mi)	Total persons 2010	Total persons 2014	Percent change 2010–2014	Persons per square mile, 2014	Foreign born	Lives in same house as previous year	Median household income (dollars)	Income of $100,000 or more	Income below poverty level	Percent in labor force	Unemployment rate	Family households	One person households
	1	2	3	4	5	6	7	8	9	10	11	12	13	14
KENTUCKY—Con.														
Middlesborough city	7.383	10,191	9,872	-3.1	1,337.2	0.9	90.4	$21,694	4.4	33.4	41.1	14.1	61.4	34.5
Mount Washington city	7.348	11,718	12,246	4.5	1,666.6	0.2	88.4	$62,799	20.5	11.9	70.1	8.2	72.9	23.1
Murray city	11.440	17,736	18,630	5.0	1,628.4	7.4	68.2	$35,041	12.2	23.4	56.4	13.5	45.9	41.9
Newport city	2.729	15,449	15,426	-0.1	5,652.1	2.9	77.7	$29,993	9.0	32.6	59.8	13.1	50.4	39.1
Nicholasville city	13.278	28,038	29,097	3.8	2,191.3	2.4	75.4	$44,213	11.1	17.7	67.4	11.2	60.4	34.0
Owensboro city	19.840	57,412	58,374	1.7	2,942.2	2.5	83.6	$38,213	10.4	17.8	59.1	7.9	53.4	34.0
Paducah city	20.157	25,027	24,978	-0.2	1,239.1	2.0	82.7	$31,338	12.7	22.9	53.6	8.8	53.4	41.8
Radcliff city	12.967	22,305	22,952	2.9	1,770.0	7.1	69.5	$45,311	13.4	17.7	66.8	12.3	68.3	27.1
Richmond city	22.835	31,369	33,556	7.0	1,469.5	2.1	69.5	$30,295	8.2	29.4	62.4	10.6	49.1	37.0
St. Matthews city	4.312	17,468	17,911	2.5	4,154.1	6.2	80.9	$53,905	21.4	7.9	72.7	4.8	44.7	44.0
Shelbyville city	8.204	14,049	14,985	6.7	1,826.6	13.3	81.7	$46,630	13.4	20.2	69.1	7.2	69.9	25.3
Shepherdsville city	11.785	11,309	11,856	4.8	1,006.0	1.0	80.2	$48,571	9.2	15.3	73.4	8.8	73.2	20.5
Shively city	4.571	15,264	15,643	2.5	3,422.1	2.5	91.9	$34,826	6.1	20.4	57.8	8.8	57.0	36.9
Somerset city	11.387	11,194	11,422	2.0	1,003.1	1.6	78.6	$24,851	4.3	33.5	54.0	6.4	55.3	39.4
Winchester city	8.792	18,370	18,443	0.4	2,097.6	1.5	72.7	$35,055	11.5	20.3	60.1	11.1	60.2	32.1
LOUISIANA	43,203.903	4,533,479	4,649,676	2.6	107.6	3.9	86.0	$44,991	18.5	18.8	61.1	8.7	65.9	28.7
Abbeville city	6.061	12,255	12,446	1.6	2,053.5	3.8	77.7	$28,939	10.8	27.5	59.7	14.7	63.2	32.7
Alexandria city	28.391	47,587	48,175	1.2	1,696.8	3.4	85.5	$35,263	11.7	23.0	55.1	11.4	61.4	35.3
Baker city	8.288	13,888	13,776	-0.8	1,662.2	3.2	86.6	$41,060	8.6	17.2	63.0	9.3	70.8	28.0
Bastrop city	8.896	11,365	10,881	-4.3	1,223.1	0.4	91.7	$22,721	2.9	37.6	53.0	15.5	59.9	35.4
Baton Rouge city	77.422	229,447	228,895	-0.2	2,956.5	5.3	80.7	$38,790	15.9	23.4	64.0	10.0	54.3	35.1
Bayou Blue CDP	23.263	12,352	NA	NA	NA	1.5	81.7	$55,193	19.4	14.7	64.5	6.2	76.8	20.0
Bayou Cane CDP	7.606	19,355	NA	NA	NA	5.2	79.6	$51,968	20.5	11.1	64.8	4.9	68.4	24.5
Belle Chasse CDP	24.916	12,679	NA	NA	NA	4.9	89.7	$63,238	26.8	9.2	67.6	3.9	74.2	20.0
Bogalusa city	9.504	12,232	11,926	-2.5	1,254.9	3.3	82.7	$25,036	7.8	36.4	49.9	23.5	62.9	34.0
Bossier City city	42.510	61,631	67,472	9.5	1,587.2	5.1	80.7	$47,103	17.2	14.4	67.6	6.4	62.3	33.2
Central city	62.247	26,867	28,119	4.7	451.7	1.0	91.8	$66,778	28.7	8.0	65.9	5.0	79.5	19.4
Chalmette CDP	7.153	16,751	NA	NA	NA	7.8	82.4	$43,039	14.1	17.2	62.9	11.1	67.2	25.3
Claiborne CDP	9.957	11,507	NA	NA	NA	1.8	88.3	$51,190	20.8	13.8	66.8	5.7	70.3	24.0
Crowley city	5.851	13,263	13,189	-0.6	2,254.1	3.2	78.2	$28,185	10.1	34.3	53.2	16.7	63.3	28.5
Denham Springs city	7.293	10,215	10,097	-1.2	1,384.5	2.6	88.2	$48,105	16.4	14.7	62.9	10.8	65.7	27.5
DeRidder city	9.228	10,578	10,799	2.1	1,170.3	5.0	79.5	$42,356	13.0	22.3	60.5	8.0	66.9	26.9
Destrehan CDP	5.909	11,535	NA	NA	NA	9.1	85.4	$70,013	34.9	6.3	71.4	8.8	79.0	17.3
Estelle CDP	5.013	16,377	NA	NA	NA	9.9	95.7	$52,659	18.0	10.9	60.6	4.2	78.0	18.0
Eunice city	5.138	10,398	10,330	-0.7	2,010.7	1.0	85.7	$31,078	6.7	28.8	53.8	7.1	58.9	33.7
Gardere CDP	3.393	10,580	NA	NA	NA	12.3	76.1	$43,162	12.3	29.6	79.8	6.2	59.6	19.2
Gonzales city	9.096	9,782	10,457	6.9	1,149.6	2.8	86.7	$51,923	23.8	18.8	63.7	9.1	62.8	29.2
Gretna city	4.004	17,734	17,845	0.6	4,457.1	13.1	82.8	$34,158	15.5	23.0	57.9	9.8	57.6	34.7
Hammond city	14.013	20,015	20,363	1.7	1,453.1	3.1	70.7	$31,753	17.2	27.8	61.6	15.6	58.8	31.1
Harvey CDP	6.599	20,348	NA	NA	NA	14.1	84.1	$39,398	17.8	23.5	60.8	4.5	65.3	30.4
Houma city	14.426	33,703	34,124	1.2	2,365.5	4.6	84.8	$47,212	19.3	19.1	60.5	7.4	67.2	27.1
Jefferson CDP	2.707	11,193	NA	NA	NA	7.0	85.9	$41,016	11.7	15.1	66.1	8.7	48.3	42.3
Jennings city	10.404	10,383	10,183	-1.9	978.7	1.1	80.4	$31,019	13.2	27.3	53.7	11.1	63.6	30.8
Kenner city	14.869	66,705	67,064	0.5	4,510.4	18.1	89.0	$49,771	19.4	13.6	66.4	8.6	66.5	29.0
Lafayette city	51.499	121,131	126,066	4.1	2,447.9	5.6	80.5	$45,682	20.6	18.2	66.4	6.4	55.7	35.2
Lake Charles city	42.144	72,033	74,889	4.0	1,777.0	3.5	75.8	$35,830	14.2	23.2	62.1	11.1	60.2	34.0
Laplace CDP	20.892	29,872	NA	NA	NA	4.5	89.9	$54,278	20.3	14.6	65.6	8.9	75.4	21.2
Luling CDP	23.301	12,119	NA	NA	NA	1.9	94.7	$62,176	30.0	10.1	67.2	7.0	74.2	18.1
Mandeville city	6.944	11,931	12,236	2.6	1,762.1	7.8	83.2	$69,451	33.3	9.7	65.0	6.9	66.2	29.3
Marrero CDP	7.937	33,141	NA	NA	NA	5.1	91.3	$32,910	11.2	24.5	56.8	8.0	65.8	30.9
Metairie CDP	23.222	138,481	NA	NA	NA	13.0	85.8	$51,808	23.0	13.4	66.5	6.9	59.4	34.3
Minden city	14.967	13,082	12,808	-2.1	855.8	0.8	82.2	$29,154	8.3	25.7	55.5	13.4	63.1	32.3
Monroe city	29.294	49,154	49,601	0.9	1,693.2	2.0	85.4	$28,565	12.5	32.6	57.6	12.1	58.3	36.7
Morgan City city	5.982	12,404	11,943	-3.7	1,996.4	4.0	85.4	$42,132	11.9	21.9	58.0	8.8	65.4	28.1
Moss Bluff CDP	15.224	11,557	NA	NA	809.8	3.0	85.8	$65,944	26.9	4.1	60.9	7.0	80.8	16.0
Natchitoches city	22.703	18,545	18,384	-0.9	809.8	1.6	80.7	$26,848	10.7	35.6	57.9	13.7	56.1	33.8
New Iberia city	11.139	30,617	30,745	0.4	2,760.1	4.5	83.8	$40,117	13.4	21.6	60.7	11.4	64.2	30.8
New Orleans city	169.418	343,829	384,320	11.8	2,268.5	6.0	82.5	$36,964	16.9	26.1	62.1	11.6	51.4	40.2
Opelousas city	7.928	16,758	16,617	-0.8	2,096.1	0.7	85.7	$21,373	4.8	38.0	47.7	10.5	64.7	32.6
Pineville city	12.590	14,508	14,425	-0.6	1,145.8	2.6	80.6	$39,375	16.3	19.0	53.7	8.6	59.5	36.7
Prairieville CDP	22.005	26,895	NA	NA	NA	3.1	91.2	$93,768	45.2	7.8	74.3	4.5	80.5	15.2
River Ridge CDP	2.795	13,494	NA	NA	NA	2.5	90.7	$60,543	26.7	10.1	61.0	4.7	68.0	28.2
Ruston city	20.916	21,907	22,301	1.8	1,066.2	6.5	68.9	$29,560	10.8	36.5	60.0	13.3	50.9	32.9
Shenandoah CDP	6.198	18,399	NA	NA	NA	3.0	88.1	$91,949	46.2	3.2	72.2	3.2	73.8	20.4
Shreveport city	107.137	200,410	198,242	-1.1	1,850.4	2.6	83.4	$38,413	15.8	20.4	60.9	8.3	60.7	34.7
Slidell city	14.843	27,071	27,622	2.0	1,860.9	4.3	84.0	$50,432	19.0	13.8	62.9	9.5	69.7	22.4
Sulphur city	10.103	20,408	20,206	-1.0	1,999.9	3.5	81.1	$46,780	18.3	17.2	58.1	8.5	67.8	26.2
Terrytown CDP	3.681	23,319	NA	NA	NA	18.1	87.6	$43,971	14.9	19.8	71.9	8.4	69.5	27.7
Thibodaux city	6.028	14,571	14,603	0.2	2,422.7	2.8	78.5	$39,534	16.3	19.8	57.2	7.3	57.9	32.1
Timberlane CDP	1.496	10,243	NA	NA	NA	14.1	92.9	$53,617	19.8	12.5	65.1	4.8	73.4	20.2
West Monroe city	7.985	13,064	12,985	-0.6	1,626.1	1.7	85.4	$32,849	9.1	27.5	60.4	7.1	57.8	39.0
Woodmere CDP	3.652	12,080	NA	NA	NA	4.7	89.6	$54,335	17.3	21.4	64.8	6.8	82.4	15.8
Zachary city	23.928	14,942	16,219	8.5	677.8	0.9	87.9	$72,012	25.9	8.5	67.1	4.6	83.0	14.2
MAINE	30,842.922	1,328,361	1,330,089	0.1	43.1	3.5	86.1	$48,804	17.4	13.9	63.9	7.4	62.9	29.1
Auburn city & MCD (Androscoggin)	59.330	23,052	22,912	-0.6	386.2	3.1	81.5	$45,279	14.3	16.1	64.0	8.6	57.8	33.0
Augusta city & MCD (Kennebec)	55.134	19,132	18,705	-2.2	339.3	3.7	82.9	$38,263	11.0	17.7	59.5	8.4	52.7	39.3
Bangor city & MCD (Penobscot)	34.259	33,037	32,568	-1.4	950.6	3.7	76.8	$36,272	12.3	21.8	62.0	8.1	48.1	38.8
Biddeford city & MCD (York)	30.084	21,277	21,337	0.3	709.2	4.9	80.1	$45,729	14.7	16.1	68.7	6.3	55.8	32.8
Brunswick CDP	14.510	15,175	NA	NA	NA	3.3	78.8	$48,176	19.3	10.7	61.3	7.0	55.1	38.5

1 Dry land or land partially or temporarily covered by water.
2 16 years old and over.

Table B. Incorporated Places, Census Designated Places (CDPs), and Minor Civil Divisions (MCDs) of 10,000 or More Population — Crime, Construction, and Local Government Finance

STATE City, town, township, borough, or CDP (county if applicable)	Serious crimes known to police, 2014[1] Total number	Rate[2] Total	Rate[2] Violent	Rate[2] Property	New residential construction authorized by building permits, 2014 Value ($1,000)	Number of housing units	Percent single family	Local government finance, 2012 General revenue Total (mil dol)	Intergovernmental Total (mil dol)	Intergovernmental Percent from state gov.	Taxes per capita[3]	General expenditure Total (mil dol)	Per capita[3] Total	Per capita[3] Capital outlays	Debt outstanding (mil dol)
	15	16	17	18	19	20	21	22	23	24	25	26	27	28	29
KENTUCKY—Con.															
Middlesborough city	673	6821	152	6669	560	7	100.0	9.4	2.2	19.4	356	9.7	967	109	0.0
Mount Washington city	NA	NA	NA	NA	NA	NA	NA	6.5	0.7	41.8	217	19.1	1,601	1,222	10.9
Murray city	588	3233	137	3095	19,132	291	13.7	262.4	1.2	99.6	369	124.2	6,703	608	63.2
Newport city	1,020	6642	501	6141	818	1	100.0	37.5	2.8	75.4	785	30.9	1,997	121	312.2
Nicholasville city	1,135	3929	183	3745	13,541	102	87.3	20.8	2.5	72.9	473	18.1	638	35	32.1
Owensboro city	2,385	4066	210	3856	26,689	320	79.4	98.3	27.0	14.9	602	105.2	1,812	630	399.8
Paducah city	1,448	5788	324	5464	13,060	92	17.4	63.2	11.9	37.1	1297	49.1	1,954	263	39.7
Radcliff city	599	2577	250	2328	568	5	100.0	13.1	2.3	55.6	407	9.9	429	75	3.0
Richmond city	1,366	4161	308	3853	11,324	171	58.5	34.6	1.4	35.9	631	25.5	785	137	104.2
St. Matthews city	724	4035	189	3845	NA	NA	NA	12.0	0.7	91.7	604	9.4	533	54	22.4
Shelbyville city	321	2151	188	1963	NA	NA	NA	8.7	0.5	58.5	492	9.5	656	176	18.4
Shepherdsville city	342	2901	212	2689	NA	NA	NA	12.3	0.5	75.0	567	7.0	604	80	7.4
Shively city	701	4474	428	4046	NA	NA	NA	10.2	0.6	100.0	557	6.7	437	40	30.9
Somerset city	682	5929	278	5651	787	14	85.7	20.3	3.7	1.3	535	22.4	1,982	245	21.6
Winchester city	881	4791	228	4563	NA	NA	NA	35.0	10.4	18.1	603	25.4	1,380	67	17.0
LOUISIANA	184,758	3974	515	3459	2,888,790	15,255	84.2	X	X	X	X	X	X	X	X
Abbeville city	668	5349	1033	4316	1,021	8	100.0	8.8	1.4	33.7	374	14.7	1,191	91	3.6
Alexandria city	4,619	9501	1765	7736	9,324	49	79.6	82.5	13.7	28.9	1121	92.8	1,936	198	94.9
Baker city	407	2947	181	2766	0	0	0.0	11.7	1.1	80.9	454	12.7	912	66	3.0
Bastrop city	1,468	13521	1299	12223	0	0	0.0	18.2	2.7	51.5	847	15.9	1,433	134	6.6
Baton Rouge city	12,390	5401	924	4477	90,321	476	48.7	959.1	199.4	55.2	1992	1203.6	5,233	1,750	1639.8
Bayou Blue CDP	NA	NA	NA	NA	NA	NA	NA	NA	NA	NA	NA	NA	NA	NA	NA
Bayou Cane CDP	NA	NA	NA	NA	NA	NA	NA	NA	NA	NA	NA	NA	NA	NA	NA
Belle Chasse CDP	NA	NA	NA	NA	NA	NA	NA	NA	NA	NA	NA	NA	NA	NA	NA
Bogalusa city	778	6505	886	5619	NA	NA	NA	18.6	4.6	33.7	847	17.8	1,473	164	12.7
Bossier City city	3,637	5391	642	4749	100,441	1,057	55.4	108.4	8.2	55.5	1090	129.1	1,975	823	360.5
Central city	NA	NA	NA	NA	31,411	134	100.0	9.1	0.3	100.0	313	4.7	169	2	0.0
Chalmette CDP	NA	NA	NA	NA	NA	NA	NA	NA	NA	NA	NA	NA	NA	NA	NA
Claiborne CDP	NA	NA	NA	NA	NA	NA	NA	NA	NA	NA	NA	NA	NA	NA	NA
Crowley city	632	4786	795	3991	800	5	100.0	19.5	4.7	17.4	873	17.0	1,291	143	12.5
Denham Springs city	867	8558	809	7748	1,531	10	100.0	21.9	2.8	54.7	1162	30.7	3,030	958	111.9
DeRidder city	317	2927	277	2650	6,588	27	100.0	10.3	1.1	39.6	711	10.6	988	74	0.2
Destrehan CDP	NA	NA	NA	NA	NA	NA	NA	NA	NA	NA	NA	NA	NA	.NA	NA
Estelle CDP	NA	NA	NA	NA	NA	NA	NA	NA	NA	NA	NA	NA	NA	NA	NA
Eunice city	783	7581	1191	6390	900	6	100.0	11.5	1.3	64.0	684	12.0	1,156	210	1.8
Gardere CDP	NA	NA	NA	NA	NA	NA	NA	NA	NA	NA	NA	NA	NA	NA	NA
Gonzales city	NA	NA	NA	NA	13,971	96	100.0	19.6	4.1	75.4	1360	25.3	2,487	819	51.7
Gretna city	541	3036	236	2801	2,593	23	73.9	33.3	9.0	70.0	819	32.6	1,833	379	16.0
Hammond city	2,392	11716	1176	10541	9,301	40	82.5	36.0	4.6	44.8	1207	34.6	1,711	179	27.8
Harvey CDP	NA	NA	NA	NA	NA	NA	NA	NA	NA	NA	NA	NA	NA	NA	NA
Houma city	1,601	4691	618	4073	NA	NA	NA	411.9	103.8	73.9	3483	430.0	12,764	2,321	213.1
Jefferson CDP	NA	NA	NA	NA	NA	NA	NA	NA	NA	NA	NA	NA	NA	NA	NA
Jennings city	336	3314	424	2890	3,164	36	100.0	11.2	1.6	31.3	686	11.0	1,075	138	2.0
Kenner city	2,577	3844	236	3608	6,259	19	100.0	77.5	40.2	21.3	332	70.3	1,050	164	61.5
Lafayette city	7,614	6085	651	5435	NA	NA	NA	402.4	70.2	47.1	1631	443.4	3,597	882	1132.6
Lake Charles city	3,733	5013	690	4323	81,511	826	17.6	116.9	27.3	9.2	952	117.0	1,590	348	92.3
Laplace CDP	NA	NA	NA	NA	NA	NA	NA	NA	NA	NA	NA	NA	NA	NA	NA
Luling CDP	NA	NA	NA	NA	NA	NA	NA	NA	NA	NA	NA	NA	NA	NA	NA
Mandeville city	274	2237	155	2081	11,586	30	100.0	22.2	0.3	72.8	1528	17.7	1,463	261	3.9
Marrero CDP	NA	NA	NA	NA	NA	NA	NA	NA	NA	NA	NA	NA	NA	NA	NA
Metairie CDP	NA	NA	NA	NA	NA	NA	NA	NA	NA	NA	NA	NA	NA	NA	NA
Minden city	298	2306	139	2167	853	4	100.0	12.5	2.3	23.0	533	18.4	1,417	219	3.1
Monroe city	6,385	12796	2579	10216	28,041	181	65.7	129.3	28.8	34.5	1564	140.8	2,843	755	177.3
Morgan City city	446	3710	324	3386	1,935	6	100.0	17.4	4.2	36.0	654	20.1	1,659	278	12.2
Moss Bluff CDP	NA	NA	NA	NA	NA	NA	NA	NA	NA	NA	NA	NA	NA	NA	NA
Natchitoches city	1,426	7815	1030	6784	2,130	8	100.0	27.1	7.2	40.2	710	29.3	1,584	168	9.5
New Iberia city	NA	NA	NA	NA	3,928	20	65.0	32.2	4.6	29.3	693	42.4	1,376	297	38.7
New Orleans city	20,152	5206	974	4232	201,755	1,026	55.9	1505.1	535.6	44.1	1349	1604.4	4,334	1,371	2018.9
Opelousas city	1,460	8873	1738	7135	2,033	8	100.0	26.7	5.6	30.8	874	25.7	1,542	113	20.9
Pineville city	980	6775	657	6119	6,016	40	95.0	21.1	3.7	80.2	916	24.1	1,662	321	7.0
Prairieville CDP	NA	NA	NA	NA	NA	NA	NA	NA	NA	NA	NA	NA	NA	NA	NA
River Ridge CDP	NA	NA	NA	NA	NA	NA	NA	NA	NA	NA	NA	NA	NA	NA	NA
Ruston city	949	4242	349	3894	5,847	26	100.0	28.9	6.1	50.1	668	26.5	1,199	124	26.3
Shenandoah CDP	NA	NA	NA	NA	NA	NA	NA	NA	NA	NA	NA	NA	NA	NA	NA
Shreveport city	10,648	5319	721	4598	70,783	270	97.8	369.6	59.6	35.0	1037	315.2	1,560	169	540.8
Slidell city	1,553	5622	300	5321	9,393	94	20.2	55.2	15.5	65.5	1001	55.1	2,012	612	25.1
Sulphur city	1,160	5776	269	5507	5,773	48	95.8	28.1	4.2	34.0	846	27.9	1,384	245	2.8
Terrytown CDP	NA	NA	NA	NA	NA	NA	NA	NA	NA	NA	NA	NA	NA	NA	7.6
Thibodaux city	691	4744	542	4202	12,766	41	100.0	19.8	3.9	34.4	785	20.3	1,393	109	2.8
Timberlane CDP	NA	NA	NA	NA	NA	NA	NA	NA	NA	NA	NA	NA	NA	NA	NA
West Monroe city	1,418	10828	2459	8369	4,530	45	51.1	35.3	8.5	80.4	1589	37.7	2,883	1,104	13.7
Woodmere CDP	NA	NA	NA	NA	NA	NA	NA	NA	NA	NA	NA	NA	NA	NA	NA
Zachary city	552	3423	403	3020	19,487	120	100.0	16.1	2.5	75.4	683	16.5	1,061	197	2.7
MAINE	28,121	2114	128	1986	612,903	3,242	83.7	X	X	X	X	X	X	X	X
Auburn city & MCD (Androscoggin)	915	3983	118	3865	4,429	23	100.0	75.3	30.9	93.8	1799	68.1	2,968	223	61.8
Augusta city & MCD (Kennebec)	1,172	6262	422	5840	1,313	9	100.0	63.2	23.2	77.5	1568	61.3	3,242	177	41.1
Bangor city & MCD (Penobscot)	1,733	5318	169	5149	3,752	17	76.5	131.1	38.3	93.4	1653	165.2	5,035	1,527	109.4
Biddeford city & MCD (York)	985	4624	488	4135	3,937	22	100.0	67.4	18.7	89.2	1901	76.2	3,577	753	66.7
Brunswick CDP	NA	NA	NA	NA	NA	NA	NA	NA	NA	NA	NA	NA	NA	NA	NA

1 Data for serious crimes have not been adjusted for underreporting. This may affect comparability between geographic areas over time.
2 Per 100,000 population estimated by the FBI.   3 Based on population estimated as of July 1 of the year shown.

Table B. Incorporated Places, Census Designated Places (CDPs), and Minor Civil Divisions (MCDs) of 10,000 or More Population — Land Area, Population, and Households, and Employment

STATE City, town, township, borough, or CDP (county if applicable)	Land area,[1] 2010 (sq mi)	Total persons 2010	Total persons 2014	Percent change 2010–2014	Persons per square mile, 2014	Foreign born	Lives in same house as previous year	Median household income (dollars)	Income of $100,000 or more	Income below poverty level	Percent in labor force	Unemploy-ment rate	Family households	One person households
	1	2	3	4	5	6	7	8	9	10	11	12	13	14
MAINE—Con.														
Brunswick town (Cumberland)..	46.727	20,278	20,441	0.8	437.5	3.1	81.5	$55,833	21.8	10.1	63.5	6.7	57.6	36.3
Falmouth town (Cumberland) ...	29.376	11,185	11,734	4.9	399.4	5.7	89.2	$99,324	49.5	4.5	66.1	3.6	68.4	26.9
Gorham town (Cumberland).....	50.616	16,380	17,024	3.9	336.3	1.8	84.5	$74,563	33.5	5.2	74.5	4.5	71.8	20.2
Kennebunk town (York)............	35.075	10,798	11,111	2.9	316.8	3.6	92.9	$72,489	33.5	4.8	64.6	6.7	68.8	26.6
Lewiston city & MCD (Androscoggin)...........	34.147	36,592	36,299	-0.8	1,063.0	4.5	80.8	$36,696	10.4	23.4	61.3	10.2	57.3	34.7
Orono town (Penobscot)..........	18.175	10,356	10,670	3.0	587.1	3.9	60.3	$43,832	20.3	26.9	54.4	9.3	42.5	35.1
Portland city & MCD (Cumberland).................	21.545	66,194	66,666	0.7	3,094.3	13.2	74.9	$45,865	18.0	20.1	70.1	6.9	45.0	39.1
Saco city & MCD (York)...........	38.464	18,482	19,014	2.9	494.3	6.6	84.5	$52,611	19.9	10.4	69.4	4.8	61.9	26.5
Sanford city & MCD (York)........	47.782	20,796	20,906	0.5	437.5	2.5	86.3	$44,123	13.4	18.8	64.4	9.3	61.7	29.3
Scarborough town (Cumberland).................	47.609	18,919	19,524	3.2	410.1	7.1	89.2	$78,359	37.8	6.6	68.6	4.0	70.7	23.8
South Portland city & MCD (Cumberland).................	12.043	25,002	25,424	1.7	2,111.1	7.0	80.9	$53,614	20.8	10.0	71.6	5.2	56.9	32.5
Waterville city & MCD (Kennebec).................	13.578	15,722	16,182	2.9	1,191.8	3.1	75.1	$31,995	14.4	24.7	56.5	16.4	50.0	39.5
Westbrook city & MCD (Cumberland).................	17.154	17,494	17,886	2.2	1,042.7	7.9	84.1	$45,041	14.3	13.7	64.2	8.2	57.4	35.5
Windham town (Cumberland)...	46.557	16,997	17,589	3.5	377.8	1.7	86.0	$66,307	26.1	9.0	69.4	3.5	68.3	20.8
York town (York)......................	54.670	12,529	12,803	2.2	234.2	3.5	85.5	$68,263	31.1	8.3	64.3	6.9	62.7	28.7
MARYLAND.........................	9,707.241	5,773,785	5,976,407	3.5	615.7	14.2	86.7	$74,149	36.1	9.4	68.9	8.0	67.1	26.9
Aberdeen city.......................	6.488	14,981	15,434	3.0	2,378.9	8.1	84.9	$50,327	19.5	13.5	67.0	9.9	65.9	29.5
Accokeek CDP........................	27.436	10,573	NA	NA	NA	4.9	93.5	$126,000	65.5	4.0	76.1	6.7	81.3	16.1
Adelphi CDP...........................	2.744	15,086	NA	NA	NA	49.5	81.3	$61,870	21.9	11.8	76.7	8.6	63.6	23.9
Annapolis city	7.197	38,274	38,856	1.5	5,399.1	15.0	83.7	$75,320	36.0	8.7	70.9	5.1	54.3	36.4
Annapolis Neck CDP................	6.937	10,950	NA	NA	NA	6.0	93.2	$117,111	58.5	2.7	64.7	4.7	68.8	26.5
Arbutus CDP..........................	6.525	20,483	NA	NA	NA	13.1	89.0	$70,221	30.0	6.9	72.1	4.9	62.8	26.1
Arnold CDP............................	10.818	23,106	NA	NA	NA	5.0	89.9	$105,250	52.9	4.4	72.8	4.3	73.7	20.5
Aspen Hill CDP.......................	9.622	48,759	NA	NA	NA	40.7	86.7	$82,030	38.5	8.0	72.1	8.3	73.1	22.1
Ballenger Creek CDP...............	10.814	18,274	NA	NA	NA	14.2	82.4	$78,000	37.8	8.1	74.5	8.8	64.0	29.0
Baltimore city........................	80.944	621,121	622,793	0.3	7,694.1	7.5	82.8	$41,819	16.3	22.2	62.1	13.9	52.0	39.0
Bel Air town	3.037	10,132	10,264	1.3	3,379.6	4.5	86.8	$67,925	29.1	8.0	66.9	6.1	61.7	34.1
Bel Air North CDP	15.961	30,568	NA	NA	NA	3.5	92.1	$99,538	49.6	4.5	71.1	4.1	80.6	15.1
Bel Air South CDP	15.662	47,709	NA	NA	NA	6.7	90.9	$89,053	42.9	4.7	72.4	6.5	70.9	24.2
Beltsville CDP.........................	7.161	16,772	NA	NA	NA	37.4	85.9	$71,326	28.1	9.9	75.5	9.4	71.2	23.7
Bensville CDP.........................	16.889	11,923	NA	NA	NA	7.2	92.9	$121,509	63.6	2.5	75.0	5.0	82.7	14.7
Bethesda CDP........................	13.251	60,858	NA	NA	NA	23.0	86.2	$145,288	65.4	3.7	68.4	3.8	64.7	29.9
Bowie city.............................	18.771	54,930	57,646	4.9	3,071.0	13.0	90.2	$106,396	54.7	3.2	74.2	7.7	71.4	23.4
Brock Hall CDP.......................	13.617	9,552	NA	NA	NA	11.5	90.2	$135,420	71.4	2.7	77.5	7.8	76.8	19.2
Brooklyn Park CDP..................	4.200	14,373	NA	NA	NA	5.8	88.6	$54,966	21.5	12.3	63.9	11.0	68.1	24.8
California CDP........................	12.778	11,857	NA	NA	NA	7.5	75.8	$91,972	44.4	6.4	75.4	5.8	68.7	25.0
Calverton CDP........................	4.584	17,724	NA	NA	NA	36.3	89.1	$76,121	35.4	4.3	64.6	6.6	62.4	33.5
Cambridge city.......................	10.540	12,382	12,569	1.5	1,192.5	3.8	82.6	$32,341	10.3	24.9	62.8	14.2	59.8	33.7
Camp Springs CDP..................	7.689	19,096	NA	NA	NA	8.9	88.5	$84,681	41.3	4.5	71.9	11.8	70.2	26.1
Carney CDP............................	6.969	29,941	NA	NA	NA	10.6	87.6	$61,338	25.2	8.0	67.2	6.1	58.0	37.0
Catonsville CDP......................	13.961	41,567	NA	NA	NA	7.8	89.6	$77,166	37.4	6.7	61.6	6.5	61.9	30.0
Chesapeake Ranch Estates CDP......	4.320	10,519	NA	NA	NA	4.6	90.0	$87,768	38.6	3.9	77.1	10.0	79.0	16.7
Chillum CDP...........................	3.417	33,513	NA	NA	NA	46.8	79.4	$56,494	20.5	13.5	75.5	8.9	65.8	23.8
Clarksburg CDP.......................	8.214	13,766	NA	NA	NA	34.0	88.1	$136,748	69.6	2.2	79.6	4.8	84.4	11.7
Clinton CDP............................	24.999	35,970	NA	NA	NA	7.7	90.7	$101,501	51.3	4.1	70.4	9.6	73.4	23.4
Cloverly CDP..........................	9.995	15,126	NA	NA	NA	29.0	92.3	$116,113	61.6	1.9	68.3	7.2	82.9	13.7
Cockeysville CDP....................	11.387	20,776	NA	NA	NA	20.6	80.9	$64,473	26.6	9.3	75.3	5.4	53.0	37.9
Colesville CDP........................	5.119	14,647	NA	NA	NA	28.3	93.8	$105,962	52.7	3.6	66.2	5.0	79.4	19.4
College Park city....................	5.632	30,413	32,256	6.1	5,727.5	18.7	61.8	$56,736	26.6	27.8	51.8	10.7	44.2	30.2
Columbia CDP........................	31.927	99,615	NA	NA	NA	18.6	87.3	$100,252	50.2	6.0	74.3	6.0	66.9	27.3
Coral Hills CDP.......................	1.507	9,895	NA	NA	NA	7.8	81.6	$58,708	20.5	8.3	73.6	13.3	62.9	32.2
Crofton CDP...........................	6.613	27,348	NA	NA	NA	6.9	87.1	$109,633	56.8	3.9	78.9	4.6	70.0	24.5
Cumberland city.....................	10.052	20,830	20,235	-2.9	2,013.1	2.1	83.5	$31,750	9.9	22.0	55.3	12.9	54.3	39.9
Damascus CDP.......................	11.556	15,257	NA	NA	NA	13.7	92.2	$115,605	61.0	4.8	74.4	5.7	81.8	12.2
Dundalk CDP..........................	13.068	63,597	NA	NA	NA	6.2	87.3	$49,225	14.4	12.5	61.8	11.4	63.7	29.7
Easton town...........................	11.243	16,190	16,675	3.0	1,483.1	7.8	86.0	$51,220	20.4	11.7	60.4	6.4	63.5	32.8
East Riverdale CDP.................	1.633	15,509	NA	NA	NA	49.7	82.8	$60,488	19.3	9.0	78.0	9.0	75.8	16.0
Edgewood CDP.......................	17.781	25,562	NA	NA	NA	6.4	91.1	$56,025	20.2	15.2	71.2	11.2	73.4	20.2
Eldersburg CDP......................	39.837	30,531	NA	NA	NA	15.0	87.2	$96,427	46.9	5.4	79.5	5.4	71.8	22.2
Elkridge CDP..........................	8.388	15,593	NA	NA	NA	23.9	88.3	$114,694	57.8	4.4	69.0	4.4	79.6	17.4
Elkton town...........................	8.726	15,515	15,852	2.2	1,816.6	7.0	83.4	$55,625	26.7	12.5	63.2	10.1	67.4	27.7
Ellicott City CDP.....................	29.955	65,834	NA	NA	NA	7.5	85.4	$50,311	17.1	12.4	67.4	10.8	61.7	32.7
Essex CDP..............................	9.258	39,262	NA	NA	NA	35.8	79.3	$67,500	32.0	9.7	75.4	10.3	68.2	25.3
Fairland CDP..........................	4.957	23,681	NA	NA	NA	14.1	84.2	$64,529	24.8	7.0	73.7	10.2	69.2	21.7
Ferndale CDP.........................	3.975	16,746	NA	NA	NA	6.6	89.5	$64,393	25.3	9.5	72.0	12.2	64.3	33.5
Forestville CDP.......................	3.928	12,353	NA	NA	NA	14.9	87.9	$107,406	54.1	4.8	68.8	8.5	77.0	19.9
Fort Washington CDP...............	13.794	23,717	NA	NA	NA	19.3	80.5	$65,967	29.5	10.0	74.0	7.1	61.0	31.4
Frederick city........................	22.939	65,287	68,400	4.8	2,981.8	40.2	83.8	$78,441	39.8	9.1	74.3	6.6	68.5	25.5
Gaithersburg city....................	10.249	59,897	66,816	11.6	6,519.4	37.1	84.1	$86,472	41.7	6.8	78.8	6.9	72.0	23.6
Germantown CDP....................	17.029	86,395	NA	NA	NA	10.6	80.8	$52,687	20.3	10.8	72.6	16.9	63.6	28.8
Glassmanor CDP.....................	2.351	17,295	NA	NA	NA	9.2	84.7	$62,447	25.0	9.0	70.2	7.7	62.3	30.5
Glen Burnie CDP.....................	17.323	67,639	NA	NA	NA	45.3	86.4	$84,386	41.2	7.9	76.0	8.1	69.9	22.7
Glenmont CDP.......................	2.796	13,529	NA	NA	NA	20.5	87.8	$106,325	52.5	7.3	72.5	7.7	81.4	17.7
Glen Dale CDP........................	7.159	13,466	NA	NA	NA	28.9	80.3	$62,685	26.8	10.0	77.5	6.9	55.9	35.0
Greenbelt city........................	6.272	23,048	24,125	4.7	3,846.3	6.8	76.3	$38,080	10.5	23.0	65.9	13.9	58.3	34.3
Hagerstown city......................	12.163	39,729	40,364	1.6	3,318.6	4.8	84.7	$56,579	16.2	6.8	68.1	6.5	68.5	27.1
Halfway CDP..........................	4.651	10,701	NA	NA	NA									

1 Dry land or land partially or temporarily covered by water.
2 16 years old and over.

Table B. Incorporated Places, Census Designated Places (CDPs), and Minor Civil Divisions (MCDs) of 10,000 or More Population — Crime, Construction, and Local Government Finance

STATE City, town, township, borough, or CDP (county if applicable)	Serious crimes known to police, 2014[1] Total number	Rate[2] Total	Rate[2] Violent	Rate[2] Property	New residential construction authorized by building permits, 2014 Value ($1,000)	Number of housing units	Percent single family	Local government finance, 2012 General revenue Total (mil dol)	Intergovernmental Total (mil dol)	Percent from state gov.	Taxes per capita[3]	General expenditure Total (mil dol)	Per capita[3] Total	Capital outlays	Debt outstanding (mil dol)
	15	16	17	18	19	20	21	22	23	24	25	26	27	28	29
MAINE—Con.															
Brunswick town (Cumberland)..	410	2014	93	1921	8,564	34	100.0	56.3	17.9	98.8	1631	52.6	2,586	212	27.4
Falmouth town (Cumberland) ...	126	1088	17	1070	16,942	101	40.6	45.0	8.7	99.4	2687	45.4	3,981	651	55.6
Gorham town (Cumberland)	210	1238	59	1179	13,822	76	100.0	49.5	22.3	97.7	1401	46.7	2,799	189	47.6
Kennebunk town (York)............	78	703	54	649	8,612	36	100.0	13.1	1.6	100.0	828	12.6	1,146	206	7.4
Lewiston city & MCD (Androscoggin)	986	2709	231	2478	2,166	10	100.0	117.7	52.6	84.0	1355	112.8	3,095	292	152.4
Orono town (Penobscot)...........	133	1236	37	1199	235	2	100.0	10.3	2.7	58.5	495	10.6	1,004	61	17.7
Portland city & MCD (Cumberland).........	2,292	3453	238	3215	16,024	100	36.0	318.6	71.3	78.7	2178	329.4	4,972	746	423.0
Saco city & MCD (York)	415	2187	195	1992	9,943	63	79.4	21.7	2.1	97.2	812	22.2	1,185	104	16.8
Sanford city & MCD (York)........	NA	NA	NA	NA	3,194	39	28.2	63.2	33.5	93.7	1278	57.5	2,753	122	10.5
Scarborough town (Cumberland).........	385	1979	77	1902	21,207	70	100.0	68.3	10.4	94.7	2568	69.6	3,629	358	82.3
South Portland city & MCD (Cumberland).........	840	3317	154	3163	6,823	50	62.0	82.8	11.7	92.5	2430	82.1	3,270	347	50.1
Waterville city & MCD (Kennebec).........	743	4637	331	4307	11,781	170	7.6	43.1	23.5	76.3	1077	46.1	2,910	568	22.9
Westbrook city & MCD (Cumberland).........	617	3465	208	3257	4,499	36	77.8	64.4	21.9	95.8	1983	55.3	3,142	164	63.8
Windham town (Cumberland)...	410	2335	97	2239	15,189	91	86.8	14.2	1.6	94.9	615	15.7	906	142	23.4
York town (York)........................	220	1727	39	1688	18,493	62	100.0	43.3	3.0	96.5	2929	45.7	3,611	288	28.6
MARYLAND....................	176,520	2954	446	2508	2,889,171	16,331	64.5	X	X	X	X	X	X	X	X
Aberdeen city............................	567	3741	468	3272	22,587	117	34.2	25.8	9.1	73.8	698	15.9	1,058	0	25.3
Accokeek CDP	NA	NA	NA	NA	NA	NA	NA	NA	NA	NA	NA	NA	NA	NA	NA
Adelphi CDP	NA	NA	NA	NA	NA	NA	NA	NA	NA	NA	NA	NA	NA	NA	NA
Annapolis city............................	1,143	2946	500	2446	52,833	372	41.9	82.8	14.6	35.6	1125	65.6	1,703	14	96.8
Annapolis Neck CDP	NA	NA	NA	NA	NA	NA	NA	NA	NA	NA	NA	NA	NA	NA	NA
Arbutus CDP............................	NA	NA	NA	NA	NA	NA	NA	NA	NA	NA	NA	NA	NA	NA	NA
Arnold CDP	NA	NA	NA	NA	NA	NA	NA	NA	NA	NA	NA	NA	NA	NA	NA
Aspen Hill CDP	NA	NA	NA	NA	NA	NA	NA	NA	NA	NA	NA	NA	NA	NA	NA
Ballenger Creek CDP	NA	NA	NA	NA	NA	NA	NA	NA	NA	NA	NA	NA	NA	NA	NA
Baltimore city............................	37,766	6057	1339	4718	94,235	821	29.4	3407.6	1720.1	81.7	1989	3659.5	5,874	527	2621.6
Bel Air town............................	346	3347	290	3057	325	2	100.0	14.2	1.8	24.5	771	15.3	1,485	213	2.9
Bel Air North CDP	NA	NA	NA	NA	NA	NA	NA	NA	NA	NA	NA	NA	NA	NA	NA
Bel Air South CDP	NA	NA	NA	NA	NA	NA	NA	NA	NA	NA	NA	NA	NA	NA	NA
Beltsville CDP............................	NA	NA	NA	NA	NA	NA	NA	NA	NA	NA	NA	NA	NA	NA	NA
Bensville CDP............................	NA	NA	NA	NA	NA	NA	NA	NA	NA	NA	NA	NA	NA	NA	NA
Bethesda CDP............................	NA	NA	NA	NA	NA	NA	NA	NA	NA	NA	NA	NA	NA	NA	NA
Bowie city	921	1610	133	1478	NA	NA	NA	46.8	10.8	16.7	491	42.1	748	0	18.0
Brock Hall CDP............................	NA	NA	NA	NA	NA	NA	NA	NA	NA	NA	NA	NA	NA	NA	NA
Brooklyn Park CDP	NA	NA	NA	NA	NA	NA	NA	NA	NA	NA	NA	NA	NA	NA	NA
California CDP............................	NA	NA	NA	NA	NA	NA	NA	NA	NA	NA	NA	NA	NA	NA	NA
Calverton CDP............................	NA	NA	NA	NA	NA	NA	NA	NA	NA	NA	NA	NA	NA	NA	NA
Cambridge city............................	902	7120	995	6125	1,430	11	100.0	24.5	11.6	80.6	643	15.9	1,274	75	23.2
Camp Springs CDP	NA	NA	NA	NA	NA	NA	NA	NA	NA	NA	NA	NA	NA	NA	NA
Carney CDP	NA	NA	NA	NA	NA	NA	NA	NA	NA	NA	NA	NA	NA	NA	NA
Catonsville CDP............................	NA	NA	NA	NA	NA	NA	NA	NA	NA	NA	NA	NA	NA	NA	NA
Chesapeake Ranch Estates CDP	NA	NA	NA	NA	NA	NA	NA	NA	NA	NA	NA	NA	NA	NA	NA
Chillum CDP............................	NA	NA	NA	NA	NA	NA	NA	NA	NA	NA	NA	NA	NA	NA	NA
Clarksburg CDP............................	NA	NA	NA	NA	NA	NA	NA	NA	NA	NA	NA	NA	NA	NA	NA
Clinton CDP............................	NA	NA	NA	NA	NA	NA	NA	NA	NA	NA	NA	NA	NA	NA	NA
Cloverly CDP............................	NA	NA	NA	NA	NA	NA	NA	NA	NA	NA	NA	NA	NA	NA	NA
Cockeysville CDP.....................	NA	NA	NA	NA	NA	NA	NA	NA	NA	NA	NA	NA	NA	NA	NA
Colesville CDP............................	NA	NA	NA	NA	NA	NA	NA	NA	NA	NA	NA	NA	NA	NA	NA
College Park city.....................	NA	NA	NA	NA	NA	NA	NA	15.3	2.1	19.1	315	14.1	451	4	8.4
Columbia CDP............................	NA	NA	NA	NA	NA	NA	NA	NA	NA	NA	NA	NA	NA	NA	NA
Coral Hills CDP............................	NA	NA	NA	NA	NA	NA	NA	NA	NA	NA	NA	NA	NA	NA	NA
Crofton CDP............................	NA	NA	NA	NA	NA	NA	NA	NA	NA	NA	NA	NA	NA	NA	NA
Cumberland city.....................	1,455	7145	732	6413	455	3	100.0	31.4	6.6	22.8	541	30.3	1,476	19	68.7
Damascus CDP............................	NA	NA	NA	NA	NA	NA	NA	NA	NA	NA	NA	NA	NA	NA	NA
Dundalk CDP............................	NA	NA	NA	NA	NA	NA	NA	NA	NA	NA	NA	NA	NA	NA	NA
Easton town............................	598	3561	464	3097	4,985	22	100.0	34.4	2.1	27.5	779	18.4	1,108	0	32.3
East Riverdale CDP	NA	NA	NA	NA	NA	NA	NA	NA	NA	NA	NA	NA	NA	NA	NA
Edgewood CDP............................	NA	NA	NA	NA	NA	NA	NA	NA	NA	NA	NA	NA	NA	NA	NA
Eldersburg CDP............................	NA	NA	NA	NA	NA	NA	NA	NA	NA	NA	NA	NA	NA	NA	NA
Elkridge CDP............................	NA	NA	NA	NA	NA	NA	NA	NA	NA	NA	NA	NA	NA	NA	NA
Elkton town............................	1,389	8808	1452	7356	2,333	13	100.0	14.9	1.9	16.9	443	15.0	956	8	19.0
Ellicott City CDP	NA	NA	NA	NA	NA	NA	NA	NA	NA	NA	NA	NA	NA	NA	NA
Essex CDP............................	NA	NA	NA	NA	NA	NA	NA	NA	NA	NA	NA	NA	NA	NA	NA
Fairland CDP............................	NA	NA	NA	NA	NA	NA	NA	NA	NA	NA	NA	NA	NA	NA	NA
Ferndale CDP............................	NA	NA	NA	NA	NA	NA	NA	NA	NA	NA	NA	NA	NA	NA	NA
Forestville CDP............................	NA	NA	NA	NA	NA	NA	NA	NA	NA	NA	NA	NA	NA	NA	NA
Fort Washington CDP	NA	NA	NA	NA	NA	NA	NA	NA	NA	NA	NA	NA	NA	NA	NA
Frederick city	1,845	2743	430	2314	72,247	672	29.5	90.8	14.2	14.9	700	84.6	1,273	9	224.2
Gaithersburg city.....................	NA	NA	NA	NA	27,241	247	60.3	54.0	13.4	7.5	495	49.4	783	40	142.6
Germantown CDP	NA	NA	NA	NA	NA	NA	NA	NA	NA	NA	NA	NA	NA	NA	NA
Glassmanor CDP	NA	NA	NA	NA	NA	NA	NA	NA	NA	NA	NA	NA	NA	NA	NA
Glen Burnie CDP	NA	NA	NA	NA	NA	NA	NA	NA	NA	NA	NA	NA	NA	NA	NA
Glenmont CDP............................	NA	NA	NA	NA	NA	NA	NA	NA	NA	NA	NA	NA	NA	NA	NA
Glenn Dale CDP............................	NA	NA	NA	NA	NA	NA	NA	NA	NA	NA	NA	NA	NA	NA	NA
Greenbelt city............................	882	3688	385	3303	NA	NA	NA	27.0	5.2	20.0	788	26.0	1,102	14	4.8
Hagerstown city.....................	1,741	4269	650	3619	10,351	106	24.5	57.3	7.1	21.8	645	50.2	1,239	16	66.0
Halfway CDP............................	NA	NA	NA	NA	NA	NA	NA	NA	NA	NA	NA	NA	NA	NA	NA

1 Data for serious crimes have not been adjusted for underreporting. This may affect comparability between geographic areas over time.
2 Per 100,000 population estimated by the FBI. 3 Based on population estimated as of July 1 of the year shown.

Table B. Incorporated Places, Census Designated Places (CDPs), and Minor Civil Divisions (MCDs) of 10,000 or More Population — **Land Area, Population, and Households, and Employment**

STATE City, town, township, borough, or CDP (county if applicable)	Land area,[1] 2010 (sq mi)	Population				Population characteristics 2010–2014		Household income and poverty, 2010–2014			Employment,[2] 2010–2014		Households, 2010–2014 (percent of households)	
		Total persons 2010	Total persons 2014	Percent change 2010–2014	Persons per square mile, 2014	Foreign born	Lives in same house as previous year	Median household income (dollars)	Income of $100,000 or more (Percent of households)	Income below poverty level (Percent of households)	Percent in labor force	Unemployment rate	Family households	One person households
	1	2	3	4	5	6	7	8	9	10	11	12	13	14
MARYLAND—Con.														
Havre de Grace city	5.464	12,982	13,512	4.1	2,473.1	6.0	85.2	$65,641	33.5	9.9	67.3	8.9	62.6	31.0
Hillcrest Heights CDP	2.487	16,469	NA	NA	NA	6.2	82.7	$56,425	21.4	7.1	69.4	11.6	55.9	38.9
Hyattsville city	2.665	17,656	18,420	4.3	6,911.2	35.2	85.5	$61,806	25.0	10.8	78.7	6.8	58.5	31.3
Ilchester CDP	10.746	23,476	NA	NA	NA	20.5	91.4	$113,372	58.0	4.1	77.8	4.8	72.9	19.7
Joppatowne CDP	6.729	12,616	NA	NA	NA	5.9	88.6	$71,174	30.5	7.4	70.2	8.5	71.4	26.0
Kemp Mill CDP	2.497	12,564	NA	NA	NA	23.1	88.8	$107,746	52.6	5.5	70.1	4.3	73.6	23.4
Kettering CDP	5.490	12,790	NA	NA	NA	11.7	90.1	$91,648	43.4	4.6	68.6	8.6	66.8	29.5
Lake Arbor CDP	3.134	9,776	NA	NA	NA	14.3	85.2	$94,898	47.2	4.6	76.2	12.2	64.5	30.9
Lake Shore CDP	13.426	19,477	NA	NA	NA	2.6	91.6	$92,823	44.3	2.8	72.8	7.0	77.7	18.2
Landover CDP	4.003	23,078	NA	NA	NA	21.4	83.0	$49,820	15.0	14.3	72.2	11.3	64.0	29.4
Langley Park CDP	0.994	18,755	NA	NA	NA	67.8	87.4	$54,671	17.1	16.0	83.5	9.0	67.6	15.2
Lanham CDP	3.528	10,157	NA	NA	NA	30.3	91.7	$71,811	36.3	5.2	68.9	9.0	81.8	14.2
Largo CDP	3.062	10,709	NA	NA	NA	10.3	84.4	$81,786	34.6	7.2	78.1	8.6	54.1	40.2
Laurel city	4.421	25,115	26,160	4.2	5,917.1	24.4	79.2	$68,230	30.2	8.5	78.5	7.2	57.1	35.3
Lexington Park CDP	5.623	11,626	NA	NA	NA	8.8	80.2	$64,103	24.8	13.5	70.8	7.3	63.3	30.1
Linthicum CDP	5.462	10,324	NA	NA	NA	5.5	93.5	$78,989	39.8	6.6	66.2	6.0	70.6	25.3
Lochearn CDP	5.590	25,333	NA	NA	NA	10.5	90.5	$55,673	21.0	8.4	63.1	9.6	66.7	29.7
Marlboro Village CDP	3.856	9,438	NA	NA	NA	6.2	81.4	$94,636	46.5	2.5	71.2	3.5	58.3	35.9
Maryland City CDP	7.735	16,093	NA	NA	NA	22.2	84.4	$96,544	48.3	1.9	80.8	6.9	61.2	28.8
Mays Chapel CDP	3.709	11,420	NA	NA	NA	12.5	91.2	$96,971	48.8	3.6	73.8	2.5	70.2	24.9
Middle River CDP	7.779	25,191	NA	NA	NA	11.1	86.3	$55,505	20.7	11.3	69.4	8.6	66.3	28.5
Milford Mill CDP	6.945	29,042	NA	NA	NA	12.8	84.5	$58,137	22.4	9.5	72.6	12.0	64.8	29.3
Mitchellville CDP	4.937	10,967	NA	NA	NA	17.6	93.2	$117,500	58.7	2.5	73.2	9.2	76.3	19.4
Montgomery Village CDP	3.994	32,032	NA	NA	NA	38.3	85.7	$77,537	37.9	7.5	75.1	6.3	68.6	25.3
New Carrollton city	1.529	12,134	12,708	4.7	8,309.8	33.5	85.8	$59,438	21.7	10.0	72.2	12.9	67.7	26.9
North Bethesda CDP	8.867	43,828	NA	NA	NA	33.4	76.7	$105,968	53.6	5.7	72.5	5.4	54.8	35.5
North Laurel CDP	6.481	4,474	NA	NA	NA	23.0	89.2	$96,601	48.2	5.2	82.9	5.4	70.2	23.2
North Potomac CDP	6.534	24,410	NA	NA	NA	35.2	91.1	$151,771	69.8	4.6	71.9	5.6	85.5	13.1
Ocean Pines CDP	6.658	11,710	NA	NA	NA	4.4	91.2	$73,310	29.9	5.3	53.8	8.2	68.9	26.4
Odenton CDP	14.771	37,132	NA	NA	NA	7.6	81.6	$98,524	49.0	3.9	76.4	6.1	65.5	27.1
Olney CDP	16.198	33,844	NA	NA	NA	19.2	92.7	$126,468	64.0	2.8	71.9	5.5	83.7	13.7
Overlea CDP	3.003	12,275	NA	NA	NA	7.5	90.7	$59,881	25.4	8.0	68.7	6.0	58.8	35.7
Owings Mills CDP	9.535	30,622	NA	NA	NA	19.1	81.5	$71,153	30.2	6.3	74.8	5.2	60.2	31.3
Oxon Hill CDP	6.615	17,722	NA	NA	NA	17.9	84.5	$66,860	24.8	6.9	72.5	13.1	61.2	33.4
Parkville CDP	4.285	30,734	NA	NA	NA	10.5	87.6	$54,430	20.2	12.1	69.5	7.8	61.8	31.7
Parole CDP	10.270	15,922	NA	NA	NA	11.0	80.6	$91,282	45.7	2.7	59.1	4.3	50.4	39.9
Pasadena CDP	14.938	24,287	NA	NA	NA	5.0	89.6	$98,657	48.7	5.1	75.8	6.8	72.4	20.6
Perry Hall CDP	6.974	28,474	NA	NA	NA	10.7	89.0	$75,964	34.7	5.6	71.6	5.2	67.9	27.7
Pikesville CDP	12.349	30,764	NA	NA	NA	20.0	89.0	$74,544	37.3	8.1	63.4	6.2	61.6	32.8
Potomac CDP	25.133	44,965	NA	NA	NA	29.3	89.6	$181,385	73.4	4.2	63.3	4.0	81.8	16.0
Randallstown CDP	10.219	32,430	NA	NA	NA	10.4	92.7	$75,766	35.2	8.6	71.1	8.4	66.2	29.6
Redland CDP	7.027	17,242	NA	NA	NA	37.4	89.7	$99,938	50.0	3.5	74.1	6.9	78.3	15.6
Reisterstown CDP	5.165	25,968	NA	NA	NA	21.5	88.3	$57,478	25.6	13.1	72.2	7.6	71.0	22.3
Riviera Beach CDP	2.633	12,677	NA	NA	NA	2.2	92.0	$77,160	31.8	5.3	73.3	8.0	77.5	18.8
Rockville city	13.559	61,285	65,937	7.6	4,863.0	34.5	84.5	$98,530	49.0	6.0	72.7	5.3	66.5	26.6
Rosaryville CDP	9.186	10,697	NA	NA	NA	5.7	94.0	$117,090	59.6	3.4	73.5	7.5	80.2	16.1
Rosedale CDP	6.893	19,257	NA	NA	NA	8.6	89.3	$55,155	23.8	8.9	65.6	10.9	70.0	24.9
Rossville CDP	5.381	15,147	NA	NA	NA	19.6	83.3	$63,389	24.4	6.4	69.5	5.0	58.7	31.9
Salisbury city	13.386	30,352	32,563	7.3	2,432.5	11.5	69.0	$37,131	11.3	23.9	60.9	10.6	52.3	34.4
Seabrook CDP	3.021	17,287	NA	NA	NA	31.6	87.3	$71,909	29.3	7.1	71.2	9.1	70.2	25.4
Severn CDP	17.735	44,231	NA	NA	NA	12.5	87.6	$91,276	45.1	6.9	74.1	7.5	72.3	22.5
Severna Park CDP	16.490	37,634	NA	NA	NA	4.8	92.9	$121,710	59.4	3.2	69.2	6.3	81.3	16.1
Silver Spring CDP	7.893	71,452	NA	NA	NA	37.3	79.4	$72,289	34.3	10.6	79.3	7.8	54.2	35.9
South Laurel CDP	8.141	26,112	NA	NA	NA	25.2	83.9	$65,042	27.2	6.3	76.0	7.2	61.7	34.6
Suitland CDP	4.247	25,825	NA	NA	NA	6.0	80.6	$56,951	18.2	11.3	75.3	12.1	64.1	32.0
Summerfield CDP	3.632	10,898	NA	NA	NA	10.5	81.2	$70,891	28.8	6.4	73.5	10.8	58.2	35.7
Takoma Park city	2.089	16,715	17,670	5.7	8,456.9	31.1	84.9	$78,106	41.1	7.7	78.2	8.1	65.7	26.8
Timonium CDP	5.354	9,925	NA	NA	NA	14.0	90.9	$81,865	41.4	4.1	60.7	6.7	65.8	30.6
Towson CDP	14.151	55,197	NA	NA	NA	9.8	80.9	$74,916	36.7	11.3	58.4	5.7	56.1	35.3
Travilah CDP	15.827	12,159	NA	NA	NA	35.1	91.8	$208,421	81.5	4.1	66.1	4.7	89.1	9.8
Waldorf CDP	36.247	67,752	NA	NA	NA	7.7	89.4	$84,809	39.6	8.2	74.3	8.3	71.5	23.0
Walker Mill CDP	3.161	11,302	NA	NA	NA	3.9	90.6	$63,750	22.4	14.1	69.1	14.3	64.2	34.1
Westminster city	6.628	18,586	18,724	0.7	2,824.9	3.3	84.1	$55,051	25.6	14.7	62.0	5.6	61.2	32.9
Wheaton CDP	6.898	48,284	NA	NA	NA	45.2	83.2	$78,742	37.1	9.1	77.6	8.4	73.1	20.2
White Oak CDP	3.780	17,403	NA	NA	NA	41.8	81.0	$63,378	28.4	11.6	77.0	12.2	60.7	28.7
Woodlawn CDP (Baltimore County)	9.539	37,879	NA	NA	NA	14.7	88.1	$65,850	25.2	8.2	71.1	10.0	65.0	27.6
MASSACHUSETTS	7,800.058	6,547,817	6,745,408	3.0	864.8	15.3	86.8	$67,846	33.2	12.0	67.6	8.4	63.6	28.8
Abington CDP & town (Plymouth)	9.948	15,988	16,197	1.3	1,628.1	5.0	90.9	$81,500	35.8	4.3	74.0	8.1	69.4	25.9
Acton town (Middlesex)	19.865	21,924	23,237	6.0	1,169.7	25.0	88.6	$120,865	57.9	5.6	70.6	5.6	72.1	24.3
Acushnet town (Bristol)	18.427	10,303	10,410	1.0	564.9	12.6	95.6	$69,570	28.7	4.9	68.6	8.1	74.2	21.7
Agawam Town city & MCD (Hampden)	23.310	28,438	28,772	1.2	1,234.3	8.0	91.7	$63,561	27.9	10.1	67.3	7.0	65.4	30.2
Amesbury Town city & MCD (Essex)	12.263	16,283	16,794	3.1	1,369.5	5.6	91.4	$76,463	34.6	5.4	76.1	6.9	63.9	29.5
Amherst town (Hampshire)	27.606	37,819	39,774	5.2	1,440.8	15.7	63.1	$52,537	27.8	28.6	55.4	10.2	46.9	26.5
Amherst Center CDP	4.940	19,065	NA	NA	NA	11.8	57.2	$37,089	20.9	29.2	48.6	12.5	39.9	30.7
Andover town (Essex)	30.849	33,209	35,085	5.6	1,137.3	15.2	91.1	$125,321	57.9	5.7	67.2	5.7	75.2	22.1
Arlington CDP & town (Middlesex)	5.146	42,844	44,461	3.8	8,640.0	17.1	88.4	$92,338	46.4	6.2	72.8	5.9	58.6	33.0
Ashland town (Middlesex)	12.330	16,593	17,312	4.3	1,404.1	13.8	89.5	$102,721	50.3	5.0	74.7	5.5	70.0	25.3
Athol town (Worcester)	32.294	11,577	11,621	0.4	359.8	2.8	86.0	$47,122	16.5	15.5	62.3	14.3	60.7	32.3
Attleboro city & MCD (Bristol)	26.811	43,593	43,970	0.9	1,640.0	9.3	88.4	$65,141	29.4	10.3	70.2	8.8	67.5	26.3

1 Dry land or land partially or temporarily covered by water.
2 16 years old and over.

Table B. Incorporated Places, Census Designated Places (CDPs), and Minor Civil Divisions (MCDs) of 10,000 or More Population — Crime, Construction, and Local Government Finance

STATE City, town, township, borough, or CDP (county if applicable)	Serious crimes known to police, 2014[1] Total number	Rate[2] Total	Rate[2] Violent	Rate[2] Property	New residential construction authorized by building permits, 2014 Value ($1,000)	Number of housing units	Percent single family	Local government finance, 2012 General revenue Total (mil dol)	Intergovernmental Total (mil dol)	Percent from state gov.	Taxes per capita[3]	General expenditure Total (mil dol)	Per capita[3] Total	Capital outlays	Debt outstanding (mil dol)
	15	16	17	18	19	20	21	22	23	24	25	26	27	28	29
MARYLAND—Con.															
Havre de Grace city	342	2510	250	2261	8,320	48	100.0	20.1	4.5	32.9	669	17.6	1,310	104	28.5
Hillcrest Heights CDP	NA	NA	NA	NA	NA	NA	NA	NA	NA	NA	NA	NA	NA	NA	NA
Hyattsville city	1,265	6966	507	6460	NA	NA	NA	13.7	1.3	64.2	649	14.6	807	219	0.0
Ilchester CDP	NA	NA	NA	NA	NA	NA	NA	NA	NA	NA	NA	NA	NA	NA	NA
Joppatowne CDP	NA	NA	NA	NA	NA	NA	NA	NA	NA	NA	NA	NA	NA	NA	NA
Kemp Mill CDP	NA	NA	NA	NA	NA	NA	NA	NA	NA	NA	NA	NA	NA	NA	NA
Kettering CDP	NA	NA	NA	NA	NA	NA	NA	NA	NA	NA	NA	NA	NA	NA	NA
Lake Arbor CDP	NA	NA	NA	NA	NA	NA	NA	NA	NA	NA	NA	NA	NA	NA	NA
Lake Shore CDP	NA	NA	NA	NA	NA	NA	NA	NA	NA	NA	NA	NA	NA	NA	NA
Landover CDP	NA	NA	NA	NA	NA	NA	NA	NA	NA	NA	NA	NA	NA	NA	NA
Langley Park CDP	NA	NA	NA	NA	NA	NA	NA	NA	NA	NA	NA	NA	NA	NA	NA
Lanham CDP	NA	NA	NA	NA	NA	NA	NA	NA	NA	NA	NA	NA	NA	NA	NA
Largo CDP	NA	NA	NA	NA	NA	NA	NA	NA	NA	NA	NA	NA	NA	NA	NA
Laurel city	1,068	4115	593	3522	0	0	0.0	29.2	4.0	20.5	800	25.4	992	3	10.1
Lexington Park CDP	NA	NA	NA	NA	NA	NA	NA	NA	NA	NA	NA	NA	NA	NA	NA
Linthicum CDP	NA	NA	NA	NA	NA	NA	NA	NA	NA	NA	NA	NA	NA	NA	NA
Lochearn CDP	NA	NA	NA	NA	NA	NA	NA	NA	NA	NA	NA	NA	NA	NA	NA
Marlboro Village CDP	NA	NA	NA	NA	NA	NA	NA	NA	NA	NA	NA	NA	NA	NA	NA
Maryland City CDP	NA	NA	NA	NA	NA	NA	NA	NA	NA	NA	NA	NA	NA	NA	NA
Mays Chapel CDP	NA	NA	NA	NA	NA	NA	NA	NA	NA	NA	NA	NA	NA	NA	NA
Middle River CDP	NA	NA	NA	NA	NA	NA	NA	NA	NA	NA	NA	NA	NA	NA	NA
Milford Mill CDP	NA	NA	NA	NA	NA	NA	NA	NA	NA	NA	NA	NA	NA	NA	NA
Mitchellville CDP	NA	NA	NA	NA	NA	NA	NA	NA	NA	NA	NA	NA	NA	NA	NA
Montgomery Village CDP	NA	NA	NA	NA	NA	NA	NA	NA	NA	NA	NA	NA	NA	NA	NA
New Carrollton city	390	3095	643	2452	NA	NA	NA	8.2	1.2	22.9	436	6.4	513	36	3.1
North Bethesda CDP	NA	NA	NA	NA	NA	NA	NA	NA	NA	NA	NA	NA	NA	NA	NA
North Laurel CDP	NA	NA	NA	NA	NA	NA	NA	NA	NA	NA	NA	NA	NA	NA	NA
North Potomac CDP	NA	NA	NA	NA	NA	NA	NA	NA	NA	NA	NA	NA	NA	NA	NA
Ocean Pines CDP	NA	NA	NA	NA	NA	NA	NA	NA	NA	NA	NA	NA	NA	NA	NA
Odenton CDP	NA	NA	NA	NA	NA	NA	NA	NA	NA	NA	NA	NA	NA	NA	NA
Olney CDP	NA	NA	NA	NA	NA	NA	NA	NA	NA	NA	NA	NA	NA	NA	NA
Overlea CDP	NA	NA	NA	NA	NA	NA	NA	NA	NA	NA	NA	NA	NA	NA	NA
Owings Mills CDP	NA	NA	NA	NA	NA	NA	NA	NA	NA	NA	NA	NA	NA	NA	NA
Oxon Hill CDP	NA	NA	NA	NA	NA	NA	NA	NA	NA	NA	NA	NA	NA	NA	NA
Parkville CDP	NA	NA	NA	NA	NA	NA	NA	NA	NA	NA	NA	NA	NA	NA	NA
Parole CDP	NA	NA	NA	NA	NA	NA	NA	NA	NA	NA	NA	NA	NA	NA	NA
Pasadena CDP	NA	NA	NA	NA	NA	NA	NA	NA	NA	NA	NA	NA	NA	NA	NA
Perry Hall CDP	NA	NA	NA	NA	NA	NA	NA	NA	NA	NA	NA	NA	NA	NA	NA
Pikesville CDP	NA	NA	NA	NA	NA	NA	NA	NA	NA	NA	NA	NA	NA	NA	NA
Potomac CDP	NA	NA	NA	NA	NA	NA	NA	NA	NA	NA	NA	NA	NA	NA	NA
Randallstown CDP	NA	NA	NA	NA	NA	NA	NA	NA	NA	NA	NA	NA	NA	NA	NA
Redland CDP	NA	NA	NA	NA	NA	NA	NA	NA	NA	NA	NA	NA	NA	NA	NA
Reisterstown CDP	NA	NA	NA	NA	NA	NA	NA	NA	NA	NA	NA	NA	NA	NA	NA
Riviera Beach CDP	NA	NA	NA	NA	NA	NA	NA	NA	NA	NA	NA	NA	NA	NA	NA
Rockville city	NA	NA	NA	NA	95,721	578	2.8	92.8	17.8	12.0	644	94.1	1,486	5	135.9
Rosaryville CDP	NA	NA	NA	NA	NA	NA	NA	NA	NA	NA	NA	NA	NA	NA	NA
Rosedale CDP	NA	NA	NA	NA	NA	NA	NA	NA	NA	NA	NA	NA	NA	NA	NA
Rossville CDP	NA	NA	NA	NA	NA	NA	NA	NA	NA	NA	NA	NA	NA	NA	NA
Salisbury city	2,121	6674	900	5774	5,428	58	3.4	51.7	5.3	32.3	725	39.7	1,279	49	70.9
Seabrook CDP	NA	NA	NA	NA	NA	NA	NA	NA	NA	NA	NA	NA	NA	NA	NA
Severn CDP	NA	NA	NA	NA	NA	NA	NA	NA	NA	NA	NA	NA	NA	NA	NA
Severna Park CDP	NA	NA	NA	NA	NA	NA	NA	NA	NA	NA	NA	NA	NA	NA	NA
Silver Spring CDP	NA	NA	NA	NA	NA	NA	NA	NA	NA	NA	NA	NA	NA	NA	NA
South Laurel CDP	NA	NA	NA	NA	NA	NA	NA	NA	NA	NA	NA	NA	NA	NA	NA
Suitland CDP	NA	NA	NA	NA	NA	NA	NA	NA	NA	NA	NA	NA	NA	NA	NA
Summerfield CDP	NA	NA	NA	NA	NA	NA	NA	NA	NA	NA	NA	NA	NA	NA	NA
Takoma Park city	654	3640	351	3289	NA	NA	NA	21.3	5.2	14.2	701	21.9	1,261	136	4.4
Timonium CDP	NA	NA	NA	NA	NA	NA	NA	NA	NA	NA	NA	NA	NA	NA	NA
Towson CDP	NA	NA	NA	NA	NA	NA	NA	NA	NA	NA	NA	NA	NA	NA	NA
Travilah CDP	NA	NA	NA	NA	NA	NA	NA	NA	NA	NA	NA	NA	NA	NA	NA
Waldorf CDP	NA	NA	NA	NA	NA	NA	NA	NA	NA	NA	NA	NA	NA	NA	NA
Walker Mill CDP	NA	NA	NA	NA	NA	NA	NA	NA	NA	NA	NA	NA	NA	NA	NA
Westminster city	833	4466	472	3994	NA	NA	NA	24.9	5.3	10.6	639	20.8	1,119	143	18.7
Wheaton CDP	NA	NA	NA	NA	NA	NA	NA	NA	NA	NA	NA	NA	NA	NA	NA
White Oak CDP	NA	NA	NA	NA	NA	NA	NA	NA	NA	NA	NA	NA	NA	NA	NA
Woodlawn CDP (Baltimore County)	NA	NA	NA	NA	NA	NA	NA	NA	NA	NA	NA	NA	NA	NA	NA
MASSACHUSETTS	151,666	2248	391	1857	3,300,622	14,486	50.6	X	X	X	X	X	X	X	X
Abington CDP & town (Plymouth)	NA	NA	NA	NA	3,198	15	86.7	45.6	12.4	99.1	1814	44.0	2,738	106	16.7
Acton town (Middlesex)	198	854	73	780	22,074	87	100.0	87.7	10.4	99.1	3145	86.5	3,820	104	41.7
Acushnet town (Bristol)	114	1097	221	876	4,751	24	100.0	26.9	8.8	99.5	1419	25.2	2,444	58	14.2
Agawam Town city & MCD (Hampden)	426	1481	181	1300	5,277	37	29.7	84.8	27.5	99.5	1745	102.8	3,589	65	25.0
Amesbury Town city & MCD (Essex)	197	1174	250	924	2,987	19	100.0	58.4	15.3	96.8	2251	54.8	3,315	206	46.7
Amherst town (Hampshire)	357	916	177	739	5,949	26	42.3	75.1	19.9	87.7	1110	77.8	1,994	155	13.3
Amherst Center CDP	NA	NA	NA	NA	NA	NA	NA	NA	NA	NA	NA	NA	NA	NA	NA
Andover town (Essex)	268	768	46	722	17,103	65	53.8	149.2	19.4	98.6	3420	139.1	4,068	269	87.7
Arlington CDP & town (Middlesex)	445	1001	142	860	15,962	119	8.4	147.2	28.4	86.3	2349	129.6	2,963	165	59.5
Ashland town (Middlesex)	152	877	87	790	7,427	79	13.9	58.2	9.9	99.9	2264	67.3	3,960	614	46.0
Athol town (Worcester)	237	2033	395	1639	893	4	100.0	19.5	5.3	100.0	946	20.0	1,717	319	13.0
Attleboro city & MCD (Bristol)...	953	2162	243	1919	11,275	84	95.2	126.9	47.0	97.8	1412	113.5	2,593	116	72.7

1 Data for serious crimes have not been adjusted for underreporting. This may affect comparability between geographic areas over time.
2 Per 100,000 population estimated by the FBI.   3 Based on population estimated as of July 1 of the year shown.

Table B. Incorporated Places, Census Designated Places (CDPs), and Minor Civil Divisions (MCDs) of 10,000 or More Population — **Land Area, Population, and Households, and Employment**

STATE City, town, township, borough, or CDP (county if applicable)	Land area,[1] 2010 (sq mi)	Total persons 2010	Total persons 2014	Percent change 2010–2014	Persons per square mile, 2014	Foreign born	Lives in same house as previous year	Median household income (dollars)	Income of $100,000 or more	Income below poverty level	Percent in labor force	Unemploy-ment rate	Family households	One person households
	1	2	3	4	5	6	7	8	9	10	11	12	13	14
MASSACHUSETTS—Con.														
Auburn town (Worcester)..........	15.482	16,188	16,387	1.2	1,058.4	6.7	93.0	$72,695	33.4	5.6	67.3	7.0	68.8	27.2
Barnstable Town city & MCD (Barnstable)	59.805	45,189	44,529	-1.5	744.6	10.0	90.7	$58,933	26.1	12.7	61.9	7.7	60.5	32.2
Bedford town (Middlesex).........	13.658	13,320	14,225	6.6	1,040.0	14.4	87.8	$114,676	55.4	5.5	66.0	7.0	73.0	24.2
Belchertown town (Hampshire)	52.643	14,649	14,846	1.3	282.0	3.8	88.2	$74,221	35.8	8.2	71.3	6.5	71.9	23.5
Bellingham town (Norfolk).........	18.349	16,336	16,770	2.7	914.0	7.1	94.4	$87,417	42.1	4.0	75.2	7.3	70.6	23.8
Belmont CDP & town (Middlesex)	4.651	24,729	25,496	3.1	5,481.9	21.9	86.9	$105,859	52.3	6.0	67.1	4.9	71.9	23.1
Beverly city & MCD (Essex)......	15.093	39,502	40,952	3.7	2,713.3	6.3	87.1	$73,980	35.9	8.8	68.3	7.0	58.4	31.4
Billerica town (Middlesex).........	25.566	40,243	42,264	5.0	1,653.1	9.1	93.3	$93,761	46.2	4.3	72.2	6.7	75.2	21.4
Boston city & MCD (Suffolk)	48.366	617,680	655,884	6.2	13,560.9	27.0	78.2	$54,485	27.8	21.7	68.2	10.0	47.7	37.4
Bourne town (Barnstable).........	40.644	19,754	19,711	-0.2	485.0	3.4	88.0	$63,664	30.6	10.8	60.9	7.2	63.7	30.2
Braintree Town city & MCD (Norfolk)	13.749	35,739	37,362	4.5	2,717.5	13.2	91.1	$87,500	43.2	6.7	69.9	8.3	69.3	25.0
Bridgewater town (Plymouth)....	27.317	26,567	27,472	3.4	1,005.7	5.5	85.0	$88,481	42.2	6.6	65.1	7.7	72.6	16.8
Brockton city & MCD (Plymouth)..................	21.328	93,810	94,779	1.0	4,443.8	25.2	86.1	$48,569	17.2	17.7	66.5	13.6	68.4	26.9
Brookline CDP & town (Norfolk)	6.750	58,618	59,334	1.2	8,789.7	25.2	80.5	$93,640	47.7	13.6	67.6	5.6	51.6	34.9
Burlington CDP & town (Middlesex)	11.735	24,498	25,683	4.8	2,188.7	19.5	88.0	$95,465	48.0	5.1	69.2	7.8	71.8	23.4
Cambridge city & MCD (Middlesex)	6.390	105,201	109,694	4.3	17,167.1	28.1	73.1	$75,909	38.2	14.2	67.6	5.8	40.9	41.3
Canton town (Norfolk)...............	18.797	21,572	22,510	4.3	1,197.6	13.7	89.9	$90,878	44.9	7.1	68.5	8.1	65.1	30.3
Carver town (Plymouth).............	37.410	11,509	11,583	0.6	309.6	2.5	94.3	$72,804	29.3	6.9	71.2	7.2	70.1	24.9
Charlton town (Worcester)........	42.183	12,981	13,312	2.5	315.6	3.8	91.5	$91,287	43.3	6.6	74.0	8.9	78.5	15.5
Chelmsford town (Middlesex)....	22.370	33,802	34,960	3.4	1,562.8	10.8	91.1	$93,643	47.4	5.4	69.0	5.7	68.7	27.5
Chelsea city & MCD (Suffolk) ...	2.212	35,177	38,861	10.5	17,566.9	44.4	85.2	$48,725	17.6	22.0	71.8	11.2	63.9	28.1
Chicopee city & MCD (Hampden)	22.831	55,298	55,795	0.9	2,443.9	8.8	87.1	$47,276	15.4	13.4	63.4	10.1	60.1	32.7
Clinton town (Worcester)	5.655	13,606	13,749	1.1	2,431.4	9.7	88.6	$64,867	26.0	11.0	72.7	7.9	59.4	34.3
Concord town (Middlesex).........	24.524	17,668	19,535	10.6	796.6	8.7	87.6	$132,385	64.3	6.3	53.7	3.8	69.6	25.3
Danvers CDP & town (Essex)...	13.276	26,493	27,460	3.7	2,068.4	6.6	89.6	$77,404	37.4	5.0	69.9	7.9	66.0	29.6
Dartmouth town (Bristol)...........	60.925	34,032	34,415	1.1	564.9	12.4	86.9	$68,684	33.1	9.4	60.2	8.6	68.8	26.6
Dedham CDP & town (Norfolk).	10.247	24,729	25,473	3.0	2,485.9	15.0	87.4	$85,558	42.0	5.7	65.4	6.8	64.6	31.4
Dennis town (Barnstable)	20.510	14,207	14,037	-1.2	684.4	5.6	89.9	$50,860	20.0	14.4	55.4	9.2	56.9	38.6
Dracut town (Middlesex)	20.635	29,457	31,079	5.5	1,506.1	7.5	90.0	$76,786	36.8	5.9	72.5	5.9	74.5	20.8
Dudley town (Worcester)...........	20.817	11,390	11,818	3.8	567.7	8.6	89.6	$68,053	29.7	9.9	70.3	8.9	68.7	24.2
Duxbury town (Plymouth)	23.738	15,059	15,384	2.2	648.1	3.5	91.4	$120,253	59.1	3.9	64.5	6.7	77.9	19.8
East Bridgewater town (Plymouth)..................	17.209	13,790	14,243	3.3	827.7	2.9	95.0	$88,534	43.3	4.3	71.3	6.2	74.1	20.5
Easthampton Town city & MCD (Hampshire)	13.330	16,053	16,036	-0.1	1,203.0	6.9	88.5	$56,927	18.1	9.9	70.7	6.1	58.2	31.7
East Longmeadow town (Hampden)	13.006	15,720	16,123	2.6	1,239.6	6.1	91.5	$84,173	41.2	5.5	68.8	6.6	71.3	25.8
Easton town (Bristol)	28.757	23,112	23,907	3.4	831.4	6.9	92.5	$95,372	48.7	3.9	70.2	6.9	77.0	19.4
Everett city & MCD (Middlesex)	3.425	41,667	44,231	6.2	12,913.5	40.6	87.3	$51,056	18.0	14.3	72.5	10.1	68.4	24.5
Fairhaven town (Bristol)	12.335	15,873	16,034	1.0	1,299.9	5.3	91.1	$60,445	24.9	12.3	65.6	7.5	58.2	33.1
Fall River city & MCD (Bristol) ..	33.133	88,857	88,712	-0.2	2,677.5	19.1	83.8	$33,763	10.1	23.4	59.7	15.0	57.0	36.1
Falmouth town (Barnstable)......	44.066	31,531	31,631	0.3	717.8	8.3	90.9	$64,070	29.1	8.1	57.4	8.7	62.0	34.5
Fitchburg city & MCD (Worcester)	27.828	40,318	40,445	0.3	1,453.4	11.5	82.0	$46,628	17.1	19.5	64.2	12.5	64.6	27.1
Foxborough town (Norfolk)	19.848	16,865	17,376	3.0	875.5	7.2	88.1	$94,538	46.8	5.6	72.6	6.7	69.4	24.2
Framingham CDP & town (Middlesex)	25.038	68,326	70,746	3.5	2,825.5	27.0	83.0	$68,881	34.8	11.9	71.0	6.9	62.8	30.3
Franklin Town city & MCD (Norfolk)	26.632	31,635	32,836	3.8	1,232.9	6.4	91.4	$101,980	50.9	4.8	72.7	6.9	75.1	20.9
Gardner city & MCD (Worcester)	22.082	20,228	20,381	0.8	923.0	8.0	82.1	$46,589	13.5	17.0	60.1	11.3	61.3	31.6
Gloucester city & MCD (Essex)	26.193	28,789	29,626	2.9	1,131.1	8.5	90.0	$60,229	28.0	10.9	65.5	10.0	63.5	30.5
Grafton town (Worcester)	22.813	17,765	18,371	3.4	805.3	10.0	92.0	$81,250	42.1	8.6	70.8	6.8	69.2	25.2
Greenfield Town city & MCD (Franklin)	21.427	17,456	17,368	-0.5	810.6	6.3	82.8	$48,493	12.1	14.4	65.9	7.4	56.0	34.5
Groton town (Middlesex)...........	32.756	10,646	11,222	5.4	342.6	7.4	94.8	$116,686	57.0	5.5	69.6	5.7	80.0	16.1
Hanover town (Plymouth)	15.609	13,879	14,360	3.5	920.0	4.3	91.8	$98,750	49.3	3.5	68.8	8.2	77.7	19.4
Hanson town (Plymouth)	15.054	10,209	10,441	2.3	693.6	2.7	94.8	$93,771	46.0	4.4	73.0	9.3	79.2	17.1
Harwich town (Barnstable)	20.884	12,243	12,188	-0.4	583.6	7.3	93.4	$67,332	23.1	6.9	58.6	9.4	62.2	31.9
Haverhill city & MCD (Essex)....	32.968	60,879	62,488	2.6	1,895.4	9.0	86.4	$61,208	27.5	11.6	68.5	9.1	64.1	29.0
Hingham town (Plymouth)	22.227	22,157	22,964	3.6	1,033.1	5.3	90.5	$103,350	51.4	4.8	61.7	5.3	72.5	25.4
Holbrook CDP & town (Norfolk)	7.251	10,802	11,026	2.1	1,520.6	10.8	90.4	$63,297	28.7	7.6	67.0	8.1	64.8	29.4
Holden town (Worcester)..........	35.084	17,346	18,476	6.5	526.6	7.6	93.3	$97,972	48.7	3.4	70.7	7.0	79.1	17.0
Holliston town (Middlesex)........	18.645	13,547	14,388	6.2	771.7	7.0	91.5	$108,350	53.4	4.9	70.3	7.1	75.6	21.3
Holyoke city & MCD (Hampden)	21.281	39,880	40,124	0.6	1,885.5	6.1	84.4	$35,550	13.8	29.6	58.7	14.4	62.0	30.2
Hopkinton town (Middlesex)	26.261	14,925	16,311	9.3	621.1	7.5	91.0	$128,267	64.1	3.0	69.9	5.2	78.8	17.1
Hudson town (Middlesex)	11.522	19,063	19,754	3.6	1,714.5	17.7	93.0	$74,082	36.6	6.6	67.4	5.9	69.4	25.7
Hudson CDP.	5.737	14,907	NA	NA	NA	20.0	91.7	$66,334	30.8	7.9	65.8	6.5	66.9	28.0
Hull CDP & town (Plymouth)	2.809	10,293	10,365	0.7	3,689.9	6.3	88.0	$77,440	34.8	7.0	66.2	6.6	55.9	37.2
Ipswich town (Essex)	32.109	13,175	13,661	3.7	425.5	3.2	88.9	$77,901	37.6	6.2	69.9	7.2	63.6	28.8
Kingston town (Plymouth).........	18.657	12,629	13,154	4.2	705.0	3.0	89.7	$86,339	43.5	5.5	68.9	9.2	73.4	21.4
Lakeville town (Plymouth).........	29.558	10,602	11,208	5.7	379.2	4.2	92.7	$82,418	39.5	5.6	71.4	5.5	76.4	18.9
Lawrence city & MCD (Essex)..	6.926	76,377	78,197	2.4	11,290.8	38.3	83.6	$34,496	10.5	29.5	63.5	13.5	69.9	24.1
Leicester town (Worcester).......	23.251	10,970	11,270	2.7	484.7	5.7	91.8	$68,790	26.4	8.0	70.3	7.4	67.4	23.9
Leominster city & MCD (Worcester)	28.815	40,759	41,150	1.0	1,428.1	12.7	87.9	$59,263	23.3	12.0	69.2	10.1	62.2	30.1
Lexington CDP & town (Middlesex)	16.434	31,394	33,075	5.4	2,012.6	24.4	91.5	$137,456	64.7	5.5	63.0	6.0	76.8	20.6

1 Dry land or land partially or temporarily covered by water.
2 16 years old and over.

Table B. Incorporated Places, Census Designated Places (CDPs), and Minor Civil Divisions (MCDs) of 10,000 or More Population — **Crime, Construction, and Local Government Finance**

STATE City, town, township, borough, or CDP (county if applicable)	Serious crimes known to police, 2014[1]				New residential construction authorized by building permits, 2014			Local government finance, 2012							
	Total number	Rate[2]			Value ($1,000)	Number of housing units	Percent single family	General revenue				General expenditure			Debt outstanding (mil dol)
		Total	Violent	Property				Total (mil dol)	Intergovernmental		Taxes per capita[3]	Total (mil dol)	Per capita[3]		
									Total (mil dol)	Percent from state gov.			Total	Capital outlays	
	15	16	17	18	19	20	21	22	23	24	25	26	27	28	29
MASSACHUSETTS—Con.															
Auburn town (Worcester)	531	3239	250	2989	3,429	25	100.0	56.3	12.7	98.6	2281	56.3	3,458	483	30.4
Barnstable Town city & MCD (Barnstable)	1,365	3058	632	2426	15,419	48	100.0	177.7	41.0	87.9	2458	175.2	3,917	633	131.5
Bedford town (Middlesex)	74	522	49	473	19,684	38	100.0	74.4	11.6	95.9	4031	73.9	5,360	55	60.3
Belchertown town (Hampshire)	178	1206	142	1064	8,613	39	100.0	48.2	21.3	97.9	1599	47.4	3,203	202	33.4
Bellingham town (Norfolk)	302	1798	179	1619	6,606	44	100.0	54.6	16.0	93.5	2037	49.7	3,003	201	36.7
Belmont CDP & town (Middlesex)	190	744	63	681	6,984	13	100.0	101.3	16.2	98.3	2911	96.7	3,835	512	60.2
Beverly city & MCD (Essex)	552	1346	190	1155	2,195	9	100.0	134.3	32.2	93.2	2083	122.1	3,027	262	89.1
Billerica town (Middlesex)	423	998	80	918	9,123	48	100.0	150.9	38.8	99.2	2463	151.4	3,649	495	87.6
Boston city & MCD (Suffolk)	22,018	3365	726	2639	687,770	2,841	1.7	3134.7	946.2	90.8	2844	3160.4	4,932	468	1572.5
Bourne town (Barnstable)	372	1881	318	1562	9,421	26	100.0	68.3	11.3	97.1	2064	59.5	3,015	200	35.5
Braintree Town city & MCD (Norfolk)	890	2401	237	2164	7,178	55	7.3	122.1	30.7	98.2	2110	126.4	3,467	261	145.9
Bridgewater town (Plymouth)	NA	NA	NA	NA	4,711	28	100.0	49.5	4.6	96.1	1452	47.6	1,803	185	21.7
Brockton city & MCD (Plymouth)	3,900	4130	1052	3079	27,765	175	30.3	341.1	188.9	94.9	1255	341.2	3,628	290	242.9
Brookline CDP & town (Norfolk)	934	1572	279	1293	5,556	13	100.0	251.1	39.1	94.2	2953	232.1	3,938	454	78.5
Burlington CDP & town (Middlesex)	527	2045	144	1902	14,373	56	100.0	138.2	33.9	99.9	3675	132.5	5,246	1,149	58.1
Cambridge city & MCD (Middlesex)	2,912	2691	279	2412	63,800	285	10.9	1412.6	295.2	74.5	3195	1310.4	12,357	887	340.3
Canton town (Norfolk)	285	1270	263	1007	8,506	116	0.9	82.8	11.6	97.0	2812	93.1	4,238	292	74.5
Carver town (Plymouth)	165	1432	243	1189	2,832	20	100.0	35.5	13.8	97.7	1726	33.6	2,924	59	7.6
Charlton town (Worcester)	115	867	113	754	7,250	32	100.0	25.7	3.6	98.4	1407	25.1	1,913	320	20.4
Chelmsford town (Middlesex)	595	1698	86	1613	2,895	11	100.0	120.3	23.7	99.8	2469	123.8	3,582	23	103.1
Chelsea city & MCD (Suffolk)	1,483	3862	1112	2750	35,894	385	0.0	149.1	80.2	94.0	1320	146.8	3,958	166	35.1
Chicopee city & MCD (Hampden)	1,693	3032	385	2647	3,276	22	81.8	183.1	93.0	88.2	1298	183.1	3,289	279	51.4
Clinton town (Worcester)	56	407	44	364	5,117	28	100.0	38.1	16.1	99.7	1484	38.9	2,845	39	26.0
Concord town (Middlesex)	171	866	51	815	30,237	117	36.8	91.0	6.8	99.6	3877	81.1	4,291	309	75.4
Danvers CDP & town (Essex)	719	2585	129	2456	6,105	28	100.0	117.9	40.8	95.2	2474	126.2	4,646	1,322	82.4
Dartmouth town (Bristol)	994	2864	207	2657	16,968	60	100.0	84.2	20.6	99.0	1552	75.3	2,184	206	63.1
Dedham CDP & town (Norfolk)	542	2126	67	2059	3,412	12	100.0	107.0	16.6	96.0	3094	103.0	4,109	858	56.6
Dennis town (Barnstable)	427	3034	469	2565	18,290	63	96.8	49.7	1.9	99.8	2875	49.9	3,542	340	18.1
Dracut town (Middlesex)	505	1626	64	1561	10,833	49	95.9	79.5	30.3	99.9	1335	78.4	2,583	337	85.5
Dudley town (Worcester)	116	1003	355	649	2,894	17	100.0	14.4	2.0	100.0	921	14.6	1,258	15	7.3
Duxbury town (Plymouth)	98	637	65	572	10,453	37	100.0	64.6	10.7	99.4	3248	74.6	4,918	940	34.4
East Bridgewater town (Plymouth)	176	1239	141	1098	5,393	28	100.0	53.1	24.4	98.7	1822	63.7	4,566	1,751	55.7
Easthampton Town city & MCD (Hampshire)	209	1310	263	1047	1,272	7	100.0	42.7	19.9	95.9	1272	51.9	3,223	932	22.6
East Longmeadow town (Hampden)	281	1746	130	1616	7,273	33	100.0	54.2	15.2	99.7	2232	55.4	3,475	183	34.7
Easton town (Bristol)	270	1128	104	1024	16,880	98	24.5	71.6	18.2	99.1	2031	77.0	3,257	533	42.3
Everett city & MCD (Middlesex)	1,045	2410	404	2006	49,605	437	3.7	159.8	65.9	97.2	2084	163.2	3,832	25	61.8
Fairhaven town (Bristol)	487	3014	402	2612	2,159	12	100.0	52.8	18.3	94.3	1625	48.7	3,047	461	20.0
Fall River city & MCD (Bristol)	3,229	3632	1167	2464	3,895	38	100.0	291.2	173.4	87.5	956	273.3	3,082	273	271.7
Falmouth town (Barnstable)	874	2752	359	2393	25,580	136	41.9	121.5	20.2	96.1	2801	113.2	3,590	214	136.3
Fitchburg city & MCD (Worcester)	1,491	3682	815	2867	4,012	24	83.3	133.3	69.5	95.2	1108	123.9	3,067	250	74.6
Foxborough town (Norfolk)	NA	NA	NA	NA	7,729	31	87.1	66.8	19.0	98.0	2407	66.9	3,910	479	92.7
Framingham CDP & town (Middlesex)	NA	NA	NA	NA	12,568	77	81.8	257.6	56.4	94.5	2476	263.6	3,765	615	186.8
Franklin Town city & MCD (Norfolk)	110	335	15	320	10,969	47	44.7	113.1	39.1	99.7	1932	108.1	3,337	214	55.4
Gardner city & MCD (Worcester)	758	3704	748	2957	4,704	34	100.0	57.0	28.6	96.7	1067	61.6	3,034	263	20.9
Gloucester city & MCD (Essex)	331	1118	307	810	16,825	65	63.1	108.7	22.2	85.3	2398	118.1	4,041	621	137.0
Grafton town (Worcester)	118	645	186	459	13,516	62	100.0	73.2	36.4	98.4	1804	91.0	5,042	2,355	42.5
Greenfield Town city & MCD (Franklin)	722	4123	828	3295	1,875	11	9.1	58.8	24.8	81.0	1583	59.9	3,406	482	24.9
Groton town (Middlesex)	61	542	9	533	3,312	14	100.0	31.2	2.1	97.6	2361	31.0	2,814	212	14.8
Hanover town (Plymouth)	193	1339	28	1311	3,361	12	100.0	54.8	12.5	99.7	2578	62.5	4,412	872	60.4
Hanson town (Plymouth)	94	906	193	713	10,093	65	49.2	19.1	2.1	93.3	1588	18.9	1,841	93	7.8
Harwich town (Barnstable)	235	1922	245	1677	13,208	43	100.0	53.4	5.7	88.0	3276	52.1	4,274	4	31.7
Haverhill city & MCD (Essex)	1,839	2940	699	2241	12,536	101	36.6	179.2	72.3	95.2	1477	178.9	2,897	125	94.2
Hingham town (Plymouth)	287	1251	74	1177	22,464	72	100.0	98.9	18.3	100.0	3186	92.7	4,118	275	80.8
Holbrook CDP & town (Norfolk)	NA	NA	NA	NA	3,410	10	100.0	34.1	8.1	99.4	2026	32.2	2,948	50	22.0
Holden town (Worcester)	113	621	71	549	11,352	57	96.5	39.1	4.0	97.9	1850	38.3	2,173	77	47.0
Holliston town (Middlesex)	67	467	35	432	7,625	34	100.0	55.5	14.2	100.0	2755	55.9	3,986	170	48.3
Holyoke city & MCD (Hampden)	2,643	6552	967	5586	650	4	50.0	180.1	108.6	96.0	1283	193.1	4,810	387	104.5
Hopkinton town (Middlesex)	44	271	6	265	20,301	104	100.0	68.8	14.0	93.1	3195	64.9	4,185	361	53.1
Hudson town (Middlesex)	201	1017	56	961	4,774	24	100.0	70.6	21.9	98.7	2172	79.1	4,061	695	64.6
Hudson CDP	NA	NA	NA	NA	NA	NA	NA	NA	NA	NA	NA	NA	NA	NA	NA
Hull CDP & town (Plymouth)	167	1610	309	1302	2,377	7	100.0	38.9	9.2	89.4	2470	38.2	3,710	205	26.6
Ipswich town (Essex)	122	890	58	832	17,369	30	100.0	45.3	9.0	99.0	2424	44.0	3,256	184	43.7
Kingston town (Plymouth)	197	1527	202	1325	13,001	69	100.0	40.6	8.2	97.9	2215	38.9	3,049	175	51.2
Lakeville town (Plymouth)	159	1409	133	1276	4,462	23	100.0	21.6	1.5	93.3	1713	20.8	1,912	62	8.2
Lawrence city & MCD (Essex)	2,897	3706	1094	2612	4,151	33	18.2	293.4	219.3	93.9	741	270.5	3,497	39	148.3
Leicester town (Worcester)	264	2328	238	2090	3,788	21	100.0	30.7	15.7	96.1	1228	32.5	2,904	190	8.0
Leominster city & MCD (Worcester)	1,442	3502	658	2844	14,212	46	95.7	137.6	72.2	98.2	1401	130.9	3,200	778	58.1
Lexington CDP & town (Middlesex)	230	696	30	666	29,700	99	100.0	179.2	20.5	99.7	4342	178.1	5,514	106	86.0

1 Data for serious crimes have not been adjusted for underreporting. This may affect comparability between geographic areas over time.
2 Per 100,000 population estimated by the FBI.   3 Based on population estimated as of July 1 of the year shown.

Table B. Incorporated Places, Census Designated Places (CDPs), and Minor Civil Divisions (MCDs) of 10,000 or More Population — Land Area, Population, and Households, and Employment

STATE City, town, township, borough, or CDP (county if applicable)	Land area,[1] 2010 (sq mi)	Total persons 2010	Total persons 2014	Percent change 2010–2014	Persons per square mile, 2014	Foreign born	Lives in same house as previous year	Median household income (dollars)	Income of $100,000 or more	Income below poverty level	Percent in labor force	Unemploy-ment rate	Family households	One person households
	1	2	3	4	5	6	7	8	9	10	11	12	13	14
MASSACHUSETTS—Con.														
Longmeadow CDP & town (Hampden)	9.119	15,784	15,882	0.6	1,741.6	9.9	93.2	$108,835	53.5	6.2	63.4	5.2	77.7	19.8
Lowell city & MCD (Middlesex)	13.583	106,519	109,945	3.2	8,094.3	25.2	83.2	$49,164	17.8	18.9	66.9	11.5	62.7	29.1
Ludlow town (Hampden)	27.205	21,103	21,436	1.6	787.9	15.4	89.6	$61,410	29.0	7.1	60.9	7.1	69.7	25.2
Lunenburg town (Worcester)	26.419	10,086	11,107	10.1	420.4	6.0	89.7	$71,055	35.9	11.3	69.0	6.2	66.7	24.7
Lynn city & MCD (Essex)	10.741	90,329	92,137	2.0	8,577.8	32.0	84.2	$47,195	20.6	20.4	67.1	10.9	66.1	28.3
Lynnfield CDP & town (Essex)	9.883	11,596	12,668	9.2	1,281.8	7.8	91.8	$114,816	57.3	1.3	71.5	5.5	80.9	15.9
Malden city & MCD (Middlesex)	5.044	59,464	60,859	2.3	12,066.2	42.4	82.3	$55,523	23.3	17.2	70.9	11.0	60.6	28.1
Mansfield town (Bristol)	20.101	23,184	23,595	1.8	1,173.8	7.4	90.0	$93,082	47.2	4.3	76.2	7.6	74.0	20.6
Marblehead CDP & town (Essex)	4.386	19,808	20,454	3.3	4,663.1	7.5	90.7	$100,709	50.4	7.0	66.8	5.0	67.9	29.2
Marlborough city & MCD (Middlesex)	20.866	38,499	39,612	2.9	1,898.4	21.6	85.4	$71,424	34.2	7.1	74.9	6.9	59.5	32.3
Marshfield town (Plymouth)	28.621	25,132	25,635	2.0	895.7	4.1	91.0	$89,702	46.5	6.5	72.8	6.0	71.1	22.6
Mashpee town (Barnstable)	23.394	14,006	14,049	0.3	600.5	4.6	91.6	$65,768	27.3	9.0	57.6	7.6	65.9	30.5
Maynard CDP & town (Middlesex)	5.213	10,110	10,474	3.6	2,009.1	12.4	89.9	$79,252	40.0	10.0	75.6	6.6	58.1	34.0
Medfield town (Norfolk)	14.402	12,024	12,394	3.1	860.6	4.9	94.1	$143,641	66.4	5.2	69.4	5.7	84.1	13.6
Medford city & MCD (Middlesex)	8.101	56,253	57,437	2.1	7,090.0	21.1	83.7	$77,868	37.2	9.4	69.6	6.7	59.2	26.6
Medway town (Norfolk)	11.543	12,758	13,184	3.3	1,142.2	6.0	92.6	$109,841	55.5	3.0	75.8	6.6	75.1	24.1
Melrose city & MCD (Middlesex)	4.679	26,983	27,969	3.7	5,977.9	12.2	87.8	$86,409	42.2	5.5	71.8	4.8	65.3	29.8
Methuen Town city & MCD (Essex)	22.250	47,255	49,112	3.9	2,207.3	15.0	90.8	$68,587	31.7	9.7	70.4	8.0	70.7	25.8
Middleborough town (Plymouth)	69.076	23,116	24,103	4.3	348.9	3.3	88.6	$75,727	34.1	8.8	68.8	10.2	75.7	18.4
Milford town (Worcester)	14.751	27,993	28,439	1.6	1,928.0	16.7	88.4	$68,007	32.9	10.3	72.5	7.4	69.1	24.3
Milford CDP	10.160	25,055	NA	NA	NA	17.6	87.5	$63,129	29.7	11.0	71.5	7.3	68.3	25.0
Millbury town (Worcester)	15.708	13,261	13,460	1.5	856.9	4.7	88.6	$71,676	33.8	6.9	70.7	6.1	70.6	24.0
Milton CDP & town (Norfolk)	13.009	27,003	27,360	1.3	2,103.2	11.5	89.0	$113,087	57.2	5.1	66.8	5.6	76.5	19.5
Nantucket town (Nantucket)	45.552	10,172	10,856	6.7	238.3	15.8	90.4	$86,529	42.7	7.5	75.7	3.2	60.0	31.0
Natick town (Middlesex)	14.954	33,002	35,523	7.6	2,375.5	13.9	87.7	$98,902	49.5	4.4	73.9	4.7	62.6	31.5
Needham CDP & town (Norfolk)	12.286	28,890	30,205	4.6	2,458.4	12.7	90.7	$129,154	60.9	5.4	68.0	5.0	75.5	22.5
New Bedford city & MCD (Bristol)	19.997	95,072	94,845	-0.2	4,743.0	19.7	86.2	$36,813	11.7	23.3	62.2	12.2	59.1	34.1
Newburyport city & MCD (Essex)	8.348	17,416	17,926	2.9	2,147.3	6.4	87.1	$83,149	42.4	6.9	68.4	8.7	58.9	34.0
Newton city & MCD (Middlesex)	17.837	85,174	88,287	3.7	4,949.6	20.9	85.2	$118,639	57.1	6.2	67.2	5.7	69.6	24.9
Norfolk town (Norfolk)	14.904	11,227	11,800	5.1	791.7	6.0	89.7	$143,682	64.1	5.0	55.1	4.6	84.0	12.4
North Adams city & MCD (Berkshire)	20.346	13,708	13,354	-2.6	656.3	3.0	83.7	$37,654	11.3	20.3	56.6	11.7	53.4	38.9
Northampton city & MCD (Hampshire)	34.245	28,549	28,554	0.0	833.8	9.5	82.5	$58,179	26.8	13.7	67.8	7.8	49.7	37.1
North Andover town (Essex)	26.307	28,352	29,478	4.0	1,120.6	11.1	90.1	$100,544	50.2	5.6	70.3	7.9	70.7	24.7
North Attleborough town (Bristol)	18.874	28,712	28,908	0.7	1,531.6	5.1	91.3	$81,847	38.8	5.2	76.0	7.6	71.2	22.9
Northborough town (Worcester)	18.476	14,155	14,834	4.8	802.9	12.7	92.6	$107,111	53.0	2.9	69.7	6.0	77.3	18.4
Northbridge town (Worcester)	17.269	15,707	16,407	4.5	950.1	4.0	90.8	$70,399	32.8	5.3	73.8	7.9	67.7	26.5
North Reading town (Middlesex)	13.140	14,892	15,509	4.1	1,180.3	7.5	91.9	$112,419	56.0	6.5	70.2	5.8	75.8	20.2
Norton town (Bristol)	27.812	19,031	19,396	1.9	697.4	5.0	88.3	$80,806	41.5	5.8	68.3	7.9	73.0	22.6
Norwell town (Plymouth)	20.928	10,506	10,817	3.0	516.9	3.3	90.6	$110,671	55.5	2.6	65.8	6.8	84.3	14.4
Norwood CDP & town (Norfolk)	10.368	28,604	29,056	1.6	2,802.4	15.0	88.1	$79,963	39.0	7.6	69.6	6.3	59.3	32.1
Oxford town (Worcester)	26.529	13,709	13,853	1.1	522.2	3.2	87.8	$70,016	28.7	6.4	75.3	7.0	66.5	31.3
Palmer Town city & MCD (Hampden)	31.578	12,140	12,174	0.3	385.5	1.7	88.5	$51,846	21.1	10.3	65.4	10.6	62.7	30.6
Peabody city & MCD (Essex)	16.212	51,251	52,376	2.2	3,230.8	15.6	90.2	$62,234	28.2	9.0	65.4	6.1	61.7	33.2
Pembroke town (Plymouth)	21.778	17,837	18,197	2.0	835.6	3.4	93.1	$89,954	45.9	3.7	74.6	6.8	78.7	18.1
Pepperell town (Middlesex)	22.600	11,497	11,975	4.2	529.9	4.4	91.0	$77,767	37.1	6.0	73.5	6.9	74.5	20.5
Pittsfield city & MCD (Berkshire)	40.469	44,737	43,697	-2.3	1,079.8	6.3	86.3	$43,489	15.9	15.5	64.7	10.8	56.6	36.9
Plymouth town (Plymouth)	96.448	56,468	58,271	3.2	604.2	5.3	89.3	$76,925	37.1	7.9	67.4	8.0	70.1	23.1
Quincy city & MCD (Norfolk)	16.569	92,271	93,397	1.2	5,636.8	29.4	83.4	$62,710	28.3	11.3	70.4	9.4	54.2	36.5
Randolph CDP & town (Norfolk)	9.831	32,108	33,629	4.7	3,420.6	29.7	89.4	$63,259	27.5	12.0	70.9	14.6	69.8	24.2
Raynham town (Bristol)	20.489	13,383	13,691	2.3	668.2	7.3	90.8	$80,056	40.2	6.2	68.5	7.8	72.2	22.7
Reading CDP & town (Middlesex)	9.953	24,733	25,508	3.1	2,562.8	8.1	91.8	$103,913	52.6	3.2	71.3	5.4	71.1	23.8
Rehoboth town (Bristol)	46.938	11,608	11,926	2.7	254.1	4.9	96.2	$85,691	42.7	4.4	73.9	7.7	79.7	13.2
Revere city & MCD (Suffolk)	5.687	51,733	54,157	4.7	9,522.6	33.1	85.8	$50,900	20.0	16.9	68.5	10.4	59.5	32.0
Rockland town (Plymouth)	10.027	17,480	17,761	1.6	1,771.2	5.4	91.9	$66,860	28.9	5.4	70.6	8.9	67.9	26.9
Salem city & MCD (Essex)	8.280	41,340	42,824	3.6	5,172.1	14.8	81.4	$59,044	24.2	14.4	68.8	9.5	53.5	37.5
Sandwich town (Barnstable)	42.743	20,675	20,536	-0.7	480.5	3.2	90.0	$84,167	39.9	5.5	68.9	8.0	76.3	20.0
Saugus CDP & town (Essex)	10.799	26,636	27,921	4.8	2,585.5	10.5	93.3	$76,141	35.7	8.4	69.5	8.8	69.8	25.3
Scituate town (Plymouth)	17.635	18,135	18,413	1.5	1,044.1	4.7	91.5	$102,577	50.7	3.6	66.2	6.7	74.7	22.7
Seekonk town (Bristol)	18.378	13,722	14,683	7.0	799.0	6.8	94.3	$74,242	35.6	6.6	68.6	7.5	77.1	17.9
Sharon town (Norfolk)	23.438	17,610	18,121	2.9	773.2	19.2	92.8	$127,413	61.1	3.1	72.3	4.8	81.4	15.3
Shrewsbury town (Worcester)	20.728	35,608	36,580	2.7	1,764.7	21.2	89.0	$97,365	48.5	5.0	70.3	6.4	73.1	23.0
Somerset CDP & town (Bristol)	7.900	18,165	18,278	0.6	2,313.6	10.7	94.5	$72,558	32.8	8.4	60.6	10.3	73.1	23.4
Somerville city & MCD (Middlesex)	4.122	75,635	78,901	4.3	19,141.1	24.3	76.7	$66,866	32.1	13.8	74.4	6.5	43.8	32.1
Southbridge Town city & MCD (Worcester)	20.280	16,719	16,825	0.6	829.6	6.4	84.3	$42,376	12.7	16.8	65.0	10.4	60.0	33.0

1 Dry land or land partially or temporarily covered by water.
2 16 years old and over.

Table B. Incorporated Places, Census Designated Places (CDPs), and Minor Civil Divisions (MCDs) of 10,000 or More Population — Crime, Construction, and Local Government Finance

STATE City, town, township, borough, or CDP (county if applicable)	Serious crimes known to police, 2014[1] Total number	Rate[2] Total	Rate[2] Violent	Rate[2] Property	New residential construction authorized by building permits, 2014 Value ($1,000)	Number of housing units	Percent single family	Local government finance, 2012 General revenue Total (mil dol)	Intergovernmental Total (mil dol)	Percent from state gov.	Taxes per capita[3]	General expenditure Total (mil dol)	Per capita[3] Total	Capital outlays	Debt outstanding (mil dol)
	15	16	17	18	19	20	21	22	23	24	25	26	27	28	29
MASSACHUSETTS—Con.															
Longmeadow CDP & town (Hampden)	146	918	57	862	1,004	4	100.0	66.8	18.1	99.7	2740	99.1	6,246	2,651	68.7
Lowell city & MCD (Middlesex)	3,399	3098	546	2552	17,531	101	64.4	379.7	222.6	91.4	1102	358.5	3,303	268	256.6
Ludlow town (Hampden)	344	1598	214	1384	5,942	26	100.0	67.3	28.6	99.5	1567	66.0	3,103	34	20.2
Lunenburg town (Worcester)	313	2785	178	2607	7,533	51	27.5	32.6	8.8	98.8	1881	32.4	2,975	116	26.5
Lynn city & MCD (Essex)	2,999	3255	777	2478	6,011	59	18.6	304.3	187.6	95.4	1179	313.0	3,429	13	67.5
Lynnfield CDP & town (Essex)	101	799	63	736	9,683	26	100.0	46.8	7.6	97.3	2973	44.5	3,768	197	29.5
Malden city & MCD (Middlesex)	1,327	2178	359	1819	1,241	12	83.3	196.5	94.6	92.6	1234	199.3	3,301	386	106.3
Mansfield town (Bristol)	287	1210	177	1033	5,405	24	83.3	88.9	28.0	98.8	2177	89.3	3,818	96	49.0
Marblehead CDP & town (Essex)	248	1220	118	1102	7,728	16	100.0	75.1	9.9	99.7	2846	87.4	4,334	512	45.1
Marlborough city & MCD (Middlesex)	829	2086	340	1746	3,854	29	100.0	132.1	30.2	96.1	2319	126.8	3,229	96	60.4
Marshfield town (Plymouth)	220	857	164	694	6,462	26	100.0	85.0	22.8	99.3	2101	89.4	3,517	369	41.7
Mashpee town (Barnstable)	283	2004	326	1678	36,310	127	77.2	53.4	9.1	94.2	2869	51.0	3,657	95	30.4
Maynard CDP & town (Middlesex)	NA	NA	NA	NA	7,655	36	27.8	37.6	6.0	98.8	2549	45.3	4,386	1,183	52.9
Medfield town (Norfolk)	65	524	32	491	9,916	111	17.1	51.1	9.3	99.6	3044	49.0	4,007	115	35.7
Medford city & MCD (Middlesex)	957	1663	184	1479	1,001	8	50.0	142.6	31.8	91.0	1650	142.2	2,492	58	45.4
Medway town (Norfolk)	61	464	23	441	5,540	26	100.0	52.9	17.0	99.4	2350	56.2	4,337	850	38.0
Melrose city & MCD (Middlesex)	296	1059	111	948	612	3	100.0	82.1	18.2	97.0	1924	86.2	3,141	285	63.4
Methuen Town city & MCD (Essex)	883	1804	194	1610	37,012	123	96.7	133.7	50.8	97.6	1469	135.9	2,829	221	66.0
Middleborough town (Plymouth)	358	1505	252	1253	15,916	139	30.2	70.2	27.5	97.2	1541	67.7	2,899	9	39.9
Milford town (Worcester)	516	1815	193	1621	6,064	42	95.2	91.7	27.5	97.4	2046	86.9	3,084	198	35.9
Milford CDP	NA	NA	NA	NA	NA	NA	NA	NA	NA	NA	NA	NA	NA	NA	NA
Millbury town (Worcester)	317	2353	200	2152	4,748	24	100.0	37.9	12.4	99.4	1605	37.5	2,818	135	30.9
Milton CDP & town (Norfolk)	280	1022	40	982	4,547	10	100.0	96.1	15.1	99.5	2481	98.0	3,601	122	41.7
Nantucket town (Nantucket)	309	2945	67	2878	107,620	149	100.0	124.7	9.9	51.2	7751	105.6	10,208	1,603	196.2
Natick town (Middlesex)	556	1550	151	1399	42,093	206	32.0	159.6	49.1	99.7	2804	170.8	5,050	1,546	111.0
Needham CDP & town (Norfolk)	199	664	13	650	44,323	106	100.0	143.3	23.1	98.1	3508	148.7	5,057	1,172	99.8
New Bedford city & MCD (Bristol)	4,564	4786	1258	3527	2,118	19	100.0	342.6	197.7	87.3	1091	319.6	3,371	394	257.5
Newburyport city & MCD (Essex)	189	1053	150	903	3,913	12	100.0	65.8	9.8	97.8	2582	74.7	4,234	425	56.9
Newton city & MCD (Middlesex)	811	912	68	845	28,106	67	82.1	352.9	45.9	82.2	3076	348.0	3,989	200	217.6
Norfolk town (Norfolk)	28	237	17	220	12,666	43	100.0	40.8	13.1	99.1	2248	51.7	4,485	1,644	28.1
North Adams city & MCD (Berkshire)	570	4231	557	3675	195	1	100.0	44.7	25.7	90.9	1080	47.6	3,501	100	12.2
Northampton city & MCD (Hampshire)	825	2898	464	2435	9,554	39	69.2	93.2	21.7	85.3	1647	100.6	3,506	673	81.7
North Andover town (Essex)	326	1105	27	1078	15,135	46	82.6	91.3	14.8	99.5	2274	76.9	2,658	117	59.1
North Attleborough town (Bristol)	532	1841	62	1778	7,686	38	100.0	90.2	34.8	99.9	1565	92.8	3,225	350	62.9
Northborough town (Worcester)	174	1168	134	1034	7,760	35	68.6	52.5	7.6	95.3	2807	49.9	3,411	182	25.2
Northbridge town (Worcester)	359	2210	197	2013	9,894	47	72.3	60.4	35.8	99.9	1237	42.2	2,612	60	9.5
North Reading town (Middlesex)	117	753	109	644	8,415	29	100.0	60.7	11.3	97.0	2560	55.3	3,619	297	84.7
Norton town (Bristol)	100	513	21	493	4,126	21	100.0	54.7	20.8	99.8	1590	55.9	2,896	338	26.3
Norwell town (Plymouth)	96	888	93	796	12,216	37	100.0	43.8	7.1	98.4	3266	42.2	3,979	173	20.5
Norwood CDP & town (Norfolk)	352	1209	79	1130	2,900	9	100.0	100.4	18.8	92.0	2254	121.1	4,199	377	145.5
Oxford town (Worcester)	259	1867	281	1586	1,936	13	76.9	49.6	28.6	99.1	1389	44.0	3,191	232	9.5
Palmer Town city & MCD (Hampden)	201	1653	370	1283	400	3	33.3	38.1	18.2	82.8	1354	40.1	3,294	156	15.6
Peabody city & MCD (Essex)	1,028	1963	267	1696	5,063	25	100.0	155.1	38.9	89.5	1894	155.3	2,995	158	45.3
Pembroke town (Plymouth)	160	879	165	714	6,346	24	100.0	60.4	22.5	99.9	1932	58.6	3,266	198	31.6
Pepperell town (Middlesex)	137	1142	158	983	3,530	13	100.0	22.9	3.2	100.0	1439	20.9	1,770	61	14.0
Pittsfield city & MCD (Berkshire)	1,539	3506	444	3062	2,926	13	100.0	156.1	75.8	92.6	1592	180.6	4,076	509	87.1
Plymouth town (Plymouth)	667	1144	178	966	51,527	236	92.1	210.5	63.7	92.1	2283	212.9	3,715	892	128.1
Quincy city & MCD (Norfolk)	1,894	2014	419	1595	13,312	119	9.2	303.7	68.6	83.6	1983	317.7	3,420	279	211.7
Randolph CDP & town (Norfolk)	601	1777	387	1390	3,795	23	100.0	93.3	28.0	99.9	1592	94.2	2,830	145	40.6
Raynham town (Bristol)	315	2310	191	2120	6,829	37	100.0	36.3	1.6	99.0	2260	33.9	2,515	55	18.2
Reading CDP & town (Middlesex)	168	658	23	634	9,030	62	19.4	89.8	23.2	97.9	2239	82.2	3,260	138	38.2
Rehoboth town (Bristol)	115	964	75	889	5,026	25	100.0	23.1	2.5	97.5	1682	22.2	1,890	24	0.5
Revere city & MCD (Suffolk)	1,389	2553	557	1996	7,531	48	12.5	167.2	86.7	75.9	1396	159.6	2,981	128	59.8
Rockland town (Plymouth)	NA	NA	NA	NA	7,680	31	74.2	77.3	42.3	97.5	1651	92.7	5,270	2,431	38.5
Salem city & MCD (Essex)	1,311	3060	359	2700	1,305	6	100.0	150.4	51.6	89.1	1818	149.1	3,528	208	62.2
Sandwich town (Barnstable)	229	1110	179	931	5,597	17	100.0	71.1	15.2	98.0	2502	70.3	3,415	50	31.4
Saugus CDP & town (Essex)	777	2767	253	2514	4,097	15	100.0	76.8	11.6	99.1	2091	77.5	2,832	205	44.9
Scituate town (Plymouth)	129	702	131	571	8,296	29	100.0	72.2	14.3	93.3	2721	71.9	3,950	420	50.7
Seekonk town (Bristol)	393	2698	137	2560	14,567	104	42.3	46.2	9.3	100.0	2456	42.8	3,060	99	24.2
Sharon town (Norfolk)	81	446	NA	446	6,568	16	100.0	76.4	18.2	99.4	3096	81.6	4,570	1,185	58.8
Shrewsbury town (Worcester)	211	577	5	571	13,139	57	100.0	133.1	44.9	98.6	1639	132.8	3,682	702	78.7
Somerset CDP & town (Bristol)	323	1759	201	1557	0	0	0.0	53.5	7.8	99.9	2376	54.5	2,983	70	19.8
Somerville city & MCD (Middlesex)	1,437	1801	267	1534	0	0	0.0	214.8	65.2	90.3	1489	222.7	2,865	243	99.6
Southbridge Town city & MCD (Worcester)	436	2586	368	2219	3,121	23	100.0	82.8	55.5	97.9	1096	94.0	5,605	2,735	54.3

1 Data for serious crimes have not been adjusted for underreporting. This may affect comparability between geographic areas over time.
2 Per 100,000 population estimated by the FBI.   3 Based on population estimated as of July 1 of the year shown.

Table B. Incorporated Places, Census Designated Places (CDPs), and Minor Civil Divisions (MCDs) of 10,000 or More Population — **Land Area, Population, and Households, and Employment**

STATE City, town, township, borough, or CDP (county if applicable)	Land area,[1] 2010 (sq mi)	Total persons 2010	Total persons 2014	Percent change 2010–2014	Persons per square mile, 2014	Foreign born	Lives in same house as previous year	Median household income (dollars)	Income of $100,000 or more	Income below poverty level	Percent in labor force	Unemploy- ment rate	Family households	One person households
	1	2	3	4	5	6	7	8	9	10	11	12	13	14
MASSACHUSETTS—Con.														
South Hadley town (Hampshire)	17.713	17,514	17,691	1.0	998.7	5.6	87.6	$62,803	26.6	10.2	65.4	6.9	60.1	34.0
South Yarmouth CDP..............	6.956	11,092	NA	NA	NA	11.2	89.8	$50,673	16.8	10.8	61.3	8.6	57.0	36.6
Spencer town (Worcester)........	32.832	11,688	11,805	1.0	359.6	3.3	87.0	$60,943	27.5	11.9	68.3	9.9	62.7	31.4
Springfield city & MCD (Hampden)	31.865	153,195	153,991	0.5	4,832.6	10.8	82.8	$34,731	11.2	28.9	58.3	15.4	64.9	29.1
Stoneham CDP & town (Middlesex)	6.019	21,275	21,886	2.9	3,636.0	10.4	91.6	$76,218	37.2	4.6	69.5	5.9	60.9	31.1
Stoughton town (Norfolk).........	16.089	26,955	28,396	5.3	1,764.9	15.2	92.9	$74,688	36.3	8.8	69.7	8.6	67.8	27.8
Sudbury town (Middlesex)........	24.272	17,659	18,766	6.3	773.2	10.6	91.8	$169,505	72.4	3.0	66.2	4.7	88.1	10.5
Swampscott CDP & town (Essex)	3.023	13,787	14,014	1.6	4,635.1	12.9	86.6	$96,494	47.6	5.2	70.6	5.6	70.4	26.1
Swansea town (Bristol)............	22.694	15,865	16,150	1.8	711.7	7.4	94.5	$77,345	37.4	5.3	72.1	7.0	73.6	20.2
Taunton city & MCD (Bristol) ...	46.702	55,874	56,544	1.2	1,210.7	11.3	88.3	$52,225	21.6	14.8	64.1	10.4	64.1	28.7
Tewksbury town (Middlesex).....	20.702	28,953	30,260	4.5	1,461.7	6.5	93.9	$87,496	43.8	4.4	70.5	6.4	71.4	25.7
Tyngsborough town (Middlesex)	16.775	11,292	12,149	7.6	724.2	7.2	93.9	$93,108	48.1	8.1	75.4	9.5	75.9	17.3
Uxbridge town (Worcester).......	29.587	13,457	13,783	2.4	465.8	3.9	92.5	$86,768	42.3	4.7	73.8	9.1	73.8	21.8
Wakefield CDP & town (Middlesex)	7.356	25,094	26,774	6.7	3,639.7	7.3	90.7	$85,156	41.1	6.1	72.6	6.6	67.1	26.7
Walpole town (Norfolk)	20.433	24,069	24,933	3.6	1,220.2	9.4	92.1	$90,332	44.2	3.8	66.5	5.4	72.0	24.5
Waltham city & MCD (Middlesex)	12.729	60,632	63,014	3.9	4,950.5	26.5	81.7	$73,162	33.5	10.6	68.3	6.3	53.7	34.6
Wareham town (Plymouth)	35.864	21,822	22,473	3.0	626.6	3.1	89.8	$62,560	23.6	9.7	65.6	11.5	63.1	31.5
Watertown Town city & MCD (Middlesex)	3.993	31,915	34,127	6.9	8,546.1	23.8	83.8	$86,461	41.5	9.3	76.2	7.7	54.3	34.4
Wayland town (Middlesex)........	15.045	12,994	13,541	4.2	900.0	15.1	94.3	$142,306	63.6	6.2	65.7	4.7	73.8	24.7
Webster town (Worcester)........	12.380	16,767	16,844	0.5	1,360.6	11.4	83.9	$48,650	19.5	12.6	65.6	10.9	63.2	30.7
Webster CDP........................	2.998	11,412	NA	NA	NA	12.4	79.5	$43,704	14.6	15.6	65.0	13.2	61.8	31.7
Wellesley CDP & town (Norfolk)	10.016	27,971	29,362	5.0	2,931.6	14.0	87.4	$159,615	67.8	3.6	59.6	5.7	77.1	20.4
Westborough town (Worcester)	20.577	18,272	18,756	2.6	911.5	21.3	84.7	$100,552	50.6	4.1	69.5	4.7	67.6	28.0
Westfield city & MCD (Hampden)	46.258	41,094	41,608	1.3	899.5	9.5	85.9	$60,845	26.9	9.7	64.8	9.5	66.1	27.9
Westford town (Middlesex)	30.252	21,951	23,678	7.9	782.7	13.4	92.2	$125,143	64.0	2.8	71.9	5.4	83.4	12.8
Weston town (Middlesex)	16.825	11,264	11,992	6.5	712.8	15.4	84.3	$201,200	74.0	3.8	58.5	4.0	79.2	18.2
Westport town (Bristol)	49.847	15,532	15,742	1.4	315.8	8.5	94.5	$80,840	37.8	4.7	65.1	8.9	70.7	25.3
West Springfield Town city & MCD (Hampden).................	16.713	28,391	28,627	0.8	1,712.8	15.0	85.4	$52,806	21.9	10.7	66.0	10.5	62.7	31.6
Westwood town (Norfolk).........	10.882	14,616	14,979	2.5	1,376.4	12.5	92.1	$128,813	60.2	4.0	67.2	4.6	75.1	21.9
Weymouth Town city & MCD (Norfolk)	16.792	53,743	55,643	3.5	3,313.6	9.9	91.4	$69,099	32.3	7.4	70.1	9.4	59.7	33.2
Whitman town (Plymouth)	6.940	14,489	14,790	2.1	2,131.2	3.6	91.2	$76,494	33.7	7.3	76.0	7.9	68.3	25.8
Wilbraham town (Hampden)......	22.164	14,219	14,509	2.0	654.6	5.7	95.1	$87,303	43.9	7.0	66.4	6.0	72.5	23.7
Wilmington CDP & town (Middlesex)	16.978	22,325	23,370	4.7	1,376.5	7.4	92.9	$100,536	50.3	3.0	73.8	7.2	80.5	15.2
Winchendon town (Worcester) .	43.025	10,300	10,615	3.1	246.7	2.4	89.0	$59,332	22.8	11.7	64.7	5.3	68.8	24.9
Winchester CDP & town (Middlesex)	6.031	21,374	22,270	4.2	3,692.8	15.1	90.8	$141,829	64.1	3.9	67.8	5.4	79.6	18.9
Winthrop Town city & MCD (Suffolk)	1.990	17,497	18,352	4.9	9,220.6	13.6	91.2	$64,169	29.7	9.9	68.8	8.9	58.1	33.9
Woburn city & MCD (Middlesex)	12.637	38,134	39,272	3.0	3,107.7	15.9	87.9	$77,883	37.4	7.2	71.7	7.0	64.1	29.3
Worcester city & MCD (Worcester)	37.371	181,041	183,016	1.1	4,897.3	21.4	84.5	$46,105	18.2	21.0	62.6	10.5	58.4	32.5
Wrentham town (Norfolk)..........	21.707	10,955	11,422	4.3	526.2	5.2	94.4	$99,302	49.7	5.3	72.9	7.4	73.6	21.7
Yarmouth town (Barnstable)	24.148	23,797	23,592	-0.9	977.0	9.5	90.9	$55,858	20.5	8.6	58.6	6.8	58.9	36.1
MICHIGAN................	56,538.899	9,884,133	9,909,877	0.3	175.3	6.2	85.3	$49,087	18.8	15.4	61.5	11.4	65.3	28.9
Ada township (Kent)	36.033	13,135	14,040	6.9	389.6	5.2	92.7	$119,286	59.9	2.1	68.9	3.7	87.9	11.1
Adrian city & MCD (Lenawee) ..	8.023	21,193	20,840	-1.7	2,597.4	3.3	74.1	$31,576	8.9	28.2	57.9	15.8	53.8	36.5
Algoma township (Kent)...........	34.174	9,932	10,663	7.4	312.0	1.2	94.8	$77,399	35.1	5.0	68.7	5.6	87.0	12.3
Allendale CDP	22.726	17,579	NA	NA	NA	3.5	63.8	$46,884	17.9	30.3	65.7	11.6	56.5	16.1
Allendale charter township (Ottawa)	31.130	20,708	21,655	4.6	695.6	3.4	65.6	$46,284	16.7	30.1	66.6	10.3	57.6	14.7
Allen Park city & MCD (Wayne)	7.004	28,210	27,566	-2.3	3,935.8	4.9	92.0	$60,655	22.4	6.7	62.4	10.0	68.3	28.0
Alpena city & MCD (Alpena).....	8.541	10,483	10,247	-2.3	1,199.7	0.9	78.3	$32,377	7.1	24.4	59.3	10.1	57.2	35.8
Alpine township (Kent)............	35.887	13,321	13,787	3.5	384.2	8.8	79.5	$44,808	14.5	16.7	71.9	10.7	66.2	25.2
Ann Arbor city & MCD (Washtenaw)	27.865	113,947	117,770	3.4	4,226.5	17.7	64.6	$56,835	28.0	18.5	61.9	7.1	43.5	37.9
Antwerp township (Van Buren)*	34.682	12,182	12,086	-0.8	348.5	2.6	92.7	$58,404	22.7	7.7	69.2	7.2	74.6	22.5
Auburn Hills city & MCD (Oakland)	16.594	21,412	21,845	2.0	1,316.4	16.0	76.4	$52,949	17.2	10.6	69.0	9.9	56.7	32.2
Bangor charter township (Bay) .	14.102	14,641	14,369	-1.9	1,019.0	1.2	82.8	$44,636	15.1	15.8	51.8	7.8	64.4	30.7
Bath charter township (Clinton)	31.866	11,616	11,946	2.8	374.9	5.6	74.5	$60,188	25.7	16.4	65.4	6.6	58.7	25.5
Battle Creek city & MCD (Calhoun)	42.598	52,347	51,833	-2.2	1,216.8	5.5	80.6	$37,885	12.6	20.0	60.1	13.6	61.0	33.9
Bay City city & MCD (Bay).......	10.166	34,932	34,149	-2.2	3,359.0	1.3	83.5	$36,179	8.1	22.3	61.5	13.5	58.1	34.5
Bedford township (Monroe)	39.197	31,085	30,944	-0.5	789.4	2.2	91.9	$63,114	23.6	7.6	64.8	9.2	71.0	25.4
Beecher CDP........................	5.882	10,232	NA	NA	NA	0.6	82.9	$22,833	1.3	38.1	45.1	31.8	69.6	26.1
Benton charter township (Berrien)	32.368	14,749	14,527	-1.5	448.8	5.3	85.8	$26,329	6.0	30.7	53.8	16.0	62.6	33.3
Benton Harbor city & MCD (Berrien)	4.427	10,038	10,018	-0.2	2,263.0	0.7	76.2	$19,359	1.5	43.3	55.4	28.4	62.4	32.6
Berkley city & MCD (Oakland)..	2.615	14,970	15,273	2.0	5,840.8	5.4	88.5	$70,625	28.1	6.9	74.1	7.3	57.5	34.5

1 Dry land or land partially or temporarily covered by water.
2 16 years old and over.

Table B. Incorporated Places, Census Designated Places (CDPs), and Minor Civil Divisions (MCDs) of 10,000 or More Population — Crime, Construction, and Local Government Finance

STATE City, town, township, borough, or CDP (county if applicable)	Serious crimes known to police, 2014[1] Total number	Rate[2] Total	Rate[2] Violent	Rate[2] Property	New residential construction authorized by building permits, 2014 Value ($1,000)	Number of housing units	Percent single family	Local government finance, 2012 General revenue Total (mil dol)	Intergovernmental Total (mil dol)	Percent from state gov.	Taxes per capita[3]	General expenditure Total (mil dol)	Per capita[3] Total	Capital outlays	Debt outstanding (mil dol)
	15	16	17	18	19	20	21	22	23	24	25	26	27	28	29
MASSACHUSETTS—Con.															
South Hadley town (Hampshire)	270	1521	180	1341	2,516	15	86.7	48.2	17.7	97.2	1326	44.3	2,483	27	24.8
South Yarmouth CDP	NA	NA	NA	NA	NA	NA	NA	NA	NA	NA	NA	NA	NA	NA	NA
Spencer town (Worcester)	176	1489	135	1354	0	0	0.0	16.7	2.5	100.0	1089	16.7	1,426	0	12.4
Springfield city & MCD (Hampden)	7,585	4933	1091	3842	8,653	43	90.7	710.6	501.8	92.6	1192	702.0	4,562	459	260.5
Stoneham CDP & town (Middlesex)	232	1059	96	963	4,899	22	90.9	70.3	15.8	99.0	1994	67.2	3,105	96	30.3
Stoughton town (Norfolk)	577	2028	334	1694	4,864	40	47.5	88.7	21.4	98.5	1963	82.4	2,957	126	32.4
Sudbury town (Middlesex)	60	323	5	317	10,305	25	100.0	86.8	10.5	98.4	4004	90.6	4,994	285	32.4
Swampscott CDP & town (Essex)	267	1903	128	1775	25,094	195	5.6	57.0	8.5	86.1	3192	55.6	4,000	305	42.2
Swansea town (Bristol)	366	2262	204	2058	5,595	43	100.0	38.6	9.4	93.6	1705	38.9	2,429	145	9.0
Taunton city & MCD (Bristol)	845	1502	371	1130	10,461	87	58.6	200.1	101.1	96.2	1394	198.2	3,540	473	120.6
Tewksbury town (Middlesex)	505	1658	282	1376	23,871	201	37.3	117.5	34.5	99.3	2321	107.2	3,587	1,085	145.6
Tyngsborough town (Middlesex)	116	946	122	824	5,967	27	100.0	37.4	10.9	99.8	1929	36.8	3,079	102	7.7
Uxbridge town (Worcester)	184	1340	138	1202	9,859	38	100.0	55.2	27.5	99.8	1865	71.4	5,259	2,197	39.8
Wakefield CDP & town (Middlesex)	321	1216	163	1053	5,150	19	100.0	83.1	14.4	97.7	2233	84.8	3,310	62	26.1
Walpole town (Norfolk)	349	1392	68	1325	21,656	61	100.0	82.0	15.2	99.5	2342	81.2	3,295	208	32.5
Waltham city & MCD (Middlesex)	872	1390	196	1194	16,246	51	80.4	215.4	26.2	94.8	2606	206.3	3,326	185	106.4
Wareham town (Plymouth)	802	3551	522	3029	5,637	31	100.0	66.7	20.7	93.8	1585	64.9	2,908	193	41.4
Watertown Town city & MCD (Middlesex)	470	1409	93	1316	2,609	13	15.4	111.0	16.6	95.8	2365	108.0	3,282	224	44.3
Wayland town (Middlesex)	20	147	44	103	11,582	39	74.4	82.7	19.7	97.8	4383	106.8	8,029	2,378	74.4
Webster town (Worcester)	427	2531	468	2063	3,155	19	100.0	44.6	18.5	91.5	1211	40.3	2,398	188	33.2
Webster CDP	NA	NA	NA	NA	NA	NA	NA	NA	NA	NA	NA	NA	NA	NA	NA
Wellesley CDP & town (Norfolk)	192	653	48	605	47,283	66	100.0	153.0	28.2	99.6	3852	172.7	5,984	1,450	115.4
Westborough town (Worcester)	208	1108	69	1039	10,132	56	100.0	92.3	16.5	92.8	3585	89.0	4,840	513	122.8
Westfield city & MCD (Hampden)	618	1495	208	1287	5,498	26	84.6	141.0	61.2	91.3	1541	132.3	3,207	439	98.9
Westford town (Middlesex)	117	495	51	444	5,769	25	100.0	95.8	24.4	98.5	2814	90.8	3,969	102	70.9
Weston town (Middlesex)	45	375	25	350	35,192	31	100.0	80.7	8.8	97.9	5699	86.9	7,414	1,300	78.5
Westport town (Bristol)	NA	NA	NA	NA	3,912	26	100.0	35.8	9.6	96.5	1531	40.6	2,595	257	10.3
West Springfield Town city & MCD (Hampden)	1,414	4915	431	4484	4,864	25	40.0	111.8	41.7	97.5	2226	122.2	4,273	802	43.5
Westwood town (Norfolk)	141	941	113	828	80,197	387	8.0	77.3	12.6	99.6	3942	75.3	5,088	629	37.8
Weymouth Town city & MCD (Norfolk)	812	1450	239	1211	13,488	75	42.7	149.6	43.6	97.1	1571	133.5	2,426	127	91.2
Whitman town (Plymouth)	230	1556	358	1197	4,048	25	100.0	27.4	2.7	99.9	1428	26.4	1,806	141	16.5
Wilbraham town (Hampden)	163	1121	76	1045	10,597	39	100.0	41.1	6.8	31.1	2234	46.0	3,201	92	16.3
Wilmington CDP & town (Middlesex)	281	1200	132	1068	6,630	34	100.0	91.4	22.6	99.9	2672	87.9	3,826	264	48.8
Winchendon town (Worcester)	274	2578	348	2230	4,657	37	100.0	33.9	19.9	90.1	1054	30.7	2,927	212	14.1
Winchester CDP & town (Middlesex)	156	699	22	677	18,095	35	88.6	97.9	15.0	97.1	3253	99.6	4,551	725	88.0
Winthrop Town city & MCD (Suffolk)	242	1321	322	999	11,328	49	0.0	48.7	12.7	93.0	1468	49.2	2,723	34	11.4
Woburn city & MCD (Middlesex)	586	1487	180	1307	16,246	67	67.2	134.2	22.5	96.5	2436	140.9	3,624	251	86.3
Worcester city & MCD (Worcester)	7,380	4027	965	3063	11,051	104	84.6	673.9	351.9	90.1	1373	681.7	3,738	461	657.7
Wrentham town (Norfolk)	216	1899	88	1811	10,936	46	100.0	35.4	6.6	99.7	2458	33.1	2,970	25	14.2
Yarmouth town (Barnstable)	783	3306	861	2445	12,183	30	100.0	73.4	4.1	85.6	2318	69.4	2,938	108	23.9
MICHIGAN	244,895	2471	427	2044	3,314,833	15,933	77.7	X	X	X	X	X	X	X	X
Ada township (Kent)	NA	NA	NA	NA	NA	NA	NA	6.0	1.1	100.0	214	8.0	589	185	6.7
Adrian city & MCD (Lenawee)	487	2343	236	2107	NA	NA	NA	19.9	5.2	85.1	321	18.0	855	68	30.1
Algoma township (Kent)	NA	NA	NA	NA	24,149	204	22.5	1.8	0.8	100.0	76	1.5	150	32	0.0
Allendale CDP	NA	NA	NA	NA	NA	NA	NA	NA	NA	NA	NA	NA	NA	NA	NA
Allendale charter township (Ottawa)	NA	NA	NA	NA	35,018	429	22.1	6.7	1.7	100.0	102	5.1	240	20	8.2
Allen Park city & MCD (Wayne)	610	2214	189	2025	0	0	0.0	38.0	4.5	94.9	707	43.2	1,545	192	85.9
Alpena city & MCD (Alpena)	267	2604	263	2341	1,135	6	16.7	14.2	4.0	56.7	458	13.3	1,288	143	10.4
Alpine township (Kent)	NA	NA	NA	NA	4,035	12	100.0	4.5	1.2	79.1	83	3.3	247	17	10.0
Ann Arbor city & MCD (Washtenaw)*	2,410	2046	166	1881	6,636	24	91.7	205.6	39.3	54.4	775	199.0	1,717	426	244.9
Antwerp township (Van Buren)*	NA	NA	NA	NA	4,061	22	100.0	1.8	0.7	89.9	89	1.5	124	8	0.0
Auburn Hills city & MCD (Oakland)	729	3335	252	3083	3,480	45	35.6	39.6	4.2	95.2	1009	39.0	1,801	181	14.2
Bangor charter township (Bay)	NA	NA	NA	NA	0	0	0.0	5.8	1.0	99.7	133	5.5	377	0	0.0
Bath charter township (Clinton)	NA	NA	NA	NA	55,941	246	8.9	6.3	1.2	77.9	246	6.8	580	156	6.9
Battle Creek city & MCD (Calhoun)	2,835	4630	786	3845	1,927	10	100.0	117.1	35.5	38.6	913	105.6	2,035	231	87.6
Bay City city & MCD (Bay)	1,187	3460	531	2929	189	1	100.0	52.3	16.3	64.9	371	52.6	1,522	200	72.6
Bedford township (Monroe)	NA	NA	NA	NA	16,117	88	100.0	10.8	2.5	90.7	127	13.2	426	166	16.0
Beecher CDP	NA	NA	NA	NA	NA	NA	NA	NA	NA	NA	NA	NA	NA	NA	NA
Benton charter township (Berrien)	359	2479	228	2251	3,556	13	100.0	13.4	3.1	40.2	417	12.9	880	64	3.5
Benton Harbor city & MCD (Berrien)	795	7939	2556	5382	1,473	9	100.0	16.4	9.0	17.5	295	16.1	1,608	95	13.4
Berkley city & MCD (Oakland)	144	940	46	894	4,026	24	100.0	16.8	2.7	80.2	489	14.3	944	18	9.9

1 Data for serious crimes have not been adjusted for underreporting. This may affect comparability between geographic areas over time.
2 Per 100,000 population estimated by the FBI. 3 Based on population estimated as of July 1 of the year shown.

Table B. Incorporated Places, Census Designated Places (CDPs), and Minor Civil Divisions (MCDs) of 10,000 or More Population — **Land Area, Population, and Households, and Employment**

STATE City, town, township, borough, or CDP (county if applicable)	Land area,[1] 2010 (sq mi)	Total persons 2010	Total persons 2014	Percent change 2010–2014	Persons per square mile, 2014	Foreign born	Lives in same house as previous year	Median household income (dollars)	Income of $100,000 or more	Income below poverty level	Percent in labor force	Unemployment rate	Family households	One person households
	1	2	3	4	5	6	7	8	9	10	11	12	13	14
MICHIGAN—Con.														
Beverly Hills village..................	4.000	10,267	10,448	1.8	2,612.2	6.1	90.3	$103,011	52.6	4.0	67.8	6.1	71.8	25.0
Big Rapids city & MCD (Mecosta)	4.355	10,432	10,443	0.1	2,398.0	3.9	58.9	$25,134	7.2	38.1	57.6	23.4	40.5	37.8
Birmingham city & MCD (Oakland)	4.792	20,103	20,757	3.3	4,331.9	8.0	83.2	$107,161	52.5	3.6	70.0	4.3	62.2	32.8
Blackman charter township (Jackson)	31.729	24,051	23,923	-0.5	754.0	1.7	71.6	$37,298	9.3	15.5	41.0	13.4	57.3	37.9
Bloomfield charter township (Oakland)	24.633	41,070	41,967	2.2	1,703.7	15.2	91.0	$108,235	54.7	5.8	60.5	6.9	73.5	23.7
Brandon charter township (Oakland)	35.107	15,175	15,572	2.6	443.6	2.1	92.1	$68,322	30.0	11.9	69.3	10.0	80.3	15.7
Bridgeport charter township (Saginaw)	34.603	10,514	10,190	-3.1	294.5	0.9	90.4	$39,249	8.0	15.2	55.0	13.3	67.7	28.5
Brighton township (Livingston) .	32.957	17,790	18,132	1.9	550.2	3.5	93.0	$94,611	46.0	4.0	65.9	6.7	82.3	14.4
Brownstown charter township (Wayne)	22.155	30,627	30,770	0.5	1,388.8	7.7	87.9	$66,601	29.2	8.3	67.7	9.2	69.8	24.1
Burton city & MCD (Genesee)..	23.355	29,999	28,974	-3.4	1,240.6	1.4	86.5	$42,002	11.4	19.1	59.9	16.3	67.1	27.8
Byron township (Kent)	36.110	20,317	22,097	8.8	611.9	4.5	90.7	$57,368	23.5	7.0	67.4	7.0	75.7	22.7
Cadillac city & MCD (Wexford) .	7.173	10,356	10,335	-0.2	1,440.7	1.3	81.7	$34,106	6.0	19.7	57.2	11.9	59.2	35.6
Caledonia township (Kent).......	34.927	12,338	13,470	9.2	385.7	3.5	87.2	$80,621	29.3	5.7	71.0	4.4	81.8	15.0
Cannon township (Kent)	35.335	13,336	14,154	6.1	400.6	3.0	95.3	$88,250	44.1	3.4	69.5	5.7	84.1	14.1
Canton charter township (Wayne)	36.109	90,173	89,701	-0.5	2,484.2	15.6	86.7	$82,243	38.9	5.5	70.7	7.6	74.9	20.3
Cascade charter township (Kent)	33.874	17,135	18,316	6.9	540.7	6.8	89.7	$107,719	54.5	3.2	66.9	6.2	80.6	17.4
Chesterfield township (Macomb)	27.543	43,381	44,385	2.3	1,611.5	4.4	88.7	$67,391	27.6	8.6	71.5	10.9	71.3	23.6
Clawson city & MCD (Oakland)	2.199	11,825	12,049	1.9	5,478.5	9.5	89.2	$54,021	20.4	9.3	71.2	9.6	52.7	39.4
Clinton charter township (Macomb)	28.104	96,796	99,084	2.4	3,525.6	7.0	84.0	$47,706	16.1	12.4	64.7	13.0	60.4	34.0
Coldwater city & MCD (Branch)	8.047	10,945	10,811	-1.2	1,343.4	5.2	87.1	$34,260	7.7	18.5	61.0	10.3	61.3	32.1
Commerce charter township (Oakland)	27.444	40,186	42,112	4.8	1,534.5	8.8	90.9	$81,489	38.9	6.0	69.2	8.1	77.5	18.6
Comstock charter township (Kalamazoo)*	33.314	14,854	15,336	3.2	460.3	4.8	87.1	$50,364	14.8	12.0	64.3	9.6	62.4	30.7
Comstock Park CDP..............	3.879	10,088	NA	NA	NA	11.1	77.8	$40,451	10.8	21.4	73.5	10.7	62.7	27.9
Cooper charter township (Kalamazoo)	36.335	10,111	10,510	3.9	289.2	4.4	89.7	$56,839	19.6	9.0	63.3	7.8	66.9	25.1
Cutlerville CDP	5.869	14,370	NA	NA	NA	5.3	81.7	$42,595	12.3	13.1	65.1	9.9	64.4	30.4
Davison township (Genesee)....	33.318	19,575	19,071	-2.6	572.4	1.4	87.0	$50,926	17.6	10.6	59.7	9.9	62.6	30.2
Dearborn city & MCD (Wayne) .	24.230	98,146	95,535	-2.7	3,942.9	26.5	86.8	$46,776	19.0	21.6	55.2	11.7	67.6	28.7
Dearborn Heights city & MCD (Wayne)	11.738	57,774	56,415	-2.4	4,806.0	18.3	88.9	$44,440	13.7	16.7	57.7	13.2	66.9	29.8
Delhi charter township (Ingham)	28.610	25,877	26,247	1.4	917.4	5.6	86.9	$59,263	27.8	8.6	67.1	8.2	68.2	26.3
Delta charter township (Eaton).	32.464	32,408	32,921	1.6	1,014.1	7.0	84.5	$60,169	21.5	8.3	66.0	7.5	57.0	37.6
Detroit city & MCD (Wayne)......	138.750	713,862	680,250	-4.7	4,902.7	5.2	83.7	$26,095	6.4	36.2	53.3	27.1	57.2	38.1
DeWitt charter township (Clinton)	28.101	14,325	14,691	2.6	522.8	3.1	90.4	$60,347	24.3	9.8	64.2	5.9	66.7	26.9
East Bay township (Grand Traverse)	39.939	10,663	11,253	5.5	281.8	1.2	87.6	$61,394	17.1	6.0	70.9	7.3	70.0	23.7
East Grand Rapids city & MCD (Kent)	2.932	10,692	11,258	5.3	3,839.2	4.4	87.6	$107,824	52.9	2.1	70.7	5.2	80.2	17.4
East Lansing city	13.553	48,557	48,648	0.2	3,589.3	15.2	44.3	$33,064	17.7	37.7	52.1	8.7	32.6	37.8
East Lansing city (Ingham).......	10.042	46,610	46,672	0.1	4,647.5	15.1	43.4	$32,379	17.5	38.3	51.4	8.5	31.7	38.5
Eastpointe city & MCD (Macomb)	5.143	32,442	32,654	0.7	6,348.7	3.3	81.5	$40,997	8.1	21.1	64.0	16.3	64.0	30.8
Emmett charter township (Calhoun)	32.000	11,770	11,686	-0.7	365.2	1.8	87.5	$50,692	18.5	12.2	60.8	7.8	67.9	26.5
Escanaba city & MCD (Delta)...	12.875	12,616	12,413	-1.6	964.1	1.0	83.6	$26,808	5.6	27.0	56.2	14.3	49.9	43.0
Farmington city & MCD (Oakland)	2.660	10,372	10,554	1.8	3,967.6	16.8	85.7	$58,908	25.6	6.7	65.6	7.3	60.0	36.5
Farmington Hills city & MCD (Oakland)	33.280	79,740	81,435	2.1	2,446.9	18.4	83.8	$71,061	33.7	7.5	65.3	5.9	62.5	32.9
Fenton city	6.678	11,756	11,463	-2.5	1,716.6	3.3	82.7	$42,153	13.7	12.8	67.0	10.1	62.0	27.8
Fenton city (Genesee)	6.555	11,746	11,453	-2.5	1,747.2	3.3	82.7	$42,153	13.7	12.8	67.0	10.1	62.0	27.8
Fenton charter township (Genesee)	23.806	15,552	15,261	-1.9	641.1	2.3	88.4	$73,801	32.8	7.9	63.7	6.9	75.4	19.1
Ferndale city & MCD (Oakland)	3.879	19,900	20,256	1.8	5,221.4	4.0	82.0	$50,590	18.2	13.9	75.1	10.5	43.0	42.7
Flint city & MCD (Genesee)......	33.397	102,400	99,002	-3.3	2,964.4	1.1	77.7	$24,679	4.6	36.2	50.3	26.3	56.4	37.0
Flint charter township (Genesee)	23.298	31,929	30,892	-3.2	1,326.0	4.6	83.3	$41,893	11.1	16.9	55.1	13.5	60.5	33.9
Flushing charter township (Genesee)	31.383	10,632	10,337	-2.8	329.4	2.3	89.7	$61,810	18.1	7.1	59.3	9.9	71.0	25.2
Forest Hills CDP	49.271	25,867	NA	NA	NA	5.7	91.0	$118,788	58.8	2.5	68.1	4.9	85.2	13.3
Fort Gratiot charter township (St. Clair)	15.957	11,115	11,095	-0.2	695.3	4.5	82.8	$50,964	20.3	10.2	56.5	9.3	65.3	28.2
Fraser city & MCD (Macomb) ...	4.141	14,480	14,622	1.0	3,530.9	4.8	91.8	$51,230	19.3	11.5	63.6	10.7	63.6	31.9
Frenchtown township (Monroe)	41.817	20,428	20,032	-1.9	479.0	2.1	84.2	$45,562	12.2	13.0	58.2	12.9	65.0	26.8
Fruitport charter township (Muskegon)	29.981	13,598	13,752	1.1	458.7	1.7	90.7	$54,836	17.9	8.5	65.6	8.7	77.9	16.1
Gaines charter township (Kent)	35.704	25,145	26,151	4.0	732.4	5.5	83.1	$57,577	21.8	7.7	71.5	6.7	70.8	22.5
Garden City city & MCD (Wayne)	5.869	27,692	27,052	-2.3	4,609.0	3.2	88.3	$51,461	14.1	10.1	64.3	11.4	67.8	26.6
Garfield charter township (Grand Traverse)	26.592	16,256	16,803	3.4	631.9	3.3	81.8	$41,429	14.0	13.7	58.3	5.6	55.8	37.3

1 Dry land or land partially or temporarily covered by water.
2 16 years old and over.

Table B. Incorporated Places, Census Designated Places (CDPs), and Minor Civil Divisions (MCDs) of 10,000 or More Population — Crime, Construction, and Local Government Finance

STATE City, town, township, borough, or CDP (county if applicable)	Serious crimes known to police, 2014[1] Total number	Rate[2] Total	Rate[2] Violent	Rate[2] Property	New residential construction authorized by building permits, 2014 Value ($1,000)	Number of housing units	Percent single family	Local government finance, 2012 General revenue Total (mil dol)	Intergovernmental Total (mil dol)	Percent from state gov.	Taxes per capita[3]	General expenditure Total (mil dol)	Per capita[3] Total	Capital outlays	Debt outstanding (mil dol)
	15	16	17	18	19	20	21	22	23	24	25	26	27	28	29
MICHIGAN—Con.															
Beverly Hills village.............	88	839	19	820	358	1	100.0	11.3	1.4	99.4	616	12.7	1,220	24	4.8
Big Rapids city & MCD (Mecosta)...........	181	1718	180	1537	NA	NA	NA	15.5	4.0	57.6	462	13.0	1,213	70	14.7
Birmingham city & MCD (Oakland)...........	217	1053	58	995	46,864	105	100.0	51.8	3.8	75.4	1459	46.8	2,297	370	38.1
Blackman charter township (Jackson)...........	NA	NA	NA	NA	145	1	100.0	8.6	2.6	68.8	99	4.0	167	12	3.6
Bloomfield charter township (Oakland)...........	350	831	40	791	40,661	61	100.0	62.3	4.0	73.4	1029	56.7	1,364	52	65.0
Brandon charter township (Oakland)...........	NA	NA	NA	NA	7,417	30	100.0	6.8	1.0	99.3	313	6.1	394	8	2.0
Bridgeport charter township (Saginaw)...........	227	2215	517	1698	0	0	0.0	4.5	1.1	96.5	147	4.2	409	52	1.2
Brighton township (Livingston) .	NA	NA	NA	NA	NA	NA	NA	6.3	1.3	100.0	82	3.2	178	3	17.1
Brownstown charter township (Wayne)...........	384	1256	144	1112	13,850	83	100.0	35.2	3.0	81.2	513	27.8	907	105	33.5
Burton city & MCD (Genesee)..	1,360	4690	476	4214	1,256	8	100.0	18.2	5.5	93.6	148	18.3	623	116	12.1
Byron township (Kent)	NA	NA	NA	NA	35,421	149	100.0	7.3	1.7	96.4	97	5.9	282	6	0.0
Cadillac city & MCD (Wexford) .	397	3869	565	3304	NA	NA	NA	13.7	3.1	68.1	504	13.8	1,347	49	11.6
Caledonia township (Kent)........	NA	NA	NA	NA	25,693	116	96.6	4.6	0.9	100.0	118	3.5	274	47	9.4
Cannon township (Kent)	NA	NA	NA	NA	17,038	64	100.0	3.7	1.0	100.0	97	2.6	193	10	4.7
Canton charter township (Wayne)...........	1,449	1627	134	1493	42,717	228	70.2	80.5	9.0	86.5	403	70.8	791	40	80.0
Cascade charter township (Kent)...........	NA	NA	NA	NA	104,309	352	64.8	9.8	1.3	98.3	416	7.3	416	76	10.6
Chesterfield township (Macomb)...........	904	2045	242	1803	28,481	122	100.0	26.6	2.3	90.9	306	23.5	537	11	34.4
Clawson city & MCD (Oakland)	95	785	66	719	600	2	100.0	14.0	2.0	88.0	663	13.0	1,083	76	27.6
Clinton charter township (Macomb)...........	2,391	2418	299	2118	28,879	361	20.2	78.2	9.2	78.9	371	67.2	687	12	78.8
Coldwater city & MCD (Branch)	247	2282	277	2004	0	0	0.0	15.7	2.6	67.1	371	16.8	1,549	73	20.0
Commerce charter township (Oakland)...........	NA	NA	NA	NA	28,387	86	100.0	24.4	3.6	72.8	318	29.0	707	182	127.6
Comstock charter township (Kalamazoo)*	NA	NA	NA	NA	6,991	29	100.0	5.6	1.3	82.2	115	4.8	320	25	1.0
Comstock Park CDP.................	NA	NA	NA	NA	NA	NA	NA	NA	NA	NA	NA	NA	NA	NA	NA
Cooper charter township (Kalamazoo)...........	NA	NA	NA	NA	2,157	9	100.0	1.7	0.8	100.0	39	1.5	141	9	1.3
Cutlerville CDP.................	NA	NA	NA	NA	NA	NA	NA	NA	NA	NA	NA	NA	NA	NA	NA
Davison city & MCD (Genesee)....	350	1837	283	1553	8,613	80	40.0	8.3	1.5	97.1	73	8.3	430	28	0.0
Dearborn city & MCD (Wayne) .	3,482	3650	359	3292	6,573	22	100.0	175.2	29.5	56.1	888	163.2	1,685	219	274.1
Dearborn Heights city & MCD (Wayne)...........	1,423	2525	380	2145	3,668	12	100.0	74.1	29.6	29.1	490	61.3	1,071	5	58.1
Delhi charter township (Ingham)...........	NA	NA	NA	NA	16,715	114	45.6	18.9	2.3	100.0	315	16.1	619	92	31.8
Delta charter township (Eaton) .	NA	NA	NA	NA	9,195	45	100.0	20.8	2.8	83.3	308	19.7	605	47	20.4
Detroit city & MCD (Wayne)......	46,617	6808	1990	4819	33,443	238	13.9	2146.1	681.0	63.6	1078	2248.4	3,227	289	8166.1
DeWitt charter township (Clinton)...........	2	14	NA	14	6,911	30	100.0	9.8	2.5	52.4	244	9.0	619	80	1.5
East Bay township (Grand Traverse)...........	NA	NA	NA	NA	NA	NA	NA	4.2	0.8	100.0	179	2.9	266	1	6.1
East Grand Rapids city & MCD (Kent)...........	140	1238	27	1212	NA	NA	NA	13.0	1.6	100.0	738	12.3	1,116	65	11.7
East Lansing city (Clinton)...........	839	1728	284	1444	842	7	100.0	62.4	13.1	74.3	455	63.0	1,296	67	60.8
East Lansing city (Ingham).......	839	1728	284	1444	842	7	100.0	NA	NA	NA	NA	NA	NA	NA	NA
Eastpointe charter township (Macomb)...........	1,295	3963	826	3137	60	1	100.0	33.6	7.4	68.2	466	35.4	1,090	71	15.3
Emmett charter township (Calhoun)...........	633	5437	498	4939	0	0	0.0	4.3	1.5	96.9	175	4.2	361	50	3.0
Escanaba city & MCD (Delta)...	556	4431	287	4144	NA	NA	NA	12.6	3.1	77.8	398	12.4	991	34	10.7
Farmington city & MCD (Oakland)...........	105	990	85	905	0	0	0.0	12.7	1.6	89.6	490	12.7	1,208	125	7.0
Farmington Hills city & MCD (Oakland)...........	1,085	1328	116	1212	14,452	43	100.0	79.0	13.9	86.1	463	81.3	1,007	37	17.7
Fenton city (Genesee)...........	239	2072	139	1934	3,378	28	21.4	11.1	1.8	97.1	458	9.3	802	44	15.9
Fenton city (Genesee)..............	239	2072	139	1934	3,378	28	21.4	NA	NA	NA	NA	NA	NA	NA	NA
Fenton charter township (Genesee)...........	NA	NA	NA	NA	12,011	48	100.0	10.2	1.2	99.6	49	8.5	551	43	31.2
Ferndale city & MCD (Oakland)	602	2959	251	2708	839	6	100.0	41.6	11.7	33.8	862	33.3	1,653	46	25.6
Flint city & MCD (Genesee)......	5,588	5635	1709	3926	786	6	100.0	502.1	117.5	72.0	321	538.2	5,357	401	170.4
Flint charter township (Genesee)...........	1,992	6447	761	5686	491	3	100.0	20.3	2.9	72.9	196	16.3	519	14	7.4
Flushing charter township (Genesee)...........	60	581	165	417	NA	NA	NA	3.0	0.8	93.3	96	2.8	265	2	0.0
Forest Hills CDP.................	NA	NA	NA	NA	NA	NA	NA	NA	NA	NA	NA	NA	NA	NA	NA
Fort Gratiot charter township (St. Clair)...........	NA	NA	NA	NA	1,599	10	100.0	5.4	0.9	100.0	187	3.9	353	15	2.8
Fraser city & MCD (Macomb) ...	372	2542	219	2324	775	4	100.0	19.9	2.4	87.3	673	20.2	1,394	253	20.3
Frenchtown township (Monroe)	NA	NA	NA	NA	3,849	21	100.0	10.4	1.8	84.0	381	8.6	424	0	3.8
Fruitport charter township (Muskegon)...........	NA	NA	NA	NA	NA	NA	NA	4.4	1.2	100.0	152	4.2	308	71	4.9
Gaines charter township (Kent)	NA	NA	NA	NA	8,300	42	95.2	6.4	1.9	97.7	25	5.0	195	4	0.0
Garden City city & MCD (Wayne)...........	443	1639	215	1424	50	1	100.0	29.5	6.1	87.6	398	24.0	874	14	50.5
Garfield charter township (Grand Traverse)...........	NA	NA	NA	NA	11,069	43	100.0	10.0	1.2	100.0	246	6.6	401	57	3.0

1 Data for serious crimes have not been adjusted for underreporting. This may affect comparability between geographic areas over time.
2 Per 100,000 population estimated by the FBI. 3 Based on population estimated as of July 1 of the year shown.

Table B. Incorporated Places, Census Designated Places (CDPs), and Minor Civil Divisions (MCDs) of 10,000 or More Population — Land Area, Population, and Households, and Employment

STATE City, town, township, borough, or CDP (county if applicable)	Land area,[1] 2010 (sq mi)	Total persons 2010	Total persons 2014	Percent change 2010–2014	Persons per square mile, 2014	Foreign born	Lives in same house as previous year	Median household income (dollars)	Income of $100,000 or more	Income below poverty level	Percent in labor force	Unemploy- ment rate	Family households	One person households
	1	2	3	4	5	6	7	8	9	10	11	12	13	14
MICHIGAN—Con.														
Genesee charter township (Genesee)	29.059	21,577	20,732	-3.9	713.5	1.6	88.9	$41,179	9.6	16.1	56.8	15.2	69.0	26.6
Genoa township (Livingston)	33.823	19,791	20,281	2.5	599.6	4.2	90.5	$74,587	33.6	5.5	66.1	7.5	73.6	21.5
Georgetown charter township (Ottawa)	33.179	46,985	49,646	5.7	1,496.3	3.0	88.8	$63,852	24.6	6.7	68.3	5.0	76.8	20.1
Grand Blanc charter township (Genesee)	32.696	37,508	36,733	-2.1	1,123.5	6.4	85.8	$58,392	25.0	10.5	62.5	10.4	67.5	26.8
Grand Haven city & MCD (Ottawa)	5.771	10,412	10,965	5.3	1,900.0	2.7	86.5	$44,235	12.8	11.2	67.0	12.0	61.2	33.2
Grand Haven charter township (Ottawa)	28.680	15,178	15,990	5.3	557.5	4.6	86.4	$67,513	29.9	6.6	69.9	7.0	78.4	15.7
Grand Rapids city & MCD (Kent)	44.409	188,051	193,792	3.1	4,363.8	9.9	76.6	$39,913	11.4	22.6	66.7	12.0	56.2	32.7
Grand Rapids charter township (Kent)	15.345	16,656	17,773	6.7	1,158.2	7.5	89.2	$82,326	39.6	2.4	64.7	3.4	77.2	21.0
Grandville city & MCD (Kent)	7.273	15,378	15,857	3.1	2,180.3	3.7	89.5	$53,490	16.3	9.0	67.1	6.3	71.2	22.1
Green Oak township (Livingston)	34.211	17,476	18,237	4.4	533.1	2.9	91.6	$76,217	35.7	6.9	67.0	7.6	74.0	22.5
Grosse Ile township (Wayne)	9.224	10,371	10,181	-1.8	1,103.8	6.6	88.6	$92,674	47.8	3.7	61.1	6.6	74.8	23.7
Grosse Pointe Park city & MCD (Wayne)	2.169	11,553	11,288	-2.3	5,204.4	6.6	90.6	$97,083	49.6	5.9	65.8	5.7	73.9	22.3
Grosse Pointe Woods city & MCD (Wayne)	3.249	16,120	15,835	-1.8	4,874.4	3.8	93.0	$89,513	42.9	5.3	65.8	7.8	74.7	22.0
Hamburg township (Livingston)	32.242	21,165	21,691	2.5	672.8	2.6	91.8	$77,209	35.5	4.2	67.4	7.2	76.3	19.4
Hamtramck city & MCD (Wayne)	2.086	22,417	22,099	-1.4	10,595.7	43.6	80.7	$25,183	5.8	42.0	50.1	19.6	69.4	25.2
Harper Woods city & MCD (Wayne)	2.610	14,236	13,907	-2.3	5,329.1	3.7	88.9	$48,111	10.7	13.8	66.0	12.8	60.7	35.0
Harrison charter township (Macomb)	14.309	24,587	24,918	1.3	1,741.4	3.8	85.8	$54,501	24.0	10.9	68.0	10.0	63.2	31.2
Hartland township (Livingston)	35.861	14,664	15,033	2.5	419.2	2.4	90.5	$82,016	38.5	4.3	70.6	8.6	82.2	15.3
Haslett CDP	15.376	19,220	NA	NA	NA	10.4	82.0	$57,203	25.5	12.6	65.8	6.7	55.3	34.9
Hazel Park city & MCD (Oakland)	2.818	16,422	16,604	1.1	5,893.1	6.4	82.6	$31,596	6.1	26.6	60.5	16.8	51.5	40.9
Highland charter township (Oakland)	34.111	19,202	19,725	2.7	578.3	2.5	90.0	$70,376	32.0	7.6	67.1	9.0	75.1	21.0
Highland Park city & MCD (Wayne)	2.971	11,776	10,375	-11.9	3,492.3	0.3	88.9	$19,391	2.7	46.8	44.7	35.0	48.1	47.4
Holland city	16.661	33,051	33,644	1.8	2,019.3	11.4	75.0	$44,619	13.1	16.2	63.6	8.6	67.1	25.8
Holland city (Ottawa)	8.395	26,035	26,571	2.1	3,165.1	11.7	73.6	$45,929	13.3	15.8	64.4	8.5	67.2	25.2
Holland charter township (Ottawa)	27.028	35,636	37,433	5.0	1,385.0	15.5	85.7	$55,208	17.5	10.8	73.1	6.3	74.4	21.6
Holly township (Oakland)*	34.380	11,362	11,570	1.8	336.5	2.1	88.7	$63,368	22.2	9.4	67.0	11.4	74.7	19.1
Holt CDP	15.674	23,973	NA	NA	NA	5.3	86.1	$58,253	27.9	8.4	67.8	8.2	67.6	26.7
Huron charter township (Wayne)	35.352	15,879	15,678	-1.3	443.5	2.2	92.0	$69,828	30.5	11.3	65.6	12.9	77.7	18.9
Independence charter township (Oakland)	34.996	34,683	36,145	4.2	1,032.8	4.3	86.9	$76,628	35.5	7.2	67.6	9.7	75.4	20.9
Inkster city & MCD (Wayne)	6.253	25,366	24,786	-2.3	3,964.0	2.8	80.6	$27,849	5.8	34.1	57.0	20.8	59.6	36.2
Ionia city & MCD (Ionia)	5.348	11,394	11,439	0.4	2,139.1	1.1	71.6	$36,006	4.6	23.3	38.7	16.6	66.4	28.9
Jackson city & MCD (Jackson)	10.844	33,534	33,200		3,061.6	1.8	76.2	$27,342	6.1	33.5	60.5	18.0	58.8	34.0
Jenison CDP	5.855	16,538	NA	NA	NA	1.9	91.7	$56,381	17.6	5.5	64.1	4.1	73.6	24.6
Kalamazoo city & MCD (Kalamazoo)	24.682	74,262	75,922	2.2	3,076.0	6.1	65.3	$32,959	10.7	30.0	63.9	12.8	46.4	35.1
Kalamazoo charter township (Kalamazoo)	11.683	21,918	22,482	2.6	1,924.3	3.0	79.9	$40,784	9.2	18.4	66.4	12.2	58.4	34.0
Kentwood city & MCD (Kent)	20.904	48,707	50,764	4.2	2,428.5	16.4	81.4	$49,201	16.1	12.9	69.5	8.4	65.4	28.1
Lansing city	39.124	114,299	114,620	0.3	2,929.7	8.1	77.0	$35,675	7.4	25.0	65.8	13.5	53.1	36.8
Lansing city (Ingham)	33.306	109,565	109,870	0.3	3,298.8	8.2	77.1	$36,045	7.5	25.1	65.8	13.3	52.9	36.9
Lenox township (Macomb)*	38.706	10,470	10,680	2.0	275.9	2.2	85.4	$54,831	16.3	11.6	57.2	12.2	75.6	21.8
Leoni township (Jackson)	48.544	13,807	13,753	-0.4	283.3	1.4	87.9	$41,073	10.5	14.3	63.5	16.6	62.8	30.5
Lincoln charter township (Berrien)	17.911	14,691	14,559	-0.9	812.8	7.7	91.9	$66,667	27.2	6.8	65.8	7.8	68.4	28.6
Lincoln Park city & MCD (Wayne)	5.872	38,144	37,231	-2.4	6,340.3	7.4	84.5	$39,871	7.9	17.8	59.5	13.8	63.5	31.8
Livonia city & MCD (Wayne)	35.695	96,942	94,958	-2.0	2,660.2	6.9	90.9	$69,386	29.6	5.9	64.0	7.6	68.9	27.7
Lyon charter township (Oakland)	30.951	14,545	17,215	18.4	556.2	3.3	85.6	$82,972	40.1	3.9	69.1	6.8	76.7	19.9
Macomb township (Macomb)	36.226	79,580	85,459	7.4	2,359.1	9.8	95.2	$84,391	41.6	4.7	70.2	6.1	80.5	16.6
Madison Heights city & MCD (Oakland)	7.087	29,694	30,267	1.9	4,270.7	16.0	85.4	$40,820	11.8	19.3	65.1	12.2	55.6	37.8
Marion township (Livingston)	34.894	9,996	10,246	2.5	293.6	1.9	90.8	$80,146	38.4	5.1	67.5	5.9	83.7	14.2
Marquette city & MCD (Marquette)	11.414	21,367	21,441	0.3	1,878.5	2.2	71.1	$35,719	13.8	26.6	56.2	8.7	47.3	38.5
Melvindale city & MCD (Wayne)	2.720	10,715	10,441	-2.6	3,838.0	12.4	83.7	$33,834	6.1	26.7	57.2	15.0	58.4	39.2
Meridian charter township (Ingham)	30.493	39,688	41,776	5.3	1,370.0	13.1	82.2	$63,067	31.2	14.1	65.8	6.5	57.1	32.9
Midland city	33.742	41,869	41,957	0.2	1,243.5	6.5	81.2	$50,433	22.4	15.3	60.8	7.7	60.8	32.2
Midland city (Midland)	33.295	41,712	41,804	0.2	1,255.6	6.5	81.0	$50,560	22.5	15.2	60.8	7.8	60.8	32.2
Milford charter township (Oakland)*A2293	32.992	15,736	16,486	4.8	499.7	4.8	90.3	$81,756	40.5	6.2	69.8	8.9	71.8	25.4
Monitor charter township (Bay)	36.779	10,735	10,623		288.8	0.9	89.3	$57,869	22.9	8.8	57.1	6.7	66.3	25.4
Monroe city & MCD (Monroe)	9.166	20,733	20,198	-2.6	2,203.6	2.5	84.0	$45,037	15.7	20.3	61.4	9.8	64.2	31.6
Monroe charter township (Monroe)	16.900	14,568	14,355	-1.5	849.4	1.8	88.7	$44,512	16.7	15.8	55.2	8.5	68.6	27.8

1 Dry land or land partially or temporarily covered by water.
2 16 years old and over.

Table B. Incorporated Places, Census Designated Places (CDPs), and Minor Civil Divisions (MCDs) of 10,000 or More Population — Crime, Construction, and Local Government Finance

STATE City, town, township, borough, or CDP (county if applicable)	Serious crimes known to police, 2014[1] Total number	Rate[2] Total	Rate[2] Violent	Rate[2] Property	New residential construction authorized by building permits, 2014 Value ($1,000)	Number of housing units	Percent single family	Local government finance, 2012 General revenue Total (mil dol)	Intergovernmental Total (mil dol)	Intergovernmental Percent from state gov.	Taxes per capita[3]	General expenditure Total (mil dol)	Per capita[3] Total	Per capita[3] Capital outlays	Debt outstanding (mil dol)
	15	16	17	18	19	20	21	22	23	24	25	26	27	28	29
MICHIGAN—Con.															
Genesee charter township (Genesee)	500	2420	508	1911	0	0	0.0	8.2	2.5	72.0	89	9.0	427	4	0.8
Genoa township (Livingston)	NA	NA	NA	NA	NA	NA	NA	7.8	1.6	100.0	82	6.6	330	45	7.6
Georgetown charter township (Ottawa)	NA	NA	NA	NA	51,628	237	100.0	13.6	3.8	97.3	79	12.6	263	0	0.0
Grand Blanc charter township (Genesee)	642	1753	158	1595	25,526	111	100.0	22.9	3.1	99.9	240	24.3	659	15	11.9
Grand Haven city & MCD (Ottawa)	237	2151	154	1996	5,367	57	12.3	21.7	5.8	41.9	992	17.6	1,646	193	37.8
Grand Haven charter township (Ottawa)	NA	NA	NA	NA	16,574	66	100.0	6.3	1.1	100.0	199	4.5	288	13	11.9
Grand Rapids city & MCD (Kent)	6,555	3390	714	2675	32,210	203	36.9	321.9	89.0	37.4	637	325.6	1,709	174	552.9
Grand Rapids charter township (Kent)	NA	NA	NA	NA	NA	NA	NA	3.5	1.3	100.0	112	3.0	173	29	0.0
Grandville city & MCD (Kent)	715	4517	183	4334	2,777	12	100.0	25.8	2.6	84.7	430	28.5	1,827	872	11.4
Green Oak township (Livingston)	207	1140	116	1025	34,232	102	100.0	9.4	1.9	70.2	273	8.6	483	29	28.0
Grosse Ile township (Wayne)	42	414	10	404	5,287	12	100.0	14.0	1.0	78.5	851	11.2	1,086	69	47.0
Grosse Pointe Park city & MCD (Wayne)	298	2642	115	2526	500	1	100.0	15.7	1.9	84.4	759	17.2	1,500	50	16.6
Grosse Pointe Woods city & MCD (Wayne)	214	1354	139	1215	1,251	4	100.0	20.8	2.2	99.6	844	19.3	1,211	13	9.4
Hamburg township (Livingston)	107	494	46	447	NA	NA	NA	9.1	1.7	97.6	197	9.1	425	55	19.8
Hamtramck city & MCD (Wayne)	892	4048	1030	3018	650	6	100.0	32.2	13.2	33.4	483	33.3	1,494	34	2.2
Harper Woods city & MCD (Wayne)	1,050	7556	1101	6455	113	1	100.0	15.6	2.5	93.5	560	16.9	1,202	7	6.9
Harrison charter township (Macomb)	NA	NA	NA	NA	2,291	8	100.0	15.6	2.2	90.8	291	15.3	619	10	9.9
Hartland township (Livingston)	NA	NA	NA	NA	NA	NA	NA	7.5	1.2	100.0	118	5.3	360	4	31.0
Haslett CDP	NA	NA	NA	NA	NA	NA	NA	NA	NA	NA	NA	NA	NA	NA	NA
Hazel Park city & MCD (Oakland)	437	2622	414	2208	0	0	0.0	21.5	4.5	67.9	475	20.3	1,229	9	13.6
Highland charter township (Oakland)	NA	NA	NA	NA	6,081	24	100.0	7.5	1.5	93.0	213	6.2	320	3	3.2
Highland Park city & MCD (Wayne)	583	5741	1733	4008	NA	NA	NA	28.9	10.4	32.9	877	24.8	2,267	1	82.0
Holland city	1,149	3421	426	2995	2,432	13	100.0	45.8	12.0	77.2	504	51.4	1,542	413	47.8
Holland city (Ottawa)	1,149	3421	426	2995	2,432	13	100.0	NA	NA	NA	NA	NA	NA	NA	NA
Holland charter township (Ottawa)	NA	NA	NA	NA	19,343	107	100.0	22.0	6.9	43.3	214	15.8	433	87	2.7
Holly township (Oakland)*	NA	NA	NA	NA	235	1	100.0	2.0	0.3	93.4	118	1.8	157	7	0.0
Holt CDP	NA	NA	NA	NA	NA	NA	NA	NA	NA	NA	NA	NA	NA	NA	NA
Huron charter township (Wayne)	205	1311	160	1151	5,497	21	100.0	9.7	1.5	83.8	310	8.2	521	12	4.6
Independence charter township (Oakland)	NA	NA	NA	NA	25,810	117	100.0	23.0	2.7	100.0	348	20.4	580	1	15.7
Inkster city & MCD (Wayne)	1,070	4324	1229	3096	75	0	0.0	43.4	14.9	32.0	537	41.5	1,654	64	48.3
Ionia city & MCD (Ionia)	218	1907	297	1609	NA	NA	NA	11.9	3.6	60.4	277	10.3	905	156	24.6
Jackson city & MCD (Jackson)	1,727	5170	895	4275	241	1	100.0	52.5	18.8	34.8	555	61.6	1,847	294	42.3
Jenison CDP	NA	NA	NA	NA	NA	NA	NA	NA	NA	NA	NA	NA	NA	NA	NA
Kalamazoo city & MCD (Kalamazoo)	3,791	4998	1165	3832	3,730	13	100.0	130.6	43.5	46.0	580	121.7	1,617	207	453.2
Kalamazoo charter township (Kalamazoo)	507	2086	296	1790	3,249	13	100.0	8.8	2.0	95.2	210	8.6	385	34	0.4
Kentwood city & MCD (Kent)	1,651	3262	358	2904	11,491	157	97.5	37.6	7.9	86.2	420	37.4	753	60	20.1
Lansing city	4,865	4271	1119	3153	4,509	14	100.0	199.5	45.8	54.5	601	191.2	1,673	175	693.1
Lansing city (Ingham)	4,865	4271	1119	3153	4,509	14	100.0	NA	NA	NA	NA	NA	NA	NA	NA
Lenox township (Macomb)*	NA	NA	NA	NA	389	2	100.0	12.9	0.4	99.0	929	2.9	277	0	26.4
Leoni township (Jackson)	NA	NA	NA	NA	450	3	100.0	6.9	1.0	100.0	67	5.6	405	52	27.7
Lincoln charter township (Berrien)	165	1137	62	1075	8,666	25	100.0	6.5	1.0	100.0	235	6.2	427	43	2.6
Lincoln Park city & MCD (Wayne)	1,428	3846	587	3259	0	0	0.0	33.8	9.0	78.1	418	38.4	1,019	22	16.7
Livonia city & MCD (Wayne)	1,899	2002	125	1877	10,247	41	100.0	124.8	25.5	60.0	586	115.2	1,199	38	52.7
Lyon charter township (Oakland)	NA	NA	NA	NA	59,938	363	96.1	15.9	1.2	96.6	291	11.9	764	261	54.8
Macomb township (Macomb)	NA	NA	NA	NA	104,017	510	89.4	32.6	6.6	94.7	150	30.5	373	23	71.7
Madison Heights city & MCD (Oakland)	779	2566	231	2335	988	11	100.0	38.4	6.7	70.4	674	43.5	1,448	121	14.5
Marion township (Livingston)	NA	NA	NA	NA	0	0	0.0	2.0	0.8	100.0	50	2.2	222	6	8.0
Marquette city & MCD (Marquette)	297	1380	139	1240	NA	NA	NA	36.0	6.4	60.5	663	34.5	1,603	299	69.4
Melvindale city & MCD (Wayne)	335	3213	690	2522	482	4	100.0	15.1	3.7	51.6	554	16.9	1,592	7	5.8
Meridian charter township (Ingham)	1,013	2463	204	2259	32,390	103	100.0	25.1	3.3	86.6	330	23.3	576	24	4.3
Midland city	598	1415	118	1297	11,801	199	22.1	69.8	10.8	85.7	874	61.2	1,460	164	35.9
Midland city (Midland)	598	1415	118	1297	11,801	199	22.1	NA	NA	NA	NA	NA	NA	NA	NA
Milford charter township (Oakland)*A2293	95	577	24	553	10,876	38	100.0	9.1	0.7	98.3	387	9.2	572	76	10.4
Monitor charter township (Bay)	NA	NA	NA	NA	2,749	10	100.0	3.9	0.8	87.8	164	3.5	329	14	0.3
Monroe city & MCD (Monroe)	565	2780	472	2307	660	4	100.0	34.5	5.5	74.3	788	45.0	2,196	395	44.2
Monroe charter township (Monroe)	NA	NA	NA	NA	1,992	12	100.0	3.3	1.1	99.8	125	2.9	203	10	1.2

1 Data for serious crimes have not been adjusted for underreporting. This may affect comparability between geographic areas over time.
2 Per 100,000 population estimated by the FBI.   3 Based on population estimated as of July 1 of the year shown.

Table B. Incorporated Places, Census Designated Places (CDPs), and Minor Civil Divisions (MCDs) of 10,000 or More Population — Land Area, Population, and Households, and Employment

STATE City, town, township, borough, or CDP (county if applicable)	Land area,[1] 2010 (sq mi)	Population				Population characteristics 2010–2014		Household income and poverty, 2010–2014			Employment,[2] 2010–2014		Households, 2010–2014 (percent of households)	
		Total persons 2010	Total persons 2014	Percent change 2010–2014	Persons per square mile, 2014	Foreign born	Lives in same house as previous year	Median household income (dollars)	Percent of households — Income of $100,000 or more	Income below poverty level	Percent in labor force	Unemployment rate	Family households	One person households
	1	2	3	4	5	6	7	8	9	10	11	12	13	14
MICHIGAN—Con.														
Mount Clemens city & MCD (Macomb)	4.068	16,314	16,408	0.6	4,033.2	2.8	81.9	$36,348	8.2	20.0	56.5	16.8	53.0	40.5
Mount Morris township (Genesee)	31.508	21,501	20,797	-3.3	660.1	2.2	86.4	$33,480	6.8	27.3	49.4	23.3	67.0	28.6
Mount Pleasant city & MCD (Isabella)	7.741	26,016	25,971	-0.2	3,355.0	6.0	51.3	$29,107	10.7	35.5	58.9	12.9	39.3	33.3
Mundy township (Genesee)	36.013	15,120	14,722	-2.6	408.8	1.9	90.5	$55,888	16.6	8.5	59.0	8.3	70.4	25.5
Muskegon city & MCD (Muskegon)	14.211	38,403	38,393	0.0	2,701.6	2.4	73.4	$25,989	5.1	33.2	50.9	22.0	55.8	37.2
Muskegon charter township (Muskegon)	23.191	17,840	17,774	-0.4	766.4	0.9	82.8	$37,317	9.8	18.6	60.2	15.6	71.1	23.5
Muskegon Heights city & MCD (Muskegon)	3.185	10,856	10,799	-0.5	3,390.3	0.2	76.3	$20,474	2.0	42.2	52.3	27.0	63.7	31.3
New Baltimore city & MCD (Macomb)	4.608	12,084	12,269	1.5	2,662.4	2.2	94.1	$80,762	34.9	6.7	68.5	5.5	74.8	23.8
Niles city	5.791	11,599	11,400	-1.7	1,968.5	2.1	81.3	$32,283	7.0	29.7	58.7	13.9	60.0	35.3
Niles city (Berrien)	5.142	11,598	11,399	-1.7	2,216.8	2.1	81.3	$32,283	7.0	29.7	58.7	13.9	60.0	35.3
Niles township (Berrien)	37.317	14,165	13,957	-1.5	374.0	3.5	85.5	$43,909	12.0	13.8	60.4	12.4	67.6	27.3
Northview CDP	10.336	14,541	NA	NA	NA	1.8	84.4	$52,965	17.6	10.0	65.2	9.3	62.1	32.3
Northville township (Wayne)	16.192	28,497	28,809	1.1	1,779.2	16.2	86.4	$101,949	50.5	3.8	63.1	5.1	69.0	28.7
Norton Shores city & MCD (Muskegon)	23.235	23,994	24,081	0.4	1,036.4	2.9	87.8	$50,266	17.6	9.3	61.5	10.7	64.7	30.8
Novi city & MCD (Oakland)	30.229	55,224	58,416	5.8	1,932.4	18.8	86.2	$80,299	40.9	6.5	69.3	6.0	63.6	31.8
Oakland charter township (Oakland)	36.300	16,779	18,820	12.2	518.5	11.1	92.0	$118,969	58.7	3.6	65.0	6.9	81.1	15.7
Oak Park city & MCD (Oakland)	5.164	29,319	29,834	1.8	5,776.9	10.5	85.8	$47,292	12.0	16.7	64.1	14.2	66.3	29.9
Oceola township (Livingston)	36.128	11,975	12,266	2.4	339.5	3.5	88.6	$83,190	36.9	2.7	68.3	5.9	79.3	17.7
Okemos CDP	16.765	21,369	NA	NA	NA	14.8	82.5	$71,678	37.1	15.0	65.7	6.6	60.3	29.6
Orion charter township (Oakland)*	33.319	35,394	36,777	3.9	1,103.8	6.9	86.8	$80,955	37.8	7.8	69.7	8.7	72.4	23.0
Oshtemo charter township (Kalamazoo)	35.864	21,701	22,458	3.5	626.2	8.6	75.6	$40,172	18.7	21.2	67.0	8.7	51.6	35.6
Owosso city & MCD (Shiawassee)	5.228	15,194	14,779	-2.7	2,826.9	0.8	84.1	$34,994	6.4	21.1	64.0	12.3	63.3	29.5
Oxford charter township (Oakland)*	33.786	20,526	21,343	4.0	631.7	4.5	88.2	$70,694	34.9	8.3	65.0	9.6	74.0	23.8
Park township (Ottawa)	19.204	17,802	18,537	4.1	965.3	3.1	88.5	$71,455	31.0	6.6	67.2	7.4	82.8	14.5
Pittsfield charter township (Washtenaw)	27.236	34,804	37,548	7.9	1,378.6	18.3	80.9	$67,183	33.9	11.7	68.1	6.9	58.6	31.2
Plainfield charter township (Kent)	35.061	30,967	32,538	5.1	928.0	2.1	87.9	$59,237	22.3	8.2	67.8	7.8	68.8	27.1
Plymouth charter township (Wayne)	15.930	27,524	27,039	-1.8	1,697.3	6.6	87.9	$80,806	40.6	5.2	64.2	6.4	69.8	26.0
Pontiac city & MCD (Oakland)	19.971	59,515	59,808	0.5	2,994.7	7.2	74.5	$27,632	5.7	33.6	60.9	21.0	59.9	33.6
Portage city & MCD (Kalamazoo)	32.223	46,287	47,837	3.3	1,484.6	4.6	84.8	$55,050	21.8	12.0	67.9	8.2	63.8	30.7
Port Huron city & MCD (St. Clair)	8.091	30,177	29,168	-3.3	3,604.8	3.4	80.3	$32,888	7.3	25.8	60.7	17.8	59.4	33.5
Port Huron charter township (St. Clair)	12.838	10,654	10,448	-1.9	813.8	2.3	71.3	$42,730	14.0	21.5	54.9	19.0	70.1	24.5
Redford charter township (Wayne)	11.239	48,362	47,446	-1.9	4,221.5	3.2	84.5	$50,006	13.7	11.6	66.2	14.2	64.6	30.5
Riverview city & MCD (Wayne)	4.395	12,486	12,222	-2.1	2,780.7	3.2	83.5	$49,583	20.4	10.7	57.8	9.5	66.7	29.9
Rochester city & MCD (Oakland)	3.825	12,711	12,995	2.2	3,397.4	12.7	85.4	$76,133	40.8	6.2	69.9	6.0	59.9	36.3
Rochester Hills city & MCD (Oakland)	32.820	70,995	73,125	3.0	2,228.1	14.8	87.2	$80,806	40.1	6.4	66.9	7.2	69.4	26.1
Romulus city & MCD (Wayne)	35.608	23,989	23,496	-2.1	659.9	4.6	83.8	$44,525	10.1	18.3	62.7	16.5	66.8	29.2
Roseville city & MCD (Macomb)	9.829	47,299	47,598	0.6	4,842.8	4.3	84.2	$40,646	8.8	15.8	63.3	13.3	60.8	34.0
Royal Oak city & MCD (Oakland)	11.784	57,236	59,069	3.2	5,012.7	7.6	83.9	$64,873	29.9	8.0	74.7	5.8	46.8	40.9
Saginaw city & MCD (Saginaw)	17.107	51,507	49,844	-3.2	2,913.7	1.7	82.2	$29,049	5.8	31.4	55.8	21.8	58.9	35.7
Saginaw charter township (Saginaw)	24.497	40,840	39,982	-2.1	1,632.1	5.4	84.3	$50,322	18.8	11.4	60.5	6.4	59.7	34.3
St. Clair Shores city & MCD (Macomb)	11.667	59,730	60,036	0.5	5,145.8	4.7	89.2	$53,252	17.8	8.6	63.2	10.2	59.3	35.5
St. Joseph charter township (Berrien)	6.648	10,028	9,919	-1.1	1,492.0	4.3	91.4	$61,082	23.3	4.7	63.9	6.6	69.9	27.0
Sault Ste. Marie city & MCD (Chippewa)	14.775	14,144	13,959	-1.3	944.8	4.0	79.0	$32,125	7.7	22.9	63.7	13.4	52.4	38.6
Scio township (Washtenaw)*	33.725	20,072	21,332	6.3	632.5	12.1	85.9	$90,100	44.9	7.2	69.5	6.5	71.9	24.0
Shelby charter township (Macomb)	34.297	73,804	76,859	4.1	2,241.0	13.8	91.3	$64,946	28.8	8.8	62.6	8.8	70.0	25.5
Southfield city & MCD (Oakland)	26.274	71,739	73,002	1.8	2,778.5	10.2	81.1	$49,548	18.5	14.2	60.3	13.5	56.8	39.4
Southfield township (Oakland)	8.046	14,547	14,829	1.9	1,843.1	6.9	91.6	$106,361	54.8	4.6	64.9	6.0	73.2	24.2
Southgate city & MCD (Wayne)	6.846	30,047	29,416	-2.1	4,296.9	5.9	85.7	$48,924	15.6	11.8	61.1	9.9	58.5	35.4
South Lyon city & MCD (Oakland)	3.734	11,327	11,713	3.4	3,136.8	3.3	86.7	$55,889	27.3	8.0	64.1	7.0	62.4	34.8
Springfield charter township (Oakland)	35.431	13,940	14,344	2.9	404.8	3.5	90.7	$82,428	41.0	5.5	68.6	11.6	79.8	17.4
Spring Lake township (Ottawa)	16.478	14,300	14,887	4.1	903.4	3.0	88.6	$56,744	25.5	8.5	64.2	8.4	69.8	26.5
Sterling Heights city & MCD (Macomb)	36.507	129,699	131,741	1.6	3,608.6	25.2	88.2	$58,800	23.9	10.9	63.7	10.2	70.1	26.6

1 Dry land or land partially or temporarily covered by water.
2 16 years old and over.

Table B. Incorporated Places, Census Designated Places (CDPs), and Minor Civil Divisions (MCDs) of 10,000 or More Population — **Crime, Construction, and Local Government Finance**

STATE City, town, township, borough, or CDP (county if applicable)	Serious crimes known to police, 2014[1] Total number	Rate[2] Total	Violent	Property	New residential construction authorized by building permits, 2014 Value ($1,000)	Number of housing units	Percent single family	Local government finance, 2012 General revenue Total (mil dol)	Intergovernmental Total (mil dol)	Percent from state gov.	Taxes per capita[3]	General expenditure Total (mil dol)	Per capita[3] Total	Capital outlays	Debt outstanding (mil dol)
	15	16	17	18	19	20	21	22	23	24	25	26	27	28	29
MICHIGAN—Con.															
Mount Clemens city & MCD (Macomb)	NA	NA	NA	NA	0	0	0.0	20.5	4.3	63.0	377	19.6	1,203	13	27.8
Mount Morris township (Genesee)	952	4573	576	3996	375	3	100.0	8.4	2.4	89.8	144	9.3	440	12	2.0
Mount Pleasant city & MCD (Isabella)	557	2124	248	1876	4,204	62	11.3	19.8	5.1	79.3	309	19.6	748	41	13.0
Mundy township (Genesee)	342	2323	177	2146	1,887	11	81.8	7.1	1.2	98.4	180	7.1	477	20	0.0
Muskegon city & MCD (Muskegon)	2,077	5619	822	4797	571	4	100.0	40.9	9.9	74.7	468	46.3	1,248	68	30.6
Muskegon charter township (Muskegon)	850	4784	338	4446	817	6	100.0	8.8	1.8	78.6	201	8.4	471	6	15.0
Muskegon Heights city & MCD (Muskegon)	1,005	9283	1746	7537	0	0	0.0	10.4	3.3	69.6	329	11.0	1,023	15	16.7
New Baltimore city & MCD (Macomb)	108	882	57	825	8,059	29	100.0	11.0	1.4	99.6	466	9.9	819	88	33.3
Niles city	396	3477	562	2915	276	2	100.0	12.1	3.5	63.3	300	12.1	1,049	56	8.3
Niles city (Berrien)	396	3477	562	2915	276	2	100.0	NA	NA	NA	NA	NA	NA	NA	NA
Niles township (Berrien)	NA	NA	NA	NA	2,310	9	100.0	5.0	1.0	99.5	137	5.3	376	52	1.3
Northview CDP	NA	NA	NA	NA	NA	NA	NA	NA	NA	NA	NA	NA	NA	NA	NA
Northville township (Wayne)	379	1316	83	1233	24,360	57	100.0	28.5	3.1	84.3	445	23.7	825	57	39.9
Norton Shores city & MCD (Muskegon)	745	3104	175	2929	11,051	54	87.0	29.2	4.7	76.2	445	20.0	836	129	1.9
Novi city & MCD (Oakland)	899	1533	78	1454	36,491	203	97.5	64.1	7.6	98.2	557	58.8	1,034	128	48.0
Oakland charter township (Oakland)	NA	NA	NA	NA	47,492	141	100.0	10.0	1.4	99.7	408	6.8	387	4	6.5
Oak Park city & MCD (Oakland)	655	2185	337	1848	171	1	100.0	34.3	6.1	77.1	515	32.4	1,094	25	45.1
Oceola township (Livingston)	NA	NA	NA	NA	NA	NA	NA	3.1	0.9	100.0	69	1.5	125	25	7.2
Okemos CDP	NA	NA	NA	NA	NA	NA	NA	NA	NA	NA	NA	NA	NA	NA	NA
Orion charter township (Oakland)*	NA	NA	NA	NA	40,318	220	54.1	16.2	2.6	89.7	181	18.8	524	150	1.4
Oshtemo charter township (Kalamazoo)	NA	NA	NA	NA	12,501	49	91.8	6.0	1.8	95.5	63	5.2	236	38	0.0
Owosso city & MCD (Shiawassee)	465	3166	572	2594	0	0	0.0	11.4	3.2	87.4	258	13.0	874	99	6.4
Oxford charter township (Oakland)*	NA	NA	NA	NA	23,142	93	100.0	11.4	1.5	93.8	329	13.0	624	2	14.6
Park township (Ottawa)	NA	NA	NA	NA	15,317	46	100.0	4.5	1.3	100.0	130	3.9	217	27	0.0
Pittsfield charter township (Washtenaw)	814	2217	234	1982	36,123	269	32.0	26.3	3.9	71.4	312	22.5	627	61	13.3
Plainfield charter township (Kent)	NA	NA	NA	NA	29,793	125	93.6	13.6	3.0	86.0	143	13.2	416	33	14.1
Plymouth charter township (Wayne)	319	1183	74	1109	6,226	28	57.1	22.6	3.3	60.9	282	26.8	982	65	10.2
Pontiac city & MCD (Oakland)	NA	NA	NA	NA	3,837	26	100.0	80.8	29.4	48.1	491	91.7	1,541	157	80.8
Portage city & MCD (Kalamazoo)	1,573	3289	157	3133	17,250	95	51.6	42.4	7.6	94.6	508	39.8	842	89	90.1
Port Huron city & MCD (St. Clair)	1,066	3658	762	2896	2,305	19	10.5	56.4	17.9	36.7	712	60.3	2,048	427	122.4
Port Huron charter township (St. Clair)	NA	NA	NA	NA	495	3	100.0	5.5	0.9	94.3	234	6.0	574	135	5.6
Redford charter township (Wayne)	1,674	3527	533	2994	7,002	54	100.0	47.0	8.5	58.4	451	44.9	935	38	29.8
Riverview city & MCD (Wayne)	193	1581	98	1483	744	3	100.0	26.0	2.3	73.8	501	30.8	2,490	257	14.6
Rochester city & MCD (Oakland)	120	919	92	827	9,120	27	100.0	15.3	1.9	87.3	677	15.8	1,226	166	3.5
Rochester Hills city & MCD (Oakland)	NA	NA	NA	NA	57,772	217	38.2	71.4	14.4	64.9	437	59.2	819	60	31.9
Romulus city & MCD (Wayne)	679	2900	564	2336	1,898	22	100.0	35.2	6.7	77.8	696	33.9	1,430	118	50.2
Roseville city & MCD (Macomb)	2,080	4368	449	3919	145	2	100.0	60.4	8.9	82.4	527	53.3	1,126	43	13.3
Royal Oak city & MCD (Oakland)	672	1132	130	1002	40,210	129	100.0	80.5	15.1	59.4	537	82.6	1,412	97	117.8
Saginaw city & MCD (Saginaw)	2,067	4132	1689	2443	5,001	39	12.8	92.8	33.0	36.6	420	92.8	1,827	78	81.9
Saginaw charter township (Saginaw)	944	2347	174	2173	6,554	50	62.0	20.4	3.3	95.2	201	20.4	501	31	10.7
St. Clair Shores city & MCD (Macomb)	883	1468	193	1275	4,126	27	100.0	68.3	10.3	86.2	546	62.0	1,037	61	53.2
St. Joseph charter township (Berrien)	201	2026	171	1855	1,564	7	100.0	5.4	0.7	100.0	323	5.0	500	5	0.8
Sault Ste. Marie city & MCD (Chippewa)	364	2584	341	2244	352	1	100.0	24.5	8.7	58.3	527	26.3	1,855	535	48.2
Scio township (Washtenaw)*	NA	NA	NA	NA	NA	NA	NA	9.1	1.4	92.1	251	7.7	373	17	20.2
Shelby charter township (Macomb)	859	1122	124	998	68,058	307	47.6	53.0	6.5	86.6	397	67.2	896	95	34.9
Southfield city & MCD (Oakland)	2,356	3213	280	2934	3,486	5	100.0	103.2	22.5	49.8	892	95.5	1,316	49	64.8
Southfield township (Oakland)	NA	NA	NA	NA	0	0	0.0	0.6	0.0	100.0	38	0.7	46	0	0.0
Southgate city & MCD (Wayne)	999	3402	310	3092	2,349	9	100.0	30.9	6.3	84.0	550	30.8	1,034	2	22.5
South Lyon city & MCD (Oakland)	75	641	94	547	2,181	15	100.0	8.7	1.6	93.3	380	9.2	797	121	14.2
Springfield charter township (Oakland)	NA	NA	NA	NA	1,670	8	100.0	6.4	1.2	86.5	288	5.1	363	7	2.8
Spring Lake township (Ottawa)	NA	NA	NA	NA	7,226	26	100.0	5.2	1.1	93.1	120	4.5	308	93	8.3
Sterling Heights city & MCD (Macomb)	2,234	1698	160	1537	22,695	108	63.9	116.0	21.5	85.9	426	126.6	970	137	63.9

1 Data for serious crimes have not been adjusted for underreporting. This may affect comparability between geographic areas over time.
2 Per 100,000 population estimated by the FBI.　3 Based on population estimated as of July 1 of the year shown.

Table B. Incorporated Places, Census Designated Places (CDPs), and Minor Civil Divisions (MCDs) of 10,000 or More Population — **Land Area, Population, and Households, and Employment**

STATE City, town, township, borough, or CDP (county if applicable)	Land area,[1] 2010 (sq mi)	Total persons 2010	Total persons 2014	Percent change 2010–2014	Persons per square mile, 2014	Foreign born	Lives in same house as previous year	Median household income (dollars)	Income of $100,000 or more	Income below poverty level	Percent in labor force	Unemploy- ment rate	Family households	One person households
	1	2	3	4	5	6	7	8	9	10	11	12	13	14
MICHIGAN—Con.														
Sturgis city & MCD (St. Joseph)	6.507	10,994	10,901	-0.8	1,675.2	8.4	87.6	$36,206	7.3	20.6	60.1	12.5	63.5	32.6
Summit township (Jackson)	29.090	22,508	22,474	-0.2	772.6	2.8	85.1	$54,485	19.8	11.1	59.1	7.2	69.3	26.1
Superior charter township (Washtenaw)	35.211	13,058	13,572	3.9	385.4	14.0	87.1	$67,529	31.4	12.3	66.7	11.1	70.5	24.4
Taylor city & MCD (Wayne)	23.597	63,131	61,594	-2.4	2,610.2	4.5	83.4	$41,742	9.6	19.0	61.0	16.4	66.6	28.4
Texas charter township (Kalamazoo)	34.763	14,701	16,162	9.9	464.9	6.0	86.6	$96,105	47.5	3.2	66.7	8.5	86.5	10.0
Thomas township (Saginaw)	30.609	11,985	11,685	-2.5	381.7	2.2	89.9	$55,827	23.6	6.9	56.8	7.7	68.8	28.5
Traverse City city	8.326	14,674	15,042	2.5	1,806.7	2.0	79.3	$47,836	20.2	13.0	68.7	8.0	52.1	38.8
Traverse City city (Grand Traverse)	7.975	14,482	14,852	2.6	1,862.3	2.0	78.9	$47,370	19.7	12.9	68.8	8.1	51.8	39.0
Trenton city & MCD (Wayne)	7.263	18,853	18,427	-2.3	2,537.1	4.0	92.4	$53,257	20.8	10.5	57.0	9.6	62.9	33.5
Troy city & MCD (Oakland)	33.468	80,980	83,107	2.6	2,483.1	27.7	87.4	$84,325	40.3	7.3	64.8	7.4	73.7	23.1
Tyrone township (Livingston)	35.440	10,020	10,265	2.4	289.6	2.5	90.1	$78,941	36.8	4.3	65.4	9.3	84.0	12.5
Union charter township (Isabella)	28.157	12,927	13,588	5.1	482.6	2.9	54.9	$26,401	9.4	42.1	69.4	11.5	41.1	29.4
Van Buren charter township (Wayne)	33.969	28,821	28,315	-1.8	833.5	4.4	82.3	$54,470	21.0	11.1	69.1	9.5	64.4	28.2
Vienna charter township (Genesee)	35.006	13,255	12,862	-3.0	367.4	2.5	89.6	$53,396	15.9	9.4	56.4	11.7	71.4	23.1
Walker city & MCD (Kent)	24.942	23,537	24,468	4.0	981.0	4.8	81.1	$49,587	15.8	12.8	69.6	6.9	57.3	34.0
Warren city & MCD (Macomb)	34.383	134,056	135,099	0.8	3,929.2	11.5	86.5	$43,500	12.4	17.1	60.7	13.2	64.1	30.0
Washington township (Macomb)*	35.523	25,143	26,469	5.3	745.1	9.7	92.8	$79,570	35.9	6.5	66.0	8.3	77.7	19.6
Waterford charter township (Oakland)	30.608	71,705	73,139	2.0	2,389.5	5.3	85.4	$55,111	20.5	11.6	67.2	9.9	63.2	30.0
Waverly CDP	9.068	23,925	NA	NA	NA	7.1	81.9	$53,360	17.2	9.3	65.5	8.8	52.8	41.6
Wayne city & MCD (Wayne)	6.020	17,593	17,091	-2.9	2,839.2	2.9	87.7	$39,333	8.2	20.2	61.6	14.5	58.6	33.8
West Bloomfield charter township (Oakland)	26.997	64,690	65,957	2.0	2,443.1	20.2	88.7	$90,317	45.8	5.6	64.9	7.6	74.2	23.0
Westland city & MCD (Wayne)	20.425	84,097	82,314	-2.1	4,030.1	6.6	84.0	$43,903	14.3	15.1	64.4	11.5	58.9	35.0
White Lake charter township (Oakland)	33.524	30,019	30,955	3.1	923.4	3.4	87.5	$71,689	33.6	6.0	68.5	7.7	75.6	19.8
Wixom city & MCD (Oakland)	9.147	13,498	13,744	1.8	1,502.5	11.5	84.4	$47,353	24.0	13.7	76.7	6.9	54.0	39.2
Woodhaven city & MCD (Wayne)	6.387	12,875	12,594	-2.2	1,971.7	5.2	84.2	$58,609	25.6	7.5	66.2	7.5	66.5	28.3
Wyandotte city & MCD (Wayne)	5.317	25,883	25,151	-2.8	4,729.9	2.6	88.6	$51,074	17.7	12.6	64.2	10.9	60.7	35.3
Wyoming city & MCD (Kent)	24.616	72,122	74,826	3.7	3,039.7	10.4	83.4	$46,672	11.8	14.8	72.7	9.4	66.8	25.9
Ypsilanti city & MCD (Washtenaw)	4.329	19,569	20,081	2.6	4,638.2	5.8	56.5	$32,148	10.7	28.5	67.3	13.2	37.1	42.7
Ypsilanti charter township (Washtenaw)	29.931	53,362	52,139	-2.3	1,742.0	5.7	80.5	$45,928	17.2	16.1	69.1	12.4	59.1	32.3
Zeeland charter township (Ottawa)	34.394	9,970	10,690	7.2	310.8	5.1	91.4	$66,326	26.6	6.7	75.2	8.5	77.5	17.3
MINNESOTA	79,626.740	5,303,925	5,457,173	2.9	68.5	7.5	85.5	$60,828	25.7	11.0	70.1	6.5	64.9	28.2
Albert Lea city & MCD (Freeborn)	13.097	18,053	17,815	-1.3	1,360.2	4.2	86.0	$37,576	12.0	14.5	61.5	6.4	56.2	38.3
Alexandria city & MCD (Douglas)	15.963	11,070	11,680	5.5	731.7	1.2	75.2	$39,167	9.4	18.5	64.9	6.6	48.9	44.6
Andover city & MCD (Anoka)	33.878	30,598	31,996	4.6	944.5	3.3	92.6	$93,314	45.5	3.5	77.4	5.2	83.3	13.7
Anoka city & MCD (Anoka)	6.696	17,142	17,276	0.8	2,580.1	4.8	82.0	$47,408	15.1	12.2	65.2	6.9	60.1	33.8
Apple Valley city & MCD (Dakota)	16.873	49,084	50,487	2.9	2,992.2	9.3	86.7	$80,609	38.1	5.3	75.7	5.8	71.0	23.9
Austin city & MCD (Mower)	11.801	24,720	24,716	0.0	2,094.5	10.6	84.5	$39,890	13.1	16.0	65.2	7.8	59.9	35.7
Bemidji city & MCD (Beltrami)	14.406	14,076	14,453	2.7	1,003.3	3.0	73.5	$33,197	6.6	21.4	60.4	9.9	51.0	39.7
Big Lake city & MCD (Sherburne)	6.906	10,060	10,360	3.0	1,500.1	5.1	87.6	$63,941	24.3	8.8	78.4	6.7	74.7	17.9
Blaine city	33.839	57,177	61,190	7.0	1,808.3	10.0	89.8	$73,496	32.9	5.8	75.7	6.6	73.8	21.4
Blaine city (Anoka)	33.654	57,177	61,190	7.0	1,818.2	10.0	89.8	$73,496	32.9	5.8	75.7	6.6	73.8	21.4
Bloomington city & MCD (Hennepin)	34.705	82,893	86,314	4.1	2,487.1	11.5	86.5	$63,053	27.2	8.0	68.3	6.7	59.7	33.0
Brainerd city & MCD (Crow Wing)	11.905	13,586	13,425	-1.2	1,127.7	3.3	78.4	$32,169	4.8	24.3	62.9	10.8	53.5	38.0
Brooklyn Center city & MCD (Hennepin)	7.956	30,130	30,729	2.0	3,862.5	23.2	83.0	$45,198	11.9	15.8	67.3	8.9	66.1	28.3
Brooklyn Park city & MCD (Hennepin)	26.098	75,784	78,728	3.9	3,016.6	21.6	86.2	$62,656	26.6	11.0	73.5	7.7	72.5	22.5
Buffalo city & MCD (Wright)	7.277	15,459	15,912	2.9	2,186.5	2.9	84.1	$61,884	24.4	13.0	70.9	5.6	63.4	30.9
Burnsville city & MCD (Dakota)	24.905	60,307	61,630	2.2	2,474.6	13.4	82.7	$63,997	26.1	9.3	73.3	6.5	63.2	28.9
Champlin city & MCD (Hennepin)	8.168	23,091	23,828	3.2	2,917.3	6.7	91.3	$86,788	38.9	2.5	80.2	3.6	72.4	22.4
Chanhassen city	20.441	22,998	24,967	8.6	1,221.4	7.0	89.1	$108,078	53.9	2.9	75.3	4.8	78.9	17.8
Chanhassen city (Carver)	20.194	22,950	24,918	8.6	1,233.9	7.0	89.0	$107,849	53.8	2.9	75.2	4.8	78.9	17.8
Chaska city & MCD (Carver)	16.970	23,770	24,838	4.5	1,463.6	8.6	85.7	$76,301	35.6	4.6	77.5	4.0	70.1	24.2
Cloquet city & MCD (Carlton)	35.202	12,124	12,081	-0.4	343.2	0.8	90.9	$46,383	13.3	17.5	63.7	7.1	61.5	31.8
Columbia Heights city & MCD (Anoka)	3.410	19,496	19,675	0.9	5,769.1	16.3	82.9	$48,857	16.4	13.1	69.3	9.6	56.0	36.1
Coon Rapids city & MCD (Anoka)	22.612	61,476	62,112	1.0	2,746.9	7.6	86.3	$64,694	26.6	8.1	74.2	7.9	67.0	25.7
Cottage Grove city & MCD (Washington)	33.621	34,589	35,630	3.0	1,059.7	6.0	91.9	$82,485	37.3	4.9	75.9	5.3	79.0	16.1
Crystal city & MCD (Hennepin)	5.781	22,142	22,605	2.1	3,910.5	10.0	86.5	$59,860	20.7	7.9	70.5	4.7	59.9	30.5

1 Dry land or land partially or temporarily covered by water.
2 16 years old and over.

Table B. Incorporated Places, Census Designated Places (CDPs), and Minor Civil Divisions (MCDs) of 10,000 or More Population — Crime, Construction, and Local Government Finance

STATE City, town, township, borough, or CDP (county if applicable)	Serious crimes known to police, 2014[1] Total number	Rate[2] Total	Rate[2] Violent	Rate[2] Property	New residential construction authorized by building permits, 2014 Value ($1,000)	Number of housing units	Percent single family	Local government finance, 2012 General revenue Total (mil dol)	Intergovernmental Total (mil dol)	Percent from state gov.	Taxes per capita[3]	General expenditure Total (mil dol)	Per capita[3] Total	Capital outlays	Debt outstanding (mil dol)
	15	16	17	18	19	20	21	22	23	24	25	26	27	28	29
MICHIGAN—Con.															
Sturgis city & MCD (St. Joseph)	368	3372	449	2923	0	0	0.0	13.0	2.6	66.2	304	13.2	1,207	125	29.0
Summit township (Jackson)	NA	NA	NA	NA	1,757	7	100.0	6.6	1.7	98.3	81	4.7	207	1	3.9
Superior charter township (Washtenaw)	NA	NA	NA	NA	17,564	37	100.0	6.8	1.1	100.0	271	6.8	515	43	6.1
Taylor city & MCD (Wayne)	2,142	3481	559	2922	1,401	7	42.9	98.5	28.2	37.2	688	96.7	1,549	17	147.4
Texas charter township (Kalamazoo)	NA	NA	NA	NA	24,028	84	100.0	3.8	1.2	100.0	93	3.3	216	29	0.4
Thomas township (Saginaw)	168	1434	111	1323	2,959	12	100.0	12.2	6.2	14.0	169	5.7	477	112	0.0
Traverse City city	323	2138	305	1834	0	0	0.0	37.8	8.4	38.4	771	34.7	2,329	328	16.8
Traverse City city (Grand Traverse)	323	2138	305	1834	0	0	0.0	NA	NA	NA	NA	NA	NA	NA	NA
Trenton city & MCD (Wayne)	247	1342	201	1141	1,712	10	100.0	30.4	3.4	86.7	887	29.6	1,587	113	35.7
Troy city & MCD (Oakland)	1,418	1703	61	1641	44,327	167	74.3	91.2	12.7	89.5	600	79.5	969	131	55.0
Tyrone township (Livingston)	NA	NA	NA	NA	439	3	100.0	2.8	0.8	100.0	62	2.1	207	5	11.5
Union charter township (Isabella)	NA	NA	NA	NA	2,602	17	100.0	5.5	1.2	90.3	149	4.8	368	66	8.0
Van Buren charter township (Wayne)	659	2331	262	2069	4,396	19	100.0	19.3	2.3	94.4	258	18.5	646	35	56.0
Vienna charter township (Genesee)	NA	NA	NA	NA	1,079	5	100.0	5.9	1.3	74.5	176	5.0	387	0	4.4
Walker city & MCD (Kent)	626	2561	131	2430	6,445	31	93.5	17.2	3.4	98.2	467	14.9	620	111	13.7
Warren city & MCD (Macomb)	4,090	3028	478	2550	4,832	69	30.4	142.5	27.4	77.3	588	136.7	1,019	40	159.2
Washington township (Macomb)*	NA	NA	NA	NA	55,340	145	100.0	12.2	2.2	90.8	229	12.2	478	52	6.0
Waterford charter township (Oakland)	NA	NA	NA	NA	7,358	60	70.0	52.4	7.1	78.1	338	58.1	801	19	27.9
Waverly CDP	NA	NA	NA	NA	NA	NA	NA	NA	NA	NA	NA	NA	NA	NA	NA
Wayne city & MCD (Wayne)	508	2977	703	2273	0	0	0.0	28.4	4.9	71.6	643	32.1	1,854	117	34.3
West Bloomfield charter township (Oakland)	573	865	77	788	13,254	32	100.0	46.0	7.0	67.1	389	64.9	991	26	32.4
Westland city & MCD (Wayne)	2,212	2689	364	2326	4,791	43	81.4	82.4	25.5	58.5	327	78.6	943	2	12.4
White Lake charter township (Oakland)	398	1286	65	1222	10,002	43	100.0	15.4	2.4	97.1	276	14.9	486	16	8.4
Wixom city & MCD (Oakland)	289	2094	116	1978	3,277	12	100.0	15.0	2.8	63.0	652	14.1	1,033	134	17.6
Woodhaven city & MCD (Wayne)	250	1987	103	1883	250	1	100.0	14.8	1.9	89.6	757	14.5	1,136	0	14.5
Wyandotte city & MCD (Wayne)	616	2456	175	2281	1,156	6	100.0	44.6	7.8	56.0	656	53.7	2,107	160	63.3
Wyoming city & MCD (Kent)	1,808	2423	389	2035	8,542	58	100.0	74.0	21.7	50.6	365	64.1	874	19	117.0
Ypsilanti city & MCD (Washtenaw)	849	4266	829	3437	0	0	0.0	22.9	8.9	38.3	590	22.6	1,143	39	56.6
Ypsilanti charter township (Washtenaw)	NA	NA	NA	NA	9,182	45	100.0	26.6	4.8	80.4	318	25.8	481	17	6.0
Zeeland charter township (Ottawa)	NA	NA	NA	NA	5,215	25	100.0	4.2	0.8	100.0	246	3.1	298	163	5.9
MINNESOTA	137,882	2527	229	2297	3,680,420	16,990	62.9	X	X	X	X	X	X	X	X
Albert Lea city & MCD (Freeborn)	427	2394	163	2232	1,978	9	100.0	27.9	13.0	88.1	384	25.5	1,420	437	17.0
Alexandria city & MCD (Douglas)	465	3970	222	3748	13,970	95	29.5	11.9	2.9	65.9	472	13.8	1,197	472	31.0
Andover city & MCD (Anoka)	NA	NA	NA	NA	14,817	52	100.0	22.9	1.9	92.9	406	18.3	588	147	55.4
Anoka city & MCD (Anoka)	616	3562	301	3261	9,130	24	100.0	19.2	2.0	95.7	572	15.8	919	149	30.0
Apple Valley city & MCD (Dakota)	1,084	2148	83	2065	54,296	368	19.3	46.2	2.4	99.7	518	38.3	766	170	71.3
Austin city & MCD (Mower)	651	2629	266	2362	1,658	11	100.0	28.6	11.4	95.6	255	31.7	1,279	392	47.2
Bemidji city & MCD (Beltrami)	1,237	8523	434	8089	8,917	124	53.2	31.8	15.1	99.8	497	48.7	3,402	2,336	104.2
Big Lake city & MCD (Sherburne)	156	1508	126	1382	1,662	9	100.0	8.1	1.6	94.8	338	11.2	1,092	481	59.0
Blaine city	1,884	3079	72	3007	96,213	343	100.0	45.6	3.0	81.8	396	44.2	746	172	51.9
Blaine city (Anoka)	1,884	3079	72	3007	96,213	343	100.0	NA	NA	NA	NA	NA	NA	NA	NA
Bloomington city & MCD (Hennepin)	3,359	3854	180	3674	2,449	11	100.0	120.6	11.3	85.5	NA	137.2	NA	NA	158.7
Brainerd city & MCD (Crow Wing)	745	5534	669	4866	1,404	8	25.0	29.9	14.9	60.0	432	29.4	2,179	829	63.2
Brooklyn Center city & MCD (Hennepin)	1,315	4261	324	3937	491	4	100.0	39.3	5.0	72.8	NA	39.3	NA	NA	47.5
Brooklyn Park city & MCD (Hennepin)	2,678	3390	386	3004	25,595	114	100.0	79.5	9.0	54.3	NA	69.8	NA	NA	95.6
Buffalo city & MCD (Wright)	317	1993	69	1923	10,112	47	100.0	14.2	1.7	63.7	329	16.5	1,048	250	114.5
Burnsville city & MCD (Dakota)	1,770	2869	115	2754	8,118	34	100.0	55.1	4.0	78.6	547	54.1	885	185	62.7
Champlin city & MCD (Hennepin)	344	1435	83	1352	2,304	10	100.0	24.7	1.3	100.0	NA	21.0	NA	NA	41.6
Chanhassen city	NA	NA	NA	NA	38,903	153	84.3	21.0	1.4	84.4	503	20.1	842	118	47.9
Chanhassen city (Carver)	NA	NA	NA	NA	38,903	153	84.3	NA	NA	NA	NA	NA	NA	NA	NA
Chaska city & MCD (Carver)	226	919	49	870	41,675	165	84.2	29.2	1.6	85.5	604	26.3	1,094	121	96.7
Cloquet city & MCD (Carlton)	519	4314	233	4081	2,287	8	100.0	12.2	3.2	96.7	232	11.5	956	144	74.8
Columbia Heights city & MCD (Anoka)	556	2821	244	2577	2,459	11	100.0	24.9	4.9	86.9	551	25.8	1,315	362	47.9
Coon Rapids city & MCD (Anoka)	1,624	2609	133	2476	3,415	12	100.0	50.6	4.4	75.2	453	69.6	1,124	385	87.0
Cottage Grove city & MCD (Washington)	694	1951	56	1894	22,751	77	100.0	32.6	4.1	86.1	391	30.2	858	186	57.0
Crystal city & MCD (Hennepin)	622	2741	154	2587	14,181	138	5.8	25.2	4.3	100.0	NA	25.0	NA	NA	30.0

1 Data for serious crimes have not been adjusted for underreporting. This may affect comparability between geographic areas over time.
2 Per 100,000 population estimated by the FBI.   3 Based on population estimated as of July 1 of the year shown.

Table B. Incorporated Places, Census Designated Places (CDPs), and Minor Civil Divisions (MCDs) of 10,000 or More Population — Land Area, Population, and Households, and Employment

STATE City, town, township, borough, or CDP (county if applicable)	Land area,[1] 2010 (sq mi)	Total persons 2010	Total persons 2014	Percent change 2010–2014	Persons per square mile, 2014	Foreign born	Lives in same house as previous year	Median household income (dollars)	Income of $100,000 or more	Income below poverty level	Percent in labor force	Unemploy-ment rate	Family households	One person households
	1	2	3	4	5	6	7	8	9	10	11	12	13	14
MINNESOTA—Con.														
Duluth city & MCD (St. Louis) ...	67.678	86,266	86,238	0.0	1,274.2	2.8	76.4	$43,518	16.6	21.2	64.5	8.0	53.8	34.7
Eagan city & MCD (Dakota)	31.118	64,205	66,084	2.9	2,123.7	11.9	85.0	$80,247	39.4	6.4	77.5	5.2	68.2	25.6
East Bethel city & MCD (Anoka)	44.802	11,626	11,642	0.1	259.9	1.3	92.5	$87,441	42.4	5.1	75.7	7.5	79.0	14.5
Eden Prairie city & MCD (Hennepin)	32.511	60,751	63,228	4.1	1,944.8	13.9	86.2	$95,697	47.9	5.5	74.7	5.1	70.3	24.3
Edina city & MCD (Hennepin)...	15.447	47,940	49,596	3.5	3,210.8	10.5	88.0	$86,968	45.0	4.7	62.7	5.1	62.8	33.1
Elk River city & MCD (Sherburne)	42.297	22,974	23,746	3.4	561.4	3.6	84.3	$74,772	31.6	6.8	74.5	5.4	73.5	22.4
Fairmont city & MCD (Martin)...	15.071	10,666	10,328	-3.2	685.3	3.3	87.1	$51,809	12.3	12.7	65.9	5.1	58.4	36.6
Faribault city & MCD (Rice)	15.294	23,352	23,594	1.0	1,542.6	9.8	80.5	$50,428	14.5	13.0	62.1	9.1	66.5	28.7
Farmington city & MCD (Dakota)	14.721	21,087	22,571	7.0	1,533.3	5.7	89.7	$87,653	39.2	3.0	80.7	4.3	76.1	17.8
Fergus Falls city & MCD (Otter Tail)	14.111	13,138	13,304	1.3	942.8	2.5	80.0	$41,977	14.6	16.0	63.6	6.9	60.3	36.0
Forest Lake city & MCD (Washington)	30.535	18,377	19,399	5.6	635.3	3.7	83.6	$71,995	28.7	8.4	73.9	6.3	73.5	21.5
Fridley city & MCD (Anoka)	10.147	27,208	27,670	1.7	2,726.8	10.9	77.7	$54,509	18.2	11.0	69.2	8.9	61.9	29.5
Golden Valley city & MCD (Hennepin)	10.226	20,351	20,866	2.5	2,040.4	9.0	85.6	$82,325	40.9	7.0	69.1	5.0	65.3	28.2
Grand Rapids city & MCD (Itasca)	22.533	10,869	11,097	2.1	492.5	0.6	83.9	$39,974	9.1	15.3	55.2	5.4	59.6	33.9
Ham Lake city & MCD (Anoka).	34.394	15,296	15,888	3.9	461.9	3.5	92.0	$89,949	43.7	4.3	72.2	7.1	83.5	11.9
Hastings city	10.317	22,174	22,566	1.8	2,187.3	1.8	84.5	$64,119	26.7	7.0	69.0	7.1	66.4	26.3
Hastings city (Dakota)	10.061	22,174	22,564	1.8	2,242.7	1.8	84.5	$64,119	26.7	7.0	69.0	7.1	66.4	26.3
Hibbing city & MCD (St. Louis) .	181.831	16,361	16,302	-0.4	89.7	2.3	84.3	$38,112	10.8	19.4	59.3	7.6	55.6	37.8
Hopkins city & MCD (Hennepin)	4.081	17,601	18,056	2.6	4,424.8	19.3	74.2	$49,418	18.3	12.6	72.2	6.5	52.8	38.3
Hugo city & MCD (Washington)	33.452	13,336	14,239	6.8	425.7	2.9	88.9	$81,773	36.1	3.9	78.8	3.7	73.6	19.6
Hutchinson city & MCD (McLeod).	8.663	14,180	13,872	-2.2	1,601.2	2.9	84.3	$49,945	15.7	8.2	66.9	3.8	63.0	32.6
Inver Grove Heights city & MCD (Dakota)	27.791	33,882	34,709	2.4	1,248.9	7.7	86.0	$64,635	30.4	8.0	73.2	7.4	66.3	26.3
Lakeville city & MCD (Dakota)..	36.049	55,954	59,866	7.0	1,660.7	6.3	91.0	$94,635	47.1	5.9	78.8	4.3	81.7	14.1
Lino Lakes city & MCD (Anoka)	28.219	20,216	20,948	3.6	742.3	1.8	89.7	$103,407	52.8	4.7	72.9	5.6	83.9	13.4
Little Canada city & MCD (Ramsey)	3.893	9,773	10,228	4.7	2,627.1	14.5	89.0	$49,518	16.6	9.5	70.6	7.4	52.2	39.3
Mankato city	18.152	39,338	40,411	2.7	2,226.3	5.3	76.4	$42,929	13.8	23.5	71.1	6.4	48.9	32.4
Mankato city (Blue Earth)	17.858	39,334	40,407	2.7	2,262.7	5.3	76.4	$42,929	13.8	23.5	71.1	6.4	48.9	32.4
Maple Grove city & MCD (Hennepin)	32.637	61,569	66,945	8.7	2,051.2	9.1	90.8	$92,267	46.6	5.0	77.1	5.5	74.4	20.6
Maplewood city & MCD (Ramsey)	16.975	38,018	40,199	5.7	2,368.1	12.4	85.8	$60,323	26.2	8.6	66.0	6.0	62.4	32.1
Marshall city & MCD (Lyon)	10.410	13,687	13,641	-0.3	1,310.4	7.6	76.5	$47,042	19.3	18.3	74.7	4.1	57.9	33.1
Mendota Heights city & MCD (Dakota)	9.150	11,071	11,222	1.4	1,226.5	4.6	91.2	$98,098	49.2	3.4	66.1	5.2	76.0	21.3
Minneapolis city & MCD (Hennepin)	54.011	382,599	407,207	6.4	7,539.3	15.1	75.0	$50,767	22.9	20.1	73.3	9.0	44.8	40.3
Minnetonka city & MCD (Hennepin)	26.904	49,723	51,486	3.5	1,913.7	8.5	84.8	$80,068	39.9	5.5	70.0	5.4	62.8	31.3
Monticello city & MCD (Wright)	8.940	12,759	13,136	3.0	1,469.3	3.3	81.5	$73,151	29.1	7.7	78.1	4.9	68.8	24.9
Moorhead city & MCD (Clay)....	19.795	38,065	39,857	4.7	2,013.5	4.3	77.8	$49,514	16.3	16.4	71.7	5.7	60.1	30.4
Mounds View city & MCD (Ramsey)	4.026	12,155	12,657	4.1	3,143.5	7.9	86.1	$59,121	21.4	9.4	71.3	7.8	65.5	26.6
New Brighton city & MCD (Ramsey)	6.457	21,456	22,266	3.8	3,448.6	9.7	83.6	$61,324	27.2	10.2	64.7	5.2	61.6	30.7
New Hope city & MCD (Hennepin)	5.065	20,346	20,792	2.2	4,105.2	13.4	85.5	$47,755	18.8	10.4	65.9	7.3	55.9	38.0
New Ulm city & MCD (Brown)...	9.982	13,522	13,258	-2.0	1,328.2	1.2	86.6	$45,911	12.9	11.0	68.8	4.5	58.1	35.6
North Branch city & MCD (Chisago)	35.593	10,125	10,160	0.3	285.4	1.4	86.3	$67,220	21.8	7.4	73.0	5.9	67.5	24.5
Northfield city............................	8.502	20,017	20,356	1.7	2,394.1	7.8	78.6	$58,375	26.4	11.5	70.6	5.7	66.2	28.6
Northfield city (Rice)	7.006	18,870	19,166	1.6	2,735.5	8.3	78.0	$56,673	25.7	11.9	70.9	5.9	65.2	29.2
North Mankato city	6.029	13,397	13,432	0.3	2,227.9	3.6	85.5	$56,488	21.0	9.2	77.9	5.0	65.2	26.4
North Mankato city (Nicollet)	6.028	13,397	13,432	0.3	2,228.4	3.6	85.5	$56,488	21.0	9.2	77.9	5.0	65.2	26.4
North St. Paul city & MCD (Ramsey)	2.849	11,460	12,224	6.7	4,291.3	7.6	85.6	$52,246	20.9	12.8	66.2	12.0	61.9	28.6
Oakdale city & MCD (Washington)	10.899	27,365	28,033	2.4	2,572.1	7.4	87.9	$67,822	28.2	7.2	74.3	6.5	66.0	27.2
Otsego city & MCD (Wright)	29.559	13,571	15,047	10.9	509.0	2.4	89.5	$72,626	30.7	4.0	79.6	5.0	78.3	18.5
Owatonna city & MCD (Steele).	14.754	25,601	25,625	0.1	1,736.9	4.9	85.8	$52,790	20.1	12.7	69.7	6.7	65.1	30.7
Plymouth city & MCD (Hennepin)	32.643	70,561	75,057	6.4	2,299.3	12.0	86.0	$84,321	42.0	5.5	71.7	5.3	67.6	26.0
Prior Lake city & MCD (Scott)...	15.956	22,908	25,039	9.3	1,569.2	5.4	87.6	$95,692	47.8	6.1	76.1	4.9	75.1	19.8
Ramsey city & MCD (Anoka)....	28.812	23,668	25,598	8.2	888.4	5.5	90.9	$83,115	37.6	2.4	77.9	6.3	80.5	15.3
Red Wing city & MCD (Goodhue)	34.598	16,459	16,470	0.1	476.0	2.8	86.6	$48,431	21.0	12.4	63.3	7.2	60.4	32.0
Richfield city & MCD (Hennepin)	6.845	35,228	36,179	2.7	5,285.5	21.1	86.0	$52,484	19.7	11.4	72.7	7.7	56.4	34.7
Robbinsdale city & MCD (Hennepin)	2.789	13,951	14,320	2.6	5,134.4	6.2	81.7	$57,012	23.7	12.0	69.9	7.7	58.7	32.7
Rochester city & MCD (Olmsted)	54.604	106,748	111,402	4.4	2,040.2	12.6	84.5	$63,472	27.1	9.3	71.8	4.8	62.1	30.6
Rogers city & MCD (Hennepin)	25.489	11,200	12,393	10.7	486.2	3.5	89.3	$100,525	50.4	2.7	75.8	3.7	80.8	13.3
Rosemount city & MCD (Dakota)	33.217	21,874	22,998	5.1	692.4	8.2	90.5	$86,845	41.7	5.1	75.8	4.0	77.6	18.8

1 Dry land or land partially or temporarily covered by water.
2 16 years old and over.

Table B. Incorporated Places, Census Designated Places (CDPs), and Minor Civil Divisions (MCDs) of 10,000 or More Population — Crime, Construction, and Local Government Finance

STATE City, town, township, borough, or CDP (county if applicable)	Serious crimes known to police, 2014[1]				New residential construction authorized by building permits, 2014			Local government finance, 2012							
	Total number	Rate[2]			Value ($1,000)	Number of housing units	Percent single family	General revenue				General expenditure			Debt outstanding (mil dol)
		Total	Violent	Property				Total (mil dol)	Intergovernmental		Taxes per capita[3]	Total (mil dol)	Per capita[3]		
									Total (mil dol)	Percent from state gov.			Total	Capital outlays	
	15	16	17	18	19	20	21	22	23	24	25	26	27	28	29
MINNESOTA—Con.															
Duluth city & MCD (St. Louis)...	3,959	4598	359	4239	26,292	180	25.6	206.7	90.6	73.8	488	223.1	2,586	972	251.3
Eagan city & MCD (Dakota)	1,201	1827	36	1790	43,450	173	90.2	55.0	3.8	90.8	442	57.4	885	201	61.1
East Bethel city & MCD (Anoka) ...	NA	NA	NA	NA	2,652	15	100.0	8.0	1.1	37.4	446	9.5	816	354	22.4
Eden Prairie city & MCD (Hennepin)	871	1382	35	1347	21,136	61	100.0	70.0	5.2	80.2	NA	67.1	NA	NA	202.7
Edina city & MCD (Hennepin)...	916	1842	54	1788	87,438	231	52.8	63.6	3.2	88.7	NA	63.8	NA	NA	119.7
Elk River city & MCD (Sherburne)	494	2098	81	2017	15,051	90	100.0	25.2	1.7	93.1	570	23.2	996	132	64.3
Fairmont city & MCD (Martin)...	347	3343	231	3112	771	3	100.0	18.1	9.5	51.8	300	15.4	1,467	336	28.4
Faribault city & MCD (Rice)	689	2941	320	2621	4,468	23	65.2	29.6	7.8	82.7	341	47.2	2,012	1,133	41.9
Farmington city & MCD (Dakota)	213	950	71	878	17,059	83	100.0	19.7	2.2	100.0	474	15.3	697	14	44.7
Fergus Falls city & MCD (Otter Tail)	518	3863	321	3543	0	0	0.0	29.9	8.7	73.2	338	36.5	2,763	953	48.4
Forest Lake city & MCD (Washington)	546	2827	171	2656	17,924	79	75.9	14.4	1.4	87.8	420	13.0	686	37	16.7
Fridley city & MCD (Anoka)	1,357	4885	245	4640	1,521	7	100.0	25.2	2.5	85.3	485	22.0	798	53	14.9
Golden Valley city & MCD (Hennepin)	500	2386	43	2343	25,155	178	7.3	39.5	1.4	32.3	NA	34.1	NA	NA	175.8
Grand Rapids city & MCD (Itasca)	411	3730	218	3512	5,220	53	34.0	25.1	6.4	70.3	577	59.1	5,417	3,644	63.5
Ham Lake city & MCD (Anoka).	NA	NA	NA	NA	13,182	55	100.0	6.7	0.4	99.5	344	6.7	432	159	0.0
Hastings city	644	2864	178	2686	10,973	42	100.0	19.9	0.9	87.3	492	22.0	986	225	30.8
Hastings city (Dakota)	644	2864	178	2686	10,973	42	100.0	NA	NA	NA	NA	NA	NA	NA	NA
Hibbing city & MCD (St. Louis) .	341	2093	295	1799	2,362	13	100.0	28.8	12.9	97.9	273	25.4	1,558	406	25.0
Hopkins city & MCD (Hennepin)	503	2774	204	2570	1,260	3	100.0	22.6	2.1	46.8	NA	21.3	NA	NA	25.7
Hugo city & MCD (Washington)	NA	NA	NA	NA	11,187	49	100.0	8.9	0.8	39.7	391	7.1	516	122	14.4
Hutchinson city & MCD (McLeod)	337	2441	101	2340	4,771	23	100.0	100.9	5.5	70.0	517	95.1	6,834	547	118.7
Inver Grove Heights city & MCD (Dakota)	748	2171	200	1971	28,336	118	44.1	31.7	4.0	89.5	466	53.2	1,557	670	55.6
Lakeville city & MCD (Dakota) ..	704	1189	42	1147	115,143	347	100.0	38.7	2.8	74.0	436	42.0	732	180	90.0
Lino Lakes city & MCD (Anoka)	132	628	71	557	9,046	33	100.0	14.6	1.3	96.9	433	16.8	809	271	25.3
Little Canada city & MCD (Ramsey)	NA	NA	NA	NA	1,931	6	100.0	9.7	0.3	94.2	387	12.9	1,287	103	10.6
Mankato city	1,536	3750	261	3489	25,259	222	34.7	77.8	20.6	42.2	539	74.6	1,863	805	117.0
Mankato city (Blue Earth)	1,536	3750	261	3489	25,259	222	34.7	NA	NA	NA	NA	NA	NA	NA	NA
Maple Grove city & MCD (Hennepin)	1,204	1815	35	1780	106,789	502	61.0	94.0	6.8	98.0	NA	87.7	NA	NA	207.8
Maplewood city & MCD (Ramsey)	1,976	4904	151	4752	4,916	25	100.0	49.5	5.8	59.6	481	51.2	1,300	407	157.8
Marshall city & MCD (Lyon)	363	2702	253	2449	3,202	22	50.0	26.6	6.3	72.2	489	26.6	1,975	732	75.4
Mendota Heights city & MCD (Dakota)	226	2019	63	1956	7,935	17	100.0	11.3	0.3	92.1	609	11.5	1,036	244	10.7
Minneapolis city & MCD (Hennepin)	23,216	5740	1012	4728	365,662	1,959	7.0	1017.5	148.8	51.2	1170	1439.6	3,663	222	3439.9
Minnetonka city & MCD (Hennepin)	814	1572	46	1526	26,124	53	100.0	66.8	15.6	62.1	NA	65.7	NA	NA	91.2
Monticello city & MCD (Wright)	NA	NA	NA	NA	10,917	65	100.0	19.9	1.6	97.9	737	28.2	2,176	1,033	69.7
Moorhead city & MCD (Clay)....	897	2259	176	2083	53,993	401	46.1	71.8	30.0	77.2	210	91.5	2,342	1,042	252.1
Mounds View city & MCD (Ramsey)	444	3511	182	3329	5,100	68	1.5	12.2	1.0	87.0	665	12.4	997	289	2.5
New Brighton city & MCD (Ramsey)	558	2505	45	2460	1,415	7	100.0	25.8	0.9	76.3	594	22.4	1,023	109	50.5
New Hope city & MCD (Hennepin)	340	1627	72	1555	10,542	100	0.0	22.8	2.1	95.7	NA	19.3	NA	NA	38.1
New Ulm city & MCD (Brown)...	272	2071	69	2002	9,284	73	39.7	26.7	5.8	83.0	660	23.8	1,798	447	41.5
North Branch city & MCD (Chisago)	280	2779	79	2699	4,505	34	100.0	8.6	1.1	97.5	479	7.0	701	13	59.6
Northfield city	289	1395	72	1323	6,443	26	100.0	86.9	3.6	85.2	368	85.1	4,157	418	76.2
Northfield city (Rice)	289	1395	72	1323	6,443	26	100.0	NA	NA	NA	NA	NA	NA	NA	NA
North Mankato city	281	2090	193	1896	10,127	47	76.6	16.5	4.7	98.6	460	15.1	1,130	315	31.8
North Mankato city (Nicollet)	281	2090	193	1896	10,127	47	76.6	NA	NA	NA	NA	NA	NA	NA	NA
North St. Paul city & MCD (Ramsey)	327	2737	84	2653	155	1	100.0	13.4	2.4	100.0	553	12.0	1,021	321	25.1
Oakdale city & MCD (Washington)	1,262	4528	187	4342	567	2	100.0	20.9	1.3	73.5	379	27.2	981	403	31.2
Otsego city & MCD (Wright)	NA	NA	NA	NA	53,156	188	98.9	8.8	0.2	97.1	297	7.5	534	83	52.4
Owatonna city & MCD (Steele).	655	2564	141	2423	3,734	21	81.0	26.3	7.8	88.0	426	25.3	995	237	49.7
Plymouth city & MCD (Hennepin)	1,113	1487	72	1415	126,495	312	100.0	77.8	8.1	86.5	NA	66.3	NA	NA	108.6
Prior Lake city & MCD (Scott)...	394	1590	93	1497	37,631	125	100.0	20.1	2.2	52.3	479	19.6	819	190	41.7
Ramsey city & MCD (Anoka)....	363	1438	59	1378	14,506	66	100.0	24.5	2.0	100.0	550	25.4	1,055	428	44.6
Red Wing city & MCD (Goodhue)	545	3297	218	3080	4,815	18	100.0	34.1	3.5	88.1	794	34.6	2,097	247	40.5
Richfield city & MCD (Hennepin)	955	2623	214	2409	1,610	6	100.0	43.3	7.0	35.4	NA	42.6	NA	NA	105.3
Robbinsdale city & MCD (Hennepin)	405	2815	195	2620	7,182	43	16.3	27.4	1.8	96.1	NA	27.8	NA	NA	238.5
Rochester city & MCD (Olmsted)	2,428	2173	184	1990	96,126	486	72.4	216.6	36.4	96.7	572	238.9	2,190	743	2086.4
Rogers city & MCD (Hennepin)	NA	NA	NA	NA	17,320	51	84.3	17.9	3.2	97.3	NA	18.8	NA	NA	22.0
Rosemount city & MCD (Dakota)	216	945	74	871	36,291	178	48.3	21.5	0.6	98.5	551	21.7	966	442	35.7

1 Data for serious crimes have not been adjusted for underreporting. This may affect comparability between geographic areas over time.
2 Per 100,000 population estimated by the FBI. 3 Based on population estimated as of July 1 of the year shown.

Table B. Incorporated Places, Census Designated Places (CDPs), and Minor Civil Divisions (MCDs) of 10,000 or More Population — **Land Area, Population, and Households, and Employment**

STATE City, town, township, borough, or CDP (county if applicable)	Land area,[1] 2010 (sq mi)	Population				Population characteristics 2010–2014		Household income and poverty, 2010–2014	Percent of households		Employment,[2] 2010–2014		Households, 2010–2014 (percent of households)	
		Total persons 2010	Total persons 2014	Percent change 2010–2014	Persons per square mile, 2014	Foreign born	Lives in same house as previous year	Median household income (dollars)	Income of $100,000 or more	Income below poverty level	Percent in labor force	Unemployment rate	Family households	One person households
	1	2	3	4	5	6	7	8	9	10	11	12	13	14
MINNESOTA—Con.														
Roseville city & MCD (Ramsey)	13.004	33,660	35,319	4.9	2,716.1	11.9	84.6	$62,464	28.3	8.8	64.0	4.4	55.5	37.7
St. Cloud city	40.039	65,946	66,389	0.7	1,658.1	6.8	69.1	$44,485	14.7	21.2	69.4	9.2	53.6	30.2
St. Cloud city (Stearns)	31.864	52,646	52,808	0.3	1,657.3	7.3	69.4	$46,756	16.0	19.8	72.1	9.1	53.9	29.7
St. Louis Park city & MCD (Hennepin)	10.616	45,241	47,502	5.0	4,474.6	10.1	80.2	$65,151	28.0	8.2	75.6	5.2	48.7	40.9
St. Michael city & MCD (Wright)	32.729	16,399	17,087	4.2	522.1	3.4	90.2	$94,318	45.1	2.2	80.4	4.1	89.9	8.8
St. Paul city & MCD (Ramsey)	51.979	285,068	297,640	4.4	5,726.2	18.2	77.9	$48,258	19.2	19.9	70.5	9.5	55.0	35.3
St. Peter city & MCD (Nicollet)	5.590	11,196	11,570	3.3	2,069.9	4.3	76.5	$56,071	14.7	14.5	66.4	3.8	61.5	29.6
Sartell city	9.867	15,951	16,523	3.6	1,674.6	2.9	82.2	$69,380	30.6	7.5	77.0	3.6	71.0	20.2
Sartell city (Stearns)	8.741	13,703	14,210	3.7	1,625.7	3.0	80.8	$81,993	36.1	5.7	80.4	2.3	75.9	14.7
Sauk Rapids city & MCD (Benton)	6.188	12,836	13,348	4.0	2,157.0	2.6	79.7	$52,164	20.0	18.4	73.7	9.1	65.9	25.8
Savage city & MCD (Scott)	15.632	26,911	29,208	8.5	1,868.5	10.4	91.9	$94,432	45.4	4.0	79.9	5.4	77.1	17.4
Shakopee city & MCD (Scott)	28.008	37,073	39,677	7.0	1,416.6	16.0	87.9	$79,670	37.1	6.1	78.6	5.9	73.8	20.2
Shoreview city & MCD (Ramsey)	10.776	25,043	26,194	4.6	2,430.7	9.5	89.8	$79,485	37.8	5.4	67.3	4.6	65.7	29.6
South St. Paul city & MCD (Dakota)	5.647	20,158	20,487	1.6	3,628.1	6.3	83.3	$55,190	16.9	13.8	72.6	9.1	62.2	29.5
Stillwater city & MCD (Washington)	6.955	18,246	18,800	3.0	2,703.1	2.7	87.5	$75,200	34.6	7.8	69.6	5.3	70.6	24.6
Vadnais Heights city & MCD (Ramsey)	6.979	12,302	13,143	6.8	1,883.0	9.7	90.5	$73,208	33.6	6.4	71.4	3.6	64.2	29.0
Waconia city & MCD (Carver)	4.425	10,697	11,774	10.1	2,661.0	2.0	85.2	$78,086	37.5	4.8	74.9	3.6	72.5	23.3
West St. Paul city & MCD (Dakota)	4.914	19,540	19,806	1.4	4,030.3	11.6	88.1	$45,392	16.7	12.4	64.3	8.7	56.0	39.3
White Bear township (Ramsey)	7.300	10,949	11,503	5.1	1,575.6	2.9	94.7	$90,297	42.3	3.5	71.3	6.3	75.8	20.6
White Bear Lake city	8.014	23,781	24,986	5.1	3,117.6	5.4	86.6	$61,672	22.8	5.2	66.3	4.4	62.2	33.2
White Bear Lake city (Ramsey)	7.940	23,394	24,591	5.1	3,097.3	5.5	86.8	$62,259	23.1	5.2	66.8	4.5	63.3	32.0
Willmar city & MCD (Kandiyohi)	14.155	19,610	19,570	-0.2	1,382.5	10.5	82.7	$42,033	12.3	18.9	68.5	8.3	59.4	32.8
Winona city & MCD (Winona)	18.842	27,595	27,384	-0.8	1,453.3	3.6	75.6	$40,113	14.6	20.6	69.6	10.8	48.6	38.8
Woodbury city & MCD (Washington)	34.912	61,965	66,807	7.8	1,913.6	10.5	87.7	$98,974	49.3	3.7	75.1	4.7	73.4	20.5
Worthington city & MCD (Nobles)	7.365	12,764	12,932	1.3	1,756.0	30.1	80.7	$46,406	13.4	19.0	65.9	9.8	67.7	29.3
MISSISSIPPI	46,923.272	2,968,103	2,994,079	0.9	63.8	2.2	86.0	$39,464	13.3	21.3	58.4	10.9	68.7	27.3
Bay St. Louis city	14.692	9,262	11,388	23.0	775.1	2.7	77.9	$41,078	11.4	19.0	56.9	8.4	60.4	34.5
Biloxi city	38.222	44,054	44,984	2.1	1,176.9	7.7	75.7	$39,374	12.2	18.9	68.0	9.8	58.6	34.6
Brandon city	25.662	22,066	23,156	4.9	902.4	2.4	84.3	$71,199	32.6	7.1	65.8	5.5	79.3	19.2
Brookhaven city	21.644	12,513	12,470	-0.3	576.1	0.9	87.2	$29,233	11.4	33.1	51.8	10.0	68.2	29.9
Byram city	18.364	11,491	11,556	0.6	629.3	0.8	85.8	$55,532	17.8	8.8	76.3	6.4	74.1	23.4
Canton city	21.352	13,195	13,713	3.9	642.2	5.6	86.8	$37,591	12.0	26.9	54.7	8.0	69.6	26.0
Clarksdale city	13.887	17,960	17,011	-5.3	1,224.9	1.0	85.4	$27,742	6.6	37.0	55.0	16.6	67.4	29.7
Cleveland city	7.303	12,334	12,412	0.6	1,699.6	1.4	83.6	$34,138	10.3	24.0	62.3	13.5	61.6	33.2
Clinton city	41.833	25,215	25,411	0.8	607.4	5.8	90.2	$60,161	23.3	13.2	65.8	4.7	71.5	24.5
Columbus city	22.090	23,640	23,248	-1.7	1,052.4	2.0	83.3	$29,335	9.3	29.4	58.2	17.6	56.1	37.4
Corinth city	30.159	14,573	14,865	2.0	492.9	2.1	79.8	$30,944	9.7	25.0	55.8	12.4	59.3	36.1
D'Iberville city	7.063	9,486	10,962	15.6	1,552.0	5.9	78.2	$45,378	7.6	11.1	68.9	7.0	63.2	29.0
Gautier city	30.229	18,572	18,596	0.1	615.2	6.9	90.0	$45,934	10.8	15.2	61.1	10.4	71.1	24.3
Greenville city	26.895	34,403	32,704	-4.9	1,216.0	1.8	81.3	$30,096	9.2	33.0	59.5	22.9	66.2	30.0
Greenwood city	12.335	16,087	15,730	-2.2	1,275.2	1.8	88.9	$26,126	9.6	37.6	48.2	16.7	62.8	35.5
Grenada city	30.007	13,092	12,956	-1.0	431.8	0.8	86.5	$29,286	10.9	26.2	54.5	10.0	65.8	32.9
Gulfport city	55.599	67,786	71,750	5.8	1,290.5	3.9	74.3	$36,658	10.6	22.9	62.7	11.7	62.0	31.5
Hattiesburg city	53.240	45,767	47,016	2.7	883.1	3.7	71.0	$27,827	8.4	34.1	63.4	14.3	51.4	36.9
Hernando city	25.732	14,060	15,290	8.7	594.2	1.9	84.5	$61,466	27.2	9.5	63.6	7.2	74.1	24.0
Horn Lake city	16.047	26,068	26,766	2.7	1,668.0	3.9	81.7	$45,817	10.2	11.8	72.4	10.5	70.3	24.4
Indianola city	8.571	10,683	10,078	-5.7	1,175.8	0.9	84.9	$27,181	9.3	28.9	58.4	19.4	66.7	30.7
Jackson city	111.049	173,593	171,155	-1.4	1,541.3	1.7	83.8	$33,080	10.5	27.1	62.0	12.6	62.6	32.1
Laurel city	16.236	18,543	18,868	1.8	1,162.1	5.8	88.2	$28,002	8.8	28.7	55.6	11.5	62.5	33.1
Long Beach city	10.005	14,792	15,448	4.4	1,544.0	3.6	77.0	$50,051	20.7	14.2	67.4	9.6	70.4	23.2
McComb city	11.576	12,790	12,703	-0.7	1,097.4	1.7	78.6	$29,798	9.4	27.3	55.0	10.0	58.2	36.3
Madison city	25.220	24,149	25,455	5.4	1,009.3	3.2	90.2	$99,109	49.3	4.7	71.4	4.6	79.6	19.3
Meridian city	53.739	41,148	40,196	-2.3	748.0	1.6	82.0	$29,531	11.3	29.5	59.3	12.8	61.4	34.6
Moss Point city	24.155	13,704	13,671	-0.2	566.0	0.4	89.0	$37,006	8.4	22.4	53.0	16.7	60.6	35.6
Natchez city	13.195	15,792	15,269	-3.3	1,157.1	1.7	90.6	$26,853	10.8	31.1	50.3	11.1	60.2	37.7
Ocean Springs city	11.524	17,442	17,530	0.5	1,521.2	4.1	82.9	$57,080	25.7	10.2	59.9	6.7	65.3	27.5
Olive Branch city	36.719	33,486	35,457	5.9	965.6	4.6	87.5	$64,253	24.0	7.5	72.7	8.2	74.6	21.3
Oxford city	15.834	18,877	21,757	15.3	1,374.0	5.1	65.8	$31,230	14.2	33.6	58.6	8.9	45.3	38.8
Pascagoula city	15.380	22,392	22,224	-0.8	1,445.0	4.2	78.6	$38,574	13.0	22.8	58.4	10.8	60.8	34.0
Pearl city	25.495	25,700	26,388	2.7	1,035.0	3.8	79.6	$41,326	12.0	14.0	65.5	9.0	69.5	25.4
Petal city	16.771	10,454	10,727	2.6	639.6	3.8	82.8	$50,955	13.0	14.5	64.5	8.2	71.3	23.6
Picayune city	12.956	10,877	10,749	-1.2	829.7	1.2	84.6	$32,969	8.8	20.8	51.9	10.3	67.8	28.7
Ridgeland city	19.653	24,040	24,221	0.8	1,232.4	6.1	81.6	$55,012	20.4	9.4	71.7	4.5	55.7	36.9
Southaven city	41.289	48,976	51,824	5.8	1,255.1	3.5	83.0	$58,712	21.3	9.3	71.5	6.8	73.3	22.5
Starkville city	25.513	23,909	24,886	4.1	975.4	4.8	74.1	$31,357	15.4	32.6	60.0	12.1	49.3	37.6
Tupelo city	51.144	34,546	35,688	3.3	697.8	2.7	85.1	$41,979	15.7	22.1	60.4	7.8	68.1	28.5
Vicksburg city	32.981	23,856	23,392	-1.9	709.3	1.8	91.6	$27,991	8.9	28.1	54.6	11.1	60.4	36.0
West Point city	20.884	11,318	11,093	-2.0	531.2	0.2	86.9	$26,784	13.1	30.9	59.7	20.0	76.0	22.8
Yazoo City city	9.838	11,403	11,366	-0.3	1,155.4	0.3	86.6	$18,566	4.7	47.2	52.4	31.0	64.4	31.6
MISSOURI	68,741.519	5,988,923	6,063,589	1.2	88.2	3.9	83.9	$47,764	17.8	14.9	63.9	8.4	64.9	29.1
Affton CDP	4.775	20,307	NA	NA	NA	10.6	90.5	$56,492	19.9	8.0	70.0	5.4	59.3	36.2
Arnold city	11.583	20,808	21,243	2.1	1,834.1	4.4	87.2	$56,329	18.8	8.4	67.6	8.4	69.6	24.3

1 Dry land or land partially or temporarily covered by water.
2 16 years old and over.

Table B. Incorporated Places, Census Designated Places (CDPs), and Minor Civil Divisions (MCDs) of 10,000 or More Population — **Crime, Construction, and Local Government Finance**

STATE City, town, township, borough, or CDP (county if applicable)	Serious crimes known to police, 2014[1] Total number	Rate[2] Total	Rate[2] Violent	Rate[2] Property	New residential construction authorized by building permits, 2014 Value ($1,000)	New residential construction Number of housing units	New residential construction Percent single family	Local government finance, 2012 General revenue Total (mil dol)	General revenue Intergovernmental Total (mil dol)	General revenue Intergovernmental Percent from state gov.	Taxes per capita[3]	General expenditure Total (mil dol)	General expenditure Per capita[3] Total	General expenditure Per capita[3] Capital outlays	Debt outstanding (mil dol)
	15	16	17	18	19	20	21	22	23	24	25	26	27	28	29
MINNESOTA—Con.															
Roseville city & MCD (Ramsey)	1,899	5375	127	5247	4,479	12	100.0	33.7	3.3	86.1	506	34.0	981	217	20.1
St. Cloud city	2,771	4175	393	3782	21,800	217	19.8	89.0	22.7	89.2	550	105.0	1,592	659	413.3
St. Cloud city (Stearns)	2,771	4175	393	3782	21,800	217	19.8	NA	NA	NA	NA	NA	NA	NA	NA
St. Louis Park city & MCD (Hennepin)	1,369	2855	136	2719	48,439	328	3.4	76.4	3.2	86.2	NA	77.7	NA	NA	499.7
St. Michael city & MCD (Wright)	NA	NA	NA	NA	10,482	34	100.0	11.7	2.9	84.1	347	9.2	550	81	43.3
St. Paul city & MCD (Ramsey)	12,357	4147	662	3484	92,655	494	14.2	510.2	119.9	59.1	602	504.8	1,733	219	770.7
St. Peter city & MCD (Nicollet)	189	1643	87	1556	4,282	21	100.0	32.4	3.4	20.9	278	32.2	2,816	240	62.4
Sartell city	350	2140	31	2109	17,466	72	100.0	17.6	0.7	99.2	373	18.5	1,136	497	95.5
Sartell city (Stearns)	350	2140	31	2109	17,466	72	100.0	NA	NA	NA	NA	NA	NA	NA	NA
Sauk Rapids city & MCD (Benton)	261	1950	82	1868	7,759	45	64.4	17.9	2.4	98.6	514	11.9	915	275	38.3
Savage city & MCD (Scott)	624	2147	93	2054	53,196	439	18.7	32.0	3.4	94.3	584	22.4	802	183	84.5
Shakopee city & MCD (Scott)	825	2082	144	1938	30,394	160	43.8	36.9	5.1	99.9	410	36.0	928	217	92.8
Shoreview city & MCD (Ramsey)	306	1168	61	1106	6,132	28	100.0	25.3	1.3	99.9	441	23.1	899	137	51.1
South St. Paul city & MCD (Dakota)	562	2741	385	2356	1,094	6	100.0	29.9	8.1	36.7	523	29.3	1,435	217	16.6
Stillwater city & MCD (Washington)	277	1476	43	1433	12,537	45	100.0	28.0	1.5	100.0	803	28.4	1,530	433	72.6
Vadnais Heights city & MCD (Ramsey)	328	2488	114	2374	1,390	5	100.0	12.0	0.6	81.2	471	11.5	898	2	0.0
Waconia city & MCD (Carver)	NA	NA	NA	NA	27,238	84	100.0	12.7	0.3	85.3	467	10.1	896	136	65.7
West St. Paul city & MCD (Dakota)	1,113	5619	353	5266	490	2	100.0	19.5	1.7	77.2	595	26.4	1,337	401	45.7
White Bear township (Ramsey)	NA	NA	NA	NA	1,836	7	100.0	7.5	0.8	94.3	324	8.4	747	175	12.8
White Bear Lake city	687	2770	125	2645	2,819	10	80.0	19.4	2.8	83.9	234	20.2	830	201	3.1
White Bear Lake city (Ramsey)	687	2770	125	2645	2,819	10	80.0	NA	NA	NA	NA	NA	NA	NA	NA
Willmar city & MCD (Kandiyohi)	606	3077	274	2803	4,305	17	64.7	123.6	6.0	98.7	317	133.0	6,759	789	152.5
Winona city & MCD (Winona)	97	352	91	261	2,168	10	100.0	24.8	11.9	97.0	284	23.2	837	90	7.0
Woodbury city & MCD (Washington)	1,213	1823	54	1769	107,121	342	86.8	61.1	3.7	75.8	475	55.7	863	229	92.0
Worthington city & MCD (Nobles)	220	1694	146	1548	5,533	56	3.6	17.5	5.8	80.9	317	18.3	1,406	305	15.4
MISSISSIPPI	95,800	3200	278	2921	1,033,059	6,871	80.7	X	X	X	X	X	X	X	X
Bay St. Louis city	NA	NA	NA	NA	56,177	455	58.9	6.3	3.6	99.6	157	4.1	395	9	16.1
Biloxi city	2,936	6523	478	6046	47,999	326	31.3	102.9	58.6	70.6	518	110.6	2,484	715	68.0
Brandon city	221	973	75	898	39,098	157	100.0	17.2	6.2	87.0	252	15.3	675	66	22.5
Brookhaven city	NA	NA	NA	NA	1,254	8	100.0	13.9	6.6	88.2	353	13.5	1,078	6	6.9
Byram city	NA	NA	NA	NA	5,048	35	100.0	5.2	1.9	99.6	265	4.3	371	167	0.0
Canton city	NA	NA	NA	NA	40	1	100.0	17.3	3.2	100.0	346	13.8	1,044	5	19.6
Clarksdale city	NA	NA	NA	NA	0	0	0.0	16.9	3.6	86.1	314	20.7	1,171	57	130.4
Cleveland city	137	1099	48	1051	1,325	6	100.0	13.7	5.1	79.0	381	15.1	1,227	238	12.2
Clinton city	NA	NA	NA	NA	16,507	74	100.0	22.4	8.4	97.4	332	20.7	810	145	36.4
Columbus city	NA	NA	NA	NA	1,336	9	100.0	31.0	11.9	86.5	471	28.1	1,195	225	53.7
Corinth city	NA	NA	NA	NA	1,248	10	100.0	171.1	8.4	97.3	270	156.9	10,582	613	148.8
D'Iberville city	NA	NA	NA	NA	12,837	196	33.7	6.6	1.8	95.0	312	7.2	719	13	8.0
Gautier city	617	3330	313	3017	1,971	9	100.0	14.5	4.7	87.9	202	13.7	740	60	24.6
Greenville city	2,450	7443	295	7148	1,412	7	100.0	30.6	10.5	67.0	368	32.5	970	190	22.8
Greenwood city	1,561	9878	563	9315	989	14	100.0	148.2	7.0	94.6	370	150.8	9,517	1,041	29.1
Grenada city	NA	NA	NA	NA	1,971	14	100.0	15.8	7.3	97.7	354	16.9	1,307	244	20.2
Gulfport city	3,706	5161	199	4961	21,120	132	98.5	510.2	92.4	40.6	466	508.4	7,267	1,373	212.6
Hattiesburg city	2,855	5957	198	5758	18,287	150	26.0	68.9	33.4	74.6	537	64.6	1,378	307	89.3
Hernando city	NA	NA	NA	NA	12,204	92	100.0	10.8	3.1	92.9	282	10.1	683	24	10.4
Horn Lake city	571	2133	112	2021	10,969	65	100.0	18.5	4.3	95.2	264	15.9	598	35	35.8
Indianola city	860	8452	1238	7214	120	2	100.0	9.4	4.6	91.7	288	9.2	877	302	9.0
Jackson city	11,975	6947	924	6023	43,524	420	100.0	222.7	65.9	65.5	452	212.1	1,210	208	322.3
Laurel city	936	4906	273	4633	2,409	19	100.0	28.3	12.6	87.4	335	25.9	1,377	204	35.4
Long Beach city	334	2145	83	2062	7,020	44	93.2	19.1	8.3	15.9	377	13.2	865	0	3.8
McComb city	899	7062	361	6700	0	0	0.0	129.5	9.0	86.1	369	121.2	9,495	925	57.2
Madison city	278	1087	59	1028	43,168	135	100.0	24.3	6.9	86.4	446	29.6	1,193	450	48.9
Meridian city	2,242	5485	587	4898	4,123	10	100.0	43.9	15.5	100.0	456	39.7	973	158	61.0
Moss Point city	NA	NA	NA	NA	1,017	15	100.0	1.6	0.6	100.0	47	1.1	83	0	25.4
Natchez city	1,132	7329	414	6914	341	3	100.0	28.2	12.1	100.0	530	27.5	1,767	491	20.0
Ocean Springs city	651	3717	160	3557	9,900	70	77.1	20.4	9.9	91.9	269	23.2	1,334	380	24.0
Olive Branch city	1,038	2939	255	2684	26,179	224	100.0	42.4	15.2	100.0	434	33.8	978	185	57.9
Oxford city	555	2597	173	2424	46,410	471	41.4	59.2	11.8	90.6	508	31.4	1,563	283	55.7
Pascagoula city	1,590	7157	531	6626	1,138	8	100.0	43.2	20.8	100.0	515	43.5	1,957	521	19.4
Pearl city	64	243	27	216	7,189	42	81.0	24.5	10.5	91.4	263	32.5	1,241	187	99.8
Petal city	85	780	18	762	2,775	15	100.0	8.9	2.8	100.0	407	11.0	1,022	164	22.5
Picayune city	628	5819	686	5133	1,509	15	46.7	14.5	6.7	90.1	379	17.9	1,656	602	16.9
Ridgeland city	739	3015	204	2811	29,021	71	100.0	30.8	11.8	93.9	474	35.0	1,441	373	57.9
Southaven city	1,596	3101	272	2829	34,894	320	96.9	49.4	12.7	100.0	512	48.7	966	118	96.2
Starkville city	877	3509	172	3337	26,555	257	18.3	19.3	9.0	80.8	182	20.8	846	178	26.4
Tupelo city	NA	NA	NA	NA	7,115	46	100.0	65.5	32.8	96.4	442	62.2	1,751	529	82.1
Vicksburg city	1,686	7187	695	6492	1,353	7	100.0	47.6	9.2	100.0	957	46.7	1,988	338	20.9
West Point city	366	3267	536	2732	867	6	100.0	9.7	3.5	76.5	382	9.4	836	62	21.3
Yazoo City city	NA	NA	NA	NA	1,089	6	100.0	10.4	2.5	97.6	345	9.4	814	73	2.0
MISSOURI	203,093	3349	443	2906	2,682,665	16,003	56.7	X	X	X	X	X	X	X	X
Affton CDP	NA	NA	NA	NA	NA	NA	NA	NA	NA	NA	NA	NA	NA	NA	NA
Arnold city	814	3838	141	3697	5,028	36	100.0	24.1	2.5	38.0	641	22.5	1,073	48	83.9

1 Data for serious crimes have not been adjusted for underreporting. This may affect comparability between geographic areas over time.
2 Per 100,000 population estimated by the FBI.   3 Based on population estimated as of July 1 of the year shown.

Table B. Incorporated Places, Census Designated Places (CDPs), and Minor Civil Divisions (MCDs) of 10,000 or More Population — **Land Area, Population, and Households, and Employment**

STATE City, town, township, borough, or CDP (county if applicable)	Land area,[1] 2010 (sq mi)	Population				Population characteristics 2010–2014		Household income and poverty, 2010–2014			Employment,[2] 2010–2014		Households, 2010–2014 (percent of households)	
		Total persons 2010	Total persons 2014	Percent change 2010–2014	Persons per square mile, 2014	Foreign born	Lives in same house as previous year	Median household income (dollars)	Percent of households		Percent in labor force	Unemploy- ment rate	Family households	One person households
									Income of $100,000 or more	Income below poverty level				
	1	2	3	4	5	6	7	8	9	10	11	12	13	14
MISSOURI—Con.														
Ballwin city	9.016	30,411	30,505	0.3	3,383.6	7.3	87.7	$82,685	39.3	3.7	69.2	5.2	77.6	18.5
Bellefontaine Neighbors city	4.433	10,852	10,807	-0.4	2,437.9	0.8	88.7	$36,823	5.6	18.7	67.7	11.7	63.6	32.4
Belton city	14.246	23,116	23,165	0.2	1,626.1	5.0	85.3	$53,316	14.2	11.1	70.2	10.2	68.3	25.4
Blue Springs city	22.310	52,637	53,573	1.8	2,401.3	2.4	87.9	$63,850	23.1	8.6	69.9	6.2	73.2	20.3
Bolivar city	8.279	10,325	10,572	2.4	1,276.9	0.5	76.6	$36,156	10.2	21.6	59.7	11.6	56.4	33.6
Branson city	20.674	10,547	11,340	7.5	548.5	8.2	66.0	$38,425	11.3	22.4	62.2	10.2	57.3	34.9
Bridgeton city	14.644	11,550	11,782	2.0	804.5	6.4	86.4	$44,822	19.7	13.5	61.6	11.0	65.7	30.2
Cameron city	6.062	9,933	9,762	-1.7	1,610.5	1.8	73.9	$35,469	8.2	18.1	35.7	13.0	59.1	35.8
Cape Girardeau city	28.872	37,995	39,167	3.1	1,356.6	4.1	75.6	$40,077	13.6	22.1	62.9	8.5	55.8	33.5
Carthage city	11.650	14,378	14,271	-0.7	1,225.0	15.7	84.0	$31,913	7.9	22.1	59.4	10.2	62.3	31.1
Chesterfield city	31.811	47,484	47,777	0.6	1,501.9	11.3	88.1	$94,263	47.0	5.0	62.7	4.7	71.2	25.3
Clayton city	2.478	15,939	15,882	-0.4	6,409.6	12.5	72.2	$95,500	47.7	8.9	57.7	5.0	57.5	36.6
Columbia city	63.833	108,835	116,906	7.4	1,831.4	7.8	67.8	$43,776	20.4	23.9	68.1	5.3	51.5	31.6
Concord CDP	5.484	16,421	NA	NA	NA	5.6	93.2	$67,834	27.0	4.9	61.7	5.3	62.8	32.6
Crestwood city	3.599	11,912	11,951	0.3	3,320.6	5.9	91.7	$66,842	30.1	5.1	66.4	7.1	65.1	28.4
Creve Coeur city	10.310	17,835	17,868	0.2	1,733.0	14.0	81.4	$92,033	47.2	5.6	64.8	3.5	64.3	28.4
Dardenne Prairie city	4.918	11,505	12,783	11.1	2,599.4	2.6	96.4	$112,663	58.4	1.6	71.3	6.0	87.1	11.5
Eureka city	10.654	10,194	10,543	3.4	989.6	4.8	82.7	$82,596	42.7	4.7	62.5	6.6	83.6	14.5
Excelsior Springs city	10.410	11,084	11,488	3.6	1,103.6	3.0	81.6	$51,634	10.4	14.9	63.9	6.6	67.7	27.3
Farmington city	9.144	16,307	17,915	9.9	1,959.2	1.4	72.9	$40,321	10.0	18.4	48.6	9.3	56.0	32.9
Ferguson city	6.197	21,203	21,086	-0.6	3,402.6	1.1	87.7	$40,660	8.7	21.0	64.7	12.3	65.6	31.4
Festus city	5.707	11,602	11,885	2.4	2,082.7	1.0	87.1	$45,752	17.5	13.2	64.5	10.2	67.3	28.6
Florissant city	12.637	52,291	52,303	0.0	4,139.0	2.6	85.7	$51,415	12.7	7.7	68.6	9.2	64.6	31.7
Fort Leonard Wood CDP	96.190	15,061	NA	NA	NA	5.6	24.5	$46,514	7.2	7.8	92.1	8.2	66.1	18.1
Fulton city	12.259	12,790	12,864	0.6	1,049.4	3.4	69.2	$40,274	7.7	21.7	47.7	9.9	50.1	42.1
Gladstone city	8.040	25,410	26,800	5.5	3,333.4	5.0	83.8	$52,783	17.6	10.8	66.0	8.1	62.5	29.6
Grain Valley city	6.075	12,853	13,236	3.0	2,178.7	1.1	86.7	$57,168	17.7	9.4	74.5	5.6	74.5	21.7
Grandview city	14.726	24,475	25,290	3.3	1,717.4	10.2	76.4	$41,559	10.1	15.8	70.0	10.0	59.3	34.3
Hannibal city	15.735	17,916	17,893	-0.1	1,137.2	1.8	84.5	$37,309	7.2	19.2	58.9	7.8	62.1	31.6
Harrisonville city	9.883	10,019	9,983	-0.4	1,010.1	0.1	76.6	$44,000	11.5	15.4	64.7	11.4	62.5	33.3
Hazelwood city	16.023	25,700	25,666	-0.1	1,601.8	6.3	83.6	$44,855	15.9	13.0	70.4	11.1	60.9	33.9
Independence city	77.806	116,828	117,494	0.6	1,510.1	4.4	89.0	$44,038	12.5	15.0	61.8	9.0	60.1	33.5
Jackson city	10.632	13,748	14,677	6.8	1,380.4	0.8	79.6	$48,471	13.8	13.9	65.2	6.0	69.8	26.3
Jefferson City city	36.081	43,088	43,132	0.1	1,195.4	3.6	79.4	$47,901	17.6	14.4	59.4	5.4	60.7	33.5
Jennings city	3.733	14,743	14,737	0.0	3,947.9	0.9	81.2	$27,785	3.4	21.4	65.1	26.4	55.6	40.1
Joplin city	36.768	50,788	51,316	1.0	1,395.7	2.5	79.3	$37,899	11.1	19.2	66.2	8.9	57.6	32.6
Kansas City city	314.954	459,787	470,800	2.4	1,494.8	7.6	80.2	$45,376	17.8	17.7	68.5	9.1	55.5	36.7
Kennett city	7.002	10,932	10,796	-1.2	1,541.9	2.0	79.1	$30,690	8.8	26.8	50.6	10.8	64.5	31.7
Kirksville city	14.386	17,505	17,633	0.7	1,225.7	4.4	61.4	$27,840	9.4	33.1	51.5	6.8	43.6	42.5
Kirkwood city	9.158	27,540	27,660	0.4	3,020.2	2.9	88.7	$77,420	38.5	6.7	66.7	3.2	60.6	34.2
Lake St. Louis city	8.031	14,558	15,014	3.1	1,869.6	2.7	82.7	$71,462	35.0	5.4	68.1	6.5	70.4	21.5
Lebanon city	14.636	14,474	14,650	1.2	1,000.9	1.9	77.9	$30,050	6.6	22.5	53.7	10.2	63.6	32.1
Lee's Summit city	63.821	91,388	93,864	2.7	1,470.7	3.8	88.4	$78,186	36.7	6.2	72.3	5.4	74.1	22.0
Lemay CDP	4.367	16,645	NA	NA	NA	13.4	86.5	$43,746	6.0	13.1	63.0	7.2	60.3	33.0
Liberty city	28.884	29,155	30,376	4.2	1,051.7	2.8	83.6	$65,106	27.9	8.7	67.4	8.8	71.9	22.2
Manchester city	5.079	18,095	18,197	0.6	3,582.9	9.4	90.5	$81,489	36.9	6.0	72.1	3.3	65.7	25.2
Marshall city	10.217	13,061	13,042	-0.1	1,276.6	8.7	82.6	$36,420	9.3	21.0	61.4	6.9	62.9	30.8
Maryland Heights city	21.889	27,473	27,405	-0.2	1,252.0	15.0	79.9	$58,744	21.0	9.9	72.9	7.3	57.8	33.2
Maryville city	5.848	11,999	12,007	0.1	2,053.3	2.4	57.9	$26,611	5.7	34.2	63.9	9.0	40.5	39.1
Mehlville CDP	7.452	28,380	NA	NA	NA	17.1	85.5	$47,360	16.4	10.6	66.6	7.5	60.0	36.7
Mexico city	12.101	11,543	11,664	1.0	963.9	1.2	84.0	$40,788	6.1	16.7	61.2	9.7	61.6	34.2
Moberly city	12.641	13,986	13,890	-0.7	1,098.8	0.7	79.9	$33,942	8.9	21.7	48.2	8.3	60.4	33.1
Neosho city	15.730	11,835	12,134	2.5	771.4	8.5	75.9	$35,276	5.4	19.6	57.9	5.5	61.0	34.1
Nixa city	8.475	19,026	20,570	8.1	2,427.0	1.7	82.1	$49,364	13.8	12.2	69.0	6.4	73.1	21.7
Oakville CDP	15.927	36,143	NA	NA	NA	3.6	89.5	$79,223	37.5	4.3	67.6	4.8	77.8	17.9
O'Fallon city	29.639	79,588	84,009	5.6	2,834.4	3.7	89.0	$78,634	35.6	5.2	75.2	5.0	75.3	20.7
Old Jamestown CDP	14.929	19,184	NA	NA	NA	3.3	93.1	$78,388	33.5	5.1	66.6	7.8	75.8	20.8
Overland city	4.364	16,062	15,985	-0.5	3,663.2	5.7	84.5	$45,246	11.1	15.3	71.0	7.3	59.7	29.4
Ozark city	11.196	17,820	18,871	5.9	1,685.6	2.7	77.1	$47,046	17.0	10.4	67.4	6.0	74.2	21.5
Poplar Bluff city	13.139	17,050	17,242	1.1	1,312.2	1.6	73.6	$29,513	6.1	27.2	52.7	10.3	56.9	38.2
Raymore city	17.282	19,205	19,963	3.9	1,155.2	1.7	88.7	$72,380	27.2	5.0	65.7	5.1	75.5	20.7
Raytown city	9.929	29,526	29,481	-0.2	2,969.3	2.0	88.5	$49,442	13.6	10.8	66.0	6.8	63.9	31.2
Republic city	14.959	14,755	15,680	6.3	1,048.2	0.7	80.9	$51,755	11.7	13.6	68.5	6.6	73.9	21.8
Rolla city	12.034	19,561	19,926	1.9	1,655.8	9.1	67.8	$32,478	10.8	26.5	51.7	7.4	49.6	36.9
St. Ann city	3.187	13,020	12,955	-0.5	4,065.1	6.6	87.3	$37,617	10.2	15.0	67.4	10.8	52.0	44.2
St. Charles city	23.751	65,846	68,090	3.4	2,866.9	6.0	82.2	$56,622	24.1	10.7	67.8	7.2	62.7	30.9
St. Joseph city	44.007	76,807	76,967	0.2	1,749.0	4.0	77.5	$42,042	12.6	19.1	63.6	9.0	60.1	33.3
St. Louis city	61.953	319,365	317,419	-0.6	5,123.5	6.8	78.5	$34,800	12.0	25.1	65.1	14.1	46.7	44.2
St. Peters city	22.376	52,626	56,076	6.6	2,506.1	3.6	89.9	$69,854	28.9	4.1	73.1	6.4	68.1	27.0
Sedalia city	13.397	21,385	21,492	0.5	1,604.2	7.1	78.3	$31,553	8.1	24.4	60.8	7.2	59.8	33.9
Sikeston city	17.468	16,322	16,370	0.3	937.1	1.2	81.9	$37,076	9.8	19.4	62.1	9.3	66.3	26.0
Spanish Lake CDP	7.368	19,650	NA	NA	NA	1.7	74.2	$32,760	9.7	20.7	69.1	22.0	62.0	34.3
Springfield city	82.004	159,500	165,378	3.7	2,016.7	3.9	73.3	$32,473	7.9	24.2	62.3	9.3	50.2	37.6
Town and Country city	11.675	10,848	10,975	1.2	940.0	11.4	87.3	$162,500	73.1	3.7	51.7	2.9	83.4	14.3
Troy city	7.736	10,590	11,355	7.2	1,467.8	1.2	83.4	$50,906	12.9	16.7	59.9	7.2	64.6	31.1
Union city	9.077	10,295	10,859	5.5	1,196.3	1.6	84.0	$42,315	14.0	9.7	70.6	10.5	63.6	32.3
University City city	5.898	35,364	35,115	-0.7	5,953.7	7.2	82.2	$53,667	26.2	15.9	66.1	8.6	52.9	37.2
Warrensburg city	8.869	18,848	19,963	5.9	2,251.0	4.7	60.4	$41,683	11.7	28.0	62.4	7.1	50.4	29.8
Washington city	9.318	13,982	14,020	0.3	1,504.6	2.2	86.3	$49,627	17.5	11.3	63.8	5.1	67.1	29.7
Webb City city	8.632	10,996	11,075	0.7	1,283.1	1.7	84.4	$37,854	7.4	19.4	65.5	7.9	60.2	31.8
Webster Groves city	5.904	22,995	23,186	0.8	3,927.2	2.9	88.6	$86,205	41.2	5.8	67.9	4.4	67.6	27.4
Wentzville city	19.736	29,347	33,912	15.6	1,718.2	1.2	89.8	$72,095	29.7	4.5	74.8	4.6	79.4	17.4
West Plains city	13.315	11,986	12,275	2.4	921.9	1.9	71.4	$30,000	8.1	28.3	55.0	8.4	60.7	35.4
Wildwood city	66.457	35,533	35,820	0.8	539.0	6.3	91.6	$123,578	62.1	4.0	69.7	4.1	85.2	13.2
MONTANA	145,545.795	989,417	1,023,579	3.5	7.0	2.0	83.5	$46,766	16.2	14.3	64.3	6.8	62.8	30.2
Billings city	43.073	104,224	108,869	4.5	2,527.6	1.9	81.0	$49,265	18.6	13.1	67.9	4.4	58.6	33.1

1 Dry land or land partially or temporarily covered by water.
2 16 years old and over.

Table B. Incorporated Places, Census Designated Places (CDPs), and Minor Civil Divisions (MCDs) of 10,000 or More Population — Crime, Construction, and Local Government Finance

STATE City, town, township, borough, or CDP (county if applicable)	Serious crimes known to police, 2014[1] Total number	Rate[2] Total	Rate[2] Violent	Rate[2] Property	New residential construction authorized by building permits, 2014 Value ($1,000)	Number of housing units	Percent single family	Local government finance, 2012 General revenue Total (mil dol)	Intergovernmental Total (mil dol)	Percent from state gov.	Taxes per capita[3]	General expenditure Total (mil dol)	Per capita[3] Total	Per capita[3] Capital outlays	Debt outstanding (mil dol)
	15	16	17	18	19	20	21	22	23	24	25	26	27	28	29
MISSOURI—Con.															
Ballwin city	218	714	26	600	11,568	37	100.0	18.7	9.4	1.9	173	18.7	613	106	17.1
Bellefontaine Neighbors city	355	3282	444	2839	125	1	100.0	4.5	0.4	91.5	295	4.7	429	0	4.9
Belton city	830	3580	362	3218	2,603	13	100.0	33.7	3.8	100.0	692	42.2	1,816	653	83.5
Blue Springs city	1,456	2725	157	2567	28,083	273	44.3	53.1	13.3	54.5	462	57.4	1,082	459	129.0
Bolivar city	580	5512	551	4961	7,440	59	100.0	7.0	1.0	96.9	387	11.0	1,054	82	6.7
Branson city	1,269	11363	663	10700	6,393	33	87.9	57.6	14.6	100.0	2489	50.2	4,603	716	259.0
Bridgeton city	907	7738	623	7115	785	6	100.0	20.2	12.2	15.0	438	21.5	1,849	288	20.2
Cameron city	NA	NA	NA	NA	1,230	7	71.4	5.1	0.8	60.3	270	6.2	629	84	4.8
Cape Girardeau city	2,019	5175	579	4596	17,031	115	79.1	57.8	5.4	100.0	921	52.2	1,349	435	56.2
Carthage city	584	4117	190	3927	2,850	24	66.7	58.8	2.1	100.0	574	50.4	3,573	18	46.1
Chesterfield city	764	1598	71	1527	NA	NA	NA	34.7	22.0	9.0	202	34.5	723	209	69.9
Clayton city	279	1758	88	1670	12,914	13	100.0	29.3	5.3	61.1	1193	34.6	2,174	711	32.5
Columbia city	4,398	3764	351	3413	216,174	1,183	37.5	138.4	19.3	25.9	563	212.6	1,877	640	354.5
Concord CDP	NA	NA	NA	NA	NA	NA	NA	NA	NA	NA	NA	NA	NA	NA	NA
Crestwood city	232	1941	25	1916	NA	NA	NA	11.7	6.7	14.1	333	11.0	920	84	1.0
Creve Coeur city	259	1449	78	1371	32,389	206	14.6	20.8	7.1	35.3	538	19.4	1,086	175	7.6
Dardenne Prairie city	NA	NA	NA	NA	7,542	39	100.0	2.7	0.5	80.1	153	1.9	161	90	0.0
Eureka city	180	1709	66	1643	5,014	23	65.2	10.5	2.0	99.2	640	12.0	1,154	379	5.9
Excelsior Springs city	429	3732	217	3514	330	2	100.0	36.2	1.3	100.0	679	35.0	3,099	102	49.9
Farmington city	833	4584	407	4177	10,013	98	45.9	14.7	1.9	77.9	470	14.1	816	170	5.5
Ferguson city	1,142	5415	545	4870	0	0	0.0	17.2	7.1	0.0	301	19.5	920	198	15.5
Festus city	304	2558	513	2045	10,788	72	33.3	14.5	0.8	100.0	699	10.7	908	212	12.6
Florissant city	1,010	1928	187	1741	140	1	100.0	33.1	18.3	15.6	161	32.8	626	96	22.1
Fort Leonard Wood CDP	NA	NA	NA	NA	NA	NA	NA	NA	NA	NA	NA	NA	NA	NA	NA
Fulton city	437	3426	337	3089	992	8	100.0	14.8	1.7	100.0	456	17.3	1,350	110	16.9
Gladstone city	812	3084	277	2807	726	6	100.0	29.7	4.2	55.7	597	27.7	1,069	194	41.1
Grain Valley city	220	1668	106	1562	13,517	65	100.0	9.3	0.6	82.8	463	6.0	458	32	27.9
Grandview city	936	3669	321	3347	1,009	7	100.0	26.1	0.7	100.0	698	30.6	1,244	0	22.7
Hannibal city	919	5141	375	4766	2,883	18	100.0	22.2	4.0	100.0	664	20.9	1,170	268	44.8
Harrisonville city	351	3512	210	3302	1,280	5	100.0	18.2	2.3	100.0	746	19.1	1,908	465	37.8
Hazelwood city	899	3503	273	3230	877	6	100.0	38.3	16.6	5.6	683	41.8	1,627	196	43.7
Independence city	7,058	6016	406	5610	9,662	64	93.8	188.3	31.9	65.8	748	191.9	1,636	278	427.5
Jackson city	261	1796	144	1651	16,593	72	100.0	11.5	6.3	100.0	215	9.5	667	0	8.4
Jefferson City city	1,464	3375	307	3069	13,208	79	70.9	59.3	4.3	100.0	838	57.9	1,340	163	62.3
Jennings city	945	6402	1450	4952	6,624	49	4.1	10.4	3.8	16.8	347	13.2	891	69	13.0
Joplin city	4,226	8327	516	7811	24,336	263	78.7	79.1	7.5	60.0	914	75.9	1,511	421	15.0
Kansas City city	28,668	6120	1258	4862	281,796	2,734	24.0	1256.7	117.6	15.8	1599	1156.0	2,489	448	2948.0
Kennett city	1,062	9732	880	8853	2,567	14	100.0	6.9	0.4	100.0	262	4.4	404	0	4.7
Kirksville city	581	3302	375	2927	9,215	54	61.1	18.8	1.2	91.8	530	18.6	1,059	284	14.4
Kirkwood city	521	1887	127	1760	20,438	61	100.0	31.5	7.3	39.6	568	30.7	1,115	279	23.0
Lake St. Louis city	316	2123	94	2028	29,763	165	49.7	10.4	1.1	44.5	549	10.2	691	93	14.7
Lebanon city	686	4630	371	4258	2,919	17	88.2	11.9	0.3	100.0	427	9.9	679	11	13.9
Lee's Summit city	1,879	2008	88	1920	117,028	571	56.2	126.6	6.4	34.2	788	116.7	1,263	277	98.3
Lemay CDP	NA	NA	NA	NA	NA	NA	NA	NA	NA	NA	NA	NA	NA	NA	NA
Liberty city	614	2025	211	1814	5,742	30	100.0	33.0	1.0	69.8	663	32.0	1,073	157	47.2
Manchester city	297	1631	44	1587	NA	NA	NA	15.6	10.4	10.7	217	14.8	816	190	59.1
Marshall city	369	2840	262	2579	4,950	41	17.1	12.3	0.8	62.7	302	12.2	930	57	0.0
Maryland Heights city	567	2067	222	1845	0	0	0.0	47.8	14.1	52.2	891	36.8	1,340	394	17.8
Maryville city	192	1590	124	1466	3,705	27	25.9	13.3	1.9	100.0	562	12.1	1,007	173	13.1
Mehlville CDP	NA	NA	NA	NA	NA	NA	NA	NA	NA	NA	NA	NA	NA	NA	NA
Mexico city	396	3433	191	3242	85	2	100.0	10.0	1.1	82.2	520	13.5	1,167	524	13.3
Moberly city	432	3158	132	3027	1,580	14	100.0	14.7	0.8	96.9	701	14.2	1,015	118	59.1
Neosho city	598	4888	245	4643	2,173	21	52.4	11.8	2.3	100.0	593	10.0	828	77	27.4
Nixa city	342	1671	117	1554	25,516	141	97.2	10.6	0.7	67.2	256	9.5	479	18	23.3
Oakville CDP	NA	NA	NA	NA	NA	NA	NA	NA	NA	NA	NA	NA	NA	NA	NA
O'Fallon city	1,139	1363	72	1291	49,889	442	77.8	65.0	5.7	97.0	478	58.2	710	117	231.0
Old Jamestown CDP	NA	NA	NA	NA	NA	NA	NA	NA	NA	NA	NA	NA	NA	NA	NA
Overland city	657	4107	344	3763	0	0	0.0	9.3	1.6	84.3	390	9.6	597	40	0.0
Ozark city	NA	NA	NA	NA	9,722	78	100.0	13.3	1.0	70.2	345	11.5	629	63	44.2
Poplar Bluff city	1,581	9115	663	8452	1,359	25	28.0	31.2	1.8	100.0	1052	25.9	1,508	144	28.8
Raymore city	372	1871	101	1771	32,880	159	89.9	16.6	1.0	67.6	568	16.6	850	148	25.5
Raytown city	1,361	4613	400	4213	665	6	66.7	24.5	1.7	100.0	468	23.7	802	108	54.1
Republic city	351	2222	184	2039	11,288	83	100.0	12.6	1.0	86.8	461	10.0	649	32	16.1
Rolla city	899	4523	548	3975	12,482	105	61.9	24.8	2.3	47.9	670	25.1	1,263	341	11.5
St. Ann city	275	2122	316	1806	0	0	0.0	11.9	1.4	96.0	443	11.3	867	47	0.4
St. Charles city	1,837	2703	184	2519	76,206	395	44.6	85.0	6.1	40.0	884	87.4	1,314	334	217.8
St. Joseph city	4,645	6011	454	5557	11,680	60	90.0	112.7	24.2	75.0	685	85.5	1,107	153	532.1
St. Louis city	25,267	7931	1679	6253	123,458	758	12.7	986.4	175.2	99.4	1706	1082.7	3,391	490	1862.1
St. Peters city	1,219	2202	170	2032	87,449	405	64.4	69.7	8.7	23.6	712	72.3	1,337	393	126.3
Sedalia city	1,504	6991	637	6354	1,710	17	76.5	114.7	1.6	100.0	822	118.0	5,499	330	69.8
Sikeston city	1,298	7852	1645	6207	2,701	41	65.9	19.0	3.0	100.0	623	24.0	1,467	441	140.1
Spanish Lake CDP	NA	NA	NA	NA	NA	NA	NA	NA	NA	NA	NA	NA	NA	NA	NA
Springfield city	14,599	8833	1186	7646	65,835	1,116	13.1	302.8	56.5	34.5	934	276.2	1,702	333	1021.0
Town and Country city	120	1097	46	1051	22,064	55	100.0	13.0	0.8	36.0	959	12.3	1,130	134	0.0
Troy city	307	2703	255	2447	4,725	42	100.0	8.7	1.5	100.0	339	9.2	835	0	14.0
Union city	583	5477	301	5176	6,373	54	100.0	9.5	1.0	41.6	595	8.8	841	96	7.7
University City city	1,532	4365	544	3821	839	3	100.0	39.5	14.2	32.7	401	40.5	1,149	172	13.5
Warrensburg city	692	3427	233	3195	5,312	72	22.2	16.7	1.0	84.7	527	17.7	897	204	38.1
Washington city	485	3454	93	3361	4,627	29	93.1	22.5	0.9	82.7	959	20.4	1,464	282	153.1
Webb City city	641	5839	91	5748	4,831	43	100.0	10.1	0.5	87.0	645	8.1	742	116	9.5
Webster Groves city	258	1109	120	989	3,986	14	100.0	21.9	9.0	10.1	395	26.8	1,163	417	15.0
Wentzville city	543	1632	129	1502	148,798	626	90.1	32.7	2.6	11.6	663	39.1	1,245	374	64.6
West Plains city	758	6152	276	5876	1,418	19	47.4	16.5	1.8	100.0	701	14.4	1,176	180	21.0
Wildwood city	NA	NA	NA	NA	NA	NA	NA	13.3	6.4	6.0	164	11.4	318	100	5.1
MONTANA	28,625	2797	324	2473	647,022	3,884	52.6	X	X	X	X	X	X	X	X
Billings city	5,381	4881	381	4500	122,415	605	78.2	139.3	26.8	53.7	356	121.4	1,134	258	108.2

1 Data for serious crimes have not been adjusted for underreporting. This may affect comparability between geographic areas over time.
2 Per 100,000 population estimated by the FBI.   3 Based on population estimated as of July 1 of the year shown.

Table B. Incorporated Places, Census Designated Places (CDPs), and Minor Civil Divisions (MCDs) of 10,000 or More Population — Land Area, Population, and Households, and Employment

STATE City, town, township, borough, or CDP (county if applicable)	Land area,[1] 2010 (sq mi)	Total persons 2010	Total persons 2014	Percent change 2010–2014	Persons per square mile, 2014	Foreign born	Lives in same house as previous year	Median household income (dollars)	Income of $100,000 or more	Income below poverty level	Percent in labor force	Unemploy- ment rate	Family households	One person households
	1	2	3	4	5	6	7	8	9	10	11	12	13	14
MONTANA—Con.														
Bozeman city	19.716	37,284	41,660	11.7	2,113.0	4.3	65.3	$46,422	14.4	18.7	72.1	8.1	45.2	33.0
Butte-Silver Bow	718.477	34,204	34,680	1.4	48.3	1.8	81.2	$37,503	12.7	20.5	62.3	7.2	56.4	35.9
Butte-Silver Bow (balance)	716.244	33,502	33,980	1.4	47.4	1.8	81.2	$37,654	12.7	20.2	62.1	7.0	56.2	36.1
Great Falls city	21.923	58,631	59,152	0.9	2,698.1	2.2	80.3	$43,374	13.8	15.2	63.8	5.6	59.6	34.4
Helena city	16.507	28,212	29,943	6.1	1,814.0	1.7	75.2	$50,311	17.7	12.6	65.7	5.1	52.7	40.3
Kalispell city	11.683	19,907	21,518	8.1	1,841.8	2.2	84.0	$40,511	9.6	16.1	65.3	8.7	55.4	37.4
Missoula city	28.865	66,877	69,821	4.4	2,418.9	2.9	73.8	$41,968	15.7	19.3	70.2	9.2	50.5	33.7
NEBRASKA	76,824.168	1,826,341	1,881,503	3.0	24.5	6.5	83.5	$52,400	19.4	12.4	70.5	5.4	65.0	28.7
Beatrice city	8.774	12,437	12,055	-3.1	1,374.0	1.7	86.0	$40,750	11.0	13.9	64.0	5.2	59.3	33.8
Bellevue city	15.891	51,022	53,936	5.7	3,394.1	8.6	81.7	$59,123	19.8	10.8	71.3	7.9	70.9	24.1
Chalco CDP	2.817	10,994	NA	NA	NA	4.6	82.9	$67,679	26.7	5.9	85.2	4.0	72.1	20.1
Columbus city	10.120	22,184	22,630	2.0	2,236.1	9.8	84.8	$51,261	14.3	9.8	74.1	5.8	63.1	32.3
Fremont city	9.242	26,413	26,500	0.3	2,867.2	7.2	82.6	$47,239	11.9	12.6	67.0	6.0	67.1	27.1
Grand Island city	29.682	48,645	51,236	5.3	1,726.1	15.8	80.7	$46,527	12.6	15.7	72.1	7.0	64.4	28.2
Hastings city	14.100	25,222	24,915	-1.2	1,767.1	6.1	82.8	$46,840	14.3	12.8	68.2	7.3	60.5	32.6
Kearney city	13.153	30,803	32,469	5.4	2,468.5	4.3	73.2	$48,433	17.9	14.7	74.9	4.5	59.1	28.7
La Vista city	4.541	15,997	17,636	10.2	3,883.7	8.0	83.9	$55,836	20.8	7.0	80.9	4.2	60.6	32.7
Lexington city	4.500	10,230	10,146	-0.8	2,254.9	38.7	84.0	$44,966	6.9	17.5	74.6	8.5	76.4	20.5
Lincoln city	90.418	258,468	272,996	5.6	3,019.3	7.9	76.7	$49,794	18.7	15.3	72.0	6.3	59.0	30.7
Norfolk city	10.690	24,210	24,444	1.0	2,286.6	6.7	81.4	$43,266	12.8	17.0	71.3	4.4	63.8	30.5
North Platte city	13.236	24,736	24,327	-1.7	1,838.0	1.8	83.6	$43,772	12.9	14.2	65.5	5.4	58.0	35.6
Omaha city	129.869	423,327	446,599	5.5	3,438.8	9.8	81.2	$48,751	19.0	15.5	70.8	7.3	59.6	33.0
Papillion city	6.639	19,223	23,270	21.1	3,505.1	3.1	86.3	$74,111	33.3	5.4	73.4	4.4	72.3	23.0
Scottsbluff city	6.215	15,039	14,875	-1.1	2,393.4	5.3	84.7	$37,813	9.5	16.0	66.2	9.0	59.0	34.5
South Sioux City city	5.706	13,353	13,360	0.1	2,341.4	25.7	80.7	$40,975	10.3	26.4	73.1	9.3	74.7	21.6
NEVADA	109,781.175	2,700,692	2,839,099	5.1	25.9	19.1	77.8	$52,205	19.9	13.6	65.1	11.8	64.5	27.7
Boulder City city	208.270	15,027	15,386	2.4	73.9	3.8	83.9	$55,583	22.5	12.3	57.2	12.3	61.2	34.3
Carson City	144.661	55,274	54,522	-1.4	376.9	11.7	76.7	$50,108	16.7	15.2	60.4	14.5	61.4	31.3
Elko city	17.723	18,317	20,300	10.8	1,145.4	10.8	81.6	$74,433	31.2	7.4	70.9	5.3	70.4	20.8
Enterprise CDP	46.457	108,481	NA	NA	NA	25.2	75.1	$68,623	29.0	7.9	73.0	8.1	67.0	22.5
Fernley city	122.585	19,368	19,204	-0.8	156.7	7.2	76.7	$54,036	19.6	9.8	61.5	17.3	73.1	19.8
Gardnerville Ranchos CDP	15.017	11,312	NA	NA	NA	4.6	83.1	$51,707	13.7	16.4	67.3	9.7	71.0	24.3
Henderson city	104.657	257,354	277,440	7.8	2,650.9	12.1	82.2	$63,830	27.6	9.4	65.1	10.3	66.9	26.1
Las Vegas city	133.127	584,240	613,599	5.0	4,609.1	21.3	76.1	$50,903	19.1	15.4	64.5	13.1	64.5	28.3
Mesquite city	35.812	15,277	16,970	11.1	473.9	10.3	84.1	$45,066	11.4	11.0	47.2	13.0	65.0	28.5
North Las Vegas city	98.016	216,700	230,788	6.5	2,354.6	21.7	75.5	$53,105	17.3	15.0	67.3	12.2	72.6	21.2
Pahrump CDP	301.729	36,441	NA	NA	NA	8.4	80.3	$41,277	11.8	15.4	43.1	18.0	68.2	25.6
Paradise CDP	46.714	223,167	NA	NA	NA	25.1	75.1	$45,390	14.4	14.7	68.8	12.1	55.1	35.4
Reno city	107.221	226,012	236,995	4.9	2,210.3	16.4	75.6	$46,489	18.2	17.1	66.7	10.5	55.8	34.7
Spanish Springs CDP	55.660	15,064	NA	NA	NA	6.7	84.6	$78,842	34.7	4.2	69.3	12.3	76.1	19.0
Sparks city	36.169	90,258	94,708	4.9	2,618.5	16.9	77.4	$53,481	20.3	11.6	68.3	10.6	65.6	27.2
Spring Creek CDP	58.769	12,361	NA	NA	NA	2.1	86.4	$94,513	47.9	2.4	74.8	1.2	78.4	14.9
Spring Valley CDP	33.250	178,395	NA	NA	NA	30.3	76.1	$50,795	16.7	11.9	69.3	10.6	59.3	30.3
Summerlin South CDP	9.656	24,085	NA	NA	NA	16.7	76.5	$91,765	45.1	5.4	62.4	8.2	69.0	26.3
Sunrise Manor CDP	33.367	189,372	NA	NA	NA	26.8	76.5	$38,994	10.1	20.4	64.7	16.7	69.9	23.6
Sun Valley CDP	14.903	19,299	NA	NA	NA	18.0	86.7	$44,017	9.0	17.1	63.1	11.6	71.4	20.6
Whitney CDP	6.714	38,585	NA	NA	NA	27.2	79.8	$47,569	13.3	13.2	69.5	12.7	66.3	25.2
Winchester CDP	4.382	27,978	NA	NA	NA	33.6	73.1	$37,059	12.9	21.2	62.3	15.0	52.6	36.7
NEW HAMPSHIRE	8,952.651	1,316,466	1,326,813	0.8	148.2	5.6	86.5	$65,986	29.5	8.8	68.7	6.5	66.8	25.4
Amherst town (Hillsborough)	34.189	11,201	11,266	0.6	329.5	4.6	92.7	$115,898	57.5	3.0	70.6	3.6	80.9	16.1
Bedford town (Hillsborough)	32.836	21,203	21,689	2.3	660.5	5.0	89.7	$123,423	62.2	2.5	67.8	5.0	81.5	13.1
Berlin city & MCD (Coos)	61.617	10,051	9,501	-5.5	154.2	3.4	83.3	$36,358	9.9	15.9	52.5	10.8	60.6	35.2
Claremont city & MCD (Sullivan)	43.121	13,355	13,074	-2.1	303.2	1.7	82.1	$45,510	13.5	14.2	64.5	9.9	61.2	30.5
Concord city & MCD (Merrimack)	64.245	42,692	42,444	-0.6	660.7	6.4	81.8	$54,182	22.2	11.4	65.2	7.1	57.4	33.8
Conway town (Carroll)	69.404	10,115	9,984	-1.3	143.9	5.7	85.6	$46,695	13.5	10.4	67.1	3.6	68.1	24.0
Derry CDP	15.224	22,015	NA	NA	NA	5.5	88.0	$57,338	22.6	10.9	73.7	7.1	63.1	27.3
Derry town (Rockingham)	35.609	33,109	33,307	0.6	935.3	4.4	89.2	$65,637	28.0	8.5	74.3	7.7	68.3	23.7
Dover city & MCD (Strafford)	26.713	29,983	30,665	2.3	1,147.9	6.5	79.1	$60,038	24.5	10.1	72.8	6.7	57.9	29.4
Durham CDP	2.696	10,345	NA	NA	NA	9.3	41.3	$44,722	21.5	34.7	60.1	7.3	41.7	29.3
Durham town (Strafford)	22.384	14,638	15,759	7.7	704.0	7.8	53.7	$67,578	34.9	20.7	61.7	5.7	59.0	22.7
Exeter town (Rockingham)	19.558	14,306	14,543	1.7	743.6	3.9	88.7	$74,071	35.0	6.3	68.1	5.5	60.6	31.7
Goffstown town (Hillsborough)	36.858	17,651	17,972	1.8	487.6	4.1	87.1	$69,123	33.1	4.6	67.5	5.0	67.2	24.7
Hampton town (Rockingham)	12.903	14,976	15,208	1.5	1,178.7	3.9	86.6	$73,750	36.1	7.1	67.2	6.5	66.2	30.2
Hanover town (Grafton)	49.023	11,260	11,379	1.1	232.1	12.0	72.3	$94,063	46.6	9.8	48.7	3.1	61.2	32.0
Hooksett town (Merrimack)	36.499	13,451	13,771	2.4	377.3	3.8	88.3	$82,725	36.3	3.4	74.7	5.9	70.0	24.2
Hudson town (Hillsborough)	28.319	24,467	24,775	1.3	874.8	5.8	91.1	$84,448	39.2	5.2	72.8	8.3	76.8	16.8
Keene city & MCD (Cheshire)	37.248	23,409	23,034	-1.6	618.4	3.6	71.2	$52,327	20.5	15.9	63.8	9.8	52.8	33.0
Laconia city & MCD (Belknap)	19.818	15,947	16,067	0.8	810.7	3.8	85.3	$49,925	19.9	14.3	62.2	9.6	60.5	32.9
Lebanon city & MCD (Grafton)	40.322	13,151	13,589	3.3	337.0	11.4	82.3	$52,825	22.6	12.1	67.3	3.4	57.5	36.1
Londonderry CDP	12.307	11,037	NA	NA	NA	1.9	93.4	$90,252	42.9	3.9	73.4	8.7	76.0	18.5
Londonderry town (Rockingham)	41.985	24,129	24,403	1.1	581.2	3.7	94.5	$91,861	45.2	3.1	76.3	6.2	76.9	17.6
Manchester city & MCD (Hillsborough)	33.101	109,571	110,448	0.8	3,336.7	13.2	80.6	$55,306	20.8	12.9	69.6	7.9	58.6	30.7
Merrimack town (Hillsborough)	32.529	25,494	25,659	0.6	788.8	4.7	93.5	$91,429	44.8	4.2	74.8	4.6	74.8	19.1
Milford town (Hillsborough)	25.320	15,115	15,153	0.3	598.5	5.5	88.0	$63,203	28.4	5.7	71.8	6.7	70.5	25.3
Nashua city & MCD (Hillsborough)	30.849	86,494	87,259	0.9	2,828.6	13.4	83.4	$66,818	30.6	11.0	71.3	8.1	63.6	28.0

1 Dry land or land partially or temporarily covered by water.
2 16 years old and over.

Table B. Incorporated Places, Census Designated Places (CDPs), and Minor Civil Divisions (MCDs) of 10,000 or More Population — Crime, Construction, and Local Government Finance

STATE City, town, township, borough, or CDP (county if applicable)	Serious crimes known to police, 2014[1] Total number	Rate[2] Total	Rate[2] Violent	Rate[2] Property	New residential construction authorized by building permits, 2014 Value ($1,000)	Number of housing units	Percent single family	Local government finance, 2012 General revenue Total (mil dol)	Intergovernmental Total (mil dol)	Percent from state gov.	Taxes per capita[3]	General expenditure Total (mil dol)	Per capita[3] Total	Capital outlays	Debt outstanding (mil dol)
	15	16	17	18	19	20	21	22	23	24	25	26	27	28	29
MONTANA—Con.															
Bozeman city	1,194	2946	188	2759	115,449	671	44.0	47.2	7.7	100.0	446	47.1	1,218	295	35.1
Butte-Silver Bow	NA	NA	NA	NA	4,887	58	55.2	75.8	25.6	85.0	803	64.6	1,874	446	42.1
Butte-Silver Bow (balance)	1,643	4740	355	4385	4,887	58	55.2	NA	NA	NA	NA	NA	NA	NA	NA
Great Falls city	2,738	4602	274	4328	43,724	356	13.5	59.8	11.2	86.2	300	59.2	1,004	125	39.4
Helena city	1,302	4350	535	3816	37,605	338	15.4	39.8	8.5	54.5	320	38.1	1,306	175	45.1
Kalispell city	1,035	4873	250	4624	19,950	94	85.1	27.2	6.7	82.1	452	24.5	1,195	51	29.4
Missoula city	3,147	4517	327	4190	30,607	494	31.4	74.2	24.8	96.6	422	74.8	1,093	151	84.9
NEBRASKA	52,754	2804	280	2523	1,205,827	7,605	62.4	X	X	X	X	X	X	X	X
Beatrice city	503	4160	753	3407	1,670	7	100.0	17.4	5.2	56.6	451	18.9	1,566	291	7.5
Bellevue city	1,003	1849	96	1753	78,929	415	29.2	47.3	5.6	93.3	589	46.0	874	117	65.0
Chalco CDP	NA	NA	NA	NA	NA	NA	NA	NA	NA	NA	NA	NA	NA	NA	NA
Columbus city	406	1795	93	1702	13,359	60	80.0	32.0	6.4	45.8	689	26.2	1,167	368	30.2
Fremont city	686	2606	220	2386	6,365	31	100.0	32.4	11.1	42.3	439	26.6	1,007	230	38.9
Grand Island city	2,354	4616	257	4359	32,482	198	71.7	57.1	7.8	100.0	468	52.8	1,053	87	50.6
Hastings city	1,026	4093	291	3801	11,033	58	81.0	28.7	7.4	57.1	446	25.1	1,005	106	56.1
Kearney city	761	2341	258	2082	43,019	265	54.7	41.2	6.7	95.0	478	40.5	1,270	106	56.1
La Vista city	295	1643	95	1548	13,204	42	100.0	21.8	4.3	100.0	679	22.2	1,281	246	60.4
Lexington city	302	2962	147	2815	2,175	22	9.1	11.2	2.8	73.4	460	11.2	1,104	292	15.5
Lincoln city	10,000	3687	338	3349	251,646	1,792	47.7	295.4	84.6	29.9	516	277.5	1,045	307	1294.9
Norfolk city	646	2627	171	2456	8,184	50	86.0	26.8	3.1	88.1	518	27.0	1,106	143	30.4
North Platte city	1,112	4541	331	4210	2,532	16	100.0	32.4	7.5	45.0	538	37.7	1,535	145	56.8
Omaha city	21,511	4906	561	4345	280,516	2,453	53.2	610.0	80.9	60.1	903	580.3	1,333	325	1049.9
Papillion city	316	1398	84	1314	79,920	322	86.6	27.0	5.3	29.5	645	25.0	1,200	120	55.5
Scottsbluff city	606	4038	313	3724	3,167	13	100.0	21.3	1.9	95.0	740	18.3	1,217	261	11.5
South Sioux City city	513	3818	156	3662	3,428	16	87.5	15.6	4.4	100.0	503	16.4	1,231	225	65.3
NEVADA	92,583	3261	636	2625	1,754,597	13,016	68.3	X	X	X	X	X	X	X	X
Boulder City city	154	1011	105	906	4,242	15	100.0	38.7	18.0	52.0	381	38.0	2,512	784	45.0
Carson City	1,035	1906	295	1611	11,679	35	94.3	111.3	36.0	61.3	701	103.8	1,902	301	282.0
Elko city	864	4209	336	3873	31,249	250	26.4	28.9	10.6	97.5	383	39.8	2,063	693	19.9
Enterprise CDP	NA	NA	NA	NA	NA	NA	NA	NA	NA	NA	NA	NA	NA	NA	NA
Fernley city	NA	NA	NA	NA	1,586	8	100.0	11.6	5.6	7.2	189	10.7	560	50	81.2
Gardnerville Ranchos CDP	NA	NA	NA	NA	NA	NA	NA	NA	NA	NA	NA	NA	NA	NA	NA
Henderson city	5,875	2143	165	1978	251,384	2,256	56.0	402.5	181.2	47.5	487	422.6	1,594	454	308.8
Las Vegas city	57,630	3764	841	2923	202,296	1,453	100.0	801.6	407.6	63.4	336	876.8	1,470	462	637.5
Mesquite city	281	1679	143	1536	34,323	196	100.0	38.8	19.1	90.2	660	50.4	3,142	1,461	57.7
North Las Vegas city	7,290	3177	777	2401	66,571	522	90.2	281.9	110.2	80.4	377	281.1	1,260	340	473.2
Pahrump CDP	NA	NA	NA	NA	NA	NA	NA	NA	NA	NA	NA	NA	NA	NA	NA
Paradise CDP	NA	NA	NA	NA	NA	NA	NA	NA	NA	NA	NA	NA	NA	NA	NA
Reno city	7,945	3380	488	2892	291,806	1,557	55.1	315.2	72.0	57.4	526	287.2	1,245	153	1243.0
Spanish Springs CDP	NA	NA	NA	NA	NA	NA	NA	NA	NA	NA	NA	NA	NA	NA	NA
Sparks city	2,801	2979	327	2653	85,609	377	97.9	93.5	28.6	69.1	378	85.8	933	92	243.8
Spring Creek CDP	NA	NA	NA	NA	NA	NA	NA	NA	NA	NA	NA	NA	NA	NA	NA
Spring Valley CDP	NA	NA	NA	NA	NA	NA	NA	NA	NA	NA	NA	NA	NA	NA	NA
Summerlin South CDP	NA	NA	NA	NA	NA	NA	NA	NA	NA	NA	NA	NA	NA	NA	NA
Sunrise Manor CDP	NA	NA	NA	NA	NA	NA	NA	NA	NA	NA	NA	NA	NA	NA	NA
Sun Valley CDP	NA	NA	NA	NA	NA	NA	NA	NA	NA	NA	NA	NA	NA	NA	NA
Whitney CDP	NA	NA	NA	NA	NA	NA	NA	NA	NA	NA	NA	NA	NA	NA	NA
Winchester CDP	NA	NA	NA	NA	NA	NA	NA	NA	NA	NA	NA	NA	NA	NA	NA
NEW HAMPSHIRE	28,643	2159	196	1963	653,428	3,403	64.3	X	X	X	X	X	X	X	X
Amherst town (Hillsborough)	199	1765	80	1685	1,858	6	100.0	11.2	0.9	91.6	841	12.1	1,078	201	2.5
Bedford town (Hillsborough)	338	1557	32	1525	23,216	165	12.7	23.1	1.8	89.2	847	19.2	892	6	15.4
Berlin city & MCD (Coos)	165	1734	221	1514	0	0	0.0	40.4	22.0	70.3	1491	32.6	3,387	128	11.2
Claremont city & MCD (Sullivan)	389	2997	293	2704	562	5	100.0	20.6	4.8	98.8	886	17.4	1,321	69	32.6
Concord city & MCD (Merrimack)	1,058	2498	203	2295	16,168	116	36.2	62.7	3.7	75.0	931	59.6	1,402	31	67.0
Conway town (Carroll)	385	3849	280	3569	6,807	26	100.0	11.1	1.1	70.7	928	9.4	933	20	0.5
Derry CDP	NA	NA	NA	NA	NA	NA	NA	NA	NA	NA	NA	NA	NA	NA	NA
Derry town (Rockingham)	671	2013	162	1851	5,937	30	93.3	38.3	3.5	90.3	865	37.5	1,129	86	13.0
Dover city & MCD (Strafford)	503	1642	134	1508	17,664	107	64.5	105.4	21.2	95.8	2139	90.6	2,982	200	72.6
Durham CDP	NA	NA	NA	NA	NA	NA	NA	NA	NA	NA	NA	NA	NA	NA	NA
Durham town (Strafford)	116	745	77	668	38,198	202	5.0	18.6	5.1	69.7	489	17.2	1,123	339	10.4
Exeter town (Rockingham)	135	924	130	794	9,123	80	11.3	18.5	1.1	95.7	934	16.6	1,152	16	10.5
Goffstown town (Hillsborough)	291	1632	123	1508	3,830	17	88.2	20.7	2.6	90.9	871	19.2	1,084	168	2.1
Hampton town (Rockingham)	311	2040	118	1922	13,903	90	32.2	25.4	1.6	74.8	1450	24.2	1,610	147	16.6
Hanover town (Grafton)	193	1702	212	1491	2,404	7	100.0	19.8	1.1	76.2	1080	24.4	2,162	442	16.6
Hooksett town (Merrimack)	414	3003	181	2822	4,286	23	82.6	16.0	1.0	90.5	892	16.8	1,223	99	6.2
Hudson town (Hillsborough)	462	1872	130	1742	6,199	47	100.0	23.5	2.0	79.5	765	23.1	943	4	16.1
Keene city & MCD (Cheshire)	997	4259	273	3986	613	4	25.0	45.0	3.5	76.9	1066	44.6	1,908	318	38.9
Laconia city & MCD (Belknap)	678	4226	424	3802	19,546	100	44.0	63.9	19.1	97.6	2434	55.9	3,485	112	29.8
Lebanon city & MCD (Grafton)	473	3449	255	3193	5,464	64	3.1	30.6	2.0	90.8	1406	35.2	2,604	820	51.7
Londonderry CDP	NA	NA	NA	NA	NA	NA	NA	NA	NA	NA	NA	NA	NA	NA	NA
Londonderry town (Rockingham)	280	1148	86	1062	14,234	54	100.0	31.5	2.0	92.2	950	29.4	1,212	61	18.5
Manchester city & MCD (Hillsborough)	4,691	4243	620	3623	19,720	114	91.2	391.9	151.9	74.0	1379	436.7	3,964	479	566.8
Merrimack town (Hillsborough)	193	753	16	738	5,854	23	100.0	31.7	3.7	87.6	733	30.7	1,204	162	4.5
Milford town (Hillsborough)	250	1651	152	1499	3,194	17	100.0	13.3	1.1	91.4	638	12.7	842	0	6.2
Nashua city & MCD (Hillsborough)	2,059	2359	234	2125	36,803	396	14.6	282.0	81.9	99.2	2033	264.6	3,055	177	156.2

1 Data for serious crimes have not been adjusted for underreporting. This may affect comparability between geographic areas over time.
2 Per 100,000 population estimated by the FBI. 3 Based on population estimated as of July 1 of the year shown.

Table B. Incorporated Places, Census Designated Places (CDPs), and Minor Civil Divisions (MCDs) of 10,000 or More Population — Land Area, Population, and Households, and Employment

STATE City, town, township, borough, or CDP (county if applicable)	Land area,[1] 2010 (sq mi)	Total persons 2010	Total persons 2014	Percent change 2010–2014	Persons per square mile, 2014	Foreign born	Lives in same house as previous year	Median household income (dollars)	Income of $100,000 or more	Income below poverty level	Percent in labor force	Unemploy-ment rate	Family households	One person households
	1	2	3	4	5	6	7	8	9	10	11	12	13	14
NEW HAMPSHIRE—Con.														
Pelham town (Hillsborough)......	26.390	12,897	13,219	2.5	500.9	4.5	91.7	$87,359	46.4	6.4	73.1	6.0	77.8	17.3
Portsmouth city & MCD (Rockingham).....................	15.635	21,233	21,598	1.7	1,381.4	7.4	80.8	$67,679	32.1	7.8	72.6	4.2	46.2	41.4
Raymond town (Rockingham) ..	28.766	10,138	10,280	1.4	357.4	2.9	83.7	$66,563	28.0	7.4	74.0	7.1	70.2	18.3
Rochester city & MCD (Strafford)........................	45.402	29,752	29,991	0.8	660.6	2.6	84.4	$48,114	15.4	13.7	65.9	6.9	58.8	30.2
Salem town (Rockingham)........	24.725	28,776	29,005	0.8	1,173.1	8.5	90.8	$78,395	35.1	4.8	72.1	7.3	71.0	21.9
Somersworth city & MCD (Strafford)........................	9.787	11,766	11,777	0.1	1,203.3	11.0	79.2	$53,094	18.4	15.2	72.4	7.0	70.7	17.4
Windham town (Rockingham)...	26.806	13,592	14,250	4.8	531.6	5.0	91.3	$111,982	58.9	3.5	72.0	5.7	79.4	17.3
NEW JERSEY	7,354.220	8,791,936	8,938,175	1.7	1,215.4	21.5	90.1	$72,062	35.6	10.4	66.3	9.7	69.3	25.8
Aberdeen township (Monmouth)	5.447	18,209	18,292	0.5	3,358.1	17.3	91.6	$88,630	42.6	5.6	70.5	9.1	69.5	24.7
Asbury Park city & MCD (Monmouth)......................	1.424	16,116	15,778	-2.1	11,082.1	24.0	78.2	$32,459	14.0	27.0	68.3	15.2	47.3	39.7
Atlantic City city & MCD (Atlantic)........................	10.747	39,558	39,415	-0.4	3,667.5	31.4	85.8	$26,936	8.0	33.3	60.4	17.4	54.3	40.0
Avenel CDP	3.517	17,011	NA	NA	NA	30.0	94.7	$71,711	28.6	8.3	50.6	6.3	71.4	25.0
Barnegat township (Ocean).....	34.377	20,936	22,303	6.5	648.8	6.4	89.0	$66,294	25.9	7.0	57.1	11.4	71.6	24.4
Bayonne city & MCD (Hudson).	5.813	63,010	65,975	4.7	11,349.2	27.9	94.0	$55,224	23.9	14.4	62.4	7.5	64.7	29.7
Beachwood borough & MCD (Ocean)............................	2.848	11,045	11,253	1.9	3,951.4	4.0	92.9	$76,279	33.4	5.8	72.7	7.2	74.1	21.3
Belleville township (Essex)	3.340	35,928	36,396	1.3	10,896.0	33.2	90.2	$65,462	25.0	8.8	71.1	9.9	62.4	31.7
Bellmawr borough & MCD (Camden).........................	2.998	11,583	11,454	-1.1	3,820.5	8.8	89.9	$50,450	19.0	11.7	66.1	12.3	63.7	29.7
Bergenfield borough & MCD (Bergen)...........................	2.876	26,764	27,406	2.4	9,528.5	40.7	91.8	$80,365	37.8	10.0	68.3	7.3	75.5	19.3
Berkeley township (Ocean).......	42.874	41,254	41,950	1.7	978.4	6.2	91.3	$43,558	16.5	7.5	42.6	12.3	56.6	40.3
Berkeley Heights township (Union)	6.211	13,183	13,542	2.7	2,180.2	14.7	95.6	$139,500	64.9	2.4	66.4	6.0	79.5	18.4
Bernards township (Somerset) ..	23.930	26,654	26,857	0.8	1,122.3	17.8	88.9	$126,667	61.7	3.5	63.8	4.3	70.0	27.9
Bloomfield township (Essex).....	5.306	47,347	47,929	1.2	9,032.8	27.9	91.3	$71,521	31.6	8.2	68.6	7.5	65.0	28.8
Bordentown township (Burlington)........................	8.515	11,367	11,604	2.1	1,362.8	13.8	90.4	$85,739	41.2	2.3	70.1	5.4	71.0	24.4
Bound Brook borough & MCD (Somerset).......................	1.659	10,402	11,116	6.9	6,700.0	33.0	92.8	$63,017	27.8	6.1	75.8	7.9	70.9	22.6
Bradley Gardens CDP	4.487	14,206	NA	NA	NA	29.2	93.6	$114,729	58.4	4.7	71.7	6.5	76.5	21.5
Branchburg township (Somerset).......................	20.044	14,459	14,552	0.6	726.0	15.3	95.0	$120,968	59.5	2.9	72.9	6.2	78.7	18.3
Brick township (Ocean)	25.714	75,072	75,911	1.1	2,952.1	6.5	92.0	$69,063	32.1	7.1	65.4	10.5	66.6	28.4
Bridgeton city & MCD (Cumberland)....................	6.179	25,349	25,347	0.0	4,102.1	23.9	82.6	$35,352	10.8	31.4	50.9	16.6	71.5	24.4
Bridgewater township (Somerset).......................	32.037	44,462	44,903	1.0	1,401.6	23.2	93.7	$114,963	58.2	4.8	67.9	6.7	76.3	20.6
Browns Mills CDP	5.367	11,223	NA	NA	NA	7.3	90.0	$56,438	20.4	13.5	65.6	11.9	65.9	26.6
Burlington township (Burlington)........................	13.415	22,598	22,673	0.3	1,690.1	12.8	93.0	$85,000	42.1	7.3	72.3	8.3	72.5	23.0
Camden city & MCD (Camden)	8.921	77,346	77,332	0.0	8,668.3	12.6	82.9	$26,201	6.6	38.5	57.1	22.0	64.8	29.4
Carteret borough & MCD (Middlesex)......................	4.418	22,844	24,114	5.6	5,458.6	31.9	87.8	$64,294	21.8	11.9	69.0	13.8	78.1	19.6
Cedar Grove township (Essex).	4.251	12,411	12,542	1.1	2,950.1	16.0	95.0	$103,384	51.7	4.0	60.9	6.1	74.8	21.4
Chatham township (Morris)	8.979	10,452	10,615	1.6	1,182.3	13.3	90.9	$135,497	61.5	3.1	61.2	5.9	69.0	28.2
Cherry Hill township (Camden)	24.097	70,876	71,417	0.8	2,963.8	16.2	90.0	$89,567	44.3	5.2	67.9	7.8	72.4	23.1
Cherry Hill Mall CDP	3.642	14,171	NA	NA	NA	20.7	85.4	$85,390	37.9	5.9	72.6	7.9	68.8	26.6
Cinnaminson township (Burlington)........................	7.505	15,569	16,840	8.2	2,243.9	6.1	94.9	$94,682	46.7	5.2	67.2	7.1	78.1	19.6
City of Orange township (Essex)	2.220	30,252	30,934	2.3	13,932.4	35.8	91.1	$32,749	11.0	25.9	65.1	16.1	55.4	40.6
Clark township (Union)	4.305	14,756	15,460	4.8	3,591.5	13.1	94.3	$91,295	46.2	3.9	66.3	8.1	72.0	25.3
Cliffside Park borough & MCD (Bergen)...........................	0.964	23,596	25,503	8.1	26,468.9	41.8	90.4	$56,171	28.4	14.1	64.3	9.0	63.8	32.3
Clifton city & MCD (Passaic)....	11.268	84,136	85,927	2.1	7,626.0	35.7	92.8	$68,096	32.6	9.6	67.2	7.6	69.8	26.5
Clinton township (Hunterdon)...	29.876	13,478	13,158	-2.4	440.4	7.8	85.6	$124,583	60.8	2.8	57.7	5.5	75.1	22.1
Collingswood borough & MCD (Camden).........................	1.823	13,933	13,962	0.2	7,659.1	6.9	86.7	$59,705	28.3	6.8	71.8	6.6	51.3	37.7
Colonia CDP	3.910	17,795	NA	NA	NA	21.0	93.7	$87,557	44.3	3.5	70.0	9.0	80.6	17.3
Colts Neck township (Monmouth)	30.731	10,142	10,065	-0.8	327.5	6.3	96.1	$136,488	63.9	4.9	58.2	3.6	85.9	12.6
Cranford township (Union)	4.830	22,625	23,907	5.7	4,950.1	8.4	93.1	$116,276	57.8	3.2	69.6	7.1	73.6	23.1
Delran township (Burlington)	6.591	16,896	16,775	-0.7	2,545.1	15.3	93.3	$92,585	45.6	6.1	73.0	8.8	72.0	20.2
Denville township (Morris)........	11.976	16,680	16,829	0.9	1,405.2	11.0	94.6	$105,135	54.5	2.4	69.3	7.5	71.7	25.0
Deptford township (Gloucester)	17.361	30,573	30,483	-0.3	1,755.8	8.0	90.6	$67,196	30.5	9.4	65.4	9.4	67.9	26.2
Dover town & MCD (Morris)......	2.679	18,143	18,313	0.9	6,836.5	49.5	89.8	$60,878	23.7	8.0	75.2	8.1	71.2	21.8
Dumont borough & MCD (Bergen)...........................	1.983	17,479	17,863	2.2	9,010.0	28.1	95.2	$91,811	44.9	5.0	70.0	6.4	73.2	24.1
East Brunswick township (Middlesex)......................	21.711	47,512	48,474	2.0	2,232.6	32.8	92.0	$97,270	49.1	5.7	67.7	8.4	77.9	20.0
East Greenwich township (Gloucester)......................	14.443	9,555	10,292	7.7	712.6	4.8	94.5	$112,697	56.5	5.9	69.1	7.4	82.6	15.2
East Hanover township (Morris)	7.877	11,156	11,289	1.2	1,433.2	20.8	96.0	$107,682	54.0	4.6	66.7	9.8	75.6	21.3
East Orange city & MCD (Essex)	3.898	64,107	65,078	1.5	16,696.5	24.5	84.8	$36,978	12.6	23.5	67.4	20.1	54.8	41.2
East Windsor township (Mercer)	15.636	27,190	27,536	1.3	1,761.1	32.4	89.5	$83,539	40.7	9.4	69.3	8.7	73.0	22.5

1 Dry land or land partially or temporarily covered by water.
2 16 years old and over.

Table B. Incorporated Places, Census Designated Places (CDPs), and Minor Civil Divisions (MCDs) of 10,000 or More Population — **Crime, Construction, and Local Government Finance**

STATE City, town, township, borough, or CDP (county if applicable)	Serious crimes known to police, 2014[1] Total number	Rate[2] Total	Rate[2] Violent	Rate[2] Property	New residential construction authorized by building permits, 2014 Value ($1,000)	Number of housing units	Percent single family	Local government finance, 2012 General revenue Total (mil dol)	Intergovernmental Total (mil dol)	Percent from state gov.	Taxes per capita[3]	General expenditure Total (mil dol)	Per capita[3] Total	Per capita[3] Capital outlays	Debt outstanding (mil dol)
	15	16	17	18	19	20	21	22	23	24	25	26	27	28	29
NEW HAMPSHIRE—Con.															
Pelham town (Hillsborough)......	152	1157	61	1096	7,050	40	75.0	12.7	0.9	100.0	836	11.8	907	0	3.7
Portsmouth city & MCD (Rockingham).................	544	2528	172	2356	6,150	21	100.0	118.4	23.8	76.7	3189	96.9	4,535	581	148.9
Raymond town (Rockingham) ..	150	1464	166	1298	5,557	24	91.7	7.7	0.7	100.0	621	6.8	671	14	1.9
Rochester city & MCD (Strafford).................	1,386	4659	407	4253	4,992	44	100.0	102.0	39.7	96.1	1835	100.7	3,371	643	80.7
Salem town (Rockingham)........	806	2787	194	2593	11,123	45	91.1	39.3	2.6	77.0	1095	33.6	1,164	19	8.0
Somersworth city & MCD (Strafford).................	530	4516	562	3954	487	3	100.0	40.7	15.1	93.1	1810	39.5	3,359	248	36.9
Windham town (Rockingham)...	103	722	28	694	36,671	95	90.5	12.4	1.1	98.7	746	12.9	925	84	0.4
NEW JERSEY	178,339	1995	261	1734	4,069,959	28,155	39.1	X	X	X	X	X	X	X	X
Aberdeen township (Monmouth)..............	241	1323	77	1246	5,610	61	100.0	22.0	2.1	96.6	694	19.7	1,084	43	29.7
Asbury Park city & MCD (Monmouth)..............	1,023	6479	1324	5155	618	5	100.0	54.4	26.7	69.1	897	55.6	3,499	431	39.4
Atlantic City city & MCD (Atlantic).................	2,973	7518	1323	6196	15,643	114	17.5	265.6	40.5	25.2	4993	225.7	5,703	269	164.0
Avenel CDP........................	NA	NA	NA	NA	NA	NA	NA	NA	NA	NA	NA	NA	NA	NA	NA
Barnegat township (Ocean)........	223	1007	104	904	9,116	73	100.0	23.6	1.5	82.4	907	25.1	1,173	51	17.1
Bayonne city & MCD (Hudson).	951	1449	226	1224	23,792	193	28.5	247.8	88.4	85.4	2113	277.8	4,287	148	460.2
Beachwood borough & MCD (Ocean).................	140	1250	71	1179	784	7	100.0	10.2	0.7	100.0	617	11.0	993	5	10.6
Belleville township (Essex)	933	2571	281	2290	257	4	100.0	55.7	6.7	100.0	1257	51.7	1,429	14	25.1
Bellmawr borough & MCD (Camden).................	218	1888	78	1810	459	0	0.0	11.6	1.4	98.9	742	10.8	938	71	15.1
Bergenfield borough & MCD (Bergen).................	127	465	40	425	2,046	8	100.0	32.3	2.9	94.6	1033	28.7	1,057	46	14.8
Berkeley township (Ocean).......	624	1487	69	1418	19,573	116	100.0	46.6	5.8	80.6	676	48.5	1,169	131	41.5
Berkeley Heights township (Union).................	64	472	7	465	4,864	21	100.0	16.3	1.9	97.1	999	14.6	1,092	79	17.5
Bernards township (Somerset) .	147	545	22	523	7,760	12	100.0	31.5	2.9	71.7	843	30.0	1,112	141	16.6
Bloomfield township (Essex).....	1,213	2542	205	2337	3,987	393	1.8	68.4	7.7	94.7	1239	67.0	1,407	86	37.3
Bordentown township (Burlington).................	166	1451	114	1338	1,592	9	100.0	10.5	1.1	79.5	613	9.0	784	6	7.7
Bound Brook borough & MCD (Somerset).................	232	2209	171	2037	14,272	265	6.8	11.4	1.2	99.0	758	12.8	1,212	245	15.4
Bradley Gardens CDP.............	NA	NA	NA	NA	NA	NA	NA	NA	NA	NA	NA	NA	NA	NA	NA
Branchburg township (Somerset).................	68	466	21	446	1,861	8	100.0	18.4	3.2	100.0	753	19.3	1,321	292	16.4
Brick township (Ocean)	1,258	1655	117	1538	43,537	166	100.0	110.2	10.5	74.8	1004	92.2	1,224	138	181.2
Bridgeton city & MCD (Cumberland).................	1,236	4896	1022	3874	1,150	14	100.0	34.1	9.2	55.7	491	34.9	1,382	155	15.0
Bridgewater township (Somerset).................	556	1233	44	1189	0	0	0.0	46.3	7.6	95.2	559	44.3	982	77	54.6
Browns Mills CDP.................	NA	NA	NA	NA	NA	NA	NA	NA	NA	NA	NA	NA	NA	NA	NA
Burlington township (Burlington).................	423	1868	102	1766	8,881	75	100.0	26.3	5.0	95.8	510	22.8	1,010	39	24.7
Camden city & MCD (Camden)	4,395	5716	2016	3700	13,285	687	0.9	232.9	174.8	71.9	391	160.2	2,073	195	77.8
Carteret borough & MCD (Middlesex).................	335	1381	185	1195	11,623	210	4.8	45.2	11.7	22.1	997	48.1	2,013	371	26.0
Cedar Grove township (Essex).	75	600	16	584	6,488	40	37.5	15.7	1.4	96.0	783	15.0	1,202	68	9.6
Chatham township (Morris)	42	393	9	383	16,096	27	100.0	16.1	1.2	86.9	1121	15.3	1,444	177	16.2
Cherry Hill township (Camden)	1,935	2685	112	2573	2,723	18	100.0	69.8	10.1	99.2	723	63.2	889	153	121.8
Cherry Hill Mall CDP	NA	NA	NA	NA	NA	NA	NA	NA	NA	NA	NA	NA	NA	NA	NA
Cinnaminson township (Burlington)	439	2572	182	2390	5,156	45	100.0	15.6	2.3	89.7	521	15.0	914	120	16.8
City of Orange township (Essex).................	1,420	4651	1042	3610	36,844	427	4.2	164.7	108.9	90.1	1572	147.6	4,841	73	48.4
Clark township (Union)...........	135	882	26	856	6,445	202	33.2	23.7	2.2	97.7	1135	21.8	1,455	11	28.6
Cliffside Park borough & MCD (Bergen).................	260	1013	136	877	34,890	157	26.1	38.5	7.0	24.4	1141	37.6	1,534	123	33.7
Clifton city & MCD (Passaic).....	1,613	1879	217	1663	13,076	121	62.8	115.4	15.5	73.5	990	103.5	1,216	37	71.7
Clinton township (Hunterdon) ...	62	468	8	460	602	3	100.0	9.5	1.4	75.7	497	10.8	811	80	22.8
Collingswood borough & MCD (Camden).................	338	2440	166	2274	4,175	64	6.3	18.1	2.6	63.5	704	16.9	1,218	106	35.2
Colonia CDP........................	NA	NA	NA	NA	NA	NA	NA	NA	NA	NA	NA	NA	NA	NA	NA
Colts Neck township (Monmouth).................	62	615	30	585	7,088	10	100.0	10.3	2.1	100.0	721	8.2	817	36	9.6
Cranford township (Union)........	177	754	21	732	12,952	194	22.7	32.3	3.1	99.4	1004	29.3	1,270	99	35.1
Delran township (Burlington)	212	1260	83	1177	437	4	100.0	19.7	1.4	98.9	811	14.5	857	60	16.2
Denville township (Morris)	116	686	53	632	6,812	39	100.0	19.1	0.5	77.7	765	19.4	1,148	0	18.1
Deptford township (Gloucester)	1,412	4609	235	4374	4,099	43	100.0	37.9	9.2	99.9	635	31.3	1,023	50	15.9
Dover town & MCD (Morris)......	297	1612	206	1406	0	0	0.0	22.3	4.7	32.6	757	21.3	1,163	84	8.6
Dumont borough & MCD (Bergen).................	90	504	45	459	1,061	5	100.0	18.3	1.4	100.0	951	16.0	904	0	25.0
East Brunswick township (Middlesex)	733	1515	74	1440	6,254	29	72.4	63.1	8.1	56.1	872	57.7	1,202	86	88.4
East Greenwich township (Gloucester).................	NA	NA	NA	NA	7,360	45	91.1	8.3	2.0	95.4	408	10.1	1,003	154	20.8
East Hanover township (Morris)	203	1790	71	1720	6,367	34	100.0	21.3	3.4	95.9	1379	21.5	1,907	75	24.9
East Orange city & MCD (Essex).................	1,558	2406	707	1699	1,776	24	29.2	399.7	273.1	95.8	1730	362.6	5,630	108	100.2
East Windsor township (Mercer).................	277	1001	58	943	3,515	19	100.0	23.5	4.4	94.6	489	23.1	841	90	45.1

1 Data for serious crimes have not been adjusted for underreporting. This may affect comparability between geographic areas over time.
2 Per 100,000 population estimated by the FBI.   3 Based on population estimated as of July 1 of the year shown.

Table B. Incorporated Places, Census Designated Places (CDPs), and Minor Civil Divisions (MCDs) of 10,000 or More Population — Land Area, Population, and Households, and Employment

STATE City, town, township, borough, or CDP (county if applicable)	Land area,[1] 2010 (sq mi)	Total persons 2010	Total persons 2014	Percent change 2010–2014	Persons per square mile, 2014	Foreign born	Lives in same house as previous year	Median household income (dollars)	Income of $100,000 or more	Income below poverty level	Percent in labor force	Unemploy-ment rate	Family households	One person households
						Population characteristics 2010–2014		Household income and poverty, 2010–2014	Percent of households		Employment,[2] 2010–2014		Households, 2010–2014 (percent of households)	
	1	2	3	4	5	6	7	8	9	10	11	12	13	14
NEW JERSEY—Con.														
Eatontown borough & MCD (Monmouth)	5.826	12,709	12,257	-3.6	2,103.9	22.3	88.7	$64,378	26.9	7.0	71.8	9.2	60.0	34.4
Echelon CDP	2.812	10,743	NA	NA	NA	22.4	77.1	$51,488	15.9	12.1	63.3	10.9	49.5	42.2
Edgewater borough & MCD (Bergen)	0.931	11,511	12,343	7.2	13,256.4	41.6	80.3	$99,609	49.8	8.5	71.3	6.4	51.6	40.7
Edison township (Middlesex)	29.970	99,971	101,970	2.0	3,402.4	43.3	87.2	$91,881	46.0	5.4	68.6	8.2	77.1	19.5
Egg Harbor township (Atlantic)	66.594	43,323	43,851	1.2	658.5	16.0	94.3	$71,868	32.9	9.2	74.5	13.0	73.9	22.2
Elizabeth city & MCD (Union)	12.317	124,969	128,705	3.0	10,449.2	47.1	85.2	$43,966	13.9	19.4	70.7	12.2	70.1	24.0
Elmwood Park borough & MCD (Bergen)	2.646	19,403	20,374	5.0	7,700.6	32.7	93.9	$67,500	30.8	10.8	66.1	6.6	73.0	21.7
Englewood city & MCD (Bergen)	4.916	27,127	27,670	2.0	5,628.3	32.2	89.2	$73,249	38.0	10.7	68.4	6.7	63.4	30.7
Evesham township (Burlington)	29.284	45,530	45,613	0.2	1,557.6	7.8	92.2	$93,732	45.5	4.2	72.9	6.9	71.8	24.1
Ewing township (Mercer)	15.250	35,790	36,546	2.1	2,396.4	10.4	84.8	$77,479	32.0	9.9	61.8	10.2	61.4	30.9
Fair Lawn borough & MCD (Bergen)	5.138	32,457	33,549	3.4	6,529.8	30.4	91.8	$100,755	50.4	5.8	69.5	8.1	75.7	21.1
Fairview borough & MCD (Bergen)	0.842	13,835	14,317	3.5	16,994.0	47.3	91.8	$51,990	19.7	20.0	64.5	10.2	62.1	29.8
Florence township (Burlington)	9.780	12,109	12,357	2.0	1,263.4	9.0	92.6	$79,987	37.3	4.1	71.5	8.6	68.9	24.6
Florham Park borough & MCD (Morris)	7.316	11,734	11,829	0.8	1,617.0	16.1	89.4	$105,368	53.3	3.9	63.6	5.7	75.1	22.7
Fords CDP	2.651	15,187	NA	NA	NA	30.8	91.7	$79,754	35.3	7.4	70.0	9.7	76.2	20.0
Fort Lee borough & MCD (Bergen)	2.536	35,336	37,026	4.8	14,601.0	51.6	90.7	$67,119	33.6	12.4	60.9	8.5	57.4	40.3
Franklin township (Gloucester)	55.907	16,820	16,702	-0.7	298.7	4.7	94.6	$76,830	33.7	7.7	68.2	10.8	80.3	16.4
Franklin township (Somerset)	46.147	62,300	65,938	5.8	1,428.9	28.6	91.0	$92,311	45.4	5.3	68.2	6.9	69.0	25.8
Franklin Lakes borough & MCD (Bergen)	9.379	10,590	10,837	2.3	1,155.4	17.8	92.4	$153,657	71.1	4.0	63.1	6.5	84.8	13.8
Franklin Park CDP	2.605	13,295	NA	NA	NA	36.0	90.9	$89,231	40.4	5.5	74.3	5.4	62.6	29.8
Freehold borough & MCD (Monmouth)	1.949	12,052	11,973	-0.7	6,144.4	32.3	92.0	$53,375	22.0	14.0	68.7	8.0	69.4	26.0
Freehold township (Monmouth)	38.504	36,184	35,812		930.1	13.1	91.9	$102,511	52.2	4.5	64.7	6.7	75.1	20.9
Galloway township (Atlantic)	89.074	37,349	37,583	0.6	421.9	13.8	85.6	$63,444	25.9	8.0	66.8	11.5	73.5	19.7
Garfield city & MCD (Bergen)	2.102	30,487	31,486	3.3	14,979.9	44.3	95.4	$46,499	15.8	15.4	64.3	9.4	73.1	22.1
Glassboro borough & MCD (Gloucester)	9.184	18,579	19,007	2.3	2,069.5	4.7	77.8	$64,136	31.2	17.2	61.3	11.8	66.8	21.3
Glen Rock borough & MCD (Bergen)	2.714	11,601	11,901	2.6	4,384.9	12.9	90.6	$154,615	69.9	3.0	71.5	6.7	86.5	10.3
Gloucester township (Camden)	22.983	64,634	64,029	-0.9	2,785.9	7.6	90.5	$72,699	31.5	9.2	70.9	9.5	71.2	24.5
Gloucester City city & MCD (Camden)	2.328	11,458	11,317	-1.2	4,861.8	4.7	84.1	$51,153	19.7	10.7	65.2	10.6	67.7	26.4
Greentree CDP	4.659	11,367	NA	NA	NA	21.0	94.6	$108,146	55.4	3.0	70.1	5.0	80.9	16.9
Guttenberg town & MCD (Hudson)	0.195	11,176	11,481	2.7	58,817.3	56.4	87.6	$52,466	21.3	16.0	69.7	10.6	59.7	33.5
Hackensack city & MCD (Bergen)	4.179	43,010	44,519	3.5	10,652.7	39.1	85.1	$53,338	25.3	14.5	66.6	7.1	55.7	36.6
Haddon township (Camden)	2.688	14,707	14,519	-1.3	5,401.6	4.5	90.1	$78,489	37.5	7.2	69.8	6.5	66.4	27.8
Haddonfield borough & MCD (Camden)	2.824	11,593	11,411	-1.6	4,040.5	3.7	86.7	$125,000	58.7	4.2	66.3	5.4	73.2	24.0
Hamilton township (Atlantic)	111.131	26,503	26,647	0.5	239.8	15.5	83.3	$61,233	23.5	10.5	69.2	11.9	71.8	24.2
Hamilton township (Mercer)	39.499	88,464	89,136	0.8	2,256.7	14.9	92.5	$71,197	32.8	6.8	68.1	9.7	68.5	26.6
Hamilton Square CDP	4.343	12,784	NA	NA	NA	7.6	95.1	$109,090	55.7	1.7	71.0	5.3	79.2	16.3
Hammonton town & MCD (Atlantic)	40.887	14,791	14,765	-0.2	361.1	12.1	90.0	$61,235	30.9	9.4	65.7	9.3	70.2	25.6
Hanover township (Morris)	10.525	13,712	14,659	6.9	1,392.8	17.1	90.2	$109,434	53.6	3.6	67.6	5.9	72.2	25.5
Harrison township (Gloucester)	19.141	12,417	12,818	3.2	669.7	3.8	96.0	$127,875	63.1	3.0	71.5	7.9	85.7	11.2
Harrison town & MCD (Hudson)	1.203	13,619	15,376	12.9	12,780.4	54.1	87.8	$53,772	19.7	13.8	65.6	11.2	68.7	22.2
Hasbrouck Heights borough & MCD (Bergen)	1.505	11,842	12,147	2.6	8,071.9	19.8	92.9	$87,705	43.8	10.1	65.0	8.8	72.0	23.7
Hawthorne borough & MCD (Passaic)	3.335	18,791	19,048	1.4	5,711.8	16.9	95.1	$81,885	41.0	5.3	73.3	8.7	71.8	24.1
Hazlet township (Monmouth)	5.567	20,334	20,166	-0.8	3,622.2	9.2	93.4	$86,867	42.3	5.8	67.0	10.8	75.3	21.3
Highland Park borough & MCD (Middlesex)	1.812	13,982	14,436	3.2	7,969.1	26.9	77.1	$66,414	34.8	13.0	73.8	8.6	57.1	31.3
Hillsborough township (Somerset)	54.537	38,303	39,544	3.2	725.1	18.7	93.8	$115,200	57.0	3.6	72.7	6.1	77.1	19.3
Hillsdale borough & MCD (Bergen)	2.953	10,223	10,482	2.5	3,549.1	16.0	95.9	$113,077	57.3	9.8	66.0	6.0	81.9	16.8
Hillside township (Union)	2.749	21,404	21,919	2.4	7,972.3	29.6	90.7	$59,720	25.2	15.1	67.5	17.9	75.7	22.4
Hoboken city & MCD (Hudson)	1.260	50,006	53,312	6.6	42,311.2	16.0	76.3	$106,875	54.4	10.6	78.0	4.1	39.6	38.3
Holiday City-Berkeley CDP	5.752	12,831	NA	NA	NA	7.5	92.5	$31,044	5.5	9.4	22.3	16.9	42.6	54.9
Holmdel township (Monmouth)	17.896	16,773	16,694	-0.5	932.8	20.9	91.1	$134,746	65.5	3.9	58.2	6.5	83.4	16.3
Hopatcong borough & MCD (Sussex)	10.854	15,147	14,684	-3.1	1,352.8	11.2	94.7	$85,357	39.0	5.1	71.9	14.5	72.9	19.5
Hopewell township (Mercer)	58.032	18,301	18,400	0.5	317.1	11.0	93.2	$144,539	67.3	3.6	69.8	6.1	79.9	17.0
Howell township (Monmouth)	60.558	51,075	51,897	1.6	857.0	10.2	94.8	$96,282	48.2	6.2	69.3	7.8	78.0	18.8
Irvington township (Essex)	2.928	53,933	54,512	1.1	18,617.6	31.7	87.0	$38,165	9.5	20.8	71.1	19.9	59.0	37.1
Iselin CDP	3.189	18,695	NA	NA	NA	44.7	88.5	$80,200	39.0	6.3	65.4	7.0	78.5	17.1
Jackson township (Ocean)	99.244	54,862	56,449	2.9	568.8	8.4	93.0	$87,629	43.3	5.7	65.9	10.5	77.7	18.7
Jefferson township (Morris)	38.893	21,311	21,483	0.8	552.4	9.2	94.9	$96,298	47.9	4.6	70.1	7.0	72.3	23.3
Jersey City city & MCD (Hudson)	14.792	247,643	262,146	5.9	17,721.6	39.8	85.4	$58,907	29.4	17.2	68.8	10.4	60.8	29.3
Keansburg borough & MCD (Monmouth)	1.069	10,105	9,872	-2.3	9,234.4	9.0	89.9	$43,696	19.4	20.4	66.8	13.8	56.5	35.6
Kearny town & MCD (Hudson)	8.781	40,684	41,837	2.8	4,764.3	41.0	89.4	$63,093	26.2	11.4	69.0	13.1	77.4	19.1

1 Dry land or land partially or temporarily covered by water.
2 16 years old and over.

Table B. Incorporated Places, Census Designated Places (CDPs), and Minor Civil Divisions (MCDs) of 10,000 or More Population — Crime, Construction, and Local Government Finance

	Serious crimes known to police, 2014[1]				New residential construction authorized by building permits, 2014			Local government finance, 2012							
		Rate[2]						General revenue				General expenditure			
									Intergovernmental				Per capita[3]		
STATE City, town, township, borough, or CDP (county if applicable)	Total number	Total	Violent	Property	Value ($1,000)	Number of housing units	Percent single family	Total (mil dol)	Total (mil dol)	Percent from state gov.	Taxes per capita[3]	Total (mil dol)	Total	Capital outlays	Debt outstanding (mil dol)
	15	16	17	18	19	20	21	22	23	24	25	26	27	28	29
NEW JERSEY—Con.															
Eatontown borough & MCD (Monmouth)	499	4089	205	3884	5,070	52	100.0	24.5	1.7	99.6	1449	24.3	1,977	296	19.6
Echelon CDP	NA	NA	NA	NA	NA	NA	NA	NA	NA	NA	NA	NA	NA	NA	NA
Edgewater borough & MCD (Bergen)	196	1590	49	1541	11,995	165	11.5	25.7	3.9	28.0	1676	27.2	2,262	517	40.2
Edison township (Middlesex)	1,203	1180	96	1084	13,288	48	100.0	345.6	47.7	85.4	2724	335.2	3,315	96	72.4
Egg Harbor township (Atlantic)	943	2144	211	1932	5,839	54	100.0	40.1	10.0	65.4	483	42.8	978	182	42.5
Elizabeth city & MCD (Union)	4,988	3886	890	2997	25,616	224	0.4	263.2	59.9	65.7	1191	254.8	2,007	251	124.1
Elmwood Park borough & MCD (Bergen)	370	1823	143	1680	4,868	54	24.1	25.2	1.7	96.8	938	22.2	1,108	67	20.2
Englewood city & MCD (Bergen)	588	2125	278	1847	43,335	542	0.6	130.4	25.5	71.3	3607	132.8	4,840	411	44.8
Evesham township (Burlington)	545	1195	75	1120	578	6	16.7	43.8	4.2	84.8	530	38.0	831	106	86.7
Ewing township (Mercer)	787	2139	185	1954	10,683	9	55.6	52.1	12.7	79.2	876	42.3	1,167	29	13.7
Fair Lawn borough & MCD (Bergen)	356	1073	75	998	5,575	66	15.2	44.1	4.4	97.6	1166	39.3	1,195	65	38.7
Fairview borough & MCD (Bergen)	211	1470	181	1289	9,407	100	5.0	16.0	1.3	97.5	935	17.1	1,207	228	12.5
Florence township (Burlington)	63	508	89	419	2,782	22	100.0	10.9	2.2	65.3	591	9.4	762	95	21.2
Florham Park borough & MCD (Morris)	104	877	17	860	10,148	27	100.0	18.8	1.2	99.8	1172	18.9	1,594	173	20.0
Fords CDP	NA	NA	NA	NA	NA	NA	NA	NA	NA	NA	NA	NA	NA	NA	NA
Fort Lee borough & MCD (Bergen)	273	754	47	707	13,157	52	28.8	75.6	8.8	24.0	1726	78.8	2,198	328	62.2
Franklin township (Gloucester)	281	1678	30	1648	2,794	21	100.0	10.4	1.6	97.4	477	10.0	599	24	6.7
Franklin township (Somerset)	982	1488	64	1424	2,794	21	100.0	61.7	8.4	60.6	650	64.2	1,005	93	69.6
Franklin Lakes borough & MCD (Bergen)	73	675	55	619	9,682	16	68.8	15.6	1.9	99.8	1165	14.3	1,329	94	14.5
Franklin Park CDP	NA	NA	NA	NA	NA	NA	NA	NA	NA	NA	NA	NA	NA	NA	NA
Freehold borough & MCD (Monmouth)	167	1387	233	1154	1,756	12	100.0	16.0	1.5	87.8	853	15.2	1,267	153	11.2
Freehold township (Monmouth)	640	1776	86	1690	0	0	0.0	44.5	8.6	92.3	627	35.9	997	0	48.9
Galloway township (Atlantic)	722	1914	141	1774	3,100	33	100.0	26.3	2.8	97.2	460	19.8	529	0	34.2
Garfield city & MCD (Bergen)	721	2295	207	2088	3,390	129	11.6	35.0	4.4	66.3	798	30.5	985	29	21.5
Glassboro borough & MCD (Gloucester)	380	1991	141	1850	7,741	68	100.0	27.0	5.4	55.1	691	26.6	1,411	194	62.1
Glen Rock borough & MCD (Bergen)	70	588	25	562	6,153	31	100.0	16.1	1.1	87.3	1176	14.0	1,187	52	14.1
Gloucester township (Camden)	1,416	2201	232	1970	5,850	59	0.0	55.3	7.4	65.0	591	49.0	761	135	61.5
Gloucester City city & MCD (Camden)	337	2954	245	2709	0	0	0.0	19.2	4.6	87.5	967	18.3	1,598	167	26.3
Greentree CDP	NA	NA	NA	NA	NA	NA	NA	NA	NA	NA	NA	NA	NA	NA	NA
Guttenberg town & MCD (Hudson)	128	1112	235	878	1,800	18	0.0	20.2	4.1	20.8	1191	19.6	1,716	72	5.0
Hackensack city & MCD (Bergen)	732	1647	202	1444	5,257	119	7.6	89.8	9.7	58.1	1693	81.7	1,851	0	36.0
Haddon township (Camden)	352	2406	116	2290	9,584	89	12.4	13.5	2.5	62.1	553	14.9	1,015	223	25.8
Haddonfield borough & MCD (Camden)	158	1373	35	1338	5,320	18	100.0	15.7	1.7	98.2	1033	19.3	1,670	633	22.1
Hamilton township (Atlantic)	1,075	4011	179	3832	1,090	14	64.3	29.3	4.7	90.6	725	26.8	998	107	19.3
Hamilton township (Mercer)	1,679	1884	166	1718	1,090	14	64.3	102.4	21.0	99.9	714	94.7	1,066	76	77.3
Hamilton Square CDP	NA	NA	NA	NA	NA	NA	NA	NA	NA	NA	NA	NA	NA	NA	NA
Hammonton town & MCD (Atlantic)	172	1162	115	1047	1,280	6	100.0	13.5	1.9	78.3	559	13.2	892	39	37.6
Hanover township (Morris)	193	1345	84	1261	9,730	102	20.6	28.8	2.9	93.3	1416	26.7	1,916	273	0.0
Harrison township (Gloucester)	153	1194	55	1140	8,676	48	100.0	8.1	0.8	100.0	423	10.0	791	175	41.9
Harrison town & MCD (Hudson)	310	1976	249	1728	35,496	468	0.4	84.4	50.3	92.9	1873	80.9	5,780	266	71.1
Hasbrouck Heights borough & MCD (Bergen)	63	521	50	472	1,125	4	100.0	18.1	1.2	89.8	1375	16.1	1,344	42	7.9
Hawthorne borough & MCD (Passaic)	187	981	16	965	0	0	0.0	17.3	0.7	100.0	813	15.6	821	0	13.7
Hazlet township (Monmouth)	253	1253	20	1233	264	2	100.0	23.9	2.6	91.6	751	22.7	1,122	66	14.6
Highland Park borough & MCD (Middlesex)	168	1160	48	1112	7,927	64	100.0	16.3	2.9	39.4	719	17.6	1,231	171	15.1
Hillsborough township (Somerset)	219	554	33	521	13,893	130	35.4	31.1	3.5	99.6	519	30.4	777	38	14.8
Hillsdale borough & MCD (Bergen)	43	410	19	391	0	0	0.0	12.3	1.4	94.7	882	12.0	1,151	71	5.0
Hillside township (Union)	651	2972	438	2533	173	1	100.0	39.5	4.5	100.0	1500	35.1	1,619	0	5.2
Hoboken city & MCD (Hudson)	1,182	2218	280	1938	133,571	475	0.8	112.1	26.1	53.1	1137	110.1	2,106	65	101.0
Holiday City-Berkeley CDP	NA	NA	NA	NA	NA	NA	NA	NA	NA	NA	NA	NA	NA	NA	NA
Holmdel township (Monmouth)	196	1174	36	1138	3,388	25	100.0	21.0	2.3	99.7	847	20.3	1,214	58	24.6
Hopatcong borough & MCD (Sussex)	100	679	41	638	2,261	13	100.0	19.3	1.3	97.1	905	15.8	1,058	73	53.5
Hopewell township (Mercer)	106	576	49	527	1,263	10	100.0	24.5	4.6	70.0	978	21.4	1,176	247	60.0
Howell township (Monmouth)	610	1176	71	1104	21,214	153	93.5	48.0	9.5	99.4	565	54.2	1,060	235	50.7
Irvington township (Essex)	2,523	4640	1263	3376	435	4	0.0	262.4	162.7	96.1	1582	240.8	4,441	30	119.4
Iselin CDP	NA	NA	NA	NA	NA	NA	NA	NA	NA	NA	NA	NA	NA	NA	NA
Jackson township (Ocean)	594	1054	66	989	12,283	61	100.0	41.5	3.7	99.3	570	39.4	709	74	46.6
Jefferson township (Morris)	180	834	51	783	844	5	100.0	22.4	2.3	100.0	873	18.9	877	1	16.7
Jersey City city & MCD (Hudson)	5,621	2162	531	1631	487,563	2,180	9.0	597.9	170.1	64.9	918	580.2	2,260	102	847.1
Keansburg borough & MCD (Monmouth)	238	2382	260	2122	4,308	27	88.9	21.6	5.2	36.4	1167	19.3	1,924	72	18.6
Kearny town & MCD (Hudson)	985	2347	207	2140	25,251	151	0.7	76.1	28.2	95.1	994	71.6	1,713	127	83.3

1 Data for serious crimes have not been adjusted for underreporting. This may affect comparability between geographic areas over time.
2 Per 100,000 population estimated by the FBI.   3 Based on population estimated as of July 1 of the year shown.

Table B. Incorporated Places, Census Designated Places (CDPs), and Minor Civil Divisions (MCDs) of 10,000 or More Population — Land Area, Population, and Households, and Employment

STATE City, town, township, borough, or CDP (county if applicable)	Land area,[1] 2010 (sq mi)	Total persons 2010	Total persons 2014	Percent change 2010–2014	Persons per square mile, 2014	Foreign born	Lives in same house as previous year	Median household income (dollars)	Income of $100,000 or more	Income below poverty level	Percent in labor force	Unemploy-ment rate	Family households	One person households
	1	2	3	4	5	6	7	8	9	10	11	12	13	14
NEW JERSEY—Con.														
Kendall Park CDP................	3.702	9,339	NA	NA	NA	23.7	92.0	$111,123	57.3	4.1	70.0	7.3	82.0	16.6
Kinnelon borough & MCD (Morris)........................	17.989	10,248	10,381	1.3	577.1	10.5	95.0	$125,000	61.7	2.1	69.7	10.1	82.3	14.8
Lacey township (Ocean)...........	83.280	27,644	28,211	2.1	338.7	3.4	94.2	$71,835	32.5	6.6	66.7	11.4	70.8	24.7
Lakewood township (Ocean)	24.577	92,837	95,177	2.5	3,872.6	13.4	88.0	$41,026	13.0	24.6	55.5	9.2	72.3	24.6
Lakewood CDP...................	7.078	53,805	NA	NA	NA	14.1	89.2	$38,025	13.7	36.1	56.6	7.4	87.3	10.9
Lawrence township (Mercer)......	21.808	33,472	33,130	-1.0	1,519.1	26.4	85.5	$88,308	43.9	6.1	69.8	7.4	63.1	30.7
Lincoln Park borough & MCD (Morris)........................	6.378	10,521	10,482	-0.4	1,643.3	17.7	92.5	$81,661	36.4	3.7	66.0	6.8	70.9	24.2
Linden city & MCD (Union).......	10.679	40,499	41,651	2.8	3,900.3	33.0	88.7	$62,778	25.3	11.3	67.7	11.9	69.4	26.3
Lindenwold borough & MCD (Camden)......................	3.892	17,613	17,417	-1.1	4,474.7	20.0	82.2	$40,578	10.4	17.0	69.0	12.7	55.0	36.5
Little Egg Harbor township (Ocean)........................	47.368	20,063	20,396	1.7	430.6	3.7	89.9	$60,259	25.0	7.9	58.4	12.0	70.5	25.1
Little Falls township (Passaic)...	2.771	14,432	14,516	0.6	5,238.0	18.7	88.7	$75,923	36.9	6.4	65.5	9.4	63.6	33.8
Little Ferry borough & MCD (Bergen).......................	1.477	10,632	10,866	2.2	7,358.8	43.7	87.8	$63,810	29.5	7.6	71.1	6.7	64.4	27.6
Livingston township (Essex)	13.774	29,361	29,931	1.9	2,173.1	22.7	95.1	$137,665	65.8	3.1	65.3	6.6	84.1	14.3
Lodi borough & MCD (Bergen) .	2.265	24,136	24,654	2.1	10,886.0	35.2	92.3	$48,914	18.2	14.1	65.9	9.7	63.5	31.2
Long Branch city & MCD (Monmouth)...................	5.274	30,719	30,522	-0.6	5,786.8	30.1	85.0	$48,736	20.9	15.8	68.1	10.9	59.6	33.6
Lower township (Cape May).....	27.742	22,866	22,262	-2.6	802.5	4.7	91.2	$53,624	19.6	10.7	63.5	11.3	63.8	30.1
Lumberton township (Burlington).....................	12.924	12,559	12,447	-0.9	963.1	10.1	88.1	$88,299	43.4	6.9	72.0	9.7	71.3	23.2
Lyndhurst township (Bergen)....	4.555	20,554	22,079	7.4	4,847.3	28.2	89.1	$71,848	32.9	10.7	61.7	8.2	68.8	27.0
Madison borough & MCD (Morris)........................	4.303	15,819	16,122	1.9	3,746.5	14.4	85.2	$109,737	54.7	3.1	63.9	7.4	70.0	26.5
Mahwah township (Bergen)......	25.697	25,890	26,500	2.4	1,031.2	15.4	91.6	$102,168	52.6	4.0	69.3	8.9	65.0	31.2
Manalapan township (Monmouth)...................	30.607	38,872	39,987	2.9	1,306.5	12.0	96.1	$110,573	56.7	4.0	65.7	8.2	81.2	16.8
Manchester township (Ocean)..	81.625	43,070	43,555	1.1	533.6	8.6	93.7	$39,826	12.8	8.7	38.0	11.3	50.8	46.2
Mantua township (Gloucester)..	15.849	15,217	15,150	-0.4	955.9	2.4	94.6	$82,204	40.8	7.6	70.3	8.0	72.7	24.2
Manville borough & MCD (Somerset).....................	2.361	10,344	10,388	0.4	4,400.6	22.1	92.3	$62,787	24.8	10.1	68.7	11.8	67.9	28.8
Maple Shade township (Burlington).....................	3.822	19,131	18,979	-0.8	4,966.3	9.9	84.3	$58,750	20.7	8.5	73.2	9.5	56.1	37.6
Maplewood township (Essex) ...	3.877	23,869	24,657	3.3	6,359.1	19.9	91.4	$116,014	57.8	4.9	73.4	7.2	77.8	19.6
Marlboro township (Monmouth)	30.361	40,191	41,000	2.0	1,350.4	20.0	94.5	$135,929	64.7	1.9	66.6	6.9	85.4	13.2
Marlton CDP....................	3.227	10,133	NA	NA	NA	7.6	91.3	$70,461	35.6	4.9	72.6	7.5	66.4	28.2
Martinsville CDP.................	12.322	11,980	NA	NA	NA	13.5	95.1	$136,959	65.9	4.2	65.1	6.3	82.1	15.8
Medford township (Burlington)..	38.921	23,033	23,357	1.4	600.1	6.5	92.8	$109,033	54.5	4.1	67.0	5.9	79.4	17.8
Mercerville CDP.................	3.696	13,230	NA	NA	NA	11.7	91.4	$79,830	36.9	2.3	66.8	7.9	72.0	23.1
Metuchen borough & MCD (Middlesex)....................	2.777	13,574	13,826	1.9	4,978.7	19.0	90.6	$109,351	55.0	4.5	69.3	6.2	71.4	24.1
Middle township (Cape May)	70.335	18,911	18,883	-0.1	268.5	8.1	92.3	$60,156	29.8	9.5	60.3	10.4	69.4	25.7
Middlesex borough & MCD (Middlesex)....................	3.518	13,635	13,888	1.9	3,948.1	17.1	94.3	$81,424	39.7	4.2	71.3	7.8	74.5	23.1
Middletown township (Monmouth)...................	40.980	66,509	66,017	-0.7	1,611.0	6.9	93.5	$103,907	51.5	4.9	67.5	8.4	74.8	22.0
Millburn township (Essex).......	9.327	20,120	20,401	1.4	2,187.2	18.5	92.3	$165,944	68.9	2.7	65.1	5.6	81.1	16.5
Millstone township (Monmouth)	36.599	10,566	10,448	-1.1	285.5	7.5	94.7	$140,038	68.5	2.4	67.1	8.0	84.6	11.5
Millville city & MCD (Cumberland)..................	42.013	28,400	28,497	0.3	678.3	3.5	86.0	$50,787	19.6	16.2	65.5	15.5	64.9	28.4
Monroe township (Gloucester) .	46.393	36,125	37,379	3.5	805.7	5.3	92.1	$71,741	32.4	8.1	68.5	11.1	74.9	20.4
Monroe township (Middlesex)...	41.980	39,132	42,810	9.4	1,019.8	18.3	94.4	$70,772	38.1	5.5	48.2	9.4	66.1	31.6
Montclair township (Essex).......	6.309	37,676	38,142	1.2	6,045.3	15.1	89.6	$97,907	49.0	7.4	69.9	7.4	64.0	29.7
Montgomery township (Somerset).....................	32.306	22,257	22,746	2.2	704.1	25.0	92.6	$154,375	70.6	4.0	66.0	6.5	83.4	14.2
Montville township (Morris).......	18.507	21,524	21,842	1.5	1,180.2	19.6	92.0	$118,761	59.2	4.2	68.6	6.7	81.6	16.1
Moorestown township (Burlington).....................	14.693	20,726	20,594	-0.6	1,401.6	7.7	91.5	$118,875	56.6	3.7	66.7	6.8	76.9	20.4
Moorestown-Lenola CDP........	7.010	14,217	NA	NA	NA	5.0	89.6	$100,643	50.5	3.9	69.1	8.0	73.5	23.2
Morris township (Morris)..........	15.700	22,434	22,573	0.6	1,437.8	11.4	92.1	$127,074	61.3	3.1	66.7	6.9	71.0	24.6
Morristown town & MCD (Morris)........................	2.909	18,324	19,085	4.2	6,560.6	34.0	86.7	$75,696	35.3	11.2	74.7	5.1	47.9	39.5
Mount Laurel township (Burlington).....................	21.692	41,864	41,743	-0.3	1,924.4	9.9	90.1	$85,301	42.4	4.7	68.9	7.6	63.4	32.4
Mount Olive township (Morris)..	29.303	28,109	28,921	2.9	987.0	15.9	92.1	$88,467	42.7	6.7	74.9	7.2	66.6	28.8
Neptune township (Monmouth)	8.182	27,935	27,721	-0.8	3,388.2	13.4	88.2	$63,881	26.3	10.7	65.1	9.6	66.2	28.3
Newark city & MCD (Essex)	24.193	277,149	280,579	1.2	11,597.3	27.9	86.2	$34,012	10.1	29.3	63.3	19.1	63.4	30.1
New Brunswick city & MCD (Middlesex)....................	5.227	54,578	57,080	4.6	10,919.7	38.6	73.0	$38,399	12.8	31.4	60.0	10.9	59.4	25.5
New Milford borough & MCD (Bergen).......................	2.274	16,341	16,678	2.1	7,334.1	29.8	92.4	$75,071	36.4	5.8	68.4	7.1	68.1	29.5
New Providence borough & MCD (Union).................	3.640	12,171	12,422	2.1	3,412.3	18.2	89.5	$139,071	61.0	2.3	67.9	5.5	76.1	19.2
North Arlington borough & MCD (Bergen).................	2.562	15,392	15,723	2.2	6,136.7	26.7	90.8	$71,750	35.4	9.8	60.9	7.2	73.1	24.1
North Bergen township (Hudson).......................	5.195	60,772	62,602	3.0	12,049.3	51.2	87.6	$54,365	21.1	15.9	70.1	13.0	66.0	27.8
North Brunswick township (Middlesex)....................	11.995	41,348	42,488	2.8	3,542.0	34.6	89.1	$80,505	39.9	7.6	71.0	8.0	70.5	23.7
North Plainfield borough & MCD (Somerset)................	2.794	21,936	22,029	0.4	7,883.3	38.0	91.7	$69,363	28.5	9.3	77.7	7.5	69.8	23.3
Nutley township (Essex)	3.384	28,370	28,700	1.2	8,480.4	18.7	94.0	$84,711	41.7	7.8	66.9	8.4	63.4	30.2

1 Dry land or land partially or temporarily covered by water.
2 16 years old and over.

Table B. Incorporated Places, Census Designated Places (CDPs), and Minor Civil Divisions (MCDs) of 10,000 or More Population — Crime, Construction, and Local Government Finance

STATE City, town, township, borough, or CDP (county if applicable)	Serious crimes known to police, 2014[1] Total number	Rate[2] Total	Rate[2] Violent	Rate[2] Property	New residential construction authorized by building permits, 2014 Value ($1,000)	Number of housing units	Percent single family	Local government finance, 2012 General revenue Total (mil dol)	Intergovernmental Total (mil dol)	Percent from state gov.	Taxes per capita[3]	General expenditure Total (mil dol)	Per capita[3] Total	Capital outlays	Debt outstanding (mil dol)
	15	16	17	18	19	20	21	22	23	24	25	26	27	28	29
NEW JERSEY—Con.															
Kendall Park CDP.................	NA	NA	NA	NA	NA	NA	NA	NA	NA	NA	NA	NA	NA	NA	NA
Kinnelon borough & MCD (Morris)..................	61	585	48	537	4,455	17	100.0	11.7	0.8	100.0	993	10.5	1,008	99	13.2
Lacey township (Ocean)..........	462	1644	64	1580	12,500	81	100.0	32.1	11.6	99.2	388	27.6	993	36	47.3
Lakewood township (Ocean)	1,285	1371	178	1193	54,452	469	71.6	88.0	22.3	36.5	608	78.8	850	41	71.9
Lakewood CDP......................	NA	NA	NA	NA	NA	NA	NA	NA	NA	NA	NA	NA	NA	NA	NA
Lawrence township (Mercer)	730	2203	139	2064	305	3	100.0	40.0	5.8	99.2	806	37.1	1,118	105	28.9
Lincoln Park borough & MCD (Morris)..................	76	727	57	669	459	0	0.0	16.3	1.4	86.0	1197	16.1	1,526	52	27.1
Linden city & MCD (Union)....	1,232	2965	366	2599	12,366	312	7.1	93.5	30.9	71.2	1345	93.7	2,288	123	46.6
Lindenwold borough & MCD (Camden)................	669	3822	663	3159	7,951	142	5.6	14.4	2.6	92.1	572	13.3	760	29	6.2
Little Egg Harbor township (Ocean).................	357	1750	88	1662	46,792	149	100.0	21.1	2.7	69.4	772	21.3	1,039	94	16.7
Little Falls township (Passaic)...	150	1030	69	961	892	5	100.0	14.4	1.6	87.4	823	14.3	987	94	18.2
Little Ferry borough & MCD (Bergen)................	79	727	147	580	148	1	100.0	13.5	1.6	69.7	1074	12.9	1,202	129	9.7
Livingston township (Essex)	325	1094	54	1041	14,757	46	100.0	42.4	3.3	97.9	1118	44.7	1,509	258	90.3
Lodi borough & MCD (Bergen) .	406	1647	174	1473	1,159	8	0.0	32.8	8.7	25.2	752	33.0	1,350	55	22.2
Long Branch city & MCD (Monmouth)..............	838	2765	320	2445	16,966	139	30.2	71.9	21.4	25.7	1241	74.6	2,445	343	70.9
Lower township (Cape May)	506	2265	175	2090	5,218	30	93.3	29.6	2.4	98.3	916	26.1	1,153	113	32.6
Lumberton township (Burlington)...............	307	2459	128	2331	792	1	100.0	8.6	2.1	86.8	484	7.5	601	83	7.0
Lyndhurst township (Bergen)....	268	1244	97	1146	27,848	416	3.1	34.1	2.3	72.9	1377	34.0	1,599	65	61.5
Madison borough & MCD (Morris)................	135	824	24	800	11,874	48	45.8	29.1	11.4	74.9	931	29.5	1,836	358	32.9
Mahwah township (Bergen)......	131	494	26	468	6,612	18	77.8	39.2	5.5	97.3	989	36.3	1,384	63	43.0
Manalapan township (Monmouth)..............	252	629	37	592	3,056	25	80.0	30.5	4.3	97.1	643	32.2	812	161	20.6
Manchester township (Ocean)..	380	876	23	853	202	5	0.0	35.4	4.9	81.4	524	30.4	705	16	44.9
Mantua township (Gloucester)..	257	1701	40	1662	761	0	0.0	14.5	2.3	77.9	576	12.3	814	12	20.1
Manville borough & MCD (Somerset)...............	267	2558	115	2443	666	6	33.3	14.5	1.8	94.6	978	13.2	1,260	42	8.0
Maple Shade township (Burlington)...............	415	2181	221	1961	3,087	37	45.9	16.5	2.9	89.0	585	16.6	870	179	54.0
Maplewood township (Essex) ...	447	1811	182	1628	3,702	162	5.6	36.0	3.0	71.6	1192	37.0	1,541	197	55.0
Marlboro township (Monmouth)	275	682	30	652	1,238	11	54.5	29.7	2.6	99.7	614	31.3	778	90	46.0
Marlton CDP.........................	NA	NA	NA	NA	NA	NA	NA	NA	NA	NA	NA	NA	NA	NA	NA
Martinsville CDP....................	NA	NA	NA	NA	NA	NA	NA	NA	NA	NA	NA	NA	NA	NA	NA
Medford township (Burlington)..	186	797	64	733	18,784	92	93.5	20.1	2.6	87.2	513	28.6	1,231	391	69.7
Mercerville CDP.....................	NA	NA	NA	NA	NA	NA	NA	NA	NA	NA	NA	NA	NA	NA	NA
Metuchen borough & MCD (Middlesex)..............	154	1114	65	1049	3,764	19	100.0	16.0	1.7	94.3	875	14.6	1,065	41	20.9
Middle township (Cape May)	673	3564	238	3326	18,340	56	91.1	25.1	5.6	90.6	755	24.4	1,291	206	34.4
Middlesex borough & MCD (Middlesex)..............	141	1016	79	937	35	0	0.0	15.5	2.0	100.0	907	14.6	1,059	77	10.4
Middletown township (Monmouth)..............	570	861	36	824	8,604	55	89.1	78.9	11.7	59.6	796	78.5	1,184	136	80.8
Millburn township (Essex)........	353	1742	44	1698	12,836	32	100.0	48.0	2.8	99.2	2000	34.4	1,711	82	9.3
Millstone township (Monmouth)	NA	NA	NA	NA	2,949	15	33.3	4.9	1.2	99.5	304	4.7	443	43	20.2
Millville city & MCD (Cumberland).............	2,133	7417	692	6725	1,971	19	100.0	50.7	12.0	68.9	765	49.8	1,738	61	39.9
Monroe township (Gloucester) .	732	1982	130	1852	4,400	37	100.0	38.2	4.5	96.0	690	32.6	890	17	36.0
Monroe township (Middlesex)..	218	515	24	491	4,400	37	100.0	41.6	2.7	94.8	677	64.9	1,586	282	85.7
Montclair township (Essex).......	612	1609	121	1488	43,636	410	2.0	192.4	15.8	91.5	4290	179.6	4,740	208	205.1
Montgomery township (Somerset)...............	118	523	9	514	14,230	74	100.0	23.3	3.0	99.8	580	24.6	1,091	95	76.6
Montville township (Morris).......	155	708	46	662	4,713	14	100.0	29.9	2.3	96.6	974	27.9	1,283	67	49.4
Moorestown township (Burlington)...............	407	1971	184	1787	15,076	55	100.0	26.9	2.6	87.5	920	22.0	1,061	97	30.6
Moorestown-Lenola CDP	NA	NA	NA	NA	NA	NA	NA	NA	NA	NA	NA	NA	NA	NA	NA
Morris township (Morris)...........	163	721	49	672	16,728	66	100.0	43.3	5.9	63.7	1274	33.7	1,491	0	28.7
Morristown town & MCD (Morris)................	381	2051	231	1820	27,177	212	5.7	57.2	10.1	32.8	1419	48.8	2,641	241	103.5
Mount Laurel township (Burlington)...............	672	1612	67	1544	2,337	19	42.1	43.3	3.1	97.8	637	34.4	820	31	76.1
Mount Olive township (Morris)..	231	800	45	755	12,736	78	100.0	31.4	2.8	92.9	773	29.3	1,029	96	26.7
Neptune township (Monmouth)	1,533	5512	485	5027	7,287	255	7.5	49.5	11.1	47.4	1034	47.2	1,693	118	30.4
Newark city & MCD (Essex)	10,967	3929	1078	2851	69,735	507	6.3	845.2	438.4	36.2	1099	860.7	3,093	368	658.6
New Brunswick city & MCD (Middlesex)..............	2,000	3559	744	2815	139,436	728	1.2	273.2	161.6	90.4	1087	308.3	5,532	930	406.3
New Milford borough & MCD (Bergen)................	80	480	12	468	4,679	14	100.0	18.0	1.7	100.0	955	18.3	1,107	139	12.0
New Providence borough & MCD (Union)............	92	743	40	702	39,218	503	4.2	16.9	1.7	93.3	1152	14.4	1,172	110	11.7
North Arlington borough & MCD (Bergen)...........	196	1248	121	1127	956	4	50.0	18.7	2.8	91.9	968	19.4	1,242	105	31.0
North Bergen township (Hudson)...............	799	1272	183	1089	0	0	0.0	109.4	16.6	44.1	998	99.2	1,587	77	134.8
North Brunswick township (Middlesex)..............	923	2170	132	2039	1,092	6	100.0	44.8	5.6	93.4	720	47.6	1,135	137	124.5
North Plainfield borough & MCD (Somerset)...........	359	1626	163	1463	0	0	0.0	23.5	2.2	76.3	825	20.7	935	45	12.1
Nutley township (Essex)	267	933	52	880	6,062	46	21.7	48.7	3.2	94.3	1544	41.9	1,466	44	8.3

1 Data for serious crimes have not been adjusted for underreporting. This may affect comparability between geographic areas over time.
2 Per 100,000 population estimated by the FBI. 3 Based on population estimated as of July 1 of the year shown.

Items 15–29

Table B. Incorporated Places, Census Designated Places (CDPs), and Minor Civil Divisions (MCDs) of 10,000 or More Population — **Land Area, Population, and Households, and Employment**

STATE City, town, township, borough, or CDP (county if applicable)	Land area,[1] 2010 (sq mi)	Total persons 2010	Total persons 2014	Percent change 2010–2014	Persons per square mile, 2014	Foreign born	Lives in same house as previous year	Median household income (dollars)	Income of $100,000 or more	Income below poverty level	Percent in labor force	Unemployment rate	Family households	One person households
	1	2	3	4	5	6	7	8	9	10	11	12	13	14
NEW JERSEY—Con.														
Oakland borough & MCD (Bergen)	8.455	12,755	13,046	2.3	1,543.0	9.5	93.3	$117,596	56.8	3.9	67.6	6.2	82.0	13.3
Ocean township (Monmouth)	10.877	27,291	27,200	-0.3	2,500.8	18.8	90.3	$78,056	39.2	9.3	69.1	7.2	71.0	24.8
Ocean Acres CDP	5.852	16,142	NA	NA	NA	4.2	92.8	$79,467	34.8	5.4	67.9	9.3	78.1	19.2
Ocean City city & MCD (Cape May)	6.337	11,701	11,374	-2.8	1,794.8	7.9	86.4	$59,522	31.1	7.6	56.2	6.6	55.7	39.5
Old Bridge CDP	7.110	23,753	NA	NA	NA	17.3	94.6	$100,484	50.3	4.9	69.0	8.0	79.9	15.4
Old Bridge township (Middlesex)	38.061	65,377	67,010	2.5	1,760.6	21.7	93.5	$84,300	42.7	4.3	70.1	7.8	70.1	24.2
Palisades Park borough & MCD (Bergen)	1.251	19,622	20,471	4.3	16,369.8	63.7	89.8	$59,429	25.6	17.1	65.1	7.4	68.3	21.8
Paramus borough & MCD (Bergen)	10.469	26,342	26,832	1.9	2,563.0	30.6	94.7	$96,454	47.8	3.2	57.3	6.4	80.7	17.6
Parsippany-Troy Hills township (Morris)	23.539	53,207	53,679	0.9	2,280.4	34.4	91.0	$87,081	42.5	6.1	68.9	8.5	70.9	25.1
Passaic city & MCD (Passaic)	3.147	69,781	71,509	2.5	22,724.6	43.3	95.8	$33,081	10.9	30.5	59.5	10.6	72.9	23.6
Paterson city & MCD (Passaic)	8.428	146,199	146,753	0.4	17,412.6	33.1	90.1	$33,964	12.1	29.0	57.2	11.5	73.8	22.7
Pemberton township (Burlington)	61.284	27,912	27,822	-0.3	454.0	8.0	89.4	$61,217	22.1	11.0	62.9	11.8	65.9	27.5
Pennsauken township (Camden)	10.435	35,885	35,561	-0.9	3,407.9	15.3	92.5	$60,433	25.3	11.3	69.9	11.4	70.7	25.3
Pennsville CDP	10.067	11,888	NA	NA	NA	3.6	89.6	$57,966	24.2	11.1	63.3	9.3	67.1	28.9
Pennsville township (Salem)	21.278	13,409	13,005	-3.0	611.2	3.8	89.9	$58,368	24.9	10.9	63.0	9.3	66.5	29.2
Pequannock township (Morris)	6.749	15,540	15,567	0.2	2,306.6	8.5	94.4	$89,435	42.2	5.5	63.4	6.6	61.3	34.4
Perth Amboy city & MCD (Middlesex)	4.702	50,814	52,328	3.0	11,128.8	39.1	93.3	$45,276	17.3	23.1	60.3	6.2	74.2	22.5
Phillipsburg town & MCD (Warren)	3.193	14,950	14,570	-2.5	4,563.1	10.0	90.5	$44,214	14.9	15.9	64.5	13.1	65.6	29.0
Pine Hill borough & MCD (Camden)	3.871	10,233	10,464	2.3	2,703.1	4.6	92.8	$50,876	19.7	13.5	67.7	9.4	66.0	29.7
Piscataway township (Middlesex)	18.839	56,042	58,982	5.2	3,130.8	33.0	85.6	$89,529	43.2	5.8	61.5	8.8	75.0	20.5
Plainfield city & MCD (Union)	6.023	49,808	50,955	2.3	8,460.6	39.2	84.1	$53,099	22.9	20.2	75.0	13.2	72.0	21.8
Plainsboro township (Middlesex)	11.785	22,999	23,429	1.9	1,988.1	46.4	83.6	$92,967	46.2	4.7	72.4	6.2	63.9	31.3
Pleasantville city & MCD (Atlantic)	5.694	20,249	20,467	1.1	3,594.8	24.9	83.8	$40,521	11.7	21.4	69.2	16.2	66.3	27.4
Point Pleasant borough & MCD (Ocean)	3.489	18,392	18,665	1.5	5,350.3	3.0	92.6	$84,163	43.9	6.7	68.8	8.8	66.9	28.4
Pompton Lakes borough & MCD (Passaic)	2.909	11,097	11,166	0.6	3,839.0	19.6	92.5	$87,284	41.2	4.4	74.9	8.8	65.9	28.6
Princeton & MCD (Mercer)	17.932	28,573	30,108	5.4	1,679.0	25.2	80.0	$116,875	56.4	6.1	64.2	7.2	64.7	26.4
Princeton Meadows CDP	2.077	13,834	NA	NA	NA	47.5	80.8	$83,518	39.8	5.6	75.5	6.9	60.5	33.4
Rahway city & MCD (Union)	3.897	27,346	28,528	4.3	7,321.1	23.1	91.7	$59,076	25.6	11.0	69.2	12.7	65.5	30.0
Ramsey borough & MCD (Bergen)	5.521	14,473	14,800	2.3	2,680.6	12.3	94.6	$122,165	63.4	2.6	68.8	5.4	76.5	21.2
Randolph township (Morris)	20.847	25,688	25,964	1.1	1,245.5	20.0	91.6	$117,560	58.6	4.6	71.7	3.1	77.4	20.0
Raritan township (Hunterdon)	37.527	22,177	22,061	-0.5	587.9	10.2	93.8	$113,214	55.5	4.5	71.4	6.7	74.2	22.2
Readington township (Hunterdon)	47.736	16,126	16,040	-0.5	336.0	8.0	92.2	$121,210	59.4	4.6	71.6	8.4	76.9	19.1
Red Bank borough & MCD (Monmouth)	1.739	12,206	12,445	2.0	7,156.6	23.7	84.8	$62,440	27.7	11.1	74.0	10.4	47.7	43.5
Ridgefield borough & MCD (Bergen)	2.552	11,032	11,289	2.3	4,424.3	47.4	92.1	$69,466	29.2	6.9	63.9	9.7	75.7	21.8
Ridgefield Park village & MCD (Bergen)	1.718	12,729	12,996	2.1	7,563.2	33.9	92.0	$64,741	29.2	8.1	69.3	6.1	71.4	26.6
Ridgewood village & MCD (Bergen)	5.752	24,958	25,496	2.2	4,432.6	21.3	91.6	$141,315	66.4	4.1	64.2	6.2	78.6	17.7
Ringwood borough & MCD (Passaic)	25.220	12,228	12,377	1.2	490.8	10.3	94.9	$106,880	57.0	1.9	69.8	6.8	84.1	13.0
River Edge borough & MCD (Bergen)	1.854	11,340	11,579	2.1	6,244.7	27.9	92.1	$104,250	51.1	1.8	67.6	4.5	78.2	18.9
Robbinsville township (Mercer)	20.316	13,642	14,112	3.4	694.6	14.9	89.0	$114,593	59.4	2.4	71.9	6.1	69.1	26.8
Robertsville CDP	5.919	11,297	NA	NA	NA	15.4	95.3	$123,405	60.7	1.5	60.8	5.8	84.0	14.4
Rockaway township (Morris)	41.648	24,161	24,441	1.2	586.8	16.7	94.0	$102,202	51.5	3.2	72.5	7.0	73.6	21.6
Roselle borough & MCD (Union)	2.651	21,085	21,551	2.2	8,128.6	29.6	90.3	$43,122	16.8	15.2	64.6	15.4	63.4	33.4
Roselle Park borough & MCD (Union)	1.232	13,297	13,595	2.2	11,036.8	28.2	92.3	$61,122	29.9	8.5	70.6	14.8	69.9	27.6
Roxbury township (Morris)	20.841	23,324	23,524	0.9	1,128.7	12.4	95.7	$104,453	53.2	4.4	70.4	6.8	79.4	17.7
Rutherford borough & MCD (Bergen)	2.813	18,061	18,464	2.2	6,563.8	24.6	91.5	$82,385	41.1	6.5	70.7	7.3	70.7	25.4
Saddle Brook township (Bergen)	2.689	13,659	13,984	2.4	5,200.9	22.9	94.0	$78,132	35.4	6.0	65.8	6.6	70.0	26.1
Sayreville borough & MCD (Middlesex)	15.835	42,702	45,262	6.0	2,858.4	27.1	94.2	$81,136	38.2	5.8	67.3	8.5	73.5	22.7
Scotch Plains township (Union)	9.019	23,510	24,086	2.5	2,670.7	17.5	91.6	$112,220	54.3	1.3	70.3	6.4	78.4	18.8
Secaucus town & MCD (Hudson)	5.762	16,260	18,416	13.3	3,195.9	36.1	87.6	$84,626	43.3	7.8	64.2	8.1	68.7	27.1
Short Hills CDP	5.251	13,165	NA	NA	NA	15.7	93.7	$235,216	80.6	2.3	62.1	3.6	87.8	11.7
Somerset CDP	6.327	22,083	NA	NA	NA	26.8	89.5	$95,667	48.1	5.2	68.3	6.8	70.1	24.6
Somers Point city & MCD (Atlantic)	4.030	10,795	10,756	-0.4	2,669.1	10.0	88.6	$47,945	18.7	13.2	66.6	8.4	58.3	34.7
Somerville borough & MCD (Somerset)	2.332	12,098	12,153	0.5	5,211.0	21.7	91.6	$72,527	30.1	5.5	71.6	6.9	63.0	32.3

1 Dry land or land partially or temporarily covered by water.
2 16 years old and over.

Table B. Incorporated Places, Census Designated Places (CDPs), and Minor Civil Divisions (MCDs) of 10,000 or More Population — **Crime, Construction, and Local Government Finance**

STATE City, town, township, borough, or CDP (county if applicable)	Serious crimes known to police, 2014[1] Total number	Rate[2] Total	Rate[2] Violent	Rate[2] Property	New residential construction authorized by building permits, 2014 Value ($1,000)	Number of housing units	Percent single family	Local government finance, 2012 General revenue Total (mil dol)	Intergovernmental Total (mil dol)	Percent from state gov.	Taxes per capita[3]	General expenditure Total (mil dol)	Per capita[3] Total	Capital outlays	Debt outstanding (mil dol)
	15	16	17	18	19	20	21	22	23	24	25	26	27	28	29
NEW JERSEY—Con.															
Oakland borough & MCD (Bergen)	160	1228	23	1205	727	2	100.0	17.8	1.5	99.0	1183	17.4	1,350	177	12.1
Ocean township (Monmouth)	779	2860	173	2687	6,100	20	100.0	38.4	3.2	94.3	919	34.1	1,252	215	48.7
Ocean Acres CDP	NA	NA	NA	NA	NA	NA	NA	NA	NA	NA	NA	NA	NA	NA	NA
Ocean City city & MCD (Cape May)	488	4284	114	4170	68,109	253	44.7	66.1	5.0	60.3	4424	68.4	5,925	953	64.3
Old Bridge CDP	NA	NA	NA	NA	NA	NA	NA	NA	NA	NA	NA	NA	NA	NA	NA
Old Bridge township (Middlesex)	819	1223	43	1180	20,234	128	50.0	70.1	6.6	98.0	551	60.7	916	32	90.3
Palisades Park borough & MCD (Bergen)	123	601	68	532	19,401	103	71.8	19.6	1.0	96.4	812	18.3	917	82	8.8
Paramus borough & MCD (Bergen)	1,219	4550	86	4464	8,515	17	100.0	60.6	4.7	91.3	1859	49.8	1,869	77	39.3
Parsippany-Troy Hills township (Morris)	485	898	68	829	5,387	24	100.0	80.4	5.3	99.2	934	86.9	1,618	406	94.2
Passaic city & MCD (Passaic)	1,601	2248	651	1596	2,181	37	18.9	116.8	43.8	42.5	840	115.2	1,634	39	18.9
Paterson city & MCD (Passaic)	5,048	3456	816	2640	11,683	147	2.7	273.4	94.3	64.3	959	265.5	1,818	72	119.6
Pemberton township (Burlington)	664	2379	362	2017	461	7	100.0	25.1	4.1	99.0	547	23.1	827	76	21.9
Pennsauken township (Camden)	1,059	2952	229	2723	897	16	37.5	40.8	8.4	80.2	636	41.8	1,169	115	26.0
Pennsville CDP	NA	NA	NA	NA	NA	NA	NA	NA	NA	NA	NA	NA	NA	NA	NA
Pennsville township (Salem)	293	2245	100	2145	538	3	100.0	17.2	5.6	99.8	504	8.8	663	21	12.3
Pequannock township (Morris)	124	791	83	708	5,606	23	100.0	19.7	2.5	72.1	782	19.3	1,241	73	13.2
Perth Amboy city & MCD (Middlesex)	1,234	2358	472	1886	547	5	60.0	99.9	23.5	45.3	1136	92.3	1,780	148	91.3
Phillipsburg town & MCD (Warren)	366	2509	178	2331	1,935	12	100.0	26.6	5.8	49.0	871	23.4	1,596	138	9.8
Pine Hill borough & MCD (Camden)	336	3175	369	2806	13,806	189	20.6	9.1	1.0	94.9	534	7.3	697	46	7.3
Piscataway township (Middlesex)	634	1073	83	990	2,899	19	73.7	62.5	7.3	99.8	737	53.2	921	139	60.7
Plainfield city & MCD (Union)	1,572	3092	710	2382	266	3	100.0	100.9	20.9	40.2	1089	102.8	2,039	6	48.0
Plainsboro township (Middlesex)	128	546	26	521	1,070	3	100.0	23.8	2.0	96.6	824	28.7	1,237	419	45.9
Pleasantville city & MCD (Atlantic)	595	2891	821	2070	32,722	247	15.4	30.8	7.7	77.4	965	27.8	1,355	64	14.3
Point Pleasant borough & MCD (Ocean)	228	1229	43	1186	15,773	124	51.6	21.4	1.6	97.2	867	18.2	988	155	26.7
Pompton Lakes borough & MCD (Passaic)	102	913	81	832	1,423	9	100.0	14.3	1.4	97.4	870	15.3	1,373	194	7.5
Princeton borough (Mercer)	290	995	69	926	11,466	20	100.0	29.7	3.9	30.0	443	28.9	1,008	147	45.4
Princeton Meadows CDP	NA	NA	NA	NA	NA	NA	NA	NA	NA	NA	NA	NA	NA	NA	NA
Rahway city & MCD (Union)	365	1273	181	1092	3,079	123	6.5	52.2	8.2	52.9	1263	40.3	1,445	119	64.7
Ramsey borough & MCD (Bergen)	166	1123	68	1055	6,031	18	100.0	23.6	1.6	99.2	1276	25.6	1,749	209	8.1
Randolph township (Morris)	188	722	27	695	19,338	71	4.2	30.2	2.6	80.2	859	28.1	1,084	90	16.1
Raritan township (Hunterdon)	163	739	50	689	7,030	36	100.0	16.3	2.4	95.3	599	15.1	681	23	24.2
Readington township (Hunterdon)	127	790	6	784	13,935	49	100.0	17.6	1.5	99.9	873	16.7	1,038	106	61.0
Red Bank borough & MCD (Monmouth)	299	2449	197	2252	4,066	95	14.7	23.3	2.7	81.3	1173	26.8	2,199	225	23.8
Ridgefield borough & MCD (Bergen)	53	470	9	461	4,422	23	56.5	13.1	6.1	100.0	560	10.7	960	0	15.3
Ridgefield Park village & MCD (Bergen)	132	1016	46	970	372	5	100.0	20.0	1.6	94.5	1328	17.7	1,377	69	13.3
Ridgewood village & MCD (Bergen)	183	718	24	695	7,168	20	90.0	42.4	3.1	76.6	1397	43.2	1,712	51	55.2
Ringwood borough & MCD (Passaic)	65	525	40	485	2,762	13	100.0	12.1	0.4	100.0	904	11.4	926	0	15.3
River Edge borough & MCD (Bergen)	70	605	17	588	2,455	12	100.0	13.4	1.3	94.0	1047	14.9	1,298	175	9.5
Robbinsville township (Mercer)	113	797	49	748	9,287	62	54.8	21.0	2.7	65.2	1142	19.6	1,409	177	54.5
Robertsville CDP	NA	NA	NA	NA	NA	NA	NA	NA	NA	NA	NA	NA	NA	NA	NA
Rockaway township (Morris)	437	1778	45	1734	6,127	146	8.9	35.5	2.2	100.0	1212	34.7	1,422	65	21.9
Roselle borough & MCD (Union)	441	2045	301	1744	8	0	0.0	33.9	2.4	100.0	1436	31.1	1,456	60	13.2
Roselle Park borough & MCD (Union)	132	971	81	890	1,386	21	100.0	16.1	1.3	98.0	901	15.8	1,174	165	15.8
Roxbury township (Morris)	288	1218	17	1201	2,486	20	100.0	33.0	2.3	100.0	1021	29.8	1,268	109	14.5
Rutherford borough & MCD (Bergen)	267	1447	43	1404	2	0	0.0	28.0	2.2	96.3	1331	24.2	1,322	53	14.2
Saddle Brook township (Bergen)	298	2133	72	2061	7,380	66	18.2	18.4	1.8	78.3	1186	17.8	1,282	0	27.0
Sayreville borough & MCD (Middlesex)	501	1115	80	1035	2,716	17	100.0	48.5	12.4	79.2	663	48.1	1,097	44	53.0
Scotch Plains township (Union)	253	1049	79	970	4,957	24	100.0	24.8	2.5	97.9	763	23.9	1,001	73	16.0
Secaucus town & MCD (Hudson)	546	2890	196	2695	35,734	632	2.1	49.1	5.6	50.7	2169	46.6	2,629	64	42.1
Short Hills CDP	NA	NA	NA	NA	NA	NA	NA	NA	NA	NA	NA	NA	NA	NA	NA
Somerset CDP	NA	NA	NA	NA	NA	NA	NA	NA	NA	NA	NA	NA	NA	NA	NA
Somers Point city & MCD (Atlantic)	358	3320	223	3098	3,599	14	100.0	14.7	1.6	68.7	950	15.4	1,428	266	13.6
Somerville borough & MCD (Somerset)	206	1691	164	1527	357	2	100.0	18.8	1.6	99.3	1114	17.5	1,436	225	21.8

1 Data for serious crimes have not been adjusted for underreporting. This may affect comparability between geographic areas over time.
2 Per 100,000 population estimated by the FBI.   3 Based on population estimated as of July 1 of the year shown.

Table B. Incorporated Places, Census Designated Places (CDPs), and Minor Civil Divisions (MCDs) of 10,000 or More Population — **Land Area, Population, and Households, and Employment**

STATE City, town, township, borough, or CDP (county if applicable)	Land area,[1] 2010 (sq mi)	Total persons 2010	Total persons 2014	Percent change 2010–2014	Persons per square mile, 2014	Foreign born	Lives in same house as previous year	Median household income (dollars)	Income of $100,000 or more	Income below poverty level	Percent in labor force	Unemploy- ment rate	Family households	One person households
	1	2	3	4	5	6	7	8	9	10	11	12	13	14
NEW JERSEY—Con.														
Southampton township (Burlington)	43.668	10,464	10,362	-1.0	237.3	4.3	95.4	$56,130	23.9	6.2	50.8	7.7	65.9	31.5
South Brunswick township (Middlesex)	40.651	43,417	45,163	4.0	1,111.0	33.7	90.9	$110,167	56.8	2.8	69.7	6.2	77.7	18.5
South Orange Village township (Essex)	2.856	16,198	16,362	1.0	5,730.0	16.4	91.7	$119,888	56.8	7.4	62.0	8.7	68.2	26.6
South Plainfield borough & MCD (Middlesex)	8.327	23,385	23,960	2.5	2,877.5	23.0	92.8	$90,880	43.6	4.7	69.3	7.8	77.8	18.0
South River borough & MCD (Middlesex)	2.769	16,008	16,334	2.0	5,898.6	28.8	94.1	$65,509	26.2	10.4	70.9	15.2	68.9	26.5
Sparta township (Sussex)	36.945	19,723	19,333	-2.0	523.3	8.6	94.3	$126,090	63.0	4.0	68.1	6.8	79.8	17.7
Springdale CDP	5.349	14,518	NA	NA	NA	14.5	93.0	$116,523	58.6	2.9	65.1	5.4	80.8	16.3
Springfield township (Union)	5.174	15,817	17,193	8.7	3,322.9	22.9	92.7	$100,461	50.5	6.3	71.4	6.2	62.9	33.0
Stafford township (Ocean)	45.848	26,535	26,809	1.0	584.7	6.3	92.1	$73,968	34.0	6.1	62.2	9.2	72.2	24.8
Summit city & MCD (Union)	5.996	21,457	22,071	2.9	3,681.3	20.6	93.3	$121,509	59.8	5.7	65.2	6.2	72.3	23.9
Teaneck township (Bergen)	6.026	39,796	40,587	2.0	6,735.2	23.5	93.9	$95,435	47.1	6.6	66.4	6.8	76.7	18.8
Tenafly borough & MCD (Bergen)	4.601	14,488	14,816	2.3	3,220.3	29.7	85.9	$140,923	64.0	9.0	61.9	6.9	82.1	16.6
Tinton Falls borough & MCD (Monmouth)	15.487	17,892	17,898	0.0	1,155.7	6.7	89.5	$73,278	36.0	6.4	58.5	9.5	52.3	43.7
Toms River CDP	38.943	88,791	NA	NA	NA	9.7	89.9	$73,321	34.9	6.5	65.0	8.6	70.0	25.1
Toms River township (Ocean)	40.489	91,238	91,250	0.0	2,253.7	9.5	89.8	$72,939	34.6	6.6	64.4	8.7	69.0	26.1
Totowa borough & MCD (Passaic)	3.997	10,804	10,937	1.2	2,736.1	19.5	96.1	$85,014	42.1	6.4	59.5	11.9	72.1	24.1
Trenton city & MCD (Mercer)	7.648	84,910	84,034	-1.0	10,987.0	23.6	84.0	$35,647	10.3	28.9	61.6	18.5	62.3	31.2
Union township (Union)	9.071	56,642	57,832	2.1	6,375.2	28.7	93.5	$73,249	33.8	8.9	66.4	9.9	70.1	27.1
Union City city & MCD (Hudson)	1.283	66,439	68,668	3.4	53,534.1	57.8	87.4	$40,939	14.4	24.0	68.2	12.5	68.7	24.9
Upper township (Cape May)	62.149	12,373	12,113	-2.1	194.9	2.2	94.0	$77,198	36.4	4.6	67.8	6.9	77.5	20.2
Upper Montclair CDP	2.538	11,565	NA	NA	NA	10.8	92.7	$167,806	68.9	3.6	70.9	5.2	74.1	20.8
Ventnor City city & MCD (Atlantic)	1.951	10,650	10,597	-0.5	5,430.3	27.0	90.8	$50,129	21.0	14.4	60.5	13.2	56.9	34.7
Vernon township (Sussex)	67.225	23,542	22,799	-3.2	339.1	6.6	92.5	$87,707	41.4	5.7	76.0	10.5	77.3	17.1
Verona township (Essex)	2.756	13,338	13,701	2.7	4,971.6	12.2	94.4	$100,503	50.3	2.6	67.0	6.9	65.5	31.0
Vineland city & MCD (Cumberland)	68.424	60,724	61,171	0.7	894.0	12.6	90.9	$50,690	20.3	15.2	63.1	11.7	70.0	24.6
Voorhees township (Camden)	11.494	29,316	29,023	-1.0	2,525.0	20.0	84.7	$75,858	37.4	7.7	62.9	8.1	64.5	29.7
Wall township (Monmouth)	30.673	26,164	26,032	-0.5	848.7	5.0	93.6	$93,768	47.3	4.7	64.8	6.4	68.7	26.1
Wallington borough & MCD (Bergen)	0.984	11,335	11,626	2.6	11,820.5	47.3	95.8	$53,502	22.2	10.5	66.4	6.7	67.2	27.6
Wanaque borough & MCD (Passaic)	8.009	11,115	11,447	3.0	1,429.2	14.5	92.7	$85,373	40.1	4.5	67.0	14.5	74.6	21.6
Wantage township (Sussex)	66.753	11,358	11,154	-1.8	167.1	4.9	95.0	$79,965	37.4	4.0	69.2	9.6	78.2	17.5
Warren township (Somerset)	19.551	15,311	15,948	4.2	815.7	20.8	97.0	$144,233	65.5	2.9	63.7	6.4	85.5	12.8
Washington township (Gloucester)	21.382	48,547	47,841	-1.5	2,237.4	6.4	93.5	$83,600	40.6	5.2	69.9	10.2	77.0	20.3
Washington township (Morris)	44.447	18,537	18,706	0.9	420.9	8.2	95.9	$125,149	60.7	3.0	70.4	6.5	79.9	15.9
Waterford township (Camden)	36.041	10,649	10,732	0.8	297.8	2.9	95.3	$71,807	32.6	4.9	67.6	11.9	76.0	19.6
Wayne township (Passaic)	23.750	54,709	55,049	0.6	2,317.8	18.6	91.5	$104,825	52.8	5.4	66.2	8.6	75.8	20.4
Weehawken township (Hudson)	0.785	12,554	13,870	10.5	17,676.0	37.5	85.5	$72,874	39.1	10.7	72.6	7.4	54.9	34.2
West Caldwell township (Essex)	5.056	10,794	11,030	2.2	2,181.5	11.2	94.7	$101,083	50.3	3.6	62.3	7.3	73.9	23.7
West Deptford township (Gloucester)	15.411	21,677	21,382	-1.4	1,387.4	4.8	90.1	$67,866	30.4	7.8	67.4	9.9	62.4	30.6
Westfield town & MCD (Union)	6.719	30,316	30,890	1.9	4,597.6	10.7	90.7	$138,165	63.8	2.0	67.8	7.2	78.3	19.5
West Freehold CDP	5.912	13,613	NA	NA	NA	11.0	95.6	$104,841	53.5	4.3	69.4	6.6	74.2	22.0
West Milford township (Passaic)	76.093	26,249	26,632	1.5	350.0	6.0	94.3	$96,773	48.4	4.4	72.4	8.9	75.5	20.9
West New York town & MCD (Hudson)	0.995	49,708	52,597	5.8	52,882.8	57.7	83.1	$45,412	19.0	22.5	71.3	13.3	63.2	27.6
West Orange township (Essex)	12.045	46,239	46,995	1.6	3,901.5	29.0	91.4	$90,031	45.8	6.1	69.3	8.0	69.4	26.9
West Windsor township (Mercer)	25.564	27,165	28,465	4.8	1,113.5	38.2	87.3	$161,716	67.9	4.8	69.1	6.1	81.2	16.1
Westwood borough & MCD (Bergen)	2.264	10,908	11,149	2.2	4,924.5	17.6	85.8	$85,588	42.2	6.6	65.7	5.9	69.0	28.3
Williamstown CDP	7.419	15,567	NA	NA	NA	4.8	90.4	$63,281	25.8	9.8	67.9	11.6	71.6	21.5
Willingboro township (Burlington)	7.738	31,625	31,804	0.6	4,109.9	14.3	91.0	$68,479	27.5	6.3	65.7	15.0	77.0	19.7
Winslow township (Camden)	57.342	39,499	38,895	-1.5	678.2	9.1	87.7	$69,312	31.7	8.6	69.2	11.9	72.5	22.9
Woodbridge CDP	3.854	19,265	NA	NA	NA	30.4	85.3	$86,506	41.5	7.0	70.2	7.8	74.5	20.6
Woodbridge township (Middlesex)	23.219	99,580	100,824	1.2	4,342.3	30.6	90.5	$80,134	37.2	6.7	65.5	8.1	76.2	19.9
Woodbury city & MCD (Gloucester)	2.009	10,174	10,016	-1.6	4,985.4	5.8	89.6	$53,359	25.1	18.3	66.4	11.3	60.1	34.6
Woodland Park borough & MCD (Passaic)	2.934	11,819	12,403	4.9	4,227.3	26.9	93.8	$79,732	41.0	5.9	66.7	8.1	72.2	23.4
Woolwich township (Gloucester)	20.909	10,200	11,783	15.5	563.5	9.5	90.8	$117,571	63.2	3.5	76.0	4.2	83.5	15.1
Wyckoff township (Bergen)	6.540	16,683	17,039	2.1	2,605.2	11.3	94.5	$141,964	64.2	2.6	61.9	6.1	79.8	19.2
NEW MEXICO	121,298.143	2,059,192	2,085,572	1.3	17.2	9.9	85.5	$44,968	17.3	18.9	60.2	9.6	65.1	28.9
Alamogordo city	21.435	30,415	31,060	2.1	1,449.0	9.6	80.3	$43,460	11.6	16.6	56.6	10.6	64.9	30.3
Albuquerque city	188.149	546,360	557,169	2.0	2,961.3	10.7	83.1	$47,413	18.9	17.0	65.3	8.5	59.9	32.7
Artesia city	9.940	11,321	11,842	4.6	1,191.4	5.3	86.6	$48,103	19.3	13.3	61.2	4.3	74.2	23.5

1 Dry land or land partially or temporarily covered by water.
2 16 years old and over.

Table B. Incorporated Places, Census Designated Places (CDPs), and Minor Civil Divisions (MCDs) of 10,000 or More Population — Crime, Construction, and Local Government Finance

STATE City, town, township, borough, or CDP (county if applicable)	Serious crimes known to police, 2014[1] Total number	Rate[2] Total	Rate[2] Violent	Rate[2] Property	New residential construction authorized by building permits, 2014 Value ($1,000)	Number of housing units	Percent single family	Local government finance, 2012 General revenue Total (mil dol)	Intergovernmental Total (mil dol)	Percent from state gov.	Taxes per capita[3]	General expenditure Total (mil dol)	Per capita[3] Total	Per capita[3] Capital outlays	Debt outstanding (mil dol)
	15	16	17	18	19	20	21	22	23	24	25	26	27	28	29
NEW JERSEY—Con.															
Southampton township (Burlington)	NA	NA	NA	NA	2,629	12	100.0	5.8	1.3	100.0	396	5.2	496	39	10.0
South Brunswick township (Middlesex)	397	880	22	858	13,735	65	100.0	59.9	7.0	90.0	792	59.0	1,330	201	95.4
South Orange Village township (Essex)	277	1697	147	1550	3,184	215	0.0	32.2	2.8	90.7	1369	30.3	1,861	101	52.7
South Plainfield borough & MCD (Middlesex)	400	1673	79	1593	6,160	107	40.2	32.1	3.7	93.5	858	30.4	1,284	57	13.8
South River borough & MCD (Middlesex)	179	1097	147	950	571	4	50.0	12.3	1.3	94.4	628	14.6	904	71	28.6
Sparta township (Sussex)	88	454	46	408	6,529	38	86.8	24.4	2.0	74.6	939	19.6	1,001	0	31.9
Springdale CDP	NA	NA	NA	NA	NA	NA	NA	NA	NA	NA	NA	NA	NA	NA	NA
Springfield township (Union)	167	976	12	965	852	4	100.0	28.4	2.7	96.3	1383	27.3	1,616	134	18.0
Stafford township (Ocean)	357	1321	63	1258	48,406	284	100.0	47.2	3.1	90.2	1243	41.0	1,522	129	139.1
Summit city & MCD (Union)	186	840	54	786	8,140	17	100.0	116.2	9.2	71.9	4436	119.1	5,438	775	65.0
Teaneck township (Bergen)	519	1281	123	1157	18,089	79	21.5	62.1	3.6	95.4	1405	61.9	1,537	125	25.2
Tenafly borough & MCD (Bergen)	94	636	7	630	2,435	10	100.0	25.3	1.2	100.0	1591	27.8	1,896	405	20.1
Tinton Falls borough & MCD (Monmouth)	308	1712	17	1696	37	2	100.0	23.8	1.7	100.0	939	22.7	1,272	128	20.9
Toms River CDP	NA	NA	NA	NA	NA	NA	NA	NA	NA	NA	NA	NA	NA	NA	NA
Toms River township (Ocean)	2,545	2777	86	2691	110,485	803	92.7	110.1	10.8	82.9	764	108.6	1,178	94	112.0
Totowa borough & MCD (Passaic)	346	3161	146	3015	2,902	15	100.0	16.0	1.9	91.2	1155	14.3	1,312	106	0.5
Trenton city & MCD (Mercer)	2,960	3510	1104	2406	55	10	0.0	505.3	395.0	94.6	938	482.0	5,714	70	390.2
Union township (Union)	1,041	1800	154	1646	1,184	4	100.0	84.8	6.4	100.0	1231	72.2	1,260	0	33.3
Union City city & MCD (Hudson)	1,425	2072	347	1724	5,836	43	0.0	355.1	263.5	96.4	1184	313.3	4,583	154	82.9
Upper township (Cape May)	NA	NA	NA	NA	3,588	13	100.0	10.3	6.4	100.0	279	8.9	723	0	5.1
Upper Montclair CDP	NA	NA	NA	NA	NA	NA	NA	NA	NA	NA	NA	NA	NA	NA	NA
Ventnor City city & MCD (Atlantic)	333	3134	132	3002	5,652	6	33.3	49.2	4.8	89.4	3831	53.3	5,010	785	38.5
Vernon township (Sussex)	321	1404	13	1391	4,765	30	50.0	23.6	2.8	95.9	868	20.6	890	95	27.3
Verona township (Essex)	69	501	29	472	8,909	83	53.0	21.5	1.4	93.1	1253	21.1	1,579	222	40.1
Vineland city & MCD (Cumberland)	2,510	4107	437	3670	7,451	71	100.0	73.4	16.1	56.5	602	67.7	1,110	67	133.2
Voorhees township (Camden)	594	2031	120	1912	4,836	21	100.0	26.4	3.0	90.8	696	31.0	1,058	281	33.6
Wall township (Monmouth)	354	1358	38	1319	8,895	40	100.0	39.2	3.8	97.3	1068	35.1	1,346	71	37.1
Wallington borough & MCD (Bergen)	125	1077	69	1008	3,190	34	100.0	10.4	0.8	92.7	710	12.5	1,085	231	13.6
Wanaque borough & MCD (Passaic)	84	747	89	658	658	8	0.0	15.4	1.1	96.9	850	14.4	1,284	86	25.1
Wantage township (Sussex)	NA	NA	NA	NA	5,402	60	26.7	7.1	1.4	98.3	435	5.0	449	37	6.2
Warren township (Somerset)	77	481	25	456	6,123	22	100.0	20.0	1.3	100.0	815	17.5	1,110	124	23.0
Washington township (Gloucester)	928	1929	64	1865	3,438	12	100.0	40.5	3.7	96.9	589	39.1	811	1	37.7
Washington township (Morris)	40	213	37	176	3,438	12	100.0	17.8	2.4	75.5	686	15.5	824	72	11.0
Waterford township (Camden)	93	858	83	775	4,402	34	100.0	9.1	1.4	100.0	578	9.6	904	72	9.8
Wayne township (Passaic)	1,090	1975	67	1908	6,862	19	100.0	83.6	5.5	91.8	1194	85.1	1,546	220	60.9
Weehawken township (Hudson)	282	2077	140	1937	41,373	403	0.0	35.5	2.2	100.0	2143	50.1	3,869	1,680	72.3
West Caldwell township (Essex)	56	513	46	467	4,839	22	100.0	18.5	2.0	71.9	1317	20.5	1,889	330	13.5
West Deptford township (Gloucester)	388	1805	51	1754	1,823	13	100.0	33.8	3.3	79.8	1082	28.8	1,337	19	126.0
Westfield town & MCD (Union)	293	945	61	883	25,608	72	100.0	37.4	4.0	79.9	967	39.3	1,283	88	20.7
West Freehold CDP	NA	NA	NA	NA	NA	NA	NA	NA	NA	NA	NA	NA	NA	NA	NA
West Milford township (Passaic)	278	1044	79	965	2,521	22	72.7	31.3	3.8	98.8	912	33.5	1,263	122	39.9
West New York town & MCD (Hudson)	717	1358	290	1068	3,673	58	0.0	209.6	134.4	93.8	986	216.0	4,160	249	52.4
West Orange township (Essex)	808	1724	218	1507	3,006	11	100.0	69.3	7.8	98.0	1192	67.4	1,443	170	50.4
West Windsor township (Mercer)	384	1338	42	1296	6,471	76	3.9	41.4	2.4	96.0	1005	38.3	1,355	0	45.2
Westwood borough & MCD (Bergen)	47	422	45	377	1,417	5	100.0	15.8	1.5	95.8	1236	15.5	1,402	158	19.6
Williamstown CDP	NA	NA	NA	NA	NA	NA	NA	NA	NA	NA	NA	NA	NA	NA	NA
Willingboro township (Burlington)	807	2526	385	2141	1,236	122	1.6	43.7	5.9	97.0	1004	41.6	1,304	198	55.6
Winslow township (Camden)	582	1487	184	1303	9,711	0	0.0	29.8	6.4	99.9	423	31.4	800	93	28.6
Woodbridge CDP	NA	NA	NA	NA	NA	NA	NA	NA	NA	NA	NA	NA	NA	NA	NA
Woodbridge township (Middlesex)	1,931	1912	115	1798	0	0	0.0	154.3	41.4	58.0	762	152.2	1,515	239	185.1
Woodbury city & MCD (Gloucester)	511	5074	308	4766	336	1	100.0	13.2	1.7	100.0	1018	13.5	1,336	76	19.3
Woodland Park borough & MCD (Passaic)	175	1412	40	1372	16,108	120	6.7	14.3	1.4	86.7	1009	13.9	1,142	125	16.4
Woolwich township (Gloucester)	55	477	17	460	8,047	71	100.0	6.1	1.1	45.5	428	6.7	612	69	7.7
Wyckoff township (Bergen)	88	517	12	506	8,470	15	100.0	19.4	1.2	100.0	837	17.6	1,042	37	0.9
NEW MEXICO	86,336	4140	597	3542	881,907	4,799	84.5	X	X	X	X	X	X	X	X
Alamogordo city	1,061	3363	295	3069	NA	NA	NA	41.0	11.2	83.4	560	39.0	1,236	363	58.7
Albuquerque city	35,371	6329	883	5446	209,154	1,416	78.4	951.2	282.5	80.4	663	827.4	1,491	292	2091.8
Artesia city	553	4801	1328	3473	9,599	46	100.0	32.4	23.7	96.7	346	26.8	2,356	411	29.8

1 Data for serious crimes have not been adjusted for underreporting. This may affect comparability between geographic areas over time.
2 Per 100,000 population estimated by the FBI.   3 Based on population estimated as of July 1 of the year shown.

Table B. Incorporated Places, Census Designated Places (CDPs), and Minor Civil Divisions (MCDs) of 10,000 or More Population — Land Area, Population, and Households, and Employment

STATE City, town, township, borough, or CDP (county if applicable)	Land area,[1] 2010 (sq mi)	Total persons 2010	Total persons 2014	Percent change 2010–2014	Persons per square mile, 2014	Foreign born	Lives in same house as previous year	Median household income (dollars)	Income of $100,000 or more	Income below poverty level	Percent in labor force	Unemploy-ment rate	Family households	One person households
	1	2	3	4	5	6	7	8	9	10	11	12	13	14
NEW MEXICO—Con.														
Carlsbad city.............	28.909	26,200	28,103	7.3	972.1	4.3	83.5	$48,058	18.2	15.6	63.0	6.7	67.1	29.0
Chaparral CDP............	59.231	14,631	NA	NA	NA	32.0	93.9	$31,726	5.8	33.7	58.4	14.5	87.4	11.3
Clovis city.................	23.498	37,790	39,860	5.5	1,696.3	8.2	77.1	$40,136	11.4	19.4	64.4	9.5	65.2	29.9
Deming city...............	16.239	14,848	14,605	-1.6	899.4	16.2	76.9	$25,526	4.4	31.1	54.4	18.8	58.2	35.6
Española city.............	7.843	10,234	10,130	-1.0	1,291.6	13.8	91.3	$30,336	9.7	28.5	59.8	13.7	58.0	37.6
Farmington city..........	32.230	45,886	44,445	-3.1	1,379.0	4.6	86.0	$55,810	23.0	16.6	63.4	6.9	70.1	25.9
Gallup city................	18.908	21,788	22,469	3.1	1,188.3	5.5	85.8	$47,177	17.6	23.8	56.5	7.0	68.8	27.6
Hobbs city................	26.078	34,133	37,118	8.7	1,423.3	16.9	87.3	$53,750	21.0	17.4	61.8	5.6	74.0	22.5
Las Cruces city..........	76.939	97,636	101,408	3.9	1,318.0	10.7	76.2	$40,658	14.3	22.4	61.9	11.4	60.4	29.9
Las Vegas city...........	7.825	14,055	13,518	-3.8	1,727.6	3.8	87.1	$21,539	8.0	36.5	40.7	7.6	46.9	45.6
Los Alamos CDP.........	11.142	12,019	NA	NA	NA	12.0	84.5	$107,031	53.2	3.9	67.3	3.7	62.6	32.0
Los Lunas village........	14.791	14,935	15,206	1.8	1,028.1	5.2	89.7	$51,635	19.1	14.4	58.6	9.6	66.2	28.8
Lovington city............	4.793	11,009	11,840	7.5	2,470.5	20.0	90.8	$47,993	12.3	21.1	58.8	7.8	77.6	17.4
North Valley CDP........	7.021	11,333	NA	NA	NA	8.3	86.6	$46,471	20.5	18.3	56.9	8.4	61.9	31.0
Portales city..............	7.036	12,265	12,233	-0.3	1,738.7	7.3	71.9	$33,642	6.2	29.8	62.8	10.8	61.2	28.7
Rio Rancho city..........	103.337	87,394	93,820	7.4	907.9	5.9	87.6	$59,243	23.5	10.8	64.1	7.6	70.6	23.1
Roswell city..............	29.857	48,411	48,608	0.4	1,628.0	13.3	81.8	$38,919	12.7	22.4	59.7	7.9	67.5	28.4
Santa Fe city.............	46.582	67,968	70,297	3.4	1,509.1	12.9	80.5	$50,213	20.9	14.9	64.5	9.1	50.9	39.8
Silver City town..........	10.129	10,315	10,172	-1.4	1,004.3	5.5	87.0	$38,258	11.7	20.8	55.8	8.5	59.2	37.6
South Valley CDP........	28.798	40,976	NA	NA	NA	17.8	89.5	$36,746	11.3	24.7	57.7	12.0	72.4	20.9
Sunland Park city........	12.614	14,140	15,400	8.9	1,220.9	37.2	92.8	$28,710	6.1	37.8	64.6	12.0	84.3	13.7
NEW YORK	47,126.397	19,378,112	19,746,227	1.9	419.0	22.3	88.9	$58,687	27.9	14.8	63.5	8.9	63.9	29.6
Albany city & MCD (Albany)	21.388	97,856	98,566	0.7	4,608.4	11.2	79.9	$41,099	15.5	23.7	61.0	8.9	42.3	43.9
Alden town (Erie)*	34.308	10,865	10,629	-2.2	309.8	2.6	83.9	$62,305	22.2	8.2	54.9	8.6	73.9	22.1
Amherst town (Erie)*	53.196	122,366	124,837	2.0	2,346.7	12.9	85.4	$68,106	32.3	9.4	62.1	5.1	61.9	31.3
Amsterdam city & MCD (Montgomery)	5.872	18,627	18,135	-2.6	3,088.1	5.5	84.1	$36,961	13.5	24.3	59.9	13.2	55.3	39.1
Arcadia town (Wayne)*	52.033	14,240	13,915	-2.3	267.4	3.2	87.1	$43,451	9.4	15.7	59.7	8.3	62.0	31.9
Auburn city & MCD (Cayuga) ...	8.336	27,688	27,019	-2.4	3,241.1	3.1	80.7	$38,399	11.8	19.6	58.1	11.0	53.4	40.5
Aurora town (Erie)*	36.394	13,782	13,839	0.4	380.3	2.7	89.6	$72,787	31.4	6.0	67.4	4.0	71.1	24.8
Babylon village	2.447	12,166	12,172	0.0	4,974.6	10.4	92.7	$101,549	51.3	5.3	69.8	6.6	66.9	24.7
Babylon town (Suffolk)*	52.343	213,603	214,191	0.3	4,092.0	19.1	93.4	$81,000	38.5	6.9	66.1	7.3	74.4	21.4
Baldwin CDP..............	2.963	24,033	NA	NA	NA	26.8	94.3	$92,990	44.7	7.0	69.6	7.5	84.9	12.0
Ballston town (Saratoga)*	29.576	9,765	10,411	6.6	352.0	2.2	89.5	$81,495	37.6	5.7	65.0	8.0	74.0	20.5
Batavia city & MCD (Genesee).	5.195	15,447	15,077	-2.4	2,902.0	3.4	81.5	$40,882	12.4	17.7	61.8	7.5	55.5	35.2
Bath town (Steuben)*	95.323	12,379	12,184	-1.6	127.8	2.0	84.2	$41,339	12.4	19.0	55.2	7.8	54.5	37.8
Bay Shore CDP...........	5.375	26,337	NA	NA	NA	23.1	88.2	$67,539	30.3	11.0	71.6	8.5	65.4	29.2
Beacon city & MCD (Dutchess)	4.739	14,604	14,238	-2.5	3,004.4	11.8	85.0	$63,284	27.4	13.2	63.0	11.5	59.4	32.6
Bedford town (Westchester)	37.176	17,335	17,910	3.3	481.8	16.3	91.7	$119,069	58.3	4.6	59.0	7.5	80.8	16.3
Beekman town (Dutchess)	29.838	14,587	14,473	-0.8	485.0	9.9	93.0	$96,970	49.1	4.6	57.6	7.0	82.9	13.9
Bellmore CDP.............	2.359	16,218	NA	NA	NA	9.4	95.2	$113,306	55.5	2.1	66.9	6.8	78.9	17.9
Bethlehem town (Albany)	49.030	33,658	34,685	3.1	707.4	6.7	90.3	$92,188	44.9	4.1	68.2	5.5	67.6	26.6
Bethpage CDP............	3.576	16,429	NA	NA	NA	12.9	97.0	$95,686	48.1	3.4	61.2	7.2	77.2	20.9
Binghamton city & MCD (Broome)	10.489	47,376	46,299	-2.3	4,414.1	9.7	79.6	$30,828	10.0	29.5	54.2	11.4	47.3	40.2
Blooming Grove town (Orange)*	34.736	18,027	17,750	-1.5	511.0	6.1	93.9	$87,500	42.8	5.4	68.7	5.9	73.4	21.3
Bohemia CDP.............	8.610	10,180	NA	NA	NA	5.6	92.5	$87,099	43.8	5.0	63.6	8.9	72.8	23.5
Brentwood CDP..........	10.967	60,664	NA	NA	NA	42.4	93.3	$69,214	30.9	10.4	70.6	9.5	82.6	12.5
Brighton CDP & town (Monroe)	15.410	36,632	36,941	0.8	2,397.2	16.6	80.8	$61,891	29.5	10.4	61.5	6.2	52.1	36.3
Bronx borough (Bronx)	42.086	1,385,108	1,438,159	3.8	34,171.7	34.0	88.5	$34,284	12.1	29.8	59.3	15.0	66.0	30.0
Brookhaven town (Suffolk)*	259.459	486,040	489,403	0.7	1,886.2	11.5	92.9	$86,828	42.4	7.4	65.7	6.6	74.5	20.6
Brooklyn borough (Kings)........	69.814	2,504,709	2,621,793	4.7	37,554.1	37.5	90.5	$46,958	21.4	22.0	62.8	10.6	63.2	28.9
Brunswick town (Rensselaer) ...	44.347	11,941	12,265	2.7	276.6	4.4	93.5	$81,568	38.8	2.2	72.2	4.4	68.6	26.0
Buffalo city & MCD (Erie)........	40.384	261,325	258,703	-1.0	6,406.1	8.6	82.3	$31,668	9.7	28.5	59.8	12.5	52.0	39.2
Camillus town (Onondaga)	34.424	24,173	24,285	0.5	705.5	6.5	92.5	$64,217	27.0	6.2	68.5	6.2	67.8	26.8
Canandaigua city & MCD (Ontario)	4.594	10,591	10,488		2,282.8	2.7	81.3	$45,036	16.2	13.9	66.3	8.4	49.3	40.5
Canandaigua town (Ontario)	56.796	9,962	10,518	5.6	185.2	2.4	86.7	$59,847	28.1	7.7	59.1	7.2	64.6	29.4
Canton town (St. Lawrence)*	104.765	10,995	11,214	2.0	107.0	6.5	73.4	$49,484	18.4	16.6	51.2	8.9	58.1	26.7
Carmel town (Putnam)............	35.907	34,305	34,387	0.2	957.7	13.0	93.7	$105,406	52.3	4.1	68.3	8.1	79.5	17.7
Catskill town (Greene)*	60.439	11,776	11,454	-2.7	189.5	4.2	87.9	$47,408	13.6	13.9	56.2	12.6	63.6	30.5
Centereach CDP	8.729	31,578	NA	NA	NA	11.5	93.3	$94,909	47.8	4.9	68.7	5.6	82.1	14.2
Central Islip CDP	7.109	34,450	NA	NA	NA	35.5	90.4	$65,695	27.7	15.1	68.9	8.5	76.3	19.1
Cheektowaga CDP	25.357	75,178	NA	NA	NA	4.8	90.3	$48,703	13.9	10.6	64.1	7.8	58.8	34.5
Cheektowaga town (Erie)*	29.432	88,226	87,840	-0.4	2,984.5	4.7	90.7	$48,643	13.4	10.4	64.1	7.8	58.8	34.5
Chenango town (Broome)	33.834	11,252	11,045	-1.8	326.4	3.4	90.7	$61,383	21.2	8.6	68.1	7.0	70.7	24.0
Chester town (Orange)*	25.049	11,981	11,872	-0.9	473.9	15.7	93.3	$88,119	41.4	3.9	67.5	6.4	74.1	22.1
Chili town (Monroe)	39.498	28,623	28,766	0.5	728.3	6.6	89.2	$62,646	25.1	5.9	69.8	6.9	70.9	24.0
Cicero town (Onondaga)*	48.279	31,632	31,608	-0.1	654.7	3.6	89.5	$67,821	27.5	7.3	69.5	7.3	70.1	24.7
Clarence town (Erie)	53.498	30,673	31,769	3.6	593.8	7.3	91.8	$89,454	44.0	4.8	66.3	3.2	74.8	21.1
Clarkstown town (Rockland)*	38.475	84,187	87,059	3.4	2,262.7	22.3	94.2	$102,311	51.4	4.9	66.3	7.6	75.8	20.7
Clay town (Onondaga)*	47.958	58,206	59,806	2.7	1,247.1	5.2	90.6	$65,956	24.5	7.5	71.0	5.5	67.2	26.1
Clifton Park town (Saratoga).....	48.202	36,734	37,030	0.8	768.2	6.2	91.3	$98,178	48.9	2.5	68.8	4.0	71.0	24.3
Cohoes city & MCD (Albany).....	3.774	16,168	16,212	0.3	4,296.3	4.7	83.3	$44,534	12.8	14.5	65.3	9.6	52.8	37.9
Colonie town (Albany)*A3319	55.948	81,591	83,015	1.7	1,483.8	10.1	88.6	$72,806	33.5	6.6	66.8	5.2	63.4	30.3
Commack CDP............	11.960	36,124	NA	NA	NA	9.9	94.8	$113,432	55.8	3.8	65.6	7.3	80.9	17.3
Copiague CDP............	3.226	22,993	NA	NA	NA	30.1	93.6	$69,008	31.0	8.3	67.6	8.0	71.5	24.3
Coram CDP................	13.825	39,113	NA	NA	NA	17.5	89.8	$78,227	39.0	7.1	68.9	7.4	68.5	24.1
Corning city & MCD (Steuben).	3.084	11,183	10,993	-1.7	3,564.8	3.2	80.2	$48,791	18.1	17.4	68.8	7.7	50.2	40.6
Cornwall town (Orange)*	26.653	12,646	12,508	-1.1	469.3	5.2	92.7	$85,117	42.7	5.9	66.4	6.7	69.5	25.5
Cortland city & MCD (Cortland)	3.894	19,192	19,164	-0.1	4,921.4	2.0	77.3	$40,229	8.9	18.6	57.2	7.5	48.8	40.4
Cortlandt town (Westchester)*	39.258	41,592	42,714	2.7	1,088.0	16.0	92.2	$95,733	48.4	4.8	66.7	8.1	74.1	23.0
Deer Park CDP............	6.168	27,745	NA	NA	NA	15.3	94.4	$84,143	42.9	7.1	67.2	6.9	74.2	21.9

1 Dry land or land partially or temporarily covered by water.
2 16 years old and over.

Table B. Incorporated Places, Census Designated Places (CDPs), and Minor Civil Divisions (MCDs) of 10,000 or More Population — Crime, Construction, and Local Government Finance

STATE City, town, township, borough, or CDP (county if applicable)	Serious crimes known to police, 2014[1] Total number	Rate[2] Total	Rate[2] Violent	Rate[2] Property	New residential construction authorized by building permits, 2014 Value ($1,000)	Number of housing units	Percent single family	Local government finance, 2012 General revenue Total (mil dol)	Intergovernmental Total (mil dol)	Intergovernmental Percent from state gov.	Taxes per capita[3]	General expenditure Total (mil dol)	Per capita[3] Total	Per capita[3] Capital outlays	Debt outstanding (mil dol)
	15	16	17	18	19	20	21	22	23	24	25	26	27	28	29
NEW MEXICO—Con.															
Carlsbad city............	1,370	4886	510	4376	34,318	290	40.7	58.1	6.7	35.3	1412	48.5	1,811	487	40.7
Chaparral CDP............	NA	NA	NA	NA	NA	NA	NA	NA	NA	NA	NA	NA	NA	NA	NA
Clovis city............	2,461	6180	362	5819	27,344	141	62.4	56.3	14.0	34.5	706	57.5	1,457	483	25.6
Deming city............	869	5973	1065	4908	1,197	7	100.0	19.1	6.8	79.9	362	17.2	1,166	151	1.5
Española city............	890	8750	2605	6145	0	0	0.0	15.0	0.7	100.0	995	12.5	1,227	107	21.9
Farmington city............	1,822	4023	665	3358	21,596	109	100.0	92.1	35.8	11.0	600	99.0	2,161	207	1802.6
Gallup city............	2,845	12724	2147	10577	1,000	4	100.0	48.7	7.2	53.1	1252	48.6	2,201	236	50.4
Hobbs city............	1,828	5002	673	4329	39,784	276	68.5	89.8	35.4	93.8	1098	69.8	1,994	1,088	58.7
Las Cruces city............	4,909	4807	289	4519	59,479	298	96.3	182.5	39.2	26.8	953	144.3	1,429	190	152.7
Las Vegas city............	588	4323	963	3360	0	0	0.0	24.0	4.0	86.3	902	24.7	1,782	184	26.0
Los Alamos CDP............	NA	NA	NA	NA	NA	NA	NA	NA	NA	NA	NA	NA	NA	NA	NA
Los Lunas village............	861	5599	806	4793	8,131	75	100.0	23.4	1.9	72.3	927	21.4	1,403	207	84.2
Lovington city............	50	428	86	342	NA	NA	NA	14.0	2.2	90.1	752	11.1	984	128	8.6
North Valley CDP............	NA	NA	NA	NA	NA	NA	NA	NA	NA	NA	NA	NA	NA	NA	NA
Portales city............	430	3433	184	3250	3,199	20	100.0	13.9	4.7	92.5	348	11.5	910	90	2.6
Rio Rancho city............	1,989	2140	188	1951	142,023	820	90.4	95.2	13.7	34.9	599	87.0	959	166	236.5
Roswell city............	3,429	7050	765	6285	7,614	44	34.8	55.1	34.8	96.0	192	56.9	1,173	255	18.0
Santa Fe city............	3,261	4630	346	4283	37,092	161	100.0	162.5	78.1	73.2	518	178.9	2,584	479	381.4
Silver City town............	144	1402	234	1168	928	4	100.0	16.7	2.8	100.0	977	14.9	1,448	242	9.5
South Valley CDP............	NA	NA	NA	NA	NA	NA	NA	NA	NA	NA	NA	NA	NA	NA	NA
Sunland Park city............	164	1074	105	969	34,715	181	100.0	8.4	1.4	85.2	362	9.7	662	73	0.1
NEW YORK	414,680	2100	382	1718	5,581,783	36,286	28.6	X	X	X	X	X	X	X	X
Albany city & MCD (Albany)	4,668	4735	803	3931	11,321	79	43.0	252.8	90.3	28.3	625	277.7	2,820	454	773.1
Alden town (Erie)*	NA	NA	NA	NA	1,410	6	100.0	4.1	1.6	18.8	228	3.9	370	32	0.8
Amherst town (Erie)*	2,194	1846	108	1738	54,114	380	22.1	147.7	47.3	11.3	644	153.1	1,239	109	135.3
Amsterdam city & MCD (Montgomery)	520	2873	166	2707	0	0	0.0	21.2	7.7	43.5	288	23.3	1,273	220	24.6
Arcadia town (Wayne)*	NA	NA	NA	NA	340	2	100.0	3.3	0.9	25.5	162	3.3	237	24	4.7
Auburn city & MCD (Cayuga) ...	1,078	3947	454	3493	9,861	114	3.5	42.1	14.9	40.5	447	47.1	1,722	251	52.9
Aurora town (Erie)*	137	993	65	928	6,926	30	100.0	8.6	2.3	32.7	365	7.4	539	32	20.5
Babylon village*	NA	NA	NA	NA	2,344	9	100.0	9.6	1.5	91.9	486	8.8	723	56	4.1
Babylon town (Suffolk)*	NA	NA	NA	NA	14,640	41	100.0	163.7	23.7	14.4	466	167.6	783	74	200.3
Baldwin CDP............	NA	NA	NA	NA	NA	NA	NA	NA	NA	NA	NA	NA	NA	NA	NA
Ballston town (Saratoga)*	NA	NA	NA	NA	17,479	106	67.9	4.8	2.4	5.0	169	4.0	408	44	4.2
Batavia city & MCD (Genesee).	675	4434	499	3935	580	6	0.0	21.6	4.4	93.7	826	18.2	1,190	56	8.9
Bath town (Steuben)*	NA	NA	NA	NA	1,137	13	100.0	3.0	1.2	30.6	138	3.0	248	22	0.0
Bay Shore CDP............	NA	NA	NA	NA	NA	NA	NA	NA	NA	NA	NA	NA	NA	NA	NA
Beacon city & MCD (Dutchess)	288	2010	300	1710	3,585	84	8.3	22.6	7.7	31.1	686	23.3	1,615	256	31.9
Bedford town (Westchester)	125	703	11	692	15,302	10	100.0	29.9	3.4	30.5	1314	39.1	2,226	757	43.5
Beekman town (Dutchess)	NA	NA	NA	NA	3,100	6	100.0	4.6	1.2	28.2	189	4.5	305	18	3.0
Bellmore CDP............	NA	NA	NA	NA	NA	NA	NA	NA	NA	NA	NA	NA	NA	NA	NA
Bethlehem town (Albany)	490	1414	104	1310	21,075	99	58.6	37.8	11.4	6.5	385	39.1	1,146	82	71.8
Bethpage CDP............	NA	NA	NA	NA	NA	NA	NA	NA	NA	NA	NA	NA	NA	NA	NA
Binghamton city & MCD (Broome)	2,355	5094	664	4430	370	3	100.0	80.6	30.7	45.7	765	75.4	1,615	190	115.0
Blooming Grove town (Orange)*	NA	NA	NA	NA	1,051	6	100.0	12.4	2.2	24.5	521	12.2	686	21	5.8
Bohemia CDP............	NA	NA	NA	NA	NA	NA	NA	NA	NA	NA	NA	NA	NA	NA	NA
Brentwood CDP............	NA	NA	NA	NA	NA	NA	NA	NA	NA	NA	NA	NA	NA	NA	NA
Brighton CDP & town (Monroe)	882	2391	70	2321	633	3	100.0	26.8	5.2	38.6	427	26.3	709	91	5.9
Bronx borough (Bronx)	NA	NA	NA	NA	185,203	1,885	0.0	NA	NA	NA	NA	NA	NA	NA	NA
Brookhaven town (Suffolk)*	NA	NA	NA	NA	55,645	244	97.5	289.0	24.2	34.2	361	361.4	740	182	607.4
Brooklyn borough (Kings).........	NA	NA	NA	NA	734,465	7,551	0.0	NA	NA	NA	NA	NA	NA	NA	NA
Brunswick town (Rensselaer) ...	NA	NA	NA	NA	4,934	110	20.0	6.6	1.8	18.0	332	6.0	491	24	2.2
Buffalo city & MCD (Erie)........	15,622	6045	1228	4817	19,388	118	55.9	1438.1	1151.5	83.0	573	1532.1	5,896	790	609.4
Camillus town (Onondaga).......	483	1987	53	1934	13,525	160	25.6	17.7	0.7	79.7	523	17.3	716	50	3.8
Canandaigua city & MCD (Ontario)............	NA	NA	NA	NA	1,828	9	100.0	16.5	4.4	51.6	868	15.6	1,483	246	19.2
Canandaigua town (Ontario)	355	3396	517	2880	22,206	117	57.3	9.5	5.7	19.3	319	8.0	774	140	2.3
Canton town (St. Lawrence)*	NA	NA	NA	NA	1,008	11	100.0	2.4	1.0	27.2	97	2.5	218	4	0.0
Carmel town (Putnam)*	218	633	35	598	10,757	53	58.5	34.8	3.9	86.1	699	32.2	936	114	30.3
Catskill town (Greene)*	NA	NA	NA	NA	1,724	15	100.0	5.3	0.2	88.8	274	5.8	497	42	0.7
Centereach CDP............	NA	NA	NA	NA	NA	NA	NA	NA	NA	NA	NA	NA	NA	NA	NA
Central Islip CDP............	NA	NA	NA	NA	NA	NA	NA	NA	NA	NA	NA	NA	NA	NA	NA
Cheektowaga CDP............	NA	NA	NA	NA	NA	NA	NA	NA	NA	NA	NA	NA	NA	NA	NA
Cheektowaga town (Erie)*	2,902	3711	260	3451	3,989	18	100.0	86.0	14.0	29.7	750	93.0	1,058	228	30.8
Chenango town (Broome)	NA	NA	NA	NA	881	5	100.0	6.2	2.7	9.0	245	6.8	610	126	13.5
Chester town (Orange)*	NA	NA	NA	NA	721	4	100.0	9.2	1.5	11.1	562	9.3	777	16	5.9
Chili town (Monroe)	NA	NA	NA	NA	10,610	58	100.0	15.0	4.7	43.7	318	13.6	474	80	3.5
Cicero town (Onondaga)*	496	1672	64	1608	2,878	14	100.0	13.9	1.3	39.0	373	13.9	440	19	2.5
Clarence town (Erie)	NA	NA	NA	NA	51,542	240	44.6	21.1	7.9	19.4	393	20.6	668	139	21.2
Clarkstown town (Rockland)*	1,536	1886	92	1794	6,494	24	100.0	126.1	13.2	17.5	1215	133.8	1,560	266	94.9
Clay town (Onondaga)	NA	NA	NA	NA	17,740	131	61.8	22.8	1.8	38.8	339	23.4	399	21	5.2
Clifton Park town (Saratoga).....	NA	NA	NA	NA	20,995	48	100.0	24.8	12.5	10.3	134	24.9	674	53	45.4
Cohoes city & MCD (Albany)....	267	1648	265	1383	14,925	187	1.6	23.6	9.9	37.3	472	24.1	1,490	214	46.8
Colonie town (Albany)*A3319	2,083	2646	93	2553	53,515	285	53.0	93.9	26.6	5.3	329	87.2	1,063	84	124.8
Commack CDP............	NA	NA	NA	NA	NA	NA	NA	NA	NA	NA	NA	NA	NA	NA	NA
Copiague CDP............	NA	NA	NA	NA	NA	NA	NA	NA	NA	NA	NA	NA	NA	NA	NA
Coram CDP............	NA	NA	NA	NA	NA	NA	NA	NA	NA	NA	NA	NA	NA	NA	NA
Corning city & MCD (Steuben) .	381	3451	353	3098	150	1	100.0	19.0	4.4	98.6	916	17.8	1,604	275	15.4
Cornwall town (Orange)*	NA	NA	NA	NA	4,337	35	11.4	9.1	2.1	21.7	491	10.8	863	113	4.7
Cortland city & MCD (Cortland)	392	2060	147	1913	185	2	0.0	23.5	8.7	36.3	468	21.3	1,110	122	16.2
Cortlandt town (Westchester)*	NA	NA	NA	NA	3,418	15	100.0	32.2	5.9	15.3	490	32.7	773	28	11.6
Deer Park CDP............	NA	NA	NA	NA	NA	NA	NA	NA	NA	NA	NA	NA	NA	NA	NA

1 Data for serious crimes have not been adjusted for underreporting. This may affect comparability between geographic areas over time.
2 Per 100,000 population estimated by the FBI. 3 Based on population estimated as of July 1 of the year shown.

Table B. Incorporated Places, Census Designated Places (CDPs), and Minor Civil Divisions (MCDs) of 10,000 or More Population — Land Area, Population, and Households, and Employment

STATE City, town, township, borough, or CDP (county if applicable)	Land area,[1] 2010 (sq mi)	Total persons 2010	Total persons 2014	Percent change 2010–2014	Persons per square mile, 2014	Foreign born	Lives in same house as previous year	Median household income (dollars)	Income of $100,000 or more	Income below poverty level	Percent in labor force	Unemployment rate	Family households	One person households
	1	2	3	4	5	6	7	8	9	10	11	12	13	14
NEW YORK—Con.														
Depew village	5.076	15,304	15,205	-0.6	2,995.2	3.6	90.2	$49,291	11.9	9.8	65.2	7.1	61.4	32.5
De Witt town (Onondaga)*	33.772	25,812	25,735	-0.3	762.0	10.0	84.5	$63,175	27.3	8.7	62.4	7.1	62.9	32.1
Dix Hills CDP	15.938	26,892	NA	NA	NA	17.3	95.6	$139,583	65.6	3.4	61.8	5.7	84.7	12.0
Dobbs Ferry village	2.429	10,875	11,098	2.1	4,568.5	18.4	85.9	$113,062	55.2	2.8	64.8	6.3	67.6	27.0
Dryden town (Tompkins)	93.640	14,436	14,978	3.8	160.0	4.0	85.6	$59,757	23.0	12.2	67.7	4.2	61.0	28.6
Dunkirk city & MCD (Chautauqua)	4.502	12,563	12,216	-2.8	2,713.6	3.4	84.3	$37,930	9.9	22.3	61.2	9.9	55.1	36.1
Eastchester CDP	3.294	19,554	NA	NA	NA	17.0	92.8	$106,030	52.5	3.6	64.3	4.8	66.8	29.9
Eastchester town (Westchester)*	4.853	32,362	33,030	2.1	6,806.0	16.8	90.5	$104,891	51.7	4.2	64.4	6.2	65.9	29.8
East Fishkill town (Dutchess)	56.504	29,033	29,332	1.0	519.1	9.2	94.7	$100,766	50.4	3.0	66.3	8.0	81.5	15.4
East Greenbush town (Rensselaer)	24.020	16,473	16,434	-0.2	684.2	5.7	90.4	$70,699	32.8	6.2	70.1	4.1	65.2	26.9
East Hampton town (Suffolk)*	74.328	21,457	21,927	2.2	295.0	18.8	93.5	$79,019	39.9	8.5	62.0	7.4	62.7	29.8
East Islip CDP	3.965	14,475	NA	NA	NA	3.0	96.6	$113,236	55.8	5.2	63.8	5.9	81.1	14.7
East Massapequa CDP	3.440	19,069	NA	NA	NA	15.1	96.3	$98,021	49.3	5.9	66.2	6.3	76.2	17.6
East Meadow CDP	6.303	38,132	NA	NA	NA	18.3	90.8	$95,071	46.9	5.0	59.6	6.6	74.3	23.4
East Northport CDP	5.161	20,217	NA	NA	NA	6.7	94.1	$102,432	51.0	6.1	68.1	7.6	77.8	20.2
East Patchogue CDP	8.352	22,469	NA	NA	NA	10.6	93.8	$68,358	32.5	11.4	61.8	6.7	64.4	30.2
Eggertsville CDP	2.861	15,019	NA	NA	NA	14.4	90.4	$64,957	29.8	11.9	69.2	6.7	61.9	30.8
Elma town (Erie)*	34.521	11,317	11,720	3.6	339.5	3.2	94.9	$74,814	31.7	5.3	61.6	3.6	73.1	23.7
Elmira city & MCD (Chemung)	7.251	29,200	28,647	-1.9	3,950.8	2.0	77.7	$29,865	8.9	27.7	50.4	9.2	54.6	34.8
Elmont CDP	3.410	33,198	NA	NA	NA	44.1	93.1	$88,915	42.5	7.8	70.6	9.1	83.2	13.0
Elwood CDP	4.781	11,177	NA	NA	NA	11.8	97.3	$108,401	54.7	3.6	67.8	8.0	82.4	15.3
Endicott village	3.194	13,392	13,083	-2.3	4,096.3	6.0	79.1	$33,070	8.5	21.4	62.4	12.4	50.6	42.8
Endwell CDP	3.744	11,446	NA	NA	NA	4.8	87.0	$54,775	23.8	7.6	64.5	4.3	61.7	33.3
Evans town (Erie)	41.530	16,356	16,300	-0.3	392.5	1.9	87.9	$60,474	19.5	11.5	65.4	9.0	65.8	27.3
Fairmount CDP	3.334	10,224	NA	NA	NA	6.3	93.4	$59,505	20.6	6.4	69.2	7.0	67.6	26.5
Fallsburg town (Sullivan)	77.622	12,870	12,845	-0.2	165.5	16.0	79.3	$46,060	16.2	21.7	54.9	13.4	65.2	28.0
Farmington town (Ontario)	39.430	11,829	12,904	9.1	327.3	7.5	85.8	$65,020	24.2	8.2	70.7	6.2	73.3	22.2
Farmingville CDP	4.121	15,481	NA	NA	NA	11.3	95.2	$96,492	45.3	5.1	68.6	5.9	87.3	9.2
Fishkill town (Dutchess)*	27.336	23,003	23,596	2.6	863.2	13.6	84.9	$81,801	38.6	7.5	61.3	10.2	60.3	34.3
Floral Park village	1.416	15,863	15,967	0.7	11,272.6	13.6	91.5	$106,134	53.4	4.0	68.1	6.5	75.8	21.1
Fort Drum CDP	14.341	12,955	NA	NA	NA	8.6	49.1	$42,141	8.3	15.3	76.9	16.0	84.2	12.1
Franklin Square CDP	2.878	29,320	NA	NA	NA	23.0	94.7	$92,123	46.0	5.7	63.4	8.4	79.8	17.7
Fredonia village	5.189	11,230	10,792	-3.9	2,079.8	3.8	77.1	$45,714	17.4	19.0	55.8	5.8	50.9	33.1
Freeport village	4.633	42,860	43,304	1.0	9,346.1	32.9	93.5	$67,056	33.0	15.1	67.9	9.7	71.2	23.1
Fulton city & MCD (Oswego)	3.755	11,896	11,648	-2.1	3,102.3	2.7	82.7	$34,856	8.9	24.9	56.8	15.7	62.7	30.2
Garden City village	5.330	22,382	22,616	1.1	4,243.2	6.4	92.9	$152,401	67.5	3.9	59.8	5.5	80.8	18.7
Gates town (Monroe)	15.199	28,400	28,592	0.7	1,881.1	10.4	88.3	$50,473	15.8	8.3	64.8	7.0	61.1	32.3
Geddes town (Onondaga)*	9.156	17,118	16,875	-1.4	1,843.0	6.1	91.5	$54,238	20.4	7.6	63.1	6.3	59.4	33.6
Geneseo town (Livingston)	43.944	10,483	10,663	1.7	242.6	7.1	68.1	$42,138	22.4	30.6	50.0	6.4	48.0	28.7
Geneva city	4.210	13,272	13,160	-0.8	3,126.1	6.6	74.2	$40,428	14.4	20.3	60.2	6.3	52.1	37.6
Geneva town (Ontario)	4.194	13,272	13,160	-0.8	3,137.5	6.6	74.2	$40,428	14.4	20.3	60.2	6.3	52.1	37.6
German Flatts town (Herkimer)	33.695	13,253	13,013	-1.8	386.2	1.9	89.0	$43,329	11.6	17.6	61.3	9.7	61.4	29.5
Glen Cove city & MCD (Nassau)	6.655	26,964	27,314	1.3	4,104.3	34.6	90.6	$65,267	32.5	12.8	64.1	5.9	66.5	27.1
Glens Falls city & MCD (Warren)	3.851	14,700	14,428	-1.9	3,747.0	2.9	86.1	$44,341	16.9	16.3	68.7	8.8	50.0	37.2
Glenville town (Schenectady)*	49.244	29,478	29,666	0.6	602.4	3.3	91.6	$67,161	28.6	6.3	65.0	6.7	64.8	31.4
Gloversville city & MCD (Fulton)	5.020	15,640	15,122	-3.3	3,012.3	1.5	80.9	$35,317	9.8	24.9	57.5	14.7	56.4	33.8
Goshen town (Orange)*	43.642	13,687	13,733	0.3	314.7	9.0	87.0	$85,061	39.4	6.2	58.4	8.9	69.3	27.5
Grand Island town (Erie)	28.274	20,374	20,734	1.8	733.3	5.7	90.1	$77,857	37.5	6.4	66.2	5.3	73.0	22.2
Great Neck village	1.333	9,975	10,118	1.4	7,589.1	36.3	93.8	$81,778	42.0	10.1	61.9	10.2	73.2	25.7
Greece CDP	4.373	14,519	NA	NA	NA	6.6	90.6	$50,590	15.8	8.9	61.9	4.6	62.8	32.8
Greece town (Monroe)	47.522	96,095	97,084	1.0	2,042.9	6.8	90.1	$55,390	20.5	7.9	64.2	5.8	64.2	30.0
Greenburgh town (Westchester)*	30.309	88,400	91,388	3.4	3,015.2	22.5	90.8	$112,216	55.0	4.5	68.2	6.6	70.0	25.9
Greenlawn CDP	3.724	13,742	NA	NA	NA	16.7	95.7	$88,119	42.8	5.4	59.9	8.3	72.5	24.0
Guilderland town (Albany)	57.902	35,303	35,818	1.5	618.6	9.4	87.4	$79,074	38.9	5.0	66.9	5.0	60.5	31.4
Halfmoon town (Saratoga)	32.580	21,517	23,369	8.6	717.3	10.6	85.1	$66,884	31.4	6.4	71.3	4.6	62.6	28.2
Hamburg town (Erie)*	41.323	56,936	57,904	1.7	1,401.3	2.8	91.1	$61,934	24.9	7.0	68.9	7.2	63.9	31.3
Hampton Bays CDP	12.948	13,603	NA	NA	NA	24.0	93.9	$72,575	28.8	5.9	63.0	5.9	66.0	26.6
Harrison village & town (Westchester)	16.763	27,471	28,151	2.5	1,679.3	25.2	85.1	$111,122	54.7	7.0	60.7	7.0	76.7	17.9
Hauppauge CDP	10.728	20,882	NA	NA	NA	9.3	94.9	$103,775	51.2	3.1	65.5	5.3	77.4	19.7
Haverstraw village	1.980	11,910	12,172	2.2	6,147.2	40.3	89.1	$56,714	28.1	14.6	70.5	9.2	73.1	18.3
Haverstraw town (Rockland)*	22.155	36,634	37,530	2.4	1,694.0	26.7	89.7	$75,901	35.7	9.0	70.3	9.2	75.8	19.0
Hempstead village	3.684	53,891	55,527	3.0	15,073.5	38.1	88.5	$51,714	23.2	21.0	67.7	10.8	68.8	24.5
Hempstead town (Nassau)*	118.676	759,933	770,116	1.3	6,489.2	21.7	93.3	$94,158	47.1	7.1	66.1	7.9	77.6	18.9
Henrietta town (Monroe)	35.349	42,581	43,639	2.5	1,234.5	9.8	82.6	$61,945	24.2	11.9	64.5	6.6	64.1	24.8
Herkimer town (Herkimer)	31.662	10,169	10,001	-1.7	315.9	4.2	84.0	$39,608	8.8	19.3	58.0	10.4	58.2	35.7
Hicksville CDP	6.791	41,547	NA	NA	NA	25.8	95.0	$93,453	47.8	5.2	66.0	7.0	81.4	14.3
Highlands town (Orange)*	30.409	12,492	12,201	-2.3	401.2	7.4	77.4	$80,038	34.3	5.8	75.4	7.8	68.7	26.6
Holbrook CDP	7.173	27,195	NA	NA	NA	6.6	93.4	$96,536	47.7	3.7	71.1	7.4	78.0	18.6
Holtsville CDP	7.108	19,714	NA	NA	NA	11.1	96.1	$92,730	44.6	6.3	67.8	5.7	77.0	18.6
Horseheads town (Chemung)*	35.606	19,485	19,613	0.7	550.8	4.5	87.2	$56,218	23.9	12.0	62.3	3.9	64.3	29.7
Huntington CDP	7.594	18,046	NA	NA	NA	10.6	94.1	$120,346	56.5	4.8	68.3	5.9	70.7	24.5
Huntington town (Suffolk)*	94.119	203,260	204,673	0.7	2,174.6	13.9	93.9	$107,323	53.5	5.8	64.7	7.2	77.0	19.6
Huntington Station CDP	5.475	33,029	NA	NA	NA	26.6	92.8	$74,371	38.4	12.5	70.9	8.3	74.2	20.8
Hyde Park town (Dutchess)	36.662	21,581	21,309	-1.3	581.2	6.5	88.8	$75,291	32.6	9.3	64.7	7.2	66.6	26.7
Irondequoit CDP & town (Monroe)	15.001	51,692	51,462	-0.4	3,430.5	7.5	92.1	$53,729	19.0	8.7	64.8	6.7	60.6	34.2
Islip CDP	4.822	18,689	NA	NA	NA	9.7	94.0	$97,723	47.7	3.1	70.1	6.4	75.2	20.9
Islip town (Suffolk)*	103.902	335,543	336,793	0.4	3,241.4	19.7	92.9	$85,281	41.6	7.0	68.8	7.7	76.8	19.0

1 Dry land or land partially or temporarily covered by water.
2 16 years old and over.

Table B. Incorporated Places, Census Designated Places (CDPs), and Minor Civil Divisions (MCDs) of 10,000 or More Population — **Crime, Construction, and Local Government Finance**

STATE City, town, township, borough, or CDP (county if applicable)	Serious crimes known to police, 2014[1] Total number	Rate[2] Total	Rate[2] Violent	Rate[2] Property	New residential construction authorized by building permits, 2014 Value ($1,000)	Number of housing units	Percent single family	Local government finance, 2012 General revenue Total (mil dol)	Intergovernmental Total (mil dol)	Percent from state gov.	Taxes per capita[3]	General expenditure Total (mil dol)	Per capita[3] Total	Capital outlays	Debt outstanding (mil dol)
	15	16	17	18	19	20	21	22	23	24	25	26	27	28	29
NEW YORK—Con.															
Depew village	266	1750	99	1651	275	1	100.0	12.9	2.0	20.9	579	12.6	829	31	4.3
De Witt town (Onondaga)*	707	3117	97	3020	4,555	18	100.0	20.1	1.6	55.5	645	19.0	737	39	4.8
Dix Hills CDP	NA	NA	NA	NA	NA	NA	NA	NA	NA	NA	NA	NA	NA	NA	NA
Dobbs Ferry village	99	892	27	865	1,104	3	100.0	17.4	2.9	38.3	1100	18.0	1,636	309	19.9
Dryden town (Tompkins)	NA	NA	NA	NA	2,042	16	75.0	6.1	2.6	20.4	188	7.2	493	76	0.3
Dunkirk city & MCD (Chautauqua)	287	2338	375	1963	0	0	0.0	20.1	5.7	40.7	416	20.3	1,641	150	13.2
Eastchester CDP	NA	NA	NA	NA	NA	NA	NA	NA	NA	NA	NA	NA	NA	NA	NA
Eastchester town (Westchester)*	NA	NA	NA	NA	234	1	100.0	34.6	7.1	6.1	626	36.6	1,121	69	15.1
East Fishkill town (Dutchess)	167	569	31	539	11,539	36	100.0	18.1	1.9	9.7	438	19.1	652	88	25.4
East Greenbush town (Rensselaer)	393	2388	134	2255	4,012	18	100.0	16.9	3.5	40.8	575	14.1	859	15	7.1
East Hampton town (Suffolk)*	294	1490	41	1450	68,604	111	100.0	83.7	18.0	5.5	2477	74.2	3,413	604	131.3
East Islip CDP	NA	NA	NA	NA	NA	NA	NA	NA	NA	NA	NA	NA	NA	NA	NA
East Massapequa CDP	NA	NA	NA	NA	NA	NA	NA	NA	NA	NA	NA	NA	NA	NA	NA
East Meadow CDP	NA	NA	NA	NA	NA	NA	NA	NA	NA	NA	NA	NA	NA	NA	NA
East Northport CDP	NA	NA	NA	NA	NA	NA	NA	NA	NA	NA	NA	NA	NA	NA	NA
East Patchogue CDP	NA	NA	NA	NA	NA	NA	NA	NA	NA	NA	NA	NA	NA	NA	NA
Eggertsville CDP	NA	NA	NA	NA	NA	NA	NA	NA	NA	NA	NA	NA	NA	NA	NA
Elma town (Erie)*	NA	NA	NA	NA	12,280	38	100.0	5.7	2.6	19.6	160	5.6	488	74	0.0
Elmira city & MCD (Chemung)	1,045	3628	281	3347	0	0	0.0	41.8	23.4	53.0	398	41.7	1,427	358	36.3
Elmont CDP	NA	NA	NA	NA	NA	NA	NA	NA	NA	NA	NA	NA	NA	NA	NA
Elwood CDP	NA	NA	NA	NA	NA	NA	NA	NA	NA	NA	NA	NA	NA	NA	NA
Endicott village	687	5246	588	4658	0	0	0.0	20.0	5.1	26.0	717	20.2	1,527	173	11.0
Endwell CDP	NA	NA	NA	NA	NA	NA	NA	NA	NA	NA	NA	NA	NA	NA	NA
Evans town (Erie)	210	1291	141	1149	4,218	13	100.0	12.0	2.4	13.8	541	13.0	795	32	0.0
Fairmount CDP	NA	NA	NA	NA	NA	NA	NA	NA	NA	NA	NA	NA	NA	NA	NA
Fallsburg town (Sullivan)	120	986	107	879	15,111	83	100.0	14.8	1.0	36.0	713	14.7	1,137	13	11.6
Farmington town (Ontario)	NA	NA	NA	NA	9,133	36	100.0	9.6	3.0	6.8	167	8.1	651	81	12.3
Farmingville CDP	NA	NA	NA	NA	NA	NA	NA	NA	NA	NA	NA	NA	NA	NA	NA
Fishkill town (Dutchess)*	220	1023	47	977	6,936	87	100.0	11.7	1.2	11.1	228	8.6	368	19	25.9
Floral Park village	56	352	57	295	317	1	100.0	24.8	0.9	55.3	1375	24.1	1,513	90	4.2
Fort Drum CDP	NA	NA	NA	NA	NA	NA	NA	NA	NA	NA	NA	NA	NA	NA	NA
Franklin Square CDP	NA	NA	NA	NA	NA	NA	NA	NA	NA	NA	NA	NA	NA	NA	NA
Fredonia village	246	2271	92	2179	499	4	25.0	7.9	2.2	10.9	279	7.4	675	43	5.2
Freeport village	1,000	2313	352	1961	1,551	8	100.0	62.3	3.3	46.3	985	67.6	1,566	34	138.4
Fulton city & MCD (Oswego)	471	4023	137	3887	0	0	0.0	23.3	6.4	55.0	1051	22.9	1,944	60	7.4
Garden City village	291	1288	53	1235	4,958	12	100.0	53.4	1.1	58.8	2074	56.7	2,512	152	22.2
Gates town (Monroe)	1,102	3861	228	3633	4,740	44	38.6	16.6	3.4	26.4	402	15.8	554	38	0.6
Geddes town (Onondaga)*	NA	NA	NA	NA	241	1	100.0	9.6	1.7	31.7	430	9.2	540	41	2.4
Geneseo town (Livingston)	NA	NA	NA	NA	2,262	14	50.0	2.5	0.6	21.4	131	2.2	213	48	1.1
Geneva city	374	2837	182	2655	0	0	0.0	22.3	3.3	70.9	750	25.5	1,931	309	97.4
Geneva town (Ontario)	374	2837	182	2655	0	0	0.0	NA	NA	NA	NA	NA	NA	NA	NA
German Flatts town (Herkimer)	NA	NA	NA	NA	320	2	100.0	2.0	0.6	41.4	99	2.0	154	1	0.4
Glen Cove city & MCD (Nassau)	103	378	22	356	4,367	36	11.1	53.4	17.4	54.0	1125	56.1	2,063	478	81.8
Glens Falls city & MCD (Warren)	364	2507	179	2328	2,227	24	100.0	26.9	5.8	68.7	877	29.8	2,042	244	56.3
Glenville town (Schenectady)*	NA	NA	NA	NA	5,239	60	16.7	13.6	3.6	11.1	300	13.1	444	15	20.4
Gloversville city & MCD (Fulton)	717	4704	262	4442	125	1	100.0	16.6	3.3	97.4	683	16.1	1,046	78	6.1
Goshen town (Orange)*	NA	NA	NA	NA	3,925	23	100.0	8.4	2.0	31.2	367	7.5	550	63	3.9
Grand Island town (Erie)	NA	NA	NA	NA	10,525	66	51.5	16.6	4.2	27.3	467	16.9	818	165	16.2
Great Neck village	NA	NA	NA	NA	1,496	4	100.0	10.8	1.9	14.4	795	11.1	1,101	139	11.8
Greece CDP	NA	NA	NA	NA	NA	NA	NA	NA	NA	NA	NA	NA	NA	NA	NA
Greece town (Monroe)	2,598	2674	174	2500	19,340	89	91.0	55.1	10.8	12.2	414	53.3	551	79	25.6
Greenburgh town (Westchester)*	NA	NA	NA	NA	24,272	101	29.7	87.1	8.4	17.7	733	83.4	922	25	60.2
Greenlawn CDP	NA	NA	NA	NA	NA	NA	NA	NA	NA	NA	NA	NA	NA	NA	NA
Guilderland town (Albany)	683	2011	65	1947	28,506	101	100.0	28.5	11.4	4.7	286	25.7	724	13	36.5
Halfmoon town (Saratoga)	NA	NA	NA	NA	35,994	174	73.0	11.4	5.5	5.1	174	12.6	566	56	42.4
Hamburg town (Erie)*	1,097	2403	120	2282	18,316	145	66.9	36.5	6.7	15.3	449	37.0	643	53	14.5
Hampton Bays CDP	NA	NA	NA	NA	NA	NA	NA	NA	NA	NA	NA	NA	NA	NA	NA
Harrison village & town (Westchester)	NA	NA	NA	NA	29,038	31	100.0	50.5	6.3	2.3	1419	55.4	1,993	6	0.0
Hauppauge CDP	NA	NA	NA	NA	NA	NA	NA	NA	NA	NA	NA	NA	NA	NA	NA
Haverstraw village	NA	NA	NA	NA	125	1	100.0	8.9	1.2	72.7	544	9.3	773	24	16.4
Haverstraw town (Rockland)*	317	847	131	716	280	2	100.0	33.9	2.7	7.0	679	32.0	864	26	41.9
Hempstead village	1,446	2595	863	1732	0	0	0.0	71.2	3.7	54.3	1013	80.4	1,463	51	47.9
Hempstead town (Nassau)*	NA	NA	NA	NA	52,372	199	100.0	472.3	69.1	19.3	449	553.8	723	54	655.0
Henrietta town (Monroe)	NA	NA	NA	NA	30,748	117	100.0	15.2	4.6	14.9	141	13.4	309	12	1.4
Herkimer town (Herkimer)	NA	NA	NA	NA	0	0	0.0	2.0	0.6	30.1	127	2.0	194	19	0.3
Hicksville CDP	NA	NA	NA	NA	NA	NA	NA	NA	NA	NA	NA	NA	NA	NA	NA
Highlands town (Orange)*	NA	NA	NA	NA	1,522	12	66.7	5.1	0.9	19.3	264	4.7	385	5	0.7
Holbrook CDP	NA	NA	NA	NA	NA	NA	NA	NA	NA	NA	NA	NA	NA	NA	NA
Holtsville CDP	NA	NA	NA	NA	NA	NA	NA	NA	NA	NA	NA	NA	NA	NA	NA
Horseheads town (Chemung)*	NA	NA	NA	NA	15,542	27	100.0	4.5	3.2	9.8	53	4.5	230	34	0.1
Huntington CDP	NA	NA	NA	NA	NA	NA	NA	NA	NA	NA	NA	NA	NA	NA	NA
Huntington town (Suffolk)*	NA	NA	NA	NA	16,122	69	100.0	194.4	24.4	49.6	636	189.7	930	114	131.9
Huntington Station CDP	NA	NA	NA	NA	NA	NA	NA	NA	NA	NA	NA	NA	NA	NA	NA
Hyde Park town (Dutchess)	151	708	66	642	0	0	0.0	8.3	1.8	23.3	270	11.4	530	147	15.4
Irondequoit CDP & town (Monroe)	1,492	2903	148	2755	649	4	100.0	32.8	6.8	27.8	451	28.5	552	58	25.0
Islip CDP	NA	NA	NA	NA	NA	NA	NA	NA	NA	NA	NA	NA	NA	NA	NA
Islip town (Suffolk)*	NA	NA	NA	NA	10,261	43	100.0	197.9	40.1	31.9	340	232.6	690	121	200.0

1 Data for serious crimes have not been adjusted for underreporting. This may affect comparability between geographic areas over time.
2 Per 100,000 population estimated by the FBI.   3 Based on population estimated as of July 1 of the year shown.

Table B. Incorporated Places, Census Designated Places (CDPs), and Minor Civil Divisions (MCDs) of 10,000 or More Population — Land Area, Population, and Households, and Employment

STATE City, town, township, borough, or CDP (county if applicable)	Land area,[1] 2010 (sq mi)	Total persons 2010	Total persons 2014	Percent change 2010–2014	Persons per square mile, 2014	Foreign born	Lives in same house as previous year	Median household income (dollars)	Income of $100,000 or more	Income below poverty level	Percent in labor force	Unemploy- ment rate	Family households	One person households
	1	2	3	4	5	6	7	8	9	10	11	12	13	14
NEW YORK—Con.														
Ithaca city & MCD (Tompkins) ..	5.388	30,020	30,720	2.3	5,701.5	17.6	55.1	$30,318	13.5	38.9	47.6	7.1	29.0	42.7
Ithaca town (Tompkins)*	28.946	19,920	20,515	3.0	708.7	22.6	70.8	$52,316	27.4	18.3	52.5	5.4	50.4	35.5
Jamestown city & MCD (Chautauqua)	8.935	31,146	30,429	-2.3	3,405.8	1.6	80.8	$31,128	7.7	26.6	59.6	12.3	57.4	35.9
Jefferson Valley-Yorktown CDP	6.926	14,142	NA	NA	NA	10.5	92.6	$104,414	51.9	1.5	63.6	7.2	76.0	22.9
Jericho CDP	3.946	13,567	NA	NA	NA	23.6	92.3	$137,463	66.7	3.3	63.6	5.3	81.2	16.1
Johnson City village..................	4.536	15,174	14,832	-2.3	3,269.6	7.4	80.5	$37,936	9.7	19.3	58.4	8.4	50.5	40.0
Kenmore village........................	1.436	15,423	15,236	-1.2	10,611.5	2.3	91.5	$50,880	18.9	10.1	69.4	5.8	55.1	39.1
Kent town (Putnam)	40.504	13,533	13,399	-1.0	330.8	13.0	95.5	$87,808	42.4	6.2	67.4	7.1	81.6	15.2
Kingsbury town (Washington)*	39.692	12,692	12,619	-0.6	317.9	2.4	81.7	$44,621	12.4	17.0	69.8	9.8	64.6	26.1
Kings Park CDP	6.216	17,282	NA	NA	NA	6.1	95.0	$101,308	51.1	4.2	64.9	7.2	76.1	20.0
Kingston city & MCD (Ulster).....	7.482	23,881	23,557	-1.4	3,148.3	12.3	81.7	$41,719	13.8	15.5	62.3	9.5	54.2	38.5
Kirkland town (Oneida)	33.762	10,315	10,263	-0.5	304.0	7.3	83.6	$60,542	25.4	6.7	58.8	4.4	59.4	34.6
Kiryas Joel (Orange)	1.109	20,175	22,246	10.3	20,066.8	6.6	94.6	$25,795	9.3	54.5	48.2	6.5	94.5	4.6
Lackawanna city & MCD (Erie).	6.571	18,141	17,955	-1.0	2,732.4	9.0	89.4	$36,640	9.6	20.2	60.3	11.9	58.8	35.9
La Grange town (Dutchess)......	39.879	15,721	15,750	0.2	394.9	7.4	92.8	$101,176	50.9	2.3	69.3	9.6	81.4	15.8
Lake Grove village	2.955	11,191	11,241	0.4	3,803.6	15.6	95.1	$92,173	46.8	10.2	64.9	5.0	76.9	20.6
Lake Ronkonkoma CDP	4.937	20,155	NA	NA	NA	10.4	93.7	$90,922	44.6	5.3	66.6	6.6	72.2	24.2
Lancaster village.....................	2.699	10,364	10,294	-0.7	3,814.6	1.5	89.4	$51,924	22.8	7.9	72.8	9.9	61.9	27.3
Lancaster town (Erie)*	37.708	41,617	42,748	2.7	1,133.6	3.0	90.4	$66,029	30.5	7.2	70.9	6.5	68.8	25.8
Lansing town (Tompkins)*	60.490	11,027	11,444	3.8	189.2	15.2	78.5	$71,067	32.6	6.4	68.7	2.6	63.9	27.7
Le Ray town (Jefferson)..........	73.626	21,782	22,416	2.9	304.5	7.8	55.2	$44,370	11.9	12.7	74.5	14.4	80.4	16.7
Levittown CDP	6.811	51,881	NA	NA	NA	11.9	94.6	$99,867	49.9	2.9	68.2	6.8	82.6	14.5
Lewisboro town (Westchester) .	27.746	12,411	12,724	2.5	458.6	9.5	94.3	$141,477	64.9	1.8	68.0	7.6	78.7	18.5
Lewiston town (Niagara)*	37.122	16,262	16,110	-0.9	434.0	5.2	86.8	$64,475	29.0	6.7	58.1	4.6	65.4	31.3
Lindenhurst village..................	3.758	27,253	27,321	0.2	7,270.6	15.5	94.2	$84,414	40.1	5.2	67.9	6.4	77.2	18.7
Lloyd town (Ulster)..................	31.266	10,863	10,620	-2.2	339.7	5.8	89.5	$64,597	29.6	10.2	67.8	10.4	67.5	25.4
Lockport city & MCD (Niagara).	8.400	21,179	20,743	-2.1	2,469.5	3.7	85.7	$40,111	11.7	18.2	60.7	9.3	57.9	34.9
Lockport town (Niagara)	44.843	20,526	20,260	-1.3	451.8	3.5	92.6	$59,332	22.3	10.2	64.0	6.7	63.8	31.6
Long Beach city & MCD (Nassau)	2.215	33,275	33,664	1.2	15,200.5	18.5	86.8	$83,396	42.4	7.6	69.0	6.2	53.1	38.5
Lynbrook village......................	2.014	19,423	19,558	0.7	9,712.6	15.8	93.1	$87,712	44.5	6.2	63.6	9.1	67.5	27.4
Lysander town (Onondaga)*	61.714	21,759	22,413	3.0	363.2	2.7	90.1	$77,353	37.3	7.4	66.5	5.4	74.3	20.6
Malone town (Franklin)*	101.519	14,545	14,377	-1.2	141.6	4.2	72.6	$48,285	17.6	19.4	38.3	5.5	64.8	27.6
Malta town (Saratoga)*	27.922	14,765	14,873	0.7	532.7	4.4	86.2	$77,953	37.1	4.1	73.9	5.6	65.7	27.7
Mamakating town (Sullivan)......	96.108	12,083	11,700	-3.2	121.7	5.3	87.3	$54,317	20.1	11.5	68.5	14.0	66.3	25.8
Mamaroneck village.................	3.170	18,930	19,302	2.0	6,089.5	24.2	89.9	$85,865	44.1	9.5	68.4	8.4	65.0	31.4
Mamaroneck town (Westchester)*	6.654	29,156	29,860	2.4	4,487.5	19.9	88.6	$116,969	56.4	6.9	67.3	7.4	69.3	27.6
Manhattan borough (New York)	22.656	1,585,873	1,636,268	3.2	72,222.9	28.9	83.6	$71,656	38.7	15.6	67.4	8.2	41.4	47.3
Manlius town (Onondaga)*	49.218	32,370	32,405	0.1	658.4	6.2	91.0	$75,609	38.2	6.0	66.2	5.5	68.3	27.4
Manorville CDP	25.406	14,314	NA	NA	NA	4.2	96.3	$107,660	52.5	3.3	65.8	5.9	77.0	19.5
Massapequa CDP	3.560	21,685	NA	NA	NA	5.4	96.9	$122,192	58.8	1.5	66.3	5.5	80.2	17.0
Massapequa Park village	2.210	17,008	17,206	1.2	7,786.2	5.4	97.1	$114,574	56.9	2.4	65.6	8.4	82.9	14.7
Massena village	4.524	10,936	10,723	-1.9	2,370.0	4.2	85.7	$39,658	10.8	20.0	61.2	14.4	56.0	37.3
Massena town (St. Lawrence) ..	44.369	12,883	12,652	-1.8	285.2	4.2	86.4	$40,019	9.6	19.6	58.9	16.3	56.6	36.9
Mastic CDP..............................	3.950	15,481	NA	NA	NA	12.0	95.5	$70,600	27.9	12.5	66.4	6.2	79.8	15.3
Mastic Beach village................	4.024	14,841	14,874	0.2	3,696.7	5.1	97.2	$64,434	29.0	16.3	67.0	11.0	78.2	15.7
Medford CDP............................	10.799	24,142	NA	NA	NA	11.3	92.9	$90,914	42.0	6.8	65.1	5.9	75.2	19.5
Melville CDP.............................	12.085	18,985	NA	NA	NA	13.5	93.5	$117,007	56.7	5.5	57.9	6.1	76.7	20.8
Merrick CDP.............................	4.019	22,097	NA	NA	NA	9.4	96.2	$133,047	67.3	3.1	67.6	7.5	86.9	11.4
Middle Island CDP....................	8.240	10,483	NA	NA	NA	9.3	92.0	$68,725	28.0	9.3	62.0	5.9	60.3	33.3
Middletown city & MCD (Orange).	5.076	28,086	27,728	-1.3	5,462.7	21.0	87.8	$50,584	18.1	17.8	67.4	11.0	61.8	33.1
Miller Place CDP	6.551	12,339	NA	NA	NA	5.2	97.3	$111,417	54.5	4.0	72.2	6.3	82.0	15.2
Milton town (Saratoga)*	35.690	18,568	18,968	2.2	531.5	1.9	87.7	$64,464	29.5	8.2	73.6	9.3	65.9	27.6
Mineola village........................	1.879	18,799	19,028	1.2	10,125.5	31.5	93.8	$81,177	39.6	5.3	66.1	4.6	66.5	29.3
Monroe town (Orange)*	19.976	39,912	42,280	5.9	2,116.5	10.9	94.0	$65,866	35.9	23.5	64.6	6.1	84.0	13.3
Monsey CDP	2.273	18,412	NA	NA	NA	13.8	93.1	$35,049	18.0	42.0	50.0	9.8	93.4	3.8
Montgomery town (Orange)*	50.256	22,606	23,523	4.1	468.1	7.1	91.0	$71,655	35.0	10.6	67.4	8.3	71.9	23.0
Moreau town (Saratoga)*	41.936	14,739	15,350	4.1	366.0	1.9	89.7	$59,317	23.8	7.6	66.5	7.4	65.1	26.0
Mount Kisco village & town (Westchester)	3.035	10,877	11,103	2.1	3,658.0	36.6	87.3	$71,727	33.4	11.2	75.0	7.9	67.1	26.3
Mount Pleasant town (Westchester)*	27.452	43,727	44,638	2.1	1,626.1	20.1	88.5	$105,820	52.4	7.6	63.7	6.7	76.4	19.6
Mount Sinai CDP	5.998	12,118	NA	NA	NA	8.4	98.1	$112,470	57.1	4.7	62.8	2.4	80.8	17.9
Mount Vernon city & MCD (Westchester)......................	4.386	67,290	68,458	1.7	15,609.4	33.4	89.6	$49,268	21.2	15.6	67.9	13.4	62.1	33.5
Nanuet CDP	5.436	17,882	NA	NA	NA	29.0	92.9	$89,901	43.1	5.6	69.2	8.3	68.7	27.8
Nesconset CDP	3.821	13,387	NA	NA	NA	12.0	92.3	$112,314	57.7	5.2	66.6	6.1	81.4	16.6
Newburgh city & MCD (Orange).	3.804	28,866	28,358	-1.8	7,454.2	24.2	86.1	$33,125	14.0	33.9	62.7	11.5	65.8	28.6
Newburgh town (Orange)	42.678	29,801	30,584	2.6	716.6	9.2	93.5	$79,775	37.4	6.5	67.4	7.5	74.2	22.2
New Cassel CDP	1.479	14,059	NA	NA	NA	41.0	96.7	$74,956	39.7	16.0	69.4	5.5	82.4	16.5
New Castle town (Westchester)	23.165	17,547	17,967	2.4	775.6	13.0	90.2	$186,493	78.3	2.0	65.6	3.3	84.5	14.7
New City CDP...........................	15.582	33,559	NA	NA	NA	18.8	95.1	$117,764	59.3	4.3	65.3	7.1	83.7	14.4
New Hartford town (Oneida)*	25.378	22,166	22,150	-0.1	872.8	6.4	89.2	$62,529	26.7	6.7	60.9	4.9	59.3	35.9
New Paltz town (Ulster)*	33.875	14,003	14,096	0.7	416.1	8.3	75.5	$66,164	29.5	16.7	58.4	11.2	50.6	33.4
New Rochelle city & MCD (Westchester)......................	10.350	77,062	79,637	3.3	7,694.2	28.2	87.4	$68,270	36.6	10.4	65.0	8.3	68.3	28.6
New Windsor town (Orange)	34.076	25,244	26,265	4.0	770.8	11.6	91.3	$69,010	33.4	4.7	68.1	6.5	69.4	25.8
New York city	301.493	8,174,959	8,491,079	3.9	28,163.4	37.1	89.0	$52,737	25.8	19.3	63.4	10.3	60.0	32.5
Niagara Falls city & MCD (Niagara)	14.086	50,172	49,219	-1.9	3,494.2	4.7	90.4	$33,009	9.2	24.9	57.9	11.6	56.8	37.6
Niskayuna town (Schenectady)	14.150	21,778	22,277	2.3	1,574.4	13.1	91.0	$95,542	47.2	4.8	64.5	4.1	72.3	23.5
North Amityville CDP................	2.354	17,862	NA	NA	NA	31.7	90.2	$66,915	26.1	9.9	61.2	5.7	71.0	25.3

1 Dry land or land partially or temporarily covered by water.
2 16 years old and over.

Table B. Incorporated Places, Census Designated Places (CDPs), and Minor Civil Divisions (MCDs) of 10,000 or More Population — Crime, Construction, and Local Government Finance

	Serious crimes known to police, 2014[1]				New residential construction authorized by building permits, 2014			Local government finance, 2012							
		Rate[2]							General revenue				General expenditure		
									Intergovernmental				Per capita[3]		
STATE City, town, township, borough, or CDP (county if applicable)	Total number	Total	Violent	Property	Value ($1,000)	Number of housing units	Percent single family	Total (mil dol)	Total (mil dol)	Percent from state gov.	Taxes per capita[3]	Total (mil dol)	Total	Capital outlays	Debt outstanding (mil dol)
	15	16	17	18	19	20	21	22	23	24	25	26	27	28	29
NEW YORK—Con.															
Ithaca city & MCD (Tompkins) ..	1,221	3985	144	3842	8,924	79	2.5	58.8	12.2	65.1	1088	57.2	1,881	235	76.9
Ithaca town (Tompkins)*	NA	NA	NA	NA	4,804	14	71.4	14.5	4.1	22.1	329	12.9	643	59	6.2
Jamestown city & MCD (Chautauqua)	1,510	4927	728	4200	0	0	0.0	70.2	29.9	76.1	487	77.7	2,528	164	36.2
Jefferson Valley-Yorktown CDP	NA	NA	NA	NA	NA	NA	NA	NA	NA	NA	NA	NA	NA	NA	NA
Jericho CDP	NA	NA	NA	NA	NA	NA	NA	NA	NA	NA	NA	NA	NA	NA	NA
Johnson City village	1,141	7697	344	7353	NA	NA	NA	20.3	6.0	14.0	657	21.4	1,432	70	38.9
Kenmore village	332	2182	112	2070	0	0	0.0	14.2	2.9	36.1	599	13.1	857	26	6.1
Kent town (Putnam)	82	612	15	597	460	2	100.0	16.7	0.7	94.5	1082	16.1	1,200	85	3.0
Kingsbury town (Washington)*	NA	NA	NA	NA	281	2	100.0	2.5	0.3	70.3	150	2.5	194	32	0.0
Kings Park CDP	NA	NA	NA	NA	NA	NA	NA	NA	NA	NA	NA	NA	NA	NA	NA
Kingston city & MCD (Ulster)....	746	3147	312	2835	1,225	7	100.0	44.2	20.5	37.1	694	44.8	1,888	225	30.5
Kirkland town (Oneida)	NA	NA	NA	NA	812	4	100.0	5.8	2.4	3.7	240	5.2	508	23	0.7
Kiryas Joel village	NA	NA	NA	NA	18,315	133	0.0	11.4	6.3	5.9	138	11.5	538	180	14.2
Lackawanna city & MCD (Erie).	494	2755	457	2298	5,200	48	100.0	24.5	14.2	53.6	519	25.9	1,433	202	6.7
La Grange town (Dutchess)......	NA	NA	NA	NA	4,034	15	100.0	9.6	1.3	30.1	352	7.2	459	3	20.2
Lake Grove village	NA	NA	NA	NA	2,122	6	100.0	4.1	0.3	83.6	208	3.9	346	21	0.0
Lake Ronkonkoma CDP	NA	NA	NA	NA	NA	NA	NA	NA	NA	NA	NA	NA	NA	NA	NA
Lancaster village	NA	NA	NA	NA	480	4	0.0	10.0	1.3	28.9	456	10.2	986	120	52.6
Lancaster town (Erie)*	446	1213	41	1172	46,081	159	93.1	31.9	7.5	24.9	509	31.6	749	89	71.2
Lansing town (Tompkins)*	NA	NA	NA	NA	8,293	58	34.5	6.6	1.6	11.5	192	5.0	446	75	3.5
Le Ray town (Jefferson)	NA	NA	NA	NA	NA	NA	NA	4.5	1.4	9.2	46	3.6	159	26	11.7
Levittown CDP	NA	NA	NA	NA	NA	NA	NA	NA	NA	NA	NA	NA	NA	NA	NA
Lewisboro town (Westchester) .	5	39	NA	39	1,587	7	14.3	11.1	2.0	20.2	559	10.9	871	25	13.9
Lewiston town (Niagara)*	132	818	37	780	4,546	44	27.3	13.6	4.6	5.5	329	13.0	804	84	8.8
Lindenhurst village	NA	NA	NA	NA	1,408	9	100.0	11.6	1.7	75.6	257	11.3	413	55	5.9
Lloyd town (Ulster)	121	1134	56	1078	3,833	41	12.2	8.3	1.3	52.2	554	15.4	1,438	742	9.1
Lockport city & MCD (Niagara).	NA	NA	NA	NA	0	0	0.0	28.4	7.7	41.2	607	29.5	1,407	103	15.1
Lockport town (Niagara)	652	3135	375	2760	4,479	23	100.0	13.2	5.5	4.4	244	11.6	569	64	12.9
Long Beach city & MCD (Nassau)	339	1009	128	881	3,000	15	100.0	66.7	9.4	52.8	1002	74.0	2,210	91	54.6
Lynbrook village	180	923	77	846	0	0	0.0	32.4	1.3	75.1	1417	33.4	1,712	138	23.4
Lysander town (Onondaga)*	NA	NA	NA	NA	16,382	160	48.8	6.2	2.0	24.8	173	5.8	261	44	3.8
Malone town (Franklin)*	NA	NA	NA	NA	0	0	0.0	2.9	0.4	45.6	142	3.1	210	50	0.2
Malta town (Saratoga)	NA	NA	NA	NA	20,435	96	52.1	9.7	4.3	5.7	137	10.5	706	147	3.1
Mamakating town (Sullivan)......	NA	NA	NA	NA	1,040	5	100.0	5.6	0.6	67.3	351	5.1	427	8	0.0
Mamaroneck village	192	994	104	891	5,620	10	40.0	33.7	6.7	3.8	1216	31.7	1,657	165	44.3
Mamaroneck town (Westchester)*	NA	NA	NA	NA	0	0	0.0	37.2	9.9	7.3	755	39.0	1,325	109	17.4
Manhattan borough (New York)	NA	NA	NA	NA	524,215	5,380	0.0	NA	NA	NA	NA	NA	NA	NA	NA
Manlius town (Onondaga)*	392	1595	65	1530	10,727	42	100.0	15.9	0.7	61.8	421	15.6	481	18	0.5
Manorville CDP	NA	NA	NA	NA	NA	NA	NA	NA	NA	NA	NA	NA	NA	NA	NA
Massapequa CDP	NA	NA	NA	NA	NA	NA	NA	NA	NA	NA	NA	NA	NA	NA	NA
Massapequa Park village	NA	NA	NA	NA	966	4	100.0	6.4	1.1	88.2	264	5.7	332	58	7.8
Massena village	387	3588	241	3347	0	0	0.0	12.0	2.7	15.1	485	11.4	1,049	62	9.5
Massena town (St. Lawrence) ..	NA	NA	NA	NA	0	0	0.0	59.2	2.7	14.2	170	56.5	4,408	155	9.9
Mastic CDP	NA	NA	NA	NA	NA	NA	NA	NA	NA	NA	NA	NA	NA	NA	NA
Mastic Beach village	NA	NA	NA	NA	241	1	100.0	4.0	0.0	0.0	127	2.8	188	11	0.0
Medford CDP	NA	NA	NA	NA	NA	NA	NA	NA	NA	NA	NA	NA	NA	NA	NA
Melville CDP	NA	NA	NA	NA	NA	NA	NA	NA	NA	NA	NA	NA	NA	NA	NA
Merrick CDP	NA	NA	NA	NA	NA	NA	NA	NA	NA	NA	NA	NA	NA	NA	NA
Middle Island CDP	NA	NA	NA	NA	NA	NA	NA	NA	NA	NA	NA	NA	NA	NA	NA
Middletown city & MCD (Orange)	953	3440	451	2989	16,658	69	100.0	41.5	13.3	24.7	681	38.9	1,397	51	84.2
Miller Place CDP	NA	NA	NA	NA	NA	NA	NA	NA	NA	NA	NA	NA	NA	NA	NA
Milton town (Saratoga)*	NA	NA	NA	NA	3,370	18	100.0	4.4	2.8	7.6	58	4.8	255	25	0.0
Mineola village	NA	NA	NA	NA	5,234	43	16.3	18.8	1.2	52.7	772	17.8	941	35	18.8
Monroe town (Orange)*	NA	NA	NA	NA	8,070	16	100.0	11.1	2.4	29.4	106	10.5	255	16	1.2
Monsey CDP	NA	NA	NA	NA	NA	NA	NA	NA	NA	NA	NA	NA	NA	NA	NA
Montgomery town (Orange)*	NA	NA	NA	NA	1,677	11	100.0	9.5	1.8	16.6	270	9.2	404	37	3.0
Moreau town (Saratoga)*	NA	NA	NA	NA	14,028	101	36.6	6.2	2.5	7.4	156	6.5	429	56	6.1
Mount Kisco village & town (Westchester)	145	1305	252	1053	750	2	100.0	23.1	4.5	14.6	1352	22.0	1,999	94	28.1
Mount Pleasant town (Westchester)*	NA	NA	NA	NA	6,058	14	100.0	40.0	6.8	8.2	591	39.5	892	23	107.2
Mount Sinai CDP	NA	NA	NA	NA	NA	NA	NA	NA	NA	NA	NA	NA	NA	NA	NA
Mount Vernon city & MCD (Westchester)	1,526	2230	722	1508	529	6	33.3	96.7	15.2	70.5	1042	104.4	1,537	169	56.4
Nanuet CDP	NA	NA	NA	NA	NA	NA	NA	NA	NA	NA	NA	NA	NA	NA	NA
Nesconset CDP	NA	NA	NA	NA	NA	NA	NA	NA	NA	NA	NA	NA	NA	NA	NA
Newburgh city & MCD (Orange)	1,285	4528	1476	3052	1,255	10	100.0	57.5	23.9	52.4	742	56.9	1,989	235	100.8
Newburgh town (Orange)	1,432	4645	101	4545	11,727	97	25.8	29.0	4.7	12.1	628	25.2	823	30	29.2
New Cassel CDP	NA	NA	NA	NA	NA	NA	NA	NA	NA	NA	NA	NA	NA	NA	NA
New Castle town (Westchester)	54	300	11	289	5,353	8	100.0	28.2	2.9	18.8	1211	29.9	1,680	133	19.7
New City CDP	NA	NA	NA	NA	NA	NA	NA	NA	NA	NA	NA	NA	NA	NA	NA
New Hartford town (Oneida)*	817	4023	123	3900	3,005	11	100.0	14.6	6.2	7.1	324	15.3	694	124	11.0
New Paltz town (Ulster)*	233	1656	213	1442	3,150	9	100.0	11.0	0.5	44.2	639	11.4	810	45	0.8
New Rochelle city & MCD (Westchester)	1,396	1744	229	1516	2,537	5	100.0	134.5	29.2	42.3	1022	133.3	1,700	146	141.5
New Windsor town (Orange)	565	2148	137	2011	20,657	152	25.7	23.6	4.3	14.5	564	22.8	891	80	10.5
New York city	186,311	2199	597	1602	185,203	1,885	0.0	85078.0	30398.8	83.5	5077	81160.8	9,701	1,196	131462.0
Niagara Falls city & MCD (Niagara)	3,228	6548	1189	5359	964	6	100.0	98.1	50.3	53.9	824	127.8	2,570	657	72.6
Niskayuna town (Schenectady)	389	1749	36	1713	5,141	23	100.0	17.3	3.8	7.0	371	15.9	724	22	9.6
North Amityville CDP	NA	NA	NA	NA	NA	NA	NA	NA	NA	NA	NA	NA	NA	NA	NA

1 Data for serious crimes have not been adjusted for underreporting. This may affect comparability between geographic areas over time.
2 Per 100,000 population estimated by the FBI.   3 Based on population estimated as of July 1 of the year shown.

Table B. Incorporated Places, Census Designated Places (CDPs), and Minor Civil Divisions (MCDs) of 10,000 or More Population — **Land Area, Population, and Households, and Employment**

STATE City, town, township, borough, or CDP (county if applicable)	Land area,[1] 2010 (sq mi)	Total persons 2010	Total persons 2014	Percent change 2010–2014	Persons per square mile, 2014	Foreign born	Lives in same house as previous year	Median household income (dollars)	Income of $100,000 or more	Income below poverty level	Percent in labor force	Unemployment rate	Family households	One person households
	1	2	3	4	5	6	7	8	9	10	11	12	13	14
NEW YORK—Con.														
North Babylon CDP	3.372	17,509	NA	NA	NA	11.8	94.6	$87,403	40.3	4.3	66.7	7.0	75.6	19.8
North Bay Shore CDP	3.214	18,944	NA	NA	NA	34.6	92.4	$69,696	36.8	9.2	72.9	9.1	86.9	10.3
North Bellmore CDP	2.620	19,941	NA	NA	NA	11.3	94.3	$105,943	53.8	3.2	64.9	7.0	81.4	15.4
North Bellport CDP	4.897	11,545	NA	NA	NA	18.1	92.6	$68,591	29.2	17.4	61.3	6.7	81.6	14.8
North Castle town (Westchester)	23.812	11,860	12,225	3.1	513.4	12.5	90.6	$159,031	70.8	2.9	65.8	5.9	83.9	13.9
North Greenbush town (Rensselaer)	18.546	12,075	12,120	0.4	653.5	4.0	86.1	$79,050	33.4	5.5	66.9	5.4	65.4	28.1
North Hempstead town (Nassau)*	53.513	226,319	229,637	1.5	4,291.2	28.5	93.3	$104,264	52.1	5.3	62.8	6.4	75.8	21.2
North Lindenhurst CDP	1.930	11,652	NA	NA	NA	24.6	90.9	$70,493	30.6	8.1	66.5	10.1	74.3	24.1
North Massapequa CDP	2.995	17,886	NA	NA	NA	6.4	96.9	$102,798	51.1	4.8	65.6	4.0	80.7	16.4
North Merrick CDP	1.719	12,272	NA	NA	NA	8.9	96.9	$109,920	55.7	3.0	67.1	3.9	83.8	12.3
North New Hyde Park CDP	1.973	14,899	NA	NA	NA	28.0	94.9	$109,813	59.2	4.3	62.5	7.5	87.5	11.2
North Tonawanda city & MCD (Niagara)	10.100	31,568	30,929	-2.0	3,062.2	2.9	88.1	$47,604	17.7	10.7	66.2	7.7	57.7	36.8
North Valley Stream CDP	1.865	16,628	NA	NA	NA	36.6	96.7	$100,882	50.8	7.0	68.5	11.2	82.7	13.8
North Wantagh CDP	1.903	11,960	NA	NA	NA	7.1	98.1	$100,313	50.1	2.8	66.8	4.0	79.6	17.6
Oceanside CDP	4.955	32,109	NA	NA	NA	11.4	96.7	$97,922	48.7	5.5	64.6	5.8	77.1	19.9
Ogden town (Monroe)*	36.478	19,856	20,225	1.9	554.4	5.7	90.9	$70,830	29.5	5.6	70.6	6.1	74.3	21.6
Ogdensburg city & MCD (St. Lawrence)	4.956	11,128	10,895	-2.1	2,198.5	4.9	77.9	$38,822	14.6	19.0	51.6	9.3	58.1	34.5
Olean city & MCD (Cattaraugus)	5.908	14,452	14,043	-2.8	2,377.1	2.1	84.7	$39,876	12.2	18.0	64.0	9.3	53.6	36.4
Oneida city & MCD (Madison)	22.053	11,406	11,192	-1.9	507.5	3.0	91.3	$46,958	15.3	18.3	58.5	7.0	62.9	32.6
Oneonta city & MCD (Otsego)	4.361	13,901	13,838	-0.5	3,172.9	4.1	62.0	$38,034	15.2	28.5	50.1	9.0	43.7	36.1
Onondaga town (Onondaga)	57.740	23,101	23,082	-0.1	399.8	4.7	88.0	$72,389	34.7	6.2	64.3	5.4	68.7	27.5
Ontario town (Wayne)	32.412	10,136	10,097	-0.4	311.5	3.7	88.9	$62,200	25.8	6.3	67.3	4.7	72.0	22.5
Orangetown town (Rockland)*	24.098	49,212	50,463	2.5	2,094.1	15.1	92.6	$97,543	49.0	7.5	63.3	6.6	68.1	28.0
Orchard Park town (Erie)*	38.437	29,054	29,545	1.7	768.7	3.6	92.4	$81,326	40.0	2.1	65.4	3.9	70.6	27.2
Ossining village	3.168	25,071	25,359	1.1	8,004.9	39.6	90.0	$68,533	33.1	15.2	70.7	8.9	70.5	23.8
Ossining town (Westchester)*	11.556	37,674	38,214	1.4	3,306.8	30.6	90.1	$82,009	43.2	11.6	67.2	7.8	72.2	23.7
Oswego city & MCD (Oswego)	7.614	18,142	17,988	-0.8	2,362.5	2.6	80.4	$39,466	13.7	24.8	57.3	9.1	52.9	36.8
Owego town (Tioga)*	104.221	19,883	19,340	-2.7	185.6	3.8	90.9	$69,777	29.2	7.1	65.1	7.1	72.0	24.1
Oyster Bay town (Nassau)*	103.752	293,219	297,896	1.6	2,871.2	15.0	94.8	$111,341	55.4	3.8	64.1	5.7	79.4	17.6
Parma town (Monroe)*	42.024	15,633	15,863	1.5	377.5	3.8	92.0	$66,793	27.7	4.3	67.9	6.2	75.4	19.8
Patchogue village	2.256	11,798	12,364	4.8	5,480.4	16.3	91.6	$70,035	29.2	16.3	68.9	5.1	61.3	29.7
Patterson town (Putnam)	32.208	12,035	12,011	-0.2	372.9	11.2	94.8	$89,901	43.4	3.9	63.8	7.4	74.8	23.0
Pearl River CDP	6.799	15,876	NA	NA	NA	11.5	96.0	$101,227	50.9	7.0	65.4	4.8	73.2	23.9
Peekskill city & MCD (Westchester)	4.368	23,583	24,058	2.0	5,508.3	27.5	85.7	$51,961	26.2	15.0	71.8	12.9	61.6	33.0
Pelham town (Westchester)	2.172	12,396	12,607	1.7	5,804.5	14.4	93.4	$140,977	64.3	2.1	67.8	3.7	82.8	14.2
Penfield town (Monroe)*	37.220	36,262	37,189	2.6	999.2	6.6	92.6	$78,329	37.3	5.8	64.7	5.4	67.7	28.6
Perinton town (Monroe)*	34.188	46,462	46,658	0.4	1,364.8	5.4	91.6	$78,702	38.1	6.7	67.5	6.1	68.9	26.2
Pittsford town (Monroe)*	23.193	29,396	29,570	0.6	1,274.9	9.9	87.7	$106,134	53.3	5.0	61.4	4.6	75.6	20.0
Plainview CDP	5.733	26,217	NA	NA	NA	15.2	95.3	$122,591	59.6	3.0	64.0	4.7	81.2	17.1
Plattekill town (Ulster)	35.111	10,499	10,336	-1.6	294.4	5.0	93.8	$60,193	26.7	13.3	65.7	8.0	66.5	28.0
Plattsburgh city & MCD (Clinton)	5.039	19,989	19,740	-1.2	3,917.8	6.9	68.6	$34,460	13.6	23.4	53.6	7.2	47.6	37.2
Plattsburgh town (Clinton)	45.901	11,870	11,839	-0.3	257.9	5.1	88.4	$56,896	20.9	13.0	61.4	6.7	67.5	23.6
Pomfret town (Chautauqua)*	43.855	14,965	14,471	-3.3	330.0	3.1	80.3	$48,108	18.3	18.1	54.4	6.7	54.6	31.8
Port Chester village	2.331	28,968	29,522	1.9	12,667.5	45.3	84.5	$56,134	25.0	15.5	73.9	7.7	71.7	21.6
Port Washington CDP	4.185	15,846	NA	NA	NA	20.0	90.5	$108,767	54.6	4.8	64.0	7.3	76.2	19.3
Potsdam town (St. Lawrence)*	101.403	16,041	16,190	0.9	159.7	8.7	69.6	$46,677	19.2	20.3	52.5	9.9	51.0	36.0
Poughkeepsie city & MCD (Dutchess)	5.145	30,900	30,513	-1.3	5,931.2	21.8	82.3	$38,973	15.2	21.7	64.1	14.5	54.7	36.1
Poughkeepsie town (Dutchess)*	28.517	45,170	44,640	-1.2	1,565.4	13.3	85.8	$68,076	31.0	10.1	63.0	8.6	67.3	27.0
Putnam Valley town (Putnam)	41.175	11,809	11,722	-0.7	284.7	11.2	96.1	$103,455	51.4	5.8	67.5	8.1	78.3	18.3
Queens borough (Queens)	108.765	2,230,539	2,321,580	4.1	21,344.8	47.8	90.3	$57,210	25.0	14.7	64.2	9.5	67.4	26.3
Queensbury town (Warren)	62.830	27,899	27,675	-0.8	440.5	3.9	88.9	$64,949	27.2	9.4	62.1	4.8	68.2	26.9
Ramapo town (Rockland)*	61.195	126,595	133,351	5.3	2,179.1	23.5	91.5	$68,701	33.7	18.3	65.1	8.8	79.2	17.9
Red Hook town (Dutchess)	36.169	11,319	11,263	-0.5	311.4	8.3	84.1	$68,424	33.8	9.4	64.2	7.3	63.5	29.6
Ridge CDP	13.202	13,336	NA	NA	NA	5.7	91.6	$57,848	29.2	7.9	56.5	6.6	62.5	32.0
Riverhead CDP	15.093	13,299	NA	NA	NA	25.3	86.0	$53,403	25.5	13.5	60.8	9.8	65.2	28.6
Riverhead town (Suffolk)	67.426	33,505	33,777	0.8	501.0	15.4	90.2	$68,422	35.2	9.1	61.4	9.5	68.7	26.9
Rochester city & MCD (Monroe)	35.771	210,512	209,983	-0.3	5,870.2	9.1	76.6	$30,784	8.3	29.5	61.2	13.9	49.8	40.4
Rockville Centre village	3.248	24,023	24,191	0.7	7,448.9	8.8	93.1	$108,456	52.3	6.0	64.6	6.6	67.4	28.9
Rocky Point CDP	11.297	14,014	NA	NA	NA	4.3	91.4	$93,542	46.5	3.8	72.6	9.5	78.3	18.7
Rome city & MCD (Oneida)	74.791	33,725	32,645	-3.2	436.5	3.5	82.8	$44,694	15.3	15.3	55.6	6.6	57.4	36.1
Ronkonkoma CDP	7.816	19,082	NA	NA	NA	9.7	93.2	$86,432	40.1	5.0	69.6	8.6	76.5	18.1
Roosevelt CDP	1.770	16,258	NA	NA	NA	30.4	93.0	$62,566	29.8	18.8	69.1	11.2	79.2	15.8
Rotterdam CDP	6.922	20,652	NA	NA	NA	4.3	95.0	$59,262	21.0	6.5	65.4	7.7	64.3	30.6
Rotterdam town (Schenectady)	35.683	29,098	29,411	1.1	824.2	3.6	94.2	$63,887	24.7	5.9	66.4	6.3	64.5	30.6
Rye city & MCD (Westchester)	5.854	15,720	16,000	1.8	2,733.3	15.5	89.5	$155,422	67.2	4.5	58.9	5.9	75.4	22.0
Rye town (Westchester)	6.919	45,930	46,837	2.0	6,769.6	35.2	86.3	$74,509	37.0	11.1	71.6	7.8	73.0	22.4
St. James CDP	4.562	13,338	NA	NA	NA	5.0	94.4	$98,576	49.5	4.8	59.8	5.1	77.9	18.2
Salina town (Onondaga)*	13.750	33,710	33,450	-0.8	2,432.7	5.4	90.9	$52,402	15.0	10.0	64.3	7.5	56.5	35.7
Salisbury CDP	1.737	12,093	NA	NA	NA	24.6	97.0	$96,875	47.9	5.2	66.8	7.5	83.6	14.0
Saratoga Springs city & MCD (Saratoga)	28.065	26,565	27,436	3.3	977.6	6.4	81.2	$67,303	30.9	9.5	63.4	7.5	47.5	39.8
Saugerties town (Ulster)*	64.574	19,482	19,235	-1.3	297.9	5.6	90.9	$60,425	25.4	7.6	67.2	9.3	68.8	26.6
Sayville CDP	5.306	16,853	NA	NA	NA	3.5	94.0	$104,427	52.0	4.2	64.3	7.2	72.4	23.7
Scarsdale village & town (Westchester)	6.660	17,166	17,729	3.3	2,661.9	22.3	90.7	$241,453	82.7	1.5	61.5	5.5	89.5	9.1

1 Dry land or land partially or temporarily covered by water.
2 16 years old and over.

Table B. Incorporated Places, Census Designated Places (CDPs), and Minor Civil Divisions (MCDs) of 10,000 or More Population — Crime, Construction, and Local Government Finance

STATE City, town, township, borough, or CDP (county if applicable)	Serious crimes known to police, 2014[1] Total number	Rate[2] Total	Rate[2] Violent	Rate[2] Property	New residential construction authorized by building permits, 2014 Value ($1,000)	Number of housing units	Percent single family	Local government finance, 2012 General revenue Total (mil dol)	Intergovernmental Total (mil dol)	Percent from state gov.	Taxes per capita[3]	General expenditure Total (mil dol)	Per capita[3] Total	Capital outlays	Debt outstanding (mil dol)
	15	16	17	18	19	20	21	22	23	24	25	26	27	28	29
NEW YORK—Con.															
North Babylon CDP	NA	NA	NA	NA	NA	NA	NA	NA	NA	NA	NA	NA	NA	NA	NA
North Bay Shore CDP	NA	NA	NA	NA	NA	NA	NA	NA	NA	NA	NA	NA	NA	NA	NA
North Bellmore CDP	NA	NA	NA	NA	NA	NA	NA	NA	NA	NA	NA	NA	NA	NA	NA
North Bellport CDP	NA	NA	NA	NA	NA	NA	NA	NA	NA	NA	NA	NA	NA	NA	NA
North Castle town (Westchester)	65	532	16	515	14,642	12	100.0	26.9	2.0	17.0	1748	26.8	2,229	175	18.2
North Greenbush town (Rensselaer)	201	1654	115	1539	7,857	30	43.3	8.3	1.6	16.7	325	6.5	538	20	22.8
North Hempstead town (Nassau)*	NA	NA	NA	NA	15,621	45	100.0	202.2	23.6	18.2	602	233.2	1,021	267	354.7
North Lindenhurst CDP	NA	NA	NA	NA	NA	NA	NA	NA	NA	NA	NA	NA	NA	NA	NA
North Massapequa CDP	NA	NA	NA	NA	NA	NA	NA	NA	NA	NA	NA	NA	NA	NA	NA
North Merrick CDP	NA	NA	NA	NA	NA	NA	NA	NA	NA	NA	NA	NA	NA	NA	NA
North New Hyde Park CDP	NA	NA	NA	NA	NA	NA	NA	NA	NA	NA	NA	NA	NA	NA	NA
North Tonawanda city & MCD (Niagara)	530	1710	155	1556	1,789	12	100.0	43.9	17.1	37.3	596	41.6	1,330	104	13.9
North Valley Stream CDP	NA	NA	NA	NA	NA	NA	NA	NA	NA	NA	NA	NA	NA	NA	NA
North Wantagh CDP	NA	NA	NA	NA	NA	NA	NA	NA	NA	NA	NA	NA	NA	NA	NA
Oceanside CDP	NA	NA	NA	NA	NA	NA	NA	NA	NA	NA	NA	NA	NA	NA	NA
Ogden town (Monroe)*	259	1282	84	1198	8,228	35	100.0	10.2	2.1	12.1	353	9.8	489	25	1.4
Ogdensburg city & MCD (St. Lawrence)	457	4158	209	3949	60	1	100.0	16.7	5.7	64.2	690	17.1	1,545	288	6.8
Olean city & MCD (Cattaraugus)	445	3160	213	2947	222	1	100.0	21.5	4.7	76.1	818	20.7	1,458	165	27.5
Oneida city & MCD (Madison)	483	4301	285	4016	361	5	20.0	14.7	3.3	69.2	691	14.3	1,267	142	13.1
Oneonta city & MCD (Otsego)	274	1963	186	1776	20,250	142	0.7	19.8	10.2	39.0	364	21.5	1,540	296	8.2
Onondaga town (Onondaga)	NA	NA	NA	NA	4,262	25	100.0	9.6	1.0	31.4	350	8.6	370	10	2.5
Ontario town (Wayne)	NA	NA	NA	NA	4,722	39	48.7	6.4	1.2	12.1	258	6.8	674	22	4.3
Orangetown town (Rockland)*	NA	NA	NA	NA	3,579	10	100.0	62.3	4.3	33.7	1013	72.2	1,450	113	73.8
Orchard Park town (Erie)*	405	1373	44	1328	20,788	72	97.2	19.7	5.4	16.6	441	19.0	646	98	11.9
Ossining village	266	1045	216	829	175	1	100.0	33.4	8.9	10.1	805	37.3	1,479	39	25.9
Ossining town (Westchester)*	NA	NA	NA	NA	1,820	12	66.7	13.5	1.1	29.2	292	13.6	358	22	7.4
Oswego city & MCD (Oswego)	687	3793	315	3478	883	11	100.0	39.3	9.3	46.1	1085	37.7	2,071	176	25.7
Owego town (Tioga)*	NA	NA	NA	NA	1,268	6	100.0	8.5	3.1	19.5	148	10.3	528	62	10.0
Oyster Bay town (Nassau)*	NA	NA	NA	NA	49,652	159	100.0	277.5	33.8	25.2	729	371.9	1,257	388	739.9
Parma town (Monroe)*	NA	NA	NA	NA	2,896	19	100.0	6.0	2.4	45.9	165	5.7	363	54	0.1
Patchogue village	NA	NA	NA	NA	16,200	57	100.0	16.0	3.5	24.9	691	12.9	1,089	199	13.9
Patterson town (Putnam)	NA	NA	NA	NA	770	4	100.0	11.8	1.9	45.3	762	11.1	922	115	8.3
Pearl River CDP	NA	NA	NA	NA	NA	NA	NA	NA	NA	NA	NA	NA	NA	NA	NA
Peekskill city & MCD (Westchester)	243	1009	224	785	0	0	0.0	47.0	19.2	38.2	675	53.1	2,226	142	94.5
Pelham town (Westchester)	NA	NA	NA	NA	NA	NA	NA	3.5	0.3	94.4	187	3.8	304	1	0.0
Penfield town (Monroe)	NA	NA	NA	NA	43,688	227	48.5	17.8	4.6	9.6	257	16.9	461	18	18.1
Perinton town (Monroe)*	NA	NA	NA	NA	10,978	59	96.6	22.9	4.4	13.4	257	24.3	522	92	22.4
Pittsford town (Monroe)*	NA	NA	NA	NA	16,597	33	100.0	15.7	3.3	9.2	364	15.0	505	36	12.8
Plainview CDP	NA	NA	NA	NA	NA	NA	NA	NA	NA	NA	NA	NA	NA	NA	NA
Plattekill town (Ulster)	NA	NA	NA	NA	1,139	5	100.0	3.5	0.5	48.6	247	3.3	318	3	0.3
Plattsburgh city & MCD (Clinton)	295	1484	156	1328	1,159	7	100.0	29.2	9.9	48.1	500	31.5	1,586	185	36.9
Plattsburgh town (Clinton)	NA	NA	NA	NA	10,689	76	15.8	10.2	4.8	5.8	302	10.5	889	111	10.6
Pomfret town (Chautauqua)*	NA	NA	NA	NA	500	3	100.0	2.5	1.0	24.5	70	2.6	177	14	0.9
Port Chester village	563	1908	213	1694	2,235	12	50.0	36.3	5.3	14.4	808	37.3	1,275	86	50.5
Port Washington CDP	NA	NA	NA	NA	NA	NA	NA	NA	NA	NA	NA	NA	NA	NA	NA
Potsdam town (St. Lawrence)*	NA	NA	NA	NA	876	4	100.0	4.1	1.5	24.5	94	3.8	233	34	0.2
Poughkeepsie city & MCD (Dutchess)	978	3201	894	2307	250	2	100.0	58.3	29.4	22.7	624	54.6	1,777	206	86.8
Poughkeepsie town (Dutchess)*	1,466	3362	119	3243	2,443	15	100.0	41.4	5.9	44.8	623	36.4	810	83	36.4
Putnam Valley town (Putnam)	NA	NA	NA	NA	0	0	0.0	11.5	0.9	55.9	828	11.4	970	84	1.3
Queens borough (Queens)	NA	NA	NA	NA	458,159	4,900	4.4	NA	NA	NA	NA	NA	NA	NA	NA
Queensbury town (Warren)	NA	NA	NA	NA	17,350	165	40.6	23.5	10.0	14.6	304	22.8	819	112	16.4
Ramapo town (Rockland)*	NA	NA	NA	NA	32,867	299	6.0	85.3	5.6	18.3	512	114.6	882	278	152.2
Red Hook town (Dutchess)	NA	NA	NA	NA	925	4	100.0	4.0	1.1	47.2	232	5.0	447	118	4.5
Ridge CDP	NA	NA	NA	NA	NA	NA	NA	NA	NA	NA	NA	NA	NA	NA	NA
Riverhead CDP	NA	NA	NA	NA	NA	NA	NA	NA	NA	NA	NA	NA	NA	NA	NA
Riverhead town (Suffolk)	946	2807	148	2659	6,185	44	100.0	69.0	4.7	50.2	1495	77.9	2,309	121	227.5
Rochester city & MCD (Monroe)	10,643	5060	850	4210	28,816	223	31.4	1215.0	931.5	73.2	859	1222.9	5,805	517	496.9
Rockville Centre village	211	875	70	804	1,300	4	100.0	40.4	5.8	35.1	1094	45.6	1,890	203	37.6
Rocky Point CDP	NA	NA	NA	NA	NA	NA	NA	NA	NA	NA	NA	NA	NA	NA	NA
Rome city & MCD (Oneida)	658	2017	101	1916	3,707	22	27.3	49.4	15.0	77.6	760	50.7	1,538	140	46.6
Ronkonkoma CDP	NA	NA	NA	NA	NA	NA	NA	NA	NA	NA	NA	NA	NA	NA	NA
Roosevelt CDP	NA	NA	NA	NA	NA	NA	NA	NA	NA	NA	NA	NA	NA	NA	NA
Rotterdam CDP	NA	NA	NA	NA	NA	NA	NA	NA	NA	NA	NA	NA	NA	NA	NA
Rotterdam town (Schenectady)	917	3125	55	3071	20,005	132	18.2	20.6	6.1	8.2	452	20.0	687	17	9.3
Rye city & MCD (Westchester)	58	362	25	337	0	0	0.0	38.0	3.8	40.9	1469	43.7	2,757	96	20.8
Rye town (Westchester)	NA	NA	NA	NA	NA	NA	NA	2.8	0.4	100.0	43	3.3	71	0	0.4
St. James CDP	NA	NA	NA	NA	NA	NA	NA	NA	NA	NA	NA	NA	NA	NA	NA
Salina town (Onondaga)*	NA	NA	NA	NA	0	0	0.0	18.1	4.3	97.8	379	24.6	729	156	26.0
Salisbury CDP	NA	NA	NA	NA	NA	NA	NA	NA	NA	NA	NA	NA	NA	NA	NA
Saratoga Springs city & MCD (Saratoga)	655	2382	236	2146	38,834	198	36.4	48.9	5.5	67.4	1193	43.3	1,605	81	36.7
Saugerties town (Ulster)*	233	1212	83	1129	3,759	18	88.9	15.6	3.8	46.8	506	14.4	745	23	10.0
Sayville CDP	NA	NA	NA	NA	NA	NA	NA	NA	NA	NA	NA	NA	NA	NA	NA
Scarsdale village & town (Westchester)	130	734	6	728	50,827	35	100.0	55.0	10.0	7.5	2100	57.3	3,283	662	17.5

1 Data for serious crimes have not been adjusted for underreporting. This may affect comparability between geographic areas over time.
2 Per 100,000 population estimated by the FBI. 3 Based on population estimated as of July 1 of the year shown.

Table B. Incorporated Places, Census Designated Places (CDPs), and Minor Civil Divisions (MCDs) of 10,000 or More Population — Land Area, Population, and Households, and Employment

STATE City, town, township, borough, or CDP (county if applicable)	Land area,[1] 2010 (sq mi)	Total persons 2010	Total persons 2014	Percent change 2010–2014	Persons per square mile, 2014	Foreign born	Lives in same house as previous year	Median household income (dollars)	Income of $100,000 or more	Income below poverty level	Percent in labor force	Unemployment rate	Family households	One person households
	1	2	3	4	5	6	7	8	9	10	11	12	13	14
NEW YORK—Con.														
Schenectady city & MCD (Schenectady)	10.792	66,134	65,936	-0.3	6,109.7	13.3	88.1	$38,916	9.8	20.1	63.2	12.0	52.6	39.9
Schodack town (Rensselaer)	61.927	12,794	13,123	2.6	211.9	1.8	91.2	$79,139	35.8	5.6	67.6	8.6	73.7	21.9
Seaford CDP	2.610	15,294	NA	NA	NA	7.4	94.3	$104,479	53.5	3.2	69.1	6.4	77.0	20.0
Selden CDP	4.321	19,851	NA	NA	NA	13.8	94.0	$87,178	37.9	7.7	68.7	6.7	78.7	16.3
Setauket-East Setauket CDP	8.506	15,477	NA	NA	NA	12.1	95.6	$124,974	62.9	2.2	69.2	4.2	79.0	18.3
Shawangunk town (Ulster)	56.056	14,332	14,174	-1.1	252.9	4.1	91.0	$86,531	42.7	4.9	55.9	7.6	74.4	20.1
Shirley CDP	11.092	27,854	NA	NA	NA	14.7	95.2	$81,258	35.7	7.6	68.3	5.5	82.0	13.4
Sleepy Hollow village	2.199	9,870	10,208	3.4	4,641.6	40.9	90.6	$58,672	29.2	16.7	67.0	8.8	70.2	26.7
Smithtown CDP	11.621	26,470	NA	NA	NA	6.2	93.5	$110,683	58.8	4.9	63.8	7.9	76.6	20.1
Smithtown town (Suffolk)*	53.694	117,801	118,446	0.5	2,205.9	7.8	94.3	$111,407	56.3	4.1	65.1	6.5	79.2	18.1
Somers town (Westchester)	29.642	20,434	21,280	4.1	717.9	10.6	93.9	$114,367	58.7	3.1	60.6	6.1	76.3	21.6
Southampton town (Suffolk)*	139.181	56,792	58,093	2.3	417.4	18.8	87.9	$77,130	38.3	7.6	58.1	5.5	67.2	26.8
Southeast town (Putnam)*	31.734	18,404	18,248	-0.8	575.0	16.4	92.1	$88,062	45.3	7.4	72.9	8.6	72.7	23.5
South Farmingdale CDP	2.218	14,486	NA	NA	NA	11.2	96.1	$105,565	54.0	3.2	66.0	7.0	83.8	13.8
Southold town (Suffolk)	53.763	21,969	22,248	1.3	413.8	8.7	93.8	$83,559	41.6	3.9	57.8	7.6	68.3	26.6
Southport town (Chemung)	46.413	10,940	10,620	-2.9	228.8	1.0	88.6	$50,642	16.9	10.6	54.9	5.3	62.0	30.1
Spring Valley village	2.012	31,275	32,510	3.9	16,158.6	44.5	85.0	$46,142	14.9	22.2	72.1	13.5	75.9	19.7
Staten Island borough (Richmond)	58.172	468,730	473,279	1.0	8,135.8	21.5	94.3	$74,043	35.6	12.3	59.5	7.6	74.2	22.6
Stony Brook CDP	5.806	13,740	NA	NA	NA	9.2	92.2	$139,674	67.6	3.5	65.9	6.0	77.3	18.7
Stony Point CDP	5.442	12,147	NA	NA	NA	12.8	94.4	$96,042	48.1	4.8	66.1	8.5	77.0	17.7
Stony Point town (Rockland)	27.625	15,059	15,463	2.7	559.7	11.4	94.8	$97,522	48.9	4.6	65.2	8.3	77.9	17.0
Suffern village	2.089	10,723	10,991	2.5	5,262.2	18.4	89.9	$80,733	37.6	7.1	70.9	8.4	63.0	33.1
Sullivan town (Madison)*	73.147	15,339	15,386	0.3	210.3	1.4	92.8	$63,261	21.1	6.3	65.0	3.6	68.4	25.9
Sweden town (Monroe)*	33.680	14,175	14,259	0.6	423.4	4.5	77.1	$49,571	21.4	16.2	58.8	7.5	58.9	27.8
Syosset CDP	4.974	18,829	NA	NA	NA	21.3	93.1	$140,915	65.3	4.9	64.5	4.1	85.0	14.0
Syracuse city & MCD (Onondaga)	25.045	145,196	144,263	-0.6	5,760.1	11.8	74.3	$31,566	10.6	30.5	56.5	12.5	49.8	39.8
Tarrytown village	2.926	11,277	11,537	2.3	3,942.5	19.1	86.2	$91,906	47.3	4.0	68.1	8.9	63.9	29.5
Terryville CDP	3.228	11,849	NA	NA	NA	13.5	89.4	$90,474	45.9	3.8	66.2	6.7	78.8	18.2
Thompson town (Sullivan)*	84.089	15,308	15,066	-1.6	179.2	11.3	80.8	$36,360	12.0	25.3	57.3	13.0	59.0	36.9
Tonawanda city & MCD (Erie)	3.803	15,130	14,976		3,937.7	4.4	91.4	$46,026	13.7	12.1	63.7	8.8	57.4	35.9
Tonawanda CDP	17.299	58,144	NA	NA	NA	5.4	89.5	$54,498	17.3	9.3	64.2	5.0	58.7	34.9
Tonawanda town (Erie)*	18.735	73,567	73,281	-0.4	3,911.4	4.8	89.9	$53,603	17.6	9.5	65.3	5.2	58.0	35.8
Troy city & MCD (Rensselaer)	10.357	50,129	49,910	-0.4	4,818.7	8.3	75.2	$39,526	13.5	23.6	62.4	12.1	50.0	37.3
Ulster town (Ulster)	26.807	12,339	12,111	-1.7	452.5	8.3	87.5	$47,925	22.0	12.5	61.9	12.7	63.6	30.2
Union town (Broome)*	35.452	56,346	55,202	-2.0	1,557.1	6.1	84.1	$45,639	15.7	14.1	62.1	8.3	57.2	36.1
Uniondale CDP	2.713	24,759	NA	NA	NA	40.5	93.9	$71,953	33.8	9.9	64.8	9.2	79.4	15.7
Utica city & MCD (Oneida)	16.759	62,235	61,332	-1.5	3,659.7	18.2	80.2	$31,173	8.6	27.3	56.8	12.9	55.9	36.8
Valley Cottage CDP	4.309	9,107	NA	NA	NA	22.1	94.8	$100,188	50.1	4.4	63.2	7.2	63.8	30.6
Valley Stream village	3.480	37,559	37,832	0.7	10,871.9	33.7	92.6	$88,145	43.7	7.7	69.3	10.3	77.9	17.4
Van Buren town (Onondaga)*	35.408	13,184	13,372	1.4	377.7	3.8	88.2	$52,696	18.3	6.1	63.1	5.8	60.7	34.1
Vestal town (Broome)	51.742	28,043	28,242	0.7	545.8	9.1	83.2	$61,206	27.3	8.4	50.6	7.5	66.3	29.0
Victor town (Ontario)*A3006	35.918	14,272	14,616	2.4	406.9	4.2	88.7	$81,591	42.1	3.0	65.5	6.7	74.2	22.6
Wallkill town (Orange)	62.107	27,426	28,176	2.7	453.7	13.3	90.7	$70,446	29.5	9.0	66.8	9.3	72.2	22.8
Wantagh CDP	3.830	18,871	NA	NA	NA	7.4	95.8	$127,953	60.6	2.5	66.4	5.2	84.1	13.6
Wappinger town (Dutchess)*	27.054	27,111	27,137	0.1	1,003.1	14.9	89.1	$77,474	34.0	4.2	71.3	8.1	68.3	25.0
Warwick town (Orange)*	101.342	32,065	31,293	-2.4	308.8	8.0	93.7	$82,196	39.9	6.3	66.4	8.3	69.6	24.6
Watertown city & MCD (Jefferson)	9.039	27,031	27,590	2.1	3,052.2	4.6	70.0	$41,197	9.6	20.3	64.4	11.4	54.4	37.4
Watervliet city & MCD (Albany)	1.345	10,254	10,233	-0.2	7,605.4	4.0	79.9	$44,159	9.9	13.2	71.9	7.7	49.2	42.6
Wawarsing town (Ulster)*	130.505	13,159	13,100	-0.4	100.4	11.2	85.1	$47,582	18.0	12.0	49.3	12.9	68.5	24.4
Webster town (Monroe)*	33.531	42,641	43,892	2.9	1,309.0	9.4	91.5	$67,201	29.4	7.1	67.3	5.4	68.8	26.0
West Babylon CDP	7.760	43,213	NA	NA	NA	14.4	94.3	$84,066	40.4	6.0	65.3	7.7	77.3	18.4
Westbury village	2.344	15,040	15,329	1.9	6,540.9	34.6	95.5	$85,086	40.8	5.7	67.0	5.0	69.1	24.3
West Haverstraw village	1.519	10,165	10,417	2.5	6,855.8	25.1	86.4	$82,320	34.8	7.0	68.6	8.2	84.6	12.4
West Hempstead CDP	2.656	18,862	NA	NA	NA	21.2	94.1	$96,879	48.6	6.3	66.0	8.2	80.0	17.8
West Islip CDP	6.323	28,335	NA	NA	NA	5.1	95.7	$104,740	52.9	4.1	68.1	5.7	81.5	15.3
West Seneca CDP & town (Erie)	21.357	44,696	45,219	1.2	2,117.3	2.8	90.1	$58,392	21.0	6.8	65.9	7.8	63.7	32.3
Wheatfield town (Niagara)	27.911	18,117	18,320	1.1	656.4	6.4	95.0	$66,250	30.8	9.5	64.4	5.9	67.4	29.6
White Plains city & MCD (Westchester)	9.768	56,853	58,035	2.1	5,941.5	32.2	86.9	$81,743	41.3	9.0	70.2	6.9	60.8	33.4
Whitestown town (Oneida)*	27.318	18,667	18,610	-0.3	681.2	2.8	91.5	$55,334	22.4	11.3	62.9	6.8	62.6	30.1
Wilton town (Saratoga)	35.834	16,154	16,638	3.0	464.3	4.9	88.3	$75,026	37.5	7.3	67.6	5.8	69.5	25.7
Woodbury village	35.602	10,686	10,814	1.2	303.7	14.7	97.0	$124,400	59.6	4.4	71.9	6.7	83.7	13.4
Woodbury town (Orange)*	36.124	11,353	11,496	1.3	318.2	15.4	96.0	$120,000	57.9	4.6	72.6	6.3	83.8	13.5
Woodmere CDP	2.582	17,121	NA	NA	NA	14.0	95.6	$127,265	60.9	5.7	63.2	5.3	80.3	18.4
Wyandanch CDP	4.473	11,647	NA	NA	NA	25.1	95.4	$60,673	25.9	12.0	65.7	12.2	81.1	16.0
Yonkers city & MCD (Westchester)	18.012	195,979	200,667	2.4	11,140.6	31.2	89.4	$61,132	27.9	15.0	62.6	9.5	64.9	31.3
Yorktown town (Westchester)	36.645	36,081	36,976	2.5	1,009.0	12.4	93.9	$100,837	50.3	2.6	65.0	6.7	74.3	22.8
NORTH CAROLINA	48,617.903	9,535,691	9,943,964	4.3	204.5	7.6	84.7	$46,693	17.6	16.1	63.2	10.5	66.4	27.9
Albemarle city	16.918	15,902	15,976	0.5	944.3	2.5	81.8	$33,318	9.4	23.5	56.5	13.3	60.6	35.7
Apex town	16.066	37,501	43,907	17.1	2,732.9	10.1	85.8	$89,392	45.0	3.7	76.9	6.4	76.7	19.2
Archdale city	8.245	11,403	11,539	1.2	1,399.5	5.4	85.0	$51,418	13.5	9.5	66.6	8.3	69.1	27.0
Asheboro city	18.705	25,195	25,886	2.7	1,383.9	15.9	83.6	$31,652	6.6	22.3	58.7	12.7	63.3	32.8
Asheville city	45.305	83,417	87,882	5.4	1,939.8	7.1	77.5	$44,077	16.4	17.1	64.4	7.9	48.5	39.7
Belmont city	10.272	10,243	10,456	2.1	1,017.9	5.8	91.7	$51,167	25.1	15.3	65.6	9.3	63.7	32.9
Boone town	6.204	17,123	18,130	5.9	2,922.4	3.3	45.5	$13,608	7.0	59.3	53.8	18.5	19.6	36.9
Burlington city	29.072	50,922	51,812	1.7	1,782.2	9.4	83.4	$37,316	11.3	18.8	62.9	10.6	61.3	33.7
Carrboro town	6.519	19,589	20,984	7.1	3,219.0	18.7	72.8	$51,310	24.8	14.6	79.1	4.8	49.8	37.0
Cary town	55.162	135,276	155,227	14.7	2,814.0	19.8	82.8	$91,481	46.1	6.0	72.4	5.1	71.6	22.8

1 Dry land or land partially or temporarily covered by water.
2 16 years old and over.

Table B. Incorporated Places, Census Designated Places (CDPs), and Minor Civil Divisions (MCDs) of 10,000 or More Population — Crime, Construction, and Local Government Finance

STATE City, town, township, borough, or CDP (county if applicable)	Serious crimes known to police, 2014[1] Total number	Rate[2] Total	Rate[2] Violent	Rate[2] Property	New residential construction authorized by building permits, 2014 Value ($1,000)	Number of housing units	Percent single family	Local government finance, 2012 General revenue Total (mil dol)	Intergovernmental Total (mil dol)	Percent from state gov.	Taxes per capita[3]	General expenditure Total (mil dol)	Per capita[3] Total	Capital outlays	Debt outstanding (mil dol)
	15	16	17	18	19	20	21	22	23	24	25	26	27	28	29
NEW YORK—Con.															
Schenectady city & MCD (Schenectady)	3,068	4660	870	3790	367	2	100.0	89.2	31.5	44.8	453	98.0	1,484	180	159.7
Schodack town (Rensselaer)....	77	660	60	600	5,060	23	100.0	8.8	1.6	8.3	474	7.8	598	70	16.0
Seaford CDP	NA	NA	NA	NA	NA	NA	NA	NA	NA	NA	NA	NA	NA	NA	NA
Selden CDP	NA	NA	NA	NA	NA	NA	NA	NA	NA	NA	NA	NA	NA	NA	NA
Setauket-East Setauket CDP ...	NA	NA	NA	NA	NA	NA	NA	NA	NA	NA	NA	NA	NA	NA	NA
Shawangunk town (Ulster)........	73	516	42	473	2,620	10	100.0	5.7	0.5	48.5	266	6.3	444	103	5.4
Shirley CDP	NA	NA	NA	NA	NA	NA	NA	NA	NA	NA	NA	NA	NA	NA	NA
Sleepy Hollow village	NA	NA	NA	NA	0	0	0.0	12.2	2.0	21.0	719	11.7	1,175	55	19.0
Smithtown CDP	NA	NA	NA	NA	NA	NA	NA	NA	NA	NA	NA	NA	NA	NA	NA
Smithtown town (Suffolk)*	NA	NA	NA	NA	7,601	40	100.0	90.4	6.7	38.4	511	94.7	800	107	14.8
Somers town (Westchester)	NA	NA	NA	NA	3,738	15	46.7	14.7	3.5	20.4	407	13.4	643	89	11.1
Southampton town (Suffolk)*	826	1625	94	1531	223,925	274	100.0	135.3	12.0	50.5	1896	142.6	2,479	941	138.3
Southeast town (Putnam)*	NA	NA	NA	NA	3,623	10	100.0	11.8	1.7	98.5	406	14.0	767	114	12.4
South Farmingdale CDP	NA	NA	NA	NA	NA	NA	NA	NA	NA	NA	NA	NA	NA	NA	NA
Southold town (Suffolk)	320	1601	55	1546	6,391	52	100.0	49.3	7.6	32.0	1542	48.9	2,207	504	47.4
Southport town (Chemung)	NA	NA	NA	NA	310	2	100.0	4.7	3.3	8.8	101	4.6	422	55	0.0
Spring Valley village	524	1608	408	1200	3,139	17	41.2	34.8	11.4	13.6	684	34.7	1,083	29	16.9
Staten Island borough (Richmond)	NA	NA	NA	NA	121,227	712	45.8	NA	NA	NA	NA	NA	NA	NA	NA
Stony Brook CDP	NA	NA	NA	NA	NA	NA	NA	NA	NA	NA	NA	NA	NA	NA	NA
Stony Point CDP	NA	NA	NA	NA	NA	NA	NA	NA	NA	NA	NA	NA	NA	NA	NA
Stony Point town (Rockland).....	116	753	84	668	2,787	16	68.8	20.3	1.1	50.2	1032	22.2	1,455	120	27.9
Suffern village	66	601	46	556	220	1	100.0	14.2	1.5	26.8	862	14.2	1,312	104	10.9
Sullivan town (Madison)*	NA	NA	NA	NA	6,816	34	100.0	5.8	0.9	31.1	298	5.5	359	67	5.6
Sweden town (Monroe)*	NA	NA	NA	NA	1,445	9	100.0	4.9	1.1	13.1	199	4.6	325	34	1.8
Syosset CDP	NA	NA	NA	NA	NA	NA	NA	NA	NA	NA	NA	NA	NA	NA	NA
Syracuse city & MCD (Onondaga)	6,927	4793	811	3982	14,798	216	6.9	822.4	598.0	72.4	668	858.4	5,950	640	1117.3
Tarrytown village	92	798	52	746	3,703	10	100.0	22.6	5.0	49.4	1334	25.8	2,263	431	44.2
Terryville CDP	NA	NA	NA	NA	NA	NA	NA	NA	NA	NA	NA	NA	NA	NA	NA
Thompson town (Sullivan)*	NA	NA	NA	NA	12,722	83	100.0	8.7	0.5	66.7	385	8.9	584	37	7.6
Tonawanda city & MCD (Erie) ..	373	2494	147	2347	0	0	0.0	22.3	9.4	49.3	702	21.9	1,454	200	11.4
Tonawanda CDP	NA	NA	NA	NA	NA	NA	NA	NA	NA	NA	NA	NA	NA	NA	NA
Tonawanda town (Erie)*	1,116	1922	176	1746	361	2	100.0	82.2	16.5	16.3	621	98.6	1,340	280	43.6
Troy city & MCD (Rensselaer) ..	2,561	5127	759	4368	1,484	12	100.0	90.3	48.5	30.6	433	91.3	1,830	238	99.0
Ulster town (Ulster)	406	3352	132	3220	20,755	87	5.7	14.9	1.2	29.2	942	12.0	979	62	8.3
Union town (Broome)*	NA	NA	NA	NA	1,330	6	100.0	21.4	10.0	11.6	175	23.6	425	75	4.8
Uniondale CDP	NA	NA	NA	NA	NA	NA	NA	NA	NA	NA	NA	NA	NA	NA	NA
Utica city & MCD (Oneida)	2,788	4518	653	3865	0	0	0.0	93.1	41.6	48.0	597	94.1	1,521	162	95.0
Valley Cottage CDP	NA	NA	NA	NA	NA	NA	NA	NA	NA	NA	NA	NA	NA	NA	NA
Valley Stream village	NA	NA	NA	NA	7,608	40	2.5	33.6	2.5	57.9	716	37.3	987	118	28.5
Van Buren town (Onondaga)*	NA	NA	NA	NA	1,605	8	100.0	6.1	1.3	17.4	321	4.7	356	49	1.5
Vestal town (Broome)	592	2113	43	2070	2,297	9	100.0	22.7	8.7	13.2	350	26.1	926	162	21.1
Victor town (Ontario)*A3006	NA	NA	NA	NA	24,619	81	100.0	9.9	5.5	7.2	220	9.3	648	52	2.8
Wallkill town (Orange)	553	1960	167	1794	15,395	101	42.6	24.9	5.9	25.3	363	21.7	783	50	22.4
Wantagh CDP	NA	NA	NA	NA	NA	NA	NA	NA	NA	NA	NA	NA	NA	NA	NA
Wappinger town (Dutchess)*	NA	NA	NA	NA	0	0	0.0	13.9	1.8	24.5	326	12.4	455	42	27.1
Warwick town (Orange)*	NA	NA	NA	NA	3,092	15	100.0	18.9	6.4	19.5	357	18.9	604	100	6.7
Watertown city & MCD (Jefferson)	1,449	5173	546	4627	0	0	0.0	42.6	26.8	23.3	316	49.0	1,746	140	24.2
Watervliet city & MCD (Albany)	223	2179	225	1954	200	3	33.3	13.2	6.6	34.3	416	14.4	1,405	173	9.2
Wawarsing town (Ulster)*	NA	NA	NA	NA	894	5	100.0	9.9	2.3	16.1	500	8.8	665	89	7.8
Webster town (Monroe)*	522	1180	59	1121	27,628	174	37.4	23.8	4.6	8.8	331	27.9	642	143	18.2
West Babylon CDP	NA	NA	NA	NA	NA	NA	NA	NA	NA	NA	NA	NA	NA	NA	NA
Westbury village	NA	NA	NA	NA	2,007	15	100.0	7.8	0.8	50.7	421	7.1	465	48	6.1
West Haverstraw village	NA	NA	NA	NA	0	0	0.0	6.4	0.7	51.8	458	7.1	693	71	3.0
West Hempstead CDP	NA	NA	NA	NA	NA	NA	NA	NA	NA	NA	NA	NA	NA	NA	NA
West Islip CDP	NA	NA	NA	NA	NA	NA	NA	NA	NA	NA	NA	NA	NA	NA	NA
West Seneca CDP & town (Erie)	805	1794	91	1703	30,158	239	18.0	40.8	6.8	18.9	652	43.5	970	82	21.0
Wheatfield town (Niagara)........	NA	NA	NA	NA	9,490	41	100.0	10.6	4.6	3.4	269	8.1	446	24	12.8
White Plains city & MCD (Westchester)	1,150	1979	179	1800	14,338	111	7.2	165.8	12.3	50.2	1897	178.6	3,112	124	106.6
Whitestown town (Oneida)*	NA	NA	NA	NA	4,168	17	100.0	6.5	2.6	10.1	180	5.6	301	22	4.5
Wilton town (Saratoga)	NA	NA	NA	NA	14,529	45	100.0	7.7	5.1	3.7	97	7.3	445	65	0.3
Woodbury village	NA	NA	NA	NA	8,277	32	100.0	4.1	0.1	0.0	361	3.6	342	31	0.5
Woodbury town (Orange)*	373	3473	37	3436	NA	NA	NA	13.9	2.3	28.3	953	12.6	1,112	32	8.0
Woodmere CDP	NA	NA	NA	NA	NA	NA	NA	NA	NA	NA	NA	NA	NA	NA	NA
Wyandanch CDP	NA	NA	NA	NA	NA	NA	NA	NA	NA	NA	NA	NA	NA	NA	NA
Yonkers city & MCD (Westchester)	2,986	1488	487	1001	20,098	81	28.4	973.8	463.3	98.2	2146	967.5	4,872	267	757.7
Yorktown town (Westchester) ...	225	608	41	568	4,542	17	100.0	47.6	8.4	17.9	827	42.3	1,160	87	34.5
NORTH CAROLINA	318,464	3203	330	2873	8,619,650	49,911	70.2	X	X	X	X	X	X	X	X
Albemarle city	876	5464	586	4877	NA	NA	NA	19.9	4.2	46.6	548	19.7	1,237	20	4.0
Apex town	490	1129	64	1064	95,823	578	100.0	41.1	5.4	89.2	575	41.1	1,016	152	63.3
Archdale city	269	2321	138	2183	NA	NA	NA	9.5	1.8	85.9	365	11.0	959	240	8.8
Asheboro city	1,628	6243	261	5982	3,150	24	100.0	28.8	4.7	94.5	623	29.2	1,140	28	9.3
Asheville city	4,778	5418	568	4850	67,125	312	80.8	115.3	28.1	51.3	775	121.5	1,415	244	110.4
Belmont city	442	4228	210	4018	NA	NA	NA	10.8	0.3	17.1	682	9.9	955	44	6.6
Boone town	382	2065	178	1887	9,336	107	4.7	17.9	2.0	95.1	612	16.1	891	48	3.8
Burlington city	2,416	4680	682	3998	17,761	147	100.0	64.2	9.0	59.4	695	62.8	1,224	7	62.0
Carrboro town	525	2472	146	2326	11,054	47	100.0	18.8	1.6	97.6	778	16.1	792	54	7.0
Cary town	1,809	1167	63	1104	281,116	1,676	67.4	187.2	16.9	75.1	687	218.0	1,496	577	243.8

1 Data for serious crimes have not been adjusted for underreporting. This may affect comparability between geographic areas over time.
2 Per 100,000 population estimated by the FBI. 3 Based on population estimated as of July 1 of the year shown.

Table B. Incorporated Places, Census Designated Places (CDPs), and Minor Civil Divisions (MCDs) of 10,000 or More Population — Land Area, Population, and Households, and Employment

STATE City, town, township, borough, or CDP (county if applicable)	Land area,[1] 2010 (sq mi)	Total persons 2010	Total persons 2014	Percent change 2010–2014	Persons per square mile, 2014	Foreign born	Lives in same house as previous year	Median household income (dollars)	Income of $100,000 or more	Income below poverty level	Percent in labor force	Unemployment rate	Family households	One person households
	1	2	3	4	5	6	7	8	9	10	11	12	13	14
NORTH CAROLINA—Con.														
Chapel Hill town	21.179	57,233	59,376	3.7	2,803.5	16.7	63.9	$62,620	34.3	19.5	57.4	7.0	52.1	33.3
Charlotte city	303.449	735,758	809,958	10.1	2,669.2	15.3	79.1	$53,274	23.1	14.8	72.1	10.8	60.6	31.2
Clayton town	13.717	16,208	18,445	13.8	1,344.7	5.1	87.9	$56,941	21.7	10.6	69.5	8.3	69.8	22.9
Clemmons village	11.843	18,623	19,522	4.8	1,648.4	9.4	89.3	$66,680	32.5	6.6	64.7	4.6	71.3	26.1
Concord city	60.905	79,195	85,560	8.0	1,404.8	10.3	84.9	$52,901	22.6	11.5	68.5	11.7	70.0	25.7
Cornelius town	11.565	24,894	27,481	10.4	2,376.2	7.7	81.7	$81,059	40.9	5.0	72.3	7.0	65.9	27.0
Davidson town	5.755	10,933	11,981	9.6	2,081.7	6.6	77.8	$94,551	47.9	5.8	64.5	6.9	64.6	32.5
Durham city	108.502	228,404	251,893	10.3	2,321.6	14.5	75.7	$49,585	20.9	16.7	68.8	8.3	57.1	33.3
Eden city	13.896	15,704	15,407	-1.9	1,108.8	3.6	83.7	$31,413	6.2	24.2	53.8	18.3	63.9	32.7
Elizabeth City city	11.171	18,635	18,047	-3.2	1,615.6	2.8	80.9	$31,188	9.8	30.4	59.7	19.3	63.4	30.2
Fayetteville city	146.822	200,582	203,948	1.7	1,389.1	6.5	75.9	$44,514	13.5	16.4	65.8	13.8	63.8	30.4
Fuquay-Varina town	12.495	17,985	22,644	25.9	1,812.3	11.8	85.0	$59,592	24.3	10.9	72.0	9.7	72.6	22.9
Garner town	14.864	25,758	27,814	8.0	1,871.3	6.7	85.2	$58,107	22.9	8.2	70.6	9.1	65.3	29.5
Gastonia city	51.559	71,741	73,698	2.7	1,429.4	8.2	83.5	$39,578	13.1	19.5	63.3	13.6	67.3	28.1
Goldsboro city	28.363	35,524	35,947	1.2	1,267.4	4.6	73.2	$35,086	9.4	23.6	56.8	18.7	60.0	36.2
Graham city	9.298	14,305	14,479	1.2	1,557.2	9.5	81.1	$32,713	7.7	25.2	62.0	11.1	63.6	33.3
Greensboro city	126.676	268,877	282,586	5.1	2,230.8	10.8	83.6	$41,518	15.0	17.7	65.0	10.0	57.3	34.5
Greenville city	34.807	84,573	89,852	6.2	2,581.4	5.4	69.1	$35,225	12.9	28.0	66.5	12.6	49.0	34.4
Harrisburg town	9.836	13,044	14,132	8.3	1,436.7	7.0	91.8	$82,135	32.4	7.4	70.8	5.6	81.7	16.0
Havelock city	16.848	20,735	20,706	-0.1	1,229.0	5.5	62.5	$44,258	9.7	15.2	77.2	11.6	76.5	17.7
Henderson city	8.512	15,415	15,265	-1.0	1,793.3	6.6	85.1	$24,167	5.9	30.8	50.0	17.8	60.1	35.8
Hendersonville city	7.126	13,109	13,650	4.1	1,915.6	9.4	76.0	$36,000	7.2	21.8	51.2	12.3	51.8	43.2
Hickory city	29.907	40,065	40,143	0.2	1,342.3	9.4	83.3	$42,393	18.2	17.5	63.2	7.7	60.5	31.5
High Point city	54.002	104,387	108,629	4.1	2,011.6	11.9	82.6	$43,015	15.9	17.8	66.0	12.6	64.7	30.0
Holly Springs town	15.125	24,676	30,157	22.2	1,993.8	6.9	87.2	$91,755	43.6	3.6	74.4	5.4	80.5	16.0
Hope Mills town	7.731	15,540	16,301	4.9	2,108.5	6.2	80.4	$47,332	13.9	14.6	63.3	9.8	69.6	26.8
Huntersville town	39.877	46,774	51,567	10.2	1,293.1	5.9	85.7	$85,258	43.5	6.9	75.5	6.6	71.5	23.2
Indian Trail town	21.768	33,608	36,360	8.2	1,670.3	8.2	86.8	$67,338	25.6	5.0	75.3	9.0	83.5	12.6
Jacksonville city	46.537	70,145	69,047	-1.6	1,483.7	5.0	66.6	$41,293	10.3	13.3	75.2	13.0	73.2	23.8
Kannapolis city	32.189	42,615	45,245	6.2	1,405.6	6.9	88.5	$41,453	11.5	16.9	65.0	13.2	67.2	27.8
Kernersville town	17.480	23,121	23,739	2.7	1,358.1	8.1	82.8	$49,066	18.3	12.0	67.1	6.4	61.8	33.8
Kings Mountain city	13.011	10,595	10,644	0.5	818.1	1.5	85.3	$36,830	10.6	21.7	62.0	15.5	62.9	32.3
Kinston city	18.351	21,677	21,392	-1.3	1,165.7	1.9	77.5	$28,608	7.3	31.0	56.1	17.8	59.2	35.3
Knightdale town	6.330	11,406	13,871	21.6	2,191.3	11.4	84.4	$72,591	30.3	7.1	77.8	4.5	68.5	29.1
Laurinburg city	12.520	15,962	15,593	-2.3	1,245.4	2.9	82.7	$28,216	8.7	30.8	48.1	17.2	62.1	35.4
Leland town	19.763	13,673	17,015	24.4	861.0	6.2	76.4	$61,823	23.1	11.0	63.9	8.5	69.7	26.2
Lenoir city	19.636	18,234	17,920	-1.7	912.6	7.3	88.7	$30,036	6.5	25.0	56.3	16.3	60.4	37.4
Lewisville town	14.093	12,710	13,342	5.0	946.7	4.2	93.5	$73,403	31.0	5.8	64.6	9.0	76.9	19.5
Lexington city	17.979	18,931	19,257	1.7	1,071.1	10.4	76.3	$30,173	4.9	24.4	51.3	18.5	62.2	34.6
Lincolnton city	8.594	10,484	10,732	2.4	1,248.8	8.7	80.2	$31,049	9.4	23.0	60.3	15.7	61.0	34.1
Lumberton city	17.894	21,548	21,716	0.8	1,213.6	9.0	84.4	$31,899	11.4	29.4	48.2	8.8	66.2	29.3
Matthews town	17.103	27,196	30,008	10.3	1,754.5	8.6	87.9	$71,361	32.4	6.2	68.9	7.5	72.8	23.8
Mebane city	8.406	11,366	13,277	16.8	1,579.5	6.4	81.3	$51,751	21.3	12.8	73.8	7.2	68.4	28.4
Mint Hill town	23.887	22,763	25,076	10.2	1,049.8	7.8	91.7	$70,530	29.9	8.4	65.5	6.5	74.6	21.3
Monroe city	29.756	32,797	34,331	4.7	1,153.7	19.7	82.5	$43,328	14.0	19.4	67.1	12.3	75.6	19.3
Mooresville town	21.605	33,651	35,300	4.9	1,633.9	6.7	83.7	$61,458	25.7	9.6	70.0	11.9	70.7	25.2
Morganton city	19.153	16,918	16,690	-1.3	871.4	11.7	83.7	$35,144	12.6	21.8	53.0	11.7	58.2	34.2
Morrisville town	8.278	18,576	22,772	22.6	2,751.0	29.8	78.9	$84,301	41.3	4.4	77.3	5.0	69.5	25.6
Mount Airy city	11.711	10,394	10,383	-0.1	886.6	5.3	88.2	$31,134	9.3	22.7	49.8	12.4	59.7	37.2
Mount Holly city	9.740	13,646	14,016	2.7	1,439.0	7.9	87.6	$48,290	19.7	13.4	68.5	10.8	61.8	33.0
Murraysville CDP	8.615	14,215	NA	NA	NA	6.1	89.3	$58,940	16.6	7.9	75.2	6.3	59.5	31.1
New Bern city	27.729	29,547	30,291	2.5	1,092.4	7.4	79.9	$41,238	12.5	20.3	63.6	15.2	59.3	36.7
Newton city	13.773	12,968	13,005	0.3	944.3	8.4	85.2	$29,884	7.2	27.0	54.1	12.7	63.6	31.2
Pinehurst village	16.580	14,669	15,434	5.2	930.9	5.5	88.4	$75,284	34.7	2.1	41.9	3.8	69.3	28.5
Piney Green CDP	13.758	13,293	NA	NA	NA	6.5	74.6	$46,935	10.9	14.5	69.1	15.5	70.3	22.3
Raleigh city	144.119	403,971	439,896	8.9	3,052.3	13.3	78.9	$54,581	23.7	13.0	70.9	8.3	56.3	33.9
Reidsville city	14.558	14,449	14,073	-2.6	966.7	2.5	83.4	$36,900	8.2	23.9	59.1	11.2	58.6	37.5
Roanoke Rapids city	9.941	15,754	15,495	-1.6	1,558.8	2.0	84.5	$36,477	12.3	21.9	55.8	10.7	65.4	31.6
Rocky Mount city	44.040	57,719	56,325	-2.4	1,279.0	3.3	82.2	$36,724	9.1	20.9	58.2	17.7	61.9	33.5
Salisbury city	22.139	33,524	33,710	0.6	1,522.7	4.7	77.6	$34,230	10.3	25.0	50.7	15.5	59.9	34.4
Sanford city	26.688	28,135	29,116	3.5	1,091.0	14.6	81.2	$44,391	13.6	21.7	64.4	12.9	67.1	28.0
Shelby city	21.097	20,326	20,276	-0.2	961.1	4.1	85.9	$32,500	10.1	24.4	57.2	16.6	59.4	36.2
Smithfield town	12.130	10,960	11,735	7.1	967.4	11.0	86.1	$32,403	8.9	24.9	50.0	13.0	66.0	31.1
Southern Pines town	16.542	12,352	13,235	7.1	800.1	5.7	85.0	$46,385	26.7	14.7	54.2	11.3	51.7	42.7
Spring Lake town	23.095	12,007	13,370	11.4	578.9	7.0	60.3	$37,154	3.8	20.3	71.5	16.1	69.2	24.2
Stallings town	7.950	13,797	14,968	8.5	1,882.7	7.3	91.1	$77,374	34.2	6.4	70.4	6.9	79.8	17.8
Statesville city	24.048	24,541	25,722	4.8	1,069.6	9.3	78.5	$32,605	10.1	27.0	63.2	16.6	65.6	29.7
Summerfield town	26.557	10,232	10,753	5.1	404.9	4.8	94.4	$102,713	50.6	4.0	66.0	6.3	79.5	15.5
Tarboro town	11.158	11,413	11,310	-0.9	1,013.7	3.7	90.2	$34,267	10.7	17.3	54.2	13.8	65.3	30.5
Thomasville city	16.771	26,772	27,002	0.9	1,610.1	8.6	82.9	$35,127	6.2	22.1	64.6	15.6	61.4	31.4
Wake Forest town	15.350	30,096	36,693	21.9	2,390.4	7.5	85.3	$77,173	38.2	7.7	70.2	6.5	75.5	19.9
Waxhaw town	11.611	9,860	12,750	29.3	1,098.1	7.2	91.3	$74,650	34.2	5.7	68.5	10.7	80.8	16.6
Wilmington city	51.608	106,478	113,657	6.7	2,202.3	6.4	75.7	$42,130	19.1	21.4	65.2	11.3	51.5	35.6
Wilson city	30.470	49,159	49,395	0.5	1,621.1	6.9	80.7	$38,030	11.7	23.1	59.9	13.7	63.5	32.2
Winston-Salem city	132.497	229,634	239,269	4.2	1,805.8	10.8	80.8	$40,480	15.1	20.2	63.4	11.4	58.7	34.9
NORTH DAKOTA	69,000.795	672,591	739,482	9.9	10.7	2.9	82.5	$55,579	21.7	12.1	70.5	3.1	60.8	31.2
Bismarck city	31.611	61,264	68,896	12.5	2,179.5	1.8	83.0	$57,660	22.5	9.8	71.4	2.4	57.7	33.1
Dickinson city	12.915	17,866	22,322	24.9	1,728.4	4.2	80.8	$69,956	27.2	10.9	74.2	2.9	59.5	29.9
Fargo city	48.942	105,549	115,863	9.8	2,367.3	7.0	72.9	$46,311	17.7	15.0	75.7	4.2	48.3	37.8
Grand Forks city	20.175	52,876	56,057	6.0	2,778.5	4.5	74.6	$44,134	16.3	21.2	71.4	4.6	49.7	36.3
Jamestown city	12.812	15,427	15,446	0.1	1,205.6	1.7	83.9	$47,985	14.6	13.3	65.7	3.2	56.1	38.9
Mandan city	11.094	18,425	20,820	13.0	1,876.7	0.7	83.1	$55,368	20.0	10.0	72.2	3.6	62.7	30.8
Minot city	24.739	40,962	47,997	17.2	1,940.2	3.5	76.0	$57,248	19.0	9.8	72.7	2.7	56.2	33.3
West Fargo city	14.437	25,830	31,771	23.0	2,200.6	5.1	85.0	$69,104	26.3	8.3	78.8	1.7	67.8	25.9

1 Dry land or land partially or temporarily covered by water.
2 16 years old and over.

Table B. Incorporated Places, Census Designated Places (CDPs), and Minor Civil Divisions (MCDs) of 10,000 or More Population — Crime, Construction, and Local Government Finance

STATE City, town, township, borough, or CDP (county if applicable)	Serious crimes known to police, 2014[1] Total number	Rate[2] Total	Rate[2] Violent	Rate[2] Property	New residential construction authorized by building permits, 2014 Value ($1,000)	Number of housing units	Percent single family	Local government finance, 2012 General revenue Total (mil dol)	Intergovernmental Total (mil dol)	Percent from state gov.	Taxes per capita[3]	General expenditure Total (mil dol)	Per capita[3] Total	Capital outlays	Debt outstanding (mil dol)
	15	16	17	18	19	20	21	22	23	24	25	26	27	28	29
NORTH CAROLINA—Con.															
Chapel Hill town	1,433	2381	143	2238	17,870	51	100.0	80.0	23.1	43.6	826	68.9	1,174	154	60.5
Charlotte city	35,619	4157	590	3567	NA	NA	NA	1401.8	250.6	43.7	803	1294.8	1,671	438	3227.6
Clayton town	441	2438	193	2244	40,376	273	100.0	20.7	2.9	100.0	629	20.0	1,166	338	27.6
Clemmons village	NA	NA	NA	NA	NA	NA	NA	5.4	1.7	95.2	155	5.4	280	39	0.0
Concord city	2,504	2961	114	2848	NA	NA	NA	109.3	19.4	51.2	682	107.7	1,311	79	100.3
Cornelius town	419	1529	120	1409	NA	NA	NA	20.1	3.1	62.9	587	17.5	666	125	12.0
Davidson town	133	1113	67	1046	NA	NA	NA	10.5	1.4	76.9	668	10.3	897	58	3.0
Durham city	12,919	5173	734	4439	238,122	1,514	76.2	303.7	47.0	61.0	717	302.6	1,262	129	398.4
Eden city	558	3615	395	3220	1,082	7	100.0	17.9	3.9	65.6	512	18.1	1,165	62	11.5
Elizabeth City city	887	4884	501	4383	4,769	39	100.0	22.8	7.9	41.3	496	19.5	1,054	57	6.4
Fayetteville city	11,563	5632	506	5126	59,897	423	81.8	208.3	50.9	51.4	472	235.1	1,166	340	204.6
Fuquay-Varina town	711	3212	258	2955	115,004	499	100.0	21.5	3.6	51.5	584	20.8	1,039	142	31.5
Garner town	1,264	4682	189	4493	16,235	94	100.0	26.6	2.9	28.3	760	24.8	926	110	13.9
Gastonia city	4,172	5670	658	5013	59,401	243	96.7	81.0	9.5	71.1	636	85.6	1,176	76	94.3
Goldsboro city	2,537	6954	899	6055	9,360	59	100.0	41.9	6.6	92.5	633	47.0	1,303	68	50.9
Graham city	643	4495	475	4020	4,355	31	100.0	12.3	1.6	98.3	487	11.0	766	36	6.5
Greensboro city	11,506	4077	477	3600	188,669	1,229	33.8	371.9	60.4	63.7	711	412.3	1,492	244	443.1
Greenville city	4,153	4604	519	4085	83,309	755	24.5	116.0	31.1	70.0	525	107.6	1,228	125	143.1
Harrisburg town	NA	NA	NA	NA	NA	NA	NA	10.5	1.4	85.1	422	10.0	742	238	9.1
Havelock city	399	1902	76	1825	908	8	100.0	15.3	3.0	74.6	282	14.0	662	29	11.9
Henderson city	1,663	10847	1494	9353	NA	NA	NA	35.7	19.1	16.8	509	19.2	1,252	191	16.3
Hendersonville city	600	4428	332	4096	NA	NA	NA	21.1	2.6	83.5	763	19.6	1,856	476	29.2
Hickory city	2,053	5077	391	4687	NA	NA	NA	61.0	10.1	62.0	844	60.2	1,500	170	38.0
High Point city	4,368	4024	465	3559	86,462	594	41.4	158.5	22.3	59.1	768	167.5	1,571	282	267.0
Holly Springs town	288	959	67	893	84,730	406	100.0	30.9	2.0	49.5	700	32.1	1,195	166	37.9
Hope Mills town	1,081	6592	427	6165	5,470	18	100.0	11.4	1.8	95.5	472	11.3	711	132	3.1
Huntersville town	1,063	2069	113	1956	NA	NA	NA	34.2	5.5	74.2	450	35.6	722	217	41.4
Indian Trail town	NA	NA	NA	NA	NA	NA	NA	10.0	2.4	32.5	182	7.7	220	16	2.4
Jacksonville city	NA	NA	NA	NA	6,566	48	58.3	66.3	10.7	56.8	458	75.1	1,079	221	103.2
Kannapolis city	1,042	2327	179	2148	NA	NA	NA	41.5	5.6	64.3	572	48.1	1,099	338	67.9
Kernersville town	998	4216	342	3874	6,422	37	100.0	25.3	4.4	96.1	711	25.8	1,101	69	10.4
Kings Mountain city	315	2958	207	2751	5,628	74	18.9	11.3	2.6	82.0	393	13.0	1,221	67	2.6
Kinston city	1,816	8394	1807	6587	4,080	26	7.7	32.3	8.1	89.5	614	35.0	1,615	303	23.2
Knightdale town	436	3165	181	2984	30,622	152	100.0	12.2	2.5	77.5	574	10.6	830	71	5.7
Laurinburg city	1,027	6529	1036	5492	NA	NA	NA	10.8	2.3	98.3	257	12.2	777	82	5.0
Leland town	349	2104	96	2008	103,712	415	100.0	9.8	1.5	74.9	445	9.7	645	75	11.4
Lenoir city	826	4590	239	4351	NA	NA	NA	20.8	5.0	98.0	617	20.9	1,164	43	7.2
Lewisville town	NA	NA	NA	NA	NA	NA	NA	4.1	1.0	96.8	236	4.0	309	48	2.1
Lexington city	729	3835	442	3393	3,024	13	100.0	23.9	5.0	89.1	617	27.1	1,429	122	18.4
Lincolnton city	528	4888	472	4415	NA	NA	NA	13.4	1.5	87.5	653	13.3	1,257	17	20.6
Lumberton city	3,376	15432	1659	13772	1,414	7	100.0	30.0	4.4	85.6	720	31.7	1,454	264	15.3
Matthews town	796	2660	150	2509	NA	NA	NA	20.9	3.5	73.5	506	19.8	691	109	6.0
Mebane city	629	4694	157	4538	16,734	147	100.0	13.3	1.2	98.8	745	13.4	1,056	132	8.0
Mint Hill town	546	2185	136	2049	NA	NA	NA	10.6	1.7	100.0	310	14.2	592	202	3.2
Monroe city	1,945	5679	455	5223	8,799	83	95.2	55.3	6.6	75.2	738	69.9	2,080	827	59.6
Mooresville town	1,112	3161	225	2936	NA	NA	NA	65.3	6.7	75.3	1034	71.2	2,068	563	220.0
Morganton city	688	4099	256	3842	1,251	9	100.0	26.4	3.3	96.1	674	26.7	1,589	149	8.0
Morrisville town	479	2101	48	2053	63,598	451	100.0	22.8	2.2	97.9	881	22.0	1,070	171	11.3
Mount Airy city	539	5173	451	4722	NA	NA	NA	14.9	2.1	85.7	884	15.1	1,444	154	16.0
Mount Holly city	250	1790	129	1661	NA	NA	NA	13.9	2.2	91.0	581	14.6	1,062	135	12.4
Murraysville CDP	NA	NA	NA	NA	NA	NA	NA	NA	NA	NA	NA	NA	NA	NA	NA
New Bern city	1,389	4573	402	4172	18,760	107	100.0	44.8	7.8	87.0	636	43.0	1,416	135	76.1
Newton city	499	3820	482	3338	NA	NA	NA	15.8	2.8	84.5	643	15.7	1,210	234	18.5
Pinehurst village	115	747	6	741	27,443	121	100.0	16.1	2.5	99.3	830	14.4	961	73	2.2
Piney Green CDP	NA	NA	NA	NA	NA	NA	NA	NA	NA	NA	NA	NA	NA	NA	NA
Raleigh city	5,183	1182	152	1030	626,797	4,655	28.3	555.4	92.1	53.9	679	527.4	1,245	199	1004.7
Reidsville city	784	5563	319	5244	0	0	0.0	18.6	2.9	91.3	726	20.8	1,461	251	6.5
Roanoke Rapids city	1,119	7172	583	6589	1,202	6	100.0	15.0	2.7	100.0	610	13.9	888	34	19.7
Rocky Mount city	3,277	5774	939	4835	1,935	17	100.0	82.1	24.8	46.4	549	81.9	1,437	161	10.0
Salisbury city	1,968	5852	711	5142	NA	NA	NA	55.5	5.3	90.5	656	64.5	1,931	175	81.1
Sanford city	1,093	3667	265	3402	10,160	42	100.0	35.2	4.6	61.9	628	34.4	1,189	24	51.3
Shelby city	862	4240	718	3522	2,134	9	100.0	22.4	3.8	88.0	548	27.0	1,329	94	29.3
Smithfield town	757	6469	726	5743	NA	NA	NA	17.3	1.0	56.7	762	16.5	1,451	133	17.8
Southern Pines town	596	4529	570	3959	31,334	137	100.0	18.3	2.2	84.9	811	18.8	1,476	137	8.0
Spring Lake town	694	5218	654	4564	554	5	100.0	8.5	2.8	89.8	232	8.9	683	50	2.2
Stallings town	204	1374	121	1253	NA	NA	NA	5.8	1.2	99.9	294	6.6	461	154	0.0
Statesville city	1,311	5113	628	4485	NA	NA	NA	30.5	4.2	100.0	709	33.7	1,345	264	22.0
Summerfield town	NA	NA	NA	NA	NA	NA	NA	1.4	0.4	100.0	53	1.1	103	19	0.0
Tarboro town	442	3902	185	3716	312	6	100.0	12.7	3.5	99.7	344	15.4	1,363	5	0.1
Thomasville city	1,160	4294	374	3920	5,740	35	88.6	26.0	4.5	82.6	525	26.2	973	39	42.9
Wake Forest town	794	2208	156	2053	83,946	548	84.7	31.1	3.1	92.3	802	34.4	1,042	231	32.8
Waxhaw town	NA	NA	NA	NA	44,103	252	100.0	7.5	0.9	88.1	583	5.6	544	27	0.0
Wilmington city	5,938	5236	675	4560	NA	NA	NA	128.8	25.2	52.9	693	132.5	1,206	224	205.6
Wilson city	2,166	4355	533	3823	22,886	134	46.3	71.8	10.0	67.7	557	70.7	1,427	69	113.0
Winston-Salem city	14,592	6129	712	5417	89,747	783	65.6	293.3	50.8	63.3	594	303.3	1,294	272	727.7
NORTH DAKOTA	17,565	2375	265	2110	1,636,051	12,178	37.2	X	X	X	X	X	X	X	X
Bismarck city	1,892	2762	270	2492	152,357	1,134	50.6	128.3	46.0	40.5	571	118.8	1,827	623	97.9
Dickinson city	697	3225	236	2989	100,846	535	50.7	27.1	6.3	100.0	663	22.2	1,124	327	1.7
Fargo city	3,478	3006	359	2648	218,628	2,170	17.4	237.9	83.4	99.5	658	229.3	2,080	749	566.3
Grand Forks city	1,685	3039	240	2800	121,309	898	23.7	100.1	20.7	28.9	709	59.4	1,106	129	382.8
Jamestown city	492	3187	266	2921	6,256	34	100.0	16.6	1.5	87.9	490	17.5	1,142	137	25.6
Mandan city	666	3288	262	3027	61,769	447	28.6	18.9	1.9	100.0	360	20.3	1,065	58	69.5
Minot city	1,367	2867	325	2542	89,936	719	25.7	75.0	19.3	56.5	849	44.2	1,005	135	41.8
West Fargo city	611	1973	194	1779	145,309	982	55.1	34.8	5.1	100.0	384	41.1	1,488	814	120.7

1 Data for serious crimes have not been adjusted for underreporting. This may affect comparability between geographic areas over time.
2 Per 100,000 population estimated by the FBI. 3 Based on population estimated as of July 1 of the year shown.

Table B. Incorporated Places, Census Designated Places (CDPs), and Minor Civil Divisions (MCDs) of 10,000 or More Population — **Land Area, Population, and Households, and Employment**

STATE City, town, township, borough, or CDP (county if applicable)	Land area,[1] 2010 (sq mi)	Total persons 2010	Total persons 2014	Percent change 2010–2014	Persons per square mile, 2014	Foreign born	Lives in same house as previous year	Median household income (dollars)	Income of $100,000 or more	Income below poverty level	Percent in labor force	Unemployment rate	Family households	One person households
	1	2	3	4	5	6	7	8	9	10	11	12	13	14
NORTH DAKOTA—Con.														
Williston city	20.356	15,910	24,562	54.4	1,206.6	2.2	75.8	$83,750	39.9	8.3	72.9	1.1	59.5	29.0
OHIO	40,860.692	11,536,725	11,594,163	0.5	283.7	4.1	85.4	$48,849	18.6	15.0	63.6	9.2	64.4	29.8
Akron city	62.033	199,092	197,859	-0.6	3,189.6	4.6	85.0	$34,139	9.0	24.5	62.4	14.1	55.2	37.1
Alliance city	9.004	22,322	22,078	-1.1	2,451.9	1.3	80.0	$31,863	8.1	24.9	56.7	16.0	55.8	38.1
Amherst city	7.062	12,021	12,143	1.0	1,719.4	3.2	87.9	$64,731	29.9	7.9	68.0	7.7	73.2	22.8
Ashland city	11.169	20,362	20,218	-0.7	1,810.1	5.0	78.5	$39,215	11.8	15.2	59.5	11.6	60.6	33.9
Ashtabula city	7.735	19,124	18,508	-3.2	2,392.8	1.6	84.2	$28,682	4.6	31.6	54.8	13.6	58.6	35.2
Athens city	9.827	23,838	24,024	0.8	2,444.7	8.8	47.6	$17,358	9.8	52.1	51.1	12.7	28.1	43.9
Aurora city	22.913	15,546	15,734	1.2	686.7	6.7	90.7	$80,831	38.4	4.6	66.5	6.9	70.2	28.7
Austintown CDP	11.619	29,677	NA	NA	NA	1.8	89.7	$41,601	10.0	12.0	61.4	9.7	61.3	35.7
Avon city	20.807	21,191	22,302	5.2	1,071.8	4.9	92.6	$78,839	40.8	6.5	65.4	6.1	73.2	23.7
Avon Lake city	11.130	22,581	23,204	2.8	2,084.9	4.4	91.0	$81,840	38.4	5.1	65.4	4.3	69.8	25.8
Barberton city	9.037	26,570	26,302		2,910.5	2.6	88.9	$37,965	7.3	17.5	63.4	11.8	62.9	32.3
Bay Village city	4.566	15,651	15,435	-1.4	3,380.7	3.1	93.7	$87,942	42.3	2.8	68.8	4.2	73.9	22.9
Beachwood city	5.272	11,953	11,797	-1.3	2,237.5	16.9	86.0	$83,125	43.7	5.3	54.9	3.4	61.1	35.8
Beavercreek city	26.427	45,193	45,934	1.6	1,738.1	7.5	86.3	$79,243	37.4	5.2	64.4	5.1	67.7	26.5
Bedford city	5.353	13,074	12,805	-2.1	2,392.0	2.8	85.4	$39,820	10.2	14.4	68.2	7.7	57.9	39.0
Bedford Heights city	4.543	10,757	10,675	-0.8	2,349.8	4.5	86.7	$36,573	9.0	16.9	61.7	14.8	59.0	39.0
Bellefontaine city	10.050	13,370	13,167	-1.5	1,310.1	1.6	81.3	$40,459	10.7	20.0	61.3	10.4	64.1	28.1
Berea city	5.709	19,093	18,986	-0.6	3,325.6	3.6	82.9	$54,534	19.0	9.5	66.2	8.9	53.5	38.6
Bexley city	2.421	13,054	13,517	3.5	5,583.1	5.8	81.6	$93,893	47.0	8.9	70.0	4.7	68.2	23.5
Blue Ash city	7.578	12,114	12,149	0.3	1,603.2	15.5	87.1	$65,991	34.2	6.2	65.2	6.9	64.5	30.9
Boardman CDP	15.121	35,376	NA	NA	NA	3.1	87.8	$47,914	16.6	10.5	66.9	6.1	58.7	36.3
Bowling Green city	12.622	30,048	31,591	5.1	2,502.8	5.0	57.1	$34,202	15.3	32.9	64.8	12.8	44.2	35.5
Brecksville city	19.524	13,659	13,469	-1.4	689.9	7.5	90.8	$93,409	47.4	3.8	64.7	5.3	70.3	26.7
Bridgetown CDP	4.323	14,407	NA	NA	NA	1.3	90.9	$58,877	19.4	7.7	65.2	5.5	67.9	28.9
Broadview Heights city	13.049	19,397	19,254	-0.7	1,475.6	12.3	90.4	$79,213	38.1	5.8	68.1	5.6	64.8	28.9
Brooklyn city	4.248	11,169	10,947	-2.0	2,577.1	11.8	88.8	$41,959	8.5	11.2	63.8	7.5	57.3	36.7
Brook Park city	7.524	19,212	18,886	-1.7	2,510.2	4.3	91.9	$49,366	12.6	9.7	63.2	8.2	63.5	32.2
Brunswick city	12.918	34,274	34,604	1.0	2,678.8	2.7	91.5	$62,417	20.7	8.0	71.8	6.2	69.3	25.1
Bucyrus city	7.422	12,362	11,973	-3.1	1,613.3	1.0	78.1	$33,999	5.7	19.7	53.9	12.9	60.2	34.7
Cambridge city	6.352	10,635	10,485	-1.4	1,650.6	1.1	87.4	$29,881	9.6	22.5	53.5	11.4	56.9	37.2
Canton city	25.510	73,017	72,297		2,834.1	2.2	81.7	$29,980	6.1	28.4	61.5	14.6	57.3	36.1
Celina city	4.982	10,407	10,373	-0.3	2,082.1	1.0	84.8	$39,659	8.1	11.5	66.9	10.4	63.3	31.5
Centerville city	10.941	23,994	23,915	-0.3	2,185.8	6.2	85.4	$59,917	27.3	6.5	59.1	6.5	61.0	33.9
Chillicothe city	10.428	21,901	21,738	-0.7	2,084.6	0.9	83.6	$38,363	11.1	17.5	56.2	15.3	57.0	38.2
Cincinnati city	77.941	296,950	298,165	0.4	3,825.5	5.1	75.5	$34,002	13.6	28.1	64.7	13.1	46.7	43.7
Circleville city	6.741	13,316	13,455	1.0	1,996.0	0.1	80.8	$38,205	10.6	16.8	53.9	9.9	64.4	31.8
Clayton city	18.506	13,209	13,170	-0.3	711.7	3.2	91.0	$66,427	25.8	6.5	67.0	10.1	72.5	23.8
Cleveland city	77.705	396,697	389,521	-1.8	5,012.8	4.7	79.8	$26,179	6.8	32.8	58.9	19.2	51.5	41.6
Cleveland Heights city	8.107	46,238	45,181	-2.3	5,573.3	8.1	83.1	$53,155	21.9	17.7	65.6	9.3	54.8	37.0
Columbus city	217.967	788,654	835,957	6.0	3,835.2	11.3	77.0	$44,774	15.3	19.0	69.8	8.9	53.5	35.8
Conneaut city	26.355	12,841	12,813	-0.2	486.2	1.1	79.5	$34,230	5.3	18.4	48.2	12.5	59.5	33.1
Coshocton city	8.071	11,216	11,107		1,376.1	0.8	80.8	$35,149	10.1	19.4	52.9	10.0	61.6	34.5
Cuyahoga Falls city	25.622	49,583	49,210	-0.8	1,920.6	3.4	90.1	$49,188	14.0	12.1	66.8	6.6	58.1	35.7
Dayton city	55.664	141,761	141,003	-0.5	2,533.1	4.0	74.8	$28,174	6.1	30.7	57.5	16.6	50.9	42.3
Defiance city	12.170	16,995	16,776	-1.3	1,378.5	1.3	81.9	$43,947	10.3	15.4	61.1	9.7	63.8	29.5
Delaware city	19.010	34,756	37,372	7.5	1,965.9	2.8	82.3	$54,683	21.9	9.2	66.9	4.3	62.6	32.3
Dent CDP	5.930	10,497	NA	NA	NA	2.4	89.4	$71,235	33.1	5.2	68.1	4.2	68.3	26.5
Dover city	5.690	12,826	12,857	0.2	2,259.7	3.6	85.9	$44,223	12.1	11.4	58.1	5.5	65.6	31.3
Dublin city	24.562	41,345	44,214	6.9	1,800.1	16.1	88.1	$117,860	60.3	2.8	72.5	4.1	78.0	18.6
East Cleveland city	3.086	17,844	17,432	-2.3	5,649.2	2.9	81.1	$20,660	2.8	43.8	49.4	28.6	48.0	48.3
Eastlake city	6.395	18,577	18,321	-1.4	2,864.9	5.7	90.8	$50,478	15.0	9.9	67.5	7.0	63.7	29.4
East Liverpool city	4.699	11,212	10,951	-2.3	2,330.5	1.2	83.5	$26,887	5.9	30.7	54.5	15.7	60.4	34.0
Elyria city	20.572	54,533	53,972		2,623.6	1.5	82.4	$42,272	10.2	18.6	65.4	11.0	63.5	29.0
Englewood city	6.551	13,465	13,457	-0.1	2,054.3	4.2	87.7	$52,321	17.2	10.0	60.9	8.7	65.3	33.1
Euclid city	10.630	48,905	47,893	-2.1	4,505.5	3.0	84.8	$36,128	8.7	19.8	63.5	14.6	52.3	43.2
Fairborn city	13.149	32,763	33,329	1.7	2,534.6	5.4	82.5	$42,545	13.4	22.6	64.8	10.6	56.7	34.4
Fairfield city	20.880	42,503	42,770	0.6	2,048.4	8.0	84.8	$55,803	19.4	8.3	71.8	8.9	66.9	26.9
Fairview Park city	4.683	16,826	16,481	-2.1	3,519.5	8.4	90.4	$53,425	20.4	9.5	67.8	7.6	55.8	39.3
Findlay city	19.140	41,186	41,098	-0.2	2,147.3	3.6	79.0	$43,948	14.0	17.8	64.7	10.1	59.4	33.7
Finneytown CDP	4.057	12,741	NA	NA	NA	5.3	87.1	$53,507	20.9	11.1	67.6	9.3	68.7	26.9
Forest Park city	6.477	18,720	18,723	0.0	2,890.8	9.6	84.9	$48,865	13.8	12.6	68.1	10.1	67.6	27.4
Forestville CDP	3.700	10,532	NA	NA	NA	8.0	88.1	$64,053	31.1	11.3	57.9	5.6	67.5	31.1
Fostoria city	7.546	13,441	13,182	-1.9	1,746.8	0.5	87.5	$34,708	4.6	23.2	60.9	14.9	61.8	34.8
Franklin city	9.174	11,769	11,811	0.4	1,287.4	1.2	82.9	$44,467	12.9	16.1	61.6	9.8	67.9	26.4
Fremont city	8.344	16,734	16,448	-1.7	1,971.3	2.4	82.0	$33,445	7.4	26.9	63.0	12.8	60.9	33.5
Gahanna city	12.427	33,233	34,257	3.1	2,756.7	5.6	87.4	$73,583	36.1	5.1	72.7	5.5	69.2	25.2
Galion city	7.621	10,510	10,175	-3.2	1,335.1	0.6	84.0	$33,176	6.3	18.7	55.7	11.1	62.3	32.2
Garfield Heights city	7.231	28,849	28,229	-2.1	3,904.1	3.4	87.3	$41,171	8.8	15.6	63.4	13.1	63.9	32.5
Green city	32.063	25,744	25,917	0.7	808.3	2.7	92.2	$61,665	26.8	8.0	66.8	6.5	68.2	27.4
Greenville city	6.626	13,227	13,037	-1.4	1,967.6	0.8	80.1	$31,904	6.9	17.7	55.8	12.2	53.7	41.8
Grove City city	16.265	35,578	38,519	8.3	2,368.2	2.6	88.5	$66,964	28.1	8.6	69.4	4.7	69.4	25.0
Hamilton city	21.467	62,272	62,486	0.3	2,910.7	3.6	82.7	$40,080	10.5	19.0	61.0	12.1	62.6	30.7
Harrison city	5.202	9,920	10,479	5.6	2,014.5	0.1	87.9	$60,529	24.9	7.7	74.2	6.9	71.8	23.4
Heath city	10.723	10,282	10,456	1.7	975.1	2.2	84.5	$43,740	13.5	11.4	62.7	7.5	62.2	32.8
Hilliard city	13.196	28,225	32,465	15.0	2,460.3	6.1	88.2	$88,203	43.8	5.1	74.3	5.6	74.5	20.9
Huber Heights city	22.273	38,102	38,162	0.2	1,713.4	3.5	84.1	$51,938	15.7	10.2	64.8	9.2	68.7	26.7
Hudson city	25.598	22,262	22,448	0.8	876.9	7.4	90.7	$123,324	59.9	3.1	63.4	5.6	81.8	16.2
Ironton city	4.161	11,129	10,995	-1.2	2,642.3	0.3	83.5	$34,301	10.8	19.9	52.1	8.3	60.5	35.5
Kent city	9.176	28,906	29,639	2.5	3,229.9	6.5	62.1	$35,210	14.3	34.9	69.6	13.3	47.8	27.8
Kettering city	18.706	56,161	55,705	-0.8	2,977.9	3.4	83.9	$49,790	16.7	11.1	65.5	7.3	57.1	37.3
Lakewood city	5.535	52,131	50,926	-2.3	9,200.9	8.1	78.6	$45,098	15.5	15.8	73.6	8.3	44.5	45.1
Lancaster city	18.845	38,781	39,595	2.1	2,101.0	1.5	78.7	$37,494	12.3	18.6	59.6	10.2	59.2	34.2

1 Dry land or land partially or temporarily covered by water.
2 16 years old and over.

Table B. Incorporated Places, Census Designated Places (CDPs), and Minor Civil Divisions (MCDs) of 10,000 or More Population — **Crime, Construction, and Local Government Finance**

STATE City, town, township, borough, or CDP (county if applicable)	Serious crimes known to police, 2014[1] Total number	Rate[2] Total	Rate[2] Violent	Rate[2] Property	New residential construction authorized by building permits, 2014 Value ($1,000)	Number of housing units	Percent single family	Local government finance, 2012 General revenue Total (mil dol)	Intergovernmental Total (mil dol)	Percent from state gov.	Taxes per capita[3]	General expenditure Total (mil dol)	Per capita[3] Total	Per capita[3] Capital outlays	Debt outstanding (mil dol)
	15	16	17	18	19	20	21	22	23	24	25	26	27	28	29
NORTH DAKOTA—Con.															
Williston city	1,319	5811	533	5278	231,754	1,630	20.4	38.2	4.6	74.1	1117	39.4	2,030	1,012	77.3
OHIO	357,558	3084	285	2799	3,753,786	19,872	63.1	X	X	X	X	X	X	X	X
Akron city	10,489	5300	690	4610	NA	NA	NA	350.3	65.6	64.3	879	337.8	1,701	101	794.0
Alliance city	1,021	4601	338	4263	972	13	100.0	25.8	4.7	66.8	517	21.6	973	193	64.6
Amherst city	199	1640	25	1615	3,297	18	100.0	9.4	0.8	99.9	468	11.5	955	247	13.0
Ashland city	513	2528	74	2454	1,480	8	50.0	24.1	3.4	100.0	486	21.5	1,046	72	16.0
Ashtabula city	NA	NA	NA	NA	0	0	0.0	19.7	4.9	96.0	424	20.6	1,094	153	3.9
Athens city	399	1657	112	1545	4,621	13	100.0	19.4	1.0	90.8	480	23.1	960	50	7.8
Aurora city	170	1091	58	1033	15,043	51	100.0	21.4	2.2	99.8	991	18.0	1,162	116	14.2
Austintown CDP	NA	NA	NA	NA	NA	NA	NA	NA	NA	NA	NA	NA	NA	NA	NA
Avon city	NA	NA	NA	NA	51,658	124	100.0	25.9	5.2	100.0	749	32.8	1,505	730	85.5
Avon Lake city	NA	NA	NA	NA	31,641	142	43.0	38.3	12.0	94.3	708	35.6	1,561	305	1.0
Barberton city	1,072	4078	259	3820	675	5	100.0	31.7	6.9	86.9	533	30.8	1,170	202	16.6
Bay Village city	101	654	19	635	4,539	15	100.0	18.3	2.9	100.0	781	19.3	1,249	127	8.7
Beachwood city	647	5477	102	5376	1,669	3	100.0	37.6	1.1	63.8	2787	35.8	3,019	166	26.1
Beavercreek city	1,037	2262	55	2208	NA	NA	NA	25.7	8.8	100.0	279	26.8	583	125	12.0
Bedford city	449	3499	187	3312	0	0	0.0	27.9	2.9	42.6	1278	29.4	2,274	211	21.8
Bedford Heights city	291	2724	318	2406	0	0	0.0	23.5	2.8	91.0	1252	23.5	2,212	161	3.5
Bellefontaine city	632	4804	220	4583	NA	NA	NA	17.3	6.0	16.7	471	18.1	1,373	265	9.5
Berea city	213	1122	100	1022	550	2	100.0	27.8	3.4	100.0	811	22.3	1,173	212	14.5
Bexley city	451	3330	111	3219	952	2	100.0	17.7	2.4	100.0	680	17.7	1,334	299	20.6
Blue Ash city	345	2840	66	2775	5,298	18	100.0	47.6	2.7	100.0	2873	48.4	3,994	1,498	65.5
Boardman CDP	NA	NA	NA	NA	NA	NA	NA	NA	NA	NA	NA	NA	NA	NA	NA
Bowling Green city	675	2100	118	1982	NA	NA	NA	36.0	6.4	100.0	667	36.9	1,161	103	24.2
Brecksville city	65	481	NA	481	6,232	10	100.0	24.9	1.6	97.6	1498	22.0	1,627	199	13.7
Bridgetown CDP	NA	NA	NA	NA	NA	NA	NA	NA	NA	NA	NA	NA	NA	NA	NA
Broadview Heights city	53	274	140	135	6,014	20	100.0	22.6	3.0	79.3	759	21.0	1,088	200	7.0
Brooklyn city	728	6640	265	6375	0	0	0.0	21.8	1.0	78.6	1679	14.2	1,291	140	8.4
Brook Park city	NA	NA	NA	NA	0	0	0.0	28.7	4.1	100.0	1077	30.2	1,588	281	2.8
Brunswick city	325	939	55	884	14,638	128	39.1	26.4	4.7	51.4	463	22.8	662	108	11.1
Bucyrus city	777	6471	242	6230	270	1	100.0	12.2	2.1	91.4	454	17.2	1,423	484	0.0
Cambridge city	623	5947	477	5470	1,500	17	70.6	12.5	1.4	100.0	758	10.0	949	105	4.9
Canton city	4,659	6436	1008	5427	1,670	12	100.0	118.3	36.4	85.3	642	113.3	1,558	208	20.1
Celina city	408	3934	183	3751	1,850	12	58.3	11.6	1.4	46.3	427	8.7	836	150	25.5
Centerville city	400	1670	96	1574	2,061	17	29.4	23.3	2.3	52.7	627	20.3	848	72	16.7
Chillicothe city	1,847	8435	370	8065	994	11	100.0	28.2	5.7	87.9	683	23.9	1,097	81	5.4
Cincinnati city	19,399	6517	913	5604	50,826	601	16.5	947.1	392.8	17.6	1400	783.9	2,641	864	917.4
Circleville city	712	5286	252	5034	0	0	0.0	92.3	2.4	61.6	487	81.8	6,113	289	44.8
Clayton city	194	1469	53	1416	NA	NA	NA	9.0	2.3	100.0	435	9.1	691	139	9.6
Cleveland city	26,421	6798	1339	5459	7,350	124	77.4	897.0	231.8	58.8	1071	897.7	2,294	222	2530.4
Cleveland Heights city	1,325	2931	234	2696	1,383	9	100.0	55.8	10.6	84.0	699	57.2	1,254	119	18.6
Columbus city	40,184	4837	558	4278	449,879	3,642	19.9	1434.3	260.4	47.1	958	1353.3	1,670	431	2555.4
Conneaut city	346	2684	419	2265	NA	NA	NA	9.9	2.1	98.8	362	10.8	844	136	0.0
Coshocton city	NA	NA	NA	NA	280	2	100.0	8.5	1.1	90.1	452	7.9	703	0	15.5
Cuyahoga Falls city	1,150	2338	100	2238	NA	NA	NA	65.4	9.3	91.5	637	59.4	1,207	245	55.8
Dayton city	9,238	6450	864	5587	630	7	100.0	304.4	74.9	66.0	832	297.8	2,099	314	131.3
Defiance city	503	2999	185	2814	1,679	7	100.0	23.7	6.4	71.5	460	22.7	1,336	319	15.7
Delaware city	861	2336	174	2163	41,671	196	83.2	45.0	6.0	28.6	578	56.6	1,578	458	89.4
Dent CDP	NA	NA	NA	NA	NA	NA	NA	NA	NA	NA	NA	NA	NA	NA	NA
Dover city	85	661	47	614	120	1	100.0	15.2	3.6	100.0	553	15.4	1,200	314	21.6
Dublin city	482	1091	18	1073	66,256	202	100.0	103.4	5.5	100.0	1739	90.8	2,117	497	57.2
East Cleveland city	518	2969	768	2201	0	0	0.0	19.3	6.9	100.0	487	22.7	1,291	10	0.0
Eastlake city	454	2470	76	2394	1,101	3	100.0	19.7	4.2	100.0	586	21.0	1,138	133	15.3
East Liverpool city	NA	NA	NA	NA	0	0	0.0	6.8	2.0	100.0	383	6.7	603	18	7.7
Elyria city	NA	NA	NA	NA	2,431	24	100.0	65.0	18.3	87.1	508	62.4	1,153	112	50.5
Englewood city	505	3750	186	3565	2,787	20	70.0	13.9	2.6	100.0	547	13.4	998	145	0.0
Euclid city	125	261	25	236	0	0	0.0	62.8	10.1	90.8	581	73.1	1,514	131	40.5
Fairborn city	1,043	3134	144	2990	9,052	35	100.0	38.1	6.6	99.9	498	37.4	1,124	168	21.9
Fairfield city	1,355	3177	230	2947	1,467	9	100.0	52.2	6.6	100.0	686	61.3	1,438	11	32.0
Fairview Park city	NA	NA	NA	NA	375	1	100.0	20.8	2.1	87.8	755	19.3	1,161	68	22.7
Findlay city	1,556	3739	192	3547	6,646	28	92.9	47.4	7.7	100.0	599	43.6	1,050	149	18.2
Finneytown CDP	NA	NA	NA	NA	NA	NA	NA	NA	NA	NA	NA	NA	NA	NA	NA
Forest Park city	664	3546	304	3242	0	0	0.0	18.6	0.7	2.2	717	19.1	1,025	105	6.5
Forestville CDP	NA	NA	NA	NA	NA	NA	NA	NA	NA	NA	NA	NA	NA	NA	NA
Fostoria city	NA	NA	NA	NA	85	1	100.0	12.9	2.2	100.0	415	12.3	926	120	1.3
Franklin city	NA	NA	NA	NA	625	3	100.0	15.8	2.2	100.0	666	14.1	1,192	46	11.8
Fremont city	1,018	6216	147	6069	0	0	0.0	34.3	17.8	8.0	557	18.8	1,131	106	10.7
Gahanna city	670	1956	70	1886	5,041	24	54.2	35.0	5.1	65.6	562	38.9	1,150	171	26.3
Galion city	588	5756	186	5570	180	1	100.0	11.5	1.3	78.7	546	11.3	1,099	157	13.1
Garfield Heights city	1,001	3540	382	3158	0	0	0.0	34.7	4.5	59.7	748	32.2	1,130	3	27.3
Green city	NA	NA	NA	NA	NA	NA	NA	27.4	4.6	79.0	800	25.0	969	123	58.3
Greenville city	368	2823	307	2516	NA	NA	NA	13.6	2.8	97.7	612	10.8	822	104	2.0
Grove City city	1,452	3827	100	3726	46,847	234	73.5	38.4	8.3	45.2	651	33.8	917	213	35.9
Hamilton city	1,168	1877	169	1708	1,474	9	100.0	89.3	12.8	82.9	618	83.9	1,348	178	315.7
Harrison city	NA	NA	NA	NA	10,423	93	60.2	13.7	2.5	100.0	566	17.4	1,717	486	26.1
Heath city	543	5179	210	4969	NA	NA	NA	13.4	3.7	100.0	640	15.0	1,448	376	7.6
Hilliard city	NA	NA	NA	NA	52,553	338	46.7	35.0	7.3	60.4	762	31.8	1,040	211	62.6
Huber Heights city	1,235	3238	197	3042	NA	NA	NA	30.3	5.3	52.2	442	34.7	911	258	57.3
Hudson city	130	577	18	559	NA	NA	NA	32.9	4.1	100.0	1035	32.4	1,453	278	44.7
Ironton city	339	3069	172	2897	564	3	100.0	11.7	4.5	100.0	228	19.1	1,728	51	5.0
Kent city	654	2007	233	1774	8,856	79	10.1	26.7	4.8	93.2	488	31.0	1,046	271	19.1
Kettering city	1,132	2029	95	1934	937	7	100.0	81.4	18.4	94.3	863	83.8	1,495	462	18.1
Lakewood city	824	1618	130	1489	1,200	1	100.0	61.0	11.1	71.9	685	53.0	1,032	61	92.2
Lancaster city	1,858	4709	276	4433	9,761	70	40.0	74.4	14.1	95.8	511	62.8	1,614	139	375.7

1 Data for serious crimes have not been adjusted for underreporting. This may affect comparability between geographic areas over time.
2 Per 100,000 population estimated by the FBI. 3 Based on population estimated as of July 1 of the year shown.

Table B. Incorporated Places, Census Designated Places (CDPs), and Minor Civil Divisions (MCDs) of 10,000 or More Population — Land Area, Population, and Households, and Employment

STATE City, town, township, borough, or CDP (county if applicable)	Land area,[1] 2010 (sq mi)	Population				Population characteristics 2010–2014		Household income and poverty, 2010–2014			Employment,[2] 2010–2014		Households, 2010–2014 (percent of households)	
		Total persons 2010	Total persons 2014	Percent change 2010–2014	Persons per square mile, 2014	Foreign born	Lives in same house as previous year	Median household income (dollars	Percent of households Income of $100,000 or more	Income below poverty level	Percent in labor force	Unemploy-ment rate	Family households	One person households
	1	2	3	4	5	6	7	8	9	10	11	12	13	14
OHIO—Con.														
Lebanon city	12.891	20,032	20,434	2.0	1,585.2	3.4	84.6	$63,520	23.8	9.2	72.7	9.9	73.7	22.3
Lima city	13.536	38,761	38,265	-1.3	2,826.9	1.0	74.2	$28,901	5.8	31.7	59.3	19.2	58.8	34.4
Lorain city	23.673	64,097	63,776	-0.5	2,694.0	3.0	83.1	$35,330	9.7	24.6	60.4	15.4	64.0	32.2
Loveland city	5.032	12,063	12,405	2.8	2,465.0	3.3	89.2	$73,225	34.8	9.0	70.7	2.1	70.1	24.7
Lyndhurst city	4.432	14,001	13,733	-1.9	3,098.5	8.5	92.2	$66,352	27.9	4.9	65.8	4.8	63.8	31.7
Macedonia city	9.663	11,133	11,579	4.0	1,198.3	5.9	92.5	$80,825	37.8	1.5	68.6	7.1	74.5	21.1
Mack CDP	9.273	11,585	NA	NA	NA	2.0	93.6	$80,797	40.4	4.6	66.0	4.6	82.3	14.8
Mansfield city	30.872	47,821	46,824	-2.1	1,516.7	1.5	77.5	$32,225	7.5	23.7	49.4	13.0	55.4	39.3
Maple Heights city	5.171	23,138	22,735	-1.7	4,396.6	2.4	88.6	$36,661	7.1	21.7	63.8	15.7	58.7	37.8
Marietta city	8.429	14,085	13,954	-0.9	1,655.4	2.8	82.8	$31,030	11.6	23.0	54.7	10.6	52.6	42.6
Marion city	11.773	36,828	36,620	-0.6	3,110.5	1.4	75.7	$33,423	7.0	22.2	48.3	12.2	63.3	30.7
Marysville city	16.285	22,098	22,708	2.8	1,394.4	2.8	77.8	$54,561	21.5	10.6	59.5	6.2	67.3	28.7
Mason city	18.646	30,857	31,613	2.5	1,695.4	11.2	89.8	$83,466	41.0	4.7	68.9	5.7	74.0	21.9
Massillon city	18.978	32,199	32,274	0.2	1,700.6	1.1	86.2	$39,390	10.4	17.6	61.8	11.3	61.1	33.4
Maumee city	9.845	14,286	14,036	-1.7	1,425.6	2.3	86.1	$56,016	19.1	10.9	67.8	6.0	63.6	30.3
Mayfield Heights city	4.170	19,155	18,849	-1.6	4,520.6	17.1	84.2	$44,828	13.6	10.0	65.1	7.3	47.1	47.5
Medina city	11.571	26,666	26,523	-0.5	2,292.1	2.5	85.7	$53,425	21.5	11.3	68.6	5.4	66.4	28.2
Mentor city	26.642	47,159	46,870	-0.6	1,759.2	3.7	93.3	$67,983	28.9	6.7	67.9	5.5	67.9	26.9
Miamisburg city	12.206	20,181	20,092	-0.4	1,646.0	1.7	86.1	$52,171	23.4	11.9	62.3	6.9	64.7	30.4
Middleburg Heights city	8.064	15,946	15,751	-1.2	1,953.2	14.2	85.9	$59,361	22.5	6.7	62.4	7.5	61.4	34.0
Middletown city	26.185	48,678	48,791	0.2	1,863.3	3.2	80.6	$35,828	9.1	21.1	61.2	15.8	61.4	32.7
Monfort Heights CDP	5.915	11,948	NA	NA	NA	1.6	90.5	$72,649	29.3	4.5	67.6	4.1	74.5	24.1
Monroe city	15.874	12,453	13,279	6.6	836.5	2.5	87.6	$69,313	26.8	7.0	69.7	5.5	73.2	23.2
Montgomery city	5.289	10,251	10,440	1.8	1,973.9	8.3	93.9	$101,675	51.7	4.6	59.3	5.3	74.3	23.1
Mount Vernon city	9.409	16,990	16,788	-1.2	1,784.2	0.9	73.0	$34,533	8.3	20.9	59.7	11.7	56.7	36.4
Newark city	20.757	47,574	47,839	0.6	2,304.7	1.2	78.9	$36,679	10.8	20.7	63.1	9.9	59.7	33.6
New Franklin city	25.036	14,222	14,292	0.5	570.8	2.3	94.1	$65,052	23.1	5.4	64.8	8.1	75.0	21.7
New Philadelphia city	8.216	17,283	17,438	0.9	2,122.5	1.6	82.4	$40,106	11.9	15.3	65.0	8.3	65.4	28.9
Niles city	8.611	19,266	18,778	-2.5	2,180.7	1.4	86.3	$38,027	8.6	19.5	55.6	11.4	57.6	37.1
Northbrook CDP	1.949	10,668	NA	NA	NA	2.7	83.3	$39,704	8.0	13.9	71.1	12.4	68.1	26.9
North Canton city	6.400	17,486	17,490	0.0	2,732.8	3.6	83.4	$52,530	17.8	6.5	62.0	6.8	57.5	35.3
North Olmsted city	11.672	32,713	32,130	-1.8	2,752.7	8.1	91.0	$60,136	22.8	5.4	67.1	8.1	64.4	30.2
North Ridgeville city	23.438	29,466	31,871	8.2	1,359.8	4.6	91.5	$66,746	25.6	5.8	67.9	9.0	71.9	25.4
North Royalton city	21.310	30,444	30,327	-0.4	1,423.2	9.5	91.0	$69,126	30.2	5.1	68.2	5.8	65.3	29.6
Norton city	20.172	12,090	12,042	-0.4	597.0	1.6	94.5	$62,161	21.9	6.1	68.6	7.1	72.6	24.4
Norwalk city	8.863	17,013	16,898	-0.7	1,906.5	3.9	84.7	$43,421	11.6	15.1	61.7	8.8	64.1	28.7
Norwood city	3.147	19,207	19,405	1.0	6,165.5	3.2	80.5	$36,075	10.6	19.4	68.0	7.8	48.5	41.2
Oregon city	29.981	20,313	20,196	-0.6	673.6	2.5	86.7	$52,423	21.8	11.1	62.9	8.3	65.0	30.8
Oxford city	7.244	21,376	21,782	1.9	3,006.8	6.0	48.4	$28,129	15.7	40.8	49.2	4.7	35.7	33.2
Painesville city	6.829	19,559	19,840	1.4	2,905.3	14.0	79.6	$33,770	10.4	23.1	64.2	9.4	62.6	30.5
Parma city	20.025	81,601	80,015	-1.9	3,995.7	10.1	88.9	$49,568	14.3	10.7	65.4	8.1	63.4	32.7
Parma Heights city	4.186	20,718	20,330	-1.9	4,857.2	11.9	79.4	$43,670	12.6	13.0	63.5	7.3	55.5	39.1
Pataskala city	28.760	14,924	15,192	1.8	528.2	1.5	83.7	$67,880	23.4	8.6	69.7	5.2	71.7	24.1
Perrysburg city	11.931	20,796	21,368	2.8	1,790.9	5.1	90.4	$74,271	35.8	8.0	70.7	6.4	62.7	32.7
Pickerington city	9.783	18,278	19,408	6.2	1,983.9	5.9	79.9	$82,247	37.7	3.9	73.6	7.5	80.4	16.3
Piqua city	11.627	20,523	20,759	1.1	1,785.4	1.1	78.8	$37,699	7.6	18.2	63.8	12.9	61.8	30.8
Portsmouth city	10.734	20,226	20,326	0.5	1,893.5	2.0	82.1	$30,114	8.4	28.2	48.7	11.6	54.0	36.8
Powell city	4.973	11,498	12,511	8.8	2,515.6	9.0	87.2	$136,250	71.2	0.4	72.5	4.1	86.1	11.0
Ravenna city	5.630	11,723	11,643	-0.7	2,068.0	0.6	83.3	$36,317	6.8	21.7	67.4	13.5	55.1	37.9
Reading city	2.892	10,385	10,354	-0.3	3,580.8	4.1	84.2	$40,480	14.9	14.5	62.5	10.5	56.0	39.3
Reynoldsburg city	11.113	35,900	36,711	2.3	3,303.4	6.8	82.8	$60,183	23.1	9.7	72.1	7.0	64.6	27.7
Richmond Heights city	4.436	10,557	10,495	-0.6	2,365.7	10.3	87.0	$47,733	16.0	10.6	64.5	9.0	54.9	39.6
Riverside city	9.720	25,201	25,040	-0.6	2,576.2	3.1	79.0	$41,734	11.3	16.0	63.1	13.4	64.9	29.4
Rocky River city	4.736	20,213	20,433	1.1	4,314.2	10.8	89.2	$63,889	31.5	5.5	63.0	5.2	57.0	39.2
Salem city	6.424	12,295	12,087	-1.7	1,881.7	1.4	81.6	$39,587	8.6	17.2	65.3	9.4	60.9	33.0
Sandusky city	9.726	25,919	25,346	-2.2	2,606.1	2.3	81.3	$34,377	8.6	19.9	62.4	11.8	53.5	41.0
Seven Hills city	4.908	11,812	11,702	-0.9	2,384.4	13.0	94.3	$67,786	29.1	5.2	62.9	7.8	67.7	27.5
Shaker Heights city	6.282	28,448	27,790	-2.3	4,423.5	8.9	89.1	$75,177	38.8	9.9	65.8	5.4	66.3	30.0
Sharonville city	9.826	13,560	13,581	0.2	1,382.2	10.6	83.7	$52,302	19.5	13.7	66.1	6.5	55.8	38.8
Sidney city	11.926	21,225	20,905	-1.5	1,752.9	2.6	82.7	$43,530	10.6	17.8	64.6	8.7	65.9	27.0
Solon city	20.361	23,348	23,075	-1.2	1,133.3	14.4	93.4	$94,925	47.8	2.9	66.8	6.0	79.8	18.9
South Euclid city	4.651	22,295	21,869	-1.9	4,702.4	5.7	89.5	$56,841	18.0	8.2	71.9	9.2	63.4	31.9
Springboro city	9.346	17,334	18,017	3.9	1,927.8	5.2	91.0	$93,292	46.2	3.5	68.9	6.5	81.7	14.3
Springdale city	4.966	11,223	11,212	-0.1	2,257.5	15.3	83.1	$49,757	16.0	18.3	60.4	7.5	63.0	31.7
Springfield city	25.549	60,608	59,956	-1.1	2,346.7	2.5	78.0	$31,327	8.0	26.4	58.1	13.8	57.2	35.9
Steubenville city	10.557	18,659	18,303	-1.9	1,737.0	2.0	81.0	$31,219	10.3	30.5	48.5	10.3	57.6	36.6
Stow city	17.093	34,837	34,773	-0.2	2,034.4	4.2	92.4	$64,073	27.2	7.0	68.2	6.2	66.2	28.5
Streetsboro city	23.487	16,029	16,238	1.3	691.4	4.3	82.8	$59,631	19.3	9.7	72.4	7.1	63.7	30.0
Strongsville city	24.622	44,750	44,654	-0.2	1,813.6	7.8	90.9	$77,849	38.2	4.6	67.7	6.4	70.7	25.5
Struthers city	3.642	10,713	10,441	-2.5	2,866.7	1.4	82.6	$36,819	5.7	16.3	60.3	13.7	63.8	30.7
Sylvania city	6.482	18,971	18,965	0.0	2,925.9	4.5	88.2	$69,051	34.3	8.4	64.0	5.9	68.2	28.1
Tallmadge city	13.982	17,572	17,527	-0.3	1,253.5	2.9	93.8	$54,200	22.2	10.6	60.8	6.7	70.3	26.1
Tiffin city	6.765	17,963	17,739	-1.2	2,622.1	2.9	77.3	$39,530	8.2	16.1	59.0	12.0	60.1	31.3
Toledo city	80.721	287,206	281,031	-2.2	3,481.5	3.4	80.7	$33,485	8.0	25.9	62.3	15.3	55.9	36.4
Trenton city	4.563	11,869	12,260	3.3	2,686.6	0.4	80.0	$59,481	15.7	12.7	71.4	7.9	74.5	18.8
Trotwood city	30.494	24,432	24,171	-1.1	792.6	1.9	81.0	$35,697	9.6	20.7	56.3	12.5	59.5	36.8
Troy city	11.761	25,235	25,564	1.3	2,173.7	3.0	81.1	$47,517	13.7	13.5	66.4	6.9	64.5	29.6
Twinsburg city	13.772	18,796	18,837	0.2	1,367.8	7.1	87.3	$69,778	34.5	5.7	68.2	4.6	69.3	27.4
University Heights city	1.820	13,539	13,203	-2.5	7,253.3	9.7	82.6	$67,971	32.8	13.0	65.9	6.6	64.0	29.9
Upper Arlington city	9.774	33,682	34,609	2.8	3,541.0	7.6	89.5	$100,736	50.4	5.1	67.6	4.5	70.7	25.3
Urbana city	7.735	11,790	11,524	-2.3	1,489.9	1.0	75.5	$37,473	7.9	15.7	57.8	15.0	61.4	31.7
Vandalia city	12.332	15,246	15,139	-0.7	1,227.6	2.1	87.3	$51,935	19.3	10.7	67.4	9.0	64.8	31.9
Van Wert city	7.353	10,846	10,768	-0.7	1,464.5	0.9	81.2	$36,783	8.1	16.8	58.8	11.3	61.8	33.6
Vermilion city	10.643	10,586	10,478	-1.0	984.5	1.1	90.5	$52,014	19.1	11.6	60.2	8.4	58.5	23.7
Wadsworth city	10.621	21,538	21,893	1.6	2,061.3	1.9	85.6	$58,007	21.8	8.1	65.8	6.2	65.9	30.2
Warren city	16.127	41,557	40,633	-2.2	2,519.6	1.8	83.0	$29,249	5.7	29.9	49.9	11.7	55.3	39.3

1 Dry land or land partially or temporarily covered by water.
2 16 years old and over.

Table B. Incorporated Places, Census Designated Places (CDPs), and Minor Civil Divisions (MCDs) of 10,000 or More Population — **Crime, Construction, and Local Government Finance**

STATE City, town, township, borough, or CDP (county if applicable)	Serious crimes known to police, 2014[1]				New residential construction authorized by building permits, 2014			Local government finance, 2012							
	Total number	Rate[2]			Value ($1,000)	Number of housing units	Percent single family	General revenue				General expenditure			Debt outstanding (mil dol)
		Total	Violent	Property				Total (mil dol)	Intergovernmental		Taxes per capita[3]	Total (mil dol)	Per capita[3]		
									Total (mil dol)	Percent from state gov.			Total	Capital outlays	
	15	16	17	18	19	20	21	22	23	24	25	26	27	28	29
OHIO—Con.															
Lebanon city	472	2296	88	2208	16,486	98	17.3	26.1	3.7	100.0	567	23.7	1,163	327	36.6
Lima city	2,221	5804	923	4882	175	2	100.0	73.9	31.0	93.2	482	56.9	1,483	345	36.5
Lorain city	2,876	4521	384	4137	7,451	72	100.0	67.9	22.6	96.7	402	56.8	890	61	48.2
Loveland city	NA	NA	NA	NA	18,024	88	54.5	12.7	0.7	62.0	555	13.3	1,092	80	14.5
Lyndhurst city	70	509	44	466	3,770	9	100.0	19.3	4.9	100.0	784	19.2	1,388	41	2.2
Macedonia city	NA	NA	NA	NA	13,218	54	100.0	15.2	3.4	100.0	851	12.4	1,092	33	11.4
Mack CDP	NA	NA	NA	NA	NA	NA	NA	NA	NA	NA	NA	NA	NA	NA	NA
Mansfield city	3,421	7414	466	6948	2,080	10	100.0	55.9	12.3	51.1	588	51.8	1,101	78	9.9
Maple Heights city	NA	NA	NA	NA	0	0	0.0	20.5	2.1	79.7	585	18.8	821	19	15.8
Marietta city	176	1253	71	1181	NA	NA	NA	12.0	1.5	100.0	510	19.4	1,379	37	10.1
Marion city	1,666	4531	286	4246	50	1	100.0	39.4	10.3	100.0	375	36.5	989	43	44.8
Marysville city	241	1073	49	1024	NA	NA	NA	32.5	3.5	67.0	704	35.2	1,589	207	212.1
Mason city	393	1251	35	1216	51,268	423	33.6	54.1	7.0	87.3	937	56.2	1,798	343	120.3
Massillon city	1,197	3718	267	3451	7,295	75	56.0	35.7	5.9	26.8	540	33.4	1,036	44	22.4
Maumee city	593	4217	128	4089	690	4	100.0	29.6	3.8	100.0	1349	29.3	2,074	486	30.4
Mayfield Heights city	127	672	5	667	8,383	39	100.0	22.4	2.4	96.3	969	21.7	1,143	14	2.8
Medina city	72	153	6	147	0	0	0.0	27.0	2.3	92.3	636	24.7	931	114	45.6
Mentor city	118	251	6	245	24,936	117	76.1	61.5	10.0	90.4	862	59.9	1,274	0	34.9
Miamisburg city	423	2104	169	1934	1,104	4	100.0	29.8	3.2	100.0	899	34.9	1,730	338	25.1
Middleburg Heights city	NA	NA	NA	NA	491	3	100.0	29.2	2.0	100.0	1342	28.9	1,831	72	47.0
Middletown city	4,088	8411	638	7773	2,801	20	100.0	84.2	23.4	47.0	501	78.5	1,612	138	241.5
Monfort Heights CDP	NA	NA	NA	NA	NA	NA	NA	NA	NA	NA	NA	NA	NA	NA	NA
Monroe city	NA	NA	NA	NA	7,131	50	100.0	18.6	4.4	100.0	744	19.0	1,480	164	19.3
Montgomery city	167	1607	29	1578	17,100	37	100.0	17.9	2.9	34.7	1271	16.0	1,558	162	3.4
Mount Vernon city	NA	NA	NA	NA	1,199	5	100.0	21.1	3.8	49.3	692	23.5	1,393	485	24.7
Newark city	2,361	4939	153	4786	NA	NA	NA	52.3	16.1	92.8	462	52.1	1,091	140	24.5
New Franklin city	86	600	28	572	NA	NA	NA	6.8	1.6	78.4	302	6.8	477	55	0.0
New Philadelphia city	254	1458	80	1377	3,674	24	75.0	13.4	1.8	5.2	482	15.2	879	6	0.0
Niles city	865	4589	340	4250	1,091	6	100.0	18.6	3.7	100.0	406	21.1	1,109	124	7.9
Northbrook CDP	NA	NA	NA	NA	NA	NA	NA	NA	NA	NA	NA	NA	NA	NA	NA
North Canton city	257	1468	80	1388	3,480	12	100.0	16.8	2.7	100.0	463	19.8	1,137	125	18.1
North Olmsted city	NA	NA	NA	NA	125	1	100.0	41.3	6.2	95.2	724	35.0	1,082	136	38.8
North Ridgeville city	237	747	35	713	34,692	310	74.5	32.6	5.0	88.6	516	29.7	972	100	34.1
North Royalton city	NA	NA	NA	NA	12,211	44	100.0	28.1	4.2	100.0	554	25.8	852	47	40.3
Norton city	45	374	17	357	1,587	11	100.0	10.1	2.2	62.9	532	8.4	698	100	8.1
Norwalk city	430	2561	125	2436	1,866	11	100.0	13.3	0.7	90.0	466	14.7	866	4	1.5
Norwood city	1,306	6864	389	6475	38,001	300	0.0	23.1	2.2	7.3	1005	18.8	987	4	20.9
Oregon city	550	2722	134	2588	4,221	23	100.0	37.3	4.7	43.3	1265	29.7	1,466	227	29.5
Oxford city	526	2455	266	2189	6,180	47	25.5	18.5	1.3	67.5	454	16.4	757	43	4.7
Painesville city	420	2097	250	1848	2,909	17	100.0	25.6	6.8	82.0	474	25.3	1,297	215	11.4
Parma city	1,293	1613	85	1528	4,500	125	0.0	80.5	21.4	100.0	599	75.6	937	31	37.5
Parma Heights city	353	1733	74	1659	0	0	0.0	17.3	2.9	86.3	599	16.3	795	83	9.0
Pataskala city	NA	NA	NA	NA	NA	NA	NA	11.5	2.0	58.9	281	9.9	656	292	11.4
Perrysburg city	248	1153	19	1134	NA	NA	NA	29.4	2.6	89.2	842	24.1	1,138	186	22.3
Pickerington city	NA	NA	NA	NA	26,468	113	96.5	13.4	1.1	100.0	406	11.1	595	35	52.6
Piqua city	1,095	5278	169	5109	NA	NA	NA	23.9	3.5	88.9	553	19.6	948	92	5.3
Portsmouth city	1,629	7956	464	7492	3,149	148	0.0	18.5	3.7	77.1	436	17.3	851	67	4.4
Powell city	110	886	16	870	27,338	124	88.7	10.1	0.7	63.6	603	7.9	659	91	21.5
Ravenna city	NA	NA	NA	NA	NA	NA	NA	15.8	3.5	100.0	686	15.0	1,293	76	5.5
Reading city	NA	NA	NA	NA	250	2	100.0	10.4	1.6	100.0	722	11.8	1,137	10	2.1
Reynoldsburg city	1,208	3294	155	3139	13,444	86	59.3	27.3	3.4	100.0	406	25.5	702	31	22.9
Richmond Heights city	323	3079	133	2945	1,405	8	100.0	11.4	0.5	99.8	953	11.1	1,056	107	11.0
Riverside city	632	2521	203	2318	NA	NA	NA	11.8	3.1	96.7	263	11.2	447	11	2.0
Rocky River city	NA	NA	NA	NA	4,297	17	100.0	35.5	6.0	100.0	809	36.2	1,808	129	14.3
Salem city	292	2416	91	2325	607	6	100.0	8.7	0.8	78.1	398	8.9	732	130	15.8
Sandusky city	1,120	4438	289	4149	1,474	3	100.0	39.2	10.7	84.2	686	32.3	1,262	169	27.6
Seven Hills city	74	632	51	581	1,841	16	100.0	13.9	3.0	100.0	680	13.5	1,153	153	18.3
Shaker Heights city	272	978	32	945	0	0	0.0	52.5	8.5	41.5	1195	57.7	2,057	258	27.3
Sharonville city	NA	NA	NA	NA	7,019	113	0.9	26.3	2.8	55.2	1583	41.0	3,030	1,207	51.7
Sidney city	947	4518	177	4341	1,620	10	80.0	29.4	7.2	78.1	718	23.6	1,125	267	16.0
Solon city	178	770	35	736	9,265	20	100.0	63.9	6.8	100.0	1882	62.7	2,709	786	4.6
South Euclid city	586	2676	100	2576	1,815	11	100.0	24.3	4.6	90.9	631	23.5	1,069	140	5.1
Springboro city	161	896	67	829	12,415	73	100.0	23.2	2.1	100.0	654	17.1	970	43	41.6
Springdale city	695	6197	490	5706	0	0	0.0	15.9	0.8	91.2	1254	14.7	1,315	50	10.6
Springfield city	4,680	7947	751	7196	1,349	8	100.0	86.7	27.8	35.7	635	79.9	1,328	177	42.8
Steubenville city	NA	NA	NA	NA	1,211	18	11.1	36.8	13.9	66.9	623	34.7	1,885	487	49.4
Stow city	687	1977	69	1908	8,956	41	100.0	35.8	7.4	100.0	623	32.9	950	128	28.9
Streetsboro city	296	1833	68	1764	7,765	45	82.2	16.9	2.2	88.1	832	17.9	1,110	184	6.0
Strongsville city	782	1748	92	1657	24,869	73	100.0	63.9	10.5	39.1	881	66.8	1,498	383	60.3
Struthers city	493	4717	297	4421	NA	NA	NA	11.7	5.7	100.0	342	12.4	1,171	518	0.0
Sylvania city	NA	NA	NA	NA	NA	NA	NA	19.2	2.1	100.0	582	22.4	1,188	236	26.4
Tallmadge city	412	2350	131	2219	NA	NA	NA	19.4	2.8	94.5	627	19.3	1,104	94	10.8
Tiffin city	390	2190	90	2100	1,178	15	100.0	19.4	3.4	78.1	502	16.4	919	125	12.4
Toledo city	8,708	3097	1091	2006	26,614	493	5.3	451.3	105.2	62.6	618	399.2	1,408	377	357.2
Trenton city	NA	NA	NA	NA	1,499	12	100.0	6.8	1.2	100.0	172	6.3	516	18	9.3
Trotwood city	1,230	5084	405	4679	448	4	100.0	20.6	4.3	73.5	451	23.1	950	235	17.0
Troy city	934	3663	161	3502	NA	NA	NA	33.3	3.4	70.1	674	30.1	1,187	140	19.5
Twinsburg city	137	726	26	699	7,238	27	100.0	33.0	3.0	100.0	1148	28.6	1,523	229	25.3
University Heights city	272	2035	217	1818	0	0	0.0	19.4	5.0	45.5	898	17.4	1,293	91	3.1
Upper Arlington city	411	1188	12	1176	20,560	23	100.0	43.7	6.5	59.0	815	52.7	1,538	476	51.9
Urbana city	426	3677	199	3479	NA	NA	NA	11.9	1.2	55.4	519	13.8	1,181	207	13.9
Vandalia city	376	2482	125	2356	1,042	6	100.0	27.8	3.8	100.0	891	34.5	2,269	687	11.6
Van Wert city	425	3949	288	3661	1,453	7	100.0	11.7	1.6	100.0	619	12.6	1,164	70	0.1
Vermilion city	170	1624	115	1509	145	1	100.0	12.4	2.1	100.0	411	12.0	1,139	28	16.8
Wadsworth city	438	2001	50	1950	12,166	58	94.8	30.0	7.3	98.8	470	27.9	1,285	140	37.8
Warren city	1,838	4528	448	4080	0	0	0.0	62.9	13.4	36.4	486	56.8	1,394	127	33.9

1 Data for serious crimes have not been adjusted for underreporting. This may affect comparability between geographic areas over time.
2 Per 100,000 population estimated by the FBI. 3 Based on population estimated as of July 1 of the year shown.

Table B. Incorporated Places, Census Designated Places (CDPs), and Minor Civil Divisions (MCDs) of 10,000 or More Population — **Land Area, Population, and Households, and Employment**

STATE City, town, township, borough, or CDP (county if applicable)		Population				Population characteristics 2010–2014		Household income and poverty, 2010–2014			Employment,[2] 2010–2014		Households, 2010–2014 (percent of households)	
									Percent of households					
	Land area,[1] 2010 (sq mi)	Total persons 2010	Total persons 2014	Percent change 2010–2014	Persons per square mile, 2014	Foreign born	Lives in same house as previous year	Median household income (dollars	Income of $100,000 or more	Income below poverty level	Percent in labor force	Unemploy-ment rate	Family households	One person households
	1	2	3	4	5	6	7	8	9	10	11	12	13	14
OHIO—Con.														
Warrensville Heights city	4.130	13,542	13,286	-1.9	3,217.2	3.1	86.2	$35,143	4.5	17.6	60.2	12.3	54.8	41.3
Washington Court House city	8.739	14,192	14,085	-0.8	1,611.8	1.6	79.9	$34,839	6.1	21.3	57.8	9.2	61.9	32.5
West Carrollton city	6.459	13,143	13,018	-1.0	2,015.5	4.5	81.5	$37,179	7.8	18.0	68.3	8.7	51.6	39.9
Westerville city	12.463	36,116	37,667	4.3	3,022.2	5.4	86.4	$81,763	40.3	6.6	68.9	4.4	69.4	26.2
Westlake city	15.926	32,729	32,424	-0.9	2,035.9	9.4	89.3	$76,250	37.8	5.9	65.7	5.6	60.9	34.8
Whitehall city	5.280	18,135	18,558	2.3	3,515.1	11.5	78.1	$34,348	6.4	23.3	68.8	13.7	57.0	35.0
White Oak CDP	6.167	19,167	NA	NA	NA	5.6	86.0	$59,668	24.5	12.5	67.1	7.5	66.9	28.5
Wickliffe city	4.634	12,747	12,584	-1.3	2,715.6	4.4	92.1	$47,954	17.2	8.2	65.1	8.8	61.2	36.5
Willoughby city	10.249	22,268	22,453	0.8	2,190.7	6.0	88.2	$51,864	16.0	7.5	68.1	6.5	55.3	38.7
Willowick city	2.536	14,175	14,009	-1.2	5,523.1	4.8	92.1	$49,718	13.0	7.2	68.0	9.3	60.3	35.2
Wilmington city	10.889	12,520	12,375	-1.2	1,136.5	0.7	77.2	$30,625	5.2	26.3	59.0	13.7	57.8	36.4
Wooster city	16.319	26,119	26,540	1.6	1,626.4	4.1	74.5	$41,143	12.7	18.4	59.9	6.2	59.5	35.1
Worthington city	5.462	13,567	14,384	6.0	2,633.3	4.1	90.0	$87,842	43.9	3.1	66.9	3.4	66.6	28.2
Xenia city	13.008	25,658	25,911	1.0	1,991.9	1.7	85.2	$37,153	10.0	22.4	56.2	10.9	60.5	36.8
Youngstown city	33.966	66,982	65,062	-2.9	1,915.5	4.2	82.7	$24,361	4.2	33.6	50.1	19.6	55.0	39.7
Zanesville city	11.768	25,484	25,372	-0.4	2,156.0	1.1	78.1	$26,240	5.2	26.8	52.6	13.3	58.3	35.7
OKLAHOMA	68,594.918	3,751,616	3,878,051	3.4	56.5	5.6	82.5	$46,235	16.6	15.9	61.9	6.8	66.5	28.1
Ada city	19.754	16,827	17,130	1.8	867.2	2.8	72.7	$33,943	10.0	23.2	63.4	8.2	52.0	39.2
Altus city	18.373	19,813	19,531	-1.4	1,063.0	7.3	79.5	$39,780	10.6	16.6	65.8	8.7	64.7	28.7
Ardmore city	49.879	24,446	25,226	3.2	505.7	3.9	84.3	$41,574	13.2	17.2	61.3	7.4	62.7	33.2
Bartlesville city	22.751	35,752	36,498	2.1	1,604.2	4.1	81.1	$48,862	19.4	13.5	59.6	5.4	63.6	32.2
Bethany city	5.228	19,051	19,580	2.8	3,745.1	8.5	78.5	$42,387	14.0	15.3	64.0	6.5	63.3	32.3
Bixby city	24.841	20,910	24,008	14.8	966.5	4.4	84.8	$71,321	33.8	8.2	68.0	4.6	77.0	19.0
Broken Arrow city	61.632	98,832	104,726	6.0	1,699.2	5.8	86.2	$66,250	26.7	6.7	71.1	5.9	75.6	20.9
Chickasha city	22.034	16,038	16,334	1.8	741.3	2.8	79.1	$40,383	11.7	18.2	57.7	6.1	62.9	32.8
Choctaw city	27.305	11,146	11,992	7.6	439.2	1.3	91.0	$66,187	27.8	9.1	60.7	5.8	75.5	21.5
Claremore city	14.785	18,581	18,971	2.1	1,283.1	2.5	79.6	$39,726	10.9	16.3	61.0	8.8	61.6	34.5
Del City city	7.518	21,332	22,008	3.2	2,927.3	3.8	77.6	$41,085	5.5	17.9	61.6	8.4	61.4	32.7
Duncan city	42.870	23,423	23,173	-1.1	540.5	3.7	75.3	$40,171	11.6	16.2	57.2	8.5	62.8	33.9
Durant city	26.708	15,861	17,041	7.4	638.1	4.3	71.3	$35,584	9.1	21.5	62.2	10.0	58.3	33.0
Edmond city	84.695	81,399	88,605	8.9	1,046.2	6.6	81.5	$71,825	35.1	10.5	68.1	4.7	70.1	23.4
Elk City city	16.233	11,706	12,680	8.3	781.1	1.9	81.3	$58,920	19.7	9.9	62.6	3.7	65.2	26.6
El Reno city	79.243	16,749	18,153	8.4	229.1	5.8	82.6	$49,259	14.1	12.4	56.7	7.6	63.4	31.2
Enid city	73.954	49,379	51,386	4.1	694.8	8.1	75.9	$44,266	12.6	12.7	64.1	6.2	67.8	28.3
Glenpool city	10.334	10,791	11,855	9.9	1,147.1	2.9	85.6	$60,800	17.0	8.5	72.6	7.9	78.4	16.7
Guthrie city	18.773	10,191	11,096	8.9	591.1	1.7	77.2	$40,122	12.0	21.5	56.1	6.9	62.7	32.2
Guymon city	7.564	11,446	12,128	6.0	1,603.4	26.3	83.5	$50,648	16.2	11.0	73.0	6.4	73.3	22.8
Jenks city	17.135	16,928	19,951	17.9	1,164.3	5.8	87.0	$84,758	39.1	3.7	74.0	3.1	81.4	14.6
Lawton city	81.034	96,867	97,017	0.2	1,197.2	6.4	67.7	$43,263	12.6	17.9	65.1	10.0	63.3	30.3
McAlester city	16.197	18,383	18,247	-0.7	1,126.6	2.7	77.2	$40,785	13.7	21.2	52.2	6.1	60.1	33.9
Miami city	10.838	13,574	13,671	0.7	1,261.4	2.7	84.2	$35,198	7.8	21.4	58.9	8.5	62.9	32.1
Midwest City city	24.403	54,371	57,039	4.9	2,337.4	3.8	83.1	$45,196	11.8	13.8	63.8	6.9	62.7	31.8
Moore city	21.830	55,081	59,196	7.5	2,711.7	5.0	82.6	$58,542	19.8	9.9	70.5	6.0	72.3	22.1
Muskogee city	43.044	39,222	38,616	-1.5	897.1	4.0	80.7	$36,322	9.6	22.9	57.3	8.1	63.1	31.3
Mustang city	11.986	17,395	19,638	12.9	1,638.4	3.0	85.5	$67,176	25.3	5.7	71.1	5.0	77.1	19.8
Norman city	178.767	110,925	118,040	6.4	660.3	6.5	73.0	$50,714	21.6	17.7	64.3	5.8	57.4	30.8
Oklahoma City city	606.690	580,008	620,602	7.0	1,022.9	12.4	79.6	$47,004	18.4	16.5	67.0	6.6	62.7	30.7
Okmulgee city	17.086	12,574	12,227	-2.8	715.6	0.8	75.8	$28,101	4.6	28.3	50.5	17.2	54.6	39.4
Owasso city	16.580	29,720	33,773	13.6	2,037.0	3.8	82.1	$65,550	24.4	7.9	73.0	5.5	72.7	22.4
Ponca City city	18.386	25,401	24,766	-2.5	1,347.0	2.9	79.7	$40,089	12.3	15.3	59.9	8.1	61.8	33.7
Sand Springs city	19.261	18,833	19,553	3.8	1,015.2	1.3	84.2	$50,920	16.6	11.4	67.0	5.4	69.5	26.6
Sapulpa city	22.492	20,076	20,432	1.8	908.4	2.8	87.2	$39,969	12.8	15.3	57.2	8.0	66.0	30.3
Shawnee city	44.135	29,857	31,254	4.7	708.1	2.2	79.5	$38,001	11.5	22.1	61.2	7.7	63.1	31.7
Stillwater city	29.536	45,688	48,406	5.9	1,638.9	8.8	63.2	$32,255	12.6	33.1	61.0	6.1	43.6	36.1
Tahlequah city	12.480	15,739	16,496	4.8	1,321.8	4.9	79.2	$29,630	10.8	29.8	55.2	10.1	54.6	38.1
Tulsa city	196.860	391,922	399,682	2.0	2,030.3	10.1	79.5	$41,957	16.1	17.9	65.6	7.7	58.1	35.1
Warr Acres city	2.813	10,043	10,408	3.6	3,700.2	16.0	85.3	$40,536	12.3	16.3	66.6	5.8	66.5	29.0
Weatherford city	6.760	10,835	11,989	10.7	1,773.4	5.4	74.9	$38,077	14.9	25.3	66.4	5.1	60.2	26.9
Woodward city	13.138	11,972	12,963	8.3	986.7	4.0	82.5	$54,133	16.5	16.2	68.2	4.4	64.4	30.8
Yukon city	26.226	22,709	25,349	11.6	966.6	3.1	83.7	$63,651	23.7	7.1	66.3	4.4	74.6	20.1
OREGON	95,988.009	3,831,073	3,970,239	3.6	41.4	9.8	81.8	$50,521	19.5	15.1	62.5	10.5	63.4	27.9
Albany city	17.537	50,158	51,980	3.6	2,964.0	5.9	81.0	$45,478	13.8	18.0	61.9	12.5	66.0	27.3
Aloha CDP	7.360	49,425	NA	NA	NA	18.3	83.9	$62,988	19.4	12.5	73.7	9.7	74.8	18.4
Altamont CDP	8.113	19,257	NA	NA	NA	4.7	85.3	$41,795	11.1	15.6	58.7	10.3	68.4	26.6
Ashland city	6.638	20,078	20,684	3.0	3,116.0	6.2	74.2	$43,500	18.8	17.5	59.0	9.5	48.9	40.6
Beaverton city	18.691	89,779	95,109	5.9	5,088.6	20.4	78.2	$57,068	24.0	12.8	70.6	9.2	59.7	30.1
Bend city	33.005	76,639	84,080	9.7	2,547.5	5.1	78.9	$52,471	20.1	12.3	66.4	8.3	61.0	29.7
Bethany CDP	5.146	20,646	NA	NA	NA	27.0	83.1	$111,023	56.8	4.1	66.6	5.6	80.9	16.1
Canby city	4.368	16,649	17,010	2.2	3,894.5	11.6	87.7	$58,653	22.9	9.4	65.3	10.3	71.3	22.4
Cedar Mill CDP	3.316	14,546	NA	NA	NA	15.7	87.7	$96,361	48.5	7.1	67.3	7.8	70.0	22.3
Central Point city	3.903	17,174	17,724	3.2	4,540.7	2.4	80.4	$46,765	11.9	10.1	60.3	10.1	70.5	23.9
Coos Bay city	10.597	15,973	16,039	0.4	1,513.5	5.9	78.4	$36,360	9.8	19.4	52.5	11.1	53.6	37.9
Cornelius city	2.005	11,869	12,185	2.7	6,077.6	25.6	84.1	$55,203	15.2	9.8	74.5	16.3	81.8	12.3
Corvallis city	14.226	54,488	54,953	0.9	3,863.0	11.5	71.1	$40,425	19.1	28.6	58.7	8.7	46.2	32.3
Dallas city	4.810	14,583	15,102	3.6	3,139.9	2.0	76.9	$50,170	14.3	16.1	56.6	14.4	70.3	24.2
Damascus city	16.035	10,547	10,893	3.3	679.3	8.2	94.4	$85,708	40.6	5.8	65.0	8.9	84.7	11.4
Eugene city	43.757	156,358	160,561	2.7	3,669.4	8.1	71.7	$42,715	17.1	22.7	60.4	10.0	51.3	32.5
Forest Grove city	5.744	21,088	23,096	9.5	4,020.7	12.7	77.8	$48,365	17.5	15.5	61.5	10.9	69.1	24.9
Four Corners CDP	2.473	15,947	NA	NA	NA	19.8	80.4	$44,254	8.5	21.1	65.7	16.3	72.6	21.5
Gladstone city	2.394	11,497	11,888	3.4	4,964.9	6.1	81.6	$54,494	17.5	14.4	63.7	9.9	65.5	26.4
Grants Pass city	10.883	34,654	35,272	1.8	3,241.1	3.2	80.0	$33,240	9.7	20.4	51.9	13.3	58.3	35.1
Gresham city	23.221	105,590	109,892	4.1	4,732.5	17.6	81.7	$47,706	16.0	18.5	65.3	12.1	66.9	25.8

1 Dry land or land partially or temporarily covered by water.
2 16 years old and over.

Table B. Incorporated Places, Census Designated Places (CDPs), and Minor Civil Divisions (MCDs) of 10,000 or More Population — **Crime, Construction, and Local Government Finance**

STATE City, town, township, borough, or CDP (county if applicable)	Serious crimes known to police, 2014[1]: Total number	Serious crimes: Rate[2]: Total	Serious crimes: Rate[2]: Violent	Serious crimes: Rate[2]: Property	New residential construction authorized by building permits, 2014: Value ($1,000)	New residential construction: Number of housing units	New residential construction: Percent single family	Local government finance, 2012: General revenue: Total (mil dol)	General revenue: Intergovernmental: Total (mil dol)	General revenue: Intergovernmental: Percent from state gov.	General revenue: Taxes per capita[3]	General expenditure: Total (mil dol)	General expenditure: Per capita[3]: Total	General expenditure: Per capita[3]: Capital outlays	Debt outstanding (mil dol)
	15	16	17	18	19	20	21	22	23	24	25	26	27	28	29
OHIO—Con.															
Warrensville Heights city	NA	NA	NA	NA	534	4	100.0	18.2	1.8	29.4	1157	17.6	1,318	24	20.6
Washington Court House city	664	4719	220	4498	965	7	100.0	14.7	3.1	100.0	501	14.2	1,007	52	19.8
West Carrollton city	395	3032	207	2825	620	2	100.0	12.4	1.7	100.0	545	12.7	968	2	8.3
Westerville city	849	2244	74	2170	20,905	187	3.7	85.6	17.7	81.5	1359	96.9	2,605	855	75.5
Westlake city	400	1234	37	1197	23,691	57	100.0	58.8	5.1	53.1	1222	49.3	1,518	310	43.8
Whitehall city	1,314	7069	694	6375	317	3	100.0	26.0	2.8	21.1	1185	23.9	1,299	2	1.4
White Oak CDP	NA	NA	NA	NA	NA	NA	NA	NA	NA	NA	NA	NA	NA	NA	NA
Wickliffe city	NA	NA	NA	NA	990	9	100.0	22.4	2.9	44.0	1341	22.4	1,765	422	1.9
Willoughby city	445	1978	98	1880	26,447	155	31.6	37.8	5.3	86.9	1011	36.2	1,619	199	44.7
Willowick city	NA	NA	NA	NA	1,810	11	100.0	15.3	4.9	100.0	519	14.6	1,036	151	2.8
Wilmington city	651	5227	153	5074	0	0	0.0	20.3	4.4	100.0	478	20.7	1,667	72	21.7
Wooster city	981	3708	276	3432	5,919	25	100.0	134.0	6.0	94.8	532	128.8	4,877	371	10.1
Worthington city	276	1985	101	1884	1,385	3	100.0	29.1	2.1	100.0	1673	25.4	1,845	0	8.5
Xenia city	893	3444	216	3228	NA	NA	NA	28.5	5.5	95.4	514	28.4	1,089	214	7.4
Youngstown city	3,623	5602	660	4942	0	0	0.0	104.6	20.7	41.1	826	89.8	1,358	37	32.0
Zanesville city	1,597	6284	405	5878	250	1	100.0	44.9	17.1	96.5	701	34.3	1,347	67	6.6
OKLAHOMA	131,726	3397	406	2991	2,457,497	14,179	72.2	X	X	X	X	X	X	X	X
Ada city	1,109	6446	738	5708	8,870	106	13.2	25.3	1.3	74.5	969	24.4	1,424	164	5.2
Altus city	685	3507	369	3139	11,336	26	100.0	21.5	2.0	42.5	551	51.6	2,622	897	30.1
Ardmore city	2,180	8682	1669	7013	6,842	50	100.0	41.9	2.2	88.8	1070	34.0	1,374	178	49.6
Bartlesville city	1,001	2753	228	2524	17,959	90	93.3	40.2	4.0	79.0	619	44.1	1,213	354	60.7
Bethany city	625	3175	381	2794	623	4	100.0	12.3	0.3	100.0	284	11.5	592	9	3.6
Bixby city	386	1621	197	1423	46,817	227	100.0	16.7	1.3	56.6	526	19.8	877	392	37.9
Broken Arrow city	1,864	1782	142	1641	116,618	622	78.1	90.6	4.1	24.8	528	91.4	896	239	183.9
Chickasha city	604	3670	541	3129	2,023	14	100.0	19.5	0.7	38.1	762	18.1	1,122	198	4.3
Choctaw city	179	1491	150	1341	16,888	71	100.0	5.4	0.2	64.4	303	7.0	605	132	17.1
Claremore city	438	2289	219	2069	5,013	39	64.1	20.3	3.0	19.6	614	26.2	1,388	279	46.1
Del City city	1,387	6264	768	5496	967	7	100.0	14.8	0.5	75.9	445	18.0	824	210	9.1
Duncan city	1,338	5721	244	5477	5,263	33	100.0	23.8	0.5	84.3	664	24.8	1,064	238	22.5
Durant city	1,183	6905	403	6502	8,911	87	90.8	29.8	5.1	22.8	950	28.0	1,699	337	104.8
Edmond city	1,619	1832	92	1740	173,217	585	95.9	93.1	6.8	73.5	651	115.9	1,364	281	136.7
Elk City city	355	2761	93	2668	3,160	15	100.0	26.1	1.5	44.3	1437	17.5	1,428	284	20.9
El Reno city	466	2571	265	2306	5,955	39	79.5	21.9	1.2	100.0	700	15.3	873	11	39.2
Enid city	2,234	4377	370	4007	14,693	63	100.0	67.3	6.0	81.8	769	80.2	1,606	728	78.5
Glenpool city	282	2388	390	1998	41,943	428	18.7	10.1	1.3	39.7	532	8.6	751	2	52.4
Guthrie city	334	3014	235	2780	2,475	15	100.0	10.3	1.1	50.0	481	10.3	972	168	20.1
Guymon city	248	1990	297	1693	645	7	42.9	13.8	0.9	68.8	698	21.3	1,779	746	29.5
Jenks city	176	923	84	839	72,132	278	100.0	18.1	1.4	91.6	468	15.9	879	89	48.1
Lawton city	5,401	5570	921	4649	10,679	62	74.2	96.6	12.3	38.3	575	92.9	943	108	141.0
McAlester city	1,032	5645	284	5361	10,829	72	51.4	104.3	1.9	67.8	934	101.6	5,541	271	64.2
Miami city	577	4180	406	3774	443	7	100.0	14.6	1.3	82.6	558	19.5	1,419	434	23.9
Midwest City city	2,778	4847	323	4524	14,781	92	100.0	69.8	4.9	68.6	646	62.1	1,107	89	106.7
Moore city	1,603	2708	132	2577	82,954	541	90.2	45.7	1.5	65.9	561	41.5	717	95	71.4
Muskogee city	1,956	5047	1102	3945	4,074	21	100.0	130.4	3.3	45.2	729	134.9	3,462	322	44.3
Mustang city	311	1594	220	1374	25,934	87	100.0	15.7	0.7	99.3	495	13.2	713	30	26.9
Norman city	3,435	2864	160	2703	168,704	1,154	46.7	443.4	6.4	56.7	687	422.1	3,646	294	372.5
Oklahoma City city	32,040	5185	774	4411	770,619	4,461	74.1	1107.5	90.6	50.5	1003	835.1	1,392	272	1318.9
Okmulgee city	506	4107	536	3571	30	1	100.0	12.9	1.5	38.3	528	12.8	1,033	70	51.1
Owasso city	538	1623	157	1466	56,709	270	98.5	32.7	0.8	93.6	658	29.0	924	98	39.4
Ponca City city	1,472	5943	787	5156	7,023	69	30.4	41.3	2.3	61.5	655	56.7	2,278	730	59.4
Sand Springs city	641	3295	175	3120	12,733	64	100.0	23.1	2.2	48.4	671	17.6	920	148	19.8
Sapulpa city	671	3211	297	2914	12,664	75	100.0	26.0	2.3	66.6	754	29.0	1,422	216	85.6
Shawnee city	2,067	6617	836	5782	9,781	51	100.0	34.1	5.6	40.8	656	30.7	1,003	220	23.5
Stillwater city	1,477	3106	320	2786	35,184	299	29.4	49.0	2.9	45.6	622	48.2	1,033	155	38.1
Tahlequah city	732	4436	255	4182	6,635	62	69.4	86.6	1.0	40.5	360	91.7	5,625	345	19.9
Tulsa city	23,521	5887	805	5082	183,107	1,365	29.5	741.9	77.4	11.3	862	712.6	1,806	561	1254.1
Warr Acres city	445	4255	421	3834	1,817	10	100.0	7.9	0.1	77.2	508	7.7	745	73	1.8
Weatherford city	233	1921	148	1772	9,050	38	94.7	9.7	2.6	5.8	350	8.3	732	241	13.1
Woodward city	461	3552	393	3159	3,970	23	60.9	24.0	5.3	39.8	1127	26.0	2,110	826	33.3
Yukon city	578	2280	130	2150	8,083	43	100.0	27.9	0.7	77.9	881	26.7	1,105	105	35.5
OREGON	123,529	3111	232	2879	3,243,361	16,645	51.5	X	X	X	X	X	X	X	X
Albany city	1,717	3309	81	3228	38,938	224	54.5	59.2	9.0	56.9	638	56.1	1,094	127	122.1
Aloha CDP	NA	NA	NA	NA	NA	NA	NA	NA	NA	NA	NA	NA	NA	NA	NA
Altamont CDP	NA	NA	NA	NA	NA	NA	NA	NA	NA	NA	NA	NA	NA	NA	NA
Ashland city	654	3134	125	3009	11,614	56	73.2	37.8	2.9	37.7	1021	37.3	1,823	217	38.7
Beaverton city	1,648	1745	135	1611	46,567	308	42.5	79.4	16.3	57.8	475	78.1	842	126	26.4
Bend city	2,312	2805	144	2661	190,056	847	93.4	88.7	15.0	54.7	558	81.1	1,029	162	92.3
Bethany CDP	NA	NA	NA	NA	NA	NA	NA	NA	NA	NA	NA	NA	NA	NA	NA
Canby city	279	1649	95	1555	NA	NA	NA	18.1	3.3	81.2	566	23.0	1,365	636	23.2
Cedar Mill CDP	NA	NA	NA	NA	NA	NA	NA	NA	NA	NA	NA	NA	NA	NA	NA
Central Point city	503	2841	158	2683	14,358	71	100.0	11.2	2.3	100.0	355	9.6	555	26	9.0
Coos Bay city	939	5891	326	5565	976	6	100.0	21.7	6.1	77.9	624	17.3	1,078	198	15.5
Cornelius city	382	3124	147	2977	452	2	100.0	8.4	1.7	78.4	276	6.9	566	24	3.3
Corvallis city	1,813	3264	131	3133	71,703	406	18.2	71.4	12.8	43.7	647	62.4	1,135	94	59.4
Dallas city	451	3037	175	2862	9,701	41	100.0	13.3	2.9	90.2	377	12.5	846	128	17.6
Damascus city	NA	NA	NA	NA	NA	NA	NA	5.2	1.5	56.3	324	3.9	363	51	0.0
Eugene city	7,224	4518	367	4151	172,793	1,032	21.7	265.1	45.3	46.0	757	254.5	1,612	275	418.2
Forest Grove city	727	3196	334	2862	29,472	136	80.9	27.4	4.3	63.0	419	27.5	1,254	108	113.2
Four Corners CDP	NA	NA	NA	NA	NA	NA	NA	NA	NA	NA	NA	NA	NA	NA	NA
Gladstone city	355	3015	399	2615	NA	NA	NA	9.1	1.7	55.8	457	8.7	745	120	2.1
Grants Pass city	2,163	6146	372	5774	15,210	75	94.7	36.2	6.8	64.2	589	35.8	1,028	164	12.2
Gresham city	5,710	5178	498	4680	14,984	63	96.8	102.2	33.7	52.1	363	106.4	979	155	82.4

1 Data for serious crimes have not been adjusted for underreporting. This may affect comparability between geographic areas over time.
2 Per 100,000 population estimated by the FBI. 3 Based on population estimated as of July 1 of the year shown.

Table B. Incorporated Places, Census Designated Places (CDPs), and Minor Civil Divisions (MCDs) of 10,000 or More Population — **Land Area, Population, and Households, and Employment**

STATE City, town, township, borough, or CDP (county if applicable)	Land area,[1] 2010 (sq mi)	Total persons 2010	Total persons 2014	Percent change 2010–2014	Persons per square mile, 2014	Foreign born	Lives in same house as previous year	Median household income (dollars	Income of $100,000 or more	Income below poverty level	Percent in labor force	Unemployment rate	Family households	One person households
	1	2	3	4	5	6	7	8	9	10	11	12	13	14
OREGON—Con.														
Happy Valley city	8.863	14,283	17,319	21.3	1,954.0	15.5	87.6	$100,438	50.2	3.9	66.6	7.5	83.8	13.4
Hayesville CDP	3.043	19,936	NA	NA	NA	23.1	85.4	$41,059	11.1	20.6	64.0	13.6	74.9	19.0
Hermiston city	7.821	16,751	17,137	2.3	2,191.1	12.8	78.9	$46,655	13.3	17.8	68.3	8.1	64.3	27.7
Hillsboro city	24.238	92,149	99,393	7.9	4,100.7	19.6	79.2	$66,668	26.6	11.9	70.9	8.4	69.1	24.8
Keizer city	7.152	36,485	37,303	2.2	5,215.9	9.5	81.1	$50,897	17.0	13.1	64.5	9.5	71.5	23.0
Klamath Falls city	19.977	20,991	21,119	0.6	1,057.2	5.0	74.1	$33,604	11.0	25.2	60.7	16.2	57.1	31.9
La Grande city	4.583	13,090	13,026	-0.5	2,842.5	3.5	76.6	$36,536	10.2	26.4	59.9	9.4	53.1	33.8
Lake Oswego city	10.690	36,654	37,999	3.7	3,554.5	11.3	82.1	$84,244	42.2	8.2	64.2	9.1	64.0	30.4
Lebanon city	6.671	15,517	15,982	3.0	2,395.8	2.4	80.9	$40,791	4.6	21.6	56.7	10.0	59.6	29.2
McMinnville city	10.576	32,187	33,393	3.7	3,157.5	12.6	82.6	$44,451	13.4	17.2	60.3	12.1	68.5	25.3
Medford city	25.762	74,943	78,557	4.8	3,049.3	7.0	78.3	$42,366	13.5	18.9	61.8	12.2	63.8	29.4
Milwaukie city	4.824	20,291	20,640	1.7	4,278.3	6.7	82.1	$55,827	15.7	11.4	66.6	10.2	58.1	31.3
Newberg city	5.802	22,123	22,692	2.6	3,911.1	8.7	77.8	$54,856	18.9	14.0	65.8	7.9	69.2	23.0
Newport city	9.051	9,989	10,116	1.3	1,117.7	9.6	78.0	$40,448	15.5	17.3	59.7	7.1	56.9	35.6
Oak Grove CDP	3.887	16,629	NA	NA	NA	6.4	83.4	$50,435	20.0	9.8	61.5	11.4	57.4	34.2
Oak Hills CDP	1.565	11,333	NA	NA	NA	23.5	80.3	$76,800	36.4	7.2	71.8	7.8	70.9	22.8
Oatfield CDP	3.395	13,415	NA	NA	NA	5.2	89.5	$67,740	29.8	8.9	64.4	8.1	71.2	24.3
Ontario city	5.166	11,366	10,982	-3.4	2,126.0	11.1	81.4	$26,512	6.8	32.7	56.1	15.1	60.3	34.8
Oregon City city	9.657	32,628	35,266	8.1	3,651.8	5.7	82.8	$59,429	22.5	11.4	65.3	9.8	69.6	23.4
Pendleton city	10.777	16,612	16,904	1.8	1,568.5	3.0	77.9	$45,930	16.9	12.9	57.7	9.7	61.7	33.6
Portland city	133.452	583,789	619,360	6.1	4,641.1	14.0	79.3	$53,230	23.3	16.5	69.4	9.4	51.4	34.5
Redmond city	16.790	26,215	27,941	6.6	1,664.2	6.4	78.2	$39,008	9.8	19.6	61.2	19.5	69.8	24.2
Roseburg city	10.434	21,884	21,903	0.1	2,099.2	3.3	81.5	$39,081	11.3	18.8	54.0	14.2	53.4	38.4
St. Helens city	4.749	13,028	13,061	0.3	2,750.3	4.9	85.7	$47,421	15.6	18.3	64.5	15.1	69.2	25.4
Salem city	48.567	154,742	161,637	4.5	3,328.2	12.0	78.2	$46,273	15.9	16.3	61.6	12.9	63.8	29.8
Sherwood city	4.310	18,194	18,978	4.3	4,402.8	6.8	88.8	$84,360	39.3	6.9	73.2	7.5	78.2	19.1
Springfield city	15.737	59,361	60,263	1.5	3,829.3	5.3	75.8	$39,355	8.9	20.4	65.3	12.9	59.8	28.5
The Dalles city	6.567	14,944	15,162	1.5	2,308.9	8.2	86.2	$41,561	9.9	13.1	56.6	8.3	65.6	30.4
Tigard city	12.250	48,085	50,787	5.6	4,145.8	13.5	83.6	$60,849	29.4	8.9	70.7	8.3	64.9	27.0
Troutdale city	5.937	15,962	16,552	3.7	2,788.1	10.0	84.1	$58,790	20.8	16.4	70.5	12.8	74.2	19.2
Tualatin city	8.214	26,049	26,907	3.3	3,275.9	12.2	87.1	$65,903	32.3	10.8	72.5	9.6	65.0	28.1
West Linn city	7.380	25,107	26,289	4.7	3,562.4	9.1	86.4	$83,933	40.7	5.8	65.5	8.1	73.9	21.7
Wilsonville city	7.200	19,509	22,026	12.9	3,059.1	9.3	71.0	$58,757	27.7	9.0	63.1	8.9	58.8	32.9
Woodburn city	5.362	24,069	24,734	2.8	4,613.2	31.3	89.5	$43,144	8.7	21.1	62.4	13.6	67.7	27.6
PENNSYLVANIA	44,742.701	12,702,884	12,787,209	0.7	285.8	6.1	88.0	$53,115	21.9	12.9	62.9	8.6	64.6	29.6
Abington township (Montgomery)	15.514	55,343	55,682	0.6	3,589.2	10.2	91.0	$75,557	36.9	6.5	68.5	7.0	71.4	25.4
Adams township (Butler)	22.402	11,652	12,930	11.0	577.2	4.6	87.5	$94,143	46.7	4.2	68.5	3.1	68.8	21.7
Allentown city & MCD (Lehigh)	17.548	118,161	119,104	0.8	6,787.5	15.5	77.0	$36,578	8.8	23.4	62.8	15.1	62.9	30.0
Allison Park CDP	13.831	21,552	NA	NA	NA	4.9	91.7	$80,572	36.7	5.3	65.1	4.1	69.7	26.3
Altoona city & MCD (Blair)	9.906	46,321	45,558	-1.6	4,599.1	1.3	87.8	$36,258	8.0	20.4	59.2	9.2	60.8	33.8
Amity township (Berks)	18.166	12,583	12,784	1.6	703.7	3.1	92.5	$81,884	40.4	7.2	70.4	8.6	76.7	18.2
Antrim township (Franklin)	70.243	14,890	15,356	3.1	218.6	2.1	90.4	$68,966	25.0	6.2	66.4	4.4	71.5	23.3
Ardmore CDP	1.970	12,455	NA	NA	NA	15.6	86.5	$74,671	34.2	8.6	71.5	6.2	55.0	35.3
Aston township (Delaware)	5.844	16,592	16,863	1.6	2,885.5	2.8	94.0	$78,956	34.0	3.3	67.0	6.1	68.9	26.0
Baldwin borough & MCD (Allegheny)	5.775	19,765	19,740	-0.1	3,418.1	5.2	91.7	$53,699	19.5	7.1	65.7	8.4	65.2	30.9
Bensalem township (Bucks)	19.835	60,427	60,420	0.0	3,046.1	15.7	92.7	$60,401	24.9	7.0	70.9	8.2	66.3	29.0
Berwick borough & MCD (Columbia)	3.076	10,475	10,316	-1.5	3,354.0	2.6	84.7	$39,098	7.6	14.0	62.1	8.4	61.6	27.9
Bethel Park municipality & MCD (Allegheny)	11.671	32,315	32,257	-0.2	2,763.9	2.5	92.1	$70,102	31.4	4.2	66.8	5.8	69.4	27.5
Bethlehem city	19.102	74,982	75,135	0.2	3,933.4	8.4	79.2	$46,902	16.2	17.5	58.7	9.3	57.4	34.9
Bethlehem city (Lehigh)	4.298	19,343	19,634	1.5	4,567.7	6.1	86.2	$48,060	16.3	12.8	64.2	8.5	55.3	38.2
Bethlehem city (Northampton)	14.803	55,639	55,501	-0.2	3,749.2	9.2	76.7	$46,422	16.1	19.4	56.8	9.6	58.3	33.5
Bethlehem township (Northampton)	14.432	23,820	23,885	0.3	1,655.1	10.7	92.5	$81,381	40.7	4.3	64.4	5.0	74.6	20.6
Bloomsburg town & MCD (Columbia)	4.350	14,855	14,727	-0.9	3,385.4	3.8	71.5	$29,694	10.8	31.5	46.8	6.0	41.9	33.8
Bristol township (Bucks)	15.957	54,582	54,160	-0.8	3,394.2	7.1	93.4	$57,128	20.8	9.2	68.6	9.7	70.0	24.7
Broomall CDP	2.890	10,789	NA	NA	NA	14.2	93.2	$70,185	34.8	5.4	65.3	5.5	70.6	24.8
Buckingham township (Bucks)	32.882	20,075	20,386	1.5	620.0	7.1	91.8	$119,620	59.1	6.9	66.8	6.5	78.5	17.8
Butler city & MCD (Butler)	2.719	13,757	13,369	-2.8	4,917.5	1.4	79.8	$29,895	7.7	27.8	58.8	10.7	56.5	38.4
Butler township (Butler)	21.622	17,248	16,877	-2.2	780.5	2.0	89.4	$55,183	18.6	8.6	62.4	5.5	62.2	31.7
Caln township (Chester)	8.856	13,815	14,168	2.6	1,599.9	9.0	87.5	$68,152	31.1	6.2	75.5	7.7	62.4	30.9
Carlisle borough & MCD (Cumberland)	5.532	18,682	18,916	1.3	3,419.1	7.4	76.3	$46,614	18.0	16.0	65.1	7.5	52.7	38.5
Carnot-Moon CDP	5.981	11,372	NA	NA	NA	10.6	81.0	$57,013	24.7	13.2	68.2	7.4	49.1	42.0
Cecil township (Washington)	26.298	11,271	11,884	5.4	451.9	2.7	92.6	$74,510	35.7	3.8	70.3	6.2	72.6	21.7
Center township (Beaver)	15.049	11,795	11,783	-0.1	783.0	1.7	90.2	$71,750	29.9	8.7	63.1	4.5	75.6	22.7
Chambersburg borough & MCD (Franklin)	6.925	20,268	20,602	1.6	2,975.1	9.9	81.5	$40,936	10.5	18.8	59.3	7.7	59.3	34.5
Cheltenham township (Montgomery)	9.035	36,756	37,024	0.7	4,097.9	11.9	87.3	$75,831	37.3	9.6	68.5	9.2	64.3	29.7
Chester city & MCD (Delaware)	4.839	33,972	34,133	0.5	7,053.5	4.3	85.1	$28,607	6.6	30.2	53.7	20.5	57.1	36.9
Chestnuthill township (Monroe)	37.388	17,164	16,732	-2.5	447.5	10.3	91.9	$62,236	26.7	6.7	65.2	11.3	72.7	19.6
Coal township (Northumberland)	26.361	10,383	10,517	1.3	399.0	1.0	85.8	$37,588	10.4	14.7	36.0	9.3	62.7	31.6
Coatesville city & MCD (Chester)	1.808	13,102	13,164	0.5	7,281.8	10.4	82.4	$35,601	11.2	31.4	68.2	15.7	64.3	30.3
Colonial Park CDP	4.757	13,229	NA	NA	NA	9.3	81.4	$50,220	16.0	9.9	68.9	6.0	55.5	35.7
Columbia borough & MCD (Lancaster)	2.414	10,400	10,383	-0.2	4,301.4	4.0	87.3	$43,410	8.6	15.5	64.2	8.4	61.0	31.6
Concord township (Delaware)	13.623	17,231	17,533	1.8	1,287.0	7.0	84.2	$84,386	41.7	4.3	50.1	4.6	66.9	30.4

1 Dry land or land partially or temporarily covered by water.
2 16 years old and over.

Table B. Incorporated Places, Census Designated Places (CDPs), and Minor Civil Divisions (MCDs) of 10,000 or More Population — Crime, Construction, and Local Government Finance

STATE City, town, township, borough, or CDP (county if applicable)	Serious crimes known to police, 2014[1] Total number	Rate[2] Total	Rate[2] Violent	Rate[2] Property	New residential construction authorized by building permits, 2014 Value ($1,000)	Number of housing units	Percent single family	Local government finance, 2012 General revenue Total (mil dol)	Intergovernmental Total (mil dol)	Percent from state gov.	Taxes per capita[3]	General expenditure Total (mil dol)	Per capita[3] Total	Per capita[3] Capital outlays	Debt outstanding (mil dol)
	15	16	17	18	19	20	21	22	23	24	25	26	27	28	29
OREGON—Con.															
Happy Valley city	NA	NA	NA	NA	105,583	354	100.0	8.4	1.9	73.1	354	6.9	441	33	4.4
Hayesville CDP	NA	NA	NA	NA	NA	NA	NA	NA	NA	NA	NA	NA	NA	NA	NA
Hermiston city	507	2951	221	2729	9,020	47	100.0	11.3	1.9	87.2	359	9.7	567	69	18.2
Hillsboro city	2,391	2424	189	2236	102,448	886	20.9	134.5	12.8	83.8	832	124.8	1,309	91	62.2
Keizer city	867	2331	175	2157	20,828	125	44.8	21.2	3.3	99.7	290	18.1	490	50	28.7
Klamath Falls city	969	4551	324	4227	NA	NA	NA	32.6	7.4	62.6	512	30.2	1,420	323	60.1
La Grande city	358	2739	115	2624	3,482	23	30.4	14.2	2.7	66.0	473	13.1	997	124	3.5
Lake Oswego city	535	1414	50	1364	41,879	105	73.3	80.7	14.9	44.5	1164	69.2	1,857	263	156.3
Lebanon city	749	4672	268	4404	6,708	45	57.8	17.6	1.7	91.4	655	20.1	1,274	414	41.2
McMinnville city	981	2940	165	2775	26,098	170	54.7	37.5	4.1	96.1	459	30.1	909	86	22.1
Medford city	5,546	7078	482	6596	89,822	407	65.6	102.4	14.5	49.3	758	104.2	1,361	306	380.1
Milwaukie city	513	2495	248	2247	1,552	6	100.0	23.0	2.2	66.3	555	24.1	1,180	52	7.0
Newberg city	425	1650	101	1549	9,580	41	100.0	24.3	3.4	54.2	473	22.9	1,018	177	28.6
Newport city	NA	NA	NA	NA	4,537	22	100.0	21.5	2.0	80.3	1463	18.9	1,878	340	38.5
Oak Grove CDP	NA	NA	NA	NA	NA	NA	NA	NA	NA	NA	NA	NA	NA	NA	NA
Oak Hills CDP	NA	NA	NA	NA	NA	NA	NA	NA	NA	NA	NA	NA	NA	NA	NA
Oatfield CDP	NA	NA	NA	NA	NA	NA	NA	NA	NA	NA	NA	NA	NA	NA	NA
Ontario city	703	6378	590	5788	1,102	10	100.0	14.2	4.4	97.4	492	15.7	1,407	454	11.4
Oregon City city	844	2404	85	2318	21,027	83	95.2	52.1	16.8	99.0	594	43.8	1,308	472	33.8
Pendleton city	521	3064	235	2828	6,690	38	100.0	22.1	4.9	66.0	601	26.6	1,574	569	34.9
Portland city	35,140	5708	473	5235	773,329	5,016	15.8	1298.8	266.5	44.2	1016	1280.8	2,124	548	3381.1
Redmond city	1,076	3880	328	3552	34,935	148	100.0	35.3	5.9	60.8	502	32.9	1,229	258	73.6
Roseburg city	1,322	6013	246	5767	NA	NA	NA	28.1	4.1	55.4	803	26.9	1,228	154	13.1
St. Helens city	402	3076	115	2961	6,920	32	100.0	9.3	1.2	99.7	238	9.9	759	126	11.5
Salem city	7,583	4680	314	4367	74,121	291	92.8	251.3	76.0	63.8	642	240.9	1,527	209	711.5
Sherwood city	286	1502	32	1471	19,865	65	100.0	21.1	5.3	28.6	569	21.6	1,151	481	54.3
Springfield city	2,950	4886	353	4533	8,042	37	94.6	103.6	9.1	99.1	549	90.7	1,514	262	151.8
The Dalles city	567	3729	112	3617	NA	NA	NA	19.8	8.3	44.9	356	20.8	1,378	543	35.9
Tigard city	1,445	2832	149	2683	19,949	63	100.0	45.1	9.8	49.5	522	43.3	870	90	131.8
Troutdale city	572	3444	175	3269	307	1	100.0	15.0	3.3	43.3	456	13.3	809	84	0.0
Tualatin city	787	2906	103	2803	5,664	16	100.0	29.9	5.6	64.3	498	27.4	1,025	191	14.5
West Linn city	260	992	31	962	13,047	38	100.0	24.0	5.0	70.0	439	22.2	865	100	21.7
Wilsonville city	38	173	14	159	51,115	242	100.0	41.8	4.2	58.4	1092	42.0	2,040	1,029	98.0
Woodburn city	736	3008	262	2746	17,645	74	100.0	24.4	2.7	98.9	555	19.8	818	166	71.0
PENNSYLVANIA	287,180	2246	314	1932	4,714,443	25,059	65.3	X	X	X	X	X	X	X	X
Abington township (Montgomery)	1,187	2134	108	2026	1,931	8	100.0	55.1	6.9	63.9	531	54.7	984	74	26.7
Adams township (Butler)	64	496	39	457	40,891	144	100.0	5.2	0.5	100.0	326	5.4	437	52	0.0
Allentown city & MCD (Lehigh)	4,432	3733	515	3219	5,594	345	6.1	129.2	30.4	47.0	477	175.0	1,471	88	119.4
Allison Park CDP	NA	NA	NA	NA	NA	NA	NA	NA	NA	NA	NA	NA	NA	NA	NA
Altoona city & MCD (Blair)	1,049	2297	348	1949	401	4	100.0	29.3	7.5	47.2	381	27.1	587	40	38.9
Amity township (Berks)	136	1061	55	1006	2,079	12	100.0	6.5	1.0	89.7	276	6.1	482	22	2.7
Antrim township (Franklin)	NA	NA	NA	NA	10,009	45	88.9	7.9	1.4	44.7	150	10.4	687	343	8.9
Ardmore CDP	NA	NA	NA	NA	NA	NA	NA	NA	NA	NA	NA	NA	NA	NA	NA
Aston township (Delaware)	253	1494	89	1406	1,191	9	100.0	10.3	1.0	98.1	439	9.8	581	58	5.3
Baldwin borough & MCD (Allegheny)	114	575	71	504	6,114	84	4.8	14.5	1.2	87.7	384	13.8	697	0	11.7
Bensalem township (Bucks)	1,857	3069	134	2935	5,499	38	100.0	48.0	18.0	88.3	306	58.0	960	128	52.2
Berwick borough & MCD (Columbia)	301	2920	233	2687	241	1	100.0	4.0	0.6	90.5	297	4.3	412	29	0.6
Bethel Park municipality & MCD (Allegheny)	288	889	77	812	610	2	100.0	24.5	2.7	71.8	427	25.6	790	60	4.8
Bethlehem city	2,034	2711	281	2430	2,016	21	100.0	101.1	27.5	100.0	632	89.6	1,193	0	228.4
Bethlehem city (Lehigh)	NA	NA	NA	NA	2,016	21	100.0	NA	NA	NA	NA	NA	NA	NA	NA
Bethlehem city (Northampton)	NA	NA	NA	NA	2,016	21	100.0	NA	NA	NA	NA	NA	NA	NA	NA
Bethlehem township (Northampton)	399	1671	54	1617	7,709	32	100.0	21.0	2.3	95.0	455	18.1	759	7	16.5
Bloomsburg town & MCD (Columbia)	283	1960	346	1614	590	4	100.0	6.7	2.1	65.5	199	6.6	454	27	1.1
Bristol township (Bucks)	1,379	2537	178	2359	171	2	100.0	40.8	6.0	77.7	479	41.4	759	113	20.1
Broomall CDP	NA	NA	NA	NA	NA	NA	NA	NA	NA	NA	NA	NA	NA	NA	NA
Buckingham township (Bucks)	85	417	15	402	4,717	15	100.0	14.7	1.2	100.0	402	12.4	612	96	23.1
Butler city & MCD (Butler)	623	4610	400	4210	0	0	0.0	8.6	2.1	60.8	420	8.5	624	25	1.8
Butler township (Butler)	497	2911	182	2729	1,665	7	100.0	6.7	1.0	100.0	298	6.2	362	3	3.5
Caln township (Chester)	352	2485	501	1984	7,726	32	100.0	8.6	1.0	100.0	355	10.1	718	208	5.9
Carlisle borough & MCD (Cumberland)	570	3004	206	2799	9,532	87	100.0	24.1	6.3	53.1	376	28.9	1,527	702	18.1
Carnot-Moon CDP	NA	NA	NA	NA	NA	NA	NA	NA	NA	NA	NA	NA	NA	NA	NA
Cecil township (Washington)	82	694	34	660	9,657	40	100.0	6.4	0.8	100.0	422	6.0	521	7	1.2
Center township (Beaver)	492	4184	238	3946	1,964	8	100.0	5.9	1.1	84.0	352	4.9	417	0	8.1
Chambersburg borough & MCD (Franklin)	833	4051	384	3667	5,223	46	4.3	25.5	3.4	76.1	319	30.0	1,470	181	19.1
Cheltenham township (Montgomery)	1,036	2810	179	2631	10,140	42	100.0	40.0	5.5	79.3	556	39.2	1,064	42	40.8
Chester city & MCD (Delaware)	1,699	4989	1536	3453	0	0	0.0	47.9	12.2	79.6	563	45.6	1,340	83	8.1
Chestnuthill township (Monroe)	NA	NA	NA	NA	1,382	6	100.0	3.9	1.0	94.4	148	3.8	224	6	5.3
Coal township (Northumberland)	314	2961	236	2726	163	1	100.0	3.5	1.3	61.1	180	4.3	402	2	20.9
Coatesville city & MCD (Chester)	460	3500	997	2504	143	4	100.0	9.3	1.3	83.5	428	10.0	765	0	0.4
Colonial Park CDP	NA	NA	NA	NA	NA	NA	NA	NA	NA	NA	NA	NA	NA	NA	NA
Columbia borough & MCD (Lancaster)	244	2351	154	2197	0	0	0.0	6.9	1.7	96.0	392	5.3	513	0	2.4
Concord township (Delaware)	NA	NA	NA	NA	298	4	100.0	8.7	0.7	97.3	199	9.0	521	66	12.8

1 Data for serious crimes have not been adjusted for underreporting. This may affect comparability between geographic areas over time.
2 Per 100,000 population estimated by the FBI.   3 Based on population estimated as of July 1 of the year shown.

Table B. Incorporated Places, Census Designated Places (CDPs), and Minor Civil Divisions (MCDs) of 10,000 or More Population — Land Area, Population, and Households, and Employment

STATE City, town, township, borough, or CDP (county if applicable)	Land area,[1] 2010 (sq mi)	Population				Population characteristics 2010–2014		Household income and poverty, 2010–2014	Percent of households		Employment,[2] 2010–2014		Households, 2010–2014 (percent of households)	
		Total persons 2010	Total persons 2014	Percent change 2010–2014	Persons per square mile, 2014	Foreign born	Lives in same house as previous year	Median household income (dollars)	Income of $100,000 or more	Income below poverty level	Percent in labor force	Unemploy-ment rate	Family households	One person households
	1	2	3	4	5	6	7	8	9	10	11	12	13	14
PENNSYLVANIA—Con.														
Coolbaugh township (Monroe) .	86.205	20,564	20,257	-1.5	235.0	12.8	91.3	$53,664	19.2	14.0	64.7	17.9	80.2	17.1
Cranberry township (Butler)......	22.823	28,098	30,170	7.4	1,321.9	3.3	91.5	$100,020	50.0	2.9	75.3	4.9	76.7	20.4
Croydon CDP......................	2.485	9,950	NA	NA	NA	5.6	92.3	$56,155	21.0	10.2	72.6	13.3	68.0	26.3
Cumru township (Berks)...........	20.901	15,147	15,192	0.3	726.9	5.1	86.7	$60,105	25.5	7.2	65.1	5.1	61.3	32.8
Darby borough & MCD (Delaware).................	0.842	10,690	10,695	0.0	12,698.4	14.2	85.3	$32,224	3.8	25.4	59.9	17.4	71.1	23.0
Derry township (Dauphin).........	27.203	24,679	24,881	0.8	914.6	8.5	81.8	$65,138	33.0	8.2	64.7	4.2	59.5	33.5
Derry township (Westmoreland)................	95.091	14,504	14,340	-1.1	150.8	0.9	89.4	$43,258	11.3	15.8	55.0	7.2	64.6	31.2
Dingman township (Pike).........	58.188	11,928	11,699	-1.9	201.1	10.5	93.2	$76,201	31.1	5.7	69.8	15.3	76.7	17.1
Douglass township (Montgomery)................	15.294	10,195	10,401	2.0	680.1	3.4	94.1	$73,230	34.5	2.9	68.9	4.0	76.8	18.8
Dover township (York)..............	41.558	21,078	21,286	1.0	512.2	2.0	91.4	$57,650	21.4	8.1	70.1	7.8	71.1	23.2
Doylestown township (Bucks)...	15.321	17,680	17,506		1,142.7	4.0	83.5	$99,333	49.5	3.9	57.1	6.3	71.3	24.7
Drexel Hill CDP....................	3.194	28,043	NA	NA	NA	7.8	89.7	$65,328	30.7	9.1	72.5	9.1	63.3	31.8
Dunmore borough & MCD (Lackawanna)................	8.918	14,057	13,791	-1.9	1,546.4	5.3	91.3	$48,422	18.9	9.2	61.4	7.1	57.4	37.2
East Cocalico township (Lancaster)..................	20.427	10,310	10,435	1.2	510.9	4.8	92.9	$62,549	25.3	8.9	66.9	4.3	75.9	18.7
East Goshen township (Chester)...................	10.046	18,026	18,198	1.0	1,811.4	4.1	90.1	$75,053	39.1	4.1	61.8	6.0	58.4	33.6
East Hempfield township (Lancaster)..................	21.069	23,522	24,139	2.6	1,145.7	6.0	86.7	$68,031	34.0	5.5	68.4	4.5	70.0	26.2
East Lampeter township (Lancaster)..................	19.658	16,453	16,909	2.8	860.2	6.7	89.6	$56,094	19.9	10.0	71.2	5.6	71.1	19.9
East Norriton township (Montgomery)	6.053	13,590	14,103	3.8	2,330.0	10.1	90.1	$79,620	37.1	4.7	65.1	6.9	63.2	31.0
Easton city & MCD (Northampton)................	4.240	26,800	27,052	0.9	6,380.4	12.2	71.2	$39,773	12.5	19.7	58.5	13.1	60.4	31.2
East Pennsboro township (Cumberland)................	10.488	20,625	21,384	3.7	2,038.9	6.9	87.2	$62,909	21.0	10.2	69.3	6.9	67.6	27.2
Easttown township (Chester)....	8.225	10,497	10,608	1.1	1,289.7	8.8	95.5	$130,577	59.0	6.2	61.0	4.8	76.8	21.0
East Whiteland township (Chester)...................	10.935	10,650	10,750	0.9	983.1	17.2	88.2	$90,327	45.2	6.8	72.9	4.6	73.9	18.4
Elizabeth township (Allegheny).	22.838	13,271	13,277	0.0	581.4	1.2	92.4	$60,342	21.1	8.6	58.1	8.6	69.7	27.1
Elizabethtown borough & MCD (Lancaster)..................	2.641	11,545	11,611	0.6	4,395.7	1.9	82.7	$55,601	18.3	10.5	64.8	5.0	67.7	25.9
Emmaus borough & MCD (Lehigh).....................	2.895	11,215	11,335	1.1	3,915.9	3.4	87.0	$55,929	15.2	7.3	69.1	5.9	62.6	32.8
Ephrata borough & MCD (Lancaster)..................	3.418	13,392	13,837	3.3	4,048.1	2.4	88.9	$50,417	12.0	9.8	74.8	7.5	63.2	31.3
Erie city & MCD (Erie)............	19.135	101,784	99,452	-2.3	5,197.4	6.6	81.0	$33,007	7.8	25.0	60.5	11.0	55.0	36.9
Exeter township (Berks)	24.227	25,550	25,768	0.9	1,063.6	3.7	92.3	$74,689	34.7	4.4	72.7	6.5	75.4	20.0
Fairview township (Erie)	28.969	10,102	10,184	0.8	351.5	2.4	89.6	$76,602	34.4	4.3	61.8	5.9	76.4	19.0
Fairview township (York).........	35.577	16,668	17,039	2.2	478.9	1.8	90.6	$77,144	35.9	5.4	71.1	3.8	74.8	20.0
Falls township (Bucks)............	21.256	34,300	33,968	-1.0	1,598.1	6.7	92.1	$64,533	25.6	8.7	69.6	8.0	68.5	25.6
Ferguson township (Centre)	47.651	17,690	18,310	3.5	384.3	16.3	75.6	$61,096	30.7	17.3	63.5	2.7	58.1	28.6
Forks township (Northampton) .	12.105	14,721	15,230	3.5	1,258.2	8.0	91.8	$92,551	46.5	4.9	69.1	7.9	78.9	16.9
Franconia township (Montgomery)	13.833	13,064	13,260	1.5	958.6	4.8	93.8	$82,500	39.7	6.3	64.1	4.5	81.2	15.6
Franklin Park borough & MCD (Allegheny)..................	13.523	13,467	14,269	6.0	1,055.2	9.4	94.6	$116,378	58.7	1.6	66.9	3.7	80.5	16.5
Fullerton CDP......................	3.672	14,925	NA	NA	NA	18.3	81.3	$53,216	16.1	11.7	67.9	9.1	62.2	32.4
Greene township (Franklin)	57.303	16,700	17,401	4.2	303.7	1.8	87.6	$56,301	23.6	11.4	60.4	7.5	72.4	23.5
Greensburg city & MCD (Westmoreland)	4.055	14,892	14,571	-2.2	3,592.9	1.9	86.5	$38,339	14.0	18.5	59.8	8.5	50.2	43.2
Guilford township (Franklin)......	51.017	14,531	14,700	1.2	288.1	4.4	92.8	$62,168	22.0	5.3	60.1	4.0	70.4	26.0
Hamilton township (Franklin)	35.540	10,791	11,054	2.4	311.0	4.1	92.1	$57,550	24.6	5.4	67.0	5.1	65.6	29.1
Hampden township (Cumberland)................	17.245	27,647	28,940	4.7	1,678.2	10.3	90.4	$80,573	38.9	3.3	70.7	4.6	67.4	28.2
Hampton township (Allegheny).	16.198	18,363	18,478	0.6	1,140.8	3.8	93.9	$84,351	38.6	4.2	67.1	3.7	70.8	26.2
Hanover township (Luzerne).....	18.866	11,076	10,976	-0.9	581.8	1.0	90.6	$38,772	14.7	18.1	57.8	8.4	58.7	37.0
Hanover township (Northampton)................	6.553	10,866	11,380	4.7	1,736.6	11.4	93.6	$81,742	38.2	5.0	64.4	6.1	73.9	23.0
Hanover borough & MCD (York).....................	3.696	15,277	15,454	1.2	4,180.9	4.2	81.6	$44,249	12.4	11.3	67.0	8.8	58.2	34.8
Harborcreek township (Erie).....	34.089	17,234	17,578	2.0	515.7	3.0	85.0	$62,236	23.0	6.3	60.2	9.8	71.6	22.4
Harrisburg city & MCD (Dauphin)....................	8.130	49,528	49,082	-0.9	6,037.3	9.8	78.6	$32,476	7.9	28.6	62.3	16.7	53.0	37.8
Harrison township (Allegheny)..	7.360	10,461	10,472	0.1	1,422.7	0.7	92.6	$47,058	9.9	13.2	61.1	9.1	66.2	30.2
Hatfield township (Montgomery)................	9.938	17,249	17,589	2.0	1,770.0	18.6	87.5	$75,182	34.6	7.0	71.1	5.5	70.7	24.3
Haverford township (Delaware)	9.945	48,484	48,909	0.9	4,917.9	7.2	93.2	$93,788	46.3	4.5	67.8	6.2	72.1	24.2
Hazleton city & MCD (Luzerne)	6.011	25,340	24,932	-1.6	4,147.5	26.1	82.9	$30,947	7.2	24.4	61.4	15.1	65.4	29.7
Hempfield township (Westmoreland)	76.728	43,247	41,733	-3.5	543.9	1.5	90.2	$58,595	24.0	7.7	59.1	5.5	67.1	28.7
Hermitage city & MCD (Mercer)	29.197	16,375	16,118	-1.6	552.0	1.3	89.6	$53,784	18.4	7.4	60.9	6.7	63.9	32.3
Hershey CDP........................	14.357	14,257	NA	NA	NA	10.1	80.3	$54,118	27.1	11.4	60.4	4.7	53.5	36.3
Hilltown township (Bucks)........	26.967	15,030	15,190	1.1	563.3	3.7	90.7	$83,810	39.7	5.2	67.6	6.9	78.2	19.3
Hopewell township (Beaver)	16.754	12,593	12,529	-0.5	747.8	2.3	89.0	$62,750	21.4	7.2	60.0	4.4	66.2	30.2
Horsham CDP.......................	5.470	14,842	NA	NA	NA	7.2	90.9	$68,843	33.4	3.6	74.3	7.0	66.8	29.6
Horsham township (Montgomery)	17.322	26,147	26,557	1.6	1,533.2	7.6	91.4	$86,233	42.6	4.6	73.4	6.5	71.6	24.4
Indiana borough & MCD (Indiana)...................	1.759	13,975	14,194	1.6	8,068.0	2.7	47.0	$27,881	7.7	40.4	55.8	14.0	35.2	38.6

1 Dry land or land partially or temporarily covered by water.
2 16 years old and over.

Table B. Incorporated Places, Census Designated Places (CDPs), and Minor Civil Divisions (MCDs) of 10,000 or More Population — Crime, Construction, and Local Government Finance

STATE City, town, township, borough, or CDP (county if applicable)	Serious crimes known to police, 2014[1] Total number	Rate[2] Total	Rate[2] Violent	Rate[2] Property	New residential construction authorized by building permits, 2014 Value ($1,000)	Number of housing units	Percent single family	Local government finance, 2012 General revenue Total (mil dol)	Intergovernmental Total (mil dol)	Intergovernmental Percent from state gov.	Taxes per capita[3]	General expenditure Total (mil dol)	Per capita[3] Total	Per capita[3] Capital outlays	Debt outstanding (mil dol)
	15	16	17	18	19	20	21	22	23	24	25	26	27	28	29
PENNSYLVANIA—Con.															
Coolbaugh township (Monroe) .	NA	NA	NA	NA	5,957	29	100.0	7.8	1.3	100.0	292	6.8	332	0	8.4
Cranberry township (Butler)......	413	1384	20	1364	49,401	170	64.7	32.2	3.7	88.0	471	32.8	1,138	87	57.1
Croydon CDP.......................	NA	NA	NA	NA	NA	NA	NA	NA	NA	NA	NA	NA	NA	NA	NA
Cumru township (Berks)..........	303	1989	79	1910	1,467	10	100.0	13.5	1.5	67.0	463	12.1	799	27	2.8
Darby borough & MCD (Delaware)........................	868	8122	3855	4267	0	0	0.0	8.0	0.8	88.0	417	7.7	718	12	2.0
Derry township (Dauphin)........	421	1692	64	1627	8,327	38	52.6	21.5	4.5	59.3	474	21.1	852	114	34.7
Derry township (Westmoreland)	NA	NA	NA	NA	8,327	38	52.6	2.7	0.7	90.7	129	2.9	198	7	0.0
Dingman township (Pike)..........	NA	NA	NA	NA	3,022	13	100.0	2.7	0.9	100.0	136	3.2	268	103	0.3
Douglass township (Montgomery)	129	1240	125	1115	275	5	100.0	4.0	0.7	99.4	255	3.7	362	6	0.0
Dover township (York).............	NA	NA	NA	NA	5,844	38	100.0	10.9	2.5	50.6	200	14.3	673	228	25.3
Doylestown township (Bucks)...	179	1016	40	976	2,494	8	100.0	10.0	1.2	96.7	430	9.5	539	69	3.5
Drexel Hill CDP.....................	NA	NA	NA	NA	NA	NA	NA	NA	NA	NA	NA	NA	NA	NA	NA
Dunmore borough & MCD (Lackawanna).................	234	1678	201	1477	750	3	100.0	9.4	1.4	99.5	467	7.4	527	1	13.4
East Cocalico township (Lancaster)......................	94	902	29	873	1,449	10	100.0	6.2	2.5	32.0	279	6.4	620	53	3.3
East Goshen township (Chester).......................	NA	NA	NA	NA	11,835	71	15.5	14.7	1.0	100.0	420	12.6	695	67	7.1
East Hempfield township (Lancaster)......................	427	1774	54	1720	12,867	56	57.1	13.4	1.6	99.7	333	12.2	514	20	3.3
East Lampeter township (Lancaster)......................	649	3845	107	3738	3,968	22	100.0	12.8	3.2	44.8	347	12.1	724	18	19.3
East Norriton township (Montgomery)	330	2327	197	2129	241	1	100.0	12.0	1.3	72.5	502	10.8	771	98	4.2
Easton city & MCD (Northampton)..................	713	2627	298	2328	0	0	0.0	52.4	14.3	75.3	546	53.4	1,967	129	33.9
East Pennsboro township (Cumberland)...................	245	1152	80	1072	7,538	26	100.0	15.7	2.9	98.5	242	29.9	1,430	773	31.9
Easttown township (Chester)....	103	974	28	945	4,402	9	100.0	12.1	0.8	100.0	562	10.3	977	37	32.1
East Whiteland township (Chester)........................	132	1234	75	1159	1,609	14	14.3	11.0	0.9	90.5	537	12.1	1,131	121	8.6
Elizabeth township (Allegheny)	131	984	53	931	1,231	7	100.0	5.0	0.6	100.0	304	5.5	415	16	2.2
Elizabethtown borough & MCD (Lancaster).................	159	1362	103	1259	1,693	13	100.0	13.1	5.2	19.5	327	14.6	1,251	321	6.7
Emmaus borough & MCD (Lehigh).......................	134	1184	62	1122	200	2	100.0	10.0	1.1	79.1	469	10.8	954	102	4.6
Ephrata borough & MCD (Lancaster)...................	234	1728	258	1469	815	3	100.0	13.9	1.1	98.0	242	18.4	1,362	148	16.0
Erie city & MCD (Erie)	3,046	3034	404	2629	185	3	100.0	113.3	23.8	46.1	464	105.0	1,039	74	189.6
Exeter township (Berks)..........	506	1964	78	1887	3,569	27	100.0	21.4	2.2	76.2	322	20.5	796	80	56.7
Fairview township (Erie)	NA	NA	NA	NA	317	1	100.0	3.6	0.9	97.3	239	2.7	262	2	0.0
Fairview township (York)..........	249	1468	142	1327	317	1	100.0	12.6	2.6	41.3	299	12.4	737	65	10.9
Falls township (Bucks)............	825	2424	170	2254	1,122	11	18.2	22.4	2.0	96.3	111	24.1	706	63	0.0
Ferguson township (Centre)	138	758	77	681	40,887	248	46.0	13.5	3.6	31.7	485	14.8	831	205	3.1
Forks township (Northampton) .	186	1222	20	1202	9,121	52	100.0	11.7	1.0	89.4	426	11.5	763	71	10.3
Franconia township (Montgomery)	71	535	23	513	210	1	100.0	6.5	1.1	88.6	320	11.4	863	205	9.8
Franklin Park borough & MCD (Allegheny).................	70	494	42	452	24,489	75	100.0	8.0	0.8	100.0	415	7.6	547	84	2.1
Fullerton CDP.......................	NA	NA	NA	NA	NA	NA	NA	NA	NA	NA	NA	NA	NA	NA	NA
Greene township (Franklin)	NA	NA	NA	NA	881	4	100.0	4.2	0.7	100.0	119	4.6	267	61	0.0
Greensburg city & MCD (Westmoreland)	433	2965	335	2629	458	1	100.0	13.6	1.9	67.8	520	11.6	789	62	7.4
Guilford township (Franklin)......	NA	NA	NA	NA	6,006	25	100.0	2.6	0.7	100.0	95	3.5	240	18	0.0
Hamilton township (Franklin)	NA	NA	NA	NA	4,311	26	100.0	1.6	0.4	97.9	98	1.4	126	12	0.0
Hampden township (Cumberland)...................	288	997	66	931	28,916	128	72.7	24.9	1.9	94.9	253	20.2	714	26	49.0
Hampton township (Allegheny).	127	686	113	572	11,221	36	100.0	13.2	1.2	90.3	431	12.3	665	16	17.1
Hanover township (Luzerne).....	302	2738	326	2412	1,544	6	100.0	7.1	1.2	100.0	509	6.6	596	28	1.5
Hanover township (Northampton)	NA	NA	NA	NA	1,544	6	100.0	9.3	1.3	76.9	513	7.4	664	14	2.3
Hanover borough & MCD (York).........................	448	2913	228	2685	2,272	20	30.0	20.7	3.9	40.5	412	25.2	1,642	547	40.1
Harborcreek township (Erie).....	NA	NA	NA	NA	5,101	24	100.0	4.9	0.8	96.0	169	4.6	270	33	0.5
Harrisburg city & MCD (Dauphin)......................	2,375	4836	1114	3722	430	3	100.0	93.9	6.2	90.0	616	78.7	1,595	121	110.0
Harrison township (Allegheny)..	86	820	86	734	2,426	18	100.0	4.6	0.6	100.0	315	5.2	492	16	4.9
Hatfield township (Montgomery)	244	1166	48	1118	233	1	100.0	10.9	1.8	87.3	398	10.9	623	38	5.7
Haverford township (Delaware)	606	1240	53	1187	17,740	63	46.0	44.4	6.2	76.6	479	51.8	1,063	272	28.3
Hazleton city & MCD (Luzerne)	694	2773	476	2298	0	0	0.0	18.6	7.2	55.0	329	13.3	528	65	11.6
Hempfield township (Westmoreland)	NA	NA	NA	NA	605	3	100.0	13.6	2.7	84.8	219	12.7	294	32	10.0
Hermitage city & MCD (Mercer)	461	2856	161	2695	1,671	11	100.0	21.3	6.4	20.6	518	24.4	1,504	301	10.6
Hershey CDP........................	NA	NA	NA	NA	NA	NA	NA	NA	NA	NA	NA	NA	NA	NA	NA
Hilltown township (Bucks).........	197	1297	105	1192	9,657	40	100.0	7.8	1.1	87.9	374	6.4	423	26	1.2
Hopewell township (Beaver)	155	1229	103	1126	913	5	20.0	9.4	0.8	100.0	329	8.5	677	31	12.4
Horsham CDP........................	NA	NA	NA	NA	NA	NA	NA	NA	NA	NA	NA	NA	NA	NA	NA
Horsham township (Montgomery)	230	869	68	801	5,738	27	100.0	16.4	2.7	99.7	457	13.6	515	26	6.3
Indiana borough & MCD (Indiana)........................	459	3262	1350	1912	200	2	100.0	11.0	1.3	86.2	229	10.7	767	49	12.9

1 Data for serious crimes have not been adjusted for underreporting. This may affect comparability between geographic areas over time.
2 Per 100,000 population estimated by the FBI.   3 Based on population estimated as of July 1 of the year shown.

Table B. Incorporated Places, Census Designated Places (CDPs), and Minor Civil Divisions (MCDs) of 10,000 or More Population — Land Area, Population, and Households, and Employment

STATE City, town, township, borough, or CDP (county if applicable)	Land area,[1] 2010 (sq mi)	Population				Population characteristics 2010–2014		Household income and poverty, 2010–2014			Employment,[2] 2010–2014		Households, 2010–2014 (percent of households)	
		Total persons 2010	Total persons 2014	Percent change 2010–2014	Persons per square mile, 2014	Foreign born	Lives in same house as previous year	Median household income (dollars)	Income of $100,000 or more	Income below poverty level	Percent in labor force	Unemployment rate	Family households	One person households
	1	2	3	4	5	6	7	8	9	10	11	12	13	14
PENNSYLVANIA—Con.														
Jefferson Hills borough & MCD (Allegheny)	16.540	10,629	11,232	5.7	679.1	2.6	92.8	$77,118	35.9	6.4	66.8	6.1	67.4	26.6
Johnstown city & MCD (Cambria)	5.893	20,975	20,184	-3.8	3,425.1	0.7	86.0	$25,376	2.5	31.4	51.1	15.3	49.2	44.2
King of Prussia CDP	8.486	19,936	NA	NA	NA	23.8	85.1	$72,942	33.2	7.5	70.5	5.8	60.2	32.9
Kingston borough & MCD (Luzerne)	2.128	13,182	12,994	-1.4	6,106.8	5.3	86.8	$48,248	17.2	14.3	59.4	7.2	54.0	38.0
Lancaster city & MCD (Lancaster)	7.225	59,322	59,302	0.0	8,208.0	9.2	81.4	$33,772	7.9	24.3	63.1	13.9	55.2	34.7
Lancaster township (Lancaster)	5.861	16,121	17,002	5.5	2,900.7	7.9	82.9	$52,535	18.4	13.0	62.6	8.3	64.3	26.1
Lansdale borough & MCD (Montgomery)	2.993	16,269	16,487	1.3	5,509.4	13.2	83.2	$61,182	21.4	7.0	70.6	6.2	59.9	32.7
Lansdowne borough & MCD (Delaware)	1.181	10,620	10,641	0.2	9,008.0	8.9	94.4	$56,020	24.9	12.3	67.4	8.5	62.3	33.1
Lebanon city & MCD (Lebanon)	4.167	25,477	25,573	0.4	6,136.6	6.7	80.3	$35,313	7.8	24.1	65.0	15.7	60.1	34.5
Lehigh township (Northampton)	29.277	10,526	10,439	-0.8	356.6	2.6	92.3	$68,194	30.0	3.6	66.5	5.8	79.4	17.1
Lehman township (Pike)	48.941	10,663	10,427	-2.2	213.1	14.9	87.6	$54,658	22.1	12.6	58.2	17.5	73.6	21.7
Levittown CDP	10.149	52,983	NA	NA	NA	4.0	93.2	$69,232	26.3	6.5	68.9	8.0	74.6	21.5
Limerick township (Montgomery)	22.507	18,074	18,756	3.8	833.3	7.5	92.8	$83,570	40.5	3.9	71.3	6.8	72.9	23.4
Logan township (Blair)	46.395	12,303	12,319	0.1	265.5	1.6	88.5	$44,969	15.5	12.5	53.1	5.0	61.8	28.2
Lower Allen township (Cumberland)	10.127	17,980	18,949	5.4	1,871.1	4.9	79.2	$54,845	19.7	7.8	47.3	4.6	56.8	38.8
Lower Burrell city & MCD (Westmoreland)	11.264	11,761	11,531	-2.0	1,023.7	0.9	92.5	$51,300	19.7	9.5	62.0	9.5	66.2	31.3
Lower Gwynedd township (Montgomery)	9.303	11,405	11,553	1.3	1,241.8	8.8	91.6	$92,987	47.0	7.7	58.3	4.9	64.5	33.0
Lower Macungie township (Lehigh)	22.347	30,629	31,639	3.3	1,415.8	9.3	93.2	$80,659	38.1	4.9	65.1	8.8	74.1	21.5
Lower Makefield township (Bucks)	17.871	32,559	32,687	0.4	1,829.1	8.3	90.3	$126,492	62.7	2.5	70.0	7.0	77.1	19.1
Lower Merion township (Montgomery)	23.671	57,837	58,273	0.8	2,461.8	14.1	87.1	$115,657	55.2	5.5	63.2	5.3	67.2	27.3
Lower Moreland township (Montgomery)	7.281	12,988	13,215	1.7	1,815.0	16.5	95.3	$105,109	52.6	4.7	61.6	5.2	79.8	18.5
Lower Paxton township (Dauphin)	28.171	47,360	48,086	1.5	1,706.9	7.4	86.5	$67,839	29.6	7.3	71.4	5.6	63.7	30.2
Lower Pottsgrove township (Montgomery)	7.920	12,059	12,192	1.1	1,539.3	4.2	94.1	$73,963	36.9	9.3	70.8	9.3	75.4	21.3
Lower Providence township (Montgomery)	15.249	25,436	25,694	1.0	1,685.0	11.5	86.7	$93,413	46.5	4.5	61.6	4.5	73.6	23.3
Lower Salford township (Montgomery)	14.442	14,959	15,348	2.6	1,062.7	6.3	90.4	$92,405	46.7	3.4	74.0	6.9	75.9	19.8
Lower Saucon township (Northampton)	24.269	10,772	10,794	0.2	444.8	3.4	92.9	$79,215	35.7	5.3	65.0	9.3	74.6	21.8
Lower Southampton township (Bucks)	6.674	18,909	19,010	0.5	2,848.3	11.2	92.3	$78,483	32.7	4.4	70.3	9.2	76.8	19.4
Loyalsock township (Lycoming)	21.151	11,026	11,201	1.6	529.6	2.1	92.9	$46,843	23.0	11.4	52.9	5.4	58.5	39.1
McCandless township (Allegheny)	16.499	28,457	28,921	1.6	1,752.9	7.5	88.4	$81,257	39.8	5.2	65.9	4.1	67.4	28.2
McKeesport city & MCD (Allegheny)	5.044	19,731	19,561	-0.9	3,877.8	2.7	84.9	$26,224	5.9	30.6	54.9	13.9	51.6	41.4
Manchester township (York)	15.884	18,161	18,439	1.5	1,160.9	6.1	91.1	$73,640	35.0	3.6	72.5	5.9	74.2	20.1
Manheim township (Lancaster)	23.862	38,167	39,341	3.1	1,648.7	7.7	87.6	$67,796	32.5	4.7	63.1	5.3	70.4	26.1
Manor township (Lancaster)	38.333	19,612	20,423	4.1	532.8	4.6	89.8	$59,860	21.0	6.7	71.0	6.6	69.7	23.3
Marple township (Delaware)	10.202	23,428	23,708	1.2	2,323.8	12.4	93.0	$75,270	38.1	5.4	61.9	5.8	73.7	23.3
Meadville city & MCD (Crawford)	4.376	13,392	13,238	-1.1	3,025.5	2.2	74.0	$32,259	10.5	23.2	55.0	9.1	54.2	37.7
Middle Smithfield township (Monroe)	53.159	16,001	15,730	-1.7	295.9	14.5	96.4	$60,396	25.7	7.5	66.1	14.1	78.6	17.4
Middletown township (Bucks)	18.904	45,436	45,332	-0.2	2,398.0	6.3	91.3	$82,288	38.4	4.9	69.6	8.0	72.9	23.2
Middletown township (Delaware)	13.466	15,807	15,945	0.9	1,184.1	6.2	90.0	$86,082	41.7	5.0	60.7	5.3	67.0	29.2
Millcreek township (Erie)	32.074	53,517	54,012	0.9	1,684.0	4.6	87.1	$55,547	23.8	11.3	65.1	6.4	64.0	31.4
Monroeville municipality & MCD (Allegheny)	19.715	28,341	28,285	-0.2	1,434.7	7.0	88.5	$56,554	24.0	7.8	61.6	5.5	59.9	35.5
Montgomery township (Montgomery)	10.630	24,790	25,946	4.7	2,440.9	16.8	92.4	$101,161	50.6	3.7	73.1	5.5	73.8	22.6
Montgomeryville CDP	4.755	12,624	NA	NA	NA	15.1	90.1	$106,360	53.1	2.9	74.4	5.1	78.3	17.6
Moon township (Allegheny)	23.826	24,167	25,524	5.6	1,071.3	7.4	87.7	$70,155	34.5	9.1	68.6	6.2	62.5	31.0
Mountain Top CDP	15.043	10,982	NA	NA	NA	5.0	91.4	$73,078	34.0	4.1	68.6	7.2	81.6	15.4
Mount Joy township (Lancaster)	27.838	9,873	10,724	8.6	385.2	4.3	90.9	$62,842	23.0	14.2	74.7	7.1	70.8	22.4
Mount Lebanon township (Allegheny)	6.078	33,137	32,922	-0.6	5,416.6	9.1	90.0	$80,914	41.0	6.9	63.9	4.6	64.0	33.2
Mount Pleasant township (Westmoreland)	55.944	10,911	10,680	-2.1	190.9	0.5	94.9	$50,915	15.6	9.6	63.7	7.1	66.9	28.3
Muhlenberg township (Berks)	11.775	19,630	19,857	1.2	1,686.3	7.2	88.6	$61,323	21.8	6.7	67.2	6.8	69.3	23.3
Munhall borough & MCD (Allegheny)	2.298	11,406	11,305	-0.9	4,920.2	2.7	86.9	$44,075	13.8	9.5	64.7	8.3	52.5	40.3
Murrysville municipality & MCD (Westmoreland)	36.838	20,079	20,162	0.4	547.3	4.6	93.1	$90,026	44.3	4.8	63.6	4.1	77.5	20.2
Nanticoke city & MCD (Luzerne)	3.456	10,465	10,301	-1.6	2,980.6	2.2	86.9	$35,723	7.7	21.3	59.2	10.6	60.8	36.1
Nether Providence township (Delaware)	4.714	13,706	13,805	0.7	2,928.7	6.7	92.4	$99,770	49.9	2.1	64.8	7.2	74.0	22.9

1 Dry land or land partially or temporarily covered by water.
2 16 years old and over.

Table B. Incorporated Places, Census Designated Places (CDPs), and Minor Civil Divisions (MCDs) of 10,000 or More Population — Crime, Construction, and Local Government Finance

STATE City, town, township, borough, or CDP (county if applicable)	Serious crimes known to police, 2014[1]				New residential construction authorized by building permits, 2014			Local government finance, 2012							
		Rate[2]						General revenue				General expenditure			
									Intergovernmental				Per capita[3]		
	Total number	Total	Violent	Property	Value ($1,000)	Number of housing units	Percent single family	Total (mil dol)	Total (mil dol)	Percent from state gov.	Taxes per capita[3]	Total (mil dol)	Total	Capital outlays	Debt outstanding (mil dol)
	15	16	17	18	19	20	21	22	23	24	25	26	27	28	29
PENNSYLVANIA—Con.															
Jefferson Hills borough & MCD (Allegheny)	81	721	80	641	17,663	78	100.0	10.6	0.7	99.6	520	9.9	900	14	5.9
Johnstown city & MCD (Cambria)	933	4289	575	3714	0	0	0.0	24.0	6.7	36.5	482	24.7	1,199	127	11.3
King of Prussia CDP	NA	NA	NA	NA	NA	NA	NA	NA	NA	NA	NA	NA	NA	NA	NA
Kingston borough & MCD (Luzerne)	338	2590	153	2437	0	0	0.0	9.2	2.5	97.9	407	8.7	663	62	3.0
Lancaster city & MCD (Lancaster)	2,694	4541	679	3862	2,503	16	100.0	69.1	11.7	71.8	522	87.4	1,472	261	221.6
Lancaster township (Lancaster)	422	2473	94	2379	3,017	10	100.0	4.9	0.6	99.1	172	4.0	237	3	0.0
Lansdale borough & MCD (Montgomery)	242	1472	189	1283	3,138	29	86.2	14.8	4.2	37.7	314	20.8	1,272	371	17.8
Lansdowne borough & MCD (Delaware)	312	2935	235	2700	266	2	100.0	8.9	1.3	96.7	402	8.2	772	78	3.0
Lebanon city & MCD (Lebanon)	700	2741	309	2432	0	0	0.0	21.7	10.2	34.6	325	26.5	1,036	259	0.3
Lehigh township (Northampton)	129	1241	164	1077	387	2	100.0	3.8	0.8	97.9	274	3.3	315	2	0.7
Lehman township (Pike)	NA	NA	NA	NA	0	0	0.0	1.9	0.6	95.8	114	2.4	231	4	0.4
Levittown CDP	NA	NA	NA	NA	NA	NA	NA	NA	NA	NA	NA	NA	NA	NA	NA
Limerick township (Montgomery)	507	2706	32	2674	3,872	27	100.0	12.6	1.3	93.4	315	12.9	698	71	12.6
Logan township (Blair)	294	2385	454	1931	2,426	12	100.0	9.1	1.5	58.7	321	8.8	709	11	26.2
Lower Allen township (Cumberland)	337	1799	85	1714	7,947	99	33.3	10.6	1.1	99.1	375	9.4	519	26	11.3
Lower Burrell city & MCD (Westmoreland)	227	1957	34	1923	647	2	100.0	8.0	0.7	97.9	369	7.4	633	7	6.1
Lower Gwynedd township (Montgomery)	164	1418	86	1332	3,014	6	100.0	10.6	1.2	86.0	479	11.3	982	61	5.3
Lower Macungie township (Lehigh)	NA	NA	NA	NA	5,481	26	100.0	15.9	1.4	100.0	223	15.4	494	47	5.2
Lower Makefield township (Bucks)	310	945	40	906	9,023	46	100.0	23.5	2.3	92.7	303	21.4	655	19	34.1
Lower Merion township (Montgomery)	965	1656	60	1596	10,632	27	100.0	87.1	11.7	45.2	921	87.2	1,499	134	107.4
Lower Moreland township (Montgomery)	143	1081	53	1028	2,414	10	100.0	12.6	0.8	96.0	512	10.8	825	27	24.9
Lower Paxton township (Dauphin)	1,033	2147	170	1976	25,591	106	100.0	20.9	3.1	100.0	262	19.8	415	9	88.6
Lower Pottsgrove township (Montgomery)	226	1854	82	1772	278	1	100.0	5.4	0.7	97.4	297	5.2	424	15	0.2
Lower Providence township (Montgomery)	335	1304	195	1110	21,139	213	6.1	11.9	2.1	79.4	315	10.6	415	29	7.6
Lower Salford township (Montgomery)	75	487	39	448	2,832	6	100.0	9.8	1.0	89.9	415	10.4	683	76	14.5
Lower Saucon township (Northampton)	124	1148	93	1055	3,400	10	100.0	9.3	1.6	97.5	478	6.4	596	49	5.4
Lower Southampton township (Bucks)	390	2058	158	1900	6,174	71	100.0	20.0	2.6	54.7	567	19.3	1,017	36	13.0
Loyalsock township (Lycoming)	NA	NA	NA	NA	7,252	26	53.8	10.9	3.7	99.5	270	8.0	713	158	3.2
McCandless township (Allegheny)	302	1040	38	1002	7,782	28	100.0	14.5	2.3	99.8	371	17.3	600	80	0.3
McKeesport city & MCD (Allegheny)	1,073	5013	1794	3219	0	0	0.0	16.8	4.3	52.1	300	18.4	934	4	25.1
Manchester township (York)	NA	NA	NA	NA	1,267	6	100.0	13.1	1.6	74.1	376	12.5	685	2	9.7
Manheim township (Lancaster)	698	1783	41	1742	25,333	97	100.0	29.3	3.3	89.6	407	38.9	1,005	487	18.5
Manor township (Lancaster)	203	1000	79	921	830	5	60.0	6.6	1.0	100.0	192	5.8	289	12	0.0
Marple township (Delaware)	341	1440	42	1398	1,838	10	100.0	19.1	1.7	97.4	452	17.2	731	29	7.6
Meadville city & MCD (Crawford)	297	2244	227	2017	559	2	100.0	10.7	2.5	78.6	362	12.7	956	155	35.8
Middle Smithfield township (Monroe)	NA	NA	NA	NA	2,451	10	100.0	5.3	0.6	100.0	161	6.3	399	85	12.5
Middletown township (Bucks)	1,047	2302	90	2211	7,782	82	100.0	26.9	3.5	69.4	335	28.6	629	70	28.4
Middletown township (Delaware)	NA	NA	NA	NA	7,782	82	100.0	5.7	0.7	97.2	227	5.6	355	31	9.7
Millcreek township (Erie)	973	1788	94	1695	422	2	100.0	33.4	4.8	95.1	320	34.1	630	37	18.0
Monroeville municipality & MCD (Allegheny)	597	2101	341	1760	1,520	7	100.0	23.1	1.7	95.3	695	30.1	1,058	116	30.2
Montgomery township (Montgomery)	446	1720	31	1690	4,390	18	55.6	15.5	1.7	94.9	499	15.6	611	65	1.1
Montgomeryville CDP	NA	NA	NA	NA	NA	NA	NA	NA	NA	NA	NA	NA	NA	NA	NA
Moon township (Allegheny)	237	929	63	866	15,321	64	100.0	13.8	1.5	97.1	458	13.3	531	14	8.2
Mountain Top CDP	NA	NA	NA	NA	NA	NA	NA	NA	NA	NA	NA	NA	NA	NA	NA
Mount Joy township (Lancaster)	NA	NA	NA	NA	2,333	12	66.7	4.7	1.0	50.7	214	5.1	496	115	0.0
Mount Lebanon township (Allegheny)	236	714	27	687	1,207	5	100.0	39.1	2.7	88.2	695	39.6	1,196	121	25.7
Mount Pleasant township (Westmoreland)	NA	NA	NA	NA	0	0	0.0	2.5	0.6	96.9	142	2.4	223	25	1.3
Muhlenberg township (Berks)	688	3456	131	3325	6,528	81	25.9	14.3	1.6	77.9	462	14.0	705	120	10.6
Munhall borough & MCD (Allegheny)	121	1067	141	926	724	3	100.0	7.4	0.7	99.7	364	7.5	656	7	0.0
Murrysville municipality & MCD (Westmoreland)	184	907	143	764	8,933	37	100.0	10.9	1.5	95.4	429	11.3	558	51	4.1
Nanticoke city & MCD (Luzerne)	284	2746	242	2504	0	0	0.0	9.0	2.7	83.9	393	10.5	1,007	248	3.8
Nether Providence township (Delaware)	152	1102	152	950	0	0	0.0	7.7	0.8	97.6	300	8.0	581	52	5.6

1 Data for serious crimes have not been adjusted for underreporting. This may affect comparability between geographic areas over time.
2 Per 100,000 population estimated by the FBI.   3 Based on population estimated as of July 1 of the year shown.

Table B. Incorporated Places, Census Designated Places (CDPs), and Minor Civil Divisions (MCDs) of 10,000 or More Population — Land Area, Population, and Households, and Employment

STATE City, town, township, borough, or CDP (county if applicable)	Land area,[1] 2010 (sq mi)	Total persons 2010	Total persons 2014	Percent change 2010–2014	Persons per square mile, 2014	Foreign born	Lives in same house as previous year	Median household income (dollars)	Income of $100,000 or more	Income below poverty level	Percent in labor force	Unemployment rate	Family households	One person households
	1	2	3	4	5	6	7	8	9	10	11	12	13	14
PENNSYLVANIA—Con.														
Newberry township (York)	30.416	15,289	15,365	0.5	505.2	0.9	90.8	$62,207	21.3	6.6	73.7	8.3	73.3	21.3
New Britain township (Bucks)	14.759	11,075	11,258	1.7	762.8	5.3	94.2	$91,227	46.1	4.1	73.1	6.4	76.3	19.8
New Castle city & MCD (Lawrence)	8.307	23,273	22,575	-3.0	2,717.5	1.4	84.9	$29,762	7.0	26.4	51.1	11.3	60.3	35.5
New Garden township (Chester)	16.113	11,988	12,098	0.9	750.8	22.9	93.7	$117,500	58.3	8.2	70.2	2.8	83.1	10.2
New Hanover township (Montgomery)	21.681	10,939	12,227	11.8	564.0	2.1	96.9	$88,848	41.9	4.5	71.5	8.2	81.8	15.5
New Kensington city & MCD (Westmoreland)	3.949	13,116	12,796	-2.4	3,240.2	1.6	88.1	$36,555	11.0	20.7	56.5	12.0	56.3	37.8
Newtown township (Bucks)	11.900	19,299	19,668	1.9	1,652.8	12.0	92.3	$109,563	55.5	4.8	69.1	6.0	75.1	21.7
Newtown township (Delaware)	10.018	12,216	12,428	1.7	1,240.6	9.1	87.5	$86,854	44.7	3.1	62.2	8.1	67.4	28.3
Norristown borough & MCD (Montgomery)	3.519	34,324	34,484	0.5	9,798.3	18.3	86.9	$42,296	12.4	19.8	69.4	12.0	58.9	33.2
Northampton township (Bucks)	25.681	39,726	39,577	-0.4	1,541.1	10.8	95.7	$106,661	53.3	2.8	68.2	7.2	80.6	17.6
North Fayette township (Allegheny)	25.184	13,934	14,377	3.2	570.9	2.9	86.9	$70,129	30.3	6.8	74.9	5.1	59.0	29.7
North Huntingdon township (Westmoreland)	27.260	30,611	30,748	0.4	1,127.9	2.3	94.2	$68,348	29.6	3.5	66.0	4.5	74.2	22.6
North Lebanon township (Lebanon)	16.748	11,429	11,686	2.2	697.8	3.5	91.2	$60,595	22.0	6.2	68.4	5.3	80.4	16.8
North Middleton township (Cumberland)	23.193	11,143	11,383	2.2	490.8	2.7	85.9	$65,061	26.3	8.9	68.7	1.8	72.1	25.8
North Strabane township (Washington)	27.264	13,408	14,076	5.0	516.3	2.0	89.1	$75,019	33.7	2.6	67.2	3.8	69.3	26.3
North Union township (Fayette)	39.020	12,726	12,488	-1.9	320.0	0.9	94.0	$35,205	9.5	18.0	51.7	7.4	61.9	33.8
North Versailles township (Allegheny)	8.027	10,217	10,154	-0.6	1,265.0	1.7	89.9	$42,112	8.6	19.2	62.9	5.5	58.2	35.9
North Whitehall township (Lehigh)	28.063	15,703	16,063	2.3	572.4	3.5	93.2	$75,192	33.5	4.9	71.4	8.7	77.1	18.9
Oil City city & MCD (Venango)	4.493	10,557	10,227	-3.1	2,276.4	1.1	79.3	$34,897	7.2	25.7	58.1	10.8	59.3	34.6
Palmer township (Northampton)	10.260	20,634	20,930	1.4	2,040.0	8.6	92.6	$74,657	32.9	5.7	63.1	6.5	74.1	21.8
Patton township (Centre)	24.531	15,311	15,808	3.2	644.4	13.7	65.9	$52,944	24.0	20.0	64.4	4.1	50.4	27.1
Penn township (Westmoreland)	30.764	20,005	19,750	-1.3	642.0	0.7	94.3	$75,645	33.9	5.6	65.4	4.9	77.6	19.7
Penn township (York)	12.976	15,618	15,928	2.0	1,227.5	2.7	90.4	$60,608	21.3	7.8	69.2	7.5	69.8	24.1
Penn Hills township (Allegheny)	19.118	42,331	42,109	-0.5	2,202.6	2.6	89.3	$46,764	13.5	10.7	65.0	9.0	59.9	34.7
Peters township (Washington)	19.547	21,213	21,975	3.6	1,124.2	5.0	91.8	$107,237	53.6	2.4	65.8	3.7	81.1	16.0
Philadelphia city & MCD (Philadelphia)	134.109	1,526,006	1,560,297	2.2	11,634.6	12.5	85.8	$37,460	14.0	24.5	59.2	14.9	53.1	39.5
Phoenixville borough & MCD (Chester)	3.510	16,440	16,599	1.0	4,729.2	13.0	85.7	$58,418	22.3	9.8	75.0	6.8	52.0	38.7
Pine township (Allegheny)	16.963	11,497	12,531	9.0	738.7	5.9	92.4	$145,504	70.3	2.2	68.7	4.9	83.3	14.0
Pittsburgh city & MCD (Allegheny)	55.376	305,702	305,412	-0.1	5,515.2	7.5	79.1	$40,009	15.8	21.4	61.9	9.4	46.9	41.2
Plum borough & MCD (Allegheny)	28.583	27,124	27,532	1.5	963.2	1.5	92.9	$67,639	26.3	5.4	67.2	6.4	68.4	26.9
Plumstead township (Bucks)	27.164	12,442	13,208	6.2	486.2	5.5	90.8	$90,670	45.8	5.2	76.1	5.1	74.7	22.5
Plymouth township (Montgomery)	8.391	16,525	16,715	1.1	1,992.0	9.2	91.2	$76,863	36.5	4.2	69.2	7.3	67.4	27.7
Pocono township (Monroe)	34.240	11,070	10,820	-2.3	316.0	8.9	91.6	$55,295	22.6	11.4	63.4	18.7	73.3	19.3
Pottstown borough & MCD (Montgomery)	4.888	22,377	22,684	1.4	4,641.1	2.6	86.8	$45,724	15.0	16.8	69.4	8.9	56.6	36.7
Pottsville city & MCD (Schuylkill)	4.166	14,324	13,940	-2.7	3,346.4	1.3	83.3	$36,768	9.2	17.1	56.0	9.7	57.8	35.8
Radnor township (Delaware)	13.776	31,531	31,480	-0.2	2,285.1	10.3	83.8	$100,129	50.1	8.2	57.6	5.1	60.9	33.4
Rapho township (Lancaster)	47.423	10,438	11,443	9.6	241.3	1.8	95.2	$73,788	27.3	4.9	69.5	3.4	71.1	22.1
Reading city & MCD (Berks)	9.884	88,080	87,812	-0.3	8,884.6	18.5	77.6	$26,867	4.9	35.9	60.4	20.0	63.9	29.2
Richland township (Allegheny)	14.630	11,100	11,522	3.8	787.6	3.0	95.7	$87,184	41.6	5.4	67.5	3.7	73.5	26.0
Richland township (Bucks)	20.648	13,052	13,100	0.4	634.4	5.0	93.6	$63,028	27.6	7.6	73.1	10.9	75.1	21.3
Richland township (Cambria)	20.593	12,814	12,346	-3.7	599.5	1.8	81.7	$46,552	19.2	11.6	51.8	7.0	63.4	32.2
Ridley township (Delaware)	5.119	30,767	31,047	0.9	6,065.4	5.8	92.6	$63,679	24.8	9.8	71.2	8.9	65.8	29.0
Robinson township (Allegheny)	15.219	13,355	13,692	2.5	899.7	6.3	86.9	$78,627	36.9	3.6	70.6	4.9	59.8	31.7
Ross township (Allegheny)	14.475	31,105	31,012	-0.3	2,142.4	5.5	88.6	$61,819	26.0	7.2	66.0	4.1	58.0	36.7
Rostraver township (Westmoreland)	32.283	11,363	11,212	-1.3	347.3	2.2	90.6	$60,595	27.8	9.8	63.1	8.8	76.0	21.9
St. Marys city & MCD (Elk)	99.322	13,070	12,793	-2.1	128.8	1.5	91.9	$48,842	13.6	11.0	60.2	4.5	67.9	30.6
Salisbury township (Lancaster)	41.760	11,062	11,264	1.8	269.7	1.3	90.8	$60,069	22.7	9.1	68.2	3.4	87.1	11.4
Salisbury township (Lehigh)	11.171	13,501	13,673	1.3	1,223.9	6.4	90.9	$69,685	29.3	7.3	64.4	7.8	75.1	22.3
Sandy township (Clearfield)	51.960	10,623	10,617	-0.1	204.3	1.1	87.9	$47,523	14.1	8.9	59.3	10.9	68.9	26.9
Scott township (Allegheny)	3.909	17,024	16,939	-0.5	4,333.9	9.3	88.3	$62,216	25.0	6.6	62.8	6.9	56.2	38.7
Scranton city & MCD (Lackawanna)	25.309	76,089	75,281	-1.1	2,974.4	9.0	82.3	$37,551	11.3	19.8	57.5	9.1	58.1	34.9
Shaler township (Allegheny)	11.075	28,757	28,641	-0.4	2,586.1	2.3	93.5	$69,816	26.9	5.1	67.2	5.7	71.1	25.6
Sharon city & MCD (Mercer)	3.770	14,038	13,669	-2.6	3,626.1	3.4	82.4	$29,213	7.6	26.8	55.3	11.6	59.4	38.2
Shiloh CDP	4.223	11,218	NA	NA	NA	4.3	87.5	$63,544	22.1	6.2	60.6	6.9	70.5	25.6
Silver Spring township (Cumberland)	32.314	13,666	15,728	15.1	486.7	5.6	91.8	$77,500	35.8	5.4	66.6	6.8	69.6	25.8
Skippack township (Montgomery)	13.837	13,715	15,204	10.9	1,098.8	5.8	86.0	$106,952	55.2	4.4	50.2	5.4	74.6	20.9
Somerset township (Somerset)	64.204	12,122	12,306	1.5	191.7	0.6	82.6	$43,552	16.0	12.3	38.0	7.0	68.6	28.7
South Fayette township (Allegheny)	20.382	14,416	15,311	6.2	751.2	6.1	92.2	$80,804	37.0	5.0	69.0	5.7	67.5	26.8
South Middleton township (Cumberland)	48.739	14,661	15,066	2.8	309.1	2.6	88.7	$69,300	30.5	4.0	67.0	5.2	70.0	23.2

1 Dry land or land partially or temporarily covered by water.
2 16 years old and over.

Table B. Incorporated Places, Census Designated Places (CDPs), and Minor Civil Divisions (MCDs) of 10,000 or More Population — **Crime, Construction, and Local Government Finance**

STATE City, town, township, borough, or CDP (county if applicable)	Serious crimes known to police, 2014[1] Total number	Rate[2] Total	Rate[2] Violent	Rate[2] Property	New residential construction authorized by building permits, 2014 Value ($1,000)	Number of housing units	Percent single family	Local government finance, 2012 General revenue Total (mil dol)	Intergovernmental Total (mil dol)	Intergovernmental Percent from state gov.	Taxes per capita[3]	General expenditure Total (mil dol)	Per capita[3] Total	Per capita[3] Capital outlays	Debt outstanding (mil dol)
	15	16	17	18	19	20	21	22	23	24	25	26	27	28	29
PENNSYLVANIA—Con.															
Newberry township (York).........	297	1941	124	1817	4,488	32	100.0	5.6	0.9	97.8	213	5.5	357	9	11.6
New Britain township (Bucks)...	64	580	18	562	0	0	0.0	6.5	0.8	95.0	462	5.3	482	20	2.4
New Castle city & MCD (Lawrence)............................	983	4344	508	3836	0	0	0.0	24.3	7.2	9.6	617	21.1	924	25	25.0
New Garden township (Chester).............................	105	869	83	786	1,127	4	100.0	10.3	2.7	29.0	305	10.6	876	228	3.2
New Hanover township (Montgomery)	121	986	73	913	23,553	103	100.0	6.3	0.7	96.1	282	12.6	1,074	329	10.4
New Kensington city & MCD (Westmoreland)	540	4198	420	3778	0	0	0.0	9.0	2.4	35.1	359	8.6	665	34	0.0
Newtown township (Bucks).......	173	760	66	694	3,633	25	100.0	12.2	1.4	97.6	445	11.5	592	34	9.6
Newtown township (Delaware) .	120	972	105	867	3,633	25	100.0	8.9	0.8	100.0	402	8.4	682	2	3.1
Norristown borough & MCD (Montgomery)	1,139	3306	746	2560	57	1	100.0	28.2	3.4	47.9	627	30.2	875	85	23.9
Northampton township (Bucks)	168	423	15	408	4,934	28	57.1	25.4	2.8	100.0	381	21.1	533	12	22.4
North Fayette township (Allegheny)...........................	336	2351	49	2302	14,921	132	39.4	12.6	1.3	88.5	534	11.4	808	0	11.4
North Huntingdon township (Westmoreland)	522	1690	68	1622	24,431	86	100.0	13.0	1.6	100.0	342	11.6	376	22	1.9
North Lebanon township (Lebanon)............................	378	3252	206	3045	NA	NA	NA	4.0	0.9	88.8	226	3.7	321	28	0.6
North Middleton township (Cumberland).........................	185	1629	106	1523	4,182	24	100.0	3.4	0.6	100.0	228	3.5	308	17	8.3
North Strabane township (Washington)........................	155	1105	71	1033	27,674	139	100.0	9.0	3.5	98.2	341	11.5	835	84	8.6
North Union township (Fayette)	NA	NA	NA	NA	NA	NA	NA	2.5	0.6	100.0	133	3.1	244	68	0.0
North Versailles township (Allegheny)...........................	257	2078	307	1771	4,851	40	0.0	6.7	0.7	97.1	450	5.0	485	12	5.4
North Whitehall township (Lehigh)..............................	NA	NA	NA	NA	7,934	23	100.0	5.0	0.8	100.0	224	4.4	278	19	2.3
Oil City city & MCD (Venango) .	216	2104	156	1948	148	1	100.0	10.0	2.8	63.8	312	13.0	1,258	167	13.0
Palmer township (Northampton)......................	359	1715	76	1639	25,681	213	13.6	17.4	1.5	92.2	429	18.0	866	22	12.9
Patton township (Centre)..........	190	1241	52	1189	6,364	19	100.0	7.7	0.7	97.9	417	9.2	593	141	7.5
Penn township (Westmoreland)	58	292	116	176	3,621	15	100.0	8.4	1.2	97.3	334	8.6	434	55	1.8
Penn township (York)...............	181	1142	133	1010	3,621	15	100.0	14.8	2.4	98.4	386	22.8	1,451	778	18.9
Penn Hills township (Allegheny)	1,088	2573	385	2187	381	2	100.0	36.7	3.7	68.6	455	35.5	837	94	90.7
Peters township (Washington)..	132	601	36	564	180	1	100.0	16.0	1.9	98.0	519	16.6	770	141	10.5
Philadelphia city & MCD (Philadelphia)......................	68,741	4409	1021	3388	879,066	3,973	19.0	6411.8	2254.7	74.3	2089	5483.2	3,537	209	7729.2
Phoenixville borough & MCD (Chester).............................	428	2589	266	2323	3,890	39	100.0	14.5	2.4	80.3	389	13.8	835	79	11.5
Pine township (Allegheny)........	NA	NA	NA	NA	44,932	96	100.0	10.3	0.9	100.0	630	9.4	791	153	5.9
Pittsburgh city & MCD (Allegheny)...........................	12,338	4011	798	3213	46,476	338	26.3	607.0	163.6	87.2	1166	548.9	1,791	25	704.7
Plum borough & MCD (Allegheny)...........................	323	1171	275	895	7,492	41	100.0	13.3	1.8	85.5	352	13.6	498	25	50.0
Plumstead township (Bucks)	86	659	31	628	15,722	120	100.0	7.2	0.9	100.0	455	9.6	759	146	18.9
Plymouth township (Montgomery)	582	3486	246	3241	400	2	100.0	24.3	2.5	99.4	926	23.8	1,430	120	0.0
Pocono township (Monroe).......	233	2154	148	2006	1,134	6	100.0	17.3	12.3	80.3	420	21.9	1,999	1,449	15.5
Pottstown borough & MCD (Montgomery)	1,315	5817	770	5048	1,547	21	100.0	30.1	5.0	71.5	509	22.9	1,017	34	1.2
Pottsville city & MCD (Schuylkill)..........................	349	2485	271	2215	195	1	100.0	11.6	4.2	39.9	432	8.1	575	17	4.8
Radnor township (Delaware)	323	1026	70	956	11,277	36	100.0	35.3	3.5	96.4	754	30.5	972	74	50.1
Rapho township (Lancaster).....	NA	NA	NA	NA	15,078	88	100.0	3.1	1.3	49.9	150	3.4	313	117	0.0
Reading city & MCD (Berks).....	3,309	3767	865	2902	0	0	0.0	139.8	30.8	89.3	488	135.9	1,543	96	256.9
Richland township (Allegheny) .	NA	NA	NA	NA	7,556	29	100.0	7.3	0.7	100.0	403	6.9	608	21	11.9
Richland township (Bucks)	358	2741	46	2695	7,556	29	100.0	5.5	0.9	98.4	309	4.7	358	4	6.9
Richland township (Cambria) ...	635	5089	80	5009	7,556	29	100.0	6.2	1.5	50.8	337	5.9	470	84	0.2
Ridley township (Delaware)......	447	1439	103	1336	593	1	100.0	22.1	2.0	85.4	432	19.7	636	23	6.2
Robinson township (Allegheny)	363	2654	146	2508	15,859	51	88.2	10.3	1.1	87.3	597	10.0	740	16	0.0
Ross township (Allegheny)........	722	2319	93	2226	1,559	10	100.0	21.7	1.4	100.0	423	18.9	605	9	3.8
Rostraver township (Westmoreland)	455	4056	232	3824	3,404	15	86.7	6.7	0.8	92.8	368	6.1	538	28	5.8
St. Marys city & MCD (Elk).......	248	1926	70	1856	2,374	14	100.0	12.8	3.5	94.7	445	15.0	1,156	299	21.7
Salisbury township (Lancaster)	NA	NA	NA	NA	6,019	49	26.5	2.6	0.6	99.7	113	2.6	232	31	2.2
Salisbury township (Lehigh)	219	1605	81	1524	6,019	49	26.5	9.4	1.2	100.0	335	10.5	774	46	2.9
Sandy township (Clearfield)......	258	2421	160	2262	7,832	58	34.5	8.1	3.0	92.7	311	5.8	546	48	9.3
Scott township (Allegheny).......	177	1041	94	947	1,200	8	50.0	11.5	1.0	92.8	412	12.0	707	12	9.2
Scranton city & MCD (Lackawanna)	2,318	3060	285	2775	365,949	1,733	100.0	67.6	10.7	95.5	593	70.2	923	3	61.9
Shaler township (Allegheny).....	372	1294	52	1241	1,197	6	100.0	15.7	1.0	100.0	308	18.3	634	36	6.0
Sharon city & MCD (Mercer)	595	4344	613	3730	0	0	0.0	10.1	2.1	46.7	475	11.0	798	2	3.4
Shiloh CDP	NA	NA	NA	NA	NA	NA	NA	NA	NA	NA	NA	NA	NA	NA	NA
Silver Spring township (Cumberland).........................	219	1418	45	1373	41,316	228	99.1	6.9	0.9	100.0	323	14.0	961	259	7.9
Skippack township (Montgomery)	NA	NA	NA	NA	5,344	42	100.0	5.9	0.5	96.7	258	4.8	337	62	4.1
Somerset township (Somerset)	NA	NA	NA	NA	768	4	100.0	2.8	0.6	100.0	116	2.6	210	0	0.0
South Fayette township (Allegheny)...........................	91	594	7	588	30,830	113	100.0	8.8	1.0	95.9	447	8.1	543	0	7.6
South Middleton township (Cumberland).........................	NA	NA	NA	NA	8,528	47	100.0	4.6	0.8	100.0	194	3.9	262	19	3.6

1 Data for serious crimes have not been adjusted for underreporting. This may affect comparability between geographic areas over time.
2 Per 100,000 population estimated by the FBI.   3 Based on population estimated as of July 1 of the year shown.

Table B. Incorporated Places, Census Designated Places (CDPs), and Minor Civil Divisions (MCDs) of 10,000 or More Population — Land Area, Population, and Households, and Employment

STATE City, town, township, borough, or CDP (county if applicable)	Land area,[1] 2010 (sq mi)	Total persons 2010	Total persons 2014	Percent change 2010–2014	Persons per square mile, 2014	Foreign born	Lives in same house as previous year	Median household income (dollars)	Income of $100,000 or more	Income below poverty level	Percent in labor force	Unemploy-ment rate	Family households	One person households
	1	2	3	4	5	6	7	8	9	10	11	12	13	14
PENNSYLVANIA—Con.														
South Park CDP & township (Allegheny)	9.270	13,416	13,498	0.6	1,456.1	3.8	90.2	$69,365	30.2	7.0	68.3	6.0	72.0	24.1
South Union township (Fayette)	16.762	10,683	10,639	-0.4	634.7	0.5	91.6	$51,034	22.2	11.1	56.2	10.0	66.1	29.4
South Whitehall township (Lehigh)	17.077	19,180	19,602	2.2	1,147.8	9.4	89.4	$71,280	32.1	4.7	62.9	7.2	67.8	27.1
Spring township (Berks)	18.480	27,128	27,443	1.2	1,485.0	6.9	88.3	$67,230	27.5	5.4	64.9	5.2	67.6	26.7
Springettsbury township (York)	16.376	26,668	26,849	0.7	1,639.5	8.8	82.7	$59,412	21.8	5.1	55.7	6.2	69.4	25.4
Springfield township (Delaware)	6.321	24,211	24,375	0.7	3,856.5	6.0	93.3	$95,373	47.9	4.1	68.3	5.8	78.2	19.1
Springfield township (Montgomery)	6.785	19,422	19,546	0.6	2,880.7	6.3	89.5	$85,074	43.2	8.6	66.2	7.9	68.2	26.7
Spring Garden township (York)	6.745	12,490	12,803	2.5	1,898.2	4.1	85.2	$72,141	33.7	4.3	61.9	6.8	72.7	22.1
State College borough & MCD (Centre)	4.560	42,034	42,100	0.2	9,232.0	11.6	43.5	$26,627	14.0	42.7	43.7	8.8	27.4	37.1
Stroud township (Monroe)	31.059	19,215	18,747	-2.4	603.6	15.7	91.9	$66,239	27.6	10.7	66.8	12.1	75.7	18.4
Susquehanna township (Dauphin)	13.339	24,036	24,482	1.9	1,835.4	7.2	87.0	$63,357	24.1	5.6	67.9	7.4	56.6	36.2
Swatara township (Dauphin)	13.051	23,362	24,474	4.8	1,875.3	9.5	82.6	$57,445	20.2	8.2	63.2	5.3	69.0	26.2
Towamencin township (Montgomery)	9.682	17,578	18,205	3.6	1,880.3	10.8	91.7	$73,056	37.2	6.9	68.4	6.4	65.8	30.6
Tredyffrin township (Chester)	19.766	29,334	29,545	0.7	1,494.8	13.5	90.8	$112,472	55.8	4.3	68.4	4.2	65.2	31.0
Uniontown city & MCD (Fayette)	2.041	10,372	10,064	-3.0	4,931.1	4.2	83.8	$26,846	7.7	29.8	48.6	14.0	49.3	42.4
Unity township (Westmoreland)	67.441	22,606	22,403	-0.9	332.2	1.2	91.0	$59,583	27.0	8.8	58.5	5.2	70.7	25.7
Upper Allen township (Cumberland)	13.198	18,056	19,193	6.3	1,454.3	5.6	80.3	$66,058	28.0	5.2	63.1	4.8	63.9	32.9
Upper Chichester township (Delaware)	6.687	16,739	16,987	1.5	2,540.4	6.0	92.1	$62,213	24.7	7.8	65.7	10.4	61.8	28.9
Upper Darby township (Delaware)	7.825	82,795	82,927	0.2	10,597.2	20.0	89.7	$50,654	20.2	13.7	68.8	10.1	64.5	30.7
Upper Dublin township (Montgomery)	13.230	25,569	26,218	2.5	1,981.7	9.3	94.0	$106,869	53.8	3.2	67.7	5.2	77.4	20.2
Upper Gwynedd township (Montgomery)	8.126	15,552	15,944	2.5	1,962.0	13.6	90.6	$89,348	42.6	4.7	64.7	6.4	70.4	25.6
Upper Macungie township (Lehigh)	26.072	20,067	22,404	11.6	859.3	11.6	93.0	$86,017	41.5	4.2	71.5	6.5	72.3	21.8
Upper Merion township (Montgomery)	16.956	28,388	28,638	0.9	1,689.0	19.8	86.8	$80,068	38.2	6.9	70.8	5.3	62.7	30.0
Upper Moreland township (Montgomery)	7.972	24,015	24,274	1.1	3,044.7	10.0	89.5	$65,208	27.8	5.1	68.5	6.7	66.2	28.8
Upper Providence township (Delaware)	5.602	10,142	10,332	1.9	1,844.2	10.0	92.5	$107,311	54.3	2.7	69.0	5.4	70.8	24.9
Upper Providence township (Montgomery)	17.809	21,219	22,667	6.8	1,272.8	9.1	92.3	$117,627	56.8	3.3	72.9	4.1	76.9	18.8
Upper St. Clair CDP & township (Allegheny)	9.818	19,229	19,335	0.6	1,969.3	9.3	93.5	$106,444	53.3	4.3	63.1	5.2	81.2	16.9
Upper Saucon township (Lehigh)	24.461	14,808	15,878	7.2	649.1	5.2	90.2	$89,034	44.7	3.2	65.8	7.4	77.5	17.8
Upper Southampton township (Bucks)	6.620	15,152	15,152	0.0	2,289.0	9.4	93.8	$72,890	37.1	4.8	65.5	5.1	69.7	26.8
Upper Uwchlan township (Chester)	10.893	11,227	11,540	2.8	1,059.4	18.0	90.4	$152,234	73.4	0.7	75.3	4.9	85.2	12.8
Uwchlan township (Chester)	10.399	18,088	18,618	2.9	1,790.3	7.2	92.9	$109,583	54.6	5.9	72.3	6.0	75.4	19.2
Warminster township (Bucks)	10.162	32,682	32,659	-0.1	3,213.8	10.9	92.3	$62,028	26.9	7.8	62.2	9.5	67.2	28.8
Warrington township (Bucks)	13.697	23,418	23,743	1.4	1,733.5	10.9	90.2	$95,795	47.8	6.8	70.7	7.3	79.3	17.4
Warwick township (Bucks)	10.972	14,437	14,694	1.8	1,339.2	7.5	95.9	$106,481	54.4	3.2	70.1	5.1	75.3	21.2
Warwick township (Lancaster)	19.778	17,778	17,945	0.9	907.3	3.9	93.0	$71,050	26.6	4.9	69.0	5.6	76.4	20.9
Washington township (Franklin)	39.050	14,009	14,454	3.2	370.1	3.1	89.3	$56,384	21.5	6.2	63.7	5.5	71.1	25.2
Washington city & MCD (Washington)	2.948	13,895	13,551	-2.5	4,597.4	1.6	78.8	$34,234	9.6	23.7	60.0	11.5	50.6	39.9
Waynesboro borough & MCD (Franklin)	3.412	10,568	10,760	1.8	3,153.4	2.8	85.3	$40,037	9.8	14.2	64.4	14.0	62.8	32.3
Weigelstown CDP	5.815	12,875	NA	NA	NA	2.2	89.9	$54,241	19.4	8.0	67.4	7.7	72.7	21.0
West Bradford township (Chester)	18.498	12,223	12,625	3.3	682.5	7.5	94.3	$105,434	53.2	2.7	72.8	3.1	83.3	11.4
West Chester borough & MCD (Chester)	1.846	18,461	19,189	3.9	10,393.8	7.4	69.9	$48,779	21.4	20.1	67.4	7.8	36.5	37.6
West Deer township (Allegheny)	28.869	11,771	11,902	1.1	412.3	0.8	93.1	$59,466	23.5	5.1	65.5	7.1	66.8	28.4
West Goshen township (Chester)	11.853	21,866	23,050	5.4	1,944.6	9.3	88.9	$91,688	44.9	8.4	73.3	6.2	69.8	19.0
West Hempfield township (Lancaster)	18.455	16,153	16,411	1.6	889.3	5.2	94.7	$70,816	31.3	6.5	74.3	7.6	76.0	19.5
West Lampeter township (Lancaster)	16.395	15,180	15,734	3.6	959.7	1.3	93.6	$66,883	25.6	5.7	53.8	8.2	68.6	26.7
West Manchester township (York)	19.942	18,894	18,861	-0.2	945.8	3.9	89.4	$58,727	20.6	6.4	63.4	8.5	66.3	29.4
West Mifflin borough & MCD (Allegheny)	14.212	20,313	20,175	-0.7	1,419.5	1.1	91.2	$47,894	14.7	13.3	63.5	9.6	63.3	31.9
West Norriton township (Montgomery)	5.886	15,663	15,805	0.9	2,685.2	10.4	89.8	$63,745	26.3	6.4	70.4	7.9	54.5	38.9
Westtown township (Chester)	8.664	10,827	10,919	0.8	1,260.2	6.4	88.2	$117,661	56.6	3.2	69.9	7.8	75.7	18.3
West Whiteland township (Chester)	12.835	18,274	18,453	1.0	1,437.7	15.1	89.7	$92,577	44.6	2.8	74.6	5.9	69.1	25.2
White township (Indiana)	42.346	15,821	16,322	3.2	385.4	3.2	82.8	$47,105	21.6	16.5	53.7	6.7	56.1	34.9

1 Dry land or land partially or temporarily covered by water.
2 16 years old and over.

Table B. Incorporated Places, Census Designated Places (CDPs), and Minor Civil Divisions (MCDs) of 10,000 or More Population — **Crime, Construction, and Local Government Finance**

STATE City, town, township, borough, or CDP (county if applicable)	Serious crimes known to police, 2014[1] Total number	Rate[2] Total	Rate[2] Violent	Rate[2] Property	New residential construction authorized by building permits, 2014 Value ($1,000)	New residential construction authorized by building permits, 2014 Number of housing units	New residential construction authorized by building permits, 2014 Percent single family	Local government finance, 2012 General revenue Total (mil dol)	Local government finance, 2012 General revenue Intergovernmental Total (mil dol)	Local government finance, 2012 General revenue Intergovernmental Percent from state gov.	Local government finance, 2012 General revenue Taxes per capita[3]	Local government finance, 2012 General expenditure Total (mil dol)	Local government finance, 2012 General expenditure Per capita[3] Total	Local government finance, 2012 General expenditure Per capita[3] Capital outlays	Local government finance, 2012 Debt outstanding (mil dol)
	15	16	17	18	19	20	21	22	23	24	25	26	27	28	29
PENNSYLVANIA—Con.															
South Park CDP & township (Allegheny)	44	324	29	295	2,353	8	100.0	9.3	0.9	98.3	337	8.3	615	29	3.2
South Union township (Fayette)	NA	NA	NA	NA	4,539	22	100.0	2.8	0.5	100.0	203	2.9	268	17	0.0
South Whitehall township (Lehigh)	645	3295	41	3254	2,984	17	100.0	15.7	1.8	93.1	587	16.6	853	106	0.9
Spring township (Berks)	267	971	58	913	4,735	24	100.0	20.7	2.6	77.5	429	22.3	813	111	22.1
Springettsbury township (York)	1,002	3739	112	3627	2,011	8	100.0	23.5	2.0	74.6	369	25.9	968	144	26.9
Springfield township (Delaware)	581	2387	78	2308	0	0	0.0	21.2	2.0	98.2	460	20.2	831	36	5.3
Springfield township (Montgomery)	209	1070	46	1024	0	0	0.0	15.6	2.0	99.6	419	16.1	825	54	0.5
Spring Garden township (York)	397	3091	179	2912	5,114	38	100.0	11.8	0.8	100.0	472	11.5	904	0	1.0
State College borough & MCD (Centre)	658	1164	46	1118	1,200	6	100.0	36.3	5.5	55.6	272	35.4	843	78	28.2
Stroud township (Monroe)	1,353	3982	194	3788	6,800	25	100.0	8.9	0.8	98.0	363	7.3	382	1	8.9
Susquehanna township (Dauphin)	409	1668	155	1513	0	0	0.0	12.9	1.7	93.2	395	12.9	528	31	6.3
Swatara township (Dauphin)	1,295	5253	373	4880	10,833	73	37.0	12.2	1.7	95.3	416	12.5	525	8	11.9
Towamencin township (Montgomery)	139	759	93	666	5,460	39	30.8	12.6	1.1	98.8	342	9.7	541	38	12.2
Tredyffrin township (Chester)	241	816	37	778	9,300	17	100.0	29.8	6.1	97.3	462	29.9	1,014	173	29.3
Uniontown city & MCD (Fayette)	509	5020	404	4616	125	1	100.0	8.9	1.6	41.2	419	8.3	807	15	6.7
Unity township (Westmoreland)	NA	NA	NA	NA	7,967	33	100.0	5.8	1.0	100.0	202	5.3	233	67	3.5
Upper Allen township (Cumberland)	155	824	11	814	26,150	125	100.0	11.5	1.1	95.7	284	15.9	864	175	19.1
Upper Chichester township (Delaware)	455	2675	194	2481	391	3	100.0	12.5	1.3	87.5	542	10.9	647	50	5.8
Upper Darby township (Delaware)	1,986	2397	427	1970	0	0	0.0	72.1	11.0	53.3	573	69.8	843	24	21.7
Upper Dublin township (Montgomery)	213	810	46	764	2,413	15	100.0	26.5	2.7	80.9	754	36.5	1,397	371	28.3
Upper Gwynedd township (Montgomery)	107	672	75	597	385	3	100.0	14.3	1.3	98.1	442	14.6	925	93	9.3
Upper Macungie township (Lehigh)	NA	NA	NA	NA	36,455	151	100.0	20.5	2.5	99.0	374	22.1	1,024	139	0.0
Upper Merion township (Montgomery)	1,158	4042	91	3951	2,145	14	100.0	34.9	4.0	73.1	789	33.9	1,186	118	27.1
Upper Moreland township (Montgomery)	549	2264	62	2202	430	3	100.0	20.3	2.4	76.9	629	18.0	746	23	5.1
Upper Providence township (Delaware)	28	270	19	251	3,807	48	100.0	5.6	0.7	94.0	423	4.7	455	6	4.6
Upper Providence township (Montgomery)	361	1626	36	1590	3,807	48	100.0	13.8	1.6	100.0	389	16.1	745	129	0.9
Upper St. Clair CDP & township (Allegheny)	114	588	41	546	18,294	152	14.5	27.4	1.8	90.2	871	29.1	1,510	59	56.8
Upper Saucon township (Lehigh)	148	943	25	918	22,694	94	100.0	11.5	1.3	76.2	464	11.2	727	101	9.7
Upper Southampton township (Bucks)	168	1107	79	1027	0	0	0.0	11.4	1.4	74.2	483	11.8	775	78	5.2
Upper Uwchlan township (Chester)	137	1184	NA	1184	480	2	100.0	7.0	0.6	100.0	409	9.8	854	223	2.3
Uwchlan township (Chester)	157	850	65	785	30,895	177	1.7	12.8	1.2	89.7	343	13.1	716	10	4.3
Warminster township (Bucks)	492	1500	73	1427	440	3	100.0	23.4	2.4	100.0	412	21.8	667	27	6.4
Warrington township (Bucks)	213	901	25	876	14,820	87	100.0	16.8	2.4	88.9	370	21.4	912	166	26.2
Warwick township (Bucks)	66	448	48	401	1,589	6	100.0	9.1	1.0	100.0	475	7.6	519	51	8.6
Warwick township (Lancaster)	NA	NA	NA	NA	1,589	6	100.0	4.8	1.0	97.1	177	4.3	243	4	0.0
Washington township (Franklin)	479	3311	76	3235	911	10	100.0	4.8	1.1	81.3	171	4.7	329	26	1.6
Washington city & MCD (Washington)	604	4413	468	3946	168	1	100.0	15.7	3.5	70.2	733	9.6	692	7	17.8
Waynesboro borough & MCD (Franklin)	330	3070	279	2791	5,167	46	13.0	5.6	0.8	65.9	245	7.3	680	94	0.5
Weigelstown CDP	NA	NA	NA	NA	NA	NA	NA	NA	NA	NA	NA	NA	NA	NA	NA
West Bradford township (Chester)	NA	NA	NA	NA	7,700	58	100.0	7.0	1.9	47.5	206	7.3	591	151	7.9
West Chester borough & MCD (Chester)	417	2184	225	1959	19,500	215	4.7	26.0	2.4	87.0	497	23.3	1,230	44	27.6
West Deer township (Allegheny)	99	834	17	817	6,909	40	100.0	4.2	0.7	100.0	274	4.0	334	9	0.1
West Goshen township (Chester)	308	1332	82	1249	6,168	40	100.0	20.5	1.6	100.0	509	20.8	915	126	7.9
West Hempfield township (Lancaster)	176	1072	67	1005	4,055	16	100.0	6.1	1.0	99.2	208	5.4	334	15	0.0
West Lampeter township (Lancaster)	154	980	13	968	9,522	53	100.0	5.6	0.7	100.0	224	4.8	309	2	3.0
West Manchester township (York)	535	2838	164	2673	795	4	100.0	14.7	2.3	96.2	288	13.5	715	55	0.8
West Mifflin borough & MCD (Allegheny)	463	2288	158	2130	421	2	100.0	14.5	1.7	89.8	560	13.5	664	21	9.2
West Norriton township (Montgomery)	427	2700	158	2542	0	0	0.0	12.3	1.2	96.7	431	10.5	667	7	11.0
Westtown township (Chester)	NA	NA	NA	NA	0	0	0.0	8.9	0.8	82.6	393	8.3	766	58	16.1
West Whiteland township (Chester)	454	2455	87	2368	0	0	0.0	13.5	1.4	100.0	456	14.2	769	97	14.8
White township (Indiana)	NA	NA	NA	NA	0	0	0.0	5.7	0.6	100.0	167	5.8	366	30	0.0

1 Data for serious crimes have not been adjusted for underreporting. This may affect comparability between geographic areas over time.
2 Per 100,000 population estimated by the FBI. 3 Based on population estimated as of July 1 of the year shown.

Table B. Incorporated Places, Census Designated Places (CDPs), and Minor Civil Divisions (MCDs) of 10,000 or More Population — Land Area, Population, and Households, and Employment

STATE City, town, township, borough, or CDP (county if applicable)	Land area,¹ 2010 (sq mi)	Total persons 2010	Total persons 2014	Percent change 2010–2014	Persons per square mile, 2014	Foreign born	Lives in same house as previous year	Median household income (dollars)	Income of $100,000 or more	Income below poverty level	Percent in labor force	Unemployment rate	Family households	One person households
	1	2	3	4	5	6	7	8	9	10	11	12	13	14
PENNSYLVANIA—Con.														
Whitehall borough & MCD (Allegheny)	3.326	13,944	13,896	-0.3	4,178.3	12.9	87.5	$56,196	23.4	9.8	64.1	5.8	60.5	35.7
Whitehall township (Lehigh)	12.567	26,738	27,214	1.8	2,165.5	14.9	85.5	$57,158	21.3	8.5	67.0	7.6	64.3	29.3
Whitemarsh township (Montgomery)	14.592	17,349	17,674	1.9	1,211.2	5.1	93.1	$112,205	56.4	3.8	68.8	6.2	68.8	25.1
Whitpain township (Montgomery)	12.846	18,875	19,180	1.6	1,493.1	12.3	89.2	$118,063	58.4	3.4	67.7	5.6	76.9	19.8
Wilkes-Barre city & MCD (Luzerne)	6.980	41,498	40,814	-1.6	5,847.0	6.1	78.5	$31,361	7.3	26.1	56.7	9.9	54.8	38.0
Wilkinsburg borough & MCD (Allegheny)	2.251	15,930	15,813	-0.7	7,024.5	3.0	79.3	$33,483	7.9	18.3	63.4	11.5	42.9	46.2
Williamsport city & MCD (Lycoming)	8.731	29,381	29,197	-0.6	3,344.1	1.7	78.7	$33,537	8.9	26.5	60.9	14.2	57.0	31.4
Willistown township (Chester)	18.109	10,497	10,823	3.1	597.7	7.6	91.5	$101,627	51.0	2.3	63.6	4.0	71.9	25.3
Willow Grove CDP	3.659	15,726	NA	NA	NA	10.6	90.6	$68,435	27.6	5.2	67.5	7.8	67.5	28.4
Windsor township (York)	27.278	17,504	17,853	2.0	654.5	2.8	91.3	$72,715	30.4	6.6	69.8	9.1	81.6	15.8
Woodlyn CDP	1.674	9,485	NA	NA	NA	4.8	95.6	$51,162	21.4	16.9	69.0	10.1	63.1	32.1
Worcester township (Montgomery)	16.220	9,750	10,326	5.9	636.6	8.5	93.0	$114,583	57.8	2.0	69.2	4.6	72.1	25.4
Wyomissing borough & MCD (Berks)	4.476	10,461	10,472	0.1	2,339.4	6.9	86.5	$73,545	34.9	4.3	61.6	5.3	60.8	30.3
Yeadon borough & MCD (Delaware)	1.595	11,443	11,525	0.7	7,226.4	17.3	93.0	$49,735	19.9	11.1	63.2	8.5	66.1	31.5
York city & MCD (York)	5.293	43,806	43,865	0.1	8,287.0	7.0	74.2	$28,819	5.1	34.1	60.7	20.9	58.2	33.4
York township (York)	25.254	27,790	28,127	1.2	1,113.8	4.8	88.5	$62,292	24.9	7.6	65.4	6.4	66.4	28.9
RHODE ISLAND	1,033.814	1,052,931	1,055,173	0.2	1,020.7	13.1	86.6	$56,423	25.2	14.2	65.9	9.5	62.5	30.2
Barrington town (Bristol)	8.215	16,314	16,236	-0.5	1,976.4	7.6	94.1	$103,937	52.3	2.3	67.5	5.8	75.9	22.5
Bristol town (Bristol)	9.817	22,955	22,332	-2.7	2,274.7	11.1	87.5	$60,988	30.2	10.6	62.1	8.4	63.9	28.6
Burrillville town (Providence)	55.035	15,955	16,246	1.8	295.2	2.7	91.7	$60,666	22.6	9.8	65.8	8.5	70.7	25.8
Central Falls city & MCD (Providence)	1.198	19,383	19,328	-0.3	16,131.6	38.1	84.0	$28,842	7.4	30.2	62.4	13.6	67.6	27.2
Coventry town (Kent)	59.054	35,020	35,021	0.0	593.0	3.0	90.3	$69,050	28.9	8.5	69.9	11.4	68.3	26.6
Cranston city & MCD (Providence)	28.340	80,386	81,037	0.8	2,859.4	13.0	89.8	$58,684	25.1	11.9	64.1	10.6	64.5	29.9
Cumberland town (Providence)	26.449	33,506	34,301	2.4	1,296.9	9.3	95.0	$74,499	32.7	6.9	68.1	4.9	68.2	27.5
East Greenwich town (Kent)	16.396	13,147	13,147	0.0	801.9	7.1	89.7	$92,727	48.3	6.2	64.1	5.1	68.4	26.5
East Providence city & MCD (Providence)	13.242	47,033	47,331	0.6	3,574.3	15.5	86.5	$51,077	19.8	12.3	65.7	10.4	59.9	34.2
Johnston town (Providence)	23.430	28,769	29,144	1.3	1,243.9	8.4	90.1	$57,457	27.6	12.6	64.9	6.8	60.0	32.6
Lincoln town (Providence)	18.120	21,104	21,507	1.9	1,186.9	6.6	93.8	$66,827	33.7	8.1	67.9	6.2	66.6	27.2
Middletown town (Newport)	12.716	16,097	16,105	0.0	1,266.5	8.4	82.4	$70,244	32.4	7.4	68.9	8.9	65.9	28.9
Narragansett town (Washington)	13.893	15,900	15,705	-1.2	1,130.5	1.9	78.3	$65,842	32.7	13.2	65.1	3.6	50.1	35.5
Newport city & MCD (Newport)	7.674	24,974	24,089	-3.5	3,139.2	8.8	75.1	$61,320	29.7	12.5	70.8	6.1	43.8	42.4
Newport East CDP	5.739	11,769	NA	NA	NA	8.0	83.8	$64,012	27.1	6.9	68.6	9.6	61.5	31.7
North Kingstown town (Washington)	43.149	26,601	26,291	-1.2	609.3	5.2	89.2	$80,506	40.2	8.9	69.4	7.5	71.8	23.5
North Providence town (Providence)	5.625	32,084	32,366	0.9	5,753.8	9.8	90.1	$53,470	20.0	12.0	65.4	8.4	58.1	35.4
North Smithfield town (Providence)	23.804	11,967	12,218	2.1	513.3	3.6	90.6	$78,163	36.8	6.0	66.0	5.2	68.8	24.5
Pawtucket city & MCD (Providence)	8.682	71,141	71,499	0.5	8,235.5	23.7	84.7	$40,578	11.1	21.3	67.3	13.8	61.1	32.8
Portsmouth town (Newport)	22.995	17,393	17,373	-0.1	755.5	5.6	89.0	$77,483	41.1	8.2	63.5	8.2	68.6	26.0
Providence city & MCD (Providence)	18.400	178,038	179,154	0.6	9,736.6	29.8	77.7	$37,514	14.9	28.5	64.2	13.7	57.3	30.9
Scituate town (Providence)	48.166	10,327	10,496	1.6	217.9	4.1	95.0	$80,802	37.3	6.3	71.3	6.5	72.3	25.5
Smithfield town (Providence)	26.306	21,430	21,507	0.4	817.6	4.4	87.2	$71,305	34.0	4.9	60.9	7.8	67.8	28.9
South Kingstown town (Washington)	56.449	30,607	30,750	0.5	544.7	5.5	82.9	$72,021	35.2	8.6	61.0	6.8	64.2	28.2
Tiverton town (Newport)	29.045	15,780	15,813	0.2	544.4	5.1	90.9	$73,438	32.9	7.7	67.6	8.1	68.3	25.8
Valley Falls CDP	3.501	11,547	NA	NA	NA	13.2	93.7	$59,878	23.9	9.0	69.7	3.9	75.2	19.3
Warren town (Bristol)	6.118	10,606	10,492	-1.1	1,714.8	6.4	80.4	$53,706	21.9	11.2	69.1	11.1	60.6	32.5
Warwick city & MCD (Kent)	35.039	82,670	81,963	-0.9	2,339.2	6.7	90.6	$62,803	25.7	8.2	68.4	9.0	60.9	32.3
Westerly CDP	15.834	17,936	NA	NA	NA	5.7	85.2	$58,620	27.0	9.5	65.4	8.4	63.4	28.0
Westerly town (Washington)	29.534	22,787	22,731	-0.2	769.7	5.4	86.8	$62,381	29.0	9.0	64.2	8.3	65.7	27.0
West Warwick town (Kent)	7.790	29,185	28,880	-1.0	3,707.2	7.7	84.1	$50,138	18.2	17.4	70.0	9.1	56.5	33.6
Woonsocket city & MCD (Providence)	7.739	41,186	41,228	0.1	5,327.4	10.8	90.5	$35,216	13.0	24.9	58.8	8.1	56.5	35.7
SOUTH CAROLINA	30,060.695	4,625,401	4,832,482	4.5	160.8	4.8	84.5	$45,033	16.4	17.1	61.2	10.6	67.1	27.8
Aiken city	20.803	29,553	30,258	2.4	1,454.5	5.0	82.9	$53,489	25.9	15.0	53.2	8.5	60.2	35.4
Anderson city	14.390	26,387	27,181	3.0	1,888.9	3.4	77.2	$28,987	10.4	25.8	54.4	12.1	56.7	38.0
Beaufort city	27.999	12,443	13,130	5.5	468.9	6.9	76.0	$46,915	19.8	15.4	67.4	4.0	65.0	29.6
Berea CDP	7.704	14,295	NA	NA	NA	12.1	86.8	$29,964	6.6	28.0	60.2	13.5	63.1	34.9
Bluffton town	51.362	13,353	15,199	13.8	295.9	17.4	82.4	$64,217	23.4	8.8	72.8	9.8	73.2	21.8
Cayce city	16.792	12,522	12,951	3.4	771.3	6.4	82.3	$43,186	10.3	20.5	65.4	8.5	54.8	31.2
Charleston city	109.035	120,246	130,113	8.2	1,193.3	3.9	77.0	$52,971	24.3	17.5	66.4	7.4	51.5	35.4
Clemson city	7.443	13,962	15,072	8.0	2,025.0	10.9	59.5	$33,632	20.2	36.2	56.9	7.6	41.0	31.9
Columbia city	133.063	130,065	132,067	1.5	992.5	5.4	64.8	$41,454	16.9	22.1	64.3	11.7	49.9	38.8
Conway city	21.748	17,295	20,175	16.7	927.7	1.8	73.9	$35,479	10.0	28.4	57.5	11.0	63.3	27.3
Dentsville CDP	6.698	14,062	NA	NA	NA	8.4	73.9	$37,339	7.7	15.2	69.2	12.4	56.6	38.2
Easley city	12.368	20,027	20,549	2.6	1,661.5	5.3	83.7	$40,453	14.4	13.7	59.5	10.2	65.8	30.6
Five Forks CDP	7.571	14,140	NA	NA	NA	7.3	89.7	$113,405	58.7	1.5	69.8	4.7	88.7	10.1

1 Dry land or land partially or temporarily covered by water.
2 16 years old and over.

Table B. Incorporated Places, Census Designated Places (CDPs), and Minor Civil Divisions (MCDs) of 10,000 or More Population — Crime, Construction, and Local Government Finance

STATE City, town, township, borough, or CDP (county if applicable)	Serious crimes known to police, 2014[1] Total number	Rate[2] Total	Rate[2] Violent	Rate[2] Property	New residential construction authorized by building permits, 2014 Value ($1,000)	Number of housing units	Percent single family	Local government finance, 2012 General revenue Total (mil dol)	Intergovernmental Total (mil dol)	Percent from state gov.	Taxes per capita[3]	General expenditure Total (mil dol)	Per capita[3] Total	Per capita[3] Capital outlays	Debt outstanding (mil dol)
	15	16	17	18	19	20	21	22	23	24	25	26	27	28	29
PENNSYLVANIA—Con.															
Whitehall borough & MCD (Allegheny)	59	423	86	337	400	1	100.0	12.2	0.9	84.0	517	14.8	1,061	24	2.9
Whitehall township (Lehigh)	1,298	4782	99	4682	834	10	100.0	19.7	2.7	77.0	486	19.2	707	39	5.5
Whitemarsh township (Montgomery)	285	1627	69	1558	2,457	11	54.5	22.2	2.3	70.5	748	22.9	1,310	193	15.1
Whitpain township (Montgomery)	274	1427	135	1292	1,931	11	100.0	19.9	1.7	100.0	710	18.0	944	64	11.4
Wilkes-Barre city & MCD (Luzerne)	1,628	3969	436	3533	850	4	100.0	52.9	20.4	46.2	583	57.3	1,386	201	73.4
Wilkinsburg borough & MCD (Allegheny)	606	3818	882	2936	0	0	0.0	11.2	1.5	95.0	383	14.5	909	4	8.4
Williamsport city & MCD (Lycoming)	1,143	3896	450	3446	9,680	99	4.0	41.3	20.3	45.8	526	30.5	1,035	151	5.4
Willistown township (Chester)	56	520	19	502	6,492	39	41.0	9.2	0.8	93.8	595	8.8	828	70	10.6
Willow Grove CDP	NA	NA	NA	NA	NA	NA	NA	NA	NA	NA	NA	NA	NA	NA	NA
Windsor township (York)	NA	NA	NA	NA	702	7	100.0	9.3	0.9	82.1	207	8.8	496	67	0.4
Woodlyn CDP	NA	NA	NA	NA	NA	NA	NA	NA	NA	NA	NA	NA	NA	NA	NA
Worcester township (Montgomery)	NA	NA	NA	NA	15,307	51	100.0	4.0	0.5	100.0	260	3.6	354	33	0.0
Wyomissing borough & MCD (Berks)	451	4301	67	4235	0	0	0.0	12.9	1.0	96.5	701	11.6	1,110	41	0.2
Yeadon borough & MCD (Delaware)	513	4452	738	3714	0	0	0.0	7.6	0.7	95.1	395	8.0	696	19	3.9
York city & MCD (York)	1,832	4168	883	3285	15,693	65	100.0	68.7	9.7	51.4	566	63.2	1,448	39	128.7
York township (York)	769	1258	154	1105	9,875	60	38.3	19.4	1.9	78.8	315	16.8	599	35	6.4
RHODE ISLAND	25,248	2393	219	2174	195,030	952	83.6	X	X	X	X	X	X	X	X
Barrington town (Bristol)	214	1309	24	1284	3,426	10	100.0	68.9	8.7	83.9	3374	69.3	4,253	225	26.2
Bristol town (Bristol)	235	1052	54	999	3,586	13	100.0	46.8	3.6	100.0	1653	46.4	2,073	188	57.2
Burrillville town (Providence)	147	908	74	833	2,439	19	100.0	51.9	18.7	99.6	1750	49.4	3,068	218	24.3
Central Falls city & MCD (Providence)	740	3795	687	3108	0	0	0.0	46.3	5.4	99.2	691	44.4	2,285	165	121.2
Coventry town (Kent)	527	1503	71	1432	6,308	44	95.5	99.8	34.5	80.1	1657	95.1	2,719	90	42.4
Cranston city & MCD (Providence)	1,703	2105	133	1971	3,439	24	100.0	282.2	60.2	92.5	2322	256.9	3,184	42	88.4
Cumberland town (Providence)	426	1242	52	1189	11,421	72	100.0	89.2	23.2	99.7	1782	84.4	2,488	110	60.8
East Greenwich town (Kent)	161	1222	30	1191	4,064	12	100.0	58.3	3.6	100.0	3470	59.0	4,498	724	91.1
East Providence city & MCD (Providence)	701	1480	112	1369	303	3	100.0	148.4	43.6	95.5	1942	155.3	3,292	150	75.2
Johnston town (Providence)	424	1451	144	1308	1,194	10	100.0	98.6	21.3	97.9	2390	97.1	3,349	144	22.7
Lincoln town (Providence)	452	2110	56	2054	11,895	58	100.0	78.4	20.2	85.2	2420	73.0	3,431	89	44.2
Middletown town (Newport)	322	1986	117	1869	2,627	10	100.0	72.3	19.3	91.7	2700	67.8	4,232	385	31.8
Narragansett town (Washington)	208	1323	32	1291	6,252	19	100.0	63.9	6.4	94.2	2918	55.3	3,513	278	27.0
Newport city & MCD (Newport)	1,071	4470	397	4074	13,639	83	15.7	126.6	24.4	92.5	2762	127.7	5,146	581	74.7
Newport East CDP	NA	NA	NA	NA	NA	NA	NA	NA	NA	NA	NA	NA	NA	NA	NA
North Kingstown town (Washington)	340	1297	111	1187	9,823	40	100.0	102.2	23.4	89.1	2696	96.9	3,677	53	48.8
North Providence town (Providence)	476	1469	151	1318	2,582	30	26.7	91.6	21.2	92.7	2106	85.9	2,665	49	30.2
North Smithfield town (Providence)	206	1678	24	1654	2,624	32	100.0	40.0	8.3	100.0	2309	37.7	3,117	55	42.7
Pawtucket city & MCD (Providence)	2,328	3259	291	2967	1,237	7	71.4	197.7	91.3	77.8	1339	192.3	2,697	24	159.7
Portsmouth town (Newport)	197	1129	75	1055	7,159	40	87.5	62.8	10.3	88.4	2713	55.8	3,220	80	18.4
Providence city & MCD (Providence)	7,793	4362	522	3840	3,318	27	51.9	747.8	292.1	91.6	1822	715.3	4,004	160	735.9
Scituate town (Providence)	57	543	29	514	2,786	13	100.0	32.4	5.3	100.0	2450	32.3	3,098	31	11.4
Smithfield town (Providence)	216	1005	28	978	3,410	17	100.0	66.6	10.0	100.0	2345	65.6	3,054	122	22.5
South Kingstown town (Washington)	294	957	46	911	12,864	48	100.0	92.0	14.2	99.0	2254	87.8	2,891	109	22.8
Tiverton town (Newport)	294	1845	119	1726	4,564	21	100.0	50.8	9.8	100.0	2415	49.5	3,133	10	35.4
Valley Falls CDP	NA	NA	NA	NA	NA	NA	NA	NA	NA	NA	NA	NA	NA	NA	NA
Warren town (Bristol)	235	2224	151	2072	1,490	7	100.0	26.8	2.7	74.9	2212	26.4	2,497	220	13.9
Warwick city & MCD (Kent)	1,952	2377	102	2275	6,450	45	80.0	318.8	59.3	98.4	2682	303.4	3,707	110	170.1
Westerly CDP	NA	NA	NA	NA	NA	NA	NA	NA	NA	NA	NA	NA	NA	NA	NA
Westerly town (Washington)	616	2712	110	2602	19,958	57	100.0	79.4	8.5	99.5	2842	78.2	3,449	142	82.3
West Warwick town (Kent)	446	1541	211	1331	2,518	28	17.9	102.3	38.0	96.5	1890	92.1	3,190	54	46.6
Woonsocket city & MCD (Providence)	1,336	3247	532	2715	764	8	100.0	147.2	67.5	95.5	1401	147.3	3,584	80	202.3
SOUTH CAROLINA	191,269	3958	498	3460	5,424,387	27,537	77.9	X	X	X	X	X	X	X	X
Aiken city	1,620	5319	348	4971	26,123	182	72.5	42.7	5.6	22.9	790	40.3	1,341	206	2.8
Anderson city	2,429	8953	992	7962	3,695	32	56.3	40.2	4.0	38.2	735	43.2	1,613	63	125.4
Beaufort city	1,005	7678	741	6937	10,549	32	100.0	23.4	1.5	15.4	1378	18.3	1,452	215	21.1
Berea CDP	NA	NA	NA	NA	NA	NA	NA	NA	NA	NA	NA	NA	NA	NA	NA
Bluffton town	494	3591	240	3352	213,544	585	100.0	14.9	2.1	31.4	786	14.7	1,068	206	17.9
Cayce city	781	6036	734	5302	6,627	36	100.0	15.6	0.2	48.8	584	12.5	987	96	57.9
Charleston city	3,257	2508	210	2298	114,237	978	61.3	207.6	27.8	72.1	1053	178.8	1,424	222	74.3
Clemson city	524	3650	181	3469	14,285	156	20.5	21.9	5.6	60.8	698	12.7	902	111	8.4
Columbia city	8,280	6173	772	5401	63,341	546	37.4	222.0	28.7	56.5	721	189.3	1,435	255	505.3
Conway city	1,175	5931	692	5240	33,422	249	76.7	20.3	3.1	39.0	515	22.4	1,204	278	2.5
Dentsville CDP	NA	NA	NA	NA	NA	NA	NA	NA	NA	NA	NA	NA	NA	NA	NA
Easley city	1,328	6522	467	6055	14,394	72	87.5	21.6	4.2	100.0	498	26.7	1,326	186	49.1
Five Forks CDP	NA	NA	NA	NA	NA	NA	NA	NA	NA	NA	NA	NA	NA	NA	NA

1 Data for serious crimes have not been adjusted for underreporting. This may affect comparability between geographic areas over time.
2 Per 100,000 population estimated by the FBI.   3 Based on population estimated as of July 1 of the year shown.

Table B. Incorporated Places, Census Designated Places (CDPs), and Minor Civil Divisions (MCDs) of 10,000 or More Population — Land Area, Population, and Households, and Employment

STATE City, town, township, borough, or CDP (county if applicable)	Land area,[1] 2010 (sq mi)	Total persons 2010	Total persons 2014	Percent change 2010–2014	Persons per square mile, 2014	Foreign born	Lives in same house as previous year	Median household income (dollars)	Income of $100,000 or more	Income below poverty level	Percent in labor force	Unemployment rate	Family households	One person households
	1	2	3	4	5	6	7	8	9	10	11	12	13	14
SOUTH CAROLINA—Con.														
Florence city	21.196	37,023	37,961	2.5	1,790.9	2.3	84.6	$43,007	16.5	19.4	65.5	12.1	66.0	30.4
Forest Acres city	4.600	10,401	10,603	1.9	2,305.1	5.2	83.7	$51,974	26.7	12.8	65.6	9.4	54.3	41.4
Fort Mill town	16.529	11,283	13,087	16.0	791.8	4.1	82.3	$61,100	30.3	11.6	69.4	6.4	68.3	30.8
Gaffney city	8.347	12,545	12,597	0.4	1,509.1	1.6	88.8	$29,943	9.4	25.6	51.0	13.4	56.6	38.1
Gantt CDP	9.914	14,229	NA	NA	NA	8.1	84.7	$30,154	8.1	26.4	57.4	14.9	64.3	30.4
Goose Creek city	40.199	36,145	40,370	11.7	1,004.2	5.8	74.8	$62,107	21.5	10.4	71.8	9.3	75.4	19.7
Greenville city	28.772	59,153	62,252	5.2	2,163.6	7.0	76.2	$41,147	19.6	19.4	65.6	9.7	49.3	42.9
Greenwood city	16.253	23,285	23,236	-0.2	1,429.6	6.7	76.7	$24,760	7.2	29.9	57.7	14.9	57.6	35.5
Greer city	19.924	25,595	27,676	8.1	1,389.1	11.9	79.8	$44,111	17.9	17.4	69.0	7.3	64.6	29.1
Hanahan city	10.597	17,994	19,865	10.4	1,874.6	10.8	81.7	$49,871	17.7	13.4	68.6	6.9	63.5	30.7
Hilton Head Island town	41.363	37,096	40,039	7.9	968.0	14.6	83.7	$68,437	31.6	8.9	54.5	5.9	65.3	28.2
Irmo town	6.542	11,118	11,893	7.0	1,818.0	2.6	90.8	$55,829	16.8	11.3	72.4	6.5	71.7	25.7
James Island town	4.743	11,217	11,630	3.7	2,452.0	2.1	91.0	$62,301	27.4	9.9	61.7	9.6	59.4	34.4
Ladson CDP	7.023	13,790	NA	NA	NA	5.3	84.0	$49,359	13.8	10.5	67.4	11.9	78.3	19.4
Lexington town	8.998	17,887	19,893	11.2	2,210.8	6.3	76.2	$61,166	26.6	10.7	64.8	5.4	63.1	31.6
Mauldin city	9.892	23,138	24,823	7.3	2,509.3	6.7	83.2	$56,619	21.2	6.8	67.2	6.6	65.9	28.9
Mount Pleasant town	45.128	67,854	77,796	14.7	1,723.9	4.6	81.0	$76,202	38.1	8.0	71.4	6.2	65.2	27.2
Myrtle Beach city	23.500	27,105	29,992	10.7	1,276.3	16.8	82.3	$37,064	14.0	18.1	65.0	11.2	54.3	35.4
Newberry city	8.607	10,281	10,268	-0.1	1,193.0	9.1	74.1	$32,759	9.4	29.9	56.3	10.0	63.6	31.9
North Augusta city	20.326	21,327	22,300	4.6	1,097.1	4.8	84.0	$50,771	20.1	10.7	61.9	8.9	67.3	29.2
North Charleston city	73.402	97,601	106,749	9.4	1,454.3	8.6	74.6	$39,446	11.5	21.0	68.4	11.8	61.9	30.5
North Myrtle Beach city	20.112	13,802	15,174	9.9	754.5	7.7	82.9	$45,780	15.7	12.8	53.0	8.8	54.1	38.9
Oak Grove CDP	6.671	10,291	NA	NA	NA	3.9	83.1	$47,804	13.0	8.1	69.3	6.3	63.4	27.9
Orangeburg city	8.982	13,960	13,553	-2.9	1,508.9	3.1	77.4	$28,967	7.4	28.7	48.4	14.5	58.4	36.4
Parker CDP	6.822	11,431	NA	NA	NA	9.8	82.6	$29,164	4.5	32.1	58.6	17.0	71.5	21.5
Port Royal town	18.988	10,689	11,870	11.0	625.1	4.3	59.6	$46,643	14.5	13.3	77.5	4.9	62.8	32.4
Red Hill CDP	11.205	13,223	NA	NA	NA	8.7	75.8	$41,291	10.9	18.0	61.4	6.0	60.6	29.4
Rock Hill city	36.520	66,474	69,967	5.3	1,915.8	4.8	78.4	$40,718	13.7	19.5	68.3	11.5	60.7	31.5
St. Andrews CDP	6.281	20,493	NA	NA	NA	4.8	69.7	$33,575	6.1	19.8	72.9	12.4	49.7	39.1
Seven Oaks CDP	7.584	15,144	NA	NA	NA	5.2	80.2	$47,341	15.6	13.4	70.1	7.4	63.6	31.0
Simpsonville city	8.472	18,401	20,125	9.4	2,375.4	8.2	83.4	$55,910	17.1	8.5	72.7	6.4	69.4	26.8
Socastee CDP	13.347	19,952	NA	NA	NA	9.3	78.8	$37,634	6.8	18.3	64.5	10.2	62.7	27.8
Spartanburg city	19.767	36,757	37,525	2.1	1,898.4	3.8	78.4	$34,092	10.5	25.6	58.2	13.7	58.4	36.9
Summerville town	17.784	42,590	46,974	10.3	2,641.3	3.5	78.1	$55,290	21.4	12.0	66.8	10.7	69.1	26.3
Sumter city	32.282	40,524	40,929	1.0	1,267.8	3.9	79.4	$39,072	13.2	20.1	60.9	14.5	63.5	31.9
Taylors CDP	10.688	21,617	NA	NA	NA	8.6	86.5	$48,871	15.1	12.0	65.0	6.8	71.1	24.3
Wade Hampton CDP	8.914	20,622	NA	NA	NA	6.4	86.5	$45,993	19.2	11.1	63.4	6.2	61.2	34.9
West Columbia city	7.178	15,262	15,920	4.3	2,217.9	14.4	79.3	$40,931	13.6	15.5	64.0	8.9	45.9	43.7
SOUTH DAKOTA	75,810.997	814,191	853,175	4.8	11.3	2.9	83.7	$50,338	17.2	13.0	69.1	4.8	64.4	29.5
Aberdeen city	15.839	26,091	27,800	6.6	1,755.2	3.4	79.8	$47,540	15.0	14.0	70.7	3.0	58.4	36.0
Brookings city	13.359	22,073	23,225	5.2	1,738.6	5.7	60.5	$41,061	13.7	19.6	70.3	4.1	52.5	32.7
Huron city	9.513	12,592	13,163	4.5	1,383.7	11.9	86.5	$39,927	9.5	18.9	67.0	3.1	58.4	36.4
Mitchell city	11.219	15,278	15,693	2.7	1,398.8	2.4	78.8	$47,622	14.0	13.1	68.8	3.7	56.2	38.1
Pierre city	13.059	13,646	14,054	3.0	1,076.2	1.6	79.2	$52,961	21.9	10.4	72.4	2.3	57.1	39.9
Rapid City city	55.438	67,964	72,638	6.9	1,310.3	1.8	77.1	$46,392	15.1	13.6	67.8	5.9	59.6	33.1
Sioux Falls city	73.333	153,897	168,586	9.5	2,298.9	7.1	81.9	$52,607	18.8	11.7	74.7	4.6	61.8	30.4
Spearfish city	16.457	10,532	11,091	5.3	673.9	2.1	74.6	$39,758	16.1	20.8	66.4	4.5	56.3	34.8
Vermillion city	4.117	10,578	10,699	1.1	2,598.9	4.0	56.5	$28,690	11.8	37.6	64.3	9.7	39.4	33.5
Watertown city	17.684	21,517	22,057	2.5	1,247.3	1.2	81.6	$45,185	11.4	12.7	71.5	3.5	57.8	34.5
Yankton city	8.284	14,454	14,552	0.7	1,756.7	1.9	81.0	$42,250	14.9	16.8	62.9	3.7	57.4	37.0
TENNESSEE	41,234.894	6,346,275	6,549,352	3.2	158.8	4.7	84.6	$44,621	16.2	16.7	61.4	9.5	66.7	28.1
Arlington town	23.059	11,517	11,634	1.0	504.5	4.0	92.6	$97,500	47.7	2.7	75.2	2.3	91.8	5.7
Athens city	15.535	13,563	13,664	0.7	879.6	7.4	72.7	$31,807	10.5	25.5	56.7	10.3	57.7	38.0
Bartlett city	32.276	56,922	58,264	2.4	1,805.2	4.0	91.1	$80,240	35.7	4.4	67.9	6.3	79.4	17.6
Brentwood city	41.195	37,060	40,982	10.6	994.8	8.0	90.1	$138,395	66.3	2.1	65.3	4.0	89.3	9.2
Bristol city	32.585	26,709	26,729	0.1	820.3	2.1	82.3	$35,959	10.7	19.7	55.7	9.4	60.9	33.4
Brownsville city	10.202	10,292	9,974	-3.1	977.6	0.9	81.2	$29,162	6.4	27.9	57.0	13.1	56.1	39.9
Chattanooga city	142.039	168,828	173,778	2.9	1,223.5	5.4	80.7	$39,683	14.0	20.6	61.6	10.7	57.3	35.4
Clarksville city	98.276	132,963	146,806	10.4	1,493.8	6.4	73.1	$47,489	12.2	16.3	66.4	10.8	71.7	22.3
Cleveland city	26.892	41,285	43,182	4.6	1,605.7	8.2	76.4	$37,325	13.2	22.7	59.7	11.1	61.5	31.4
Collierville town	36.023	45,604	48,655	6.7	1,350.7	6.4	89.6	$106,783	53.6	3.2	70.5	6.2	84.3	14.3
Columbia city	31.805	34,685	36,071	4.0	1,134.1	4.9	81.4	$34,325	9.2	20.3	61.5	10.7	61.5	33.3
Cookeville city	32.732	30,557	31,335	2.5	957.3	8.0	77.8	$29,240	10.6	32.6	53.3	13.7	51.3	34.1
Crossville city	20.159	10,832	11,330	4.6	562.0	3.9	75.9	$27,946	9.0	24.8	50.7	10.1	63.9	31.4
Dickson city	20.144	14,658	14,993	2.3	744.3	2.2	82.5	$34,869	10.9	17.9	58.8	7.2	68.4	27.7
Dyersburg city	17.351	17,145	16,839	-1.8	970.5	2.2	81.2	$34,444	10.8	21.1	53.6	10.0	64.7	30.7
East Ridge city	8.281	20,979	21,317	1.6	2,574.1	7.3	79.8	$39,445	6.3	13.4	65.0	6.4	59.2	36.1
Elizabethton city	9.769	14,308	14,271	-0.3	1,460.9	1.0	83.7	$28,721	8.5	23.3	49.9	10.4	62.3	36.0
Farragut town	16.022	20,673	21,687	4.9	1,353.6	7.2	89.8	$104,715	52.1	3.3	61.5	5.4	78.7	19.5
Franklin city	41.302	62,601	70,612	12.8	1,709.6	9.5	81.4	$81,432	41.1	7.2	70.8	5.3	69.5	27.3
Gallatin city	31.635	30,399	33,347	9.7	1,054.1	6.6	78.2	$46,279	17.6	13.1	62.5	7.7	70.3	25.6
Germantown city	19.979	38,844	39,267	1.1	1,965.4	7.1	91.1	$110,169	55.8	3.3	63.6	4.2	78.2	19.1
Goodlettsville city	14.206	15,921	16,991	6.7	1,196.0	4.0	84.8	$52,648	19.6	12.0	64.0	9.8	65.5	29.5
Greeneville town	17.014	15,062	15,035	-0.2	883.7	4.6	84.0	$32,869	9.0	26.0	51.0	10.0	61.3	35.2
Hendersonville city	31.429	51,328	55,153	7.5	1,754.8	4.8	84.3	$61,514	25.9	8.1	69.9	5.6	73.2	23.2
Jackson city	58.613	66,929	67,319	0.6	1,148.5	4.3	82.9	$37,988	14.1	21.7	60.2	11.7	62.9	32.3
Johnson City city	42.825	63,476	65,813	3.7	1,536.8	5.2	81.1	$39,121	17.7	22.8	59.9	6.2	56.1	33.6
Kingsport city	53.202	52,777	53,028	0.5	996.7	2.2	83.7	$38,333	14.4	18.3	54.3	10.1	62.3	34.0
Knoxville city	98.524	178,764	184,281	3.1	1,870.4	5.6	81.7	$33,494	10.1	21.8	61.0	7.9	46.6	44.0
Lakeland city	23.518	12,430	12,564	1.1	534.2	7.4	90.7	$91,620	45.7	3.9	71.1	4.6	74.2	21.6
La Vergne city	24.934	32,588	34,274	5.2	1,374.6	13.2	86.1	$53,672	15.7	8.0	74.5	8.8	76.0	19.1
Lawrenceburg city	12.648	10,407	10,498	0.9	830.0	4.1	82.5	$27,100	6.8	23.9	53.3	17.6	57.2	37.5

1 Dry land or land partially or temporarily covered by water.
2 16 years old and over.

624 SC(Florence city)—TN(Lawrenceburg city)   Items 1–14

Table B. Incorporated Places, Census Designated Places (CDPs), and Minor Civil Divisions (MCDs) of 10,000 or More Population — **Crime, Construction, and Local Government Finance**

STATE City, town, township, borough, or CDP (county if applicable)	Serious crimes known to police, 2014[1] Total number	Rate[2] Total	Rate[2] Violent	Rate[2] Property	New residential construction authorized by building permits, 2014 Value ($1,000)	Number of housing units	Percent single family	Local government finance, 2012 General revenue Total (mil dol)	Intergovernmental Total (mil dol)	Intergovernmental Percent from state gov.	Taxes per capita[3]	General expenditure Total (mil dol)	Per capita[3] Total	Per capita[3] Capital outlays	Debt outstanding (mil dol)
	15	16	17	18	19	20	21	22	23	24	25	26	27	28	29
SOUTH CAROLINA—Con.															
Florence city	3,128	8242	843	7399	NA	NA	NA	47.5	3.6	40.8	603	40.8	1,086	63	139.9
Forest Acres city	493	4652	727	3925	4,271	17	100.0	6.5	0.3	7.3	536	5.1	484	33	0.0
Fort Mill town	264	2085	245	1841	106,505	253	100.0	11.4	0.9	53.3	586	8.6	725	35	9.3
Gaffney city	586	4621	662	3958	NA	NA	NA	11.1	1.9	18.0	658	10.5	837	39	1.8
Gantt CDP	NA	NA	NA	NA	NA	NA	NA	NA	NA	NA	NA	NA	NA	NA	NA
Goose Creek city	988	2425	248	2177	20,045	124	100.0	19.6	0.7	100.0	298	20.5	528	67	1.4
Greenville city	3,397	5486	809	4677	116,948	1,037	18.0	95.3	5.9	100.0	1066	99.6	1,643	290	94.3
Greenwood city	1,671	7142	996	6146	NA	NA	NA	16.3	5.3	53.0	405	16.2	694	106	35.8
Greer city	903	3279	356	2923	41,896	230	100.0	28.9	2.8	31.9	593	45.5	1,711	36	93.7
Hanahan city	380	1900	215	1685	42,553	734	11.4	8.5	2.5	100.0	249	8.5	445	40	2.4
Hilton Head Island town	NA	NA	NA	NA	73,028	146	100.0	89.1	35.5	16.2	1261	94.8	2,471	1,299	127.7
Irmo town	394	3314	530	2784	NA	NA	NA	4.3	0.3	100.0	244	4.6	402	35	0.0
James Island town	NA	NA	NA	NA	NA	NA	NA	NA	NA	NA	NA	NA	NA	NA	NA
Ladson CDP	NA	NA	NA	NA	NA	NA	NA	NA	NA	NA	NA	NA	NA	NA	NA
Lexington town	754	3770	320	3450	10,179	80	100.0	19.1	1.0	82.9	422	36.7	1,915	1,158	60.7
Mauldin city	578	2324	181	2143	6,789	68	100.0	17.5	0.8	70.9	574	16.4	682	113	6.3
Mount Pleasant town	1,502	1958	180	1778	326,540	1,332	55.5	114.5	34.1	60.2	833	106.8	1,486	667	99.4
Myrtle Beach city	5,171	17419	1438	15981	137,719	452	98.0	161.3	12.2	83.8	2918	123.3	4,360	375	216.4
Newberry city	613	5982	498	5485	180	2	100.0	15.0	4.9	15.0	460	15.1	1,469	438	18.7
North Augusta city	864	3850	138	3712	25,405	115	100.0	28.9	5.5	29.7	521	26.6	1,212	313	12.5
North Charleston city	6,538	6192	724	5468	45,780	450	85.8	122.2	14.2	23.7	915	119.1	1,168	208	186.0
North Myrtle Beach city	1,899	12596	677	11920	67,935	287	95.1	50.3	5.7	77.9	1767	41.6	2,877	422	31.4
Oak Grove CDP	NA	NA	NA	NA	NA	NA	NA	NA	NA	NA	NA	NA	NA	NA	NA
Orangeburg city	760	5476	656	4821	225	4	100.0	17.2	0.8	62.3	552	20.7	1,493	217	8.7
Parker CDP	NA	NA	NA	NA	NA	NA	NA	NA	NA	NA	NA	NA	NA	NA	NA
Port Royal town	342	2911	306	2604	21,635	91	100.0	6.1	0.3	100.0	413	6.8	604	114	1.1
Red Hill CDP	NA	NA	NA	NA	NA	NA	NA	NA	NA	NA	NA	NA	NA	NA	NA
Rock Hill city	2,733	3918	515	3403	139,828	834	28.1	88.3	12.8	15.4	525	102.2	1,502	271	186.9
St. Andrews CDP	NA	NA	NA	NA	NA	NA	NA	NA	NA	NA	NA	NA	NA	NA	NA
Seven Oaks CDP	NA	NA	NA	NA	NA	NA	NA	NA	NA	NA	NA	NA	NA	NA	NA
Simpsonville city	886	4448	296	4152	32,216	201	100.0	16.6	2.9	16.8	576	13.2	687	95	6.8
Socastee CDP	NA	NA	NA	NA	NA	NA	NA	NA	NA	NA	NA	NA	NA	NA	NA
Spartanburg city	2,806	7424	960	6464	3,547	15	100.0	53.3	13.1	6.6	895	42.1	1,130	160	205.6
Summerville town	1,773	3788	299	3489	101,302	594	56.1	29.5	3.1	88.8	494	26.9	608	53	7.9
Sumter city	2,253	5450	779	4671	NA	NA	NA	43.8	6.9	24.7	587	40.1	980	178	45.0
Taylors CDP	NA	NA	NA	NA	NA	NA	NA	NA	NA	NA	NA	NA	NA	NA	NA
Wade Hampton CDP	NA	NA	NA	NA	NA	NA	NA	NA	NA	NA	NA	NA	NA	NA	NA
West Columbia city	902	5665	1017	4648	9,136	55	100.0	11.6	1.2	48.1	437	17.1	1,090	274	34.9
SOUTH DAKOTA	18,688	2190	327	1864	689,248	4,722	59.3	X	X	X	X	X	X	X	X
Aberdeen city	623	2255	279	1976	7,623	119	52.1	39.6	5.1	70.4	900	38.1	1,414	18	63.9
Brookings city	377	1629	99	1529	16,958	153	47.1	96.9	1.1	58.7	639	93.9	4,149	763	31.3
Huron city	NA	NA	NA	NA	2,651	15	100.0	18.6	0.6	73.5	815	14.9	1,141	99	8.3
Mitchell city	650	4167	436	3731	3,204	25	68.0	26.7	2.4	31.3	1025	25.7	1,659	172	22.4
Pierre city	486	3456	348	3108	9,928	103	19.4	27.2	9.2	81.8	719	29.4	2,116	734	30.2
Rapid City city	3,140	4393	599	3794	47,733	323	62.2	138.0	19.9	85.8	1077	126.9	1,813	706	113.7
Sioux Falls city	5,694	3403	445	2958	233,076	1,878	44.8	226.3	20.3	62.2	933	225.7	1,408	474	307.2
Spearfish city	346	3077	222	2854	28,191	155	56.1	15.5	1.2	72.4	862	13.1	1,219	207	23.8
Vermillion city	268	2499	308	2192	3,090	40	30.0	12.0	0.6	85.0	542	9.7	898	105	25.0
Watertown city	549	2482	262	2220	13,698	127	40.2	32.2	4.0	51.0	809	36.1	1,655	640	58.7
Yankton city	498	3406	376	3030	7,311	56	42.9	19.8	1.4	50.4	770	19.5	1,344	248	29.8
TENNESSEE	240,295	3669	608	3061	4,550,319	27,632	64.7	X	X	X	X	X	X	X	X
Arlington town	NA	NA	NA	NA	NA	NA	NA	13.4	6.4	84.0	330	9.1	784	280	9.7
Athens city	1,112	8152	1151	7001	1,861	21	52.4	24.1	16.3	74.4	407	28.8	2,114	189	13.0
Bartlett city	1,155	1973	268	1705	39,831	202	100.0	55.6	18.3	51.6	361	47.7	820	25	40.8
Brentwood city	376	923	47	876	98,465	251	100.0	49.5	19.7	38.7	463	45.0	1,153	330	29.8
Bristol city	1,094	4112	459	3654	6,011	32	87.5	75.0	35.6	60.9	999	74.6	2,797	336	50.2
Brownsville city	606	6086	1426	4660	403	4	100.0	9.8	5.0	32.4	308	10.5	1,049	1	0.0
Chattanooga city	12,697	7278	973	6306	133,327	1,127	31.0	485.4	165.9	19.7	809	396.3	2,300	197	733.3
Clarksville city	5,255	3633	671	2963	104,767	987	86.1	137.4	38.8	51.1	262	103.9	725	103	870.1
Cleveland city	2,960	6862	858	6004	25,554	330	21.2	109.5	65.6	56.3	464	96.6	2,278	237	130.0
Collierville town	857	1795	157	1637	50,351	142	100.0	56.6	15.9	37.4	547	51.4	1,107	164	60.9
Columbia city	1,452	4060	624	3437	9,246	77	100.0	41.4	15.4	53.0	360	40.7	1,166	252	73.5
Cookeville city	1,525	4879	400	4479	24,777	209	63.2	277.1	19.0	22.5	303	277.4	8,954	919	143.9
Crossville city	1,079	9516	847	8669	33,329	246	81.7	19.6	11.8	42.2	373	19.6	1,762	574	32.7
Dickson city	925	6158	746	5412	12,386	102	37.3	15.5	7.1	36.8	416	12.3	833	5	35.3
Dyersburg city	1,589	9364	1273	8091	1,245	7	100.0	64.5	39.1	68.5	651	56.9	3,342	271	34.0
East Ridge city	1,179	5489	764	4726	1,048	12	100.0	13.4	5.0	54.7	277	12.1	567	40	6.3
Elizabethton city	897	6240	410	5830	1,053	5	100.0	36.7	22.5	73.2	564	44.0	3,075	110	59.6
Farragut town	NA	NA	NA	NA	37,875	111	100.0	9.0	7.1	40.7	58	8.2	386	89	0.0
Franklin city	1,101	1562	139	1423	203,262	801	59.6	87.6	39.1	37.2	368	85.2	1,285	230	172.8
Gallatin city	570	1740	317	1423	78,927	368	100.0	34.4	11.7	42.9	376	33.1	1,045	154	47.2
Germantown city	480	1215	81	1134	NA	NA	NA	61.8	21.1	73.1	627	65.4	1,661	429	32.1
Goodlettsville city	755	4432	346	4086	4,959	14	100.0	17.8	6.4	38.0	295	18.0	1,097	266	14.2
Greeneville town	740	4930	553	4377	5,144	19	63.2	56.7	32.8	55.3	892	43.8	2,923	99	50.7
Hendersonville city	853	1559	181	1378	32,797	198	100.0	35.8	16.0	45.5	260	34.8	655	51	11.8
Jackson city	3,802	5602	1083	4519	31,835	149	100.0	87.7	28.3	31.7	609	83.5	1,243	137	119.1
Johnson City city	2,611	3984	366	3618	53,862	462	46.3	163.0	78.4	55.6	732	167.9	2,594	204	422.8
Kingsport city	2,957	5578	604	4975	20,288	105	84.8	166.0	83.1	48.9	1080	164.5	3,118	644	225.1
Knoxville city	13,656	7407	875	6532	83,013	861	21.0	351.6	81.3	38.7	898	318.2	1,747	425	920.7
Lakeland city	NA	NA	NA	NA	NA	NA	NA	6.2	2.9	83.7	46	5.8	464	131	11.3
La Vergne city	768	2231	502	1728	9,922	56	100.0	25.4	7.8	50.3	306	18.7	553	55	25.9
Lawrenceburg city	687	6575	881	5695	1,604	10	60.0	14.3	5.3	31.2	387	13.0	1,241	89	53.5

1 Data for serious crimes have not been adjusted for underreporting. This may affect comparability between geographic areas over time.
2 Per 100,000 population estimated by the FBI.   3 Based on population estimated as of July 1 of the year shown.

Table B. Incorporated Places, Census Designated Places (CDPs), and Minor Civil Divisions (MCDs) of 10,000 or More Population — **Land Area, Population, and Households, and Employment**

STATE City, town, township, borough, or CDP (county if applicable)	Land area,[1] 2010 (sq mi)	Population Total persons 2010	Total persons 2014	Percent change 2010–2014	Persons per square mile, 2014	Population characteristics 2010–2014 Foreign born	Lives in same house as previous year	Household income and poverty, 2010–2014 Median household income (dollars)	Percent of households Income of $100,000 or more	Income below poverty level	Employment,[2] 2010–2014 Percent in labor force	Unemploy-ment rate	Households, 2010–2014 (percent of households) Family households	One person households
	1	2	3	4	5	6	7	8	9	10	11	12	13	14
TENNESSEE—Con.														
Lebanon city	38.365	26,156	29,427	12.5	767.0	6.6	79.1	$41,051	14.9	16.5	61.5	11.1	64.1	31.9
Lewisburg city	13.376	11,100	11,371	2.4	850.1	6.0	83.6	$32,348	7.5	22.3	58.9	14.3	66.1	28.4
McMinnville city	11.066	13,605	13,620	0.1	1,230.8	6.9	83.2	$28,535	7.3	26.7	50.3	7.0	56.7	37.0
Manchester city	14.190	10,113	10,349	2.3	729.3	7.3	80.3	$38,063	6.7	24.8	56.6	8.5	64.3	30.6
Martin city	12.685	11,468	11,322	-1.3	892.6	1.9	66.4	$30,189	10.8	37.0	56.3	16.2	52.4	32.4
Maryville city	16.801	27,466	28,329	3.1	1,686.2	3.5	83.6	$52,120	20.8	14.3	59.2	7.5	66.0	31.2
Memphis city	317.373	651,858	656,861	0.8	2,069.7	6.2	80.2	$37,099	12.6	23.4	64.0	13.4	59.4	34.5
Middle Valley CDP	10.653	12,684	NA	NA	NA	4.4	92.0	$58,813	23.3	8.0	62.8	7.2	76.1	20.0
Millington city	33.245	11,149	11,080	-0.6	333.3	3.8	77.6	$48,779	15.1	21.2	63.0	8.5	60.1	31.7
Morristown city	27.320	28,988	29,304	1.1	1,072.6	10.8	83.5	$31,082	8.0	27.4	54.8	12.7	66.1	29.0
Mount Juliet city	23.244	24,760	29,387	18.7	1,264.3	5.4	87.3	$73,512	29.4	8.7	70.7	6.3	76.1	20.3
Murfreesboro city	55.876	109,046	120,954	10.9	2,164.7	6.7	73.1	$50,337	19.3	16.7	68.8	8.4	60.9	27.8
Nashville-Davidson metropolitan government	504.032	626,663	668,347	6.7	1,326.0	11.8	79.4	$47,434	18.2	16.0	69.0	8.2	55.7	35.4
Nashville-Davidson metropolitan government (balance)	475.932	603,506	644,014	6.7	1,353.2	12.1	79.2	$46,758	17.4	16.2	69.2	8.2	55.2	35.8
Oak Ridge city	85.273	29,330	29,303	-0.1	343.6	6.7	82.2	$52,534	24.3	14.3	61.3	9.5	59.6	35.5
Paris city	13.013	10,166	10,156	-0.1	780.5	1.8	71.5	$29,705	8.5	28.8	54.4	15.7	60.7	35.4
Portland city	14.258	11,486	12,218	6.4	856.9	1.8	77.3	$51,027	9.6	14.3	65.4	10.0	73.8	22.2
Red Bank city	6.555	11,653	11,784	1.1	1,797.8	7.2	76.6	$37,678	11.1	19.9	69.1	8.2	55.0	36.9
Sevierville city	24.136	14,788	16,355	10.6	677.6	12.4	77.6	$34,167	12.4	22.3	64.8	8.1	61.9	29.7
Seymour CDP	12.629	10,919	NA	NA	NA	2.3	84.5	$54,386	10.4	8.1	63.6	7.4	71.1	24.3
Shelbyville city	18.600	20,334	21,037	3.5	1,131.0	14.6	84.2	$27,743	5.1	27.5	54.6	8.7	71.1	22.6
Smyrna town	29.590	39,976	45,274	13.3	1,530.0	8.3	81.8	$52,516	17.9	12.7	71.6	7.6	65.6	28.2
Soddy-Daisy city	23.221	12,934	13,190	2.0	568.0	0.9	85.7	$42,937	16.3	9.6	58.5	9.7	76.4	20.8
Springfield city	13.443	16,478	16,752	1.7	1,246.1	8.3	82.6	$39,980	10.4	18.6	62.5	10.2	66.8	28.5
Spring Hill city	27.070	29,038	34,269	18.0	1,265.9	4.3	86.9	$76,840	30.7	3.3	75.1	3.4	78.9	18.0
Tullahoma city	23.495	18,655	18,899	1.3	804.4	2.1	82.7	$35,665	11.4	17.9	57.8	12.5	66.5	30.7
Union City city	12.327	10,912	10,666	-2.3	865.3	2.1	81.3	$35,051	9.4	24.9	54.1	16.5	69.1	24.5
White House city	11.134	10,273	11,042	7.5	991.7	2.9	90.5	$68,284	17.0	6.2	70.4	7.1	73.2	24.5
TEXAS	261,231.700	25,146,104	26,956,958	7.2	103.2	16.5	83.0	$52,576	22.8	15.7	64.9	7.7	69.6	24.9
Abilene city	106.577	117,463	120,958	3.0	1,134.9	5.9	73.4	$42,766	13.7	17.6	60.1	6.7	64.1	28.6
Addison town	4.379	13,056	15,457	18.4	3,530.1	21.8	60.6	$60,456	27.3	9.5	81.0	3.7	34.9	54.0
Alamo city	7.548	18,518	19,224	3.8	2,547.0	24.0	89.8	$35,188	10.9	24.6	51.6	12.2	75.3	21.7
Aldine CDP	7.900	15,869	NA	NA	NA	40.5	84.3	$35,152	6.9	29.6	61.3	13.2	83.3	14.2
Alice city	11.992	19,109	19,395	1.5	1,617.3	4.6	87.8	$41,621	19.8	21.8	59.5	5.8	73.4	23.1
Allen city	26.388	84,290	94,179	11.7	3,569.1	17.1	87.0	$102,120	51.8	5.1	75.9	5.2	81.4	15.0
Alton city	7.132	13,900	15,497	11.5	2,172.9	35.3	87.2	$28,512	4.3	39.8	59.7	8.9	86.9	10.5
Alvin city	24.291	24,223	25,525	5.4	1,050.8	9.4	82.6	$45,164	17.0	17.3	63.7	7.4	71.2	24.2
Amarillo city	99.898	190,672	197,254	3.5	1,974.6	10.5	80.9	$47,053	17.2	15.5	67.8	5.4	65.4	28.9
Andrews city	5.093	11,083	13,245	19.5	2,600.8	11.1	85.9	$60,579	27.1	10.9	65.6	4.2	73.0	23.9
Angleton city	11.272	18,862	19,472	3.2	1,727.4	9.8	89.8	$53,638	22.1	11.3	64.4	5.5	70.3	24.0
Arlington city	95.896	365,361	383,204	4.9	3,996.0	19.7	79.9	$53,055	21.3	14.9	71.1	8.8	67.9	26.0
Atascocita CDP	25.225	65,844	NA	NA	NA	9.5	82.8	$82,361	39.3	5.6	68.9	6.0	80.6	15.6
Athens city	16.794	12,708	12,819	0.9	763.3	15.1	78.5	$33,470	14.7	23.8	56.4	5.7	65.0	32.2
Austin city	312.424	811,458	912,791	12.5	2,921.6	18.4	74.3	$55,216	24.9	15.7	73.2	6.8	52.5	34.0
Azle city	8.821	10,947	11,530	5.3	1,307.1	2.6	80.6	$54,171	18.4	13.8	60.6	4.4	65.9	30.8
Balch Springs city	8.990	23,876	25,120	5.2	2,794.2	22.7	85.9	$39,874	9.1	24.2	61.5	8.9	78.7	17.4
Bay City city	8.776	17,618	17,368	-1.4	1,979.0	9.7	86.0	$38,859	16.6	22.1	61.1	7.6	67.6	29.4
Baytown city	38.558	72,024	76,127	5.7	1,974.4	17.9	79.5	$46,776	16.6	19.0	60.9	11.7	71.7	24.4
Beaumont city	82.134	117,267	117,585	0.3	1,431.6	9.9	84.4	$39,191	15.7	21.5	59.9	10.6	61.5	33.3
Bedford city	10.017	46,979	48,908	4.1	4,882.7	8.6	82.6	$60,373	25.4	7.7	71.0	6.1	60.1	34.3
Beeville city	6.173	12,863	13,303	3.4	2,154.9	4.0	81.5	$36,989	7.5	24.8	58.2	8.1	66.3	28.6
Bellaire city	3.592	16,855	18,252	8.3	5,080.7	19.9	88.9	$169,663	69.0	3.2	66.4	3.6	76.8	21.0
Bellmead city	6.833	9,901	10,184	2.9	1,490.4	14.8	79.2	$34,213	8.2	26.1	64.1	10.2	69.0	23.4
Belton city	18.813	18,223	20,128	10.5	1,069.9	8.1	81.7	$51,742	19.9	17.3	59.3	6.7	67.1	27.4
Benbrook city	11.511	21,234	22,419	5.6	1,947.6	5.0	87.0	$64,553	28.2	6.9	64.9	5.0	65.7	31.1
Big Spring city	19.100	27,282	28,472	4.4	1,490.7	12.1	78.8	$43,750	13.3	17.1	47.9	7.9	62.8	31.0
Boerne city	10.490	10,603	12,835	21.1	1,223.6	8.4	78.8	$57,027	26.5	11.8	60.6	6.0	64.7	30.1
Bonham city	9.833	10,127	10,058	-0.7	1,022.9	8.5	67.0	$33,449	7.4	23.7	38.6	16.8	57.1	37.0
Borger city	8.789	13,350	12,978	-2.8	1,476.6	9.2	87.0	$42,792	14.8	18.9	62.8	6.1	64.3	32.2
Brenham city	12.041	15,716	16,297	3.7	1,353.5	6.9	81.7	$43,506	16.1	19.0	54.0	5.1	66.1	28.5
Brownsville city	132.444	174,982	183,046	4.6	1,382.1	29.7	88.3	$32,348	10.7	33.9	57.5	10.9	81.1	17.3
Brownwood city	14.832	19,287	18,972	-1.6	1,279.2	6.5	90.2	$37,933	9.7	21.1	56.0	5.2	66.1	28.1
Brushy Creek CDP	6.931	21,764	NA	NA	NA	18.0	83.5	$99,775	49.9	3.3	74.1	7.2	80.7	14.9
Bryan city	45.273	76,218	80,913	6.2	1,787.2	15.0	72.6	$39,231	12.4	24.9	66.5	8.8	59.9	29.9
Burkburnett city	11.331	10,811	11,142	3.1	983.3	2.4	83.5	$50,958	15.0	6.9	64.8	4.7	67.0	29.8
Burleson city	26.020	36,696	41,818	14.0	1,607.1	2.5	83.8	$69,088	27.5	7.8	73.4	6.5	75.2	21.1
Canyon city	6.978	13,312	14,432	8.4	2,068.1	4.7	73.7	$41,080	18.7	25.7	67.5	3.2	59.9	29.6
Canyon Lake CDP	143.332	21,262	NA	NA	NA	3.9	88.1	$53,281	24.6	10.4	54.2	8.8	66.4	26.8
Carrollton city	36.267	119,100	128,353	7.8	3,539.1	26.2	85.1	$69,282	32.6	7.5	75.4	5.6	72.4	22.1
Cedar Hill city	35.843	45,030	48,084	6.8	1,341.5	9.7	88.5	$67,913	27.8	8.4	74.3	7.4	73.9	22.5
Cedar Park city	23.754	51,743	63,574	22.9	2,676.3	11.8	80.9	$79,323	37.1	6.0	72.5	6.6	74.0	20.5
Channelview CDP	14.789	38,289	NA	NA	NA	23.8	85.9	$49,355	16.7	18.3	68.7	11.0	77.1	18.4
Cibolo city	15.113	20,091	25,280	25.8	1,672.7	7.7	85.1	$87,613	42.2	5.0	70.9	4.8	83.9	15.0
Cinco Ranch CDP	4.845	18,274	NA	NA	NA	27.1	86.3	$130,645	63.2	2.7	67.9	3.2	83.0	15.4
Cleburne city	36.257	29,763	29,848	0.3	823.2	11.3	78.0	$48,260	15.0	14.8	60.9	7.3	70.1	23.6
Cloverleaf CDP	3.314	22,942	NA	NA	NA	33.3	83.6	$37,410	13.0	24.3	66.7	13.7	77.6	17.2
Clute city	5.362	11,211	11,392	1.6	2,124.4	19.6	80.9	$43,689	11.4	17.5	67.2	8.6	65.7	28.5
College Station city	50.641	94,061	103,483	10.0	2,043.5	13.1	60.2	$33,434	17.2	34.9	60.2	7.6	46.1	27.7
Colleyville city	13.103	22,805	24,952	9.4	1,904.3	8.7	92.5	$151,169	70.7	1.7	67.7	4.8	89.3	9.6
Conroe city	54.491	56,992	65,871	15.6	1,208.8	21.5	79.6	$46,109	17.6	17.1	64.0	5.2	65.7	27.6
Converse city	6.981	18,198	21,054	15.7	3,016.0	7.9	80.5	$62,627	23.0	9.3	68.0	5.8	76.3	17.8

1 Dry land or land partially or temporarily covered by water.
2 16 years old and over.

Table B. Incorporated Places, Census Designated Places (CDPs), and Minor Civil Divisions (MCDs) of 10,000 or More Population — Crime, Construction, and Local Government Finance

STATE City, town, township, borough, or CDP (county if applicable)	Serious crimes known to police, 2014[1] Total number	Rate[2] Total	Violent	Property	New residential construction authorized by building permits, 2014 Value ($1,000)	Number of housing units	Percent single family	Local government finance, 2012 General revenue Total (mil dol)	Intergovernmental Total (mil dol)	Percent from state gov.	Taxes per capita[3]	General expenditure Total (mil dol)	Per capita[3] Total	Capital outlays	Debt outstanding (mil dol)
	15	16	17	18	19	20	21	22	23	24	25	26	27	28	29
TENNESSEE—Con.															
Lebanon city	1,175	4057	763	3294	56,610	428	63.6	28.1	13.4	31.2	218	31.0	1,113	106	61.0
Lewisburg city	443	3888	1255	2633	NA	NA	NA	18.4	1.4	100.0	304	20.5	1,827	534	30.4
McMinnville city	624	4560	943	3618	635	8	75.0	15.4	4.6	59.7	451	16.9	1,244	227	13.5
Manchester city	NA	NA	NA	NA	5,424	44	63.6	25.7	13.3	72.0	595	28.3	2,767	24	52.6
Martin city	273	2410	256	2154	1,260	13	100.0	2.4	1.3	94.6	78	2.9	254	0	0.0
Maryville city	706	2511	135	2376	18,208	102	100.0	74.6	37.7	68.6	1027	71.2	2,571	85	130.5
Memphis city	50,683	7739	1744	5995	NA	NA	NA	2270.7	1329.3	61.2	789	2276.9	3,451	425	2500.9
Middle Valley CDP	NA	NA	NA	NA	NA	NA	NA	NA	NA	NA	NA	NA	NA	NA	NA
Millington city	593	5345	496	4849	342	2	100.0	26.3	17.4	71.8	318	27.3	2,441	1,223	6.7
Morristown city	1,666	5666	653	5013	5,367	28	100.0	51.1	16.0	22.3	440	46.1	1,582	230	126.8
Mount Juliet city	601	2065	213	1852	163,340	835	43.4	22.7	11.2	42.1	171	17.4	649	72	17.0
Murfreesboro city	4,630	3891	535	3355	195,878	1,734	47.3	157.1	75.8	58.2	422	168.1	1,476	135	318.3
Nashville-Davidson metropolitan government	32,658	4886	1120	3767	953,546	6,367	39.9	2398.7	624.4	98.0	1952	2431.3	3,888	403	4895.0
Nashville-Davidson metropolitan government (balance)	30,909	4772	1125	3647	NA	NA	NA	NA	NA	NA	NA	NA	NA	NA	NA
Oak Ridge city	NA	NA	NA	NA	2,573	19	100.0	134.1	83.4	33.6	1182	107.5	3,666	210	170.4
Paris city	552	5430	423	5007	1,124	13	84.6	12.7	5.3	32.0	235	19.2	1,890	812	16.9
Portland city	402	3319	570	2750	7,883	41	100.0	12.3	4.0	52.4	352	10.6	896	189	13.4
Red Bank city	579	4877	573	4304	2,527	17	100.0	7.6	2.8	65.8	224	6.9	581	80	5.4
Sevierville city	820	5024	558	4467	6,512	34	100.0	47.3	22.4	29.4	383	46.9	3,004	256	245.4
Seymour CDP	NA	NA	NA	NA	NA	NA	NA	NA	NA	NA	NA	NA	NA	NA	NA
Shelbyville city	732	3509	647	2862	9,485	86	25.6	20.3	6.3	45.3	362	28.0	1,362	670	26.0
Smyrna town	1,290	2944	331	2613	30,814	314	77.4	53.2	16.9	24.7	269	50.3	1,205	109	71.6
Soddy-Daisy city	384	2916	243	2673	3,534	20	100.0	6.5	3.1	46.0	233	5.7	432	42	0.0
Springfield city	963	5768	1000	4768	2,455	28	71.4	18.4	6.7	31.9	286	19.0	1,150	164	40.7
Spring Hill city	376	1123	111	1013	101,627	575	99.3	19.8	7.0	49.1	182	26.7	857	343	21.6
Tullahoma city	864	4575	561	4013	5,399	50	100.0	53.5	28.7	70.7	571	58.8	3,139	242	67.0
Union City city	741	6921	560	6360	1,849	6	100.0	25.0	14.8	75.6	513	28.0	2,595	222	9.9
White House city	NA	NA	NA	NA	5,754	52	100.0	11.0	4.0	47.4	307	9.3	880	189	10.3
TEXAS	923,348	3425	406	3019	26,295,841	166,982	59.7	X	X	X	X	X	X	X	X
Abilene city	5,915	4901	473	4428	57,115	278	100.0	137.0	15.0	30.9	697	116.5	972	130	132.7
Addison town	753	4688	417	4271	3,675	18	50.0	61.8	14.1	31.7	2200	72.8	4,793	1,954	66.5
Alamo city	1,389	7290	761	6529	4,032	59	100.0	11.9	1.5	76.0	352	9.2	487	21	14.1
Aldine CDP	NA	NA	NA	NA	NA	NA	NA	NA	NA	NA	NA	NA	NA	NA	NA
Alice city	1,172	5953	726	5226	3,088	24	100.0	26.8	1.1	13.0	995	25.1	1,286	326	24.7
Allen city	1,201	1279	78	1201	231,799	1,333	37.7	117.2	4.4	12.3	873	125.1	1,390	272	179.7
Alton city	263	1718	65	1652	7,734	70	84.3	14.8	9.7	100.0	138	4.5	304	7	6.6
Alvin city	764	3026	265	2760	25,250	132	100.0	23.3	0.3	90.9	605	23.2	930	144	30.9
Amarillo city	10,742	5433	684	4749	164,302	853	55.0	243.2	33.1	39.3	614	262.0	1,339	339	366.9
Andrews city	390	2965	608	2357	16,964	155	34.2	8.7	1.0	2.9	433	7.0	572	56	0.0
Angleton city	473	2487	273	2213	3,104	25	100.0	14.8	0.4	100.0	466	12.8	676	42	19.5
Arlington city	15,316	3999	484	3515	127,751	870	54.0	460.5	35.2	25.8	644	480.0	1,275	145	2154.5
Atascocita CDP	NA	NA	NA	NA	NA	NA	NA	NA	NA	NA	NA	NA	NA	NA	NA
Athens city	585	4562	343	4219	765	4	100.0	13.3	0.5	82.8	765	12.4	966	59	7.9
Austin city	41,025	4539	396	4142	1,105,477	9,442	29.7	1410.8	92.8	27.1	709	1511.5	1,746	382	5572.8
Azle city	NA	NA	NA	NA	6,124	43	100.0	14.5	0.8	8.5	651	14.7	1,308	282	31.5
Balch Springs city	1,312	5185	921	4264	1,530	11	100.0	15.1	1.4	44.8	482	20.2	810	333	10.3
Bay City city	781	4468	315	4153	13,564	150	100.0	17.8	0.3	100.0	514	17.1	976	143	18.2
Baytown city	3,398	4456	316	4140	25,391	190	100.0	105.9	8.6	14.0	589	126.1	1,710	339	189.8
Beaumont city	6,580	5581	891	4690	45,300	354	100.0	168.9	28.1	23.8	782	178.4	1,526	395	353.3
Bedford city	1,540	3144	457	2687	7,435	30	100.0	41.1	0.8	100.0	562	42.9	889	121	61.2
Beeville city	451	3366	209	3157	1,203	11	100.0	11.9	0.0	0.0	531	10.0	762	11	0.6
Bellaire city	356	1968	138	1829	71,977	120	100.0	24.4	0.9	6.8	980	23.5	1,342	213	71.5
Bellmead city	NA	NA	NA	NA	3,880	34	100.0	7.5	0.2	100.0	558	6.7	671	152	0.9
Belton city	1,000	5036	201	4834	19,425	94	93.6	18.3	2.2	45.6	499	19.0	979	281	17.2
Benbrook city	410	1827	125	1702	16,379	48	100.0	18.5	0.0	100.0	679	14.8	675	11	14.1
Big Spring city	1,549	5466	762	4704	3,694	33	87.9	26.6	1.5	86.7	521	29.9	1,081	134	23.3
Boerne city	328	2552	241	2311	56,131	242	100.0	18.3	1.2	43.7	1031	22.1	1,911	601	74.9
Bonham city	253	2536	90	2446	866	21	33.3	11.0	0.3	100.0	465	10.6	1,065	135	0.0
Borger city	581	4478	871	3607	0	0	0.0	14.7	0.8	42.0	591	14.5	1,107	77	16.7
Brenham city	540	3336	327	3008	8,693	85	97.6	23.4	1.3	39.5	863	32.1	2,012	81	55.0
Brownsville city	8,063	4396	304	4091	64,924	609	90.1	224.1	50.4	11.0	415	175.9	976	181	528.4
Brownwood city	855	4526	360	4166	1,783	16	62.5	27.7	1.7	81.0	752	24.2	1,271	163	17.3
Brushy Creek CDP	NA	NA	NA	NA	NA	NA	NA	NA	NA	NA	NA	NA	NA	NA	NA
Bryan city	2,859	3607	426	3180	52,867	251	92.8	85.5	6.5	55.6	522	96.3	1,235	236	362.9
Burkburnett city	321	2909	190	2719	2,264	12	100.0	7.1	0.2	100.0	423	8.4	771	59	11.1
Burleson city	983	2355	165	2190	95,002	593	69.6	54.3	0.2	84.0	897	43.5	1,115	101	130.3
Canyon city	115	818	64	754	8,283	60	36.7	9.4	0.3	100.0	365	7.6	554	36	5.6
Canyon Lake CDP	NA	NA	NA	NA	NA	NA	NA	NA	NA	NA	NA	NA	NA	NA	NA
Carrollton city	2,950	2294	129	2165	206,458	1,586	22.9	128.2	6.2	86.1	708	119.3	951	184	168.5
Cedar Hill city	1,532	3256	198	3058	22,755	106	100.0	54.5	2.8	12.5	748	54.1	1,163	158	156.9
Cedar Park city	1,032	1621	105	1515	130,686	639	93.3	71.9	5.6	100.0	732	67.0	1,156	349	214.5
Channelview CDP	NA	NA	NA	NA	NA	NA	NA	NA	NA	NA	NA	NA	NA	NA	NA
Cibolo city	298	1199	60	1139	87,411	379	100.0	13.7	0.3	87.5	360	14.5	645	208	34.4
Cinco Ranch CDP	NA	NA	NA	NA	NA	NA	NA	NA	NA	NA	NA	NA	NA	NA	NA
Cleburne city	1,079	3629	256	3373	3,975	31	80.6	51.2	3.4	11.5	884	43.9	1,472	106	132.4
Cloverleaf CDP	NA	NA	NA	NA	NA	NA	NA	NA	NA	NA	NA	NA	NA	NA	NA
Clute city	177	1566	133	1433	4,929	30	100.0	11.0	0.5	64.8	486	13.7	1,216	319	0.0
College Station city	2,534	2497	188	2309	201,458	1,535	47.0	94.1	3.3	25.7	549	101.4	1,036	172	242.2
Colleyville city	152	610	40	570	63,233	109	100.0	34.1	0.6	100.0	1070	27.7	1,157	110	30.2
Conroe city	2,463	3822	321	3501	196,962	1,111	78.4	70.6	1.0	16.8	824	74.4	1,211	375	196.2
Converse city	508	2438	422	2016	50,673	230	100.0	12.2	0.6	22.3	392	12.0	609	49	5.5

1 Data for serious crimes have not been adjusted for underreporting. This may affect comparability between geographic areas over time.
2 Per 100,000 population estimated by the FBI. 3 Based on population estimated as of July 1 of the year shown.

Table B. Incorporated Places, Census Designated Places (CDPs), and Minor Civil Divisions (MCDs) of 10,000 or More Population — **Land Area, Population, and Households, and Employment**

STATE City, town, township, borough, or CDP (county if applicable)	Land area,[1] 2010 (sq mi)	Population — Total persons 2010	Total persons 2014	Percent change 2010–2014	Persons per square mile, 2014	Population characteristics 2010–2014 — Foreign born	Lives in same house as previous year	Household income and poverty, 2010–2014 — Median household income (dollars)	Percent of households — Income of $100,000 or more	Income below poverty level	Employment,[2] 2010–2014 — Percent in labor force	Unemployment rate	Households, 2010–2014 (percent of households) — Family households	One person households
	1	2	3	4	5	6	7	8	9	10	11	12	13	14
TEXAS—Con.														
Coppell city	14.438	38,659	40,678	5.2	2,817.5	20.8	85.7	$111,325	56.4	4.4	73.3	4.1	79.0	18.7
Copperas Cove city	17.681	32,169	32,943	2.4	1,863.2	7.4	80.2	$52,948	17.8	9.6	63.1	12.2	75.0	21.9
Corinth city	7.792	19,796	20,836	5.3	2,674.1	6.4	86.1	$85,170	40.6	7.8	73.3	8.3	77.0	19.5
Corpus Christi city	160.536	305,215	320,434	5.0	1,996.0	8.1	79.6	$49,675	19.8	16.7	65.0	7.2	68.2	25.0
Corsicana city	22.230	23,835	23,989	0.6	1,079.1	15.1	80.2	$38,536	9.6	20.4	62.6	12.9	69.7	24.5
Crowley city	7.255	12,838	14,572	13.5	2,008.4	6.6	82.7	$64,836	25.2	7.1	74.3	6.4	77.8	19.8
Dallas city	341.364	1,197,792	1,281,047	7.0	3,752.7	24.2	80.8	$43,359	18.6	20.1	67.8	8.9	57.6	34.4
Deer Park city	10.456	32,010	33,719	5.3	3,224.8	7.5	85.0	$77,612	34.9	7.7	67.7	7.1	80.2	16.9
Del Rio city	20.343	35,926	36,079	0.4	1,773.6	24.8	85.5	$41,110	14.0	21.6	60.7	9.6	73.4	24.6
Denison city	23.034	22,697	22,907	0.9	994.5	3.4	80.6	$36,472	11.4	20.9	57.0	10.2	63.8	31.3
Denton city	93.112	116,207	128,205	10.3	1,376.9	13.5	69.3	$48,518	19.5	21.4	67.6	9.5	57.8	27.9
DeSoto city	21.615	49,027	51,934	5.9	2,402.7	5.1	89.0	$56,911	24.2	12.0	68.2	10.1	70.7	27.0
Dickinson city	9.870	18,679	19,595	4.9	1,985.4	13.1	85.0	$67,083	31.8	10.7	69.5	7.5	78.5	17.9
Donna city	8.292	15,759	16,448	4.4	1,983.6	22.7	87.7	$30,049	6.3	32.7	57.4	17.1	81.3	16.8
Dumas city	5.523	14,691	14,937	1.7	2,704.3	24.8	82.5	$46,475	14.6	15.9	71.4	4.6	78.5	18.8
Duncanville city	11.238	38,544	39,707	3.0	3,533.4	14.2	90.1	$55,100	18.8	11.7	68.1	7.4	74.2	23.7
Eagle Pass city	9.611	26,247	28,329	7.9	2,947.4	32.7	89.0	$35,590	11.7	25.8	58.5	10.5	80.1	19.3
Edinburg city	39.016	74,565	83,014	11.3	2,127.7	19.7	81.8	$42,498	15.6	25.1	64.9	9.1	76.4	17.8
Eidson Road CDP	7.047	8,960	NA	NA	NA	36.6	93.4	$32,668	6.2	28.7	61.8	16.7	84.2	15.0
El Campo city	8.287	11,602	11,577	-0.2	1,397.0	10.7	88.5	$42,491	15.6	19.7	64.9	6.0	69.0	26.9
El Paso city	256.571	649,133	679,036	4.6	2,645.1	24.9	84.6	$42,037	15.1	20.9	60.7	8.6	73.4	23.1
Ennis city	28.116	18,511	18,823	1.7	669.5	13.3	77.5	$43,634	12.0	21.2	67.4	8.9	71.7	22.7
Euless city	16.206	51,295	53,630	4.6	3,309.3	19.3	79.3	$54,619	21.4	11.7	75.4	8.7	60.0	31.8
Farmers Branch city	11.794	28,616	32,560	13.8	2,760.7	23.3	82.1	$58,666	22.3	9.7	69.2	7.7	66.4	28.4
Flower Mound town	41.899	64,685	69,650	7.7	1,662.3	11.4	88.9	$121,549	62.2	2.5	74.1	4.3	85.6	12.4
Forest Hill city	4.245	12,355	12,795	3.6	3,013.9	20.5	89.7	$43,949	7.4	19.3	63.1	11.1	76.5	19.9
Forney city	13.893	14,608	17,536	20.0	1,262.2	4.3	90.1	$72,681	34.4	7.6	74.9	11.2	80.7	14.4
Fort Hood CDP	15.507	29,589	NA	NA	NA	4.6	56.8	$42,603	4.6	12.0	79.0	20.9	96.3	3.2
Fort Worth city	340.703	742,060	812,238	9.5	2,384.0	17.5	81.8	$52,492	20.3	16.9	67.2	8.6	67.3	27.2
Four Corners CDP	2.541	12,382	NA	NA	NA	44.5	95.3	$63,814	29.5	15.9	64.6	5.4	94.1	4.3
Fredericksburg city	8.600	10,530	10,886	3.4	1,265.8	6.0	82.9	$50,645	21.0	13.4	54.6	6.9	60.2	35.0
Freeport city	14.945	12,049	12,191	1.2	815.7	17.6	82.4	$36,341	13.3	24.2	64.0	11.6	69.0	26.9
Fresno CDP	8.786	19,069	NA	NA	NA	14.5	91.4	$66,705	30.6	9.2	71.4	7.4	86.1	11.9
Friendswood city	20.724	35,803	38,248	6.8	1,845.6	8.7	87.7	$95,120	48.5	5.6	64.9	5.7	76.4	20.5
Frisco city	66.389	117,084	145,035	23.9	2,184.6	15.9	84.7	$112,155	57.0	3.6	76.1	4.9	81.1	15.6
Gainesville city	19.010	16,002	16,095	0.6	846.7	15.2	81.3	$37,807	10.6	21.1	67.0	10.2	68.1	28.4
Galena Park city	4.858	10,916	11,178	2.4	2,300.8	37.3	81.6	$43,586	10.1	19.9	59.5	9.3	81.3	14.5
Galveston city	41.147	47,745	49,608	3.9	1,205.6	14.8	70.7	$38,008	14.3	23.5	59.8	10.7	51.6	40.6
Garland city	57.037	226,871	235,501	3.8	4,128.9	27.4	84.7	$51,997	17.8	13.9	70.5	9.8	75.6	20.4
Gatesville city	8.901	15,745	15,872	0.8	1,783.1	6.9	81.7	$40,480	7.7	22.0	29.8	8.1	70.9	24.0
Georgetown city	49.558	47,455	59,102	24.5	1,192.6	10.3	83.8	$62,219	26.1	8.1	50.5	7.6	67.8	28.9
Glenn Heights city	7.217	11,278	11,915	5.6	1,650.9	4.8	90.5	$61,983	25.3	10.3	67.9	8.1	82.2	13.8
Grand Prairie city	72.237	175,468	185,453	5.7	2,567.3	21.4	86.4	$55,336	21.4	13.0	71.8	8.7	74.4	21.4
Grapevine city	31.930	46,334	50,844	9.7	1,592.4	12.9	81.1	$75,931	36.2	9.4	76.2	4.3	66.6	27.1
Greatwood CDP	2.626	11,538	NA	NA	NA	10.4	95.7	$145,912	72.4	1.7	66.0	2.2	88.7	10.6
Greenville city	32.630	25,557	26,180	2.4	802.3	10.9	77.8	$36,960	12.1	21.7	58.7	12.3	59.8	34.9
Groves city	5.173	16,144	15,753	-2.4	3,045.0	7.3	84.8	$48,807	16.6	13.0	60.1	12.3	65.3	31.5
Haltom City city	12.345	42,409	43,913	3.5	3,557.2	23.2	80.8	$43,792	12.3	14.8	68.0	8.4	65.2	29.4
Harker Heights city	15.389	26,718	28,526	6.8	1,853.6	10.0	77.8	$63,878	26.6	12.6	64.9	8.9	76.7	19.9
Harlingen city	39.918	64,918	65,914	1.5	1,651.2	16.2	89.1	$34,868	13.5	27.2	51.2	8.9	74.4	22.3
Henderson city	11.951	13,712	13,604	-0.8	1,138.3	7.4	64.0	$41,509	20.0	14.3	44.4	3.2	65.1	31.7
Hereford city	6.138	15,370	15,216	-1.0	2,479.2	15.2	85.1	$40,924	8.2	21.0	62.3	7.0	74.0	24.3
Hewitt city	6.940	13,548	14,166	4.6	2,041.2	4.6	86.7	$70,300	24.1	5.1	70.3	3.5	78.9	15.9
Hidalgo city	7.390	12,522	13,497	7.8	1,826.3	40.7	88.4	$41,386	7.2	26.0	59.0	9.1	92.9	4.3
Highland Village city	5.526	15,085	15,995	6.0	2,894.3	6.1	90.5	$133,161	69.1	1.5	72.6	3.7	90.3	6.9
Horizon City city	8.714	16,730	19,332	15.6	2,218.5	17.2	91.2	$52,030	17.3	19.3	64.8	8.6	86.5	8.9
Houston city	599.739	2,096,661	2,239,558	6.8	3,734.2	28.4	79.4	$45,728	20.6	19.4	68.1	8.9	60.8	32.2
Humble city	9.865	15,127	15,616	3.2	1,583.0	24.2	73.7	$42,129	13.9	12.2	67.8	11.1	64.1	30.0
Huntsville city	35.848	38,550	40,435	4.9	1,128.0	8.2	72.6	$29,257	10.2	36.2	34.7	7.6	51.3	31.8
Hurst city	9.966	37,335	38,733	3.7	3,886.4	12.2	83.6	$53,488	23.9	11.7	68.1	7.7	68.5	27.7
Hutto city	8.024	16,459	21,170	28.6	2,638.3	6.7	83.5	$70,519	24.4	4.8	74.4	6.8	87.2	11.3
Irving city	67.041	216,287	232,406	7.5	3,466.6	34.2	77.2	$50,942	20.2	13.6	73.4	7.5	64.3	29.7
Jacinto City city	1.869	10,553	10,809	2.4	5,784.5	32.2	88.5	$30,484	5.1	29.9	59.5	24.9	72.6	24.2
Jacksonville city	14.191	14,537	14,675	0.9	1,034.1	15.9	83.6	$30,996	8.4	30.9	59.3	7.7	72.1	24.0
Katy city	11.255	14,121	15,591	10.4	1,385.3	13.0	84.4	$73,006	28.2	8.3	66.2	4.5	68.0	24.9
Keller city	18.455	39,633	43,924	10.8	2,380.1	6.7	86.7	$114,266	57.1	5.3	66.8	4.9	82.1	15.5
Kerrville city	20.828	22,384	22,905	2.3	1,099.7	7.1	78.3	$39,095	12.9	13.7	51.5	8.4	58.0	37.2
Kilgore city	18.563	13,478	14,948	10.9	805.2	8.7	79.4	$49,766	16.3	18.2	60.9	6.4	64.2	31.5
Killeen city	53.541	127,911	138,154	8.0	2,580.4	8.8	70.9	$48,283	12.4	14.7	70.9	11.8	71.2	23.6
Kingsville city	13.824	26,213	26,529	1.2	1,919.1	7.2	79.7	$36,500	12.0	29.5	60.9	11.8	64.0	25.0
Kyle city	19.087	28,016	32,881	17.4	1,722.7	8.3	81.0	$75,182	28.9	6.1	74.7	4.4	79.8	14.2
La Homa CDP	6.741	11,985	NA	NA	NA	35.5	92.7	$28,352	5.4	39.0	57.6	16.8	90.6	8.4
Lake Jackson city	19.441	26,830	27,604	2.9	1,419.9	7.3	83.1	$72,645	31.4	6.9	64.6	5.3	69.2	25.3
Lakeway city	10.535	11,673	13,685	17.2	1,299.0	10.7	86.0	$109,628	55.0	5.4	61.1	7.1	76.3	19.9
La Marque city	13.951	14,511	15,521	7.0	1,115.4	9.0	84.4	$44,040	15.7	16.8	60.4	12.8	66.5	29.0
Lancaster city	33.228	36,655	38,453	4.9	1,157.2	7.3	88.7	$49,590	14.5	14.5	66.9	10.3	70.8	26.5
La Porte city	18.634	33,800	35,039	3.7	1,880.4	8.7	86.4	$67,806	30.4	9.9	70.0	8.2	76.4	17.8
Laredo city	92.278	236,058	252,309	6.9	2,734.2	27.2	84.8	$39,408	13.8	28.4	58.6	6.5	82.1	15.1
League City city	51.258	83,560	94,403	13.0	1,841.7	9.4	85.4	$90,972	43.9	4.5	73.1	4.5	73.5	21.0
Leander city	23.017	26,262	34,172	30.1	1,484.7	8.2	80.3	$75,983	35.1	4.3	77.7	8.0	81.3	14.5
Leon Valley city	3.432	10,152	11,015	8.5	3,209.5	12.6	76.7	$60,040	20.0	11.1	69.9	4.7	62.0	31.2
Levelland city	10.179	13,555	13,954	2.9	1,370.9	7.6	74.8	$45,701	15.9	18.0	63.2	7.2	72.5	22.4
Lewisville city	36.431	95,309	102,889	8.0	2,824.2	19.8	75.3	$58,559	22.9	7.7	78.3	5.9	62.5	29.2
Little Elm city	14.583	25,896	35,414	36.8	2,428.5	13.5	87.1	$81,866	36.7	5.2	75.9	6.9	82.9	13.7
Live Oak city	4.751	13,131	15,116	15.1	3,181.5	9.1	84.9	$59,286	20.3	11.3	67.4	6.6	61.3	31.1
Lockhart city	15.575	12,698	13,232	4.2	849.6	5.2	80.2	$47,859	15.5	13.7	56.5	6.4	66.7	28.2

1 Dry land or land partially or temporarily covered by water.
2 16 years old and over.

Table B. Incorporated Places, Census Designated Places (CDPs), and Minor Civil Divisions (MCDs) of 10,000 or More Population — Crime, Construction, and Local Government Finance

STATE City, town, township, borough, or CDP (county if applicable)	Serious crimes known to police, 2014[1] Total number	Rate[2] Total	Rate[2] Violent	Rate[2] Property	New residential construction authorized by building permits, 2014 Value ($1,000)	Number of housing units	Percent single family	Local government finance, 2012 General revenue Total (mil dol)	Intergovernmental Total (mil dol)	Percent from state gov.	Taxes per capita[3]	General expenditure Total (mil dol)	Per capita[3] Total	Capital outlays	Debt outstanding (mil dol)
	15	16	17	18	19	20	21	22	23	24	25	26	27	28	29
TEXAS—Con.															
Coppell city	518	1271	56	1215	39,386	118	100.0	72.0	0.3	100.0	1451	65.6	1,638	306	93.5
Copperas Cove city	1,069	3204	336	2868	14,817	114	86.0	25.8	0.6	100.0	425	73.0	2,187	1,475	98.1
Corinth city	210	1009	91	918	11,950	23	100.0	22.1	0.1	100.0	600	25.5	1,246	310	32.2
Corpus Christi city	16,204	5076	656	4420	285,268	2,342	50.5	357.9	29.6	42.3	614	389.3	1,246	290	1152.6
Corsicana city	1,243	5184	501	4684	2,314	11	100.0	28.9	1.6	75.0	642	29.4	1,222	143	58.5
Crowley city	379	2630	229	2401	9,006	64	100.0	11.4	0.5	4.8	556	15.9	1,170	523	27.1
Dallas city	54,126	4254	665	3589	801,685	7,856	15.0	2544.8	172.7	56.8	872	2543.0	2,045	435	7943.6
Deer Park city	730	2178	137	2040	16,000	59	100.0	42.3	0.3	34.3	585	36.3	1,097	77	44.9
Del Rio city	975	2742	135	2607	7,829	63	87.3	34.7	4.3	47.7	418	37.0	1,026	201	64.8
Denison city	802	3512	385	3126	1,515	11	100.0	24.4	0.6	6.1	568	27.1	1,195	104	20.4
Denton city	3,388	2705	270	2435	201,483	830	78.9	169.7	11.5	79.7	765	149.1	1,207	175	501.7
DeSoto city	1,920	3690	282	3407	34,277	164	100.0	50.0	1.3	100.0	640	48.8	954	113	130.8
Dickinson city	580	2985	278	2707	16,848	84	100.0	15.7	2.3	49.7	500	14.8	776	71	15.8
Donna city	1,107	6761	1014	5747	3,588	33	100.0	12.5	0.6	1.6	396	11.4	706	137	48.6
Dumas city	395	2632	253	2378	2,096	13	100.0	8.5	0.0	100.0	330	10.4	688	109	7.2
Duncanville city	1,531	3841	314	3527	3,860	14	100.0	37.1	1.0	60.3	573	42.9	1,085	220	19.1
Eagle Pass city	875	3121	128	2993	9,610	99	70.7	32.1	2.3	62.3	387	32.6	1,184	237	61.2
Edinburg city	4,716	5727	359	5367	54,221	495	57.0	72.5	6.4	81.8	518	71.1	903	197	98.1
Eidson Road CDP	NA	NA	NA	NA	NA	NA	NA	NA	NA	NA	NA	NA	NA	NA	NA
El Campo city	346	3021	436	2584	1,640	6	100.0	12.7	1.0	10.9	578	12.4	1,082	121	10.4
El Paso city	17,241	2534	393	2142	416,264	2,798	72.2	743.5	92.0	24.8	572	621.6	920	181	1534.1
Ennis city	698	3724	299	3425	6,776	27	100.0	20.5	0.9	96.8	802	16.1	861	37	49.5
Euless city	1,313	2446	119	2327	24,795	104	100.0	66.2	1.7	13.5	806	61.4	1,162	109	51.8
Farmers Branch city	1,000	3079	188	2891	8,898	28	100.0	55.4	0.8	73.5	1395	53.3	1,813	185	24.3
Flower Mound town	691	993	55	939	160,319	355	100.0	74.2	2.2	6.5	800	76.4	1,125	247	129.5
Forest Hill city	443	3466	250	3216	543	3	100.0	9.3	0.0	100.0	552	8.8	695	60	6.0
Forney city	281	1637	151	1485	28,299	135	100.0	20.2	0.2	100.0	918	34.0	2,138	1,123	81.6
Fort Hood CDP	NA	NA	NA	NA	NA	NA	NA	NA	NA	NA	NA	NA	NA	NA	NA
Fort Worth city	36,693	4559	558	4001	749,094	5,923	52.7	1108.5	81.2	53.9	783	1116.7	1,434	341	2401.8
Four Corners CDP	NA	NA	NA	NA	NA	NA	NA	NA	NA	NA	NA	NA	NA	NA	NA
Fredericksburg city	247	2266	64	2202	7,738	39	100.0	19.2	0.3	95.0	884	17.2	1,603	137	4.9
Freeport city	339	2801	330	2470	1,739	6	100.0	14.2	0.2	12.0	423	14.4	1,188	70	6.7
Fresno CDP	NA	NA	NA	NA	NA	NA	NA	NA	NA	NA	NA	NA	NA	NA	NA
Friendswood city	350	921	55	866	70,813	189	100.0	32.1	3.1	8.8	562	35.6	963	285	66.6
Frisco city	2,653	1869	83	1786	688,442	3,188	67.9	214.9	32.8	2.5	977	202.2	1,572	466	640.8
Gainesville city	833	5195	486	4708	2,830	18	100.0	26.6	1.5	39.6	872	24.6	1,524	284	27.6
Galena Park city	247	2213	251	1963	305	5	60.0	7.6	0.2	0.0	477	6.3	569	40	7.3
Galveston city	2,310	4718	523	4195	71,859	279	100.0	180.4	62.3	54.6	1217	182.3	3,769	1,529	316.3
Garland city	8,339	3527	272	3255	50,237	329	54.7	228.5	19.9	12.3	457	234.9	1,004	127	905.7
Gatesville city	287	1795	94	1701	3,820	32	50.0	6.2	0.3	100.0	197	6.1	376	53	10.7
Georgetown city	785	1382	118	1264	378,129	1,724	70.1	65.1	3.9	87.5	675	70.7	1,345	298	168.4
Glenn Heights city	320	2696	371	2325	3,794	23	100.0	8.0	0.2	38.7	372	9.0	765	134	6.0
Grand Prairie city	5,117	2762	260	2502	100,024	593	66.4	252.2	40.5	30.9	723	217.4	1,195	147	447.1
Grapevine city	1,265	2474	121	2353	40,004	122	96.7	125.9	3.7	100.0	1953	92.9	1,916	312	142.7
Greatwood CDP	NA	NA	NA	NA	NA	NA	NA	NA	NA	NA	NA	NA	NA	NA	NA
Greenville city	1,336	5142	550	4591	7,446	47	93.6	39.6	2.4	41.3	762	43.8	1,690	468	148.3
Groves city	589	3745	604	3141	2,372	11	100.0	13.4	1.4	100.0	483	13.1	826	130	12.6
Haltom City city	1,314	2996	246	2750	651	4	100.0	42.3	2.2	23.7	565	38.1	878	131	60.4
Harker Heights city	886	3111	267	2844	43,524	203	100.0	24.0	0.5	27.3	558	26.5	951	239	50.6
Harlingen city	2,205	3351	222	3129	13,916	123	100.0	87.2	13.1	29.3	615	112.2	1,703	650	118.7
Henderson city	536	3914	453	3462	278	3	100.0	14.7	0.6	100.0	641	11.3	815	110	10.7
Hereford city	444	2929	310	2619	837	10	20.0	57.2	0.2	100.0	309	55.3	3,600	34	1477.3
Hewitt city	156	1101	113	988	12,158	47	100.0	7.7	0.1	100.0	396	9.4	677	258	25.1
Hidalgo city	290	2157	364	1792	5,554	56	100.0	18.9	2.5	98.6	320	17.2	1,313	221	14.6
Highland Village city	115	723	44	679	5,537	18	100.0	18.8	0.2	37.1	897	16.4	1,048	42	32.7
Horizon City city	294	1503	46	1457	3,366	33	100.0	4.1	0.2	100.0	181	3.4	181	10	1.9
Houston city	126,205	5685	991	4694	2,399,526	20,304	26.6	3667.9	315.0	27.9	888	3697.9	1,708	274	13983.7
Humble city	1,739	11156	680	10476	4,033	31	61.3	30.2	5.8	3.6	1014	22.9	1,480	143	10.0
Huntsville city	1,167	2913	527	2386	22,744	222	36.0	32.1	1.0	50.9	376	30.5	766	52	38.9
Hurst city	1,848	4774	369	4405	2,814	15	73.3	51.1	2.4	26.0	911	49.1	1,285	225	57.6
Hutto city	172	836	63	773	135,978	429	100.0	12.7	0.1	100.0	411	13.8	734	141	47.4
Irving city	6,803	2936	221	2715	284,366	1,553	31.6	281.4	21.9	71.5	839	289.2	1,281	200	567.8
Jacinto City city	306	2835	93	2742	60	1	100.0	9.4	1.6	100.0	469	7.8	723	146	6.2
Jacksonville city	720	4880	712	4168	380	3	100.0	14.0	0.9	100.0	557	12.0	817	37	11.1
Katy city	NA	NA	NA	NA	64,938	183	100.0	29.8	4.6	100.0	1481	26.1	1,765	203	30.6
Keller city	398	911	55	856	114,560	526	64.4	52.3	5.6	60.6	765	46.9	1,117	201	128.2
Kerrville city	660	2904	312	2592	31,241	91	71.4	28.8	0.8	9.2	871	23.3	1,035	0	43.6
Kilgore city	588	3976	345	3631	3,337	22	100.0	24.4	0.4	84.2	1222	20.4	1,444	200	9.6
Killeen city	5,549	3986	608	3378	131,283	963	86.1	120.2	5.4	5.6	466	125.1	928	204	238.9
Kingsville city	1,168	4436	725	3711	5,809	36	100.0	22.9	0.6	12.6	464	21.7	825	89	28.3
Kyle city	584	1789	205	1584	84,325	751	67.2	18.5	1.7	25.7	346	21.9	709	200	69.4
La Homa CDP	NA	NA	NA	NA	NA	NA	NA	NA	NA	NA	NA	NA	NA	NA	NA
Lake Jackson city	570	2070	127	1943	1,509	8	100.0	29.0	0.4	54.4	543	25.6	942	152	42.1
Lakeway city	150	1107	133	974	70,564	244	100.0	10.8	0.2	34.2	653	10.9	855	58	6.0
La Marque city	1,054	6888	490	6397	24,315	144	100.0	16.0	2.9	54.5	501	17.2	1,150	201	13.3
Lancaster city	1,387	3612	276	3336	18,977	89	100.0	48.5	11.5	23.8	649	46.9	1,238	111	96.3
La Porte city	654	1877	201	1676	19,067	62	100.0	56.7	0.9	100.0	769	48.6	1,407	246	45.1
Laredo city	10,663	4248	389	3859	186,839	1,719	55.5	394.6	81.6	35.0	516	350.9	1,429	400	576.1
League City city	1,905	2053	106	1947	218,186	1,358	72.9	86.5	3.8	100.0	658	73.3	829	130	210.1
Leander city	403	1217	115	1102	261,740	1,079	100.0	26.5	2.2	9.7	606	29.0	981	234	176.0
Leon Valley city	748	6824	374	6450	1,592	9	100.0	9.5	0.1	100.0	638	8.9	836	23	3.1
Levelland city	548	3903	434	3468	3,512	13	100.0	12.5	1.2	44.6	533	12.0	874	108	12.9
Lewisville city	2,806	2739	196	2543	40,307	201	90.0	95.9	2.2	49.8	628	100.9	1,013	207	244.1
Little Elm city	330	954	118	835	304,835	892	100.0	30.5	4.2	98.1	629	39.3	1,357	641	74.2
Live Oak city	541	3569	218	3351	3,066	17	100.0	14.7	0.2	46.9	766	15.2	1,069	139	16.5
Lockhart city	421	3193	190	3003	8,110	80	100.0	12.0	0.6	72.9	459	13.3	1,031	46	16.4

1 Data for serious crimes have not been adjusted for underreporting. This may affect comparability between geographic areas over time.
2 Per 100,000 population estimated by the FBI.   3 Based on population estimated as of July 1 of the year shown.

Table B. Incorporated Places, Census Designated Places (CDPs), and Minor Civil Divisions (MCDs) of 10,000 or More Population — Land Area, Population, and Households, and Employment

STATE City, town, township, borough, or CDP (county if applicable)	Land area,[1] 2010 (sq mi)	Population Total persons 2010	Total persons 2014	Percent change 2010–2014	Persons per square mile, 2014	Population characteristics 2010–2014 Foreign born	Lives in same house as previous year	Household income and poverty 2010–2014 Median household income (dollars)	Percent of households Income of $100,000 or more	Income below poverty level	Employment,[2] 2010–2014 Percent in labor force	Unemployment rate	Households, 2010–2014 (percent of households) Family households	One person households
	1	2	3	4	5	6	7	8	9	10	11	12	13	14
TEXAS—Con.														
Longview city	55.692	80,455	81,593	1.4	1,465.1	9.8	78.6	$43,767	16.1	17.1	62.6	7.2	66.2	29.4
Lubbock city	122.419	229,399	243,839	6.3	1,991.8	5.9	73.0	$44,139	16.3	19.8	66.9	6.4	59.9	30.0
Lufkin city	33.412	35,064	36,141	3.1	1,081.7	10.7	76.2	$39,606	12.4	17.7	61.6	9.9	69.0	26.7
Lumberton city	13.409	11,972	12,312	2.8	918.2	1.4	85.9	$62,166	25.3	8.4	66.9	6.0	76.3	21.3
McAllen city	49.309	130,289	138,596	6.4	2,810.8	28.6	85.8	$43,476	17.7	24.1	61.3	7.8	75.8	20.4
McKinney city	62.171	131,025	156,767	19.6	2,521.5	12.3	84.2	$82,988	40.5	6.6	71.3	4.0	79.0	16.8
Mansfield city	36.395	56,373	62,246	10.4	1,710.3	9.1	88.6	$89,774	45.9	6.3	73.2	5.3	81.1	16.1
Marshall city	29.594	23,523	24,701	5.0	834.7	9.4	83.7	$34,336	10.4	22.7	59.1	8.8	66.5	30.3
Mercedes city	11.799	15,677	16,591	5.8	1,406.1	18.1	86.5	$30,644	4.6	36.9	56.0	18.3	77.5	21.1
Mesquite city	47.231	139,629	144,416	3.4	3,057.7	16.2	83.4	$49,837	17.3	13.0	71.4	7.6	74.5	22.0
Midland city	73.008	111,127	128,037	15.2	1,753.7	9.9	82.4	$67,144	30.9	10.2	70.1	4.3	70.0	24.2
Midlothian city	50.261	18,311	20,934	14.3	416.5	3.8	82.6	$72,126	30.0	6.2	72.3	6.9	82.1	14.1
Mineral Wells city	20.399	16,790	15,362	-8.5	753.1	7.0	73.4	$35,508	11.4	23.6	51.5	9.8	64.1	31.1
Mission city	35.540	77,665	82,431	6.1	2,319.4	27.4	91.1	$43,592	15.5	23.3	57.8	8.5	82.1	15.8
Mission Bend CDP	4.897	36,501	NA	NA	NA	38.4	93.3	$60,085	21.1	10.8	68.2	6.3	85.4	12.8
Missouri City city	28.817	66,825	71,710	7.3	2,488.4	22.3	91.6	$84,662	41.2	5.5	70.4	7.8	81.6	16.7
Mount Pleasant city	15.571	15,985	16,021	0.2	1,028.9	25.8	85.0	$37,957	11.2	22.2	65.0	7.4	73.5	22.3
Murphy city	5.683	17,862	20,230	13.3	3,559.8	22.5	97.1	$121,360	66.4	3.8	73.6	5.1	91.4	6.1
Nacogdoches city	27.017	32,899	33,687	2.4	1,246.9	10.9	68.5	$31,442	9.1	29.9	57.4	10.9	54.7	35.1
Nederland city	5.924	16,993	17,108	0.7	2,888.0	2.0	86.5	$56,990	21.8	8.4	66.0	7.0	67.7	28.1
New Braunfels city	44.867	57,727	66,394	15.0	1,479.8	7.1	81.1	$59,083	20.9	10.8	66.9	6.1	71.1	23.6
New Territory CDP	4.528	15,186	NA	NA	NA	39.4	93.1	$123,445	59.4	4.1	66.6	3.9	89.6	9.6
North Richland Hills city	18.131	63,343	68,529	8.2	3,779.6	9.6	83.5	$62,927	26.6	7.4	71.1	6.2	70.1	25.6
Odessa city	45.172	99,880	114,597	14.7	2,536.9	13.1	80.3	$56,119	23.4	13.0	68.0	5.0	69.2	25.3
Orange city	21.308	18,612	18,913	1.6	887.6	1.7	81.1	$41,494	14.8	22.2	56.4	9.0	65.2	31.7
Palestine city	19.422	18,774	18,393	-2.0	947.0	9.8	82.3	$38,146	12.0	20.8	59.3	5.7	69.1	28.1
Pampa city	9.016	17,994	18,399	2.3	2,040.7	9.3	83.9	$44,237	14.0	13.5	62.7	5.2	63.8	32.6
Paris city	36.405	25,163	24,895	-1.1	683.8	3.7	76.5	$33,557	8.7	25.8	58.8	10.5	62.3	33.5
Pasadena city	43.493	149,300	153,887	3.1	3,538.2	25.4	80.3	$46,585	17.0	18.4	64.5	10.7	72.1	23.6
Pearland city	46.092	89,891	103,441	15.1	2,244.2	16.5	89.9	$94,653	46.9	4.9	73.7	4.9	79.1	18.4
Pecan Grove CDP	8.635	15,963	NA	NA	NA	5.1	90.7	$101,131	50.6	2.9	72.4	4.4	83.0	14.8
Pflugerville city	22.705	48,356	54,644	13.0	2,406.7	15.3	89.8	$74,196	33.6	8.7	74.5	5.3	75.4	19.3
Pharr city	23.552	70,470	75,382	7.0	3,200.6	32.4	88.0	$34,655	8.8	33.6	58.7	10.6	83.2	14.3
Plainview city	13.794	22,200	21,166	-4.7	1,534.5	11.1	77.5	$42,419	9.5	23.2	64.2	9.0	70.7	25.7
Plano city	71.670	259,841	278,480	7.2	3,885.6	24.1	86.6	$82,944	41.1	7.1	71.5	5.9	71.0	24.4
Port Arthur city	76.922	54,376	54,548	0.3	709.1	20.7	85.3	$31,736	11.3	27.8	58.6	12.5	61.0	34.5
Portland city	6.992	15,102	15,915	5.4	2,276.1	4.9	80.9	$66,662	27.4	6.7	66.6	3.2	77.7	19.7
Port Lavaca city	10.151	12,248	12,399	1.2	1,221.5	11.6	84.0	$42,598	14.9	22.2	64.7	11.4	69.5	23.0
Port Neches city	8.630	13,040	12,755	-2.2	1,478.0	4.6	82.4	$61,600	28.1	10.1	65.9	7.2	72.3	24.7
Prosper town	24.749	9,523	14,416	51.4	582.5	7.2	82.5	$111,641	54.3	10.4	67.6	3.8	86.5	10.8
Raymondville city	4.115	11,277	11,117	-1.4	2,701.9	18.6	79.5	$24,150	6.3	42.2	30.6	12.3	78.9	18.0
Red Oak city	15.189	10,769	11,560	7.3	761.1	9.6	85.6	$67,132	26.2	9.3	68.9	4.2	74.1	21.4
Rendon CDP	24.637	12,552	NA	NA	NA	10.4	89.4	$66,784	33.3	10.1	66.2	8.3	77.9	16.9
Richardson city	28.563	99,223	108,617	9.5	3,802.8	23.0	82.4	$70,959	34.0	9.7	69.0	7.5	67.1	25.4
Richmond city	4.064	11,588	12,018	3.7	2,957.3	21.8	79.5	$47,110	20.1	16.5	58.1	6.3	73.2	21.0
Rio Grande City city	11.351	13,803	14,227	3.1	1,253.4	27.0	80.4	$29,974	14.4	33.5	55.4	8.7	73.1	22.8
Robinson city	31.240	10,508	11,416	8.6	365.4	3.7	89.5	$71,215	27.1	7.4	67.1	4.2	84.0	13.2
Robstown city	15.503	11,487	11,657	1.5	751.9	2.6	83.7	$31,435	14.6	28.3	55.9	15.5	77.9	18.0
Rockwall city	29.282	37,572	41,785	11.2	1,427.0	9.1	85.5	$86,627	41.2	5.0	69.2	5.6	78.3	17.4
Rosenberg city	26.156	31,383	34,468	9.8	1,317.8	18.9	82.1	$44,318	14.3	17.8	64.1	4.9	73.0	22.9
Round Rock city	34.231	99,990	112,744	12.8	3,293.6	13.6	76.9	$70,952	32.0	7.7	74.1	7.1	72.6	21.3
Rowlett city	20.422	56,242	58,407	3.8	2,860.0	13.4	92.0	$83,442	38.4	4.9	71.6	7.7	84.1	12.4
Sachse city	9.783	20,329	23,681	16.5	2,420.5	17.4	86.3	$91,543	44.4	2.9	74.4	5.7	82.5	13.4
Saginaw city	7.561	19,806	21,703	9.6	2,870.2	5.6	86.7	$74,521	28.6	6.6	74.4	7.8	81.4	16.7
San Angelo city	59.518	93,227	98,975	6.2	1,662.9	6.7	73.4	$42,855	13.7	16.9	63.8	6.4	62.6	31.4
San Antonio city	460.985	1,327,556	1,436,697	8.2	3,116.6	14.2	80.5	$46,317	17.2	18.5	64.6	8.4	65.7	28.3
San Benito city	15.792	24,253	24,506	1.0	1,551.8	16.8	90.1	$27,880	7.1	36.8	53.5	12.3	75.4	21.6
San Elizario CDP	10.273	13,603	NA	NA	NA	35.6	89.2	$22,574	2.4	48.1	49.2	14.6	87.2	11.8
San Juan city	11.448	33,856	36,174	6.8	3,159.9	30.1	90.3	$34,518	10.3	31.3	58.9	8.4	85.9	12.1
San Marcos city	30.234	45,068	58,892	30.7	1,947.9	5.5	59.2	$27,261	7.2	33.4	62.3	9.5	38.8	32.8
Santa Fe city	17.397	12,347	12,860	4.2	739.2	3.5	90.0	$61,552	29.3	7.6	62.4	12.2	72.1	23.6
Schertz city	31.777	31,793	36,896	16.1	1,161.1	7.4	86.5	$72,463	33.5	7.0	67.1	7.0	77.8	19.6
Seabrook city	5.325	11,952	12,792	7.0	2,402.2	11.8	86.3	$79,308	42.8	6.4	72.1	5.2	62.8	32.1
Seagoville city	18.847	14,915	15,723	5.4	834.2	16.5	88.0	$43,713	11.7	13.8	50.5	5.6	76.3	22.7
Seguin city	34.533	25,173	27,041	7.4	783.1	9.1	85.5	$36,755	10.8	20.9	60.8	9.5	63.8	32.4
Sherman city	43.952	38,340	39,943	4.2	908.8	10.7	75.6	$42,820	13.0	19.0	63.4	11.0	64.4	28.8
Sienna Plantation CDP	13.259	13,721	NA	NA	NA	11.2	88.1	$130,300	64.6	6.5	64.7	6.5	93.4	5.9
Snyder city	8.713	11,202	11,571	3.3	1,328.0	7.3	79.8	$46,250	17.8	14.5	61.0	3.6	69.3	27.2
Socorro city	22.034	32,031	32,909	2.7	1,493.5	36.1	91.7	$30,416	5.2	34.7	58.0	13.1	86.4	12.4
South Houston city	3.052	16,988	17,536	3.2	5,745.5	38.3	83.9	$37,483	7.3	25.2	63.4	10.1	82.2	14.0
Southlake city	21.877	26,576	29,086	9.4	1,329.5	9.4	90.9	$170,742	73.0	4.1	63.3	4.8	87.8	10.9
Spring CDP	23.201	54,298	NA	NA	NA	11.4	85.6	$67,252	27.2	7.9	72.2	7.7	76.6	19.3
Stafford city	6.997	17,698	18,344	3.7	2,621.8	34.9	81.9	$58,519	22.7	11.2	68.7	5.3	67.0	28.2
Stephenville city	11.888	17,093	19,374	13.3	1,629.8	4.3	71.3	$35,015	10.6	33.4	62.3	6.0	48.5	32.0
Sugar Land city	33.591	78,592	86,777	10.4	2,583.3	34.0	89.4	$105,400	53.5	5.0	65.0	5.3	83.7	14.9
Sulphur Springs city	20.219	15,450	15,975	3.4	790.1	7.4	75.2	$39,936	13.1	21.5	59.7	10.1	72.1	24.0
Sweetwater city	10.193	10,906	10,805	-0.9	1,060.0	4.3	80.0	$34,013	10.4	22.4	60.0	9.3	63.8	30.4
Taylor city	18.382	15,281	16,483	7.9	896.7	9.9	81.9	$46,568	12.5	14.8	65.3	10.5	70.5	26.1
Temple city	69.797	66,315	70,765	6.7	1,014.3	8.3	83.6	$47,962	18.2	14.9	62.0	7.0	66.2	29.4
Terrell city	19.814	15,816	16,561	4.7	835.8	15.3	74.3	$41,154	11.1	19.0	65.2	13.2	68.7	26.3
Texarkana city	29.044	36,409	37,225	2.2	1,281.7	5.3	85.6	$38,810	14.1	23.3	57.2	10.3	62.0	33.6
Texas City city	64.288	45,091	46,639	3.4	725.5	6.6	78.1	$44,659	15.2	18.7	59.6	12.2	68.8	26.1
The Colony city	13.974	36,328	41,352	13.8	2,959.3	14.6	82.7	$71,425	31.8	5.4	79.8	7.7	65.1	26.1
The Woodlands CDP	43.299	93,847	NA	NA	NA	15.1	81.1	$108,635	53.6	5.4	64.8	4.9	75.7	21.7
Timberwood Park CDP	21.022	13,447	NA	NA	NA	12.6	84.2	$110,725	55.5	4.3	72.6	4.4	83.2	13.3
Tomball city	11.938	10,753	11,299	5.1	946.5	8.8	72.6	$42,070	21.5	16.2	57.3	6.9	55.2	37.1

1 Dry land or land partially or temporarily covered by water.
2 16 years old and over.

630 TX(Longview city)—TX(Tomball city)

Items 1–14

Table B. Incorporated Places, Census Designated Places (CDPs), and Minor Civil Divisions (MCDs) of 10,000 or More Population — Crime, Construction, and Local Government Finance

STATE City, town, township, borough, or CDP (county if applicable)	Serious crimes known to police, 2014[1] — Total number	Rate[2] Total	Rate[2] Violent	Rate[2] Property	New residential construction authorized by building permits, 2014 — Value ($1,000)	Number of housing units	Percent single family	Local government finance, 2012 — General revenue Total (mil dol)	Intergovernmental Total (mil dol)	Percent from state gov.	Taxes per capita[3]	General expenditure Total (mil dol)	Per capita[3] Total	Capital outlays	Debt outstanding (mil dol)
	15	16	17	18	19	20	21	22	23	24	25	26	27	28	29
TEXAS—Con.															
Longview city	3,982	4876	460	4416	35,566	235	71.5	103.8	12.8	28.3	798	94.8	1,166	149	160.6
Lubbock city	12,701	5252	862	4390	275,162	2,049	43.3	270.7	38.4	30.0	538	310.3	1,313	386	1342.1
Lufkin city	2,173	5982	432	5550	10,255	56	85.7	50.9	0.7	59.9	716	52.9	1,468	203	179.5
Lumberton city	201	1644	213	1431	12,453	89	100.0	4.0	2.0	100.0	156	1.8	152	0	0.0
McAllen city	5,128	3713	131	3582	99,003	608	67.8	185.3	20.0	21.5	727	201.4	1,488	430	182.6
McKinney city	3,071	2010	147	1863	626,257	2,237	76.4	171.7	14.0	23.8	764	184.3	1,284	234	313.4
Mansfield city	991	1600	95	1505	118,436	532	42.1	76.9	0.3	100.0	894	67.5	1,136	167	183.2
Marshall city	1,040	4202	618	3584	3,447	18	100.0	25.4	1.2	91.6	630	25.4	1,034	216	28.8
Mercedes city	942	5713	619	5095	2,532	27	85.2	18.3	2.9	93.5	672	24.3	1,486	600	30.2
Mesquite city	6,278	4348	299	4049	2,085	18	61.1	149.0	15.9	19.4	571	164.5	1,147	212	242.0
Midland city	3,673	2884	320	2565	235,573	1,553	59.0	147.3	7.4	38.3	790	126.0	1,052	145	125.3
Midlothian city	370	1818	138	1681	39,058	278	100.0	38.4	2.1	11.1	1533	40.3	2,079	139	159.2
Mineral Wells city	706	4210	262	3948	1,064	5	100.0	15.0	1.1	100.0	484	12.5	746	14	19.8
Mission city	2,500	3054	116	2938	36,968	299	100.0	73.0	7.2	12.2	478	68.7	850	112	387.2
Mission Bend CDP	NA	NA	NA	NA	NA	NA	NA	NA	NA	NA	NA	NA	NA	NA	NA
Missouri City city	1,288	1818	178	1640	130,193	783	57.0	57.5	9.1	36.1	524	66.1	963	354	174.1
Mount Pleasant city	737	4567	483	4084	2,606	22	100.0	15.2	0.1	100.0	522	18.6	1,153	287	31.1
Murphy city	162	813	65	748	30,959	94	100.0	15.5	0.0	100.0	607	16.7	870	235	48.1
Nacogdoches city	1,331	3904	323	3581	7,445	68	47.1	37.5	1.3	98.2	514	34.0	1,005	86	62.8
Nederland city	502	2857	359	2498	10,095	47	87.2	15.7	0.2	45.0	629	13.5	797	176	20.6
New Braunfels city	2,283	3533	282	3251	257,981	1,506	70.1	75.8	2.4	48.3	754	79.1	1,294	279	122.5
New Territory CDP	NA	NA	NA	NA	NA	NA	NA	NA	NA	NA	NA	NA	NA	NA	NA
North Richland Hills city	1,662	2433	176	2257	25,541	95	100.0	83.8	11.2	100.0	705	93.1	1,424	490	95.6
Odessa city	5,285	4652	940	3712	108,454	556	77.3	103.9	3.9	38.2	580	93.2	877	116	124.0
Orange city	567	2985	379	2606	16,182	244	11.5	26.5	4.2	78.6	525	27.0	1,423	249	21.5
Palestine city	874	4704	587	4118	232	2	100.0	22.7	0.8	62.1	728	22.4	1,200	111	27.3
Pampa city	925	4995	567	4428	770	3	100.0	19.4	0.1	100.0	549	20.7	1,136	351	19.6
Paris city	1,226	4935	559	4375	2,462	28	50.0	30.9	2.2	100.0	722	29.3	1,166	79	25.2
Pasadena city	5,221	3400	385	3016	10,600	78	97.4	146.5	20.4	12.6	497	138.9	910	167	223.9
Pearland city	2,228	2173	156	2017	304,884	2,076	51.4	113.9	0.6	58.8	794	118.6	1,230	308	497.5
Pecan Grove CDP	NA	NA	NA	NA	NA	NA	NA	NA	NA	NA	NA	NA	NA	NA	NA
Pflugerville city	913	1657	111	1546	100,322	873	68.4	42.9	1.9	93.4	509	44.6	858	248	167.6
Pharr city	2,676	3589	390	3199	24,169	364	68.7	63.4	5.8	5.1	422	59.7	815	150	103.3
Plainview city	884	4062	244	3818	546	3	100.0	17.1	0.6	64.8	440	14.9	670	53	15.8
Plano city	5,967	2148	165	1983	287,925	2,017	26.0	386.2	19.2	55.2	907	338.6	1,240	181	352.8
Port Arthur city	2,472	4563	629	3933	36,670	430	57.2	104.3	23.2	53.0	652	92.8	1,701	263	88.1
Portland city	558	3514	139	3376	24,066	95	100.0	15.0	0.6	51.1	620	13.7	893	154	25.6
Port Lavaca city	437	3520	532	2989	2,033	16	75.0	11.2	0.1	100.0	531	9.5	774	83	11.7
Port Neches city	294	2310	440	1870	4,301	19	100.0	13.5	0.0	100.0	621	11.1	868	23	12.5
Prosper town	NA	NA	NA	NA	228,512	557	100.0	10.7	0.0	100.0	685	6.1	515	93	29.2
Raymondville city	687	6182	1107	5075	7,723	54	100.0	6.3	1.6	100.0	257	5.6	495	58	6.0
Red Oak city	350	3083	106	2977	22,653	135	100.0	10.6	0.6	2.7	553	7.4	667	72	15.1
Rendon CDP	NA	NA	NA	NA	NA	NA	NA	NA	NA	NA	NA	NA	NA	NA	NA
Richardson city	2,584	2444	169	2274	90,964	627	15.2	156.9	3.8	94.5	1020	174.7	1,684	269	311.9
Richmond city	380	3188	403	2785	5,433	28	100.0	15.6	0.7	72.1	635	18.8	1,600	332	30.1
Rio Grande City city	380	2702	242	2460	NA	NA	NA	8.6	0.9	67.7	403	9.4	670	139	26.5
Robinson city	149	1297	252	1045	6,872	41	100.0	6.0	0.0	0.0	346	5.5	493	0	15.7
Robstown city	646	5502	1133	4369	NA	NA	NA	8.7	0.0	0.0	349	6.0	520	0	16.1
Rockwall city	802	1924	98	1825	64,327	266	100.0	44.0	0.7	30.2	910	49.9	1,249	367	163.4
Rosenberg city	817	2432	274	2158	70,988	339	73.2	36.1	5.0	24.6	665	29.5	906	207	52.3
Round Rock city	2,329	2076	125	1951	78,638	797	52.6	146.3	3.6	66.0	1050	119.5	1,120	243	260.2
Rowlett city	878	1502	127	1375	75,057	562	20.3	58.1	2.1	65.8	587	55.7	965	142	119.6
Sachse city	NA	NA	NA	NA	81,709	280	100.0	32.6	0.4	9.8	1359	32.7	1,514	852	41.4
Saginaw city	530	2453	227	2226	20,030	77	100.0	20.9	3.1	100.0	610	21.4	1,026	285	26.2
San Angelo city	4,191	4256	332	3924	69,568	629	36.4	93.6	7.0	10.4	575	98.6	1,026	216	234.6
San Antonio city	85,096	5957	539	5418	745,110	5,638	40.3	1748.6	300.5	51.3	534	1743.3	1,258	188	8830.9
San Benito city	1,168	4788	279	4510	3,947	48	100.0	17.2	0.8	0.6	375	15.9	649	43	40.7
San Elizario CDP	NA	NA	NA	NA	NA	NA	NA	NA	NA	NA	NA	NA	NA	NA	NA
San Juan city	1,335	3710	542	3168	7,443	110	100.0	18.0	1.1	32.3	275	18.5	524	97	24.6
San Marcos city	1,933	3414	318	3096	39,493	243	100.0	67.7	3.7	100.0	769	82.3	1,643	440	264.7
Santa Fe city	290	2283	173	2110	8,101	51	100.0	6.6	2.0	99.2	345	5.2	414	64	0.0
Schertz city	719	1945	176	1769	80,094	299	100.0	37.4	1.3	65.0	611	31.5	902	81	73.9
Seabrook city	192	1498	70	1428	38,032	434	4.1	15.6	0.1	100.0	869	16.9	1,354	202	13.6
Seagoville city	587	3748	140	3608	4,983	45	100.0	10.5	0.4	51.9	430	10.0	644	27	6.7
Seguin city	1,083	4007	351	3655	14,634	87	100.0	116.5	6.1	85.0	529	116.4	4,428	511	172.6
Sherman city	1,292	3269	359	2910	16,890	119	100.0	47.8	2.7	3.7	704	48.9	1,254	120	23.5
Sienna Plantation CDP	NA	NA	NA	NA	NA	NA	NA	NA	NA	NA	NA	NA	NA	NA	NA
Snyder city	520	4479	646	3833	1,200	8	100.0	11.4	0.3	100.0	532	11.9	1,050	234	5.6
Socorro city	427	1309	129	1180	14,187	161	96.3	7.7	0.5	0.0	185	9.8	298	92	12.3
South Houston city	681	3893	463	3430	977	13	69.2	13.2	1.2	100.0	463	12.0	693	60	4.2
Southlake city	421	1470	24	1446	138,278	202	100.0	68.2	0.6	38.4	1972	66.5	2,398	864	179.6
Spring CDP	NA	NA	NA	NA	NA	NA	NA	NA	NA	NA	NA	NA	NA	NA	NA
Stafford city	805	4417	428	3989	8,258	32	100.0	32.1	11.9	28.5	921	29.4	1,631	682	23.3
Stephenville city	463	2444	190	2254	8,297	85	49.4	14.9	0.3	100.0	582	14.0	763	52	22.9
Sugar Land city	1,499	1762	116	1646	89,475	429	40.8	160.2	31.2	93.8	948	161.5	1,972	729	363.3
Sulphur Springs city	246	1541	225	1315	899	8	100.0	21.8	4.8	100.0	596	21.1	1,352	492	19.1
Sweetwater city	303	2826	504	2322	0	0	0.0	15.6	0.4	100.0	660	12.1	1,134	20	18.4
Taylor city	506	3076	371	2705	4,279	33	100.0	18.5	1.7	24.5	026	18.7	1,160	287	50.5
Temple city	2,630	3702	251	3451	109,120	622	99.5	85.5	3.7	93.7	666	91.2	1,319	299	177.8
Terrell city	659	4002	559	3443	3,202	34	100.0	25.5	5.6	43.6	899	24.1	1,497	444	28.6
Texarkana city	2,718	7212	862	6350	6,660	82	100.0	47.9	0.8	78.3	853	49.1	1,322	277	69.8
Texas City city	1,802	3894	324	3570	44,903	364	100.0	68.4	8.3	43.2	944	58.5	1,280	147	91.3
The Colony city	439	1091	134	957	36,902	77	100.0	38.4	2.1	73.4	652	46.1	1,181	397	97.6
The Woodlands CDP	NA	NA	NA	NA	NA	NA	NA	NA	NA	NA	NA	NA	NA	NA	NA
Timberwood Park CDP	NA	NA	NA	NA	NA	NA	NA	NA	NA	NA	NA	NA	NA	NA	NA
Tomball city	570	5083	375	4708	27,075	107	100.0	20.2	0.3	15.1	1263	15.8	1,428	76	25.3

1 Data for serious crimes have not been adjusted for underreporting. This may affect comparability between geographic areas over time.
2 Per 100,000 population estimated by the FBI. 3 Based on population estimated as of July 1 of the year shown.

Table B. Incorporated Places, Census Designated Places (CDPs), and Minor Civil Divisions (MCDs) of 10,000 or More Population — Land Area, Population, and Households, and Employment

STATE City, town, township, borough, or CDP (county if applicable)	Land area,[1] 2010 (sq mi)	Total persons 2010	Total persons 2014	Percent change 2010–2014	Persons per square mile, 2014	Foreign born	Lives in same house as previous year	Median household income (dollars)	Income of $100,000 or more	Income below poverty level	Percent in labor force	Unemploy-ment rate	Family households	One person households
	1	2	3	4	5	6	7	8	9	10	11	12	13	14
TEXAS—Con.														
Tyler city	56.639	96,945	101,421	4.6	1,790.6	12.0	76.0	$42,752	16.8	17.4	62.8	7.2	60.8	32.7
Universal City city	5.579	18,530	19,721	6.4	3,535.0	10.6	80.1	$60,934	21.3	9.4	67.4	4.9	69.6	24.3
University Park city	3.686	23,068	24,396	5.8	6,619.0	5.3	77.5	$176,836	72.3	6.4	60.6	5.8	80.0	14.9
Uvalde city	7.651	15,753	16,412	4.2	2,145.2	14.0	85.2	$35,940	9.9	20.8	58.6	11.8	73.1	22.6
Vernon city	7.895	11,002	10,531	-4.3	1,333.8	5.3	78.0	$38,953	6.8	19.4	62.7	7.4	61.9	33.6
Victoria city	35.855	62,601	66,094	5.6	1,843.3	6.4	79.6	$46,745	17.6	16.9	65.2	7.5	68.0	27.6
Vidor city	12.015	10,710	10,920	2.0	908.8	1.7	89.1	$42,066	11.4	15.3	64.9	7.8	70.7	26.6
Waco city	89.028	124,810	130,194	4.3	1,462.4	11.2	74.7	$32,864	10.4	27.2	58.8	8.5	59.0	32.4
Watauga city	4.162	23,497	24,345	3.6	5,849.9	11.2	86.2	$61,716	19.7	8.9	73.5	7.7	75.9	18.6
Waxahachie city	47.607	29,603	32,344	9.3	679.4	7.8	76.7	$53,336	18.8	13.1	66.9	7.9	72.6	22.8
Weatherford city	24.858	25,250	27,769	10.0	1,117.1	5.7	79.7	$52,532	19.7	12.1	62.0	7.2	66.0	29.0
Webster city	6.390	10,622	11,115	4.6	1,739.4	23.5	63.1	$44,107	9.7	14.9	75.4	8.6	44.1	44.1
Wells Branch CDP	2.527	12,120	NA	NA	NA	19.6	71.1	$46,780	17.2	14.0	80.6	5.5	48.4	40.0
Weslaco city	14.444	35,437	37,601	6.1	2,603.3	21.1	84.7	$37,057	10.1	27.3	55.4	10.9	77.4	20.4
West Odessa CDP	62.722	22,707	NA	NA	NA	17.3	86.7	$50,938	17.3	16.5	62.4	7.0	75.6	20.1
West University Place city	2.004	14,787	15,604	5.5	7,786.1	12.8	91.3	$207,429	75.6	2.5	65.7	3.1	80.1	17.4
White Settlement city	5.040	16,116	16,896	4.8	3,352.5	10.7	78.6	$39,747	7.7	18.1	62.8	6.9	65.6	27.2
Wichita Falls city	72.212	104,724	105,114	0.4	1,455.6	8.2	79.0	$43,751	14.5	17.9	62.4	7.2	62.6	31.6
Wylie city	21.123	41,393	45,913	10.9	2,173.6	11.6	87.0	$83,594	38.2	5.3	74.3	6.4	80.7	15.8
UTAH	82,169.616	2,763,885	2,942,902	6.5	35.8	8.4	82.8	$59,846	22.9	11.9	68.0	6.9	75.1	19.5
American Fork city	9.298	26,439	28,152	6.5	3,027.7	4.2	86.2	$66,687	26.0	11.9	66.1	6.5	81.3	16.1
Bountiful city	13.454	42,561	43,385	1.9	3,224.8	3.9	85.8	$64,630	27.0	7.3	62.6	5.4	78.4	18.0
Brigham City city	24.514	17,908	18,631	4.0	760.0	2.0	82.3	$51,856	13.8	9.2	62.8	6.0	77.2	20.7
Cedar City city	35.846	28,862	29,483	2.2	822.5	4.2	79.6	$40,061	11.4	24.8	64.7	12.6	68.5	21.7
Cedar Hills city	2.704	9,756	10,261	5.2	3,795.2	4.9	90.8	$93,125	45.8	5.5	66.8	5.8	89.7	9.6
Centerville city	5.980	15,326	16,819	9.7	2,812.4	2.7	88.8	$76,478	34.1	6.2	67.2	3.8	79.0	19.6
Clearfield city	7.637	30,117	30,484	1.2	3,991.4	5.9	78.2	$48,158	13.2	13.6	72.6	7.0	73.7	22.1
Clinton city	5.848	20,426	21,104	3.3	3,608.5	5.3	89.2	$71,865	25.4	3.8	72.2	4.7	87.1	11.4
Cottonwood Heights city	8.738	33,435	34,166	2.2	3,910.1	7.8	86.1	$76,630	33.3	5.7	70.3	5.6	76.0	19.5
Draper city	30.097	42,272	46,202	9.3	1,535.1	6.9	84.5	$94,852	46.6	4.1	64.7	4.4	85.1	11.8
Eagle Mountain city	44.852	21,415	25,593	19.5	570.6	4.1	84.5	$68,091	22.2	7.3	71.9	4.9	92.3	6.6
Farmington city	9.855	18,275	22,159	21.3	2,248.4	4.0	86.9	$84,110	36.9	4.0	68.9	3.0	85.4	12.5
Heber city	8.469	11,378	13,599	19.5	1,605.8	15.0	83.7	$60,275	20.4	10.4	73.2	7.0	76.8	18.5
Herriman city	20.273	21,738	28,556	31.4	1,408.6	4.6	80.9	$78,141	36.1	5.3	74.8	5.6	90.6	7.8
Highland city	8.506	15,507	17,456	12.6	2,052.3	3.0	88.8	$107,121	53.5	3.8	59.8	5.6	97.0	3.0
Holladay city	7.913	26,472	27,129	2.5	3,428.4	6.2	87.0	$72,827	37.9	6.4	63.2	4.8	68.1	27.6
Hurricane city	51.367	13,749	15,032	9.3	292.6	1.4	81.2	$45,213	11.7	13.0	52.2	3.4	78.6	19.4
Kaysville city	10.480	27,410	29,494	7.6	2,814.4	2.3	89.1	$86,982	41.8	7.2	68.9	4.0	85.2	12.3
Kearns CDP	4.634	35,731	NA	NA	NA	15.6	89.0	$57,097	10.5	11.2	75.6	8.7	81.8	14.0
Layton city	21.883	67,297	72,231	7.3	3,300.8	6.6	83.7	$66,665	26.0	9.8	69.0	4.6	80.0	15.5
Lehi city	27.099	47,735	56,275	17.9	2,076.7	4.2	86.1	$74,200	29.6	6.0	69.6	6.1	88.5	9.3
Lindon city	8.381	10,082	10,723	6.4	1,279.4	4.8	86.3	$83,182	41.1	7.2	65.1	5.9	92.9	5.8
Logan city	17.787	48,203	48,997	1.6	2,754.6	11.2	67.0	$35,770	9.6	23.7	69.3	7.1	64.6	21.2
Magna CDP	7.918	26,505	NA	NA	NA	12.8	86.8	$55,913	15.6	13.5	73.8	9.8	82.0	12.9
Midvale city	5.914	27,983	31,725	13.4	5,364.8	15.2	77.6	$51,077	12.8	13.7	74.3	7.4	61.3	29.4
Millcreek CDP	13.652	62,139	NA	NA	NA	10.4	82.4	$57,429	24.0	9.0	66.7	5.3	59.9	31.3
Murray city	12.291	46,695	48,822	4.6	3,972.2	7.5	81.1	$53,797	20.9	11.4	70.3	6.6	63.9	28.2
North Ogden city	7.236	17,324	18,172	4.9	2,511.3	2.1	90.0	$75,054	26.4	4.2	66.6	4.6	84.3	13.6
North Salt Lake city	8.549	16,322	19,193	17.6	2,245.1	10.4	82.2	$69,945	30.1	11.6	74.4	5.9	74.9	17.3
Ogden city	27.170	82,827	84,316	1.8	3,103.3	12.8	77.8	$40,937	9.9	21.0	65.6	10.0	65.1	27.1
Orem city	18.154	88,323	91,781	3.9	5,055.8	10.8	79.7	$54,048	19.2	16.0	67.0	7.7	79.0	14.8
Payson city	9.576	18,330	19,331	5.5	2,018.7	7.6	83.2	$59,591	18.4	12.2	67.1	6.6	84.6	13.9
Pleasant Grove city	9.183	33,540	37,064	10.5	4,036.2	3.8	77.6	$62,660	22.2	8.7	69.6	6.5	84.1	12.9
Provo city	41.663	112,494	114,801	2.1	2,755.5	11.1	60.8	$40,359	12.9	27.7	68.3	7.4	70.3	14.7
Riverton city	12.659	38,801	41,457	6.8	3,275.0	2.8	90.1	$84,718	40.4	3.0	76.3	3.9	90.2	8.6
Roy city	7.918	36,884	37,877	2.7	4,783.7	5.9	87.4	$60,100	18.2	9.8	68.6	5.7	77.3	19.7
St. George city	74.434	72,763	78,505	7.9	1,054.7	8.5	79.9	$48,188	15.4	13.4	57.0	9.5	72.1	22.3
Salt Lake City city	111.199	186,452	190,884	2.4	1,716.6	17.5	77.7	$45,833	18.4	18.5	70.1	8.2	52.3	36.3
Sandy city	23.065	87,720	91,148	3.9	3,951.7	6.9	87.5	$78,048	36.0	6.7	70.8	5.6	78.7	17.0
Saratoga Springs city	21.594	17,802	24,356	36.8	1,127.9	4.1	81.6	$76,682	32.2	2.4	71.8	5.3	91.0	7.1
Smithfield city	5.129	9,628	11,014	14.4	2,147.4	5.3	87.0	$57,697	20.3	6.5	69.1	6.2	86.1	13.5
South Jordan city	22.011	50,420	62,781	24.5	2,852.2	4.5	84.0	$91,228	44.6	3.8	70.2	5.3	84.4	11.8
South Ogden city	3.681	16,532	16,852	1.9	4,578.0	5.3	86.9	$54,685	16.8	9.7	67.0	4.8	70.5	25.7
South Salt Lake city	6.944	23,615	24,748	4.8	3,563.7	26.6	71.1	$37,238	7.4	23.1	65.0	8.5	56.3	32.4
Spanish Fork city	15.511	34,740	37,527	8.0	2,419.3	6.2	82.8	$63,376	19.2	6.0	68.2	6.6	85.1	12.5
Springville city	14.411	29,500	31,464	6.7	2,183.3	6.8	83.6	$59,375	18.9	6.9	69.9	5.6	84.8	12.9
Syracuse city	9.477	24,369	26,639	9.3	2,810.9	2.0	89.4	$86,158	38.4	2.7	74.8	3.4	90.4	7.8
Taylorsville city	10.848	58,644	60,433	3.1	5,571.0	14.3	84.3	$57,779	20.2	10.6	73.0	7.5	71.5	22.9
Tooele city	24.035	31,605	32,573	3.1	1,355.2	3.4	84.2	$56,370	17.5	9.7	67.3	9.0	77.0	19.3
Washington city	32.278	18,761	23,360	24.5	723.7	7.9	83.6	$49,995	12.9	11.2	61.4	9.0	82.0	15.6
West Haven city	10.303	10,275	11,582	12.7	1,124.2	5.6	85.9	$71,802	31.4	4.6	75.0	6.6	75.7	18.1
West Jordan city	32.465	103,708	110,920	7.0	3,416.6	9.6	87.1	$69,404	25.7	8.1	76.1	6.8	80.8	15.5
West Valley City city	35.561	129,475	134,495	3.9	3,782.1	22.0	82.0	$52,814	14.5	16.8	72.8	9.2	80.3	15.8
Woods Cross city	3.882	9,761	11,097	13.7	2,858.5	6.0	87.8	$69,825	24.9	8.4	76.6	3.7	85.5	10.7
VERMONT	9,216.656	625,745	626,562	0.1	68.0	4.2	86.7	$54,447	20.8	12.0	67.2	6.2	62.5	28.5
Bennington town (Bennington)	42.249	15,764	15,431	-2.1	365.2	2.6	82.9	$36,990	12.0	20.7	60.0	10.6	61.5	31.4
Brattleboro town (Windham)	31.828	12,046	11,765	-2.3	369.6	5.2	86.3	$46,899	12.1	14.5	67.4	9.0	51.9	35.8
Burlington city & MCD (Chittenden)	10.306	42,417	42,211	-0.5	4,095.6	10.2	67.5	$42,745	16.3	24.5	64.7	8.8	41.3	36.1
Colchester town (Chittenden)	36.327	17,067	17,384	1.9	478.5	4.7	84.4	$68,440	30.5	8.6	73.9	3.9	69.2	20.1
Essex town (Chittenden)*	38.824	19,593	20,724	5.8	533.8	7.5	87.0	$73,530	33.0	6.2	74.4	4.6	65.5	26.8
Milton town (Chittenden)	51.380	10,352	10,667	3.0	207.6	3.6	91.8	$65,857	25.3	4.8	76.7	6.5	71.0	20.4

1 Dry land or land partially or temporarily covered by water.
2 16 years old and over.

632   TX(Tyler city)—VT(Milton town (Chittenden))

Items 1–14

Table B. Incorporated Places, Census Designated Places (CDPs), and Minor Civil Divisions (MCDs) of 10,000 or More Population — Crime, Construction, and Local Government Finance

STATE City, town, township, borough, or CDP (county if applicable)	Serious crimes known to police, 2014[1] Total number	Rate[2] Total	Rate[2] Violent	Rate[2] Property	New residential construction authorized by building permits, 2014 Value ($1,000)	Number of housing units	Percent single family	Local government finance, 2012 General revenue Total (mil dol)	Intergovernmental Total (mil dol)	Percent from state gov.	Taxes per capita[3]	General expenditure Total (mil dol)	Per capita[3] Total	Per capita[3] Capital outlays	Debt outstanding (mil dol)
	15	16	17	18	19	20	21	22	23	24	25	26	27	28	29
TEXAS—Con.															
Tyler city	4,557	4513	463	4051	97,026	280	95.7	128.9	15.0	13.7	623	120.1	1,209	168	428.2
Universal City city	450	2299	230	2069	1,615	7	100.0	16.5	0.1	100.0	523	16.2	842	131	36.0
University Park city	306	1263	17	1247	92,591	126	84.9	51.8	0.1	100.0	1037	47.8	2,007	171	407.4
Uvalde city	858	5228	457	4771	1,241	13	100.0	13.4	2.7	99.5	367	15.6	969	365	19.8
Vernon city	318	3003	217	2786	285	2	100.0	7.7	0.1	3.3	350	9.0	833	7	8.9
Victoria city	2,649	4030	516	3515	85,491	835	19.5	78.7	5.7	39.9	773	89.3	1,386	576	179.1
Vidor city	475	4336	475	3862	1,280	11	100.0	7.1	0.0	50.0	491	6.8	619	20	1.0
Waco city	5,585	4298	443	3855	156,358	1,245	30.9	359.0	127.8	9.2	762	344.8	2,700	343	8413.1
Watauga city	455	1869	94	1774	677	6	100.0	19.5	0.4	100.0	531	20.2	839	164	24.6
Waxahachie city	1,013	3160	90	3070	46,444	314	100.0	40.4	0.2	100.0	928	33.9	1,090	82	170.0
Weatherford city	740	2698	171	2527	35,312	195	100.0	34.6	3.2	80.9	782	43.0	1,627	441	117.6
Webster city	608	5478	252	5226	5,648	22	100.0	23.7	0.6	74.5	1769	22.7	2,084	390	38.6
Wells Branch CDP	NA	NA	NA	NA	NA	NA	NA	NA	NA	NA	NA	NA	NA	NA	NA
Weslaco city	3,105	8289	1207	7083	14,309	199	71.9	37.6	0.7	25.3	599	35.9	972	114	115.6
West Odessa CDP	NA	NA	NA	NA	NA	NA	NA	NA	NA	NA	NA	NA	NA	NA	NA
West University Place city	171	1103	13	1090	48,344	67	100.0	25.3	0.4	2.3	1172	24.3	1,592	306	84.0
White Settlement city	521	3091	178	2913	5,094	35	100.0	16.2	0.2	37.3	648	12.6	760	0	16.3
Wichita Falls city	4,684	4463	406	4057	19,442	122	60.7	120.3	13.6	34.0	633	114.0	1,088	129	168.4
Wylie city	548	1209	108	1101	59,932	251	100.0	43.1	1.6	92.9	688	53.2	1,199	374	119.8
UTAH	91,057	3094	216	2878	3,360,911	17,510	64.4	X	X	X	X	X	X	X	X
American Fork city	842	2192	55	2137	19,693	93	86.0	30.4	2.8	100.0	497	29.8	1,092	170	62.3
Bountiful city	884	2050	90	1960	17,976	65	63.1	25.9	3.0	48.4	320	21.6	504	27	18.1
Brigham City city	489	2632	145	2487	5,149	29	100.0	18.4	1.4	52.9	402	24.0	1,317	282	33.8
Cedar City city	845	2892	267	2625	23,285	142	71.8	26.1	3.3	64.2	465	21.4	736	103	21.1
Cedar Hills city	NA	NA	NA	NA	5,086	10	100.0	6.0	0.3	85.3	299	9.6	962	313	15.2
Centerville city	571	3368	319	3050	1,807	7	100.0	10.5	0.7	78.0	457	10.7	663	62	12.5
Clearfield city	686	2247	128	2119	5,433	40	100.0	27.3	4.4	91.5	387	21.4	704	59	24.6
Clinton city	239	1137	43	1094	8,632	39	100.0	11.1	0.9	79.9	279	9.3	449	8	2.6
Cottonwood Heights city	801	2326	122	2204	7,401	21	100.0	14.9	1.2	96.8	374	16.8	494	109	0.0
Draper city	1,221	2653	156	2496	58,084	219	78.5	36.2	2.5	98.9	544	32.8	742	114	33.1
Eagle Mountain city	NA	NA	NA	NA	91,726	355	100.0	14.3	1.6	66.4	239	16.9	727	62	50.3
Farmington city	292	1299	71	1228	31,365	115	100.0	13.1	0.7	82.2	326	15.5	747	312	0.0
Heber city	124	932	68	864	40,594	141	100.0	8.9	1.3	53.2	490	9.8	793	365	1.4
Herriman city	NA	NA	NA	NA	90,825	611	85.9	15.2	2.5	100.0	345	22.2	909	253	44.6
Highland city	NA	NA	NA	NA	46,169	139	100.0	10.0	0.7	100.0	290	9.8	598	28	15.1
Holladay city	NA	NA	NA	NA	10,732	26	100.0	17.7	2.0	70.1	434	15.0	555	0	20.8
Hurricane city	222	1502	101	1400	35,001	209	94.3	34.6	0.9	75.4	397	10.9	760	78	13.2
Kaysville city	210	719	51	667	53,969	184	100.0	15.6	1.7	75.8	236	10.3	364	62	2.6
Kearns CDP	NA	NA	NA	NA	NA	NA	NA	NA	NA	NA	NA	NA	NA	NA	NA
Layton city	1,596	2228	123	2105	69,947	452	57.1	45.3	3.8	61.6	375	40.3	587	14	4.9
Lehi city	749	1336	68	1268	140,201	719	63.0	47.8	1.8	100.0	552	36.9	718	82	97.2
Lindon city	226	2105	75	2031	14,671	52	100.0	11.2	0.4	81.2	712	10.9	1,048	21	22.7
Logan city	819	1670	71	1598	35,706	260	38.8	58.6	7.2	21.6	408	49.7	1,011	194	43.8
Magna CDP	NA	NA	NA	NA	NA	NA	NA	NA	NA	NA	NA	NA	NA	NA	NA
Midvale city	NA	NA	NA	NA	59,790	385	43.9	17.3	1.8	50.9	368	17.2	568	9	50.8
Millcreek CDP	NA	NA	NA	NA	NA	NA	NA	NA	NA	NA	NA	NA	NA	NA	NA
Murray city	2,644	5387	454	4932	33,465	179	34.1	52.5	4.5	36.2	604	48.5	1,005	89	36.9
North Ogden city	199	1095	83	1012	14,895	60	100.0	9.6	0.7	88.6	295	8.6	484	44	4.3
North Salt Lake city	451	2627	82	2545	42,807	219	79.9	15.3	0.5	93.1	569	13.0	766	252	10.4
Ogden city	4,169	4930	538	4392	29,763	321	17.8	102.4	13.2	30.0	578	114.7	1,367	205	115.6
Orem city	1,992	2156	43	2112	149,896	1,028	22.9	78.3	6.3	49.6	427	65.7	725	49	67.1
Payson city	497	2570	78	2493	8,875	55	74.5	14.5	1.0	69.3	328	13.5	714	130	24.9
Pleasant Grove city	275	779	42	736	62,953	365	44.1	23.6	2.0	81.2	261	21.4	621	39	62.2
Provo city	2,388	2038	131	1907	40,136	291	44.0	87.3	11.8	35.6	339	98.1	850	250	115.1
Riverton city	NA	NA	NA	NA	28,619	116	64.7	19.6	1.5	82.4	264	34.9	864	199	482.2
Roy city	806	2125	111	2015	1,452	11	100.0	21.0	1.5	77.3	279	16.4	436	23	7.2
St. George city	1,631	2095	145	1950	120,943	792	95.1	76.3	3.8	65.5	504	76.8	1,020	221	157.4
Salt Lake City city	17,728	9216	755	8461	47,290	340	27.9	529.4	30.7	31.4	1062	382.9	2,021	145	393.2
Sandy city	2,714	2987	175	2812	51,544	503	15.7	79.3	5.3	56.3	502	64.8	724	74	93.6
Saratoga Springs city	196	812	54	759	61,837	320	72.5	21.2	1.0	100.0	488	21.1	999	226	11.9
Smithfield city	NA	NA	NA	NA	20,038	209	11.5	8.4	0.6	74.3	318	7.6	749	38	4.0
South Jordan city	1,424	2312	78	2234	213,288	1,130	71.3	55.2	2.4	79.1	614	50.1	895	75	71.6
South Ogden city	319	1894	142	1751	5,021	15	100.0	12.0	0.6	80.4	411	11.4	683	37	10.0
South Salt Lake city	1,892	7580	849	6730	4,203	43	25.6	31.2	3.1	70.1	948	52.6	2,160	1,143	17.0
Spanish Fork city	497	1327	24	1303	53,945	190	100.0	37.6	1.4	82.8	277	31.9	880	170	24.7
Springville city	650	2057	108	1950	23,970	328	18.3	25.9	1.1	90.9	325	30.3	989	165	37.6
Syracuse city	274	1050	54	996	39,671	178	84.3	13.7	0.9	93.1	337	10.3	410	23	14.7
Taylorsville city	NA	NA	NA	NA	7,629	34	100.0	24.7	2.8	76.1	287	28.5	473	69	10.9
Tooele city	1,469	4520	314	4206	17,324	157	54.1	20.4	1.8	85.9	358	20.7	645	92	36.8
Washington city	530	2332	119	2213	99,250	393	100.0	19.9	1.3	100.0	556	16.6	798	86	39.7
West Haven city	NA	NA	NA	NA	18,528	97	73.2	3.6	0.4	100.0	235	3.0	274	75	0.0
West Jordan city	2,288	2050	191	1859	75,647	364	77.2	65.0	6.3	62.5	329	59.0	544	60	23.2
West Valley City city	6,620	4919	473	4446	61,239	563	24.5	134.8	12.6	33.4	507	154.8	1,168	359	149.0
Woods Cross city	NA	NA	NA	NA	9,283	44	86.4	7.3	0.3	100.0	442	5.4	526	30	5.4
VERMONT	10,173	1624	99	1524	281,490	1,546	63.3	X	X	X	X	X	X	X	X
Bennington town (Bennington)	405	2619	213	2405	500	3	100.0	15.4	4.5	100.0	550	17.1	1,101	47	10.9
Brattleboro town (Windham)	475	4047	349	3698	1,285	8	100.0	20.6	2.3	55.2	1129	28.0	2,361	1,020	33.9
Burlington city & MCD (Chittenden)	1,455	3444	137	3306	612	4	100.0	110.0	17.7	38.0	908	92.8	2,192	417	192.6
Colchester town (Chittenden)	134	773	46	726	7,868	40	60.0	17.3	3.9	84.8	608	19.1	1,109	359	8.8
Essex town (Chittenden)*	358	1725	39	1686	4,088	17	76.5	11.8	0.8	100.0	460	11.8	586	0	0.7
Milton town (Chittenden)	152	1431	66	1365	7,498	90	13.3	7.0	0.5	97.8	472	7.2	682	104	8.4

1 Data for serious crimes have not been adjusted for underreporting. This may affect comparability between geographic areas over time.
2 Per 100,000 population estimated by the FBI. 3 Based on population estimated as of July 1 of the year shown.

Table B. Incorporated Places, Census Designated Places (CDPs), and Minor Civil Divisions (MCDs) of 10,000 or More Population — Land Area, Population, and Households, and Employment

STATE City, town, township, borough, or CDP (county if applicable)	Land area,[1] 2010 (sq mi)	Population Total persons 2010	Total persons 2014	Percent change 2010–2014	Persons per square mile, 2014	Population characteristics 2010–2014 Foreign born	Lives in same house as previous year	Household income and poverty, 2010–2014 Median household income (dollars)	Percent of households Income of $100,000 or more	Income below poverty level	Employment,[2] 2010–2014 Percent in labor force	Unemployment rate	Households, 2010–2014 (percent of households) Family households	One person households
	1	2	3	4	5	6	7	8	9	10	11	12	13	14
VERMONT—Con.														
Rutland city & MCD (Rutland)..	7.558	16,495	15,942	-3.4	2,109.4	2.7	87.0	$38,558	11.7	17.1	62.7	8.9	56.8	34.7
South Burlington city & MCD (Chittenden)	16.492	17,902	18,743	4.7	1,136.5	10.1	84.4	$67,396	29.3	5.2	70.9	4.7	55.5	32.6
VIRGINIA	39,490.084	8,001,023	8,326,289	4.1	210.8	11.6	84.7	$64,792	30.8	11.0	66.4	6.9	67.3	26.5
Alexandria city	15.049	140,006	150,575	7.5	10,005.4	26.6	78.2	$87,319	43.6	6.8	79.2	4.7	47.6	42.7
Annandale CDP	7.848	41,008	NA	NA	NA	44.7	85.8	$78,780	38.9	10.6	71.1	6.6	71.1	23.9
Arlington CDP	25.992	207,627	NA	NA	NA	22.9	78.7	$105,120	53.1	6.5	78.7	3.6	46.3	40.1
Ashburn CDP	17.048	43,511	NA	NA	NA	22.5	86.8	$122,687	62.5	3.0	75.9	4.1	77.6	18.3
Bailey's Crossroads CDP	2.051	23,643	NA	NA	NA	50.6	84.9	$67,465	30.3	14.3	68.3	7.4	57.0	35.7
Blacksburg town	19.894	42,607	43,985	3.2	2,211.0	17.0	55.1	$29,271	16.7	41.2	51.2	8.8	34.4	29.7
Bon Air CDP	8.336	16,366	NA	NA	NA	8.4	87.6	$68,561	30.4	6.5	68.5	8.0	65.3	29.1
Brambleton CDP	5.755	9,845	NA	NA	NA	23.9	80.0	$171,156	83.0	2.1	82.6	3.3	84.9	9.1
Brandermill CDP	6.163	13,173	NA	NA	NA	6.6	85.9	$75,657	34.7	2.2	66.8	6.0	67.4	29.6
Bristol city	13.013	17,841	17,184	-3.7	1,320.5	1.6	77.2	$33,616	7.8	19.2	57.1	11.0	64.5	30.3
Broadlands CDP	3.271	12,313	NA	NA	NA	17.3	88.2	$163,800	84.8	1.0	82.1	3.8	87.1	10.1
Buckhall CDP	20.199	16,293	NA	NA	NA	15.9	92.5	$125,372	67.4	4.1	74.4	6.8	81.7	15.6
Bull Run CDP	2.599	14,983	NA	NA	NA	37.0	80.3	$64,781	22.0	12.2	79.5	3.6	61.4	27.5
Burke CDP	8.627	41,055	NA	NA	NA	22.1	89.7	$132,066	68.2	2.2	72.8	3.2	84.4	12.0
Burke Centre CDP	3.133	17,326	NA	NA	NA	25.6	85.1	$100,086	50.1	4.8	71.6	4.5	77.5	17.9
Cascades CDP	3.687	11,912	NA	NA	NA	23.6	89.2	$141,750	70.2	2.3	73.5	2.8	73.5	21.7
Cave Spring CDP	11.911	24,922	NA	NA	NA	7.5	84.1	$65,053	27.9	7.2	68.3	5.8	61.3	33.7
Centreville CDP	11.945	71,135	NA	NA	NA	33.5	84.0	$103,696	52.9	4.7	77.7	5.5	73.2	19.8
Chantilly CDP	12.000	23,039	NA	NA	NA	32.5	90.2	$118,991	59.1	8.0	76.4	8.1	83.1	11.4
Charlottesville city	10.238	43,435	45,593	5.0	4,453.3	11.8	72.8	$47,218	22.1	23.7	61.9	5.0	43.6	37.0
Cherry Hill CDP	7.796	16,000	NA	NA	NA	27.9	79.8	$80,574	38.0	7.2	77.0	6.9	75.7	18.6
Chesapeake city	340.785	222,209	233,371	5.0	684.8	4.7	85.9	$70,176	30.5	8.6	67.6	7.6	74.9	20.9
Chester CDP	13.158	20,987	NA	NA	NA	6.1	89.0	$60,570	21.9	11.5	65.6	8.6	68.3	26.4
Christiansburg town	14.123	20,961	21,805	4.0	1,543.9	3.0	83.3	$51,508	16.7	12.2	67.9	3.6	60.3	32.5
Colonial Heights city	7.522	17,413	17,731	1.8	2,357.3	5.6	89.9	$52,529	20.3	7.8	61.8	7.2	64.8	28.6
Countryside CDP	2.574	10,072	NA	NA	NA	17.4	86.7	$111,646	59.3	0.8	81.3	3.1	72.0	20.0
Culpeper town	7.221	16,651	17,411	4.6	2,411.1	11.8	86.1	$54,791	22.4	14.0	67.8	7.2	69.9	25.0
Dale City CDP	14.232	65,969	NA	NA	NA	26.1	84.1	$85,383	40.6	6.4	74.7	8.3	82.0	14.2
Danville city	42.968	43,066	42,444	-1.4	987.8	3.4	82.3	$32,173	8.8	24.4	55.8	14.7	59.6	35.9
Dranesville CDP	3.843	11,921	NA	NA	NA	16.8	92.0	$166,775	77.0	4.9	72.1	3.2	85.4	14.1
East Highland Park CDP	8.811	14,796	NA	NA	NA	3.9	90.8	$47,085	12.2	11.7	66.6	10.4	60.2	36.6
Fairfax city	6.240	22,542	24,483	8.6	3,923.7	25.0	83.5	$100,584	50.4	7.1	69.5	5.5	65.8	21.7
Fairfax Station CDP	9.087	12,030	NA	NA	NA	16.2	89.5	$163,796	73.2	2.2	70.5	4.2	83.5	13.5
Fair Oaks CDP	4.999	30,223	NA	NA	NA	33.7	72.9	$102,072	51.3	5.7	81.4	4.1	54.6	33.1
Falls Church city	1.987	12,289	13,601	10.7	6,844.1	17.9	79.9	$120,500	57.8	4.0	77.3	5.0	63.1	32.2
Fort Hunt CDP	5.851	16,045	NA	NA	NA	8.9	89.1	$166,506	76.3	1.2	64.4	3.0	83.0	14.8
Franconia CDP	3.474	18,245	NA	NA	NA	25.4	88.1	$113,039	59.0	2.5	78.8	4.2	62.9	28.8
Franklin Farm CDP	4.753	19,288	NA	NA	NA	18.0	91.5	$170,037	83.1	3.0	73.4	4.0	89.4	8.3
Fredericksburg city	10.439	24,023	28,350	18.0	2,715.7	8.3	69.5	$49,454	22.9	17.2	64.6	10.4	55.2	35.7
Front Royal town	9.242	14,440	15,038	4.1	1,627.1	3.9	87.0	$46,609	16.2	14.7	65.2	9.4	64.8	30.1
Gainesville CDP	10.126	11,481	NA	NA	NA	18.6	86.8	$130,944	66.1	3.8	77.5	3.7	80.5	14.3
Glen Allen CDP	8.791	14,774	NA	NA	NA	8.7	88.9	$68,101	30.5	6.3	71.6	5.1	68.9	28.0
Great Falls CDP	25.357	15,427	NA	NA	NA	24.5	91.5	$229,200	84.3	2.2	60.6	4.4	90.5	6.4
Groveton CDP	4.347	14,598	NA	NA	NA	31.0	84.7	$66,786	34.5	10.4	77.1	6.3	68.9	23.9
Hampton city	51.441	137,508	136,879	-0.5	2,660.9	4.9	84.1	$49,879	17.6	13.9	64.9	10.5	62.8	30.9
Harrisonburg city	17.332	48,907	52,478	7.3	3,027.8	15.5	67.3	$38,807	11.2	27.2	57.8	6.8	50.7	26.3
Herndon town	4.276	23,292	24,554	5.4	5,741.6	43.2	87.2	$100,399	50.4	4.2	80.6	4.7	71.8	21.6
Highland Springs CDP	7.998	15,711	NA	NA	NA	3.4	86.0	$40,045	10.5	16.7	69.0	13.6	72.5	21.4
Hollins CDP	8.611	14,673	NA	NA	NA	5.0	86.7	$56,534	18.4	8.3	60.9	5.8	59.0	35.8
Hopewell city	10.278	22,591	22,196	-1.7	2,159.5	4.9	88.0	$39,156	10.1	18.4	60.9	13.7	62.1	33.5
Huntington CDP	1.090	11,267	NA	NA	NA	23.0	79.7	$85,807	38.8	5.9	80.0	3.5	42.9	47.5
Hybla Valley CDP	2.053	15,801	NA	NA	NA	31.4	86.6	$56,165	28.0	18.0	71.6	4.3	63.4	30.6
Idylwood CDP	2.864	17,288	NA	NA	NA	37.4	82.6	$98,040	49.1	6.3	78.3	5.7	60.2	27.7
Kings Park West CDP	2.957	13,390	NA	NA	NA	22.7	86.8	$134,762	68.2	4.6	68.6	5.8	79.7	14.6
Kingstowne CDP	2.863	15,556	NA	NA	NA	22.1	80.9	$124,259	66.1	1.6	79.8	3.3	60.9	31.4
Lake Ridge CDP	9.351	41,058	NA	NA	NA	20.3	83.6	$101,737	51.0	3.6	75.3	5.6	74.2	21.3
Lakeside CDP	4.328	11,849	NA	NA	NA	12.7	85.8	$44,589	13.1	14.5	73.8	11.3	59.4	33.2
Lansdowne CDP	3.980	11,253	NA	NA	NA	24.1	78.3	$124,291	58.1	1.1	72.6	4.0	67.8	24.5
Laurel CDP	5.388	16,713	NA	NA	NA	12.5	73.9	$50,509	13.2	11.0	72.1	8.2	58.8	32.9
Leesburg town	12.389	42,616	49,496	16.1	3,995.3	22.5	84.6	$101,719	50.9	4.5	77.7	4.7	75.0	18.7
Lincolnia CDP	4.740	22,855	NA	NA	NA	44.1	83.7	$93,352	47.1	8.0	74.8	5.6	65.3	26.0
Linton Hall CDP	12.727	35,725	NA	NA	NA	14.0	89.3	$134,219	73.6	1.2	80.4	3.4	88.1	8.9
Lorton CDP	5.298	18,610	NA	NA	NA	34.9	83.6	$90,820	45.3	3.1	79.1	8.4	73.6	22.2
Lowes Island CDP	3.017	10,756	NA	NA	NA	25.1	88.0	$138,973	76.4	1.7	72.4	4.0	82.1	14.5
Lynchburg city	49.128	75,613	79,047	4.5	1,609.0	5.1	74.2	$39,391	13.6	22.1	58.4	9.6	57.0	34.7
McLean CDP	24.780	48,115	NA	NA	NA	23.6	89.9	$188,639	77.0	2.7	62.0	4.5	80.3	17.3
McNair CDP	2.046	17,513	NA	NA	NA	43.5	69.0	$106,769	57.1	2.9	81.7	3.6	61.0	29.2
Madison Heights CDP	19.193	11,285	NA	NA	NA	1.7	88.9	$40,177	8.7	11.2	60.2	7.3	59.0	36.6
Manassas city	9.881	37,839	42,081	11.2	4,258.9	26.9	84.4	$71,215	33.5	9.2	75.1	8.0	74.7	20.3
Manassas Park city	2.539	14,241	15,174	6.6	5,976.5	32.4	83.7	$73,460	32.6	7.6	72.5	3.7	72.8	23.8
Manchester CDP	5.926	10,804	NA	NA	NA	10.0	87.4	$54,513	22.3	7.2	69.8	9.6	60.2	32.8
Martinsville city	10.956	13,821	13,711	-0.8	1,251.4	3.5	85.2	$27,746	9.2	26.8	52.3	14.2	55.5	41.4
Marumsco CDP	7.421	35,036	NA	NA	NA	36.9	82.3	$71,892	29.4	9.4	77.7	6.7	71.8	22.4
Meadowbrook CDP	8.131	18,312	NA	NA	NA	12.5	91.6	$56,910	19.6	8.6	67.6	11.8	72.4	23.1
Mechanicsville CDP	28.317	36,348	NA	NA	NA	4.4	89.0	$72,170	30.9	5.6	68.4	5.2	73.2	21.2
Merrifield CDP	2.697	15,212	NA	NA	NA	42.7	73.6	$112,049	57.6	4.1	81.9	4.9	55.4	28.4
Montclair CDP	6.005	19,570	NA	NA	NA	13.0	89.4	$119,105	62.2	2.3	72.8	4.4	81.3	16.5
Mount Vernon CDP	5.226	12,416	NA	NA	NA	22.2	89.9	$122,407	55.7	8.1	66.3	4.0	78.4	18.0
Neabsco CDP	4.609	12,068	NA	NA	NA	23.2	83.7	$124,089	60.8	3.0	76.6	4.4	79.7	17.5
Newington CDP	4.549	12,943	NA	NA	NA	27.9	89.1	$133,456	65.4	3.7	76.4	5.8	82.6	13.3

1 Dry land or land partially or temporarily covered by water.
2 16 years old and over.

Table B. Incorporated Places, Census Designated Places (CDPs), and Minor Civil Divisions (MCDs) of 10,000 or More Population — Crime, Construction, and Local Government Finance

STATE City, town, township, borough, or CDP (county if applicable)	Serious crimes known to police, 2014[1] Total number	Rate[2] Total	Rate[2] Violent	Rate[2] Property	New residential construction authorized by building permits, 2014 Value ($1,000)	Number of housing units	Percent single family	Local government finance, 2012 General revenue Total (mil dol)	Intergovernmental Total (mil dol)	Intergovernmental Percent from state gov.	Taxes per capita[3]	General expenditure Total (mil dol)	Per capita[3] Total	Per capita Capital outlays	Debt outstanding (mil dol)
	15	16	17	18	19	20	21	22	23	24	25	26	27	28	29
VERMONT—Con.															
Rutland city & MCD (Rutland) ..	681	4245	349	3896	465	3	100.0	22.7	2.9	90.8	862	21.6	1,328	40	14.1
South Burlington city & MCD (Chittenden)	552	2939	107	2833	18,217	68	72.1	26.0	1.4	80.8	777	24.1	1,309	251	42.5
VIRGINIA	177,060	2127	196	1930	4,655,664	28,682	65.7	X	X	X	X	X	X	X	X
Alexandria city	3,263	2160	185	1975	170,552	1,324	13.1	694.5	112.0	62.0	3394	697.3	4,746	514	580.7
Annandale CDP....................	NA	NA	NA	NA	NA	NA	NA	NA	NA	NA	NA	NA	NA	NA	NA
Arlington CDP.....................	NA	NA	NA	NA	NA	NA	NA	NA	NA	NA	NA	NA	NA	NA	NA
Ashburn CDP......................	NA	NA	NA	NA	NA	NA	NA	NA	NA	NA	NA	NA	NA	NA	NA
Bailey's Crossroads CDP	NA	NA	NA	NA	NA	NA	NA	NA	NA	NA	NA	NA	NA	NA	NA
Blacksburg town	424	967	73	894	21,969	117	55.6	40.4	14.5	48.6	382	36.6	855	218	23.1
Bon Air CDP	NA	NA	NA	NA	NA	NA	NA	NA	NA	NA	NA	NA	NA	NA	NA
Brambleton CDP...................	NA	NA	NA	NA	NA	NA	NA	NA	NA	NA	NA	NA	NA	NA	NA
Brandermill CDP...................	NA	NA	NA	NA	NA	NA	NA	NA	NA	NA	NA	NA	NA	NA	NA
Bristol city	537	3118	313	2804	900	10	80.0	72.8	36.6	91.5	1513	81.7	4,611	452	57.6
Broadlands CDP...................	NA	NA	NA	NA	NA	NA	NA	NA	NA	NA	NA	NA	NA	NA	NA
Buckhall CDP......................	NA	NA	NA	NA	NA	NA	NA	NA	NA	NA	NA	NA	NA	NA	NA
Bull Run CDP	NA	NA	NA	NA	NA	NA	NA	NA	NA	NA	NA	NA	NA	NA	NA
Burke CDP.........................	NA	NA	NA	NA	NA	NA	NA	NA	NA	NA	NA	NA	NA	NA	NA
Burke Centre CDP	NA	NA	NA	NA	NA	NA	NA	NA	NA	NA	NA	NA	NA	NA	NA
Cascades CDP	NA	NA	NA	NA	NA	NA	NA	NA	NA	NA	NA	NA	NA	NA	NA
Cave Spring CDP	NA	NA	NA	NA	NA	NA	NA	NA	NA	NA	NA	NA	NA	NA	NA
Centreville CDP	NA	NA	NA	NA	NA	NA	NA	NA	NA	NA	NA	NA	NA	NA	NA
Chantilly CDP	NA	NA	NA	NA	NA	NA	NA	NA	NA	NA	NA	NA	NA	NA	NA
Charlottesville city................	1,550	3477	431	3047	30,030	173	35.8	233.9	98.5	67.6	2089	229.9	5,163	617	117.7
Cherry Hill CDP	NA	NA	NA	NA	NA	NA	NA	NA	NA	NA	NA	NA	NA	NA	NA
Chesapeake city..................	7,428	3195	430	2765	182,896	886	95.5	886.7	369.8	97.8	1852	865.4	3,792	475	635.5
Chester CDP.......................	NA	NA	NA	NA	NA	NA	NA	NA	NA	NA	NA	NA	NA	NA	NA
Christiansburg town...............	482	2225	97	2128	9,177	71	100.0	26.8	3.8	88.9	732	27.4	1,277	138	18.8
Colonial Heights city..............	905	5111	215	4897	1,694	13	100.0	74.5	26.0	91.9	2293	72.5	4,139	472	39.8
Countryside CDP..................	NA	NA	NA	NA	NA	NA	NA	NA	NA	NA	NA	NA	NA	NA	NA
Culpeper town	520	3013	238	2775	NA	NA	NA	17.4	2.3	100.0	486	16.4	975	70	39.7
Dale City CDP	NA	NA	NA	NA	NA	NA	NA	NA	NA	NA	NA	NA	NA	NA	NA
Danville city	1,965	4577	447	4129	1,638	12	100.0	173.3	85.4	95.4	1186	179.2	4,189	318	152.0
Dranesville CDP...................	NA	NA	NA	NA	NA	NA	NA	NA	NA	NA	NA	NA	NA	NA	NA
East Highland Park CDP	NA	NA	NA	NA	NA	NA	NA	NA	NA	NA	NA	NA	NA	NA	NA
Fairfax city	464	1906	74	1832	7,183	54	100.0	123.4	23.1	79.4	3711	115.6	4,925	176	257.2
Fairfax Station CDP	NA	NA	NA	NA	NA	NA	NA	NA	NA	NA	NA	NA	NA	NA	NA
Fair Oaks CDP.....................	NA	NA	NA	NA	NA	NA	NA	NA	NA	NA	NA	NA	NA	NA	NA
Falls Church city	239	1733	130	1602	108,237	547	6.8	85.0	11.1	80.6	4486	76.6	5,828	246	71.0
Fort Hunt CDP	NA	NA	NA	NA	NA	NA	NA	NA	NA	NA	NA	NA	NA	NA	NA
Franconia CDP	NA	NA	NA	NA	NA	NA	NA	NA	NA	NA	NA	NA	NA	NA	NA
Franklin Farm CDP	NA	NA	NA	NA	NA	NA	NA	NA	NA	NA	NA	NA	NA	NA	NA
Fredericksburg city	1,333	4572	449	4122	5,648	23	100.0	127.4	33.7	69.0	2501	119.9	4,422	416	349.9
Front Royal town	445	2965	153	2812	NA	NA	NA	13.8	2.6	98.8	389	14.2	973	175	12.0
Gainesville CDP...................	NA	NA	NA	NA	NA	NA	NA	NA	NA	NA	NA	NA	NA	NA	NA
Glen Allen CDP....................	NA	NA	NA	NA	NA	NA	NA	NA	NA	NA	NA	NA	NA	NA	NA
Great Falls CDP...................	NA	NA	NA	NA	NA	NA	NA	NA	NA	NA	NA	NA	NA	NA	NA
Groveton CDP	NA	NA	NA	NA	NA	NA	NA	NA	NA	NA	NA	NA	NA	NA	NA
Hampton city.......................	4,790	3507	256	3251	7,087	160	100.0	525.3	220.7	90.2	1599	516.8	3,777	217	359.9
Harrisonburg city..................	1,257	2416	198	2218	14,080	152	47.4	165.0	51.6	74.2	1238	166.3	3,246	275	500.6
Herndon town	361	1461	194	1266	2,572	14	100.0	38.6	7.2	73.5	831	37.7	1,549	116	20.0
Highland Springs CDP............	NA	NA	NA	NA	NA	NA	NA	NA	NA	NA	NA	NA	NA	NA	NA
Hollins CDP	NA	NA	NA	NA	NA	NA	NA	NA	NA	NA	NA	NA	NA	NA	NA
Hopewell city	764	3464	381	3083	10,409	90	100.0	102.4	46.9	88.6	1441	115.7	5,185	1,010	93.0
Huntington CDP....................	NA	NA	NA	NA	NA	NA	NA	NA	NA	NA	NA	NA	NA	NA	NA
Hybla Valley CDP..................	NA	NA	NA	NA	NA	NA	NA	NA	NA	NA	NA	NA	NA	NA	NA
Idylwood CDP......................	NA	NA	NA	NA	NA	NA	NA	NA	NA	NA	NA	NA	NA	NA	NA
Kings Park West CDP.............	NA	NA	NA	NA	NA	NA	NA	NA	NA	NA	NA	NA	NA	NA	NA
Kingstowne CDP...................	NA	NA	NA	NA	NA	NA	NA	NA	NA	NA	NA	NA	NA	NA	NA
Lake Ridge CDP...................	NA	NA	NA	NA	NA	NA	NA	NA	NA	NA	NA	NA	NA	NA	NA
Lakeside CDP......................	NA	NA	NA	NA	NA	NA	NA	NA	NA	NA	NA	NA	NA	NA	NA
Lansdowne CDP...................	NA	NA	NA	NA	NA	NA	NA	NA	NA	NA	NA	NA	NA	NA	NA
Laurel CDP	NA	NA	NA	NA	NA	NA	NA	NA	NA	NA	NA	NA	NA	NA	NA
Leesburg town	788	1611	121	1490	NA	NA	NA	59.3	13.1	95.3	693	58.7	1,273	249	126.9
Lincolnia CDP......................	NA	NA	NA	NA	NA	NA	NA	NA	NA	NA	NA	NA	NA	NA	NA
Linton Hall CDP	NA	NA	NA	NA	NA	NA	NA	NA	NA	NA	NA	NA	NA	NA	NA
Lorton CDP.........................	NA	NA	NA	NA	NA	NA	NA	NA	NA	NA	NA	NA	NA	NA	NA
Lowes Island CDP.................	NA	NA	NA	NA	NA	NA	NA	NA	NA	NA	NA	NA	NA	NA	NA
Lynchburg city.....................	2,372	3016	472	2545	17,863	92	100.0	266.8	110.8	87.0	1510	268.3	3,449	589	330.4
McLean CDP	NA	NA	NA	NA	NA	NA	NA	NA	NA	NA	NA	NA	NA	NA	NA
McNair CDP........................	NA	NA	NA	NA	NA	NA	NA	NA	NA	NA	NA	NA	NA	NA	NA
Madison Heights CDP.............	NA	NA	NA	NA	NA	NA	NA	NA	NA	NA	NA	NA	NA	NA	NA
Manassas city	866	2031	326	1705	17,617	125	100.0	181.8	62.5	84.3	2049	169.8	4,168	200	130.5
Manassas Park city................	177	1065	150	915	2,050	11	100.0	58.7	24.8	93.0	1685	60.1	3,985	30	123.4
Manchester CDP...................	NA	NA	NA	NA	NA	NA	NA	NA	NA	NA	NA	NA	NA	NA	NA
Martinsville city	437	3175	356	2819	95	1	100.0	57.1	31.6	71.5	1147	56.8	4,132	290	24.5
Marumsco CDP	NA	NA	NA	NA	NA	NA	NA	NA	NA	NA	NA	NA	NA	NA	NA
Meadowbrook CDP................	NA	NA	NA	NA	NA	NA	NA	NA	NA	NA	NA	NA	NA	NA	NA
Mechanicsville CDP...............	NA	NA	NA	NA	NA	NA	NA	NA	NA	NA	NA	NA	NA	NA	NA
Merrifield CDP.....................	NA	NA	NA	NA	NA	NA	NA	NA	NA	NA	NA	NA	NA	NA	NA
Montclair CDP	NA	NA	NA	NA	NA	NA	NA	NA	NA	NA	NA	NA	NA	NA	NA
Mount Vernon CDP................	NA	NA	NA	NA	NA	NA	NA	NA	NA	NA	NA	NA	NA	NA	NA
Neabsco CDP......................	NA	NA	NA	NA	NA	NA	NA	NA	NA	NA	NA	NA	NA	NA	NA
Newington CDP....................	NA	NA	NA	NA	NA	NA	NA	NA	NA	NA	NA	NA	NA	NA	NA

1 Data for serious crimes have not been adjusted for underreporting. This may affect comparability between geographic areas over time.
2 Per 100,000 population estimated by the FBI.   3 Based on population estimated as of July 1 of the year shown.

Table B. Incorporated Places, Census Designated Places (CDPs), and Minor Civil Divisions (MCDs) of 10,000 or More Population — Land Area, Population, and Households, and Employment

STATE City, town, township, borough, or CDP (county if applicable)	Land area,[1] 2010 (sq mi)	Total persons 2010	Total persons 2014	Percent change 2010–2014	Persons per square mile, 2014	Foreign born	Lives in same house as previous year	Median household income (dollars)	Income of $100,000 or more	Income below poverty level	Percent in labor force	Unemployment rate	Family households	One person households
	1	2	3	4	5	6	7	8	9	10	11	12	13	14
VIRGINIA—Con.														
Newington Forest CDP	3.306	12,442	NA	NA	NA	21.9	91.4	$120,380	62.7	2.4	80.2	5.7	73.3	21.7
Newport News city	68.855	180,918	182,965	1.1	2,657.3	7.7	76.4	$51,000	17.0	14.0	69.5	9.6	62.3	31.5
Norfolk city	54.085	242,831	245,428	1.1	4,537.8	6.8	77.3	$44,150	15.3	18.6	68.8	11.6	57.9	32.6
Oakton CDP	9.760	34,166	NA	NA	NA	33.1	85.2	$121,250	57.3	4.8	72.6	4.5	69.7	22.3
Petersburg city	22.934	32,420	32,701	0.9	1,425.9	3.6	81.2	$33,927	7.1	23.6	55.5	15.1	57.5	35.2
Poquoson city	15.385	12,157	12,048	-0.9	783.1	4.3	88.3	$83,460	39.9	6.3	64.4	4.7	75.8	21.0
Portsmouth city	33.802	95,535	96,004	0.5	2,840.1	2.6	81.1	$46,239	13.5	16.1	63.7	10.5	64.4	30.4
Radford city	9.872	16,408	17,646	7.5	1,787.6	4.0	65.7	$30,284	11.5	36.1	50.4	9.4	46.0	33.1
Reston CDP	15.319	58,404	NA	NA	NA	23.6	81.3	$110,321	55.3	6.1	76.8	5.1	57.2	33.8
Richmond city	59.824	204,246	217,853	6.7	3,641.6	7.0	76.4	$41,331	16.0	22.3	65.1	10.7	47.0	41.4
Roanoke city	42.526	96,919	99,428	2.6	2,338.1	7.3	81.0	$39,530	10.9	19.8	63.5	8.0	55.9	37.4
Rose Hill CDP (Fairfax County)	5.548	20,226	NA	NA	NA	22.8	89.2	$104,766	52.3	4.9	70.8	6.0	70.1	25.2
Salem city	14.440	24,848	25,483	2.6	1,764.7	4.9	79.6	$50,590	18.7	12.7	62.9	5.9	62.3	32.1
Short Pump CDP	8.950	24,729	NA	NA	NA	18.3	77.6	$109,770	55.6	3.1	75.2	3.2	73.6	21.8
South Riding CDP	6.898	24,256	NA	NA	NA	27.5	87.8	$142,088	73.5	2.5	77.8	3.6	84.8	12.2
Springfield CDP	7.863	30,484	NA	NA	NA	43.7	91.0	$89,516	43.4	7.3	67.1	5.8	68.0	26.8
Staunton city	19.973	23,746	24,538	3.3	1,228.5	3.6	81.7	$39,982	12.2	16.9	60.4	6.4	56.3	37.7
Sterling CDP	5.486	27,822	NA	NA	NA	35.6	87.9	$86,968	41.1	8.5	77.1	4.6	70.7	23.0
Sudley CDP	2.771	16,203	NA	NA	NA	32.6	85.8	$68,298	30.5	8.1	79.1	7.2	67.9	24.3
Suffolk city	400.185	84,596	86,806	2.6	216.9	3.3	86.7	$66,822	28.1	10.5	67.8	8.9	73.4	22.6
Sugarland Run CDP	2.009	11,799	NA	NA	NA	34.1	91.3	$94,211	44.2	7.4	77.5	7.0	84.3	10.3
Timberlake CDP	11.199	12,183	NA	NA	NA	3.0	83.3	$48,697	13.4	14.2	65.3	7.5	68.4	25.3
Tuckahoe CDP	20.477	44,990	NA	NA	NA	14.4	83.7	$65,420	32.3	8.4	65.5	6.6	62.8	30.4
Tysons Corner CDP	4.265	19,627	NA	NA	NA	43.7	73.0	$101,587	50.9	5.2	74.6	6.1	55.4	37.6
Vienna town	4.407	15,685	16,459	4.9	3,734.4	22.8	87.8	$133,776	65.8	2.9	69.8	3.6	78.5	17.2
Virginia Beach city	249.714	437,966	450,980	3.0	1,806.0	8.9	82.0	$67,001	28.9	7.8	70.7	6.2	69.0	23.9
Wakefield CDP	3.773	11,275	NA	NA	NA	24.1	89.4	$153,421	74.5	2.4	66.5	4.3	85.8	12.4
Waynesboro city	15.030	21,020	21,366	1.6	1,421.5	4.1	83.8	$45,499	9.2	17.7	60.6	7.8	63.0	32.2
West Falls Church CDP	4.988	29,207	NA	NA	NA	38.1	87.5	$89,071	44.9	7.5	78.2	5.5	67.2	25.3
West Springfield CDP	4.798	22,460	NA	NA	NA	23.0	88.6	$114,375	57.3	3.2	71.3	5.2	71.0	23.6
Williamsburg city	8.918	13,673	14,691	7.4	1,647.3	10.1	59.6	$48,057	20.4	15.4	49.6	6.2	50.7	40.0
Winchester city	9.235	26,203	27,543	5.1	2,982.5	11.2	78.1	$44,731	18.5	14.3	63.6	7.2	57.3	33.2
Wolf Trap CDP	9.797	16,131	NA	NA	NA	16.9	91.9	$203,952	81.3	1.5	65.0	4.2	91.7	6.5
Woodlawn CDP (Fairfax County)	2.307	20,804	NA	NA	NA	43.9	88.3	$66,718	23.4	9.3	78.5	8.4	66.7	27.4
Wyndham CDP	3.655	9,785	NA	NA	NA	13.8	87.1	$146,667	71.2	1.0	70.1	3.2	84.6	13.5
WASHINGTON	66,455.518	6,724,543	7,061,530	5.0	106.3	13.3	82.6	$60,294	26.2	12.2	64.7	8.8	64.5	27.8
Aberdeen city	10.653	16,894	16,255	-3.8	1,525.9	10.8	83.4	$39,735	12.3	22.1	57.7	12.9	61.6	31.2
Anacortes city	11.737	15,766	16,232	3.0	1,383.0	6.7	82.8	$59,369	23.8	11.0	55.2	6.8	65.1	28.3
Arlington city	9.299	17,951	18,808	4.8	2,022.6	6.9	83.1	$61,131	19.9	11.2	64.4	10.4	67.5	27.5
Artondale CDP	13.586	12,653	NA	NA	NA	4.5	92.7	$87,850	42.4	3.9	65.8	4.7	83.6	12.4
Auburn city	29.615	70,172	76,347	8.8	2,578.0	18.3	82.5	$57,635	23.0	13.5	65.6	9.5	66.5	26.7
Bainbridge Island city	27.614	23,025	23,293	1.2	843.5	7.4	82.8	$95,976	48.5	6.2	61.7	7.2	71.4	24.4
Battle Ground city	7.944	17,682	18,930	7.1	2,382.8	11.1	84.2	$57,347	18.7	12.4	65.5	8.7	75.0	19.9
Bellevue city	33.480	127,887	136,426	6.7	4,074.9	34.6	79.1	$92,524	45.7	6.9	66.6	7.1	65.4	26.8
Bellingham city	27.069	80,867	83,365	3.1	3,079.7	10.2	75.8	$42,440	15.5	22.6	64.9	9.6	49.1	33.7
Bonney Lake city	7.942	17,374	18,809	8.3	2,368.3	5.4	86.5	$79,725	37.9	7.1	72.9	8.0	77.8	15.9
Bothell city	12.104	33,522	36,567	9.1	3,021.0	16.7	83.0	$75,643	38.0	7.0	70.3	7.8	64.7	26.9
Bothell West CDP	4.216	16,607	NA	NA	NA	15.8	89.1	$85,258	40.5	3.8	72.5	7.3	73.2	21.7
Bremerton city	28.422	37,830	38,572	2.0	1,357.1	8.0	70.2	$43,527	12.0	18.8	65.2	11.2	51.6	38.0
Bryn Mawr-Skyway CDP	2.837	15,645	NA	NA	NA	27.6	86.9	$57,575	26.6	12.4	68.4	8.5	66.2	26.2
Burien city	10.055	48,072	50,188	4.4	4,991.2	24.0	81.7	$52,140	20.3	16.2	66.3	8.5	63.0	29.2
Camano CDP	39.762	NA	NA	NA	NA	3.4	91.4	$66,890	28.4	5.5	54.4	10.6	74.0	21.7
Camas city	13.740	19,395	21,220	9.4	1,544.4	9.7	86.6	$84,643	42.4	4.8	66.9	7.0	77.4	18.1
Centralia city	7.487	16,553	16,623	0.4	2,220.4	8.5	76.6	$37,230	8.1	20.0	56.1	15.4	57.4	34.8
Cheney city	4.347	10,590	11,420	7.8	2,626.8	6.3	56.6	$28,194	10.9	44.0	57.9	12.5	45.9	27.0
Cottage Lake CDP	22.662	22,494	NA	NA	NA	11.1	92.6	$134,802	67.6	3.5	67.2	4.5	84.1	11.7
Covington city	5.812	17,565	19,134	8.9	3,292.1	12.1	86.4	$87,315	40.2	6.5	75.2	7.0	75.8	16.7
Des Moines city	6.495	29,673	31,011	4.5	4,774.6	24.0	83.4	$58,308	22.8	11.1	64.3	8.9	61.7	30.4
Eastmont CDP	5.096	20,101	NA	NA	NA	15.0	85.8	$89,931	44.3	4.1	69.5	7.4	77.3	16.4
East Renton Highlands CDP	11.218	11,140	NA	NA	NA	8.1	90.7	$92,556	45.9	3.8	64.6	7.1	80.9	14.4
East Wenatchee city	3.801	13,190	13,505	2.4	3,552.7	14.6	82.4	$52,989	16.8	12.2	65.1	10.4	70.4	22.6
Edmonds city	8.903	39,698	40,896	3.0	4,593.6	13.9	88.0	$72,926	35.8	8.0	63.6	6.3	62.9	30.9
Elk Plain CDP	7.691	14,205	NA	NA	NA	6.5	87.6	$65,830	19.5	8.5	64.5	12.5	76.2	18.4
Ellensburg city	7.032	18,251	18,774	2.9	2,669.6	8.0	53.0	$28,341	7.6	41.9	60.3	9.6	39.4	35.1
Enumclaw city	5.157	11,092	11,548	4.1	2,239.5	6.7	83.1	$56,764	21.3	11.0	69.2	7.4	61.0	29.8
Everett city	33.109	103,022	106,736	3.6	3,223.8	18.1	78.4	$48,562	17.2	16.0	68.6	10.9	53.9	36.6
Fairwood CDP (King County)	4.734	19,102	NA	NA	NA	15.8	83.1	$93,402	44.7	4.5	72.6	6.1	73.0	19.7
Federal Way city	22.265	89,306	93,425	4.6	4,196.0	23.7	80.2	$54,186	23.0	13.6	66.8	8.7	68.0	25.0
Ferndale city	7.025	11,431	12,704	11.1	1,808.4	13.2	88.0	$51,944	17.0	17.2	62.3	10.0	73.8	21.7
Five Corners CDP	5.903	18,159	NA	NA	NA	13.4	82.3	$65,645	19.7	9.7	67.3	12.5	76.0	18.3
Fort Lewis CDP	10.269	11,046	NA	NA	NA	4.3	55.3	$44,949	6.6	9.8	77.2	9.4	96.0	2.3
Frederickson CDP	11.554	18,719	NA	NA	NA	10.1	85.6	$69,250	24.2	8.1	67.1	9.3	76.1	17.7
Graham CDP	34.989	23,491	NA	NA	NA	3.3	89.1	$71,951	28.8	5.7	70.4	6.7	76.1	19.1
Grandview city	6.235	10,862	11,140	2.6	1,786.6	29.0	87.8	$37,012	6.1	23.4	61.4	15.3	77.5	18.7
Hazel Dell CDP	4.837	19,435	NA	NA	NA	9.7	79.9	$48,545	17.2	14.5	63.8	10.1	65.0	28.2
Issaquah city	11.405	30,434	34,056	11.9	2,986.1	19.2	78.7	$88,770	45.0	5.7	70.4	6.0	62.8	30.9
Kelso city	8.141	11,925	11,788	-1.1	1,448.0	6.9	79.7	$33,492	7.7	28.8	50.6	22.5	64.8	25.1
Kenmore city	6.165	20,460	21,839	6.7	3,542.5	17.3	86.9	$88,472	43.2	9.0	68.4	7.1	69.3	22.2
Kennewick city	26.873	73,874	77,421	4.8	2,881.0	12.3	80.1	$51,739	20.2	15.2	64.2	6.5	66.8	27.6
Kent city	33.759	118,593	125,560	5.9	3,719.4	26.7	82.0	$57,490	24.4	14.8	67.2	9.4	67.3	26.5
Kirkland city	17.818	80,585	85,763	6.4	4,813.3	20.0	81.7	$90,611	45.6	6.5	72.3	7.0	62.4	29.9
Klahanie CDP	1.926	10,674	NA	NA	NA	23.3	83.5	$116,830	61.3	3.3	77.5	6.6	81.2	18.0
Lacey city	16.059	42,395	45,446	7.2	2,830.0	11.6	76.2	$59,885	18.0	9.1	62.2	9.4	65.8	28.8

1 Dry land or land partially or temporarily covered by water.
2 16 years old and over.

Table B. Incorporated Places, Census Designated Places (CDPs), and Minor Civil Divisions (MCDs) of 10,000 or More Population — Crime, Construction, and Local Government Finance

STATE City, town, township, borough, or CDP (county if applicable)	Serious crimes known to police, 2014[1] Total number	Rate[2] Total	Rate[2] Violent	Rate[2] Property	New residential construction authorized by building permits, 2014 Value ($1,000)	Number of housing units	Percent single family	Local government finance, 2012 General revenue Total (mil dol)	Intergovernmental Total (mil dol)	Percent from state gov.	Taxes per capita[3]	General expenditure Total (mil dol)	Per capita[3] Total	Capital outlays	Debt outstanding (mil dol)
	15	16	17	18	19	20	21	22	23	24	25	26	27	28	29
VIRGINIA—Con.															
Newington Forest CDP	NA	NA	NA	NA	NA	NA	NA	NA	NA	NA	NA	NA	NA	NA	NA
Newport News city	6,334	3473	429	3044	19,582	330	33.0	774.9	330.7	85.5	1785	806.2	4,467	333	797.6
Norfolk city	10,981	4444	520	3924	62,419	650	60.5	1105.0	447.5	74.8	1691	1153.5	4,686	548	1752.2
Oakton CDP	NA	NA	NA	NA	NA	NA	NA	NA	NA	NA	NA	NA	NA	NA	NA
Petersburg city	1,036	3183	593	2590	1,145	8	100.0	125.4	70.3	87.3	1406	129.9	4,039	140	34.6
Poquoson city	103	851	91	760	4,298	24	100.0	38.9	15.6	95.0	1571	39.1	3,219	172	37.8
Portsmouth city	5,451	5653	610	5043	29,789	153	92.2	430.0	216.4	85.2	1669	514.7	5,331	1,170	519.2
Radford city	477	2744	598	2146	1,830	10	100.0	37.3	20.0	90.7	661	46.1	2,747	70	26.7
Reston CDP	NA	NA	NA	NA	NA	NA	NA	NA	NA	NA	NA	NA	NA	NA	NA
Richmond city	9,690	4471	583	3887	58,844	551	33.0	1063.0	471.0	79.9	1951	1029.3	4,866	638	1340.2
Roanoke city	4,476	4524	344	4180	5,918	49	71.4	385.6	172.3	96.1	1766	378.3	3,865	222	544.5
Rose Hill CDP (Fairfax County)	NA	NA	NA	NA	NA	NA	NA	NA	NA	NA	NA	NA	NA	NA	NA
Salem city	530	2085	114	1971	5,148	38	100.0	98.9	33.3	90.7	1976	103.6	4,136	420	83.6
Short Pump CDP	NA	NA	NA	NA	NA	NA	NA	NA	NA	NA	NA	NA	NA	NA	NA
South Riding CDP	NA	NA	NA	NA	NA	NA	NA	NA	NA	NA	NA	NA	NA	NA	NA
Springfield CDP	NA	NA	NA	NA	NA	NA	NA	NA	NA	NA	NA	NA	NA	NA	NA
Staunton city	623	2543	127	2416	12,766	137	16.8	77.4	34.6	96.9	1349	83.6	3,495	229	66.3
Sterling CDP	NA	NA	NA	NA	NA	NA	NA	NA	NA	NA	NA	NA	NA	NA	NA
Sudley CDP	NA	NA	NA	NA	NA	NA	NA	NA	NA	NA	NA	NA	NA	NA	NA
Suffolk city	2,485	2890	272	2618	56,647	348	85.3	304.8	145.8	82.7	1577	324.3	3,808	436	538.4
Sugarland Run CDP	NA	NA	NA	NA	NA	NA	NA	NA	NA	NA	NA	NA	NA	NA	NA
Timberlake CDP	NA	NA	NA	NA	NA	NA	NA	NA	NA	NA	NA	NA	NA	NA	NA
Tuckahoe CDP	NA	NA	NA	NA	NA	NA	NA	NA	NA	NA	NA	NA	NA	NA	NA
Tysons Corner CDP	NA	NA	NA	NA	NA	NA	NA	NA	NA	NA	NA	NA	NA	NA	NA
Vienna town	172	1041	48	992	NA	NA	NA	26.6	3.7	94.5	1111	25.9	1,598	136	12.4
Virginia Beach city	10,532	2335	148	2187	158,800	1,208	57.0	1602.6	600.6	84.2	1817	1799.1	4,036	628	1698.8
Wakefield CDP	NA	NA	NA	NA	NA	NA	NA	NA	NA	NA	NA	NA	NA	NA	NA
Waynesboro city	688	3227	155	3072	6,962	48	91.7	77.9	33.7	86.1	1574	75.1	3,558	368	88.8
West Falls Church CDP	NA	NA	NA	NA	NA	NA	NA	NA	NA	NA	NA	NA	NA	NA	NA
West Springfield CDP	NA	NA	NA	NA	NA	NA	NA	NA	NA	NA	NA	NA	NA	NA	NA
Williamsburg city	205	1323	161	1162	28,521	258	12.0	40.6	6.4	87.4	2045	37.5	2,563	268	14.7
Winchester city	1,171	4261	313	3948	3,220	23	91.3	116.1	39.1	89.9	2267	112.7	4,147	231	201.0
Wolf Trap CDP	NA	NA	NA	NA	NA	NA	NA	NA	NA	NA	NA	NA	NA	NA	NA
Woodlawn CDP (Fairfax County)	NA	NA	NA	NA	NA	NA	NA	NA	NA	NA	NA	NA	NA	NA	NA
Wyndham CDP	NA	NA	NA	NA	NA	NA	NA	NA	NA	NA	NA	NA	NA	NA	NA
WASHINGTON	281,842	3991	285	3706	7,016,518	33,898	52.8	X	X	X	X	X	X	X	X
Aberdeen city	1,051	6470	634	5836	288	1	100.0	24.3	3.0	61.1	739	21.3	1,291	123	18.6
Anacortes city	439	2723	143	2581	15,617	56	100.0	27.0	3.2	38.6	800	22.5	1,417	183	60.9
Arlington city	1,142	6063	181	5882	705	3	100.0	24.1	2.5	83.6	563	24.0	1,311	413	55.7
Artondale CDP	NA	NA	NA	NA	NA	NA	NA	NA	NA	NA	NA	NA	NA	NA	NA
Auburn city	4,900	6446	397	6048	85,126	362	100.0	109.0	17.7	41.8	598	107.6	1,464	393	68.3
Bainbridge Island city	348	1498	43	1455	17,539	53	92.5	28.9	4.5	98.7	675	24.1	1,035	256	37.7
Battle Ground city	348	1886	125	1762	18,482	83	100.0	14.1	1.1	79.7	405	17.5	971	291	37.1
Bellevue city	4,750	3507	106	3401	266,975	1,292	18.2	284.5	33.1	23.5	1157	257.3	1,947	276	176.9
Bellingham city	4,934	5941	270	5671	73,475	541	25.0	120.9	15.0	39.1	825	118.7	1,446	280	92.2
Bonney Lake city	531	2867	108	2759	63,734	385	51.2	19.8	2.8	94.2	515	22.8	1,269	373	33.8
Bothell city	1,130	3131	72	3059	46,633	151	68.9	54.5	14.0	63.8	848	61.1	1,763	521	43.3
Bothell West CDP	NA	NA	NA	NA	NA	NA	NA	NA	NA	NA	NA	NA	NA	NA	NA
Bremerton city	2,025	5145	528	4616	20,808	136	47.8	57.7	6.4	49.1	646	58.3	1,484	236	75.6
Bryn Mawr-Skyway CDP	NA	NA	NA	NA	NA	NA	NA	NA	NA	NA	NA	NA	NA	NA	NA
Burien city	2,632	5234	511	4723	17,475	57	100.0	28.1	4.7	75.2	378	34.9	705	215	33.0
Camano CDP	NA	NA	NA	NA	NA	NA	NA	NA	NA	NA	NA	NA	NA	NA	NA
Camas city	311	1462	75	1387	54,754	178	100.0	32.8	5.7	75.5	753	32.3	1,575	519	35.3
Centralia city	780	4677	486	4191	1,913	11	100.0	18.3	3.6	77.3	293	18.2	1,089	284	63.2
Cheney city	321	2819	246	2573	2,857	12	66.7	12.2	1.2	56.9	475	16.5	1,497	311	11.5
Cottage Lake CDP	NA	NA	NA	NA	NA	NA	NA	NA	NA	NA	NA	NA	NA	NA	NA
Covington city	775	4048	214	3834	0	0	0.0	13.7	1.6	93.9	474	11.7	641	56	14.9
Des Moines city	1,274	4120	388	3731	13,107	50	66.0	29.2	4.6	73.5	412	26.8	881	214	14.4
Eastmont CDP	NA	NA	NA	NA	NA	NA	NA	NA	NA	NA	NA	NA	NA	NA	NA
East Renton Highlands CDP	NA	NA	NA	NA	NA	NA	NA	NA	NA	NA	NA	NA	NA	NA	NA
East Wenatchee city	388	2866	111	2755	794	6	16.7	7.8	0.6	83.5	461	6.6	492	34	1.3
Edmonds city	1,231	3004	134	2870	23,105	99	46.5	45.6	4.4	75.7	693	42.6	1,054	137	37.6
Elk Plain CDP	NA	NA	NA	NA	NA	NA	NA	NA	NA	NA	NA	NA	NA	NA	NA
Ellensburg city	660	3590	136	3454	13,842	79	79.7	18.8	4.6	79.1	477	19.8	1,078	274	22.5
Enumclaw city	379	3275	156	3120	3,117	15	86.7	17.7	3.1	66.7	503	16.3	1,424	393	34.2
Everett city	7,311	6903	344	6559	33,889	270	51.9	182.2	16.6	67.5	1033	170.4	1,629	324	252.3
Fairwood CDP (King County)	NA	NA	NA	NA	NA	NA	NA	NA	NA	NA	NA	NA	NA	NA	NA
Federal Way city	5,944	6354	386	5968	88,474	559	13.8	65.3	12.0	93.7	435	59.1	643	167	13.7
Ferndale city	391	3111	215	2896	14,712	72	86.1	14.7	2.8	96.0	620	14.9	1,245	470	23.0
Five Corners CDP	NA	NA	NA	NA	NA	NA	NA	NA	NA	NA	NA	NA	NA	NA	NA
Fort Lewis CDP	NA	NA	NA	NA	NA	NA	NA	NA	NA	NA	NA	NA	NA	NA	NA
Frederickson CDP	NA	NA	NA	NA	NA	NA	NA	NA	NA	NA	NA	NA	NA	NA	NA
Graham CDP	NA	NA	NA	NA	NA	NA	NA	NA	NA	NA	NA	NA	NA	NA	NA
Grandview city	260	2327	125	2202	1,545	11	100.0	10.4	1.8	92.8	423	11.0	908	222	8.2
Hazel Dell CDP	NA	NA	NA	NA	NA	NA	NA	NA	NA	NA	NA	NA	NA	NA	NA
Issaquah city	1,103	3209	52	3157	181,984	855	22.1	59.7	10.5	71.1	949	53.3	1,633	344	38.5
Kelso city	704	5975	280	5695	175	2	100.0	15.2	1.9	70.2	531	15.3	1,297	179	9.9
Kenmore city	321	1467	87	1380	19,910	51	100.0	12.6	0.9	88.9	436	15.2	714	210	0.2
Kennewick city	2,617	3382	246	3136	78,409	328	92.1	68.6	6.5	69.3	550	69.4	914	179	63.3
Kent city	6,634	5272	288	4984	84,780	375	48.0	137.7	20.6	82.9	511	140.6	1,143	354	164.6
Kirkland city	2,122	2486	100	2387	136,067	671	35.9	106.7	9.7	53.2	731	105.7	1,267	159	53.5
Klahanie CDP	NA	NA	NA	NA	NA	NA	NA	NA	NA	NA	NA	NA	NA	NA	NA
Lacey city	1,507	3310	182	3128	77,888	314	100.0	56.2	9.1	68.1	611	60.0	1,365	347	24.6

1 Data for serious crimes have not been adjusted for underreporting. This may affect comparability between geographic areas over time.
2 Per 100,000 population estimated by the FBI.   3 Based on population estimated as of July 1 of the year shown.

Table B. Incorporated Places, Census Designated Places (CDPs), and Minor Civil Divisions (MCDs) of 10,000 or More Population — Land Area, Population, and Households, and Employment

STATE City, town, township, borough, or CDP (county if applicable)	Land area,[1] 2010 (sq mi)	Total persons 2010	Total persons 2014	Percent change 2010–2014	Persons per square mile, 2014	Foreign born	Lives in same house as previous year	Median household income (dollars)	Income of $100,000 or more	Income below poverty level	Percent in labor force	Unemploy- ment rate	Family households	One person households
	1	2	3	4	5	6	7	8	9	10	11	12	13	14
WASHINGTON—Con.														
Lake Forest Park city	3.533	12,599	13,184	4.6	3,731.6	9.7	88.9	$90,495	45.3	6.8	66.4	7.3	69.5	24.6
Lakeland North CDP	3.246	12,942	NA	NA	NA	19.4	91.6	$70,005	28.8	9.1	68.6	9.0	68.9	26.7
Lakeland South CDP	4.970	11,574	NA	NA	NA	12.9	91.5	$77,554	32.5	6.1	68.5	8.4	74.1	19.8
Lake Stevens city	8.875	28,060	30,284	7.9	3,412.4	6.3	85.7	$70,345	30.4	7.8	72.2	8.5	73.9	18.7
Lake Tapps CDP	12.399	11,859	NA	NA	NA	2.9	91.2	$103,065	51.5	4.7	70.2	6.5	79.8	13.8
Lakewood city	17.181	58,163	59,610	2.5	3,469.4	15.9	76.5	$44,667	15.3	17.4	60.2	14.1	57.2	36.9
Longview city	14.538	36,834	36,483	-1.0	2,509.4	5.7	78.5	$37,827	12.7	21.4	53.8	15.0	57.5	35.5
Lynden city	5.258	12,002	13,165	9.7	2,503.9	12.1	85.5	$59,021	19.4	7.7	59.0	6.2	71.4	26.6
Lynnwood city	7.850	35,845	36,687	2.3	4,673.6	28.4	83.6	$50,562	20.5	14.6	64.8	8.1	60.0	30.7
Maltby CDP	19.401	10,830	NA	NA	NA	6.0	93.5	$107,535	54.8	4.0	67.0	5.6	84.5	11.7
Maple Valley city	5.730	22,684	25,125	10.8	4,384.5	6.2	86.4	$97,809	49.0	4.2	73.5	8.5	76.6	18.1
Martha Lake CDP	4.548	15,473	NA	NA	NA	21.2	81.8	$77,229	32.1	9.2	71.0	9.8	75.9	17.0
Marysville city	20.691	60,024	65,087	8.4	3,145.6	9.6	83.4	$64,328	24.9	8.7	68.8	10.3	71.0	23.5
Mercer Island city	6.320	22,691	24,326	7.2	3,849.0	17.4	87.1	$125,651	59.4	5.3	58.8	4.5	72.2	24.7
Mill Creek city	4.660	18,229	19,200	5.3	4,120.3	21.5	83.1	$88,770	41.9	5.4	67.7	4.8	70.7	24.5
Mill Creek East CDP	4.447	15,709	NA	NA	NA	22.3	88.3	$98,998	49.2	6.1	72.8	7.3	75.4	19.8
Monroe city	6.046	17,304	17,899	3.4	2,960.6	12.8	79.1	$66,649	28.0	8.6	57.3	8.3	75.0	19.7
Moses Lake city	17.837	20,366	21,713	6.6	1,217.3	11.1	81.1	$47,914	13.2	14.1	65.0	11.3	65.7	28.7
Mountlake Terrace city	4.057	19,884	20,817	4.7	5,131.3	17.2	82.2	$61,477	21.3	9.1	72.5	7.5	62.3	30.0
Mount Vernon city	12.218	31,762	33,132	4.3	2,711.7	17.5	80.2	$44,404	15.4	18.0	61.5	9.4	67.6	24.4
Mukilteo city	6.340	20,254	20,993	3.6	3,311.1	19.0	82.5	$89,942	45.7	5.8	70.8	6.1	71.0	22.8
Newcastle city	4.447	10,368	11,201	8.0	2,518.8	26.4	81.6	$110,456	53.7	4.0	73.1	5.0	71.3	20.0
North Lynnwood CDP	3.121	16,574	NA	NA	NA	24.4	73.6	$60,292	22.6	10.0	74.1	8.7	58.8	28.2
Oak Harbor city	9.651	22,130	22,306	0.8	2,311.2	13.0	72.6	$48,362	12.3	13.6	67.7	9.8	63.8	30.5
Olympia city	17.821	46,476	49,218	5.9	2,761.8	8.3	78.1	$52,834	21.3	16.7	66.0	9.0	52.3	37.1
Orchards CDP	5.401	19,556	NA	NA	NA	10.5	83.9	$60,184	18.7	8.5	70.7	10.6	77.0	18.4
Parkland CDP	8.636	35,803	NA	NA	NA	14.4	79.9	$47,647	10.8	15.9	64.4	13.0	62.1	29.9
Pasco city	32.312	61,083	68,648	12.4	2,124.5	25.7	83.7	$54,700	16.5	19.5	67.6	7.7	76.6	18.8
Port Angeles city	10.699	19,038	19,256	1.1	1,799.8	3.4	80.4	$39,524	12.3	17.7	54.7	12.6	54.1	37.3
Port Orchard city	9.683	12,200	13,266	8.7	1,370.1	6.6	76.6	$55,521	22.6	16.3	53.6	12.0	69.3	26.4
Prairie Ridge CDP	4.088	11,464	NA	NA	NA	2.2	89.0	$70,905	24.6	7.4	66.9	9.5	78.6	15.3
Pullman city	9.882	29,799	31,682	6.3	3,206.0	14.0	51.1	$24,487	15.4	44.0	55.1	9.1	39.2	29.8
Puyallup city	14.112	37,028	39,105	5.6	2,771.1	6.5	79.2	$63,009	26.3	8.7	67.3	10.4	62.5	29.4
Redmond city	16.467	54,313	59,285	9.2	3,600.3	37.3	76.3	$99,586	49.7	7.4	71.2	5.8	61.0	30.7
Renton city	23.373	91,819	98,404	7.2	4,210.2	28.5	78.6	$65,223	27.2	10.3	71.7	7.5	59.9	31.3
Richland city	38.555	48,104	53,019	10.2	1,375.1	8.1	81.8	$69,372	33.2	9.4	64.5	6.5	66.2	28.7
Salmon Creek CDP	6.347	19,686	NA	NA	NA	6.6	80.2	$68,231	28.6	10.7	64.6	13.8	72.1	22.6
Sammamish city	18.407	46,763	51,229	9.6	2,783.2	24.7	90.6	$144,775	72.7	3.3	68.8	4.4	87.8	9.3
SeaTac city	10.031	26,909	28,126	4.5	2,803.9	37.6	77.3	$45,573	13.5	17.3	63.7	10.1	59.0	32.3
Seattle city	83.837	608,658	668,342	9.8	7,971.9	18.0	77.2	$67,365	33.5	12.7	72.4	6.5	44.6	41.1
Sedro-Woolley city	3.925	10,596	10,764	1.6	2,742.2	4.3	79.8	$44,014	10.6	14.7	65.4	11.8	60.9	28.7
Shoreline city	11.673	53,031	55,174	4.0	4,726.5	19.7	84.8	$64,096	29.9	10.1	66.0	8.7	61.2	30.8
Silverdale CDP	12.632	19,204	NA	NA	NA	10.5	70.8	$59,260	24.8	8.6	63.3	10.6	61.8	29.9
Silver Firs CDP	6.860	20,891	NA	NA	NA	13.8	90.5	$102,480	53.6	3.1	77.6	5.2	82.6	12.1
Snoqualmie city	7.218	10,670	12,630	18.4	1,749.8	9.3	82.7	$130,060	70.1	0.4	79.2	4.7	82.3	15.5
South Hill CDP	18.359	52,431	NA	NA	NA	9.1	84.8	$74,010	30.8	6.7	70.1	10.1	78.0	16.3
Spanaway CDP	8.774	27,227	NA	NA	NA	9.6	84.5	$59,988	20.9	9.7	62.0	8.9	73.2	19.8
Spokane city	68.736	209,440	212,052	1.2	3,085.0	7.0	81.0	$42,814	13.8	18.3	61.4	9.5	56.9	34.1
Spokane Valley city	37.712	89,745	91,729	2.2	2,432.4	4.7	84.6	$48,274	14.3	13.9	63.1	9.6	64.1	28.9
Sunnyside city	6.633	15,855	16,140	1.8	2,433.3	31.1	86.3	$32,641	8.3	23.8	62.9	11.8	82.0	16.2
Tacoma city	49.733	198,397	205,159	3.4	4,125.2	13.4	80.5	$51,269	19.8	15.9	64.6	11.3	57.2	33.5
Tukwila city	9.171	19,107	19,920	4.3	2,171.9	39.7	76.6	$44,820	15.5	19.2	68.7	11.1	58.4	33.8
Tumwater city	14.360	17,371	18,820	8.3	1,310.6	6.8	77.0	$62,258	21.1	10.0	65.6	6.3	60.7	31.7
Union Hill-Novelty Hill CDP	24.227	18,805	NA	NA	NA	20.8	89.1	$124,606	62.5	2.7	64.6	6.1	78.6	15.7
University Place city	8.425	31,146	32,282	3.6	3,831.7	13.0	83.7	$59,164	27.3	9.8	67.2	12.5	67.6	28.0
Vancouver city	46.777	161,849	169,294	4.6	3,619.1	13.1	80.0	$50,379	17.1	13.6	64.6	11.3	61.3	30.2
Vashon CDP	36.926	10,624	NA	NA	NA	6.3	90.5	$72,568	34.5	6.6	65.7	6.0	59.8	33.6
Walla Walla city	12.800	31,731	31,910	0.6	2,493.0	12.3	80.9	$42,348	12.2	19.4	54.8	8.8	55.4	38.4
Walnut Grove CDP	3.829	9,790	NA	NA	NA	10.0	85.5	$56,448	21.8	7.0	59.9	10.9	61.1	29.7
Washougal city	5.467	14,102	14,999	6.4	2,743.3	4.9	84.6	$60,353	23.4	10.3	65.8	12.1	70.1	23.2
Wenatchee city	7.856	32,105	33,261	3.6	4,233.9	12.9	87.0	$47,168	17.4	12.9	61.2	7.9	65.6	29.7
West Richland city	21.974	11,832	13,351	12.8	607.6	4.0	89.1	$81,778	37.0	8.6	66.3	8.0	78.2	17.5
White Center CDP	2.257	13,495	NA	NA	NA	32.0	80.5	$42,763	13.3	24.1	68.9	9.6	61.9	27.5
Woodinville city	5.601	10,938	11,372	4.0	2,030.5	13.4	87.1	$97,604	48.5	4.6	73.7	5.3	63.1	31.2
Yakima city	27.625	91,276	93,357	2.3	3,379.4	17.4	79.1	$40,189	12.3	20.1	62.0	11.2	64.9	29.4
WEST VIRGINIA	24,038.209	1,853,033	1,850,326	-0.1	77.0	1.5	88.3	$41,576	13.7	17.8	54.3	8.2	64.9	29.9
Beckley city	9.499	17,614	17,238	-2.1	1,814.6	4.4	81.2	$33,616	13.1	23.5	57.1	7.9	56.3	37.2
Bluefield city	8.789	10,443	10,448	0.0	1,188.7	1.9	88.2	$35,354	12.4	21.7	53.5	4.9	63.3	33.8
Charleston city	31.501	51,347	50,404	-1.8	1,600.1	3.0	82.6	$48,959	21.4	16.6	61.9	6.6	52.5	41.2
Clarksburg city	9.731	16,570	16,242	-2.0	1,669.2	1.1	90.9	$36,353	9.4	18.1	58.7	7.8	55.1	39.6
Cross Lanes CDP	6.379	9,995	NA	NA	NA	3.3	90.6	$55,538	21.0	13.6	69.7	6.1	66.9	27.8
Fairmont city	8.590	18,709	18,740	0.2	2,181.7	1.2	82.3	$36,731	13.3	22.1	59.6	5.9	57.6	35.0
Huntington city	16.219	49,135	48,807	-0.7	3,009.2	2.6	78.0	$28,673	9.9	30.1	52.5	9.0	49.9	40.1
Martinsburg city	6.650	17,227	17,743	3.0	2,667.9	7.1	79.1	$36,736	10.6	23.9	60.7	14.3	60.6	33.7
Morgantown city	9.983	28,827	31,073	7.8	3,112.4	5.7	63.6	$32,400	16.1	36.7	53.9	8.1	37.1	45.0
Parkersburg city	11.776	31,381	30,981	-1.3	2,630.9	0.6	88.2	$33,247	8.8	20.9	55.7	10.5	57.4	37.7
St. Albans city	3.615	11,039	10,835	-1.8	2,997.3	1.4	89.9	$47,134	13.8	8.3	62.4	6.5	60.6	35.4
South Charleston city	7.886	13,508	13,214	-2.2	1,675.6	1.4	86.4	$44,610	14.8	13.3	60.0	4.0	56.8	39.3
Teays Valley CDP	7.186	13,175	NA	NA	NA	1.9	92.3	$70,361	29.6	9.4	60.7	4.4	75.0	21.4
Vienna city	3.789	10,751	10,562	-1.8	2,787.8	1.7	89.0	$42,055	17.1	9.8	59.2	6.2	61.8	34.7
Weirton city	18.054	19,745	19,362	-1.9	1,072.4	1.4	84.0	$39,326	11.7	14.1	57.2	6.7	59.9	35.7
Wheeling city	13.791	28,479	27,790	-2.4	2,015.1	1.5	86.5	$36,085	12.7	20.1	57.6	6.1	53.4	42.1
WISCONSIN	54,157.803	5,687,289	5,757,564	1.2	106.3	4.7	85.8	$52,738	19.6	12.4	67.4	7.2	64.1	29.0
Allouez village & MCD (Brown)	4.610	13,975	13,943	-0.2	3,024.5	4.6	87.6	$65,101	22.5	5.6	60.8	6.2	68.5	26.6

1 Dry land or land partially or temporarily covered by water.
2 16 years old and over.

Table B. Incorporated Places, Census Designated Places (CDPs), and Minor Civil Divisions (MCDs) of 10,000 or More Population — Crime, Construction, and Local Government Finance

STATE City, town, township, borough, or CDP (county if applicable)	Serious crimes known to police, 2014[1] Total number	Rate[2] Total	Rate[2] Violent	Rate[2] Property	New residential construction authorized by building permits, 2014 Value ($1,000)	Number of housing units	Percent single family	Local government finance, 2012 General revenue Total (mil dol)	Intergovernmental Total (mil dol)	Percent from state gov.	Taxes per capita[3]	General expenditure Total (mil dol)	Per capita[3] Total	Per capita[3] Capital outlays	Debt outstanding (mil dol)
	15	16	17	18	19	20	21	22	23	24	25	26	27	28	29
WASHINGTON—Con.															
Lake Forest Park city	350	2650	68	2582	4,011	9	100.0	12.5	1.8	37.9	481	10.9	839	81	5.6
Lakeland North CDP	NA	NA	NA	NA	NA	NA	NA	NA	NA	NA	NA	NA	NA	NA	NA
Lakeland South CDP	NA	NA	NA	NA	NA	NA	NA	NA	NA	NA	NA	NA	NA	NA	NA
Lake Stevens city	830	2731	165	2567	41,041	148	98.6	14.7	2.9	47.3	333	9.2	318	2	22.3
Lake Tapps CDP	NA	NA	NA	NA	NA	NA	NA	NA	NA	NA	NA	NA	NA	NA	NA
Lakewood city	2,860	4822	644	4178	11,589	49	57.1	45.5	9.7	66.3	480	49.0	831	168	12.0
Longview city	2,453	6728	365	6363	3,063	13	100.0	58.1	10.3	61.4	685	58.2	1,593	375	34.6
Lynden city	149	1135	61	1074	14,863	90	52.2	17.4	3.4	96.5	606	14.1	1,116	332	38.1
Lynnwood city	2,654	7245	273	6972	11,460	34	100.0	66.8	5.6	76.9	1065	58.4	1,610	230	46.2
Maltby CDP	NA	NA	NA	NA	NA	NA	NA	NA	NA	NA	NA	NA	NA	NA	NA
Maple Valley city	379	1496	51	1445	49,883	159	100.0	15.9	1.5	97.3	454	15.2	628	172	6.5
Martha Lake CDP	NA	NA	NA	NA	NA	NA	NA	NA	NA	NA	NA	NA	NA	NA	NA
Marysville city	2,897	4522	175	4347	62,755	477	20.1	60.6	3.7	74.9	483	58.8	943	114	92.8
Mercer Island city	384	1571	25	1546	65,762	272	23.2	36.4	1.9	59.3	883	34.3	1,449	197	20.5
Mill Creek city	467	2462	132	2330	48,638	301	14.0	12.8	1.0	88.7	518	12.0	641	39	1.1
Mill Creek East CDP	NA	NA	NA	NA	NA	NA	NA	NA	NA	NA	NA	NA	NA	NA	NA
Monroe city	767	4303	353	3949	9,815	69	31.9	20.1	1.4	90.7	463	21.8	1,244	390	40.2
Moses Lake city	1,562	7238	468	6770	19,121	120	71.7	35.4	1.4	87.4	847	28.3	1,337	199	30.8
Mountlake Terrace city	746	3574	192	3383	3,145	18	100.0	21.9	1.3	80.1	577	22.0	1,088	113	9.3
Mount Vernon city	1,595	4862	265	4597	18,729	114	100.0	38.0	3.3	70.9	552	33.3	1,033	107	37.4
Mukilteo city	572	2724	124	2600	10,602	35	100.0	18.2	1.9	99.3	658	18.8	912	178	11.7
Newcastle city	350	3115	62	3053	17,601	50	100.0	8.2	0.9	93.7	560	8.8	813	251	2.6
North Lynnwood CDP	NA	NA	NA	NA	NA	NA	NA	NA	NA	NA	NA	NA	NA	NA	NA
Oak Harbor city	417	1885	167	1718	14,736	61	100.0	23.7	3.1	64.1	421	25.3	1,136	263	5.3
Olympia city	2,389	4899	410	4489	41,543	191	77.0	99.6	9.9	54.8	1045	116.3	2,434	673	95.1
Orchards CDP	NA	NA	NA	NA	NA	NA	NA	NA	NA	NA	NA	NA	NA	NA	NA
Parkland CDP	NA	NA	NA	NA	NA	NA	NA	NA	NA	NA	NA	NA	NA	NA	NA
Pasco city	1,657	2397	255	2143	58,315	261	83.9	56.3	7.4	83.9	414	43.0	644	84	48.6
Port Angeles city	959	4990	546	4443	4,963	32	100.0	39.4	7.0	39.1	581	41.3	2,165	354	36.3
Port Orchard city	929	7067	601	6466	11,237	49	100.0	13.9	1.9	93.9	551	13.9	1,096	227	12.3
Prairie Ridge CDP	NA	NA	NA	NA	NA	NA	NA	NA	NA	NA	NA	NA	NA	NA	NA
Pullman city	550	1729	211	1518	24,340	190	25.8	28.8	6.2	79.9	450	23.2	740	102	7.0
Puyallup city	2,901	7435	282	7153	29,785	116	100.0	56.2	6.0	83.5	756	45.2	1,184	149	75.3
Redmond city	1,788	3066	57	3010	111,736	480	45.0	132.9	19.1	27.4	1298	135.8	2,399	780	82.8
Renton city	5,459	5557	233	5324	114,261	605	35.5	182.1	40.0	23.2	844	161.6	1,687	421	184.1
Richland city	1,307	2446	170	2275	85,061	343	67.3	85.1	16.9	69.5	682	81.3	1,579	382	147.2
Salmon Creek CDP	NA	NA	NA	NA	NA	NA	NA	NA	NA	NA	NA	NA	NA	NA	NA
Sammamish city	394	772	16	757	107,616	278	100.0	38.6	2.0	89.9	638	30.6	623	115	7.7
SeaTac city	1,682	5985	637	5348	1,271	11	9.1	44.1	5.0	93.3	1224	38.5	1,392	195	5.8
Seattle city	44,776	6749	604	6146	1,109,041	7,445	12.1	1849.1	193.2	68.5	1438	1658.2	2,611	430	4163.6
Sedro-Woolley city	496	4653	159	4494	1,773	11	100.0	12.6	2.6	78.9	442	12.3	1,161	345	16.5
Shoreline city	1,778	3221	170	3050	17,413	53	96.2	64.6	27.8	75.5	527	61.5	1,129	532	38.3
Silverdale CDP	NA	NA	NA	NA	NA	NA	NA	NA	NA	NA	NA	NA	NA	NA	NA
Silver Firs CDP	NA	NA	NA	NA	NA	NA	NA	NA	NA	NA	NA	NA	NA	NA	NA
Snoqualmie city	164	1327	81	1246	56,923	173	100.0	18.9	1.6	51.4	969	15.4	1,330	243	16.1
South Hill CDP	NA	NA	NA	NA	NA	NA	NA	NA	NA	NA	NA	NA	NA	NA	NA
Spanaway CDP	NA	NA	NA	NA	NA	NA	NA	NA	NA	NA	NA	NA	NA	NA	NA
Spokane city	19,218	9107	548	8559	112,488	519	43.0	360.6	46.8	62.8	641	346.3	1,653	310	189.9
Spokane Valley city	5,542	6065	325	5740	62,156	491	30.3	47.6	9.5	74.7	379	44.6	492	104	7.9
Sunnyside city	478	2968	130	2838	4,261	29	100.0	15.5	1.9	55.7	487	14.5	906	36	19.4
Tacoma city	14,412	7040	798	6242	170,709	1,059	24.6	497.4	82.6	61.5	792	525.2	2,597	668	1587.6
Tukwila city	3,465	17394	818	16575	6,030	17	100.0	81.3	27.4	81.3	2054	76.7	3,906	1,533	31.4
Tumwater city	735	3910	319	3590	29,661	122	98.4	29.6	2.8	25.8	936	25.1	1,386	140	6.7
Union Hill-Novelty Hill CDP	NA	NA	NA	NA	NA	NA	NA	NA	NA	NA	NA	NA	NA	NA	NA
University Place city	785	2433	214	2219	28,186	207	24.2	20.3	3.7	81.0	386	19.2	607	164	55.9
Vancouver city	5,840	3462	344	3118	70,593	818	23.1	216.2	36.9	48.3	622	188.0	1,138	228	263.9
Vashon CDP	NA	NA	NA	NA	NA	NA	NA	NA	NA	NA	NA	NA	NA	NA	NA
Walla Walla city	1,668	5240	330	4910	13,679	89	94.4	47.0	7.8	77.4	512	48.0	1,505	391	62.5
Walnut Grove CDP	NA	NA	NA	NA	NA	NA	NA	NA	NA	NA	NA	NA	NA	NA	NA
Washougal city	402	2697	127	2570	21,378	82	100.0	18.7	5.1	96.6	595	19.5	1,337	555	30.7
Wenatchee city	1,220	3717	192	3525	7,414	55	67.3	35.6	3.6	70.5	627	31.6	972	109	42.9
West Richland city	232	1748	121	1627	32,112	106	100.0	9.8	0.8	67.7	326	7.9	625	77	12.1
White Center CDP	NA	NA	NA	NA	NA	NA	NA	NA	NA	NA	NA	NA	NA	NA	NA
Woodinville city	446	3910	70	3839	38,418	165	13.9	12.7	1.2	94.8	883	11.5	1,022	314	3.6
Yakima city	5,042	5383	438	4945	26,013	137	89.1	108.8	28.2	59.7	539	101.0	1,085	250	60.7
WEST VIRGINIA	43,236	2337	302	2035	395,354	2,677	71.3	X	X	X	X	X	X	X	X
Beckley city	1,471	8360	1080	7280	2,270	8	100.0	36.6	10.5	2.2	939	36.9	2,090	662	19.7
Bluefield city	295	2816	716	2100	0	0	0.0	13.3	1.2	70.0	447	13.9	1,322	0	5.7
Charleston city	3,985	7861	1243	6618	5,117	18	100.0	119.9	8.4	43.3	1461	118.2	2,318	327	118.0
Clarksburg city	NA	NA	NA	NA	0	0	0.0	22.0	1.4	9.7	814	20.6	1,252	3	7.2
Cross Lanes CDP	NA	NA	NA	NA	NA	NA	NA	NA	NA	NA	NA	NA	NA	NA	NA
Fairmont city	310	1646	170	1476	205	2	100.0	19.8	0.7	33.8	507	14.0	746	21	44.3
Huntington city	NA	NA	NA	NA	383	10	0.0	66.4	5.5	20.3	561	69.9	1,422	172	44.1
Martinsburg city	226	1272	96	1176	998	8	100.0	22.4	1.3	33.2	675	21.8	1,243	90	19.3
Morgantown city	894	2874	260	2614	4,063	57	19.3	47.5	3.6	18.6	602	57.9	1,916	338	120.1
Parkersburg city	1,160	3725	286	3439	1,279	11	100.0	38.3	2.2	14.9	512	37.9	1,214	142	67.9
St. Albans city	497	4548	430	4118	110	1	100.0	9.2	0.2	32.1	543	8.7	796	0	20.2
South Charleston city	958	7131	849	6282	0	0	0.0	29.6	0.2	36.6	1292	29.8	2,223	0	13.0
Teays Valley CDP	NA	NA	NA	NA	NA	NA	NA	NA	NA	NA	NA	NA	NA	NA	NA
Vienna city	210	1981	38	1943	415	4	50.0	8.8	0.3	25.1	562	8.1	764	76	0.0
Weirton city	297	1525	92	1433	479	4	100.0	19.4	2.6	100.0	359	19.4	995	24	40.2
Wheeling city	929	3331	782	2549	6,189	55	5.5	68.9	4.3	9.3	776	77.9	2,759	267	49.6
WISCONSIN	136,952	2379	290	2088	2,599,187	14,622	58.7	X	X	X	X	X	X	X	X
Allouez village & MCD (Brown)	NA	NA	NA	NA	360	2	100.0	11.4	2.5	97.8	416	11.6	830	77	23.9

1 Data for serious crimes have not been adjusted for underreporting. This may affect comparability between geographic areas over time.
2 Per 100,000 population estimated by the FBI. 3 Based on population estimated as of July 1 of the year shown.

Table B. Incorporated Places, Census Designated Places (CDPs), and Minor Civil Divisions (MCDs) of 10,000 or More Population — Land Area, Population, and Households, and Employment

STATE City, town, township, borough, or CDP (county if applicable)	Land area,[1] 2010 (sq mi)	Population Total persons 2010	Population Total persons 2014	Population Percent change 2010–2014	Population characteristics 2010–2014 Persons per square mile, 2014	Population characteristics 2010–2014 Foreign born	Population characteristics 2010–2014 Lives in same house as previous year	Household income and poverty, 2010–2014 Median household income (dollars)	Percent of households Income of $100,000 or more	Percent of households Income below poverty level	Employment,[2] 2010–2014 Percent in labor force	Employment,[2] 2010–2014 Unemployment rate	Households, 2010–2014 (percent of households) Family households	Households, 2010–2014 (percent of households) One person households
	1	2	3	4	5	6	7	8	9	10	11	12	13	14
WISCONSIN—Con.														
Appleton city	24.445	72,628	73,971	1.8	3,026.0	6.6	85.4	$53,439	17.8	11.8	69.9	4.5	62.4	30.1
Appleton city (Calumet)	3.308	11,082	11,256	1.6	3,402.2	8.1	92.0	$66,453	22.4	9.9	76.2	2.4	70.1	19.4
Appleton city (Outagamie)	20.748	60,056	61,190	1.9	2,949.2	6.3	84.5	$52,320	17.4	11.7	69.1	5.0	61.9	31.1
Ashwaubenon village & MCD (Brown)	12.395	16,943	17,111	1.0	1,380.4	3.7	82.3	$52,914	19.6	9.9	68.7	8.1	64.5	29.8
Baraboo city & MCD (Sauk)	7.397	12,050	12,085	0.3	1,633.7	1.8	80.9	$39,923	11.0	13.8	69.0	8.9	59.3	30.2
Beaver Dam city & MCD (Dodge)	7.137	16,214	16,536	2.0	2,316.9	3.0	84.2	$45,840	11.7	9.5	67.4	7.1	57.9	36.3
Bellevue village & MCD (Brown)	14.375	14,710	15,215	3.4	1,058.4	7.2	84.9	$51,913	18.0	11.2	70.7	4.9	62.1	26.9
Beloit city & MCD (Rock)	17.318	37,004	36,881	-0.3	2,129.6	9.3	83.2	$36,384	9.5	21.2	63.6	14.5	63.4	30.0
Brookfield city & MCD (Waukesha)	27.195	37,931	37,982	0.1	1,396.7	6.7	91.7	$91,485	45.2	4.4	63.1	5.3	74.7	22.4
Brown Deer village & MCD (Milwaukee)	4.396	12,000	12,102	0.9	2,752.8	6.8	89.3	$55,396	17.9	10.0	67.2	7.5	60.2	36.0
Burlington city	7.576	10,529	10,541	0.1	1,391.5	3.1	89.1	$50,548	15.8	12.4	71.7	8.6	57.5	35.1
Burlington city (Racine)	7.427	10,529	10,541	0.1	1,419.3	3.1	89.1	$50,548	15.8	12.4	71.7	8.6	57.5	35.1
Caledonia village & MCD (Racine)	45.401	24,705	24,708	0.0	544.2	3.8	94.0	$68,936	32.0	6.8	65.4	7.4	74.2	21.4
Cedarburg city & MCD (Ozaukee)	4.832	11,461	11,506	0.4	2,381.4	3.5	89.0	$71,813	33.9	7.6	69.6	6.2	64.8	29.5
Chippewa Falls city & MCD (Chippewa)	11.310	13,727	13,965	1.7	1,234.7	0.7	80.8	$36,170	8.0	16.5	59.3	9.6	50.1	43.6
Cudahy city & MCD (Milwaukee)	4.765	18,271	18,341	0.4	3,849.5	6.7	90.7	$46,657	12.7	15.6	61.9	10.5	58.1	35.1
De Pere city & MCD (Brown)	11.763	23,806	24,555	3.1	2,087.5	2.9	81.8	$56,834	20.1	7.1	69.7	6.5	65.0	29.6
Eau Claire city	32.122	66,190	67,684	2.3	2,107.1	3.5	77.2	$43,295	14.7	18.0	71.3	6.0	52.4	34.1
Eau Claire city (Eau Claire)	28.135	64,216	65,682	2.3	2,334.6	3.4	76.8	$43,090	15.0	18.2	71.2	5.9	52.1	34.1
Elkhorn city & MCD (Walworth)	8.042	10,084	9,975	-1.1	1,240.4	4.1	86.0	$50,910	12.7	9.2	71.7	10.1	66.6	28.8
Fitchburg city & MCD (Dane)	34.922	25,163	27,154	7.9	777.6	16.9	77.7	$62,832	28.1	12.7	73.8	6.2	62.7	29.1
Fond du Lac city & MCD (Fond du Lac)	18.926	43,023	42,917	-0.2	2,267.6	5.1	82.1	$45,914	13.7	14.3	66.9	8.9	58.7	34.5
Fort Atkinson city & MCD (Jefferson)	5.654	12,393	12,430	0.3	2,198.3	6.3	82.4	$47,868	14.9	12.0	66.8	6.3	62.5	30.3
Franklin city & MCD (Milwaukee)	34.583	35,451	36,278	2.3	1,049.0	7.4	83.9	$73,122	35.7	6.0	61.4	4.6	69.6	26.1
Germantown village & MCD (Washington)	34.373	19,753	19,901	0.7	579.0	3.4	91.0	$74,865	35.2	5.1	74.2	6.4	74.8	20.7
Glendale city & MCD (Milwaukee)	5.783	12,879	12,887	0.1	2,228.5	9.2	85.6	$61,296	27.1	11.4	59.6	4.9	55.9	38.5
Grafton village & MCD (Ozaukee)	5.017	11,477	11,531	0.5	2,298.5	4.9	87.2	$61,887	29.3	6.1	69.9	3.6	64.8	30.8
Grand Chute town (Outagamie)	23.458	20,908	22,097	5.7	942.0	7.7	84.4	$53,531	19.5	10.5	70.2	2.9	57.5	34.1
Green Bay city & MCD (Brown)	45.430	103,913	104,891	0.9	2,308.9	8.2	82.9	$43,063	12.9	16.5	67.0	8.3	58.0	33.6
Greendale village & MCD (Milwaukee)	5.562	14,046	14,332	2.0	2,576.6	6.3	88.6	$63,480	28.7	8.5	63.3	6.8	66.8	29.2
Greenfield city & MCD (Milwaukee)	11.515	36,746	37,157	1.1	3,226.7	8.7	88.4	$50,311	16.7	10.1	63.1	6.8	53.3	39.6
Greenville town (Outagamie)	35.719	10,309	11,235	9.0	314.5	2.5	91.0	$85,806	39.1	3.4	75.2	4.0	80.7	13.1
Hartford city	7.959	14,221	14,280	0.4	1,794.3	4.7	86.3	$56,536	20.4	8.7	72.1	4.5	64.4	30.3
Hartford city (Washington)	7.416	14,221	14,280	0.4	1,925.5	4.7	86.3	$56,536	20.4	8.7	72.1	4.5	64.4	30.3
Howard village	18.113	17,399	18,987	9.1	1,048.3	3.2	86.7	$57,599	22.0	8.1	75.2	6.2	71.7	22.5
Howard village (Brown)	18.096	17,399	18,987	9.1	1,049.2	3.2	86.7	$57,599	22.0	8.1	75.2	6.2	71.7	22.5
Hudson city & MCD (St. Croix)	6.536	12,715	13,415	5.5	2,052.3	2.0	83.4	$62,554	27.6	6.6	73.5	5.1	59.2	32.5
Janesville city & MCD (Rock)	33.748	63,606	64,009	0.6	1,896.7	3.6	82.7	$49,372	16.6	14.5	67.3	9.2	64.5	28.4
Kaukauna city	7.678	15,460	15,799	2.2	2,057.6	1.9	89.2	$54,945	17.7	9.6	74.9	5.5	65.2	27.3
Kaukauna city (Outagamie)	7.663	15,460	15,799	2.2	2,061.6	1.9	89.2	$54,945	17.7	9.6	74.9	5.5	65.2	27.3
Kenosha city & MCD (Kenosha)	27.022	99,228	99,894	0.7	3,696.8	7.6	82.6	$48,181	16.8	17.7	66.4	12.0	63.7	28.8
La Crosse city & MCD (La Crosse)	20.484	51,323	52,440	2.2	2,560.0	3.1	71.2	$40,340	10.0	19.5	66.6	6.2	47.0	35.6
Lisbon town (Waukesha)	27.537	10,182	10,333	1.5	375.2	2.5	95.5	$80,606	36.7	2.4	69.6	5.8	82.4	15.3
Little Chute village & MCD (Outagamie)	5.430	10,450	10,813	3.5	1,991.2	1.3	90.4	$57,161	15.4	6.7	70.4	5.5	71.6	23.3
Madison city & MCD (Dane)	76.689	233,059	245,691	5.4	3,203.7	10.7	71.9	$53,933	23.0	17.4	72.5	5.8	48.7	35.7
Manitowoc city & MCD (Manitowoc)	17.716	33,740	33,102	-1.9	1,868.5	3.4	91.4	$41,280	13.6	11.9	64.1	8.2	57.0	37.2
Marinette city & MCD (Marinette)	6.828	10,968	10,897	-0.6	1,595.8	2.0	85.3	$34,602	7.7	18.2	62.3	8.1	48.0	45.8
Marshfield city	13.350	19,079	18,691	-2.0	1,400.1	3.1	85.4	$42,619	11.9	10.8	67.6	5.9	56.4	37.0
Marshfield city (Wood)	11.475	18,178	17,790	-2.1	1,550.3	3.2	85.8	$42,744	11.9	10.9	67.8	5.5	57.1	36.0
Menasha city	6.030	17,351	17,604	1.5	2,919.6	4.3	88.2	$46,001	14.6	11.3	68.8	6.3	61.8	32.6
Menasha city (Winnebago)	4.488	15,144	15,369	1.5	3,424.3	4.7	88.1	$42,429	9.9	12.5	67.9	7.2	59.9	34.2
Menasha town (Winnebago)	12.172	18,498	18,867	2.0	1,550.0	3.6	86.9	$56,828	18.3	9.2	71.6	6.0	62.8	29.9
Menomonee Falls village & MCD (Waukesha)	32.994	35,625	35,974	1.0	1,090.3	5.4	89.9	$73,936	32.8	4.9	67.1	4.9	68.0	28.0
Menomonie city & MCD (Dunn)	13.692	16,284	16,237	-0.3	1,185.9	4.2	58.2	$37,155	9.6	23.3	60.9	7.1	47.6	34.3
Mequon city & MCD (Ozaukee)	46.355	23,139	23,509	1.6	507.2	8.3	91.6	$106,813	52.3	4.3	60.5	5.3	73.5	22.6
Middleton city & MCD (Dane)	8.851	17,547	18,671	6.4	2,109.4	9.4	79.4	$62,238	26.9	5.9	72.6	5.7	58.2	34.2
Milwaukee city	96.105	594,738	599,642	0.8	6,239.4	9.8	78.9	$35,489	10.0	25.6	65.1	13.1	56.3	35.0
Milwaukee city (Milwaukee)	96.083	594,738	599,642	0.8	6,240.8	9.8	78.9	$35,489	10.0	25.6	65.1	13.1	56.3	35.0
Monroe city & MCD (Green)	4.807	10,817	10,781	-0.3	2,242.6	3.5	84.4	$39,441	12.3	13.9	65.4	5.2	57.9	34.3
Mount Pleasant village & MCD (Racine)	33.686	26,197	26,293	0.4	780.5	5.2	89.8	$65,347	29.3	6.5	64.8	7.8	63.9	29.9
Muskego city & MCD (Waukesha)	31.595	24,135	24,621	2.0	779.3	3.3	92.7	$83,033	40.0	2.8	74.7	4.0	77.7	20.1

1 Dry land or land partially or temporarily covered by water.
2 16 years old and over.

Table B. Incorporated Places, Census Designated Places (CDPs), and Minor Civil Divisions (MCDs) of 10,000 or More Population — Crime, Construction, and Local Government Finance

STATE City, town, township, borough, or CDP (county if applicable)	Serious crimes known to police, 2014[1] Total number	Rate[2] Total	Rate[2] Violent	Rate[2] Property	New residential construction authorized by building permits, 2014 Value ($1,000)	Number of housing units	Percent single family	Local government finance, 2012 General revenue Total (mil dol)	Intergovernmental Total (mil dol)	Percent from state gov.	Taxes per capita[3]	General expenditure Total (mil dol)	Per capita[3] Total	Capital outlays	Debt outstanding (mil dol)
	15	16	17	18	19	20	21	22	23	24	25	26	27	28	29
WISCONSIN—Con.															
Appleton city	1,603	2171	269	1901	31,639	198	29.3	105.8	35.3	66.9	547	95.4	1,306	185	159.0
Appleton city (Calumet)	NA	NA	NA	NA	31,639	198	29.3	NA	NA	NA	NA	NA	NA	NA	NA
Appleton city (Outagamie)	NA	NA	NA	NA	31,639	198	29.3	NA	NA	NA	NA	NA	NA	NA	NA
Ashwaubenon village & MCD (Brown)	NA	NA	NA	NA	6,607	29	72.4	19.9	3.9	83.4	601	20.1	1,176	69	17.4
Baraboo city & MCD (Sauk)	377	3113	91	3022	2,268	12	83.3	16.5	5.3	85.2	658	16.3	1,357	229	25.1
Beaver Dam city & MCD (Dodge)	449	2740	55	2686	4,034	45	28.9	21.2	6.3	91.8	567	25.3	1,552	575	34.6
Bellevue village & MCD (Brown)	NA	NA	NA	NA	5,674	49	42.9	9.3	1.4	92.5	220	9.3	624	110	18.5
Beloit city & MCD (Rock)	1,388	3764	404	3360	719	7	100.0	62.8	26.8	88.2	542	62.9	1,709	281	93.8
Brookfield city & MCD (Waukesha)	1,034	2720	58	2662	22,245	56	100.0	58.1	9.5	75.4	977	58.2	1,531	164	66.3
Brown Deer village & MCD (Milwaukee)	546	4503	165	4338	140	1	100.0	15.3	2.7	84.5	747	16.9	1,402	115	22.9
Burlington city	221	2100	48	2053	7,856	52	46.2	17.8	3.2	73.0	864	15.5	1,479	188	40.2
Burlington city (Racine)	221	2100	48	2053	7,856	52	46.2	NA	NA	NA	NA	NA	NA	NA	NA
Caledonia village & MCD (Racine)	314	1269	150	1119	0	0	0.0	24.4	3.6	92.5	513	25.4	1,029	92	40.0
Cedarburg city & MCD (Ozaukee)	104	905	NA	905	5,526	17	100.0	12.7	2.1	80.3	633	12.9	1,120	111	5.8
Chippewa Falls city & MCD (Chippewa)	170	1238	197	1041	6,162	64	10.9	19.5	6.8	90.4	490	16.8	1,223	91	23.4
Cudahy city & MCD (Milwaukee)	524	2854	191	2664	1,107	13	7.7	27.1	8.0	90.1	709	25.2	1,377	148	73.6
De Pere city & MCD (Brown)	261	1066	49	1017	8,173	55	63.6	28.6	5.7	94.3	512	27.5	1,138	214	29.1
Eau Claire city	1,837	2704	162	2542	10,958	65	100.0	86.2	27.3	65.5	536	88.9	1,320	274	99.4
Eau Claire city (Eau Claire)	NA	NA	NA	NA	10,958	65	100.0	NA	NA	NA	NA	NA	NA	NA	NA
Elkhorn city & MCD (Walworth)	143	1439	70	1369	1,107	6	100.0	12.5	2.5	71.2	616	13.9	1,387	183	33.8
Fitchburg city & MCD (Dane)	486	1822	277	1544	41,443	371	9.4	30.2	5.5	88.9	718	39.3	1,517	661	29.6
Fond du Lac city & MCD (Fond du Lac)	1,344	3129	328	2801	9,007	52	57.7	60.5	20.6	71.8	490	63.0	1,465	223	203.2
Fort Atkinson city & MCD (Jefferson)	195	1559	104	1455	543	3	100.0	14.3	3.4	82.4	522	13.8	1,110	178	17.5
Franklin city & MCD (Milwaukee)	788	2158	55	2103	14,893	51	96.1	41.4	6.9	92.4	747	36.9	1,030	91	32.5
Germantown village & MCD (Washington)	NA	NA	NA	NA	14,213	60	100.0	24.5	3.7	88.4	673	21.2	1,072	93	30.9
Glendale city & MCD (Milwaukee)	864	6683	232	6451	0	0	0.0	33.9	5.2	100.0	1799	33.3	2,583	164	160.2
Grafton village & MCD (Ozaukee)	146	1266	87	1179	4,797	20	100.0	15.1	2.5	96.7	788	14.0	1,215	74	41.6
Grand Chute town (Outagamie)	924	4170	95	4076	16,717	66	100.0	23.7	3.5	76.5	500	19.5	910	143	29.8
Green Bay city & MCD (Brown)	2,836	2701	497	2204	19,446	180	38.9	138.7	46.3	79.3	512	133.7	1,276	218	209.5
Greendale village & MCD (Milwaukee)	512	3552	49	3504	696	2	100.0	14.5	2.1	96.6	631	30.8	2,153	256	17.5
Greenfield city & MCD (Milwaukee)	1,015	2724	150	2574	9,815	96	10.4	36.7	6.5	88.9	556	41.0	1,106	190	32.8
Greenville town (Outagamie)	NA	NA	NA	NA	20,994	158	51.9	3.3	0.6	100.0	181	3.0	278	56	2.1
Hartford city	251	1761	42	1719	7,666	48	87.5	23.3	6.3	79.1	655	28.0	1,968	649	54.8
Hartford city (Washington)	251	1761	42	1719	7,666	48	87.5	NA	NA	NA	NA	NA	NA	NA	NA
Howard village	NA	NA	NA	NA	16,411	108	72.2	13.1	2.7	95.7	300	11.9	644	95	4.4
Howard village (Brown)	NA	NA	NA	NA	16,411	108	72.2	NA	NA	NA	NA	NA	NA	NA	NA
Hudson city & MCD (St. Croix)	481	3619	135	3483	13,517	55	76.4	14.2	2.9	52.7	503	13.9	1,070	92	11.5
Janesville city & MCD (Rock)	2,238	3503	254	3250	15,897	73	89.0	81.1	21.4	60.8	488	86.4	1,359	476	106.9
Kaukauna city	213	1349	139	1210	6,302	42	85.7	19.0	4.7	94.7	487	20.8	1,326	219	75.3
Kaukauna city (Outagamie)	213	1349	139	1210	6,302	42	85.7	NA	NA	NA	NA	NA	NA	NA	NA
Kenosha city & MCD (Kenosha)	2,701	2700	288	2412	5,989	47	40.4	136.7	40.5	74.7	666	121.2	1,213	141	179.5
La Crosse city & MCD (La Crosse)	1,638	3177	202	2975	4,496	26	92.3	96.0	32.3	81.3	801	83.2	1,597	241	98.7
Lisbon town (Waukesha)	NA	NA	NA	NA	60	1	100.0	5.8	0.9	83.6	333	5.2	506	61	6.5
Little Chute village & MCD (Outagamie)	NA	NA	NA	NA	6,874	97	13.4	14.5	4.8	64.2	510	14.9	1,427	287	26.6
Madison city & MCD (Dane)	7,835	3188	344	2844	233,692	1,680	14.0	476.1	163.1	64.2	802	469.3	1,956	262	526.8
Manitowoc city & MCD (Manitowoc)	1,003	3017	223	2794	5,457	65	13.8	48.5	17.0	90.1	469	54.5	1,630	246	154.4
Marinette city & MCD (Marinette)	325	2975	92	2883	535	3	100.0	15.2	6.7	93.9	466	13.4	1,231	92	22.5
Marshfield city	350	1875	43	1832	4,988	52	19.2	30.7	9.6	91.7	668	36.1	1,914	260	83.3
Marshfield city (Wood)	NA	NA	NA	NA	4,988	52	19.2	NA	NA	NA	NA	NA	NA	NA	NA
Menasha city	416	2358	210	2149	7,356	40	100.0	24.4	8.7	74.1	616	30.1	1,720	83	81.2
Menasha city (Winnebago)	416	2358	210	2149	7,356	40	100.0	NA	NA	NA	NA	NA	NA	NA	NA
Menasha town (Winnebago)	200	1052	105	946	9,200	115	27.0	16.3	2.3	89.8	398	16.4	876	158	38.3
Menomonee Falls village & MCD (Waukesha)	451	1253	22	1231	21,820	103	45.6	46.2	6.0	94.8	698	54.6	1,523	188	94.1
Menomonie city & MCD (Dunn)	460	2853	242	2611	1,621	11	100.0	19.9	7.4	82.2	405	19.0	1,174	112	30.3
Mequon city & MCD (Ozaukee)	154	658	34	624	45,991	151	43.0	27.9	3.8	94.4	853	29.8	1,276	194	48.9
Middleton city & MCD (Dane)	297	1593	64	1528	30,084	152	76.3	36.1	5.8	79.2	1161	28.8	1,579	313	55.9
Milwaukee city	36,461	6073	1485	4588	17,811	206	16.5	1070.1	483.1	64.8	505	1000.4	1,671	211	1306.0
Milwaukee city (Milwaukee)	36,461	6073	1485	4588	17,811	206	16.5	NA	NA	NA	NA	NA	NA	NA	NA
Monroe city & MCD (Green)	283	2612	166	2446	380	3	33.3	15.6	3.5	91.6	641	13.1	1,216	111	14.1
Mount Pleasant village & MCD (Racine)	811	3092	61	3031	6,667	29	86.2	34.1	6.0	62.3	601	36.3	1,387	0	47.2
Muskego city & MCD (Waukesha)	221	896	28	868	21,223	78	100.0	25.5	3.1	90.8	559	28.3	1,158	244	44.9

1 Data for serious crimes have not been adjusted for underreporting. This may affect comparability between geographic areas over time.
2 Per 100,000 population estimated by the FBI. 3 Based on population estimated as of July 1 of the year shown.

Table B. Incorporated Places, Census Designated Places (CDPs), and Minor Civil Divisions (MCDs) of 10,000 or More Population — **Land Area, Population, and Households, and Employment**

STATE City, town, township, borough, or CDP (county if applicable)	Land area,[1] 2010 (sq mi)	Total persons 2010	Total persons 2014	Percent change 2010–2014	Persons per square mile, 2014	Foreign born	Lives in same house as previous year	Median household income (dollars)	Income of $100,000 or more	Income below poverty level	Percent in labor force	Unemployment rate	Family households	One person households
	1	2	3	4	5	6	7	8	9	10	11	12	13	14
WISCONSIN—Con.														
Neenah city & MCD (Winnebago)	9.208	25,504	25,855	1.4	2,807.8	3.3	84.7	$52,271	18.0	9.7	69.5	4.9	61.0	31.5
New Berlin city & MCD (Waukesha)	36.466	39,584	39,842	0.7	1,092.6	5.3	91.1	$74,203	34.9	4.4	67.6	5.1	66.0	29.1
Oak Creek city & MCD (Milwaukee)	28.451	34,452	35,053	1.7	1,232.1	6.7	88.6	$64,570	28.2	7.9	72.0	6.2	63.3	29.8
Oconomowoc city & MCD (Waukesha)	11.515	15,759	16,319	3.6	1,417.2	3.5	88.3	$70,204	32.0	7.3	72.0	5.5	69.2	26.1
Onalaska city & MCD (La Crosse)	10.206	17,790	18,385	3.3	1,801.4	4.7	86.3	$53,813	22.6	8.6	68.9	5.5	67.8	25.4
Oshkosh city & MCD (Winnebago)	25.653	66,083	66,621	0.8	2,597.0	2.5	78.9	$42,860	11.7	17.6	63.3	6.5	51.7	35.2
Pewaukee city & MCD (Waukesha)	19.509	13,204	13,942	5.6	714.6	4.5	90.0	$81,976	39.9	3.2	67.9	4.1	72.2	22.8
Platteville city & MCD (Grant)	5.363	11,255	12,281	9.1	2,290.1	1.8	58.5	$39,756	7.5	31.2	62.8	4.2	44.8	28.7
Pleasant Prairie village & MCD (Kenosha)	33.376	19,719	20,400	3.5	611.2	4.7	89.4	$72,520	32.2	6.9	65.8	8.7	69.1	24.6
Plover village & MCD (Portage)	10.509	12,123	12,326	1.7	1,172.9	3.7	80.3	$58,409	23.4	15.3	69.1	7.3	64.8	26.7
Portage city & MCD (Columbia)	8.824	10,324	10,178	-1.4	1,153.4	2.0	75.3	$44,150	13.0	15.5	64.8	6.4	60.9	31.8
Port Washington city & MCD (Ozaukee)	5.805	11,290	11,586	2.6	1,995.9	2.2	86.4	$61,978	23.3	4.5	73.6	5.5	65.1	27.6
Racine city & MCD (Racine)	15.487	78,860	78,065	-1.0	5,040.6	7.7	86.9	$39,623	11.5	21.0	64.6	13.2	59.9	33.1
Richfield village & MCD (Washington)	35.910	11,300	11,460	1.4	319.1	3.4	95.7	$91,014	46.1	2.8	73.6	6.1	85.1	12.7
River Falls city	6.517	15,003	15,175	1.1	2,328.7	1.8	60.4	$49,742	17.5	17.5	71.0	5.8	52.4	27.4
River Falls city (Pierce)	4.018	11,854	11,897	0.4	2,961.0	1.8	57.2	$44,460	17.4	20.5	70.6	5.8	50.2	26.9
Salem town (Kenosha)	29.141	12,061	12,184	1.0	418.1	3.2	92.2	$65,447	24.9	7.5	73.7	9.4	75.3	22.1
Sheboygan city & MCD (Sheboygan)	13.975	49,290	48,775		3,490.1	10.4	83.6	$43,107	10.0	13.0	69.4	8.6	59.8	32.2
Shorewood village & MCD (Milwaukee)	1.594	13,162	13,331	1.3	8,363.2	11.9	80.4	$63,550	31.3	13.5	74.2	4.9	52.6	36.6
South Milwaukee city & MCD (Milwaukee)	4.799	21,155	21,236	0.4	4,425.5	5.0	88.9	$51,499	17.5	11.9	67.5	9.8	62.9	31.2
Stevens Point city & MCD (Portage)	17.176	26,703	26,658	-0.2	1,552.1	4.0	68.3	$40,081	10.6	24.2	67.4	9.7	48.3	34.8
Stoughton city & MCD (Dane)	5.389	12,649	13,039	3.1	2,419.5	2.0	87.1	$57,813	21.1	8.7	71.8	5.6	62.2	31.6
Suamico village & MCD (Brown)	36.341	11,346	11,878	4.7	326.8	1.0	94.8	$85,403	38.3	2.9	78.3	5.6	85.5	12.9
Sun Prairie city & MCD (Dane)	12.011	29,541	31,752	7.5	2,643.6	4.3	84.3	$66,956	26.9	7.7	76.6	5.6	67.2	24.5
Superior city & MCD (Douglas)	36.963	27,244	26,705	-2.0	722.5	2.6	81.9	$39,503	12.2	20.9	66.5	8.6	55.8	37.6
Sussex village & MCD (Waukesha)	7.518	10,518	10,740	2.1	1,428.6	3.5	85.3	$73,958	35.1	5.9	75.7	3.6	75.0	20.6
Two Rivers city & MCD (Manitowoc)	6.078	11,723	11,437	-2.4	1,881.8	1.3	91.9	$39,529	10.2	12.1	59.9	6.3	61.7	33.2
Verona city & MCD (Dane)	6.697	10,678	12,003	12.4	1,792.4	3.0	88.7	$81,474	36.8	4.9	73.3	3.3	59.5	35.4
Watertown city	12.047	23,855	23,891	0.2	1,983.2	2.1	86.7	$49,926	13.3	11.1	69.6	11.4	65.2	31.8
Watertown city (Jefferson)	7.980	15,394	15,504	0.7	1,942.9	2.9	87.0	$46,747	11.2	13.9	71.4	9.8	64.8	31.4
Waukesha city & MCD (Waukesha)	24.798	70,706	71,489	1.1	2,882.9	7.8	81.9	$58,126	22.7	10.8	73.1	6.0	61.0	30.6
Waunakee village & MCD (Dane)	6.895	12,099	13,067	8.0	1,895.0	3.5	89.6	$90,365	43.5	4.1	76.5	4.2	78.4	18.3
Waupun city	4.650	11,352	11,377	0.2	2,446.6	1.5	81.3	$46,807	8.7	9.5	49.4	4.4	64.9	33.6
Wausau city & MCD (Marathon)	18.838	39,114	39,302	0.5	2,086.3	7.9	79.5	$40,464	13.3	17.4	66.2	9.3	55.7	37.1
Wauwatosa city & MCD (Milwaukee)	13.245	46,449	47,102	1.4	3,556.2	4.5	86.6	$69,467	30.7	6.3	71.4	4.6	57.8	36.0
West Allis city & MCD (Milwaukee)	11.387	60,419	60,624	0.3	5,324.0	5.4	86.3	$44,475	12.4	13.3	69.5	7.9	51.6	40.0
West Bend city & MCD (Washington)	15.070	31,199	31,692	1.6	2,102.9	2.8	85.7	$56,829	18.9	8.2	70.8	6.7	64.7	29.2
Weston village & MCD (Marathon)	21.547	14,868	14,988	0.8	695.6	3.7	86.0	$50,657	17.4	10.7	71.3	7.7	68.2	27.5
Whitefish Bay village & MCD (Milwaukee)	2.126	14,110	14,122	0.1	6,643.6	7.2	88.9	$102,576	51.4	3.5	71.7	4.8	71.1	24.7
Whitewater city	8.761	14,390	15,040	4.5	1,716.8	7.8	53.3	$30,281	9.2	39.1	65.4	7.6	45.0	31.8
Whitewater city (Walworth)	5.969	11,150	11,945	7.1	2,001.3	7.4	56.2	$29,226	9.0	38.4	66.0	7.1	44.4	32.6
Wisconsin Rapids city & MCD (Wood)	13.845	18,371	17,966	-2.2	1,297.7	2.9	82.0	$36,299	7.2	13.1	60.4	7.8	53.7	40.9
WYOMING	97,093.136	563,767	584,153	3.6	6.0	3.4	81.6	$58,252	23.5	10.9	68.4	5.2	65.3	27.7
Casper city	25.991	55,323	60,086	8.6	2,311.8	2.4	81.1	$57,511	22.1	8.5	69.9	4.9	63.1	29.5
Cheyenne city	25.202	59,631	62,845	5.4	2,493.6	2.9	79.0	$54,845	22.5	10.1	68.0	5.8	62.0	31.6
Evanston city	10.287	12,387	12,190	-1.6	1,185.0	5.4	76.0	$49,333	19.3	15.5	70.5	6.9	71.3	24.2
Gillette city	19.634	29,812	31,971	7.2	1,628.3	4.3	78.1	$73,426	32.5	9.7	76.4	4.6	68.5	23.0
Green River city	13.725	12,515	12,630	0.9	920.2	5.4	83.6	$71,766	33.8	8.3	71.5	7.6	73.3	20.8
Laramie city	17.739	30,815	32,081	4.1	1,808.5	5.9	64.7	$38,451	14.4	30.9	66.0	6.0	45.2	32.4
Riverton city	10.011	10,695	10,953	2.4	1,094.1	0.2	79.9	$42,208	14.7	15.1	67.0	9.3	55.7	35.7
Rock Springs city	19.339	23,036	24,045	4.4	1,243.3	6.0	75.9	$70,918	31.2	11.0	72.8	5.8	66.4	27.0
Sheridan city	10.958	17,450	17,916	2.7	1,635.0	4.0	76.7	$49,314	16.8	11.4	62.8	4.5	57.5	36.8

1 Dry land or land partially or temporarily covered by water.
2 16 years old and over.

Table B. Incorporated Places, Census Designated Places (CDPs), and Minor Civil Divisions (MCDs) of 10,000 or More Population — Crime, Construction, and Local Government Finance

STATE City, town, township, borough, or CDP (county if applicable)	Serious crimes known to police, 2014[1] Total number	Rate[2] Total	Violent	Property	New residential construction authorized by building permits, 2014 Value ($1,000)	Number of housing units	Percent single family	Local government finance, 2012 General revenue Total (mil dol)	Intergovernmental Total (mil dol)	Percent from state gov.	Taxes per capita[3]	General expenditure Total (mil dol)	Per capita[3] Total	Capital outlays	Debt outstanding (mil dol)
	15	16	17	18	19	20	21	22	23	24	25	26	27	28	29
WISCONSIN—Con.															
Neenah city & MCD (Winnebago)	514	1978	142	1835	10,698	54	96.3	34.2	7.5	78.2	681	35.3	1,374	110	75.6
New Berlin city & MCD (Waukesha)	NA	NA	NA	NA	9,825	31	100.0	42.8	4.9	98.3	591	43.8	1,103	116	45.0
Oak Creek city & MCD (Milwaukee)	1,015	2889	125	2763	12,713	81	25.9	39.6	9.3	95.7	591	40.8	1,169	139	112.6
Oconomowoc city & MCD (Waukesha)	241	1474	67	1407	9,553	38	94.7	23.1	4.4	54.3	801	22.9	1,443	327	34.4
Onalaska city & MCD (La Crosse)	410	2224	33	2191	11,585	58	70.7	18.0	3.5	80.7	559	18.1	993	157	43.7
Oshkosh city & MCD (Winnebago)	1,588	2371	233	2139	15,564	157	9.6	88.9	26.0	83.5	554	92.9	1,393	336	221.7
Pewaukee city & MCD (Waukesha)	NA	NA	NA	NA	29,280	100	96.0	20.4	3.8	52.2	639	18.8	1,379	152	16.0
Platteville city & MCD (Grant)	268	2347	201	2146	1,318	10	40.0	14.2	5.5	92.9	460	16.2	1,441	534	31.4
Pleasant Prairie village & MCD (Kenosha)	405	1997	84	1913	21,297	138	36.2	43.1	6.0	91.3	788	36.9	1,852	157	108.4
Plover village & MCD (Portage)	182	1478	81	1397	5,252	19	100.0	13.0	2.7	99.9	500	12.2	1,000	206	30.6
Portage city & MCD (Columbia)	72	710	148	562	6,590	112	3.6	11.4	3.7	95.6	479	12.4	1,217	229	17.0
Port Washington city & MCD (Ozaukee)	103	906	106	801	5,561	27	92.6	14.6	4.6	93.0	443	15.5	1,356	201	30.9
Racine city & MCD (Racine)	3,040	3895	406	3488	415	3	100.0	138.3	56.9	78.9	627	139.8	1,787	186	233.6
Richfield village & MCD (Washington)	NA	NA	NA	NA	14,328	40	100.0	3.4	0.8	99.8	214	3.3	293	83	0.3
River Falls city	321	2105	85	2020	NA	NA	NA	17.3	5.4	84.6	360	16.9	1,125	107	20.6
River Falls city (Pierce)	321	2105	85	2020	8,903	57	100.0	NA	NA	NA	NA	NA	NA	NA	NA
Salem town (Kenosha)	NA	NA	NA	NA	7,493	22	100.0	8.6	1.0	73.7	278	9.4	781	139	25.7
Sheboygan city & MCD (Sheboygan)	1,422	2926	317	2609	1,346	7	100.0	64.8	24.2	81.4	549	58.7	1,204	114	62.5
Shorewood village & MCD (Milwaukee)	281	2100	164	1936	0	0	0.0	17.0	3.0	86.6	843	22.0	1,668	470	28.0
South Milwaukee city & MCD (Milwaukee)	515	2423	245	2178	NA	NA	NA	23.5	6.7	86.9	533	24.0	1,130	87	37.2
Stevens Point city & MCD (Portage)	595	2231	158	2074	5,585	40	55.0	34.5	13.5	80.1	519	34.2	1,272	140	44.4
Stoughton city & MCD (Dane)	NA	NA	NA	NA	3,179	17	88.2	15.4	3.1	83.2	551	15.6	1,202	267	31.4
Suamico village & MCD (Brown)	NA	NA	NA	NA	18,349	115	38.3	8.5	1.2	97.6	423	8.8	756	154	31.1
Sun Prairie city & MCD (Dane)	767	2455	90	2366	38,354	266	42.9	36.3	6.6	89.6	700	33.4	1,092	159	70.0
Superior city & MCD (Douglas)	1,813	6771	276	6494	395	3	100.0	47.8	19.7	86.8	488	43.1	1,604	221	54.2
Sussex village & MCD (Waukesha)	NA	NA	NA	NA	3,651	12	100.0	10.1	1.2	98.7	471	14.5	1,361	408	38.7
Two Rivers city & MCD (Manitowoc)	228	1985	174	1811	134	1	100.0	17.3	6.5	87.1	432	16.6	1,435	134	29.8
Verona city & MCD (Dane)	181	1499	50	1449	41,743	224	38.4	20.9	3.4	85.6	1249	16.1	1,431	279	36.6
Watertown city	483	2017	209	1808	NA	NA	NA	28.2	7.5	93.7	507	25.9	1,084	125	67.9
Watertown city (Jefferson)	NA	NA	NA	NA	5,756	18	88.9	NA	NA	NA	NA	NA	NA	NA	NA
Waukesha city & MCD (Waukesha)	1,296	1823	129	1694	31,448	319	24.5	94.8	23.2	75.8	753	92.3	1,297	257	127.7
Waunakee village & MCD (Dane)	105	807	100	707	34,858	93	100.0	15.4	2.2	89.2	683	15.2	1,199	312	46.8
Waupun city	130	1148	132	1015	NA	NA	NA	9.5	4.0	98.4	229	14.2	1,246	473	26.1
Wausau city & MCD (Marathon)	851	2162	221	1941	5,172	22	100.0	59.2	21.8	72.8	667	52.5	1,340	306	50.1
Wauwatosa city & MCD (Milwaukee)	1,604	3391	159	3232	26,525	309	1.0	76.5	14.7	62.5	891	68.2	1,451	107	100.8
West Allis city & MCD (Milwaukee)	2,936	4832	360	4471	1,519	23	17.4	89.6	27.7	67.2	652	88.3	1,455	97	78.5
West Bend city & MCD (Washington)	955	3018	164	2853	5,198	32	68.8	37.8	8.6	79.5	714	36.4	1,152	223	79.7
Weston village & MCD (Marathon)	NA	NA	NA	NA	4,202	59	30.5	22.5	9.2	37.7	568	23.1	1,545	361	66.4
Whitefish Bay village & MCD (Milwaukee)	185	1309	42	1267	2,520	4	100.0	16.3	2.6	86.4	750	19.5	1,382	295	42.0
Whitewater city	293	1977	121	1856	NA	NA	NA	16.4	8.0	68.7	315	16.4	1,102	259	25.8
Whitewater city (Walworth)	NA	NA	NA	NA	3,620	43	2.3	NA	NA	NA	NA	NA	NA	NA	NA
Wisconsin Rapids city & MCD (Wood)	767	4271	67	4204	4,986	49	10.2	28.8	9.3	83.0	631	30.4	1,669	348	48.3
WYOMING	12,619	2160	195	1965	502,643	1,901	84.9	X	X	X	X	X	X	X	X
Casper city	1,716	2824	138	2685	40,956	146	100.0	90.9	48.4	57.4	185	91.8	1,586	372	19.5
Cheyenne city	1,884	2983	141	2842	40,981	283	65.4	102.2	45.4	60.0	231	84.7	1,372	240	86.1
Evanston city	369	3006	73	2932	3,871	17	64.7	14.4	9.7	66.4	132	13.9	1,136	164	0.0
Gillette city	1,008	3123	158	2965	66,417	163	100.0	102.0	79.8	46.5	129	73.4	2,334	563	91.7
Green River city	193	1503	241	1262	6,385	25	72.0	29.3	23.6	50.3	102	25.8	2,020	637	0.0
Laramie city	753	2350	150	2201	8,407	51	100.0	40.4	21.5	68.2	162	47.7	1,503	636	44.3
Riverton city	479	4332	280	4052	2,857	17	64.7	15.5	7.7	74.3	175	14.3	1,298	316	3.6
Rock Springs city	607	2485	274	2210	28,575	188	40.4	48.9	33.3	63.9	151	45.8	1,911	466	9.8
Sheridan city	443	2472	218	2254	10,851	53	81.1	31.8	21.0	65.4	215	28.0	1,579	421	8.0

1 Data for serious crimes have not been adjusted for underreporting. This may affect comparability between geographic areas over time.
2 Per 100,000 population estimated by the FBI. 3 Based on population estimated as of July 1 of the year shown.

TABLE C.

Incorporated Places, Census Designated Places (CDPs), and Minor Civil Divisions (MCDs) of 10,000 or More Population— Economic Census

(For explanation of symbols see page xvi)

Table C. Incorporated Places, Census Designated Places (CDPs), and Minor Civil Divisions (MCDs) of 10,000 or More Population — Economic Census

STATE City, town, township, borough, or CDP (county if applicable)	Utilities Number of establishments	Number of employees	Manufacturing Number of establishments	Number of employees	Wholesale trade[1] Number of establishments	Number of employees	Retail trade Number of establishments	Number of employees	Transportation and warehousing Number of establishments	Number of employees	Information Number of establishments	Number of employees	Finance and insurance Number of establishments	Number of employees	Real estate and rental and leasing Number of establishments
	1	2	3	4	5	6	7	8	9	10	11	12	13	14	15
United States...................	17,595	651,234	297,191	11,214,165	355,983	4,880,666	1,062,083	14,703,529	213,809	4,305,464	138,341	3,321,226	468,183	6,040,880	354,106
ALABAMA......................	424	15,454	4,283	232,650	4,600	60,332	18,211	218,531	2,836	57,835	1,574	35,102	7,294	72,763	3,858
Alabaster city..................	1	D	26	1,145	44	579	92	1,773	11	D	8	123	32	127	17
Albertville city..............	NA	NA	34	4,107	27	597	131	1,199	14	279	11	175	56	308	21
Alexander City city...........	2	D	17	1,413	8	82	100	1,016	8	D	8	79	31	246	17
Anniston city..................	7	D	45	3,187	38	701	158	2,051	19	266	10	235	89	487	35
Athens city....................	NA	NA	23	1,961	20	283	152	1,967	8	D	14	D	73	306	38
Atmore city....................	3	D	8	791	6	D	68	541	7	D	9	152	21	163	5
Auburn city....................	4	D	60	3,523	34	217	206	3,180	11	117	24	414	77	625	54
Bessemer city.................	1	D	41	1,549	58	944	194	2,746	31	1,545	11	239	58	326	27
Birmingham city..............	28	D	249	10,654	500	9,168	943	12,300	193	6,838	172	5,015	538	12,913	281
Calera city....................	12	D	9	446	11	D	47	759	17	356	5	D	17	97	7
Center Point city.............	NA	NA	NA	NA	3	D	47	460	4	7	1	D	19	85	11
Chelsea city..................	NA	NA	NA	NA	7	36	25	395	NA	NA	4	D	14	74	NA
Cullman city..................	2	D	45	2,228	34	392	210	2,328	25	1,081	16	193	97	700	31
Daphne city...................	NA	NA	4	37	34	277	110	2,225	7	32	13	137	57	368	48
Decatur city..................	2	D	82	4,735	77	1,316	332	4,256	28	300	19	241	153	1,796	57
Dothan city...................	2	D	78	D	148	D	501	7,114	56	1,020	45	D	193	1,181	94
Enterprise city...............	2	D	18	844	11	38	155	1,802	6	D	16	D	73	D	40
Eufaula city..................	8	D	22	D	11	D	75	747	16	217	4	D	34	D	14
Fairfield city................	NA	NA	13	2,532	11	143	48	727	NA	NA	NA	NA	7	63	2
Fairhope city.................	1	D	17	241	15	89	108	856	10	34	7	54	50	247	30
Florence city.................	NA	NA	53	2,616	49	584	302	4,139	15	216	15	D	131	788	77
Foley city....................	NA	NA	15	1,140	13	60	231	2,897	6	35	7	68	47	288	30
Forestdale CDP...............	NA	NA	NA	NA	NA	NA	29	521	3	5	2	D	19	90	8
Fort Payne city..............	NA	NA	45	3,133	13	126	113	1,332	15	D	8	D	52	239	12
Gadsden city.................	3	D	48	3,839	39	351	229	3,037	16	246	21	283	95	681	39
Gardendale city..............	2	D	3	17	9	31	66	1,016	9	40	8	163	37	179	12
Gulf Shores city.............	1	D	8	35	8	14	78	1,085	10	62	11	94	31	156	45
Hartselle city...............	1	D	15	D	9	125	68	772	6	D	4	D	27	178	8
Helena city..................	NA	NA	14	223	7	47	15	227	4	D	5	37	14	55	3
Homewood city................	NA	NA	24	1,121	65	775	224	3,152	16	684	38	1,480	113	5,056	59
Hoover city..................	5	D	25	345	80	1,134	384	7,578	22	217	58	2,609	238	6,243	95
Hueytown city................	1	D	9	82	17	127	69	977	4	D	1	D	25	D	7
Huntsville city..............	1	D	173	13,598	225	3,051	999	14,677	96	1,324	119	5,217	412	3,049	311
Irondale city................	NA	NA	14	326	58	985	40	747	13	366	8	D	25	208	16
Jacksonville city............	NA	NA	6	166	1	D	35	611	2	D	1	D	12	65	12
Jasper city..................	6	D	25	1,199	24	177	155	1,858	13	D	11	105	61	366	28
Leeds city...................	1	D	25	801	13	89	95	1,445	5	D	1	D	21	D	14
Madison city.................	NA	NA	32	977	52	728	131	2,356	29	1,962	19	323	74	410	56
Millbrook city...............	1	D	4	13	8	31	45	623	1	D	3	D	22	106	12
Mobile city..................	16	616	152	8,817	353	4,191	968	14,109	178	3,703	126	2,717	496	4,959	310
Montgomery city..............	12	631	172	10,902	274	4,739	874	11,871	100	3,670	108	D	414	4,129	219
Moody city...................	NA	NA	11	244	16	704	28	224	3	D	3	13	16	60	2
Mountain Brook city..........	NA	NA	7	87	24	97	99	967	2	D	11	D	82	695	43
Muscle Shoals city...........	NA	NA	38	2,731	23	204	96	1,601	12	182	3	D	54	376	14
Northport city...............	NA	NA	21	345	28	465	152	1,900	18	42	3	D	67	362	29
Opelika city.................	1	D	34	2,067	32	373	206	2,732	26	1,550	14	202	75	D	40
Oxford city..................	1	D	18	262	35	336	167	2,622	14	378	12	458	50	256	12
Ozark city...................	4	D	8	105	7	69	72	729	8	D	5	D	30	184	14
Pelham city..................	3	138	42	1,464	153	1,644	170	2,074	18	243	19	D	77	391	47
Pell City city...............	4	50	31	1,730	16	222	78	1,204	9	38	7	60	35	271	12
Phenix City city.............	2	D	31	D	10	D	125	1,683	12	90	4	D	68	327	34
Pleasant Grove city..........	NA	NA	NA	NA	1	D	10	97	5	D	NA	NA	7	33	2
Prattville city..............	2	D	15	839	19	84	152	2,669	11	D	9	D	74	D	35
Prichard city................	4	D	15	280	11	270	60	487	20	591	3	D	11	44	8
Saks CDP.....................	NA	NA	3	D	1	D	11	57	2	D	3	D	3	D	3
Saraland city................	1	D	13	560	10	188	64	923	12	356	5	66	39	164	13
Scottsboro city..............	NA	NA	37	3,616	10	D	121	1,499	10	D	11	D	44	218	21
Selma city...................	1	D	30	2,219	18	146	125	1,280	1	D	7	D	50	315	24
Sylacauga city...............	NA	NA	23	1,018	12	126	87	1,075	7	129	7	D	41	226	13
Talladega city...............	3	D	18	787	9	97	85	942	2	D	5	81	29	153	9
Tillmans Corner CDP	1	D	5	36	5	34	27	290	5	43	1	D	9	26	8
Troy city....................	NA	NA	16	996	16	275	110	1,232	14	D	7	D	39	262	23
Trussville city..............	2	D	23	942	33	244	115	1,728	9	D	6	48	42	175	15
Tuscaloosa city..............	6	D	53	4,454	77	955	475	6,821	47	1,152	29	658	173	1,285	124
Vestavia Hills city..........	1	D	15	47	39	220	156	1,659	8	118	30	712	114	1,472	81
ALASKA.......................	86	2,025	527	12,450	638	7,734	2,508	33,721	1,091	18,957	399	6,523	740	7,215	872
Anchorage municipality	15	D	182	2,049	336	5,228	860	15,253	327	10,425	177	4,355	390	4,803	383
Badger CDP...................	1	D	7	32	4	4	12	93	12	119	1	D	NA	NA	7
College CDP..................	1	D	7	54	2	D	29	595	12	179	4	D	13	63	16
Fairbanks city...............	4	D	37	239	47	531	208	3,630	46	956	25	478	76	639	88
Juneau city and borough ..	2	D	26	236	36	265	142	1,821	58	932	22	249	49	366	61
Knik-Fairview CDP............	NA	NA	NA	NA	1	D	3	D	4	17	1	D	1	D	6
ARIZONA......................	265	12,185	4,269	131,941	5,570	73,496	17,479	286,184	3,110	80,725	2,117	48,994	9,196	128,762	8,089
Anthem CDP...................	2	D	3	7	10	43	23	623	5	4	4	D	32	129	25
Apache Junction city.........	1	D	13	85	11	D	90	1,591	10	26	5	47	31	160	40
Avondale city	1	D	9	29	15	161	113	3,480	15	95	8	402	42	146	42
Buckeye town.................	3	D	11	203	15	106	50	597	27	1,025	4	13	28	102	19
Bullhead City city...........	8	147	6	39	9	64	119	2,195	16	567	9	120	41	196	52
Camp Verde town	2	D	10	104	7	35	40	476	11	86	NA	NA	10	44	10

1 Merchant wholesalers, except manufacturers' sales branches and offices.

Table C. Incorporated Places, Census Designated Places (CDPs), and Minor Civil Divisions (MCDs) of 10,000 or More Population — **Economic Census**

STATE City, town, township, borough, or CDP (county if applicable)	Real estate and rental and leasing — Number of employees	Professional, scientific, and technical services — Number of establishments	Number of employees	Administration and support and waste management and mediation services — Number of establishments	Number of employees	Educational services — Number of establishments	Number of employees	Health care and social assistance — Number of establishments	Number of employees	Arts, entertainment, and recreation — Number of establishments	Number of employees	Accommodation and food services — Number of establishments	Number of employees	Other services (except public administration) — Number of establishments	Number of employees
	16	17	18	19	20	21	22	23	24	25	26	27	28	29	30
United States	1,923,770	856,463	8,203,735	386,387	9,774,262	67,960	642,334	831,303	18,414,757	124,591	2,081,668	662,489	12,007,689	529,691	3,430,711
ALABAMA	22,852	9,109	89,988	4,118	133,280	554	3,858	10,305	243,194	1,086	17,170	8,339	157,337	6,087	37,291
Alabaster city	54	58	528	30	706	9	26	89	2,366	6	86	48	1,162	38	D
Albertville city	488	43	215	21	D	2	D	62	973	3	D	28	D	21	98
Alexander City city	42	25	128	23	D	NA	NA	69	D	4	D	33	547	27	D
Anniston city	151	108	657	34	785	3	D	174	4,116	9	D	72	1,481	88	371
Athens city	105	73	516	26	178	2	D	93	D	9	D	71	1,385	50	284
Atmore city	19	13	59	3	D	NA	NA	26	491	3	D	23	D	16	68
Auburn city	299	125	1,074	56	714	14	115	115	1,370	13	D	198	3,581	92	436
Bessemer city	159	73	564	26	489	2	D	91	2,461	8	D	95	1,734	49	478
Birmingham city	3,076	842	9,399	330	12,916	41	395	748	38,487	69	1,525	564	11,239	411	4,354
Calera city	13	5	38	8	84	2	D	17	126	4	D	25	371	13	D
Center Point city	D	9	47	6	33	NA	NA	25	D	2	D	15	289	14	D
Chelsea city	NA	18	77	12	65	1	D	18	D	2	D	22	D	11	D
Cullman city	164	69	317	27	695	3	D	131	1,857	4	54	86	1,636	49	D
Daphne city	125	92	368	37	431	8	53	92	1,131	11	202	69	1,384	50	278
Decatur city	218	139	978	66	1,857	9	D	274	4,610	14	D	140	2,847	99	D
Dothan city	D	193	1,098	101	D	13	D	301	9,062	29	D	223	4,538	166	D
Enterprise city	198	49	425	21	D	6	D	83	1,535	11	D	73	1,202	50	D
Eufaula city	D	32	88	8	D	NA	NA	37	658	6	D	42	D	16	59
Fairfield city	D	6	D	3	D	1	D	14	299	NA	NA	20	280	11	59
Fairhope city	98	89	320	27	162	3	D	97	2,101	10	50	65	1,607	32	203
Florence city	309	136	674	34	756	11	D	215	3,875	13	D	129	3,445	85	D
Foley city	99	44	305	22	704	2	D	76	1,658	5	486	69	1,685	27	170
Forestdale CDP	41	11	58	7	22	NA	NA	10	95	1	D	19	D	8	D
Fort Payne city	36	50	278	15	342	1	D	67	1,178	6	D	53	1,006	29	D
Gadsden city	182	99	1,065	34	4,069	2	D	231	5,841	9	D	90	2,203	68	D
Gardendale city	34	36	331	12	51	1	D	42	587	3	29	30	D	29	D
Gulf Shores city	933	48	159	25	236	NA	NA	26	167	13	198	67	1,865	35	121
Hartselle city	26	20	168	8	136	NA	NA	40	D	3	6	33	D	23	131
Helena city	2	26	D	12	47	3	D	20	128	4	D	15	192	14	D
Homewood city	362	157	1,291	70	3,201	14	201	193	5,609	9	66	117	2,294	89	1,636
Hoover city	675	282	D	113	4,675	28	147	229	3,408	29	363	187	4,241	91	498
Hueytown city	23	14	61	11	D	3	7	18	268	1	D	29	490	31	D
Huntsville city	D	1,006	28,897	265	9,382	45	459	723	19,108	83	1,585	527	11,685	337	2,856
Irondale city	171	35	319	33	352	1	D	16	211	3	D	17	205	27	141
Jacksonville city	70	15	41	6	D	NA	NA	22	575	2	D	29	621	15	D
Jasper city	135	74	401	19	109	3	18	112	2,250	4	D	56	971	46	D
Leeds city	48	18	71	12	63	NA	NA	17	134	3	D	32	530	18	D
Madison city	266	151	D	47	2,329	12	132	120	1,830	11	105	109	1,795	58	D
Millbrook city	D	14	79	7	9	1	D	24	266	1	D	29	459	26	D
Mobile city	1,554	704	7,962	291	15,029	49	283	589	19,251	68	1,866	488	10,868	384	2,545
Montgomery city	1,890	581	6,099	259	12,027	28	D	652	16,295	51	D	471	9,716	411	2,833
Moody city	D	12	307	7	D	NA	NA	13	D	NA	NA	16	281	14	D
Mountain Brook city	943	93	214	26	150	3	10	60	1,099	16	717	59	1,208	44	260
Muscle Shoals city	89	21	104	15	D	NA	NA	48	996	10	150	48	816	24	D
Northport city	D	57	367	25	519	5	40	111	D	10	140	69	1,622	55	D
Opelika city	149	63	281	55	3,329	6	D	95	4,412	5	D	98	2,049	61	D
Oxford city	35	29	174	20	D	1	D	44	827	4	D	85	2,291	35	D
Ozark city	47	29	98	8	35	3	D	45	1,018	4	D	45	D	21	100
Pelham city	358	109	744	65	2,873	7	45	60	668	11	213	68	1,510	77	574
Pell City city	27	48	203	14	579	3	D	40	796	3	D	43	822	27	94
Phenix City city	95	46	170	22	D	6	D	66	D	5	D	67	1,285	52	269
Pleasant Grove city	D	5	7	2	D	NA	NA	9	269	2	D	3	D	7	15
Prattville city	138	54	276	14	56	2	D	87	1,456	12	D	85	2,148	53	D
Prichard city	83	4	15	13	169	1	D	34	D	2	D	14	179	14	D
Saks CDP	5	1	D	2	D	NA	NA	3	D	3	5	3	D	5	38
Saraland city	62	24	138	12	803	1	D	20	D	2	D	38	638	29	232
Scottsboro city	71	47	137	22	132	1	D	86	1,412	5	D	51	965	27	D
Selma city	73	44	D	7	117	1	D	92	1,936	6	44	41	767	31	145
Sylacauga city	37	22	63	7	D	2	D	65	D	1	D	30	503	19	110
Talladega city	114	21	106	9	D	NA	NA	49	1,010	5	D	30	454	21	67
Tillmans Corner CDP	19	9	34	9	129	3	33	6	76	3	D	8	133	11	68
Troy city	85	25	631	13	188	2	D	59	1,021	7	D	60	D	33	D
Trussville city	48	60	219	36	423	4	40	54	754	11	218	54	1,301	48	365
Tuscaloosa city	1,192	235	D	89	3,736	15	D	279	9,665	24	D	284	6,941	139	1,210
Vestavia Hills city	1,191	174	2,191	50	2,599	20	252	127	2,162	18	317	77	1,770	67	610
ALASKA	4,212	1,898	17,648	1,131	19,836	188	1,365	2,432	48,701	545	5,055	2,126	26,836	1,355	7,238
Anchorage municipality	2,403	1,141	13,516	576	15,710	91	548	1,165	25,616	141	2,799	788	14,957	580	3,863
Badger CDP	16	9	28	15	103	1	D	7	26	2	D	6	47	11	D
College CDP	41	29	168	16	149	4	21	43	303	5	D	32	471	20	D
Fairbanks city	468	140	1,298	71	1,123	14	179	207	5,171	47	506	138	2,215	114	528
Juneau city and borough	249	89	514	54	328	10	173	144	2,458	35	286	119	1,329	82	406
Knik-Fairview CDP	3	8	31	7	D	NA	NA	7	D	2	D	4	D	2	D
ARIZONA	40,479	16,198	121,381	8,051	216,880	1,301	12,809	16,872	315,107	1,764	42,407	11,669	251,455	8,503	62,073
Anthem CDP	53	44	101	25	74	5	14	49	356	5	D	28	443	22	138
Apache Junction city	141	22	76	26	159	NA	NA	70	1,405	5	34	45	665	40	260
Avondale city	118	47	197	37	316	11	D	113	1,106	7	D	86	1,658	62	421
Buckeye town	59	37	196	19	124	1	D	18	189	4	163	46	798	15	54
Bullhead City city	187	46	160	40	736	1	D	125	2,127	10	D	85	1,091	48	290
Camp Verde town	16	14	31	13	67	3	6	25	366	2	D	31	411	11	38

Table C. Incorporated Places, Census Designated Places (CDPs), and Minor Civil Divisions (MCDs) of 10,000 or More Population — Economic Census

Economic activity by sector, 2012

STATE City, town, township, borough, or CDP (county if applicable)	Utilities Number of establishments	Utilities Number of employees	Manufacturing Number of establishments	Manufacturing Number of employees	Wholesale trade[1] Number of establishments	Wholesale trade[1] Number of employees	Retail trade Number of establishments	Retail trade Number of employees	Transportation and warehousing Number of establishments	Transportation and warehousing Number of employees	Information Number of establishments	Information Number of employees	Finance and insurance Number of establishments	Finance and insurance Number of employees	Real estate and rental and leasing Number of establishments
	1	2	3	4	5	6	7	8	9	10	11	12	13	14	15
ARIZONA—Con.															
Casa Grande city	5	184	37	1,753	25	403	190	3,440	27	847	13	256	64	462	52
Casas Adobes CDP	1	D	14	147	26	62	179	2,196	18	59	21	182	128	627	86
Catalina Foothills CDP	NA	NA	10	30	19	69	126	1,298	9	D	17	115	98	569	162
Chandler city	1	D	165	7,413	228	4,007	658	13,607	85	1,126	88	3,284	383	8,610	304
Chino Valley town	2	D	13	109	5	50	38	388	7	58	2	D	14	57	15
Coolidge city	2	D	5	40	8	209	30	471	3	D	2	D	8	D	8
Cottonwood city	2	D	12	55	11	85	77	1,319	6	85	8	34	31	144	31
Douglas city	2	D	NA	NA	7	17	68	894	12	133	5	10	13	82	13
Drexel Heights CDP	NA	NA	NA	NA	2	D	28	418	2	D	1	D	10	36	2
El Mirage city	NA	NA	13	251	4	36	26	498	9	112	NA	NA	6	D	10
Eloy city	NA	NA	9	225	1	D	21	192	2	D	1	D	1	D	4
Flagstaff city	3	D	58	3,453	68	554	322	5,224	57	878	19	497	125	728	129
Florence town	1	D	NA	NA	1	D	12	142	3	4	2	D	8	38	4
Flowing Wells CDP	NA	NA	19	354	21	190	34	356	11	235	2	D	6	D	10
Fort Mohave CDP	1	D	4	35	10	41	37	458	4	D	2	D	15	45	13
Fortuna Foothills CDP	2	D	NA	NA	3	D	22	172	3	D	1	D	12	69	9
Fountain Hills town	1	D	8	51	23	69	77	781	5	13	11	76	45	150	45
Gilbert town	2	D	118	1,887	143	1,264	470	9,470	64	415	53	881	296	1,527	292
Glendale city	2	D	134	2,988	118	1,188	674	12,710	80	622	34	607	289	3,419	215
Goodyear city	NA	NA	22	1,220	23	D	141	3,318	23	1,186	11	130	78	357	62
Green Valley CDP	2	D	8	19	4	D	51	508	2	D	2	D	40	157	26
Kingman city	5	D	11	133	22	211	128	2,586	27	361	17	247	50	309	35
Lake Havasu City city	3	D	65	916	48	223	215	2,843	24	148	19	151	70	387	80
Marana town	2	D	30	1,028	20	108	114	2,868	15	121	11	254	49	220	31
Maricopa city	NA	NA	11	148	7	16	26	729	7	D	9	D	32	141	15
Mesa city	3	D	245	7,319	292	3,313	1,315	22,342	132	2,727	112	1,570	686	4,683	547
New Kingman-Butler CDP	NA	NA	NA	NA	5	23	8	30	5	D	1	D	2	D	NA
New River CDP	NA	NA	8	24	15	25	17	76	7	D	4	9	2	D	7
Nogales city	2	D	17	172	95	719	160	2,001	113	1,004	10	D	39	238	31
Oro Valley town	NA	NA	10	2,279	23	57	90	2,092	7	29	6	67	77	306	60
Paradise Valley town	NA	NA	3	D	8	34	11	61	1	D	4	D	31	306	52
Payson town	3	D	12	D	9	78	79	980	9	32	4	D	32	141	38
Peoria city	5	60	49	874	60	289	387	8,515	47	182	19	322	205	962	156
Phoenix city	30	6,459	1,338	38,642	1,853	30,877	3,712	60,797	815	42,188	643	20,074	2,545	56,886	1,894
Prescott city	5	165	61	1,457	62	557	279	4,290	25	201	32	435	130	602	127
Prescott Valley town	1	D	31	603	31	430	100	1,348	26	185	9	126	45	221	36
Queen Creek town	NA	NA	5	27	7	14	50	973	12	59	5	D	27	115	24
Rio Rico CDP	1	D	4	D	44	D	9	146	40	501	NA	NA	3	D	7
Sahuarita town	1	D	3	D	3	D	23	730	5	13	4	50	11	D	10
San Luis city	NA	NA	5	D	8	233	36	591	21	132	1	D	9	35	5
San Tan Valley CDP	1	D	6	49	6	D	21	642	6	10	1	D	21	57	4
Scottsdale city	3	18	216	7,082	505	4,707	1,218	18,728	129	1,228	228	4,395	1,154	12,933	983
Sedona city	3	D	15	62	13	58	188	1,144	15	261	15	98	30	124	53
Show Low city	4	D	8	86	9	71	92	1,637	16	115	12	348	21	109	26
Sierra Vista city	6	177	11	57	12	86	160	2,810	18	152	16	229	56	330	60
Sierra Vista Southeast CDP	NA	NA	4	8	1	D	25	178	3	3	1	D	2	D	5
Somerton city	NA	NA	NA	NA	5	13	31	299	7	14	NA	NA	7	40	3
Sun City CDP	5	D	7	45	8	26	71	911	4	5	4	24	75	606	25
Sun City West CDP	NA	NA	NA	NA	2	D	28	393	1	D	3	D	39	172	10
Sun Lakes CDP	NA	NA	NA	NA	4	D	11	200	3	D	1	D	15	90	17
Surprise city	1	D	19	281	27	401	169	4,396	26	329	16	275	114	572	63
Tanque Verde CDP	NA	NA	8	16	9	13	11	38	1	D	5	5	7	D	22
Tempe city	4	D	373	15,660	436	8,635	755	14,805	126	4,021	145	4,765	408	18,291	407
Tucson city	9	D	393	6,648	446	4,468	1,883	30,599	220	4,928	210	5,465	742	7,203	735
Tucson Estates CDP	NA	NA	NA	NA	NA	NA	7	36	4	D	1	D	1	D	4
Vail CDP	1	D	NA	NA	1	D	4	D	1	D	2	D	4	7	5
Valencia West CDP	NA	NA	NA	NA	NA	NA	4	20	3	D	NA	NA	1	D	1
Verde Village CDP	NA	NA	4	12	4	D	3	D	7	26	NA	NA	5	5	5
Yuma city	4	D	42	1,800	80	1,615	302	5,503	68	674	36	D	110	1,009	124
ARKANSAS	320	7,065	2,688	153,706	2,884	34,492	10,923	135,448	2,356	50,798	1,020	23,729	4,319	35,504	2,802
Arkadelphia city	3	D	10	190	5	D	69	923	2	D	6	D	28	187	26
Batesville city	2	D	17	3,078	13	169	105	1,267	6	D	8	D	42	D	14
Bella Vista town	1	D	NA	NA	12	20	25	307	3	D	7	31	30	128	24
Benton city	2	D	35	561	23	138	127	1,859	20	203	9	D	53	281	26
Bentonville city	1	D	21	304	86	1,135	119	2,488	34	D	38	818	75	526	67
Blytheville city	4	62	20	1,644	21	202	82	772	20	510	7	54	28	167	16
Bryant city	1	D	10	176	20	180	83	1,666	14	72	2	D	34	153	17
Cabot city	NA	NA	11	194	15	97	81	1,421	8	76	7	D	39	164	30
Camden city	4	73	10	400	13	127	82	975	11	D	5	D	31	D	14
Centerton city	NA	NA	NA	NA	NA	NA	11	88	3	D	1	D	4	D	3
Conway city	4	D	54	3,479	57	618	284	4,730	35	419	20	D	126	847	94
El Dorado city	2	D	20	883	31	D	151	1,798	22	270	11	D	58	439	34
Fayetteville city	4	D	57	4,106	54	550	419	7,043	36	D	53	799	142	1,132	137
Forrest City city	3	D	3	D	9	D	83	924	8	116	7	61	26	D	18
Fort Smith city	5	D	148	13,228	171	2,184	521	7,161	88	1,369	55	1,202	207	1,394	156
Harrison city	4	D	35	1,541	22	343	116	1,542	19	899	16	D	53	397	30
Helena-West Helena city	3	D	9	295	13	180	59	624	11	93	6	D	14	86	10
Hope city	1	D	16	719	7	D	68	847	9	D	7	49	22	161	16
Hot Springs city	5	D	33	800	43	409	364	4,655	23	260	25	617	142	884	73
Hot Springs Village CDP	NA	NA	NA	NA	3	D	24	417	4	D	4	32	28	99	15
Jacksonville city	4	D	23	543	10	84	89	1,404	6	14	6	D	32	381	44
Jonesboro city	2	D	80	4,781	94	1,133	406	6,053	73	965	32	574	137	1,168	110
Little Rock city	28	D	166	8,152	358	6,552	994	14,533	154	5,289	199	8,660	712	11,364	377
Magnolia city	3	D	21	1,624	18	D	81	853	7	111	8	D	34	235	27
Malvern city	3	D	17	896	6	D	62	819	8	154	5	D	29	D	9
Marion city	1	D	7	303	10	142	25	290	10	139	1	D	13	D	4

1 Merchant wholesalers, except manufacturers' sales branches and offices.

Table C. Incorporated Places, Census Designated Places (CDPs), and Minor Civil Divisions (MCDs) of 10,000 or More Population — Economic Census

STATE / City, town, township, borough, or CDP (county if applicable)	Real estate and rental and leasing — No. employees (16)	Professional, scientific, and technical services — No. establishments (17)	No. employees (18)	Administration and support and waste management and mediation services — No. establishments (19)	No. employees (20)	Educational services — No. establishments (21)	No. employees (22)	Health care and social assistance — No. establishments (23)	No. employees (24)	Arts, entertainment, and recreation — No. establishments (25)	No. employees (26)	Accommodation and food services — No. establishments (27)	No. employees (28)	Other services (except public administration) — No. establishments (29)	No. employees (30)
ARIZONA—Con.															
Casa Grande city	198	60	533	36	1,216	5	D	168	3,257	9	122	114	D	71	437
Casas Adobes CDP	D	210	1,209	107	1,854	21	145	373	6,903	20	D	117	2,754	86	371
Catalina Foothills CDP	746	239	1,517	71	436	25	148	154	1,928	25	745	68	3,564	65	733
Chandler city	896	643	D	288	4,329	93	945	715	10,378	68	2,506	474	10,996	275	2,149
Chino Valley town	23	14	75	11	60	NA	NA	20	D	2	D	21	258	17	D
Coolidge city	17	10	32	8	D	2	D	13	118	2	D	17	D	10	44
Cottonwood city	103	42	238	17	D	1	D	98	1,835	3	D	51	596	34	177
Douglas city	D	8	25	2	D	NA	NA	17	275	1	D	30	409	12	D
Drexel Heights CDP	D	9	26	11	21	2	D	16	109	2	D	10	198	9	D
El Mirage city	D	7	18	15	219	NA	NA	8	D	NA	NA	11	128	14	D
Eloy city	16	2	D	6	D	3	D	6	161	1	D	12	180	9	D
Flagstaff city	450	253	1,364	93	906	14	D	319	5,419	39	587	300	6,034	161	1,023
Florence town	D	8	23	14	D	NA	NA	18	606	4	D	24	D	10	D
Flowing Wells CDP	64	12	120	26	610	1	D	12	63	3	D	11	140	25	83
Fort Mohave CDP	43	12	68	10	D	2	D	26	460	4	47	24	285	13	D
Fortuna Foothills CDP	20	6	55	8	13	NA	NA	13	D	4	D	33	461	18	D
Fountain Hills town	75	107	226	46	238	6	D	59	534	20	178	51	D	54	250
Gilbert town	787	534	3,357	278	3,642	43	293	641	8,675	52	1,083	287	6,139	226	1,399
Glendale city	820	309	D	229	4,472	31	345	627	11,126	43	D	381	8,050	275	1,558
Goodyear city	136	88	480	47	801	12	69	138	3,586	13	D	113	2,899	56	301
Green Valley CDP	D	34	194	17	80	NA	NA	66	1,401	23	238	31	459	38	175
Kingman city	94	49	233	38	748	4	22	120	2,846	8	47	92	1,681	50	360
Lake Havasu City city	277	96	319	89	573	5	D	176	2,579	12	D	134	2,333	146	549
Marana town	81	58	325	41	415	9	53	52	583	14	454	96	2,178	73	402
Maricopa city	29	38	94	22	182	1	D	35	226	3	D	30	479	26	106
Mesa city	2,280	1,024	5,218	524	28,839	76	776	1,253	21,915	87	2,113	733	14,688	619	3,803
New Kingman-Butler CDP	NA	3	D	7	25	1	D	5	44	1	D	6	36	6	D
New River CDP	5	29	60	23	122	2	D	11	D	5	10	7	112	11	D
Nogales city	D	42	129	20	D	5	D	54	1,043	4	D	60	820	27	101
Oro Valley town	D	123	447	48	420	14	D	126	1,866	17	363	67	1,998	56	D
Paradise Valley town	90	74	177	25	196	5	18	100	581	7	258	9	D	13	130
Payson town	79	42	119	20	84	2	D	72	D	5	D	55	D	32	134
Peoria city	621	221	1,012	165	1,301	34	244	399	6,732	35	652	243	5,889	176	1,084
Phoenix city	13,507	4,864	44,364	2,275	78,764	308	3,640	3,877	88,736	368	8,726	2,493	57,339	2,031	18,982
Prescott city	254	219	694	81	782	14	61	359	6,148	25	223	154	2,390	132	649
Prescott Valley town	99	42	336	56	287	4	D	116	1,982	11	241	75	1,112	64	275
Queen Creek town	D	52	136	42	134	3	1	75	710	5	D	38	698	24	112
Rio Rico CDP	9	8	17	7	43	NA	NA	5	D	1	D	11	76	4	D
Sahuarita town	17	14	34	21	78	1	D	20	169	2	D	19	438	9	D
San Luis city	D	6	D	2	D	NA	NA	17	186	1	D	14	206	3	6
San Tan Valley CDP	10	23	41	28	50	1	D	29	684	5	53	21	335	11	D
Scottsdale city	5,713	1,990	14,258	644	18,088	141	1,516	1,471	22,335	169	5,203	746	22,062	644	6,128
Sedona city	239	75	185	27	290	6	146	62	298	18	106	93	1,856	40	280
Show Low city	79	28	87	14	166	1	D	86	1,434	3	24	46	D	26	150
Sierra Vista city	317	104	2,494	46	1,164	6	D	154	2,587	10	D	100	2,058	56	301
Sierra Vista Southeast CDP	5	10	47	10	37	3	D	13	104	4	14	8	66	9	58
Somerton city	D	4	D	5	25	NA	NA	10	D	NA	NA	6	D	5	15
Sun City CDP	202	54	429	16	61	3	34	156	4,471	17	305	37	420	46	417
Sun City West CDP	14	21	96	13	772	2	D	109	2,576	12	D	12	142	17	193
Sun Lakes CDP	31	17	33	5	5	2	D	19	D	2	D	7	95	7	D
Surprise city	148	82	269	90	648	6	45	175	1,407	11	210	140	3,145	95	538
Tanque Verde CDP	44	74	133	20	63	4	23	28	201	7	100	3	D	13	47
Tempe city	3,684	973	12,489	406	21,043	77	633	569	10,089	67	1,372	563	12,672	342	2,631
Tucson city	3,966	1,585	11,128	670	23,445	153	1,087	1,805	41,707	166	2,539	1,214	26,136	944	6,631
Tucson Estates CDP	9	3	8	4	19	NA	NA	4	20	1	D	12	109	7	39
Vail CDP	10	8	23	6	23	2	D	5	23	2	D	4	150	4	12
Valencia West CDP	D	2	D	2	D	NA	NA	1	D	NA	NA	NA	NA	4	33
Verde Village CDP	11	15	17	16	53	3	1	7	D	2	D	4	59	4	D
Yuma city	513	173	1,064	109	3,297	11	D	300	6,412	19	D	227	4,641	137	817
ARKANSAS	12,867	5,678	32,210	2,601	52,676	373	2,206	7,485	166,455	781	8,881	5,473	95,854	3,961	21,830
Arkadelphia city	D	26	D	6	25	3	D	45	865	4	22	30	D	21	85
Batesville city	68	46	169	21	1,449	1	D	85	2,836	5	D	49	969	39	D
Bella Vista town	D	34	65	14	65	2	D	29	412	6	D	20	D	15	202
Benton city	53	62	250	23	D	4	D	98	2,710	12	D	62	1,080	57	D
Bentonville city	286	226	3,747	76	1,111	14	93	117	2,023	15	D	123	2,365	77	582
Blytheville city	65	23	84	20	647	1	D	73	1,293	6	30	51	840	26	100
Bryant city	31	44	195	15	167	5	D	61	D	6	33	62	1,351	31	D
Cabot city	77	50	210	19	115	3	19	52	604	5	43	46	841	31	D
Camden city	29	19	D	10	71	NA	NA	54	1,213	3	21	28	D	21	175
Centerton city	11	9	13	3	D	NA	NA	10	D	NA	NA	8	97	3	24
Conway city	402	169	D	67	D	13	166	240	4,573	15	196	172	4,248	110	621
El Dorado city	192	60	230	24	D	2	D	113	2,077	10	D	61	899	64	299
Fayetteville city	2,012	365	D	89	996	27	166	347	8,702	39	642	326	6,288	155	954
Forrest City city	45	30	D	7	D	NA	NA	50	961	2	D	33	522	17	D
Fort Smith city	813	273	1,310	132	D	18	124	358	10,478	25	262	245	5,188	176	D
Harrison city	56	48	238	22	903	2	D	111	2,239	6	D	59	1,053	38	183
Helena-West Helena city	28	25	D	5	34	NA	NA	56	D	4	D	14	D	22	85
Hope city	52	7	D	8	D	NA	NA	46	D	2	D	30	D	26	D
Hot Springs city	302	148	735	60	1,244	8	D	239	6,336	37	1,489	194	4,178	101	531
Hot Springs Village CDP	24	21	27	10	18	NA	NA	14	D	4	D	16	D	10	D
Jacksonville city	170	34	191	16	D	3	37	69	1,537	7	41	61	1,010	27	129
Jonesboro city	469	158	835	82	2,107	15	D	335	8,401	20	299	193	4,134	106	722
Little Rock city	2,450	1,185	7,681	431	12,233	84	576	971	31,677	82	1,178	593	12,849	494	3,744
Magnolia city	D	25	203	17	278	4	6	63	851	3	D	38	D	35	D
Malvern city	36	21	76	5	D	5	6	37	1,217	3	D	28	D	19	101
Marion city	D	14	D	7	D	2	D	25	D	5	9	18	D	11	D

Table C. Incorporated Places, Census Designated Places (CDPs), and Minor Civil Divisions (MCDs) of 10,000 or More Population — Economic Census

STATE City, town, township, borough, or CDP (county if applicable)	Utilities Number of establishments (1)	Number of employees (2)	Manufacturing Number of establishments (3)	Number of employees (4)	Wholesale trade[1] Number of establishments (5)	Number of employees (6)	Retail trade Number of establishments (7)	Number of employees (8)	Transportation and warehousing Number of establishments (9)	Number of employees (10)	Information Number of establishments (11)	Number of employees (12)	Finance and insurance Number of establishments (13)	Number of employees (14)	Real estate and rental and leasing Number of establishments (15)
ARKANSAS—Con.															
Maumelle city	1	D	9	1,698	14	D	21	513	12	176	6	D	36	108	21
Mountain Home city	3	46	25	1,649	10	D	151	1,857	7	29	17	D	55	469	25
North Little Rock city	NA	NA	62	1,978	196	3,234	417	6,092	63	2,332	31	398	150	957	89
Paragould city	1	D	37	3,299	26	378	130	1,608	11	104	8	D	51	578	30
Pine Bluff city	5	D	48	4,258	40	354	248	3,072	16	227	9	D	75	701	53
Rogers city	3	D	53	5,462	60	510	297	5,130	31	D	27	364	128	814	83
Russellville city	11	D	40	4,067	47	384	216	2,815	29	970	21	279	86	835	59
Searcy city	3	D	30	2,010	34	325	174	2,488	25	1,569	13	133	68	489	40
Sherwood city	NA	NA	17	D	30	188	94	1,899	9	19	2	D	48	312	28
Siloam Springs city	1	D	16	2,378	10	75	72	1,141	6	D	9	50	27	194	21
Springdale city	1	D	101	7,619	144	1,569	247	3,448	74	2,556	21	446	103	855	74
Texarkana city	3	D	26	2,303	37	D	113	1,324	31	D	5	D	50	D	27
Van Buren city	1	D	39	3,410	41	600	79	1,140	26	4,099	8	56	43	259	22
West Memphis city	1	D	25	815	38	717	102	1,660	39	1,932	5	D	23	136	30
CALIFORNIA	1,143	66,836	38,741	1,163,341	52,664	723,526	106,419	1,540,055	21,218	441,734	21,925	561,399	48,523	601,858	49,276
Adelanto city	1	D	42	1,108	7	114	19	286	14	D	2	D	7	41	9
Agoura Hills city	NA	NA	20	71	66	574	103	1,136	9	121	58	754	100	2,146	59
Alameda city	2	D	50	3,006	63	2,252	155	1,956	32	350	41	634	94	858	95
Alamo CDP	NA	NA	3	24	16	50	29	355	2	D	4	5	41	365	49
Albany city	NA	NA	9	39	11	53	47	709	2	D	12	D	21	114	27
Alhambra city	4	D	76	1,252	234	999	233	3,923	65	297	35	469	125	1,251	117
Aliso Viejo city	1	D	30	378	74	1,311	82	1,210	11	927	39	981	98	2,016	79
Alpine CDP	NA	NA	NA	NA	8	7	34	255	9	6	5	32	14	78	26
Altadena CDP	3	27	9	44	6	9	61	479	7	D	28	55	22	115	28
Alum Rock CDP	NA	NA	NA	NA	NA	NA	6	D	NA	NA	NA	NA	2	D	NA
American Canyon city	NA	NA	12	747	17	170	29	704	23	263	1	D	13	48	15
Anaheim city	8	504	693	19,991	799	9,520	826	13,333	132	3,896	118	2,477	365	5,846	381
Anderson city	2	D	14	103	9	37	60	774	6	111	3	20	17	106	11
Antelope CDP	NA	NA	NA	NA	2	D	37	1,554	18	63	4	D	17	50	14
Antioch city	1	D	22	235	23	316	216	3,781	29	129	10	156	60	392	60
Apple Valley town	4	D	25	319	10	32	113	2,311	32	1,125	6	97	44	326	37
Arcadia city	1	D	47	905	284	1,066	295	4,276	30	587	26	199	178	1,024	175
Arcata city	NA	NA	46	832	18	268	103	952	12	157	7	33	22	130	26
Arden-Arcade CDP	NA	NA	30	190	32	229	382	6,290	15	26	44	1,886	202	2,273	216
Arroyo Grande city	NA	NA	11	152	13	51	83	1,215	6	51	10	112	60	440	37
Artesia city	NA	NA	19	279	31	73	81	654	7	25	2	D	29	193	26
Arvin city	1	D	NA	NA	6	D	24	227	3	D	NA	NA	3	15	9
Ashland CDP	NA	NA	4	D	4	D	41	385	5	D	1	D	6	D	21
Atascadero city	2	D	26	109	30	210	116	1,230	7	37	10	73	42	213	27
Atwater city	NA	NA	13	368	8	D	74	1,314	8	27	2	D	30	157	12
Auburn city	NA	NA	25	240	22	D	90	992	10	237	21	314	52	250	45
Avenal city	1	D	NA	NA	NA	NA	13	71	2	D	NA	NA	1	D	6
Avocado Heights CDP	NA	NA	36	315	119	849	50	293	19	206	NA	NA	1	D	10
Azusa city	3	D	100	4,979	75	1,416	94	1,147	10	82	5	163	21	101	22
Bakersfield city	11	679	143	2,541	274	3,933	960	18,130	173	2,117	96	4,165	403	5,418	343
Baldwin Park city	1	D	85	1,533	151	860	130	2,106	46	926	6	D	34	173	22
Banning city	2	D	22	326	11	347	58	616	8	58	5	26	22	114	29
Barstow city	3	D	3	8	9	138	129	1,934	11	246	8	D	21	104	29
Bay Point CDP	1	D	4	290	NA	NA	16	125	4	D	NA	NA	1	D	8
Beaumont city	3	D	14	361	9	27	57	1,297	13	93	2	D	19	86	24
Bell city	NA	NA	30	1,711	71	1,564	51	458	26	467	5	D	18	197	12
Bellflower city	4	21	33	254	34	226	174	1,970	26	552	18	297	47	252	78
Bell Gardens city	1	D	50	863	39	474	79	1,127	16	58	5	4	13	68	10
Belmont city	NA	NA	20	352	19	D	57	761	4	8	16	D	29	D	49
Benicia city	NA	NA	70	2,579	66	1,134	71	844	37	456	8	98	27	D	43
Berkeley city	1	D	152	3,744	94	1,175	497	5,449	16	143	121	1,939	101	662	198
Beverly Hills city	NA	NA	57	348	158	778	429	5,382	18	80	360	15,108	283	2,988	481
Big Bear City CDP	NA	NA	3	6	2	D	18	70	1	D	4	12	1	D	6
Bloomington CDP	1	D	11	62	10	D	33	164	30	329	6	D	4	D	7
Blythe city	7	D	NA	NA	7	57	50	673	14	64	6	23	13	58	9
Bonita CDP	NA	NA	4	44	13	62	10	32	1	D	2	D	18	103	31
Bostonia CDP	NA	NA	15	97	15	74	33	158	6	20	NA	NA	3	19	18
Brawley city	NA	NA	4	D	16	170	42	611	10	57	4	D	20	142	19
Brea city	6	97	152	5,251	263	3,865	321	6,133	42	1,289	37	989	145	7,676	97
Brentwood city	1	D	17	232	14	59	142	2,263	10	17	17	181	65	385	55
Buena Park city	NA	NA	109	3,966	204	3,037	202	3,987	49	1,980	19	371	77	773	57
Burbank city	1	D	191	5,031	208	2,987	399	7,310	83	1,634	525	37,263	196	2,141	242
Burlingame city	3	D	49	1,679	136	978	159	2,011	112	3,936	53	D	143	827	149
Calabasas city	NA	NA	12	1,306	48	823	80	1,076	15	141	96	666	150	2,288	96
Calexico city	NA	NA	12	265	58	403	136	1,997	60	526	6	39	37	220	24
California City city	NA	NA	NA	NA	NA	NA	17	109	NA	NA	2	D	6	D	8
Camarillo city	2	D	134	4,292	147	2,132	313	5,248	32	623	55	1,260	124	961	87
Cameron Park CDP	NA	NA	8	104	5	20	48	563	6	D	4	D	31	D	30
Campbell city	1	D	92	1,840	74	D	182	2,925	14	335	57	937	165	961	85
Camp Pendleton South CDP	NA	NA	NA	NA	NA	NA	NA	NA	NA	NA	NA	NA	NA	NA	NA
Canyon Lake city	NA	NA	NA	NA	9	30	14	43	4	10	2	D	13	34	16
Capitola city	NA	NA	8	42	12	135	154	2,203	2	D	7	D	56	382	56
Carlsbad city	8	301	160	12,711	292	5,465	485	7,796	59	1,155	118	2,619	316	2,240	314
Carmichael CDP	1	D	27	95	30	148	130	1,522	21	160	NA	NA	58	208	89
Carpinteria city	NA	NA	31	2,080	23	287	53	466	6	26	8	D	25	285	15
Carson city	1	D	230	9,808	337	6,718	210	4,267	329	6,459	14	453	52	518	64
Casa de Oro-Mount Helix CDP	NA	NA	11	55	7	77	41	431	6	44	1	D	17	77	37
Castaic CDP	NA	NA	3	8	4	1	26	333	7	71	7	D	6	D	15
Castro Valley CDP	NA	NA	7	15	18	D	102	1,073	14	98	10	99	43	212	63
Cathedral City city	3	D	13	29	24	127	145	2,002	8	38	12	299	32	124	38

1 Merchant wholesalers, except manufacturers' sales branches and offices.

STATE City, town, township, borough, or CDP (county if applicable)	Real estate and rental and leasing	Professional, scientific, and technical services		Administration and support and waste management and mediation services		Educational services		Health care and social assistance		Arts, entertainment, and recreation		Accommodation and food services		Other services (except public administration)	
	Number of employees	Number of establishments	Number of employees	Number of establishments	Number of employees	Number of establishments	Number of employees	Number of establishments	Number of employees	Number of establishments	Number of employees	Number of establishments	Number of employees	Number of establishments	Number of employees
	16	17	18	19	20	21	22	23	24	25	26	27	28	29	30
ARKANSAS—Con.															
Maumelle city	84	29	81	19	250	6	D	42	D	6	57	29	401	20	D
Mountain Home city	D	53	312	21	162	6	D	137	3,207	9	D	62	1,069	55	D
North Little Rock city	440	175	1,435	99	3,951	20	146	243	5,930	25	603	227	4,536	158	1,349
Paragould city	D	47	423	16	172	2	D	91	1,545	6	D	61	D	37	D
Pine Bluff city	173	59	433	32	808	5	D	192	4,077	8	D	102	D	67	D
Rogers city	322	216	1,644	54	760	11	51	178	3,545	13	237	145	3,735	74	381
Russellville city	174	106	371	44	1,336	5	D	138	2,870	11	D	103	2,256	71	418
Searcy city	121	73	407	28	D	2	D	122	3,954	15	D	83	1,883	56	377
Sherwood city	80	43	539	37	1,415	2	D	72	920	4	D	43	673	46	211
Siloam Springs city	55	33	113	16	D	4	D	52	856	5	D	47	784	25	D
Springdale city	254	137	D	81	1,443	15	108	164	5,133	21	D	134	2,345	103	845
Texarkana city	D	41	D	20	D	2	D	65	D	5	D	69	D	42	D
Van Buren city	147	50	169	21	D	5	D	53	1,269	6	D	50	929	42	D
West Memphis city	168	38	194	18	465	2	D	88	1,823	8	D	68	1,158	43	293
CALIFORNIA	273,511	114,321	1,303,232	41,820	1,109,518	9,240	105,142	103,207	1,776,440	21,191	303,838	78,560	1,394,984	57,009	395,836
Adelanto city	21	7	75	7	200	1	D	8	D	1	D	14	D	6	80
Agoura Hills city	537	218	D	57	630	15	156	114	932	60	194	62	D	46	216
Alameda city	382	234	2,323	66	D	25	226	206	2,454	34	666	208	2,505	132	801
Alamo CDP	149	66	190	22	141	3	D	38	317	5	D	23	D	22	83
Albany city	73	64	D	15	D	5	21	64	D	6	D	55	515	55	D
Alhambra city	396	222	894	90	1,010	30	370	282	3,288	16	256	196	3,107	112	516
Aliso Viejo city	D	288	3,609	74	5,422	20	260	122	3,596	16	D	68	1,335	51	392
Alpine CDP	D	43	126	22	97	2	D	25	394	3	11	21	D	18	72
Altadena CDP	D	107	D	24	98	12	89	96	1,439	35	D	26	287	30	83
Alum Rock CDP	NA	4	D	7	30	NA	NA	18	D	1	D	4	34	6	D
American Canyon city	89	17	52	14	D	1	D	31	D	6	183	30	338	19	66
Anaheim city	3,684	684	4,391	419	21,930	65	721	892	15,700	79	D	692	23,526	397	3,128
Anderson city	28	13	85	10	193	1	D	21	348	4	23	28	435	20	109
Antelope CDP	81	24	54	23	89	2	D	22	169	5	D	22	378	16	75
Antioch city	266	92	600	79	D	15	D	244	5,414	17	319	129	1,981	97	542
Apple Valley town	179	68	339	37	407	8	23	201	3,061	8	D	85	D	44	287
Arcadia city	483	259	1,920	79	645	41	261	394	4,953	72	1,935	212	3,593	113	648
Arcata city	68	47	1,026	18	144	8	53	73	1,401	7	110	85	1,421	44	304
Arden-Arcade CDP	1,237	360	1,860	147	3,180	24	235	370	10,024	27	559	225	3,957	190	1,184
Arroyo Grande city	134	66	206	27	296	5	D	104	1,127	9	97	47	866	33	189
Artesia city	56	36	75	20	110	8	155	81	1,088	4	D	85	D	39	D
Arvin city	13	3	D	NA	NA	2	D	8	183	1	D	8	83	3	D
Ashland CDP	35	8	D	10	D	1	D	14	571	NA	NA	18	171	21	D
Atascadero city	D	75	365	31	220	4	D	114	2,848	9	127	70	926	40	191
Atwater city	32	10	27	8	99	NA	NA	27	468	4	D	35	532	20	D
Auburn city	190	115	632	23	377	4	28	82	664	8	48	46	733	49	235
Avenal city	D	NA	NA	1	D	2	D	7	D	NA	NA	3	D	1	D
Avocado Heights CDP	54	12	118	12	649	1	D	12	240	2	D	25	268	40	123
Azusa city	46	35	309	33	893	5	D	49	571	3	D	73	895	69	315
Bakersfield city	1,907	800	6,042	328	10,808	53	561	1,101	21,024	76	2,798	675	12,835	440	2,869
Baldwin Park city	119	31	143	40	763	6	D	85	4,474	2	D	85	1,201	37	D
Banning city	216	14	145	12	160	1	D	54	852	1	D	46	751	31	188
Barstow city	137	23	235	13	146	3	6	55	904	2	D	92	1,626	33	286
Bay Point CDP	16	5	5	8	D	1	D	14	D	1	D	11	110	5	15
Beaumont city	77	19	45	18	144	2	D	48	803	5	D	45	629	43	D
Bell city	D	16	405	17	D	1	D	35	363	1	D	54	580	28	201
Bellflower city	249	60	317	59	D	3	D	167	4,416	8	170	117	1,294	126	547
Bell Gardens city	36	10	153	11	312	1	D	32	800	2	D	53	669	38	348
Belmont city	533	107	508	26	435	9	41	57	388	6	93	62	716	53	D
Benicia city	187	98	580	55	711	8	35	54	311	11	130	60	767	66	573
Berkeley city	744	623	4,143	144	D	91	1,308	501	7,983	90	1,287	437	6,068	297	2,228
Beverly Hills city	2,312	1,022	5,287	208	3,019	31	713	1,099	6,037	866	3,843	200	8,518	345	2,561
Big Bear City CDP	23	15	36	11	26	1	D	10	D	NA	NA	9	48	9	38
Bloomington CDP	D	1	D	9	23	NA	NA	9	D	1	D	13	154	36	D
Blythe city	23	12	53	9	95	1	D	28	D	4	D	40	486	18	44
Bonita CDP	111	30	140	18	94	6	40	29	218	3	4	22	269	12	85
Bostonia CDP	61	11	31	18	151	NA	NA	9	D	2	D	14	143	43	187
Brawley city	61	17	75	8	182	3	D	53	1,358	3	D	41	469	33	161
Brea city	536	289	2,382	113	4,293	19	1,174	161	2,030	18	221	160	4,045	91	955
Brentwood city	173	84	280	49	D	12	94	109	927	12	380	102	1,623	81	464
Buena Park city	218	110	960	73	1,878	11	386	182	1,816	14	D	185	2,924	86	483
Burbank city	2,976	609	248,625	211	35,467	62	1,343	501	9,152	312	1,738	325	6,840	281	2,578
Burlingame city	935	274	2,039	103	6,441	28	424	197	D	22	259	145	4,340	131	819
Calabasas city	401	315	1,699	69	1,657	10	55	104	542	116	232	52	921	47	251
Calexico city	104	42	112	13	113	1	D	24	274	2	D	53	852	16	61
California City city	40	6	D	4	D	NA	NA	9	D	1	D	9	D	6	20
Camarillo city	608	302	2,530	86	4,709	20	146	263	3,257	23	D	165	3,099	125	991
Cameron Park CDP	97	64	246	20	242	3	D	49	397	4	D	35	454	40	D
Campbell city	448	314	2,979	113	4,264	31	435	206	2,591	22	D	133	2,474	186	1,214
Camp Pendleton South CDP	NA	NA	NA	NA	NA	NA	NA	NA	NA	NA	NA	NA	NA	NA	NA
Canyon Lake city	37	31	99	18	74	NA	NA	12	128	1	D	10	D	9	156
Capitola city	D	50	282	13	80	5	D	55	724	4	102	78	1,336	31	231
Carlsbad city	1,571	899	6,385	241	3,372	58	921	322	4,331	67	2,483	251	7,216	191	1,804
Carmichael CDP	571	105	D	62	1,215	17	108	229	5,867	14	254	88	1,191	78	488
Carpinteria city	52	35	205	30	D	6	14	26	102	6	17	50	669	29	D
Carson city	625	101	970	92	6,717	9	90	173	1,874	17	D	158	2,289	113	1,076
Casa de Oro-Mount Helix CDP	D	50	135	28	314	2	D	34	427	4	D	27	302	31	D
Castaic CDP	28	29	47	9	13	1	D	12	D	5	16	26	347	18	D
Castro Valley CDP	193	103	D	43	D	17	104	179	6,683	20	167	85	1,044	69	230
Cathedral City city	182	40	99	71	413	5	45	72	744	12	346	85	1,365	91	752

Table C. Incorporated Places, Census Designated Places (CDPs), and Minor Civil Divisions (MCDs) of 10,000 or More Population — **Economic Census**

STATE City, town, township, borough, or CDP (county if applicable)	Utilities		Manufacturing		Wholesale trade[1]		Retail trade		Transportation and warehousing		Information		Finance and insurance		Real estate and rental and leasing
	Number of establish-ments	Number of employees	Number of establish-ments	Number of employees	Number of establish-ments	Number of employees	Number of establish-ments	Number of employees	Number of establish-ments	Number of employees	Number of establish-ments	Number of employees	Number of establish-ments	Number of employees	Number of establish-ments
	1	2	3	4	5	6	7	8	9	10	11	12	13	14	15
CALIFORNIA—Con.															
Ceres city	1	D	21	391	22	335	89	1,606	23	855	2	D	25	141	30
Cerritos city	1	D	88	2,532	254	5,230	233	7,278	60	2,244	35	1,901	96	2,356	79
Cherryland CDP	NA	NA	6	53	2	D	19	182	5	17	NA	NA	6	23	9
Chico city	3	D	71	1,549	84	831	419	6,368	43	620	49	890	205	1,659	137
Chino city	2	D	220	5,480	457	5,476	266	4,563	139	1,951	19	155	87	625	78
Chino Hills city	1	D	10	72	90	248	140	2,399	20	78	14	157	64	764	66
Chowchilla city	NA	NA	6	296	7	D	26	251	5	15	NA	NA	10	48	11
Chula Vista city	3	D	126	4,237	299	1,793	616	11,228	98	1,605	47	666	200	1,610	241
Citrus CDP	NA	NA	NA	NA	NA	NA	3	D	1	D	NA	NA	2	D	3
Citrus Heights city	NA	NA	12	31	16	58	263	4,698	14	48	14	139	119	579	79
Claremont city	1	D	20	620	20	86	80	1,102	6	47	14	63	51	348	58
Clayton city	NA	NA	NA	NA	1	D	14	207	4	9	1	D	12	35	11
Clearlake city	4	D	NA	NA	3	D	35	682	2	D	2	D	7	53	10
Clovis city	NA	NA	42	2,866	47	190	267	5,059	43	303	18	394	102	511	79
Coachella city	NA	NA	11	773	22	460	49	671	8	126	1	D	15	93	17
Coalinga city	1	D	4	14	4	D	30	415	7	148	3	18	5	32	9
Colton city	1	D	53	2,758	44	770	103	1,508	23	120	10	93	31	154	34
Commerce city	1	D	224	10,130	398	10,317	188	3,483	112	4,063	23	520	27	179	43
Compton city	2	D	129	4,001	141	2,276	160	1,571	117	2,023	11	111	26	211	21
Concord city	2	D	106	1,779	116	896	423	7,650	55	1,104	55	1,626	222	6,256	148
Corcoran city	NA	NA	11	D	12	146	28	201	8	99	2	D	1	D	4
Corona city	1	D	341	12,813	288	5,898	450	8,115	132	1,379	50	708	178	1,450	175
Coronado city	4	D	7	48	10	18	65	451	6	154	11	D	30	135	84
Costa Mesa city	5	108	232	6,196	288	4,160	748	13,371	58	833	86	1,390	285	4,361	298
Coto de Caza CDP	NA	NA	5	31	19	D	10	117	1	D	6	13	19	43	20
Country Club CDP	NA	NA	NA	NA	1	D	11	53	NA	NA	NA	NA	NA	NA	1
Covina city	4	224	89	1,490	67	405	154	2,746	25	119	13	329	106	988	94
Cudahy city	2	D	24	476	12	91	29	489	5	46	NA	NA	3	D	5
Culver City city	1	D	53	1,612	110	2,279	287	5,510	32	330	203	12,185	93	656	107
Cupertino city	1	D	35	927	71	1,507	121	D	5	59	40	D	106	667	104
Cypress city	NA	NA	35	1,287	101	3,164	103	1,617	21	361	29	716	56	2,887	65
Daly City city	NA	NA	20	283	35	D	193	3,738	34	175	20	1,265	68	D	54
Dana Point city	NA	NA	24	155	51	232	102	1,042	12	97	11	102	71	214	78
Danville town	1	D	11	125	44	173	124	1,610	8	27	21	45	99	606	103
Davis city	NA	NA	22	627	16	256	124	2,061	10	D	19	270	70	D	116
Del Aire CDP	NA	NA	4	D	9	66	4	16	11	174	3	D	4	D	6
Delano city	1	D	11	85	20	180	80	1,045	19	387	2	D	24	131	19
Desert Hot Springs city	NA	NA	NA	NA	1	D	40	549	8	24	4	D	12	63	10
Diamond Bar city	1	D	14	231	249	634	113	1,062	45	260	17	52	118	2,072	98
Diamond Springs CDP	NA	NA	44	263	21	124	65	1,012	6	D	10	141	22	D	19
Dinuba city	1	D	8	D	12	152	63	1,018	8	D	4	D	19	80	15
Discovery Bay CDP	1	D	NA	NA	2	D	8	139	NA	NA	3	14	6	24	10
Dixon city	1	D	16	632	12	230	40	1,152	12	235	4	D	14	169	22
Downey city	3	D	79	1,968	97	813	275	4,421	74	1,991	20	242	136	1,123	153
Duarte city	NA	NA	33	969	52	719	54	1,285	11	61	3	D	17	89	15
Dublin city	2	D	18	1,281	64	323	175	3,862	23	97	25	1,161	70	457	55
East Hemet CDP	NA	NA	NA	NA	1	D	5	24	1	D	NA	NA	2	D	7
East Los Angeles CDP	1	D	102	1,640	77	753	199	1,346	35	383	13	152	52	290	30
East Palo Alto city	2	D	6	D	5	D	24	926	5	D	3	D	12	159	20
East Rancho Dominguez CDP	NA	NA	NA	NA	2	D	13	158	2	D	NA	NA	1	D	NA
East San Gabriel CDP	NA	NA	NA	NA	18	32	20	264	7	14	3	6	7	D	13
Eastvale city	NA	NA	7	225	53	212	46	1,067	43	810	6	D	14	65	14
East Whittier CDP	NA	NA	NA	NA	NA	NA	3	D	1	D	NA	NA	1	D	4
El Cajon city	2	D	162	4,472	134	1,080	445	6,280	37	615	29	367	115	821	158
El Centro city	2	D	16	204	53	433	200	4,172	35	295	26	291	52	491	46
El Cerrito city	NA	NA	8	54	10	16	66	1,495	7	28	11	83	30	828	20
El Dorado Hills CDP	1	D	30	1,468	41	317	69	890	12	D	25	347	87	D	58
Elk Grove city	NA	NA	30	532	42	347	280	5,913	62	605	19	399	147	769	110
El Monte city	4	D	142	2,558	294	1,887	274	3,254	99	1,560	15	343	76	2,455	72
El Paso de Robles (Paso Robles) city	1	D	67	2,175	47	328	151	2,429	23	173	14	211	63	453	55
El Segundo city	4	D	77	32,971	86	2,758	96	2,302	64	1,438	132	10,686	153	2,613	94
El Sobrante CDP (Contra Costa County)	NA	NA	3	23	4	8	25	190	3	7	3	D	9	30	3
El Sobrante CDP (Riverside County)	NA	NA	NA	NA	1	D	5	26	5	28	NA	NA	3	D	7
Emeryville city	NA	NA	51	2,935	53	1,733	111	2,814	11	176	45	3,149	27	D	31
Encinitas city	NA	NA	41	186	96	462	282	3,927	19	55	60	307	146	567	181
Escondido city	4	D	165	2,794	132	1,165	541	9,200	45	437	49	767	166	1,216	180
Eureka city	NA	NA	29	541	42	388	233	3,186	19	264	19	220	77	590	61
Exeter city	NA	NA	7	323	6	126	22	204	5	29	5	D	11	68	8
Fairfield city	1	D	60	2,638	69	1,393	311	5,307	54	761	31	948	109	1,802	99
Fair Oaks CDP	NA	NA	5	21	15	40	67	723	3	D	8	44	67	292	59
Fallbrook CDP	NA	NA	36	339	30	241	71	731	11	92	8	58	31	154	35
Farmersville city	1	D	4	24	3	D	14	93	NA	NA	NA	NA	4	12	5
Fillmore city	6	20	4	84	7	142	33	294	8	105	6	D	9	D	6
Florence-Graham CDP	NA	NA	90	810	45	350	91	681	18	107	1	D	14	103	8
Florin CDP	NA	NA	21	2,342	23	197	107	2,070	26	497	2	D	29	189	38
Folsom city	1	D	26	674	44	374	282	5,534	12	24	52	1,789	195	1,782	103
Fontana city	4	D	105	4,084	145	3,620	321	5,905	189	4,911	17	223	90	628	88
Foothill Farms CDP	NA	NA	5	24	13	394	33	356	3	D	1	D	10	42	18
Fortuna city	NA	NA	7	96	6	16	67	672	7	14	NA	NA	19	87	22
Foster City city	1	D	11	817	60	D	31	876	12	75	27	2,043	53	D	50
Fountain Valley city	NA	NA	86	2,752	105	1,076	221	3,205	23	185	23	139	110	620	106
Fremont city	1	D	328	18,254	458	9,470	411	7,229	101	1,249	82	1,235	212	1,778	240
French Valley CDP	NA	NA	5	197	5	D	5	D	6	61	2	D	10	38	13
Fresno city	4	D	335	12,295	514	7,741	1,539	22,005	308	5,342	169	3,673	711	8,642	506
Fullerton city	4	D	195	6,326	236	2,434	374	5,211	82	2,200	34	320	171	1,035	172

1 Merchant wholesalers, except manufacturers' sales branches and offices.

Table C. Incorporated Places, Census Designated Places (CDPs), and Minor Civil Divisions (MCDs) of 10,000 or More Population — Economic Census

STATE City, town, township, borough, or CDP (county if applicable)	Real estate and rental and leasing — Number of employees	Professional, scientific, and technical services — Number of establishments	Number of employees	Administration and support and waste management and mediation services — Number of establishments	Number of employees	Educational services — Number of establishments	Number of employees	Health care and social assistance — Number of establishments	Number of employees	Arts, entertainment, and recreation — Number of establishments	Number of employees	Accommodation and food services — Number of establishments	Number of employees	Other services (except public administration) — Number of establishments	Number of employees
	16	17	18	19	20	21	22	23	24	25	26	27	28	29	30
CALIFORNIA—Con.															
Ceres city	110	25	311	22	612	5	D	48	560	6	D	58	1,188	44	D
Cerritos city	226	189	4,693	63	1,535	26	220	207	2,908	11	94	146	D	66	542
Cherryland CDP	18	3	D	8	D	NA	NA	28	513	1	D	10	30	22	D
Chico city	769	293	1,900	119	3,126	21	155	432	7,595	30	585	247	4,730	172	1,528
Chino city	289	148	1,068	113	4,536	23	140	209	2,537	29	D	149	2,564	135	1,369
Chino Hills city	116	169	428	47	1,016	19	97	111	D	13	324	116	2,267	56	D
Chowchilla city	23	5	D	6	D	1	D	10	D	2	D	21	D	8	13
Chula Vista city	987	360	2,921	177	1,798	41	293	565	9,163	43	1,445	385	6,198	239	1,732
Citrus CDP	D	2	D	3	D	1	D	6	61	NA	NA	3	34	3	4
Citrus Heights city	408	122	1,252	69	1,041	17	163	168	1,915	19	421	126	2,343	92	455
Claremont city	180	134	775	30	152	11	75	164	2,605	12	376	97	1,667	43	176
Clayton city	32	20	63	7	D	NA	NA	15	88	3	D	10	166	14	33
Clearlake city	30	7	45	7	29	NA	NA	38	777	NA	NA	29	251	11	D
Clovis city	276	155	894	76	1,006	18	175	206	4,332	19	258	197	3,352	122	758
Coachella city	58	7	30	24	74	1	D	18	117	1	D	46	753	18	D
Coalinga city	35	8	28	5	36	NA	NA	12	259	1	D	20	277	6	13
Colton city	222	50	510	31	1,108	5	D	97	4,337	4	D	85	1,150	61	564
Commerce city	557	57	427	51	4,200	3	D	34	691	7	D	60	1,025	45	1,037
Compton city	61	16	D	33	962	6	D	91	801	5	D	94	1,207	62	D
Concord city	996	298	3,084	205	9,243	39	513	410	6,994	44	834	247	3,850	244	1,334
Corcoran city	6	2	D	2	D	NA	NA	11	235	NA	NA	16	D	4	9
Corona city	641	319	1,877	197	5,505	40	256	335	4,906	30	398	276	4,993	232	1,458
Coronado city	275	109	564	17	189	11	75	68	947	15	194	90	3,342	40	291
Costa Mesa city	3,347	687	8,743	221	8,428	37	364	390	4,505	59	1,187	422	8,168	356	2,330
Coto de Caza CDP	31	78	107	12	28	2	D	19	D	3	D	4	23	5	19
Country Club CDP	D	5	21	4	D	2	D	9	D	2	D	4	74	5	9
Covina city	479	148	946	77	3,121	9	66	221	3,811	13	308	114	1,803	116	538
Cudahy city	D	4	D	2	D	NA	NA	15	246	1	D	22	D	10	D
Culver City city	1,251	427	5,790	119	5,332	31	296	211	5,864	135	673	183	3,434	165	1,292
Cupertino city	401	444	2,980	62	1,327	54	646	204	2,188	19	D	150	2,728	83	317
Cypress city	277	118	979	50	1,351	16	D	121	1,721	26	393	105	1,460	70	682
Daly City city	273	69	291	50	689	9	57	264	4,168	16	233	145	2,549	93	365
Dana Point city	163	168	548	48	266	8	D	101	626	21	D	111	3,674	69	414
Danville town	379	223	956	62	D	18	142	148	1,416	22	335	96	1,576	60	273
Davis city	619	209	1,511	57	227	28	202	148	2,401	22	302	182	D	87	530
Del Aire CDP	D	15	447	13	219	NA	NA	16	83	NA	NA	5	39	9	D
Delano city	69	21	89	7	D	3	D	74	1,601	4	D	43	432	24	71
Desert Hot Springs city	D	8	215	17	53	NA	NA	32	258	3	D	36	353	21	59
Diamond Bar city	D	235	1,242	65	1,046	32	220	169	1,339	6	114	123	1,370	71	309
Diamond Springs CDP	45	30	240	18	133	1	D	44	744	3	D	29	292	35	D
Dinuba city	36	14	56	5	16	1	D	26	374	3	11	32	D	17	D
Discovery Bay CDP	63	12	34	8	D	2	D	6	61	7	88	10	130	5	D
Dixon city	78	19	108	15	145	4	D	26	198	8	D	39	611	19	D
Downey city	1,051	147	712	82	1,703	12	74	314	8,934	15	245	213	4,046	141	837
Duarte city	78	23	D	17	240	3	1	52	693	4	D	47	585	24	113
Dublin city	214	190	1,452	53	D	17	94	137	1,518	16	278	141	2,588	89	744
East Hemet CDP	15	8	24	8	22	NA	NA	15	247	2	D	7	D	2	D
East Los Angeles CDP	226	59	343	50	1,686	5	D	172	3,690	4	19	101	1,163	90	D
East Palo Alto city	92	20	404	12	30	2	D	30	D	4	44	14	660	15	135
East Rancho Dominguez CDP	NA	NA	NA	1	D	NA	NA	11	118	NA	NA	4	35	4	D
East San Gabriel CDP	16	20	44	5	8	3	19	18	126	3	D	8	D	2	D
Eastvale city	47	52	116	33	455	1	D	28	86	3	26	34	698	19	D
East Whittier CDP	D	3	D	7	11	NA	NA	4	19	NA	NA	5	D	1	D
El Cajon city	625	199	2,323	95	1,472	23	350	257	4,879	16	301	236	3,169	187	1,338
El Centro city	207	92	476	38	889	4	28	142	2,410	6	44	116	1,870	63	276
El Cerrito city	D	69	210	24	D	6	59	69	481	5	D	47	635	33	223
El Dorado Hills CDP	155	205	1,073	69	604	16	133	106	978	16	337	55	940	53	294
Elk Grove city	427	199	1,084	108	D	41	446	308	3,082	18	401	206	3,919	150	755
El Monte city	390	107	783	80	974	16	83	184	2,836	5	40	164	1,488	137	450
El Paso de Robles (Paso Robles) city	178	77	273	43	431	5	19	84	823	16	122	114	2,080	54	290
El Segundo city	1,452	358	10,365	110	5,091	16	204	70	705	46	D	128	2,655	73	D
El Sobrante CDP (Contra Costa County)	6	18	60	13	D	2	D	28	161	4	27	15	95	19	123
El Sobrante CDP (Riverside County)	4	16	25	12	61	NA	NA	9	D	1	D	1	D	2	D
Emeryville city	256	182	4,562	43	D	5	377	38	1,565	13	613	104	2,598	44	D
Encinitas city	428	529	1,667	145	1,438	44	304	385	4,573	56	843	214	4,943	164	929
Escondido city	937	338	D	194	3,672	23	383	385	7,449	28	803	263	4,164	250	1,343
Eureka city	263	107	591	33	640	9	D	157	3,198	19	216	135	1,649	93	559
Exeter city	16	9	32	12	D	1	D	24	202	1	D	21	D	11	124
Fairfield city	406	158	1,037	86	2,040	16	172	267	6,255	21	430	211	3,101	143	975
Fair Oaks CDP	D	122	439	40	454	12	32	117	1,025	10	181	51	811	51	318
Fallbrook CDP	87	80	408	39	248	5	19	85	1,491	14	D	55	779	55	241
Farmersville city	10	2	D	3	D	NA	NA	8	45	NA	NA	9	99	6	15
Fillmore city	13	11	38	5	14	NA	NA	18	279	1	D	25	D	9	D
Florence-Graham CDP	29	8	43	6	D	1	D	24	337	1	D	38	426	33	152
Florin CDP	181	16	144	16	140	3	D	74	957	1	D	65	984	45	D
Folsom city	489	328	3,161	73	644	22	239	238	3,331	26	501	180	3,470	108	797
Fontana city	538	89	411	95	1,802	13	91	183	7,134	19	309	219	3,451	179	986
Foothill Farms CDP	D	9	31	12	30	NA	NA	16	83	1	D	17	196	20	196
Fortuna city	44	21	83	11	71	NA	NA	40	631	3	D	30	314	22	74
Foster City city	352	151	2,145	44	1,065	16	125	81	996	5	337	59	1,120	26	170
Fountain Valley city	346	232	1,873	79	466	23	312	395	5,842	24	D	146	2,203	94	616
Fremont city	1,052	1,051	13,424	211	D	103	1,338	624	11,109	41	761	381	5,412	299	2,058
French Valley CDP	21	18	91	7	D	3	17	13	60	5	D	5	D	6	D
Fresno city	3,269	1,127	8,491	514	13,324	78	1,592	1,616	32,532	93	3,018	927	16,854	653	5,622
Fullerton city	684	378	3,338	135	2,358	41	251	407	7,269	32	508	323	5,151	207	2,187

Table C. Incorporated Places, Census Designated Places (CDPs), and Minor Civil Divisions (MCDs) of 10,000 or More Population — **Economic Census**

Economic activity by sector, 2012

STATE City, town, township, borough, or CDP (county if applicable)	Utilities Number of establishments	Number of employees	Manufacturing Number of establishments	Number of employees	Wholesale trade[1] Number of establishments	Number of employees	Retail trade Number of establishments	Number of employees	Transportation and warehousing Number of establishments	Number of employees	Information Number of establishments	Number of employees	Finance and insurance Number of establishments	Number of employees	Real estate and rental and leasing Number of establishments
	1	2	3	4	5	6	7	8	9	10	11	12	13	14	15
CALIFORNIA—Con.															
Galt city	NA	NA	14	217	4	D	37	529	9	D	2	D	14	70	9
Gardena city	2	D	224	4,643	164	1,540	177	2,197	58	1,176	12	110	49	395	54
Garden Acres CDP	NA	NA	7	285	4	D	11	80	6	260	1	D	NA	NA	2
Garden Grove city	1	D	272	7,436	232	2,465	402	5,005	64	527	47	810	146	913	138
Gilroy city	1	D	54	1,346	41	D	313	5,155	25	365	11	186	50	310	40
Glendale city	1	D	198	4,473	254	1,911	731	11,330	105	785	198	3,639	372	5,442	310
Glendora city	NA	NA	41	827	34	362	131	2,471	13	89	20	508	71	544	63
Goleta city	NA	NA	109	5,347	52	999	127	2,317	21	415	33	2,302	50	730	52
Grand Terrace city	2	D	9	D	12	107	23	216	6	42	2	D	11	53	10
Granite Bay CDP	1	D	7	21	16	58	34	312	6	16	9	D	51	452	56
Grass Valley city	2	D	44	587	14	293	165	2,209	10	D	11	194	73	516	34
Greenfield city	NA	NA	3	18	7	139	28	255	10	D	1	D	5	35	6
Grover Beach city	NA	NA	24	333	13	154	52	414	3	11	2	D	17	64	20
Hacienda Heights CDP	NA	NA	13	31	103	314	63	664	42	74	7	15	44	212	48
Half Moon Bay city	NA	NA	8	D	10	D	52	622	3	D	6	29	18	D	15
Hanford city	4	D	29	894	26	325	168	2,905	19	231	8	204	55	407	50
Hawaiian Gardens city	NA	NA	11	32	11	35	27	236	2	D	NA	NA	9	25	5
Hawthorne city	2	D	67	3,043	67	1,209	183	3,443	89	1,530	29	305	39	435	64
Hayward city	1	D	315	10,345	457	6,380	399	5,840	200	3,195	34	708	95	1,187	171
Healdsburg city	NA	NA	37	740	24	260	99	908	5	35	5	42	33	164	31
Hemet city	1	D	21	748	21	124	203	3,658	9	32	22	621	71	428	74
Hercules city	NA	NA	9	1,352	11	D	16	272	4	D	3	D	11	276	5
Hermosa Beach city	NA	NA	11	300	27	127	67	653	6	30	42	146	46	155	52
Hesperia city	NA	NA	53	392	42	186	173	2,101	34	558	6	81	41	280	54
Highland city	1	D	9	168	14	D	59	836	11	116	5	25	17	86	20
Hillsborough town	NA	NA	NA	NA	7	D	4	D	NA	NA	2	D	13	24	37
Hollister city	NA	NA	38	1,274	20	212	88	1,192	18	259	7	D	42	D	32
Home Gardens CDP	NA	NA	6	152	7	81	11	37	2	D	1	D	2	D	3
Huntington Beach city	3	D	320	12,880	403	4,714	556	8,069	58	529	77	870	319	2,137	319
Huntington Park city	4	87	100	2,565	55	740	182	2,196	22	107	10	122	44	277	21
Imperial city	NA	NA	NA	NA	19	176	21	249	18	188	2	D	3	103	12
Imperial Beach city	1	D	NA	NA	6	9	30	224	3	D	1	D	12	78	20
Indio city	1	D	25	329	35	373	162	2,624	23	148	16	174	38	197	45
Inglewood city	1	D	68	2,175	81	2,277	257	3,440	219	2,656	28	355	49	316	65
Irvine city	10	D	427	27,718	986	18,431	593	9,845	97	3,466	370	17,255	1,014	19,247	647
Isla Vista CDP	NA	NA	NA	NA	NA	NA	12	157	NA	NA	2	D	1	D	17
Jurupa Valley city	2	D	86	2,923	83	1,822	122	1,370	146	4,117	6	241	29	175	42
Kerman city	NA	NA	4	D	10	84	26	253	5	6	3	D	7	32	6
King City city	3	69	7	71	6	83	42	432	5	95	4	18	13	68	4
Kingsburg city	NA	NA	7	205	4	14	25	350	10	69	NA	NA	20	144	12
La Cañada Flintridge city	3	D	9	22	13	41	54	827	3	D	25	113	42	211	58
La Crescenta-Montrose CDP	NA	NA	5	12	30	138	37	360	9	34	15	50	28	155	28
Ladera Ranch CDP	NA	NA	4	20	14	14	33	512	4	7	8	42	38	108	28
Lafayette city	NA	NA	15	107	38	182	92	1,089	9	41	21	284	102	659	59
Laguna Beach city	NA	NA	16	105	36	D	167	975	10	33	26	136	63	296	102
Laguna Hills city	NA	NA	49	426	94	623	186	2,324	17	150	26	265	171	991	93
Laguna Niguel city	NA	NA	24	209	63	264	133	2,959	9	39	26	250	123	655	108
Laguna Woods city	NA	NA	NA	NA	2	D	26	596	NA	NA	2	D	10	58	7
La Habra city	NA	NA	57	829	72	416	173	3,158	22	1,174	8	126	62	484	48
Lake Arrowhead CDP	3	9	7	40	7	24	36	311	2	D	8	39	13	66	14
Lake Elsinore city	NA	NA	65	790	37	272	157	2,732	21	99	12	107	37	237	39
Lake Forest city	1	D	96	5,765	187	3,004	205	3,212	29	358	46	787	140	2,027	115
Lakeland Village CDP	NA	NA	3	17	4	13	9	29	4	21	1	D	1	D	3
Lake Los Angeles CDP	NA	NA	NA	NA	1	D	2	D	3	D	NA	NA	NA	NA	NA
Lakeside CDP	NA	NA	14	283	14	129	28	169	18	113	3	D	5	D	35
Lakewood city	NA	NA	10	238	32	142	228	4,820	32	130	22	279	75	548	36
La Mesa city	NA	NA	21	115	23	192	229	3,846	17	186	15	158	153	852	133
La Mirada city	2	D	58	2,267	125	3,047	88	1,375	55	968	12	127	43	273	56
Lamont CDP	1	D	NA	NA	2	D	29	264	5	27	NA	NA	1	D	2
Lancaster city	8	D	57	983	68	867	300	4,983	54	1,565	28	386	109	2,410	132
La Palma city	1	D	11	987	28	252	21	204	5	D	6	57	21	D	10
La Presa CDP	NA	NA	10	174	3	D	47	587	6	49	2	D	10	39	15
La Puente city	NA	NA	13	105	24	110	92	1,111	17	24	2	D	33	211	19
La Quinta city	NA	NA	4	6	17	33	93	2,204	5	22	12	59	48	211	87
La Riviera CDP	NA	NA	NA	NA	4	D	16	73	2	D	2	D	13	45	9
Larkspur city	1	D	12	86	16	181	60	695	9	99	19	156	96	752	53
Lathrop city	1	D	25	1,572	12	606	24	416	33	1,819	1	D	8	54	15
La Verne city	NA	NA	55	1,093	66	691	74	1,298	11	135	5	50	36	165	34
Lawndale city	NA	NA	18	239	15	111	87	774	13	56	NA	NA	32	168	22
Lemon Grove city	NA	NA	9	81	9	46	77	1,227	11	73	2	D	20	119	16
Lemon Hill CDP	NA	NA	3	D	4	D	23	262	2	D	NA	NA	7	28	6
Lemoore city	1	D	6	D	5	D	40	470	11	D	2	D	16	D	19
Lennox CDP	NA	NA	4	48	9	38	28	225	49	372	NA	NA	3	D	7
Lincoln city	NA	NA	10	601	16	151	52	975	15	146	7	44	52	219	38
Linda CDP	NA	NA	5	92	1	D	26	197	8	97	NA	NA	4	D	9
Lindsay city	NA	NA	5	498	6	D	23	189	3	D	1	D	5	30	10
Live Oak CDP	NA	NA	22	176	26	298	55	383	6	D	5	98	7	D	23
Livermore city	5	89	132	3,690	162	3,292	281	3,560	41	835	27	1,830	95	574	99
Livingston city	NA	NA	8	D	2	D	16	189	8	D	1	D	3	20	7
Lodi city	NA	NA	80	2,124	39	265	209	3,353	30	551	16	240	102	1,687	77
Loma Linda city	1	D	7	50	13	D	33	427	6	10	1	D	14	46	22
Lomita city	NA	NA	3	6	17	42	68	594	12	42	4	19	13	61	28
Lompoc city	1	D	23	573	9	51	111	1,395	12	68	4	20	40	188	31
Long Beach city	11	963	234	8,027	318	4,469	957	13,033	333	20,506	134	3,046	405	4,868	502
Los Alamitos city	1	D	50	1,760	76	621	74	543	13	D	11	195	66	344	52
Los Altos city	1	D	23	189	17	D	102	D	4	D	31	D	79	344	98
Los Angeles city	40	2,672	5,034	101,103	8,552	83,938	11,359	133,706	1,938	59,557	5,526	78,511	4,978	85,836	5,948
Los Banos city	NA	NA	9	553	11	131	74	1,197	16	70	7	D	24	127	23

1 Merchant wholesalers, except manufacturers' sales branches and offices.

Table C. Incorporated Places, Census Designated Places (CDPs), and Minor Civil Divisions (MCDs) of 10,000 or More Population — Economic Census

| | Real estate and rental and leasing | Professional, scientific, and technical services | | Administration and support and waste management and mediation services | | Educational services | | Health care and social assistance | | Arts, entertainment, and recreation | | Accommodation and food services | | Other services (except public administration) | |
| STATE City, town, township, borough, or CDP (county if applicable) | Number of employees | Number of establishments | Number of employees | Number of establishments | Number of employees | Number of establishments | Number of employees | Number of establishments | Number of employees | Number of establishments | Number of employees | Number of establishments | Number of employees | Number of establishments | Number of employees |
	16	17	18	19	20	21	22	23	24	25	26	27	28	29	30
CALIFORNIA—Con.															
Galt city	22	20	62	7	15	3	D	25	D	7	52	30	360	22	D
Gardena city	332	69	364	55	1,600	7	D	145	2,371	10	1,403	202	2,258	130	794
Garden Acres CDP	D	1	D	7	46	NA	NA	NA	NA	NA	NA	3	15	3	D
Garden Grove city	495	248	1,570	153	3,789	33	324	495	5,331	24	D	396	6,025	243	1,482
Gilroy city	136	73	382	53	617	6	39	135	2,027	9	383	127	2,168	92	745
Glendale city	2,740	891	7,769	242	17,177	43	399	1,030	13,657	167	952	403	6,449	350	2,314
Glendora city	256	114	692	62	624	13	117	203	3,282	18	421	88	1,402	90	541
Goleta city	278	159	2,023	57	1,218	8	49	128	1,940	8	D	102	1,752	63	618
Grand Terrace city	35	16	135	15	179	3	28	30	317	1	D	9	D	8	21
Granite Bay CDP	D	81	337	28	301	9	90	49	D	10	175	36	374	26	D
Grass Valley city	136	78	409	31	563	6	34	156	2,719	15	118	87	1,139	63	218
Greenfield city	17	3	D	1	D	NA	NA	13	95	1	D	10	D	5	12
Grover Beach city	44	40	183	22	222	4	35	26	633	2	D	30	420	22	76
Hacienda Heights CDP	D	78	221	38	343	18	131	121	659	6	9	88	1,122	41	110
Half Moon Bay city	73	51	207	19	138	2	D	27	D	9	199	58	1,261	27	D
Hanford city	200	52	268	29	234	6	141	170	4,110	7	D	91	1,597	52	213
Hawaiian Gardens city	44	5	18	6	156	1	D	27	566	1	D	24	257	22	79
Hawthorne city	427	72	514	59	777	6	174	144	2,290	15	D	124	1,650	101	D
Hayward city	1,330	266	2,793	136	D	29	314	279	7,803	21	327	297	3,731	225	1,764
Healdsburg city	115	67	196	12	426	5	8	55	704	10	132	72	1,040	33	114
Hemet city	345	75	333	46	447	7	73	236	4,157	12	190	144	2,179	98	429
Hercules city	13	27	200	7	D	NA	NA	40	214	1	D	28	361	11	D
Hermosa Beach city	192	134	398	29	493	13	72	86	597	33	146	107	1,859	48	247
Hesperia city	187	51	450	49	451	8	54	81	813	6	D	104	1,773	95	399
Highland city	57	24	113	29	439	4	9	50	1,467	3	D	56	753	35	219
Hillsborough town	D	42	82	8	15	2	D	13	39	5	D	6	55	3	D
Hollister city	81	46	147	26	646	8	D	75	1,147	7	D	53	645	60	D
Home Gardens CDP	19	2	D	4	D	1	D	5	17	1	D	2	D	10	D
Huntington Beach city	1,411	770	4,393	258	5,239	59	391	631	4,894	77	841	441	8,517	351	2,225
Huntington Park city	104	26	240	26	1,646	6	70	130	1,651	2	D	99	1,374	54	D
Imperial city	45	10	58	11	185	NA	NA	16	D	2	D	8	D	9	47
Imperial Beach city	D	21	88	9	26	2	D	28	493	4	28	33	351	31	148
Indio city	232	74	308	96	880	3	16	126	1,965	22	D	106	2,965	74	501
Inglewood city	939	74	800	69	766	10	186	270	4,271	32	1,156	168	2,570	138	1,006
Irvine city	10,154	2,780	34,213	566	24,612	167	2,404	1,032	11,437	247	8,666	606	14,173	382	3,566
Isla Vista CDP	92	1	D	1	D	NA	NA	3	D	2	D	35	517	5	20
Jurupa Valley city	345	41	307	55	1,044	3	D	72	1,209	15	D	90	D	77	492
Kerman city	28	8	17	4	D	NA	NA	17	178	2	D	13	195	11	19
King City city	13	9	35	6	37	NA	NA	19	D	6	D	33	326	12	32
Kingsburg city	21	14	314	9	D	2	D	27	259	1	D	35	291	12	D
La Cañada Flintridge city	140	89	189	16	113	5	28	102	664	42	519	47	731	38	198
La Crescenta-Montrose CDP	D	79	222	21	290	13	66	51	215	15	11	27	271	25	111
Ladera Ranch CDP	28	91	211	21	118	8	25	39	262	6	D	21	D	18	78
Lafayette city	209	230	1,395	37	D	22	272	128	1,507	29	400	66	1,420	59	374
Laguna Beach city	371	213	610	56	299	11	103	124	D	23	D	123	3,249	76	349
Laguna Hills city	631	335	1,852	89	964	21	111	350	5,320	11	141	94	1,905	82	495
Laguna Niguel city	446	298	872	93	681	16	62	222	1,736	28	441	119	1,929	101	542
Laguna Woods city	35	23	D	6	10	2	D	33	986	1	D	14	372	9	66
La Habra city	128	80	381	46	755	19	D	108	1,053	8	D	136	1,866	104	624
Lake Arrowhead CDP	40	22	53	22	82	6	76	26	309	10	D	20	248	19	52
Lake Elsinore city	103	55	235	30	121	8	33	64	414	10	296	98	1,432	69	D
Lake Forest city	1,051	412	3,461	135	3,954	39	208	200	5,169	28	D	181	2,897	118	764
Lakeland Village CDP	16	3	3	2	D	NA	NA	2	D	NA	NA	5	14	5	D
Lake Los Angeles CDP	NA	NA	NA	1	D	NA	NA	2	D	NA	NA	1	D	1	D
Lakeside CDP	209	17	54	25	179	2	D	28	349	4	28	22	300	26	65
Lakewood city	147	67	367	29	1,364	9	21	175	2,216	10	205	156	3,191	81	570
La Mesa city	884	229	1,068	83	2,501	17	116	342	7,662	15	341	167	3,198	122	937
La Mirada city	501	67	355	23	272	7	32	110	1,417	11	135	98	1,486	37	149
Lamont CDP	D	3	D	4	D	1	D	8	140	NA	NA	15	165	7	D
Lancaster city	545	151	1,020	83	3,020	16	272	417	9,693	14	D	205	3,762	182	910
La Palma city	47	38	760	17	283	7	17	57	1,082	NA	NA	37	357	8	D
La Presa CDP	D	12	49	21	445	NA	NA	34	393	2	D	28	256	32	120
La Puente city	62	15	239	12	517	1	D	58	426	1	D	68	734	35	121
La Quinta city	190	89	339	54	366	11	70	79	453	21	839	73	3,254	48	276
La Riviera CDP	30	16	231	9	D	4	38	19	365	3	D	21	168	8	D
Larkspur city	D	118	629	20	216	9	81	113	1,142	7	120	41	799	25	D
Lathrop city	106	8	56	14	631	NA	NA	17	D	2	D	27	393	14	D
La Verne city	153	72	290	43	382	9	67	70	915	12	195	78	1,240	40	D
Lawndale city	295	44	229	38	264	4	40	68	366	4	11	46	610	67	D
Lemon Grove city	71	23	119	21	535	2	D	45	855	3	38	48	643	50	162
Lemon Hill CDP	25	3	D	2	D	1	D	9	37	NA	NA	10	36	14	D
Lemoore city	58	21	119	7	45	1	D	29	161	5	D	38	D	14	D
Lennox CDP	11	8	40	11	86	1	D	15	131	2	D	8	66	6	33
Lincoln city	86	44	216	25	104	4	30	76	795	9	106	50	D	40	348
Linda CDP	23	4	13	2	D	NA	NA	6	D	NA	NA	13	133	6	D
Lindsay city	19	4	17	4	D	NA	NA	14	D	NA	NA	10	D	8	D
Live Oak CDP	82	47	301	28	413	9	D	141	4,098	7	56	20	149	52	309
Livermore city	525	205	8,175	115	D	24	285	180	2,316	29	D	180	2,541	134	830
Livingston city	16	1	D	1	D	NA	NA	6	130	NA	NA	16	185	2	D
Lodi city	403	104	656	60	907	8	23	194	3,131	13	290	127	1,893	111	646
Loma Linda city	133	32	144	15	D	2	D	144	12,106	NA	NA	38	404	22	71
Lomita city	74	44	173	19	207	9	69	68	621	2	D	58	655	46	185
Lompoc city	146	36	263	24	D	4	D	78	1,542	5	D	82	1,055	50	319
Long Beach city	3,660	1,047	7,779	371	11,988	99	1,116	1,209	25,677	110	2,268	877	16,971	655	5,748
Los Alamitos city	266	130	894	42	886	8	196	217	2,752	8	D	47	1,010	38	330
Los Altos city	304	280	1,992	47	481	33	184	146	1,344	20	D	85	1,252	70	527
Los Angeles city	36,498	14,452	135,867	4,307	96,069	945	10,748	11,169	205,046	7,863	39,472	8,009	138,886	6,567	47,913
Los Banos city	59	18	86	14	83	1	D	51	710	3	D	57	804	26	105

Table C. Incorporated Places, Census Designated Places (CDPs), and Minor Civil Divisions (MCDs) of 10,000 or More Population — **Economic Census**

STATE City, town, township, borough, or CDP (county if applicable)	Utilities Number of establish-ments	Number of employees	Manufacturing Number of establish-ments	Number of employees	Wholesale trade[1] Number of establish-ments	Number of employees	Retail trade Number of establish-ments	Number of employees	Transportation and warehousing Number of establish-ments	Number of employees	Information Number of establish-ments	Number of employees	Finance and insurance Number of establish-ments	Number of employees	Real estate and rental and leasing Number of establish-ments
	1	2	3	4	5	6	7	8	9	10	11	12	13	14	15
CALIFORNIA—Con.															
Los Gatos town	NA	NA	32	488	28	D	176	D	5	14	37	D	103	712	105
Los Osos CDP	2	D	12	167	6	D	23	270	2	D	5	D	15	80	13
Lynwood city	NA	NA	51	1,057	39	580	118	1,386	22	208	2	D	33	169	16
McFarland city	NA	NA	NA	NA	1	D	21	156	3	11	1	D	1	D	2
McKinleyville CDP	NA	NA	7	47	7	D	35	528	12	57	2	D	12	94	20
Madera city	1	D	35	1,055	22	250	173	2,163	24	151	7	D	54	285	35
Magalia CDP	3	D	3	D	NA	NA	11	100	NA	NA	1	D	1	D	1
Malibu city	NA	NA	6	58	24	323	101	754	2	D	68	288	41	145	78
Manhattan Beach city	1	D	19	82	40	D	178	2,924	8	51	70	329	120	1,813	127
Manteca city	NA	NA	22	972	26	393	177	3,440	50	719	11	292	51	D	56
Marina city	NA	NA	15	169	4	39	48	977	7	39	4	16	12	62	25
Martinez city	NA	NA	18	907	23	D	57	1,031	21	208	7	37	39	277	41
Marysville city	1	D	10	78	11	419	55	821	8	128	6	D	30	182	15
Maywood city	2	D	16	228	20	432	54	472	12	204	NA	NA	13	37	3
Mead Valley CDP	NA	NA	10	693	4	28	10	201	12	D	NA	NA	NA	NA	1
Mendota city	1	D	NA	NA	3	D	22	176	8	D	NA	NA	1	D	3
Menifee city	1	D	16	266	14	57	87	1,672	17	218	8	D	29	199	50
Menlo Park city	3	D	56	2,390	33	468	122	1,502	14	478	53	D	191	3,048	84
Merced city	1	D	28	1,234	37	742	227	3,728	23	536	15	D	84	593	69
Millbrae city	NA	NA	9	129	23	D	62	661	13	D	6	105	38	D	30
Mill Valley city	NA	NA	12	76	18	61	72	832	2	D	23	94	46	171	38
Milpitas city	NA	NA	157	8,969	143	4,902	307	5,295	36	569	45	D	87	544	72
Mission Viejo city	1	D	51	440	107	576	356	6,275	18	219	37	340	229	1,186	161
Modesto city	NA	NA	91	7,104	113	1,977	683	10,639	65	1,200	56	797	271	2,169	207
Monrovia city	3	D	94	2,885	89	709	109	1,951	14	130	22	276	48	909	58
Montclair city	NA	NA	85	938	82	593	243	4,021	12	78	7	118	25	154	32
Montebello city	3	70	71	2,433	114	1,826	203	3,498	75	1,029	11	D	53	349	55
Monterey city	2	D	44	717	36	382	199	2,265	21	394	43	657	93	977	88
Monterey Park city	4	D	42	593	207	1,082	202	1,671	71	343	21	300	86	3,872	89
Moorpark city	1	D	52	1,349	53	774	55	890	7	33	22	407	32	373	35
Moraga town	NA	NA	5	31	7	21	26	414	3	3	8	15	24	122	9
Moreno Valley city	2	D	23	802	30	663	311	5,600	71	2,247	22	D	83	594	73
Morgan Hill city	1	D	79	3,047	58	1,873	105	D	7	23	19	D	60	398	65
Morro Bay city	NA	NA	16	55	3	D	74	579	7	36	6	89	19	84	18
Mountain House CDP	1	D	NA	NA	NA	NA	3	D	3	D	NA	NA	3	16	NA
Mountain View city	2	D	121	3,230	106	2,330	244	4,078	19	457	191	27,874	77	1,032	121
Murrieta city	2	D	63	609	97	667	218	3,873	34	212	25	161	120	582	118
Muscoy CDP	1	D	NA	NA	NA	NA	7	20	6	41	1	D	NA	NA	1
Napa city	1	D	110	1,899	69	437	315	4,374	36	424	27	334	135	899	101
National City city	1	D	70	1,045	87	1,198	304	5,393	34	951	10	D	48	316	50
Newark city	NA	NA	67	2,348	61	1,443	168	2,856	26	617	17	495	41	203	42
Newman city	NA	NA	6	564	4	25	16	170	7	D	1	D	4	18	5
Newport Beach city	1	D	86	3,739	190	1,183	441	6,409	44	803	87	588	672	10,021	698
Nipomo CDP	NA	NA	10	78	11	165	26	288	3	23	1	D	13	56	10
Norco city	NA	NA	33	449	27	469	86	1,093	28	80	2	D	30	166	38
North Auburn CDP	NA	NA	8	145	10	108	84	1,585	6	22	5	D	30	149	24
North Fair Oaks CDP	1	D	53	480	12	D	41	252	8	D	4	37	10	D	7
North Highlands CDP	NA	NA	33	272	49	473	151	1,658	31	402	10	1,514	42	549	61
North Tustin CDP	NA	NA	3	8	15	D	9	36	7	49	7	31	15	D	38
Norwalk city	4	43	52	698	88	639	178	3,078	39	1,391	11	353	50	506	44
Novato city	NA	NA	52	557	73	579	162	2,538	22	194	52	887	123	2,389	105
Oakdale city	NA	NA	31	1,647	18	138	78	857	13	91	3	27	32	239	21
Oak Hills CDP	NA	NA	NA	NA	NA	NA	3	9	8	45	NA	NA	NA	NA	5
Oakland city	4	D	333	6,555	376	4,921	1,014	10,458	261	14,685	172	4,534	380	9,064	482
Oakley city	1	D	7	201	9	D	38	366	12	35	1	D	9	50	18
Oak Park CDP	NA	NA	3	16	6	D	6	33	3	1	5	D	13	D	16
Oceanside city	NA	NA	164	4,715	149	1,476	389	6,742	46	822	38	515	129	801	157
Oildale CDP	2	D	7	93	5	37	52	544	11	202	1	D	7	49	23
Olivehurst CDP	NA	NA	6	98	3	D	18	140	6	D	NA	NA	1	D	4
Ontario city	6	D	391	11,003	681	11,341	579	13,650	276	15,436	63	2,087	185	2,309	182
Orange city	3	D	287	6,122	333	3,442	558	7,821	63	1,121	71	892	317	5,539	259
Orangevale CDP	1	D	14	31	10	D	49	794	4	16	2	D	56	166	36
Orcutt CDP	NA	NA	NA	NA	4	9	38	334	9	37	3	D	23	110	17
Orinda city	NA	NA	6	29	11	119	25	241	4	23	12	D	46	306	43
Oroville city	2	D	31	1,043	12	96	100	1,289	9	64	8	D	41	194	19
Oxnard city	9	220	172	6,057	183	3,805	430	6,729	101	1,330	44	896	168	1,154	139
Pacifica city	NA	NA	9	139	7	D	61	699	8	D	7	27	29	146	28
Pacific Grove city	3	D	5	22	8	D	65	534	1	D	7	22	21	77	23
Palmdale city	2	D	35	4,686	28	128	299	6,423	41	313	35	574	94	572	102
Palm Desert city	1	D	40	196	74	389	453	6,199	24	259	41	794	136	824	144
Palm Springs city	3	D	27	624	35	535	184	2,480	25	1,005	36	582	74	403	123
Palo Alto city	NA	NA	81	6,683	76	D	317	5,759	21	223	187	11,791	241	2,903	197
Palos Verdes Estates city	NA	NA	6	147	18	58	15	84	2	D	5	5	23	84	59
Paradise town	NA	NA	16	85	6	D	77	791	3	D	9	136	32	183	25
Paramount city	1	D	205	4,348	212	1,709	110	1,202	41	787	10	56	21	201	33
Parkway CDP	NA	NA	7	70	11	D	42	534	11	370	1	D	5	35	12
Parlier city	NA	NA	3	220	1	D	18	161	3	10	1	D	3	16	3
Pasadena city	3	D	89	1,016	163	1,382	594	9,409	35	551	172	5,084	469	10,861	322
Patterson city	1	D	6	317	10	357	36	408	8	944	6	D	13	58	9
Perris city	1	D	39	1,034	20	265	92	2,151	35	1,393	5	D	22	133	32
Petaluma city	NA	NA	100	3,106	101	2,055	262	3,233	35	801	39	380	120	946	70
Phelan CDP	1	D	3	17	1	D	15	278	5	11	1	D	6	32	7
Pico Rivera city	2	D	60	1,446	84	1,923	113	2,571	48	1,193	7	96	40	287	34
Piedmont city	NA	NA	NA	NA	NA	NA	5	97	NA	NA	1	D	12	73	17
Pinole city	NA	NA	4	44	9	D	67	1,344	1	D	2	D	28	148	18
Pittsburg city	6	D	40	2,175	32	324	99	2,084	25	182	9	164	31	218	25
Placentia city	2	D	108	3,097	108	923	96	1,099	19	226	5	9	61	311	61
Placerville city	NA	NA	12	49	2	D	100	1,051	2	D	7	104	32	D	17
Pleasant Hill city	1	D	17	78	29	172	146	2,490	18	114	17	195	77	829	46

1 Merchant wholesalers, except manufacturers' sales branches and offices.

Table C. Incorporated Places, Census Designated Places (CDPs), and Minor Civil Divisions (MCDs) of 10,000 or More Population — Economic Census

STATE City, town, township, borough, or CDP (county if applicable)	Real estate and rental and leasing — Number of employees	Professional, scientific, and technical services — Number of establishments	Number of employees	Administration and support and waste management and mediation services — Number of establishments	Number of employees	Educational services — Number of establishments	Number of employees	Health care and social assistance — Number of establishments	Number of employees	Arts, entertainment, and recreation — Number of establishments	Number of employees	Accommodation and food services — Number of establishments	Number of employees	Other services (except public administration) — Number of establishments	Number of employees
	16	17	18	19	20	21	22	23	24	25	26	27	28	29	30
CALIFORNIA—Con.															
Los Gatos town	366	277	1,637	44	215	28	184	314	2,829	21	691	124	2,447	102	461
Los Osos CDP	D	24	78	19	84	2	D	33	186	3	D	25	174	13	89
Lynwood city	100	15	96	15	D	NA	NA	126	3,759	NA	NA	79	1,053	54	D
McFarland city	D	2	D	3	D	NA	NA	7	58	NA	NA	6	27	1	D
McKinleyville CDP	54	21	114	15	51	1	D	32	254	4	55	20	338	14	47
Madera city	148	39	173	29	1,086	8	D	129	2,410	6	75	79	1,081	50	223
Magalia CDP	D	8	21	9	12	NA	NA	12	76	NA	NA	4	31	3	22
Malibu city	222	131	993	36	413	14	237	64	587	87	177	67	1,807	36	157
Manhattan Beach city	430	308	1,384	81	787	28	151	189	1,347	78	288	154	3,688	90	721
Manteca city	231	54	319	55	752	7	D	127	2,611	11	D	117	1,839	81	320
Marina city	79	18	126	28	142	3	D	26	374	5	55	50	666	23	D
Martinez city	171	80	373	52	D	7	D	68	4,197	9	48	79	753	59	219
Marysville city	50	46	205	13	D	NA	NA	53	1,902	5	73	48	752	25	D
Maywood city	4	4	D	8	578	NA	NA	24	340	NA	NA	39	425	29	D
Mead Valley CDP	D	4	8	6	D	NA	NA	11	235	NA	NA	2	D	2	D
Mendota city	7	1	D	1	D	NA	NA	5	76	1	D	14	70	3	D
Menifee city	242	52	174	31	191	7	44	97	1,683	8	D	67	1,348	53	258
Menlo Park city	374	339	6,175	79	1,152	33	375	154	1,446	18	222	104	1,790	91	773
Merced city	322	85	544	47	647	5	D	285	4,465	15	D	131	2,340	80	433
Millbrae city	96	61	172	20	191	8	44	52	696	6	123	85	1,571	36	D
Mill Valley city	D	131	414	21	72	8	68	97	697	27	400	48	706	47	264
Milpitas city	394	266	3,741	72	1,562	34	387	227	2,528	22	288	282	4,613	128	1,168
Mission Viejo city	775	470	1,598	150	1,341	35	246	484	6,479	29	424	193	3,372	183	1,199
Modesto city	925	391	2,911	166	3,635	44	448	657	16,671	39	732	394	7,262	271	1,517
Monrovia city	202	152	2,436	53	1,069	7	65	92	1,681	16	92	108	1,787	77	584
Montclair city	179	25	217	36	639	7	47	108	2,578	8	D	83	1,650	75	D
Montebello city	309	66	375	52	1,899	7	D	186	3,159	7	142	130	1,741	87	628
Monterey city	312	239	4,045	74	1,113	15	D	304	5,011	34	818	212	5,518	87	748
Monterey Park city	296	159	1,274	92	2,813	33	464	273	3,624	9	354	177	2,613	87	401
Moorpark city	137	94	313	32	304	11	49	45	666	11	62	41	835	31	170
Moraga town	30	80	185	14	D	4	14	27	295	4	D	25	327	25	167
Moreno Valley city	312	85	509	84	460	18	452	238	5,177	12	D	213	3,468	131	504
Morgan Hill city	232	142	2,207	47	633	15	784	105	D	12	240	113	1,457	75	368
Morro Bay city	37	29	62	17	166	2	D	35	459	6	71	81	1,009	25	117
Mountain House CDP	NA	7	7	4	20	1	D	6	D	NA	NA	NA	NA	NA	NA
Mountain View city	668	594	17,221	114	2,114	44	697	326	7,444	28	900	314	4,218	160	884
Murrieta city	326	206	873	122	795	22	137	266	4,201	33	475	148	2,672	153	991
Muscoy CDP	D	NA	NA	5	84	NA	NA	8	D	NA	NA	2	D	2	D
Napa city	472	214	971	124	2,898	33	275	283	5,857	25	431	205	3,698	151	866
National City city	288	46	473	41	492	5	D	171	3,189	11	D	169	2,512	113	578
Newark city	132	132	1,882	38	D	17	163	81	529	7	D	162	2,273	69	412
Newman city	8	11	72	3	D	NA	NA	11	137	NA	NA	13	75	3	9
Newport Beach city	4,870	1,249	8,089	268	3,973	64	483	902	11,307	107	1,304	369	11,543	265	1,795
Nipomo CDP	38	18	50	22	257	NA	NA	26	242	6	D	21	246	6	22
Norco city	108	75	1,221	35	523	6	14	43	384	8	108	72	1,532	66	318
North Auburn CDP	83	58	283	20	117	7	54	107	1,930	9	D	61	1,095	38	D
North Fair Oaks CDP	30	30	156	33	359	3	56	33	D	6	50	32	247	44	D
North Highlands CDP	337	63	342	61	1,139	3	29	66	1,745	7	124	88	1,590	79	633
North Tustin CDP	110	84	194	26	82	7	13	51	315	8	D	7	188	14	D
Norwalk city	194	68	400	44	2,283	5	109	151	3,908	7	198	138	1,902	82	389
Novato city	D	237	3,005	129	1,886	23	480	188	2,569	22	303	122	1,804	112	1,037
Oakdale city	218	40	247	15	68	3	5	43	363	5	D	52	656	30	D
Oak Hills CDP	5	5	9	8	20	1	D	1	D	1	D	2	D	6	15
Oakland city	2,716	1,451	11,503	386	7,358	151	2,316	1,151	25,852	106	3,542	967	13,126	855	6,680
Oakley city	78	25	102	29	150	2	D	27	228	3	D	25	D	26	61
Oak Park CDP	27	52	90	8	20	1	D	15	D	20	27	4	D	3	5
Oceanside city	562	313	2,342	171	2,818	33	360	336	5,557	39	1,083	306	5,216	205	1,263
Oildale CDP	241	21	65	13	162	1	D	19	639	2	D	35	396	16	39
Olivehurst CDP	6	1	D	1	D	NA	NA	10	D	NA	NA	3	24	4	D
Ontario city	1,205	257	2,680	222	20,118	21	1,048	232	4,757	21	366	332	6,564	201	2,656
Orange city	1,787	715	4,833	277	13,397	40	346	655	19,946	40	425	398	6,959	307	2,479
Orangevale CDP	158	64	242	38	175	4	13	63	947	5	D	32	399	45	D
Orcutt CDP	49	38	92	21	D	7	25	49	316	4	17	36	566	15	D
Orinda city	D	115	358	22	D	3	D	63	D	12	211	34	363	16	116
Oroville city	68	27	155	12	D	NA	NA	85	2,075	9	75	56	D	43	195
Oxnard city	694	214	1,981	187	5,564	19	81	445	5,050	34	473	282	4,397	195	1,198
Pacifica city	64	72	272	27	D	10	80	52	601	9	103	67	633	38	D
Pacific Grove city	D	36	133	25	96	4	4	54	704	4	47	71	836	28	139
Palmdale city	326	96	909	67	242	15	310	192	2,037	13	351	206	4,388	100	484
Palm Desert city	713	260	862	148	2,793	14	95	255	2,721	53	2,297	194	5,547	155	1,003
Palm Springs city	573	191	664	75	1,076	8	36	264	4,692	38	1,249	262	6,904	113	840
Palo Alto city	1,214	853	12,347	111	4,690	68	513	405	22,834	48	919	280	6,048	176	2,619
Palos Verdes Estates city	D	86	248	14	68	8	D	54	169	16	D	10	47	8	29
Paradise town	204	34	107	20	78	3	D	111	2,476	10	145	40	D	54	168
Paramount city	192	38	384	34	1,583	3	D	78	1,276	2	D	73	683	71	616
Parkway CDP	58	11	30	10	89	2	D	28	602	1	D	21	268	30	131
Parlier city	D	2	D	1	D	NA	NA	8	205	NA	NA	6	55	1	D
Pasadena city	1,704	1,224	16,414	276	7,564	76	820	1,016	17,831	176	1,997	473	9,619	410	2,995
Patterson city	91	10	52	10	43	NA	NA	21	181	4	21	23	D	10	42
Perris city	110	29	133	29	271	2	D	44	704	6	D	68	1,017	34	D
Petaluma city	347	211	1,468	114	1,148	24	139	189	3,281	33	D	162	2,080	126	751
Phelan CDP	18	10	42	4	8	1	D	14	D	4	D	15	233	5	11
Pico Rivera city	214	30	229	39	1,104	4	D	82	1,375	4	D	118	1,627	72	541
Piedmont city	35	46	D	3	D	3	D	23	D	4	D	1	D	12	33
Pinole city	D	33	124	20	D	4	14	100	865	4	D	61	1,002	31	D
Pittsburg city	231	49	310	42	D	5	D	84	1,102	4	76	84	1,394	51	557
Placentia city	362	112	377	66	970	13	66	140	2,227	9	D	91	1,268	70	461
Placerville city	D	39	127	18	181	3	D	91	2,645	4	15	57	655	34	177
Pleasant Hill city	233	135	779	51	D	17	135	130	1,851	20	361	93	1,540	69	475

Table C. Incorporated Places, Census Designated Places (CDPs), and Minor Civil Divisions (MCDs) of 10,000 or More Population — Economic Census

	Utilities		Manufacturing		Wholesale trade¹		Retail trade		Transportation and warehousing		Information		Finance and insurance		Real estate and rental and leasing
STATE City, town, township, borough, or CDP (county if applicable)	Number of establishments	Number of employees	Number of establishments	Number of employees	Number of establishments	Number of employees	Number of establishments	Number of employees	Number of establishments	Number of employees	Number of establishments	Number of employees	Number of establishments	Number of employees	Number of establishments
	1	2	3	4	5	6	7	8	9	10	11	12	13	14	15
CALIFORNIA—Con.															
Pleasanton city	2	D	78	1,560	135	5,394	330	6,278	34	362	107	5,512	224	3,141	176
Pomona city	5	D	212	4,462	301	3,224	293	3,308	93	2,274	28	805	84	934	76
Porterville city	4	D	16	868	24	127	147	2,231	22	1,234	9	141	49	572	33
Port Hueneme city	1	D	3	D	6	D	29	359	17	158	NA	NA	18	D	15
Poway city	1	D	117	9,014	96	2,136	144	2,679	36	805	29	537	63	2,067	89
Prunedale CDP	1	D	NA	NA	6	38	21	193	3	D	2	D	9	36	13
Quartz Hill CDP	1	D	NA	NA	NA	NA	22	134	4	D	1	D	6	D	8
Ramona CDP	1	D	18	90	7	65	66	821	20	87	5	42	18	88	34
Rancho Cordova city	5	D	115	4,676	173	2,537	218	3,332	38	493	62	3,485	154	9,791	108
Rancho Cucamonga city	4	D	246	8,056	322	3,710	436	8,160	148	2,678	41	606	225	2,777	177
Rancho Mirage city	1	D	5	12	6	17	75	1,053	7	15	13	274	43	234	41
Rancho Palos Verdes city	NA	NA	11	63	53	163	46	388	10	33	15	59	46	161	66
Rancho San Diego CDP	NA	NA	3	27	11	43	46	851	7	25	4	56	25	123	25
Rancho Santa Margarita city	NA	NA	42	2,892	59	550	72	1,504	5	9	23	1,052	68	338	65
Red Bluff city	NA	NA	10	201	7	D	84	885	8	D	7	D	33	180	21
Redding city	2	D	83	757	115	1,223	444	7,061	62	692	41	662	200	1,717	148
Redlands city	7	D	58	1,140	56	495	240	4,676	36	731	22	2,572	130	798	72
Redondo Beach city	3	D	35	183	64	311	274	3,969	34	677	53	282	96	632	111
Redwood City city	NA	NA	75	1,834	65	1,049	204	4,486	30	274	119	15,953	145	1,423	129
Reedley city	NA	NA	10	337	16	77	63	574	10	287	4	D	27	125	17
Rialto city	3	D	70	1,567	54	698	152	2,173	100	4,626	8	44	38	221	48
Richmond city	1	D	118	3,925	99	1,431	238	3,600	68	2,176	24	306	50	414	72
Ridgecrest city	1	D	4	22	4	D	82	1,246	7	43	8	92	23	204	25
Rio Linda CDP	NA	NA	9	97	8	D	18	151	5	10	NA	NA	1	D	5
Ripon city	NA	NA	16	816	9	D	28	384	12	166	NA	NA	9	40	8
Riverbank city	NA	NA	9	442	10	13	46	936	7	51	4	D	12	52	7
Riverside city	7	121	264	9,041	293	4,399	829	13,943	154	5,441	87	2,214	319	3,280	341
Rocklin city	1	D	45	916	65	1,562	149	1,824	14	377	28	1,484	83	1,300	104
Rohnert Park city	NA	NA	38	791	41	692	106	2,088	11	53	18	684	43	D	49
Rosamond CDP	2	D	3	15	6	33	20	227	2	D	2	D	2	D	16
Rosedale CDP	NA	NA	8	D	13	73	20	192	16	D	NA	NA	7	38	12
Rosemead city	13	D	53	670	107	450	172	1,583	32	297	11	106	53	407	28
Rosemont CDP	1	D	7	138	5	D	24	209	10	39	NA	NA	29	377	7
Roseville city	NA	NA	69	1,325	108	1,597	588	13,555	50	781	58	1,677	424	5,661	238
Rossmoor CDP	NA	NA	NA	NA	5	D	10	52	1	D	3	6	3	D	14
Rowland Heights CDP	NA	NA	19	145	143	493	149	1,541	52	149	9	37	59	298	73
Sacramento city	16	1,132	322	7,890	488	7,125	1,200	18,041	249	5,239	237	5,681	579	6,608	573
Salida CDP	NA	NA	10	439	19	506	37	653	6	67	5	79	14	91	10
Salinas city	2	D	77	2,255	123	1,861	428	6,955	116	1,210	50	901	125	1,327	116
San Anselmo town	NA	NA	7	34	16	57	54	447	5	22	4	4	17	82	16
San Bernardino city	4	373	122	2,811	128	2,392	526	8,518	95	4,704	35	557	175	3,324	125
San Bruno city	NA	NA	13	D	36	798	149	2,508	39	254	19	D	53	464	44
San Buenaventura (Ventura) city	2	D	157	2,717	167	1,531	517	6,814	55	863	54	518	198	1,086	190
San Carlos city	NA	NA	90	1,460	103	885	142	1,828	24	452	25	D	50	D	55
San Clemente city	4	D	99	1,448	162	1,826	204	2,501	18	58	35	437	128	536	138
San Diego city	41	D	1,137	41,655	1,823	35,353	4,119	61,044	859	13,330	807	26,707	2,617	37,000	2,764
San Diego Country Estates CDP	NA	NA	6	12	4	5	6	22	5	8	1	D	5	7	5
San Dimas city	8	1,160	71	1,267	75	704	112	1,792	16	112	11	78	72	760	55
San Fernando city	1	D	69	1,912	41	1,018	77	671	15	110	8	D	38	311	21
San Francisco city	19	D	693	7,506	1,066	12,056	3,573	43,378	372	7,089	1,331	49,681	2,150	48,893	1,828
San Gabriel city	NA	NA	43	389	128	479	211	1,577	43	183	9	43	81	561	81
Sanger city	1	D	18	600	10	64	47	710	6	21	2	D	13	68	10
San Jacinto city	1	D	30	354	13	59	50	861	13	59	2	D	10	46	22
San Jose city	10	985	897	32,421	1,023	42,254	2,297	40,525	301	5,739	432	14,483	1,006	16,219	1,045
San Juan Capistrano city	NA	NA	28	792	62	339	128	1,795	11	73	14	50	90	458	74
San Leandro city	NA	NA	182	4,777	249	3,095	305	5,619	113	2,606	42	848	88	1,021	129
San Lorenzo CDP	NA	NA	9	675	11	D	19	476	9	D	NA	NA	12	D	6
San Luis Obispo city	3	D	73	1,170	83	1,001	365	4,892	32	1,036	48	928	142	1,104	137
San Marcos city	NA	NA	157	4,276	133	1,494	246	4,005	36	767	23	256	85	494	103
San Marino city	NA	NA	5	30	35	122	36	143	5	10	6	20	51	212	74
San Mateo city	3	D	46	601	87	839	378	6,587	49	D	127	5,680	247	6,944	182
San Pablo city	NA	NA	10	50	8	30	77	947	6	27	NA	NA	20	117	17
San Rafael city	NA	NA	76	632	124	1,151	344	5,031	38	525	73	2,433	190	1,948	161
San Ramon city	NA	NA	27	302	98	1,095	117	2,015	22	205	70	5,938	237	4,177	131
Santa Ana city	8	D	771	19,771	555	6,699	822	11,680	109	2,166	116	2,862	418	6,338	316
Santa Barbara city	7	D	96	998	110	1,641	531	6,881	51	495	115	1,912	267	1,990	287
Santa Clara city	2	D	508	15,935	378	12,811	352	5,045	84	1,446	166	6,826	114	1,591	177
Santa Clarita city	9	408	231	8,930	198	3,225	535	9,774	56	D	132	1,366	252	1,823	233
Santa Cruz city	1	D	90	1,324	59	1,181	255	3,098	19	323	42	377	74	539	87
Santa Fe Springs city	4	D	518	14,276	656	12,262	146	1,994	153	3,430	20	316	55	453	76
Santa Maria city	3	D	89	2,996	109	1,108	367	5,362	81	1,029	30	456	112	821	100
Santa Monica city	4	D	88	807	159	1,317	682	10,986	37	458	662	14,567	292	3,647	418
Santa Paula city	1	D	23	433	16	D	55	705	17	174	6	D	26	D	22
Santa Rosa city	5	14	153	4,862	166	1,963	654	10,479	57	644	75	985	321	2,930	254
Santee city	NA	NA	84	1,353	46	410	123	2,861	26	117	13	D	34	408	58
Saratoga city	NA	NA	14	252	25	D	34	D	1	D	17	D	45	177	85
Scotts Valley city	NA	NA	26	919	19	D	58	685	3	D	14	257	32	D	17
Seal Beach city	NA	NA	9	839	15	362	87	1,299	3	D	7	59	75	424	31
Seaside city	NA	NA	10	85	13	D	98	1,427	5	20	4	D	15	72	12
Selma city	1	D	9	333	12	174	72	1,258	9	D	3	D	17	92	16
Shafter city	NA	NA	15	616	18	533	30	253	20	987	1	D	9	35	8
Shasta Lake city	NA	NA	11	349	3	D	16	130	1	D	1	D	2	D	1
Sierra Madre city	NA	NA	10	30	11	38	16	85	2	D	8	15	16	D	18
Signal Hill city	1	D	68	892	86	699	80	2,501	30	272	12	74	31	1,056	33
Simi Valley city	3	85	130	3,504	144	1,371	413	5,841	37	242	74	839	213	5,780	118
Solana Beach city	NA	NA	20	85	30	378	91	787	4	D	27	683	76	408	85

1 Merchant wholesalers, except manufacturers' sales branches and offices.

Table C. Incorporated Places, Census Designated Places (CDPs), and Minor Civil Divisions (MCDs) of 10,000 or More Population — **Economic Census**

STATE City, town, township, borough, or CDP (county if applicable)	Real estate and rental and leasing Number of employees	Professional, scientific, and technical services Number of establishments	Professional, scientific, and technical services Number of employees	Administration and support and waste management and mediation services Number of establishments	Administration and support and waste management and mediation services Number of employees	Educational services Number of establishments	Educational services Number of employees	Health care and social assistance Number of establishments	Health care and social assistance Number of employees	Arts, entertainment, and recreation Number of establishments	Arts, entertainment, and recreation Number of employees	Accommodation and food services Number of establishments	Accommodation and food services Number of employees	Other services (except public administration) Number of establishments	Other services (except public administration) Number of employees
	16	17	18	19	20	21	22	23	24	25	26	27	28	29	30
CALIFORNIA—Con.															
Pleasanton city	748	553	7,366	216	7,359	53	381	292	5,117	44	915	240	3,856	150	1,082
Pomona city	475	114	708	74	1,590	15	271	319	9,084	16	337	195	2,940	146	861
Porterville city	115	45	185	19	638	3	D	151	2,790	6	D	81	1,268	42	188
Port Hueneme city	70	42	301	16	116	3	D	24	249	3	6	41	540	28	203
Poway city	353	252	1,442	76	1,052	22	255	163	2,510	25	374	105	1,280	101	623
Prunedale CDP	35	17	41	18	65	1	D	16	D	NA	NA	13	152	12	39
Quartz Hill CDP	31	11	34	15	361	3	27	9	10	1	D	12	114	10	99
Ramona CDP	97	47	148	21	180	2	D	43	321	4	D	39	529	53	207
Rancho Cordova city	532	237	4,297	116	3,384	21	208	114	4,827	18	405	144	2,383	101	747
Rancho Cucamonga city	1,031	402	2,547	220	12,830	39	514	413	5,171	35	D	312	7,074	234	1,249
Rancho Mirage city	91	78	305	28	232	2	D	244	5,209	18	977	70	4,200	37	256
Rancho Palos Verdes city	D	138	585	25	90	17	81	123	865	14	327	38	1,388	29	120
Rancho San Diego CDP	D	39	109	16	56	3	D	31	412	6	104	42	D	25	D
Rancho Santa Margarita city	148	191	1,525	58	1,379	23	327	85	637	17	D	83	1,423	57	D
Red Bluff city	86	31	107	15	153	NA	NA	88	D	5	19	60	794	34	232
Redding city	550	281	1,659	125	2,815	21	287	531	9,221	30	D	254	4,374	213	1,336
Redlands city	293	209	1,046	87	2,037	30	164	325	5,729	22	D	174	3,257	135	934
Redondo Beach city	309	330	D	97	1,075	35	227	218	1,536	43	332	212	4,099	140	843
Redwood City city	628	451	7,803	135	1,610	26	260	318	5,668	37	903	216	2,841	148	2,111
Reedley city	D	19	61	7	D	2	D	50	1,354	3	D	28	D	19	53
Rialto city	204	32	208	36	391	7	41	95	828	6	98	89	1,287	70	338
Richmond city	370	152	1,899	73	D	16	305	184	5,690	22	1,089	123	1,053	113	620
Ridgecrest city	141	53	1,267	21	D	2	D	62	1,056	8	D	60	939	40	152
Rio Linda CDP	12	4	19	15	D	1	D	9	47	NA	NA	9	81	11	D
Ripon city	D	20	99	8	25	NA	NA	19	D	4	13	23	349	23	D
Riverbank city	D	9	63	10	123	1	D	22	239	3	6	37	561	17	63
Riverside city	1,685	631	4,442	281	10,631	54	572	868	17,360	63	910	535	9,620	415	2,615
Rocklin city	407	170	1,185	61	740	22	161	143	D	15	391	80	1,274	77	498
Rohnert Park city	248	67	424	56	679	7	D	83	868	13	343	87	1,698	64	360
Rosamond CDP	29	8	31	5	D	1	D	6	33	6	175	17	205	8	D
Rosedale CDP	40	36	225	29	214	4	D	17	96	1	D	7	119	11	59
Rosemead city	70	78	389	35	552	15	140	136	1,719	6	155	157	2,023	97	253
Rosemont CDP	27	34	126	28	560	2	D	31	703	2	D	25	288	5	23
Roseville city	1,902	494	8,360	178	3,729	40	223	488	12,724	43	855	365	7,478	209	2,446
Rossmoor CDP	32	28	D	4	24	3	9	13	D	2	D	2	D	4	12
Rowland Heights CDP	203	89	322	45	244	35	184	116	636	9	D	141	1,328	75	230
Sacramento city	3,255	1,803	16,894	520	16,161	107	1,733	1,288	40,520	123	3,349	1,093	20,289	982	8,189
Salida CDP	98	19	257	14	617	7	206	15	D	2	D	19	328	9	27
Salinas city	586	229	1,649	120	D	18	D	344	6,406	15	245	253	3,746	199	1,218
San Anselmo town	D	80	272	24	122	14	D	44	236	8	30	39	532	36	118
San Bernardino city	514	241	2,003	138	8,932	24	668	449	13,338	29	D	342	5,741	236	1,864
San Bruno city	156	82	1,002	49	1,057	5	97	115	1,236	9	D	129	1,868	106	722
San Buenaventura (Ventura) city	1,046	470	2,745	173	3,713	29	334	494	9,570	55	932	327	5,534	248	1,225
San Carlos city	277	206	922	68	1,123	23	122	105	889	20	117	116	1,498	94	977
San Clemente city	386	382	1,467	105	1,477	19	103	210	1,442	38	D	162	2,475	110	651
San Diego city	17,178	7,468	105,870	1,973	75,831	501	5,788	4,180	85,519	513	14,534	3,527	80,688	2,511	24,385
San Diego Country Estates CDP	D	12	24	9	51	NA	NA	3	D	3	36	4	8	9	159
San Dimas city	535	135	1,890	54	1,010	11	134	111	1,980	17	183	77	1,183	59	867
San Fernando city	116	30	103	17	235	4	9	53	608	NA	NA	54	801	61	334
San Francisco city	15,000	6,295	84,841	1,342	35,608	386	6,223	3,119	62,075	510	13,573	4,059	73,417	2,411	20,361
San Gabriel city	209	144	483	73	426	15	44	219	3,293	5	127	176	1,866	106	451
Sanger city	23	14	62	4	D	1	D	42	428	NA	NA	32	354	16	82
San Jacinto city	63	15	126	16	28	2	D	38	353	NA	NA	40	628	37	141
San Jose city	5,858	2,974	39,615	1,043	35,513	245	2,428	2,437	34,064	190	5,893	1,916	31,023	1,374	9,094
San Juan Capistrano city	237	219	993	62	534	17	257	125	1,289	17	D	73	1,257	60	268
San Leandro city	905	125	718	100	D	12	75	279	5,289	15	241	191	2,329	182	1,274
San Lorenzo CDP	40	7	D	8	D	1	D	29	136	2	D	23	294	11	64
San Luis Obispo city	693	340	2,872	76	1,995	25	291	360	5,465	21	219	218	4,125	145	656
San Marcos city	377	235	911	131	4,613	30	317	164	2,195	23	216	169	2,973	134	776
San Marino city	218	98	227	22	68	10	76	65	D	9	D	20	276	24	141
San Mateo city	789	535	D	191	5,728	38	255	469	6,602	33	720	313	4,808	240	1,770
San Pablo city	59	12	95	15	189	4	D	41	D	1	D	60	739	36	D
San Rafael city	794	501	2,379	119	1,680	50	1,580	347	6,206	73	479	224	2,841	235	1,952
San Ramon city	D	523	7,408	120	D	39	351	287	2,783	22	535	148	2,324	129	996
Santa Ana city	2,685	1,020	9,025	468	27,280	56	1,723	837	13,396	36	819	542	7,493	439	2,649
Santa Barbara city	1,101	657	3,836	268	2,953	62	486	562	8,733	97	1,508	421	8,143	287	1,734
Santa Clara city	1,396	922	19,150	200	9,579	44	375	250	8,359	43	2,653	400	7,151	265	1,827
Santa Clarita city	1,129	513	3,036	213	5,750	69	601	501	6,700	122	1,340	327	6,766	291	1,939
Santa Cruz city	286	288	1,341	83	809	44	282	227	2,536	34	1,059	256	4,446	136	1,229
Santa Fe Springs city	1,096	110	1,045	107	5,954	12	474	71	1,414	10	D	98	1,170	130	1,321
Santa Maria city	522	149	1,072	88	1,759	11	D	336	5,368	22	277	178	2,596	143	1,003
Santa Monica city	3,011	1,170	10,092	179	3,726	86	1,873	902	9,745	698	1,995	454	12,289	454	3,626
Santa Paula city	111	21	146	16	45	2	D	46	342	7	D	42	D	34	D
Santa Rosa city	1,131	613	4,461	205	4,641	45	404	712	13,671	73	1,568	389	5,764	313	2,079
Santee city	270	73	439	57	417	8	270	88	682	14	D	108	1,620	98	577
Saratoga city	219	170	523	24	122	16	192	108	D	13	302	64	883	39	185
Scotts Valley city	74	84	723	19	144	10	63	42	805	8	D	51	D	35	148
Seal Beach city	D	112	1,765	26	402	8	24	90	1,048	7	D	85	1,792	33	495
Seaside city	66	19	D	31	180	1	D	21	D	6	D	71	1,005	57	254
Selma city	59	15	61	12	67	3	13	46	907	3	D	44	678	28	D
Shafter city	36	6	27	4	D	3	D	16	320	1	D	16	D	8	29
Shasta Lake city	D	1	D	6	39	2	D	14	159	2	D	12	82	4	8
Sierra Madre city	25	34	108	17	107	6	7	36	677	11	26	14	231	15	D
Signal Hill city	D	76	799	61	2,114	4	D	50	632	7	51	35	485	57	448
Simi Valley city	557	369	2,804	183	2,566	25	152	361	3,989	48	602	251	3,984	167	D
Solana Beach city	490	198	1,006	43	497	15	76	108	617	25	344	54	1,237	49	334

Table C. Incorporated Places, Census Designated Places (CDPs), and Minor Civil Divisions (MCDs) of 10,000 or More Population — Economic Census

Economic activity by sector, 2012

STATE City, town, township, borough, or CDP (county if applicable)	Utilities Number of establishments	Utilities Number of employees	Manufacturing Number of establishments	Manufacturing Number of employees	Wholesale trade[1] Number of establishments	Wholesale trade[1] Number of employees	Retail trade Number of establishments	Retail trade Number of employees	Transportation and warehousing Number of establishments	Transportation and warehousing Number of employees	Information Number of establishments	Information Number of employees	Finance and insurance Number of establishments	Finance and insurance Number of employees	Real estate and rental and leasing Number of establishments
	1	2	3	4	5	6	7	8	9	10	11	12	13	14	15
CALIFORNIA—Con.															
Soledad city	NA	NA	4	73	7	70	27	259	10	D	1	D	6	28	12
Sonoma city	1	D	28	800	24	218	104	1,002	4	D	8	D	54	335	41
Soquel CDP	NA	NA	15	170	14	D	50	831	7	113	6	16	19	52	13
South El Monte city	2	D	402	5,184	487	2,988	139	1,076	26	106	3	D	14	48	21
South Gate city	NA	NA	121	4,380	79	1,000	165	2,220	49	1,069	9	104	30	209	41
South Lake Tahoe city	3	D	9	D	7	20	139	1,447	7	67	8	68	26	D	65
South Pasadena city	NA	NA	13	86	36	130	56	720	9	22	24	135	44	433	58
South San Francisco city	1	D	111	10,909	330	5,622	187	3,063	278	5,778	28	3,439	60	461	76
South San Jose Hills CDP	NA	NA	6	45	37	242	26	123	4	22	2	D	NA	NA	10
South Whittier CDP	NA	NA	4	46	21	47	40	285	10	39	4	D	8	11	12
Spring Valley CDP (San Diego County)	NA	NA	25	359	16	148	27	115	9	D	NA	NA	7	D	22
Stanford CDP	1	D	NA	NA	3	D	11	D	NA	NA	4	D	3	D	2
Stanton city	1	D	63	702	28	D	104	1,162	15	84	1	D	12	53	19
Stevenson Ranch CDP	NA	NA	6	15	14	48	35	876	6	15	11	D	21	96	27
Stockton city	3	D	166	5,937	239	4,944	695	10,893	198	3,827	57	1,158	287	3,529	253
Suisun City city	1	D	7	22	5	D	31	316	7	19	1	D	10	D	10
Sunnyvale city	NA	NA	225	25,088	210	13,280	279	5,005	36	1,026	170	11,570	111	1,293	153
Sun Village CDP	NA	NA	NA	NA	2	D	5	24	6	11	NA	NA	NA	NA	NA
Susanville city	NA	NA	NA	NA	3	D	51	679	1	D	7	58	19	80	14
Tamalpais-Homestead Valley CDP	NA	NA	4	10	6	11	16	92	2	D	14	25	6	D	7
Tehachapi city	4	56	11	138	1	D	35	573	2	D	4	27	15	66	12
Temecula city	NA	NA	125	5,024	150	2,522	439	8,208	54	423	42	734	190	1,125	184
Temescal Valley CDP	NA	NA	11	245	17	399	17	136	15	85	2	D	7	35	6
Temple City city	NA	NA	24	149	91	352	99	1,152	25	70	5	59	47	233	41
Thousand Oaks city	6	255	124	3,346	158	2,474	545	9,016	36	564	128	1,674	457	4,825	279
Torrance city	6	D	248	12,560	607	5,653	663	11,780	161	1,760	113	1,631	365	3,827	343
Tracy city	2	D	52	2,358	62	1,275	235	3,772	73	2,767	14	312	80	428	76
Truckee town	1	D	15	133	9	69	92	839	12	64	6	D	21	109	52
Tulare city	3	D	27	1,940	50	515	181	2,794	38	426	7	138	55	313	46
Turlock city	1	D	71	2,986	64	696	209	3,514	43	513	11	201	90	595	58
Tustin city	NA	NA	98	3,270	192	2,126	282	6,234	22	255	59	2,368	214	2,150	172
Twentynine Palms city	NA	NA	NA	NA	4	17	31	312	4	105	5	25	10	59	11
Ukiah city	NA	NA	19	301	14	220	128	1,761	11	147	16	108	41	406	45
Union City city	NA	NA	81	3,879	139	3,705	107	2,198	54	1,005	22	284	41	D	40
Upland city	2	D	95	981	120	664	240	3,685	32	617	24	118	117	646	102
Vacaville city	NA	NA	44	2,425	36	332	323	5,699	26	647	17	264	87	669	106
Valinda CDP	NA	NA	NA	NA	2	D	16	71	9	25	1	D	4	D	2
Vallejo city	1	D	32	356	28	794	233	3,910	39	592	16	204	78	587	73
Valle Vista CDP	NA	NA	NA	NA	2	D	11	195	1	D	1	D	3	D	10
Victorville city	4	D	18	1,222	32	241	318	6,108	55	1,120	33	1,025	92	730	88
View Park-Windsor Hills CDP	NA	NA	NA	NA	NA	NA	12	66	2	D	5	D	2	D	7
Vincent CDP	NA	NA	NA	NA	2	D	13	39	1	D	1	D	NA	NA	NA
Vineyard CDP	NA	NA	NA	NA	4	D	11	178	9	39	1	D	8	28	7
Visalia city	4	D	67	2,417	126	1,321	396	6,664	68	1,886	33	635	183	2,112	131
Vista city	NA	NA	178	7,380	201	3,510	252	4,089	25	198	32	653	78	459	138
Walnut city	NA	NA	30	318	229	925	105	1,008	32	118	7	18	36	233	56
Walnut Creek city	NA	NA	32	591	68	595	308	6,753	15	140	63	2,064	379	5,644	224
Walnut Park CDP	1	D	NA	NA	3	D	27	185	3	D	NA	NA	17	D	NA
Wasco city	NA	NA	6	104	3	D	41	426	6	28	NA	NA	8	35	14
Watsonville city	NA	NA	57	1,381	54	1,108	146	2,398	39	449	15	207	59	392	60
West Carson CDP	NA	NA	31	381	27	123	62	670	18	179	6	40	11	60	24
West Covina city	2	D	16	632	88	433	292	5,618	49	372	24	351	106	835	82
West Hollywood city	1	D	36	225	103	527	331	3,472	5	27	228	1,641	58	439	146
Westminster city	10	D	93	775	118	533	453	5,841	37	193	31	335	97	782	93
Westmont CDP	NA	NA	NA	NA	1	D	25	77	3	D	NA	NA	2	D	5
West Puente Valley CDP	NA	NA	3	28	7	22	6	34	8	94	NA	NA	1	D	1
West Rancho Dominguez CDP	NA	NA	168	4,601	137	2,358	63	879	93	2,289	4	D	5	39	18
West Sacramento city	NA	NA	64	3,118	140	3,579	124	2,110	95	2,872	22	1,209	48	836	77
West Whittier-Los Nietos CDP	NA	NA	14	289	10	75	24	323	8	17	NA	NA	3	D	9
Whittier city	2	D	47	732	71	342	200	2,993	34	250	20	145	97	569	102
Wildomar city	2	D	8	75	8	31	39	377	12	24	4	D	13	44	15
Willowbrook CDP	NA	NA	4	D	5	D	21	195	2	D	1	D	2	D	1
Windsor town	NA	NA	26	570	23	441	52	1,077	16	290	6	D	24	D	23
Winter Gardens CDP	NA	NA	3	13	5	D	36	294	7	9	1	D	6	27	14
Winton CDP	NA	NA	NA	NA	NA	NA	13	72	4	17	1	D	NA	NA	4
Woodcrest CDP	NA	NA	NA	NA	8	27	16	225	12	D	3	3	6	18	9
Woodland city	2	D	57	2,002	77	829	154	2,515	47	1,716	13	125	66	D	60
Yorba Linda city	1	D	54	1,386	124	1,029	114	1,557	14	22	20	151	103	471	102
Yuba City city	5	D	43	1,144	44	372	247	4,003	57	285	12	D	99	762	78
Yucaipa city	1	D	20	326	15	62	89	995	8	82	7	37	34	131	45
Yucca Valley town	3	117	9	56	5	15	79	1,253	5	38	7	83	23	124	21
COLORADO	365	8,498	4,898	114,632	5,733	75,717	18,474	245,704	3,443	61,976	3,023	81,953	9,828	98,761	9,295
Arvada city	5	D	110	2,139	83	880	259	3,832	43	248	25	190	172	840	125
Aurora city	2	D	122	2,400	230	5,173	908	15,374	209	3,548	87	1,321	384	2,259	298
Berkley CDP	NA	NA	16	779	14	72	38	224	7	63	8	D	3	D	13
Black Forest CDP	1	D	6	D	7	D	11	22	7	7	4	5	14	18	21
Boulder city	6	D	216	7,153	187	3,538	574	8,079	27	401	170	3,167	310	2,140	316
Brighton city	3	D	22	697	25	462	100	2,136	26	290	10	116	48	269	34
Broomfield city	1	D	82	3,087	52	D	261	4,606	21	319	53	2,108	113	1,838	96
Cañon City city	3	D	13	161	10	D	88	1,273	10	116	9	99	40	178	26
Castle Pines city	NA	NA	4	10	6	82	26	429	3	8	6	D	29	74	20
Castle Rock town	1	D	16	221	30	D	189	2,800	4	D	22	135	74	287	78

1 Merchant wholesalers, except manufacturers' sales branches and offices.

Table C. Incorporated Places, Census Designated Places (CDPs), and Minor Civil Divisions (MCDs) of 10,000 or More Population — Economic Census

STATE City, town, township, borough, or CDP (county if applicable)	Real estate and rental and leasing — Number of employees	Professional, scientific, and technical services — Number of establishments	Number of employees	Administration and support and waste management and mediation services — Number of establishments	Number of employees	Educational services — Number of establishments	Number of employees	Health care and social assistance — Number of establishments	Number of employees	Arts, entertainment, and recreation — Number of establishments	Number of employees	Accommodation and food services — Number of establishments	Number of employees	Other services (except public administration) — Number of establishments	Number of employees
	16	17	18	19	20	21	22	23	24	25	26	27	28	29	30
CALIFORNIA—Con.															
Soledad city	45	4	32	9	31	NA	NA	16	D	NA	NA	21	D	4	16
Sonoma city	184	63	260	29	D	8	23	81	1,353	12	D	79	1,654	36	161
Soquel CDP	24	61	182	15	126	5	D	42	440	8	45	28	312	25	282
South El Monte city	47	47	328	32	239	2	D	31	777	3	D	57	815	64	D
South Gate city	202	28	402	34	553	6	D	82	862	6	D	108	1,192	82	263
South Lake Tahoe city	393	50	181	34	104	9	D	103	1,139	14	D	161	2,682	56	352
South Pasadena city	D	142	587	39	218	13	44	110	789	44	225	61	882	48	210
South San Francisco city	666	191	4,329	126	5,143	12	224	186	3,052	19	231	204	3,673	123	1,401
South San Jose Hills CDP	57	NA	NA	9	47	NA	NA	9	77	NA	NA	4	115	11	D
South Whittier CDP	34	22	70	17	76	1	D	53	713	2	D	24	272	48	D
Spring Valley CDP (San Diego County)	118	30	100	26	239	2	D	38	434	3	5	17	170	20	151
Stanford CDP	D	28	409	33	D	10	57	6	D	3	10	24	D	3	D
Stanton city	84	31	D	20	D	NA	NA	35	D	6	D	82	924	56	307
Stevenson Ranch CDP	81	57	159	18	53	3	D	31	99	15	35	28	883	15	D
Stockton city	1,338	373	2,436	208	6,437	28	457	706	16,417	45	915	424	6,912	344	2,542
Suisun City city	23	18	89	17	D	1	D	21	100	4	D	31	426	28	D
Sunnyvale city	960	810	18,824	107	3,902	55	680	419	4,276	36	638	346	4,781	179	997
Sun Village CDP	NA	NA	NA	6	31	NA	NA	1	D	NA	NA	2	D	1	D
Susanville city	28	19	D	7	25	3	D	45	686	7	D	31	545	22	60
Tamalpais-Homestead Valley CDP	D	69	113	20	183	4	D	23	D	10	27	10	D	14	D
Tehachapi city	43	11	66	9	D	3	D	22	D	1	D	40	468	19	129
Temecula city	706	370	1,569	134	4,702	43	481	333	2,698	32	724	281	9,653	199	1,170
Temescal Valley CDP	D	17	43	10	83	NA	NA	15	58	6	D	7	96	4	31
Temple City city	D	76	235	24	125	23	169	97	1,355	4	8	64	836	60	220
Thousand Oaks city	971	809	D	237	4,454	52	361	669	7,077	106	999	317	6,760	230	1,271
Torrance city	1,992	881	6,823	275	8,731	90	637	1,075	16,066	60	1,193	419	8,055	280	1,998
Tracy city	181	108	504	70	1,121	16	60	174	2,115	17	220	137	2,191	106	479
Truckee town	470	97	289	49	236	8	25	66	928	22	407	70	2,539	40	232
Tulare city	149	47	322	30	323	3	D	113	D	10	D	80	1,403	61	333
Turlock city	280	75	502	46	832	7	65	186	3,796	16	303	146	2,528	100	670
Tustin city	853	550	3,508	130	3,155	30	380	373	3,950	23	D	232	4,167	142	1,153
Twentynine Palms city	77	16	144	8	89	1	D	18	242	4	D	49	661	21	111
Ukiah city	195	80	319	18	D	3	27	126	2,029	7	22	80	864	60	234
Union City city	162	109	D	49	D	18	105	143	2,179	7	D	113	1,771	74	645
Upland city	876	209	1,306	104	2,368	22	113	370	5,872	26	458	145	D	148	770
Vacaville city	542	114	632	80	1,607	19	215	198	6,039	21	443	168	3,293	128	635
Valinda CDP	D	6	25	11	20	NA	NA	17	178	1	D	7	D	2	D
Vallejo city	300	96	667	61	849	12	45	270	8,425	22	1,351	167	2,623	131	629
Valle Vista CDP	37	9	26	5	D	1	D	2	D	1	D	3	70	4	20
Victorville city	465	104	574	48	1,303	13	D	221	4,314	12	D	175	3,245	103	551
View Park-Windsor Hills CDP	22	14	23	8	42	2	D	21	97	4	2	15	D	10	30
Vincent CDP	NA	7	12	4	30	NA	NA	5	42	1	D	3	19	7	36
Vineyard CDP	22	13	44	13	77	1	D	25	180	5	16	14	126	7	34
Visalia city	834	246	1,543	125	4,416	19	178	407	9,018	19	654	234	4,245	184	1,118
Vista city	738	230	1,448	120	1,762	7	11	254	3,410	13	D	171	2,150	129	836
Walnut city	D	107	340	31	379	18	168	92	767	7	10	48	539	50	D
Walnut Creek city	1,209	691	6,364	166	D	32	238	474	12,296	47	567	202	4,358	203	2,590
Walnut Park CDP	NA	10	51	10	44	NA	NA	38	282	NA	NA	14	D	7	D
Wasco city	37	4	20	4	D	NA	NA	16	D	1	D	28	D	15	D
Watsonville city	256	74	535	53	948	8	37	182	2,817	9	D	90	1,218	79	304
West Carson CDP	82	23	D	17	494	1	D	47	5,826	2	D	36	640	26	229
West Covina city	421	145	761	95	5,172	17	403	336	6,389	13	397	196	3,421	96	529
West Hollywood city	820	398	2,286	103	D	16	D	259	1,231	488	1,220	229	7,741	199	1,462
Westminster city	300	145	635	70	1,126	21	142	301	2,959	16	D	245	2,672	149	826
Westmont CDP	35	4	D	5	18	1	D	20	164	1	D	15	164	10	D
West Puente Valley CDP	D	1	D	3	3	2	D	13	79	NA	NA	1	D	3	D
West Rancho Dominguez CDP	266	11	126	27	607	NA	NA	20	437	NA	NA	26	395	25	287
West Sacramento city	604	84	955	52	1,619	11	D	75	D	10	455	91	D	102	876
West Whittier-Los Nietos CDP	21	5	D	8	D	NA	NA	16	148	NA	NA	30	382	17	76
Whittier city	338	166	755	71	1,107	15	783	320	8,204	17	388	177	2,662	119	579
Wildomar city	123	24	73	25	176	2	D	56	1,335	7	D	31	402	21	171
Willowbrook CDP	D	NA	NA	2	D	NA	NA	12	1,268	NA	NA	10	224	7	D
Windsor town	160	57	335	32	268	9	D	44	280	6	D	52	D	32	249
Winter Gardens CDP	D	15	45	15	161	NA	NA	21	155	1	D	19	214	29	D
Winton CDP	7	NA	NA	4	9	NA	NA	3	D	NA	NA	3	15	6	22
Woodcrest CDP	34	21	56	26	474	4	19	18	211	2	D	10	88	9	51
Woodland city	300	82	D	52	624	4	D	124	2,683	15	153	104	D	88	D
Yorba Linda city	293	247	1,406	89	642	22	138	170	1,275	27	429	92	1,710	83	560
Yuba City city	420	103	484	68	D	8	D	225	3,116	16	201	124	2,121	91	D
Yucaipa city	152	59	175	36	299	6	13	88	1,028	12	D	55	764	46	186
Yucca Valley town	75	24	142	18	45	4	D	72	D	3	D	42	772	33	115
COLORADO	38,706	23,872	180,064	8,354	210,408	1,911	14,615	14,869	257,898	2,433	51,235	12,744	240,484	10,246	64,398
Arvada city	276	382	1,535	168	1,810	32	215	231	2,830	26	D	186	3,172	184	900
Aurora city	1,233	640	D	339	8,433	66	563	654	13,962	50	856	577	10,728	463	3,256
Berkley CDP	60	9	D	9	128	NA	NA	1	D	3	D	9	45	18	84
Black Forest CDP	38	75	165	29	D	5	22	9	22	4	D	8	46	11	30
Boulder city	1,091	1,363	17,924	215	3,822	120	714	642	7,932	119	1,373	429	8,834	327	2,248
Brighton city	114	51	173	32	517	6	27	83	1,488	8	24	83	1,338	55	253
Broomfield city	313	325	6,060	92	1,474	30	229	145	1,611	22	496	143	2,944	109	704
Cañon City city	127	40	123	12	271	2	D	77	1,884	8	D	59	745	26	152
Castle Pines city	52	72	154	11	D	4	D	22	D	2	D	17	234	13	68
Castle Rock town	202	196	559	71	447	24	127	119	1,005	18	D	103	1,843	112	591

Table C. Incorporated Places, Census Designated Places (CDPs), and Minor Civil Divisions (MCDs) of 10,000 or More Population — **Economic Census**

STATE City, town, township, borough, or CDP (county if applicable)	Utilities Number of establish-ments	Utilities Number of employees	Manufacturing Number of establish-ments	Manufacturing Number of employees	Wholesale trade[1] Number of establish-ments	Wholesale trade[1] Number of employees	Retail trade Number of establish-ments	Retail trade Number of employees	Transportation and warehousing Number of establish-ments	Transportation and warehousing Number of employees	Information Number of establish-ments	Information Number of employees	Finance and insurance Number of establish-ments	Finance and insurance Number of employees	Real estate and rental and leasing Number of establish-ments
	1	2	3	4	5	6	7	8	9	10	11	12	13	14	15
COLORADO—Con.															
Centennial city	3	D	69	1,750	189	3,340	264	4,771	51	D	121	3,132	417	4,290	250
Cherry Creek CDP	NA	NA	NA	NA	4	7	6	9	1	D	7	9	15	D	15
Cimarron Hills CDP	NA	NA	30	519	28	276	41	427	10	D	NA	NA	12	24	17
Clifton CDP	NA	NA	5	30	10	120	30	404	19	77	NA	NA	9	63	9
Colorado Springs city	3	14	351	8,351	325	3,638	1,621	24,923	161	3,061	247	9,109	917	9,139	845
Columbine CDP	NA	NA	9	27	15	13	46	532	4	10	12	D	30	149	27
Commerce City city	1	D	87	2,851	140	2,530	105	1,333	130	6,011	7	67	35	158	48
Dakota Ridge CDP	NA	NA	6	D	16	18	35	439	4	7	6	18	32	121	17
Denver city	28	1,984	759	17,032	1,175	17,997	2,282	26,469	446	23,110	582	16,362	1,625	25,980	1,451
Durango city	3	D	33	407	32	369	241	2,673	18	309	33	255	71	811	78
Englewood city	1	D	128	2,688	100	1,489	203	2,525	18	D	17	432	91	1,042	87
Erie town	NA	NA	12	159	6	D	24	174	5	D	6	D	17	D	16
Evans city	NA	NA	9	90	13	167	33	377	11	57	1	D	7	D	6
Federal Heights city	NA	NA	NA	NA	7	D	47	579	4	9	3	D	20	114	21
Firestone town	NA	NA	NA	NA	1	D	28	589	13	D	NA	NA	11	D	5
Fort Carson CDP	NA	NA	NA	NA	1	D	8	41	NA	NA	NA	NA	5	35	3
Fort Collins city	4	D	109	5,760	108	D	617	9,667	37	440	89	1,293	325	1,975	298
Fort Morgan city	1	D	18	2,945	12	85	51	652	14	94	7	D	30	191	15
Fountain city	1	D	7	145	3	D	37	1,021	17	D	1	D	20	100	9
Fruita city	NA	NA	8	69	11	128	27	288	8	D	NA	NA	11	43	8
Golden city	6	D	62	2,215	52	929	90	1,434	10	168	21	289	55	440	41
Grand Junction city	7	D	93	1,938	167	1,556	477	6,718	97	1,745	55	1,119	190	1,595	195
Greeley city	8	115	53	4,235	77	1,110	291	4,986	61	1,267	33	930	169	2,832	119
Greenwood Village city	2	D	15	D	71	638	119	1,964	16	180	95	6,749	429	10,179	204
Highlands Ranch CDP	NA	NA	31	384	57	889	190	3,465	23	82	55	1,344	171	2,083	148
Johnstown town	1	D	13	140	7	44	17	385	8	D	4	D	14	D	3
Ken Caryl CDP	5	D	12	574	24	170	74	869	7	14	16	117	97	550	64
Lafayette city	NA	NA	46	780	26	D	70	854	5	D	10	13	54	154	37
Lakewood city	8	216	99	1,112	129	930	669	10,547	52	815	81	1,020	374	4,335	251
Littleton city	1	D	32	4,492	60	901	244	4,098	10	182	41	5,209	125	685	89
Lone Tree city	NA	NA	10	51	18	109	199	5,542	4	9	21	1,385	46	234	29
Longmont city	1	D	118	2,180	69	775	270	3,932	33	559	31	1,592	149	745	121
Louisville city	1	D	53	2,313	41	995	73	1,415	5	18	21	788	55	224	43
Loveland city	NA	NA	99	2,619	79	1,202	320	5,233	39	1,296	31	1,161	143	1,227	110
Montrose city	6	D	43	952	33	260	131	1,868	22	292	8	79	57	281	39
Northglenn city	1	D	26	425	18	201	105	1,817	10	D	3	D	48	236	31
Parker town	NA	NA	27	399	30	228	153	2,728	18	85	12	73	97	396	71
Pueblo city	6	D	54	1,733	58	704	406	6,473	34	924	34	1,103	178	958	108
Pueblo West CDP	2	D	14	164	13	169	48	658	8	190	3	D	19	45	23
Security-Widefield CDP	1	D	3	D	2	D	20	136	10	D	1	D	17	53	13
Sherrelwood CDP	NA	NA	NA	NA	2	D	21	171	3	12	2	D	1	D	7
Steamboat Springs city	2	D	20	110	21	185	182	1,491	21	182	19	136	48	203	105
Sterling city	2	D	13	205	15	196	88	1,067	15	128	9	D	33	204	12
Superior town	NA	NA	NA	NA	4	D	36	853	1	D	7	60	21	145	11
The Pinery CDP	NA	NA	NA	NA	7	D	7	11	3	24	2	D	11	9	12
Thornton city	2	D	16	250	29	213	189	4,625	42	125	27	1,811	97	474	81
Welby CDP	NA	NA	16	274	17	293	23	178	5	D	1	D	4	6	23
Westminster city	1	D	53	747	72	1,572	322	6,329	33	88	43	869	200	1,391	157
Wheat Ridge city	2	D	42	1,007	68	680	163	2,222	17	242	11	76	65	323	53
Windsor town	1	D	25	1,890	24	D	57	534	12	104	8	D	39	D	25
CONNECTICUT	153	10,545	4,350	163,847	3,675	58,814	12,597	182,528	1,595	44,003	1,675	37,338	6,108	119,326	3,219
Ansonia city & town (New Haven)	NA	NA	16	355	9	D	44	567	3	67	1	D	10	D	4
Avon town (Hartford)	2	D	9	630	15	133	83	1,137	3	D	9	D	58	358	25
Berlin town (Hartford)	4	D	78	2,292	50	742	81	1,388	10	510	12	D	29	210	14
Bethel town (Fairfield)	NA	NA	48	1,174	31	D	56	833	12	263	3	107	29	222	10
Bloomfield town (Hartford)	NA	NA	71	3,357	52	1,175	62	988	27	1,185	16	D	42	D	31
Branford town (New Haven)	NA	NA	52	1,087	57	D	153	1,998	14	189	21	253	52	287	35
Bridgeport city & town (Fairfield)	6	506	139	3,274	138	D	266	3,050	36	625	58	809	196	5,986	94
Bristol city & town (Hartford)	NA	NA	130	2,827	38	342	170	2,867	13	325	29	D	55	556	40
Brookfield town (Fairfield)	1	D	26	1,062	33	D	88	1,358	10	273	6	71	29	128	7
Canton town (Hartford)	NA	NA	8	32	11	51	84	1,242	NA	NA	7	32	24	104	6
Cheshire town (New Haven)	1	D	50	1,788	58	1,894	78	1,547	15	655	12	134	56	937	27
Clinton town (Middlesex)	1	D	18	376	9	D	120	1,600	4	68	10	48	12	57	6
Colchester town (New London)	NA	NA	9	156	4	D	51	839	2	D	4	31	17	70	11
Conning Towers Nautilus Park CDP	NA	NA	NA	NA	NA	NA	NA	NA	NA	NA	NA	NA	NA	NA	NA
Coventry town (Tolland)	NA	NA	6	21	1	D	17	187	3	51	2	D	3	D	5
Cromwell town (Middlesex)	NA	NA	14	335	16	D	47	1,161	3	71	8	134	20	91	19
Danbury city & town (Fairfield)	1	D	93	5,623	109	1,316	454	8,144	45	493	32	623	128	1,899	84
Darien CDP & town (Fairfield)	1	D	7	112	18	247	105	1,425	9	134	13	108	91	886	19
Derby city & town (New Haven)	NA	NA	19	159	8	D	59	1,429	4	6	5	31	9	D	7
East Hampton town (Middlesex)	2	D	14	76	1	D	27	324	2	D	4	D	6	D	3
East Hartford CDP & town (Hartford)	2	D	61	15,769	84	1,953	136	2,274	31	1,167	16	D	79	1,141	56
East Haven CDP & town (New Haven)	NA	NA	26	459	21	388	72	1,179	18	216	6	31	15	D	12

1 Merchant wholesalers, except manufacturers' sales branches and offices.

Table C. Incorporated Places, Census Designated Places (CDPs), and Minor Civil Divisions (MCDs) of 10,000 or More Population — **Economic Census**

STATE City, town, township, borough, or CDP (county if applicable)	Real estate and rental and leasing — Number of employees	Professional, scientific, and technical services — Number of establish-ments	Number of employees	Administration and support and waste management and mediation services — Number of establish-ments	Number of employees	Educational services — Number of establish-ments	Number of employees	Health care and social assistance — Number of establish-ments	Number of employees	Arts, entertainment, and recreation — Number of establish-ments	Number of employees	Accommodation and food services — Number of establish-ments	Number of employees	Other services (except public administration) — Number of establish-ments	Number of employees
	16	17	18	19	20	21	22	23	24	25	26	27	28	29	30
COLORADO—Con.															
Centennial city	998	695	3,802	222	5,153	67	1,188	402	4,300	39	D	207	3,322	207	1,186
Cherry Creek CDP	19	55	D	5	D	5	D	11	57	1	D	3	D	3	4
Cimarron Hills CDP	64	25	157	34	350	4	D	11	69	5	74	19	227	34	D
Clifton CDP	87	17	37	8	D	NA	NA	5	D	4	93	21	509	11	39
Colorado Springs city	2,875	1,919	17,333	673	20,100	175	1,496	1,676	26,896	169	2,772	1,040	23,240	885	7,414
Columbine CDP	D	94	181	28	87	8	17	67	627	9	D	35	501	43	D
Commerce City city	531	43	293	63	1,167	7	D	35	569	2	D	58	926	97	752
Dakota Ridge CDP	D	103	195	33	137	8	26	38	237	4	D	19	226	30	104
Denver city	9,373	4,291	42,123	1,178	59,033	308	2,489	2,093	54,161	313	9,279	1,982	42,906	1,607	13,247
Durango city	298	227	892	73	472	10	75	188	2,490	29	144	147	2,730	97	452
Englewood city	377	162	1,140	121	1,708	15	48	219	D	10	137	95	1,448	133	905
Erie town	20	102	209	22	87	6	D	37	D	5	D	20	D	15	D
Evans city	D	15	51	9	D	NA	NA	8	D	1	D	16	243	13	65
Federal Heights city	313	16	149	6	28	2	D	17	D	NA	NA	25	467	13	D
Firestone town	11	26	71	4	7	NA	NA	8	36	4	D	19	258	8	28
Fort Carson CDP	D	30	410	8	D	1	D	3	D	NA	NA	6	129	6	47
Fort Collins city	1,258	882	6,238	242	3,463	76	839	630	11,402	84	1,057	427	8,329	318	1,804
Fort Morgan city	31	20	85	14	D	NA	NA	39	D	3	D	33	428	20	74
Fountain city	47	20	97	17	79	4	D	28	186	1	D	45	967	18	D
Fruita city	20	29	55	12	D	3	D	16	D	4	80	27	398	8	17
Golden city	207	205	1,406	38	313	22	94	58	771	15	142	76	1,226	57	385
Grand Junction city	663	369	2,139	141	D	24	137	362	9,166	27	566	211	4,578	231	1,662
Greeley city	518	183	827	96	1,624	19	D	271	5,812	33	328	184	3,501	143	784
Greenwood Village city	1,062	523	5,662	138	10,882	31	321	204	2,362	16	507	163	3,187	100	906
Highlands Ranch CDP	384	502	2,148	135	779	52	297	186	1,954	31	797	130	2,676	137	1,009
Johnstown town	10	24	110	9	37	NA	NA	15	D	3	D	16	D	13	69
Ken Caryl CDP	383	168	883	46	178	16	156	100	881	14	254	65	1,287	64	287
Lafayette city	D	171	1,034	37	180	19	109	110	3,373	8	248	56	674	50	218
Lakewood city	791	827	7,444	253	10,157	51	690	542	10,860	51	680	378	7,456	304	1,986
Littleton city	410	346	4,994	80	2,549	24	285	246	3,909	25	D	135	D	124	887
Lone Tree city	97	94	491	24	547	9	36	129	2,012	7	206	88	2,319	30	212
Longmont city	362	379	4,846	131	D	29	244	284	4,397	37	371	187	3,623	182	964
Louisville city	151	214	1,970	38	565	18	106	129	1,538	15	89	65	1,209	42	413
Loveland city	577	260	1,265	109	1,555	21	162	257	5,353	34	166	194	4,019	152	902
Montrose city	98	84	380	36	D	2	D	155	2,232	11	D	69	966	68	304
Northglenn city	107	59	256	39	656	6	D	60	680	8	239	45	922	52	D
Parker city	118	220	687	65	782	31	293	172	2,176	17	D	106	2,252	129	791
Pueblo city	523	187	1,443	97	3,078	13	205	379	10,868	33	661	286	4,992	178	967
Pueblo West CDP	D	28	D	21	229	2	D	35	D	7	D	37	368	39	159
Security-Widefield CDP	20	20	65	21	47	1	D	20	164	3	D	12	129	24	69
Sherrelwood CDP	24	14	D	7	D	1	D	9	101	1	D	12	256	7	D
Steamboat Springs city	478	158	487	73	D	10	145	110	D	33	D	125	4,642	65	368
Sterling city	D	26	96	13	D	NA	NA	58	965	5	D	40	549	39	135
Superior town	60	79	307	13	32	6	23	25	185	7	24	25	381	20	89
The Pinery CDP	15	55	84	11	71	3	D	9	D	3	D	1	D	6	D
Thornton city	487	171	1,048	88	707	12	57	171	3,058	24	193	164	3,197	111	831
Welby CDP	77	11	D	14	144	NA	NA	6	D	1	D	11	119	25	D
Westminster city	568	379	3,724	151	5,303	48	295	271	5,270	31	D	231	5,395	158	1,006
Wheat Ridge city	272	190	1,365	71	1,265	11	30	190	4,519	19	89	91	1,347	121	594
Windsor town	84	88	647	33	D	7	D	55	697	11	149	43	D	32	157
CONNECTICUT	19,778	9,220	97,578	5,186	92,994	1,062	10,435	10,296	271,272	1,610	26,476	8,263	134,546	7,282	43,384
Ansonia city & town (New Haven)	11	18	58	14	52	3	2	31	886	1	D	22	115	22	83
Avon town (Hartford)	54	88	582	35	169	6	16	115	1,718	12	D	41	660	43	344
Berlin town (Hartford)	92	40	203	42	1,148	6	D	56	927	11	110	57	534	59	261
Bethel town (Fairfield)	177	40	D	40	355	9	D	40	933	8	D	55	549	41	216
Bloomfield town (Hartford)	150	52	444	42	478	6	40	113	2,116	9	140	47	613	49	446
Branford town (New Haven)	1,150	100	749	53	584	12	196	112	2,008	18	D	103	1,407	100	619
Bridgeport city & town (Fairfield)	406	209	4,324	127	2,718	19	196	312	13,333	38	736	227	2,202	202	1,177
Bristol city & town (Hartford)	151	67	302	54	504	4	53	141	3,745	19	553	108	1,222	89	446
Brookfield town (Fairfield)	19	65	300	35	310	10	69	66	D	13	223	43	512	48	D
Canton town (Hartford)	15	45	198	17	148	7	22	20	556	7	90	33	467	43	D
Cheshire town (New Haven)	D	85	803	40	653	12	45	97	2,197	10	D	48	523	57	D
Clinton town (Middlesex)	D	22	64	22	110	5	21	31	330	8	83	30	271	27	D
Colchester town (New London)	D	21	D	16	36	6	19	45	678	3	D	24	415	28	119
Conning Towers Nautilus Park CDP	NA	NA	NA	NA	NA	NA	NA	NA	NA	NA	NA	NA	NA	NA	NA
Coventry town (Tolland)	8	15	33	10	D	1	D	12	D	3	D	13	122	6	D
Cromwell town (Middlesex)	121	27	282	22	237	8	19	49	1,932	8	139	45	919	42	253
Danbury city & town (Fairfield)	1,711	226	2,662	140	2,802	25	200	266	8,624	27	389	211	3,531	178	1,123
Darien CDP & town (Fairfield)	50	81	655	45	561	6	57	64	553	22	790	64	924	71	483
Derby city & town (New Haven)	D	17	127	17	158	4	6	52	1,996	2	D	38	551	27	87
East Hampton town (Middlesex)	3	16	70	12	D	NA	NA	16	246	4	D	15	D	12	D
East Hartford CDP & town (Hartford)	336	89	2,234	76	3,548	8	D	104	3,271	12	99	77	1,018	95	713
East Haven CDP & town (New Haven)	D	37	254	20	113	2	D	44	928	5	D	50	656	54	194

Table C. Incorporated Places, Census Designated Places (CDPs), and Minor Civil Divisions (MCDs) of 10,000 or More Population — **Economic Census**

STATE City, town, township, borough, or CDP (county if applicable)	Utilities Number of establishments	Utilities Number of employees	Manufacturing Number of establishments	Manufacturing Number of employees	Wholesale trade[1] Number of establishments	Wholesale trade[1] Number of employees	Retail trade Number of establishments	Retail trade Number of employees	Transportation and warehousing Number of establishments	Transportation and warehousing Number of employees	Information Number of establishments	Information Number of employees	Finance and insurance Number of establishments	Finance and insurance Number of employees	Real estate and rental and leasing Number of establishments
	1	2	3	4	5	6	7	8	9	10	11	12	13	14	15
CONNECTICUT—Con.															
East Lyme town (New London)..............	NA	NA	16	202	9	177	60	714	6	103	5	D	19	D	20
East Windsor town (Hartford)..................	2	D	30	804	33	552	56	937	16	166	2	D	21	106	11
Ellington town (Tolland)	NA	NA	19	426	5	D	30	573	1	D	3	D	9	35	10
Enfield town (Hartford)......	3	D	43	1,197	39	2,668	186	3,671	19	1,146	18	639	44	D	20
Fairfield town (Fairfield)	NA	NA	30	617	60	D	245	3,481	29	455	28	201	172	982	80
Farmington town (Hartford)..................	1	D	38	2,455	35	693	209	3,850	7	121	24	561	165	4,339	51
Glastonbury town (Hartford)..................	1	D	44	743	31	468	113	2,015	6	180	35	605	156	1,752	39
Granby town (Hartford).....	NA	NA	4	48	3	D	31	510	2	D	2	D	17	56	3
Greenwich town (Fairfield)	2	D	37	949	82	1,031	347	4,198	32	1,435	42	1,344	451	5,936	143
Greenwich CDP...............	NA	NA	NA	NA	NA	NA	NA	NA	NA	NA	NA	NA	NA	NA	NA
Griswold town (New London)*..............	NA	NA	NA	NA	1	D	19	121	3	170	1	D	3	D	2
Groton town (New London)*..............	NA	NA	16	332	16	D	130	1,650	12	351	9	275	27	303	28
Guilford town (New Haven)	NA	NA	32	943	41	D	100	1,008	9	385	14	150	70	371	19
Hamden town (New Haven)..................	NA	NA	65	1,227	46	563	180	2,775	19	648	21	272	78	513	45
Hartford city & town (Hartford)..................	5	D	68	1,013	112	2,244	357	3,053	49	2,860	77	2,081	249	29,426	164
Killingly town (Windham)*.	1	D	30	1,534	10	593	49	706	11	992	2	D	15	104	7
Ledyard town (New London)..................	NA	NA	5	40	2	D	17	152	2	D	2	D	6	D	7
Madison town (New Haven)..................	1	D	11	131	20	D	63	607	5	86	13	115	35	160	14
Manchester CDP..............	NA	NA	NA	NA	NA	NA	NA	NA	NA	NA	NA	NA	NA	NA	NA
Manchester town (Hartford)..................	NA	NA	69	2,573	53	894	347	6,681	19	717	27	727	60	370	51
Mansfield town (Tolland)...	1	D	3	D	2	D	51	841	1	D	6	D	19	119	16
Meriden city & town (New Haven)..................	1	D	66	2,433	38	306	228	3,081	20	470	22	1,142	48	516	44
Middletown city & town (Middlesex)	4	D	52	3,583	44	1,087	120	1,690	12	224	29	316	52	1,059	39
Milford city & town (New Haven)..................	3	49	151	3,305	98	1,476	323	5,819	20	299	26	785	91	857	51
Milford city (balance)	3	49	151	3,305	98	1,476	323	5,819	20	299	26	785	91	857	51
Monroe town (Fairfield).....	NA	NA	24	622	21	D	73	1,102	5	133	6	D	35	165	15
Montville town (New London)..................	2	D	8	448	9	65	66	929	7	D	4	D	12	D	10
Naugatuck borough & town (New Haven).........	2	D	47	1,168	21	480	66	1,031	5	116	3	31	23	335	14
New Britain city & town (Hartford)..................	1	D	94	2,959	39	402	146	1,691	17	631	6	119	42	774	40
New Canaan town (Fairfield)..................	NA	NA	6	107	22	D	93	776	12	D	14	157	71	512	27
New Fairfield town (Fairfield)..................	NA	NA	5	247	8	18	14	309	3	D	4	D	12	44	4
New Haven city & town (New Haven)	5	D	70	2,250	74	D	322	3,135	33	1,257	61	2,289	113	2,864	128
Newington CDP & town (Hartford)..................	4	D	78	1,996	39	679	128	2,826	10	45	14	252	57	426	29
New London city & town (New London)	2	D	15	212	13	D	101	1,343	15	560	14	549	39	257	24
New Milford town (Litchfield)	4	D	53	856	37	D	107	1,416	11	187	8	74	30	135	20
Newtown town (Fairfield)*.	3	D	16	632	27	D	51	510	12	180	16	519	19	203	8
North Branford town (New Haven)..................	NA	NA	18	919	15	D	33	454	10	108	3	D	6	D	5
North Haven CDP & town (New Haven)..................	2	D	44	3,601	57	1,264	140	2,265	25	769	19	D	58	D	32
Norwalk city & town (Fairfield)..................	11	339	100	1,733	129	2,445	343	5,913	41	1,087	86	2,463	193	3,416	95
Norwich city & town (New London)..................	NA	NA	25	699	20	571	125	2,053	18	945	13	271	43	599	35
Old Saybrook town (Middlesex)	NA	NA	26	420	20	175	103	1,609	8	94	7	250	26	128	21
Orange CDP & town (New Haven)..................	5	D	11	663	23	667	124	2,133	12	359	7	D	30	289	18
Oxford town (New Haven).	NA	NA	39	605	14	87	21	131	23	312	4	D	10	D	4
Plainfield town (Windham)	NA	NA	25	589	6	24	48	509	8	603	4	14	10	56	8
Plainville town (Hartford) ..	3	D	66	1,345	32	472	64	1,281	12	154	5	D	23	161	23
Plymouth town (Litchfield)	NA	NA	32	406	9	D	22	251	5	154	NA	NA	4	30	3
Ridgefield town (Fairfield) .	1	D	12	130	14	D	101	957	5	77	16	198	61	D	39
Rocky Hill town (Hartford).	2	D	13	102	38	1,032	64	1,193	15	712	28	751	73	1,221	28
Seymour town (New Haven)..................	3	18	23	906	7	D	31	448	5	282	6	140	13	86	7
Shelton city & town (Fairfield)..................	7	587	64	2,951	56	D	90	1,821	9	D	27	915	89	2,232	38
Simsbury town (Hartford)..	1	D	13	474	15	57	59	1,092	2	D	15	45	60	D	28
Somers town (Tolland)......	NA	NA	15	151	11	73	24	152	3	48	1	D	8	40	5
Southbury town (New Haven)..................	2	D	16	108	14	72	74	914	7	102	11	119	36	209	15
Southington town (Hartford)..................	1	D	77	1,550	35	503	150	2,681	24	D	10	D	64	649	28
South Windsor town (Hartford)..................	1	D	85	2,935	68	1,202	114	1,329	25	549	8	503	53	497	15

1 Merchant wholesalers, except manufacturers' sales branches and offices.

Table C. Incorporated Places, Census Designated Places (CDPs), and Minor Civil Divisions (MCDs) of 10,000 or More Population — Economic Census

STATE / City, town, township, borough, or CDP (county if applicable)	Real estate and rental and leasing	Professional, scientific, and technical services		Administration and support and waste management and mediation services		Educational services		Health care and social assistance		Arts, entertainment, and recreation		Accommodation and food services		Other services (except public administration)	
	Number of employees	Number of establishments	Number of employees	Number of establishments	Number of employees	Number of establishments	Number of employees	Number of establishments	Number of employees	Number of establishments	Number of employees	Number of establishments	Number of employees	Number of establishments	Number of employees
	16	17	18	19	20	21	22	23	24	25	26	27	28	29	30
CONNECTICUT—Con.															
East Lyme town (New London)	40	38	D	20	73	11	53	54	676	13	105	54	D	35	141
East Windsor town (Hartford)	72	19	172	31	1,481	4	D	20	287	3	D	43	750	32	D
Ellington town (Tolland)	38	18	38	18	142	4	23	22	192	5	56	21	D	15	55
Enfield town (Hartford)	154	55	606	38	636	12	111	144	2,209	11	231	83	1,949	72	400
Fairfield town (Fairfield)	322	281	1,523	135	1,857	34	273	247	4,295	49	819	184	2,892	155	915
Farmington town (Hartford)	312	153	2,227	73	2,318	10	52	122	5,446	16	359	84	1,996	71	992
Glastonbury town (Hartford)	122	165	2,433	59	1,281	16	D	166	2,550	21	279	71	1,440	97	566
Granby town (Hartford)	11	16	92	14	D	1	D	25	367	2	D	20	156	13	D
Greenwich town (Fairfield)	1,098	314	1,399	149	856	40	223	231	4,474	67	1,538	159	2,543	206	1,173
Greenwich CDP	NA	NA	NA	NA	NA	NA	NA	NA	NA	NA	NA	NA	NA	NA	NA
Griswold town (New London)*	D	6	D	6	D	2	D	3	19	2	D	9	D	7	28
Groton town (New London)*	D	41	392	16	56	8	78	75	1,413	19	199	84	D	47	291
Guilford town (New Haven)	D	90	674	37	117	11	115	98	1,792	14	105	53	634	61	320
Hamden town (New Haven)	D	131	913	92	1,847	24	220	199	4,405	23	230	125	1,967	115	608
Hartford city & town (Hartford)	1,337	399	5,678	114	5,808	38	632	428	23,437	39	1,322	326	4,429	330	2,154
Killingly town (Windham)*	18	12	82	22	106	2	D	39	983	4	D	25	307	16	D
Ledyard town (New London)	D	17	D	16	128	1	D	25	356	6	12	30	D	12	101
Madison town (New Haven)	D	65	297	29	215	5	32	61	901	8	49	39	482	38	240
Manchester CDP	NA	NA	NA	NA	NA	NA	NA	NA	NA	NA	NA	NA	NA	NA	NA
Manchester town (Hartford)	268	106	1,051	51	564	15	128	197	5,496	18	156	158	3,091	118	591
Mansfield town (Tolland)	66	28	D	10	D	6	D	53	D	4	15	50	1,432	19	243
Meriden city & town (New Haven)	505	76	760	61	2,274	9	80	138	4,576	8	274	116	1,292	94	512
Middletown city & town (Middlesex)	248	110	1,185	54	870	14	107	172	7,956	14	317	110	1,311	104	557
Milford city & town (New Haven)	D	178	2,832	87	2,174	18	120	162	3,622	24	322	172	2,632	144	856
Milford city (balance)	D	178	2,832	87	2,174	18	120	162	3,622	24	322	172	2,632	144	856
Monroe town (Fairfield)	47	51	D	47	371	9	D	50	393	6	56	50	662	51	207
Montville town (New London)	38	15	D	15	127	2	D	27	538	1	D	41	D	27	D
Naugatuck borough & town (New Haven)	D	32	213	12	D	4	11	43	850	5	D	51	474	45	164
New Britain city & town (Hartford)	184	85	810	42	1,578	6	D	170	7,478	16	315	91	1,195	100	503
New Canaan town (Fairfield)	76	91	D	43	253	17	D	46	D	19	490	51	D	49	238
New Fairfield town (Fairfield)	D	31	D	12	76	2	D	18	D	8	D	18	183	15	34
New Haven city & town (New Haven)	751	375	3,436	92	2,089	28	932	446	21,688	41	519	337	4,119	246	1,541
Newington CDP & town (Hartford)	133	75	964	64	839	9	118	75	2,359	12	D	76	1,414	83	552
New London city & town (New London)	147	97	D	26	464	8	84	123	4,112	21	171	89	1,217	71	401
New Milford town (Litchfield)	57	69	329	45	388	13	D	82	1,589	18	291	60	620	66	273
Newtown town (Fairfield)*	26	71	470	48	212	12	D	35	623	7	104	43	406	36	256
North Branford town (New Haven)	D	19	98	37	435	3	19	16	328	4	140	28	248	22	91
North Haven CDP & town (New Haven)	294	76	514	48	656	6	64	74	1,361	12	D	78	1,630	72	426
Norwalk city & town (Fairfield)	327	340	3,538	219	5,156	36	218	254	6,307	68	1,388	251	2,845	228	1,366
Norwich city & town (New London)	D	63	894	24	227	10	91	164	4,959	10	103	93	D	73	514
Old Saybrook town (Middlesex)	56	48	271	28	401	5	27	59	1,106	15	110	59	862	44	209
Orange CDP & town (New Haven)	D	45	180	34	249	6	46	48	688	15	D	67	1,289	45	312
Oxford town (New Haven)	D	20	93	25	115	1	D	13	308	2	D	20	251	21	D
Plainfield town (Windham)	16	13	73	7	83	2	D	24	717	4	15	32	344	32	D
Plainville town (Hartford)	56	39	423	24	691	4	25	54	1,170	7	210	56	746	40	257
Plymouth town (Litchfield)	5	5	D	10	176	NA	NA	13	D	1	D	14	183	10	D
Ridgefield town (Fairfield)	D	121	D	46	791	25	82	90	959	32	273	63	578	60	469
Rocky Hill town (Hartford)	239	100	1,698	47	703	11	170	77	1,969	6	127	59	940	74	444
Seymour town (New Haven)	D	32	104	17	309	8	65	26	350	3	D	34	295	33	D
Shelton city & town (Fairfield)	605	140	1,681	83	4,005	10	375	119	2,769	14	175	112	1,915	76	459
Simsbury town (Hartford)	D	82	492	36	186	8	65	54	932	15	285	66	948	48	221
Somers town (Tolland)	6	19	95	16	65	2	D	15	D	5	24	10	114	17	D
Southbury town (New Haven)	D	62	229	27	341	11	70	78	1,366	15	D	37	653	39	D
Southington town (Hartford)	107	73	454	50	378	6	175	115	2,143	19	387	130	2,246	89	374
South Windsor town (Hartford)	32	63	488	61	850	7	D	78	1,062	13	218	45	717	66	552

Table C. Incorporated Places, Census Designated Places (CDPs), and Minor Civil Divisions (MCDs) of 10,000 or More Population — **Economic Census**

	Utilities		Manufacturing		Wholesale trade[1]		Retail trade		Transportation and warehousing		Information		Finance and insurance		Real estate and rental and leasing
STATE City, town, township, borough, or CDP (county if applicable)	Number of establish-ments	Number of employees	Number of establish-ments	Number of employees	Number of establish-ments	Number of employees	Number of establish-ments	Number of employees	Number of establish-ments	Number of employees	Number of establish-ments	Number of employees	Number of establish-ments	Number of employees	Number of establish-ments
	1	2	3	4	5	6	7	8	9	10	11	12	13	14	15
CONNECTICUT—Con.															
Stafford town (Tolland)......	NA	NA	16	992	6	D	37	401	8	94	1	D	13	92	4
Stamford city & town (Fairfield)	7	960	104	1,959	213	5,498	482	6,199	109	1,924	121	3,616	491	13,818	217
Stonington town (New London)	2	D	30	782	14	D	129	1,157	5	107	12	171	33	162	14
Storrs CDP	NA	NA	NA	NA	NA	NA	NA	NA	NA	NA	NA	NA	NA	NA	NA
Stratford CDP & town (Fairfield)	1	D	74	12,700	86	D	140	2,097	41	1,589	15	679	68	453	41
Suffield town (Hartford).....	NA	NA	12	375	17	365	18	181	14	218	4	8	15	77	6
Tolland town (Tolland)	2	D	18	623	8	D	32	353	3	D	4	D	9	31	7
Torrington city & town (Litchfield)	3	D	65	1,870	32	D	159	2,832	6	152	7	93	46	412	25
Trumbull CDP & town (Fairfield)	NA	NA	20	629	33	D	164	3,021	10	526	20	252	49	1,305	30
Vernon town (Tolland).......	NA	NA	31	454	11	D	123	1,789	3	D	5	78	42	245	29
Wallingford town (New Haven)	NA	NA	100	3,750	105	2,055	142	2,882	32	834	38	1,467	69	1,550	40
Wallingford Center CDP ...	NA	NA	NA	NA	NA	NA	NA	NA	NA	NA	NA	NA	NA	NA	NA
Waterbury city & town (New Haven)	3	D	153	3,206	80	803	425	6,035	30	665	26	786	87	755	72
Waterford town (New London)	2	D	8	D	15	D	175	3,475	14	620	15	D	24	154	17
Watertown town (Litchfield)	NA	NA	62	2,226	14	80	70	1,281	7	690	5	72	27	151	9
West Hartford CDP & town (Hartford)	1	D	50	2,488	43	406	251	4,096	12	561	28	D	148	948	66
West Haven city & town (New Haven)	NA	NA	49	1,411	60	1,248	110	1,361	27	721	8	D	28	D	43
Weston town (Fairfield).....	NA	NA	NA	NA	9	20	7	68	3	D	9	D	13	D	7
Westport CDP & town (Fairfield)	1	D	11	95	51	237	242	2,824	22	307	35	700	205	2,889	66
Wethersfield CDP & town (Hartford)	NA	NA	17	179	15	122	96	1,257	10	62	5	D	48	367	27
Willimantic CDP..............	NA	NA	NA	NA	NA	NA	NA	NA	NA	NA	NA	NA	NA	NA	NA
Wilton town (Fairfield)	NA	NA	8	D	32	729	68	979	10	175	17	204	75	831	37
Winchester town (Litchfield)	NA	NA	34	713	9	D	34	339	4	D	6	77	13	93	9
Windham town (Windham)	2	D	17	680	16	210	72	1,628	5	87	8	200	16	217	11
Windsor town (Hartford) ...	3	D	44	6,504	45	765	61	1,124	44	1,283	14	606	90	7,662	37
Windsor Locks CDP & town (Hartford)	NA	NA	22	1,186	13	D	30	267	47	1,964	4	34	14	176	20
Wolcott town (New Haven)	NA	NA	31	310	13	105	33	262	8	63	2	D	7	D	10
DELAWARE.....................	48	2,622	573	26,355	835	7,653	3,616	51,711	612	11,938	417	6,964	1,920	36,438	1,111
Bear CDP	NA	NA	4	D	3	54	32	560	8	12	1	D	13	59	7
Brookside CDP................	NA	NA	17	351	9	129	22	371	9	D	1	D	7	28	13
Dover city......................	6	D	19	1,518	38	296	205	3,883	24	D	41	647	103	789	75
Glasgow CDP..................	NA	NA	5	42	4	19	37	674	8	48	3	85	11	64	5
Hockessin CDP................	NA	NA	NA	NA	12	D	44	564	2	D	3	8	28	194	15
Middletown town..............	NA	NA	9	872	8	70	64	1,547	6	66	6	66	23	135	11
Newark city....................	4	D	25	932	41	195	176	2,877	11	95	15	78	105	2,809	49
Pike Creek Valley CDP	NA	NA	NA	NA	6	9	18	332	NA	NA	2	D	11	90	10
Smyrna town...................	1	D	5	29	3	D	47	680	6	D	2	D	20	87	6
Wilmington city	12	463	66	999	114	878	303	2,882	51	1,238	97	1,099	523	14,960	204
DISTRICT OF COLUMBIA	47	D	113	1,361	335	3,415	1,710	19,780	193	8,483	741	22,144	999	18,080	1,112
Washington city	47	D	113	1,361	335	3,415	1,710	19,780	193	8,483	741	22,144	999	18,080	1,112
FLORIDA......................	699	27,343	12,890	277,089	27,109	252,418	71,189	947,877	13,280	209,381	8,030	152,775	30,653	338,872	29,845
Alafaya CDP	2	D	NA	NA	18	38	155	3,435	17	81	20	197	31	506	56
Altamonte Springs city......	NA	NA	40	307	77	1,929	342	5,824	20	64	54	2,414	150	1,265	109
Apollo Beach CDP............	NA	NA	7	50	11	34	24	232	5	6	2	D	27	85	30
Apopka city....................	2	D	27	360	67	724	155	2,058	26	133	13	D	59	299	34
Atlantic Beach city	1	D	7	33	11	D	46	203	12	D	5	D	23	D	29
Auburndale city...............	NA	NA	25	1,487	11	65	78	1,000	23	582	4	D	21	D	18
Aventura city...................	NA	NA	13	149	142	476	375	9,146	16	48	39	245	141	1,057	206
Azalea Park CDP..............	NA	NA	3	8	8	39	41	366	5	5	1	D	9	52	10
Bartow city.....................	4	D	22	1,154	9	72	68	1,223	12	104	7	53	35	D	12
Bayonet Point CDP	NA	NA	NA	NA	1	D	57	992	3	8	NA	NA	24	165	11
Bayshore Gardens CDP ...	NA	NA	NA	NA	2	D	56	1,004	3	D	3	D	30	163	9
Bellair-Meadowbrook Terrace CDP...............	NA	NA	13	87	20	D	172	2,327	6	D	9	168	30	138	17
Belle Glade city...............	1	D	5	D	23	D	64	438	10	43	3	D	17	103	10
Bellview CDP...................	NA	NA	NA	NA	7	33	33	325	1	D	7	D	10	D	7
Bloomingdale CDP............	NA	NA	5	9	9	15	47	550	5	9	3	7	32	98	17
Boca Raton city	5	D	153	2,052	379	4,030	652	9,944	69	682	180	3,740	639	8,560	432
Bonita Springs city...........	5	140	24	146	43	525	187	2,067	14	84	21	343	120	581	119
Boynton Beach city..........	NA	NA	64	735	105	828	377	5,602	37	493	32	328	200	1,123	116
Bradenton city................	2	D	30	1,819	43	288	265	3,701	12	32	21	461	122	1,109	79
Brandon CDP..................	NA	NA	45	607	118	1,580	484	9,938	54	399	47	685	214	3,834	141
Brent CDP......................	NA	NA	20	104	74	846	144	1,968	31	291	9	145	30	279	29
Brownsville CDP..............	NA	NA	24	325	59	667	37	147	22	280	4	26	4	17	11
Buenaventura Lakes CDP	NA	NA	4	9	1	D	35	447	12	17	NA	NA	10	78	16
Callaway city...................	NA	NA	NA	NA	1	D	39	622	1	D	2	D	9	42	8
Cape Coral city...............	2	D	85	548	100	294	404	6,381	59	145	32	362	180	872	292
Carrollwood CDP..............	NA	NA	16	D	38	292	113	1,253	15	20	9	D	93	778	69

[1] Merchant wholesalers, except manufacturers' sales branches and offices.

Table C. Incorporated Places, Census Designated Places (CDPs), and Minor Civil Divisions (MCDs) of 10,000 or More Population — Economic Census

STATE City, town, township, borough, or CDP (county if applicable)	Real estate and rental and leasing — Number of employees	Professional, scientific, and technical services — Number of establishments	Number of employees	Administration and support and waste management and mediation services — Number of establishments	Number of employees	Educational services — Number of establishments	Number of employees	Health care and social assistance — Number of establishments	Number of employees	Arts, entertainment, and recreation — Number of establishments	Number of employees	Accommodation and food services — Number of establishments	Number of employees	Other services (except public administration) — Number of establishments	Number of employees
	16	17	18	19	20	21	22	23	24	25	26	27	28	29	30
CONNECTICUT—Con.															
Stafford town (Tolland)......	10	15	65	8	D	1	D	17	1,011	4	D	16	166	23	57
Stamford city & town (Fairfield)..................	1,369	642	7,795	420	7,624	52	644	454	8,225	68	1,678	389	5,995	343	1,994
Stonington town (New London)................	D	71	590	26	212	8	24	57	859	26	735	90	D	49	250
Storrs CDP	NA	NA	NA	NA	NA	NA	NA	NA	NA	NA	NA	NA	NA	NA	NA
Stratford CDP & town (Fairfield).................	134	101	647	73	1,727	11	96	132	3,130	17	268	105	1,097	113	713
Suffield town (Hartford).....	29	25	157	23	81	3	68	21	D	4	D	17	146	14	D
Tolland town (Tolland).......	17	17	221	14	D	4	30	30	598	2	D	12	127	15	116
Torrington city & town (Litchfield)................	102	61	463	50	611	8	40	155	3,519	17	221	79	959	78	486
Trumbull CDP & town (Fairfield)................	98	114	1,029	45	1,886	11	91	138	3,922	18	D	63	869	52	331
Vernon town (Tolland).......	136	43	281	22	D	7	22	95	2,203	7	206	62	1,150	61	418
Wallingford town (New Haven).................	230	115	1,939	67	1,424	15	86	127	4,838	16	313	118	1,851	128	947
Wallingford Center CDP ..	NA	NA	NA	NA	NA	NA	NA	NA	NA	NA	NA	NA	NA	NA	NA
Waterbury city & town (New Haven)	293	147	925	62	1,643	14	129	315	10,914	17	391	231	3,063	166	1,089
Waterford town (New London)................	44	40	550	34	548	5	33	62	1,814	10	126	54	D	36	D
Watertown town (Litchfield)	47	30	151	25	219	5	D	50	840	3	D	47	451	48	D
West Hartford CDP & town (Hartford)................	288	201	1,187	70	1,127	23	222	241	4,883	29	475	154	2,968	147	844
West Haven city & town (New Haven)	132	63	348	36	1,347	8	139	71	3,836	5	11	110	1,471	87	387
Weston town (Fairfield).....	7	39	D	12	48	9	D	5	D	12	112	5	D	3	D
Westport CDP & town (Fairfield)................	D	293	1,595	67	628	31	277	148	1,521	39	518	97	D	110	1,131
Wethersfield CDP & town (Hartford)................	84	69	479	33	363	8	59	87	1,635	10	186	62	753	47	271
Willimantic CDP..............	NA	NA	NA	NA	NA	NA	NA	NA	NA	NA	NA	NA	NA	NA	NA
Wilton town (Fairfield)	D	142	5,709	52	1,606	11	D	69	1,001	15	397	46	524	48	339
Winchester town (Litchfield)	24	14	65	12	18	1	D	33	469	4	D	16	131	19	D
Windham town (Windham)	44	30	130	13	171	3	21	87	2,780	4	D	54	906	41	178
Windsor town (Hartford) ...	149	74	2,778	49	1,104	6	161	88	2,207	6	D	62	1,017	43	582
Windsor Locks CDP & town (Hartford)............	405	16	52	16	554	2	D	18	259	4	D	49	1,136	42	480
Wolcott town (New Haven)	D	14	58	12	94	3	24	36	570	3	D	28	231	21	D
DELAWARE...................	5,402	2,543	D	1,369	22,885	190	D	2,524	61,897	409	8,102	1,987	35,609	1,513	9,841
Bear CDP	29	13	58	11	D	4	D	19	129	2	D	22	332	14	D
Brookside CDP	59	25	812	27	197	NA	NA	12	431	3	25	11	135	12	D
Dover city.......................	286	160	1,129	64	2,342	15	D	238	6,619	24	397	151	4,280	80	585
Glasgow CDP	14	30	238	17	81	4	20	46	D	4	12	24	633	14	134
Hockessin CDP................	91	71	242	29	225	8	25	53	1,070	9	370	32	495	33	174
Middletown town..............	20	31	185	10	75	5	D	57	656	7	59	51	974	30	D
Newark city.....................	192	117	1,334	44	740	11	D	159	10,058	16	195	133	3,183	66	527
Pike Creek Valley CDP	23	21	96	9	66	5	51	22	255	6	69	13	218	9	85
Smyrna town....................	17	10	39	9	30	2	D	38	D	4	D	30	D	21	129
Wilmington city	805	587	9,319	182	3,636	31	D	395	9,974	52	728	197	2,964	203	1,553
DISTRICT OF COLUMBIA	10,103	5,061	97,555	1,079	28,946	338	5,311	2,065	67,742	301	7,510	2,371	60,370	3,357	58,982
Washington city	10,103	5,061	97,555	1,079	28,946	338	5,311	2,065	67,742	301	7,510	2,371	60,370	3,357	58,982
FLORIDA	139,955	70,785	440,858	33,177	1,212,420	4,661	38,075	56,659	991,254	7,562	169,796	37,118	786,082	34,843	195,176
Alafaya CDP	183	137	387	60	309	19	45	94	593	13	D	77	2,252	38	D
Altamonte Springs city......	1,328	293	1,495	145	6,829	21	81	256	4,950	22	289	140	3,730	120	817
Apollo Beach CDP...........	36	54	141	23	D	9	29	25	163	6	47	13	64	15	45
Apopka city.....................	90	96	354	81	482	7	D	85	1,190	8	131	67	D	67	328
Atlantic Beach city	D	62	D	41	528	2	D	33	D	12	35	36	D	26	D
Auburndale city................	97	28	104	17	157	2	D	27	487	4	26	35	584	22	D
Aventura city...................	737	362	944	68	D	38	1,353	294	3,344	23	168	109	3,319	121	1,685
Azalea Park CDP.............	38	13	75	12	438	NA	NA	12	85	4	38	13	79	26	D
Bartow city......................	106	72	544	34	495	6	38	66	1,482	3	4	37	712	30	154
Bayonet Point CDP	14	21	72	12	D	2	D	51	924	1	D	22	D	24	138
Bayshore Gardens CDP ...	38	30	D	20	397	3	5	35	365	1	D	33	398	11	56
Bellair-Meadowbrook Terrace CDP	82	37	1,377	19	137	5	32	72	988	10	D	70	1,544	48	D
Belle Glade city...............	18	18	51	9	D	1	D	43	604	NA	NA	17	240	20	D
Bellview CDP	18	16	51	11	D	3	D	16	110	1	D	19	315	19	D
Bloomingdale CDP	38	56	140	30	177	7	8	36	289	7	D	26	395	18	68
Boca Raton city...............	3,486	1,459	D	441	12,853	65	319	760	10,391	99	1,725	362	10,342	419	2,390
Bonita Springs city...........	399	198	962	118	D	15	D	125	1,142	36	1,305	116	D	115	502
Boynton Beach city...........	610	353	1,510	176	1,693	16	66	353	6,284	29	744	197	4,235	189	1,270
Bradenton city.................	390	221	1,011	104	D	15	96	334	8,863	31	D	134	2,396	105	708
Brandon CDP...................	546	307	4,111	159	6,579	25	209	450	6,675	40	612	237	D	180	957
Brent CDP	160	34	760	29	5,765	3	D	51	910	4	D	38	684	53	347
Brownsville CDP..............	88	11	55	12	D	2	D	18	327	2	D	7	D	30	98
Buenaventura Lakes CDP	39	7	10	12	23	1	D	13	77	3	D	19	D	18	D
Callaway city...................	13	7	37	6	D	NA	NA	15	277	NA	NA	20	458	11	D
Cape Coral city................	534	349	1,081	297	1,112	25	D	286	2,900	37	D	212	3,797	247	1,126
Carrollwood CDP..............	201	198	722	60	616	12	143	101	1,106	19	107	83	1,655	66	336

Table C. Incorporated Places, Census Designated Places (CDPs), and Minor Civil Divisions (MCDs) of 10,000 or More Population — Economic Census

STATE City, town, township, borough, or CDP (county if applicable)	Utilities		Manufacturing		Wholesale trade[1]		Retail trade		Transportation and warehousing		Information		Finance and insurance		Real estate and rental and leasing
	Number of establish-ments	Number of employees	Number of establish-ments	Number of employees	Number of establish-ments	Number of employees	Number of establish-ments	Number of employees	Number of establish-ments	Number of employees	Number of establish-ments	Number of employees	Number of establish-ments	Number of employees	Number of establish-ments
	1	2	3	4	5	6	7	8	9	10	11	12	13	14	15
FLORIDA—Con.															
Casselberry city	2	D	26	298	26	111	128	2,264	6	D	7	23	62	395	46
Cheval CDP	NA	NA	NA	NA	4	D	8	41	2	D	3	6	22	43	2
Citrus Park CDP	NA	NA	8	17	15	D	107	1,979	10	41	6	63	26	132	15
Clearwater city	4	D	97	1,674	143	1,373	647	9,790	66	1,341	62	602	339	2,751	280
Clermont city	2	D	9	65	21	82	147	2,818	25	98	14	98	79	405	83
Cocoa city	4	D	43	693	22	161	143	1,613	13	178	7	D	36	167	27
Cocoa Beach city	NA	NA	4	11	4	D	58	700	7	D	5	7	25	111	30
Coconut Creek city	NA	NA	14	216	58	237	153	3,213	17	31	19	119	53	242	46
Conway CDP	NA	NA	3	5	5	D	16	205	4	5	3	3	11	40	5
Cooper City city	NA	NA	7	21	39	D	81	1,450	15	18	10	10	66	370	42
Coral Gables city	NA	NA	28	447	180	1,576	297	4,154	49	473	107	1,346	409	5,016	359
Coral Springs city	1	D	59	775	239	1,345	455	7,810	67	158	50	542	294	2,360	217
Coral Terrace CDP	2	D	7	61	27	139	71	420	8	27	6	8	24	104	19
Country Club CDP	NA	NA	13	96	84	316	68	1,216	24	39	2	D	33	350	20
Country Walk CDP	NA	NA	22	266	69	309	33	311	11	53	5	19	7	D	12
Crestview city	1	D	5	32	9	41	102	1,403	11	D	5	47	32	209	20
Cutler Bay town	NA	NA	4	9	28	116	165	2,223	8	D	3	D	42	187	28
Cypress Lake CDP	NA	NA	NA	NA	7	18	24	401	4	16	4	D	31	157	25
Dania Beach city	1	D	44	696	129	857	183	1,613	37	674	13	108	29	117	58
Davie town	4	D	88	1,879	262	1,782	405	5,802	79	466	36	474	169	993	196
Daytona Beach city	5	D	63	1,532	79	627	461	6,387	34	607	44	845	128	1,070	143
DeBary city	5	154	17	263	18	57	35	176	4	D	4	38	27	D	19
Deerfield Beach city	1	D	107	2,166	218	2,314	298	3,593	59	2,256	54	1,316	142	1,861	122
DeLand city	NA	NA	57	1,798	45	209	175	2,527	17	449	16	573	87	490	56
Delray Beach city	2	D	73	585	112	564	380	4,553	42	283	45	494	160	980	152
Deltona city	NA	NA	3	D	10	D	97	1,566	20	27	14	51	33	200	18
Destin city	3	D	10	40	25	284	194	2,915	33	87	18	191	51	393	102
Doctor Phillips CDP	NA	NA	3	6	20	D	42	1,021	8	31	15	60	49	253	52
Doral city	NA	NA	127	2,765	1,540	13,960	445	6,595	627	10,704	106	3,421	217	2,988	212
Dunedin city	NA	NA	18	234	29	265	123	1,010	7	90	7	65	60	294	42
East Lake CDP	NA	NA	13	406	17	26	35	618	9	24	7	45	44	135	46
East Lake-Orient Park CDP	1	D	55	1,433	152	2,761	74	629	50	1,507	19	459	87	6,217	41
East Milton CDP	1	D	3	19	3	D	10	57	10	67	1	D	1	D	2
Edgewater city	NA	NA	21	388	10	81	60	468	13	28	4	19	17	D	18
Egypt Lake-Leto CDP	1	D	7	132	28	401	87	1,886	23	98	17	131	62	1,313	52
Elfers CDP	NA	NA	5	11	8	16	59	690	7	52	NA	NA	19	165	11
Englewood CDP	2	D	12	24	6	46	85	1,299	6	11	7	40	43	264	42
Ensley CDP	1	D	21	115	26	204	88	1,518	10	78	5	43	28	183	25
Estero CDP	NA	NA	5	10	13	32	241	3,537	9	22	9	140	43	211	55
Eustis city	4	54	14	143	13	D	88	999	5	D	9	D	32	196	37
Fairview Shores CDP	NA	NA	15	143	12	89	57	608	3	D	3	D	20	99	19
Fernandina Beach city	1	D	13	902	12	86	102	1,070	12	D	8	62	38	178	35
Ferry Pass CDP	1	D	19	753	34	282	108	1,331	19	431	16	622	38	353	46
Fish Hawk CDP	NA	NA	NA	NA	3	D	13	311	4	18	NA	NA	18	57	12
Fleming Island CDP	1	D	3	6	16	34	66	1,419	10	9	11	381	33	334	40
Florida City city	NA	NA	5	55	14	104	66	1,333	1	D	5	D	8	40	11
Florida Ridge CDP	NA	NA	9	98	7	D	29	440	3	D	1	D	7	38	3
Forest City CDP	NA	NA	5	16	10	D	33	414	7	10	9	26	17	73	13
Fort Lauderdale city	5	D	282	3,899	571	5,787	1,161	12,021	418	6,291	234	6,808	673	7,978	708
Fort Myers city	7	D	93	1,720	167	2,206	688	9,914	75	1,356	68	2,475	275	1,711	212
Fort Pierce city	2	D	26	495	35	360	220	2,803	24	962	12	435	60	434	61
Fort Walton Beach city	1	D	32	1,488	39	279	151	1,861	20	824	13	234	63	490	53
Fountainebleau CDP	5	D	9	18	50	100	117	2,311	23	74	25	D	54	493	50
Four Corners CDP	NA	NA	NA	NA	8	D	24	384	8	D	1	D	5	15	62
Fruit Cove CDP	NA	NA	3	D	12	25	35	628	8	11	6	D	29	113	16
Fruitville CDP	NA	NA	43	573	60	592	79	1,460	17	124	14	263	31	444	33
Gainesville city	3	D	86	1,558	135	1,457	547	8,426	41	525	102	1,460	203	2,986	201
Gibsonton CDP	4	D	8	100	7	52	22	490	7	D	1	D	6	11	9
Gladeview CDP	NA	NA	33	467	60	752	39	352	30	458	2	D	6	7	7
Glenvar Heights CDP	NA	NA	58	528	134	606	135	1,503	15	246	19	138	34	154	79
Golden Gate CDP	NA	NA	5	12	2	D	42	548	7	7	7	D	27	102	13
Golden Glades CDP	NA	NA	9	29	13	D	84	521	10	7	7	7	14	49	21
Goldenrod CDP	NA	NA	13	148	18	127	29	345	5	D	7	40	11	76	8
Gonzalez CDP	1	D	6	69	4	27	8	35	2	D	3	D	2	D	4
Goulds CDP	NA	NA	NA	NA	3	7	21	104	2	D	1	D	1	D	4
Greenacres city	NA	NA	4	56	27	108	94	1,481	14	108	5	53	33	179	22
Gulf Gate Estates CDP	1	D	10	25	6	D	87	1,292	3	D	1	D	32	188	16
Gulfport city	NA	NA	11	52	6	45	16	66	2	D	1	D	10	43	17
Haines City city	NA	NA	16	489	13	46	67	1,035	15	281	3	D	20	D	30
Hallandale Beach city	NA	NA	34	334	80	429	137	1,858	24	45	19	52	54	352	92
Hialeah city	6	D	436	4,833	515	3,886	1,060	10,595	236	2,550	41	1,016	231	1,118	250
Hialeah Gardens city	NA	NA	42	367	61	267	97	1,421	31	133	3	D	20	52	12
Highland City CDP	NA	NA	NA	NA	3	12	4	14	3	2	NA	NA	1	D	3
Hobe Sound CDP	NA	NA	7	33	7	24	47	385	13	20	1	D	24	98	16
Holiday CDP	1	D	10	28	14	213	63	787	6	D	2	D	22	112	16
Holly Hill city	1	D	28	421	39	209	93	736	2	D	5	20	20	D	20
Hollywood city	4	D	96	1,125	285	2,279	573	6,316	98	1,970	82	856	286	2,319	297
Homestead city	4	D	19	221	41	288	182	2,386	24	67	9	80	57	394	43
Homosassa Springs CDP	1	D	3	25	1	D	37	524	1	D	1	D	6	D	9
Horizon West CDP	NA	NA	NA	NA	7	7	11	D	4	5	6	9	6	D	23
Hudson CDP	2	D	NA	NA	8	63	48	387	8	24	1	D	14	72	18
Hunters Creek CDP	NA	NA	NA	NA	8	15	30	301	9	9	3	4	19	99	35
Immokalee CDP	2	D	NA	NA	23	400	50	347	8	25	3	20	10	74	7
Iona CDP	NA	NA	7	34	12	35	83	873	5	177	5	40	21	81	30
Ives Estates CDP	NA	NA	14	51	64	388	30	224	10	91	11	D	7	23	15
Jacksonville city	14	D	579	21,616	1,075	18,668	3,011	43,471	902	23,125	443	8,692	1,679	52,738	1,093
Jacksonville Beach city	NA	NA	12	50	31	304	139	1,520	13	207	16	127	67	335	67
Jasmine Estates CDP	NA	NA	5	10	4	30	44	629	NA	NA	2	D	22	114	9

1 Merchant wholesalers, except manufacturers' sales branches and offices.

Table C. Incorporated Places, Census Designated Places (CDPs), and Minor Civil Divisions (MCDs) of 10,000 or More Population — Economic Census

STATE City, town, township, borough, or CDP (county if applicable)	Real estate and rental and leasing — Number of employees	Professional, scientific, and technical services — Number of establishments	Number of employees	Administration and support and waste management and mediation services — Number of establishments	Number of employees	Educational services — Number of establishments	Number of employees	Health care and social assistance — Number of establishments	Number of employees	Arts, entertainment, and recreation — Number of establishments	Number of employees	Accommodation and food services — Number of establishments	Number of employees	Other services (except public administration) — Number of establishments	Number of employees
	16	17	18	19	20	21	22	23	24	25	26	27	28	29	30
FLORIDA—Con.															
Casselberry city	329	89	414	69	938	12	104	74	683	10	85	70	873	68	248
Cheval CDP	D	32	51	15	D	3	25	12	65	3	D	4	D	3	D
Citrus Park CDP	63	75	358	45	231	4	5	70	616	7	56	37	686	34	273
Clearwater city	1,132	696	4,344	232	38,338	40	407	516	9,548	61	1,366	346	7,252	239	1,770
Clermont city	205	105	340	62	641	10	54	163	2,788	19	314	91	1,932	71	413
Cocoa city	105	72	363	26	347	3	D	45	D	5	36	46	643	48	258
Cocoa Beach city	129	66	196	23	237	3	3	49	D	10	D	83	1,886	60	294
Coconut Creek city	1,730	166	725	98	692	13	D	106	1,565	22	D	80	1,383	84	636
Conway CDP	12	37	92	22	107	4	8	22	104	2	D	2	D	10	38
Cooper City city	91	180	404	68	226	18	658	140	930	14	D	49	687	51	331
Coral Gables city	1,144	1,506	7,941	167	D	44	342	541	5,142	61	779	246	5,972	193	1,136
Coral Springs city	765	753	D	317	D	59	390	483	3,744	76	D	275	4,612	261	960
Coral Terrace CDP	61	61	157	37	D	4	101	126	4,884	2	D	20	D	43	D
Country Club CDP	87	62	213	33	D	1	D	73	644	6	D	34	542	34	129
Country Walk CDP	563	38	161	18	D	1	D	13	72	7	47	2	D	23	D
Crestview city	58	49	272	18	D	6	23	86	1,738	4	42	67	1,230	32	130
Cutler Bay town	68	72	344	46	D	6	19	71	1,137	8	63	66	D	40	164
Cypress Lake CDP	D	55	296	19	D	2	D	56	D	5	D	27	445	25	125
Dania Beach city	301	138	632	67	686	5	D	51	353	26	D	83	1,723	104	1,177
Davie town	604	539	1,639	236	2,802	46	244	270	2,079	50	540	195	D	266	1,282
Daytona Beach city	667	313	2,948	103	2,522	17	231	290	10,799	42	2,017	256	5,862	174	1,461
DeBary city	49	60	191	43	262	4	4	32	333	2	D	20	273	29	75
Deerfield Beach city	846	338	2,736	180	4,551	17	D	182	4,282	42	D	155	2,717	191	665
DeLand city	207	131	573	30	358	8	32	139	2,583	21	248	94	1,414	86	351
Delray Beach city	673	467	1,971	169	D	25	199	405	5,926	57	584	211	4,061	239	1,056
Deltona city	24	67	193	92	227	8	8	90	822	8	91	40	500	37	D
Destin city	400	97	366	50	3,716	6	8	46	481	21	280	111	3,749	80	364
Doctor Phillips CDP	D	95	417	40	208	11	28	70	476	12	158	62	1,778	32	190
Doral city	1,180	562	3,701	196	D	33	541	224	3,020	43	305	228	3,851	169	1,366
Dunedin city	87	154	544	58	322	13	75	127	2,214	13	84	100	1,271	74	257
East Lake CDP	D	150	243	44	101	5	25	82	377	8	259	21	308	28	175
East Lake-Orient Park CDP	469	97	4,924	83	17,939	10	D	42	1,208	7	D	43	D	57	887
East Milton CDP	D	3	D	7	D	NA	NA	2	D	NA	NA	5	D	2	D
Edgewater city	36	26	81	21	635	3	4	27	130	3	D	20	351	36	122
Egypt Lake-Leto CDP	341	93	1,509	74	D	11	89	125	2,394	5	23	41	383	35	322
Elfers CDP	27	18	94	25	D	NA	NA	53	D	NA	NA	18	237	27	D
Englewood CDP	D	47	200	32	371	2	D	60	531	11	95	42	582	51	201
Ensley CDP	90	34	177	27	183	2	D	33	318	5	53	40	663	47	440
Estero CDP	128	81	265	38	D	3	D	53	569	11	603	57	1,682	45	374
Eustis city	99	48	199	31	152	1	D	88	1,105	9	27	55	821	49	198
Fairview Shores CDP	D	57	314	34	211	6	D	39	1,279	4	D	27	343	36	194
Fernandina Beach city	D	78	243	22	126	8	80	66	700	14	289	70	D	39	D
Ferry Pass CDP	178	60	389	46	12,990	8	37	124	3,174	8	101	78	1,239	40	253
Fish Hawk CDP	13	39	98	15	32	3	D	18	139	2	D	15	456	8	16
Fleming Island CDP	D	72	229	26	140	11	49	75	648	8	256	41	896	32	202
Florida City city	29	4	14	4	15	1	D	28	302	3	D	33	696	11	41
Florida Ridge CDP	3	24	55	36	420	NA	NA	13	97	6	11	14	181	24	78
Forest City CDP	27	33	145	18	39	4	9	34	D	6	68	21	D	25	D
Fort Lauderdale city	3,644	2,319	14,924	752	46,872	93	741	938	20,654	161	1,286	710	20,279	805	4,822
Fort Myers city	1,133	489	6,695	167	3,348	31	D	423	10,677	41	1,365	282	5,994	286	1,640
Fort Pierce city	221	138	682	43	499	15	281	187	3,646	16	D	126	2,222	94	539
Fort Walton Beach city	321	94	604	56	1,420	2	D	95	D	13	136	96	2,111	66	465
Fountainebleau CDP	276	142	494	29	D	2	D	155	1,577	5	D	53	D	72	200
Four Corners CDP	774	12	22	33	69	NA	NA	8	D	5	12	33	1,286	9	71
Fruit Cove CDP	25	90	179	43	108	6	26	41	391	4	7	12	163	20	D
Fruitville CDP	136	93	943	84	649	8	22	52	1,135	6	27	26	450	55	251
Gainesville city	1,076	480	2,807	171	3,707	42	492	440	17,841	53	1,047	380	8,375	246	2,034
Gibsonton CDP	16	12	37	12	93	NA	NA	7	36	11	D	14	D	9	21
Gladeview CDP	22	8	54	9	D	NA	NA	12	100	NA	NA	14	203	15	D
Glenvar Heights CDP	232	213	1,117	42	D	11	37	121	872	13	33	43	534	92	430
Golden Gate CDP	49	22	60	45	244	2	D	29	D	1	D	33	D	17	D
Golden Glades CDP	D	30	65	20	D	6	17	71	1,227	3	1	16	D	29	146
Goldenrod CDP	12	26	110	14	111	7	17	23	D	2	D	8	D	17	D
Gonzalez CDP	5	9	20	9	31	NA	NA	5	29	NA	NA	1	D	8	9
Goulds CDP	D	2	D	7	28	2	D	10	120	NA	NA	5	35	6	D
Greenacres city	55	96	629	49	D	8	13	90	681	11	56	58	939	58	229
Gulf Gate Estates CDP	62	59	175	27	85	2	D	51	1,113	5	42	56	858	37	160
Gulfport city	25	32	45	18	25	1	D	16	D	3	D	20	232	14	D
Haines City city	111	16	57	15	98	2	D	46	459	5	92	40	560	23	97
Hallandale Beach city	188	183	663	63	D	10	D	150	1,036	31	D	85	2,230	141	632
Hialeah city	682	348	1,631	224	D	33	297	821	10,640	35	180	347	3,876	445	1,526
Hialeah Gardens city	34	29	262	38	D	1	D	37	752	5	11	30	326	68	D
Highland City CDP	3	18	32	13	22	NA	NA	9	229	3	D	1	D	4	D
Hobe Sound CDP	D	35	108	36	214	2	D	20	477	14	172	21	203	36	128
Holiday CDP	63	27	96	29	D	2	D	29	D	4	24	30	D	32	208
Holly Hill city	61	42	185	24	181	2	D	26	D	7	66	30	259	56	238
Hollywood city	3,294	905	3,385	303	4,230	44	153	568	11,497	97	1,240	330	5,683	319	1,934
Homestead city	141	80	344	57	D	9	87	181	3,526	8	D	93	1,813	63	244
Homosassa Springs CDP	29	10	12	23	D	NA	NA	15	183	1	D	9	94	11	D
Horizon West CDP	33	38	73	17	59	3	D	10	D	8	D	12	88	11	68
Hudson CDP	43	16	40	13	D	NA	NA	83	1,870	6	D	22	183	26	92
Hunters Creek CDP	D	38	74	25	71	5	14	43	584	7	94	26	425	25	141
Immokalee CDP	28	10	D	9	D	NA	NA	30	643	1	D	24	D	18	186
Iona CDP	D	40	107	26	374	2	D	21	D	10	150	24	285	36	124
Ives Estates CDP	D	30	117	12	D	1	D	14	D	4	14	9	66	15	40
Jacksonville city	6,806	2,871	28,701	1,472	50,205	210	2,444	2,302	53,374	247	6,388	1,765	33,931	1,478	D
Jacksonville Beach city	182	185	779	75	1,125	9	D	154	D	19	701	109	2,641	92	D
Jasmine Estates CDP	16	20	84	19	D	2	D	30	319	1	D	28	721	20	D

Table C. Incorporated Places, Census Designated Places (CDPs), and Minor Civil Divisions (MCDs) of 10,000 or More Population — **Economic Census**

STATE City, town, township, borough, or CDP (county if applicable)	Utilities — Number of establishments	Utilities — Number of employees	Manufacturing — Number of establishments	Manufacturing — Number of employees	Wholesale trade[1] — Number of establishments	Wholesale trade[1] — Number of employees	Retail trade — Number of establishments	Retail trade — Number of employees	Transportation and warehousing — Number of establishments	Transportation and warehousing — Number of employees	Information — Number of establishments	Information — Number of employees	Finance and insurance — Number of establishments	Finance and insurance — Number of employees	Real estate and rental and leasing — Number of establishments
	1	2	3	4	5	6	7	8	9	10	11	12	13	14	15
FLORIDA—Con.															
Jensen Beach CDP	NA	NA	10	58	9	65	156	2,493	14	29	5	D	33	210	24
Jupiter town	10	D	57	777	100	669	257	2,886	32	804	28	308	176	879	160
Jupiter Farms CDP	1	D	6	16	7	D	19	204	6	14	4	4	5	17	16
Kendale Lakes CDP	NA	NA	8	16	39	79	95	1,228	29	200	7	D	41	166	20
Kendall CDP	NA	NA	43	321	179	719	489	10,610	30	96	45	391	232	2,677	178
Kendall West CDP	NA	NA	NA	NA	9	17	42	526	15	21	2	D	15	70	15
Key Biscayne village	NA	NA	5	16	29	67	47	299	5	12	7	14	40	127	76
Key Largo CDP	1	D	11	23	9	D	80	952	18	42	6	27	27	90	40
Keystone CDP	1	D	22	583	30	173	44	305	9	15	9	29	27	63	27
Key West city	NA	NA	11	63	18	29	321	2,682	50	611	17	230	42	347	115
Kissimmee city	NA	NA	28	125	49	D	366	4,823	58	275	22	172	110	696	147
Lady Lake town	1	D	4	39	5	D	85	1,728	7	76	4	D	24	107	16
Lake Butler CDP	NA	NA	3	D	9	14	14	195	5	7	3	D	14	25	29
Lake City city	4	D	21	466	31	446	196	2,543	19	749	11	111	55	480	36
Lakeland city	1	D	82	3,922	156	2,930	559	8,370	90	5,118	39	857	260	4,747	194
Lakeland Highlands CDP	NA	NA	3	7	10	85	25	220	2	D	1	D	16	D	15
Lake Magdalene CDP	3	D	5	16	23	166	109	1,699	7	18	11	216	63	368	49
Lake Mary city	4	D	16	667	56	692	73	1,173	7	211	78	1,761	152	5,197	63
Lakeside CDP	2	D	8	37	13	55	101	1,548	10	26	9	D	30	114	28
Lake Wales city	3	D	13	1,015	11	170	125	1,905	9	153	6	56	47	D	22
Lakewood Park CDP	NA	NA	NA	NA	NA	NA	15	153	3	3	1	D	2	D	3
Lake Worth city	NA	NA	45	244	43	331	120	888	23	153	14	D	35	127	43
Land O' Lakes CDP	NA	NA	15	44	36	183	98	1,136	16	42	6	32	58	239	36
Lantana town	NA	NA	12	93	8	18	97	985	8	106	4	D	24	127	19
Largo city	3	D	107	2,541	102	D	330	4,311	27	173	38	222	131	778	115
Lauderdale Lakes city	NA	NA	8	32	20	102	73	1,072	11	51	4	D	23	156	20
Lauderhill city	NA	NA	19	158	41	D	198	1,478	18	D	7	D	43	222	56
Lealman CDP	NA	NA	28	355	26	241	76	394	11	117	3	D	10	36	17
Leesburg city	1	D	23	548	51	348	226	3,075	21	475	12	536	68	413	47
Lehigh Acres CDP	2	D	13	83	15	D	96	1,430	19	79	1	D	33	227	46
Leisure City CDP	NA	NA	NA	NA	4	1	28	258	3	D	1	D	8	D	9
Lighthouse Point city	NA	NA	5	36	23	D	48	767	7	8	2	D	33	162	34
Lockhart CDP	NA	NA	25	1,204	25	158	37	279	13	53	1	D	7	D	12
Longwood city	2	D	66	1,324	92	493	166	1,458	13	639	14	56	63	477	38
Lutz CDP	1	D	12	69	22	D	68	1,098	10	25	8	16	39	173	34
Lynn Haven city	NA	NA	11	890	9	204	52	1,026	5	175	2	D	26	230	21
Maitland city	NA	NA	12	138	38	D	52	681	5	D	71	3,351	213	5,680	89
Mango CDP	NA	NA	NA	NA	7	21	23	439	6	D	NA	NA	4	13	10
Marco Island city	2	D	4	19	17	46	97	890	18	120	7	66	41	149	95
Margate city	1	D	30	154	62	411	171	2,476	21	88	12	91	90	586	51
Meadow Woods CDP	NA	NA	NA	NA	7	D	14	228	17	30	2	D	2	D	8
Melbourne city	4	D	96	5,615	102	1,461	464	6,067	46	448	60	1,499	173	1,583	170
Merritt Island CDP	1	D	17	351	27	99	185	2,898	16	D	14	117	64	432	55
Miami city	7	D	343	3,948	1,440	8,474	2,398	21,175	492	16,573	381	4,917	1,192	14,594	1,169
Miami Beach city	1	D	29	99	151	415	561	5,912	40	139	114	1,002	193	1,304	457
Miami Gardens city	1	D	68	1,871	180	3,106	302	4,416	36	516	33	748	68	1,163	69
Miami Lakes town	NA	NA	24	2,155	113	1,305	72	1,372	45	328	26	352	128	2,266	85
Miami Shores village	NA	NA	NA	NA	15	172	30	458	4	5	9	8	21	93	13
Miami Springs city	NA	NA	6	20	18	91	38	178	18	153	10	44	16	106	18
Middleburg CDP	NA	NA	3	7	6	D	38	877	9	23	2	D	10	54	8
Midway CDP (Santa Rosa County)	2	D	9	75	8	14	39	313	2	D	6	46	13	44	24
Miramar city	NA	NA	33	825	198	2,748	198	3,297	78	1,459	66	2,521	109	2,411	72
Mount Dora city	NA	NA	9	141	16	D	85	1,623	5	22	3	D	38	274	27
Myrtle Grove CDP	NA	NA	NA	NA	4	7	25	309	NA	NA	1	D	6	D	6
Naples city	6	D	32	422	50	292	671	9,282	43	601	50	1,195	268	1,648	289
Navarre CDP	2	D	7	19	6	46	42	758	4	D	2	D	26	105	26
New Port Richey city	1	D	16	547	24	69	117	1,887	3	D	6	35	63	346	50
New Smyrna Beach city	1	D	17	142	16	73	133	1,957	10	D	8	38	56	251	58
Niceville city	1	D	5	D	6	25	53	682	7	42	2	D	30	141	25
Northdale CDP	NA	NA	13	43	16	26	49	896	10	10	5	30	34	157	34
North Fort Myers CDP	1	D	23	291	17	126	141	1,473	16	54	15	163	39	537	53
North Lauderdale city	1	D	11	44	7	D	70	961	18	D	4	D	16	92	18
North Miami city	NA	NA	27	468	76	364	188	1,749	21	121	26	283	65	339	90
North Miami Beach city	1	D	23	247	57	156	191	2,470	15	143	20	261	76	640	72
North Palm Beach village	NA	NA	5	24	13	71	45	236	7	12	4	31	38	186	33
North Port city	1	D	12	247	23	133	80	1,454	16	21	12	56	35	164	29
Oakland Park city	2	D	103	724	114	811	252	2,047	38	328	17	146	108	804	96
Oakleaf Plantation CDP	NA	NA	NA	NA	1	D	8	8	3	D	NA	NA	3	4	6
Oak Ridge CDP	NA	NA	7	515	17	662	42	948	13	106	4	9	18	D	19
Ocala city	7	D	105	3,819	166	2,285	631	9,325	88	1,758	44	1,101	232	1,760	171
Ocoee city	NA	NA	13	192	32	632	160	2,639	30	225	11	173	43	222	30
Ojus CDP	NA	NA	11	47	35	114	41	131	4	17	5	3	26	122	42
Oldsmar city	2	D	63	1,138	62	565	74	1,002	10	D	19	421	40	737	29
Olympia Heights CDP	NA	NA	3	11	10	20	44	291	5	D	1	D	24	132	11
Opa-locka city	NA	NA	67	1,077	95	883	110	533	51	571	5	D	8	30	32
Orange City city	NA	NA	13	170	24	114	117	2,136	3	19	10	79	40	275	24
Orlando city	4	D	253	11,032	634	8,653	1,580	27,103	324	15,788	236	6,268	668	7,416	762
Ormond Beach city	4	D	40	820	44	767	195	2,299	16	164	12	69	93	566	74
Oviedo city	NA	NA	13	44	31	D	148	2,331	9	24	9	101	73	369	66
Pace CDP	1	D	5	88	9	D	67	1,306	7	86	5	D	35	147	18
Palatka city	3	D	19	1,442	11	93	122	1,629	11	151	12	108	37	264	26
Palm Bay city	1	D	39	8,936	32	202	170	2,500	38	D	9	305	53	285	54
Palm Beach Gardens city	1	D	24	489	68	341	348	6,747	30	419	43	635	230	2,088	138
Palm City CDP	1	D	14	225	29	D	36	521	14	D	7	D	53	224	38
Palm Coast city	1	D	21	428	36	100	140	2,406	39	92	16	D	82	450	98
Palmetto city	3	D	24	143	14	71	60	928	12	266	3	4	23	140	17
Palmetto Bay village	1	D	9	36	44	176	112	2,135	9	7	17	82	65	419	49
Palmetto Estates CDP	NA	NA	NA	NA	5	12	25	280	3	6	1	D	5	19	3

1 Merchant wholesalers, except manufacturers' sales branches and offices.

Table C. Incorporated Places, Census Designated Places (CDPs), and Minor Civil Divisions (MCDs) of 10,000 or More Population — **Economic Census**

Economic activity by sector, 2012

STATE City, town, township, borough, or CDP (county if applicable)	Real estate and rental and leasing — Number of employees	Professional, scientific, and technical services — Number of establishments	Professional... — Number of employees	Administration and support and waste management and mediation services — Number of establishments	Admin... — Number of employees	Educational services — Number of establishments	Educational — Number of employees	Health care and social assistance — Number of establishments	Health — Number of employees	Arts, entertainment, and recreation — Number of establishments	Arts — Number of employees	Accommodation and food services — Number of establishments	Accommodation — Number of employees	Other services (except public administration) — Number of establishments	Other — Number of employees
	16	17	18	19	20	21	22	23	24	25	26	27	28	29	30
FLORIDA—Con.															
Jensen Beach CDP	110	52	219	35	1,222	4	27	40	453	8	D	65	1,245	38	136
Jupiter town	862	453	2,227	171	2,671	26	94	338	3,821	49	1,356	151	3,307	187	1,191
Jupiter Farms CDP	36	54	83	43	D	2	D	12	31	9	31	7	78	27	D
Kendale Lakes CDP	48	84	230	70	D	9	41	102	663	10	43	48	D	48	93
Kendall CDP	530	666	D	144	D	38	807	540	9,503	24	211	179	3,546	173	1,012
Kendall West CDP	32	35	46	33	D	4	4	31	141	5	9	20	219	19	45
Key Biscayne village	142	109	157	22	D	12	D	41	125	16	99	34	972	46	375
Key Largo CDP	70	37	104	27	140	6	37	27	D	20	240	59	1,115	43	137
Keystone CDP	D	141	374	60	757	5	21	38	133	8	51	25	D	25	67
Key West city	520	145	530	59	245	10	37	102	1,245	49	380	262	5,760	60	268
Kissimmee city	584	177	811	135	1,787	16	88	294	5,389	22	957	209	5,035	125	630
Lady Lake town	26	21	90	18	801	4	15	52	854	3	D	36	900	21	D
Lake Butler CDP	D	76	218	32	453	5	27	29	61	10	55	15	D	10	33
Lake City city	164	84	337	34	1,246	1	D	153	4,227	10	D	93	1,751	49	196
Lakeland city	1,027	358	2,657	166	4,493	18	88	417	13,181	33	693	246	5,649	171	971
Lakeland Highlands CDP	25	54	238	25	1,239	1	D	22	D	1	D	12	246	18	89
Lake Magdalene CDP	144	141	406	58	512	16	237	120	1,639	7	D	48	767	45	D
Lake Mary city	247	190	2,161	65	2,573	18	136	161	1,656	11	120	89	2,121	41	271
Lakeside CDP	82	53	264	43	329	15	79	73	983	6	D	54	945	56	199
Lake Wales city	73	44	175	14	212	2	D	68	1,125	6	D	50	867	35	124
Lakewood Park CDP	D	6	6	10	23	1	D	6	40	6	25	8	143	6	D
Lake Worth city	88	121	555	78	D	7	22	81	1,122	18	84	63	683	78	334
Land O' Lakes CDP	219	103	738	47	D	11	68	92	881	17	187	40	749	62	279
Lantana town	33	34	105	25	D	3	13	32	422	5	10	51	769	38	D
Largo city	569	220	2,075	148	2,876	22	105	261	8,586	31	219	183	2,788	188	906
Lauderdale Lakes city	282	28	D	29	614	2	D	97	2,075	1	D	35	391	41	142
Lauderhill city	635	98	342	40	391	11	85	140	1,830	16	D	82	944	113	431
Lealman CDP	41	19	73	31	D	5	30	45	1,191	3	D	21	321	31	169
Leesburg city	235	79	348	50	721	6	36	202	4,685	12	D	81	1,482	70	517
Lehigh Acres CDP	151	61	234	94	D	4	D	74	1,300	7	112	46	643	47	172
Leisure City CDP	50	4	11	7	D	1	D	22	277	2	D	13	165	16	44
Lighthouse Point city	92	98	251	23	D	7	D	54	309	13	124	24	356	30	147
Lockhart CDP	37	22	165	36	123	1	D	11	D	3	D	9	D	23	87
Longwood city	508	139	847	76	1,595	12	91	115	2,560	16	287	59	596	104	512
Lutz CDP	86	106	501	50	438	6	18	79	691	4	D	29	407	36	104
Lynn Haven city	56	30	186	18	92	2	D	37	516	3	D	28	476	21	D
Maitland city	741	335	4,000	80	4,892	10	124	142	3,222	12	1,051	45	749	66	437
Mango CDP	64	5	46	5	34	NA	NA	2	D	1	D	12	126	11	D
Marco Island city	327	81	207	49	223	4	10	38	176	11	197	78	2,380	76	586
Margate city	171	133	648	95	2,096	12	265	162	2,286	14	D	98	D	113	399
Meadow Woods CDP	11	7	5	22	32	4	11	12	56	2	D	5	D	9	D
Melbourne city	628	399	3,608	166	4,820	34	419	444	11,805	35	478	213	4,009	196	1,033
Merritt Island CDP	224	134	603	57	1,549	12	48	148	1,855	17	65	83	1,663	66	289
Miami city	4,273	3,527	22,110	815	D	120	967	1,874	39,678	236	4,798	1,267	26,462	1,070	6,835
Miami Beach city	1,556	662	2,072	154	D	33	253	426	6,701	125	1,063	626	23,117	290	2,156
Miami Gardens city	266	78	335	46	D	11	321	180	1,916	24	D	100	1,628	83	385
Miami Lakes town	607	270	1,165	92	D	12	148	200	2,817	17	109	54	1,634	59	677
Miami Shores village	22	80	148	20	D	4	D	48	259	10	247	14	225	24	62
Miami Springs city	76	36	82	20	D	6	D	52	698	9	215	42	759	19	106
Middleburg CDP	13	10	51	16	55	NA	NA	10	D	3	D	15	145	20	D
Midway CDP (Santa Rosa County)	23	37	132	29	92	6	D	33	342	3	D	15	214	20	100
Miramar city	466	271	1,455	131	3,117	19	318	225	D	26	D	118	1,660	114	520
Mount Dora city	99	61	228	19	43	2	D	78	1,507	12	87	45	862	29	150
Myrtle Grove CDP	19	12	45	6	30	1	D	20	D	2	D	12	177	10	30
Naples city	936	443	1,955	131	1,272	23	66	420	8,184	53	893	335	8,915	286	1,657
Navarre CDP	43	45	D	26	72	1	D	35	315	3	74	33	493	24	D
New Port Richey city	154	92	660	33	D	8	87	198	3,179	10	25	66	853	58	257
New Smyrna Beach city	179	88	241	43	293	5	3	94	1,307	17	D	76	1,359	103	454
Niceville city	104	45	266	19	135	2	D	48	D	6	32	37	634	23	107
Northdale CDP	D	90	242	45	252	8	27	84	848	8	331	36	534	17	D
North Fort Myers CDP	246	58	236	56	D	3	D	48	617	14	D	67	1,125	64	316
North Lauderdale city	70	40	D	35	D	3	D	49	694	6	23	28	364	35	189
North Miami city	276	158	521	57	D	11	71	149	3,350	20	D	104	1,478	115	683
North Miami Beach city	239	213	734	78	D	22	211	222	4,772	16	280	124	1,833	96	453
North Palm Beach village	D	114	374	35	D	1	D	63	337	11	67	24	374	41	142
North Port city	50	62	137	66	322	5	10	60	736	6	91	38	682	44	141
Oakland Park city	430	221	964	134	1,863	18	173	164	1,438	15	158	100	1,691	179	574
Oakleaf Plantation CDP	3	13	20	12	44	1	D	6	D	NA	NA	2	D	NA	NA
Oak Ridge CDP	93	7	D	21	454	3	D	14	77	NA	NA	20	D	9	D
Ocala city	897	383	1,854	169	3,934	23	140	579	12,993	21	294	251	5,431	216	1,383
Ocoee city	241	92	412	58	900	10	45	106	2,660	17	D	77	904	59	D
Ojus CDP	D	68	168	24	D	6	12	55	740	5	D	25	237	49	151
Oldsmar city	135	90	836	47	918	13	26	37	D	9	D	51	953	44	D
Olympia Heights CDP	13	42	158	26	D	4	10	46	D	3	3	17	224	22	224
Opa-locka city	140	17	126	19	D	7	47	29	193	2	D	17	149	54	369
Orange City city	75	36	133	20	250	6	50	126	2,619	7	101	61	1,315	40	D
Orlando city	7,122	2,019	22,472	678	33,664	104	1,472	989	33,440	163	17,181	999	26,376	677	5,817
Ormond Beach city	338	172	654	87	613	14	66	231	2,606	32	D	118	2,321	99	642
Oviedo city	186	141	637	64	313	13	103	126	1,054	14	115	62	1,202	55	D
Pace CDP	54	37	156	18	69	1	D	26	D	4	26	35	623	21	D
Palatka city	97	43	136	16	103	1	D	109	1,789	5	49	42	763	39	212
Palm Bay city	143	100	636	147	661	9	42	143	1,816	18	110	108	1,820	95	360
Palm Beach Gardens city	730	501	2,429	138	D	22	142	329	3,918	48	714	143	4,820	132	1,050
Palm City CDP	323	125	443	48	506	8	42	66	502	19	343	33	D	47	293
Palm Coast city	D	128	288	106	D	6	D	156	2,325	19	490	91	D	75	332
Palmetto city	41	42	206	18	488	5	13	37	543	9	129	25	348	38	176
Palmetto Bay village	113	162	455	54	D	15	124	101	D	15	73	48	D	50	223
Palmetto Estates CDP	D	10	42	19	D	2	D	29	254	NA	NA	14	88	9	76

Table C. Incorporated Places, Census Designated Places (CDPs), and Minor Civil Divisions (MCDs) of 10,000 or More Population — Economic Census

Economic activity by sector, 2012

STATE City, town, township, borough, or CDP (county if applicable)	Utilities Number of establish-ments	Utilities Number of employees	Manufacturing Number of establish-ments	Manufacturing Number of employees	Wholesale trade[1] Number of establish-ments	Wholesale trade[1] Number of employees	Retail trade Number of establish-ments	Retail trade Number of employees	Transportation and warehousing Number of establish-ments	Transportation and warehousing Number of employees	Information Number of establish-ments	Information Number of employees	Finance and insurance Number of establish-ments	Finance and insurance Number of employees	Real estate and rental and leasing Number of establish-ments
	1	2	3	4	5	6	7	8	9	10	11	12	13	14	15
FLORIDA—Con.															
Palm Harbor CDP	1	D	29	223	41	283	185	2,259	22	47	23	235	108	486	95
Palm River-Clair Mel CDP	2	D	28	399	63	2,035	56	849	35	491	7	388	15	317	26
Palm Springs village	NA	NA	9	24	14	197	93	1,198	7	19	7	39	34	240	22
Palm Valley CDP	NA	NA	3	6	23	106	35	319	10	26	12	53	50	240	33
Panama City city	1	D	39	1,448	68	765	338	4,441	37	610	33	567	126	1,218	98
Panama City Beach city	1	D	4	17	18	85	165	2,330	5	11	10	575	28	225	54
Parkland city	NA	NA	NA	NA	40	D	25	242	12	D	11	21	33	62	44
Pembroke Pines city	NA	NA	46	249	202	702	577	10,690	85	325	64	958	200	1,967	159
Pensacola city	14	D	49	766	67	641	418	6,109	40	662	50	669	218	1,887	122
Pine Castle CDP	NA	NA	13	231	16	100	34	170	10	15	4	D	4	17	8
Pinecrest village	NA	NA	NA	NA	26	61	42	426	3	25	9	D	34	205	47
Pine Hills CDP	NA	NA	4	21	7	38	108	1,183	27	23	4	112	24	125	26
Pinellas Park city	3	D	238	7,383	166	2,065	284	3,773	46	877	18	364	90	1,668	67
Pinewood CDP	NA	NA	NA	NA	3	12	45	446	1	D	NA	NA	3	43	7
Plantation city	7	D	41	268	120	490	348	5,590	65	1,075	58	771	246	2,746	198
Plant City city	2	D	49	1,795	79	1,769	157	2,140	31	603	10	D	71	411	46
Poinciana CDP	NA	NA	NA	NA	NA	NA	21	643	18	21	NA	NA	10	D	9
Pompano Beach city	4	D	250	5,908	454	6,291	624	8,020	139	2,207	53	741	157	923	228
Port Charlotte CDP	1	D	22	101	35	146	266	3,689	11	D	13	138	86	448	53
Port Orange city	1	D	18	210	34	D	164	2,608	27	72	10	149	69	423	94
Port St. John CDP	1	D	NA	NA	2	D	23	325	4	7	NA	NA	6	D	4
Port St. Lucie city	6	D	48	840	81	489	334	8,054	71	215	34	466	143	687	139
Port Salerno CDP	NA	NA	NA	NA	7	11	18	274	3	7	2	D	8	54	8
Princeton CDP	1	D	NA	NA	14	99	28	149	14	307	4	D	4	14	3
Punta Gorda city	1	D	7	38	25	87	74	966	7	129	6	25	51	251	47
Richmond West CDP	NA	NA	NA	NA	24	38	23	383	12	15	4	D	7	17	12
Riverview CDP	NA	NA	5	D	25	385	129	1,734	41	155	10	D	75	1,080	38
Riviera Beach city	5	D	69	1,424	102	2,211	106	878	46	1,376	14	157	22	96	44
Rockledge city	NA	NA	40	872	34	305	79	784	14	236	8	45	42	223	21
Royal Palm Beach village	3	D	5	15	32	184	154	3,525	18	91	9	124	51	265	23
Ruskin CDP	1	D	12	312	9	59	46	397	6	D	3	D	21	90	14
Safety Harbor city	NA	NA	26	559	26	D	40	257	3	D	13	34	43	454	24
St. Augustine city	NA	NA	26	199	22	119	264	2,030	14	231	11	37	65	325	57
St. Cloud city	1	D	15	163	12	D	127	1,765	10	28	6	28	31	160	43
St. Petersburg city	9	D	148	4,906	187	2,580	905	13,444	79	391	104	5,979	540	13,763	347
San Carlos Park CDP	1	D	6	32	8	33	34	178	8	9	2	D	13	44	18
Sanford city	1	D	59	1,596	88	1,374	358	5,781	33	577	19	189	75	433	70
Sarasota city	4	D	57	552	88	651	505	5,274	23	429	52	1,397	287	2,355	242
Sarasota Springs CDP	NA	NA	4	18	6	30	23	225	9	19	3	4	17	79	15
Satellite Beach city	1	D	NA	NA	8	D	21	255	NA	NA	1	D	24	63	11
Sebastian city	1	D	12	50	11	D	68	975	7	30	4	12	29	122	28
Sebring city	4	D	18	296	20	D	146	2,516	8	D	10	99	53	336	29
Seminole city	NA	NA	6	11	5	D	96	1,845	4	8	8	104	55	249	30
Shady Hills CDP	1	D	NA	NA	2	D	13	67	7	14	1	D	2	D	2
South Bradenton CDP	NA	NA	12	66	10	71	88	1,155	5	26	10	62	26	138	30
Southchase CDP	NA	NA	10	250	25	175	55	860	13	137	6	74	14	45	17
South Daytona city	NA	NA	14	73	12	D	70	568	2	D	5	D	19	D	15
South Miami city	NA	NA	9	19	21	53	126	992	5	4	10	245	36	236	53
South Miami Heights CDP	NA	NA	NA	NA	11	33	49	834	5	15	3	D	29	D	16
South Venice CDP	NA	NA	NA	NA	7	D	49	809	4	10	3	D	17	58	6
Spring Hill CDP	NA	NA	41	765	46	151	202	3,428	31	82	20	103	110	486	71
Stuart city	1	D	56	956	57	360	307	4,299	17	135	29	599	144	1,167	86
Sun City Center CDP	NA	NA	NA	NA	1	D	36	603	3	3	NA	NA	36	135	10
Sunny Isles Beach city	NA	NA	NA	NA	44	92	58	662	12	27	13	48	28	104	80
Sunrise city	4	D	71	495	262	2,458	544	10,882	64	619	56	1,941	162	3,511	122
Sunset CDP	NA	NA	5	18	30	79	50	441	10	21	5	D	39	606	31
Sweetwater city	NA	NA	8	24	71	457	156	2,913	25	162	NA	NA	31	167	22
Tallahassee city	8	D	77	1,297	176	1,987	854	13,278	71	1,044	169	3,203	448	4,201	331
Tamarac city	NA	NA	20	370	60	1,056	131	2,294	34	127	18	342	86	552	63
Tamiami CDP	1	D	9	26	56	90	114	994	36	97	11	13	47	225	49
Tampa city	12	1,361	303	5,894	646	9,863	1,878	24,934	274	9,857	327	10,878	1,160	23,171	856
Tarpon Springs city	1	D	27	335	35	210	130	1,109	11	35	12	136	52	166	40
Tavares city	NA	NA	13	110	7	D	46	361	5	44	2	D	22	101	20
Temple Terrace city	NA	NA	8	538	26	226	76	1,074	8	55	26	D	49	698	35
The Acreage CDP	2	D	16	34	25	D	23	249	27	41	5	4	15	25	17
The Crossings CDP	NA	NA	4	8	31	122	45	715	12	16	7	D	18	72	26
The Hammocks CDP	1	D	8	D	51	67	68	903	15	24	6	9	34	125	27
The Villages CDP	NA	NA	NA	NA	10	20	67	1,494	5	D	4	D	38	322	43
Thonotosassa CDP	NA	NA	NA	NA	12	100	25	539	10	D	4	8	1	D	8
Three Lakes CDP	1	D	71	1,366	203	1,248	90	484	31	224	24	174	52	266	57
Titusville city	3	D	37	433	21	236	168	2,468	24	286	15	201	60	281	35
Town 'n' Country CDP	2	D	84	2,402	182	2,446	244	4,205	75	951	57	2,385	111	3,779	87
Trinity CDP	NA	NA	NA	NA	6	14	18	414	10	35	1	D	28	183	24
Union Park CDP	NA	NA	NA	NA	5	16	25	147	4	D	NA	NA	11	D	8
University CDP (Hillsborough County)	NA	NA	7	48	21	77	134	1,347	6	18	6	D	12	73	40
University CDP (Orange County)	2	D	14	554	14	271	55	701	3	D	20	1,307	45	871	33
University Park CDP	NA	NA	5	9	18	52	96	1,176	11	17	5	15	37	371	31
Upper Grand Lagoon CDP	NA	NA	10	108	10	70	39	300	15	151	4	D	22	127	24
Valrico CDP	NA	NA	4	12	15	37	52	609	11	59	3	2	28	54	36
Venice city	1	D	23	1,264	29	123	158	1,753	9	57	12	129	66	447	64
Vero Beach city	NA	NA	19	927	40	D	215	1,697	17	113	19	416	137	857	84
Vero Beach South CDP	NA	NA	12	34	20	D	88	1,726	11	34	7	148	37	202	28
Viera East CDP	NA	NA	NA	NA	3	22	10	72	3	D	NA	NA	14	587	7
Villas CDP	NA	NA	16	79	27	156	82	1,369	3	D	11	168	33	221	46
Warrington CDP	1	D	8	42	4	D	43	474	3	9	4	D	6	D	12
Wekiwa Springs CDP	NA	NA	4	D	20	63	20	158	9	19	8	48	41	284	42
Wellington village	1	D	22	191	78	239	243	3,279	21	43	21	99	93	427	117

1 Merchant wholesalers, except manufacturers' sales branches and offices.

Table C. Incorporated Places, Census Designated Places (CDPs), and Minor Civil Divisions (MCDs) of 10,000 or More Population — **Economic Census**

	Real estate and rental and leasing	Professional, scientific, and technical services		Administration and support and waste management and mediation services		Educational services		Health care and social assistance		Arts, entertainment, and recreation		Accommodation and food services		Other services (except public administration)	
STATE City, town, township, borough, or CDP (county if applicable)	Number of employees	Number of establishments	Number of employees	Number of establishments	Number of employees	Number of establishments	Number of employees	Number of establishments	Number of employees	Number of establishments	Number of employees	Number of establishments	Number of employees	Number of establishments	Number of employees
	16	17	18	19	20	21	22	23	24	25	26	27	28	29	30
FLORIDA—Con.															
Palm Harbor CDP	241	256	1,726	120	538	21	143	242	3,528	30	350	116	2,482	121	425
Palm River-Clair Mel CDP	273	27	421	18	227	NA	NA	15	73	NA	NA	16	D	35	D
Palm Springs village	86	51	253	37	D	4	D	117	1,019	1	D	43	521	43	126
Palm Valley CDP	D	129	343	43	865	10	47	59	D	14	831	22	845	44	D
Panama City city	488	200	1,542	64	1,648	18	138	326	7,615	20	243	167	3,198	103	629
Panama City Beach city	387	40	483	33	1,004	2	D	30	238	26	D	123	3,677	55	434
Parkland city	D	161	234	48	241	11	D	67	D	13	D	13	123	12	D
Pembroke Pines city	506	563	1,725	229	2,612	50	224	592	7,016	60	D	285	5,958	212	1,163
Pensacola city	590	452	4,625	130	7,416	22	111	417	13,681	25	804	212	5,204	153	1,134
Pine Castle CDP	26	15	D	23	314	2	D	9	56	1	D	13	177	15	D
Pinecrest village	94	166	626	24	D	13	40	63	D	13	28	21	402	19	D
Pine Hills CDP	103	28	67	36	201	7	9	121	760	5	D	45	927	41	172
Pinellas Park city	263	168	1,250	124	2,274	14	137	170	2,951	16	126	106	1,876	148	867
Pinewood CDP	33	9	33	3	D	NA	NA	45	1,768	1	D	16	185	12	69
Plantation city	1,034	724	4,448	257	6,420	48	350	603	7,234	53	D	188	3,356	206	1,002
Plant City city	146	92	394	44	642	4	11	134	2,083	9	604	76	D	60	349
Poinciana CDP	D	15	36	22	104	1	D	10	D	4	43	17	D	13	46
Pompano Beach city	930	471	1,768	247	3,459	25	142	332	4,348	53	D	249	3,807	340	2,048
Port Charlotte CDP	189	123	453	77	4,082	10	D	262	4,559	21	287	93	2,169	109	366
Port Orange city	362	120	901	112	671	15	29	137	1,404	23	327	103	2,310	96	424
Port St. John CDP	12	8	53	11	15	1	D	16	D	2	D	21	349	12	31
Port St. Lucie city	353	279	1,264	272	2,202	23	130	384	5,477	40	654	204	3,628	171	735
Port Salerno CDP	D	19	30	20	38	3	D	10	D	5	33	15	270	16	103
Princeton CDP	19	7	6	12	38	NA	NA	13	200	NA	NA	8	44	4	11
Punta Gorda city	146	89	306	32	167	1	D	88	1,705	11	102	48	943	40	283
Richmond West CDP	18	32	42	27	D	NA	NA	31	158	2	D	14	151	23	34
Riverview CDP	D	124	443	60	605	12	25	79	D	17	154	86	1,254	55	366
Riviera Beach city	312	49	464	38	D	7	72	57	2,203	10	289	39	836	87	625
Rockledge city	101	81	419	51	498	4	D	118	3,314	13	124	46	734	39	D
Royal Palm Beach village	38	117	547	71	D	13	30	124	1,039	14	140	95	1,883	70	435
Ruskin CDP	64	15	42	23	D	NA	NA	25	317	1	D	21	295	27	124
Safety Harbor city	61	118	331	49	240	5	11	103	3,088	6	13	40	467	43	276
St. Augustine city	250	129	557	51	509	13	41	91	1,318	30	D	191	3,464	70	D
St. Cloud city	132	53	163	48	165	6	D	76	1,514	5	D	61	1,042	46	198
St. Petersburg city	1,614	1,166	11,552	427	73,004	74	850	945	18,690	95	2,447	525	9,116	476	2,450
San Carlos Park CDP	32	34	58	43	D	2	D	10	D	1	D	16	294	17	37
Sanford city	417	130	849	78	2,248	13	D	131	2,124	16	201	119	2,238	111	578
Sarasota city	768	626	3,193	168	2,616	19	62	510	10,958	64	1,672	286	6,049	247	1,437
Sarasota Springs CDP	45	53	D	42	1,063	4	8	58	944	4	D	18	222	26	96
Satellite Beach city	32	50	313	22	50	3	18	31	D	4	D	20	267	17	28
Sebastian city	D	55	182	53	155	6	11	50	D	9	D	38	D	37	192
Sebring city	78	51	267	26	974	5	5	128	1,335	11	D	69	1,347	53	241
Seminole city	170	80	279	33	166	7	36	99	5,339	11	D	54	742	61	304
Shady Hills CDP	D	17	55	19	D	1	D	9	44	NA	NA	1	D	15	43
South Bradenton CDP	113	36	154	32	431	2	D	56	691	3	D	39	848	41	126
Southchase CDP	126	15	59	31	341	3	6	23	154	7	121	25	D	26	132
South Daytona city	64	34	244	25	340	4	D	37	D	5	D	35	384	39	117
South Miami city	D	160	530	35	D	8	62	239	2,314	9	D	53	1,200	83	500
South Miami Heights CDP	112	14	32	23	D	NA	NA	30	492	1	D	20	253	25	49
South Venice CDP	13	23	79	25	D	3	16	42	352	5	13	23	260	17	D
Spring Hill CDP	155	152	594	105	D	11	74	335	4,689	21	223	139	2,068	105	414
Stuart city	786	276	1,715	85	659	15	23	311	5,111	19	183	132	2,466	125	543
Sun City Center CDP	37	24	110	11	D	3	D	78	2,257	8	167	19	427	15	166
Sunny Isles Beach city	367	84	114	28	D	7	17	30	D	18	68	68	2,132	58	381
Sunrise city	492	364	2,464	215	10,092	38	133	272	4,625	39	829	187	4,135	145	705
Sunset CDP	D	114	364	27	D	5	D	184	1,624	8	D	27	315	20	71
Sweetwater city	161	25	143	21	D	5	22	54	D	1	D	42	413	34	199
Tallahassee city	1,808	1,165	10,454	274	4,043	85	696	699	16,073	76	1,188	588	13,051	531	4,150
Tamarac city	250	166	553	110	2,344	7	D	222	3,112	20	187	63	926	75	240
Tamiami CDP	191	114	248	45	D	4	5	203	1,195	6	24	64	780	74	186
Tampa city	5,003	2,684	32,804	763	50,214	122	2,667	1,488	34,012	182	7,391	1,087	25,033	957	7,966
Tarpon Springs city	125	106	318	61	671	7	36	88	1,472	14	131	82	1,142	60	236
Tavares city	49	54	239	17	138	3	14	90	D	7	107	29	257	40	139
Temple Terrace city	76	112	783	37	D	7	57	94	1,680	14	181	68	D	26	D
The Acreage CDP	20	56	86	142	D	5	11	32	72	5	D	9	66	43	135
The Crossings CDP	64	49	59	26	D	8	24	39	139	8	55	25	485	24	104
The Hammocks CDP	D	75	146	41	D	9	39	72	644	9	84	45	501	34	D
The Villages CDP	D	85	263	24	105	6	D	84	2,214	7	6	42	D	12	D
Thonotosassa CDP	22	13	99	20	D	2	D	11	92	1	D	7	193	13	100
Three Lakes CDP	207	174	613	58	D	16	100	102	777	12	15	26	373	81	262
Titusville city	121	95	565	52	1,164	10	D	160	3,340	9	180	95	1,730	84	463
Town 'n' Country CDP	654	226	2,244	154	5,359	17	88	179	2,651	26	D	104	D	99	576
Trinity CDP	33	49	133	22	D	2	D	46	1,178	6	D	20	417	16	127
Union Park CDP	42	6	35	10	18	2	D	14	64	4	D	11	134	12	37
University CDP (Hillsborough County)	335	29	134	22	D	6	42	161	10,244	3	D	35	557	46	193
University CDP (Orange County)	194	144	4,038	46	3,914	15	517	30	866	3	D	100	2,183	22	263
University Park CDP	105	50	138	32	D	8	40	117	633	10	150	54	D	44	D
Upper Grand Lagoon CDP	63	43	647	25	175	5	D	16	50	8	54	25	714	28	140
Valrico CDP	72	91	185	49	D	4	22	43	165	8	188	15	225	35	154
Venice city	169	121	417	51	558	8	15	154	3,828	17	220	88	1,299	87	488
Vero Beach city	487	220	925	55	782	12	231	162	1,560	12	235	99	1,835	106	537
Vero Beach South CDP	101	64	141	38	D	1	D	33	665	13	161	38	D	43	194
Viera East CDP	12	39	217	10	41	1	D	30	863	2	D	3	73	3	14
Villas CDP	114	71	442	32	D	2	D	60	749	5	69	35	D	44	302
Warrington CDP	49	19	85	6	D	2	D	10	90	3	D	19	338	12	53
Wekiwa Springs CDP	D	122	305	41	1,421	9	25	27	D	4	D	10	135	19	116
Wellington village	203	319	776	151	D	40	124	247	2,497	65	540	105	2,479	97	494

Table C. Incorporated Places, Census Designated Places (CDPs), and Minor Civil Divisions (MCDs) of 10,000 or More Population — Economic Census

STATE City, town, township, borough, or CDP (county if applicable)	Utilities		Manufacturing		Wholesale trade[1]		Retail trade		Transportation and warehousing		Information		Finance and insurance		Real estate and rental and leasing
	Number of establish-ments	Number of employees	Number of establish-ments	Number of employees	Number of establish-ments	Number of employees	Number of establish-ments	Number of employees	Number of establish-ments	Number of employees	Number of establish-ments	Number of employees	Number of establish-ments	Number of employees	Number of establish-ments
	1	2	3	4	5	6	7	8	9	10	11	12	13	14	15
FLORIDA—Con.															
Wesley Chapel CDP	NA	NA	6	22	16	57	112	2,481	15	55	11	102	30	134	25
Westchase CDP	NA	NA	6	170	17	165	35	433	4	6	9	D	27	84	27
Westchester CDP	NA	NA	8	26	27	D	118	1,703	21	66	7	D	51	272	33
West Lealman CDP	NA	NA	6	303	13	37	44	286	6	13	NA	NA	10	32	7
West Little River CDP	NA	NA	6	96	25	190	106	546	21	215	1	D	12	70	10
West Melbourne city	1	D	32	516	30	252	137	2,186	9	25	12	148	28	157	15
Weston city	NA	NA	20	153	279	1,712	134	2,210	41	191	44	D	170	854	165
West Palm Beach city	13	D	103	1,822	146	1,663	535	8,040	109	1,831	103	4,199	294	3,367	260
West Park city	1	D	15	67	22	93	30	191	9	49	2	D	11	40	5
West Pensacola CDP	NA	NA	14	92	10	171	80	622	6	16	6	D	9	D	9
West Perrine CDP	NA	NA	3	41	1	D	25	226	1	D	1	D	4	22	2
Westview CDP	NA	NA	15	832	38	1,244	17	147	29	906	NA	NA	NA	NA	3
Westwood Lakes CDP	NA	NA	NA	NA	4	3	10	55	4	8	NA	NA	3	15	4
Wilton Manors city	NA	NA	12	36	14	D	64	546	6	D	8	D	20	76	40
Winter Garden city	3	D	26	470	41	446	158	2,483	34	246	14	110	49	245	63
Winter Haven city	2	D	28	513	45	1,427	201	2,939	41	2,285	17	155	100	D	59
Winter Park city	1	D	32	185	52	335	232	2,936	4	24	42	1,031	201	1,729	134
Winter Springs city	NA	NA	13	82	28	125	43	453	14	21	8	34	41	128	42
World Golf Village CDP	NA	NA	NA	NA	4	D	11	75	2	D	NA	NA	3	25	6
Wright CDP	NA	NA	10	31	12	61	73	1,432	4	9	9	248	24	127	35
Yulee CDP	NA	NA	9	206	7	28	49	879	11	67	2	D	11	55	6
Zephyrhills city	NA	NA	15	488	6	47	62	961	5	D	5	54	22	123	18
GEORGIA	599	22,615	7,456	333,837	10,637	150,168	33,426	433,840	5,972	154,248	4,155	123,145	14,434	164,422	10,484
Acworth city	NA	NA	14	169	15	58	92	1,484	9	190	6	56	38	213	13
Albany city	4	D	60	2,943	111	1,406	458	6,179	55	D	30	671	170	1,184	130
Alpharetta city	1	D	21	412	161	3,714	372	7,362	47	2,026	221	15,848	449	10,357	203
Americus city	2	D	13	561	19	298	108	1,260	9	108	8	D	42	D	19
Athens-Clarke County unified government	6	D	78	5,115	99	1,801	516	6,963	46	843	38	541	171	1,136	190
Athens-Clarke County unified government (balance)	6	D	78	5,115	99	1,801	516	6,963	46	843	38	541	171	1,136	190
Atlanta city	36	D	295	7,404	698	11,556	1,875	24,977	259	29,338	685	27,297	1,291	29,542	1,121
Augusta-Richmond County consolidated government	12	257	111	7,884	182	1,856	812	10,830	113	2,210	73	2,850	250	2,795	201
Augusta-Richmond County consolidated government (balance)	11	D	111	7,884	182	1,856	785	10,587	112	D	72	D	237	2,734	194
Bainbridge city	2	D	21	644	17	202	106	1,175	7	35	8	D	46	224	20
Belvedere Park CDP	NA	NA	NA	NA	4	12	54	463	3	D	2	D	13	66	9
Brookhaven city	NA	NA	NA	NA	NA	NA	NA	NA	NA	NA	NA	NA	NA	NA	NA
Brunswick city	4	D	20	1,480	24	153	154	1,967	27	741	14	221	71	391	36
Buford city	1	D	68	1,521	81	1,450	214	4,653	20	652	18	150	69	396	46
Calhoun city	1	D	66	5,539	39	1,009	140	1,391	13	150	10	D	57	314	30
Candler-McAfee CDP	NA	NA	3	8	5	15	54	241	2	D	3	D	6	D	13
Canton city	2	D	25	1,637	23	109	132	2,703	6	D	17	207	66	338	39
Carrollton city	4	D	50	3,083	36	307	188	2,604	12	550	17	871	92	643	41
Cartersville city	1	D	53	3,618	51	586	173	2,332	24	732	12	D	94	497	53
Chamblee city	4	D	51	1,083	73	642	143	1,812	22	178	21	408	40	279	40
College Park city	NA	NA	19	500	28	1,187	68	268	86	4,978	4	D	24	397	29
Columbus city	8	D	122	6,977	157	1,843	796	11,371	72	904	68	1,255	354	11,182	237
Conyers city	3	D	53	3,209	35	318	169	3,259	20	397	17	324	68	487	41
Cordele city	1	D	14	444	22	181	102	1,106	11	104	7	77	40	D	23
Covington city	NA	NA	42	3,196	29	344	124	1,487	11	59	16	198	64	464	32
Cusseta-Chattahoochee County unified government	1	D	NA	NA	1	D	18	126	2	D	3	28	6	36	NA
Dallas city	1	D	19	222	22	135	82	1,189	6	10	5	72	25	127	11
Dalton city	1	D	147	10,548	108	1,489	259	2,644	34	1,353	20	D	112	555	41
Decatur city	2	D	10	51	16	53	80	562	8	D	31	230	30	164	43
Doraville city	1	D	27	205	83	484	105	1,129	28	430	8	D	33	193	23
Douglas city	2	D	27	2,170	29	347	141	1,523	22	1,032	10	98	54	303	23
Douglasville city	2	D	20	D	20	146	253	4,228	17	229	18	130	73	498	50
Druid Hills CDP	NA	NA	NA	NA	1	D	8	61	1	D	10	D	7	31	15
Dublin city	3	D	23	1,634	20	239	167	1,980	9	255	9	93	61	D	32
Duluth city	1	D	39	1,549	127	3,067	199	2,792	29	312	32	668	142	1,813	98
Dunwoody city	5	D	14	54	60	978	250	5,168	17	171	60	2,508	211	3,064	123
East Point city	NA	NA	24	648	30	640	90	1,196	22	665	9	207	27	D	33
Evans CDP	NA	NA	10	D	14	172	85	2,193	7	37	9	76	40	321	24
Fairburn city	2	D	11	1,061	17	930	43	325	35	1,028	1	D	10	33	11
Fayetteville city	1	D	15	74	38	287	165	3,042	21	163	10	203	68	492	46
Forest Park city	9	D	20	902	80	2,281	89	959	63	3,055	6	227	24	D	22
Gainesville city	4	D	86	8,909	92	D	299	3,927	38	755	19	472	156	1,476	71
Georgetown CDP	NA	NA	NA	NA	3	D	18	205	4	20	7	D	8	18	8
Griffin city	NA	NA	41	1,718	29	345	169	2,261	14	223	10	D	72	440	31
Grovetown city	NA	NA	NA	NA	7	396	26	460	4	D	NA	NA	8	21	6
Hinesville city	3	D	4	D	6	D	127	1,682	11	D	7	D	47	359	41
Jesup city	4	D	8	D	9	D	85	1,039	7	91	5	D	32	D	13
Johns Creek city	1	D	14	D	67	231	149	1,831	20	90	35	D	122	3,924	99
Kennesaw city	2	D	51	1,225	80	1,153	189	3,621	35	637	16	170	70	593	43
Kingsland city	2	D	3	D	3	D	65	830	NA	NA	3	D	26	168	19
LaGrange city	2	D	57	5,180	32	609	184	2,600	16	1,169	17	D	80	779	42
Lawrenceville city	2	D	67	2,258	115	1,926	309	3,550	42	817	27	911	102	622	71
Lilburn city	NA	NA	31	298	33	215	120	1,690	6	68	8	89	45	238	13
Lithia Springs CDP	3	D	27	1,128	45	1,048	70	1,773	21	578	5	292	18	84	24
Loganville city	NA	NA	9	D	20	99	79	1,557	8	18	7	67	33	158	23

1 Merchant wholesalers, except manufacturers' sales branches and offices.

Table C. Incorporated Places, Census Designated Places (CDPs), and Minor Civil Divisions (MCDs) of 10,000 or More Population — **Economic Census**

STATE City, town, township, borough, or CDP (county if applicable)	Real estate and rental and leasing — Number of employees	Professional, scientific, and technical services — Number of establishments	Number of employees	Administration and support and waste management and mediation services — Number of establishments	Number of employees	Educational services — Number of establishments	Number of employees	Health care and social assistance — Number of establishments	Number of employees	Arts, entertainment, and recreation — Number of establishments	Number of employees	Accommodation and food services — Number of establishments	Number of employees	Other services (except public administration) — Number of establishments	Number of employees
	16	17	18	19	20	21	22	23	24	25	26	27	28	29	30
FLORIDA—Con.															
Wesley Chapel CDP	65	82	160	42	D	9	D	58	577	9	65	49	D	32	D
Westchase CDP	D	108	209	31	1,082	8	29	64	373	10	172	32	430	24	166
Westchester CDP	92	109	294	50	D	11	18	172	850	4	3	48	604	55	186
West Lealman CDP	22	8	20	22	90	3	21	24	223	1	D	19	278	16	92
West Little River CDP	78	8	22	8	D	NA	NA	27	285	2	D	18	D	22	D
West Melbourne city	63	43	219	29	522	1	D	45	1,037	5	D	57	1,151	58	277
Weston city	346	485	1,320	129	1,608	40	207	262	3,367	27	493	97	2,066	97	568
West Palm Beach city	1,144	1,122	7,455	279	10,840	43	203	622	12,742	69	1,695	356	6,424	337	1,943
West Park city	23	2	D	17	D	NA	NA	9	D	2	D	12	93	31	D
West Pensacola CDP	61	14	84	13	55	1	D	15	97	5	52	26	325	19	D
West Perrine CDP	D	8	D	4	D	1	D	11	50	NA	NA	2	D	19	D
Westview CDP	14	3	11	6	D	NA	NA	8	16	NA	NA	7	38	5	D
Westwood Lakes CDP	D	15	19	11	D	1	D	21	136	2	D	1	D	9	12
Wilton Manors city	57	110	274	34	D	7	29	64	851	8	D	55	701	50	137
Winter Garden city	199	110	377	60	515	8	28	86	993	27	180	62	D	59	366
Winter Haven city	305	120	497	62	3,901	16	79	182	7,135	14	621	119	1,878	80	379
Winter Park city	416	476	2,577	96	2,362	28	154	325	5,515	47	D	153	3,518	147	731
Winter Springs city	D	101	230	56	2,059	4	D	42	D	21	147	36	497	36	125
World Golf Village CDP	52	16	42	13	58	1	D	8	461	3	D	5	D	8	D
Wright CDP	145	45	D	33	D	1	D	94	1,945	2	D	22	374	46	157
Yulee CDP	27	7	57	20	59	2	D	19	D	4	28	21	D	19	D
Zephyrhills city	58	24	121	16	D	3	D	78	1,589	7	D	36	834	29	125
GEORGIA	55,551	28,112	D	11,678	328,304	2,064	14,080	22,734	448,460	2,733	42,851	18,815	353,638	13,828	89,302
Acworth city	30	58	384	27	341	9	33	47	438	6	35	65	1,233	37	D
Albany city	493	199	D	90	2,433	9	D	294	8,854	22	D	211	D	141	929
Alpharetta city	1,412	847	13,182	296	13,737	41	126	404	3,895	36	1,263	286	6,486	157	1,135
Americus city	D	35	230	15	D	4	14	68	D	4	D	52	846	35	164
Athens-Clarke County unified government	926	303	1,697	129	2,959	36	200	439	8,443	37	558	342	6,927	192	1,261
Athens-Clarke County unified government (balance)	926	303	1,697	129	2,959	36	200	439	8,443	37	558	342	6,927	192	1,261
Atlanta city	9,940	3,531	53,178	825	33,071	173	1,190	1,632	37,406	360	8,828	1,618	42,124	1,242	14,930
Augusta-Richmond County consolidated government	1,069	478	4,251	205	6,970	31	340	645	24,184	53	1,333	424	9,448	275	1,816
Augusta-Richmond County consolidated government (balance)	1,056	472	4,225	201	D	31	340	636	24,118	53	1,333	412	9,279	263	D
Bainbridge city	67	31	121	12	416	2	D	48	871	4	45	37	530	32	125
Belvedere Park CDP	42	18	58	5	28	1	D	26	188	1	D	24	D	11	34
Brookhaven city	NA	NA	NA	NA	NA	NA	NA	NA	NA	NA	NA	NA	NA	NA	NA
Brunswick city	130	106	355	37	1,936	7	12	139	3,035	13	D	82	1,545	59	353
Buford city	D	127	769	43	576	11	81	81	821	16	D	111	2,372	82	663
Calhoun city	85	41	294	17	589	4	10	58	1,498	4	D	78	1,286	32	D
Candler-McAfee CDP	D	8	20	5	D	NA	NA	22	464	1	D	24	D	13	104
Canton city	103	105	436	33	405	7	D	92	1,885	16	177	90	2,078	45	223
Carrollton city	201	77	466	26	1,103	6	D	137	3,356	12	210	108	2,000	50	D
Cartersville city	161	86	371	29	1,227	7	149	93	1,695	13	201	94	1,797	72	482
Chamblee city	181	150	827	55	1,402	12	65	57	755	11	131	80	875	82	539
College Park city	463	52	543	23	1,473	7	D	66	1,232	2	D	91	2,600	29	D
Columbus city	1,461	350	2,520	193	4,973	29	226	590	14,823	49	1,037	442	10,453	322	2,293
Conyers city	190	85	565	39	1,548	6	D	136	2,831	6	87	112	2,440	72	413
Cordele city	184	22	D	15	D	1	D	66	1,123	3	38	39	725	21	87
Covington city	111	50	238	21	234	4	11	82	1,732	7	111	77	1,298	41	D
Cusseta-Chattahoochee County unified government	NA	28	232	6	D	2	D	5	20	3	D	9	42	5	D
Dallas city	D	35	125	23	273	6	23	41	805	5	28	34	600	38	148
Dalton city	158	124	5,071	40	2,215	7	D	157	D	11	88	120	D	71	649
Decatur city	134	319	1,490	35	422	28	169	111	1,461	26	108	79	1,383	66	276
Doraville city	201	46	243	37	874	5	17	35	377	4	28	67	537	74	D
Douglas city	89	51	198	17	D	2	D	96	1,846	7	42	55	1,135	31	D
Douglasville city	204	113	604	29	441	6	15	129	2,828	5	D	129	2,867	86	385
Druid Hills CDP	D	51	242	13	287	3	123	29	D	5	14	39	D	12	62
Dublin city	119	59	280	17	732	5	D	116	4,090	6	D	75	1,325	47	D
Duluth city	459	279	2,539	107	4,351	44	292	179	2,386	20	74	144	1,624	142	874
Dunwoody city	1,450	572	6,017	162	9,568	31	323	212	3,437	23	533	141	3,952	88	522
East Point city	301	52	275	30	1,910	9	39	100	2,002	15	D	72	1,504	45	772
Evans CDP	59	75	465	43	D	11	96	98	1,571	10	D	74	1,602	38	241
Fairburn city	D	12	36	16	149	3	9	16	291	5	17	24	321	19	229
Fayetteville city	214	107	394	44	361	9	109	156	3,191	10	89	80	1,886	74	345
Forest Park city	133	23	136	21	965	2	D	36	D	2	D	40	613	31	D
Gainesville city	254	179	888	74	2,383	10	70	297	D	20	D	151	2,837	111	533
Georgetown CDP	32	6	58	9	76	2	D	5	38	1	D	14	247	4	D
Griffin city	137	61	288	17	584	5	D	112	2,585	12	D	103	1,635	52	239
Grovetown city	34	8	15	8	D	1	D	5	129	3	D	15	259	11	47
Hinesville city	159	42	458	21	137	2	D	60	1,022	3	D	80	1,307	48	326
Jesup city	55	27	D	5	D	3	5	60	D	3	D	42	D	25	149
Johns Creek city	D	581	1,819	111	3,411	61	935	160	2,402	24	925	137	2,100	87	D
Kennesaw city	220	145	980	67	1,161	10	D	88	1,336	17	453	111	2,319	101	D
Kingsland city	80	12	36	9	16	1	D	38	D	3	D	42	999	22	89
LaGrange city	193	65	746	37	2,082	4	20	100	D	14	D	86	1,738	58	D
Lawrenceville city	367	232	D	101	9,395	10	51	277	6,827	16	D	128	2,022	151	846
Lilburn city	55	61	198	45	651	12	86	72	565	6	39	69	916	49	D
Lithia Springs CDP	258	20	133	34	2,076	2	D	33	329	1	D	33	656	26	144
Loganville city	94	42	163	32	1,321	5	32	49	294	5	13	54	934	37	D

STATE City, town, township, borough, or CDP (county if applicable)	Utilities Number of establish-ments	Utilities Number of employees	Manufacturing Number of establish-ments	Manufacturing Number of employees	Wholesale trade[1] Number of establish-ments	Wholesale trade[1] Number of employees	Retail trade Number of establish-ments	Retail trade Number of employees	Transportation and warehousing Number of establish-ments	Transportation and warehousing Number of employees	Information Number of establish-ments	Information Number of employees	Finance and insurance Number of establish-ments	Finance and insurance Number of employees	Real estate and rental and leasing Number of establish-ments
	1	2	3	4	5	6	7	8	9	10	11	12	13	14	15
GEORGIA—Con.															
Mableton CDP	NA	NA	23	260	42	878	93	930	22	502	3	D	30	130	27
McDonough city	4	D	16	1,046	27	720	105	2,189	44	2,135	8	118	53	340	37
Macon-Bibb County	6	D	71	D	122	D	629	7,527	60	D	33	607	227	D	126
Marietta city	7	D	109	3,408	275	3,494	447	6,196	63	2,394	58	1,210	222	1,818	186
Martinez CDP	3	D	25	930	23	153	128	2,060	11	59	7	45	69	362	45
Milledgeville city	3	D	16	1,808	16	D	133	1,950	6	24	11	D	54	326	32
Milton city	3	D	6	16	20	147	56	916	4	D	16	159	43	269	24
Monroe city	NA	NA	21	1,022	22	367	88	1,046	8	D	7	53	41	244	15
Moultrie city	2	D	19	940	23	194	143	1,457	6	D	13	D	54	301	32
Mountain Park CDP	NA	NA	7	32	22	80	33	813	3	D	1	D	9	38	12
Newnan city	5	55	31	1,019	33	D	200	3,261	15	665	19	474	88	445	68
Norcross city	1	D	90	2,299	245	4,424	192	1,845	47	1,090	55	2,050	131	1,493	89
North Decatur CDP	NA	NA	9	37	8	20	97	1,447	1	D	9	D	22	90	31
North Druid Hills CDP	1	D	10	363	12	71	65	1,028	6	D	32	210	30	156	40
Peachtree City city	NA	NA	39	1,864	75	1,037	145	2,641	27	2,209	18	307	70	455	74
Peachtree Corners city	NA	NA	NA	NA	NA	NA	NA	NA	NA	NA	NA	NA	NA	NA	NA
Perry city	3	39	9	629	9	86	69	858	6	206	2	D	28	140	17
Pooler city	1	D	18	536	39	770	68	1,500	32	354	2	D	29	204	19
Powder Springs city	NA	NA	11	141	17	120	32	573	10	69	8	D	9	64	8
Redan CDP	NA	NA	6	324	2	D	32	419	8	D	1	D	11	D	2
Richmond Hill city	NA	NA	4	D	5	D	62	801	6	D	5	D	24	74	24
Riverdale city	4	D	NA	NA	3	D	89	1,418	3	D	3	37	27	D	24
Rome city	9	D	61	3,069	54	693	283	3,352	13	309	19	481	114	774	61
Roswell city	4	D	57	636	177	1,786	324	5,202	36	716	65	1,297	241	1,279	179
St. Marys city	1	D	4	D	6	D	66	1,282	4	D	6	D	21	109	14
St. Simons CDP	2	D	5	D	9	41	98	492	4	34	5	D	28	110	44
Sandy Springs city	6	D	30	529	147	3,515	252	3,933	32	600	142	6,186	475	10,524	334
Savannah city	14	354	104	3,234	180	1,884	869	11,121	167	4,877	85	1,262	320	2,342	246
Smyrna city	4	D	40	1,132	73	2,229	189	2,894	23	614	40	1,269	116	1,265	87
Snellville city	NA	NA	6	19	21	104	164	3,106	21	55	16	169	58	343	18
Statesboro city	6	D	26	1,163	23	141	202	2,828	17	636	10	D	81	541	56
Stockbridge city	1	D	12	D	11	38	95	1,819	18	375	9	282	68	700	38
Sugar Hill city	NA	NA	13	285	12	47	33	522	9	118	4	D	10	30	19
Suwanee city	1	D	47	1,149	123	1,922	121	1,514	14	450	21	83	73	455	56
Thomasville city	1	D	29	1,639	45	376	167	1,839	14	150	8	68	68	576	34
Tifton city	4	D	17	334	35	304	168	1,485	24	1,019	10	D	73	398	26
Tucker CDP	4	691	48	1,447	98	1,508	111	1,589	27	1,484	27	D	61	1,250	47
Union City city	2	D	6	666	9	111	64	1,889	12	734	4	D	18	109	23
Valdosta city	14	D	65	2,208	85	822	370	4,978	47	1,742	19	447	124	858	100
Vidalia city	6	D	23	D	16	D	100	875	9	D	7	D	41	217	17
Villa Rica city	1	D	22	1,996	17	161	64	953	13	121	5	D	28	126	17
Vinings CDP	1	D	4	D	21	402	25	721	5	58	37	834	95	1,189	60
Warner Robins city	4	D	25	519	22	221	291	4,392	5	25	15	287	119	841	79
Waycross city	6	75	16	454	22	D	171	2,170	15	346	10	D	49	D	25
Wilmington Island CDP	2	D	NA	NA	4	D	24	307	12	104	2	D	16	75	15
Winder city	1	D	24	190	20	D	96	1,451	5	D	6	80	49	273	21
Woodstock city	1	D	34	608	55	486	142	2,567	15	67	11	109	96	707	46
HAWAII	54	3,379	796	11,440	1,561	16,686	4,643	68,360	847	26,839	543	8,329	1,401	18,686	1,919
East Honolulu CDP	1	D	3	9	33	65	55	962	11	26	14	D	32	104	49
Ewa Beach CDP	NA	NA	NA	NA	2	D	12	373	1	D	1	D	5	23	NA
Ewa Gentry CDP	1	D	NA	NA	1	D	7	128	2	D	NA	NA	1	D	4
Halawa CDP	NA	NA	6	94	28	258	16	64	4	16	2	D	5	D	11
Hawaiian Paradise Park CDP	NA	NA	NA	NA	2	D	NA	NA	1	D	NA	NA	1	D	1
Hilo CDP	2	D	46	425	71	839	228	3,849	42	671	19	336	68	660	80
Kahului CDP	1	D	18	95	52	637	194	4,127	56	1,995	23	388	47	323	52
Kailua CDP (Hawaii County)	1	D	14	183	26	138	145	2,239	43	763	16	209	38	432	50
Kailua CDP (Honolulu County)	1	D	13	47	17	62	96	1,388	10	123	10	22	40	200	54
Kalaoa CDP	NA	NA	7	53	22	218	30	570	22	186	5	D	1	D	9
Kaneohe CDP	NA	NA	15	120	12	19	119	1,597	10	72	9	133	27	158	26
Kaneohe Station CDP	NA	NA	NA	NA	1	D	6	26	NA	NA	2	D	2	D	2
Kapaa CDP	NA	NA	4	9	11	80	50	572	4	D	4	4	7	D	15
Kapolei CDP	NA	NA	3	D	7	149	21	1,067	11	D	5	83	21	455	15
Kihei CDP	NA	NA	7	18	12	65	68	867	10	154	10	61	27	245	60
Lahaina CDP	2	D	5	10	5	D	166	1,247	23	370	10	51	15	69	32
Makakilo CDP	NA	NA	NA	NA	5	14	5	D	1	D	1	D	1	D	4
Mililani Mauka CDP	NA	NA	3	21	5	D	5	D	5	D	9	956	5	D	2
Mililani Town CDP	NA	NA	NA	NA	9	16	34	974	3	4	6	89	22	152	6
Nanakuli CDP	NA	NA	NA	NA	1	D	14	171	2	D	2	D	1	D	3
Ocean Pointe CDP	NA	NA	NA	NA	NA	NA	6	43	NA	NA	NA	NA	1	D	6
Pearl City CDP	1	D	12	171	38	463	65	2,081	11	813	10	125	29	144	21
Royal Kunia CDP	NA	NA	NA	NA	1	D	8	458	1	D	2	D	4	24	1
Schofield Barracks CDP	NA	NA	NA	NA	NA	NA	5	39	NA	NA	1	D	2	D	1
Urban Honolulu CDP	9	D	351	5,599	782	9,002	1,851	26,485	312	17,375	265	4,877	716	13,345	825
Wahiawa CDP	1	D	5	57	6	30	43	461	4	D	2	D	14	79	14
Waianae CDP	NA	NA	NA	NA	NA	NA	20	430	6	46	1	D	7	34	9
Wailuku CDP	1	D	27	309	36	285	58	502	13	197	8	96	30	158	38
Waimalu CDP	NA	NA	6	51	10	125	115	2,144	2	D	8	120	16	184	29
Waipahu CDP	NA	NA	20	359	56	790	106	2,248	19	149	2	D	26	582	34
Waipio CDP	NA	NA	11	383	27	741	15	164	9	147	8	D	8	101	6
IDAHO	204	3,709	1,759	52,084	1,739	21,470	5,815	72,980	1,736	17,195	654	12,264	2,793	21,698	2,033
Ammon city	NA	NA	9	D	3	D	40	995	7	8	4	D	30	121	15
Blackfoot city	1	D	13	D	18	239	61	775	7	9	2	D	35	228	12

1 Merchant wholesalers, except manufacturers' sales branches and offices.

Table C. Incorporated Places, Census Designated Places (CDPs), and Minor Civil Divisions (MCDs) of 10,000 or More Population — Economic Census

STATE City, town, township, borough, or CDP (county if applicable)	Real estate and rental and leasing — Number of employees	Professional, scientific, and technical services — Number of establishments	Professional — Number of employees	Administration and support and waste management and mediation services — Number of establishments	Administration — Number of employees	Educational services — Number of establishments	Educational — Number of employees	Health care and social assistance — Number of establishments	Health — Number of employees	Arts, entertainment, and recreation — Number of establishments	Arts — Number of employees	Accommodation and food services — Number of establishments	Accommodation — Number of employees	Other services (except public administration) — Number of establishments	Other — Number of employees
	16	17	18	19	20	21	22	23	24	25	26	27	28	29	30
GEORGIA—Con.															
Mableton CDP	108	76	194	38	319	5	36	57	326	6	23	39	D	35	267
McDonough city	198	75	359	34	1,947	3	D	78	947	5	50	80	1,390	64	298
Macon-Bibb County	575	287	2,013	106	2,934	20	89	406	12,378	22	322	266	4,795	192	1,025
Marietta city	884	559	5,368	183	3,411	34	255	418	10,547	31	228	289	4,708	244	1,475
Martinez CDP	184	88	D	49	1,526	11	84	79	1,007	12	D	59	D	63	D
Milledgeville city	D	44	741	31	552	3	D	99	D	8	58	81	1,293	45	D
Milton city	D	205	4,498	62	451	14	67	29	170	17	171	44	635	33	194
Monroe city	55	40	152	19	D	2	D	56	927	5	D	48	736	26	73
Moultrie city	83	45	153	19	407	4	D	82	1,692	4	D	54	839	31	D
Mountain Park CDP	34	51	168	28	209	6	8	26	247	6	13	29	483	20	D
Newnan city	185	92	514	32	939	6	D	106	D	9	D	112	2,784	78	D
Norcross city	578	269	4,269	106	3,806	14	68	122	2,441	15	152	154	2,084	101	781
North Decatur CDP	D	87	234	28	166	12	29	168	4,199	10	28	60	886	37	196
North Druid Hills CDP	D	126	783	37	375	13	73	89	4,197	16	284	71	1,479	56	728
Peachtree City city	158	173	869	59	709	25	150	122	1,138	22	335	100	2,410	95	811
Peachtree Corners city	NA	NA	NA	NA	NA	NA	NA	NA	NA	NA	NA	NA	NA	NA	NA
Perry city	44	32	507	13	254	1	D	47	890	5	D	60	1,117	15	D
Pooler city	81	34	196	45	982	6	D	37	248	7	98	81	1,606	25	246
Powder Springs city	19	28	80	20	93	5	24	41	D	4	D	20	324	20	60
Redan CDP	D	19	66	8	D	1	D	17	77	3	13	18	282	12	60
Richmond Hill city	D	40	183	12	94	1	D	44	D	4	D	62	D	31	282
Riverdale city	83	19	91	10	105	1	D	83	1,076	1	D	52	773	37	D
Rome city	202	146	700	51	2,324	10	D	243	7,521	17	158	138	3,070	74	637
Roswell city	787	752	4,280	215	8,952	60	442	389	5,501	61	805	237	4,531	225	D
St. Marys city	43	25	125	15	D	5	D	53	358	5	D	43	513	27	107
St. Simons CDP	107	91	238	28	129	3	D	37	488	7	D	62	1,359	22	55
Sandy Springs city	2,561	971	D	265	14,848	52	218	666	17,618	42	880	266	4,373	221	1,456
Savannah city	1,266	498	5,013	201	7,494	22	D	584	16,631	62	780	571	12,766	274	1,990
Smyrna city	297	280	8,545	95	4,525	18	213	221	2,490	19	291	161	2,788	113	589
Snellville city	60	97	303	32	102	9	36	192	3,337	9	128	75	D	81	D
Statesboro city	266	88	469	23	1,000	8	D	162	2,639	4	D	124	D	65	D
Stockbridge city	151	73	454	39	293	6	89	146	3,247	9	136	83	1,205	40	D
Sugar Hill city	50	37	106	32	363	9	45	24	214	8	D	14	173	30	D
Suwanee city	141	186	824	73	2,012	22	118	95	D	19	365	99	1,869	82	410
Thomasville city	D	57	257	23	1,292	3	D	125	3,553	10	D	63	1,056	52	D
Tifton city	99	67	470	16	1,600	7	D	89	D	6	D	79	1,860	48	D
Tucker CDP	128	187	1,527	78	2,967	15	165	148	1,807	11	84	86	1,470	108	636
Union City city	D	17	70	10	172	2	D	31	705	NA	NA	42	666	18	D
Valdosta city	1,363	174	915	71	2,096	11	D	306	6,937	18	351	214	4,519	111	619
Vidalia city	45	41	391	16	248	1	D	88	1,698	5	38	45	834	28	159
Villa Rica city	37	23	70	13	191	2	D	56	992	5	D	48	689	27	161
Vinings CDP	726	134	1,348	53	2,278	3	D	28	1,439	6	12	41	810	35	239
Warner Robins city	303	160	2,400	54	1,323	14	D	201	4,486	13	D	157	3,608	91	519
Waycross city	D	52	237	24	274	3	D	110	2,798	3	D	58	1,281	41	197
Wilmington Island CDP	41	32	67	22	49	1	D	12	138	5	78	20	324	9	27
Winder city	48	45	330	14	D	2	D	60	888	3	D	52	D	30	D
Woodstock city	175	152	901	68	1,176	12	82	151	1,251	13	D	101	2,020	85	393
HAWAII	11,369	3,226	21,629	1,799	47,307	347	2,410	3,559	66,772	495	10,623	3,518	98,364	2,808	19,348
East Honolulu CDP	105	110	282	50	D	9	14	78	980	14	434	65	D	49	252
Ewa Beach CDP	NA	3	D	8	22	1	D	17	365	2	D	10	172	13	D
Ewa Gentry CDP	21	3	D	9	D	1	D	2	D	1	D	7	104	6	D
Halawa CDP	46	16	42	19	187	NA	NA	14	D	4	D	12	160	18	145
Hawaiian Paradise Park CDP	D	3	D	3	D	NA	NA	1	D	NA	NA	1	D	1	D
Hilo CDP	358	101	653	62	1,669	7	36	225	4,286	11	144	146	2,239	96	464
Kahului CDP	535	43	258	53	2,052	10	39	96	1,533	13	478	84	1,703	60	501
Kailua CDP (Hawaii County)	431	62	233	41	D	9	87	69	642	12	538	103	3,508	59	391
Kailua CDP (Honolulu County)	176	96	D	43	348	7	39	139	1,985	13	194	86	1,446	65	440
Kalaoa CDP	17	22	125	28	727	NA	NA	9	57	2	D	3	D	9	38
Kaneohe CDP	89	51	299	28	186	7	45	103	1,952	14	236	74	1,140	67	352
Kaneohe Station CDP	D	15	74	3	D	NA	NA	NA	NA	NA	NA	2	D	5	D
Kapaa CDP	30	17	49	11	D	3	14	26	288	4	D	39	619	15	113
Kapolei CDP	D	11	102	12	297	2	D	26	1,441	9	266	33	915	20	164
Kihei CDP	184	51	258	41	307	9	45	42	307	14	185	91	1,622	71	270
Lahaina CDP	211	21	80	20	969	5	31	24	194	14	D	93	3,748	45	191
Makakilo CDP	3	7	15	10	72	1	D	7	D	NA	NA	4	13	11	D
Mililani Mauka CDP	D	15	58	11	67	3	35	8	D	1	D	6	87	11	47
Mililani Town CDP	28	18	81	16	70	4	22	25	246	3	119	41	1,055	32	480
Nanakuli CDP	D	3	15	5	D	1	D	7	118	NA	NA	6	134	7	17
Ocean Pointe CDP	23	6	40	1	D	NA	NA	4	D	2	D	16	268	5	20
Pearl City CDP	101	36	224	29	488	3	25	84	885	3	146	74	1,346	61	292
Royal Kunia CDP	D	6	D	8	D	1	D	5	D	1	D	18	223	8	33
Schofield Barracks CDP	D	20	244	5	132	1	D	1	D	NA	NA	1	D	2	D
Urban Honolulu CDP	5,335	1,709	14,263	706	25,562	163	1,399	1,513	32,660	137	2,747	1,471	38,426	1,346	10,410
Wahiawa CDP	53	22	149	16	D	6	34	39	871	3	D	44	704	25	146
Waianae CDP	28	9	43	5	D	1	D	30	826	1	D	24	353	8	D
Wailuku CDP	125	129	524	48	746	3	D	122	3,326	9	85	47	438	59	273
Waimalu CDP	92	24	193	17	423	9	70	90	D	4	165	70	1,480	40	363
Waipahu CDP	182	20	226	32	572	6	32	98	826	4	D	77	1,007	70	474
Waipio CDP	15	15	121	14	283	4	48	8	356	2	D	15	492	19	133
IDAHO	6,268	4,198	32,076	2,185	33,714	293	1,763	4,865	83,505	712	8,944	3,564	54,257	2,553	12,188
Ammon city	63	27	69	15	D	1	D	56	633	1	D	26	D	15	99
Blackfoot city	35	26	120	16	64	4	D	71	1,677	4	D	37	D	21	160

Table C.   Incorporated Places, Census Designated Places (CDPs), and Minor Civil Divisions (MCDs) of 10,000 or More Population — **Economic Census**

STATE City, town, township, borough, or CDP (county if applicable)	Utilities Number of establishments	Utilities Number of employees	Manufacturing Number of establishments	Manufacturing Number of employees	Wholesale trade[1] Number of establishments	Wholesale trade[1] Number of employees	Retail trade Number of establishments	Retail trade Number of employees	Transportation and warehousing Number of establishments	Transportation and warehousing Number of employees	Information Number of establishments	Information Number of employees	Finance and insurance Number of establishments	Finance and insurance Number of employees	Real estate and rental and leasing Number of establishments
	1	2	3	4	5	6	7	8	9	10	11	12	13	14	15
IDAHO—Con.															
Boise City city	27	1,952	216	12,584	376	5,188	916	13,392	180	3,407	191	5,664	635	5,762	452
Burley city	1	D	21	1,234	22	278	98	1,218	26	D	8	D	32	206	19
Caldwell city	1	D	53	D	29	299	121	1,512	36	694	8	D	52	263	36
Chubbuck city	NA	NA	3	38	6	58	60	1,205	11	74	4	280	19	593	12
Coeur d'Alene city	2	D	63	1,116	50	612	309	4,575	26	236	34	590	147	1,494	103
Eagle city	2	D	19	79	21	190	57	618	8	D	17	78	84	308	64
Garden City city	2	D	55	568	40	380	119	1,249	8	D	4	D	40	239	37
Hayden city	1	D	38	287	15	222	65	954	10	149	8	86	31	171	20
Idaho Falls city	2	D	80	1,528	114	1,210	362	5,209	63	597	31	873	181	1,060	101
Jerome city	1	D	15	1,250	19	198	57	687	28	493	5	D	19	D	18
Kuna city	1	D	4	32	1	D	19	211	6	30	1	D	11	28	5
Lewiston city	2	D	27	D	37	472	191	2,163	31	D	14	347	82	D	35
Meridian city	1	D	55	1,143	93	2,282	246	4,537	44	608	31	1,119	181	3,652	101
Moscow city	1	D	12	44	9	166	110	1,711	4	20	19	158	43	210	38
Mountain Home city	5	D	5	D	2	D	54	869	15	D	3	D	24	140	7
Nampa city	2	D	78	3,627	78	939	300	5,210	73	1,152	27	775	140	791	77
Pocatello city	1	D	33	1,499	69	656	219	2,935	42	365	18	223	126	1,197	69
Post Falls city	1	D	49	1,109	27	143	99	1,762	20	84	8	D	55	247	33
Rexburg city	4	D	18	415	20	285	105	1,542	19	226	10	D	46	240	46
Twin Falls city	8	D	59	1,669	75	810	314	4,308	71	718	21	308	126	814	87
ILLINOIS	492	29,968	13,868	542,004	16,036	255,531	39,947	592,942	13,251	230,695	5,404	124,859	22,230	296,035	12,035
Addison village	1	D	310	5,793	198	3,798	96	1,807	118	2,886	15	296	39	295	42
Algonquin village	NA	NA	23	391	23	95	158	3,492	23	97	11	51	48	200	23
Alsip village	1	D	80	3,761	91	1,757	59	832	51	930	8	158	22	113	18
Alton city	7	587	22	1,105	27	284	150	2,233	14	42	17	217	52	D	34
Antioch village	NA	NA	36	520	10	D	57	1,208	12	31	5	21	33	186	18
Arlington Heights village	1	D	71	1,902	151	3,104	203	3,354	84	169	46	1,509	176	1,187	96
Aurora city	3	D	138	8,689	150	2,943	566	9,344	123	2,810	44	318	210	2,930	130
Barrington village	NA	NA	21	293	29	198	66	640	10	197	14	D	77	498	25
Bartlett village	NA	NA	29	999	57	751	41	615	46	86	10	26	38	159	22
Batavia city	1	D	88	3,758	78	799	90	1,634	27	643	13	143	45	216	26
Beach Park village	NA	NA	5	24	1	D	18	100	8	D	NA	NA	3	D	4
Belleville city	7	D	38	1,347	42	549	188	2,333	26	734	14	312	115	904	55
Bellwood village	1	D	31	2,058	11	124	29	243	24	127	3	D	10	D	7
Belvidere city	NA	NA	39	6,985	12	91	86	1,140	23	376	7	86	45	183	15
Bensenville village	NA	NA	195	4,444	162	2,404	81	851	218	2,902	6	D	26	136	28
Berwyn city	NA	NA	15	486	12	37	112	836	48	109	4	D	43	243	27
Bloomingdale village	NA	NA	31	1,724	53	918	190	3,601	49	259	11	121	56	417	30
Bloomington city	3	D	49	1,525	73	D	360	5,463	44	974	40	734	165	D	95
Blue Island city	NA	NA	31	756	32	655	46	269	12	66	3	D	15	117	9
Bolingbrook village	4	209	54	3,763	103	3,334	214	5,088	114	2,586	22	1,767	60	372	39
Bourbonnais village	NA	NA	6	176	13	157	120	2,506	12	98	5	75	54	1,530	24
Bradley village	1	D	13	891	17	181	80	1,251	1	D	1	D	19	D	12
Bridgeview village	NA	NA	68	2,811	67	574	76	1,489	57	811	4	D	26	230	14
Brookfield village	NA	NA	15	137	11	36	27	218	24	D	3	D	14	D	13
Buffalo Grove village	1	D	53	3,097	122	2,672	128	1,340	72	512	24	205	108	1,554	47
Burbank city	NA	NA	6	47	6	25	90	1,363	51	210	3	25	28	D	7
Burr Ridge village	1	D	36	1,250	62	915	53	776	16	158	17	D	51	561	31
Cahokia village	NA	NA	6	39	4	D	44	602	11	171	2	D	19	64	7
Calumet City city	NA	NA	10	485	12	D	173	2,769	22	89	8	51	40	D	17
Campton Hills village	NA	NA	5	29	7	D	6	D	9	16	2	D	9	31	19
Canton city	2	D	4	33	3	D	68	969	5	27	4	33	25	D	10
Carbondale city	1	D	13	276	10	108	157	2,760	12	177	16	303	63	417	51
Carol Stream village	NA	NA	95	4,421	109	2,642	91	1,508	78	2,068	18	623	37	262	36
Carpentersville village	NA	NA	24	1,720	14	D	52	882	52	44	5	82	27	137	22
Cary village	NA	NA	46	2,044	25	D	39	371	7	101	5	69	34	104	12
Centralia city	1	D	11	D	14	114	80	812	7	D	9	123	40	D	12
Champaign city	3	D	55	1,692	66	1,267	394	6,538	34	1,126	62	2,002	175	1,698	108
Channahon village	1	D	14	1,339	9	118	17	178	35	414	1	D	8	52	11
Charleston city	1	D	16	435	5	45	70	960	6	D	2	D	31	D	24
Chatham village	NA	NA	4	136	3	4	25	329	2	D	4	22	20	117	5
Chicago city	57	4,983	1,870	58,435	2,310	37,189	7,285	85,388	1,732	53,117	1,530	52,959	4,907	102,751	3,076
Chicago Heights city	NA	NA	52	2,462	37	1,028	68	758	34	2,351	15	428	36	D	15
Chicago Ridge village	NA	NA	12	69	12	82	126	2,068	22	370	9	87	4	D	10
Cicero town	1	D	70	2,847	37	638	134	2,028	69	370	12	117	54	525	14
Collinsville city	1	D	11	98	27	201	89	1,754	12	254	15	D	56	D	26
Country Club Hills city	NA	NA	NA	NA	1	D	28	553	9	26	2	D	18	95	3
Crest Hill city	NA	NA	17	391	13	71	45	592	26	252	3	D	18	67	17
Crestwood village	2	D	26	508	30	308	67	1,564	22	821	8	123	18	87	13
Crystal Lake city	2	D	76	2,902	68	662	210	3,601	41	226	19	290	114	717	44
Danville city	3	D	48	3,425	42	D	150	2,342	18	768	9	215	85	1,022	31
Darien city	1	D	12	349	26	121	49	1,033	54	100	5	D	44	981	17
Decatur city	9	D	81	7,384	83	1,104	296	4,330	54	3,062	21	470	146	1,211	73
Deerfield village	NA	NA	15	127	58	3,874	71	1,180	5	D	29	516	100	1,337	59
DeKalb city	1	D	27	987	15	D	133	2,587	15	D	18	577	43	342	41
Des Plaines city	2	D	127	5,811	138	2,522	171	3,047	144	3,100	34	837	121	1,035	82
Dixon city	2	D	20	1,586	4	D	64	699	7	D	4	D	32	D	11
Dolton village	NA	NA	9	631	3	D	50	560	10	132	2	D	17	D	6
Downers Grove village	3	D	62	3,257	113	2,190	227	4,336	61	1,964	51	1,622	181	4,471	104
East Moline city	NA	NA	29	3,376	15	240	41	663	8	D	5	D	17	111	9
East Peoria city	1	D	22	3,695	46	882	91	1,660	22	876	8	130	33	268	22
East St. Louis city	3	D	11	169	20	201	61	378	26	643	9	D	14	61	14
Edwardsville city	1	D	12	156	22	284	104	1,754	26	1,498	13	193	92	D	31
Effingham city	1	D	35	1,731	26	628	139	2,454	22	721	14	D	55	481	29
Elgin city	3	D	182	7,541	193	3,654	240	3,813	152	883	32	1,457	184	4,175	78
Elk Grove Village village	NA	NA	406	13,764	447	7,000	116	2,416	357	4,417	33	533	92	1,288	59
Elmhurst city	1	D	75	1,574	130	3,294	158	2,107	43	470	39	993	110	1,627	65

1   Merchant wholesalers, except manufacturers' sales branches and offices.

Table C.   Incorporated Places, Census Designated Places (CDPs), and Minor Civil Divisions (MCDs) of 10,000 or More Population — **Economic Census**

	Economic activity by sector, 2012														
STATE City, town, township, borough, or CDP (county if applicable)	Real estate and rental and leasing	Professional, scientific, and technical services		Administration and support and waste management and mediation services		Educational services		Health care and social assistance		Arts, entertainment, and recreation		Accommodation and food services		Other services (except public administration)	
	Number of employees	Number of establishments	Number of employees	Number of establishments	Number of employees	Number of establishments	Number of employees	Number of establishments	Number of employees	Number of establishments	Number of employees	Number of establishments	Number of employees	Number of establishments	Number of employees
	16	17	18	19	20	21	22	23	24	25	26	27	28	29	30
IDAHO—Con.															
Boise City city	1,905	1,155	9,787	458	11,884	76	507	902	23,150	85	2,455	617	11,334	492	2,707
Burley city	26	36	113	8	80	3	D	75	1,231	5	D	40	D	29	D
Caldwell city	183	50	208	33	639	6	D	110	1,878	8	D	65	1,007	54	317
Chubbuck city	D	16	87	13	49	3	10	45	529	3	28	25	458	17	D
Coeur d'Alene city	404	245	D	95	1,497	16	59	308	6,130	37	305	184	3,531	95	490
Eagle city	117	121	438	33	913	11	D	88	D	13	D	46	762	52	D
Garden City city	198	56	378	34	742	6	D	31	D	7	55	50	D	79	424
Hayden city	51	47	204	28	288	4	7	45	640	6	103	32	D	32	D
Idaho Falls city	366	287	8,144	80	3,081	16	82	443	6,869	19	593	191	3,578	120	D
Jerome city	D	17	93	13	D	1	D	31	D	1	D	22	294	23	D
Kuna city	D	18	40	12	D	1	D	20	142	1	D	21	228	11	D
Lewiston city	D	78	496	63	1,051	6	D	137	D	16	137	95	D	77	D
Meridian city	236	197	1,595	119	1,774	18	169	287	4,996	29	470	178	3,513	103	594
Moscow city	150	66	461	20	196	4	46	73	1,306	7	D	106	1,700	45	355
Mountain Home city	D	9	48	10	22	NA	NA	41	D	5	D	43	555	19	D
Nampa city	186	141	798	92	D	12	86	216	4,462	20	291	159	2,965	110	622
Pocatello city	D	140	1,196	56	1,403	7	D	274	3,236	20	232	151	2,633	94	D
Post Falls city	91	57	275	35	221	4	99	95	1,549	8	65	57	735	52	243
Rexburg city	149	59	719	26	597	3	D	88	1,375	7	60	48	840	27	D
Twin Falls city	259	175	924	74	D	8	D	264	5,063	24	179	140	2,486	106	693
ILLINOIS	76,794	38,673	364,336	16,849	459,740	2,927	29,233	33,055	770,484	4,520	77,153	27,117	469,870	23,334	165,366
Addison village	347	94	455	75	3,428	11	D	63	1,308	9	D	73	D	123	809
Algonquin village	D	111	340	41	687	11	76	91	D	18	D	82	1,821	72	374
Alsip village	132	25	155	37	1,942	2	D	27	691	6	62	40	703	57	D
Alton city	109	64	555	34	446	3	D	132	4,380	13	D	92	1,842	55	296
Antioch village	31	32	93	23	147	1	D	26	D	9	D	37	539	30	141
Arlington Heights village	633	489	3,105	116	3,227	30	413	379	8,784	34	483	148	2,732	165	1,110
Aurora city	676	450	2,399	196	12,047	38	286	370	9,114	43	1,274	257	4,005	202	1,610
Barrington village	131	150	808	30	387	16	105	85	1,127	12	168	44	D	62	319
Bartlett village	61	148	319	42	1,069	8	67	52	876	8	D	36	460	35	D
Batavia city	100	139	2,360	46	555	15	57	67	D	5	D	63	1,094	61	519
Beach Park village	9	10	13	26	43	NA	NA	8	D	1	D	8	D	7	D
Belleville city	169	154	1,074	47	1,879	14	D	197	8,659	22	D	142	D	114	722
Bellwood village	17	9	24	11	205	NA	NA	23	372	NA	NA	16	87	22	D
Belvidere city	45	31	D	21	250	4	D	55	D	6	D	49	D	38	D
Bensenville village	329	63	795	54	2,668	2	D	25	D	7	37	45	317	61	D
Berwyn city	68	71	1,276	32	655	2	D	138	3,909	6	42	86	D	63	361
Bloomingdale village	D	126	528	48	869	12	90	120	1,882	10	D	79	1,920	55	592
Bloomington city	439	241	2,107	136	3,927	25	329	249	5,109	42	942	223	4,927	172	1,709
Blue Island city	39	19	78	27	1,274	NA	NA	52	2,914	2	D	43	512	37	202
Bolingbrook village	190	154	1,517	122	7,233	15	38	144	3,156	19	569	154	3,230	88	457
Bourbonnais village	69	35	165	23	420	3	D	107	1,546	4	D	60	1,461	37	D
Bradley village	69	17	101	21	169	4	D	29	1,089	6	130	48	991	26	D
Bridgeview village	229	32	456	36	1,222	2	D	26	594	8	171	54	1,032	68	D
Brookfield village	D	39	98	21	273	3	2	32	362	3	D	29	254	43	D
Buffalo Grove village	261	313	3,419	67	3,012	29	254	180	1,717	14	D	101	1,514	95	540
Burbank city	19	28	92	19	205	2	D	38	825	3	D	50	742	40	D
Burr Ridge village	283	122	D	43	2,376	7	165	90	D	15	502	20	551	24	182
Cahokia village	28	5	D	6	33	NA	NA	12	D	4	D	25	351	18	D
Calumet City city	95	31	168	14	126	1	D	65	881	3	37	79	1,238	39	131
Campton Hills village	51	47	105	15	53	1	D	20	183	7	15	7	113	16	38
Canton city	D	21	113	6	D	1	D	48	1,625	6	24	37	D	27	191
Carbondale city	287	61	480	20	D	4	16	113	2,611	7	53	95	D	54	202
Carol Stream village	267	90	494	65	2,149	9	D	63	948	9	62	76	991	68	277
Carpentersville village	91	37	108	49	494	1	D	25	D	4	D	37	859	34	201
Cary village	12	66	168	28	147	5	33	33	302	10	D	28	397	40	D
Centralia city	D	22	133	8	66	NA	NA	69	2,297	8	62	36	555	30	123
Champaign city	1,117	247	1,760	90	1,685	26	223	209	3,908	31	352	301	6,636	150	1,321
Channahon village	70	14	47	13	132	1	D	24	D	4	D	25	297	17	89
Charleston city	D	29	149	18	520	3	D	90	D	7	48	51	804	43	D
Chatham village	14	19	71	13	99	4	D	18	D	5	11	17	303	15	D
Chicago city	23,960	10,164	150,662	2,933	107,618	642	9,379	6,556	179,570	914	19,132	6,022	115,965	4,997	44,783
Chicago Heights city	164	26	149	31	669	NA	NA	81	2,904	5	49	46	576	44	224
Chicago Ridge village	53	16	69	16	D	1	D	29	712	3	D	38	684	34	D
Cicero town	70	36	206	59	5,358	4	14	76	1,282	5	34	86	1,040	74	267
Collinsville city	158	83	621	35	439	6	37	58	D	10	D	67	1,471	48	278
Country Club Hills city	3	9	22	5	20	2	D	18	218	1	D	21	215	17	D
Crest Hill city	170	18	123	23	977	5	D	37	428	5	100	33	317	43	326
Crestwood village	193	21	113	34	1,336	2	D	25	654	11	272	39	746	39	D
Crystal Lake city	197	204	763	75	1,594	27	324	200	2,275	23	385	120	2,615	123	804
Danville city	114	59	349	30	691	6	D	114	D	11	216	87	1,544	66	339
Darien city	D	87	657	35	181	7	100	71	D	8	106	45	820	39	D
Decatur city	432	126	1,036	72	1,635	14	147	258	7,729	23	520	179	3,415	130	D
Deerfield village	402	233	4,476	59	1,512	24	144	86	D	15	197	62	1,337	38	352
DeKalb city	340	48	146	35	576	6	32	75	2,424	7	66	99	1,677	55	362
Des Plaines city	1,134	274	D	155	1,717	25	309	241	7,963	15	D	163	2,001	184	1,444
Dixon city	64	22	157	19	D	1	D	53	1,395	4	110	55	605	33	D
Dolton village	24	9	42	10	261	2	D	33	672	4	D	26	D	20	D
Downers Grove village	504	343	3,641	165	5,550	30	260	241	5,423	20	567	154	3,004	138	1,380
East Moline city	85	25	624	10	72	5	D	33	D	10	88	42	D	34	167
East Peoria city	107	41	366	33	690	5	D	41	D	6	12	91	2,856	41	D
East St. Louis city	45	14	110	18	133	3	D	61	1,032	1	D	35	D	19	123
Edwardsville city	117	130	876	28	869	14	60	82	607	16	D	80	1,650	48	331
Effingham city	162	42	270	30	475	4	D	103	D	10	D	79	1,844	61	D
Elgin city	298	275	1,441	170	6,969	24	142	301	7,727	29	D	185	3,061	169	1,484
Elk Grove Village village	695	179	1,872	108	6,234	8	D	139	5,661	16	65	114	1,739	125	1,061
Elmhurst city	367	244	1,290	87	1,643	19	234	228	6,636	24	334	108	1,721	113	840

Table C. Incorporated Places, Census Designated Places (CDPs), and Minor Civil Divisions (MCDs) of 10,000 or More Population — Economic Census

STATE City, town, township, borough, or CDP (county if applicable)	Utilities Number of establishments (1)	Utilities Number of employees (2)	Manufacturing Number of establishments (3)	Manufacturing Number of employees (4)	Wholesale trade[1] Number of establishments (5)	Wholesale trade[1] Number of employees (6)	Retail trade Number of establishments (7)	Retail trade Number of employees (8)	Transportation and warehousing Number of establishments (9)	Transportation and warehousing Number of employees (10)	Information Number of establishments (11)	Information Number of employees (12)	Finance and insurance Number of establishments (13)	Finance and insurance Number of employees (14)	Real estate and rental and leasing Number of establishments (15)
ILLINOIS—Con.															
Elmwood Park village	NA	NA	13	74	7	40	40	533	38	73	7	D	25	D	16
Evanston city	NA	NA	48	1,051	53	529	213	3,480	21	426	67	1,020	118	762	106
Evergreen Park village	NA	NA	8	106	9	30	87	1,475	6	20	8	52	45	313	12
Fairview Heights city	NA	NA	3	19	12	55	262	4,316	6	20	12	149	46	D	21
Forest Park village	NA	NA	17	728	23	440	54	1,086	8	42	5	20	18	D	11
Fox Lake village	1	D	9	83	6	D	45	792	10	19	5	D	22	154	10
Frankfort village	1	D	43	1,116	38	280	91	1,592	21	229	8	28	68	367	32
Franklin Park village	NA	NA	217	6,239	70	1,566	51	588	74	2,116	7	301	18	110	14
Freeport city	2	D	36	1,727	22	161	111	1,665	12	78	10	100	64	D	20
Gages Lake CDP	NA	NA	NA	NA	NA	NA	9	32	5	D	1	D	1	D	3
Galesburg city	NA	NA	30	732	23	362	153	3,184	26	447	12	230	67	D	27
Geneva city	NA	NA	43	1,616	37	D	212	2,812	14	509	12	242	86	468	31
Glen Carbon village	NA	NA	5	103	5	23	31	887	6	326	NA	NA	31	D	10
Glendale Heights village	NA	NA	47	3,195	66	1,605	68	1,459	50	225	4	D	29	130	15
Glen Ellyn village	NA	NA	9	D	32	340	95	1,154	12	D	15	69	83	411	44
Glenview village	1	D	47	635	100	1,478	159	3,471	43	400	24	867	141	5,813	85
Godfrey village	NA	NA	8	58	7	35	41	798	12	225	3	D	34	D	14
Granite City city	1	D	30	4,619	27	311	88	1,361	20	241	3	D	40	D	30
Grayslake village	NA	NA	24	578	26	226	54	602	21	375	14	30	37	167	22
Gurnee village	NA	NA	67	2,485	64	869	255	4,991	23	363	20	D	61	571	37
Hanover Park village	NA	NA	11	645	29	1,122	68	872	34	263	4	D	32	278	13
Harvey city	NA	NA	22	1,384	22	320	64	362	26	645	3	D	11	54	9
Hazel Crest village	NA	NA	8	406	4	32	24	141	9	37	3	D	12	71	10
Herrin city	NA	NA	4	37	11	112	75	1,177	11	179	1	D	19	D	11
Hickory Hills city	NA	NA	7	87	12	59	28	560	31	293	5	D	22	296	11
Highland Park city	NA	NA	24	115	48	172	166	2,543	12	47	19	77	86	487	61
Hinsdale village	1	D	8	56	27	202	71	785	13	57	7	D	79	490	40
Hoffman Estates village	NA	NA	25	824	80	1,536	116	2,421	49	439	45	3,521	78	1,170	32
Homer Glen village	NA	NA	15	59	13	34	56	882	53	148	1	D	34	147	25
Homewood village	1	D	NA	NA	18	D	92	1,859	11	71	12	382	52	D	27
Huntley village	1	D	30	1,046	40	355	65	1,048	25	144	5	5	26	124	13
Jacksonville city	1	D	21	1,491	16	D	118	1,652	10	238	11	146	47	803	23
Joliet city	6	963	73	3,592	93	1,662	408	6,796	168	2,833	29	502	146	1,159	83
Justice village	NA	NA	3	54	8	44	22	86	36	72	1	D	2	D	5
Kankakee city	2	D	29	1,347	31	591	84	1,152	21	480	11	289	43	D	26
Kewanee city	1	D	13	823	9	38	54	865	6	D	5	54	25	182	10
La Grange village	1	D	21	938	28	208	53	377	11	347	12	98	44	232	24
La Grange Park village	NA	NA	4	37	8	48	9	185	5	6	1	D	16	D	12
Lake Forest city	NA	NA	9	110	34	6,402	81	727	7	75	15	19	108	1,674	39
Lake in the Hills village	NA	NA	18	133	21	D	43	708	36	164	5	D	32	131	10
Lake Zurich village	NA	NA	44	2,696	65	736	108	2,409	14	75	11	220	64	1,298	25
Lansing village	NA	NA	29	1,427	31	310	103	1,840	32	313	6	74	40	308	25
Lemont village	NA	NA	21	1,077	26	645	48	782	54	453	4	16	37	D	20
Libertyville village	2	D	50	1,590	65	939	103	1,613	16	223	17	115	73	1,062	48
Lincoln city	3	D	10	436	9	230	68	961	7	188	5	D	38	D	21
Lincolnwood village	NA	NA	31	1,050	40	423	110	1,761	16	91	12	390	41	246	46
Lindenhurst village	NA	NA	NA	NA	4	D	17	90	10	15	NA	NA	15	84	7
Lisle village	1	D	26	696	74	1,167	64	944	28	334	39	1,357	110	1,627	46
Lockport city	NA	NA	16	383	17	42	55	954	36	214	4	D	36	171	12
Lombard village	3	D	58	895	106	1,333	239	4,273	49	657	44	785	124	1,900	76
Loves Park city	NA	NA	91	3,391	53	793	137	1,393	16	154	10	309	50	D	25
Lyons village	NA	NA	12	110	23	229	29	375	36	111	3	D	9	60	10
McHenry city	NA	NA	58	1,296	50	2,143	130	1,633	23	300	13	647	79	430	31
Machesney Park village	NA	NA	57	1,234	35	388	66	1,508	16	53	11	140	15	D	7
Macomb city	2	D	9	952	6	D	83	1,236	5	89	9	D	36	D	22
Marion city	3	D	21	1,584	26	346	126	2,137	23	496	18	198	83	1,139	25
Markham city	NA	NA	3	72	14	309	38	338	31	1,130	NA	NA	7	31	8
Matteson village	NA	NA	3	D	4	D	102	2,566	7	106	9	48	27	D	6
Mattoon city	2	D	14	862	26	D	113	1,610	12	140	20	D	51	D	21
Maywood village	2	D	20	445	6	D	38	198	10	347	2	D	10	36	8
Melrose Park village	NA	NA	97	4,615	59	1,157	100	2,887	56	1,809	4	88	31	D	20
Midlothian village	NA	NA	6	124	6	D	40	407	8	6	1	D	21	D	7
Minooka village	1	D	11	157	12	D	24	352	30	593	3	D	15	71	5
Mokena village	NA	NA	44	615	66	537	68	835	29	135	11	120	61	374	24
Moline city	2	D	39	2,353	34	D	259	4,706	29	1,099	28	789	116	1,390	56
Montgomery village	NA	NA	28	1,634	24	1,205	53	1,111	37	578	1	D	17	117	5
Morris city	NA	NA	15	286	18	173	82	1,221	13	387	8	83	42	225	16
Morton village	NA	NA	30	2,482	21	D	59	1,151	28	2,141	2	D	32	348	18
Morton Grove village	NA	NA	39	2,843	54	1,034	92	1,034	19	112	12	38	29	D	11
Mount Prospect village	NA	NA	39	1,541	81	1,167	162	3,666	80	507	23	506	91	926	45
Mount Vernon city	3	D	15	D	36	D	147	2,150	12	D	14	261	62	D	18
Mundelein village	2	D	59	1,625	69	698	110	1,413	28	141	11	53	45	227	23
Naperville city	8	D	82	1,751	224	2,764	518	9,553	107	1,463	81	1,964	396	5,581	207
New Lenox village	1	D	20	385	16	163	66	1,521	23	338	7	85	58	D	22
Niles village	NA	NA	55	1,914	100	2,067	273	6,549	48	885	21	493	72	D	46
Normal town	1	D	16	1,881	24	D	131	2,949	24	1,271	16	D	63	D	34
Norridge village	NA	NA	11	376	9	111	128	2,418	27	40	8	69	21	D	9
North Aurora village	NA	NA	18	1,104	14	D	54	1,045	7	61	3	41	23	107	9
Northbrook village	1	D	79	2,299	188	3,410	259	4,718	42	880	45	457	265	D	152
North Chicago city	NA	NA	15	6,797	11	415	35	124	9	43	3	15	11	187	4
Northlake city	NA	NA	17	2,149	17	317	35	516	33	841	8	145	11	D	5
Oak Forest city	NA	NA	14	366	21	89	59	630	26	245	4	63	39	230	14
Oak Lawn village	NA	NA	27	436	28	89	162	3,509	49	78	7	D	116	968	38
Oak Park village	NA	NA	18	158	22	46	154	1,491	14	53	26	307	71	446	83
O'Fallon city	2	D	11	276	15	68	84	2,087	15	186	10	187	65	D	37
Orland Park village	NA	NA	33	414	51	350	371	8,020	74	574	27	449	181	1,583	74
Oswego village	NA	NA	23	477	25	117	94	2,158	23	329	8	109	48	316	25
Ottawa city	1	D	24	826	18	209	109	1,512	16	1,116	11	128	51	D	23
Palatine village	1	D	43	1,882	69	446	186	3,623	78	1,746	19	155	126	716	72

1 Merchant wholesalers, except manufacturers' sales branches and offices.

Table C. Incorporated Places, Census Designated Places (CDPs), and Minor Civil Divisions (MCDs) of 10,000 or More Population — **Economic Census**

	Economic activity by sector, 2012														
	Real estate and rental and leasing	Professional, scientific, and technical services		Administration and support and waste management and mediation services		Educational services		Health care and social assistance		Arts, entertainment, and recreation		Accommodation and food services		Other services (except public administration)	
STATE City, town, township, borough, or CDP (county if applicable)	Number of employees	Number of establish-ments	Number of employees	Number of establish-ments	Number of employees	Number of establish-ments	Number of employees	Number of establish-ments	Number of employees	Number of establish-ments	Number of employees	Number of establish-ments	Number of employees	Number of establish-ments	Number of employees
	16	17	18	19	20	21	22	23	24	25	26	27	28	29	30
ILLINOIS—Con.															
Elmwood Park village	D	35	142	23	688	3	D	60	679	3	D	33	401	29	D
Evanston city	443	416	2,219	90	652	46	545	331	11,035	54	880	238	3,779	199	1,648
Evergreen Park village	85	30	133	15	131	8	41	105	3,244	5	82	37	724	37	D
Fairview Heights city	124	49	949	35	401	2	D	52	732	9	D	85	D	49	D
Forest Park village	37	35	124	13	323	10	79	34	793	5	25	63	684	42	283
Fox Lake village	26	17	94	12	132	3	17	16	121	14	72	40	553	26	D
Frankfort village	77	108	401	39	1,263	8	35	87	664	10	129	63	1,108	50	406
Franklin Park village	109	21	116	34	1,068	4	22	41	463	2	D	40	415	51	D
Freeport city	68	59	345	29	D	5	D	91	2,386	11	122	64	889	60	481
Gages Lake CDP	2	17	14	11	17	NA	NA	14	101	2	D	13	164	10	45
Galesburg city	107	56	285	33	D	3	D	110	3,555	11	185	92	1,464	64	461
Geneva city	54	183	680	41	528	15	64	138	2,846	13	D	96	1,931	65	484
Glen Carbon village	19	33	259	11	295	1	D	53	D	5	D	20	458	23	D
Glendale Heights village	151	43	142	25	509	5	26	35	993	10	169	45	706	42	D
Glen Ellyn village	278	180	484	49	328	17	92	104	1,223	11	473	61	959	58	332
Glenview village	475	280	2,042	111	1,030	31	319	271	5,037	40	586	158	2,761	142	774
Godfrey village	106	21	113	17	50	3	D	37	D	4	D	26	411	32	154
Granite City city	150	32	214	20	312	3	16	86	D	8	112	67	1,011	58	439
Grayslake village	56	91	434	44	574	10	48	81	638	13	D	51	791	46	211
Gurnee village	175	126	488	72	1,887	14	163	174	1,691	18	D	136	3,217	71	552
Hanover Park village	D	38	151	33	2,218	7	88	36	332	3	73	36	446	36	D
Harvey city	63	8	48	17	305	1	D	57	D	NA	NA	40	744	19	77
Hazel Crest village	142	12	32	7	84	NA	NA	60	2,253	NA	NA	16	162	8	D
Herrin city	39	24	122	11	82	3	D	59	1,998	6	31	26	360	23	121
Hickory Hills city	45	35	143	21	218	3	D	28	310	4	25	30	D	14	64
Highland Park city	186	233	1,039	97	1,129	28	298	174	2,604	41	684	90	1,506	123	656
Hinsdale village	191	141	465	44	D	17	D	182	4,554	13	D	39	D	45	376
Hoffman Estates village	123	223	1,756	69	882	19	411	239	4,895	17	324	117	1,993	67	466
Homer Glen village	54	68	260	38	195	3	30	51	582	10	71	31	427	45	263
Homewood village	86	68	361	28	444	11	71	89	1,652	11	169	60	1,114	45	268
Huntley village	28	40	141	28	229	5	47	38	353	5	192	22	248	33	D
Jacksonville city	87	30	605	23	155	2	D	112	2,482	14	220	69	1,140	47	D
Joliet city	400	236	1,485	148	2,350	17	D	407	8,575	24	480	235	5,812	180	1,558
Justice village	20	14	44	9	D	NA	NA	17	D	NA	NA	16	101	21	196
Kankakee city	75	54	293	29	162	2	D	113	3,937	7	207	53	D	48	265
Kewanee city	24	14	57	6	7	1	D	40	856	3	89	21	D	28	78
La Grange village	80	90	252	21	280	6	52	90	2,068	7	D	50	D	40	228
La Grange Park village	D	34	65	7	11	2	D	28	658	7	155	11	108	11	146
Lake Forest city	213	171	796	38	429	10	54	89	2,599	22	868	55	D	49	213
Lake in the Hills village	22	53	236	31	1,929	5	50	51	583	8	D	29	524	44	D
Lake Zurich village	100	117	447	51	2,490	16	111	64	606	12	127	57	D	54	D
Lansing village	95	46	169	39	420	4	D	61	533	7	D	62	1,206	55	605
Lemont village	75	61	130	26	199	8	68	58	1,503	12	D	44	D	35	186
Libertyville village	288	213	1,079	43	908	16	121	207	4,469	15	D	86	1,242	92	700
Lincoln city	81	27	124	6	27	4	D	50	1,211	6	D	44	689	43	177
Lincolnwood village	129	112	713	40	3,864	3	D	90	1,274	5	112	42	662	39	207
Lindenhurst village	22	26	79	7	35	3	7	29	D	1	D	12	165	10	38
Lisle village	406	221	4,947	65	2,506	16	250	81	1,550	5	45	64	1,272	68	361
Lockport city	71	37	147	24	145	7	43	32	294	11	100	49	484	56	305
Lombard village	2,385	222	2,198	100	6,835	12	144	165	2,796	15	D	148	3,359	131	913
Loves Park city	102	44	221	43	1,083	7	62	60	1,251	13	368	65	921	53	409
Lyons village	19	18	48	14	71	2	D	15	D	5	102	30	315	15	113
McHenry city	D	78	398	52	411	7	40	104	3,392	7	55	83	1,267	76	396
Machesney Park village	125	23	360	21	265	2	D	17	D	1	D	37	658	42	D
Macomb city	96	35	227	16	123	2	D	61	1,532	6	147	80	1,469	40	174
Marion city	114	72	324	32	717	5	D	106	3,468	12	70	81	1,785	37	271
Markham city	105	5	41	10	61	NA	NA	18	153	2	D	19	D	14	60
Matteson village	9	36	129	19	419	4	17	54	729	1	D	55	1,197	23	D
Mattoon city	92	30	245	23	467	2	D	48	D	5	52	71	1,400	44	220
Maywood village	20	14	36	20	667	2	D	37	D	4	D	20	170	18	136
Melrose Park village	106	23	83	44	2,208	1	D	117	2,803	7	183	72	D	44	D
Midlothian village	42	10	33	9	72	4	8	23	194	2	D	36	377	20	D
Minooka village	D	19	D	11	62	2	D	17	D	4	D	21	326	9	D
Mokena village	100	111	572	46	585	20	346	58	911	13	81	45	D	65	328
Moline city	286	113	990	64	5,180	14	69	194	3,190	15	382	156	2,771	107	710
Montgomery village	15	28	187	26	969	1	D	13	D	3	D	22	387	25	74
Morris city	D	45	186	16	50	9	D	79	D	10	D	52	869	53	D
Morton village	59	37	281	23	239	5	D	62	1,279	10	94	47	840	47	265
Morton Grove village	25	87	346	30	326	7	61	68	839	9	215	49	662	47	216
Mount Prospect village	235	176	2,613	72	1,464	10	59	136	2,433	10	234	112	1,568	96	672
Mount Vernon city	62	61	455	16	813	1	D	133	D	12	D	70	1,548	62	344
Mundelein village	66	107	590	68	511	7	26	52	310	12	D	75	1,082	74	D
Naperville city	731	1,077	9,792	258	5,702	90	540	616	11,118	79	1,322	361	7,975	285	2,227
New Lenox village	D	55	294	39	267	6	66	68	2,754	6	D	45	1,006	59	D
Niles village	319	89	472	44	578	10	92	156	3,290	10	437	135	D	85	500
Normal town	256	69	552	37	D	7	D	93	2,939	12	91	106	2,742	58	D
Norridge village	31	16	75	29	D	NA	NA	26	725	4	D	42	D	26	D
North Aurora village	26	38	86	21	404	4	D	43	408	4	D	18	380	30	D
Northbrook village	2,172	579	10,747	174	5,222	35	216	285	3,834	38	911	96	2,082	117	774
North Chicago city	29	17	163	19	151	6	D	21	D	1	D	31	390	15	73
Northlake city	151	14	320	16	732	NA	NA	18	518	1	D	24	279	18	59
Oak Forest city	64	48	131	36	1,007	4	96	52	D	4	D	37	593	42	184
Oak Lawn village	162	96	385	70	1,061	8	79	249	9,138	15	165	108	2,406	100	765
Oak Park village	352	290	994	65	1,978	26	191	300	5,810	36	497	101	1,703	132	680
O'Fallon city	143	85	1,347	27	196	8	123	70	D	9	D	69	D	50	324
Orland Park village	201	237	1,155	71	1,439	22	D	303	D	22	674	170	4,254	130	1,077
Oswego village	D	72	154	46	1,268	13	286	72	785	10	108	60	1,375	61	D
Ottawa city	152	55	539	26	421	5	25	84	1,893	7	D	61	918	49	334
Palatine village	198	349	1,385	118	1,335	27	260	147	1,988	20	D	111	1,558	158	860

Table C. Incorporated Places, Census Designated Places (CDPs), and Minor Civil Divisions (MCDs) of 10,000 or More Population — Economic Census

STATE City, town, township, borough, or CDP (county if applicable)	Utilities — Number of establishments (1)	Utilities — Number of employees (2)	Manufacturing — Number of establishments (3)	Manufacturing — Number of employees (4)	Wholesale trade[1] — Number of establishments (5)	Wholesale trade[1] — Number of employees (6)	Retail trade — Number of establishments (7)	Retail trade — Number of employees (8)	Transportation and warehousing — Number of establishments (9)	Transportation and warehousing — Number of employees (10)	Information — Number of establishments (11)	Information — Number of employees (12)	Finance and insurance — Number of establishments (13)	Finance and insurance — Number of employees (14)	Real estate and rental and leasing — Number of establishments (15)
ILLINOIS—Con.															
Palos Heights city	NA	NA	8	38	14	42	36	398	10	181	3	D	54	285	21
Palos Hills city	NA	NA	8	36	7	25	37	227	59	113	2	D	22	142	13
Park Forest village	NA	NA	6	259	2	D	13	81	9	17	5	D	13	D	7
Park Ridge city	NA	NA	10	358	52	191	93	1,009	36	89	23	147	110	773	68
Pekin city	2	D	30	1,003	15	D	125	2,127	10	79	11	177	59	955	20
Peoria city	9	D	84	3,270	150	2,501	502	7,845	58	1,262	76	1,969	290	3,000	152
Peru city	1	D	18	997	27	263	112	2,518	21	773	6	106	41	199	18
Plainfield village	NA	NA	21	620	28	361	97	1,781	41	234	11	218	71	324	29
Plano city	NA	NA	10	675	2	D	26	127	14	D	2	D	14	82	2
Pontiac city	2	D	12	1,303	7	77	54	965	8	87	4	44	29	D	9
Prospect Heights city	NA	NA	18	105	26	111	27	638	32	86	2	D	14	83	11
Quincy city	3	D	45	1,744	71	1,290	256	4,452	17	266	26	458	116	D	50
Rantoul village	NA	NA	16	1,448	5	42	41	602	3	7	9	501	19	172	15
Richton Park village	NA	NA	NA	NA	2	D	13	96	2	D	1	D	5	24	8
Riverdale village	NA	NA	9	475	4	105	14	131	8	220	3	10	4	23	1
River Forest village	NA	NA	5	16	7	17	27	622	1	D	7	12	24	D	22
River Grove village	NA	NA	14	156	11	D	20	286	28	136	2	D	9	28	3
Rockford city	4	D	340	15,649	187	2,468	551	8,326	87	4,064	51	1,007	295	2,833	144
Rock Island city	3	D	39	1,390	64	1,280	79	969	30	1,025	12	305	48	1,128	22
Rolling Meadows city	NA	NA	40	2,268	76	1,147	58	1,245	32	317	24	465	101	1,856	36
Romeoville village	2	D	50	1,642	67	1,833	59	1,194	100	3,373	20	540	30	198	22
Roscoe village	NA	NA	19	382	7	45	32	336	5	D	2	D	22	D	7
Roselle village	NA	NA	38	1,017	45	760	62	592	49	673	4	16	43	189	27
Round Lake village	NA	NA	9	246	5	6	18	171	23	37	1	D	14	35	6
Round Lake Beach village	NA	NA	7	67	6	18	54	1,518	20	13	2	D	19	155	9
St. Charles city	NA	NA	93	5,614	102	1,005	160	3,016	23	358	24	352	130	670	79
Sauk Village village	NA	NA	NA	NA	4	81	7	70	7	D	NA	NA	3	14	NA
Schaumburg village	1	D	151	3,929	270	4,850	483	11,457	140	1,089	109	3,892	294	6,813	148
Schiller Park village	NA	NA	69	2,320	32	841	38	409	76	1,154	2	D	14	157	8
Shiloh village	NA	NA	NA	NA	3	3	36	801	2	D	2	D	18	D	10
Shorewood village	NA	NA	13	308	10	65	53	1,391	14	D	NA	NA	27	114	13
Skokie village	1	D	134	5,070	122	D	334	5,566	58	1,067	37	585	153	892	103
South Elgin village	NA	NA	51	1,593	40	243	46	906	18	86	3	D	26	155	13
South Holland village	NA	NA	46	2,148	45	855	41	509	31	1,559	2	D	39	D	16
Springfield city	8	D	66	2,116	130	2,845	586	10,451	42	1,043	81	2,127	301	5,802	152
Sterling city	1	D	12	813	15	175	91	1,688	2	D	7	159	34	D	12
Streamwood village	2	D	34	764	21	83	88	1,637	52	316	3	22	47	D	21
Streator city	2	D	16	490	15	386	53	759	7	122	4	D	35	252	10
Summit village	NA	NA	10	310	13	D	27	157	40	367	6	D	15	53	5
Swansea village	1	D	8	86	9	28	39	503	10	64	4	D	44	316	21
Sycamore city	1	D	29	1,587	12	142	54	1,156	7	598	6	D	38	251	15
Taylorville city	1	D	7	233	8	D	62	945	4	56	10	D	38	D	14
Tinley Park village	NA	NA	38	1,063	64	739	157	3,495	57	340	10	D	88	644	35
Urbana city	2	D	21	D	27	D	83	1,532	14	234	8	D	37	D	31
Vernon Hills village	NA	NA	24	1,696	68	2,464	214	5,361	27	D	17	329	70	632	24
Villa Park village	NA	NA	47	592	40	775	119	1,706	28	605	10	D	36	136	13
Warrenville city	NA	NA	15	174	33	1,207	30	561	9	33	11	D	52	1,312	16
Washington city	1	D	6	268	7	D	58	1,151	10	D	7	39	23	D	13
Waterloo city	NA	NA	5	64	5	20	40	824	7	108	9	D	31	D	9
Wauconda village	NA	NA	65	973	40	721	42	336	6	6	4	D	12	55	14
Waukegan city	4	D	81	4,911	65	1,228	209	3,534	48	1,600	9	322	80	597	52
Westchester village	NA	NA	11	73	17	371	21	297	10	17	6	169	58	913	17
West Chicago city	NA	NA	94	4,848	61	1,725	77	1,098	48	503	8	28	35	203	19
Western Springs village	NA	NA	NA	NA	8	14	19	280	4	D	2	D	28	99	15
Westmont village	1	D	30	654	70	714	102	1,947	44	D	27	428	68	832	31
Wheaton city	1	D	21	440	50	D	176	2,564	17	79	32	303	142	1,571	66
Wheeling village	NA	NA	141	7,219	143	2,705	90	1,437	76	970	10	34	36	619	30
Wilmette village	NA	NA	11	95	33	69	98	1,255	4	6	9	38	68	D	38
Winnetka village	NA	NA	4	14	9	21	48	398	1	D	8	14	38	199	26
Wood Dale city	NA	NA	84	2,222	112	2,367	49	1,289	149	1,786	8	234	23	202	9
Woodridge village	2	D	40	1,714	64	2,715	98	2,039	70	2,259	15	717	54	681	31
Wood River city	2	D	9	56	10	149	59	1,079	10	236	1	D	27	D	9
Woodstock city	1	D	53	2,903	35	D	85	1,582	17	D	9	252	35	242	28
Worth village	NA	NA	NA	NA	6	8	34	317	14	18	2	D	23	D	7
Yorkville city	1	D	13	546	14	90	49	865	16	D	3	D	25	160	13
Zion city	3	D	18	280	8	D	48	841	12	187	2	D	10	72	7
INDIANA	538	15,558	8,141	452,513	6,460	91,474	21,601	309,552	5,096	118,242	2,183	42,361	9,692	96,927	5,729
Anderson city	2	D	48	982	36	D	234	3,713	29	1,411	20	1,100	85	483	58
Auburn city	1	D	34	2,454	7	D	66	1,016	4	D	9	D	41	232	17
Avon town	NA	NA	11	850	11	D	113	2,490	16	249	8	68	45	207	24
Bedford city	3	D	28	967	14	152	103	1,419	7	57	13	134	47	332	14
Beech Grove city	NA	NA	37	766	34	515	46	1,007	9	D	4	D	25	D	12
Bloomington city	9	D	40	1,182	40	444	386	6,729	19	305	46	1,079	141	1,090	134
Brownsburg town	NA	NA	26	663	19	D	88	1,773	20	1,676	3	D	52	236	21
Carmel city	3	D	61	827	135	1,253	289	5,860	24	146	70	2,071	387	8,428	200
Cedar Lake town	NA	NA	4	D	2	D	29	333	2	D	NA	NA	4	17	7
Chesterton town	1	D	13	D	12	D	56	607	12	286	4	30	43	189	10
Clarksville town	6	110	24	544	16	158	192	4,323	30	1,389	8	D	44	243	23
Columbus city	8	D	100	10,319	53	895	193	3,316	29	454	21	D	101	807	60
Connersville city	3	D	26	1,185	12	D	64	925	8	D	8	D	28	139	18
Crawfordsville city	1	D	38	3,510	19	111	98	1,440	10	149	11	D	50	244	24
Crown Point city	2	D	36	838	38	D	75	895	10	114	13	196	63	460	32
Dyer town	NA	NA	9	222	18	25	45	554	10	56	NA	NA	27	138	9
East Chicago city	1	D	42	7,628	35	D	47	356	24	346	3	D	17	147	12
Elkhart city	4	D	314	16,342	144	2,148	258	3,871	45	990	20	313	129	1,097	76
Evansville city	15	D	173	7,490	219	4,224	730	11,717	104	8,765	72	2,407	285	3,836	178
Fishers town	1	D	37	685	83	1,279	185	3,340	35	827	45	1,374	181	2,991	86

1 Merchant wholesalers, except manufacturers' sales branches and offices.

STATE City, town, township, borough, or CDP (county if applicable)	Real estate and rental and leasing — Number of employees	Professional, scientific, and technical services — Number of establishments	Number of employees	Administration and support and waste management and mediation services — Number of establishments	Number of employees	Educational services — Number of establishments	Number of employees	Health care and social assistance — Number of establishments	Number of employees	Arts, entertainment, and recreation — Number of establishments	Number of employees	Accommodation and food services — Number of establishments	Number of employees	Other services (except public administration) — Number of establishments	Number of employees
	16	17	18	19	20	21	22	23	24	25	26	27	28	29	30
ILLINOIS—Con.															
Palos Heights city	78	88	258	17	64	5	35	176	5,774	4	40	37	540	44	238
Palos Hills city	29	63	891	26	155	3	D	58	743	4	D	29	328	26	72
Park Forest village	38	8	27	9	D	2	D	35	420	4	D	9	160	17	108
Park Ridge city	D	252	874	70	1,000	12	82	262	7,344	13	185	66	887	84	820
Pekin city	57	41	251	32	255	5	29	92	2,147	12	98	86	1,460	71	318
Peoria city	778	358	4,947	134	7,271	20	243	441	21,289	41	1,123	326	6,429	212	4,345
Peru city	73	31	238	13	511	NA	NA	67	1,508	4	186	60	1,203	40	244
Plainfield village	128	134	801	58	561	11	65	119	1,104	9	265	85	1,610	66	448
Plano city	D	11	43	11	D	NA	NA	9	42	1	D	19	109	12	45
Pontiac city	29	19	72	10	D	2	D	38	1,436	2	D	33	413	25	178
Prospect Heights city	64	55	126	39	2,535	9	60	17	153	4	21	22	484	27	109
Quincy city	201	116	693	52	1,126	10	94	131	5,288	24	358	126	2,186	112	D
Rantoul village	96	17	49	7	D	NA	NA	23	D	6	D	27	446	11	D
Richton Park village	30	5	D	4	D	1	D	14	314	3	D	15	250	8	34
Riverdale village	D	4	30	3	D	NA	NA	11	238	1	D	4	9	10	84
River Forest village	27	61	101	11	56	7	90	60	D	8	30	15	266	17	105
River Grove village	D	12	91	13	88	3	D	10	D	2	D	22	235	30	D
Rockford city	1,187	422	2,885	178	8,715	27	289	488	16,868	46	845	336	7,122	302	1,967
Rock Island city	66	114	1,041	35	540	7	D	114	3,686	15	161	62	1,356	71	457
Rolling Meadows city	D	188	2,196	72	3,656	9	D	58	940	5	D	73	1,264	41	355
Romeoville village	435	38	346	43	1,542	7	36	33	D	10	420	61	1,259	46	537
Roscoe village	25	19	58	9	71	2	D	29	D	6	158	23	401	35	D
Roselle village	73	97	262	38	358	6	47	49	358	5	70	55	437	52	337
Round Lake village	46	28	46	24	149	NA	NA	20	101	4	D	21	237	21	D
Round Lake Beach village	25	20	74	40	45	1	D	28	348	7	87	31	484	29	122
St. Charles city	456	214	D	85	1,366	20	163	160	1,707	27	D	114	2,960	102	791
Sauk Village village	NA	5	41	4	10	NA	NA	9	D	NA	NA	8	98	4	5
Schaumburg village	1,064	713	10,430	255	13,867	40	284	273	3,649	35	917	265	7,508	238	2,419
Schiller Park village	104	23	99	11	D	2	D	14	344	3	22	57	1,521	34	D
Shiloh village	29	15	137	6	38	2	D	18	D	3	D	23	D	4	17
Shorewood village	31	24	140	11	188	4	D	25	290	1	D	35	564	24	225
Skokie village	670	384	2,644	125	2,442	32	281	391	5,968	25	480	155	3,453	181	1,430
South Elgin village	35	46	124	25	324	4	29	37	683	6	D	38	522	45	D
South Holland village	75	47	367	30	365	4	6	76	1,586	2	D	34	481	50	D
Springfield city	676	420	3,992	167	5,448	27	351	371	19,230	62	1,134	402	8,032	362	2,870
Sterling city	38	24	119	9	380	2	D	46	1,653	3	D	39	822	30	191
Streamwood village	247	81	236	47	256	9	20	56	1,304	4	D	64	991	57	D
Streator city	27	14	55	11	1,044	1	D	41	874	5	D	51	440	28	141
Summit village	27	8	75	6	129	1	D	16	87	1	D	20	272	25	D
Swansea village	156	62	610	21	116	3	17	79	1,331	3	D	21	434	28	259
Sycamore city	D	54	311	25	192	6	69	66	1,009	9	64	50	851	38	427
Taylorville city	80	37	437	12	165	2	D	39	D	4	D	38	D	34	199
Tinley Park village	135	140	990	65	1,144	12	76	175	3,098	18	216	130	2,621	71	421
Urbana city	1,483	73	539	18	464	6	D	72	6,743	13	82	108	1,781	51	605
Vernon Hills village	D	160	1,632	30	671	17	145	111	1,182	19	508	95	1,717	40	401
Villa Park village	D	57	199	36	1,024	5	D	42	D	4	28	61	816	83	418
Warrenville city	D	67	850	51	2,618	2	D	34	D	5	D	42	1,045	25	149
Washington city	29	26	111	14	52	3	22	24	D	5	24	34	515	25	D
Waterloo city	D	25	D	12	53	1	D	29	D	5	D	34	D	19	D
Wauconda village	43	42	242	36	2,429	3	25	18	309	3	D	26	375	38	254
Waukegan city	239	163	961	142	7,938	12	44	131	3,120	18	358	133	1,955	100	411
Westchester village	101	69	527	41	1,819	2	D	87	1,455	4	24	30	264	33	304
West Chicago city	129	78	800	86	4,747	11	58	43	535	8	104	46	567	46	255
Western Springs village	114	84	296	8	40	4	43	31	275	6	47	14	228	18	D
Westmont village	150	128	902	64	2,298	9	80	94	1,661	11	217	74	1,036	77	1,292
Wheaton city	209	415	D	92	675	17	70	199	3,535	22	393	111	1,954	104	664
Wheeling village	116	124	976	93	2,794	20	68	75	1,456	4	D	57	D	78	383
Wilmette village	D	174	390	37	162	15	83	131	1,192	19	225	50	D	81	503
Winnetka village	82	78	149	15	80	9	23	46	255	11	D	22	305	31	156
Wood Dale city	D	56	185	43	1,734	2	D	28	D	4	46	32	591	42	632
Woodridge village	303	115	924	69	D	7	42	83	495	12	231	55	965	48	451
Wood River city	34	15	66	5	D	1	D	24	D	1	D	41	581	23	111
Woodstock city	112	65	266	33	482	3	D	76	2,122	8	D	57	720	58	272
Worth village	18	21	76	8	52	1	D	21	157	2	D	20	235	21	116
Yorkville city	D	42	278	22	754	8	16	55	D	8	D	42	699	35	184
Zion city	18	10	53	17	356	NA	NA	31	1,692	1	D	39	502	27	D
INDIANA	31,715	12,829	99,962	7,106	178,946	1,127	9,664	15,156	396,923	2,069	33,726	13,057	255,223	10,777	72,937
Anderson city	276	107	513	43	1,367	10	49	174	5,181	23	D	148	2,940	113	739
Auburn city	72	44	184	22	654	3	D	62	1,235	10	187	54	1,135	33	160
Avon town	113	37	147	18	354	4	30	91	2,565	11	D	77	2,118	36	D
Bedford city	49	49	716	10	D	1	D	65	1,836	8	33	48	D	51	289
Beech Grove city	D	31	152	15	616	1	D	24	957	5	D	24	D	43	D
Bloomington city	709	225	1,647	90	4,669	34	204	277	8,020	24	413	340	7,466	150	1,622
Brownsburg town	54	65	247	24	138	1	D	58	D	17	322	68	1,415	41	227
Carmel city	1,684	575	3,523	183	4,298	46	621	414	9,019	64	868	185	3,477	187	1,056
Cedar Lake town	20	15	54	6	D	1	D	7	D	4	D	25	385	14	D
Chesterton town	44	52	198	16	D	4	23	37	D	2	D	58	1,014	36	398
Clarksville town	127	29	101	18	144	2	D	51	1,110	13	299	84	D	45	D
Columbus city	218	139	3,462	54	1,659	13	D	206	4,641	18	D	167	3,488	87	583
Connersville city	D	24	D	9	D	3	6	49	1,508	5	43	40	D	34	D
Crawfordsville city	60	37	141	22	670	3	5	73	1,189	8	D	70	1,040	56	D
Crown Point city	105	102	724	30	360	12	61	106	3,370	12	D	69	1,271	85	606
Dyer town	11	27	198	17	D	3	D	48	1,756	6	D	45	748	28	D
East Chicago city	173	16	193	24	652	1	D	35	1,638	3	D	39	D	31	212
Elkhart city	452	138	880	52	3,344	10	57	166	5,529	12	D	161	3,011	115	849
Evansville city	1,359	357	3,195	177	10,232	33	260	499	16,977	59	D	403	9,956	309	2,477
Fishers town	267	341	1,893	116	5,812	28	275	218	3,437	39	785	175	3,719	109	1,064

Table C. Incorporated Places, Census Designated Places (CDPs), and Minor Civil Divisions (MCDs) of 10,000 or More Population — **Economic Census**

STATE City, town, township, borough, or CDP (county if applicable)	Utilities		Manufacturing		Wholesale trade[1]		Retail trade		Transportation and warehousing		Information		Finance and insurance		Real estate and rental and leasing
	Number of establish-ments	Number of employees	Number of establish-ments	Number of employees	Number of establish-ments	Number of employees	Number of establish-ments	Number of employees	Number of establish-ments	Number of employees	Number of establish-ments	Number of employees	Number of establish-ments	Number of employees	Number of establish-ments
	1	2	3	4	5	6	7	8	9	10	11	12	13	14	15
INDIANA—Con.															
Fort Wayne city	12	D	352	14,791	412	5,926	1,096	18,193	168	4,431	119	2,639	578	8,364	307
Frankfort city	NA	NA	22	2,004	10	66	73	788	7	229	4	41	25	170	9
Franklin city	7	D	46	2,613	27	392	71	1,274	11	269	9	144	41	267	17
Gary city	17	D	42	6,100	44	928	173	1,321	48	4,001	6	D	35	170	40
Goshen city	3	D	103	14,551	30	825	162	2,853	12	200	8	104	69	623	36
Granger CDP	NA	NA	25	339	22	153	80	1,239	3	D	5	28	29	112	17
Greencastle city	2	D	10	1,239	4	D	65	873	8	D	3	D	29	159	14
Greenfield city	2	D	20	2,269	12	240	93	1,506	6	102	8	D	39	229	23
Greensburg city	2	D	30	3,410	19	241	89	1,062	12	D	7	D	35	263	14
Greenwood city	6	D	41	1,175	45	1,444	327	6,283	41	850	19	217	137	849	67
Griffith town	NA	NA	18	332	23	D	43	511	23	328	1	D	25	128	14
Hammond city	9	D	59	3,013	81	D	196	3,401	68	2,193	18	273	59	424	38
Highland town	NA	NA	20	169	22	98	121	2,561	15	352	5	D	51	325	20
Hobart city	NA	NA	19	816	26	D	224	4,767	21	143	9	91	36	198	22
Huntington city	2	D	47	2,849	12	177	85	1,048	11	308	8	D	43	243	19
Indianapolis city	25	2,283	813	41,099	1,210	22,417	2,725	42,887	687	34,548	499	12,920	1,515	27,324	1,177
Indianapolis city (balance)	25	2,283	811	D	1,209	D	2,716	42,551	684	D	499	12,920	1,511	27,306	1,176
Jasper city	1	D	44	4,779	41	797	124	2,463	14	413	10	D	55	422	19
Jeffersonville city	4	D	77	5,491	49	686	120	1,524	49	1,944	9	255	76	1,396	41
Kokomo city	8	165	62	D	50	498	297	4,441	28	538	15	D	117	665	64
Lafayette city	4	D	81	11,970	81	1,088	416	7,125	53	1,204	27	453	167	D	103
Lake Station city	NA	NA	5	84	3	D	29	378	11	77	NA	NA	9	35	1
La Porte city	5	D	51	2,721	25	207	109	1,469	13	157	13	D	49	324	24
Lawrence city	NA	NA	25	363	45	780	120	1,957	19	D	10	D	65	375	40
Lebanon city	2	D	31	871	21	504	70	963	24	638	8	D	33	147	22
Logansport city	1	D	25	1,494	16	218	91	1,283	8	186	10	D	37	243	13
Madison city	4	D	24	1,939	11	89	94	864	7	40	8	D	24	157	19
Marion city	2	D	38	3,034	21	206	176	2,595	19	1,007	6	424	68	D	29
Martinsville city	4	D	15	402	5	33	79	1,043	7	53	5	D	32	154	14
Merrillville town	11	D	25	452	37	D	204	3,524	20	181	17	590	128	1,143	66
Michigan City city	2	D	59	2,978	36	448	250	3,669	12	D	14	177	42	453	29
Mishawaka city	1	D	85	2,618	61	679	371	6,956	28	D	35	644	128	1,479	56
Muncie city	4	D	64	1,955	53	551	355	5,605	29	487	13	D	125	1,193	71
Munster town	NA	NA	13	455	24	D	76	1,132	24	459	1	D	49	330	30
New Albany city	5	D	83	4,966	48	509	144	2,129	21	205	16	175	101	546	35
New Castle city	3	D	14	696	5	D	91	832	3	D	7	64	31	261	17
New Haven city	2	D	35	1,515	32	1,255	58	615	17	266	1	D	31	127	13
Noblesville city	6	114	46	2,056	68	634	231	4,179	26	94	23	372	101	770	57
Peru city	NA	NA	19	914	15	D	63	670	6	D	4	D	34	194	8
Plainfield town	2	D	21	582	32	2,638	135	2,794	67	4,359	10	105	44	190	30
Plymouth city	4	D	45	2,588	8	114	88	1,384	1	D	13	92	34	243	18
Portage city	1	D	20	2,252	24	481	91	1,828	41	357	8	D	43	216	30
Purdue University CDP	1	D	NA	NA	NA	NA	6	65	NA	NA	NA	NA	1	D	2
Richmond city	2	D	70	4,238	38	352	208	3,244	27	509	18	D	79	689	38
St. John town	NA	NA	6	17	12	44	46	921	9	45	NA	NA	29	136	13
Schererville town	NA	NA	12	374	19	130	105	2,289	17	58	11	129	62	376	34
Seymour city	3	D	37	4,453	19	300	128	1,791	28	1,337	10	D	55	270	34
Shelbyville city	3	D	51	3,832	18	370	89	1,197	10	521	9	79	43	209	22
South Bend city	4	D	164	7,099	154	2,577	315	5,010	85	1,899	61	2,217	165	2,076	107
Speedway town	NA	NA	6	581	6	54	52	801	8	D	4	28	31	158	13
Terre Haute city	6	D	74	6,131	77	971	330	4,709	45	1,232	29	D	117	1,155	72
Valparaiso city	2	D	46	1,909	42	550	193	3,356	18	178	18	188	93	552	62
Vincennes city	5	89	19	1,348	18	110	127	1,802	16	125	8	72	50	389	29
Wabash city	4	44	32	1,847	12	138	80	962	3	D	11	D	29	240	10
Warsaw city	4	D	40	5,799	32	D	148	2,492	8	90	17	201	78	600	30
Washington city	4	D	9	969	3	54	64	663	10	295	4	D	35	167	14
Westfield city	2	D	19	1,092	30	722	85	1,872	11	124	13	D	34	113	24
West Lafayette city	1	D	15	488	5	15	61	1,350	3	D	12	346	40	D	36
Yorktown town	NA	NA	11	144	6	18	14	74	5	D	3	D	9	D	8
Zionsville town	NA	NA	17	187	17	114	61	458	17	D	9	D	52	153	24
IOWA	272	7,656	3,598	203,722	4,302	58,872	12,046	174,556	3,499	55,762	1,545	30,342	6,071	91,750	2,742
Altoona city	NA	NA	8	273	16	600	46	1,823	12	109	4	52	22	D	10
Ames city	1	D	43	3,163	35	204	212	4,054	18	519	36	921	84	561	72
Ankeny city	NA	NA	27	3,429	40	1,385	142	3,622	26	498	17	178	69	D	58
Bettendorf city	3	D	27	3,277	42	466	95	1,525	19	245	10	132	81	528	45
Boone city	2	D	13	228	5	D	53	842	7	D	5	D	33	167	11
Burlington city	1	D	26	2,687	24	377	114	1,524	17	154	7	158	58	430	25
Carroll city	2	D	17	936	21	203	105	1,312	18	245	11	149	44	683	15
Cedar Falls city	NA	NA	43	1,523	48	961	154	2,884	23	D	24	317	86	849	49
Cedar Rapids city	10	D	120	15,535	219	3,999	489	11,220	114	7,302	95	4,248	297	8,395	159
Clinton city	3	D	30	2,803	22	155	127	2,161	20	176	14	417	46	336	26
Clive city	NA	NA	14	625	38	286	103	2,345	12	93	16	185	84	1,131	47
Coralville city	NA	NA	13	1,332	20	360	183	3,968	15	243	17	491	45	632	29
Council Bluffs city	3	D	39	3,878	67	1,010	236	5,340	56	851	14	225	102	549	70
Davenport city	8	D	98	6,751	180	2,928	478	8,922	63	1,182	55	1,539	202	1,954	121
Des Moines city	12	D	155	6,111	270	4,570	647	9,121	139	6,467	128	5,658	406	23,431	212
Dubuque city	4	D	87	3,472	81	883	336	6,175	51	1,901	40	1,276	141	2,881	80
Fort Dodge city	3	D	33	1,006	36	544	151	2,488	33	1,508	21	D	63	375	35
Fort Madison city	1	D	16	1,935	5	D	45	748	7	76	3	D	24	162	9
Indianola city	1	D	9	189	12	281	56	1,103	5	D	6	D	25	D	15
Iowa City city	1	D	42	2,852	34	676	247	4,188	20	319	20	D	100	867	75
Johnston city	1	D	9	72	20	158	35	754	11	129	5	78	57	1,872	21
Keokuk city	1	D	29	1,834	12	67	62	995	9	141	5	62	28	150	10
Marion city	2	D	39	633	29	257	120	1,894	13	116	5	D	57	368	24
Marshalltown city	2	D	30	4,891	23	346	125	1,923	16	160	10	155	46	294	27
Mason City city	1	D	37	2,333	45	584	179	3,317	32	784	18	314	69	924	44
Muscatine city	NA	NA	32	3,881	23	255	103	1,695	26	550	6	68	43	336	35

1 Merchant wholesalers, except manufacturers' sales branches and offices.

Table C. Incorporated Places, Census Designated Places (CDPs), and Minor Civil Divisions (MCDs) of 10,000 or More Population — **Economic Census**

	Economic activity by sector, 2012														
STATE City, town, township, borough, or CDP (county if applicable)	Real estate and rental and leasing — Number of employees	Professional, scientific, and technical services — Number of establishments	Number of employees	Administration and support and waste management and mediation services — Number of establishments	Number of employees	Educational services — Number of establishments	Number of employees	Health care and social assistance — Number of establishments	Number of employees	Arts, entertainment, and recreation — Number of establishments	Number of employees	Accommodation and food services — Number of establishments	Number of employees	Other services (except public administration) — Number of establishments	Number of employees
	16	17	18	19	20	21	22	23	24	25	26	27	28	29	30
INDIANA—Con.															
Fort Wayne city	1,715	721	4,884	367	8,085	73	626	838	26,588	103	1,734	614	14,022	548	4,052
Frankfort city	D	29	85	15	801	5	48	40	791	1	D	39	592	33	D
Franklin city	57	56	236	16	590	5	D	84	2,455	8	D	63	1,319	40	287
Gary city	347	45	228	38	1,131	7	24	127	3,230	7	D	87	1,078	78	473
Goshen city	126	67	397	28	575	4	4	102	3,121	6	80	88	1,742	71	371
Granger CDP	D	61	299	30	155	6	D	39	551	11	D	37	D	33	254
Greencastle city	39	26	115	10	202	3	D	45	941	3	3	47	876	36	D
Greenfield city	115	45	1,282	19	595	5	11	92	2,065	10	D	63	1,341	46	202
Greensburg city	D	21	108	14	1,089	3	7	53	D	5	19	40	820	28	D
Greenwood city	247	121	819	84	5,186	17	D	168	3,761	14	217	152	4,007	112	921
Griffith town	62	20	110	14	436	4	D	19	D	1	D	37	435	44	D
Hammond city	284	93	1,037	52	1,427	13	225	103	4,179	10	D	145	D	124	818
Highland town	82	74	326	35	362	7	59	83	1,650	7	D	59	982	60	379
Hobart city	79	45	347	28	557	8	154	67	2,586	12	D	73	1,440	71	496
Huntington city	55	28	154	13	515	3	D	48	D	8	D	60	948	53	D
Indianapolis city	11,003	2,587	31,610	1,240	44,707	208	2,427	2,278	80,905	284	6,669	1,988	45,071	1,479	16,352
Indianapolis city (balance)	D	2,580	31,600	1,236	44,689	208	2,427	2,268	80,875	284	6,669	1,984	45,009	1,473	16,336
Jasper city	83	57	267	22	256	4	D	90	2,716	6	57	55	1,301	41	219
Jeffersonville city	313	100	642	56	2,395	8	17	131	4,010	13	210	90	D	81	672
Kokomo city	300	100	600	55	D	13	96	210	5,235	25	D	175	3,811	118	888
Lafayette city	496	179	1,094	84	4,581	19	D	291	9,184	34	378	222	4,819	176	1,280
Lake Station city	D	6	D	2	D	1	D	7	D	1	D	21	299	22	135
La Porte city	78	46	207	19	779	3	8	75	2,511	12	D	70	D	61	419
Lawrence city	217	100	1,046	92	1,178	5	D	68	1,021	13	D	81	D	71	353
Lebanon city	61	32	142	20	466	2	D	50	1,462	4	17	49	707	33	218
Logansport city	56	32	178	26	901	2	D	64	D	8	D	62	930	40	D
Madison city	36	32	213	12	173	2	D	56	1,720	11	D	54	1,045	32	D
Marion city	121	54	292	35	D	4	D	145	4,792	7	D	84	1,540	64	310
Martinsville city	33	25	120	8	52	3	D	41	D	5	27	27	548	33	D
Merrillville town	525	179	1,403	66	1,267	20	282	259	4,308	10	213	132	3,016	83	591
Michigan City city	131	61	333	37	1,211	3	D	111	2,698	9	121	100	3,199	71	370
Mishawaka city	374	109	D	67	2,276	19	130	167	4,502	18	D	200	4,928	106	679
Muncie city	314	125	1,213	60	859	13	94	263	7,729	28	444	171	3,804	131	837
Munster town	79	78	511	18	143	9	100	208	D	13	D	56	1,175	50	955
New Albany city	133	118	791	43	1,662	7	D	171	4,816	8	D	85	D	79	632
New Castle city	64	26	114	14	D	2	D	58	D	8	20	40	738	45	D
New Haven city	48	28	121	17	D	NA	NA	19	315	5	20	32	433	31	179
Noblesville city	170	182	708	64	590	14	D	150	2,842	29	276	107	2,503	93	560
Peru city	22	20	69	5	8	NA	NA	30	856	7	104	38	590	30	D
Plainfield town	252	51	387	43	2,823	6	39	54	D	7	D	89	1,947	55	602
Plymouth city	67	35	223	13	761	3	D	48	1,266	4	D	43	795	39	195
Portage city	140	40	239	30	D	2	D	77	1,205	11	163	81	1,687	59	489
Purdue University CDP	D	NA	NA	2	D	NA	NA	2	D	NA	NA	13	134	2	D
Richmond city	158	62	323	45	2,536	10	59	141	4,284	15	68	119	2,480	68	318
St. John town	26	27	104	18	156	6	99	33	D	5	D	25	482	31	166
Schererville town	201	89	463	31	230	7	D	88	949	7	D	96	2,116	68	D
Seymour city	93	32	199	19	695	4	D	89	2,346	8	57	65	1,371	49	338
Shelbyville city	75	36	182	14	443	2	D	60	1,582	7	D	62	1,324	46	370
South Bend city	659	272	2,276	110	1,942	18	116	329	10,310	26	D	234	4,026	224	1,811
Speedway town	D	25	D	16	139	3	D	41	D	3	D	33	D	29	291
Terre Haute city	414	163	1,035	67	2,305	18	76	265	7,415	25	181	231	4,616	127	871
Valparaiso city	346	150	850	52	D	15	D	185	3,661	15	D	117	2,468	105	753
Vincennes city	D	38	165	28	340	5	D	81	2,761	8	D	68	1,362	46	224
Wabash city	82	33	302	15	352	1	D	47	991	8	D	40	729	36	251
Warsaw city	92	67	264	28	1,261	7	147	94	2,541	11	63	77	1,532	57	491
Washington city	48	24	107	11	40	2	D	57	1,177	5	D	38	627	34	D
Westfield city	131	72	234	46	438	9	84	60	750	15	320	63	1,494	49	307
West Lafayette city	182	60	950	12	D	3	D	57	1,096	7	D	129	2,599	32	387
Yorktown town	18	16	51	11	53	2	D	18	388	1	40	9	141	8	D
Zionsville town	86	105	399	51	490	9	33	56	781	18	107	37	491	36	235
IOWA	12,031	6,204	48,521	3,560	73,721	451	4,935	8,131	206,906	1,466	21,233	7,047	115,134	5,866	30,672
Altoona city	31	22	89	6	16	1	D	22	535	8	D	39	1,017	28	243
Ames city	364	136	877	64	1,076	15	118	134	3,975	24	356	195	3,976	105	860
Ankeny city	148	91	463	55	554	13	130	96	1,296	17	D	100	2,414	75	527
Bettendorf city	D	103	431	59	1,272	6	D	118	2,646	13	210	70	1,919	60	310
Boone city	22	24	121	11	60	1	D	36	1,019	12	130	28	D	29	D
Burlington city	623	45	238	31	356	2	D	92	D	16	399	80	1,689	56	D
Carroll city	D	32	130	21	196	3	11	79	D	3	D	37	602	32	D
Cedar Falls city	224	98	2,726	46	1,191	9	53	96	2,187	24	89	110	2,719	60	473
Cedar Rapids city	744	363	4,009	184	5,332	30	302	417	12,740	56	1,487	372	7,177	257	2,043
Clinton city	89	47	221	32	1,213	2	D	90	2,731	14	193	76	1,377	59	224
Clive city	324	108	858	50	D	7	79	94	1,103	8	D	81	1,696	75	512
Coralville city	132	58	739	29	527	7	126	84	1,119	6	77	104	2,646	40	258
Council Bluffs city	329	104	615	53	679	6	43	199	4,803	20	D	159	4,908	118	613
Davenport city	566	274	1,980	149	5,870	18	D	316	8,715	39	1,015	285	6,066	199	1,636
Des Moines city	1,470	557	6,111	246	7,704	34	265	496	22,872	80	1,361	537	9,062	443	2,959
Dubuque city	318	131	2,782	87	2,018	15	100	225	7,267	40	1,743	181	3,760	145	933
Fort Dodge city	D	64	1,039	33	400	1	D	107	2,707	14	115	79	1,347	47	D
Fort Madison city	33	17	57	8	501	3	D	33	805	4	33	33	356	28	101
Indianola city	58	27	141	12	209	3	D	45	780	9	50	40	659	34	150
Iowa City city	326	151	950	75	1,787	24	D	251	13,993	26	345	214	D	126	1,062
Johnston city	44	78	618	34	D	9	113	49	1,687	12	D	41	743	29	476
Keokuk city	37	21	85	15	426	NA	NA	55	1,164	6	103	44	623	27	70
Marion city	D	55	357	33	315	6	D	72	942	11	D	53	880	53	281
Marshalltown city	D	37	306	26	327	1	D	70	1,646	8	D	79	1,049	52	D
Mason City city	116	61	372	56	1,142	6	D	112	4,092	19	184	83	1,464	73	435
Muscatine city	179	45	639	32	D	3	D	75	1,485	8	199	72	1,066	50	268

Table C. Incorporated Places, Census Designated Places (CDPs), and Minor Civil Divisions (MCDs) of 10,000 or More Population — **Economic Census**

STATE City, town, township, borough, or CDP (county if applicable)	Utilities Number of establishments	Utilities Number of employees	Manufacturing Number of establishments	Manufacturing Number of employees	Wholesale trade[1] Number of establishments	Wholesale trade[1] Number of employees	Retail trade Number of establishments	Retail trade Number of employees	Transportation and warehousing Number of establishments	Transportation and warehousing Number of employees	Information Number of establishments	Information Number of employees	Finance and insurance Number of establishments	Finance and insurance Number of employees	Real estate and rental and leasing Number of establishments
	1	2	3	4	5	6	7	8	9	10	11	12	13	14	15
IOWA—Con.															
Newton city	2	D	18	1,379	9	133	69	966	5	55	9	263	28	252	19
North Liberty city	1	D	8	592	9	109	30	305	8	D	3	D	17	D	9
Oskaloosa city	2	D	17	567	17	317	85	1,096	7	58	8	103	32	D	9
Ottumwa city	3	116	17	D	24	177	119	2,164	20	319	11	D	53	364	20
Pella city	1	D	21	5,103	18	255	70	817	7	D	7	D	24	166	16
Sioux City city	4	D	77	4,428	129	2,034	388	6,950	70	1,060	35	774	158	1,429	83
Spencer city	4	52	20	D	36	D	98	1,339	15	187	10	166	30	228	24
Storm Lake city	3	42	18	3,207	9	80	72	1,011	8	44	11	D	42	236	14
Urbandale city	4	D	35	1,403	96	1,331	148	2,686	20	1,051	47	980	155	3,931	43
Waterloo city	5	D	98	11,343	80	1,370	300	5,413	62	1,413	17	525	139	1,975	83
Waukee city	NA	NA	4	D	10	245	23	465	7	43	3	12	19	D	18
West Des Moines city	3	D	32	1,031	63	723	389	8,652	27	574	69	1,917	348	17,793	120
KANSAS	230	7,263	2,875	152,423	3,790	52,168	10,548	145,480	2,510	50,019	1,406	34,052	5,976	59,099	2,999
Andover city	NA	NA	7	218	10	114	42	534	5	D	1	D	24	97	7
Arkansas City city	2	D	11	1,142	8	74	60	716	3	D	6	60	24	161	8
Atchison city	2	D	17	D	11	D	42	622	6	D	8	D	23	111	8
Coffeyville city	1	D	23	1,672	18	136	46	610	9	743	5	D	31	159	16
Derby city	NA	NA	15	172	5	D	76	1,467	2	D	9	51	37	170	19
Dodge City city	2	D	17	D	44	535	108	1,697	28	378	22	D	55	267	21
El Dorado city	3	D	12	323	13	D	65	797	14	85	8	58	41	167	24
Emporia city	5	D	33	2,706	15	367	149	1,752	16	199	13	D	62	D	34
Garden City city	3	D	12	D	27	199	149	2,259	43	251	14	159	57	452	26
Gardner city	1	D	6	228	8	17	31	664	5	D	7	D	22	D	10
Great Bend city	4	D	20	442	25	174	97	1,450	18	D	10	105	44	856	24
Hays city	3	181	22	559	34	313	152	2,008	27	182	16	D	69	690	34
Haysville city	2	D	8	342	2	D	19	155	2	D	1	D	7	31	7
Hutchinson city	2	D	41	1,579	50	630	202	2,967	21	D	21	535	101	686	52
Junction City city	2	D	7	655	7	D	88	1,264	29	450	11	D	43	D	34
Kansas City city	1	D	161	10,043	197	4,909	405	6,193	149	5,244	23	D	121	806	128
Lansing city	NA	NA	5	341	1	D	17	147	5	81	NA	NA	12	56	8
Lawrence city	4	D	45	2,467	53	413	333	5,800	34	884	36	2,556	163	886	141
Leavenworth city	2	D	17	685	9	D	110	1,589	12	181	13	D	49	834	25
Leawood city	NA	NA	14	189	34	407	137	2,931	8	63	13	D	198	2,122	102
Lenexa city	1	D	135	6,020	289	4,625	200	3,850	62	7,031	82	3,028	111	1,468	105
Liberal city	2	D	7	D	31	D	87	1,230	22	751	11	D	33	D	19
McPherson city	NA	NA	27	D	19	D	79	901	10	115	5	42	33	490	18
Manhattan city	2	D	34	673	31	480	260	5,438	18	224	28	D	107	797	102
Merriam city	NA	NA	25	326	29	420	61	1,646	11	1,054	8	163	20	691	18
Newton city	1	D	29	1,083	13	58	76	1,117	8	D	8	42	37	225	19
Olathe city	2	D	100	5,995	154	3,054	336	6,935	74	1,637	45	1,024	180	2,262	131
Ottawa city	1	D	19	575	4	D	68	934	7	D	5	67	26	133	9
Overland Park city	6	D	84	2,007	248	7,767	739	13,517	73	1,863	210	10,348	914	16,629	362
Parsons city	3	D	23	1,566	5	D	59	747	5	D	7	D	30	D	8
Pittsburg city	2	D	29	1,556	22	392	113	1,625	10	55	10	D	39	210	31
Prairie Village city	NA	NA	13	432	25	140	57	967	4	D	12	D	76	500	47
Salina city	2	D	55	3,944	72	898	243	3,949	48	592	29	D	103	D	59
Shawnee city	2	D	46	1,586	58	805	175	3,243	37	1,173	20	D	112	499	77
Topeka city	9	D	84	4,722	120	1,342	574	8,921	79	1,524	54	1,898	338	5,244	173
Wichita city	9	D	442	25,801	515	7,443	1,477	24,136	221	6,693	181	4,591	863	9,471	478
Winfield city	NA	NA	15	1,222	14	88	50	671	11	100	7	D	30	D	9
KENTUCKY	340	8,685	3,782	213,545	3,690	57,630	15,224	202,615	2,910	84,757	1,552	33,009	6,346	67,888	3,534
Ashland city	5	D	18	D	35	579	190	3,334	12	175	20	D	72	D	29
Bardstown city	3	D	30	3,113	21	239	107	1,518	20	279	9	D	52	307	16
Berea city	1	D	17	1,292	3	D	55	736	5	D	5	17	28	177	10
Bowling Green city	2	D	95	7,873	108	1,303	449	6,831	49	1,337	32	D	179	1,521	102
Burlington CDP	NA	NA	4	25	3	D	17	347	5	D	1	D	17	81	6
Campbellsville city	2	D	8	296	14	D	97	1,189	2	D	8	D	38	171	10
Covington city	3	D	28	746	26	D	121	1,297	21	386	17	154	49	344	32
Danville city	5	112	18	D	18	D	121	1,643	13	D	16	D	58	359	20
Elizabethtown city	4	D	51	4,727	36	319	264	4,076	24	601	22	817	99	1,066	61
Erlanger city	1	D	25	1,487	41	534	47	713	45	4,833	11	262	17	72	28
Florence city	1	D	38	3,293	40	D	295	6,297	27	3,983	15	619	128	3,227	49
Fort Campbell North CDP	NA	NA	NA	NA	NA	NA	NA	NA	NA	NA	NA	NA	NA	NA	NA
Fort Knox CDP	1	D	NA	NA	NA	NA	4	D	2	D	2	D	6	D	NA
Fort Thomas city	NA	NA	4	18	9	D	25	211	5	15	9	47	29	141	16
Frankfort city	2	D	15	550	22	D	137	1,965	6	26	16	319	76	831	27
Georgetown city	1	D	22	7,150	18	D	107	1,687	9	499	9	D	49	259	32
Glasgow city	2	D	24	2,563	22	324	133	1,838	9	D	9	D	56	402	19
Henderson city	4	D	54	2,214	34	D	152	2,089	19	D	10	201	70	D	36
Hopkinsville city	2	D	49	4,305	50	739	169	2,369	22	D	14	D	78	608	44
Independence city	NA	NA	NA	NA	5	D	32	417	14	D	4	7	19	72	7
Jeffersontown city	NA	NA	93	3,786	163	2,822	145	2,960	33	1,118	34	968	117	2,317	85
Lawrenceburg city	NA	NA	14	830	4	D	43	700	5	D	4	D	16	D	10
Lexington-Fayette urban county	24	581	224	8,005	352	7,283	1,192	19,820	147	5,355	174	7,262	600	5,531	431
Louisville/Jefferson County metro government	28	D	718	40,666	1,006	15,867	2,659	41,294	526	29,694	394	9,381	1,572	29,965	926
Louisville/Jefferson County metro government (balance)	25	D	560	34,648	711	11,176	1,996	30,358	451	27,423	295	6,644	1,126	24,760	678
Lyndon city	3	D	NA	NA	18	353	29	427	3	D	23	1,450	87	1,420	28
Madisonville city	2	D	24	1,660	29	225	125	1,943	9	119	14	114	59	295	34
Mayfield city	2	D	11	121	12	345	68	1,017	3	D	7	D	40	276	23
Middlesborough city	2	D	15	1,064	14	D	95	1,252	5	D	8	60	27	216	14
Mount Washington city	NA	NA	NA	NA	3	D	33	410	4	D	NA	NA	15	D	3

1 Merchant wholesalers, except manufacturers' sales branches and offices.

Table C. Incorporated Places, Census Designated Places (CDPs), and Minor Civil Divisions (MCDs) of 10,000 or More Population — Economic Census

STATE City, town, township, borough, or CDP (county if applicable)	Real estate and rental and leasing Number of employees	Professional, scientific, and technical services Number of establishments	Number of employees	Administration and support and waste management and mediation services Number of establishments	Number of employees	Educational services Number of establishments	Number of employees	Health care and social assistance Number of establishments	Number of employees	Arts, entertainment, and recreation Number of establishments	Number of employees	Accommodation and food services Number of establishments	Number of employees	Other services (except public administration) Number of establishments	Number of employees
	16	17	18	19	20	21	22	23	24	25	26	27	28	29	30
IOWA—Con.															
Newton city	53	31	405	14	201	NA	NA	64	1,339	6	D	43	677	35	188
North Liberty city	31	24	167	14	188	5	21	30	316	4	12	28	387	12	D
Oskaloosa city	D	30	131	12	54	2	D	40	963	9	111	31	456	26	120
Ottumwa city	86	42	250	22	D	2	D	86	2,520	12	251	71	1,188	43	227
Pella city	39	30	249	16	192	1	D	50	1,177	8	93	38	542	30	133
Sioux City city	496	178	915	117	2,642	14	D	300	8,054	39	733	232	D	153	D
Spencer city	D	34	171	20	431	2	D	57	1,468	10	149	50	624	30	181
Storm Lake city	66	31	173	9	159	1	D	32	1,081	5	9	36	708	25	D
Urbandale city	245	178	1,832	63	12,079	19	176	83	1,855	21	D	81	1,762	92	712
Waterloo city	387	115	995	88	2,300	5	30	248	8,211	34	594	169	3,684	129	901
Waukee city	D	33	89	19	D	6	D	30	396	9	454	18	323	15	D
West Des Moines city	906	359	4,625	132	5,291	21	D	273	4,861	31	713	214	4,793	123	1,317
KANSAS	14,256	7,110	60,989	3,442	70,236	475	3,998	7,934	192,272	1,000	14,341	5,943	106,850	5,147	29,521
Andover city	11	32	179	11	92	3	D	45	D	5	D	26	483	14	203
Arkansas City city	D	23	97	4	D	1	D	36	665	3	D	30	D	20	82
Atchison city	D	17	D	9	D	1	D	45	D	9	D	33	D	17	D
Coffeyville city	62	14	52	9	866	NA	NA	39	829	3	D	33	630	27	104
Derby city	D	25	145	14	69	2	D	45	618	5	D	44	1,076	32	D
Dodge City city	D	43	D	28	D	1	D	88	D	11	D	71	D	52	261
El Dorado city	46	31	153	10	D	1	D	68	1,488	4	D	41	613	28	110
Emporia city	139	44	D	22	174	5	14	91	D	6	D	82	D	54	D
Garden City city	69	54	D	28	160	1	D	94	2,006	7	D	66	1,333	51	246
Gardner city	15	18	69	10	33	6	D	27	D	4	12	28	D	18	D
Great Bend city	98	44	266	14	152	3	D	93	1,303	8	D	46	D	41	183
Hays city	95	71	289	37	260	4	D	102	3,084	6	70	90	1,872	68	D
Haysville city	18	3	D	10	109	NA	NA	6	D	1	D	10	D	13	D
Hutchinson city	145	83	588	60	1,387	5	18	150	4,337	9	D	99	1,867	82	417
Junction City city	D	24	D	20	D	NA	NA	50	D	8	D	47	1,208	47	D
Kansas City city	519	175	2,553	132	5,070	12	D	296	12,969	27	D	227	4,773	199	1,225
Lansing city	14	13	24	7	12	NA	NA	22	D	2	D	19	D	10	66
Lawrence city	D	251	1,714	99	1,019	29	247	262	6,222	31	478	270	6,211	164	1,361
Leavenworth city	130	75	634	27	349	3	D	86	D	7	D	59	974	55	D
Leawood city	D	238	1,715	68	3,344	17	D	163	D	19	D	73	2,185	63	842
Lenexa city	588	321	5,102	149	11,597	23	D	156	5,329	20	540	106	1,884	84	620
Liberal city	D	22	139	14	D	2	D	72	D	6	D	45	789	41	D
McPherson city	52	35	169	20	460	1	D	72	1,249	6	111	45	721	49	185
Manhattan city	D	118	790	46	432	19	D	174	3,257	13	D	168	3,912	109	1,032
Merriam city	186	39	536	28	565	NA	NA	70	D	3	35	28	504	46	D
Newton city	50	34	183	7	30	1	D	90	2,173	9	D	40	723	34	D
Olathe city	585	342	1,676	177	3,317	36	D	269	6,408	40	722	234	5,437	174	1,252
Ottawa city	28	24	D	15	D	3	D	52	1,508	3	23	41	698	32	D
Overland Park city	2,042	1,221	17,166	430	12,149	79	D	707	15,861	81	1,653	456	10,355	378	2,608
Parsons city	29	12	53	4	D	NA	NA	72	3,910	3	D	28	413	18	108
Pittsburg city	96	48	301	14	300	2	D	103	2,355	5	104	56	1,139	40	190
Prairie Village city	D	105	512	33	230	6	D	116	D	14	D	34	776	38	369
Salina city	199	102	D	62	817	5	D	175	4,669	21	D	132	2,986	107	D
Shawnee city	306	168	929	80	1,271	12	D	126	D	14	D	109	2,166	88	596
Topeka city	803	387	3,638	157	3,717	28	D	473	15,241	45	D	330	6,636	330	3,268
Wichita city	3,607	1,008	8,937	519	11,801	76	970	1,220	31,393	114	2,483	962	19,526	673	5,193
Winfield city	19	30	87	12	176	1	D	76	1,404	3	D	27	497	27	103
KENTUCKY	18,250	8,101	62,851	3,925	93,839	569	4,024	11,425	251,878	1,242	17,360	7,678	156,965	5,849	38,364
Ashland city	133	68	476	24	554	3	D	206	D	7	165	92	2,217	66	D
Bardstown city	43	38	203	19	917	1	D	75	1,468	15	D	56	D	30	159
Berea city	20	23	58	7	649	1	D	55	987	3	D	37	D	23	116
Bowling Green city	363	182	1,761	92	3,047	25	D	343	7,509	27	656	243	5,498	159	913
Burlington CDP	12	14	44	7	28	1	D	17	129	3	D	23	495	15	141
Campbellsville city	62	38	75	14	D	NA	NA	48	D	8	29	39	699	27	D
Covington city	203	125	930	35	482	7	37	90	2,172	13	114	125	1,793	85	421
Danville city	D	44	238	27	557	6	D	122	2,900	7	106	57	D	49	200
Elizabethtown city	304	111	577	38	2,455	11	D	237	4,939	12	D	112	2,798	78	516
Erlanger city	198	52	287	18	932	2	D	25	D	3	D	32	704	44	493
Florence city	260	102	1,559	66	2,435	14	72	153	3,801	21	500	161	3,755	71	D
Fort Campbell North CDP	NA	1	D	NA	NA	NA	NA	2	D	NA	NA	NA	NA	1	D
Fort Knox CDP	NA	40	454	10	357	2	D	2	D	NA	NA	7	97	7	D
Fort Thomas city	118	30	203	12	60	1	D	46	2,014	7	D	16	163	15	D
Frankfort city	154	102	714	28	505	4	D	133	1,515	10	D	88	1,698	85	522
Georgetown city	D	53	261	31	2,560	4	29	103	1,231	7	53	80	D	42	D
Glasgow city	D	38	248	15	1,479	4	D	89	D	6	D	55	D	38	175
Henderson city	D	62	364	26	D	3	16	128	D	10	D	81	1,388	53	D
Hopkinsville city	124	59	374	31	D	3	D	138	2,684	8	153	77	1,524	54	298
Independence city	12	13	70	5	6	2	D	19	121	NA	NA	15	305	12	57
Jeffersontown city	586	180	3,598	121	3,725	16	292	109	2,954	18	397	108	2,931	93	815
Lawrenceburg city	D	19	64	3	D	2	D	25	293	2	D	30	403	20	D
Lexington-Fayette urban county	2,128	1,072	10,073	426	10,484	83	918	1,048	29,625	130	2,194	772	17,490	553	4,405
Louisville/Jefferson County metro government	7,168	2,197	22,198	1,137	29,367	169	1,383	2,390	65,785	283	5,776	1,651	39,711	1,307	11,226
Louisville/Jefferson County metro government (balance)	4,611	1,649	15,773	846	19,658	114	835	1,704	47,438	229	4,329	1,289	29,962	973	8,724
Lyndon city	D	65	773	21	663	4	D	54	835	3	D	25	366	31	196
Madisonville city	103	48	302	28	287	3	10	94	2,855	8	D	60	1,302	43	D
Mayfield city	49	35	326	6	22	1	D	67	1,282	5	D	36	D	19	111
Middlesborough city	51	19	86	8	D	NA	NA	48	817	3	D	31	642	25	D
Mount Washington city	10	13	41	9	98	NA	NA	23	230	4	D	17	314	23	D

Table C. Incorporated Places, Census Designated Places (CDPs), and Minor Civil Divisions (MCDs) of 10,000 or More Population — Economic Census

STATE City, town, township, borough, or CDP (county if applicable)	Utilities Number of establish-ments	Utilities Number of employees	Manufacturing Number of establish-ments	Manufacturing Number of employees	Wholesale trade¹ Number of establish-ments	Wholesale trade¹ Number of employees	Retail trade Number of establish-ments	Retail trade Number of employees	Transportation and warehousing Number of establish-ments	Transportation and warehousing Number of employees	Information Number of establish-ments	Information Number of employees	Finance and insurance Number of establish-ments	Finance and insurance Number of employees	Real estate and rental and leasing Number of establish-ments
	1	2	3	4	5	6	7	8	9	10	11	12	13	14	15
KENTUCKY—Con.															
Murray city	3	10	20	2,340	27	227	134	1,737	5	D	12	D	54	D	31
Newport city	NA	NA	25	652	15	187	88	1,238	9	382	5	206	17	84	15
Nicholasville city	2	D	51	2,245	27	D	117	1,996	11	87	11	D	44	196	21
Owensboro city	3	D	64	3,644	67	943	336	4,944	31	856	15	D	161	2,526	63
Paducah city	2	D	36	D	72	D	320	5,310	37	2,271	23	D	102	1,014	58
Radcliff city	1	D	4	120	8	D	82	1,111	5	D	5	D	33	228	35
Richmond city	5	36	32	1,896	18	99	199	2,976	7	D	21	418	95	459	42
St. Matthews city	NA	NA	8	45	19	334	254	4,660	5	D	14	122	77	547	47
Shelbyville city	4	D	11	707	11	D	84	1,288	3	D	11	87	39	252	23
Shepherdsville city	1	D	13	823	10	D	57	757	21	2,406	5	34	29	176	17
Shively city	NA	NA	18	800	9	98	64	570	10	D	5	33	20	D	13
Somerset city	5	199	35	1,423	34	617	180	2,632	13	120	14	152	82	572	33
Winchester city	4	D	28	1,978	16	512	103	1,414	8	D	11	157	39	250	19
LOUISIANA	517	11,132	3,308	136,327	4,823	64,259	16,743	220,257	3,764	70,059	1,426	24,743	7,716	64,813	4,500
Abbeville city	2	D	14	327	16	144	86	1,184	9	71	8	D	48	305	13
Alexandria city	NA	NA	37	1,826	73	914	385	5,698	24	368	27	493	182	1,171	98
Baker city	NA	NA	8	243	7	194	52	725	3	D	2	D	21	82	12
Bastrop city	6	55	7	45	5	71	58	579	2	D	4	D	42	176	14
Baton Rouge city	18	D	185	4,968	306	3,894	1,146	16,570	127	1,933	131	2,430	636	7,709	339
Bayou Blue CDP	NA	NA	6	143	4	D	6	52	8	43	NA	NA	5	19	5
Bayou Cane CDP	NA	NA	14	102	15	83	154	2,595	12	77	5	99	59	428	33
Belle Chasse CDP	1	D	33	1,446	38	929	37	275	52	1,227	1	D	19	D	29
Bogalusa city	3	D	7	D	4	D	61	628	1	D	6	D	36	D	8
Bossier City city	1	D	47	1,018	77	1,165	379	5,660	50	662	20	D	137	889	79
Central city	1	D	21	155	9	33	40	867	12	D	4	13	22	88	15
Chalmette CDP	2	D	22	877	17	D	81	1,114	15	D	1	D	25	148	13
Claiborne CDP	NA	NA	NA	NA	6	18	30	226	2	D	2	D	15	65	4
Crowley city	3	D	12	413	13	144	79	1,272	8	D	9	95	44	235	12
Denham Springs city	3	D	17	D	14	D	104	2,097	7	93	11	126	74	470	21
DeRidder city	4	D	6	287	7	41	82	1,234	3	D	4	D	47	686	18
Destrehan CDP	3	D	NA	NA	9	D	16	160	10	D	3	D	14	57	7
Estelle CDP	NA	NA	NA	NA	2	D	17	194	7	D	NA	NA	4	D	2
Eunice city	6	D	11	296	11	D	78	D	11	142	5	D	34	177	12
Gardere CDP	NA	NA	NA	NA	NA	NA	13	48	1	D	1	D	1	D	1
Gonzales city	2	D	13	80	39	533	167	2,600	8	D	12	172	60	291	20
Gretna city	8	D	18	297	27	D	144	2,110	13	301	8	130	38	229	26
Hammond city	8	D	26	933	31	787	208	3,106	22	253	18	357	115	2,290	54
Harvey CDP	NA	NA	34	649	55	698	129	2,514	35	900	6	D	51	270	19
Houma city	1	D	32	1,045	68	686	167	2,292	57	929	9	144	95	537	61
Jefferson CDP	1	D	14	D	36	723	41	534	14	362	2	D	9	210	15
Jennings city	4	52	7	D	11	82	76	1,066	12	69	2	D	41	D	13
Kenner city	7	D	54	1,074	113	883	266	4,356	102	2,048	17	230	115	750	86
Lafayette city	5	D	129	3,831	276	3,728	808	12,699	110	2,685	90	2,515	478	3,385	334
Lake Charles city	8	D	39	1,224	72	847	442	6,000	46	1,607	34	556	202	1,407	117
Laplace CDP	3	D	7	537	13	D	92	1,402	21	D	10	D	52	513	25
Luling CDP	1	D	6	D	5	D	30	213	7	150	2	D	17	51	7
Mandeville city	6	79	7	91	33	243	125	1,660	14	101	9	55	96	754	30
Marrero CDP	1	D	11	D	13	201	130	1,826	12	113	8	111	41	201	19
Metairie CDP	6	D	69	787	194	1,968	699	11,710	107	1,108	84	1,501	479	5,417	229
Minden city	NA	NA	9	646	9	128	91	1,395	8	33	4	37	44	222	22
Monroe city	5	86	41	1,356	81	1,211	400	5,914	38	682	48	2,041	227	3,774	119
Morgan City city	NA	NA	19	784	39	659	82	888	33	1,223	9	114	45	291	38
Moss Bluff CDP	1	D	3	8	4	13	37	313	4	14	1	D	16	84	6
Natchitoches city	2	D	8	D	16	100	115	1,537	4	D	17	D	56	319	36
New Iberia city	4	D	49	1,703	54	695	208	2,791	16	74	13	D	111	817	56
New Orleans city	23	D	144	6,049	256	3,794	1,275	12,371	200	6,218	179	2,737	517	6,576	379
Opelousas city	3	21	15	440	13	D	120	1,879	9	720	10	99	69	487	26
Pineville city	10	D	9	1,106	8	94	78	1,342	6	D	4	53	46	186	13
Prairieville CDP	2	D	30	358	28	288	62	962	6	D	1	D	24	119	20
River Ridge CDP	NA	NA	3	6	4	13	26	277	1	D	3	D	13	42	10
Ruston city	NA	NA	15	D	23	373	135	2,043	6	118	13	D	86	620	38
Shenandoah CDP	NA	NA	NA	NA	8	12	38	454	1	D	3	D	39	167	18
Shreveport city	24	D	145	4,796	294	D	875	12,231	154	3,915	86	D	474	3,059	285
Slidell city	2	D	26	1,895	27	158	282	4,263	22	178	16	256	124	618	37
Sulphur city	NA	NA	18	480	23	282	94	1,435	25	266	7	47	40	203	26
Terrytown CDP	2	D	7	D	4	6	71	451	5	55	1	D	22	176	15
Thibodaux city	NA	NA	12	619	17	213	122	1,688	6	8	11	132	74	394	21
Timberlane CDP	NA	NA	NA	NA	2	D	31	326	5	6	1	D	13	63	3
West Monroe city	4	D	31	D	49	409	150	1,999	14	149	16	321	73	416	36
Woodmere CDP	NA	NA	NA	NA	1	D	14	D	4	D	NA	NA	7	37	NA
Zachary city	3	D	10	88	6	46	70	1,214	9	60	5	D	36	178	13
MAINE	99	2,363	1,650	49,238	1,344	14,753	6,351	80,155	1,175	14,908	845	11,952	1,899	25,688	1,580
Auburn city & MCD (Androscoggin)	NA	NA	44	2,457	42	500	159	3,117	29	790	9	D	50	912	44
Augusta city & MCD (Kennebec)	5	D	16	505	24	1,182	162	3,528	18	299	26	464	63	687	29
Bangor city & MCD (Penobscot)	2	D	37	775	63	849	310	6,147	37	1,103	41	1,158	104	1,010	90
Biddeford city & MCD (York)	4	105	53	1,559	18	D	109	1,840	6	16	14	241	29	309	22
Brunswick CDP	NA	NA	NA	NA	NA	NA	NA	NA	NA	NA	NA	NA	NA	NA	NA
Brunswick town (Cumberland)	2	D	24	484	10	48	120	1,982	6	18	16	279	40	361	35
Falmouth town (Cumberland)	NA	NA	7	64	15	103	57	951	2	D	4	D	34	871	22

1 Merchant wholesalers, except manufacturers' sales branches and offices.

Table C. Incorporated Places, Census Designated Places (CDPs), and Minor Civil Divisions (MCDs) of 10,000 or More Population — Economic Census

STATE / City, town, township, borough, or CDP (county if applicable)	Real estate and rental and leasing — Number of employees	Professional, scientific, and technical services — Number of establishments	Professional, scientific, and technical services — Number of employees	Administration and support and waste management and mediation services — Number of establishments	Administration and support and waste management and mediation services — Number of employees	Educational services — Number of establishments	Educational services — Number of employees	Health care and social assistance — Number of establishments	Health care and social assistance — Number of employees	Arts, entertainment, and recreation — Number of establishments	Arts, entertainment, and recreation — Number of employees	Accommodation and food services — Number of establishments	Accommodation and food services — Number of employees	Other services (except public administration) — Number of establishments	Other services (except public administration) — Number of employees
	16	17	18	19	20	21	22	23	24	25	26	27	28	29	30
KENTUCKY—Con.															
Murray city	112	53	250	15	123	7	D	94	D	7	D	77	1,650	42	D
Newport city	119	51	286	14	567	3	6	33	469	11	372	84	D	32	D
Nicholasville city	87	52	286	33	270	4	49	76	619	10	135	53	D	49	178
Owensboro city	427	129	1,362	51	2,490	14	D	288	7,048	24	452	134	3,481	120	D
Paducah city	252	141	908	48	1,654	8	12	211	5,905	15	217	174	3,615	97	D
Radcliff city	164	26	383	5	D	3	6	53	D	4	36	50	1,307	25	D
Richmond city	150	78	522	25	543	8	D	159	2,482	14	D	113	2,762	55	262
St. Matthews city	D	103	620	51	664	18	117	329	10,590	11	345	104	2,971	80	586
Shelbyville city	99	43	149	15	342	2	D	65	936	3	D	40	899	40	D
Shepherdsville city	82	31	167	13	819	1	D	44	561	4	D	40	874	22	D
Shively city	53	15	177	14	310	NA	NA	50	744	3	13	30	939	28	110
Somerset city	157	74	288	31	1,121	5	D	175	3,801	9	D	69	1,499	39	D
Winchester city	48	41	239	14	868	2	D	105	1,263	4	12	51	1,075	33	156
LOUISIANA	31,298	11,728	88,093	4,576	103,246	673	6,248	11,999	284,979	1,376	23,386	9,019	193,928	6,293	43,500
Abbeville city	64	56	172	14	63	1	D	57	1,041	6	38	32	637	26	D
Alexandria city	472	206	1,346	86	1,769	12	D	341	8,580	20	119	165	3,114	114	641
Baker city	53	10	45	3	D	NA	NA	26	439	3	D	16	277	15	35
Bastrop city	46	15	76	2	D	NA	NA	60	1,308	5	D	23	D	22	D
Baton Rouge city	1,827	1,146	12,827	366	10,786	74	D	886	25,275	98	2,349	699	15,983	588	6,467
Bayou Blue CDP	D	5	7	8	190	NA	NA	3	68	NA	NA	3	22	7	31
Bayou Cane CDP	179	44	700	21	784	6	33	49	D	6	52	82	2,305	39	170
Belle Chasse CDP	323	39	297	23	340	2	D	18	D	5	56	41	607	38	D
Bogalusa city	27	17	51	1	D	1	D	42	1,129	4	D	34	422	15	62
Bossier City city	508	117	711	67	1,090	12	D	175	3,661	23	935	202	7,287	110	668
Central city	42	25	75	15	132	3	D	40	512	5	30	15	363	24	115
Chalmette CDP	41	29	141	17	180	4	D	41	D	2	D	56	D	26	D
Claiborne CDP	6	14	56	9	36	1	D	20	220	5	13	16	242	11	D
Crowley city	72	43	124	8	136	1	D	59	893	4	15	34	D	19	133
Denham Springs city	68	62	379	22	514	4	D	63	777	7	108	75	1,450	41	237
DeRidder city	D	29	107	11	73	3	20	61	D	3	D	36	686	17	60
Destrehan CDP	14	31	130	11	D	2	D	21	D	8	D	20	323	11	61
Estelle CDP	D	7	28	7	D	1	D	5	101	3	D	14	144	6	23
Eunice city	68	29	139	5	114	1	D	63	724	5	D	29	446	21	124
Gardere CDP	D	3	D	3	20	NA	NA	7	D	1	D	5	14	4	D
Gonzales city	92	37	219	22	519	5	D	76	1,937	7	172	73	1,602	34	174
Gretna city	307	73	406	28	655	2	D	66	D	8	D	74	870	49	267
Hammond city	306	96	409	22	1,017	8	37	174	5,499	16	D	116	2,717	66	645
Harvey CDP	147	48	756	22	319	4	73	40	D	2	D	71	1,509	62	D
Houma city	589	145	925	45	656	10	68	159	3,558	9	78	90	1,690	67	560
Jefferson CDP	141	24	291	21	256	1	D	22	D	2	D	22	389	22	D
Jennings city	296	43	235	3	D	NA	NA	64	1,307	5	D	28	478	24	91
Kenner city	622	159	1,862	102	2,824	15	52	171	2,896	25	D	184	3,718	116	873
Lafayette city	2,352	1,009	7,293	235	5,110	45	421	829	20,259	59	979	542	12,372	290	2,665
Lake Charles city	480	279	1,794	90	1,559	19	156	370	9,775	34	D	197	6,132	126	904
Laplace CDP	149	49	281	32	D	4	D	56	1,200	11	175	65	1,160	28	D
Luling CDP	D	23	D	9	276	NA	NA	24	842	6	D	19	223	9	D
Mandeville city	D	118	624	24	336	10	D	115	1,248	8	42	86	1,422	43	275
Marrero CDP	114	32	193	22	397	1	D	128	3,587	3	D	54	1,067	38	D
Metairie CDP	1,724	768	5,622	305	10,932	37	392	668	8,045	45	D	399	7,571	297	1,946
Minden city	D	31	166	15	D	1	D	55	1,616	3	D	37	D	22	D
Monroe city	811	293	1,979	90	2,088	12	156	408	8,766	29	468	167	3,761	111	766
Morgan City city	808	53	278	25	446	1	D	58	800	8	D	49	D	39	D
Moss Bluff CDP	16	17	D	6	29	NA	NA	15	119	3	D	17	D	6	D
Natchitoches city	206	55	237	19	1,991	3	D	95	1,667	8	74	76	1,574	29	D
New Iberia city	311	100	400	37	1,614	8	D	179	3,270	12	D	81	D	77	D
New Orleans city	2,156	1,450	13,212	405	11,816	88	717	861	21,761	181	5,158	1,300	35,510	578	4,297
Opelousas city	D	71	226	13	138	4	23	157	3,866	10	D	51	830	30	D
Pineville city	34	35	249	16	77	5	D	65	2,126	3	D	43	D	35	183
Prairieville CDP	57	60	382	32	1,399	5	49	50	541	6	53	37	706	38	D
River Ridge CDP	108	36	79	7	D	2	D	20	128	1	D	16	152	11	D
Ruston city	208	76	597	25	D	6	D	95	2,924	7	D	82	1,720	39	D
Shenandoah CDP	D	38	89	19	169	4	27	36	515	6	D	26	650	25	D
Shreveport city	2,266	578	3,926	228	10,004	48	D	798	D	67	816	460	12,644	335	2,455
Slidell city	365	139	583	65	842	8	D	218	4,559	5	107	180	3,220	94	430
Sulphur city	138	48	1,035	13	229	4	D	62	1,288	5	D	67	1,378	34	D
Terrytown CDP	68	41	411	23	499	5	62	64	1,430	6	58	38	701	23	121
Thibodaux city	100	73	426	15	90	2	D	105	2,289	7	D	75	1,423	38	295
Timberlane CDP	7	7	D	8	56	NA	NA	49	D	2	D	16	308	8	44
West Monroe city	280	65	436	40	791	7	51	137	3,428	2	D	81	1,918	55	371
Woodmere CDP	NA	6	23	11	212	1	D	8	D	1	D	7	70	6	50
Zachary city	32	31	123	10	57	4	D	58	D	7	122	35	801	24	D
MAINE	6,242	3,492	22,943	1,958	22,395	341	2,659	4,730	109,231	849	7,305	3,958	49,672	2,786	13,755
Auburn city & MCD (Androscoggin)	114	57	694	43	1,664	2	D	119	1,943	11	130	78	1,502	70	400
Augusta city & MCD (Kennebec)	129	99	D	47	841	15	182	160	6,189	8	131	94	1,774	105	596
Bangor city & MCD (Penobscot)	404	159	1,008	65	1,479	15	207	310	11,124	15	228	139	3,366	100	646
Biddeford city & MCD (York)	71	40	337	32	334	4	D	111	2,267	7	99	62	956	44	235
Brunswick CDP	NA	NA	NA	NA	NA	NA	NA	NA	NA	NA	NA	NA	NA	NA	NA
Brunswick town (Cumberland)	86	103	436	39	377	5	8	135	3,292	22	186	85	1,087	59	436
Falmouth town (Cumberland)	38	55	684	26	579	6	D	67	783	18	284	21	386	24	D

Table C. Incorporated Places, Census Designated Places (CDPs), and Minor Civil Divisions (MCDs) of 10,000 or More Population — **Economic Census**

STATE City, town, township, borough, or CDP (county if applicable)	Utilities Number of establishments	Utilities Number of employees	Manufacturing Number of establishments	Manufacturing Number of employees	Wholesale trade[1] Number of establishments	Wholesale trade[1] Number of employees	Retail trade Number of establishments	Retail trade Number of employees	Transportation and warehousing Number of establishments	Transportation and warehousing Number of employees	Information Number of establishments	Information Number of employees	Finance and insurance Number of establishments	Finance and insurance Number of employees	Real estate and rental and leasing Number of establishments
	1	2	3	4	5	6	7	8	9	10	11	12	13	14	15
MAINE—Con.															
Gorham town (Cumberland)	NA	NA	23	495	19	420	45	487	8	D	3	D	19	185	12
Kennebunk town (York)	NA	NA	11	366	17	D	58	526	1	D	14	359	34	314	18
Lewiston city & MCD (Androscoggin)	2	D	65	1,507	37	657	157	1,935	23	1,066	25	1,355	60	2,011	48
Orono town (Penobscot)	NA	NA	5	82	4	3	19	184	1	D	4	24	11	277	7
Portland city & MCD (Cumberland)	6	D	101	2,425	174	2,511	395	4,893	78	1,150	149	2,895	278	6,646	226
Saco city & MCD (York)	1	D	24	821	18	345	60	1,157	13	164	6	63	32	296	26
Sanford city & MCD (York)	1	D	38	1,209	11	D	96	1,367	7	114	6	20	25	211	20
Scarborough town (Cumberland)	NA	NA	28	610	43	538	106	2,273	21	576	11	95	48	300	46
South Portland city & MCD (Cumberland)	NA	NA	33	1,452	50	811	244	4,606	27	1,195	28	390	84	3,340	48
Waterville city & MCD (Kennebec)	NA	NA	9	D	13	93	118	2,009	7	128	14	109	44	289	21
Westbrook city & MCD (Cumberland)	1	D	33	1,652	53	1,033	62	1,300	23	286	16	600	40	851	21
Windham town (Cumberland)	NA	NA	32	369	17	89	83	1,499	9	16	13	56	29	130	15
York town (York)	NA	NA	15	145	16	83	68	562	4	27	2	D	28	129	24
MARYLAND	130	9,484	3,096	100,079	4,768	73,369	18,179	281,678	3,348	64,906	2,381	56,781	7,583	100,204	6,001
Aberdeen city	NA	NA	8	247	16	D	66	1,425	9	393	3	D	24	151	16
Accokeek CDP	NA	NA	NA	NA	4	D	12	234	5	103	NA	NA	3	D	4
Adelphi CDP	NA	NA	NA	NA	NA	NA	14	288	2	D	4	D	3	35	4
Annapolis city	1	D	37	324	62	404	488	7,230	25	255	64	1,370	135	898	98
Annapolis Neck CDP	NA	NA	3	D	3	D	14	199	2	D	4	85	11	27	11
Arbutus CDP	1	D	32	784	70	884	67	1,364	23	323	12	D	16	101	19
Arnold CDP	1	D	NA	NA	12	23	32	563	2	D	3	D	22	80	15
Aspen Hill CDP	NA	NA	NA	NA	10	12	47	1,042	12	30	6	25	22	D	22
Ballenger Creek CDP	NA	NA	34	1,832	55	594	173	4,154	16	727	11	157	54	1,011	47
Baltimore city	29	D	409	11,748	544	8,592	1,839	15,747	346	9,245	264	5,324	685	18,909	596
Bel Air town	1	D	14	94	19	133	187	3,424	4	49	12	D	86	773	41
Bel Air North CDP	1	D	11	51	17	127	39	655	10	30	5	D	26	177	15
Bel Air South CDP	NA	NA	3	11	15	D	82	2,262	11	25	7	60	45	219	42
Beltsville CDP	NA	NA	49	1,677	101	1,321	114	1,318	36	920	27	366	36	230	37
Bensville CDP	NA	NA	NA	NA	NA	NA	3	6	2	D	1	D	2	D	1
Bethesda CDP	5	D	23	172	48	356	272	4,650	11	46	92	2,444	324	6,900	270
Bowie city	NA	NA	6	19	14	168	149	3,864	12	41	13	125	77	D	28
Brock Hall CDP	NA	NA	9	563	21	1,590	21	278	8	356	7	210	3	D	8
Brooklyn Park CDP	NA	NA	5	119	7	D	41	455	16	144	3	D	5	D	8
California CDP	NA	NA	4	D	2	D	72	2,135	4	D	3	D	23	214	22
Calverton CDP	NA	NA	6	89	12	191	26	1,738	4	D	31	1,522	23	D	21
Cambridge city	1	D	20	729	12	135	64	935	8	63	9	73	30	216	22
Camp Springs CDP	NA	NA	3	D	2	D	34	685	5	20	NA	NA	15	D	16
Carney CDP	1	D	7	39	12	33	79	2,103	6	D	2	D	37	193	16
Catonsville CDP	NA	NA	11	103	21	132	118	1,773	8	D	11	70	46	203	45
Chesapeake Ranch Estates CDP	NA	NA	NA	NA	1	D	1	D	NA	NA	NA	NA	1	D	1
Chillum CDP	NA	NA	NA	NA	4	D	42	886	7	39	2	D	7	38	26
Clarksburg CDP	NA	NA	3	D	3	4	5	52	3	D	1	D	7	13	17
Clinton CDP	NA	NA	16	209	11	120	80	1,698	27	105	9	155	31	D	11
Cloverly CDP	NA	NA	3	6	4	16	19	169	4	13	6	20	5	18	8
Cockeysville CDP	NA	NA	51	5,068	55	1,887	143	4,198	10	173	43	2,274	187	5,601	60
Colesville CDP	NA	NA	5	35	2	D	30	278	1	D	8	23	19	95	6
College Park city	1	D	6	101	11	55	69	1,686	5	2	14	300	21	D	19
Columbia CDP	1	D	56	1,036	130	3,100	405	9,143	39	394	85	2,127	298	5,124	159
Coral Hills CDP	NA	NA	NA	NA	NA	NA	24	157	NA	NA	NA	NA	2	D	3
Crofton CDP	NA	NA	9	131	13	85	33	421	3	6	4	92	21	100	20
Cumberland city	2	D	16	543	25	239	102	1,124	25	373	17	344	47	D	29
Damascus CDP	NA	NA	4	7	2	D	29	251	5	22	2	D	13	D	10
Dundalk CDP	1	D	30	566	29	378	200	3,340	43	265	7	76	50	270	39
Easton town	NA	NA	21	446	32	241	141	2,099	9	176	20	262	69	566	34
East Riverdale CDP	NA	NA	NA	NA	NA	NA	19	76	4	5	NA	NA	5	17	5
Edgewood CDP	NA	NA	21	995	24	461	62	1,167	12	138	NA	NA	11	81	16
Eldersburg CDP	NA	NA	15	267	25	78	80	1,549	20	D	10	112	25	D	29
Elkridge CDP	NA	NA	28	988	71	1,436	43	397	42	1,438	10	D	12	67	25
Elkton town	1	D	10	1,509	6	25	82	1,610	14	659	3	D	37	227	20
Ellicott City CDP	NA	NA	14	217	40	194	187	3,121	20	120	18	151	106	657	79
Essex CDP	NA	NA	6	88	7	25	83	925	10	81	10	140	25	134	23
Fairland CDP	NA	NA	3	7	6	8	33	1,060	5	36	3	3	10	91	15
Ferndale CDP	NA	NA	10	175	30	586	42	702	17	302	2	D	16	163	14
Forestville CDP	1	D	7	74	24	259	96	1,463	14	329	3	D	13	66	12
Fort Washington CDP	1	D	NA	NA	4	38	45	610	9	55	4	13	15	70	20
Frederick city	1	D	59	2,045	78	844	320	5,293	26	343	43	738	188	5,352	99
Gaithersburg city	NA	NA	35	1,039	76	1,339	337	6,863	16	333	45	1,309	138	D	95
Germantown CDP	NA	NA	20	2,723	31	157	138	3,164	16	88	32	1,269	52	430	41
Glassmanor CDP	NA	NA	NA	NA	2	D	31	481	3	4	1	D	4	29	7
Glen Burnie CDP	NA	NA	34	373	51	840	339	6,283	42	1,046	16	240	85	581	55
Glenmont CDP	NA	NA	NA	NA	2	D	15	207	1	D	NA	NA	6	D	3
Glenn Dale CDP	NA	NA	NA	NA	6	28	10	66	6	39	7	208	6	D	8
Greenbelt city	NA	NA	6	572	16	D	92	1,464	4	D	18	376	50	528	25
Hagerstown city	2	D	61	3,335	51	463	207	4,043	39	1,443	29	589	96	3,734	65
Halfway CDP	3	D	NA	NA	11	222	97	1,761	3	5	10	121	17	108	13
Havre de Grace city	NA	NA	9	720	7	D	47	396	5	D	3	D	19	74	11
Hillcrest Heights CDP	NA	NA	NA	NA	1	D	28	402	1	D	NA	NA	3	18	14
Hyattsville city	NA	NA	NA	NA	19	71	118	2,140	7	376	8	455	24	D	17

1 Merchant wholesalers, except manufacturers' sales branches and offices.

Table C. Incorporated Places, Census Designated Places (CDPs), and Minor Civil Divisions (MCDs) of 10,000 or More Population — Economic Census

STATE City, town, township, borough, or CDP (county if applicable)	Real estate and rental and leasing — Number of employees	Professional, scientific, and technical services — Number of establishments	Number of employees	Administration and support and waste management and mediation services — Number of establishments	Number of employees	Educational services — Number of establishments	Number of employees	Health care and social assistance — Number of establishments	Number of employees	Arts, entertainment, and recreation — Number of establishments	Number of employees	Accommodation and food services — Number of establishments	Number of employees	Other services (except public administration) — Number of establishments	Number of employees
	16	17	18	19	20	21	22	23	24	25	26	27	28	29	30
MAINE—Con.															
Gorham town (Cumberland)	D	49	120	47	280	6	5	35	700	5	24	19	274	25	118
Kennebunk town (York)	56	60	288	17	74	3	25	51	869	10	74	51	701	32	162
Lewiston city & MCD (Androscoggin)	222	85	799	46	1,228	6	36	178	6,817	15	183	74	1,015	84	452
Orono town (Penobscot)	46	20	97	4	D	2	D	15	D	1	D	24	345	13	85
Portland city & MCD (Cumberland)	1,453	593	5,308	169	4,035	52	685	453	16,376	65	908	330	5,887	275	1,732
Saco city & MCD (Cumberland)	D	65	322	34	306	3	4	76	1,360	15	171	58	627	32	184
Sanford city & MCD (York)	58	41	188	17	132	4	D	100	2,156	4	32	53	768	47	285
Scarborough town (Cumberland)	188	95	873	58	676	9	74	114	3,523	22	242	70	1,106	55	409
South Portland city & MCD (Cumberland)	459	101	686	60	1,189	16	142	147	3,440	13	35	124	2,729	75	652
Waterville city & MCD (Kennebec)	128	51	223	13	146	8	29	117	4,504	11	187	74	1,275	39	245
Westbrook city & MCD (Cumberland)	86	57	332	37	709	10	85	68	1,753	15	59	38	555	36	307
Windham town (Cumberland)	30	38	134	37	207	2	D	53	D	4	34	37	D	45	234
York town (York)	D	46	201	35	115	NA	NA	55	1,520	15	125	75	970	32	225
MARYLAND	42,838	19,714	244,710	7,950	182,659	1,517	D	16,000	359,734	1,960	35,932	11,344	204,222	9,978	79,391
Aberdeen city	95	46	466	15	733	3	D	51	529	2	D	59	1,339	36	D
Accokeek CDP	D	11	47	10	169	3	D	6	25	3	D	9	122	10	77
Adelphi CDP	19	12	29	10	107	1	D	14	283	1	D	15	287	14	48
Annapolis city	449	373	2,143	63	614	21	180	188	2,422	43	683	194	4,975	208	2,381
Annapolis Neck CDP	18	46	89	15	56	4	D	5	D	6	18	8	76	16	202
Arbutus CDP	143	69	747	44	1,052	4	34	36	2,396	1	D	51	D	51	429
Arnold CDP	29	73	273	35	392	6	D	54	1,154	7	241	17	263	29	150
Aspen Hill CDP	D	68	145	43	223	4	7	90	1,014	10	425	42	789	31	147
Ballenger Creek CDP	230	98	1,514	49	1,250	2	D	31	783	8	289	81	2,104	48	511
Baltimore city	4,055	1,555	21,994	569	18,782	112	2,698	1,471	79,915	167	6,131	1,541	21,832	939	8,989
Bel Air town	144	156	1,144	39	327	8	79	112	3,594	6	301	71	1,954	72	609
Bel Air North CDP	39	55	219	42	313	4	8	67	1,127	9	128	34	432	46	D
Bel Air South CDP	D	75	952	44	266	8	51	110	1,342	8	106	43	1,010	37	202
Beltsville CDP	561	87	1,708	63	1,575	6	31	46	885	2	D	49	606	76	1,176
Bensville CDP	D	13	18	5	22	1	D	3	3	NA	NA	1	D	1	D
Bethesda CDP	3,986	853	11,118	164	14,362	79	1,134	365	8,912	54	1,005	238	5,701	252	3,353
Bowie city	170	169	4,213	75	590	14	88	222	2,120	20	D	72	1,969	53	327
Brock Hall CDP	88	33	334	16	949	6	D	13	292	2	D	4	D	7	D
Brooklyn Park CDP	39	14	94	7	116	NA	NA	19	305	7	D	26	562	32	D
California CDP	95	52	2,351	8	D	6	D	34	259	6	49	48	1,340	23	123
Calverton CDP	169	47	970	22	469	3	38	35	2,272	2	D	26	D	16	D
Cambridge city	45	36	111	14	75	1	D	68	1,466	9	D	40	1,045	37	292
Camp Springs CDP	87	23	139	10	193	4	23	25	285	NA	NA	23	351	26	123
Carney CDP	D	44	266	32	180	5	44	61	1,812	5	80	46	810	33	D
Catonsville CDP	146	116	862	52	601	9	D	165	5,226	14	294	65	1,029	74	438
Chesapeake Ranch Estates CDP	D	4	D	3	3	NA	NA	NA	NA	NA	NA	NA	NA	1	D
Chillum CDP	158	11	26	16	187	1	D	30	960	NA	NA	18	231	26	D
Clarksburg CDP	72	66	123	19	202	2	D	17	124	NA	NA	4	7	2	D
Clinton CDP	40	47	342	37	684	5	D	125	3,885	5	D	47	1,007	62	399
Cloverly CDP	10	55	132	23	187	8	D	22	123	4	10	11	D	10	99
Cockeysville CDP	992	175	3,791	85	4,029	17	262	89	1,962	19	397	105	2,032	98	1,150
Colesville CDP	14	44	107	22	192	2	D	44	456	4	13	18	D	17	77
College Park city	77	80	605	29	631	7	D	36	263	6	81	111	1,966	57	475
Columbia CDP	1,419	888	D	191	8,558	79	900	448	8,380	52	1,701	241	5,575	203	2,099
Coral Hills CDP	38	2	D	2	D	NA	NA	2	D	NA	NA	11	65	14	D
Crofton CDP	74	73	692	23	525	6	31	47	655	9	145	28	480	21	D
Cumberland city	113	59	301	18	D	5	D	147	D	9	D	62	988	58	329
Damascus CDP	14	45	125	31	165	5	10	22	210	4	52	21	298	19	D
Dundalk CDP	314	39	459	39	655	2	D	98	1,491	12	215	97	1,420	79	476
Easton town	133	89	1,444	35	1,048	5	15	134	3,152	18	264	81	1,664	69	347
East Riverdale CDP	D	5	7	7	D	2	D	8	D	NA	NA	11	56	4	D
Edgewood CDP	73	34	553	19	235	3	3	33	222	1	D	43	804	29	230
Eldersburg CDP	123	101	568	54	611	9	D	78	2,192	10	181	57	1,168	51	294
Elkridge CDP	150	63	648	41	1,816	9	D	25	452	7	67	39	588	39	D
Elkton town	67	65	281	15	223	2	D	109	2,392	8	D	51	1,038	51	327
Ellicott City CDP	304	398	D	81	705	38	D	264	3,288	28	369	127	2,553	121	765
Essex CDP	D	36	162	32	489	3	36	46	470	8	75	60	702	62	311
Fairland CDP	81	32	124	13	131	4	1	48	845	1	D	12	221	8	61
Ferndale CDP	128	22	226	23	349	3	D	19	726	4	69	28	618	17	252
Forestville CDP	97	7	72	22	650	2	D	9	254	2	D	28	512	20	D
Fort Washington CDP	D	43	248	22	277	8	92	67	1,112	11	264	31	341	24	D
Frederick city	462	382	3,747	110	5,030	28	252	378	8,025	24	721	218	4,153	179	1,343
Gaithersburg city	514	419	9,653	111	2,146	33	191	196	3,371	25	445	204	3,774	168	1,487
Germantown CDP	D	274	3,618	98	886	16	107	158	1,320	13	253	118	2,076	68	453
Glassmanor CDP	69	1	D	1	D	1	D	2	D	NA	NA	11	131	3	24
Glen Burnie CDP	403	146	1,191	83	1,547	16	91	257	6,519	12	149	144	2,575	145	899
Glenmont CDP	D	24	56	12	26	3	3	14	66	1	D	8	120	9	D
Glenn Dale CDP	24	53	1,319	16	321	3	D	31	183	2	D	5	D	9	D
Greenbelt city	1,405	167	6,948	56	2,646	3	D	151	1,117	5	11	46	1,074	29	203
Hagerstown city	251	113	1,009	55	1,630	10	D	210	3,313	17	409	127	2,416	113	627
Halfway CDP	53	8	79	13	190	NA	NA	17	109	2	D	33	888	20	D
Havre de Grace city	29	27	190	4	22	3	2	58	D	10	173	38	646	33	145
Hillcrest Heights CDP	73	1	D	2	D	NA	NA	4	36	1	D	14	112	7	9
Hyattsville city	109	51	383	27	572	10	86	76	905	2	D	59	1,092	34	125

STATE City, town, township, borough, or CDP (county if applicable)	Utilities Number of establishments	Utilities Number of employees	Manufacturing Number of establishments	Manufacturing Number of employees	Wholesale trade[1] Number of establishments	Wholesale trade[1] Number of employees	Retail trade Number of establishments	Retail trade Number of employees	Transportation and warehousing Number of establishments	Transportation and warehousing Number of employees	Information Number of establishments	Information Number of employees	Finance and insurance Number of establishments	Finance and insurance Number of employees	Real estate and rental and leasing Number of establishments
	1	2	3	4	5	6	7	8	9	10	11	12	13	14	15
MARYLAND—Con.															
Ilchester CDP	2	D	NA	NA	11	135	19	264	9	37	10	D	18	277	15
Joppatowne CDP	NA	NA	4	8	4	D	12	216	3	D	2	D	6	35	5
Kemp Mill CDP	NA	NA	NA	NA	2	D	5	D	3	6	4	5	7	D	10
Kettering CDP	NA	NA	NA	NA	NA	NA	28	874	2	D	NA	NA	8	D	4
Lake Arbor CDP	NA	NA	NA	NA	2	D	12	266	6	35	5	D	20	114	13
Lake Shore CDP	NA	NA	6	D	5	26	44	649	11	119	3	21	9	48	13
Landover CDP	NA	NA	12	772	33	1,533	55	514	27	985	10	114	4	21	15
Langley Park CDP	NA	NA	NA	NA	2	D	51	479	4	D	2	D	5	D	12
Lanham CDP	NA	NA	8	522	15	309	52	1,628	8	223	9	296	14	D	17
Largo CDP	NA	NA	NA	NA	NA	NA	22	331	1	D	6	D	3	54	4
Laurel city	NA	NA	12	115	11	195	138	2,078	13	192	14	112	50	D	42
Lexington Park CDP	NA	NA	NA	NA	2	D	40	454	6	D	6	43	11	69	17
Linthicum CDP	NA	NA	18	D	43	860	51	562	24	658	12	394	32	839	20
Lochearn CDP	NA	NA	NA	NA	10	185	20	136	5	D	NA	NA	3	8	8
Marlboro Village CDP	NA	NA	NA	NA	NA	NA	6	48	NA	NA	1	D	1	D	3
Maryland City CDP	NA	NA	NA	NA	4	D	40	1,740	5	D	1	D	11	45	10
Mays Chapel CDP	NA	NA	NA	NA	4	7	21	131	2	D	2	D	27	246	19
Middle River CDP	NA	NA	22	1,511	17	171	61	1,012	29	243	NA	NA	13	92	14
Milford Mill CDP	NA	NA	12	344	14	319	48	800	19	742	8	D	19	222	21
Mitchellville CDP	NA	NA	NA	NA	14	506	15	109	7	27	15	1,249	7	D	11
Montgomery Village CDP	NA	NA	NA	NA	7	D	48	669	NA	NA	8	15	28	D	15
New Carrollton city	NA	NA	NA	NA	NA	NA	24	737	4	D	3	D	4	28	3
North Bethesda CDP	NA	NA	30	281	51	635	232	4,607	25	300	46	1,232	165	1,682	133
North Laurel CDP	NA	NA	15	570	16	149	31	986	8	49	1	D	5	42	18
North Potomac CDP	NA	NA	4	14	14	18	25	93	5	6	2	D	8	D	15
Ocean Pines CDP	NA	NA	NA	NA	3	1	1	D	2	D	NA	NA	4	12	12
Odenton CDP	1	D	8	162	14	462	63	855	14	276	4	D	24	123	30
Olney CDP	NA	NA	6	22	10	46	66	1,052	3	D	5	16	36	D	30
Overlea CDP	NA	NA	3	D	4	34	44	810	5	42	7	D	26	156	7
Owings Mills CDP	NA	NA	33	1,003	55	856	119	1,977	15	52	21	410	88	3,924	55
Oxon Hill CDP	NA	NA	3	12	7	24	83	1,369	6	22	6	102	19	206	16
Parkville CDP	NA	NA	5	10	11	34	99	1,067	4	20	8	34	25	126	15
Parole CDP	NA	NA	21	164	25	258	114	2,382	10	195	24	928	110	827	55
Pasadena CDP	NA	NA	16	582	17	D	66	983	15	419	2	D	18	74	16
Perry Hall CDP	2	D	NA	NA	8	23	57	715	17	54	6	20	44	355	16
Pikesville CDP	NA	NA	13	37	22	100	133	1,700	12	53	14	118	94	471	66
Potomac CDP	NA	NA	5	14	20	D	187	3,773	3	D	37	243	61	D	62
Randallstown CDP	NA	NA	4	10	15	82	53	667	9	31	1	D	20	71	16
Redland CDP	NA	NA	4	24	12	D	16	364	5	38	2	D	12	D	7
Reisterstown CDP	NA	NA	6	89	10	181	72	1,258	12	31	4	D	37	202	18
Riviera Beach CDP	NA	NA	3	6	3	5	18	269	2	D	1	D	5	D	3
Rockville city	1	D	61	1,516	74	1,661	321	5,420	37	381	88	2,524	240	5,007	131
Rosaryville CDP	NA	NA	NA	NA	NA	NA	2	D	3	38	1	D	NA	NA	NA
Rosedale CDP	NA	NA	22	553	46	1,205	64	754	18	505	3	10	12	71	15
Rossville CDP	NA	NA	18	353	29	518	68	1,973	17	361	6	45	13	259	16
Salisbury city	3	D	46	2,713	58	707	234	4,178	26	330	28	851	117	896	77
Seabrook CDP	NA	NA	NA	NA	2	D	24	448	3	D	3	D	7	47	3
Severn CDP	NA	NA	10	848	15	618	185	4,289	15	D	20	551	20	D	16
Severna Park CDP	1	D	15	46	37	104	115	1,280	14	122	10	87	88	441	51
Silver Spring CDP	2	D	29	324	47	780	206	2,538	15	50	88	5,730	77	947	100
South Laurel CDP	NA	NA	7	36	9	63	52	456	12	101	2	D	12	58	27
Suitland CDP	NA	NA	NA	NA	2	D	43	848	NA	NA	4	D	6	21	14
Summerfield CDP	NA	NA	NA	NA	1	D	11	172	1	D	NA	NA	3	D	5
Takoma Park city	NA	NA	NA	NA	10	33	66	457	3	16	7	37	15	D	18
Timonium CDP	1	D	25	643	32	226	122	2,555	8	D	17	281	109	1,174	37
Towson CDP	1	D	25	330	48	287	371	6,787	14	224	43	762	211	2,135	105
Travilah CDP	NA	NA	NA	NA	10	16	7	51	4	26	8	64	3	D	16
Waldorf CDP	1	D	24	249	41	D	348	6,736	24	564	19	311	86	D	62
Walker Mill CDP	NA	NA	NA	NA	NA	NA	5	17	2	D	NA	NA	NA	NA	24
Westminster city	1	D	21	616	33	349	166	3,254	5	72	17	302	57	367	31
Wheaton CDP	NA	NA	5	16	11	D	177	2,605	10	44	12	51	39	215	27
White Oak CDP	NA	NA	NA	NA	2	D	32	679	4	21	2	D	11	55	24
Woodlawn CDP (Baltimore County)	NA	NA	14	303	24	139	193	3,234	18	69	12	197	46	350	32
MASSACHUSETTS	274	13,305	6,806	234,168	6,619	114,195	24,311	351,598	3,558	77,843	3,673	115,614	9,384	202,811	6,485
Abington CDP & town (Plymouth)	NA	NA	13	347	10	D	50	1,241	12	209	NA	NA	12	101	12
Acton town (Middlesex)	2	D	29	759	29	227	116	1,679	5	45	20	200	29	153	16
Acushnet town (Bristol)	NA	NA	7	D	7	D	18	74	7	50	NA	NA	2	D	7
Agawam Town city & MCD (Hampden)	2	D	54	2,280	49	729	75	922	11	95	3	D	24	D	20
Amesbury Town city & MCD (Essex)	2	D	33	1,039	20	356	36	364	6	20	7	35	18	224	10
Amherst town (Hampshire)	NA	NA	10	59	7	10	66	846	6	72	14	83	34	D	30
Amherst Center CDP	NA	NA	NA	NA	NA	NA	NA	NA	NA	NA	NA	NA	NA	NA	NA
Andover town (Essex)	2	D	27	8,851	58	1,571	79	967	8	40	42	1,617	82	2,817	36
Arlington CDP & town (Middlesex)	NA	NA	11	51	13	D	102	1,047	8	78	23	176	41	395	34
Ashland town (Middlesex)	1	D	22	837	20	D	43	927	8	141	5	D	11	D	11
Athol town (Worcester)	1	D	9	976	4	D	36	375	8	106	3	42	12	146	9
Attleboro city & MCD (Bristol)	2	D	88	3,518	32	496	134	2,277	16	106	9	23	36	187	26
Auburn town (Worcester)	2	D	23	726	49	1,609	140	2,747	7	340	7	95	35	434	21
Barnstable Town city & MCD (Barnstable)	1	D	46	897	47	444	384	4,724	36	718	41	810	99	D	70
Bedford town (Middlesex)	NA	NA	28	2,130	22	1,319	47	876	9	221	26	2,827	25	191	9

1 Merchant wholesalers, except manufacturers' sales branches and offices.

Table C. Incorporated Places, Census Designated Places (CDPs), and Minor Civil Divisions (MCDs) of 10,000 or More Population — **Economic Census**

STATE City, town, township, borough, or CDP (county if applicable)	Real estate and rental and leasing	Professional, scientific, and technical services		Administration and support and waste management and mediation services		Educational services		Health care and social assistance		Arts, entertainment, and recreation		Accommodation and food services		Other services (except public administration)	
	Number of employees	Number of establish-ments	Number of employees	Number of establish-ments	Number of employees	Number of establish-ments	Number of employees	Number of establish-ments	Number of employees	Number of establish-ments	Number of employees	Number of establish-ments	Number of employees	Number of establish-ments	Number of employees
	16	17	18	19	20	21	22	23	24	25	26	27	28	29	30
MARYLAND—Con.															
Ilchester CDP	109	98	2,214	23	404	5	17	22	D	6	102	17	320	13	104
Joppatowne CDP	D	5	D	14	D	NA	NA	18	88	2	D	11	131	5	10
Kemp Mill CDP	73	34	137	5	14	3	7	36	504	3	3	7	51	13	78
Kettering CDP	D	12	55	3	D	1	D	12	235	NA	NA	15	201	13	D
Lake Arbor CDP	48	66	570	22	1,114	7	66	61	1,622	5	37	14	623	9	46
Lake Shore CDP	D	27	123	25	108	3	D	27	237	3	20	25	D	32	D
Landover CDP	384	22	162	21	286	NA	NA	12	517	2	D	24	386	22	D
Langley Park CDP	88	9	30	7	34	NA	NA	5	143	NA	NA	27	D	14	72
Lanham CDP	152	47	1,316	24	2,660	7	41	42	882	5	D	26	543	29	475
Largo CDP	26	14	109	2	D	2	D	22	568	NA	NA	18	479	8	21
Laurel city	655	74	930	37	1,437	4	6	98	1,260	22	709	79	1,725	59	493
Lexington Park CDP	80	67	D	9	D	1	D	18	322	2	D	34	596	19	D
Linthicum CDP	321	55	1,361	25	1,905	5	D	29	503	6	47	76	1,966	29	416
Lochearn CDP	50	10	36	16	345	NA	NA	36	491	1	D	6	41	19	D
Marlboro Village CDP	D	6	D	3	D	2	D	5	D	NA	NA	6	65	2	D
Maryland City CDP	85	22	72	16	211	2	D	19	261	6	D	20	392	17	D
Mays Chapel CDP	100	59	123	16	D	4	23	64	D	5	26	7	153	9	17
Middle River CDP	113	32	260	23	295	3	D	21	414	5	28	41	715	29	D
Milford Mill CDP	228	62	2,042	32	474	6	D	88	3,672	4	22	40	475	24	D
Mitchellville CDP	48	62	1,224	33	1,922	7	230	30	850	2	D	14	262	14	70
Montgomery Village CDP	82	83	391	22	196	6	55	71	1,353	2	D	34	358	32	146
New Carrollton city	D	1	D	5	46	1	D	8	144	1	D	20	D	9	82
North Bethesda CDP	1,914	440	7,933	116	2,401	43	457	386	5,743	26	496	120	2,491	175	2,181
North Laurel CDP	244	49	350	16	296	6	32	16	63	2	D	17	308	25	D
North Potomac CDP	38	164	403	20	205	5	41	51	322	5	D	17	252	8	52
Ocean Pines CDP	32	18	28	13	35	1	D	8	60	1	D	8	138	12	198
Odenton CDP	98	60	349	20	154	5	41	65	930	8	177	53	1,000	33	257
Olney CDP	135	127	667	46	2,030	16	103	129	2,421	14	272	49	845	40	316
Overlea CDP	34	24	138	18	392	3	26	37	415	4	55	29	607	18	166
Owings Mills CDP	683	159	2,869	73	1,234	11	173	94	1,916	12	D	95	D	43	627
Oxon Hill CDP	128	17	248	20	300	2	D	74	489	1	D	47	1,463	30	252
Parkville CDP	D	36	272	21	376	4	9	76	998	7	D	53	524	63	377
Parole CDP	607	211	3,644	45	1,994	10	D	174	6,229	7	107	69	1,690	54	289
Pasadena CDP	69	38	302	26	210	5	23	51	484	6	273	42	661	44	D
Perry Hall CDP	43	50	258	46	320	7	114	73	1,054	6	153	48	958	45	D
Pikesville CDP	400	231	1,056	72	1,126	20	331	207	2,425	18	D	66	1,068	85	543
Potomac CDP	D	323	1,223	36	442	22	124	131	1,020	20	670	79	1,387	55	364
Randallstown CDP	57	21	81	30	200	4	D	88	1,196	4	58	27	338	31	D
Redland CDP	39	40	129	24	120	5	15	21	D	3	62	25	280	13	D
Reisterstown CDP	80	65	343	36	149	7	39	59	538	4	D	37	565	41	D
Riviera Beach CDP	D	8	D	11	62	3	D	15	83	3	6	19	267	20	D
Rockville city	1,785	875	18,891	189	7,155	34	372	337	6,441	41	1,035	252	4,133	244	3,160
Rosaryville CDP	NA	12	31	5	52	3	5	9	D	2	D	1	D	2	D
Rosedale CDP	109	17	40	28	336	1	D	22	149	4	D	41	356	18	D
Rossville CDP	78	21	502	25	314	1	D	95	1,511	3	D	33	799	25	D
Salisbury city	478	157	1,428	59	1,410	14	D	211	6,691	13	D	143	2,552	106	843
Seabrook CDP	D	14	38	12	62	NA	NA	60	2,187	2	D	34	D	12	D
Severn CDP	105	54	216	41	1,375	2	D	26	359	4	D	59	1,945	36	D
Severna Park CDP	483	172	990	61	2,286	13	113	95	1,356	17	D	60	935	75	483
Silver Spring CDP	628	421	6,320	154	4,178	31	525	307	4,349	33	482	172	2,909	241	2,636
South Laurel CDP	152	45	163	11	88	2	D	55	D	1	D	23	268	31	105
Suitland CDP	D	21	199	6	28	1	D	16	125	3	23	20	210	17	D
Summerfield CDP	30	12	117	4	158	1	D	14	205	1	D	5	67	13	D
Takoma Park city	124	85	363	14	D	10	79	93	2,450	3	15	27	330	44	365
Timonium CDP	D	104	963	51	959	14	121	76	1,918	19	485	47	1,207	41	487
Towson CDP	736	595	4,189	113	3,277	23	306	493	15,217	36	590	199	4,067	150	1,156
Travilah CDP	D	102	283	13	599	4	D	28	130	1	D	8	146	9	D
Waldorf CDP	304	115	967	52	656	17	D	223	2,133	11	146	136	D	129	845
Walker Mill CDP	48	3	18	1	D	1	D	4	37	NA	NA	1	D	4	17
Westminster city	104	108	562	31	332	9	73	101	1,722	11	216	76	1,929	72	584
Wheaton CDP	D	105	458	68	690	14	140	146	1,800	5	6	91	912	59	317
White Oak CDP	D	34	94	13	67	1	D	90	919	5	27	17	202	16	99
Woodlawn CDP (Baltimore County)	301	78	727	48	1,934	6	D	113	2,750	7	D	106	D	59	339
MASSACHUSETTS	42,788	21,422	255,022	9,998	192,242	2,180	22,879	18,386	587,485	3,130	55,585	16,898	273,185	14,008	93,489
Abington CDP & town (Plymouth)	21	23	81	24	D	3	14	23	339	7	54	40	722	35	D
Acton town (Middlesex)	57	145	1,230	32	301	19	204	67	1,014	20	184	44	695	56	283
Acushnet town (Bristol)	15	10	27	7	2	2	D	8	D	1	D	16	189	15	D
Agawam Town city & MCD (Hampden)	77	65	707	53	498	3	D	61	1,578	9	D	58	618	55	254
Amesbury Town city & MCD (Essex)	21	46	287	23	69	9	51	48	741	8	100	35	486	38	117
Amherst town (Hampshire)	D	80	369	20	93	31	117	82	11,022	16	126	84	1,317	61	375
Amherst Center CDP	NA	NA	NA	NA	NA	NA	NA	NA	NA	NA	NA	NA	NA	NA	NA
Andover town (Essex)	D	224	4,269	71	2,171	21	97	107	1,839	18	D	81	1,227	60	427
Arlington CDP & town (Middlesex)	D	138	321	48	416	15	60	132	1,768	20	318	73	847	102	459
Ashland town (Middlesex)	75	58	686	25	166	6	50	26	D	3	5	43	469	41	291
Athol town (Worcester)	26	12	42	6	D	3	D	30	698	4	51	17	185	14	55
Attleboro city & MCD (Bristol)	115	59	342	55	722	10	52	131	4,694	15	D	83	D	78	331
Auburn town (Worcester)	189	39	327	35	829	9	84	60	1,137	6	56	51	1,122	39	281
Barnstable Town city & MCD (Barnstable)	227	204	695	113	627	25	162	227	6,557	40	518	196	2,834	153	869
Bedford town (Middlesex)	D	134	2,621	23	229	8	47	54	3,869	4	33	34	D	33	194

Table C. Incorporated Places, Census Designated Places (CDPs), and Minor Civil Divisions (MCDs) of 10,000 or More Population — Economic Census

STATE City, town, township, borough, or CDP (county if applicable)	Utilities		Manufacturing		Wholesale trade[1]		Retail trade		Transportation and warehousing		Information		Finance and insurance		Real estate and rental and leasing
	Number of establishments	Number of employees	Number of establishments	Number of employees	Number of establishments	Number of employees	Number of establishments	Number of employees	Number of establishments	Number of employees	Number of establishments	Number of employees	Number of establishments	Number of employees	Number of establishments
	1	2	3	4	5	6	7	8	9	10	11	12	13	14	15
MASSACHUSETTS—Con.															
Belchertown town (Hampshire)	1	D	9	154	15	D	26	279	6	548	2	D	10	D	6
Bellingham town (Norfolk)	4	D	24	447	15	D	75	1,889	9	65	8	75	13	64	5
Belmont CDP & town (Middlesex)	NA	NA	6	79	8	D	71	727	5	59	14	50	33	232	24
Beverly city & MCD (Essex)	3	D	56	2,099	41	274	139	2,099	18	222	45	622	77	1,151	40
Billerica town (Middlesex)	NA	NA	89	4,601	79	2,086	112	2,267	46	968	17	503	20	D	29
Boston city & MCD (Suffolk)	25	D	284	6,965	517	9,559	2,161	28,148	400	17,162	571	24,881	1,737	90,141	1,030
Bourne town (Barnstable)	1	D	26	352	17	118	86	737	22	224	14	159	17	D	26
Braintree Town city & MCD (Norfolk)	2	D	27	1,842	62	1,246	283	5,695	37	874	48	737	109	1,845	73
Bridgewater town (Plymouth)	NA	NA	17	173	18	D	67	756	14	325	5	10	24	274	18
Brockton city & MCD (Plymouth)	10	D	68	2,022	60	1,117	331	4,816	52	1,333	24	388	89	1,047	51
Brookline CDP & town (Norfolk)	NA	NA	21	288	27	130	154	1,683	7	26	44	383	53	431	96
Burlington CDP & town (Middlesex)	3	171	42	3,313	67	1,415	285	5,830	18	405	107	7,281	99	1,196	50
Cambridge city & MCD (Middlesex)	3	D	68	1,810	75	2,383	455	6,195	21	180	198	8,641	161	2,023	159
Canton town (Norfolk)	NA	NA	55	2,386	79	1,777	91	1,461	21	556	11	96	40	3,104	28
Carver town (Plymouth)	NA	NA	7	158	7	D	20	273	6	58	1	D	9	36	6
Charlton town (Worcester)	NA	NA	12	855	8	80	27	273	12	94	6	D	11	54	8
Chelmsford town (Middlesex)	NA	NA	69	3,811	39	1,615	112	2,248	17	1,931	26	2,466	48	255	23
Chelsea city & MCD (Suffolk)	NA	NA	37	1,604	83	D	95	1,884	62	1,117	6	D	17	354	33
Chicopee city & MCD (Hampden)	NA	NA	70	3,014	36	1,193	158	2,538	30	637	10	418	49	D	43
Clinton town (Worcester)	NA	NA	25	1,358	9	180	40	450	5	72	3	26	10	118	9
Concord town (Middlesex)	NA	NA	24	190	27	385	86	847	7	D	22	1,306	47	231	31
Danvers CDP & town (Essex)	NA	NA	66	3,344	37	566	192	5,360	14	224	29	964	80	921	30
Dartmouth town (Bristol)	NA	NA	31	1,292	19	451	206	3,961	9	176	11	122	28	214	28
Dedham CDP & town (Norfolk)	1	D	12	166	25	400	170	3,864	14	35	25	593	70	1,069	34
Dennis town (Barnstable)	NA	NA	13	57	10	80	103	1,060	7	222	12	72	26	154	29
Dracut town (Middlesex)	NA	NA	14	201	13	174	56	881	11	381	6	D	20	125	16
Dudley town (Worcester)	NA	NA	16	711	6	26	20	208	3	D	NA	NA	7	D	3
Duxbury town (Plymouth)	NA	NA	5	28	14	D	31	158	4	120	7	35	24	80	10
East Bridgewater town (Plymouth)	NA	NA	15	280	9	D	33	196	10	58	1	D	8	28	7
Easthampton Town city & MCD (Hampshire)	NA	NA	30	791	9	D	46	419	5	D	5	35	8	186	12
East Longmeadow town (Hampden)	NA	NA	29	2,080	23	376	60	800	4	34	7	89	39	D	17
Easton town (Bristol)	1	D	34	763	30	338	85	1,285	25	402	10	87	41	232	23
Everett city & MCD (Middlesex)	1	D	45	705	46	1,375	118	1,880	36	411	5	31	39	1,572	23
Fairhaven town (Bristol)	NA	NA	11	385	9	35	72	1,256	8	58	7	244	21	257	8
Fall River city & MCD (Bristol)	7	280	133	4,419	67	1,218	284	3,310	42	453	15	436	109	1,476	75
Falmouth town (Barnstable)	NA	NA	28	424	11	29	162	1,834	18	152	16	231	41	263	47
Fitchburg city & MCD (Worcester)	1	D	58	1,701	34	292	114	1,234	18	712	6	122	29	D	29
Foxborough town (Norfolk)	1	D	19	945	30	537	92	1,299	15	172	19	574	28	229	20
Framingham CDP & town (Middlesex)	1	D	54	1,481	79	D	264	4,796	23	447	72	2,447	105	785	83
Franklin Town city & MCD (Norfolk)	NA	NA	55	3,313	45	1,609	106	1,651	25	700	8	43	34	336	29
Gardner city & MCD (Worcester)	2	D	34	1,016	6	49	83	1,176	7	205	6	209	16	151	8
Gloucester city & MCD (Essex)	1	D	47	2,248	47	385	129	1,514	26	247	13	94	30	245	28
Grafton town (Worcester)	NA	NA	15	816	10	55	34	295	10	63	4	4	10	101	7
Greenfield Town city & MCD (Franklin)	2	D	27	579	22	369	108	1,683	5	D	9	100	32	D	18
Groton town (Middlesex)	1	D	6	214	7	D	23	309	5	31	6	22	7	50	6
Hanover town (Plymouth)	3	D	30	525	20	D	159	2,087	5	65	9	87	24	181	13
Hanson town (Plymouth)	NA	NA	11	117	7	D	27	308	5	D	NA	NA	10	D	5
Harwich town (Barnstable)	NA	NA	8	59	11	22	68	687	7	77	6	79	10	D	14
Haverhill city & MCD (Essex)	2	D	82	2,653	48	626	146	2,420	22	276	9	51	55	488	46
Hingham town (Plymouth)	1	D	20	563	42	498	144	2,286	12	134	14	161	79	2,197	29
Holbrook CDP & town (Norfolk)	1	D	24	428	14	255	33	303	17	131	NA	NA	9	58	7
Holden town (Worcester)	NA	NA	8	251	10	D	38	431	2	D	3	13	19	66	13
Holliston town (Middlesex)	NA	NA	41	949	28	D	37	251	4	D	5	D	15	D	7
Holyoke city & MCD (Hampden)	3	D	63	1,672	25	483	229	4,017	12	519	11	94	57	702	39
Hopkinton town (Middlesex)	NA	NA	17	976	29	D	26	326	5	67	7	23	17	155	14
Hudson town (Middlesex)	1	D	72	2,451	34	D	67	1,405	9	111	5	62	17	297	16
Hudson CDP	NA	NA	NA	NA	NA	NA	NA	NA	NA	NA	NA	NA	NA	NA	NA

1 Merchant wholesalers, except manufacturers' sales branches and offices.

Table C. Incorporated Places, Census Designated Places (CDPs), and Minor Civil Divisions (MCDs) of 10,000 or More Population — **Economic Census**

	Economic activity by sector, 2012														
	Real estate and rental and leasing	Professional, scientific, and technical services		Administration and support and waste management and mediation services		Educational services		Health care and social assistance		Arts, entertainment, and recreation		Accommodation and food services		Other services (except public administration)	
STATE City, town, township, borough, or CDP (county if applicable)	Number of employees	Number of establish-ments	Number of employees	Number of establish-ments	Number of employees	Number of establish-ments	Number of employees	Number of establish-ments	Number of employees	Number of establish-ments	Number of employees	Number of establish-ments	Number of employees	Number of establish-ments	Number of employees
	16	17	18	19	20	21	22	23	24	25	26	27	28	29	30
MASSACHUSETTS—Con.															
Belchertown town (Hampshire)	D	22	108	19	59	6	D	26	D	3	5	15	196	21	87
Bellingham town (Norfolk)	17	31	125	23	372	1	D	14	261	5	D	41	663	33	177
Belmont CDP & town (Middlesex)	56	94	272	30	376	9	152	86	2,544	8	D	44	515	51	356
Beverly city & MCD (Essex)	226	175	1,223	78	1,697	14	118	171	5,187	25	913	115	D	87	702
Billerica town (Middlesex)	1,958	127	2,908	70	1,427	9	D	54	956	13	175	73	1,037	91	453
Boston city & MCD (Suffolk)	10,940	3,091	59,828	954	34,590	252	3,748	1,632	112,776	325	10,384	2,276	52,474	1,830	16,979
Bourne town (Barnstable)	105	64	487	27	280	10	84	51	629	14	D	71	816	45	239
Braintree Town city & MCD (Norfolk)	1,395	207	1,787	88	4,144	13	147	108	3,245	19	D	124	2,474	110	1,095
Bridgewater town (Plymouth)	115	49	473	26	137	5	14	28	D	6	85	48	1,032	38	162
Brockton city & MCD (Plymouth)	183	135	780	85	2,116	19	156	292	11,734	14	266	153	2,206	167	1,106
Brookline CDP & town (Norfolk)	D	216	1,019	46	469	26	223	306	4,377	32	356	170	2,420	137	794
Burlington CDP & town (Middlesex)	781	232	7,775	127	7,830	16	211	92	5,556	12	67	102	3,041	79	1,345
Cambridge city & MCD (Middlesex)	983	926	28,522	131	3,127	89	1,588	338	10,230	63	943	466	9,912	279	2,745
Canton town (Norfolk)	D	114	1,261	60	910	14	145	67	2,874	16	296	60	785	70	474
Carver town (Plymouth)	20	11	34	19	D	1	D	20	166	3	D	17	164	17	94
Charlton town (Worcester)	8	27	157	23	61	2	D	18	D	5	D	23	367	13	66
Chelmsford town (Middlesex)	142	140	1,953	60	912	17	171	149	2,972	14	148	79	1,332	81	881
Chelsea city & MCD (Suffolk)	184	33	1,405	29	1,712	4	67	78	2,109	2	D	71	746	45	D
Chicopee city & MCD (Hampden)	164	47	544	40	559	11	142	80	1,917	9	66	115	1,553	93	540
Clinton town (Worcester)	41	22	108	12	61	1	D	19	D	2	D	30	222	33	156
Concord town (Middlesex)	D	156	938	33	191	13	65	139	3,207	31	518	42	D	50	202
Danvers CDP & town (Essex)	165	130	782	47	1,654	14	119	138	9,393	22	D	100	2,307	78	481
Dartmouth town (Bristol)	76	53	431	47	616	8	D	121	2,836	16	295	92	2,084	67	532
Dedham CDP & town (Norfolk)	D	103	565	50	1,695	11	55	89	2,511	12	D	70	2,014	77	476
Dennis town (Barnstable)	76	39	108	42	199	3	10	37	478	15	88	103	864	43	133
Dracut town (Middlesex)	67	42	186	27	75	11	31	55	D	7	49	53	704	63	226
Dudley town (Worcester)	13	6	28	9	97	1	D	9	202	4	19	17	189	19	190
Duxbury town (Plymouth)	20	56	200	26	77	7	76	45	546	9	71	17	182	14	238
East Bridgewater town (Plymouth)	23	18	143	18	94	5	D	19	313	5	194	28	430	22	D
Easthampton Town city & MCD (Hampshire)	39	27	66	23	351	5	D	37	708	4	8	37	439	35	159
East Longmeadow town (Hampden)	D	48	349	34	124	6	24	58	1,480	7	204	37	D	51	407
Easton town (Bristol)	59	76	314	57	1,101	13	D	76	1,070	23	271	43	768	58	319
Everett city & MCD (Middlesex)	85	32	D	30	636	5	15	49	D	5	109	91	D	79	449
Fairhaven town (Bristol)	13	25	157	17	170	1	D	41	1,844	5	29	56	D	31	162
Fall River city & MCD (Bristol)	292	150	858	71	986	18	151	284	10,853	17	315	182	D	176	882
Falmouth town (Barnstable)	D	99	1,965	82	332	9	101	133	2,555	47	313	127	1,866	83	379
Fitchburg city & MCD (Worcester)	98	46	227	39	D	6	D	118	2,604	6	52	83	1,145	61	310
Foxborough town (Norfolk)	D	63	744	50	1,188	7	39	50	586	16	D	57	1,708	41	207
Framingham CDP & town (Middlesex)	350	305	3,960	147	4,463	20	210	265	7,537	17	512	159	3,258	126	1,143
Franklin Town city & MCD (Norfolk)	123	106	944	47	253	13	87	59	839	17	342	68	1,532	65	D
Gardner city & MCD (Worcester)	38	28	171	17	149	4	34	70	2,090	7	67	46	781	38	157
Gloucester city & MCD (Essex)	D	86	265	43	181	4	14	86	1,693	25	310	117	1,078	70	317
Grafton town (Worcester)	8	37	184	21	82	8	D	26	371	2	D	25	243	30	D
Greenfield Town city & MCD (Franklin)	50	58	260	24	309	5	51	107	2,566	15	208	51	879	47	229
Groton town (Middlesex)	11	27	76	21	75	3	18	28	D	5	18	13	280	13	D
Hanover town (Plymouth)	44	65	354	32	D	9	56	52	964	5	125	42	D	54	D
Hanson town (Plymouth)	6	10	55	12	D	2	D	10	D	2	D	16	210	19	D
Harwich town (Barnstable)	D	27	D	54	200	NA	NA	37	451	14	54	53	520	32	139
Haverhill city & MCD (Essex)	263	91	621	65	885	9	D	157	4,080	29	803	131	1,829	97	486
Hingham town (Plymouth)	68	144	562	39	347	16	179	78	2,158	22	321	49	1,293	55	346
Holbrook CDP & town (Norfolk)	D	12	80	18	134	1	D	20	177	2	D	17	206	33	D
Holden town (Worcester)	29	37	155	21	110	7	D	38	585	4	29	25	433	22	D
Holliston town (Middlesex)	9	48	1,338	41	577	4	D	31	D	4	12	15	160	29	D
Holyoke city & MCD (Hampden)	316	68	585	24	437	14	100	142	5,575	17	180	92	1,516	58	337
Hopkinton town (Middlesex)	93	99	D	26	216	7	D	35	D	13	92	21	248	15	112
Hudson town (Middlesex)	62	54	D	34	537	2	D	27	D	8	39	47	585	38	277
Hudson CDP	NA	NA	NA	NA	NA	NA	NA	NA	NA	NA	NA	NA	NA	NA	NA

Table C. Incorporated Places, Census Designated Places (CDPs), and Minor Civil Divisions (MCDs) of 10,000 or More Population — **Economic Census**

STATE City, town, township, borough, or CDP (county if applicable)	Utilities		Manufacturing		Wholesale trade[1]		Retail trade		Transportation and warehousing		Information		Finance and insurance		Real estate and rental and leasing
	Number of establish-ments	Number of employees	Number of establish-ments	Number of employees	Number of establish-ments	Number of employees	Number of establish-ments	Number of employees	Number of establish-ments	Number of employees	Number of establish-ments	Number of employees	Number of establish-ments	Number of employees	Number of establish-ments
	1	2	3	4	5	6	7	8	9	10	11	12	13	14	15
MASSACHUSETTS—Con.															
Hull CDP & town (Plymouth)	1	D	NA	NA	4	D	19	126	8	65	1	D	7	26	4
Ipswich town (Essex)	NA	NA	40	1,146	20	278	45	349	NA	NA	3	D	15	141	11
Kingston town (Plymouth)	NA	NA	11	89	12	D	97	1,675	2	D	7	97	17	120	8
Lakeville town (Plymouth)	NA	NA	13	164	16	137	23	208	10	248	5	24	12	D	12
Lawrence city & MCD (Essex)	3	D	91	4,080	57	1,311	196	1,593	31	349	18	293	36	247	42
Leicester town (Worcester)	NA	NA	11	81	7	113	22	402	4	D	3	3	5	27	4
Leominster city & MCD (Worcester)	4	D	88	2,714	45	541	234	4,584	25	344	11	146	57	D	43
Lexington CDP & town (Middlesex)	1	D	19	703	29	593	65	826	5	86	31	1,998	64	376	28
Longmeadow CDP & town (Hampden)	NA	NA	3	18	5	24	37	479	1	D	5	D	25	D	15
Lowell city & MCD (Middlesex)	5	D	76	3,530	58	945	225	2,474	26	171	23	979	79	1,648	68
Ludlow town (Hampden)	3	D	37	746	7	118	55	638	9	D	5	86	19	D	15
Lunenburg town (Worcester)	NA	NA	5	105	8	78	33	685	2	D	3	D	10	42	13
Lynn city & MCD (Essex)	2	D	36	3,277	38	381	221	2,345	33	293	17	188	49	798	47
Lynnfield CDP & town (Essex)	NA	NA	NA	NA	13	D	23	417	8	473	5	76	32	222	12
Malden city & MCD (Middlesex)	7	D	40	1,439	36	398	133	1,280	27	426	17	835	41	693	46
Mansfield town (Bristol)	NA	NA	26	1,406	41	1,138	83	1,889	16	358	13	221	31	257	21
Marblehead CDP & town (Essex)	NA	NA	13	76	15	D	80	562	6	28	12	35	31	263	16
Marlborough city & MCD (Middlesex)	6	121	66	3,867	79	1,587	221	3,452	32	309	53	1,739	64	1,396	51
Marshfield town (Plymouth)	NA	NA	16	278	25	330	63	1,010	9	50	11	133	31	190	21
Mashpee town (Barnstable)	NA	NA	6	21	16	107	91	1,097	4	15	6	32	13	57	17
Maynard CDP & town (Middlesex)	NA	NA	9	110	7	D	27	182	3	D	10	335	9	D	14
Medfield town (Norfolk)	NA	NA	6	115	13	D	28	405	2	D	6	D	14	92	11
Medford city & MCD (Middlesex)	NA	NA	39	450	44	789	163	2,317	31	373	27	219	66	1,563	34
Medway town (Norfolk)	1	D	15	598	8	D	45	463	4	30	9	D	16	114	4
Melrose city & MCD (Middlesex)	NA	NA	9	84	4	D	57	664	4	29	3	D	23	133	20
Methuen Town city & MCD (Essex)	1	D	42	1,448	33	D	110	2,240	26	1,582	13	234	44	309	38
Middleborough town (Plymouth)	3	13	21	1,049	19	D	78	633	21	329	3	D	18	501	13
Milford town (Worcester)	2	D	25	4,109	25	867	124	2,358	14	204	16	141	31	319	20
Milford CDP	NA	NA	NA	NA	NA	NA	NA	NA	NA	NA	NA	NA	NA	NA	NA
Millbury town (Worcester)	NA	NA	31	679	9	146	69	1,730	6	131	8	D	7	103	2
Milton CDP & town (Norfolk)	NA	NA	3	30	9	D	31	286	3	5	5	13	31	120	19
Nantucket town (Nantucket)	1	D	18	75	7	D	155	998	16	84	16	86	17	D	53
Natick town (Middlesex)	NA	NA	26	309	51	411	335	6,445	16	401	30	2,039	38	887	37
Needham CDP & town (Norfolk)	NA	NA	35	1,023	54	664	103	1,330	10	D	39	1,615	107	1,252	59
New Bedford city & MCD (Bristol)	5	D	109	4,990	98	1,933	287	3,185	65	1,054	22	486	94	782	81
Newburyport city & MCD (Essex)	1	D	64	1,843	40	689	114	1,197	15	83	22	167	37	316	22
Newton city & MCD (Middlesex)	NA	NA	51	685	102	1,642	322	4,523	46	317	94	3,078	182	2,204	155
Norfolk town (Norfolk)	NA	NA	5	53	8	104	14	97	6	454	3	5	10	23	5
North Adams city & MCD (Berkshire)	1	D	11	462	4	D	62	911	9	82	14	151	15	D	12
Northampton city & MCD (Hampshire)	3	D	27	1,072	26	D	176	2,277	11	165	35	366	43	421	36
North Andover town (Essex)	3	D	29	946	32	998	74	1,409	10	176	11	411	71	425	27
North Attleborough town (Bristol)	NA	NA	56	1,145	27	241	228	4,125	5	31	11	216	33	259	31
Northborough town (Worcester)	2	D	16	272	26	254	62	1,666	13	687	7	60	30	133	14
Northbridge town (Worcester)	2	D	18	342	9	D	44	783	3	6	2	D	16	200	12
North Reading town (Middlesex)	NA	NA	11	389	25	445	48	942	17	289	11	D	24	218	11
Norton town (Bristol)	NA	NA	23	525	14	1,674	33	431	10	49	7	D	6	D	12
Norwell town (Plymouth)	NA	NA	12	195	20	305	50	861	5	D	12	225	48	589	23
Norwood CDP & town (Norfolk)	1	D	51	2,424	77	1,825	147	3,038	24	1,169	41	2,060	51	890	46
Oxford town (Worcester)	NA	NA	25	867	20	390	47	1,132	14	152	7	169	15	97	7
Palmer Town city & MCD (Hampden)	1	D	32	693	16	D	51	596	10	97	5	D	11	D	5
Peabody city & MCD (Essex)	NA	NA	58	2,187	59	1,497	298	5,204	41	716	18	140	67	761	41
Pembroke town (Plymouth)	1	D	29	291	33	235	90	1,080	5	40	4	5	16	99	13
Pepperell town (Middlesex)	1	D	10	100	5	D	24	287	5	40	4	D	6	D	5

1 Merchant wholesalers, except manufacturers' sales branches and offices.

Table C. Incorporated Places, Census Designated Places (CDPs), and Minor Civil Divisions (MCDs) of 10,000 or More Population — Economic Census

STATE City, town, township, borough, or CDP (county if applicable)	Real estate and rental and leasing — Number of employees	Professional, scientific, and technical services — Number of establishments	Number of employees	Administration and support and waste management and mediation services — Number of establishments	Number of employees	Educational services — Number of establishments	Number of employees	Health care and social assistance — Number of establishments	Number of employees	Arts, entertainment, and recreation — Number of establishments	Number of employees	Accommodation and food services — Number of establishments	Number of employees	Other services (except public administration) — Number of establishments	Number of employees
	16	17	18	19	20	21	22	23	24	25	26	27	28	29	30
MASSACHUSETTS—Con.															
Hull CDP & town (Plymouth)	8	17	33	13	D	NA	NA	8	D	9	D	30	267	11	23
Ipswich town (Essex)	27	43	208	23	103	6	30	27	266	7	250	36	418	37	133
Kingston town (Plymouth)	32	27	108	24	D	5	D	28	676	10	259	37	D	30	141
Lakeville town (Plymouth)	44	36	133	29	165	4	D	25	345	9	117	17	245	21	82
Lawrence city & MCD (Essex)	220	70	348	54	1,124	12	100	164	7,559	7	109	119	D	103	776
Leicester town (Worcester)	20	7	14	18	96	1	D	11	398	3	D	14	193	15	58
Leominster city & MCD (Worcester)	298	96	554	64	795	7	47	120	2,292	18	128	107	2,048	79	327
Lexington CDP & town (Middlesex)	D	301	5,573	56	1,676	27	152	156	2,448	29	453	74	1,174	65	405
Longmeadow CDP & town (Hampden)	53	35	58	15	55	4	4	45	868	6	103	19	243	9	D
Lowell city & MCD (Middlesex)	315	134	939	100	3,642	12	127	219	8,911	23	231	218	D	176	895
Ludlow town (Hampden)	47	25	166	32	234	8	17	29	466	5	D	40	461	38	205
Lunenburg town (Worcester)	39	19	49	15	23	5	54	12	D	5	6	17	192	9	56
Lynn city & MCD (Essex)	222	85	494	60	707	12	48	192	5,733	21	254	140	D	121	726
Lynnfield CDP & town (Essex)	D	82	248	28	168	4	13	28	259	3	122	15	219	15	47
Malden city & MCD (Middlesex)	174	64	300	61	705	14	171	112	D	6	54	95	1,129	113	850
Mansfield town (Bristol)	88	78	653	29	609	10	69	49	651	9	D	49	1,010	57	330
Marblehead CDP & town (Essex)	D	85	241	34	109	14	35	47	684	21	598	39	350	39	195
Marlborough city & MCD (Middlesex)	206	199	5,950	76	1,666	8	50	108	2,752	17	374	133	2,397	83	834
Marshfield town (Plymouth)	D	56	211	35	139	5	31	61	827	20	163	47	844	46	223
Mashpee town (Barnstable)	D	38	147	35	199	2	D	36	439	14	D	38	596	33	263
Maynard CDP & town (Middlesex)	37	47	388	26	D	3	16	17	D	3	20	28	463	25	94
Medfield town (Norfolk)	15	54	168	38	329	3	D	31	382	4	D	18	D	26	135
Medford city & MCD (Middlesex)	148	119	497	64	436	11	114	122	3,088	13	D	102	1,323	120	691
Medway town (Norfolk)	11	24	109	21	124	6	D	33	357	5	D	32	478	20	D
Melrose city & MCD (Middlesex)	72	75	253	33	263	7	29	84	2,592	10	182	40	467	51	257
Methuen Town city & MCD (Essex)	D	85	374	60	1,123	7	58	116	3,290	11	234	104	1,800	67	425
Middleborough town (Plymouth)	36	44	241	30	165	NA	NA	54	926	3	D	45	765	42	312
Milford town (Worcester)	78	89	674	42	769	5	D	117	3,066	12	190	84	1,337	71	D
Milford CDP	NA	NA	NA	NA	NA	NA	NA	NA	NA	NA	NA	NA	NA	NA	NA
Millbury town (Worcester)	D	18	95	20	194	3	24	15	411	4	2	40	610	18	D
Milton CDP & town (Norfolk)	62	77	297	17	282	1	D	67	1,231	13	D	27	376	26	149
Nantucket town (Nantucket)	157	56	176	115	558	4	D	35	392	28	247	111	849	44	155
Natick town (Middlesex)	158	194	1,222	79	1,212	17	118	119	2,000	27	D	106	1,836	108	703
Needham CDP & town (Norfolk)	369	235	3,047	57	761	20	128	143	3,589	22	244	64	D	88	519
New Bedford city & MCD (Bristol)	296	161	855	73	3,085	17	D	236	8,500	28	626	216	D	174	1,011
Newburyport city & MCD (Essex)	66	115	619	32	509	8	41	93	2,462	25	168	65	1,144	50	277
Newton city & MCD (Middlesex)	2,297	614	4,854	199	4,894	68	853	444	10,794	60	1,198	191	4,920	228	1,519
Norfolk town (Norfolk)	1	41	107	20	D	3	D	13	72	4	8	8	D	15	D
North Adams city & MCD (Berkshire)	73	22	116	11	55	NA	NA	48	1,304	7	154	40	460	25	165
Northampton city & MCD (Hampshire)	108	129	661	39	325	22	215	176	4,378	25	434	105	1,982	86	528
North Andover town (Essex)	141	154	1,359	49	2,810	19	208	132	2,101	18	204	64	1,238	56	433
North Attleborough town (Bristol)	102	86	250	36	224	12	461	50	802	14	948	70	1,203	70	417
Northborough town (Worcester)	65	66	885	21	151	8	113	44	741	9	114	39	D	43	263
Northbridge town (Worcester)	57	25	92	16	345	3	3	35	850	7	172	25	332	18	85
North Reading town (Middlesex)	D	77	477	32	448	6	25	29	D	9	113	33	599	51	D
Norton town (Bristol)	24	31	157	23	304	7	D	48	1,115	14	144	39	D	30	98
Norwell town (Plymouth)	127	88	1,024	47	1,998	8	74	52	1,474	13	212	22	412	43	D
Norwood CDP & town (Norfolk)	430	146	2,714	64	1,721	18	199	145	4,074	15	152	97	1,802	103	647
Oxford town (Worcester)	62	21	87	8	D	4	D	11	177	4	49	24	338	25	92
Palmer Town city & MCD (Hampden)	17	30	168	12	185	6	12	25	D	3	D	29	317	31	104
Peabody city & MCD (Essex)	393	101	1,263	98	1,547	15	118	155	5,028	12	249	141	2,605	128	689
Pembroke town (Plymouth)	27	51	405	30	332	3	34	27	561	9	106	39	640	45	241
Pepperell town (Middlesex)	D	21	D	17	163	3	D	13	D	NA	NA	13	124	18	D

Table C. Incorporated Places, Census Designated Places (CDPs), and Minor Civil Divisions (MCDs) of 10,000 or More Population — **Economic Census**

STATE City, town, township, borough, or CDP (county if applicable)	Utilities		Manufacturing		Wholesale trade[1]		Retail trade		Transportation and warehousing		Information		Finance and insurance		Real estate and rental and leasing
	Number of establish-ments	Number of employees	Number of establish-ments	Number of employees	Number of establish-ments	Number of employees	Number of establish-ments	Number of employees	Number of establish-ments	Number of employees	Number of establish-ments	Number of employees	Number of establish-ments	Number of employees	Number of establish-ments
	1	2	3	4	5	6	7	8	9	10	11	12	13	14	15
MASSACHUSETTS—Con.															
Pittsfield city & MCD (Berkshire)	4	D	51	2,555	54	655	186	2,985	24	330	24	529	68	D	40
Plymouth town (Plymouth)	6	D	42	1,188	39	347	234	4,113	25	552	29	779	79	514	44
Quincy city & MCD (Norfolk)	2	D	42	593	65	1,188	234	4,022	26	850	49	1,879	147	10,037	84
Randolph CDP & town (Norfolk)	NA	NA	28	869	34	833	71	942	25	702	8	161	24	226	18
Raynham town (Bristol)	NA	NA	15	841	27	223	96	2,497	11	257	3	15	20	330	15
Reading CDP & town (Middlesex)	NA	NA	11	184	6	12	58	2,142	7	33	10	87	30	373	18
Rehoboth town (Bristol)	NA	NA	7	D	12	60	15	130	9	D	4	16	9	37	7
Revere city & MCD (Suffolk)	1	D	12	D	25	D	117	1,717	42	429	6	D	31	183	18
Rockland town (Plymouth)	1	D	32	636	40	466	53	556	13	204	5	D	30	405	13
Salem city & MCD (Essex)	3	D	33	734	36	274	164	2,242	21	112	15	94	57	721	42
Sandwich town (Barnstable)	1	D	8	42	10	90	81	703	6	23	5	D	22	D	27
Saugus CDP & town (Essex)	NA	NA	21	281	16	D	206	3,950	14	70	19	264	30	285	19
Scituate town (Plymouth)	1	D	8	90	9	D	47	350	7	40	3	8	16	127	15
Seekonk town (Bristol)	NA	NA	16	195	25	179	139	2,773	19	432	6	D	14	129	11
Sharon town (Norfolk)	NA	NA	7	275	26	154	21	414	6	D	8	D	23	112	14
Shrewsbury town (Worcester)	NA	NA	32	814	44	429	121	1,851	35	1,831	12	113	31	333	43
Somerset CDP & town (Bristol)	4	D	7	376	6	16	61	934	5	93	5	42	19	168	7
Somerville city & MCD (Middlesex)	2	D	53	1,142	39	489	183	3,203	30	982	36	405	42	370	63
Southbridge Town city & MCD (Worcester)	2	D	26	968	15	119	64	792	4	34	6	D	14	215	10
South Hadley town (Hampshire)	NA	NA	10	242	5	D	33	538	6	D	4	D	22	D	9
South Yarmouth CDP	NA	NA	NA	NA	NA	NA	NA	NA	NA	NA	NA	NA	NA	NA	NA
Spencer town (Worcester)	1	D	16	959	2	D	30	492	6	133	4	D	12	131	5
Springfield city & MCD (Hampden)	6	491	98	4,029	105	1,487	468	5,777	74	1,716	51	1,364	155	D	109
Stoneham CDP & town (Middlesex)	NA	NA	15	148	16	D	73	962	12	85	2	D	32	274	16
Stoughton town (Norfolk)	2	D	45	930	73	936	112	2,174	28	238	8	21	43	326	31
Sudbury town (Middlesex)	NA	NA	8	120	23	748	64	907	3	D	15	140	33	179	16
Swampscott CDP & town (Essex)	NA	NA	3	5	7	D	40	789	NA	NA	2	D	15	104	13
Swansea town (Bristol)	NA	NA	13	D	14	68	130	1,700	13	39	4	62	15	91	11
Taunton city & MCD (Bristol)	1	D	49	4,336	59	2,147	220	3,261	41	1,099	21	D	51	607	36
Tewksbury town (Middlesex)	2	D	29	379	27	587	80	2,201	23	888	9	91	19	151	22
Tyngsborough town (Middlesex)	NA	NA	15	192	19	D	32	221	4	25	5	58	8	D	12
Uxbridge town (Worcester)	NA	NA	13	528	18	237	35	453	14	417	1	D	5	D	6
Wakefield CDP & town (Middlesex)	NA	NA	32	607	35	627	77	822	11	78	23	1,040	75	1,314	23
Walpole town (Norfolk)	1	D	34	830	41	719	80	1,415	13	94	9	19	23	178	15
Waltham city & MCD (Middlesex)	9	D	95	4,122	94	D	232	3,100	32	1,187	131	6,276	189	4,128	106
Wareham town (Plymouth)	1	D	36	646	26	D	129	2,076	21	427	10	65	21	126	20
Watertown Town city & MCD (Middlesex)	NA	NA	46	1,161	31	391	144	2,660	16	633	58	4,387	36	D	31
Wayland town (Middlesex)	1	D	3	14	9	D	37	414	2	D	7	18	17	D	15
Webster town (Worcester)	1	D	19	317	14	232	58	819	6	36	4	15	15	D	23
Webster CDP	NA	NA	NA	NA	NA	NA	NA	NA	NA	NA	NA	NA	NA	NA	NA
Wellesley CDP & town (Norfolk)	NA	NA	12	33	31	203	119	1,575	7	32	15	147	185	4,574	58
Westborough town (Worcester)	5	93	37	1,099	37	630	100	1,855	14	467	36	842	85	2,621	32
Westfield city & MCD (Hampden)	1	D	92	3,103	43	1,006	123	1,944	35	1,221	8	D	39	D	32
Westford town (Middlesex)	NA	NA	27	1,037	25	D	65	857	12	78	14	257	29	164	17
Weston town (Middlesex)	NA	NA	7	64	12	D	20	141	3	6	6	11	31	D	14
Westport town (Bristol)	NA	NA	16	120	13	168	53	512	12	175	1	D	17	76	13
West Springfield Town city & MCD (Hampden)	NA	NA	59	1,657	58	830	194	3,483	23	670	11	199	55	D	34
Westwood town (Norfolk)	1	D	9	491	23	351	33	895	9	D	3	D	38	669	22
Weymouth Town city & MCD (Norfolk)	1	D	33	495	51	343	198	2,472	18	391	12	41	70	2,833	46
Whitman town (Plymouth)	NA	NA	18	219	9	D	38	493	4	D	1	D	14	D	4
Wilbraham town (Hampden)	NA	NA	7	492	7	34	38	646	8	232	2	D	23	D	11
Wilmington CDP & town (Middlesex)	1	D	69	4,831	89	2,805	75	1,140	35	899	13	308	32	315	25
Winchendon town (Worcester)	NA	NA	16	122	11	92	22	234	2	D	1	D	6	D	2
Winchester CDP & town (Middlesex)	NA	NA	11	264	14	D	51	465	2	D	14	169	37	465	28
Winthrop Town city & MCD (Suffolk)	NA	NA	NA	NA	5	26	38	216	8	50	3	D	12	112	12
Woburn city & MCD (Middlesex)	NA	NA	131	4,341	201	4,360	185	3,843	56	1,775	52	1,824	106	1,693	84

1 Merchant wholesalers, except manufacturers' sales branches and offices.

Table C. Incorporated Places, Census Designated Places (CDPs), and Minor Civil Divisions (MCDs) of 10,000 or More Population — Economic Census

STATE City, town, township, borough, or CDP (county if applicable)	Real estate and rental and leasing — Number of employees	Professional, scientific, and technical services — Number of establishments	— Number of employees	Administration and support and waste management and mediation services — Number of establishments	— Number of employees	Educational services — Number of establishments	— Number of employees	Health care and social assistance — Number of establishments	— Number of employees	Arts, entertainment, and recreation — Number of establishments	— Number of employees	Accommodation and food services — Number of establishments	— Number of employees	Other services (except public administration) — Number of establishments	— Number of employees
	16	17	18	19	20	21	22	23	24	25	26	27	28	29	30
MASSACHUSETTS—Con.															
Pittsfield city & MCD (Berkshire)	244	135	1,939	60	895	12	141	235	6,430	34	393	141	1,849	93	743
Plymouth town (Plymouth)	401	174	D	95	3,938	14	182	197	5,473	31	1,093	167	3,059	98	555
Quincy city & MCD (Norfolk)	455	268	2,311	109	2,575	17	106	287	24,029	28	D	241	3,168	211	1,521
Randolph CDP & town (Norfolk)	D	44	351	31	225	5	16	89	1,435	4	D	55	1,066	58	333
Raynham town (Bristol)	57	42	265	25	460	2	D	45	590	4	68	47	935	46	191
Reading CDP & town (Middlesex)	D	71	D	27	183	15	173	73	D	7	285	42	780	53	305
Rehoboth town (Bristol)	5	24	86	35	D	3	5	13	81	10	29	22	D	15	D
Revere city & MCD (Suffolk)	219	46	146	45	439	9	55	75	1,021	9	56	96	1,142	83	D
Rockland town (Plymouth)	36	49	419	23	D	11	72	19	487	8	D	36	795	33	199
Salem city & MCD (Essex)	206	168	770	46	425	9	68	141	7,718	26	639	132	1,707	117	657
Sandwich town (Barnstable)	107	61	250	48	208	9	34	62	1,175	12	125	53	873	26	142
Saugus CDP & town (Essex)	74	49	224	35	207	5	19	63	686	14	174	98	2,258	73	441
Scituate town (Plymouth)	26	49	108	29	160	7	30	35	514	15	D	31	752	33	174
Seekonk town (Bristol)	25	30	186	42	377	8	64	33	177	13	182	69	1,456	47	D
Sharon town (Norfolk)	44	102	226	28	91	7	D	59	430	14	183	18	183	28	183
Shrewsbury town (Worcester)	248	107	553	36	181	18	D	66	1,102	12	334	65	1,014	55	335
Somerset CDP & town (Bristol)	39	26	102	16	59	2	D	37	985	8	76	40	D	37	D
Somerville city & MCD (Middlesex)	267	178	895	55	946	17	79	160	4,402	22	210	195	2,436	132	1,461
Southbridge Town city & MCD (Worcester)	69	24	84	16	196	3	4	66	1,915	4	9	37	311	40	267
South Hadley town (Hampshire)	43	21	72	18	99	4	D	31	529	6	29	33	395	27	143
South Yarmouth CDP	NA	NA	NA	NA	NA	NA	NA	NA	NA	NA	NA	NA	NA	NA	NA
Spencer town (Worcester)	8	17	74	11	72	3	21	15	160	5	16	24	363	14	D
Springfield city & MCD (Hampden)	658	329	2,914	150	3,065	28	854	459	19,893	25	331	268	4,663	248	2,471
Stoneham CDP & town (Middlesex)	159	78	527	47	805	2	D	100	1,417	9	104	54	697	52	290
Stoughton town (Norfolk)	224	103	540	63	780	13	81	77	3,036	11	124	66	1,149	67	396
Sudbury town (Middlesex)	56	117	1,610	28	248	3	24	54	1,381	15	D	28	D	34	206
Swampscott CDP & town (Essex)	97	39	99	25	98	3	36	39	370	7	41	30	D	28	116
Swansea town (Bristol)	40	31	158	21	159	3	14	42	661	15	104	42	D	33	162
Taunton city & MCD (Bristol)	109	101	1,018	55	768	16	61	146	3,336	9	99	111	D	92	477
Tewksbury town (Middlesex)	69	65	583	33	153	10	107	61	1,555	8	79	62	1,067	63	D
Tyngsborough town (Middlesex)	34	35	319	19	1,020	3	17	14	D	10	177	33	815	26	D
Uxbridge town (Worcester)	9	21	108	17	66	6	38	9	172	5	40	24	191	35	143
Wakefield CDP & town (Middlesex)	D	137	1,904	75	2,805	13	77	89	1,653	6	27	60	737	95	378
Walpole town (Norfolk)	D	73	418	57	1,144	7	114	56	803	10	161	52	903	68	367
Waltham city & MCD (Middlesex)	894	389	11,343	142	10,470	27	814	218	4,727	37	756	304	3,249	177	1,159
Wareham town (Plymouth)	108	32	408	17	D	3	19	55	1,474	9	41	66	1,145	48	240
Watertown Town city & MCD (Middlesex)	183	137	2,905	45	973	18	205	109	1,618	26	360	84	996	101	1,602
Wayland town (Middlesex)	86	73	293	28	242	4	27	37	D	15	365	21	D	26	122
Webster town (Worcester)	88	24	96	10	51	1	D	38	1,081	7	36	42	D	35	148
Webster CDP	NA	NA	NA	NA	NA	NA	NA	NA	NA	NA	NA	NA	NA	NA	NA
Wellesley CDP & town (Norfolk)	D	292	1,570	47	799	21	172	183	2,055	17	333	73	D	69	474
Westborough town (Worcester)	135	166	4,328	70	2,308	17	246	93	2,381	10	476	90	1,640	52	280
Westfield city & MCD (Hampden)	144	59	640	36	305	5	29	97	2,243	12	D	78	1,356	68	354
Westford town (Middlesex)	81	111	2,483	28	D	6	224	48	806	13	406	44	873	41	167
Weston town (Middlesex)	112	66	D	13	82	4	D	50	D	11	263	15	147	8	54
Westport town (Bristol)	19	29	98	30	114	5	D	25	181	11	D	33	D	30	105
West Springfield Town city & MCD (Hampden)	90	78	498	56	1,237	9	44	101	2,397	13	339	105	2,119	76	590
Westwood town (Norfolk)	169	67	511	31	288	6	92	45	1,160	6	D	26	279	27	D
Weymouth Town city & MCD (Norfolk)	182	120	1,165	81	1,175	10	81	173	7,229	14	D	102	1,520	119	615
Whitman town (Plymouth)	4	11	25	15	D	1	D	11	114	3	19	24	418	33	D
Wilbraham town (Hampden)	22	32	130	17	108	6	45	38	651	5	D	19	285	30	144
Wilmington CDP & town (Middlesex)	193	73	1,466	41	1,006	9	116	56	1,256	7	55	54	683	48	D
Winchendon town (Worcester)	D	4	7	6	24	1	D	13	172	1	D	21	215	12	D
Winchester CDP & town (Middlesex)	D	114	283	31	342	10	120	99	3,052	12	197	33	350	50	222
Winthrop Town city & MCD (Suffolk)	23	18	35	7	35	5	39	31	368	10	D	26	281	30	D
Woburn city & MCD (Middlesex)	859	305	4,871	175	6,323	28	325	154	4,511	27	530	102	2,048	127	1,248

Table C. Incorporated Places, Census Designated Places (CDPs), and Minor Civil Divisions (MCDs) of 10,000 or More Population — Economic Census

	Economic activity by sector, 2012														
	Utilities		Manufacturing		Wholesale trade[1]		Retail trade		Transportation and warehousing		Information		Finance and insurance		Real estate and rental and leasing
STATE City, town, township, borough, or CDP (county if applicable)	Number of establishments	Number of employees	Number of establishments	Number of employees	Number of establishments	Number of employees	Number of establishments	Number of employees	Number of establishments	Number of employees	Number of establishments	Number of employees	Number of establishments	Number of employees	Number of establishments
	1	2	3	4	5	6	7	8	9	10	11	12	13	14	15
MASSACHUSETTS—Con.															
Worcester city & MCD (Worcester)	7	428	163	7,061	178	2,454	564	7,853	89	1,848	55	2,003	246	4,135	152
Wrentham town (Norfolk)	1	D	10	245	11	D	170	2,906	7	61	5	D	14	47	11
Yarmouth town (Barnstable)	4	D	23	164	20	136	123	1,116	11	307	13	238	22	D	27
MICHIGAN	389	23,036	12,444	514,058	9,392	132,490	34,858	441,190	5,699	106,324	3,294	67,232	13,181	151,712	7,826
Ada township (Kent)	NA	NA	12	D	23	D	28	D	5	D	8	195	54	395	27
Adrian city & MCD (Lenawee)	1	D	25	1,024	12	D	118	2,092	9	289	9	149	40	D	24
Algoma township (Kent)	NA	NA	7	71	16	98	23	340	2	D	1	D	6	18	10
Allendale CDP	NA	NA	NA	NA	NA	NA	NA	NA	NA	NA	NA	NA	NA	NA	NA
Allendale charter township (Ottawa)	NA	NA	14	459	5	73	24	300	6	89	2	D	12	D	8
Allen Park city & MCD (Wayne)	NA	NA	19	158	15	145	110	1,877	8	110	7	147	34	202	21
Alpena city & MCD (Alpena)	3	67	26	1,022	17	91	75	997	9	65	14	146	30	275	9
Alpine township (Kent)	NA	NA	26	1,073	23	630	61	1,195	8	269	8	D	19	81	6
Ann Arbor city & MCD (Washtenaw)	6	D	66	1,132	77	452	507	8,042	22	291	101	5,285	221	3,766	146
Antwerp township (Van Buren)*	3	D	11	371	6	D	24	159	8	40	4	29	8	28	2
Auburn Hills city & MCD (Oakland)	NA	NA	95	6,639	85	1,976	221	3,964	16	361	13	388	71	2,548	42
Bangor charter township (Bay)	1	D	10	110	12	198	109	1,963	5	20	4	D	23	177	13
Bath charter township (Clinton)	NA	NA	4	106	2	D	12	60	2	D	2	D	5	D	10
Battle Creek city & MCD (Calhoun)	2	D	57	7,973	31	440	247	3,200	24	1,115	17	267	90	627	42
Bay City city & MCD (Bay)	NA	NA	50	1,974	36	614	145	1,187	10	56	7	19	53	559	24
Bedford township (Monroe)	1	D	34	1,144	18	170	57	697	8	155	2	D	32	D	18
Beecher CDP	NA	NA	NA	NA	NA	NA	NA	NA	NA	NA	NA	NA	NA	NA	NA
Benton charter township (Berrien)	2	D	48	1,534	18	152	104	2,138	13	104	7	108	19	181	20
Benton Harbor city & MCD (Berrien)	NA	NA	18	611	16	164	60	476	4	40	4	D	6	D	6
Berkley city & MCD (Oakland)	NA	NA	10	35	16	93	66	649	4	D	2	D	18	72	12
Beverly Hills village	NA	NA	NA	NA	7	11	14	87	NA	NA	2	D	9	D	6
Big Rapids city & MCD (Mecosta)	2	D	12	1,447	5	D	68	972	2	D	7	450	35	153	18
Birmingham city & MCD (Oakland)	NA	NA	22	231	48	153	155	1,341	8	40	33	610	136	1,751	91
Blackman charter township (Jackson)	6	D	55	2,166	25	364	147	2,945	19	296	6	70	29	154	24
Bloomfield charter township (Oakland)	1	D	11	148	51	143	102	1,692	6	44	18	360	97	691	80
Brandon charter township (Oakland)	NA	NA	6	47	7	D	31	270	7	23	5	31	7	28	7
Bridgeport charter township (Saginaw)	NA	NA	23	751	13	189	26	270	9	37	1	D	12	65	3
Brighton township (Livingston)	NA	NA	15	393	34	340	80	962	15	101	6	56	48	320	17
Brownstown charter township (Wayne)	1	D	16	649	15	228	50	589	35	1,307	1	D	24	D	12
Burton city & MCD (Genesee)	NA	NA	32	334	24	723	153	2,299	15	81	5	93	32	260	21
Byron township (Kent)	NA	NA	42	1,163	59	1,600	61	648	37	2,477	6	D	32	241	13
Cadillac city & MCD (Wexford)	4	D	31	3,651	11	316	76	704	12	159	12	D	30	D	18
Caledonia township (Kent)	1	D	11	542	21	349	45	740	5	59	3	D	25	D	14
Cannon township (Kent)	1	D	8	18	11	54	9	66	4	10	4	3	13	D	8
Canton charter township (Wayne)	NA	NA	46	1,176	65	2,463	220	4,803	66	1,727	24	360	73	381	42
Cascade charter township (Kent)	1	D	52	5,360	54	1,751	69	1,655	37	1,161	35	1,310	76	1,722	37
Chesterfield township (Macomb)	1	D	115	3,648	31	376	130	2,438	20	97	9	73	44	201	28
Clawson city & MCD (Oakland)	NA	NA	22	382	24	237	51	404	7	22	4	133	10	193	10
Clinton charter township (Macomb)	3	301	181	4,292	83	729	359	5,597	54	258	14	540	139	1,136	90
Coldwater city & MCD (Branch)	1	D	33	1,522	17	208	65	976	8	D	4	48	35	305	21
Commerce township (Oakland)	NA	NA	53	1,119	50	489	107	2,600	17	49	17	237	48	206	25
Comstock charter township (Kalamazoo)*	NA	NA	23	951	29	307	43	890	18	213	5	52	18	87	6
Comstock Park CDP	NA	NA	NA	NA	NA	NA	NA	NA	NA	NA	NA	NA	NA	NA	NA
Cooper charter township (Kalamazoo)	NA	NA	11	328	4	6	4	14	4	21	NA	NA	NA	NA	3
Cutlerville CDP	NA	NA	NA	NA	NA	NA	NA	NA	NA	NA	NA	NA	NA	NA	NA
Davison township (Genesee)	NA	NA	7	125	7	D	51	1,062	7	49	2	D	17	82	10

1 Merchant wholesalers, except manufacturers' sales branches and offices.

Table C. Incorporated Places, Census Designated Places (CDPs), and Minor Civil Divisions (MCDs) of 10,000 or More Population — Economic Census

STATE / City, town, township, borough, or CDP (county if applicable)	Real estate and rental and leasing — Number of employees	Professional, scientific, and technical services — Number of establishments	Number of employees	Administration and support and waste management and mediation services — Number of establishments	Number of employees	Educational services — Number of establishments	Number of employees	Health care and social assistance — Number of establishments	Number of employees	Arts, entertainment, and recreation — Number of establishments	Number of employees	Accommodation and food services — Number of establishments	Number of employees	Other services (except public administration) — Number of establishments	Number of employees
	16	17	18	19	20	21	22	23	24	25	26	27	28	29	30
MASSACHUSETTS—Con.															
Worcester city & MCD (Worcester)	707	424	3,713	179	3,660	43	553	635	31,458	44	1,194	441	6,201	309	2,346
Wrentham town (Norfolk)	58	34	103	26	648	4	13	23	593	1	D	26	622	15	D
Yarmouth town (Barnstable)	288	56	258	60	467	8	16	104	1,975	26	251	131	1,764	59	503
MICHIGAN	48,706	21,650	D	11,260	314,917	1,674	D	26,231	585,530	3,369	46,255	19,491	347,337	15,919	96,150
Ada township (Kent)	116	73	303	26	176	4	14	46	568	4	D	15	186	17	95
Adrian city & MCD (Lenawee)	89	42	171	23	659	4	D	108	1,826	5	D	71	1,376	49	366
Algoma township (Kent)	25	9	37	8	19	1	D	8	D	1	D	6	106	12	D
Allendale CDP	NA	NA	NA	NA	NA	NA	NA	NA	NA	NA	NA	NA	NA	NA	NA
Allendale charter township (Ottawa)	29	12	85	4	D	3	D	19	205	1	D	25	647	14	D
Allen Park city & MCD (Wayne)	399	55	593	35	292	7	63	81	1,117	9	105	68	1,258	48	289
Alpena city & MCD (Alpena)	91	31	D	11	D	2	D	58	765	6	D	36	459	36	159
Alpine township (Kent)	23	16	40	11	141	4	23	10	49	7	89	22	D	20	D
Ann Arbor city & MCD (Washtenaw)	1,591	650	5,934	136	2,703	56	488	387	21,619	65	771	381	8,311	239	1,691
Antwerp township (Van Buren)*	D	6	D	8	21	2	D	15	343	1	D	7	74	18	65
Auburn Hills city & MCD (Oakland)	307	158	11,427	85	4,903	6	D	59	2,343	11	D	121	3,255	47	668
Bangor charter township (Bay)	34	23	270	14	409	2	D	44	1,143	7	D	40	663	39	D
Bath charter township (Clinton)	29	15	47	14	D	1	D	9	114	4	D	8	172	7	48
Battle Creek city & MCD (Calhoun)	247	95	748	59	2,391	10	96	185	6,426	20	383	140	D	97	767
Bay City city & MCD (Bay)	113	91	650	29	288	6	45	141	4,251	19	65	102	1,744	84	486
Bedford township (Monroe)	D	36	218	21	174	2	D	51	713	9	75	57	654	34	D
Beecher CDP	NA	NA	NA	NA	NA	NA	NA	NA	NA	NA	NA	NA	NA	NA	NA
Benton charter township (Berrien)	89	22	383	19	471	NA	NA	25	632	4	D	39	924	34	266
Benton Harbor city & MCD (Berrien)	72	6	D	10	348	2	D	24	368	4	32	12	166	17	68
Berkley city & MCD (Oakland)	36	46	216	21	92	4	36	54	D	4	30	35	449	37	D
Beverly Hills village	14	37	150	8	22	2	D	41	349	5	D	7	218	6	D
Big Rapids city & MCD (Mecosta)	60	30	198	9	412	2	D	47	1,038	5	D	47	947	26	123
Birmingham city & MCD (Oakland)	D	284	2,246	53	551	15	145	138	1,233	26	255	77	1,772	102	797
Blackman charter township (Jackson)	141	28	386	20	476	2	D	39	D	4	52	59	1,524	40	282
Bloomfield charter township (Oakland)	D	278	1,776	73	979	19	120	217	2,404	17	416	59	1,337	58	402
Brandon charter township (Oakland)	23	21	86	18	47	1	D	25	183	1	D	13	192	18	65
Bridgeport charter township (Saginaw)	14	14	62	6	40	NA	NA	17	305	3	D	19	398	20	67
Brighton township (Livingston)	58	95	707	28	2,573	5	D	57	D	10	D	28	348	49	268
Brownstown charter township (Wayne)	D	28	D	23	426	1	D	81	821	6	37	30	598	32	D
Burton city & MCD (Genesee)	98	42	240	37	10,379	2	D	97	1,131	9	117	56	1,191	59	289
Byron township (Kent)	81	54	201	47	1,926	NA	NA	38	638	8	82	36	515	48	D
Cadillac city & MCD (Wexford)	51	33	176	16	955	NA	NA	54	1,557	9	106	42	565	36	D
Caledonia township (Kent)	26	32	481	36	10,689	5	16	25	D	6	41	28	618	20	D
Cannon township (Kent)	11	25	56	13	88	NA	NA	11	D	4	66	9	D	13	D
Canton charter township (Wayne)	D	219	1,195	85	1,094	31	380	223	2,408	22	D	162	3,114	110	604
Cascade charter township (Kent)	541	130	1,209	54	2,868	10	79	40	608	14	89	57	1,456	52	560
Chesterfield township (Macomb)	D	57	237	42	407	6	62	94	984	13	99	68	1,603	54	D
Clawson city & MCD (Oakland)	86	32	87	16	69	3	10	40	455	2	D	40	490	24	111
Clinton charter township (Macomb)	469	198	1,808	121	3,720	14	218	366	8,184	21	244	182	3,633	190	1,090
Coldwater city & MCD (Branch)	70	28	D	12	348	1	D	64	1,276	7	47	49	796	35	175
Commerce charter township (Oakland)	201	100	507	75	1,369	7	107	104	2,158	19	336	92	1,456	54	D
Comstock charter township (Kalamazoo)*	33	22	116	25	468	1	D	23	246	3	D	41	870	18	84
Comstock Park CDP	NA	NA	NA	NA	NA	NA	NA	NA	NA	NA	NA	NA	NA	NA	NA
Cooper charter township (Kalamazoo)	5	8	22	6	42	NA	NA	11	153	3	D	2	D	7	D
Cutlerville CDP	NA	NA	NA	NA	NA	NA	NA	NA	NA	NA	NA	NA	NA	NA	NA
Davison township (Genesee)	45	27	161	11	D	4	D	61	D	2	D	28	688	21	117

Table C. Incorporated Places, Census Designated Places (CDPs), and Minor Civil Divisions (MCDs) of 10,000 or More Population — **Economic Census**

STATE City, town, township, borough, or CDP (county if applicable)	Utilities		Manufacturing		Wholesale trade[1]		Retail trade		Transportation and warehousing		Information		Finance and insurance		Real estate and rental and leasing
	Number of establish-ments	Number of employees	Number of establish-ments	Number of employees	Number of establish-ments	Number of employees	Number of establish-ments	Number of employees	Number of establish-ments	Number of employees	Number of establish-ments	Number of employees	Number of establish-ments	Number of employees	Number of establish-ments
	1	2	3	4	5	6	7	8	9	10	11	12	13	14	15
MICHIGAN—Con.															
Dearborn city & MCD (Wayne)	4	117	79	9,205	140	1,314	539	6,554	199	1,109	35	505	127	4,539	95
Dearborn Heights city & MCD (Wayne)	NA	NA	24	172	44	157	181	1,602	62	127	7	D	55	223	46
Delhi charter township (Ingham)	NA	NA	19	980	21	D	52	617	13	89	8	D	24	D	19
Delta charter township (Eaton)	1	D	21	4,704	28	753	165	3,292	22	D	16	549	80	3,320	39
Detroit city & MCD (Wayne)	29	D	382	17,613	409	7,378	2,092	11,850	265	6,695	156	7,123	479	13,228	266
DeWitt charter township (Clinton)	NA	NA	7	75	8	D	35	499	11	226	NA	NA	21	D	21
East Bay township (Grand Traverse)	1	D	5	75	7	D	25	385	4	D	3	6	12	D	12
East Grand Rapids city & MCD (Kent)	NA	NA	NA	NA	8	13	18	174	1	D	2	D	15	90	17
East Lansing city	NA	NA	5	D	8	45	85	1,293	1	D	21	441	101	D	54
East Lansing city (Ingham)	NA	NA	4	D	8	45	84	D	1	D	21	441	100	D	54
Eastpointe city & MCD (Macomb)	NA	NA	14	137	14	47	126	1,120	9	14	5	D	21	119	13
Emmett charter township (Calhoun)	NA	NA	13	330	7	D	48	1,033	6	D	3	34	13	72	8
Escanaba city & MCD (Delta)	2	D	28	1,933	25	195	121	1,818	19	307	16	D	48	632	20
Farmington city & MCD (Oakland)	NA	NA	11	116	5	67	59	381	2	D	7	14	33	294	14
Farmington Hills city & MCD (Oakland)	2	D	88	1,849	182	2,605	298	4,091	26	305	72	1,644	255	5,316	168
Fenton city	NA	NA	27	1,018	12	115	97	1,567	6	20	5	45	39	303	28
Fenton city (Genesee)	NA	NA	27	1,018	12	115	97	1,567	6	20	5	45	39	303	27
Fenton charter township (Genesee)	NA	NA	18	449	12	66	26	507	4	22	2	D	10	49	10
Ferndale city & MCD (Oakland)	NA	NA	51	1,403	53	859	88	765	8	21	10	88	16	184	22
Flint city & MCD (Genesee)	3	D	70	6,444	62	885	377	3,419	45	1,909	29	492	78	1,182	67
Flint charter township (Genesee)	NA	NA	25	338	35	524	258	4,362	19	534	6	112	81	1,535	39
Flushing charter township (Genesee)	NA	NA	3	D	2	D	12	65	5	19	NA	NA	4	11	4
Forest Hills CDP	NA	NA	NA	NA	NA	NA	NA	NA	NA	NA	NA	NA	NA	NA	NA
Fort Gratiot charter township (St. Clair)	NA	NA	7	29	3	9	125	2,590	5	14	4	46	22	138	15
Fraser city & MCD (Macomb)	NA	NA	127	3,692	48	502	43	637	7	35	3	D	16	73	12
Frenchtown township (Monroe)	2	D	7	1,202	10	D	96	1,939	5	9	4	50	19	84	13
Fruitport charter township (Muskegon)	NA	NA	21	639	8	D	83	1,376	5	42	5	31	10	38	5
Gaines charter township (Kent)	NA	NA	23	891	13	124	32	401	5	3	5	91	20	95	9
Garden City city & MCD (Wayne)	NA	NA	18	204	12	D	103	906	5	22	3	5	25	98	11
Garfield charter township (Grand Traverse)	NA	NA	53	1,482	44	290	200	3,813	22	314	14	160	27	137	35
Genesee charter township (Genesee)	1	D	4	76	7	D	39	312	7	36	1	D	8	46	12
Genoa township (Livingston)	NA	NA	38	979	27	157	42	522	7	D	7	78	18	66	14
Georgetown charter township (Ottawa)	NA	NA	45	548	43	390	92	1,242	21	250	7	72	49	287	20
Grand Blanc charter township (Genesee)	NA	NA	26	726	24	329	66	1,349	9	14	8	143	55	291	27
Grand Haven city & MCD (Ottawa)	1	D	57	1,892	16	278	104	1,041	4	D	15	195	38	202	22
Grand Haven charter township (Ottawa)	NA	NA	31	2,370	11	37	26	582	4	68	2	D	17	61	9
Grand Rapids city & MCD (Kent)	3	D	293	17,974	218	5,550	545	6,140	59	1,041	89	1,827	357	4,906	194
Grand Rapids charter township (Kent)	NA	NA	12	489	16	D	54	810	6	16	17	311	83	1,161	42
Grandville city & MCD (Kent)	1	D	43	1,613	44	718	222	4,124	10	129	11	166	55	487	31
Green Oak township (Livingston)	NA	NA	56	1,651	39	794	73	1,161	12	515	4	49	16	121	10
Grosse Ile township (Wayne)	NA	NA	6	60	4	D	11	133	3	13	2	D	8	D	11
Grosse Pointe Park city & MCD (Wayne)	NA	NA	3	6	3	D	16	65	1	D	3	1	10	36	6
Grosse Pointe Woods city & MCD (Wayne)	NA	NA	6	34	7	D	48	453	2	D	2	D	31	192	14
Hamburg township (Livingston)	NA	NA	11	231	8	9	15	89	8	13	2	D	6	18	4
Hamtramck city & MCD (Wayne)	NA	NA	10	304	10	87	122	558	21	40	NA	NA	17	D	8
Harper Woods city & MCD (Wayne)	NA	NA	NA	NA	3	D	83	1,534	1	D	2	D	20	114	9
Harrison charter township (Macomb)	NA	NA	50	582	14	D	49	299	15	73	5	4	9	31	21

1 Merchant wholesalers, except manufacturers' sales branches and offices.

Table C. Incorporated Places, Census Designated Places (CDPs), and Minor Civil Divisions (MCDs) of 10,000 or More Population — **Economic Census**

STATE City, town, township, borough, or CDP (county if applicable)	Real estate and rental and leasing	Professional, scientific, and technical services		Administration and support and waste management and mediation services		Educational services		Health care and social assistance		Arts, entertainment, and recreation		Accommodation and food services		Other services (except public administration)	
	Number of employees	Number of establishments	Number of employees	Number of establishments	Number of employees	Number of establishments	Number of employees	Number of establishments	Number of employees	Number of establishments	Number of employees	Number of establishments	Number of employees	Number of establishments	Number of employees
	16	17	18	19	20	21	22	23	24	25	26	27	28	29	30
MICHIGAN—Con.															
Dearborn city & MCD (Wayne)	D	267	11,832	158	9,763	15	418	410	9,865	22	D	257	4,444	214	D
Dearborn Heights city & MCD (Wayne)	D	75	257	45	167	5	12	116	1,275	5	79	97	1,408	91	307
Delhi charter township (Ingham)	D	53	268	29	530	5	15	66	966	7	46	33	D	37	D
Delta charter township (Eaton)	241	90	610	52	2,207	13	D	108	D	12	119	96	2,585	74	792
Detroit city & MCD (Wayne)	1,293	701	15,390	417	14,341	72	1,118	1,022	46,219	76	4,024	933	20,452	777	5,524
DeWitt charter township (Clinton)	79	43	254	18	486	5	12	32	244	3	39	27	346	19	155
East Bay township (Grand Traverse)	106	21	123	18	184	1	D	19	239	5	5	36	1,320	12	104
East Grand Rapids city & MCD (Kent)	44	43	121	12	33	3	15	26	302	6	D	16	137	8	37
East Lansing city	D	132	1,571	32	768	11	81	123	3,223	7	D	121	2,411	52	752
East Lansing city (Ingham)	D	131	D	30	D	11	81	121	D	6	D	120	D	52	752
Eastpointe city & MCD (Macomb)	49	31	D	32	200	3	8	84	419	6	28	47	704	59	270
Emmett charter township (Calhoun)	23	24	52	10	40	3	10	28	169	3	19	24	D	15	D
Escanaba city & MCD (Delta)	55	56	433	18	244	5	D	67	1,256	14	D	62	892	53	D
Farmington city & MCD (Oakland)	70	59	483	16	172	8	39	51	D	9	127	45	499	32	172
Farmington Hills city & MCD (Oakland)	3,544	736	10,653	172	3,634	15	211	422	9,375	33	735	175	2,826	184	1,897
Fenton city	D	37	143	17	91	7	42	54	730	4	25	48	1,113	35	172
Fenton city (Genesee)	135	37	143	14	D	7	42	54	730	3	D	48	1,113	35	172
Fenton charter township (Genesee)	391	31	79	16	D	3	D	26	186	4	107	14	353	14	D
Ferndale city & MCD (Oakland)	72	57	272	32	315	4	21	39	D	10	41	75	D	48	217
Flint city & MCD (Genesee)	440	136	705	60	1,982	13	73	223	9,230	12	366	179	2,260	137	1,147
Flint charter township (Genesee)	244	102	686	44	2,844	9	67	330	3,805	9	D	106	2,565	59	419
Flushing charter township (Genesee)	11	14	42	16	D	3	D	22	147	1	D	4	23	12	30
Forest Hills CDP	NA	NA	NA	NA	NA	NA	NA	NA	NA	NA	NA	NA	NA	NA	NA
Fort Gratiot charter township (St. Clair)	48	26	120	10	173	1	D	44	720	3	D	32	976	17	94
Fraser city & MCD (Macomb)	34	24	D	31	327	5	19	40	685	7	47	36	437	37	149
Frenchtown township (Monroe)	33	16	60	17	728	2	D	55	863	5	56	42	905	22	124
Fruitport charter township (Muskegon)	16	16	68	15	65	5	D	17	178	6	43	45	1,022	21	D
Gaines charter township (Kent)	32	26	101	36	286	NA	NA	39	1,900	1	D	22	442	30	D
Garden City city & MCD (Wayne)	D	20	103	20	82	1	D	82	2,006	3	D	46	740	54	261
Garfield charter township (Grand Traverse)	127	67	491	40	378	6	21	85	D	10	D	31	D	55	D
Genesee charter township (Genesee)	63	14	D	14	197	NA	NA	24	D	4	D	23	240	21	127
Genoa township (Livingston)	121	68	334	26	437	6	16	45	690	9	D	14	294	26	D
Georgetown charter township (Ottawa)	D	65	370	44	905	7	42	62	1,154	13	109	33	701	64	321
Grand Blanc charter township (Genesee)	113	63	387	41	1,383	4	34	143	4,753	11	235	46	908	35	138
Grand Haven city & MCD (Ottawa)	163	69	344	21	844	4	17	64	1,313	10	D	64	1,013	45	249
Grand Haven charter township (Ottawa)	D	18	36	17	225	1	D	23	D	3	D	15	159	9	D
Grand Rapids city & MCD (Kent)	1,027	574	6,116	245	9,779	45	298	586	27,827	80	2,142	408	8,881	347	2,494
Grand Rapids charter township (Kent)	501	100	756	36	276	9	44	154	2,887	5	D	39	929	43	381
Grandville city & MCD (Kent)	113	74	394	36	521	6	43	62	D	10	100	63	2,178	56	705
Green Oak township (Livingston)	52	41	106	29	128	3	D	16	D	3	D	17	657	24	D
Grosse Ile township (Wayne)	D	15	27	9	38	2	D	16	D	6	94	10	98	6	18
Grosse Pointe Park city & MCD (Wayne)	D	42	166	7	34	4	D	14	D	4	D	18	128	7	23
Grosse Pointe Woods city & MCD (Wayne)	D	56	100	19	26	5	4	68	734	4	D	38	730	30	233
Hamburg township (Livingston)	D	50	88	27	105	2	D	16	263	7	86	9	153	14	68
Hamtramck city & MCD (Wayne)	D	10	D	9	17	1	D	29	374	2	D	46	354	25	D
Harper Woods city & MCD (Wayne)	57	30	195	13	299	3	D	38	D	5	D	21	336	16	D
Harrison charter township (Macomb)	70	36	D	22	68	5	51	15	73	17	D	35	432	33	D

Table C. Incorporated Places, Census Designated Places (CDPs), and Minor Civil Divisions (MCDs) of 10,000 or More Population — **Economic Census**

STATE City, town, township, borough, or CDP (county if applicable)	Utilities		Manufacturing		Wholesale trade[1]		Retail trade		Transportation and warehousing		Information		Finance and insurance		Real estate and rental and leasing
	Number of establish-ments	Number of employees	Number of establish-ments	Number of employees	Number of establish-ments	Number of employees	Number of establish-ments	Number of employees	Number of establish-ments	Number of employees	Number of establish-ments	Number of employees	Number of establish-ments	Number of employees	Number of establish-ments
	1	2	3	4	5	6	7	8	9	10	11	12	13	14	15
MICHIGAN—Con.															
Hartland township (Livingston)	2	D	9	107	16	D	25	615	3	D	4	D	21	117	9
Haslett CDP	NA	NA	NA	NA	NA	NA	NA	NA	NA	NA	NA	NA	NA	NA	NA
Hazel Park city & MCD (Oakland)	NA	NA	30	335	19	266	60	455	1	D	4	4	14	59	11
Highland charter township (Oakland)	1	D	22	222	9	D	54	942	8	D	5	D	25	63	17
Highland Park city & MCD (Wayne)	NA	NA	10	494	8	577	76	566	5	D	2	D	10	D	5
Holland city	1	D	96	7,866	36	373	158	2,040	17	569	10	196	71	540	46
Holland city (Ottawa)	1	D	34	2,006	16	130	121	1,595	6	90	10	196	58	488	34
Holland charter township (Ottawa)	1	D	130	8,102	77	1,100	202	3,312	28	578	9	128	63	523	39
Holly township (Oakland)*	NA	NA	5	149	4	13	6	16	4	22	NA	NA	4	D	2
Holt CDP	NA	NA	NA	NA	NA	NA	NA	NA	NA	NA	NA	NA	NA	NA	NA
Huron charter township (Wayne)	NA	NA	11	390	6	D	19	126	20	921	NA	NA	8	D	3
Independence charter township (Oakland)	2	D	27	242	29	248	65	807	3	3	9	29	55	288	36
Inkster city & MCD (Wayne)	NA	NA	14	185	5	D	53	278	5	19	NA	NA	7	20	13
Ionia city & MCD (Ionia)	NA	NA	5	D	2	D	27	189	NA	NA	1	D	16	244	4
Jackson city & MCD (Jackson)	8	D	92	2,477	58	1,008	173	1,735	11	176	10	100	65	635	31
Jenison CDP	NA	NA	NA	NA	NA	NA	NA	NA	NA	NA	NA	NA	NA	NA	NA
Kalamazoo city & MCD (Kalamazoo)	2	D	107	3,950	86	1,218	271	2,495	31	794	28	580	117	1,107	82
Kalamazoo charter township (Kalamazoo)	NA	NA	31	1,583	25	371	49	369	4	67	2	D	4	D	16
Kentwood city & MCD (Kent)	2	D	122	9,987	128	2,727	284	4,399	59	901	24	345	85	2,152	48
Lansing city	8	D	90	4,856	107	1,728	430	6,033	32	2,027	65	1,140	121	D	94
Lansing city (Ingham)	7	D	89	D	106	D	424	*5,976	31	D	65	1,140	121	D	91
Lenox township (Macomb)*	NA	NA	6	53	2	D	9	242	7	D	NA	NA	3	D	2
Leoni township (Jackson)	NA	NA	27	670	14	69	53	892	9	107	5	29	7	42	6
Lincoln charter township (Berrien)	NA	NA	29	1,017	10	97	38	539	7	35	2	D	19	74	15
Lincoln Park city & MCD (Wayne)	NA	NA	15	178	10	D	123	1,315	8	20	3	D	19	D	11
Livonia city & MCD (Wayne)	2	D	251	9,447	244	3,484	467	7,544	99	2,161	56	1,686	212	3,213	105
Lyon charter township (Oakland)	1	D	25	538	36	883	51	1,090	8	D	3	D	17	D	14
Macomb township (Macomb)	NA	NA	51	2,040	31	122	108	1,782	38	D	3	D	55	320	34
Madison Heights city & MCD (Oakland)	1	D	156	3,674	107	1,638	178	3,280	20	810	21	558	32	228	41
Marion township (Livingston)	NA	NA	4	9	5	D	7	25	6	6	1	D	2	D	1
Marquette city & MCD (Marquette)	2	D	21	378	14	107	129	1,949	12	97	20	191	62	574	34
Melvindale city & MCD (Wayne)	2	D	11	229	12	115	35	185	23	266	1	D	9	D	4
Meridian charter township (Ingham)	2	D	13	128	11	77	201	3,642	11	49	16	89	90	D	43
Midland city	3	D	47	5,897	29	219	241	3,558	10	206	27	256	82	D	52
Midland city (Midland)	3	D	45	D	28	D	241	3,558	10	206	27	256	82	D	51
Milford charter township (Oakland)*A2293	1	D	19	357	15	126	12	43	9	71	NA	NA	9	D	7
Monitor charter township (Bay)	NA	NA	16	836	6	60	25	626	7	D	4	D	12	124	6
Monroe city & MCD (Monroe)	1	D	31	1,474	18	365	77	693	10	129	5	89	29	D	13
Monroe charter township (Monroe)	2	D	10	238	10	D	52	576	4	110	4	D	25	D	15
Mount Clemens city & MCD (Macomb)	1	D	37	1,405	18	D	75	591	9	80	6	D	32	193	15
Mount Morris township (Genesee)	1	D	9	66	13	D	69	569	10	70	2	D	24	143	11
Mount Pleasant city & MCD (Isabella)	1	D	24	434	24	292	114	2,381	10	252	11	162	58	537	32
Mundy township (Genesee)	NA	NA	12	223	24	195	41	734	9	314	3	D	31	282	12
Muskegon city & MCD (Muskegon)	2	D	63	3,241	34	808	126	1,911	23	481	11	D	38	276	18
Muskegon charter township (Muskegon)	NA	NA	19	810	15	D	68	1,001	10	69	3	D	31	136	13
Muskegon Heights city & MCD (Muskegon)	1	D	29	690	12	D	31	180	2	D	7	65	4	12	4
New Baltimore city & MCD (Macomb)	NA	NA	10	332	8	D	31	449	2	D	2	D	8	36	6
Niles city	NA	NA	23	699	8	112	40	459	4	91	4	70	26	128	15
Niles city (Berrien)	NA	NA	21	D	8	112	40	459	4	91	4	70	26	128	15
Niles township (Berrien)	1	D	18	475	13	73	43	777	8	44	3	D	17	78	18
Northview CDP	NA	NA	NA	NA	NA	NA	NA	NA	NA	NA	NA	NA	NA	NA	NA
Northville township (Wayne)	1	D	10	339	15	133	42	1,276	7	14	4	46	29	155	24

1 Merchant wholesalers, except manufacturers' sales branches and offices.

Table C. Incorporated Places, Census Designated Places (CDPs), and Minor Civil Divisions (MCDs) of 10,000 or More Population — **Economic Census**

STATE City, town, township, borough, or CDP (county if applicable)	Real estate and rental and leasing — Number of employees	Professional, scientific, and technical services — Number of establishments	Number of employees	Administration and support and waste management and mediation services — Number of establishments	Number of employees	Educational services — Number of establishments	Number of employees	Health care and social assistance — Number of establishments	Number of employees	Arts, entertainment, and recreation — Number of establishments	Number of employees	Accommodation and food services — Number of establishments	Number of employees	Other services (except public administration) — Number of establishments	Number of employees
	16	17	18	19	20	21	22	23	24	25	26	27	28	29	30
MICHIGAN—Con.															
Hartland township (Livingston)	31	29	63	14	113	4	26	31	D	8	D	22	D	19	D
Haslett CDP	NA	NA	NA	NA	NA	NA	NA	NA	NA	NA	NA	NA	NA	NA	NA
Hazel Park city & MCD (Oakland)	40	16	96	20	113	1	D	12	58	4	D	32	234	39	D
Highland charter township (Oakland)	37	45	224	34	152	3	16	37	D	5	D	24	448	28	125
Highland Park city & MCD (Wayne)	D	7	D	7	D	1	D	26	917	2	D	14	D	3	D
Holland city	225	83	D	45	D	5	D	142	3,140	11	221	79	1,893	74	631
Holland city (Ottawa)	D	58	D	27	D	2	D	109	2,326	10	D	57	1,441	54	D
Holland charter township (Ottawa)	186	70	744	56	3,289	10	149	101	1,443	16	144	81	2,019	83	477
Holly township (Oakland)*	D	8	9	6	9	NA	NA	8	D	3	7	3	58	5	29
Holt CDP	NA	NA	NA	NA	NA	NA	NA	NA	NA	NA	NA	NA	NA	NA	NA
Huron charter township (Wayne)	D	10	D	11	D	1	D	20	133	4	6	9	105	19	D
Independence charter township (Oakland)	152	83	313	43	290	7	22	146	1,664	16	328	53	1,105	46	283
Inkster city & MCD (Wayne)	D	11	D	8	149	1	D	39	509	NA	NA	22	187	15	74
Ionia city & MCD (Ionia)	23	11	34	3	D	1	D	29	525	3	D	17	D	13	62
Jackson city & MCD (Jackson)	150	92	866	34	966	6	D	190	6,524	15	D	96	1,480	73	534
Jenison CDP	NA	NA	NA	NA	NA	NA	NA	NA	NA	NA	NA	NA	NA	NA	NA
Kalamazoo city & MCD (Kalamazoo)	669	205	1,700	81	2,168	21	198	261	13,606	44	877	210	4,849	186	1,438
Kalamazoo charter township (Kalamazoo)	87	15	61	19	297	1	D	44	568	4	40	19	324	19	127
Kentwood city & MCD (Kent)	254	124	1,622	80	7,752	7	58	131	5,835	18	505	106	2,408	77	796
Lansing city	511	242	2,302	106	D	22	183	293	13,826	37	862	233	4,028	279	D
Lansing city (Ingham)	D	239	D	101	D	22	183	291	D	36	D	230	4,000	278	2,524
Lenox township (Macomb)*	D	3	3	8	D	NA	NA	10	38	3	D	3	D	6	31
Leoni township (Jackson)	D	7	D	7	31	1	D	17	252	5	22	23	373	23	171
Lincoln charter township (Berrien)	42	32	157	18	176	5	31	30	208	4	27	28	554	13	D
Lincoln Park city & MCD (Wayne)	D	26	237	17	1,566	2	D	60	844	4	16	67	895	64	357
Livonia city & MCD (Wayne)	607	377	7,899	229	12,634	26	248	522	8,989	28	D	259	5,903	244	1,781
Lyon charter township (Oakland)	57	30	316	37	227	3	18	30	293	7	D	30	540	20	109
Macomb township (Macomb)	72	85	181	87	600	13	41	116	1,031	9	142	76	1,395	61	429
Madison Heights city & MCD (Oakland)	489	109	2,800	57	1,231	12	86	107	2,942	13	116	101	1,743	98	638
Marion township (Livingston)	D	17	D	13	D	NA	NA	7	88	1	D	2	D	11	D
Marquette city & MCD (Marquette)	D	67	371	32	272	6	D	160	4,084	18	133	81	1,623	61	287
Melvindale city & MCD (Wayne)	D	10	230	10	456	NA	NA	7	D	2	D	30	376	28	146
Meridian charter township (Ingham)	343	163	699	47	928	19	86	143	1,347	20	379	112	2,218	75	475
Midland city	242	113	672	59	D	13	D	210	5,944	24	D	111	2,562	108	769
Midland city (Midland)	D	113	672	58	D	13	D	209	D	24	D	111	2,562	108	769
Milford charter township (Oakland)*A2293	17	44	279	32	1,296	NA	NA	24	552	2	D	10	96	18	D
Monitor charter township (Bay)	9	7	228	8	46	1	D	25	456	3	D	17	439	7	D
Monroe city & MCD (Monroe)	60	48	211	30	963	1	D	89	2,703	8	144	54	1,052	34	175
Monroe charter township (Monroe)	31	16	230	8	78	6	D	39	773	11	D	20	317	17	90
Mount Clemens city & MCD (Macomb)	D	125	519	35	654	1	D	78	3,181	6	25	56	D	55	316
Mount Morris township (Genesee)	36	10	48	14	161	4	8	47	D	6	D	30	893	30	189
Mount Pleasant city & MCD (Isabella)	980	68	388	22	393	7	D	134	2,138	5	23	73	D	51	351
Mundy township (Genesee)	50	37	248	26	856	4	D	37	D	1	D	29	780	9	47
Muskegon city & MCD (Muskegon)	121	80	838	23	515	4	24	138	8,584	14	D	72	1,276	61	408
Muskegon charter township (Muskegon)	66	17	83	15	D	1	D	26	227	7	65	45	848	20	D
Muskegon Heights city & MCD (Muskegon)	17	6	D	7	57	1	D	13	430	I	D	11	109	23	111
New Baltimore city & MCD (Macomb)	17	17	D	5	D	3	D	33	696	4	5	16	253	19	D
Niles city	52	20	174	14	216	NA	NA	43	495	2	D	33	449	21	161
Niles city (Berrien)	52	20	174	14	216	NA	NA	43	495	1	D	32	D	21	161
Niles township (Berrien)	58	19	87	17	99	NA	NA	21	359	3	27	19	D	16	67
Northview CDP	NA	NA	NA	NA	NA	NA	NA	NA	NA	NA	NA	NA	NA	NA	NA
Northville township (Wayne)	D	98	722	32	137	5	D	49	D	8	147	48	1,093	41	217

Table C. Incorporated Places, Census Designated Places (CDPs), and Minor Civil Divisions (MCDs) of 10,000 or More Population — Economic Census

STATE City, town, township, borough, or CDP (county if applicable)	Utilities		Manufacturing		Wholesale trade[1]		Retail trade		Transportation and warehousing		Information		Finance and insurance		Real estate and rental and leasing
	Number of establish-ments	Number of employees	Number of establish-ments	Number of employees	Number of establish-ments	Number of employees	Number of establish-ments	Number of employees	Number of establish-ments	Number of employees	Number of establish-ments	Number of employees	Number of establish-ments	Number of employees	Number of establish-ments
	1	2	3	4	5	6	7	8	9	10	11	12	13	14	15
MICHIGAN—Con.															
Norton Shores city & MCD (Muskegon)	NA	NA	52	2,575	28	D	89	1,638	14	214	13	161	36	218	21
Novi city & MCD (Oakland)	2	D	73	1,726	147	2,514	355	6,929	38	1,565	34	708	122	876	81
Oakland charter township (Oakland)	NA	NA	NA	NA	12	33	19	185	3	3	4	D	11	87	8
Oak Park city & MCD (Oakland)	NA	NA	45	812	63	600	121	980	15	128	12	133	19	69	30
Oceola township (Livingston)	NA	NA	8	22	7	18	7	41	4	8	1	D	4	D	1
Okemos CDP	NA	NA	NA	NA	NA	NA	NA	NA	NA	NA	NA	NA	NA	NA	NA
Orion charter township (Oakland)*	NA	NA	35	3,042	32	625	78	1,304	18	207	8	129	26	150	23
Oshtemo charter township (Kalamazoo)	NA	NA	11	62	14	341	79	2,457	5	18	9	111	59	491	23
Owosso city & MCD (Shiawassee)	NA	NA	21	512	11	150	39	299	2	D	7	135	25	119	10
Oxford charter township (Oakland)*	NA	NA	26	1,184	11	D	26	461	5	D	1	D	17	88	10
Park township (Ottawa)	NA	NA	7	480	8	48	15	69	6	10	3	D	7	8	14
Pittsfield charter township (Washtenaw)	2	D	50	1,449	62	1,194	125	2,900	23	368	26	887	38	300	30
Plainfield charter township (Kent)	1	D	51	1,699	44	310	106	1,641	12	68	5	18	62	342	33
Plymouth charter township (Wayne)	NA	NA	60	2,945	57	1,516	57	1,260	16	400	12	41	47	606	41
Pontiac city & MCD (Oakland)	3	D	43	984	43	D	190	1,572	27	1,107	15	664	33	188	45
Portage city & MCD (Kalamazoo)	2	D	56	6,306	46	903	302	5,471	24	237	22	258	140	2,368	52
Port Huron city & MCD (St. Clair)	3	D	45	2,633	20	194	115	1,145	29	326	17	D	55	783	23
Port Huron charter township (St. Clair)	NA	NA	27	933	15	D	51	801	18	273	3	D	5	22	10
Redford charter township (Wayne)	1	D	77	1,865	55	551	176	1,427	15	65	7	168	41	204	24
Riverview city & MCD (Wayne)	1	D	13	172	10	105	34	209	13	83	NA	NA	12	D	12
Rochester city & MCD (Oakland)	NA	NA	22	660	12	60	72	737	6	166	4	35	47	252	21
Rochester Hills city & MCD (Oakland)	NA	NA	97	4,059	89	959	247	5,126	21	97	23	247	92	499	48
Romulus city & MCD (Wayne)	NA	NA	68	3,544	63	1,237	74	698	193	16,947	6	D	8	D	29
Roseville city & MCD (Macomb)	NA	NA	128	3,854	45	593	250	4,380	24	133	14	107	36	284	46
Royal Oak city & MCD (Oakland)	2	D	66	1,118	55	590	224	2,496	12	81	41	690	75	643	65
Saginaw city & MCD (Saginaw)	NA	NA	57	2,770	35	544	146	874	13	198	23	911	43	608	20
Saginaw charter township (Saginaw)	1	D	24	506	37	198	253	4,131	11	259	20	442	123	758	52
St. Clair Shores city & MCD (Macomb)	NA	NA	39	1,191	38	187	174	2,098	9	D	7	45	83	513	41
St. Joseph charter township (Berrien)	NA	NA	8	231	8	D	27	364	2	D	1	D	16	134	7
Sault Ste. Marie city & MCD (Chippewa)	2	D	17	341	15	223	94	1,400	13	34	11	149	36	261	13
Scio township (Washtenaw)*	NA	NA	60	2,512	43	576	82	1,268	8	71	14	986	30	219	10
Shelby charter township (Macomb)	1	D	151	4,249	86	881	251	3,693	42	201	6	55	107	521	60
Southfield city & MCD (Oakland)	1	D	72	3,434	149	2,717	421	5,634	48	611	179	6,241	351	10,141	219
Southfield township (Oakland)	NA	NA	NA	NA	NA	NA	NA	NA	NA	NA	NA	NA	NA	NA	NA
Southgate city & MCD (Wayne)	NA	NA	7	D	7	D	130	2,593	12	61	5	244	38	456	21
South Lyon city & MCD (Oakland)	NA	NA	14	458	2	D	33	236	1	D	3	7	17	72	9
Springfield charter township (Oakland)	NA	NA	18	292	14	44	19	323	2	D	NA	NA	4	13	3
Spring Lake township (Ottawa)	NA	NA	37	2,354	16	81	35	259	7	11	2	D	11	42	8
Sterling Heights city & MCD (Macomb)	1	D	254	15,436	151	1,914	449	7,490	114	742	41	1,381	178	1,401	93
Sturgis city & MCD (St. Joseph)	NA	NA	38	2,318	14	D	71	821	6	40	5	51	31	181	10
Summit township (Jackson)	NA	NA	19	1,006	8	39	51	496	9	116	1	D	33	251	13
Superior charter township (Washtenaw)	NA	NA	NA	NA	3	7	8	78	3	9	NA	NA	7	13	7
Taylor city & MCD (Wayne)	NA	NA	80	2,506	66	1,096	326	5,342	88	1,660	11	222	53	318	45
Texas charter township (Kalamazoo)	NA	NA	5	85	9	D	16	140	6	D	1	D	10	D	8
Thomas township (Saginaw)	NA	NA	5	D	3	D	35	721	8	29	NA	NA	15	103	9
Traverse City city	5	141	76	2,207	44	408	233	2,297	18	D	44	D	119	1,467	78
Traverse City city (Grand Traverse)	5	141	75	D	44	408	228	2,208	18	D	43	D	115	1,442	75

1 Merchant wholesalers, except manufacturers' sales branches and offices.

Table C. Incorporated Places, Census Designated Places (CDPs), and Minor Civil Divisions (MCDs) of 10,000 or More Population — Economic Census

STATE City, town, township, borough, or CDP (county if applicable)	Real estate and rental and leasing — Number of employees	Professional, scientific, and technical services — Number of establishments	Professional... — Number of employees	Administration and support and waste management and mediation services — Number of establishments	Administration... — Number of employees	Educational services — Number of establishments	Educational services — Number of employees	Health care and social assistance — Number of establishments	Health care... — Number of employees	Arts, entertainment, and recreation — Number of establishments	Arts... — Number of employees	Accommodation and food services — Number of establishments	Accommodation... — Number of employees	Other services (except public administration) — Number of establishments	Other services... — Number of employees
	16	17	18	19	20	21	22	23	24	25	26	27	28	29	30
MICHIGAN—Con.															
Norton Shores city & MCD (Muskegon)	138	44	219	18	763	5	32	89	1,090	9	121	51	997	36	263
Novi city & MCD (Oakland)	388	314	4,877	96	2,687	15	99	242	4,914	21	D	161	3,802	108	973
Oakland charter township (Oakland)	D	40	477	14	73	6	10	24	D	1	D	18	322	6	D
Oak Park city & MCD (Oakland)	D	39	317	38	1,004	4	6	94	927	2	D	43	D	38	D
Oceola township (Livingston)	D	16	55	9	27	3	4	6	62	2	D	3	D	3	10
Okemos CDP	NA	NA	NA	NA	NA	NA	NA	NA	NA	NA	NA	NA	NA	NA	NA
Orion charter township (Oakland)*	113	67	374	48	362	8	91	82	943	9	296	42	916	39	241
Oshtemo charter township (Kalamazoo)	200	62	267	32	1,056	7	137	71	1,321	7	44	48	1,240	36	323
Owosso city & MCD (Shiawassee)	29	27	155	11	87	NA	NA	54	1,718	5	D	37	509	38	237
Oxford charter township (Oakland)*	51	29	60	24	129	5	25	30	D	3	55	14	223	21	D
Park township (Ottawa)	D	34	97	11	48	1	D	19	D	8	D	9	D	13	57
Pittsfield charter township (Washtenaw)	347	134	1,649	45	2,045	13	100	108	D	12	120	72	1,411	45	336
Plainfield charter township (Kent)	178	94	617	43	1,115	14	207	65	716	16	417	59	1,013	52	258
Plymouth charter township (Wayne)	245	120	1,803	40	924	5	23	57	683	11	145	49	1,082	50	186
Pontiac city & MCD (Oakland)	221	41	370	53	1,097	6	D	165	6,493	10	D	102	1,226	63	480
Portage city & MCD (Kalamazoo)	1,240	139	1,131	73	3,759	13	164	175	2,063	18	D	142	D	99	795
Port Huron city & MCD (St. Clair)	71	68	334	23	411	4	D	165	4,489	13	D	64	1,016	46	243
Port Huron charter township (St. Clair)	41	8	46	16	178	4	50	17	D	3	16	25	516	17	92
Redford charter township (Wayne)	D	45	413	43	1,413	6	33	91	2,258	9	98	76	967	74	360
Riverview city & MCD (Wayne)	D	11	D	5	D	6	50	38	1,044	1	D	19	249	26	D
Rochester city & MCD (Oakland)	D	109	1,213	32	251	6	10	104	2,416	11	327	49	1,398	53	348
Rochester Hills city & MCD (Oakland)	199	250	2,652	98	2,600	19	230	309	3,647	23	142	105	2,490	95	507
Romulus city & MCD (Wayne)	469	22	233	51	1,328	1	D	59	862	1	D	79	3,206	34	475
Roseville city & MCD (Macomb)	301	52	288	46	813	4	D	111	1,281	9	133	109	2,763	81	441
Royal Oak city & MCD (Oakland)	284	290	2,099	82	966	19	203	202	14,877	17	142	157	3,304	134	788
Saginaw city & MCD (Saginaw)	61	83	798	40	1,171	4	22	170	10,702	11	229	76	948	64	354
Saginaw charter township (Saginaw)	278	120	720	47	2,704	13	143	240	3,765	17	207	93	2,352	97	645
St. Clair Shores city & MCD (Macomb)	130	161	781	80	1,639	8	39	214	2,847	24	227	116	D	116	709
St. Joseph charter township (Berrien)	36	14	481	8	370	2	D	36	D	4	86	20	334	16	78
Sault Ste. Marie city & MCD (Chippewa)	56	27	190	9	52	1	D	65	1,865	12	49	67	1,955	29	149
Scio township (Washtenaw)*	D	106	813	39	4,503	12	77	41	D	8	201	36	796	45	360
Shelby charter township (Macomb)	D	187	2,880	132	6,998	24	323	199	1,884	20	394	163	2,782	136	690
Southfield city & MCD (Oakland)	3,050	732	D	288	21,742	37	468	753	13,703	27	307	240	4,113	167	985
Southfield township (Oakland)	NA	NA	NA	NA	NA	NA	NA	NA	NA	NA	NA	NA	NA	NA	NA
Southgate city & MCD (Wayne)	D	32	230	16	749	4	71	111	1,851	5	172	92	2,179	55	D
South Lyon city & MCD (Oakland)	23	13	47	6	8	2	D	21	265	7	53	21	272	15	D
Springfield charter township (Oakland)	3	28	55	23	122	2	D	25	D	5	11	8	49	9	69
Spring Lake township (Ottawa)	D	22	111	11	118	2	D	26	D	5	D	19	378	24	D
Sterling Heights city & MCD (Macomb)	549	266	8,887	150	7,518	20	149	374	4,669	28	311	226	4,510	193	1,065
Sturgis city & MCD (St. Joseph)	30	24	D	10	277	NA	NA	39	974	4	84	24	322	24	96
Summit township (Jackson)	85	38	233	11	D	2	D	53	839	9	D	27	497	23	D
Superior charter township (Washtenaw)	22	27	238	16	D	1	D	31	D	3	D	6	33	6	D
Taylor city & MCD (Wayne)	312	95	788	72	2,285	16	72	153	3,480	15	D	143	2,257	116	1,023
Texas charter township (Kalamazoo)	49	28	54	13	185	3	19	16	122	4	D	25	545	16	D
Thomas township (Saginaw)	20	12	40	11	118	4	D	15	295	9	D	21	358	31	D
Traverse City city	216	213	1,325	63	569	13	85	234	6,598	17	208	129	2,435	100	740
Traverse City city (Grand Traverse)	214	211	D	61	D	13	85	229	6,555	17	208	128	D	99	D

Table C. Incorporated Places, Census Designated Places (CDPs), and Minor Civil Divisions (MCDs) of 10,000 or More Population — **Economic Census**

	Utilities		Manufacturing		Wholesale trade[1]		Retail trade		Transportation and warehousing		Information		Finance and insurance		Real estate and rental and leasing
STATE City, town, township, borough, or CDP (county if applicable)	Number of establishments	Number of employees	Number of establishments	Number of employees	Number of establishments	Number of employees	Number of establishments	Number of employees	Number of establishments	Number of employees	Number of establishments	Number of employees	Number of establishments	Number of employees	Number of establishments
	1	2	3	4	5	6	7	8	9	10	11	12	13	14	15
MICHIGAN—Con.															
Trenton city & MCD (Wayne)	1	D	13	931	6	61	48	333	7	106	4	D	31	153	14
Troy city & MCD (Oakland)	NA	NA	251	5,912	331	6,106	550	10,978	54	681	141	5,254	414	9,440	152
Tyrone township (Livingston)	NA	NA	6	D	3	D	7	43	5	28	NA	NA	3	D	5
Union charter township (Isabella)	NA	NA	9	D	8	55	42	516	6	102	7	D	13	107	12
Van Buren charter township (Wayne)	1	D	33	1,864	23	689	54	1,205	34	1,100	2	D	19	D	16
Vienna charter township (Genesee)	NA	NA	5	51	6	D	38	867	2	D	5	109	14	67	6
Walker city & MCD (Kent)	NA	NA	110	4,406	75	2,221	115	3,156	33	2,203	9	778	50	278	31
Warren city & MCD (Macomb)	1	D	320	13,623	165	3,181	460	5,305	129	3,020	29	1,034	113	1,954	99
Washington township (Macomb)*	NA	NA	10	68	8	D	59	838	7	59	3	D	26	112	15
Waterford charter township (Oakland)	NA	NA	41	432	60	479	275	3,166	44	750	14	107	103	596	60
Waverly CDP	NA	NA	NA	NA	NA	NA	NA	NA	NA	NA	NA	NA	NA	NA	NA
Wayne city & MCD (Wayne)	NA	NA	17	5,310	17	197	74	736	22	493	2	D	15	79	8
West Bloomfield charter township (Oakland)	NA	NA	19	77	54	200	156	1,842	18	31	21	79	88	610	93
Westland city & MCD (Wayne)	1	D	67	1,690	51	477	305	4,569	30	296	18	273	64	378	52
White Lake charter township (Oakland)	1	D	8	41	16	78	66	1,667	11	31	1	D	25	112	11
Wixom city & MCD (Oakland)	1	D	100	3,403	123	2,347	46	869	23	291	9	232	22	241	18
Woodhaven city & MCD (Wayne)	NA	NA	5	D	9	99	63	2,084	16	220	9	120	12	D	12
Wyandotte city & MCD (Wayne)	NA	NA	31	1,430	14	D	86	467	13	525	5	D	30	238	9
Wyoming city & MCD (Kent)	1	D	155	6,340	166	3,842	257	4,053	56	2,844	23	225	97	678	73
Ypsilanti city & MCD (Washtenaw)	NA	NA	15	437	6	D	55	398	12	1,458	7	10	20	67	15
Ypsilanti charter township (Washtenaw)	2	D	19	659	15	688	119	1,472	23	535	4	D	30	140	38
Zeeland charter township (Ottawa)	2	D	19	541	17	248	15	59	15	278	1	D	3	D	7
MINNESOTA	320	12,802	7,313	297,884	6,569	108,467	19,109	288,888	4,617	82,311	2,655	63,187	9,266	157,494	6,300
Albert Lea city & MCD (Freeborn)	2	D	41	2,501	16	255	103	1,649	24	225	9	D	47	437	21
Alexandria city & MCD (Douglas)	2	D	43	2,421	22	753	137	2,323	18	124	17	227	65	374	28
Andover city & MCD (Anoka)	NA	NA	12	165	11	36	37	601	15	223	3	D	31	232	45
Anoka city & MCD (Anoka)	NA	NA	42	3,832	20	D	64	635	5	210	4	D	42	657	19
Apple Valley city & MCD (Dakota)	NA	NA	13	506	22	83	119	3,499	13	80	18	214	77	703	53
Austin city & MCD (Mower)	1	D	24	3,620	6	D	99	1,573	12	258	6	74	44	271	17
Bemidji city & MCD (Beltrami)	3	93	12	149	24	335	154	2,669	20	222	11	343	49	351	19
Big Lake city & MCD (Sherburne)	NA	NA	12	314	4	30	23	328	2	D	3	D	10	D	6
Blaine city	NA	NA	160	2,730	72	1,059	222	4,265	70	1,303	16	317	74	463	61
Blaine city (Anoka)	NA	NA	146	2,217	67	1,021	219	D	68	D	16	317	73	D	61
Bloomington city & MCD (Hennepin)	1	D	120	4,999	193	5,005	522	12,250	67	1,057	93	2,713	390	10,246	199
Brainerd city & MCD (Crow Wing)	3	D	38	1,035	20	180	130	1,063	13	204	8	167	46	739	22
Brooklyn Center city & MCD (Hennepin)	NA	NA	26	1,719	25	508	72	1,863	8	D	9	125	25	543	32
Brooklyn Park city & MCD (Hennepin)	NA	NA	113	5,330	80	1,488	155	3,311	36	816	10	D	53	442	55
Buffalo city & MCD (Wright)	NA	NA	25	333	6	D	65	1,324	2	D	7	114	40	179	14
Burnsville city & MCD (Dakota)	1	D	94	3,051	159	D	333	5,998	36	1,218	29	647	119	895	118
Champlin city & MCD (Hennepin)	NA	NA	12	233	13	D	40	746	9	D	6	35	21	107	23
Chanhassen city	NA	NA	36	3,502	62	1,694	74	1,435	5	8	15	384	42	336	36
Chanhassen city (Carver)	NA	NA	33	D	60	D	74	1,435	5	8	15	384	42	336	36
Chaska city & MCD (Carver)	1	D	56	4,875	22	413	42	826	9	134	14	81	34	340	24
Cloquet city & MCD (Carlton)	2	D	15	1,322	7	D	55	898	5	93	6	66	27	214	11
Columbia Heights city & MCD (Anoka)	NA	NA	20	874	11	D	45	534	7	10	6	24	17	87	11
Coon Rapids city & MCD (Anoka)	2	D	50	2,992	24	331	180	4,610	30	652	15	D	79	542	62
Cottage Grove city & MCD (Washington)	NA	NA	11	1,173	11	D	48	956	19	263	5	D	20	95	21
Crystal city & MCD (Hennepin)	NA	NA	13	114	15	247	77	983	8	D	5	D	14	76	15

1 Merchant wholesalers, except manufacturers' sales branches and offices.

Table C. Incorporated Places, Census Designated Places (CDPs), and Minor Civil Divisions (MCDs) of 10,000 or More Population — Economic Census

STATE City, town, township, borough, or CDP (county if applicable)	Real estate and rental and leasing	Professional, scientific, and technical services		Administration and support and waste management and mediation services		Educational services		Health care and social assistance		Arts, entertainment, and recreation		Accommodation and food services		Other services (except public administration)	
	Number of employees	Number of establishments	Number of employees	Number of establishments	Number of employees	Number of establishments	Number of employees	Number of establishments	Number of employees	Number of establishments	Number of employees	Number of establishments	Number of employees	Number of establishments	Number of employees
	16	17	18	19	20	21	22	23	24	25	26	27	28	29	30
MICHIGAN—Con.															
Trenton city & MCD (Wayne)	D	31	310	18	153	2	D	86	1,714	3	D	38	626	40	143
Troy city & MCD (Oakland)	1,427	870	D	438	24,989	51	866	512	11,273	36	514	269	6,231	226	2,105
Tyrone township (Livingston)	3	16	D	10	D	NA	NA	8	88	2	D	3	22	5	D
Union charter township (Isabella)	40	16	227	10	114	1	D	31	539	6	82	28	D	28	177
Van Buren charter township (Wayne)	120	29	461	25	354	3	10	33	D	12	D	45	1,011	28	148
Vienna charter township (Genesee)	16	10	48	9	D	1	D	43	596	4	35	17	356	18	D
Walker city & MCD (Kent)	119	55	348	44	1,039	6	37	75	1,319	5	107	73	1,885	61	674
Warren city & MCD (Macomb)	605	192	13,153	147	4,363	13	70	366	8,284	24	247	296	5,058	236	1,648
Washington township (Macomb)*	D	50	265	25	276	3	D	55	341	5	39	35	664	26	168
Waterford charter township (Oakland)	215	152	609	93	641	16	59	197	2,319	26	235	140	2,537	161	806
Waverly CDP	NA	NA	NA	NA	NA	NA	NA	NA	NA	NA	NA	NA	NA	NA	NA
Wayne city & MCD (Wayne)	D	14	134	14	757	2	D	61	2,269	1	D	41	379	40	D
West Bloomfield charter township (Oakland)	466	241	681	77	540	17	73	282	5,656	40	669	91	1,496	97	595
Westland city & MCD (Wayne)	D	64	308	65	1,008	6	47	176	2,684	18	238	151	2,695	122	830
White Lake charter township (Oakland)	33	44	190	41	111	5	23	34	206	5	42	32	663	33	D
Wixom city & MCD (Oakland)	114	76	870	39	708	5	22	21	D	4	38	36	480	31	285
Woodhaven city & MCD (Wayne)	D	13	D	2	D	1	D	40	502	5	D	34	802	22	D
Wyandotte city & MCD (Wayne)	D	43	138	13	156	3	9	56	2,880	5	27	60	604	48	210
Wyoming city & MCD (Kent)	669	109	D	75	2,143	12	296	140	4,606	13	489	128	2,271	122	868
Ypsilanti city & MCD (Washtenaw)	D	44	460	16	385	3	D	59	D	7	62	49	828	26	D
Ypsilanti charter township (Washtenaw)	D	48	893	42	218	10	281	104	6,569	12	187	68	923	52	334
Zeeland charter township (Ottawa)	13	11	D	21	1,106	3	4	11	D	NA	NA	9	79	12	D
MINNESOTA	34,499	16,348	140,927	7,238	162,828	1,275	11,961	15,107	440,195	2,714	42,320	11,345	221,859	10,832	72,715
Albert Lea city & MCD (Freeborn)	D	30	168	22	335	2	D	60	2,459	10	96	56	902	49	325
Alexandria city & MCD (Douglas)	111	59	D	28	696	2	D	105	3,185	15	64	63	1,429	64	315
Andover city & MCD (Anoka)	162	64	129	32	D	5	23	46	D	9	260	19	339	34	D
Anoka city & MCD (Anoka)	47	61	267	21	709	4	11	47	1,047	7	D	40	672	36	258
Apple Valley city & MCD (Dakota)	201	163	462	50	258	19	414	132	1,839	14	136	72	1,751	66	588
Austin city & MCD (Mower)	120	31	233	25	431	2	D	71	2,734	8	68	55	962	62	449
Bemidji city & MCD (Beltrami)	D	48	D	22	130	6	39	94	3,282	13	D	59	1,327	53	275
Big Lake city & MCD (Sherburne)	17	12	D	7	21	1	D	20	D	3	D	18	347	15	77
Blaine city	190	113	735	83	6,027	12	134	114	1,825	25	537	109	2,569	123	965
Blaine city (Anoka)	D	113	735	83	6,027	9	D	113	D	25	537	105	D	120	D
Bloomington city & MCD (Hennepin)	4,195	566	7,374	236	12,610	38	482	279	7,009	29	725	266	8,597	191	1,921
Brainerd city & MCD (Crow Wing)	72	43	329	26	359	5	15	89	3,311	12	149	51	756	51	225
Brooklyn Center city & MCD (Hennepin)	131	60	438	29	1,673	2	D	96	1,745	6	118	48	1,089	33	194
Brooklyn Park city & MCD (Hennepin)	299	129	1,205	97	2,314	17	D	124	3,253	20	260	84	1,407	88	546
Buffalo city & MCD (Wright)	28	60	166	25	342	4	20	58	2,216	7	D	30	D	37	243
Burnsville city & MCD (Dakota)	503	289	1,438	106	1,965	20	182	234	5,517	37	952	129	2,756	134	907
Champlin city & MCD (Hennepin)	72	61	197	19	35	5	21	34	D	7	219	26	665	25	D
Chanhassen city	335	126	1,980	45	896	14	207	54	601	20	467	47	D	64	483
Chanhassen city (Carver)	335	126	1,980	45	896	14	207	54	601	20	467	47	D	64	483
Chaska city & MCD (Carver)	D	73	273	28	281	7	28	56	1,009	6	D	36	477	28	203
Cloquet city & MCD (Carlton)	43	23	110	10	68	1	D	47	1,067	10	D	33	590	33	148
Columbia Heights city & MCD (Anoka)	19	33	234	23	701	2	D	41	D	1	D	33	444	27	157
Coon Rapids city & MCD (Anoka)	199	113	842	78	1,103	3	D	159	6,076	20	646	110	2,581	88	697
Cottage Grove city & MCD (Washington)	D	33	94	34	198	4	13	48	708	5	59	32	652	44	251
Crystal city & MCD (Hennepin)	68	27	74	24	806	3	24	66	D	3	10	30	507	44	297

Table C. Incorporated Places, Census Designated Places (CDPs), and Minor Civil Divisions (MCDs) of 10,000 or More Population — **Economic Census**

STATE City, town, township, borough, or CDP (county if applicable)	Utilities Number of establish-ments	Utilities Number of employees	Manufacturing Number of establish-ments	Manufacturing Number of employees	Wholesale trade[1] Number of establish-ments	Wholesale trade[1] Number of employees	Retail trade Number of establish-ments	Retail trade Number of employees	Transportation and warehousing Number of establish-ments	Transportation and warehousing Number of employees	Information Number of establish-ments	Information Number of employees	Finance and insurance Number of establish-ments	Finance and insurance Number of employees	Real estate and rental and leasing Number of establish-ments
	1	2	3	4	5	6	7	8	9	10	11	12	13	14	15
MINNESOTA—Con.															
Duluth city & MCD (St. Louis)	7	D	89	2,381	93	1,063	427	6,141	58	1,228	67	1,174	163	2,242	120
Eagan city & MCD (Dakota)	NA	NA	86	3,073	143	2,815	163	3,258	129	5,030	68	11,342	138	6,233	106
East Bethel city & MCD (Anoka)	NA	NA	13	80	6	41	15	51	11	55	1	D	4	24	5
Eden Prairie city & MCD (Hennepin)	NA	NA	110	7,861	177	2,957	242	5,876	37	1,604	75	1,979	200	5,667	124
Edina city & MCD (Hennepin)	4	53	62	3,155	129	1,086	299	6,044	15	D	51	1,002	264	3,890	195
Elk River city & MCD (Sherburne)	NA	NA	53	1,304	19	100	84	1,609	24	342	8	D	46	334	40
Fairmont city & MCD (Martin)	1	D	25	1,062	18	D	70	1,043	10	148	7	83	35	D	13
Faribault city & MCD (Rice)	1	D	34	2,618	16	D	98	1,505	18	464	10	147	36	229	27
Farmington city & MCD (Dakota)	2	D	21	538	15	D	27	248	11	312	4	D	14	D	10
Fergus Falls city & MCD (Otter Tail)	4	D	30	1,715	17	205	95	1,659	14	211	13	126	47	233	24
Forest Lake city & MCD (Washington)	NA	NA	28	427	7	14	100	1,791	6	D	8	72	45	261	32
Fridley city & MCD (Anoka)	NA	NA	113	5,972	70	9,569	86	2,040	30	1,191	7	D	30	125	36
Golden Valley city & MCD (Hennepin)	1	D	54	4,804	75	1,222	74	1,556	15	853	35	1,136	126	5,942	62
Grand Rapids city & MCD (Itasca)	3	D	19	827	15	65	111	1,792	6	75	14	135	50	294	21
Ham Lake city & MCD (Anoka)	NA	NA	47	531	20	131	32	235	15	D	4	D	13	38	19
Hastings city	1	D	25	1,110	13	62	65	1,193	9	189	9	D	35	D	19
Hastings city (Dakota)	1	D	25	1,110	13	62	65	1,193	9	189	9	D	35	D	19
Hibbing city & MCD (St. Louis)	NA	NA	26	944	38	476	93	1,171	12	81	11	155	34	181	15
Hopkins city & MCD (Hennepin)	1	D	44	1,446	42	1,090	80	868	10	D	12	204	33	1,022	45
Hugo city & MCD (Washington)	NA	NA	17	539	7	88	19	217	5	8	NA	NA	10	32	8
Hutchinson city & MCD (McLeod)	NA	NA	28	3,244	12	253	91	1,506	10	146	5	82	41	261	21
Inver Grove Heights city & MCD (Dakota)	2	D	27	832	20	D	69	1,520	24	504	7	D	32	343	27
Lakeville city & MCD (Dakota)	2	D	55	2,932	45	D	120	2,125	35	501	14	D	82	378	64
Lino Lakes city & MCD (Anoka)	NA	NA	24	571	23	308	29	573	12	228	NA	NA	21	96	20
Little Canada city & MCD (Ramsey)	NA	NA	22	455	21	D	36	474	6	239	7	D	34	118	27
Mankato city	6	D	49	2,644	55	980	271	5,743	21	250	24	1,358	113	867	70
Mankato city (Blue Earth)	6	D	49	2,644	55	980	269	D	21	250	24	1,358	113	867	70
Maple Grove city & MCD (Hennepin)	2	D	95	6,410	86	935	183	4,073	20	1,122	34	1,396	126	1,241	86
Maplewood city & MCD (Ramsey)	NA	NA	24	541	38	425	229	4,308	17	305	17	212	50	463	43
Marshall city & MCD (Lyon)	1	D	28	1,562	22	393	96	1,698	19	547	13	185	41	D	28
Mendota Heights city & MCD (Dakota)	1	D	18	750	27	D	21	185	17	474	11	D	47	1,406	9
Minneapolis city & MCD (Hennepin)	27	D	427	12,837	483	7,802	1,123	14,533	203	15,599	390	9,632	843	36,604	684
Minnetonka city & MCD (Hennepin)	NA	NA	81	4,523	131	3,457	294	5,982	17	D	75	2,231	246	9,804	140
Monticello city & MCD (Wright)	3	D	21	1,106	12	284	51	1,289	10	137	5	69	29	170	16
Moorhead city & MCD (Clay)	NA	NA	21	699	31	433	113	1,992	32	251	9	D	54	302	30
Mounds View city & MCD (Ramsey)	NA	NA	10	559	13	799	29	382	6	D	1	D	5	D	6
New Brighton city & MCD (Ramsey)	NA	NA	41	2,300	44	913	39	677	24	471	5	75	41	265	38
New Hope city & MCD (Hennepin)	NA	NA	53	2,864	53	818	44	868	8	D	12	118	31	D	27
New Ulm city & MCD (Brown)	NA	NA	18	1,919	11	D	69	1,248	18	527	7	209	31	276	12
North Branch city & MCD (Chisago)	1	D	11	216	14	196	59	748	6	D	3	D	14	73	10
Northfield city	1	D	24	1,482	15	562	68	919	9	D	7	39	32	215	18
Northfield city (Rice)	1	D	22	D	14	D	66	D	9	D	7	39	31	D	17
North Mankato city	NA	NA	27	3,110	21	287	22	358	10	290	6	D	18	81	11
North Mankato city (Nicollet)	NA	NA	NA	NA	NA	NA	22	358	NA	NA	NA	NA	NA	NA	NA
North St. Paul city & MCD (Ramsey)	NA	NA	12	115	7	D	25	328	5	15	4	D	7	92	9
Oakdale city & MCD (Washington)	NA	NA	28	673	40	480	64	1,514	15	691	13	215	63	1,134	27
Otsego city & MCD (Wright)	NA	NA	10	20	7	30	14	429	12	D	1	D	7	18	8
Owatonna city & MCD (Steele)	2	D	36	4,139	22	323	103	2,096	24	397	13	456	54	D	20

1 Merchant wholesalers, except manufacturers' sales branches and offices.

Table C. Incorporated Places, Census Designated Places (CDPs), and Minor Civil Divisions (MCDs) of 10,000 or More Population — **Economic Census**

STATE City, town, township, borough, or CDP (county if applicable)	Real estate and rental and leasing — Number of employees	Professional, scientific, and technical services — Number of establishments	Number of employees	Administration and support and waste management and mediation services — Number of establishments	Number of employees	Educational services — Number of establishments	Number of employees	Health care and social assistance — Number of establishments	Number of employees	Arts, entertainment, and recreation — Number of establishments	Number of employees	Accommodation and food services — Number of establishments	Number of employees	Other services (except public administration) — Number of establishments	Number of employees
	16	17	18	19	20	21	22	23	24	25	26	27	28	29	30
MINNESOTA—Con.															
Duluth city & MCD (St. Louis)	657	234	D	76	2,486	24	101	415	16,618	56	879	227	5,656	186	1,428
Eagan city & MCD (Dakota)	799	338	3,631	89	1,345	26	440	179	7,047	21	617	153	3,503	132	1,558
East Bethel city & MCD (Anoka)	6	14	21	19	40	2	D	4	27	4	57	6	53	19	67
Eden Prairie city & MCD (Hennepin)	916	430	4,020	103	2,360	41	239	165	2,983	33	D	149	3,143	133	1,099
Edina city & MCD (Hennepin)	1,617	495	4,222	135	14,690	37	215	390	9,328	37	D	104	2,811	131	1,463
Elk River city & MCD (Sherburne)	102	76	403	40	312	5	19	68	1,842	16	213	54	D	53	296
Fairmont city & MCD (Martin)	30	31	176	9	191	1	D	47	D	12	D	30	699	35	119
Faribault city & MCD (Rice)	139	41	302	22	401	3	D	89	1,953	14	D	51	810	53	260
Farmington city & MCD (Dakota)	8	39	117	19	210	2	D	30	D	8	D	19	339	27	D
Fergus Falls city & MCD (Otter Tail)	54	39	246	13	175	4	D	94	2,907	14	125	42	638	51	237
Forest Lake city & MCD (Washington)	D	44	191	21	343	4	55	58	678	12	73	46	1,019	54	402
Fridley city & MCD (Anoka)	D	77	302	40	1,413	3	D	84	D	10	D	48	D	53	485
Golden Valley city & MCD (Hennepin)	512	245	4,775	75	2,125	9	68	140	4,725	13	193	74	1,350	64	745
Grand Rapids city & MCD (Itasca)	D	48	586	11	131	4	D	101	2,437	16	D	44	893	46	256
Ham Lake city & MCD (Anoka)	35	53	190	31	390	2	D	23	D	9	97	14	205	31	172
Hastings city	76	39	244	22	311	5	31	53	1,554	7	199	48	835	50	317
Hastings city (Dakota)	76	39	244	22	311	5	31	53	1,554	6	D	48	835	50	317
Hibbing city & MCD (St. Louis)	50	46	364	18	353	2	D	63	2,385	9	38	34	566	29	229
Hopkins city & MCD (Hennepin)	235	84	1,583	30	442	8	26	57	4,226	9	250	41	727	80	505
Hugo city & MCD (Washington)	D	17	48	17	114	NA	NA	24	208	1	D	10	200	17	D
Hutchinson city & MCD (McLeod)	70	35	196	10	393	2	D	76	1,732	8	D	38	D	32	307
Inver Grove Heights city & MCD (Dakota)	168	84	398	57	556	4	25	67	1,254	7	D	52	971	50	305
Lakeville city & MCD (Dakota)	122	167	523	75	976	29	133	104	1,167	15	486	65	1,687	86	591
Lino Lakes city & MCD (Anoka)	37	57	143	14	39	3	D	27	D	5	D	12	591	20	135
Little Canada city & MCD (Ramsey)	232	40	627	25	1,603	4	57	37	726	6	D	23	414	29	193
Mankato city	539	119	1,027	48	1,069	11	D	190	8,498	21	505	140	3,421	91	D
Mankato city (Blue Earth)	539	117	D	46	D	11	D	190	8,498	21	505	138	D	89	D
Maple Grove city & MCD (Hennepin)	191	275	1,183	89	2,163	20	199	161	3,137	16	D	113	3,337	117	908
Maplewood city & MCD (Ramsey)	176	93	374	37	1,176	9	76	193	4,836	18	120	108	2,244	80	464
Marshall city & MCD (Lyon)	D	32	305	21	D	4	9	57	1,590	10	D	48	1,032	30	171
Mendota Heights city & MCD (Dakota)	86	89	1,083	49	1,428	7	129	53	1,253	7	D	16	1,085	26	604
Minneapolis city & MCD (Hennepin)	4,056	2,362	31,765	608	19,174	157	2,214	1,250	54,418	248	5,962	1,141	27,424	992	8,871
Minnetonka city & MCD (Hennepin)	1,091	439	3,648	148	6,076	32	227	206	4,569	34	619	112	2,594	111	835
Monticello city & MCD (Wright)	D	28	81	11	347	2	D	42	D	4	143	39	D	27	197
Moorhead city & MCD (Clay)	145	49	D	38	D	2	D	140	3,685	15	D	57	1,584	76	415
Mounds View city & MCD (Ramsey)	6	24	197	8	D	NA	NA	16	D	2	D	14	D	15	D
New Brighton city & MCD (Ramsey)	160	88	690	26	625	5	15	71	1,508	6	84	28	545	41	263
New Hope city & MCD (Hennepin)	D	66	486	15	D	7	26	50	2,362	6	D	35	563	30	D
New Ulm city & MCD (Brown)	46	31	358	14	83	5	D	42	1,636	13	148	38	723	41	179
North Branch city & MCD (Chisago)	27	10	D	10	42	3	7	38	605	3	8	21	D	23	129
Northfield city	D	64	229	19	229	9	66	54	D	9	D	47	1,077	39	222
Northfield city (Rice)	D	62	D	17	D	9	66	52	D	9	D	45	D	37	D
North Mankato city	113	18	D	11	100	3	D	37	649	2	D	19	284	24	D
North Mankato city (Nicollet)	NA	NA	NA	NA	NA	NA	NA	NA	NA	NA	NA	NA	NA	NA	NA
North St. Paul city & MCD (Ramsey)	19	16	62	15	82	NA	NA	28	664	3	D	19	141	25	167
Oakdale city & MCD (Washington)	D	87	877	35	951	7	78	53	861	14	316	40	963	39	179
Otsego city & MCD (Wright)	17	29	89	13	82	2	D	18	1,032	5	45	9	177	15	81
Owatonna city & MCD (Steele)	235	46	158	23	651	5	27	107	2,288	12	D	66	1,448	67	447

Table C. Incorporated Places, Census Designated Places (CDPs), and Minor Civil Divisions (MCDs) of 10,000 or More Population — Economic Census

STATE City, town, township, borough, or CDP (county if applicable)	Utilities		Manufacturing		Wholesale trade[1]		Retail trade		Transportation and warehousing		Information		Finance and insurance		Real estate and rental and leasing
	Number of establish-ments	Number of employees	Number of establish-ments	Number of employees	Number of establish-ments	Number of employees	Number of establish-ments	Number of employees	Number of establish-ments	Number of employees	Number of establish-ments	Number of employees	Number of establish-ments	Number of employees	Number of establish-ments
	1	2	3	4	5	6	7	8	9	10	11	12	13	14	15
MINNESOTA—Con.															
Plymouth city & MCD (Hennepin)	NA	NA	167	10,038	203	5,086	183	3,279	35	D	57	646	204	4,018	137
Prior Lake city & MCD (Scott)	NA	NA	15	395	10	D	44	371	10	70	7	D	42	155	16
Ramsey city & MCD (Anoka)	1	D	76	2,051	29	358	65	583	12	128	5	D	19	D	21
Red Wing city & MCD (Goodhue)	4	D	33	3,111	12	77	111	1,466	13	156	8	91	37	203	25
Richfield city & MCD (Hennepin)	NA	NA	15	46	15	285	116	2,488	9	D	10	77	36	D	27
Robbinsdale city & MCD (Hennepin)	NA	NA	4	10	3	27	32	243	1	D	5	D	8	138	16
Rochester city & MCD (Olmsted)	3	D	56	7,887	71	905	507	9,720	58	1,373	57	D	194	1,696	149
Rogers city & MCD (Hennepin)	1	D	57	1,652	44	1,046	56	1,522	25	D	4	D	21	89	23
Rosemount city & MCD (Dakota)	2	D	19	1,440	21	D	34	347	20	706	4	D	16	D	9
Roseville city & MCD (Ramsey)	2	D	56	1,644	68	1,075	304	6,393	57	1,990	35	1,285	76	1,777	53
St. Cloud city	2	D	59	4,810	75	2,002	326	6,280	48	2,432	27	1,071	161	2,481	104
St. Cloud city (Stearns)	2	D	47	4,112	66	1,873	287	5,535	41	2,342	25	D	151	2,444	89
St. Louis Park city & MCD (Hennepin)	4	D	64	1,517	108	1,486	205	4,325	19	450	60	1,146	147	2,046	131
St. Michael city & MCD (Wright)	1	D	26	262	12	82	34	325	13	D	NA	NA	14	D	13
St. Paul city & MCD (Ramsey)	7	D	225	6,867	270	4,879	739	9,230	127	1,674	131	5,775	302	13,148	349
St. Peter city & MCD (Nicollet)	NA	NA	10	367	5	D	35	355	3	39	3	D	15	D	9
Sartell city	NA	NA	5	D	1	D	28	464	5	D	3	D	29	143	9
Sartell city (Stearns)	NA	NA	5	D	1	D	27	D	3	D	3	D	29	143	7
Sauk Rapids city & MCD (Benton)	NA	NA	26	1,213	17	464	36	653	11	60	4	D	17	80	13
Savage city & MCD (Scott)	NA	NA	42	1,165	33	594	83	1,069	15	D	2	D	26	112	41
Shakopee city & MCD (Scott)	3	D	43	2,790	54	1,186	116	2,294	26	686	7	D	40	216	44
Shoreview city & MCD (Ramsey)	NA	NA	34	1,368	23	D	38	696	7	D	15	514	37	1,582	25
South St. Paul city & MCD (Dakota)	NA	NA	37	1,715	29	487	44	1,003	16	177	1	D	18	568	16
Stillwater city & MCD (Washington)	NA	NA	19	554	16	D	97	1,060	13	74	10	60	36	270	34
Vadnais Heights city & MCD (Ramsey)	NA	NA	42	1,223	30	585	43	1,278	15	204	3	D	22	115	21
Waconia city & MCD (Carver)	1	D	18	1,139	9	D	36	780	7	125	7	D	19	74	14
West St. Paul city & MCD (Dakota)	NA	NA	15	484	12	49	100	1,931	11	273	9	D	31	182	30
White Bear township (Ramsey)	NA	NA	32	1,552	11	D	17	229	4	D	4	D	12	D	15
White Bear Lake city	2	D	37	946	39	452	82	1,415	10	111	7	68	59	347	57
White Bear Lake city (Ramsey)	2	D	37	946	39	452	77	1,364	10	111	7	68	57	D	57
Willmar city & MCD (Kandiyohi)	1	D	33	2,397	38	636	144	2,461	20	209	20	248	45	371	31
Winona city & MCD (Winona)	NA	NA	65	3,317	33	354	113	2,298	28	837	18	732	40	476	33
Woodbury city & MCD (Washington)	1	D	22	686	38	D	232	4,979	21	366	23	793	110	3,119	74
Worthington city & MCD (Nobles)	1	D	16	2,751	16	256	78	1,273	12	191	8	94	35	208	12
MISSISSIPPI	592	8,803	2,252	132,789	2,484	30,351	11,594	136,032	2,019	33,100	926	13,879	4,692	34,472	2,374
Bay St. Louis city	2	D	15	502	5	11	41	218	7	31	4	D	24	196	13
Biloxi city	5	D	20	265	37	417	209	2,470	14	109	17	307	72	713	69
Brandon city	2	D	13	D	24	375	91	1,533	9	66	10	113	58	D	28
Brookhaven city	3	D	21	1,015	22	D	145	1,653	11	D	11	D	58	330	24
Byram city	2	D	6	170	4	D	39	541	5	17	2	D	18	84	10
Canton city	1	D	13	4,252	18	D	83	715	11	575	6	D	23	109	12
Clarksdale city	1	D	14	661	21	245	110	1,006	8	53	9	83	46	D	34
Cleveland city	4	D	8	1,053	13	190	112	1,267	8	D	8	D	44	D	27
Clinton city	5	D	8	D	13	96	84	960	6	D	11	212	50	216	33
Columbus city	6	D	49	2,768	55	995	250	3,211	40	624	14	D	102	479	46
Corinth city	2	D	28	820	26	431	150	1,578	12	125	9	D	55	286	18
D'Iberville city	NA	NA	6	75	11	54	89	1,768	2	D	7	D	35	152	17
Gautier city	1	D	4	D	5	14	59	874	3	81	6	21	24	165	13
Greenville city	3	D	23	740	40	333	168	1,891	35	505	10	232	65	289	35
Greenwood city	3	D	23	1,333	28	381	139	1,582	15	82	11	D	63	362	32
Grenada city	2	D	23	2,216	17	D	100	1,153	10	83	8	77	45	215	16
Gulfport city	25	D	57	1,788	84	869	385	5,435	67	1,064	30	586	144	1,477	121
Hattiesburg city	9	D	57	2,861	85	866	453	7,195	39	546	38	612	195	1,506	99
Hernando city	3	33	14	337	6	D	67	919	8	D	3	D	32	162	7
Horn Lake city	2	D	14	683	17	D	70	1,069	9	D	1	D	26	113	22
Indianola city	4	26	3	17	11	D	66	674	14	578	5	D	30	174	6
Jackson city	27	D	103	2,717	244	3,355	700	9,327	87	2,200	119	2,377	419	5,270	232
Laurel city	5	D	24	4,664	50	506	174	2,511	14	189	11	154	82	420	43
Long Beach city	1	D	3	6	6	46	37	339	2	D	NA	NA	18	350	17

1 Merchant wholesalers, except manufacturers' sales branches and offices.

Table C. Incorporated Places, Census Designated Places (CDPs), and Minor Civil Divisions (MCDs) of 10,000 or More Population — **Economic Census**

STATE / City, town, township, borough, or CDP (county if applicable)	Real estate and rental and leasing — Number of employees	Professional, scientific, and technical services — Number of establishments	Number of employees	Administration and support and waste management and mediation services — Number of establishments	Number of employees	Educational services — Number of establishments	Number of employees	Health care and social assistance — Number of establishments	Number of employees	Arts, entertainment, and recreation — Number of establishments	Number of employees	Accommodation and food services — Number of establishments	Number of employees	Other services (except public administration) — Number of establishments	Number of employees
	16	17	18	19	20	21	22	23	24	25	26	27	28	29	30
MINNESOTA—Con.															
Plymouth city & MCD (Hennepin)	710	500	6,498	138	3,850	41	428	243	3,620	23	D	131	2,863	114	918
Prior Lake city & MCD (Scott)	D	77	D	42	106	4	1	45	559	13	D	21	D	32	157
Ramsey city & MCD (Anoka)	41	42	162	28	355	3	D	28	D	7	58	16	250	19	D
Red Wing city & MCD (Goodhue)	87	34	154	21	424	10	D	77	2,345	9	178	50	2,452	44	230
Richfield city & MCD (Hennepin)	384	100	450	58	950	11	40	107	2,724	8	D	62	1,172	61	423
Robbinsdale city & MCD (Hennepin)	22	26	177	12	D	5	22	57	5,230	7	49	18	269	20	D
Rochester city & MCD (Olmsted)	676	230	10,733	138	2,312	30	267	363	19,539	45	D	292	7,130	193	1,637
Rogers city & MCD (Hennepin)	62	46	639	40	1,049	8	19	37	585	8	11	33	806	38	D
Rosemount city & MCD (Dakota)	14	55	94	23	207	8	D	36	393	12	87	29	466	34	D
Roseville city & MCD (Ramsey)	352	213	2,187	70	1,700	10	101	168	4,241	17	185	118	3,330	118	1,124
St. Cloud city	478	151	D	77	2,628	16	D	236	12,960	41	551	163	3,714	132	1,302
St. Cloud city (Stearns)	437	145	D	63	2,186	13	D	204	10,933	37	520	138	3,283	110	977
St. Louis Park city & MCD (Hennepin)	2,014	371	3,127	121	6,154	20	234	233	10,678	31	473	96	2,413	139	1,015
St. Michael city & MCD (Wright)	15	36	88	24	D	2	D	20	177	8	56	8	108	15	110
St. Paul city & MCD (Ramsey)	2,485	885	6,742	329	10,575	90	1,232	1,040	40,511	138	3,733	599	11,383	603	5,303
St. Peter city & MCD (Nicollet)	D	16	85	5	D	2	D	35	1,630	4	D	23	404	16	D
Sartell city	26	21	389	16	D	5	22	58	1,706	13	278	16	D	20	192
Sartell city (Stearns)	D	20	D	13	D	5	22	52	D	13	278	15	D	19	D
Sauk Rapids city & MCD (Benton)	33	21	99	8	D	2	D	37	739	7	29	14	290	20	D
Savage city & MCD (Scott)	81	109	D	43	372	9	D	50	455	9	203	43	D	58	542
Shakopee city & MCD (Scott)	110	121	D	51	1,271	12	31	81	2,503	19	713	78	D	70	394
Shoreview city & MCD (Ramsey)	D	112	340	34	424	6	50	79	930	13	360	30	629	22	D
South St. Paul city & MCD (Dakota)	93	34	239	30	583	5	36	37	D	8	90	23	227	32	210
Stillwater city & MCD (Washington)	D	109	394	18	112	8	46	65	2,266	12	201	64	1,282	43	321
Vadnais Heights city & MCD (Ramsey)	D	27	344	18	685	3	D	40	786	7	D	26	622	21	D
Waconia city & MCD (Carver)	38	32	180	16	D	1	D	41	2,104	5	36	18	D	25	115
West St. Paul city & MCD (Dakota)	D	53	157	28	371	5	D	69	1,468	10	351	56	1,152	59	417
White Bear township (Ramsey)	17	38	255	19	136	2	D	18	D	2	D	7	D	18	D
White Bear Lake city	173	87	640	31	1,050	10	122	89	1,306	15	D	55	1,047	78	1,426
White Bear Lake city (Ramsey)	173	87	640	31	1,050	10	122	86	D	12	D	54	D	75	D
Willmar city & MCD (Kandiyohi)	94	65	442	32	447	3	D	145	4,552	11	180	57	1,031	50	379
Winona city & MCD (Winona)	100	62	D	23	463	3	19	90	2,840	20	321	88	1,902	53	304
Woodbury city & MCD (Washington)	D	266	1,287	62	660	25	535	204	4,004	26	566	114	2,800	94	874
Worthington city & MCD (Nobles)	D	28	D	9	D	1	D	58	1,234	11	D	29	515	30	251
MISSISSIPPI	10,235	4,747	30,205	2,215	47,990	284	1,870	6,211	157,620	656	8,840	5,177	116,238	3,540	19,232
Bay St. Louis city	D	31	149	9	84	NA	NA	29	D	2	D	39	1,118	11	D
Biloxi city	279	136	931	39	1,485	6	21	150	5,322	29	1,512	127	10,835	62	369
Brandon city	153	82	309	36	161	4	7	63	D	6	87	60	1,031	32	134
Brookhaven city	D	42	244	12	95	4	D	62	1,744	5	D	53	D	36	D
Byram city	23	16	135	10	D	NA	NA	13	D	2	D	33	D	14	D
Canton city	29	17	126	14	D	1	D	48	949	2	D	42	493	15	D
Clarksdale city	236	35	D	11	76	2	D	74	1,680	7	47	43	D	31	127
Cleveland city	72	35	148	13	135	4	36	61	1,209	7	59	43	800	37	144
Clinton city	D	58	353	30	D	4	36	52	878	11	103	56	1,270	39	193
Columbus city	162	79	427	39	1,540	6	D	135	2,815	14	183	103	1,945	67	D
Corinth city	166	46	349	14	D	4	19	97	D	8	78	62	1,066	35	147
D'Iberville city	76	16	117	6	D	3	22	20	149	5	47	51	1,337	25	130
Gautier city	80	21	129	12	358	1	D	30	264	8	D	29	430	12	D
Greenville city	127	59	261	33	800	3	13	138	2,633	10	233	71	1,709	65	D
Greenwood city	100	43	D	15	D	4	D	72	D	0	78	68	D	42	D
Grenada city	D	20	D	15	888	1	D	73	D	5	D	56	D	24	93
Gulfport city	598	186	982	100	2,512	8	67	242	6,270	17	175	197	5,065	132	817
Hattiesburg city	424	188	1,263	58	1,751	13	68	242	9,732	19	D	232	5,570	104	657
Hernando city	16	39	108	7	39	3	D	30	D	3	D	37	D	26	127
Horn Lake city	106	14	102	9	96	1	D	17	D	6	264	52	1,260	22	D
Indianola city	16	16	61	2	D	1	D	33	529	3	D	24	289	22	129
Jackson city	1,458	557	D	205	5,852	33	D	653	26,004	44	970	370	7,443	333	2,406
Laurel city	153	61	371	12	107	4	28	85	3,064	5	D	81	D	51	291
Long Beach city	41	17	58	8	46	3	8	24	181	1	D	32	430	14	65

Table C. Incorporated Places, Census Designated Places (CDPs), and Minor Civil Divisions (MCDs) of 10,000 or More Population — Economic Census

STATE / City, town, township, borough, or CDP (county if applicable)	Utilities — Number of establishments	Utilities — Number of employees	Manufacturing — Number of establishments	Manufacturing — Number of employees	Wholesale trade¹ — Number of establishments	Wholesale trade¹ — Number of employees	Retail trade — Number of establishments	Retail trade — Number of employees	Transportation and warehousing — Number of establishments	Transportation and warehousing — Number of employees	Information — Number of establishments	Information — Number of employees	Finance and insurance — Number of establishments	Finance and insurance — Number of employees	Real estate and rental and leasing — Number of establishments
	1	2	3	4	5	6	7	8	9	10	11	12	13	14	15
MISSISSIPPI—Con.															
McComb city	4	20	7	61	24	170	160	2,100	9	81	6	113	68	343	29
Madison city	2	D	9	575	23	D	77	1,574	5	56	10	1,053	70	365	32
Meridian city	10	217	46	1,331	58	1,362	344	4,598	27	558	23	D	159	1,500	69
Moss Point city	2	D	10	431	7	68	40	243	5	16	2	D	16	145	3
Natchez city	3	D	15	623	25	211	164	2,071	10	432	15	143	67	409	30
Ocean Springs city	2	D	16	242	11	87	107	1,262	5	28	10	D	42	200	30
Olive Branch city	NA	NA	54	1,854	51	1,000	122	1,896	60	1,877	7	102	57	263	19
Oxford city	2	D	9	54	19	175	192	2,423	8	32	21	D	72	410	38
Pascagoula city	4	D	27	14,085	28	322	124	1,724	15	226	3	D	63	406	30
Pearl city	4	D	25	628	68	1,095	115	1,947	23	310	6	111	62	D	43
Petal city	3	D	3	12	2	D	54	782	5	44	1	D	21	86	16
Picayune city	4	71	18	318	9	126	94	769	8	122	4	36	46	236	14
Ridgeland city	1	D	18	278	71	D	286	4,039	13	256	48	1,364	212	2,645	76
Southaven city	3	D	15	D	38	1,464	214	3,945	41	2,393	9	158	79	424	40
Starkville city	2	D	19	1,200	12	431	138	1,711	10	D	17	181	67	D	51
Tupelo city	3	D	72	3,811	113	1,169	374	6,061	54	1,240	30	634	155	2,208	77
Vicksburg city	4	D	30	2,539	33	230	192	2,467	14	619	14	202	73	396	38
West Point city	2	D	18	D	10	D	66	742	8	D	6	D	33	D	8
Yazoo City city	2	D	5	77	13	181	74	641	6	66	6	D	26	133	16
MISSOURI	361	16,131	6,097	243,208	6,557	96,683	21,456	302,568	4,543	82,336	2,422	59,607	10,876	132,479	6,165
Affton CDP	1	D	15	693	16	304	37	383	7	12	2	D	26	D	11
Arnold city	NA	NA	21	775	17	194	89	2,088	15	139	6	150	67	406	26
Ballwin city	NA	NA	7	50	16	49	88	1,585	8	33	4	D	52	D	22
Bellefontaine Neighbors city	NA	NA	5	120	4	52	13	109	5	36	NA	NA	2	D	3
Belton city	1	D	11	686	11	184	74	1,179	6	111	8	73	31	155	22
Blue Springs city	1	D	35	905	42	304	160	3,296	20	369	9	198	108	D	69
Bolivar city	3	D	9	239	8	461	75	926	7	57	6	D	31	D	7
Branson city	1	D	15	114	11	D	313	3,953	10	119	20	314	47	300	71
Bridgeton city	NA	NA	47	2,372	69	1,208	105	2,375	40	2,782	16	771	50	1,782	31
Cameron city	3	D	4	D	2	D	44	599	3	D	2	D	24	269	11
Cape Girardeau city	5	D	40	1,959	88	1,141	299	4,617	26	330	33	D	138	706	89
Carthage city	NA	NA	19	2,774	3	D	62	925	9	D	7	D	42	322	16
Chesterfield city	NA	NA	57	1,345	146	2,241	315	5,198	37	689	47	839	351	4,403	129
Clayton city	NA	NA	6	85	35	1,244	77	1,377	6	D	18	222	288	4,777	114
Columbia city	3	D	72	2,930	98	1,158	537	10,468	52	1,292	76	1,455	269	6,321	192
Concord CDP	NA	NA	9	52	7	41	65	1,266	15	187	6	D	50	D	16
Crestwood city	NA	NA	16	518	11	191	39	947	4	14	5	D	40	D	22
Creve Coeur city	7	D	19	490	54	703	134	2,610	26	823	46	1,506	212	2,619	81
Dardenne Prairie city	NA	NA	NA	NA	7	D	19	426	2	D	2	D	9	24	6
Eureka city	NA	NA	15	699	14	66	47	752	8	8	6	23	27	D	9
Excelsior Springs city	1	D	15	1,051	3	D	49	738	9	329	5	48	21	94	13
Farmington city	1	D	13	446	14	D	100	1,964	12	219	14	191	57	709	32
Ferguson city	NA	NA	10	67	17	645	67	1,635	8	22	4	D	21	D	13
Festus city	3	D	8	158	5	D	51	1,235	5	35	6	D	38	D	19
Florissant city	1	D	10	49	18	55	176	3,083	16	309	10	129	78	D	28
Fort Leonard Wood CDP	1	D	NA	NA	1	D	11	58	1	D	NA	NA	5	83	2
Fulton city	2	D	16	677	1	D	69	766	6	D	5	D	35	349	13
Gladstone city	NA	NA	7	D	16	43	82	1,845	13	48	5	D	82	325	48
Grain Valley city	NA	NA	19	956	12	94	22	237	4	8	4	D	15	D	15
Grandview city	2	D	44	2,151	40	427	81	1,038	17	438	4	D	27	222	28
Hannibal city	2	D	27	1,996	13	143	96	1,338	9	54	9	D	48	261	13
Harrisonville city	NA	NA	13	521	11	105	58	938	8	200	3	D	28	137	14
Hazelwood city	NA	NA	35	3,589	53	1,573	142	3,422	47	978	16	383	38	D	29
Independence city	1	D	72	4,011	71	473	456	8,382	48	356	37	628	195	2,023	105
Jackson city	1	D	26	701	18	147	78	986	10	D	5	D	47	207	12
Jefferson City city	7	D	35	2,574	60	2,030	258	4,881	23	482	46	D	153	1,681	54
Jennings city	NA	NA	9	233	2	D	43	374	1	D	2	D	14	D	11
Joplin city	5	D	83	5,204	99	1,568	378	6,152	54	4,208	23	1,013	150	868	77
Kansas City city	16	D	374	17,035	614	10,628	1,458	24,531	354	10,542	274	13,553	880	25,685	578
Kennett city	NA	NA	6	441	14	163	66	759	13	71	5	71	34	190	15
Kirksville city	2	D	12	625	15	121	102	1,467	10	97	15	D	41	228	20
Kirkwood city	NA	NA	28	643	35	228	128	2,693	7	D	22	341	74	D	43
Lake St. Louis city	1	D	5	D	19	D	68	1,353	5	15	4	D	41	194	18
Lebanon city	1	D	33	3,850	20	257	137	1,603	18	110	10	98	52	D	24
Lee's Summit city	3	D	71	D	98	1,351	290	5,326	48	670	37	911	226	1,888	120
Lemay CDP	NA	NA	20	336	7	116	37	317	4	42	NA	NA	11	D	9
Liberty city	NA	NA	22	927	23	235	86	1,299	20	1,022	10	93	77	381	35
Manchester city	NA	NA	5	10	21	40	77	1,738	8	35	5	14	42	D	15
Marshall city	NA	NA	12	1,619	20	253	67	754	7	81	4	D	36	210	9
Maryland Heights city	4	D	107	3,658	235	5,339	117	2,674	28	608	48	2,241	75	6,161	57
Maryville city	1	D	13	D	5	65	56	1,010	7	D	9	D	31	164	15
Mehlville CDP	NA	NA	8	93	14	D	206	4,066	12	108	10	57	59	D	21
Mexico city	3	81	21	1,341	7	110	71	608	6	41	8	D	35	198	11
Moberly city	2	D	20	996	12	235	84	1,047	12	841	13	D	49	D	16
Neosho city	5	D	24	1,481	9	D	75	1,029	15	245	6	D	56	275	13
Nixa city	1	D	23	334	19	165	67	1,022	16	97	4	D	43	209	22
Oakville CDP	3	D	16	464	18	96	39	574	20	165	4	15	47	D	26
O'Fallon city	1	D	56	4,204	72	D	199	3,400	36	418	17	134	154	6,688	80
Old Jamestown CDP	NA	NA	3	9	3	D	25	469	8	28	1	D	11	D	3
Overland city	NA	NA	49	1,386	44	842	73	852	16	572	6	D	20	D	15
Ozark city	3	D	37	602	14	149	91	1,278	4	D	7	84	42	221	24
Poplar Bluff city	1	D	20	2,046	25	149	156	2,305	18	133	12	D	62	461	34
Raymore city	NA	NA	3	8	3	D	27	797	11	D	6	D	27	126	10
Raytown city	2	D	26	302	22	162	92	1,528	10	64	5	D	45	207	23
Republic city	1	D	9	103	10	D	45	863	7	32	6	16	25	108	8
Rolla city	2	D	20	517	21	257	136	2,058	23	255	20	211	59	320	29

1 Merchant wholesalers, except manufacturers' sales branches and offices.

Table C. Incorporated Places, Census Designated Places (CDPs), and Minor Civil Divisions (MCDs) of 10,000 or More Population — **Economic Census**

STATE / City, town, township, borough, or CDP (county if applicable)	Real estate and rental and leasing — Number of employees	Professional, scientific, and technical services — Number of establishments	Professional... — Number of employees	Administration and support and waste management and mediation services — Number of establishments	Admin... — Number of employees	Educational services — Number of establishments	Educational... — Number of employees	Health care and social assistance — Number of establishments	Health care... — Number of employees	Arts, entertainment, and recreation — Number of establishments	Arts... — Number of employees	Accommodation and food services — Number of establishments	Accommodation... — Number of employees	Other services (except public administration) — Number of establishments	Other services... — Number of employees
	16	17	18	19	20	21	22	23	24	25	26	27	28	29	30
MISSISSIPPI—Con.															
McComb city	108	49	193	12	84	4	20	91	D	4	D	62	1,330	38	213
Madison city	393	118	555	35	192	11	D	86	2,193	14	199	57	D	38	230
Meridian city	242	120	961	58	1,523	11	D	197	7,487	17	130	154	3,512	111	D
Moss Point city	D	13	185	9	432	2	D	21	D	2	D	34	628	17	D
Natchez city	109	48	220	21	D	2	D	83	1,880	15	D	83	1,586	36	170
Ocean Springs city	152	67	303	16	206	3	34	103	D	12	D	79	1,288	43	219
Olive Branch city	56	40	176	39	3,235	3	D	59	679	13	D	70	1,581	50	D
Oxford city	91	93	781	21	201	5	D	108	2,448	13	D	110	2,272	41	D
Pascagoula city	123	78	825	31	1,241	6	D	87	2,578	8	D	60	958	46	300
Pearl city	218	30	169	22	252	3	D	33	D	6	82	73	1,563	48	235
Petal city	D	20	70	6	D	1	D	21	199	6	D	20	399	12	83
Picayune city	39	28	247	14	48	NA	NA	60	D	8	37	50	D	26	224
Ridgeland city	442	201	2,141	44	2,461	18	214	106	1,429	13	D	121	2,737	90	787
Southaven city	135	75	538	39	1,527	5	D	152	4,355	9	D	125	3,105	57	338
Starkville city	156	62	381	26	819	4	25	81	1,656	7	D	90	2,283	49	D
Tupelo city	343	162	1,025	88	4,226	9	D	224	7,458	16	102	165	4,002	96	D
Vicksburg city	181	84	827	29	D	4	9	104	D	11	D	104	4,036	46	D
West Point city	20	21	D	8	38	1	D	27	696	3	D	36	D	24	D
Yazoo City city	D	18	157	3	D	NA	NA	38	D	2	D	22	D	19	D
MISSOURI	33,447	13,279	137,981	7,221	148,318	979	9,427	17,766	399,940	2,095	38,190	12,459	239,264	10,357	62,825
Affton CDP	49	21	75	25	185	2	D	28	D	4	26	24	291	30	D
Arnold city	98	32	187	32	1,512	2	D	60	836	5	D	73	1,790	54	304
Ballwin city	57	66	132	37	102	4	22	45	396	13	364	42	774	45	D
Bellefontaine Neighbors city	7	6	20	3	D	1	D	23	255	NA	NA	2	D	4	12
Belton city	65	32	D	26	268	1	D	43	D	2	D	48	1,035	39	180
Blue Springs city	199	110	564	79	622	16	D	136	2,235	26	272	114	2,209	88	478
Bolivar city	45	29	D	9	159	1	D	56	1,585	3	D	40	753	25	177
Branson city	790	62	266	58	754	1	D	75	1,791	77	D	237	5,427	55	321
Bridgeton city	218	63	917	54	2,219	4	49	141	4,087	6	83	64	1,618	59	D
Cameron city	38	14	D	9	D	NA	NA	41	D	3	D	22	350	17	D
Cape Girardeau city	263	109	D	71	1,992	10	D	269	10,438	17	D	123	3,435	103	631
Carthage city	73	18	127	10	128	2	D	46	1,039	4	D	47	739	30	107
Chesterfield city	673	394	13,252	130	3,735	33	265	274	7,749	37	673	175	4,601	138	1,122
Clayton city	2,026	487	4,837	51	1,195	8	305	122	907	18	283	100	2,295	103	738
Columbia city	852	350	3,333	162	2,684	35	275	541	16,053	49	717	367	8,566	282	1,861
Concord CDP	46	51	306	28	109	3	21	66	866	6	148	38	879	43	D
Crestwood city	61	54	146	15	150	5	29	37	314	10	66	21	502	22	D
Creve Coeur city	1,006	249	3,814	116	7,987	17	465	454	13,504	19	178	88	1,862	94	1,109
Dardenne Prairie city	4	20	83	9	119	NA	NA	17	279	2	D	5	93	7	48
Eureka city	20	30	68	17	80	2	D	32	410	6	D	34	677	29	D
Excelsior Springs city	D	7	D	9	254	2	D	36	D	5	6	31	595	23	109
Farmington city	126	51	204	16	870	4	D	124	3,624	5	31	56	1,106	37	186
Ferguson city	26	12	46	14	26	1	D	68	D	6	D	46	651	14	D
Festus city	59	26	75	13	138	4	29	65	688	5	D	39	951	29	D
Florissant city	170	56	318	35	201	10	61	189	2,313	10	D	108	2,211	86	514
Fort Leonard Wood CDP	D	24	370	3	D	1	D	2	D	NA	NA	4	847	7	41
Fulton city	55	16	79	12	86	1	D	44	2,118	6	55	41	511	32	119
Gladstone city	345	75	D	31	921	8	103	78	725	6	108	41	756	50	252
Grain Valley city	43	12	D	23	89	4	8	11	153	2	D	13	122	17	66
Grandview city	194	23	144	41	587	1	D	50	554	4	13	41	D	34	244
Hannibal city	33	32	208	18	250	3	D	110	D	11	61	58	894	40	D
Harrisonville city	24	30	D	13	64	1	D	43	1,034	3	D	30	466	27	77
Hazelwood city	193	47	746	54	3,204	NA	NA	76	1,044	7	D	69	1,138	43	335
Independence city	593	225	1,035	102	771	18	170	296	6,432	21	D	223	5,275	174	960
Jackson city	57	30	200	14	120	3	D	34	383	5	63	32	D	29	D
Jefferson City city	207	204	1,520	81	1,444	16	D	237	6,354	21	272	152	3,034	194	D
Jennings city	25	6	60	3	D	NA	NA	49	D	NA	NA	10	218	18	112
Joplin city	407	147	977	51	6,362	9	40	295	10,020	19	313	194	4,298	130	884
Kansas City city	4,517	1,523	21,888	615	15,614	107	960	1,452	42,718	181	5,247	1,098	25,669	844	6,987
Kennett city	D	19	91	7	D	1	D	57	2,583	3	D	23	D	20	61
Kirksville city	D	39	680	17	169	7	33	98	1,921	6	74	56	D	51	D
Kirkwood city	D	134	D	49	419	15	76	118	1,402	19	576	65	1,509	57	390
Lake St. Louis city	43	49	199	28	84	2	D	47	1,548	8	140	30	573	23	D
Lebanon city	64	34	147	12	267	5	D	66	1,439	6	90	66	984	36	D
Lee's Summit city	370	306	D	132	1,212	23	438	284	5,621	29	D	183	3,599	148	924
Lemay CDP	49	5	35	22	223	NA	NA	29	D	2	D	29	511	32	154
Liberty city	160	115	D	40	283	12	D	128	3,705	12	93	63	1,380	54	323
Manchester city	73	43	236	24	274	10	69	47	D	10	80	33	368	32	186
Marshall city	16	24	80	13	D	2	D	60	1,306	7	D	28	479	26	D
Maryland Heights city	371	157	3,597	99	4,561	9	117	78	3,240	12	171	94	3,434	57	595
Maryville city	28	19	93	14	D	1	D	40	1,137	6	D	40	1,051	26	128
Mehlville CDP	110	52	302	27	548	4	12	70	1,685	7	139	76	1,600	42	D
Mexico city	D	18	138	13	D	3	D	53	1,166	5	D	28	342	32	201
Moberly city	D	19	82	12	D	1	D	66	1,450	4	D	48	D	34	D
Neosho city	32	26	116	12	D	2	D	38	D	4	D	36	583	25	D
Nixa city	67	48	204	20	129	2	D	45	405	6	31	41	703	38	D
Oakville CDP	47	52	212	53	946	7	D	50	619	12	56	33	611	43	226
O'Fallon city	339	124	791	85	983	13	66	188	2,915	27	697	155	D	123	919
Old Jamestown CDP	D	15	26	20	135	3	10	41	469	3	D	8	73	11	42
Overland city	89	33	277	42	792	2	D	72	1,348	2	D	36	529	52	316
Ozark city	D	38	325	20	124	1	D	38	721	5	D	46	D	33	166
Poplar Bluff city	147	39	303	18	D	2	D	158	3,853	7	78	65	1,615	42	225
Raymore city	31	38	D	21	96	5	D	37	D	1	D	16	288	22	100
Raytown city	108	58	318	29	899	5	8	51	D	5	105	47	658	55	368
Republic city	10	18	78	12	60	2	D	23	247	4	6	26	D	16	D
Rolla city	128	49	270	18	210	5	17	108	3,230	8	D	92	1,505	43	189

Table C. Incorporated Places, Census Designated Places (CDPs), and Minor Civil Divisions (MCDs) of 10,000 or More Population — **Economic Census**

Economic activity by sector, 2012

STATE City, town, township, borough, or CDP (county if applicable)	Utilities		Manufacturing		Wholesale trade[1]		Retail trade		Transportation and warehousing		Information		Finance and insurance		Real estate and rental and leasing
	Number of establish-ments	Number of employees	Number of establish-ments	Number of employees	Number of establish-ments	Number of employees	Number of establish-ments	Number of employees	Number of establish-ments	Number of employees	Number of establish-ments	Number of employees	Number of establish-ments	Number of employees	Number of establish-ments
	1	2	3	4	5	6	7	8	9	10	11	12	13	14	15
MISSOURI—Con.															
St. Ann city	NA	NA	NA	NA	7	28	36	326	3	D	NA	NA	16	D	7
St. Charles city	2	D	66	1,654	82	1,620	257	4,047	50	897	27	348	175	911	104
St. Joseph city	4	D	88	D	92	1,627	321	5,412	72	1,482	22	D	178	1,739	92
St. Louis city	17	D	484	17,422	452	7,692	923	9,422	208	8,059	185	7,096	429	13,516	411
St. Peters city	1	D	49	1,365	74	D	325	6,097	28	376	21	408	143	1,060	64
Sedalia city	2	D	29	2,094	26	250	142	2,086	17	395	13	241	68	400	32
Sikeston city	2	D	26	1,543	27	669	123	1,635	17	335	16	D	61	429	30
Spanish Lake CDP	NA	NA	3	41	3	D	21	287	6	8	1	D	9	D	16
Springfield city	2	D	239	10,927	328	6,097	967	16,828	162	7,662	108	4,256	538	7,003	342
Town and Country city	NA	NA	3	16	21	D	27	368	7	43	33	3,193	79	1,538	33
Troy city	1	D	9	574	10	D	80	1,026	6	21	3	D	34	215	17
Union city	2	D	34	1,806	14	D	53	730	13	123	3	D	29	176	17
University City city	NA	NA	13	112	23	298	86	781	4	11	11	198	33	D	39
Warrensburg city	3	D	7	970	5	D	90	1,406	5	D	9	96	46	223	24
Washington city	NA	NA	48	2,852	25	222	110	1,777	12	281	8	198	68	403	15
Webb City city	NA	NA	20	D	10	124	36	713	8	85	3	D	28	109	6
Webster Groves city	NA	NA	8	26	16	84	72	666	6	20	13	78	53	D	32
Wentzville city	2	D	21	2,315	26	D	100	2,179	14	367	14	252	49	D	12
West Plains city	NA	NA	23	1,395	19	145	149	1,502	11	56	11	114	56	284	27
Wildwood city	NA	NA	4	12	30	82	35	452	8	326	8	75	41	D	29
MONTANA	204	2,925	1,237	15,729	1,288	13,034	4,831	55,418	1,475	11,861	615	9,160	1,944	16,206	1,726
Billings city	10	260	128	2,078	236	3,832	618	9,047	148	2,120	97	1,706	343	4,005	231
Bozeman city	4	D	79	932	60	549	357	5,153	28	447	51	454	148	1,110	162
Butte-Silver Bow	7	D	35	492	37	348	172	2,203	41	439	19	277	56	336	47
Butte-Silver Bow (balance)	7	D	35	492	37	348	172	2,203	41	439	19	277	56	336	47
Great Falls city	10	188	43	832	92	1,011	314	4,496	60	676	25	552	158	1,685	104
Helena city	3	D	38	380	49	425	220	3,292	41	399	39	563	119	1,696	79
Kalispell city	2	D	28	704	32	404	174	2,828	19	170	21	364	96	1,116	69
Missoula city	5	170	64	573	104	1,372	476	6,831	55	1,373	70	1,983	224	1,836	158
NEBRASKA	115	930	1,844	92,409	2,720	34,409	7,279	105,953	2,283	26,879	954	20,647	4,201	62,434	2,001
Beatrice city	1	D	20	897	19	252	84	859	12	53	9	93	30	162	11
Bellevue city	NA	NA	13	578	15	68	110	2,318	13	34	14	246	68	D	50
Chalco CDP	NA	NA	14	291	25	386	19	D	13	184	2	D	5	D	6
Columbus city	2	D	41	2,305	21	206	134	1,930	27	248	12	D	77	457	35
Fremont city	NA	NA	35	1,126	30	395	131	2,220	13	277	10	117	66	385	33
Grand Island city	NA	NA	58	6,981	75	1,089	273	4,710	62	1,249	24	317	123	1,163	73
Hastings city	1	D	39	2,069	38	429	132	1,808	20	161	13	175	60	317	57
Kearney city	1	D	29	710	46	698	190	3,245	26	465	25	401	95	522	50
La Vista city	1	D	5	35	19	246	35	624	11	76	5	28	30	557	16
Lexington city	1	D	6	D	7	73	58	685	7	32	3	57	19	106	5
Lincoln city	4	D	210	11,045	242	3,927	946	16,644	143	4,085	144	4,681	570	D	323
Norfolk city	1	D	33	506	39	1,187	173	2,757	40	552	15	D	95	543	53
North Platte city	NA	NA	10	184	32	307	163	1,978	30	771	15	207	69	424	37
Omaha city	14	D	381	16,879	667	10,205	1,634	33,150	299	9,354	318	10,349	1,196	35,921	605
Papillion city	1	D	8	166	14	D	99	2,470	8	55	6	88	48	282	20
Scottsbluff city	3	D	14	369	29	440	132	2,013	26	182	13	199	55	912	35
South Sioux City city	NA	NA	24	D	9	D	55	806	14	331	4	D	17	619	9
NEVADA	123	4,991	1,706	38,123	2,501	27,649	8,135	129,977	1,409	43,720	1,234	17,216	4,053	34,396	3,866
Boulder City city	2	D	16	148	8	125	53	425	12	333	3	6	17	138	15
Carson City	4	D	122	2,798	89	519	212	3,139	34	282	59	271	124	1,032	111
Elko city	2	D	14	149	47	639	115	1,775	32	446	12	135	37	237	29
Enterprise CDP	2	D	41	977	80	944	337	5,357	35	1,310	39	686	72	566	95
Fernley city	1	D	16	637	7	542	27	676	15	833	3	D	15	56	13
Gardnerville Ranchos CDP	1	D	NA	NA	1	D	10	41	3	1	NA	NA	1	D	4
Henderson city	4	179	122	3,591	196	1,314	721	13,600	89	1,383	120	1,228	417	3,374	395
Las Vegas city	7	D	197	2,631	431	3,801	1,705	29,614	189	4,915	273	4,950	1,000	12,331	904
Mesquite city	NA	NA	8	223	9	D	51	681	8	170	6	77	29	127	42
North Las Vegas city	10	D	107	3,260	160	2,944	291	6,155	104	5,294	32	438	101	595	103
Pahrump CDP	4	D	11	D	6	D	91	1,215	9	37	15	D	25	D	28
Paradise CDP	10	D	260	3,890	504	5,702	1,545	23,272	230	11,828	207	2,900	541	4,593	595
Reno city	15	1,147	231	7,327	302	4,234	975	15,952	176	4,183	172	4,010	524	5,513	454
Spanish Springs CDP	NA	NA	NA	NA	9	D	11	238	10	D	2	D	4	D	3
Sparks city	3	D	171	5,510	227	3,506	304	4,346	132	4,135	20	272	107	541	108
Spring Creek CDP	NA	NA	3	D	2	D	13	188	2	D	1	D	6	11	5
Spring Valley CDP	4	D	32	708	97	513	391	6,909	35	186	60	779	340	2,331	358
Summerlin South CDP	NA	NA	NA	NA	8	17	9	19	2	D	8	D	22	241	34
Sunrise Manor CDP	1	D	34	473	50	562	206	3,522	51	862	23	304	62	550	101
Sun Valley CDP	NA	NA	3	8	NA	NA	12	109	2	D	1	D	5	39	3
Whitney CDP	1	D	6	91	5	23	37	359	5	29	3	D	8	44	14
Winchester CDP	1	D	9	16	25	48	125	1,960	9	7	29	292	261	589	70
NEW HAMPSHIRE	120	3,329	1,851	66,636	1,543	21,140	6,127	95,660	804	13,787	802	13,731	1,889	24,252	1,338
Amherst town (Hillsborough)	1	D	36	569	22	100	69	992	5	D	7	D	16	78	10
Bedford town (Hillsborough)	NA	NA	20	412	37	319	80	1,430	15	266	20	251	126	1,309	39
Berlin city & MCD (Coos)	3	D	9	139	7	D	36	278	5	52	6	20	12	162	8
Claremont city & MCD (Sullivan)	4	11	32	486	21	263	82	1,512	10	D	6	64	18	158	20
Concord city & MCD (Merrimack)	2	D	63	1,332	53	934	279	5,383	18	463	39	480	101	1,875	66

1 Merchant wholesalers, except manufacturers' sales branches and offices.

Table C. Incorporated Places, Census Designated Places (CDPs), and Minor Civil Divisions (MCDs) of 10,000 or More Population — **Economic Census**

STATE City, town, township, borough, or CDP (county if applicable)	Real estate and rental and leasing — Number of employees	Professional, scientific, and technical services — Number of establishments	Number of employees	Administration and support and waste management and mediation services — Number of establishments	Number of employees	Educational services — Number of establishments	Number of employees	Health care and social assistance — Number of establishments	Number of employees	Arts, entertainment, and recreation — Number of establishments	Number of employees	Accommodation and food services — Number of establishments	Number of employees	Other services (except public administration) — Number of establishments	Number of employees
	16	17	18	19	20	21	22	23	24	25	26	27	28	29	30
MISSOURI—Con.															
St. Ann city	29	5	22	16	326	2	D	21	72	3	6	31	427	16	D
St. Charles city	519	245	3,406	98	2,437	8	51	249	4,852	29	368	209	5,808	147	1,001
St. Joseph city	323	146	978	92	1,932	11	93	303	D	25	573	177	3,925	158	D
St. Louis city	2,432	1,009	17,461	416	18,245	61	733	1,219	35,572	140	7,147	1,036	22,069	629	4,529
St. Peters city	235	140	755	96	3,352	17	243	258	3,719	31	669	181	3,751	145	965
Sedalia city	295	62	1,527	34	1,317	3	D	121	2,701	7	D	68	1,356	72	D
Sikeston city	D	52	328	22	615	4	D	105	2,826	8	D	42	D	35	225
Spanish Lake CDP	85	4	32	10	50	1	D	49	436	1	D	13	D	13	93
Springfield city	2,232	667	5,518	304	9,953	47	313	729	D	83	D	646	13,397	486	3,800
Town and Country city	312	86	1,113	29	855	4	40	187	5,449	8	356	26	D	30	228
Troy city	54	26	104	5	31	2	D	44	D	3	D	35	748	29	D
Union city	49	41	D	12	317	1	D	38	516	2	D	29	535	29	155
University City city	404	86	241	30	229	13	269	183	1,994	10	118	82	1,295	57	515
Warrensburg city	78	40	186	16	D	4	11	81	1,846	3	D	67	1,328	39	187
Washington city	129	55	332	30	596	1	D	121	1,985	9	D	57	1,199	41	227
Webb City city	17	10	68	7	50	2	D	25	469	4	54	30	D	19	D
Webster Groves city	199	117	691	36	180	9	108	83	2,057	16	D	49	1,110	35	216
Wentzville city	44	40	159	46	1,288	6	28	89	1,060	5	75	73	D	58	381
West Plains city	110	44	235	12	D	2	D	112	2,898	6	D	56	895	30	D
Wildwood city	D	112	364	52	242	5	17	63	939	6	288	28	D	27	D
MONTANA	5,207	3,545	16,660	1,675	20,448	269	1,642	3,512	65,657	1,126	10,903	3,458	46,251	2,278	10,917
Billings city	828	523	3,198	230	8,558	38	171	510	11,940	117	1,529	346	7,362	301	1,847
Bozeman city	420	416	1,652	116	677	31	232	270	3,776	60	813	190	3,550	145	837
Butte-Silver Bow	137	107	654	52	485	10	67	159	3,303	37	356	147	2,244	72	289
Butte-Silver Bow (balance)	137	107	654	52	485	10	67	159	3,303	37	356	147	2,244	72	289
Great Falls city	296	175	1,116	97	D	9	98	249	6,013	72	748	210	3,656	124	754
Helena city	265	206	1,588	60	1,138	23	104	246	D	46	571	149	2,758	165	1,006
Kalispell city	213	139	607	44	1,531	10	64	190	4,149	26	324	108	1,860	83	424
Missoula city	818	420	2,666	141	2,651	42	335	434	9,004	80	1,127	275	5,444	232	1,704
NEBRASKA	10,068	4,448	74,514	2,569	57,034	312	2,226	5,410	125,469	842	13,090	4,326	70,128	3,989	21,832
Beatrice city	22	24	D	21	239	1	D	49	1,583	8	129	39	549	44	D
Bellevue city	167	86	969	48	320	5	29	111	1,976	12	D	104	1,961	77	427
Chalco CDP	9	10	77	18	132	2	D	2	D	4	89	23	D	10	D
Columbus city	116	56	436	39	1,379	4	27	75	1,519	11	D	64	918	62	D
Fremont city	167	38	152	35	1,254	4	D	97	2,321	9	96	75	1,208	65	253
Grand Island city	293	100	610	75	1,480	9	D	176	4,421	26	393	139	2,398	132	D
Hastings city	129	53	273	45	D	3	D	111	D	15	D	74	1,311	51	D
Kearney city	146	80	536	52	1,165	6	47	155	3,745	23	541	123	2,815	90	551
La Vista city	40	23	96	21	154	4	45	39	342	5	D	34	865	21	D
Lexington city	8	18	98	8	D	NA	NA	30	490	6	48	31	418	24	53
Lincoln city	1,561	791	8,757	368	6,650	76	542	927	22,689	106	2,466	635	12,813	622	3,938
Norfolk city	D	72	639	32	673	6	60	139	2,183	13	D	78	1,510	77	D
North Platte city	90	68	393	28	424	3	D	132	2,417	14	82	83	1,589	70	372
Omaha city	5,464	1,478	54,730	808	34,792	107	819	1,590	44,466	187	4,860	1,164	23,447	961	7,661
Papillion city	D	49	310	30	191	5	75	91	1,723	10	223	43	1,139	46	273
Scottsbluff city	88	48	300	25	297	2	D	96	2,447	11	96	62	999	49	339
South Sioux City city	58	24	D	7	D	NA	NA	24	390	4	116	32	495	28	D
NEVADA	22,412	8,102	47,934	3,998	93,727	537	5,506	6,308	108,585	1,290	26,705	5,815	296,762	3,538	25,386
Boulder City city	33	49	130	18	96	8	33	37	531	15	D	45	462	33	136
Carson City	304	295	1,180	140	1,458	12	D	224	3,744	48	D	159	2,740	126	660
Elko city	225	80	594	32	528	4	22	104	1,369	17	D	88	1,715	51	D
Enterprise CDP	2,895	215	1,782	118	6,683	15	158	76	560	48	127	189	6,960	60	968
Fernley city	38	22	61	17	694	1	D	14	D	10	202	32	364	13	D
Gardnerville Ranchos CDP	3	7	7	14	39	1	D	6	D	4	32	8	64	1	D
Henderson city	1,468	930	D	386	4,367	67	461	729	9,527	141	2,814	478	14,087	350	2,469
Las Vegas city	5,221	2,339	13,382	908	15,193	121	1,075	1,803	30,509	284	4,611	1,140	40,393	771	6,155
Mesquite city	D	43	121	18	233	NA	NA	35	D	10	265	34	2,185	20	D
North Las Vegas city	630	137	D	167	4,691	19	387	224	6,342	28	1,146	224	7,028	141	1,825
Pahrump CDP	64	45	146	24	342	1	D	53	D	15	D	50	980	42	D
Paradise CDP	4,622	936	9,608	653	26,292	68	911	564	11,014	195	5,997	1,057	144,631	506	3,668
Reno city	2,345	1,178	7,075	473	15,626	73	607	918	19,211	125	2,425	697	21,617	481	3,427
Spanish Springs CDP	6	24	36	19	37	2	D	11	D	1	D	8	97	7	20
Sparks city	561	147	1,113	147	1,610	22	159	183	3,074	36	938	193	4,855	173	1,021
Spring Creek CDP	D	11	D	7	18	1	D	9	D	2	D	11	D	9	D
Spring Valley CDP	1,740	558	3,253	224	7,877	54	239	560	8,223	69	1,471	422	6,319	224	1,428
Summerlin South CDP	D	70	172	21	47	3	5	47	253	5	D	21	D	15	D
Sunrise Manor CDP	510	66	289	101	1,400	5	60	57	D	13	185	156	4,618	95	354
Sun Valley CDP	4	4	17	5	11	NA	NA	7	41	2	D	7	98	1	D
Whitney CDP	84	11	34	13	291	1	D	5	D	5	194	29	1,292	16	D
Winchester CDP	270	173	1,064	77	1,223	11	110	198	4,792	24	329	125	8,334	48	283
NEW HAMPSHIRE	7,044	3,825	30,159	2,178	45,153	392	3,988	3,578	87,099	724	12,946	3,606	54,047	2,879	16,603
Amherst town (Hillsborough)	141	67	396	24	86	9	D	38	D	5	60	20	319	26	D
Bedford town (Hillsborough)	398	128	1,089	68	1,227	13	136	91	2,677	8	57	38	936	28	209
Berlin city & MCD (Coos)	23	10	42	5	52	NA	NA	37	1,139	5	D	13	126	24	D
Claremont city & MCD (Sullivan)	218	15	79	16	377	1	D	49	724	3	12	31	D	35	93
Concord city & MCD (Merrimack)	330	231	1,947	57	983	23	194	229	9,549	26	430	120	2,629	222	1,183

Table C. Incorporated Places, Census Designated Places (CDPs), and Minor Civil Divisions (MCDs) of 10,000 or More Population — Economic Census

STATE City, town, township, borough, or CDP (county if applicable)	Utilities Number of establishments	Utilities Number of employees	Manufacturing Number of establishments	Manufacturing Number of employees	Wholesale trade[1] Number of establishments	Wholesale trade[1] Number of employees	Retail trade Number of establishments	Retail trade Number of employees	Transportation and warehousing Number of establishments	Transportation and warehousing Number of employees	Information Number of establishments	Information Number of employees	Finance and insurance Number of establishments	Finance and insurance Number of employees	Real estate and rental and leasing Number of establishments
	1	2	3	4	5	6	7	8	9	10	11	12	13	14	15
NEW HAMPSHIRE—Con.															
Conway town (Carroll)	NA	NA	27	399	12	D	178	2,095	7	39	25	192	25	D	27
Derry CDP	NA	NA	NA	NA	NA	NA	NA	NA	NA	NA	NA	NA	NA	NA	NA
Derry town (Rockingham).	1	D	25	459	26	172	91	1,228	18	186	9	91	19	105	20
Dover city & MCD (Strafford)	NA	NA	44	919	34	445	96	1,391	9	506	15	316	54	D	35
Durham CDP	NA	NA	NA	NA	NA	NA	NA	NA	NA	NA	NA	NA	NA	NA	NA
Durham town (Strafford) ..	NA	NA	NA	NA	3	1	15	193	1	D	6	26	9	D	12
Exeter town (Rockingham)	NA	NA	21	1,225	19	321	85	790	11	361	9	60	34	D	15
Goffstown town (Hillsborough)..............	NA	NA	15	171	8	70	45	653	4	196	2	D	12	52	6
Hampton town (Rockingham)..............	3	D	21	564	14	87	60	419	12	66	6	9	30	221	24
Hanover town (Grafton)	NA	NA	7	D	5	10	48	463	1	D	11	125	27	176	15
Hooksett town (Merrimack)	1	D	23	999	29	623	78	2,073	12	123	6	74	28	1,083	18
Hudson town (Hillsborough)..............	NA	NA	73	2,819	42	579	73	1,709	17	181	7	D	16	94	19
Keene city & MCD (Cheshire)	5	D	37	2,178	26	229	165	3,008	7	212	22	322	63	1,399	36
Laconia city & MCD (Belknap)	1	D	37	1,404	13	D	86	871	5	D	11	102	24	D	20
Lebanon city & MCD (Grafton)	2	D	31	1,858	31	373	166	3,097	18	188	30	809	35	303	46
Londonderry CDP............	NA	NA	NA	NA	NA	NA	NA	NA	NA	NA	NA	NA	NA	NA	NA
Londonderry town (Rockingham)..............	NA	NA	56	3,306	58	946	68	2,059	34	1,136	7	169	32	224	28
Manchester city & MCD (Hillsborough).............	13	D	116	5,175	192	3,297	464	7,470	68	1,710	137	3,935	262	3,947	132
Merrimack town (Hillsborough)..............	1	D	34	1,782	35	431	123	1,892	14	198	15	258	26	149	18
Milford town (Hillsborough)	1	D	36	1,759	13	104	80	1,146	10	152	3	7	18	107	12
Nashua city & MCD (Hillsborough)..............	4	83	117	8,970	127	1,591	455	9,973	43	1,130	80	1,868	120	883	109
Pelham town (Hillsborough)..............	NA	NA	24	521	11	104	37	380	6	18	5	15	8	37	4
Portsmouth city & MCD (Rockingham)..............	7	217	39	1,948	77	777	254	3,860	29	657	55	1,693	150	3,178	63
Raymond town (Rockingham)..............	1	D	5	98	6	25	28	444	8	D	NA	NA	8	D	4
Rochester city & MCD (Strafford)	1	D	34	1,135	14	D	123	2,506	9	D	10	202	37	272	22
Salem town (Rockingham)	2	D	49	1,383	85	2,117	326	6,649	21	320	26	337	56	1,009	36
Somersworth city & MCD (Strafford)	1	D	19	829	11	D	84	1,538	4	D	5	D	10	D	12
Windham town (Rockingham)..............	NA	NA	14	167	19	141	42	442	10	52	13	70	17	49	9
NEW JERSEY	406	20,304	7,758	230,697	12,760	208,830	31,722	436,299	7,004	160,321	3,705	119,179	11,927	198,724	8,749
Aberdeen township (Monmouth)...............	NA	NA	11	112	16	D	56	732	11	86	9	186	31	178	13
Asbury Park city & MCD (Monmouth)...............	1	D	9	68	8	78	64	337	8	30	4	29	11	48	26
Atlantic City city & MCD (Atlantic)................	8	91	6	54	12	388	330	3,060	14	501	3	D	28	160	47
Avenel CDP	NA	NA	NA	NA	NA	NA	NA	NA	NA	NA	NA	NA	NA	NA	NA
Barnegat township (Ocean)	NA	NA	5	16	10	D	40	326	5	D	2	D	11	72	8
Bayonne city & MCD (Hudson)	1	D	32	931	48	1,157	190	1,864	72	1,505	7	81	55	458	40
Beachwood borough & MCD (Ocean)............	NA	NA	NA	NA	6	16	16	84	2	D	NA	D	2	D	3
Belleville township (Essex)	1	D	46	433	36	274	88	844	37	211	5	D	17	D	22
Bellmawr borough & MCD (Camden)................	1	D	16	545	18	117	27	190	15	489	4	150	4	29	9
Bergenfield borough & MCD (Bergen).............	NA	NA	17	158	32	202	88	702	15	123	7	59	18	76	15
Berkeley township (Ocean).....................	5	D	12	142	9	D	57	602	11	70	3	D	21	130	16
Berkeley Heights township (Union).....................	1	D	12	107	16	235	30	356	8	63	8	D	28	342	10
Bernards township (Somerset).................	NA	NA	9	37	25	315	45	383	8	D	42	D	55	1,899	22
Bloomfield township (Essex).....................	NA	NA	27	311	34	493	122	1,761	21	88	9	D	48	468	50
Bordentown township (Burlington)...............	2	D	6	470	12	D	42	715	13	195	2	D	15	83	9
Bound Brook borough & MCD (Somerset).........	NA	NA	6	58	8	D	27	342	10	50	1	D	8	D	4
Bradley Gardens CDP	NA	NA	NA	NA	NA	NA	NA	NA	NA	NA	NA	NA	NA	NA	NA
Branchburg township (Somerset).................	1	D	50	3,351	64	1,583	34	640	16	513	10	D	22	137	7
Brick township (Ocean)	NA	NA	27	209	43	266	222	4,118	30	127	18	329	69	488	57
Bridgeton city & MCD (Cumberland)...............	1	D	11	627	18	249	92	842	6	D	5	D	16	D	13
Bridgewater township (Somerset).................	2	D	16	374	74	3,125	251	6,469	45	1,548	31	D	84	2,302	49
Browns Mills CDP	NA	NA	NA	NA	NA	NA	NA	NA	NA	NA	NA	NA	NA	NA	NA
Burlington township (Burlington)...............	2	D	24	917	22	699	87	1,608	26	806	5	123	21	202	21

1 Merchant wholesalers, except manufacturers' sales branches and offices.

Table C. Incorporated Places, Census Designated Places (CDPs), and Minor Civil Divisions (MCDs) of 10,000 or More Population — **Economic Census**

STATE City, town, township, borough, or CDP (county if applicable)	Real estate and rental and leasing — Number of employees	Professional, scientific, and technical services — Number of establishments	— Number of employees	Administration and support and waste management and mediation services — Number of establishments	— Number of employees	Educational services — Number of establishments	— Number of employees	Health care and social assistance — Number of establishments	— Number of employees	Arts, entertainment, and recreation — Number of establishments	— Number of employees	Accommodation and food services — Number of establishments	— Number of employees	Other services (except public administration) — Number of establishments	— Number of employees
	16	17	18	19	20	21	22	23	24	25	26	27	28	29	30
NEW HAMPSHIRE—Con.															
Conway town (Carroll)	103	34	225	19	106	4	D	56	1,182	17	740	103	1,467	36	141
Derry CDP	NA	NA	NA	NA	NA	NA	NA	NA	NA	NA	NA	NA	NA	NA	NA
Derry town (Rockingham)	D	52	329	45	246	5	32	80	1,897	11	103	54	765	52	347
Dover city & MCD (Strafford)	358	104	D	51	849	6	D	128	3,487	12	82	88	1,552	68	409
Durham CDP	NA	NA	NA	NA	NA	NA	NA	NA	NA	NA	NA	NA	NA	NA	NA
Durham town (Strafford)	70	29	183	12	44	2	D	17	154	3	D	35	368	11	D
Exeter town (Rockingham)	155	48	236	24	442	10	27	90	3,225	14	237	45	718	40	226
Goffstown town (Hillsborough)	11	29	116	26	162	3	D	32	D	8	194	26	294	31	D
Hampton town (Rockingham)	D	64	488	27	329	3	D	31	196	10	75	104	886	31	117
Hanover town (Grafton)	53	32	253	11	63	8	D	39	760	6	17	33	722	15	60
Hooksett town (Merrimack)	D	25	216	26	286	6	D	32	255	10	122	35	656	44	227
Hudson town (Hillsborough)	38	47	228	42	298	11	92	31	515	10	116	44	547	60	220
Keene city & MCD (Cheshire)	163	79	404	37	557	9	71	99	3,428	15	335	87	1,694	62	588
Laconia city & MCD (Belknap)	D	54	389	28	380	3	D	63	2,722	17	178	79	711	56	234
Lebanon city & MCD (Grafton)	136	95	698	38	429	14	71	80	7,213	12	292	52	1,113	52	460
Londonderry CDP	NA	NA	NA	NA	NA	NA	NA	NA	NA	NA	NA	NA	NA	NA	NA
Londonderry town (Rockingham)	222	98	760	60	877	8	53	78	D	12	287	55	949	53	D
Manchester city & MCD (Hillsborough)	1,348	440	4,313	169	19,959	34	629	353	11,906	47	1,148	304	5,518	283	2,246
Merrimack town (Hillsborough)	142	74	422	51	410	11	58	54	814	9	291	59	D	52	290
Milford town (Hillsborough)	42	28	114	30	306	2	D	39	525	3	D	46	608	41	256
Nashua city & MCD (Hillsborough)	414	325	3,402	130	2,437	30	487	326	8,728	33	608	232	4,426	176	1,540
Pelham town (Hillsborough)	D	19	104	22	D	1	D	15	D	4	21	15	211	27	D
Portsmouth city & MCD (Rockingham)	232	275	3,327	79	2,448	16	145	196	4,310	43	441	159	3,965	100	580
Raymond town (Rockingham)	27	8	65	11	27	2	D	17	139	2	D	17	209	19	83
Rochester city & MCD (Strafford)	75	39	389	35	395	8	D	76	1,750	5	D	80	969	58	331
Salem town (Rockingham)	D	127	1,254	74	3,529	11	93	102	1,400	21	734	104	1,725	91	552
Somersworth city & MCD (Strafford)	28	17	349	12	108	1	D	40	729	6	249	25	266	22	221
Windham town (Rockingham)	19	46	202	21	104	5	36	35	473	6	85	27	D	28	179
NEW JERSEY	53,751	29,390	307,549	13,580	282,090	2,659	32,465	26,935	540,875	3,421	56,427	20,127	291,933	18,327	108,216
Aberdeen township (Monmouth)	110	49	364	19	77	5	38	33	370	9	162	35	506	39	163
Asbury Park city & MCD (Monmouth)	139	28	171	5	131	2	D	33	508	7	18	74	1,011	36	244
Atlantic City city & MCD (Atlantic)	475	70	D	32	828	4	15	85	3,174	16	148	228	38,593	68	934
Avenel CDP	NA	NA	NA	NA	NA	NA	NA	NA	NA	NA	NA	NA	NA	NA	NA
Barnegat township (Ocean)	68	17	89	14	63	1	D	26	318	4	17	22	175	27	85
Bayonne city & MCD (Hudson)	203	83	685	29	263	8	26	177	2,844	10	D	125	1,247	117	470
Beachwood borough & MCD (Ocean)	3	9	58	4	8	NA	NA	9	D	NA	NA	9	63	14	38
Belleville township (Essex)	88	31	D	42	407	2	D	101	3,222	11	172	67	659	80	464
Bellmawr borough & MCD (Camden)	45	21	246	12	361	1	D	11	D	2	D	22	202	18	115
Bergenfield borough & MCD (Bergen)	24	46	154	29	168	7	D	75	684	4	D	42	284	54	139
Berkeley township (Ocean)	19	31	73	44	103	2	D	57	1,333	10	D	55	566	60	273
Berkeley Heights township (Union)	D	67	674	29	241	10	90	40	1,730	8	334	31	394	34	141
Bernards township (Somerset)	D	130	5,937	32	531	15	909	73	2,581	8	579	60	1,478	35	D
Bloomfield township (Essex)	140	114	3,567	59	714	11	75	139	1,970	19	131	96	D	90	312
Bordentown township (Burlington)	23	31	216	7	37	4	51	17	134	3	D	29	741	24	144
Bound Brook borough & MCD (Somerset)	D	20	D	12	26	2	D	33	D	2	D	31	339	25	D
Bradley Gardens CDP	NA	NA	NA	NA	NA	NA	NA	NA	NA	NA	NA	NA	NA	NA	NA
Branchburg township (Somerset)	17	69	1,299	36	1,328	3	10	44	682	5	164	42	529	40	D
Brick township (Ocean)	275	154	588	104	782	22	D	257	5,987	34	919	132	D	161	691
Bridgeton city & MCD (Cumberland)	109	31	142	10	141	NA	NA	52	974	1	D	41	364	25	D
Bridgewater township (Somerset)	D	294	3,608	95	1,954	27	306	163	2,819	22	D	122	2,561	87	605
Browns Mills CDP	NA	NA	NA	NA	NA	NA	NA	NA	NA	NA	NA	NA	NA	NA	NA
Burlington township (Burlington)	134	38	468	17	699	4	13	57	1,865	3	D	57	810	41	189

Table C. Incorporated Places, Census Designated Places (CDPs), and Minor Civil Divisions (MCDs) of 10,000 or More Population — **Economic Census**

STATE City, town, township, borough, or CDP (county if applicable)	Utilities Number of establishments	Utilities Number of employees	Manufacturing Number of establishments	Manufacturing Number of employees	Wholesale trade[1] Number of establishments	Wholesale trade[1] Number of employees	Retail trade Number of establishments	Retail trade Number of employees	Transportation and warehousing Number of establishments	Transportation and warehousing Number of employees	Information Number of establishments	Information Number of employees	Finance and insurance Number of establishments	Finance and insurance Number of employees	Real estate and rental and leasing Number of establishments
	1	2	3	4	5	6	7	8	9	10	11	12	13	14	15
NEW JERSEY—Con.															
Camden city & MCD (Camden)	2	D	47	1,487	53	1,070	211	1,129	30	616	14	63	28	165	37
Carteret borough & MCD (Middlesex)	NA	NA	10	782	36	1,547	38	533	42	1,353	5	27	9	D	9
Cedar Grove township (Essex)	NA	NA	29	1,158	25	270	30	328	4	5	5	D	22	122	8
Chatham township (Morris)	NA	NA	3	41	7	D	16	121	2	D	3	D	16	50	9
Cherry Hill township (Camden)	4	D	54	1,624	125	1,274	450	9,254	53	193	50	2,090	178	2,325	118
Cherry Hill Mall CDP	NA	NA	NA	NA	NA	NA	NA	NA	NA	NA	NA	NA	NA	NA	NA
Cinnaminson township (Burlington)	NA	NA	44	860	39	577	62	1,281	16	321	5	21	25	178	16
City of Orange township (Essex)	3	D	17	235	17	217	127	650	24	165	4	28	11	D	39
Clark township (Union)	NA	NA	12	496	19	200	48	1,360	10	175	3	D	41	D	24
Cliffside Park borough & MCD (Bergen)	1	D	10	53	30	63	55	155	9	44	6	10	12	87	20
Clifton city & MCD (Passaic)	4	D	144	5,418	181	2,492	281	4,593	73	1,418	23	271	97	813	95
Clinton township (Hunterdon)	NA	NA	3	D	13	29	27	246	4	97	7	50	31	D	14
Collingswood borough & MCD (Camden)	1	D	4	63	10	70	43	201	3	27	10	40	24	125	8
Colonia CDP	NA	NA	NA	NA	NA	NA	NA	NA	NA	NA	NA	NA	NA	NA	NA
Colts Neck township (Monmouth)	1	D	6	41	13	32	27	351	4	20	6	17	24	88	23
Cranford township (Union)	2	D	28	536	43	987	50	430	25	332	15	316	75	1,238	29
Delran township (Burlington)	2	D	10	100	20	D	74	1,214	15	490	2	D	14	128	12
Denville township (Morris)	1	D	31	782	37	359	88	1,150	5	D	8	67	30	208	15
Deptford township (Gloucester)	1	D	21	147	22	D	238	5,533	15	115	16	169	22	219	18
Dover town & MCD (Morris)	5	D	22	509	26	298	66	814	29	316	6	D	19	110	16
Dumont borough & MCD (Bergen)	NA	NA	9	99	11	29	27	266	5	16	2	D	20	81	13
East Brunswick township (Middlesex)	1	D	41	888	98	832	246	4,049	42	726	26	406	78	1,120	50
East Greenwich township (Gloucester)	NA	NA	6	192	9	D	12	65	8	52	2	D	5	18	5
East Hanover township (Morris)	2	D	36	978	48	712	115	2,395	13	405	9	122	34	284	19
East Orange city & MCD (Essex)	1	D	12	112	16	169	133	1,073	25	354	5	24	15	103	59
East Windsor township (Mercer)	NA	NA	8	147	21	D	74	1,484	17	94	14	517	26	369	19
Eatontown borough & MCD (Monmouth)	NA	NA	25	1,540	41	787	163	3,060	12	271	13	321	34	251	36
Echelon CDP	NA	NA	NA	NA	NA	NA	NA	NA	NA	NA	NA	NA	NA	NA	NA
Edgewater borough & MCD (Bergen)	NA	NA	7	15	29	105	82	1,643	7	D	10	136	13	78	23
Edison township (Middlesex)	8	146	89	2,863	356	6,581	426	8,428	176	5,425	61	2,289	151	2,648	100
Egg Harbor township (Atlantic)	4	D	20	434	44	453	146	2,945	27	527	17	380	32	460	44
Elizabeth city & MCD (Union)	6	D	69	2,138	118	3,077	540	6,663	243	8,357	16	157	71	464	98
Elmwood Park borough & MCD (Bergen)	1	D	30	1,483	46	899	55	577	29	393	6	D	22	259	12
Englewood city & MCD (Bergen)	NA	NA	54	1,240	88	1,119	163	1,915	19	391	11	121	39	222	67
Evesham township (Burlington)	NA	NA	15	351	47	474	184	3,485	15	187	24	287	140	2,233	59
Ewing township (Mercer)	NA	NA	50	786	43	729	117	1,387	19	416	24	893	40	3,348	34
Fair Lawn borough & MCD (Bergen)	NA	NA	35	1,421	51	376	94	1,142	41	473	13	87	60	741	35
Fairview borough & MCD (Bergen)	NA	NA	21	149	42	338	59	431	18	53	3	D	7	50	13
Florence township (Burlington)	NA	NA	10	925	9	D	17	106	5	D	1	D	5	23	3
Florham Park borough & MCD (Morris)	NA	NA	10	739	23	457	26	350	7	18	23	581	101	2,271	26
Fords CDP	NA	NA	NA	NA	NA	NA	NA	NA	NA	NA	NA	NA	NA	NA	NA
Fort Lee borough & MCD (Bergen)	1	D	14	203	147	950	127	917	40	210	30	557	115	781	118
Franklin township (Gloucester)	NA	NA	3	7	20	D	32	269	15	106	5	D	7	44	4
Franklin township (Somerset)	5	D	73	3,895	118	4,702	125	1,834	53	838	34	1,330	81	3,225	47
Franklin Lakes borough & MCD (Bergen)	NA	NA	16	543	24	367	29	D	3	D	6	63	30	D	17
Franklin Park CDP	NA	NA	NA	NA	NA	NA	NA	NA	NA	NA	NA	NA	NA	NA	NA
Freehold borough & MCD (Monmouth)	2	D	9	158	12	189	60	896	9	56	4	D	34	231	19
Freehold township (Monmouth)	2	D	14	828	41	438	260	5,935	22	383	29	659	69	484	32
Galloway township (Atlantic)	NA	NA	3	D	9	36	60	674	13	385	3	D	17	108	18

1 Merchant wholesalers, except manufacturers' sales branches and offices.

Table C. Incorporated Places, Census Designated Places (CDPs), and Minor Civil Divisions (MCDs) of 10,000 or More Population — **Economic Census**

STATE City, town, township, borough, or CDP (county if applicable)	Real estate and rental and leasing — Number of employees	Professional, scientific, and technical services — Number of establishments	Number of employees	Administration and support and waste management and mediation services — Number of establishments	Number of employees	Educational services — Number of establishments	Number of employees	Health care and social assistance — Number of establishments	Number of employees	Arts, entertainment, and recreation — Number of establishments	Number of employees	Accommodation and food services — Number of establishments	Number of employees	Other services (except public administration) — Number of establishments	Number of employees
	16	17	18	19	20	21	22	23	24	25	26	27	28	29	30
NEW JERSEY—Con.															
Camden city & MCD (Camden)	D	53	785	42	2,431	8	D	156	10,670	11	238	87	723	67	550
Carteret borough & MCD (Middlesex)	38	23	420	12	309	1	D	21	D	1	D	24	275	25	93
Cedar Grove township (Essex)	13	48	206	31	109	6	48	51	D	6	27	23	322	27	D
Chatham township (Morris)	89	44	93	13	D	6	21	25	463	6	304	13	161	12	71
Cherry Hill township (Camden)	620	510	4,946	177	6,865	38	D	382	8,968	40	611	207	4,694	200	1,550
Cherry Hill Mall CDP	NA	NA	NA	NA	NA	NA	NA	NA	NA	NA	NA	NA	NA	NA	NA
Cinnaminson township (Burlington)	46	47	507	36	483	3	17	38	531	5	D	47	834	42	D
City of Orange township (Essex)	98	16	D	31	607	2	D	69	775	1	D	41	421	53	201
Clark township (Union)	D	79	1,074	23	782	2	D	77	795	3	D	35	593	36	217
Cliffside Park borough & MCD (Bergen)	D	50	173	19	60	4	3	70	455	3	D	50	236	47	200
Clifton city & MCD (Passaic)	586	253	1,866	110	2,873	20	642	397	4,500	20	216	159	2,027	178	995
Clinton township (Hunterdon)	55	70	964	31	267	6	24	45	D	6	160	20	306	21	D
Collingswood borough & MCD (Camden)	34	61	412	14	155	4	148	43	635	2	D	43	610	39	163
Colonia CDP	NA	NA	NA	NA	NA	NA	NA	NA	NA	NA	NA	NA	NA	NA	NA
Colts Neck township (Monmouth)	61	62	226	24	130	4	27	33	222	12	311	22	199	11	D
Cranford township (Union)	155	121	1,148	51	1,182	6	24	90	1,950	10	88	50	402	50	218
Delran township (Burlington)	132	16	83	43	248	7	19	30	378	7	58	35	738	38	220
Denville township (Morris)	49	104	640	38	513	16	D	119	3,302	11	155	62	773	63	359
Deptford township (Gloucester)	151	35	186	36	303	2	D	40	878	9	197	73	2,105	51	245
Dover town & MCD (Morris)	42	40	231	29	D	6	90	50	1,174	1	D	56	370	51	D
Dumont borough & MCD (Bergen)	D	30	96	20	107	3	D	30	178	1	D	33	193	37	D
East Brunswick township (Middlesex)	302	343	2,030	114	3,023	29	208	272	4,329	20	426	97	1,821	102	758
East Greenwich township (Gloucester)	56	17	66	8	94	1	D	11	106	2	D	7	D	12	124
East Hanover township (Morris)	120	86	2,526	68	1,146	11	199	26	909	9	D	69	972	51	D
East Orange city & MCD (Essex)	323	41	D	25	273	6	114	150	6,317	6	10	44	593	66	280
East Windsor township (Mercer)	D	114	975	35	975	8	D	57	D	10	195	57	953	45	248
Eatontown borough & MCD (Monmouth)	1,232	106	4,095	34	618	6	D	82	1,750	11	150	58	1,427	41	351
Echelon CDP	NA	NA	NA	NA	NA	NA	NA	NA	NA	NA	NA	NA	NA	NA	NA
Edgewater borough & MCD (Bergen)	107	65	270	9	D	5	6	43	593	13	D	49	D	51	239
Edison township (Middlesex)	1,297	831	16,486	174	10,201	45	343	410	10,299	29	241	252	3,825	180	1,012
Egg Harbor township (Atlantic)	285	85	1,617	77	762	12	D	106	2,029	20	D	93	1,404	79	352
Elizabeth city & MCD (Union)	447	118	455	92	3,361	20	365	236	6,245	11	80	249	2,725	204	1,291
Elmwood Park borough & MCD (Bergen)	51	52	1,427	35	2,010	4	13	43	D	4	39	40	372	43	185
Englewood city & MCD (Bergen)	538	117	650	43	501	15	102	230	4,782	19	325	63	787	103	460
Evesham township (Burlington)	350	246	3,237	108	5,144	19	D	237	4,443	17	D	92	1,888	85	832
Ewing township (Mercer)	155	93	1,119	57	637	10	D	91	2,038	10	194	90	D	86	580
Fair Lawn borough & MCD (Bergen)	D	197	1,219	58	D	15	110	190	2,466	13	191	65	673	86	440
Fairview borough & MCD (Bergen)	49	9	84	17	123	3	D	11	78	2	D	36	224	34	D
Florence township (Burlington)	D	6	25	13	26	3	8	10	116	1	D	15	121	6	18
Florham Park borough & MCD (Morris)	118	144	5,243	42	D	3	44	77	749	10	D	37	614	35	399
Fords CDP	NA	NA	NA	NA	NA	NA	NA	NA	NA	NA	NA	NA	NA	NA	NA
Fort Lee borough & MCD (Bergen)	499	269	1,142	78	508	24	85	195	1,120	14	37	116	1,113	132	578
Franklin township (Gloucester)	6	13	56	25	673	NA	NA	10	110	4	22	23	247	26	D
Franklin township (Somerset)	173	310	7,062	94	2,211	19	97	233	3,009	19	D	134	1,823	100	551
Franklin Lakes borough & MCD (Bergen)	47	62	389	33	2,044	4	D	45	D	11	172	17	203	20	D
Franklin Park CDP	NA	NA	NA	NA	NA	NA	NA	NA	NA	NA	NA	NA	NA	NA	NA
Freehold borough & MCD (Monmouth)	102	87	319	37	184	2	D	41	698	4	14	40	511	42	138
Freehold township (Monmouth)	181	146	809	56	1,496	14	103	229	4,716	23	940	109	2,281	85	805
Galloway township (Atlantic)	132	41	273	36	165	7	D	128	4,231	12	D	84	1,371	64	421

Table C. Incorporated Places, Census Designated Places (CDPs), and Minor Civil Divisions (MCDs) of 10,000 or More Population — Economic Census

STATE City, town, township, borough, or CDP (county if applicable)	Utilities Number of establish-ments	Utilities Number of employees	Manufacturing Number of establish-ments	Manufacturing Number of employees	Wholesale trade¹ Number of establish-ments	Wholesale trade¹ Number of employees	Retail trade Number of establish-ments	Retail trade Number of employees	Transportation and warehousing Number of establish-ments	Transportation and warehousing Number of employees	Information Number of establish-ments	Information Number of employees	Finance and insurance Number of establish-ments	Finance and insurance Number of employees	Real estate and rental and leasing Number of establish-ments
	1	2	3	4	5	6	7	8	9	10	11	12	13	14	15
NEW JERSEY—Con.															
Garfield city & MCD (Bergen)	NA	NA	56	576	42	407	81	825	29	104	4	D	18	121	12
Glassboro borough & MCD (Gloucester)	2	D	12	238	18	D	84	1,217	4	42	4	D	12	84	8
Glen Rock borough & MCD (Bergen)	NA	NA	5	19	25	505	37	332	NA	NA	5	284	21	131	15
Gloucester township (Camden)	1	D	27	1,083	38	298	104	1,405	28	148	5	D	37	216	26
Gloucester City city & MCD (Camden)	NA	NA	16	99	12	D	32	212	14	856	2	D	3	26	4
Greentree CDP	NA	NA	NA	NA	NA	NA	NA	NA	NA	NA	NA	NA	NA	NA	NA
Guttenberg town & MCD (Hudson)	NA	NA	8	D	10	D	27	D	10	D	NA	NA	7	D	5
Hackensack city & MCD (Bergen)	6	D	83	1,190	182	1,678	259	3,895	54	543	36	538	100	747	126
Haddon township (Camden)	NA	NA	8	82	9	50	54	622	5	14	1	D	13	162	6
Haddonfield borough & MCD (Camden)	NA	NA	5	35	5	22	58	249	1	D	10	51	34	216	16
Hamilton township (Atlantic)	2	D	7	68	10	D	178	3,495	5	D	12	166	13	68	10
Hamilton township (Mercer)	2	D	56	2,730	84	794	294	4,468	61	1,995	26	597	113	1,462	70
Hamilton Square CDP	NA	NA	NA	NA	NA	NA	NA	NA	NA	NA	NA	NA	NA	NA	NA
Hammonton town & MCD (Atlantic)	2	D	11	208	23	529	93	1,044	14	77	3	9	29	1,155	11
Hanover township (Morris)	NA	NA	20	936	53	921	43	1,138	21	280	16	268	38	956	28
Harrison township (Gloucester)	1	D	NA	NA	11	D	38	653	9	105	NA	NA	11	71	10
Harrison town & MCD (Hudson)	1	D	13	338	15	429	39	534	20	340	2	D	12	D	8
Hasbrouck Heights borough & MCD (Bergen)	NA	NA	8	27	31	341	36	320	22	372	7	54	35	235	20
Hawthorne borough & MCD (Passaic)	NA	NA	44	867	33	521	70	619	18	216	6	D	28	129	16
Hazlet township (Monmouth)	1	D	13	187	19	96	77	1,398	16	278	7	125	30	156	10
Highland Park borough & MCD (Middlesex)	NA	NA	9	40	9	D	36	264	6	D	2	D	8	D	22
Hillsborough township (Somerset)	4	D	42	492	67	705	79	1,205	22	265	16	D	36	D	25
Hillsdale borough & MCD (Bergen)	NA	NA	5	14	9	D	28	406	3	D	4	D	13	63	10
Hillside township (Union)	NA	NA	43	1,069	73	1,099	67	921	34	548	NA	NA	10	77	20
Hoboken city & MCD (Hudson)	3	D	22	184	48	269	164	1,297	30	1,922	41	2,337	93	1,235	81
Holiday City-Berkeley CDP	NA	NA	NA	NA	NA	NA	NA	NA	NA	NA	NA	NA	NA	NA	NA
Holmdel township (Monmouth)	2	D	NA	NA	25	114	63	1,361	5	D	13	D	34	257	17
Hopatcong borough & MCD (Sussex)	3	D	4	17	2	D	19	152	10	30	2	D	1	D	3
Hopewell township (Mercer)	NA	NA	8	193	20	D	17	213	3	D	5	D	8	D	7
Howell township (Monmouth)	4	D	45	334	72	458	182	2,599	31	324	15	D	56	280	28
Irvington township (Essex)	1	D	40	1,199	32	332	193	901	22	91	9	D	15	94	25
Iselin CDP	NA	NA	NA	NA	NA	NA	NA	NA	NA	NA	NA	NA	NA	NA	NA
Jackson township (Ocean)	1	D	19	215	21	99	154	2,154	23	80	6	D	32	196	33
Jefferson township (Morris)	1	D	12	51	25	131	47	476	7	D	4	7	16	76	6
Jersey City city & MCD (Hudson)	5	D	99	2,493	191	4,740	807	9,038	217	3,942	109	4,448	369	30,055	233
Keansburg borough & MCD (Monmouth)	NA	NA	5	42	2	D	10	79	6	D	NA	NA	4	D	NA
Kearny town & MCD (Hudson)	1	D	47	1,272	75	1,611	104	1,643	130	2,170	5	D	38	227	34
Kendall Park CDP	NA	NA	NA	NA	NA	NA	NA	NA	NA	NA	NA	NA	NA	NA	NA
Kinnelon borough & MCD (Morris)	NA	NA	5	26	11	28	12	194	7	38	8	100	11	48	3
Lacey township (Ocean)	1	D	9	68	17	63	79	1,375	15	103	4	D	27	164	17
Lakewood township (Ocean)	10	364	89	3,570	146	1,539	308	2,954	45	1,389	19	283	85	416	169
Lakewood CDP	NA	NA	NA	NA	NA	NA	NA	NA	NA	NA	NA	NA	NA	NA	NA
Lawrence township (Mercer)	6	D	21	527	34	315	216	3,723	6	58	16	814	74	881	39
Lincoln Park borough & MCD (Morris)	NA	NA	11	158	17	266	21	465	10	331	5	D	11	61	8
Linden city & MCD (Union)	1	D	105	3,184	119	1,875	183	2,770	123	1,860	14	244	34	231	34
Lindenwold borough & MCD (Camden)	NA	NA	3	29	6	85	27	208	1	D	3	3	4	D	12
Little Egg Harbor township (Ocean)	NA	NA	3	6	9	31	22	224	6	116	3	D	7	59	12
Little Falls township (Passaic)	NA	NA	22	250	22	129	47	859	6	51	12	1,150	34	323	18
Little Ferry borough & MCD (Bergen)	NA	NA	18	461	62	940	55	318	16	266	4	D	5	D	12
Livingston township (Essex)	NA	NA	14	243	48	318	195	2,588	10	39	16	D	96	1,448	52

1 Merchant wholesalers, except manufacturers' sales branches and offices.

Table C. Incorporated Places, Census Designated Places (CDPs), and Minor Civil Divisions (MCDs) of 10,000 or More Population — Economic Census

STATE City, town, township, borough, or CDP (county if applicable)	Real estate and rental and leasing — Number of employees	Professional, scientific, and technical services — Number of establishments	Number of employees	Administration and support and waste management and mediation services — Number of establishments	Number of employees	Educational services — Number of establishments	Number of employees	Health care and social assistance — Number of establishments	Number of employees	Arts, entertainment, and recreation — Number of establishments	Number of employees	Accommodation and food services — Number of establishments	Number of employees	Other services (except public administration) — Number of establishments	Number of employees
	16	17	18	19	20	21	22	23	24	25	26	27	28	29	30
NEW JERSEY—Con.															
Garfield city & MCD (Bergen)	110	35	183	31	134	5	20	36	463	2	D	43	343	67	D
Glassboro borough & MCD (Gloucester)	32	14	91	12	301	4	D	48	689	4	77	49	808	33	194
Glen Rock borough & MCD (Bergen)	84	76	311	18	57	1	D	43	242	5	27	28	201	27	230
Gloucester township (Camden)	132	98	482	71	577	14	224	83	789	17	105	84	1,236	68	708
Gloucester City city & MCD (Camden)	D	11	D	7	23	2	D	14	104	NA	NA	28	176	10	69
Greentree CDP	NA	NA	NA	NA	NA	NA	NA	NA	NA	NA	NA	NA	NA	NA	NA
Guttenberg town & MCD (Hudson)	7	33	77	10	D	4	8	21	D	2	D	19	D	23	135
Hackensack city & MCD (Bergen)	573	427	2,772	136	3,664	17	309	384	19,023	16	397	120	D	162	934
Haddon township (Camden)	40	22	77	14	33	3	25	20	D	6	57	30	459	32	D
Haddonfield borough & MCD (Camden)	D	145	1,102	22	188	7	D	69	707	8	87	29	283	36	195
Hamilton township (Atlantic)	83	40	305	22	114	4	16	56	666	12	148	84	D	45	202
Hamilton township (Mercer)	328	242	2,444	147	2,745	31	D	322	7,427	21	749	193	D	215	1,424
Hamilton Square CDP	NA	NA	NA	NA	NA	NA	NA	NA	NA	NA	NA	NA	NA	NA	NA
Hammonton town & MCD (Atlantic)	23	38	224	28	470	2	D	62	648	10	D	36	417	41	D
Hanover township (Morris)	104	106	5,416	54	1,476	14	272	51	1,201	17	360	44	938	39	561
Harrison township (Gloucester)	33	33	182	16	240	1	D	39	478	4	95	18	216	11	D
Harrison town & MCD (Hudson)	23	21	72	10	41	4	D	25	D	3	153	34	D	29	66
Hasbrouck Heights borough & MCD (Bergen)	155	47	503	21	327	8	51	37	304	7	151	34	D	29	D
Hawthorne borough & MCD (Passaic)	359	53	171	36	286	5	72	51	D	4	D	38	233	47	D
Hazlet township (Monmouth)	83	69	544	22	96	7	28	72	695	5	145	60	960	53	210
Highland Park borough & MCD (Middlesex)	157	45	263	6	D	6	D	69	827	1	D	24	157	41	147
Hillsborough township (Somerset)	150	178	698	72	359	18	137	137	1,768	12	241	60	762	83	540
Hillsdale borough & MCD (Bergen)	28	27	65	33	182	5	70	18	148	3	8	20	256	31	149
Hillside township (Union)	48	18	325	20	301	1	D	22	331	3	D	25	262	30	D
Hoboken city & MCD (Hudson)	472	209	1,148	40	1,129	16	104	136	2,267	26	D	219	D	123	735
Holiday City-Berkeley CDP	NA	NA	NA	NA	NA	NA	NA	NA	NA	NA	NA	NA	NA	NA	NA
Holmdel township (Monmouth)	89	93	602	23	132	8	56	105	2,327	4	D	29	D	25	220
Hopatcong borough & MCD (Sussex)	D	13	68	13	20	2	D	7	51	2	D	14	48	19	D
Hopewell township (Mercer)	38	70	D	37	210	7	D	30	D	12	67	14	164	17	121
Howell township (Monmouth)	83	102	515	100	1,103	20	118	111	1,419	21	342	82	1,075	94	554
Irvington township (Essex)	187	14	D	16	D	NA	NA	92	905	3	D	54	417	63	D
Iselin CDP	NA	NA	NA	NA	NA	NA	NA	NA	NA	NA	NA	NA	NA	NA	NA
Jackson township (Ocean)	161	96	328	76	525	16	52	61	1,190	21	D	68	332	74	361
Jefferson township (Morris)	11	50	270	30	D	3	D	40	294	14	53	43	530	27	85
Jersey City city & MCD (Hudson)	1,129	588	7,013	160	8,236	41	945	511	12,274	53	D	471	4,941	385	2,090
Keansburg borough & MCD (Monmouth)	NA	3	D	4	D	NA	NA	13	281	6	D	18	119	8	14
Kearny town & MCD (Hudson)	227	47	227	43	1,488	5	7	80	796	3	D	56	532	59	D
Kendall Park CDP	NA	NA	NA	NA	NA	NA	NA	NA	NA	NA	NA	NA	NA	NA	NA
Kinnelon borough & MCD (Morris)	4	48	176	17	D	2	D	24	121	1	D	8	84	13	108
Lacey township (Ocean)	63	48	252	31	134	9	40	76	D	8	56	48	609	58	D
Lakewood township (Ocean)	1,065	179	1,547	101	1,699	34	632	266	6,692	19	D	78	737	124	737
Lakewood CDP	NA	NA	NA	NA	NA	NA	NA	NA	NA	NA	NA	NA	NA	NA	NA
Lawrence township (Mercer)	278	183	2,615	72	7,100	23	D	178	2,559	15	406	85	1,426	63	531
Lincoln Park borough & MCD (Morris)	90	27	71	18	154	2	D	25	1,580	4	63	16	123	18	D
Linden city & MCD (Union)	187	53	1,152	50	811	5	45	68	1,540	6	74	95	986	107	659
Lindenwold borough & MCD (Camden)	56	8	39	12	92	NA	NA	18	D	2	D	16	150	21	D
Little Egg Harbor township (Ocean)	52	10	27	12	40	2	D	19	384	5	134	18	130	29	124
Little Falls township (Passaic)	52	53	513	28	191	2	D	33	186	2	D	41	562	36	160
Little Ferry borough & MCD (Bergen)	65	10	84	13	54	NA	NA	8	61	1	D	21	280	21	D
Livingston township (Essex)	D	213	1,458	69	3,321	26	212	243	2,649	17	596	79	1,336	79	583

Items 16–30

Table C. Incorporated Places, Census Designated Places (CDPs), and Minor Civil Divisions (MCDs) of 10,000 or More Population — **Economic Census**

STATE City, town, township, borough, or CDP (county if applicable)	Utilities Number of establishments	Utilities Number of employees	Manufacturing Number of establishments	Manufacturing Number of employees	Wholesale trade[1] Number of establishments	Wholesale trade[1] Number of employees	Retail trade Number of establishments	Retail trade Number of employees	Transportation and warehousing Number of establishments	Transportation and warehousing Number of employees	Information Number of establishments	Information Number of employees	Finance and insurance Number of establishments	Finance and insurance Number of employees	Real estate and rental and leasing Number of establishments
	1	2	3	4	5	6	7	8	9	10	11	12	13	14	15
NEW JERSEY—Con.															
Lodi borough & MCD (Bergen)	1	D	27	310	41	460	89	1,048	25	63	5	97	24	132	27
Long Branch city & MCD (Monmouth)	NA	NA	17	250	20	113	89	1,000	12	61	3	8	21	117	29
Lower township (Cape May)	1	D	9	145	8	24	45	490	18	99	1	D	11	54	18
Lumberton township (Burlington)	NA	NA	7	D	14	D	22	520	14	1,229	1	D	7	48	10
Lyndhurst township (Bergen)	NA	NA	24	764	54	975	61	1,079	28	472	6	198	28	280	21
Madison borough & MCD (Morris)	NA	NA	5	42	7	52	78	945	8	D	8	93	37	363	19
Mahwah township (Bergen)	1	D	40	5,588	87	1,781	65	1,522	19	752	25	465	59	696	34
Manalapan township (Monmouth)	1	D	22	276	71	303	128	1,708	34	116	12	181	45	224	21
Manchester township (Ocean)	1	D	4	57	9	23	52	1,048	11	141	1	D	28	180	14
Mantua township (Gloucester)	NA	NA	11	89	11	D	39	954	15	540	6	13	22	208	6
Manville borough & MCD (Somerset)	NA	NA	8	39	1	D	32	406	7	D	1	D	8	D	2
Maple Shade township (Burlington)	NA	NA	16	281	18	288	74	1,190	7	15	5	42	9	65	26
Maplewood township (Essex)	1	D	21	299	13	102	76	454	15	144	12	90	26	121	17
Marlboro township (Monmouth)	2	D	25	245	98	793	78	1,038	27	291	11	73	51	440	38
Marlton CDP	NA	NA	NA	NA	NA	NA	NA	NA	NA	NA	NA	NA	NA	NA	NA
Martinsville CDP	NA	NA	NA	NA	NA	NA	NA	NA	NA	NA	NA	NA	NA	NA	NA
Medford township (Burlington)	NA	NA	12	232	27	D	92	1,745	12	25	7	100	49	326	23
Mercerville CDP	NA	NA	NA	NA	NA	NA	NA	NA	NA	NA	NA	NA	NA	NA	NA
Metuchen borough & MCD (Middlesex)	NA	NA	22	565	34	D	51	337	15	173	7	D	37	250	22
Middle township (Cape May)	2	D	15	172	16	D	110	2,204	6	13	9	123	28	298	20
Middlesex borough & MCD (Middlesex)	NA	NA	63	1,248	55	613	54	549	19	226	1	D	10	D	11
Middletown township (Monmouth)	3	D	15	376	27	101	162	2,516	23	630	38	D	97	1,923	38
Millburn township (Essex)	3	D	9	93	27	579	225	4,713	6	181	18	145	82	1,956	70
Millstone township (Monmouth)	1	D	5	78	14	104	16	110	9	41	5	D	12	D	5
Millville city & MCD (Cumberland)	4	D	43	2,425	27	468	88	1,798	15	D	7	151	20	146	12
Monroe township (Gloucester)	NA	NA	32	375	20	D	95	1,156	18	337	6	D	23	136	17
Monroe township (Middlesex)	NA	NA	14	983	51	518	66	522	62	1,507	4	D	41	229	16
Montclair township (Essex)	NA	NA	15	80	25	69	150	1,185	19	180	43	209	49	314	65
Montgomery township (Somerset)	NA	NA	12	462	22	66	47	592	11	D	9	D	30	D	15
Montville township (Morris)	2	D	33	1,028	102	1,616	46	442	23	649	9	D	37	255	24
Moorestown township (Burlington)	2	D	48	6,513	59	1,481	136	2,267	16	291	16	498	72	948	34
Moorestown-Lenola CDP	NA	NA	NA	NA	NA	NA	NA	NA	NA	NA	NA	NA	NA	NA	NA
Morris township (Morris)	2	D	8	D	15	93	28	444	6	D	14	D	51	2,165	24
Morristown town & MCD (Morris)	5	D	11	125	32	D	110	1,219	17	288	23	445	99	862	55
Mount Laurel township (Burlington)	10	D	19	677	72	1,881	134	3,562	23	544	52	2,458	153	9,919	55
Mount Olive township (Morris)	NA	NA	31	1,397	49	648	81	1,576	21	1,023	8	178	32	288	17
Neptune township (Monmouth)	1	D	18	723	27	287	88	1,488	11	222	12	861	29	527	20
Newark city & MCD (Essex)	16	D	251	6,686	335	5,162	913	5,918	381	26,933	123	4,692	345	14,480	214
New Brunswick city & MCD (Middlesex)	2	D	52	842	60	839	121	736	29	675	13	325	37	D	46
New Milford borough & MCD (Bergen)	NA	NA	3	10	10	34	24	280	6	13	1	D	11	68	8
New Providence borough & MCD (Union)	NA	NA	7	79	9	164	25	292	8	42	11	D	28	214	9
North Arlington borough & MCD (Bergen)	NA	NA	11	163	14	160	44	299	17	435	4	D	21	121	13
North Bergen township (Hudson)	NA	NA	50	1,193	128	2,249	165	2,717	115	1,892	16	215	33	209	59
North Brunswick township (Middlesex)	NA	NA	27	2,990	70	681	122	2,351	33	470	10	109	39	391	47
North Plainfield borough & MCD (Somerset)	NA	NA	7	75	14	66	65	672	12	D	5	14	18	D	14
Nutley township (Essex)	NA	NA	17	130	24	201	68	782	8	28	8	198	37	267	25
Oakland borough & MCD (Bergen)	1	D	26	723	27	507	47	810	11	289	10	D	22	177	8
Ocean township (Monmouth)	NA	NA	25	188	31	181	123	2,817	15	190	11	200	28	219	35
Ocean Acres CDP	NA	NA	NA	NA	NA	NA	NA	NA	NA	NA	NA	NA	NA	NA	NA

1 Merchant wholesalers, except manufacturers' sales branches and offices.

Table C. Incorporated Places, Census Designated Places (CDPs), and Minor Civil Divisions (MCDs) of 10,000 or More Population — **Economic Census**

STATE City, town, township, borough, or CDP (county if applicable)	Real estate and rental and leasing	Professional, scientific, and technical services		Administration and support and waste management and mediation services		Educational services		Health care and social assistance		Arts, entertainment, and recreation		Accommodation and food services		Other services (except public administration)	
	Number of employees	Number of establish-ments	Number of employees	Number of establish-ments	Number of employees	Number of establish-ments	Number of employees	Number of establish-ments	Number of employees	Number of establish-ments	Number of employees	Number of establish-ments	Number of employees	Number of establish-ments	Number of employees
	16	17	18	19	20	21	22	23	24	25	26	27	28	29	30
NEW JERSEY—Con.															
Lodi borough & MCD (Bergen)	89	36	96	23	317	3	D	23	D	1	D	48	324	59	D
Long Branch city & MCD (Monmouth)	76	46	183	32	83	5	13	108	3,038	10	145	93	1,567	64	286
Lower township (Cape May)	42	15	91	25	74	3	D	25	458	12	D	55	649	33	205
Lumberton township (Burlington)	115	21	75	23	295	3	D	42	905	6	42	11	92	21	82
Lyndhurst township (Bergen)	121	87	2,225	47	2,516	10	308	52	471	6	293	57	561	56	D
Madison borough & MCD (Morris)	78	61	310	28	D	9	81	55	668	14	D	45	655	44	230
Mahwah township (Bergen)	108	102	1,077	81	1,288	9	68	47	346	13	403	59	1,089	43	242
Manalapan township (Monmouth)	96	172	626	73	337	7	47	142	1,204	27	560	66	696	96	658
Manchester township (Ocean)	114	17	106	28	227	2	D	68	1,743	3	13	30	419	53	316
Mantua township (Gloucester)	24	34	300	31	315	5	43	49	851	2	D	28	379	40	D
Manville borough & MCD (Somerset)	D	8	28	23	173	NA	NA	23	D	1	D	23	128	23	D
Maple Shade township (Burlington)	175	22	263	21	218	6	53	26	436	5	66	47	883	39	D
Maplewood township (Essex)	72	76	D	22	117	9	89	74	768	21	374	48	D	49	282
Marlboro township (Monmouth)	83	266	918	79	981	30	305	150	1,046	21	281	47	566	79	481
Marlton CDP	NA	NA	NA	NA	NA	NA	NA	NA	NA	NA	NA	NA	NA	NA	NA
Martinsville CDP	NA	NA	NA	NA	NA	NA	NA	NA	NA	NA	NA	NA	NA	NA	NA
Medford township (Burlington)	46	125	621	57	354	16	242	120	1,530	15	275	57	673	67	352
Mercerville CDP	NA	NA	NA	NA	NA	NA	NA	NA	NA	NA	NA	NA	NA	NA	NA
Metuchen borough & MCD (Middlesex)	D	141	919	29	308	16	D	82	1,151	2	D	38	215	51	281
Middle township (Cape May)	61	44	239	51	388	5	D	130	2,846	16	221	81	610	59	266
Middlesex borough & MCD (Middlesex)	51	51	377	32	239	5	39	29	156	1	D	31	184	41	D
Middletown township (Monmouth)	116	172	1,750	79	957	26	185	138	1,556	27	441	103	1,444	107	521
Millburn township (Essex)	D	169	2,055	40	885	11	84	154	4,349	17	450	60	1,220	73	388
Millstone township (Monmouth)	8	61	337	29	239	3	23	17	D	9	51	14	203	20	97
Millville city & MCD (Cumberland)	51	44	213	12	99	2	D	91	1,534	7	289	56	673	41	185
Monroe township (Gloucester)	82	48	143	43	449	7	82	40	603	7	151	41	553	63	D
Monroe township (Middlesex)	209	149	524	48	1,593	9	71	91	1,312	15	337	40	224	55	392
Montclair township (Essex)	D	210	911	45	290	24	221	210	2,918	48	889	139	1,449	126	632
Montgomery township (Somerset)	134	244	1,207	53	4,347	20	131	66	1,367	13	D	32	376	44	574
Montville township (Morris)	59	169	1,212	63	723	9	44	64	D	11	D	48	519	41	199
Moorestown township (Burlington)	177	224	5,932	61	1,831	13	D	153	3,023	11	43	59	1,004	50	308
Moorestown-Lenola CDP	NA	NA	NA	NA	NA	NA	NA	NA	NA	NA	NA	NA	NA	NA	NA
Morris township (Morris)	156	102	2,188	31	348	8	89	79	1,185	17	238	33	774	21	394
Morristown town & MCD (Morris)	696	246	1,645	67	579	12	86	210	8,826	14	D	101	1,733	94	559
Mount Laurel township (Burlington)	1,645	244	4,388	111	2,931	15	D	142	2,364	21	909	123	2,648	71	472
Mount Olive township (Morris)	208	99	677	47	848	6	84	64	D	13	105	58	717	46	D
Neptune township (Monmouth)	74	57	405	36	524	10	71	87	5,146	9	100	57	824	59	462
Newark city & MCD (Essex)	2,108	415	6,676	225	7,838	34	545	497	17,437	28	1,845	536	7,920	501	5,449
New Brunswick city & MCD (Middlesex)	263	132	1,060	71	4,059	16	271	129	10,044	9	227	161	2,009	102	1,040
New Milford borough & MCD (Bergen)	20	33	99	24	76	2	D	18	363	3	D	22	217	24	D
New Providence borough & MCD (Union)	35	67	1,114	28	307	3	20	36	777	8	100	33	D	23	D
North Arlington borough & MCD (Bergen)	60	20	56	15	382	1	D	40	298	3	D	36	285	35	D
North Bergen township (Hudson)	324	77	209	55	1,782	2	D	102	2,119	9	78	123	1,674	103	521
North Brunswick township (Middlesex)	360	222	1,280	62	5,276	13	58	133	1,878	8	256	87	1,331	86	444
North Plainfield borough & MCD (Somerset)	112	22	93	28	132	3	D	36	523	1	D	31	182	40	D
Nutley township (Essex)	62	78	D	44	1,539	9	48	93	D	10	15	55	463	85	253
Oakland borough & MCD (Bergen)	24	59	387	39	265	5	15	53	637	8	117	34	328	27	D
Ocean township (Monmouth)	D	86	540	62	577	11	60	132	1,700	10	141	66	781	58	D
Ocean Acres CDP	NA	NA	NA	NA	NA	NA	NA	NA	NA	NA	NA	NA	NA	NA	NA

Table C. Incorporated Places, Census Designated Places (CDPs), and Minor Civil Divisions (MCDs) of 10,000 or More Population — Economic Census

STATE City, town, township, borough, or CDP (county if applicable)	Utilities		Manufacturing		Wholesale trade[1]		Retail trade		Transportation and warehousing		Information		Finance and insurance		Real estate and rental and leasing
	Number of establish-ments	Number of employees	Number of establish-ments	Number of employees	Number of establish-ments	Number of employees	Number of establish-ments	Number of employees	Number of establish-ments	Number of employees	Number of establish-ments	Number of employees	Number of establish-ments	Number of employees	Number of establish-ments
	1	2	3	4	5	6	7	8	9	10	11	12	13	14	15
NEW JERSEY—Con.															
Ocean City city & MCD (Cape May)	NA	NA	8	62	5	12	111	671	4	18	10	53	26	238	44
Old Bridge CDP	NA	NA	NA	NA	NA	NA	NA	NA	NA	NA	NA	NA	NA	NA	NA
Old Bridge township (Middlesex)	2	D	19	448	49	D	171	2,314	48	238	12	40	53	439	36
Palisades Park borough & MCD (Bergen)	NA	NA	11	223	78	234	96	435	21	41	10	171	19	141	27
Paramus borough & MCD (Bergen)	NA	NA	17	265	112	2,436	618	15,076	29	1,343	51	1,633	130	2,166	73
Parsippany-Troy Hills township (Morris)	3	D	56	1,477	120	3,457	146	2,140	52	2,531	70	3,030	218	7,882	116
Passaic city & MCD (Passaic)	NA	NA	101	1,388	80	768	260	2,083	32	340	8	D	37	214	44
Paterson city & MCD (Passaic)	1	D	225	4,649	194	2,269	541	3,169	74	558	18	239	66	389	70
Pemberton township (Burlington)	NA	NA	5	100	5	D	39	390	5	37	1	D	6	D	10
Pennsauken township (Camden)	NA	NA	77	3,932	123	2,945	128	1,561	55	1,323	11	62	15	88	33
Pennsville CDP	NA	NA	NA	NA	NA	NA	NA	NA	NA	NA	NA	NA	NA	NA	NA
Pennsville township (Salem)	2	D	4	D	4	D	50	639	2	D	NA	NA	9	71	9
Pequannock township (Morris)	NA	NA	12	52	32	401	60	869	10	54	5	28	20	112	11
Perth Amboy city & MCD (Middlesex)	4	15	37	1,099	34	1,109	208	1,281	51	571	8	D	24	189	30
Phillipsburg town & MCD (Warren)	8	D	17	891	11	D	57	926	11	184	4	D	6	55	3
Pine Hill borough & MCD (Camden)	NA	NA	NA	NA	1	D	15	87	4	D	1	D	1	D	5
Piscataway township (Middlesex)	1	D	56	4,148	110	2,646	85	1,471	39	800	64	2,609	51	822	37
Plainfield city & MCD (Union)	6	D	23	390	25	D	125	633	18	141	8	D	18	71	18
Plainsboro township (Middlesex)	2	D	19	1,401	32	D	25	237	NA	NA	23	864	39	1,532	20
Pleasantville city & MCD (Atlantic)	2	D	14	91	27	388	73	1,202	7	249	7	367	9	D	18
Point Pleasant borough & MCD (Ocean)	1	D	15	42	15	48	56	529	6	17	5	14	25	191	15
Pompton Lakes borough & MCD (Passaic)	NA	NA	11	80	12	D	36	235	4	6	2	D	13	75	7
Princeton & MCD (Mercer)	1	D	4	264	7	D	101	1,414	2	D	15	153	71	1,209	40
Princeton Meadows CDP	NA	NA	NA	NA	NA	NA	NA	NA	NA	NA	NA	NA	NA	NA	NA
Rahway city & MCD (Union)	NA	NA	40	3,169	67	808	70	651	26	224	4	11	12	D	20
Ramsey borough & MCD (Bergen)	3	2	10	163	55	880	106	2,084	15	D	12	136	41	355	15
Randolph township (Morris)	NA	NA	29	476	53	602	65	871	15	223	9	234	32	189	25
Raritan township (Hunterdon)	4	D	30	1,151	25	195	80	2,155	12	84	8	D	34	D	15
Readington township (Hunterdon)	NA	NA	25	579	24	241	40	389	13	166	2	D	27	D	14
Red Bank borough & MCD (Monmouth)	NA	NA	16	232	11	60	105	769	9	51	22	203	105	1,053	37
Ridgefield borough & MCD (Bergen)	1	D	33	1,229	75	574	63	518	27	147	5	D	18	98	18
Ridgefield Park village & MCD (Bergen)	NA	NA	12	545	35	D	27	163	11	102	4	D	12	106	19
Ridgewood village & MCD (Bergen)	NA	NA	6	22	32	122	111	954	5	11	10	48	62	450	39
Ringwood borough & MCD (Passaic)	NA	NA	10	136	20	176	16	152	4	D	8	D	11	41	3
River Edge borough & MCD (Bergen)	1	D	NA	NA	12	45	22	170	2	D	6	70	21	261	12
Robbinsville township (Mercer)	1	D	16	548	26	1,645	44	681	17	302	10	D	12	D	15
Robertsville CDP	NA	NA	NA	NA	NA	NA	NA	NA	NA	NA	NA	NA	NA	NA	NA
Rockaway township (Morris)	2	D	22	1,437	34	1,747	101	2,010	15	296	12	229	22	166	14
Roselle borough & MCD (Union)	NA	NA	27	549	32	D	55	334	17	245	1	D	14	106	9
Roselle Park borough & MCD (Union)	NA	NA	12	95	13	D	32	146	6	D	2	D	8	57	6
Roxbury township (Morris)	1	D	19	371	37	357	121	2,179	19	114	14	189	26	195	20
Rutherford borough & MCD (Bergen)	NA	NA	5	D	29	115	43	385	18	367	15	D	32	272	27
Saddle Brook township (Bergen)	NA	NA	38	1,388	66	1,027	59	790	22	1,205	10	355	51	657	27
Sayreville borough & MCD (Middlesex)	6	D	32	1,262	57	511	104	1,185	62	469	9	55	21	110	20
Scotch Plains township (Union)	NA	NA	18	88	19	D	45	200	7	43	1	D	29	132	13
Secaucus town & MCD (Hudson)	2	D	19	861	152	4,999	107	3,264	105	8,088	28	1,974	40	644	50
Short Hills CDP	NA	NA	NA	NA	NA	NA	NA	NA	NA	NA	NA	NA	NA	NA	NA
Somerset CDP	NA	NA	NA	NA	NA	NA	NA	NA	NA	NA	NA	NA	NA	NA	NA

1 Merchant wholesalers, except manufacturers' sales branches and offices.

Table C. Incorporated Places, Census Designated Places (CDPs), and Minor Civil Divisions (MCDs) of 10,000 or More Population — **Economic Census**

STATE City, town, township, borough, or CDP (county if applicable)	Real estate and rental and leasing — Number of employees	Professional, scientific, and technical services — Number of establishments	Number of employees	Administration and support and waste management and mediation services — Number of establishments	Number of employees	Educational services — Number of establishments	Number of employees	Health care and social assistance — Number of establishments	Number of employees	Arts, entertainment, and recreation — Number of establishments	Number of employees	Accommodation and food services — Number of establishments	Number of employees	Other services (except public administration) — Number of establishments	Number of employees
	16	17	18	19	20	21	22	23	24	25	26	27	28	29	30
NEW JERSEY—Con.															
Ocean City city & MCD (Cape May)	110	49	195	18	88	5	D	33	D	20	81	131	618	48	142
Old Bridge CDP	NA	NA	NA	NA	NA	NA	NA	NA	NA	NA	NA	NA	NA	NA	NA
Old Bridge township (Middlesex)	276	161	840	76	640	15	75	161	2,554	8	164	102	1,342	100	D
Palisades Park borough & MCD (Bergen)	71	55	129	29	71	13	57	46	241	7	85	80	475	67	226
Paramus borough & MCD (Bergen)	692	217	2,256	110	2,025	23	237	217	5,440	25	557	156	3,372	73	645
Parsippany-Troy Hills township (Morris)	2,523	452	D	187	10,892	19	156	192	3,956	27	D	170	2,611	75	470
Passaic city & MCD (Passaic)	124	60	360	54	3,336	9	74	123	2,848	13	D	115	674	98	301
Paterson city & MCD (Passaic)	382	76	351	117	1,799	15	75	232	8,840	14	210	232	D	210	1,350
Pemberton township (Burlington)	D	12	D	12	13	1	D	24	1,214	NA	NA	27	215	20	D
Pennsauken township (Camden)	732	65	910	50	1,013	4	58	80	1,380	6	43	55	D	69	D
Pennsville CDP	NA	NA	NA	NA	NA	NA	NA	NA	NA	NA	NA	NA	NA	NA	NA
Pennsville township (Salem)	25	19	47	10	D	2	D	41	D	1	D	27	706	26	D
Pequannock township (Morris)	45	44	357	27	491	9	71	54	D	4	126	33	D	46	D
Perth Amboy city & MCD (Middlesex)	135	48	328	39	1,947	6	65	78	1,910	5	39	102	614	92	765
Phillipsburg town & MCD (Warren)	6	32	D	15	96	4	D	53	741	4	D	34	311	26	D
Pine Hill borough & MCD (Camden)	25	2	D	5	12	1	D	9	99	1	D	14	120	9	D
Piscataway township (Middlesex)	550	287	6,976	82	4,089	18	93	97	2,720	12	D	84	1,318	61	1,622
Plainfield city & MCD (Union)	60	38	192	36	467	6	46	104	1,835	5	D	75	613	79	280
Plainsboro township (Middlesex)	170	273	3,563	34	703	17	351	60	661	4	D	47	975	20	125
Pleasantville city & MCD (Atlantic)	124	36	191	21	188	3	D	58	980	NA	NA	35	355	51	D
Point Pleasant borough & MCD (Ocean)	93	53	191	27	92	4	9	48	451	9	96	42	D	50	222
Pompton Lakes borough & MCD (Passaic)	13	27	138	20	47	2	D	36	D	4	30	23	176	34	115
Princeton & MCD (Mercer)	267	137	818	19	229	18	D	32	D	18	533	72	D	67	803
Princeton Meadows CDP	NA	NA	NA	NA	NA	NA	NA	NA	NA	NA	NA	NA	NA	NA	NA
Rahway city & MCD (Union)	257	29	264	26	338	2	D	46	1,440	7	D	53	524	44	D
Ramsey borough & MCD (Bergen)	61	102	601	107	1,035	5	23	66	D	28	307	65	1,069	53	577
Randolph township (Morris)	D	120	501	55	525	17	170	79	762	21	463	42	D	50	285
Raritan township (Hunterdon)	87	86	298	34	579	11	190	112	3,531	12	399	30	329	42	263
Readington township (Hunterdon)	102	77	610	50	497	7	41	27	D	6	D	33	289	31	191
Red Bank borough & MCD (Monmouth)	127	171	1,282	57	909	14	146	146	3,242	18	586	77	1,293	76	434
Ridgefield borough & MCD (Bergen)	39	50	164	26	115	5	23	36	D	5	38	33	286	37	D
Ridgefield Park village & MCD (Bergen)	151	25	267	11	73	1	D	20	94	NA	NA	16	164	27	D
Ridgewood village & MCD (Bergen)	D	134	480	32	649	15	148	193	5,463	19	410	73	678	60	396
Ringwood borough & MCD (Passaic)	D	46	202	27	225	3	D	31	317	10	28	18	146	25	D
River Edge borough & MCD (Bergen)	133	56	254	26	270	5	14	40	646	5	14	18	213	21	D
Robbinsville township (Mercer)	127	49	453	27	561	10	D	25	219	6	33	28	D	35	430
Robertsville CDP	NA	NA	NA	NA	NA	NA	NA	NA	NA	NA	NA	NA	NA	NA	NA
Rockaway township (Morris)	62	62	526	41	657	1	D	36	365	6	D	41	580	28	291
Roselle borough & MCD (Union)	34	10	39	17	445	3	D	28	379	2	D	34	340	38	D
Roselle Park borough & MCD (Union)	D	16	62	11	51	5	46	36	D	2	D	25	219	21	D
Roxbury township (Morris)	48	70	207	52	508	14	80	80	875	9	52	70	1,055	71	394
Rutherford borough & MCD (Bergen)	98	96	703	31	1,622	8	442	67	D	10	56	52	414	50	127
Saddle Brook township (Bergen)	255	59	708	31	1,089	3	D	56	959	4	D	30	523	34	D
Sayreville borough & MCD (Middlesex)	95	103	857	40	444	9	D	52	575	10	203	82	677	94	417
Scotch Plains township (Union)	78	78	277	56	937	11	.73	63	1,025	10	346	38	500	50	208
Secaucus town & MCD (Hudson)	709	92	940	74	2,478	3	D	61	1,408	8	670	90	1,794	39	146
Short Hills CDP	NA	NA	NA	NA	NA	NA	NA	NA	NA	NA	NA	NA	NA	NA	NA
Somerset CDP	NA	NA	NA	NA	NA	NA	NA	NA	NA	NA	NA	NA	NA	NA	NA

Table C. Incorporated Places, Census Designated Places (CDPs), and Minor Civil Divisions (MCDs) of 10,000 or More Population — **Economic Census**

STATE City, town, township, borough, or CDP (county if applicable)	Utilities Number of establishments	Utilities Number of employees	Manufacturing Number of establishments	Manufacturing Number of employees	Wholesale trade[1] Number of establishments	Wholesale trade[1] Number of employees	Retail trade Number of establishments	Retail trade Number of employees	Transportation and warehousing Number of establishments	Transportation and warehousing Number of employees	Information Number of establishments	Information Number of employees	Finance and insurance Number of establishments	Finance and insurance Number of employees	Real estate and rental and leasing Number of establishments
	1	2	3	4	5	6	7	8	9	10	11	12	13	14	15
NEW JERSEY—Con.															
Somers Point city & MCD (Atlantic)	NA	NA	3	5	6	35	69	1,080	1	D	3	6	14	73	5
Somerville borough & MCD (Somerset)	NA	NA	18	318	14	184	58	662	9	D	11	D	38	228	12
Southampton township (Burlington)	3	D	10	150	7	45	33	272	10	463	6	D	7	56	6
South Brunswick township (Middlesex)	NA	NA	50	2,035	130	3,426	77	1,484	93	4,002	33	1,706	44	800	30
South Orange Village township (Essex)	NA	NA	5	24	7	D	41	437	3	40	8	39	21	124	28
South Plainfield borough & MCD (Middlesex)	3	D	78	3,134	130	2,893	126	2,123	53	1,128	17	372	26	205	32
South River borough & MCD (Middlesex)	NA	NA	17	330	22	D	34	118	24	234	2	D	8	D	8
Sparta township (Sussex)	NA	NA	17	212	29	378	47	475	21	244	11	D	38	D	15
Springdale CDP	NA	NA	NA	NA	NA	NA	NA	NA	NA	NA	NA	NA	NA	NA	NA
Springfield township (Union)	2	D	37	825	50	848	78	1,626	13	150	10	101	41	354	31
Stafford township (Ocean)	1	D	8	53	6	D	121	2,884	9	49	11	D	25	167	26
Summit city & MCD (Union)	4	529	14	D	19	D	103	693	7	84	14	120	100	1,144	36
Teaneck township (Bergen)	NA	NA	21	496	54	351	97	638	17	D	18	490	47	480	54
Tenafly borough & MCD (Bergen)	NA	NA	6	30	32	73	42	614	4	D	9	21	28	177	26
Tinton Falls borough & MCD (Monmouth)	NA	NA	16	602	33	483	142	1,901	7	533	11	273	28	408	18
Toms River CDP	NA	NA	NA	NA	NA	NA	NA	NA	NA	NA	NA	NA	NA	NA	NA
Toms River township (Ocean)	3	D	43	428	57	315	393	7,733	32	161	28	593	139	1,184	94
Totowa borough & MCD (Passaic)	NA	NA	33	1,612	58	1,445	82	1,807	22	891	18	794	34	282	36
Trenton city & MCD (Mercer)	4	37	53	1,273	49	733	242	1,208	20	179	31	451	52	D	52
Union township (Union)	3	D	71	2,190	102	1,933	265	5,022	53	774	27	1,191	70	527	75
Union City city & MCD (Hudson)	1	D	42	339	48	203	270	1,209	52	136	13	189	50	D	50
Upper township (Cape May)	1	D	6	44	6	D	48	650	3	D	11	D	20	D	13
Upper Montclair CDP	NA	NA	NA	NA	NA	NA	NA	NA	NA	NA	NA	NA	NA	NA	NA
Ventnor City city & MCD (Atlantic)	NA	NA	NA	NA	3	D	35	301	2	D	2	D	7	32	9
Vernon township (Sussex)	NA	NA	9	46	9	D	27	295	10	96	3	D	13	D	6
Verona township (Essex)	NA	NA	6	191	11	D	42	431	6	D	6	109	27	138	24
Vineland city & MCD (Cumberland)	NA	NA	86	3,864	78	1,429	271	3,918	46	2,557	20	502	69	757	76
Voorhees township (Camden)	12	D	11	388	32	354	107	1,691	14	128	19	1,109	72	575	30
Wall township (Monmouth)	10	D	38	1,111	70	934	130	1,757	22	155	22	294	116	1,409	48
Wallington borough & MCD (Bergen)	NA	NA	9	381	14	344	37	247	6	D	3	D	10	63	9
Wanaque borough & MCD (Passaic)	NA	NA	17	113	6	D	24	430	3	D	2	D	5	D	2
Wantage township (Sussex)	2	D	5	45	1	D	29	279	11	114	1	D	7	D	2
Warren township (Somerset)	1	D	15	1,056	24	612	32	334	6	D	21	D	60	3,010	21
Washington township (Gloucester)	1	D	13	131	39	330	172	3,627	21	282	11	172	55	413	39
Washington township (Morris)	NA	NA	11	397	17	56	14	76	8	107	5	15	14	70	13
Waterford township (Camden)	NA	NA	4	124	10	38	17	154	6	66	NA	NA	6	44	2
Wayne township (Passaic)	NA	NA	52	2,550	86	2,934	331	7,151	40	958	23	257	106	1,757	79
Weehawken township (Hudson)	NA	NA	NA	NA	8	D	30	319	12	78	11	75	24	D	19
West Caldwell township (Essex)	NA	NA	23	1,667	41	1,157	43	912	6	20	9	193	40	207	30
West Deptford township (Gloucester)	NA	NA	32	1,970	39	2,045	31	650	22	660	6	443	21	84	14
Westfield town & MCD (Union)	NA	NA	7	85	23	D	131	1,394	14	97	16	64	67	547	29
West Freehold CDP	NA	NA	NA	NA	NA	NA	NA	NA	NA	NA	NA	NA	NA	NA	NA
West Milford township (Passaic)	NA	NA	16	160	20	D	50	598	8	61	9	22	18	263	13
West New York town & MCD (Hudson)	1	D	40	188	33	D	213	1,141	25	D	4	D	29	D	57
West Orange township (Essex)	NA	NA	22	150	36	350	108	1,394	19	176	19	384	63	367	64
West Windsor township (Mercer)	4	D	15	442	44	491	76	2,638	7	350	22	800	113	1,415	39
Westwood borough & MCD (Bergen)	1	D	17	158	18	67	80	673	12	362	8	147	30	169	21
Williamstown CDP	NA	NA	NA	NA	NA	NA	NA	NA	NA	NA	NA	NA	NA	NA	NA
Willingboro township (Burlington)	NA	NA	3	D	3	D	56	1,613	7	71	3	D	14	130	8
Winslow township (Camden)	4	110	20	407	21	230	69	1,070	15	584	6	26	17	122	16
Woodbridge CDP	NA	NA	NA	NA	NA	NA	NA	NA	NA	NA	NA	NA	NA	NA	NA

1 Merchant wholesalers, except manufacturers' sales branches and offices.

Table C. Incorporated Places, Census Designated Places (CDPs), and Minor Civil Divisions (MCDs) of 10,000 or More Population — Economic Census

STATE City, town, township, borough, or CDP (county if applicable)	Real estate and rental and leasing — Number of employees	Professional, scientific, and technical services — Number of establishments	Number of employees	Administration and support and waste management and mediation services — Number of establishments	Number of employees	Educational services — Number of establishments	Number of employees	Health care and social assistance — Number of establishments	Number of employees	Arts, entertainment, and recreation — Number of establishments	Number of employees	Accommodation and food services — Number of establishments	Number of employees	Other services (except public administration) — Number of establishments	Number of employees
	16	17	18	19	20	21	22	23	24	25	26	27	28	29	30
NEW JERSEY—Con.															
Somers Point city & MCD (Atlantic)	12	25	81	14	69	1	D	70	2,421	8	123	58	995	36	D
Somerville borough & MCD (Somerset)	33	121	685	35	326	3	31	93	3,530	5	D	47	389	39	D
Southampton township (Burlington)	39	10	63	20	211	2	D	8	159	3	D	11	191	22	D
South Brunswick township (Middlesex)	370	426	3,235	94	3,000	17	207	101	1,184	16	304	64	878	70	331
South Orange Village township (Essex)	D	79	D	21	343	10	69	79	D	17	126	48	541	36	122
South Plainfield borough & MCD (Middlesex)	362	136	2,770	59	1,971	14	198	88	1,160	8	D	74	1,208	86	D
South River borough & MCD (Middlesex)	52	25	74	12	213	1	D	13	D	NA	NA	23	111	30	99
Sparta township (Sussex)	D	97	381	41	389	14	64	81	1,190	8	186	41	507	41	D
Springdale CDP	NA	NA	NA	NA	NA	NA	NA	NA	NA	NA	NA	NA	NA	NA	NA
Springfield township (Union)	D	131	1,026	49	1,613	8	41	106	D	8	306	42	601	71	401
Stafford township (Ocean)	55	41	146	37	155	6	25	93	1,833	9	116	57	D	58	323
Summit city & MCD (Union)	196	114	3,515	59	656	14	D	128	4,820	23	685	60	D	65	560
Teaneck township (Bergen)	155	130	4,509	39	257	15	139	225	4,708	16	161	78	910	81	280
Tenafly borough & MCD (Bergen)	61	59	161	19	79	14	59	85	D	20	223	42	492	49	231
Tinton Falls borough & MCD (Monmouth)	D	68	1,001	50	1,348	7	D	87	2,245	9	111	44	552	22	140
Toms River CDP	NA	NA	NA	NA	NA	NA	NA	NA	NA	NA	NA	NA	NA	NA	NA
Toms River township (Ocean)	349	301	1,884	161	1,107	30	181	469	9,438	44	D	223	3,017	226	1,439
Totowa borough & MCD (Passaic)	203	85	1,050	42	958	2	D	63	1,297	5	55	39	484	39	183
Trenton city & MCD (Mercer)	352	116	901	55	1,048	13	D	167	8,112	16	313	140	D	154	1,008
Union township (Union)	430	172	3,194	95	1,874	16	230	210	3,632	15	529	124	D	144	970
Union City city & MCD (Hudson)	147	87	314	53	983	11	44	182	2,242	6	D	126	831	113	281
Upper township (Cape May)	71	35	199	16	73	4	44	33	291	9	28	39	469	27	85
Upper Montclair CDP	NA	NA	NA	NA	NA	NA	NA	NA	NA	NA	NA	NA	NA	NA	NA
Ventnor City city & MCD (Atlantic)	17	18	73	11	58	2	D	21	D	2	D	35	D	36	181
Vernon township (Sussex)	D	30	62	39	378	4	25	30	198	9	D	28	542	37	121
Verona township (Essex)	69	59	D	29	252	7	78	70	1,084	8	121	27	212	45	338
Vineland city & MCD (Cumberland)	276	120	613	72	1,376	11	D	226	5,216	11	60	128	2,165	126	755
Voorhees township (Camden)	142	152	916	47	1,203	7	D	276	6,735	9	217	84	D	59	428
Wall township (Monmouth)	237	179	2,175	74	780	14	273	172	3,231	22	D	65	674	91	506
Wallington borough & MCD (Bergen)	34	11	D	12	119	1	D	21	D	4	65	26	105	14	56
Wanaque borough & MCD (Passaic)	D	15	26	16	D	4	15	13	625	2	D	13	85	15	D
Wantage township (Sussex)	D	14	25	16	59	2	D	13	D	5	25	16	154	11	D
Warren township (Somerset)	91	151	2,824	56	198	10	45	104	791	13	194	55	D	46	D
Washington township (Gloucester)	150	83	404	60	389	16	D	184	3,737	22	366	93	1,519	98	910
Washington township (Morris)	33	71	241	36	241	6	19	31	D	8	85	11	212	14	59
Waterford township (Camden)	D	12	55	14	69	3	39	17	D	4	D	19	D	15	51
Wayne township (Passaic)	382	236	1,763	152	5,693	16	290	291	4,649	31	769	170	2,946	122	906
Weehawken township (Hudson)	52	28	409	16	107	1	D	13	D	7	D	28	520	18	75
West Caldwell township (Essex)	D	83	581	29	331	2	D	61	626	5	D	25	385	38	D
West Deptford township (Gloucester)	73	39	648	41	1,266	1	D	43	1,233	9	98	24	270	32	158
Westfield town & MCD (Union)	119	153	830	51	448	15	132	164	2,165	19	666	74	D	98	558
West Freehold CDP	NA	NA	NA	NA	NA	NA	NA	NA	NA	NA	NA	NA	NA	NA	NA
West Milford township (Passaic)	D	48	185	59	188	5	D	57	571	8	D	46	399	61	220
West New York town & MCD (Hudson)	405	70	167	45	196	11	205	103	2,187	10	26	87	669	80	D
West Orange township (Essex)	D	173	1,161	70	525	10	D	275	5,035	24	623	88	1,532	87	275
West Windsor township (Mercer)	160	400	9,328	59	1,306	23	D	86	1,605	15	109	49	1,177	48	628
Westwood borough & MCD (Bergen)	80	57	303	36	374	8	133	93	972	10	167	29	319	44	D
Williamstown CDP	NA	NA	NA	NA	NA	NA	NA	NA	NA	NA	NA	NA	NA	NA	NA
Willingboro township (Burlington)	39	12	102	12	32	2	D	67	1,776	1	D	29	370	37	81
Winslow township (Camden)	47	24	168	41	247	7	D	69	2,584	6	50	57	842	42	D
Woodbridge CDP	NA	NA	NA	NA	NA	NA	NA	NA	NA	NA	NA	NA	NA	NA	NA

Table C. Incorporated Places, Census Designated Places (CDPs), and Minor Civil Divisions (MCDs) of 10,000 or More Population — **Economic Census**

STATE City, town, township, borough, or CDP (county if applicable)	Utilities Number of establishments	Utilities Number of employees	Manufacturing Number of establishments	Manufacturing Number of employees	Wholesale trade[1] Number of establishments	Wholesale trade[1] Number of employees	Retail trade Number of establishments	Retail trade Number of employees	Transportation and warehousing Number of establishments	Transportation and warehousing Number of employees	Information Number of establishments	Information Number of employees	Finance and insurance Number of establishments	Finance and insurance Number of employees	Real estate and rental and leasing Number of establishments
	1	2	3	4	5	6	7	8	9	10	11	12	13	14	15
NEW JERSEY—Con.															
Woodbridge township (Middlesex)	7	D	65	1,952	153	4,063	496	8,502	168	5,084	58	956	161	4,472	118
Woodbury city & MCD (Gloucester)	NA	NA	13	151	8	D	54	758	6	D	7	217	15	104	12
Woodland Park borough & MCD (Passaic)	NA	NA	21	585	22	216	39	692	4	D	7	560	22	574	9
Woolwich township (Gloucester)	NA	NA	3	43	11	D	8	D	7	170	1	D	1	D	9
Wyckoff township (Bergen)	NA	NA	20	121	31	177	70	709	7	43	6	D	33	146	26
NEW MEXICO	234	4,880	1,389	26,731	1,646	17,448	6,590	90,792	1,384	17,510	764	12,516	2,674	22,709	2,369
Alamogordo city	2	D	10	118	11	D	136	1,966	14	144	10	266	42	294	43
Albuquerque city	11	D	482	10,810	700	8,712	1,885	31,702	257	4,989	276	7,054	981	11,279	851
Artesia city	3	D	10	481	17	D	58	834	12	66	9	166	21	215	17
Carlsbad city	2	D	16	252	21	148	118	1,753	30	398	13	99	43	D	28
Chaparral CDP	2	D	3	D	3	D	15	123	3	D	NA	NA	2	D	2
Clovis city	5	D	17	120	30	297	176	2,391	24	329	14	D	76	461	57
Deming city	2	D	10	D	11	D	65	922	14	113	7	63	20	D	22
Española city	1	D	8	D	6	D	51	903	5	25	5	D	27	225	16
Farmington city	2	D	46	519	103	921	319	4,848	45	595	30	365	112	724	82
Gallup city	4	D	19	252	39	D	176	2,622	22	436	19	D	70	389	36
Hobbs city	3	D	29	479	69	877	146	2,271	74	740	14	213	56	348	59
Las Cruces city	9	148	55	948	66	473	398	6,973	53	1,107	36	450	190	1,638	160
Las Vegas city	2	D	5	26	5	28	68	862	6	87	7	D	28	D	12
Los Alamos CDP	1	D	4	32	3	D	23	346	2	D	11	D	17	281	21
Los Lunas village	NA	NA	4	D	NA	NA	57	1,323	11	711	5	D	45	171	21
Lovington city	2	D	NA	NA	11	108	38	333	29	333	6	D	19	92	14
North Valley CDP	1	D	40	533	41	1,111	36	332	21	366	3	D	5	13	15
Portales city	4	D	12	D	9	D	47	634	11	D	4	80	21	D	9
Rio Rancho city	2	D	29	3,562	24	D	115	2,593	22	336	23	D	72	689	58
Roswell city	2	D	25	95	33	336	211	2,992	39	361	23	D	102	615	71
Santa Fe city	8	110	87	456	81	683	714	7,979	41	486	71	598	194	1,761	229
Silver City town	2	D	9	98	9	81	77	978	8	30	14	D	25	168	28
South Valley CDP	3	44	20	368	21	222	64	621	38	342	1	D	18	116	13
Sunland Park city	1	D	5	26	4	D	11	97	6	32	1	D	6	27	7
NEW YORK	616	42,612	16,475	426,621	28,853	325,663	77,463	905,325	12,312	240,587	11,335	286,744	27,518	539,761	32,033
Albany city & MCD (Albany)	6	D	63	1,500	115	1,234	477	7,460	56	1,531	97	2,817	176	5,374	146
Alden town (Erie)*	NA	NA	12	175	3	D	10	110	3	99	NA	NA	3	D	2
Amherst town (Erie)*	4	D	70	2,364	157	3,799	501	11,724	59	862	71	1,187	344	12,240	147
Amsterdam city & MCD (Montgomery)	1	D	38	1,293	16	123	63	1,214	10	185	5	108	25	120	11
Arcadia town (Wayne)*	NA	NA	5	67	3	12	19	388	4	D	1	D	3	6	4
Auburn city & MCD (Cayuga)	1	D	49	2,185	20	209	130	2,095	9	165	16	399	37	212	40
Aurora town (Erie)*	NA	NA	10	D	7	63	8	34	3	D	2	D	3	36	4
Babylon village	2	D	11	27	14	D	67	332	15	77	4	D	27	D	25
Babylon town (Suffolk)*	NA	NA	601	12,675	622	8,540	765	9,771	208	4,088	60	1,109	146	1,048	191
Baldwin CDP	NA	NA	NA	NA	NA	NA	NA	NA	NA	NA	NA	NA	NA	NA	NA
Ballston town (Saratoga)*	NA	NA	15	262	14	206	27	509	2	D	1	D	15	D	8
Batavia city & MCD (Genesee)	2	D	33	1,215	37	468	99	954	5	110	15	126	34	260	16
Bath town (Steuben)*	NA	NA	3	D	3	D	24	297	3	D	2	D	3	20	2
Bay Shore CDP	NA	NA	NA	NA	NA	NA	NA	NA	NA	NA	NA	NA	NA	NA	NA
Beacon city & MCD (Dutchess)	1	D	18	255	7	D	37	250	3	D	10	D	11	84	9
Bedford town (Westchester)	1	D	13	60	32	193	105	986	10	137	32	249	47	208	56
Beekman town (Dutchess)	1	D	NA	NA	2	D	13	165	4	5	NA	NA	6	18	4
Bellmore CDP	NA	NA	NA	NA	NA	NA	NA	NA	NA	NA	NA	NA	NA	NA	NA
Bethlehem town (Albany)	1	D	17	903	19	120	93	1,960	18	287	11	D	48	839	27
Bethpage CDP	NA	NA	NA	NA	NA	NA	NA	NA	NA	NA	NA	NA	NA	NA	NA
Binghamton city & MCD (Broome)	5	D	49	1,261	61	658	183	2,279	25	508	15	563	88	1,029	61
Blooming Grove town (Orange)*	1	D	NA	NA	5	40	11	51	6	25	1	D	1	D	9
Bohemia CDP	NA	NA	NA	NA	NA	NA	NA	NA	NA	NA	NA	NA	NA	NA	NA
Brentwood CDP	NA	NA	NA	NA	NA	NA	NA	NA	NA	NA	NA	NA	NA	NA	NA
Brighton CDP & town (Monroe)	1	D	20	707	50	680	100	947	7	108	31	397	128	1,903	74
Bronx borough (Bronx)	4	D	323	6,197	676	10,510	3,932	27,777	403	8,332	186	3,924	467	4,033	2,235
Brookhaven town (Suffolk)*	16	199	257	4,906	427	5,465	1,289	16,945	242	4,134	106	1,542	428	2,434	289
Brooklyn borough (Kings)	44	5,485	1,756	18,296	3,457	28,586	9,931	65,979	1,430	19,476	895	9,307	1,530	23,567	4,327
Brunswick town (Rensselaer)	1	D	4	7	8	D	36	726	4	37	9	76	19	D	7
Buffalo city & MCD (Erie)	4	D	321	11,225	253	3,776	939	10,760	130	4,043	117	3,536	271	8,880	257
Camillus town (Onondaga)	1	D	3	D	12	66	78	1,724	5	4	9	78	30	145	15
Canandaigua city & MCD (Ontario)	1	D	14	286	7	151	78	1,149	1	D	6	137	27	312	24
Canandaigua town (Ontario)	NA	NA	11	863	5	13	53	876	7	59	2	D	10	37	6
Canton town (St. Lawrence)*	1	D	3	D	6	116	16	183	2	D	NA	NA	NA	NA	1
Carmel town (Putnam)	1	D	20	115	30	115	134	1,360	20	173	18	120	49	226	32
Catskill town (Greene)*	NA	NA	NA	NA	5	37	19	206	3	D	4	D	4	D	8

1 Merchant wholesalers, except manufacturers' sales branches and offices.

STATE City, town, township, borough, or CDP (county if applicable)	Real estate and rental and leasing — Number of employees	Professional, scientific, and technical services — Number of establishments	Number of employees	Administration and support and waste management and mediation services — Number of establishments	Number of employees	Educational services — Number of establishments	Number of employees	Health care and social assistance — Number of establishments	Number of employees	Arts, entertainment, and recreation — Number of establishments	Number of employees	Accommodation and food services — Number of establishments	Number of employees	Other services (except public administration) — Number of establishments	Number of employees
	16	17	18	19	20	21	22	23	24	25	26	27	28	29	30
NEW JERSEY—Con.															
Woodbridge township (Middlesex)	1,001	518	7,204	175	10,510	19	189	226	4,088	17	376	242	3,604	204	1,079
Woodbury city & MCD (Gloucester)	58	97	415	35	2,237	1	D	85	2,933	6	136	27	440	38	D
Woodland Park borough & MCD (Passaic)	27	52	288	21	118	1	D	50	499	8	70	34	334	34	D
Woolwich township (Gloucester)	102	20	161	12	88	6	18	21	194	2	D	4	D	6	73
Wyckoff township (Bergen)	81	77	195	45	335	12	55	60	1,408	8	D	32	429	37	D
NEW MEXICO	9,754	4,687	44,175	1,835	34,485	427	3,028	4,967	116,557	652	12,259	4,177	82,601	2,962	17,464
Alamogordo city	136	48	219	23	245	2	D	86	2,090	9	D	75	D	51	315
Albuquerque city	4,012	2,040	16,802	647	19,582	191	1,268	1,762	46,890	185	D	1,281	29,238	974	6,645
Artesia city	55	20	163	15	D	5	D	32	821	5	40	32	624	23	D
Carlsbad city	142	47	401	19	D	3	D	77	2,024	6	37	69	1,320	50	322
Chaparral CDP	D	3	D	8	D	1	D	10	D	NA	NA	3	D	5	12
Clovis city	204	68	439	31	894	2	D	112	D	7	42	78	1,927	67	432
Deming city	D	19	D	9	45	1	D	47	D	4	D	53	D	25	D
Española city	38	19	D	6	165	2	D	50	1,496	3	D	38	D	22	D
Farmington city	592	176	1,030	69	709	12	66	223	5,500	14	202	129	3,091	138	1,092
Gallup city	133	35	D	12	97	1	D	89	3,032	5	24	135	D	65	413
Hobbs city	459	56	403	47	691	4	D	95	D	8	D	98	1,703	71	632
Las Cruces city	563	258	D	108	1,993	21	102	422	10,232	20	D	276	6,189	180	933
Las Vegas city	35	28	D	5	11	NA	NA	65	2,719	NA	NA	43	635	23	82
Los Alamos CDP	D	55	D	23	D	3	D	58	1,030	8	D	32	384	23	D
Los Lunas village	50	35	154	9	D	NA	NA	44	1,000	5	D	47	852	15	D
Lovington city	66	11	49	6	84	NA	NA	12	D	5	D	21	391	14	D
North Valley CDP	54	25	D	28	799	3	29	17	304	4	D	13	212	35	259
Portales city	D	15	D	5	D	1	D	28	D	3	D	29	D	13	D
Rio Rancho city	157	101	D	70	D	19	D	144	2,486	15	D	91	2,066	82	490
Roswell city	201	94	954	44	266	7	48	160	3,694	12	107	119	2,281	64	328
Santa Fe city	847	482	2,255	131	873	60	617	441	7,268	89	585	349	7,896	289	1,683
Silver City town	D	29	D	7	18	3	D	67	1,597	5	D	55	734	30	D
South Valley CDP	47	18	D	24	231	1	D	39	543	NA	NA	34	419	31	85
Sunland Park city	22	5	D	7	34	1	D	9	267	3	D	6	119	9	D
NEW YORK	166,315	59,302	588,820	25,642	544,193	5,485	64,810	56,734	1,468,987	11,615	162,729	49,731	679,146	45,646	271,689
Albany city & MCD (Albany)	951	439	8,135	144	3,314	35	657	388	21,421	42	1,209	453	5,990	301	2,332
Alden (Erie)*	D	7	D	11	D	NA	NA	5	30	3	D	7	63	10	93
Amherst town (Erie)*	1,312	437	4,920	290	11,750	47	680	621	11,715	54	1,001	387	7,992	230	1,444
Amsterdam city & MCD (Montgomery)	43	29	106	9	33	2	D	95	2,559	6	14	50	403	30	D
Arcadia town (Wayne)*	10	2	D	5	D	1	D	2	D	2	D	2	D	7	D
Auburn city & MCD (Cayuga)	121	55	356	25	902	5	D	163	3,713	19	434	94	1,291	71	323
Aurora town (Erie)*	23	18	77	16	39	2	D	12	D	1	D	9	D	10	37
Babylon village	144	95	425	26	904	8	D	85	972	8	124	46	847	50	259
Babylon town (Suffolk)*	1,120	373	2,605	317	4,219	46	336	316	4,628	65	568	313	4,390	467	3,018
Baldwin CDP	NA	NA	NA	NA	NA	NA	NA	NA	NA	NA	NA	NA	NA	NA	NA
Ballston town (Saratoga)*	18	42	279	18	261	3	D	14	136	2	D	18	173	23	92
Batavia city & MCD (Genesee)	77	33	157	12	D	6	21	92	2,307	8	D	55	864	47	366
Bath town (Steuben)*	D	5	D	4	10	NA	NA	12	1,082	NA	NA	10	52	11	D
Bay Shore CDP	NA	NA	NA	NA	NA	NA	NA	NA	NA	NA	NA	NA	NA	NA	NA
Beacon city & MCD (Dutchess)	80	37	150	12	59	3	21	30	520	8	89	32	213	28	94
Bedford town (Westchester)	D	118	626	74	472	20	95	88	957	27	323	51	500	70	342
Beekman town (Dutchess)	5	11	19	15	D	2	D	15	49	2	D	16	D	15	D
Bellmore CDP	NA	NA	NA	NA	NA	NA	NA	NA	NA	NA	NA	NA	NA	NA	NA
Bethlehem town (Albany)	126	75	330	47	171	11	41	104	1,881	15	254	69	801	71	339
Bethpage CDP	NA	NA	NA	NA	NA	NA	NA	NA	NA	NA	NA	NA	NA	NA	NA
Binghamton city & MCD (Broome)	245	123	1,466	52	725	10	64	153	6,854	23	D	171	3,078	111	648
Blooming Grove town (Orange)*	20	19	59	8	15	4	8	10	D	1	D	4	D	14	D
Bohemia CDP	NA	NA	NA	NA	NA	NA	NA	NA	NA	NA	NA	NA	NA	NA	NA
Brentwood CDP	NA	NA	NA	NA	NA	NA	NA	NA	NA	NA	NA	NA	NA	NA	NA
Brighton CDP & town (Monroe)	595	168	1,717	59	1,802	19	D	268	7,106	12	206	82	1,371	70	495
Bronx borough (Bronx)	8,856	671	3,704	423	6,830	124	1,391	2,145	98,945	141	3,698	1,735	15,924	1,757	8,242
Brookhaven town (Suffolk)*	1,102	877	9,782	683	4,145	121	670	1,236	22,909	161	1,768	811	10,228	930	4,048
Brooklyn borough (Kings)	15,248	4,346	23,391	1,615	43,561	558	6,109	6,394	184,851	739	7,454	4,809	34,099	4,675	18,153
Brunswick town (Rensselaer)	53	22	D	6	11	2	D	28	D	7	69	23	275	20	D
Buffalo city & MCD (Erie)	2,117	679	16,028	307	6,929	41	438	690	36,513	85	1,916	660	11,300	436	2,818
Camillus town (Onondaga)	38	37	176	19	74	5	14	65	718	12	107	45	D	43	D
Canandaigua city & MCD (Ontario)	65	40	133	20	1,052	4	D	62	2,754	12	77	54	855	31	311
Canandaigua town (Ontario)	66	21	175	11	168	NA	NA	21	382	9	109	16	225	21	D
Canton town (St. Lawrence)*	D	4	D	4	D	NA	NA	7	97	1	D	6	D	4	15
Carmel town (Putnam)	98	117	406	81	623	18	68	115	2,597	24	219	84	716	102	339
Catskill town (Greene)*	43	10	49	6	11	1	D	25	541	4	21	18	180	17	D

Table C. Incorporated Places, Census Designated Places (CDPs), and Minor Civil Divisions (MCDs) of 10,000 or More Population — Economic Census

STATE City, town, township, borough, or CDP (county if applicable)	Utilities Number of establishments	Utilities Number of employees	Manufacturing Number of establishments	Manufacturing Number of employees	Wholesale trade[1] Number of establishments	Wholesale trade[1] Number of employees	Retail trade Number of establishments	Retail trade Number of employees	Transportation and warehousing Number of establishments	Transportation and warehousing Number of employees	Information Number of establishments	Information Number of employees	Finance and insurance Number of establishments	Finance and insurance Number of employees	Real estate and rental and leasing Number of establishments
	1	2	3	4	5	6	7	8	9	10	11	12	13	14	15
NEW YORK—Con.															
Centereach CDP	NA	NA	NA	NA	NA	NA	NA	NA	NA	NA	NA	NA	NA	NA	NA
Central Islip CDP	NA	NA	NA	NA	NA	NA	NA	NA	NA	NA	NA	NA	NA	NA	NA
Cheektowaga CDP	NA	NA	NA	NA	NA	NA	NA	NA	NA	NA	NA	NA	NA	NA	NA
Cheektowaga town (Erie)*	1	D	83	3,607	138	2,887	295	5,395	107	3,548	31	760	88	722	64
Chenango town (Broome)	NA	NA	8	168	5	D	30	386	5	46	2	D	13	49	6
Chester town (Orange)*	NA	NA	8	221	16	103	12	208	9	135	1	D	4	D	6
Chili town (Monroe)	1	D	23	2,077	29	513	58	1,441	31	806	5	D	21	240	23
Cicero town (Onondaga)*	3	D	21	825	30	647	122	3,097	29	1,569	7	31	52	322	36
Clarence town (Erie)	2	D	35	1,595	35	420	109	1,404	13	90	9	48	59	D	27
Clarkstown town (Rockland)*	3	253	75	1,275	135	1,244	471	7,639	46	461	52	1,038	146	929	128
Clay town (Onondaga)*	5	D	29	1,652	46	750	150	3,902	27	1,169	15	286	48	205	46
Clifton Park town (Saratoga)	2	D	22	368	36	584	139	2,598	13	101	20	1,228	86	669	46
Cohoes city & MCD (Albany)	1	D	14	442	9	D	42	365	4	12	2	D	8	D	14
Colonie town (Albany)*A3319	1	D	60	2,162	163	2,147	416	8,008	69	2,007	79	2,015	298	5,702	136
Commack CDP	NA	NA	NA	NA	NA	NA	NA	NA	NA	NA	NA	NA	NA	NA	NA
Copiague CDP	NA	NA	NA	NA	NA	NA	NA	NA	NA	NA	NA	NA	NA	NA	NA
Coram CDP	NA	NA	NA	NA	NA	NA	NA	NA	NA	NA	NA	NA	NA	NA	NA
Corning city & MCD (Steuben)	1	D	8	539	5	14	47	657	NA	NA	8	100	29	375	15
Cornwall town (Orange)*	NA	NA	6	24	7	16	18	219	9	39	2	D	12	40	11
Cortland city & MCD (Cortland)	1	D	28	981	6	D	69	730	6	D	9	94	31	227	23
Cortlandt town (Westchester)*	4	D	18	490	29	271	79	1,334	19	115	13	D	25	D	28
Deer Park CDP	NA	NA	NA	NA	NA	NA	NA	NA	NA	NA	NA	NA	NA	NA	NA
Depew village	NA	NA	22	1,634	32	566	96	2,109	13	111	5	D	32	870	10
De Witt town (Onondaga)*	1	D	113	4,543	168	3,203	210	4,176	53	1,274	50	2,739	131	3,540	65
Dix Hills CDP	NA	NA	NA	NA	NA	NA	NA	NA	NA	NA	NA	NA	NA	NA	NA
Dobbs Ferry village	NA	NA	4	42	7	18	27	173	8	D	3	D	7	D	6
Dryden town (Tompkins)	1	D	12	196	7	129	38	323	8	84	6	65	12	D	7
Dunkirk city & MCD (Chautauqua)	3	D	18	1,545	5	52	40	400	9	88	6	120	11	101	7
Eastchester CDP	NA	NA	NA	NA	NA	NA	NA	NA	NA	NA	NA	NA	NA	NA	NA
Eastchester town (Westchester)*	NA	NA	5	12	24	79	122	2,028	14	108	4	D	52	251	69
East Fishkill town (Dutchess)	NA	NA	18	4,081	23	D	61	413	10	40	5	21	35	146	22
East Greenbush town (Rensselaer)	1	D	9	1,495	7	D	69	1,417	9	246	4	D	26	D	15
East Hampton town (Suffolk)*	1	D	14	104	18	97	136	631	21	85	20	104	26	D	56
East Islip CDP	NA	NA	NA	NA	NA	NA	NA	NA	NA	NA	NA	NA	NA	NA	NA
East Massapequa CDP	NA	NA	NA	NA	NA	NA	NA	NA	NA	NA	NA	NA	NA	NA	NA
East Meadow CDP	NA	NA	NA	NA	NA	NA	NA	NA	NA	NA	NA	NA	NA	NA	NA
East Northport CDP	NA	NA	NA	NA	NA	NA	NA	NA	NA	NA	NA	NA	NA	NA	NA
East Patchogue CDP	NA	NA	NA	NA	NA	NA	NA	NA	NA	NA	NA	NA	NA	NA	NA
Eggertsville CDP*	NA	NA	NA	NA	NA	NA	NA	NA	NA	NA	NA	NA	NA	NA	NA
Elma town (Erie)*	2	D	11	759	9	72	27	236	7	70	1	D	7	19	6
Elmira city & MCD (Chemung)	NA	NA	29	1,823	38	448	86	1,051	12	339	11	254	37	795	34
Elmont CDP	NA	NA	NA	NA	NA	NA	NA	NA	NA	NA	NA	NA	NA	NA	NA
Elwood CDP	NA	NA	NA	NA	NA	NA	NA	NA	NA	NA	NA	NA	NA	NA	NA
Endicott village	NA	NA	12	1,286	16	275	58	539	3	44	7	192	28	229	11
Endwell CDP	NA	NA	NA	NA	NA	NA	NA	NA	NA	NA	NA	NA	NA	NA	NA
Evans town (Erie)	1	D	7	542	4	54	29	294	7	43	3	D	14	D	7
Fairmount CDP	NA	NA	NA	NA	NA	NA	NA	NA	NA	NA	NA	NA	NA	NA	NA
Fallsburg town (Sullivan)	NA	NA	9	400	8	D	34	169	10	290	5	D	9	62	18
Farmington town (Ontario)	1	D	9	343	17	272	19	372	9	292	1	D	2	D	7
Farmingville CDP	NA	NA	NA	NA	NA	NA	NA	NA	NA	NA	NA	NA	NA	NA	NA
Fishkill town (Dutchess)*	1	D	5	48	6	248	52	1,346	12	28	15	243	29	426	12
Floral Park village	NA	NA	11	97	31	200	53	334	19	80	8	D	39	221	33
Fort Drum CDP	NA	NA	NA	NA	NA	NA	NA	NA	NA	NA	NA	NA	NA	NA	NA
Franklin Square CDP	NA	NA	NA	NA	NA	NA	NA	NA	NA	NA	NA	NA	NA	NA	NA
Fredonia village	1	D	6	D	3	D	29	589	4	204	5	72	19	79	14
Freeport village	1	D	77	1,736	75	737	192	1,963	48	1,070	13	D	44	197	38
Fulton city & MCD (Oswego)	2	D	18	1,114	4	38	71	979	5	92	2	D	19	161	13
Garden City village	4	D	17	175	60	676	172	3,366	13	417	17	240	176	2,323	75
Gates town (Monroe)	1	D	64	2,305	48	839	86	1,761	29	1,705	7	122	33	247	36
Geddes town (Onondaga)*	NA	NA	16	504	18	D	34	557	6	148	1	D	9	41	10
Geneseo town (Livingston)	NA	NA	NA	NA	NA	NA	NA	NA	NA	NA	NA	NA	NA	NA	NA
Geneva city	1	D	16	765	6	43	68	1,288	3	131	4	136	24	204	10
Geneva city (Ontario)	NA	NA	NA	NA	NA	NA	68	1,288	NA	NA	NA	NA	NA	NA	NA
German Flatts town (Herkimer)	NA	NA	NA	NA	NA	NA	NA	NA	NA	NA	NA	NA	NA	NA	NA
Glen Cove city & MCD (Nassau)	1	D	22	254	36	140	115	1,192	13	72	15	46	32	176	24
Glens Falls city & MCD (Warren)	3	D	25	1,941	17	233	67	1,048	8	99	14	434	43	1,044	19
Glenville town (Schenectady)*	NA	NA	15	332	12	169	61	1,649	12	211	1	D	23	D	8
Gloversville city & MCD (Fulton)	1	D	34	664	14	184	51	591	7	D	6	D	17	95	8
Goshen town (Orange)*	NA	NA	12	167	18	255	21	234	7	131	1	D	7	32	11
Grand Island town (Erie)	NA	NA	17	1,491	15	D	42	398	8	79	4	24	20	81	13

1 Merchant wholesalers, except manufacturers' sales branches and offices.

Table C. Incorporated Places, Census Designated Places (CDPs), and Minor Civil Divisions (MCDs) of 10,000 or More Population — Economic Census

STATE City, town, township, borough, or CDP (county if applicable)	Real estate and rental and leasing — Number of employees	Professional, scientific, and technical services — Number of establishments	— Number of employees	Administration and support and waste management and mediation services — Number of establishments	— Number of employees	Educational services — Number of establishments	— Number of employees	Health care and social assistance — Number of establishments	— Number of employees	Arts, entertainment, and recreation — Number of establishments	— Number of employees	Accommodation and food services — Number of establishments	— Number of employees	Other services (except public administration) — Number of establishments	— Number of employees
	16	17	18	19	20	21	22	23	24	25	26	27	28	29	30
NEW YORK—Con.															
Centereach CDP	NA	NA	NA	NA	NA	NA	NA	NA	NA	NA	NA	NA	NA	NA	NA
Central Islip CDP	NA	NA	NA	NA	NA	NA	NA	NA	NA	NA	NA	NA	NA	NA	NA
Cheektowaga CDP	NA	NA	NA	NA	NA	NA	NA	NA	NA	NA	NA	NA	NA	NA	NA
Cheektowaga town (Erie)*	759	121	1,458	141	3,767	13	87	170	5,308	19	D	200	4,614	139	1,269
Chenango town (Broome)	D	10	53	10	212	2	D	18	D	6	26	15	277	10	D
Chester town (Orange)*	D	14	30	13	205	2	D	6	D	2	D	4	D	11	D
Chili town (Monroe)	125	46	408	34	494	3	18	56	935	10	60	48	558	46	D
Cicero town (Onondaga)*	221	39	D	48	269	8	D	41	329	26	315	67	1,123	67	D
Clarence town (Erie)	D	91	359	76	489	11	94	99	1,354	20	D	58	1,146	73	384
Clarkstown town (Rockland)*	524	492	1,938	213	3,349	45	249	385	6,836	58	D	240	2,996	247	1,173
Clay town (Onondaga)*	267	68	673	60	735	12	104	124	2,022	12	500	80	1,800	47	D
Clifton Park town (Saratoga)	254	174	1,120	54	614	15	225	123	1,568	17	685	86	1,847	52	381
Cohoes city & MCD (Albany)	D	13	100	9	356	3	D	35	655	5	25	23	155	25	D
Colonie town (Albany)*A3319	944	368	4,195	163	7,436	41	418	234	4,926	36	796	271	5,371	242	2,162
Commack CDP	NA	NA	NA	NA	NA	NA	NA	NA	NA	NA	NA	NA	NA	NA	NA
Copiague CDP	NA	NA	NA	NA	NA	NA	NA	NA	NA	NA	NA	NA	NA	NA	NA
Coram CDP	NA	NA	NA	NA	NA	NA	NA	NA	NA	NA	NA	NA	NA	NA	NA
Corning city & MCD (Steuben)	103	35	242	19	251	1	D	67	1,915	15	D	59	976	31	168
Cornwall town (Orange)*	22	27	120	17	292	2	D	26	D	5	47	17	113	21	D
Cortland city & MCD (Cortland)	83	42	321	14	352	3	26	84	2,664	13	214	72	1,972	50	242
Cortlandt town (Westchester)*	85	88	265	53	331	9	81	80	4,848	23	D	54	483	57	198
Deer Park CDP	NA	NA	NA	NA	NA	NA	NA	NA	NA	NA	NA	NA	NA	NA	NA
Depew village	57	31	343	34	555	3	D	47	696	11	149	59	1,162	54	351
De Witt town (Onondaga)*	516	153	1,656	80	4,949	21	163	124	2,237	12	271	123	2,774	110	1,280
Dix Hills CDP	NA	NA	NA	NA	NA	NA	NA	NA	NA	NA	NA	NA	NA	NA	NA
Dobbs Ferry village	17	42	155	14	24	6	D	39	1,094	11	168	36	412	21	137
Dryden town (Tompkins)	33	24	135	23	93	1	D	25	D	5	6	19	225	16	170
Dunkirk city & MCD (Chautauqua)	D	11	40	7	229	3	D	43	1,102	6	D	22	214	32	153
Eastchester CDP	NA	NA	NA	NA	NA	NA	NA	NA	NA	NA	NA	NA	NA	NA	NA
Eastchester town (Westchester)*	D	117	307	47	244	22	123	97	583	20	285	56	672	123	518
East Fishkill town (Dutchess)	56	96	605	37	376	16	71	72	810	13	126	69	D	51	D
East Greenbush town (Rensselaer)	60	49	1,829	15	72	4	6	46	1,013	5	234	62	806	40	395
East Hampton town (Suffolk)*	176	114	284	152	869	11	12	41	419	59	425	140	1,342	62	257
East Islip CDP	NA	NA	NA	NA	NA	NA	NA	NA	NA	NA	NA	NA	NA	NA	NA
East Massapequa CDP	NA	NA	NA	NA	NA	NA	NA	NA	NA	NA	NA	NA	NA	NA	NA
East Meadow CDP	NA	NA	NA	NA	NA	NA	NA	NA	NA	NA	NA	NA	NA	NA	NA
East Northport CDP	NA	NA	NA	NA	NA	NA	NA	NA	NA	NA	NA	NA	NA	NA	NA
East Patchogue CDP	NA	NA	NA	NA	NA	NA	NA	NA	NA	NA	NA	NA	NA	NA	NA
Eggertsville CDP*	NA	NA	NA	NA	NA	NA	NA	NA	NA	NA	NA	NA	NA	NA	NA
Elma town (Erie)*	8	21	130	15	127	3	D	21	280	8	D	13	226	31	99
Elmira city & MCD (Chemung)	137	52	303	29	1,158	1	D	115	4,378	15	259	63	995	45	245
Elmont CDP	NA	NA	NA	NA	NA	NA	NA	NA	NA	NA	NA	NA	NA	NA	NA
Elwood CDP	NA	NA	NA	NA	NA	NA	NA	NA	NA	NA	NA	NA	NA	NA	NA
Endicott village	185	43	473	16	206	6	104	41	862	3	D	55	D	29	213
Endwell CDP	NA	NA	NA	NA	NA	NA	NA	NA	NA	NA	NA	NA	NA	NA	NA
Evans town (Erie)	D	12	23	16	59	1	D	31	575	5	D	34	360	27	D
Fairmount CDP	NA	NA	NA	NA	NA	NA	NA	NA	NA	NA	NA	NA	NA	NA	NA
Fallsburg town (Sullivan)	74	11	31	10	69	2	D	46	648	4	D	28	73	37	118
Farmington town (Ontario)	35	18	71	11	102	2	D	15	D	12	D	19	375	12	D
Farmingville CDP	NA	NA	NA	NA	NA	NA	NA	NA	NA	NA	NA	NA	NA	NA	NA
Fishkill town (Dutchess)*	61	44	274	19	496	4	24	49	D	6	D	49	823	39	132
Floral Park village	113	96	580	31	1,006	7	15	47	455	9	123	34	329	52	199
Fort Drum CDP	NA	NA	NA	NA	NA	NA	NA	NA	NA	NA	NA	NA	NA	NA	NA
Franklin Square CDP	NA	NA	NA	NA	NA	NA	NA	NA	NA	NA	NA	NA	NA	NA	NA
Fredonia village	41	24	152	9	233	1	D	27	342	8	D	34	935	13	D
Freeport village	176	119	447	73	417	4	D	134	2,110	20	92	95	638	119	581
Fulton city & MCD (Oswego)	36	24	53	8	D	NA	NA	55	1,431	5	119	44	519	26	83
Garden City village	311	567	3,653	73	1,432	10	168	162	3,608	26	486	89	1,856	83	494
Gates town (Monroe)	1,003	45	436	58	1,097	10	D	90	1,784	9	423	92	1,379	57	534
Geddes town (Onondaga)*	69	15	57	8	40	4	17	24	773	6	D	36	D	18	D
Geneseo town (Livingston)	NA	NA	NA	NA	NA	NA	NA	NA	NA	NA	NA	NA	NA	NA	NA
Geneva city	36	27	128	16	269	4	D	57	2,265	4	D	53	836	29	107
Geneva city (Ontario)	NA	NA	NA	NA	NA	NA	NA	NA	NA	NA	NA	NA	NA	NA	NA
German Flatts town (Herkimer)	NA	NA	NA	NA	NA	NA	NA	NA	NA	NA	NA	NA	NA	NA	NA
Glen Cove city & MCD (Nassau)	93	87	335	109	323	3	11	133	3,469	13	D	82	D	81	272
Glens Falls city & MCD (Warren)	71	66	399	21	1,937	3	D	129	4,325	13	283	54	507	32	281
Glenville town (Schenectady)*	20	30	D	27	152	6	14	48	853	9	184	34	448	23	D
Gloversville city & MCD (Fulton)	40	26	137	10	111	1	D	63	1,832	1	D	31	148	23	222
Goshen town (Orange)*	30	21	93	12	41	6	10	31	292	4	38	16	144	9	D
Grand Island town (Erie)	D	38	414	21	80	1	D	29	396	10	D	37	D	32	97

Table C. Incorporated Places, Census Designated Places (CDPs), and Minor Civil Divisions (MCDs) of 10,000 or More Population — Economic Census

STATE City, town, township, borough, or CDP (county if applicable)	Utilities		Manufacturing		Wholesale trade[1]		Retail trade		Transportation and warehousing		Information		Finance and insurance		Real estate and rental and leasing
	Number of establish-ments	Number of employees	Number of establish-ments	Number of employees	Number of establish-ments	Number of employees	Number of establish-ments	Number of employees	Number of establish-ments	Number of employees	Number of establish-ments	Number of employees	Number of establish-ments	Number of employees	Number of establish-ments
	1	2	3	4	5	6	7	8	9	10	11	12	13	14	15
NEW YORK—Con.															
Great Neck village	NA	NA	6	19	42	D	36	271	3	4	NA	NA	15	93	38
Greece CDP	NA	NA	NA	NA	NA	NA	NA	NA	NA	NA	NA	NA	NA	NA	NA
Greece town (Monroe)	2	D	30	1,900	30	236	264	6,346	18	42	19	179	78	478	69
Greenburgh town (Westchester)*	NA	NA	28	1,163	107	1,619	150	2,504	51	1,056	47	1,204	112	1,763	84
Greenlawn CDP	NA	NA	NA	NA	NA	NA	NA	NA	NA	NA	NA	NA	NA	NA	NA
Guilderland town (Albany)	4	133	19	271	32	374	122	1,471	22	143	12	209	67	366	39
Halfmoon town (Saratoga)	1	D	15	287	26	759	61	1,135	9	76	13	214	39	D	26
Hamburg town (Erie)*	1	D	28	1,247	22	407	175	4,013	21	492	6	D	30	D	39
Hampton Bays CDP	NA	NA	NA	NA	NA	NA	NA	NA	NA	NA	NA	NA	NA	NA	NA
Harrison village & town (Westchester)	NA	NA	NA	NA	NA	NA	53	423	NA	NA	NA	NA	NA	NA	NA
Hauppauge CDP	NA	NA	NA	NA	NA	NA	NA	NA	NA	NA	NA	NA	NA	NA	NA
Haverstraw village	NA	NA	5	18	5	D	21	66	2	D	1	D	3	10	4
Haverstraw town (Rockland)*	1	D	5	33	7	15	22	261	8	45	3	D	5	25	12
Hempstead village	NA	NA	19	221	31	297	198	1,830	19	80	13	D	50	266	51
Hempstead town (Nassau)*	14	D	277	3,256	650	3,704	2,032	27,859	416	7,012	176	3,433	728	9,131	488
Henrietta town (Monroe)	2	D	80	4,412	107	2,901	229	6,773	38	1,002	44	2,469	68	681	55
Herkimer town (Herkimer)	NA	NA	NA	NA	NA	NA	NA	NA	NA	NA	NA	NA	NA	NA	NA
Hicksville CDP	NA	NA	NA	NA	NA	NA	NA	NA	NA	NA	NA	NA	NA	NA	NA
Highlands town (Orange)*	NA	NA	NA	NA	2	D	13	56	NA	NA	2	D	1	D	2
Holbrook CDP	NA	NA	NA	NA	NA	NA	NA	NA	NA	NA	NA	NA	NA	NA	NA
Holtsville CDP	NA	NA	NA	NA	NA	NA	NA	NA	NA	NA	NA	NA	NA	NA	NA
Horseheads town (Chemung)*	NA	NA	9	197	9	234	32	282	3	D	1	D	6	15	8
Huntington CDP	NA	NA	NA	NA	NA	NA	NA	NA	NA	NA	NA	NA	NA	NA	NA
Huntington town (Suffolk)*	16	D	136	5,075	362	4,376	944	11,849	164	2,117	130	4,731	647	9,459	292
Huntington Station CDP	NA	NA	NA	NA	NA	NA	NA	NA	NA	NA	NA	NA	NA	NA	NA
Hyde Park town (Dutchess)	1	D	10	66	9	D	51	453	4	D	4	D	15	96	16
Irondequoit CDP & town (Monroe)	NA	NA	14	128	20	79	128	2,699	16	337	5	39	41	279	38
Islip CDP	NA	NA	NA	NA	NA	NA	NA	NA	NA	NA	NA	NA	NA	NA	NA
Islip town (Suffolk)*	11	D	613	15,901	747	11,373	1,137	12,465	298	5,306	107	5,507	429	3,542	280
Ithaca city & MCD (Tompkins)	2	D	32	397	13	98	177	3,072	13	303	29	374	56	554	53
Ithaca town (Tompkins)*	NA	NA	11	973	4	D	11	239	3	23	5	16	6	22	9
Jamestown city & MCD (Chautauqua)	1	D	62	1,733	39	221	126	1,462	12	117	12	194	54	278	26
Jefferson Valley-Yorktown CDP	NA	NA	NA	NA	NA	NA	NA	NA	NA	NA	NA	NA	NA	NA	NA
Jericho CDP	NA	NA	NA	NA	NA	NA	NA	NA	NA	NA	NA	NA	NA	NA	NA
Johnson City village	1	D	8	111	18	99	133	2,745	2	D	8	127	32	206	12
Kenmore village	NA	NA	10	75	7	D	38	396	2	D	2	D	14	D	4
Kent town (Putnam)	NA	NA	6	45	4	D	21	98	8	D	2	D	7	33	7
Kingsbury town (Washington)*	NA	NA	3	23	4	D	19	234	1	D	NA	NA	4	35	1
Kings Park CDP	NA	NA	NA	NA	NA	NA	NA	NA	NA	NA	NA	NA	NA	NA	NA
Kingston city & MCD (Ulster)	1	D	41	831	25	D	212	3,163	20	474	27	556	65	728	51
Kirkland town (Oneida)	NA	NA	6	580	6	63	26	266	3	D	3	18	13	D	7
Kiryas Joel village	NA	NA	31	323	49	111	77	398	9	30	4	13	20	76	32
Lackawanna city & MCD (Erie)	NA	NA	23	312	11	275	50	443	13	330	1	D	10	37	7
La Grange town (Dutchess)	NA	NA	16	167	15	163	37	407	15	261	3	D	15	118	17
Lake Grove village	NA	NA	4	32	5	D	170	4,150	5	D	6	D	11	D	3
Lake Ronkonkoma CDP	NA	NA	NA	NA	NA	NA	NA	NA	NA	NA	NA	NA	NA	NA	NA
Lancaster village	1	D	26	992	13	182	21	165	8	194	5	D	11	76	3
Lancaster town (Erie)*	NA	NA	33	1,094	31	1,232	46	954	20	653	5	D	18	D	16
Lansing town (Tompkins)*	2	D	9	208	NA	NA	15	88	4	D	4	D	1	D	6
Le Ray town (Jefferson)	1	D	NA	NA	2	D	25	480	4	D	1	D	7	D	13
Levittown CDP	NA	NA	NA	NA	NA	NA	NA	NA	NA	NA	NA	NA	NA	NA	NA
Lewisboro town (Westchester)	NA	NA	8	41	17	43	36	278	NA	NA	7	28	15	D	7
Lewiston town (Niagara)*	NA	NA	NA	NA	3	D	13	110	8	36	1	D	6	D	8
Lindenhurst village	NA	NA	37	368	39	D	118	804	21	61	5	D	22	D	13
Lloyd town (Ulster)	NA	NA	13	381	14	99	28	394	2	D	3	D	20	84	13
Lockport city & MCD (Niagara)	NA	NA	37	940	19	D	66	498	17	425	11	137	34	227	20
Lockport town (Niagara)	3	D	17	1,481	15	128	84	1,727	10	255	3	D	21	188	12
Long Beach city & MCD (Nassau)	NA	NA	6	15	30	443	85	629	12	49	8	D	35	411	49
Lynbrook village	1	D	23	112	55	255	108	833	39	262	11	D	50	413	32
Lysander town (Onondaga)*	NA	NA	8	896	7	D	27	280	14	480	3	19	7	23	6
Malone town (Franklin)*	2	D	4	D	5	112	33	470	5	37	NA	NA	12	70	2
Malta town (Saratoga)	1	D	3	D	13	77	28	171	2	D	4	D	13	D	8
Mamakating town (Sullivan)	NA	NA	NA	NA	5	D	25	150	7	383	NA	NA	10	33	7
Mamaroneck village	NA	NA	30	294	29	139	104	758	10	15	13	170	45	232	51
Mamaroneck town (Westchester)*	NA	NA	NA	NA	14	42	31	494	9	147	9	79	19	D	11
Manhattan borough (New York)	31	D	2,063	21,220	7,678	84,273	11,691	148,493	803	18,539	4,540	160,097	7,430	293,087	9,627
Manlius town (Onondaga)*	NA	NA	6	85	21	D	45	1,132	3	D	NA	NA	23	88	23
Manorville CDP	NA	NA	NA	NA	NA	NA	NA	NA	NA	NA	NA	NA	NA	NA	NA

1 Merchant wholesalers, except manufacturers' sales branches and offices.

Table C. Incorporated Places, Census Designated Places (CDPs), and Minor Civil Divisions (MCDs) of 10,000 or More Population — **Economic Census**

	Economic activity by sector, 2012														
	Real estate and rental and leasing	Professional, scientific, and technical services		Administration and support and waste management and mediation services		Educational services		Health care and social assistance		Arts, entertainment, and recreation		Accommodation and food services		Other services (except public administration)	
STATE City, town, township, borough, or CDP (county if applicable)	Number of employees	Number of establishments	Number of employees	Number of establishments	Number of employees	Number of establishments	Number of employees	Number of establishments	Number of employees	Number of establishments	Number of employees	Number of establishments	Number of employees	Number of establishments	Number of employees
	16	17	18	19	20	21	22	23	24	25	26	27	28	29	30
NEW YORK—Con.															
Great Neck village	127	51	156	21	D	9	D	49	D	10	97	17	67	42	148
Greece CDP	NA	NA	NA	NA	NA	NA	NA	NA	NA	NA	NA	NA	NA	NA	NA
Greece town (Monroe)	270	113	1,123	95	599	18	93	201	7,496	24	659	143	2,863	87	474
Greenburgh town (Westchester)*	703	260	1,229	80	1,572	20	210	165	2,929	46	826	106	1,628	115	719
Greenlawn CDP	NA	NA	NA	NA	NA	NA	NA	NA	NA	NA	NA	NA	NA	NA	NA
Guilderland town (Albany)	D	122	806	41	1,138	7	D	167	3,045	15	323	86	1,383	66	472
Halfmoon town (Saratoga)	153	43	552	27	792	6	57	32	303	12	171	37	415	40	D
Hamburg town (Erie)*	189	56	297	57	379	7	33	89	1,440	22	D	109	2,149	69	529
Hampton Bays CDP	NA	NA	NA	NA	NA	NA	NA	NA	NA	NA	NA	NA	NA	NA	NA
Harrison village & town (Westchester)	NA	NA	NA	NA	NA	NA	NA	NA	NA	NA	NA	NA	NA	NA	NA
Hauppauge CDP	NA	NA	NA	NA	NA	NA	NA	NA	NA	NA	NA	NA	NA	NA	NA
Haverstraw village	8	8	D	15	26	1	D	23	456	1	D	23	84	28	D
Haverstraw town (Rockland)*	30	25	58	16	89	NA	NA	48	402	8	148	24	234	21	54
Hempstead village	275	98	D	51	335	13	120	164	2,634	6	D	121	983	106	638
Hempstead town (Nassau)	1,700	1,729	8,649	944	6,779	159	1,063	1,568	25,765	243	4,660	1,105	14,045	1,215	5,790
Henrietta town (Monroe)	387	135	1,679	72	8,084	16	548	63	3,238	18	598	138	3,642	86	700
Herkimer town (Herkimer)	NA	NA	NA	NA	NA	NA	NA	NA	NA	NA	NA	NA	NA	NA	NA
Hicksville CDP	NA	NA	NA	NA	NA	NA	NA	NA	NA	NA	NA	NA	NA	NA	NA
Highlands town (Orange)*	D	14	134	1	D	1	D	3	D	NA	NA	10	430	7	D
Holbrook CDP	NA	NA	NA	NA	NA	NA	NA	NA	NA	NA	NA	NA	NA	NA	NA
Holtsville CDP	NA	NA	NA	NA	NA	NA	NA	NA	NA	NA	NA	NA	NA	NA	NA
Horseheads town (Chemung)*	76	8	57	9	73	1	D	17	1,038	1	D	16	169	16	D
Huntington CDP	NA	NA	NA	NA	NA	NA	NA	NA	NA	NA	NA	NA	NA	NA	NA
Huntington town (Suffolk)*	923	1,510	10,391	581	14,986	98	650	804	14,194	152	1,846	499	6,920	603	3,084
Huntington Station CDP	NA	NA	NA	NA	NA	NA	NA	NA	NA	NA	NA	NA	NA	NA	NA
Hyde Park town (Dutchess)	44	22	96	22	D	7	10	49	612	10	25	41	510	37	D
Irondequoit CDP & town (Monroe)	137	74	457	45	464	10	139	112	1,910	19	110	100	1,508	60	261
Islip CDP	NA	NA	NA	NA	NA	NA	NA	NA	NA	NA	NA	NA	NA	NA	NA
Islip town (Suffolk)*	1,302	981	10,700	622	10,197	83	1,120	865	22,253	108	1,559	648	7,742	736	3,540
Ithaca city & MCD (Tompkins)	372	129	1,017	25	295	12	99	105	1,314	24	155	203	2,774	77	541
Ithaca town (Tompkins)*	44	28	132	9	D	5	D	44	2,188	6	159	19	413	8	D
Jamestown city & MCD (Chautauqua)	D	67	338	18	587	7	D	88	4,646	18	288	72	733	72	447
Jefferson Valley-Yorktown CDP	NA	NA	NA	NA	NA	NA	NA	NA	NA	NA	NA	NA	NA	NA	NA
Jericho CDP	NA	NA	NA	NA	NA	NA	NA	NA	NA	NA	NA	NA	NA	NA	NA
Johnson City village	40	26	D	15	997	1	D	82	4,601	4	81	53	726	35	D
Kenmore village	8	26	78	29	696	7	54	30	665	4	D	34	403	32	D
Kent town (Putnam)	6	17	42	23	71	1	D	21	270	4	D	13	35	20	72
Kingsbury town (Washington)*	D	1	D	3	D	NA	NA	10	99	2	D	11	89	7	26
Kings Park CDP	NA	NA	NA	NA	NA	NA	NA	NA	NA	NA	NA	NA	NA	NA	NA
Kingston city & MCD (Ulster)	175	113	D	43	536	7	197	192	4,054	25	380	127	1,477	72	366
Kirkland town (Oneida)	8	18	85	10	8	5	D	33	771	4	39	36	D	21	93
Kiryas Joel village	71	42	130	19	344	1	D	12	515	5	12	12	D	12	D
Lackawanna city & MCD (Erie)	24	16	84	18	324	NA	NA	40	1,152	5	D	38	494	33	186
La Grange town (Dutchess)	73	40	151	25	109	5	33	64	684	7	146	23	355	31	92
Lake Grove village	35	26	96	13	163	6	15	22	D	2	D	28	767	14	63
Lake Ronkonkoma CDP	NA	NA	NA	NA	NA	NA	NA	NA	NA	NA	NA	NA	NA	NA	NA
Lancaster village	15	16	48	8	28	3	D	22	248	3	D	16	272	16	98
Lancaster town (Erie)*	105	39	482	43	353	3	D	53	1,441	14	132	38	564	32	D
Lansing town (Tompkins)*	4	13	148	11	42	1	D	7	D	6	28	10	91	8	26
Le Ray town (Jefferson)	157	27	390	7	79	1	D	15	76	1	D	29	D	18	80
Levittown CDP	NA	NA	NA	NA	NA	NA	NA	NA	NA	NA	NA	NA	NA	NA	NA
Lewisboro town (Westchester)	11	68	203	37	131	10	37	41	787	10	D	20	182	29	93
Lewiston town (Niagara)*	28	13	19	21	D	1	D	27	D	3	D	23	311	9	D
Lindenhurst village	54	67	221	55	609	7	49	55	D	9	42	80	893	107	308
Lloyd town (Ulster)	26	32	127	10	D	7	37	37	772	5	52	34	351	26	D
Lockport city & MCD (Niagara)	89	66	229	23	538	2	D	94	1,700	11	102	58	D	43	228
Lockport town (Niagara)	48	22	83	25	D	6	45	32	680	9	86	36	631	28	D
Long Beach city & MCD (Nassau)	129	102	203	39	125	7	35	104	D	11	97	91	1,052	94	272
Lynbrook village	112	105	3,726	57	541	7	43	106	1,053	9	138	63	653	93	441
Lysander town (Onondaga)*	21	25	118	20	62	2	D	20	228	8	55	9	86	18	85
Malone town (Franklin)*	D	6	27	9	D	NA	NA	12	D	2	D	20	273	13	42
Malta town (Saratoga)	46	33	283	13	30	2	D	33	615	10	151	29	478	13	65
Mamakating town (Sullivan)	20	17	88	15	46	NA	NA	14	82	2	D	18	78	8	24
Mamaroneck village	D	85	233	83	948	13	75	83	1,121	23	713	75	603	105	486
Mamaroneck town (Westchester)*	45	63	160	20	109	3	D	18	D	5	D	14	161	23	88
Manhattan borough (New York)	70,399	17,504	289,103	4,444	199,782	1,230	26,447	8,106	251,513	4,253	62,572	9,634	206,517	9,778	92,777
Manlius town (Onondaga)*	86	38	158	21	101	2	D	80	1,288	7	412	19	476	21	D
Manorville CDP	NA	NA	NA	NA	NA	NA	NA	NA	NA	NA	NA	NA	NA	NA	NA

Table C. Incorporated Places, Census Designated Places (CDPs), and Minor Civil Divisions (MCDs) of 10,000 or More Population — Economic Census

	Economic activity by sector, 2012														
STATE City, town, township, borough, or CDP (county if applicable)	Utilities		Manufacturing		Wholesale trade[1]		Retail trade		Transportation and warehousing		Information		Finance and insurance		Real estate and rental and leasing
	Number of establishments	Number of employees	Number of establishments	Number of employees	Number of establishments	Number of employees	Number of establishments	Number of employees	Number of establishments	Number of employees	Number of establishments	Number of employees	Number of establishments	Number of employees	Number of establishments
	1	2	3	4	5	6	7	8	9	10	11	12	13	14	15
NEW YORK—Con.															
Massapequa CDP	NA	NA	NA	NA	NA	NA	NA	NA	NA	NA	NA	NA	NA	NA	NA
Massapequa Park village	NA	NA	5	16	20	D	47	388	7	18	3	D	29	119	11
Massena village	1	D	15	1,128	9	68	93	1,421	2	D	5	41	21	170	9
Massena town (St. Lawrence)	NA	NA	NA	NA	NA	NA	NA	NA	NA	NA	NA	NA	NA	NA	NA
Mastic CDP	NA	NA	NA	NA	NA	NA	NA	NA	NA	NA	NA	NA	NA	NA	NA
Mastic Beach village	NA	NA	NA	NA	5	10	16	82	6	D	1	D	NA	NA	1
Medford CDP	NA	NA	NA	NA	NA	NA	NA	NA	NA	NA	NA	NA	NA	NA	NA
Melville CDP	NA	NA	NA	NA	NA	NA	NA	NA	NA	NA	NA	NA	NA	NA	NA
Merrick CDP	NA	NA	NA	NA	NA	NA	NA	NA	NA	NA	NA	NA	NA	NA	NA
Middle Island CDP	NA	NA	NA	NA	NA	NA	NA	NA	NA	NA	NA	NA	NA	NA	NA
Middletown city & MCD (Orange)	1	D	29	685	25	247	133	2,251	8	216	11	649	23	201	26
Miller Place CDP	NA	NA	NA	NA	NA	NA	NA	NA	NA	NA	NA	NA	NA	NA	NA
Milton town (Saratoga)*	NA	NA	5	76	6	D	23	257	3	D	NA	NA	10	D	10
Mineola village	1	D	44	711	57	496	126	1,104	14	39	11	D	74	699	38
Monroe town (Orange)*	1	D	6	32	18	105	55	1,215	7	25	3	D	14	54	14
Monsey CDP	NA	NA	NA	NA	NA	NA	NA	NA	NA	NA	NA	NA	NA	NA	NA
Montgomery town (Orange)*	NA	NA	11	293	21	856	30	384	27	1,489	2	D	11	119	11
Moreau town (Saratoga)*	NA	NA	8	91	4	28	15	108	5	D	NA	NA	1	D	6
Mount Kisco village & town (Westchester)	1	D	15	188	28	309	125	1,766	13	58	16	248	54	410	22
Mount Pleasant town (Westchester)*	1	D	18	245	68	2,299	91	1,546	31	996	30	1,521	53	481	43
Mount Sinai CDP	NA	NA	NA	NA	NA	NA	NA	NA	NA	NA	NA	NA	NA	NA	NA
Mount Vernon city & MCD (Westchester)	NA	NA	99	2,363	91	1,605	227	2,427	37	1,185	9	45	37	D	133
Nanuet CDP	NA	NA	NA	NA	NA	NA	NA	NA	NA	NA	NA	NA	NA	NA	NA
Nesconset CDP	NA	NA	NA	NA	NA	NA	NA	NA	NA	NA	NA	NA	NA	NA	NA
Newburgh city & MCD (Orange)	2	D	47	696	47	378	114	2,067	22	410	12	D	25	195	27
Newburgh town (Orange)	3	D	14	516	40	997	137	1,712	43	767	19	373	56	362	24
New Cassel CDP	NA	NA	NA	NA	NA	NA	NA	NA	NA	NA	NA	NA	NA	NA	NA
New Castle town (Westchester)	1	D	9	60	17	43	51	412	7	274	11	27	27	D	21
New City CDP	NA	NA	NA	NA	NA	NA	NA	NA	NA	NA	NA	NA	NA	NA	NA
New Hartford town (Oneida)*	3	D	14	2,483	13	122	148	3,124	10	118	12	219	47	1,096	19
New Paltz town (Ulster)*	NA	NA	4	122	8	68	37	559	4	D	6	D	10	D	9
New Rochelle city & MCD (Westchester)	3	D	46	744	85	821	252	2,869	46	222	25	331	88	447	202
New Windsor town (Orange)	2	D	30	755	39	812	85	1,076	29	626	10	138	39	311	43
New York city	114	18,553	5,572	68,953	15,124	148,956	34,215	318,004	5,155	112,043	6,215	182,826	11,276	342,605	19,341
Niagara Falls city & MCD (Niagara)	2	D	43	1,662	30	D	261	3,751	33	443	15	449	45	235	44
Niskayuna town (Schenectady)	NA	NA	8	214	6	D	50	1,497	2	D	5	D	24	D	20
North Amityville CDP	NA	NA	NA	NA	NA	NA	NA	NA	NA	NA	NA	NA	NA	NA	NA
North Babylon CDP	NA	NA	NA	NA	NA	NA	NA	NA	NA	NA	NA	NA	NA	NA	NA
North Bay Shore CDP	NA	NA	NA	NA	NA	NA	NA	NA	NA	NA	NA	NA	NA	NA	NA
North Bellmore CDP	NA	NA	NA	NA	NA	NA	NA	NA	NA	NA	NA	NA	NA	NA	NA
North Bellport CDP	NA	NA	NA	NA	NA	NA	NA	NA	NA	NA	NA	NA	NA	NA	NA
North Castle town (Westchester)	NA	NA	10	296	38	600	54	481	32	496	12	89	66	2,244	48
North Greenbush town (Rensselaer)	NA	NA	NA	NA	8	D	28	406	1	D	8	462	20	D	4
North Hempstead town (Nassau)*	4	D	141	3,144	438	6,378	736	10,420	105	1,467	93	1,467	319	3,264	332
North Lindenhurst CDP	NA	NA	NA	NA	NA	NA	NA	NA	NA	NA	NA	NA	NA	NA	NA
North Massapequa CDP	NA	NA	NA	NA	NA	NA	NA	NA	NA	NA	NA	NA	NA	NA	NA
North Merrick CDP	NA	NA	NA	NA	NA	NA	NA	NA	NA	NA	NA	NA	NA	NA	NA
North New Hyde Park CDP	NA	NA	NA	NA	NA	NA	NA	NA	NA	NA	NA	NA	NA	NA	NA
North Tonawanda city & MCD (Niagara)	2	D	62	1,440	27	640	80	804	11	546	3	D	30	113	12
North Valley Stream CDP	NA	NA	NA	NA	NA	NA	NA	NA	NA	NA	NA	NA	NA	NA	NA
North Wantagh CDP	NA	NA	NA	NA	NA	NA	NA	NA	NA	NA	NA	NA	NA	NA	NA
Oceanside CDP	NA	NA	NA	NA	NA	NA	NA	NA	NA	NA	NA	NA	NA	NA	NA
Ogden town (Monroe)*	NA	NA	18	858	14	223	20	86	10	28	4	66	2	D	5
Ogdensburg city & MCD (St. Lawrence)	2	D	7	367	10	146	44	818	5	D	6	28	18	110	6
Olean city & MCD (Cattaraugus)	4	D	15	3,230	11	56	113	1,774	9	87	10	189	29	422	25
Oneida city & MCD (Madison)	NA	NA	9	458	6	D	57	1,165	5	33	6	77	23	344	17
Oneonta city & MCD (Otsego)	3	D	9	259	13	117	83	869	3	55	7	224	20	D	17
Onondaga town (Onondaga)	NA	NA	9	89	10	D	32	305	6	118	4	37	7	51	11
Ontario town (Wayne)	1	D	20	616	14	93	38	261	8	9	1	D	8	21	7
Orangetown town (Rockland)*	1	D	67	4,600	74	1,661	87	959	23	298	35	D	57	358	36
Orchard Park town (Erie)*	2	D	39	2,488	33	377	92	1,987	9	146	11	306	44	251	12
Ossining village	NA	NA	5	D	14	70	78	542	11	55	11	69	35	175	21
Ossining town (Westchester)*	NA	NA	3	9	6	53	7	43	3	7	3	D	5	D	8

1 Merchant wholesalers, except manufacturers' sales branches and offices.

Table C. Incorporated Places, Census Designated Places (CDPs), and Minor Civil Divisions (MCDs) of 10,000 or More Population — **Economic Census**

STATE City, town, township, borough, or CDP (county if applicable)	Real estate and rental and leasing — Number of employees	Professional, scientific, and technical services — Number of establishments	Number of employees	Administration and support and waste management and mediation services — Number of establishments	Number of employees	Educational services — Number of establishments	Number of employees	Health care and social assistance — Number of establishments	Number of employees	Arts, entertainment, and recreation — Number of establishments	Number of employees	Accommodation and food services — Number of establishments	Number of employees	Other services (except public administration) — Number of establishments	Number of employees
	16	17	18	19	20	21	22	23	24	25	26	27	28	29	30
NEW YORK—Con.															
Massapequa CDP	NA	NA	NA	NA	NA	NA	NA	NA	NA	NA	NA	NA	NA	NA	NA
Massapequa Park village	29	45	95	28	D	5	18	31	171	2	D	39	497	27	D
Massena village	35	15	64	11	69	NA	NA	39	912	2	D	47	518	30	142
Massena town (St. Lawrence)	NA	NA	NA	NA	NA	NA	NA	NA	NA	NA	NA	NA	NA	NA	NA
Mastic CDP	NA	NA	NA	NA	NA	NA	NA	NA	NA	NA	NA	NA	NA	NA	NA
Mastic Beach village	D	9	11	13	23	1	D	8	D	1	D	13	118	15	D
Medford CDP	NA	NA	NA	NA	NA	NA	NA	NA	NA	NA	NA	NA	NA	NA	NA
Melville CDP	NA	NA	NA	NA	NA	NA	NA	NA	NA	NA	NA	NA	NA	NA	NA
Merrick CDP	NA	NA	NA	NA	NA	NA	NA	NA	NA	NA	NA	NA	NA	NA	NA
Middle Island CDP	NA	NA	NA	NA	NA	NA	NA	NA	NA	NA	NA	NA	NA	NA	NA
Middletown city & MCD (Orange)	76	50	209	18	245	10	42	98	3,315	7	D	67	616	61	398
Miller Place CDP	NA	NA	NA	NA	NA	NA	NA	NA	NA	NA	NA	NA	NA	NA	NA
Milton town (Saratoga)*	26	16	87	16	120	2	D	23	221	5	23	20	301	13	D
Mineola village	133	272	1,810	70	521	11	54	98	8,511	10	64	60	776	88	410
Monroe town (Orange)*	20	27	86	18	148	2	D	34	D	5	72	19	167	24	117
Monsey CDP	NA	NA	NA	NA	NA	NA	NA	NA	NA	NA	NA	NA	NA	NA	NA
Montgomery town (Orange)*	83	19	170	19	541	1	D	13	200	4	45	18	D	30	170
Moreau town (Saratoga)*	17	9	35	6	27	1	D	9	66	8	27	9	98	4	D
Mount Kisco village & town (Westchester)	103	87	389	53	238	12	78	115	3,472	8	298	80	703	78	334
Mount Pleasant town (Westchester)*	193	172	2,137	76	2,224	16	121	131	8,604	19	160	69	971	72	473
Mount Sinai CDP	NA	NA	NA	NA	NA	NA	NA	NA	NA	NA	NA	NA	NA	NA	NA
Mount Vernon city & MCD (Westchester)	468	102	337	79	986	12	190	152	3,002	17	D	104	692	150	865
Nanuet CDP	NA	NA	NA	NA	NA	NA	NA	NA	NA	NA	NA	NA	NA	NA	NA
Nesconset CDP	NA	NA	NA	NA	NA	NA	NA	NA	NA	NA	NA	NA	NA	NA	NA
Newburgh city & MCD (Orange)	127	61	371	37	793	3	D	117	3,312	8	D	87	1,121	74	549
Newburgh town (Orange)	56	87	774	57	840	10	36	85	1,099	10	D	80	1,183	62	402
New Cassel CDP	NA	NA	NA	NA	NA	NA	NA	NA	NA	NA	NA	NA	NA	NA	NA
New Castle town (Westchester)	44	103	385	28	125	9	D	58	344	29	144	28	363	57	204
New City CDP	NA	NA	NA	NA	NA	NA	NA	NA	NA	NA	NA	NA	NA	NA	NA
New Hartford town (Oneida)*	57	46	305	26	1,341	3	38	84	3,640	7	67	81	D	30	179
New Paltz town (Ulster)*	39	31	105	14	208	5	17	29	493	8	D	31	1,042	15	D
New Rochelle city & MCD (Westchester)	770	229	2,292	181	1,183	27	180	282	5,774	39	426	208	1,949	212	1,021
New Windsor town (Orange)	319	54	1,715	38	667	7	10	81	801	9	D	66	684	58	263
New York city	107,333	26,642	333,026	8,570	283,713	2,479	39,778	23,000	688,569	5,697	82,892	21,506	304,855	21,724	142,379
Niagara Falls city & MCD (Niagara)	223	85	364	39	1,028	7	D	125	3,084	16	186	171	5,873	78	485
Niskayuna town (Schenectady)	D	61	D	26	D	4	D	73	1,654	7	65	27	321	23	62
North Amityville CDP	NA	NA	NA	NA	NA	NA	NA	NA	NA	NA	NA	NA	NA	NA	NA
North Babylon CDP	NA	NA	NA	NA	NA	NA	NA	NA	NA	NA	NA	NA	NA	NA	NA
North Bay Shore CDP	NA	NA	NA	NA	NA	NA	NA	NA	NA	NA	NA	NA	NA	NA	NA
North Bellmore CDP	NA	NA	NA	NA	NA	NA	NA	NA	NA	NA	NA	NA	NA	NA	NA
North Bellport CDP	NA	NA	NA	NA	NA	NA	NA	NA	NA	NA	NA	NA	NA	NA	NA
North Castle town (Westchester)	198	123	768	42	394	11	169	44	660	14	325	44	D	44	177
North Greenbush town (Rensselaer)	D	32	389	16	58	2	D	18	866	4	28	21	328	20	72
North Hempstead town (Nassau)*	1,412	740	5,486	271	3,789	69	754	775	D	74	1,378	324	5,264	465	3,153
North Lindenhurst CDP	NA	NA	NA	NA	NA	NA	NA	NA	NA	NA	NA	NA	NA	NA	NA
North Massapequa CDP	NA	NA	NA	NA	NA	NA	NA	NA	NA	NA	NA	NA	NA	NA	NA
North Merrick CDP	NA	NA	NA	NA	NA	NA	NA	NA	NA	NA	NA	NA	NA	NA	NA
North New Hyde Park CDP	NA	NA	NA	NA	NA	NA	NA	NA	NA	NA	NA	NA	NA	NA	NA
North Tonawanda city & MCD (Niagara)	48	35	429	35	D	4	19	71	521	15	110	55	642	62	183
North Valley Stream CDP	NA	NA	NA	NA	NA	NA	NA	NA	NA	NA	NA	NA	NA	NA	NA
North Wantagh CDP	NA	NA	NA	NA	NA	NA	NA	NA	NA	NA	NA	NA	NA	NA	NA
Oceanside CDP	NA	NA	NA	NA	NA	NA	NA	NA	NA	NA	NA	NA	NA	NA	NA
Ogden town (Monroe)*	19	21	130	22	405	1	D	15	D	4	30	9	140	16	39
Ogdensburg city & MCD (St. Lawrence)	20	9	37	8	D	NA	NA	53	1,733	1	D	33	299	16	112
Olean city & MCD (Cattaraugus)	124	38	277	13	D	5	D	98	2,223	4	40	58	816	33	253
Oneida city & MCD (Madison)	56	25	70	17	189	1	D	67	1,567	7	142	40	434	24	D
Oneonta city & MCD (Otsego)	72	44	339	8	40	5	D	74	1,791	9	46	70	903	37	239
Onondaga town (Onondaga)	39	31	110	30	148	3	4	47	1,956	8	44	24	289	11	D
Ontario town (Wayne)	20	11	56	16	D	1	D	13	97	1	D	16	204	18	D
Orangetown town (Rockland)*	120	149	1,344	68	595	16	92	122	2,819	34	418	133	1,454	96	D
Orchard Park town (Erie)*	102	60	352	55	606	11	D	105	3,020	13	D	46	1,109	51	288
Ossining village	60	56	228	60	1,903	9	91	53	1,141	6	31	44	417	51	154
Ossining town (Westchester)*	29	40	188	12	130	1	D	20	617	3	D	11	119	21	D

Table C. Incorporated Places, Census Designated Places (CDPs), and Minor Civil Divisions (MCDs) of 10,000 or More Population — Economic Census

STATE City, town, township, borough, or CDP (county if applicable)	Utilities Number of establishments	Utilities Number of employees	Manufacturing Number of establishments	Manufacturing Number of employees	Wholesale trade[1] Number of establishments	Wholesale trade[1] Number of employees	Retail trade Number of establishments	Retail trade Number of employees	Transportation and warehousing Number of establishments	Transportation and warehousing Number of employees	Information Number of establishments	Information Number of employees	Finance and insurance Number of establishments	Finance and insurance Number of employees	Real estate and rental and leasing Number of establishments
	1	2	3	4	5	6	7	8	9	10	11	12	13	14	15
NEW YORK—Con.															
Oswego city & MCD (Oswego)	6	D	11	743	8	D	95	1,392	7	34	10	108	31	234	20
Owego town (Tioga)*	NA	NA	15	713	5	69	27	339	5	D	2	D	8	61	4
Oyster Bay town (Nassau)*	18	1,921	236	4,877	767	10,004	1,200	16,468	234	4,282	197	6,785	660	11,032	417
Parma town (Monroe)*	1	D	10	67	5	27	30	237	4	D	3	D	3	5	5
Patchogue village	3	D	16	318	9	D	151	2,146	8	68	7	D	35	308	15
Patterson town (Putnam)	2	D	10	179	12	D	26	222	6	118	2	D	11	55	7
Pearl River CDP	NA	NA	NA	NA	NA	NA	NA	NA	NA	NA	NA	NA	NA	NA	NA
Peekskill city & MCD (Westchester)	NA	NA	17	288	30	277	98	977	18	114	14	D	25	D	25
Pelham town (Westchester)	NA	NA	NA	NA	NA	NA	NA	NA	NA	NA	NA	NA	NA	NA	NA
Penfield town (Monroe)	1	D	21	1,209	32	155	129	2,900	4	8	9	73	66	348	34
Perinton town (Monroe)*	1	D	40	1,125	58	487	64	1,210	9	64	35	338	136	1,838	75
Pittsford town (Monroe)*	NA	NA	21	670	21	124	75	2,001	4	D	18	139	70	737	34
Plainview CDP	NA	NA	NA	NA	NA	NA	NA	NA	NA	NA	NA	NA	NA	NA	NA
Plattekill town (Ulster)	NA	NA	3	22	8	21	9	126	3	D	4	20	1	D	2
Plattsburgh city & MCD (Clinton)	3	D	27	1,555	30	550	115	1,449	20	310	16	307	45	231	31
Plattsburgh town (Clinton)	NA	NA	23	996	19	461	139	2,821	15	165	5	113	20	110	19
Pomfret town (Chautauqua)*	NA	NA	NA	NA	NA	NA	17	197	1	D	NA	NA	3	10	1
Port Chester village	NA	NA	33	874	44	428	140	1,997	15	140	19	227	23	D	40
Port Washington CDP	NA	NA	NA	NA	NA	NA	NA	NA	NA	NA	NA	NA	NA	NA	NA
Potsdam town (St. Lawrence)*	NA	NA	7	123	2	D	32	517	3	8	5	D	10	43	6
Poughkeepsie city & MCD (Dutchess)	1	D	27	2,474	23	D	158	2,246	11	45	18	274	54	502	61
Poughkeepsie town (Dutchess)*	4	D	26	297	40	377	238	4,322	19	605	23	351	65	960	56
Putnam Valley town (Putnam)	NA	NA	4	13	3	D	19	59	6	12	4	D	5	15	7
Queens borough (Queens)	24	2,864	1,294	22,240	2,971	24,171	7,388	59,829	2,214	61,395	492	7,607	1,468	19,466	2,840
Queensbury town (Warren)	1	D	32	1,602	29	212	189	3,525	14	436	12	527	39	213	25
Ramapo town (Rockland)*	1	D	27	136	74	381	151	1,015	14	37	8	D	48	192	74
Red Hook town (Dutchess)	NA	NA	6	15	8	49	36	301	4	24	8	D	15	59	13
Ridge CDP	NA	NA	NA	NA	NA	NA	NA	NA	NA	NA	NA	NA	NA	NA	NA
Riverhead CDP	NA	NA	NA	NA	NA	NA	NA	NA	NA	NA	NA	NA	NA	NA	NA
Riverhead town (Suffolk)	7	D	46	1,096	54	403	350	6,003	25	169	21	338	69	616	49
Rochester city & MCD (Monroe)	12	D	417	19,217	279	3,486	783	7,561	116	3,394	118	4,610	225	3,380	261
Rockville Centre village	2	D	12	138	32	305	122	1,078	13	108	8	D	71	458	94
Rocky Point CDP	NA	NA	NA	NA	NA	NA	NA	NA	NA	NA	NA	NA	NA	NA	NA
Rome city & MCD (Oneida)	1	D	37	1,439	20	148	134	2,050	25	1,554	13	283	40	536	41
Ronkonkoma CDP	NA	NA	NA	NA	NA	NA	NA	NA	NA	NA	NA	NA	NA	NA	NA
Roosevelt CDP	NA	NA	NA	NA	NA	NA	NA	NA	NA	NA	NA	NA	NA	NA	NA
Rotterdam CDP	NA	NA	NA	NA	NA	NA	NA	NA	NA	NA	NA	NA	NA	NA	NA
Rotterdam town (Schenectady)	NA	NA	15	395	17	145	133	2,244	20	1,294	13	D	33	D	20
Rye city & MCD (Westchester)	1	D	3	22	24	172	66	384	7	D	13	201	53	593	42
Rye town (Westchester)	NA	NA	NA	NA	NA	NA	NA	NA	NA	NA	NA	NA	NA	NA	NA
St. James CDP	NA	NA	NA	NA	NA	NA	NA	NA	NA	NA	NA	NA	NA	NA	NA
Salina town (Onondaga)*	3	10	45	1,029	51	1,514	88	1,044	26	420	19	336	39	1,077	36
Salisbury CDP	NA	NA	NA	NA	NA	NA	NA	NA	NA	NA	NA	NA	NA	NA	NA
Saratoga Springs city & MCD (Saratoga)	3	D	22	1,441	28	278	154	2,059	13	242	32	607	91	D	51
Saugerties town (Ulster)*	NA	NA	19	644	15	160	38	403	11	125	9	30	10	D	7
Sayville CDP	NA	NA	NA	NA	NA	NA	NA	NA	NA	NA	NA	NA	NA	NA	NA
Scarsdale village & town (Westchester)	NA	NA	7	27	24	105	83	776	3	11	10	39	42	205	40
Schenectady city & MCD (Schenectady)	3	D	53	2,742	34	354	203	1,642	18	166	19	490	72	D	55
Schodack town (Rensselaer)	NA	NA	11	294	12	D	32	231	5	389	1	D	11	D	11
Seaford CDP	NA	NA	NA	NA	NA	NA	NA	NA	NA	NA	NA	NA	NA	NA	NA
Selden CDP	NA	NA	NA	NA	NA	NA	NA	NA	NA	NA	NA	NA	NA	NA	NA
Setauket-East Setauket CDP	NA	NA	NA	NA	NA	NA	NA	NA	NA	NA	NA	NA	NA	NA	NA
Shawangunk town (Ulster)	NA	NA	8	150	5	D	16	55	10	477	1	D	7	30	6
Shirley CDP	NA	NA	NA	NA	NA	NA	NA	NA	NA	NA	NA	NA	NA	NA	NA
Sleepy Hollow village	NA	NA	NA	NA	4	5	26	48	4	D	2	D	10	D	8
Smithtown CDP	NA	NA	NA	NA	NA	NA	NA	NA	NA	NA	NA	NA	NA	NA	NA
Smithtown town (Suffolk)*	2	D	161	9,171	305	5,129	408	6,078	98	849	64	1,238	249	1,558	152
Somers town (Westchester)	1	D	3	9	18	47	36	535	10	24	6	13	40	221	33
Southampton town (Suffolk)*	10	D	46	269	58	D	303	2,648	31	268	32	240	65	D	105
Southeast town (Putnam)*	1	D	18	981	35	532	75	872	11	65	7	100	36	256	22
South Farmingdale CDP	NA	NA	NA	NA	NA	NA	NA	NA	NA	NA	NA	NA	NA	NA	NA
Southold town (Suffolk)	3	D	36	433	27	D	144	918	12	207	18	169	37	277	45
Southport town (Chemung)	NA	NA	6	142	4	72	28	225	2	D	NA	NA	5	D	3
Spring Valley village	2	D	20	159	52	259	102	1,146	16	635	11	75	42	331	65
Staten Island borough (Richmond)	11	D	136	999	342	1,416	1,273	15,926	305	4,301	102	1,891	381	2,452	312

1 Merchant wholesalers, except manufacturers' sales branches and offices.

Table C. Incorporated Places, Census Designated Places (CDPs), and Minor Civil Divisions (MCDs) of 10,000 or More Population — **Economic Census**

STATE City, town, township, borough, or CDP (county if applicable)	Real estate and rental and leasing — Number of employees	Professional, scientific, and technical services — Number of establishments	Number of employees	Administration and support and waste management and mediation services — Number of establishments	Number of employees	Educational services — Number of establishments	Number of employees	Health care and social assistance — Number of establishments	Number of employees	Arts, entertainment, and recreation — Number of establishments	Number of employees	Accommodation and food services — Number of establishments	Number of employees	Other services (except public administration) — Number of establishments	Number of employees
	16	17	18	19	20	21	22	23	24	25	26	27	28	29	30
NEW YORK—Con.															
Oswego city & MCD (Oswego)	80	46	181	13	46	5	12	79	2,716	14	213	95	1,208	46	219
Owego town (Tioga)*	D	21	D	13	139	NA	NA	24	250	8	D	29	D	13	D
Oyster Bay town (Nassau)*	2,206	1,547	10,934	651	12,356	142	1,048	1,111	21,570	185	2,291	698	8,975	787	4,437
Parma town (Monroe)*	11	9	D	12	68	1	D	5	20	6	D	8	D	10	D
Patchogue village	38	64	208	26	216	3	48	61	947	16	D	74	1,032	78	301
Patterson town (Putnam)	7	22	189	18	61	2	D	12	134	5	143	13	D	22	190
Pearl River CDP	NA	NA	NA	NA	NA	NA	NA	NA	NA	NA	NA	NA	NA	NA	NA
Peekskill city & MCD (Westchester)	98	45	161	50	438	7	50	64	865	13	99	59	511	70	741
Pelham town (Westchester)	NA	NA	NA	NA	NA	NA	NA	NA	NA	NA	NA	NA	NA	NA	NA
Penfield town (Monroe)	152	95	805	61	536	16	90	139	2,302	17	957	77	1,223	52	D
Perinton town (Monroe)*	411	191	2,009	60	1,600	17	D	128	2,045	24	256	70	D	52	405
Pittsford town (Monroe)*	191	122	1,310	24	826	9	430	75	1,243	20	912	41	1,110	36	442
Plainview CDP	NA	NA	NA	NA	NA	NA	NA	NA	NA	NA	NA	NA	NA	NA	NA
Plattekill town (Ulster)	D	7	D	16	52	NA	NA	6	D	1	D	9	425	7	18
Plattsburgh city & MCD (Clinton)	95	84	591	22	883	3	D	120	4,187	11	171	84	1,331	45	223
Plattsburgh town (Clinton)	108	15	86	19	156	NA	NA	51	593	2	D	38	925	24	175
Pomfret town (Chautauqua)*	D	3	D	4	D	NA	NA	5	163	2	D	13	139	3	11
Port Chester village	119	61	187	68	544	13	D	54	883	9	64	98	948	85	312
Port Washington CDP	NA	NA	NA	NA	NA	NA	NA	NA	NA	NA	NA	NA	NA	NA	NA
Potsdam town (St. Lawrence)*	13	7	26	5	D	1	D	16	264	1	D	15	85	17	D
Poughkeepsie city & MCD (Dutchess)	263	132	1,034	38	2,485	9	D	165	5,837	12	226	126	D	96	477
Poughkeepsie town (Dutchess)*	292	91	377	56	638	11	55	146	3,906	17	140	119	1,566	81	460
Putnam Valley town (Putnam)	17	23	31	15	86	6	D	17	87	9	85	8	D	17	D
Queens borough (Queens)	11,679	3,248	13,293	1,654	29,855	468	4,477	5,047	122,646	435	7,623	4,558	40,510	4,645	19,428
Queensbury town (Warren)	116	64	336	46	310	8	40	119	1,715	26	368	105	2,069	61	376
Ramapo town (Rockland)*	250	129	474	60	395	15	56	144	2,176	10	117	58	413	88	1,295
Red Hook town (Dutchess)	35	40	124	12	D	3	D	38	693	11	45	38	366	16	44
Ridge CDP	NA	NA	NA	NA	NA	NA	NA	NA	NA	NA	NA	NA	NA	NA	NA
Riverhead CDP	NA	NA	NA	NA	NA	NA	NA	NA	NA	NA	NA	NA	NA	NA	NA
Riverhead town (Suffolk)	189	118	824	78	763	10	58	173	3,858	41	657	129	1,741	98	442
Rochester city & MCD (Monroe)	2,499	646	7,611	244	8,111	67	664	503	29,731	91	2,591	570	7,114	370	2,717
Rockville Centre village	211	176	653	52	1,693	16	111	217	2,696	24	252	105	1,468	109	450
Rocky Point CDP	NA	NA	NA	NA	NA	NA	NA	NA	NA	NA	NA	NA	NA	NA	NA
Rome city & MCD (Oneida)	152	77	1,333	19	252	3	D	113	2,348	21	204	81	D	72	300
Ronkonkoma CDP	NA	NA	NA	NA	NA	NA	NA	NA	NA	NA	NA	NA	NA	NA	NA
Roosevelt CDP	NA	NA	NA	NA	NA	NA	NA	NA	NA	NA	NA	NA	NA	NA	NA
Rotterdam CDP	NA	NA	NA	NA	NA	NA	NA	NA	NA	NA	NA	NA	NA	NA	NA
Rotterdam town (Schenectady)	126	19	D	26	164	4	D	47	620	9	D	62	823	42	D
Rye city & MCD (Westchester)	113	95	347	26	154	14	154	60	1,281	16	664	38	507	45	260
Rye town (Westchester)	NA	NA	NA	NA	NA	NA	NA	NA	NA	NA	NA	NA	NA	NA	NA
St. James CDP	NA	NA	NA	NA	NA	NA	NA	NA	NA	NA	NA	NA	NA	NA	NA
Salina town (Onondaga)*	218	68	1,323	59	6,344	4	D	52	1,839	10	75	76	1,269	68	479
Salisbury CDP	NA	NA	NA	NA	NA	NA	NA	NA	NA	NA	NA	NA	NA	NA	NA
Saratoga Springs city & MCD (Saratoga)	209	155	945	48	767	12	78	153	3,941	56	1,322	170	3,198	79	369
Saugerties town (Ulster)*	24	22	123	15	47	3	24	20	D	18	97	32	341	26	D
Sayville CDP	NA	NA	NA	NA	NA	NA	NA	NA	NA	NA	NA	NA	NA	NA	NA
Scarsdale village & town (Westchester)	105	89	273	17	133	9	123	99	554	15	203	39	526	48	306
Schenectady city & MCD (Schenectady)	225	148	D	66	1,547	11	117	233	7,968	20	718	182	1,857	104	636
Schodack town (Rensselaer)	49	15	71	18	160	2	D	33	307	3	8	19	271	22	D
Seaford CDP	NA	NA	NA	NA	NA	NA	NA	NA	NA	NA	NA	NA	NA	NA	NA
Selden CDP	NA	NA	NA	NA	NA	NA	NA	NA	NA	NA	NA	NA	NA	NA	NA
Setauket-East Setauket CDP	NA	NA	NA	NA	NA	NA	NA	NA	NA	NA	NA	NA	NA	NA	NA
Shawangunk town (Ulster)	12	9	20	16	25	2	D	15	145	5	6	11	53	14	D
Shirley CDP	NA	NA	NA	NA	NA	NA	NA	NA	NA	NA	NA	NA	NA	NA	NA
Sleepy Hollow village	25	24	47	12	22	5	30	35	D	7	45	23	D	21	D
Smithtown CDP	NA	NA	NA	NA	NA	NA	NA	NA	NA	NA	NA	NA	NA	NA	NA
Smithtown town (Suffolk)*	557	629	3,994	283	3,690	56	991	370	7,912	53	849	250	3,536	290	1,574
Somers town (Westchester)	D	95	537	57	354	6	26	58	1,076	14	145	46	340	29	81
Southampton town (Suffolk)*	185	227	751	305	1,745	17	67	126	1,775	66	699	168	1,565	141	643
Southeast town (Putnam)*	50	72	343	38	242	4	D	56	1,694	17	210	33	390	41	222
South Farmingdale CDP	NA	NA	NA	NA	NA	NA	NA	NA	NA	NA	NA	NA	NA	NA	NA
Southold town (Suffolk)	90	71	222	88	574	4	7	69	1,123	34	318	112	671	65	235
Southport town (Chemung)	D	4	D	5	D	NA	NA	14	276	2	D	15	170	7	38
Spring Valley village	212	71	167	32	217	5	8	65	1,240	6	23	46	D	49	572
Staten Island borough (Richmond)	1,151	873	3,535	434	3,685	99	1,354	1,308	30,614	129	1,545	770	7,805	869	3,779

Table C. Incorporated Places, Census Designated Places (CDPs), and Minor Civil Divisions (MCDs) of 10,000 or More Population — **Economic Census**

STATE / City, town, township, borough, or CDP (county if applicable)	Utilities — Number of establishments	Utilities — Number of employees	Manufacturing — Number of establishments	Manufacturing — Number of employees	Wholesale trade[1] — Number of establishments	Wholesale trade[1] — Number of employees	Retail trade — Number of establishments	Retail trade — Number of employees	Transportation and warehousing — Number of establishments	Transportation and warehousing — Number of employees	Information — Number of establishments	Information — Number of employees	Finance and insurance — Number of establishments	Finance and insurance — Number of employees	Real estate and rental and leasing — Number of establishments
	1	2	3	4	5	6	7	8	9	10	11	12	13	14	15
NEW YORK—Con.															
Stony Brook CDP	NA	NA	NA	NA	NA	NA	NA	NA	NA	NA	NA	NA	NA	NA	NA
Stony Point CDP	NA	NA	NA	NA	NA	NA	NA	NA	NA	NA	NA	NA	NA	NA	NA
Stony Point town (Rockland)	NA	NA	7	119	16	75	28	333	6	21	5	22	20	114	11
Suffern village	NA	NA	5	D	19	142	38	557	6	15	7	D	39	199	15
Sullivan town (Madison)*	NA	NA	6	164	9	105	15	61	8	18	1	D	1	D	2
Sweden town (Monroe)*	NA	NA	3	D	5	37	36	1,180	7	69	1	D	9	D	8
Syosset CDP	NA	NA	NA	NA	NA	NA	NA	NA	NA	NA	NA	NA	NA	NA	NA
Syracuse city & MCD (Onondaga)	7	D	111	3,772	145	2,316	573	7,928	49	1,408	88	1,650	253	5,368	258
Tarrytown village	2	D	11	82	23	1,674	30	304	3	D	10	D	52	592	31
Terryville CDP	NA	NA	NA	NA	NA	NA	NA	NA	NA	NA	NA	NA	NA	NA	NA
Thompson town (Sullivan)*	1	D	5	40	4	D	31	539	6	16	1	D	13	206	16
Tonawanda city & MCD (Erie)	NA	NA	34	909	30	386	57	944	14	329	6	D	17	D	21
Tonawanda CDP	NA	NA	NA	NA	NA	NA	NA	NA	NA	NA	NA	NA	NA	NA	NA
Tonawanda town (Erie)*	4	D	72	3,739	75	1,334	158	1,462	62	2,065	10	376	53	255	50
Troy city & MCD (Rensselaer)	2	D	32	620	30	D	148	1,648	14	253	14	323	36	D	45
Ulster town (Ulster)	NA	NA	13	214	11	86	71	1,585	11	309	3	D	22	1,191	26
Union town (Broome)*	NA	NA	28	2,169	24	157	65	894	12	241	8	D	20	331	19
Uniondale CDP	NA	NA	NA	NA	NA	NA	NA	NA	NA	NA	NA	NA	NA	NA	NA
Utica city & MCD (Oneida)	NA	NA	68	1,708	63	877	180	2,547	16	636	32	2,007	75	2,063	52
Valley Cottage CDP	NA	NA	NA	NA	NA	NA	NA	NA	NA	NA	NA	NA	NA	NA	NA
Valley Stream village	NA	NA	25	92	68	432	203	2,570	137	2,139	11	80	68	699	48
Van Buren town (Onondaga)*	NA	NA	7	149	6	D	21	318	14	482	NA	NA	4	D	8
Vestal town (Broome)	1	D	13	507	31	383	145	3,436	8	169	32	751	40	471	26
Victor town (Ontario)*A3006	NA	NA	44	1,758	28	422	127	2,784	7	60	10	517	17	70	10
Wallkill town (Orange)	NA	NA	29	1,145	28	255	213	3,820	23	466	20	826	47	917	35
Wantagh CDP	NA	NA	NA	NA	NA	NA	NA	NA	NA	NA	NA	NA	NA	NA	NA
Wappinger town (Dutchess)*	1	D	7	287	19	313	51	905	17	107	7	D	15	68	23
Warwick town (Orange)*	NA	NA	11	78	16	128	32	659	9	28	12	19	10	25	14
Watertown city & MCD (Jefferson)	4	D	15	818	21	290	185	3,253	12	487	23	658	61	456	43
Watervliet city & MCD (Albany)	NA	NA	12	258	6	80	27	285	5	39	2	D	9	D	8
Wawarsing town (Ulster)*	NA	NA	NA	NA	4	D	15	96	6	19	2	D	2	D	2
Webster town (Monroe)*	NA	NA	24	635	27	94	102	2,608	12	81	14	569	31	165	24
West Babylon CDP	NA	NA	NA	NA	NA	NA	NA	NA	NA	NA	NA	NA	NA	NA	NA
Westbury village	NA	NA	15	474	33	520	84	1,691	17	422	17	260	31	490	26
West Haverstraw village	1	D	8	31	7	37	31	275	5	16	3	D	11	D	7
West Hempstead CDP	NA	NA	NA	NA	NA	NA	NA	NA	NA	NA	NA	NA	NA	NA	NA
West Islip CDP	NA	NA	NA	NA	NA	NA	NA	NA	NA	NA	NA	NA	NA	NA	NA
West Seneca CDP & town (Erie)	1	D	32	1,430	30	502	153	2,767	23	449	22	D	71	828	32
Wheatfield town (Niagara)	NA	NA	38	1,425	22	376	42	581	18	223	1	D	23	78	15
White Plains city & MCD (Westchester)	6	D	33	338	100	1,551	422	7,482	38	601	73	2,893	277	4,932	187
Whitestown town (Oneida)*	NA	NA	19	1,009	5	35	20	384	5	62	3	D	10	D	8
Wilton town (Saratoga)	NA	NA	9	49	15	557	111	2,347	8	D	5	54	22	D	21
Woodbury village	NA	NA	6	22	9	25	212	5,184	4	3	NA	NA	11	39	17
Woodbury town (Orange)*	NA	NA	NA	NA	1	D	1	D	NA	NA	NA	NA	1	D	NA
Woodmere CDP	NA	NA	NA	NA	NA	NA	NA	NA	NA	NA	NA	NA	NA	NA	NA
Wyandanch CDP	NA	NA	NA	NA	NA	NA	NA	NA	NA	NA	NA	NA	NA	NA	NA
Yonkers city & MCD (Westchester)	1	D	88	2,755	161	1,348	657	9,473	100	2,501	42	1,147	171	1,222	363
Yorktown town (Westchester)	NA	NA	20	184	32	240	176	2,649	19	371	26	455	60	262	44
NORTH CAROLINA	478	20,114	8,953	403,593	9,713	136,174	34,288	446,373	5,393	108,760	3,570	79,833	13,088	168,278	10,140
Albemarle city	NA	NA	35	900	17	114	136	1,604	2	D	7	100	44	271	26
Apex town	3	D	34	1,042	44	753	131	2,427	13	77	14	127	47	251	27
Archdale city	NA	NA	28	2,097	27	516	34	308	12	191	1	D	22	148	12
Asheboro city	NA	NA	63	6,915	33	313	196	2,375	10	86	17	155	83	761	38
Asheville city	3	D	130	4,595	155	1,477	776	11,310	52	885	86	1,395	287	2,170	244
Belmont city	NA	NA	13	399	16	D	58	1,089	7	151	5	D	30	147	9
Boone town	NA	NA	27	576	14	96	165	2,350	4	D	14	161	44	291	49
Burlington city	3	D	92	3,671	81	1,025	367	5,655	28	668	22	389	123	1,207	66
Carrboro town	NA	NA	12	D	13	90	60	703	2	D	10	D	12	D	26
Cary town	7	D	68	1,693	144	1,776	495	9,194	34	495	145	14,961	243	1,505	218
Chapel Hill town	1	D	17	D	27	141	199	2,833	6	37	48	492	127	2,166	88
Charlotte city	32	D	643	21,152	1,540	25,446	2,600	39,240	679	30,683	590	18,683	2,049	66,375	1,372
Clayton town	NA	NA	11	659	8	74	77	1,119	2	D	6	D	30	137	20
Clemmons village	2	D	14	863	23	309	72	746	6	11	7	20	33	D	17
Concord city	2	D	87	4,261	113	1,941	489	9,070	42	486	36	738	105	575	103
Cornelius town	1	D	24	371	41	289	90	1,291	19	126	11	80	82	471	82
Davidson town	NA	NA	5	D	10	58	27	327	4	9	7	55	27	97	21
Durham city	6	D	144	7,368	173	5,168	871	13,896	93	2,413	159	3,435	325	4,740	275
Eden city	2	D	11	1,476	8	325	104	1,094	8	D	6	D	24	134	25
Elizabeth City city	2	D	18	220	19	334	166	2,169	9	58	9	D	51	D	31
Fayetteville city	6	166	63	2,169	104	2,032	825	12,882	82	1,005	67	1,787	252	1,720	264
Fuquay-Varina town	NA	NA	18	728	12	222	105	1,669	5	D	10	71	44	313	19
Garner town	4	D	22	684	57	1,381	112	1,911	19	235	9	164	47	287	33
Gastonia city	10	D	104	5,248	86	848	378	5,774	29	661	18	406	110	D	90

1 Merchant wholesalers, except manufacturers' sales branches and offices.

Table C. Incorporated Places, Census Designated Places (CDPs), and Minor Civil Divisions (MCDs) of 10,000 or More Population — Economic Census

STATE City, town, township, borough, or CDP (county if applicable)	Real estate and rental and leasing — Number of employees	Professional, scientific, and technical services — Number of establishments	Professional, scientific, and technical services — Number of employees	Administration and support and waste management and mediation services — Number of establishments	Administration and support and waste management and mediation services — Number of employees	Educational services — Number of establishments	Educational services — Number of employees	Health care and social assistance — Number of establishments	Health care and social assistance — Number of employees	Arts, entertainment, and recreation — Number of establishments	Arts, entertainment, and recreation — Number of employees	Accommodation and food services — Number of establishments	Accommodation and food services — Number of employees	Other services (except public administration) — Number of establishments	Other services (except public administration) — Number of employees
	16	17	18	19	20	21	22	23	24	25	26	27	28	29	30
NEW YORK—Con.															
Stony Brook CDP	NA	NA	NA	NA	NA	NA	NA	NA	NA	NA	NA	NA	NA	NA	NA
Stony Point CDP	NA	NA	NA	NA	NA	NA	NA	NA	NA	NA	NA	NA	NA	NA	NA
Stony Point town (Rockland)	20	22	57	20	350	2	D	42	308	5	D	42	368	23	D
Suffern village	48	48	229	27	290	4	18	63	D	3	D	38	327	38	D
Sullivan town (Madison)*	D	10	35	10	45	1	D	5	39	5	D	4	24	5	D
Sweden town (Monroe)*	25	5	D	6	17	NA	NA	11	D	3	6	16	D	12	D
Syosset CDP	NA	NA	NA	NA	NA	NA	NA	NA	NA	NA	NA	NA	NA	NA	NA
Syracuse city & MCD (Onondaga)	2,011	482	6,872	146	5,083	32	203	490	24,142	51	1,181	386	6,146	277	2,009
Tarrytown village	118	134	2,484	24	168	7	D	65	1,287	20	D	49	856	39	199
Terryville CDP	NA	NA	NA	NA	NA	NA	NA	NA	NA	NA	NA	NA	NA	NA	NA
Thompson town (Sullivan)*	81	17	41	12	66	1	D	34	2,820	9	D	21	197	21	58
Tonawanda city & MCD (Erie)	119	32	191	29	308	3	D	31	325	1	D	43	821	33	D
Tonawanda CDP	NA	NA	NA	NA	NA	NA	NA	NA	NA	NA	NA	NA	NA	NA	NA
Tonawanda town (Erie)*	307	90	1,784	89	2,887	11	70	167	3,594	11	302	118	1,549	118	D
Troy city & MCD (Rensselaer)	214	113	809	30	292	11	69	195	6,714	13	D	146	1,747	83	538
Ulster town (Ulster)	117	24	D	14	461	4	16	31	1,509	8	D	33	478	33	152
Union town (Broome)*	82	35	306	14	290	3	D	43	584	8	104	57	627	43	D
Uniondale CDP	NA	NA	NA	NA	NA	NA	NA	NA	NA	NA	NA	NA	NA	NA	NA
Utica city & MCD (Oneida)	213	141	1,076	62	2,068	9	291	240	9,877	13	86	158	D	112	2,196
Valley Cottage CDP	NA	NA	NA	NA	NA	NA	NA	NA	NA	NA	NA	NA	NA	NA	NA
Valley Stream village	218	146	1,088	67	404	8	23	140	1,032	14	62	82	1,147	122	D
Van Buren town (Onondaga)*	34	6	D	11	63	1	D	5	D	5	28	22	296	8	D
Vestal town (Broome)	137	37	374	42	1,460	9	D	64	D	11	209	85	1,948	57	362
Victor town (Ontario)*A3006	53	60	762	26	456	2	D	25	D	9	141	45	1,245	27	183
Wallkill town (Orange)	123	46	309	42	365	5	23	98	4,457	13	116	96	1,843	65	552
Wantagh CDP	NA	NA	NA	NA	NA	NA	NA	NA	NA	NA	NA	NA	NA	NA	NA
Wappinger town (Dutchess)*	137	42	170	39	730	6	D	41	417	10	64	36	366	36	135
Warwick town (Orange)*	20	39	145	37	138	4	22	30	185	13	234	19	82	30	90
Watertown city & MCD (Jefferson)	232	58	437	32	899	4	11	167	4,638	14	D	105	2,206	66	403
Watervliet city & MCD (Albany)	33	11	77	4	D	NA	NA	13	65	2	D	20	186	15	72
Wawarsing town (Ulster)*	D	5	D	2	D	NA	NA	9	122	3	D	17	63	7	15
Webster town (Monroe)*	75	69	419	48	348	8	65	70	1,425	14	179	51	869	51	193
West Babylon CDP	NA	NA	NA	NA	NA	NA	NA	NA	NA	NA	NA	NA	NA	NA	NA
Westbury village	52	77	458	82	353	6	5	88	909	4	5	60	D	64	295
West Haverstraw village	23	7	D	7	23	1	D	27	910	3	18	19	141	22	D
West Hempstead CDP	NA	NA	NA	NA	NA	NA	NA	NA	NA	NA	NA	NA	NA	NA	NA
West Islip CDP	NA	NA	NA	NA	NA	NA	NA	NA	NA	NA	NA	NA	NA	NA	NA
West Seneca CDP & town (Erie)	236	78	352	67	1,213	8	55	144	2,079	12	384	91	1,395	92	517
Wheatfield town (Niagara)	54	30	363	36	D	3	D	60	1,323	4	29	35	385	27	D
White Plains city & MCD (Westchester)	892	637	5,517	180	4,127	44	413	424	10,975	41	715	203	3,100	231	2,493
Whitestown town (Oneida)*	35	8	78	5	18	2	D	6	D	7	29	7	184	15	96
Wilton town (Saratoga)	57	30	115	23	141	2	D	28	429	5	150	32	630	22	118
Woodbury village	117	30	55	18	83	2	D	23	110	3	D	41	D	20	D
Woodbury town (Orange)*	NA	NA	NA	1	D	1	D	NA	NA	NA	NA	NA	NA	NA	NA
Woodmere CDP	NA	NA	NA	NA	NA	NA	NA	NA	NA	NA	NA	NA	NA	NA	NA
Wyandanch CDP	NA	NA	NA	NA	NA	NA	NA	NA	NA	NA	NA	NA	NA	NA	NA
Yonkers city & MCD (Westchester)	1,099	257	1,533	174	3,640	24	427	515	11,787	53	1,251	351	3,484	431	1,744
Yorktown town (Westchester)	135	135	D	64	699	20	123	169	2,205	22	D	97	D	102	585
NORTH CAROLINA	47,155	22,855	196,287	11,712	255,584	1,891	16,069	22,977	529,570	3,471	58,185	19,496	358,602	13,716	80,710
Albemarle city	105	43	223	21	375	5	D	130	2,833	7	211	67	1,025	43	D
Apex town	74	158	611	56	1,035	18	115	108	1,352	11	202	90	1,635	68	454
Archdale city	24	20	73	13	D	2	D	25	543	3	20	32	478	20	D
Asheboro city	152	76	358	26	1,532	5	26	144	3,405	10	151	102	1,875	53	296
Asheville city	785	583	3,523	187	4,845	46	183	645	17,386	93	2,218	541	11,795	286	1,735
Belmont city	23	27	94	14	114	3	D	37	D	1	D	37	711	27	D
Boone town	215	91	502	26	182	2	D	114	D	17	109	104	2,322	43	239
Burlington city	419	107	828	57	2,847	17	D	258	6,648	20	489	188	4,010	100	552
Carrboro town	99	84	343	14	84	11	D	55	D	12	126	40	705	27	129
Cary town	681	908	8,770	210	4,814	86	828	498	6,572	65	1,797	372	7,249	241	2,421
Chapel Hill town	381	297	D	51	554	44	296	258	11,207	42	378	220	4,078	105	1,334
Charlotte city	8,759	3,212	43,368	1,405	60,472	250	1,779	2,023	52,599	303	9,732	1,888	40,752	1,352	10,894
Clayton town	63	51	194	20	450	3	8	82	949	11	146	47	852	31	D
Clemmons village	D	72	254	36	202	6	D	44	D	12	220	60	D	36	187
Concord city	464	208	D	100	2,389	22	117	234	3,877	54	2,105	233	6,309	147	749
Cornelius town	200	162	920	50	1,383	14	D	72	D	31	362	75	1,113	64	D
Davidson town	37	73	566	16	436	12	50	35	D	11	125	30	505	18	47
Durham city	1,601	992	D	296	7,132	95	1,652	716	24,293	92	1,366	645	12,968	401	3,868
Eden city	90	28	162	20	556	1	D	46	1,477	6	74	47	683	31	146
Elizabeth City city	160	54	283	27	187	2	D	120	2,344	8	D	90	D	48	D
Fayetteville city	1,622	449	5,635	168	5,681	41	789	674	18,940	55	760	480	10,965	284	1,621
Fuquay-Varina town	36	49	193	27	172	5	13	58	1,063	7	125	68	D	49	293
Garner town	128	76	558	39	358	10	107	89	970	8	108	66	1,528	56	354
Gastonia city	546	171	824	88	3,340	8	D	322	9,083	28	455	191	3,998	145	884

Table C. Incorporated Places, Census Designated Places (CDPs), and Minor Civil Divisions (MCDs) of 10,000 or More Population — Economic Census

	Economic activity by sector, 2012														
	Utilities		Manufacturing		Wholesale trade[1]		Retail trade		Transportation and warehousing		Information		Finance and insurance		Real estate and rental and leasing
STATE City, town, township, borough, or CDP (county if applicable)	Number of establish-ments	Number of employees	Number of establish-ments	Number of employees	Number of establish-ments	Number of employees	Number of establish-ments	Number of employees	Number of establish-ments	Number of employees	Number of establish-ments	Number of employees	Number of establish-ments	Number of employees	Number of establish-ments
	1	2	3	4	5	6	7	8	9	10	11	12	13	14	15
NORTH CAROLINA—Con.															
Goldsboro city	3	D	49	3,089	56	1,306	311	4,058	25	316	18	250	100	856	44
Graham city	NA	NA	24	668	18	200	60	680	1	D	3	D	24	132	15
Greensboro city	5	D	308	16,855	541	7,993	1,232	19,426	207	10,030	175	5,087	618	8,327	455
Greenville city	NA	NA	35	424	70	700	421	6,355	28	242	39	753	186	1,238	125
Harrisburg town	NA	NA	23	484	18	174	36	688	11	110	2	D	18	80	9
Havelock city	NA	NA	4	67	4	D	72	772	6	154	4	D	15	109	22
Henderson city	2	D	24	770	17	337	146	1,940	12	218	10	406	43	D	45
Hendersonville city	2	D	21	859	32	234	232	2,961	3	D	15	225	88	617	45
Hickory city	5	165	161	5,444	129	4,126	454	6,897	39	799	47	1,099	157	914	100
High Point city	1	D	241	12,901	298	4,852	410	4,792	46	955	37	969	153	4,129	115
Holly Springs town	NA	NA	9	116	14	D	40	786	1	D	5	D	30	122	23
Hope Mills town	NA	NA	NA	NA	6	D	44	854	5	179	NA	NA	21	105	15
Huntersville town	1	D	25	706	66	621	161	2,686	15	66	18	140	104	1,099	62
Indian Trail town	1	D	53	830	84	838	91	1,494	30	641	5	5	39	122	21
Jacksonville city	1	D	12	D	26	109	340	5,936	29	250	23	442	91	1,004	100
Kannapolis city	4	D	28	468	25	178	158	1,596	24	905	7	D	51	243	33
Kernersville town	2	D	47	1,805	71	1,100	154	2,305	39	1,812	12	81	60	D	39
Kings Mountain city	2	D	24	2,104	8	D	56	523	9	D	3	D	22	95	12
Kinston city	2	D	22	D	36	575	177	2,274	12	277	10	D	70	496	34
Knightdale town	1	D	8	68	5	D	65	1,378	3	11	4	26	26	500	18
Laurinburg city	1	D	17	938	8	D	112	1,335	6	D	13	117	34	D	18
Leland town	1	D	16	464	14	149	46	820	15	D	1	D	21	84	13
Lenoir city	2	D	52	4,304	27	140	121	1,338	10	193	10	D	42	270	. 30
Lewisville town	1	D	NA	NA	7	D	24	658	5	D	2	D	12	D	5
Lexington city	2	D	55	1,382	36	620	156	2,003	14	171	11	113	55	425	38
Lincolnton city	NA	NA	27	995	14	97	101	1,594	8	83	7	80	43	245	20
Lumberton city	2	D	29	2,098	37	655	210	3,080	17	213	12	163	69	872	34
Matthews town	1	D	34	713	53	549	170	3,135	14	D	23	546	59	231	50
Mebane city	1	D	18	2,803	7	145	111	1,604	9	199	5	D	21	93	21
Mint Hill town	NA	NA	15	53	25	169	48	633	13	71	11	28	34	163	15
Monroe city	1	D	89	6,657	76	1,328	230	3,076	25	229	21	182	87	408	43
Mooresville town	2	D	73	2,277	81	690	226	3,734	9	D	24	219	103	499	64
Morganton city	2	D	39	4,095	21	143	148	1,728	9	D	7	D	56	298	30
Morrisville town	NA	NA	35	670	82	3,417	75	1,267	44	982	34	796	29	D	43
Mount Airy city	2	D	30	1,370	22	378	148	1,707	16	358	13	108	39	270	33
Mount Holly city	4	D	17	2,348	8	21	20	255	10	100	2	D	13	59	13
Murraysville CDP	NA	NA	NA	NA	5	11	18	182	10	35	NA	NA	4	14	10
New Bern city	1	D	34	2,008	33	D	248	3,073	17	230	20	332	86	470	51
Newton city	NA	NA	53	2,733	14	D	67	609	10	676	7	54	32	264	16
Pinehurst village	NA	NA	5	19	10	44	33	156	1	D	3	D	36	D	18
Piney Green CDP	NA	NA	NA	NA	1	D	11	35	1	D	1	D	NA	NA	7
Raleigh city	31	D	267	5,229	570	8,627	1,698	27,148	162	3,908	299	8,744	930	15,869	735
Reidsville city	2	D	25	2,219	16	188	107	1,297	8	36	5	46	44	240	15
Roanoke Rapids city	4	D	13	752	7	D	125	1,633	5	D	10	92	36	D	29
Rocky Mount city	NA	NA	43	4,002	74	1,406	331	4,143	33	791	32	D	117	1,852	77
Salisbury city	1	D	66	1,904	47	945	203	2,948	20	1,111	19	D	89	457	44
Sanford city	4	D	44	4,754	22	D	192	2,658	8	D	12	D	63	D	38
Shelby city	2	D	35	1,098	20	D	184	2,242	14	D	15	198	66	471	55
Smithfield town	1	D	23	1,304	14	141	193	2,621	5	D	12	97	67	367	29
Southern Pines town	NA	NA	15	395	5	15	101	1,759	6	151	13	133	40	256	40
Spring Lake town	NA	NA	3	23	6	29	50	743	NA	NA	1	D	13	D	15
Stallings town	2	D	27	566	14	46	38	419	6	19	NA	NA	12	29	16
Statesville city	2	D	89	4,471	53	439	217	2,759	21	667	15	139	83	503	42
Summerfield town	NA	NA	4	D	7	D	18	163	2	D	1	D	8	26	14
Tarboro town	1	D	19	2,159	6	D	70	907	8	80	12	D	26	132	18
Thomasville city	NA	NA	86	2,096	30	453	128	1,458	22	1,196	4	28	37	174	24
Wake Forest town	1	D	14	111	26	139	87	1,725	10	17	9	74	44	187	33
Waxhaw town	NA	NA	5	14	9	42	36	564	3	9	1	D	25	76	9
Wilmington city	6	D	91	3,247	139	1,191	764	10,389	96	1,246	97	2,520	325	2,224	249
Wilson city	1	D	59	6,692	76	742	263	3,268	34	712	17	231	94	D	65
Winston-Salem city	4	D	200	8,322	239	3,943	1,008	15,129	85	1,787	85	1,783	460	9,908	293
NORTH DAKOTA	124	D	745	23,541	1,430	18,880	3,185	47,186	1,641	18,847	361	7,052	1,755	17,199	912
Bismarck city	11	D	57	824	115	1,967	357	6,779	98	2,605	55	815	219	2,201	122
Dickinson city	2	D	16	360	40	526	142	1,929	58	357	15	D	58	432	34
Fargo city	3	D	126	6,087	251	5,114	518	11,065	153	2,054	81	3,026	352	7,231	238
Grand Forks city	3	289	42	2,015	59	965	279	5,654	72	1,142	24	D	110	939	73
Jamestown city	2	D	19	644	21	342	87	1,250	32	D	12	D	44	391	24
Mandan city	2	D	26	824	20	D	82	1,085	46	217	6	D	38	275	36
Minot city	4	D	26	346	68	1,285	250	5,160	88	742	22	480	122	1,564	68
West Fargo city	1	D	42	2,294	41	477	91	1,133	42	682	8	D	38	253	21
Williston city	3	D	22	199	59	806	83	1,594	82	1,107	11	D	53	362	50
OHIO	627	26,222	14,482	627,124	11,744	182,791	36,531	549,152	6,966	158,891	3,956	90,083	17,443	241,719	9,932
Akron city	22	D	269	8,672	217	2,998	612	7,731	109	1,951	92	1,898	237	3,016	167
Alliance city	1	D	39	1,669	17	236	112	1,959	5	28	9	138	44	229	17
Amherst city	NA	NA	6	648	7	40	58	886	3	6	2	D	20	127	10
Ashland city	NA	NA	45	2,134	21	299	84	1,440	14	105	8	479	38	236	18
Ashtabula city	3	D	24	1,221	11	140	101	1,565	7	100	8	112	36	165	20
Athens city	2	D	20	97	9	D	107	1,922	4	D	18	132	45	287	44
Aurora city	NA	NA	24	1,254	27	1,180	102	2,178	8	42	5	31	29	93	11
Austintown CDP	NA	NA	19	477	35	273	112	2,111	15	308	5	25	46	257	23
Avon city	1	D	28	1,125	34	586	86	2,469	11	281	4	D	37	149	12
Avon Lake city	1	D	31	2,880	13	42	36	596	9	D	7	62	29	204	17
Barberton city	NA	NA	50	1,938	22	523	71	780	7	37	4	53	27	128	6
Bay Village city	NA	NA	8	55	18	134	12	230	2	D	3	D	16	D	10
Beachwood city	NA	NA	23	227	54	413	156	2,710	14	D	31	635	143	2,749	108

1 Merchant wholesalers, except manufacturers' sales branches and offices.

STATE / City, town, township, borough, or CDP (county if applicable)	Real estate and rental and leasing — Number of employees	Professional, scientific, and technical services — Number of establishments	Professional, scientific, and technical services — Number of employees	Administration and support and waste management and mediation services — Number of establishments	Administration and support and waste management and mediation services — Number of employees	Educational services — Number of establishments	Educational services — Number of employees	Health care and social assistance — Number of establishments	Health care and social assistance — Number of employees	Arts, entertainment, and recreation — Number of establishments	Arts, entertainment, and recreation — Number of employees	Accommodation and food services — Number of establishments	Accommodation and food services — Number of employees	Other services (except public administration) — Number of establishments	Other services (except public administration) — Number of employees
	16	17	18	19	20	21	22	23	24	25	26	27	28	29	30
NORTH CAROLINA—Con.															
Goldsboro city	216	104	614	29	1,135	9	D	186	5,477	17	D	144	2,625	85	D
Graham city	60	48	153	12	186	3	D	32	366	6	D	40	D	30	D
Greensboro city	3,181	937	D	427	27,157	82	876	879	23,135	107	2,247	789	16,835	516	3,316
Greenville city	546	229	1,225	82	1,882	26	442	390	14,056	29	506	288	6,910	121	762
Harrisburg town	8	30	77	24	310	1	D	32	502	13	D	36	453	39	288
Havelock city	64	33	573	14	152	3	D	22	D	3	D	51	899	27	110
Henderson city	196	41	184	15	107	5	D	86	2,323	8	169	60	D	31	140
Hendersonville city	107	96	460	34	322	4	D	169	4,238	10	D	122	1,998	80	473
Hickory city	324	199	1,198	80	2,630	16	114	266	D	24	592	219	4,748	118	912
High Point city	754	274	D	121	3,072	24	D	290	8,553	29	455	229	D	185	1,311
Holly Springs town	D	81	224	30	361	6	D	67	498	8	D	39	575	29	106
Hope Mills town	66	19	149	6	49	3	D	26	502	8	80	43	D	19	D
Huntersville town	160	183	856	88	829	22	129	152	1,482	28	703	99	2,246	75	D
Indian Trail town	55	59	174	69	727	5	7	43	337	11	114	55	887	62	D
Jacksonville city	390	154	1,239	55	1,595	13	160	200	4,778	21	280	219	4,593	121	873
Kannapolis city	142	57	523	23	157	3	D	62	1,379	11	D	74	D	51	D
Kernersville town	125	81	468	51	1,285	6	D	77	1,238	16	229	81	D	65	421
Kings Mountain city	22	21	165	8	127	1	D	33	D	2	D	35	477	7	D
Kinston city	D	46	400	28	1,053	6	D	141	3,568	12	D	75	1,521	56	D
Knightdale town	73	40	393	20	335	6	15	36	571	3	D	46	914	24	D
Laurinburg city	33	25	D	17	782	3	D	97	2,029	5	55	53	D	26	91
Leland town	23	27	109	11	89	2	D	34	503	5	20	39	D	14	D
Lenoir city	87	42	185	12	294	3	24	76	1,496	5	71	72	D	36	D
Lewisville town	10	26	42	22	48	2	D	12	130	9	D	12	214	14	D
Lexington city	D	69	333	17	490	5	32	82	D	6	D	87	1,620	49	231
Lincolnton city	52	26	134	13	445	NA	NA	70	D	5	74	52	1,004	42	129
Lumberton city	129	69	356	21	1,582	6	73	143	5,235	9	D	104	2,014	37	D
Matthews town	236	144	690	62	404	20	D	137	3,056	27	603	104	2,147	73	321
Mebane city	61	22	120	6	D	3	19	30	505	5	D	40	839	12	71
Mint Hill town	D	59	404	32	494	9	55	37	391	6	118	25	372	31	D
Monroe city	135	90	422	42	784	2	D	149	3,553	10	113	105	1,927	88	418
Mooresville town	191	147	1,618	70	1,683	19	220	158	2,542	45	1,056	159	2,948	87	539
Morganton city	82	67	325	17	558	4	D	117	2,744	14	68	80	1,484	43	D
Morrisville town	441	162	4,435	79	2,899	15	156	50	808	7	53	87	1,337	33	260
Mount Airy city	128	37	182	19	454	1	D	78	2,054	10	78	84	1,387	32	218
Mount Holly city	36	21	89	11	207	1	D	19	D	3	D	17	D	11	D
Murraysville CDP	24	12	39	13	56	NA	NA	6	64	2	D	9	140	8	30
New Bern city	223	112	719	43	880	9	D	171	4,923	16	D	123	2,528	75	452
Newton city	37	33	125	12	709	1	D	37	963	4	32	23	264	25	D
Pinehurst village	D	62	176	18	94	2	D	71	D	6	D	27	1,498	13	38
Piney Green CDP	18	3	5	7	40	NA	NA	1	D	NA	NA	5	35	5	D
Raleigh city	5,229	2,206	23,220	843	25,760	155	1,172	1,501	31,918	185	6,675	1,145	24,150	959	7,601
Reidsville city	39	25	171	25	221	2	D	82	1,325	9	103	58	896	39	165
Roanoke Rapids city	118	32	179	22	516	3	4	69	1,131	7	33	57	1,127	39	252
Rocky Mount city	357	125	803	74	D	10	107	232	4,199	22	193	146	3,442	105	601
Salisbury city	205	97	529	44	911	10	D	187	6,931	21	282	138	2,714	57	393
Sanford city	144	66	D	26	1,292	9	D	139	2,204	9	126	92	1,665	62	341
Shelby city	216	82	499	31	596	6	D	151	3,870	9	D	91	1,462	58	355
Smithfield town	222	64	248	24	529	6	15	91	2,495	7	D	73	1,514	34	162
Southern Pines town	107	70	787	24	363	9	63	88	D	22	418	74	1,476	40	276
Spring Lake town	60	14	162	5	D	2	D	10	98	NA	NA	49	790	23	90
Stallings town	18	32	100	22	159	3	D	8	D	8	62	18	251	32	D
Statesville city	194	87	627	47	1,701	4	D	185	2,735	10	152	132	2,419	72	448
Summerfield town	99	33	62	20	125	3	6	13	138	2	D	13	205	4	6
Tarboro town	48	24	94	6	D	NA	NA	53	D	6	D	32	D	16	D
Thomasville city	D	44	141	27	529	2	D	43	D	8	D	72	D	46	D
Wake Forest town	76	117	594	43	205	20	135	96	D	20	279	57	1,050	51	D
Waxhaw town	D	38	114	16	36	2	D	18	D	5	7	29	386	17	105
Wilmington city	1,574	654	4,462	215	3,389	34	314	616	10,095	67	1,031	440	9,326	283	1,821
Wilson city	229	98	D	45	1,989	10	D	185	4,946	18	215	124	2,521	86	512
Winston-Salem city	1,575	674	5,725	296	10,224	45	289	625	19,638	86	1,624	539	11,157	367	2,256
NORTH DAKOTA	5,157	1,722	13,715	990	12,715	85	749	1,856	56,639	421	4,901	1,935	35,698	1,716	9,232
Bismarck city	389	277	1,912	120	D	12	D	257	10,532	39	D	162	4,873	236	D
Dickinson city	159	61	395	36	297	3	12	83	1,863	14	D	65	1,281	61	D
Fargo city	1,613	417	5,297	207	4,884	26	270	368	14,344	72	1,497	316	8,386	291	2,044
Grand Forks city	481	118	1,419	87	1,211	13	126	146	6,502	39	D	174	4,076	118	731
Jamestown city	72	27	149	21	D	2	D	55	2,405	11	102	45	855	45	D
Mandan city	D	50	D	23	D	3	D	53	D	9	D	39	D	48	238
Minot city	D	120	702	58	829	9	D	131	D	26	406	150	3,741	108	D
West Fargo city	D	39	D	36	406	3	3	48	729	10	39	38	D	60	390
Williston city	484	76	469	30	508	1	D	55	1,294	10	86	59	1,468	51	D
OHIO	60,966	23,961	233,876	13,081	362,944	1,943	15,568	28,237	798,770	3,810	60,704	23,432	437,293	18,851	127,366
Akron city	1,062	452	5,794	205	4,805	29	291	504	24,064	52	1,160	407	5,634	357	2,147
Alliance city	79	32	161	12	438	3	11	84	2,063	4	D	66	1,261	58	352
Amherst city	43	25	121	11	71	2	D	43	584	8	59	45	956	32	189
Ashland city	99	36	745	20	240	1	D	83	1,825	8	48	45	830	53	327
Ashtabula city	76	33	191	21	841	3	48	83	2,394	10	D	50	659	43	186
Athens city	185	47	448	11	133	8	D	100	2,097	4	9	111	2,393	48	292
Aurora city	46	47	313	24	134	4	D	31	9	11	212	31	D	29	171
Austintown CDP	140	27	297	25	967	2	D	94	1,731	8	58	81	1,353	45	308
Avon city	97	62	248	36	518	5	23	64	1,101	10	282	54	1,118	43	D
Avon Lake city	425	49	262	34	555	5	37	47	488	6	D	41	483	33	D
Barberton city	19	27	D	16	170	2	D	85	2,390	4	D	46	D	48	260
Bay Village city	16	35	104	16	96	2	43	25	360	3	D	13	104	19	75
Beachwood city	1,402	239	1,860	76	4,131	25	198	183	5,125	18	419	62	1,729	51	499

Table C. Incorporated Places, Census Designated Places (CDPs), and Minor Civil Divisions (MCDs) of 10,000 or More Population — Economic Census

STATE City, town, township, borough, or CDP (county if applicable)	Utilities Number of establishments	Utilities Number of employees	Manufacturing Number of establishments	Manufacturing Number of employees	Wholesale trade¹ Number of establishments	Wholesale trade¹ Number of employees	Retail trade Number of establishments	Retail trade Number of employees	Transportation and warehousing Number of establishments	Transportation and warehousing Number of employees	Information Number of establishments	Information Number of employees	Finance and insurance Number of establishments	Finance and insurance Number of employees	Real estate and rental and leasing Number of establishments
	1	2	3	4	5	6	7	8	9	10	11	12	13	14	15
OHIO—Con.															
Beavercreek city	NA	NA	28	D	23	167	216	4,600	8	110	18	241	65	279	46
Bedford city	NA	NA	27	1,589	24	245	62	1,856	10	119	2	D	18	394	19
Bedford Heights city	NA	NA	48	1,409	57	1,634	36	523	20	436	1	D	15	D	22
Bellefontaine city	2	D	15	773	10	D	88	1,217	9	72	9	83	36	175	18
Berea city	NA	NA	30	1,131	21	143	47	657	18	D	5	D	28	121	13
Bexley city	NA	NA	NA	NA	2	D	25	160	3	9	2	D	26	129	15
Blue Ash city	NA	NA	75	3,306	141	2,761	83	1,255	19	185	48	1,438	153	2,035	57
Boardman CDP	3	D	45	831	43	416	281	4,682	16	192	20	317	104	630	41
Bowling Green city	1	D	35	1,906	15	116	99	1,599	8	208	21	261	53	222	38
Brecksville city	4	D	12	393	43	804	35	515	9	116	21	815	65	1,558	27
Bridgetown CDP	NA	NA	10	110	7	73	59	934	7	41	8	89	29	156	20
Broadview Heights city	1	D	11	288	24	418	37	602	4	D	14	97	38	183	14
Brooklyn city	NA	NA	28	1,721	14	568	49	1,432	16	D	6	D	26	761	13
Brook Park city	NA	NA	60	2,905	42	516	41	676	38	876	4	D	16	D	11
Brunswick city	NA	NA	49	969	48	532	93	1,759	14	237	9	108	49	D	22
Bucyrus city	NA	NA	21	1,233	11	D	66	729	6	94	6	65	30	417	12
Cambridge city	3	D	20	1,024	14	D	79	979	6	76	6	87	33	280	24
Canton city	6	D	136	8,020	89	1,263	249	3,432	26	456	20	485	111	2,981	71
Celina city	NA	NA	15	768	4	53	68	979	4	116	8	122	34	375	14
Centerville city	1	D	18	146	11	D	90	1,897	6	56	4	D	57	508	36
Chillicothe city	6	D	14	1,410	15	D	158	2,975	10	179	14	D	58	316	39
Cincinnati city	28	2,245	363	12,881	358	5,890	941	13,549	153	4,509	174	4,774	537	20,445	405
Circleville city	NA	NA	11	D	8	D	59	586	4	29	4	D	40	209	17
Clayton city	NA	NA	13	234	6	D	29	736	4	D	1	D	14	30	9
Cleveland city	14	959	805	22,075	577	9,142	1,206	10,637	233	7,714	167	4,615	543	16,568	349
Cleveland Heights city	NA	NA	8	46	8	43	97	1,340	7	28	13	168	46	D	50
Columbus city	31	D	518	19,881	807	17,060	2,566	46,211	507	23,782	378	13,835	1,155	47,985	904
Conneaut city	NA	NA	18	784	2	D	30	372	1	D	2	D	13	71	4
Coshocton city	2	D	17	1,053	7	D	79	1,056	9	214	12	108	31	216	11
Cuyahoga Falls city	NA	NA	76	2,565	39	573	171	3,313	14	105	14	313	78	407	42
Dayton city	9	D	266	9,794	158	3,063	375	3,791	73	1,773	71	2,789	139	2,973	136
Defiance city	2	D	22	2,821	12	158	104	1,854	9	236	14	207	41	364	19
Delaware city	1	D	38	2,755	14	120	118	1,738	23	2,898	16	84	50	213	36
Dent CDP	NA	NA	6	136	6	18	24	664	2	D	2	D	19	95	12
Dover city	NA	NA	33	2,303	14	D	70	898	7	D	5	D	35	266	12
Dublin city	5	52	33	1,051	88	1,426	118	2,215	14	599	70	3,531	241	7,927	75
East Cleveland city	NA	NA	8	81	4	D	46	302	3	10	2	D	12	D	8
Eastlake city	2	D	74	1,558	29	393	58	706	5	D	5	15	36	68	15
East Liverpool city	1	D	12	279	9	50	40	353	11	165	2	D	9	52	3
Elyria city	NA	NA	100	4,869	56	309	219	3,567	21	372	19	380	70	445	48
Englewood city	NA	NA	18	223	10	D	47	724	8	D	NA	NA	24	123	14
Euclid city	2	D	75	5,059	34	533	84	993	14	25	12	143	99	241	49
Fairborn city	2	D	12	443	11	330	78	1,061	10	D	3	D	31	432	35
Fairfield city	3	D	82	3,088	72	1,793	175	3,937	42	1,108	6	D	67	D	50
Fairview Park city	NA	NA	4	14	10	29	58	1,053	4	12	5	31	26	191	20
Findlay city	4	D	56	5,654	40	638	205	3,287	27	1,456	21	407	100	480	50
Finneytown CDP	NA	NA	NA	NA	2	D	45	469	3	D	NA	NA	7	D	3
Forest Park city	NA	NA	26	585	36	670	56	1,525	8	29	5	95	22	D	12
Forestville CDP	NA	NA	3	8	4	8	59	1,130	3	D	6	26	44	227	21
Fostoria city	2	D	26	2,031	7	D	35	484	6	298	5	23	24	128	6
Franklin city	1	D	46	2,031	14	210	43	722	3	D	2	D	16	D	9
Fremont city	NA	NA	45	2,691	19	200	104	1,553	16	260	14	179	46	356	15
Gahanna city	5	D	27	754	38	619	87	1,378	21	383	11	135	71	1,494	40
Galion city	NA	NA	24	1,030	9	104	41	410	3	D	5	D	22	D	8
Garfield Heights city	NA	NA	18	838	27	404	78	960	23	544	9	316	33	188	20
Green city	1	D	37	1,479	31	457	55	1,490	35	1,886	10	226	61	421	22
Greenville city	1	D	26	1,835	14	167	89	1,215	7	235	8	56	41	339	16
Grove City city	NA	NA	29	1,545	32	869	121	3,256	38	3,225	9	D	55	565	34
Hamilton city	NA	NA	69	1,827	43	800	213	3,262	24	409	15	348	74	432	31
Harrison city	NA	NA	30	1,339	11	599	72	1,123	1	D	1	D	20	100	14
Heath city	2	D	18	1,428	9	D	109	2,319	12	225	9	126	29	196	20
Hilliard city	NA	NA	28	1,506	51	700	85	1,405	16	208	21	1,181	49	444	39
Huber Heights city	NA	NA	31	2,494	20	394	98	2,020	18	1,140	4	D	35	165	25
Hudson city	NA	NA	27	897	56	550	73	932	7	D	20	579	89	1,636	32
Ironton city	4	55	10	439	8	89	57	481	2	D	5	D	26	150	6
Kent city	2	D	59	1,435	13	D	78	1,344	6	100	7	169	29	200	22
Kettering city	NA	NA	45	1,601	26	D	158	3,328	11	66	21	D	84	1,503	57
Lakewood city	NA	NA	33	587	22	D	110	1,149	15	289	7	121	60	690	58
Lancaster city	2	D	45	2,844	27	368	235	3,240	23	170	19	198	84	539	54
Lebanon city	NA	NA	40	2,187	19	D	97	1,447	4	23	12	D	36	D	21
Lima city	3	D	37	1,724	49	663	125	1,634	19	350	14	227	68	672	29
Lorain city	1	D	40	2,533	27	786	121	1,836	18	130	12	196	50	522	36
Loveland city	1	D	14	262	20	531	38	673	4	D	7	33	30	120	9
Lyndhurst city	NA	NA	5	27	6	21	76	1,204	3	7	1	D	45	136	16
Macedonia city	4	D	37	1,267	26	657	62	1,188	16	414	9	69	16	71	9
Mack CDP	NA	NA	NA	NA	2	D	6	105	3	10	1	D	7	37	6
Mansfield city	4	D	96	5,359	56	1,001	185	2,073	23	468	26	792	101	613	58
Maple Heights city	NA	NA	21	270	21	645	83	1,039	13	122	4	D	34	112	13
Marietta city	5	D	32	1,071	33	562	120	1,490	7	86	7	112	56	507	24
Marion city	5	D	31	2,001	18	286	112	1,762	6	D	15	681	62	328	25
Marysville city	2	D	18	958	12	D	73	1,473	14	212	12	133	38	163	26
Mason city	NA	NA	32	3,399	51	1,783	105	1,864	11	D	11	D	62	594	30
Massillon city	3	D	60	5,519	29	419	119	2,488	12	197	7	177	49	386	24
Maumee city	1	D	39	1,300	47	807	106	2,223	19	1,786	14	172	96	1,008	32
Mayfield Heights city	NA	NA	4	D	19	D	100	2,003	2	D	11	117	95	1,496	29
Medina city	2	D	61	3,036	50	526	111	1,813	19	178	17	197	55	D	30
Mentor city	3	91	213	8,675	97	944	303	5,884	27	360	24	558	146	782	49
Miamisburg city	1	D	37	1,982	29	307	62	1,292	5	117	27	572	28	D	10
Middleburg Heights city	2	D	24	672	41	449	100	2,762	57	2,613	11	515	61	566	23

1 Merchant wholesalers, except manufacturers' sales branches and offices.

Table C. Incorporated Places, Census Designated Places (CDPs), and Minor Civil Divisions (MCDs) of 10,000 or More Population — **Economic Census**

STATE City, town, township, borough, or CDP (county if applicable)	Real estate and rental and leasing — Number of employees	Professional, scientific, and technical services — Number of establishments	Professional — Number of employees	Administration and support and waste management and mediation services — Number of establishments	Admin — Number of employees	Educational services — Number of establishments	Educational — Number of employees	Health care and social assistance — Number of establishments	Health care — Number of employees	Arts, entertainment, and recreation — Number of establishments	Arts — Number of employees	Accommodation and food services — Number of establishments	Accommodation — Number of employees	Other services (except public administration) — Number of establishments	Other — Number of employees
	16	17	18	19	20	21	22	23	24	25	26	27	28	29	30
OHIO—Con.															
Beavercreek city	176	190	4,057	51	397	14	90	128	1,961	9	165	105	2,738	60	489
Bedford city	83	21	102	15	100	2	D	48	1,317	8	69	29	D	44	299
Bedford Heights city	297	24	286	19	270	1	D	13	343	10	64	15	307	26	D
Bellefontaine city	96	25	125	11	715	1	D	69	D	6	D	46	837	35	372
Berea city	62	44	300	24	93	5	37	41	1,285	5	D	39	695	38	206
Bexley city	44	33	73	5	57	4	9	15	D	1	D	24	420	18	83
Blue Ash city	666	248	5,809	135	5,480	19	213	129	2,780	6	213	78	1,612	71	800
Boardman CDP	1,657	121	767	75	5,229	13	93	218	4,970	14	320	99	2,231	78	454
Bowling Green city	159	52	312	16	265	10	D	96	2,350	12	D	117	2,586	53	259
Brecksville city	D	99	873	31	498	5	41	34	D	7	30	27	422	30	200
Bridgeton CDP	89	32	135	10	53	3	32	43	696	6	118	41	1,230	30	174
Broadview Heights city	D	71	274	40	595	5	35	51	640	9	93	30	517	43	286
Brooklyn city	104	13	31	10	103	1	D	28	D	3	D	44	1,063	18	D
Brook Park city	69	36	810	26	341	1	D	27	661	10	100	38	502	36	D
Brunswick city	92	56	390	38	448	5	43	56	905	11	62	63	1,072	67	430
Bucyrus city	36	19	D	13	54	1	D	38	924	5	D	31	475	28	120
Cambridge city	67	26	D	15	507	4	D	92	D	2	D	53	1,125	41	195
Canton city	248	156	723	72	1,530	17	121	216	11,054	25	385	170	2,652	148	1,089
Celina city	46	22	152	6	D	1	D	34	595	2	D	41	789	35	185
Centerville city	D	90	525	34	237	7	22	84	1,185	14	96	53	D	45	409
Chillicothe city	162	56	335	26	792	2	D	112	3,568	9	D	91	2,204	62	421
Cincinnati city	2,489	1,127	19,429	393	11,485	63	406	950	48,741	139	4,343	738	15,321	582	4,694
Circleville city	63	34	333	15	D	1	D	57	1,845	7	D	29	530	27	105
Clayton city	23	13	62	16	65	1	D	55	770	3	61	15	261	17	86
Cleveland city	3,895	1,164	17,185	399	14,444	63	811	727	69,208	107	4,578	980	16,885	744	5,847
Cleveland Heights city	166	105	279	29	117	14	71	109	1,829	14	76	80	1,005	71	367
Columbus city	6,933	2,072	29,166	863	36,605	149	1,416	1,998	75,569	193	5,644	1,959	42,063	1,289	11,730
Conneaut city	16	14	36	10	566	2	D	22	489	5	D	30	329	16	68
Coshocton city	37	19	82	17	319	3	D	63	1,359	6	D	36	657	41	D
Cuyahoga Falls city	197	108	867	65	2,049	10	D	156	3,174	10	90	119	2,339	111	744
Dayton city	713	309	3,898	157	4,654	26	295	425	24,302	34	924	276	4,570	235	1,702
Defiance city	74	35	203	8	196	4	28	62	1,878	6	D	55	984	42	297
Delaware city	117	54	355	25	1,678	3	D	123	3,301	10	D	87	1,313	57	D
Dent CDP	42	20	50	7	28	1	D	17	240	5	14	15	D	18	D
Dover city	45	30	206	5	23	3	D	82	2,790	7	167	32	436	26	144
Dublin city	673	369	3,381	124	5,179	22	243	213	5,977	32	694	123	3,294	57	1,468
East Cleveland city	40	6	D	6	24	NA	NA	33	863	1	D	23	268	7	27
Eastlake city	55	36	217	18	102	3	D	17	97	10	98	30	392	41	D
East Liverpool city	3	9	49	7	D	1	D	51	977	3	59	20	307	28	104
Elyria city	223	80	393	43	1,443	2	D	145	4,400	9	D	118	2,230	77	451
Englewood city	55	24	273	10	55	1	D	40	673	5	175	43	1,014	35	D
Euclid city	355	42	361	40	401	3	D	117	4,067	8	71	71	D	62	184
Fairborn city	161	77	1,397	25	1,149	9	52	49	700	8	120	74	1,535	45	212
Fairfield city	299	83	453	71	2,661	7	70	146	3,063	11	198	104	1,990	91	699
Fairview Park city	220	70	287	26	238	6	43	70	498	1	D	46	D	37	D
Findlay city	382	108	649	50	1,603	14	65	157	4,434	16	238	147	3,530	105	744
Finneytown CDP	D	12	42	10	359	2	D	28	280	3	36	22	532	22	101
Forest Park city	116	30	923	20	634	3	D	45	847	4	36	39	865	35	D
Forestville CDP	85	47	178	15	105	2	D	98	2,643	5	D	36	990	30	236
Fostoria city	18	18	69	10	D	1	D	42	801	4	127	31	457	27	134
Franklin city	30	18	117	13	271	1	D	21	422	4	D	21	320	28	472
Fremont city	86	39	178	23	644	2	D	70	1,859	6	137	48	694	42	185
Gahanna city	159	143	973	67	2,020	20	330	152	3,009	15	261	104	1,861	68	705
Galion city	21	17	D	5	D	NA	NA	34	1,063	3	54	29	387	27	135
Garfield Heights city	69	48	360	35	2,418	4	D	72	2,760	4	10	46	654	36	D
Green city	176	77	958	36	1,300	6	20	77	1,919	12	D	54	949	48	576
Greenville city	44	29	156	15	86	4	D	55	1,661	7	D	50	696	49	196
Grove City city	164	46	389	57	1,697	6	54	101	1,488	15	539	110	2,387	66	1,089
Hamilton city	165	97	412	34	869	9	74	151	3,779	12	100	129	2,433	92	667
Harrison city	35	15	67	8	D	1	D	24	225	5	D	37	991	29	D
Heath city	78	17	243	13	206	2	D	22	804	5	D	60	1,446	24	D
Hilliard city	256	85	778	61	1,003	11	89	96	1,338	19	385	70	1,572	53	391
Huber Heights city	124	32	495	25	836	7	50	74	1,130	8	175	78	1,638	57	311
Hudson city	114	140	634	57	619	12	32	78	1,072	15	256	52	1,124	48	367
Ironton city	21	19	113	10	102	2	D	50	865	3	17	22	D	22	D
Kent city	93	45	347	24	D	4	5	58	729	7	D	89	1,426	51	293
Kettering city	197	112	2,815	57	560	12	115	186	5,922	18	580	107	D	85	936
Lakewood city	322	116	388	44	790	16	169	128	2,720	16	269	115	1,820	74	568
Lancaster city	215	71	D	40	544	6	D	169	4,517	16	D	108	2,393	81	D
Lebanon city	84	60	331	15	261	3	15	67	D	9	D	46	785	38	238
Lima city	186	75	379	40	1,594	7	45	177	7,559	9	136	77	1,196	72	489
Lorain city	118	52	225	37	538	4	D	138	4,102	17	D	71	1,107	78	565
Loveland city	31	43	188	23	D	6	D	25	D	6	24	31	575	23	D
Lyndhurst city	72	36	82	18	123	6	100	73	866	7	D	35	1,187	32	230
Macedonia city	48	34	131	19	169	1	D	28	396	4	D	38	929	25	D
Mack CDP	15	11	19	10	D	NA	NA	10	D	1	D	6	100	6	D
Mansfield city	295	117	668	59	2,341	4	43	217	5,937	16	298	111	2,022	113	729
Maple Heights city	60	9	62	17	238	3	D	46	950	4	19	29	347	33	D
Marietta city	150	64	422	23	D	5	D	84	4,887	8	116	69	1,405	56	290
Marion city	93	42	144	24	336	3	D	131	3,750	9	D	66	1,259	61	505
Marysville city	117	34	D	20	5,455	3	D	63	1,598	7	D	54	1,115	42	237
Mason city	86	110	587	49	1,284	14	D	124	2,436	18	1,038	98	2,588	43	250
Massillon city	88	44	236	20	442	5	26	90	2,963	6	66	79	1,175	69	466
Maumee city	364	72	1,830	37	1,416	10	41	88	3,006	12	174	91	2,284	55	349
Mayfield Heights city	194	63	800	30	1,180	2	D	95	3,424	3	D	65	1,532	44	411
Medina city	110	109	531	51	3,867	6	35	97	2,305	8	57	59	1,182	75	520
Mentor city	163	169	899	108	2,407	12	121	181	3,025	12	D	174	3,813	135	908
Miamisburg city	21	46	706	27	852	4	25	41	1,654	9	54	52	982	26	226
Middleburg Heights city	163	93	730	43	1,311	7	22	129	5,924	3	60	70	1,537	44	281

Table C. Incorporated Places, Census Designated Places (CDPs), and Minor Civil Divisions (MCDs) of 10,000 or More Population — Economic Census

STATE City, town, township, borough, or CDP (county if applicable)	Utilities Number of establishments	Number of employees	Manufacturing Number of establishments	Number of employees	Wholesale trade[1] Number of establishments	Number of employees	Retail trade Number of establishments	Number of employees	Transportation and warehousing Number of establishments	Number of employees	Information Number of establishments	Number of employees	Finance and insurance Number of establishments	Number of employees	Real estate and rental and leasing Number of establishments
	1	2	3	4	5	6	7	8	9	10	11	12	13	14	15
OHIO—Con.															
Middletown city	NA	NA	53	4,040	33	D	153	3,372	17	D	12	92	71	363	53
Monfort Heights CDP	NA	NA	3	7	3	D	15	440	1	D	1	D	17	185	6
Monroe city	5	D	22	875	30	632	104	1,462	19	691	53	D	12	47	16
Montgomery city	NA	NA	NA	NA	10	49	48	704	2	D	1	D	46	D	23
Mount Vernon city	2	D	31	4,031	15	134	101	1,519	4	18	13	D	51	342	23
Newark city	4	D	41	2,302	34	514	145	1,825	20	383	15	315	89	3,070	42
New Franklin city	1	D	9	168	7	67	19	118	8	23	2	D	12	64	7
New Philadelphia city	4	D	30	1,484	18	136	129	1,967	8	119	14	267	33	182	23
Niles city	2	D	29	988	15	184	158	2,379	6	D	9	100	28	183	21
Northbrook CDP	NA	NA	3	D	7	24	19	330	3	D	6	D	12	64	7
North Canton city	NA	NA	11	172	13	181	66	1,209	12	231	3	9	49	303	23
North Olmsted city	NA	NA	16	208	22	166	250	4,827	17	113	19	258	78	771	36
North Ridgeville city	NA	NA	42	1,305	30	442	58	647	21	417	7	5	25	106	12
North Royalton city	NA	NA	73	779	52	478	63	484	27	180	18	224	38	283	26
Norton city	NA	NA	23	898	14	202	37	719	15	D	2	D	19	76	4
Norwalk city	1	D	33	1,537	18	246	73	1,035	4	62	11	153	29	213	21
Norwood city	NA	NA	24	1,260	18	182	92	1,591	7	D	21	D	62	577	16
Oregon city	2	D	15	1,728	9	D	64	1,777	11	80	5	39	33	176	21
Oxford city	2	D	8	227	5	D	51	725	4	D	4	13	25	121	15
Painesville city	NA	NA	43	1,484	17	191	57	367	4	13	7	12	41	154	11
Parma city	NA	NA	32	1,923	44	851	270	3,793	29	356	9	213	122	783	57
Parma Heights city	NA	NA	7	21	3	D	54	454	6	11	3	D	30	D	14
Pataskala city	3	D	7	1,142	9	D	36	780	12	387	2	D	23	D	11
Perrysburg city	NA	NA	36	1,621	48	613	95	1,307	12	193	13	115	66	331	28
Pickerington city	2	D	3	D	7	D	51	924	9	D	2	D	31	129	21
Piqua city	NA	NA	57	3,048	16	145	117	1,707	11	267	8	70	34	281	19
Portsmouth city	1	D	14	422	12	90	105	1,034	9	74	11	168	39	310	30
Powell city	NA	NA	11	D	15	D	52	431	3	6	6	D	30	127	16
Ravenna city	1	D	27	1,222	8	187	43	588	7	D	3	56	30	237	8
Reading city	NA	NA	20	910	14	131	40	375	6	109	2	D	11	65	13
Reynoldsburg city	1	D	15	243	8	D	119	2,127	11	80	7	64	60	327	39
Richmond Heights city	NA	NA	5	392	8	50	75	842	7	D	4	139	28	153	13
Riverside city	1	D	5	90	9	D	57	516	9	316	NA	NA	11	49	16
Rocky River city	NA	NA	13	50	29	95	83	1,078	13	175	8	D	76	439	34
Salem city	1	D	49	1,749	17	234	77	1,280	4	D	6	100	33	176	8
Sandusky city	4	5	41	1,644	31	380	101	1,277	10	75	9	246	49	282	35
Seven Hills city	NA	NA	8	21	11	159	15	194	4	9	1	D	34	316	3
Shaker Heights city	NA	NA	NA	NA	10	20	47	494	3	D	6	44	40	192	36
Sharonville city	4	D	61	5,109	103	2,514	80	1,146	56	2,183	11	351	52	431	55
Sidney city	1	D	56	4,744	20	751	92	1,478	16	481	10	127	44	274	25
Solon city	2	D	88	11,638	143	3,216	89	1,436	20	282	18	974	101	962	53
South Euclid city	NA	NA	14	480	11	64	46	629	9	92	6	22	26	D	14
Springboro city	1	D	29	1,157	19	716	56	810	5	47	3	D	42	D	16
Springdale city	NA	NA	13	1,947	18	248	170	3,368	10	196	18	606	50	701	24
Springfield city	4	D	79	2,767	50	1,628	221	3,643	26	1,620	10	115	92	2,302	58
Steubenville city	2	D	11	188	17	254	102	1,905	4	56	17	217	36	162	17
Stow city	4	D	47	1,336	47	590	102	2,184	9	109	5	65	56	233	38
Streetsboro city	NA	NA	37	2,663	28	846	63	1,582	10	D	3	D	23	96	22
Strongsville city	4	D	72	2,434	70	1,636	240	4,775	30	455	18	292	101	1,439	53
Struthers city	1	D	14	567	4	D	21	274	4	51	1	D	7	45	1
Sylvania city	NA	NA	12	D	10	26	76	1,161	5	72	3	D	45	345	10
Tallmadge city	NA	NA	47	1,148	24	155	46	1,545	15	134	6	17	26	101	12
Tiffin city	3	D	31	2,180	14	420	83	1,083	9	63	6	24	37	218	18
Toledo city	8	D	295	11,821	249	3,832	935	13,004	136	2,915	90	2,231	316	3,086	237
Trenton city	NA	NA	4	D	2	D	19	118	1	D	NA	NA	6	23	NA
Trotwood city	NA	NA	12	95	8	57	69	1,189	8	245	8	D	18	73	21
Troy city	3	D	49	5,461	18	253	79	1,695	9	430	11	62	61	259	21
Twinsburg city	NA	NA	64	2,858	113	2,125	55	1,403	14	260	10	652	55	D	23
University Heights city	NA	NA	3	16	1	D	49	1,029	1	D	1	D	16	D	5
Upper Arlington city	NA	NA	11	61	14	D	85	891	3	15	19	299	94	494	42
Urbana city	1	D	26	2,387	6	D	58	762	5	229	3	D	30	170	11
Vandalia city	NA	NA	41	2,520	34	694	51	1,031	27	748	4	21	45	195	21
Van Wert city	3	D	23	2,493	11	102	66	1,020	9	203	2	D	40	717	8
Vermilion city	NA	NA	8	D	5	D	36	451	1	D	2	D	14	46	9
Wadsworth city	NA	NA	48	1,478	20	397	74	2,048	14	293	7	15	32	D	19
Warren city	4	D	45	5,428	28	712	155	1,907	18	716	16	363	58	356	32
Warrensville Heights city	NA	NA	38	886	48	519	47	489	16	220	2	D	16	D	29
Washington Court House city	1	D	18	970	6	D	75	1,038	4	D	5	D	30	155	10
West Carrollton city	NA	NA	37	1,283	23	334	61	1,146	4	D	6	D	21	106	17
Westerville city	2	D	34	1,218	52	494	108	1,683	14	46	22	356	160	6,179	54
Westlake city	2	D	49	1,200	82	1,308	161	2,377	19	D	30	1,373	147	1,185	64
Whitehall city	NA	NA	4	12	9	D	107	1,837	5	D	4	26	37	795	37
White Oak CDP	2	D	15	455	6	15	53	417	9	66	1	D	32	249	10
Wickliffe city	2	D	43	1,494	16	213	39	300	5	53	2	D	25	114	9
Willoughby city	NA	NA	161	3,475	67	741	103	1,581	15	218	6	149	79	296	39
Willowick city	NA	NA	NA	NA	3	3	37	585	2	D	NA	NA	28	57	4
Wilmington city	1	D	15	885	10	142	72	1,025	9	D	9	D	29	383	19
Wooster city	1	D	36	3,603	36	476	165	2,606	18	374	10	230	72	733	31
Worthington city	4	D	37	795	42	581	73	840	17	259	14	D	104	1,368	46
Xenia city	NA	NA	27	493	14	263	79	1,259	7	D	6	64	41	205	16
Youngstown city	5	D	90	3,310	89	1,488	219	2,454	23	527	30	1,183	67	849	54
Zanesville city	2	D	28	D	24	251	210	3,093	20	1,152	18	502	84	529	29
OKLAHOMA	345	8,202	3,610	133,064	3,909	50,660	13,051	168,839	2,641	44,502	1,497	28,890	6,691	57,760	4,000
Ada city	5	140	24	988	33	352	143	1,694	11	119	10	D	66	D	36
Altus city	1	D	9	D	18	180	91	1,192	17	115	8	D	40	D	18
Ardmore city	4	D	30	2,166	39	696	195	2,384	33	1,172	13	174	90	613	57

1 Merchant wholesalers, except manufacturers' sales branches and offices.

Table C. Incorporated Places, Census Designated Places (CDPs), and Minor Civil Divisions (MCDs) of 10,000 or More Population — Economic Census

STATE City, town, township, borough, or CDP (county if applicable)	Real estate and rental and leasing — Number of employees	Professional, scientific, and technical services — Number of establishments	Professional, scientific, and technical services — Number of employees	Administration and support and waste management and mediation services — Number of establishments	Administration and support and waste management and mediation services — Number of employees	Educational services — Number of establishments	Educational services — Number of employees	Health care and social assistance — Number of establishments	Health care and social assistance — Number of employees	Arts, entertainment, and recreation — Number of establishments	Arts, entertainment, and recreation — Number of employees	Accommodation and food services — Number of establishments	Accommodation and food services — Number of employees	Other services (except public administration) — Number of establishments	Other services (except public administration) — Number of employees
	16	17	18	19	20	21	22	23	24	25	26	27	28	29	30
OHIO—Con.															
Middletown city	219	63	579	51	1,182	8	34	136	3,504	10	D	91	2,064	77	553
Monfort Heights CDP	16	18	76	14	40	1	D	34	952	1	D	13	322	7	28
Monroe city	184	19	120	10	196	NA	NA	13	460	8	33	26	277	12	126
Montgomery city	62	48	146	10	221	8	66	111	3,926	4	D	34	609	32	231
Mount Vernon city	85	31	281	12	379	6	D	86	2,276	4	29	62	1,193	49	389
Newark city	158	83	455	62	1,457	8	58	153	5,389	17	D	97	1,672	81	529
New Franklin city	32	15	36	22	D	1	D	15	D	3	D	9	181	14	63
New Philadelphia city	115	54	364	26	646	4	16	58	887	6	76	60	992	65	343
Niles city	133	28	156	20	2,650	5	78	54	988	8	72	68	D	37	289
Northbrook CDP	26	8	40	7	14	NA	NA	12	165	2	D	11	215	8	60
North Canton city	260	64	663	27	528	3	16	69	2,268	6	167	61	1,169	42	263
North Olmsted city	156	68	2,306	44	828	10	53	84	1,320	7	58	119	2,387	110	712
North Ridgeville city	46	43	240	44	272	2	D	42	541	6	64	43	611	50	209
North Royalton city	141	93	308	59	475	10	96	66	1,127	10	48	39	398	63	307
Norton city	11	20	91	29	334	4	D	19	D	3	44	20	324	20	D
Norwalk city	83	45	228	18	212	4	D	52	1,781	8	D	46	730	37	232
Norwood city	117	54	691	33	765	6	96	44	1,095	8	D	52	1,375	38	449
Oregon city	89	15	76	20	156	2	D	95	2,798	3	D	59	1,154	45	228
Oxford city	D	18	78	6	44	4	25	33	645	6	D	65	1,637	40	272
Painesville city	28	44	289	16	146	2	D	43	724	4	D	30	409	33	291
Parma city	314	91	638	89	1,716	6	15	201	6,344	12	136	163	2,484	144	889
Parma Heights city	80	32	207	13	90	1	D	58	583	6	D	44	493	27	D
Pataskala city	39	14	D	18	263	1	D	18	328	9	D	27	438	21	D
Perrysburg city	144	85	554	36	462	7	65	72	1,658	8	D	77	1,855	49	418
Pickerington city	54	32	124	19	150	6	40	53	490	8	144	68	1,341	31	D
Piqua city	81	23	108	11	434	NA	NA	44	D	5	D	50	971	35	159
Portsmouth city	102	51	259	20	317	5	39	137	4,688	7	35	66	1,313	45	D
Powell city	36	69	294	19	120	11	140	47	D	13	132	36	616	35	203
Ravenna city	24	38	184	8	45	2	D	77	2,954	3	5	28	491	33	363
Reading city	89	28	437	12	D	NA	NA	17	332	1	D	27	D	19	90
Reynoldsburg city	185	74	464	37	729	5	36	111	1,829	7	47	74	D	50	290
Richmond Heights city	D	35	197	29	120	2	D	42	1,316	3	D	29	341	29	D
Riverside city	82	38	617	15	824	2	D	34	D	6	92	51	D	23	111
Rocky River city	D	101	401	34	277	7	39	77	835	9	265	59	1,158	62	364
Salem city	29	25	112	14	348	1	D	70	2,163	5	D	45	647	37	178
Sandusky city	135	57	305	29	831	4	D	83	3,732	23	D	72	865	49	197
Seven Hills city	4	27	259	28	3,073	2	D	21	D	3	D	15	270	15	D
Shaker Heights city	D	95	459	34	411	8	44	70	1,835	17	271	33	362	39	131
Sharonville city	759	94	2,201	44	2,591	10	402	46	1,265	4	D	72	1,387	62	592
Sidney city	D	38	318	20	900	4	D	75	D	9	135	51	1,068	37	228
Solon city	193	140	1,521	71	2,437	14	128	95	1,202	8	72	60	1,296	53	D
South Euclid city	96	36	108	22	47	7	37	60	698	3	D	35	423	37	250
Springboro city	44	49	456	20	157	3	D	60	688	8	D	31	D	29	164
Springdale city	215	56	1,239	35	4,196	9	72	91	1,726	4	73	62	1,767	27	226
Springfield city	324	103	817	38	1,774	7	D	246	8,785	19	194	154	3,174	122	792
Steubenville city	98	55	202	26	658	2	D	101	3,332	6	92	61	1,063	40	296
Stow city	169	100	864	48	564	11	98	81	1,303	21	167	86	1,724	64	429
Streetsboro city	322	19	75	16	524	1	D	21	376	2	D	54	969	33	269
Strongsville city	439	121	402	56	430	13	D	109	1,806	17	201	122	2,951	81	775
Struthers city	D	11	40	7	10	1	D	16	272	4	32	13	210	20	D
Sylvania city	D	62	487	20	797	6	86	113	2,226	9	215	54	D	49	418
Tallmadge city	D	33	384	38	810	3	84	55	899	2	D	27	415	39	D
Tiffin city	45	34	200	22	D	3	19	82	1,314	7	37	48	806	49	281
Toledo city	1,823	452	4,173	290	8,457	33	154	694	23,389	84	3,387	632	11,286	431	3,072
Trenton city	NA	5	27	1	D	NA	NA	14	125	4	6	12	148	12	D
Trotwood city	70	10	73	9	137	1	D	24	1,034	6	D	15	298	17	D
Troy city	105	59	411	32	1,113	1	D	90	D	12	134	75	1,906	63	328
Twinsburg city	129	77	670	41	1,780	8	68	53	2,032	6	56	53	D	44	D
University Heights city	26	21	69	15	38	3	D	24	D	4	14	27	545	16	88
Upper Arlington city	D	119	766	38	723	11	30	80	1,752	8	D	66	1,333	39	335
Urbana city	35	27	218	10	D	1	D	39	1,167	7	139	36	616	29	104
Vandalia city	190	32	380	24	613	6	76	42	988	6	D	38	719	38	375
Van Wert city	33	23	94	5	D	2	D	49	1,370	7	D	33	696	33	D
Vermilion city	D	12	54	8	8	1	D	23	344	14	D	29	390	26	130
Wadsworth city	51	46	343	21	211	4	17	71	1,914	5	D	53	1,003	43	210
Warren city	175	98	425	41	1,081	2	D	192	5,005	14	116	89	6,193	82	421
Warrensville Heights city	240	29	540	14	156	5	25	55	2,299	2	D	33	510	17	131
Washington Court House city	D	19	D	9	215	NA	NA	49	1,323	5	D	34	631	30	159
West Carrollton city	87	14	119	12	545	4	62	21	684	4	114	43	1,015	27	D
Westerville city	D	206	2,231	65	2,738	14	183	237	5,835	11	D	102	D	79	1,057
Westlake city	258	230	1,534	103	2,074	15	48	262	5,914	15	532	99	2,797	83	731
Whitehall city	134	39	346	16	1,032	4	37	74	1,453	3	D	60	981	64	D
White Oak CDP	28	30	175	23	185	3	12	53	446	8	96	25	477	29	169
Wickliffe city	24	25	101	28	310	1	D	21	470	6	85	34	430	42	235
Willoughby city	D	90	610	49	1,196	6	102	124	3,071	8	D	90	1,735	76	418
Willowick city	6	13	86	10	46	NA	NA	11	83	5	D	26	355	18	D
Wilmington city	147	23	D	13	587	2	D	68	D	6	71	43	D	31	D
Wooster city	107	76	746	32	730	5	D	132	3,407	11	268	85	1,683	60	354
Worthington city	140	133	1,548	60	2,476	14	196	126	2,725	9	53	37	856	41	219
Xenia city	43	29	118	6	125	1	D	81	1,575	8	95	50	1,003	39	190
Youngstown city	357	117	1,594	54	1,059	7	55	183	7,844	15	236	117	D	118	1,017
Zanesville city	170	69	318	24	534	3	D	145	5,236	11	142	100	2,215	89	797
OKLAHOMA	21,261	9,470	71,997	4,415	93,335	535	4,679	10,654	213,226	1,052	26,375	7,403	143,561	5,411	32,388
Ada city	D	71	318	33	452	3	D	120	D	5	D	66	D	34	166
Altus city	D	36	D	15	105	3	D	43	1,353	7	D	52	1,052	26	140
Ardmore city	201	111	651	36	478	12	D	181	3,490	18	D	96	2,250	61	690

Table C. Incorporated Places, Census Designated Places (CDPs), and Minor Civil Divisions (MCDs) of 10,000 or More Population — Economic Census

STATE City, town, township, borough, or CDP (county if applicable)	Utilities		Manufacturing		Wholesale trade[1]		Retail trade		Transportation and warehousing		Information		Finance and insurance		Real estate and rental and leasing
	Number of establishments	Number of employees	Number of establishments	Number of employees	Number of establishments	Number of employees	Number of establishments	Number of employees	Number of establishments	Number of employees	Number of establishments	Number of employees	Number of establishments	Number of employees	Number of establishments
	1	2	3	4	5	6	7	8	9	10	11	12	13	14	15
OKLAHOMA—Con.															
Bartlesville city	4	86	25	D	21	D	161	D	14	D	14	D	90	693	39
Bethany city	NA	NA	5	26	13	73	52	359	16	D	9	D	32	155	11
Bixby city	1	D	26	333	29	132	61	725	6	D	6	D	23	183	18
Broken Arrow city	2	D	132	5,570	125	1,347	253	4,115	39	D	40	618	145	768	92
Chickasha city	4	D	33	769	31	446	101	1,243	23	118	9	D	48	334	22
Choctaw city	NA	NA	NA	NA	3	D	20	126	4	D	5	18	11	D	6
Claremore city	2	D	38	2,129	10	D	115	1,743	5	D	11	D	46	388	31
Del City city	NA	NA	10	567	9	D	62	1,047	7	D	1	D	46	250	12
Duncan city	4	D	34	1,799	32	218	138	1,516	17	473	12	153	59	450	20
Durant city	3	D	24	899	20	472	87	1,211	7	D	12	D	54	582	22
Edmond city	2	D	38	410	96	D	327	4,505	22	251	44	461	277	1,498	181
Elk City city	3	D	12	D	25	464	102	1,265	26	544	11	85	26	186	27
El Reno city	2	D	14	512	24	172	63	842	17	148	3	D	30	188	14
Enid city	4	D	50	2,172	58	690	251	3,289	45	447	23	D	102	713	72
Glenpool city	1	D	8	130	3	D	22	155	5	D	NA	NA	8	34	4
Guthrie city	1	D	13	290	5	D	51	699	6	D	8	D	32	157	21
Guymon city	NA	NA	9	D	20	249	62	803	11	D	5	D	32	193	11
Jenks city	4	D	14	933	2	D	38	470	7	D	10	58	31	208	21
Lawton city	6	D	39	3,367	49	378	352	4,956	35	567	24	D	159	1,588	118
McAlester city	5	D	20	632	26	201	131	1,777	22	371	13	209	96	D	37
Miami city	1	D	23	1,131	9	81	59	754	4	D	7	D	36	D	18
Midwest City city	4	D	12	280	19	D	176	4,097	18	104	11	100	107	680	74
Moore city	1	D	25	808	33	D	147	2,442	17	D	13	D	64	386	47
Muskogee city	3	D	46	3,200	45	806	215	2,855	25	362	15	215	98	540	48
Mustang city	1	D	7	51	9	D	45	720	14	D	10	174	29	D	20
Norman city	4	D	69	2,255	59	746	419	7,006	48	477	49	910	214	1,422	210
Oklahoma City city	37	1,927	645	21,675	1,025	17,349	2,186	31,326	440	9,865	330	9,043	1,341	16,487	893
Okmulgee city	3	D	11	D	11	76	59	767	2	D	5	D	33	175	12
Owasso city	NA	NA	23	633	15	D	115	2,434	9	D	12	D	60	291	40
Ponca City city	NA	NA	34	1,373	23	157	126	1,576	17	320	11	143	64	309	27
Sand Springs city	2	D	28	D	13	189	67	1,203	12	D	6	D	44	219	21
Sapulpa city	3	D	35	1,428	33	810	98	1,380	16	388	8	D	44	350	16
Shawnee city	4	D	30	2,564	29	D	191	2,675	8	100	19	251	75	578	33
Stillwater city	2	D	28	946	22	158	202	3,157	24	351	27	311	89	663	66
Tahlequah city	NA	NA	8	33	8	D	101	1,490	5	D	11	D	55	248	25
Tulsa city	31	D	629	22,012	770	11,810	1,708	26,411	293	5,872	280	8,528	1,033	13,108	715
Warr Acres city	1	D	5	37	7	32	57	561	4	D	2	D	32	173	15
Weatherford city	4	D	13	56	8	D	72	1,023	15	D	5	D	28	162	22
Woodward city	5	D	16	274	35	D	105	1,154	39	432	6	D	48	297	27
Yukon city	1	D	25	653	20	160	85	1,637	21	64	8	66	60	357	34
OREGON	286	8,069	5,289	151,990	4,393	59,523	13,879	187,402	2,991	52,351	2,010	38,799	5,812	57,422	5,644
Albany city	3	D	61	D	39	369	187	2,812	23	724	6	118	84	586	58
Aloha CDP	NA	NA	27	1,023	11	D	82	853	17	99	3	10	25	116	25
Altamont CDP	NA	NA	6	79	13	229	58	526	16	84	2	D	18	D	20
Ashland city	NA	NA	53	494	23	211	140	1,230	7	44	27	120	41	186	39
Beaverton city	1	D	115	6,475	185	2,640	391	7,600	40	723	111	3,429	246	3,555	208
Bend city	15	142	162	2,444	136	908	503	6,406	57	991	71	1,380	247	1,562	257
Bethany CDP	NA	NA	NA	NA	11	26	18	206	NA	NA	7	40	13	37	14
Canby city	1	D	34	1,171	19	573	53	762	13	225	7	139	30	130	17
Cedar Mill CDP	NA	NA	4	13	2	D	19	297	4	D	7	110	25	63	14
Central Point city	NA	NA	20	145	9	44	30	327	17	178	3	D	17	71	10
Coos Bay city	1	D	21	186	14	159	83	1,486	26	705	10	162	26	174	23
Cornelius city	NA	NA	20	336	8	213	24	614	5	13	3	D	8	34	5
Corvallis city	NA	NA	47	974	26	D	212	3,138	16	380	42	635	73	537	86
Dallas city	1	D	8	371	4	D	36	627	6	17	5	28	22	92	15
Damascus city	NA	NA	7	64	5	37	13	180	6	18	1	D	5	21	11
Eugene city	3	D	263	5,512	241	3,013	726	10,971	99	1,262	106	1,859	364	3,118	286
Forest Grove city	NA	NA	26	1,372	7	84	44	417	9	31	5	D	20	D	25
Four Corners CDP	NA	NA	3	D	4	47	51	614	4	19	2	D	14	79	15
Gladstone city	NA	NA	3	19	8	D	32	716	4	49	1	D	17	57	9
Grants Pass city	4	D	68	1,632	25	307	241	3,637	18	237	24	333	102	615	72
Gresham city	2	D	73	4,848	55	1,615	270	3,677	58	983	32	1,629	106	2,230	119
Happy Valley city	NA	NA	6	56	12	35	19	337	9	27	2	D	13	36	16
Hayesville CDP	NA	NA	8	64	2	D	36	360	4	D	3	D	16	65	14
Hermiston city	2	D	12	467	18	251	66	1,157	18	1,373	8	73	26	185	21
Hillsboro city	2	D	149	13,248	99	1,315	303	5,624	46	561	59	2,947	117	3,182	116
Keizer city	NA	NA	7	46	11	25	83	1,213	5	23	11	89	42	156	36
Klamath Falls city	7	D	24	573	20	155	127	2,040	18	207	14	D	45	958	34
La Grande city	2	D	11	580	6	65	63	810	14	144	15	105	35	192	14
Lake Oswego city	2	D	36	674	94	1,457	126	D	9	D	24	335	276	2,564	127
Lebanon city	NA	NA	15	585	2	D	55	920	4	D	6	D	31	151	19
McMinnville city	NA	NA	63	1,915	20	111	144	2,005	17	D	16	128	51	477	35
Medford city	8	D	91	1,599	112	1,139	479	7,401	82	1,238	55	984	241	2,014	145
Milwaukie city	NA	NA	49	2,007	43	543	67	1,051	16	149	15	283	25	585	25
Newberg city	2	D	51	2,046	16	51	61	902	11	D	9	42	31	163	38
Newport city	1	D	21	381	16	92	99	1,107	10	85	10	75	24	143	26
Oak Grove CDP	NA	NA	17	313	11	D	62	1,098	6	D	3	D	17	101	19
Oak Hills CDP	NA	NA	3	7	2	D	2	D	1	D	6	18	4	4	8
Oatfield CDP	NA	NA	4	D	6	6	12	119	3	D	1	D	17	59	10
Ontario city	1	D	22	D	18	302	90	1,570	14	225	5	D	29	175	14
Oregon City city	1	D	47	586	14	163	98	1,607	19	D	12	93	43	237	37
Pendleton city	2	D	18	733	14	323	67	940	13	D	11	133	45	211	18
Portland city	49	D	978	26,432	1,139	20,024	2,527	32,426	582	18,396	540	10,512	1,119	17,243	1,221
Redmond city	2	D	59	951	33	206	113	1,962	26	172	13	755	50	242	42
Roseburg city	3	104	25	417	22	160	200	3,018	12	348	17	236	80	725	56
St. Helens city	NA	NA	14	496	5	30	44	574	9	D	5	31	19	146	10
Salem city	4	D	182	5,324	141	1,652	604	9,646	103	1,320	58	1,546	282	2,740	271

1 Merchant wholesalers, except manufacturers' sales branches and offices.

Table C. Incorporated Places, Census Designated Places (CDPs), and Minor Civil Divisions (MCDs) of 10,000 or More Population — Economic Census

STATE City, town, township, borough, or CDP (county if applicable)	Real estate and rental and leasing	Professional, scientific, and technical services		Administration and support and waste management and mediation services		Educational services		Health care and social assistance		Arts, entertainment, and recreation		Accommodation and food services		Other services (except public administration)	
	Number of employees	Number of establishments	Number of employees	Number of establishments	Number of employees	Number of establishments	Number of employees	Number of establishments	Number of employees	Number of establishments	Number of employees	Number of establishments	Number of employees	Number of establishments	Number of employees
	16	17	18	19	20	21	22	23	24	25	26	27	28	29	30
OKLAHOMA—Con.															
Bartlesville city	D	81	1,313	41	1,091	7	40	154	2,866	18	423	100	D	71	448
Bethany city	58	45	129	23	249	4	15	56	1,454	5	D	31	D	39	200
Bixby city	D	50	184	34	108	5	13	46	335	5	98	32	D	25	103
Broken Arrow city	227	228	1,457	155	2,317	21	99	213	3,741	34	533	169	D	149	921
Chickasha city	140	67	219	21	220	NA	NA	70	D	7	D	47	1,124	41	D
Choctaw city	14	15	47	14	37	2	D	13	179	4	D	11	280	9	D
Claremore city	80	57	278	28	455	7	D	119	2,149	6	46	67	D	40	183
Del City city	37	27	145	10	121	1	D	39	558	2	D	41	D	36	227
Duncan city	85	67	348	22	169	5	D	83	1,831	8	D	61	892	50	223
Durant city	62	53	347	19	216	5	D	105	1,827	6	D	63	D	25	D
Edmond city	642	430	2,414	171	1,188	36	277	433	4,227	39	586	202	4,394	179	961
Elk City city	378	60	238	20	D	1	D	73	932	4	21	59	806	26	D
El Reno city	160	20	D	12	D	NA	NA	43	584	4	D	35	513	25	246
Enid city	312	107	563	60	998	7	D	199	D	20	272	120	2,183	111	555
Glenpool city	10	12	28	10	50	NA	NA	21	199	4	D	17	D	10	D
Guthrie city	67	26	84	16	D	1	D	37	D	4	63	37	D	30	D
Guymon city	29	29	D	12	D	NA	NA	36	D	4	D	43	607	23	95
Jenks city	85	58	413	24	226	1	D	48	D	2	D	27	D	17	D
Lawton city	D	129	951	88	1,463	11	165	252	D	21	D	195	4,445	119	D
McAlester city	174	81	291	25	455	2	D	102	2,235	5	D	76	1,348	42	D
Miami city	D	36	190	16	D	2	D	54	D	3	D	44	D	21	D
Midwest City city	374	95	734	41	307	4	11	203	3,463	11	60	121	2,544	64	463
Moore city	172	64	412	45	D	12	D	102	1,074	5	D	105	2,398	65	D
Muskogee city	196	76	526	39	804	5	11	196	5,071	11	D	106	2,011	71	D
Mustang city	160	44	D	20	D	1	D	39	D	2	D	35	578	23	D
Norman city	975	453	1,928	157	6,450	44	268	457	8,244	46	D	312	7,292	166	954
Oklahoma City city	5,794	2,370	19,816	1,051	35,124	125	2,153	2,227	48,353	182	3,679	1,361	30,537	1,099	7,787
Okmulgee city	34	27	108	10	D	NA	NA	74	1,191	4	D	33	D	22	D
Owasso city	125	83	452	38	175	7	36	96	1,567	13	D	76	1,812	47	162
Ponca City city	97	67	377	28	687	3	6	107	1,893	9	184	54	932	46	244
Sand Springs city	96	43	296	21	218	2	D	37	551	8	D	45	727	25	D
Sapulpa city	62	44	139	27	D	7	D	54	1,283	7	D	66	1,150	38	162
Shawnee city	139	84	640	39	738	6	D	128	2,011	10	D	98	2,180	52	281
Stillwater city	263	102	D	48	375	10	35	127	2,966	11	64	146	3,143	81	677
Tahlequah city	128	36	118	18	366	7	44	93	2,370	5	D	69	1,119	29	250
Tulsa city	5,522	1,877	16,470	743	22,239	99	872	1,602	41,344	154	D	1,099	D	871	6,385
Warr Acres city	D	39	131	16	D	1	D	34	383	1	D	37	923	22	93
Weatherford city	275	26	118	14	77	1	D	39	D	5	D	35	673	25	128
Woodward city	D	47	183	19	276	3	D	75	787	6	D	53	D	33	D
Yukon city	87	78	263	27	D	6	D	77	1,199	8	83	63	1,488	56	342
OREGON	26,016	11,663	84,493	5,299	83,420	1,024	7,810	12,475	217,584	1,636	24,031	10,610	150,482	6,894	37,941
Albany city	203	100	555	63	1,978	5	10	131	2,882	16	255	119	1,905	76	512
Aloha CDP	61	43	D	65	D	6	26	110	D	4	D	53	711	52	196
Altamont CDP	62	24	118	16	168	2	D	45	268	2	D	43	511	26	D
Ashland city	79	102	454	31	147	14	62	159	D	25	843	146	1,601	36	179
Beaverton city	904	452	D	195	5,965	51	417	407	5,089	56	697	317	5,077	213	1,417
Bend city	701	503	1,776	170	2,345	41	360	435	7,508	58	1,380	303	4,684	210	1,050
Bethany CDP	172	49	D	20	76	15	189	24	D	5	D	23	199	11	D
Canby city	D	30	88	15	81	NA	NA	48	457	8	82	39	500	32	D
Cedar Mill CDP	47	53	D	15	D	7	52	36	D	4	D	11	162	8	64
Central Point city	69	25	85	15	51	NA	NA	30	305	3	14	25	227	19	68
Coos Bay city	132	44	199	29	900	3	D	88	2,376	7	D	54	677	41	267
Cornelius city	12	5	D	19	131	NA	NA	28	D	4	30	9	112	15	D
Corvallis city	D	211	1,731	48	653	22	129	230	4,626	22	D	179	2,837	113	792
Dallas city	42	19	116	10	68	1	D	59	D	5	D	41	D	16	D
Damascus city	25	26	110	23	144	1	D	12	D	3	D	11	131	11	31
Eugene city	1,256	687	4,203	221	4,571	78	620	733	11,120	75	1,304	526	8,479	368	2,462
Forest Grove city	D	28	D	20	249	4	D	67	D	6	43	40	581	31	82
Four Corners CDP	45	10	58	13	24	1	D	31	D	2	D	36	734	17	D
Gladstone city	43	29	D	8	46	NA	NA	25	421	4	54	15	169	6	D
Grants Pass city	248	92	434	50	876	4	D	219	3,987	21	290	145	2,089	75	385
Gresham city	445	128	D	101	1,309	20	164	359	5,038	25	394	221	3,294	131	533
Happy Valley city	D	28	70	16	99	6	D	27	213	3	30	18	285	15	D
Hayesville CDP	267	6	17	16	388	1	D	30	D	3	51	23	D	13	D
Hermiston city	58	36	D	12	333	NA	NA	74	1,195	3	D	46	D	24	D
Hillsboro city	914	220	D	141	2,309	17	289	301	5,334	27	284	237	3,789	131	996
Keizer city	218	43	207	45	487	7	19	82	D	15	133	56	D	38	209
Klamath Falls city	88	80	473	22	195	7	D	135	2,615	13	D	79	1,111	57	284
La Grande city	63	39	205	20	91	4	D	80	1,265	3	D	49	739	37	D
Lake Oswego city	627	372	3,174	85	1,086	16	106	196	2,073	26	279	113	1,928	98	462
Lebanon city	49	18	121	8	33	1	D	50	1,412	3	43	46	D	23	151
McMinnville city	120	87	D	38	513	4	5	132	2,265	10	280	86	1,138	48	D
Medford city	642	245	1,516	134	1,909	24	132	382	9,401	35	424	262	4,049	169	1,142
Milwaukie city	124	63	308	42	709	8	51	100	2,406	8	190	47	605	37	D
Newberg city	D	47	220	23	127	7	30	91	D	8	D	55	1,041	41	119
Newport city	64	47	174	21	165	3	D	67	D	11	158	100	1,277	51	251
Oak Grove CDP	40	23	81	22	D	4	37	38	D	3	16	38	480	32	D
Oak Hills CDP	28	26	D	2	D	2	D	16	138	1	D	8	76	5	18
Oatfield CDP	330	23	45	11	24	2	D	39	309	NA	NA	10	99	14	D
Ontario city	35	31	133	15	53	2	D	94	1,389	6	D	60	859	39	D
Oregon City city	109	96	373	53	372	9	D	139	2,251	12	75	79	1,044	58	D
Pendleton city	47	41	225	15	225	1	D	94	1,386	11	74	73	1,048	37	156
Portland city	8,268	3,464	30,345	976	21,778	285	3,033	2,551	56,678	384	6,193	2,522	38,496	1,699	11,796
Redmond city	164	43	D	38	606	4	D	105	1,568	6	42	93	1,231	47	204
Roseburg city	168	87	557	48	1,386	8	23	199	4,025	13	219	118	1,454	71	380
St. Helens city	54	21	50	9	D	3	D	61	926	4	24	32	451	20	D
Salem city	1,130	498	3,127	200	3,617	39	241	680	13,717	51	750	405	6,360	321	1,720

Table C. Incorporated Places, Census Designated Places (CDPs), and Minor Civil Divisions (MCDs) of 10,000 or More Population — **Economic Census**

STATE / City, town, township, borough, or CDP (county if applicable)	Utilities — Number of establishments	Utilities — Number of employees	Manufacturing — Number of establishments	Manufacturing — Number of employees	Wholesale trade[1] — Number of establishments	Wholesale trade[1] — Number of employees	Retail trade — Number of establishments	Retail trade — Number of employees	Transportation and warehousing — Number of establishments	Transportation and warehousing — Number of employees	Information — Number of establishments	Information — Number of employees	Finance and insurance — Number of establishments	Finance and insurance — Number of employees	Real estate and rental and leasing — Number of establishments
	1	2	3	4	5	6	7	8	9	10	11	12	13	14	15
OREGON—Con.															
Sherwood city	2	D	26	782	20	D	43	780	9	80	5	54	19	D	18
Springfield city	1	D	85	2,380	39	873	209	3,545	37	677	14	D	87	1,211	64
The Dalles city	2	D	22	252	17	604	108	1,417	9	88	16	D	40	D	34
Tigard city	1	D	93	1,716	148	2,255	327	7,093	36	500	79	2,671	225	3,454	121
Troutdale city	NA	NA	16	521	8	39	69	1,014	27	D	2	D	11	D	13
Tualatin city	4	D	121	6,893	107	1,685	109	1,837	31	851	19	1,116	50	254	59
West Linn city	1	D	10	264	29	93	54	473	8	157	11	76	57	177	41
Wilsonville city	4	D	59	3,924	83	1,961	71	2,033	29	540	16	239	46	278	43
Woodburn city	1	D	21	616	17	254	172	2,289	9	D	7	104	31	166	19
PENNSYLVANIA	757	30,687	13,988	543,641	12,568	195,004	43,952	643,903	8,175	209,798	5,109	130,606	17,733	266,764	9,438
Abington township (Montgomery)	NA	NA	24	115	34	201	249	4,495	16	83	11	72	87	633	43
Adams township (Butler)	NA	NA	16	997	20	216	18	168	3	D	1	D	6	D	5
Allentown city & MCD (Lehigh)	15	D	140	2,442	144	2,072	366	5,377	58	1,069	22	712	124	1,377	95
Allison Park CDP	NA	NA	NA	NA	NA	NA	NA	NA	NA	NA	NA	NA	NA	NA	NA
Altoona city & MCD (Blair)	3	D	45	1,006	47	803	248	4,693	27	434	23	383	90	996	41
Amity township (Berks)	NA	NA	13	495	11	112	27	356	9	151	NA	NA	10	D	6
Antrim township (Franklin)	NA	NA	26	2,284	8	92	21	311	9	53	5	D	8	D	3
Ardmore CDP	NA	NA	NA	NA	NA	NA	NA	NA	NA	NA	NA	NA	NA	NA	NA
Aston township (Delaware)	NA	NA	27	801	24	288	34	447	10	193	9	D	25	D	12
Baldwin borough & MCD (Allegheny)	NA	NA	3	15	5	16	17	202	4	D	4	D	5	12	2
Bensalem township (Bucks)	NA	NA	102	2,709	152	2,462	372	6,580	65	721	32	1,299	92	1,214	74
Berwick borough & MCD (Columbia)	1	D	22	1,556	10	148	43	614	5	D	5	83	19	D	9
Bethel Park municipality & MCD (Allegheny)	5	D	30	441	32	257	109	2,824	8	415	18	183	59	406	30
Bethlehem city	3	D	53	3,306	59	D	214	3,511	39	1,532	31	876	128	1,911	62
Bethlehem city (Lehigh)	1	D	16	1,776	27	1,141	64	1,129	8	221	7	D	36	1,147	19
Bethlehem city (Northampton)	2	D	37	1,530	32	D	150	2,382	31	1,311	24	D	92	764	43
Bethlehem township (Northampton)	NA	NA	24	884	29	D	53	936	26	1,113	9	120	21	203	18
Bloomsburg town & MCD (Columbia)	2	D	14	1,673	11	129	67	1,221	3	16	7	69	21	D	17
Bristol township (Bucks)	2	D	90	3,600	100	1,517	177	1,632	56	2,217	15	1,104	51	308	41
Broomall CDP	NA	NA	NA	NA	NA	NA	NA	NA	NA	NA	NA	NA	NA	NA	NA
Buckingham township (Bucks)	NA	NA	19	92	29	170	101	721	9	353	9	D	32	139	16
Butler city & MCD (Butler)	1	D	21	253	19	200	66	769	5	184	8	D	24	167	18
Butler township (Butler)	NA	NA	13	1,659	13	217	94	2,513	5	D	6	171	34	292	27
Caln township (Chester)	1	D	6	109	5	154	33	703	2	D	2	D	13	74	3
Carlisle borough & MCD (Cumberland)	NA	NA	22	1,126	8	205	112	2,017	23	2,023	11	211	50	325	28
Carnot-Moon CDP	NA	NA	NA	NA	NA	NA	NA	NA	NA	NA	NA	NA	NA	NA	NA
Cecil township (Washington)	5	206	19	1,152	25	1,037	6	7	3	D	8	D	31	174	19
Center township (Beaver)	1	D	4	D	4	D	50	1,213	4	D	3	80	11	D	4
Chambersburg borough & MCD (Franklin)	NA	NA	31	1,505	36	820	133	2,317	15	1,669	19	309	56	631	34
Cheltenham township (Montgomery)	NA	NA	34	239	32	251	103	1,169	5	D	14	62	61	648	25
Chester city & MCD (Delaware)	2	D	26	1,401	18	163	61	340	11	116	6	D	3	27	15
Chestnuthill township (Monroe)	NA	NA	7	D	9	D	54	757	7	16	3	25	14	73	9
Coal township (Northumberland)	NA	NA	6	95	4	D	23	449	5	D	NA	NA	1	D	3
Coatesville city & MCD (Chester)	1	D	10	859	2	D	39	241	6	48	3	D	7	62	11
Colonial Park CDP	NA	NA	NA	NA	NA	NA	NA	NA	NA	NA	NA	NA	NA	NA	NA
Columbia borough & MCD (Lancaster)	1	D	10	773	13	215	26	338	4	36	1	D	9	34	6
Concord township (Delaware)	NA	NA	6	373	15	397	83	2,079	3	D	6	D	32	D	15
Coolbaugh township (Monroe)	1	D	NA	NA	4	48	11	85	7	D	NA	NA	2	D	4
Cranberry township (Butler)	NA	NA	38	2,619	86	1,462	159	3,547	21	715	23	1,237	64	1,210	37
Croydon CDP	NA	NA	NA	NA	NA	NA	NA	NA	NA	NA	NA	NA	NA	NA	NA
Cumru township (Berks)	NA	NA	8	407	3	D	22	194	5	22	2	D	14	77	10
Darby borough & MCD (Delaware)	NA	NA	NA	NA	6	33	24	587	2	D	1	D	6	D	4
Derry township (Dauphin)	3	D	10	D	15	31	122	1,804	2	3	13	100	49	266	26
Derry township (Westmoreland)	NA	NA	32	1,306	10	58	12	65	8	72	1	D	3	6	4
Dingman township (Pike)	1	D	NA	NA	1	D	1	D	4	5	NA	NA	2	D	2
Douglass township (Montgomery)	1	D	19	424	7	D	40	543	1	D	2	D	7	D	8
Dover township (York)	NA	NA	15	279	9	63	28	487	13	104	2	D	10	34	6
Doylestown township (Bucks)	1	D	8	143	17	55	35	935	10	27	8	D	52	348	23
Drexel Hill CDP	NA	NA	NA	NA	NA	NA	NA	NA	NA	NA	NA	NA	NA	NA	NA
Dunmore borough & MCD (Lackawanna)	2	D	14	601	25	515	48	639	13	633	6	851	26	382	8

1 Merchant wholesalers, except manufacturers' sales branches and offices.

Table C. Incorporated Places, Census Designated Places (CDPs), and Minor Civil Divisions (MCDs) of 10,000 or More Population — **Economic Census**

STATE / City, town, township, borough, or CDP (county if applicable)	Real estate and rental and leasing — Number of employees	Professional, scientific, and technical services — Number of establishments	— Number of employees	Administration and support and waste management and mediation services — Number of establishments	— Number of employees	Educational services — Number of establishments	— Number of employees	Health care and social assistance — Number of establishments	— Number of employees	Arts, entertainment, and recreation — Number of establishments	— Number of employees	Accommodation and food services — Number of establishments	— Number of employees	Other services (except public administration) — Number of establishments	— Number of employees
	16	17	18	19	20	21	22	23	24	25	26	27	28	29	30
OREGON—Con.															
Sherwood city	67	50	D	24	275	4	17	48	446	6	D	40	564	38	261
Springfield city	274	87	572	67	1,226	18	73	194	7,058	21	184	168	2,503	93	444
The Dalles city	88	39	249	22	145	6	D	69	1,725	5	38	61	911	43	D
Tigard city	615	363	3,238	166	5,376	29	281	226	2,654	18	218	167	2,707	131	845
Troutdale city	56	22	D	18	77	5	D	20	228	NA	NA	35	756	20	D
Tualatin city	595	108	1,279	57	D	8	96	141	D	12	418	80	1,542	89	542
West Linn city	172	122	290	38	165	8	44	96	558	14	73	45	645	47	D
Wilsonville city	222	72	1,651	46	1,504	7	34	65	2,036	5	127	68	974	50	283
Woodburn city	133	26	124	19	296	2	D	55	D	9	120	55	D	21	83
PENNSYLVANIA	58,585	29,297	316,658	15,046	310,656	2,315	22,560	36,552	955,479	4,402	99,568	27,646	439,159	25,231	154,319
Abington township (Montgomery)	198	134	598	89	490	14	83	239	10,498	21	390	105	D	105	581
Adams township (Butler)	14	31	D	17	253	4	22	37	879	5	27	15	347	18	D
Allentown city & MCD (Lehigh)	498	215	1,823	108	3,206	25	261	399	9,074	32	365	255	3,394	251	1,659
Allison Park CDP	NA	NA	NA	NA	NA	NA	NA	NA	NA	NA	NA	NA	NA	NA	NA
Altoona city & MCD (Blair)	193	88	791	78	1,149	9	95	217	5,724	21	142	137	2,176	125	728
Amity township (Berks)	12	15	D	20	99	3	D	20	251	7	32	15	247	24	D
Antrim township (Franklin)	22	9	52	9	65	1	D	9	61	5	D	10	D	19	118
Ardmore CDP	NA	NA	NA	NA	NA	NA	NA	NA	NA	NA	NA	NA	NA	NA	NA
Aston township (Delaware)	62	37	329	31	594	8	D	33	246	3	D	37	612	36	D
Baldwin borough & MCD (Allegheny)	D	14	283	17	80	6	23	25	809	2	D	14	172	20	132
Bensalem township (Bucks)	682	170	1,382	105	1,876	16	47	174	2,265	34	D	178	3,689	141	781
Berwick borough & MCD (Columbia)	22	18	115	5	20	NA	NA	45	D	3	15	28	301	25	95
Bethel Park municipality & MCD (Allegheny)	104	92	391	46	181	6	73	124	1,738	11	145	65	1,589	85	644
Bethlehem city	306	176	1,009	57	3,363	13	58	247	6,248	20	327	217	4,921	140	1,015
Bethlehem city (Lehigh)	102	34	224	18	558	2	D	99	4,129	5	71	36	598	42	408
Bethlehem city (Northampton)	204	142	785	39	2,805	11	D	148	2,119	15	256	181	4,323	98	607
Bethlehem township (Northampton)	81	45	401	26	383	7	41	84	1,696	6	99	37	725	28	D
Bloomsburg town & MCD (Columbia)	95	44	245	13	347	4	D	47	D	8	126	54	1,042	37	205
Bristol township (Bucks)	845	58	610	61	899	4	6	101	1,882	11	296	104	1,085	120	823
Broomall CDP	NA	NA	NA	NA	NA	NA	NA	NA	NA	NA	NA	NA	NA	NA	NA
Buckingham township (Bucks)	52	105	377	39	198	6	26	38	320	8	154	30	565	28	D
Butler city & MCD (Butler)	61	52	402	19	212	2	D	101	2,878	3	D	36	425	40	195
Butler township (Butler)	108	38	504	18	822	4	D	83	1,829	14	92	51	1,271	55	294
Caln township (Chester)	8	19	34	10	68	NA	NA	46	2,853	NA	NA	20	484	17	D
Carlisle borough & MCD (Cumberland)	99	75	490	21	353	6	46	84	1,957	10	D	88	1,559	66	440
Carnot-Moon CDP	NA	NA	NA	NA	NA	NA	NA	NA	NA	NA	NA	NA	NA	NA	NA
Cecil township (Washington)	115	55	955	34	1,430	2	D	14	332	2	D	9	78	18	96
Center township (Beaver)	10	17	75	16	813	2	D	46	888	3	16	25	759	23	123
Chambersburg borough & MCD (Franklin)	103	90	1,288	31	1,503	7	46	160	5,406	10	203	99	1,599	76	463
Cheltenham township (Montgomery)	139	136	1,254	55	507	18	140	127	2,275	15	165	61	552	66	D
Chester city & MCD (Delaware)	D	15	271	19	328	7	D	67	2,000	4	D	40	D	39	D
Chestnuthill township (Monroe)	14	17	D	14	43	4	8	33	418	4	17	22	303	20	60
Coal township (Northumberland)	11	5	29	4	D	NA	NA	17	1,261	1	D	17	213	4	D
Coatesville city & MCD (Chester)	40	9	50	7	D	1	D	29	288	4	32	15	99	21	D
Colonial Park CDP	NA	NA	NA	NA	NA	NA	NA	NA	NA	NA	NA	NA	NA	NA	NA
Columbia borough & MCD (Lancaster)	14	7	D	5	24	NA	NA	17	D	1	D	21	221	21	104
Concord township (Delaware)	19	59	399	36	1,529	8	41	59	1,251	10	D	51	1,553	29	D
Coolbaugh township (Monroe)	9	7	D	10	19	1	D	13	D	1	D	8	22	14	70
Cranberry township (Butler)	158	119	4,873	58	1,694	9	131	131	1,940	5	D	84	2,476	72	740
Croydon CDP	NA	NA	NA	NA	NA	NA	NA	NA	NA	NA	NA	NA	NA	NA	NA
Cumru township (Berks)	84	24	200	19	135	NA	NA	31	771	4	65	21	D	18	D
Darby borough & MCD (Delaware)	38	2	D	3	D	1	D	37	2,189	2	D	20	151	9	28
Derry township (Dauphin)	D	58	391	19	143	9	38	99	1,899	19	D	86	2,988	48	936
Derry township (Westmoreland)	D	4	D	8	104	1	D	23	1,013	5	D	12	94	19	98
Dingman township (Pike)	D	7	16	5	25	1	D	1	D	1	D	NA	NA	5	D
Douglass township (Montgomery)	37	16	82	12	189	NA	NA	12	152	4	81	28	286	20	D
Dover township (York)	8	14	85	23	223	NA	NA	25	415	4	82	19	222	15	35
Doylestown township (Bucks)	65	101	556	43	D	7	D	101	3,573	6	D	39	623	28	387
Drexel Hill CDP	NA	NA	NA	NA	NA	NA	NA	NA	NA	NA	NA	NA	NA	NA	NA
Dunmore borough & MCD (Lackawanna)	47	44	297	28	715	1	D	65	1,256	4	D	48	543	29	D

Table C. Incorporated Places, Census Designated Places (CDPs), and Minor Civil Divisions (MCDs) of 10,000 or More Population — **Economic Census**

STATE / City, town, township, borough, or CDP (county if applicable)	Utilities		Manufacturing		Wholesale trade[1]		Retail trade		Transportation and warehousing		Information		Finance and insurance		Real estate and rental and leasing
	Number of establishments	Number of employees	Number of establishments	Number of employees	Number of establishments	Number of employees	Number of establishments	Number of employees	Number of establishments	Number of employees	Number of establishments	Number of employees	Number of establishments	Number of employees	Number of establishments
	1	2	3	4	5	6	7	8	9	10	11	12	13	14	15
PENNSYLVANIA—Con.															
East Cocalico township (Lancaster)	NA	NA	36	2,021	12	759	24	186	21	D	3	5	6	47	5
East Goshen township (Chester)	NA	NA	7	725	15	71	25	D	5	12	7	D	22	70	20
East Hempfield township (Lancaster)	NA	NA	55	3,728	65	1,126	94	1,453	20	791	15	129	43	319	25
East Lampeter township (Lancaster)	NA	NA	56	3,217	44	784	203	2,654	17	249	12	215	31	288	12
East Norriton township (Montgomery)	NA	NA	4	33	13	D	68	983	6	24	6	55	34	217	14
Easton city & MCD (Northampton)	1	D	26	505	28	D	143	1,730	14	358	9	253	42	388	21
East Pennsboro township (Cumberland)	NA	NA	5	25	3	D	36	560	6	9	5	28	40	1,404	12
Easttown township (Chester)	4	D	8	45	11	D	38	606	2	D	2	D	34	247	20
East Whiteland township (Chester)	1	D	32	808	63	3,570	92	1,140	12	232	34	1,800	78	679	29
Elizabeth township (Allegheny)	1	D	15	421	9	105	21	295	8	140	2	D	9	42	2
Elizabethtown borough & MCD (Lancaster)	NA	NA	9	353	7	101	41	753	3	D	5	75	15	80	10
Emmaus borough & MCD (Lehigh)	1	D	21	329	5	D	61	799	3	D	9	D	21	99	8
Ephrata borough & MCD (Lancaster)	NA	NA	25	530	14	251	59	620	3	D	8	D	24	202	10
Erie city & MCD (Erie)	6	D	148	5,832	110	1,629	374	5,516	49	569	38	837	152	4,109	66
Exeter township (Berks)	1	D	14	1,035	14	231	61	1,664	14	381	8	105	33	163	9
Fairview township (Erie)	1	D	41	1,899	3	103	21	131	6	120	NA	NA	11	D	5
Fairview township (York)	1	D	18	316	20	264	27	683	23	984	4	41	12	124	7
Falls township (Bucks)	4	D	58	1,696	65	1,104	126	2,172	46	1,483	8	214	26	217	34
Ferguson township (Centre)	1	D	14	467	7	52	55	1,174	4	63	10	348	35	224	23
Forks township (Northampton)	2	D	22	1,613	8	88	25	504	6	D	1	D	13	D	8
Franconia township (Montgomery)	NA	NA	23	2,265	19	191	10	154	6	273	1	D	6	D	9
Franklin Park borough & MCD (Allegheny)	2	D	5	13	10	36	14	189	4	7	7	D	34	224	8
Fullerton CDP	NA	NA	NA	NA	NA	NA	NA	NA	NA	NA	NA	NA	NA	NA	NA
Greene township (Franklin)	NA	NA	16	561	9	92	48	423	3	D	4	D	7	44	7
Greensburg city & MCD (Westmoreland)	4	D	31	598	29	257	250	4,343	15	261	25	843	71	506	39
Guilford township (Franklin)	NA	NA	17	602	17	219	67	1,229	12	136	1	D	19	88	10
Hamilton township (Franklin)	NA	NA	6	D	7	D	24	315	10	126	2	D	6	D	2
Hampden township (Cumberland)	NA	NA	19	1,068	33	355	126	2,137	36	3,654	9	115	66	461	36
Hampton township (Allegheny)	NA	NA	13	44	22	195	55	544	5	29	3	14	29	219	23
Hanover township (Luzerne)	1	D	21	1,220	19	582	38	489	10	548	7	230	14	D	7
Hanover township (Northampton)	NA	NA	20	785	26	409	18	538	7	D	12	558	34	2,343	9
Hanover borough & MCD (York)	NA	NA	38	4,170	17	187	165	2,706	5	77	10	156	47	311	24
Harborcreek township (Erie)	NA	NA	15	452	6	86	50	1,100	8	89	9	166	15	71	14
Harrisburg city & MCD (Dauphin)	13	D	32	1,432	58	1,349	233	2,682	37	537	47	965	93	4,368	44
Harrison township (Allegheny)	NA	NA	12	257	5	28	48	769	5	139	1	D	20	84	7
Hatfield township (Montgomery)	NA	NA	74	5,018	64	2,097	73	1,319	15	905	8	126	22	D	20
Haverford township (Delaware)	1	D	22	182	33	169	93	1,138	9	D	17	182	55	250	26
Hazleton city & MCD (Luzerne)	3	D	47	2,606	33	499	112	1,124	28	1,059	13	292	41	164	19
Hempfield township (Westmoreland)	4	D	37	911	29	888	69	1,738	18	251	10	100	40	248	21
Hermitage city & MCD (Mercer)	NA	NA	20	1,286	13	233	125	2,516	8	69	10	118	45	792	23
Hershey CDP	NA	NA	NA	NA	NA	NA	NA	NA	NA	NA	NA	NA	NA	NA	NA
Hilltown township (Bucks)	NA	NA	33	1,388	35	280	58	1,381	13	135	2	D	13	97	7
Hopewell township (Beaver)	1	D	8	529	8	43	43	654	10	153	1	D	6	D	5
Horsham CDP	NA	NA	NA	NA	NA	NA	NA	NA	NA	NA	NA	NA	NA	NA	NA
Horsham township (Montgomery)	NA	NA	39	2,323	60	D	77	1,354	12	D	27	2,988	104	4,008	28
Indiana borough & MCD (Indiana)	1	D	10	552	9	D	67	961	4	16	6	197	38	1,109	19
Jefferson Hills borough & MCD (Allegheny)	NA	NA	10	465	9	D	11	44	3	D	NA	NA	8	20	7
Johnstown city & MCD (Cambria)	2	D	37	2,010	27	195	102	1,589	7	D	21	622	54	708	29
King of Prussia CDP	NA	NA	NA	NA	NA	NA	NA	NA	NA	NA	NA	NA	NA	NA	NA

1 Merchant wholesalers, except manufacturers' sales branches and offices.

Table C. Incorporated Places, Census Designated Places (CDPs), and Minor Civil Divisions (MCDs) of 10,000 or More Population — **Economic Census**

STATE City, town, township, borough, or CDP (county if applicable)	Real estate and rental and leasing — Number of employees	Professional, scientific, and technical services — Number of establishments	Number of employees	Administration and support and waste management and mediation services — Number of establishments	Number of employees	Educational services — Number of establishments	Number of employees	Health care and social assistance — Number of establishments	Number of employees	Arts, entertainment, and recreation — Number of establishments	Number of employees	Accommodation and food services — Number of establishments	Number of employees	Other services (except public administration) — Number of establishments	Number of employees
	16	17	18	19	20	21	22	23	24	25	26	27	28	29	30
PENNSYLVANIA—Con.															
East Cocalico township (Lancaster)	39	14	90	14	434	NA	NA	14	124	2	D	24	379	25	162
East Goshen township (Chester)	94	57	506	25	257	6	D	28	623	3	D	14	230	29	D
East Hempfield township (Lancaster)	201	64	368	49	807	7	134	106	2,722	10	166	43	982	45	326
East Lampeter township (Lancaster)	80	48	507	33	564	2	D	34	1,305	7	271	118	2,609	40	310
East Norriton township (Montgomery)	130	58	659	38	252	5	47	71	2,069	8	207	40	D	40	305
Easton city & MCD (Northampton)	D	87	369	28	653	3	D	85	1,080	11	354	110	1,447	66	321
East Pennsboro township (Cumberland)	33	37	1,291	13	265	4	16	78	3,608	2	D	42	641	27	196
Easttown township (Chester)	141	64	506	15	110	9	43	50	2,034	9	512	28	402	22	D
East Whiteland township (Chester)	161	187	2,571	62	1,020	7	80	48	605	13	302	62	1,509	47	D
Elizabeth township (Allegheny)	D	6	69	14	163	3	D	24	210	7	D	20	152	24	99
Elizabethtown borough & MCD (Lancaster)	16	24	132	9	271	1	D	24	1,569	6	D	20	180	27	115
Emmaus borough & MCD (Lehigh)	29	28	161	24	319	2	D	35	343	4	D	26	309	30	358
Ephrata borough & MCD (Lancaster)	35	27	183	21	1,645	1	D	57	D	5	120	37	625	44	268
Erie city & MCD (Erie)	427	197	1,798	103	2,523	14	91	451	17,754	42	D	222	3,551	225	1,448
Exeter township (Berks)	86	42	186	32	349	3	6	45	889	9	D	46	931	36	D
Fairview township (Erie)	34	6	15	6	19	NA	NA	23	755	5	D	15	131	15	D
Fairview township (York)	39	38	471	32	397	4	D	16	199	5	21	26	375	30	203
Falls township (Bucks)	178	62	685	73	610	6	50	65	555	11	D	69	890	84	361
Ferguson township (Centre)	161	82	1,412	25	205	7	86	46	442	5	78	27	763	37	220
Forks township (Northampton)	23	17	158	14	128	4	D	18	197	6	27	25	171	18	D
Franconia township (Montgomery)	59	32	95	26	426	2	D	16	821	4	D	13	179	18	D
Franklin Park borough & MCD (Allegheny)	29	51	340	17	340	3	11	26	279	4	D	6	96	10	61
Fullerton CDP	NA	NA	NA	NA	NA	NA	NA	NA	NA	NA	NA	NA	NA	NA	NA
Greene township (Franklin)	29	19	128	15	368	3	13	9	100	8	45	16	205	22	D
Greensburg city & MCD (Westmoreland)	142	131	678	29	446	6	D	178	6,221	17	257	92	1,755	88	495
Guilford township (Franklin)	47	18	112	14	148	1	D	21	446	5	68	26	416	33	D
Hamilton township (Franklin)	D	5	26	7	64	NA	NA	6	D	4	17	15	D	16	61
Hampden township (Cumberland)	219	127	1,570	45	847	11	51	68	2,085	11	D	62	1,493	52	469
Hampton township (Allegheny)	113	58	593	37	328	5	61	64	525	9	187	35	620	40	215
Hanover township (Luzerne)	58	12	938	24	621	3	41	17	173	1	D	30	310	29	D
Hanover township (Northampton)	93	50	1,386	13	571	4	D	69	1,447	4	24	26	D	10	D
Hanover borough & MCD (York)	73	62	271	19	957	3	D	113	D	5	D	62	1,558	62	478
Harborcreek township (Erie)	46	10	130	14	50	2	D	31	668	5	188	29	588	28	D
Harrisburg city & MCD (Dauphin)	381	263	3,113	86	1,383	10	28	187	7,663	24	D	183	2,537	200	1,217
Harrison township (Allegheny)	21	12	76	4	D	NA	NA	54	D	4	5	21	377	29	81
Hatfield township (Montgomery)	110	51	526	27	808	3	35	76	1,683	8	158	31	378	49	391
Haverford township (Delaware)	242	140	490	64	367	15	164	166	2,973	21	534	64	652	88	365
Hazleton city & MCD (Luzerne)	51	54	472	31	1,700	4	D	110	2,999	7	D	60	553	48	150
Hempfield township (Westmoreland)	74	61	215	42	598	4	46	109	1,956	8	D	60	1,785	53	238
Hermitage city & MCD (Mercer)	97	47	301	27	462	2	D	153	2,666	12	234	62	1,442	45	263
Hershey CDP	NA	NA	NA	NA	NA	NA	NA	NA	NA	NA	NA	NA	NA	NA	NA
Hilltown township (Bucks)	24	24	68	35	395	2	D	23	370	6	D	27	298	31	112
Hopewell township (Beaver)	15	13	755	11	63	1	D	33	341	3	11	26	451	20	136
Horsham CDP	NA	NA	NA	NA	NA	NA	NA	NA	NA	NA	NA	NA	NA	NA	NA
Horsham township (Montgomery)	280	132	2,075	72	2,774	7	58	58	3,253	22	421	80	1,189	52	D
Indiana borough & MCD (Indiana)	62	48	262	14	168	1	D	60	1,087	3	D	54	1,240	33	185
Jefferson Hills borough & MCD (Allegheny)	21	17	87	13	70	1	D	52	2,749	3	12	10	75	10	101
Johnstown city & MCD (Cambria)	200	82	919	32	796	4	14	161	6,057	7	176	69	869	63	353
King of Prussia CDP	NA	NA	NA	NA	NA	NA	NA	NA	NA	NA	NA	NA	NA	NA	NA

Table C. Incorporated Places, Census Designated Places (CDPs), and Minor Civil Divisions (MCDs) of 10,000 or More Population — **Economic Census**

STATE City, town, township, borough, or CDP (county if applicable)	Utilities Number of establish-ments	Number of employees	Manufacturing Number of establish-ments	Number of employees	Wholesale trade[1] Number of establish-ments	Number of employees	Retail trade Number of establish-ments	Number of employees	Transportation and warehousing Number of establish-ments	Number of employees	Information Number of establish-ments	Number of employees	Finance and insurance Number of establish-ments	Number of employees	Real estate and rental and leasing Number of establish-ments
	1	2	3	4	5	6	7	8	9	10	11	12	13	14	15
PENNSYLVANIA—Con.															
Kingston borough & MCD (Luzerne)	NA	NA	15	72	27	222	72	690	6	43	1	D	33	225	23
Lancaster city & MCD (Lancaster)	4	16	74	3,363	60	719	364	5,382	18	1,671	31	892	81	1,331	48
Lancaster township (Lancaster)	1	D	6	D	5	43	45	616	1	D	5	186	13	170	7
Lansdale borough & MCD (Montgomery)	NA	NA	37	782	22	D	67	836	12	190	10	450	32	229	15
Lansdowne borough & MCD (Delaware)	NA	NA	NA	NA	7	71	20	232	2	D	4	D	9	D	4
Lebanon city & MCD (Lebanon)	NA	NA	55	1,140	18	D	107	1,260	7	55	14	254	41	357	27
Lehigh township (Northampton)	NA	NA	7	30	4	28	20	103	2	D	1	D	6	20	1
Lehman township (Pike)	2	D	NA	NA	1	D	1	D	3	D	NA	NA	NA	NA	3
Levittown CDP	NA	NA	NA	NA	NA	NA	NA	NA	NA	NA	NA	NA	NA	NA	NA
Limerick township (Montgomery)	1	D	18	966	25	D	190	3,544	25	692	2	D	37	176	11
Logan township (Blair)	NA	NA	12	505	18	359	81	1,186	9	391	13	494	9	47	16
Lower Allen township (Cumberland)	2	D	18	582	32	355	109	2,107	14	317	9	270	54	1,146	21
Lower Burrell city & MCD (Westmoreland)	1	D	7	100	2	D	41	432	1	D	2	D	14	D	10
Lower Gwynedd township (Montgomery)	NA	NA	5	D	18	158	27	369	3	6	10	62	30	195	19
Lower Macungie township (Lehigh)	NA	NA	18	2,228	25	285	37	380	17	562	10	80	31	176	32
Lower Makefield township (Bucks)	1	D	3	23	26	334	32	692	9	38	8	5	48	308	11
Lower Merion township (Montgomery)	5	D	36	395	76	488	311	4,199	12	113	101	2,199	242	4,589	130
Lower Moreland township (Montgomery)	1	D	30	678	45	758	53	311	15	102	9	78	44	300	29
Lower Paxton township (Dauphin)	1	D	22	231	46	832	197	4,234	14	159	32	833	84	698	49
Lower Pottsgrove township (Montgomery)	NA	NA	NA	NA	4	D	25	557	4	79	1	D	16	267	10
Lower Providence township (Montgomery)	2	D	23	840	23	186	65	1,131	11	206	18	231	37	643	15
Lower Salford township (Montgomery)	1	D	27	1,368	20	304	45	677	4	D	2	D	31	1,271	17
Lower Saucon township (Northampton)	NA	NA	6	97	8	78	19	259	3	D	NA	NA	3	D	4
Lower Southampton township (Bucks)	1	D	54	1,827	77	917	154	1,519	50	147	17	823	98	529	41
Loyalsock township (Lycoming)	NA	NA	13	467	12	218	61	825	6	27	6	54	33	230	18
McCandless township (Allegheny)	NA	NA	7	22	20	161	72	1,204	6	21	5	185	61	276	32
McKeesport city & MCD (Allegheny)	1	D	13	282	19	252	81	952	8	348	4	D	27	104	10
Manchester township (York)	1	D	72	3,720	48	1,029	38	502	22	723	6	171	29	130	18
Manheim township (Lancaster)	2	D	40	2,017	53	622	165	3,823	25	733	17	229	140	1,353	78
Manor township (Lancaster)	NA	NA	8	D	6	D	33	627	3	D	2	D	14	75	11
Marple township (Delaware)	NA	NA	24	479	39	371	83	1,436	7	100	11	D	38	631	14
Meadville city & MCD (Crawford)	3	D	43	1,185	13	129	76	1,066	5	84	11	202	41	246	19
Middle Smithfield township (Monroe)	NA	NA	NA	NA	NA	NA	13	155	1	D	NA	NA	3	D	2
Middletown township (Bucks)	NA	NA	17	399	35	299	117	3,208	19	98	16	211	54	374	35
Middletown township (Delaware)	2	D	11	243	7	28	28	372	6	D	6	16	13	D	7
Millcreek township (Erie)	4	D	97	2,696	69	921	216	3,761	30	793	18	226	89	521	58
Monroeville municipality & MCD (Allegheny)	NA	NA	17	549	46	520	276	5,452	11	17	25	289	84	712	58
Montgomery township (Montgomery)	NA	NA	52	2,170	41	477	90	2,488	13	255	15	218	35	239	17
Montgomeryville CDP	NA	NA	NA	NA	NA	NA	NA	NA	NA	NA	NA	NA	NA	NA	NA
Moon township (Allegheny)	2	D	11	187	34	365	75	1,381	50	2,570	18	1,316	48	994	44
Mountain Top CDP	NA	NA	NA	NA	NA	NA	NA	NA	NA	NA	NA	NA	NA	NA	NA
Mount Joy township (Lancaster)	NA	NA	4	551	8	288	28	670	17	D	1	D	6	23	4
Mount Lebanon township (Allegheny)	NA	NA	7	14	13	157	80	696	3	D	8	61	36	191	26
Mount Pleasant township (Westmoreland)	NA	NA	29	841	13	163	46	623	8	318	3	D	12	47	7
Muhlenberg township (Berks)	1	D	42	2,330	42	1,130	116	2,591	23	788	8	D	29	136	15
Munhall borough & MCD (Allegheny)	NA	NA	3	D	5	D	19	402	3	8	2	D	10	70	6
Murrysville municipality & MCD (Westmoreland)	1	D	28	2,196	27	D	54	695	9	76	6	110	36	346	23

1 Merchant wholesalers, except manufacturers' sales branches and offices.

Table C. Incorporated Places, Census Designated Places (CDPs), and Minor Civil Divisions (MCDs) of 10,000 or More Population — **Economic Census**

STATE City, town, township, borough, or CDP (county if applicable)	Real estate and rental and leasing — Number of employees	Professional, scientific, and technical services — Number of establishments	Number of employees	Administration and support and waste management and mediation services — Number of establishments	Number of employees	Educational services — Number of establishments	Number of employees	Health care and social assistance — Number of establishments	Number of employees	Arts, entertainment, and recreation — Number of establishments	Number of employees	Accommodation and food services — Number of establishments	Number of employees	Other services (except public administration) — Number of establishments	Number of employees
	16	17	18	19	20	21	22	23	24	25	26	27	28	29	30
PENNSYLVANIA—Con.															
Kingston borough & MCD (Luzerne)	84	80	388	21	592	3	9	127	2,622	5	D	44	547	35	D
Lancaster city & MCD (Lancaster)	394	224	1,836	57	891	15	109	208	9,829	23	399	162	2,948	142	814
Lancaster township (Lancaster)	D	26	111	10	76	3	D	37	1,507	5	D	24	508	18	D
Lansdale borough & MCD (Montgomery)	153	50	233	25	186	7	32	61	1,798	5	D	53	463	65	339
Lansdowne borough & MCD (Delaware)	7	18	46	10	149	1	D	25	291	3	D	14	257	12	37
Lebanon city & MCD (Lebanon)	128	54	334	18	824	2	D	98	2,847	6	D	58	609	72	273
Lehigh township (Northampton)	D	10	69	12	102	3	2	12	87	2	D	12	D	17	D
Lehman township (Pike)	D	4	9	5	22	2	D	NA	NA	4	116	4	42	8	196
Levittown CDP	NA	NA	NA	NA	NA	NA	NA	NA	NA	NA	NA	NA	NA	NA	NA
Limerick township (Montgomery)	50	57	330	33	342	5	36	44	D	13	596	55	1,014	49	D
Logan township (Blair)	70	19	49	13	386	1	D	31	1,414	9	159	37	853	25	234
Lower Allen township (Cumberland)	210	79	1,062	37	747	6	43	75	1,908	5	D	49	886	55	527
Lower Burrell city & MCD (Westmoreland)	48	18	86	10	27	5	41	40	403	6	52	20	224	36	181
Lower Gwynedd township (Montgomery)	D	69	1,083	23	657	5	27	56	1,503	7	93	22	357	21	D
Lower Macungie township (Lehigh)	70	71	471	30	442	8	53	61	831	6	37	36	520	37	212
Lower Makefield township (Bucks)	22	129	2,895	35	490	14	41	62	570	6	96	25	414	20	D
Lower Merion township (Montgomery)	753	442	2,710	110	2,041	42	582	474	9,898	50	768	186	D	209	1,945
Lower Moreland township (Montgomery)	D	90	302	31	389	6	166	108	1,156	6	165	31	257	53	284
Lower Paxton township (Dauphin)	247	118	1,097	78	2,005	17	167	205	4,644	16	119	106	2,359	109	694
Lower Pottsgrove township (Montgomery)	63	26	208	21	1,582	4	D	57	866	4	23	15	259	14	94
Lower Providence township (Montgomery)	77	86	1,983	55	667	8	109	46	1,832	8	D	54	756	42	D
Lower Salford township (Montgomery)	D	62	751	20	D	6	56	38	696	4	D	24	280	30	D
Lower Saucon township (Northampton)	D	23	135	20	D	1	D	9	163	1	D	20	503	18	68
Lower Southampton township (Bucks)	323	174	1,119	72	1,045	11	D	110	2,786	21	317	65	1,353	106	500
Loyalsock township (Lycoming)	186	33	302	16	219	2	D	58	1,438	6	114	48	1,186	27	D
McCandless township (Allegheny)	132	89	781	30	591	10	68	142	4,464	10	50	40	962	61	D
McKeesport city & MCD (Allegheny)	37	24	85	16	195	2	D	105	2,637	6	22	40	336	38	196
Manchester township (York)	194	24	459	27	857	4	D	21	304	8	134	36	960	33	681
Manheim township (Lancaster)	464	119	1,050	70	3,502	17	206	180	5,845	12	D	104	2,457	89	909
Manor township (Lancaster)	87	28	472	25	162	1	D	20	158	6	84	14	263	29	D
Marple township (Delaware)	144	86	620	36	509	10	202	89	2,848	15	D	46	603	61	338
Meadville city & MCD (Crawford)	79	50	280	16	186	8	D	113	2,374	4	D	42	682	50	270
Middle Smithfield township (Monroe)	D	2	D	2	D	1	D	5	175	2	D	14	D	2	D
Middletown township (Bucks)	130	115	836	74	1,162	13	D	205	6,133	6	8	69	1,528	56	507
Middletown township (Delaware)	14	35	249	25	185	2	D	87	4,680	8	336	21	298	16	D
Millcreek township (Erie)	317	100	570	59	2,339	15	193	176	4,053	18	D	135	2,691	115	868
Monroeville municipality & MCD (Allegheny)	546	100	1,194	53	901	13	118	214	3,739	19	204	128	2,852	87	526
Montgomery township (Montgomery)	63	102	524	44	548	12	101	39	466	3	D	46	1,153	26	D
Montgomeryville CDP	NA	NA	NA	NA	NA	NA	NA	NA	NA	NA	NA	NA	NA	NA	NA
Moon township (Allegheny)	407	91	2,564	54	2,387	7	30	122	1,384	10	140	80	2,114	50	433
Mountain Top CDP	NA	NA	NA	NA	NA	NA	NA	NA	NA	NA	NA	NA	NA	NA	NA
Mount Joy township (Lancaster)	13	19	153	10	122	1	D	12	190	4	46	16	D	25	D
Mount Lebanon township (Allegheny)	89	130	427	32	398	9	69	131	2,707	10	69	47	815	47	316
Mount Pleasant township (Westmoreland)	47	11	63	10	70	NA	NA	25	173	6	19	30	459	33	197
Muhlenberg township (Berks)	38	25	172	32	993	NA	NA	38	586	11	69	47	771	49	320
Munhall borough & MCD (Allegheny)	62	11	133	8	169	NA	NA	26	538	1	D	24	218	18	D
Murrysville municipality & MCD (Westmoreland)	83	81	491	36	372	7	23	62	666	12	85	28	695	43	D

Table C. Incorporated Places, Census Designated Places (CDPs), and Minor Civil Divisions (MCDs) of 10,000 or More Population — Economic Census

STATE City, town, township, borough, or CDP (county if applicable)	Utilities Number of establish-ments	Utilities Number of employees	Manufacturing Number of establish-ments	Manufacturing Number of employees	Wholesale trade[1] Number of establish-ments	Wholesale trade[1] Number of employees	Retail trade Number of establish-ments	Retail trade Number of employees	Transportation and warehousing Number of establish-ments	Transportation and warehousing Number of employees	Information Number of establish-ments	Information Number of employees	Finance and insurance Number of establish-ments	Finance and insurance Number of employees	Real estate and rental and leasing Number of establish-ments
	1	2	3	4	5	6	7	8	9	10	11	12	13	14	15
PENNSYLVANIA—Con.															
Nanticoke city & MCD (Luzerne)...............	NA	NA	5	52	2	D	28	286	3	D	2	D	14	51	4
Nether Providence township (Delaware)	NA	NA	NA	NA	4	8	7	62	3	D	3	D	7	17	10
Newberry township (York).	NA	NA	6	172	6	133	16	108	10	49	1	D	5	D	7
New Britain township (Bucks)......................	NA	NA	18	957	16	263	18	210	1	D	2	D	17	D	6
New Castle city & MCD (Lawrence)...............	9	D	51	1,102	34	D	79	601	12	244	12	D	25	196	18
New Garden township (Chester)...................	NA	NA	7	137	22	660	21	322	12	454	3	D	7	38	5
New Hanover township (Montgomery)	1	D	5	8	2	D	9	109	1	D	NA	NA	9	D	2
New Kensington city & MCD (Westmoreland) ...	NA	NA	20	507	24	172	46	826	1	D	7	146	23	104	11
Newtown township (Bucks)	1	D	15	442	34	380	70	825	8	6	11	141	78	761	24
Newtown township (Delaware)...................	NA	NA	10	114	23	198	59	664	5	222	13	D	63	1,897	24
Norristown borough & MCD (Montgomery)	3	D	16	470	43	732	92	614	9	114	11	212	20	163	29
Northampton township (Bucks)......................	1	D	68	1,222	91	846	89	1,141	39	76	7	D	70	459	28
North Fayette township (Allegheny).................	1	D	10	725	13	195	26	386	4	22	2	D	15	D	5
North Huntingdon township (Westmoreland)	NA	NA	44	1,142	23	392	98	1,445	10	347	3	D	33	151	30
North Lebanon township (Lebanon)...................	NA	NA	14	294	5	D	48	953	11	675	5	D	8	D	4
North Middleton township (Cumberland)...............	NA	NA	NA	NA	3	D	20	228	4	44	2	D	6	D	9
North Strabane township (Washington)..............	NA	NA	14	1,106	18	D	31	380	7	D	4	D	15	68	5
North Union township (Fayette).....................	1	D	18	895	8	D	49	358	14	133	1	D	10	62	7
North Versailles township (Allegheny).................	NA	NA	7	160	12	54	46	D	10	205	2	D	9	39	9
North Whitehall township (Lehigh)......................	NA	NA	12	103	11	93	38	425	12	260	4	D	13	92	8
Oil City city & MCD (Venango)	4	D	10	482	5	30	30	297	6	60	3	D	16	104	8
Palmer township (Northampton)..............	NA	NA	20	1,227	15	D	60	1,170	8	210	5	96	21	122	14
Patton township (Centre)..	NA	NA	3	21	3	D	22	1,054	1	D	7	78	19	96	14
Penn township (Westmoreland)	NA	NA	17	475	9	72	21	122	9	75	NA	NA	18	84	5
Penn township (York)........	1	D	26	2,557	10	133	52	886	11	259	1	D	18	105	6
Penn Hills township (Allegheny).................	1	D	24	874	20	180	97	1,628	12	122	8	111	30	150	30
Peters township (Washington).................	2	D	12	194	39	174	105	1,491	3	D	10	43	62	276	22
Philadelphia city & MCD (Philadelphia)................	17	1,928	765	22,558	1,047	16,940	4,506	50,185	473	24,174	540	22,421	1,443	38,784	1,079
Phoenixville borough & MCD (Chester).............	3	D	14	226	18	191	58	925	5	69	4	10	27	236	22
Pine township (Allegheny)	NA	NA	3	30	21	259	71	1,695	2	D	8	78	80	463	19
Pittsburgh city & MCD (Allegheny).................	18	1,389	295	7,303	399	6,843	1,202	17,411	114	3,623	330	11,013	803	34,290	473
Plum borough & MCD (Allegheny).................	1	D	26	320	29	227	51	658	9	659	4	D	15	103	17
Plumstead township (Bucks)......................	NA	NA	24	674	23	438	44	1,146	6	77	1	D	14	54	8
Plymouth township (Montgomery)	2	D	16	499	66	1,543	141	4,106	20	537	23	611	122	2,158	52
Pocono township (Monroe)	3	D	7	D	10	D	156	2,376	5	72	5	18	16	84	15
Pottstown borough & MCD (Montgomery)	1	D	43	1,333	36	D	122	1,697	10	173	20	321	29	318	11
Pottsville city & MCD (Schuylkill)...................	NA	NA	11	1,096	20	288	69	978	10	D	8	304	38	279	16
Radnor township (Delaware)...................	3	D	13	63	24	D	138	1,293	5	D	34	792	206	2,737	47
Rapho township (Lancaster)...................	NA	NA	12	528	18	381	21	167	10	161	1	D	2	D	4
Reading city & MCD (Berks).......................	8	1,223	94	7,270	47	973	227	3,321	30	714	21	642	65	1,844	60
Richland township (Allegheny).................	2	D	17	245	10	58	49	1,290	10	668	8	D	16	77	13
Richland township (Bucks)	NA	NA	38	961	16	342	77	1,245	8	118	NA	NA	9	185	7
Richland township (Cambria)...................	3	D	16	1,408	21	246	129	2,188	16	503	10	136	47	729	12
Ridley township (Delaware)...................	NA	NA	20	194	18	103	94	1,397	16	90	5	D	29	D	13
Robinson township (Allegheny).................	NA	NA	20	448	53	862	100	2,120	13	364	18	949	39	307	28
Ross township (Allegheny)	NA	NA	17	225	40	372	257	4,794	7	13	23	202	66	319	26
Rostraver township (Westmoreland)	NA	NA	4	32	6	80	48	1,277	9	174	1	D	12	105	9
St. Marys city & MCD (Elk)	3	D	74	4,286	13	68	69	666	12	214	5	51	22	148	5

1 Merchant wholesalers, except manufacturers' sales branches and offices.

Table C. Incorporated Places, Census Designated Places (CDPs), and Minor Civil Divisions (MCDs) of 10,000 or More Population — **Economic Census**

STATE City, town, township, borough, or CDP (county if applicable)	Real estate and rental and leasing — No. of employees (16)	Professional, scientific, and technical services — No. of establishments (17)	No. of employees (18)	Administration and support and waste management and mediation services — No. of establishments (19)	No. of employees (20)	Educational services — No. of establishments (21)	No. of employees (22)	Health care and social assistance — No. of establishments (23)	No. of employees (24)	Arts, entertainment, and recreation — No. of establishments (25)	No. of employees (26)	Accommodation and food services — No. of establishments (27)	No. of employees (28)	Other services (except public administration) — No. of establishments (29)	No. of employees (30)
PENNSYLVANIA—Con.															
Nanticoke city & MCD (Luzerne)	14	5	28	5	35	NA	NA	27	377	1	D	16	122	17	72
Nether Providence township (Delaware)	37	60	313	12	192	1	D	49	822	9	94	7	117	5	34
Newberry township (York)	26	8	37	12	30	1	D	6	48	1	D	14	223	17	D
New Britain township (Bucks)	30	29	142	29	328	2	D	22	546	4	D	14	264	20	96
New Castle city & MCD (Lawrence)	188	46	221	15	387	4	D	101	3,765	4	95	51	508	64	302
New Garden township (Chester)	3	23	242	23	417	2	D	12	121	NA	NA	10	91	16	D
New Hanover township (Montgomery)	D	18	31	10	59	1	D	13	135	5	85	8	43	10	D
New Kensington city & MCD (Westmoreland)	28	27	235	13	259	3	7	56	568	6	131	38	467	31	348
Newtown township (Bucks)	92	134	1,545	43	402	12	D	88	1,562	10	373	41	D	37	147
Newtown township (Delaware)	D	79	3,129	47	3,151	10	69	71	2,037	8	D	30	526	49	615
Norristown borough & MCD (Montgomery)	108	95	701	46	1,685	2	D	129	3,554	9	D	59	D	53	217
Northampton township (Bucks)	87	195	517	64	455	11	D	112	1,195	14	251	58	D	63	331
North Fayette township (Allegheny)	12	20	54	11	108	3	2	20	322	3	D	29	426	25	166
North Huntingdon township (Westmoreland)	119	69	314	48	280	3	D	85	1,236	8	109	46	983	57	D
North Lebanon township (Lebanon)	9	10	45	5	10	3	21	9	D	2	D	10	178	13	D
North Middleton township (Cumberland)	39	4	2	4	30	NA	NA	5	60	3	D	10	72	14	47
North Strabane township (Washington)	48	18	157	27	329	4	29	41	1,422	5	D	21	596	13	81
North Union township (Fayette)	26	15	244	6	D	3	D	33	1,511	1	D	21	198	28	132
North Versailles township (Allegheny)	71	14	122	10	96	2	D	21	479	3	51	29	723	29	D
North Whitehall township (Lehigh)	27	20	65	22	79	3	D	45	D	7	D	21	229	25	D
Oil City city & MCD (Venango)	13	9	15	9	238	2	D	33	587	3	D	31	237	22	123
Palmer township (Northampton)	53	30	115	10	116	2	D	56	914	6	71	40	D	38	D
Patton township (Centre)	103	28	221	6	14	2	D	15	D	5	D	19	D	16	D
Penn township (Westmoreland)	7	35	108	26	116	4	12	31	750	6	73	17	204	17	D
Penn township (York)	19	9	72	11	84	2	D	33	940	8	223	41	718	32	D
Penn Hills township (Allegheny)	132	54	336	54	1,277	4	D	110	1,690	10	187	54	751	90	349
Peters township (Washington)	81	84	279	42	1,441	14	68	129	1,284	8	D	54	1,238	64	551
Philadelphia city & MCD (Philadelphia)	8,856	2,845	47,158	1,016	26,053	270	4,141	3,920	152,972	373	18,608	3,669	53,533	2,493	17,972
Phoenixville borough & MCD (Chester)	121	41	196	23	160	4	21	61	1,788	4	D	51	743	41	D
Pine township (Allegheny)	67	82	453	26	326	10	D	98	1,197	5	D	52	1,180	54	392
Pittsburgh city & MCD (Allegheny)	3,628	1,523	27,408	479	20,500	99	1,052	1,343	59,171	163	9,131	1,234	22,377	900	7,411
Plum borough & MCD (Allegheny)	57	37	539	49	369	NA	NA	31	608	9	D	36	527	46	D
Plumstead township (Bucks)	27	28	96	31	159	4	D	26	454	4	20	25	320	24	D
Plymouth township (Montgomery)	1,026	165	3,783	73	3,117	10	58	97	2,406	8	92	65	1,643	45	264
Pocono township (Monroe)	90	21	70	26	333	NA	NA	32	245	5	D	68	1,845	25	109
Pottstown borough & MCD (Montgomery)	47	54	267	26	383	5	7	81	2,086	9	432	65	977	67	286
Pottsville city & MCD (Schuylkill)	62	55	524	17	182	2	D	114	4,288	7	29	47	629	50	349
Radnor township (Delaware)	665	226	1,511	79	1,688	23	147	146	2,125	22	491	118	2,300	78	754
Rapho township (Lancaster)	7	13	208	17	82	2	D	3	155	5	67	14	182	24	174
Reading city & MCD (Berks)	436	130	1,995	41	848	8	82	157	4,905	18	446	149	1,822	117	809
Richland township (Allegheny)	145	23	94	25	255	2	D	52	932	9	151	28	666	39	200
Richland township (Bucks)	62	20	185	14	68	NA	NA	21	138	5	43	20	343	16	D
Richland township (Cambria)	76	40	1,660	25	611	2	D	97	1,700	8	61	60	1,468	42	248
Ridley township (Delaware)	90	31	503	32	516	3	6	50	555	5	D	65	907	82	357
Robinson township (Allegheny)	175	46	802	35	815	3	10	75	1,783	4	D	53	1,295	47	354
Ross township (Allegheny)	189	105	832	69	737	7	24	87	1,444	13	D	78	1,814	80	412
Rostraver township (Westmoreland)	43	7	31	17	76	3	4	30	259	4	48	34	D	22	100
St. Marys city & MCD (Elk)	16	18	120	20	194	3	D	55	1,610	4	7	38	494	43	169

Table C. Incorporated Places, Census Designated Places (CDPs), and Minor Civil Divisions (MCDs) of 10,000 or More Population — Economic Census

STATE City, town, township, borough, or CDP (county if applicable)	Utilities		Manufacturing		Wholesale trade[1]		Retail trade		Transportation and warehousing		Information		Finance and insurance		Real estate and rental and leasing
	Number of establishments	Number of employees	Number of establishments	Number of employees	Number of establishments	Number of employees	Number of establishments	Number of employees	Number of establishments	Number of employees	Number of establishments	Number of employees	Number of establishments	Number of employees	Number of establishments
	1	2	3	4	5	6	7	8	9	10	11	12	13	14	15
PENNSYLVANIA—Con.															
Salisbury township (Lancaster)	NA	NA	21	141	12	83	44	326	9	143	NA	NA	5	33	8
Salisbury township (Lehigh)	NA	NA	5	D	8	76	43	685	3	D	7	249	18	D	6
Sandy township (Clearfield)	3	D	12	308	11	D	70	1,391	12	141	5	D	9	40	4
Scott township (Allegheny)	NA	NA	10	144	13	309	31	700	NA	NA	6	50	32	339	14
Scranton city & MCD (Lackawanna)	2	D	77	2,100	96	1,385	340	4,493	37	1,275	33	754	112	2,956	54
Shaler township (Allegheny)	1	D	16	228	17	115	53	982	9	369	6	D	17	166	24
Sharon city & MCD (Mercer)	1	D	19	497	14	195	42	427	7	D	5	298	18	139	8
Shiloh CDP	NA	NA	NA	NA	NA	NA	NA	NA	NA	NA	NA	NA	NA	NA	NA
Silver Spring township (Cumberland)	3	D	22	602	21	254	77	3,056	14	530	5	D	19	165	9
Skippack township (Montgomery)	NA	NA	9	474	6	D	29	169	5	D	2	D	14	46	4
Somerset township (Somerset)	3	D	22	656	21	158	68	1,098	21	D	2	D	15	276	14
South Fayette township (Allegheny)	1	D	11	304	37	546	26	512	5	40	12	D	11	61	13
South Middleton township (Cumberland)	NA	NA	7	598	6	28	40	606	15	928	5	D	26	D	9
South Park CDP & township (Allegheny)	NA	NA	NA	NA	8	28	15	245	7	148	2	D	10	63	3
South Union township (Fayette)	1	D	4	56	5	D	72	1,337	4	57	1	D	9	79	6
South Whitehall township (Lehigh)	5	D	14	590	17	215	92	1,872	6	D	7	86	78	1,434	35
Spring township (Berks)	2	D	17	216	14	575	40	963	9	41	4	D	65	911	24
Springettsbury township (York)	1	D	31	1,770	28	920	193	4,266	7	D	9	122	69	707	35
Springfield township (Delaware)	2	D	5	D	16	62	172	4,303	6	32	15	D	45	243	17
Springfield township (Montgomery)	NA	NA	16	122	11	D	62	610	7	43	7	D	30	159	17
Spring Garden township (York)	1	D	24	1,389	15	358	31	252	12	321	3	12	11	42	14
State College borough & MCD (Centre)	1	D	5	169	9	51	138	1,883	10	74	16	185	59	312	56
Stroud township (Monroe)	NA	NA	7	35	8	D	37	608	5	D	6	89	9	65	8
Susquehanna township (Dauphin)	NA	NA	6	105	17	950	76	1,199	8	126	28	889	74	3,191	21
Swatara township (Dauphin)	NA	NA	24	903	74	1,935	105	2,352	32	2,213	12	249	33	599	29
Towamencin township (Montgomery)	NA	NA	14	798	18	240	18	437	6	30	3	D	18	89	10
Tredyffrin township (Chester)	1	D	12	1,004	57	1,738	109	1,943	9	95	71	2,995	216	17,836	63
Uniontown city & MCD (Fayette)	1	D	19	389	18	94	107	1,616	6	115	9	346	28	200	23
Unity township (Westmoreland)	1	D	28	886	10	55	32	987	10	60	2	D	15	67	7
Upper Allen township (Cumberland)	NA	NA	6	174	11	474	29	765	8	256	6	384	33	1,249	14
Upper Chichester township (Delaware)	NA	NA	14	560	31	572	47	792	14	234	6	D	18	153	14
Upper Darby township (Delaware)	NA	NA	26	346	38	353	244	3,191	18	66	20	258	71	461	40
Upper Dublin township (Montgomery)	NA	NA	13	171	41	554	67	1,072	6	D	30	521	88	5,735	36
Upper Gwynedd township (Montgomery)	1	D	14	4,114	20	D	34	610	4	2	5	48	31	109	14
Upper Macungie township (Lehigh)	1	D	60	4,427	59	1,700	75	1,694	62	5,545	12	189	45	1,164	26
Upper Merion township (Montgomery)	2	D	38	1,270	123	2,736	375	9,023	29	719	105	4,120	176	4,466	80
Upper Moreland township (Montgomery)	1	D	56	950	52	611	108	2,929	11	280	11	153	44	172	35
Upper Providence township (Delaware)	NA	NA	NA	NA	13	194	16	66	6	D	1	D	22	171	11
Upper Providence township (Montgomery)	NA	NA	28	892	30	482	35	969	15	665	11	255	23	D	11
Upper St. Clair CDP & township (Allegheny)	1	D	9	155	19	109	122	2,051	8	D	9	277	40	582	20
Upper Saucon township (Lehigh)	NA	NA	5	D	15	D	51	635	8	428	5	109	29	146	13
Upper Southampton township (Bucks)	NA	NA	36	1,371	37	272	63	766	22	49	9	177	59	321	32
Upper Uwchlan township (Chester)	1	D	5	14	11	131	9	71	4	D	3	D	13	D	2
Uwchlan township (Chester)	NA	NA	30	936	37	573	52	990	7	68	35	1,230	70	1,452	20
Warminster township (Bucks)	1	D	71	1,836	67	1,249	114	2,508	19	100	15	503	60	379	23
Warrington township (Bucks)	1	D	31	586	34	463	102	2,490	6	25	13	136	44	773	14
Warwick township (Bucks)	NA	NA	36	361	43	407	28	302	19	118	2	D	24	87	11

1 Merchant wholesalers, except manufacturers' sales branches and offices.

Table C. Incorporated Places, Census Designated Places (CDPs), and Minor Civil Divisions (MCDs) of 10,000 or More Population — **Economic Census**

STATE City, town, township, borough, or CDP (county if applicable)	Real estate and rental and leasing — Number of employees	Professional, scientific, and technical services — Number of establishments	— Number of employees	Administration and support and waste management and mediation services — Number of establishments	— Number of employees	Educational services — Number of establishments	— Number of employees	Health care and social assistance — Number of establishments	— Number of employees	Arts, entertainment, and recreation — Number of establishments	— Number of employees	Accommodation and food services — Number of establishments	— Number of employees	Other services (except public administration) — Number of establishments	— Number of employees
	16	17	18	19	20	21	22	23	24	25	26	27	28	29	30
PENNSYLVANIA—Con.															
Salisbury township (Lancaster)	21	15	96	10	52	1	D	10	111	1	D	21	D	15	D
Salisbury township (Lehigh)	28	29	144	15	397	2	D	126	D	5	D	22	442	13	D
Sandy township (Clearfield)	39	14	124	9	25	NA	NA	21	792	2	D	26	D	14	D
Scott township (Allegheny)	56	55	412	18	616	4	47	60	3,145	2	D	34	576	31	200
Scranton city & MCD (Lackawanna)	333	209	1,280	60	1,423	11	31	316	11,267	23	483	217	2,965	153	785
Shaler township (Allegheny)	98	34	164	37	222	2	D	38	329	6	31	39	545	55	224
Sharon city & MCD (Mercer)	41	26	152	14	363	1	D	55	2,603	3	D	25	262	39	206
Shiloh CDP	NA	NA	NA	NA	NA	NA	NA	NA	NA	NA	NA	NA	NA	NA	NA
Silver Spring township (Cumberland)	121	29	184	21	119	4	D	25	229	4	D	34	846	33	214
Skippack township (Montgomery)	4	45	198	23	266	3	D	30	206	4	42	16	151	24	D
Somerset township (Somerset)	52	17	252	14	145	NA	NA	44	623	4	38	20	D	25	178
South Fayette township (Allegheny)	90	51	290	24	389	1	D	42	900	6	69	17	296	30	654
South Middleton township (Cumberland)	16	26	176	24	998	3	D	64	1,717	6	D	28	400	25	165
South Park CDP & township (Allegheny)	D	23	D	10	D	4	17	21	377	4	32	20	200	16	62
South Union township (Fayette)	17	13	D	10	D	NA	NA	60	1,481	8	D	35	753	14	D
South Whitehall township (Lehigh)	266	77	1,412	44	1,125	8	26	134	3,035	8	D	70	1,546	56	339
Spring township (Berks)	87	79	814	26	316	7	60	60	1,163	6	94	29	522	27	D
Springettsbury township (York)	180	61	495	28	877	8	D	102	2,218	12	461	98	1,984	63	486
Springfield township (Delaware)	61	55	254	50	339	9	144	86	1,787	10	D	65	1,505	55	D
Springfield township (Montgomery)	63	59	157	31	198	8	45	73	2,117	12	321	35	366	54	252
Spring Garden township (York)	72	29	432	18	281	2	D	70	D	3	D	27	269	25	D
State College borough & MCD (Centre)	401	91	512	26	549	11	214	127	3,061	16	294	135	3,042	57	333
Stroud township (Monroe)	20	20	D	6	32	1	D	28	421	6	125	24	D	22	D
Susquehanna township (Dauphin)	255	93	1,517	44	1,673	6	D	118	8,578	11	214	66	1,233	63	503
Swatara township (Dauphin)	125	36	758	34	1,688	3	10	52	1,226	6	77	65	1,183	74	461
Towamencin township (Montgomery)	D	34	143	15	55	1	D	24	559	1	D	17	148	12	D
Tredyffrin township (Chester)	592	308	4,117	107	6,979	17	140	157	3,152	17	196	72	1,196	86	740
Uniontown city & MCD (Fayette)	130	50	307	22	326	3	D	111	2,720	6	21	63	D	45	205
Unity township (Westmoreland)	34	22	195	24	192	1	D	58	736	6	81	26	644	34	174
Upper Allen township (Cumberland)	58	64	1,500	34	629	3	D	56	D	4	D	29	693	33	616
Upper Chichester township (Delaware)	136	25	168	26	269	4	6	31	614	4	D	31	396	33	D
Upper Darby township (Delaware)	224	116	479	81	2,771	10	24	206	3,670	15	144	155	D	145	586
Upper Dublin township (Montgomery)	184	175	5,273	78	1,136	13	166	102	2,567	7	134	49	421	36	361
Upper Gwynedd township (Montgomery)	D	55	580	20	128	6	39	57	1,109	4	25	38	630	25	D
Upper Macungie township (Lehigh)	131	100	1,303	45	1,792	9	38	50	871	8	186	59	1,239	41	D
Upper Merion township (Montgomery)	1,034	291	7,098	163	9,688	18	108	132	1,918	24	343	130	4,178	84	721
Upper Moreland township (Montgomery)	271	88	429	67	1,292	8	55	115	2,735	9	150	57	950	65	414
Upper Providence township (Delaware)	50	49	173	14	140	3	4	37	388	5	D	10	140	19	D
Upper Providence township (Montgomery)	77	76	368	30	251	4	7	41	358	9	323	29	392	26	D
Upper St. Clair CDP & township (Allegheny)	250	93	494	22	432	5	23	59	1,059	10	155	38	703	22	D
Upper Saucon township (Lehigh)	45	38	438	25	D	3	72	30	337	14	212	29	789	16	D
Upper Southampton township (Bucks)	108	94	502	52	569	6	D	84	1,151	7	D	34	442	52	D
Upper Uwchlan township (Chester)	D	76	D	12	188	3	D	12	87	2	D	7	163	12	72
Uwchlan township (Chester)	151	119	1,285	30	1,408	15	263	49	516	9	132	40	D	40	292
Warminster township (Bucks)	152	66	1,104	49	262	8	D	98	1,682	8	D	66	841	74	D
Warrington township (Bucks)	71	77	817	57	504	3	12	76	1,519	12	D	65	1,349	52	D
Warwick township (Bucks)	24	66	204	26	1,050	2	D	28	408	5	D	17	213	33	D

Table C. Incorporated Places, Census Designated Places (CDPs), and Minor Civil Divisions (MCDs) of 10,000 or More Population — Economic Census

STATE City, town, township, borough, or CDP (county if applicable)	Utilities Number of establish-ments	Number of employees	Manufacturing Number of establish-ments	Number of employees	Wholesale trade[1] Number of establish-ments	Number of employees	Retail trade Number of establish-ments	Number of employees	Transportation and warehousing Number of establish-ments	Number of employees	Information Number of establish-ments	Number of employees	Finance and insurance Number of establish-ments	Number of employees	Real estate and rental and leasing Number of establish-ments
	1	2	3	4	5	6	7	8	9	10	11	12	13	14	15
PENNSYLVANIA—Con.															
Warwick township (Lancaster)	2	D	19	1,298	12	291	33	842	16	173	4	18	10	38	10
Washington township (Franklin)	NA	NA	9	94	2	D	38	379	7	114	2	D	5	27	10
Washington city & MCD (Washington)	1	D	23	333	16	184	173	2,773	4	16	12	233	48	395	18
Waynesboro borough & MCD (Franklin)	3	D	23	1,327	3	D	42	923	1	D	2	D	18	88	10
Weigelstown CDP	NA	NA	NA	NA	NA	NA	NA	NA	NA	NA	NA	NA	NA	NA	NA
West Bradford township (Chester)	NA	NA	7	142	8	D	12	223	5	D	5	6	5	D	2
West Chester borough & MCD (Chester)	NA	NA	16	227	23	227	66	761	2	D	17	268	59	423	26
West Deer township (Allegheny)	NA	NA	13	142	12	69	26	296	5	9	2	D	5	12	3
West Goshen township (Chester)	2	D	61	2,056	97	1,165	100	3,902	25	3,090	17	374	70	487	35
West Hempfield township (Lancaster)	NA	NA	25	868	9	208	33	581	10	169	1	D	8	50	7
West Lampeter township (Lancaster)	NA	NA	9	248	6	49	44	722	5	215	2	D	23	106	5
West Manchester township (York)	NA	NA	19	2,908	19	103	114	2,176	12	610	10	229	39	302	12
West Mifflin borough & MCD (Allegheny)	NA	NA	13	4,135	13	D	168	3,771	14	310	11	112	19	129	10
West Norriton township (Montgomery)	NA	NA	14	271	29	947	41	948	6	195	16	266	10	47	10
Westtown township (Chester)	NA	NA	NA	NA	6	8	21	324	1	D	11	D	27	171	7
West Whiteland township (Chester)	NA	NA	32	1,270	53	724	218	3,877	10	385	18	496	75	D	28
White township (Indiana)	6	D	16	419	23	D	119	2,702	13	208	8	D	25	174	12
Whitehall borough & MCD (Allegheny)	NA	NA	NA	NA	9	32	14	95	4	D	NA	NA	13	64	16
Whitehall township (Lehigh)	NA	NA	21	445	23	195	275	5,673	18	174	15	166	35	248	31
Whitemarsh township (Montgomery)	1	D	25	1,838	32	D	42	610	7	D	23	1,843	62	901	33
Whitpain township (Montgomery)	NA	NA	9	102	33	D	57	731	11	74	14	177	130	3,616	45
Wilkes-Barre city & MCD (Luzerne)	8	541	26	1,099	46	546	260	5,744	15	368	34	1,311	80	2,009	34
Wilkinsburg borough & MCD (Allegheny)	1	D	6	65	9	106	21	127	5	10	8	194	8	D	15
Williamsport city & MCD (Lycoming)	2	D	51	3,612	40	1,077	109	1,683	27	651	16	415	61	667	28
Willistown township (Chester)	NA	NA	6	27	17	130	6	32	NA	NA	2	D	20	222	7
Willow Grove CDP	NA	NA	NA	NA	NA	NA	NA	NA	NA	NA	NA	NA	NA	NA	NA
Windsor township (York)	1	D	8	273	2	D	23	613	5	18	1	D	16	86	4
Woodlyn CDP	NA	NA	NA	NA	NA	NA	NA	NA	NA	NA	NA	NA	NA	NA	NA
Worcester township (Montgomery)	1	D	8	28	14	276	14	62	2	D	4	29	15	40	5
Wyomissing borough & MCD (Berks)	2	D	7	565	18	202	167	2,946	3	D	9	94	82	1,674	22
Yeadon borough & MCD (Delaware)	NA	NA	14	246	16	95	20	153	1	D	NA	NA	4	19	2
York city & MCD (York)	5	235	76	3,422	60	1,005	138	2,077	16	747	17	756	52	374	36
York township (York)	NA	NA	25	3,002	27	497	105	1,396	13	296	9	174	51	968	34
RHODE ISLAND	39	1,217	1,509	39,608	1,158	15,697	3,795	47,688	610	11,271	435	7,236	1,311	25,216	1,058
Barrington town (Bristol)	NA	NA	9	33	6	D	40	298	2	D	5	D	17	83	12
Bristol town (Bristol)	NA	NA	52	1,052	25	D	60	682	8	D	2	D	20	115	20
Burrillville town (Providence)	1	D	12	637	13	D	18	201	7	D	3	32	4	D	5
Central Falls city & MCD (Providence)	NA	NA	30	564	4	D	44	238	3	D	1	D	7	D	8
Coventry town (Kent)	NA	NA	32	524	21	D	90	1,705	9	502	5	D	17	140	14
Cranston city & MCD (Providence)	1	D	156	4,275	129	D	288	4,488	52	901	27	445	106	2,606	66
Cumberland town (Providence)	3	D	36	1,645	37	D	75	958	20	595	11	80	28	D	31
East Greenwich town (Kent)	NA	NA	17	211	22	D	51	754	6	21	11	D	37	259	27
East Providence city & MCD (Providence)	2	D	89	2,304	81	D	150	1,954	32	250	22	426	81	2,773	57
Johnston town (Providence)	5	D	80	1,138	31	D	129	1,606	41	568	6	17	29	D	35
Lincoln town (Providence)	2	D	36	1,845	41	D	56	737	19	440	11	343	28	2,409	22
Middletown town (Newport)	1	D	16	319	14	D	103	1,586	7	495	9	242	33	886	36
Narragansett town (Washington)	NA	NA	15	313	20	166	50	717	6	D	2	D	10	61	31
Newport city & MCD (Newport)	1	D	25	102	18	71	213	1,578	37	219	17	187	34	283	52
Newport East CDP	NA	NA	NA	NA	NA	NA	NA	NA	NA	NA	NA	NA	NA	NA	NA
North Kingstown town (Washington)	3	D	56	4,944	47	573	117	1,976	34	579	16	160	34	228	17

1 Merchant wholesalers, except manufacturers' sales branches and offices.

Table C. Incorporated Places, Census Designated Places (CDPs), and Minor Civil Divisions (MCDs) of 10,000 or More Population — **Economic Census**

STATE City, town, township, borough, or CDP (county if applicable)	Real estate and rental and leasing Number of employees	Professional, scientific, and technical services Number of establishments	Number of employees	Administration and support and waste management and mediation services Number of establishments	Number of employees	Educational services Number of establishments	Number of employees	Health care and social assistance Number of establishments	Number of employees	Arts, entertainment, and recreation Number of establishments	Number of employees	Accommodation and food services Number of establishments	Number of employees	Other services (except public administration) Number of establishments	Number of employees
	16	17	18	19	20	21	22	23	24	25	26	27	28	29	30
PENNSYLVANIA—Con.															
Warwick township (Lancaster)	224	21	109	14	67	2	D	30	708	0	D	19	497	12	D
Washington township (Franklin)	23	17	137	15	74	1	D	16	125	5	56	18	271	16	D
Washington city & MCD (Washington)	122	93	883	27	844	1	D	165	4,525	6	D	71	1,614	62	325
Waynesboro borough & MCD (Franklin)	43	26	150	6	36	2	D	42	1,084	5	200	25	351	27	219
Weigelstown CDP	NA	NA	NA	NA	NA	NA	NA	NA	NA	NA	NA	NA	NA	NA	NA
West Bradford township (Chester)	D	38	111	22	103	2	D	15	120	7	118	12	264	11	D
West Chester borough & MCD (Chester)	77	169	1,460	23	276	2	D	54	1,065	5	247	91	1,894	63	D
West Deer township (Allegheny)	D	18	44	23	116	2	D	11	181	4	15	12	D	17	D
West Goshen township (Chester)	204	157	1,553	70	7,219	12	42	139	4,801	16	432	46	929	97	849
West Hempfield township (Lancaster)	20	28	D	11	54	4	23	23	999	5	16	20	284	19	64
West Lampeter township (Lancaster)	48	20	D	20	80	3	11	33	1,411	5	159	17	559	25	102
West Manchester township (York)	65	26	114	21	1,098	1	D	54	1,595	11	D	53	D	59	391
West Mifflin borough & MCD (Allegheny)	115	23	D	19	200	6	154	37	828	12	D	61	1,042	34	220
West Norriton township (Montgomery)	23	32	118	24	218	3	D	29	D	3	D	20	286	33	D
Westtown township (Chester)	21	48	177	18	103	1	D	36	356	4	38	8	59	14	D
West Whiteland township (Chester)	D	176	3,122	58	2,318	10	107	146	1,919	7	133	86	1,688	48	D
White township (Indiana)	51	37	460	17	153	5	D	112	2,753	7	113	46	1,037	47	427
Whitehall borough & MCD (Allegheny)	165	26	136	27	1,541	1	D	22	498	4	D	7	206	11	D
Whitehall township (Lehigh)	244	49	410	23	214	8	52	61	1,330	11	132	80	1,846	72	378
Whitemarsh township (Montgomery)	182	120	2,127	46	726	9	D	82	2,094	10	295	38	684	45	306
Whitpain township (Montgomery)	498	222	3,793	76	1,939	11	D	75	1,951	9	184	63	D	45	D
Wilkes-Barre city & MCD (Luzerne)	237	120	1,486	46	1,159	3	D	158	5,976	13	D	126	2,784	90	545
Wilkinsburg borough & MCD (Allegheny)	D	14	932	10	96	1	D	50	1,565	1	D	15	298	15	54
Williamsport city & MCD (Lycoming)	204	75	1,194	26	463	6	48	121	5,121	13	336	101	1,570	83	660
Willistown township (Chester)	11	44	171	22	377	3	D	65	1,582	5	97	8	82	19	D
Willow Grove CDP	NA	NA	NA	NA	NA	NA	NA	NA	NA	NA	NA	NA	NA	NA	NA
Windsor township (York)	13	16	42	23	176	1	D	26	446	3	D	17	217	18	D
Woodlyn CDP	NA	NA	NA	NA	NA	NA	NA	NA	NA	NA	NA	NA	NA	NA	NA
Worcester township (Montgomery)	6	48	135	15	57	2	D	17	555	6	62	10	80	13	D
Wyomissing borough & MCD (Berks)	D	79	930	21	1,141	7	D	132	3,203	8	315	75	2,212	46	349
Yeadon borough & MCD (Delaware)	D	5	4	5	D	NA	NA	10	D	3	D	10	85	10	66
York city & MCD (York)	297	138	1,344	34	713	11	226	113	7,013	13	247	113	1,581	81	731
York township (York)	301	59	400	37	276	7	26	134	3,236	10	281	79	1,637	40	255
RHODE ISLAND	5,615	2,997	21,165	1,651	21,201	295	1,942	3,236	84,067	537	8,798	2,973	44,063	2,276	13,046
Barrington town (Bristol)	D	49	112	30	53	11	D	50	1,612	14	275	23	270	29	83
Bristol town (Bristol)	D	39	165	29	117	5	30	45	753	10	D	58	735	52	230
Burrillville town (Providence)	6	16	49	15	D	4	21	20	550	5	D	25	383	21	49
Central Falls city & MCD (Providence)	49	8	23	11	D	1	D	27	474	NA	NA	33	217	20	59
Coventry town (Kent)	D	40	214	45	167	11	D	40	824	8	D	60	970	55	188
Cranston city & MCD (Providence)	366	222	1,893	135	2,063	32	156	292	5,049	31	427	182	D	181	1,121
Cumberland town (Providence)	99	70	335	44	230	9	41	79	877	10	109	59	671	75	468
East Greenwich town (Kent)	D	72	275	32	316	3	D	99	1,270	11	D	75	1,211	46	234
East Providence city & MCD (Providence)	376	129	1,318	70	692	9	30	173	4,401	24	688	114	1,746	111	584
Johnston town (Providence)	192	46	160	88	1,060	9	14	106	1,926	15	D	79	D	83	401
Lincoln town (Providence)	97	77	448	44	311	10	156	75	955	16	D	53	998	35	133
Middletown town (Newport)	D	76	1,655	35	361	7	32	84	1,789	11	95	96	1,576	54	313
Narragansett town (Washington)	D	40	93	25	110	3	5	44	464	14	56	70	955	35	153
Newport city & MCD (Newport)	197	118	1,060	58	362	6	74	87	1,784	45	757	175	3,514	73	368
Newport East CDP	NA	NA	NA	NA	NA	NA	NA	NA	NA	NA	NA	NA	NA	NA	NA
North Kingstown town (Washington)	56	108	528	50	536	11	48	74	1,665	25	D	66	882	51	261

Table C. Incorporated Places, Census Designated Places (CDPs), and Minor Civil Divisions (MCDs) of 10,000 or More Population — **Economic Census**

STATE City, town, township, borough, or CDP (county if applicable)	Utilities Number of establishments	Utilities Number of employees	Manufacturing Number of establishments	Manufacturing Number of employees	Wholesale trade[1] Number of establishments	Wholesale trade[1] Number of employees	Retail trade Number of establishments	Retail trade Number of employees	Transportation and warehousing Number of establishments	Transportation and warehousing Number of employees	Information Number of establishments	Information Number of employees	Finance and insurance Number of establishments	Finance and insurance Number of employees	Real estate and rental and leasing Number of establishments
	1	2	3	4	5	6	7	8	9	10	11	12	13	14	15
RHODE ISLAND—Con.															
North Providence town (Providence)...............	NA	NA	35	345	14	100	93	1,000	11	D	5	24	25	D	28
North Smithfield town (Providence)...............	NA	NA	23	534	16	D	39	981	16	570	2	D	11	D	10
Pawtucket city & MCD (Providence)...............	1	D	132	3,327	64	D	176	1,604	33	340	11	95	53	544	55
Portsmouth town (Newport)	NA	NA	17	1,376	12	D	50	481	7	79	5	80	16	85	15
Providence city & MCD (Providence)...............	9	D	217	3,165	184	1,942	646	6,835	75	1,124	134	2,591	332	6,113	208
Scituate town (Providence)	NA	NA	7	D	6	60	17	D	5	D	3	23	3	D	4
Smithfield town (Providence)...............	NA	NA	58	1,198	45	D	111	1,982	19	168	17	169	36	1,095	23
South Kingstown town (Washington)	1	D	22	232	21	122	124	1,256	10	113	15	119	33	169	22
Tiverton town (Newport) ...	NA	NA	9	41	16	91	48	431	8	131	1	D	9	D	5
Valley Falls CDP	NA	NA	NA	NA	NA	NA	NA	NA	NA	NA	NA	NA	NA	NA	NA
Warren town (Bristol)........	1	D	31	548	17	D	45	375	5	301	5	104	13	71	11
Warwick city & MCD (Kent)	1	D	130	3,281	140	1,919	429	7,656	76	2,343	43	583	175	3,838	111
Westerly CDP	NA	NA	NA	NA	NA	NA	NA	NA	NA	NA	NA	NA	NA	NA	NA
Westerly town (Washington)...............	3	D	27	465	19	253	129	1,780	8	37	7	81	35	543	28
West Warwick town (Kent)	NA	NA	31	1,293	25	D	92	936	7	321	8	D	25	746	23
Woonsocket city & MCD (Providence)...............	1	D	43	853	33	D	129	1,366	11	720	9	66	27	D	40
SOUTH CAROLINA.........	333	11,956	3,854	207,396	4,337	54,949	17,586	220,438	2,497	48,696	1,436	34,056	7,204	66,331	4,692
Aiken city	7	D	22	1,506	19	92	233	3,420	10	D	17	299	99	708	42
Anderson city....................	4	D	50	1,956	35	253	279	4,031	14	432	12	151	118	578	47
Beaufort city	2	D	6	72	9	49	111	922	6	41	9	89	55	275	32
Berea CDP	NA	NA	NA	NA	3	D	20	314	3	D	1	D	9	39	8
Bluffton town	2	D	9	32	20	116	90	1,154	7	9	9	82	44	1,158	32
Cayce city	16	D	16	625	23	308	54	678	12	167	7	143	31	398	15
Charleston city.................	7	D	77	1,335	137	1,331	733	10,061	108	2,615	78	4,425	297	2,281	278
Clemson city	1	D	4	51	2	D	51	621	2	D	4	D	28	130	15
Columbia city	17	D	69	1,172	206	3,094	657	10,186	58	942	146	2,681	516	14,225	227
Conway city	1	D	19	537	27	238	163	1,815	6	107	5	83	74	470	33
Dentsville CDP	2	D	15	190	19	324	121	1,627	4	D	8	115	50	738	20
Easley city	1	D	20	970	21	95	125	1,852	17	45	9	74	69	274	20
Five Forks CDP	NA	NA	4	44	10	14	19	362	NA	NA	5	11	13	D	15
Florence city	4	D	20	1,773	59	973	382	5,058	23	258	21	397	179	2,959	79
Forest Acres city..............	NA	NA	3	D	10	61	73	1,449	3	D	8	66	51	255	15
Fort Mill town	4	D	10	132	23	D	43	742	8	270	10	716	53	1,363	12
Gaffney city......................	1	D	8	D	6	D	156	2,107	5	D	5	35	57	277	28
Gantt CDP	NA	NA	20	748	36	378	29	120	12	403	5	D	4	17	9
Goose Creek city	4	D	13	755	9	D	74	1,511	11	51	2	D	46	235	22
Greenville city	6	D	104	3,863	173	2,302	777	12,402	63	1,796	112	2,952	491	5,160	243
Greenwood city................	2	D	15	1,734	14	D	170	2,255	4	9	10	D	83	461	26
Greer city	1	D	39	849	42	309	138	2,345	31	541	10	46	71	514	35
Hanahan city.....................	NA	NA	9	D	16	364	19	244	21	425	1	D	4	11	19
Hilton Head Island town....	2	D	28	186	54	188	259	2,750	44	211	33	611	106	716	223
Irmo town..........................	NA	NA	6	88	12	72	68	1,221	7	13	4	12	42	183	19
James Island town............	NA	NA	NA	NA	NA	NA	NA	NA	NA	NA	NA	NA	NA	NA	NA
Ladson CDP	NA	NA	14	2,781	18	213	26	275	12	112	3	D	4	8	11
Lexington town..................	6	D	16	305	20	D	131	2,608	9	50	12	137	78	609	31
Mauldin city	1	D	27	1,057	37	330	75	784	6	34	13	D	41	704	18
Mount Pleasant town	2	D	35	D	69	388	360	5,269	69	1,135	51	762	195	1,584	183
Myrtle Beach city	2	D	27	758	82	616	683	9,822	31	376	45	697	130	1,149	211
Newberry city....................	NA	NA	9	64	9	D	71	791	4	34	8	28	38	174	7
North Augusta city	2	D	8	350	11	69	105	1,871	15	667	7	158	66	468	22
North Charleston city........	15	D	122	11,200	219	3,399	580	8,363	163	2,069	61	2,424	183	2,093	148
North Myrtle Beach city	NA	NA	8	43	4	D	168	1,871	13	43	7	34	54	260	77
Oak Grove CDP................	1	D	NA	NA	8	102	32	240	7	61	1	D	2	D	13
Orangeburg city	NA	NA	20	D	23	164	152	1,850	12	103	7	D	62	494	25
Parker CDP	NA	NA	7	151	9	156	22	233	2	D	3	D	8	22	2
Port Royal town	NA	NA	NA	NA	1	D	15	202	2	D	NA	NA	6	19	6
Red Hill CDP	NA	NA	4	32	9	29	16	357	7	62	1	D	6	D	7
Rock Hill city	NA	NA	60	2,691	68	1,091	322	4,914	22	404	25	956	148	873	77
St. Andrews CDP	1	D	7	D	17	150	68	749	4	63	16	291	53	205	32
Seven Oaks CDP..............	NA	NA	8	340	11	125	68	981	8	130	7	D	65	506	21
Simpsonville city	2	D	22	558	13	109	75	1,634	8	43	5	D	46	221	21
Socastee CDP	1	D	NA	NA	4	7	55	412	4	15	4	86	15	71	10
Spartanburg city	2	D	32	1,002	63	508	355	5,853	17	873	31	1,835	182	982	82
Summerville town	3	D	27	1,055	39	339	196	3,764	25	415	22	D	118	695	67
Sumter city........................	5	D	29	D	31	278	289	3,599	19	283	15	D	111	775	57
Taylors CDP	NA	NA	15	285	16	229	35	277	4	12	7	101	19	75	14
Wade Hampton CDP	NA	NA	15	170	23	231	98	1,280	3	20	4	D	45	367	23
West Columbia city..........	2	D	20	935	46	519	132	1,491	17	928	5	17	59	240	27
SOUTH DAKOTA............	158	2,216	1,025	41,931	1,317	15,827	3,843	49,867	1,146	9,549	446	6,750	1,958	26,472	962
Aberdeen city....................	2	D	31	2,351	42	698	176	2,778	30	229	15	D	89	916	55
Brookings city	NA	NA	29	4,318	18	D	105	1,593	14	144	16	D	47	386	39
Huron city	1	D	22	1,509	19	D	70	1,010	10	79	7	D	48	345	28
Mitchell city	3	D	29	1,291	21	229	120	1,962	16	79	9	D	56	318	23
Pierre city..........................	1	D	5	D	20	219	96	1,316	22	267	17	D	49	D	29
Rapid City city..................	10	D	93	1,766	139	1,600	475	7,691	74	547	46	D	217	2,844	141

1 Merchant wholesalers, except manufacturers' sales branches and offices.

Table C. Incorporated Places, Census Designated Places (CDPs), and Minor Civil Divisions (MCDs) of 10,000 or More Population — **Economic Census**

STATE City, town, township, borough, or CDP (county if applicable)	Real estate and rental and leasing Number of employees	Professional, scientific, and technical services Number of establishments	Professional, scientific, and technical services Number of employees	Administration and support and waste management and mediation services Number of establishments	Administration and support and waste management and mediation services Number of employees	Educational services Number of establishments	Educational services Number of employees	Health care and social assistance Number of establishments	Health care and social assistance Number of employees	Arts, entertainment, and recreation Number of establishments	Arts, entertainment, and recreation Number of employees	Accommodation and food services Number of establishments	Accommodation and food services Number of employees	Other services (except public administration) Number of establishments	Other services (except public administration) Number of employees
	16	17	18	19	20	21	22	23	24	25	26	27	28	29	30
RHODE ISLAND—Con.															
North Providence town (Providence)..............	150	57	576	55	301	4	11	80	2,662	7	D	76	832	63	231
North Smithfield town (Providence)..............	22	37	232	21	145	3	D	53	530	6	52	26	508	23	D
Pawtucket city & MCD (Providence)..............	311	107	763	86	2,027	15	87	180	4,972	21	348	139	1,384	126	753
Portsmouth town (Newport)................	D	52	205	27	140	7	18	40	865	17	114	35	321	32	D
Providence city & MCD (Providence)..............	1,126	798	6,387	209	6,342	54	625	594	28,579	54	1,951	566	9,893	427	3,455
Scituate town (Providence)	D	19	77	15	D	NA	NA	18	130	2	D	16	183	10	D
Smithfield town (Providence)..............	97	70	414	44	380	9	38	69	1,469	15	114	79	1,330	45	249
South Kingstown town (Washington).............	D	87	351	73	313	14	64	113	2,747	31	242	99	1,378	67	501
Tiverton town (Newport) ...	373	31	105	17	36	1	D	26	300	4	25	29	326	29	81
Valley Falls CDP............	NA	NA	NA	NA	NA	NA	NA	NA	NA	NA	NA	NA	NA	NA	NA
Warren town (Bristol)........	D	21	104	17	55	4	D	31	483	6	D	43	491	40	136
Warwick city & MCD (Kent)	1,102	345	2,268	164	3,304	16	78	378	8,920	34	603	248	4,910	207	1,435
Westerly CDP............	NA	NA	NA	NA	NA	NA	NA	NA	NA	NA	NA	NA	NA	NA	NA
Westerly town (Washington).............	92	60	236	37	92	9	49	103	2,030	32	280	107	1,334	64	276
West Warwick town (Kent)	D	32	117	21	183	7	48	43	621	12	D	65	683	54	210
Woonsocket city & MCD (Providence)..............	131	44	262	25	638	8	99	110	4,054	6	D	93	1,218	73	368
SOUTH CAROLINA.........	23,189	9,721	79,824	5,487	156,401	767	4,278	9,848	212,444	1,525	24,918	9,828	185,282	6,666	44,374
Aiken city	168	126	D	39	D	9	14	192	4,505	26	421	134	3,030	62	343
Anderson city...............	178	134	617	43	1,186	6	45	183	5,020	12	D	165	3,355	74	481
Beaufort city...............	95	89	395	27	163	3	D	86	1,267	5	36	90	1,767	45	256
Berea CDP	27	7	45	7	68	1	D	14	440	NA	NA	16	80	3	D
Bluffton town	75	65	935	37	311	8	45	60	870	8	315	60	1,273	33	350
Cayce city	108	39	301	18	532	2	D	18	D	5	D	37	736	30	341
Charleston city..............	1,716	662	4,179	183	3,755	34	252	471	17,331	94	1,417	517	11,876	279	1,902
Clemson city	D	25	160	8	D	5	20	40	324	6	D	74	1,506	23	168
Columbia city	1,594	846	9,340	240	8,690	49	305	549	19,715	48	D	505	11,042	329	3,373
Conway city	109	99	388	22	627	6	D	88	2,647	8	D	86	1,220	48	241
Dentsville CDP	546	31	262	27	934	7	31	54	931	9	108	59	1,121	35	187
Easley city	124	51	403	25	1,545	4	20	81	1,761	8	152	79	1,409	45	208
Five Forks CDP	26	27	72	19	153	3	24	22	268	3	D	19	241	13	61
Florence city	398	133	1,553	70	2,680	10	30	256	D	15	D	192	3,845	83	675
Forest Acres city............	D	46	360	21	384	5	D	57	576	9	223	49	1,142	35	267
Fort Mill town	D	55	366	19	788	3	13	39	286	6	D	39	403	36	183
Gaffney city.................	122	35	131	10	D	4	D	40	526	9	110	50	1,227	44	D
Gantt CDP	48	9	38	13	177	NA	NA	23	521	3	D	20	273	12	197
Goose Creek city	90	60	1,152	30	267	4	D	45	404	6	121	69	1,254	47	245
Greenville city..............	1,308	811	7,890	244	17,965	47	374	493	8,205	65	1,112	448	10,151	269	1,857
Greenwood city	109	72	840	21	1,038	3	35	103	4,299	8	D	97	2,073	49	260
Greer city	146	66	334	34	388	3	26	85	975	10	74	74	1,172	43	D
Hanahan city...............	53	22	548	21	254	4	25	8	266	2	D	8	D	12	D
Hilton Head Island town....	1,158	245	1,028	165	1,885	24	165	166	2,304	66	1,407	226	5,252	135	1,147
Irmo town	62	53	223	21	242	8	D	71	757	8	D	47	747	49	337
James Island town	NA	NA	NA	NA	NA	NA	NA	NA	NA	NA	NA	NA	NA	NA	NA
Ladson CDP	79	9	62	12	121	2	D	13	99	2	D	18	343	9	D
Lexington town..............	55	136	744	27	875	4	19	66	769	17	D	97	2,182	70	501
Mauldin city.................	158	52	1,215	34	1,492	6	120	59	691	7	D	51	D	34	D
Mount Pleasant town	384	416	2,412	163	D	37	D	325	4,665	44	546	220	4,417	140	896
Myrtle Beach city	2,259	218	1,141	121	1,924	15	55	236	3,045	85	1,725	546	13,643	150	1,069
Newberry city	37	24	87	7	98	1	D	37	910	1	D	40	629	20	D
North Augusta city	58	33	D	11	D	6	24	59	1,066	8	D	56	937	27	146
North Charleston city........	1,039	348	8,196	215	10,384	25	304	321	6,798	14	1,218	322	6,364	208	1,716
North Myrtle Beach city	770	51	138	33	829	3	D	33	318	33	D	184	4,370	43	359
Oak Grove CDP..............	49	7	24	15	75	1	D	11	326	NA	NA	9	143	12	86
Orangeburg city	173	49	227	24	504	4	13	86	999	4	D	67	1,452	37	180
Parker CDP.................	D	2	D	3	D	1	D	8	210	NA	NA	5	103	13	D
Port Royal town	19	14	48	4	31	NA	NA	24	467	2	D	24	306	10	D
Red Hill CDP	95	13	20	15	D	NA	NA	33	618	1	D	10	152	6	D
Rock Hill city...............	319	161	941	79	1,860	12	105	261	6,390	18	278	196	4,123	105	876
St. Andrews CDP............	161	38	192	25	1,225	4	15	38	456	3	D	52	751	42	281
Seven Oaks CDP............	206	61	835	47	2,116	9	74	46	663	3	D	36	648	37	245
Simpsonville city	52	39	159	24	1,056	4	21	60	669	11	D	57	1,056	24	100
Socastee CDP	23	20	62	24	112	1	D	25	436	NA	NA	23	215	23	D
Spartanburg city	404	193	1,296	52	2,019	14	81	209	4,306	25	202	200	4,453	117	1,052
Summerville town	248	117	494	53	D	6	28	147	2,357	16	322	146	2,968	97	597
Sumter city.................	208	99	517	37	2,080	7	41	170	4,929	7	D	128	2,635	87	717
Taylors CDP	42	33	111	20	144	4	5	22	195	5	25	17	238	20	D
Wade Hampton CDP	D	70	332	39	1,740	5	28	59	1,611	9	D	61	950	33	248
West Columbia city..........	245	50	261	28	692	4	9	72	1,705	4	D	75	1,352	64	372
SOUTH DAKOTA.............	3,526	1,822	11,144	1,085	11,555	128	750	2,298	63,494	668	6,204	2,363	37,974	1,805	8,371
Aberdeen city................	D	67	378	50	967	2	D	101	2,756	30	286	90	1,833	60	D
Brookings city	157	58	304	23	217	11	9	67	1,325	15	111	70	1,444	54	D
Huron city	D	27	D	16	115	2	D	48	D	14	112	39	487	39	143
Mitchell city................	82	44	519	22	380	2	D	76	2,166	15	73	64	1,340	41	219
Pierre city..................	D	50	277	26	D	3	D	58	1,269	17	D	44	885	71	337
Rapid City city..............	528	273	1,864	125	1,460	24	153	316	9,119	78	738	247	5,808	235	1,444

Table C. Incorporated Places, Census Designated Places (CDPs), and Minor Civil Divisions (MCDs) of 10,000 or More Population — **Economic Census**

STATE City, town, township, borough, or CDP (county if applicable)	Utilities		Manufacturing		Wholesale trade¹		Retail trade		Transportation and warehousing		Information		Finance and insurance		Real estate and rental and leasing
	Number of establishments	Number of employees	Number of establishments	Number of employees	Number of establishments	Number of employees	Number of establishments	Number of employees	Number of establishments	Number of employees	Number of establishments	Number of employees	Number of establishments	Number of employees	Number of establishments
	1	2	3	4	5	6	7	8	9	10	11	12	13	14	15
SOUTH DAKOTA—Con.															
Sioux Falls city	5	D	147	9,836	324	5,257	751	14,515	200	3,720	110	2,934	542	15,202	236
Spearfish city	2	D	24	330	5	D	90	1,104	10	193	12	D	36	228	39
Vermillion city	2	D	8	D	3	D	42	659	7	D	5	15	13	D	10
Watertown city	NA	NA	67	3,357	50	723	171	2,597	38	246	9	135	76	D	44
Yankton city	2	D	20	1,950	23	161	103	1,470	19	152	14	190	50	630	19
TENNESSEE	144	3,256	5,823	293,646	5,828	92,537	22,615	306,078	4,047	132,825	2,489	48,231	9,726	112,241	5,470
Arlington town	NA	NA	11	1,301	7	D	23	219	4	D	5	D	13	36	3
Athens city	NA	NA	30	2,834	14	181	111	1,548	9	107	10	D	54	440	22
Bartlett city	1	D	34	920	64	1,097	124	2,019	14	D	24	410	69	448	35
Brentwood city	NA	NA	18	173	59	785	175	3,254	15	126	91	1,738	288	5,867	94
Bristol city	NA	NA	47	2,255	40	394	118	1,872	14	D	14	289	86	D	34
Brownsville city	1	D	12	D	6	60	50	D	5	D	6	63	29	D	7
Chattanooga city	11	D	323	18,889	374	4,859	1,123	16,813	189	14,119	122	3,280	481	12,300	290
Clarksville city	3	D	45	3,378	68	952	489	7,756	38	421	24	395	174	1,264	137
Cleveland city	NA	NA	80	5,481	41	D	297	4,319	25	1,281	14	280	151	1,461	55
Collierville town	NA	NA	38	2,236	50	671	213	3,540	23	204	17	155	73	408	41
Columbia city	2	D	40	856	39	496	221	2,817	15	203	13	D	100	1,487	50
Cookeville city	1	D	76	2,976	50	887	274	4,064	30	460	22	D	112	1,034	54
Crossville city	2	D	20	1,749	25	158	183	2,381	18	689	15	358	63	383	30
Dickson city	NA	NA	29	2,758	18	431	130	1,790	3	D	11	148	54	D	23
Dyersburg city	NA	NA	23	1,985	24	198	140	1,740	7	D	8	73	52	409	21
East Ridge city	NA	NA	19	221	16	93	74	695	9	D	3	36	43	220	23
Elizabethton city	2	D	19	802	8	157	90	1,526	4	19	4	81	49	338	19
Farragut town	1	D	NA	NA	10	205	72	1,304	6	36	13	114	53	249	38
Franklin city	7	D	68	1,770	134	1,764	477	8,372	33	420	90	2,985	289	5,904	120
Gallatin city	1	D	61	2,257	37	530	144	2,057	22	948	10	195	76	348	38
Germantown city	NA	NA	9	D	33	D	140	1,977	14	D	12	85	83	488	42
Goodlettsville city	NA	NA	19	1,701	24	D	153	2,133	14	D	10	124	57	692	28
Greeneville town	1	D	55	3,120	20	275	156	2,250	16	D	9	D	87	658	32
Hendersonville city	NA	NA	48	810	50	D	198	2,898	13	74	25	233	108	496	68
Jackson city	3	67	77	7,033	117	1,383	426	6,689	50	947	30	566	183	D	90
Johnson City city	4	D	74	3,902	93	1,048	436	7,306	22	345	41	1,275	194	D	99
Kingsport city	4	D	38	10,628	75	904	337	5,487	41	729	21	553	156	D	59
Knoxville city	NA	NA	208	D	411	5,879	1,326	22,849	138	3,972	137	4,298	620	8,102	396
Lakeland city	NA	NA	NA	NA	2	D	22	289	2	D	2	D	8	19	6
La Vergne city	1	D	46	3,289	74	4,419	61	667	37	1,530	8	D	13	48	17
Lawrenceburg city	NA	NA	25	1,277	16	110	110	1,188	14	D	7	D	46	D	17
Lebanon city	1	D	47	2,115	42	1,219	213	2,781	42	2,583	16	210	85	597	58
Lewisburg city	1	D	33	2,495	6	47	77	833	4	58	5	D	26	D	14
McMinnville city	1	D	25	765	11	D	118	1,411	5	17	10	200	50	D	19
Manchester city	1	D	15	551	7	40	95	1,096	8	D	5	25	34	D	11
Martin city	NA	NA	5	D	9	64	60	770	3	20	6	124	26	128	13
Maryville city	1	D	31	3,037	29	271	174	2,749	19	444	14	D	91	1,669	32
Memphis city	2	D	450	18,847	980	20,551	2,365	35,878	872	50,263	306	5,694	1,221	17,982	745
Middle Valley CDP	NA	NA	3	D	2	D	9	63	3	D	2	D	4	7	2
Millington city	NA	NA	8	147	7	D	70	1,183	4	D	7	141	30	150	17
Morristown city	2	D	84	8,441	42	D	248	3,728	25	D	18	296	101	D	49
Mount Juliet city	1	D	34	488	22	368	133	2,410	22	457	15	131	59	430	27
Murfreesboro city	4	D	99	5,030	88	925	554	8,860	54	957	34	1,904	249	3,482	134
Nashville-Davidson metropolitan government	7	259	552	18,154	923	17,595	2,575	37,506	438	18,582	593	14,161	1,217	18,920	897
Nashville-Davidson metropolitan government (balance)	7	259	517	16,082	870	16,559	2,362	34,827	416	17,977	545	13,787	1,141	18,293	844
Oak Ridge city	NA	NA	44	5,527	21	D	107	1,720	8	69	16	224	65	D	42
Paris city	NA	NA	15	D	14	474	111	1,416	7	D	5	D	38	305	23
Portland city	1	D	33	2,582	8	D	45	320	21	1,353	2	D	17	147	8
Red Bank city	NA	NA	7	87	5	D	41	323	NA	NA	2	D	13	58	8
Sevierville city	1	D	15	159	8	26	281	4,329	10	150	12	147	77	646	49
Seymour CDP	NA	NA	NA	NA	4	8	25	453	8	25	3	47	17	68	10
Shelbyville city	3	D	33	3,786	19	D	127	1,379	18	D	9	D	41	D	30
Smyrna town	2	D	31	6,099	31	831	149	2,386	43	959	10	72	65	280	26
Soddy-Daisy city	NA	NA	17	173	11	144	32	511	2	D	1	D	14	66	9
Springfield city	1	D	35	4,802	17	641	90	1,419	9	D	3	D	49	D	20
Spring Hill city	NA	NA	9	D	11	423	64	1,105	15	142	13	46	29	D	18
Tullahoma city	NA	NA	42	D	15	195	137	1,574	10	151	14	275	55	D	24
Union City city	1	D	20	1,759	20	357	107	1,506	13	191	9	D	46	297	16
White House city	NA	NA	14	560	1	D	34	648	5	D	6	D	19	D	9
TEXAS	1,953	52,894	19,782	767,024	27,752	408,692	78,281	1,150,148	16,998	386,767	9,221	230,781	39,037	481,749	26,639
Abilene city	23	228	83	1,991	131	1,619	533	7,619	83	1,474	52	981	240	2,599	162
Addison town	1	D	55	1,330	121	1,737	121	1,476	63	1,029	53	1,886	260	11,505	163
Alamo city	NA	NA	8	59	21	D	56	975	7	90	3	D	11	86	9
Aldine CDP	1	D	93	3,606	44	401	66	330	15	D	3	D	9	46	15
Alice city	3	D	12	530	28	D	109	1,466	45	659	9	D	55	320	29
Allen city	NA	NA	27	987	58	D	281	5,344	15	D	34	1,579	115	822	77
Alton city	NA	NA	NA	NA	1	D	19	165	3	D	NA	NA	6	18	4
Alvin city	3	D	31	1,222	29	335	99	1,713	17	291	7	D	49	238	31
Amarillo city	15	1,308	159	12,263	216	3,356	841	12,920	136	2,348	67	1,411	433	5,139	272
Andrews city	3	11	5	D	11	D	30	344	29	468	5	D	19	117	11
Angleton city	NA	NA	16	603	9	D	67	1,099	15	187	6	47	40	189	25
Arlington city	7	D	224	9,679	333	5,752	1,147	17,817	133	1,616	117	2,654	484	8,428	379
Atascocita CDP	2	D	6	15	14	58	57	850	19	42	3	D	35	128	19
Athens city	11	D	36	1,383	17	164	88	1,011	5	15	11	100	40	253	30
Austin city	45	817	616	20,866	942	19,901	3,091	49,905	317	7,619	850	25,007	2,002	25,966	1,548
Azle city	1	D	7	D	7	D	41	664	4	D	4	D	19	74	22

1 Merchant wholesalers, except manufacturers' sales branches and offices.

Table C. Incorporated Places, Census Designated Places (CDPs), and Minor Civil Divisions (MCDs) of 10,000 or More Population — **Economic Census**

STATE / City, town, township, borough, or CDP (county if applicable)	Real estate and rental and leasing — Number of employees	Professional, scientific, and technical services — Number of establishments	Number of employees	Administration and support and waste management and mediation services — Number of establishments	Number of employees	Educational services — Number of establishments	Number of employees	Health care and social assistance — Number of establishments	Number of employees	Arts, entertainment, and recreation — Number of establishments	Number of employees	Accommodation and food services — Number of establishments	Number of employees	Other services (except public administration) — Number of establishments	Number of employees
	16	17	18	19	20	21	22	23	24	25	26	27	28	29	30
SOUTH DAKOTA—Con.															
Sioux Falls city	1,231	477	4,279	268	4,213	42	345	498	21,983	137	2,424	409	10,412	352	2,354
Spearfish city	D	39	153	24	161	4	20	65	1,168	10	D	61	1,074	34	137
Vermillion city	D	12	D	7	264	2	D	28	D	3	D	40	D	20	D
Watertown city	D	69	D	34	D	2	D	87	D	27	D	78	1,576	66	D
Yankton city	D	43	D	27	167	5	D	71	D	12	52	52	964	48	203
TENNESSEE	30,593	10,863	104,552	6,572	213,874	878	8,362	14,897	380,453	2,326	32,490	12,004	241,348	8,117	55,990
Arlington town	D	18	82	18	129	NA	NA	13	D	3	D	20	286	12	D
Athens city	101	35	168	18	443	NA	NA	84	1,521	4	23	65	1,238	37	D
Bartlett city	145	104	921	79	1,389	10	48	128	4,132	11	144	84	1,282	71	674
Brentwood city	D	307	3,299	150	8,118	28	414	234	3,795	63	1,181	92	1,834	84	610
Bristol city	93	64	569	39	1,042	1	D	130	3,994	17	D	83	1,431	58	D
Brownsville city	D	13	D	10	D	NA	NA	26	D	1	D	28	283	19	D
Chattanooga city	1,898	625	7,031	287	14,896	42	383	846	23,520	95	2,085	651	14,791	447	3,286
Clarksville city	605	158	1,564	93	D	22	D	316	6,758	18	D	319	5,879	173	D
Cleveland city	254	125	786	56	4,171	6	D	200	4,378	12	D	163	D	80	811
Collierville town	149	105	416	67	738	12	130	106	D	14	579	97	2,332	67	544
Columbia city	175	71	458	40	551	5	34	169	4,753	13	175	101	1,771	71	D
Cookeville city	156	116	484	48	1,152	9	D	199	5,291	12	D	137	D	94	D
Crossville city	113	46	158	17	781	3	D	115	2,700	6	104	71	D	36	D
Dickson city	56	33	114	13	D	2	D	95	D	7	71	69	D	31	D
Dyersburg city	67	37	181	28	661	2	D	96	1,910	7	71	52	858	37	165
East Ridge city	57	29	305	23	355	2	D	52	978	1	D	56	979	26	257
Elizabethton city	D	32	120	16	D	1	D	67	D	3	D	50	D	23	244
Farragut town	129	78	460	35	457	5	42	81	D	7	219	58	1,146	36	238
Franklin city	753	373	3,940	164	5,234	33	124	322	6,702	104	1,044	281	6,519	171	1,276
Gallatin city	456	54	693	31	995	5	D	106	2,364	8	53	58	905	58	285
Germantown city	D	115	418	68	732	11	D	198	5,475	16	D	70	1,454	60	563
Goodlettsville city	D	62	467	29	1,582	4	D	71	900	10	97	77	1,341	37	188
Greeneville town	D	65	241	27	D	3	9	120	3,607	6	37	83	1,302	43	215
Hendersonville city	251	121	951	57	674	16	D	154	2,118	29	D	112	2,638	92	462
Jackson city	431	158	951	103	D	12	64	300	11,683	23	332	210	4,703	112	643
Johnson City city	494	172	2,348	84	3,171	20	111	296	12,798	24	340	239	5,668	133	D
Kingsport city	264	143	966	55	944	13	36	269	8,007	20	D	193	4,387	108	D
Knoxville city	2,635	720	6,771	320	21,245	44	D	894	30,343	78	1,425	714	17,958	500	4,419
Lakeland city	D	11	105	14	138	3	D	9	69	5	35	16	376	15	D
La Vergne city	136	18	233	27	470	3	6	15	143	1	D	29	412	25	D
Lawrenceburg city	D	29	D	10	D	1	D	66	1,066	6	D	37	616	26	94
Lebanon city	228	87	366	52	1,750	9	D	164	2,810	12	129	108	2,239	68	705
Lewisburg city	D	20	68	11	605	NA	NA	47	D	4	D	31	D	20	93
McMinnville city	48	30	77	13	563	3	15	88	1,175	4	D	46	698	34	D
Manchester city	51	32	D	17	547	3	D	60	957	3	D	48	850	24	D
Martin city	47	13	53	5	399	2	D	58	1,365	1	D	39	667	11	D
Maryville city	88	98	642	30	946	12	94	162	4,506	15	136	94	1,644	64	307
Memphis city	5,964	1,313	14,700	835	48,358	100	2,200	1,766	55,137	134	3,829	1,243	28,822	906	8,079
Middle Valley CDP	D	6	14	9	40	2	D	3	D	NA	NA	4	25	3	D
Millington city	75	35	240	8	925	NA	NA	31	319	4	D	55	863	30	179
Morristown city	162	61	269	43	1,975	4	D	157	4,178	9	D	106	D	64	329
Mount Juliet city	242	51	495	27	190	7	34	80	D	9	114	84	1,934	50	D
Murfreesboro city	715	227	1,261	104	2,089	28	246	364	11,206	29	D	314	7,922	199	1,277
Nashville-Davidson metropolitan government	6,348	1,930	24,182	1,066	31,875	169	2,032	1,819	62,989	735	8,254	1,714	40,106	1,225	11,665
Nashville-Davidson metropolitan government (balance)	6,079	1,805	23,449	1,014	29,827	161	D	1,718	61,932	694	7,752	1,600	37,958	1,158	11,271
Oak Ridge city	152	150	9,308	66	D	11	D	134	3,017	9	140	74	1,604	61	D
Paris city	D	32	239	11	785	3	D	75	1,416	6	D	44	683	32	117
Portland city	27	8	89	7	D	NA	NA	27	D	3	D	18	D	12	D
Red Bank city	D	12	63	10	61	1	D	18	D	NA	NA	17	305	18	D
Sevierville city	359	60	257	36	294	3	D	85	1,678	13	D	129	3,630	49	262
Seymour CDP	D	18	150	8	68	2	D	31	223	3	D	23	399	15	D
Shelbyville city	D	39	176	13	644	1	D	80	892	3	D	46	766	30	D
Smyrna city	111	53	650	43	2,513	10	28	126	1,875	8	205	109	2,367	48	D
Soddy-Daisy city	20	9	53	10	47	NA	NA	16	226	2	D	32	400	20	D
Springfield city	60	38	108	19	616	3	D	75	D	7	170	45	885	36	114
Spring Hill city	64	27	89	31	264	4	15	39	D	9	19	57	1,188	28	D
Tullahoma city	88	44	D	16	774	4	D	131	2,026	6	D	56	1,015	39	166
Union City city	50	24	101	20	D	NA	NA	68	1,171	6	18	40	701	26	89
White House city	D	12	79	8	87	1	D	27	D	4	D	32	552	15	D
TEXAS	169,941	62,322	639,561	26,076	929,661	4,530	39,957	61,342	1,345,664	6,304	119,132	48,721	976,390	34,116	259,128
Abilene city	881	256	1,716	141	D	24	145	375	D	52	D	284	D	205	1,707
Addison town	1,652	399	5,370	159	9,877	28	242	83	1,194	16	D	200	5,026	75	1,208
Alamo city	110	12	62	4	12	1	D	35	776	1	D	29	556	14	D
Aldine CDP	125	9	54	15	228	NA	NA	8	91	3	16	6	56	32	157
Alice city	229	46	228	21	D	NA	NA	99	3,972	6	D	61	1,147	45	D
Allen city	413	280	1,169	88	1,822	25	173	265	3,593	24	462	170	3,771	89	729
Alton city	D	2	D	3	D	NA	NA	15	D	NA	NA	2	D	NA	NA
Alvin city	197	40	152	26	1,129	NA	NA	55	D	7	46	62	1,172	43	246
Amarillo city	1,247	464	4,066	234	D	33	362	652	16,512	73	944	500	10,147	350	2,614
Andrews city	60	20	D	8	D	1	D	26	475	3	D	26	372	19	D
Angleton city	149	47	269	11	64	3	10	65	1,485	8	26	36	524	31	119
Arlington city	1,915	737	5,727	351	10,880	59	678	928	19,213	79	4,325	684	15,492	445	3,004
Atascocita CDP	D	64	184	36	293	3	D	40	451	6	378	40	620	29	D
Athens city	149	40	D	23	270	NA	NA	83	1,590	10	80	52	804	31	D
Austin city	10,167	4,852	57,317	1,307	51,056	371	4,562	2,603	53,771	382	6,539	2,517	55,702	1,875	17,532
Azle city	76	23	83	11	51	NA	NA	47	684	2	D	28	445	22	115

Table C. Incorporated Places, Census Designated Places (CDPs), and Minor Civil Divisions (MCDs) of 10,000 or More Population — **Economic Census**

STATE City, town, township, borough, or CDP (county if applicable)	Utilities Number of establishments	Number of employees	Manufacturing Number of establishments	Number of employees	Wholesale trade[1] Number of establishments	Number of employees	Retail trade Number of establishments	Number of employees	Transportation and warehousing Number of establishments	Number of employees	Information Number of establishments	Number of employees	Finance and insurance Number of establishments	Number of employees	Real estate and rental and leasing Number of establishments
	1	2	3	4	5	6	7	8	9	10	11	12	13	14	15
TEXAS—Con.															
Balch Springs city	1	D	25	589	8	D	68	1,185	8	29	3	D	16	D	5
Bay City city	3	D	12	83	15	D	81	983	10	48	7	44	37	202	25
Baytown city	4	D	55	5,545	41	460	276	4,460	58	1,579	12	112	91	620	79
Beaumont city	13	D	103	4,671	180	2,151	611	9,166	110	1,461	64	867	236	1,651	176
Bedford city	2	D	13	111	33	211	119	1,747	20	142	15	533	107	1,864	55
Beeville city	2	D	4	53	6	D	63	896	6	43	8	D	31	165	19
Bellaire city	5	D	6	84	35	270	49	695	13	144	14	D	80	489	41
Bellmead city	NA	NA	5	80	4	9	41	1,228	2	D	1	D	9	87	2
Belton city	1	D	26	751	18	272	76	1,119	7	339	5	27	28	137	17
Benbrook city	1	D	11	369	14	D	47	684	5	D	7	39	38	156	11
Big Spring city	7	67	16	495	21	D	99	1,309	14	117	12	185	47	D	37
Boerne city	NA	NA	22	760	24	D	106	1,833	4	10	7	D	54	362	23
Bonham city	3	D	9	368	3	D	42	434	2	D	5	31	22	107	8
Borger city	2	D	15	834	17	D	62	762	8	D	5	50	27	D	9
Brenham city	3	D	28	2,339	28	472	120	1,807	10	186	13	D	51	720	31
Brownsville city	2	D	103	2,705	175	1,681	563	8,869	150	1,772	31	1,154	223	1,704	142
Brownwood city	4	D	16	D	22	D	121	1,478	11	120	11	135	45	292	25
Brushy Creek CDP	2	D	3	D	2	D	12	359	4	D	1	D	5	9	10
Bryan city	1	D	69	3,967	83	1,126	299	3,842	46	620	38	D	114	757	92
Burkburnett city	NA	NA	5	194	8	D	28	311	5	D	3	D	11	38	5
Burleson city	3	D	32	920	22	138	154	3,015	21	156	6	125	77	399	32
Canyon city	1	D	11	69	5	D	36	570	6	D	3	D	20	D	16
Canyon Lake CDP	3	D	10	D	11	26	38	298	8	D	2	D	12	37	21
Carrollton city	5	130	187	11,424	394	6,422	406	4,850	104	1,659	79	3,697	200	3,666	143
Cedar Hill city	1	D	27	782	12	94	146	3,056	18	D	11	141	43	D	23
Cedar Park city	1	D	39	1,200	44	D	232	3,735	14	54	20	317	100	D	65
Channelview CDP	NA	NA	30	2,181	26	D	61	424	48	1,462	2	D	15	86	18
Cibolo city	NA	NA	11	210	5	24	9	91	6	109	NA	NA	10	40	2
Cinco Ranch CDP	2	D	3	4	16	26	19	242	3	6	4	15	15	77	16
Cleburne city	3	52	32	1,433	35	498	155	2,084	29	D	10	154	68	336	37
Cloverleaf CDP	NA	NA	8	28	5	D	25	205	6	19	1	D	21	105	4
Clute city	2	D	8	855	17	159	45	480	8	196	3	D	17	141	21
College Station city	1	D	13	241	34	344	309	5,876	23	874	33	815	126	793	120
Colleyville city	1	D	14	91	30	100	80	1,131	9	D	4	107	86	392	47
Conroe city	5	D	104	3,733	111	1,352	382	6,345	40	751	17	311	162	952	83
Converse city	NA	NA	20	393	11	D	27	249	7	D	4	D	12	43	5
Coppell city	NA	NA	35	1,485	70	2,125	75	1,605	62	2,297	30	552	78	4,013	47
Copperas Cove city	NA	NA	4	7	1	D	70	1,004	3	D	4	129	34	232	29
Corinth city	3	D	3	D	6	D	27	537	7	D	4	D	14	69	10
Corpus Christi city	26	D	168	5,412	326	4,376	1,043	16,228	188	3,410	123	2,007	529	D	370
Corsicana city	9	D	46	2,754	25	D	136	1,906	25	791	9	117	64	D	45
Crowley city	NA	NA	6	D	6	21	29	413	3	33	1	D	18	116	10
Dallas city	59	D	1,125	42,824	1,934	28,244	4,022	57,240	658	30,845	773	22,962	3,000	44,954	2,162
Deer Park city	5	D	41	4,605	40	898	57	1,014	19	304	3	D	37	271	32
Del Rio city	3	D	15	176	21	D	142	1,984	39	395	18	145	60	D	32
Denison city	NA	NA	24	1,958	14	184	92	1,143	8	47	7	66	48	1,582	25
Denton city	4	D	93	5,210	93	1,231	399	6,463	47	3,241	31	575	179	1,195	149
DeSoto city	3	D	27	733	25	368	80	1,395	28	596	11	148	51	315	39
Dickinson city	1	D	6	49	16	D	70	669	11	32	4	D	22	116	23
Donna city	NA	NA	8	278	14	188	45	411	15	14	NA	NA	14	94	9
Dumas city	1	D	5	11	15	D	62	817	12	150	5	D	34	D	11
Duncanville city	NA	NA	22	1,137	16	D	130	1,521	15	66	6	34	66	275	38
Eagle Pass city	3	D	14	339	38	D	150	2,425	79	567	11	D	58	D	26
Edinburg city	5	D	29	625	73	1,425	216	3,856	47	968	17	214	101	680	60
Eidson Road CDP	NA	NA	NA	NA	3	5	6	36	10	12	NA	NA	NA	NA	NA
El Campo city	5	D	15	393	23	D	75	892	19	167	7	D	41	197	17
El Paso city	13	D	432	11,607	884	9,548	2,064	32,405	666	11,436	180	9,075	843	6,501	671
Ennis city	3	D	44	2,808	20	D	86	1,122	10	410	4	26	36	166	24
Euless city	2	D	37	832	48	418	135	1,595	26	279	17	145	46	271	40
Farmers Branch city	5	121	80	2,707	207	5,093	150	2,360	44	1,459	80	2,804	137	2,688	70
Flower Mound town	1	D	20	636	58	698	153	2,668	23	D	27	320	123	781	66
Forest Hill city	NA	NA	12	65	15	137	44	434	5	99	NA	NA	7	39	2
Forney city	4	D	17	511	13	D	44	839	7	55	5	24	22	122	10
Fort Hood CDP	NA	NA	NA	NA	NA	NA	15	92	4	D	NA	NA	9	D	2
Fort Worth city	16	677	645	39,747	696	16,814	2,047	31,491	507	33,599	265	7,621	1,213	20,455	704
Four Corners CDP	NA	NA	5	34	2	D	9	28	1	D	NA	NA	1	D	NA
Fredericksburg city	2	D	41	437	15	D	147	1,372	11	D	7	D	38	249	28
Freeport city	2	D	18	4,573	21	D	40	346	29	651	2	D	10	60	11
Fresno CDP	NA	NA	6	221	1	D	14	88	6	34	NA	NA	1	D	1
Friendswood city	2	D	16	175	15	D	96	1,743	14	43	11	75	66	276	44
Frisco city	1	D	36	533	96	D	437	9,421	33	436	63	2,811	222	6,428	135
Gainesville city	3	8	33	2,585	28	346	111	1,547	15	D	10	D	37	275	19
Galena Park city	NA	NA	12	814	12	D	12	72	19	336	NA	NA	2	D	3
Galveston city	2	D	29	948	36	D	208	2,523	43	1,141	13	195	65	1,370	75
Garland city	3	D	264	9,585	184	2,917	608	9,210	82	1,560	37	492	257	1,450	173
Gatesville city	3	D	8	176	3	D	42	654	5	D	7	29	17	D	7
Georgetown city	1	D	48	1,541	33	D	190	3,460	33	326	22	265	87	D	63
Glenn Heights city	NA	NA	NA	NA	3	D	27	256	2	D	NA	NA	7	D	2
Grand Prairie city	2	D	181	12,084	267	5,982	343	5,605	167	5,220	25	489	141	1,387	126
Grapevine city	NA	NA	43	1,942	93	1,933	315	4,979	167	2,252	54	1,589	94	565	77
Greatwood CDP	NA	NA	NA	NA	6	9	3	5	1	D	NA	NA	4	5	3
Greenville city	3	D	39	6,681	23	249	139	2,206	6	D	20	568	50	237	38
Groves city	NA	NA	3	D	7	55	40	308	7	D	1	D	14	157	6
Haltom City city	NA	NA	90	2,612	96	1,072	144	1,370	22	374	10	246	49	416	38
Harker Heights city	2	D	4	23	4	24	58	1,136	2	D	1	D	20	109	32
Harlingen city	4	158	49	903	75	738	298	4,835	60	1,304	39	1,877	148	1,328	97
Henderson city	3	D	17	842	14	102	89	1,211	5	D	6	D	39	349	15
Hereford city	3	D	15	189	16	D	60	D	23	D	4	D	25	D	14
Hewitt city	NA	NA	11	214	19	204	22	166	5	D	NA	NA	10	28	8

1 Merchant wholesalers, except manufacturers' sales branches and offices.

Table C. Incorporated Places, Census Designated Places (CDPs), and Minor Civil Divisions (MCDs) of 10,000 or More Population — Economic Census

	Economic activity by sector, 2012													
	Real estate and rental and leasing	Professional, scientific, and technical services		Administration and support and waste management and mediation services		Educational services		Health care and social assistance		Arts, entertainment, and recreation		Accommodation and food services		Other services (except public administration)	
STATE City, town, township, borough, or CDP (county if applicable)	Number of employees	Number of establishments	Number of employees	Number of establishments	Number of employees	Number of establishments	Number of employees	Number of establishments	Number of employees	Number of establishments	Number of employees	Number of establishments	Number of employees	Number of establishments	Number of employees
	16	17	18	19	20	21	22	23	24	25	26	27	28	29	30
TEXAS—Con.															
Balch Springs city	26	5	D	20	283	NA	NA	11	D	2	D	35	451	24	96
Bay City city	139	39	148	12	D	1	D	65	1,052	5	D	52	831	39	160
Baytown city	444	97	2,249	48	1,087	8	35	233	4,518	16	174	174	3,836	94	D
Beaumont city	1,179	373	4,944	155	6,925	21	154	557	13,380	46	623	283	6,727	223	2,008
Bedford city	209	162	805	64	2,261	17	95	198	5,807	10	108	93	1,993	63	419
Beeville city	81	26	75	7	D	2	D	48	D	4	D	48	D	33	D
Bellaire city	140	197	3,261	47	805	13	77	213	5,314	7	D	44	D	48	163
Bellmead city	D	7	23	4	23	1	D	18	291	2	D	31	544	14	D
Belton city	59	40	185	17	270	2	D	46	D	8	D	52	961	34	209
Benbrook city	43	54	287	34	339	3	3	49	712	5	D	37	593	31	266
Big Spring city	146	34	169	13	567	2	D	66	D	5	D	71	1,057	37	D
Boerne city	63	82	D	26	288	6	27	97	1,380	10	D	67	1,219	50	D
Bonham city	108	17	94	3	D	NA	NA	33	924	3	D	25	D	15	D
Borger city	D	30	D	15	D	NA	NA	39	470	6	67	37	D	28	178
Brenham city	91	40	263	23	399	6	24	90	1,880	9	75	64	896	40	D
Brownsville city	537	264	1,273	104	6,035	21	153	463	14,745	31	467	299	5,246	143	709
Brownwood city	81	40	D	15	324	4	18	114	2,821	7	D	51	923	48	241
Brushy Creek CDP	22	56	588	20	103	7	19	22	231	4	6	4	D	10	D
Bryan city	558	191	1,166	87	D	7	D	234	4,976	19	444	139	2,436	146	D
Burkburnett city	18	8	76	3	D	1	D	14	207	4	D	21	309	14	63
Burleson city	106	77	321	35	245	7	49	102	1,111	9	40	105	2,511	68	D
Canyon city	111	24	80	15	D	1	D	34	402	1	D	38	605	20	D
Canyon Lake CDP	237	32	71	14	21	2	D	14	D	7	D	30	450	28	106
Carrollton city	1,629	407	3,355	218	10,767	53	D	342	3,957	32	541	244	3,204	187	1,961
Cedar Hill city	69	55	D	27	301	6	37	87	1,269	7	89	86	2,068	36	D
Cedar Park city	185	155	912	49	566	23	134	167	2,544	25	792	137	2,517	111	733
Channelview CDP	114	16	124	22	533	1	D	30	588	1	D	43	422	24	D
Cibolo city	D	14	21	7	D	1	D	6	D	NA	NA	9	115	11	D
Cinco Ranch CDP	D	67	131	13	70	11	100	22	301	7	D	16	228	14	96
Cleburne city	120	72	434	28	752	2	D	107	2,035	8	D	81	1,365	60	356
Cloverleaf CDP	10	11	39	9	83	1	D	13	154	1	D	15	269	19	159
Clute city	74	10	259	5	103	3	246	6	169	1	D	33	508	25	149
College Station city	638	168	1,324	88	D	25	246	149	2,957	24	353	287	6,966	96	969
Colleyville city	109	155	506	54	343	13	85	116	747	17	347	40	836	58	457
Conroe city	578	205	998	88	12,204	9	59	223	4,039	15	D	164	3,450	118	738
Converse city	38	16	82	10	45	3	13	26	469	3	D	26	551	30	D
Coppell city	482	208	2,604	60	1,629	21	212	109	1,615	11	D	73	1,538	56	980
Copperas Cove city	D	31	138	15	D	3	D	37	D	3	D	50	934	47	271
Corinth city	47	40	96	19	137	3	D	28	D	1	D	22	D	7	68
Corpus Christi city	2,602	790	5,728	308	11,727	53	D	1,017	26,176	73	1,604	749	15,806	467	4,086
Corsicana city	128	49	284	23	447	4	12	118	2,195	8	D	59	994	56	199
Crowley city	22	12	61	9	D	3	D	20	D	3	15	18	425	12	D
Dallas city	20,336	5,425	68,091	1,890	104,433	295	3,187	3,892	105,321	364	9,313	2,687	59,649	1,850	16,611
Deer Park city	421	51	1,007	38	1,710	6	27	48	746	3	13	44	769	61	D
Del Rio city	114	38	D	16	D	2	D	90	D	10	D	87	1,613	45	D
Denison city	80	47	272	12	34	NA	NA	96	3,006	7	49	56	872	29	137
Denton city	585	264	1,295	104	2,793	21	236	418	7,845	24	D	283	5,961	180	1,112
DeSoto city	162	48	199	29	1,133	6	D	173	3,664	5	89	60	1,240	45	173
Dickinson city	120	25	86	20	57	4	12	39	366	7	25	34	567	25	149
Donna city	75	6	12	10	212	1	D	44	453	1	D	21	286	9	20
Dumas city	D	15	D	8	D	1	D	40	D	2	D	41	D	22	91
Duncanville city	173	54	196	21	302	10	40	110	2,216	6	D	60	1,406	72	338
Eagle Pass city	71	37	D	11	D	2	D	91	3,998	8	D	65	D	32	132
Edinburg city	205	150	739	52	1,040	7	D	347	9,489	13	162	120	1,970	77	330
Eidson Road CDP	NA	1	D	NA	NA	NA	NA	1	D	NA	NA	2	D	1	D
El Campo city	81	22	120	12	D	1	D	27	609	6	D	28	D	36	D
El Paso city	2,969	1,124	D	557	28,693	97	D	1,461	39,853	113	D	1,362	27,187	822	5,203
Ennis city	105	23	121	13	386	3	D	64	D	5	D	45	688	36	207
Euless city	267	86	D	38	2,612	5	41	82	629	6	80	89	1,538	63	D
Farmers Branch city	929	308	4,575	185	10,976	21	99	144	2,554	6	D	99	1,493	77	1,051
Flower Mound town	400	272	1,413	87	1,562	39	416	183	2,024	27	516	118	2,866	94	D
Forest Hill city	D	9	65	14	142	1	D	13	D	NA	NA	31	599	10	D
Forney city	22	29	215	12	51	3	19	40	479	6	41	45	703	36	175
Fort Hood CDP	D	56	1,609	9	254	NA	NA	18	D	1	D	7	288	7	D
Fort Worth city	4,977	1,658	22,117	773	35,758	129	1,062	1,807	45,055	177	5,362	1,288	28,324	850	8,281
Four Corners CDP	NA	11	18	7	342	1	D	18	132	NA	NA	6	27	3	D
Fredericksburg city	87	50	170	22	112	2	D	79	D	13	D	88	1,351	39	218
Freeport city	58	12	83	11	D	2	D	9	D	NA	NA	19	267	15	236
Fresno CDP	D	6	33	7	225	2	D	15	127	NA	NA	2	D	3	21
Friendswood city	314	128	447	33	242	17	52	115	1,066	12	153	70	1,121	63	331
Frisco city	672	552	4,343	166	5,993	56	D	402	4,835	50	1,747	254	6,182	149	1,090
Gainesville city	62	36	171	16	163	NA	NA	63	D	6	D	61	D	41	D
Galena Park city	D	3	D	6	48	NA	NA	5	16	NA	NA	10	67	3	D
Galveston city	403	109	566	42	689	6	D	108	5,417	37	646	212	6,605	114	554
Garland city	1,113	280	3,620	187	5,286	31	261	447	8,949	36	567	309	5,540	251	1,249
Gatesville city	D	16	127	3	D	NA	NA	19	621	3	D	26	374	21	71
Georgetown city	228	161	616	34	336	4	39	167	2,803	18	203	103	2,188	86	508
Glenn Heights city	D	2	D	3	D	NA	NA	7	D	1	D	10	211	7	26
Grand Prairie city	1,945	169	1,299	122	3,753	17	120	259	2,739	23	D	216	3,855	160	1,155
Grapevine city	785	219	1,265	94	1,758	23	154	193	3,663	17	379	175	7,278	83	729
Greatwood CDP	D	34	76	8	35	2	D	13	122	2	D	4	40	4	27
Greenville city	115	47	281	20	483	10	36	124	2,502	7	45	68	1,304	45	255
Groves city	73	9	57	6	D	1	D	24	683	2	D	22	D	14	D
Haltom City city	350	56	687	48	2,326	4	40	38	324	7	49	72	735	71	506
Harker Heights city	127	28	138	16	88	8	226	36	D	16	91	63	951	40	188
Harlingen city	443	147	788	62	2,050	9	51	371	12,970	18	205	170	3,749	118	740
Henderson city	D	43	D	13	529	1	D	54	1,102	3	D	52	D	28	207
Hereford city	53	24	D	9	D	NA	NA	20	D	3	26	25	D	30	130
Hewitt city	16	16	68	10	58	2	D	17	827	NA	NA	12	D	17	122

Table C. Incorporated Places, Census Designated Places (CDPs), and Minor Civil Divisions (MCDs) of 10,000 or More Population — **Economic Census**

STATE City, town, township, borough, or CDP (county if applicable)	Utilities Number of establishments	Number of employees	Manufacturing Number of establishments	Number of employees	Wholesale trade[1] Number of establishments	Number of employees	Retail trade Number of establishments	Number of employees	Transportation and warehousing Number of establishments	Number of employees	Information Number of establishments	Number of employees	Finance and insurance Number of establishments	Number of employees	Real estate and rental and leasing Number of establishments
	1	2	3	4	5	6	7	8	9	10	11	12	13	14	15
TEXAS—Con.															
Hidalgo city	NA	NA	6	52	67	D	66	519	62	693	NA	NA	23	235	15
Highland Village city	NA	NA	3	6	12	D	64	1,142	3	2	8	D	26	D	12
Horizon City city	1	D	9	187	5	20	15	124	14	D	1	D	9	46	2
Houston city	215	13,214	2,436	86,899	4,501	77,057	8,592	130,540	1,814	72,253	1,075	33,977	5,018	74,564	3,435
Humble city	1	D	40	1,495	56	399	301	6,496	35	551	19	439	88	470	54
Huntsville city	6	D	17	347	22	D	138	2,258	5	46	13	212	68	D	48
Hurst city	1	D	31	467	37	234	282	5,108	24	243	17	293	85	490	52
Hutto city	NA	NA	5	70	6	D	19	414	5	21	NA	NA	15	D	6
Irving city	13	1,190	160	6,926	356	11,506	606	11,927	185	7,405	257	14,693	603	23,001	339
Jacinto City city	NA	NA	8	308	5	11	29	238	7	62	1	D	10	55	2
Jacksonville city	3	D	39	1,688	15	D	84	1,023	14	509	13	D	44	234	20
Katy city	2	D	47	1,811	63	548	313	6,745	20	70	22	210	127	983	72
Keller city	NA	NA	17	87	26	93	104	1,435	10	D	14	50	67	305	35
Kerrville city	1	D	25	343	25	D	177	2,778	13	D	16	D	72	487	57
Kilgore city	2	D	31	D	69	1,147	86	1,055	32	D	7	D	33	209	35
Killeen city	4	68	15	94	22	D	402	6,119	32	554	36	821	112	872	144
Kingsville city	2	D	13	D	4	D	100	1,397	5	D	6	D	56	306	26
Kyle city	1	D	7	353	8	D	47	997	6	17	5	D	24	94	13
La Homa CDP	NA	NA	NA	NA	NA	NA	NA	NA	3	D	NA	NA	1	D	NA
Lake Jackson city	1	D	3	10	12	63	111	2,489	5	9	8	96	51	553	21
Lakeway city	1	D	7	35	21	79	47	356	6	D	6	44	64	241	29
La Marque city	NA	NA	10	321	6	121	54	638	6	D	7	60	12	D	7
Lancaster city	1	D	24	949	18	D	63	995	22	2,176	8	D	27	D	20
La Porte city	1	D	39	2,483	50	833	70	508	70	2,115	2	D	29	225	38
Laredo city	7	D	68	D	356	D	782	D	1,126	13,940	60	779	271	D	199
League City city	2	D	26	113	47	D	181	3,492	33	394	18	246	101	1,301	60
Leander city	NA	NA	17	174	9	D	36	807	6	D	5	D	21	73	14
Leon Valley city	1	D	12	71	15	88	71	1,156	4	D	2	D	31	207	8
Levelland city	2	D	14	D	13	154	52	738	9	282	6	49	44	201	9
Lewisville city	4	D	99	2,046	105	2,322	411	7,286	46	1,433	53	1,414	167	6,743	112
Little Elm city	NA	NA	7	188	8	D	31	585	7	D	2	D	11	39	7
Live Oak city	NA	NA	3	18	6	D	29	369	4	D	2	D	14	D	7
Lockhart city	1	D	9	593	5	D	42	540	5	187	4	D	20	121	11
Longview city	9	D	120	8,520	170	2,233	508	7,547	65	1,456	45	837	239	1,635	149
Lubbock city	12	D	197	4,181	317	4,844	946	15,727	146	3,131	84	2,982	512	5,219	367
Lufkin city	5	76	43	3,980	47	684	271	4,094	33	523	17	285	102	631	67
Lumberton city	NA	NA	8	D	3	D	52	820	NA	NA	1	D	27	102	12
McAllen city	3	D	96	2,207	348	3,131	870	14,085	160	2,516	76	1,082	315	2,952	206
McKinney city	4	D	70	5,938	93	771	330	6,634	36	440	37	340	201	2,003	121
Mansfield city	NA	NA	82	2,745	65	1,523	141	2,807	26	751	8	119	86	441	39
Marshall city	5	D	28	D	18	125	139	1,699	14	290	10	D	76	804	38
Mercedes city	1	D	11	158	9	72	161	2,105	3	D	3	D	17	100	12
Mesquite city	3	D	66	2,300	63	674	431	7,326	65	3,300	23	278	128	787	97
Midland city	13	381	77	D	164	2,436	453	7,059	128	2,278	48	816	325	D	225
Midlothian city	1	D	18	1,469	10	D	47	733	22	820	2	D	24	122	24
Mineral Wells city	3	D	31	1,464	18	232	80	848	9	D	7	42	26	152	17
Mission city	NA	NA	26	312	68	410	231	3,721	31	341	10	D	120	659	55
Mission Bend CDP	1	D	NA	NA	6	12	17	43	10	16	NA	NA	4	5	2
Missouri City city	NA	NA	26	550	52	316	147	2,936	14	76	10	35	74	379	41
Mount Pleasant city	5	D	26	4,703	28	D	118	1,662	11	D	11	D	49	405	24
Murphy city	NA	NA	NA	NA	5	D	31	507	5	D	6	15	20	D	5
Nacogdoches city	4	D	43	3,753	34	D	210	2,763	14	110	17	D	82	534	49
Nederland city	1	D	12	D	17	D	95	585	15	267	8	197	38	146	19
New Braunfels city	2	D	60	2,039	58	D	276	4,435	30	1,257	15	200	127	772	101
New Territory CDP	NA	NA	3	24	9	19	28	107	NA	NA	NA	NA	8	23	8
North Richland Hills city	1	D	20	1,003	29	188	150	3,641	20	234	7	78	93	2,377	66
Odessa city	7	D	122	2,282	184	2,717	401	6,849	121	1,680	24	D	210	D	136
Orange city	2	D	28	3,167	16	D	105	1,168	22	348	10	109	52	344	27
Palestine city	6	D	17	108	27	D	134	1,737	20	1,593	10	119	53	244	32
Pampa city	1	D	15	521	25	D	89	1,034	13	192	7	D	49	D	29
Paris city	6	D	35	2,757	34	D	178	2,252	29	253	16	D	79	D	43
Pasadena city	8	D	102	4,633	137	1,665	440	6,288	78	1,240	29	344	149	985	128
Pearland city	1	D	62	1,502	59	481	262	5,120	42	332	18	157	120	684	86
Pecan Grove CDP	NA	NA	NA	NA	4	39	10	151	2	D	1	D	8	D	6
Pflugerville city	1	D	19	389	41	511	86	1,515	25	768	11	201	48	162	17
Pharr city	3	D	25	333	142	1,208	179	2,374	98	1,503	11	66	79	508	41
Plainview city	5	D	16	D	27	331	98	1,366	25	1,230	8	D	51	280	27
Plano city	8	D	150	4,601	420	7,367	1,064	20,770	67	732	187	7,134	780	20,720	398
Port Arthur city	4	71	40	4,687	24	D	187	3,169	33	770	11	D	60	346	35
Portland city	1	D	NA	NA	2	D	36	813	6	29	7	D	27	142	15
Port Lavaca city	2	D	6	184	10	42	48	800	7	D	7	45	27	186	14
Port Neches city	NA	NA	13	743	9	115	22	410	9	107	3	D	19	193	15
Prosper town	NA	NA	7	52	6	D	21	99	1	D	4	D	13	D	10
Raymondville city	NA	NA	3	12	5	31	23	370	5	39	3	D	18	90	5
Red Oak city	1	D	3	66	6	D	18	300	10	25	1	D	10	48	8
Rendon CDP	NA	NA	11	172	10	D	16	89	12	90	2	D	7	22	7
Richardson city	3	D	138	7,059	220	8,348	353	4,650	34	441	167	8,247	337	11,771	172
Richmond city	2	D	10	325	13	D	71	1,388	3	5	4	40	26	151	18
Rio Grande City city	3	D	3	D	7	D	72	1,176	8	72	7	D	34	206	9
Robinson city	NA	NA	5	15	8	91	23	267	8	D	1	D	3	19	4
Robstown city	2	D	8	D	17	228	34	417	11	359	3	D	21	D	6
Rockwall city	3	D	41	936	41	D	202	3,754	24	636	20	207	82	458	52
Rosenberg city	4	D	22	823	23	498	161	2,925	6	59	14	214	72	345	36
Round Rock city	8	D	77	2,828	104	D	398	8,410	32	342	25	1,542	191	D	119
Rowlett city	NA	NA	42	592	33	123	92	1,508	16	62	9	D	51	290	25
Sachse city	NA	NA	6	17	3	D	13	43	8	D	2	D	10	D	4
Saginaw city	1	D	39	1,935	19	263	39	909	19	670	1	D	21	116	12
San Angelo city	7	D	88	3,166	94	853	398	5,806	43	479	44	D	180	1,274	127
San Antonio city	9	36	742	27,947	1,287	D	4,211	72,437	579	15,209	518	16,436	2,215	54,169	1,500

1 Merchant wholesalers, except manufacturers' sales branches and offices.

Table C. Incorporated Places, Census Designated Places (CDPs), and Minor Civil Divisions (MCDs) of 10,000 or More Population — **Economic Census**

STATE City, town, township, borough, or CDP (county if applicable)	Real estate and rental and leasing — Number of employees	Professional, scientific, and technical services — Number of establishments	Professional, scientific, and technical services — Number of employees	Administration and support and waste management and mediation services — Number of establishments	Administration and support and waste management and mediation services — Number of employees	Educational services — Number of establishments	Educational services — Number of employees	Health care and social assistance — Number of establishments	Health care and social assistance — Number of employees	Arts, entertainment, and recreation — Number of establishments	Arts, entertainment, and recreation — Number of employees	Accommodation and food services — Number of establishments	Accommodation and food services — Number of employees	Other services (except public administration) — Number of establishments	Other services (except public administration) — Number of employees
	16	17	18	19	20	21	22	23	24	25	26	27	28	29	30
TEXAS—Con.															
Hidalgo city	109	11	44	8	133	NA	NA	8	44	2	D	15	337	7	39
Highland Village city	24	63	448	22	58	2	D	44	519	7	98	37	906	14	D
Horizon City city	D	6	D	5	D	NA	NA	8	73	2	D	13	177	5	D
Houston city	28,791	9,288	160,107	3,453	212,070	526	5,184	7,043	175,483	584	18,692	5,645	122,643	3,873	37,491
Humble city	214	104	618	36	327	12	120	162	3,110	19	D	144	4,620	92	1,287
Huntsville city	175	68	393	30	252	2	D	92	D	9	D	94	D	48	D
Hurst city	240	167	1,037	60	562	12	96	138	1,559	15	D	103	2,129	77	D
Hutto city	22	15	51	6	D	NA	NA	18	D	2	D	22	371	13	70
Irving city	4,857	1,009	29,098	371	35,866	41	389	547	10,780	50	939	545	11,557	304	4,504
Jacinto City city	D	5	16	2	D	2	D	17	235	NA	NA	18	D	10	D
Jacksonville city	50	31	86	17	528	1	D	69	D	1	D	37	D	25	136
Katy city	269	154	1,660	76	1,318	20	246	248	3,355	13	386	183	4,066	99	D
Keller city	219	152	562	38	318	17	108	121	1,238	11	210	81	1,232	61	394
Kerrville city	140	110	D	49	304	3	D	166	3,474	19	153	93	1,746	77	465
Kilgore city	405	44	366	20	680	1	D	39	720	4	41	49	674	34	D
Killeen city	580	105	1,036	62	818	16	93	185	2,143	23	452	248	5,406	166	1,203
Kingsville city	D	29	160	13	D	6	D	66	D	4	27	70	D	42	D
Kyle city	16	12	34	14	191	3	10	47	1,095	6	47	39	461	20	D
La Homa CDP	NA	1	D	4	8	NA	NA	1	D	NA	NA	3	D	2	D
Lake Jackson city	113	47	202	19	349	6	22	134	1,724	8	D	58	1,421	33	199
Lakeway city	D	87	438	34	202	10	59	60	571	9	91	38	717	26	159
La Marque city	21	13	118	10	69	NA	NA	20	D	5	D	31	565	20	D
Lancaster city	75	17	D	16	351	5	34	47	931	3	D	32	646	27	171
La Porte city	469	55	1,954	34	1,270	5	27	40	358	4	4	68	1,241	46	5,941
Laredo city	692	317	1,803	165	5,189	24	125	534	D	37	D	388	D	203	1,129
League City city	182	175	1,646	68	524	13	82	159	D	22	D	121	2,047	99	693
Leander city	36	37	134	21	D	7	17	41	D	4	D	27	405	29	159
Leon Valley city	33	23	299	17	394	5	38	43	789	6	98	39	D	42	D
Levelland city	59	21	D	4	8	NA	NA	41	1,084	4	D	37	D	21	D
Lewisville city	551	216	1,997	155	5,756	29	155	242	4,652	32	587	232	4,707	159	1,085
Little Elm city	23	26	64	24	73	4	9	18	160	4	85	23	D	12	44
Live Oak city	23	5	21	11	90	NA	NA	73	1,594	2	D	22	D	8	D
Lockhart city	26	21	77	4	D	2	D	38	D	NA	NA	29	514	20	D
Longview city	792	316	2,719	142	3,148	14	D	367	9,154	24	318	239	5,463	182	1,365
Lubbock city	1,524	580	3,658	283	6,918	58	411	799	21,494	68	1,043	597	13,817	408	3,242
Lufkin city	299	121	642	46	1,102	6	45	250	6,839	17	171	122	2,852	93	D
Lumberton city	26	11	34	4	D	2	D	23	223	3	D	27	D	12	D
McAllen city	810	456	2,520	156	10,561	30	339	767	16,328	32	437	402	8,909	184	1,496
McKinney city	1,027	349	1,370	121	1,008	39	208	358	5,542	34	D	229	4,652	145	1,143
Mansfield city	140	116	545	63	1,590	18	133	185	D	17	571	118	D	72	573
Marshall city	120	80	317	23	D	1	D	92	1,629	5	15	83	1,479	52	D
Mercedes city	109	9	89	5	D	2	D	25	374	2	D	23	369	12	96
Mesquite city	413	106	764	108	1,743	13	84	326	6,614	25	D	217	5,218	128	966
Midland city	1,243	447	4,345	177	2,596	21	D	380	6,987	38	782	279	6,352	227	1,846
Midlothian city	66	31	136	21	314	5	15	41	419	4	10	35	D	29	108
Mineral Wells city	76	33	224	11	D	1	D	47	677	3	D	54	671	28	D
Mission city	219	75	438	34	335	15	70	276	8,989	13	D	135	2,294	84	486
Mission Bend CDP	D	20	38	23	158	1	D	33	332	NA	NA	6	D	6	25
Missouri City city	93	131	D	44	375	21	138	169	1,577	12	221	101	1,540	76	459
Mount Pleasant city	D	27	D	12	D	2	D	86	D	5	41	60	D	35	189
Murphy city	14	53	111	19	80	4	D	28	D	4	D	33	D	20	D
Nacogdoches city	154	80	405	43	393	3	D	193	D	14	D	105	2,457	66	374
Nederland city	72	39	198	27	619	8	D	62	616	2	D	36	D	32	192
New Braunfels city	423	153	670	83	1,658	13	118	240	4,809	37	D	228	4,685	125	1,405
New Territory CDP	42	53	116	10	45	2	D	22	251	4	12	12	D	8	D
North Richland Hills city	280	142	875	77	2,489	8	20	133	2,763	22	250	127	2,539	79	474
Odessa city	815	181	1,430	99	1,886	8	D	299	7,394	35	533	230	5,893	175	1,515
Orange city	190	47	227	17	1,362	6	33	75	786	5	45	72	990	38	399
Palestine city	D	60	183	23	D	3	D	127	1,992	7	97	60	1,139	49	D
Pampa city	D	41	398	19	D	1	D	55	D	5	D	33	692	38	143
Paris city	152	47	326	35	613	3	D	168	3,537	10	D	93	1,462	74	D
Pasadena city	762	160	3,249	91	2,745	10	86	328	7,134	13	194	202	3,882	146	1,432
Pearland city	418	190	842	65	682	35	262	253	2,607	18	450	180	4,226	137	931
Pecan Grove CDP	18	41	158	13	D	1	D	11	65	3	D	15	218	15	D
Pflugerville city	59	59	185	32	339	12	89	61	927	7	100	61	1,266	55	D
Pharr city	264	60	770	41	2,597	8	94	154	3,934	7	10	95	1,721	61	467
Plainview city	90	40	D	17	207	2	D	71	952	7	34	47	954	40	312
Plano city	3,742	1,494	21,497	470	14,352	119	908	1,366	19,401	78	1,659	681	14,581	462	3,987
Port Arthur city	282	48	471	36	623	5	21	128	2,560	9	215	102	1,890	48	199
Portland city	47	27	164	12	148	3	D	31	626	6	103	31	666	18	D
Port Lavaca city	109	17	91	6	D	NA	NA	34	582	3	D	44	478	21	D
Port Neches city	48	19	127	6	316	3	D	25	160	4	D	16	D	18	D
Prosper town	63	28	49	15	282	3	2	27	D	5	9	20	279	7	25
Raymondville city	10	9	D	4	D	NA	NA	26	412	1	D	16	236	10	D
Red Oak city	25	12	33	11	54	2	D	14	285	1	D	16	D	10	D
Rendon CDP	D	13	24	11	46	NA	NA	5	D	4	7	5	D	8	58
Richardson city	756	682	9,109	236	7,549	47	380	505	6,469	36	D	322	5,202	182	1,654
Richmond city	100	53	177	19	122	4	D	106	1,872	9	512	41	734	39	183
Rio Grande City city	23	25	D	5	34	NA	NA	69	4,593	1	D	28	470	13	D
Robinson city	D	4	16	10	75	2	D	8	63	1	D	16	172	6	26
Robstown city	D	6	D	10	D	1	D	21	1,950	NA	NA	25	D	20	171
Rockwall city	D	156	838	71	3,961	12	D	172	2,101	18	D	124	3,006	62	D
Rosenberg city	123	39	167	23	137	1	D	59	644	4	D	92	1,713	55	D
Round Rock city	402	311	1,693	109	2,631	39	212	310	6,735	37	908	278	6,112	162	1,521
Rowlett city	52	76	502	47	258	11	D	103	1,988	9	D	70	990	80	422
Sachse city	D	21	54	20	59	5	8	12	102	2	D	12	156	16	D
Saginaw city	57	19	150	10	59	3	D	21	250	1	D	41	D	20	D
San Angelo city	D	193	1,232	107	D	7	35	262	D	33	539	210	4,220	193	989
San Antonio city	10,878	3,361	37,364	1,505	74,125	257	4,007	3,790	102,675	339	D	3,209	79,964	2,055	14,973

Table C. Incorporated Places, Census Designated Places (CDPs), and Minor Civil Divisions (MCDs) of 10,000 or More Population — **Economic Census**

STATE / City, town, township, borough, or CDP (county if applicable)	Utilities — Number of establishments	Utilities — Number of employees	Manufacturing — Number of establishments	Manufacturing — Number of employees	Wholesale trade[1] — Number of establishments	Wholesale trade[1] — Number of employees	Retail trade — Number of establishments	Retail trade — Number of employees	Transportation and warehousing — Number of establishments	Transportation and warehousing — Number of employees	Information — Number of establishments	Information — Number of employees	Finance and insurance — Number of establishments	Finance and insurance — Number of employees	Real estate and rental and leasing — Number of establishments
	1	2	3	4	5	6	7	8	9	10	11	12	13	14	15
TEXAS—Con.															
San Benito city	2	D	17	251	15	D	73	1,198	10	195	3	20	41	234	12
San Elizario CDP	NA	NA	NA	NA	2	D	9	40	8	D	NA	NA	2	D	NA
San Juan city	1	D	9	99	15	D	60	887	12	504	3	D	20	101	10
San Marcos city	3	88	40	D	26	D	405	7,099	24	1,116	17	513	97	D	75
Santa Fe city	NA	NA	9	75	11	101	29	172	4	D	2	D	12	57	7
Schertz city	1	D	25	773	56	D	50	1,220	16	566	2	D	31	220	27
Seabrook city	NA	NA	8	153	11	84	41	447	10	D	1	D	17	87	16
Seagoville city	NA	NA	12	242	8	57	38	594	9	D	3	D	10	D	15
Seguin city	2	D	48	3,995	25	D	139	1,826	10	79	8	D	60	329	34
Sherman city	4	D	46	4,317	47	425	207	3,645	21	447	18	382	83	578	50
Sienna Plantation CDP	NA	NA	NA	NA	2	D	3	D	3	3	1	D	4	4	4
Snyder city	4	D	11	83	17	215	57	709	7	127	6	56	22	D	12
Socorro city	1	D	14	79	14	140	58	695	31	221	1	D	16	77	8
South Houston city	NA	NA	45	783	45	406	79	1,075	12	D	2	D	26	129	7
Southlake city	NA	NA	28	295	59	591	229	5,140	24	D	26	976	138	837	92
Spring CDP	2	D	37	1,248	49	538	144	2,713	19	80	7	88	62	379	37
Stafford city	NA	NA	113	5,075	157	1,934	149	2,848	21	1,286	28	206	60	238	41
Stephenville city	4	68	26	2,199	15	149	140	1,691	15	550	9	115	48	257	29
Sugar Land city	6	229	57	3,099	164	1,983	475	8,226	36	394	44	748	248	1,880	167
Sulphur Springs city	7	D	32	1,570	24	857	130	1,554	24	184	11	D	45	D	27
Sweetwater city	6	D	7	313	11	D	47	D	7	37	6	42	28	D	9
Taylor city	2	D	20	900	13	D	60	722	7	D	9	91	28	D	10
Temple city	5	D	59	4,222	59	1,974	286	4,130	36	1,464	29	1,970	133	1,343	80
Terrell city	4	D	34	1,917	22	D	138	1,746	19	1,396	6	42	36	336	17
Texarkana city	3	D	26	814	57	742	309	5,047	39	1,844	24	D	152	1,146	78
Texas City city	4	167	25	4,126	28	211	186	1,575	25	402	9	110	57	644	34
The Colony city	NA	NA	NA	NA	17	D	69	987	6	D	6	D	32	140	17
The Woodlands CDP	8	D	37	1,132	119	1,140	338	7,315	34	539	40	929	282	2,476	179
Timberwood Park CDP	NA	NA	6	26	18	39	14	39	3	6	4	D	5	D	13
Tomball city	3	3	40	867	37	512	136	2,678	9	31	18	254	73	375	29
Tyler city	11	216	88	4,002	114	1,433	632	9,824	70	1,030	60	2,383	388	2,697	208
Universal City city	1	D	6	119	7	59	55	669	4	D	6	138	32	163	20
University Park city	1	D	8	92	14	117	85	850	4	D	9	D	52	185	44
Uvalde city	3	D	14	392	20	D	86	1,133	31	278	11	115	36	267	25
Vernon city	2	D	9	D	10	D	44	D	3	D	7	D	24	120	9
Victoria city	5	D	55	1,062	82	1,085	353	5,240	45	644	21	453	168	D	110
Vidor city	3	D	6	D	5	16	66	757	10	138	4	D	21	82	10
Waco city	7	D	134	12,060	130	2,062	589	7,888	70	1,710	74	1,108	265	3,884	162
Watauga city	NA	NA	NA	NA	NA	NA	88	1,344	5	16	5	58	26	123	7
Waxahachie city	3	D	54	3,534	31	D	138	2,364	29	1,092	23	239	63	364	46
Weatherford city	1	D	31	825	25	274	198	3,255	17	D	14	128	78	469	37
Webster city	NA	NA	11	210	28	458	154	2,362	14	208	18	415	63	352	46
Wells Branch CDP	NA	NA	16	379	32	D	18	108	19	179	8	86	3	D	15
Weslaco city	1	D	12	92	37	417	160	2,807	9	279	16	338	84	423	49
West Odessa CDP	NA	NA	21	184	23	308	23	206	43	496	1	D	2	D	9
West University Place city	NA	NA	5	15	4	3	25	325	1	D	6	16	27	203	15
White Settlement city	NA	NA	13	1,354	7	79	33	278	2	D	4	D	19	171	12
Wichita Falls city	6	D	97	3,045	116	981	434	6,851	58	882	46	1,033	186	1,475	153
Wylie city	1	D	32	1,788	14	D	62	1,258	3	D	6	D	28	143	17
UTAH	214	4,319	3,163	108,264	3,015	43,523	9,095	133,535	2,177	45,945	1,414	37,498	4,865	52,959	4,446
American Fork city	4	D	27	591	28	439	137	2,331	14	361	36	1,406	62	713	60
Bountiful city	NA	NA	42	797	42	263	146	1,951	27	723	17	50	96	431	81
Brigham City city	1	D	26	1,800	9	97	70	973	14	213	4	D	37	205	18
Cedar City city	2	D	57	1,212	24	183	140	1,698	27	146	15	114	63	361	57
Cedar Hills city	NA	NA	5	10	3	D	5	D	6	10	NA	NA	10	17	13
Centerville city	NA	NA	17	287	21	142	49	1,277	10	56	6	141	23	132	22
Clearfield city	NA	NA	47	5,724	21	302	58	549	24	232	5	16	41	225	25
Clinton city	NA	NA	4	21	2	D	30	855	6	8	1	D	15	76	6
Cottonwood Heights city	1	D	23	250	41	914	70	1,589	20	218	18	485	172	2,382	232
Draper city	5	D	41	1,216	51	772	186	3,580	17	367	35	838	122	1,168	104
Eagle Mountain city	NA	NA	4	D	4	5	14	42	7	3	4	D	6	6	12
Farmington city	NA	NA	5	38	9	D	32	602	4	14	8	11	33	175	25
Heber city	NA	NA	19	162	3	D	64	860	16	67	7	51	25	D	22
Herriman city	NA	NA	6	D	5	D	15	239	17	56	2	D	18	D	12
Highland city	NA	NA	4	8	11	47	30	220	7	12	3	D	25	80	31
Holladay city	2	D	11	445	25	189	75	784	4	D	19	130	76	404	80
Hurricane city	1	D	20	198	17	D	40	604	20	813	4	40	17	87	21
Kaysville city	NA	NA	15	180	22	269	62	707	9	47	13	106	36	119	36
Kearns CDP	NA	NA	15	363	4	D	30	447	10	56	4	40	10	D	7
Layton city	1	D	43	870	47	321	295	4,761	34	1,052	25	532	117	1,130	111
Lehi city	NA	NA	32	518	22	303	144	2,159	20	91	28	627	68	255	58
Lindon city	NA	NA	59	1,517	38	585	55	962	12	140	14	849	15	137	23
Logan city	1	D	112	7,049	67	606	248	3,710	25	409	30	649	121	482	108
Magna CDP	1	D	8	864	5	74	23	354	15	86	1	D	8	D	5
Midvale city	1	D	34	435	48	604	149	2,153	11	D	18	564	88	603	69
Millcreek CDP	1	D	51	382	82	741	178	2,600	18	86	22	203	134	1,357	124
Murray city	NA	NA	118	1,590	109	1,032	353	5,656	40	296	42	1,388	206	2,581	134
North Ogden city	1	D	3	D	4	D	15	290	4	4	2	D	17	72	26
North Salt Lake city	NA	NA	44	1,119	33	562	39	337	25	1,138	3	42	23	62	33
Ogden city	8	D	134	7,939	100	1,412	344	3,839	47	2,602	26	871	153	1,654	100
Orem city	2	D	122	2,729	102	1,421	451	7,296	43	641	84	2,318	156	1,058	185
Payson city	1	D	12	926	9	85	48	1,117	12	31	5	D	24	87	7
Pleasant Grove city	2	D	30	238	19	75	65	675	9	101	13	97	49	261	48
Provo city	1	D	81	1,908	55	1,506	317	4,334	31	687	78	4,530	159	1,265	120
Riverton city	NA	NA	8	D	21	76	68	1,184	15	71	10	93	54	223	41
Roy city	NA	NA	17	65	7	D	72	906	7	D	3	D	46	502	19
St. George city	4	D	87	1,376	106	D	425	5,477	64	1,570	50	602	194	1,077	218

1 Merchant wholesalers, except manufacturers' sales branches and offices.

STATE City, town, township, borough, or CDP (county if applicable)	Real estate and rental and leasing — Number of employees	Professional, scientific, and technical services — Number of establishments	Professional, scientific, and technical services — Number of employees	Administration and support and waste management and mediation services — Number of establishments	Administration and support and waste management and mediation services — Number of employees	Educational services — Number of establishments	Educational services — Number of employees	Health care and social assistance — Number of establishments	Health care and social assistance — Number of employees	Arts, entertainment, and recreation — Number of establishments	Arts, entertainment, and recreation — Number of employees	Accommodation and food services — Number of establishments	Accommodation and food services — Number of employees	Other services (except public administration) — Number of establishments	Other services (except public administration) — Number of employees
	16	17	18	19	20	21	22	23	24	25	26	27	28	29	30
TEXAS—Con.															
San Benito city	58	18	105	17	477	2	D	54	1,680	2	D	38	534	20	77
San Elizario CDP	NA	2	D	3	11	NA	NA	7	210	NA	NA	3	18	2	D
San Juan city	38	12	46	3	D	NA	NA	60	1,301	3	D	28	363	15	D
San Marcos city	338	96	823	45	1,149	11	64	147	3,321	9	D	212	4,456	85	D
Santa Fe city	20	18	D	8	88	1	D	12	D	3	D	22	220	21	78
Schertz city	D	31	275	24	518	8	70	47	748	5	84	58	1,287	40	D
Seabrook city	88	32	313	14	100	4	34	24	D	8	88	44	969	23	D
Seagoville city	38	14	149	11	56	1	D	12	167	2	D	20	D	14	84
Seguin city	192	49	198	23	750	4	16	107	1,986	11	D	81	1,368	59	394
Sherman city	178	114	395	47	2,137	7	D	225	5,171	17	D	102	2,593	55	429
Sienna Plantation CDP	3	19	16	4	3	2	D	12	24	3	D	2	D	1	D
Snyder city	D	15	102	6	D	NA	NA	22	538	4	D	47	D	25	D
Socorro city	33	7	41	13	D	1	D	13	D	1	D	24	263	24	112
South Houston city	28	10	76	12	53	1	D	9	D	5	49	33	434	30	D
Southlake city	599	229	1,624	80	3,649	29	295	196	2,335	23	D	111	D	73	604
Spring CDP	143	90	672	40	443	8	58	86	936	14	569	77	1,894	50	371
Stafford city	281	116	1,759	65	3,045	7	31	103	2,230	10	D	78	1,575	54	D
Stephenville city	97	49	269	28	506	1	D	61	1,699	15	105	84	1,547	62	303
Sugar Land city	483	521	4,603	131	2,457	52	373	571	7,582	34	855	328	7,038	143	988
Sulphur Springs city	D	40	D	24	475	2	D	72	1,367	7	D	47	768	40	D
Sweetwater city	D	27	D	6	D	NA	NA	31	D	5	D	35	506	12	D
Taylor city	23	20	78	12	255	NA	NA	28	D	2	D	31	398	20	125
Temple city	409	118	929	66	1,172	5	56	188	14,832	23	184	170	3,451	125	1,027
Terrell city	73	26	130	16	327	1	D	56	1,812	7	D	59	1,110	22	D
Texarkana city	385	124	705	59	1,377	7	31	245	6,693	21	D	134	3,369	108	761
Texas City city	281	43	D	23	696	4	16	99	D	3	D	74	1,229	49	307
The Colony city	177	51	276	32	135	5	37	48	386	10	136	47	1,083	34	D
The Woodlands CDP	766	539	4,681	120	2,413	41	294	333	D	39	1,378	240	5,619	117	1,366
Timberwood Park CDP	28	39	76	17	266	2	D	18	D	3	D	10	16	14	D
Tomball city	90	72	342	30	323	4	31	138	2,990	6	44	84	1,653	50	D
Tyler city	953	461	3,511	156	2,685	26	D	543	19,843	45	994	310	7,298	222	1,759
Universal City city	68	28	252	15	D	7	15	25	219	6	108	46	D	53	276
University Park city	D	116	228	24	91	8	26	46	316	3	D	62	1,134	28	207
Uvalde city	85	33	D	9	D	1	D	71	D	4	D	53	884	28	D
Vernon city	D	17	D	6	D	1	D	32	D	2	D	38	484	24	D
Victoria city	714	143	832	77	1,385	17	D	285	6,447	41	D	176	3,538	126	866
Vidor city	22	13	118	7	D	1	D	19	D	3	D	23	D	21	D
Waco city	1,293	274	2,145	164	6,482	21	299	434	14,275	47	823	350	7,672	243	1,695
Watauga city	22	19	118	12	D	5	33	22	181	5	61	50	1,273	30	D
Waxahachie city	149	64	274	29	546	5	24	106	1,686	8	D	80	1,902	51	287
Weatherford city	174	87	323	25	280	3	D	139	2,358	8	56	116	2,114	76	632
Webster city	298	119	3,071	32	2,215	12	99	253	5,361	11	305	114	3,332	69	596
Wells Branch CDP	56	33	1,083	26	417	4	3	16	D	4	28	17	220	17	D
Weslaco city	201	60	534	21	299	5	D	187	6,809	12	D	84	1,781	58	482
West Odessa CDP	52	16	57	10	376	NA	NA	3	D	1	D	16	176	20	D
West University Place city	39	83	225	14	115	6	51	54	D	1	D	20	401	5	45
White Settlement city	43	15	103	7	59	1	D	22	757	4	26	16	D	21	D
Wichita Falls city	759	210	1,304	89	D	14	D	350	10,307	28	506	236	5,370	184	1,021
Wylie city	54	49	153	37	341	5	D	51	802	5	42	42	D	35	D
UTAH	16,197	9,009	76,345	4,007	108,970	763	6,822	7,285	126,175	923	20,749	5,108	95,933	4,259	26,026
American Fork city	167	118	1,593	49	D	14	245	132	2,186	8	159	82	1,558	58	D
Bountiful city	170	193	716	76	1,898	12	95	221	3,144	13	110	69	D	78	582
Brigham City city	D	29	132	18	D	5	20	80	D	6	53	29	445	28	D
Cedar City city	140	83	385	45	615	12	D	127	1,537	10	D	82	1,224	52	199
Cedar Hills city	12	29	40	7	D	1	D	9	D	2	D	3	49	4	D
Centerville city	33	57	135	21	67	12	48	28	206	5	49	23	568	27	139
Clearfield city	102	59	1,259	29	504	1	D	52	1,240	5	D	32	611	37	204
Clinton city	33	13	57	20	142	NA	NA	16	144	1	D	22	300	8	68
Cottonwood Heights city	745	210	1,225	56	654	12	124	126	1,814	14	144	54	799	31	170
Draper city	334	245	1,348	109	2,026	23	707	135	1,011	17	240	94	1,494	84	508
Eagle Mountain city	9	28	43	11	D	3	D	9	D	3	7	7	46	4	22
Farmington city	48	69	447	29	203	4	9	47	426	8	D	14	128	14	D
Heber city	D	61	175	27	105	6	D	43	D	7	D	34	D	29	D
Herriman city	9	40	138	27	74	4	D	33	118	3	1	15	D	14	D
Highland city	46	75	110	17	D	8	20	36	135	4	D	27	591	10	71
Holladay city	D	160	488	37	215	10	115	98	D	13	D	51	578	50	174
Hurricane city	31	31	67	17	75	NA	NA	25	393	5	8	30	220	21	D
Kaysville city	77	90	647	30	310	5	24	55	445	6	239	16	354	30	D
Kearns CDP	30	4	D	18	104	2	D	9	D	2	D	15	164	14	D
Layton city	313	179	1,135	85	650	18	122	168	3,101	20	196	149	3,414	120	758
Lehi city	70	174	1,914	58	D	14	145	64	646	18	452	50	1,117	45	261
Lindon city	65	54	446	40	D	9	110	30	155	8	71	20	335	24	113
Logan city	396	180	1,552	61	2,172	17	134	199	3,772	24	335	120	2,287	95	542
Magna CDP	14	10	D	7	D	NA	NA	19	D	3	16	20	254	18	D
Midvale city	468	93	626	47	498	12	147	72	1,311	7	94	94	1,572	66	354
Millcreek CDP	467	275	1,647	106	4,313	21	116	365	5,093	21	258	93	1,201	119	779
Murray city	1,271	300	2,624	131	3,029	14	124	323	10,174	15	344	113	2,538	171	1,246
North Ogden city	37	25	75	21	44	6	D	37	364	3	31	8	162	14	42
North Salt Lake city	136	48	820	34	2,121	3	D	11	D	5	D	22	196	20	D
Ogden city	413	247	3,023	115	4,088	11	52	316	6,831	19	406	184	3,206	157	1,108
Orem city	566	358	7,806	181	3,953	45	286	256	5,144	47	441	152	3,262	163	818
Payson city	13	23	100	8	D	2	D	59	775	3	11	26	D	26	D
Pleasant Grove city	98	99	670	40	D	13	77	62	495	11	35	29	280	41	D
Provo city	569	348	2,723	135	12,596	40	D	309	9,316	35	D	186	3,335	140	928
Riverton city	95	89	191	49	237	10	58	84	D	5	10	48	758	37	D
Roy city	54	29	249	23	318	4	D	56	751	5	55	40	661	40	D
St. George city	541	325	D	167	1,790	23	112	410	6,315	35	D	216	3,957	130	822

Table C. Incorporated Places, Census Designated Places (CDPs), and Minor Civil Divisions (MCDs) of 10,000 or More Population — **Economic Census**

STATE City, town, township, borough, or CDP (county if applicable)	Utilities Number of establishments	Number of employees	Manufacturing Number of establishments	Number of employees	Wholesale trade[1] Number of establishments	Number of employees	Retail trade Number of establishments	Number of employees	Transportation and warehousing Number of establishments	Number of employees	Information Number of establishments	Number of employees	Finance and insurance Number of establishments	Number of employees	Real estate and rental and leasing Number of establishments
	1	2	3	4	5	6	7	8	9	10	11	12	13	14	15
UTAH—Con.															
Salt Lake City city	49	1,872	457	24,316	603	12,541	918	14,096	335	19,201	300	8,248	675	14,561	528
Sandy city	1	D	103	2,619	130	1,173	382	6,580	51	353	86	4,386	279	3,616	202
Saratoga Springs city	NA	NA	5	8	4	3	20	206	6	19	1	D	10	38	17
Smithfield city	2	D	14	386	2	D	23	245	8	27	1	D	13	43	8
South Jordan city	3	D	23	D	38	1,231	112	2,249	20	77	28	1,317	138	1,739	93
South Ogden city	NA	NA	3	8	9	70	77	1,234	4	6	2	D	51	455	40
South Salt Lake city	NA	NA	160	3,344	223	3,887	216	2,706	32	404	15	196	47	1,026	60
Spanish Fork city	NA	NA	39	1,771	19	186	88	1,077	19	331	8	48	52	259	29
Springville city	2	D	46	3,092	25	639	74	1,095	9	D	8	133	25	96	19
Syracuse city	NA	NA	3	6	5	11	17	595	9	30	3	D	16	39	17
Taylorsville city	1	D	17	601	18	76	101	1,695	17	D	13	D	94	D	48
Tooele city	3	D	19	729	7	D	75	1,334	12	D	6	76	32	150	19
Washington city	NA	NA	8	73	13	D	50	1,000	23	107	4	D	13	56	36
West Haven city	NA	NA	23	302	8	95	17	181	7	15	2	D	4	4	19
West Jordan city	NA	NA	106	2,439	76	1,201	207	3,971	58	299	17	206	112	1,108	82
West Valley City city	1	D	156	4,762	143	2,669	280	5,549	83	3,771	57	3,524	102	4,488	73
Woods Cross city	NA	NA	32	403	22	408	36	411	16	158	3	D	13	69	9
VERMONT......................	65	D	1,013	31,487	696	9,464	3,509	38,910	486	5,731	507	6,775	990	9,039	741
Bennington town (Bennington)	NA	NA	30	1,545	7	D	115	1,628	8	112	16	251	27	219	18
Brattleboro town (Windham)	4	D	34	1,214	27	D	138	1,508	10	256	17	153	34	426	26
Burlington city & MCD (Chittenden)	1	D	24	613	48	539	224	3,271	18	251	60	1,312	123	1,590	61
Colchester town (Chittenden)	1	D	21	582	21	626	57	897	12	221	17	547	37	271	27
Essex town (Chittenden)* .	NA	NA	14	485	16	620	54	727	6	99	4	164	17	62	14
Milton town (Chittenden)...	NA	NA	16	718	8	151	29	339	11	184	4	D	7	34	7
Rutland city & MCD (Rutland)	3	D	26	403	27	259	148	1,640	9	99	19	182	59	428	26
South Burlington city & MCD (Chittenden)	1	D	29	818	48	834	191	3,235	12	362	35	1,311	72	756	57
VIRGINIA.........................	314	15,065	5,101	228,197	6,232	88,353	27,415	410,918	4,779	90,068	3,916	101,402	11,190	153,274	8,862
Alexandria city	5	315	72	1,332	82	1,139	480	7,180	65	1,491	120	1,736	226	D	240
Annandale CDP.................	NA	NA	11	44	23	D	120	1,188	10	36	23	309	106	1,136	60
Arlington CDP....................	8	D	34	220	85	1,090	613	9,610	52	D	182	6,698	249	D	404
Ashburn CDP.....................	1	D	18	413	34	624	75	2,318	28	136	76	5,804	63	D	46
Bailey's Crossroads CDP .	NA	NA	9	40	7	D	107	2,350	10	98	15	179	30	221	33
Blacksburg town	NA	NA	20	1,473	14	D	97	1,363	9	57	27	D	48	D	50
Bon Air CDP	NA	NA	10	8	12	39	142	2,154	1	D	11	147	65	D	22
Brambleton CDP	NA	NA	NA	NA	3	D	8	156	NA	NA	3	D	2	D	3
Brandermill CDP	NA	NA	NA	NA	11	51	24	368	4	D	5	47	32	D	16
Bristol city	NA	NA	23	1,057	34	802	157	1,732	14	330	12	1,048	53	D	23
Broadlands CDP................	NA	NA	NA	NA	2	D	9	329	2	D	3	D	6	D	9
Buckhall CDP	NA	NA	NA	NA	6	20	6	27	2	D	NA	NA	NA	NA	11
Bull Run CDP	NA	NA	NA	NA	3	D	82	1,735	5	4	4	22	24	D	29
Burke CDP	NA	NA	6	14	13	D	45	660	8	43	8	21	40	138	23
Burke Centre CDP.............	NA	NA	3	18	2	D	35	729	5	D	1	D	14	64	16
Cascades CDP	NA	NA	NA	NA	4	D	36	1,162	1	D	5	26	15	D	12
Cave Spring CDP	NA	NA	12	123	35	464	130	1,954	13	D	16	D	101	1,817	45
Centreville CDP	NA	NA	7	41	25	D	98	1,161	14	38	11	D	69	287	38
Chantilly CDP....................	1	D	57	1,028	112	2,580	152	3,073	33	1,502	46	1,656	71	1,901	72
Charlottesville city............	2	D	46	455	48	513	331	3,925	12	233	63	1,547	114	D	99
Cherry Hill CDP.................	NA	NA	NA	NA	3	D	9	515	7	14	1	D	3	9	5
Chesapeake city	5	D	130	3,965	239	3,447	789	15,088	206	2,963	68	2,532	290	3,799	273
Chester CDP	1	D	14	709	11	133	90	1,789	10	389	8	D	31	138	29
Christiansburg town...........	1	D	21	819	23	D	181	3,305	10	60	8	D	53	D	26
Colonial Heights city.........	NA	NA	8	129	10	53	180	3,498	3	D	9	157	52	D	27
Countryside CDP...............	NA	NA	NA	NA	1	D	16	148	NA	NA	6	88	13	D	7
Culpeper town	1	D	11	606	9	D	106	1,329	5	D	11	546	42	D	27
Dale City CDP	3	74	NA	NA	8	D	69	914	16	41	9	D	24	123	18
Danville city	1	D	46	4,635	50	545	306	4,165	18	326	19	D	101	D	64
Dranesville CDP................	NA	NA	NA	NA	4	D	3	29	2	D	4	10	5	D	5
East Highland Park CDP ..	NA	NA	5	111	7	128	40	445	3	D	1	D	5	D	8
Fairfax city	1	D	29	158	40	372	251	5,526	12	D	47	544	155	D	60
Fairfax Station CDP...........	NA	NA	NA	NA	2	D	8	D	2	D	3	8	3	D	8
Fair Oaks CDP..................	1	D	3	D	12	D	156	3,667	4	D	18	315	72	1,355	38
Falls Church city...............	NA	NA	17	74	18	D	92	1,010	11	D	16	347	43	D	35
Fort Hunt CDP	1	D	NA	NA	2	D	9	136	1	D	9	32	5	17	10
Franconia CDP	NA	NA	11	284	17	D	31	304	17	371	4	D	21	84	23
Franklin Farm CDP	NA	NA	NA	NA	6	D	26	577	1	D	3	D	12	45	14
Fredericksburg city	1	D	26	221	21	224	253	4,098	12	D	20	554	92	D	70
Front Royal town	NA	NA	15	365	4	31	101	1,434	10	192	10	83	45	D	12
Gainesville CDP................	1	D	5	68	5	292	83	2,143	3	D	5	35	27	D	21
Glen Allen CDP	NA	NA	4	69	14	D	136	2,738	7	19	11	80	45	2,386	20
Great Falls CDP................	NA	NA	5	25	14	D	30	273	3	D	9	D	33	121	33
Groveton CDP	NA	NA	NA	NA	1	D	18	694	2	D	3	D	11	D	6
Hampton city	2	D	68	2,189	71	886	436	6,791	43	328	33	1,199	121	1,020	114
Harrisonburg city	NA	NA	46	2,556	57	1,006	334	5,664	26	261	34	492	130	857	72
Herndon town	1	D	20	163	25	D	89	967	17	832	56	1,787	65	D	70
Highland Springs CDP......	NA	NA	4	142	11	D	30	290	8	D	2	D	11	D	11
Hollins CDP	NA	NA	16	1,600	21	368	44	620	7	252	1	D	27	D	16
Hopewell city	6	115	16	1,338	11	84	73	586	7	42	3	D	25	D	22
Huntington CDP................	NA	NA	3	12	NA	NA	20	339	2	D	NA	NA	4	D	6
Hybla Valley CDP..............	NA	NA	NA	NA	3	D	62	1,352	1	D	5	D	11	72	14

1 Merchant wholesalers, except manufacturers' sales branches and offices.

Table C.   Incorporated Places, Census Designated Places (CDPs), and Minor Civil Divisions (MCDs) of 10,000 or More Population — **Economic Census**

STATE City, town, township, borough, or CDP (county if applicable)	Real estate and rental and leasing — Number of employees	Professional, scientific, and technical services — Number of establishments	Number of employees	Administration and support and waste management and mediation services — Number of establishments	Number of employees	Educational services — Number of establishments	Number of employees	Health care and social assistance — Number of establishments	Number of employees	Arts, entertainment, and recreation — Number of establishments	Number of employees	Accommodation and food services — Number of establishments	Number of employees	Other services (except public administration) — Number of establishments	Number of employees
	16	17	18	19	20	21	22	23	24	25	26	27	28	29	30
UTAH—Con.															
Salt Lake City city	3,093	1,459	16,999	450	22,917	94	1,288	719	23,555	104	2,538	735	16,057	634	5,422
Sandy city	654	443	2,500	185	3,187	38	356	288	3,709	36	798	188	3,696	133	886
Saratoga Springs city	45	32	53	11	D	4	D	20	153	6	18	5	60	6	16
Smithfield city	10	20	35	15	34	2	D	23	135	5	D	9	132	8	67
South Jordan city	253	230	1,478	97	1,483	15	119	125	1,631	13	D	68	1,569	59	318
South Ogden city	81	47	280	25	D	3	D	78	1,012	4	406	30	566	28	130
South Salt Lake city	466	121	1,407	72	2,042	8	41	55	1,554	12	D	81	958	134	806
Spanish Fork city	60	80	381	36	D	15	75	60	D	8	113	40	664	39	D
Springville city	21	66	320	23	D	8	60	66	565	8	D	39	D	34	D
Syracuse city	20	36	76	21	121	6	68	28	D	5	34	16	238	14	55
Taylorsville city	157	86	D	64	4,709	5	13	111	1,225	12	168	83	1,618	44	262
Tooele city	61	32	165	18	D	4	D	64	D	6	60	45	755	40	D
Washington city	96	33	60	24	86	1	D	31	193	8	20	20	D	23	100
West Haven city	158	24	109	21	199	1	D	9	85	2	D	14	368	29	136
West Jordan city	181	154	555	113	1,894	20	152	192	3,532	14	230	116	2,362	102	686
West Valley City city	525	119	1,512	113	2,762	15	90	137	2,694	20	D	179	2,987	129	673
Woods Cross city	36	36	377	20	269	6	62	3	D	5	D	14	190	19	194
VERMONT	3,092	2,113	15,948	1,046	7,347	249	1,689	2,096	44,198	451	7,147	1,920	31,365	1,588	7,211
Bennington town (Bennington)	82	36	135	20	269	6	50	110	2,300	11	61	58	694	41	170
Brattleboro town (Windham)	114	51	260	19	182	17	137	112	2,155	16	68	87	993	59	243
Burlington city & MCD (Chittenden)	347	271	2,422	60	429	27	80	178	8,210	27	673	151	2,846	112	717
Colchester town (Chittenden)	51	57	573	41	208	6	29	51	1,623	12	164	37	590	30	155
Essex town (Chittenden)*	57	37	100	30	393	8	39	32	317	9	327	18	D	23	86
Milton town (Chittenden)	15	9	49	14	34	NA	NA	14	D	2	D	10	157	16	D
Rutland city & MCD (Rutland)	92	91	410	37	393	8	D	143	4,051	14	D	92	1,197	72	369
South Burlington city & MCD (Chittenden)	386	116	1,602	43	968	21	217	131	1,939	18	354	83	2,020	94	587
VIRGINIA	54,246	29,368	429,690	10,385	249,802	2,100	19,327	18,774	411,108	2,744	54,248	16,832	320,514	14,726	112,430
Alexandria city	1,475	1,238	18,505	276	16,326	67	759	397	7,356	55	766	387	8,051	584	9,997
Annandale CDP	494	274	D	91	3,668	19	85	154	1,888	18	D	111	D	111	488
Arlington CDP	5,188	1,829	42,070	291	9,361	94	2,307	484	8,987	97	2,463	647	17,342	642	10,355
Ashburn CDP	D	360	3,524	50	4,841	39	D	111	1,551	18	D	100	1,585	68	875
Bailey's Crossroads CDP	127	136	2,232	41	1,654	10	D	49	872	4	159	76	1,085	64	368
Blacksburg town	393	154	2,267	23	266	14	D	104	D	11	109	100	2,054	57	347
Bon Air CDP	D	81	493	28	2,301	3	2	90	1,222	10	176	41	1,181	39	267
Brambleton CDP	D	72	122	13	56	3	2	14	D	2	D	9	177	8	D
Brandermill CDP	105	45	133	20	221	12	51	40	459	5	83	15	D	20	253
Bristol city	69	44	239	15	D	6	D	48	654	8	D	82	1,811	46	D
Broadlands CDP	16	97	247	4	13	5	23	13	62	3	32	24	434	13	D
Buckhall CDP	19	40	120	21	98	4	3	6	D	5	40	6	33	12	D
Bull Run CDP	131	45	293	18	D	3	D	60	586	1	D	26	442	23	D
Burke CDP	58	132	321	35	169	9	38	84	857	9	D	35	524	40	199
Burke Centre CDP	45	48	184	9	28	2	D	29	686	3	132	25	356	17	207
Cascades CDP	26	85	300	15	95	5	D	63	D	4	D	21	582	13	135
Cave Spring CDP	D	110	384	47	D	12	150	115	D	8	D	61	1,440	56	260
Centreville CDP	111	283	1,599	61	1,247	21	114	123	D	8	302	116	1,700	76	455
Chantilly CDP	767	504	22,251	110	5,697	25	178	76	2,453	19	D	130	2,434	101	1,938
Charlottesville city	502	322	2,555	89	1,183	30	349	175	D	40	D	293	5,199	151	1,444
Cherry Hill CDP	13	8	20	4	D	NA	NA	5	D	3	D	11	154	4	D
Chesapeake city	1,227	510	D	343	8,383	60	955	497	9,693	52	1,199	466	10,267	399	2,990
Chester CDP	110	38	154	21	714	6	63	42	439	7	257	72	1,475	44	D
Christiansburg town	95	66	356	28	263	4	D	76	D	7	D	80	2,093	59	D
Colonial Heights city	151	50	491	18	240	5	19	108	1,746	8	182	82	2,180	50	357
Countryside CDP	19	33	181	9	84	5	D	30	325	3	25	27	364	9	94
Culpeper town	117	46	256	17	199	2	D	63	1,471	7	D	61	870	40	D
Dale City CDP	75	60	264	59	229	4	15	82	1,153	6	53	45	696	32	D
Danville city	339	74	522	42	1,602	14	D	194	4,803	16	218	139	2,850	101	535
Dranesville CDP	20	79	133	6	36	1	D	8	71	3	D	NA	NA	5	12
East Highland Park CDP	35	4	30	10	59	1	D	15	131	2	D	18	309	14	65
Fairfax city	261	647	6,022	117	2,187	33	236	265	3,637	26	583	192	3,608	146	1,531
Fairfax Station CDP	59	66	154	14	121	3	D	8	D	4	D	3	23	9	89
Fair Oaks CDP	D	284	5,456	33	2,144	13	96	122	3,529	6	D	45	1,247	45	438
Falls Church city	192	157	1,798	47	824	11	127	108	D	16	130	119	1,098	93	588
Fort Hunt CDP	14	64	266	13	82	7	32	20	262	2	D	6	74	11	52
Franconia CDP	271	100	2,699	27	622	3	D	62	D	1	D	26	437	34	312
Franklin Farm CDP	26	131	222	16	100	11	42	22	D	5	D	26	361	17	105
Fredericksburg city	308	180	1,390	38	551	16	D	189	5,216	17	373	165	3,718	104	860
Front Royal town	44	46	193	13	D	4	D	55	1,103	8	D	62	845	50	336
Gainesville CDP	59	76	351	20	D	6	42	57	612	9	169	57	1,088	23	D
Glen Allen CDP	105	66	450	36	784	4	43	37	401	5	97	69	1,841	28	271
Great Falls CDP	50	178	923	29	187	13	68	26	231	14	221	33	474	32	229
Groveton CDP	D	22	89	17	D	NA	NA	19	169	2	D	19	623	17	D
Hampton city	750	279	3,711	127	3,024	24	D	265	7,739	37	D	250	5,380	176	1,056
Harrisonburg city	351	139	924	56	925	12	D	163	2,860	19	D	186	4,468	127	690
Herndon town	383	339	6,977	61	796	18	178	115	1,164	12	D	124	1,738	88	632
Highland Springs CDP	33	11	16	1	D	NA	NA	15	294	2	D	12	188	13	162
Hollins CDP	66	42	456	18	826	2	D	55	1,903	4	22	26	518	24	125
Hopewell city	97	35	184	14	220	1	D	49	1,450	3	6	52	728	38	200
Huntington CDP	48	21	830	5	D	2	D	14	D	1	D	23	D	20	145
Hybla Valley CDP	81	18	121	16	250	1	D	72	D	2	D	32	516	17	149

Table C. Incorporated Places, Census Designated Places (CDPs), and Minor Civil Divisions (MCDs) of 10,000 or More Population — Economic Census

STATE City, town, township, borough, or CDP (county if applicable)	Utilities Number of establishments	Utilities Number of employees	Manufacturing Number of establishments	Manufacturing Number of employees	Wholesale trade[1] Number of establishments	Wholesale trade[1] Number of employees	Retail trade Number of establishments	Retail trade Number of employees	Transportation and warehousing Number of establishments	Transportation and warehousing Number of employees	Information Number of establishments	Information Number of employees	Finance and insurance Number of establishments	Finance and insurance Number of employees	Real estate and rental and leasing Number of establishments
	1	2	3	4	5	6	7	8	9	10	11	12	13	14	15
VIRGINIA—Con.															
Idylwood CDP	NA	NA	3	D	1	D	16	232	2	D	7	26	14	D	13
Kings Park West CDP	NA	NA	NA	NA	3	5	14	240	1	D	3	36	10	D	8
Kingstowne CDP	NA	NA	NA	NA	2	D	23	892	2	D	4	95	9	D	7
Lake Ridge CDP	NA	NA	3	19	2	D	41	586	6	D	5	47	28	D	17
Lakeside CDP	NA	NA	16	540	23	583	46	442	11	161	4	D	14	D	8
Lansdowne CDP	NA	NA	NA	NA	5	D	9	134	1	D	6	D	4	27	8
Laurel CDP	NA	NA	8	85	32	316	50	839	11	39	21	D	20	647	21
Leesburg town	2	D	11	347	27	366	266	5,403	21	139	27	405	108	807	64
Lincolnia CDP	NA	NA	15	140	35	D	73	1,014	21	217	17	267	29	D	24
Linton Hall CDP	NA	NA	4	48	11	D	7	50	5	D	6	13	10	25	10
Lorton CDP	NA	NA	20	318	37	D	40	366	28	386	1	D	10	D	15
Lowes Island CDP	NA	NA	NA	NA	3	D	6	87	2	D	2	D	7	16	2
Lynchburg city	4	D	83	8,339	69	877	385	7,371	42	695	36	573	166	D	109
McLean CDP	NA	NA	9	40	33	D	240	3,503	2	D	30	338	108	D	119
McNair CDP	1	D	NA	NA	12	1,282	15	411	4	D	55	7,263	13	D	25
Madison Heights CDP	NA	NA	8	169	7	D	53	886	8	D	1	D	20	D	7
Manassas city	NA	NA	32	4,012	41	D	194	2,778	33	420	23	681	73	D	52
Manassas Park city	1	D	12	237	23	281	31	240	4	D	4	D	6	D	9
Manchester CDP	NA	NA	6	D	9	46	42	562	6	112	9	204	51	D	16
Martinsville city	2	D	24	1,041	16	D	111	1,578	5	D	14	D	50	D	31
Marumsco CDP	1	D	18	450	9	D	82	1,283	28	402	4	22	12	D	21
Meadowbrook CDP	NA	NA	NA	NA	2	D	38	388	9	48	1	D	13	D	4
Mechanicsville CDP	NA	NA	30	607	40	1,189	157	3,167	22	352	8	84	70	D	43
Merrifield CDP	NA	NA	25	229	28	D	90	2,065	16	79	28	428	40	D	35
Montclair CDP	NA	NA	NA	NA	2	D	15	274	1	D	NA	NA	5	D	4
Mount Vernon CDP	NA	NA	3	11	4	D	21	150	3	17	4	5	6	22	5
Neabsco CDP	NA	NA	NA	NA	1	D	20	765	5	23	2	D	5	D	4
Newington CDP	1	D	24	610	62	D	39	640	24	975	8	670	8	49	19
Newington Forest CDP	NA	NA	NA	NA	1	D	4	D	3	4	2	D	NA	NA	4
Newport News city	1	D	91	26,503	110	1,438	686	9,879	87	1,645	54	2,236	242	1,740	254
Norfolk city	7	D	130	6,866	209	3,287	867	12,440	198	6,766	239	3,151	310	D	291
Oakton CDP	NA	NA	3	D	8	23	25	269	4	15	24	D	39	D	37
Petersburg city	2	D	28	1,646	21	570	145	1,426	15	260	4	D	38	D	32
Poquoson city	NA	NA	3	D	4	D	28	305	2	D	2	D	13	D	12
Portsmouth city	2	D	56	2,196	48	688	273	3,081	57	1,711	14	293	83	528	71
Radford city	1	D	18	2,794	8	51	39	537	2	D	5	32	27	D	21
Reston CDP	NA	NA	13	150	35	1,062	112	2,445	20	D	164	9,604	169	3,685	124
Richmond city	18	D	187	5,882	269	3,767	808	8,666	139	2,870	132	3,552	362	10,830	258
Roanoke city	7	D	100	3,869	180	2,727	535	9,912	101	3,446	69	1,542	218	3,579	155
Rose Hill CDP (Fairfax County)	NA	NA	3	25	2	D	18	196	4	18	4	D	6	D	4
Salem city	1	D	61	3,558	77	1,567	145	1,995	26	325	11	D	70	D	35
Short Pump CDP	NA	NA	3	14	11	62	169	4,310	5	4	15	781	45	D	27
South Riding CDP	1	D	3	7	4	19	20	287	4	9	3	D	9	D	13
Springfield CDP	1	D	19	649	29	D	199	3,587	22	534	24	1,162	57	D	54
Staunton city	3	D	23	430	22	200	134	1,862	11	210	11	D	54	D	43
Sterling CDP	NA	NA	15	230	16	150	100	1,590	40	2,895	13	224	18	D	14
Sudley CDP	2	D	NA	NA	1	D	46	902	4	4	4	18	17	D	7
Suffolk city	3	D	46	1,996	54	961	226	3,536	55	1,291	21	256	79	745	67
Sugarland Run CDP	NA	NA	NA	NA	4	6	5	108	4	12	NA	NA	3	D	5
Timberlake CDP	NA	NA	11	220	12	D	48	352	9	D	2	D	25	D	20
Tuckahoe CDP	NA	NA	4	12	24	87	108	1,459	8	64	10	112	79	577	54
Tysons Corner CDP	NA	NA	12	105	63	D	221	6,499	11	34	135	5,181	263	D	175
Vienna town	NA	NA	13	126	18	D	100	1,079	2	D	9	27	55	D	34
Virginia Beach city	5	D	207	5,616	391	6,893	1,500	22,723	201	1,617	202	4,493	783	15,589	649
Wakefield CDP	NA	NA	NA	NA	1	D	2	D	1	D	1	D	1	D	6
Waynesboro city	NA	NA	28	1,856	16	253	123	2,123	21	214	24	D	35	D	30
West Falls Church CDP	NA	NA	5	21	8	D	64	1,004	4	D	11	D	32	D	17
West Springfield CDP	NA	NA	4	37	5	9	28	500	1	D	4	D	13	D	19
Williamsburg city	NA	NA	3	D	7	49	119	1,931	1	D	6	D	34	D	24
Winchester city	NA	NA	23	2,197	39	677	283	4,126	13	141	18	243	91	576	59
Wolf Trap CDP	NA	NA	NA	NA	3	D	4	30	NA	NA	8	44	7	21	15
Woodlawn CDP (Fairfax County)	NA	NA	NA	NA	1	D	27	285	1	D	2	D	6	D	13
Wyndham CDP	NA	NA	NA	NA	2	D	7	D	1	D	NA	NA	6	4	6
WASHINGTON	297	9,213	6,992	248,192	7,733	103,307	21,588	307,089	4,840	87,862	3,281	128,014	9,737	97,245	9,913
Aberdeen city	1	D	16	D	19	229	99	1,679	16	126	12	149	35	313	26
Anacortes city	NA	NA	31	1,296	5	D	81	768	17	73	10	86	36	173	31
Arlington city	NA	NA	80	2,014	26	375	75	1,341	20	429	7	19	37	D	43
Artondale CDP	NA	NA	NA	NA	9	15	10	D	2	D	NA	NA	6	D	7
Auburn city	NA	NA	159	9,859	174	3,739	281	4,676	94	2,496	24	D	66	348	86
Bainbridge Island city	2	D	26	299	26	188	80	686	12	68	21	378	52	184	39
Battle Ground city	NA	NA	14	306	13	D	58	740	20	D	7	60	28	132	13
Bellevue city	5	D	115	1,733	324	4,333	673	12,225	52	1,107	240	20,990	596	9,821	517
Bellingham city	4	D	126	3,061	147	D	532	8,805	32	518	58	1,740	201	1,694	199
Bonney Lake city	NA	NA	6	11	3	3	61	1,504	7	18	4	35	26	112	13
Bothell city	NA	NA	38	3,273	63	1,357	100	1,451	10	216	66	3,820	102	1,275	75
Bothell West CDP	NA	NA	3	D	4	D	7	25	2	D	1	D	6	22	8
Bremerton city	2	D	21	578	27	191	134	1,704	19	352	10	324	54	520	67
Bryn Mawr-Skyway CDP	NA	NA	3	5	2	D	12	D	5	10	1	D	4	17	11
Burien city	NA	NA	28	82	23	138	163	2,013	31	247	10	D	50	243	72
Camano CDP	5	14	11	71	11	D	15	104	9	29	1	D	4	15	9
Camas city	NA	NA	19	2,228	16	D	44	313	11	48	11	67	29	135	11
Centralia city	NA	NA	33	483	18	120	111	1,169	7	52	4	70	32	166	24
Cheney city	NA	NA	5	353	1	D	25	319	2	D	4	46	9	49	11
Cottage Lake CDP	NA	NA	11	104	21	47	17	184	5	4	5	D	8	17	25
Covington city	NA	NA	NA	NA	10	52	50	1,368	7	6	5	D	10	59	15

1 Merchant wholesalers, except manufacturers' sales branches and offices.

Table C. Incorporated Places, Census Designated Places (CDPs), and Minor Civil Divisions (MCDs) of 10,000 or More Population — Economic Census

STATE City, town, township, borough, or CDP (county if applicable)	Real estate and rental and leasing — Number of employees	Professional, scientific, and technical services — Number of establishments	Professional, scientific, and technical services — Number of employees	Administration and support and waste management and mediation services — Number of establishments	Administration and support and waste management and mediation services — Number of employees	Educational services — Number of establishments	Educational services — Number of employees	Health care and social assistance — Number of establishments	Health care and social assistance — Number of employees	Arts, entertainment, and recreation — Number of establishments	Arts, entertainment, and recreation — Number of employees	Accommodation and food services — Number of establishments	Accommodation and food services — Number of employees	Other services (except public administration) — Number of establishments	Other services (except public administration) — Number of employees
	16	17	18	19	20	21	22	23	24	25	26	27	28	29	30
VIRGINIA—Con.															
Idylwood CDP	63	83	860	15	1,217	7	D	24	D	2	D	18	331	24	136
Kings Park West CDP	48	54	160	13	46	1	D	16	177	3	14	20	456	10	56
Kingstowne CDP	37	64	1,859	17	169	3	2	7	D	3	62	17	433	10	134
Lake Ridge CDP	55	100	599	44	769	8	158	66	1,049	10	D	35	543	32	383
Lakeside CDP	39	36	263	14	220	3	14	29	453	7	205	17	205	48	279
Lansdowne CDP	10	57	D	17	444	7	42	80	D	3	22	17	1,257	12	249
Laurel CDP	87	46	514	17	D	2	D	73	1,307	4	44	32	634	36	D
Leesburg town	288	305	2,439	59	419	21	D	182	2,150	15	287	118	2,305	98	664
Lincolnia CDP	203	103	1,714	37	987	12	203	57	2,340	6	92	38	396	50	374
Linton Hall CDP	7	92	311	23	66	3	17	11	D	4	28	6	55	10	34
Lorton CDP	70	52	1,439	41	595	2	D	39	717	6	D	20	204	28	D
Lowes Island CDP	D	72	186	13	49	2	D	17	123	2	D	9	166	7	35
Lynchburg city	447	200	3,395	94	D	34	401	268	9,339	33	562	215	5,071	173	1,161
McLean CDP	D	513	7,036	79	1,294	30	515	218	1,637	26	D	123	D	113	876
McNair CDP	255	277	13,852	21	2,119	10	D	13	D	4	92	42	720	12	140
Madison Heights CDP	27	14	68	10	46	1	D	21	D	3	3	27	D	29	91
Manassas city	229	213	3,462	72	867	20	D	174	3,297	13	135	109	1,587	141	848
Manassas Park city	33	23	153	32	430	3	5	5	D	2	D	14	89	52	D
Manchester CDP	94	49	2,020	30	411	2	D	53	1,352	5	133	23	D	26	156
Martinsville city	104	48	241	22	1,267	2	D	109	2,135	12	135	46	718	46	231
Marumsco CDP	80	21	120	32	247	3	D	103	D	3	D	43	713	73	366
Meadowbrook CDP	20	13	51	9	D	2	D	32	D	3	D	16	D	11	D
Mechanicsville CDP	163	93	524	55	505	14	92	157	3,726	17	267	97	1,899	110	731
Merrifield CDP	339	194	5,521	68	5,874	11	110	135	2,391	5	D	62	1,288	68	644
Montclair CDP	22	28	156	12	73	3	D	9	69	2	D	17	D	13	97
Mount Vernon CDP	13	33	158	10	202	4	44	15	162	2	D	19	217	23	97
Neabsco CDP	3	11	13	4	14	3	D	28	235	5	145	9	110	14	D
Newington CDP	141	119	3,241	36	1,187	7	53	19	615	2	D	22	223	70	D
Newington Forest CDP	4	19	32	4	48	NA	NA	8	84	NA	NA	NA	NA	4	D
Newport News city	1,672	364	4,971	199	6,129	44	493	390	13,476	51	946	386	6,621	289	1,963
Norfolk city	2,496	708	12,065	251	13,302	42	D	533	18,651	66	1,655	593	11,264	374	3,245
Oakton CDP	D	214	5,486	33	493	11	34	62	552	4	D	27	334	43	248
Petersburg city	223	36	175	24	535	2	D	126	4,740	11	102	79	885	74	554
Poquoson city	20	22	85	12	73	5	8	14	204	NA	NA	21	278	26	D
Portsmouth city	332	147	3,227	116	3,227	9	D	207	7,793	25	388	172	2,624	148	1,100
Radford city	83	25	196	14	60	2	D	39	507	4	D	49	934	29	D
Reston CDP	487	869	26,593	134	11,741	35	1,415	249	5,678	26	D	129	3,643	127	2,485
Richmond city	1,539	856	10,406	280	5,981	52	693	597	25,804	99	2,427	618	11,470	516	3,904
Roanoke city	950	328	2,920	137	3,836	25	190	314	12,451	36	406	320	6,509	250	2,083
Rose Hill CDP (Fairfax County)	41	54	164	28	252	NA	NA	17	127	6	D	10	183	27	D
Salem city	176	75	552	31	717	7	D	114	5,223	13	D	92	1,825	101	563
Short Pump CDP	D	99	310	25	212	8	42	40	D	7	360	78	D	43	498
South Riding CDP	46	173	485	17	486	9	93	21	224	3	D	16	272	15	115
Springfield CDP	325	145	2,845	79	2,399	6	29	102	2,525	6	71	117	2,301	82	844
Staunton city	D	52	295	21	171	7	D	86	2,194	15	D	80	1,433	85	436
Sterling CDP	67	82	336	62	564	7	26	36	440	7	260	55	1,040	62	400
Sudley CDP	46	22	926	19	199	3	D	23	270	2	D	34	D	14	58
Suffolk city	243	123	D	71	643	12	D	177	4,087	16	359	147	2,477	94	593
Sugarland Run CDP	32	26	156	10	28	1	D	5	74	1	D	9	D	7	31
Timberlake CDP	D	22	D	26	304	4	D	33	320	7	27	30	864	22	86
Tuckahoe CDP	177	138	616	35	213	13	98	128	2,545	21	418	53	971	88	482
Tysons Corner CDP	3,321	875	48,948	142	11,389	40	771	163	2,192	34	D	157	4,296	123	1,338
Vienna town	102	165	1,209	36	693	20	114	117	D	10	D	91	1,235	83	485
Virginia Beach city	6,165	1,395	17,405	675	12,066	133	940	997	18,362	183	2,435	1,153	21,910	829	4,778
Wakefield CDP	9	46	103	14	106	3	21	9	43	5	D	4	27	4	5
Waynesboro city	D	42	761	22	752	7	D	48	875	11	136	68	1,330	52	364
West Falls Church CDP	218	98	1,423	37	741	9	65	77	1,113	5	24	51	D	50	347
West Springfield CDP	192	73	297	13	47	8	53	58	650	10	186	21	420	20	195
Williamsburg city	D	39	154	18	138	5	28	44	D	7	D	143	4,043	29	276
Winchester city	260	131	1,122	44	1,357	8	31	261	6,460	17	246	130	2,518	85	506
Wolf Trap CDP	26	116	247	17	121	4	9	12	116	6	D	2	D	8	D
Woodlawn CDP (Fairfax County)	71	11	D	15	27	NA	NA	15	D	3	24	14	122	25	98
Wyndham CDP	18	34	65	7	D	3	4	14	D	3	D	3	D	1	D
WASHINGTON	45,209	20,047	167,512	9,045	141,235	2,069	16,424	19,833	374,227	2,744	58,770	16,333	234,145	12,425	69,976
Aberdeen city	84	35	206	18	333	3	D	112	1,688	5	74	60	552	42	D
Anacortes city	110	55	269	25	148	5	27	72	1,287	10	D	59	D	59	293
Arlington city	140	30	131	16	77	10	D	73	1,393	9	127	72	853	44	201
Artondale CDP	5	18	31	17	62	3	4	17	67	4	16	2	D	3	D
Auburn city	344	121	630	81	1,474	15	112	190	2,920	31	D	145	1,859	157	849
Bainbridge Island city	D	212	D	42	218	18	232	97	818	27	325	40	D	50	182
Battle Ground city	D	30	158	17	75	3	8	42	427	5	26	43	616	31	D
Bellevue city	3,594	1,266	14,910	387	17,145	138	1,537	958	12,412	88	2,449	432	8,993	410	2,745
Bellingham city	847	436	2,022	124	1,581	44	342	486	8,267	66	704	325	5,589	243	1,531
Bonney Lake city	37	17	79	15	66	5	44	39	D	4	D	49	846	45	D
Bothell city	269	202	2,875	66	1,389	16	152	165	1,720	8	415	140	1,982	77	443
Bothell West CDP	8	23	43	15	39	1	D	14	70	1	D	4	23	12	D
Bremerton city	218	86	671	38	545	9	50	146	5,220	10	253	108	1,440	81	377
Bryn Mawr-Skyway CDP	14	8	D	11	112	1	D	21	166	3	D	4	41	9	D
Burien city	226	95	477	40	184	12	56	199	3,161	13	283	103	1,221	114	D
Camano CDP	16	22	50	18	52	1	D	13	D	4	46	9	D	11	34
Camas city	29	76	751	17	78	3	D	40	260	5	83	35	296	24	D
Centralia city	58	35	188	25	324	2	D	81	2,120	4	D	65	867	38	157
Cheney city	55	10	33	4	13	NA	NA	22	D	1	D	31	311	9	D
Cottage Lake CDP	D	94	212	31	164	7	27	22	D	8	104	4	D	18	D
Covington city	D	29	129	18	68	4	6	45	288	NA	NA	44	719	32	D

Table C. Incorporated Places, Census Designated Places (CDPs), and Minor Civil Divisions (MCDs) of 10,000 or More Population — Economic Census

STATE City, town, township, borough, or CDP (county if applicable)	Utilities		Manufacturing		Wholesale trade[1]		Retail trade		Transportation and warehousing		Information		Finance and insurance		Real estate and rental and leasing
	Number of establishments	Number of employees	Number of establishments	Number of employees	Number of establishments	Number of employees	Number of establishments	Number of employees	Number of establishments	Number of employees	Number of establishments	Number of employees	Number of establishments	Number of employees	Number of establishments
	1	2	3	4	5	6	7	8	9	10	11	12	13	14	15
WASHINGTON—Con.															
Des Moines city	NA	NA	6	18	15	116	38	360	19	108	4	D	22	118	16
Eastmont CDP	NA	NA	NA	NA	4	18	12	27	8	35	1	D	10	D	5
East Renton Highlands CDP	1	D	5	105	8	55	10	20	3	D	2	D	4	D	7
East Wenatchee city	NA	NA	4	60	15	156	75	1,433	5	20	3	D	24	138	12
Edmonds city	NA	NA	19	214	39	201	133	1,449	18	95	18	76	87	D	76
Elk Plain CDP	1	D	NA	NA	2	D	6	180	5	4	2	D	3	D	4
Ellensburg city	5	D	15	432	19	134	94	1,205	13	106	8	110	32	151	28
Enumclaw city	1	D	19	495	10	73	59	699	9	34	6	D	26	512	14
Everett city	1	D	134	43,136	134	2,108	449	6,782	81	2,309	53	1,517	176	1,568	168
Fairwood CDP (King County)	NA	NA	3	34	5	D	16	295	3	3	NA	NA	11	60	11
Federal Way city	NA	NA	25	347	54	450	257	4,441	53	451	33	2,300	148	1,208	101
Ferndale city	1	D	40	2,071	23	D	45	555	11	226	6	42	22	D	13
Five Corners CDP	NA	NA	9	23	10	59	27	311	12	74	1	D	10	54	6
Fort Lewis CDP	NA	NA	NA	NA	NA	NA	16	105	1	D	NA	NA	6	116	2
Frederickson CDP	2	D	11	1,896	10	72	10	177	13	82	1	D	4	8	4
Graham CDP	1	D	5	24	11	90	20	209	13	42	3	D	6	16	9
Grandview city	NA	NA	7	276	7	D	31	313	12	646	NA	NA	11	46	13
Hazel Dell CDP	NA	NA	21	198	17	115	82	1,295	17	135	7	111	46	320	33
Issaquah city	2	D	27	1,407	44	272	136	3,108	11	290	26	D	87	456	77
Kelso city	1	D	23	939	12	153	66	838	11	258	5	D	13	57	17
Kenmore city	NA	NA	22	108	17	126	43	450	4	D	9	D	23	107	24
Kennewick city	3	D	45	714	67	659	378	6,113	25	227	36	660	153	954	117
Kent city	1	D	247	14,012	430	8,772	340	4,711	248	4,624	34	1,131	122	1,088	155
Kirkland city	2	D	50	668	104	1,023	216	4,128	13	69	74	3,531	195	1,186	182
Klahanie CDP	NA	NA	NA	NA	7	10	11	99	1	D	4	D	6	D	12
Lacey city	1	D	17	415	23	493	148	3,567	15	443	14	2,194	81	706	54
Lake Forest Park city	NA	NA	4	14	4	D	23	214	4	7	1	D	3	D	19
Lakeland North CDP	NA	NA	NA	NA	1	D	4	21	9	D	1	D	NA	NA	5
Lakeland South CDP	NA	NA	NA	NA	5	5	5	25	6	9	NA	NA	NA	NA	3
Lake Stevens city	NA	NA	12	D	6	40	45	848	10	27	5	32	29	D	30
Lake Tapps CDP	NA	NA	5	13	6	24	10	64	11	20	2	D	3	1	11
Lakewood city	1	D	36	585	67	834	227	2,725	33	444	15	179	87	969	102
Longview city	2	D	37	2,469	39	637	175	3,043	27	315	15	240	78	695	55
Lynden city	NA	NA	20	621	14	D	71	789	10	202	8	68	35	D	21
Lynnwood city	NA	NA	48	675	95	794	425	7,823	25	147	34	1,067	167	1,315	90
Maltby CDP	1	D	40	1,065	26	427	28	431	15	36	2	D	8	D	9
Maple Valley city	NA	NA	8	42	11	47	38	694	9	99	2	D	33	106	15
Martha Lake CDP	NA	NA	8	17	5	11	14	77	5	20	2	D	5	D	19
Marysville city	NA	NA	55	1,672	34	236	172	3,450	13	59	13	136	60	D	63
Mercer Island city	1	D	10	51	27	74	36	383	10	47	22	D	65	830	79
Mill Creek city	NA	NA	7	D	18	39	55	903	5	11	3	69	44	D	29
Mill Creek East CDP	NA	NA	9	262	7	154	14	79	2	D	5	D	12	22	10
Monroe city	NA	NA	58	1,111	31	196	98	1,056	9	37	6	47	27	D	23
Moses Lake city	1	D	21	1,204	39	294	130	1,799	29	357	8	138	48	262	35
Mountlake Terrace city	NA	NA	12	132	13	83	31	414	10	88	3	D	20	D	14
Mount Vernon city	2	D	32	673	32	385	135	2,017	22	355	11	165	63	335	56
Mukilteo city	NA	NA	74	2,221	55	642	40	318	4	36	6	37	29	D	30
Newcastle city	NA	NA	6	42	9	52	14	219	6	D	3	D	16	57	11
North Lynnwood CDP	NA	NA	8	32	13	D	34	477	2	D	2	D	13	D	19
Oak Harbor city	2	D	9	170	3	D	74	988	5	57	7	D	40	278	31
Olympia city	2	D	32	514	39	390	367	5,515	15	99	54	825	147	1,428	114
Orchards CDP	NA	NA	19	184	27	234	31	500	15	56	1	D	13	80	15
Parkland CDP	2	D	11	221	9	79	63	670	18	D	1	D	23	D	22
Pasco city	1	D	37	D	77	939	157	2,051	81	1,049	19	174	41	D	46
Port Angeles city	NA	NA	28	761	11	D	117	1,035	21	205	5	D	42	310	26
Port Orchard city	NA	NA	6	32	8	84	67	1,181	5	26	6	56	32	273	33
Prairie Ridge CDP	NA	NA	NA	NA	2	D	1	D	1	D	NA	NA	3	4	2
Pullman city	1	D	12	D	11	177	51	1,027	8	102	7	54	22	114	40
Puyallup city	1	D	43	954	39	652	239	5,078	41	1,930	19	686	89	605	86
Redmond city	2	D	127	6,634	173	3,101	251	3,923	12	1,406	121	D	114	1,053	128
Renton city	2	D	71	13,466	110	3,308	264	5,284	86	1,064	23	D	131	1,325	115
Richland city	1	D	39	1,839	19	186	143	2,531	27	222	18	D	60	656	89
Salmon Creek CDP	NA	NA	21	421	30	198	46	743	9	25	5	35	30	111	23
Sammamish city	NA	NA	6	14	31	52	47	413	11	43	11	D	42	125	41
SeaTac city	NA	NA	15	130	19	177	71	943	94	2,645	8	D	20	D	40
Seattle city	10	179	859	20,323	1,093	16,045	2,530	34,652	478	26,393	862	26,680	1,466	22,649	1,966
Sedro-Woolley city	NA	NA	20	538	6	D	39	325	7	25	1	D	11	56	12
Shoreline city	NA	NA	17	147	33	135	121	2,364	14	90	21	D	57	283	70
Silverdale CDP	2	D	11	85	7	47	194	3,373	4	D	18	182	73	475	56
Silver Firs CDP	1	D	NA	NA	11	D	7	55	1	D	NA	NA	7	D	14
Snoqualmie city	2	D	5	228	13	147	15	112	1	D	7	D	16	39	11
South Hill CDP	1	D	10	48	8	54	65	1,261	20	60	7	53	42	D	40
Spanaway CDP	1	D	10	114	7	D	55	945	13	171	1	D	16	70	23
Spokane city	5	D	200	4,292	249	3,330	862	13,166	132	2,012	117	2,683	496	7,172	281
Spokane Valley city	3	D	189	6,500	202	2,963	476	7,626	74	1,159	36	361	166	1,580	147
Sunnyside city	NA	NA	19	550	16	224	74	1,077	5	D	6	97	25	156	25
Tacoma city	1	D	194	6,347	210	2,967	744	11,177	136	2,850	59	934	281	3,781	297
Tukwila city	NA	NA	75	2,695	164	2,588	282	4,783	75	2,130	34	D	68	1,121	86
Tumwater city	NA	NA	41	1,068	33	330	72	1,493	16	367	5	19	40	235	37
Union Hill-Novelty Hill CDP	1	D	3	5	9	39	15	163	4	9	6	D	9	D	24
University Place city	NA	NA	17	87	12	75	51	728	9	26	9	D	48	269	55
Vancouver city	3	D	182	6,379	185	2,441	555	10,131	133	2,045	82	2,431	385	3,855	273
Vashon city	4	16	21	231	6	8	39	363	4	18	13	D	11	44	17
Walla Walla city	6	D	83	1,043	54	483	150	1,667	10	139	19	341	64	630	42
Walnut Grove CDP	NA	NA	25	573	24	142	20	379	23	207	4	D	1	D	7
Washougal city	NA	NA	20	618	12	91	28	264	9	49	3	D	13	43	9

1 Merchant wholesalers, except manufacturers' sales branches and offices.

Table C. Incorporated Places, Census Designated Places (CDPs), and Minor Civil Divisions (MCDs) of 10,000 or More Population — Economic Census

STATE City, town, township, borough, or CDP (county if applicable)	Real estate and rental and leasing Number of employees	Professional, scientific, and technical services Number of establish-ments	Number of employees	Administration and support and waste management and mediation services Number of establish-ments	Number of employees	Educational services Number of establish-ments	Number of employees	Health care and social assistance Number of establish-ments	Number of employees	Arts, entertainment, and recreation Number of establish-ments	Number of employees	Accommodation and food services Number of establish-ments	Number of employees	Other services (except public administration) Number of establish-ments	Number of employees
	16	17	18	19	20	21	22	23	24	25	26	27	28	29	30
WASHINGTON—Con.															
Des Moines city	36	32	106	20	72	5	44	67	1,298	3	48	55	744	32	81
Eastmont CDP	6	23	60	13	65	2	D	23	67	NA	NA	3	15	6	13
East Renton Highlands CDP	16	15	25	18	D	3	21	9	32	5	D	6	56	7	20
East Wenatchee city	33	22	162	26	122	1	D	46	D	7	D	41	781	29	100
Edmonds city	205	174	755	74	710	24	80	220	3,356	18	404	113	1,426	85	435
Elk Plain CDP	10	3	D	9	40	1	D	7	D	1	D	7	141	9	33
Ellensburg city	64	39	167	18	86	3	D	71	1,480	12	D	86	1,282	42	D
Enumclaw city	D	25	130	9	78	5	26	50	476	4	D	42	416	32	D
Everett city	1,056	315	2,792	142	2,773	31	289	416	11,682	38	670	343	4,457	232	1,468
Fairwood CDP (King County)	32	23	37	11	46	5	28	21	118	3	D	18	256	14	75
Federal Way city	442	167	1,491	132	4,179	26	216	342	6,393	24	445	221	3,085	160	744
Ferndale city	33	24	122	19	443	5	34	41	D	4	59	33	375	16	71
Five Corners CDP	8	18	71	29	595	4	D	30	D	2	D	18	111	17	D
Fort Lewis CDP	D	40	467	6	257	NA	NA	3	D	NA	NA	10	167	7	83
Frederickson CDP	8	5	21	20	104	3	D	11	D	1	D	6	89	7	D
Graham CDP	16	6	10	10	15	3	17	26	158	6	51	12	143	22	D
Grandview city	40	6	11	5	D	2	D	16	346	1	D	11	118	3	D
Hazel Dell CDP	114	70	368	24	137	9	D	60	D	6	98	54	D	55	D
Issaquah city	311	189	1,046	48	744	30	178	215	2,634	17	518	109	1,729	93	661
Kelso city	57	17	291	15	145	2	D	32	471	2	D	35	574	24	D
Kenmore city	33	60	183	43	508	4	19	59	380	13	206	43	356	30	D
Kennewick city	683	204	D	111	2,669	16	D	269	D	25	608	195	3,554	139	849
Kent city	866	220	1,858	162	3,405	16	96	327	3,467	26	443	272	3,198	245	1,412
Kirkland city	867	460	4,487	109	2,764	43	268	348	6,424	51	932	191	2,958	179	835
Klahanie CDP	18	34	66	11	32	4	21	14	166	2	D	10	109	8	D
Lacey city	210	74	2,388	42	478	7	D	125	D	12	324	122	1,852	89	548
Lake Forest Park city	D	36	127	16	76	3	D	22	93	2	D	4	D	5	19
Lakeland North CDP	6	9	17	11	113	NA	NA	13	D	2	D	3	37	5	16
Lakeland South CDP	D	10	21	20	91	NA	NA	7	D	1	D	2	D	6	D
Lake Stevens city	D	20	69	18	109	7	31	43	D	5	D	42	621	30	D
Lake Tapps CDP	14	18	45	10	28	1	D	8	D	1	D	9	107	10	64
Lakewood city	445	111	544	64	1,100	14	89	207	D	25	934	179	2,433	145	670
Longview city	208	85	461	35	1,461	13	90	167	4,697	15	D	104	1,490	85	525
Lynden city	100	53	197	23	87	3	D	33	445	10	75	34	463	24	108
Lynnwood city	307	156	1,410	102	1,970	20	107	216	2,971	11	199	204	3,092	149	1,018
Maltby CDP	16	32	115	31	701	3	D	14	37	2	D	4	D	19	D
Maple Valley city	D	32	100	23	79	14	106	43	350	10	142	42	378	42	D
Martha Lake CDP	52	20	37	19	56	1	D	23	143	2	D	10	177	13	68
Marysville city	218	60	336	48	189	13	82	125	1,352	10	167	104	1,365	106	D
Mercer Island city	400	135	399	39	150	20	108	78	817	19	D	40	433	47	D
Mill Creek city	D	62	158	34	427	6	33	77	D	9	D	60	894	39	D
Mill Creek East CDP	16	31	126	15	64	3	21	12	49	1	D	7	24	13	46
Monroe city	74	33	149	21	130	6	35	70	D	11	D	65	772	47	220
Moses Lake city	104	57	D	27	492	2	D	88	1,762	4	D	73	1,236	62	D
Mountlake Terrace city	130	33	254	21	173	7	60	48	1,065	9	445	38	322	22	96
Mount Vernon city	143	117	512	37	623	12	107	140	4,127	12	315	83	915	78	352
Mukilteo city	107	68	629	32	176	9	196	57	630	10	D	55	647	45	D
Newcastle city	31	42	149	20	330	1	D	25	209	2	D	13	139	12	41
North Lynnwood CDP	37	30	95	18	73	1	D	14	133	1	D	24	263	27	D
Oak Harbor city	130	41	251	22	98	7	43	68	751	10	D	63	744	37	177
Olympia city	428	287	D	79	841	27	242	443	8,280	24	438	215	3,316	203	1,411
Orchards CDP	40	34	272	17	177	3	17	42	496	4	5	18	239	27	D
Parkland CDP	94	23	79	25	240	6	19	47	D	3	24	51	619	42	138
Pasco city	224	62	D	63	629	10	D	101	1,630	13	317	88	1,288	80	D
Port Angeles city	97	66	D	36	177	4	D	133	2,425	14	71	87	966	53	D
Port Orchard city	76	64	D	17	D	3	34	55	1,061	10	78	53	D	40	D
Prairie Ridge CDP	D	3	D	10	20	1	D	2	D	NA	NA	1	D	3	5
Pullman city	180	36	304	11	105	1	D	69	1,308	7	105	103	1,302	36	166
Puyallup city	417	119	627	48	717	13	67	204	4,684	19	650	151	2,421	102	834
Redmond city	1,207	386	7,439	115	4,335	42	408	232	3,076	35	554	244	4,597	149	D
Renton city	610	208	2,109	118	1,866	36	412	336	7,101	21	1,071	241	3,787	171	951
Richland city	268	182	7,386	56	5,311	14	125	227	D	22	591	127	2,055	77	544
Salmon Creek CDP	D	71	378	24	177	8	112	58	D	9	141	38	555	35	D
Sammamish city	D	197	405	45	301	29	291	74	469	20	355	30	488	36	D
SeaTac city	312	17	243	37	1,057	3	D	38	1,050	3	D	96	2,996	56	726
Seattle city	11,652	4,695	55,416	1,158	19,762	409	3,908	2,711	72,737	485	10,159	2,823	45,976	1,946	14,902
Sedro-Woolley city	40	14	D	4	46	1	D	29	D	3	D	32	D	20	76
Shoreline city	282	114	428	68	580	16	71	206	2,654	28	957	100	1,054	84	D
Silverdale CDP	212	86	807	32	1,247	8	49	142	2,176	8	438	93	1,579	54	324
Silver Firs CDP	43	23	78	21	94	2	D	16	102	1	D	10	137	8	49
Snoqualmie city	26	41	129	13	19	8	D	30	D	6	137	34	455	20	D
South Hill CDP	118	32	166	40	231	7	48	75	683	4	23	60	1,131	62	D
Spanaway CDP	57	11	78	16	42	1	D	24	96	2	D	34	350	21	D
Spokane city	1,580	748	5,605	272	5,424	65	611	899	24,925	87	1,751	601	10,256	439	2,687
Spokane Valley city	814	189	1,245	185	4,065	23	127	321	5,920	27	491	216	3,468	196	1,306
Sunnyside city	174	22	139	15	102	4	9	73	D	2	D	35	407	23	D
Tacoma city	1,748	507	D	252	4,331	43	357	686	23,046	70	2,543	501	7,220	414	3,045
Tukwila city	941	108	1,052	73	3,884	12	189	96	1,331	17	1,008	128	3,170	60	639
Tumwater city	101	57	325	29	2,225	6	56	86	D	13	D	64	788	55	329
Union Hill-Novelty Hill CDP	D	72	132	25	303	3	D	21	105	6	109	7	89	13	D
University Place city	D	66	251	32	429	10	67	93	746	10	D	41	459	52	308
Vancouver city	1,384	574	4,115	243	6,883	56	387	616	14,435	47	823	428	6,939	363	D
Vashon CDP	D	51	134	22	58	8	35	27	D	19	128	19	155	28	D
Walla Walla city	128	79	356	44	252	2	D	128	3,945	20	310	114	1,746	63	D
Walnut Grove CDP	22	14	82	13	28	1	D	13	285	3	D	8	111	14	D
Washougal city	22	24	79	14	83	3	D	21	116	5	38	22	206	17	D

Table C. Incorporated Places, Census Designated Places (CDPs), and Minor Civil Divisions (MCDs) of 10,000 or More Population — Economic Census

	Economic activity by sector, 2012														
	Utilities		Manufacturing		Wholesale trade[1]		Retail trade		Transportation and warehousing		Information		Finance and insurance		Real estate and rental and leasing
STATE City, town, township, borough, or CDP (county if applicable)	Number of establishments	Number of employees	Number of establishments	Number of employees	Number of establishments	Number of employees	Number of establishments	Number of employees	Number of establishments	Number of employees	Number of establishments	Number of employees	Number of establishments	Number of employees	Number of establishments
	1	2	3	4	5	6	7	8	9	10	11	12	13	14	15
WASHINGTON—Con.															
Wenatchee city	2	D	23	401	52	587	185	2,635	21	330	17	320	94	603	61
West Richland city	1	D	5	62	2	D	14	125	2	D	NA	NA	6	D	12
White Center CDP	NA	NA	17	109	5	30	35	430	1	D	NA	NA	9	91	6
Woodinville city	NA	NA	102	3,158	75	1,066	86	1,294	8	65	11	D	46	224	39
Yakima city	4	D	99	2,981	108	2,196	346	5,078	63	578	41	735	157	1,143	146
WEST VIRGINIA	221	5,849	1,245	48,686	1,334	16,906	6,393	85,305	1,234	15,705	673	10,945	2,148	17,875	1,405
Beckley city	4	D	21	433	33	336	153	2,753	19	130	17	431	54	336	32
Bluefield city	4	D	14	181	27	226	99	1,164	7	117	17	333	25	D	10
Charleston city	18	745	39	528	121	1,588	358	5,805	31	620	89	2,022	233	4,365	135
Clarksburg city	3	D	22	419	26	365	92	1,916	17	D	8	317	44	196	15
Cross Lanes CDP	NA	NA	NA	NA	3	D	33	852	5	D	4	D	15	250	9
Fairmont city	5	D	32	611	28	439	93	1,329	11	183	14	229	50	358	25
Huntington city	7	D	52	3,170	73	1,250	211	2,788	19	160	29	668	120	970	74
Martinsburg city	2	D	19	770	18	323	137	2,644	12	468	13	237	54	340	34
Morgantown city	3	D	22	446	26	142	260	4,385	23	233	26	542	86	797	79
Parkersburg city	1	D	25	657	40	338	203	3,074	27	305	22	784	83	717	53
St. Albans city	4	D	9	D	4	16	56	983	3	D	3	20	25	119	11
South Charleston city	3	D	12	561	27	D	76	1,206	7	396	6	D	35	204	16
Teays Valley CDP	NA	NA	3	D	12	297	23	283	6	71	4	D	17	111	13
Vienna city	NA	NA	5	D	2	D	106	2,154	1	D	2	D	20	120	8
Weirton city	3	D	15	1,728	13	148	78	1,105	10	238	4	D	28	D	20
Wheeling city	4	114	37	D	62	D	142	1,690	11	D	22	D	76	D	49
WISCONSIN	323	14,046	8,995	436,777	5,990	97,040	19,272	296,956	5,251	97,724	2,295	52,807	9,177	140,391	4,509
Allouez village & MCD (Brown)	NA	NA	NA	NA	5	48	15	269	10	141	2	D	33	D	14
Appleton city (Calumet)	3	D	104	7,600	98	1,432	291	4,865	40	762	49	996	198	4,795	60
Appleton city (Calumet)	NA	NA	NA	NA	4	D	25	755	3	D	5	D	19	D	4
Appleton city (Outagamie)	3	D	99	D	92	1,396	259	4,013	37	D	40	929	173	3,839	54
Ashwaubenon village & MCD (Brown)	5	D	83	4,716	90	1,997	221	3,822	45	1,046	26	390	92	1,380	31
Baraboo city & MCD (Sauk)	1	D	21	1,686	10	D	115	1,493	6	111	7	72	31	D	24
Beaver Dam city & MCD (Dodge)	1	D	27	1,829	10	213	80	1,504	12	840	12	198	44	315	18
Bellevue village & MCD (Brown)	NA	NA	26	713	12	61	44	1,435	16	418	7	D	28	D	9
Beloit city & MCD (Rock)	1	D	52	2,599	19	456	115	1,756	16	390	7	185	37	502	17
Brookfield city & MCD (Waukesha)	NA	NA	56	1,544	108	1,733	301	5,576	21	390	84	2,376	315	5,234	94
Brown Deer village & MCD (Milwaukee)	NA	NA	17	906	20	352	35	625	8	18	8	1,164	21	597	6
Burlington city	2	D	35	2,539	22	115	71	1,403	3	D	3	74	43	228	8
Burlington city (Racine)	2	D	35	2,539	21	D	70	D	3	D	3	74	43	228	8
Caledonia village & MCD (Racine)	1	D	30	1,037	15	121	43	605	22	D	4	7	23	D	8
Cedarburg city & MCD (Ozaukee)	NA	NA	32	813	17	136	61	540	2	D	7	52	27	255	9
Chippewa Falls city & MCD (Chippewa)	1	D	42	3,335	10	166	85	2,403	13	170	8	161	37	287	8
Cudahy city & MCD (Milwaukee)	NA	NA	40	3,291	16	151	36	648	42	813	NA	NA	19	136	18
De Pere city & MCD (Brown)	4	D	60	4,073	40	866	63	1,263	18	371	7	D	61	3,822	16
Eau Claire city	6	D	79	3,823	79	1,509	340	6,565	47	682	37	597	168	2,866	94
Eau Claire city (Eau Claire)	5	D	62	3,322	64	1,296	333	6,528	34	508	34	D	168	2,866	88
Elkhorn city & MCD (Walworth)	1	D	39	1,226	19	176	52	556	8	94	7	56	31	169	10
Fitchburg city & MCD (Dane)	NA	NA	30	3,154	25	967	58	614	16	157	26	392	48	416	42
Fond du Lac city & MCD (Fond du Lac)	2	D	72	4,252	41	812	211	3,688	27	417	21	D	101	1,305	31
Fort Atkinson city & MCD (Jefferson)	2	D	18	1,721	10	558	53	713	16	314	6	352	31	177	10
Franklin city & MCD (Milwaukee)	2	D	52	3,383	35	402	75	2,107	39	673	5	77	34	161	25
Germantown village & MCD (Washington)	2	D	96	3,704	57	1,301	53	1,447	19	241	7	54	47	233	17
Glendale city & MCD (Milwaukee)	NA	NA	26	1,919	23	680	133	2,740	13	96	22	326	50	644	29
Grafton village & MCD (Ozaukee)	NA	NA	39	2,207	10	D	55	1,245	3	D	4	52	27	132	14
Grand Chute town (Outagamie)	NA	NA	46	2,453	66	694	270	6,005	18	212	19	270	76	692	31
Green Bay city & MCD (Brown)	9	D	130	10,215	106	2,190	340	5,909	88	2,224	40	1,805	203	2,219	94
Greendale village & MCD (Milwaukee)	NA	NA	21	327	6	D	118	1,851	4	7	3	D	22	93	10
Greenfield city & MCD (Milwaukee)	NA	NA	17	106	14	192	149	3,100	22	72	18	280	65	388	38
Greenville town (Outagamie)	NA	NA	37	1,108	28	1,190	23	182	17	2,216	3	D	18	D	11
Hartford city	NA	NA	44	3,787	6	D	55	789	11	177	5	111	21	158	5
Hartford city (Washington)	NA	NA	43	D	6	D	55	789	11	177	5	111	21	158	5
Howard village	NA	NA	43	1,252	24	345	61	845	13	202	3	D	31	D	16

1 Merchant wholesalers, except manufacturers' sales branches and offices.

Table C. Incorporated Places, Census Designated Places (CDPs), and Minor Civil Divisions (MCDs) of 10,000 or More Population — **Economic Census**

STATE City, town, township, borough, or CDP (county if applicable)	Real estate and rental and leasing Number of employees	Professional, scientific, and technical services Number of establishments	Number of employees	Administration and support and waste management and mediation services Number of establishments	Number of employees	Educational services Number of establishments	Number of employees	Health care and social assistance Number of establishments	Number of employees	Arts, entertainment, and recreation Number of establishments	Number of employees	Accommodation and food services Number of establishments	Number of employees	Other services (except public administration) Number of establishments	Number of employees
	16	17	18	19	20	21	22	23	24	25	26	27	28	29	30
WASHINGTON—Con.															
Wenatchee city	211	104	554	47	306	15	73	155	4,305	16	175	112	1,622	92	D
West Richland city	18	13	D	10	64	1	D	11	D	2	D	12	91	4	12
White Center CDP	25	11	49	16	97	1	D	30	200	4	163	36	199	31	D
Woodinville city	133	97	786	44	513	21	126	82	872	10	D	75	1,121	62	D
Yakima city	587	215	D	96	1,694	24	118	357	9,490	36	706	239	3,527	174	1,032
WEST VIRGINIA	6,011	2,974	24,816	1,427	31,878	166	1,139	4,939	129,075	756	8,349	3,629	66,302	2,661	16,583
Beckley city	152	65	323	21	817	4	23	174	5,089	13	D	91	1,965	51	D
Bluefield city	D	30	130	11	221	1	D	84	1,660	11	D	31	481	30	145
Charleston city	663	391	4,210	116	3,765	14	105	405	12,611	33	806	225	4,651	208	1,700
Clarksburg city	D	70	D	17	415	4	D	65	1,630	17	D	70	1,422	52	326
Cross Lanes CDP	42	20	262	9	1,782	3	60	32	212	7	33	25	366	13	D
Fairmont city	82	86	868	18	1,190	5	D	102	2,182	10	D	67	1,190	65	443
Huntington city	259	139	1,756	58	2,287	7	29	266	10,487	24	D	172	2,964	103	597
Martinsburg city	145	74	338	26	344	2	D	145	3,480	10	107	94	1,739	56	325
Morgantown city	435	131	2,026	38	1,543	10	50	116	8,776	29	200	207	4,596	78	612
Parkersburg city	239	91	603	54	1,271	5	D	201	5,441	27	345	130	2,121	100	645
St. Albans city	30	26	162	3	D	2	D	42	522	5	D	31	506	22	D
South Charleston city	104	42	529	26	654	6	15	128	2,950	8	26	55	970	43	249
Teays Valley CDP	89	33	240	13	119	NA	NA	33	348	1	D	14	250	23	D
Vienna city	24	13	34	7	65	1	D	41	519	6	52	41	1,009	16	D
Weirton city	101	37	363	12	64	1	D	94	2,180	24	D	68	D	28	125
Wheeling city	D	139	1,658	49	2,086	10	D	222	6,309	32	D	103	2,033	106	854
WISCONSIN	23,762	11,301	99,162	6,786	139,859	1,005	8,819	14,659	386,141	2,655	43,555	14,137	221,567	10,210	62,054
Allouez village & MCD (Brown)	64	27	303	16	158	1	D	48	1,317	8	D	18	308	19	95
Appleton city	D	193	1,791	79	2,403	21	104	284	7,818	29	967	211	4,363	145	1,095
Appleton city (Calumet)	D	8	D	4	D	NA	NA	19	D	NA	NA	24	519	11	D
Appleton city (Outagamie)	303	182	1,744	72	2,366	21	104	259	D	29	967	183	3,762	130	D
Ashwaubenon village & MCD (Brown)	175	82	1,304	51	2,246	12	D	85	1,880	19	D	103	2,918	70	D
Baraboo city & MCD (Sauk)	76	31	450	12	264	1	D	57	1,570	10	59	38	D	36	120
Beaver Dam city & MCD (Dodge)	49	29	182	18	496	3	D	87	1,825	10	D	52	831	30	124
Bellevue village & MCD (Brown)	22	26	168	21	199	1	D	35	875	7	D	26	411	26	D
Beloit city & MCD (Rock)	88	38	212	19	543	2	D	63	2,538	9	172	90	1,338	59	270
Brookfield city & MCD (Waukesha)	1,075	306	3,589	118	2,148	22	353	319	4,798	27	471	124	3,114	128	1,400
Brown Deer village & MCD (Milwaukee)	18	26	227	18	572	4	44	40	403	8	D	25	548	18	D
Burlington city	11	36	202	21	125	3	D	56	1,466	5	46	44	614	38	D
Burlington city (Racine)	11	35	D	21	125	3	D	56	1,466	5	46	43	D	38	D
Caledonia village & MCD (Racine)	27	35	165	26	507	2	D	26	411	13	62	27	D	28	180
Cedarburg city & MCD (Ozaukee)	43	47	488	20	213	7	74	34	360	14	D	38	573	28	158
Chippewa Falls city & MCD (Chippewa)	D	45	230	20	377	1	D	76	D	8	D	68	839	40	D
Cudahy city & MCD (Milwaukee)	59	16	44	17	407	NA	NA	31	951	6	D	24	355	32	D
De Pere city & MCD (Brown)	113	51	273	27	240	7	D	33	730	14	D	60	966	37	269
Eau Claire city	462	145	1,527	101	3,722	25	335	307	10,382	41	814	229	D	146	1,012
Eau Claire city (Eau Claire)	D	142	1,503	94	3,587	24	D	303	D	40	D	227	4,714	141	905
Elkhorn city & MCD (Walworth)	38	31	205	19	543	5	D	41	846	5	D	36	623	29	114
Fitchburg city & MCD (Dane)	247	85	556	30	392	17	169	42	1,490	18	323	43	930	44	460
Fond du Lac city & MCD (Fond du Lac)	144	91	1,050	47	1,381	2	D	186	4,706	24	384	125	2,424	106	716
Fort Atkinson city & MCD (Jefferson)	23	28	195	15	464	3	D	70	1,891	9	314	48	452	33	162
Franklin city & MCD (Milwaukee)	127	58	424	49	280	7	94	96	1,602	13	285	60	768	52	352
Germantown village & MCD (Washington)	D	56	560	53	460	7	54	31	D	14	71	44	997	41	252
Glendale city & MCD (Milwaukee)	D	114	1,212	43	450	14	125	133	2,378	8	D	54	1,601	37	237
Grafton village & MCD (Ozaukee)	D	26	135	9	D	4	22	41	D	8	139	29	509	22	120
Grand Chute town (Outagamie)	251	91	640	49	2,568	9	80	72	1,618	10	D	102	2,449	72	775
Green Bay city & MCD (Brown)	610	228	1,901	117	4,088	16	D	276	13,073	39	D	272	5,414	174	1,288
Greendale village & MCD (Milwaukee)	50	26	154	7	D	1	D	22	278	4	D	26	364	13	D
Greenfield city & MCD (Milwaukee)	182	80	589	41	223	6	D	147	3,734	19	422	72	D	72	493
Greenville town (Outagamie)	41	23	140	18	626	4	118	18	D	4	6	13	211	20	429
Hartford city	12	21	D	12	203	6	29	34	791	3	14	36	627	27	D
Hartford city (Washington)	12	21	D	12	203	6	29	34	791	3	14	36	627	26	D
Howard village	116	33	367	36	486	2	D	37	468	10	D	36	650	45	171

Table C. Incorporated Places, Census Designated Places (CDPs), and Minor Civil Divisions (MCDs) of 10,000 or More Population — Economic Census

Economic activity by sector, 2012

STATE City, town, township, borough, or CDP (county if applicable)	Utilities — Number of establishments	Number of employees	Manufacturing — Number of establishments	Number of employees	Wholesale trade[1] — Number of establishments	Number of employees	Retail trade — Number of establishments	Number of employees	Transportation and warehousing — Number of establishments	Number of employees	Information — Number of establishments	Number of employees	Finance and insurance — Number of establishments	Number of employees	Real estate and rental and leasing — Number of establishments
	1	2	3	4	5	6	7	8	9	10	11	12	13	14	15
WISCONSIN—Con.															
Howard village (Brown)	NA	NA	43	1,252	24	345	61	845	13	202	3	D	31	D	16
Hudson city & MCD (St. Croix)	2	D	27	821	32	473	103	2,001	12	D	11	111	57	354	29
Janesville city & MCD (Rock)	2	D	82	3,985	75	1,941	276	5,678	43	787	27	818	105	683	53
Kaukauna city	1	D	34	1,779	28	491	39	777	13	D	NA	NA	17	159	10
Kaukauna city (Outagamie)	1	D	34	1,779	28	491	39	777	13	D	NA	NA	17	159	10
Kenosha city & MCD (Kenosha)	NA	NA	99	2,044	56	763	295	5,162	50	1,233	13	235	124	739	67
La Crosse city & MCD (La Crosse)	4	D	93	4,666	61	1,690	251	4,879	55	1,256	36	1,479	111	978	74
Lisbon town (Waukesha)	NA	NA	11	165	7	60	6	20	9	D	1	D	7	D	7
Little Chute village & MCD (Outagamie)	NA	NA	32	2,396	13	D	25	187	3	53	3	D	13	D	4
Madison city & MCD (Dane)	7	1,587	182	8,788	270	4,849	972	17,918	100	2,360	206	4,622	455	13,359	369
Manitowoc city & MCD (Manitowoc)	NA	NA	75	6,299	27	461	146	2,436	20	328	12	179	64	474	19
Marinette city & MCD (Marinette)	1	D	30	4,991	9	100	89	1,293	11	349	9	91	28	219	8
Marshfield city	1	D	40	2,274	26	662	116	3,231	22	D	16	D	56	736	23
Marshfield city (Wood)	1	D	37	2,547	22	502	97	2,547	22	D	16	D	53	726	23
Menasha city	NA	NA	28	2,128	12	125	31	470	7	255	2	D	21	D	10
Menasha city (Winnebago)	NA	NA	26	D	12	125	26	444	7	255	2	D	21	D	10
Menasha town (Winnebago)	NA	NA	42	2,948	16	153	32	226	22	824	3	D	18	D	8
Menomonee Falls village & MCD (Waukesha)	2	D	176	8,361	89	1,425	126	2,741	30	295	13	429	73	1,860	20
Menomonie city & MCD (Dunn)	1	D	27	2,117	10	192	76	1,494	15	1,367	5	D	43	451	19
Mequon city & MCD (Ozaukee)	1	D	46	2,450	79	829	88	1,161	10	119	11	281	95	1,035	46
Middleton city & MCD (Dane)	NA	NA	47	2,191	46	918	109	3,209	10	422	39	1,050	96	1,512	45
Milwaukee city	24	D	540	22,779	485	11,513	1,368	15,652	293	7,927	208	7,866	691	32,904	460
Milwaukee city (Milwaukee)	24	D	539	D	485	11,513	1,367	D	293	7,927	208	7,866	691	32,904	460
Monroe city & MCD (Green)	2	D	34	D	15	543	88	1,902	13	118	8	415	33	218	18
Mount Pleasant village & MCD (Racine)	NA	NA	35	2,073	21	346	64	1,331	27	120	13	136	55	D	20
Muskego city & MCD (Waukesha)	NA	NA	38	1,182	21	133	47	837	18	330	3	D	31	173	14
Neenah city & MCD (Winnebago)	NA	NA	60	5,008	24	278	82	1,520	16	992	5	D	59	671	17
New Berlin city & MCD (Waukesha)	NA	NA	130	6,222	119	2,332	96	2,375	36	1,315	22	597	67	828	27
Oak Creek city & MCD (Milwaukee)	8	D	55	3,412	32	1,429	80	2,059	59	2,425	5	97	46	383	38
Oconomowoc city & MCD (Waukesha)	NA	NA	36	1,837	16	D	69	1,164	16	1,207	7	45	38	321	22
Onalaska city & MCD (La Crosse)	NA	NA	14	368	16	D	85	2,543	12	147	18	D	66	926	21
Oshkosh city & MCD (Winnebago)	2	D	115	11,025	50	1,198	250	4,856	34	819	23	D	109	1,326	53
Pewaukee city & MCD (Waukesha)	5	D	58	2,631	94	1,527	38	981	14	288	24	D	57	810	33
Platteville city & MCD (Grant)	NA	NA	12	454	10	43	57	1,082	4	D	8	122	25	211	25
Pleasant Prairie village & MCD (Kenosha)	1	D	27	2,427	12	607	111	2,511	11	473	3	D	12	98	19
Plover village & MCD (Portage)	2	D	20	1,612	13	250	66	1,443	14	582	3	D	29	112	11
Portage city & MCD (Columbia)	1	D	22	1,637	13	D	56	1,010	12	149	9	95	32	125	12
Port Washington city & MCD (Ozaukee)	5	D	21	1,153	10	123	26	250	7	D	4	44	15	239	8
Racine city & MCD (Racine)	NA	NA	143	4,602	42	448	281	3,410	26	643	14	245	72	919	37
Richfield village & MCD (Washington)	NA	NA	25	559	18	D	26	581	12	D	3	3	11	D	9
River Falls city	1	D	22	477	5	79	45	581	2	D	5	27	24	192	15
River Falls city (Pierce)	1	D	7	111	2	D	26	347	1	D	3	D	15	131	12
Salem town (Kenosha)	NA	NA	7	75	10	88	17	171	12	126	NA	NA	2	D	7
Sheboygan city & MCD (Sheboygan)	3	D	89	6,676	41	451	197	3,362	23	869	14	230	97	D	31
Shorewood village & MCD (Milwaukee)	NA	NA	3	D	4	11	31	373	1	D	4	D	16	93	20
South Milwaukee city & MCD (Milwaukee)	NA	NA	21	2,874	7	19	23	252	9	30	NA	NA	15	83	7
Stevens Point city & MCD (Portage)	1	D	30	1,791	32	332	120	2,003	17	1,379	18	190	81	4,638	19
Stoughton city & MCD (Dane)	NA	NA	18	1,674	12	146	48	544	10	181	4	22	20	96	15
Suamico village & MCD (Brown)	NA	NA	10	435	10	34	23	117	14	D	NA	NA	4	21	2
Sun Prairie city & MCD (Dane)	1	D	29	1,020	33	822	70	1,155	18	458	15	D	50	D	25

1 Merchant wholesalers, except manufacturers' sales branches and offices.

Table C. Incorporated Places, Census Designated Places (CDPs), and Minor Civil Divisions (MCDs) of 10,000 or More Population — **Economic Census**

STATE City, town, township, borough, or CDP (county if applicable)	Real estate and rental and leasing — Number of employees	Professional, scientific, and technical services — Number of establishments	Number of employees	Administration and support and waste management and mediation services — Number of establishments	Number of employees	Educational services — Number of establishments	Number of employees	Health care and social assistance — Number of establishments	Number of employees	Arts, entertainment, and recreation — Number of establishments	Number of employees	Accommodation and food services — Number of establishments	Number of employees	Other services (except public administration) — Number of establishments	Number of employees
	16	17	18	19	20	21	22	23	24	25	26	27	28	29	30
WISCONSIN—Con.															
Howard village (Brown)	D	33	367	36	486	2	D	37	468	10	D	36	650	45	171
Hudson city & MCD (St. Croix)	61	82	517	26	212	7	30	68	948	12	281	61	1,419	38	307
Janesville city & MCD (Rock)	260	107	624	63	1,825	9	57	167	5,772	25	391	162	3,046	119	733
Kaukauna city	52	20	343	17	147	3	D	23	542	5	12	32	292	33	140
Kaukauna city (Outagamie)	52	20	343	17	147	3	D	23	542	5	12	32	292	33	140
Kenosha city & MCD (Kenosha)	289	125	816	70	2,169	12	69	332	6,802	26	537	235	3,801	162	1,148
La Crosse city & MCD (La Crosse)	475	172	1,430	61	2,294	11	D	156	8,924	38	1,166	222	3,923	132	1,047
Lisbon town (Waukesha)	13	10	48	13	D	NA	NA	7	D	6	135	5	65	9	10
Little Chute village & MCD (Outagamie)	24	15	136	9	371	NA	NA	14	D	7	24	24	338	16	52
Madison city & MCD (Dane)	2,871	1,034	14,030	299	11,717	90	742	693	33,154	121	2,115	743	15,474	621	5,591
Manitowoc city & MCD (Manitowoc)	D	58	453	33	544	6	21	115	3,722	17	344	86	1,544	65	330
Marinette city & MCD (Marinette)	D	24	149	9	134	NA	NA	64	1,839	3	D	53	726	30	163
Marshfield city	91	34	270	17	341	3	D	70	6,985	8	D	68	913	47	D
Marshfield city (Wood)	91	31	D	15	D	3	D	63	6,702	8	D	61	785	45	320
Menasha city	D	30	168	21	355	2	D	47	D	7	D	42	483	26	301
Menasha city (Winnebago)	D	29	D	18	D	2	D	46	D	6	D	41	D	24	D
Menasha town (Winnebago)	21	27	352	22	846	3	D	38	930	8	182	17	268	25	D
Menomonee Falls village & MCD (Waukesha)	260	91	1,294	63	1,116	10	74	78	3,407	14	178	66	1,248	71	756
Menomonie city & MCD (Dunn)	D	47	284	15	503	NA	NA	67	2,542	10	49	57	1,032	43	D
Mequon city & MCD (Ozaukee)	D	168	826	68	1,564	19	D	124	2,465	20	305	55	985	59	414
Middleton city & MCD (Dane)	D	110	1,960	41	1,351	10	29	83	939	13	310	77	2,111	47	230
Milwaukee city	3,036	1,102	16,734	745	28,417	109	1,373	1,546	50,163	151	7,083	1,106	D	842	6,544
Milwaukee city (Milwaukee)	3,036	1,102	16,734	745	28,417	109	1,373	1,546	50,163	151	7,083	1,104	21,146	842	6,544
Monroe city & MCD (Green)	D	23	180	11	519	3	D	43	D	12	D	42	571	39	167
Mount Pleasant village & MCD (Racine)	80	50	387	25	817	3	D	92	1,385	6	D	56	1,290	35	D
Muskego city & MCD (Waukesha)	116	38	129	51	480	5	80	31	353	10	84	34	510	34	179
Neenah city & MCD (Winnebago)	142	51	476	21	1,598	4	D	101	1,806	17	427	70	1,153	57	414
New Berlin city & MCD (Waukesha)	263	109	2,193	81	1,983	7	73	92	1,466	18	362	65	1,345	79	698
Oak Creek city & MCD (Milwaukee)	405	35	414	32	373	5	62	57	612	13	D	68	1,366	44	D
Oconomowoc city & MCD (Waukesha)	107	49	171	20	55	8	39	92	2,973	10	54	50	957	32	197
Onalaska city & MCD (La Crosse)	75	26	156	23	882	5	64	69	1,518	9	D	49	1,539	41	300
Oshkosh city & MCD (Winnebago)	306	101	1,378	58	1,416	10	52	184	6,035	22	207	187	3,495	91	969
Pewaukee city & MCD (Waukesha)	225	91	1,295	39	473	5	D	65	965	9	301	33	564	36	298
Platteville city & MCD (Grant)	D	16	302	13	303	1	D	36	747	NA	NA	34	591	32	103
Pleasant Prairie village & MCD (Kenosha)	D	32	162	27	358	4	D	28	1,450	3	D	36	731	15	D
Plover village & MCD (Portage)	D	18	185	14	66	1	D	32	485	4	14	40	704	19	D
Portage city & MCD (Columbia)	89	30	198	17	219	1	D	53	1,382	7	39	45	694	36	214
Port Washington city & MCD (Ozaukee)	15	24	404	13	107	5	D	35	D	4	32	31	482	20	D
Racine city & MCD (Racine)	121	119	745	56	2,770	10	D	199	5,695	39	370	161	D	134	855
Richfield village & MCD (Washington)	16	18	42	18	149	1	D	7	204	6	73	20	287	19	D
River Falls city	33	33	370	13	235	4	D	34	1,002	8	D	39	757	29	127
River Falls city (Pierce)	26	21	83	8	D	4	D	20	215	6	D	31	D	21	D
Salem town (Kenosha)	7	21	69	10	26	NA	NA	10	D	5	117	21	255	16	56
Sheboygan city & MCD (Sheboygan)	181	95	716	42	1,377	2	D	193	4,892	21	470	132	1,976	101	613
Shorewood village & MCD (Milwaukee)	D	37	94	11	158	6	16	38	496	5	D	27	478	20	116
South Milwaukee city & MCD (Milwaukee)	38	18	69	17	132	2	D	33	801	3	D	35	356	28	D
Stevens Point city & MCD (Portage)	D	57	635	30	397	8	D	105	3,222	15	551	112	1,748	77	518
Stoughton city & MCD (Dane)	D	24	116	15	64	5	24	36	D	6	68	31	302	34	194
Suamico village & MCD (Brown)	D	14	20	15	49	2	D	14	117	4	D	13	250	7	20
Sun Prairie city & MCD (Dane)	70	60	404	26	392	10	60	59	862	9	D	50	844	41	240

Table C. Incorporated Places, Census Designated Places (CDPs), and Minor Civil Divisions (MCDs) of 10,000 or More Population — **Economic Census**

STATE City, town, township, borough, or CDP (county if applicable)	Utilities Number of establishments	Utilities Number of employees	Manufacturing Number of establishments	Manufacturing Number of employees	Wholesale trade[1] Number of establishments	Wholesale trade[1] Number of employees	Retail trade Number of establishments	Retail trade Number of employees	Transportation and warehousing Number of establishments	Transportation and warehousing Number of employees	Information Number of establishments	Information Number of employees	Finance and insurance Number of establishments	Finance and insurance Number of employees	Real estate and rental and leasing Number of establishments
	1	2	3	4	5	6	7	8	9	10	11	12	13	14	15
WISCONSIN—Con.															
Superior city & MCD (Douglas)	4	D	40	1,200	39	669	113	1,835	32	D	12	D	46	D	34
Sussex village & MCD (Waukesha)	NA	NA	41	2,889	16	538	28	476	6	D	4	D	17	145	3
Two Rivers city & MCD (Manitowoc)	2	D	27	838	6	60	35	395	10	138	5	D	18	108	8
Verona city & MCD (Dane)	1	D	22	667	18	497	24	463	6	171	9	D	23	122	3
Watertown city	2	D	41	1,923	17	310	87	1,345	17	279	5	72	41	243	12
Watertown city (Jefferson)	2	D	36	1,517	14	295	72	1,105	14	D	4	D	40	D	9
Waukesha city & MCD (Waukesha)	4	D	142	9,474	115	2,148	213	4,314	43	1,398	20	802	146	1,797	56
Waunakee village & MCD (Dane)	NA	NA	20	1,118	9	476	30	367	4	60	7	246	21	160	11
Waupun city.....................	NA	NA	10	428	3	D	29	357	6	43	NA	NA	20	103	7
Wausau city & MCD (Marathon)	4	D	64	4,486	44	817	187	4,576	28	909	24	469	141	3,731	39
Wauwatosa city & MCD (Milwaukee)..................	2	D	51	3,718	56	1,033	293	5,436	24	626	31	647	149	1,821	45
West Allis city & MCD (Milwaukee).................	4	D	92	3,448	107	1,830	243	4,249	35	659	27	456	101	1,697	43
West Bend city & MCD (Washington)...............	2	D	52	1,779	25	201	120	2,163	17	234	11	150	70	529	18
Weston village & MCD (Marathon)	NA	NA	26	1,215	38	559	42	771	11	222	2	D	27	146	10
Whitefish Bay village & MCD (Milwaukee)..........	NA	NA	6	42	8	D	25	372	NA	NA	5	D	17	99	11
Whitewater city	NA	NA	15	1,476	9	D	34	570	8	33	2	D	21	179	18
Whitewater city (Walworth)	NA	NA	14	D	9	D	34	570	7	D	2	D	21	179	18
Wisconsin Rapids city & MCD (Wood)	3	D	29	1,808	15	105	110	1,764	21	324	13	1,144	57	D	25
WYOMING	138	2,435	553	10,094	709	7,003	2,681	30,088	988	10,133	331	3,998	992	6,707	1,076
Casper city......................	8	D	27	471	80	841	299	4,299	74	644	20	346	124	965	124
Cheyenne city..................	8	D	51	1,132	93	782	321	4,632	70	2,427	65	1,138	195	1,590	112
Evanston city	3	D	18	208	15	D	72	843	17	207	7	D	25	D	32
Gillette city	7	D	27	482	49	813	160	2,202	42	684	7	150	48	412	61
Green River city...............	NA	NA	9	147	7	47	35	295	9	89	5	D	12	D	16
Laramie city	5	30	21	141	19	95	131	1,671	16	104	13	159	49	D	50
Riverton city...................	3	D	15	129	20	170	80	1,300	27	223	15	100	35	190	35
Rock Springs city.............	2	D	20	191	38	432	146	2,040	60	748	11	115	37	232	49
Sheridan city...................	2	D	18	294	21	128	128	1,488	21	157	11	128	51	D	47

1 Merchant wholesalers, except manufacturers' sales branches and offices.

	Economic activity by sector, 2012														
	Real estate and rental and leasing	Professional, scientific, and technical services		Administration and support and waste management and mediation services		Educational services		Health care and social assistance		Arts, entertainment, and recreation		Accommodation and food services		Other services (except public administration)	
STATE City, town, township, borough, or CDP (county if applicable)	Number of employees	Number of establish-ments	Number of employees	Number of establish-ments	Number of employees	Number of establish-ments	Number of employees	Number of establish-ments	Number of employees	Number of establish-ments	Number of employees	Number of establish-ments	Number of employees	Number of establish-ments	Number of employees
	16	17	18	19	20	21	22	23	24	25	26	27	28	29	30
WISCONSIN—Con.															
Superior city & MCD (Douglas)	106	55	323	23	348	4	39	90	1,806	17	130	107	1,625	64	556
Sussex village & MCD (Waukesha)..................	15	17	127	13	73	4	18	18	273	8	66	15	246	18	D
Two Rivers city & MCD (Manitowoc)	22	9	49	3	D	NA	NA	27	D	8	D	24	328	18	D
Verona city & MCD (Dane)	D	40	176	23	264	3	37	30	418	10	59	25	D	20	D
Watertown city	61	35	233	20	749	3	D	97	1,997	13	97	53	759	49	191
Watertown city (Jefferson)	D	28	202	15	735	3	D	68	D	8	D	45	688	37	148
Waukesha city & MCD (Waukesha)..................	321	188	1,794	96	1,810	18	294	269	6,573	29	584	153	3,185	138	1,102
Waunakee village & MCD (Dane).........................	20	36	132	26	270	3	D	24	410	9	57	20	363	23	86
Waupun city	10	13	78	NA	NA	3	D	33	536	5	D	22	336	17	D
Wausau city & MCD (Marathon)	D	131	1,005	30	777	15	86	227	7,158	25	388	111	1,690	77	519
Wauwatosa city & MCD (Milwaukee)..................	268	238	2,310	146	6,036	14	75	378	16,592	20	532	142	3,107	95	986
West Allis city & MCD (Milwaukee)..................	293	86	925	104	4,598	11	68	191	6,515	16	253	159	D	130	789
West Bend city & MCD (Washington)...............	D	50	380	31	1,396	5	19	122	1,854	17	572	66	1,326	93	546
Weston village & MCD (Marathon)	53	14	106	12	666	1	D	39	D	8	D	34	439	35	D
Whitefish Bay village & MCD (Milwaukee)..........	24	39	64	12	D	3	8	36	D	5	5	9	D	15	D
Whitewater city	D	17	49	8	437	1	D	30	508	6	D	38	929	24	110
Whitewater city (Walworth)	D	16	D	6	D	1	D	30	508	6	D	38	929	23	D
Wisconsin Rapids city & MCD (Wood)	D	42	258	24	312	3	D	85	D	12	D	68	861	56	390
WYOMING	4,546	2,141	9,134	954	6,450	142	1,201	1,898	31,340	428	3,971	1,799	27,580	1,373	6,655
Casper city......................	649	216	1,146	106	1,055	15	D	285	4,941	31	335	158	3,224	159	937
Cheyenne city	390	416	1,758	135	1,054	22	107	290	6,289	25	D	176	3,518	158	812
Evanston city	143	35	219	12	72	3	10	54	1,203	3	D	34	709	20	D
Gillette city	265	95	502	49	749	8	D	91	1,720	12	110	94	1,529	89	D
Green River city	21	31	102	10	D	1	D	19	147	2	D	22	D	25	D
Laramie city	132	96	737	33	179	12	D	121	D	14	72	103	1,976	79	402
Riverton city	210	52	205	17	61	2	D	58	860	5	26	51	712	39	155
Rock Springs city.............	227	75	358	32	499	4	D	85	1,138	10	D	75	D	48	294
Sheridan city	173	91	565	35	170	2	D	110	D	13	162	69	1,019	61	267

APPENDIX A
GEOGRAPHIC CONCEPTS

This volume presents data for places and Minor Civil Divisions (MCDs). These two types of geographic areas are similar and often represent the same location. Although they are presented separately in most data sources, this volume combines them to simplify analysis in the twelve states where MCDs serve as general-purpose local governments.

Table A includes data for all places and MCDs, regardless of size. Table B and Table C include incorporated places, census designated places (CDPs) and MCDs with a 2010 census population of 10,000 or more, or a population of 10,000 or more as estimated in the 5-year American Community Survey (ACS).

The places for which data are presented in this volume include incorporated places, Census Designated Places (CDPs), consolidated cities, minor civil divisions (MCDs), and Economic Places.

Incorporated Places

Incorporated places included in this volume are generally those reported to the Census Bureau as being legally in existence on January 1, 2014, under the laws of their respective states as cities, boroughs, municipalities, towns, and villages, with the following exceptions: the towns in the New England states, New York, and Wisconsin and the boroughs in New York are recognized as minor civil divisions (MCDs) for decennial census purposes; the boroughs in Alaska are county equivalents for decennial census statistical presentation purposes. There are a few incorporated places that do not have a legal description. An incorporated place is established to provide governmental functions for a concentration of people, as opposed to a minor civil division, which generally is created to provide services or administer an area without regard, necessarily, to population. Places always are within a single state or equivalent entity, but may extend across county and county subdivision boundaries. MCDs are sometimes called County Subdivisions and each MCD is wholly within a named county. When an incorporated place extends across county boundaries, there are several MCDs within that single incorporated city.

Census Designated Place (CDP)

Census designated places (CDPs) are delineated for each decennial census as the statistical counterparts of incorporated places. CDPs are delineated to provide census data for concentrations of population, housing, and commercial structures that are identifiable by name but not legally incorporated under the laws of the state in which they are located. CDP boundaries usually are defined in cooperation with state, local, and tribal officials. These boundaries, which usually coincide with visible features or the boundary of an adjacent incorporated place or other legal entity boundary, have no legal status, nor any officials elected to serve traditional municipal functions. CDP boundaries may change from one decennial census to the next with changes in the settlement pattern; a CDP with the same name as a CDP in an earlier census does not necessarily have the same boundary. The ACS includes CDPs, generally the same as those in the 2010 census, but some have become incorporated places.[1] Other data sources sometimes have different definitions of places and towns and may include places that the Census Bureau has categorized as CDPs. However, CDPs are generally not included in other data sources.

Beginning with the 2000 census, CDPs did not need to meet a minimum population threshold to qualify for tabulation of census data. For the 1990 census and earlier censuses, the Census Bureau required CDPs to qualify on the basis of various minimum population size criteria.

Hawaii is the only state that has no incorporated places recognized by the U.S. Census Bureau. All places shown in the data products for Hawaii are CDPs. Honolulu county was divided into Urban Honolulu CDP and East Honolulu CDP for the first time in the 2010 census.

Consolidated City

A consolidated city is a unit of local government for which the functions of an incorporated place and its county or MCD have merged. The legal aspects of this action may result in both the primary incorporated place and the county or MCD continuing to exist as legal entities, even though the county or MCD performs few or no governmental functions and has few or no elected officials. In places where this occurs, and in places where one or more other incorporated places in the county or MCD continue to function as separate governments (even though they have been included in the consolidated government), the primary incorporated place is referred to as a consolidated city.

---

1 For a list of places that changed after the 2010 census, see https://www.census.gov/geo/partnerships/docs/bas/2010-2014entitychanges.xls

This volume contains data for eight consolidated cities: Milford, CT; Athens-Clarke County, GA; Augusta-Richmond County, GA; Greeley County Unified Government, KS; Indianapolis, IN; Louisville/Jefferson County, KY; Butte-Silver Bow, MT; and Nashville-Davidson, TN.

Within the consolidated city, there is usually a large core city that is the principal city of the consolidated city. This principal city is referred to as the "balance" in census tabulations. Table A, B, and C include both the consolidated city and the "balance". Some data sources include both, while others are not clear about which entity is identified.

Minor Civil Division (MCD)

The primary political divisions of most states are termed counties. Minor civil divisions (MCDs) are the primary governmental or administrative divisions of a county in many states (parish in Louisiana). MCDs represent many different kinds of legal entities with a wide variety of governmental and/or administrative functions. MCDs are variously designated as American Indian reservations, assessment districts, boroughs, charter townships, election districts, election precincts, gores, grants, locations, magisterial districts, parish governing authority districts, plantations, precincts, purchases, road districts, supervisors' districts, towns, townships, and unorganized territories. In some states, all or some incorporated places are not located in any MCD (independent places) and thus serve as MCDs in their own right. In other states, incorporated places are part of the MCDs in which they are located (dependent places), or the pattern is mixed—some incorporated places are independent of MCDs and others are included within one or more MCDs. In Maine and New York, there are American Indian reservations and off-reservation trust lands that serve as MCD equivalents; a separate MCD is created when the American Indian area crosses a county boundary.

The MCDs in 12 states (Connecticut, Maine, Massachusetts, Michigan, Minnesota, New Hampshire, New Jersey, New York, Pennsylvania, Rhode Island, Vermont, and Wisconsin) also serve as general-purpose local governments that typically can perform the same governmental functions as incorporated places. The Census Bureau presents data for these MCDs in all data products providing information for places. In this volume, MCDs are included for these 12 states.

The name of each MCD is followed by its county name in parentheses. Where an MCD is co-extensive with an incorporated place or a CDP, only a single listing is included, with the county name in parentheses and a notation that specifies the two types of entities.

Economic Place

Table C includes data from the 2012 Economic Census. The Economic Census uses a concept called the "Economic Place" that includes incorporated places, census designated places, and minor civil divisions with populations of 2,500 or more. Table C includes only those Economic Places with populations of 10,000 or more. In some states, incorporated cities or villages are within towns or MCDs. In the Economic Census data, the "balance" of the town that is outside of incorporated cities or villages is identified as a separate place.[2] In the decennial census, the American Community Survey, and other sources, data represent these entire towns, while the Economic Census data represent only the portion of the town that is not within an incorporated place inside the town. The component incorporated places are not in Table C if their populations are below 10,000.

2 Details about specific places in the Economic Census can be found at http://www.census.gov//econ/census/help/geography/2012_geochanges.html#

APPENDIX B
SOURCE NOTES AND EXPLANATIONS

TABLE A
ALL PLACES

Table A presents data from the 2010 Census of Population and Housing, the annual Population Estimates Program, and the American Community Survey. Data are included for all incorporated places, consolidated cities, and census designated places (CDPs), as well as for minor civil divisions (MCDs) in the 12 states where MCDs serve as general purpose local governments. This table includes 19,534 incorporated places; 8 consolidated cities; 9,762 CDPs, and 11,963 MCDs (in the 12 applicable states). In Table A, the number of geographic entities has been reduced to 38,145 by eliminating duplicate entities. Where an MCD is co-extensive with an incorporated place or a CDP, only a single listing is included.

All data were retrieved through the Census Bureau's American FactFinder at factfinder2.census.gov, or from the downloadable datasets of the Population Estimates Program.

POPULATION, Item 1 through 4
Source: U.S. Census Bureau—Population Estimates Program, Incorporated Places and Minor Civil Divisions Datasets: Subcounty Resident Population Estimates: April 1, 2010 to July 1, 2014; American Community Survey, 2010–2014 5-year estimates; 2010 SF1, Table P1

The population total for 2010 is from the decennial census and represents the resident population as of April 1 in the census year. However, where possible, item 1 shows the 2010 census *base* population, rather than the actual enumerated population. The base population may differ from the census count due to legal boundary updates, other geographic program changes, and Count Question Resolution actions. The base population serves as the starting point for the annual estimates. The 2014 annual estimates and the percent change since 2010 are shown in items 2 and 3. All Census Designated Places and some Minor Civil Divisions are not available in the 2014 Population Estimates dataset. Their 2010 population totals are from the 2010 SF1 data

and there is no measure of population change from 2010 to 2014.

Column 4 shows the total population estimate for each area from the American Community Survey 5-year file for the years 2010 through 2014. This total is derived from the census and the population estimates and represents the population over that 5-year time period. The population characteristics in columns 5 through 16 are based on this total population.

POPULATION BY RACE AND HISPANIC ORIGIN, Items 5 through 9
Source: U.S. Census Bureau—American Community Survey, 2010–2014 5-year estimates, Table B03002

The U.S. Census Bureau collects race data in accordance with guidelines provided by the U.S. Office of Management and Budget (OMB), and these data are based on self-identification. The racial categories included in the census questionnaire generally reflect a social definition of race recognized in this country and not an attempt to define race biologically, anthropologically, or genetically. In addition, it is recognized that the categories of the race item include racial and national origin or sociocultural groups. People may choose to report more than one race to indicate their racial mixture, such as "American Indian" and "White." People who identify their origin as Hispanic, Latino, or Spanish may be any race.

Respondents were offered the option of selecting one or more races. In this table, Columns 5 through 7 refer to individuals who identified with only one racial category and who were not Hispanic or Latino. Column 8 combines the racial categories American Indian and Alaska native alone; Native Hawaiian and Other Pacific Islander alone; some other race alone; and two or more races, all not Hispanic or Latino. Column 9 includes all persons who were of Hispanic or Latino origin.

The **White** population is defined as persons having origins in any of the original peoples of Europe, the Middle East, or North Africa. It includes those who indicated their race as White, as well as persons who did not classify themselves in one of the specific race categories listed on the questionnaire but entered a nationality such as Irish, German, Italian, Lebanese, Near Easterner, Arab, or Polish.

The **Black** population includes persons having origins in any of the Black racial groups of Africa. It includes those who indicated their race as "Black, African Am., or Negro", as well as persons who did not classify themselves in one of the specific race categories but reported entries such as African American, Afro American, Kenyan, Nigerian, or Haitian.

The **Asian** population includes persons having origins in any of the original peoples of the Far East, Southeast Asia, or the Indian subcontinent, including, for example, Cambodia, China, India, Japan, Korea, Malaysia, Pakistan, the Philippine Islands, Thailand, and Vietnam. It includes persons who indicated their race as Asian Indian, Chinese, Filipino, Japanese, Korean, Vietnamese, or "Other Asian," as well as persons who provided write-in entries of such groups as Cambodian, Laotian, Hmong, Pakistani, or Taiwanese.

The **American Indian or Alaska Native** population includes persons having origins in any of the original peoples of North and South America (including Central America) and who maintain tribal affiliation or community attachment. It includes those who indicated their race as American Indian or Alaska Native, as well as persons who did not classify themselves in one of the specific race categories but reported entries such as Canadian Indian, French-American Indian, Spanish-American Indian, Eskimo, Aleut, Alaska Indian, or any of the American Indian or Alaska Native tribes.

The **Native Hawaiian or Other Pacific Islander** population includes persons having origins in any of the original peoples of Hawaii, Guam, Samoa, or other Pacific Islands. It includes those who indicated their race as "Native Hawaiian", "Guamanian or Chamorro", "Samoan," or "Other Pacific Islander", as well as persons who reported entries such as Part Hawaiian, American Samoan, Fijian, Melanesian, or Tahitian.

The Hispanic population is based on a question that asked respondents "Is this person Spanish/Hispanic/Latino?" Persons marking any one of the four Hispanic categories (i.e., Mexican, Puerto Rican, Cuban, or other Hispanic, Latino, or Spanish origin) are collectively referred to as Hispanic.

In the American Community Survey, people who identify with the terms "Hispanic" or "Latino" are those who classify themselves in one of the specific Hispanic or Latino categories listed on the ACS questionnaire—"Mexican," "Puerto Rican," or "Cuban"—as well as those who indicate

that they are "other Spanish, Hispanic, or Latino." Origin can be viewed as the heritage, nationality group, lineage, or country of birth of the person or the person's parents or ancestors before their arrival in the United States. People who identify their origin as Spanish, Hispanic, or Latino may be of any race.

AGE, Items 10 through 12
Source: U.S. Census Bureau—American Community Survey, 2010–2014 5-year estimates, Table B01001

Age is defined as age at last birthday, as of the date of the ACS interview or questionnaire. The ACS also asked for the specific date of birth of the respondent, and ACS procedures used the birth date for deriving age data.

HOUSEHOLDS, Items 13 and 14
Source: U.S. Census Bureau—American Community Survey, 2010–2014 5-year estimates, Table B25003

A household consists of persons occupying a single housing unit. A housing unit is a house, an apartment, a group of rooms, or a single room occupied as separate living quarters. The occupants may be a single family, one person living alone, two or more families living together, or any other group of related or unrelated persons who share a housing unit. The number of households is the same as the number of year-round occupied housing units.

A housing unit is **owner occupied** if the owner or co-owner lives in the unit even if it is mortgaged or not fully paid for. The owner or co-owner must live in the unit and usually is Person 1 on the ACS questionnaire. Column 14 shows the percentage of **households** (occupied housing units) that are owner occupied.

EDUCATIONAL ATTAINMENT OF HOUSEHOLDERS, Items 15 and 16
Source: U.S. Census Bureau—American Community Survey, 2010–2014 5-year estimates, Table B25013

Educational attainment data are tabulated for people 18 years old and over. Items 15 and 16 include householders. Respondents are classified according to the highest degree or the highest level of school completed. The question included instructions for persons currently enrolled in school to report the level of the previous grade attended or the highest degree received.

High School Diploma or less: this category includes people whose highest degree was a high school diploma or its equivalent, people who reported completing the 12th grade but not receiving a diploma, people whose highest grade attended was less than 12th grade, and people who never attended school.

Bachelor's degree or more: this category includes people who have received a bachelor's, master's, or professional or doctorate degree.

TABLE B
PLACES AND MINOR CIVIL DIVISIONS OF 10,000 OR MORE POPULATION

Table B presents data from several sources for incorporated places, consolidated cities, census designated places, and minor civil divisions (in the 12 states where MCDs serve as general purpose local governments), and Economic Places with 10,000 or more population. There are 4,808 geographic entities in Table B, including the United States, the states, and the District of Columbia. Where an MCD is co-extensive with a place, only a single listing is included.

LAND AREA, Items 1 and 5
Source: U.S. Census Bureau—2014 U.S. Gazetteer Files

Land area measurements are shown to the nearest square mile. Land area includes dry land and land temporarily or partially covered by water, such as marshlands, swamps, and river floodplains. Square miles may be multiplied by 2.59 to convert these area measurements into square kilometers.

POPULATION, Item 2 through 4
Source: U.S. Census Bureau—Population Estimates Program, Incorporated Places and Minor Civil Divisions Datasets: Subcounty Resident Population Estimates: April 1, 2010 to July 1, 2014; 2010 SF1, Table P1

The population total for 2010 is from the decennial census and represents the resident population as of April 1 in the census year. However, where possible, item 2 shows the 2010 census *base* population, rather than the actual enumerated population. The base population may differ from the census count due to legal boundary updates, other geographic program changes, and Count Question Resolution actions. The base population serves as the starting point

for the annual estimates. All Census Designated Places and some Minor Civil Divisions are not available in the 2014 Population Estimates dataset. Their 2010 population totals are from the 2010 SF1 data and there is no measure of population change from 2010 to 2014.

The 2014 annual estimates and the percent change since 2010 are shown in items 3 and 4.

FOREIGN-BORN POPULATION, 2010–2014, Item 6
Source: U.S. Census Bureau—2010–2014 American Community Survey 5-year estimates, Table B05002

The **foreign-born population** includes anyone who was not a U.S. citizen or a U.S. national at birth. This includes respondents who indicated they were a U.S. citizen by naturalization or not a U.S. citizen.

RESIDENCE ONE YEAR AGO, 2010–2014, Item 7
Source: U.S. Census Bureau—2010–2014 American Community Survey 5-year estimates, Table B07003

The data on residence 1 year ago were derived from answers to a question that was asked of the population 1 year and older. People who had moved from another residence in the United States or Puerto Rico 1 year earlier were asked to report the exact address (number and street name); the name of the city, town, or post office; the name of the U.S. county or municipio in Puerto Rico; state or Puerto Rico; and the ZIP Code where they lived 1 year ago. People living outside the United States and Puerto Rico were asked to report the name of the foreign country or U.S. Island Area where they were living 1 year ago. Column 7 shows the proportion of all residents 1 year and older who lived in the same house where they had lived one year before the interview date.

HOUSEHOLD INCOME, 2010-2014, Items 8 through 10.
Source: U.S. Census Bureau—2010–2014 American Community Survey 5-year estimates, Tables B17017, B19001, and B19013

Household Income includes the income of the householder and all other individuals 15 years old and over in the household, whether they are related to the householder or not.

Because many households consist of only one person, average household income is usually less than average family income. Although the household income statistics cover the past 12 months, the characteristics of individuals and the composition of households refer to the time of interview. Thus, the income of the household does not include amounts received by individuals who were members of the household during all or part of the past 12 months if these individuals no longer resided in the household at the time of interview. Similarly, income amounts reported by individuals who did not reside in the household during the past 12 months but who were members of the household at the time of interview are included. However, the composition of most households was the same during the past 12 months as at the time of interview.

Total income is the sum of the amounts reported separately for wage or salary income; net self-employment income; interest, dividends, or net rental or royalty income or income from estates and trusts; Social Security or railroad retirement income; Supplemental Security Income (SSI); public assistance or welfare payments; retirement, survivor, or disability pensions; and all other income.

Receipts from the following sources are not included as income: capital gains, money received from the sale of property (unless the recipient was engaged in the business of selling such property); the value of income "in kind" from food stamps, public housing subsidies, medical care, employer contributions for individuals; withdrawal of bank deposits; money borrowed; tax refunds; exchange of money between relatives living in the same household; and gifts and lump-sum inheritances, insurance payments, and other types of lump-sum receipts.

Median income divides the income distribution into two equal parts: half of the cases fall below the median income and half above the median. For households, the median income is based on the distribution of the total number of households including those with no income. Median income for households is computed on the basis of a standard distribution with the minimum value less than $2,500 and the maximum value $250,000 or more. Median income is rounded to the nearest whole dollar. Median income figures are calculated using linear interpolation if the width of the interval containing the estimate is $2,500 or less. If the width of the interval containing the estimate is greater than $2,500, Pareto interpolation is used.

Income components were reported for the 12 months preceding the interview month. Monthly Consumer Price Indices (CPI) factors were used to inflation-adjust these components to a reference calendar year (January through December). For example, a household interviewed in March 2010 reports their income for March 2009 through February 2010. Their income is adjusted to the 2010 reference calendar year by multiplying their reported income by 2010

average annual CPI (January-December 2010) and then dividing by the average CPI for March 2009-February 2010.

In order to inflate income amounts from previous years, the dollar values on individual records are inflated to the latest year's dollar values by multiplying by a factor equal to the average annual CPI-U-RS factor for the current year, divided by the average annual CPI-U-RS factor for the earlier/earliest year

Poverty statistics in ACS products adhere to the standards specified by the Office of Management and Budget in Statistical Policy Directive 14. The Census Bureau uses a set of dollar value thresholds that vary by family size and composition to determine who is in poverty. Further, poverty thresholds for people living alone or with nonrelatives (unrelated individuals) vary by age (under 65 years or 65 years and older). The poverty thresholds for two-person families also vary by the age of the householder. If a family's total income is less than the dollar value of the appropriate threshold, then that family and every individual in it are considered to be in poverty. Similarly, if an unrelated individual's total income is less than the appropriate threshold, then that individual is considered to be in poverty.

In determining the poverty status of families and unrelated individuals, the Census Bureau uses thresholds (income cutoffs) arranged in a two-dimensional matrix. The matrix consists of family size (from one person to nine or more people) cross-classified by presence and number of family members under 18 years old (from no children present to eight or more children present). Unrelated individuals and two-person families are further differentiated by age of reference person (RP) (under 65 years old and 65 years old and over).

To determine a person's poverty status, one compares the person's total family income in the last 12 months with the poverty threshold appropriate for that person's family size and composition. If the total income of that person's family is less than the threshold appropriate for that family, then the person is considered "below the poverty level," together with every member of his or her family. If a person is not living with anyone related by birth, marriage, or adoption, then the person's own income is compared with his or her poverty threshold. The total number of people below the poverty level is the sum of people in families and the number of unrelated individuals with incomes in the last 12 months below the poverty threshold.

Since ACS is a continuous survey, people respond throughout the year. Because the income questions specify a period covering the last 12 months, the appropriate poverty thresholds are adjusted with monthly inflation factors for the 12 months preceding the data collection, and further adjusted to represent the 5-year period covered by the 2010–2014 data.

Poverty Thresholds for 2014 by Size of Family and Number of Related Children Under 18 Years

Size of family unit	Weighted average thresholds	Related children under 18 years								
		None	One	Two	Three	Four	Five	Six	Seven	Eight or more
One person (unrelated individual)	12,071									
Under 65 years	12,316	12,316								
65 years and over	11,354	11,354								
Two people	15,379									
Householder under 65 years	15,934	15,853	16,317							
Householder 65 years and over............	14,326	14,309	16,256							
Three people	18,850	18,518	19,055	19,073						
Four people	24,230	24,418	24,817	24,008	24,091					
Five people...	28,695	29,447	29,875	28,960	28,252	27,820				
Six people...	32,473	33,869	34,004	33,303	32,631	31,633	31,041			
Seven people	36,927	38,971	39,214	38,375	37,791	36,701	35,431	34,036		
Eight people	40,968	43,586	43,970	43,179	42,485	41,501	40,252	38,953	38,622	
Nine people or more...............................	49,021	52,430	52,685	51,984	51,396	50,430	49,101	47,899	47,601	45,768

Source: U.S. Census Bureau.

EMPLOYMENT STATUS, 2010–2014, Items 11 and 12
Source: U.S. Census Bureau—2010–2014 American Community Survey 5-year estimates, Table B23025

The data on **employment status** refer to work during the week preceding the interview. The employment status data tabulations include people 16 years old and over.

Employed. All civilians 16 years old and over who were either (1) "at work"—those who did any work at all during the reference week as paid employees, worked in their own business or profession, worked on their own farm, or worked 15 hours or more as unpaid workers on a family farm or in a family business; or (2) were "with a job but not at work"—those who did not work during the reference week, but who had jobs or businesses from which they were temporarily absent because of illness, bad weather, industrial dispute, vacation, or other personal reasons. Excluded from the employed are people whose only activity consisted of work around their own house (e.g., painting, repairing, or housework) or unpaid volunteer work for religious, charitable, and similar organizations. Also excluded are all institutionalized people and people on active duty in the United States Armed Forces.

Unemployed. All civilians 16 years old and over were classified as unemployed if they were neither "at work" nor "with a job but not at work" during the reference week, were looking for work during the last 4 weeks, and were available to start a job. Also included as unemployed were civilians 16 years old and over who: did not work at all during the reference week, were on temporary layoff from a job, had been informed that they would be recalled to work within the next 6 months or had been given a date to return to work, and were available to return to work during the reference week, except for temporary illness. Examples of job seeking activities were:

- Registering at a public or private employment office
- Meeting with prospective employers
- Investigating possibilities for starting a professional practice or opening a business
- Placing or answering advertisements
- Writing letters of application
- Being on a union or professional register

Civilian Labor force. All people classified as "employed" and "unemployed".

Not in labor force. All people 16 years old and over who are not classified as members of the labor force. This category consists mainly of students, individuals taking care of home or family, retired workers, seasonal workers enumerated in an off-season who were not looking for work, institutionalized people (all institutionalized people are placed in this category regardless of any work activities they may have done in the reference week), and people doing only incidental unpaid family work (fewer than 15 hours during the reference week).

HOUSEHOLDS, 2010-2014, Items 13 and 14.
Source: U.S. Census Bureau—2010–2014 American Community Survey 5-year estimates, Table B11001

A **household** includes all of the people who occupy a housing unit. (People not living in households are classified as living in group quarters.) A housing unit is a house, an apartment, a mobile home, a group of rooms, or a single room occupied (or if vacant, intended for occupancy) as separate living quarters. Separate living quarters are those in which the occupants live separately from any other people in the building and that have direct access from the outside of the building or through a common hall. The occupants may be a single family, one person living alone, two or more families living together, or any other group of related or unrelated people who share living quarters.

A family includes a householder and one or more other people living in the same household who are related to the householder by birth, marriage, or adoption. All people in a household who are related to the householder are regarded as members of his or her family. A **family household** may contain people not related to the householder. Thus, family households may include more members than do families. A household can contain only one family for purposes of census tabulations. Not all households contain families since a household may comprise a group of unrelated people or of one person living alone.

CRIME, Items 15 through 18
Source: U.S. Federal Bureau of Investigation—Uniform Crime Reports

Crime data are as reported to the FBI by law enforcement agencies and have not been adjusted for under-reporting. This may affect comparability between geographic areas or over time.

Through the voluntary contribution of crime statistics by law enforcement agencies across the United States, the Uniform Crime Reporting (UCR) Program provides periodic assessments of crime in the nation as measured by those offenses that come to the attention of the law enforcement community. The Committee on Uniform Crime Records of the International Association of Chiefs of Police initiated this voluntary national data-collection effort in 1930. UCR Program contributors compile and submit their crime data in one of two manners: either directly to the FBI or through the State UCR Programs.

Seven offenses, because of their seriousness, frequency of occurrence, and likelihood of being reported to police, were initially selected to serve as an index for evaluating fluctuations in the volume of crime. These serious crimes were murder and nonnegligent manslaughter, forcible rape, robbery, aggravated assault, burglary, larceny-theft, and motor vehicle theft. By congressional mandate, arson was added as the eighth index offense in 1979. The totals shown in this volume do not include arson.

In 2004, the FBI discontinued the use of the Crime Index in the UCR Program and its publications, stating that the Crime Index was driven upward by the offense with the highest number of cases (in this case, larceny-theft) creating a bias against jurisdictions with a high number of larceny-thefts but a low number of other serious crimes, such as murder and forcible rape. The FBI is currently publishing a violent crime total and a property crime total until a more viable index is developed.

In 2013, the FBI adopted a new definition of rape. Rape is now defined as, "Penetration, no matter how slight, of the vagina or anus with any body part or object, or oral penetration by a sex organ of another person, without the consent of the victim." The new definition updated the 80-year-old historical definition of rape which was "carnal knowledge of a female forcibly and against her will." Effectively, the revised definition expands rape to include both male and female victims and offenders, and reflects the various forms of sexual penetration understood to be rape, especially nonconsenting acts of sodomy, and sexual assaults with objects.

Violent crimes include four categories of offenses: (1) Murder and nonnegligent manslaughter, as defined in the UCR Program, is the willful (nonnegligent) killing of one human being by another. This offense excludes deaths caused by negligence, suicide, or accident; justifiable homicides; and attempts to murder or assaults to murder. (2) Rape is the penetration, no matter how slight, of the vagina or anus with any body part or object, or oral penetration by a sex organ of another person, without the consent of the victim. Assaults or attempts to commit rape by force or threat of force are also included; however, statutory rape (without force) and other sex offenses are excluded. (3) Robbery is the taking or attempting to take anything of value from the care, custody, or control of a person or persons by force or threat of force or violence and/or by putting the victim in fear. (4) Aggravated assault is an unlawful attack by one person upon another for the purpose of inflicting severe or aggravated bodily injury. This type of assault is usually accompanied by the use of a weapon or by other means likely to produce death or great bodily harm. Attempts are included, since injury does not necessarily have to result when a gun, knife, or other weapon is used, as these incidents could and probably would result in a serious personal injury if the crime were successfully completed.

Property crimes include three categories: (1) Burglary, or breaking and entering, is the unlawful entry of a structure to commit a felony or theft, even though no force was used to gain entrance. (2) Larceny/theft is the unauthorized taking of the personal property of another, without the use of force. (3) Motor vehicle theft is the unauthorized taking of any motor vehicle.

Rates are based on population estimates provided by the FBI. If a city is not in the UCR database, or if the population of the crime-reporting unit is less than 75 percent of the city's 2014 estimated population, the data for that area are considered not available. For some states, reporting is not sufficiently complete to be representative of the state as a whole, and state totals for those states have been estimated by the FBI.

The FBI website for the Uniform Crime Reports is: http://www.fbi.gov/about-us/cjis/ucr. Data for the cities were compiled from the individual agency data in the Crime by County text file obtained from FBI's Criminal Justice Information Division.

CONSTRUCTION—BUILDING PERMITS, Items 19 through 21
Source: U. S. Census Bureau—Building Permits Survey

Figures represent private residential construction authorized by building permits in approximately 19,000 places in the United States. Valuation represents the cost of construction as recorded on the building permit. This figure usually excludes the cost of on-site and off-site development and improvements and the cost of heating, plumbing, electrical, and elevator installations.

Most of the permit-issuing jurisdictions are municipalities; the remainder are counties, townships, or unincorporated towns. For the municipalities, and townships or towns, the area subject to building permit requirements to which the figures pertain is normally that of the governmental jurisdictions. A small number of municipalities have authority to issue building or zoning permits for areas extending beyond their corporate limits. In such cases, the data relate to the entire area within which the permit-issuing authority is exercised. Similarly, a small number of townships issue permits for only a part of the township and the data normally cover only the area subject to the township's permit system. The portion of construction measurable from building permit records is inherently limited since such records obviously do not reflect construction activity outside of the area subject to local permit requirements. For the nation as a whole, less than 2 percent of all privately owned housing units built are construction in areas that do not require building permits.

If a city or town was not matched as a permit-issuing place covered by the Census Bureau, an "NA" is shown. Cities that are permit-issuing places but that issued no permits during the period are represented by a "0." State totals were obtained by summing the data for permit-issuing places within each jurisdiction.

Residential building permits include buildings with any number of housing units. Hotels, apartment hotels, dormitories, fraternity houses, and other non-housekeeping residential buildings are not included.

The building permits data were compiled from the place level files available from the Census Bureau at http://www.census.gov/construction/bps/sample.html.

LOCAL GOVERNMENT FINANCES, Items 22 through 29
Source: U. S. Census Bureau—2012 Census of Governments

Total **general revenue** includes all governmental revenue except utility, liquor store, and employee-retirement or other insurance trust revenue. It includes all tax collections and intergovernmental revenue, even if designated for employee-retirement or local utility purposes.

Intergovernmental revenue consists of amounts received from other governments as fiscal aid in the form of shared revenues and grants-in-ad, as reimbursements for performance of general expenditure functions, and specific services for the paying government (e.g., care of prisoners or contractual research) of amounts in lieu of taxes. It excludes amounts received from other governments for sale of property, commodities, and utility services. All intergovernmental revenue is classified as general revenue. Intergovernmental revenue from the state government includes amounts originally from the federal government but channeled through the state.

Taxes are compulsory contributions exacted by a government for public purposes, and exclude employee and employer assessments for retirement and social insurance purposes, which are classified as insurance trust revenue. All tax revenue is classified as general revenue and comprises amounts received (including interest and penalties but excluding protested amounts and refunds) from all taxes imposed by a government Note that local government tax revenue excludes any amounts from shares of state-imposed and collected taxes, which are classified as intergovernmental revenue.

Total **general expenditure** includes all city expenditure other than the specifically enumerated kinds of expenditure classified as utility, liquor store, and employee retirement and other insurance trust expenditures.

Capital outlays are direct expenditures for contract of force account construction of buildings, roads, and other improvements, and for purchases of equipment, land, and existing structures. They include amounts for additions, replacements, and major alterations to fixed works and structures. However, expenditure for repair to such works and structures is classified as current operation expenditure.

A major portion of capital outlay is commonly financed by borrowing, while government revenue does not include receipts from borrowing. Among other things, this distorts the relationship between the totals presented for revenue and expenditure and renders this relationship useless as a direct measure of the degree of budgetary "balance," as that term is generally applied.

Total **debt** outstanding is the total of all debt obligations remaining unpaid on the date specified.

Information about the 2012 Census of Governments is available at http://www.census.gov/govs/cog/index.html, The data in this volume were compiled from the "Finances of Individual Governments" files obtained from the Governments Division of the Census Bureau.

TABLE C
PLACES AND MINOR CIVIL DIVISIONS OF 10,000 OR MORE POPULATION— ECONOMIC CENSUS

ECONOMIC ACTIVITY BY SECTOR, Items 1 through 30
Source: U.S. Census Bureau, 2012 Economic Census

Table C presents data from the 2012 Economic Census for incorporated places, consolidated cities, census designated places, and minor civil divisions (in the 12 states where MCDs serve as general purpose local governments), and Economic Places with 10,000 or more population. There are 4,808 geographic entities in Table C, including the United States, the states, and the District of Columbia. Where an MCD is co-extensive with a place, only a single listing is included. The Economic Census uses a geographic concept called the "Economic Place". In this volume, the economic places have been matched to the standard categories to enable consistency between Table B and Table C. In some states, incorporated cities or villages are within towns or MCDs. In the Economic Census data, the "balance" of the town that is outside of incorporated cities or villages is identified as a separate place. In the decennial census, the American Community Survey, and other sources, data represent these entire towns, while the Economic Census data represent only the portion of the town that is not within an incorporated place inside the town.

The Economic Census provides a detailed portrait of the nation's economy once every five years, from the national to the local level. The 2012 Economic Census covers nearly all of the U.S. economy in its basic collection of establishment statistics. In 1997, it began use of the new North American Industry Classification System (NAICS) and therefore data are not comparable to economic data from prior years, which were based on the Standard Industrial Classification (SIC) system.

NAICS, developed in cooperation with Canada and Mexico, classifies North America's economic activities at 2-, 3-, 4-,

and 5-digit levels of detail, and the U.S. version of NAICS further defines industries to a sixth digit. The Economic Census takes advantage of this hierarchy to publish data at these successive levels of detail: sector (2-digit); subsector (3-digit); industry group (4-digit); industry (5-digit); and U.S. industry (6-digit). This volume includes data at the 2-digit (sector) level.

The following industry categories are not included in the Economic Census: Agriculture, Forestry, Fishing and Hunting; Rail Transportation; Postal Service; Funds, Trusts, and Other Financial Vehicles; Elementary and Secondary Schools; Junior Colleges; Colleges, Universities, and Professional Schools; Religious Organizations; Labor Unions and Similar Labor Organizations; Political Organizations; Private Households; and Public Administration.

The economic census does not generally include government-owned establishments, even when their primary activity would be classified in industries covered by the economic census. Because of these exclusions, economic census data for industries in many sectors might appear to be incomplete, as illustrated below.

At the same time, exceptions have been made to *include* the following governmental activities in the economic census: Hospitals; Government-owned liquor stores; University press publishers; and Federal Reserve Banks. In addition, the economic census does *include* the activities of private contractors that may be carrying out governmental functions on contract. Examples are highway construction contractors; privately operated prisons; private firms contracting to provide services to government; and Government-owned/ contractor-operated (GOCO) plants.

Aside from the above exceptions, the 2012 Economic Census includes private nonfarm establishments in 18 sectors. Three sectors are only published at the state level: Mining, quarrying, and oil and gas extraction; Construction; and Management of companies and enterprises. For the remaining 15 sectors, Table B shows the number of establishments and the number of employees in each sector.

Number of establishments. An establishment is a single physical location at which business is conducted and/or

Sector	Illustrative Governmental Activities Excluded
Utilities	Public electric, gas, water and sewer utilities
Construction	Highway construction performed by government employees
Retail Trade	Post exchanges, ship stores and similar establishments operated on military posts by agencies of the federal government
Transportation and Warehousing	Publicly-operated buses and subway systems
Information	Public libraries
Administrative and Support and Waste Management and Remediation Services	Municipal trash removal
Health Care and Social Assistance	Municipal ambulance services and County or city nursing care services
Arts, Entertainment, and Recreation	Public museums or zoos

services are provided. It is not necessarily identical with a company or enterprise, which may consist of one establishment or more.

Economic census figures represent a summary of reports for individual establishments rather than companies. For cases where a census report was received, separate information was obtained for each location where business was conducted. When administrative records of other federal agencies were used instead of a census report, no information was available on the number of locations operated. Each economic census establishment was tabulated according to the physical location at which the business was conducted. The count of establishments represents those in business at any time during the census year.

When two activities or more were carried on at a single location under a single ownership, all activities generally were grouped together as a single establishment. The entire establishment was classified on the basis of its major activity and all data for it were included in that classification. However, when distinct and separate economic activities (for which different industry classification codes were appropriate) were conducted at a single location under a single ownership, separate establishment reports for each of the different activities were obtained in the census.

Number of Employees. Paid employees consist of full- and part-time employees. Included are employees on paid sick leave, paid holidays, and paid vacations; not included are full- and part-time leased employees whose payroll was filed under an employee leasing company's Employer Identification Number (EIN), and temporary staffing obtained from a staffing service. The definition of paid employees is the same as that used by the Internal Revenue Service (IRS) on Form 941.

The following sectors are included in Table C:

Utilities. The Utilities sector comprises establishments engaged in the provision of the following utility services: electric power, natural gas, steam supply, water supply, and sewage removal. Within this sector, the specific activities associated with the utility services provided vary by utility: electric power includes generation, transmission, and distribution; natural gas includes distribution; steam supply includes provision and/or distribution; water supply includes treatment and distribution; and sewage removal includes collection, treatment, and disposal of waste through sewer systems and sewage treatment facilities.

Excluded from this sector are establishments primarily engaged in waste management services classified in Waste Management and Remediation Services. These establishments also collect, treat, and dispose of waste materials; however, they do not use sewer systems or sewage treatment facilities.

Public electric, gas, water, and sewer utilities are not included.

Manufacturing. The Manufacturing sector comprises establishments engaged in the mechanical, physical, or chemical transformation of materials, substances, or components into new products. The assembling of component parts of manufactured products is considered manufacturing, except in cases where the activity is appropriately classified in Construction.

Establishments in the Manufacturing sector are often described as plants, factories, or mills and characteristically use power-driven machines and materials-handling equipment. However, establishments that transform materials or substances into new products by hand or in the worker's home and those engaged in selling to the general public products made on the same premises from which they are sold, such as bakeries, candy stores, and custom tailors, may also be included in this sector. Manufacturing establishments may process materials or may contract with other establishments to process their materials for them. Both types of establishments are included in manufacturing.

The materials, substances, or components transformed by manufacturing establishments are raw materials that are products of agriculture, forestry, fishing, mining, or quarrying as well as products of other manufacturing establishments. The materials used may be purchased directly from producers, obtained through customary trade channels, or secured without recourse to the market by transferring the product from one establishment to another, under the same ownership.

The new product of a manufacturing establishment may be finished in the sense that it is ready for utilization or consumption, or it may be semifinished to become an input for an establishment engaged in further manufacturing. For example, the product of the alumina refinery is the input used in the primary production of aluminum; primary aluminum is the input to an aluminum wire drawing plant; and aluminum wire is the input for a fabricated wire product manufacturing establishment.

The subsectors in the Manufacturing sector generally reflect distinct production processes related to material inputs, production equipment, and employee skills. In the machinery area, where assembling is a key activity, parts and accessories for manufactured products are classified in the industry of the finished manufactured item when they are made for separate sale. For example, a replacement refrigerator door would be classified with refrigerators and an attachment for a piece of metal working machinery would be classified with metal working machinery. However, components, input from other manufacturing establishments, are classified based on the production function of the component manufacturer. For example, electronic components are classified in Computer and Electronic Product Manufacturing and stampings are classified in Fabricated Metal Product Manufacturing.

Manufacturing establishments often perform one or more activities that are classified outside the Manufacturing sector of NAICS. For instance, almost all manufacturing has some captive research and development or administrative operations, such as accounting, payroll, or management. These captive services are treated the same as captive manufacturing activities. When the services are provided by separate establishments, they are classified to the NAICS sector where such services are primary, not in manufacturing.

Wholesale Trade. The Wholesale Trade sector comprises establishments engaged in wholesaling merchandise, generally without transformation, and rendering services incidental to the sale of merchandise. The merchandise described in this sector includes the outputs of agriculture, mining, manufacturing, and certain information industries, such as publishing.

The wholesaling process is an intermediate step in the distribution of merchandise. Wholesalers are organized to sell or arrange the purchase or sale of (a) goods for resale (i.e., goods sold to other wholesalers or retailers), (b) capital or durable nonconsumer goods, and (c) raw and intermediate materials and supplies used in production.

Wholesalers sell merchandise to other businesses and normally operate from a warehouse or office. These warehouses and offices are characterized by having little or no display of merchandise. In addition, neither the design nor the location of the premises is intended to solicit walk-in traffic. Wholesalers do not normally use advertising directed to the general public. Customers are generally reached initially via telephone, in-person marketing, or by specialized advertising that may include Internet and other electronic means. Follow-up orders are either vendor-initiated or client-initiated, generally based on previous sales, and typically exhibit strong ties between sellers and buyers. In fact, transactions are often conducted between wholesalers and clients that have long-standing business relationships.

This sector comprises two main types of wholesalers: merchant wholesalers that sell goods on their own account and business-to-business electronic markets, agents, and brokers that arrange sales and purchases for others generally for a commission or fee. In this book, only the merchant wholesalers are included.

(1) Establishments that sell goods on their own account are known as wholesale merchants, distributors, jobbers, drop shippers, and import/export merchants. Also included as wholesale merchants are sales offices and sales branches (but not retail stores) maintained by manufacturing, refining, or mining enterprises apart from their plants or mines for the purpose of marketing their products. Merchant wholesale establishments typically maintain their own warehouse, where they receive and handle goods for their customers. Goods are generally sold without transformation, but may include integral functions, such as sorting, packaging, labeling, and other marketing services.

(2) (*not included in this book*) Establishments arranging for the purchase or sale of goods owned by others or purchasing goods, generally on a commission basis are known as business-to-business electronic markets, agents and brokers, commission merchants, import/export agents and brokers, auction companies, and manufacturers' representatives. These establishments operate from offices and generally do not own or handle the goods they sell.

Some wholesale establishments may be connected with a single manufacturer and promote and sell the particular manufacturers' products to a wide range of other wholesalers or retailers. Other wholesalers may be connected to a retail chain, or limited number of retail chains, and only provide a variety of products needed by that particular retail operation(s). These wholesalers may obtain the products from a wide range of manufacturers. Still other wholesalers may not take title to the goods, but act as agents and brokers for a commission.

Retail trade. The Retail Trade sector comprises establishments engaged in retailing merchandise, generally without transformation, and rendering services incidental to the sale of merchandise.

The retailing process is the final step in the distribution of merchandise; retailers are, therefore, organized to sell merchandise in small quantities to the general public. This sector comprises two main types of retailers: store and non-store retailers.

1. Store retailers operate fixed point-of-sale locations, located and designed to attract a high volume of walk-in customers. In general, retail stores have extensive displays of merchandise and use mass-media advertising to attract customers. They typically sell merchandise to the general public for personal or household consumption, but some also serve business and institutional clients. These include establishments, such as office supply stores, computer and software stores, building materials dealers, plumbing supply stores, and electrical supply stores. Catalog showrooms, gasoline stations, automotive dealers, and mobile home dealers are treated as store retailers.

In addition to retailing merchandise, some types of store retailers are also engaged in the provision of after-sales services, such as repair and installation. For example, new automobile dealers, electronics and appliance stores, and musical instrument and supplies stores often provide repair services. As a general rule, establishments engaged in retailing merchandise and providing after-sales services are classified in this sector.

The first eleven subsectors of retail trade are store retailers. The establishments are grouped into industries and industry groups typically based on one or more of the following criteria:

(a) The merchandise line or lines carried by the store; for example, specialty stores are distinguished from general-line stores.

(b) The usual trade designation of the establishments. This criterion applies in cases where a store type is well recognized by the industry and the public, but difficult to define strictly in terms of merchandise lines carried; for example, pharmacies, hardware stores, and department stores.

(c) Capital requirements in terms of display equipment; for example, food stores have equipment requirements not found in other retail industries.

(d) Human resource requirements in terms of expertise; for example, the staff of an automobile dealer requires knowledge in financing, registering, and licensing issues that are not necessary in other retail industries.

2. Nonstore retailers, like store retailers, are organized to serve the general public, but their retailing methods differ. The establishments of this subsector reach customers and market merchandise with methods, such as the broadcasting of "infomercials," the broadcasting and publishing of direct-response advertising, the publishing of paper and electronic catalogs, door-to-door solicitation, in-home demonstration, selling from portable stalls (street vendors, except food), and distribution through vending machines. Establishments engaged in the direct sale (nonstore) of products, such as home heating oil dealers and home delivery newspaper routes are included here.

The buying of goods for resale is a characteristic of retail trade establishments that particularly distinguishes them from establishments in the agriculture, manufacturing, and construction industries. For example, farms that sell their products at or from the point of production are not classified in retail, but rather in agriculture. Similarly, establishments that both manufacture and sell their products to the general public are not classified in retail, but rather in manufacturing. However, establishments that engage in processing activities incidental to retailing are classified in retail. This includes establishments, such as optical goods stores that do in-store grinding of lenses, and meat and seafood markets.

Wholesalers also engage in the buying of goods for resale, but they are not usually organized to serve the general public. They typically operate from a warehouse or office and neither the design nor the location of these premises is intended to solicit a high volume of walk-in traffic. Wholesalers supply institutional, industrial, wholesale, and retail clients; their operations are, therefore, generally organized to purchase, sell, and deliver merchandise in larger quantities. However, dealers of durable nonconsumer goods, such as farm machinery and heavy duty trucks, are included in wholesale trade even if they often sell these products in single units.

Retail establishments operated by agencies of the federal government, such as military post exchanges and ship stores, are not included.

Transportation and Warehousing. The Transportation and Warehousing sector includes industries providing transportation of passengers and cargo, warehousing and storage for goods, scenic and sightseeing transportation, and support activities related to modes of transportation. Establishments in these industries use transportation equipment or transportation related facilities as a productive asset. The type of equipment depends on the mode of transportation. The modes of transportation are air, rail, water, road, and pipeline.

The Transportation and Warehousing sector distinguishes three basic types of activities: subsectors for each mode of transportation, a subsector for warehousing and storage, and a subsector for establishments providing support activities for transportation. In addition, there are subsectors for establishments that provide passenger transportation for scenic and sightseeing purposes, postal services, and courier services.

A separate subsector for support activities is established in the sector because, first, support activities for transportation are inherently multimodal, such as freight transportation arrangement, or have multimodal aspects. Secondly, there are production process similarities among the support activity industries.

One of the support activities identified in the support activity subsector is the routine repair and maintenance of transportation equipment (e.g., aircraft at an airport, railroad rolling stock at a railroad terminal, or ships at a harbor or port facility). Such establishments do not perform complete overhauling or rebuilding of transportation equipment (i.e., periodic restoration of transportation equipment to original design specifications) or transportation equipment conversion (i.e., major modification to systems). An establishment that primarily performs factory (or shipyard) overhauls, rebuilding, or conversions of aircraft, railroad rolling stock, or a ship is classified in Subsector 336, Transportation Equipment Manufacturing according to the type of equipment.

Many of the establishments in this sector often operate on networks, with physical facilities, labor forces, and equipment spread over an extensive geographic area.

Warehousing establishments in this sector are distinguished from merchant wholesaling in that the warehouse establishments do not sell the goods.

Excluded from this sector are establishments primarily engaged in providing travel agent services that support transportation and other establishments, such as hotels, businesses, and government agencies. These establishments are classified in Administrative and Support and Waste Management and Remediation Services. Also, establishments primarily engaged in providing rental and leasing of transportation equipment without operator are classified in Rental and Leasing Services.

For the 2012 Economic Census, Rail Transportation and Postal Service are not included. Publicly-operated buses and subway systems are not included.

Information. The Information sector comprises establishments engaged in the following processes: (a) producing and distributing information and cultural products, (b) providing the means to transmit or distribute these products as well as data or communications, and (c) processing data.

The main components of this sector are the publishing industries, including software publishing, and both traditional publishing and publishing exclusively on the Internet; the motion picture and sound recording industries; the broadcasting industries, including traditional broadcasting and those broadcasting exclusively over the Internet; the telecommunications industries; web search portals, data processing industries, and the information services industries.

The expressions ''information age'' and ''global information economy'' are used with considerable frequency today. The general idea of an ''information economy'' includes both the notion of industries primarily producing, processing, and distributing information, as well as the idea that every industry is using available information and information technology to reorganize and make themselves more productive.

For the purposes of NAICS, it is the transformation of information into a commodity that is produced and distributed by a number of growing industries that is at issue. The Information sector groups three types of establishments: (1) those engaged in producing and distributing information and cultural products; (2) those that provide the means to transmit or distribute these products as well as data or communications; and (3) those that process data. Cultural products are those that directly express attitudes, opinions, ideas, values, and artistic creativity; provide entertainment; or offer information and analysis concerning the past and present. Included in this definition are popular, mass-produced products as well as cultural products that normally have a more limited audience, such as poetry books, literary magazines, or classical records.

The unique characteristics of information and cultural products, and of the processes involved in their production and distribution, distinguish the Information sector from the goods-producing and service-producing sectors. Some of these characteristics are:

1. Unlike traditional goods, an "information or cultural product," such as a newspaper on-line or television program, does not necessarily have tangible qualities, nor is it necessarily associated with a particular form. A movie can be shown at a movie theater, on a television broadcast, through video-on-demand or rented at a local video store. A sound recording can be aired on radio, embedded in multimedia products, or sold at a record store.
2. Unlike traditional services, the delivery of these products does not require direct contact between the supplier and the consumer.
3. The value of these products to the consumer lies in their informational, educational, cultural, or entertainment content, not in the format in which they are distributed. Most of these products are protected from unlawful reproduction by copyright laws.
4. The intangible property aspect of information and cultural products makes the processes involved in their production and distribution very different from goods and services. Only those possessing the rights to these works are authorized to reproduce, alter, improve, and distribute them. Acquiring and using these rights often involves significant costs. In addition, technology is revolutionizing the distribution of these products. It is possible to distribute them in a physical form, via broadcast, or on-line.
5. Distributors of information and cultural products can easily add value to the products they distribute. For instance, broadcasters add advertising not contained in the original product. This capacity means that unlike traditional distributors, they derive revenue not from sale of the distributed product to the final consumer, but from those who pay for the privilege of adding information to the original product. Similarly, a directory and mailing list publisher can acquire the rights to thousands of previously published newspaper and periodical articles and add new value by providing search and software and organizing the information in a way that facilitates research and retrieval. These products often command a much higher price than the original information.

The distribution modes for information commodities may either eliminate the necessity for traditional manufacture, or reverse the conventional order of manufacture-distribute: A newspaper distributed on-line, for example, can be printed locally or by the final consumer. Similarly, packaged software, which at the time of the 2012 Economic Census was mainly bought through the traditional retail channels, is already becoming available mainly on-line. The NAICS Information sector is designed to make such economic changes transparent as they occur, or to facilitate designing surveys that will monitor the new phenomena and provide data to analyze the changes.

Many of the industries in the NAICS Information sector are engaged in producing products protected by copyright law, or in distributing them (other than distribution by traditional wholesale and retail methods). Examples are traditional publishing industries, software and directory and mailing list publishing industries, and film and sound industries. Broadcasting and telecommunications industries and information providers and processors are also included in the Information sector, because their technologies are so closely linked to other industries in the Information sector.

Public libraries are not included.

Finance and Insurance. The Finance and Insurance sector comprises establishments primarily engaged in financial transactions (transactions involving the creation, liquidation, or change in ownership of financial assets) and/or in facilitating financial transactions. Three principal types of activities are identified:

1. Raising funds by taking deposits and/or issuing securities and, in the process, incurring liabilities. Establishments engaged in this activity use raised funds to acquire financial assets by making loans and/or purchasing securities. Putting themselves at risk, they channel funds from lenders to borrowers and transform or repackage the funds with respect to maturity, scale, and risk. This activity is known as financial intermediation.
2. Pooling of risk by underwriting insurance and annuities. Establishments engaged in this activity collect fees, insurance premiums, or annuity considerations; build up reserves; invest those reserves; and make contractual payments. Fees are based on the expected incidence of the insured risk and the expected return on investment.
3. Providing specialized services facilitating or supporting financial intermediation, insurance, and employee benefit programs.

In addition, monetary authorities charged with monetary control are included in this sector.

The subsectors, industry groups, and industries within the NAICS Finance and Insurance sector are defined on the basis of their unique production processes. As with all industries, the production processes are distinguished by their use of specialized human resources and specialized physical capital. In addition, the way in which these establishments acquire and allocate financial capital, their source of funds, and the use of those funds provides a third basis for distinguishing characteristics of the production process. For

instance, the production process in raising funds through deposit-taking is different from the process of raising funds in bond or money markets. The process of making loans to individuals also requires different production processes than does the creation of investment pools or the underwriting of securities.

Most of the Finance and Insurance subsectors contain one or more industry groups of (1) intermediaries with similar patterns of raising and using funds and (2) establishments engaged in activities that facilitate, or are otherwise related to, that type of financial or insurance intermediation. Industries within this sector are defined in terms of activities for which a production process can be specified, and many of these activities are not exclusive to a particular type of financial institution. To deal with the varied activities taking place within existing financial institutions, the approach is to split these institutions into components performing specialized services. This requires defining the units engaged in providing those services and developing procedures that allow for their delineation. These units are the equivalents for finance and insurance of the establishments defined for other industries.

The output of many financial services, as well as the inputs and the processes by which they are combined, cannot be observed at a single location and can only be defined at a higher level of the organizational structure of the enterprise. Additionally, a number of independent activities that represent separate and distinct production processes may take place at a single location belonging to a multilocation financial firm. Activities are more likely to be homogeneous with respect to production characteristics than are locations, at least in financial services. The classification defines activities broadly enough that it can be used both by those classifying by location and by those employing a more top-down approach to the delineation of the establishment.

Establishments engaged in activities that facilitate, or are otherwise related to, the various types of intermediation have been included in individual subsectors, rather than in a separate subsector dedicated to services alone because these services are performed by intermediaries, as well as by specialist establishments, the extent to which the activity of the intermediaries can be separately identified is not clear.

The Finance and Insurance sector has been defined to encompass establishments primarily engaged in financial transactions; that is, transactions involving the creation, liquidation, change in ownership of financial assets; or in facilitating financial transactions. Financial industries are extensive users of electronic means for facilitating the verification of financial balances, authorizing transactions, transferring funds to and from transactors' accounts, notifying banks (or credit card issuers) of the individual transactions, and providing daily summaries. Since these transaction processing activities are integral to the production of finance and insurance services, establishments that principally provide a financial transaction processing service are classified to this sector, rather than to the data processing industry in the Information sector.

Legal entities that hold portfolios of assets on behalf of others are significant and data on them are required for a variety of purposes. Thus for NAICS, these funds, trusts, and other financial vehicles are the fifth subsector of the Finance and Insurance sector. These entities earn interest, dividends, and other property income, but have little or no employment and no revenue from the sale of services. Separate establishments and employees devoted to the management of funds are classified in Other Financial Investment Activities.

Real Estate and Rental and Leasing. The Real Estate and Rental and Leasing sector comprises establishments primarily engaged in renting, leasing, or otherwise allowing the use of tangible or intangible assets, and establishments providing related services. The major portion of this sector comprises establishments that rent, lease, or otherwise allow the use of their own assets by others. The assets may be tangible, as is the case of real estate and equipment, or intangible, as is the case with patents and trademarks.

This sector also includes establishments primarily engaged in managing real estate for others, selling, renting and/or buying real estate for others, and appraising real estate. These activities are closely related to this sector's main activity, and it was felt that from a production basis they would best be included here. In addition, a substantial proportion of property management is self-performed by lessors.

The main components of this sector are the real estate lessors industries (including equity real estate investment trusts (REITs)); equipment lessors industries (including motor vehicles, computers, and consumer goods); and lessors of nonfinancial intangible assets (except copyrighted works).

Excluded from this sector are establishments primarily engaged in renting or leasing equipment with operators. Establishments renting or leasing equipment with operators are classified in various subsectors of NAICS depending on the nature of the services provided (e.g., transportation, construction, agriculture). These activities are excluded from this sector because the client is paying for the expertise and knowledge of the equipment operator, in addition to the rental of the equipment. In many cases, such as the rental of heavy construction equipment, the operator is essential to operate the equipment.

Professional, Scientific, and Technical Services. The Professional, Scientific, and Technical Services sector comprises establishments that specialize in performing professional, scientific, and technical activities for others. These activities require a high degree of expertise and training. The establishments in this sector specialize according to expertise and provide these services to clients in a variety of industries and, in some cases, to households. Activities performed include: legal advice and representation; accounting, bookkeeping, and payroll services; architectural, engineering, and specialized design services; computer services; consulting services; research services; advertising services; photographic services; translation and interpretation services; veterinary services; and other professional, scientific, and technical services.

This sector excludes establishments primarily engaged in providing a range of day-to-day office administrative services, such as financial planning, billing and recordkeeping, personnel, and physical distribution and logistics. These establishments are classified in Administrative and Support and Waste Management and Remediation Services.

Administrative and Support and Waste Management and Remediation Services. The Administrative and Support and Waste Management and Remediation Services sector comprises establishments performing routine support activities for the day-to-day operations of other organizations. These essential activities are often undertaken in-house by establishments in many sectors of the economy. The establishments in this sector specialize in one or more of these support activities and provide these services to clients in a variety of industries and, in some cases, to households. Activities performed include: office administration, hiring and placing of personnel, document preparation and similar clerical services, solicitation, collection, security and surveillance services, cleaning, and waste disposal services.

The administrative and management activities performed by establishments in this sector are typically on a contract or fee basis. These activities may also be performed by establishments that are part of the company or enterprise. However, establishments involved in administering, overseeing, and managing other establishments of the company or enterprise, are classified in Management of Companies and Enterprises. Those establishments normally undertake the strategic and organizational planning and decision making role of the company or enterprise.

Municipal trash removal is not included.

Educational Services. The Educational Services sector comprises establishments that provide instruction and training in a wide variety of subjects. This instruction and training is provided by specialized establishments, such as schools, colleges, universities, and training centers. These establishments may be privately owned and operated for profit or not for profit, or they may be publicly owned and operated. They may also offer food and/or accommodation services to their students.

Educational services are usually delivered by teachers or instructors that explain, tell, demonstrate, supervise, and direct learning. Instruction is imparted in diverse settings, such as educational institutions, the workplace, or the home, and through diverse means, such as correspondence, television, the Internet, or other electronic and distance-learning methods. The training provided by these establishments may include the use of simulators and simulation methods. It can be adapted to the particular needs of the students, for example sign language can replace verbal language for teaching students with hearing impairments. All industries in the sector share this commonality of process, namely, labor inputs of instructors with the requisite subject matter expertise and teaching ability.

For the 2012 Economic Census, Elementary and Secondary Schools; Junior Colleges; and Colleges, Universities, and Professional Schools are not included.

Health Care and Social Assistance. The Health Care and Social Assistance sector comprises establishments providing health care and social assistance for individuals. The sector includes both health care and social assistance because it is sometimes difficult to distinguish between the boundaries of these two activities. The industries in this sector are arranged on a continuum starting with those establishments providing medical care exclusively, continuing with those providing health care and social assistance, and finally finishing with those providing only social assistance. The services provided by establishments in this sector are delivered by trained professionals. All industries in the sector share this commonality of process, namely, labor inputs of health practitioners or social workers with the requisite expertise. Many of the industries in the sector are defined based on the educational degree held by the practitioners included in the industry.

Excluded from this sector are aerobic classes (in Amusement, Gambling and Recreation Industries) and non-medical diet and weight reducing centers (in Personal and Laundry Services). Although these can be viewed as health services, these services are not typically delivered by health practitioners.

Municipal ambulance services, and county or city nursing care services are not included.

Arts, Entertainment, and Recreation. The Arts, Entertainment, and Recreation sector includes a wide range of establishments that operate facilities or provide services to meet varied cultural, entertainment, and recreational interests of their patrons. This sector comprises (1) establishments that are involved in producing, promoting, or participating in live performances, events, or exhibits intended for public viewing; (2) establishments that preserve and exhibit objects and sites of historical, cultural, or educational interest; and (3) establishments that operate facilities or provide services that enable patrons to participate in recreational activities or pursue amusement, hobby, and leisure-time interests.

Some establishments that provide cultural, entertainment, or recreational facilities and services are classified in other sectors. Excluded from this sector are: (1) establishments that provide both accommodations and recreational facilities, such as hunting and fishing camps and resort and casino hotels are classified in Accommodation; (2) restaurants and night clubs that provide live entertainment in addition to the sale of food and beverages are classified in Food Services and Drinking Places; (3) motion picture theaters, libraries and archives, and publishers of newspapers, magazines, books, periodicals, and computer software are classified in Information; and (4) establishments using transportation equipment to provide recreational and entertainment services, such as those operating sightseeing buses, dinner cruises, or helicopter rides, are classified in Scenic and Sightseeing Transportation.

Public museums and zoos are not included.

Accommodation and Food Services. The Accommodation and Food Services sector comprises establishments providing customers with lodging and/or preparing meals, snacks, and beverages for immediate consumption. The sector includes both accommodation and food services establishments because the two activities are often combined at the same establishment.

Excluded from this sector are civic and social organizations; amusement and recreation parks; theaters; and other recreation or entertainment facilities providing food and beverage services.

Other Services (except Public Administration). The Other Services (except Public Administration) sector comprises establishments engaged in providing services not specifically provided for elsewhere in the classification system. Establishments in this sector are primarily engaged in activities, such as equipment and machinery repairing, promoting or administering religious activities, grantmaking, advocacy, and providing drycleaning and laundry services, personal care services, death care services, pet care services, photofinishing services, temporary parking services, and dating services.

Private households that engage in employing workers on or about the premises in activities primarily concerned with the operation of the household are included in this sector.

Excluded from this sector are establishments primarily engaged in retailing new equipment and also performing repairs and general maintenance on equipment. These establishments are classified Retail Trade.

The following sectors are not included in Table B because they are only available at the state level. The definitions are included because they are in Table 4 in the Introduction. In a few states, these sectors represent significant numbers of employees.

Mining, Quarrying, and Oil and Gas Extraction. The Mining, Quarrying, and Oil and Gas Extraction sector comprises establishments that extract naturally occurring mineral solids, such as coal and ores; liquid minerals, such as crude petroleum; and gases, such as natural gas. The term mining is used in the broad sense to include quarrying, well operations, beneficiating (e.g., crushing, screening, washing, and flotation), and other preparation customarily performed at the mine site, or as a part of mining activity.

The Mining, Quarrying, and Oil and Gas Extraction sector distinguishes two basic activities: mine operation and mining support activities. Mine operation includes establishments operating mines, quarries, or oil and gas wells on their own account or for others on a contract or fee basis. Mining support activities include establishments that perform exploration (except geophysical surveying) and/or other mining services on a contract or fee basis (except mine site preparation and construction of oil/gas pipelines).

Establishments in the Mining, Quarrying, and Oil and Gas Extraction sector are grouped and classified according to the natural resource mined or to be mined. Industries include establishments that develop the mine site, extract the natural resources, and/or those that beneficiate (i.e., prepare) the mineral mined. Beneficiation is the process whereby the extracted material is reduced to particles that can be separated into mineral and waste, the former suitable for further processing or direct use. The operations that take place in beneficiation are primarily mechanical, such as grinding, washing, magnetic separation, and centrifugal separation. In contrast, manufacturing operations primarily use chemical and electrochemical processes, such as electrolysis and distillation. However, some treatments, such as heat treatments, take place in both the beneficiation and the manufacturing (i.e., smelting/refining) stages. The range of preparation activities varies by mineral and the purity of any given ore deposit. While some minerals, such as petroleum and natural gas, require little or no preparation, others are washed and screened, while yet others, such as gold and silver, can be transformed into bullion before leaving the mine site.

Mining, beneficiating, and manufacturing activities often occur in a single location. Separate receipts will be collected for these activities whenever possible. When receipts cannot be broken out between mining and manufacturing, establishments that mine or quarry nonmetallic minerals, and then beneficiate the nonmetallic minerals into more finished manufactured products are classified based on the primary activity of the establishment. A mine that manufactures a small amount of finished products will be classified in Mining, Quarrying, and Oil and Gas Extraction. An establishment that mines whose primary output is a more finished manufactured product will be classified in Manufacturing.

Construction. The Construction sector comprises establishments primarily engaged in the construction of buildings or engineering projects (e.g., highways and utility systems). Establishments primarily engaged in the preparation of sites for new construction and establishments primarily engaged in subdividing land for sale as building sites also are included in this sector.

Construction work done may include new work, additions, alterations, or maintenance and repairs. Activities of these establishments generally are managed at a fixed place of business, but they usually perform construction activities at multiple project sites. Production responsibilities for establishments in this sector are usually specified in (1) contracts with the owners of construction projects (prime contracts) or (2) contracts with other construction establishments (subcontracts).

Establishments primarily engaged in contracts that include responsibility for all aspects of individual construction projects are commonly known as general contractors, but also may be known as design-builders, construction managers, turnkey contractors, or (in cases where two or more establishments jointly secure a general contract) joint-venture contractors. Construction managers that provide oversight and scheduling only (i.e., agency) as well as construction managers that are responsible for the entire project (i.e., at risk) are included as general contractor type establishments. Establishments of the "general contractor type" frequently arrange construction of separate parts of their projects through subcontracts with other construction establishments.

Establishments primarily engaged in activities to produce a specific component (e.g., masonry, painting, and electrical work) of a construction project are commonly known as specialty trade contractors. Activities of specialty trade contractors are usually subcontracted from other construction establishments, but especially in remodeling and repair construction, the work may be done directly for the owner of the property.

Establishments primarily engaged in activities to construct buildings to be sold on sites that they own are known as for-sale builders, but also may be known as speculative builders or merchant builders. For-sale builders produce buildings in a manner similar to general contractors, but their production processes also include site acquisition and securing of financial backing. For-sale builders are most often associated with the construction of residential buildings. Like general contractors, they may subcontract all or part of the actual construction work on their buildings.

There are substantial differences in the types of equipment, work force skills, and other inputs required by establishments in this sector. To highlight these differences and variations in the underlying production functions, this sector is divided into three subsectors.

Construction of Buildings, comprises establishments of the general contractor type and for-sale builders involved in the construction of buildings. Heavy and Civil Engineering Construction, comprises establishments involved in the construction of engineering projects. Specialty Trade Contractors, comprises establishments engaged in specialty trade activities generally needed in the construction of all types of buildings.

Force account construction is construction work performed by an enterprise primarily engaged in some business other than construction for its own account, using employees of the enterprise. This activity is not included in the construction sector unless the construction work performed is the primary activity of a separate establishment of the enterprise. The installation and the ongoing repair and maintenance of telecommunications and utility networks is excluded from construction when the establishments performing the work are not independent contractors. Although a growing proportion of this work is subcontracted to independent contractors in the Construction Sector, the operating units of telecommunications and utility companies performing this work are included with the telecommunications or utility activities.

Management of Companies and Enterprises. The Management of Companies and Enterprises sector comprises (1) establishments that hold the securities of (or other equity interests in) companies and enterprises for the purpose of owning a controlling interest or influencing management decisions or (2) establishments (except government establishments) that administer, oversee, and manage establishments of the company or enterprise and that normally undertake the strategic or organizational planning and decision making role of the company or enterprise. Establishments that administer, oversee, and manage may hold the securities of the company or enterprise.

Establishments in this sector perform essential activities that are often undertaken in-house by establishments in many sectors of the economy. By consolidating the performance of these activities of the enterprise at one establishment, economies of scale are achieved.

Government establishments primarily engaged in administering, overseeing, and managing governmental programs are classified in Public Administration and are not included in the Economic Census. Establishments primarily engaged in providing a range of day-to-day office administrative services, such as financial planning, billing and recordkeeping, personnel, and physical distribution and logistics are classified in Office Administrative Services.